THE OFFICIAL® PRICE GUIDE TO Records 2002

Sixteenth Edition

JERRY OSBORNE

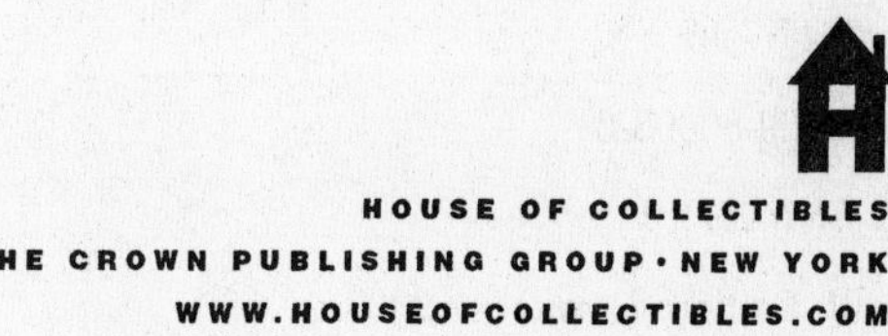
HOUSE OF COLLECTIBLES
THE CROWN PUBLISHING GROUP • NEW YORK
WWW.HOUSEOFCOLLECTIBLES.COM

Important Notice: All of the information, including valuations, in this book has been compiled from the most reliable sources, and every effort has been made to eliminate errors and questionable data. Nevertheless, the possibility of error in a work of such immense scope always exists. The publisher will not be held responsible for losses that may occur in the purchase, sale, or other transaction of items because of information contained herein. Readers who feel they have discovered errors are invited to *write* and inform us, so any errors may be corrected in subsequent editions. Those seeking further information on the topics covered in this book are advised to refer to the complete line of *Official Price Guides* published by the House of Collectibles.

Published by: House of Collectibles
The Crown Publishing Group
New York, New York

www.houseofcollectibles.com

Distributed by the Crown Publishing Group, a division of Random House, Inc., New York, and simultaneously in Canada by Random House of Canada Limited, Toronto.

www.randomhouse.com

Printed in the United States of America

ISSN: 0747-7392

ISBN: 0-609-80908-3

10 9 8 7 6 5 4 3 2 1

Sixteenth Edition: November 2002

CONTENTS

ACKNOWLEDGMENTS

The single most important element in the updating and revision of a price and reference guide is reader input. From dealers and collectors, located in every state and in nearly every country, we receive suggestions, additions and corrections.

Every single piece of data we acquire from readers is carefully reviewed, with all the appropriate and usable information utilized in a future printing of this guide — though not necessarily in the very next edition.

As enthusiastically as we encourage your contributions, let us suggest that when you mail to us you will type or print your name clearly, on both the envelope and its contents. It is as frustrating for us to receive a packet of information, and not be able to credit the sender, as it probably is for the sender to not see his or her name in the Acknowledgments. For those with fairly common names, using a middle name or initial is a plus.

Specifically for this edition, we are grateful for the information and assistance supplied by those whose names appear below. To these good folks, our deepest gratitude is extended. The amount of data and investment of time varied, but without each and every one of them this book and its value would have been something less than it is.

Rob Abson
Bob Alaniz
Carol Alaniz
Davie Allan
Ronnie Allen
Bill Amey
Marti Anderson
Stephen M. Anderson
Mike Andrews
Annette
Jungle Jim Arslanian
Moo Avvento
Ben Baarsma
James Baird
Richard Banker
Darren Baumgartner
Russ C. Bell
Jocelyn Bellanger
Tony Bellus
Lee Bendgen
Pat Benti
Dennis Benzer
Don & Dian Berger
Lionel Bernhard
Greg Berry
Bob Biddle
Thomas Bintz
Dave Blackstone
Charles Blair
Wendy Bleistein
Tom Boggs
Don Borkowski
Ray Bourdeaux
Dennis G. Bowers
Chris G. Bowman
Susan Kim Bowman
David Breese
Martin Brooks
Denise M. Brown
Kip Brown
Pat Brown
John. M. Brusselman
Chris Burgess
James Burton
Gary Calkins
Jim Callahan
Wilson Callan
Douglas Cantrell
James Carlson
Trace Carpenter
William R. Cashdollar
Frank Castillo
Rich Centalla
Howard Champion
Fred Charlton
Dawn Halloran
Charouhas
Knox Christie
Lorena Christie
Dick Clark
Fred Clemens
Bob Clere
Patrick Conklin
Hardy Cook
Daniel Costa
Pat Cottle
Perry Cox
Anthony Craft
Joel Crigler
James Cullen
Pat Cummings
Dick Dale
Nicky D'Andrea
Jeff Dam
Bobby Darnell
Brian Davis
Charles Dawson
Devon Dawson
Sandra Derliunas
Thomas Diehl
Dutch Dilluvio
James Doidge
Mike Donlin
Bud Donovan
Earl Douglass
Dennis Dow
Joe Dowell
James Drennan
Don Dressel
Jack Dunham
Judith M. Ihnken Ebner
Ragnar Ebsen
Douglas Edwards
Edmond I. Edwards
Ron Englehart
Barbara Ericson
Frank Faccioli
Dennis Favreau
Frank Fazio
George Fedoruk
Mike Fitzgerald
Jim Flanagan
Richard Floyd
D.J. Fontana
Jerry Ford
Göran Forsberg
Sven Forsberg
Mark Fortin
Larry Forward
David Foster
Connie Francis
Rob Friedman
Arnie Ganem
Bernie Gardzalla
Jean-Marc Gargiulo
Richard Gesner
Jim Gibbons
Gregory L. Gillis
Walter Gladwin
Bobby Goldsboro

Jimmy Goode
William Gourd
Charles T. Gray
Ori Grosz
Buck Hafeman
Marshall Hall
Michael Harrah
Charles N. Hellinger
Big Richie Henchar
Larry Henley
Bruce P. Henningsgaard
Bob Henry
Douglas Herrman
Jack Herwig
Ersel Hickey
Michael B. Hill
Tom Holland
Clarence "Chuck" Holmes
Rick Horvath
Brian Hoyle
Fred L. Hoyt
Len Hruszowy
Pauline Hubbard
Bruce Huffman
David Huisman
James Hurst
Stefan Jadefjord
Michael A. Janowski
John & Verna
Betty Johnson
Jeffrey E. Johnson
Wilma L. Jones
Daniel F. Joyce
Steve Joyce
Dave Jurgensmeier
George Kane
William D. Katz
Bob Keen
Tapio Keihanen
Frank Kelley
Scott Kelley
Al Kelly
Joe Knapp
Tony Kolodziej
Tracy Kolodziej
Douglas H. Koppenhofer
Brian Korn
Frank Kovacs
Milt Krantz
Colin Kreitzer
Rocky Kruegel
Ronald Kunkin
Bruce Kuramoto
Jack Land
George J. Lapata
Ken Larimore
Tom Lascari
Stephen Lawrence
Brian Lee
Ronald Lees
Susan Lehmkuhl
Linda Gail Lewis
Chuck Lezotte
Dave Liss
Dale Little
Jennifer LoGalbo
Wayne London
Edward Lopez
René Lucas
David Ludwig
Curt Lundgren
Jack Macklin
Stephen Macleod
Pat Maguire
Chas Mannell
Cary Mansfield
Anthony Marchesani
Ed Marcus
Franklin Markowitz
Bob Marovich
Dan Martin
S. Martz
Craig Masters
Harold D. Mathews
Peter McCullough
Ronnie McDowell
Jim McLaughlin
Melanie McMillan
Dale "Satch" McQuaid
Dave Melton
Stephen Miller
Vincent P. Miller
Larry Mitchell
Valerie Mongue
Hugo Montoya
Scotty Moore
Howard Moser
David W. Mozey
Tony J. Muñoz
Brian Murphy
Dan Murphy
Gary E. Myers
Shawn Nagy
Ryan Nakhleh
Marty Neer
Wayne G. Nielander
Fred Ninomiya, Jr.
Norman Nonnweiler
Jay Notartomaso
Larry Nuding
Gerald Ognjan
Geoff Olive
Linda Ann Osborne
Jim Osmialowski
Frank Owens
Bob Pareti
Richard Paul
Victor Pearlin
Alex Peavey
Ryan Pershon
Dan Pettem
Gary Phillips
Ben Piper
Tom Pokladowski
Jared Poppel
J.J. Powell
Shawn Powers
Tom Prestopnik
Jim Price
Ray Price
Steve Propes
Chester Prudhomme
Jim Pucel
Bob Ramsdell
Ray Reed
John Lewis Reeder
Todd Reichl
Ellis Reida
Jack Ricks
Robert G. Ritter
Dick Rosemont
Kevin Ross
Everett Salinas
Robert P. Santee
Tom Schoeck
Phillip J. Schwartz
Angelo Sciacca
Joe Scibetta
Paul Setzler
Michael Sharritt
Alan Sheppard
Doug Siegel
Tom Silverthorn
Andrew P. Smith
Richard C. Sneathen
Jan Solgas
John Speakman
John Sprecher
Mike Stewart
Eddie Sulik Jr.
Bo Svensson
John Swartz
Howard A. Sweet
Howard Sweitzer
Yumi Takeuchi
Bill Taylor
Charles W. Taylor III
Robert Termorshuizen
Henry Thome
Chet Torres
George G. Trabant
Charles A. Trimble
Howard Tring
Joe Trojanowski
Hugh Turner
Jesse Lee Turner
David Uren
Tom Vaughn
J. Walsh
Jan Warner
Jim Warner
Harry Warren
Bob Waters
Jim Weaver
Larry J. Weinecke
Allen F. Weitzel
Joel Whitburn
Gary Whitehead
Graham Whitehead
Danny A. White
Vicki Wightman
Joseph Wilbur
Dennis Wilson
Eric Wincentsen
Doug Winslow
David Wood
Rita Lyn Woodby
Bob Young
Tom Zagryn
Fred Zerega
Perry Zmolek

THE OFFICIAL® PRICE GUIDE TO

Records 2002

Sixteenth Edition

INTRODUCTION

The New Look

Between the 15th edition, published in 2001, and this 16th *Official Price Guide to Records,* the publisher (House of Collectibles) reformatted and resized most of their books, including this title.

To meet these new specifications, approximately 25% of the contents of the 15th edition needed to be honorably discharged.

Deciding what to keep and what to leave out presented quite a challenge. Most important is that we retain all of the most collectible items. Usually these are also the most valuable items..

To that end, we created a set of somewhat complicated specifications to guide us in making the final cuts. Be assured the deletions are not random, nor are they based on anyone's particular favorites.

The method chosen ensures that any artist, having just one record meeting the formula's minimum value requirement, is represented in their entirety — as we have done in previous editions. There are no artists whose listings appear only in part.

Fortunately we managed to trim the book to the new size by dropping only listings of very low value. Thus no recordings of collectible consequence are missing.

As for those listings no longer found in the guide, they have not vanished into a black hole. They can likely be evaluated by consulting *the Guidelines for Pricing Records Not in This Edition* section of this Introduction.

Also, our complete data base can easily be had on the *Music Tracker* software CD-ROM.

How Prices Are Determined

Record values shown in the price guide are averaged using information derived from a number of reliable, proven sources.

The preferred form of communication by dealers and collectors is now e-mail. When it's time to prepare a revised edition, all of the e-mail we receive are carefully analyzed.

Since scanned images can easily be attached to an e-mail, we especially appreciate having them when possible. The actual label and cover art is still the most reliable source of the information we need for a complete listing.

For those who prefer to send photocopies of record labels and covers, simply use the U.S. mail.

Our e-mail address is **jpo@olympus.net.** Add it to your e-mail Address Book. Remember to provide your full name separately since Internet letters normally transmit only the sender's e-mail address.

If you help, we want to credit you properly. Just make sure we have — and can read — the information with which to do it.

Please send all additions, corrections, and suggestions to

Jerry Osborne
Box 255
Port Townsend, WA 98368
e-mail: jpo@olympus.net

Printed marketplace publications and online Internet sales are also extremely important sources of pricing information. Through these, hobbyists buy, sell, and trade music collectibles. We painstakingly review those periodicals and sites, carefully comparing prices being asked to those shown in our most recent edition. Keep in mind, however, that while *asking* prices are considered, greater weight is given to actual *sales* prices.

If active trading indicates prices in the guide need to be increased or decreased, those changes are made. With our frequent publishing schedule, it is never long before the corrections appear in print.

What makes this step in the pricing process so vital is that nothing more verifiably illustrates the out-of-print record marketplace than everyday sales lists placed by dealers from around the country and around the globe.

Also of great assistance to price tracking are the individual sales catalogs and auction results lists we routinely receive from dealers. Auction results are especially useful, so keep 'em coming.

Record prices, as with most collectibles, can vary drastically from one area of the country to another. Having reviewers and annotators in every state — as well as in Europe, Asia, and beyond — enables us to present a realistic average of the highest and lowest current trading prices for an identically graded copy of each record.

Other sources of consequential information include private set sale and auction lists, record convention trading, personal visits with collectors and to retail locations around the country, and hundreds of hours on the telephone with key advisors.

Although the record marketplace information in this edition was believed accurate at press time, it is ever subject to market changes. At any time, major bulk discoveries, quantity dumps, sudden increases brought about by an artist's death, overnight stardom that creates a greater demand for earlier material, and other such events and trends can easily affect scarcity and demand. With our constant research, keeping track of the day-to-day changes and discoveries taking place in the fascinating world of record collecting is a relatively simple and ongoing procedure.

To ensure the greatest possible accuracy, our prices are averaged from data culled from all of the aforementioned sources.

We can never get too much input or have too many reviewers. We wholeheartedly encourage you to submit anything and everything you feel would be useful in building a better record guide. The quantity of information is not a factor — no amount is too little or too much.

The extensive list of names always found in the Acknowledgments chapter indicates the development of our board of advisors. We want *you* to join the team.

When preparing additions for *Records* please try to list records in generally the same format as is used in the guide: artist's name, label, selection number, title, year of release (if known), and price range. Since our database is stored alphabetically by artist, there is no need to reference *Records* book page numbers.

Please be very careful to submit information accurately, exactly as it appears on the label. Incomplete copying, especially of artist names, is the reason for embarrassing duplications in the guide. If the credit reads "Winston and the Aardvarks," list it that way. Do not simply tell us it's by the Aardvarks! This oversight can easily create duplicate listings — one under "W" and another under "A." Thank you.

About the Format

Our arrangement of listings is the most logical way to present so much information in a single volume. In use since 1984, our format is a proven success that offers unlimited potential for expansion.

The structure of *Records* allows us to include all of the following in one multipurpose guidebook. Included are 7-inch singles, both 33 rpm and 45 rpm; 78 rpm singles; 12-inch singles, both 33 and 45 rpm; 33 and 45 rpm EPs (extended plays); 78 rpm albums, 10-inch and 12-inch LPs (long plays); picture sleeves; promotional issues, picture discs, and more.

Once you locate an artist's section, their records are listed alphabetically by LABEL. Individual listings for each label appear in numerical order. In many instances, listings that are numerical by selection number are also chronological in sequence of release, but there are times when this is not the case. This format is especially helpful when using the guide along with an artist or label discography. Since the year of release is also provided for each listing, the reader knows immediately the pattern being followed by the label at the time.

Once familiar with the format, you'll find it easy and functional. See the "Sample" page for more information. New users should take time to familiarize themselves with the array. Reading all of the introductory pages should answer most reader questions.

The documenting and pricing of so many recordings is made possible by selectively economizing on space, listing individual titles when necessary but not when it's possible to group a number of equally valuable releases together on one line. Still, *any time* it is necessary to have a separate listing on a record in order to clearly and accurately present the information, we will do it. When a specific selection number is noted, whether listed as an exception or not, the title will also be given for easy identification.

One troubling facet of our approach is the artist who had one or more records of a value indicated for a particular label or series, but who also had one release (or more) that is a notable exception. Every effort has been made to separately document such exceptions, however, due to the sheer bulk of information herein, some may be missed. If you know of any, let us know about them.

You will find that the expansion of an artist's section, moving more toward individual rather than grouped listings, will be as commonplace in subsequent volumes of this series as with this edition. There are hundreds of artists with revised sections in this volume, listing many more individual titles and selection numbers than ever before. With some performers, it is, or perhaps soon will be, necessary to list every single record separately.

The ever-increasing number of pages in the guide are but one indication of how many artists' sections are expanded with individual title listings, over previous editions. Every year thousands of records are listed and priced individually that previously were not.

The decision to expand a section is partly based on reader input. Many examples of individual pricing in this edition can be directly attributed to a letter or call suggesting the need to do so.

Non-Rock Guidelines

Since some parameters are necessary to decide which non-rock performers to include in *Records,* the following guideline is used.

If a non-rock artist had either a single or album on the Billboard charts, all *vinyl* recordings known to us by that artist will be found in the guide. This allows for the most popular performers of country, western, jazz, personality, easy listening or other music style to be included, without trying to incorporate every record ever made into one book (although many want us to provide exactly that).

Though these are the parameters, exceptions are not uncommon. You will find many in this edition who had no charted recordings, but were chosen because of their overall significance in the collectors' marketplace. There are others included simply because we received requests from readers to add them. If there is someone you feel needs to be in this guide, who is not at this time, please write with that suggestion. We are always listening to your suggestions.

Remember, we're only talking about records and artists that are not particularly in demand here! If you have a *collectible* record not currently listed, we want it in the guide. What it sounds like or whether or not it charted anywhere is of no importance.

Grading and the Price Range

The pricing shown in this edition represents the price *range* for near-mint condition copies. The value range allows for the countless variables that affect record pricing. Often, the range will widen as the dollar amount increases, making a $500 to $1,000 range as logical as a $5.00 to $10.00 range.

One standardized system of record grading, used and endorsed by Osborne Enterprises as well as buyers and sellers worldwide, is as follows:

MINT: A *mint* item must be absolutely perfect. Nothing less can be honestly described as mint. Even brand new purchases can easily be flawed in some manner and not qualify as mint. To allow for tiny blemishes, the highest grade used in our record guide series is *near-mint.* An absolutely pristine mint, or still sealed, item may carry a slight premium above the near-mint range shown in this guide.

VERY GOOD: Records in *very good* condition should have a minimum of visual or audible imperfections, which should not detract much from your enjoyment of owning them. This grade is halfway between good and near-mint.

GOOD: Practically speaking, the grade of *good* means that the item may be good enough to fill a gap in your collection until a better copy becomes available. Good condition merchandise will show definite signs of wear and tear, probably evidencing that no protective care was given the item. Even so, records in good condition should play all the way through without skipping.

Most older records are going to be in something less than near-mint, or "excellent" condition. It is very important to use the near-mint price range in this guide only as a starting point in record appraising. Be honest about actual condition. Apply the same standards to the records you trade or sell as you would want one from whom you were buying to observe. Visual grading may be unreliable. Accurate grading may require playing the record (play-grading).

Use the following formula to determine values on lesser condition copies:

For **VERY GOOD** condition, figure about 25% to 50% of the near-mint price range given in this guide.

With many of the older pieces that cannot be found in near-mint, VG or VG+ may be the highest grade available. This significantly narrows the gap between VG and the near-mint range.

For **GOOD** condition, figure about 10% to 25% of the near-mint price range given in this guide.

It will surprise no one to learn that the gulch between good and mint is becoming a canyon. The drift toward widening the grading gap that began about 10 years ago shows no signs of slowing. To keep pace with this phenomenon, changes have been made in the guide to reflect the ever-increasing premiums being paid for mint condition items.

We know of no industry observers who forecast a reversal of this trend.

The 10-Point Grading System

Another recommended grading system is based on the often-used 10-point scale. Many feel that grading with the 10-point system allows for a more precise description of records that are in less than mint condition. Instead of vague terms, such as VG++ and M-- (is "very good plus, plus" the same as "mint minus, minus"?), assigning a specific number provides a more accurate classification of condition.

Most of the records you are likely to buy or sell will no doubt be graded somewhere between 5 and 10.

After using this system ourselves for a few years, agree that it is more precise. Customers who have purchased records from us have, without exception, been pleased with this way of grading.

10: MINT
9: NEAR-MINT
8: Better than VG but below NM
7: VERY GOOD
6: Better than G but below VG
5: GOOD
4: Better than POOR but below G
3: POOR
2: Really trashed
1: It hurts to think about it

This table shows how the 10-point system equates with the more established terms.

The Bottom Line

All the price guides and reporting of previous sales in the world won't change the fundamental fact that true value is nothing more than what one person is willing to accept and what another is prepared to pay. Actual value is based on scarcity and demand. It has always been that way and always will be.

A recording — or anything for that matter — can be 50 or 100 years old, but if no one wants it, the actual value will certainly be minimal. Just because something is old does not necessarily make it valuable. Someone has to want it!

On the other hand, a recent release, perhaps just weeks old, can have exceptionally high value if it has already become scarce and is by an artist whose following has created a demand. A record does not have to be old to be valuable.

Record Types Defined

With the inconsistent language used by the record companies in describing an EP or an LP, we've determined that a language guideline of some kind is needed in order to compile a useful record guide.

Some labels call a 10-inch album an "EP" if it has something less than the prescribed number of tracks found on their LPs. Others call an EP a "Little LP." A few companies have even created special names, associated only with their own label, for the basic record formats.

Having carefully analyzed all of this, we have adopted the following classifications of record configurations, which consistently categorize all types, sizes, and speeds in one section or another:

Singles: 78 rpm are those that play at 78 rpm. Though 78s are almost always 10-inch discs, a few 7-inch 78 rpm singles have been made.

Singles: 7-Inch can be either 45 rpm or 331/3 (always referred to simply as "33") speed singles. If a 7-inch single has more than one track on either side we consider it an EP.

Singles are priced strictly as a disc, with a separate section devoted to picture sleeves (which are often traded separately). If we know that picture sleeves exist for a given artist, a separate grouping will appear for the label, price, and applicable year of release. Should you know of picture sleeves not documented in this edition, please advise us accordingly.

There have been a few 5- and 6-inch discs manufactured, but for the sake of keeping singles with singles (and since we don't want to establish a "Singles: 5-inch" category), such curios will be tossed in with the 7-inch singles, with an explanatory note.

EPs: 7-Inch are 7-inch discs that have more than one track on one or both sides. Even if labeled an "EP" by the manufacturer, if it's pressed on a 10- or 12-inch disc it's an LP in our book. Unless so noted, all EPs are presumed to be accompanied by their original covers, in a condition about equal to the disc. An appropriate adjustment in value should be made to compensate for any differences in this area. Exceptions, such as EPs with paper sleeves or no sleeve at all, are designated as such when known.

LPs: 10/12-Inch is self-explanatory. The only possible confusion that might exist here is with 12-inch singles. If it's 10 or 12 inches in diameter, and labeled, priced, and marketed as a 12-inch single (Maxi-Single, etc.), then that's where you'll find it in this guide, regardless of its speed. Often, 12-inch singles will have a 12-inch die-cut cardboard sleeve or jacket; but many have covers that are exactly like LP jackets, with photos of the artist, etc. Unless so noted, all LPs are presumed to be accompanied by their original covers, in a condition about equal to the disc. An appropriate adjustment in value should be made to compensate for any differences in this area.

Other record type headings used such as Picture Sleeves, Promotional Singles, etc., should be clear.

Cross-Referencing and Multiple Artists' Recordings

The cross-referencing in *Records* should provide the easiest possible method of discovering other sections of the book where a particular artist is featured or appears in any capacity.

We've tried to hold to a minimum unexplained cross-references, opting to concentrate more on those cross-references for which the reader can effortlessly understand the rationalization. Minimized is the unnecessary duplication of cross-references. For example, it is not necessary to list every group in which Eric Clapton played under each and every one of those sections. What we've done is simply indicate "Also see Eric Clapton," where you will find complete cross-referencing to all other sections where he appears.

Some artists have several sections, one right after the other, because they were involved in different duets and/or compilation releases. In such instances, the primary artist (whose section begins first) is not cross-referenced after each and every subsequent section, but only after the last section wherein that artist is involved. This in effect blocks the beginning and the end of releases pertaining to that performer. If you don't find the listing you're searching for right away, remember to check the sections that follow, as the artist may have been joined by someone else on that recording causing it to appear in a separate section.

Cross-references in bold typeface are charted artists; those in normal typeface did not chart.

Artist headings and resultant cross-referencing appear in two different formats in this guide. For example:

LEWIS, Jerry Lee, Carl Perkins & Johnny Cash

Listings under this type heading are those wherein the artists perform *together*. Often these releases will also include solo tracks by one or all of the performers in addition to those on which they collaborate.

LEWIS, Jerry Lee / Carl Perkins / Johnny Cash

This heading, with names separated by a slash, indicates there are selections on *separate* tracks by each of the named artists, but they do not perform together.

ISLEY BROTHERS & DAVE "BABY" CORTEZ

This heading, with all names in upper case letters and no slash, indicates the artists perform *together*.

ISLEY BROTHERS / Brooklyn Bridge

This heading, with names after a slash that are in upper and lower case, indicates artists that perform *separately* — usually each being heard on one side of the disc.

Though exceptions do exist, the general parameter set for such releases is four different performers or less. Compilations containing five or more individual performers are deemed as Various Artists issues, to be dealt with in a separate publication.

Whenever more than one act is featured on a record, cross-references appear under all of the other artists on the disc, who have a section of their own in this edition, directing the reader to the location of the listing in question. If you're looking up a record with a different artist on each side, and you don't find it under one artist, be sure to try looking for the flip-side artist.

Not all releases containing more than one artist are given separate sections. In some cases it makes more sense to include such records in the primary section for the most important artist. We will rarely create separate sections for multiple artist discs when the other performers on the issue do not have a section of their own in this edition.

To illustrate this point, Hank Williams Jr. had several duet issues with Lois Johnson; Gene Ammons shared an LP with Sonny Stitt. Even though Johnson and Stitt do not have individual sections in this book (they didn't make the Billboard pop singles or LPs charts), such recordings may be important to collectors of Williams and Ammons. For that reason, they are included in their respective artist's section.

On the other hand, a duet by Brenda Lee and Willie Nelson requires a separate section, since either or both may be of interest to the researcher. Also, both are individually pop-charted artists. There are a few isolated exceptions to this policy, simply because every section in this edition was separately prepared and customized in whatever manner necessary to provide the user with the most usable information.

Promotional Issues

Separate documenting and pricing of promotional issues is, in most cases, unnecessary. Because most of the records issued during the primary four decades covered in this guide were simultaneously pressed for promotional purposes, a separate listing of them would theoretically double the size of an already large book.

Rather, we've chosen to list promotional copies separately when we have the knowledge that an alternate price (either higher or lower) consistently is asked for them. For the most part, promos of everyday releases will fall into the same range — usually toward the high end — given for store stock copies. Some may stretch the range slightly, but not enough to warrant separate pricing. Premiums may be paid for promos that have different (longer, shorter, differently mixed, etc.) versions of tunes, even though the artist may not be particularly hot in the collecting marketplace.

When identified as a "Promotional issue," we are usually describing a record with a special promotional ("Not For Sale," "Dee Jay Copy," etc.) label or sleeve, and not a *designate* promo. Designate promos are identical to commercial releases, except they have been rubber or mechanically stamped, stickered, written on by hand, or in some way altered to accommodate their use for promotional purposes. There are very few designate promos listed in this edition, and those that are (such as in the Elvis Presley section) are clearly identified as such.

Colored Vinyl Pressings

Records known to exist on both black vinyl and colored vinyl (vinyl is the term used regardless of whether it's polystyrene or vinyl) are listed separately since there is usually a value difference. However, some colored vinyl releases were never pressed on black vinyl, and since there is no way to have the record other than on colored vinyl, it may or may not be specifically noted as being on colored vinyl.

Because the true color of some colored vinyl pressings may be a judgment call, we once used "colored vinyl" to indicate discs that are not standard black vinyl.

We are gradually replacing "colored" with the specific color used. If you know the exact color of any records still shown in the guide as "colored," please send us that information.

Foreign Releases

Originally, *Records* listed only U.S. releases. Now, there are many exceptions. A handful of records that were widely distributed in the United States or sold via widespread U.S. advertising, even though manufactured outside the country, are included. Such anomalies would appear only in the more sophisticated sections of the guide.

There are also numerous Canadian releases included, with more being added to each new edition. The collectors' market for out-of-print Canadian records is mostly a U.S. market. The trading of rare Canadian discs between Canadian collectors is not quite as widespread as those instances that involve a U.S. buyer or seller. Yet it is from Canadian collectors that we receive most of our information on those releases, and we expect to have more listed in future editions.

Thanks to a team of Canadian collectors — especially Peter McCullough — our number of Canadian listings increases with each edition.

Beyond North America, there are millions of overseas releases with collector value to fans in those countries as well as to stateside collectors. Unfortunately, the tremendous volume of material and the variances in pricing make it impossible to comprehensively document and price imports.

Bootlegs and Counterfeits

Bootleg and counterfeit records are not priced in this guide, though a few are cited, along with information on how to distinguish them from an original.

For the record, a bootleg recording is one illegally manufactured, usually containing material not previously available in a legitimate form. Often, with the serious collector in mind, a boot will package previously issued tracks that have achieved some degree of value or scarcity. If the material is easily available, legally, then there would be no gain for the bootlegger.

The counterfeit record is one manufactured as close as possible in sound and appearance to the source disc from which it was inspired. Not all counterfeits were created to fool an unsuspecting buyer into thinking he or she was buying an authentic issue, but some were. Many were designated in some way, such as a slight marking or variance, so as not to allow them to be confused with originals. Such a fake record primarily exists to fill a gap in the collector's file until the real thing comes along.

With both bootleg and with counterfeit records, the appropriate and deserving recipients of royalties are, of course, denied remuneration for their works.

Since most of the world's valuable records have been counterfeited, it is always a good idea to consult with an expert when there is any doubt. The trained eye can usually spot a fake.

This is not to say *unauthorized* releases are excluded from the book. There are many legitimate releases that are unauthorized by one entity or another; records that are neither bootleg nor counterfeit. Unauthorized does not necessarily mean illegal.

Group Names and Personnel

One problem that we'll never completely solve involves the many instances where groups using the exact same name are lumped together with other groups who are completely different. Whenever known to be different, these groups are given separate sections; however, there are times when we simply do not know. If you can shed any light in this area, we'd love to hear from you. Thanks to readers, many such groups have been sorted since our last edition.

The listing sequence for artists using the same name is chronological. Thus the ABC group, Silk, who had a release in 1969, is listed ahead of the Philadelphia International group, Silk, that first recorded in 1979.

As often as not, there will have been group members that have come and gone over the years. Reflecting this turnover in our listing of members' names may cause some confusion, when the reader sees 12 different members shown for a group named the Five Satins. We've tried, whenever possible, to list the original line-up first, followed by later members. Also, the lead singer is usually listed first. We welcome additional information on group members from readers. One of the most reliable sources of this data is the LP covers, which often list members. If you can fill in the members' names on any groups where we don't list that information, we'll see that it gets into our next edition.

When group members' names are given, there is a likelihood that not all of the members named appear on *all* of the releases documented. It is also possible that not all of the members named ever recorded with all of the other members shown at the same time.

When names are given for a solo performer, those named are likely noteworthy sidemen.

As more and more group members are named in future editions, there will be added cross-referencing to reflect the constant shuffle of performers from one group to another.

Parenthetical Notes

Some of the information that may be found in parentheses following the artist heading has already been covered. However, other uses of this space include:

• Complete artist and group or artist and band names. Some artists were shown as being with one group on a few releases, solo on some, and with yet another group on other issues. We've tried to present the information the way, or ways, that it is shown on the actual record label. When encased in quote marks, it means that this particular wording or credit variation is exactly as shown on the label.

• Variations of spelling or names for the same artist. With some artists, it's convenient to have everything in one section; however, when it is illogical to combine listings, perhaps because the performer was popular under more than one name (such as Johnny Cymbal and Derek), you'll find individual sections for each name. Cross-references will be used to help you locate things easily. Having "Kenneth Rogers" in parentheses is not intended to mean that Kenneth is Kenny's real name. Rather, we're letting you know that on at least one of his records he is credited as Kenneth Rogers instead of Kenny Rogers. Same goes for Tony Perkins, who may also be credited as "Anthony Perkins." We may at times provide real names of artists, but only when we feel they need to be given. While we have no desire to give the real names of everyone who has recorded under a pseudonym, there are times when you do need this information. This is especially true when they have also recorded under their real name or when more than one person has recorded under the same pseudonym. To help sort things out, we will, when known, give you the real name of someone who has recorded under a nom de guerre, such as Guitar Slim (a.k.a. Johnny Winter).

• Names of guest performers who may or may not be credited on the actual label, but who we feel you should know were involved in some of the records listed in that section.

Oldies Labels and Reissues

An effort has been made to include many "oldies" or reissue records in the guide. Though many reissues of this type are of no value beyond their current retail cost, some are. Look at some of the early RCA Victor Gold Standard Series Elvis Presley releases, for example. Once in a blue moon a tune will turn up in true stereo on a reissue label that was previously hard to find in stereo. Otherwise, it's just our desire to report comprehensively on all artists that prompted the listing of reissues.

The main reason we've included these reissues is to eliminate confusion, especially among younger collectors. Often, they'll discover a hit tune on a label like Lana or Lost-Nite, and think it's an original release predating the label that had the hit.

If there are reissues numbered as part of a label's standard release series, and not documented in this edition, please tell us about them.

Using This Guide: Some Additional Points

• A few of the more prolific labels with lengthy names are abbreviated in this guide. They are:

ABC-PAR .... ABC-Paramount
GNP .... GNP/Crescendo
MFSL .... Mobile Fidelity Sound Lab
RCA .... RCA Victor
SSS/SUN .... Shelby Singleton's Sun
(Sometimes shown as SSS INT'L.)
20TH FOX .... 20th Century-Fox
U.A. .... United Artists
W.B. .... Warner Brothers

Notes: The short-lived (1959) Warner records label is shown as "Warner." Excelsior's old United Artist (singular) label is spelled out. The late-'60s Minnesota label "UA" is not shown with periods, as is United Artists. Records on the old Memphis Sun label are of course identified simply as "Sun."

The alphabetization in *Records* makes finding any artist or label easy, but a few guidelines may speed the process along for you:

• Names that are simply letters (and are not intended to be pronounced as a word) are found at the beginning of the listings under each letter of the alphabet (i.e., **ABC, AC-DC, GQ, SSQ,** etc.). The same rule applies to acronyms (i.e. **B.R.A.T.T.S.,** etc.) and to initialisms (i.e. **MFSB,** etc.). If a series of letters that stand for a longer name can be pronounced as a word, such as "Bratts," it is an acronym. If not, as with MFSB, it is an initialism. When known, we'll parenthetically tell you what the abbreviation represents.

• Names are listed in the alphabetical order of the first word. This means you'll find **Rock Squad** before **Rocket.** Hyphenated words are looked upon as whole words (i.e., **Mello-Kings** is treated the same as **Mellokings**). Divided names or names with Spanish articles (i.e., **De Vorzon, Del Satins, El Dorados; Las Vegas, Los Lobos,** etc.) are alphabetically listed as though they were a one-word name.

• Possessive names precede similarly spelled names that are not possessive. For example, **KNIGHT'S** would be found before **KNIGHTS,** regardless of what follows the comma.

• It is flabbergasting to discover how many of the people responsible for crediting bands and groups on record labels have no understanding (or schooling) regarding when to use a possessive apostrophe. This is by far the most frequently found mistake on labels — one which we refuse to blindly copy for our artist headings, lest anyone think that we don't know better. However, for those labels that do credit groups like — to use an actual example — the Capitols (on Gateway) as **CAPITOL'S**, we will indicate that senseless variation under the artist's heading, in parentheses.

• The articles "A" or "The" have been dropped from group names in this guide even though they may appear on the records as part of the name.

• With record labels, listings appear in 1) alphabetical, 2) numerical, and 3) chronological order. Selection prefixes are generally not used (they make it more difficult to scan the numbers) unless they are necessary for identification. With some artists (Beatles, Elvis, etc.) it is essential at times because of constant reissues.

• Some sections make use of the label prefixes to sort things out, but most use a number series. If the numbers are duplicated by the label, or if any of a variety of confusing similarities exist, we may resort to the prefixes for clarity.

• Regarding 78 rpms. As to which late '50s and early '60s tunes came out on 78s, we cannot safely assume much of anything. If you know of 78s from the end of the 78 rpm era that we do not list, please advise us accordingly. We would be especially happy to learn of charted hits issued after 1957.

• Whenever possible, records priced in the $25.00 to $35.00 range and up are listed individually with label, selection number, and title.

• Anytime we find that the monaural or the stereo issue of a particular record is in need of a separate listing (because there is a price difference for one that is outside the boundaries of the price range of the other), we will gladly provide same. If there is but one listing, this indicates that we have no reason to believe there is much difference in the two forms. A little application of the known variables will help in this area. For example, if the range is $20.00 to $40.00 for a 1960 LP and you know that the stereo issue is in true stereo, it's safe to place the mono at the low end of the range ($20.00 to $30.00) and the stereo at the high end ($30.00 to $40.00). The calculation may be reversed for late '60s and for most electronically reprocessed issues.

• Singles picture sleeves are listed and priced separately, when known. However, EPs and LPs are presumed to have their original covers. Evaluate the condition of EP and LP covers just as critically as you would the discs, making appropriate allowances for flaws.

• We believe the year or years of release given in the far-right column to be accurate. If we don't know the correct year, the column is left blank. In some cases the record may have been released in one year and debuted on the nation's music charts the following year. This is common for year-end issues and explains why you may remember a hit as being from 1966, although we list it as a 1965 release.

• Entering the 21st century created a slight problem with the two digit indication of year of issue: how to know at a glance whether "01" is 1901 or 2001. We therefore indicate present century years using all four digits (i.e. 2000, 2001, etc.).

• If you have delta (Δ) numbers for records we do not have release years for, please send them to us. From those numbers we can usually determine year of issue. Delta numbers are found etched in the record's vinyl trail-off area.

• When multiple years are indicated, such as "64-66," it means the records described on that line spanned the years 1964 through 1966. They may have had one issue in 1964 and another in 1966, or may have had eight releases during those years. It does *not* mean that we believe the release came out sometime between 1964 and 1966. If the exact year is not known but the decade of release is, then we will provide that ('50s, '60s, '70s, etc.)

• When a selection number series, such as a "4000 series," is shown, it includes numbers 4000 through 4999. If it were meant to indicate only 4000 through 4099, then separate listings would be found for 4100, 4200, etc.

• Goofy as it seems, a few records have been issued with neither artist nor label name shown. You will find this on both singles and albums. These items are filed here by title.

• There are hundreds of multi-disc albums priced in the guide, though some may not be identified as having more than one disc. They are, nevertheless, included in the price range. Feel free to inform us of any unidentified multi-disc sets you catch.

• Mislabeled records are usually no big deal. We constantly hear from folks who think they have struck gold because one of their records has its labels screwed up in some manner. Either they are reversed, with each side bearing the label intended for the other side, or mislabeled altogether with a label from an entirely different record — perhaps even by a completely different artist. Generally, production errors of this kind do not increase value. They may, in some cases, make the disc even less attractive to a collector. For those very, very few exceptions, the necessary information is already noted in *Records*.

• While this guide makes no attempt to fully document gospel recordings per se, the wonderful, soulful harmony of groups like the Swan Silvertones and Soul Stirrers make their records popular among rhythm and blues collectors. For that reason they are included. Others are being added on an as-requested basis.

• To conserve space, when the same title is listed as both 45 and 78, we may not list the title in both sections if it requires more than one line. You may therefore find only the label name in the 78 section, whereas the complete number and title will be in the 45 section.

• In most cases, we have no specifics regarding which 78s came on both black and colored plastic. Lacking comments to the contrary, all 78s are presumed to be black plastic.

• With all recently added listings, when two (or more) releases came out in the same calendar year, a note reading "First issue" will indicate which came first. Most examples of this occurred with independent labels whose records got picked up by one of the major companies, and issued on their own label. Of course, if the years of release differ from one label to the other there is no need for the note. As we run across them, we will make a similar notation to the older listings in the guide.

• When an artist is shown as making their chart debut on the LP charts, but we list no albums and only singles by them — it is because we have yet to confirm any *vinyl* albums. If you find vinyl LPs which we do not list, please let us know of them.

Guidelines for Pricing Records Not in This Edition

Since it is impossible for us to include *every* record ever produced, a few guidelines may assist you in evaluating records *not found* in this edition:

• Rock Singles: Most pre-1970 Rock and Roll, R&B, Rockabilly, and Blues singles are in the guide. We would like to know of any that are missing so they can be added. There are too many variables to generalize regarding pricing recordings in these fields of music. Rock singles from the '70s to present are seldom going to sell for over $10.00, with most being available for less than $5.00.

• Most pre-1970 Rock and Roll, R&B, Rockabilly, and Blues albums are in the guide. We would like to know of any that are missing so they can be added. There are too many variables to generalize regarding pricing recordings in these fields of music. Rock LPs from the '70s to present can usually be found for $10.00 to $20.00. Those from 1980 to present should be under $10.00.

• Pop Singles on 45 rpm: Most Pop (i.e. non-Rock) vocal and instrumental 45s from the '50s are available for under $15.00. From many Rock-oriented dealers, Pop singles can often be bought for under $10.00. The few exceptions are likely to be folks with charted hits, and those will be found in the guide.

• Pop music singles from the '60s to present are seldom going to sell for over $10.00. Many are available for $3.00 to $6.00.

• Pop Singles on 78 rpm: Most are available for under $10.00. Albums of 78s — usually in a gatefold binder with individual paper sleeves — will vary, but most are in the $10.00 to $30.00 range.

• Pop Long Play Albums: From the '50s, 12-inch Pop LPs generally are found for under $40.00. Ten-inch LPs may go for up to $75.00

• Most Pop LPs from the '60s and '70s can usually be found for $10.00 to $20.00. Those from 1980 to present should be under $10.00.

• Pop Extended Play Albums: Pop EPs are scarce, as are all EPs, but many are still very reasonable. Most can be found for $10.00 to $20.00, often for even less.

• Easy Listening Music: The average easy listening record will be worth about half of the price ranges shown for Pop Music. Some exceptions, with higher values, are LPs by certain lounge music performers and virtually any with female models pictured in exotic settings and in alluring poses on their covers.

• Country Music on 45 rpm: Most Country vocal and instrumental 45s from the '50s are available for under $15.00; many for less than $10.00. Obvious exceptions are any that border on Rockabilly. Don't take any Country record for granted! Play both sides of every disc, as it is always possible you'll discover a great country rocker.

• Country music singles from the '60s to present are seldom going to sell for more than $10.00. Many are available for $4.00 to $6.00.

• Country Music on 78 rpm: Most of the Country 78s should fall into the $10.00 to $40.00 range. There are, however, many older 78s with prices well into three figures; some even higher.

• Country Music Long Play Albums: From the '50s, 12-inch LPs generally are found for around $30.00 to $60.00. Ten-inch LPs may go for from $50 to $100. As always, the range will vary widely depending on the following and collectibility of the artist.

• Most Country LPs from the '60s to present can be found for $15.00 to $25.00. Again, there are exceptions.

• Country Music Extended Play Albums: Very, very few Country music EPs were big sellers, which means nearly all are rare. You may find they are in the same price range as the '50s LPs above; some will bring even more than LPs from the same time period.

• Jazz Singles on 45 rpm: Most Jazz 45s from the '50s are available for under $15.00. The few exceptions are likely to be artists with charted hits, which will be found in the guide.

• Jazz singles from the '60s to present are seldom going to sell for more than $10.00. Many are available for $3.00 to $6.00.

• Jazz Singles on 78 rpm: Most Jazz 78s are available for under $20.00. Until the late '40s or early '50s, an *album* was a gatefold binder with a number of 78s, usually in individual paper sleeves. Prices on these Jazz albums will vary, but most will fall in the $25.00 to $75.00 range.

- Jazz Long Play Albums: From the '50s, 12-inch jazz LPs generally are found for under $50 to $100. Ten-inch LPs may go for $75 to $200.
- Most Jazz LPs from the '60s to present can still be found for $20.00 to $40.00.
- Jazz Extended Play Albums: As with Country, very few Jazz EPs were big sellers. While all are rare, there is not as much demand for them from jazz collectors as for long-play albums. Of course, outside Jazz circles there is virtually no demand for them. You may find they are, in general, worth little more than the prices shown above for Jazz singles from the same time period.
- Comedy, Personality, and Spoken Word Long Play Albums: From the '50s and '60s, 12-inch Comedy and Personality (not Soundtrack or Original Cast) LPs generally are found for under $20.00 to $40.00.
- Most Comedy and Personality LPs from the '70s to present can be had for $10.00 to $15.00.
- If we really wanted to add another 100,000 or so listings, we could open the door wider to pre-war Blues 78s. While that is not possible, you will indeed find quite a number of pre-war Blues records in the guide, but that's usually because those artists either charted or continued to record during the post-war years and are included here for that reason.
- In summary, there is no way these few paragraphs can constitute a complete price guide for the millions of non-Rock records that exist. If such generic generalizations were possible, while guaranteeing unerring accuracy, the entire price guide would be about ten pages. It is the exceptions that make record pricing so complicated and difficult to document. Our goal here is simply to provide a rough idea of the value of recordings that are outside the parameters of the guide.

What to Expect When Selling Your Records to a Dealer

As most know, there is a noteworthy difference between the prices reported in this guide and the prices that one can expect a dealer to pay when buying records for resale. Unless a dealer is buying for a personal collection and without thoughts of resale, he or she is simply not in a position to pay full price. Dealers work on a percentage basis, largely determined by the total dollar investment, quality, and quantity of material offered as well as the financial condition and inventory of the dealer at the time.

Another very important consideration is the length of time it will take the dealer to recover at least the amount of the original investment. The greater the demand for the stock and the better the condition, the quicker the return and therefore the greater the percentage that can be paid. Our experience has shown that, day-in and day-out, most dealers will pay from 25% to 50% of *guide* prices. And that's assuming they are planning to resell at guide prices. If they traditionally sell below guide, that will be reflected in what they can pay for stock.

If you have records to sell, it would be wise to check with several shops. In doing so you'll begin to get a good idea of the value of your collection to a dealer.

Also, consult the Directory of Buyers and Sellers in this guide for the names of many dealers who not only might be interested in buying, but from whom many collectible records are available for purchase.

Buy and Sell on the Internet

More and more folks are accessing the Internet for every conceivable purpose, including buying and selling stuff.

Being able to shop and sell online from one's home is understandably becoming more popular every month. If you have internet access, and have yet to explore electronic buying and selling, you should consider joining the fun.

Auction sites are plentiful; however, ones for those who prefer set prices are not.

To meet that need, we created Osborne Collectibles. Our site provides a surprisingly inexpensive way to offer collectibles to the online world.

All terms and conditions are self-explanatory. Log on soon.

www.JerryOsborne.com/collectibles.htm

Concluding Thoughts

The purpose of this guide is to report as accurately as possible the most recent prices asked and paid for records within the area of its coverage. There are two key words here that deserve emphasis: **Guide** and **Report**.

We cannot stress enough that this book is only a guide. There always have been and always will be instances of records selling well above and below the prices shown within these pages. These extremes are recognized in the final averaging process; but it's still important to understand that just because we've reported a 30-year-old record as having a $25.00 to $50.00 near-mint value, doesn't mean that a collector of that material should be hesitant to pay $75.00 for it. How badly he or she wants it and how often it's possible to purchase it *at any price* should be the prime factors considered, not that we last reported it at a lower price. Of course, we'd like to know about sales of this sort so that the next edition can reflect the new pricing information.

We may report a record for $500 to $1,000, which may have been an accurate appraisal at press time. However, before the new edition hits the streets, the price might be $1,000 to $2,000. One or two transactions and six months later it jumps to $2,000 to $4,000. By the time we're close to the following year's guide, this same disc may be considered a bargain at $5,000.

At that point, people may look at the book and wonder how we could show $500 to $1,000 for a $5,000 record. "Our price is a joke," you'll hear. And at that point it is.

As in other areas of living, inflation is an undeniable factor in rapidly rising prices of music collectibles

Another component in the inflation equation, however, is the trend for auctioneers to pick the high end of the price range shown in the guide — and make that the *minimum* bid.

Anyone wanting that particular record will likely end up paying more than the posted minimum amount.

Then the results get reported to us.

Some dealers send us only the winning bids, others also submit an average of bids received. A few even send along all of the bid amounts they get.

When we learn *only* of the winning bid, we'll do one of two things:

1. If the item is extremely rare and another sale is unlikely any time soon, we will probably position the winning bid in the middle of our price range. This allows for price movement in either direction.

2. If the item is not so scarce, and other sales are likely, we'll put the winning bid at the high end of the range. This usually provides a realistic price range, since the winning bid is by no means the medium offering — merely the top dollar bid. The average sale price is going to be something less.

Regardless of what the range is in our next edition, the cycle begins anew: a new auction is held, using our top price as the new minimum bid.

We mention this truism, not to infer there is anything unethical about the practice, but merely to share one explanation for constantly rising prices.

Meanwhile, please keep in mind that any of the world's more valuable records now have the potential to be worth considerably more in the near future than on the day when work ended on this edition. The key is simply this: Is it a money record in the first place? If so, remain open to surprising price increases.

Our objective is to report and reflect record marketplace activity — not to *establish* prices. For that reason, and if given the choice, we'd prefer to be a bit behind the times rather than ahead. With this guide being regularly revised, it will never be long before the necessary changes are reported within these pages.

We encourage record companies, artist management organizations, talent agencies, publicists, and performers to make certain that we are on the active mailing list for new release information, press releases, bios, publicity photos, and anything pertaining to recordings.

There is an avalanche of helpful information in this guide to aid the collector in determining what is valuable and what may not be worth fooling with.

Still, the wise fan will also keep abreast of current trends and news, either online or through the pages of publications devoted to his or her favorite forms of music.

SAMPLE LISTING

Artist's primary heading.

FLAMINGOS ***R&B '56***

(With Red Holloway's Orchestra)

May also be shown on some releases as ...

Chart or charts and year this artist FIRST appeared on Billboard. For this group, they first hit the R&B chart in 1956.

Singles: 78 rpm

CHANCE (1133 " If I Can't Have You")............... 100-200 53
CHANCE (1145 "Golden Teardrops")............... 200-300 53
PARROT (808 "Dream of a Lifetime") 100-150 54
PARROT (812 "I'm Yours") 150-200 55

Singles: 7-inch

CHANCE (1133 "If I Can't Have You")............... 500-750 53
(Black vinyl.)
CHANCE (1133 "If I Can't Have You")............ 1000-2000 53
(Red vinyl.)
CHANCE (1145 "Golden Teardrops")............... 500-750 53
(Black vinyl.)
CHANCE (1145 "Golden Teardrops")............ 2000-3000 53
(Red vinyl.)

Near-mint price range.

Helpful explanatory notes.

END (1035 "Please Wait for Me")........................... 30-50 58
(Title later changed to *Lovers Never Say Goodbye*.)
END (1035 "Lovers Never Say Goodbye") 10-20 58
END (1046 "I Only Have Eyes for You"/ "Goodnight Sweetheart")... 20-30 59
END (1046 "I Only Have Eyes for You"/ "At the Prom").. 10-20 59
(Note different flip.)
END (1046 "I Only Have Eyes for You") 40-50 59
(Stereo.)

Year or years of release.

Label names, selection numbers, and titles.

PARROT (808 "Dream of a Lifetime") 500-1000 54
(Black vinyl.)
PARROT (808 "Dream of a Lifetime") 2000-3000 54
(Red vinyl.)
PARROT (811 "I Really Don't Want to Know")... 1500-2500 55
(Black vinyl.)
PARROT (811 "I Really Don't Want to Know")... 5000-7000 55
(Red vinyl.)

EPs: 7-inch

END (205 "Goodnight Sweetheart") 40-60 59
(Monaural.)
END (205 "Goodnight Sweetheart") 50-85 59
(Stereo.)

Category or type of items listed in each section.

LPs: 10/12-inch

CHECKER (1433 "Flamingos") 75-125 59
(Monaural.)
CHECKER (3005 "Flamingos") 25-50 66
(Stereo.)
END (304 "Flamingo Serenade")........................... 50-100 59
(Monaural.)
END (304 "Flamingo Serenade")........................... 75-125 59
(Stereo.)
END (316 "The Sound of the Flamingos") 40-60 62
(Monaural.)
END (316 "The Sound of the Flamingos") 50-75 62
(Stereo.)

Members: Sollie McElroy; John Carter; Zeke Carey; Jake Carey; Paul Wilson; Nate Nelson; Tommy Hunt; Terry Johnson.

Also see HUNT, Tommy
Also see McELROY, Sollie
Also see NELSON, Nate

Names of group members and/or recording session participants.

References to other, related, sections in the guide.

A

A. DEBBIE

Singles: 7-inch

J-RUDE (1401 "Here Is My Heart")...... 100-200 65
(Identification number shown since no selection number is used.)

A GO-GOS

Singles: 7-inch

DB (3665 "Just a Little Bit of Soul")......... 15-25 65
PEE VEE (2000 "Shake & Fingerpop").... 15-25 66
Members: Dave Winter; Chuck Wisner; Terry Berkheimer; Harold Winter.

AC/DC *LP '77*

Singles: 12-inch

ATLANTIC...8-12 79
(Promotional only.)

Singles: 7-inch

ATCO...5-10 77
ATLANTIC...3-6 78-83

Promotional Singles

ATCO (7068 "It's a Long Way to the Top".. 15-25 77
ATCO (7086 "Problem Child"................. 15-25 77
ATLANTIC (3499 "Rock 'N' Roll Damnation")...................................... 10-20 78
ATLANTIC (3553 "Whole Lotta Rosie")... 10-20 79
ATLANTIC (3617 "Highway to Hell")........ 10-20 79
ATLANTIC (3644 "Touch Too Much").........8-12 80
ATLANTIC (3761 "You Shook Me All Night Long")...8-12 80
ATLANTIC (3787 "Back in Black")..............5-10 80
ATLANTIC (3894 "Let's Get It Up")............5-10 81
ATLANTIC (89136 "Heatseeker")................3-5 88
ATLANTIC (89614 "Jailbreak")...................5-10 82
ATLANTIC (89774 "Guns for Hire")............5-10 83

Picture Sleeves

ATLANTIC (3894 "Let's Get It Up")..............4-8 81
ATLANTIC (89774 "Guns for Hire")..............4-8 83

LPs: 10/12-inch

ATCO (142 "High Voltage")...................... 15-25 76
ATCO (151 "Let There Be Rock").............. 15-25 77
ATLANTIC (001 "Live from the Atlantic Studios").. 20-30 77
(Promotional issue only.)
ATLANTIC (562 "Interviews").................. 15-20 83
ATLANTIC...5-10 81-88
EAST/WEST...5-10 '90s
Members: Bon Scott; Angus Young; Mark Evans; Malcolm Young; Phil Rudd; Cliff Williams; Brian Johnson; Chris Slade; Simon Wright.
Also see DIO, Ronnie

A-C D-C CURRENT SWINGERS

Singles: 7-inch

J-GEMS (415 "Time to Dance")............... 10-15 63

A.F.O. EXECUTIVES & TAMI LYNN

LPs: 10/12-inch

A.F.O. (0002 "A Compendium")............. 75-125
Also see LYNN, Tami

AF-TABS

Singles: 7-inch

JET.. 10-20 65
FIVE STAR...5-10 69

A-440

Singles: 7-inch

CINEMA (006 "When I Get Out")................8-12 67
CINEMA (008 "Santa Claus Is Comin' Yeah")...8-12 67
SOMA (103 "It's Just Your Mind")........... 10-15 67

ARS NOVA

Singles: 7-inch

ATLANTIC...5-10 69
ELEKTRA..5-10 68

LPs: 10/12-inch

ATLANTIC.. 10-15 69
ELEKTRA... 10-15 68
Members: Mavry Baker; Sam Brown; Wyatt Day; Bill Fowell; Joe Hunt; Art Koenig; Jimmy Owens; Giovanni Papalia; John Pierson; Jonathan Raskin.

AARDVARK

Singles: 7-inch

ZOOLOGICAL GARDENS (80606 "Wish I Could Tell You")...30-40 67

AARDVARKS

Singles: 7-inch

BELL (1059 "Josephine").........................20-30 65
FORTE (2021 "Let's Move Together")......10-15 67
TALPA (68101 "Let's Move Together").....10-15 68
Member: David Waggoner.
Also see CROW
Also see SOUTH 40

AARDVARKS

Singles: 7-inch

ARCH...15-25 '60s
FENTON (2090 "I Don't Believe")............20-30 66
VARK (2058 "I'm Higher Than I'm Down")..30-50 66

AARON, Lee

LPs: 10/12-inch

VISUAL VINYL (1001 "Lee Aaron Project")..30-40 82
(Picture disc.)

ABANDONED

Singles: 7-inch

ABANDONED ("Come Along Mary")....100-200 '60s
(Selection number not known.)

ABBA *P&R/LP '74*

Singles: 12-inch

ATLANTIC...4-8 77-79

Singles: 7-inch

ATLANTIC...3-6 75-82

Picture Sleeves

ATLANTIC...3-6 77-82

LPs: 10/12-inch

ATLANTIC (Except 300)........................10-20 74-84
ATLANTIC (300 "Abba")..........................15-25 78
(Promotional issue only.)
CBS INT'L...8-12 80
EPIC...5-8 79
K-TEL...8-10 80
NAUTILUS (20 "Arrival")........................15-25 82
(Half-speed mastered.)
SILVER EAGLE......................................8-10 84
Members: Anni-frid Lyngstad; Bjorn Ulvaeus; Benny Andersson; Agnetha Faltskog.

ABBA / Spinners / Firefall / England Dan & John Ford Coley

EPs: 7-inch

W.B. SPECIAL PRODUCTS.......................5-10 78
(Coca-Cola/Burger King promotional issue. Issued with paper sleeve.)
Also see ABBA
Also see SPINNERS

ABBEY TAVERN SINGERS *P&R '66*

Singles: 7-inch

HBR (498 "Off to Dublin in the Green")......5-10 66
V.I.P. (25048 "Off to Dublin in the Green").5-10 66

EPs: 7-inch

V.I.P. (60402 "Off to Dublin in the Green")..15-25 66

LPs: 10/12-inch

V.I.P. (402 "Off to Dublin in the Green")...30-60 66

ABBOTT, Billy, & Jewels *P&R '63*

Singles: 7-inch

PARKWAY (874 "Groovy Baby").............15-20 63
PARKWAY (905 "It Isn't Fair")...............10-15 64

ABBOTT, Jay

Singles: 7-inch

SULTAN (1001 "Latanya").......................10-20 60
BOMBAY (1313 "Latanya").......................10-20 60

ABBOTT, Tony

Singles: 7-inch

DEB (232 "Sidewalks of New York Cha Cha")..15-25 59
WYE (1005 "Sidewalks of New York Cha Cha")..8-15 61

ABBOTT & COSTELLO

Singles: 78 rpm

DECCA (187 "Jack and the Beanstalk").....8-12 52
ENTERPRISE (501 "Who's on First").......15-25

Singles: 7-inch

CAMPBELL (1001 "Who's on First")..........5-10 60
DECCA (187 "Jack & the Beanstalk")......10-20 52

Picture Sleeves

DECCA (187 "Jack & the Beanstalk")......25-40 52
(Sleeve for either 45 or 78 rpm.)
Members: Bud Abbott; Lou Costello.

ABBOTT SINGERS

Singles: 78 rpm

FABOR (4003 "We're Gonna Bop")............5-10 55

Singles: 7-inch

FABOR (4003 "We're Gonna Bop").........10-15 55

ABEL & STARLINERS

Singles: 7-inch

CHICO (18 "Chicken Hop")......................10-20 62

ABERNATHY, Lee Roy

Singles: 78 rpm

KING (4223 "Gospel Boogie")..................10-15 48

Singles: 7-inch

KING (4223 "Gospel Boogie")..................20-40 '50s

ABERNATHY, Marion

Singles: 78 rpm

FEDERAL...10-15 51
KING...10-15 47-49
Also see BLUES WOMAN
Also see PAGE, Hot Lips

ABNEY, Bob

Singles: 7-inch

PIK (12 "Ghost Riders in the Sky")..........10-15 67

ABNOR, Jon
(Howard Abnor; Jon Howard Abnor Involvement)

Singles: 7-inch

ABNAK...5-10 64-70
ATCO (6358 "Don't")...............................5-10 65

LPs: 10/12-inch

ABNAK (2072 "Intro to Change").............10-20 68
Also see JON & ROBIN

ABOOTAYS

Singles: 7-inch

VIM (504 "Abootay")...............................10-15 60

ABRAHAM

Singles: 7-inch

HY SIGN (3511 "Hook & Boogie")...........15-30 73
HY SIGN (3514 "Scaredfly")....................10-20 74
WAND (11217 "Kangaroo")........................4-8 70

ABRAM, J.D.
(With the Handicappers Band)

Singles: 7-inch

REENA (1028 "Doctor of Love")..............30-50 68

ABRAMS, Ray, Band

Singles: 7-inch

JAX (311 "Late Freight")..........................25-35 53
(Red vinyl.)
Also see GAYTEN, Paul

ABSHIRE, Nathan, & Pine Grove Boys

Singles: 7-inch

KHOURY'S..10-15 61

ABSTRACT REALITY

Singles: 7-inch

SPORT (104 "Love Burns")..................100-150

ABSTRACT SOUND

Singles: 7-inch

GRAY SOUNDS (006 "Blacked Out Mind")..20-30
SOS (1002 "Blacked Out Mind")..............20-30 '60s

ABSTRACTS

Singles: 7-inch

POMPEII (66679 "Smell of Incense").......10-15 68

LPs: 10/12-inch

POMPEII (6002 "The Abstracts")............20-30 68
Members: Henri Dondini; Tony Francesco Peluso; Michael Thatcher; Pierie Vigeant

ABSTRAK SOUND

Singles: 7-inch

CBM ("You're Gonna Break My Heart") ...20-30 66
(No selection number used.)

ACADEMICS
(With the Kingsmen Quintet)

Singles: 7-inch

ANCHO (101 "Too Good to Be True")..150-200 57
ANCHO (103 "Darla, My Darlin' ")........150-200 57
ANCHO (104 "I Often Wonder")..................3-5
(Previously unreleased.)
ANCHOR (101 "Too Good to Be True")..500-750 57
(First issue.)
ELMONT (1001 "Somethin' Cool")...........50-60 58
NU=DISC (8001 "Somethin' Cool")..........10-20 '60s
(Blue vinyl.)
RELIC (509 "At My Front Door")................ 5-10 64
RELIC (510 "Too Good to Be True")........10-15 64
Members: Dave Fisher; Ron Marone; Marty Ganter; Bill Greenberg; Goose Greenberg.
Also see KINGSMEN
Also see PASSENGERS

ACADEMICS / Premiers

LPs: 10/12-inch

PREMAX ("Academics Meet the Premiers")..40-60
(Selection number not known.)
Also see ACADEMICS

ACCENT

Singles: 7-inch

PARROT (40022 "Winds of Change")...... 10-20 67

ACCENTS
(With Jackie Allen)

Singles: 78 rpm

ACCENT...10-15 55-56
BLUE MILL...15-20 55

Singles: 7-inch

ACCENT (1025 "Cool-a-Roo")..................15-25 55
ACCENT (1037 "Name Song")..................15-25 56
BLUE MILL (111 "Baby Blue")..................40-50 55

ACCENTS *P&R '58*
(Featuring Robert Draper Jr.)

Singles: 7-inch

BRUNSWICK (55100 "Wiggle Wiggle")...10-20 58
BRUNSWICK (55123 "Ching a Ling")......20-30 59
CORAL (62151 "Autumn Leaves")...........10-15 59
JUBILEE (5353 "Red Light")....................10-15 59
Members: Robert Draper Jr.; James Jackson; Robert Armstrong; Billy Hood; Arvid Garrett; Israel Goudeau Jr.
Also see THREE SHARPS & FLAT

ACCENTS

Singles: 7-inch

JOKER (200 "Cassius Clay")................200-300 62
(Red vinyl.)
SULTAN (5500 "Rags to Riches")..........50-100 61
Also see CALLENDER, Bobby
Also see ENGLISH, Scott

ACCENTS

Singles: 7-inch

JIVE!! (888 "100 Wailin' Cats")................15-25 62
(Pictures well-dressed cat with signboard.)
JIVE!! (888 "100 Wailin' Cats")................10-20 62
(Cat not shown on label.)
MATT (0001 "Little Boy Blue")..................10-20 62
VEE-JAY (484 "100 Wailin' Cats")............. 8-12 63

ACCENTS

Singles: 7-inch

MERCURY (72154 "Enchanted Garden")...30-40 63

ACCENTS

Singles: 7-inch

M-PAC (7216 "New Girl")........................20-30 64
ONE-DERFUL (4833 "You Better Think Again")..10-20 65
Member: Clifford Curry.
Also see CURRY, Clifford

ACCENTS
("Featuring Ron Petersen")

Singles: 7-inch

JERDEN (728 "Linda Lu").......................15-25 64
Members: Ron Petersen; Laurie Vitt; Vic Bundy; Pat Jerns; George Palmerton.
Also see FRANTICS

ACCENTS

Singles: 7-inch

BANGAR..15-25 63-66
BEAR (1977 "No One Heard You Cry")...25-35 66
GARRETT..15-25 64-65
TWIN TOWN..15-25 65

ACCENTS

Singles: 7-inch

GAZARRI (90931 "People Are Funny")....25-35

ACE, Buddy — R&B '66
Singles: 78 rpm
DUKE ... 10-15 56-57
PEACOCK ... 10-15 55
Singles: 7-inch
DUKE (100 series) ... 15-25 56-58
DUKE (300 & 400 series) ... 10-15 60-69
FIDELITY (3011 "Something New") ... 10-20 59
PAULA ... 4-6 70-72
PEACOCK (1659 "I Told You So") ... 20-30 55
SPECIALTY (699 "Oh Why") ... 10-20 59

ACE, Johnny — R&B '52
(With the Beale Streeters; with Johnny Otis Orchestra; with Johnny Board Orchestra)
Singles: 78 rpm
DUKE ... 15-25 52-55
QUALITY ... 15-25 54
(Canadian.)
Singles: 7-inch
ABC ... 4-6 73
DUKE (102 "My Song") ... 30-50 52
DUKE (107 "Cross My Heart") ... 30-50 53
DUKE (112 "The Clock") ... 30-50 53
DUKE (128 "Please Forgive Me") ... 30-50 54
DUKE (132 "Never Let Me Go") ... 30-50 54
DUKE (136 "Pledging My Love"/"No Money") ... 30-50 55
DUKE (136 "Pledging My Love"/"Anymore") ... 20-30 60
(Different flip. Also has added voices and orchestration.)
DUKE (144 "Anymore") ... 30-50 55
DUKE (148 "So Lonely") ... 30-50 55
DUKE (154 "Don't You Know") ... 30-50 55
DUKE (155 "Back Home") ... 30-50 55
MCA ... 3-5 84
QUALITY (1353 "Pledging My Love") ... 25-50 54
(Canadian.)
EPs: 7-inch
DUKE (71 "Johnny Ace") ... 15-25 63
(Six-track juke box issue. Includes title strips.)
DUKE (80 "Memorial Album") ... 150-200 55
DUKE (81 "Tribute Album") ... 150-200 55
LPs: 10/12-inch
DUKE (70 "Memorial Album") ... 550-650 55
(10-inch LP.)
DUKE (71 "Memorial Album") ... 150-250 57
(No playing card shown on cover.)
DUKE (71 "Memorial Album") ... 60-80 61
(Playing card shown on cover.)
DUKE (X-71 "Memorial Album") ... 8-10 74
MCA ... 4-6 83
Also see BLAND, Bobby
Also see OTIS, Johnny

ACE, Johnny / Earl Forrest
Singles: 78 rpm
FLAIR ... 100-200 53
Singles: 7-inch
FLAIR (1015 "Midnight Hours Journey") ... 500-750 53
Also see FORREST, Earl

ACE, Johnny, & Willie Mae Thornton
Singles: 78 rpm
DUKE ... 15-25 53
Singles: 7-inch
DUKE (118 "Yes Baby"/"Saving My Love for You") ... 30-50 53
Also see ACE, Johnny
Also see THORNTON, Willie Mae

ACE, Sonny
(With the Del Sharps; with Twisters)
Singles: 7-inch
ATLANTIC (2364 "Chili Peppers") ... 5-10 66
COBRA (214 "Amor Que Malo") ... 5-10 65
COBRA (224 "Chili Peppers") ... 8-12 65
COBRA (1113 "Anymore") ... 15-25 65
RIVAL (01 "Tamales") ... 5-10
TNT (153 "If My Teardrops Could Talk") ... 400-500 58

ACEY, Johnny
Singles: 7-inch
ARROW (740 "Our Love Is Over") ... 20-30 58
D.J.L. (616 "My Home") ... 10-20
FALEW (101 "Stay Away Love") ... 10-20 63
FALEW (105 "Don't Deceived Me") ... 10-20 64
FIRE (1015 "Please Don't Go") ... 15-25 60
FLING (728 "I Go Into Orbit") ... 15-25 62

ACKLIN, Barbara — P&R/R&B/LP '68
Singles: 7-inch
BRUNSWICK ... 8-12 67-73
CAPITOL ... 4-6 74-75
ERIC ... 3-5 83
Picture Sleeves
BRUNSWICK (55388 "Just Ain't No Love") ... 10-15 68
LPs: 10/12-inch
BRUNSWICK ... 15-20 68-71
CAPITOL ... 8-12 75
Session: Chi-Lites.
Also see ALLEN, Barbara
Also see CHANDLER, Gene, and Barbara Acklin
Also see CHI-LITES

ACORN, Bobby, & Leaves
(Bobby Mizzell)
Singles: 7-inch
DIAMOND JIM ... 10-15 62
Also see MIZZELL, Bobby

ACORN SISTERS
Singles: 7-inch
ACORN (159 "Alpha & Omega") ... 15-25 62
ACORN (593 "Real Gone") ... 75-125 59
BOONE (1033 "After All") ... 10-20 65
BOONE (1048 "Wait Until Tomorrow") ... 10-20 66
EPs: 7-inch
STARDAY (119 "Acorn Sisters") ... 15-25 59

ACORNS
Singles: 7-inch
UNART (2006 "Angel") ... 15-25 58
UNART (2015 "Your Name and Mine") ... 15-20 59

ACOUSTICS
Singles: 7-inch
CANALTOWN (254 "My Rights") ... 20-30 66
CHERRY BLOSSOM ... 5-10

ACQUINETTS
(Carl Green's Acquinetts)
Singles: 7-inch
LILLY (508 "Apple of My Heart") ... 30-40 61

ACT IV
Singles: 7-inch
CUB (9150 "A Better Man Than I") ... 10-20 65

ACTIONEERS
Singles: 7-inch
SHANE (57 "No One Wants Me") ... 15-25 65

ACUFF, Roy — P&R '38/C&W '44
(With the Smoky Mountain Boys; with Crazy Tennesseans)
Singles: 78 rpm
BANNER ... 10-20
CAPITOL ... 4-8 53-55
COLUMBIA ... 5-10 45-49
CONQUEROR ... 10-20
DECCA ... 4-8 55
MGM ... 5-10 51
MELOTONE ... 10-20
OKEH ... 5-10 40-45
ORIOLE ... 10-20
PERFECT ... 10-20
ROMEO ... 10-20
VOCALION ... 8-12 38-40
Singles: 7-inch
CAPITOL (2385 thru 3209) ... 5-10 53-55
COLUMBIA (20000 series) ... 10-20 52
DECCA ... 5-10 55
ELEKTRA ... 4-6 78
HICKORY (314 thru 362) ... 4-6 73-75
HICKORY (1073 thru 1664) ... 4-8 58-72
MGM ... 10-20 51
EPs: 7-inch
CAPITOL (617 "Songs of the Smokey Mountains") ... 10-15 55
(Price is for any of three volumes.)
COLUMBIA (Except 2895) ... 10-20 51-59
COLUMBIA (2895 "Roy Acuff EP") ... 30-50 '50s
LPs: 10/12-inch
CAPITOL (617 "Songs of the Smokey Mountains") ... 20-40 55
CAPITOL (2276 "The Voice of Country Music") ... 10-20 65
CAPITOL (T-1870 "Country Music Hall of Fame's Roy Acuff") ... 10-20 63
(Monaural.)
CAPITOL (SM-1870 "Country Music Hall of Fame's Roy Acuff") ... 5-10 79
(Reprocessed stereo.)
COLUMBIA (9004 "Songs of the Smokey Mountains") ... 30-50 50
(10-inch LP.)
COLUMBIA (9010 "Old Time Barn Dance") ... 30-50 50
(10-inch LP.)
COLUMBIA (CS-1034 "Roy Acuff's Greatest Hits") ... 8-12 70
COLUMBIA (PC-1034 "Roy Acuff's Greatest Hits") ... 8-12 70
COLUMBIA (39998 "Roy Acuff") ... 5-8 85
ELEKTRA ... 5-10 78-82
CAPITOL (2103 "The Great Roy Acuff") ... 20-30 64
GOLDEN COUNTRY ... 5-10
HARMONY ... 8-20 58-70
HICKORY (101 thru 119) ... 20-35 61-65
HICKORY (125 thru 162) ... 15-30 65-70
HICKORY/MGM ... 8-12 74-75
METRO ... 10-20 65
MGM (3707 "Favorite Hymns") ... 30-40 58
MGM (4044 "Hymn Time") ... 15-25 62
PICKWICK ... 5-10 '70s
PICKWICK/HILLTOP ... 8-15 65-69
ROUNDER ... 5-8 85
SEARS (123 "Take My Hand, Precious Lord") ... 15-20
TIME-LIFE ... 5-10 '80s
Session: Jordanaires.
Also see JORDANAIRES
Also see WILLIAMS, Hank / Roy Acuff
Also see NITTY GRITTY DIRT BAND & ROY ACUFF

ACUFF, Roy, & Kitty Wells
Singles: 78 rpm
DECCA ... 4-6 56
Singles: 7-inch
DECCA ... 10-15 56
Also see ACUFF, Roy
Also see WELLS, Kitty

AD LIBS — P&R/R&B '65
Singles: 7-inch
A.G.P. (100 "New York in the Dark") ... 100-150 66
BLUE CAT (102 "The Boy from New York City") ... 10-15 65
BLUE CAT (114 "He Ain't No Angel") ... 15-25 65
BLUE CAT (119 "On the Corner") ... 5-10 65
BLUE CAT (123 "Johnny My Boy") ... 5-10 66
CAPITOL (2944 "Love Me") ... 4-8 70
ESKEE ("New York in the Dark") ... 200-300 66
(Selection number not known.)
JOHNNIE BOY (1 "I Stayed Home") ... 3-5 88
KAREN (1527 "Think of Me") ... 15-25 66
PHILIPS (40461 "You're in Love") ... 5-10 67
SHARE (106 "The Boy from New York City") ... 5-10 69
STOOP SOUNDS (513 "Human") ... 100-125 99
Members: Mary Ann Thomas; Danny Austin; Hugh Harris; J.T. Taylor; Norm Donegan; Dave Watts.
Also see CREATORS

AD LIBS / Atlantics / Hudsons / Variations
LPs: 10/12-inch
ACAPPELLA (1001 "New York City to L.A. Acappella All the Way") ... 100-200
(Dark blue label.)

AD LIBS
Singles: 7-inch
VE ("Think of Me") ... 20-30 '60s
(Selection number not known.)

ADAIR, Robin
Singles: 7-inch
POWERTREE (150 "Alone Alone") ... 10-15 64

ADAM'S APPLES
Singles: 7-inch
BRUNSWICK (55330 "Don't Take It Out on This World") ... 50-100 67
BRUNSWICK (55367 "You're the One I Love") ... 25-45 68

ADAMS, Al
Singles: 7-inch
FRISCO (101 "Baby It's Love") ... 10-15 62
FRISCO (102 "To Know") ... 10-15 62

ADAMS, Alberta
Singles: 78 rpm
CHESS (1551 "This Morning") ... 5-10 53
Singles: 7-inch
CHESS (1551 "This Morning") ... 15-25 53
THELMA (2282 "I Got a Feeling") ... 20-40 62

ADAMS, Alicia
(With Ray Stanley & Orchestra)
Singles: 7-inch
CAPITOL (4444 "Ballad of Ronnie") ... 10-15 60
CAPITOL (4545 "Love Bandit") ... 10-15 61
Also see STANLEY, Ray

ADAMS, Armond
Singles: 7-inch
FORTUNE (572 "The Storm") ... 10-20 65

ADAMS, Art, & Rhythm Knights
Singles: 7-inch
CHERRY (1005 "Rock Crazy Baby") ... 100-150 60
CHERRY (1019 "Dancin' Doll") ... 200-300 60

ADAMS, Arthur K.
(Arthur Adams)
Singles: 7-inch
CHISA (8003 "Let's Make Some Love") ... 5-10 69
(Black vinyl.)
CHISA (8003 "Let's Make Some Love") ... 10-20 69
(Colored vinyl. Promotional issue only.)
CHISA (8008 "My Baby's Love") ... 8-12 70
CHISA (8011 "Can't Wait to See You") ... 8-12 71
DUCHESS (1009 "I Had a Dream") ... 10-15 61
JAMIE (1180 "Willin' to Die") ... 10-15 61
MODERN (1034 "Drives Me Out of My Mind") ... 5-10 67
MODERN (1050 "I'm Lonely for You") ... 5-10 68

ADAMS, Billy
(With the Rock-A-Teers; with Georgia & Teens; with Paramounts)
Singles: 7-inch
AMY (893 "You and Me") ... 8-12 63
APT (25072 "My Happiness") ... 8-12 62
ARC (2002 "I Don't Want to Be Me") ... 5-10 68
CAPITOL (4308 "Count Every Star") ... 10-20 59
CAPITOL (4373 "Can't Get Enough") ... 10-20 60
DECCA (30724 "Baby I'm Bugged") ... 30-50 58
DOT (15689 "You Heard Me Knocking") ... 10-20 58
FERN (807 "Darling, Take My Hand") ... 50-75 61
FERN (808 "Tattle Tale") ... 20-30 61
FERN (812 "Rip Van Winkle") ... 20-30 61
FERN (813 "Call Me") ... 20-30 61
HOME OF THE BLUES (239 "Looking for My Baby") ... 8-12 63
HOME OF THE BLUES (242 "My Happiness") ... 8-12 63
KO KO (8801 "Bicycle Hop") ... 8-12 62
NAU-VOO (802 "You Gotta Have a Duck Tail") ... 100-200 58
NAU-VOO (805 "Return of the All American Boy") ... 50-75 59
NAU-VOO (808 "Blue Eyed Ella") ... 25-50 59
QUINCY (932 "Rock, Pretty Mama") ... 1500-2000 59
SUN (389 "Betty & Dupree") ... 10-15 64
SUN (391 "Trouble in Mind") ... 10-15 64
SUN (394 "Reconsider Baby") ... 10-15 64
SUN (401 "Open the Door, Richard") ... 10-15 66
WAND (133 "Billy Boy") ... 10-15 63

ADAMS, Bobby — R&B '70
(Bobby Grier Adams)
Singles: 7-inch
BATTLE (45914 "Better Days Ahead") ... 5-10 63
BIG B. (778 "The Kind of Man") ... 100-200
COED (604 "Save Those Teardrops") ... 5-10 65
COLPIX (195 "Here Is One") ... 10-20 61
COLPIX (604 "I Think You Want My Girl") ... 20-30 61
HOME-TOWN (101 "Love Ain't Nothing But a Business") ... 4-8 70
MAY (113 "Who Knows What Might Have Been") ... 10-20 62
PET (803 "I Want My Lovin'") ... 15-25 58
PURDY (102 "Don't You Feel It") ... 10-20 64
SYMBOL (902 "This Feeling") ... 10-20 59
SYMBOL (905 "Don't Leave") ... 10-20 59
SYMBOL (908 "Little Miss America") ... 10-20 60
SYMBOL (911 "Let Me Love You") ... 10-20 61

ADAMS, Bobby, & Norma Jean Carpenter
Singles: 7-inch
KINGSTAR ... 4-6 71
Also see ADAMS, Bobby

ADAMS, Bryan *P&R/LP '82*
(B.G. Adams)
Singles: 12-inch
A&M (Except "Let Me Take You Dancing") ..4-8 82-87
(Black vinyl.)
A&M ("Let Me Take You Dancing")......... 10-20 79
(Black vinyl. Selection number not known.)
A&M (Colored vinyl)..............................5-10 84
Singles: 7-inch
A&M (0422 "Please Forgive Me") 3-5 93
A&M (1567 "I Do It for You").........................3-5 91
A&M (1576 "Can't Stop This Thing We Started")..3-5 91
A&M (1578 "The Only Thing That Looks Good on Me Is You"/"Hey Elvis")...........................4-6 96
A&M (1588 thru 1611)..............................3-5 91-92
A&M (2163 "Let Me Take You Dancing") 4-6 79
(Black vinyl.)
A&M (2163 "Let Me Take You Dancing") ...8-12 79
(Colored vinyl.)
A&M (2220 "Hidin' from Love").....................4-6 80
A&M (2249 "Give Me Your Love")...................4-6 80
A&M (2359 thru 2964)..............................3-5 82-87
A&M (8651 "Christmastime")........................3-5 85
Picture Sleeves
A&M (1578 "The Only Thing That Looks Good on Me Is You"/"Hey Elvis")..4-8 96
A&M (2163 "Let Me Take You Dancing") 10-15 79
A&M (2536 thru 2964) 3-6 83-87
LPs: 10/12-inch
A&M..5-10 80-87
Also see DION
Also see SWEENEY TODD

ADAMS, Bryan, & Tina Turner
Singles: 7-inch
A&M (2791 "It's Only Love")........................3-5 85
Picture Sleeves
A&M (2791 "It's Only Love").........................3-5 85
Also see ADAMS, Bryan
Also see TURNER, Tina

ADAMS, Charlie
Singles: 78 rpm
DECCA (28397 "TT Boogie").................. 10-15 52
Singles: 7-inch
DECCA (28397 "TT Boogie").................. 15-25 52

ADAMS, Easy
Singles: 78 rpm
TNT (1007 "New Bandera Waltz") 10-15 53
Singles: 7-inch
TNT (1007 "New Bandera Waltz") 15-25 53

ADAMS, Edie
Singles: 78 rpm
UNIQUE...5-10 56-57
Singles: 7-inch
UNIQUE.. 10-20 56-57
LPs: 10/12-inch
MGM (3751 "Music to Listen to Records By").. 15-25 59
RKO UNIQUE (135 "Edie Adams")......... 40-60 58

ADAMS, Faith
Singles: 7-inch
SAVOY (1606 "Cry, You Crazy Heart") ... 10-20 61

ADAMS, Faye *R&B '53*
(With Jimmy Mundy & Orchestra; with Joe Morris Orchestra; Faye Scruggs)
Singles: 78 rpm
ATLANTIC.. 10-25 53
HERALD.. 10-25 53-57
IMPERIAL.. 10-15 57
Singles: 7-inch
ABC...4-6 73
ATLANTIC (1007 "Sweet Talk") 50-75 53
COLLECTABLES 3-5 82
HERALD (416 "Shake a Hand").............. 20-30 53
(Black vinyl.)
HERALD (416 "Shake a Hand")............ 75-125 53
(Red vinyl.)
HERALD (419 "I'll Be True").................... 30-40 53
(Black vinyl.)
HERALD (419 "I'll Be True").................. 75-125 53
(Red vinyl.)
HERALD (423 "Every Day") 20-30 54
HERALD (429 "Crazy Mixed-Up World"). 30-40 54
HERALD (434 "Hurts Me to My Heart")... 15-25 54
HERALD (439 "I Owe My Heart")............ 15-25 54
HERALD (444 "Your Love")..................... 15-25 55
HERALD (450 "You Ain't Been True") 15-25 55
HERALD (457 "Angels Tell Me")..............10-20 55
HERALD (462 "No Way Out")..................10-20 55
HERALD (470 "Teenage Heart")..............10-20 56
HERALD (480 "Takin' You Back")............10-20 56
HERALD (489 "Anytime, Anyplace, Anywhere")..10-20 56
HERALD (512 "Shake a Hand")..................8-12 57
IMPERIAL (5443 "Keeper of My Heart")...15-20 57
IMPERIAL (5456 "You're Crazy")............50-75 57
IMPERIAL (5471 "I Have a Twinkle in My Eye")..10-15 57
IMPERIAL (5525 "When We Kiss")..........10-15 58
LIDO (603 "It Made Me Cry") 10-15 59
LIDO (606 "I Can't Be Wrong")..................10-15 60
PRESTIGE (224 "You Can Trust in Me") .10-15 62
WARWICK (550 "Look Around")................10-15 60
WARWICK (590 "Shake a Hand") 10-15 60
WARWICK (620 "Johnny, Don't Believe Her")..10-15 61
WARWICK (638 "It Can't Be Wrong").......10-15 61
LPs: 10/12-inch
COLLECTABLES..6-8 88
SAVOY (14398 "Faye Adams")..................8-10 76
WARWICK (2031 "Shake a Hand") 150-250 61
Also see MORRIS, Joe, & His Orchestra

ADAMS, Faye / Little Esther / Maxine Brown
LPs: 10/12-inch
MUSICTONE (7001 "Great Female R&B Package")..20-30 65
Also see BROWN, Maxine

ADAMS, Faye / Little Esther / Shirley & Lee
LPs: 10/12-inch
ALMOR (103 "Golden Souvenirs")...........10-20
Also see LITTLE ESTHER
Also see MORRIS, Joe, & His Orchestra
Also see SHIRLEY & LEE

ADAMS, Faye / Jimmy McGriff
Singles: 7-inch
COLLECTABLES..3-5 82
Also see McGRIFF, Jimmy

ADAMS, Faye / Jay McShann
Singles: 7-inch
OLDIES 45 (109 "Shake a Hand")...............4-8 '60s
Also see ADAMS, Faye
Also see McSHANN, Jay

ADAMS, Harry
Singles: 7-inch
KENTUCKY (521 "Milk Bucket Boogie")..50-100

ADAMS, J.T., & Shirley Griffith
LPs: 10/12-inch
PRESTIGE BLUESVILLE (1077 "The Blues of J.T. Adams and Shirley Griffith")....................50-75 64

ADAMS, Jerri
Singles: 7-inch
COLUMBIA...10-15 57-59
FRATERNITY (874 "Ivory Tower")..............5-10 61
EPs: 7-inch
COLUMBIA..8-12 58-59
LPs: 10/12-inch
COLUMBIA (1258 "Play for Keeps").........15-20 59

ADAMS, Jerry
Singles: 7-inch
KRASH (5002 "It Doesn't Matter Anymore")..8-12
UNIVERSE (502 "Party Doll") 50-75
WHEEL (1003 "Old Black Joe") 150-200 59
(Features Leon Russell on piano.)
Also see RUSSELL, Leon

ADAMS, Jo Jo
(Dr. Jo Jo Adams)
Singles: 78 rpm
ALLADIN...10-15 46
ARISTOCRAT..10-15 47
CHANCE (1127 "Didn't I Tell You")..........25-50 53
HY-TONE...10-15 47
MELODY LANE...10-15 46
PARROT (788 "Call My Baby")..................20-40 54
Singles: 7-inch
CHANCE (1127 "Didn't I Tell You")......100-150 53
PARROT (788 "Call My Baby")..............75-125 54
(Black vinyl.)
PARROT (788 "Call My Baby")............200-300 54
(Colored vinyl.)

ADAMS, Johnny *R&B '62*
(John Adams)
Singles: 7-inch
ARIOLA AMERICA..4-6 78
ATLANTIC..4-6 71-72
GAMMA (101 "Best of Luck to You") ....4-6 '70s
GONE (5147 "I'm Grateful")......................30-50 64
HEP ME...4-8 74-76
J.B...4-6 76
MODERN (1044 "One Day")........................5-10 67
PACEMAKER (240 "A Place Called Home")..10-15 65
PACEMAKER (249 "When I'll Stop Loving You")..10-15 65
PACEMAKER (255 "Let Them Talk").......10-15 65
PAID...3-5 84
RIC 10-20 59-63
RON 8-12 64-65
SSS INT'L..10-15 68-74
(Black vinyl.)
SSS INT'L (809 "I Won't Cry")..................15-20 70
(Green vinyl.)
TOWNHOUSE..4-6
WATCH (6333 "Part of Me")......................20-30 63
LPs: 10/12-inch
ARIOLA AMERICAN (50036 "After All the Good Is Gone")..5-10 78
CHELSEA 10-20 77
HEP ME...8-10 74-76
ROUNDER (2044 "From the Heart") 5-10 84
ROUNDER (2049 "After Dark")..................5-10 86
ROUNDER (2059 "Room with a View of the Blues")...5-10 88
ROUNDER (2095 "Walking on a Tightrope")...5-10 89
SSS INT'L (5 "Heart and Soul") 10-15 70

ADAMS, Johnny, & Gondoliers
Singles: 7-inch
RIC (963 "Nowhere to Go")......................10-20 59
Also see ADAMS, Johnny
Also see GONDOLIERS

ADAMS, Kay *C&W '66*
(With the Cliffie Stone Group)
Singles: 7-inch
TOWER...8-12 65-68
Picture Sleeves
TOWER (445 "Gonna Have a Good Time")...8-12 68
LPs: 10/12-inch
FRONTLINE...8-12
TOWER..10-15 66-68
Also see STONE, Cliffie

ADAMS, Kerry
Singles: 7-inch
CALLA (103 "Fast Talking Lover")...........10-15 65
CHANCELLOR (1060 "Hideaway") 10-15 60

ADAMS, Lindy
Singles: 7-inch
TRI DISC (108 "A Bird in the Hand")........10-15 62

ADAMS, Link
Singles: 7-inch
A-OKAY (111 "Angel Or Not")..................40-50 61

ADAMS, Little Johnnie
Singles: 7-inch
MELATONE (1029 "No In-Between").......10-20

ADAMS, Marie *R&B '52*
(With Bill Harvey's Band; with Three Tons of Joy)
Singles: 78 rpm
PEACOCK..10-15 51-54
Singles: 7-inch
CAPITOL (4108 "A Fool in Love") 15-25 58
PEACOCK..20-40 51-54
VANTAGE...4-6 73
Also see OTIS, Johnny

ADAMS, Marvin, & Boppers
Singles: 7-inch
ROJAC (8172 "I'm on My Way")..............20-30

ADAMS, Mike, & Red Jackets
Singles: 7-inch
KENT (377 "Red River Twist")....................5-10 62
LPs: 10/12-inch
CROWN (312 "Surfers Beat")..................30-40 63
(Black vinyl.)
CROWN (312 "Surfers Beat")................75-100 63
(Colored vinyl.)
Members: Mike Adams; Norm Eiserman; Johnny Jones; Kaye Klassy.

ADAMS, Nick
Singles: 7-inch
MERCURY (71579 "Born a Rebel") 10-20 60
MERCURY (71607 "Johnny Yuma, the Rebel")..10-20 60
RCA (8073 "Tired & Lonely Rebel") 8-12 62

ADAMS, Pepper
(Pepper Adams Five; with Jimmy Knepper)
LPs: 10/12-inch
INTERLUDE (502 "Pepper Adams Five")..30-40 59
(Monaural.)
INTERLUDE (1002 "Pepper Adams Five")..40-50 59
(Stereo.)
METROJAZZ (1004 "Pepper-Knepper Quintet")..50-75 59
MODE (112 "Pepper Adams") 50-100 57
REGENT (6066 "Cool Sound")................50-75 58
RIVERSIDE (265 "10 to 4 at the 5 Spot").50-75 58
(Monaural.)
RIVERSIDE (1104 "10 to 4 at the 5 Spot")...65-85 58
(Stereo.)
SAVOY...5-10 84-85
WARWICK (2041 "Out of This World").....50-75 61
WORKSHOP JAZZ (219 "Compositions of Charlie Mingus")..30-50 63
WORLD PACIFIC (407 "Critic's Choice").40-60 58
Also see BYRD, Donald

ADAMS, Ray
Singles: 7-inch
RAINBOW (348 "I'm Gone") 40-50 57

ADAMS, Richie
(Ritchie Adams)
Singles: 7-inch
BELTONE (1001 "Right Away")...............10-20 61
BELTONE (1011 "Two Initials")...............10-20 61
CONGRESS (217 "I Understand") 10-15 64
CONGRESS (226 "The King")..................10-15 64
CONGRESS (232 "What Am I")................10-15 65
CONGRESS (248 "I Ain't Gonna Make It Without You")..10-15 65
CONGRESS (256 "I Can't Escape from You")..25-50 65
IMPERIAL (5806 "I Got Eyes")................10-15 62
IMPERIAL (5838 "Pakistan")...................10-15 62
MCA...3-5 80
MGM (13629 "You Were Mine") 5-10 66
P.I.P. (6519 "Mamacita")..............................4-6 76
RIBBON (6910 "Lonely One")..................10-20 60
RIBBON (6913 "Back to School")............10-20 60
Also see ARCHIES
Also see FIREFLIES

ADAMS, Rusty
Singles: 7-inch
BRIAR..5-10
D..4-6 71
HARVARD (812 "Flame in My Heart") 8-12 60
ZEPHYR (014 "Kisses")...........................10-15 57
Also see McCORMICK, George / Rusty Adams

ADAMS, T. Carl
Singles: 7-inch
DORE (541 "Guitar Safari") 15-25 59

ADAMS, Woodrow
(With the Three Bs; with Boogie Blues Blasters)
Singles: 78 rpm
CHECKER (757 "Pretty Baby Blues") .. 150-200 52
METEOR (5018 "Wine Head Woman")..100-200 55
Singles: 7-inch
HOME OF THE BLUES (109 "Something on My Mind") 15-25 60
METEOR (5018 "Wine Head Woman")..800-1000 55

ADAPTERS
Singles: 7-inch
MONTGOMERY (003 "Why")...................15-25 66
MOONGLOW (5015 "Why")......................15-25 66
MOONGLOW (5022 "I Want to Know")....15-25 67

ADDEO, Nicky
(With the Darchaes; with Counts; with Plazas; "Uniques Featuring Nickie Addeo")
Singles: 7-inch
EARL'S (1533 "Gloria")...5-10 '70s
MELODY (1417 "Where There Is Love"). 15-20 64
NOBELL (7001 "Danny Boy")...5-10 83
(Red vinyl.)
REVELATION VII (101 "Danny Boy").. 100-200 64
(Reportedly 200 made.)
SAVOY (200 "Gloria")... 50-100 63
(Black vinyl)
SAVOY (200 "Gloria")... 100-150 63
(Green vinyl)
SAVOY (200 "Gloria")... 75-125 63
(Red vinyl)
SELSOM (104 "Over the Rainbow").... 150-250 65
VIK... 15-25 '50s
Picture Sleeves
REVELATION VII (101 "Danny Boy").. 100-200 64
EPs: 7-inch
VIK... 30-50 '50s
Also see BARBAROSO & HISTORIANS
Also see SPRINGSTEEN, Bruce
Also see UNIQUES
Also see WHITE, Ben, & Darchaes

ADDERLEY, Julian "Cannonball" *P&R/R&B '61*
(Cannonball Adderley Orchestra; Cannonball Adderley Quintet; Cannonball Adderley Sextet)
Singles: 7-inch
BLUE NOTE (1738 "Somethin' Else")...5-10 59
BLUE NOTE (1739 "One for Daddy-O")...5-10 59
CAPITOL...4-8 61-73
LIMELIGHT (3055 "Limehouse Blues")...4-6 65
MERCURY (71712 "Limehouse Blues")...5-10 60
RIVERSIDE...8-12 61-64
Picture Sleeves
CAPITOL (3406 "Taurus/Scorpio")...4-8 72
EPs: 7-inch
EMARCY... 10-20 55
LPs: 10/12-inch
BLUE NOTE... 20-30 58
(Label reads "Blue Note Records Inc. - New York, U.S.A.")
BLUE NOTE... 15-25 66
(Label reads "Blue Note Records - A Division Of Liberty Records Inc.")
CAPITOL (Except 2200 and 2300 series)..8-15 66-80
CAPITOL (2200 and 2300 series)... 12-25 64-65
DOBRE...5-8 77
EMARCY (400 series)...8-12 76
EMARCY (36000 series)... 30-40 55-59
EMARCY (80018 "Cannonball's Sharpshooters")... 40-50 59
EVEREST...8-12 71
FANTASY...8-12 73-75
LIMELIGHT... 10-20 66
MERCURY (1000 series)...5-10 81
MERCURY (20000 and 60000 series)..... 15-30 61-62
MILESTONE...6-12 73-82
PACIFIC JAZZ... 15-25 62
RIVERSIDE (032 thru 142)...5-8 82-85
RIVERSIDE (200 thru 400 series)... 15-30 58-63
RIVERSIDE (1100 series)... 20-30 59-60
RIVERSIDE (3000 series)... 10-15 68
RIVERSIDE (9000 series)... 15-25 60-63
SAVOY (2200 series)...8-12 76
SAVOY (12018 "Presenting Cannonball")... 50-75 55
TRIP...5-10 75
VSP... 10-20 65
WING...8-12 68
Also see WILSON, Nancy, & Cannonball Adderley

ADDERLEY, Julian "Cannonball," & John Coltrane
LPs: 10/12-inch
LIMELIGHT... 10-20 65
MERCURY... 20-30 61
Also see COLTRANE, John

ADDERLEY, Julian "Cannonball," & Sergio Mendes
LPs: 10/12-inch
CAPITOL... 10-15 68-71
EVEREST...5-10 73
Also see ADDERLEY, Julian "Cannonball"
Also see MENDES, Sergio

ADDERLEY, Tommy
(With the Meteors)
Singles: 7-inch
LEXIAN (10 "I'm Comin' Home")...15-25
MAR-MAR (314 "Whole Lotta Shakin' Goin' On")...15-25 60

ADDRISI BROTHERS *P&R '59*
Singles: 7-inch
BELL (45434 "Who Do I Think I Am")...4-6 74
BRAD (003 "I'll Be True")...15-20 58
BUDDAH...4-6 77
COLUMBIA...5-8 72-73
DEL-FI (4116 "Cherrystone")...20-25 59
DEL-FI (4120 "Saving My Kisses")...10-20 59
DEL-FI (4125 "It's Love")...10-20 59
DEL-FI (4130 "Gonna See My Baby")...10-20 59
ELEKTRA...3-5 81
IMPERIAL (5715 "Four Little Girls")...8-12 60
POM POM (3374 "Dance Is Over")...5-10 62
PRIVATE STOCK...4-6 75
SCOTTI BROTHERS...4-6 79
VALIANT (720 "Mr. Love")...5-10 65
VALIANT (6047 "Love Me Baby")...5-10 64
VALIANT (6058 "Little Miss Sad")...15-25 64
W.B....5-10 62-68
Picture Sleeves
SCOTTI BROTHERS (500 "Ghost Dancer")...4-6 79
(Promotional issue only.)
LPs: 10/12-inch
BUDDAH...5-10 77
COLUMBIA...5-10 72
Members: Dick Addrisi; Don Addrisi.

ADELPHIS
(With Teacho Wiltshire's Orchestra; Adelphies)
Singles: 7-inch
RIM (2020 "Darlin' It's You")...75-125 58
(Mistakenly credits "Adelphies.")
RIM (2020 "Darlin' It's You")...50-75 58
(Properly credits "Adelphis.")
RIM (2022 "[The Sun Will] Shine Again") .50-75 58
(With parenthetical subtitle.)
RIM (2022 "Shine Again")...20-30 61
(Subtitle omitted.)
20TH FOX (543 "Free Fall")...10-20 64
Also see WILTSHIRE, Teacho

ADENO, Bobby
(Bobby Adano)
Singles: 7-inch
BACK BEAT (552 "It's a Sad World")...10-15 65
BACK BEAT (579 "I'll Give up the World")...10-15 67
BACK BEAT (5104 "Hands of Time")...5-8 74
IMPERIAL (5628 "Eager Beaver Heart")..10-15 59
REVUE (552 "Hands of Time")...15-25 '60s

ADKINS, Hasil
Singles: 7-inch
AIR (5045 "She's Mine")...300-400 58
ARC...10-15
AVENUE (102 "Get Out My Car")...150-200 57
AVENUE (103 "Slow Hunch")...75-125 57
FEASIBLE...5-10 68
HUB (4561 "My Blue Star")...40-60 66
JODY (1000 "She Said")...100-200 '60s
NORTON...3-5 90
ROXIE (5134 "The Hunch")...300-350 63
Picture Sleeves
ARC...10-15
NORTON...3-5 90
EPs: 7-inch
NORTON...6-8 83
LPs: 10/12-inch
NORTON...8-10 86-87

ADKINS, Mike
(With Lemon Extract)
Singles: 7-inch
RCA...5-10 67-69
LPs: 10/12-inch
MIKE ADKINS (1061 "Mike Adkins")...15-25

ADKINSON, Billy
Singles: 7-inch
GALA (112 "Rock-A-Mo")...350-400 60

ADMIRAL ICE
(Admiral Shohn Ice)
Singles: 7-inch
ADMIRAL ICE ("My Carolina Girl")...20-30
(No selection number used.)
ADMIRAL ICE (3219 "Beach Bum")...20-30

ADMIRAL TONES
("Featuring Johnny Johns")
Singles: 7-inch
FELSTED (8563 "Rocksville, Pa.")...15-25 59
FUTURE (1006 "Rocksville, Pa.")...50-75 59
HI MAR (1001 "Stompin' U.S.A.")...10-20 62
Members: Paul Gottschall Jr.; George "Desi" Desmond; Ernie Howry; Johnny Johns.
Also see JOHNS, Johnny, & Three Jays
Also see THOMAS, Paul

ADMIRALS
Singles: 78 rpm
KING...20-30 55
Singles: 7-inch
KING (4772 "Oh Yes")...100-200 55
KING (4782 "Close Your Eyes")...100-200 55
Members: Richard Beasley; James Farmer; Willie Barnes; Wesley Devereaux; Eugene McDaniels.
Also see BARNES, Billy
Also see MILLINDER, Lucky, & Admirals
Also see SULTANS

ADMIRALS
Singles: 7-inch
VALMOR (15 "Mr. Blue")...10-20 62

ADMIRALS
Singles: 7-inch
VOLT (125 "King of Love")...15-25 65

ADMIRATIONS
Singles: 7-inch
APOLLO (753 "My Baby")...15-25 61

ADMIRATIONS
(With Sammy Lowe Orchestra)
Singles: 7-inch
ATOMIC (12871 "Dear Lady")...75-100
BRUNSWICK (55332 "Hey Mama")...10-20 67
JASON SCOTT (05 "To the Aisle")...3-5 80
(500 made.)
KELWAY (107 "Over the Rainbow")...4-8 74
(Red vinyl.)
MERCURY (71521 "Bells of Rosa Rita")..20-30 59
MERCURY (71883 "To the Aisle")...125-150 61
POPULAR REQUEST (107 "Bells of Rosa Rita")...3-5 94
Members: Joseph Lorello; John Mallon.
Also see DEDICATIONS

ADMIRATIONS / Bel Mars
Singles: 7-inch
CANDLELITE (414 "Gonna Find My Pretty Baby"/"Li'l Li'l Lulu")...5-10 63
(Red vinyl.)
Also see HEARTSPINNERS / Admirations
Also see NUTMEGS / Admirations

ADMIRATIONS
Singles: 7-inch
TARX (1000 "I'm Going to Get You")...40-50 62

ADMIRATIONS
Singles: 7-inch
HULL (1202 "Moonlight")...400-500 67

ADMIRATIONS
Singles: 7-inch
ONE-DERFUL (4849 "Wait 'Til I Get to Know You")...5-10 67
ONE-DERFUL (4851 "Don't Leave Me")...5-10 67
PEACHES (6721 "You Left Me")...100-200
(Also issued as by the Aspirations.)
Also see ASPIRATIONS

ADRIAN, Lee
(With the Rochester Collegiates; with Chaperones)
Singles: 7-inch
RCA (7201 "26 Men")...10-20 58
RICHCRAFT (5006 "I'm So Lonely")...10-20 59
SMC (1385 "I'm So Lonely")...10-15 59
SMC (1386 "School Is Over")...30-40 59

ADRIAN & SUNSETS
Singles: 7-inch
SUNSET (602 "Breakthrough")...25-35 63
Picture Sleeves
SUNSET (602 "Breakthrough")...35-45 63
LPs: 10/12-inch
SUNSET (601 "Breakthrough")...50-75 63
(Black vinyl.)
SUNSET (601 "Breakthrough")...200-300 63
(Multi-colored vinyl.)
Members: Adrian Lloyd; Dick Lambert; Bruce Riddar; Ron Eglit; Clyde Brown; Bobby Forest.
Also see HOLLYWOOD SUNSETS BAND
Also see RUMBLERS

ADVANCEMENT
LPs: 10/12-inch
PHILIPS (600328 "Advancement")...30-50 69
Members: Lynne Blessing; Colin Bailey; Hal Gordon.

ADVENTURERS
Singles: 7-inch
CAPITOL (4292 "Rip Van Winkle")...10-15 59
COLUMBIA (3-42227 "Rock and Roll Uprising")...75-100 61
(Compact 33 Single.)
COLUMBIA (4-42227 "Rock and Roll Uprising")...40-50 61
JERDEN (105 "Little Genie")...10-15 60
MECCA (11 "Shaggin' ")...10-20 60
MIRACLE (1 "2 O'Clock Express")...10-15 60
READING (602 "Lover Doll")...10-20 66
LPs: 10/12-inch
COLUMBIA (1747 "Can't Stop Twistin' ") .20-30 61
(Monaural.)
COLUMBIA (8547 "Can't Stop Twistin' ") .30-40 61
(Stereo.)

ADVENTURERS
Singles: 7-inch
BLUE ROCK 4071 "Something Bad")...4-8 69
COMPASS (7010 "Easy Baby")...5-8 67
RAN-DEE (106 "It's Alright")...10-15 62

ADVENTURERS
Singles: 7-inch
MUSIC WORLD (110 "Darlin' ")...15-25

AEROSMITH *P&R/LP '73*
Singles: 7-inch
COLUMBIA...3-6 73-80
GEFFEN...3-5 85-91
Picture Sleeves
GEFFEN...3-5 85-89
LPs: 10/12-inch
COLUMBIA (Except KC-32005 and quad issues)...5-15 73-86
COLUMBIA (KC-32005 "Aerosmith")...20-25 73
(Orange cover. Incorrectly shows *Walking the Dog* as "Walking the Dig.")
COLUMBIA (KC-32005 "Aerosmith")...20-25 73
(Blue cover. Incorrectly shows *Walking the Dog* as "Walking the Dig." Promotional issue only.)
COLUMBIA (KC-32005 "Aerosmith")...10-12 73
(Blue cover. Correctly lists *Walking the Dog.*)
COLUMBIA (KCQ-32847 "Get Your Wings")...20-30 74
(Quadraphonic.)
COLUMBIA (PCQ-33479 "Toys in the Attic")...20-30 75
(Quadraphonic.)
COLUMBIA (PCQ-34165 "Rocks")...20-30 76
(Quadraphonic.)
GEFFEN...5-10 85-87
Promotional LPs
COLUMBIA (187 "Pure Gold")...50-55 76
(Boxed set of the group's first three LPs.)
Members: Steve Tyler; Tom Hamilton; Joey Kramer; Joe Perry; Brad Whitford; Rick Dufay; Jimmy Crespo.
Also see CHAIN REACTION

AFDEM, Jeff, & Springfield Flute
Singles: 7-inch
BURDETTE (5 "Who Will Ever Know")...10-15 68
BURDETTE (8 "Ever On My Mind")...10-15 68
BURDETTE (489 "Scarborough Fair")...10-15 69
JERDEN (923 "Something")...5-8 71
PICCADILLY (250 "Mellow Yellow")...10-15 67
LPs: 10/12-inch
BURDETTE (5162 "Something")...30-50 69
Also see SPRINGFIELD RIFLE

AFFECTION COLLECTION
Singles: 7-inch
EVOLUTION...8-12 69
MAUDZ (001 "Time Rests Heavy on My Hands")...20-30 '60s
U.A....5-10 68
LPs: 10/12-inch
EVOLUTION...10-15 69

Members: Mike Doggett; Hal Rowberry; Don Christensen; Tim Comeau; Ray Hassell.

AFFECTIONS

Singles: 7-inch

CHATTAHOOCHEE (698 "Hey Girl") 10-20 65
(Previously issued as by the Fabulous Chancellors.)
Members: Rich Crowley; Terry Call; Dale Rich; Tom Lowe; Monty Saxton; Dennis Swindle.
Also see FABULOUS CHANCELLORS

AFFINITY

Singles: 7-inch

PARAMOUNT 4-8 70

LPs: 10/12-inch

PARAMOUNT 15-25 70
Members: Linda Boyle; Lynton Naiff; Mike Jopp; Mo Foster; Grant Serpell.

AFFLUENTS

Singles: 7-inch

CUCA ("I Feel Free") 10-20 67
(Selection number not known.)
USA (901 "Get Ready") 10-20 68
Members: Ted Pfeffer; Jim Morris; Tom Pilizak; Russ Engelwire; Dan Carson; Jeff Schmus; George Shuput.

AFTER ALL

LPs: 10/12-inch

ATHENA (6006 "After All") 15-25 70
Members: Bill Moon; Charles Short; Alan Gold; Mark Ellerbee.

AFTERGLOW

LPs: 10/12-inch

MTA (5010 "Afterglow") 75-100 67

AGAFON

Singles: 7-inch

GOLDEN NORTH (101 "Walkin' the Dog") 10-15

AGAN, Larry

Singles: 7-inch

SQUIRE (103 "Frankie's New Lover") 30-50 62

AGAPE

LPs: 10/12-inch

MARK (2170 "Gospel Hard Rock") 75-100 71
RENRUT ("Victims of Tradition") 50-80 72

AGBAY, Tony, & Continentals

Singles: 7-inch

NEW GLO 20-30

AGE OF BRONZE

Singles: 7-inch

GUAVA (102 "I'm Gonna Love You") .... 40-60 '60s

AGE OF REASON

Singles: 7-inch

ASCOT (2230 "Magnet") 30-50 67
GEORGETOWNE ("Magnet") 40-60 67
(Selection number not known.)

LPs: 10/12-inch

GEORGETOWNE ("Age of Reason") .. 150-250 69
(No selection number used.)

AGEE, Don

Singles: 7-inch

TROPHY INT'L (1501 "My Car Is Faster Than Yours") 50-75

AGEE, Ray

(With the Four Kings; with Teenetts)

Singles: 78 rpm

ALADDIN (3161 "Deep Trouble") 30-40 52
CASH 8-12 56
MODERN 10-20 52
QUEEN (101 "Brought It All By Myself") .. 15-25 52
R&B 10-20 55
RECORDED IN HOLLYWOOD 10-20 52
SPARK 10-20 55
TAN 10-15 55

Singles: 7-inch

ALADDIN (3161 "Deep Trouble") 50-75 52
BORN AGAIN 3-5 84
BRANDIN (210 "Feel So Good") 5-10 66
BRANDIN (211 "Love of Life") 5-10 66
CASH (1032 "Till Death Do Us Part") 15-25 56
CELESTE (612 "I'm the Gambler") 8-12 64
CELESTE (616 "Merry Xmas Time") 8-12 64
CELESTE (617 "Till Death Do Us Part") 8-12 65
CELESTE (619 "Your Precious Love") 8-12 66
CHECK (102 "Pray for Me") 40-50 59
EBB (111 "True Lips") 15-25 57
ELKO (109 "Black Night Is Gone") 10-20 59
FAT BACK (101 "I Can't Work and Watch You") 8-12
HIGHLAND (1192 "Keep Smiling") .... 5-10 '60s
JEWEL (784 "Hard Working Man") 5-10 67
KRAFTON 5-8 67-72
MAR JAN (001 "These Things Are True") 10-20 63
MODERN (883 "Flirtin' Blues") 50-75 52
MODERN (891 "My Lonesome Days Are Gone") 50-75 52
PLAID (105 "Pray for Me") 30-40 59
PROWLIN' 4-6 76
R&B (1311 "Without a Friend") 40-50 55
RECORDED IN HOLLYWOOD (240 "Troubles Bring Me Down") 50-75 52
ROMARK (118 "It's Hard to Explain") .... 4-8 '70s
SHIRLEY (108 "I Wanna Know Why") 25-35 63
SHIRLEY (109 "Open Up Your Heart") 10-15 63
SHIRLEY (111 "You Hit Me Where It Hurts") 15-25 63
SOLID SOUL (802 "Boy and Girl Thing") . 10-15 69
SOUL TOWN 10-15 66
SPARK (119 "Wobble-Lou") 25-35 55
TAN (307 "How Could You Say Goodbye") 25-35 55
TAN (3004 "Hey Hey Lovie Du") 25-35 55
VELTONE 10-20 60
WATTS WAY (642 "My So Called Friend") 5-10

LPs: 10/12-inch

J.W. 8-12
KRAFTON 10-15 68
WHITE 5-10 83
Also see ISOM RAY

AGEE, Ray, & Elly Johnson

Singles: 7-inch

EBB (111 "My Silent Prayer") 20-25 57

AGEE, Ray, & Mary Ann Miles

Singles: 7-inch

CELESTE (611 "Baby's Coming Home") 8-12 64
Also see AGEE, Ray
Also see MILES, Mary Ann

AGENTS

Singles: 7-inch

P&L (1001 "You Were Meant for Me") ...... 20-30 '60s
RALLY (504 "Gotta Help Me") 20-30 66

AGENTS

LPs: 10/12-inch

SUNSET 15-20 67

AGENTS

Singles: 7-inch

LIBERTY BELL (3260 "The Love I Hold") 30-40

AGGREGATION

Singles: 7-inch

LHI (1209 "Sunshine Superman") 15-25 68

LPs: 10/12-inch

LHI (12008 "Mind Oydssey") 300-500 68

AGRATI, Don

(Don Grady)

Singles: 7-inch

ELEKTRA 4-6 73

LPs: 10/12-inch

ELEKTRA 10-15 73
Also see GRADY, Don
Also see YELLOW BALLOON

AH-MOORS

Singles: 78 rpm

RAINBOW (10060 "Honey, Honey, Honey") 30-40 48

AH QUIN, Joe

LPs: 10/12-inch

LEHUA (7041 "Oceans Away") 10-20
NORTH SHORE (1001 "Nostalgic Hawaiiana") 10-20

AIKEN, Ben

Singles: 7-inch

LOMA (2069 "You Were Meant to Be My Baby") 10-15 67
LOMA (2076 "Callin' ") 10-15 67
LOMA (2084 "Satisfied") 10-15 67
LOMA (2100 "Baby You Move Me") 10-15 68
PHILLY GROOVE 5-10 71-72
ROULETTE (4649 "Hurry On Home") 5-10 65
SQUIRE 4-8

AIMEE, Joyce

Singles: 7-inch

CRYSTALETTE (744 "Playboy Lover") 10-20 61
CRYSTALETTE (746 "Fickle Heart") 10-20 62

AIMES, Steward

Singles: 7-inch

H&W (100 "Angelina") 20-25

AIR SUPPLY P&R/LP '80

Singles: 7-inch

ARISTA 3-5 80-86
FLASHBACK 3-5 82

Picture Sleeves

ARISTA 3-5 80-86

LPs: 10/12-inch

ARISTA 5-10 80-86
COLUMBIA 10-15 77
MFSL (113 "The One That You Love") 40-60 84
NAUTILUS (31 "Lost in Love") 15-25 82
Members: Graham Russell; Russell Hitchcock; David Moyse; Criston Barker; Ralph Cooper; David Green; Frank Esler-Smith; Rex Goh.

AIRES, Jimmy / Barry Winston / Billy Logan / Michael Reed

EPs: 7-inch

PROMENADE (14 "Whispering Bells") 15-25 57
(Title shown is of the Aires track. If there is an actual EP title, we're not yet aware of it.)

A-JACKS

Singles: 7-inch

VALIANT (6048 "Knight Ride") 15-20 64

AKENS, Jewel P&R/R&B '65

("Mr. Birds & Bees")

Singles: 7-inch

AMERICAN INT'L ARTISTS 4-6 75
CAPEHART (5007 "Wee Bit More of Your Lovin' ") 15-20 61
COLGEMS (1009 "Born a Loser") 5-10 67
COLGEMS (1025 "You Better Move On") .. 5-10 68
CREST (1098 "Wee Bit More of Your Lovin' ") 10-15 62
ERA 10-15 64-69
ICEPAC (303 "What Would You Do") 10-15
MDM ("Christine") 4-6 88
(No selection number used.)
MINASA (6716 "Wee Bit More of Your Lovin' ") 5-10 65
PAULA (337 "Blue Eyed Soul Brother") 4-6 70
RTV 4-6 72
WEST-ONE 4-6

LPs: 10/12-inch

ERA (110 "The Birds & Bees") 20-35 65
Also see FOUR DOTS
Also see JEWEL & EDDIE

A'KIES

Singles: 7-inch

PAN WORLD (515/516 "Haunted Sax"/"Haunted Piano") 15-25 59
Members: Aki Aleong; Sandy Nelson.
Also see ALEONG, Aki
Also see NELSON, Sandy

AKIM & AKTONES

(With the Hank Levine Orchestra; Aki Aleong)

Singles: 7-inch

PAN WORLD (520 "Fall in Love with Me") 25-35 60
Also see ALEONG, Aki

AKINS, Audrey

Singles: 7-inch

KARATE (515 "What Can You Lose") 8-12 65
PETAL (1030 "Down Came My Tears") ... 15-25 65

AKINS, J.C., & Dukes

Singles: 7-inch

BOUNTY (5589 "You Upset My Very Soul") 10-20

AKINS, Jerry, & Rockin' Obsidians

Singles: 7-inch

HI MAR (103/104 "Sherry My Love"/"All Our Friends Would Know") 15-25 62

AKINS, Jim

Singles: 7-inch

MARLO (1517 "Floating on a Cloud") 15-20 61
MARLO (1530 "Answer from Heaven") 10-15 63
MARLO (1532 "Lonely Weekend") 10-15 63
MARLO (1547 "I'm Gone") 10-15 63

AL & EDDIE

Singles: 7-inch

FABULOUS (201 "Really I Love You") 30-40 59

AL & JIM

Singles: 7-inch

LOGAN (3117 "Rock-A-Billy Music") 75-125 59

AL & NETTIE

(With the Nat Hendrix Band; Al & Nattie)

Singles: 7-inch

ART-TONE (829 "Now You Know") 10-20 62
CHRISTY (106 "Move Baby Move") 50-75 58
GEDINSON'S (6159 "Now You Know") ... 10-20 61

AL & TINY

Singles: 7-inch

HURRICANE (6994 "I'm Going Crazy") ... 15-25

AL'S UNTOUCHABLES

Singles: 7-inch

HUNT (6007 "Come on Baby") 20-30 66
Member: Al Huntzinger.
Also see UNTOUCHABLES

ALABAMA C&W '77

(Alabama Band)

Singles: 7-inch

GRT 8-12 77
LIMBO INT'L ("I Wanna Come Over") ...... 10-20 '70s
(Selection number not known.)
MDJ 4-8 79-80
RCA 3-5 80-93
RCA GOLD STANDARD 3-5 82
SSS INT'L (Colored vinyl) 5-10 81

Picture Sleeves

GRT (129 "I Wanna Be with You Tonight") 10-20 77
RCA 3-5 80-90

LPs: 10/12-inch

ACCORD 5-10 81
ALABAMA RECORDS (78 9-01 "The Alabama Band") 200-400 78
PLANTATION (44 "Wild Country") 40-60 81
RCA 5-10 80-90
SONNY 30-50 79
Members: Randy Owen; Jeff Cook; Teddy Gentry; Rick Scott; Mark Herndon.
Also see WILD COUNTRY

ALABAMA KID

Singles: 7-inch

VARSITY (83 "Rockin' Jalopy") 200-300 58

ALABAMA SLIM

(Ralph Willis)

Singles: 78 rpm

SAVOY 10-20 48
Also see WILLIS, Ralph

ALABAMA STATE TROUPERS

LPs: 10/12-inch

ELEKTRA 10-15 72
Members: Furry Lewis; Jeannie Greene; Lonnie Mack; Don Nix.
Also see LEWIS, Furry
Also see MACK, Lonnie

ALADDIN, Johnny

(With the Passions)

Singles: 7-inch

JAMA 4-8
CHIP (1001 "Why Did You Go") 40-50 60

Picture Sleeves

JAMA 5-10
Also see PASSIONS

ALADDIN, Russ

Singles: 7-inch

ALPINE (65 "Little Miss America") 10-20 60
CHARM (103 "Me and My Lover") 50-75 59

ALADDIN & GENIES

Singles: 7-inch

DRUMMOND (5001 "Amazon") 20-30 61

ALADDINS

Singles: 7-inch

ALADDIN (3275 "Cry Cry Baby") 150-250 55
ALADDIN (3298 "Get off My Feet") 100-150 55
ALADDIN (3314 "All of My Life") 150-250 56
ALADDIN (3358 "Help Me") 75-150 56

Members: Ed Williams; Alfred Harper; Ted Harper; Gaylord Green.

ALADDINS
Singles: 7-inch
FRANKIE (6 "Dot, My Love")............... 300-400 58

ALADDINS
Singles: 7-inch
WITCH (109 "Please Love Me")............. 30-40 62
WITCH (111 "Our Love Will Be")............ 20-30 62

ALAIMO, Chuck P&R '57
(Chuck Alaimo Quartet)
Singles: 7-inch
KEN (311 "Leap Frog")........................... 15-25 57
MGM (12449 "Leap Frog")..................... 10-20 57
MGM (12508 "How I Love You")............ 10-20 58
MGM (12589 "Where's My Baby")........... 10-20 58
MGM (12636 "Hop in My Jalop")............ 10-20 58
Members: Chuck Alaimo; Tommy Rossi; Pat Magnolia; Bill Irvine.

ALAIMO, Steve P&R '62
(With the Redcoats)
Singles: 7-inch
ABC..5-10 66-67
ABC-PAR...5-10 64-66
ATCO...5-8 67-71
CHECKER.. 10-15 61-63
DADE (1805 "Love Letters").................. 15-25 59
DICKSON (6445 "Blue Fire").................. 10-15 60
ENTRANCE...4-6 71-72
ERIC..3-5 83
IMPERIAL...5-10 60-63
LIFETIME 30-40 58
MARLIN (6064 "I Want You to Love Me").. 10-20 59
MARLIN (6065 "The Weekend's Over")... 10-20 59
MARLIN (6067 "She's My Baby")........... 20-30 59
EPs: 7-inch
ABC-PAR (531 "Where the Action Is")..... 10-20 65
(Juke box issue only.)
LPs: 10/12-inch
ABC-PAR (501 "Starring Steve Alaimo"). 15-20 65
(Monaural.)
ABC-PAR (S-501 "Starring Steve Alaimo")... 20-30 65
(Stereo.)
ABC-PAR (531 "Where the Action Is")..... 15-20 65
(Monaural.)
ABC-PAR (S-531 "Where the Action Is"). 20-30 65
(Stereo.)
ABC-PAR (551 "Steve Alaimo Sings & Swings")... 15-20 66
(Monaural.)
ABC-PAR (S-551 "Steve Alaimo Sings & Swings")... 20-30 66
(Stereo.)
CHECKER (2981 "Twist").................... 25-40 63
CHECKER (2983 "Mashed Potatoes") 25-40 62
CHECKER (2986 "Everyday I Have to Cry") 25-50 63
CROWN (5382 "Steve Alaimo")............. 10-20 63
Also see DELMIRAS
Also see RED COATS
Also see RIVERS, Johnny / Steve Alaimo
Also see UNKNOWNS

ALAIMO, Steve, & Betty Wright
Singles: 7-inch
ATCO (6659 "I'm Thankful")......................5-10 69
Also see ALAIMO, Steve
Also see WRIGHT, Betty

ALAMOS
Singles: 7-inch
HI-Q (5030 "Donkey Walk")..................... 10-20 63

ALAN
LPs: 10/12-inch
ALAN ("A Tribute to Elvis")..................... 30-40 75
(No selection number used.)

ALAN, Buddy C&W '68
(With Don Rich & Buckaroos)
Singles: 7-inch
CAPITOL 5-10 68-75
SUN DEVIL (1001 "Ride 'Em Cowboy") 4-8 78
LPs: 10/12-inch
CAPITOL... 10-15 70-75
Also see BUCKAROOS
Also see OWENS, Buck, & Buddy Alan

ALAN, Denni
Singles: 7-inch
ACADEMY (434 "Sixth Solid Baby").....100-125 59

ALAN, Edgar, & Po' Boys
Singles: 7-inch
RUST (5053 "Panic Button")....................10-15 62

ALAN, Lee
Singles: 7-inch
LEE ALAN PRESENTS ("A Trip to Miami")..400-500 64
(No selection number used. Includes insert sheet. DJ Lee Alan interviews the Beatles.)
LEE ALAN PRESENTS ("A Trip to Miami")..300-400 64
(Without insert sheet.)
Also see BEATLES

ALAN, Lee, & Vandellas
Singles: 7-inch
YMCA/WXYZ (94472 "Set Me Free").......50-75 '60s
(Promotional, fund-raising issue.)
Also see ALAN, Lee
Also see MARTHA & VANDELLAS

ALAN, Phil, & Ardees
(Phil Alan & Ardee's)
Singles: 7-inch
KO CO BO (1010 "Tell Me Why") 400-500

ALAN, Terry
Singles: 7-inch
HART-VAN (0129 "Stompin' Time")..........10-20 63

ALAN & ALPINES
Singles: 7-inch
ELKO (16 "Ginger Bread") 75-100

ALARM CLOCKS
Singles: 7-inch
AWAKE (107 "Yeah")...............................50-75 66

ALBAM, Manny
(With the Jerry Duane Singers; Manny Albam Orchestra)
Singles: 7-inch
COLPIX 5-10 62
IMPULSE..5-10 62
LPs: 10/12-inch
DOT..10-20 59
IMPULSE...10-20 62
RCA...10-20 61-62
TOP RANK...10-20 60
U.A. 10-20 60
VOCALION...10-15 60

ALBANO, Frankie
Singles: 7-inch
ANOTHER FEATURE 5-10 66
DONDEE (1922 "School Girl").................10-20 '60s
TOWER (153 "She'll Never Know") 5-10 65
Session: Davie Allan.
Also see ALLAN, Davie

ALBEE & CASUALS
Singles: 7-inch
DESTINATION (609 "Your [sic] the Kind of Girl")..15-25 65

ALBERT, Eddie
Singles: 78 rpm
KAPP...5-10 54-56
Singles: 7-inch
BELL...4-6 69
COLUMBIA..4-6 68
HICKORY..5-10 64-65
KAPP...10-20 54-56
LPs: 10/12-inch
COLUMBIA..8-12 68
DOT..8-12
HAMILTON (103 "Oh What a Beautiful Mornin' ")..10-20 59
(Monaural.)
HAMILTON (12103 "Oh What a Beautiful Mornin' ")..15-25 59
(Stereo.)

ALBERT, Eddie, & Sondra Lee P&R '56
Singles: 78 rpm
KAPP (134 "Little Child") 5-10 56
Singles: 7-inch
KAPP (134 "Little Child")...........................10-20 56
Picture Sleeves
KAPP (134 "Little Child") 20-30 56
Also see ALBERT, Eddie

ALBERT, Urel C&W '73
Singles: 7-inch
CINNAMON (786 "Just Wait").......................4-6 74
TOAST 4-6 73
LPs: 10/12-inch
SPAR (3016 "Saturday Night in Nashville") 20-30
CINNAMON 20-30

ALBERT & CHARLES
Singles: 7-inch
PIONEER (1005 "Weird")......................100-150

ALBERTI, Willy P&R '59
Singles: 7-inch
EPIC (9352 "Julia")......................................5-10 59
LONDON (1888 "Marina")..............................5-10 59
PHILIPS (40280 "My Diary of Love")..........5-10 65
LPs: 10/12-inch
LONDON (3662 "Marina")...............................5-15 59

ALBERTO COMBO
Singles: 7-inch
TAMMY (1025 "Green Monster")...............10-20 61

ALBERTS, Al
Singles: 7-inch
COLUMBIA (42737 "Before Tomorrow Is Yesterday")..5-10 63
CORAL...5-10 59
JAGUAR (100 "When I Lost You")................5-10 66
MGM..5-10 59-60
PRESIDENT (711 thru 715).......................10-15 61
PRESIDENT (719 "Before Tomorrow Is Yesterday")..10-20 63
SWAN...5-10 61-64
VEE-JAY (568 "One Has My Name").........5-10 63
LPs: 10/12-inch
CORAL (57259 "Man Has Got to Sing")...15-25 59
(Monaural.)
CORAL (757259 "Man Has Got to Sing").25-35 59
(Stereo.)
Also see FOUR ACES

ALBERTS, Al / 3 Of A Kind
Singles: 7-inch
TODD (1087 "Yoshiko"/"Only on Sunday") 5-10 63
Also see ALBERTS, Al

ALBIN, Hollis
Singles: 7-inch
HAMMOND (106 "V-8 Ford Boogie") ...100-150 59

ALBRIGHT, Lola
EPs: 7-inch
COLUMBIA (13271 "Dreamsville")............8-12 59
LPs: 10/12-inch
COLUMBIA (1327 "Dreamsville") 10-15 59
(Monaural.)
COLUMBIA (8133 "Dreamsville") 15-20 59
(Stereo.)

ALCATRAZZ LP '84
Singles: 7-inch
ROCSHIRE...4-8 83
Picture Sleeves
ROCSHIRE...8-15 83
LPs: 10/12-inch
CAPITOL..15-25 85
ROCSHIRE..15-25 83-84
Members: Graham Bonnet; Steve Vai; Yngwie Malmsteen; Gary Shea; Jan Uvena; Jimmy Waldo.

ALCONS
Singles: 7-inch
BRUNSWICK (55128 "One Note Samba")...10-15 59
CORAL (62201 "Mambo Jambo")..............10-15 60

ALDA, Alex
(Nick Massi)
Singles: 7-inch
TOPIX (6007 "Little Pony")......................40-60 62
(Promotional issue only.)
Also see 4 SEASONS

ALDEN, Roy, & Aldenaires
Singles: 7-inch
GLOLITE (106 "Crazy Memories") 30-40

ALDEN & ONE-NIGHTERS
Singles: 7-inch
RCA (7490 "Love-O-Meter") 15-25 59

ALDON & EC'S
Singles: 7-inch
GAITY (174 "Endsville")...........................40-60 59
Members: Al Fremstad; Don Cronkhite; Tex Hanson; Art Hestekin; Kip McFaul; Tom O'Brien.

ALDRICH, Ronnie LP '61
(With the Squadcats)
LPs: 10/12-inch
LONDON PHASE 4......................................5-15 60-71
RICHMOND (20058 "All Time Jazz Hits")..10-20 59
(Monaural.)
RICHMOND (30058 "All Time Jazz Hits")..15-25 59
(Stereo.)

ALDRIDGE, Jim
Singles: 7-inch
RAZORBACK (110 "The Frog")...............15-20 61

ALEONG, Aki
(With the Nobels; with Teen Twenty; with His Licorice Twisters; Aki)
Singles: 7-inch
MONA-LEE (130 "How Do I Stand with You?")...400-500 59
REPRISE 8-12 61-62
VEE-JAY (520 "Body Surf") 8-12 63
VEE-JAY (527 "Love Is Funny")..................8-12 63
LPs: 10/12-inch
REPRISE (6011 "Twistin' the Hits")..........30-40 62
REPRISE (6020 "C'mon Baby, Let's Dance")..30-40 62
VEE-JAY (1060 "Come Surf with Me").......40-50 63
Session: Ralph Geddes; Paul Geddes; Marty Smith; Ron Smith; Louis Abella; Rick Gardner.
Also see A'KIES
Also see AKIM & AKTONES
Also see EXPRESSOS

ALEXANDER, Arthur P&R/R&B '62
Singles: 7-inch
AT YOU...4-6
BUDDAH..4-8 75-78
DOT..15-20 62-64
GORDA 4-8
MONUMENT..5-10 68
MUSIC MILL 4-8 77
SOUND STAGE 7 ....5-8 65-70
W.B. 4-6 72-73
EPs: 7-inch
DOT (434 "You Better Move On") 25-35 62
(Stereo. Juke box issue only.)
LPs: 10/12-inch
DOT (3434 "You Better Move On") 35-45 62
(Monaural.)
DOT (25434 "You Better Move On") 40-55 62
(Stereo.)
W.B. 8-15 72
Also see ALEXANDER, June

ALEXANDER, Bob, & Coaxials
Singles: 7-inch
TUNE (206 "Treehouse").......................175-225

ALEXANDER, C., & Natural 3
Singles: 7-inch
GUY JIM (588 "Pay Them No Mind").......15-25 '60s
LEO...30-40 '60s

ALEXANDER, Charles
Singles: 7-inch
CB (302 "Pretty Blue")..........................100-200

ALEXANDER, Jeff
(Jeff Alexander Quartet)
Singles: 78 rpm
AARDELL (0001 "Dr. Geek")....................10-15 55
Singles: 7-inch
AARDELL (0001 "Dr. Geek") 40-50 55
LPs: 10/12-inch
FH...10-20

ALEXANDER, Joe
(Joe Alexander's Highlanders)
Singles: 78 rpm
CAPITOL...10-20 46-48
EXCELSIOR 5-15 46
Also see BROOKS, Dusty

ALEXANDER, Joe, & Cubans
Singles: 78 rpm
BALLAD (1008 "Oh Maria") 400-600 55

Singles: 7-inch
BALLAD (1008 "Oh Maria")............ 1000-1500 55
Members: Joe Alexander; Chuck Berry; Faith Douglas; Freddy Golden.
Also see ALEXANDER, Joe
Also see BERRY, Chuck

ALEXANDER, June
(Arthur Alexander)
Singles: 7-inch
JUDD (1020 "Sally Sue Brown") 25-35 60
Also see ALEXANDER, Arthur

ALEXANDER, Keith
Singles: 7-inch
GEMINI (901 "Poor Orphan Boy").......... 30-40 62

ALEXANDER, Max
Singles: 7-inch
CAPROCK (116 "Little Rome") 75-125 59

ALEXANDER, Mike, & Visions
Singles: 7-inch
RICHIE (673 "Pop Goes Love") 20-30 67

ALEXANDER, Norm
(Norman Alexander)
Singles: 78 rpm
HOLLYWOOD.................................... 15-25 53
Singles: 7-inch
FIFTY-FOUR (5424 "Danny Boy") 15-25 59
HOLLYWOOD (1004 "My Baby Left Me").. 25-35 53
HONEE B (106 "Trusting You") 15-25 59

ALEXANDER, Texas, & Benton's Busy Bees
Singles: 78 rpm
FREEDOM (1538 "Bottoms Blues") 75-125 50

ALEXANDER, Van
Singles: 7-inch
CAPITOL (4258 "Big Operator").............. 10-15 59
LPs: 10/12-inch
CAPITOL (1243 "Home of Happy Feet") . 15-20 59

ALEXANDER & BANDSMEN
Singles: 7-inch
JAY (5267 "Everybody Rock")............... 75-125

ALEXANDER & GREATS
Singles: 7-inch
ARVEE (5064 "Swanee Stomp")............ 10-20 62
LIMELIGHT (3040 "Hot Dang Mustang"). 15-25 64

ALEXANDER'S ROCK TIME BAND
Singles: 7-inch
J&T (2022 "Number One Hippie on the Village Scene") 10-15 67
Members: Jeff Travis; Craig Perkins, Kelly Kotera, Frank Elia; Bruce Watson.
Also see COACHMEN

ALEXANDER'S TIMELESS BLOOZBAND
Singles: 7-inch
KAPP 5-10 69
MATAMAT.. 15-20 67
UNI (55044 "Love So Strong") 10-15 67
LPs: 10/12-inch
UNI (73021 "For Sale")........................ 30-50 68
SMACK (1001 "Alexander's Timeless Bloozband") 150-250 67

ALEXANDERS
Singles: 7-inch
FILM CITY (1004 "Snap Your Fingers") .. 40-50

ALFI & HARRY *P&R '56*
(David Seville)
Singles: 78 rpm
LIBERTY...5-10 55-57
Singles: 7-inch
LIBERTY (55008 "The Trouble with Harry")... 15-20 55
LIBERTY (55016 "Persian on Excursion").. 10-15 56
LIBERTY (55066 "Closing Time") 10-15 57
Also see SEVILLE, David

ALFORD, Annie
Singles: 78 rpm
GROOVE (0172 "It's Heavenly") 10-20 56
Singles: 7-inch
GROOVE (0172 "It's Heavenly")............ 30-40 56
VIK (0288 "Easy Baby")......................... 20-30 57
Also see FORD, Ann

ALFRED, Chuz
Singles: 78 rpm
SAVOY 5-10 55
Singles: 7-inch
SAVOY (1158 "Buckeye Bounce")...........15-25 55
SAVOY (1175 "Rock Along")....................15-25 55

ALGERE, Ray
Singles: 7-inch
TOU-SEA (126 "In My Corner") 20-30

ALHONA, Richie
Singles: 7-inch
FANTASY (553 "One Desire") 8-12 61
(Black vinyl.)
FANTASY (553 "One Desire") 20-30 61
(Red vinyl. Promotional issue only. May include dee jay insert letter.)
FANTASY (556 "Mama Mama")..................8-12 61
FANTASY (561 "Fool")...............................8-12 62
Picture Sleeves
FANTASY (553 "One Desire") 20-30 61

ALI, Muhammad
(With Frank Sinatra, Richie Havens, Jayne Kennedy, Ossie Davis, Arthur Morrison, Howard Cosell)
LPs: 10/12-inch
ST. JOHN'S (1 "The Adventures of Ali and His Gang vs. Mr. Tooth Decay") 20-40 76
(Made for the St. John's Fruit and Vegetable Co. Promotional issue only.)
Also see CLAY, Cassius
Also see HAVENS, Richie
Also see SINATRA, Frank

ALICE IN CHAINS *LP '91*
LPs: 10/12-inch
COLUMBIA (2192 "Face Lift")..................50-75 90
(Promotional issue only.)
COLUMBIA (46075 "Face Lift")..................5-10 91
COLUMBIA (52475 "Face Lift")..................5-10 92
COLUMBIA (57804 "Jar of Flies")............12-18 94
(Promotional issue only.)
COLUMBIA (67248 "Jar of Flies"/"Sap") ..10-15 94
(Two colored vinyl discs.)

ALICE JEAN & MONDELLOS
("15 Year Old Alice Jean")
Singles: 7-inch
RHYTHM (102 "100 Years from Today") 250-350 57
Also see MONDELLOS

ALICE WONDER LAND *P&R '63*
Singles: 7-inch
BARDELL (774 "He's Mine")....................15-25 63
UNITED INT'L...10-15
Also see SWANS

ALICIA & ROCKAWAYS
Singles: 78 rpm
EPIC 10-20 56
Singles: 7-inch
EPIC (9191 "Why Can't I Be Loved")........20-25 56

ALICIA & ROCKAWAYS / Ken Darrell & Rockaways
Singles: 78 rpm
EPIC 10-15 57
Singles: 7-inch
EPIC (9226 "I'm Not Goin' Steady"/ "Faleroo")...15-20 57
Also see ALICIA & ROCKAWAYS

ALIENS
Singles: 7-inch
SON OF A WITCH (1801 "Season of the Witch") 10-20

ALIOTTA, HAYNES & JEREMIAH
Singles: 7-inch
ALIOTTA, HAYNES & JEREMIAH ("Lake Shore Drive")..8-10 78
(Yellow label. Shows only title, artist and A/B sides.)
SNOW QUEEN (1000 "Snow Queen"/"Lake Shore Drive")..15-20 73
LPs: 10/12-inch
AMPEX (10119 "Jeremiah")....................10-20 71
BIG FOOT 20-25 78
LITTLE FOOT 8-10 77
Members: Ted Aliotta; Mitch Aliotta; Skip Haynes; John Jeremiah.
Also see ROTARY CONNECTION

ALIVE 'N KICKING *P&R/LP '70*
(Alive 'N Kickin')
Singles: 7-inch
A&M...4-6
ROULETTE...4-6 70-71
Picture Sleeves
A&M...4-6
LPs: 10/12-inch
ROULETTE (42052 "Alive 'N Kickin' ")......20-30 70
(Commercial issue.)
ROULETTE (42052 "Alive 'N Kickin' ")......40-60 70
(Promotional issue.)
Members: Pepe Cardona; Sandy Toder; John Parisio; Bruce Sudano; Thomas "Woody" Wilson; Vito Albano.

ALL NIGHT WORKERS
Singles: 7-inch
CAMEO (420 "Honey & Wine")................30-40 66
MERCURY (72833 "Collector")................15-25 68
ROUND SOUND (1 "Don't Put All Your Eggs in One Basket") 350-450 65
Member: Lou Reed.
Also see REED, Lou

ALL STARS
Singles: 7-inch
VON (704 "2-2-5 Special") ....40-60 '60s

ALL STARS
LPs: 10/12-inch
GRAMOPHONE (20192 "Boogie Woogie")..40-50

ALLADINS
Singles: 7-inch
PRISM (6001 "Then")..........................500-600 60

ALLAN, Chad
(With the Expressions)
Singles: 7-inch
MALA (12033 "Thru the Looking Glass") 4-8 68
REPRISE...4-6 71
LPs: 10/12-inch
SCEPTER (533 "Guess Who's Chad Allan and the Expressions")..25-35 66
Also see ALLEN, Chad
Also see GUESS WHO

ALLAN, Davie *P&R '65*
(With the Arrows; "The Arrows Featuring Davie Allen")
Singles: 7-inch
ARTISTS OF AMERICA 4-6 76
CUDE (101 "War Path")..........................30-40 63
MARC (3223 "War Path")........................20-30 63
MGM...4-6 71-73
MRC..3-5 84
PRIVATE STOCK......................................4-6 74
SIDEWALK (1 "Apache '65")....................20-30 64
TOWER..10-15 65-68
WHAT..3-5 82
LPs: 10/12-inch
ALKOR 5-10 84
ARROW DYNAMICS....................................8-12 85
DIONYSUS 5-10
TOWER (5002 "Apache '65").....................25-50 65
TOWER (5078 "Blues Theme")..................25-50 67
TOWER (5094 "Cycle-Ddelic Sounds")......25-50 67
TOWER (5139 "Wild in the Street")......100-150 68
WHAT (601 "Stoked on Surf")..................10-15 83
Members: Davie Allan; Steve Pugh; Larry Brown; Paul Johnson; Don Manning; Tony Allwine.
Also see ALBANO, Frankie
Also see ANNETTE
Also see BROOKINS, Doug
Also see CURB, Mike
Also see DALE, Dick
Also see FASTEST GROUP ALIVE
Also see FROST, Max, & Troopers
Also see GRADS
Also see GREEN BEANS
Also see HANDS OF TIME
Also see HEYBURNERS
Also see HONDELLS
Also see MOORE & MOORE
Also see NAYLOR, Jerry
Also see PARIS SISTERS
Also see PEWTER, Jim
Also see PRISCILLA
Also see RONSTADT, Linda
Also see SHARLETS
Also see SINNERS
Also see STAFFORD, Terry
Also see STARLETS
Also see STREAMERS
Also see 13TH COMMITTEE
Also see TONY & VIZITORS
Also see VIOT, Russ
Also see VISITORS
Also see ZANIES

ALLAN, Davie / Eternity's Children / Main Attraction / Sunrays
EPs: 7-inch
TOWER (4557 "Selections from April Albums")..25-50 68
(Promotional issue only.)
Also see ALLAN, Davie
Also see ETERNITY'S CHILDREN
Also see SUNRAYS

ALLAN, Johnnie
(Johnnie Allen; Johnny Allen)
Singles: 7-inch
AMY (814 "Everybody's Got a Girl But Me")...8-12 61
JIN (100 series, except 181)..................10-20 59-66
JIN (181 "Let's Do It")............................50-75 65
JIN (200 & 300 series) 5-10 66-76
MERCURY (71567 "Angel Love") 8-12 60
MGM (12799 "Lonely Days, Lonely Nights")...5-10 59
PIC-1 (102 "Love Fever")..........................5-10 64
VIKING (1016 "Unfaithful One")..............10-15 61
LPs: 10/12-inch
JIN 15-20

ALLAN, Kent
Singles: 7-inch
ALON (9008 "What Have I Done") 25-35 63

ALLAN, Kirby
Singles: 7-inch
MAZE (140 "Mother Don't Allow Rock & Roll") ....75-125 '50s
(Black vinyl.)
MAZE (140 "Mother Don't Allow Rock & Roll") 5-10
(Colored vinyl.)
MAZE (1002 "Don't You Remember")......10-20 55

ALLAN & FLAMES
Singles: 7-inch
CAMPBELL (225 "Till the End of Time")..50-60 59
COLONIAL (7006 "Till the End of Time").30-40 60

ALLEGRO, Joe
Singles: 7-inch
CHAM (001 "Teen-age Clementine") 8-12
END (1013 "Web of Dreams") 50-75 58
LAURIE (3307 "You Know").......................5-10 65
LAURIE (3650 "Sound of the Wild") 4-6 77
LIBERTY (55064 "I Found a Dream") 10-20 57

ALLEN, Adrienne
Singles: 7-inch
RUST (5058 "Dancing with Tears in My Eyes")..8-12 63
U.A. (758 "One Boy in My Life") 8-12 64
YALE (240 "When Love Comes Knocking")...75-125 60
Also see FIVE DISCS

ALLEN, Al, & Drags
Singles: 7-inch
CARLTON (511 "Egghead") 15-25 59
RADIANT (1506 "The Drag") 15-25 62

ALLEN, Annisteen *R&B '53*
(With Her Home Town Boys; with Gene Redd Orchestra)
Singles: 78 rpm
CAPITOL..10-15 54-55
DECCA...10-15 56-57
FEDERAL 10-20 51-52
KING (4115 thru 4128)............................10-20 46
KING (4608 thru 4691)..............................8-12 53-54
Singles: 7-inch
CAPITOL..20-30 54-55
DECCA...10-20 56-57
KING..25-35 53-54
WIG (104 "Sweet William") 10-20 59
Also see ALLEN, Ernestine
Also see GREER, John

ALLEN, Annisteen, & Melvin Moore
(With the Lucky Millinder Orchestra)
Singles: 7-inch
TODD (1037 "Trouble in Mind")..................5-10 59

Also see ALLEN, Annisteen

ALLEN, Barbara
Singles: 7-inch
DECCA (30598 "Sweet Willie") 10-20 58
FELSTED (8537 "Never Let Me Go") 10-20 59
FELSTED (8545 "He Loves Me") 10-20 59
FELSTED (8556 "Rockin' Charleston") 10-20 59
FELSTED (8583 "Say the Magic Words") 10-20 59
FELSTED (8594 "My Problem") 10-20 59

ALLEN, Barbara
Singles: 7-inch
SPECIAL AGENT (203 "I'm Not Mad Anymore") 25-50 66
Also see ACKLIN, Barbara

ALLEN, Beau
Singles: 7-inch
HFA (1016 "Give Me Your Love") 15-25 65
SCEPTER (12247 "My Time") 5-10 69
EPs: 7-inch
HFA 25-35

ALLEN, Bernie
Singles: 7-inch
CHECKER (862 "You Can Run, But You Can't Hide") 15-25 57

ALLEN, Bill, Trio
Singles: 7-inch
VEE-JAY (542 "Money") 10-20 63

ALLEN, Billy
(With the Keynotes; with Back Beats; Bill Allen)
Singles: 7-inch
ELDORADO (505 "Butterfly") 10-15 57
IMPERIAL (5500 "Please Give Me Something") 75-100 58

ALLEN, Billy, & Nomads
Singles: 7-inch
SOMA (1112 "Ryders in the Sky") 30-40 59
SOMA (1415 "Ryders in the Sky") 10-15 64

ALLEN, Blinky
(Blinky Allen Orchestra; with Star Dusters)
Singles: 78 rpm
FLAIR 10-20 54
SWING TIME 15-25 53
Singles: 7-inch
FLAIR 20-30 54
PERSONALITY (3502 "Battle of Beatnik Bay") 10-15 61
SWING TIME 25-35 53
Also see ANNA MARIA & BLINKY ALLEN STAR DUSTERS

ALLEN, Bob
Singles: 7-inch
CLASS (250 "After Shock") 30-40 59
DIAMOND (197 "I'm Alone Again") 10-15 66

ALLEN, Chad
(With the Reflections)
Singles: 7-inch
CANADIAN AMERICAN (802 "Tribute to Buddy Holly"/"Back and Forth") 30-50 64
CANADIAN AMERICAN (802 "I Just Didn't Have the Heart"/"Back and Forth") 15-20 64
LAMA (7779 "Little Lonely") 30-40 61
QUALITY (1559 "Shy Guy") 15-20 '60s
(Canadian.)
QUALITY (1644 "Stop Teasing Me") 20-30 '60s
(Canadian.)
RADIANT (1508 "Come on Linda") 8-12 62
SMASH (1720 "Little Lonely") 10-15 61
Also see ALLAN, Chad
Also see ASHLEY, Bob

ALLEN, Charlie
Singles: 7-inch
PORTRAIT (107 "Sweetie Pie") 10-20 61

ALLEN, Chip, & Chipettes
Singles: 7-inch
CORSICAN (100 "Tell Me Today") 10-15 63

ALLEN, Chip, & Pictures
Singles: 7-inch
ASTRO (117 "Let the Good Times Roll") 10-15 67

ALLEN, Chris
Singles: 7-inch
HOLLYWOOD (1098 "Saxophone Pete") 75-100 59
HOLLYWOOD (1101 "Tick Tock") 40-60 60

ALLEN, Chris & Peter
Singles: 7-inch
ABC 5-10 66
MERCURY 5-10 68
LPs: 10/12-inch
MERCURY 10-20 68

ALLEN, Clay
Singles: 78 rpm
TNT 10-15 53
Singles: 7-inch
TNT (102 "How Many Hearts Have You Broken") 15-25 53

ALLEN, Connee
(With Leon Washington's Orchestra)
Singles: 78 rpm
THERON 15-25 55
Singles: 7-inch
THERON (114 "I Haven't Got the Heart") 50-75 55
THERON (115 "Saving My Love") 50-75 55
Also see RHODES, Todd

ALLEN, Cordia
Singles: 7-inch
DALE (104 "Lovers Call") 15-25 58

ALLEN, Dale, & Rebel Rousers
Singles: 7-inch
VAMPIRE (10762 "Hideaway") 60-80 62
Also see TITANS

ALLEN, Danny
Singles: 7-inch
VALLEY 15-25 58

ALLEN, Dave "The Man"
Singles: 7-inch
TIFFANY 4-6 71
LPs: 10/12-inch
INT'L ARTISTS (11 "Color Blind") 60-75 69
(Green label.)
INT'L ARTISTS (11 "Color Blind") 75-100 69
(White label. Promotional issue only.)
INT'L ARTISTS (11 "Color Blind") 15-25
(Reissue. Green label. With "RE2" etched in the vinyl trail-off.)

ALLEN, Dayton *LP '60*
LPs: 10/12-inch
GRAND AWARD (424 "Why Not!") 20-30 60

ALLEN, Dick, & Fairlanes
Singles: 7-inch
CUCA (63114 "Dreamin'") 15-25 63
Also see NIGHT OWLS

ALLEN, Dickie
Singles: 7-inch
IMPERIAL (5701 "Sally Ann") 15-25 60

ALLEN, Duane
Singles: 7-inch
KEYNOTE (25 "Surf Around the World") 15-25 63

ALLEN, Ernestine
(Annisteen Allen)
Singles: 7-inch
TRU SOUND (405 "Let It Roll") 10-20 61
LPs: 10/12-inch
TRU SOUND (15004 "Let It Roll") 35-50 62
Also see ALLEN, Annisteen

ALLEN, Frankie
Singles: 7-inch
ADONIS (104 "If You Make a Wish") 10-20 60

ALLEN, George
(George Smith)
Singles: 7-inch
SOTOPLAY (0010 "Tight Dress") 10-15 61
SOTOPLAY (0031 "I Must Be Crazy") 10-20 62
Also see HARMONICA KING
Also see LITTLE WALTER, JR.
Also see SMITH, George

ALLEN, Harold
Singles: 7-inch
MAR-VEL (1200 "Honky Tonk Women") 30-40 57
MAR-VEL (1201 "If You Were Mine Again") 50-75 57

ALLEN, Ira
Singles: 7-inch
MAV-RICK (105 "Nursery Rock") 350-400

ALLEN, Jesse
Singles: 78 rpm
ALADDIN 25-50 52
BAYOU 10-20 53
CORAL 25-50 51
IMPERIAL 25-50 53-55
Singles: 7-inch
ALADDIN (3129 "Rock This Morning") 75-150 52
BAYOU (011 "Dragnet") 50-75 53
CORAL (65078 "My Suffering") 75-150 51
DUPLEX (9003 "Love My Baby") 150-250
IMPERIAL (5256 "Gotta Call That Number") 75-150 53
IMPERIAL (5285 "Sittin' and Wonderin'") 100-200 54
IMPERIAL (5305 "Things I'm Gonna Do") 75-150 53
IMPERIAL (5315 "Rockin' & Rollin'") 75-150 55
VIN (1002 "Goodbye Blues") 30-50 58

ALLEN, Jimmy
(With the Two Jays; Jimmie Allen)
Singles: 78 rpm
MGM 10-15 52
Singles: 7-inch
AL-BRITE (1200 "My Girl Is a Pearl") 75-100 58
KOOL (1008 "These Lonely Blues") 10-15 60
MGM 20-30 52

ALLEN, Jimmy, & Tommy Bartella
Singles: 7-inch
AL-BRITE (1300 "When Santa Comes Over the Brooklyn Bridge") 15-25 59
Also see ALLEN, Jimmy

ALLEN, Joe, & His Alley Cats
Singles: 7-inch
JALO (201 "Baby, Baby, Baby") 50-75 58
JALO (202 "I Want to Thrill You") 50-75 58

ALLEN, Judy
Singles: 7-inch
LAURIE (3017 "No More") 15-25 58
LAURIE (3018 "Six Little Men") 15-25 58
LAURIE (3025 "Sentimental Me") 15-25 59

ALLEN, Lee *P&R '58*
Singles: 78 rpm
ALADDIN 10-20 56
EMBER 20-40 58
Singles: 7-inch
ALADDIN 15-25 56
COLLECTABLES 3-5 82
EMBER 10-20 57-62
WAND 5-10 '60s
EPs: 7-inch
EMBER (103 "Walkin' with Mr. Lee") 50-75 58
LPs: 10/12-inch
COLLECTABLES (5083 "Walkin' with Mr. Lee") 5-10 87
EMBER (200 "Walkin' with Mr. Lee") 75-125 58
(Red label.)
EMBER (200 "Walkin' with Mr. Lee") 60-80 58
("Logs" label. Ember logo is formed with logs.)
EMBER (200 "Walkin' with Mr. Lee") 25-40 60
(Black label.)
Also see BIRDSONG, Larry
Also see DOMINO, Fats
Also see BLASTERS
Also see GAYTEN, Paul
Also see LITTLE RICHARD
Also see NEWSOM, Chubby, & Her Hip Shakers
Also see SMITH, Huey

ALLEN, Levinsky
Singles: 7-inch
VITAL (321 "Layed Off") 40-50 60

ALLEN, Little Joe
Singles: 7-inch
MCM (411 "Tiger") 100-150

ALLEN, Little Johnny
Singles: 78 rpm
BULLSEYE 10-20 56
Singles: 7-inch
BULLSEYE (105 "She's the Girl for Me") 20-30 56

ALLEN, Little Marie
Singles: 7-inch
TRIUMPH (603 "Humdinger") 10-20 59
Also see WARNER, Sonny, & Marie Allen

ALLEN, Lonnie
Singles: 7-inch
VAL-HILL (1005 "You'll Never Change Me") 50-75

ALLEN, Mike
Singles: 7-inch
MAR-RAY (7001 "Love Is Just a Game") 10-20

ALLEN, Mills
Singles: 7-inch
BLACK GOLD (303 "This Is It") 15-25 62
BLACK GOLD (304 "This Is It") 10-20 62
(Alternate track reissue.)

ALLEN, Milton
(With the Goldens & Paradons)
Singles: 78 rpm
RCA (6994 "Love a, Love a Lover") 15-25 57
ROBIN (61824 "My Song") 25-35 56
Singles: 7-inch
RCA (6994 "Love a, Love a Lover") 15-25 57
RCA (7116 "Don't Bug Me Baby") 50-75 58
ROBIN (61824 "My Song") 150-200 56

ALLEN, Mimi
(With the Miles Grayson Orchestra)
Singles: 7-inch
THREE SPEED (711 "Do You Miss Me") 25-35 61
LPs: 10/12-inch
DECCA (8825 "There Goes My Harp") 5-10 59

ALLEN, Pat
JOSIE (772 "Please Be Kind") 5-10 55
Singles: 7-inch
JOSIE (772 "Please Be Kind") 10-20 55

ALLEN, Pete
Singles: 7-inch
GLORY (300 "Sweet of You") 10-20 59

ALLEN, Ray
(With the Upbeats; with Vinny Catalano & Orchestra)
Singles: 7-inch
BLAST (204 "Peggy Sue") 8-12 62
DCP (1007 "He Don't Love You Anymore") 8-12 64
DCP (1103 "No Top Suit") 8-12 64
MALA (504 "That Is My Love") 5-10 65
MALA (522 "Dondi") 5-10 66
ROULETTE (4721 "Al Di La") 5-10 67
ROULETTE (4737 "Roselina") 5-10 67
SINCLAIR (1004 "Let Them Talk") 20-30 61
LPs: 10/12-inch
BLAST (6804 "A Tribute to Six") 75-125 62
Also see CATALANO, Vinny

ALLEN, Ray, & Carnations
Singles: 7-inch
ACE (130 "A Fool in Love") 50-75 59
Also see CARNATIONS

ALLEN, Ray, & Trendells
Singles: 7-inch
CUCA (6544 "Look at Me") 15-25 65
CUCA (6562 "Shake a Tail Feather") 15-25 65
CUCA (63104 "Who's Gonna Cry") 15-25 63
Members: Ray Allen Harbach; Danny Riccio; Larry Rongsvoog; Dick Simon; John Verbraken; Ted Riccio; Duane Gauger; Damon Lee.

ALLEN, Rex *C&W '49*
(With the Arizona Wranglers & Jerry Byrd)
Singles: 78 rpm
DECCA (Except 30651) 5-10 52-57
DECCA (30651 "Knock Knock, Rattle") 10-20 56
MERCURY 5-10 49-55
Singles: 7-inch
BUENA VISTA 10-15 59-60
DECCA (Except 28000 thru 30000 series) 4-8 56-72
DECCA (28000 & 29000 series) 5-10 52-56
DECCA (30000 series except 30651) 5-10 56
DECCA (30651 "Knock Knock, Rattle") 15-20 56
JAMIE 4-6 76
MCA 4-6 79
MERCURY 5-10 53-63
WILDCAT 4-6
Picture Sleeves
MERCURY 10-15 63

EPs: 7-inch
DECCA.................10-20 56
MERCURY.................10-20 53-56
LPs: 10/12-inch
BUENA VISTA (3307 "Rex Allen Sings 16 Favorites")..........40-50 61
COLLECTOR'S CLASSICS..........5-10
CORAL..........5-10 73
DECCA (5000 series)..........10-15 68-70
(Decca LP numbers in this series preceded by a "7" or a "DL-7" are stereo issues.)
DECCA (8000 series)..........20-30 56-59
DESIGN..........10-15 62
DISNEYLAND..........6-10 70
HACIENDA (101 "Country Songs I Love")..........50-60
JMI (4003 "Rex Allen Sings")..........20-30
MCA..........5-10
MERCURY (20719 "Faith of a Man")..........15-25 62
(Monaural.)
MERCURY (20752 "Rex Allen Sings and Tells Tales")..........15-25 62
(Monaural.)
MERCURY (60719 "Faith of a Man")..........20-30 62
(Stereo.)
MERCURY (60752 "Rex Allen Sings and Tells Tales")..........20-30 62
(Stereo.)
PICKWICK/HILLTOP..........10-15 65
VOCALION..........6-10 70
WING..........10-15 64-66
Session: Jud Conlon Singers; Anita Kerr Singers; Merry Melody Singers.
Also see KERR, Anita
Also see CURTIS, Ken / Rex Allen & Arizona Wranglers

ALLEN, Richie P&R '60
(With the Pacific Surfers)
Singles: 7-inch
ERA (3058 "Blue Holiday")..........8-12 61
IMPERIAL..........10-20 60-63
TOWER (273 "Nothing Good")..........5-10 66
LPs: 10/12-inch
IMPERIAL..........50-75 63-64
Members: Richie Allen; Ron Lloyd; Jim MacMurdo; Bill Cooper; Ray Pohlman; Sandy Nelson; Les Weiser.
Session: Richie Podolor.
Also see NELSON, Sandy
Also see PODOLOR, Dickie

ALLEN, Ricky R&B '63
(With the Allen Dolls)
Singles: 7-inch
AGE (29102 "You'd Better Be Sure")..........25-35 61
AGE (29104 "From You")..........15-25 61
AGE (29105 thru 29125)..........10-20 62-64
APOGEE (103 "It's Love Baby")..........8-10 64
BRIGHT STAR..........5-10 66-69
FOUR BROTHERS (401 "I Can't Stand No Signifying")..........10-15 65
FOUR BROTHERS (402 "Keep It to Yourself")..........8-12 65
(Retitled reissue of *I Can't Stand No Signifying.*)
MEL-LON (1004 "Help Me Mama")..........10-15 '60s
TAM-BOO (6720 "Cut You Loose")..........5-10 68
USA..........8-10 65
Session: Elites.

ALLEN, Rockin' Dave
(With Thunderbirds)
Singles: 7-inch
JIN (130 "My Broken Heart")..........10-15 60

ALLEN, Ronnie
Singles: 7-inch
SAN (208 "Juvenile Delinquent")..........50-75 59
SAN (209 "High School Love")..........50-75 59
SAN (300 "Gonna Get My Baby")..........50-75 59
ALLEN, Ronnie
(Alan Ronald Kaltman)
Singles: 7-inch
DAPT (205 "Flip Over You")..........50-75 61

ALLEN, Rosalie C&W '46
(With the Black River Riders; with Sons of the Purple Sage; with Tex Fletcher)
Singles: 78 rpm
BLUEBIRD..........5-10 49-50
GRAND AWARD..........12-25 56-57
RCA..........5-10 46-50

Singles: 7-inch
RCA (48-0068 thru 48-0403)..........10-20 49-51
(Green vinyl.)
LPs: 10/12-inch
GRAND AWARD (330 "Songs of the Golden West")..........30-40 56
GRAND AWARD (350 "Rodeo")..........25-35 57
WALDORF (150 "C&W Hits")..........25-45 56
Also see BRITT, Elton, Rosalie Allen & Skytoppers

ALLEN, Steve P&R/LP '55
(With Donn Trenner & Orchestra)
Singles: 78 rpm
BRUNSWICK..........4-8 53
CORAL..........4-8 55-56
Singles: 7-inch
BRUNSWICK..........10-20 53
CORAL..........10-20 55-56
DOT..........5-15 59-66
DUNHILL (Except 4097)..........5-10 67-68
DUNHILL (4097 "Here Comes Sgt. Pepper")..........8-12 67
SIGNATURE..........8-12 59-60
Picture Sleeves
DOT..........10-15 65
EPs: 7-inch
BRUNSWICK..........10-20 53
COLUMBIA..........10-15 '50s
CORAL..........10-20 55-56
DECCA..........15-20 55
WOODBURY'S..........10-20
LPs: 10/12-inch
COLUMBIA (2554 "Steve Allen")..........30-40 56
(10-inch LP.)
CORAL (100 "Jazz Story")..........35-45 59
(Narration by Steve Allen, music by various artists.)
CORAL (57000 series, except 57099)......15-25 55-56
CORAL (57099 "James Dean Story")..........40-60 56
(With Bill Randle.)
CORAL (57400 series)..........10-20 63
(Monaural.)
CORAL (7-57400 series)..........15-25 63
(Stereo.)
DECCA..........20-30 55
DOT (Except 3472 & 3517)..........10-20 59-66
DOT (3472 "Steve Allen's Funny Fone Calls")..........15-25 63
DOT (3517 "More Funny Fone Calls")..........15-25 63
DUNHILL..........8-10 67
EMARCY..........15-25 58
HAMILTON..........10-20 59-64
MERCURY..........10-15 61
PETE..........5-10 69
ROULETTE (25053 "At the Roundtable").15-25 59
SIGNATURE (Except 1004)..........15-25 59
SIGNATURE (1004 "Man on the Street").30-40 59
(With Louis Nye, Tom Poston and Don Knotts.)
Session: Copacabana Trio.
Also see FOSTER, Phil
Also see KEROUAC, Jack, & Steve Allen
Also see NYE, Louis
Also see PRESLEY, Elvis

ALLEN, Steve, with George Cates Orchestra & Chorus P&R '55
Singles: 78 rpm
CORAL (61485 "Autumn Leaves")..........5-10 55
Singles: 7-inch
CORAL (61485 "Autumn Leaves")..........10-15 55

ALLEN, Steve, & Jayne Meadows
Singles: 78 rpm
CORAL..........5-10 55
Singles: 7-inch
CORAL..........10-20 55
SIGNATURE (12003 "Flattery")..........8-12 59

ALLEN, Steve, & Ricky Vera
(With George Cates & Orchestra)
Singles: 78 rpm
CORAL..........5-10 53
Singles: 7-inch
CORAL (61098 "Can I Wait Up for Santa")..........10-15 53
Also see ALLEN, Steve
Also see VERA, Ricky

ALLEN, Sue
(With the Four Students)
Singles: 78 rpm
GROOVE..........8-12 55

Singles: 7-inch
GROOVE (0130 "Think of Tomorrow")..........20-30 55
WORLD WIDE (8002 "Hurry Back")..........10-20 60
Also see BLACK, Oscar, & Sue Allen
Also see FOUR STUDENTS

ALLEN, Tony
(With the Chimes; with Champs; with Twilighters; with Wanderers; with Wonders; with Night Owls; with Originals; with Arthur Wright Combo; Tony & Barbara)
Singles: 78 rpm
DIG (104 "It Hurts Me So")..........15-25 56
(Reissue of Ultra 104.)
DIG (109 "I Found an Angel")..........20-30 56
EBB (115 "Come Back")..........10-20 57
SPECIALTY (560 "Nite Owl")..........15-20 55
SPECIALTY (570 "Especially")..........10-15 56
ULTRA (104 "It Hurts Me So")..........10-15 55
Singles: 7-inch
BETHLEHEM (3002 "Come-A, Come-A Baby")..........10-20 61
BETHLEHEM (3004 "It Hurts Me So")......10-20 62
BIG TIME (157 "Be My Love")..........30-40 58
CLASSIC ARTISTS (102 "The Back Door").5-8 88
(Black vinyl. 1000 made.)
DIG (104 "It Hurts Me So")..........20-30 56
DIG (109 "I Found an Angel")..........50-60 56
(Maroon label.)
DIG (109 "I Found an Angel")..........15-25 56
(Maroon and silver label.)
EBB (115 "Come Back")..........30-40 57
IMPERIAL (5523 "Call My Name")..........10-15 58
JAMIE (1119 "Looking for My Baby")..........10-15 59
JAMIE (1143 "Train of Love")..........10-15 59
KENT (356 "Everybody's Somebody's Fool")..........75-100 61
KENT (364 "Dreamin'")..........30-40 61
ORIGINAL SOUND (13 "Little Lonely Girl")..........30-40 60
SPECIALTY (560 "Nite Owl")..........40-50 55
SPECIALTY (570 "Especially")..........25-35 56
TAMPA (157 "Be My Love")..........40-50 58
ULTRA (104 "It Hurts Me So")..........15-25 56
(First issue.)
U.A. (50190 "Now Is Forever")..........5-10 67
LPs: 10/12-inch
CROWN (5231 "Rock 'n Roll")..........50-100 60
Also see CHIMES
Also see JAGUARS
Also see ORIGINALS
Also see OTIS, Johnny
Also see SHIELDS
Also see STARR, Bobby
Also see TWILIGHTERS
Also see WONDERS

ALLEN, Van
Singles: 7-inch
AMERICAN BARN DANCE (606 "I Don't Believe I'll Fall in Love Today")..........40-60 '60s

ALLEN, Woody LP '64
Singles: 7-inch
U.A...........4-6 72
Picture Sleeves
U.A...........4-6 72
LPs: 10/12-inch
BELL..........10-15 67
CAPITOL..........8-12 68
CASABLANCA..........8-12 79
COLPIX..........20-30 64-65
U.A. (800 series)..........6-10 77
U.A. (9900 series)..........8-12 72

ALLEN BROTHERS
Singles: 7-inch
COLPIX (165 "First Kiss")..........10-15 60

ALLEN TRIO / Five Dips
Singles: 7-inch
ORIGINAL (1005 "That's What I Like").250-300 55

ALLENS, Arvee
(Ritchie Valens)
Singles: 7-inch
DEL-FI (4111 "Fast Freight")..........25-35 59
(Reissued as by Ritchie Valens.)
Also see VALENS, Ritchie

ALLEY, Jim C&W '68
Singles: 7-inch
AVCO (606 "If I Didn't Have a Dime")..........4-6 75
DOT (17051 "Only Daddy That'll Walk the Line")..........10-15 68

PEARL (1111 "The Great Pretender")......50-75 '50s
PEARL (4447 "Dig That Rock & Roll")...75-125 '50s
TOWER (227 "Fifty a Week")..........5-10 '66

ALLEY CATS P&R/R&B '63
Singles: 7-inch
EPIC (9778 "Lily of the West")..........10-15 65
PHILLES (108 "Puddin N' Tain")..........15-25 62
WHIPPET (202 "This Thing Called Love")..........15-25 56
WHIPPET (209 "Last Night")..........15-25 57
Members: Chester Pipkin; Gary Pipkin; Bobby Sheen; Sheridan Spencer; Brice Coefield; James Barker.
Session: Jack Nitzsche.
Also see NITZSCHE, Jack
Also see SHEEN, Bobby

ALLEY KATS
Singles: 7-inch
P-C (101 "Alley Kats")..........15-25 56
Member: Sax Kari.
Also see KARI, Sax

ALLEYNE, Gloria
Singles: 78 rpm
JOSIE (767 "When I Say My Prayer")..........10-20 54
Singles: 7-inch
JOSIE (767 "When I Say My Prayer")......25-35 54
Also see LYNNE, Gloria

ALLIE OOP'S GROUP
Singles: 7-inch
CAPRICE (102 "Bloop Bloop")..........30-40 61

ALLIES
Singles: 7-inch
VALIANT (748 "I'll Sell My Soul")..........20-30 66

ALLIES
Singles: 7-inch
DEE DAY (120182 "Heartbroken Man")..........4-6 82
Picture Sleeves
DEE DAY (120182 "Heartbroken Man")..........5-8 82
EPs: 7-inch
VICTORIA (100183 "Emma Peel")..........15-25 83
Members: David Kincaid; Carl Funk; Larry Mason; Andy Pederson; Jerry Battista; Steve Adamek; Gary Shelton.

ALLISON, Dave
Singles: 7-inch
TERRY (112 "Hep Cat Rock-A-Bye")..........50-75 '50s

ALLISON, Dick, & Broughams
Singles: 7-inch
DREEM (1003 "Dream World of Love")...20-25 60
Also see THOMPSON, Ron, & Broughams

ALLISON, Fran
(With Wayne King & Orchestra; with Tony Mottola & Orchestra; Dewey Bergman & Orchestra)
Singles: 78 rpm
DECCA..........5-10 55
MERCURY (70806 "Galway Bay")..........5-10 56
RCA..........5-10 50-51
Singles: 7-inch
DECCA (29452 "Water Tumbler Tune")...10-15 55
MERCURY (70806 "Galway Bay")..........10-15 56
RCA (0253 "Punky Punkin")..........10-15 50
RCA (8767 "The Girls in My Little Boy's Life")..........5-8 66
Also see MOTTOLA, Tony

ALLISON, Gene P&R/R&B '57
Singles: 78 rpm
CALVERT..........10-15 56
DECCA..........10-15 57
VEE-JAY..........10-20 57
Singles: 7-inch
ABNER (1036 "Why Do You Treat Me So Cold")..........5-10 60
CALVERT (106 "You're My Baby")..........20-30 56
CHAMPION (1008 "Goodbye My Love")..10-15 59
CHEROKEE (1019 "I Understand")..........10-15 59
DECCA (30185 "You're My Baby")..........10-15 56
MONUMENT (876 "Walkin' in the Park")...5-10 65
REF-O-REE..........5-10
VALDOT (7000 "Stay a Little Longer")......10-15 62
VEE-JAY..........15-25 57-60
LPs: 10/12-inch
VEE-JAY (1009 "Gene Allison")..........100-200 59
(Maroon label.)
VEE-JAY (1009 "Gene Allison")..........50-75 59
(Black label.)

Also see BOB & EARL / Gene Allison

ALLISON, Jerry, & Crickets

Singles: 7-inch

LIBERTY (55742 "We Gotta Get Together") 10-20 64
LIBERTY (55767 "Now Hear This") 10-20 65
Also see CRICKETS
Also see IVAN
Also see PEWTER, Jim

ALLISON, Keith
(Guitar Keith Allison)

Singles: 7-inch

AMY (11024 "Who Do You Love") 10-20 68
COLUMBIA 10-15 66-70
W.B. (5681 "Sweet Little Rock & Roller") 10-20 65

Picture Sleeves

COLUMBIA (44028 "Louise") 8-12 67
W.B. (5681 "Sweet Little Rock & Roller") 10-20 65

LPs: 10/12-inch

COLUMBIA 15-20 67
Also see EZBA, Denny
Also see REVERE, Paul, & Raiders
Also see UNKNOWNS

ALLISON, Leevert
(Levert Allison)

Singles: 7-inch

ELBEJAY (103 "You Made a World") 10-15
PONCELLO (7004 "I Want to Give My Heart") .... 15-25 '60s
TUPELO SOUND (003 "Loving On My Mind") 75-125

ALLISON, Mose

Singles: 7-inch

ATLANTIC (5021 "Your Mind Is on Vacation") 10-20 62
COLUMBIA (41717 "Deed I Do") 8-12 60
PRESTIGE 8-15 57-64

LPs: 10/12-inch

ATLANTIC (1389 "I Don't Worry") 25-35 62
ATLANTIC (1398 "Swingin' Machine") 25-35 63
ATLANTIC (1424 "Word from Mose") 25-35 64
ATLANTIC (1450 "Mose Alive") 20-30 66
ATLANTIC (1456 "Wild Man on the Loose") 20-30 66
COLUMBIA (1444 "Transfiguration of Hiram Brown") 35-50 60
COLUMBIA (1565 "I Love the Life I Live") 35-50 60
(Monaural.)
COLUMBIA (8367 "I Love the Life I Live") 40-55 60
(Stereo.)
EPIC (16031 "Mose Allison Takes to the Hills") 30-40 62
(Monaural.)
EPIC (17031 "Mose Allison Takes to the Hills") 35-45 62
(Stereo.)
EPIC (24183 "V-8 Ford Blues") 15-25 66
(Monaural.)
EPIC (26183 "V-8 Ford Blues") 15-25 66
(Stereo.)
PRESTIGE (7091 "Back Country Suite") .. 40-60 57
PRESTIGE (7121 "Local Color") 40-60 58
PRESTIGE (7137 "Young Man Mose") 40-60 58
PRESTIGE (7152 "Creek Bank") 40-60 58
PRESTIGE (7189 "Autumn Song") 40-60 59
PRESTIGE (7215 "Ramblin'") 40-60 59
PRESTIGE (7279 "Sing") 35-50 63
PRESTIGE (7423 "Down Home Piano") .. 15-25 65
PRESTIGE (7446 "For Lovers") 15-25 66

ALLISONS — P&R '63

Singles: 7-inch

COLUMBIA (42034 "Blue Tears") 5-10 61
SMASH (1749 "Lessons in Love") 5-10 62
TIP (1011 "Surfer Street") 20-30 63

ALLMAN, Duane & Gregg — LP '72

Singles: 7-inch

BOLD 5-8 73

LPs: 10/12-inch

BOLD (301 "Duane & Gregg Allman") 20-25 72
(Gatefold cover.)
BOLD (301 "Duane & Gregg Allman") 8-10 73
(Standard cover.)
SPRINGBOARD 8-10 75
Also see ALLMAN, Duane
Also see ALLMAN, Gregg
Also see ALLMAN BROTHERS BAND
Also see ALLMAN JOYS

ALLMAN, Gregg — P&R/LP '73
(Gregg Allman Band)

Singles: 7-inch

CAPRICORN 4-6 73-77
EPIC 3-5 87-89

LPs: 10/12-inch

CAPRICORN 8-12 73-77
EPIC 5-10 87-89
ROBERT KLEIN ("Interview") 40-60 81
(Promotional issue only.)
Also see ALLMAN, Duane & Gregg
Also see ALLMAN BROTHERS BAND
Also see ALLMAN JOYS
Also see HOUR GLASS

ALLMAN, Sheldon

Singles: 7-inch

HI-FI (593 "Walk on the Ground") 5-10 60
ORIGINAL SOUND (25 "Heartbreak Boulevard") 5-10 63

LPs: 10/12-inch

DEL-FI 20-30 61
HI-FI (415 "Folk Songs for the 21st Century") 15-25 60

ALLMAN BROTHERS BAND — LP '70

Singles: 7-inch

ARISTA 3-5 80-81
CAPRICORN 5-8 70-79
EPIC 3-5 90

Picture Sleeves

ARISTA (0618 "Straight from the Heart") 3-5 81

EPs: 7-inch

ATLANTIC (805) 10-20 73
(Juke box issue only.)
CAPRICORN 10-20 73
(Juke box issue only.)

LPs: 10/12-inch

ARISTA 5-10 80-81
ATCO 15-20 69-73
CAPRICORN (Except 802) 8-15 72-79
CAPRICORN (802 "The Allman Brothers Band at the Fillmore East") 15-20 71
EPIC 5-8 90
K-TEL 5-10
MFSL (2-157 "Eat a Peach") 40-60 85
MFSL (213 "Brothers and Sisters") 30-40 94
NAUTILUS (30 "Live at the Fillmore") 50-100
(Half-speed mastered.)
POLYDOR (6339 "Best of the Allman Brothers Band") 5-10 89
POLYDOR (839-417 "The Allman Brothers Band") 25-35 89
(Six-LP boxed set, with booklet.)
Members: Duane Allman; Gregg Allman; Dicky Betts; Berry Oakley; Les Dudek; Butch Trucks; Johnny Johanson; Chuck Leavell; Dan Toler; David Goldflies; Paul Hornsby.
Also see ALLMAN, Duane & Gregg
Also see HOUR GLASS
Also see 31ST OF FEBRUARY

ALLMAN JOYS

Singles: 7-inch

DIAL (4046 "Spoonful") 25-35 66

LPs: 10/12-inch

DIAL (6005 "Early Allman") 10-15 73
Members: Duane Allman; Gregg Allman; Bob Keller; Maynard Portwood; Ralph Balinger; Ronnie Wilkin; Tommy Amato; Jack Jackson; Bobby Dennis; Bill Connell.
Also see ALLMAN, Duane & Gregg
Also see RUBBER BAND

ALL-NITERS

Singles: 7-inch

ERIE (001 "Hey Baby") 15-25 65
ERIE (002 "Girl Don't Go") 15-25 65
GMA (1 "Summertime Blues") 20-30 64
Members: Jay Milhelich; Don Hermanson; Greg Coby; Lloyd Hugo; Tony Defranco; Jimmy Lenten.

ALLSUP, Tommy
(With His Fir Kings)

Singles: 7-inch

GRT 4-6 71
POST (1000 "Yas Yas Yas") 5-8

LPs: 10/12-inch

REPRISE (6182 "The Buddy Holly Songbook") 40-50 65

ALLURES

Singles: 7-inch

MELRON (5009 "King Love") 50-100 64
STARLIGHT (48 "Our Songs of Love") 5-10 86
STARLIGHT (71 "Lovers Never Say Goodbye") 3-5 89

ALMA-KEYS
(With the Citations Band)

Singles: 7-inch

KISKI (2056 "Please Come Back to Me") 400-500 62
(Flexible disc.)
KISKI (2056 "Please Come Back to Me"). 15-25
(Rigid disc.)
Also see CITATIONS

ALMANAC SINGERS

Singles: 78 rpm

GENERAL 8-12 41-43

Albums: 78 rpm

COMMODORE ("Deep Sea Chanteys & Whaling Ballads") 15-25
(Selection number not known.)
COMMODORE (10 "Sod Buster Ballads") 15-25

LPs: 10/12-inch

COMMODORE (002 "Deep Sea Chanteys & Whaling Ballads" & "Sod Buster Ballads") 20-30 51
FOLKWAYS (85 "Labor Union Songs") 15-25 55
W.B. (1330 "Sing Along – Country Style") 10-15 59
Members: Pete Seeger; Woody Guthrie; Peter Hawes; Millard Lampell.
Also see SEEGER, Pete
Also see WEAVERS

ALMEIDA, Laurindo — LP '62
(With the Modern Jazz Quartet; with Bossa Nova All Stars)

Singles: 7-inch

CAPITOL 4-8 55-65
PACIFIC JAZZ 5-8 55

EPs: 7-inch

CAPITOL 5-15 56-59
CORAL 5-10 54-56
PACIFIC JAZZ 10-15 54

LPs: 10/12-inch

CAPITOL (Except 8000 series) 15-25 59-65
CAPITOL (8000 series) 20-35 56-58
CORAL 25-45 54-56
CRYSTAL CLEAR 5-8 80
DAYBREAK 5-10 73
DOBRE 5-10 76-77
INNER CITY 5-8 79
PACIFIC JAZZ (7 "Laurindo Almeida Quartet") 50-75 54
(10-inch LP.)
PACIFIC JAZZ (13 "Laurindo Almeida Quartet, Vol. 2") 50-75 54
(10-inch LP.)
SURREY 10-20 65
WORLD PACIFIC 25-40 56-62
Also see BYRD, Charlie
Also see DAVIS, Sammy, Jr., & Laurindo Almeida
Also see GETZ, Stan, & Laurindo Almeida
Also see MODERN JAZZ QUARTET
Also see SOMMERS, Joanie, & Laurindo Almeida
Also see VERA, Ricky

ALMEIDA, Laurindo / Chico Hamilton

LPs: 10/12-inch

JAZZTONE 10-20 64
Also see ALMEIDA, Laurindo
Also see HAMILTON, Chico

ALMEIDA, Laurindo, & Modern Jazz Quartet

Singles: 7-inch

ATLANTIC 4-8 64-65

LPs: 10/12-inch

ATLANTIC (1429 "Collaboration") 10-20 64
Also see ALMEIDA, Laurindo
Also see MODERN JAZZ QUARTET

ALMOND, Herschel

Singles: 7-inch

ACE (558 "Let's Get It On") 10-20 59
CHALLENGE (59054 "You Are the One") 15-25 59

ALMOND, Lucky Joe
(L.J. Almond)

Singles: 78 rpm

GLOBE 25-35 55

TRUMPET (Except 199 & 221) 10-15 55
TRUMPET (199 "Rock Me") 20-40 53
TRUMPET (221 "Gonna Rock and Roll"). 25-50 54

Singles: 7-inch

GLOBE (240 "Oo Oo Anything Goes"). 100-200 55
TRUMPET (Except 199 & 221) 15-25 55
TRUMPET (199 "Rock Me") 50-75 53
TRUMPET (221 "Gonna Rock and Roll") .. 50-75 54

ALONZO & BOPPERS

Singles: 7-inch

ROJAC (8172 "I'm on My Way") 30-50 63

ALPACAS

Singles: 7-inch

DOUBLE TAKE (2172 "Sometimes I Love You Girl") 20-25
M.M.I. (1237 "Time Marches On") 75-100 58

ALPERT, Herb — P&R/LP '62
(With Tijuana Brass; Herbie Alpert Sextet)

Singles: 12-inch

A&M (Black vinyl.) 4-6 79-84
A&M (Colored vinyl.) 5-8 84

Singles: 7-inch

A&M (703 "The Lonely Bull") 8-10 62
A&M (706 thru 964) 5-10 63-68
A&M (1001 thru 1526) 4-8 68-74
A&M (2000 series) 3-5 79-87
ANDEX (4036 "Summer School") 8-12 59
CAROL (700 "Sweet Georgia Brown") 8-12 59
ROWE/AMI 5-10 66
("Play Me" Sales Stimulator promotional issue.)

Picture Sleeves

A&M (792 thru 1225) 5-10 66-70
A&M (2000 series) 4-8 79-87

EPs: 7-inch

A&M 5-10 65-66
(Juke box issues only.)

LPs: 10/12-inch

A&M (100 series) 10-20 62-66
A&M (3000 series) 5-8 73-82
A&M (4114 thru 4521) 6-12 66-75
A&M (4790 thru 4949) 5-8 79-83
A&M (5000 series) 5-8 84-87
MFSL (053 "Rise") 40-60 81
Members: Lou Pagani; John Pisano; Bob Edmondson; Tonni Kalash; Nick Ceroli; Pat Senatore.
Also see GRAYSON, Milton
Also see LOU, Herb B.

ALPERT, Herb, & Hugh Masekela — LP '78

Singles: 7-inch

A&M/HORIZON 4-6 78

Picture Sleeves

A&M/HORIZON 4-6 78

LPs: 10/12-inch

A&M/HORIZON 5-10 78
Also see ALPERT, Herb
Also see MASEKELA, Hugh

ALSTON, Eddie

Singles: 7-inch

BARRY (109 "Gonna Get Me a Watchdog") 50-75 63

ALSTON, Henry

Singles: 7-inch

COLPIX (731 "Hey Everybody") 10-15 64
SKYLINE (500 "Once in a Beautiful Life"/"I Dare You Baby") 15-25 58
SKYLINE (551 "Once in a Beautiful Life"/"What Is There Left for Me") 10-20 59

ALSTON, Jo-Ann
(With Gene Redd Jr. & Orchestra)

Singles: 7-inch

VEST (8001 "He Left Me Crying") 25-35 63

ALSTON, Shirley
(Shirley Alston-Reeves)

Singles: 7-inch

PRODIGAL (0616 "I'd Rather Not Be Loving You") 4-8 75

LPs: 10/12-inch

STRAWBERRY 5-10 77
PRODIGAL (10008 "Shirley Alston with (a Little Help from My Friends") 10-15 75
(With the Drifters, Flamingos, Fred Parris & Five Satins, Belmonts, Herman's Hermits, Shep & Limelites, Danny & Juniors, and La La Brooks.)
Also see BELMONTS
Also see CHOLLI MAYE
Also see CRYSTALS

Also see DANNY & JUNIORS
Also see DRIFTERS
Also see FIVE SATINS
Also see FLAMINGOS
Also see HERMAN'S HERMITS
Also see SHEP & LIMELITES
Also see SHIRELLES

ALTAIRS

Singles: 7-inch

AMY (803 "If You Love Me") 10-20 60
Member: George Benson.
Also see BENSON, George

ALTAR, Rosalie
(Rosalie Alter)

Singles: 7-inch

ARCHIE (38 "I Had a Dream") 8-12
HARMON (1006 "Be True") 15-25 62

ALTECS

Singles: 7-inch

CLOISTER 10-20 60
DORE (649 "All Ashore") 8-12 62
FELSTED (8618 "Recess") 10-15 61
PAMELA (206 "Happy Sax") 10-15 62

ALTEERS

Singles: 7-inch

G-CLEF (705 "This Lovely Night") 30-40 64
LAURIE (3097 "Words Can't Explain") 15-25 61
Also see GARDNER, Don

ALTON, Johnnie

Singles: 7-inch

ALPHA (8 "Boys Have Feelings Too") 10-20
CHESNUT (204 "Please Love Me") 10-15 61

ALTON & JIMMY

Singles: 7-inch

SUN (323 "No More Crying the Blues") ... 10-20 59
Members: Alton Lott; Jimmy Harrell.
Also see RILEY, Billy Lee

ALVANS

Singles: 7-inch

MAY (102 "Love Is a Game") 50-75 61

ALVEY, Randy, & Green Fuzz

Singles: 7-inch

BIG TEX (445 "Green Fuzz") 50-100 66

ALVIN & BILL

Singles: 7-inch

FERNWOOD (124 "Typing Jive") 50-75 60

AMAKER, Donald

Singles: 7-inch

RAINES (22 "Don't Let Me Shed Anymore Tears") 75-100 59

AMARO, Tony
(With the Chariots)

Singles: 7-inch

LOMA (2068 "Hey Baby") 8-10 67
STACY (920 "Heart and Soul") 25-35 60

AMATO, Frankie
(Frankie "Tex" Amato)

Singles: 7-inch

COOL (161 "You Made a Fool Out of Me") 10-15 60
COUNSELLOR (001 "Next Time We Love") .... 30-40 '60s
Session: Magics.

AMATO, Jerry

Singles: 7-inch

TACIT (109 "Dream on Little Fool") .... 40-50 '60s

AMATO, Larry

Singles: 7-inch

RCA (7411 "He Made a Miracle") 10-15 58

AMATO, Tony

Singles: 7-inch

PEDDY (1003 "Brenda") .... 10-20 '60s

AMAZERS

Singles: 7-inch

BANGAR (639 "Come Back Baby") 10-20 66
THOMAS (1638 "It's You for Me") 8-12 68

AMBASSADORS

Singles: 78 rpm

TIMELY (1001 "Darling I'm Sorry") 200-300 54

AMBASSADORS
(With Andre Brummer & His Orchestra)

Singles: 78 rpm

MOTIF 10-15 56

Singles: 7-inch

MOTIF (004 "Goo Goo Bird Mambo") 25-35 56

AMBASSADORS
(With Johnny L. Chapman Orchestra)

Singles: 7-inch

AIR (5065 "Keep On Trying") 1500-2000 56
(Reportedly 50 made.)
BON (001 "Power of Love") 30-50 62
(First issue.)
REEL (117 "Power of Love") 20-30 62

AMBASSADORS

Singles: 7-inch

FLEET (3500 "Pork Chops") 10-20 61

AMBASSADORS

Singles: 7-inch

FEDERAL (12469 "I Have to Cry") 10-20 62

AMBASSADORS

Singles: 7-inch

BAY (210 "Ambassador Blues") 100-150 63

AMBASSADORS

Singles: 7-inch

PLAYBOX (202 "Lorraine") 1000-1500 63

AMBASSADORS

Singles: 7-inch

DOT (16528 "Big Breaker") 10-15 63

AMBASSADORS

Singles: 7-inch

PEE VEE (1000 "Too Much of a Good Thing") 100-200 66
Members: Don Hodgen; Lenny Clawges; Charlie Evans; Rick Reardon; Don Senft; Eric Spitzer; Tony Purcell; Bob Weaver; Bud Hill.

AMBASSADORS

Singles: 7-inch

UPTOWN (734 "I Need Someone") 10-20 66

AMBASSADORS

Singles: 7-inch

DEBROUSSARD (5831 "Do You Ever Think About Me") .... 15-25 '60s

AMBER, Jan

Singles: 7-inch

CLEFF-TONE (157/158 "Waiting"/"The Little Martian") 50-75 59
CLEFF-TONE (1011 "Pick It Up") 20-30 59

AMBERS
("Featuring Ralph Mathis")

Singles: 7-inch

EBB (142 "Never Let You Go") 30-40 58
TODD (1042 "All of My Darling") 20-30 59
Member: Ralph Mathis.

AMBERS

Singles: 7-inch

JEAN 4-6 73
NEW ART (104 "Baby I Need You") 15-25 61
SMASH (2111 "Another Love") 10-20 67
VERVE (10436 "I Love You Baby") 10-20 66
Members: Robert Rhoney; Robert Taylor; Billy Chinn; Ozzie Beek; Jerry White.

AMBERS

Singles: 7-inch

GREEZIE (501 "Listen to Your Heart") 15-25 59

AMBERTONES

Singles: 7-inch

DOTTIE (1129 "One Summer Night") 10-20 65
DOTTIE (1130 "I Need Summer") 10-20 65
GNP (329 "Bandido") 10-20 64
RAYJACK (1001 "Cruise") 20-40 65
RAYJACK (1002 "I Can Only Give You Everything") 20-40 65
NEWMAN (601 "Cruise") 10-20 65
TREASURE CHEST (1001 "I Can Only Give You Everything") 20-30 65
WHITE WHALE (242 "99 1/2") 8-12 67
WHITE WHALE (302 "Million Tears") 8-12 68

AMBITIONS

Singles: 7-inch

CROSS (1005 "Traveling Stranger") 100-150 62

AMBOY DUKES *P&R/LP '68*

Singles: 7-inch

MAINSTREAM 10-15 67-69

LPs: 10/12-inch

AUDIOFIDELITY (1005 "Journey to the Center of the Mind") 20-25 83
(Picture disc.)
DISCREET 10-20
MAINSTREAM (801 "Journeys and Migrations") 15-20 74
MAINSTREAM (6104 "Amboy Dukes") 35-55 68
MAINSTREAM (6112 "Journey to the Center of the Mind") 35-55 68
MAINSTREAM (6118 "Migration") 30-40 68
MAINSTREAM (6125 "Best of the Original Amboy Dukes") 25-35 69
POLYDOR 10-20 70
Members: Ted Nugent; Greg Arama; Rusty Day; John Drake; Steve Farmer; Dave Palmer; Andy Solomon; Rod Grange; K.J. Knight; John Angelos.
Also see DAY, Rusty
Also see KNIGHT, K.J.
Also see NUGENT, Ted

AMBROSE, Amanda

Singles: 7-inch

B.T. PUPPY (539 "Amanda's Man") 10-15 68
RCA (8167 "Crawdad Song") 5-10 63

LPs: 10/12-inch

B.T. PUPPY (539 "Green Plant") 10-20 68
DUNWICH (140 "This Door Swings Both Ways") 10-20 66
RCA (2696 "Recorded Live") 10-20 63
RCA (2742 "Amazing") 10-20 63
STEPHENY (4007 "Swings at the Black Orchid") 10-20 59

AMBROSE, Kenny

Singles: 7-inch

HAMILTON (50019 "Come On and Marry Me") 15-25 58
WILLET (109 "Your Love Is My Love") 40-50 59

AMBROSE, Sammy
(Sam Ambrose & Friend)

Singles: 7-inch

CRAZY HORSE (1315 "Ram Ram") 5-10 69
MALA (460 "Soul Shout Limbo") 5-10 63
MUSICOR (1061 "This Diamond Ring") ... 10-20 64
MUSICOR (1072 "Welcome to Dreamsville") 25-50 64

AMBROSE SLADE

LPs: 10/12-inch

FONTANA (67598 "Ballzy") 30-50 69
Also see SLADE

AMBURN, Fredde

Singles: 7-inch

TEEN (1009 "Girl in Pink Chiffon") 100-200

AMECHE, Don, & Frances Langford *LP '62*

EPs: 7-inch

COLUMBIA 8-15 61
(Promotional only.)

LPs: 10/12-inch

COLUMBIA (1000 & 8000 series) 15-20 61-62
COLUMBIA (30000 series) 8-12 71

AMELIO, Johnny
(With Bill Paradis & His Downbeats)

Singles: 7-inch

BLUE MOON (405 "Jugue"/"Downbeat") 200-300 57
(Blue vinyl copies exist; however, we have not yet determined their authenticity.)
BLUE MOON (408 "Jo Ann Jo Ann"/"I'll Forever Love You") 175-250 58
BLUE MOON (410 "Jugue"/"Jo Ann Jo Ann") 250-350 59

AMERICA *P&R/LP '72*

Singles: 7-inch

AMERICAN INT'L 4-6 79
CAPITOL 3-6 79-85
W.B. 4-6 72-77

Picture Sleeves

AMERICAN INT'L 4-6 79
CAPITOL 3-5 82-83
W.B. 4-6 72-74

LPs: 10/12-inch

CAPITOL 5-10 79-85
W.B. (Except 2576) 8-12 72-77
W.B. (2576 "America") 15-25 71
(Does NOT include *A Horse with No Name.*)
W.B. (2576 "America") 8-12 72
(Has *A Horse with No Name.*)
Members: Gerry Beckley; Dan Peek; Dewey Bunnell.

AMERICAN BEETLES
(American Beatles)

Singles: 7-inch

BYP (1001 "She's Mine") 15-25 64
ROULETTE (4550 "Don't Be Unkind") 5-10 64
ROULETTE (4559 "School Days") 5-10 64
Members: Bill Ande; Tom Condra; Dave Hieronymous; Jim Tolliver; Vic Gray.
Also see ARDELLS
Also see RAZOR'S EDGE

AMERICAN BLUES

Singles: 7-inch

AMY (997 "Your Love Is True") 15-25 67
KARMA (101 "If I Were a Carpenter") 20-30 67

LPs: 10/12-inch

KARMA (1001 "The American Blues Is Here") 250-350 67
UNI (73044 "The American Blues Do Their Thing") 35-55 69
Members: Dusty Hill; Rocky Hill; Doug Davis; Frank Beard.
Also see WARLOCKS
Also see ZZ TOP

AMERICAN BLUES EXCHANGE
(A*B*E)

LPs: 10/12-inch

TAYLUS (1 "Blueprints") 500-750 69
Members: Roy Dudley; Roger Briggs; Pete Hartman; Dan Mixer.

AMERICAN BREED *P&R '67*

Singles: 7-inch

ABC 4-6 75
ACTA 5-10 67-69
MCA 3-5 84
PARAMOUNT (0040 "Can't Make It Without You") 4-8 70

Picture Sleeves

ACTA (821 "Green Light") 8-12 68

LPs: 10/12-inch

ACTA (38002 "American Breed") 15-25 67
ACTA (38003 "Bend Me, Shape Me") 20-30 68
ACTA (38006 "Pumpkin, Powder, Scarlet & Green") 15-25 68
ACTA (38008 "Lonely Side of the City") ... 15-25 68
Members: Gary Loizzo; Chuck Colbert; Lee Graziano; Al Ciner; Kevin Murphy.
Also see GARY & NITE LITES
Also see RUFUS

AMERICAN CHEESE

Singles: 7-inch

SEAWEST (101 "When the Morning Comes") 20-30 69
Also see GENESIS
Also see KING BISCUIT ENTERTAINERS

AMERICAN DREAM *LP '70*

Singles: 7-inch

AMPEX (11001 "Good News") 4-6 70
DEMIK (101 "Tioga") 5-10 68

Picture Sleeves

AMPEX (11001 "Good News") 4-8 70

LPs: 10/12-inch

AMPEX (10101 "American Dream") 15-20 70
Members: Nick Jameson; Dooley Van Winkle; Nicky Indelicato; Don Ferris; Mickey Brook.

AMERICAN EXPRESS

Singles: 7-inch

TEEN TOWN (111 "You & Me") 10-20 69
VAULT (920 "Peggy Sue") 25-35

AMERICAN FOUR

Singles: 7-inch

SELMA (2001 "Luci Baines") 30-50 64
Members: Arthur Lee; John Echols.
Also see LOVE

AMERICAN REVOLUTION

Singles: 7-inch

FLICK DISC (902 "Come On and Get It") .. 5-10 68

LPs: 10/12-inch

FLICK DISC (002 "American Revolution") 15-25 68

Members: Richard Barcellona; Daniel Derda; Eddie Haddad; John Keith.
Also see EDGE

AMERICAN SPRING
Singles: 7-inch
COLUMBIA (45834 "Shyin' Away")..........20-30 73
Picture Sleeves
COLUMBIA (45834 "Shyin' Away")..........50-80 73
Also see SPRING

AMERICAN TEA COMPANY
Singles: 7-inch
GOLDEN VOICE (2327 "Don't Leave Your Love")..........20-30 69
Members: Gary Testrake; Ken Rogers; Mark Nelson; Tim Haley; Jim Schuh.

AMERICAN ZOO
Singles: 7-inch
REENA (1026 "Mr. Brotherhood")..........20-30 68

AMERICANS
Singles: 78 rpm
CREST (1025 "Teenage Goodnight")........5-10 56
Singles: 7-inch
CREST (1025 "Teenage Goodnight")......10-15 56

AMERSON, Doug
Singles: 7-inch
G&G (105 "Bop Man Bop")..........100-150 58
INTRASTATE (25 "Bop Man Bop")..........50-75 55

AMES, Stacey
Singles: 7-inch
RANDOM (604 "Calendar Boy")..........15-25 61

AMES, Stewart
(With Richard Wylie)
Singles: 7-inch
J&W (1000 "King for a Day")..........125-175 '60s
Also see WYLIE, Richard

AMES BROTHERS *P&R '49*
Singles: 78 rpm
CORAL..........5-15 50-56
RCA (Except E3-VB-291)..........5-10 53-57
RCA (E3-VB-291 "The Man with the Banjo")..........10-20 54
(Special "National Banjo Week" issue, "Commemorating the Invention of the Banjo. The First Native American Musical Instrument." Promotional issue only.)
Singles: 7-inch
CORAL (60140 thru 65515)..........10-20 50-56
CORAL (65554 "Good Fellow Medley")......5-10 62
EPIC..........5-10 62-63
MCA..........4-6 73
RCA (5325 thru 7046)..........10-20 53-57
RCA (7142 thru 7836)..........8-12 58-61
RCA GOLD STANDARD SERIES..........4-8 '60s
Picture Sleeves
EPIC (9530 "Love Me with All Your Heart")..........10-15 62
RCA (7655 "China Doll")..........10-15 60
RCA (7801 "Where the Hot Wind Blows")..........25-50 60
(Sleeve pictures film's stars Gina Lollobrigida and Yves Montand. Promotional issue only.)
EPs: 7-inch
CORAL..........15-25 50-53
RCA..........15-25 53-61
RCA SPECIAL PRODUCTS (48 "French's Platter Party")..........15-25 '50s
(Promotional issue. Made for French's Mustard Co. Paper sleeve.)
LPs: 10/12-inch
CAMDEN (571 "Sweet & Swing")..........10-20 60
CORAL (56014 "Sing a Song of Christmas")..........20-40 50
(10-inch LP.)
CORAL (56017 "In the Evening by the Moonlight")..........20-40 50
(10-inch LP.)
CORAL (56024 "Sentimental Me")..........20-30 51
(10-inch LP.)
CORAL (56025 Hoop-De-Doo")..........20-30 51
(10-inch LP.)
CORAL (56042 "Sweet Leilani")..........20-30 51
(10-inch LP.)
CORAL (56050 "Favorite Spirituals")..........20-30 52
(10-inch LP.)
CORAL (56079 "Home on the Range")....20-30 52
(10-inch LP.)
CORAL (56080 "Merry Christmas")..........20-30 52
(10-inch LP.)
CORAL (56097 "Favorite Songs")..........20-30 53
(10-inch LP.)
CORAL (57031 "Concert")..........20-30 56
CORAL (57054 "Love's Old Sweet Song")..........20-30 56
CORAL (57338 "Our Golden Favorites")..........20-30 60
EPIC (24036 "Hello Italy")..........10-15 63
(Monaural.)
EPIC (24069 "Ames Brothers")..........10-15 63
(Monaural.)
EPIC (26036 "Hello Italy")..........10-15 63
(Stereo.)
EPIC (26069 "Ames Brothers")..........10-15 63
(Stereo.)
MCA..........5-8 82
RCA (1000 series)..........5-10 75
RCA (1200 thru 2200 series)..........25-50 55-61
RCA (2800 series)..........10-20 64
RCA (6000 series)..........5-10 72
RCA SPECIAL PRODUCTS (0207 "Ames Brothers")..........5-10
VOCALION (3617 "Ames Brothers")..........10-20 58
VOCALION (3788 "Christmas Harmony")..........10-15 66
(Monaural.)
VOCALION (73788 "Christmas Harmony")..........10-15 66
(Stereo.)
Members: Ed; Joe; Gene; Vic.
Also see COMO, Perry / Ames Brothers / Harry Belafonte / Radio City Music Hall Orch.
Also see LEWIS, Monica, & Ames Bros.
Also see MOONEY, Art, & His Orchestra
Also see ROSS, Lanny, with Stephen Kisley, His Orchestra & Amory Brothers

AMICO, John
Singles: 7-inch
TONER (2306 "Summertime Twist")..........20-30 '60s

AMMONS, Albert *R&B '47*
(With His Rhythm Kings)
Singles: 78 rpm
COMMODORE..........10-20 44-47
MERCURY..........10-20 45-50
Singles: 7-inch
MERCURY (8053 "Shufflin' the Boogie")..45-55 51
(We have not yet verified any other specific titles on 45.)
EPs: 7-inch
MERCURY (3044 "Boogie Woogie Piano")..........50-100 54
LPs: 10/12-inch
BLUES CLASSICS..........5-10 83
COMMODORE (20002 "Boogie Woogie and the Blues")..........100-200 52
MERCURY (25012 "Boogie Woogie Piano")..........100-200 54
(10-inch LP.)

AMMONS, Albert / Jack Cooley
Singles: 78 rpm
MERCURY (70158 "Swanee River Boogie"/"I Don't Want to See You")..........5-10 53
Singles: 7-inch
MERCURY (70158 "Swanee River Boogie"/"I Don't Want to See You")..........10-20 53
Also see COOLEY, Jack

AMMONS, Albert, & Pete Johnson
(Pete Johnson & Albert Ammons)
Singles: 78 rpm
RCA..........5-10 41
EPs: 7-inch
RCA ("EPB" series)..........10-20 '50s
Also see AMMONS, Albert
Also see JOHNSON, Pete

AMMONS, Gene *R&B '47*
(With the All Stars)
Singles: 78 rpm
CHESS..........10-15 50
DECCA..........5-10 54
MERCURY..........5-15 47-53
PRESTIGE..........5-10 51-57
Singles: 7-inch
ARGO (5417 "My Babe")..........5-10 62
DECCA..........5-10 54
MERCURY..........5-10 50-53
PRESIDENT (717 "Gravy")..........5-10 62
PRESTIGE (100 thru 400 series)..........5-10 58-68
PRESTIGE (700 series)..........4-8 69-73
(This "700" series can easily be distinguished from the early fifties "700" series that follows. The company address is shown as in New Jersey. In the '50s the company was in New York.)
PRESTIGE (713 thru 921)..........5-10 51-57
(Black vinyl.)
PRESTIGE (713 thru 921)..........10-20 51-57
(Colored vinyl.)
RAY BRA..........4-6
SAVOY..........5-10 60
UNITED..........5-10 53-54
EPs: 7-inch
EMARCY (6052/3 "With Or Without")..........25-50 54
(Price for either of two volumes.)
PRESTIGE..........25-50 51
LPs: 10/12-inch
ARGO (698 "Just Jug")..........20-30 62
CHESS (1442 "Soulful Saxophone")..........30-40 59
EMARCY (400 series)..........8-12 76
EMARCY (26031 "With Or Without")......50-100 54
(10-inch LP.)
ENJA..........5-10 81
MERCURY..........20-30 60-63
OLYMPIC..........5-10 74
PRESTIGE (014 thru 192)..........5-10 82-85
PRESTIGE (7010 thru 7132)..........25-50 55-58
(Each of the following LPs in this series was reissued using the original selection number but a different title: Prestige 7050, *All Star Jam Session*, was reissued as *Woofin' & Tweetin'*; Prestige 7039, *Hi-Fi Jam Session*, was reissued as *Happy Blues*, and Prestige 7060, *Jammin' with Gene*, was reissued as *Not Really the Blues*. These three 1960 reissues are valued in the $20 to $35 range.)
PRESTIGE (7146 thru 7287)..........20-40 59-64
PRESTIGE (7300 & 7400 series)..........10-20 65-68
PRESTIGE (7500 thru 7800 series)..........8-15 68-70
PRESTIGE (10000 series)..........5-10 71-74
PRESTIGE (24000 series)..........8-12 73-81
ROOTS..........5-10 76
SAVOY..........15-25 61
TRIP..........5-10 73-75
VEE-JAY..........15-25 60-62
WING..........10-20 60-63
Also see McDUFF, Brother Jack, & Gene Ammons

AMMONS, Gene, & Richard "Groove" Holmes
LPs: 10/12-inch
PACIFIC JAZZ (32 "Groovin' with Jug")...15-25 61
Also see HOLMES, Richard "Groove"

AMMONS, Gene, & Sonny Stitt
Singles: 78 rpm
PRESTIGE..........5-10 50-51
Singles: 7-inch
PRESTIGE (700 series)..........5-10 50-51
(Black vinyl.)
PRESTIGE (700 series)..........10-20 50-51
(Colored vinyl.)
EPs: 7-inch
PRESTIGE..........25-50 51
LPs: 10/12-inch
ARGO (697 "Dig Him")..........25-35 63
CADET (785 "Jug and Sonny")..........10-20 67
CHESS..........30-40 60
PRESTIGE (107 "Gene Ammons")..........75-100 51
(10-inch LP.)
PRESTIGE (112 "Gene Ammons with Sonny Stitt")..........75-100 51
(10-inch LP.)
PRESTIGE (127 "The Gene Ammons Band")..........75-100 52
(10-inch LP.)
PRESTIGE (149 "The Gene Ammons Quartet")..........75-100 51
(10-inch LP.)
PRESTIGE (7600 series)..........6-10 69
PRESTIGE (10000 series)..........5-10 76
VERVE (8400 series)..........15-20 61-62
(Reads "MGM Records - a Division of Metro-Goldwyn-Mayer, Inc." at bottom of label.)
VERVE (8800 series)..........8-12 72
(Reads "Manufactured By MGM Record Corp.," or mentions either Polydor or Polygram at bottom of label.)
Also see AMMONS, Gene

AMMONS, Lew
Singles: 7-inch
ROYCE (5106 "Cab Driver's Blues")......50-100

AMON DUUL
LPs: 10/12-inch
PROPHESY..........25-30 70

AMON DUUL II
Singles: 7-inch
LIBERTY (56196 "Soda Shop Rock")......10-20 70
LPs: 10/12-inch
ATCO..........8-10 75
U.A. (017 "Wolf City")..........12-15 73
U.A. (198 "Vive La Trance")..........10-12 73
U.A. (5586 "Carnival in Babylon")..........15-20 72
U.A. (9954 "Dance of the Lemmings")......20-25 71
Members: Renate Knaup Kroetenschwanz; Danny Fischelscher; Dave Anderson; Chris Karrer; Reb Heibl; Kalle Housmann; Lother Meid; Falk Rogner.

AMORY, John
Singles: 7-inch
GULFSTREAM (1065 "Bad")..........50-75

AMOS, Ira
Singles: 78 rpm
MODERN..........10-20 50
OCTIVE..........10-20 51

AMOS, Tori
LPs: 10/12-inch
ATLANTIC (81845 "Y Tori Kant Read")...60-90 88
ATLANTIC (82862 "Boys for Pele")..........10-15 96
(Two colored vinyl discs.)

AMOS & ANDY *P&R '29*
Singles: 78 rpm
COLUMBIA..........10-15 '50s
VICTOR..........50-75 29
Singles: 7-inch
COLUMBIA (48002 "The Lord's Prayer").15-25 '50s

ANASTASIA
(With the Nocturnes Orchestra)
Singles: 7-inch
LAURIE (3066 "That's My Kind of Love").20-30 60
STASI (1001 "Seven Days a Week")....400-500 61
STASI (1002 "Every Road")..........1000-1500 62

ANCIENT GREASE
LPs: 10/12-inch
MERCURY (61305 "Women and Children First")..........25-35 70
Members: John Weathers; Phil Ryan; Gary Pickford Hopkins.

ANDANTES
Singles: 7-inch
DOT (16495 "My Baby's Gone")..........10-15 63
V.I.P. (25006 "Nightmare")..........1000-2000 64

ANDERKIN, Lonnie
Singles: 7-inch
LADS (700 "Teenage Baby")..........300-400 59

ANDERS, Bernie
Singles: 78 rpm
KING (4833 "My Heart Believes")..........10-20 55
Singles: 7-inch
KING (4833 "My Heart Believes")..........40-50 55

ANDERS, Lisa, with Victory Five
(Liz Anderson)
Singles: 7-inch
SENATOR (711 "Old Enough")..........30-40 60
Also see ANDERSON, Liz

ANDERS, Russ
Singles: 7-inch
ANBEE (3026 "Redheaded, Blue-Eyed Baby Doll")..........50-75

ANDERS, Terri
Singles: 7-inch
CHIEF (7027 "All in My Mind")..........10-15 61

ANDERS, Vernon
Singles: 78 rpm
MONEY (221 "All Messed Up")..........10-15 56
Singles: 7-inch
MONEY (221 "All Messed Up")..........20-30 56

ANDERS & PONCIA
Singles: 7-inch
KAMA SUTRA (240 "So It Goes")..........5-10 67
W.B...........5-10 68-69

LPs: 10/12-inch

W.B. 10-15 69

Members: Peter Anders; Vinnie Poncia.
Also see INNOCENCE
Also see PENNY ARCADE
Also see PETE & VINNIE
Also see TRADEWINDS
Also see TREASURES
Also see VIDELS

ANDERSEN, Eric LP '72

Singles: 7-inch

ARISTA........ 4-6 75-77
COLUMBIA........ 4-6 72
W.B. 4-6 68-71

LPs: 10/12-inch

ARISTA........ 5-10 75-77
COLUMBIA........ 8-10 72
VANGUARD........ 15-20 65-70
W.B. 10-15 68-70

ANDERSON, Andy
(With the Dawnbreakers; with Rolling Stones)

Singles: 7-inch

APOLLO (535 "You Shake Me Up") 75-125 59
CENTURY LTD. (601 "Gimmie a Lock of Your Hair") 50-100 60
CENTURY LTD. (602 "Gonna Sit Right Down and Cry") 75-125 60
CENTURY LTD. (603 "Promise Me")..... 75-125 60
DOT 15-20 59
FELSTED (8508 "Johnny Valentine")...... 15-25 58
ZYNN (510 I Wanna Boogie") 40-50 59

ANDERSON, Andy

Singles: 7-inch

HERMITAGE (821 "All By Myself")...... 100-200 60

ANDERSON, Anita, & Traits

Singles: 7-inch

CONTACT (502 "Secretly") .... 15-25 '60s

ANDERSON, B.K.

Singles: 7-inch

SWIRL (106 "Momma Get the Hammer") 15-25 61
SWIRL (111 "Mininum Wage") 15-25 62
SWIRL (112 "Mother-in-Law Cha Cha") .. 15-25 63

ANDERSON, Bennie, & Teals

Singles: 7-inch

KING (5893 "Little School Girl") 10-20 64

ANDERSON, Bill C&W '58
(With the Po' Boys; with Po' Folks; with Jordanaires; Whispering Bill Anderson)

Singles: 12-inch

MCA........ 4-8 78

Singles: 7-inch

DECCA (30000 series) 10-15 58-59
DECCA (31000 series) 5-10 60-66
DECCA (32000 & 33000 series) 4-8 67-72
MCA........ 3-6 73-81
PICKWICK........ 5-10 '70s
SOUTHERN TRACKS........ 3-5 82-87
SWANEE........ 3-5 85
TNT (146 "Empty Room") 20-30 57
TNT (165 "Empty Room") 10-20 59
TNT (9015 "No Song to Sing") 100-150 58

Picture Sleeves

DECCA (31521 "8 X 10") 5-10 63
DECCA (32417 "Po' Folks Christmas") 5-10 69

EPs: 7-inch

DECCA........ 5-15 63-65

LPs: 10/12-inch

BILL ANDERSON LABEL (11316 "On the Road") 15-25
(Promotional issue only.)
CORAL 4-6 73
DECCA (4192 thru 4686) 15-20 62-65
DECCA (4771 thru 5344) 10-15 66-72
(Decca LP numbers in this series preceded by a "7" or a "DL-7" are stereo issues.)
DECCA (7100 series) 15-20 69
DECCA (7200 series) 10-12 72
EPIC........ 5-10 82-85
MCA........ 5-10 73-80
SOUTHERN TRACKS........ 5-10 84
VOCALION........ 8-12 68-71

Session: Jordanaires.
Also see COE, David Allan, & Bill Anderson
Also see JORDANAIRES
Also see KERR, Anita
Also see WELLS, Kitty / Bill Anderson

ANDERSON, Bill / Jimmie Burton

EPs: 7-inch

TNT (147 "Bill Anderson/Jimmie Burton") 30-40 57
(Likely issued without special cover.)
Also see BURTON, James

ANDERSON, Bill, & Jan Howard C&W '66

Singles: 7-inch

DECCA........ 4-6 66-71

LPs: 10/12-inch

DECCA........ 6-12 68-72
Also see HOWARD, Jan

ANDERSON, Bill, & Mary Lou Turner C&W '78

Singles: 7-inch

MCA........ 4-6 78

LPs: 10/12-inch

MCA........ 5-10 76-77
Also see ANDERSON, Bill

ANDERSON, Bob

Singles: 78 rpm

WING........ 5-8 55

Singles: 7-inch

ALLAN 8-12 59
BALLY (1012 "For Only You") 10-15 56
BALLY (1019 "Sentimental Journey") 10-15 56
BALLY (1031 "Rip Tide") 10-15 57
U.A. (372 "Rose, Mose, and Me") 10-20 61
WING (90025 "Understand") 10-15 55
WING (90044 "When Your Lover Has Gone") 10-15 55

ANDERSON, Brother James

Singles: 7-inch

SUN (406 "I'm Gonna Move in the Room with the Lord") 40-60 68
Also see JANES, Roland

ANDERSON, Casey

Singles: 7-inch

AMOS (126 "Monsoon Season Hungries") 5-10 69
AMOS (137 "Sunday Joe") 4-8 70
ATCO........ 5-10 63-65
GREENE MOUNTAIN (410 "Where Will I Find a Place to Sleep This Evening") 4-6 73
REPRISE........ 5-10 68-69
URANIA (9024 "Draper Prison") 5-10 59

LPs: 10/12-inch

ATCO........ 15-20 62-65
ELEKTRA (192 "Goin' Places") 15-20 60
(Monaural.)
ELEKTRA (7192 "Goin' Places") 20-30 60
(Stereo.)
SUPERSTAR 5-10
URANIA (2028 "Casey Sings Out") 20-30 59
(Stereo.)
URANIA (9024 "Casey Sings Out") 15-20 59
(Monaural.)

ANDERSON, Cat

LPs: 10/12-inch

EMARCY (36142 "Cat On a Hot Tin Roof") 20-30 59
(Monaural.)
EMARCY (80008 "Cat On a Hot Tin Roof") 25-35 59
(Stereo.)

ANDERSON, Dot

Singles: 7-inch

DJ ("Walkin' Papers") 50-75
(Selection number not known.)

ANDERSON, Elton P&R/R&B '60

Singles: 7-inch

CAPITOL........ 8-12 62
LANOR........ 10-15 62-63
MERCURY........ 10-20 59-61
TREY (1002 "I Love You So") 15-25 59
VIN (1001 "Roll On Train") 15-25 58

Session: Mac Rebennack; Sid Lawrence Combo.
Also see REBENNACK, Mac

ANDERSON, Ernestine LP '58

Singles: 7-inch

MERCURY (Except 71772) 5-10 59-62
MERCURY (71772 "Lover's Question").... 20-30 61
OMEGA DISK (136 "Azure Te") 5-10 59
SUE 5-10 63-65

EPs: 7-inch

MERCURY........ 10-15 59

LPs: 10/12-inch

CONCORD 8-12 76-86
MERCURY 20-40 58-60
SUE (1015 "New Sound of...") 15-25 63
WING (12281 "My Kinda Swing") 10-20 64
(Monaural.)
WING (16281 "My Kinda Swing") 10-20 64
(Stereo.)

ANDERSON, Gail

Singles: 7-inch

GALAXY (760 "Born to Be Loved") 5-10 68
GAMBLE (206 "Let's Fall in Love All Over") 5-10 67
SHELL (102 "They're Laughing at Me") ... 20-30 64

ANDERSON, Gene
(With the Dynamic Psychedelics; with Keynotes; with International Hook-Up)

Singles: 7-inch

CANDIX (333 "Old Folks Party") 5-10 62
HI 4-6 72-75
ROYAL-TONE (1000 "Baby, I Dig You") .. 25-35 '60s
STAR (246 "Pains in My Heart") .... 10-20 '60s
TOP TEN (252 "Susie") 25-35 62

ANDERSON, Herb Oscar
(With the Frank De Vol Orchestra)

Singles: 78 rpm

CAPITOL........ 4-8 52

Singles: 7-inch

CAPITOL........ 10-20 52
COLUMBIA (41704 "Hello Again") 10-20 60
LAURIE (3553 "I'm Going Home") 4-8 70
LAURIE (3591 "Only a Moment") 4-8 72
ROYAL CROWN ("Hello Again") .... 4-8 '60s
(Selection number not known.)
VERVE (10481 "What Would I Be") 10-15 67
VERVE (10527 "Green Green Grass of Home") 10-15 67

LPs: 10/12-inch

VERVE (5021 "What Would I Be") 15-25 67
Also see DE VOL, Frank

ANDERSON, Ivie C&W '44
(With Ceelle Burke's Orchestra)

Singles: 78 rpm

EXCLUSIVE (3113 "Mexico Joe") 25-35 44
Also see ELLINGTON, Duke

ANDERSON, Jimmy
(With His Joy Jumpers)

Singles: 7-inch

DOT (16341 "I Wanna Boogie") 15-25 62
EXCELLO (2220 "Naggin' ") 10-15 62
EXCELLO (2227 "Going Through the Park") 10-15 63
EXCELLO (2257 "Love Me Babe") 10-15 64
ZYNN (1014 "I Wanna Boogie") 40-50 62
(First issue.)

ANDERSON, Jon LP '76

Singles: 12-inch

ATLANTIC........ 4-6 82

Singles: 7-inch

ATLANTIC........ 3-5 76-82
COLUMBIA........ 3-5 88
ELEKTRA (Except 69580) 3-5 84-85
ELEKTRA (69580 "Save All Your Love") 3-5 85
(Black vinyl.)
ELEKTRA (69580 "Save All Your Love") 4-8 85
(Colored vinyl. Special Christmas edition.)

LPs: 10/12-inch

ATLANTIC........ 5-10 76-82
COLUMBIA 5-10 88
ELEKTRA........ 5-10 85

Promotional LPs

ATLANTIC ("An Evening with Jon Anderson") 20-30 76
(Jon Anderson interviews, and music from his *Olias of Sunhillow* LP, as well as selections by Yes. Number not known.)
Also see YES

ANDERSON, Keith

Singles: 7-inch

COZY (514 "Hot Guitars") 125-150
COZY (517 "One Step Behind") 50-75
COZY (572 "It's Wrong Loving You") 50-75

ANDERSON, Kip

Singles: 7-inch

ABC-PAR (10578 "I Done You Wrong")..... 8-12 64
ALA........ 5-10
CHECKER........ 5-10 66-67
DERRICK (1000 "I Want to Be the Only One") 30-50
EVERLAST (5021 "I Feel Good") 10-20 63
EXCELLO 5-10 67-69
SHARP (102 "Oh My Linda") 15-25 60
TOMORROW (501 "I Get Carried Away").. 8-12 65
TRUE SPOT (71001 "Woman, How Do You Make Love") 10-20
VEE-JAY (325 "I Wanna Be the Only One") 10-20 59

ANDERSON, Lale P&R '61

Singles: 7-inch

KING........ 5-10 61-62

LPs: 10/12-inch

FIESTA........ 15-25
UNIVERSE........ 10-20 61

ANDERSON, Laurie LP '82
(With John Giorno & William S. Burroughs)

Singles: 12-inch

W.B. 4-6 81

Singles: 7-inch

W.B. 3-5 81-89

EPs: 7-inch

W.B. 3-5 81

LPs: 10/12-inch

GIORNO POETRY (20 "You're the Guy I Want to Share My Money With") 8-12 84
W.B. (Except 25192) 5-10 82-89
W.B. (25192 "United States Live") 35-45 85
(Five discs.)
Also see JARRE, Jean-Michael

ANDERSON, Leona

Singles: 78 rpm

COLUMBIA........ 5-10 55
UNIQUE (330 "Indian Love Call") 5-10 56

Singles: 7-inch

COLUMBIA (40403 "The Mama Doll Song") 10-15 55
COLUMBIA (40459 "Limburger Lover") ... 10-15 55
UNIQUE (330 "Indian Love Call") 10-15 56

ANDERSON, Liz C&W '66

Singles: 7-inch

EPIC........ 4-6 71-73
RCA (8000 & 9000 series) 4-8 64-70
SCORPION........ 4-6 78

LPs: 10/12-inch

CAMDEN 10-15 66
RCA........ 10-20 67-70
TUDOR........ 5-8 83
Also see ANDERS, Lisa, & Victory Five
Also see BARE, Bobby, Liz Anderson & Norma Jean

ANDERSON, Liz & Lynn C&W '68

Singles: 7-inch

RCA (9445 "Mother, May I") 4-8 68
Also see ANDERSON, Liz
Also see ANDERSON, Lynn

ANDERSON, Lynn C&W '66

Singles: 7-inch

CBS (165211 "Isn't It Always Love") 30-50 79
(Picture disc. Promotional issue only. 1200 made.)
CHART........ 4-6 66-71
COLUMBIA........ 3-6 70-80
MERCURY........ 3-5 86-89
PERMIAN........ 3-5 83
RCA........ 4-6 68

Picture Sleeves

COLUMBIA........ 4-6 70-72

EPs: 7-inch

COLUMBIA........ 4-8 72
(Promotional only.)

LPs: 10/12-inch

ALBUM GLOBE........ 5-10 76
CHART........ 10-20 67-72
COLUMBIA........ 5-10 70-80
COLUMBIA HOUSE (6033 "Lynn Anderson Treasury") 30-40 73
(Boxed, six-disc set. Mail order offer.)
COLUMBIA HOUSE (6034 "The Ways to Love a Man") 5-10 73
COLUMBIA SPECIAL PRODUCTS........ 5-10 83
ERA........ 5-8 82

51 WEST 5-8 82
HARMONY 5-10 71-73
MOUNTAIN DEW 5-10
PERMIAN 5-10 83
PICKWICK 5-10
TIME-LIFE 5-10 81
Session: Jordanaires.
Also see ANDERSON, Liz & Lynn
Also see JORDANAIRES

ANDERSON, Lynn, & Jerry Lane *C&W '67*
Singles: 7-inch
CHART (1003 "Keeping up Appearances") 4-6 67
CHART (1300 "We're Different") 4-6 65
CHART (1425 "Keeping up Appearances") 4-6 67

ANDERSON, Lynn / Ray Price
LPs: 10/12-inch
COLUMBIA HOUSE (5658 "Heart to Heart") 15-25 72
(Boxed, four-disc set. Mail order offer.)
Also see PRICE, Ray

ANDERSON, Rita
Singles: 7-inch
STUDIO ONE ("Hey Senorita") 100-200 '50s
(Selection number not known.)

ANDRÉ, Jan, & Five Crowns
Singles: 78 rpm
EMERALD (2007 "It's Funny to Everyone but Me") 30-40 55
Singles: 7-inch
EMERALD (2007 "It's Funny to Everyone but Me") 50-150 55

ANDREA, Charles, & Hi Tones
Singles: 7-inch
TORI LTD. (T-2X "Didn't We Have a Nice Time") 1500-2000 61
TORI LTD. (T-2X "Didn't We Have a Nice Time") 10-15 95

ANDREW, Danny
Singles: 7-inch
VERVE (10115 "Bongo Boy") 20-30 57

ANDREWS, Debbie, & Muskateers
Singles: 78 rpm
UNITED (144 "Don't Make Me Cry") 10-15 53
Singles: 7-inch
UNITED (144 "Don't Make Me Cry") 50-75 53

ANDREWS, Ernie
(Ernie Andrews Quintet)
Singles: 78 rpm
ALADDIN (175 "Be Nice") 15-25 47
ALADDIN (176 "So Good to Say Forgive Me") 15-25 47
ALADDIN (185 "Don't Blame Me") 15-25 47
ALADDIN (186 "Rest Yourself") 15-25 47
SPARK (118 "Soft Winds") 8-12 55
Singles: 7-inch
CAPITOL (5448 "Where Were You") 10-20 65
CAPITOL (5530 "Fine Young Girl") 10-20 65
GNP (125 "But Now I Know") 10-20 57
PHIL-L.A. OF SOUL 4-6 70-71
ROULETTE (4139 "So Hard to Laugh, So Easy to Cry") 10-15 59
SPARK (118 "Soft Winds") 15-25 55
WHIPPET (213 "My Mother's Eyes") 10-20 58
LPs: 10/12-inch
DOT (Mono and Stereo) 10-15 67
GNP 20-30 57

ANDREWS, Gary
Singles: 7-inch
ARCTIC ("Rockin' the Blues") 100-200
(Selection number not known.)

ANDREWS, Harold
Singles: 7-inch
EARLY BIRD (9663 "You're a Winner") 10-15
MRM (401 "Party Time") 10-20 62

ANDREWS, Jimmy
Singles: 7-inch
BLUE JAY (5003 "Big City Playboy") 200-300 65
GLORY (288 "Just a Walk with You") 10-15 58

ANDREWS, Johnny
Singles: 78 rpm
UNIQUE (367 "Stephanie") 5-10 56
Singles: 7-inch
UNIQUE (367 "Stephanie") 10-15 56

ANDREWS, Julie *P&R '62*
Singles: 7-inch
COLUMBIA 4-8 67
DECCA 4-8 67
LONDON (1924 "Lazy Afternoon") 5-10 60
RCA 4-6 70
20TH FOX (6712 "Star!") 4-8 68
EPs: 7-inch
RCA 10-20 56
LPs: 10/12-inch
ANGEL 15-25 58
COLUMBIA (mono and stereo) 15-25 62
COLUMBIA (31000 series) 8-12 72
HARMONY 8-10 70-72
RCA (1000 series) 8-12 70
RCA (1400 thru 1600 series) 20-30 56-58
RCA (3800 series) 8-15 67
20TH FOX (5102 "Star!") 8-15 68

ANDREWS, Julie, & Carol Burnett *LP '62*
LPs: 10/12-inch
COLUMBIA (2240 "Julie and Carol at Carnegie Hall") 15-20 62
(Monaural.)
COLUMBIA (5840 "Julie and Carol at Carnegie Hall") 20-25 62
(Stereo.)
COLUMBIA (31000 series) 8-15 72

ANDREWS, Julie, & Andre Previn / Vic Damone / Jack Jones / Marian Anderson
EPs: 7-inch
RCA (277 "We Wish You a Merry Christmas") 4-8 69
(Radio Shack "Special Collector's Edition.")
Also see ANDREWS, Julie
Also see DAMONE, Vic
Also see JONES, Jack
Also see PREVIN, Andre

ANDREWS, Julie, & Dick Van Dyke
Singles: 7-inch
BUENA VISTA (434 "Super-Cali-Fragil-Istic-Expi-Ali-Docious") 5-10 65
Picture Sleeves
BUENA VISTA (434 "Super-Cali-Fragil-Istic-Expi-Ali-Docious") 8-12 65
Also see ANDREWS, Julie
Also see VAN DYKE, Dick

ANDREWS, Lee *P&R/R&B '57*
(With the Hearts; with Frank Slay Orchestra; Pancho Villa Orchestra)
Singles: 78 rpm
ARGO (1000 "Tear Drops") 150-200 57
CHESS (1665 "Long Lonely Nights") 50-100 57
CHESS (1675 "Tear Drops") 50-100 57
GOTHAM 50-100 56
RAINBOW 100-200 54
Singles: 7-inch
ARGO (1000 "Tear Drops") 40-50 57
CASINO (110 "Baby, Come Back") 15-25 59
CASINO (452 "Try the Impossible") 300-400 58
(Red and white label, with playing cards at top.)
CASINO (452 "Try the Impossible") 75-125 58
(Black label.)
CHESS (1665 "Long Lonely Nights") 15-25 57
(Silver top label with chess pieces.)
CHESS (1665 "Long Lonely Nights") 5-10 '60s
(Blue label.)
CHESS (1675 "Tear Drops") 20-30 57
(Silver top label with chess pieces.)
CHESS (1675 "Tear Drops") 5-10 '60s
(Blue label.)
CHESS (9000 series) 4-6
COLLECTABLES 3-5 82
CRIMSON (1002 "Island of Love") 10-15 63
CRIMSON 5-10 67-68
GOTHAM (318 "Bluebird of Happiness") 100-150 56
GOTHAM (320 "Lonely Room") 150-200 56
GOTHAM (321 "Just Suppose") 100-150 56
GOTHAM (323 "Sipping a Cup of Coffee") 4-6 81
(Red vinyl.)
GOTHAM (324 "Long Lonely Nights") 4-6 81
GOTHAM (325 "I Miss My Baby") 4-6 81
GOWEN (1403 "Together Again") 10-15 62
GRAND (156 "Tear Drops") 10-15 62
GRAND (157 "Long Lonely Nights") 10-15 62
JORDAN 15-25 60
LANA (111 "Try the Impossible") 4-8 64
LOST NITE 5-10 68
MAIN LINE (102 "Long Lonely Nights") 150-250 57
(Green label.)
MAIN LINE (102 "Long Lonely Nights") 75-125 57
(Black label, with Philadelphia address shown.)
MAIN LINE (102 "Long Lonely Nights") 15-25 62
(Black label, no address shown.)
MAIN LINE (105 "Tear drops") 5-10 62
PARKWAY (860 "Gee, But I'm Lonesome") 20-30 62
PARKWAY (866 "Looking Back") 20-30 63
RAINBOW (252 "Maybe You'll Be There") 250-500 54
(Black vinyl.)
RAINBOW (252 "Maybe You'll Be There") 1000-1500 54
(Red vinyl. Print is small, with the title line being about 1½" long.)
RAINBOW (252 "Maybe You'll Be There") 20-30 62
(Red vinyl. Print is noticeably larger than on 1954 issue.)
RAINBOW (256 "The White Cliffs of Dover") 1000-1500 54
(Yellow label.)
RAINBOW (256 "The White Cliffs of Dover") 15-25 62
(Blue label.)
RAINBOW (259 "The Bells of St. Mary's") 500-750 54
(Yellow label.)
RAINBOW (259 "The Bells of St. Mary's") 15-25 62
(Blue label.)
RCA (8929 "Quiet As It's Kept") 10-15 66
RIVIERA (965 "Maybe You'll Be There") 4000-6000 54
(Red vinyl.)
SWAN (4065 "I Miss You So") 50-150 60
SWAN (4076 "A Night Like Tonight") 200-300 61
SWAN (4087 "P.S. I Love You") 300-400 61
U.A. (123 "Try the Impossible") 10-20 58
U.A. (136 "Why Do I") 10-20 58
U.A. (151 "Maybe You'll Be There") 10-20 58
U.A. (162 "Just Suppose") 10-20 59
U.A. (592 "Try the Impossible") 5-10 63
LPs: 10/12-inch
COLLECTABLES 8-12 81-85
LOST NITE (1 "Lee Andrews and the Hearts") 10-20 81
(10-inch LP. Red vinyl. 1000 made.)
LOST NITE (2 "Lee Andrews and the Hearts") 10-20 81
(10-inch LP. Red vinyl. 1000 made.)
LOST NITE (100 series) 15-25 65
POST 10-15 '70s
Members: Lee Andrews; Arthur Thompson; Roy Calhoun; Wendell Calhoun; Butch Curry; Ted Weems.
Also see FAMOUS HEARTS
Also see FIVE HEARTS
Also see HEARTS
Also see SLAY, Frank, & His Orchestra

ANDREWS SISTERS *P&R '38*
Singles: 78 rpm
CAPITOL 5-10 56-57
DECCA (Except 3598) 5-10 38-57
DECCA (3598 "Boogie Woogie Bugle Boy") 30-50 41
Singles: 7-inch
ABC 4-6 74
CAPITOL 10-15 56-59
DECCA 10-20 50-57
DOT 4-8 63-64
KAPP (309 "I've Got to Pass Your House") 10-15 59
MCA 4-6 73-78
PARAMOUNT 4-6 73
Picture Sleeves
DECCA 10-20 57
KAPP (309 "I've Got to Pass Your House") 10-15 59
EPs: 7-inch
CAPITOL (973 "Dancing '20s") 10-20 56
DECCA 10-20 51-58
LPs: 10/12-inch
ABC 5-10 74
CAPITOL 10-20 64
DECCA (4000 series) 10-15 67
(Decca LP numbers in this series preceded by a "7" or a "DL-7" are stereo issues.)
DECCA (5000 series) 20-50 49-54
(10-inch LPs.)
DECCA (8000 series) 15-25 55-58
DOT 10-20 61-67
HAMILTON 10-20 64-65
MCA 8-12 73
PARAMOUNT 5-10 73-74
VOCALION 5-10
Members: Patty Andrews; Maxene Andrews; Laverne Andrews.
Also see CROSBY, Bing

ANDREWS SISTERS & LES PAUL
Singles: 78 rpm
DECCA (23656 "Rumors Are Flying") 4-8 46
Also see PAUL, Les

ANDREWS SISTERS & ERNEST TUBB
(With the Texas Troubadors) *C&W '49*
Singles: 78 rpm
DECCA (24592 "I'm Biting My Fingernails and Thinking of You") 15-20 49
Also see TUBB, Ernest

ANDREWS SISTERS & THURL RAVENSCROFT
Singles: 7-inch
DOT (16497 "Mr. Bass Man") 8-10 63
Also see ANDREWS SISTERS
Also see RAVENSCROFT, Thurl

ANDY, Randy, & Candymen
LPs: 10/12-inch
DIPLOMAT (114 "Let's Do the Twist") 15-25 62
(Includes one track by Joey Dee & Starlighters.)
Also see DEE, Joey, & Starlighters

ANDY & CLASSICS
Singles: 7-inch
KAMA (786 "Yaba Da Ba do") 5-10 66
Picture Sleeves
KAMA (786 "Yaba Da Ba do") 10-15 66

ANDY & GIGOLOS
Singles: 7-inch
DANDY (1001 "Bo Diddie Widdie") 50-75
UNIVERSAL (10158 "The Bug") 8-12

ANDY & LIVE WIRES
Singles: 7-inch
APPLAUSE (1249 "Maggie") 15-20 61
(First issue.)
LIBERTY (55321 "Maggie") 5-10 61
Also see ANDY & MANHATTANS
Also see ANDY & PLAYBOYS
Also see BUGGS

ANDY & MANHATTANS
Singles: 7-inch
CARDON (1000 "Double Mirror, Wrap-Around Shades") 30-40
MUSICOR (1053 "Should've I") 15-25 64
MUSICOR (1112 "Skinny Minnie") 15-25 65
Also see ANDY & LIVE WIRES
Also see ANDY & PLAYBOYS
Also see BUGGS

ANDY & PLAYBOYS
Singles: 7-inch
DAWN CORY (1001 "Your Pretty Lies") 15-25 '60s
Also see ANDY & LIVE WIRES
Also see ANDY & MANHATTANS
Also see BUGGS

ANDY & WHEELS
Singles: 7-inch
STATE (700 "Grinding Wheels") 30-40

ANGEL *LP '75*
Singles: 7-inch
CASABLANCA 4-6 75-80
LPs: 10/12-inch
CASABLANCA (7021 "Angel") 10-20 75
CASABLANCA (7028 "Helluva Band") 10-20 76
CASABLANCA (7043 "On Earth As It Is in Heaven") 10-20 77
CASABLANCA (7085 "White Hot") 10-20 75
CASABLANCA (7127 "Bad Publicity") 75-125 79
(First issue.)
CASABLANCA (7127 "Sinful") 10-20 79
(Retitled.)
CASABLANCA (7203 "Live Without a Net") 10-20 75

Members: Barry Brandt; Frank DiMino; Greg Giuffria; Mickey Jones; Punky Meadows; Felix Robinson.

ANGEL, Bobby
(With the Hillsiders; with Nutrockers)

Singles: 7-inch

ASTRA (300 "Submarine Races")... 10-15 62
LAP (1003 "Savannah")... 20-30 62
(Colored vinyl. Also issued as by Bobby Lake.)
RENDEZVOUS (162 "Dorene")...5-10 62
RENDEZVOUS (169 "Dorene")...5-10 62
RHUM (101 "Baby-O")... 10-20 61
Also see LAKE, Bobby

ANGEL, Gary

Singles: 7-inch

KAMA (501 "Oh Judy")... 20-30 61

ANGEL, Ginny

Singles: 7-inch

BOW (303 "Tra La La La I'm Yours Tonight")... 15-25 58
MAY (122 "Forever Goodbye Love")... 10-15 62
RCA (7793 "There'll Be Some Changes Made")... 10-15 61

ANGEL, Johnny

Singles: 78 rpm

EXCELLO (2077 "I Realize")... 10-20 56

Singles: 7-inch

EXCELLO (2077 "I Realize")... 30-40 56
POWER (250 "Starlight")... 125-150 58
VIN (1004 "Teenage Wedding")... 15-25 58

ANGEL, Johnny
(With the Halos)

Singles: 7-inch

FELSTED (8633 "Without Her Heart")... 20-30 61
FELSTED (8646 "One More Tomorrow") 10-15 62
FELSTED (8659 "Looking for a Fool")... 10-15 62
GARDENA (117 "All Night Party")... 10-15 61
IMPERIAL (5673 "Falling Teardrops")... 15-25 60
JAF (2024 "Lonely Nights")... 15-25 61
JOSIE (936 "I Put a Spell on You")...5-10 65
LIBERTY (55895 "Summertime Blues")...5-10 66
MARKEE (113 "Johnny Angel")...8-12 63
PARLIMENT...8-12 63
SKYWAY (117 "Come On Pretty Baby")... 150-200 '60s
SWAN (4263 "This Is the Night for Love")... 40-50 66
Also see FRANKIE & JOHNNY

ANGEL, Tommy

Singles: 7-inch

NASCO (6022 "Honey Bee")... 10-15 58

ANGEL FACE
(With the Swingmasters)

Singles: 7-inch

DC (0420 "Listen Baby")... 10-20 59
GEM (210 "Keep Your Head Up High")... 15-25 53
OKEH (7071 "I Can't Look Back")... 10-20 56
SPECIALTY (684 "I Know")... 10-15 60
Also see MOTLEY, Frank, / Angel Face

ANGEL VOICES

Singles: 78 rpm

METEOR (5015 "Tell the Angels")... 10-15 54

Singles: 7-inch

METEOR (5015 "Tell the Angels")... 20-30 54

ANGELENOS

Singles: 7-inch

PEEPERS (2824 "As Long As I Have You")... 20-25 61
PEEPERS (2827 "Come on Baby")... 15-20 61
Also see BROWN, Camille, & Angelenos

ANGELETTES

Singles: 7-inch

JOSIE (813 "Mine and Mine Alone")... 20-30 57

ANGELINE & TEEN TOWNERS

Singles: 7-inch

BERTRAM INT'L (202 "Hula Rock & Roll")... 15-25 57

ANGELLE, Bobby
(Bobby Relf)

Singles: 7-inch

MONEY... 15-25 66-67
Also see RELF, Bobby

ANGELO, Don

Singles: 7-inch

MERCURY (71580 "My Love for You")...10-20 60

ANGELO'S ANGELS

Singles: 7-inch

BONNY (101 "Mach 9")...10-15 63
ERMINE...5-10 64
NEW BREED (0001 "New Dog")...5-10 '60s
TABB (3230 "Mach 9")...10-15 63

ANGELOS

Singles: 7-inch

TOLLIE (9003 "Bad Motorcycle")...8-10 64
VEE-JAY (531 "Just Like Taking Candy from a Baby")...10-20 63

ANGELS
(With Jimmy Wright & His Orchestra; with Sonny Gordon)

Singles: 78 rpm

GEE...20-30 56
GRAND...50-100 54

Singles: 7-inch

GEE (1024 "Glory of Love")...50-75 56
(Red and black label. 45 RPM only on right side of label.)
GEE (1024 "Glory of Love")...20-30 56
(Red and black label. 45 RPM on both left and right sides of label.)
GEE (1024 "Glory of Love")...10-15 60
(Gray label.)
GRAND (115 "Wedding Bells Are Ringing in My Ears")...500-750 54
(Glossy yellow label. Rigid disc. No company address shown.)
GRAND (115 "Wedding Bells Are Ringing in My Ears")...50-75 61
(Yellow label. Flexible disc. No company address shown.)
GRAND (115 "Wedding Bells Are Ringing in My Ears")...15-25 '60s
(Yellow label. Company address is shown.)
GRAND (121 "Lovely Way to Spend an Evening")... 750-1000 55
(Glossy yellow label. Rigid disc. No company address shown.)
GRAND (121 "Lovely Way to Spend an Evening")...50-75 61
(Yellow label. Flexible disc. No company address shown.)
GRAND (121 "Lovely Way to Spend an Evening")...25-35 '60s
(Yellow label. Company address is shown.)
Note: Not all of the Grand variations may exist with all of their titles; however, they are listed in case they do exist.
Also see WRIGHT, Jimmy

ANGELS

Singles: 7-inch

AUDIO (203 "A Real Sensation")...150-250 61

ANGELS

Singles: 7-inch

TAWNY (101 "A Lover's Poem")...40-60 59
Also see SAFARIS

ANGELS — P&R '61
(With the Hutch Davie Orchestra)

Singles: 7-inch

ASCOT (2139 "Irresistible")...8-12 63
CAMEO (250 "You Turn Me On")...8-10 63
CAPRICE...10-20 61-62
COLLECTABLES...3-5 82
ERIC...3-6 74
MERCURY (810 325-7 "My Boyfriend's Back")...3-5 '80s
POLYDOR (14222 "You're All I Need to Get By")...4-6 74
RCA...5-10 67-68
SMASH...10-15 63-64

Picture Sleeves

SMASH (1854 "I Adore Him")...10-20 63
SMASH (1915 "Dream Boy")...50-75 64

EPs: 7-inch

CAPRICE (1001 "The Angels")...20-30 62

LPs: 10/12-inch

ASCOT (13009 "The Angels Sing 12 of Their Greatest Hits")...20-30 64
(Monaural.)
ASCOT (16009 "The Angels Sing 12 of Their Greatest Hits")...30-40 64
(Stereo.)
CAPRICE (LP-1001 "And the Angels Sing")...40-50 62
(Monaural.)
CAPRICE (SLP-1001 "And the Angels Sing")...50-75 62
(Stereo.)
COLLECTABLES...5-8 '80s
SMASH (27039 "My Boyfriend's Back")...30-40 63
(Monaural.)
SMASH (67039 "My Boyfriend's Back")...50-75 63
(Stereo.)
SMASH (27048 "A Halo to You")...30-40 63
(Monaural.)
SMASH (67048 "A Halo to You")...40-60 63
(Stereo.)
Members: Linda Jansen; Peggy Santiglia; Barbara Allbut; Phyllis "Jiggs" Allbut; Debra Swisher.
Also see DAVIE, Hutch
Also see DELICATES
Also see POWDER PUFFS
Also see SEDAKA, Neil, & Tokens / Angels / Jimmy Gilmer & Fireballs
Also see STARLETS
Also see SWISHER, Debra

ANGELYNE

Singles: 7-inch

ERIKA (124 "Skin Tight")...40-50 83
(Five-inch picture disc. Includes poster.)
JAEVI...3-5 81

Picture Sleeves

JAEVI...3-5 81

LPs: 10/12-inch

ERIKA (9654 "Angelyne")...40-60 82
(Picture disc.)
PINK KITTEN...10-25 85

ANGIE & CHICKLETTES

Singles: 7-inch

APT (25080 "Treat Him [Ringo] Tender, Maureen")...10-20 65
Member: Jean Thomas.
Also see RAG DOLLS

ANGIE & CITATIONS

Singles: 7-inch

ANGELA (102 "Dance Her By Me")...20-30

ANGIE & MONOCOS

Singles: 7-inch

WHITETOP (1000 "Sad As I Can Be").100-200 63

ANGLO-AMERICANS

Singles: 7-inch

CHATTAHOOCHEE (705 "The Music Never Stops")...15-25 66

ANGLOS

Singles: 7-inch

SCEPTER (12204 "A Small Town Boy")..10-20 67

ANGLO-SAXON

Singles: 7-inch

TOWER (401 "Ruby")...15-20 68
TOWER (491 "Ruby")...15-20 69

ANGLO-SAXONS

Singles: 7-inch

SQUIRE (603 "Brown-Eyed Handsome Man")...30-40

ANGORIANS

Singles: 7-inch

DONNA (1388 "Raindrops")...10-15 63
TISHMAN (907 "Lullaby")...15-25 64
(One-sided.)
TISHMAN (907 "Lullaby"/"Raindrops")...20-30 64

ANGRY MEN

Singles: 7-inch

TORCH (1002 "Come with Me")...20-30 67

ANIMALS — P&R '64
(Eric Burdon & the Animals; Original Animals)

Singles: 7-inch

ABKCO...4-6 75
CAPITOL (72171 "The House of the Rising Sun")...25-45 64
(Canadian. Full-length [4:28], LP version. Edited [2:58] version is on original MGM single.)
COLLECTABLES...3-5 82
I.R.S...3-5 83
JET...4-6 77
MGM...8-15 64-71
STARDUST (1230 "The House of the Rising Sun")...4-6 94
(Full-length [4:28] version. U.S.-made Canadian reissue.)

Promotional Singles

ABKCO...4-6 75
I.R.S...4-6 83
JET...4-6 77
MGM...10-30 64-71
MGM CELEBRITY SCENE ("Animals")...40-60 66
(Boxed set of five singles with bio insert and title strips.)

Picture Sleeves

MGM (13264 "House of the Rising Sun"). 10-20 64
MGM (13274 "I'm Crying")...10-15 64
MGM (13298 "Boom Boom")...10-15 64
MGM (13339 "Bring It on Home to Me")...8-12 65
MGM (13769 "San Franciscan Nights")...5-10 67
MGM (13868 "Monterey")...5-10 67

LPs: 10/12-inch

ABKCO...8-12 73-76
ACCORD...5-10 82
I.R.S...5-10 83-85
MGM...15-30 64-69
PICKWICK...5-10 71
SCEPTER/CITATION...5-10 76
SPRINGBOARD...5-10 72
U.A....5-10 77
WAND...8-12 70
Members: Eric Burdon; Alan Price; Hilton Valentine; Chas Chandler; John Steel; John Weider.
Also see PRICE, Alan
Also see VALENTINE, Hilton

ANIMATED EGG

LPs: 10/12-inch

ALSHIRE (5104 "Animated Egg")...40-60 67

ANITA & TH' SO-AND-SO'S — P&R '62
(Anita Kerr Singers)

Singles: 7-inch

RCA (7974 "Joey Baby")...10-15 62
RCA (8050 "To Each His Own")...8-12 62
Also see KERR, Anita

ANKA, Marty

Singles: 7-inch

IMPERIAL (2187 "Tell Me")...10-20 60

ANKA, Paul — P&R/R&B '57
(With the Don Costa Orchestra)

Singles: 78 rpm

ABC-PAR (Except 9880)...15-30 57
ABC-PAR (9880 "You Are My Destiny")...25-50 57
RPM...15-20 56
SPARTON/ABC (457 "Diana")...10-20 57
(10-inch LP.)

Singles: 12-inch

COLUMBIA...4-6 83

Singles: 7-inch

ABC-PAR (104 "Share Your Love")...15-25 58
(Promotional, fan club issue.)
ABC-PAR (296-1 "My Heart Sings")...25-35 58
(Stereo Compact 33 Single.)
ABC-PAR (9831 thru 9956)...10-20 57-58
ABC-PAR (9987 "My Heart Sings")...10-15 58
(Monaural.)
ABC-PAR (9987 "My Heart Sings")...25-50 58
(Stereo.)
ABC-PAR (10011 "I Miss You So")...10-15 59
(Monaural.)
ABC-PAR (S-10011 "I Miss You So")...25-50 59
(Stereo.)
ABC-PAR (10022 "Lonely Boy")...10-15 59
(Monaural.)
ABC-PAR (S-10022 "Lonely Boy")...25-50 59
(Stereo.)
ABC-PAR (10040 "Put Your Head on My Shoulder")...10-15 59
(Monaural.)
ABC-PAR (S-10040 "Put Your Head on My Shoulder")...25-50 59
(Stereo.)
ABC-PAR (10064 "Time to Cry")...10-15 59
(Monaural.)
ABC-PAR (S-10064 "Time to Cry")...25-50 59
(Stereo.)
ABC-PAR (10082 "Puppy Love")...10-15 60
(Monaural.)
ABC-PAR (S-10082 "Puppy Love")...25-50 60
(Stereo.)

ABC-PAR (10106 "My Home Town")....... 10-15 60
(Monaural.)
ABC-PAR (S-10106 "My Home Town")... 25-50 60
(Stereo.)
ABC-PAR (10132 "Hello Young Lovers") 10-15 60
(Monaural.)
ABC-PAR (10132 "Hello Young Lovers") 25-50 60
(Stereo.)
ABC-PAR (10147 "Summer's Gone")...... 10-15 60
(Monaural.)
ABC-PAR (S-10147 "Summer's Gone") .. 25-50 60
(Stereo.)
ABC-PAR (10168 "Story of My Love")..... 10-15 60
(Monaural.)
ABC-PAR (S-10168 "Story of My Love") . 25-50 60
(Stereo.)
ABC-PAR (10169 "It's Christmas Everywhere") 10-15 60
ABC-PAR (10194 thru 10338)........8-15 61-62
BARNABY (2027 "You're Some Kind of Friend") 4-6 71
BUCCANEER........5-10 '60s
BUDDAH........4-6 72-73
CBS (7133 "You're Some Kind of Friend") ...4-6 71
COLUMBIA........3-5 83-85
ERIC........4-6 76
FAME (345 "Let Me Get to Know You")........4-6 73
RCA (Except 2000, 8000, 9000 and 10000 series) 4-8 67-79
RCA (2000 series) 10-20 62
(With "VLP" or "VP" prefix. Stereo Compact 33 series.)
RCA (37-7977 "Love Me Warm and Tender") 15-25 62
(Compact 33 Single.)
RCA (47-7977 "Love Me Warm and Tender")........5-10 62
RCA (8000 series, except 8893)........5-10 62-66
RCA (8893 "I Can't Help Lovin' You")..... 15-25 66
RCA (9000 series) 5-10 67-69
RCA (10000 series) 3-6 78-81
RPM (472 "I Confess")........ 40-50 56
RPM (499 "I Confess")........ 20-30 57
SPARTON/ABC (457 "Diana")........ 10-20 57
(Canadian. Maroon and silver label.)
SPARTON/ABC (457 "Diana")........5-10 '60s
(Canadian. Pink and black label.)
U.A. 4-6 75-77

Picture Sleeves

ABC-PAR (Except 9831 & 9956) 20-30 58-61
ABC-PAR (9831 "Diana")........5-10 '90s
ABC-PAR (9956 "Just Young")........ 50-75 58
COLUMBIA........3-5 83
ERIC........4-6 74
RCA (Except 8662 & 11000 series)........8-15 62-65
RCA (8662 "Everyday a Heart Is Broken")........ 20-25 65
RCA (11000 series) 4-6 78
U.A. 4-6 75

EPs: 7-inch

ABC........ 15-25 '60s
(Juke box issue only.)
ABC-PAR........ 25-50 59
SIRE........ 10-12 74
(Juke box issue only.)

LPs: 10/12-inch

ABC-PAR (ABC-240 "Paul Anka")........ 25-35 58
(Monaural.)
ABC-PAR (ABCS-240 "Paul Anka")........ 35-50 58
(Stereo.)
ABC-PAR (ABC-296 "My Heart Sings")... 25-35 59
(Monaural.)
ABC-PAR (ABCS-296 "My Heart Sings") 35-45 59
(Stereo.)
ABC-PAR (ABC-323 "Big 15")........ 25-35 60
(Monaural.)
ABC-PAR (ABCS-323 "Big 15") 35-45 60
(Stereo.)
ABC-PAR (ABC-347 "For Young Lovers")........ 25-30 60
(Monaural.)
ABC-PAR (ABCS-347 "For Young Lovers")........ 30-35 60
(Stereo.)
ABC-PAR (ABC-353 "Anka at the Copa")........ 25-30 60
(Monaural.)
ABC-PAR (ABCS-353 "Anka at the Copa")........ 30-35 60
(Stereo.)
ABC-PAR (ABC-360 "It's Christmas Everywhere") 25-30 60
(Monaural.)
ABC-PAR (ABCS-360 "It's Christmas Everywhere") 30-35 60
(Stereo.)
ABC-PAR (ABC-371 "Strictly Instrumental") 20-30 61
(Monaural.)
ABC-PAR (ABCS-371 "Strictly Instrumental") 25-35 61
(Stereo.)
ABC-PAR (ABC-390 "His Big 15, Vol. 2").20-30 61
(Monaural.)
ABC-PAR (ABCS-390 "His Big 15, Vol. 2") 25-35 61
(Stereo.)
ABC-PAR (ABC-409 "His Big 15, Vol. 3").20-30 62
(Monaural.)
ABC-PAR (ABCS-409 "His Big 15, Vol. 3") 25-35 62
(Stereo.)
ABC-PAR (ABC-420 "Diana") 20-30 62
(Monaural.)
ABC-PAR (ABCS-420 "Diana")........25-30 62
(Stereo.)
ACCORD........5-10 81
BARNABY........8-12
BUDDAH........8-12 71-76
CAMDEN........5-10 74
COLUMBIA........5-10 83-85
LIBERTY........5-10 81-83
EMUS (12036 "My Way") 5-10 78
PICKWICK........5-10 75
RCA (Except "LPM" & "LSP" series)........5-10 75-81
RCA (2000 thru 4000" series) 10-25 62-70
(With "LPM" prefix. Monaural.)
RCA (2000 thru 4000" series) 15-30 62-70
(With "LSP" prefix. Stereo.)
RANWOOD........5-10 81
RIVERA (0047 "Paul Anka and Others") ..25-40 63
(Has two tracks by Paul Anka.)
RHINO........5-10 86
SIRE........10-12 74-78
U.A. 5-10 74-78
Also see ANN-MARGRET
Also see COSTA, Don, Orchestra
Also see MARLO, Micki

ANKA, Paul, & Odia Coates

Singles: 12-inch

EPIC 4-6 77

Singles: 7-inch

EPIC (50298 "Make It Up to Me in Love") 4-6 76
U.A. 4-6 74-75

ANKA, Paul / Sam Cooke / Neil Sedaka

LPs: 10/12-inch

RCA (2720 "Three Great Guys")........20-25 64
Also see COOKE, Sam
Also see SEDAKA, Neil

ANKA, Paul, & Karla DeVito

Singles: 12-inch

COLUMBIA........4-6 83

Singles: 7-inch

COLUMBIA........3-5 83

ANKA, Paul, George Hamilton IV & Johnny Nash — P&R '58

Singles: 7-inch

ABC-PAR (9974 "The Teen Commandments") 10-20 58
Also see HAMILTON, George
Also see NASH, Johnny

ANKA, Paul / Lloyd Price

EPs: 7-inch

ABC-PAR (14 "Rockin' on 5th Ave.")........40-50 61
(Promotional issue made for Luden's, makers of 5th Avenue candy bars.)
Also see ANKA, Paul
Also see PRICE, Lloyd

ANN, Margaret, & Ja-Das

Singles: 7-inch

W.B. (5064 "The Girl That Johnny Walked Home") 5-10 59
W.B. (5124 "Bill Bailey, Won't You Please Come Home") 5-10 59

LPs: 10/12-inch

W.B. (1285 "It's the Most Happy Sound") 15-25 59
Note: This is not the same singer as Ann-Margret.
Also see JA DA QUARTETTE

ANNA MARIA & BLINKY ALLEN STAR DUSTERS

Singles: 78 rpm

FLAIR (1047 "An Angel Cried") 8-12 54

Singles: 7-inch

FLAIR (1047 "An Angel Cried") 15-25 54
Also see ALLEN, Blinky

ANNETTE — P&R '59

(Annette Funicello; with the Afterbeats; with Upbeats; with Camarata & His Orchestra; with Marzocchi)

Singles: 78 rpm

DISNEYLAND (102 "How Will I Know")..50-100 58

Singles: 7-inch

BUENA VISTA (336, "Jo-Jo the Dog Faced Boy"/"Lonely Guitar") 15-20 59
BUENA VISTA (336, "Jo-Jo the Dog Faced Boy"/"Love Me Forever")........10-15 59
(Note different flip side.)
BUENA VISTA (339 "Lonely Guitar") 10-20 59
BUENA VISTA (344 "My Heart Became of Age") 10-20 59
BUENA VISTA (349 "First Name Initial")..10-20 59
BUENA VISTA (354 "O Dio Mio") 10-20 59
BUENA VISTA (359 "Tell Me Who's the Girl") 15-25 60
BUENA VISTA (362 "Pineapple Princess") 15-25 60
BUENA VISTA (369 "Talk to Me Baby")...15-25 60
BUENA VISTA (374 "Dream Boy") 15-25 61
BUENA VISTA (375 "Mama Mama Rosa") 15-25 61
BUENA VISTA (384 "Blue Muu Muu")......15-25 61
BUENA VISTA (394 "The Truth About Youth") 15-25 62
BUENA VISTA (400 "My Little Grass Shack") 15-25 62
BUENA VISTA (405 "He's My Ideal") 15-25 62
BUENA VISTA (407 "Bella Bella Florence") 15-25 62
BUENA VISTA (414 "Teenage Wedding") 20-30 63
BUENA VISTA (427 "Promise Me Anything") 15-25 63
BUENA VISTA (432 "Rebel Rider") 15-25 64
BUENA VISTA (433 "Muscle Beach Party") 20-30 64
BUENA VISTA (436 "Bikini Beach Party") 20-30 64
BUENA VISTA (437 "The Wah Watusi")..10-15 64
BUENA VISTA (438 "Something Borrowed") 15-25 65
BUENA VISTA (440 "The Monkey's Uncle") 10-20 65
(With the Beach Boys.)
BUENA VISTA (442 "A Boy to Love") 10-20 65
BUENA VISTA (450 "Crystal Ball") 10-20 66
BUENA VISTA (475 "Merlin Jones") 10-15 69
DISNEYLAND (102 "How Will I Know My Love") 20-30 58
DISNEYLAND (114 "That Crazy Place from Outer Space") 20-30 58
DISNEYLAND (118 "Tall Paul") 15-25 58
JUGGY........8-10
STARVIEW........5-10 83
TOWER (326 "What's a Girl to Do") 20-25 67
(Name misspelled, shown as "Annettte.")

Picture Sleeves

BUENA VISTA (339 "Lonely Guitar") 20-30 59
BUENA VISTA (349 "First Name Initial")..20-30 59
BUENA VISTA (354 "O Dio Mio") 20-30 59
BUENA VISTA (359 "Tell Me Who's the Girl") 20-30 60
BUENA VISTA (362 "Pineapple Princess") 20-30 60
BUENA VISTA (369 "Talk to Me Baby")...20-30 60
BUENA VISTA (374 "Dream Boy") 20-30 61
BUENA VISTA (375 "Mama Mama Rosa") 20-30 61
BUENA VISTA (384 "Blue Muu Muu")......40-60 62
BUENA VISTA (394 "The Truth About Youth") 20-30 62
BUENA VISTA (400 "My Little Grass Shack") 20-30 62
BUENA VISTA (405 "He's My Ideal") 20-30 62
BUENA VISTA (407 "Bella Bella Florence") 50-75 62
BUENA VISTA (414 "Teenage Wedding") 75-100 63
BUENA VISTA (427 "Promise Me Anything") 50-75 63
BUENA VISTA (432 "Rebel Rider") 25-35 64
BUENA VISTA (433 "Muscle Beach Party") 30-40 64
BUENA VISTA (436 "Bikini Beach Party") 30-40 64
BUENA VISTA (438 "Something Borrowed") 50-75 65
BUENA VISTA (440 "The Monkey's Uncle") 25-35 65
BUENA VISTA (475 "Merlin Jones) 20-30 69
DISNEYLAND (102 "How Will I Know My Love") 25-45 58
DISNEYLAND (105 "Meetin' at the Malt Shop") 25-45 58

EPs: 7-inch

BUENA VISTA (3301 "Annette") 50-75 59
DISNEYLAND (04 "Tall Paul") 50-75 58
DISNEYLAND (69 "Mickey Mouse Club Featuring Annette") 50-75 58

LPs: 10/12-inch

BUENA VISTA (3301 "Annette") 150-200 59
BUENA VISTA (3302 "Annette Sings Anka") 100-150 60
(With bonus color photo.)
BUENA VISTA (3302 "Annette Sings Anka") 50-75 60
(Without bonus photo.)
BUENA VISTA (3303 "Hawaiiannette – Songs of Hawaii") 50-75 60
BUENA VISTA (3304 "Italiannette – Songs with Italian Flavor") 50-75 60
BUENA VISTA (3305 "Dance Annette")...50-75 61
BUENA VISTA (3312 "Story of My Teens") 50-75 62
BUENA VISTA (3316 "Annette's Beach Party") 50-75 63
BUENA VISTA (3320 "Annette on Campus") 50-75 64
BUENA VISTA (3324 "Annette at Bikini Beach") 50-75 64
BUENA VISTA (3325 "Annette's Pajama Party") 50-75 64
BUENA VISTA (3327 "Annette Sings Golden Surfin' Hits") 50-75 65
BUENA VISTA (3328 "Something Borrowed, Something Blue") 50-75 64
BUENA VISTA (4037 "Annette Funicello") 15-25 72
DISNEYLAND (Except 3906) 15-30 62-75
(Various Mouseketeer cast albums that include or feature Annette.)
DISNEYLAND (3906 "Snow White – As Told By Annette") 40-60
MICKEY MOUSE (12 thru 24) 40-60 57-58
(Various Mouseketeer cast albums that include or feature Annette.)
RHINO (Except 702) 8-10 84
RHINO (702 "Best of Annette") 25-35 84
(Picture disc.)
SILHOUETTE........10-15 81
STARVIEW (4001 "Country Album") 8-12 84
(Standard issue.)
STARVIEW (4001 "Country Album") 15-20 84
(Limited Edition series.)
Session: Davie Allan; Phil Baugh; Allan Reuss; Howard Roberts; Tommy Tedesco; Cliff Hils; Ed Hall; Jackie Kelso; Camarata.
Also see ALLAN, Davie
Also see AVALON, Frankie, & Annette
Also see BAUGH, Phil
Also see BEACH BOYS
Also see HONEYS
Also see MacMURRAY, Fred
Also see MOUSEKETEERS
Also see TEDESCO, Tommy
Also see WOOD, Gloria, & Afterbeats

ANNETTE / Jimmy Dodd

Singles: 78 rpm

DISNEYLAND (758 "How Will I Know"/"Annette") 30-40 62
(Six-inch single.)

Singles: 7-inch

DISNEYLAND (758 "How Will I Know"/"Annette") 30-40 62

Picture Sleeves

DISNEYLAND (758 "How Will I Know"/ "Annette")........ 40-60 62

ANNETTE & TOMMY KIRK / Annette & Wellingtons

Singles: 7-inch

BUENA VISTA (431 "Scrambled Egghead"/ "Merlin Jones")........ 15-25 63

Picture Sleeves

BUENA VISTA (431 "Scrambled Egghead"/ "Merlin Jones")........ 25-35 63

ANNETTE / Hayley Mills

LPs: 10/12-inch

BUENA VISTA/DISNEYLAND (3508 "Annette & Hayley Mills")........ 750-1000 64
(Cover reads Buena Vista but label is Disneyland. Issued with paper cover. Mail order only offer. One side by each artist.)
Also see MILLS, Hayley

ANNETTE & TOMMY SANDS
(With Camarata & His Orchestra)

Singles: 7-inch

BUENA VISTA (802 "The Parent Trap").. 20-30 61
(45 single.)
BUENA VISTA (802 "The Parent Trap")........ 200-300 61
(Compact 33 Single.)

Picture Sleeves

BUENA VISTA (802 "The Parent Trap").. 20-25 61
Also see ANNETTE
Also see SANDS, Tommy

ANNETTE / Dany Saval & Tom Tryon

Singles: 7-inch

BUENA VISTA (392 "That Crazy Place in Outer Space"/"Seven Moons")........ 15-25 62

Picture Sleeves

BUENA VISTA (392 "That Crazy Place in Outer Space"/"Seven Moons")........5-10 62
(Annette is not on picture sleeve.)

ANNETTE & VONNAIR SISTERS

Singles: 7-inch

BUENA VISTA (388 "Dreamin' About You")........ 15-25 61

Picture Sleeves

BUENA VISTA (388 "Dreamin' About You")........ 20-30 61
Also see ANNETTE
Also see VONNAIR SISTERS

ANNIE & ORPHANS

Singles: 7-inch

CAPITOL (5144 "My Girl's Been Bitten By the Beatle Bug")........ 10-20 64

Picture Sleeves

CAPITOL (5144 "My Girl's Been Bitten By the Beatle Bug")........ 15-25 64

ANN-MARGRET *P&R '61*

Singles: 12-inch

AVCO EMBASSY (4547 "Today")........ 10-15 70
FIRST AMERICAN (1207 "Everybody Needs Somebody Sometime")........5-10 81
MCA (1867 "Midnight Message")........5-10 80
(Promotional issue only.)
MCA (1867 "What I Do to Men")........5-10 80
OCEAN/ARIOLA AMERICA........4-8 79-80
RAM (1001 "Everybody Needs Somebody Sometime")........5-10 81
RAM........4-8 81

Singles: 7-inch

FIRST AMERICAN........3-5 81
MCA........3-5 79-80
OCEAN/ARIOLA AMERICA........3-5 79-80
RCA (VLP-2251 "Vivacious One")........ 30-50 62
(Five-disc, juke box set. With title strips.)
RCA (37-7857 "Lost Love")........ 20-40 61
(Compact 33 Single.)
RCA (47-7857 "Lost Love")........ 10-15 61
RCA (37-7894 "I Just Don't Understand")........ 20-30 61
(Compact 33 Single.)
RCA (47-7894 "I Just Don't Understand")........ 10-15 61
RCA (37-7952 "It Do Me So Good")........ 20-40 61
(Compact 33 Single.)
RCA (47-7952 "It Do Me So Good")........ 10-15 61
RCA (7986 thru 9109)........ 10-15 61-66

Picture Sleeves

RCA (7894 "I Just Don't Understand")......15-25 61
RCA (7952 "It Do Me So Good")........15-25 61
RCA (7986 "What Am I Supposed to Do")........15-25 61
RCA (8130 "No More")........15-25 62
RCA (8061 "Jim Dandy")........15-25 62
RCA (8168 "Bye Bye Birdie")........15-25 63

EPs: 7-inch

RCA (2251 "The Vivacious One")........15-25 62
RCA (2659 "Mr. Wonderful")........15-25 63
RCA (4358 "On the Way Up")........15-25 62
RCA (9058 "On the Way Up")........15-25 62

LPs: 10/12-inch

LHI........10-20 68-69
LAGNIAPPE 1959 ("Be My Guest")......200-300 59
(Cast LP produced by the Boys Tri-Ship Club of New Trier High School. Includes *Tropical Heat Wave* by Ann-Margret Olson.)
MCA........5-10 80
NORTHWESTERN UNIVERSITY/RCA (5760 "Among Friends")........100-150 60
(Cast LP for the *Waa-Mu Show of 1960* from Northwestern University. Lists Ann-Margret Olson as a dancer.)
RCA (LPM-2399 "And Here She Is")........10-20 61
(Monaural.)
RCA (LSP-2399 "And Here She Is")........15-25 61
(Stereo.)
RCA (LPM-2453 "On the Way Up")........10-20 62
(Monaural.)
RCA (LSP-2453 "On the Way Up")........15-25 62
(Stereo.)
RCA (LPM-2551 "Vivacious One")........10-20 62
(Monaural.)
RCA (LSP-2551 "Vivacious One")........15-25 62
(Stereo.)
RCA (LPM-2659 "Bachelor's Paradise")...10-20 63
(Monaural.)
RCA (LSP-2659 "Bachelor's Paradise")...15-25 63
(Stereo.)
RCA/NARM ("Tenth Anniversary Convention")........40-60 68
(Has *Bye Bye Birdie* by Ann-Margret, plus tracks by the Limeliters, Al Hirt, Paul Anka, Homer & Jethro, Peter Nero, Eddy Arnold, John Gary, Chet Atkins, Floyd Cramer, Anita Kerr Singers, Boots Randolph, Myron Cohen, Barry Sadler, Henry Mancini, Jack Jones, and Harry Belafonte. Promotional, souvenir issue only.)
Also see ANKA, Paul
Also see ARNOLD, Eddy
Also see ATKINS, Chet
Also see BELAFONTE, Harry
Also see CRAMER, Floyd
Also see HOMER & JETHRO
Also see JONES, Jack
Also see KERR, Anita
Also see LIMELITERS
Also see MANCINI, Henry
Also see RANDOLPH, Boots
Also see SADLER, Barry
Also see SEDAKA, Neil / Ann-Margret / Browns / Sam Cooke

ANN-MARGRET & JOHN GARY *LP '64*

LPs: 10/12-inch

RCA (LPM-2947 "Broadway Hits")........10-20 64
(Monaural.)
RCA (LSP-2947 "Broadway Hits")........15-25 64
(Stereo.)
Also see GARY, John

ANN-MARGRET & LEE HAZLEWOOD

Singles: 7-inch

LHI........5-10 68-69

LPs: 10/12-inch

LHI (12007 "The Cowboy & the Lady")......15-20 69

ANN-MARGRET & AL HIRT

Singles: 7-inch

RCA (VLP-2690 "Beauty & the Beard")....25-50 64
(Five-disc, juke box set. With title strips.)
RCA (9524 "Slowly")........5-10 68

EPs: 7-inch

RCA (LSP-2690 "Beauty & the Beard")....15-25 64

LPs: 10/12-inch

RCA (LPM-2690 "Beauty & the Beard") ...10-20 64
(Monaural.)
RCA (LSP-2690 "Beauty & the Beard")....15-25 64
(Stereo.)

ANN-MARGRET / Kitty Kallen / Della Reese

LPs: 10/12-inch

RCA (2724 "Three Great Girls")........15-20 63
Also see ANN-MARGRET
Also see KALLEN, Kitty
Also see REESE, Della

ANNUALS

Singles: 7-inch

CONN (2 "Once in a Lifetime")........200-300 59
MARCONN (1 "Once in a Lifetime").....150-200 59

ANONYMOUS

Singles: 7-inch

FLAT........15-20

LPs: 10/12-inch

MAJOR (1002 "Inside the Shadow")......200-300 76
Members: Marsha Rollings; Glenn Weaver; Ron Matelic; John Medvescek.

ANSWERS

Singles: 7-inch

UNITED (212 "Keeps Me Worried All the Time")........75-125 57

ANT TRIP CEREMONY

LPs: 10/12-inch

CRC (2129 "24 Hours")........400-500 67
RESURRECTION ("24 Hours")........50-75
(Selection number not known.)
Members: Roger Goodman; Gary Rosen; Steve DeTray; George Galt; Mark Stein; Jeff Williams.

ANTELL, Peter *P&R '62*
(Pete Antell)

Singles: 7-inch

BOUNTY (103 "The Times They Are A-Changin'")........15-25 65
CAMEO (234 "Night Time")........10-20 62
(Big print. Dull label.)
CAMEO (234 "Night Time")........5-10 63
(Small print. Shiny label.)
CAMEO (264 "Keep It Up")........5-10 63
NEW VOICE (818 "Wanting")........5-10 67
Also see JAYWALKER & PEDESTRIANS
Also see WILD ONES

ANTELLECTS

Singles: 7-inch

FLODAVIEUR (804 "Don't Let It Happen")........100-200 64

ANTHONY, Joy, & Dreamers

Singles: 7-inch

SINCLAIR (1001 "Earth Angel")........40-60 61

ANTHONY, Lamont
(La Mont Anthony; Lamont Dozier)

Singles: 7-inch

ANNA (1125 "Popeye")........100-200 60
ANNA (1125-G "Benny the Skinny Man")........25-50 60
(Number at bottom has a "G.")
ANNA (1125 "Benny the Skinny Man").....15-25 60
(Number at bottom has no "G.")
CHECK MATE (1001 "Just to Be Loved")........100-150 61
Also see DOZIER, Lamont

ANTHONY, Marc

Singles: 7-inch

AXTEL (100 "Penny")........30-40 60
AXTEL (102 "Party Doll")........30-40 61
DIAMOND (140 "Why Do I Love You").......5-10 63

ANTHONY, Mark

Singles: 7-inch

LA BELLE (779 "I Saw Mama Twistin' with Santa Claus")........5-10 62
PORTER (1005 "Wolf Call")........25-35 58

ANTHONY, Mike

Singles: 7-inch

IMPERIAL (5813 "Little Linda")........15-25 61

ANTHONY, Nick

Singles: 7-inch

ABC-PAR (9919 "More Than Ever")........15-25 58
ABC-PAR (9985 "Forbidden Love")........15-25 58
CARAVAN (1001 "Just a Fool")........10-20
CINDY (3001 "Sugar Baby")........15-25 57

ANTHONY, Paul

Singles: 7-inch

FIREFLY ("My Promise to You")........50-75 58
(First issue. Selection number not known.)
GAMBIT (1103 "Hello Teardrops, Goodbye Love")........25-35 63
METRO INT'L (1003 "Step Up")........30-40 '50s
ROULETTE (4099 "My Promise to You").20-30 58

ANTHONY, Ray, & His Orchestra *P&R '49*

Singles: 78 rpm

CAPITOL........3-5 49-57

Singles: 7-inch

CAPITOL........5-15 50-62
RANWOOD........4-6 68

Picture Sleeves

CAPITOL (2427 "The Bunny Hop")........15-25 53

EPs: 7-inch

CAPITOL........5-15 52-59

LPs: 10/12-inch

CAPITOL........15-30 52-62
Also see BEACH BOYS / Ray Anthony
Also see SINATRA, Frank

ANTHONY, Richard
(With the Blue Notes)

Singles: 7-inch

AMY (992 "I'm Not a Fool Anymore")........5-10 67
CAPITOL (5247 "If I Loved You")........5-10 64
FAYETTE (1622 "London Beat")........5-10 64
SWAN (4257 "No Good")........25-45 66
V.I.P. (25022 "I Don't Know What to Do")........10-15 65
VIRTUE (189 "Keep on Livin'")........100-150 '60s

ANTHONY, Vince *C&W '82*
(With the Country Blue Notes)

Singles: 7-inch

HILTON (80 "Watch My Smoke")........50-75 59
HILTON (0007 "Too Hot to Handle")........50-75 59
MIDNIGHT GOLD........3-5 82
VIKING (1018 "All Over Again")........10-15 61

ANTHONY, Wayne
(Little Wayne Anthony)

Singles: 7-inch

ROULETTE (4662 "A Thousand Miles Away")........10-15 65
ROULETTE (4672 "Little Miss Lonely")....10-15 66
ROULETTE (4694 "Out of Sight, Out of Mind")........10-15 66
VEE-JAY (557 "Here Comes Your Mama")........8-12 63
VEE-JAY (583 "Freedom to Love")........8-12 64
WALANA (102 "Blow Me a Kiss")........150-250

ANTHONY & AQUA LADS

Singles: 7-inch

GOLD BEE (1650 "I Remember")........30-40 '60s

ANTHONY & SOPHOMORES
(Anthony & Sophmores)

Singles: 7-inch

ABC-PAR (10737 "Gee")........10-15 65
ABC-PAR (10770 "Get Back to You")........5-10 66
ABC-PAR (10844 "Heartbreak")........5-10 66
COLLECTABLES........3-5 82
GRAND (163 "Embraceable You")........50-60 63
(Label shows spelling as "Embracable.")
JAMIE (1330 "Serenade")........15-25 67
JAMIE (1340 "One Summer Night")......75-125 67
JASON SCOTT (18 "Beautiful Dreamer")....3-5 82
(500 made.)
MERCURY (72103 "Play Those Oldies Mr. Dee Jay")........30-40 63
(Black label.)
MERCURY (72103 "Play Those Oldies Mr. Dee Jay")........40-50 63
(White label. Promotional issue only.)
MERCURY (72103 "Play Those Oldies Mr. Dee Jay")........10-15 65
(Red label.)
MERCURY (72168 "Better Late Than Never")........10-15 63
Member: Anthony "Tony" Maresco.
Also see DYNAMICS Featuring Tony Maresco
Also see TONY & TWILIGHTS

ANTIQUES

Singles: 7-inch

HI (2105 "So Many Ways")........20-30 66
LASALLE (69 "Go for Yourself")........300-400

ANTWINETTS
Singles: 7-inch
RCA (7398 "Johnny")....20-30 58

AORTA — LP '69
Singles: 7-inch
ATLANTIC (2545 "Strange")....10-20 68
COLUMBIA (44870 "Strange")....5-10 69
HAPPY TIGER (567 "Sandcastles")....10-15 70
LPs: 10/12-inch
COLUMBIA (9785 "Aorta")....15-25 69
COLUMBIA (38000 series)....5-10
HAPPY TIGER (1010 "Aorta 2")....35-55 70
Members: Bill Herman; Jim Donlinger; Jim Nyeholt; Billy Jones.

APACHES
Singles: 7-inch
HI (2061 "Skippin' ")....8-12 63
MERCURY (72231 "Geronimo")....30-50 64

APHRODITES CHILD
Singles: 7-inch
PHILIPS (40536 "Other People")....10-20 68
PHILIPS (40549 "Rain & Tears")....10-20 68
PHILIPS (40587 "End of the World")....10-20 68
POLYDOR (15005 "Magic Mirror")....5-10 69
VERTIGO (107 "Babylon")....4-6 72
LPs: 10/12-inch
VERTIGO (500 "Apocalypse of John")....15-25 72
Members: Demis Roussos; Lucas Sideras; Vangelis Papatharassiou; Silver Koulouris.

APOLLAS
Singles: 7-inch
LOMA (2019 "Lock Me in Your Heart")....10-15 65
LOMA (2025 "Nobody's Baby")....8-12 66
LOMA (2039 "Pretty Red Balloons")....8-12 66
LOMA (2053 "Sorry Mama")....8-12 66
W.B. (5893 "Mr. Creator")....40-60 67
W.B. (7060 "Jive Cat")....10-15 67
W.B. (7086 "Who Would Want Me Now")....10-15 67
W.B. (7181 "Seven Days")....10-15 68

APOLLO'S APACHES
Singles: 7-inch
ANYBODY'S (6088 "Cry Me a Lie")....50-75

APOLLOS
Singles: 7-inch
GALAXY (707 "I Can't Believe It")....20-30 62
GALAXY (708 "Say a Prayer")....10-15 62
HARVARD (803 "I Love You Darling")....100-200 59

APOLLOS
Singles: 7-inch
GLO (5218 "Walk By Myself")....100-200 61
Session: Rocky Hart.
Also see HART, Rocky

APOLLOS
LPs: 10/12-inch
CALIFORNIA (101 "Battle of the Beat")....20-30 64

APOLLOS
Singles: 7-inch
DELTA (183 "That's the Breaks")....20-30 65
MONTGOMERY....20-30 65

APOSTLE, Johnny, & Willows
Singles: 7-inch
POWER (01 "I Love Ya Honey")....100-150

APOSTLES
Singles: 7-inch
WGW (18702 "I'm a Lucky Guy")....30-50 66

APOSTLES
Singles: 7-inch
WELHAVEN (125935 "Help Me Find a Way")....40-60 67

APPEGGIOS
Singles: 7-inch
ARIES (001 "I'll Be Singing")....200-300 63
Also see ARROWS
Also see CONVINCERS

APPELL, Dave
(Dave Appell Trio; Dave Appell Orchestra; Dave Appell Ensemble)
Singles: 78 rpm
LONDON....5-8 50
PRESIDENT....8-12 55-56
Singles: 7-inch
B.T. PUPPY (554 "Girl of the Skies")....4-6 70
CAMEO (184 "The Young Ones")....8-12 60
CAMEO (207 "Happy Jose")....8-12 61
LONDON....10-15 50
PRESIDENT (1005 "Ring Around My Baby")....15-20 55
PRESIDENT (1006 "Teenage Meeting")....15-20 55
LPs: 10/12-inch
CAMEO (1004 "Alone Together")....35-50 58
Also see APPLEJACKS

APPLEJACKS — P&R '58
Singles: 78 rpm
CAMEO....15-25 57-58
DECCA....5-10 54
PRESIDENT....5-10 55-56
TONE-CRAFT....5-10 55
Singles: 7-inch
CAMEO (100 series)....10-20 57-60
CAMEO (200 & 300 series)....8-12 61-64
DECCA....10-15 54
PRESIDENT....10-20 55-56
TONE-CRAFT....10-20 55
Member: Dave Appell.
Also see APPELL, Dave

APPLETREE THEATRE CO.
Singles: 7-inch
VERVE FORECAST....5-10 67-68
LPs: 10/12-inch
VERVE FORECAST (3042 "Playback")....15-25 68
Members: Chuck Rainey; Herb Lovell; Terence Boylan; John Boylan; Larry Coryell; Rick Nelson.
Also see BOYLAN, Terence
Also see NELSON, Rick

APPOINTMENTS
Singles: 7-inch
DE-LITE (520 "I Saw You There")....200-300 63

APPOLLO BROTHERS
Singles: 7-inch
CLEVELAND (108 "My Beloved One")....40-50 60
LOCKET (108 "My Beloved One")....20-30 60
Member: Ruben Guevara.
Also see GUEVARA, Reuben

APPRECIATIONS
Singles: 7-inch
AWARE (1066 "I Can't Hide It")....400-500 '60s
JUBILEE (5525 "Afraid of Love")....10-15 66
SPORT (108 "There's a Place in My Heart")....50-100 67
SPORT (111 "It's Better to Cry")....100-200 67

APRIL, Johnny
LPs: 10/12-inch
APOLLO (485 "If You Are Not Plucked You Die")....20-30 59

AQUANAUTS
Singles: 7-inch
SAFARI (1005 "Rumble on the Docks")....20-30 63
SAFARI (1008 "High Divin' ")....20-30 63
SANDE (104 "High Divin' ")....10-15 64
Members: Tom Harding; Steve Harding.

AQUA-NITES
Singles: 7-inch
ASTRA (1000 "Carioca")....5-10 65
ASTRA (2001 "Christy")....75-100 65
ASTRA (2003 "Carioca")....40-50 65

AQUATONES — P&R/R&B '58
Singles: 78 rpm
FARGO (1001 "You")....25-50 58
Singles: 7-inch
DEBRA (1000 "Crazy for You")....8-10 2002
(Blue vinyl.)
FARGO (1001 "You")....25-30 58
FARGO (1002 thru 1005)....15-20 58-59
FARGO (1015 thru 1022)....10-15 60-62
FARGO (1111 "My Darling")....20-30 62
LPs: 10/12-inch
FARGO (3001 "The Aquatones Sing for You")....250-350 64
RELIC/FARGO (5033 "The Aquatones Sing for You")....8-10 '80s
Members: Lynn Nixon; Larry Vannata; Gene McCarthy; David Goddard.

ARABIANS
(With Earl Williams & His Globes)
Singles: 7-inch
CARRIE (1516 "My One Possession")....100-200 61
CARRIE (1606 "You Upset Me Baby")....50-75 62
JAM (3738 "Heaven Sent You")....200-300 60
(First issue.)
LANROD (1606 "You Upset Me Baby")....50-75 60
LE-MANS (004 "You Upset Me Baby")....40-50 64
MAGNIFICANT (102 "Crazy Little Fever")....50-75 60
(Note spelling:"Magnificant" rather than Magnificent.)
MAGNIFICENT (102 "Crazy Little Fever")....500-750 60
(Correct label spelling. Black vinyl. Red vinyl copies are bootlegs.)
MAGNIFICENT (114 "Teardrops in the Night")....50-100 61
(Black vinyl.)
MAGNIFICENT (114 "Teardrops in the Night")....100-200 61
(Red vinyl.)
TWIN STAR (1018 "Heaven Sent You")....25-35 60
Also see HAMILTON, Edward

ARABIANS
Singles: 7-inch
STAFF (1808 "Let Me Try")....30-40 '60s

ARBOGAST & ROSS
Singles: 7-inch
LIBERTY (55197 "Chaos")....10-15 59
Picture Sleeves
LIBERTY (55197 "Chaos")....40-50 59
Members: Bob Arbogast; Stan Ross.
Also see ROSS, Stan

ARCADES
Singles: 7-inch
COLLECTABLES....3-5 82
GUYDEN (2015 "Blackmail")....10-15 59
JOHNSON (116 "Fine Little Girl")....10-15 63
JOHNSON (320 "Fine Little Girl")....50-75 59
Also see ARKADES

ARCADES
Singles: 7-inch
TRIAD (502 "There's Got to Be a Loser")....75-125 '60s

ARCADOS
Singles: 7-inch
FAM (502 "When You Walked Out")....3000-4000 63

ARC-ANGELS
Singles: 7-inch
LAN-CET (142 "Goddess")....75-100 61
(Identification number shown since no selection number is used.)

ARCHANGEL
Singles: 7-inch
ANDROMEDA TOUR (145 "Barrier")....25-35 '70s

ARCHER, Frances
LPs: 10/12-inch
DISNEYLAND (1347/1348 "A Child's Garden of Verses")....125-150 55
(10-inch LP. Identification number used.)
DISNEYLAND (3006 "Folk Songs from Far Corners")....15-25 57

ARCHIBALD — R&B '50
(With Dave Bartholomew's Band)
Singles: 78 rpm
COLONY (105 "Little Miss Muffett")....50-75 51
IMPERIAL (5068 "Stack-A-Lee")....75-125 50
IMPERIAL (5082 "Shake, Baby, Shake")....40-60 50
IMPERIAL (5089 "Frantic Chick")....40-60 50
IMPERIAL (5101 "My Gal")....40-60 50
IMPERIAL (5212 "Early Morning Blues")....40-60 52
IMPERIAL (5358 "Stack-A-Lee")....50-75 55
IMPERIAL (5563 "Stack-A-Lee")....25-50 59
Singles: 7-inch
IMPERIAL (5212 "Early Morning Blues")....150-250 52
IMPERIAL (5358 "Stack-A-Lee")....75-125 55
IMPERIAL (5563 "Stack-A-Lee")....25-50 59
Also see BARTHOLOMEW, Dave

ARCHIES — P&R/LP '68
Singles: 7-inch
CALENDAR....5-10 68-69
ERIC....3-5 81
KIRSHNER (Except picture discs)....4-8 69-72
KIRSHNER....6-12 70
(5½" picture discs cut-out from cereal boxes. At least seven different songs are on two different picture styles.)
RCA....4-8 72
Picture Sleeves
CALENDAR (1006 "Bang-Shang-A-Lang")....8-15 68
CALENDAR (1007 "Feelin' So Good")....8-15 68
LPs: 10/12-inch
ACCORD (7149 "Straight A's")....8-10 81
BACK-TRAC....5-10 85
BRYLEN (4415 "The Archies")....10-20 82
CALENDAR (101 "The Archies")....50-100 68
(With "Everything's Archie" promotional pack, including: red balloon; blue button; *Archie's Laugh-In Joke Book*; blue sticker; "Letter of Introduction" poster; Don "This Man" Kirshner poster; CBS-TV flyer; "Dealer Imprint" flyer; black and white photo of John Goldwater and Don Kirshner; black and white photo of Filmations animated TV production team; Archies record and 8-track flyer; Archies bio sheet; Don Kirshner bio; September 1968 Calendar LP releases flyer.
CALENDAR (101 "The Archies")....15-25 68
(Album only.)
CALENDAR (103 "Everything's Archie")....15-25 69
CALENDAR (103 "Sugar Sugar")....10-15 70
51 WEST (16002 "The Archies")....5-10 79
KIRSHNER (105 thru 110)....15-25 69-71
RCA (0221 "The Archies")....15-25 70
(Promotional issue only.)
Members: Ron Dante, Jeff Barry; Toni Wine, plus assorted guests.
Also see ADAMS, Ritchie
Also see FASCINATORS
Also see GREENWICH, Ellie
Also see STEVENS, Ray
Also see TEMPO, Nino
Also see WINE, Toni

ARCHIES / Johnny Thunder
Singles: 7-inch
COLLECTABLES....3-5 '80s
Also see THUNDER, Johnny

ARDELLS
Singles: 7-inch
EPIC (9621 "Lonely Valley")....8-12 63
MARCO (102 "Every Day of the Week")....20-25 61
SELMA (4001 "You Can Fall in Love")....10-20 63
Picture Sleeves
EPIC (9621 "Lonely Valley")....15-25 63
Members: Bill Ande; Tom Condra; Dave Hieronymous; Johnny Burgess; Jim Tolliver; Vic Gray.
Also see AMERICAN BEETLES
Also see R DELLS
Also see RAZOR'S EDGE
Also see TONES

ARDELS
Singles: 7-inch
CAN-CUT (8888 "So Glad You're Mine")....20-30 66
(Canadian.)
CAN-CUT (8963 "Piece of Jewelry")....20-30 66
(Canadian.)

ARDEN, Toni — P&R '49
Singles: 78 rpm
COLUMBIA....3-6 49-54
DECCA....3-6 57-57
RCA....3-6 55-56
Singles: 7-inch
COLUMBIA....8-12 50-54
DECCA....10-20 57-59
MISHAWAKA....4-6
RCA....8-12 55-56
EPs: 7-inch
DECCA....10-20 58
COLUMBIA....10-20 56
LPs: 10/12-inch
DECCA....12-25 57-59
HARMONY (7212 "The Exciting Toni Arden")....10-20 59
TIARA....10-15

ARGENT — P&R/LP '72
Singles: 7-inch
DATE (1659 "Liar")....8-10 69
EPIC....5-8 69-74

LPs: 10/12-inch
EPIC.. 10-20 69-75
U.A. 5-10 76
Members: Rod Argent; Russ Ballard; Robert Henrit; Jim Rodford; John Verity.
Also see KINKS
Also see VERITY, John
Also see WINTER, Johnny / Argent / Chambers Brothers / John Hammond
Also see ZOMBIES

ARGYLES
Singles: 78 rpm
BALLY (1030 "Moonbeam") 10-20 57
Singles: 7-inch
BALLY (1030 "Moonbeam") 15-25 57

ARIEL
Singles: 7-inch
BRENT (7060 "Feels Like I'm Cryin'") 30-50 66
Also see BANSHEES

ARISTOCATS
Singles: 7-inch
SUE (714 "So in Love with You") 20-30 59
LPs: 10/12-inch
HI-FI (610 "Boogie and Blues") 30-40 59

ARISTOCRATS
Singles: 78 rpm
ESSEX (366 "Believe Me")...................... 10-15 54
Singles: 7-inch
ARISTOCRAT.................................. 15-25
ESSEX (366 "Believe Me")...................... 20-30 54
Member: Lee Raymond.

ARISTOCRATS
Singles: 7-inch
ARGO (5275 "Vagabonds")..................... 15-20 57

ARISTOCRATS
Singles: 7-inch
HOME OF THE BLUES (237 "Don't Go") 10-15 62

ARIST-O-KATS
Singles: 7-inch
VITA (168 "Chasin' the Blues") 50-75 57

ARKADES
Singles: 7-inch
JULIA (1100 "Our Love") 20-40 60
Also see ARCADES

ARLEN, Harold, & "Friend"
LPs: 10/12-inch
COLUMBIA (OL-6520 "Harold Sings Arlen") 25-35 66
(Monaural.)
COLUMBIA (OS-2920 "Harold Sings Arlen") 20-40 66
(Stereo.)
COLUMBIA (CSP-2920 "Harold Sings Arlen") 5-10
Members: Harold Arlen; Barbra Streisand.
Also see STREISAND, Barbra

ARLINGTON, Sue, & Arlisles
Singles: 7-inch
AGAR (776 "The Flip")........................ 100-150 '60s

ARLO, Ray
Singles: 7-inch
CASTLE (501 "She's My Steady Date") .. 15-25 58

ARMEN, Kay P&R '43
(With the Balladiers)
Singles: 78 rpm
DECCA...4-8 42-58
FEDERAL..4-8 51
Singles: 7-inch
DECCA...5-12 55-59
EPs: 7-inch
MGM 10-20 54-55
LPs: 10/12-inch
DECCA (5000 series) 20-40 54
(10-inch LP)
DECCA (8000 series) 10-20 59
DECCA (78000 series) 15-25 59
MGM (200 series) 20-40 54
MGM (3000 series) 15-30 55

ARMSTRONG, Dick
Singles: 7-inch
BART (22 "I Wanna Go Steady with You") 75-125

ARMSTRONG, Don
Singles: 7-inch
DON RAY (596 "Tough Luck") 50-75 60

ARMSTRONG, Jimmy
Singles: 7-inch
BROTHERS THREE (1001 "You're Getting Next to Me Baby") 40-60
ENJOY (1016 "Count the Tears") 10-20 64
JET SET (768 "I Won't Believe It Till I See It")..20-30
SHRINE (102 "Mystery") 200-300 65
STOP (105 "Close to You") 15-25 65
ZELL'S...15-25 63
Session: Thomas Bowles.

ARMSTRONG, Lil
Singles: 78 rpm
DECCA (1092 "Brown Gal") 30-50 36
EASTWOOD (101 "East Town Boogie") ..10-20
Singles: 7-inch
TREND (30017 "Let's Have a Ball")...........5-10 59

ARMSTRONG, Louis P&R '26
(With His All Stars)
Singles: 78 rpm
CAPITOL..5-10 56
COLUMBIA (2500 thru 2700 series).........15-25 32
COLUMBIA (40000 series)......................5-10 56-66
DECCA...5-15 35-58
OKEH 20-30 26-31
RCA...5-10 56
VICTOR..10-20 33
VOCALION..10-20 36
Singles: 7-inch
A&M...3-5 88
ABC 4-8 67-73
AMSTERDAM 4-6 71
AUDIO FIDELITY.......................................4-6 71
AVCO EMBASSY 4-6 71
BRUNSWICK..5-10 67-68
BUENA VISTA 5-10 67-68
CAPITOL..10-20 56
COLUMBIA (40000 series)........................5-15 56-66
CONTINENTAL..4-6 71
DECCA (24752 "That Lucky Old Sun").....25-35 49
DECCA (25000 series)...............................5-10 61-64
DECCA (27000 thru 29000 series) 15-25 50-56
DECCA (30000 thru 31000 series) 10-20 56-59
DOT..10-15 59
EPIC 4-8 69
KAPP 4-8 64-69
MCA...4-6 73
MGM..10-15 59-60
MERCURY..5-10 64-66
RCA..15-20 56
U.A. 4-6 68-69
VERVE 10-15 59-60
Picture Sleeves
A&M..3-5 88
BUENA VISTA 5-8 68
CONTINENTAL...4-6 71
KAPP 5-10 64
MGM..10-15 59
MERCURY..5-10 64
Note: Multi-disc, 1950s boxed sets are in the $15 to $25 range. At this time we do not have specific numbers and titles.
EPs: 7-inch
COLUMBIA..5-15 55-59
DECCA..8-15 55-57
RCA...10-20 53-59
LPs: 10/12-inch
ABC 5-10 68-76
ACCORD (7161 "Mr. Music") 5-10 82
AMSTERDAM 5-10 70
AUDIO FIDELITY...15-25 60-64
AUDIO FIDELITY (6241 "Louis Armstrong")..8-12 71
BIOGRAPH 5-10 73
BRUNSWICK (58004 "Jazz Classics") ...50-100 50
(10-inch LP.)
BRUNSWICK (750000 series) 8-15 68-71
BUENA VISTA 8-12 68
BULLDOG (2007 "20 Golden Pieces") 5-10 81
CHIAROSCURO 5-10 77
COLUMBIA (500 thru 900 series) 25-50 54-57
COLUMBIA (2600 series)...............................8-15 67
COLUMBIA (9400 series)...............................8-15 67
COLUMBIA (30000 series)..............................5-12 71-80
COLUMBIA (44000 series)..............................5-10 88-89
CORAL..5-10 73
DECCA (155 "Satchmo")............................50-100 65
(Boxed four-disc set. Includes booklet.)
DECCA (183 "Best of Louis Armstrong") 25-50 65
(Two discs.)
DECCA (195 "Satchmo at Symphony Hall")..30-50 66
(Boxed, two-disc set.)
DECCA (4000 series)................................10-20 61-63
DECCA (5000 series)................................25-50 50-54
(10-inch LPs.)
DECCA (8000 series)................................15-25 55-59
DECCA (9000 series)...................................8-15 67
(Decca LP numbers in this series preceded by a "7" or a "DL-7" are stereo issues.)
EPIC 10-15 69
EVEREST...5-10 71-76
GNP...8-12 77
GUEST STAR 5-10 64
HARMONY...5-10 69
JAZZ HERITAGE...5-10 80
JAZZ PANORAMA (1204 "Fireworks").....15-20
JEMI 5-10
KAPP 10-15 64
MCA..6-10 73-82
MERCURY..10-15 66
METRO 10-15 65
MILESTONE 5-10 74-75
MOSAIC (146 "Complete Decca Studio Recordings")......................................100-120 '90s
(Boxed, eight-disc audiophile set. 7,500 made.)
OLYMPIC 5-10 74
PABLO (2310 941 "Mack the Knife").........5-10 90
PAUSA...5-10 83
PICKWICK (3229 "Mame") 8-12 70
RCA (1300 & 1400 series) 25-50 53-56
RCA (2300 thru 2900 series) 10-20 61-64
(With "LPM" or "LSP" prefix.)
RCA (2600 series) 5-10 77
(With "CPL1" prefix.)
RCA (5500 series) 8-12 77
RCA (6000 series) 8-12 71
SAGA...5-10 72
STORYVILLE..5-10 80
TRIP 5-10 72
U.A. 8-15 68-69
VANGUARD..8-12 76
VERVE 15-20 60-64
VOCALION..5-10 68-69
Session: Cozy Cole; Joe Darensbourg; Jimmy Dorsey Orchestra; Lonnie Johnson; Pee Wee Hunt.
Also see BRUBECK, Dave
Also see CROSBY, Bing, Louis Armstrong, Rosemary Clooney & Hi-Los
Also see FITZGERALD, Ella, & Louis Armstrong
Also see KAYE, Danny, & Louis Armstrong
Also see JENKINS, Gordon
Also see MILLS BROTHERS & LOUIS ARMSTRONG

ARMSTRONG, Louis, & Gary Crosby
(With Jud Conlon's Rhythmaires)
Singles: 78 rpm
DECCA..5-10 55-56
Singles: 7-inch
DECCA (29420 "Ko Ko Mo") 10-15 55
DECCA (29921 "Lazy Bones")....................10-15 56
Also see CONLON, Jud
Also see CROSBY, Gary

ARMSTRONG, Louis, & Duke Ellington
Singles: 7-inch
ROULETTE (4390 "Duke's Place")..............5-10 61
LPs: 10/12-inch
MFSL (155 "Recording for the First Time") 40-60 85
ROULETTE (100 series) 8-12 71
ROULETTE (52103 "Great Reunion of Louis Armstrong & Duke Ellington")...................15-25 63
Also see ELLINGTON, Duke

ARMSTRONG, Louis, & Louis Jordan
Singles: 78 rpm
DECCA (27212 "Life Is So Peculiar").........5-10 50
Singles: 7-inch
DECCA (27212 "Life Is So Peculiar").......15-25 50
Also see JORDAN, Louis

ARMSTRONG, Louis, & Guy Lombardo
Singles: 7-inch
CAPITOL (5716 "Mumbo Jumbo")...............4-8 66
Also see LOMBARDO, Guy

ARMSTRONG, Louis, Red Nichols, & Danny Kaye
Singles: 7-inch
DOT (15991 "Battle Hymn of the Republic")..8-12 59
Picture Sleeves
DOT (15991 "Battle Hymn of the Republic")..15-25 59
Also see KAYE, Danny

ARMSTRONG, Louis, & Oscar Peterson
LPs: 10/12-inch
VERVE (6062 "Louis Armstrong Meets Oscar Peterson")...15-25 59
(Monaural.)
VERVE (8322 "Louis Armstrong Meets Oscar Peterson")...20-30 59
(Stereo.)
Also see PETERSON, Oscar

ARMSTRONG, Louis / Ma Rainey / Trixie Smith
LPs: 10/12-inch
RIVERSIDE (101 "Young Louis Armstrong") 100-200 56
Also see RAINEY, Ma

ARMSTRONG, Louis / Della Reese / Wild Bill Davidson
EPs: 7-inch
AURAVISION/COLUMBIA ("Jazz from Bourbon Street")...5-8
(Promotional bonus cardboard disc, made for Ancient Age bourbon.)
Also see ARMSTRONG, Louis
Also see REESE, Della

ARNELL, Billy
Singles: 7-inch
HOLLY (1001 "Tough Girl") 200-400

ARNELL, Ginny P&R '63
Singles: 7-inch
DECCA (31033 "Brand New")....................8-12 60
DECCA (31104 "We") 8-12 60
DECCA (31190 "Look Who's Talkin' ")........8-12 60
MGM..5-15 63-65
WARWICK (671 "No One Cares")............15-25 61
WARWICK (680 "Married to You") 10-20 62
LPs: 10/12-inch
MGM (4228 "Meet Ginny Arnell")............20-30 64
Also see JAMIE & JANE

ARNOLD, Billy "Boy"
(With Bob Carter's Orchestra)
Singles: 78 rpm
COOL (103 "I Ain't Got No Money") 10-20 53
Singles: 7-inch
COOL (103 "I Ain't Got No Money") 25-50 53
LPs: 10/12-inch
PRESTIGE BLUESVILLE (1072 "See What You've Done")...25-35 63
PRESTIGE (7389 "Blues on the South")..25-35 65
Also see BILLY BOY

ARNOLD, Clyde
Singles: 7-inch
BELLE (2205 "I've Got a Baby") 150-200

ARNOLD, Eddy C&W '45
("The Tennessee Plowboy"; with His Tennessee Plowboys)
Singles: 78 rpm
BLUEBIRD (0520 "Mommie Please Stay Home with Me") 50-75 45
BLUEBIRD (0527 "Each Minute Seems Like a Million Years")..30-60 45
RCA..10-30 46-57
Singles: 7-inch
DIAMOND P (1009 "If the Whole World Stopped Lovin' ")..5-10 73
(Promotional issue only.)
MGM...4-6 73-76
RCA (48-0001 thru 48-0390) 40-60 49-50
(Green vinyl.)
RCA (0001 thru 0476)................................20-30 49-50
(Black vinyl. Black or turquoise labels.)
RCA (0120 thru 0747) 4-6 69-72
(Orange labels.)
RCA (2000 series)...................................... 10-15 62
(Stereo Compact 33.)
RCA (3800 thru 6905) 10-20 50-57
RCA (7040 thru 8296)................................. 8-15 57-64
RCA (8363 thru 9993)................................. 4-8 64-71

RCA (10701 thru 13452) 3-6 76-83
RCA GOLD STANDARD 4-8 59-76
(With "447" prefix.)

Picture Sleeves

RCA 10-20 56-66

EPs: 7-inch

RCA (100 series).... 10-12 61
(With "LPC" prefix. Compact 33 Double.)
RCA (280 "Best Wishes") 10-20
(Promotional issue only.)
RCA (200 thru 900 series).... 10-15 52-56
(With "EPA" prefix.)
RCA (1100 & 1200 series).... 15-20 55-56
(With "EPB" prefix.)
RCA (1400 & 1500 series)....8-12 57
(With "EPA" prefix.)
RCA (3000 series) 20-40 52-54
(With "EPB" prefix.)
RCA (4000 & 5000 series)....8-15 57-59
(With "EPA" prefix.)

LPs: 10/12-inch

CAMDEN (Except "ACL1" series) 8-18 59-72
CAMDEN ("ACL1" series) 5-10 72-76
GREEN VALLEY 8-10 76
K-TEL....8-10 74
MGM....8-12 74-76
RCA ("AHL1," "ANL1," "APL1," & "AYL1" series) 5-10 73-81
RCA ("CPL1" series)....8-12 83
RCA (0051 "Greatest Hits") 8-12
(Mail order offer.)
RCA (115 "Eddy Arnold Sings Them Again") 15-25 61
RCA (168 "Welcome to My World") 10-20 75
RCA (209 "Eddy Arnold") 15-20 66
(Promotional issue only.)
RCA (1100 thru 2200 series).... 20-30 55-60
(Monaural. with "LPM" prefix.)
RCA (2300 thru 2900 series).... 12-20 60-64
(Monaural. with "LPM" prefix.)
RCA (3027 "Country Classics").... 50-75 52
(10-inch LP.)
RCA (3031 "All-Time Hits from the Hills") 50-75 52
(10-inch LP.)
RCA (3117 "All-Time Favorites").... 50-75 53
(10-inch LP.)
RCA (3219 "Chapel on the Hill") 50-75 54
(10-inch LP.)
RCA (3230 "An American Institution") 50-75 54
(10-inch LP.)
RCA (3000 series) 8-12 64-68
(12-inch LPs. with "LPM" prefix.)
RCA (1900 thru 3400 series).... 15-25 60-65
(Stereo. with "LSP" prefix. "LSP" numbers below 1900 were reprocessed stereo issues of '50s LPs. They were issued in the '60s and are in the $10-$15 range.)
RCA (3500 thru 4800 series).... 10-20 66-73
RCA (6000 series) 8-12 70
RCA SPECIAL PRODUCTS (0051 "Eddy Arnold") 8-12 73
RCA SPECIAL PRODUCTS (0934 "Best of Eddy Arnold") 8-12 90
(Two discs.)
SUNRISE....5-10 79
TIME-LIFE 5-10 81
Also see ANN-MARGRET
Also see PRESLEY, Elvis / Hank Snow / Eddy Arnold / Jim Reeves

ARNOLD, Eddy, & Jaye P. Morgan

Singles: 78 rpm

RCA....5-10 56

Singles: 7-inch

RCA 10-15 56

ARNOLD, Eddy, & Jaye P. Morgan / Dorothy Olsen ("The Singing School Teacher")

EPs: 7-inch

RCA (DJ-21 "If 'N").... 10-20 56
Also see ARNOLD, Eddy
Also see MORGAN, Jaye P.

ARNOLD, Jerry
(With the Rhythm Captains)

Singles: 7-inch

CAMEO (120 "Race for Time").... 100-150 57
CHALLENGE (59017 "Little Boy Blue") ... 15-25 58
M.O.C. (659 "Honey Babe") 8-12 65
SECURITY (106 "Race for Time") 250-300 57
(First issue.)
SECURITY (107 "High-Classed Baby")....250-300 58

ARNOLD, Kay

Singles: 7-inch

LIBERTY (55554 "The Gypsy and the Tea Leaves")....5-10 63
SIMS (223 "I'll Walk Alone")....5-10 65
SIMS (242 "My Love Is True")....5-10 65

ARNOLD, Kokomo

Singles: 78 rpm

DECCA....25-50 34-38

ARNOLD, Lloyd

Singles: 7-inch

AVET....10-15 63
K-ARK (1060 "Cold Duck Blues") 10-15 63
KATCHE (1201 "Hang Out") 750-1000
MEMPHIS (109 "Next to Me")....20-30 64
MYERS (113 "Hang Out") 100-150 60
RECORD-O-RAMA....10-20

ARNOLD, Murray

Singles: 78 rpm

CARDINAL (1016 "Boo Boo Boogie")....10-15 54

Singles: 7-inch

CARDINAL (1016 "Boo Boo Boogie")....20-30 54

ARNOLD, Ralph

Singles: 7-inch

ARNOLDS (4297 "Hound Dog Boogie") 75-125

ARNOLD, Vance, & Avengers

Singles: 7-inch

PHILIPS (40255 "I'll Cry Instead")....15-25 64
Member: Joe Cocker.
Also see COCKER, Joe

ARP, James, & Tempest

Singles: 7-inch

VELLEZ (1515 "Let It Rock")....75-125 64
Also see TEMPESTS

ARRIBIANS

Singles: 7-inch

J.O.B. (1116 "To Look at a Star").... 1500-2000 58

ARROGANTS

Singles: 7-inch

BIG A (12184 "Tom Boy") 15-25 60
CANDLELITE (425 "Mirror Mirror")....5-10 64
LUTE (6226 "Mirror Mirror") 50-75 62
STOOP SOUNDS (112 "Hold Me, Thrill Me, Kiss Me")....100-150 97
VANESSA (200 "Take Life Easy") 15-25 62
Member: Ray Morrow.

ARROWS

Singles: 78 rpm

HOLLYWOOD (1065 "Honey Child")....50-100 56
HOLLYWOOD (1071 "One Too Many Times")....75-125 56

Singles: 7-inch

HOLLYWOOD (1065 "Honey Child")....100-200 56
HOLLYWOOD (1071 "One Too Many Times")....150-250 56
Also see LYONS, Joe, & Arrows

ARROWS

Singles: 7-inch

FLASH (132 "Annie Mae")....150-200 58
Also see APPEGGIOS
Also see CONVINCERS

ART OF LOVIN'

LPs: 10/12-inch

MAINSTREAM (6113 "Art of Lovin' ") 30-50 68
Member: Gail Winnick.

ARTHUR

LPs: 10/12-inch

LHI (12000 "Dreams & Images")....30-40 68

ARTHUR, Charline
(With the Knights)

Singles: 78 rpm

BULLET (707 "Is Love a Game") 5-10 50
RCA (Except 6297)....5-10 54-55
RCA (6297 "Burn That Candle") 10-15 55

Singles: 7-inch

COIN (104 "Hello Baby")....25-35
ELDORADO (653 "Golden Record") 5-10 66
RCA (Except 6297)....10-20 54-55
RCA (6297 "Burn That Candle") 20-30 55

ARTHUR, Wayne

Singles: 7-inch

PEAK (1705 "Big Daddy") 50-75

ARTHUR & CORVETS
(Arthur Conley & Corvets)

Singles: 7-inch

NA-R-CO (203 "Darling I Love You")....15-25 64
NA-R-CO (232 "Miracles") 15-25 64
NA-R-CO (234 "Aritha")....15-25 64
NRC (2781 "Miracles") 20-30 59
NRC (2871 "Aritha") 50-75 59
Also see CONLEY, Arthur
Also see CORVETTS

ARTIE & MUSTANGS

Singles: 7-inch

ARC (1088 "Skip, Hop & Wobble")....50-75

ARTIS, Ray

Singles: 7-inch

A (111 "Art of Love")....75-125 61
BUNDY (222 "Dear Liza") 15-25 62

ARTISTICS

Singles: 7-inch

S&G (302 "Life Begins at Sixteen") 200-300 62

ARTISTICS *R&B '65*

Singles: 7-inch

BRUNSWICK....5-10 66-73
OKEH 10-15 63-66

LPs: 10/12-inch

BRUNSWICK....10-20 67-73
OKEH 15-25 67
Members: Marvin Smith; Bernard Reed; Larry Johnson; Tommy Green; Aaron Floyd; Morris Williams.
Also see DUKAYS
Also see SMITH, Marvin

ARTISTICS

Singles: 7-inch

CHA CHA (731 "Just Enough of You")....10-20 64
Also see EASTER, Jim

ARZACHEL

LPs: 10/12-inch

ROULETTE (42036 "Arzachel")....40-50 69
Members: Steve Hillage; Dave Stewart; Mort Campbell; Clive Brooks.

ASCENDORS

Singles: 7-inch

LEE (101 "I Won't Be Home") 20-30 65

ASCOTS

Singles: 7-inch

ARROW (736 "Is It Really You")....10-20 58

ASCOTS

Singles: 7-inch

J&S (1628 "What Love Can Do")....40-50 58

ASCOTS

Singles: 7-inch

DUAL-TONE (1119 "Acapulco Run") 15-25 63
Member: Derry Weaver.
Also see GAMBLERS

ASCOTS

Singles: 7-inch

ACE (650 "Perfect Love")....10-20 62
BETHLEHEM (3046 "She Did") 5-10 62
KING (5679 "Darling I'll See You Tonight")....20-30 62

ASCOTS

Singles: 7-inch

BLUE FIN (101 "I Won't Cry") ....25-35 '60s
LIVERPOOL....15-25 '60s
SUPER....15-30 66-67

ASCOTS

Singles: 7-inch

TEEK ("A Love Like Ours")....50-100
(No selection number used.)

ASHBY, Irving
(Irvin Ashby)

Singles: 7-inch

IMPERIAL (5426 "Loco-Motion") 10-20 57
IMPERIAL (5485 "Big Guitar")....10-20 58
KNIGHT (2004 "Feelin' Blue")....15-25 58

LPs: 10/12-inch

ACCENT 8-10 77
Also see FREEMAN, Ernie

ASHCROFT, Johnny

Singles: 7-inch

CAPITOL (4387 "Little Boy Lost")....25-35 60
FELSTED (8543 "Bouquet for the Bride")....10-20 59

ASHES

Singles: 7-inch

VAULT (924 "Is There Anything I Can Do")....5-10 66
VAULT (936 "Dark on You Now")....5-10 67
VAULT (973 "Homeward Bound") 5-10 71

LPs: 10/12-inch

VAULT (125 "Ashes")....35-55 68
Members: Pat Taylor; John Merrill; Jim Voight; Alan Brackett.
Also see PEANUT BUTTER CONSPIRACY
Also see PEANUT BUTTER CONSPIRACY / Ashes / Chambers Brothers

ASHFORD & SIMPSON *R&B/LP '73*

Singles: 12-inch

CAPITOL....4-6 82-86
W.B. 4-6 79

Singles: 7-inch

CAPITOL....3-5 82-89
EMI AMERICA....3-5 84-85
W.B. 3-6 73-81

Picture Sleeves

CAPITOL....3-5 80-86
W.B. ....4-6 '70s

LPs: 10/12-inch

CAPITOL....5-10 82-89
W.B. (Except HS series) 5-10 73-81
W.B. (HS-3357 "Stay Free") 15-25 79
(Half-speed mastered.)
Members: Nick Ashford; Valerie Simpson.
Also see JONES, Quincy
Also see SIMPSON, Valerie
Also see VALERIE & NICK

ASHLEY, Bob
(With the Reflections)

Singles: 7-inch

REO (8735 "Made in England")....15-25 '60s
(Canadian.)
Also see ALLEN, Chad

ASHLEY, Del
(David Gates)

Singles: 7-inch

MANCHESTER (101 "There's a Heaven")....30-40 '60s
PLANETARY (103 "Little Miss Stuck-Up") 15-25 65
Also see GATES, David

ASHLEY, John

Singles: 7-inch

CAPEHART (5006 "Little Lou")....50-75 61
DOT (15775 "Born to Rock")....50-100 58
DOT (15878 "Let the Good Times Roll")....15-25 58
DOT (15942 "Hangman")....15-25 59
INTRO (6097 "Let Yourself Go, Go, Go") 25-50
SILVER (1002 "Seriously in Love") 20-30 59
SILVER (1005 "One Love")....20-30 60

Picture Sleeves

INTRO (6097 "Let Yourself Go, Go, Go")....50-75

ASHLEY, Robert

Singles: 7-inch

MERCURY (71365 "Comic Strip Rock and Roll")....30-50 58

ASHLEY, Tony

Singles: 7-inch

DECCA (32342 "We Must Have Love") ... 10-20 69
DECCA (32520 "I'll Go Crazy")....30-60 69

ASIATICS

Singles: 7-inch

CANTON (1784 "Flu Bug") 15-25 57

ASPIRATIONS

Singles: 7-inch

PEACHES (6721 "You Left Me") 100-200
(Also issued as by the Admirations.)
Also see ADMIRATIONS

ASSOCIATION P&R/LP '66

Singles: 7-inch

COLUMBIA 4-6 72
ELEKTRA 3-5 81
JUBILEE (5505 "Babe, I'm Gonna Leave You") 5-10 65
MUMS (6016 "Rainbows Bent") 4-6 73
RCA (10217 "One Sunday Morning") 4-6 75
VALIANT 5-10 65-67
W.B. 4-6 67-71

Picture Sleeves

VALIANT 5-10 66

LPs: 10/12-inch

COLUMBIA 8-12 72
VALIANT (5002 "And Then, Along Comes the Association") 10-20 66
(Monaural.)
VALIANT (25002 "And Then, Along Comes the Association") 15-25 66
(Stereo.)
W.B. 10-15 67-71
Members: Gary Alexander; Ted Bluechel Jr; Brian Cole; Russ Giguere; Terry Kirkman; Cliff Nivison; Larry Ramos; Richard Thompson; Jim Yester.
Also see MAMAS & PAPAS / Association / Fifth Dimension
Also see MIKE & DEAN
Also see NEW CHRISTY MINSTRELS
Also see PEDESTRIANS / Association / Five Americans / Soulblenders

ASSOCIATION / Bobby Vee / Mike Love / Mary MacGregor

LPs: 10/12-inch

HITBOUND (1005 "New Memories") 10-15 83
Also see VEE, Bobby

ASSORTMENT

Singles: 7-inch

SOUNDSPOT (2224 "Bless Our Hippie Home") ...... 30-40 '60s

ASTAIRE, Fred P&R '29

Singles: 78 rpm

BRUNSWICK 10-20 35-38
COLUMBIA 15-25 29-34
DECCA 5-10 43
MGM 4-8 51-53
MERCURY 3-6 53
RCA 3-5 55
VERVE 3-5 56
VICTOR 15-20 31-33

Singles: 7-inch

ÄVA (125 "It Happens Every Spring") 4-8 63
CHOREO (104 "The Notorious Landlady") 4-8 62
CLEF 5-10 57
KAPP (311 "I'll Walk Alone") 5-10 59
MGM 5-10 51-52
MERCURY 5-10 53
RCA 5-10 55
VERVE 5-10 56

EPs: 7-inch

CLEF 10-15 57
EPIC 10-15 57
MGM 10-20 51-53
VERVE (5058 "Spectacular Fred Astaire") 10-15 59

LPs: 10/12-inch

CAMDEN 10-20 59-60
CHOREO 10-20 61
CLEF 15-30 57
EPIC (3000 series) 15-30 57
EPIC (13000 & 15000 series) 8-15 66
KAPP (1165 "Now Fred Astaire") 15-25 59
(Monaural.)
KAPP (3049 "Now Fred Astaire") 25-35 59
(Stereo.)
LION (70121 "Fred Astaire") 10-20 59
MCA (1552 "Sings") 5-10 83
MGM (100 series) 25-50 52
MGM (3000 series) 15-30 52-55
MONMOUTH EVERGREEN 10-20 71
VERVE 15-30 56-59
VOCALION 8-15 64
"X" 20-25 57
Also see CROSBY, Bing, & Fred Astaire

ASTAIRE, Fred, & Jane Powell P&R '51

Singles: 78 rpm

MGM 4-8 51

Singles: 7-inch

MGM 10-15 51

ASTAIRE, Fred, & Red Skelton / Helen Kane

(With Andre Previn)

EPs: 7-inch

MGM 10-15 50
(Not issued with cover, actually a three-track single.)
Also see ASTAIRE, Fred
Also see PREVIN, Andre

ASTEROIDS

Singles: 7-inch

RODEO (182 "Shh, Blast Off") 100-200

ASTORS P&R/R&B '65

Singles: 7-inch

STAX (139 "What Can It Be") 150-200 63
STAX (170 "Candy") 15-25 65
STAX (179 "Mystery Woman") 10-15 65
STAX (232 "Daddy Didn't Tell You") 8-12 67
Members: Curtis Johnson; Richard Harris; Eddie Stanbeck; Sam Byrnes.
Also see CHIPS

ASTRONAUTS

Singles: 7-inch

TRIAL (3521 "Farewell") 150-200 60

ASTRONAUTS P&R/LP '63

Singles: 7-inch

PALLADIUM (610 "Come Along Baby") 75-125 61
RCA 10-20 63-65

Picture Sleeves

RCA 20-30 63

EPs: 7-inch

RCA 25-40 63
RCA WURLITZER DISCOTHEQUE (100 "Discotheque Music") 30-40 64
(Promotional issue only.)

LPs: 10/12-inch

RCA 35-45 63-67
Members: Rich Fifield; Jon "Stormy" Patterson; Robert Demmon; Dennis Lindsey; James Gallagher.

ASTRONAUTS / Liverpool Five

LPs: 10/12-inch

RCA (251 "Stereo Festival") 35-45 67
(The one rock LP from a boxed set of 10. Others in this promotional set are by: Al Hirt/John Gary; Henry Mancini/Ann-Margret; Eddy Arnold/Chet Atkins; Harry Belafonte/Peter Nero; Leontyne Price/Boston Pops; Melachrino Strings/Esquivel; Neal Hefti/Derek & Ray; Morton Gould/Mario Lanza; Living Brass/Claus Ogerman.)
RCA (251 "Stereo Festival") 50-100 67
(Boxed set of all 10 LPs. Box also bears the number TVA-85.
Also see ASTRONAUTS
Also see LIVERPOOL FIVE

ASTROS

Singles: 7-inch

ANDERSON (125 "Music Maker") ...... 40-50 '60s

ATCHER, Bob C&W '46

(With the Countrymen; with Bonnie Blue Eyes)

Singles: 78 rpm

COLUMBIA 5-10 46-49
TIFFANY 5-10
VOCALION 8-12

EPs: 7-inch

COLUMBIA ...... 10-20 '50s

LPs: 10/12-inch

COLUMBIA (9006 "Early American Folk Songs") ...... 30-50 '50s
(10-inch LP.)
COLUMBIA (9013 "Songs of the Saddle") ...... 30-50 '50s
(10-inch LP.)
COLUMBIA (2232 "Dean of Cowboy Singers") 20-30 64
(Monaural.)
COLUMBIA (9032 "Dean of Cowboy Singers") 15-25 64
(Stereo.)
HARMONY (7313 "Early American Folk Songs") 15-20 64

ATELLO, Don

(Bernie Schwartz)

Singles: 7-inch

TIDE (1099 "She'll Break Your Heart") 10-20 63
TIDE (2002 "Questions I Can't Answer") 20-30 64
Also see COMFORTABLE CHAIR
Also see PRIDE, Adrian
Also see WHEEL

ATHA, Chuck

Singles: 7-inch

C-FLAT 8-12
FOX (006 "Just Me & My Baby") 50-75 57
STARS (506 "Ooh-Eee") 50-100
VOTE (001 "Wallace for '72"/"I'm a Sick American") ...... 5-10 '70s
(B-side by Frank Morris.)

ATKINS, Ben

(With the Nomads; Benny Atkins)

Singles: 7-inch

ENTERPRISE 4-6 72
JOSIE 10-20 69-70
MERCURY (71686 "I'm Following You") 15-25 60
STATUE (7001 "It Would Take a Miracle") 75-125 67
YOUNGSTOWN (609 "Come On Over") 75-125 66

ATKINS, Chet C&W '55

(With the Anita Kerr Singers)

Singles: 78 rpm

BLUEBIRD (0072 "I Know When I'm Blue") 10-20 50
BULLET (617 "Guitar Blues") 50-100 46
RCA 5-15 47-57

Singles: 7-inch

RCA (48-0089 "Telling My Trouble to My Old Guitar") 20-40 49
(Green vinyl.)
RCA (0100 thru 0400 series) 12-25 50-51
(Black or turquoise labels.)
RCA (0100 thru 0700 series) 4-6 71-74
(Orange labels.)
RCA (4000 & 5000 series) 10-20 51-55
RCA (6000 & 7000 series) 5-15 55-62
RCA (8000 & 9000 series) 4-8 62-71
RCA (10000 thru 13000 series) 3-6 75-83

Picture Sleeves

RCA 5-10 61-67

EPs: 7-inch

RCA (100 series) 8-12 61
(With "LPC" prefix. Compact 33 Double.)
RCA (500 thru 900 series) 8-15 55-56
(With "EPA" prefix.)
RCA (1100 & 1200 series) 10-20 55-56
(With "EPB" prefix.)
RCA (1300 thru 1500 series) 8-15 56-57
(With "EPA" prefix.)
RCA (3000 series) 15-25 52-54
(With "EPB" prefix.)
RCA (4000 & 5000 series) 5-10 58-60
SESAC (13 "Mr. Atkins, If You Please") 20-30 59

LPs: 10/12-inch

CAMDEN 8-12 61-72
CANDLELITE 10-15
COLUMBIA 5-10 83-85
DOLTON 15-20 67
PICKWICK/CAMDEN 8-10 75
RCA (AHL1, ANL1, APL1, & AYL1 series) 5-10 73-83
RCA (CPL1 series) 8-12 77
RCA (1000 series) 25-35 54
(With "LPM" prefix.)
RCA (1100 thru 2200 series, except 1236) 15-25 55-60
(With "LPM" prefix.)
RCA (1236 "Stringin' Along with Chet Atkins") 30-40 55
(With "LPM" prefix.)
RCA (2300 thru 2900 series) 10-15 60-64
(With "LPM" prefix.)
RCA (3079 "Gallopin' Guitar") 150-200 53
(10-inch LP.)
RCA (3163 "Stringing Along") 75-125 53
(10-inch LP.)
RCA (3000 series) 8-12 64-68
(12-inch LPs. With "LPM" prefix.)
RCA (2000 & 3000 series) 10-15 66-69
(With "LSC" prefix.)
RCA (1900 thru 3500 series) 10-20 60-66
(Stereo. With "LSP" prefix. LSP numbers below 1900 were reprocessed stereo issues of '50s LPs. They were issued in the '60s are in the $10 to $15 range.)
RCA (3500 thru 4800 series) 8-15 68-73
RCA (6000 series) 8-12 70-72
SESAC ("Chet Atkins") 75-100 59
(Exact title and selection number not known.)
TIME-LIFE 5-10 81
Session: Floyd Cramer; Bob Moore; Jack Shook; Murrey Harman; Anita Kerr Singers.
Also see ANN-MARGRET
Also see CHARLES, Ray, George Jones, & Chet Atkins
Also see COUNTRY HAMS
Also see CRAMER, Floyd
Also see EVERLY BROTHERS
Also see GIBSON, Don
Also see KERR, Anita
Also see MOORE, Bob
Also see NASHVILLE ALL-STARS
Also see NELSON, Willie
Also see PRESLEY, Elvis
Also see REED, Jerry, & Chet Atkins
Also see RHYTHM ROCKERS
Also see SNOW, Hank, & Chet Atkins

ATKINS, Chet, & Boston Pops

LPs: 10/12-inch

RCA 10-20 66-69
Also see BOSTON POPS ORCHESTRA

ATKINS, Chet, Floyd Cramer & Danny Davis

(Chet, Floyd & Danny)

Singles: 7-inch

RCA 4-6 77

LPs: 10/12-inch

RCA 5-10 77
Also see DAVIS, Danny

ATKINS, Chet, Floyd Cramer & Boots Randolph

LPs: 10/12-inch

PICKWICK 5-10 71
Also see CRAMER, Floyd
Also see RANDOLPH, Boots

ATKINS, Chet, & Mark Knopfler

LPs: 10/12-inch

COLUMBIA 5-8 90

ATKINS, Chet, & Les Paul

Singles: 7-inch

RCA 4-6 78

LPs: 10/12-inch

RCA 5-10 76-80
Also see PAUL, Les

ATKINS, Chet, Faron Young, & Anita Kerr Singers

EPs: 7-inch

SESAC (48 "No Greater Love") 25-50 59
Also see KERR, Anita
Also see YOUNG, Faron

ATKINS, Chet, & Doc Watson

LPs: 10/12-inch

RCA 5-10 80
Also see WATSON, Doc
Also see ATKINS, Chet

ATKINS, Dave

(With His Offbeats)

Singles: 7-inch

BACK BEAT (511 "Shake-Kum-Down") 40-60 58
VIV 10-15 63

ATKINS, Larry

Singles: 7-inch

HIGHLAND (1193 "Ain't That Love Enough") ...... 25-35 '60s
ROMARK 5-10 68

ATLANTA RHYTHM SECTION P&R/LP '74/C&W '79

Singles: 7-inch

COLUMBIA 3-5 81
DECCA 4-6 72
MCA 4-6 73-77
POLYDOR 3-6 74-80

LPs: 10/12-inch

COLUMBIA 5-10 81
DECCA (75265 "Atlanta Rhythm Section") 15-20 72
DECCA (75390 "Back Up Against the Wall") 15-20 72
MCA (4114 "Atlanta Rhythm Section") 8-12 77
(Two discs. Repackage of Decca LPs.)
MFSL (038 "Champagne Jam") 40-60 79
POLYDOR 5-10 74-80

Members: Ronnie Hammond; Rodney Justo; Robert Nix; Barry Bailey; James Cobb; Dean Daughtry; Paul Goddard.
Also see CANDYMEN
Also see CLASSICS IV
Also see MANILOW, Barry / Atlanta Rhythm Section

ATLANTICS

Singles: 7-inch

COLUMBIA (42877 "Bombora")....................5-10 63
COLUMBIA (43023 "Bow Man")....................5-10 64
LINDA (103 "Boo Hoo Hoo")....................10-20 61
(Reissued as by the Vikings.)
LINDA (107 "Remember the Night")....100-150 63
RAMPART (643 "Beaver Shot")....................5-10 65
RAMPART (647 "Sloop Dance")....................5-10 65

Picture Sleeves

RAMPART....................10-20 65
Also see VIKINGS
Also see WHITE, Barry, & Atlantics

ATLANTICS

Singles: 7-inch

AMON (90590 "Heartburn")....................40-60 64

ATLANTICS

Singles: 7-inch

CHERRY HILL (2771 "Duke of Earl")......15-20

ATTILA

LPs: 10/12-inch

BACK-TRAC....................5-10 85
D&J....................5-8 80
EPIC (30030 "Attila")....................40-50 70
Members: Billy Joel; Jon Small.
Also see JOEL, Billy

ATTILA & HUNS

Singles: 7-inch

MAGIC TOUCH....................15-25 67-69
SARA (6511 "Cheryl")....................15-25 65
Members: Mike Peace (Pease); Doug Deuel; Barry Berdal; Walter Staniec; Dennis Lewan; Barb Spence; Benny Wisniewski; Rich Legault.
Also see FILET OF SOUL
Also see HUNS OF TIME

ATWOOD, Eddie, & His Goodies

Singles: 7-inch

SURF (5028 "Hot Saki")....................15-25 58
Session: Danny Flores.
Also see FLORES, Danny

AU GO-GO SINGERS

Singles: 7-inch

ROULETTE (4577 "Pink Polemoniums"). 10-15 64

LPs: 10/12-inch

ROULETTE (R-25280 "They Call Us Au Go-Go Singers")....................30-40 64
(Monaural.)
ROULETTE (SR-25280 "They Call Us Au Go-Go Singers")....................40-50 64
(Stereo.)
Members: Richie Furay; Steven (Stephen) Stills.
Also see STILLS, Stephen

AUDREY *P&R '56*

Singles: 78 rpm

PLUS (104 "Dear Elvis")....................25-50 56

Singles: 7-inch

PLUS (104 "Dear Elvis")....................25-50 56
(Break-in novelty with excerpts of several Elvis Sun tracks.)
Also see PRESLEY, Elvis

AUGUST, Art

Singles: 7-inch

BRAD....................8-12 '50s
SOUND-O-RAMA (112 "Hold Out Your Hand")....................20-30 62
TRANS CONTINENTAL (1014 "Hold Out Your Hand")....................40-50 60

AUGUST, Joseph
("Mr. Google Eyes"; with René Hall's Orchestra; with Billy Ford & Orchestra; with Johnny Otis Band)

Singles: 78 rpm

COLEMAN (123 "Rough and Rocky Road")....................25-50 49
COLUMBIA (30179 "For You My Love").. 20-30 50
DOMINO (350 "Cryin' for You")....................50-75 50
DOMINO (352 "Japoline")....................50-75 50
DOMINO (360 "Rock My Soul")....................50-75 50
DUKE....................20-40 54-56
FLIP (1001 "Strange Things Happening in the Dark")....................75-125 54
LEE (209 "My Old Love")....................50-75 51
OKEH....................25-50 51

Singles: 7-inch

DUKE (117 "O What a Fool")....................40-60 54
DUKE (156 "Lead Us On")....................40-60 56
FLIP (1001 "Strange Things Happen in the Dark")....................100-200 54
INSTANT (3239 "Everything Happens At Night")....................20-30 61
OKEH (1620 "No Wine, No Women").....50-100 51
Also see FORD, Billy
Also see HALL, René
Also see OTIS, Johnny

AUGUST & DENEEN

Singles: 7-inch

ABC (11082 "We Go Together")....................40-50 68

AUM

Singles: 7-inch

FILLMORE....................5-10 69-70

LPs: 10/12-inch

FILLMORE (30002 "Resurrection")....................20-30 69
SAN FRANCISCO....................10-15 69
SIRE (97007 "Bluesvibes")....................30-40 69
Members: Wayne Ceballos; Boots Houston; Reese Marin; Larry Martin; Sean Silverman; Steve Bowman.

AUSTIN, Augie
(With the Chromatics; Little Augie Austin; with Eddie Singleton & Orchestra)

Singles: 7-inch

PONTIAC (101 "My Love for You")..........15-25 60
Also see SINGLETON, Eddie, & Chromatics / Augie Austin & Chromatics

AUSTIN, Billy, & Hearts
(With Charlie Ferguson His Tenor and Orchestra)

Singles: 78 rpm

APOLLO (444 "Angel Baby")....................150-250 52

Singles: 7-inch

APOLLO (444 "Angel Baby")....................500-750 52
(Black vinyl.)
APOLLO (444 "Angel Baby")...........4000-5000 52
(Red vinyl.)

AUSTIN, Charlotte
(With Bill Cunningham; with Daniel Darby Orchestra)

Singles: 7-inch

MATTEL (12564-12566 "Barbie Sings")...25-35 61
(Three discs.)

LPs: 10/12-inch

MATTEL ("Barbie Sings")....................100-150 61
(Demonstration record sent to Mattel dealers as a sample of the *Barbie Sings* release. Price ranges are based on value to Barbie collectors more than record collectors.)

AUSTIN, Patti *R&B '69*

Singles: 12-inch

QWEST....................4-6 84-86

Singles: 7-inch

ABC....................5-10 68
CTI....................3-6 76-80
COLUMBIA....................4-8 71-73
CORAL (62455 "He's Good Enough for Me")....................10-20 65
CORAL (62471 "I Wanna Be Loved")......10-20 65
CORAL (62478 "Someone's Gonna Cry")....................50-100 66
CORAL (62491 thru 62541)....................10-20 66-67
CORAL (62548 "All My Love")....................75-125 68
QWEST....................3-5 81-88
U.A.....................4-6 69-70

LPs: 10/12-inch

CTI....................5-10 77-80
GRP....................5-8 90
QWEST....................5-10 81-88
Also see JONES, Quincy

AUSTIN, Patti, & Jerry Butler

Singles: 7-inch

CTI (59 "In My Life")....................3-5 83
Also see BUTLER, Jerry

AUSTIN, Patti, & James Ingram *P&R '82*

Singles: 7-inch

QWEST....................3-5 82-84
Also see AUSTIN, Patti
Also see INGRAM, James

AUTRY, Gene *P&R '33/C&W '44*
(With the Cass County Boys & the Pinafores; Gene Autry & Jimmy Long)

Singles: 78 rpm

BRUNSWICK (12936 "There's An Empty Cot in the Bunkhouse Tonight")....................100-200 '30s
(Flip side, #12899, is credited to "Gene Autry & Jimmy Long.")
CHAMPION (16096 "Cowboy Yodel")..100-150 '30s
CHAMPION (16119 "Texas Blues")......100-150 '30s
CHAMPION (16141 "In the Jailhouse Now, No. 2")....................100-150 '30s
CHAMPION (16210 "Mean Mama Blues")....................100-150 '30s
CHAMPION (16228 "Pistol Packin' Papa")....................100-150 '30s
CHAMPION (16245 "Blue Days")........100-150 '30s
CHAMPION (16275 "T.B. Blues")........100-150 '30s
CLARION (5025 "Hobo Yodel")..........75-125 '30s
CLARION (5026 "No One to Call Me Darling")....................75-125 '30s
CLARION (5058 "I'll Be Thinking of You Little Girl")....................75-125 '30s
CLARION (5075 "Cowboy Yodel")..........75-125 '30s
CLARION (5154 "Dust Pan Blues")........75-125 '30s
CLARION (5155 "Waiting for a Train")...75-125 '30s
CLARION (5239 "Left My Gal in the Mountains")....................75-125 '30s
CLARION (5240 "Daddy and Home").....75-125 '30s
CLARION (5243 "Lullaby Yodel")..........75-125 '30s
CLARION (5272 "True Blue Bill")..........75-125 '30s
CLARION (5308 "A Gangster's Warning")....................75-125 '30s
CONQUEROR....................30-90 '30s
COLUMBIA....................5-15 45-56
DECCA (5426 "Blue Days")....................50-100 '30s
DECCA (5464 "In the Shadow of the Pine")....................50-100 '30s
DECCA (5488 "Bear Cat Papa Blues")..50-100 '30s
DECCA (5501 "My Carolina Sunshine Girl")....................50-100 '30s
DECCA (5426 "Blue Days")....................50-100 '30s
DECCA (5517 "T.B. Blues")....................50-100 '30s
DECCA (5527 "Yodeling Hobo")............50-100 '30s
DECCA (5544 "Pistol Packin' Mama")....50-100 '30s
DIVA (6030 "Hobo Yodel")....................50-100 '30s
DIVA (6031 "Waiting for a Train")........50-100 '30s
DIVA (6032 "Blue Yodel No. 4")............50-100 '30s
DIVA (6033 "Lullaby Yodel")....................50-100 '30s
DIVA (6035 "No One to Call Me Darling")....................50-100 '30s
DIVA (6037 "Frankie & Johnny")............50-100 '30s
DIVA (6049 "My Rough and Rowdy Ways")....................50-100 '30s
DIVA (6057 "Cowboy Yodel")....................50-100 '30s
HARMONY (1046 "Blue Yodel No. 5").....25-50 49
MONTGOMERY WARD (4242 "Bear Cat Papa Blues")....................100-200 '30s
MONTGOMERY WARD (4243 "My Carolina Sunshine Girl")....................100-200 '30s
MONTGOMERY WARD (4243 "Don't Do Me That Way")....................100-200 '30s
MONTGOMERY WARD (4244 "High-Steppin' Mama Blues")....................100-200 '30s
MONTGOMERY WARD (4245 "Rheumatism Blues")....................100-200 '30s
MONTGOMERY WARD (4275 "Wildcat Mama")....................150-250 '30s
MONTGOMERY WARD (4326 "That Ramshackle Shack")....................100-200 '30s
MONTGOMERY WARD (4333 "I'm Always Dreaming of You")....................100-200 '30s
MONTGOMERY WARD (4767 "Old Woman and the Cow")....................200-300 '30s
MONTGOMERY WARD (4767 "There's a Gal in the Mountains")....................100-200 '30s
MONTGOMERY WARD (4768 "She Wouldn't Do It")....................100-200 '30s
MONTGOMERY WARD (4768 "She's a Low Down Mama")....................150-250 '30s
MONTGOMERY WARD (4931 "Pictures of My Mother")....................100-200 '30s
MONTGOMERY WARD (4932 "Yodeling Hobo")....................100-200 '30s
MONTGOMERY WARD (4933 "In the Shadow of the Pine")....................100-200 '30s
MONTGOMERY WARD (4975 "In the Jailhouse Now, No. 2")....................100-200 '30s
MONTGOMERY WARD (4975 "T.B. Blues")....................150-250 '30s
MONTGOMERY WARD (4976 "True Blue Bill")....................100-200 '30s
MONTGOMERY WARD (4977 "Jailhouse Blues")....................100-200 '30s
MONTGOMERY WARD (4977 "Pistol Packin' Mama")....................100-200 '30s
MONTGOMERY WARD (4978 "Whisper Your Mother's Name")....................150-250 '30s
MONTGOMERY WARD (4978 "My Carolina Sunshine Girl")....................100-200 '30s
MONTGOMERY WARD (8016 "Money Ain't No Use Anyway")....................100-200 '30s
MONTGOMERY WARD (8017 "Cowboy Yodel")....................100-200 '30s
MONTGOMERY WARD (8017 "Yodeling Hobo")....................100-200 '30s
MONTGOMERY WARD (8034 "Train Whistle Blues")....................150-250 '30s
MONTGOMERY WARD (8034 "Texas Blues")....................150-250 '30s
Note: Some Montgomery Ward numbers appear to have been used twice, with different titles, and often slightly different pricing. Since this information came from the same source, we are assuming it to be accurate until proven otherwise.)
OKEH....................10-20 40-45
ORIOLE (8109 "Silver Haired Daddy of Mine")....................300-500 32
(Flip side, "Mississippi Valley Blues," is credited to "Gene Autry & Jimmy Long.")
PERFECT....................30-60
QRS (1044 "I'll Be Thinking of You, Little Gal"/"Living in the Mountains")....................3000-5000 29
ROMEO (5109 "Silver Haired Daddy of Mine")....................300-500 32
ROMEO (5110 "Jailhouse Blues")........300-500 32
SUPERTONE (9705 "I'll Be Thinking of You, Little Gal"/"Whisper Your Mother's Name")....................3000-5000 29
VELVET TONE (2338 "True Blue Bill")..50-100 '30s
VELVET TONE (2374 "A Gangster's Warning")....................50-100 '30s
VELVET TONE (7056 "Hobo Yodel").....50-100 '30s
VELVET TONE (7057 "Waiting for a Train")....................50-100 '30s
VELVET TONE (7058 "Blue Yodel No. 4")....................50-100 '30s
VELVET TONE (7059 "Lullaby Yodel")..50-100 '30s
VELVET TONE (7061 "No One to Call Me Darling")....................50-100 '30s
VELVET TONE (7063 "Frankie and Johnny")....................50-100 '30s
VELVET TONE (7075 "My Rough and Rowdy Ways")....................50-100 '30s
VELVET TONE (7083 "Cowboy Yodel")....................50-100 '30s
VOCALION....................25-50 35-40

Singles: 7-inch

COLUMBIA (56 "Rudolph, the Red-Nosed Reindeer")....................10-15 50
COLUMBIA (68 "Peter Cottontail")..........10-15 50
COLUMBIA (06189 "Statue in the Bay")......3-5 86
COLUMBIA (20700 thru 21500 series)......5-10 50-56
COLUMBIA (38700 thru 40500 series)......5-10 50-55
COLUMBIA (44000 series)....................4-6 68
MISTLETOE....................4-6 74
REPUBLIC....................4-8 59-76

Picture Sleeves

COLUMBIA (56 "Rudolph, the Red-Nosed Reindeer")....................15-25 50
COLUMBIA (68 "Peter Cottontail")..........15-25 50
COLUMBIA (121 "Three Little Dwarfs")...15-25 51
(May have been a 78 rpm sleeve only.)
COLUMBIA HALL OF FAME (33165 "Rudolph the Red-Nosed Reindeer")....................4-6 69
REPUBLIC (2002 "Santa's Comin' in a Whirlybird")....................5-10 59

EPs: 7-inch

COLUMBIA....................40-50 51-56

LPs: 10/12-inch

BIRCHMOUNT....................8-12
BULLDOG....................5-10
CHALLENGE....................25-30 58
COLUMBIA (55 thru 154)....................80-100 51-55
(10-inch LPs.)
COLUMBIA (600 series)....................80-100 55
COLUMBIA (1000 series)....................8-10 70-82
COLUMBIA (1500 series)....................10-20 61
COLUMBIA (2547 "Merry Christmas").....40-60 56
(10-inch LP.)

COLUMBIA (2568 "Easter Favorites")..... 40-60 57
(10-inch LP.)
COLUMBIA (6020 "Gene Autry Western Classics")..... 40-60 49
(10-inch LP.)
COLUMBIA (6137 "Merry Christmas")..... 40-60 50
(10-inch LP.)
COLUMBIA (8000 series)..... 80-100
COLUMBIA (9001 "Western Classics, Vol. 1")..... 40-60 51
(10-inch LP.)
COLUMBIA (9002 "Western Classics, Vol. 2")..... 40-60 51
(10-inch LP.)
COLUMBIA (15000 series)..... 8-10 81
COLUMBIA (37000 series)..... 5-10 82
DESIGN..... 8-10
ENCORE..... 6-10 80
GRT..... 10-15 77
GOLDEN AGE..... 5-10 77
GRAND PRIX..... 8-10
HALLMARK..... 8-12
HARMONY (7100 thru 7300 series)..... 20-30 56-65
HARMONY (9500 series)..... 15-25 59-64
HARMONY (11000 series)..... 10-15 64-66
HURRAH..... 5-10
INTERNATIONAL AWARD..... 5-10
MELODY RANCH (101 "Melody Ranch")..... 30-50 65
MISTLETOE..... 8-12 74
MURRAY HILL (61072 "The Gene Autry Collection")..... 45-55 83
(Four-LP set.)
MURRAY HILL (897296 "Melody Ranch Radio Show")..... 45-55 '80s
(Four-LP set.)
RCA (2600 series)..... 25-30 62
RADIOLA..... 5-10 75
REPUBLIC (1900 series)..... 5-10
REPUBLIC (6000 series)..... 5-15 76-78
STARDAY..... 6-10 78
TIMELESS TREASURES..... 5-8 83
Also see BOND, Johnny
Also see CLAYTON, Bob
Also see CLAYTON & BREEN
Also see DODDS, Johnny
Also see HANDY, John
Also see HATFIELD, Overton
Also see HILL, Sam
Also see JOHNSON, Gene
Also see LONG, Tom
Also see PARKER, Fess, & Buddy Ebsen / Gene Autry
Also see SMITH, Jimmy

AUTUMN PEOPLE

LPs: 10/12-inch

SOUNDTECH (3020 "Autumn People"). 75-100 76
Members: Lary Clark; Dan Poff; Steve Barazza; Cliff Spiegel.

AVAK, George

Singles: 7-inch

CINATONE (501 "Lindy Lou")..... 50-75

AVALANCHES

Singles: 7-inch

W.B. 10-15 63-64

LPs: 10/12-inch

W.B. (W-1525 "Ski Surfin'")..... 30-40 63
(Monaural.)
W.B. (WS-1525 "Ski Surfin'")..... 40-50 63
(Stereo.)
Members: Billy Strange; David Gates; Tommy Tedesco; Hal Blaine; Al DeLory; Wayne Burdick.
Also see BLAINE, Hal
Also see GATES, David
Also see STRANGE, Billy
Also see TEDESCO, Tommy

AVALON, Frankie P&R/R&B '58

("11 Year Old Frankie Avalon")

Singles: 78 rpm

CHANCELLOR..... 25-50 57-58
"X"..... 10-20 54

Singles: 7-inch

ABC..... 4-6 74
AMOS (127 "The Star")..... 5-10 69
BOBCAT..... 3-5 83
CHANCELLOR (1 "Shy Guy")..... 20-40
(Acnecare promotional special products issue.)
CHANCELLOR (1004 "Cupid")..... 20-30 57
CHANCELLOR (1006 thru 1026)..... 15-25 57-58
CHANCELLOR (1031 "Venus")..... 10-20 58
(Monaural)
CHANCELLOR (S-1031 "Venus")..... 25-50 59
(Stereo.)
CHANCELLOR (1036 "Bobby Sox to Stockings")..... 10-20 59
(Monaural.)
CHANCELLOR (S-1036 "Bobby Sox to Stockings")..... 25-50 59
(Stereo.)
CHANCELLOR (1040 "Just Ask Your Heart")..... 10-20 59
(Monaural.)
CHANCELLOR (S-1040 "Just Ask Your Heart")..... 25-50 59
(Stereo.)
CHANCELLOR (1045 "Why")..... 10-20 59
(Monaural.)
CHANCELLOR (S-1045 "Why")..... 25-50 59
(Stereo.)
CHANCELLOR (1048 "Don't Throw Away All Those Teardrops")..... 10-20 60
CHANCELLOR (1052 "Where Are You")..... 10-20 60
CHANCELLOR (1056 "Togetherness")..... 10-20 60
CHANCELLOR (1065 "A Perfect Love")..... 10-20 60
CHANCELLOR (1071 "All of Everything")..... 10-20 61
CHANCELLOR (1077 "Who Else But You")..... 10-20 61
CHANCELLOR (1081 "Voyage to the Bottom of the Sea")..... 10-20 61
CHANCELLOR (1087 "True True Love")..... 10-20 61
CHANCELLOR (1095 "Sleeping Beauty")..... 10-20 61
CHANCELLOR (1101 "After You've Gone")..... 10-20 62
CHANCELLOR (1107 "You Are Mine")..... 10-20 62
CHANCELLOR (1114 "Venus")..... 5-10 62
CHANCELLOR (1115 "A Miracle")..... 10-20 62
CHANCELLOR (1125 "Welcome Home")..... 10-20 62
CHANCELLOR (1131 "First Love Never Dies")..... 10-20 63
CHANCELLOR (1134 "Come Fly with Me")..... 15-25 63
CHANCELLOR (1135 "Cleopatra")..... 10-20 63
CHANCELLOR (1139 "Beach Party")..... 10-20 63
CHANCELLOR (5022 "...and Now About Mr. Avalon")..... 40-60 61
(Set of five stereo singles, numbered 5022-1 through 5022-5. Only cover has title "...and Now About Mr. Avalon. Includes cover.")
CHANCELLOR (5022-1 "The Music Stopped")..... 8-12 61
(Stereo. One of a set of five.)
CHANCELLOR (5022-2 "Lotta Livin' to Do")..... 8-12 61
(Stereo. One of a set of five.)
CHANCELLOR (5022-3 "Sail a Crooked Ship")..... 8-12 61
(Stereo. One of a set of five.)
CHANCELLOR (5022-4 "The Lonely Bit")..... 8-12 61
(Stereo. One of a set of five.)
CHANCELLOR (5022-5 "What Is This Thing Called Love")..... 8-12 61
(Stereo. One of a set of five.)
COLLECTABLES..... 3-5 81
DE LITE..... 4-6 76-78
ERIC..... 4-6 73
MCA..... 3-5 84
METROMEDIA..... 4-6 70
REGALIA (5508 "I'm in the Mood for Love")..... 4-6 72
REPRISE..... 5-10 68-69
U.A. 8-12 64-65
"X" (0006 "Trumpet Sorrento")..... 20-30 54
"X" (0026 "Trumpet Tarantella")..... 20-30 54

Picture Sleeves

CHANCELLOR (1021 thru 1045)..... 20-30 58-59
CHANCELLOR (1048 thru 1125)..... 10-20 60-63
DE LITE..... 4-8 78
U.A. 10-15 64

EPs: 7-inch

CHANCELLOR (300 "Sincerely")..... 20-40 59
CHANCELLOR (302 "Guns of Timberland")..... 20-40 60
CHANCELLOR (303 "Ballad of the Alamo")..... 20-40 60
(Without publicity kit.)
CHANCELLOR (5001 "Frankie Avalon")..20-40 58
CHANCELLOR (5002-A/B "Young Frankie Avalon")..... 20-40 59
(Price is for either of two volumes.)
CHANCELLOR (5004-A/B/C "Swingin on a Rainbow")..... 20-40 59
(Price is for any of three volumes.)
CHANCELLOR (5011-A/B/C "A Summer Scene")..... 20-40 60
(Price is for any of three volumes.)
CHANCELLOR (5012 "Good Old Summertime")..... 20-40 60
"X" (20 "A Very Young Man with a Horn")..... 20-40 55

Promotional EPs

CHANCELLOR (303 "Ballad of the Alamo")..... 50-100 60
(With complete publicity kit.)
CHANCELLOR (5004 "Swingin' on a Rainbow")..... 25-50 59
(White label. Includes paper sleeve with note from Frankie, thanking dee jays for their support.)

LPs: 10/12-inch

ABC..... 5-10 73
CHANCELLOR (5001 "Frankie Avalon")..35-50 58
CHANCELLOR (5002 "Young Frankie Avalon")..... 35-45 59
(Black vinyl.)
CHANCELLOR (5002 "Young Frankie Avalon")..... 75-100 59
(Colored vinyl.)
CHANCELLOR (5004 "Swingin' on a Rainbow")..... 40-60 59
(With bound-in photo page.)
CHANCELLOR (CHL-5011 "Summer Scene")..... 30-40 60
(Monaural.)
CHANCELLOR (CHLS-5011 "Summer Scene")..... 35-45 60
(Stereo.)
CHANCELLOR (CHL-5018 "A Whole Lot of Frankie")..... 25-35 61
CHANCELLOR (CHL-5022 "...and now about Mr. Avalon")..... 20-30 61
(Monaural.)
CHANCELLOR (CHLS-5022 "...and now about Mr. Avalon")..... 25-35 61
(Stereo.)
CHANCELLOR (CHL-5025 "Frankie Avalon Italiano")..... 20-25 62
(Monaural.)
CHANCELLOR (CHLS-5025 "Frankie Avalon Italiano")..... 20-30 62
(Stereo.)
CHANCELLOR (CHL-5027 "You Are Mine")..... 20-25 62
(Monaural.)
CHANCELLOR (CHLS-5027 "You Are Mine")..... 20-30 62
(Stereo.)
CHANCELLOR (CHL-5031 "Christmas Album")..... 20-25 62
(Monaural.)
CHANCELLOR (CHLS-5031 "Christmas Album")..... 20-30 62
(Stereo.)
CHANCELLOR (CHL-5032 "Cleopatra")..20-25 62
(Monaural.)
CHANCELLOR (CHLS-5032 "Cleopatra")..... 20-30 62
(Stereo.)
CHANCELLOR (69801 "Young and in Love")..... 50-75 60
(LP with felt cover and 3-D portrait, suitable for hanging, in a special box.)
CHANCELLOR (69801 "Young and in Love")..... 25-40 60
(LP without the box.)
DE-LITE..... 5-10 76-78
EVEREST..... 5-10 82
KOALA..... 8-15
51 WEST..... 5-10
LIBERTY..... 5-10 82
MCA..... 5-10 85
METROMEDIA..... 5-10 70
SUNSET..... 8-12 69
TRIP..... 5-10 77
U.A. 20-30 64
(With "UAL" or "UAS" prefix.)
U.A. 5-10 75
(With "UA-LA" prefix.)
Also see FABIAN / Frankie Avalon

AVALON, Frankie, & Annette

Singles: 12-inch

PACIFIC STAR (5698 "Merry Christmas")..... 20-40 81
(Picture disc.)

Singles: 7-inch

PACIFIC STAR (569 "Merry Christmas")..... 3-6 81
(Black vinyl.)
PACIFIC STAR (569 "Merry Christmas"). 15-20 81
(Colored vinyl.)

Picture Sleeves

PACIFIC STAR (569 "Merry Christmas")..... 4-8 81

LPs: 10/12-inch

BUENA VISTA (BV-3314 "Muscle Beach Party")..... 25-50 64
(Monaural. Soundtrack.)
BUENA VISTA (STER-3314 "Muscle Beach Party")..... 50-100 64
(Stereo. Soundtrack.)
RHINO (205 "Muscle Beach Party")..... 15-20 84
(Soundtrack.)
Also see ANNETTE
Also see AVALON, Frankie

AVALONS

(With Pancho Villa Orchestra; with Joseph Thomas Orchestra)

Singles: 78 rpm

GROOVE..... 50-75 56

Singles: 7-inch

BIM BAM BOOM (106 "You Do Something to Me")..... 4-8 72
CASINO (108 "You Do Something to Me")..... 250-350 59
GROOVE (0014 "Where We Going")..... 10-20 63
GROOVE (0141 "Chains Around My Heart")..... 150-250 56
GROOVE (0174 "It's Funny But It's True")..... 200-300 56
NPC (302 "Begin the Beguine")..... 15-25 64
OLIMPIC (240 "Begin the Beguine")..... 75-100 63
SANDRYON (27503 "You Are My Heart's Desire")..... 200-300 58
(Canadian.)
UNART (2007 "Hearts Desire")..... 100-125 58
Members: Ray Ingram; Charles Crowley; Jim Dozier; Bernie Purdie; George Cox.

AVALONS

Singles: 7-inch

DICE (90/91 "You Broke Our Hearts"/"Louella")..... 40-50 58

AVALONS

Singles: 7-inch

KEN-GREN (243 "Picture of You")..... 50-75 60

AVANTIES

(Gregory Dee & Avanties)

Singles: 7-inch

APEX (76931 "The Grind")..... 25-35 64
(First issue.)
BANGAR (602 "Olds Mo William")..... 15-25 64
BANGAR (620 "The Grind")..... 15-25 64
BANGAR (646 "I Want to Be with You")..... 10-20 66
BANGAR (658 "The Slide")..... 10-20 66
FOX (422 "Watusi Once More")..... 20-25 66
GARRETT (4007 "Olds Mo William")..... 15-25 64
GARRETT (4011 "The Grind")..... 15-25 64
TWIN TOWN (705 "Love Or Magic")..... 15-25 '60s
TWIN TOWN (717 "Because of You")..... 15-25 '60s
Also see JODY & BOOGIEMEN

AVENGERS

Singles: 7-inch

CURRENT (1001 "It's Hard to Hide")..... 20-30 66
F-G (104 "When It's Over")..... 10-15 65
STARBURST..... 30-50 65-66

AVENGERS

EPs: 7-inch

DANGERHOUSE (400 "We Are the One")..... 75-125 77
(Pictures one group member hanging above the other three.)
DANGERHOUSE (400 "We Are the One")..... 15-25 77
(Group member not hanging above the other three.)

AVENGERS VI
Singles: 7-inch
MARK 56 (202 "Time Bomb") 30-40 66
LPs: 10/12-inch
MARK 56 ("Good Humor Presents Real Cool Hits") 125-175 66
(Selection number not known. Promotional issue, available only through the Good Humor Ice Cream Company.)

AVERSA, Mickey, & Invaders
Singles: 7-inch
LAP (108 "Blast Off") 20-30 65

AVERY, Netti Dady, & Florida Gators
Singles: 78 rpm
ASCO (1009 "Reality Blues") 30-40

AVERY & COUNTRY BOYS
Singles: 7-inch
JAM (903 "Grandpa's Twist") 30-50

AVON & RAVE-ONS
Singles: 7-inch
TOWNE HOUSE (6 "Teen Queen") 300-400

AVONS
Singles: 78 rpm
HULL 20-50 56-57
Singles: 7-inch
ASTRA (1023 "Baby") 10-20 66
HULL (717 "Our Love Will Never End") 75-125 56
(Black label.)
HULL (717 "Our Love Will Never End") 30-40 56
(Red label.)
HULL (722 "Baby") 50-100 57
(Red label with circle around label.)
HULL (722 "Baby") 20-30
(Red label without circle.)
HULL (726 "So Close to Me") 50-100 58
HULL (728 "What Will I Do") 50-100 58
HULL (731 "What Love Can Do") 40-50 59
HULL (744 "Whisper") 50-75 61
(White label.)
HULL (744 "Whisper") 40-50 61
(Pink label.)
HULL (744 "Whisper") 30-40
(Brown label.)
HULL (754 "The Grass Is Greener") 50-100 62
(White label.)
HULL (754 "The Grass Is Greener") 40-60 62
(Brown label.)
ROULETTE 4-6 71
LPs: 10/12-inch
HULL (1000 "Hull Records Cordially Invite You to Meet the Avons") 750-1000 60
Members: Robert Lee; Wendell Lee; William Lee; Irv Watson; Curtis Norris; Franklin Cole; George Coleman.

AVONS
Singles: 7-inch
GROOVE (0022 "Oh Gee Baby") 10-15 63
GROOVE (0033 "Rolling Stone") 10-15 64
GROOVE (0039 "Whatever Happened to Our Love") 10-15 64
Picture Sleeves
GROOVE (0022 "Oh Gee Baby") 25-40 63

AXIDENTALS
LPs: 10/12-inch
ABC-PAR (138 "Hello, We're the Axidentals") 50-75 55
Member: Maynard Ferguson.
Also see FERGUSON, Maynard

AXTON, Hoyt *C&W/P&R '74*
(With the Sherwood Singers)
Singles: 7-inch
A&M 4-6 73-76
BRIAR (100 "Drinking Gourd") 5-10 61
CAPITOL 4-6 71-72
COLGEMS (1005 "San Fernando") 4-8 67
COLPIX (802 "Speed-Trap") 4-8 66
COLUMBIA 4-8 69
ELEKTRA 3-5 81
HORIZON 5-10 62-63
JEREMIAH 3-5 79-83
MCA 4-6 77-78
20TH FOX (6648 "Five Dollar Bill") 4-8 66
VEE-JAY 5-10 64-65
Picture Sleeves
A&M 4-6 73-74
LPs: 10/12-inch
A&M 5-10 73-77
ACCORD 5-10 82
ALLEGIANCE 5-10 84
BRYLEN 5-10 82
CAPITOL 8-10 71
COLUMBIA 8-12 69
EXODUS 10-15 66
HORIZON 15-25 62-63
JEREMIAH 8-10 79-82
LAKE SHORE 5-10 81
MCA 5-10 77-78
SURREY 10-20 65
VEE-JAY 10-20 64-65
VEE-JAY INT'L (Except 1000 series) 5-10 74-77
VEE-JAY INT'L (1000 series) 10-12 74
Session: Linda Ronstadt; Tanya Tucker; Ronee Blakley.
Also see RONSTADT, Linda

AXTON, Hoyt, & Chambers Brothers
Singles: 7-inch
HORIZON (360 "Gypsy Woman") 8-10 62
HORIZON (361 "This Little Light") 8-10 62
HORIZON (362 "Greenback Dollar") 8-10 62
LPs: 10/12-inch
HORIZON (1613 "Thunder 'N' Lightnin' ") 15-25 63
Also see AXTON, Hoyt
Also see CHAMBERS BROTHERS

AYERS, Cliff
(With the Dick Quigley Orchestra; with Continentals; with Crowns)
Singles: 78 rpm
EMERALD 10-15 55-56
GEM (203 "Smiling Through the Tears") 8-12 53
Singles: 7-inch
EMERALD (2004 "Lopsided Love") 50-100 55
EMERALD (2014 "Rock Baby Rock") 40-50 56
EMERALD (3000 "I Wonder Why") 50-100 59
GEM (203 "Smiling Through the Tears") 15-25 53
LINCOLN 4-8
Picture Sleeves
LINCOLN 5-10

AYERS, Roy *LP '74*
(Roy Ayers' Ubiquity)
Singles: 12-inch
COLUMBIA 4-6 84-85
POLYDOR 4-6 79
Singles: 7-inch
COLUMBIA 3-5 84-86
POLYDOR 3-6 73-81
LPs: 10/12-inch
ATLANTIC 8-12 68-76
COLUMBIA 5-10 84-86
ELEKTRA 5-10 78
POLYDOR (4049 "Ubiquity") 60-100 70
POLYDOR (5022 "He's Coming") 60-100 72
POLYDOR (5045 "Red, Black and Green") 20-40 73
POLYDOR (6016 thru 6108) 20-40 73-77
POLYDOR (6126 thru 6348) 10-20 78-82
Also see MANN, Herbie

AYO, Zena
Singles: 7-inch
CASE (1004 "Dumb Bell") 15-25 59

AYRES, Cesta
Singles: 78 rpm
IMPERIAL 10-15 53
Singles: 7-inch
IMPERIAL (5255 "You Got a Time") 25-35 53

AZALEAS
Singles: 7-inch
ROMULUS (3001 "Hands Off") 20-30 63

AZITIS
LPs: 10/12-inch
ELCO (5555 "Help") 1200-1600 71
Members: Steve Nelson; Don Lower; Michael Welch; Dennis Sullivan.

AZTECS
Singles: 7-inch
SULTAN (2 "Dreamy") 10-20 59
Picture Sleeves
SULTAN (2 "Dreamy") 40-60 59

AZTECS
Singles: 7-inch
ZIN-A-SPIN (002 "The Answer to My Prayer") 100-125 62

AZTECS
Singles: 7-inch
CARD (901 "Teenage Hall of Fame") 10-20 64
WORLD ARTISTS (1029 "Da Doo Ron Ron") 8-12 64
LPs: 10/12-inch
WORLD ARTISTS (2001 "Live at the Ad-Lib Club of London") 50-100 64

AZTEX
Singles: 7-inch
STAFF (194 "I Said Move") 75-125 67
(150 made.)

B

B., Graham
Singles: 7-inch
SPEAKS (101 "Rock and Roll Fever") 500-750

B., Ty, & Johnny
Singles: 7-inch
RED WING (705 "Meaner Than an Alligator") 25-50
Picture Sleeves
RED WING (705 "Meaner Than an Alligator") 40-50

B-B
(B.B. Cunningham Jr.)
Singles: 7-inch
COVER (3 "Humbinger") 10-20
COVER (1961 "Ivory Marbles") 10-20 61
COVER (5931 "Trip to Bandstand") 20-30 59
COVER (5981 "Scratchin' ") 15-25 59

B-B / Lyn Vernon
Singles: 7-inch
COVER (4622 "High Pockets Twist") 8-12 62
Also see B-B
Also see VERNON, Lynn

B. BUMBLE & STINGERS *P&R '61*
Singles: 7-inch
DYMO 5-10
HIGHLAND 5-10 '60s
MERCURY 5-10 66-67
RENDEZVOUS 10-20 61-63
TRIAD 4-6 74
WAX 5-10 64
Members: Billy Brumble; Ernie Freeman; Ron Brady; Fred Richard.
Also see FREEMAN, Ernie

B.C.s
Singles: 7-inch
RUFF (1015 "Oh Yeow!") 15-25 66

B-52s *LP '79*
Singles: 12-inch
W.B. 4-6 86
Singles: 7-inch
B-52s (52 "Rock Lobster") 15-20 78
REPRISE 3-5 89-91
W.B. (Except 927) 3-5 79-86
W.B. (927 "Give Me Back My Man") 3-5 81
(Promotional issue only.)
Picture Sleeves
B-52s (52 "Rock Lobster") 25-50 78
REPRISE 3-5 89
W.B. 3-5 80-83
LPs: 10/12-inch
REPRISE 5-8 89-91
W.B. 5-10 79-86
Members: Cindy Wilson; Keith Strickland; Fred Schneider III; Ricky Wilson; Kate Pierson.

B.G. RAMBLERS
Singles: 7-inch
SPARKLE (1297 "Exit Stage Left") 10-20 63

B.J. & GEMINIS
Singles: 7-inch
ATCO (6364 "Scratch My Back") 10-20 65

B + 3
Singles: 7-inch
CANADIAN AMERICAN (200 "Why Oh Why") 15-25 66
CANADIAN AMERICAN (205 "My Babe") 15-25 67

B.W. & EMERALDS
Singles: 7-inch
RUMBLE (1348 "I Need Your Love") 200-300 61

B. WILLIE & FEVERS
Singles: 7-inch
TARA (1001 "After Hours") 10-20 62

BABBITT, Harry / Tony Martin
Singles: 78 rpm
MERCURY/SAV-WAY (3055 "To Me") 100-150 47
(Picture disc. Promotional issue only.)
Also see MARTIN, Tony

BABE & LOU
("The Home Run Twins")
Singles: 78 rpm
PERFECT (12382 "Babe & Lou") 50-75 '20s
Members: Babe Ruth; Lou Gehrig.
Also see RUTH, Babe

BABES
Singles: 7-inch
DEAN (1752 "Buck Fever") 15-25 60

BABETTES
Singles: 7-inch
HOPE (0001 "We Can Life Off Love") 100-200 '60s

BABIES
Singles: 7-inch
DUNHILL (4085 "You Make Me Feel Like Someone") 10-15 67
Picture Sleeves
DUNHILL (4085 "You Make Me Feel Like Someone") 20-30 67

BABY DEE
Singles: 7-inch
AMBER (208 "Pretty-Eyed Baby") 10-15 62
ZEBRA (120 "I Cried the Last Time") 50-75 58

BABY DOLLS
Singles: 7-inch
BOOM (60002 "I Will Do It") 5-10 66
ELGIN (021 "Is This the End") 40-50 59
GAMBLE (213 "There You Are") 5-10 68
HOLLYWOOD (1111 "Why Can't I Love Him Like You") 15-25 66
MASKE (103 "I'm Lonely") 15-25 61
MASKE (701 "Thanks Mr. Dee-Jay") 30-40 61
RCA (7296 "Cause I'm in Love") 10-15 58
W.B. (5086 "Hey Baby") 10-15 59
Also see BAKER, Bill
Also see ROSIE'S BABY DOLLS

BABY FACE
(Baby Face Leroy; Baby Face Leroy Trio; with the Sunnyland Trio; with Birds; Leroy Foster;)
Singles: 78 rpm
CHESS (1447 "My Head Can't Rest Anymore") 75-125 50
J.O.B. (100 "My Head Can't Rest Anymore") 100-200 52
J.O.B. (1002 "Pet Rabbit") 100-200 52
PARKWAY (104 "Boll Weevil") 200-300 50
PARKWAY (501 "Rollin' and Tumblin' ") 2000-4000 50
SAVOY (1122 "Red Headed Woman") 25-50 54
Singles: 7-inch
SAVOY (1122 "Red Headed Woman") 50-100 54
SAVOY (1501 "Red Headed Woman") 25-50 58
Session: Muddy Waters; Little Walter.
Also see FOSTER, Leroy, & Muddy Waters
Also see LITTLE WALTER
Also see SUNNYLAND SLIM
Also see SUNNYLAND TRIO

BABY JANE & ROCK-A-BYES *P&R '63*
(Baby Jane)
Singles: 7-inch
SPOKANE (4001 "Hickory Dickory Dock") 10-20 63
(First issue.)
SPOKANE (4004 "Get Me to the Church on Time") 10-20 63
(First issue.)
U.A. (505 "Oh Johnny") 8-12 62

U.A. (560 "Doggie in the Window")..........10-15 63
U.A. (593 "Hickory Dickory Dock")..............8-12 63

BABY LLOYD
("The Baby")

Singles: 7-inch

ATCO (6175 "Wait and See")......................8-12 60
DADE (1809 "Wait and See")..................25-35 60
LOMA (2014 "There's Something on Your Mind")..5-10 65

BABY RAY — P&R '66
(Ray Eddlemon)

Singles: 7-inch

CAPACITY (116 "Dance My Tears Away")....................................10-15 '60s
IMPERIAL..8-15 66-67
ZELL'S (260 "I Cried to Be Free")...........30-40 62

LPs: 10/12-inch

IMPERIAL..15-20 67

BABY RAY & FERNS

Singles: 7-inch

DONNA (1378 "How's Your Bird")...........25-35 63
Member: Frank Zappa.
Also see ZAPPA, Frank

BACHELOR THREE
(With Hank Levine & Orchestra)

Singles: 7-inch

VI-WAY (288 "Lover Man")....................25-50 61
VI-WAY (289 "Whisper")........................25-50 61

BACHELORS

Singles: 7-inch

MERCURY (8159 "Yesterday's Roses")..150-250 49
Members: Joe Van Loan; Elijah Harvey; Allen Scott; Jim Miller.
Also see VAN LOAN, Joe

BACHELORS

Singles: 78 rpm

ALADDIN (3210 "Can't Help Loving You")..200-300 53
POPLAR (101 "After")..............................30-40 57
ROYAL ROOST (620 "You've Lied").....75-125 56

Singles: 7-inch

ALADDIN (3210 "Can't Help Loving You")...2500-3000 53
POPLAR (101 "After")..............................30-40 57
ROYAL ROOST (620 "You've Lied")...600-800 56
Members: Walt Taylor; Jim Walton; Herb Fisher; John Bowie.
Also see JETS
Also see LINKS

BACHELORS

Singles: 7-inch

EARL (101 "Dolores")......................200-300 56
Also see BARLOW, Dean, & Bachelors

BACHELORS

Singles: 78 rpm

PALACE (140 "Selfish")...........................10-15 55

Singles: 7-inch

PALACE (140 "Selfish")...........................30-40 55

BACHELORS

Singles: 7-inch

MGM (12668 "Teenage Memory")...........10-15 58
NATIONAL (104 "A Million Teardrops")...15-25 57
NATIONAL (115 "I Want a Girl")............15-25 58
TERRY-TONE (201 "Every Night")..........40-50 59

BACHELORS

Singles: 7-inch

EPIC (9369 "Do the Madison")...................5-10 60
INTERNATIONAL (777 "Is This Goodbye")...50-75 61
SMASH (1723 "Day I Met You")..................5-10 61

BACHS

LPs: 10/12-inch

("Out of the Bachs")........................1500-2500 68
(No label name or number used.)
Members: John Peterman; Black Allison; Ben Harrison.

BACK PORCH BOYS

Singles: 78 rpm

APOLLO..15-25 47
Members: Alec Seward; Louis Hayes.
Also see SEWARD, Alec, & Louis Hayes
Also see BLUES BOY

BACK STREET CRAWLER — LP '75
(Crawler)

Singles: 7-inch

EPIC..4-6 77-78

LPs: 10/12-inch

ATCO..10-12 75-76
EPIC (Except PAL-349001)......................5-10 77-78
EPIC (PAL-349001 "Crawler")..................35-45 78
(Picture disc. Promotional issue only.)
Members: Tony Braunagel; Mike Montgomery; John Bundrick; Paul Kossoff; Geoff Whitehorn; Terry Wilson Slesser.
Also see FREE

BACKGROUNDS

Singles: 7-inch

CENCO (110 "Baby Please Take Me").....20-30 61

BACKUS, Gus

Singles: 7-inch

CARLTON (471 "You Can't Go It Alone")..30-40 58
DICO..4-8
FONO-GRAF (1238 "Priscilla")..................20-30 61
GENERAL AMERICAN..............................8-10 63
MGM (13134 "Short on Love")....................8-10 63
Also see DEL-VIKINGS

BACKUS, Jim — P&R '58
("Jim Backus with Friend"; Mr. McGoo & Dennis Farnon Orchestra; Jim Bakus; with Appleknocker & His Group; with Mort Garson & Orchestra)

Singles: 7-inch

JUBILEE (5330 "Delicious").....................15-25 58
JUBILEE (5351 "Cave Man").....................15-25 58
JUBILEE (5361 "Cave Man").....................15-25 59
(Reissued with different flip side.)

EPs: 7-inch

RCA (1362 "McGoo in Hi-Fi")....................25-35 56

LPs: 10/12-inch

DORE..8-10 74
RCA (1362 "McGoo in Hi-Fi")..................50-100 56
Also see HOPE, Bob

BACKUS, Jim, & Daws Butler

Singles: 7-inch

DICO (101 "I Was a Teenage Reindeer")...25-50 59
Also see BACKUS, Jim
Also see BUTLER, Daws

BACON, Gar

Singles: 7-inch

BATON (248 "There's Gonna Be Rockin' Tonight")..30-40 57
BATON (250 "Pucker Up")........................30-40 58
DALE (105 "Chains of Love")....................15-25 57
DALE (108 "Dutch Treat").........................15-25 58
OKEH (7115 "To You to Love")...................8-12 59
RKO UNIQUE (395 "You & Your Love").....8-15 57

BACON, Shorty
(Charles "Shorty" Bacon)

Singles: 7-inch

IMPACT (17 "What's Wrong with You")....15-25 63
KELLEY (103 "Only a Dream")..................10-15 59
MOHAWK (101 "My Friend Old River")....25-50 56
MOHAWK (102 "Juvenile Blues")............25-50 56
MOHAWK (103 "Only a Dream")................25-50 57
MOHAWK (104 "My Aunt Sue")................25-50 57
OZARK (1237 "Fire of Love")....................50-75
TSM (7345 "Talk to Me")...........................50-75

BACON, Woody

Singles: 7-inch

MARBILL (101 "Round House Boogie")...10-20 61

BACON FAT

LPs: 10/12-inch

BLUE HORIZON (4807 "Grease One for Me")..25-45 70
Members: George Smith; Buddy Reed; Dick Innes; Greg Schaefer; Jerry Smith; Rod Piazz; J.D. Nicholson.

BAD & GOOD BOYS

Singles: 7-inch

M.O.C. (668 "Fire")..................................20-30 68

BAD OMENS

Singles: 7-inch

TWIN TOWN (724 "He Was a Friend").....10-20 67

BAD ROADS

Singles: 7-inch

JIN (21 "Too Bad")..................................30-50 67
RAIN TYRE (1000 "Til the End of the Day")..30-50 66

EPs: 7-inch

SUNDAZED (143 "Bad Roads")....................5-8 99

BAD SEEDS

Singles: 7-inch

J-BECK (1002 "Taste of the Same").........30-50 65
J-BECK (1003 "Zilch")...............................15-25 66
J-BECK (1005 "All Night Long")................30-50 66

BADD BOYS

Singles: 7-inch

EPIC (10119 "Never Going Back to Georgia")..30-40 67
EPIC (10165 "I Told You So")...................40-50 67

BADFINGER — P&R '69

Singles: 7-inch

APPLE (1815 "Come and Get It")..............5-15 70
APPLE (1822 "No Matter What")...............5-15 70
APPLE (1841 "Day After Day")..................5-15 71
APPLE (1844 "Baby Blue")........................5-15 72
APPLE (1864 "Apple of My Eye")............10-20 73
ATLANTIC..3-5 81
ELEKTRA..4-6 79
RADIO..3-5 81
W.B. (7801 "I Miss You")..........................4-6 74

Promotional Singles

APPLE (1841 "Day After Day")............100-125 71
White label.)
APPLE (1844 "Baby Blue")..................100-125 72
(White label.)
APPLE (1864 "Apple of My Eye").............20-25 73

Picture Sleeves

APPLE (1844 "Baby Blue")......................10-15 72

LPs: 10/12-inch

APPLE (3364 "Magic Christian Music")....20-30 70
APPLE (3367 "No Dice")..........................15-25 70
APPLE (3387 "Straight Up")......................40-60 71
APPLE (3411 "Ass")................................15-25 73
ELEKTRA (175 "Airwaves").......................10-15 79
RADIO (16030 "Say No More")...................5-10 81
RYKODISC (0189 "Day After Day")..........15-25 90
(Clear vinyl.)
W.B. (2762 "Badfinger")..........................15-20 74
W.B. (2827 "Wish You Were Here").........20-30 74
Members: Tom Evans; Joey Molland; Peter Clarke; Mike Gibbons; Pete Ham; Tony Kaye.
Also see IVEYS

BAEZ, Joan — LP '61

Singles: 7-inch

A&M..4-6 72-77
DECCA..4-6 72
PORTRAIT...4-6 77-79
RCA..4-6 72
VANGUARD (6 "Maria Dolores")...............5-10 70
(Stereo. Promotional issue, included as a bonus with the LP *The First Ten Years.*)
VANGUARD (35000 series)......................5-10 63-69
VANGUARD (35100 series)........................4-6 70-71

Picture Sleeves

A&M..4-6 72
PORTRAIT...4-6 79
RCA..4-6 72
VANGUARD (6 "Maria Dolores")...............5-10 70
(Promotional issue, included as a bonus with the LP *The First Ten Years.*)
VANGUARD (35031 "There But for Fortune")..15-25 65

LPs: 10/12-inch

A&M (Except 8375)................................6-10 72-77
A&M (8375 "Joan Baez - Radio Airplay Album")...10-15 76
(Promotional issue only.)
EMUS..5-10 79
FANTASY (5015 "Joan Baez in San Francisco")..15-25 64
MFSL (238 "Diamonds & Rust")...............30-50 94
NAUTILUS..25-35 81
(Half-speed mastered.)
PICKWICK..5-10 73
PORTRAIT..5-10 77-79
SQUIRE...10-20 63
VANGUARD (41/42 "Ballad Book")...........10-15 72
VANGUARD (49/50 "Contemporary Ballad Book")..10-15 '70s
VANGUARD (105/106 "Country Music Album")..10-20 79
VANGUARD (077 thru 123)......................25-40 60-63
VANGUARD (160 thru 306)......................15-25 64-69
VANGUARD (308 thru 332)........................8-12 69-73
VANGUARD (400 series)...........................5-10
(Vanguard numbers 077 through 446 may be preceded by a "2," "9" or "79." "VRM" prefix indicates mono, "VRS" is for stereo.)
VANGUARD (6560/61 "The First Ten Years")..15-20 70
(Two discs. Includes photo book and bonus 45, *Maria Dolores* with picture sleeve.)
VANGUARD (6570/71 "Blessed Are")......10-15 71
(Two discs.)
Also see WILSON, Dennis / Ram Jam / Joan Baez

BAEZ, Joan, Bill Wood & Ted Alevizos

LPs: 10/12-inch

VERITAS (62202 "Folksingers 'Round Harvard Square")..100-200 60
(Without text in upper right corner reading: "This is the historic album featuring the original first recordings of America's Most Exciting Folk Singer — The Best of Joan Baez." A limited, numbered edition.)
VERITAS (62202 "Folksingers 'Round Harvard Square")..50-100 61
(Cover has "This is the historic album featuring the original first recordings of America's Most Exciting Folk Singer — The Best of Joan Baez.")
Also see BAEZ, Joan

BAGBY, Doc — P&R '57

Singles: 78 rpm

GOTHAM..10-20 52
KING...10-20 55
OKEH..10-20 57

Singles: 7-inch

END (1075 "Drifting")..............................8-12 60
GATOR (Pony Walk")................................5-10 61
GONE (5087 "Pancake Hop")......................8-12 60
GOTHAM "Jumpin' at Smalls")..................25-40 52
HUNT (323 "Muscle Tough")......................15-25 58
KAISER (383 "Home Run")........................20-30 54
KING (4804 "Grinding")............................20-30 55
OKEH (7080 "Joyride Special")...................5-10 57
OKEH (7089 "Dumplins")...........................5-10 57
OKEH (7098 "Happy Feet")........................5-10 58
PERRI (1000 "Cornbread")........................5-10 62
RED TOP (107 "Rusty")............................10-20 58
RED TOP (111 "Muscle Tough").................10-20 58
RED TOP (117 "Hoppie")..........................10-20 58
RED TOP (120 "Organ Grinder Rock")....10-20 59
TALLEY-HO (104 "Little Geech")................5-10 61
TIFTON (200 "Do the Getaway")................5-10 '60s
VIM (517 "Dumplins")...............................5-10 63

EPs: 10/12-inch

EPIC (7190 "Dumplins")..........................50-75 57
Also see SELLERS, Johnny
Also see TERRY, Sonny

BAGBY, Doc / Luis Rivera

LPs: 10/12-inch

KING (631 "Battle of the Organs")...........25-35 59
Also see BAGBY, Doc

BAGDASARIAN, Ross

Singles: 78 rpm

MERCURY...5-10 54

Singles: 7-inch

IMPERIAL...5-10 69
LIBERTY (55013 thru 55275)..................10-15 56-60
LIBERTY (55462 thru 56165)....................5-8 62-70
MERCURY..10-20 54

LPs: 10/12-inch

LIBERTY..20-30 66
Also see SEVILLE, David

BAGELS

Singles: 7-inch

W.B. (5420 "I Wanna Hold Your Hair").....10-15 64

BAGGESE, Charles

Singles: 7-inch

BCS (102 "Tuff")....................................10-20 62

BAGGYS

Singles: 7-inch

PIPELINE (501 "El Surfer")......................25-35 63
Members: Russ Regan; Joe Saraceno; Gene Weed.
Also see WEED, Gene

BAHAM, Roy

Singles: 7-inch

RIFF ("Hard to Get Along With") 100-200
(Selection number not known.)

BAILEY, David

Singles: 7-inch

BANNER (60202 "My Share of Heartaches") 10-15
(Promotional issue.)
BANNER (60204 "Caney") 75-125
(Promotional issue.)

BAILEY, Don

Singles: 7-inch

USA (723 "Be My Own") 25-35 62

BAILEY, Herb

Singles: 7-inch

MOVIN' (126 "Precious Lillie") 40-50 64

BAILEY, Jack
(With the Naturals)

Singles: 7-inch

FORD (105 "Beneath the Moonlight") 75-100 61
FORD (113 "Your Magic Touch") 40-60 62
FORD (121 "I Cried") 10-20 62
MALA (432 "Memories of You") 10-20 61

BAILEY, Jimmy
(J.R. Bailey; Jim Bailey)

Singles: 7-inch

COLUMBIA (43260 "Everytime") 5-10 65
COLUMBIA (43340 "Happy Train") 8-12 66
COLUMBIA (43408 "Hush") 5-10 65
COLUMBIA (43530 "Keep on Running") 5-10 66
COLUMBIA (43602 "Happy Train") 5-10 66
WYNNE (103 "Constantly") 50-75 59
(Also issued as by Jimmy Lane & the Sugartones. We're not sure which came first.)
Also see LANE, Jimmy, & Sugartones

BAILEY, Little Maxie

Singles: 78 rpm

EXCELLO 15-25 53

Singles: 7-inch

EXCELLO (2007 "Brown Skin Woman Blues") 40-60 53
EXCELLO (2016 "Drive, Soldiers, Drive") 40-60 53

BAILEY, Max
(Max "Scatman" Bailey; Max "Blues" Bailey)

Singles: 78 rpm

BULLET (306 "Sting-a-Ree") 50-100 49
CORAL (65065 "Betty Jane") 50-75 51
DOMINO (380 "Leave It Alone") 30-40 51
FEDERAL (12003 "My, Oh My") 30-40 51

BAILEY, Mildred, & Charioteers

Singles: 78 rpm

COLUMBIA (80 "Rockin' Chair") 10-15 50
OKEH 5-10 40
VOCALION 8-12 37-40

Singles: 7-inch

COLUMBIA (80 "Rockin' Chair") 15-25 50

LPs: 10/12-inch

ALLEGRO .... 10-20 '50s
COLUMBIA (6094 "Serenade") 30-50 50
(10-inch LP.)
Also see CHARIOTEERS

BAILEY, Mildred, & Delta Rhythm Boys

Singles: 78 rpm

DECCA 5-10 54

Singles: 7-inch

DECCA (25462 "Ev'rything Depends on You") 15-25 54
Also see BAILEY, Mildred, & Charioteers
Also see DELTA RHYTHM BOYS

BAILEY, Morris, & Thomas Boys

Singles: 7-inch

BAILEY 30-45
Also see INFORMERS

BAILEY, Pearl R&B '46
(With Jackie Mabley)

Singles: 78 rpm

COLUMBIA 4-8 46-50
CORAL 3-6 52-55
MERCURY 3-6 56
ROULETTE 3-6 57
SUNSET 3-6 56
VERVE 3-6 56

Singles: 7-inch

COLUMBIA (38000 series) 10-20 50
COLUMBIA (43000 series) 4-6 66
CORAL 10-20 52-55
DECCA 4-6 64
MERCURY 10-15 56
PROJECT 3 .... 4-6 68-70
RCA (500 series) 4-6 71
RCA (9400 series) 4-6 67
ROULETTE 5-10 57-67
SUNSET 10-15 56
VERVE 10-15 56

EPs: 7-inch

COLUMBIA 15-25 52-56
CORAL 15-25 54
ROULETTE 15-25 57

LPs: 10/12-inch

ACCORD 5-10 83
COLUMBIA (900 series) 20-40 57
COLUMBIA (2600 series) 25-50 56
(10-inch LPs.)
COLUMBIA (6000 series) 25-50 50
(10-inch LPs.)
CORAL (56000 series) 25-50 54
(10-inch LPs.)
CORAL (57000 series) 25-50 57
CORONET (231 "Pearl Bailey on Stage") 10-15 64
CO-STAR 15-25 58
GUEST STAR 5-10
HARMONY (7184 "Pearl Bailey Sings") ... 10-15 59
MERCURY (Except 100 series) 20-40 56-58
MERCURY (100 series) 8-12 69
MUSICO 10-15 69
PROJECT 3 .... 5-10 70
RCA (4500 series) 5-10 71
ROULETTE (100 series) 8-12 71
ROULETTE (25000 & 25100 series) 15-30 57-63
ROULETTE (25200 & 25300 series) 10-20 64-65
ROULETTE (42002 "Back on Broadway") .... 10-20 '60s
VOCALION 15-25 58
WING 15-25 59-63

BAILEY, Pearl, & Margie Anderson

LP: 10/12-inch

CORONET (148 "Singing & Swinging") .... 10-20 '60s

BAILEY, Pearl, & Mike Douglas

Singles: 7-inch

PROJECT 3 (1335 "Young At Heart") 5-10 68

BAILEY, Pearl / Rose Murphy / Ivie Anderson

LPs: 10/12-inch

GRAND PRIX .... 10-15 '60s
Also see BAILEY, Pearl
Also see MURPHY, Rose

BAILEY, Ramblin' Red

Singles: 7-inch

BETHLEHEM (3008 "Pretty Juke Box") 8-12 62
PEACH (653 "The Hardest Rain") 10-20
PEACH (725 "Take Off Like a Bird") 100-200

BAILEY, Razzy P&R '74/C&W '76
(Razzie Bailey; Razzy; featuring the Rebelaires)

Singles: 7-inch

ABC-PAR 5-10 67
B&K (103 "Once We Loved") 75-100 59
CAPRICORN (0238 "Peanut Butter") 4-6 75
ERASTUS 4-6 76
MCA 3-5 84-86
MGM 4-6 74
1-2-3 (1717 "Beautiful Room") 5-10 69
RCA 3-6 77-84
SOUNDS OF AMERICA 3-5 86-89

Picture Sleeves

RCA 3-5 80-81

LPs: 10/12-inch

MCA 5-10 85-86
PLANTATION 5-8 81
RCA 5-10 79-84
Also see AQUARIANS

BAILEY, Thomas

Singles: 7-inch

FEDERAL (12559 "Fran") 5-10 70
FEDERAL (12567 "Wish I Was Back") ... 50-100 71

BAILY, "June Bug"

Singles: 7-inch

JO (2180 "Louisiana Twist") 50-75

BAIN, Bob

Singles: 7-inch

CAPITOL (3931 "Fender Bender") 15-25 58
CAPITOL (4109 "The Old Spinning Wheel") 15-25 58
RADIANT (1509 "Soft Guitar") 10-15 62
RADIANT (1514 "Whatever Happened to Baby Jane") 10-15 62

LPs: 10/12-inch

CAPITOL (965 "Rockin' Rollin' Strollin' ") .. 50-75 58
CAPITOL (1201 "Latin Love") 15-25 59
CAPITOL (1500 "Guitar De Amor") 15-25 61
Also see PILTDOWN MEN

BAINES, Houston
(Houston Boines)

Singles: 78 rpm

BLUES & RHYTHM 150-250 51
Also see BOINES, Houston

BAINES, Vickie

Singles: 7-inch

LOMA (2078 "We Can Find That Love") 5-10 67
PARKWAY (957 "Losing You") 10-20 65
PARKWAY (966 "Country Girl") 75-125 66

BAKER, Bill
(With the Chestnuts; Bill Baker & Del Satins; Bill Baker's Five Satins; Billy Baker & Five Satins)

Singles: 7-inch

AUDICON (115 "Is It a Dream") 50-60 61
AUDICON (118 "Just to Be Near You") 10-15 61
CORAL (62171 "Wonderful Girl") 10-20 60
ETC (227 "There's a Small Hotel") 10-20 63
ELGIN (007 "Won't You Tell Me, My Heart") 20-30 59
ELGIN (013 "Wonderful Girl") 30-40 59
JANUS GOLD 4-6 77
MUSICNOTE (119 "Teenage Triangle") ... 25-35 63
MUSICTONE (1108 "To the Aisle") 10-15 61
(Some sources show this as by Bill Baker, others as by the 5 Satins.)
PARNASO (110 "Another Sleepless Night") 15-25 65
RECORD GUILD (20593 "Won't You Tell Me My Heart") 3-5
TREASURE ISLE ("Teenage Triangle") 4-6 94
(Selection number not known.)
VIM (515 "Thank Heaven") 100-150 60
(Credits only Bill Baker.)
VIM (515-A "Thank Heaven") 5-10
(Credits "Bill Baker and Group.")

LPs: 10/12-inch

DEL CAM (1000 "I'll Be Seeing You") 8-10 87
Also see BABY DOLLS
Also see CHESTNUTS
Also see DAVID & GOLIATH
Also see DEL SATINS
Also see FIVE SATINS
Also see HOOD, Darla

BAKER, Bill, & Hong Kong Bossa Nova Band

Singles: 7-inch

ARWIN (129 "Sampan Girl") 5-10 64

BAKER, Bill, & Twitchers

Singles: 7-inch

DORE (606 "Twitchin' ") 8-12 61
KNICK (172 "Caramba") 15-25 58

BAKER, Bob

Singles: 7-inch

VEEDA (4002 "Kitty Kat Korner") 100-200 59
VEEDA (4004 "I Miss You") 75-125 59

BAKER, C.B.

Singles: 78 rpm

SITTIN' IN WITH (625 "Skin to Skin") 25-35 51

BAKER, Charlie
(Charles Baker)

Singles: 7-inch

FURY (1049 "Darling, Here You Are") 25-35 61
LIBERTY (55226 "Star of Wonder") 15-25 59
MUN RAB (106 "Star of Wonder") 75-100 59
(First issue.)

BAKER, Dick, Combo

Singles: 7-inch

KIT KAT (711 "Heartless Lover") 200-300
Also see GREENE, Hazel, & Dick Baker

BAKER, Donny, & Dimensions

Singles: 78 rpm

RAINBOW 20-30 53

Singles: 7-inch

RAINBOW (219 "Drinkin' Pop Sodee Odee") 50-75 53
(Red vinyl.)

BAKER, George

Singles: 78 rpm

RCA ("How Doth the Little Crocodile") . 150-200 38
(Picture disc. Selection number not known.)

BAKER, Jane

Singles: 78 rpm

RCA (6425 "Boom-De-De-Boom") 8-12 56

Singles: 7-inch

RCA (6425 "Boom-De-De-Boom") 15-20 56

BAKER, Jeanette
(Jeanette & Decky)

Singles: 7-inch

ALADDIN (3443 "Everything Reminds Me of You") 10-20 59
CLASS (260 "He Really Belongs to Me") . 10-15 59
DUB-TONE (2581 "Johnny") 20-30 60
IMPERIAL (5964 "Everything Reminds Me of You") 8-12 63
Session: Dots.
Also see DOTS
Also see McLOLLIE, Oscar, & Jeanette Baker

BAKER, LaVern R&B '55
(With the Gliders; with Cookies; with Billy Sebastian Orch. & Chorus; with Ray Ellis & Orchestra; Lavern Baker; La Verne Baker)

Singles: 78 rpm

ATLANTIC (1004 thru 1136) 20-50 53-57
ATLANTIC (1189 "Whipper Snapper") 20-30 58
ATLANTIC (2001 "It's So Fine") 25-35 58
ATLANTIC (2007 "I Cried a Tear") 50-100 58
ATLANTIC (2021 "I Waited Too Long") .. 75-125 59
ATLANTIC (2033 "So High, So Low") 75-125 59
ATLANTIC (2041 "Tiny Tim") 100-150 59

Singles: 7-inch

ATLANTIC (1004 "Soul on Fire") 50-100 53
ATLANTIC (1047 "Tweedle Dee") 30-50 55
ATLANTIC (1057 "Bop-Ting-a-Ling") 30-50 55
ATLANTIC (1075 "Play It Fair") 50-75 55
ATLANTIC (1087 "My Happiness Forever") 20-30 56
ATLANTIC (1093 "Fee Fee Fi Fo Fum") .. 20-30 56
ATLANTIC (1104 "Still") 20-30 56
ATLANTIC (1116 "Jim Dandy") 20-30 56
ATLANTIC (1136 "Jim Dandy Got Married") 20-30 57
ATLANTIC (1150 "Humpty Dumpty Heart") 20-30 57
ATLANTIC (1163 "St. Louis Blues") 20-30 57
ATLANTIC (1176 "Learning to Love") 20-30 57
ATLANTIC (1189 "Whipper Snapper") 15-25 58
ATLANTIC (2001 "It's So Fine") 15-25 58
ATLANTIC (2007 "I Cried a Tear") 15-25 58
ATLANTIC (2021 "I Waited Too Long") 15-25 59
ATLANTIC (2033 "So High, So Low") 10-20 59
ATLANTIC (2041 "Tiny Tim") 10-20 59
ATLANTIC (2048 "Shake a Hand") 10-20 60
ATLANTIC (2059 "Wheel of Fortune") 10-20 60
ATLANTIC (2077 "Bumble Bee") 10-20 60
ATLANTIC (2099 "Saved") 10-20 61
ATLANTIC (2109 "Hurtin' Inside") 10-20 61
ATLANTIC (2119 "Hey, Memphis") 10-20 61
ATLANTIC (2137 "Must I Cry Again") 10-20 62
ATLANTIC (2167 "See See Rider") 8-15 62
ATLANTIC (2186 "Trouble in Mind") 8-15 63
ATLANTIC (2203 "Itty Bitty Girl") 8-15 63
ATLANTIC (2234 "Go Away") 8-12 64
ATLANTIC (2267 "Fly Me to the Moon") 8-12 65
BRUNSWICK (55291 "Baby") 10-20 66
BRUNSWICK (55297 "Call Me Darling") .. 10-20 66
BRUNSWICK (55311 "Wrapped, Tied and Tangled") 25-35 67

EPs: 7-inch

ATLANTIC (566 "LaVern Baker - Tweedle Dee") 75-125 56
ATLANTIC (588 "LaVern Baker - Jim Dandy") 75-125 57
ATLANTIC (617 "LaVern Baker - I Cried a Tear") 50-100 58

LPs: 10/12-inch

ATCO (372 "Her Greatest Recordings") ... 10-15 71

ATLANTIC (1281 "LaVern Baker Sings Bessie Smith")....50-100 58
ATLANTIC (8002 "LaVern")....150-200 57
(Black label.)
ATLANTIC (8002 "LaVern")....25-50 59
(Red label.)
ATLANTIC (8007 "LaVern Baker")....100-150 57
ATLANTIC (8030 "Blues Ballads")....50-75 59
(Black label.)
ATLANTIC (8030 "Blues Ballads")....50-75 59
(White label.)
ATLANTIC (8030 "Blues Ballads")....30-60 59
(Red label.)
ATLANTIC (8036 "Precious Memories")..40-60 59
ATLANTIC (8050 "Saved")....40-60 61
ATLANTIC (8071 "See See Rider")....25-50 63
ATLANTIC (8078 "Best of LaVern Baker")....25-50 63
BRUNSWICK (54160 "Let Me Belong to You")....10-15 70
Session: King Curtis.
Also see ELLIS, Ray, Orchestra
Also see KING CURTIS
Also see RHODES, Todd
Also see WILSON, Jackie, & LaVern Baker

BAKER, LaVern, & Ben E. King

Singles: 7-inch

ATLANTIC (2067 "How Often")....10-20 60
Also see KING, Ben E.

BAKER, LaVern, & Jimmy Ricks

Singles: 7-inch

ATLANTIC (2090 "I'll Never Be Free")....10-20 61
Also see BAKER, LaVern
Also see RICKS, Jimmy

BAKER, Mickey
(Mickey "Guitar" Baker & His House Rockers)

Singles: 78 rpm

RAINBOW....15-25 55
SAVOY....15-25 52-53

Singles: 7-inch

ATLANTIC (2042 "Third Man Theme")....10-15 59
KING....10-15 63-64
MGM (12418 "Spinnin' Rock Boogie")....10-20 57
RAINBOW....25-35 55
SAVOY....35-45 52-53

LPs: 10/12-inch

ATLANTIC (8035 "Wildest Guitar")....75-125 59
KICKING MULE....5-10 78
KING (839 "But Wild")....50-75 63
Also see BONNIE SISTERS
Also see CRITERIONS
Also see DARNELL, Larry
Also see DUPREE, Champion Jack, & Mickey Baker
Also see HUMPHRIES, Teddy
Also see McGHEE, Brownie
Also see McHOUSTON, Big Red
Also see MICKEY & KITTY
Also see MICKEY & SYLVIA
Also see MR. BEAR
Also see PAIGE, Hal
Also see PRICE, Sam
Also see RIFF, Eddie
Also see SELLERS, John
Also see TERRY, Sonny
Also see 3 FRIENDS
Also see TURNER, Titus
Also see VALENTINE, Billy
Also see WASHBOARD BILL

BAKER, Penny, & Pillows

Singles: 7-inch

WITCH (123 "Bring Back the Beatles")....20-25 64

BAKER, Robert

LPs: 10/12-inch

GNP (2027 "Pardon Me for Being So Friendly But This Is My First L.S.D. Trip")....25-50 66

BAKER, Rodney, & Chantiers

Singles: 7-inch

JAN ELL (8 "Teenage Wedding Song")....15-25 61

BAKER, Ronnie
(With the Beltones)

Singles: 7-inch

JELL (200 "This Big Wide World")....20-30
LAURIE (3128 "I Want to Be Loved")....15-25 62
(First issued as by the Beltones.)
LAURIE (3164 "Land of Love")....10-15 63
LAURIE (3250 "Young at Heart")....10-15 64
Also see BELTONES
Also see BELL-TONES

BAKER, Roy "Boy"

Singles: 7-inch

DESS (7011 "I Thought I Heard You Call My Name")....75-125 57

BAKER, Sam
(With Johnny Behrens; with Jay-Bees)

Singles: 7-inch

ATHENS....10-20 61
COPA (200-3 "So Long")....600-800 60
DONNA (1332 "Island of Regret")....15-20 61
HOLLYWOOD (1126 "Slow Down")....5-10 68
JAY-KAY (112 "Island of Regret")....40-50
SAABIA....5-10
SOUND STAGE 7....5-10 65-69
USA (113 "You'd Better Check What You Got")....5-10 '60s
VAY KAY (112 "Island of Regret")....8-12 60

BAKER, Tex

Singles: 7-inch

ABC (1073 "Ontario Valley Rock")....40-50
CROSS WINDS (102 "Honky Tonk Blues")....50-60
CROSS WINDS (104 "Ontario Valley Rock")....50-60

BAKER, Virgle
(Virgil Baker)

Singles: 7-inch

RANGER (404 "Oohee Wee You're Sweet")....200-300
SMITTY (55784 "Dissatisfied")....200-300
ZONE (105 "The Game for Me")....100-200

BAKER, W.C.

Singles: 78 rpm

ESSEX (304 "Politics Boogie")....8-12 52
ROCKIN' (501 "Rumors About My Baby")....10-20 52
ROCKIN' (503 "Bessie Lou")....10-20 52

Singles: 7-inch

ESSEX (304 "Politics Boogie")....15-25 52

BAKER, Willie

Singles: 78 rpm

DELUXE....25-50 53
ROCKIN'....50-75 53

Singles: 7-inch

DELUXE (6023 "Before She Leaves Town")....75-100 53
ROCKIN' (527 "Before She Leaves Town")....100-200 53

BAKER, Yvonne
(With the Sensations)

Singles: 7-inch

ARGO (5412 "That's My Desire")....10-15 62
ARGO (5420 "Party Across the Hall")....10-15 62
ARGO (5446 "Father Dear")....8-12 63
JAMIE (1290 "What a Difference Love Makes")....8-12 64
JUNIOR (987 "Foolishly Yours")....15-25 63
MODERN (1055 "My Baby Needs Me")....5-10 68
PARKWAY (140 "You Didn't Say a Word")....50-75 67
Also see SENSATIONS

BALCOM, Bill
("Handsome" Jim Balcom; Jim Balcolm; with Shades of Rhythm)

Singles: 78 rpm

STARLA (7 "Corrido Rock")....25-50 58

Singles: 7-inch

CADDY (106 "Tribal Dance")....15-25 57
CLASS (249 "Bag Pipe Rock")....10-15 59
CLASS (259 "St. Louis Blues")....10-15 59
DOT (15711 "Corrido Rock")....10-20 58
NORWOOD (102 "Strollin'")....10-15 59
STARLA (7 "Corrido Rock")....20-30 58
(First issue.)
Also see HERRERA, Little Julian

BALDO, Frankie, & Noveltones

Singles: 7-inch

DANDY (10 "Strange Guitar")....30-40 61
(First issue.)
IMPERIAL (5755 "Strange Guitar")....10-20 61

BALDWIN, Tony

Singles: 7-inch

REM (301 "I Know")....100-150 59

BALIN, Marty *P&R/LP '81*

Singles: 7-inch

CHALLENGE (9146 "Nobody But You")...20-30 62
EMI AMERICA....3-5 81-84

Picture Sleeves

EMI AMERICA....3-5 81

LPs: 10/12-inch

EMI AMERICA....8-10 81-83
Also see JEFFERSON AIRPLANE
Also see JEFFERSON STARSHIP

BALL, Earl

Singles: 7-inch

PARTHENON (102 "2nd and San Antone")....50-75

BALL, Eugene, & Hearts

Singles: 7-inch

MELATONE (1001 "Why Oh Why")....200-300 57

BALLADEERS

Singles: 78 rpm

RCA (4612 "Goodbye Little Girl")....15-25 52

Singles: 7-inch

RCA (4612 "Goodbye Little Girl")....25-45 52

BALLADEERS

Singles: 7-inch

DEL-FI (4123 "Morning Star")....10-15 59
DEL-FI (4127 "Turtle Dove")....10-15 59
DEL-FI (4138 "Hurtin' ")....10-15 60

LPs: 10/12-inch

DEL-FI (1204 "Alive-O")....20-40 59
(Monaural.)
DEL-FI (1204 "Alive-O")....30-50 59
(Stereo.)
Members: Fred Darian; Joe Van Winkle; Al De Lory.
Also see DARIAN, Fred

BALLADIERS

Singles: 78 rpm

ALADDIN (3008 "Keep Me with You")....75-125 48
ALADDIN (3123 "Forget Me Not")....75-100 52
ANTHRACITE....20-30 55

Singles: 7-inch

ALADDIN (3123 "Forget Me Not")....550-650 52
ANTHRACITE (109 "Starlight Souvenirs")....50-75 55

BALLADS
(With Jimmy Cris Orchestra)

Singles: 78 rpm

FRANWIL....20-30 56

Singles: 7-inch

FRANWIL (5028 "Before You Fall in Love")....50-60 56
RON-CRIS (1003 "Somehow")....75-125 60
Members: Dick Arnold; Jack McCoy; Sonny Manzo; Phil Babin; Jack Knect.

BALLADS

Singles: 7-inch

TINA (102 "This Is Magic")....20-30 64

BALLARD, Florence

Singles: 7-inch

ABC (11074 "It Doesn't Matter How I Say It")....15-25 68
ABC (11144 "Love Ain't Love")....15-25 68

Picture Sleeves

ABC (11144 "Love Ain't Love")....20-30 68
Also see SUPREMES

BALLARD, Frank
(With the Philip Reynolds Band)

LPs: 10/12-inch

PHILLIPS INT'L (1985 "Rhythm & Blues Party")....800-1200 62

BALLARD, Hank, & Midnighters *R&B '59*

Singles: 78 rpm

KING (5171 "The Twist")....150-250 59
KING (5195 "Kansas City")....175-275 59
KING (5215 "Sugaree")....200-300 59

Singles: 7-inch

GUSTO....4-6 78
KING (5171 "The Twist")....20-30 59
KING (5195 "Kansas City")....15-25 59
KING (5215 "Sugaree")....10-20 59
(Monaural.)
KING (S-5215 "Sugaree")....30-40 59
(Stereo.)
KING (5245 thru 6131)....10-20 59-67
KING (6177 "I'm Back to Stay")....25-35 68
LE JOINT....4-6 79

Picture Sleeves

KING (5491 "The Continental Walk")....20-30 61

EPs: 7-inch

FEDERAL (333 "Their Greatest Hits")..200-300 54
KING (333 "Their Greatest Hits")....25-50 58
KING (435 "Singin' and Swingin, Vol. 1").25-35 59
KING (435 "Singin' and Swingin, Vol. 2").25-35 59
KING (793 "Jumpin' Hank Ballard")....25-35 62
KING (7815 "1963 Sound of Hank Ballard and Midnighters")....15-25 59

LPs: 10/12-inch

FEDERAL (295-90 "Their Greatest Hits")....10000-15000 54
(10-inch LP.)
FEDERAL (541 "Their Greatest Hits")....750-1000 57
(White cover.)
FEDERAL (541 "Their Greatest Hits")..400-600 57
(Tan or red cover.)
Note: Copies of Federal **571** are bootlegs.
KING (541 "Their Greatest Jukebox Hits")....600-800 58
KING (581 "Midnighters, Volume Two")....200-300 58
KING (618 "Singin' and Swingin'")....75-125 59
KING (674 "The One and Only")....50-75 60
KING (700 "Mr. Rhythm and Blues")....50-75 60
KING (K-740 "Spotlight on Hank Ballard")....50-75 61
(Monaural.)
KING (KS-740 "Spotlight on Hank Ballard")....75-125 61
(Stereo.)
KING (748 "Let's Go Again")....25-50 61
KING (759 "Sing Along")....25-50 61
KING (781 "Twistin' Fools")....25-50 61
KING (793 "Jumpin'")....25-50 62
KING (815 "1963 Sound")....25-50 63
KING (867 "Biggest Hits")....25-50 63
KING (896 "A Star in Your Eyes")....20-40 64
KING (913 "Those Lazy Lazy Days")....20-40 65
KING (927 "Glad Songs, Sad Songs")....15-25 66
KING (950 "24 Hit Tunes")....15-25 66
KING (981 "24 Great Songs")....15-25 68
KING (5000 "20 Hits")....8-10 77
POWER PAK (276 "Mr. Rhythm and Blues")....10-15
Also see BALLARD, Hank
Also see JOHN, Little Willie / Hank Ballard & Midnighters
Also see MIDNIGHTERS
Also see MOORE, Henry
Also see ROYALS

BALLARD, Hank, & Midnighters / Viceroys

Singles: 7-inch

KING/BETHLEHEM (5719 "That Low Down Move")....10-15 63
(The Viceroys side has a Bethlehem label. Promotional issue only.)
Also see BALLARD, Hank, & Midnighters
Also see VICEROYS

BALLARD, Jerry

Singles: 7-inch

SKIPPY (120-60 "Pinch Me")....50-75 60

BALLARD, Jimmie Lee

Singles: 7-inch

REM (305 "Say You'll Be Mine"....150-250 60

BALLARD, Kenny
(With the Fabulous Soul Brothers)

Singles: 7-inch

GENIE (101 "Lady of Stone")....15-25 '60s
KAPP (602 "Mr. Magic")....10-20 64
ROULETTE (4716 "Your Letter")....5-10 66
TOY (105 "I Wanna Love You")....10-20 63

BALLARD, Lil' Willie

LPs: 10/12-inch

KING (737 "Hit Makers and Record Breakers")....40-50 60

BALLARDS

Singles: 7-inch

VELTONE (1738 "I Hope I Never Fall in Love")....75-125 '60s

BALLENGER, Paul, & Flares

Singles: 7-inch

REED (711 "I Still Love You")....50-100 58

REED (1030 "I Hear Thunder") 150-250 59

BALLENTINES

Singles: 7-inch

DEBONAIR (190 "I Feel Your Love") 15-25
LEDO (902 "I Feel Your Love") 20-30

BALLOU, Classie, & His Tempo Kings

Singles: 7-inch

EXCELLO (2134 "Dream Love") 10-20 58
GOLDBAND (1037 "Dirty Deal") 15-20 56
LANOR (583 "C'est Si Bon") .... 4-6 '70s
LANOR (593 "All Night Man") .... 4-6 '70s
NASCO (6000 "Crazy Mambo") 10-20 57

BALTINEERS

Singles: 78 rpm

TEENAGE 50-75 56

Singles: 7-inch

LOST NITE (114 "Tears in My Eyes") ...... 15-25 '60s
(Red vinyl.)
TEENAGE (1000 "Moments Like This") 150-200 56
TEENAGE (1002 "Tears in My Eyes") . 450-550 56

BANCHEE

Singles: 7-inch

ATLANTIC (2708 "I Just Don't Know") 10-20 70

LPs: 10/12-inch

ATLANTIC (8240 "Banchee") 15-25 69
POLYDOR (4066 "Thinkin' ") 50-75 71
Members: Victor Digilio; Michael Marino; Jose Dejesus; Peter Alongi.

BAND, The P&R/LP '68

Singles: 7-inch

CAPITOL 8-12 67-68
CAPITOL 5-10 69-76
W.B. (8592 "The Well") 4-8 78

Picture Sleeves

CAPITOL (2705 "Rag Mama Rag") 5-10 70

LPs: 10/12-inch

CAPITOL (Except 2955) 10-15 69-85
CAPITOL (2955 "Music from Big Pink") ... 15-20 68
MFSL (039 "Music from Big Pink") 100-125 80
W.B. (737 "The Last Waltz") 20-30 78
(Promotional issue only.)
W.B. (3146 "The Last Waltz") 15-20 78
(Three-LP set.)
Members: Levon Helm; Rick Danko; Garth Hudson; Richard Manuel; Robbie Robertson.
Also see DYLAN, Bob
Also see HAWKINS, Ronnie
Also see LEVON & HAWKS
Also see MILLER, Steve / Band / Quicksilver Messenger Service

BANDITS / Dynamics

Singles: 7-inch

EMJAY (1928 "Nothing Can Change My Love for You"/"That's Bad") 30-40 63
EMJAY (1935 "Nothing Can Change My Love for You"/"This Love of Ours") 10-20 63

BANDLONS

Singles: 7-inch

SONIC (82661 "Miserlou") 20-30 61

BANDMASTERS

Singles: 7-inch

NASHVILLE PROD. ("Stump Jumper") . 50-100
(Selection number not known.)

BANDY, Moe C&W '74
(With Janie Fricke)

Singles: 7-inch

COLUMBIA 3-6 75-85
CURB 3-5 88-89
FOOTPRINT 5-10 74
GRC 4-6 74-75
MCA/CURB 3-5 86-87

LPs: 10/12-inch

COLUMBIA 5-10 76-85
FANFARE 5-10
GRC 10-15 74-75
MCA/CURB 5-8 86
Session: Janie Fricke; Jordanaires; Merle Haggard; Bobby Wood; Johnny Gimble; Laverna Moore; Pig Robbins; Terry McMillan.
Also see FRICKE, Janie
Also see HAGGARD, Merle
Also see JORDANAIRES

BANDY, Moe, & Becky Hobbs C&W '83

Singles: 7-inch

COLUMBIA 3-5 83

BANDY, Moe, & Joe Stampley
(Moe & Joe) C&W '79

Singles: 7-inch

COLUMBIA 3-5 79-85

LPs: 10/12-inch

COLUMBIA 5-10 81-84
Also see BANDY, Moe
Also see STAMPLEY, Joe

BANES, Jerry

Singles: 7-inch

PACE (1020 "Won't You Be My Baby") 150-250

BANGERS

Singles: 7-inch

R&B (101 "Baby, Let Me Bang Your Box") 15-25 65

BANGS

Singles: 7-inch

DOWNKIDDIE (001 "Getting Out of Hand") 25-35 81

Picture Sleeves

DOWNKIDDIE (001 "Getting Out of Hand") 40-60 81
Members: Vicki Peterson; Debbi Peterson; Susanna Hoffs.

BANISTER, James, & His Combo

Singles: 78 rpm

STATES (141 "Gold Digger") 50-75 55

Singles: 7-inch

STATES (141 "Gold Digger") 150-200 55

BANJO JO'S

Singles: 7-inch

DATE (1008 "Roving Gambler") 10-20 58

BANKS, Barbara

Singles: 7-inch

MGM (13786 "Sonny Boy") 8-10 67
SMASH (2011 "Livin' Love") 10-15 65
VEEP (1247 "Living in the Past") 10-15 66

BANKS, Bessie

Singles: 7-inch

BLUE CAT (106 "Go Now") 5-10 65
QUALITY 4-6 76
SPOKANE (4009 "Do It Now") 10-15 64
(First issue.)
TIGER (102 "Go Now") 10-15 64
VERVE (10519 "I Can't Make It") 5-8 67
VOLT (4112 "Ain't No Easy Way") 4-6 74
WAND (163 "Do It Now") 8-12 64
Also see JONES, Linda / Bessie Banks

BANKS, Buddy
(With Baby Davis)

Singles: 78 rpm

SPECIALTY (336 "Happy Home Blues") .. 15-25 49

BANKS, Darrell P&R/R&B '66

Singles: 7-inch

ATCO (6471 "Here Come the Tears") 10-20 67
ATCO (6484 "Angel Baby") 15-25 67
COTILLION (44006 "I Wanna Go Home") .. 5-10 68
REVILOT (201 "Our Love") 30-50 66
REVILOT (203 "Baby Whatcha Got") 30-50 66
SOULTOWN 5-10 66
VOLT (4014 "Just Because Your Love Has Gone") 5-10 69

LPs: 10/12-inch

ATCO (216 "Darrell Banks Is Here") 15-25 67
(Monaural.)
ATCO (216 "Darrell Banks Is Here") 25-30 67
(Stereo.)
VOLT (6002 "Here to Stay") 10-15 69

BANKS, Dick

Singles: 7-inch

LIBERTY (55145 "Dirty Dog") 25-35 58
LIBERTY (55507 "Just Like You") 8-12 62

BANKS, Douglas
(Doug Banks)

Singles: 7-inch

ARGO (5483 "I Just Kept on Dancing") 25-50 64
GUYDEN (2082 "Ain't That Just Like a Woman") 25-50 63

BANKS, Eddie
(With the Five Dreamers)

Singles: 78 rpm

GALE (1000 "I Didn't Know") 15-20 57
JOSIE (804 "Rock a Bye Blues") 10-15 56

Singles: 7-inch

GALE (1000 "I Didn't Know") 15-20 57
JOSIE (804 "Rock a Bye Blues") 30-40 56

BANKS, Homer

Singles: 7-inch

GENIE (1000 "Hooked By Love") 25-50
MINIT (32000 "A Lot of Love") 15-25 66
MINIT (32008 "Sixty Minutes of Your Love") 15-25 66
MINIT (32020 "Hooked By Love") 15-25 67
MINIT (32036 "Foolish Hearts Break First") 15-25 68
MINIT (32056 "I Know You Know") 15-25 69

BANKS, Johnny, & Everglades

Singles: 7-inch

BPV ("While Sitting in the Corner") 800-1200 63
(No selection number used.)

BANKS, Larry
(Larry Banks / Sam Jackson)

Singles: 7-inch

DCP (1133 "I'm Comin' Home") 10-15 65
KAPP (865 "I'm Not the One") 15-25 67
SELECT (722 "Will You Wait") 15-25 63
SPRING (105 "We Got a Problem") 10-15 70

BANKS, Mack
(With His Drifting Troubadours; Mac Banks)

Singles: 7-inch

FAME (580 "Be-Boppin' Daddy") 500-750 59
(500 made.)
VEE-EIGHT (131 "Sloopy Drunk") 80-120 61
Also see MR. M.B.

BANKS, Otis
(With the Majors)

Singles: 7-inch

BOW (304 " She's My Baby") 15-25 58
GALE (1002 "Don't Take My Word") 15-25 58

BAN-LONS

Singles: 7-inch

FIDELITY (4051 "Hey Baby") 100-150 62
FIDELITY (4056 "I Like It") 100-150 62

BANSHEES

Singles: 7-inch

DUNWICH (129 "Project Blue") 15-25 66
Also see ARIEL

BANSHEES

Singles: 7-inch

SOLO (1 "They Prefer Blondes") 20-30 66

BANTA, Benny

Singles: 7-inch

SOLA (4 "You're Still My Baby") 20-30
VIV (101 "Cry Little Girlie") 50-75 59

BANTAMS

Singles: 7-inch

DECCA (31040 "My Swing Is Broke") 10-15 60
DECCA (31040 "My Swing Is Broke") 20-30 60
(Pink promotional issue.)

BARAKAT, Johnny, & Vestells

Singles: 7-inch

DELL STAR (103 "Happy Time") 25-35 64
Session: Johnny Barakat; Dave Tunno; Dan Bilbery; Danny Poore; Mark Piscatelli; Terry Gibbon.

BARB, Gerry

Singles: 7-inch

ATB (4135 "About the Beetles") .... 25-35 '60s

BARBARA & BROWNS P&R/R&B '64

Singles: 7-inch

CADET (5544 "Plenty of Room") 5-10 66
SOUND OF MEMPHIS 4-6 72
STAX (150 "Big Party") 10-20 64
STAX (158 "In My Heart") 10-20 64
Members: Barbara Brown; Roberta Brown; Betty Brown; Maurice Brown.
Also see BROWN, Barbara

BARBARA & SILVER SLIPPERS

Singles: 7-inch

LESCAY (3001 "Laughing at Me") 50-75 61

BARBARA JEAN
(With the Lyrics)

Singles: 7-inch

BIG HIT (107 "Any Two Can Play") 30-50
COMET (2162 "Don't Remind Me of Tommy") 5-10 64

BARBARA JEAN & TEENS

Singles: 7-inch

ALLISON (920 "Reflection of You") 20-30 62

BARBARIANS P&R '65

Singles: 7-inch

JOY (290 "Hey Little Bird") 20-30 64
LAURIE (3308 "Are You a Boy or Are You a Girl") 15-20 65
LAURIE (3321 "What the New Breed Say") 10-15 65
LAURIE (3326 "Moulty") 20-25 65

LPs: 10/12-inch

LAURIE (2033 "The Barbarians") 50-70 66
RHINO 5-10 79
Also see ELEGANTS

BARBAROSO & HISTORIANS

Singles: 7-inch

JADE (110/120 "When I Fall in Love"/"Zoom") 50-75 64
Also see ADDEO, Nicky

BARBATA, Johnny

LPs: 10/12-inch

DEL-FI 25-35 63
Also see FULLER, Bobby
Also see SENTINELS

BARBEES

Singles: 7-inch

STEPP (236 "The Wind") 50-75 60
Members: Carolyn Gill, Sandra Tilley; Betty Kelly.
Also see VELVELETTES

BARBER, Chris P&R/R&B '59
(Chris Barber's Jazz Band)

Singles: 7-inch

ATLANTIC (2016 "Hush-A-Bye") 5-10 59
LAURIE 5-10 58-63
LONDON 5-10 62

Picture Sleeves

LAURIE (3022 "Petite Fleur") 10-20 59

LPs: 10/12-inch

ARCHIVE OF FOLK MUSIC 8-12 68
ATLANTIC (1292 "Here Is") 15-25 59
COLPIX (404 "Petite But Great") 15-25 59
LAURIE 20-30 59-62

BARBER, Don, & Dukes

Singles: 7-inch

PERSONALITY (3505 "I'll Be Blue") 75-100 62
THUNDERBIRD (105 "What's Your Name") 25-35 60

BARBER, Glenn C&W '64

Singles: 78 rpm

STARDAY (Except 166 & 249) 5-10 54-56
STARDAY (166 "Ice Water") 10-20 54
STARDAY (249 "Shadow My Baby") 15-25 56

Singles: 7-inch

CENTURY 21 .... 4-6 78-79
D (1069 "Most Beautiful") 8-12 59
D (1098 "Go Home Letter") 8-12 59
GROOVY 4-6 77
HICKORY 5-8 68-74
MMI 4-6 79
PIC-1 (137 "We'll Take Our Last Walk Tonight") 10-20 62
SIMS (148 "How Can I Forget You") 5-10 63
SKILL (002 "April Fool") 8-12 62
STARDAY (Except 166, 196, 249 & 600 series) 8-12 54-56
STARDAY (166 "Ice Water") 200-300 54
STARDAY (196 "Poor Man's Baby") 200-300 54
STARDAY (249 "Shadow My Baby") 200-300 56
STARDAY (600 series) 5-10 64
SUNBIRD 3-5 80

LPs: 10/12-inch

BRYLEN 5-10 83-84
HICKORY 8-12 70-72
HICKORY/MGM 5-10 74
TUDOR 5-10 83

BARCLAY, Eddie *P&R '55*
(Eddie Barclay & His Orchestra)
Singles: 78 rpm
MERCURY 10-20 57
RAMA 5-10 55
TICO 5-10 55
Singles: 7-inch
MERCURY (71098 "Ten Little Tears") 10-20 57
RAMA (66 "The Bandit") 5-10 55
TICO (249 "The Bandit") 15-20 55
U.A. (155 "Paris Blues") 5-10 59
LPs: 10/12-inch
MONUMENT (8055 "Plays Paris") 10-20 66
(Monaural.)
MONUMENT (18055 "Plays Paris") 10-20 66
(Stereo.)
U.A. (3023 "Americans in Paris") 15-25 59

BARCLAY, Phil
Singles: 7-inch
DOKE (101 "Young Long John") 100-200 59
DOKE (102 "Short Fat Ben") 100-200 59
DOKE (104 "Loving Baby") 100-125 59

BARCLAY STARS
LPs: 10/12-inch
ATCO (194 "Guitars Unlimited") 20-30 66

BARD, Annette
Singles: 7-inch
IMPERIAL (5643 "What Difference Does It Make") 20-25 60
Also see CONNORS, Carol

BARDI, Dick, & Orchids
Singles: 7-inch
MAESTRO (409 "Stormy Weather") 15-25

BARDOT, Brigitte
Singles: 7-inch
MGM (13099 "Sidonie") 5-10 62
LPs: 10/12-inch
BURLINGTON CAMEO (1000 "Special Bardot") 75-125 68
(TV soundtrack. Promotional issue made for Burlington Cameo.)
DECCA (8685 "And God Created Woman") 60-75 58
(Soundtrack.)
PHILIPS 15-25 63
POPLAR (1002 "Girl in the Bikini") 175-225 59
(Soundtrack.)
U.A. (4135 "Viva Maria") 12-15 66
(Soundtrack. Monaural.)
U.A. (5135 "Viva Maria") 15-25 66
(Soundtrack. Stereo.)
W.B. 10-20
Also see RUGOLO, Pete, & His Orchestra

BARDS
Singles: 78 rpm
DAWN 30-40 54
Singles: 7-inch
DAWN (208 "I'm a Wine Drinker") 100-150 54
DAWN (209 "Gravy") 50-75 54

BARDS
Singles: 7-inch
BURDETTE (103 "I Want You") 5-10 71
CAPITOL 10-15 67-68
JERDEN (907 "Tunesmith") 5-10 69
MERIDIAN (100 "Surrey with a Fringe on Top") 10-20 65
NO LABEL NAME (2148 "The Owl and the Pussycat"/"Light of Love") 15-25 67
(No label name shown.
PARROT 8-12 69-70
PICCADILLY (232 "Jabberwocky") 10-20 66
PICCADILLY (242 "Light of Love") 10-20 67
Picture Sleeves
CAPITOL (2148 "The Owl and the Pussycat") 10-20 67
MERIDIAN (100 "Surrey with a Fringe on Top") 20-30 65
LPs: 10/12-inch
PICCADILLY/FIRST AMERICAN (3419 "The Bards") 30-50 80

BARDS
Singles: 7-inch
EMCEE (13 "Alibis") 20-30 66

BARE, Bobby *C&W/P&R '62*
(With the All American Boys; with Hillsiders; with Bobby Bare Jr; Bobby Bare & Family; with Jeannie Bare)
Singles: 78 rpm
CAPITOL 5-10 57
Singles: 7-inch
CAPITOL 10-15 57
COLUMBIA 3-6 78-85
EMI AMERICA 3-5 85-86
FRATERNITY (848 "Sputnik No. 2") 10-20 59
FRATERNITY (861 "I'm Hanging Up My Rifle") 10-20 59
FRATERNITY (867 "More Than a Poor Boy Can Give") 10-20 60
FRATERNITY (871 "Lynchin' Party") 10-20 60
FRATERNITY (878 "Lorena") 15-25 61
FRATERNITY (885 "Island of Love") 10-20 61
FRATERNITY (890 "Brooklyn Bridge") 10-20 61
FRATERNITY (892 "That Mean Old Clock") 10-20 61
JACKPOT (48010 "Tender Years") 10-20 58
MERCURY 4-6 70-72
RCA (Except 8000 & 9000 series) 4-6 69-77
RCA (8000 & 9000 series) 5-10 62-68
RICE 4-6 73-74
Picture Sleeves
RCA 8-15 62-65
LPs: 10/12-inch
CAMDEN 8-12 68-73
COLUMBIA 5-10 78-85
MERCURY 10-15 70-72
OVATION 5-10 80
PHONORAMA 5-8 82
PICKWICK 5-10 75-80
PICKWICK/HILLTOP 10-15 65
RCA (ANL1 & APL1 series) 8-12 73-77
RCA (AYL1 series) 5-10 81
RCA (0079 "Singin' in the Kitchen") 15-25 74
(Promotional issue only.)
RCA (LPM-2776 thru LPM-3994) 10-20 63-68
(Monaural.)
RCA (LSP-2776 thru LSP-3994) 15-25 63-68
(Stereo.)
RCA (4000 series) 10-15 69-71
RCA (6000 series) 8-15 73
SEARS 10-15
SUN (136 "Bobby Bare's Greatest Hits") .. 15-25 74
U.A. 8-12 75-76
Session: Anita Kerr Singers; Floyd Cramer; Lacy J. Dalton; Charlie Daniels; Waylon Jennings.
Also see CRAMER, Floyd
Also see DANIELS, Charlie
Also see JENNINGS, Waylon
Also see KERR, Anita
Also see ORBISON, Roy / Bobby Bare / Joey Powers
Also see PARSONS, Bill
Also see STEWART, Wynn

BARE, Bobby, Liz Anderson & Norma Jean *C&W '66*
Singles: 7-inch
RCA (8963 "Game of Triangles") 5-10 66
LPs: 10/12-inch
BARE TRACKS 8-12
RCA 15-20 67
Also see ANDERSON, Liz
Also see NORMA JEAN

BARE, Bobby, & Skeeter Davis *C&W '65*
(Skeeter Davis & Bobby Bare)
Singles: 7-inch
RCA (8000 & 9000 series) 4-6 65-70
LPs: 10/12-inch
RCA 15-20 65-70
Also see DAVIS, Skeeter

BARE, Bobby, / Donna Fargo / Jerry Wallace
LPs: 10/12-inch
OUT OF TOWN DIST 5-10 82
Also see BARE, Bobby
Also see WALLACE, Jerry

BARE, Spence
(With Jim Wilcox)
Singles: 78 rpm
LIBERTY BELL 20-30 54
MCI 15-25 56
Singles: 7-inch
LIBERTY BELL (9004 "Shouldn't Be Seeing You") 30-40 54
MCI (1001 "Boogie Billy") 25-35 56

BARE FACTS
Singles: 7-inch
JOSIE (978 "To Think") 10-15 67
JUBILEE (5544 "Bad Part of Town") 15-25 66

BARGE, Gene
Singles: 78 rpm
CHECKER 10-20 54
LEGION 5-10
Singles: 7-inch
CHECKER (839 "Way Down Home") 20-30 54
CHECKER (1110 "Fine Twine") 5-10 65
LEGION 8-10
LEGRAND (1006 "Thinking of You") 15-25 61
PARAMOUNT (0160 "Gina") 4-6 72
LPs: 10/12-inch
CHECKER (2994 "Dance with Daddy G") 20-30 65
Also see BONDS, Gary "U.S."
Also see CHURCH STREET FIVE
Also see DADDY G
Also see WILLIS, Chuck

BARIN, Pete
(With the Pete Bennett Orchestra; Peter Barin)
Singles: 7-inch
SABINA (504 "Broken Heart") 30-40 62
SABINA (512 "Look Out for Cindy") 10-20 63
Session: Belmonts.
Also see BELMONTS

BARITONES
Singles: 7-inch
DORE (501 "After School Rock") 75-125 58

BARKDULL, Wiley
(Wiley & Jessie Barkdull)
Singles: 7-inch
ALL STAR 8-12 61-65
HICKORY (1074 "Hey Honey") 25-50 58

BARKER, Blue Lu *R&B '48*
Singles: 78 rpm
APOLLO 5-10 46-48
CAPITOL 10-15 48-50
DECCA 10-20 39-40
Singles: 7-inch
CAPITOL 20-30 50

BARKER, Delbert
Singles: 78 rpm
KING 10-15 56
TOP TUNES 5-10 54
Singles: 7-inch
GATEWAY (11602 "Blue Suede Shoes") .30-50
KING (4951 "No Good Robin Hood") 50-75 56
TOP TUNES 8-12 54

BARKER BROTHERS
Singles: 7-inch
DECCA (30811 "Lovin' Honey") 10-20 59
KENT (302 "Hey Little Mama") 75-100 58
RCA (8405 "Shh! Don't Wake Me Up") 10-20 64
VALIANT (6018 "Drifter") 8-12 62

BARKLE, Al
(With the Tritones; with Starliners; with Rosie & Romella)
Singles: 7-inch
FRANTIC (108 "Muscle Beach") 25-50 58
FRANTIC (110 "Soda Date") 25-50 59
FRANTIC (111 "Come Summer") 25-50 59
KOO-KOO (1001 "Wait 'Till the Commercial") 15-25
M&M (4041 "Jumpin' from Six to Six") .. 250-350 '50s
VITA (171 "Teen-Age Angel") 15-25 58
VITA (173 "With This Ring") 10-20 58

BARLOW, Dean
(With the Crickets; with Charles Shirley & Orchestra)
Singles: 78 rpm
DAVIS 50-75 56
JAY-DEE 50-75 54-55
Singles: 7-inch
BEACON (463 "True Love") 15-25 59
DAVIS (444 "Hi Ya Honey") 75-125 56
DAVIS (446 "Truthfully") 75-125 57
DAVIS (450 "True Love") 75-125 57
JAY-DEE (785 "Your Love") 200-300 54
(Pink label.)
JAY-DEE (785 "Your Love") 50-100 54
(Yellow label.)
JAY-DEE (786 "Just You") 100-150 54
JAY-DEE (789 "Are You Looking for a Sweetheart") 100-150 54
JAY-DEE (795 "I'm Going to Live My Life Alone") 75-125 54
JAY-DEE (799 "I'll String Along with You") 75-125 55
JAY-DEE (803 "Forever") 100-150 55
JAY-DEE (805 "True Love") 100-150 55
LESCAY (3004 "Third Window from the Right") 100-150 61
LESCAY (3010 "The Night Before Last") 15-25 61
RUST (5068 "Don't Let Him Take My Baby") 10-15 63
7 ARTS (704 "Little Sister") 50-75 61
TCF (12 "Glory of Love") 15-25 64
U.T. (4001 "You're Mine") 75-125 59
WARWICK (556 "Come Back") 10-15 60
WARWICK (618 "It's All in Your Mind") 10-20 61
Also see BACHELORS
Also see CRICKETS

BARLOW, Dean, & Bachelors
Singles: 7-inch
EARL (102 "Baby") 800-1000 57
(White label. Promotional issue only.)
EARL (102 "Baby") 600-800 57
(Orange label.)
Members: Dean Barlow; Bill Lindsay; Joe Dias.
Also see BACHELORS

BARLOW, Dean, & Crickets / Deep River Boys
Singles: 78 rpm
BEACON 30-50 54
Singles: 7-inch
BEACON (104 "Be Faithful"/"Sleepy Little Cowboy") 75-125 54
Also see CRICKETS
Also see DEEP RIVER BOYS

BARLOW, Dean, & Montereys
Singles: 78 rpm
ONYX 20-40 57
Singles: 7-inch
ONYX (513 "Dearest One") 75-100 57
ONYX (517 "Angel") 5-10 74
(Black vinyl. Previously unreleased.)
ONYX (517 "Angel") 10-15 74
(Blue vinyl. Previously unreleased.)
RELIC (511 "Dearest One") 5-10 64
Also see BARLOW, Dean
Also see MONTEREYS

BARNARD, Hubert
Singles: 7-inch
BURDETTE (787 "Boy Has She Gone") .. 50-75

BARNER, Juke Boy, & Group
(Juke Boy Bonner)
Singles: 7-inch
IRMA (111 "Rock with Me Baby") 200-300 58
Also see BONNER, Juke Boy

BARNES, Benny *C&W '56*
(Ben E. Barnes)
Singles: 78 rpm
STARDAY 10-20 56-57
Singles: 7-inch
D (1052 "Gold Records in the Snow") 25-50 59
GUYDEN 4-6 72
HALLWAY 5-10 62-65
MEGA 8-12 72
MERCURY 15-25 58-61
MUSICOR 4-6 65-66
PLAYBOY 4-8 76-77
STARDAY (200 series) 20-40 56-57
STARDAY (400 series) 15-25 58
LPs: 10/12-inch
CRAZY CAJUN 5-10
Also see JONES, George / Benny Barnes

BARNES, Billy
(Willie Barnes)
Singles: 7-inch
LIBERTY (55421 "Until") 15-25 62
U.A. (148 "If You But Knew") 20-30 58
U.A. (157 "I'm Coming to See You") 15-25 59
U.A. (311 "C.C. Rider") 10-20 61
Session: Sultans.
Also see ADMIRALS
Also see SULTANS

BARNES, Chet, & Skylarks
Singles: 7-inch
EMBASSY (201 "Everytime It Rains") 40-50 61

BARNES, David
Singles: 7-inch
SAN (302 "Lovin' On My Mind") 50-75

BARNES, Dena
Singles: 7-inch
INFERNO (2002 "Who Am I") 150-200 62

BARNES, Dorothy
Singles: 7-inch
MILKY WAY 20-30 64
Members: Arlie Neaville; Dave Marten.
Also see NEAVILLE, Arlie

BARNES, Eddie
Singles: 7-inch
CLOCK (1008 "Sweet Girl of Mine") 15-25 58
FIESTA (001 "Sweet Lover") 25-35 58

BARNES, George
Singles: 78 rpm
DECCA 10-15 52
Singles: 7-inch
DECCA (27939 "State Street Boogie") 15-25 52
MERCURY (71968 "Spooky") 15-25 62
PLEASURE (1002 "Hot Shortnin' Bread") 15-25 59
LPs: 10/12-inch
MERCURY (2011 "Guitar Galaxies") 15-25 61
(Monaural.)
MERCURY (2020 "Guitars Galore") 15-25 62
(Monaural.)
MERCURY (6011 "Guitar Galaxies") 20-30 61
(Stereo.)
MERCURY (6020 "Guitars Galore") 20-30 62
(Stereo.)

BARNES, J.J. P&R/R&B '66
(With the Dell Fi's)
Singles: 7-inch
BUDDAH (120 "I'll Keep Coming Back") .. 10-15 69
GROOVESVILLE 10-15 67
INVASION (1001 "My Baby") 8-10 70
KABLE (913 "Won't You Let Me Know") 75-125 60
MAGIC TOUCH (1000 "Cloudy Days") 5-10 70
MICKAY'S 50-75 62-63
PERCEPTION (546 "You Are Just a Living Doll") 5-10 73
REVILOT (Except 222) 10-20 68-69
REVILOT (222 "Our Love Is in the Pocket") 50-75 68
RICH (1737 "Won't You Let Me Know"). 50-100 62
RIC-TIC 10-20 65-66
RING (101 "She Ain't Ready") 20-30 64
SCEPTER (1266 "Just One More Time") 20-30 64
VOLT (4027 "Snowflakes") 10-15 69
LPs: 10/12-inch
PERCEPTION 10-20 74

BARNES, J.J., & Steve Mancha
LPs: 10/12-inch
VOLT (6001 "Rare Stamps") 10-20 69
Also see BARNES, J.J.
Also see HOLIDAYS
Also see MANCHA, Steve

BARNES, Jennie
Singles: 78 rpm
ALADDIN (3300 "My Love Song") 8-12 55
Singles: 7-inch
ALADDIN (3300 "My Love Song") 15-25 55

BARNES, Jimmy
(With the Gibralters)
Singles: 7-inch
GIBRALTAR (101 "No Regrets") 10-15 59
GIBRALTAR (102 "I Need You So Much") 10-15 59
GIBRALTAR (106 "Don't Let Nothing Stand in Your Way") 10-15 59
SAVOY (1581 "Our Wedding Day") 10-15 59
SAVOY (1590 "You Thrill Me So Much") . 10-15 60
SUE (771 "If By Any Chance") 10-15 62

BARNES, Johnny
(Johnny Barness)
Singles: 7-inch
ADONIS (105 "Did She Ask About Me") 5-10 60
CAP CITY (122 "Real Nice") .... 15-25 '60s
FLIPPIN' (105 "No Love for Me") 15-25 61
JABA (801 "Nothing Without Your Love") 150-250

BARNES, Mae
EPs: 7-inch
ATLANTIC (502 "Mae Barnes Sings") 30-50 53
LPs: 10/12-inch
ATLANTIC (404 "Fun with Mae Barnes") 150-200 53
(With the Three Flames. 10-inch LP.)
VANGUARD 20-30 58
Also see THREE FLAMES

BARNES, Orthea
(Orthela Barnes)
Singles: 7-inch
ABC-PAR (10434 "Your Picture on the Wall") 10-15 63
CORAL (62529 "Waiting for Joey") 8-12 67
MICKAY'S (350 "Your Picture on the Wall 40-50 62

BARNES, Sidney
Singles: 12-inch
PARACHUTE 4-6 78
Singles: 7-inch
BLUE CAT (125 "I Hurt on the Other Side") 75-125 66
BLUE STONE (402 "Shindig") .... 10-15 '60s
CHESS (2094 "Baloney") 6-10 65
GEMINI (101 "Wait") 10-15 61
PARACHUTE (521 "Hold on I'm Coming") ... 4-6 78
RED BIRD (039 "You'll Always Be in Style") 25-35 65
RED BIRD (054 "I Hurt on the Other Side") 5-10 65
LPs: 10/12-inch
PARACHUTE 5-10 78
Also see ROTARY CONNECTION
Also see SERENADERS

BARNETT, Billy
Singles: 7-inch
KSS (8701 "Rock It Billy") 40-60

BARNETT, Billy
Singles: 7-inch
DOUBLE B (1113 "Romp & Stomp") 150-200
PARKWAY (826 "Marlene") 20-30 61
TEX (105 "Tired of Your Honky Tonk Love") 150-200

BARNETT, Bobby C&W '60
Singles: 7-inch
BANNISTER 4-6 73
CIN KAY (128 "Burn Atlanta Down") 4-6 78
COLUMBIA 4-6 68-69
HERITAGE 4-6 74
K-ARK 5-10 67-68
PRESTA .... 4-6 '60s
RAZORBACK (012 "Brother, I've Had It") 5-10 59
RAZORBACK (306 "This Old Heart") 10-20 60
SIMS (Except 177) 10-15 63-67
SIMS (177 "John Said") 40-60 64
LPs: 10/12-inch
COLUMBIA (9790 "Lyin' Lovin' and Leavin' ") 8-15 69
HERITAGE 5-10 74
SIMS (118 "At the Crystal Palace") 15-25 64

BARNETT, James
Singles: 7-inch
FAME (1001 "Take a Good Look") 10-20 66

BARNETT, Julian, & Talents
Singles: 7-inch
HERALD (519 "Come Back to Me") 30-40 58

BARNETTE, Billy
(With the Searchers; with Divots and Ron Sunshine Orchestra)
Singles: 7-inch
MT. VERNON (500 "Don't Let Our Love Go Wrong") 500-750 62
MT. VERNON (501 "Billy the Kid") .... ?
(We're listing this because we have seen it; however, we have no opinions yet as to value. We cannot automatically assume it to be in the price range of Mt. Vernon 500. What say you?)

BARNETTE, Johnny
Singles: 7-inch
VANCE (481 "Shadow My Baby") 500-750

BARNEY & GOOGLES
Singles: 7-inch
SHIMMY (1055 "Doin' the Shimmy") 200-300 60

BARNHILL, Shorty
Singles: 7-inch
ISLAND EMPIRE (779 "I'm a Sad Sack") 75-125

BARNICOAT, Alan
Singles: 7-inch
ROCKET (105 "Savage") 50-75 59

BARNUM, H.B. P&R '61
Singles: 7-inch
CAPITOL (Except 5932) 5-10 65-68
CAPITOL (5932 "Heartbreaker") 20-40 67
DECCA 4-6 71
ELDO (111 "Lost Love") 10-20 60
IMPERIAL (5583 "Blue Moon") 10-15 58
IMPERIAL (66011 "Backstage") 8-12 64
IMPERIAL (66046 "Ska Drums") 8-12 64
IMPERIAL (66063 "Calypso Blues") 8-12 64
IMPERIAL (66074 "So What") 8-12 64
MUN RAB (103 "Don't-Cha Know") 8-12 59
RCA (7960 "Baby Baby Baby") 8-12 61
RCA (8014 "Call On Me") 8-12 62
RCA (8112 "It Hurts Too Much to Cry") 40-60 62
RCA (8155 "Take Me Out to the Ball Game") 8-12 63
ULTRA SONIC (107 "Just Goofin' ") 8-12 60
U.A. 4-6 73
Picture Sleeves
RCA (8112 "It Hurts Too Much to Cry") ... 50-75 62
LPs: 10/12-inch
CAPITOL (2278 "Golden Boy") 15-20 65
CAPITOL (2289 "Big Hits of Detroit") 15-20 65
RCA (2462 "Big Voice of Barnum – H.B. That Is") 15-20 62
RCA (2553 "Everybody Loves H.B.") 15-20 62
TROPIC ISLE (1001 "Learn to Dance the Cha Cha Cha") 15-25 59
Also see DON & DEWEY / H.B. Barnum
Also see JONE, Romeo
Also see NORMAN, Jimmy
Also see MAD LADS
Also see ROBINS

BARON, Bill
(With the Song Spinners)
Singles: 7-inch
YES (18 "Love Came to Me") 25-50 63
YES (24 "Ruby Baby") 25-50 63

BARON, Bobby
Singles: 7-inch
APT (25012 "When I Found You") 15-25 58

BARON, Elliott
Singles: 7-inch
GOLDEN WORLD (11 "The Spare Rib") .. 15-25 64

BARONS
Singles: 78 rpm
MODERN (818 "Forever") 35-50 51

BARONS
Singles: 78 rpm
DECCA 35-50 54
Singles: 7-inch
DECCA (29293 "Exactly Like You") 75-100 54
DECCA (48323 "Year and a Day") 75-100 54
Members: Leon Harrison; Roger Wainwright; Maurice Hicks; Luther Dixon.
Also see BUDDIES
Also see FOUR BUDDIES

BARONS / Mel Williams & Montclairs
EPs: 7-inch
DECCA 75-100 56
LPs: 10/12-inch
DECCA (8315 "He's a Rug Cutter") 100-150 56
Also see WILLIAMS, Mel

BARONS
Singles: 7-inch
DEMON (1520 "The Fight") 8-12 59
KEY (1001 "If You Want a Little Lovin' ") .. 15-25 59

BARONS R&B '56
Singles: 78 rpm
IMPERIAL 25-75 55-56
Singles: 7-inch
IMPERIAL (5343 "Eternally Yours") 50-100 55
(Black vinyl.)
IMPERIAL (5343 "Eternally Yours") 300-400 55
(Purple vinyl. Promotional issue only.)
IMPERIAL (5359 "My Dream My Love") 100-150 55
(Promotional issue only. DJ issue.)
IMPERIAL (5359 "My Dream My Love") 50-100 55
(Red label.)
IMPERIAL (5359 "My Dream My Love") .. 30-40 55
(Blue label.)
IMPERIAL (5370 "Cold Kisses") 75-125 55
IMPERIAL (5383 "So Long My Darling") .. 50-75 56
IMPERIAL (5397 "Don't Walk Out") 50-75 56
IMPERIAL (66057 "Silence") 10-15 64

BARONS
Singles: 7-inch
BELLAIRE (103 "Bandit") 10-20 63
DART (126 "Lonely Loretta") 10-20 60
DART (134 "Perfect Love") 10-20 61
EPIC (9586 "Pledge of a Fool") 20-30 63
EPIC (9747 "Remember Rita") 250-350 64
EPIC (10093 "Pledge of a Fool") 8-12 66

BARONS
("Formerly the Peppermints")
Singles: 7-inch
SOUL (837 "Money Don't Grow on Trees") 15-25 61
SPARTAN (400 "I've Been Hurt") 15-25 61
SPARTAN (402 "Money Don't Grow on Trees") 15-25 61
(We're not yet certain whether Soul or Spartan is the first issue.)
Also see PEPPERMINTS

BARONS
Singles: 7-inch
MIDNITE (1002 "Teenage Years") 10-20 62

BARONS
Singles: 7-inch
JAFES (985 "Try a Little Love with Me") 200-300 65
TENER (1011 "Lovin' Man") 15-25 66
TENER (1021 "Colors of Love") 15-25 67
Also see CHANCE, Larry
Also see LONNIE & CAROLLONS / Barons

BARONS
Singles: 7-inch
BROWNFIELD (1035 "Don't Burn It") 30-50 66
TORCH (101 "You're Gonna Cry") 15-20 65
TORCH (102 "I'll Never Be Happy") 10-15 65
TORCH (103 "Live and Die") 20-30 66

BARONS
Singles: 7-inch
RCA (9034 "Since You're Gone") 10-20 66

BARONS
Singles: 7-inch
MONOCLE (001 "Come to Me") 20-30 67
Also see LONNIE & CAROLLONS / Barons

BARONS
Singles: 7-inch
E&M (2901 "Dianna") 50-75
SUN-Y 10-15

BAROQUES
Singles: 7-inch
BAROQUE (53/54 "I Will Not Touch You"/ "Remember") 15-25 68
CHESS (2001 "Iowa, a Girl's Name") 10-15 67
LPs: 10/12-inch
BAROQUE (9005 "The Baroques") .... 8-12 '90s
CHESS (1516 "The Baroques") 40-60 67
Members: Rick Bieniewski; Jay Borkenhagen; Jacques Hutchinson; Dean Nimmer.
Also see MAJOR ARCANA

BAROQUES
Singles: 7-inch
VAN GOGH (2020 "Bad Girl") 20-30 67

BARR, Chuck
(With the Playboys)
Singles: 7-inch
ELSAN (1001 "Susie or Mary Lou") 50-75 58
RPC 10-15

BARR, Gloria
Singles: 7-inch
ALTA (100 "Ain't That a Crying Shame") . 25-35

BARR, Rico, & Boston Barristers

Singles: 7-inch

BOSSTOWN (1113 "I Need You Babe") . 15-25

BARRACUDA

Singles: 7-inch

RCA (9660 "The Dance at St. Francis") .. 10-20 68
RCA (9743 "Julie") 5-10 69

Picture Sleeves

RCA (9660 "The Dance at St. Francis") .. 20-35 68

BARRACUDAS

Singles: 7-inch

CUDA ("I Can't Believe") 10-20 66
(No selection number used.)
CUDA ("Days of a Quiet Sun") 8-12 69
(No selection number used.)

LPs: 10/12-inch

JUSTICE (143 "Plane View") 250-350 68

BARRACUDAS

Singles: 7-inch

ZUNDAK (101 "Baby Get Lost") 15-25 66

BARRACUDAS

Singles: 7-inch

THUNDERBIRD (877 "Saturn") ...... 20-30 '60s

BARRAN, Rob

Singles: 7-inch

SILVER STREAK (311 "Mother Goose Hop") 100-150 60

BARRELHOUSE SAMMY
(Willie Samuel)

Singles: 78 rpm

ATLANTIC (891 "Broke Down Engine Blues") 75-125 49
Also see McTELL, Blind Willie

BARRELL HOUSE BLOTT & LEE
(With the St. Louisians)

Singles: 78 rpm

CHANCE 15-25 53

Singles: 7-inch

CHANCE (1136 "Brand New Man") 75-125 53
(Black vinyl.)
CHANCE (1136 "Brand New Man") 300-400 53
(Red vinyl.)

BARRETT, Hugh
(With the Victors)

Singles: 7-inch

DYNAMIC SOUND (2003 "Another Lonely Soldier Boy") 15-25 66
LUCKY FOUR (1015 "Devil's Love") 75-125 61
LUCKY FOUR (1020 "Choo Choo Twist") 15-25 61
MADISON (164 "Got the Bull by the Horns") 30-50 61

BARRETT, Richard P&R '58
(With the Chantels; with Sevilles; with Morty Craft Orchestra; Richie Barrett)

Singles: 7-inch

ATLANTIC (2142 "Some Other Guy") 10-20 62
CRACKERJACK (4012 "Summer's Love") .8-12 63
GONE (5056 "Come Softly to Me") 15-25 59
GONE (5060 "Summer's Love") 50-75 59
MGM (12616 "Remember Me") 10-15 58
MGM (12659 "Body and Soul") 15-20 58
METRO (20006 "Only One Way") 15-20 58
ORCHID (5004 "Come Softly to Me") 10-15 58
SEVILLE (104 "Dream On") 10-20 60
20TH FOX (150 "Lovely One") 10-15 59
Also see CHANTELS
Also see CRAFT, Morty
Also see IMPERIALS
Also see VALENTINES

BARRETT, Ron
(With the Duals; with Buckskins)

Singles: 7-inch

MAGNUM (715 "Louie Louie") 10-20 64
RENDEZVOUS (215 "Spooky Movies") 8-12 63
Also see DUALS

BARRETT, Susan

Singles: 7-inch

PHILIPS (40147 "Between Two Loves") .. 10-20 63
PHILIPS (40247 "No One But You") 10-20 64
RCA (8888 "Grain of Sand") 10-20 66
RCA (9017 "Walking Happy") 10-20 66
RCA (9296 "What's It Gonna Be") 25-35 67
RCA (9384 "Sunny") 10-20 67

LPs: 10/12-inch

CAPITOL (1266 "Mixed Emotions") 10-20 59
CAPITOL (1412 "A Little Travelin' Music") 10-20 60
RCA (3738 "Susan Barrett") 20-40 67

BARRETTO, Ray P&R/R&B '63

Singles: 78 rpm

TICO (419 "El Watusi") 150-250 63

Singles: 7-inch

ASCOT (2202 "Viva Maria") 5-10 66
ATLANTIC 4-6 77-78
FANIA 5-15 68-72
RIVERSIDE 5-10 61
ROULETTE ......4-6 '70s
TICO 5-10 63
U.A. 5-10 65-67

LPs: 10/12-inch

ATLANTIC 5-10 76-78
CTI 5-10 81
FANIA 5-10 68-73
FANTASY 8-10 73
RIVERSIDE 10-15 61-66
TICO 10-15 62-63
U.A. 8-15 65-67
Also see LYTLE, Johnny, & Ray Barretto

BARRI, Steve
(Steve Barrie)

Singles: 7-inch

RONA (1003 "Please Let It Be You") 10-20 61
RONA (1004 "Story of the Ring") 20-30 61
RONA (1005 "Two Different Worlds") 10-20 62
RONA (1006 "Never Before") 10-20 62
TABB (103 "Flowers Mean Forgiveness") ......10-20 '60s
Also see FANTASTIC BAGGYS
Also see LIFEGUARDS
Also see STORYTELLERS

BARRIES

Singles: 7-inch

DI-NAN (101 "When You're Out of School") 40-50 65
EMBER (1101 "Tonight Tonight") 20-30 64
VERNON (102 "Why Don't You Write Me") 50-75 63
Members: Joe Marturiello; Al Battista; Guy Villano; Jimmy O'Connor; Nick Delano; Andy Smith.
Also see CHOSEN FEW

BARRIX, Billy

Singles: 78 rpm

CHESS (1662 "Cool Off Baby") 500-1000 57

Singles: 7-inch

CHESS (1662 "Cool Off Baby") 3500-5000 57
SHREVEPORT ("Cool Off Baby") .. 7500-10000 57
(Selection number not known.)

BARRON, Lonnie

Singles: 7-inch

SAGE (230 "Teenage Queen") 75-125 57

BARRON, Ronnie

Singles: 7-inch

SOUNDEX (604 "It's All in the Past") 10-20 65
WHEELER DEALERS (505 "The Grass Looks Greener") 5-8

BARRONS

Singles: 7-inch

KRCO (101 "Song of Songs") 50-75 59

BARRY, Bolean

Singles: 7-inch

FABOR (137 "Long Sideburns") 50-75 56

BARRY, Dave, & Sara Berner

Singles: 78 rpm

RPM 8-12 56

Singles: 7-inch

RPM (469 "Out of This World with Flying Saucers") 15-25 56
Session: Jacks.
Also see JACKS

BARRY, Jack
(With Ray Charles Singers; with Winky Dink)

Singles: 78 rpm

DECCA (88173 "Winko") ......5-10 '50s
DECCA (88174 "Winky Dink & You") ......5-10 '50s

Singles: 7-inch

DECCA (143/296 "Winko") ......10-15 '50s
DECCA (9-88173 "Winko") ......10-15 '50s
DECCA (144/297 "Winky Dink & You") ....10-15 '50s
DECCA (9-88174 "Winky Dink & You") ....10-15 '50s
(We have located these different numbers for the same titles.)
DECCA ("Huckleberry Finn") ......10-15 '50s
(Selection number not known.)

Picture Sleeves

DECCA ("Huckleberry Finn") ......15-20 '50s
Also see CHARLES, Ray, Singers

BARRY, Jeff

Singles: 7-inch

A&M (1422 "Walkin' in the Sun") 4-6 73
BELL (45140 "Love Has Never Let Me Down") 4-6 71
DECCA (31037 "It Won't Hurt") 15-20 60
DECCA (31089 "Lenore") 15-20 60
RCA (7477 "It's Called Rock and Roll") 20-30 59
RCA (7797 "Lonely Lips") 15-25 60
RCA (7821 "Teen Quartet") 10-20 60
RED BIRD (026 "I'll Still Love You") 8-10 65
UA (440 "Welcome Home") 10-15 62
UA (50529 "Where It's At") 8-10 69

LPs: 10/12-inch

A&M (4393 "Walkin' in the Sun") 10-12 73
Session: King Curtis.
Also see KING CURTIS
Also see RAINDROPS
Also see REDWOODS

BARRY, Joe P&R/R&B '61

Singles: 7-inch

ABC/DOT 4-6 77
JIN (132 "Heartbroken Love") 15-25 60
JIN (144 "I'm a Fool to Care") 15-25 61
JIN (150 "Je Suis Bet Pour T'Aimer") 10-20 61
JIN (152 "Teardrops in My Heart") 15-25 61
NUGGET 5-10 68-69
PRINCESS (4005 thru 4027) ......8-12 '60s
SHOW-BIZ (2001 "I Can't Do Without You") 20-30 59
SMASH 8-12 61-62

Picture Sleeves

SMASH (1710 "Teardrops in My Heart") .. 10-20 61

LPs: 10/12-inch

ABC/DOT 5-10 77

BARRY, Len P&R/R&B/LP '65

Singles: 7-inch

AMY (11026 "4-5-6") 5-10 68
AMY (11037 "Christopher Columbus") 5-10 68
AMY (11047 "The Child Is Born") 5-10 68
BUDDAH 4-8 72
CAMEO (303 "Don't Come Back") 5-10 64
CAMEO (318 "Little White House") 5-10 64
DECCA 8-12 65-66
DOWNEY (134 "I Don't Need It") 5-10 66
MCA 3-6 73-83
MERCURY (72299 "Happy Days") 8-10 64
PARAMOUNT (0206 "Heaven Plus Earth") . 4-8 73
PARKWAY (969 "Little White House") 5-10 66
RCA 5-10 67-68
SCEPTER 5-10 69-70

EPs: 7-inch

DECCA (74720 "1-2-3") 8-15 65
(Juke box issue only.)

LPs: 10/12-inch

BUDDAH (5105 "Ups & Downs") 10-15 72
CAMEO (C-1082 "Len Barry Sings with the Dovells") 20-25 64
(Monaural.)
CAMEO (SC-1082 "Len Barry Sings with the Dovells") 25-30 64
(Stereo.)
DECCA (4720 "1-2-3") 20-25 65
(Monaural.)
DECCA (74720 "1-2-3") 25-30 65
(Stereo.)
RCA (LPM-3823 "My Kind of Soul") 15-20 67
(Monaural.)
RCA (LSP-3823 "My Kind of Soul") 15-25 67
(Stereo.)
Also see DOVELLS

BARRY, Steve

Singles: 7-inch

VERSUS (506 "The Nightmare") 50-75

BARRY & DEANS

Singles: 7-inch

APAX (1001 "Rock with Me Baby") 50-75
ZIRKON (1001 "Rock with Me Baby") 75-125 60

BARRY & HIGHLIGHTS

Singles: 7-inch

AIRMASTER (700 "Xmas Bell Rock") 10-20 60
BAYE (511 "Xmas Bell Rock") 30-40 60
(First issue.)
PLANET (1048 "The Wonderful Years") 750-1000 61

BARRY & TAMERLANES P&R/R&B '63

Singles: 7-inch

VALIANT 10-15 63-65

LPs: 10/12-inch

A&M 10-15
VALIANT (406 "I Wonder What She's Doing Tonight") 50-75 63
Members: Barry DeVorzon; Terry Smith; Bodie Chandler.

BARRY & VI-COUNTS

Singles: 7-inch

FINE (102 "Love Forever") ......200-300 '50s

BARSANTI, Tom, & Invaders

Singles: 7-inch

DELTA (2134 "You Can't Sit Down") 20-30 65

BARTEL, Johnny, & Soul Masters

Singles: 7-inch

SOLID STATE (2514 "I Waited Too Long") 50-75 70

BARTEL, Lou
(With Don Costa & Orchestra)

Singles: 78 rpm

APOLLO (473 "I Pray") 25-35 55

Singles: 7-inch

ABC-PAR (9877 "I'm Gonna Kiss My Baby Goodnight") 15-25 57
APOLLO (473 "I Pray") 75-125 55

BARTHOLOMEW, Dave R&B '50

Singles: 78 rpm

BAYOU 20-30 53
DECCA 20-40 51
DELUXE 10-20 47-50
IMPERIAL 20-50 50-57
JAX (1 "Gold Jax Boogie") 10-20 50
KING 25-50 51-52
TRUMPET (101 "Wild As a Tiger") 10-20 50

Singles: 7-inch

BAYOU (005 "Snatchin' Back") 100-125 53
DECCA (48216 "Tra-La-La") 100-125 51
IMPERIAL (5210 "Who Drank My Beer While I Was in the Rear") 100-125 52
IMPERIAL (5249 "No More Black Nights") 100-125 51
IMPERIAL (5273 "Texas Hop") 100-125 53
IMPERIAL (5322 "Another Mule") 40-60 54
IMPERIAL (5350 "Four Winds") 40-60 55
IMPERIAL (5373 "Shrimp and Gumbo") .. 40-60 56
IMPERIAL (5390 "Turn Your Lamps Down Low") 40-60 56
IMPERIAL (5408 "Lovin' You") 30-40 56
IMPERIAL (5481 "Hard Times") 30-40 56
IMPERIAL (5500 thru 5800 series) 15-30 56-61
KING (4482 "Sweet Home Blues") 100-150 51
KING (4508 "In the Alley") 100-200 52
KING (4523 "Lawdy, Lawdy Lord") 100-150 52
(Black vinyl.)
KING (4523 "Lawdy, Lawdy Lord") 200-300 52
(Red vinyl.)
KING (4544 "My Ding-A-Ling") 100-200 52
KING (4559 "The Golden Rule") 50-100 52
KING (4585 "High Flying Woman") 50-100 53

LPs: 10/12-inch

IMPERIAL (9162 "Fats Domino Presents Dave Bartholomew & His Great Big Band") 40-50 61
(Monaural.)
IMPERIAL (9217 "New Orleans House Party") 40-50 63
(Monaural.)
IMPERIAL (12076 "Fats Domino Presents Dave Bartholomew & His Great Big Band") 40-50 61
(Stereo.)
IMPERIAL (12217 "New Orleans House Party") 40-50 63
(Stereo.)
Also see ARCHIBALD
Also see DOMINO, Fats
Also see KING, Jewel
Also see LEWIS, Smiley
Also see RHODES, Todd
Also see SHIRLEY & LEE

BARTON, Bart

Singles: 7-inch

E&M (1651 "Ain't I a Mess") ... 50-75

BARTON, Billy

(Billy Boy Barton)

Singles: 78 rpm

ABBOTT ... 10-15 53

Singles: 7-inch

ABBOTT (113 "My Darlin' Liza Lou") ... 15-25 53
ABBOTT (117 "You Will Always Be in My Heart") ... 15-25 53
BILLY BARTON (1007 "A Day Late and a Dollar Short") ... 50-75
BILLY BARTON ("Crazy Lover") ... 50-75
(No label name other than "Billy Barton" used.)
GULF REEF (1001 "Monkey Business") . 10-15 61
KING ... 10-15
RADIO (117 "Doorway to Heaven") ... 10-20 58
SIMS (176 "Even Steven") ... 10-15 64
SIMS (209 "Easy Street") ... 10-15 64
VIDOR (1007 "Crazy Lover") ... 30-50

BARTON, Dick

Singles: 7-inch

ANTHEM (60726 "Yes Baby I'm Scared") ... 100-150
ANTHEM (61712 "I Get the Blues") ... 100-150

BARTON, Eileen *P&R '50*

(With the New Yorkers; with George Cates & Orchestra; with Lawrence Welk)

Singles: 78 rpm

CORAL ... 5-10 51-56
MERCURY ... 5-10 53
NATIONAL ... 5-10 50

Singles: 7-inch

CORAL ... 10-20 51-56
CREST (1107 "Oh, Love") ... 5-10 62
MGM (12758 "If I Knew You Were Comin' I'd've Baked a Cake") ... 5-10 59
MERCURY ... 8-12 53
NATIONAL (9103 "If I Knew You Were Comin' I'd've Baked a Cake") ... 25-50 50
NATIONAL (9109 "Honey, Won't You Honeymoon with Me") ... 15-25 50
NATIONAL (9112 "May I Take Two Giant Steps") ... 15-25 50
20TH FOX (417 "Earth Stood Still") ... 5-10 63
U.A. (182 "The Joke") ... 15-25 59
U.A. (206 "The Joke") ... 10-20 60

EPs: 7-inch

CORAL ... 5-10 54

LPs: 10/12-inch

CORAL ... 15-25 54
Also see BREWER, Teresa / Eileen Barton
Also see DESMOND, Johnny, Eileen Barton & McGuire Sisters
Also see WELK, Lawrence, & His Orchestra

BARTON, Eileen, & Jimmy Wakely

Singles: 78 rpm

CORAL ... 5-10 54

Singles: 7-inch

CORAL (61175 "Bright Eyed and Bushy Tailed") ... 10-15 54
CORAL (61324 "This-a Way, That-a-Way") ... 10-15 54
Also see BARTON, Eileen
Also see WAKELY, Jimmy

BARTON, Ernie

Singles: 7-inch

PHILLIPS INT'L (3528 "Stairway to Nowhere") ... 10-15 58
PHILLIPS INT'L (3541 "Open the Door Richard") ... 100-125 59
Also see JANES, Roland

BARTON, Rod

EPs: 7-inch

AIR (508 "Rock & Roll Blues") ... 200-300 '50s

BASCOMB, Dud

Singles: 7-inch

CLOCK (1023 "Swing Along") ... 10-20 60
SAVOY (1580 "Geechie Blues") ... 15-25 59
SHARP (111 "Grumpy") ... 10-20 60

BASCOMB, Paul

(Bad Bascomb; with His 11 Star Band)

Singles: 78 rpm

ALERT ... 8-12 46
LONDON ... 5-10 51
MANOR ... 8-12 46-47
MERCURY ... 5-10 52
PARROT ... 10-20 54-55
STATES ... 8-12 52-53
UNITED (192 "Mathilda") ... 5-10 55

Singles: 7-inch

MERCURY (8299 "Nona") ... 25-50 52
PARAMOUNT ... 4-6 73
PARROT (792 "Jan") ... 40-60 54
PARROT (817 "Alley B on Fifth Avenue") ... 40-60 55
STATES (102 "Blackout") ... 30-40 52
STATES (110 "Coquette") ... 30-40 52
STATES (121 "Body & Soul") ... 30-40 53
UNITED (192 "Mathilda") ... 15-25 55

LPs: 10/12-inch

DELMARK ... 5-10 77
PARAMOUNT ... 8-10 73
PARROT ("Paul Bascomb") ... 1500-2500 55
(Selection number not known, though it's likely close to 245.)

BASCOMB, Paul, & Five Arrows / Gloria Valdez

Singles: 78 rpm

PARROT ... 50-100 55

Singles: 7-inch

PARROT (816 "Pretty Little Thing"/"You've Got Me Losing My Mind") ... 250-300 55
Also see BASCOMB, Paul

BASEBALL ("HOW TO" SERIES)

Singles: 7-inch

MARS CANDY (1 "How to Hit") ... 10-20 62
(Promotional issue, made for Mars Candy.)
MARS CANDY (2 "How to Pitch") ... 10-20 62
(Promotional issue, made for Mars Candy.)
MARS CANDY (3 "How to Field") ... 10-20 62
(Promotional issue, made for Mars Candy.)

Picture Sleeves

MARS CANDY (1 "How to Hit") ... 25-50 62
(Pictures MLB players, such as Stan Musial, Ernie Banks, Duke Snider and Ken Boyer. Promotional issues, made for Mars Candy.)
MARS CANDY (2 "How to Pitch") ... 25-50 62
(Pictures MLB players, such as Don Drysdale, Warren Spahn, Joey Jay and Johnny Padres. Promotional issues, made for Mars Candy.)
MARS CANDY (3 "How to Field") ... 25-50 62
(Pictures MLB players, such as Johnny Roseboro, Willie Mays, Gil Hodges and Don Hoak. Promotional issues, made for Mars Candy.)
Also see DRYSDALE, Don
Also see MAYS, Willie

BASEMAN, M.R., & Symbols / Marty & Symbols

Singles: 7-inch

GRAPHIC ARTS (1000 "Rip Van Winkle") ... 50-100 63
Session: Richie Cordell.
Also see CORDELL, Richie

BASEMENT WALL

Singles: 7-inch

SENATE (2109 "Never Existed") ... 25-35 68

BASH, Otto

Singles: 78 rpm

HIDS ... 5-10 56
RCA ... 10-15 56

Singles: 7-inch

HIDS (2008 "My Babe") ... 10-15 56
RCA (6426 "Later Alligator") ... 15-25 56
RCA (6585 "The Elvis Blues") ... 15-25 56
Also see MARTIN, Janis / Otto Bash

BASIE, Count *P&R '37*

Singles: 78 rpm

COLUMBIA ... 5-10 43-51
CLEF ... 4-8 52-56
CORAL ... 5-10 49
DECCA (Except 1300 thru 3000 series) ... 5-10 41-53
DECCA (1300 thru 3000 series) ... 8-15 37-40
MERCURY ... 4-8 52-53
OKEH ... 4-8 52
RCA (2127 "Open the Door, Richard") ... 5-10 47

Singles: 7-inch

ABC-PAR ... 4-6 66
BRUNSWICK ... 4-6 67
CLEF ... 5-10 52-56
COLISEUM (2709 "Fortuosity") ... 5-10 68
COLUMBIA (33000 series) ... 4-6 76
COLUMBIA (38000 & 39000 series) ... 5-10 50-51
COMMAND ... 4-8 67
CORAL (60037 "Jumpin' at the Woodside") ... 15-25 49
DECCA ... 5-10 53
DOT (17201 "That Warm Feeling") ... 4-8 68
HAPPY TIGER ... 4-6 70
MERCURY ... 5-10 52-53
OKEH ... 5-10 52
REPRISE ... 4-8 63
ROULETTE (Except "SSR" series) ... 4-8 58-62
ROULETTE ("SSR" series) ... 8-15 59
(Stereo.)
U.A. ... 4-6 66
VERVE ... 4-6 60-67

EPs: 7-inch

BRUNSWICK ... 10-15 54
CAMDEN ... 8-15 58
CLEF ... 10-20 52-55
COLUMBIA ... 10-20 50
CORAL ... 10-20
DECCA ... 10-20 53
EPIC ... 10-20 55
RCA (Except 5000 series) ... 10-20 54
RCA (5000 series) ... 8-12 59
ROULETTE ... 8-12 58-60
VERVE (5062 "Jamboree") ... 30-40 57
(Soundtrack. With Joe Williams.)

LPs: 10/12-inch

ABC ... 5-10 76
ACCORD ... 5-10 82-83
AMERICAN ... 15-25 57
BRIGHT ORANGE ... 5-10 73
BRUNSWICK (54000 series) ... 10-20 63-67
BRUNSWICK (58000 series) ... 25-35 54
(10-inch LPs.)
CAMDEN ... 10-20 58-60
CIRCLE ... 40-50 54
CLEF (120 "Count Basie & His Orchestra") ... 100-200 52
(10-inch LP.)
CLEF (148 "Count Basie Big Band") ... 100-200 52
(10-inch LP.)
CLEF (164 "Count Basie Sextet") ... 100-200 52
(10-inch LP.)
CLEF (626 "Dance Session") ... 50-100 53
CLEF (647 "Dance Session, Vol. 2") ... 50-100 53
CLEF (633 "Basieana") ... 50-100 53
CLEF (666 "Basie") ... 50-100 54
CLEF (678 "Basie Swings – Joe Williams Sings") ... 50-100 55
CLEF (685 "Count Basie") ... 50-80 56
CLEF (700 series) ... 20-30 56
COLISEUM ... 8-12 67
COLUMBIA (700 & 900 series) ... 20-30 56-57
COLUMBIA (6079 "Dance Parade") ... 25-35 49
(10-inch LPs)
COLUMBIA (31000 series) ... 10-12 72
COMMAND ... 10-20 66-71
CORAL ... 10-20
CROWN (143 "Compositions of Count Basie and Others") ... 15-20 59
(Stereo. Credits: "Members of the Count Basie Orchestra – B.B. King Guest Vocalist.")
CROWN (143 "Compositions of Count Basie and Others") ... 20-30 59
(Stereo. Red vinyl. Credits: "Members of the Count Basie Orchestra – B.B. King Guest Vocalist.")
CROWN (5111 "Compositions of Count Basie and Others") ... 10-15 59
(Monaural.)
DAYBREAK ... 6-10 71
DECCA (170 "Best Of") ... 15-25 64
DECCA (5000 series) ... 25-35 50-53
(10-inch LPs.)
DECCA (8049 "Count Basie and His Orchestra") ... 10-15 65
DOCTOR JAZZ ... 5-10 85-86
DOT (25834 "Half a Sixpence") ... 8-12 68
DOT (25902 "Basie – Straight Ahead") ... 8-12 68
EMARCY (26000 series) ... 30-45 54
(10-inch LPs.)
EMUS ... 5-10 79
EPIC (1000 & 1100 series) ... 25-35 54
(10-inch LPs.)
EPIC ... 25-35 55
FANFARE (118 "1938 Live") ... 8-12 78
FLYING DUTCHMAN ... 6-10 71
HAPPY TIGER ... 8-12 70
HARMONY (7229 "Basie's Best") ... 10-20 60
HARMONY (11000 series) ... 5-10 67-69
IMPULSE ... 10-20 62
JAZZ ARCHIVES (41 "At the Famous Door 1938-1939") ... 10-15 78
JAZZ PANORAMA ... 50-75 52
MCA ... 8-12 77-82
MGM ... 6-10 70
MFSL (129 "Basie Plays Hefti") ... 40-60 85
MFSL (237 "April in Paris") ... 30-50 94
MPS ... 10-12 72
MERCURY (25000 series) ... 25-35 50-51
(10-inch LPs.)
METRO (516 "Count Basie") ... 6-12 65
METRO (592 "Frankly Speaking") ... 6-12 66
MOSAIC (135 "Complete Roulette Live Recordings of Count Basie") ... 100-125 '90s
(12 LP boxed set. 7500 made.)
MOSAIC (149 "Complete Roulette Studio Recordings of Count Basie") ... 200-225 '90s
(15 audiophile LP boxed set. 3500 made.)
OLYMPIC ... 5-10 74
PABLO ... 5-10 74-83
PAUSA ... 5-10 83
PRESTIGE ... 5-10 82
RCA (514 "Basie in Kansas City") ... 10-15 65
RCA (1100 series) ... 25-35 54
REPRISE ... 10-15 63-65
ROULETTE (100 series) ... 12-18 71
ROULETTE (52003 thru 52106) ... 15-20 58-64
ROULETTE (52111/12/13 "The World of Count Basie") ... 30-40 64
(Three-disc set.)
SCEPTER ... 5-10 74
SOLID STATE (18032 "Basie Meets Bond") ... 8-12 68
TRIP ... 5-10 75
U.A. (3480 "Basie Meets Bond") ... 10-15 66
(Monaural.)
U.A. (6480 "Basie Meets Bond") ... 15-20 66
(Stereo.)
UPFRONT ... 5-10 '70s
VSP (12 "Inside – Outside") ... 10-15 66
VANGUARD ... 15-25 57
VERVE ... 5-10 73-84
(Reads "Manufactured By MGM Record Corp.," or mentions either Polydor or Polygram at bottom of label.)
VERVE (2000 series) ... 20-30 56
(Reads "Verve Records, Inc." at bottom of label.)
VERVE (2500 series) ... 8-12 77-82
VERVE (2600 series) ... 5-10 82
VERVE (6000 series) ... 20-30 56
(Reads "Verve Records, Inc." at bottom of label.)
VERVE (8000 & 8100 series) ... 15-25 56-57
(Reads "Verve Records, Inc." at bottom of label.)
VERVE (8200 thru 8400) ... 15-20 58-61
(Reads "Verve Records, Inc." at bottom of label.)
VERVE (8500 thru 8600 series) ... 10-15 62-67
(Reads "MGM Records - a Division of Metro-Goldwyn-Mayer, Inc." at bottom of label.)
VERVE (8700 series) ... 6-10 69
(Reads "MGM Records - a Division of Metro-Goldwyn-Mayer, Inc." at bottom of label.)
VERVE (68000 series) ... 10-20 63-65
(Reads "MGM Records - a Division of Metro-Goldwyn-Mayer, Inc." at bottom of label.)
Session: Harry Edison; Bill Johnson; Jimmy Rushing.
Also see BENNETT, Tony, & Count Basie
Also see BREWER, Teresa, & Count Basie
Also see CROSBY, Bing, & Count Basie
Also see DAVIS, Sammy, Jr., & Count Basie
Also see FITZGERALD, Ella, & Count Basie
Also see JACQUET, Illinois, & Count Basie
Also see KING, B.B.
Also see MILLS BROTHERS & COUNT BASIE
Also see PRYSOCK, Arthur, & Count Basie
Also see SINATRA, Frank, & Count Basie
Also see STARR, Kay, & Count Basie
Also see WILLIAMS, Joe
Also see WILSON, Jackie, & Count Basie
Also see YOUNG, Lester

BASIE, Count, & Tony Bennett

EPs: 7-inch

ROULETTE ... 8-12 59

LPs: 10/12-inch

ROULETTE ... 10-20 59-63
Also see BENNETT, Tony

BASIE, Count, & Alan Copeland Singers

Singles: 7-inch

ABC-PAR (570 "Basie Swingin', Voices Singin' ") 10-15 66

LPs: 10/12-inch

ABC-PAR (10830 "Happiness Is") 15-20 66

BASIE, Count, & Billy Eckstine

Singles: 7-inch

ROULETTE (Except "SSR" series) 5-10 59
ROULETTE ("SSR" series) 10-15 59

LPs: 10/12-inch

ROULETTE (52029 "Basie/Eckstine, Inc.") 15-20 59
Also see ECKSTINE, Billy

BASIE, Count, & Duke Ellington

Singles: 7-inch

COLUMBIA 4-6 62

LPs: 10/12-inch

ACCORD 5-10 82
COLUMBIA 15-20 62
Also see ELLINGTON, Duke

BASIE, Count, & Maynard Ferguson

LPs: 10/12-inch

ROULETTE 10-20 65
Also see FERGUSON, Maynard

BASIE, Count, & Benny Goodman

LPs: 10/12-inch

ABC 8-12 73
VANGUARD 15-25 59
Also see GOODMAN, Benny

BASIE, Count, & Oscar Peterson

LPs: 10/12-inch

PABLO 5-10 75-83
VERVE 15-20 59
Also see PETERSON, Oscar

BASIE, Count, & Sarah Vaughan

LPs: 10/12-inch

ROULETTE (52061 "Count Basie and Sarah Vaughan") 15-20 61

BASIE, Count, Sarah Vaughan & Joe Williams

Singles: 7-inch

ROULETTE (4273 "Teach Me Tonight") 5-10 60

LPs: 10/12-inch

ROULETTE 15-20 60
Note: Joe Williams is also a featured vocalist on many of the recordings included in the section of listings for Count Basie.
Also see BASIE, Count
Also see VAUGHAN, Sarah

BASIL, Toni *P&R/LP '82*

Singles: 12-inch

CHRYSALIS 4-6 82-85

Singles: 7-inch

A&M (791 "Breakaway") 100-200 66
CHRYSALIS 3-5 82-85
CHRYSALIS/VIRGIN (2638 "Mickey") 4-6 81
(With Radialchoice logo.)

Picture Sleeves

CHRYSALIS 3-5 82-84

LPs: 10/12-inch

CHRYSALIS 5-10 82-84

BASIN STREET BOYS

Singles: 78 rpm

EXCLUSIVE 20-40 46-49
FLAME (1002 "I Sold My Heart to the Junkman") 20-30 53
Also see BROWN, Charles / Basin Street Boys
Also see WILSON, Ormond, & Basin Street Boys

BASKERVILLE, Hayes, & Five Chestnuts / Norven Baskerville & Five Chestnuts

Singles: 7-inch

DRUM (003/004 "Billy"/"My One and Only Love") 600-800 58
Also see FIVE CHESTNUTS

BASKERVILLE, Marvin, & Five Chestnuts

Singles: 7-inch

DRUM (001/002 "Chapel in the Moonlight"/"Chi Chi") 300-500 58

BASKERVILLE, Marvin, & Five Chestnuts / Hayes Baskerville & Five Chestnuts

Singles: 7-inch

DRUM (002/003 "Chi Chi"/"Billy") 150-250 58
Also see BASKERVILLE, Marvin, & Five Chestnuts

BASKERVILLE, Norven, & Admirations

Singles: 7-inch

X-TRA (100 "Gonna Find My Pretty Baby") 40-60 '50s
Also see BASKERVILLE, Hayes, & Five Chestnuts / Norven Baskerville & Five Chestnuts

BASKERVILLE HOUNDS *P&R '69*

Singles: 7-inch

AVCO EMBASSY (4504 "Hold Me") 4-6 69
BUDDAH (17 "Caroline") 5-10 67
DOT 5-10 67
TEMA 10-15 66-68

Picture Sleeves

TEMA (131 "Christmas Is Here") 10-15 67

LPs: 10/12-inch

DOT (3823 "Baskerville Hounds") 15-20 67
(Monaural.)
DOT (25823 "Baskerville Hounds") 20-25 67
(Stereo.)
Also see TULU BABIES

BASS, Fontella *P&R/R&B '65*

Singles: 7-inch

ABC 4-6 74
BOBBIN (134 "Brand New Love") 10-15 62
CHECKER 6-12 65-67
CHESS 3-8 75-85
EPIC (50341 "Soon As I Touched Him") 4-6 77
GUSTO 4-6
MCA 3-5 83
PAULA 4-6 72-74
PRANN (5005 "My Good Lovin' ") 8-12 63
SONJA (2006 "Poor Little Fool") 10-15 70
(First issue credits Fontella Bass & Tina Turner.)

LPs: 10/12-inch

CHECKER (2997 "New Look") 15-25 66
CHESS 5-10 '70s
PAULA (2203 "Free") 8-12 71

BASS, Fontella, & Bobby McClure *P&R/R&B '65*

Singles: 7-inch

CHECKER (1097 "Don't Mess Up a Good Thing") 8-12 65
CHECKER (1111 "You'll Miss Me") 8-12 65
Also see McCLURE, Bobby

BASS, Fontella, & Oliver Sain

Singles: 7-inch

BOBBIN (140 "Honey Bee") 10-15 63

BASS, Fontella, & Tina Turner / Tina Turner

Singles: 7-inch

VESUVIUS (1002 "Poor Little Fool"/"This Would Make Me Happy") 15-20 63
(Reissue of *Poor Little Fool* on Sonja credits only Fontella Bass.)
Also see BASS, Fontella
Also see TURNER, Tina

BASS, Leon

Singles: 7-inch

TUNE (209 "Come On Baby") 50-75 60
WHIRL AWAY (1058 "Country Hix") 125-150

BASS, Sid
(Sid Bass Orchestra)

LPs: 10/12-inch

VIK (1053 "From Another World") 25-50 56

BASSETT, Tony

Singles: 7-inch

ORCHID (873 "Rockin' Little Mama") 25-50 61

BASSEY, Shirley *P&R/LP '65*

Singles: 12-inch

U.A. 4-6 79

Singles: 7-inch

COLUMBIA (40848 "Tonight My Heart Is Crying") 5-10 57
EPIC (9303 "Honey, Honey") 5-10 59
MGM (12919 "S'Wonderful") 5-10 60
U.A. 4-6 61-79

LPs: 10/12-inch

EPIC 10-20 62
LIBERTY 4-6 81-82
MGM (3862 "Fabulous Shirley Bassey") 12-20 60
PHILIPS 10-15 65
SPRINGBORAD 5-10 75
U.A. (With "LM" prefix.) 4-6 80
U.A. (With "UAL" or "UAS" prefix.) 10-15 62-72
U.A. (With "UA-LA" prefix.) 5-10 73-79
Also see NELSON, Willie / Nat "King" Cole / Johnny Mathis / Shirley Bassey

BASSMEN

Singles: 7-inch

GALLANTRY (745 "Last Laugh") 15-25
VAUGHN LTD (101 "I Need You") 20-30

BATEMAN, Carroll

Singles: 7-inch

TWIN TOWN (8033 "Look at Me") 20-25 67
Also see CARROL, Evans, & Tempos

BATEMAN, Gil

Singles: 7-inch

JERDEN (779 "Daddy Walked in Darkness") 10-20 65
PANORAMA (12 "Wicked Love") 15-25 65
PICCADILLY (227 "Wicked Love") 10-20 66
PICCADILLY (249 "The Night Before") 10-20 67

BATEMON, June
(June Bateman)

Singles: 78 rpm

HOLIDAY (2606 "Yes I Will") 10-20 57

Singles: 7-inch

ARRAWAK 10-15
CLAMIKE 8-12 '60s
FURY (1030 "Believe Me My Darling") 15-25 60
HOLIDAY (2606 "Yes I Will") 20-30 57
ODESSA (307 "I Still Love Him") 10-15 61
Also see MARQUIS
Also see WATTS, Noble, & June Bateman

BATES, Deacon L.J.
(Blind Lemon Jefferson)

Singles: 78 rpm

PARAMOUNT (12386 "I Want to Be Like Jesus in My Heart") 150-200 26
(Also issued as by Deacon Jackson.)
Also see JACKSON, Deacon
Also see JEFFERSON, Blind Lemon

BATES, Lefty Guitar
(With "His Recording Band")

Singles: 7-inch

APEX (951 "Rock Alley") 15-25 59
APEX (952 "Ena") 15-25 59
BOXER (203 "Say Whoa") 10-20
MAD (1011 "Back Ground") 25-35 58
STATES (164 "Look Me Straight in the Eye") 15-25 57
UNITED (206 "Chicago Cha Cha") 15-25 57
Also see KINGS MEN
Also see PALM, Horace M., with Lefty Bates Orchestra
Also see FOSTER BROTHERS
Also see MOROCCOS
Also see STROLLERS

BATS

Singles: 7-inch

FLAME (5155 "Batmobile") 20-25 64
HBR (445 "Nothing at All") 5-10 65
Member: Gene Moles.
Also see MOLES, Gene

BATTIN, Skip
(Skip Battyn & Group; Clyde Battin; Skip Batten Combo)

Singles: 7-inch

AURORA (159 "Dating Game") 10-15 66
GROOVE (0055 "Searchin") 25-35 65
GROOVE (0065 "What's Mine Is Mine") 25-35 65
INDIGO (143 "Can't Stop Twistin' ") 10-20 62
MAY (108 "Twister") 10-20 61
SIGNPOST 4-6 73

LPs: 10/12-inch

SIGNPOST 8-10 72
Also see BYRDS
Also see NEW RIDERS OF THE PURPLE SAGE
Also see SKIP & FLIP
Also see VINCENT, Gene

BATTISTE, Rose

Singles: 7-inch

GOLDEN WORLD (33 "Sweetheart Darling") 15-25 66
REVILOT (204 "Hit and Run") 40-60 66
REVILOT (206 "Come Back in a Hurry") 15-25 66
RIC-TIC (105 "Holding Hands") 10-15 65
THELMA (102 "Someday") 75-125 64

BATTS, Ray

Singles: 78 rpm

EXCELLO (2028 "Stealin' Sugar") 20-30 54

Singles: 7-inch

EXCELLO (2028 "Stealin' Sugar") 100-150 54

BAUGH, Phil *C&W '65*

Singles: 7-inch

CREST (1105 "Moon Magic") 10-15 62
ERA (3202 "Jesse's Theme") 5-10 69
LONGHORN (559 "Country Guitar") 10-15 65
LONGHORN (563 "One Man Band") 10-15 65

LPs: 10/12-inch

ERA (801 "California Guitar") 10-15 69
LONGHORN (002 "Country Guitar") 30-50 65
TORO (502 "Country Guitar II") 15-25 74
Also see ANNETTE

BAUM, Allen
(Alden Bunn)

Singles: 78 rpm

RED ROBIN 50-100 54

Singles: 7-inch

RED ROBIN (124 "My Kinda Woman") 200-300 54
Also see BUNN, Allen

BAXTER, Duke *P&R '69*

Singles: 7-inch

MERCURY 5-10 70
VMC (740 "Everybody Knows Matilda") 10-15 69
VMC (749 "Superstition Bend") 10-15 69
VMC (750 "Don't Hurt Us") 10-15 69

LPs: 10/12-inch

VMC (138 "Everybody Knows Matilda") 15-20 69

BAXTER, Harmon / Betty Baxter
(With the Baxters)

Singles: 7-inch

HI FI (103 "Wild Bill") 30-50 64

BAXTER, Les *P&R '51*
(With His Orchestra & Chorus; Les Baxter Balladeers; Leslie Baxter; with Notables)

Singles: 78 rpm

CAPITOL 4-6 50-57

Singles: 7-inch

A/S 4-6 70
CAPITOL 10-20 50-61
GNP 5-10 64-69
HBR (456 "Michelle") 5-10 65
LINK (313 "Linin' Track") 5-10 64
METEOR (5012 "Heartaches") 8-12 53
REPRISE 5-10 62-63
SIDEWALK (946 "Wheels") 5-10 68

Picture Sleeves

REPRISE (20120 "Theme from *The Manchurian Candidate*") 40-60 62
(A Frank Sinatra collectible, as his name is shown on this cover.)

EPs: 7-inch

CAPITOL 5-15 51-56
GNP 5-10 67-69
RCA 5-10 52
REPRISE 5-10 64

LPs: 10/12-inch

ALSHIRE 5-10 70-85
AMERICAN INT'L (1028 "Dunwich Horror") 20-25 70
(Soundtrack.)
CAPITOL (200 thru 900 series) 10-20 51-58
CAPITOL (1000 thru 1800 series) 5-15 58-63
CAPITOL (11000 series) 4-6 77-79
GNP 5-10 69
RCA 15-25 52
REPRISE 10-15 62-63
VARESE SARABANDE (81103 "Dunwich Horror") 8-10 79
Also see CHEERS
Also see CROSBY, Bing, & Bob Hope
Also see HOFFMAN, Samuel J.
Also see JOE & EDDIE
Also see SINATRA, Frank
Also see WAKELY, Jimmy

BAXTER, Ronnie

Singles: 7-inch

ATCO (6093 "Drivin' Me Out of My Mind") 20-30 57
GONE (5036 "Gates of Heaven"/"Someone to Love Me") 15-25 58

GONE (5041 "Gates of Heaven"/"Prisoner of Love")........................ 15-25 58
GONE (5050 "Is It Because")................... 15-25 58
GONE (5058 "Is It Because")................... 15-25 59
GONE (5084 "It's Magic")........................ 15-25 60
MARK-X (8001 "It's Magic")...................... 10-20 59
Also see RIGHTEOUS BROTHERS / Ronnie Baxter

BAXTER, Tony, & Manhattan Twisters

Singles: 7-inch

DING DONG (349 "How Long")............ 75-100 61

BAY BOPS

Singles: 7-inch

CORAL (61975 "Follow the Rock")......... 15-25 58
CORAL (62004 "To the Party")............... 15-25 58
Member: Barney Zarzana.
Also see DINO
Also see ZIP, Danny

BAY CITY FIVE
(With Luigi Martini)

Singles: 78 rpm

JAGUAR.. 50-75 54

Singles: 7-inch

JAGUAR (3001 "Basin Street Blues").. 150-250 54
JAGUAR (3002 "Oh Marie")................ 150-250 54

BAYOU BOYS

Singles: 78 rpm

CHECKER (765 "Dinah")......................... 50-75 52

Singles: 7-inch

CHECKER (765 "Dinah")..................... 100-150 52

BAYSIDERS

Singles: 7-inch

EVEREST..8-12 60-61

LPs: 10/12-inch

EVEREST (5124 "Over the Rainbow").... 50-75 61

BEACH, Bill

Singles: 78 rpm

KING (4940 "Peg Pants")........................ 10-15 56

Singles: 7-inch

KING (4940 "Peg Pants").................... 100-150 56

BEACH, Ray

Singles: 7-inch

("Walking Blues")................................. 50-100
(No label name or selection number used.)

BEACH BOYS *P&R/LP '62*

Singles: 12-inch

CAPITOL (9711 "Rock & Roll to the Rescue")................................... 10-15 86
(Promotional issue only.)
CAPITOL (9796 "California Dreamin'").... 10-15 86
(Promotional issue only.)
CAPITOL (15234 "Rock & Roll to the Rescue")...5-10 86
CARIBOU (2080 "Getcha Back")............ 10-15 86
(Promotional issue only.)
CARIBOU (9028 "Here Comes the Night").8-12 79
CARIBOU (9028 "Here Comes the Night").. 20-30 79
(Promotional issue only.)

Singles: 7-inch

BROTHER (1001 "Heroes & Villains")..... 10-15 67
BROTHER/REPRISE (0101 thru 0107").......4-6 73
("Back to Back" reissue series.)
BROTHER/REPRISE (0894 "Add Some Music to Your Day")...5-10 70
BROTHER/REPRISE (0929 "Slip On Through")..5-10 70
BROTHER/REPRISE (0957 "Tears in the Morning").. 12-15 70
BROTHER/REPRISE (0998 "Cool, Cool Water").. 60-75 71
BROTHER/REPRISE (1015 "Long Promised Road").. 20-30 71
BROTHER/REPRISE (1047 "Long Promised Road").. 20-30 71
BROTHER/REPRISE (1058 "Surf's Up"). 45-50 71
BROTHER/REPRISE (1091 "Cuddle Up").. 25-35 72
BROTHER/REPRISE (1101 "Marcella").. 25-35 72
BROTHER/REPRISE (1138 "Sail On Sailor")..8-12 73
BROTHER/REPRISE (1156 "California Saga")... 10-15 73
BROTHER/REPRISE (1310 "I Can Hear Music")..4-6 74
BROTHER/REPRISE (1321 "Child of Winter")..20-30 74
BROTHER/REPRISE (1325 "Sail On Sailor")..8-10 75
BROTHER/REPRISE (1336 "Wouldn't It Be Nice")..5-10 75
BROTHER/REPRISE (1354 "Rock & Roll Music")..4-6 76
BROTHER/REPRISE (1368 "It's O.K.")........4-6 76
BROTHER/REPRISE (1394 "Peggy Sue")...4-6 78
CANDIX (301 "Surfin'")..........................300-350 60
(No mention of Era distribution.)
CANDIX (301 "Surfin'")..........................150-250 60
(Reads "Distributed by Era Record Sales Inc.")
CANDIX (331 "Surfin'")..........................125-175 62
CAPITOL (2028 "Wild Honey")................10-20 67
CAPITOL (2068 "Darlin' ")........................10-20 67
CAPITOL (2160 "Friends")........................10-20 68
CAPITOL (2239 "Do It Again")..................10-20 68
CAPITOL (2360 "Bluebirds Over the Mountain")...10-20 68
CAPITOL (2432 "I Can Hear Music")........10-20 69
CAPITOL (2530 "Break Away")..................10-20 69
CAPITOL (2765 "Cottonfields")..................15-25 70
CAPITOL (3924 "Surfin' USA")....................4-8 74
(Some copies indicate "Stereo" but play mono; others indicate "Mono" but play stereo.)
CAPITOL (4777 "Surfin' Safari")...............20-30 62
CAPITOL (4880 "Ten Little Indians")........30-40 62
CAPITOL (4932 "Surfin' U.S.A.")..............15-20 62
CAPITOL (5009 "Surfer Girl")...................10-20 63
CAPITOL (5030 "Beach Boys Medley")........4-8 81
CAPITOL (5069 "Be True to Your School")..15-20 63
CAPITOL (5096 "Little Saint Nick")...........20-30 63
CAPITOL (5118 "Fun Fun Fun")................10-15 64
CAPITOL (5174 "I Get Around")................20-30 64
CAPITOL (5245 "When I Grow Up").........10-15 64
CAPITOL (5306 "Dance Dance Dance")..10-15 64
CAPITOL (5312 "The Man with All the Toys")..25-35 64
CAPITOL (5372 "Do You Wanna Dance")...30-40 65
CAPITOL (5395 "Help Me Rhonda")........10-15 65
CAPITOL (5464 "California Girls")...........10-15 65
CAPITOL (5540 "The Little Girl I Once Knew")..10-15 65
CAPITOL (5595 "Rock 'N' Roll to the Rescue")..4-8 86
CAPITOL (5561 "Barbara Ann")...............10-15 65
CAPITOL (5602 "Sloop John B")..............10-15 66
CAPITOL (5630 "California Dreamin' ")......5-10 86
CAPITOL (5676 "Good Vibrations")...........8-12 66
CAPITOL (5706 "Wouldn't It Be Nice").....10-15 66
CAPITOL (6000 series).................................4-8 67-74
(Capitol "Starline" Series.)
CAPITOL (18205 "Santa's Beard")............5-10 '90s
(Green vinyl.)
CAPITOL (44445 "Still Cruisin' ")..................4-6 89
CARIBOU (9026 "Here Comes the Night")...4-8 79
CARIBOU (9028 "Here Comes the Night")...4-8 79
(Vocal on one side, instrumental on the other.)
CARIBOU (9029 "Good Timin' ")..................4-8 79
CARIBOU (9030 "Lady Lynda")....................4-8 79
CARIBOU (9031 "Sumahama")......................4-8 79
CARIBOU (9032 "Goin' On")..........................4-6 80
CARIBOU (9033 "Santa Ana Winds")...........4-6 80
CARIBOU (9034 "School Day")......................4-6 80
CARIBOU (02633 "Goin' On").........................4-6 81
CARIBOU (04913 "Getcha' Back")................4-6 85
CARIBOU (05433 "It's Gettin' Late")............4-6 85
CARIBOU (05624 "She Believes in Love Again")..4-6 85
COLLECTABLES......................................5-10 92-95
ERA (043 "Surfin' Safari")...........................4-6 69
TRIP (51 "Surfin' ")......................................4-6 70
X (301 "Surfin'").....................................600-700 61

Promotional Singles

BROTHER/REPRISE (557-2 "Sail On Sailor")..75-100 73
BROTHER/REPRISE (0998 "Cool, Cool Water")...45-50 71
BROTHER/REPRISE (1310 "I Can Hear Music")...30-50 74
BROTHER/REPRISE (1321 "Child of Winter")...20-30 74
CAPITOL (2360 "Bluebirds over the Mountain")...15-20 69
CAPITOL (2936/7 "Salt Lake City")......200-250 65
CAPITOL (4093 "Little Honda")................15-20 75
CAPITOL (57724381976579 "The Man with All the Toys")..5-10 97
CAPITOL CUSTOM ("Spirit of America")..125-150 63
(No selection number used.)
CARIBOU (557 "Here Comes the Night") 10-12 79
(Blue vinyl.)
CARIBOU (557 "Here Comes the Night") 50-60 79
(Special Edition autographed copies. Blue vinyl.)
CARIBOU (9026 "Here Comes the Night")...10-15 79
CARIBOU (9027 thru 9034).........................3-6 79-80
CARIBOU (02633 "Goin' On")....................5-10 81
CARIBOU (04913 "Getcha Back")............5-10 85
CARIBOU (05433 "It's Gettin' Late")..........5-10 85
CARIBOU (05624 "She Believes in Love Again")...5-10 85
EVA-TONE (0300 "Living Doll")...................3-5 87
(Barbie Doll promotional issue.)
ODE (66016 "Wouldn't It Be Nice-Live Version")...35-40 71
WHAT'S IT ALL ABOUT (449/450 & 507/508)...20-25
(Public service radio station issues. Program disc 449/450 has the Beach Boys on one side and Dr. Hook on the flip. 507/508 features the Beach Boys on one side and the Rolling Stones on the other.)
Note: Promo singles *not* listed separately are presumed to fall into the same price range as commercial issues.

Picture Sleeves

BROTHER (1001 "Heroes and Villains")..40-80 67
CAPITOL (1001 "Heroes and Villains")...250-500 66
(Canadian. Made in the US before it was known that the single would not be on Capitol, then exported to Canada. As issued there, the Capitol number 5826, is covered, and the Canadian number added.)
CAPITOL (2068 "Darlin' ")........................10-20 67
CAPITOL (4777 "Surfin' Safari")...............30-40 62
CAPITOL (4880 "Ten Little Indians")......75-100 62
CAPITOL (5118 "Fun, Fun, Fun")............10-20 64
CAPITOL (5174 "I Get Around")...............30-40 64
CAPITOL (5245 "When I Grow Up").........50-60 64
CAPITOL (5306 "Dance, Dance, Dance")...10-20 64
CAPITOL (5372 "Do You Wanna Dance")...10-20 65
CAPITOL (5395 "Help Me Rhonda")........10-20 65
CAPITOL (5464 "California Girls")............50-60 65
CAPITOL (5540 "The Little Girl I Once Knew")...10-20 65
CAPITOL (5561 "Barbara Ann")..........100-125 65
CAPITOL (5595 "Rock 'N' Roll to the Rescue")..3-5 86
CAPITOL (5602 "Sloop John B.")............50-60 66
CAPITOL (5676 "Good Vibrations")..........10-20 66
CAPITOL (5826 "Heroes and Villains")...300-500 66
(Not issued with the Brother disc, which has its own sleeve. Made before it was known that the single would not be on Capitol, then exported to Canada and elsewhere – some of which worked their way back to the US.)
CARIBOU (04913 "Getcha Back")..............8-12 85
CARIBOU (05433 "It's Gettin' Late")...........8-12 85
CARIBOU (05624 "She Believes in Love Again")...8-12 85

EPs: 7-inch

BROTHER (1 "Radio Spot Backing Tracks")...225-250 73
(Promotional issue only.)
CAPITOL (189 "Best of the Beach Boys")...15-25 66
(With "LLP" prefix. Juke box issue only.)
CAPITOL (1981 "Surfer Girl")................50-100 63
CAPITOL (2027 "Shut Down, Vol. 2").....50-100 64
CAPITOL (2269 "The Beach Boys Today")...50-100 65
(Juke box issue only.)
CAPITOL (2293/94 "Beach Boys' Party")...125-175 65
(Juke box issue only.)
CAPITOL (DU-2545 "Best of the Beach Boys")...75-100 66
(Juke box issue only.)
CAPITOL (SU-2545 "Best of the Beach Boys")...50-75 66
("Little LP," LLP-189.)
CAPITOL (2754/55 "Brian Wilson Introduces Selections")..350-450 64
(Promotional issue only. Includes selections from *Beach Boys Concert* and *Beach Boys Songbook*.)
CAPITOL (5267 "4 by the Beach Boys")..30-50 66
BROTHER/REPRISE (2118 "Mount Vernon and Fairway")...8-12 73
(Packaged with *Holland* LP 2118)
ROCK SHOPPE ("The Beach Years")...75-125 75
(Demo disc for "A Six Hour Radio Special." Also contains excerpts by Jan & Dean, Dick Dale, and the Surfaris. Narrated by Roger Christian. Promotional issue. 200 made.)
SUB-POP ("I Just Wasn't Made for These Times")...5-8 96
(Three tracks.)
W.B. (422 "Sunflower Promotional Spots")...100-125 70
W.B. (534 "Vote '72")...............................35-45 72
(Promotional issue only.)

LPs: 10/12-inch

ACCORD (7234 "For Collectors Only")......5-10 83
AUDIO FIDELITY (335 "Beach Boys").......8-12 84
(Picture disc.)
AXIS/CAPITOL (8 "Their 22 Greatest Hits")...6-12 73
BROTHER (9001 "Smiley Smile")...........15-25 67
BROTHER/REPRISE (2083 "Carl & Passions: So Tough"/"Pet Sounds")..............................15-20 72
(Two discs.)
BROTHER/REPRISE (2118 "Holland")....20-30 73
(Includes *Mount Vernon & Fairway* EP.)
BROTHER/REPRISE (2118 "Holland")....10-15 73
(Without *Mount Vernon & Fairway* EP.)
BROTHER/REPRISE (2166 "Wild Honey"/"20-20")...10-15 74
(Two discs.)
BROTHER/REPRISE (2167 "Friends"/"Smiley Smile")...8-10 74
(Two discs.)
BROTHER/REPRISE (2197 "Pet Sounds")...8-10 74
BROTHER/REPRISE (2223 "Good Vibrations"/ "Best of the Beach Boys")................................8-10 75
BROTHER/REPRISE (2251 "15 Big Ones")...8-10 76
BROTHER/REPRISE (2258 "The Beach Boys Love You")...8-10 77
BROTHER/REPRISE (2268 "M.I.U. Album")...8-10 78
BROTHER/REPRISE (6382 "Sunflower")...10-15 70
BROTHER/REPRISE (6453 "Surf's Up")...20-30 71
BROTHER/REPRISE (6484 "The Beach Boys in Concert")...10-15 73
(Two discs.)
BROTHER/REPRISE (113793 "Surf's Up")...20-30 71
(Record Club issue.)
BROTHER/SUNKIST (9431 "25 Years of Good Vibrations")...10-20 86
(Includes tour booklet. Sold at Beach Boys concerts.)
CANDLELITE/CAPITOL (6994 "Golden Years of the Beach Boys")...25-30 75
(TV mail-order offer. Two discs.)
CAPITOL (SKAO-133 "20/20")................10-20 69
CAPITOL (SKAO8-33 "20/20")................30-35 69
(Capitol Record Club issue.)
CAPITOL (SWBB-253 "Close Up")...........35-45 69
(Two discs. Gatefold cover.)
CAPITOL (ST-442 "Good Vibrations").....20-30 70
CAPITOL (STBB-500 "All Summer Long"/ "California Girls")...8-12 70
(Two discs. Gatefold cover.)
CAPITOL (STBB-701 "Dance, Dance, Dance"/ "Fun, Fun, Fun")...8-12 71
(Two discs. Gatefold cover.)
CAPITOL (702 "Fun, Fun, Fun")..................5-8 71
CAPITOL (T-1808 "Surfin' Safari")..........25-35 62
(Monaural.)
CAPITOL (DT-1808 "Surfin' Safari").........20-25 63
(Duophonic.)
CAPITOL (SM-1808 "Surfin' Safari").........8-10 76
CAPITOL (T-1890 "Surfin' USA")............25-30 63
(Monaural.)
CAPITOL (ST-1890 "Surfin' USA")..........25-30 63
(Stereo.)
CAPITOL (SM-1890 "Surfin' USA")...........8-10 76

CAPITOL (T-1918 "Shut Down")............. 25-30 63
(Monaural. Various artists collection with two Beach Boys' tracks.)
CAPITOL (DT-1918 "Shut Down") 25-30 63
(Duophonic. Various artists collection with two Beach Boys' tracks.)
CAPITOL (T-1981 "Surfer Girl") 25-30 63
(Monaural.)
CAPITOL (ST-1981 "Surfer Girl")............ 25-30 63
(Stereo.)
CAPITOL (SM-1981 "Surfer Girl")..............8-10 76
CAPITOL (T-1998 "Little Deuce Coupe") 25-30 63
(Monaural.)
CAPITOL (ST-1998 "Little Deuce Coupe").................. 25-30 63
(Stereo.)
CAPITOL (ST-8-1998 "Little Deuce Coupe")............................ 100-200 63
(Capitol Record Club issue.)
CAPITOL (T-2027 "Shut Down, Vol. 2") .. 25-30 64
(Monaural.)
CAPITOL (ST-2027 "Shut Down, Vol. 2") 25-30 63
(Stereo.)
CAPITOL (T-2110 "All Summer Long").... 30-40 64
(With "Don't Back Down" incorrectly shown as "Don't Break Down.")
CAPITOL (ST-2110 "All Summer Long"). 30-40 64
(With "Don't Back Down" incorrectly shown as "Don't Break Down.")
CAPITOL (T-2110 "All Summer Long").... 15-25 64
("Don't Back Down" is shown correctly.)
CAPITOL (ST-2110 "All Summer Long"). 15-25 64
("Don't Back Down" is shown correctly.)
CAPITOL (T-2164 "Beach Boys' Christmas Album") 20-35 64
(Monaural.)
CAPITOL (ST-2164 "Beach Boys' Christmas Album") 20-35 75
(Stereo.)
CAPITOL (SM-2164 "Beach Boys' Christmas Album") 8-10 75
CAPITOL (T-2198 "Beach Boys' Concert") 15-20 64
(Monaural.)
CAPITOL (ST-2198 "Beach Boys' Concert") 15-20 64
(Stereo.)
CAPITOL (SM-2198 "Beach Boys' Concert") 8-10 76
CAPITOL (T-2269 "The Beach Boys Today!") 15-20 65
(Monaural.)
CAPITOL (DT-2269 "The Beach Boys Today!") 15-20 65
(Duophonic.)
CAPITOL (T-2354 "Summer Days")......... 20-35 65
(Monaural.)
CAPITOL (DT-2354 "Summer Days")...... 20-35 65
(Duophonic.)
CAPITOL (MAS-2398 "Beach Boys Party") 60-80 65
(Price includes 15 bonus photos. Deduct $25 to $50 if these photos are missing.)
CAPITOL (SMAS-2398 "Beach Boys Party") 60-80 65
(Price includes 15 bonus photos. Deduct $25 to $50 if these photos are missing.)
CAPITOL (T-2458 "Pet Sounds")............ 15-20 66
(Monaural.)
CAPITOL (DT-2458 "Pet Sounds") 15-20 66
(Duophonic.)
CAPITOL (T-2545 "Best of the Beach Boys").................................. 10-15 66
(Monaural.)
CAPITOL (DT-2545 "Best of the Beach Boys").................................. 10-15 66
(Duophonic.)
CAPITOL (T-2706 "Best of the Beach Boys, Vol. 2").................................. 10-15 67
(Monaural.)
CAPITOL (DT-2706 "Best of the Beach Boys, Vol. 2").................................. 10-15 67
(Duophonic.)
CAPITOL (TCL-2813 "Beach Boys Deluxe Set") 100-150 67
(Monaural. Three discs.)
CAPITOL (DTCL-2813 "Beach Boys Deluxe Set") 35-40 67
(Stereo. Three discs.)
CAPITOL (T-2859 "Wild Honey")..............15-25 67
(Monaural.)
CAPITOL (ST-2859 "Wild Honey") 10-20 67
(Stereo.)
CAPITOL (ST8-2891 "Smiley Smile").....75-100 69
(Capitol Record Club issue.)
CAPITOL (DKAO-2893 "Stack-o-Tracks")..125-200 68
(With music-lyrics booklet. Gatefold cover.)
CAPITOL (DKAO-2893 "Stack-o-Tracks")..75-125 68
(Without music-lyrics booklet. Gatefold cover.)
CAPITOL (ST8-2893 "Stack-o-Tracks")..100-125 69
(Capitol Record Club issue.)
CAPITOL (ST-2895 "Friends")................10-20 68
CAPITOL (ST-82895 "Friends")...............15-25 68
(Capitol Record Club issue.)
CAPITOL (DKAO-2945 "Best of the Beach Boys, Vol. 3") 35-45 68
CAPITOL (SKAO9-3352 "Sunflower")......30-40 70
(Capitol Record Club issue.)
CAPITOL (11307 "Endless Summer")......15-20 74
(Two discs. Gatefold.)
CAPITOL (11384 "Spirit of America").......15-20 75
(Two discs. Gatefold.)
CAPITOL (11584 "Beach Boys '69")...........8-12 76
CAPITOL (12011 "Beach Boys '69")...........5-10 79
CAPITOL (12220 "Sunshine Dream").........8-10 82
(Two discs.)
CAPITOL (12396 "Made in USA") 8-10 86
(Two discs.)
CAPITOL (16012 "Surfin' Safari") 5-8 80
CAPITOL (16014 "Surfer Girl") 5-8 80
CAPITOL (16015 "Surfin' USA")......................5-8 80
CAPITOL (16016 "All Summer Long")..........5-8 80
CAPITOL (16017 "California Girls")..............5-8 80
CAPITOL (16018 "Fun, Fun, Fun")................5-8 80
CAPITOL (16019 "Dance, Dance, Dance")..5-8 80
CAPITOL (16134 "Beach Boys '69")............5-8 80
CAPITOL (16154 "Beach Boys' Concert")....5-8 81
CAPITOL (16156 "Pet Sounds") 5-8 81
CAPITOL (16157 "Friends")..........................5-8 81
CAPITOL (16161 "Pet Sounds") 5-8 81
CAPITOL (29600 series)...........................10-15 96
(Digitally remastered.)
CAPITOL (48421 "Pet Sounds")......................5-8 90
CAPITOL (90427 "Beach Boys Concert") 10-15 96
CAPITOL (92639 "Still Cruisin' ")................5-10 89
CAPITOL (123946 "Best of the Beach Boys, Vol. 1") 20-25 74
(RCA Record Club issue.)
CAPITOL (153477 "Rarities")....................20-25 75
(RCA Record Club issue.)
CAPITOL (233559 "Endless Summer")....20-25 74
(RCA Record Club issue.)
CAPITOL (233593 "American Summer") .20-25 75
(RCA Record Club issue. Two discs.)
CAPITOL STARLINE...............................10-15 '60s
CARIBOU (35752 "L.A. – Light Album").....8-10 79
CARIBOU (36293 "Keepin' the Summer Alive")..8-10 80
CARIBOU (37445 "Ten Years of Harmony")..8-12 81
(Two discs.)
CARIBOU (39946 "Beach Boys") 5-8 85
HIGHLIGHT (9926 "Beach Boys") ....5-8 '80s
MFSL (116 "Surfer Girl")..........................30-50 84
PAIR...10-12 84
PICKWICK (2059 "High Water") 10-20 73
(Two discs.)
PICKWICK (3221 "The Beach Boys").......10-15 70
(Also issued as Sears 608.)
PICKWICK (3269 "Good Vibrations") 8-12 71
PICKWICK (3309 "Wow! Great Concert") ..8-12 72
PICKWICK (3351 "Surfer Girl") 8-12 73
PICKWICK (3562 "Little Deuce Coupe") 8-12 76
RONCO/CAPITOL (2230/8114 "Beach Boys Super Hits") 8-10 78
SEARS (608 "Summertime Blues") 100-125 70
(Sold only at Sears retail stores. Also issued as Pickwick 3221.)
SESSIONS (8134 "Beach Boys") 15-20 80
(Two discs.)
SPRINGBOARD (4021 "Greatest Hits: 1961-1963")..10-15 72
SPRINGBOARD (4021 "The Beach Boys, 1961")..8-10 77
(Repackage.)
SUNDAZED (5005 "Lost & Found")..........10-15
(Colored vinyl.)

Promotional LPs

BROTHER (9431 "Good Vibrations from the Beach Boys")..10-20 86
(Sunkist promotional issue.)
CAPITOL (1 "Open House")..................200-250 78
CAPITOL (2754/5 "Beach Boys' Concert")..300-400 64
CAPITOL (3133 "Silver Platter Service") 150-250 64
("Beach Boys Christmas Special.")
CAPITOL (3266 "Silver Platter Service") 100-150 67
CARIBOU (1024 "Keepin' the Summer Alive")..50-60 80
CRAWDADDY ("Brian Wilson Interview")..100-125 77
(Issued to radio stations only.)
MORE MUSIC (03-179-72 "Good Vibrations from London") 50-60
MUTUAL RADIO ("Dick Clark Presents the Beach Boys") 150-200 81
(Boxed, three-disc set.)
BROTHER/REPRISE ("Radio Backing Tracks for Beach Boys in Concert")......................250-300 73
TIME-LIFE..10-15 86
Members: Brian Wilson; Carl Wilson; Dennis Wilson; Mike Love; Al Jardine; David Marks; Bruce Johnston; Blondie Chaplin; Ricky Fataar.
Note: Promos NOT listed separately are priced in the same range as commercial issues.
Also see ANNETTE
Also see BEATLES / Beach Boys / Buddy Holly
Also see CAMPBELL, Glen
Also see CAPTAIN & TENNILLE
Also see CHICAGO
Also see CHRISTIAN, Roger
Also see DALE, Dick / Surfaris / Surf Kings
Also see EVERLY BROTHERS & BEACH BOYS
Also see HONEYS
Also see JAN & DEAN / Beach Boys
Also see JETT, Joan
Also see JOHNSTON, Bruce
Also see KENNY & CADETS
Also see MARKS, David
Also see PETERSEN, Paul
Also see ROLLING STONES
Also see SURVIVORS
Also see WILSON, Brian
Also see WILSON, Brian, & Mike Love
Also see WILSON, Dennis

BEACH BOYS / Ray Anthony

EPs: 7-inch

CAPITOL (2186/2185 "Complete Selections from *Surfin' Safari* by the Beach Boys") 800-1200 62
(Promotional issue only.)
Also see ANTHONY, Ray

BEACH BOYS / Merry Clayton

Singles: 7-inch

ODE (66016 "Wouldn't It Be Nice"/"The Times They Are A-Changing")..15-20 71
Also see CLAYTON, Merry

BEACH BOYS / Hollyridge Strings

LPs: 10/12-inch

CAPITOL (3123 "Silver Platter Service")..75-125 64
(Promotional issue only.)
Also see HOLLYRIDGE STRINGS

BEACH BOYS / Jan & Dean

LPs: 10/12-inch

CAPITOL (8149 "The Beach Boys/Jan & Dean")..10-20 81
(Sold only at Radio Shack stores. Realistic #S1-7010.)
EXACT 5-8 81
Also see JAN & DEAN

BEACH BOYS / Little Richard

(Beach Boys & Little Richard / Beach Boys) ***P&R '88***

Singles: 7-inch

CRITIQUE (99392 "Happy Endings")..........3-5 87
ELEKTRA (69385 "Kokomo")........................3-5 88

Picture Sleeves

CRITIQUE (99392 "Happy Endings")..........3-5 87
Also see LITTLE RICHARD

BEACH BOYS / Marketts / Frogmen

LPs: 10/12-inch

GATEWAY (10104 "Surfin' ") 8-10 77
Also see FROGMEN
Also see MARKETTS

BEACH BOYS / Surfin' Six

LPs: 10/12-inch

EVEREST (4108 "Rare, Early Recordings")..5-10 81
ORBIT (688 "Greatest Hits: 1961-1963"). 10-15 72
SCEPTER (18004 "Best of the Beach Boys")..10-15 72
(Same contents as Orbit and Wand LPs.)
WAND (688 "Greatest Hits: 1961-1963"). 10-15 72

BEACH BOYS / Tony & Joe

Singles: 7-inch

ERA (042 "Surfer Girl"/"The Freeze")..........4-6 70
Also see TONY & JOE

BEACH BOYS / Tornadoes

LPs: 10/12-inch

ERA (805 "Biggest Beach Hits")..............15-20 69
Also see TORNADOES

BEACH BOYS / Trade Winds

Singles: 7-inch

TRIP (52 "Surfer Girl"/"New York's a Lonely Town")..4-6 70
Also see TRADE WINDS

BEACH BOYS with FRANKIE VALLI & 4 SEASONS

Singles: 7-inch

FBI..3-5 84
Also see 4 SEASONS

BEACH BUMS

Singles: 7-inch

ARE YOU KIDDING ME? (1010 "The Ballad of the Yellow Baret")..25-35 66
Members: Bob Seger; Doug Brown.
Also see BROWN, Doug
Also see SEGER, Bob

BEACH GIRLS

Singles: 7-inch

DYNO VOX (202 "Skiing in the Snow")....10-20 65
VAULT (905 "He's My Surfin' Guy") 15-25 63

BEACH NUTS

Singles: 7-inch

BANG (504 "Out in the Sun")....................25-35 65
Member: Lou Reed.
Also see REED, Lou

BEACH NUTS

Singles: 7-inch

CORONADO (131 "Surf Beat '65")...........10-20 65

Picture Sleeves

CORONADO (131 "Surf Beat '65")...........25-35 65

BEACHAM, Rufus

(With His Tampa Tappers; "Mr. Soul")

Singles: 78 rpm

CHART..8-12 56
KING..10-15 55

Singles: 7-inch

CHART (617 "Good Woman") 10-20 56
CHART (627 "I Can't Believe") 10-20 56
JAX (300 "Since I Fell for You") 50-100 52
(Red vinyl.)
KING (4807 "Love Have Mercy")..............25-50 55
KING (4820 "Let Me Be")..........................25-50 55
SCEPTER (1209 "I Need Your Love") 10-20 60
SCEPTER (1214 "Take It Easy Baby") 5-10 60
SCEPTER (1215 "Just One More Chance")..5-10 61

BEACHCOMBERS

Singles: 7-inch

BIG AL ("Memories")..............................75-100 62
(No selection number used.)
Also see KRAFTONES

BEACHCOMBERS

Singles: 7-inch

JERDEN (719 "Purple Peanuts")...............8-12 63
PANORAMA (11 "The Wheeley")............15-25 63

BEACON STREET UNION ***LP '68***

Singles: 7-inch

MGM..5-10 67-69
RTP..5-10 69

LPs: 10/12-inch

MGM (4517 "The Eyes of the Beacon Street Union")..15-25 68

MGM (4568 "The Clown Died in Marvin Gardens")... 15-25 68
Members: John Lincoln Wright; Wayne Ulaky; Paul Tartachny; Richard Weisberg; Robert Rhodes.

BEAD GAME

Singles: 7-inch

AVCO EMBASSY (4539 "Sweet Medusa")...5-10 70

LPs: 10/12-inch

AVCO EMBASSY (33009 "Welcome") ... 30-50 70
Members: Jim Hodder; John Sheldon.
Also see STEELY DAN

BEAL, Billy

Singles: 7-inch

RAYNARD (10027 "Foolish Me")... 15-25 65

BEALE STREET BOYS

Singles: 78 rpm

MGM (10141 "Teach Me Baby")... 20-30 48
MGM (10197 "Wedding Bells")... 20-30 48
MGM (10273 "Home")... 20-30 48
MGM (10505 "I Wish I Had a Dime")... 20-30 49
PARADISE (100 "There Is Nothing Greater Than a Prayer")... 25-35 55
SAVOY (731 "Back Alley Blues")... 20-25 50

Singles: 7-inch

OBA (102 "There's Nothing Greater Than a Prayer")... 75-125 60
OBA (109 "As High as My Heart")... 75-125 60
PARADISE (100 "There Is Nothing Greater Than a Prayer")... 200-300 55

BEAM, Tommy "Jim"

(With the Four Fifths)

Singles: 7-inch

100 PROOF (101 "My Little Jewel")... 200-300 58
SPARKETTE (1004 "Golden Boy")... 40-60 59

BEAR FAX

Singles: 7-inch

FUZZ (0901 "Love Is a Beautiful Thing"). 15-25 66
FUZZ (4141 "Out of Our Tree")... 20-30 66

BEARD, Dean

(With the Rhythm Rebels; with Crew Cats)

Singles: 78 rpm

ATLANTIC... 50-100 57
FOX... 35-55 55

Singles: 7-inch

ATLANTIC (1137 "Rakin' & Scrapin'")... 50-100 57
ATLANTIC (1162 "Party Party")... 50-100 57
ATLANTIC (1182 "Hold Me Close")... 10-20 58
BOOTS & SADDLE ("Judy Judy")... 25-35 66
(No selection number used.)
CANDIX (341 "The Day That I Lost You") ..5-10 62
CHALLENGE (59033 "Keeper of the Key")... 10-20 58
CHALLENGE (59048 "Little Lover")... 10-20 59
EDMORAL (1011 "Rakin & Scrapin")... 150-175 57
FOX (405 "Red Rover")... 75-125 55
GAYLO (112 "The Day That I Lost You") 10-20 62
GINA (1116 "Strawberry Shake")...5-10 64
INTERNATIONAL (107 "Big D")...5-10 63
JOED (715 "Tropical Nights")... 10-15 62
SANGELO (55 "Party Party")... 100-150 58
SIMS (299 "Honky Tonks in Heaven")...5-10 66
WINSTON... 10-15 62-63
Session: Champs; Jordanaires.
Also see CHAMPS
Also see JORDANAIRES
Also see SIKES, Bobby, & Rhythm Rebels
Also see SIKES, Rick, & Rhythm Rebels

BEARD, Herbert

Singles: 78 rpm

COOL (101 "Gal! You Need a Whippin'") 35-50 53

BEARINGS

Singles: 7-inch

PYRAMID (6953 "Anything You Want")... 20-40 66
Members: Dave Britt; George Pittman; Lance Walters.

BEASLEY, Billy

Singles: 7-inch

DEE CAL (500 "A Million Teardrops")... 15-25 59

BEASLEY, Good Rockin' Sam

(Good Rockin' Beasley)

Singles: 78 rpm

EXCELLO... 15-20 53-55

Singles: 7-inch

EXCELLO (2011 "Happy Go Lucky")... 35-50 53
EXCELLO (2059 "Baby, I'm Fool Proof"). 25-35 55
EXCELLO (2070 "Funny Funny Feeling")...25-35 55

BEASLEY, Good Rockin' Sam / Kid King's Combo

Singles: 78 rpm

EXCELLO...15-20 55

Singles: 7-inch

EXCELLO (2051 "Now Listen Baby")...25-35 55
Also see BEASLEY, Good Rockin' Sam
Also see KING, Kid

BEASLEY, Jimmy

(With the Rockets)

Singles: 78 rpm

MODERN...8-12 56-57
SILHOUETTE...8-12 56

Singles: 7-inch

MODERN...15-25 56-57
SILHOUETTE...15-25 56
UNITED MODERN (103 "You're My Only Love")...5-10

LPs: 10/12-inch

CROWN (5014 "The Fabulous Jimmy Beasley")...50-75 57
CROWN (5247 "Twist with Jimmy Beasley")...20-30 61
MODERN (1214 "The Fabulous Jimmy Beasley")...75-125 56
Also see ROCKETS

BEASTIE BOYS *P&R/R&B/LP '86*

Singles: 12-inch

DEF JAM...4-6 86-87

Singles: 7-inch

CAPITOL (44454 "Hey Ladies"/"Shake Your Rump")...3-4 89
CAPITOL (PRO-79698 "Hey Ladies"/"Hey Ladies")...3-4 89
(Promotional issue.)
DEF JAM...3-5 86-87

LPs: 10/12-inch

CAPITOL (Except 79461)...5-8 89
CAPITOL (79461 "Hip Hop Sampler")...35-45 89
(Promotional issue only.)
DEF JAM...5-10 86-87
Members: Adam Horovitz; Michael Diamond; Adam Yaunch.

BEAT OF EARTH

LPs: 10/12-inch

RADISH (0001 "The Beat of the Earth")...250-350 68
Members: Morgan Chapman; Karen Darby; J.R. Nichols; Ron Collins; Bill Phillips; Sherry Phillips.

BEATIN' PATH

Singles: 7-inch

FONTANA (1583 "The Original Nothing People")...20-30 67
JUBILEE (5556 "Doctor Stone")...10-15 66
Also see STARLITES

BEATLE BUDDIES

LPs: 10/12-inch

DIPLOMAT (2313 "The Beatle Buddies").15-25 64
Also see STEWART, Judy, & Her Beatle Buddies

BEATLETTES

Singles: 7-inch

ASSAULT (1893 "Yes, You Can Hold My Hand")...10-20 64
JAMIE (1270 "Dance, Beatle Dance")...8-12 64

BEATLES *P&R '64*

Singles: 12-inch

CAPITOL (SPRO-9758 "Movie Medley")..40-50 81
(Promotional issue only.)
ULTIMIX (120 "Twist and Shout")...100-125 88
(Promotional issue only.)

Singles: 7-inch

APPLE (2056 "Hello Goodbye")...25-35 71
(With black star on label.)
APPLE (2056 "Hello Goodbye")...10-20 71
(No black star on label.)
APPLE (2138 "Lady Madonna")...25-35 71
(With black star on label.)
APPLE (2138 "Lady Madonna")...10-20 75
(No black star, but has "All Rights Reserved, etc." on label.)
APPLE (2276 "Hey Jude")...10-15 68
(Apple label with Capitol logo.)
APPLE (2276 "Hey Jude")...5-10 71
(Apple label with "Mfd by Apple, etc." on perimeter.)
APPLE (2276 "Hey Jude")...15-20 75
(Apple label with "All Rights Reserved, etc.")
APPLE (2490 "Get Back")...6-10 69
(Apple label with Capitol logo, or with "Mfd by Apple, etc." perimeter print.)
APPLE (2490 "Get Back")...15-20 75
(Apple label with "All Rights Reserved, etc.")
APPLE (2531 "Ballad of John & Yoko")....10-15 69
(Apple label with Capitol logo, or with "Mfd by Apple, etc." perimeter print.)
APPLE (2531 "Ballad of John & Yoko")....15-20 75
(Apple label with "All Rights Reserved, etc.")
APPLE (2654 "Something")...75-100 69
(Apple label with Capitol logo.)
APPLE (2654 "Something")...8-12 71
(Apple label with "Mfd by Apple, etc." perimeter print.)
APPLE (2654 "Something")...15-20 75
(Apple label with "All Rights Reserved, etc.")
APPLE (2764 "Let It Be")...8-12 69
(Apple label with Capitol logo, or with "Mfd by Apple, etc." perimeter print.)
APPLE (2764 "Let It Be")...15-20 75
(Apple label with "All Rights Reserved, etc.")
APPLE (2832 "Long and Winding Road") 15-20 69
(Apple label with Capitol logo.)
APPLE (2832 "Long and Winding Road") ..6-10 71
(Apple label with "Mfd by Apple, etc." perimeter print.)
APPLE (2832 "Long and Winding Road") 15-20 75
(Apple label with "All Rights Reserved, etc.")
APPLE (5112 "I Want to Hold Your Hand")...30-40 71
(Has black star on label.)
APPLE (5112 "I Want to Hold Your Hand")...10-15 71
(No black star on label.)
APPLE (5112 "I Want to Hold Your Hand")...15-20 75
(Apple label with "All Rights Reserved, etc.")
APPLE (5150 "Can't Buy Me Love")...25-35 71
(Has black star on label.)
APPLE (5150 "Can't Buy Me Love")...10-15 71
(No black star on label.)
APPLE (5150 "Can't Buy Me Love")...15-20 75
(Apple label with "All Rights Reserved, etc.")
APPLE (5222 "A Hard Day's Night")...25-35 71
(With black star on label.)
APPLE (5222 "A Hard Day's Night")...10-15 71
(No black star on label.)
APPLE (5222 "A Hard Day's Night")...15-20 75
(Apple label with "All Rights Reserved, etc.")
APPLE (5327 "I Feel Fine")...25-35 71
(With black star on label.)
APPLE (5327 "I Feel Fine")...10-15 71
(No black star on label.)
APPLE (5327 "I Feel Fine")...15-20 75
(Apple label with "All Rights Reserved, etc.")
APPLE (5234 "I'll Cry Instead")...25-35 71
(With black star on label.)
APPLE (5234 "I'll Cry Instead")...10-15 71
(No black star on label.)
APPLE (5234 "I'll Cry Instead")...15-20 75
(Apple label with "All Rights Reserved, etc.")
APPLE (5235 "And I Love Her")...25-35 71
(With black star on label.)
APPLE (5235 "And I Love Her")...10-15 71
(No black star on label.)
APPLE (5235 "And I Love Her")...15-20 75
(Apple label with "All Rights Reserved, etc.")
APPLE (5255 "Matchbox")...25-35 71
(With black star on label.)
APPLE (5255 "Matchbox")...10-15 71
(No black star on label.)
APPLE (5255 "Matchbox")...15-20 75
(Apple label with "All Rights Reserved, etc.")
APPLE (5371 "Eight Days a Week")...25-35 71
(Has black star on label.)
APPLE (5371 "Eight Days a Week")...10-15 71
(No black star on label.)
APPLE (5371 "Eight Days a Week")...15-20 75
(Apple label with "All Rights Reserved, etc.")
APPLE (5407 "Ticket to Ride")...25-35 71
(With black star on label.)
APPLE (5407 "Ticket to Ride")...10-15 71
(No black star on label.)
APPLE (5407 "Ticket to Ride")...15-20 75
(Apple label with "All Rights Reserved, etc.")
APPLE (5476 "Help!")...25-35 71
(With black star on label.)
APPLE (5476 "Help!")...10-15 71
(No black star on label.)
APPLE (5476 "Help!")...15-20 75
(Apple label with "All Rights Reserved, etc.")
APPLE (5498 "Yesterday")...25-35 71
(With black star on label.)
APPLE (5498 "Yesterday")...10-15 71
(No black star on label.)
APPLE (5498 "Yesterday")...15-20 75
(Apple label with "All Rights Reserved, etc.")
APPLE (5555 "We Can Work It Out")...25-35 71
(With black star on label.)
APPLE (5555 "We Can Work It Out")...10-15 71
(No black star on label.)
APPLE (5555 "We Can Work It Out")...15-20 75
(Apple label with "All Rights Reserved, etc.")
APPLE (5587 "Nowhere Man")...25-35 71
(With black star on label.)
APPLE (5587 "Nowhere Man")...10-15 71
(No black star on label.)
APPLE (5587 "Nowhere Man")...15-20 75
(Apple label with "All Rights Reserved, etc.")
APPLE (5651 "Paperback Writer")...25-35 71
(With black star on label.)
APPLE (5651 "Paperback Writer")...10-15 71
(No black star on label.)
APPLE (5651 "Paperback Writer")...15-20 75
(Apple label with "All Rights Reserved, etc.")
APPLE (5715 "Yellow Submarine")...25-35 71
(With black star on label.)
APPLE (5715 "Yellow Submarine")...10-15 71
(No black star on label.)
APPLE (5715 "Yellow Submarine")...15-20 75
(Apple label with "All Rights Reserved, etc.")
APPLE (5810 "Penny Lane")...25-35 71
(With black star on label.)
APPLE (5810 "Penny Lane")...10-15 71
(No black star on label.)
APPLE (5810 "Penny Lane")...15-20 75
(Apple label with "All Rights Reserved, etc.")
APPLE (5964 "All You Need Is Love")...25-35 71
(With black star on label.)
APPLE (5964 "All You Need Is Love")...10-15 71
(No black star on label.)
APPLE (5964 "All You Need Is Love")...15-20 75
(Apple label with "All Rights Reserved, etc.")
ATCO (6302 "Sweet Georgia Brown") .175-200 64
(Shown as by "The Beatles with Tony Sheridan.")
ATCO (6308 "Ain't She Sweet")...50-60 64
(Yellow and white label. Without cut-out hole.)
ATCO (6308 "Ain't She Sweet")...25-35 64
(Yellow and white label. With cut-out hole.)
ATCO (6308 "Ain't She Sweet")...30-40 69
(Yellow and white label with "Mfg by Atlantic.." print.)
ATLANTIC (13243 "Ain't She Sweet")... 10-15 83
(Gold and black label.)
ATLANTIC (13243 "Ain't She Sweet")...20-25 85
(Silver, black and red label.)
BRS (1/2 "Murray the 'K' and the Beatles As It Happened")...30-40 64
CAPITOL (2056 "Hello Goodbye")...20-30 67
(Yellow/orange swirl label without "Subsidiary of Capitol, etc." perimeter print.)
CAPITOL (2056 "Hello Goodbye")...40-50 68
(Yellow/orange swirl label with "Subsidiary of Capitol, etc." perimeter print.)
CAPITOL (2056 "Hello Goodbye")...55-65 69
(Red/orange label with dome logo.)
CAPITOL (2056 "Hello Goodbye")... 15-20 69
(Red/orange label with round logo.)
CAPITOL (2056 "Hello Goodbye")...5-8 76
(Orange label.)
CAPITOL (2056 "Hello Goodbye")... 10-15 78
(Purple or black label.)
CAPITOL (2138 "Lady Madonna")...20-30 68
(Yellow/orange swirl label without "Subsidiary of Capitol, etc." perimeter print.)
CAPITOL (2138 "Lady Madonna")...40-50 68
(Yellow/orange swirl label with "Subsidiary of Capitol, etc." perimeter print.)
CAPITOL (2138 "Lady Madonna")...55-65 69
(Red/orange label with dome logo.)
CAPITOL (2138 "Lady Madonna")... 15-20 69
(Red/orange label with round logo.)
CAPITOL (2138 "Lady Madonna")... 5-8 76
(Orange or purple or black label.)
CAPITOL (2276 "Hey Jude")...5-8 76
(Orange or purple or black label.)
CAPITOL (2490 "Get Back")...5-8 76
(Orange or purple or black label.)

CAPITOL (2531 "Ballad of John & Yoko")....5-8 78
(Purple or black label.)
CAPITOL (2654 "Something").....................5-8 76
(Orange or purple or black label.)
CAPITOL (2764 "Let It Be")..........................5-8 76
(Orange or purple or black label.)
CAPITOL (2832 "Long and Winding Road").5-8 76
(Orange or purple or black label.)
CAPITOL (4274 "Got to Get You into My
Life")...5-10 76
(Orange or purple or black label.)
CAPITOL (4347 "Ob-La-Di, Ob-La-Da").....5-10 76
(Orange or purple or black label.)
CAPITOL (4612 "Sgt. Pepper's Lonely Hearts Club
Band" & "With A Little Help From My
Friends")...5-8 78
(Purple or black label.)
CAPITOL (B-5100 "Movie Medley"/"Fab Four on
Film")... 40-50 82
(First issued with *Movie Medley* backed with *Fab Four on Film*, the Beatles talking about the film *A Hard Day's Night*.)
CAPITOL (B-5107 "Movie Medley"/"I'm Happy Just to
Dance with You")......................................3-5 82
CAPITOL (5112 "I Want to Hold Your
Hand").. 35-45 64
(Yellow/orange swirl label without "Subsidiary of Capitol, etc." perimeter print. Perimeter has *white* print. Reissue in 1984 has *black* perimeter print.)
CAPITOL (5112 "I Want to Hold Your
Hand").. 60-70 68
(Yellow/orange swirl label with "Subsidiary of Capitol, etc." perimeter print.)
CAPITOL (5112 "I Want to Hold Your
Hand").. 65-75 69
(Red/orange label with dome logo.)
CAPITOL (5112 "I Want to Hold Your
Hand").. 15-25 69
(Red/orange label with round logo.)
CAPITOL (5112 "I Want to Hold Your
Hand")...5-10 76
(Orange label.)
CAPITOL (5112 "I Want to Hold Your
Hand").. 10-15 78
(Purple label "Mfd. by Capitol, etc." perimeter print.)
CAPITOL (5112 "I Want to Hold Your
Hand")...3-5 84
(Yellow/orange swirl label with *black* perimeter print. Original 1964 issue has *white* perimeter print.)
CAPITOL (5112 "I Want to Hold Your
Hand")...5-8 86
(Black label.)
CAPITOL (5112 "I Want to Hold Your
Hand")...4-6 84
(Purple label with "Manufactured by Capitol, etc." perimeter print.)
CAPITOL (5112 "I Want to Hold Your
Hand")...3-5 94
(Yellow/orange swirl label. Has "NR-58123" in trail-off area.)
CAPITOL (5150 "Can't Buy Me Love").... 25-35 64
(Yellow/orange swirl label without "Subsidiary of Capitol, etc." perimeter print.)
CAPITOL (5150 "Can't Buy Me Love").... 40-50 68
(Yellow/orange swirl label with "Subsidiary of Capitol, etc." perimeter print.)
CAPITOL (5150 "Can't Buy Me Love").... 60-70 69
(Red/orange label with dome logo.)
CAPITOL (5150 "Can't Buy Me Love").... 15-20 69
(Red/orange label with round logo.)
CAPITOL (5150 "Can't Buy Me Love").........5-8 76
(Orange label.)
CAPITOL (5150 "Can't Buy Me Love").... 10-15 78
(Purple label.)
CAPITOL (B-5189 "Love Me Do")................4-6 82
(Yellow/orange or black or purple label.)
CAPITOL (5222 "A Hard Day's Night").... 25-35 64
(Yellow/orange swirl label without "Subsidiary of Capitol, etc." perimeter print.)
CAPITOL (5222 "A Hard Day's Night").... 40-50 64
(Yellow/orange swirl label with "Subsidiary of Capitol, etc." in *white* perimeter print.)
CAPITOL (5222 "A Hard Day's Night").. 75-100 64
(Yellow/orange swirl label with "Subsidiary of Capitol, etc." in *black* perimeter print.)
CAPITOL (5222 "A Hard Day's Night").... 60-70 69
(Red/orange label with dome logo.)
CAPITOL (5222 "A Hard Day's Night").... 15-20 69
(Red/orange label with round logo.)
CAPITOL (5222 "A Hard Day's Night").........5-8 76
(Orange label.)
CAPITOL (5222 "A Hard Day's Night").....10-15 78
(Purple label.)
CAPITOL (5234 "I'll Cry Instead")............25-35 64
(Yellow/orange swirl label without "Subsidiary of Capitol, etc." perimeter print.)
CAPITOL (5234 "I'll Cry Instead")............50-70 64
(Yellow/orange swirl label with "Subsidiary of Capitol, etc." perimeter print.)
CAPITOL (5234 "I'll Cry Instead")............60-75 69
(Red/orange label with dome logo.)
CAPITOL (5234 "I'll Cry Instead")............15-20 69
(Red/orange label with round logo.)
CAPITOL (5234 "I'll Cry Instead")................5-8 76
(Orange label.)
CAPITOL (5234 "I'll Cry Instead")............10-15 78
(Purple label.)
CAPITOL (5235 "And I Love Her")...........25-35 64
(Yellow/orange swirl label without "Subsidiary of Capitol, etc." perimeter print.)
CAPITOL (5235 "And I Love Her")...........40-50 64
(Yellow/orange swirl label with "Subsidiary of Capitol, etc." in *white* perimeter print.)
CAPITOL (5235 "And I Love Her").........75-100 64
(Yellow/orange swirl label with "Subsidiary of Capitol, etc." in *black* perimeter print.)
CAPITOL (5235 "And I Love Her")...........60-70 69
(Red/orange label with dome logo.)
CAPITOL (5235 "And I Love Her")...........15-20 69
(Red/orange label with round logo.)
CAPITOL (5235 "And I Love Her")...............5-8 76
(Orange label.)
CAPITOL (5235 "And I Love Her")...........10-15 78
(Purple label.)
CAPITOL (5255 "Matchbox")....................25-35 64
(Yellow/orange swirl label without "Subsidiary of Capitol, etc." perimeter print.)
CAPITOL (5255 "Matchbox")....................40-50 64
(Yellow/orange swirl label with "Subsidiary of Capitol, etc." perimeter print.)
CAPITOL (5255 "Matchbox")....................60-70 69
(Red/orange label with dome logo.)
CAPITOL (5255 "Matchbox")....................15-20 69
(Red/orange label with round logo.)
CAPITOL (5255 "Matchbox").........................5-8 76
(Orange label.)
CAPITOL (5255 "Matchbox")....................10-15 78
(Purple label.)
CAPITOL (5327 "I Feel Fine")..................25-35 64
(Yellow/orange swirl label without "Subsidiary of Capitol, etc." perimeter print.)
CAPITOL (5327 "I Feel Fine")..................40-50 64
(Yellow/orange swirl label with "Subsidiary of Capitol, etc." perimeter print.)
CAPITOL (5327 "I Feel Fine")..................60-70 69
(Red/orange label with dome logo.)
CAPITOL (5327 "I Feel Fine")..................15-20 69
(Red/orange label with round logo.)
CAPITOL (5327 "I Feel Fine").......................5-8 76
(Orange label.)
CAPITOL (5327 "I Feel Fine")..................10-15 78
(Purple label.)
CAPITOL (5371 "Eight Days a Week").....25-35 65
(Yellow/orange swirl label without "Subsidiary of Capitol, etc." perimeter print.)
CAPITOL (5371 "Eight Days a Week").....40-50 68
(Yellow/orange swirl label with "Subsidiary of Capitol, etc." perimeter print.)
CAPITOL (5371 "Eight Days a Week").....60-70 69
(Red/orange label with dome logo.)
CAPITOL (5371 "Eight Days a Week").....15-20 69
(Red/orange label with round logo.)
CAPITOL (5371 "Eight Days a Week").........5-8 76
(Orange label.)
CAPITOL (5371 "Eight Days a Week").....10-15 78
(Purple label.)
CAPITOL (5407 "Ticket to Ride").............25-35 64
(Yellow/orange swirl label without "Subsidiary of Capitol, etc." perimeter print.)
CAPITOL (5407 "Ticket to Ride").............40-50 64
(Yellow/orange swirl label with "Subsidiary of Capitol, etc." in *white* perimeter print.)
CAPITOL (5407 "Ticket to Ride")...........75-100 68
(Yellow/orange swirl label with "Subsidiary of Capitol, etc." in *black* perimeter print.)
CAPITOL (5407 "Ticket to Ride").............60-70 69
(Red/orange label with dome logo.)
CAPITOL (5407 "Ticket to Ride").............15-20 69
(Red/orange label with round logo.)
CAPITOL (5407 "Ticket to Ride") 5-8 76
(Orange label.)
CAPITOL (5407 "Ticket to Ride") 10-15 78
(Purple label.)
CAPITOL (5476 "Help!")..........................25-35 65
(Yellow/orange swirl label without "Subsidiary of Capitol, etc." perimeter print.)
CAPITOL (5476 "Help!")..........................40-50 68
(Yellow/orange swirl label with "Subsidiary of Capitol, etc." in *white* perimeter print.)
CAPITOL (5476 "Help!")........................75-100 68
(Yellow/orange swirl label with "Subsidiary of Capitol, etc." in *black* perimeter print.)
CAPITOL (5476 "Help!")..........................60-70 69
(Red/orange label with dome logo.)
CAPITOL (5476 "Help!")..........................15-20 69
(Red/orange label with round logo.)
CAPITOL (5476 "Help!")...............................5-8 76
(Orange label.)
CAPITOL (5476 "Help!")..........................10-15 78
(Purple label.)
CAPITOL (5498 "Yesterday") 20-30 64
(Yellow/orange swirl label without "Subsidiary of Capitol, etc." perimeter print.)
CAPITOL (5498 "Yesterday") 40-50 68
(Yellow/orange swirl label with "Subsidiary of Capitol, etc." in *white* perimeter print.)
CAPITOL (5498 "Yesterday") 75-100 68
(Yellow/orange swirl label with "Subsidiary of Capitol, etc." in *black* perimeter print.)
CAPITOL (5498 "Yesterday") 60-70 69
(Red/orange label with dome logo.)
CAPITOL (5498 "Yesterday") 15-20 69
(Red/orange label with round logo.)
CAPITOL (5498 "Yesterday") 5-8 76
(Orange label.)
CAPITOL (5498 "Yesterday") 10-15 78
(Purple label.)
CAPITOL (5555 "We Can Work It Out")...20-30 66
(Yellow/orange swirl label without "Subsidiary of Capitol, etc." perimeter print.)
CAPITOL (5555 "We Can Work It Out")...40-50 68
(Yellow/orange swirl label with "Subsidiary of Capitol, etc." perimeter print.)
CAPITOL (5555 "We Can Work It
Out")...1200-1500 69
(Red and white label. "Starline" series.)
CAPITOL (5555 "We Can Work It Out")...60-75 69
(Red/orange label with dome logo.)
CAPITOL (5555 "We Can Work It Out")...15-20 69
(Red/orange label with round logo.)
CAPITOL (5555 "We Can Work It Out").......5-8 76
(Orange label.)
CAPITOL (5555 "We Can Work It Out")...10-15 78
(Purple label.)
CAPITOL (5587 "Nowhere Man")............25-50 66
(Yellow/orange swirl label without "Subsidiary of Capitol, etc." perimeter print.)
CAPITOL (5587 "Nowhere Man")............40-50 68
(Yellow/orange swirl label with "Subsidiary of Capitol, etc." perimeter print.)
CAPITOL (5587 "Nowhere Man")............60-75 69
(Red/orange label with dome logo.)
CAPITOL (5587 "Nowhere Man")............15-20 69
(Red/orange label with round logo.)
CAPITOL (5587 "Nowhere Man")................5-8 76
(Orange label.)
CAPITOL (5587 "Nowhere Man")............10-15 78
(Purple label.)
CAPITOL (B-5624 "Twist and Shout")..........4-6 86
(Black or purple label.)
CAPITOL (5651 "Paperback Writer") 25-50 66
(Yellow/orange swirl label without "Subsidiary of Capitol, etc." perimeter print.)
CAPITOL (5651 "Paperback Writer") 40-50 68
(Yellow/orange swirl label with "Subsidiary of Capitol, etc." in *white* perimeter print.)
CAPITOL (5651 "Paperback Writer") 75-100 68
(Yellow/orange swirl label with "Subsidiary of Capitol, etc." in *black* perimeter print.)
CAPITOL (5651 "Paperback Writer") 60-75 69
(Red/orange label with dome logo.)
CAPITOL (5651 "Paperback Writer") 15-20 69
(Red/orange label with round logo.)
CAPITOL (5651 "Paperback Writer")...........5-8 76
(Orange label.)
CAPITOL (5651 "Paperback Writer") 10-15 78
(Purple label.)
CAPITOL (5715 "Yellow Submarine")......20-30 66
(Yellow/orange swirl label without "Subsidiary of Capitol, etc." perimeter print.)
CAPITOL (5715 "Yellow Submarine")......40-50 68
(Yellow/orange swirl label with "Subsidiary of Capitol, etc." perimeter print.)
CAPITOL (5715 "Yellow Submarine")......60-70 69
(Red/orange label with dome logo.)
CAPITOL (5715 "Yellow Submarine")......15-20 69
(Red/orange label with round logo.)
CAPITOL (5715 "Yellow Submarine").........5-8 76
(Orange label.)
CAPITOL (5715 "Yellow Submarine")......10-15 78
(Purple label.)
CAPITOL (5810 "Penny Lane")...............25-35 66
(Yellow/orange swirl label without "Subsidiary of Capitol, etc." perimeter print.)
CAPITOL (5810 "Penny Lane")...............40-50 68
(Yellow/orange swirl label with "Subsidiary of Capitol, etc." perimeter print.)
CAPITOL (5810 "Penny Lane")...............60-70 69
(Red/orange label with dome logo.)
CAPITOL (5810 "Penny Lane")...............15-20 69
(Red/orange label with round logo.)
CAPITOL (5810 "Penny Lane")....................5-8 76
(Orange label.)
CAPITOL (5810 "Penny Lane")...............10-15 78
(Purple label.)
CAPITOL (5964 "All You Need Is Love").20-30 67
(Yellow/orange swirl label without "Subsidiary of Capitol, etc." perimeter print.)
CAPITOL (5964 "All You Need Is Love").40-50 68
(Yellow/orange swirl label with "Subsidiary of Capitol, etc." perimeter print.)
CAPITOL (5964 "All You Need Is Love").60-75 69
(Red/orange label with dome logo.)
CAPITOL (5964 "All You Need Is Love").15-20 69
(Red/orange label with round logo.)
CAPITOL (5964 "All You Need Is Love").....5-8 76
(Orange label.)
CAPITOL (5964 "All You Need Is Love").10-15 78
(Purple label.)
CAPITOL (6061 "Twist and Shout").....100-125 65
(Green label. "Starline" series.)
CAPITOL (6062 "Love Me Do")...........100-125 65
(Green label. "Starline" series.)
CAPITOL (6063 "Please Please Me")..100-125 65
(Green label. "Starline" series.)
CAPITOL (6064 "Do You Want to Know a
Secret")...100-125 65
(Green label. "Starline" series.)
CAPITOL (6065 "Misery")....................100-125 65
(Green label. "Starline" series.)
CAPITOL (6065 "Misery").........................20-30 71
(Red/orange label. "Starline" series.)
CAPITOL (6066 "Kansas City")...............70-90 65
(Green label. "Starline" series.)
CAPITOL (6066 "Kansas City")...............20-30 71
(Red/orange label. "Starline" series.)
CAPITOL (A-6278 "I Want to Hold Your
Hand")..15-25 81
(Blue label reads "stereo" but plays mono. "Starline" series.)
CAPITOL (A-6278 "I Want to Hold Your
Hand")..20-30 81
(Blue label reads "mono." "Starline" series.)
CAPITOL (X-6278 "I Want to Hold Your
Hand")..10-15 81
(Blue label reads "mono." "Starline" series. .)
CAPITOL (A-6279 "Can't Buy Me Love").....5-8 81
(Blue label reads "stereo" but plays mono. "Starline" series.)
CAPITOL (A-6279 "Can't Buy Me Love").15-25 81
(Blue label reads "mono." "Starline" series.)
CAPITOL (X-6279 "Can't Buy Me Love").....4-6 81
(Blue label reads "mono." "Starline" series. .)
CAPITOL (6279 "Can't Buy Me Love").........4-6 86
(Black or purple label. "Starline" series.)
CAPITOL (A-6281 "A Hard Day's Night")......5-8 81
(Blue label reads "stereo" but plays mono. "Starline" series.)
CAPITOL (A-6281 "A Hard Day's Night").15-25 81
(Blue label reads "mono." "Starline" series.)
CAPITOL (X-6281 "A Hard Day's Night").....4-6 81
(Blue label reads "mono." "Starline" series.)
CAPITOL (6281 "A Hard Day's Night").........4-6 86
(Black or purple label "Starline" series.)
CAPITOL (A-6282 "I'll Cry Instead")............5-8 81
(Blue label reads "stereo" but plays mono. "Starline" series.)

CAPITOL (A-6282 "I'll Cry Instead") 15-25 81
(Blue label reads "mono." "Starline" series.)
CAPITOL (X-6282 "I'll Cry Instead") 4-6 81
(Blue label reads "mono." "Starline" series.)
CAPITOL (6282 "I'll Cry Instead") 4-6 86
(Black or purple label "Starline" series.)
CAPITOL (A-6283 "And I Love Her") 5-8 81
(Blue label reads "stereo" but plays mono. "Starline" series.)
CAPITOL (A-6283 "And I Love Her") 15-25 81
(Blue label reads "mono." "Starline" series.)
CAPITOL (X-6283 "And I Love Her") 4-6 81
(Blue label reads "mono." "Starline" series.)
CAPITOL (6283 "And I Love Her") 4-6 86
(Black or purple label. "Starline" series.)
CAPITOL (A-6284 "Matchbox") 5-8 81
(Blue label reads "stereo" but plays mono. "Starline" series.)
CAPITOL (A-6284 "Matchbox") 15-25 81
(Blue label reads "mono." "Starline" series.)
CAPITOL (X-6284 "Matchbox") 4-6 81
(Blue label reads "mono." "Starline" series.)
CAPITOL (6284 "Matchbox") 4-6 86
(Black or purple label. "Starline" series.)
CAPITOL (A-6286 "I Feel Fine") 5-8 81
(Blue label reads "stereo" but plays mono. "Starline" series.)
CAPITOL (A-6286 "I Feel Fine") 15-25 81
(Blue label reads "mono." "Starline" series.)
CAPITOL (X-6286 "I Feel Fine") 4-6 81
(Blue label reads "mono." "Starline" series.)
CAPITOL (6286 "I Feel Fine") 4-6 86
(Black or purple label. "Starline" series.)
CAPITOL (A-6287 "Eight Days a Week") 5-8 81
(Blue label reads "stereo" but plays mono. "Starline" series.)
CAPITOL (A-6287 "Eight Days a Week") 15-25 81
(Blue label reads "mono." "Starline" series.)
CAPITOL (X-6287 "Eight Days a Week") 4-6 81
(Blue label reads "mono." "Starline" series.)
CAPITOL (6287 "Eight Days a Week") 4-6 86
(Black or purple label. "Starline" series.)
CAPITOL (A-6288 "Ticket to Ride") 5-8 81
(Blue label reads "stereo" but plays mono. "Starline" series.)
CAPITOL (A-6288 "Ticket to Ride") 15-25 81
(Blue label reads "mono." "Starline" series.)
CAPITOL (X-6288 "Ticket to Ride") 4-6 81
(Blue label reads "mono." "Starline" series.)
CAPITOL (6288 "Ticket to Ride") 4-6 86
(Black or purple label. "Starline" series.)
CAPITOL (A-6290 "Help!") 5-8 81
(Blue label reads "stereo" but plays mono. "Starline" series.)
CAPITOL (A-6290 "Help!") 15-25 81
(Blue label reads "mono." "Starline" series.)
CAPITOL (X-6290 "Help!") 4-6 81
(Blue label reads "mono." "Starline" series.)
CAPITOL (6290 "Help!") 4-6 86
(Black or purple label "Starline" series.)
CAPITOL (A-6291 "Yesterday") 5-8 81
(Blue label reads "stereo" but plays mono. "Starline" series.)
CAPITOL (A-6291 "Yesterday") 15-25 81
(Blue label reads "mono." "Starline" series.)
CAPITOL (X-6291 "Yesterday") 4-6 81
(Blue label reads "mono." "Starline" series.)
CAPITOL (6291 "Yesterday") 4-6 86
(Black or purple label "Starline" series.)
CAPITOL (A-6293 "We Can Work It Out") 5-8 81
(Blue label reads "stereo" but plays mono. "Starline" series.)
CAPITOL (A-6293 "We Can Work It Out") 15-25 81
(Blue label reads "mono." "Starline" series.)
CAPITOL (X-6293 "We Can Work It Out") 4-6 81
(Blue label reads "mono." "Starline" series.)
CAPITOL (6293 "We Can Work It Out") 4-6 86
(Black or purple label "Starline" series.)
CAPITOL (A-6294 "Nowhere Man") 5-8 81
(Blue label reads "stereo" but plays mono. "Starline" series.)
CAPITOL (A-6294 "Nowhere Man") 15-25 81
(Blue label reads "mono." "Starline" series.)
CAPITOL (X-6294 "Nowhere Man") 4-6 81
(Blue label reads "mono." "Starline" series.)
CAPITOL (6294 "Nowhere Man") 4-6 86
(Black or purple label "Starline" series.)

CAPITOL (A-6296 "Paperback Writer") 5-8 81
(Blue label reads "stereo" but plays mono. "Starline" series.)
CAPITOL (A-6296 "Paperback Writer") 15-25 81
(Blue label reads "mono." "Starline" series.)
CAPITOL (X-6296 "Paperback Writer") 4-6 81
(Blue label reads "mono." "Starline" series.)
CAPITOL (6296 "Paperback Writer") 4-6 86
(Black or purple label "Starline" series.)
CAPITOL (A-6297 "Yellow Submarine") 5-8 81
(Blue label reads "stereo" but plays mono. "Starline" series.)
CAPITOL (A-6297 "Yellow Submarine") ...15-25 81
(Blue label reads "mono." "Starline" series.)
CAPITOL (X-6297 "Yellow Submarine") 4-6 81
(Blue label reads "mono." "Starline" series.)
CAPITOL (6297 "Yellow Submarine") 4-6 86
(Black or purple label "Starline" series.)
CAPITOL (A-6299 "Penny Lane") 5-8 81
(Blue label reads "stereo" but plays mono. "Starline" series.)
CAPITOL (A-6299 "Penny Lane") 15-25 81
(Blue label reads "mono." "Starline" series.)
CAPITOL (X-6299 "Penny Lane") 4-6 81
(Blue label reads "mono." "Starline" series.)
CAPITOL (6299 "Penny Lane") 4-6 86
(Black or purple label "Starline" series.)
CAPITOL (A-6300 "All You Need Is Love") ..5-8 81
(Blue label reads "stereo" but plays mono. "Starline" series.)
CAPITOL (A-6300 "All You Need Is Love") 15-25 81
(Blue label reads "mono." "Starline" series.)
CAPITOL (X-6300 "All You Need Is Love") ..4-6 81
(Blue label reads "mono." "Starline" series.)
CAPITOL (6300 "All You Need Is Love") ..15-20 86
(Black label. "Starline" series.)
CAPITOL (17488 "Birthday") 40-50 94
(Black vinyl, 30th Anniversary juke box issue.)
CAPITOL (17488 "Birthday") 5-10 94
(Green vinyl, 30th Anniversary juke box issue.)
CAPITOL (17688 "She Loves You") 5-10 94
(Red vinyl, 30th Anniversary juke box issue.)
CAPITOL (17689 "I Want to Hold Your Hand") 5-10 94
(Clear vinyl, 30th Anniversary juke box issue.)
CAPITOL (17690 "Can't Buy Me Love") 5-10 94
(Green vinyl, 30th Anniversary juke box issue.)
CAPITOL (17691 "Help!") 5-10 94
(White vinyl, 30th Anniversary juke box issue.)
CAPITOL (17692 "A Hard Day's Night") 5-10 94
(White vinyl, 30th Anniversary juke box issue.)
CAPITOL (17693 "All You Need Is Love") ..5-10 94
(Pink vinyl, 30th Anniversary juke box issue.)
CAPITOL (17694 "Hey Jude") 5-10 94
(Blue vinyl, 30th Anniversary juke box issue.)
CAPITOL (17695 "Let It Be") 5-10 94
(Yellow vinyl, 30th Anniversary juke box issue.)
CAPITOL (17696 "Yellow Submarine") 5-10 94
(Yellow vinyl, 30th Anniversary juke box issue.)
CAPITOL (17697 "Penny Lane") 5-10 94
(Red vinyl, 30th Anniversary juke box issue.)
CAPITOL (17698 "Something") 5-10 94
(Blue vinyl, 30th Anniversary juke box issue.)
CAPITOL (17699 "Twist & Shout") 5-10 94
(Pink vinyl, 30th Anniversary juke box issue.)
CAPITOL (17700 "Here Comes the Sun") 3-5 94
(Orange vinyl, 30th Anniversary juke box issue.)
CAPITOL (17701 "Sgt. Pepper's Lonely Hearts Club Band") 3-5 94
(Clear vinyl, 30th Anniversary juke box issue.)
CAPITOL (18888 "Norwegian Wood") 80-100 95
(Green vinyl. Juke box issue.)
CAPITOL (18889 "You've Got to Hide Your Love Away") 10-15 96
(Orange vinyl. Juke box issue.)
CAPITOL (18890 "Magical Mystery Tour") 10-15 96
(Yellow vinyl. Juke box issue.)
CAPITOL (18891 "Across the Universe") .10-15 96
(Clear vinyl. Juke box issue.)
CAPITOL (18892 "While My Guitar Gently Weeps") 10-15 96
(Blue vinyl. Juke box issue.)
CAPITOL (18893 "It's All Too Much") 10-15 96
(Blue vinyl. Juke box issue.)
CAPITOL (18894 "Nowhere Man") 10-15 96
(Green vinyl. Juke box issue.)
CAPITOL (18895 "Can't Buy Me Love") ...10-15 96
(Pink vinyl. Juke box issue.)

CAPITOL (18896 "Lucy in the Sky with Diamonds") 10-15 96
(Red vinyl. Juke box issue.)
CAPITOL (18897 "Here, There and Everywhere") 10-15 96
(Yellow vinyl. Juke box issue.)
CAPITOL (18898 "The Long and Winding Road") 10-15 96
(Blue vinyl. Juke box issue.)
CAPITOL (18899 "Got to Get You into My Life") 10-15 96
(Yellow vinyl. Juke box issue.)
CAPITOL (18900 "Ob-La-Di, Ob-La-Da"). 10-15 96
(Clear vinyl. Juke box issue.)
CAPITOL (18901 "Yesterday") 10-15 96
(Pink vinyl. Juke box issue.)
CAPITOL (18902 "Paperback Writer") 10-15 96
(Red vinyl. Juke box issue.)
CAPITOL (19341 "Norwegian Wood") 10-15 96
(Black vinyl. Juke box issue.)
CAPITOL (56785 "Love Me Do") 25-30 92
(Intended to be black vinyl but issued on red vinyl by mistake. Reportedly 1,500 made. 30th Anniversary juke box issue.)
CAPITOL (56785 "Love Me Do") 3-5 92
(Black vinyl. 30th Anniversary juke box issue.)
CAPITOL (58123 "I Want to Hold Your Hand") 3-5 96
CAPITOL (58497 "Free As a Bird") 3-5 96
CAPITOL (58544 "Real Love") 3-5 96
CAPITOL (72076 "Love Me Do") 100-200 62
(Canadian. First Capitol Beatles issue anywhere.)
CAPITOL (72090 "Please Please Me") 200-400 62
(Canadian.)
CAPITOL (72101 "From Me to You") 400-600 63
CAPITOL (72125 "She Loves You") 30-60 63
(Canadian.)
CAPITOL (72133 "Roll Over Beethoven") 30-40 64
(Canadian.)
CAPITOL (72144 "All My Loving") 30-40 64
(Canadian.)
CAPITOL (72144 "All My Loving") 80-100 71
(An error in production created a U.S. pressing of the Canadian release, *All My Loving/This Boy*.)
CAPITOL (72146 "Twist and Shout") ...200-400 64
(Canadian.)
CAPITOL (72159 "Do You Want to Know a Secret") 30-40 64
(Canadian.)
CAPITOL (72162 "Sie Liebt Dich") 500-800 64
(Canadian.)
CAPITOL (79551 "Love Me Do") 20-25 92
(White label. Mail-order promo only.)
CARROLL JAMES (3301 "The Carroll James Interview with the Beatles") 4-8 84
CICADELIC/BIODISC (001 "A Hard Day's Night") 15-20 90
(Open-end interview picture disc. With script.)
CICADELIC/BIODISC (001 "A Hard Day's Night") 25-35 90
(Open-end interview picture disc. With script. Promotional only issue made for "Records, Etc. of Payson, Az." 55 made.)
CICADELIC/BIODISC (002 "Help!: Open-end Interview") 5-8 90
(With script.)
COLLECTABLES 3-5 82
CREATIVE RADIO (B-1 "The Beatle Invasion") ....10-20 '80s
(Radio show demo. Flip side is "Inside Paul McCartney.")
DECCA (31382 "My Bonnie") 8000-12000 62
(Shown as by Tony Sheridan & Beat Brothers.) **Note:** Price is for a *COMMERCIAL*, not promotional, issue. Commercial copies are on Decca's black label with silver print and a multi-color stripe across the center of the label. Black and silver Decca labels without the other colors are bootlegs.
IBC (0082 "Murray the 'K' and the Beatles As It Happened") 8-10 76
MGM (13213 "My Bonnie") 40-50 64
(Shown as by the Beatles with Tony Sheridan.)
MGM (13227 "Why") 100-125 64
(Shown as by the Beatles with Tony Sheridan.)
MURRAY the "K" & BEATLES 20-25 64
(33 Single. Reissued in 1976 as IBC 0082.)
OLDIES 45 ....8-15 65
SILHOUETTE (1451 "Timeless 2 ½") 10-15 83
(Picture disc.)

SWAN (4152 "She Loves You") 600-650 63
(White label, with red or blue print.)
SWAN (4152 "She Loves You") 25-50 64
(Black label.)
SWAN (4182 "Sie Liebt Dich") 125-150 64
(White label with red print.)
SWAN (4182 "Sie Liebt Dich") 150-175 64
(White label with orange print.)
TOLLIE (9001 "Twist and Shout") 60-70 64
(Black label.)
TOLLIE (9001 "Twist and Shout") 60-80 64
(Yellow label with purple print.)
TOLLIE (9001 "Twist and Shout") 50-60 64
(Yellow label with blue print.)
TOLLIE (9001 "Twist and Shout") 50-75 64
(Yellow label with black print.)
TOLLIE (9001 "Twist and Shout") 60-80 64
(Yellow label with green print has logo in box.)
TOLLIE (9001 "Twist and Shout") 40-50 64
(Yellow label with green print has logo without box.)
TOLLIE (9008 "Love Me Do") 50-60 64
(Black label.)
TOLLIE (9008 "Love Me Do") 40-50 64
(Yellow label.)
TOPAZ (1353 "Seattle Press Conference"). 4-6 89
VEE-JAY (498 "Please Please Me"). 1400-1600 63
(Credits "BEATTLES." Black label with rainbow circle. Has thin lettering and oval logo.)
VEE-JAY (498 "Please Please Me")...800-1000 63
(Credits "BEATTLES." Black label with rainbow circle. Has bold lettering and oval logo.)
VEE-JAY (498 "Please Please Me"). 1500-1800 63
(Credits "BEATLES." Black label with rainbow circle. Has thin lettering and oval label logo.)
VEE-JAY (498 "Please Please Me") 700-900 63
(Credits "BEATLES." Black label with rainbow circle. Has bold lettering and oval label logo.)
VEE-JAY (498 "Please Please Me"). 1800-2000 63
(Credits "BEATLES." Black label with rainbow circle. Has brackets label logo.)
VEE-JAY (522 "From Me to You") 700-800 63
(Black label with horizontal silver lines.)
VEE-JAY (522 "From Me to You") 800-900 63
(Black label with rainbow circle and brackets logo.)
VEE-JAY (522 "From Me to You") 500-700 63
(Black label with rainbow circle and oval logo.)
VEE-JAY (581 "Please Please Me") 200-250 64
(Purple label.)
VEE-JAY (581 "Please Please Me") 140-160 64
(White label. Not a promotional issue.)
VEE-JAY (581 "Please Please Me") 60-75 64
(Yellow label.)
VEE-JAY (581 "Please Please Me") 35-45 64
(Black label with horizontal silver lines.)
VEE-JAY (581 "Please Please Me") 50-75 64
(Black label. No rainbow circle.)
VEE-JAY (581 "Please Please Me") 50-60 64
(Black label with rainbow circle.)
VEE-JAY (587 "Do You Want to Know a Secret") 35-45 64
(Solid black label with horizontal silver lines.)
VEE-JAY (587 "Do You Want to Know a Secret") 50-65 64
(Solid black label or yellow label.)
VEE-JAY (587 "Do You Want to Know a Secret") 40-50 64
(Black label with rainbow circle.)

Picture Sleeves

APPLE (2531 "Ballad of John & Yoko") ... 60-80 69
APPLE (2764 "Let It Be") 60-80 70
APPLE (2832 "Long and Winding Road") 60-80 70
ATCO (6308 "Ain't She Sweet") 350-500 64
BRS (1/2 "Murray the 'K' and the Beatles As It Happened") 150-200 64
CAPITOL/HOLIDAY INN 800-1000 64
(Promotional sleeve/flyer, pictures the four Beatles on front and their first three Capitol LPs on the back. Not known to have been issued containing any particular single. Folded over and stapled around a commercial copy Beatles single.)
CAPITOL (2056 "Hello Goodbye") 60-80 67
CAPITOL (2138 "Lady Madonna") 70-90 68
CAPITOL (2138 "Lady Madonna") 15-20 68
(Fan Club flyer insert.)
CAPITOL (4274 "Got to Get You into My Life") 3-6 88
CAPITOL (4347 "Ob-La-Di, Ob-La-Da") 5-8 76
CAPITOL (4506 "Girl") 10-15 78

CAPITOL (4612 "Sgt. Pepper's Lonely Hearts Club Band" & "With A Little Help From My Friends")...15-20 78
CAPITOL (B-5100 "Movie Medley"/"Fab Four on Film")...15-20 82
CAPITOL (B-5107 "Movie Medley"/"I'm Happy Just to Dance with You")...3-5 82
CAPITOL (B-5189 "Love Me Do")...3-5 82
CAPITOL (5112 "I Want to Hold Your Hand")...50-75 64
(This original sleeve has no periods placed at end of the small print in "Reg. U.S. Pat. Off." in Capitol logo. Reissue in 1994 has periods.)
CAPITOL (5112 WMCA Radio Promotional Sleeve)...2500-3000 64
(Back side of this sleeve pictures WMCA dee jays. Front side is identical to standard commercial issue.)
CAPITOL (5112 "I Want to Hold Your Hand")...4-6 84
(This reissue sleeve is clearly dated "1984" in lower left corner.)
CAPITOL (5112 "I Want to Hold Your Hand")...6-8 94
(This reissue sleeve has periods placed at end of the small print in "Reg. U.S. Pat. Off." in Capitol logo. Original in 1964 has no periods.)
CAPITOL (5150 "Can't Buy Me Love") 550-650 64
CAPITOL CUSTOM (2637 "Music City KFWBeatles")...800-1000 64
(Promotional sleeve/mailer for the "Souvenir Record" from KFWB and Wallichs Music City.)
CAPITOL (5222 "A Hard Day's Night")...50-75 64
CAPITOL (5234 "I'll Cry Instead")...140-160 64
CAPITOL (5235 "And I Love Her")...125-150 64
CAPITOL (5255 "Slow Down")...50-75 64
CAPITOL (5327 "I Feel Fine")...50-70 64
CAPITOL (5371 "Eight Days a Week")...25-50 65
CAPITOL (5407 "Ticket to Ride")...75-100 65
CAPITOL (5439 "Leave My Kitten Alone")...35-45 85
CAPITOL (5476 "Help!")...50-75 65
CAPITOL (5498 "Yesterday")...50-75 65
CAPITOL (5555 "We Can Work It Out")...50-75 65
CAPITOL (5587 "Nowhere Man")...40-50 66
CAPITOL (5651 "Paperback Writer")...50-75 66
CAPITOL (5715 "Yellow Submarine")...75-100 66
CAPITOL (5810 "Penny Lane")...75-100 67
CAPITOL (5964 "All You Need Is Love"). 40-50 67
CAPITOL (6066 "Kansas City")...4-6 '90s
CAPITOL (58123 "I Want to Hold Your Hand")...3-5 96
CAPITOL (58497 "Free As a Bird")...3-5 96
CAPITOL (58544 "Real Love")...3-5 96
CAPITOL (79551 "Love Me Do")...15-20 92
CARROLL JAMES (3301 "The Carroll James Interview with the Beatles")...4-8 84
CICADELIC/BIODISC (002 "Help!: Open-end Interview")...5-8 90
COLLECTABLES...3-5 82
IBC (0082 "Murray the 'K' and the Beatles As It Happened")...6-10 76
MGM (13213 "My Bonnie")...75-100 64
MGM (13227 "Why")...300-400 64
SWAN (4152 "She Loves You")...100-125 63
TOLLIE (9008 "Love Me Do")...100-125 64
TOPAZ...4-6 89
U.A. (42370 "Let It Be")...100-150 70
(Custom mailer envelope for promo radio spots single.)
VEE-JAY SPECIAL CHRISTMAS SLEEVE...75-100 64
(Standard center-cut paper sleeve printed with the Beatles' faces and "We Wish You a Merry Christmas and a Happy New Year." Issued with assorted Vee-Jay singles during the holiday season.)
VEE-JAY (581 "Please Please Me")...400-500 64
(Pictures the four Beatles.)
VEE-JAY (581 "Please Please Me") 2000-3000 64
(Promotional only sleeve. Reads "The Record That Started Beatlemania" across the top. Does not picture the group.)
VEE-JAY (587 "Do You Want to Know a Secret")...100-125 64

Promotional Singles

APPLE ("Let It Be Dialogue")...50-60 70
(Identified as "Beatles Promo 1970." Single-sided promo issue.)
ATCO (6302 "Sweet Georgia Brown"..200-250 64
(White label with black print)
ATCO (6308 "Ain't She Sweet")...250-300 64
(White label with black print)
BACKSTAGE (1111 "Like Dreamers Do")...30-40 82
(White or gray vinyl. Promotional issue only.)
BACKSTAGE (1112 "Oui Presents the Silver Beatles")...20-25 82
(*Oui* magazine promotional giveaway. Features a *Like Dreamers Do/Love of the Loved* montage. Mailing also included *Oui* News Release and subscription form. This is not a picture disc single, as the other Backstage 1100 series singles are.)
BACKSTAGE (1122 "Love of the Loved")...20-25 83
(Picture disc. Promotional issue only.)
BACKSTAGE (1133 "Like Dreamers Do")...20-25 83
(Picture disc. Promotional issue only.)
BACKSTAGE (1133 "Like Dreamers Do")...40-50 83
(Picture disc, with photo of *Penthouse* "Pet." Promotional issue only.)
CAPITOL (2056 "Hello Goodbye")...200-250 67
CAPITOL (2138 "Lady Madonna")...150-200 68
CAPITOL (4274 "Got to Get You Into My Life")...30-40 76
CAPITOL (4274 "Helter Skelter")...30-40 76
CAPITOL (4347 "Ob-La-Di, Ob-La-Da")...30-40 76
CAPITOL (4506 "Girl")...175-200 78
CAPITOL (4612 "Sgt. Pepper's Lonely Hearts Club Band" & "With a Little Help From My Friends")...30-40 78
CAPITOL (PB-5100 "Movie Medley"/"Fab Four on Film")...20-25 82
CAPITOL (P-5112/PRO-9076 "I Want to Hold Your Hand")...10-15 84
CAPITOL (PB-5150 "Can't Buy Me Love")...4000-6000
(Yellow vinyl. Experimental pressing only.)
CAPITOL (PB-5150 "Can't Buy Me Love")...2000-3000
(Black and yellow vinyl. Experimental pressing only.)
CAPITOL (PB-5189 "Love Me Do")...10-15 82
CAPITOL (PB-5624 "Twist and Shout")...10-15 86
CAPITOL (5810 "Penny Lane")...250-300 67
CAPITOL (5964 "All You Need Is Love")...200-250 67
(This promo – as with many issues by other Capitol artists – shipped with a five-inch "Rush" paper insert/flyer with information on the A and B-sides. Insert is valued separately at $100.)
CAPITOL CUSTOM (2637 "Music City KFWBeatles")...800-1000 64
(Radio KFWB and Wallichs Music City promo disc, "The Beatles Talking"/"You Can't Do That.")
CARROLL JAMES (3301 "The Carroll James Interview with the Beatles")...6-8 84
DECCA (31382 "My Bonnie")...1500-2000 62
(Shown as by Tony Sheridan & Beat Brothers. Pink label with black lettering.)
MGM (13213 "My Bonnie")...200-250 64
(Shown as by the Beatles with Tony Sheridan.)
MGM (13227 "Why")...200-250 64
(Shown as by the Beatles with Tony Sheridan.)
SWAN (4152 "She Loves You")...450-500 63
SWAN (4152 "I'll Get You")...550-650 64
(Single-sided pressing. Flip side has blank grooves.)
SWAN (4182 "Sie Liebt Dich")...400-450 64
TOLLIE (9001 "Twist and Shout")...100-125 64
TOLLIE (9008 "Love Me Do")...400-450 64
TOPAZ (1353 "Seattle Press Conference")..4-8 89
U.A. (2357 "A Hard Day's Night")...2000-3000 64
(Theater lobby advertisements. Orange label.)
U.A. (10029 "A Hard Day's Night")...2250-3500 64
(Open-end interview. Has small play hole. With five-page script.)
U.A. (10029 "A Hard Day's Night")...2000-3000 64
(Open-end interview. Has small play hole. Without five-page script.)
U.A. (42370 "Let It Be")...1000-1200 70
(Plays three radio spots for the film.)
VEE-JAY (Special DJ No. 8 "Anna"/"Ask Me Why")...10000-12000 64
VEE-JAY (498 "Please Please Me")..500-1000 63
VEE-JAY (522 "From Me to You")...400-500 63
VEE-JAY (581 "Please Please Me")...500-600 64
(Blue and white label.)
VEE-JAY (587 "Do You Want to Know a Secret")...550-650 64
WHAT'S IT ALL ABOUT...15-20

Plastic Soundsheets/Flexi-Discs

AMERICOM ("Yellow Submarine")...1500-1800 69
(Plastic "Pocket Disc" soundsheet. Number not known.)
AMERICOM (221 "Hey Jude")...250-300 69
(Plastic "Pocket Disc" soundsheet.)
AMERICOM (335 "Get Back")...800-1000 69
(Plastic "Pocket Disc" soundsheet.)
AMERICOM (382 "Ballad of John & Yoko")...600-800 69
(Plastic "Pocket Disc" soundsheet.)
EVA-TONE (830771 "Till There Was You") .4-6 83
EVA-TONE (420826 "All My Loving")...5-10 82
(Back side reads "Compliments of Musicland.")
EVA-TONE (420826 "All My Loving")...15-25 82
(Back side reads "Compliments of Sam Goody" or "Compliments of Discount.")
EVA-TONE (420827 "Magical Mystery Tour")...5-10 82
(Back side reads "Compliments of Musicland")
EVA-TONE (420827 "Magical Mystery Tour")...15-25 82
(Back side reads "Compliments of Sam Goody" or "Compliments of Discount.")
EVA-TONE (420828 "Rocky Raccoon")...5-10 82
(Back side reads "Compliments of Musicland".)
EVA-TONE (420828 "Rocky Raccoon")...15-25 82
(Back side reads "Compliments of Sam Goody" or "Compliments of Discount.")
EVA-TONE (1214825 "The Beatles German Medley")...50-60 83
OFFICIAL BEATLES FAN CLUB ("1964 Season's Greetings from the Beatles")...250-300 64
OFFICIAL BEATLES FAN CLUB ("1965 Beatles Christmas Record")...150-175 65
(Includes picture sleeve.)
OFFICIAL BEATLES FAN CLUB ("1966 Season's Greetings from the Beatles")...125-150 66
OFFICIAL BEATLES FAN CLUB ("1967 Christmas Time Is Here Again")...125-150 67
OFFICIAL BEATLES FAN CLUB ("1968 Beatles Christmas Record")...100-125 68
(Includes picture sleeve.)
OFFICIAL BEATLES FAN CLUB ("1969 Happy Christmas")...75-100 69
(Includes picture sleeve.)

EPs: 7-Inch

CAPITOL (EAP 1-2121 "Four by the Beatles")...300-400 64
CAPITOL (R-5365 "4-by the Beatles") .200-250 65
CAPITOL (58348 "Baby It's You")...4-6 95
CAPITOL COMPACT 33 (2047 "Meet the Beatles")...500-700 64
(Juke box issue only. Add $15 to 25 for each insert, which includes five title strips and three mini-LP cover photos.)
CAPITOL COMPACT 33 (2080 "The Beatles' Second Album")...500-700 64
(Juke box issue only. Add $15 to 25 for each insert, which includes five title strips and three mini-LP cover photos.)
CAPITOL COMPACT 33 (2108 "Something New")...700-900 64
(Juke box issue only. Add $15 to 25 for each insert, which includes five title strips and three mini-LP cover photos.)
VEE-JAY (VJEP 1-903 "Souvenir of Their Visit to America")...200-225 64
(Solid black label with either oval or brackets or block style Vee-Jay logo.)
VEE-JAY (VJEP 1-903 "Souvenir of Their Visit to America")...80-100 64
(Black label with rainbow color-band with oval logo.)
VEE-JAY (VJEP 1-903 "Souvenir of Their Visit to America")...200-225 64
(Black label with rainbow color-band with brackets logo.)

Promotional EPs

CAPITOL COMPACT 33 (2548/49 "Open-End Interview")...1200-1500 64
(Issued with a paper sleeve/script, which represents about $700-$800 of the value.)
CAPITOL COMPACT 33 (2598/99 "Second Open-End Interview")...1200-1400 64
(Issued with a paper sleeve/script, which represents about $600-$700 of the value.)
CAPITOL (2720/21 "The Beatles Introduce New Songs")...1500-2000 64
(45 rpm EP with John Lennon talking about Cilla Black's *It's for You*, and Paul talking about Peter & Gordon's *I Don't Want to See You Again*.)
CAPITOL 33 COMPACT (2905/06 "The Capitol Souvenir Record")...400-500 64
(Issued with a paper sleeve and script, which represents about $200-$250 of the value. Contains excerpts of 15 different songs by 15 artists, including *I Want to Hold Your Hand* by the Beatles.)
POLYGRAM (PRO-1113 "Backbeat")...40-50 94
(Soundtrack.)
VEE-JAY (903 "Souvenir of Their Visit to America")...300-350 64
(White label with blue print. Price is for disc only.)
VEE-JAY (VJEP 1-903 "Ask Me Why")...7500-8500 64
(The high price is for the paper, EP sleeve promoting *Ask Me Why* but still with the same Vee-Jay EP number as *Souvenir of Their Visit to America*.)

LPs: 10/12-Inch

ADIRONDACK (8146 "Happy Michaelmas")...15-20 81
(Has the Beatles Christmas messages)
APPLE ("Beatles Special Limited Edition")...1000-1200 74
(Boxed, 10-disc set.)
APPLE (101 "The Beatles")...200-250 68
(Two discs. With Capitol logo at bottom of label. Limited numbered edition. Includes four photos and one poster, which represent $25 to $35 of the value.)
APPLE (101 "The Beatles")...75-100 71
(Two discs. Without Capitol logo at bottom of label. Includes four photos and one poster, which represent $25 to $35 of the value.)
APPLE (101 "The Beatles")...65-75 75
(Two discs. Has "All Rights Reserved" at top. Includes four photos and one poster, which represent $25 to $35 of the value.)
APPLE (153 "Yellow Submarine")...20-30 69
(With Capitol logo at bottom of label.)
APPLE (153 "Yellow Submarine")...15-20 71
(Without Capitol logo at bottom of label.)
APPLE (153 "Yellow Submarine")...20-30 75
(Has "All Rights Reserved" at top.)
APPLE (383 "Abbey Road")...40-60 69
(With "Her Majesty" printed on label [Side 2, track 11]. Has "Manufactured By Apple" at bottom of label.)
APPLE (383 "Abbey Road")...70-90 69
(Without "Her Majesty" printed on label. Has "Manufactured By Apple" on label.)
APPLE (383 "Abbey Road")...20-30 69
(Has "Mfd. By Apple" on label.)
APPLE (383 "Abbey Road")...20-30 75
(Has "All Rights Reserved" at top.)
APPLE (385 "Hey Jude")...30-35 70
(Has title, *The Beatles Again* on label. Cover has "SW" prefix, label has "SO" prefix.)
APPLE (385 "Hey Jude")...30-35 70
(Has title, *The Beatles Again* on label. Cover and disc both have "SW" prefix.)
APPLE (385 "Hey Jude")...75-85 70
(With Capitol logo at bottom of label.)
APPLE (385 "Hey Jude")...20-30 75
(Has "All Rights Reserved" at top.)
APPLE (ST-2047 "Meet the Beatles")...25-35 68
(With Capitol logo at bottom of label.)
APPLE (ST-2047 "Meet the Beatles")...15-20 71
(Without Capitol logo at bottom of label.)
APPLE (ST-2047 "Meet the Beatles")...20-25 75
(Has "All Rights Reserved" at top.)
APPLE (ST-2080 "The Beatles' Second Album")...25-35 68
(With Capitol logo at bottom of label.)
APPLE (ST-2080 "The Beatles' Second Album")...15-20 71
(Without Capitol logo at bottom of label.)
APPLE (ST-2080 "The Beatles' Second Album")...20-25 75
(Has "All Rights Reserved" at top.)
APPLE (ST-2108 "Something New")...25-35 68
(With Capitol logo at bottom of label.)
APPLE (ST-2108 "Something New")...15-20 71
(Without Capitol logo at bottom of label.)
APPLE (ST-2108 "Something New")...20-25 75
(Has "All Rights Reserved" at top.)
APPLE (ST-2222 "The Beatles' Story")...40-50 68
(Two discs. With Capitol logo at bottom of label.)
APPLE (ST-2222 "The Beatles' Story")...30-40 71
(Two discs. Without Capitol logo at bottom of label.)
APPLE (ST-2228 "Beatles '65")...25-35 68
(With Capitol logo at bottom of label.)

APPLE (ST-2228 "Beatles '65") 15-25 71
(Without Capitol logo at bottom of label.)

APPLE (ST-2228 "Beatles '65") 20-25 75
(Has "All Rights Reserved" at top.)

APPLE (ST-2309 "Early Beatles")........... 25-35 68
(With Capitol logo at bottom of label.)

APPLE (ST-2309 "Early Beatles")........... 15-20 71
(Has "Mfd. By Apple" on label.)

APPLE (ST-2309 "Early Beatles")........... 20-25 75
(Has "All Rights Reserved" at top.)

APPLE (ST-2358 "Beatles VI")................ 25-35 68
(With Capitol logo at bottom of label.)

APPLE (ST-2358 "Beatles VI")................ 15-25 71
(Without Capitol logo at bottom of label.)

APPLE (ST-2358 "Beatles VI")................ 20-25 75
(Has "All Rights Reserved" at top.)

APPLE (ST-2386 "Help!")........................ 30-35 68
(With Capitol logo at bottom of label.)

APPLE (ST-2386 "Help!")........................ 15-20 71
(Without Capitol logo at bottom of label.)

APPLE (ST-2386 "Help!")........................ 20-25 75
(Has "All Rights Reserved" at top.)

APPLE (ST-2442 "Rubber Soul")............ 25-35 68
(With Capitol logo at bottom of label.)

APPLE (ST-2442 "Rubber Soul")............ 15-25 71
(Without Capitol logo at bottom of label.)

APPLE (2553 "Yesterday and Today").... 25-35 68
(With Capitol logo at bottom of label.)

APPLE (2553 "Yesterday and Today").... 15-20 71
(Without Capitol logo at bottom of label.)

APPLE (2553 "Yesterday and Today").... 20-25 75
(Has "All Rights Reserved" at top.)

APPLE (ST-2576 "Revolver").................. 25-35 68
(With Capitol logo at bottom of label.)

APPLE (ST-2576 "Revolver").................. 15-20 71
(Without Capitol logo at bottom of label.)

APPLE (ST-2576 "Revolver").................. 20-25 75
(Has "All Rights Reserved" at top.)

APPLE (SMAS-2653 "Sgt. Pepper's Lonely Hearts Club Band").. 30-40 68
(With Capitol logo at bottom of label.)

APPLE (SMAS-2653 "Sgt. Pepper's Lonely Hearts Club Band").. 15-25 71
(Without Capitol logo at bottom of label.)

APPLE (SMAS-2653 "Sgt. Pepper's Lonely Hearts Club Band").. 20-25 75
(Has "All Rights Reserved" at top.)

APPLE (SMAL-2835 "Magical Mystery Tour") 30-40 68
(With Capitol logo at bottom of label.)

APPLE (SMAL-2835 "Magical Mystery Tour") 15-20 71
(Without Capitol logo at bottom of label.)

APPLE (SMAL-2835 "Magical Mystery Tour") 20-25 75
(Has "All Rights Reserved" at top.)

APPLE (3403 "1962-1966")..................... 30-35 73
(Two discs. Gatefold. With "All Rights Reserved" at top.)

APPLE (3403 "1962-1966")..................... 30-40 75
(Two discs. Gatefold. Without "All Rights Reserved" at top.)

APPLE (3404 "1967-1970")..................... 25-30 73
(Two discs. Gatefold. With "All Rights Reserved" at top.)

APPLE (3404 "1967-1970")..................... 30-40 75
(Two discs. Gatefold. Without "All Rights Reserved" at top.)

APPLE (34001 "Let It Be")...................... 25-35 70

ATCO (169 "Ain't She Sweet") 275-325 64
(Monaural. Also contains selections by the Swallows.)

ATCO (169 "Ain't She Sweet") 800-1200 64
(White label. Also contains selections by the Swallows. Promotional issue only.)

ATCO (169 "Ain't She Sweet") 350-450 64
(Stereo. Tan and lavender label. Also contains selections by the Swallows.)

ATCO (169 "Ain't She Sweet") 300-400 69
(Stereo. Yellow label.)

AUDIO FIDELITY (339 "First Movement")..8-12 82

AUDIO FIDELITY (339 "First Movement")... 15-20 82
(Picture disc.)

AUDIO RARITIES (2452 "The Complete Silver Beatles) 10-15 82

AUDIO RARITIES (30003 "The Silver Beatles) 20-25 82
(Picture disc.)

BACKSTAGE (201 "Like Dreamers Do"). 40-60 82
(Two-disc set. One picture disc and one colored vinyl.)

BACKSTAGE (1111 "Like Dreamers Do")..30-40 82
(Three-disc set. Contains two picture discs and a white vinyl LP.)

BACKSTAGE (1111 "Like Dreamers Do")..70-90 82
(Three-disc set. Contains two picture discs and a GRAY vinyl LP.)

BACKSTAGE (1111 "Like Dreamers Do")..50-60 82
(Three-disc set. Includes any of the custom issues, which had various logos printed on the reverse side of the picture discs.)

BACKSTAGE (1111 "Like Dreamers Do")..30-40 82
(Three-disc set. No custom artwork on picture disc. With gatefold cover.)

BACKSTAGE (1165 "Beatles Talk with Jerry G. Volume 1") 15-20 82
(Picture disc.)

BACKSTAGE (1175 "Beatles Talk with Jerry G. Volume 2") 15-20 82
(Picture disc.)

CAPITOL ("The Platinum Beatles Collection") 550-650 84
(Boxed, 18-disc set. No selection number used.)

CAPITOL (101 "The Beatles")..................35-50 76
(Two discs. Orange label. Includes four photos and one poster, which represent $15 to $25 of the value.)

CAPITOL (101 "The Beatles")..................35-50 78
(Two discs. Purple label with "Mfd. By Capitol, etc." Includes four photos and one poster, which represent $15 to $25 of the value.)

CAPITOL (101 "The Beatles")..................40-55 83
(Two discs. Black label. Includes four photos and one poster, which represent $15 to $25 of the value.)

CAPITOL (153 "Yellow Submarine") 10-15 76
(Orange label.)

CAPITOL (153 "Yellow Submarine") 8-12 78
(Purple label.)

CAPITOL (153 "Yellow Submarine") 10-15 84
(Black label.)

CAPITOL (383 "Abbey Road")..................10-15 76
(Orange label.)

CAPITOL (383 "Abbey Road")..................10-15 78
(Purple label with "Mfd. By Capitol, etc.")

CAPITOL (383 "Abbey Road")..................20-30 83
(Black label.)

CAPITOL (385 "Hey Jude")......................10-15 76
(Orange label.)

CAPITOL (385 "Hey Jude")..........................8-12 78
(Purple label with "Mfd. by Capitol, etc." perimeter print.)

CAPITOL (SW-385 "Hey Jude")...............40-60 83
(Black label.)

CAPITOL (SJ-385 "Hey Jude") 20-30 84
(Black label.)

CAPITOL (T-2047 "Meet the Beatles").250-350 64
(Monaural.)

CAPITOL (ST-2047 "Meet the Beatles")..250-350 64
(Stereo. Black label with white print around border. Does not have "Subsidiary of Capitol, etc." perimeter print.)

CAPITOL (ST8-2047 "Meet the Beatles") 200-250 64
(Capitol Record Club issue, black label.)

CAPITOL (ST8-2047 "Meet the Beatles") 100-150 69
(Capitol Record Club issue, green label.)

CAPITOL (ST-2047 "Meet the Beatles")...40-50 69
(Stereo. Black label with white print around border. Has "Subsidiary of Capitol, etc." print.)

CAPITOL (ST-2047 "Meet the Beatles")...30-40 69
(Green label.)

CAPITOL (ST-2047 "Meet the Beatles")...10-15 76
(Orange label.)

CAPITOL (ST-2047 "Meet the Beatles")....8-12 78
(Purple label with "Mfd. by Capitol, etc.")

CAPITOL (ST-2047 "Meet the Beatles")...10-15 83
(Black label.)

CAPITOL (T-2080 "The Beatles' Second Album") 200-250 64
(Monaural.)

CAPITOL (ST-2080 "The Beatles' Second Album") 100-150 64
(Stereo. Black label with white print around border. Does not have "Subsidiary of Capitol, etc." perimeter print.)

CAPITOL (ST-8-2080 "The Beatles' Second Album") 500-750 64
(Capitol Record Club issue, black label.)

CAPITOL (ST-2080 "The Beatles' Second Album") 40-50 69
(Stereo. Black label with white print around border. Has "Subsidiary of Capitol, etc." print.)

CAPITOL (ST-2080 "The Beatles' Second Album") 30-40 69
(Green label.)

CAPITOL (ST-8-2080 "The Beatles' Second Album") 550-650 69
(Capitol Record Club issue, green label.)

CAPITOL (ST-2080 "The Beatles' Second Album") 10-15 76
(Orange label.)

CAPITOL (ST-2080 "The Beatles' Second Album") 8-12 78
(Purple label with "Mfd. by Capitol, etc.")

CAPITOL (ST-2080 "The Beatles' Second Album") 10-15 83
(Black label.)

CAPITOL (T-2108 "Something New") ..150-175 64
(Monaural.)

CAPITOL (ST-2108 "Something New") 100-125 64
(Stereo. Black label with white print around border. Does not have "Subsidiary of Capitol, etc." perimeter print.)

CAPITOL (ST8-2108 "Something New") 200-250 64
(Record Club issue, black label.)

CAPITOL (ST-2108 "Something New")....40-50 69
(Stereo. Black label with white print around border. Has "Subsidiary of Capitol, etc." print.)

CAPITOL (ST-2108 "Something New")....30-40 69
(Green label.)

CAPITOL (ST8-2108 "Something New") 100-125 69
(Record Club issue, green label.)

CAPITOL (ST8-2108 "Something New") 200-250 69
(Record Club issue, green label. Reads "Manufactured by Longines.")

CAPITOL (ST-2108 "Something New")....10-15 76
(Orange label.)

CAPITOL (ST-2108 "Something New")......8-12 78
(Purple label with "Mfd. by Capitol, etc.")

CAPITOL (ST-2108 "Something New") 1000-1500 78
(Clear vinyl. Purple label with "Mfd." perimeter print. Experimental issue only.)

CAPITOL (ST-2108 "Something New")....10-15 83
(Black label.)

CAPITOL (TBO-2222 "The Beatles' Story") 200-250 64
(Two discs. Monaural.)

CAPITOL (STBO-2222 "The Beatles' Story") 200-250 64
(Two discs. Stereo. Black label with white print around border. Does not have "Subsidiary of Capitol, etc." perimeter print.)

CAPITOL (STBO-2222 "The Beatles' Story") 50-60 69
(Two discs. Stereo. Black label with white print around border. Has "Subsidiary of Capitol, etc." print.)

CAPITOL (STBO-2222 "The Beatles' Story") 40-50 69
(Two discs. Green label.)

CAPITOL (STBO-2222 "The Beatles' Story") 15-20 76
(Two discs. Orange label.)

CAPITOL (STBO-2222 "The Beatles' Story") 15-20 78
(Two discs. Purple label.)

CAPITOL (STBO-2222 "The Beatles' Story") 40-50 83
(Two discs. Black label with black print around border.)

CAPITOL (T-2228 "Beatles '65") 100-150 64
(Monaural.)

CAPITOL (ST-2228 "Beatles '65").......100-125 64
(Stereo. Black label with white print around border. Does not have "Subsidiary of Capitol, etc." perimeter print.)

CAPITOL (ST-2228 "Beatles 65")............50-60 69
(Stereo. Black label with white print around border. Has "Subsidiary of Capitol, etc." print.)

CAPITOL (ST-2228 "Beatles '65")...........30-40 69
(Green label.)

CAPITOL (ST-2228 "Beatles '65")...........10-15 76
(Orange label.)

CAPITOL (ST-2228 "Beatles '65")............8-12 78
(Purple label.)

CAPITOL (ST-2228 "Beatles '65")...........10-15 83
(Black label with black print around border.)

CAPITOL (T-2309 "The Early Beatles") 150-200 65
(Monaural.)

CAPITOL (ST-2309 "The Early Beatles") 100-150 65
(Stereo. Black label with white print around border. Does not have "Subsidiary of Capitol, etc." perimeter print.)

CAPITOL (ST-2309 "The Early Beatles").40-50 69
(Stereo. Black label with white print around border. Has "Subsidiary of Capitol, etc." print.)

CAPITOL (ST-2309 "The Early Beatles").30-40 69
(Green label.)

CAPITOL (ST-2309 "The Early Beatles"). 10-15 76
(Orange label.)

CAPITOL (ST-2309 "The Early Beatles")...8-12 78
(Purple label.)

CAPITOL (ST-2309 "The Early Beatles").20-25 83
(Black label with black print around border.)

CAPITOL (T-2358 "Beatles VI")...........100-150 65
(Monaural.)

CAPITOL (ST-2358 "Beatles VI") 100-125 65
(Stereo. Black label with white print around border. Does not have "Subsidiary of Capitol, etc." perimeter print.)

CAPITOL (ST-2358 "Beatles VI") 100-125 69
(Stereo. Black label with white print around border. Has "Subsidiary of Capitol, etc." print.)

CAPITOL (ST-2358 "Beatles VI") 30-40 69
(Green label.)

CAPITOL (ST-2358 "Beatles VI") 10-15 76
(Orange label.)

CAPITOL (ST-2358 "Beatles VI") 1200-1500 78
(Clear vinyl. Purple label with "Mfd." perimeter print. Experimental issue only.)

CAPITOL (ST-2358 "Beatles VI") 8-12 78
(Purple label with "Mfd." perimeter print.)

CAPITOL (ST-2358 "Beatles VI") 10-15 83
(Black label with black print around border.)

CAPITOL (ST-2358 "Beatles VI")..........75-125 88
(Purple label with "Manufactured by Capitol, etc." perimeter print.)

CAPITOL (ST-8-2358 "Beatles VI")......350-450 69
(Green label. Capitol Record Club issue.)

CAPITOL (MAS-2386 "Help!")..............150-200 65
(Monaural.)

CAPITOL (SMAS-2386 "Help!")...........100-150 65
(Stereo. Black label with white print around border. Does not have "Subsidiary of Capitol, etc." perimeter print.)

CAPITOL (SMAS-2386 "Help!")...............40-50 69
(Stereo. Black label with white print around border. Has "Subsidiary of Capitol, etc." print.)

CAPITOL (SMAS-2386 "Help!")...............30-40 69
(Green label.)

CAPITOL (SMAS-2386 "Help!")...............10-15 76
(Orange label.)

CAPITOL (SMAS-2386 "Help!").................8-12 78
(Purple label with "Mfd. By Capitol, etc.")

CAPITOL (SMAS-2386 "Help!")...............10-15 83
(Black label with black print around border.)

CAPITOL (90454 "Help") 20-25 88
(Purple label with "Manufactured by Capitol, etc." perimeter print.)

CAPITOL (SMAS-8-2386 "Help!") 300-500 65
(Capitol Record Club, or Longines Symphonette Record Club issue, black label.)

CAPITOL (SMAS-8-2386 "Help!") 200-300 69
(Capitol Record Club issue, green label.)

CAPITOL (T-2442 "Rubber Soul")........125-175 65
(Monaural. Add $75 to $100 if with "Hear Paul Sing *Michelle*" cover sticker. Add $200 to $300 if with "The Beatles Latest Album ... Featuring *Michelle*.")

CAPITOL (ST-2442 "Rubber Soul") 100-125 65
(Stereo. Black label with white print around border. Does not have "Subsidiary of Capitol, etc." perimeter print. Add $75 to $100 if with "Hear Paul Sing *Michelle*" cover sticker. Add $200 to $300 if with "The Beatles Latest Album ... Featuring *Michelle*.")

CAPITOL (ST8-2442 "Rubber Soul") ...200-250 65
(Capitol Record Club issue, black label.)

CAPITOL (ST-2442 "Rubber Soul") 40-50 69
(Stereo. Black label with white print around border. Has "Subsidiary of Capitol, etc." print.)

CAPITOL (ST-2442 "Rubber Soul")........ 30-40 69
(Green label.)
CAPITOL (ST8-2442 "Rubber Soul")... 100-150 69
(Capitol Record Club issue, green label.)
CAPITOL (ST8-2442 "Rubber Soul")... 200-250 69
(Capitol Record Club issue, green label. Label reads "Manufactured by Longines.")
CAPITOL (ST-2442 "Rubber Soul")........ 10-15 76
(Orange label.)
CAPITOL (SW-2442 "Rubber Soul")..........8-12 78
(Purple label with "Mfd. By Capitol, etc.")
CAPITOL (SW-2442 "Rubber Soul")....... 10-15 83
(Black label.)
CAPITOL (T-2553 "Yesterday and Today")............................3000-4000 66
(Monaural. FIRST STATE "Butcher cover" issues.)
CAPITOL (ST-2553 "Yesterday and Today")............................6000-8000 66
(Stereo. FIRST STATE "Butcher Cover" issues.)
CAPITOL (T-2553 "Yesterday and Today")............................ 500-750 66
(Monaural. PASTE OVER or PEELED "Butcher cover" copies.)
CAPITOL (ST-2553 "Yesterday and Today")............................ 1200-1600 66
(Stereo. PASTE OVER or PEELED "Butcher cover" copies.)
Note: the wide range of values exists here due to varied opinions on the practice of peeling the "Trunk cover" from the "Butcher cover." The expertise used in the peeling is also a major factor affecting the value of these LPs.
CAPITOL (T-2553 "Yesterday and Today")............................ 125-175 66
(Monaural. "Trunk cover.")
CAPITOL (ST-2553 "Yesterday and Today")............................ 100-150 66
(Stereo. Black label with white print around border. Does not have "Subsidiary of Capitol, etc." perimeter print.)
CAPITOL (ST-8-2553 "Yesterday and Today")............................ 250-300 66
(Capitol Record Club issue, black label.)
CAPITOL (ST-2553 "Yesterday and Today")............................ 40-50 69
(Stereo. Black label with white print around border. Has "Subsidiary of Capitol, etc." print. "Trunk cover.")
CAPITOL (ST-2553 "Yesterday and Today")............................ 30-40 69
(Green label.)
CAPITOL (ST-8-2553 "Yesterday and Today")............................ 100-150 69
(Capitol Record Club issue, green label.)
CAPITOL (ST-2553 "Yesterday and Today")............................ 10-15 76
(Orange label.)
CAPITOL (ST-2553 "Yesterday and Today")............................8-12 78
(Purple label with "Mfd. By Capitol, etc.")
CAPITOL (ST-2553 "Yesterday and Today")............................ 10-15 83
(Black label.)
CAPITOL (T-2576 "Revolver") 150-175 66
(Monaural. Add $75 to $100 if with "*Yellow Submarine* and *Eleanor Rigby*" cover sticker.)
CAPITOL (ST-2576 "Revolver")........ 100-125 66
(Stereo. Black label with white print around border. Does not have "Subsidiary of Capitol, etc." perimeter print. Add $75 to $100 if with "*Yellow Submarine* and *Eleanor Rigby*" cover sticker.)
CAPITOL (ST-2576 "Revolver")........... 40-50 66
(Stereo. Black label with white print around border. Has "Subsidiary of Capitol, etc." print.)
CAPITOL (ST8-2576 "Revolver")........ 200-225 66
(Capitol Record Club issue, black label.)
CAPITOL (ST-2576 "Revolver").............. 30-40 69
(Green label.)
CAPITOL (ST8-2576 "Revolver")..........75-100 69
(Capitol Record Club issue, green label.)
CAPITOL (ST-2576 "Revolver")........... 400-500 71
(Red label.)
CAPITOL (ST-2576 "Revolver").............. 10-15 76
(Orange label.)
CAPITOL (ST8-2576 "Revolver")......... 200-250 76
(Capitol Record Club issue, orange label.)
CAPITOL (ST-2576 "Revolver")..................8-12 78
(Purple label with "Mfd. By Capitol, etc.")
CAPITOL (ST-2576 "Revolver").............. 10-15 83
(Black label.)
CAPITOL (MAS-2653 "Sgt. Pepper's Lonely Hearts Club Band") 250-300 67
(Monaural. Gatefold. Add $20 if with custom inner sleeve and Sgt. Pepper cut-outs.)
CAPITOL (SMAS-2653 "Sgt. Pepper's Lonely Hearts Club Band") 150-175 67
(Stereo. Black label with white print around border. Does not have "Subsidiary of Capitol, etc." perimeter print. Add $20 if with custom inner sleeve and Sgt. Pepper cut-outs.)
CAPITOL (SMAS-2653 "Sgt. Pepper's Lonely Hearts Club Band") 50-60 69
(Stereo. Black label with white print around border. Has "Subsidiary of Capitol, etc." print.)
CAPITOL (SMAS-2653 "Sgt. Pepper's Lonely Hearts Club Band") 40-50 69
(Green label.)
CAPITOL (SMAS-2653 "Sgt. Pepper's Lonely Hearts Club Band") 10-15 76
(Orange label.)
CAPITOL (SMAS-2653 "Sgt. Pepper's Lonely Hearts Club Band") 8-12 78
(Purple label with "Mfd. By Capitol, etc.")
CAPITOL (SMAS-2653 "Sgt. Pepper's Lonely Hearts Club Band") 10-15 83
(Black label.)
CAPITOL (MAL-2835 "Magical Mystery Tour")..250-300 67
(Monaural. Gatefold.)
CAPITOL (SMAL-2835 "Magical Mystery Tour")..80-100 67
(Stereo. Black label with white print around border. Does not have "Subsidiary of Capitol, etc." perimeter print.)
CAPITOL (SMAL-2835 "Magical Mystery Tour")..40-50 69
(Stereo. Black label with white print around border. Has "Subsidiary of Capitol, etc." print.)
CAPITOL (SMAL-2835 "Magical Mystery Tour")..40-50 69
(Green label.)
CAPITOL (SMAL-2835 "Magical Mystery Tour")..10-15 76
(Orange label.)
CAPITOL (SMAL-2835 "Magical Mystery Tour")..8-12 78
(Purple label with "Mfd. By Capitol, etc.")
CAPITOL (SMAL-2835 "Magical Mystery Tour")..10-15 83
(Black label.)
CAPITOL (SMAL-2835 "Magical Mystery Tour")..20-25 88
(Purple label with "Manufactured By Capitol, etc.")
CAPITOL (3403 "The Beatles/ 1962-1966")..15-20 76
(Two discs. Gatefold. Red Label.)
CAPITOL (3403 "The Beatles/ 1962-1966")..25-30 76
(Two discs. Gatefold. Blue Label.)
CAPITOL (3404 "The Beatles/ 1967-1970")..15-20 76
(Two discs. Gatefold. Blue Label.)
CAPITOL (SPRO-8969 "Rarities")...........40-50 78
(Bonus LP in *Beatles Collection* boxed set.)
CAPITOL (11537 "Rock 'n' Roll Music")...40-60 76
(Two discs. Gatefold.)
CAPITOL (SMAS-11638 "Beatles at the Hollywood Bowl")..15-25 77
(Without bar code [UPC] symbol.)
CAPITOL (SMAS-11638 "Beatles at the Hollywood Bowl")..300-400 77
(Tan label "Advance Pressing." Plain white cover. Promotional issue only.)
CAPITOL (SMAS-11638 "Beatles at the Hollywood Bowl")..40-50 89
(With bar code [UPC] symbol.)
CAPITOL (11711 "Love Songs")..............30-40 77
CAPITOL (11840 "Sgt. Pepper's Lonely Hearts Club Band")..20-30 78
(Picture disc.)
CAPITOL (11841 "The Beatles") 800-1200 78
(Clear vinyl. Experimental item only.)
CAPITOL (11841 "The Beatles") 750-1000 78
(Gray splash-colored vinyl. Experimental item only.)
CAPITOL (11841 "The Beatles") 55-75 78
(White vinyl. Includes four photos and one poster, which represent $15 to $25 of the value.)
CAPITOL (11842 "The Beatles/ 1962-1966")..30-40 78
(Two discs. Gatefold. Red vinyl.)
CAPITOL (11843 "The Beatles/ 1967-1970")..30-40 78
(Two discs. Gatefold. Blue vinyl.)
CAPITOL (11843 "The Beatles/ 1967-1970")...................................1000-1200 78
(Two discs. Gatefold. Clear vinyl. Experimental issue only.)
CAPITOL (11900 "Abbey Road").............35-45 78
(Picture disc.)
CAPITOL (11921 "A Hard Day's Night").....8-12 80
(Purple label with "Mfd..." perimeter print.)
CAPITOL (11921 "A Hard Day's Night")...10-15 83
(Black label.)
CAPITOL (11921 "A Hard Day's Night")...20-25 88
(Purple label with "Manufactured..." perimeter print.)
CAPITOL (11922 "Let It Be") 1200-1500 78
(Clear vinyl. Purple label with "Mfd." perimeter print. Experimental issue only.)
CAPITOL (11922 "Let It Be") 8-12 79
(Purple label with "Mfd..." perimeter print.)
CAPITOL (11922 "Let It Be") 10-15 83
(Black label.)
CAPITOL (11922 "Let It Be") 20-25 88
(Purple label with "Manufactured by Capitol, etc." perimeter print.)
CAPITOL (12009 "Rarities")..................250-300 78
(Green label. Issued in a plain white cover.)
CAPITOL (12080 "Rarities")....................20-25 80
(Black label. Cover photo not embossed.)
CAPITOL (12080 "Rarities")......................15-20 80
(Black label. Cover photo embossed.)
CAPITOL (12199 "Reel Music")..................8-12 82
(Black vinyl.)
CAPITOL (12199 "Reel Music")...............40-50 82
(Yellow vinyl. Promotional issue only.)
CAPITOL (12245 "The Beatles 20 Greatest Hits") 15-25 82-88
(Purple or black label.)
CAPITOL (16020 "Rock 'N' Roll Music, Volume I")..5-10 80
CAPITOL (16021 "Rock 'N' Roll Music, Volume II")..5-10 80
CAPITOL (31796 "Live at the BBC") 40-60 94
CAPITOL (34445 "Anthology I").............30-40 95
CAPITOL (34448 "Anthology II")..............20-30 96
CAPITOL (34451 "Anthology III")..............20-30 96
CAPITOL (46435 "Please Please Me") 25-30 87
CAPITOL (46436 "With the Beatles") 25-30 87
CAPITOL (46437 "A Hard Day's Night")...15-20 87
(Black label.)
CAPITOL (46437 "A Hard Day's Night")...20-25 90
(Purple label.)
CAPITOL (46437 "A Hard Day's Night")...25-30 95
(Purple label. With "Limited Edition" sticker.)
CAPITOL (46438 "Beatles for Sale")........15-20 87
(Black label.)
CAPITOL (46438 "Beatles for Sale")........20-25 90
(Purple label.)
CAPITOL (46438 "Beatles for Sale")........25-30 95
(Purple label. With "Limited Edition" sticker.)
CAPITOL (46439 "Help")..........................15-20 87
(Black label.)
CAPITOL (46439 "Help")..........................20-25 90
(Purple label.)
CAPITOL (46439 "Help")..........................25-30 95
(Purple label. With "Limited Edition" sticker.)
CAPITOL (46440 "Rubber Soul") 15-20 87
(Black label.)
CAPITOL (46440 "Rubber Soul") 20-25 90
(Purple label.)
CAPITOL (46440 "Rubber Soul") 25-30 95
(Purple label. With "Limited Edition" sticker.)
CAPITOL (46441 "Revolver")....................15-20 87
(Black label.)
CAPITOL (46441 "Revolver")....................20-25 90
(Purple label.)
CAPITOL (46441 "Revolver")....................25-30 95
(Purple label. With "Limited Edition" sticker.)
CAPITOL (46442 "Sgt. Pepper's Lonely Hearts Club Band")..20-25 90
(Purple label.)
CAPITOL (46442 "Sgt. Pepper's Lonely Hearts Club Band")..25-30 95
(Purple label. With "Limited Edition" sticker.)
CAPITOL (46443 "The Beatles") 55-65 88
(Two discs. Purple label with "Manufactured by Capitol, etc." perimeter print. Includes four photos and one poster, which represent $15 to $25 of the value.)
CAPITOL (46443 "The Beatles") 55-65 95
(Two discs. Custom Apple label. Includes four photos and one poster, which represent $15 to $25 of the value.)
CAPITOL (46445 "Yellow Submarine")....25-30 88
(Purple label with "Manufactured by Capitol, etc." perimeter print.)
CAPITOL (46445 "Yellow Submarine")....25-30 95
(Custom Apple label. Reads "Limited Edition.")
CAPITOL (46446 "Abbey Road").............25-30 88
(Purple label.)
CAPITOL (46446 "Abbey Road").............25-30 95
(Custom Apple label. Reads "Limited Edition.")
CAPITOL (46447 "Let It Be")....................25-30 95
(Custom Apple label. Reads "Limited Edition.")
CAPITOL (48062 "Magical Mystery Tour")..15-25 87
CAPITOL (90043 "Past Masters, Vol. 1")...6-10 88
CAPITOL (90044 "Past Masters, Vol. 2")...6-10 88
CAPITOL (90435 "The Beatles/ 1962-1966")..30-35 88
(Two discs. Gatefold. Purple label with "Manufactured by Capitol, etc." perimeter print.)
CAPITOL (90438 "The Beatles/ 1967-1970")..30-35 88
(Two discs. Gatefold. Purple label with "Manufactured by Capitol, etc." perimeter print.)
CAPITOL (90441 "Meet the Beatles") 20-30 88
CAPITOL (90443 "Something New")........20-30 88
CAPITOL (90444 "The Beatles' Second Album") 20-30 88
CAPITOL (90445 "Beatles VI")................20-30 88
CAPITOL (90446 "Beatles '65")................20-30 88
CAPITOL (90447 "Yesterday and Today")..20-30 88
CAPITOL (90452 "Revolver") 20-30 88
(Purple label with "Manufactured by Capitol, etc." perimeter print.)
CAPITOL (90453 "Rubber Soul") 20-30 88
(Purple label with "Manufactured by Capitol, etc." perimeter print.)
CAPITOL (91302 "Beatles Deluxe Box Set")..225-275 88
(Boxed, 14-disc set.)
CICADELIC (1960 "Moviemania")...........10-15 87
CICADELIC (1961 "Not a Second Time") 10-15 86
CICADELIC (1962 "Things We Said Today")..10-15 86
CICADELIC (1963 "All Our Loving").........10-15 86
CICADELIC (1964 "East Coast Invasion")..10-15 85
CICADELIC (1965 "Round the World") 10-15 86
CICADELIC (1966 "West Coast Invasion")..10-15 85
CICADELIC (1967 "From Britain with a Beat")..10-15 87
CICADELIC (1968 "Here, There and Everywhere")..10-15 88
CLARION (601 "The Amazing Beatles & Other Great English Sounds")................................100-150 66
(Monaural. Also contains selections by the Swallows.)
CLARION (601 "The Amazing Beatles & Other Great English Sounds")................................175-225 66
(Stereo. Back cover lists song titles. Also contains selections by the Swallows.)
CLARION (601 "The Amazing Beatles & Other Great English Sounds")................................200-250 66
(Stereo. Back cover does NOT list song titles. Also contains selections by the Swallows.)
CREATIVE RADIO ("The Beatle Invasion")..35-45 '80s
(Three-LP set, includes 12" x 19" poster. Promotional issue only.)
DESERT VIBRATIONS (HSRD SP1 "Christmas Reflections") 20-25 82
GREAT NORTHWEST MUSIC CO. (4007 "Beatle Talk")..5-10 78
GREAT NORTHWEST MUSIC CO. (4007 "Beatle Talk") 40-50 78
(Columbia Record Club issue.)
HALL OF MUSIC (HMI 2200 "Live 1962 Hamburg Germany") 30-40 81
I-N-S RADIO NEWS ("American Tour with Ed Rudy #2")..15-25 80
LINGASONG (7001 "Live at the Starclub in Hamburg Germany-1962")..15-20 77
(Black vinyl.)
LINGASONG (7001 "Live at the Starclub in Hamburg Germany-1962")..30-40 77
(Promotional issue. Black vinyl.)

LINGASONG (7001 "Live at the Starclub in Hamburg Germany-1962") ... 250-350 77
(Promotional issue only. Blue vinyl.)
LINGASONG (7001 "Live at the Starclub in Hamburg Germany-1962") ... 250-350 77
(Promotional issue only. Red vinyl.)
LLOYDS (AG-8146 "The Great American Tour 1965 Live Beatlemania Concert") ... 500-700 65
(With selections by the Liverpool Lads.)
METRO (M-563 "This Is Where It Started") ... 80-100 66
(Monaural. Also contains selections by Tony Sheridan and by the Titans.)
METRO (MS-563 "This Is Where It Started") ... 175-225 66
(Stereo. Also contains selections by Tony Sheridan and by the Titans.)
MFSL (1 "The Collection") ... 400-500 82
(Boxed, 13-disc set. Includes booklet and alignment tool. Half-speed mastered.)
MFSL (023 "Abbey Road") ... 30-40 78
(Half-speed mastered.)
MFSL (047 "Magical Mystery Tour") ... 55-65 81
(Half-speed mastered.)
MFSL (2-072 "The Beatles") ... 50-75 82
(Half-speed mastered.)
MFSL (UHQR 100 "Sgt. Pepper's Lonely Hearts Club Band") ... 250-350 82
(Boxed, numbered set. Silver label. Half-speed mastered. Includes inserts.)
MFSL (100 "Sgt. Pepper's Lonely Hearts Club Band") ... 30-40 85
(White label. Half-speed mastered.)
MFSL (101 "Please Please Me") ... 25-35 86
(Half-speed mastered.)
MFSL (102 "With the Beatles") ... 150-200 86
(Half-speed mastered.)
MFSL (103 "A Hard Day's Night") ... 30-40 87
(Half-speed mastered.)
MFSL (104 "Beatles for Sale") ... 30-40 87
(Half-speed mastered.)
MFSL (105 "Help!") ... 30-40 85
(Half-speed mastered.)
MFSL (106 "Rubber Soul") ... 30-40 84
(Half-speed mastered.)
MFSL (107 "Revolver") ... 30-40 86
(Half-speed mastered.)
MFSL (108 "Yellow Submarine") ... 50-60 87
(Half-speed mastered.)
MFSL (109 "Let It Be") ... 30-40 87
(Gatefold cover. Half-speed mastered.)
MFSL (109 "Let It Be") ... 300-350 87
(Single pocket cover. Half-speed mastered.)
MGM (E-4215 "The Beatles with Tony Sheridan and Guests") ... 225-250 64
(Monaural. With selections by Tony Sheridan and by the Titans.)
MGM (SE-4215 "The Beatles with Tony Sheridan and Guests") ... 600-800 64
(Stereo. With selections by Tony Sheridan and by the Titans.)
MUSIC INTERNATIONAL (4007 "Beatle Talk") ... 40-50 85
(White cover with embossed print.)
ORANGE (12880 "Silver Beatles") ... 250-350 85
(Half-speed mastered.)
PAC (2333 "Dawn of the Silver Beatles") 30-50 81
PBR INT'L (7005/6 "David Wigg Interviews [The Beatles]") ... 50-60 78
(Black vinyl. Two discs. With booklet)
PBR INT'L (7005/6 "David Wigg Interviews [The Beatles]") ... 40-50 78
(Black vinyl. Two discs. Without booklet)
PBR INT'L (7005/6 "David Wigg Interviews [The Beatles]") ... 70-90 78
(Blue vinyl. Two discs. With booklet.)
PBR INT'L (7005/6 "David Wigg Interviews [The Beatles]") ... 60-80 78
(Blue vinyl. Two discs. Without booklet.)
PHOENIX 10 (352 "The Silver Beatles, Vol. 1") ... 8-12 82
PHOENIX 10 (353 "The Silver Beatles, Vol. 2") ... 8-12 82
PHOENIX 20 (623 "20 Hits") ... 15-20 82
PHOENIX 20 (629 "20 Hits") ... 15-20 82
PICKWICK (2098 "Historic First Live Recordings") ... 20-30 78
PICKWICK (3661 "First Live Recordings, Vol. 1") ... 20-30 79
PICKWICK (3662 "First Live Recordings, Vol. 2") ... 20-30 79
PICKWICK (90051 "Recorded Live in Hamburg, 1962, Volume 1") ... 30-40 78
PICKWICK (90061 "Recorded Live in Hamburg, 1962, Volume 2") ... 30-40 78
PICKWICK (90071 "Recorded Live in Hamburg, 1962, Volume 3") ... 30-40 78
POLYDOR (4504 "In the Beginning, Circa 1960") ... 20-30 70
(Gatefold cover.)
POLYDOR (4504 "In the Beginning, Circa 1960") ... 8-12 81
(Standard cover. Label reads "Manufactured By Polydor Incorporated.")
POLYDOR (4504 "In the Beginning, Circa 1960") ... 5-10 84
(Standard cover. Label reads "Manufactured and Marketed By Polygram.")
POLYDOR (93199 "In the Beginning, Circa 1960") ... 20-30 70
(Capitol Record Club issue.)
POLYDOR (825-073 "In the Beginning, Circa 1960") ... 15-20 88
RPN (RADIO PULSEBEAT NEWS) ("American Tour with Ed Rudy #2") ... 75-100 64
(This LP was occasionally issued with a "Teen Talk" booklet. The value of the booklet is approximately the same as for the LP. This edition has NO pictures of the Beatles on the LP cover.)
RPN (RADIO PULSEBEAT NEWS) ("1965 Talk Album, Ed Rudy/New US Tour") ... 150-175 65
RAVEN (8911 "Talk Down Under") ... 10-20 81
RAVEN (8911 "Talk Down Under") ... 60-80 81
(Promotional issue only.)
RING AROUND TH E POPS (1966 "Beatle-Views, 1966 American Tour") ... 200-300 66
RING AROUND TH E POPS (1966 "Beatle-Views, 1966 American Tour") ... 200-300 69
(Reissue "Authorized By Capitol.")
SAVAGE (69 "The Savage Young Beatles") ... 1200-1500 68
(Label is yellow. Cover is glossy orange.)
SAVAGE (69 "The Savage Young Beatles") ... 100-125 68
(Label is orange. Cover is yellow.)
SILHOUETTE (10004 "Timeless") ... 20-30 81
(Picture disc.)
SILHOUETTE (10010 "Timeless II") ... 20-30 82
(Picture disc.)
SILHOUETTE (10013 "The British Are Coming") ... 10-15 84
(Black vinyl.)
SILHOUETTE (10013 "The British Are Coming") ... 60-80 84
(Red vinyl.)
SILHOUETTE (10015 "The Golden Beatles") ... 10-15 85
(Black vinyl.)
SILHOUETTE (10015 "The Golden Beatles") ... 40-80 85
(Colored vinyl.)
STERLING PRODUCTIONS (6481 "I Apologize") ... 300-350 66
(Price includes bonus 8" x 10" photo, which represents $15 to $25 of the value.)
U.A. (UAL-3366 "A Hard Day's Night") .200-225 64
(Monaural. Shows *I'll Cry Instead* as "I Cry Instead.")
U.A. (UAL-3366 "A Hard Day's Night") .175-200 64
(Monaural. Correctly shows *I'll Cry Instead.*)
U.A. (UAL-3366 "A Hard Day's Night") ... 2500-3000 64
(Monaural. White label. Promotional issue only.)
U.A. (UAS-6366 "A Hard Day's Night") ... 250-275 64
(Stereo. Black label. Black vinyl. Shows *I'll Cry Instead* as "I Cry Instead.")
U.A. (UAS-6366 "A Hard Day's Night") ... 225-250 64
(Stereo. Black label. Black vinyl. Correctly shows *I'll Cry Instead.*)
U.A. (UAS-6366 "A Hard Day's Night") 50-60 68
(Stereo. Pink and orange label.)
U.A. (UAS-6366 "A Hard Day's Night") 50-60 70
(Stereo. Black and orange label.)
U.A. (UAS-6366 "A Hard Day's Night") 15-25 71
(Stereo. Tan label.)
U.A. (UAS-6366 "A Hard Day's Night") 15-20 77
(Stereo. Orange and yellow label.)
U.A. (T-90828 "A Hard Day's Night") ... 1000-1500 65
(Monaural. Capitol Record Club issue.)
U.A. (ST-90828 "A Hard Day's Night") .500-750 65
(Stereo. Capitol Record Club issue.)
VEE-JAY (PRO-202 "Hear the Beatles Tell All") ... 200-250 64
(Monaural. Black label with rainbow color-band.)
VEE-JAY (202 "Hear the Beatles Tell All") ... 250-300 64
(Monaural. Black label with rainbow color-band. Does not have PRO prefix.)
VEE-JAY (202 "Hear the Beatles Tell All") ... 8000-10000 64
(Label reads "Promotional" on left and "Not For Sale" on right.)
VEE-JAY (202 "Hear the Beatles Tell All") . 5-10 79
(Stereo.)
VEE-JAY (202 "Hear the Beatles Tell All") ... 20-25 87
(Shaped picture disc.)
VEE-JAY (1062 "Introducing the Beatles") ... 2200-2500 64
(Monaural. Black label with oval logo. Has *Love Me Do* and *P.S. I Love You.* Back cover pictures 25 other Vee-Jay albums.)
VEE-JAY (1062 "Introducing the Beatles") ... 7000-9000 64
(Stereo. Black label with oval logo. Has *Love Me Do* and *P.S. I Love You.* Back cover pictures 25 other Vee-Jay albums.)
VEE-JAY (1062 "Introducing the Beatles") ... 1500-2000 64
(Monaural. Black label with oval logo. Has *Love Me Do* and *P.S. I Love You.* Back cover is blank.)
VEE-JAY (1062 "Introducing the Beatles") ... 5000-7000 64
(Stereo. Black label with oval logo. Has *Love Me Do* and *P.S. I Love You.* Back cover is blank.)
VEE-JAY (1062 "Introducing the Beatles") ... 900-1200 64
(Monaural. Black label oval logo.Has *Love Me Do* and *P.S. I Love You.* Back cover lists contents.)
VEE-JAY (1062 "Introducing the Beatles") ... 1000-1500 64
(Monaural. Black label with brackets logo.Has *Love Me Do* and *P.S. I Love You.* Back cover lists contents.)
VEE-JAY (1062 "Introducing the Beatles") ... 17000-19000 64
(Stereo. Black label with brackets logo. Has *Love Me Do* and *P.S. I Love You.* Back cover lists contents.)
VEE-JAY (1062 "Introducing the Beatles") ... 16000-18000 64
(Stereo. Black label with oval logo. Has *Love Me Do* and *P.S. I Love You.* Back cover lists contents.)
VEE-JAY (1062 "Introducing the Beatles") ... 400-500 64
(Monaural. Black label with oval logo. Has *Ask Me Why* and *Please Please Me.* Back cover lists contents.)
VEE-JAY (1062 "Introducing the Beatles") ... 2000-2500 64
(Stereo. With *Ask Me Why* and *Please Please Me.* For any of the label styles or logo designs. Back cover lists contents.)
VEE-JAY (1062 "Introducing the Beatles") ... 250-350 64
(Monaural. Black label, brackets logo, rainbow color-band. Has *Ask Me Why* and *Please Please Me.* Back cover lists contents.)
VEE-JAY (1062 "Introducing the Beatles") ... 250-350 64
(Monaural. Solid black label. Has *Ask Me Why* and *Please Please Me.* With "Vee-Jay Records" printed under "VJ" logo. Back cover lists contents.)
VEE-JAY (1062 "Introducing the Beatles") ... 1800-2200 64
(Stereo. Solid black label. Has *Ask Me Why* and *Please Please Me.* With "Vee-Jay Records" printed under "VJ" logo. Back cover lists contents.)
VEE-JAY (1062 "Introducing the Beatles") ... 3000-5000 64
(Monaural. Solid black label with oval logo. Has *Ask Me Why* and *Please Please Me.* Back cover lists contents.)
VEE-JAY (1062 "Introducing the Beatles") ... 1000-1500 64
(Monaural. Solid black label with brackets logo. Has *Ask Me Why* and *Please Please Me.* Back cover lists contents.)

Note: All original copies of *Introducing the Beatles* have the title and artist credit, "The Beatles," printed above the hole. Counterfeits have that text divided by the hole.
Add $50 to $75 to any monaural copies of *Introducing the Beatles* (with *Ask Me Why* and *Please Please Me*) if accompanied by a sticker "Featuring *Twist and Shout* and *Please Please Me.*" We have yet to find a stereo copy with this sticker.

VEE-JAY (1092 "Songs, Pictures and Stories") ... 350-450 64
(Monaural. Gatefold cover. Black label with colorband and brackets Vee-Jay logo.)
VEE-JAY (1092 "Songs, Pictures and Stories") ... 450-550 64
(Monaural. Gatefold cover. Black label with colorband and oval Vee-Jay logo.)
VEE-JAY (1092 "Songs, Pictures and Stories") ... 500-600 64
(Monaural. Gatefold cover. Solid black label with oval Vee-Jay logo.)
VEE-JAY (1092 "Songs, Pictures and Stories") ... 350-450 64
(Monaural. Gatefold cover. Solid black label with sans-serif Vee-Jay logo.)
VEE-JAY (1092 "Songs, Pictures and Stories") ... 2500-3000 64
(Stereo. Gatefold cover. Black label with colorband and oval Vee-Jay logo.)
VEE-JAY (1092 "Songs, Pictures and Stories") ... 2000-2500 64
(Stereo. Gatefold cover. Black label with colorband and brackets Vee-Jay logo.)
VEE-JAY (1092 "Songs, Pictures and Stories") ... 2000-2500 64
(Stereo. Gatefold cover. Solid black label with sans-serif Vee-Jay logo.)

Note: Counterfeits of Vee-Jay 1092 do not have gatefold covers.

Promotional Only LPs

APPLE (SBC-100 "The Beatles' Christmas Album") ... 200-250 70
(Special issue for Beatles fan club members.)
APPLE (SPRO 11206/207 "College Radio Sampler") ... 75-125 96
APPLE FILMS (KAL 1004 "The Yellow Submarine") ... 900-1200 69
(Contains the advertisements used on radio stations to promote the film.)
CAPITOL ("10th Anniversary Box Set: 1964-1974") ... 1500-1800 74
(Boxed, 17-disc set. No selection number used.)
CAPITOL/EMI (BC-13 "The Beatles Collection") ... 200-300 78
(Boxed, 14-disc set.)
I-N-S RADIO NEWS (DOC-1 "Beatlemania Tour Coverage") ... 900-1200 64
(Open-end interview. Includes script.)
U.A. (UA-HELP "United Artists Presents *Help!*") ... 800-900 65
(Contains the advertisements used on radio stations to promote the film.)
U.A. (UA-HELP INT "Special Open-End Interview") ... 1000-1200 65
(Price includes script and programming information, which represents about $75-100 of the value.)
U.A. (UA-HELP-SHOW "United Artists Presents *Help!*") ... 2000-2200 65
(Single-sided open-end interview. Price includes script which represents about $75 to $100 of the value.)
U.A. (2298 "Hard Day's Night Transatlantic Open-end Interview") ... 6000-7500 64
(Price includes 5-pages of script and programming information, which represents about $100 to $150 of the value.)
U.A. (2359/60 "Special Beatles Half Hour Open End Interview") ... 1000-1500 64
(Price includes 12-pages of script and programming information, which represents about $100 to $150 of the value.)
U.A. (2362/63 "United Artists Presents *A Hard Day's Night*") ... 800-1200 64
(Contains the advertisements used on radio stations to promote the film.)
U.A. (UAL-6366 "A Hard Day's Night") ... 10000-12000 64
(Pink vinyl. Likely an experimental pressing.)
Members: John Lennon; Paul McCartney; George Harrison; Pete Best; Ringo Starr.

Note: Nearly every valuable Beatles record has been counterfeited. If in doubt, have potential purchases authenticated by an expert.
Also see ALAN, Lee
Also see BEST, Pete
Also see BUDDY
Also see CLAY, Tom
Also see HARRISON, George
Also see LENNON, John
Also see MARTIN, George
Also see McCARTNEY, Paul
Also see MOORE, Harv
Also see NICOL, Jimmy, & Shubdubs
Also see PRESLEY, Elvis / Beatles
Also see PRESTON, Billy
Also see RESIDENTS
Also see SHANKAR, Ravi
Also see SILKIE
Also see STARR, Ringo

BEATLES / Beach Boys / Buddy Holly
LPs: 10/12-inch
CREATIVE RADIO SHOWS (Demo of "Specials")...75-100 79
(Promotional issue only.)
Also see HOLLY, Buddy

BEATLES / Beach Boys / Kingston Trio
Plastic Soundsheets/Flexi-Discs:
EVA-TONE (8464 "Surprise Gift from the Beatles, Beach Boys & Kingston Trio")...450-550 64
(Seven-inch tri-fold card.)
EVA-TONE (8464 "Surprise Gift from the Beatles, Beach Boys & Kingston Trio")...300-350 64
(Five-inch round plastic soundsheet.)
EVA-TONE (8464 "Surprise Gift from the Beatles, Beach Boys & Kingston Trio")...2000-2500 64
(Mailer envelope for five-inch round plastic soundsheet.)
Also see BEACH BOYS
Also see KINGSTON TRIO

BEATLES / Jerry Blabber
Singles: 7-inch
QUEST (101 "Girl I Love")...5-10 65

BEATLES / 4 Seasons LP '64
LPs: 10/12-inch
VEE-JAY (DX-30 "Beatles Vs. the Four Seasons")...800-1000 64
(Two discs. Monaural. With bonus Beatles poster.)
VEE-JAY (DX-30 "Beatles Vs. the Four Seasons")...600-800 64
(Two discs. Monaural. Without bonus Beatles poster.)
VEE-JAY (DXS-30 "Beatles Vs. the Four Seasons")...1800-2200 64
(Two discs. Stereo. With bonus Beatles poster.)
VEE-JAY (DXS-30 "Beatles Vs. the Four Seasons")...1600-2000 64
(Two discs. Stereo. Without bonus Beatles poster.)
Also see 4 SEASONS

BEATLES / Frank Ifield LP '64
LPs: 10/12-inch
VEE-JAY (1085 "Jolly What! the Beatles & Frank Ifield")...250-275 64
(Monaural. Drawing of an Englishman on cover.)
VEE-JAY (1085 "Jolly What! the Beatles & Frank Ifield")...500-600 64
(Stereo. Drawing of an Englishman on cover.)
VEE-JAY (1085 "The Beatles & Frank Ifield")...3000-3500 64
(Monaural. Pictures the Beatles on cover.)
VEE-JAY (1085 "The Beatles & Frank Ifield")...8000-9000 64
(Stereo. Pictures the Beatles on cover.)
Also see IFIELD, Frank

BEATLES / Loretta Lynn
Singles: 7-inch
VEE-JAY (581 "Please Please Me"/"Before I'm Over You")...50-100 64
(This pairing is the result of a production error.)
Also see BEATLES
Also see LYNN, Loretta

BEATLES BLAST AT STADIUM ("Described by Erupting Fans")
LPs: 10/12-inch
AUDIO JOURNAL (1 "Beatles Blast at [Shea] Stadium")...10-20 66
(Contains only noise made by fans at a Shea Stadium concert. No artist is credited.

BEATNICKS
Singles: 7-inch
KEY-LOCK (913 "Blue Angel")...500-1000 60

BEATNIKS
(Beat-Niks)
Singles: 7-inch
PERFORMANCE (500 "Get Yourself a-Ready")...10-20 59
RHYTHM (116 "Just Me and You")...400-500 58
TAMPA (160 "Foolish Fool")...10-20 58
Also see RAYE, Patsy

BEATS
Singles: 7-inch
DESIGN (827 "Bagdad Daddy")...8-12 64
LPs: 10/12-inch
DESIGN/STEREO SPECTRUM (170 "New Merseyside Sound")...25-35 64
RONDO (2026 "New Merseyside Sound")...25-35 64
(Also issued as by the Liverpool Beats.)
Also see LIVERPOOL BEATS

BEAU, Kenny
(With the Whirlwinds; Kenny Bolognese)
Singles: 7-inch
PL (1015 "You're the Right One")...100-200 59
Member: Kenny Chandler.
Also see CHANDLER, Kenny

BEAU-BELLES
Singles: 7-inch
ARROW (729 "Wonderful You")...15-25 58
PLANET (1004 "My Heart Keeps A-Rockin' ")...15-25 58

BEAU BRUMMELS P&R/LP '65
Singles: 7-inch
AUTUMN (8 "Laugh Laugh")...8-12 64
(White label.)
AUTUMN (8 "Laugh Laugh")...5-10 64
(Orange label. Different edit than on white label.)
AUTUMN (10 thru 24)...5-10 65
PEP...3-5
RHINO...3-5 82
W.B. ...4-8 66-75
Picture Sleeves
PEP...3-5
RHINO...3-5 82
LPs: 10/12-inch
ACCORD...5-10 82
AUTUMN (103 "Introducing the Beau Brummels")...40-50 65
AUTUMN (104 "Beau Brummels, Vol. 2")...40-50 65
JAS...8-10
POST...8-10
RHINO...5-10 81-82
VAULT (114 "Best of the Beau Brummels")...25-30 67
VAULT (121 "Beau Brummels, Vol. 44")...15-20 68
W.B. (Except 1644)...20-25 67-75
W.B. (1644 "Beau Brummels '66")...30-35 66
Members: Sal Valentino; Ron Elliott; Ron Meagher; Declan Mulligan; John Petersen.
Session: Van Dyke Parks.
Also see VALENTINO, Sal
Also see PARKS, Van Dyke

BEAU JENS
Singles: 7-inch
SOUND OF THE SCREEM (2162 "She Was Mine")...30-40 67

BEAU JIVES
(Beau-Jives)
Singles: 7-inch
LORD BINGO (102 "Brightest Star in the Sky")...50-75 62
LORD BINGO (103 "Dip Dip")...75-100 62
LORD BINGO (107 "Brightest Star in the Sky")...40-50 63
LORD BINGO (108 "Here We Go")...15-25 63
LORD BINGO (111 "Dip Dip")...50-75 63
SHEPHERD (2202 "I'll Never Be the Same")...40-50 61
VISION (111 "Dip Dip")...75-100 62

BEAUBIENS
Singles: 7-inch
MALIBU (67001 "Time's Passed")...100-200

BEAU-MARKS P&R '60
Singles: 7-inch
MAINSTREAM (688 "Clap Your Hands")...5-10 68
PORT (70029 "Lovely Little Lady")...10-15 62
QUALITY (014 "Clap Your Hands")...10-20 '60s
(Reissue. Canadian.)
QUALITY (1219 thru 1404)...20-30 60-62
(Canadian.)
QUALITY (1423 thru 1532)...15-25 62
(Canadian.)
QUALITY (1966 "Clap Your Hands")...30-40 60
(Canadian.)
RUST (5035 "School Is Out")...15-20 61
RUST (5050 "Tender Years")...10-15 62
SHAD (5017 "Clap Your Hands")...8-12 60
SHAD (5021 "Billy, Billy Went a Walking")...10-15 60
TIME (1032 "Rockin' Blues")...50-75 61
(Previously issued in Canada only, credited to the Del Tones.)
LPs: 10/12-inch
BIRCHMOUNT (505 "High Flying Beau-Marks")...35-50 69
(Canadian.)
Also see DEL TONES

BEAUMONT, Ashley
(Ashley Beaumont the 18th)
Singles: 7-inch
WORTHY (1003 "Shimmy Doll")...50-75 58

BEAUMONT, Jimmy P&R '61
(With the Skyliners; Jimmie Beaumont)
Singles: 7-inch
BANG (510 "Please Send Me Someone to Love")...10-20 65
BANG (525 "You Got Too Much Going for You")...15-25 66
CAPITOL (3979 "Where Have They Gone")...4-8 74
COLPIX (607 "End of the Story")...10-20 61
DOC...5-10
DRIVE (6520 "The Day the Clown Cried")...4-8 76
GALLANT (3007 "There's No Other")...10-15 64
GALLANT (3012 "Love Is a Dangerous Game")...8-12 64
MAY (112 "Ev'rybody's Cryin' ")...15-25 61
MAY (115 "I Shoulda Listened to Mama")...15-25 62
MAY (120 "Never Say Goodbye")...15-25 62
MAY (136 "Give Her My Best")...40-60 63
Also see SKYLINERS

BEAUREGARDE
(Beauregard)
Singles: 7-inch
INT'L ARTISTS (123 "Popcorn Popper")..15-20 67
LPs: 10/12-inch
EMPIRE ("Beauregarde")...75-100 69
(No selection number used.)
SOUND (7104 "Beauregarde")...50-75 69
Members: Greg Sage; Dave Kopel.

BEAUTIFUL APOLLO
Singles: 7-inch
BARRA-DONNA ("Why I")...30-50
(Selection number not known.)

BEAUTIFUL DAZE
Singles: 7-inch
RPR (101 "City Jungle")...20-30 67
SPREAD CITY (101 "City Jungle")...10-15 68

BEAUX JENS
Singles: 7-inch
SOUND OF THE SCEEN (2162 "She Was Mine")...25-35 67

BEAVER, Stan
Singles: 7-inch
KASH (1006 "Got a Rocket in My Pocket")...30-40 65
PETAL (1012 "Got a Rocket in My Pocket")...50-75 60

BEAVER & TRAPPERS
Singles: 7-inch
WHITE CLIFFS (236 "Happiness")...40-60 66

BEAVERS
Singles: 78 rpm
CORAL...50-100 49-50
Singles: 7-inch
CORAL (65018 "If You See Tears in My Eyes")...250-300 49
CORAL (65026 "Big Mouth Mama")...250-300 50
Members: Fred Hamilton; Richard Palmer; Ray Johnson; John Wilson.
Also see LANCE, Herb

BEAVERS
Singles: 7-inch
CAPITOL (3956 "Sack Dress")...15-25 58
CAPITOL (4015 "Low As I Can Be")...10-20 58

BEAVERS, Clyde C&W '60
(Clyde Beavers / Jim Martin)
Singles: 7-inch
DECCA...10-15 60
HICKORY...5-8 65-66
KA$H...5-10 65
TEMPWOOD...5-10 63
WONDER (105 "Black Knee Socks")...100-200 58
LPs: 10/12-inch
KASH COUNTRY...5-10
SOMERSET...8-12

BEAVERS, Clyde, & Red Sovine
LPs: 10/12-inch
ALSHIRE (5130 "Million Seller – Hits Made Famous By Roy Acuff and Tennessee Ernie Ford")...8-12 69
Also see BEAVERS, Clyde
Also see SOVINE, Red

BEAVERS, Jackey
(With the Fam Gang; Jackey Beavers Show)
Singles: 7-inch
CHECKER (1119 "I Need Somebody")...10-20 65
GRAND LAND (9000 "Bring Me All Your Heartaches")...15-25 '60s
MAINSTREAM (713 "When Something Is Wrong with My Baby")...5-10 69
NATION ("Come Back My Love")...20-40 '60s
(No selection number used.)
REVILOT (208 "I Need My Baby")...150-250 66
SEVENTY-SEVEN...4-6 72-73
SOUND PLUS...4-6 72
SOUND STAGE 7...5-8 69-72
W.B. ...4-6 72
Also see JOHNNY & JACKEY

BE-BOP DELUXE LP '76
Singles: 7-inch
HARVEST...4-6 75-78
LPs: 10/12-inch
HARVEST (Black vinyl)...5-10 76-78
HARVEST (Colored vinyl)...15-20 77-78
Promotional LPs
HARVEST (8531 "Be Bop's Biggest")...25-35 75
Members: Richard Brown; Robert Bryan; Paul Jeffreys; Nicholas Chatterton-Dew; Simon Fox; Andrew Clarke; Milton R. James; Bill Nelson; Ian Parkin; Charles Tumahai.

BECK, Carlton
Singles: 7-inch
HIT (1000 "The Girl I Left Behind")...3-5 '90s
TROY (100 "The Girl I Left Behind")...600-800 62
(First issued as by "Carlton.")
Also see CARLTON

BECK, Elder
Singles: 78 rpm
CHART (624 "Rock & Roll Sermon")...10-15 56
GOTHAM (603 "There's a Dead Cat on the Line")...15-25 49
Singles: 7-inch
CHART (624 "Rock and Roll Sermon")...20-30 56

BECK, Jeff P&R/LP '68
(Jeff Beck Group; with Terry Bozzio & Tony Hymas; with Jan Hammer)
Singles: 7-inch
EPIC (10000 series)...5-10 67-69
EPIC (50000 series)...4-6 75-76
LPs: 10/12-inch
ACCORD (7141 "Early Anthology")...5-10 81
EPIC (151 "Everything You Always Wanted to Hear")...20-30 76
(Promotional issue only.)
EPIC (796 "Musical Montage")...20-30 79
(Promotional issue only.)
EPIC (850 "Then and Now")...25-35 80
(Two discs. Promotional issue only.)
EPIC (26413 "Truth")...10-15 68
EPIC (26478 "Bec-Ola")...10-15 69

EPIC (KE-30973 "Rough and Ready")..... 10-15 71
EPIC (EQ-30973 "Rough and Ready") 20-30 74
(Quadraphonic.)
EPIC (KE-31331 "Jeff Beck Group")........ 10-15 72
EPIC (EQ-31331 "Jeff Beck Group") 20-30 72
(Quadraphonic.)
EPIC (PE-33409 "Blow By Blow") 10-15 75
EPIC (PEQ-33409 "Blow By Blow") 10-15 75
(Quadraphonic.)
EPIC (PE-33849 "Wired")......................... 10-15 75
EPIC (33779 "Truth"/"Beck-Ola") 10-15 75
(Two discs.)
EPIC (PEQ-33849 "Wired") 10-15 75
(Quadraphonic.)
EPIC (34433 "Live").................................8-12 77
EPIC (35684 "There and Back")................8-12 80
EPIC (39483 "Flash")...............................8-12 85
EPIC (44313 "Guitar Shop")......................8-12 89
EPIC (43409 "Blow By Blow") 15-25 75
(Half-speed mastered.)
EPIC (43849 "Wired") 10-15 75
(Half-speed mastered.)
MFP (5219 "Most of Jeff Beck") 8-10
SPRINGBOARD (4039 "Shapes of Things")..5-10 75
Members: Rod Stewart; Ronnie Wood; Nicky Hopkins; Tony Newman; Max Middleton; Bob Tench; Cozy Powell. Session: Jan Hammer; Jimmy Hall; Terry Bozzio; Tony Hymas.
Also see CLAPTON, Eric, Jeff Beck & Jimmy Page
Also see DONOVAN & JEFF BECK GROUP
Also see G.T.O.
Also see HARRISON, George / Jeff Beck / Dave Edmunds
Also see LORD SUTCH
Also see STEWART, Rod
Also see WOOD, Ron
Also see YARDBIRDS

BECK, Jeff, & Rod Stewart — P&R '85
Singles: 7-inch
EPIC (05416 "People Get Ready") 3-5 85
Picture Sleeves
EPIC (05416 "People Get Ready") 3-5 85
Also see BECK, Jeff
Also see STEWART, Rod

BECK, Jimmy — P&R '59
(With His Orchestra)
Singles: 7-inch
ASTRA (1015 "Pipe Dreams")....................5-10 65
CHAMPION (1002 "Pipe Dreams")........... 10-20 59
ZIL (9004 "Carnival")............................ 15-25 58

BECK, Joe — LP '75
(With the Highlites; with Edith Fellows)
Singles: 7-inch
CHARLES (160 "Don't Pass Me By")....... 30-50
CHARLES (478 "I've Got to Win Your Love")... 15-25
CHARLES (577 "Daddy Cool")................ 10-20
POLYDOR..4-6 77
RADAR (2614 "Cool Moose")................. 10-20 62
LPs: 10/12-inch
KUDU...8-10 75
POLYDOR..5-10 77
VERVE FORECAST.................................. 10-15 69

BECK, Johnny
Singles: 78 rpm
SITTIN' IN WITH (531 "Locked in Jail Blues").. 75-125 50

BECK BROTHERS
Singles: 7-inch
MID WEST (787 "Big Rocker")................ 50-75 59

BECKER, Lee
Singles: 7-inch
DEE's (80 "Betty Lou")......................... 150-250

BECKHAM, Tommy
(With Harold Cavallero's Orchestra)
Singles: 7-inch
TAB (28 "Gang's House")..................... 200-300
(Also issued as by Mark Evans.)
Also see EVANS, Mark

BED OF ROSES
Singles: 7-inch
DELTRON 5-10 66
TEA (2577 "Quiet") 50-100

BEDIENT, Jack
(With the Chessmen)
Singles: 7-inch
COLUMBIA..5-10 67-68
ERA (3050 "The Mystic One")....................5-10 61
EXECUTIVE PRODUCTIONS ....8-12 '60s
FANTASY (595 "Double Whammy").........15-25 65
PALOMAR (2212 "Dream Boy")................15-20 65
R-E-V (104 "Glimmer Sunshine").............15-25 66
TROPHY (1001 "Pretty One")..................10-15 65
LPs: 10/12-inch
EXECUTIVE PRODUCTIONS ("Jack Bedient") ....50-75 '60s
(Selection number not known.)
FANTASY (3365 "Live at Harvey's").........40-50 65
SATORI (1001 "Where Did She Go") 40-60 66
TROPHY (101 "Two Sides")....................40-60 64
Also see CHESSMEN

BEDLAM FOUR
Singles: 7-inch
ARMADA (001 "Hydrogen Atom")........200-300 67
LE JAC (3006 "Watch It Baby")................40-60 66
Also see ECHOMEN

BEDPOST ORACLE
Singles: 7-inch
CORBY (230 "Break of Dawn")..................20-30 68
ORACLE (29002 "Somebody to Love") 20-30 68

BEDWELL, Tommy
Singles: 7-inch
ACE (626 "Cry") 8-12 61
DEBUT (7674 "I Met an Angel")...............50-75 60

BEE, Davey, & Sonics
Singles: 7-inch
PEARL (408 "Linda Lee")........................50-75 58
(Blue vinyl.)

BEE, Jackie
Singles: 7-inch
SALEM (190 "Moments of Infatuation") 50-75 64

BEE, Jay, & Kats
Singles: 7-inch
BANGAR (606 "When School Is Through")...15-25 62

BEE GEES — P&R/LP '67
Singles: 12-inch
RSO (Except PRO 033)...............................3-6 73-84
RSO (PRO 033 "Saturday Night Fever") ..10-15 78
W.B. ....5-15 '70s
Singles: 7-inch
ATCO (6487 thru 6657).............................8-12 67-69
ATCO (6682 "Tomorrow Tomorrow"/"Sun in My Morning") 8-12 69
ATCO (6682 "Tomorrow Tomorrow Long Version]"/"Tomorrow Tomorrow [Short Version") 10-20 69
(Promotional issue only.)
ATCO (6702 thru 6909)..............................8-12 69-72
ATLANTIC 3-6
RSO...4-8 73-83
W.B. 3-5 87-89
Picture Sleeves
RSO (813173 "The Woman in You") 4-6 83
RSO (815235 "Someone Belonging to Someone")..4-6 83
W.B. (22899 "One") 3-5 89
W.B. (28351 "You Win Again")....................3-5 87
EPs: 7-inch
ATCO (4523 Horizontal").........................15-25 68
(Promotional issue only. Tracks are from *Horizontal*, though shown only as "Atco LP 33-233" on this label.)
ATCO (4535 Odessa")..............................10-20 69
(Promotional issue only.)
ATCO (37264 "Rare, Precious and Beautiful") 8-15 69
(Promotional issue only.)
RSO (200 "Greatest Hits")..........................5-10 79
(Promotional issue only.)
LPs: 10/12-inch
ATCO (Except TL-ST-142).......................15-25 67-72
ATCO (TL-ST-142 "Odessa")...................30-50 69
(Promotional issue only.)
NAUTILUS..15-25
(Half-speed mastered.)
RSO (Except 1 & 3042)..............................5-10 73-84
RSO (1 "Words and Music")......................40-60
(Promotional issue only.)
RSO (3042 "Spirits Having Flown") 10-15 79
(Picture disc.)
W.B. 5-10 87-89
Members: Barry Gibb; Maurice Gibb; Robin Gibb; Vince Melouney; Colin Petersen. Session: Alan Kendall; Blue Weaver; Dennis Bryon.
Also see GIBB, Barry

BEE GEES / Dave Brubeck
Singles: 7-inch
WHAT'S IT ALL ABOUT (1417 "Bee Gees – Their Hits and an Interview with Barry Gibb")...........10-20
(Issued only to radio stations.)
Also see BEE GEES
Also see BRUBECK, Dave, Quartet

BEE HIVES
Singles: 7-inch
FLEETWOOD (215 "Beatnik Baby").........50-75 61
KING (5881 "She Loves You") 8-12 64

BEE JAY
Singles: 7-inch
CLOCK (1743 "I'll Go On").......................25-35 61
SMASH (1743 "I'll Go On").......................15-25 62

BEE JAYS
(With Bob Swanson)
Singles: 78 rpm
MERCURY...10-15 57
Singles: 7-inch
MERCURY (71068 "Rock On")................15-25 57
PRIME (1001 "I'll Find You") 100-200 65
Also see SWANSON, Bob, & Bee Jays

BEE JEE
(With the Living Dolls)
Singles: 78 rpm
VITA..5-10 56-57
Singles: 7-inch
VITA (139 "Too Young Blues") 30-40 56
VITA (167 "Whisper Waltz")......................10-20 57

BEECHER, Johnny, & His Buckingham Road Quintet — P&R '63
(Plas Johnson)
Singles: 7-inch
ASTRA (1019 "Sax 5th Avenue") 5-10 65
CHARTER (6 "Summit Ridge Drive") 5-10 63
CHARTER (10 "She's Gone Away")...........5-10 63
CHARTER (1019 "Sax 5th Avenue")..........10-20 64
OMEGA (116 "Sax 5th Avenue")..............15-25 58
W.B. (5341 "Sax 5th Avenue")...................5-10 63
LPs: 10/12-inch
CHARTER (102 "Sax 5th Avenue") 20-40 63
CHARTER (104 "On the Scene") 20-30 63
Session: Bert Kendricks.
Also see JOHNSON, Plas

BEEFEATERS
Singles: 7-inch
ELEKTRA (45013 "Please Let Me Love You")..50-75 64
Members: David Crosby; Gene Clark; Jim McGuinn.
Also see BYRDS

BEEHLER, Doug, & Wig-Wags
Singles: 7-inch
WIG-WAG (102 "Have You No Pity On Me") 50-75

BEEMAN, Johnny
Singles: 7-inch
AMY (809 "Rockin' Beatnik")....................10-20 60

BEEP BEEP & ROADRUNNERS
Singles: 7-inch
AUDIO DYNAMICS (162 "Don't Run") 10-15 67
VINCENT (222 "Shiftin' Gears")...............40-60 65

BEER GARDEN FOUR PLUS ONE
Singles: 7-inch
SMASH (1778 "New Generation") 10-20 62

BEERS, Mackey, & Rockitts
Singles: 7-inch
MARK (113 "Lorie Lee") 100-150 58

BEES
Singles: 78 rpm
IMPERIAL (5314 "Toy Bell") 100-150 54
IMPERIAL (5320 "Get Away Baby") 300-400 54
Singles: 7-inch
IMPERIAL (5314 "Toy Bell") 250-350 54
(Glossy red label.)
IMPERIAL (5314 "Toy Bell") 30-40 54
(Flat red label.)
IMPERIAL (5320 "Get Away Baby") .1000-2000 54
Member: Billy Bland.

BEES
Singles: 7-inch
FINCH (7321 "Oh Yes") 75-125 59

BEES
Singles: 7-inch
LIVERPOOL (62225 "Voices Green and Purple")..50-75 66
Picture Sleeves
LIVERPOOL (62225 "Voices Green and Purple")..75-100 66

BEETHOVEN 4
Singles: 7-inch
DON LEE (0003 "Oh Pretty Baby") 15-25 66

BEETHOVEN 4
(Beethoven Four; Beethovens)
Singles: 7-inch
TAG (4000 "Don't Call on Me")............250-350 66
(300 made.)
TAG ("Hairy Dog") ....100-200 '60s
(Selection number not known.)
TALOS (1313 "She Don't Care") 50-75 67
Members: Joey Hall; Hayward Fowler; Larry McBrayer; Larry Butler. Session: Bill Johnson.
Also see JOHNSON, Bill

BEGINNING OF THE END — P&R/R&B '71
Singles: 7-inch
ALSTON...4-6 71-72
LPs: 10/12-inch
ALSTON (Except 379) 10-15 71-76
ALSTON (379 "Funky Nassau") 40-60 71

BEGLEY, Suzie
Singles: 7-inch
RUBY (380 "Peppermint Stick")...............10-20 57

BEGLEY SISTERS
Singles: 7-inch
RUBY (410 "If I'm Easy to Love")............10-20 57
Member: Suzie Begley.
Also see BEGLEY, Suzie

BEHRKE, Richard, Trio
LPs: 10/12-inch
ATCO (141 "Bobby Darin Presents the Richard Behrke Trio: West Side Story") 15-25 62
Also see DARIN, Bobby

BEL AIRS
(With Gates Intino)
Singles: 7-inch
AEGIS (1001 "You Left Me")................150-250
Member: Gates Intino.

BELAFONTE, Harry — P&R '52
(Harry Belafonté with the Belafonté Singers)
Singles: 78 rpm
JUBILEE...8-12 54
RCA...5-10 57
ROOST (501 "Lean on Me") 10-15 49
Singles: 7-inch
COLUMBIA..3-5 81
JUBILEE (5048 "Annabelle Lee") 10-20 54
RCA (0300 series).....................................5-10 57
RCA (0400 thru 0600 series) 4-6 71-72
RCA (4000 & 5000 series)........................10-20 52-55
RCA (6000 & 7000 series).........................5-10 55-62
RCA (8000 & 9000 series)...........................4-6 62-67
Picture Sleeves
RCA (Except 9200 series) 10-15 55-59
RCA (9200 series)......................................4-8 69
EPs: 7-inch
CAPITOL (619 "Close You Eyes")...........15-20 55
JUBILEE..20-30 54
RCA (Except 24)......................................10-20 54-61
RCA (SPD-24 "Best of Belafonte") 40-60 56
(Ten-EP boxed set, with inserts.)
LPs: 10/12-inch
BOOK OF THE MONTH 15-20 83
CAMDEN 5-10 73-74
COLUMBIA..5-10 81
CORONET..8-15
RCA (0000 thru 0900 series).....................5-10 73
RCA (1000 thru 1900 series)..................15-25 54-59
(With "LOP," "LPM" or "LSP" prefix.)
RCA (2400 series).......................................5-10 78-81
(With "AYL1 or "CPL1" prefix.)
RCA (2000 & 3000 series, except 2449)..10-20 60-67
(With "LPM" or "LSP" prefix.)

RCA (2449 "The Midnight Special")......... 20-40 62
(Has Bob Dylan playing harmonica on the title track—his first appearance on record.)
RCA (1000 series) 5-10
RCA (3800 series) 5-10 75
RCA (4000 series) 10-15 68-71
RCA (6000 series) 15-25 59-72
Also see ANN-MARGRET
Also see COMO, Perry / Ames Brothers / Harry Belafonte / Radio City Music Hall Orch.
Also see DYLAN, Bob
Also see ROBINSON, Sugar "Chile" / Harry Belafonte

BELAFONTE, Harry, & Lena Horne *LP '59*
LPs: 10/12-inch
RCA.. 15-25 59
Also see HORNE, Lena

BELAFONTE, Harry / Islanders
LPs: 10/12-inch
CELEBRITY...................................... 10-20
Also see ISLANDERS

BELAFONTE, Harry, & Miriam Makeba *LP '65*
LPs: 10/12-inch
RCA.. 10-15 65
Also see MAKEBA, Miriam

BELAFONTE, Harry, & Nana Mouskouri *LP '66*
LPs: 10/12-inch
RCA.. 10-15 66
Also see BELAFONTE, Harry

BEL-AIR FIVE
Singles: 7-inch
USA (764 "Time Has Come").................. 15-25 64

BEL-AIRE GIRLS
Singles: 7-inch
EVEREST (19333 "Blue Moon") 8-12 60
LPs: 10/12-inch
EVEREST (1081 "Sing Along with the Teen-Agers")................................ 30-40 60
(Stereo.)
EVEREST (5081 "Sing Along with the Teen-Agers")................................ 20-30 60
(Monaural.)

BEL-AIRES
Singles: 78 rpm
FLIP 25-50 54-55
Singles: 7-inch
FLIP (303 "This Paradise")..................... 50-100 54
(Maroon label.)
FLIP (303 "This Paradise")...................... 35-45 54
(Blue label.)
FLIP (304 "White Port and Lemon Juice")....................................... 100-150 55
Members: Donald Woods; Randy Bryant; Ira Foley.
Also see GREEN, Vernon, & Medallions
Also see VEL-AIRES
Also see WOODS, Donald

BEL-AIRES
Singles: 7-inch
ARC (4451 "Space Walk")...................... 20-30 59
Also see MILO, Skip

BEL-AIRES
Singles: 7-inch
LUCKY TOKEN (107 "Baggies")............ 10-20 62
NU SOUND (1022 "Pony Rock")................5-10 62
PIV..5-10
RAFT (604 "Are You My Girl")................. 50-75 62
SPARTAN...5-10

BEL-AIRES
Singles: 7-inch
DISCOTHEQUE (1004 "Ya Ha Be Be")... 25-35 67
PLANET (58 "Ya Ha Be Be")................... 15-25 67

BEL-AIRES
Singles: 7-inch
BEL-AIRE ("I'm in Love Again") 100-200
(No selection number used.)

BELAIRS
Singles: 7-inch
ARVEE (5034 "Mr. Moto") 15-25 61
ARVEE (5054 "Volcanic Action") 15-25 61
TRIUMPH (54 "Kami-Kaze")..................... 10-20 63
Members: Richard Delvy; Eddie Bertrand; Jim Roberts; Paul Johnson; Chaz Stewart.
Also see CHALLENGERS
Also see DELVY, Richard
Also see EDDIE & SHOWMEN
Also see EVERPRESENT FULLNESS
Also see GOOD GUYS

BEL-AIRS
Singles: 7-inch
SARA (6431 "Forever Loving You")......500-750 63
Members: Wayne Demmer; Dennis Gehrke; Bob Wickert; Pete Miller.

BELEW, Carl *C&W '59*
(With His Riff Riders)
Singles: 7-inch
BRUNSWICK.......................................5-10 58
DECCA (Except 30947)........................4-8 59-72
DECCA (30947 "Cool Gator Shoes").......25-35 59
4 STAR (1700 series) 10-20 58-59
MCA...4-6 74
RCA...5-10 62-68
SOWDER (248 "I'm Long Gone") 500-1000 57
EPs: 7-inch
DECCA..8-12 60
4 STAR (34 "Carl Belew") ....8-12 '50s
LPs: 10/12-inch
BUCKBOARD 5-10
DECCA (4074 "Carl Belew") 20-25 60
(Monaural.)
DECCA (7-4074 "Carl Belew") 25-35 60
(Stereo.)
FORUM 5-10
PICKWICK/HILLTOP 10-20 65
PLANTATION.......................................5-10 81
RCA...10-20 64-68
VOCALION...10-15 66-67
WRANGLER (1007 "Carl Belew")............15-25 62

BELEW, Carl, & Betty Jean Robinson *C&W '71*
Singles: 7-inch
DECCA..4-8 71-72
LPs: 10/12-inch
DECCA..8-12 71
Also see BELEW, Carl

BELGIANETTES
Singles: 7-inch
CHEER (1009 "You Gotta Pay")..............10-15 64
OKEH (7172 "My Blue Heaven")...............15-25 63
USA (731 "You're Far from Home") 10-20 62
Also see BAKER, Jo-An

BELGIANS
(With Benny & the Sportsman)
Singles: 7-inch
TEEK (3/4 "Pray Tell Me")....................100-200 64
SEAGRAVE (1 "Blabbermouth Monkey")...5-10

BELL, Archie *P&R/R&B/LP '68*
(With the Drells)
Singles: 12-inch
PHILA. INT'L 4-8 79
PLAYHOUSE 4-8 84
Singles: 7-inch
ATLANTIC...5-8 68-72
BECKETT..3-5 81-84
GLADES...4-6 73
OVIDE (228 "Tighten Up")......................50-75 67
PHILA. INT'L 4-6 76-79
TSOP..4-6 75-76
LPs: 10/12-inch
ATLANTIC...10-20 68-69
BECKETT..5-10 81-84
PHILA. INT'L 8-10 75-79
TSOP..5-8 75
Members: Archie Bell; Huey Butler; Lee Bell; James Wise; Joe Cross; Willie Parnell.

BELL, Archie & Drells with T.S.U. Toronados
Singles: 7-inch
ATLANTIC (2478 "Tighten Up") 5-10 68
Also see T.S.U. TORONADOS

BELL, Bill
(With the 4 Unknowns)
Singles: 7-inch
MIDA (112 "Little Bitty Girl") 50-75 59

BELL, Bonnie Blue
Singles: 7-inch
BAKERSFIELD (105 "Let's Go")...........200-300 56

BELL, Brother
Singles: 78 rpm
BLUES & RHYTHM (7002 "If You Feel Froggish")...25-50 51

BELL, Carey
LPs: 10/12-inch
BLUESWAY (6079 "Last Night")................8-12 73
DELMARK (622 "Blues Harp")..................10-20 69
Also see COTTON, James, Carey Bell, Junior Wells, & Billy Branch
Also see HORTON, Big Walter

BELL, Carl
(With the Novairs)
Singles: 7-inch
LAURIE (3014 "Open House in Your Heart")..40-50 58
MOHAWK (117 "Greatest Treasure").........5-10 60

BELL, Dwain
Singles: 7-inch
SUMMIT (110 "Rock & Roll on Saturday Night")..500-750 59

BELL, Eddie
(With the Rock-A-Fellas; with Bel-Aires)
Singles: 7-inch
BEL-AIRE (956 "He's a Square")............75-100
COED (512 "Countin' the Days")..............25-35 59
LUCKY FOUR (1005 "Johnny B. Goode Is in Hollywood")...75-100 61
LUCKY FOUR (1012 "The Great Great Pumpkin")..10-20 61
MERCURY (71677 "The Masked Man")...10-20 60
MERCURY (71763 "Knock, Knock, Knock")...15-25 61
Also see BELVEDERES
Also see ROCK-A-FELLAS

BELL, Freddie, & Bell Boys
(Freddy Bell)
Singles: 78 rpm
TEEN..15-25 55
MERCURY (Except 70919).....................10-20 56
MERCURY (70919 "Stay Loose, Mother Goose")..25-35 56
WING...10-20 56
Singles: 7-inch
AUDICON (103 "A Heart for a Heart")........8-12 59
MERCURY...15-25 56-57
TEEN (101 "Hound Dog").........................40-60 55
TEEN (103 "5-10-15 Hours")....................25-35 55
WING...15-25 56
LPs: 10/12-inch
MERCURY (20289 "Rock & Roll...All Flavors") 50-100 57
20TH FOX (4146 "Bells Are Swinging") ...20-30 64
(With Roberta Linn.)

BELL, Gwenn, & Brown Dots
Singles: 78 rpm
MANOR (1171 "After Awhile") 15-25 49
Also see WATSON, Deek, & Brown Dots

BELL, Hugh, & Twiggs
Singles: 78 rpm
BLAZE (109 "Redcap")...........................10-20 55
Singles: 7-inch
BLAZE (109 "Redcap")...........................20-40 55
Also see MOORE, Johnny

BELL, Joey, & Chick Foster
Singles: 7-inch
ROCK (1000 "Don't Be Late")...................10-20 59

BELL, Johnny
(Johnny Bell Tones; Johnny Bell Quartet)
Singles: 7-inch
BRUNSWICK (55142 "Flip, Flop and Fly")...75-100 59
CECIL (5050 "Ev'ry Day") 50-75 57
FLEETWOOD (1001 "Ev'ry Day")............15-25 58
UNIVERSAL (104 "Cricket Rock") 15-25 59

BELL, Kay
(Kay Bell & Spacemen)
Singles: 7-inch
BUENA VISTA (428 "Surfer's Blues").......10-20 63
Also see TUFFS

BELL, Madeline *P&R/R&B '68*
Singles: 7-inch
ASCOT...5-10 64-65
BRUT (808 "A Touch of Class")...................4-6 73
MOD (1007 "I'm Gonna Make You Love Me")...15-25 67
PHILIPS..5-10 68
PYE...4-6 76
LPs: 10/12-inch
PHILIPS..15-20 68
PYE...8-10 76
Also see MANN, Manfred

BELL, Ray
Singles: 7-inch
FRIENDLY (853 "Yodelin' Catfish Blues")...200-300
QUEEN (24006 "Loveless Island")...........10-20 61

BELL, Reuben *R&B '72*
Singles: 7-inch
ALARM..4-6 75-77
DELUXE...4-6 72-73
HOUSE OF ORANGE (2403 "I Can't Feel This Way at Home")..5-10
MURCO (1035 "It's Not That Easy").........15-25 68
MURCO (1046 "You're Gonna Miss Me")...25-50 68
SILVER FOX (8 "Too Late")......................5-10 69

BELL, Tommy
Singles: 7-inch
ZIL (9001 "Swamp Gal") 75-125 59
Also see GAMBLE, Kenny

BELL, Vincent *P&R/LP '70*
(With the Bell Men; Vinnie Bell)
Singles: 7-inch
DECCA..5-8 67-70
INDEPENDENT (102 "Quicksand")..........20-30 60
INDEPENDENT (1214 "Caravan")............20-30 60
MUSICOR (1068 "Just a Little Kiss")..........5-10 65
VERVE (10308 "Shindig")..........................8-12 63
LPs: 10/12-inch
DECCA..10-15 67-70
INDEPENDENT (8012 "Soundtronic Guitar of Vincent Bell") 20-30 60
MUSICOR...10-20 64-65
VERVE (8574 "Whistle Stop")...................10-20 64
Also see FERRANTE & TEICHER
Also see GALLAHADS

BELL BOYS
Singles: 7-inch
JAMAR (728 "I Don't Want to Lose You")...50-100
(At least one source shows this number as 101. We don't know yet who's right.)

BELL HOPS
Singles: 78 rpm
DECCA..50-75 51
Singles: 7-inch
DECCA (48208 "For the Rest of My Life")...150-200 51
DECCA (48239 "I'm All Yours")............100-150 51

BELL NOTES *P&R/R&B '59*
Singles: 7-inch
AUTOGRAPH (204 "Little Girl in Blue") ...10-15 60
ERIC..4-6 73
MADISON (136 "Shortnin' Bread") 15-25 60
MADISON (141 "Real Wild Child") 10-20 60
TIME (1004 "I've Had It")........................15-25 58
(Blue label.)
TIME (1010 "Old Spanish Town")............15-25 59
(Red label.)
TIME (1013 "Betty Dear")........................10-15 59
TIME (1015 "Don't Ask Me Why")............10-15 59
TIME (1017 "No Dice")............................10-15 59
Picture Sleeves
TIME (1004 "I've Had It")........................5-10 '90s
EPs: 7-inch
TIME (100 "I've Had It")..........................75-100 59
Members: Carl Bonura; Lenny Giambalvo; Pete Kane; Ray Ceroni; John Casey.

BELL TONES
Singles: 78 rpm
RAMA (170 "Heart to Heart")....................25-35 55
Singles: 7-inch
RAMA (170 "Heart to Heart")....................50-75 55

BELLAIRES
Singles: 78 rpm
RUBY 40-60 55

Singles: 7-inch

RUBY (103 "I'd Never Forgive Myself") 300-350 55

BEL-LARKS

(With the Eternals; with Eternals Orchestra)

Singles: 7-inch

HAMMER (6313 " A Million and One Dreams ") 1000-2000 63
RANSOM (5001 "A Million and One Dreams") 150-250 63
(Opinions vary as to which is the first issue, though the Hammer is the rarer disc.)
STOOP SOUNDS (508 "A Million and One Dreams") 50-100 97
Also see STARR, Richie

BELLATONES

Singles: 7-inch

BELLA (2204/5 "Baby, Oh Baby") 20-30 59
BELLA (2206/7 "Cupid's Arrow") 20-30 59

BELLE, Jewel / Tommy Dean & Gloom Raiders

Singles: 78 rpm

STATES (106 "Lonely Monday") 8-12 52
STATES (111 "Raining") 8-12 52
STATES (120 "Scammon Boogie") 8-12 53

Singles: 7-inch

STATES (106 "Lonely Monday") 15-25 52
STATES (111 "Raining") 15-25 52
STATES (120 "Scammon Boogie") 15-25 53

BELLE & SEBASTIAN

LPs: 10/12-inch

ELECTRIC HONEY (5 "Tigermilk") 300-500 96

BELLES

Singles: 7-inch

CHOICE 10-15 61-63
MIRWOOD (5505 "Don't Pretend") 10-15 65
TIARA (100 "Melvin") 200-300 66
TIARA (703 "La Bamba") .... 10-20 '60s
Members: Debbie Teaver; Marina Perez; May Perez; Pan Kent.

BELLINE, Denny

(With the Dwellers; with Rich Kids)

Singles: 7-inch

COLUMBIA (45123 "Living Without You") .. 5-10 70
RCA (8665 "Little Lonely Girl") 8-12 65
RCA (8883 "Money Isn't Everything") 8-12 66
RCA (9041 "Gray City Pay") 8-12 66
RCA (10171 "Rosemary Blue") 4-8 75

LPs: 10/12-inch

RCA (3655 "Denny Belline and the Rich Kids") 25-45 66
Members: Denny Belline; Richard Supa.

BELLS

Singles: 78 rpm

RAMA 200-300 55

Singles: 7-inch

RAMA (166 "What Can I Tell Her Now") 1000-1200 55
Members: Joe Van Loan; Willis Sanders; Bob Kornegay; Willie Ray.
Also see DIXIEAIRES
Also see DU DROPPERS
Also see RAVENS
Also see VALIANTS

BELLTONES

Singles: 78 rpm

COLONIAL (1 "Way Up in North Carolina") 100-125 53

BELLTONES

Singles: 78 rpm

GRAND (102 "Estelle") 250-500 54

Singles: 7-inch

GRAND (102 "Estelle") 3000-4000 54
(Black vinyl. Blue label. 500 made.)
GRAND (102 "Estelle") 1500-2500 54
(Black vinyl. Yellow label. 500 made.)
GRAND (102 "Estelle") 5000-7500 54
(Red vinyl.)
Members: Fred Walker; Estelle Powell; Harry Pascall; Irv Natson; Don Burnett; Hardy Hull Jr.
Also see MADISON BROTHERS

BELL-TONES

(With the Shytone 5 Orchestra; Belltones)

Singles: 78 rpm

SCATT 50-100 56

Singles: 7-inch

J&S (1610/1609 "I Love You"/"The Merengue") 75-125 58
SCATT (1610/1609 "I Love You"/"The Merengue") 400-500 56
Members: Ronnie Baker; Al Brandon; Billy Lee; Joe Raguso; Paul Fernandez.
Also see BAKER, Ronnie
Also see CAPRIS

BELL-TONES

Singles: 7-inch

CLOCK (71889 "There She Goes") 50-60 61
(Clock disc has the Mercury selection number.)
MERCURY (71889 "There She Goes") 15-25 61

BELLTONES

Singles: 7-inch

ITZY (1 "To Understand Me") 10-20 64
OLIMPIC (241 "To Understand Me") 30-50 63
Also see MAJORS / Belltones

BELLUS, Tony — P&R '59

(With Twin Tones-Delights; with Cathy Bellus [daughter]; T.J. Bellus)

Singles: 7-inch

ABC 4-6 73
COLLECTABLES 3-5 81
KING (5973 "Mustang") 5-10 65
MMP (187 "Mackinac Island") 3-6 86
MMP (227 "Proud to Be an American") 3-6 85
NRC (023 "Robbin' the Cradle") 15-25 59
(Three known variations: Title in black, blue, or orange print.)
NRC (035 "Hey Little Darlin'"/"Only Your Heart") 10-20 59
NRC (040 "Young Girls"/"Little Dreams") . 10-20 59
NRC (045 "Young Girls"/"Hey Little Darlin' ") 10-15 59
NRC (051 "The End of My Love") 20-30 60
NRC (058 "Give Me a Heart") 10-20 60
SHI-FI (128-10/128-15 "Fancy Free"/"Lovely Little Lady") 40-50 58
SHI-FI (040 "Kiss Those Shores Again for Me") 5-10 65
SOUTHERN TRACKS (2017 "Florida Beach Girls") 3-6 93

Picture Sleeves

MMP (187 "Mackinac Island") 4-8 86
NRC (035 "Hey Little Darlin' ") 30-40 59
NRC (051 "The End of My Love") 20-30 60

LPs: 10/12-inch

NRC (8 "Robbin' the Cradle with Tony Bellus") 50-100 60
SHI-FI (11 "Gems of Tony Bellus") 20-40 64

BELMONTS — P&R '61

("The Belmonts with Dion")

Singles: 12-inch

STRAWBERRY (1107 "I'll Never Fall in Love Again") 5-10 76

Singles: 7-inch

COLLECTABLES 3-5 81
DOT (17173 "Reminiscences") 5-8 68
DOT (17257 "Answer Me My Love") 5-8 68
LAURIE (3080 "We Belong Together") 10-20 61
LAURIE (3631 "Brand New Song") 4-8 75
MOHAWK (106 "Teenage Clementine") ... 30-40 57
ROULETTE GOLDEN GOODIES .... 4-6 '70s
SABINA (502 "I Need Someone") 20-30 61
SABINA (503 thru 513) 15-25 62-63
SABINA (517 thru 519) 30-40 64
SABINA (521 "Nothing in Return") 75-125 64
SABRINA (500 "Tell Me Why") 20-30 61
SABRINA (501 "Don't Get Around Much Anymore") 20-30 61
(In 1961, after #501, Sabrina changed its name, slightly, to Sabina.)
STRAWBERRY (106 "Cheek to Cheek") 4-6 76
SURPRISE (1000 "Tell Me Why") 75-125 61
U.A. (809 "I Don't Know Why") 30-40 64
U.A. (904 "Then I Walked Away") 10-15 65
U.A. (966 "I Got a Feeling") 10-15 66
U.A. (50007 "Come with Me") 15-20 66

LPs: 10/12-inch

BUDDAH (5123 "Cigars, Acappella, Candy") 25-50 72
CRYSTAL BALL (102 "Just for You – The Belmonts") 10-15 81
(Black vinyl. 2000 made.)
CRYSTAL BALL (102 "Just for You – The Belmonts") 25-35 81
(Colored vinyl. 25 made.)
CRYSTAL BALL (102 "Just for You – The Belmonts") 55-65 81
(Picture disc. No cover. 25 made.)
DOT (25949 "Summer Love") 25-30 69
SABINA (5001 "Carnival of Hits") 100-150 62
STRAWBERRY 10-15 76
UPTOWN 5-10 88
Members: Carlo Mastrangelo; Angelo D'Aleo; Fred Milano; Frank Lyndon.
Also see ALSTON, Shirley
Also see BARIN, Pete
Also see CARLO
Also see CLINTON, Buddy
Also see DION
Also see DION & BELMONTS
Also see LYNDON, Frank
Also see SHEPPARD, Buddy, & Holidays
Also see SOUL, Jimmy / Belmonts
Also see THOMAS, Bob

BELMONTS, Freddy Cannon & Bo Diddley

Singles: 12-inch

ROCK & ROLL TRAVELLING SHOW 4-6

LPs: 10/12-inch

DOWNTOWN 5-10
Also see BELMONTS
Also see CANNON, Freddy
Also see DIDDLEY, Bo

BELOVED ONES

Singles: 7-inch

BOYD (157 "Peep Peep Pop Pop") 20-30 66
Also see DEARLY BELOVEDS
Also see INTRUDERS

BELTONES

Singles: 78 rpm

HULL (721 "I Talk to My Echo") 25-50 57

Singles: 7-inch

COLLECTABLES 3-5 81
HULL (721 "I Talk to My Echo") 100-150 57
(Black label.)
HULL (721 "I Talk to My Echo") 25-50 58
(Red label. Shadow printing.)
ROULETTE 4-6 73

BELTONES

Singles: 7-inch

JELL (188 "I Want to Be Loved") 25-35 62
(Reissued as by Ronnie Baker & the Deltones.)
Also see BAKER, Ronnie

BEL-TONES

Singles: 7-inch

DEL AMO (4647 "Break Time") 15-25 64
DEL AMO (4648 "Little Boy Blue") 200-250 64

BELVADERES

Singles: 78 rpm

HUDSON 50-75 55

Singles: 7-inch

HUDSON (4 "Don't Leave Me to Cry") . 400-500 55
(Reissued as by the Dusters.)
Also see DUSTERS

BELVEDERES FEATURING DICK DAWSON

Singles: 7-inch

JOPZ (1771 "Buona Sera") 250-300 59

BELVEDERES

Singles: 7-inch

COUNT ("From Out of Nowhere") 10-20 61
(No selection number used.)
LUCKY FOUR (1003 "He's a Square"). 100-150 61
Members: Eddie Bell.
Also see BELL, Eddie

BELVEDERES

(With Jimmy Morris)

Singles: 78 rpm

BATON 8-12 55

Singles: 7-inch

BATON (214 "Come to Me Baby") 10-20 55
BATON (217 "We Too") 10-15 55
DOT (15852 "Hey Honey") 10-20 58
POPLAR (114 "Lost Love") 30-40 62

BELVEDERES

Singles: 7-inch

RHAPSODY (5163 "The McCoy") 15-25
TREND (30009 "Let's Get Married") 30-40 58

BELVEDERES

Singles: 7-inch

VALE (101 "Good Luck to You") 40-60

BELVIN, Andy

Singles: 7-inch

ATCO (6289 "Travelin' Mood") 8-12 64
CAL STATE (3200 "With All My Heart") ... 10-20
CANDIX (338 "Walking the Blues") 8-12 62
DEL-RE-VAU (504 "Your Hero") 5-10
GEE KAY (1002 "Hello My Lover") .... 15-25 '60s
VAULT (908 "Travelin' Mood") 10-15 64
(First issue.)
Also see VOWELS

BELVIN, Jesse — R&B '56

(With the Sharptones; with Laurels)

Singles: 78 rpm

CASH 25-50 57
MODERN 20-30 56-57
MONEY 20-30 55
RECORDED IN HOLLYWOOD (120 "Dream Girl") 50-100 50
RECORDED IN HOLLYWOOD (412 "Love Comes Tumbling Down") 50-75 53
SPECIALTY (435 "Confusin' Blues") 40-60 52
SPECIALTY 10-20 55

Singles: 7-inch

ALADDIN (3431 "Let Me Dream") 50-60 58
CASH (1056 "Beware") 75-125 57
(Orange and black label. Reissued in 1959 as by the Capris.)
CASH (1056 "Beware") 20-30 57
(Black and silver label.)
CLASS (267 "Deep in My Heart") 10-15 60
COLLECTABLES 3-5 81
CUSTOM 4-8
ERIC 4-6 73
HOLLYWOOD (1059 "Betty My Darling" 500-750 56
IMPACT (23 "Tonight My Love") 10-15 64
JAMIE (1145 "Goodnight My Love") 10-15 59
KENT (326 "Sentimental Reasons") 10-20 59
KNIGHT (2012 "Little Darling") 10-20 59
MODERN (1005 "Goodnight My Love") ... 30-40 56
MODERN (1013 thru 1027) 20-30 57
MONEY (208 "I'm Only a Fool") 35-50 55
RCA (7310 thru 7675, except 7469) 15-25 58-60
RCA (47-7469 "Guess Who") 15-25 59
(Monaural.)
RCA (61-7469 "Guess Who") 25-35 59
(Stereo.)
RCA (8040 "Guess Who") 8-12 62
RECORDED IN HOLLYWOOD (412 "Love Comes Tumbling Down") 200-400 53
SPECIALTY (435 "Confusin' Blues") 75-125 52
SPECIALTY (550 "Gone") 30-40 55
SPECIALTY (559 "Where's My Girl") 10-20 55
TENDER (518 "Beware") 35-50 59

EPs: 7-inch

RCA (2089 "Just Jesse Belvin") 35-50 59
RCA (2105 "Mr. Easy") 35-50 60

LPs: 10/12-inch

CAMDEN (960 "Jesse Belvin's Best") 15-20 66
CORONET .... 8-12 '60s
CROWN (5145 "Jesse Belvin Sings") 25-35 60
CROWN (5187 "Unforgettable") 25-35 60
RCA (0966 "Yesterdays") 8-12 75
RCA (LPM-2089 "Just Jesse Belvin") 30-50 59
(Monaural.)
RCA (LSP-2089 "Just Jesse Belvin") 30-60 59
(Stereo.)
RCA (LPM-2105 "Mr. Easy") 30-50 60
(Monaural.)
RCA (LSP-2105 "Mr. Easy") 30-60 60
(Stereo.)
UNITED (7220 "Jesse Belvin ... But Not Forgotten") .... 10-15 '60s
Also see BENTON, Brook / Jesse Belvin
Also see CAPRIS
Also see CHARGERS
Also see CLIQUES
Also see GASSERS
Also see JESSE & MARVIN
Also see LAURELS

Also see McNEELY, Big Jay, with Jesse Belvin & Three Dots and A Dash
Also see SHIELDS
Also see T-BIRDS

BELVIN, Jesse, & Five Keys / Feathers
Singles: 7-inch
CANDLELITE (427 "Love Song") 10-20 63
Also see FEATHERS
Also see FIVE KEYS

BELVIN, Jesse / Doc Starks
Singles: 7-inch
EXCALIBUR (509 "Heartless"/"Apple Cider") 3-5 88
Also see STARKS, Doc, & Nite Riders

BEN, LaBrenda
(With the Vandellas; with Beljeans; with Andantes)
Singles: 7-inch
GORDY (7009 "Camel Walk") 15-25 62
GORDY (7021 "Just Be Yourself") 15-25 63
MOTOWN (1033 "Camel Walk") 200-400 63
(First issued as by Saundra Mallett & the Vandellas.)
Also see MARTHA & VANDELLAS
Also see MALLETT, Saundra, & Vandellas

BENATAR, Pat *P&R/LP '79*
Singles: 12-inch
CHRYSALIS 4-8 79-86
COLUMBIA ("Le Bel Age") 10-15
(No selection number used. Promotional issue only.)
Singles: 7-inch
CHRYSALIS 4-8 79-89
SUNSHINE 8-12 78
TRACE (5293 "Day Gig") 20-30 74
Picture Sleeves
CHRYSALIS 4-8 79-89
LPs: 10/12-inch
CHRYSALIS 5-10 79-91
MFSL (057 "In the Heat of the Night") 40-60 81
Also see COXON'S ARMY

BENDER, D.C.
(D.C. Bendy)
Singles: 7-inch
IVORY 15-25 58
Also see TILLIS, Big Son
Also see WASHINGTON, D.C.

BENDERS
Singles: 7-inch
JAMAKA (1927 "Sharpest Little Girl") .. 250-350 59

BENDERS
Singles: 7-inch
BIG SOUND (3006 "Can't Tame Me") 40-60 66
Picture Sleeves
BIG SOUND (3006 "Can't Tame Me") 50-75 66
Members: Gerry Cain; Tom Noffke; Paul Barry; Geno Jansen.

BENDIX, Ralf
Singles: 7-inch
ABC-PAR (10340 "Baby Sittin' Boogie").. 15-20 62
LPs: 10/12-inch
CAPITOL (10197 "Auf Wiedersehn") 10-20 59

BENE, Chuck
Singles: 7-inch
ROCK ("Come Back Baby") 200-300
(Selection number not known.)

BENEFIELD, Marvin
(Vince Everett)
Singles: 7-inch
ROYALTY (505 "I'm Snowed") 40-60 58
Also see EVERETT, Vince

BENET, Vicki
(Miss Vicki Benet)
Singles: 78 rpm
MGM 5-10 53-54
Singles: 7-inch
LIBERTY (55100 "After My Laughter Came Tears") 5-10 57
LIBERTY (55186 "Heartstring Melody") 5-10 59
MGM 10-15 53-54
LPs: 10/12-inch
DECCA (8233 "Woman of Paris") 30-50 56
DECCA (8381 "The French Touch") 30-50 56

BENFIELD, Benny
Singles: 7-inch
K-ARK (690 "Flip Side of Your Heart") ..... 15-25 '50s

BENITEZ, Marga, & Mello-Tones
Singles: 78 rpm
DECCA 30-40 54
Singles: 7-inch
DECCA (48318 "Man Loves Woman") .100-200 54
Also see MELLO-TONES

BENNET, Connie, Bill Smyth, & Harlem-Aires
LPs: 10/12-inch
HOLLYWOOD (30 "Rhythm & Blues in the Night") 50-100 55
Also see HARLEMAIRES

BENNET, Ron
Singles: 7-inch
TA-RAH (1 "Dingle Dangle Doll") 50-75 61
(Previously issued as by Mike & the Jays.)
Also see MIKE & JAYS

BENNETT, Barbara
Singles: 7-inch
SWADE (101 "You Can Make It if You Try") 20-30 59

BENNETT, Bobby "Guitar"
Singles: 7-inch
JUNIOR (1009 "You Did It Again") 30-50 64
WORLD ARTISTS (1035 "She's So Fine"). 8-12 64

BENNETT, Boyd *P&R/R&B '55*
(With the Rockets; with Southlanders)
Singles: 78 rpm
KING 15-25 54-57
Singles: 7-inch
DELTA (3028 "Click Clack") 15-25 58
(Canadian.)
KING (1201 "I'm Wasting My Time") 20-30 53
KING (1413 "Waterloo") 20-30 54
KING (1432 "Poison Ivy") 30-40 55
KING (1443 "Everlovin'") 30-40 55
KING (1470 "Seventeen") 40-50 55
(White label. Promotional issue.)
KING (1470 "Seventeen") 30-40 55
(Maroon label.)
KING (1470 "Seventeen") 20-30 55
(Blue label.)
KING (1475 "Tennessee Rock and Roll"). 20-30 55
KING (1494 "My Boy Flat Top") 30-40 55
KING (4853 thru 4985) 20-30 55-56
KING (5021 thru 5282) 15-25 57-59
MERCURY (71409 thru 71813) 10-20 59-61
EPs: 7-inch
KING (377 "Boyd Bennett") 300-400 56
KING (383 "Rock & Roll with Boyd Bennett & His Rockets") 300-400 56
LPs: 10/12-inch
KING (594 "Boyd Bennett") 2500-3000 58
(Counterfeits exist.)

BENNETT, Buddy
(With the Margilators)
Singles: 7-inch
BLUE MOON (412 "Baby Don't Go") 40-60 59

BENNETT, Cliff, & Rebel Rousers
Singles: 7-inch
ABC (10842 "Got to Get You into My Life") 5-10 66
AMY (930 "If Only You'd Reply") 8-12 65
ASCOT (2146 "My Old Stand By") 8-12 64
CAPITOL (4621 "I'm in Love with You") ... 40-60 61
Also see TOE FAT

BENNETT, Harvert
Singles: 7-inch
B&F (1354 "Jack, You're Dead") 50-75

BENNETT, Joe, & Sparkletones *P&R/R&B '57*
Singles: 78 rpm
ABC-PAR 25-50 57-58
Singles: 7-inch
ABC 4-6 73
ABC-PAR (9837 thru 9885) 20-30 57-58
ABC-PAR (9929 "We've Had It") 30-40 58
PARIS 15-25 59-60
LPs: 10/12-inch
MCA 5-10 83
Members: Joe Bennett; Wayne Arthur; Howard Childress; Irving Denton.

BENNETT, Joe, & Sparkletones / Royal Teens
Singles: 7-inch
MCA (2402 "Black Slacks"/"Short Shorts") .. 3-5 83
ROULETTE (126 "Black Slacks"/"Short Shorts") .... 4-6 '70s

BENNETT, Ronnie, & Royals
Singles: 7-inch
JIN (143 "True Love True Love") 15-25 61

BENNETT, Tony *P&R '51*
Singles: 78 rpm
COLUMBIA 4-8 50-57
Singles: 7-inch
BRUT (813 "All That Love Went to Waste"). 4-6 74
COLUMBIA (1600 series) 5-10
(Colored vinyl. Promotional issue only.)
COLUMBIA (06000 series) 3-5 86
COLUMBIA (38000 thru 41000 series) 10-20 50-61
COLUMBIA (42000 thru 45000 series) 5-10 61-70
COLUMBIA/AUROVISION ("Ca C'est L'Amour") .... 5-10 '60s
(Square cardboard picture disc. Promotional issue made for Waterman Pens.)
IMPROV 4-6 75-77
MGM 4-6 73
VERVE 4-6 72-73
Picture Sleeves
COLUMBIA (1600 series) 5-10
(Promotional issue only.)
COLUMBIA (40000 & 41000 series) 5-15 53-61
COLUMBIA (42000 thru 44000 series) 5-10 61-67
IMPROV 4-6 75
EPs: 7-inch
COLUMBIA 5-15 55-59
LPs: 10/12-inch
COLUMBIA (Except 600 thru 1200 series) 6-12 59-86
COLUMBIA (600 thru 1200 series) 10-25 55-59
FANTASY 8-12
GUEST STAR 5-10
HARMONY 5-10 69-73
IMPROV 5-10 75-78
MGM 6-10 73
MGM/VERVE 6-10 72
MFSL 30-50 84
Also see GETZ, Stan
Also see MATHIS, Johnny / Tony Bennett / North Carolina Ramblers / Ray Conniff & Jerry Vale with Eugene Ormandy
Also see SHARON, Ralph

BENNETT, Tony, & Count Basie
EPs: 7-inch
COLUMBIA 6-10 59
LPs: 10/12-inch
COLUMBIA 10-20 59
Also see BASIE, Count

BENNETT, Tony, & Bill Evans
LP: 10/12-inch
MFSL (117 "Tony Bennett & Bill Evans") .35-45 84

BENNETT, Tony / Al Tornello
LPs: 10/12-inch
GUEST STAR 5-10 64
Also see BENNETT, Tony

BENNY & BEDBUGS
Singles: 7-inch
DCP (1008 "The Beatle Beat") 8-10 64
Picture Sleeves
DCP (1008 "The Beatle Beat") 15-25 64

BENSON, Al, & Leon Abbey Trio / Leon Abbey Trio
Singles: 78 rpm
PARROT (6000 "If You Were the Only Girl"/"Abbey's Boogie") 200-300 51

BENSON, Curley Ray
Singles: 7-inch
BLACK PEARL (101 "Prison Blues") 50-75 67

BENSON, Eddie
Singles: 7-inch
TRU STAR (1501 "Lonesome Tavern Blues") 50-75

BENSON, George *LP '69*
(George "Bad" Benson)
Singles: 78 rpm
GROOVE 10-15 54
Singles: 12-inch
W.B. 4-6 80-83
Singles: 7-inch
A&M (Except 1076) 4-6 68-70
A&M (1076 "My Woman's Good to Me") .. 50-75 69
ARISTA 4-6 77
CTI 4-6 75-78
COLUMBIA 5-10 66-67
GROOVE (0024 "It Should Have Been Me #2") 20-40 54
PRESTIGE 5-10 64
W.B. 3-6 76-89
Picture Sleeves
ARISTA 4-6 77
W.B. 4-6 78-89
LPs: 10/12-inch
A&M 8-12 68-76
CTI 8-10 71-78
COLUMBIA 8-10 66-67
(With "CL" or "CS" prefix.)
COLUMBIA 5-10 76
(With "CG" or "PC" prefix.)
MFSL (011 "Breezin'") 40-60 78
POLYDOR 5-10 76
VERVE 10-12 69
W.B. 5-10 75-89
Also see ALTAIRS
Also see FRANKLIN, Aretha, & George Benson
Also see McDUFF, Brother Jack

BENSON, George, & Earl Klugh *LP '87*
LPs: 10/12-inch
W.B. 5-8 87
Also see BENSON, George
Also see KLUGH, Earl

BENSON, Jackie
Singles: 7-inch
D&W ("Gotta Get You Off My Mind") 100-200
(Selection number not known.)

BENSON, Joe
Singles: 7-inch
DELUXE (6146 "Rock n' Roll Jungle") 50-75 59

BENSON – OGLETREE
(Al Benson & Louis Ogletree)
Singles: 78 rpm
PARROT (822 "Uptown Stomp") 10-15 55
Singles: 7-inch
PARROT (822 "Uptown Stomp") 20-25 55

BENTLEYS
Singles: 7-inch
SMASH (1967 "She's My Hot Rod Queen") 10-20 65
SMASH (1988 "Why Didn't I Listen to Mother") 25-50 65
(Previously issued as by the Vampires.)
Also see VAMPIRES

BENTLEYS
Singles: 7-inch
DEVLET (444 "Now It's Gone") 35-55

BENTON, Brook *P&R '58*
(With the Sandmen; with Dixie Flyers; with Merry Melody Singers)
Singles: 78 rpm
EPIC 8-15 56
OKEH 8-15 55
Singles: 7-inch
ALL PLATINUM (2364 "Can't Take My Eyes Off You") 4-6 76
BRUT 4-6 73-74
COTILLION 5-10 68-72
EPIC (9177 "Love Made Me Your Fool") . 15-25 56
EPIC (9199 "The Wall") 15-25 57
MGM 4-6 72
MERCURY (10019 "So Many Ways") 20-30 59
(Stereo.)
MERCURY (10030 "The Ties That Bind") 15-25 60
(Stereo.)
MERCURY (10037 "Kiddio") 15-25 60
(Stereo.)
MERCURY (71394 "It's Just a Matter of Time") 15-25 59
(Blue label.)
MERCURY (71394 "It's Just a Matter of Time") 10-20 59
(Black label.)
MERCURY (71443 thru 72446) 10-15 59-65

MUSICOR ... 4-6 77
OKEH (7058 "The Kentuckian Song") ... 15-25 55
OKEH (7065 "Bring Me Love") ... 15-25 55
OLDE WORLD ... 4-6 77-78
POLYDOR ... 4-6 79
RCA ... 8-12 65-67
REPRISE ... 5-10 67-68
STAX ... 4-6 74
VIK ... 10-20 57-58

Picture Sleeves

MERCURY ... 10-20 60-64
RCA ... 10-15 65

EPs: 7-inch

MERCURY (3394 "Brook Benton") ... 15-25 59
MERCURY (4033 "It's Just a Matter of Time") ... 15-25 61
MERCURY (4046 "The Boll Weevil Song") ... 15-25 61

LPs: 10/12-inch

ALL PLATINUM ... 8-10 76
CAMDEN (Except 564) ... 8-10 70
CAMDEN (564 "Brook Benton") ... 15-20 60
COTILLION ... 8-10 69-72
EPIC (3573 "Brook Benton at His Best") . 15-25 59
HARMONY ... 8-12 65
MGM ... 8-10 73
MERCURY (20000 series) ... 15-30 59-65
(Monaural.)
MERCURY (60000 series) ... 20-35 59-65
(Stereo.)
MERCURY (822321 "Greatest Hits") ... 5-8 84
MUSICOR ... 8-10 77
OLDE WORLD ... 5-10 77
RCA (APL1 series) ... 8-10 75
(With "APL1" prefix.)
RCA (LPM/LSP series) ... 10-12 66
(With "LPM" or "LSP" prefix.)
REPRISE ... 8-12 67-68
TEE VEE ... 5-10
WING ... 8-10 66
Session: King Curtis; Ray Stevens.
Also see KING CURTIS
Also see SANDMEN
Also see STEVENS, Ray
Also see TROGGS / Brook Benton

BENTON, Brook / Jesse Belvin

LPs: 10/12-inch

CROWN (350 "Brook Benton and Jesse Belvin") ... 15-25 63
Also see BELVIN, Jesse

BENTON, Brook, & Damita Jo

Singles: 7-inch

MERCURY (72207 "Stop Foolin' ") ... 5-10 63
Also see DAMITA JO

BENTON, Brook, & Bruce Darrel Jazz Orchestra

LPs: 10/12-inch

PALACE (773 "Sings Blues Favorites with the Bruce Darrel Jazz Orchestra") ... 10-20 64

BENTON, Brook / Chuck Jackson / Jimmy Soul

LPs: 10/12-inch

ALMOR (106 "Stargazing") ... 10-20 '60s
Also see JACKSON, Chuck
Also see SOUL, Jimmy

BENTON, Brook / Jackie Jocko

LPs: 10/12-inch

STRAND (1121 "The Dynamic Brook Benton Sings") ... 15-25 63

BENTON, Brook, & Dinah Washington *P&R '60*

Singles: 7-inch

MERCURY (10032 "A Rockin' Good Way") ... 20-30 60
(Stereo.)
MERCURY (71565 "Baby") ... 10-20 60
MERCURY (71629 "A Rockin' Good Way") ... 10-20 60
(Monaural.)

Picture Sleeves

MERCURY (71629 "A Rockin' Good Way") ... 15-20 60

EPs: 7-inch

MERCURY (4028 "Two of Us") ... 15-25 60

LPs: 10/12-inch

MERCURY (20588 "Two of Us") ... 25-35 60
(Monaural.)
MERCURY (60244 "Two of Us") ... 30-40 60
(Stereo.)
Also see BENTON, Brook
Also see WASHINGTON, Dinah

BENTON, Merv

Singles: 7-inch

MARVEL (401 "20-Flight Rock") ... 50-75 66

BENTON, Walt
(With the Snappers)

Singles: 7-inch

SCOTTIE (1321 "Summer School Blues") ... 40-60 60
STARO (2 "Do It Again") ... 300-400
20TH FOX (143 "Stuck Up") ... 50-75 59

BERBERIAN, John
(With the Rock East Ensemble)

LPs: 10/12-inch

MAINSTREAM (6123 "Impressions East") ... 75-100 69
VERVE FORECAST (3073 "Middle Eastern Rock") ... 30-40 69

BERK, Sammy
(Sammy Berk "At the Piano")

Singles: 7-inch

TRIPLE A (98 "Cool Cat Crawl") ... 15-25 58

BERKELEY FIVE

Singles: 7-inch

BOSS (004 "You're Gonna Cry") ... 15-25 66

BERKELEY KITES

Singles: 7-inch

MINARET (132 "Hang-Up City") ... 20-35 66
MINARET (140 "Alice in Wonderland") ... 10-20 67
MINARET (145 "Willow Run") ... 10-20 67

BERLIN *P&R/D&D/LP '83*

Singles: 12-inch

GEFFEN ... 4-6 83-84

Singles: 7-inch

COLUMBIA ... 3-5 86
GEFFEN ... 3-5 82-86
I.R.S. ... 3-5 80

Picture Sleeves

COLUMBIA ... 3-5 86
GEFFEN ... 3-5 83-86

LPs: 10/12-inch

ENIGMA ("Pleasure Victim") ... 50-100 82
(Selection number not known.)
GEFFEN ... 5-10 82-86
Members: John Crawford; Rob Brill; Terri Nunn.

BERLIN / Madonna

Singles: 7-inch

GEFFEN ... 3-5 85

Picture Sleeves

GEFFEN ... 3-5 85
Also see BERLIN
Also see MADONNA

BERLIN, Joey, & Jades

Singles: 7-inch

CHRISTY (122 "With Hope in My Heart") . 20-30 60
Also see JADES

BERNADETTE
(With Her Swingin' Bears; Bernadette Castro)

Singles: 7-inch

BEACH (5 "The Slosh") ... 10-12 61
BEACH (1001 "When You're Dancin' with Me") ... 15-20 61
BEACH (19750 "The Slosh") ... 8-10 61
GOLD COAST ... 8-10
JULIA (1106 "My Heart Stood Still") ... 8-10 62

Picture Sleeves

BEACH (5 "The Slosh") ... 20-25 61
(Sleeve liner notes indicate Bernadette had three previous singles and an LP before this release. Obviously we're missing some titles.)
Also see CASTRO, Bernadette

BERNAL, Gil

Singles: 78 rpm

AMERICAN ... 5-10 56
SPARK ... 10-20 54

Singles: 7-inch

AMERICAN ... 10-20 56
RCA (9261 "This Is Worth Fighting For") ... 8-10 67
SPARK (102 "The Whip") ... 20-30 54
SPARK (106 "Strawberry Stomp") ... 20-30 54
VERVE ... 5-10

BERNARD, Chuck *R&B '66*
(Chuck Benard; with Blue Notes)

Singles: 7-inch

JOYCE (305 "Calling Your Name") ... 200-300 58
MAVERICK (1009 "Indian Giver") ... 5-10 69
(Different recording than issued on Satellite.)
MI BOUTE ... 8-12 '60s
NEW BREED (502 "Hall of Soul") ... 10-20 '60s
ST. LAWRENCE ... 5-10 67
SATELLITE ... 10-12 65-66
ZODIAC ... 4-8 70-71

BERNARD, Rod *P&R/R&B '59*
(With the Twisters)

Singles: 78 rpm

ARGO (5327 "This Should Go On Forever") ... 40-60 59

Singles: 7-inch

ABC ... 4-6 74
ARBEE ... 5-15 65-66
ARGO (5327 "This Should Go On Forever") ... 15-25 59
ARGO (5338 "You're on My Mind") ... 10-15 59
CARL (1229 "All Night in Jail") ... 40-60 57
CARL (2441 "Linda Gail") ... 50-100 57
COLLECTABLES ... 3-5 81
COPYRIGHT ... 4-6 68
CRAZY CAJUN ... 4-6 78
HALLWAY ... 5-10 62-64
JIN (105 "This Should Go On Forever") ... 10-20 59
JIN (200 & 300 series) ... 4-6 74-76
MERCURY (71507 "One More Chance") . 15-20 59
MERCURY ... 8-12 60-61
SCEPTER (12195 "Recorded in England") ... 10-15 67
TEARDROP ... 5-10 64-65

LPs: 10/12-inch

JIN (4007 "Rod Bernard") ... 50-100 '60s
Also see MIZZELL, Bobby
Also see SHONDELLS / Rod Bernard / Warren Storm / Skip Stewart

BERNARD, Rod / Clifton Chenier

Singles: 7-inch

JIN (9014 "Boogie in Black") ... 10-15
Also see BERNARD, Rod
Also see CHENIER, Clifton

BERNDT, Robert

Singles: 7-inch

CUCA (1041 "False Dreams") ... 15-25 61

BERNIE & LEE

Singles: 7-inch

MATT (801 "Soldier Boy") ... 8-12 61
TODD (1041 "Soldier Boy") ... 10-20 59

BERNSTEIN, Leonard, & Orchestra *LP '60*

LPs: 10/12-inch

CAMDEN ... 8-15 55-56
COLUMBIA (919 "What Is Jazz") ... 20-40 56
COLUMBIA (31000 series) ... 5-10 71
COLUMBIA MASTERWORKS ... 10-20

BERNSTEIN, Leonard, & Dave Brubeck

LPs: 10/12-inch

COLUMBIA ... 12-25 60
Also see BERNSTEIN, Leonard, & His Orchestra
Also see BRUBECK, Dave

BERRIES

Singles: 7-inch

IGL (133 "Baby, That's All") ... 15-25 67

BERRY, Al, & Furness Bros.
(With Max Dickman & Orchestra)

Singles: 7-inch

MELMAR (115 "King of the Blues") ... 15-20 56
PREP (107 "King of the Blues") ... 10-15 57
Also see FURNESS BROTHERS

BERRY, Bill
(Bill Berry Quartet)

Singles: 7-inch

GMA (7 "Heavenly Angel") ... 50-75 64

LPs: 10/12-inch

DIRECTIONAL SOUND ... 15-20 67

BERRY, Brooks, & Scrapper Blackwell

LPs: 10/12-inch

PRESTIGE BLUESVILLE (1074 "My Heart Struck Sorrow") ... 20-30 64
Also see BERRY, Brooks
Also see BLACKWELL, Francis "Scrapper"

BERRY, Chuck *P&R/R&B '55*

Singles: 78 rpm

CHESS (1600 series, except 1604, 1671 & 1691) ... 30-60 55-58
CHESS (1604 "Maybellene ") ... 50-100 55
CHESS (1671 "Rock and Roll Music") ... 50-100 57
CHESS (1691 "Johnny B. Goode") ... 75-125 58
CHESS (1700 "Carol") ... 50-100 58
CHESS (1709 "Sweet Little Rock and Roller") ... 75-125 58
CHESS (1714 "Run Rudolph Run") ... 75-125 58
CHESS (1722 "Almost Grown") ... 50-100 59
CHESS (1729 "Memphis, Tennessee") .. 75-125 59
CHESS (1737 "My Childhood Sweetheart") ... 75-125 59
CHESS (1747 "Too Pooped to Pop") ... 200-300 60
QUALITY ... 20-40 55
(Canadian.)

Singles: 7-inch

ATCO (7203 "Oh What a Thrill") ... 4-6 79
BUENA VISTA (1061 "Little Queenie"/"Almost Grown") ... 100-200 62
(Red vinyl. Country of origin unknown; however, because no mention of this is made on label we will list it until we learn otherwise.)
CHESS (1604 "Maybellene") ... 40-60 55
CHESS (1610 thru 1729) ... 30-40 55-59
CHESS (1737 "Childhood Sweetheart") ... 15-25 59
CHESS (1747 "Too Pooped to Pop") ... 15-25 60
CHESS (1754 thru 2169) ... 10-20 60-75
CHESS (9000 series) ... 4-8 73
ERIC ... 4-6 73
MERCURY (72643 thru 72963) ... 5-10 66-69
QUALITY (1413 "Maybelline") ... 50-100 55
(Canadian. Note slightly different spelling.)
QUALITY (1467 "No Money Down") ... 50-100 56
(Canadian.)

Picture Sleeves

CHESS (1653 "School Day") ... 5-10 '90s
CHESS (1898 "No Particular Place to Go") ... 10-20 64
CHESS (1906 "You Never Can Tell") ... 10-20 64
CHESS (1912 "Little Marie") ... 10-20 64
CHESS (1916 "Promised Land") ... 10-20 64

EPs: 7-inch

CHESS (5118 "After School Session") . 100-200 57
CHESS (5118 "Head Over Heels") ... 150-250 57
CHESS (5119 "Rock and Roll Music") . 100-150 58
CHESS (5121 "Sweet Little 16") ... 100-150 58
CHESS (5124 "Pickin' Berries") ... 100-150 58
CHESS (5126 "Sweet Little Rock and Roller") ... 100-150 58

LPs: 10/12-inch

ACCORD (7171 "Toronto Rock 'N' Roll Revival, Vol. 2") ... 8-10 82
ACCORD (7172 "Toronto Rock 'N' Roll Revival, Vol. 3") ... 8-10 82
ATCO (118 "Rock It") ... 8-10 79
AUDIO FIDELITY (351 "ChuckBerry") ... 8-12 84
(Picture disc.)
BROOKVILLE (1274 "Chuck Berry and His Friends") ... 15-20 73
CHESS (706 "Chuck Berry" ... 15-20 76
(Two discs.)
CHESS (1426 "After School Session") ... 50-75 57
CHESS (1432 "One Dozen Berrys") ... 50-75 58
CHESS (1435 "Chuck Berry's On Top") ... 50-75 59
CHESS (1448 "Rockin' at the Hops") ... 50-75 59
CHESS (1456 "Chuck Berry's New Juke Box Hits") ... 25-40 61
CHESS (1465 "More Chuck Berry") ... 30-40 62
CHESS (1465 "Chuck Berry Twist") ... 20-25 62
(Reissue with title change.)
CHESS (1480 "Chuck Berry on Stage") ... 20-25 63
CHESS (1485 "Chuck Berry's Greatest Hits") ... 25-30 64
CHESS (1488 "St. Louis to Liverpool") ... 20-25 64
CHESS (1495 "Chuck Berry in London") . 25-30 65
CHESS (1498 "Fresh Berrys") ... 20-25 65
CHESS (LPS-1514 "Golden Decade") ... 15-20 67
(Two discs.)
CHESS (2CH-1514 "Golden Decade") ... 10-15 70
(Two discs.)

CHESS (1550 "Back Home") ... 10-15 70
CHESS (9000 series) ... 5-10 85
CHESS (50008 "San Francisco Dues") ... 10-15 71
CHESS (60020 "The London Chuck Berry Sessions") ... 15-25 72
CHESS (60023 "Golden Decade, Vol. 2") ... 15-20 73
(Two discs.)
CHESS (60028 "Golden Decade, Vol. 3") ... 15-20 74
(Two discs.)
CHESS (60032 "Chuck Berry") ... 10-15 75
CHESS/MCA ... 5-8 89
EVEREST (321 "Greatest Hits") ... 8-12 76
GUSTO (0004 "Best of Chuck Berry") ... 5-10 78
MCA ... 8-12 86-87
MAGNUM (703 "Chuck Berry Live in Concert [Toronto Rock 'N' Roll Revival]") ... 10-15 69
MERCURY (6501 "St. Louis to Frisco to Memphis") ... 10-20 72
(Two discs.)
MERCURY (61103 "Golden Hits") ... 15-25 67
MERCURY (61123 "Chuck Berry in Memphis") ... 15-25 67
MERCURY (61138 "Live at the Fillmore Auditorium") ... 15-25 67
MERCURY (61176 "From St. Louis to Frisco") ... 15-25 68
MERCURY (61223 "Concerto in B Goode") ... 15-25 69
PICKWICK (2061 "Flashback") ... 10-15 72
(Two discs.)
PICKWICK (3327 "Johnny B Goode") ... 8-12 71
PICKWICK (3345 "Sweet Little Rock & Roller") ... 8-12 71
PICKWICK (3392 "Wild Berrys") ... 8-12 71
TRIP (16-55 "16 Greatest Hits") ... 8-10 78
UPFRONT (199 "All-Time Hits") ... 5-10 79
Session: Ingrid Gibson.
Also see ALEXANDER, Joe, & Cubans
Also see DIDDLEY, Bo, & Chuck Berry
Also see MILLER, Steve

BERRY, Chuck, & Elephants Memory

LPs: 10/12-inch

CHESS (50043 "Chuck Berry Bio") ... 10-15 73
Also see ELEPHANTS MEMORY

BERRY, Chuck, & Howlin' Wolf

LPs: 10/12-inch

CHESS (1544 "Pop Origins") ... 15-25 69
Also see BERRY, Chuck
Also see HOWLIN' WOLF

BERRY, Dorothy
(With the Swans)

Singles: 7-inch

BIG THREE (401 "Don't Give Me Love") . 15-25 '60s
CHALLENGE (59221 "Cryin' on My Pillow") ... 10-15 63
DOT ... 5-10 64
LITTLE STAR ... 10-15 62
PLANETARY ... 10-15 65
TANGERINE ... 4-6 71
VANCE ... 5-10
Also see NORMAN, Jimmy, & Dorothy Berry

BERRY, Dorothy, & Jimmy Norman

Singles: 7-inch

LITTLE STAR (122 "Your Love"/"I'm with You All The Way") ... 10-15 62
Also see BERRY, Dorothy
Also see NORMAN, Jimmy

BERRY, Gordon

Singles: 7-inch

SPORT (103 "How Lonely") ... 15-25 67

BERRY, Jan
(Jan; Jan Barry)

Singles: 7-inch

A&M ... 5-10 77-78
LIBERTY (55845 "The Universal Coward") ... 10-15 65
ODE (Except 66023 & 66034) ... 15-20 72-77
ODE (66023 "Mother Earth") ... 20-40 72
(With insert note from Jan. Promotional issue only.)
ODE (66023 "Mother Earth") ... 20-30 72
(Without insert note from Jan.)
ODE (66034 "Don't You Just Know It") ... 30-40 73
(With Brian Wilson.)
RIPPLE (6101 "Tomorrow's Teardrops") . 30-45 61

Picture Sleeves

LIBERTY (55845 "The Universal Coward") ... 100-125 65
Also see JAN & ARNIE
Also see JAN & DEAN
Also see WILSON, Brian

BERRY, Red, & Bel Raves

Singles: 7-inch

DREEM (1001 "Hot Rod") ... 300-400 59
(First issue.)
20TH FOX (169 "Hot Rod") ... 100-200 59
Members: Red Berry; Lou Berry.

BERRY, Richard
(With the Dreamers; with Pharaohs; with Lockettes; with Soul Searchers; with Soul Serchers; with Silks)

Singles: 78 rpm

FLAIR ... 15-25 55
FLIP ... 15-25 56-57
RPM ... 20-30 55-56

Singles: 7-inch

AMC (616 "Go Go Girl") ... 10-15
ARC (7463 "Soulin' in C-Minor") ... 5-10
BOLD SOUL ... 4-6 71
CIRAY ... 4-6
FLAIR (1016 "One Little Prayer") ... 75-100 53
FLAIR (1052 "At Last") ... 30-40 55
FLAIR (1055 "The Big Break") ... 30-40 55
FLAIR (1058 "Daddy, Daddy") ... 40-50 55
FLAIR (1064 "Get Out of the Car") ... 40-50 55
FLAIR (1068 "God Gave Me You") ... 25-35 55
FLAIR (1071 "Next Time") ... 25-35 55
FLAIR (1075 "Jelly Roll") ... 40-50 55
FLIP (318 "Take the Key") ... 30-40 56
FLIP (321 "Louie Louie"/"You Are My Sunshine") ... 40-50 57
FLIP (321 "Louie Louie"/"Rock Rock Rock") ... 20-40 57
FLIP (327 "Rock Rock Rock") ... 15-25 57
FLIP (331 "You're the Girl") ... 20-30 58
FLIP (336 "Heaven on Wheels") ... 15-25 58
FLIP (339 "Besame Mucho") ... 15-25 58
FLIP (349 "Have Love Will Travel") ... 15-25 60
FLIP (352 "I'll Never Ever Love Again") ... 25-35 61
FLIP (360 "You Look So Good") ... 10-15 62
JONCO (51 "Doin' It") ... 5-10
K&G (9001 "I'm Your Fool") ... 50-75 61
PAXLEY (751 "Give It Up") ... 10-15 61
(Both Paxley [PAXton and FowLEY] and K&G [Kim & Gary] were owned by Kim Fowley and Gary Paxton.)
RPM (448 "Rockin' Man") ... 40-60 55
(With the Ike Turner Orchestra.)
RPM (452 "Pretty Brown Eyes") ... 40-60 56
RPM (465 "Yama Yama Pretty Mama") ... 40-60 56
RPM (477 "Wait for Me") ... 20-30 56
SMASH ... 8-12 62-63
UNITY ... 3-6
W.B. (5164 "Walk Right In") ... 40-60 60

LPs: 10/12-inch

CROWN (5371 "Richard Berry and the Dreamers") ... 20-25 63
KENT ... 5-10 86
PAM (1001 "Live from H.D. Hover Century Restaurant") ... 20-25 68
PAM (1002 "Wild Berry Live") ... 20-25
Also see BLOSSOMS
Also see DREAMERS
Also see FLAIRS
Also see FOWLEY, Kim
Also see JAMES, Etta
Also see LOCKETTES
Also see MAYE, Arthur Lee
Also see PAXTON, Gary
Also see PHARAOHS
Also see RICKIE & JENNELL
Also see ROBINS
Also see SIX TEENS / Donald Woods / Richard Berry
Also see TURNER, Ike

BERRY, Ron, & Dreamers

Singles: 7-inch

KEN-H (11290 "I'll Give You All My Love") ... 200-300 63
(Identification number shown since no selection number is used.)
PIXIE (4864 "I'm Crazy 'Bout That Woman") ... 100-200 65

BERRY KIDS

Singles: 78 rpm

MGM ... 25-50 56-57

Singles: 7-inch

MGM (12379 "Go, Go, Go Right Into Town") ... 40-80 56
MGM (12496 "Rootie Tootie") ... 40-80 57

BERWICK, Brad

Singles: 7-inch

CLINTON (1012 "I'm Better Than the Beatles") ... 10-15 65
DEEM (1125 "Are You Glad") ... 5-10 65

Picture Sleeves

CLINTON (1012 "I'm Better Than the Beatles") ... 25-35 65

BESAW, Ron, & Mojo Men

Singles: 7-inch

TARGET (2002 "I'm Sorry") ... 10-20 71
Members: Ronnie (Besaw) Fuller; Jesse Vasquez; Bobby Borlee.
Also see NEW RAGING STORMS

BEST, Peter
("Pete Best Formerly of the Beatles"; "Best of the Beatles, Peter Best"; Pete Best Combo; Pete Best Band)

Singles: 7-inch

BEATLES BEST (800 "I'll Try Anyway") ... 150-175 64
CAMEO (391 "Boys") ... 50-75 66
CAMEO (391 "Boys") ... 60-70 66
(Promotional issue.)
CAPITOL (2092 "Carousel of Love") ... 25-35 67
CAPITOL (2092 "Carousel of Love") ... 15-25 67
(Promotional issue.)
COLLECTABLES ... 4-8 87
HAPPENING (1117 "If You Can't Get Her") ... 125-150 66
HAPPENING (405 "Don't Play with Me Little Girl") ... 150-175 66
MR. MAESTRO (711 "I Can't Do Without You Now") ... 200-250 65
(Colored vinyl. With photo insert flyer. Promotional issue only.)
MR. MAESTRO (711 "I Can't Do Without You Now") ... 100-150 65
(Blue vinyl. Without photo insert flyer.)
MR. MAESTRO (711 "I Can't Do Without You Now") ... 150-200 65
(Black vinyl.)
MR. MAESTRO (712 "Casting My Spell") ... 125-150 65
(Black vinyl.)
MR. MAESTRO (712 "Casting My Spell") ... 150-200 65
(Blue vinyl. Promotional issue only.)
ORIGINAL BEATLES DRUMMER (800 "I'll Try Anyway") ... 40-50 64

Picture Sleeves

CAMEO (391 "Boys") ... 75-100 66

LPs: 10/12-inch

PB (22 "The Beatle That Time Forgot") ... 15-25 81
PB (44 "Rebirth") ... 15-25 81
PHOENIX 10 (340 "The Beatle That Time Forgot") ... 10-20 82
SAVAGE (71 "Best of the Beatles") ... 275-325 65
Also see BEATLES

BETHEA & CAP-TANS

Singles: 7-inch

LOOP (100 "Revenue Man") ... 15-25 62
SABU (102 "Whenever I Look at You") ... 40-50 63
SABU (501 "You Better Mind") ... 30-40 63
Also see CAP-TANS
Also see WAILING BETHEA & CAP-TANS

BETTER DAYS

LPs: 10/12-inch

EXIT ... 10-20 69
Members: Lynn Weyts; Joe Mendyk; Phil Salvaggio; Jerry Warner.
Also see FRONTIERS

BETTER SWEET

Singles: 7-inch

M.O.C. (667 "Like the Flowers") ... 20-30 67

BETTY JANE & TEENETTES

Singles: 7-inch

CARELLEN (101 "Show Your Love") ... 15-25 61
CARELLEN (107 "I'm No Longer Jimmy's Girl") ... 15-25 61
Also see JONES, Billy, & Teenettes

BEVERLY, Buddy

Singles: 7-inch

CYPRESS ("In Gear") ... 100-200
(Selection number not known.)

BEVERLY, Frankie
(With the Butlers; with Raw Soul; Frankie Beverley)

Singles: 7-inch

FAIRMOUNT (1012 "She Kissed Me") ... 15-25 67
FAIRMOUNT (1017 "Because of My Heart") ... 150-250 67
GAMBLE (220 "Your Pain Goes Deep") .. 15-25 68
GREGAR (108 thru 115) ... 15-25 71-72
GREGAR (220 "If That's What You Wanted") ... 50-75 72
ROUSER (1017 "Because of My Heart") ... 200-300
SASSY (1002 "If That's What You Wanted") ... 20-30
Also see BUTLERS

BEVERLY, Stan, & Hollywood Saxons
(With the "Hollywood Saxon's")

Singles: 7-inch

ENTRA (1214 "Diamonds") ... 75-100 '60s
(Red label.)
ENTRA (1214 "Diamonds") ... 20-30 '60s
(Black label.)
Also see HOLLYWOOD SAXONS

BEVERLY HILLS PAINTERS

Singles: 7-inch

GATEWAY (700 "Believe Me") ... 30-40 62
ME-MEOW (2325 "I Know Why") ... 30-40

BEY SISTERS

Singles: 78 rpm

DECCA ... 5-10 56
JAGUAR ... 10-15 55-56

Singles: 7-inch

DECCA (29960 "Dedicated to You") ... 10-20 56
DECCA (30853 "Captain Johnson") ... 10-20 59
FLIP (328 "Sugar Cookie") ... 10-15 57
JAGUAR (3016 "Patience") ... 30-40 56
JAGUAR (3018 "Sugar Cookie") ... 15-25 57
Members: Salome Bey; Geraldine Bey.
Session: Andy Bey.

BIANCO, Cappy
(Joe Oliver)

Singles: 7-inch

ABC-PAR (10044 "Cat") ... 10-15 59
CASA BLANCA (5501 "Cat") ... 20-30 59
DR (16 "Cat") ... 20-30 59
Also see HALEY, Bill

BIAS, Joan

Singles: 7-inch

WAY-OUT (5564 "I Don't Know What's Right Anymore") ... 300-400 63

BIBB, Leon
(With Gloria Foster; with Robert DeCormier & Orchestra)

Singles: 7-inch

LIBERTY (55663 "Little Boxes") ... 10-15 64
VERVE FOLKWAYS (5020 "Tar and Cement") ... 5-10 66

LPs:10/12-inch

COLUMBIA (1762 "Leon Bibb Sings") ... 15-20 62
(Monaural.)
COLUMBIA (8562 "Leon Bibb Sings") ... 10-15 62
(Stereo.)
LIBERTY (3358 "Cherries and Plums") ... 15-20 64
(Monaural.)
LIBERTY (7358 "Cherries and Plums") ... 20-25 64
(Stereo.)
VANGUARD ... 15-25
VERVE FOLKWAYS (9040 "The Hand Is on the Gate") ... 10-20 66
WASHINGTON ... 10-15

BIBLE, Fred

Singles: 7-inch

ALECIA (5503 "C'mon Baby") ... 50-75

BIG BARNEY

Singles: 7-inch

GRANDVILLE (100 "The Whole Thing") .. 25-35 '60s

BIG BEATS

Singles: 7-inch

COLUMBIA (41072 "Clark's Expedition") . 10-20 58
COLUMBIA (41199 "Rush Me") ... 10-20 58
PLAY ... 10-20 59
Member: Trini Lopez.

Also see LOPEZ, Trini

BIG BEATS

Singles: 7-inch

LIBERTY (55827 "Work Song")....5-10 65

LPs: 10/12-inch

LIBERTY (3407 "Live, At the Off-Broadway")....15-25 65
(Monaural.)
LIBERTY (7407 "Live, At the Off-Broadway")....25-35 65
(Stereo.)
Member: Arlin Harmon.

BIG BOB & DOLLARS

Singles: 7-inch

GLOBE (400 "You")....50-75 63
(Canadian.)
Also see DAVIS, Bob

BIG BOPPER *P&R/R&B '58*
(Jape Richardson; Jiles Perry Richardson Jr.)

Singles: 7-inch

D (1008 "Chantilly Lace")....200-250 58
MERCURY (71343 "Chantilly Lace")....20-30 58
MERCURY (71375 "Big Bopper's Wedding")....20-30 58
MERCURY (71416 "Walking Through My Dreams")....30-40 59
(Black label.)
MERCURY (71416 "Walking Through My Dreams")....50-60 59
(White label. Has alternate take of A-side. Promotional issue only.)
MERCURY (71451 "It's the Truth Ruth"). 25-35 59
MERCURY (71451 "It's the Truth Ruth"). 50-75 59
(White label. Promotional issue only.)
MERCURY (71482 "Pink Petticoats")....10-20 59
MERCURY CELEBRITY SERIES (30072 "Chantilly Lace")....8-10 60
WING (17000 "Chantilly Lace")....5-10 '60s

Picture Sleeves

MERCURY (71343 "Chantilly Lace")....3-5 '90s

LPs: 10/12-inch

MERCURY (20402 "Chantilly Lace")....250-300 59
(Black label.)
MERCURY (20402 "Chantilly Lace")....250-300 59
(White or pink label. Promotional issue only.)
MERCURY (20402 "Chantilly Lace")....75-100 64
(Red label.)
MERCURY (20402 "Chantilly Lace")....10-15 81
(Chicago "skyline" label.)
PICKWICK....20-30 73
RHINO....5-8 89
Also see DAMERON, Donna
Also see DEL-VIKINGS / Diamonds / Big Bopper / Gaylords
Also see RICHARDSON, Jape

BIG BOYS

Singles: 78 rpm

MELMAR....5-10 55
ROB RECS....5-10 55

Singles: 7-inch

MELMAR (113 "If I Had My Chance")....10-20 55
ROB RECS (9999 "If I Had My Chance") 40-50 55
(First issue.)

BIG BROTHER
(Featuring Ernie Joseph)

Singles: 7-inch

ALL AMERICAN (5718 "E.S.P.")....20-30 69

LPs: 10/12-inch

ALL AMERICAN (5770 "Big Brother")....75-125 70

BIG BROTHER & HOLDING CO. *LP '67*
(Big Brother)

Singles: 7-inch

COLUMBIA....5-10 68-71
MAINSTREAM....8-15 67-68

Picture Sleeves

COLUMBIA (44626 "Piece of My Heart") 15-20 68

LPs: 10/12-inch

COLUMBIA (2900 "Cheap Thrills")....100-150 68
(Monaural.)
COLUMBIA (9700 "Cheap Thrills")....25-35 68
(Stereo.)
COLUMBIA (30631 "Big Brother and the Holding Company")....15-25 71
COLUMBIA (30738 "How Hard It Is")....15-25 71
MADE TO LAST....5-10 84
MAINSTREAM (6099 "Big Brother and the Holding Company")....35-50 67
Members: Janis Joplin; David Getz; Peter Albin; Sam Andrew; Jim Gurley; David Schallock; Nick Gravenites; Kathi McDonald.
Also see JOPLIN, Janis

BIG CHENIER
(With the R&B Orchestra; Big Chenier & His Night Owls; Morris Chenier)

Singles: 7-inch

GOLDBAND (1051 "Let Me Hold Your Hand"/"Please Try to Realize")....15-25 58
GOLDBAND (1131 "The Dog and His Puppies"/ "Let Me Hold Your Hand")....10-20 61
Also see CHENIER, Clifton

BIG CHIEF TRIO
(Big Chief & His Trio; Wilbert Ellis)

Singles: 78 rpm

SITTIN' IN WITH (523 "She's Gone")....25-35 49
SITTIN' IN WITH (530 "Poor Man's Blues")....25-35 49
Also see ELLIS, Big Boy

BIG DADDY
(Frankie Brunson)

Singles: 7-inch

CRAKERJACK (4002 "Teacher")....10-15 61
GEE (1051 "Walking Her Home")....10-20 59
PMB (7220 "Hard Top")....15-25 59
WYNNE (106 "I Think You're Lying")....8-12 59

LPs: 10/12-inch

GEE (704 "Big Daddy's Blues")....35-55 60
(Red label)
GEE (704 "Big Daddy's Blues")....25-35 61
(Gray label)
REGENT (6106 "Twist Party")....20-25 62
Also see BRUNSON, Frankie

BIG DAVE
(With the Hard Tops)

Singles: 78 rpm

CAPITOL (2742 thru 2884)....10-15 54
CAPITOL (3028 "Rock & Roll Party")....20-25 55

Singles: 7-inch

CAPITOL (2742 "One Stop")....15-25 54
CAPITOL (2794 "Cat from Coos Bay")....15-25 54
CAPITOL (2884 "Big Goof")....15-25 54
CAPITOL (3028 "Rock & Roll Party")....25-50 55
CHORD (11865 "Goin' On Baby")....75-100

BIG DOG

Singles: 7-inch

JOEY (501 "Doris")....50-75 62

BIG DUKE

Singles: 78 rpm

FLAIR....10-20 53

Singles: 7-inch

FLAIR (1018 "Hey, Dr. Kinsey")....25-50 53
FLAIR (1029 "Beggin' and Pleadin'")....25-50 54

BIG ED & HIS COMBO
(Eddie Burns)

Singles: 78 rpm

CHECKER....100-200 54

Singles: 7-inch

CHECKER (790 "Biscuit Baking Mama")....750-1000 54
Also see BURNS, Eddie

BIG FIVE

Singles: 7-inch

JUNIOR (5000 "Wob-Ding-A-Ling")....50-75 61
SHAD (5019 "Stardust in Her Eyes")....50-75 60

BIG FRANK & ESSENCE

Singles: 7-inch

BLUE ROCK (4012 "Secret")....150-250 65
PHILIPS (40283 "Secret")....50-100 65

BIG GUYS

Singles: 7-inch

W.B. (7047 "Hang My Head")....25-45 67

BIG JEFF & PLAYBOYS

Singles: 78 rpm

DOT (1088 "Move on Baby")....20-40 52

Singles: 7-inch

DOT (1088 "Move on Baby")....40-60 52

BIG JIM & SUNDOWNERS

Singles: 7-inch

CHIP (1008 "Poor Little Sad-Eyed Sue")..40-60 61
MIRACLE (1301 "G-Stringer")....5-10 65

BIG JOHN & BUZZARDS

Singles: 78 rpm

COLUMBIA....10-15 54
OKEH....10-15 54

Singles: 7-inch

COLUMBIA (40345 "Hey Little Girl")....30-40 54
OKEH (7045 "Oop Shoop")....20-30 54

BIG JOHN & FABULOUS BLENDS

Singles: 7-inch

CASA GRANDE (5001 "Baby You're Wrong")....10-20 64
(Black vinyl.)
CASA GRANDE (5001 "Baby You're Wrong")....20-30 64
(Red vinyl.)
Also see BLENDS

BIG JOHN & PHILADELPHIANS / Vince Montana

Singles: 7-inch

GUYDEN (2093 "My Love, My Love"/"Cleo's Theme")....30-40 63
Also see PHILADELPHIANS

BIG JOHN'S SWING CARAVAN

Singles: 7-inch

J.F.J (600 "Lila Cha-Cha")....50-100 '60s

BIG LOST RAINBOW

LPs: 10/12-inch

("Big Lost Rainbow")....300-400 73
(Approximately 200 made. No label or number used.)

BIG MACEO *R&B '45*
(Major Merriweather)

Singles: 78 rpm

BLUEBIRD....15-30 42-45
FORTUNE (137 "Leavin' Blues")....25-50 52
FORTUNE (805 "Worried Life Blues, No. 2")....20-40 52
GROOVE....10-20 54
RCA....15-25 47-48
SPECIALTY (320 "Do You Remember")..10-20 49
SPECIALTY (346 "One Sunday Morning")....10-20 49

Singles: 7-inch

GROOVE (5001 "Chicago Breakdown")....30-50 54
RCA (50-0002 "Chicago Breakdown")....75-125 49
(Red vinyl.)

LPs: 10/12-inch

BLUEBIRD....10-12 75
Also see BRIM, John
Also see TAMPA RED

BIG MACEO & JOHN LEE HOOKER

LPs: 10/12-inch

FORTUNE (3002 "Together")....50-100 '50s
Also see BIG MACEO
Also see HOOKER, John Lee

BIG MACK & SHUFFLERS

Singles: 7-inch

TRI-MAC (501 "Out of My Mind")....15-25 58

BIG MAYBELLE *R&B '53*
(Mable Smith)

Singles: 78 rpm

KING....10-20 48-49
OKEH....10-20 53-56
SAVOY....10-20 56-58

Singles: 7-inch

BRUNSWICK....5-10 63
CHESS....5-10 66
OKEH....20-40 53-56
PARAMOUNT....4-6 73
PORT....5-10 65
ROJAC....10-15 64-69
SAVOY....10-20 56-61
SCEPTER....10-15 65

EPs: 7-inch

EPIC (7071 "Big Maybelle Sings the Blues")....40-60 57

LPs: 10/12-inch

BRUNSWICK....15-25 62-68
ENCORE....10-15 67
EPIC....8-10 83
PARAMOUNT....8-10 73
ROJAC....10-12 67-69
SAVOY (14005 "Big Maybelle Sings")....50-100 57
SAVOY (14011 "Blues, Candy and Big Maybelle")....50-100 57
SCEPTER....15-20 64
UPFRONT....8-10 73
Also see CHATMAN, Christine

BIG MIKE
(Mike Gordon)

Singles: 78 rpm

SAVOY (1152 "Rain Or Shine")....8-12 55

Singles: 7-inch

SAVOY (1152 "Rain Or Shine")....25-35 55
Session: El Tempos.
Also see GORDON, Mike, & El Tempos

BIG ROCKER
(With His 1950s Rock & Roll Band)

Singles: 7-inch

CRALEN (3001 "Rock & Roll Romance")..5-10
LUCKY FOUR (1002 "No Privacy")....10-15 61
LUCKY FOUR (1009 "Rock and Roll Romance")....40-60 62
Member: Lenny LaCour.
Also see LACOUR, Lenny

BIG SHEBA

Singles: 78 rpm

DERBY (745 "Soft Soapin' Mama")....25-35 50

BIG STAR

Singles: 7-inch

ARDENT....15-25 72-74
PRIVILEGE....4-6

LPs: 10/12-inch

ARDENT....20-25 72-74
BIG STAR FAN CLUB....15-20
(Promotional fan club issues only.)
PVC....8-10 78
PEACEABLE (1 "Peaceable")....30-45 74
Members: Alex Chilton; Andy Hummell; Jody Stepenson; Chris Bell.
Also see BOX TOPS
Also see CHILTON, Alex

BIG 3
(Big Three; "Big 3 Featuring Cass Elliot")

Singles: 7-inch

FM (3003 "Banjo Song")....8-12 63
FM (9001 "Come Away")....8-12 63
ROULETTE (4689 "Nora's Dove")....5-10 66
TOLLIE (9006 "Banjo Song")....5-10 64

Picture Sleeves

ROULETTE (4689 "Nora's Dove")....15-20 66

LPs: 10/12-inch

ACCORD (7180 "Distant Reflections")....5-10 82
FM (304 "Big Three")....15-25 63
FM (311 "Live at the Recording Studio")..15-25 64
ROULETTE (42000 "The Big 3 Featuring Cass Elliot")....15-20 68
Members: Cass Elliot; Denny Dougherty; Tim Rose.
Also see ELLIOT, Cass
Also see MAMAS & PAPAS
Also see ROSE, Tim

BIG THREE TRIO *R&B '48*

Singles: 78 rpm

BULLET (275 "Signifying Monkey")....25-35 47
COLUMBIA....20-30 47-51
DELTA....20-30 49
DOT....15-25 52
OKEH....20-30 51-53

Singles: 7-inch

COLUMBIA (30239 "Blip Blip")....50-75 51
OKEH (6807 thru 6944)....50-75 51-53
Members: Willie Dixon; Leonard "Baby Doo" Caston; Bernard Dennis.
Also see DIXON, Willie
Also see HOWARD, Rosetta

BIG TOPS

Singles: 7-inch

WARNER (1017 "I'm in Love")....150-200 58

BIG VERNON
(Joe Turner)

Singles: 78 rpm

STAG (508 "Around the Clock Blues")....25-45 47
Also see TURNER, Joe

BIG WALTER
(Walter Horton)

Singles: 78 rpm

STATES....50-100 55

Singles: 7-inch

STATES (145 "Hard Hearted Woman")....150-200 55
Also see HORTON, Big Walter

BIG WALTER
(With the Thunderbirds; Walter Price)
Singles: 78 rpm
PEACOCK ... 10-20 56-57
TNT ... 25-35 55
Singles: 7-inch
GLOBAL (409 "Watusi Freeze") ... 10-15 62
GOLDBAND ... 10-15 58-59
JET STREAM (742 "Love Me One More Time") ... 10-15 69
MYRL (406 "It's How You Treat Me") ... 10-20 61
MYRL (409 "Watusi Freeze") ... 15-25 62
(First issue.)
PEACOCK (1661 thru 1680) ... 50-75 56-57
TNT (8005 thru 8009) ... 75-125 55
Also see YOUNG, Johnny, & Big Walter

BIG WILLIE
(Willie Mabon)
Singles: 78 rpm
APOLLO (450 "Bogy Man") ... 50-100 53
Singles: 7-inch
APOLLO (450 "Bogy Man") ... 150-250 53
Also see MABON, Willie

BIGGIE RATT
(Vernon Garrett)
Singles: 7-inch
APT (26001 "We Don't Need No Music"). 10-20 69
WATTS U.S.A. (2003 "We Don't Need No Music") ... 30-40 68
Also see GARRETT, Vernon

BIKINIS
Singles: 7-inch
DOT (15808 "Kitchy Koo") ... 20-30 58
DOT (15872 "Chop Stick Rock") ... 20-30 58
ROULETTE (4073 "Boogie Rock and Roll") ... 10-15 58
TOP RANK (2032 "Spunky") ... 8-12 60

BILL & LORETTA & SADDLEMEN
Singles: 78 rpm
HOLIDAY (110 "I'm Crying") ... 800-1200 51
Members: Bill Haley; Loretta Glendenning.
Also see HALEY, Bill

BILLARD, Doug, & Soul Patrol
Singles: 7-inch
PARKWAY (126 "Emily") ... 15-25 67

BILLBOARDS
(With the Red Julian Orchestra)
Singles: 7-inch
VISTONE (2023 "With All My Heart") .. 200-400 61
(Black vinyl.)
VISTONE (2023 "With All My Heart") 500-1000 61
(Yellow vinyl.)
Also see WADE, Iona, & Billboards

BILLIE & MARK
Singles: 7-inch
DEMON (1513 "Deep Down") ... 10-20 59

BILLIE JEAN
Singles: 7-inch
DORE (675 "Teenage Time") ... 10-15 63

BILLINGSLEY, Lynn
Singles: 7-inch
BAKERSFIELD (107 "Childhood Boogie") ... 200-300 56

BILLS, Dick
Singles: 7-inch
CREST (1089 "Rockin' & Rollin' ") ... 50-75 61
Session: Glen Campbell.
Also see CAMPBELL, Glen

BILLUPS, Eddie
(Eddie Billips & the C.C.C.'s; with Gigs)
Singles: 7-inch
GAR•PAX (123 "Shake Off That Dream") 4-6 77
JOSIE (960 "My Girl") ... 5-10 66
JOSIE (971 "Feel It") ... 5-10 67
MAXX (336 "New York Kangaroo") ... 15-25 65
PEACHTREE (104 "Soldier's Prayer")... 50-100

BILLY & CLIFF
(Billy Mize & Cliff Crofford)
Singles: 7-inch
BEECEE ... 50-75
(Label, selection number and title not known.)
CHALLENGE (59089 "The Gun, the Gold and the Girl") ... 10-15 60
DORE (534 "Big Spender from the East") ... 10-15 59
LIBERTY (55560 "Louisiana Sand") ... 8-12 63
Picture Sleeves
DORE (534 "Big Spender from the East") ... 15-25 59
Members: Billy Mize; Cliff Crofford. Session: Jerry Hayes.
Also see CROFFORD, Cliff
Also see MIZE, Billy

BILLY & EDDIE
Singles: 7-inch
TOP RANK (2017 "The King Is Coming Back") ... 20-30 59

BILLY & ESSENTIALS
(Little Billy & Essentials; featuring Billy Carl)
Singles: 7-inch
CAMEO (344 "The Actor") ... 100-200 64
CHELTENHAM (1001 "The Actor").... 800-1000 64
(First issue.)
JAMIE (1229 "Steady Girl") ... 10-15 62
JAMIE (1239 "Maybe You'll Be There")....15-25 62
LANDA (691 "Steady Girl") ... 30-40 62
(First issue.)
MERCURY (72127 "Lonely Weekend")....25-35 63
MERCURY (72210 "Last Dance") ... 30-40 63
SSS INT'L (706 "I Wrote the Song") ... 5-10 67
SMASH (2045 "Babalu's Wedding Day")..10-15 66
SMASH (2071 "Don't Cry") ... 30-40 66
LPs: 10/12-inch
CRYSTAL BALL (127 "Billy and the Essentials") ... 10-15 88
(Black vinyl. 2000 made.)
Members: Billy Carlucci; Phil D'Antonio; Pete Torres; Mike Lenihan; Johnny Caulfield; Jim Sofia; Richie Grasso.
Also see FOUR-EVERS / Billy & Essentials
Also see KAY, Gary
Also see LITTLE BILLY
Also see MARSHMALLOW WAY

BILLY & FLEET
Singles: 7-inch
ARLEN (514 "Power Shift") ... 15-20 63

BILLY & GLENS
Singles: 7-inch
JARO (77006 "I Believe in You") ... 15-25 59

BILLY & KIDS
Singles: 7-inch
LINIPHONE ("Only You") ... 15-25 '60s
(No selection number used.)
LUTE (6016 "Take a Chance on Love") .50-100 61

BILLY & KIDS
(Chapelles)
Singles: 7-inch
HARMIKE (1300 "Nightrider") ... 20-30 62
TRIANGLE (2 "Nightrider") ... 20-30 62
(First issued as by the Chapelles.)
Also see CHAPELLES

BILLY & KIDS
Singles: 7-inch
JULIAN (104 "Say You Love Me") ... 20-30 65
JULIAN (109 "When I See You") ... 20-30 66

BILLY & KIDS
EPs: 7-inch
HURRAH (502 "Billy & Kids") ... 20-30 '60s

BILLY & LILLIE P&R/R&B '58
(Billy Ford & the Thunderbirds with "Vocal by Freddie Pinkard")
Singles: 78 rpm
SWAN (4002 "La Dee Dah") ... 25-50 57
Singles: 7-inch
ABC ... 4-6 73
ABC-PAR (10421 "Love Me Sincerely")...20-30 63
ABC-PAR (10489 "Carry Me 'Cross the Threshold") ... 10-20 63
CAMEO (412 "Nothing Moves") ... 5-10 66
CAMEO (435 "You Got Me by the Heart")..5-10 66
CASINO (105 "La Dee Dah"/"Lucky Ladybug") ... 10-15 59
COLLECTABLES ... 3-5 81
CROSS ROADS (101 "Baby, You Just Don't Know") ... 8-10
RIC (144 "Tic-Tac-Toe") ... 8-10 64
STACY (928 "My Pledge of Love") ... 8-12 62
SWAN (4002 "La Dee Dah") ... 15-25 57
SWAN (4005 thru 4020) ... 15-20 58
SWAN (4030 thru 4069) ... 10-20 59-61
Members: Billy Ford; Lillie Bryant.
Also see BRYANT, Lillie
Also see FORD, Billy

BILLY & LOVERS
Singles: 7-inch
DRAGON (4403 "Hold Me Close") ... 25-35 65

BILLY & MOONLIGHTERS
Singles: 7-inch
CRYSTAL BALL (101 "You Made Me Cry") ... 4-8 77
(Black vinyl. 500 made.)
CRYSTAL BALL (101 "You Made Me Cry") ... 10-20 77
(Red vinyl. 25 made.)
CRYSTAL BALL (101 "You Made Me Cry") ... 30-40 77
(Multi-color vinyl.)

BILLY & PATIOS
Singles: 7-inch
LITE (9002 "Love Is a Story") ... 100-150 61
Member: Billy Galante.

BILLY BOY
Singles: 78 rpm
VEE-JAY ... 15-25 55-57
Singles: 7-inch
VEE-JAY (146 thru 260) ... 20-40 55-57
VIVID (109 "Prisoner's Plea") ... 10-20 64
Also see ARNOLD, Billy "Boy"

BILLY JOE & CONFIDENTIALS
Singles: 7-inch
B-J (64 "Feeling Blue") ... 100-150 65

BINDER, Dennis
(Long Man Binder & His Thin Men)
Singles: 7-inch
COTTONWOOD (101 "Crawdad Song") ... 100-200
MODERN ... 25-50 54
UNITED (194 "The Long Man") ... 20-40 55

BINGHAMPTON BLUES BOYS
Singles: 7-inch
EASTSIDE ("Cross Cut Saw") ... 75-100 64
FORD ("Cross Cut Saw") ... 75-100 64
XL (901 "Cross Cut Saw") ... 60-90 64
(We're not yet certain in which order these three came out.)

BINK & BILL
Singles: 7-inch
HU-SE-CO ("Do and Don't Blues") ... 50-75
(Selection number not known.)

BINKLEY, Jimmy
(Jimmy Binkley Jazz Quintet; with Teasers)
Singles: 78 rpm
ALADDIN ... 25-50 53
CHANCE ... 50-75 53
CHECKER (789 "Wine Wine Wine") ... 75-100 55
CHECKER (835 "Messin' Around") ... 50-75 56
DOT (1183 "Blue, Blue Night") ... 10-15 53
Singles: 7-inch
ALADDIN (3193 "Night Life") ... 75-100 53
CHANCE (1134 "Hey, Hey Sugar Ray") ... 100-150 53
CHECKER (789 "Wine Wine Wine")....100-150 55
CHECKER (835 "Messin' Around") ... 50-100 56
DOT (1183 "Blue, Blue Night") ... 20-30 53
NOTE (10002 "Why Oh Why") ... 200-300 57
Also see GREEN, George, & Jimmy Binkley Jazz Quintet
Also see TEASERS

BIONDI, Dick
Singles: 7-inch
IRC (6904 "The Pizza Song") ... 10-20 62
(Promotional issue, made for WLS Radio and Pepsi Cola.)
MINUTEMAN (210 "Too Big to Cry") ... 5-10 67
Picture Sleeves
IRC (6904 "The Pizza Song") ... 20-30 62
(Promotional issue, made for WLS Radio and Pepsi Cola.)

BIRCH, Sadie
(With Kelly Owens & Band)
Singles: 78 rpm
RED ROBIN (121 "The Man I Crave") ... 10-15 53
Singles: 7-inch
RED ROBIN (121 "The Man I Crave") ... 15-25 53

BIRCHETT, Tony
Singles: 7-inch
L.B.J. (293 "You're Good People") ... 20-30 '60s

BIRDLAND QUINTET
Singles: 7-inch
JAX (5001 "You Belong to Me") ... 50-75 '50s
(Red vinyl.)
JAX (5005 "Sleepy Time Gal") ... 50-75 '50s
(Red vinyl.)
Members: Eugene Rainey; Gus Johnson Jr.; Freddie Green; Kenny Drew; Vice Prez.

BIRDLEGS & PAULINE & THEIR VERSATILITY BIRDS P&R/R&B '63
Singles: 7-inch
CUCA (1125 "Spring") ... 30-40 63
(Credits "Birdlegs & His Versatility Birds.")
OLDIES 45 (131 "Spring") ... 5-10 '60s
VEE-JAY (510 "Spring") ... 8-12 63
LPs: 10/12-inch
CUCA (4000 "Birdlegs & Pauline") ... 50-100 64
Members: Sidney Banks; Pauline Shivers Banks.
Also see PAULINE & BOBBY

BIRDMEN
Singles: 7-inch
ROCK-IT (1003 "Dance the Jaybird") ... 10-20 61

BIRDS
Singles: 7-inch
BINGO (1000 "Foggy River") ... 15-25 59

BIRDSONG, Larry R&B '56
(With Louis Brooks & His Hi-Toppers)
Singles: 78 rpm
CALVERT ... 10-20 56
DECCA ... 10-15 56
EXCELLO ... 10-15 55-56
Singles: 7-inch
ACE (589 "Who Do You Love") ... 10-20 60
CALVERT (102 "Now That We're Together") ... 20-30 56
CALVERT (104 "Three Times Seven") ... 20-30 56
CHAMPION (1003 thru 1018) ... 10-15 58-59
CHEROKEE (1018 "Young and Fancy Free") ... 15-25 59
DECCA (30186 "Let's Try It Again") ... 15-25 56
EXCELLO ... 15-25 56
HOME OF THE BLUES ... 8-12 61-62
REF-O-REE ... 5-10
SUR-SPEED (218 thru 226) ... 5-10 67-68
VEE-JAY (254 "I'm Pleading Just for You") ... 10-20 57
VEE-JAY (262 "My Darling") ... 10-20 57
VEE-JAY (277 "Fannie's Place") ... 30-40 58
Session: Lee Allen.
Also see ALLEN, Lee
Also see BROOKS, Louis

BIRDWATCHERS
Singles: 7-inch
GEMINX ... 10-15 66-67
LAURIE (3399 "You Got It") ... 5-10 67
MALA (527 thru 555) ... 15-25 66-67
SCOTT (27 thru 30) ... 25-45 66-67
LPs: 10/12-inch
FLORIDA ROCK (4001 "Birdwatchers")... 10-15 80
Member: Jerry Schils; Bobby Puccetti; Sammy Hall; Eddie Martinez; Jim Tolliver; Joey Murcia; Dave Chiodo; Craig Caraglior.
Also see LEGENDS

BIRMINGHAM SAM & HIS MAGIC GUITAR
(John Lee Hooker)
Singles: 78 rpm
SAVOY (5558 "Low Down Midnight Boogie") ... 25-50 49
Also see HOOKER, John Lee

BISCAYNE BAY SURFERS
(With Professor Marcell & Collegians)
Singles: 7-inch
MAYHAMS (214 "Surfing Is a Sight to See") ... 15-25 64
Also see PROFESSOR MARCELL & COLLEGIANS

BISCAYNES
Singles: 7-inch
RIDGE (6601 "Mis-Beat") ... 50-100 '60s
VPM (1006 "Yellow Moon") ... 15-25 61

(Same number used on a Viscaynes release.)
Also see VISCAYNES

BISCOE, Joey
Singles: 7-inch
DECCA (30414 "My Lovin' Doll") ... 15-20 57

BISHOP, Bob — C&W '68
(Bobby Bishop; Bobby Sykes)
Singles: 7-inch
ABC (11132 "Roses to Reno") ... 4-6 68
GOLDISC (3027 "Ann Marie") ... 15-20 61
MALA (423 "Anybody") ... 10-15 60
WAYSIDE (1004 "My Crying Chair") ... 5-10 67
Also see ROBBINS, Marty
Also see SYKES, Bobby

BISHOP, Dickie
Singles: 7-inch
LONDON (1784 "Jumpin' Judy") ... 10-20 57

BISHOP, Eddie
Singles: 7-inch
ABC (10799 "Call Me") ... 25-50 65
ABC (10858 "Hanky Panky") ... 10-20 66

BISHOPS
Singles: 7-inch
CAPITOL (5357 "Hollywood Scene") ... 5-10 65
CAPITOL (5487 "Out of Sight") ... 5-10 65
LUTE (6010 "Open Your Heart") ... 40-50 61
RALSTON ... 10-15

BISHOPS & MELLOWTONES
Singles: 7-inch
BRIDGES (1105 "The Wedding") ... 100-150 61
Also see REO, Walt, & Bishops

BIT'A SWEET
Singles: 7-inch
ABC (11125 "2086") ... 10-15 68
MGM (13695 "Out of Sight Out of Mind") 10-20 67
LPs: 10/12-inch
ABC (640 "Hypnotic 1") ... 30-40 68
Members: Mitch London; Russ Leslie.

BI-TONES
Singles: 7-inch
BLUEJAY (1000 "Oh How I Love You So") ... 10-20 60
Also see CHIMES

BITS 'N' PIECES
Singles: 7-inch
BITS 'N' PIECES ... 10-15
DEE GEE (2005 "Look Out Linda") ... 20-30

BITTLE, Walter "Arkie"
Singles: 7-inch
CLAUDRA (110 "Teenage Blues") ... 75-100 59
CLAUDRA (200 "Jitterbug Drag") ... 200-300 60

BIXLER, Barbara, & Goodtimes
Singles: 7-inch
SULLY (202 "Dust Bowl Baby") ... 400-500 64

BLACK, Alan
Singles: 78 rpm
CANDLELIGHT ... 5-10 56
Singles: 7-inch
ABC-PAR (9784 "Harmonica Rock") ... 15-25 57
ARGO (5486 "We Will Make Love") ... 8-12 65
CANDLELIGHT (1001 "On Bended Knee") ... 10-20 56
CANDLELIGHT (1007 "Don't Make Me Promises") ... 10-20 56
GONE (5080 "Teenage Lullaby") ... 10-15 59
RADAR (777 "Teenage Lullaby") ... 15-20 59
(First issue.)
LPs: 10/12-inch
GRAND AWARD (395 "Harmonica Spectacular") ... 15-20 59
(Monaural.)
GRAND AWARD (231 "Harmonica Spectacular") ... 20-25 59

BLACK, Bill — P&R/R&B '59
(Bill Black's Combo)
Singles: 7-inch
COLUMBIA ... 4-6 70
ECHO (8020 "Country Roads") ... 4-6 72
GUSTO ... 3-5 83
HI (2018 thru 2115) ... 10-20 59-66
HI (2124 thru 2317) ... 5-10 67-76
HI (78508 "Cashin' In") ... 4-8 78
LONDON ... 3-5 84
MEGA ... 4-6 71-74
MOTOWN ... 3-5 83
Picture Sleeves
HI (2022 "Josephine") ... 15-25 60
HI (2026 "Don't Be Cruel") ... 15-25 60
HI (2027 "Blue Tango") ... 15-25 60
HI (2036 "Ole Buttermilk Sky") ... 10-20 61
HI (2052 "Twistin' White Silver Sands") ... 10-15 62
EPs: 7-inch
HI (52 "King of the Road") ... 10-20 64
HI (22001 "Dee J. Special") ... 15-25 '60s
(Promotional only issue.)
MEGA (192 "Juke box Favorites") ... 5-10 72
(Juke box issue.)
LPs: 10/12-inch
COLUMBIA ... 8-10 69-70
51 WEST ... 5-10 84
HI (6000 & 8000 series) ... 5-10 77-78
HI (12001 "Smokie") ... 30-60 60
HI (12002 thru 12005) ... 20-40 60-62
HI (12006 thru 12041) ... 10-20 62-68
(Monaural.)
HI (32000 thru 32010) ... 15-30 61-63
(Stereo.)
HI (32011 thru 32110) ... 10-20 63-77
(Stereo.)
MEGA ... 5-10 71-74
ZODIAC ... 8-12 77
Members: Bill Black; Carl McVoy; Jerry Arnold; Hank Hankins; Martin Willis.
Also see CANNON, Ace
Also see LOYD, Jay B.
Also see POINDEXTER, Doug, & Starlite Wranglers
Also see PRESLEY, Elvis

BLACK, Cilla — P&R '64
Singles: 7-inch
BELL (726 "Step Inside Love") ... 4-6 68
CAPITOL ... 6-12 64-66
DJM ... 4-6 68-70
EMI AMERICA ... 4-6 74
PRIVATE STOCK ... 4-6 75-76
LPs: 10/12-inch
CAPITOL (T-2308 "Is It Love") ... 25-35 65
(Monaural.)
CAPITOL (ST-2308 "Is It Love") ... 35-45 65
(Stereo.)
Also see BUDDY

BLACK, Cody
Singles: 7-inch
D-TOWN (1057 "You Must Be in Love") ... 25-50 65
D-TOWN (1066 "Too Many Irons") ... 25-50 66
GIG (201 "It's Our Time to Fall in Love") ... 200-300
RAM BROCK (2002 "Going, Going, Gone") ... 15-25 '60s
STON-ROC ... 5-10 70

BLACK, Jay — P&R '80
Singles: 12-inch
MILLENNIUM (20614 "Love Is in the Air") ... 15-20 78
(Single-sided disc. Promotional issue only.)
MILLENNIUM (20614 "Love Is in the Air"/"Please Stay") ... 8-12 78
ROULETTE (7198DDJ "One Night Affair [6:55]"/"One Night Affair [6:55]") ... 10-15 76
(Promotional issue only. For the issue with Caress on flip side, see section that follows.)
Singles: 7-inch
ATLANTIC/MIGRATION (3273 "Running Scared") ... 4-6 75
MIDSONG (72012 "Part of Me That Needs Your Most") ... 3-5 80
MILLENNIUM (618 "Love Is in the Air") ... 4-6 78
PRIVATE STOCK (45058 "Every Time You Walk in the Room") ... 4-6 75
ROULETTE (7198 "One Night Affair"/"Between Two Worlds") ... 4-6 76
ROULETTE (7198 "One Night Affair [3:27]"/"One Night Affair [6:55]") ... 10-15 76
(Promotional issue only.)
ROULETTE (7198 "One Night Affair [6:55]"/"One Night Affair [6:55]") ... 10-15 76
(Promotional issue only.)
U.A. (50116 "What Will My Mary Say") ... 5-10 67
Picture Sleeves
U.A. (50116 "What Will My Mary Say") ... 8-10 67
LPs: 10/12-inch
K-TEL (562 "This Magic Moment") ... 30-40 82
(Canadian. Credits: "Jay Black of Jay and the Americans.")
Also see EMPIRES
Also see JAY & AMERICANS
Also see TWO CHAPS

BLACK, Jay / Caress
Singles: 12-inch
ROULETTE (2005 "One Night Affair"/"Fill Me Up") ... 10-15 76
(For the issue with Jay Black on both sides, see his section above.)
Also see BLACK, Jay

BLACK, Joe
(With the His Boogie Woogie Boys)
Singles: 78 rpm
CORAL ... 15-25 51
DERBY ... 5-10 49
Singles: 7-inch
CORAL (65067 "Flag Wavin' Boogie") ... 25-35 51
Also see MITCHELL, Freddie, & Orchestra

BLACK, Marjorie
Singles: 7-inch
SUE (132 "One More Hurt") ... 15-25 65

BLACK, Oscar — P&R '61
Singles: 78 rpm
ATLANTIC ... 25-50 51
Singles: 7-inch
ATLANTIC (956 "Troubled Mind Blues") ... 50-100 51
SAVOY (1600 "I'm a Fool to Care") ... 8-12 61

BLACK, Oscar, & Sue Allen
Singles: 78 rpm
GROOVE ... 15-25 54-56
Singles: 7-inch
GROOVE ... 25-50 54-56
Also see ALLEN, Sue
Also see BLACK, Oscar

BLACK, Terry — P&R '64
Singles: 7-inch
ARC ... 8-12 64-66
(Canadian.)
DUNHILL ... 8-12 65-66
TOLLIE ... 8-12 64-65
LPs: 10/12-inch
ARC (5001 "Only 16") ... 50-75 65
(Canadian.)
ARC (5002 "The Black Plague") ... 50-75 65
(Canadian.)

BLACK, Terry, & Laurel Ward — P&R '72
Singles: 7-inch
KAMA SUTRA (540 "Goin' Down") ... 4-6 72
Picture Sleeves
KAMA SUTRA (540 "Goin' Down") ... 4-8 72
Also see BLACK, Terry

BLACK, Wally
Singles: 7-inch
FABLE (629 "Rock and Roll Mama") ... 75-125 58
FEDORA (1002 "Hurt Inside") ... 10-20 61
TOPPA ... 10-20 59-63

BLACK & BLUE
Singles: 7-inch
GAME (395 "Of All the Hearts to Break") . 30-50
MERCURY ... 4-8 70

BLACK DEATH
Singles: 7-inch
CATHEDRAL (417 "Rock & Roll with Ork") ... 40-60 '60s

BLACK DIAMOND
(James Butler)
Singles: 78 rpm
JAXYSON (6 "Lonesome Blues") ... 75-125 49

BLACK DIAMOND / Goldrush
Singles: 78 rpm
JAXYSON (50 "T.P. Railer") ... 75-125 48
Also see BLACK DIAMOND

BLACK EARTH PLUS
Singles: 7-inch
CALGAR (0001 "How Can You Say You Love Me") ... 15-30 73

BLACK MAGIC & HOWARD STRUTT
Single
ERIKA (8663 "Good Ole Boys") ... 15-20 84
(Shaped picture disc. Includes poster.)
LP: 10/12-inch
VISUAL VINYL (1002 "Spellbound") ... 30-40 83
(Picture disc.)

BLACK MERDA
Singles: 7-inch
CHESS (2095 "Reality") ... 5-10 70
LPs: 10/12-inch
CHESS (1551 "Black Merda") ... 30-50 70

BLACK RAVENS
Singles: 7-inch
B&R (201,131 "Young Love") ... 15-25
Members: Sonny; Willy; Mickey; Ray; Dick.

BLACK ROSE
Singles: 7-inch
MICHIGAN NICKEL (001 "Love Handles") ... 10-20 67

BLACK SABBATH — P&R/LP '70
Singles: 7-inch
I.R.S. ... 3-5 89
W.B. ... 4-6 70-76
EPs: 7-inch
W.B. (241 "Sabbath Bloody Sabbath") ... 15-25 74
(Juke box EP.)
LPs: 10/12-inch
I.R.S. ... 5-8 89
NEMS (6003 "Paranoid") ... 8-10
W.B. (PRO-417 "Radio Spots") ... 150-200 69
W.B. (Except 1000 & 2000 series) ... 5-10 76-84
W.B. (1000 & 2000 series, except 2562) . 15-20 70-76
W.B. (2562 "Master of Reality") ... 100-200 71
(With poster insert.)
W.B. (2562 "Master of Reality") ... 25-50 71
(Without poster insert.)
W.B. ... 5-10 87
Members: Ozzy Osbourne; Tony Iommi; Kip Treavor; Bill Ward; Ronnie Dio; Terry "Geezer" Butler.
Also see DIO, Ronnie
Also see OSBOURNE, Ozzy

BLACK SATIN — R&B '75
(Featuring Fred Parris)
Singles: 7-inch
BUDDAH ... 4-6 75
LPs: 10/12-inch
BUDDAH (5654 "Black Satin") ... 8-10 76
BUDDAH (5654 "Black Satin") ... 25-35 76
(Promotional issue.)
Members: Fred Parris; Rich Freeman; Jimmy Curtis; Nate Marshall.
Also see FIVE SATINS

BLACK TIE — C&W '90
Singles: 7-inch
BENCH ... 3-5 90
LPs: 10/12-inch
BENCH ("When the Night Falls") ... 20-30 85
(Selection number not known.)
Members: James Griffin; T-Bone Burnett; Billy Swan; Randy Meisner; Robb Royer.
Also see GRIFFIN, James

BLACK WATCH
Singles: 7-inch
FENTON (2508 "Left Behind") ... 25-50 67

BLACKBEARD & PIRATES
Singles: 7-inch
AD PRESENTS (101 "Lovers Never Say Goodbye") ... 75-125 58
MAIN MAN (50 "Lovers Never Say Goodbye") ... 50-100 61

BLACKFOOT, J.D. — R&B '83
(With Ann Hines; J. Blackfoot)
Singles: 7-inch
EDGE ... 3-5 86-87
FANTASY ... 4-8 74
PHILIPS ... 8-12 69-70
SOUND TOWN ... 3-5 83-86
LPs: 10/12-inch
FANTASY (9468 "Song of Crazy Horse") 15-25 74
FANTASY (9487 "Southbound & Gone") . 15-25 75
MERCURY (61288 "The Ultimate Prophecy") ... 40-60 70
SOUND TOWN ... 5-10 84-85
Also see SOUL CHILDREN

BLACKMAN, Hank, & Killers
Singles: 7-inch
BRENT (7030 "Itchy Koo") 30-40 62

BLACKMAN, Hank / Tip Tops
Singles: 7-inch
HALO (1003 "Everyone Has Someone") 20-30
Also see BLACKMAN, Hank, & Killers
Also see TIP TOPS

BLACKSTONE
Singles: 7-inch
BLACKSTONE (14203 "Hot Blues") .... 20-40 '60s
EPIC (10728 "Freedom Rider") 4-8 71
LPs: 10/12-inch
EPIC (30470 "Blackstone") 10-12 71

BLACKWELL, Bumps, Orchestra
Singles: 7-inch
KEEN (4010 "Sumpin' Jumpin' ") 10-20 58
Also see COOKE, Sam

BLACKWELL, Francis "Scrapper"
LPs: 10/12-inch
PRESTIGE BLUESVILLE (1047 "Mr. Scrapper's Blues") 50-100 62
Also see BERRY, Brooks, & Scrapper Blackwell

BLACKWELL, George
Singles: 7-inch
SMOKE (100 "Mister Loser") 25-50 65
SMOKE (200 "Can't Lose My Head")... 100-200 66

BLACKWELL, Joe, & Individuals / Andrew Taylor & Individuals
Singles: 7-inch
MUSIC CITY (838 "Beverly My Darling"/"April Love") 1000-1200 61
Also see TAYLOR, Andrew

BLACKWELL, Lou
(With Al Smith Orchestra)
Singles: 78 rpm
CHANCE 50-75 53
Singles: 7-inch
CHANCE (1130 "How Blue the Night") 100-200 53
Also see SMITH, Al

BLACKWELL, Otis
Singles: 78 rpm
ATLANTIC 10-15 57-58
GALE 20-30 57
GROOVE 15-25 55
JAY-DEE 15-25 53-55
RCA 20-30 52-53
Singles: 7-inch
ATLANTIC 10-15 57-58
CUB 8-12 61-62
DATE (1006 "Don't Run Away") 15-20 58
DAVIS (455 "Daddy Rolling Stone") 15-25 57
EPIC (10654 "It's All Over") 20-30 70
FEVER 3-5 80
GALE (102 "It's Love and It's Real") 15-25 57
GROOVE (0034 "Oh What a Babe") 30-50 54
JAY-DEE (784 thru 808) 30-50 53-55
MGM (13090 "Kiss Away") 10-15 62
RCA 45-65 52-53
LPs: 10/12-inch
DAVIS (109 "Singin' the Blues") 200-300 56
INNER CITY (1032 "These Are My Songs") 8-12 77
Also see ROCK, Jimmy
Also see WATKINS, Viola

BLACKWELL TWINS
Singles: 7-inch
BAYNE (501 "That's My Baby") 50-100

BLACKWELLS
Singles: 7-inch
G&G (126 "Please Don't Come Crying").. 15-20 59
G&G (131 "Oh My Love") 10-15 59
GUYDEN (2020 "Oh My Love") 8-12 59
HICKORY (1241 thru 1319) 5-10 64-65
JAMIE (1141 thru 1170) 10-15 59-60
JAMIE (1173 thru 1199) 8-12 60-61
LIBERTY (55750 "Show Me Around") 5-10 64
Picture Sleeves
JAMIE (1150 "Honey Honey") 15-25 60
Members: Dewayne Blackwell; Ronald Blackwell.

BLACKWOOD APOLOGY
LPs: 10/12-inch
FONTANA (67591 "House of Leather") 15-20 69
Also see CASTAWAYS

BLADES, Carol
(With the Harptones)
Singles: 78 rpm
GEE (1029 "When Will I Know") 50-75 57
Singles: 7-inch
GEE (1029 "When Will I Know") 250-300 57
Also see HARPTONES

BLADES, Emery
Singles: 7-inch
ARVIS (110 "I Feel Like a Million") 40-60 60
RUBY (120 "Rock and Roll Carpenter") ...50-75 57
RUBY (230 "Look What You Done to Me") 25-50 57
RUBY (340 "Try, Try Again") 20-35 57

BLADES OF GRASS P&R '67
Singles: 7-inch
FINE (57027 "It Isn't Easy") 20-30 67
JUBILEE 5-10 67-68
LPs: 10/12-inch
JUBILEE 12-20 67
Members: Bruce Ames; Frank DiChiara; Marc Black; Dave Gordon.

BLAINE, Hal
(With the Young Cougars; Col. with Hollywood Raiders)
Singles: 7-inch
DUNHILL 5-10 65-69
MELODY HOUSE (100 "Slow Gate") 10-20 62
RCA 10-15 63
ROCK-IT (1000 "Alamo Rock") 20-30 59
LPs: 10/12-inch
DUNHILL 15-25 65-67
RCA (2834 "Deuces, T's Roadsters and Drums") 40-60 63
Also see AVALANCHES
Also see CATALINAS
Also see DENVER, John
Also see FABARES, Shelley
Also see GOOD GUYS
Also see KNIGHTS
Also see JAN & DEAN
Also see MONTEZ, Chris
Also see RIP CHORDS
Also see SANDS, Tommy
Also see PRESLEY, Elvis

BLAIR, Rufus
Singles: 7-inch
RIVERMONT (506 "Lowdown Feelin' ") ...50-75

BLAIR, Sandy
Singles: 7-inch
BOBBY (111 "When the Bells Stop Ringing") ....30-40 '60s

BLAIR, Sunny
Singles: 78 rpm
RPM (354 "Five Foot Three Blues") 100-200 52
Singles: 7-inch
METEOR (5006 "Please Send My Baby Back") 250-350 53
(Though credited to Blair, the flip, *Gonna Let You Go*, is reportedly by Baby Face Turner.)
Also see TURNER, Baby Face

BLAIR, Tom
(With the West Coasters; Tommy Blair)
Singles: 7-inch
DECCA (31223 "West Coast") 15-25 61
DOT (16095 "Rock It") 25-40 60
TEEN-TUNES (767 "Rock It") 50-100 60

BLAKE, Cicero
Singles: 7-inch
BRAINSTORM ....10-20 '60s
MAR-V-LUS (6004 "Sad Feeling") 5-10 64
PAULA 4-6
RAINBOWS END 5-10
RENEE 8-12 64
SOUND PLUS 4-8
SUCCESS (107 "See What Tomorrow Brings") 25-35 63
SUE 3-5 85
TOWER (454 "Here Comes the Heartache") 5-10 68

BLAKE, Dick
Singles: 7-inch
BLAKE (001 "The Robbie") 10-15 65
(No mention on label of Robbie Rivers.)
Picture Sleeves
BLAKE (001 "The Robbie") 15-20 65
(Reads: "Robbie Rivers Invites You to Do the Robbie with Dick Blake.")

BLAKE, Johnny, & Clippers
Singles: 78 rpm
GEE (1027 "I'm Yours") 30-40 57
Singles: 7-inch
GEE (1027 "I'm Yours") 50-75 57

BLAKE, Melvin
Singles: 7-inch
RODNEY (13173 "Judy") 300-400

BLAKE, Tommy
(With the Rhythm Rebels)
Singles: 78 rpm
EKKO (1006 "The Hanging Judge") 10-15 55
SUN (278 "Flat Foot Sam") 100-150 57
Singles: 7-inch
BUDDY (107 "Koolit") 700-900 58
CHANCELLOR (101 "I Gotta Be Somewhere") 8-10 62
EKKO (1006 "The Hanging Judge") 30-40 55
RCA (6925 "Mister Hoody") 50-75 57
RECCO (1006 "Folding Money") 15-20 60
SUN (278 "Flat Foot Sam") 150-200 57
SUN (300 "I Dig You Baby") 400-600 58

BLAKELY, Cliff
Singles: 7-inch
STARDAY (352 "High Steppin' ") 75-125 58
STARDAY (369 "Get off My Toes") 30-50 58

BLAKELY, Cornell
(Bouncing Cornell Blakely)
Singles: 7-inch
CARRIE (013 "Don't Touch the Moon") 4-6 70
CARRIE (1503 "Tell Me More") 50-100 60
FULTON (2453 "Don't Touch the Moon") 75-100 58
RICH (1007 "You Ain't Gonna Find") 50-75 61
(No mention of distribution by Mercury.)
RICH (71853 "You Ain't Gonna Find") 15-25 61
(With "Distributed by Mercury.")
RICH (1747 "You Broke My Heart") 40-60 62

BLAKELY, Jimmy
Singles: 7-inch
D (1175 "Honky Tonk Princess") 20-25 61
U.A. (334 "Honky Tonk Princess") 10-15 61

BLAKELY, Virginia
Singles: 7-inch
MAJO (101 "Let Nobody Love You") 150-250

BLAKELY, Wellington
Singles: 78 rpm
VEE-JAY (104 "Sailor Joe") 50-100 53
Singles: 7-inch
VEE-JAY (104 "Sailor Joe") 200-400 53

BLANC, Mel P&R '48
(With the Sportsmen & Billy May; with Alan Reed)
Singles: 78 rpm
CAPITOL (5221 "Seasons Greetings from Capitol") 10-20 49
(Promotional issue only. Also contains greetings from other Capitol artists.)
CAPITOL 10-20 48-54
Singles: 7-inch
CAPITOL (Except PRO-15) 20-30 50-54
CAPITOL (PRO-15 "I Taut I Taw a Record Dealer") 30-50 51
(Mel Blanc provides the voice of assorted cartoon characters, though he is not credited on label. Promotional issue only.)
PETER PAN 4-6 72
W.B. (5129 "Tweety's Twistmas Twouble") 5-10 59
W.B. (5156 "Blimey") 5-10 60
EPs: 7-inch
CAPITOL (436 "Party Panic") 40-60 53
LPs: 10/12-inch
CAPITOL (436 "Party Panic") 50-100 53
(10-inch LP.)
CAPITOL (3251 "Woody Woodpecker & His Talent Show") 15-25 61
CAPITOL (3257 "Bugs Bunny & His Friends") 25-35 61
CAPITOL (3261 "Tweety Pie") 15-25 63
CAPITOL (3266 "Bugs Bunny in Storyland") 15-25 63
CAPITOL (6686 "Bozo & His Pals") 15-25
COLPIX (302 "The Flintstones") 75-150 61
(TV Soundtrack.)
GOLDEN (66 "Songs of the Flintstones") 125-175 61
Also see HUNT, Pee Wee
Also see LE BLANC

BLANCHARD, Babe
Singles: 78 rpm
NESTOR (26 "One More Time") 10-15 55
Singles: 7-inch
NESTOR (26 "One More Time") 40-50 55

BLANCHARD, Bonnie, & Andy Aaron & Mean Machine
Singles: 7-inch
CRS (2 "You're the Only One") ....10-20 '60s

BLANCHARD, Edgar
Singles: 78 rpm
SPECIALTY 10-15 56
Singles: 7-inch
RIC (954 "Lonesome Guitar") 10-20 58
SPECIALTY 15-25 56
Also see GAYTEN, Paul

BLANCHARD, Jack, & Misty Morgan C&W '69
(Misty Morgan & Jack Blanchard)
Singles: 7-inch
EPIC 4-6 73-75
MEGA 4-6 71-73
WAYSIDE 4-6 69-70
LPs: 10/12-inch
EARTH (3478 "The Early Years") 125-150 70
(Promotional issue only.)
MEGA 8-12 72
WAYSIDE 10-15 70

BLANCHARD, Jackie
Singles: 7-inch
MIDA (111 "King of Hearts") 100-200 58

BLANCHARD, Red
Singles: 78 rpm
COLUMBIA 10-15 57
Singles: 7-inch
COLUMBIA (40280 "Dig That Crazy Mixed-Up Kid") 15-20 57
DOT (15901 "Open the Door Richard") 8-12 59
Also see NERVOUS NORVUS

BLAND, Billy P&R/R&B '60
Singles: 78 rpm
OLD TOWN 10-20 55-57
Singles: 7-inch
ATLANTIC 3-5 84
COLLECTABLES 3-5 81
TIP TOP 10-20 58
OLD TOWN (1016 thru 1036) 20-30 56-57
OLD TOWN (1076 "Let the Little Girl Dance") 15-25 60
OLD TOWN (1082 thru 1109) 10-20 60-61
OLD TOWN (1114 thru 1151) 10-15 62-63
Also see BEES

BLAND, Bobby R&B '57
(Bobby "Blue" Bland)
Singles: 78 rpm
CHESS (1489 "Crying") 20-40 52
DUKE (105 "I.O.U. Blues") 40-60 54
DUKE (115 "No Blow No Show") 25-50 54
DUKE (141 "It's My Life, Baby") 20-40 56
DUKE (146 thru 196) 15-30 57-58
DUKE (303 "Wishing Well") 100-200 59
DUKE (310 "Is It Real") 200-300 59
MODERN (848 "Crying All Night Long") ... 15-25 52
MODERN (868 "Good Lovin' ") 15-25 52
Singles: 7-inch
ABC 4-6 73-78
DUKE (105 "I.O.U. Blues") 75-125 54
DUKE (115 "No Blow No Show") 50-100 54
DUKE (141 "It's My Life, Baby") 40-60 56
DUKE (146 thru 196) 25-35 57-58
DUKE (300 series) 5-15 59-66
DUKE (400 series) 5-8 66-73
DUNHILL 4-6 73-74
FAIRWAY 8-10 79

MCA....3-5 79-84
MALACO....3-5 85-86

EPs: 7-inch

DUKE (75 "Here's the Man")....20-30 62
(Juke box issue only. Includes title strips.)
DUKE (78 "Ain't Nothing You Can Do")...20-30 64
(Juke box issue only. Includes title strips.)

LPs: 10/12-inch

ABC....5-10 75-78
ABC/DUKE....5-10 73
BLUESWAY (6065 "Call On Me")....5-10 73
DUKE (74 "Two Steps from the Blues")...50-75 61
DUKE (75 "Here's the Man")....45-55 62
DUKE (77 "Call On Me – That's the Way Love Is")....35-50 63
DUKE (78 "Ain't Nothing You Can Do")...35-50 64
DUKE (79 "Soul of the Man")....25-45 66
DUKE (84 "Best of Bobby Bland")....25-40 67
DUKE (86 "Best of Bobby Bland, Vol. 2") 25-40 68
DUKE (88 "Touch of the Blues")....25-40 68
DUKE (89 "Spotlighting the Man")....20-40 69
DUKE (90 "If Loving You Is Wrong")....15-25 70
DUKE (92 "Introspective")....20-25 74
DUNHILL....8-15 73-74
MCA....5-10 79-84
Also see ACE, Johnny
Also see GUNNER, Bob

BLAND, Bobby, & B.B. King *R&B '76*

Singles: 7-inch

ABC....4-6 78
IMPULSE....4-6 76

LPs: 10/12-inch

DUNHILL....10-12 74
IMPULSE....8-10 76
MCA....5-10 82
Also see KING, B.B.

BLAND, Bobby / Little Junior Parker

LPs: 10/12-inch

DUKE (DLP-72 "Bare Foot Rock and I Got You")....100-150 58
DUKE (X-72 "Bare Foot Rock and I Got You")....10-12 74
Also see PARKER, Little Junior

BLAND, Bobby, & Ike Turner

Singles: 7-inch

KENT (378 "Love You Baby")....5-10 62
Also see TURNER, Ike

BLAND, Bobby / Johnny Guitar Watson

LPs: 10/12-inch

CROWN (5358 "2 in Blues")....20-30 63
Also see BLAND, Bobby
Also see WATSON, Johnny

BLAND, Glenn

Singles: 7-inch

SARG (159 "Mean Jean")....50-75 58
SARG (164 "When My Baby Passes By")....50-75 59

BLANDERS

Singles: 7-inch

SMASH (2005 "Jitterbug")....50-75 58

BLANK, Bill

Singles: 7-inch

SHO-BIZ (1006 "Hard Luck")....50-75 59

BLANKENSHIP BROTHERS

Singles: 78 rpm

SKYLINE....25-75 56

Singles: 7-inch

BLUEGRASS (773 "Tears I Cried for You")....50-75
BLUEGRASS (816 "Lonesome Old Jail")....100-200
BLUEGRASS (870 "You Went and Broke My Heart")....50-75
SKYLINE (105 "Don't Tell Me You're Sorry")....50-100 56
SKYLINE (106 "That's Why I'm Blue").300-500 56
SKYLINE (107 "Waitin' for a Train")....400-600 56

BLANQUE, Bobby

Singles: 7-inch

ARGO (5269 "Lonely and Blue")....20-30 57

BLANTEN, Marvin

Singles: 7-inch

BI-JO (660 "She's Gone Again")....10-20
CAPO (3 "I'm Sailing a Dreamboat")....50-100

BLARNEYS

Singles: 7-inch

ROMULUS (3006 "My Little Miss America")....20-30 64

BLASERS

(Featuring Tommy "Mary Jo" Braden)

Singles: 78 rpm

UNITED....10-20 55

Singles: 7-inch

UNITED (191 "She Needs to Be Loved").15-25 55
(Previously issued as by the Four Blazes.)
Member: Tommy Braden.
Also see BRADEN, Tommy
Also see FOUR BLAZES

BLASTERS *LP '82*

Singles: 7-inch

MCA....3-5 84
SLASH....3-5 81-85

Picture Sleeves

SLASH....3-5 81-85

LPs: 10/12-inch

ROLLIN' ROCK (021 "American Music")..50-75 80
SLASH....8-12 81-85
Members: David Alvin; Phil Alvin; John Bazz; Gene Taylor; Bill Bateman; Steve Berlin; Lee Allen.
Also see ALLEN, Lee
Also see X

BLATTNER, Jules

(With His Teen Tones; with Warren Groovy Band; Warren Groovy All Stars)

Singles: 7-inch

BLUE RIBBON....5-10 76
BOBBIN (105 "Rock and Roll Blues")...125-150 59
BOBBIN (113 "Green Stuff")....40-60 59
BUDDAH....5-10 71
CINE VISTA....10-20 69
CORAL (62437 "No Money Down")....8-12 64
DMA....5-10 69
GASLIGHT....10-20 62
K-ARK (609 "Till I'm with You")....20-30 60
K-ARK (612 "One More Time")....20-30 60
METROMEDIA....5-10 73
MGM....10-20 72
NORMAN (509 thru 538)....10-20 61-62
NORMAN (1020 "New Orleans")....3-5 89
TARGET....8-12 71
TEE PEE (19/20 "Pledging My Love"/"Summertime Blues")....10-20 67

LPs: 10/12-inch

BUDDAH....10-20 71
DESMOND....5-10 79
MOUNTAIN....10-20 74
Also see J.B.G. & JULES

BLAZE, Johnny / Eddie Konecnik

(With Eddie Konecnik Orchestra)

Singles: 7-inch

APON (2142 "Oh Lovin' Baby")....15-25 59

BLAZER BOY

(James Locks)

Singles: 78 rpm

IMPERIAL....25-50 52-53

Singles: 7-inch

IMPERIAL (5199 "Morning Train")....75-100 52
IMPERIAL (5244 "Surprise Blues")....75-100 53
IMPERIAL (5801 "New Orleans Twist")....10-15 62
Also see LOCKS, James

BLAZERS

(Featuring Frankie Tucker)

LPs: 10/12-inch

HARMONY (7103 "Rock & Roll by the Blazers")....25-35 59
Also see HARMONY BLAZERS

BLAZERS

Singles: 7-inch

ACREE (101 "Beaver Patrol")....25-35 63
ACREE (102 "Sound of Mecca")....25-35 63
BRASS (306 "I Don't Need You")....15-25 63
Members: Vernon Acree; Larry Robbins; Chris Holguin; John Morris.

BLAZONS

Singles: 7-inch

BRAVURA (5001 "Magic Lamp")....200-300 58
(First issue.)
FANFARE (5001 "Magic Lamp")....100-200 58

BLEACH BOYS

Singles: 7-inch

STUDIO CITY (1030 "Wine Wine Wine").50-60 64

BLEDSOE, Steve

(With the Blue Jays)

Singles: 7-inch

SCOPE (1961 "Stan the Man")....8-12 61
SCOPE (8266 "Cool Steppin' Baby")....150-200
SUPERSTAR....4-6 73
VEM (2227 "After Hours")....10-20 60
WITCH (102 "Dumb Dumb Bunny")....50-75 61

BLENDAIRES

Singles: 7-inch

EMPIRE (5 "You Are the One")....150-200 62

BLENDAIRS

Singles: 7-inch

TIN PAN ALLEY (252 "My Love Is Just for You")....150-200 58

BLEN-DELLS

Singles: 7-inch

BELLA (608 "Forever")....100-150 62

BLENDELLS *P&R '64*

Singles: 7-inch

COLLECTABLES....3-5 81
COTILLION (44020 "Night After Night")...10-15 68
ERA....4-6 73
RAMPART (641 "La La La La La")....15-20 64
REPRISE....5-10 64-65
Also see SONNY & CHER / Bill Medley / Lettermen / Blendells

BLENDELLS

Singles: 7-inch

CAPTOWN (4029 "Night After Night")..200-300 68
DON-TEE ("You Need Love")....20-30 '60s
(Selection number not known.)

BLENDERS

Singles: 78 rpm

DECCA (27403 "I'm Afraid the Masquerade Is Over")....75-125 51
DECCA (27587 "Busiest Corner in My Home Town")....75-125 51
DECCA (28092 "I'd Be a Fool Again")....75-125 52
DECCA (28241 "Never in a Million Years")....75-125 52
DECCA (48156 "Gone")....50-100 50
DECCA (48158 "Count Every Star")....50-100 50
DECCA (48183 "I'm So Crazy for Love")....50-100 50
DECCA (48244 "My Heart Will Never Forget")....50-100 51
JAY-DEE (780 "Don't Play Around with Love")....40-60 53
MGM (11488 "I Don't Miss You Anymore")....50-100 53
MGM (11531 "Please Take Me Back")...50-100 53
NATIONAL (9092 "I Can Dream, Can't I")....50-75 49

Singles: 7-inch

DECCA (27403 thru 28241)....300-400 51-52
DECCA (48156 thru 48244)....300-400 50-51
DECCA (48158 "Count Every Star")....300-400 50
JAY-DEE (780 "Don't Play Around with Love")....100-200 53
MGM)....100-200 53
Members: Ollie Jones; Tommy Adams; Dick Palmer; Abe DeCosta; James DeLoach; Ernie Brown; Ray Johnson; Nappy Allen.
Also see BLENDERS / Sparrows
Also see MILLIONAIRES

BLENDERS / Sparrows

Singles: 78 rpm

("Don't F#*K Around with Love")....10-15
(Label is blank.)

Singles: 7-inch

KELWAY (101 "Don't F#*K Around with Love"/"I'm Gonna Do That Woman In")....5-10 71
Also see BLENDERS
Also see SPARROWS

BLENDERS

Singles: 78 rpm

RCA....10-20 56

Singles: 7-inch

RCA (6591 "I've Told Every Little Star")...25-50 56
RCA (6712 "Wake Up to the Music")....15-25 56

BLENDERS

Singles: 7-inch

ALADDIN (3449 "Two Loves")....2500-3000 59
CLASS (236 "Little Rose")....100-125 58
WANGER (189 "Angel")....30-40 59

BLENDERS

Singles: 7-inch

PARADISE (111 "I Won't Tell the World")....15-25 59
Member: Herman Dunham.
Also see VOCALEERS

BLENDERS

Singles: 7-inch

A.F.O. (305 "It Takes Time")....300-350 62

BLENDERS *P&R '63*

(Goldie Coates & Blenders)

Singles: 7-inch

CORTLAND (102 "Love Is a Treasure")...15-25 62
CORTLAND (103 "Prison of Love")....8-12 62
MAR-V-LUS (6010 "Your Love Has Got Me Down")....100-200 66
VISION (1000 "I Asked for Your Hand").75-125 57
WITCH (114 "Daughter")....15-25 63
WITCH (117 "Every Girl Is the Same")....8-12 63
WITCH (122 "One Time")....10-20 64
Members: Hilliard "Johnny" Jones; Albert Hunter; Goldie Coates; Delores Johnson; Gail Mapp.
Also see CANDLES
Also see FIVE CHANCES

BLENDORS

Singles: 7-inch

DECCA (31284 "Tell Me What's On Your Mind Baby")....15-25 61

BLENDS

(With the Eden Rockers; with Frank Paul's Orchestra)

Singles: 7-inch

CASA GRANDE (3037 "Now It's Your Turn")....15-25 60
CASA GRANDE (5000 "A Thousand Miles Away")....10-20 61
SKYLARK (108 "Tell Me")....20-30 61
TALENT (110 "Tell Me")....40-60 60
(Reads: "Music by the Eden Rockers.")
TALENT (110 "Tell Me")....15-25 60
(No mention of the Eden Rockers.")
Also see BIG JOHN & FABULOUS BLENDS

BLENDTONES

(Blend-Tones; Blend Tones)

Singles: 7-inch

CHIC-CAR (100 "She's Gone")....10-15 61
CLIFTON (36 "She's Gone")....3-5 79
DON-EL (106 "She's Gone")....30-40 61
(First issue.)
IMPERIAL (5758 "She's Gone")....10-15 61
SUCCESS (101 "Lovers")....10-15 63
SUCCESS (105 "Come on Home")....10-15 63

BLESSED END

LPs: 10/12-inch

TNS (248 "Movin' On")....200-300 71
Members: Doug Teti; Jim Shugarts; Ken Carson.

BLESSING, Michael

(Michael Nesmith)

Singles: 7-inch

COLPIX (787 "The New Recruit")....15-25 65
COLPIX (792 "Until It's Time for You to Go")....15-25 65
Also see NESMITH, Michael

BLEU LIGHTS

Singles: 7-inch

BAY SOUND (67003 "Forever")....50-100 68
(Promotional issue only.)
BAY SOUND (67003 "Forever")....50-75 68
BAY SOUND (67007 "Lonely Man's Prayer")....10-15 68
BAY SOUND (67010 "Yes I Do")....15-20 69
BAY SOUND (67013 "I Guess I'm in Love")....30-40 69

BLEVINS, Bill

Singles: 78 rpm

TRUMPET....15-25 53

Singles: 7-inch

N.H.F. (101 "Crazy Blues")....75-100 58
TRUMPET (200 "Honeymoon Waltz")....20-30 53
TRUMPET (201 "Heart for Sale")....20-30 53

BLEVINS, Chuck

Singles: 7-inch

FOXIE (7006 "Sleighbell Rock")............75-125 59

BLEVINS, Gene

Singles: 7-inch

RUBY (150 "Forever My Darling")........... 10-15 57

BLEVINS, Wendy Boy

Singles: 7-inch

IMPERIAL (5516 "A Girl in Her Teens")... 10-15 58

BLEYER, Archie P&R '54

(With Maria Alba)

Singles: 78 rpm

ARC.........8-15 35
CADENCE.........5-10 54-57
VOCALION.........8-15 34

Singles: 7-inch

CADENCE......... 10-20 54-62
SCHOLASTIC (2701 "Bedtime for Francis").........4-6 74
(Compact 33 single.)

LPs: 10/12-inch

CADENCE (3044 "Moonlight Serenade") 15-25 62
(Monaural.)
CADENCE (25044 "Moonlight Serenade")......... 20-30 62
(Stereo.)
Also see CHORDETTES
Also see HAYES, Bill

BLIHOVDE, Marv

Singles: 7-inch

KAY BEE (6001 "Been Away Too Long")......... 200-300 60
LINDY (1113 "Cigarette and Coffee Blues")......... 75-100 59
LINDY (1551 "Sweet Little Wife")............ 25-35 59
Also see DENNIS, Marv
Also see MINNESOTA MARV & VANGUARDS

BLIND FAITH LP '69

Singles: 7-inch

ATLANTIC ("In the Presence of the Lord")......... 40-60 69
(Promotional issue only.)
RSO (873 "Can't Find My Way Home")........4-6 77

LPs: 10/12-inch

ATCO (304A "Blind Faith")......... 30-40 69
(Front cover pictures a topless young girl.)
ATCO (304B "Blind Faith")......... 10-15 69
(Front cover pictures the group.)
MFSL (186 "Blind Faith")......... 40-60 69
(Half-speed mastered.)
RSO (3016 "Blind Faith").........5-10 76
(Reissue. Pictures nude girl.)
Members: Eric Clapton; Ginger Baker; Steve Winwood; Rick Grech.
Also see CLAPTON, Eric
Also see WINWOOD, Steve

BLINKY

(Sandra Williams)

Singles: 7-inch

MOTOWN (Except 1168).........4-6 68-73
MOTOWN (1168 "How You Gonna Keep It")......... 50-100 68
MOWEST.........4-6 72-73
SOUL (35089 "How You Gonna Keep It")....4-6 71
Also see STARR, Edwin, & Blinky

BLISS

Singles: 7-inch

CANYON (34 "Gangster of Love")........... 10-20 68

LPs: 10/12-inch

CANYON (7707 "Bliss")......... 75-100 68

BLOCH, Ray, & Orchestra P&R '46

Singles: 78 rpm

CORAL.........4-8 52-57
SIGNATURE.........4-8 47

Singles: 7-inch

CORAL.........6-12 53
SIGNATURE.........4-6 60-61

Picture Sleeves

CORAL (9-1327 "From Here to Eternity")......... 300-500 53
(Pictures Frank Sinatra, Burt Lancaster, Montgomery Clift, Donna Reed, and Deborah Kerr.)

LPs: 10/12-inch

AMBASSADOR.........8-12
CORAL......... 10-25 52-57
Also see LEWIS, Monica
Also see SINATRA, Frank

BLOCKBUSTERS

Singles: 78 rpm

ALADDIN (3319 "Why Baby Why")..........10-15 56
INTRO (6093 "All the Way").........10-15 56

Singles: 7-inch

ALADDIN (3319 "Why Baby Why")..........25-35 56
INTRO (6093 "All the Way").........20-30 56

BLOCKBUSTERS

Singles: 78 rpm

ANTLER.........10-20 57-58

Singles: 7-inch

ANTLER (4006 "Fulltime Baby")..............50-75 57
ANTLER (4008 "Nobody to Love")...........30-40 58
Also see NEW BLOCKBUSTERS
Also see OLENN, Johnny

BLOCKER, Dan

(With John Mitchum)

LPs: 10/12-inch

RCA (2896 "Our Land, Our Heritage")......15-25 64
TREY (903 "Tales for Young Uns")..........20-30 61

BLOKES

Singles: 7-inch

DANTE (2545 "All American Girl")...........20-40 66

BLONDE BOMBER

Singles: 7-inch

HULL (737 "Strollie Bun").........60-75 60
HULL (763 "Strollie Bun").........30-45 64
Member: Walter Rhodes.

BLONDIE LP '78

Singles: 12-inch

CHRYSALIS.........5-10 78-84

Singles: 7-inch

CHRYSALIS.........3-6 77-84
PRIVATE STOCK.........6-10 76-77

Picture Sleeves

CHRYSALIS.........3-8 79-82

LPs: 10/12-inch

CAPITOL (32748 "Remix Project")..........10-15 '90s
CHRYSALIS (Except 5001).........5-10 76-84
CHRYSALIS (5001 "Parallel Lines").........15-25 78
(Picture disc.)
MFSL (050 "Parallel Lines").........30-50 81
PRIVATE STOCK.........15-20 75
Members: Deborah Harry; Clem Burke; Jimmy Destri; Chris Stein; Gary Valentine; Fred Smith; Nigel Harrison.
Also see LITTLE GIRLS

BLOOD, SWEAT & TEARS LP '68

Singles: 7-inch

ABC (12310 "Somebody I Trusted")............4-6 78
COLUMBIA.........4-6 69-77

Picture Sleeves

COLUMBIA.........4-6 70-72

LPs: 10/12-inch

ABC.........5-10 77
COLUMBIA (Except 9619 & 49619).........10-15 69-76
COLUMBIA (9619 "Child Is Father to the Man").........20-30 68
COLUMBIA (49619 "Child Is Father to the Man").........25-35 68
(Half-speed mastered.)
L.A. (1864 "Nuclear Blues").........5-10 80
(Black vinyl.)
L.A. (1864 "Nuclear Blues").........10-12 80
(Colored vinyl. Promotional issue only.)
MFSL (251 "Blood, Sweat & Tears") 30-50
Members: David Clayton-Thomas; Al Kooper; Jerry Hyman; Fred Lipsius; Dick Halligan; Bobby Colomby; Lew Soloff; Chuck Winfield; Steve Katz; James Thomas Fielder; Dave Bargeron; Georg Wadenius; Lou Matini Jr.; Bobby Doyle; Jerry Fisher.
Also see DOYLE, Bobby
Also see FRANKLIN, Aretha / Union Gap / Blood, Sweat & Tears / Moby Grape
Also see STREISAND, Barbra
Also see THOMAS, David Clayton

BLOOMFIELD, Mike LP '69

LPs: 10/12-inch

CLOUDS.........5-10 78
COLUMBIA (9000 series).........12-15 69
COLUMBIA (37000 series).........6-10 81-83
GUITAR PLAYER.........8-10 77
HARMONY.........8-10 71
TAKOMA.........5-10 77-81
W.B. (7674 "Steelyard Blues").........4-8 73
WATERHOUSE.........5-10 81
Also see DYLAN, Bob

BLOOMFIELD, Mike, Dr. John & John Paul Hammond LP '73

LPs: 10/12-inch

COLUMBIA.........8-10 73

BLOOMFIELD, Mike, & Nick Gravenites

LPs: 10/12-inch

COLUMBIA.........10-12 69

BLOOMFIELD, Mike, & Al Kooper LP '69

Singles: 7-inch

COLUMBIA (44678 "The Weight").............5-10 68

LPs: 10/12-inch

COLUMBIA (6 "The Live Adventures of Mike Bloomfield and Al Kooper").........20-25 69
Also see MOBY GRAPE

BLOOMFIELD, Mike, Al Kooper & Steve Stills LP '68

Singles: 7-inch

COLUMBIA (44657 "Albert's Shuffle")........5-10 68

LPs: 10/12-inch

COLUMBIA (9701 "Super Session").........15-20 68
MFSL (178 "Super Session").........30-50 85
Also see BLOOMFIELD, Mike
Also see STILLS, Stephen

BLOOMSBURY PEOPLE

Singles: 7-inch

MGM (14158 "Witch Helen").........10-15 70
PAGE (1119 "Have You Seen Them Cry").........10-15 69

LPs: 10/12-inch

MGM (2184 "Bloomsbury People")..........15-25 70
Members: Sigmund Snopek III; Jon Wyderka; Dennis Lanting; Michael Lorenz; Greg Janick; Rick Harris; Michael DuJardin.
Also see MAJOR ARCANA

BLOOS PHASE

Singles: 7-inch

TEE PEE (37/38 "Will You Love Me"/"The Basic Works of Father Timothy") 15-25 67

BLOSSOMS P&R '61

Singles: 7-inch

BELL (780 thru 937).........5-10 69-70
CAPITOL (3822 thru 4072).........10-20 57-58
CHALLENGE (9138 "Big Talking Jim") 10-15 62
CHALLENGE (59122 "Write Me a Letter").........15-25 62
CLASSIC ARTISTS (110 "Lonely Friday Night").........5-8 88
(Black vinyl. 1000 made.)
EEOC (8172 "Things Are Changing").....75-100 65
(Equal Employment Opportunity Center promotional issue.)
EPIC.........4-6 77
LION.........4-6 72
MGM (13964 "Tweedle Dee").........8-12 68
ODE (101 thru 125).........5-10 67-69
OKEH (7162 "I'm in Love").........15-25 62
REPRISE (0436 thru 0639).........5-10 65-67

Picture Sleeves

EEOC (8172 "Things Are Changing").....75-100 65
(Promotional issue only.)

LPs: 10/12-inch

LION.........8-12 72
Members: Darlene "Love" Wright; Annette Williams; Gloria Jones; Fanita James-Barrett; Nanette Williams-Jackson; Grazia Nitzsche; Jean King.
Also see BERRY, Richard
Also see BOB B. SOXX & BLUE JEANS
Also see DON & DEWEY
Also see EDDY, Duane
Also see EVERETT, Betty
Also see FABARES, Shelley
Also see HALE & HUSHABYES
Also see LOVE, Darlene
Also see NELSON, Rick
Also see PLAYGIRLS
Also see PRESLEY, Elvis
Also see TYNES, Maria
Also see WILDCATS
Also see WILSON, Brian

BLOSSOMS / Coeds

Singles: 7-inch

CHALLENGE (9109 "Son-in-Law")..........10-15 61
Also see BLOSSOMS

BLOX

Singles: 7-inch

SOLAR (235 "Say Those Magic Words")...5-10 67
SOLAR (237 "Hangin' Out").........20-30 67

BLUE, Jay

Singles: 7-inch

IMPERIAL (5587 "Get off My Back")....100-200 59

BLUE, Katie, & Peppermints

Singles: 7-inch

HOUSE OF BEAUTY (114 "Doing All Right").........10-20 60
Also see PEPPERMINTS
Also see WATKINS, Katie / Texas Red & Jimmy

BLUE ANGEL

Singles: 7-inch

POLYDOR.........3-5 81

LPs: 10/12-inch

POLYDOR (6300 "Blue Angel").........15-25 80
POLYDOR (6300 "Blue Angel").........50-100 80
(White label. Promotional issue only.)
Members: Cyndi Lauper; John Morelli; Ron Halee; John Turi; Art Neilson; Lee Brovitz.
Also see LAUPER, Cyndi

BLUE ANGELS

Singles: 7-inch

CRAZY (100 "To-Geth-Er").........200-250 '50s

BLUE ANGELS

Singles: 7-inch

EDSEL (781 "Deserie").........50-75 59
PALETTE.........10-20 59-61

BLUE ANGELS

Singles: 7-inch

CAP (076 "Quicksand").........50-100
CAP (077 "Shake a Tail Feather")............10-20

BLUE BANANA

Singles: 7-inch

KANWIC (152 "Spicks & Specks")..........20-30 67

Picture Sleeves

KANWIC (152 "Spicks & Specks")..........40-60 67

BLUE BARRONS

LPs: 10/12-inch

PHILIPS (200017 "Twist to the Great Blues Hits").........20-25 62
(Monaural.)
PHILIPS (600017 "Twist to the Great Blues Hits").........25-30 62
(Stereo.)

BLUE BEARDS

(With the Jacks)

Singles: 7-inch

GUIDE (1002 "Romance").........50-75 58

BLUE BEATS

Singles: 7-inch

BEOWOLF ("Superman").........20-30 66
(No selection number used.)
COLUMBIA (43790 "Extra Girl")..............15-25 66
COLUMBIA (44098 "Born in Chicago")....20-30 67

Picture Sleeves

COLUMBIA (43790 "Extra Girl")..............60-80 66
(Promotional issue only.)

LPs: 10/12-inch

A.A. (133 "Beatle Beat").........20-30 64
Members: Lance Drake; Peter Robbins; Jack Lee; Louie Mazza.
Also see ONE

BLUE BELLES

Singles: 78 rpm

ATLANTIC.........25-50 53

Singles: 7-inch

ATLANTIC (987 "Cancel the Call").........75-125 53

BLUE BELLES

(Blue-Belles; Blue Bells; Starlets)

Singles: 7-inch

PEAK (7042 "I Sold My Heart to the Junkman").........10-20 62
RAINBOW (1903 "You're Just Fooling Yourself").........10-20
(Selection number may be something other than

"1903," which we suspect is just an identification number.)

Picture Sleeves

PEAK (7042 "I Sold My Heart to the Junkman")................................ 15-25 62

Also see STARLETS

BLUE BOYS C&W '67

Singles: 7-inch

RCA..5-10 65-68

LPs: 10/12-inch

RCA.. 15-25 65-68

Members: Bud Logan; Leo Jackson; Bunky Keels; Mel Rogers.

Also see REEVES, Jim

BLUE CHARLIE

Singles: 7-inch

NASCO (6002 "I'm Gonna Kill That Hen")...................................... 50-75 57

BLUE CHEER P&R/LP '68

Singles: 7-inch

MERCURY.......................................4-6 76

PHILIPS..8-12 68-70

Picture Sleeves

PHILIPS (40516 "Summertime Blues").... 10-15 68

LPs: 10/12-inch

MEGAFORCE....................................5-10 85

PHILIPS (9001 "Vincebus Eruption")..........5-10 80

PHILIPS (200264 "Vincebus Eruption")... 50-75 68

(Monaural.)

PHILIPS (600264 "Vincebus Eruption")... 30-50 68

(Stereo.)

PHILIPS (600278 "Outside Inside")........ 50-75 68

PHILIPS (600305 "New! Improved!")... 100-150 69

PHILIPS (600333 "Blue Cheer")............. 30-50 70

PHILIPS (600347 "Original Human Being")... 30-50 70

PHILIPS (600350 "Oh Pleasant Hope")... 40-60 71

Members: Leigh Stephens; Paul Whaley; Dick Peterson; Randy Holden; Tony Rainer; Bruce Stephens; Ralph Kellogg; Gary Yoder.

Also see GROUP B

Also see HOLDEN, Randy

Also see KAK

Also see MINT TATTOO

Also see OXFORD CIRCLE

Also see PILOT

Also see STEPHENS, Leigh

BLUE CHEER / H.P. Lovecraft / Hello People

LPs: 10/12-inch

PHILIPS (5 "Philips Dealer Demonstration Record")....................................... 50-100 68

(Promotional issue only.)

Also see BLUE CHEER

BLUE CHIPS

Singles: 78 rpm

DELUXE (6100 "Come Back")............. 50-100 56

Singles: 7-inch

DELUXE (6100 "Come Back")........... 400-500 56

(Black label.)

DELUXE (6100 "Come Back")........... 500-600 56

(White label with bio. Promotional issue only.)

Member: Carlton Lankford.

BLUE CHIPS

Singles: 7-inch

GROOVE (0006 "Promise").......................8-12 62

LAUREL (1026 "Double Dutch Twist")..... 15-25 61

RCA (7923 "Puddle of Tears")............... 10-20 61

RCA (7935 "Let It Ride")....................... 10-20 61

ROARING (804 "Where")..........................5-10 67

SHASTAIN (001 "Dynamo")..................... 20-30 58

WREN (302 "I'm So in Love with You")... 10-15 59

WREN (304 "Little Street")..................... 10-15 59

WREN (305 "A Song and a Prayer")........ 10-15 60

BLUE CHIPS

Singles: 7-inch

SPARTA (001 "Wishing Well")............ 200-300 62

(Similar selection number [Sparta 001-BB] used for an Ivorys release.)

Also see IVORYS

BLUE DIAMONDS

Singles: 78 rpm

SAVOY (1134 "Honey Baby")................. 10-15 54

Singles: 7-inch

SAVOY (1134 "Honey Baby")................. 20-30 54

Member: Ernie Kador.

Also see K-DOE, Ernie

BLUE DOTS

Singles: 78 rpm

DE LUXE..15-25 54

Singles: 7-inch

ACE (526 "Please Don't Tell 'Em")..........20-30 57

DE LUXE (6052 "Don't Do That Baby")....40-50 54

DE LUXE (6055 "Don't Hold It")...............50-75 54

DE LUXE (6061 "God Loves You")..........50-75 54

DE LUXE (6067 "Hold Me Tight")............30-40 54

BLUE ECHOES

Singles: 7-inch

ALDERAY (4156 "Rebel Train")...............10-15

ALDERAY (5178 "Maharajah of Magador")......................................10-15

BON (2112 "Debbie")..........................300-400 58

GILSTEN (3134 "Cool Guitar")...............75-125 63

BLUE ECHOES

Singles: 7-inch

B.E.P. (103 "Rosanne")...........................8-12 64

B.E.P. (104 "Respectable")......................50-75 65

(500 made.)

BRISTOL (101 "Blue Bell Bounce")..........10-15 63

ITZY (11 "Blue Bell Bounce").....................8-12 68

LAWN (225 "Blue Bell Bounce")...............10-15 64

Members: Tom Zagryn; Tom Collins; Eric Gulliksen.

BLUE ECHOES

Singles: 7-inch

RAYNARD (10019 "Moonride")................15-20 65

RAYNARD (4005 "Moonride")..................10-15 68

BLUE EYED SOUL

Singles: 7-inch

CAMEO (401 "The Shadow of Your Love")...10-20 66

CAMEO (423 Something New")...............10-20 66

SAND CITY...5-10

Member: Billy Vera.

Also see VERA, Billy

BLUE FALCONS

Singles: 7-inch

BELMONT (4005 "Run Like the Wind")....10-20 62

BLUE FEELING

Singles: 7-inch

NIGHT OWL (6861 "Tell Her No")...........15-25 68

Members: Ross Baldock; Steve Fuedner; Jack Westfall; Tommy Raml.

BLUE FLAMERS

Singles: 78 rpm

EXCELLO..25-50 54

Singles: 7-inch

EXCELLO (2026 "Driving Down the Highway")..50-75 54

BLUE FLAMES

Singles: 7-inch

STRAND (25023 "Possum")....................10-15 60

BLUE FLAMES

Singles: 7-inch

SPRY (113 "That Crazy Little House")...75-100 61

SPRY (115 "Close to Me")....................75-125 62

BLUE JAYS

Singles: 78 rpm

CHECKER (782 "White Cliffs of Dover")..250-350 53

Singles: 7-inch

CHECKER (782 "White Cliffs of Dover").. 1500-2500 53

BLUE JAYS

EPs: 7-inch

DIG THIS RECORD (777 "Earth Angel")...200-300 56

DIG THIS RECORD (778 "Tweedlee Dee")...100-200 56

(With vocals by Bernie Bridges. Includes one Diggers instrumental.)

Members: Chester Pipkin; Lee Goudreau; Dewey Terry; Don Harris.

Also see DON & DEWEY

Also see SQUIRES

BLUE JAYS

("Music By Nat Sledge")

Singles: 7-inch

BLUJAY (1002 "Write Me a Letter"). 2000-2500 61

Also see SLEDGE, Nat

BLUE JAYS P&R '61

("Lead Vocal - Leon Peels"; Leon Peels & the Bluejays)

Singles: 7-inch

CLASSIC ARTISTS (111 "Once Upon a Love")...5-8 89

(Black vinyl. 1000 made.)

CLASSIC ARTISTS (111 "Once Upon a Love")..8-10 89

(Red vinyl. 1000 made.)

COLLECTABLES..3-5 81

ERA..4-6 72

MILESTONE (2008 "Lover's Island")........15-20 61

(Blue label. Opinions differ as to which came first – the dark blue, or light blue and white label.)

MILESTONE (2008 "Lover's Island")........10-15 61

(Green label.)

MILESTONE (2009 "Tears Are Falling") ..20-30 61

MILESTONE (2010 "Let's Make Love")....10-15 62

MILESTONE (2012 "Rock, Rock, Rock").15-20 62

MILESTONE (2014 "Venus My Love").....50-75 62

Member: Leon Peels.

Also see PEELS, Leon

BLUE JAYS / Little Caesar & Romans

LPs: 10/12-inch

MILESTONE (1001 "Blue Jays Meet Little Caesar & Romans")......................................50-100 62

(Black vinyl.)

MILESTONE (1001 "Blue Jays Meet Little Caesar & Romans")....................................150-200 62

(Colored vinyl.)

Also see BLUE JAYS

Also see LITTLE CAESAR & ROMANS

BLUE KATS

Singles: 7-inch

GAITY (674 "Oh Yeah").......................100-200 '60s

(Colored vinyl.)

BLUE KNIGHTS

Singles: 7-inch

KITTEN (6970 "Madness").......................15-25 59

STRATFORD (6502 "Take the Last Train Home")...10-20

BLUE NOTES

(With Melino & His Orchestra)

Singles: 78 rpm

RAMA (25 "If You'll Be Mine")..................40-50 53

TICO (1083 "Charlotte Amalie")...............10-15 54

Singles: 7-inch

RAMA (25 "If You'll Be Mine")..............100-150 53

TICO (1083 "Charlotte Amalie")...............50-75 54

BLUE NOTES P&R '60

(Blue-Notes)

Singles: 78 rpm

JOSIE..40-50 56-57

Singles: 7-inch

COLLECTABLES..3-5 81

DASH (5005 "Hot Chills and Cold Thrills") .5-10 69

GAMUT (100 "My Heart Crys [sic] for You")..10-15 61

HARTHON (136 "Needless to Say")...........8-12 64

JALYNNE (135 "My Hero").......................20-40 60

JOSIE (800 "If You Love Me")..............100-150 56

JOSIE (823 "Retribution Blues")............75-125 57

LAST CHANCE (103 "If You Love Me").....5-10

LOST NITE...4-8

PORT (70021 "If You Love Me")..............10-15 58

RED TOP (132 "Blue Star").........................4-8 75

(Previously unissued.)

RED TOP (135 "My Hero")........................10-15 63

3 SONS (103 "W-P-L-J")........................75-125 62

UNI (55132 "Hot Chills and Cold Thrills")...5-10 69

VAL-UE (213 "My Hero").........................30-40 60

(Black vinyl. Address is P.O. Box 3885.)

VAL-UE (213 "My Hero").......................75-100 60

(Blue vinyl.)

VAL-UE (213 "My Hero")............................5-10 60

(Black vinyl. Address is P.O. Box 2630.)

VAL-UE (215 "O Holy Night")...................25-35 60

LPs: 10/12-inch

COLLECTABLES..5-10 82

Members: Harold Melvin; Jesse Gillis Jr.; Frank Peaker; Roosevelt Brodie; Lawrence Brown; Bernard Williams; John Atkins.

Also see MELVIN, Harold, & Blue Notes

Also see RANDALL, Todd

BLUE NOTES

Singles: 7-inch

COLONIAL (434 "Page One")..................15-25 58

COLONIAL (7779 "Let Her Know")...........15-25 58

COLONIAL (9999 "Never Never Land")...15-25 58

DOT (15720 "Darling of Mine")................10-15 58

TNT (150 "Darling of Mine")................100-150 58

Members: Joe Tanner; Pat Patterson; Tom Underwood.

BLUE NOTES

Singles: 7-inch

INSTANT ACTION (101 "She Is Mine") ... 10-20 '60s

LOST (104 "She Is Mine")....................500-600 60

(First issue.)

BLUE NOTES

Singles: 7-inch

ACCENT (1069 "Your Tender Lips")........ 10-20 61

TWENTIETH CENTURY (1213 "Blue Star")..10-20 61

BLUE OYSTER CULT LP '72

Singles: 12-inch

COLUMBIA..4-6 80

Singles: 7-inch

COLUMBIA..3-6 72-84

WHAT'S IT ALL ABOUT.............................8-12

(Promotional issue only.)

Picture Sleeves

COLUMBIA (02000 & 04000 series)............3-5 81-84

COLUMBIA (45000 series)..........................4-8 72

EPs: 7-inch

COLUMBIA (40 "Bootleg EP")..................20-25 72

LPs: 10/12-inch

ABC RADIO ("A Night on the Road").......35-50 81

(Promotional issue only.)

COLUMBIA (Except 31000 thru 33000 series)...5-10 76-84

COLUMBIA (31000 thru 33000 series)......6-12 72-75

Members: Al Bouchard; Joe Bouchard; Eric Bloom; Alan Lanier; Donald "Buck Dharma" Roeser.

Also see SOFT WHITE UNDERBELLY

BLUE SANDLEWOOD SOAP

Singles: 7-inch

AESOP'S LABEL (103 "Friends I Haven't Met Yet")...25-35 68

BLUE SMITTY & HIS STRING MEN

(Clarence Smith)

Singles: 78 rpm

CHESS (1522 "Crying")...........................25-50 52

Singles: 7-inch

CHESS (1522 "Crying")..........................75-100 52

BLUE SONNETS

Singles: 7-inch

COLUMBIA (42793 "Thank You Mr. Moon")...30-40 63

Member: Eric Nathanson.

Also see VOCALAIRES

BLUE TONES

Singles: 7-inch

BLUE JAY..5-10

KING (5088 "Shake Shake").....................20-30 57

KUSTOM (200 "Baby Oh Baby").............75-125

REGENCY (670 "Shake Shake")..............50-60 57

Member: Billy Gayles.

Also see GAYLES, Billy

BLUEBEARDS

Singles: 7-inch

DATE (1547 "I'm Home")............................5-10 67

GUIDE (1002 "Romance")........................50-75 58

BLUEBELLS

Singles: 7-inch

TREND (30002 "Squeegie")......................15-25 58

20TH FOX (249 "Snow White and the Three Stooges")..8-12 61

BLUEBIRDS

Singles: 78 rpm

RAINBOW (199 "Can't Help But Sing the Blues")..200-300 53

BLUEDOTS

Singles: 7-inch

HURRICANE (104 "My Very Own")..1500-2000 59

BLUENOTES *P&R '59*
("Featuring Ralph Harrington")
Singles: 7-inch
BROOKE 10-20 59-60
Picture Sleeves
BROOKE 25-45 60
Members: Tom Underwood; Joe Tanner; Pat Patterson; Ralph Harrington.
Also see FRANKLIN, Doug
Also see HAMILTON, George, IV

BLUENOTES / Five Echoes / Five Chances
LPs: 10/12-inch
CONSTELLATION (5 "Collectors Showcase, Groups Three") 20-25 64
Also see BLUENOTES
Also see FIVE CHANCES
Also see FIVE ECHOES

BLUES BOY
(Guitar Slim & Jelly Belly)
Singles: 78 rpm
SUPER DISC (1053 "In Love Blues") 20-40 48
TRU-BLUE (101 "Smilin' Blues") 25-50 47
TRUE BLUES (102 "Ungrateful Woman Blues") 25-50 47
LPs: 10/12-inch
ARHOOLIE 10-15
Also see BACK PORCH BOYS
Also see BLUES KING
Also see SEWARD, Slim, & Fat Boy Hayes

BLUES CLIMAX
LPs: 10/12-inch
HORNE (333 "Blues Climax") 50-75 69
HORNE (888 "The Alan Franklin Explosion") 50-75 70
Members: Alan Franklin; Chris Russel; Dave Dix; Buzzy Meekins; Bill Vermillion.

BLUES COMPANY
Singles: 7-inch
GREAT LAKES (3002 "Experiment in Color") 10-20
PEAR ("Love Machine") 25-35
(No selection number used.)
PEAR ("You're Dead My Friend") 25-35
(No selection number used.)

BLUES EXPRESS ORCHESTRA
Singles: 78 rpm
GEM (206 "Honkin' Away") 15-20 53
Singles: 7-inch
GEM (206 "Honkin' Away") 30-40 53

BLUES INC.
Singles: 7-inch
POWER (19362 "Out of the Darkness") 15-25 '60s
UNITED AUDIO ("7 and 7 Is") 25-35 '60s
(Selection number not known.)

BLUES KING
Singles: 78 rpm
SOLO (10-003 "Me & My Baby") 35-50 46
Members: Alec Seward; Louis Hayes.
Also see BLUES BOY
Also see SEWARD, Alec, & Louis Hayes

BLUES KINGS
Singles: 7-inch
D (1061 "Lover Come Back") 30-40 59

BLUES MAGOOS *P&R/LP '66*
Singles: 7-inch
ABC 4-8 68-70
GANIM (1000 "Who Do You Love") 20-40 69
MERCURY (30000 series) 4-6 76
MERCURY (70000 series) 8-12 66-68
VERVE FOLKWAYS (5006 "So I'm Wrong") 20-30 66
VERVE FOLKWAYS (5044 "So I'm Wrong") 15-25 67
Picture Sleeves
MERCURY (72660 "Pipe Dream") 10-20 67
MERCURY (72692 "One by One") 10-20 67
LPs: 10/12-inch
ABC 8-10 69-70
MERCURY (21096 "Psychedelic Lollipop") 40-50 66
(Monaural.)
MERCURY (21104 "Electric Comic Book") 30-40 67
(Monaural. Add $5 to $10 if accompanied by comic book insert.)
MERCURY (61096 "Psychedelic Lollipop") 25-40 66
(Red label. Stereo.)
MERCURY (61096 "Psychedelic Lollipop") 8-10
(Chicago "skyline" label.)
MERCURY (61104 "Electric Comic Book") 30-45 67
(Stereo. Add $5 to $10 if accompanied by comic book insert.)
MERCURY (61167 "Basic Blues Magoos") 20-30 68
Members: Geoff Daking; Mike Esposito; Ron Gilbert; Ralph Scala; Emil Thielhelm.
Also see FELIX & ESCORTS

BLUES PROJECT *LP '66*
Singles: 7-inch
CAPITOL 5-8 72
MCA 4-6 73
VERVE FOLKWAYS 10-15 66-67
VERVE FORECAST 10-15 67
LPs: 10/12-inch
CAPITOL 10-15 72
ELEKTRA 5-10 80
MCA 8-10 73
MGM 8-12 70-74
VERVE FOLKWAYS 15-25 66
VERVE FORECAST 12-20 67-70
Members: Al Kooper; Roy Blumenfeld; David Cohen; Tommy Flanders; Richard Green; John Gregory; Don Gretmar; Danny Kalb; Steve Katz; Andy Kulbert; Bill Lussenden; Chicken Hirsch.

BLUES ROCKERS
Singles: 78 rpm
ARISTOCRAT (407 "Trouble in My Home") 25-50 50
ARISTOCRAT (413 "When Times Are Getting Better") 25-50 50
CHESS (1483 "Little Boy, Little Boy") 25-50 50
EXCELLO (2062 "Calling All Cows") 15-25 55
Singles: 7-inch
EXCELLO (2062 "Calling All Cows") 30-50 55

BLUES WOMAN *R&B '46*
(Marion Abernathy)
Singles: 78 rpm
JUKE BOX (502 "Voo-It! Voo-It!") 20-30 46
Also see ABERNATHY, Marion

BLUESBOY BILL
Singles: 78 rpm
BLUESMAN (101 "Come On Baby") 50-100 48

BLUETHINGS
(Blue Things)
Singles: 7-inch
RCA (8692 thru 9308) 15-25 65-67
RUFF 25-35 65
Picture Sleeves
RCA (8692 "La Do Da Da") 25-40 66
LPs: 10/12-inch
CICADELIC 8-10 87
RCA (LPM-3603 "Blue Things") 60-80 66
(Monaural.)
RCA (LSP-3603 "Blue Things") 75-100 66
(Stereo.)
Members: Van Stoecklein; Richard Scott; Mike Chapman; Robert Day; Larry Burton.
Also see STOECKLEIN, Val

BLUETONES
(With "Lead Vocal By Joe Villa")
Singles: 7-inch
BLUEJAY (101 "I'll Love You") 300-400 65
(Reissued on Swan as by the Royal Teens.)
Also see ROYAL TEENS
Also see VILLA, Joey

BLUJAYS
Singles: 7-inch
BLUJAY (1002 "Write Me a Letter") 300-400 61

BLUM, Bob
Singles: 7-inch
ORBIT (103 "Rompin' Stompin' Good Time") 75-125

BO, Eddie *P&R/R&B '69*
Singles: 78 rpm
ACE (515 "I'm So Tired") 10-20 56
APOLLO (486 thru 504) 10-20 55-56
APOLLO (509 "Dearest One") 30-60 57
Singles: 7-inch
ACE (515 "I'm So Tired") 25-35 56
ACE (555 "I'll Keep on Trying") 15-25 59
APOLLO (486 "I'm Wise") 30-50 56
APOLLO (496 "Please Forget Me") 30-50 56
APOLLO (499 "I Cry Oh") 30-50 56
APOLLO (504 "Tell Me Why") 40-60 56
APOLLO (509 "Dearest One") 40-60 57
AT LAST 8-12 63
BLUE JAY (154 "Come to Me") 5-10 64
BO-SOUND 4-6 71
CAPITOL (4617 "Dinky Doo") 8-10 61
CHECKER (877 "Indeed I Do") 10-15 58
CHESS (1698 "Oh Oh") 40-60 58
CHESS (1833 "You Are the Only One") 8-10 62
CINDERELLA (1203 "Shake, Rock & Soul") 8-12 63
NOLA (704 "Everybody's Somebody's Fool") 5-10 64
RIC (156 "You Are the Only One") 10-15 62
RIC (962 thru 981) 10-15 59-61
RIC (985 "I Got to Know") 8-12 61
RIC (987 "Now Let's Popeye") 10-15 62
RIP 10-20
SEVEN B 5-10 66-68
SCRAM (117 "Hook and Sling") 5-10 69
SWAN (4099 "Now Let's Popeye") 8-10 62
ZIP (803 "You Are the Only One") 10-15 62
LPs: 10/12-inch
ROUNDER 5-10
Also see LITTLE BO
Also see PARKER, Robert

BO, Eddie, & Inez Cheatham
Singles: 7-inch
SEVEN B (7017 "A Lover and a Friend") 5-10 68
Also see BO, Eddie

BO, Little
(Eddie Bo)
Singles: 78 rpm
ACE (501 "Baby") 25-50 55
Singles: 7-inch
ACE (501 "Baby") 50-75 55
Also see BO, Eddie

BO & WEEVILS
Singles: 7-inch
ALLEN (1001 "My Time") 20-30 69
ALLEN (1004 "Love Hurts") 20-30 69
SAHARA (513 "Rosalee") 20-30

BO GRUMPUS
LPs: 10/12-inch
ATCO (246 "Before the War") 15-20 68
Members: Ronnie Blake; Jim Colegrove; Joe Hutchinson; Ed Mottau.

BO PETE
(Harry Nilsson)
Singles: 7-inch
CRUSADER (103 "Baa Baa Black Sheep") 20-30 64
TRY (501 "Groovy Little Suzy") 20-40 64
Also see NILSSON

BO STREET RUNNERS
Singles: 7-inch
KR (104 "Aladdin") 25-35
(Single-sided promotional issue.)

BO WEEVELS
(Carl Lertzman & Bo-Weevels)
Singles: 7-inch
UNITED STATES (1934 "The Beetles Will Getcha") 10-15 64
Picture Sleeves
UNITED STATES (1934 "The Beetles Will Getcha") 15-25 64

BOA
LPs: 10/12-inch
SNAKEFIELD (001 "Wrong Road") 200-300 69
Members: Bob Maledon; Brian Walton.

BOATMAN, Tooter
Singles: 7-inch
GAYLO 10-15 62
REBEL (108 "Poor Gal") 150-200 58
TWINKLE (501 "Thunder and Lightning") 200-300 58
Also see CHAPARRALS

BOATNER, Joe
Singles: 7-inch
ABEL (227 "Everytime") 20-30 59

BOAZEMAN, Harmon
Singles: 7-inch
SARG (145 "No Love in You") 75-100 58

BOB & DEBONAIRES
Singles: 7-inch
DEBONAIR ("So Blue") 50-75 61
(No selection number used.)

BOB & DELCADES
Singles: 7-inch
FOX (107 "A New Day") 40-50 59

BOB & DENNY
Singles: 7-inch
HEP (2145 "Hush, Hush Little Baby") 50-75 58

BOB & EARL
Singles: 7-inch
CLASS (213 "That's My Desire") 20-30 57
CLASS (231 "Gee Whiz") 15-25 58
CLASS (232 "Chains of Love") 15-25 58
CLASS (247 "That's My Desire") 10-20 59
HI OLDIES 4-6
MALYNN (232 "Chains of Love") 10-20 59
Members: Bobby Byrd; Earl Nelson.
Also see BYRD, Bobby
Also see HOLLYWOOD FLAMES
Also see LEE, Jackie
Also see NELSON, Earl

BOB & EARL *P&R '62*
(With René Hall Orchestra)
Singles: 7-inch
ABC (2458 "Harlem Shuffle") 4-6 73
CHENE (103 "Sissy Baby") 5-10 64
CRESTVIEW (9011 "Dancing Everywhere") 5-10 69
ISLAND 4-6
LOMA (2004 "Everybody Jerk") 5-10 64
MARC (104 "Harlem Shuffle") 8-12 63
MARC (105 "Puppet on a String") 10-15 64
MARC (106 "Baby, Your Time Is My Time") 10-15 64
MIRWOOD (5507 "It's Over") 10-15 65
MIRWOOD (5517 "Baby, It's Over") 5-10 66
(Reissue. Note slight title change.)
MIRWOOD (5526 "Baby, Your Time Is My Time") 5-10 66
TEMPE 15-25 62
TIP (1013 "As We Dance") 8-12 64
UNI 4-8 70
WHITE WHALE (310 "Harlem Shuffle") 10-15 69
LPs: 10/12-inch
CRESTVIEW (3055 "Bob & Earl") 15-20 69
TIP (9011 "Harlem Shuffle") 20-30 64
UPFRONT (118 "Bob & Earl") 10-15
Members: Bobby Relf; Earl Nelson; Earl Wilson.
Also see HALL, René
Also see NELSON, Earl
Also see WHITE, Barry

BOB & EARL / Gene Allison
Singles: 7-inch
TRIP (75 "Harlem Shuffle"/"You Can Make It if You Try") 4-6 75
Also see ALLISON, Gene

BOB & EARL / Embers
Singles: 7-inch
COLLECTABLES (3070 "Harlem Shuffle"/"Solitaire") 3-5 81
Also see BOB & EARL
Also see EMBERS

BOB & EARL
Singles: 7-inch
BIG MACK (6101 "I'll Be on My Way") 100-200

BOB & JERRY
Singles: 7-inch
COLUMBIA (42162 "We're the Guys") 25-35 61
MUSICOR (1018 "Mr. Moon, Mr. Cupid and I") 8-10 62
RENDEZVOUS (100 "Ghost Satellite") 8-10 58
Members: Bob Feldman; Jerry Goldstein.

BOB & JOE
Singles: 7-inch
A (112 "Little Girl of My Dreams") 10-20 61
A (318 "Suzie Q") 10-20 61

SANDY (1008 "Jungle Rock") 50-75 58

BOB & LUCILLE

Singles: 7-inch

DITTO (121 "Eeny Meeny Miney Moe") 300-400 59
(First issue.)
DITTO (126 "What's the Password") 50-75 60
KING (5631 "Eeny Meeny Miney Moe") 100-200 62
Members: Bob Regan; Lucille Starr.
Also see CANADIAN SWEETHEARTS
Also see STARR, Lucille

BOB & RAY

Singles: 78 rpm

ACE ("Mule Train") 10-20 49
(With Mary McGoon.)
CORAL 5-10 56

Singles: 7-inch

CORAL (61338 "This Is Your Bed") 10-15 56

LPs: 10/12-inch

B&R CLASSICS 10-20
COLUMBIA (30412 "The Two & Only") ... 10-15 71
(Original cast.)
GEG 8-12 76
GENESIS 8-12 73-76
GOULDING-ELLIOT-GREYBAR (112301 "Mary Backstage, Nobel Wife") 30-40
RCA (1773 "Stereo Spectactular") 30-40 58
RCA (2131 "Bob & Ray on a Platter") 20-30 59
U.S. ENVIRONMENTAL PROTECTION SOCIETY (72435 "Bob & Ray") 25-35
(Promotional issue only.)
UNICORN (1001 "Write If You Get Work") 20-40 54
(10-inch LP.)
Members: Bob Elliott; Ray Goulding.

BOB & RAY

Singles: 7-inch

MODERN SOUND 10-20 58
NASCO (6023 "Shorty Shorty") 10-15 58
NASCO (6029 "Sweet Nancy") 10-15 59

BOB & ROCKBILLIES

Singles: 7-inch

BLUE CHIP (11 "Your Kind of Love") 30-50 57

BOB & SHERI

Singles: 7-inch

SAFARI (101 "Surfer Moon") 600-800 61
(Brian Wilson's first record production. Original commercial copies have a light blue label and promotional copies a white label. Beware! Near-perfect counterfeits exist.)
Members: Bob Norberg; Sheri Pomeroy.
Also see SHARON MARIE
Also see SURVIVORS
Also see WILSON, Brian

BOB & SHIRLEY
(With the Valiants)

Singles: 7-inch

BAND BOX (225 "Your True Love") 20-30 60
BAND BOX (282 "Brigitte Bardot") 10-15 61

BOB & VIC

Singles: 7-inch

SKY (115 "Cross-Eyed Susie, Wake Up") 150-250

BOB B. SOXX & BLUE JEANS *P&R/R&B '62*

Singles: 7-inch

PHILLES (107 thru 113) 15-25 62-63

LPs: 10/12-inch

PHILLES (4002 "Zip-a-Dee Doo-Dah") 100-150 63
Members: Bobby Sheen; Darlene Love; Carolyn Willis; Fanita James-Barrett.
Also see BLOSSOMS
Also see LOVE, Darlene
Also see RONETTES / Crystals / Darlene Love / Bob B. Soxx & Blue Jeans
Also see SHEEN, Bobby

BOBBETTES *P&R/R&B '57*
(Bobettes)

Singles: 78 rpm

ATLANTIC 25-50 57

Singles: 7-inch

ATLANTIC (1144 "Mr. Lee") 20-30 57
ATLANTIC (1159 thru 2069) 15-25 57-60
DIAMOND (133 "Teddy") 10-15 62
DIAMOND (142 thru 189) 8-12 63-65
END (1093 "Teach Me Tonight") 8-12 61
END (1095 "I Don't Like It Like That") 20-30 61
(First issue.)
GALLIANT (1006 "I Cried") 8-12 60
GONE (5112 "I Don't Like It Like That") ... 15-25 61
JUBILEE 8-12 62
KING 8-12 61-62
MAYHEW 4-6 71-74
RCA 10-20 66
TRIPLE-X 15-25 60
Members: Emma Pought; Jannie Pought; Heather Dixon; Laura Webb; Helen Gathers.
Session: King Curtis.
Also see KING, Ben E.
Also see KING CURTIS

BOBBIE & BOBBIE

Singles: 7-inch

DICE (480 "Teenage Party") 100-150

BOBBY & BENGALS

Singles: 7-inch

B-W (502 "Double Rock") 75-125 60
B-W (601 "No Parking!") 10-15 60

BOBBY & BUDDY

Singles: 78 rpm

FURY 20-40 58

Singles: 7-inch

FURY (1008 "What's the Word, Thunderbird") 15-25 58
HIT (180 "Bless You Little Girl") 8-12
Member: Buddy Barnes.

BOBBY & CONSOLES
(Bobby Pedrick Jr.)

Singles: 7-inch

DIAMOND (141 "My Jelly Bean") 75-100 63
(Brown vinyl.)
VERVE (10402 "Karine") 40-60 66
Also see PEDRICK, Bobby, Jr.

BOBBY & COUNTS
("Vocal by Fred Ciaschi"; Bobby Comstock)

Singles: 7-inch

COUNT (6985 "Three Signs of Love") ..200-300 58
MARLEE (104 "Tra-La-La") 100-150 61
Also see COMSTOCK, Bobby

BOBBY & DEMONS

Singles: 7-inch

MCI (1028 "The Woo") 100-150 56

BOBBY & ORBITS

Singles: 7-inch

GONE (5126 "Your Cheatin' Heart") 10-20 62
SEECO (6005 "Felicia") 15-25 58
SEECO (6030 "Teenage Love") 10-20 59
SEECO (6067 "Felicia") 10-20 60

BOBBY & RHYTHM ROCKERS

Singles: 7-inch

EL DORADO (665 "Rhythm Rock") 400-600

BOBBY & TEASERS

Singles: 7-inch

FLEETWOOD (1012 "She's a Tease") 20-30 60

BOBBY & VELVETS

Singles: 7-inch

RASON (501 "I Promised") 75-125 59
Member: Bobby Sanders.
Also see EXTREMES
Also see SANDERS, Bobby

BOBBY JO

Singles: 7-inch

FLAG (5001 "Hayfever") 50-60

BOBBY PINS
(Bobbi-Pins)

Singles: 7-inch

MERCURY 5-10 63-65
OKEH (7110 "I Want You") 20-30 59

BOBBY SUE & FREELOADERS

Singles: 78 rpm

HARLEM 50-75 55

Singles: 7-inch

HARLEM (2335 "It Takes a Lot of Love") 100-150 55

BOBO, Bobby

Singles: 7-inch

DECCA (31219 "Battle of Gettysburg") 10-15 61
SAGE (239 "Doggone Long-Gone Blues") 40-60 56

BOBO, Jim

Singles: 7-inch

EKO (506 "Jungle Rock") 600-800 58
(Labels crediting Bobo may or may not have a sticker indicating singer is Hank Mizell.)
Also see MIZELL, Hank, & Jim Bobo

BOBO, Willie *LP '66*
(With the Bo-Gents)

Singles: 7-inch

BLUE NOTE 4-6 77
CAPITOL 4-6 76
COLUMBIA (10862 "Always There") 4-6 78
JUPITER JAZZ 4-6 75
TICO 8-12 59
VERVE 5-10 65-69

LPs: 10/12-inch

BLUE NOTE 5-10 77
COLUMBIA 8-10 78-79
MGM 5-10
ROULETTE (25272 "Let's Go") 15-25 64
ROULETTE (52097 "Bobo's Beat") 15-25 63
SUSSEX 8-10
TICO 10-20
TRIP 5-10
VERVE 10-20 65-69

BOBOLINKS

Singles: 7-inch

KEY (Except 573 & 574) 10-20 59
KEY (573 "Elvis Presley's Sergeant") 30-40 57
KEY (574 "You Dreamer You") 30-40 57
TUNE (226 "Lonesome Wind") 10-15 61

BOB-O-LINKS

Singles: 7-inch

HI-HO (101 "I Promise") 30-40 62
(Is this the same recording as on Way-Lin 101, credited to the Memories?)
Also see MEMORIES

BOCEPHUS
(Hank Williams Jr.)

Singles: 7-inch

VERVE (10540 "Meter Reader Maid") 20-30 67
VERVE (10572 "Splish Splash") 20-30 67
(May have been issued only as a promo.)
Also see WILLIAMS, Hank, Jr.

BOCKY & VISIONS
(Bocky)

Singles: 7-inch

CLEVETOWN (230 "Here Is My Heart") ... 15-25 66
PHILIPS (40224 thru 40279) 10-20 64-65
REDDA (1501 thru 1505 .... 15-25 64-66
Member: Bocky Dipasquale.

BODAFORD, Bill, & Rockets

Singles: 7-inch

BACK BEAT (507 "Little Girl") 15-25 58

BOENZEE CRYQUE

Singles: 7-inch

CHICORY (406 "Sky Gone Gray") 15-25 67
UNI (55012 "Sky Gone Gray") 10-15 67
Members: Sam Bush; Mort Mitchell; Rusty Young; George Grantham; Jed Neddo.
Also see POCO

BOGART, Humphrey

Singles: 7-inch

MARK 56 ("The Enforcer") 60-80
(Picture disc. Selection number not known.)

BOGGS, Lucky

Singles: 7-inch

BUDDY (110 "You Can't Stop Her?") 50-75
SHAWNEE (101 "Drillin' Rig Boogie") .. 100-200

BOGGS, Lucky / Howard Perkins

Singles: 7-inch

BISHOP (1012 "Drillin' Rig Boogie") 4-8 81
Also see PERKINS, Howard

BOGGS, Prof. Harold

Singles: 78 rpm

KING 15-25 53

Singles: 7-inch

KING (4643 "Inside the Beautiful Gate") .. 25-50 53
KING (4660 "I Want to Live Right") 25-50 53
NASHBORO 5-15 58-76

BOGIS CHIMES

Singles: 7-inch

CHAMP (3403 "I Think You'll Find") 10-15 66
Members: Jimmy Dentici; Glen Frank; Rick Skow; Dave Frasheski; Mike Kowaleski.
Also see ROAD RUNNERS

BOGLE, Jim, & Beaumen

Singles: 7-inch

TEXAS RECORD CO. (2629 "Letter to My Love") 200-300 62

BOHANON, George, Quartet

Singles: 7-inch

WORKSHOP JAZZ (2006 "Bobbie") 15-25 63

LPs: 10/12-inch

WORKSHOP JAZZ (207 "Boss Bossa Nova") 40-60 63
WORKSHOP JAZZ (214 "Bold") 40-60 64

BOHEMIAN VENDETTA

Singles: 7-inch

MAINSTREAM (681 "Riddles and Fairytales") 10-15 68
U.A. (50174 "Enough") 10-20 67

LPs: 10/12-inch

MAINSTREAM (6106 "Bohemian Vendetta") 75-100 68
Members: Brian Cooke; Nick Manzi.

BOHET, Nal

Singles: 7-inch

KARATE (532 "Jelly Belly") 5-10 66

LPs: 10/12-inch

KARATE (1403 "Belly Go Go") 15-20 67
(Monaural.)
KARATE (5403 "Belly Go Go") 20-25 67
(Stereo.)

BOICE, Wes

Singles: 7-inch

TERON (425 "Don't Come Runnin' ") ... 100-200

BOINES, Houston
("With Rhythm Acc.")

Singles: 78 rpm

RPM (364 "Monkey Motion") 150-200 52
(7-inch 78 rpm single.)
RPM (364 "Monkey Motion") 50-75 52
(10-inch single.)
Also see BAINES, Houston
Also see GILMORE, Boyd /Houston Boines / Charlie Booker

BOLAN, Marc

LPs: 10/12-inch

REPRISE (511 "Interview with Marc Bolan of T-Rex") 50-75 71
(Promotional issue only.)
RHINO (Picture disc) 8-10
WHAT 5-10 82
Also see T. REX

BOLD

Singles: 7-inch

CAMEO (430 "Gotta Get Some") 15-20 66
Also see WALKER, Steve, & Bold

BOLES, Calvin

Singles: 7-inch

YUCCA (Except 141 & 161) 10-20 59-64
YUCCA (141 "If You've Got a Lot of Dough") 20-25 62
YUCCA (161 "Stompin' on a Hardwood Floor") 50-75 63

BOLING, Wayne

Singles: 7-inch

SPOT (1111 "Please Cry") 15-25 64

BOLL WEEVIL

Singles: 7-inch

FUNN (1001 "Free-Dumb Riders") 15-20 62

BOLLIN, Zu Zu

Singles: 78 rpm

TORCH (6910 "Why Don't You Eat Where You Slept Last Night") 40-60 52
TORCH (6912 "Cry Cry Cry") 40-60 52

BOMBERS

Singles: 78 rpm

ORPHEUS 15-25 55-56

Singles: 7-inch
ORPHEUS (1101 "I'll Never Tire of You") 30-40 55
(Black vinyl.)
ORPHEUS (1101 "I'll Never Tire of You") 50-75 55
(Red vinyl.)
ORPHEUS (1105 "Two-Time Heart") 30-40 56
(Black vinyl.)
ORPHEUS (1105 "Two-Time Heart") 50-75 56
(Red vinyl.)

BON BONS
Singles: 7-inch
CORAL (62402 "What's Wrong with Ringo") 10-15 64
CORAL (62435 "Everybody Wants My Boyfriend") 8-12 64

BON BONS
Singles: 7-inch
SAMSON (3001 "Listen My Heart") 15-25 64

BONAFEDE, Carl
(With Gem-Tones; with Rhythm Jets; Carl Bonn)
Singles: 7-inch
TEK (101 "Were Wolf") 100-150
EPs: 7-inch
IMPALA (2123 "Carl Bonafede") 100-200 79
Also see SCREAMING WILDMAN

BON-AIRES
Singles: 7-inch
CATAMOUNT (130 "New Me") 4-6 76
FLAMINGO 4-8 76-77
RUST (3 "Blue Beat") 200-300 62
RUST (5077 "My Love My Love") 50-75 64
RUST (5097 "Jeanie Baby") 75-100 65

BONAIRS / Ernie Tavares Trio
Singles: 78 rpm
DOOTONE 75-100 53
Singles: 7-inch
DOOTONE (325 "It's Christmas"/"I'm Alone Tonight") 400-500 53

BOND, Bobby — C&W '72
Singles: 7-inch
DANCELAND (1000 "Livin' Doll") 25-35 61
(First issue.)
HICKORY 4-6 72
JAMIE (1185 "Livin' Doll") 10-20 61
MGM 4-6 68
PARROT (10830 "Twenty Men") 5-10 66
WAND (1102 "You've Got Time") 5-10 65
W.B. 5-10 69
LPs: 10/12-inch
ALSHIRE 8-10 69
SOMERSET/STEREO FIDELITY 10-20 '60s
TIME 15-25 64

BOND, Bryce
(With Bernadette)
LPs: 10/12-inch
LOBO (102 "Seduction Bachelor Style") 20-30 '60s
STRAND (1019 "Bachelor Apartment") 20-30 61

BOND, Eddie
(With the Stompers; with Legend Makers)
Singles: 78 rpm
EKKO 50-75 55
MERCURY 25-50 56-57
Singles: 7-inch
ADVANCE 4-6 76
AMERICAN IMAGE 3-6 89-91
CORAL (62200 "Little Black Book") 10-20 60
D (1016 "Standing in Your Window") 15-25 58
DECCER 4-8 75-78
DIPLOMAT (8566 "The Monkey and the Baboon") 50-75 63
EKKO (1015 "Talking Off the Wall") 100-200 55
EKKO (1016 "Love Makes a Fool") 75-125 55
ENTERPRISE 4-8 72
ERWIN (2001 "Here Comes The Train") 10-15 75
(Opinions vary about the year of release. Though reported to us as accurate, some question it, saying this version predates the Memphis one from 1965. We do know that year is right. If the Erwin came first, then its price would likely be in the $30 to $50 range.)
GOLDWAX (107 "Now and Then") 5-10 65
HIGH COURT 3-5 80
MEMPHIS (105 "Make the Parting Sweet") 10-15 64
MEMPHIS (114 "Cold Dark Waters") 10-15 65
MEMPHIS (115 "Here Comes the Train") 20-30 65
MERCURY (70826 "Rockin' Daddy") 50-75 56
MERCURY (70882 "Slip, Slip, Slipin' In") 50-75 56
MERCURY (70941 "Boppin' Bonnie") 75-100 56
MERCURY (71000 series) 10-20 57
MILLIONAIRE 5-10 65-67
PEN 8-10 62
ROCK IT (104 "One Way Ticket") 4-8 79
SPA (1001 "I Walk Alone") 10-15 61
STARGEM 3-6 91
STOMPER TIME (1156 "You'll Never Be a Stranger") 40-60 59
TAB (677 "Rocking Daddy") 10-20 68
TAB (669 "Juke Joint Johnnie") 10-20 68
TAGG 5-10 67
THREE STARS 4-6 78
UNITED SOUTHERN ARTISTS (506 "Second Chance") 10-15 61
WILDCAT (58 "Can't Win for Losing") 15-25 61
XL 5-10 68
LPs: 10/12-inch
COUNTRY CIRCLE (6605 "My Choice Is Eddie Bond") 15-25 73
ENTERPRISE (1038 "The Legend of Buford Pusser") 10-20 73
(Includes bonus single, booklet and music sheet.)
M.C.C.R. 25-35 69
MILLIONAIRE 25-35 67
PHILLIPS INT'L (1980 "Greatest Country Gospel Hits") 200-300 62
ROCK IT (1002 "The Soul of Memphis") 8-12 79

BOND, Johnny — C&W '47
(With the Red River Valley Boys)
Singles: 78 rpm
COLUMBIA (Except 21521) 5-15 45-56
(Columbia 20545 through 20787 also exist on 7-inch 33 singles, any of which may be in the $15 to $25 range.)
COLUMBIA (21521 "The Little Rock Roll") 8-12 56
Singles: 7-inch
COLUMBIA (Except 21521) 10-20 51-56
COLUMBIA (21521 "The Little Rock Roll") 30-45 56
CONQUEROR 10-25
DITTO (120 "The Tijuana Jail") 5-10 59
GILLETTE 4-6
KING 4-6
LAMB & LION 4-6 74
LONDON 4-6
MGM 4-6 73
OKEH 8-15 41-45
REPUBLIC (2000 series) 5-10 60
SMASH (1761 "Mister Sun") 4-6 62
STARDAY (618 thru 951) 4-8 63-72
STARDAY (7021 thru 9292) 4-6 72-74
20TH FOX 5-10 60
EPs: 7-inch
COLUMBIA 10-20 58
REPUBLIC 10-20 60
STARDAY 10-15 63
LPs: 10/12-inch
CMH 5-10 77
CAPITOL 8-12 69
CATTLE 15-20
DANNY 15-20
HARMONY 10-20 64-65
LAMB & LION 5-10 74
NASHVILLE 5-10 71
SHASTA 10-15
STARDAY (147 thru 298) 20-30 61-64
STARDAY (333 "Ten Little Bottles") 15-20 65-66
STARDAY (354 "Famous Hot Rodders I Have Known") 25-30 65
STARDAY (368 thru 472) 20-30 66-71
STARDAY (900 series) 6-10 74
Also see AUTRY, Gene
Also see HANK & FRANK
Also see TRAVIS, Merle, & Johnny Bond

BOND, Johnny, & Lefty Frizzell
Singles: 78 rpm
COLUMBIA 5-10 56-57
Singles: 7-inch
COLUMBIA 10-15 56-57
Also see BOND, Johnny
Also see FRIZZELL, Lefty

BOND, Luther
(With the Emeralds)
Singles: 78 rpm
SAVOY 20-30 55
Singles: 7-inch
FEDERAL (12368 "Old Mother Nature") 10-15 59
SAVOY (1124 "What If") 30-50 55
SAVOY (1131 "Starlight Starbright") 40-60 55
SAVOY (1159 "Written in the Stars") 50-75 55
SHOWBOAT (1501 "Gold Will Never Do") 5-10 59
SHOWBOAT (1505 "Someone to Love Me") 50-60 60
Also see EMERALDS

BONDS, Gary "U.S." — P&R/R&B '60
(U.S. Bonds; Gary Bonds)
Singles: 12-inch
EMI (9666 "Gary U.S. Bonds") 25-30 81
(Promotional issue only.)
Singles: 7-inch
ABC 4-6 73
ATCO (6689 "Star") 5-10 69
BLUFF CITY (221 "My Love Song") 4-6 74
BOTANIC (1002 "Funky Lies") 5-10 68
COLLECTABLES 3-5 81
EMI AMERICA 3-5 81-82
LEGRAND (1003 thru 1012) 15-25 60-61
(Purple label.)
LEGRAND (1003 thru 1012) 10-15 62-63
(Multi-color label.)
LEGRAND (1015 thru 1020) 10-15 61-62
LEGRAND (1022 thru 1046) 10-20 62-67
MCA 3-5 84
PRODIGAL (0612 "Believing You") 4-6 75
SKY DISC (641 "Joy to the World") 4-6 '70s
SUE (17 "One Broken Heart") 4-6 70
Picture Sleeves
EMI AMERICA 4-8 81-82
LEGRAND (1008 "Quarter to Three") 15-25 61
LEGRAND (1009 "School Is Out") 30-50 61
LPs: 10/12-inch
EMI AMERICA 5-10 81-82
LEGRAND (1000 series) 5-10 79-86
LEGRAND (3001 "Dance 'Till Quarter to Three") 40-60 61
LEGRAND (3002 "Twist Up Calypso") 40-60 62
LEGRAND (3003 "Greatest Hits") 40-60 62
MCA 5-10 84
PHOENIX 5-10 84
RHINO 5-10 84
Session: Bruce Springsteen.
Also see BARGE, Gene
Also see BONDSMEN
Also see CHECKER, Chubby / Gary U.S. Bonds
Also see CHURCH STREET FIVE
Also see GREENWICH, Ellie
Also see JACKSON, Chuck
Also see KING, Ben E.
Also see SPRINGSTEEN, Bruce

BONDS, Lee
Singles: 78 rpm
CAPITOL 10-20 54
DECCA 10-15 54
REPUBLIC 10-20 52
TENNESSEE 20-30 52
Singles: 7-inch
CAPITOL (2692 "Done Gone Crazy") 20-30 54
DECCA (29338 "I'm Looking for Some Lovin'") 15-25 54
REPUBLIC (7007 "How About a Date") 25-40 52
TENNESSEE (804 "Uh-Huh Honey") 50-75 52
TENNESSEE (826 "Wild Cattin' Woman") 50-75 52
TODD (1003 "One More Time") 10-20 59
TODD (1055 "Walking with the Blues") 10-20 60

BONDSMEN
Singles: 7-inch
AMH (6704 "I See the Light") 20-30 67
GUILLOTINE 10-15 66

BONDSMEN / Derbys
Singles: 7-inch
DAWN (303 "Wipe Out '66") 25-35 66
(Brown vinyl.)
USA (887 "Shotgun") 10-20 68

BONE, Jimmy, & Jokers
Singles: 7-inch
GRACE (510 "Little Mama") 75-125

BONGO
(Georgie Bongo)
Singles: 7-inch
DORE (573 "Outer Space") 10-20 60

BONGOS
Singles: 7-inch
SPLASH (803 "That's All") 10-20 59

BONNAVILLES
Singles: 7-inch
QUESTION MARK (101 "High Noon Stomp") 15-25 62
QUESTION MARK (103 "Bonnavilles Stomp") 15-25 62
Picture Sleeves
QUESTION MARK (101 "High Noon Stomp") 20-35 62

BONNER, Juke Boy
Singles: 7-inch
GOLDBAND (1102 "Call Me Juke Boy") 20-30 60
LPs: 10/12-inch
ARHOOLIE 5-10
Also see BARNER, Juke Boy, & Group

BONNER, Lil' Joe, & Idols
(With the Fabulous Playboys)
Singles: 78 rpm
B&S B-DISC-S 100-200 55
Singles: 7-inch
B&S B-DISC-S (1570 "Tell Me Baby") 750-1000 55

BONNEVILLES
Singles: 7-inch
DRUM BOY (45101 "Bacardi") 10-20 62
DRUM BOY (45102 "Don't You Dare") 10-20 62
FENWAY (7000 "Sky Dive") 10-20 60
CORAL (62273 "Johnny") 10-20 61
Picture Sleeves
DRUM BOY 10-20 62
LPs: 10/12-inch
DRUM BOY (1001 "Meet the Bonnevilles") 50-75 62
Members: John Cerniglia; Larry Lynne; Teddy Peplinski; Dennis Madigan; Pete Funck; Vince Megna; Tony Kolp; Howard Wales; Bob Merkt; Rick Allen; Johnny Edwards; Paul Frederick; Tom Hahn.
Also see COLBY, Wendy, & Bonnevilles
Also see CONTINENTALS
Also see ELLIS, Herb, & Vince Megna.
Also see SKUNKS

BONNEVILLES
Singles: 7-inch
BARRY (104 "Zu Zu") 15-25 62
CAPRI (102 "Give Me Your Love") 100-200 59
COLLECTABLES 3-5 81
MUNICH (103 "Zu Zu") 200-300 60
(Red label.)
MUNICH (103 "Zu Zu") 75-125 60
(Black label.)
WHITEHALL (30,002 "I Do") 50-75 59

BONNEVILLES
Singles: 7-inch
SCOTTY (643 "Let's Go") 10-20 '60s
SPOTLIGHT (102 "I'm Walking the Dog") 100-150 '60s

BONNEVILLES
Singles: 7-inch
PRIVATE STOCK (101 "Don't Break the Spell of Love") 20-30 68

BONNIE & LITTLE BOYS BLUE
Singles: 7-inch
NIKKO (611 "Bells") 2000-3000 58
STAR VILL (1002 "Bells") 3-5 '90s

BONNIE & RUSTY
Singles: 7-inch
KING (5110 "La Dee Dah") 10-20 58

BONNIE & TREASURES — P&R '65
(Featuring Charlott O'Hara)
Singles: 7-inch
PHI DAN (5005 "Home of the Brave") 35-50 65
Also see MID AMERICANS / Bonnie & Treasures

BONNIE SISTERS — P&R '56
(With Mickey "Guitar" Baker Orch; with Randy Carlos Cha Cha Rhythms)
Singles: 78 rpm
RAINBOW 15-20 56

Singles: 7-inch
RAINBOW (328 "Cry Baby") 40-50 56
Members: Jean; Pat; Sylvia. Session: Mickey Baker.
Also see BAKER, Mickey

BONNIWELL'S MUSIC MACHINE
Singles: 7-inch
W.B. 8-12 67-68
Picture Sleeves
W.B (7093 "Bottom of the Soul") 15-25 67
LPs: 10/12-inch
W.B. 12-15 67
Member: Sean Bonniwell.
Also see FRIENDLY TORPEDOS
Also see MUSIC MACHINE

BONNY, Billy
Singles: 7-inch
MARK 56 (830 "Bootleg Rock") 200-300 59

BONSALL, Joe
(Vocal by Perry LaPointe; with Orange Playboys)
Singles: 7-inch
CRAZY CAJUN (502 "La Valse de Temp") 15-25 60
GOLDBAND .... 5-10 '60s
Also see LaPOINTE, Perry
Also see OAK RIDGE BOYS

BONTY, Jay
Singles: 7-inch
M&R (5 "The Shape") 10-20 67

BONZO DOG BAND *LP '72*
(Bonzo Dog Doo-Dah Band)
Singles: 7-inch
IMPERIAL 4-6 69
U.A. 4-6 71-72
LPs: 10/12-inch
IMPERIAL 15-20 68-70
LIBERTY 5-10 83
U.A. 10-15 71-74
Members: Vivian Stanshall; Neil Innes; Roger Ruskin Spear; Hughie Flint; Tony Kaye; Dave Richards; Andy Roberts.
Also see RUTLES

BOOGALOO *R&B '56*
(With the Gallant Crew; Kent Harris)
Singles: 78 rpm
CREST 10-20 55-56
Singles: 7-inch
CREST (1014 "Big Fat Lie") 15-25 55
CREST (1030 "Cops & Robbers") 15-25 56
(Black vinyl.)
CREST (1030 "Cops & Robbers") 35-55 56
(Colored vinyl.)

BOOGIE JAKE
(Matthew Jacobs)
Singles: 7-inch
CHESS (1746 "Bad Luck and Trouble") .. 20-30 59
INSTANT (3314 "Bad Luck and Trouble") 4-6 71
MINIT (602 "Bad Luck and Trouble") 15-20 59

BOOGIE KINGS
Singles: 7-inch
MONTEL (939 "Crying Man") 5-10 65
MONTEL (984 "Philly Walk") 5-10 66
PAULA (260 "Philly Walk") 5-10 67
PAULA (272 "Bonie Maronie") 5-10 67
PIC 1 (129 "This Is Blue-Eyed Soul") 10-15 66
PIC 1 (133 "That's Really Some Good") .. 10-15 67
LPs: 10/12-inch
MONTEL (104 "Boogie Kings") 30-50 66
MONTEL (109 "Blue-Eyed Soul") 30-50 66
Members: Gee Gee Shin; Jerry Lacroix.

BOOGIE MAN
(John Lee Hooker)
Singles: 78 rpm
ACORN (308 "Morning Blues") 30-50 50
Also see HOOKER, John Lee

BOOGIE RAMBLERS
Singles: 78 rpm
GOLDBAND (1130 "Cindy Lou") 20-30 57
Singles: 7-inch
GOLDBAND (1130 "Cindy Lou") 15-25 57
Member: Huey Thierry.
Also see COOKIE & CUPCAKES

BOOK OF CHANGES
Singles: 7-inch
TOWER (337 "I Stole the Goodyear Blimp") 15-25 67
Members: Bob Bailey; Frank Smith; Joseph Bracket; Arthur Penthollow; Roland Stone.

BOOKENDS
Singles: 7-inch
CAPITOL (4667 "Let Me Walk with You") 15-25 61

BOOKER, Bea
Singles: 7-inch
PEACOCK (1682 "If I Had Known") 10-20 58

BOOKER, Charley
(Charlie Booker)
Singles: 78 rpm
BLUES & RHYTHM (7003 "Rabbit Blues") 150-200 51
(7-inch 78 rpm single.)
BLUES & RHYTHM 50-75 51
(10-inch single.)
MODERN (878 "Moonrise Blues") 50-75 51
Singles: 7-inch
MODERN (878 "Moonrise Blues") 100-200 51
Also see GILMORE, Boyd /Houston Boines / Charlie Booker

BOOKER, John Lee
(John L. Booker; John Lee Hooker)
Singles: 78 rpm
CHANCE 300-500 51-52
CHESS (1462 "Mad Man Blues") 75-125 51
DELUXE 50-75 53
GONE (60 "Mad Man Blues") 300-500 51
MODERN 25-50 51
ROCKIN' 25-50 53
Singles: 7-inch
CHANCE (1108 "Miss Lorraine") 1200-1800 51
CHANCE (1110 "Graveyard Blues") 1200-1800 51
CHANCE (1122 "609 Boogie") 800-1200 51
DELUXE (6004 "Blue Monday") 100-200 53
DELUXE (6032 "Pouring Down Rain") . 100-200 53
DELUXE (6046 "My Baby Don't Love Me") 100-200 53
MODERN (852 "Ground Hog Blues") ... 100-200 51
ROCKIN' (524 "Blue Monday") 100-200 53
ROCKIN' (525 "Pouring Down Rain") ... 100-200 53
Also see HOOKER, John Lee

BOOKER, Ronnie, & Boardwalkers
Singles: 7-inch
REX (103 "She Won't Go Steady") 400-500 61

BOOKER T. & MGs *P&R/R&B/LP '62*
Singles: 12-inch
A&M 4-8 82-84
Singles: 7-inch
A&M 3-5 81-82
ASYLUM 4-6 77
EPIC 4-6 75
STAX (Except 100 series) 4-8 67-71
STAX (100 series) 5-10 62-66
VOLT (102 "Green Onions") 20-30 62
LPs: 10/12-inch
A&M 8-10 72-81
ASYLUM 5-10 77
ATLANTIC 10-12 68
ATLANTIC/ATCO (133 "Excerpts from *In the Christmas Spirit*") 15-20 66
(Promotional issue only. One side is excerpts from *Soul Christmas*, a various artists LP.)
EPIC 8-10 74
PICKWICK 5-10
STAX (700 series, except 701 & 713) 20-30 65-68
STAX (701 "Green Onions") 25-40 62
STAX (713 "In the Christmas Spirit") 200-300 66
(Hands and keyboard drawing on front cover. Back has 1966 copyright date.)
STAX (713 " In the Christmas Spirit ") 15-25 67
(Christmas ornament cover. Back has 1967 copyright date.)
STAX (2000 series) 10-20 68-71
STAX (8000 series) 5-10 81-84
Members: Booker T. Jones; Steve Cropper; Al Jackson Jr.; Louis Steinberg; Willie Hall; Donald "Duck" Dunn.
Also see MAR-KEYS / Booker T. & MGs
Also see REDDING, Otis
Also see SANTANA
Also see SIMON, Paul
Also see TRIUMPHS

BOOMERANGS
Singles: 7-inch
BANDERA (689 "Telling Lies") 75-100 64
(First issue.)
CHECKER (1095 "Telling Lies") 30-40 64

BOONE, Pat *P&R/R&B '55*
(With Billy Vaughn & Orchestra; with Lew Douglas & Orchestra)
Singles: 78 rpm
DOT 10-25 55-58
REPUBLIC 10-15 54
Singles: 7-inch
ABC 4-6 74-75
BUENA VISTA (487 "Sounds of Christmas") 4-6 73
CAPITOL 4-6 70
CHEVROLET/RCA (4988 "June Is Bustin' Out All Over") 10-20 58
(Promotional issue. Made for Chevrolet dealers. Narration by Bob Lund.)
DOT (9 "Walking the Floor Over You") ...... 5-10 '60s
DOT (200 series) 15-25 59-60
DOT (15338 thru 15490) 20-25 55-56
(Maroon label.)
DOT (15521 thru 15982) 10-20 57-59
(Black label.)
DOT (16006 thru 16641) 8-15 59-64
DOT (16658 "Beach Girl") 30-40 64
(With Bruce Johnston and Terry Melcher.)
DOT (16668 thru 16998) 5-10 64-67
DOT (17000 series) 4-8 67-75
HITSVILLE 4-6 76-77
LION 4-6 72
MC 4-6 77
MCA 3-5 84
MGM 4-6 71-73
MELODYLAND 4-6 74-76
ORCHID 3-5 89
REPUBLIC (7049 "Until You Tell Me So") 20-30 54
REPUBLIC (7062 "Remember to Be Mine") 20-30 54
REPUBLIC (7084 "I Need Someone") 20-30 54
REPUBLIC (7119 "I Need Someone") 20-30 54
SRG 3-5 88
TETRAGRAMMATON 4-6 69
W.B. 3-5 80-81
Picture Sleeves
DOT 12-25 57-62
EPs: 7-inch
DOT 15-25 57-60
LPs: 10/12-inch
ABC 5-10 74
BIBLE VOICE 5-10 70
CANDLELITE 5-10
(Mail-order offer.)
DOT (3000 series) 25-45 55-56
(Maroon label.)
DOT (3000 series, except 3501) 12-25 57-67
(Black label. Monaural series.)
DOT (3501 "Pat Boone Sings Guess Who") 30-40 63
(Monaural.)
DOT (9000 "April Love") 30-40 57
(Soundtrack.)
DOT (25000 series, except 25270 & 25501) 10-25 58-68
(Stereo series.)
DOT (25270 "Moonglow") 10-20 60
(Black vinyl.)
DOT (25270 "Moonglow") 50-100 60
(Colored vinyl.)
DOT (25501 "Pat Boone Sings Guess Who") 35-45 63
(Stereo.)
FAMOUS TWINSET 5-8 74
HAMILTON 10-12 65
HITSVILLE 8-10 76
LAMB & LION 5-10 73-81
MC 5-10 77
MCA 5-10 82
MGM 5-10 73
PARAMOUNT 5-10 74
PICKWICK 5-10 79
SEECO (3012 "Pat Boone") .... 40-60 '50s
SUPREME 5-10 70
TETRAGRAMMATON 10-12 69
WORD 5-10 75-84
Also see BRUCE & TERRY
Also see DOUGLAS, Lew
Also see FONTANE SISTERS
Also see HUSKY, Ferlin / Pat Boone
Also see JENKINS, Gordon, & His Orchestra
Also see VAUGHN, Billy, Orchestra
Also see WARD, Robin

BOONE, Pat & Shirley
(Pat Boone Family)
Singles: 7-inch
DOT 4-6 62-64
MGM 4-6 72
MELODYLAND 4-6 75
MOTOWN 4-6 74
W.B. 4-6 79
EPs: 7-inch
DOT 5-10 59
LPs: 10/12-inch
DOT (3199 "Side by Side") 10-20 59
(Monaural.)
DOT (25199 "Side by Side") 15-25 59
(Stereo.)
LION 5-10 72
WORD 5-10 71

BOONE, Pat, & Boone Girls
Singles: 7-inch
LION 4-6 72
Also see BOONE, Pat & Shirley

BOONE'S JUMPIN' JACKS *R&B '43*
Singles: 78 rpm
DECCA (8644 "Please Be Careful") 25-50 43
Members: Chester Boone; George Johnson; Chauncey Graham; Vernon King; Buster Smith; Lloyd Phillips.

BOOT, Joe, & Fabulous Winds
(With the Floyd Standifer Orchestra)
Singles: 7-inch
CELESTIAL (111 "Rock and Roll Radio") 30-40 58

BOOTH, Charlie
Singles: 7-inch
LORI (9534 "Fishin' Fits") 50-60 62
LORI (9537 "Lord Made Man") 20-30 62
LORI (9538 "Give Me a Chance") 20-30 63

BOOTH, Chico
(With Upsetters; Quintet)
Singles: 7-inch
LEN (1012 "Skippin") 10-20 61
PALM (200 "Hot Peppers") 10-15 60
TRIEST ("Hot Pepper") 15-25 60
(First issue. Selection number not known.)

BOOTH, Henry
Singles: 7-inch
DELUXE (6190 "Starting from Tonight") .. 15-20 61
Also see MIDNIGHTERS
Also see ROYALS

BOOTMEN
Singles: 7-inch
ETIQUETTE (10 "Black Widow") 10-20 64
RIVERTON (104 "Wherever You Hide") .. 25-50 66
Members: F. Dickerson; D. McCaslin; M. Moore.

BOOTS, Don
Singles: 7-inch
BUDDY (114 "Big Fat Annie") 200-300

BOOTS, Joe
Singles: 7-inch
CONTINENTAL 30-50

BOP KATS
EPs: 7-inch
("Bop Kats") 300-500
(No label name or selection number used.)

BOP SHOO BOPS
Singles: 7-inch
CENPRO (45005 "Play Those Oldies Mr. DJ") 30-50 75

BOP-CHORDS
("Featuring Ernest Harriston")
Singles: 78 rpm
HOLIDAY 30-40 56
Singles: 7-inch
HOLIDAY (2601 "Castle in the Sky") 75-125 56
(Black label.)
HOLIDAY (2601 "Castle in the Sky") 50-100 56
(Orange label.)
HOLIDAY (2601 "Castle in the Sky") .... 15-25 '60s
(Glossy red label. Has double horizontal lines.)

HOLIDAY (2601 "Castle in the Sky") .... 10-15 '60s
(Flat red label. Has single horizontal line.)
HOLIDAY (2603 "When I Woke Up This Morning") 75-125 57
(Black label.)
HOLIDAY (2603 "When I Woke Up This Morning") .... 15-25 '60s
(Glossy red label. Has double horizontal lines.)
HOLIDAY (2603 "When I Woke Up This Morning") .... 10-15 '60s
(Flat red label. Has single horizontal line.)
HOLIDAY (2608 "Baby") 400-500 57
(Glossy red label.)
LOST NITE .... 3-5 '80s
SIOUX (8260 "Hi-Voltage") 10-20 60

LPs: 10/12-inch

LOST NITE (11 "Bop-Chords") 10-20 81
(10-inch LP. Red vinyl. 1000 made.)
Members: Ernest Harriston; Kenny "Butch" Hamilton; Morris "Mickey" Smarr; Leon Ivey; William Dailey; Peggy Jones; Skip Boyd.
Also see CHARTS / Bop - Chords / Ladders / Harmonaires
Also see 5 WINGS

BOPPERS

Singles: 7-inch

CHA CHA (701 "Be-Bop-a Jean") 200-300 59
(Reissued as by Ron Haydock & Boppers.)
Also see HAYDOCK, Ron, & Boppers

BOPPIN' BILLIES

Singles: 7-inch

MOPIC (9682 "Greens Rock") 15-25 59
(Identification number used since no selection number is shown. Has group photo on label.)
Member: Bill Green.

BOPTONES

Singles: 7-inch

EMBER (1043 "I Had a Love") 50-60 58

BORDERS, Tony

Singles: 7-inch

DELTA (1902 "Counting on You") 10-15 61
HALL/HALLWAY 8-12 63-65
QUINVY (001 "For My Woman's Love") .. 10-15
REVUE 5-10 68-69
SOUTH CAMP (7009 "You Better Believe It") 10-15
TCF (124 "Stay By My Side") 8-12 65

BORDERSONG

Singles: 7-inch

GREAT NORTHWEST (704 "She's a Good Woman") 10-20 76

LPs: 10/12-inch

REAL GOOD (1001 "Morning") 75-100 75
Members: Ann Wilson; Nancy Wilson.
Also see HEART

BORN, Mike

Singles: 7-inch

ABEL (230 "I Love You Baby") 30-40 59

BOSS FIVE

Singles: 7-inch

IMPACT (1003 "You Cheat Too Much") .. 15-25 66

BOSS FOUR

Singles: 7-inch

RIM (2025 "Walkin' By") 15-25 59

BOSS TWEADS

Singles: 7-inch

STUDIO CITY (1056 "Goin' Away") 100-150 66

BOSSMEN

Singles: 7-inch

SCORE (1001 "Mashed Potatoes") 15-25 64
SCORE (1003 "I'm Ready") 15-25 64
Members: Jesse Perales; Pete Perez; Vince Nares.
Also see MANDO & CHILI PEPPERS

BOSSMEN
(Boss-Men)

Singles: 7-inch

BECK (112 "Take a Look") .... 10-20 '60s
DICTO 10-20 65
LUCKY ELEVEN (001 "Tina Marie") .... 8-12 '60s
LUCKY ELEVEN (227 thru 231) 8-12 66
M&L (1809 "Help Me Baby") 8-12
SOFT (121 "Take a Look") .... 10-20 '60s

BOSSTONES
(Boss-Tones)

Singles: 7-inch

BOSS (401 "Mope-Itty Mope") 50-100 59
(Credits "Boss-Tones.")
BOSS (501 "Moptity Mope") 100-150 59
(Despite higher selection number, this seems to be the first pressing. Certainly copies of 401 with "Dist. Nationally - Ember" are later issues. Each has a differently spelled title and artist.)
LOST NITE .... 4-6 '70s
V-TONE (208 "Mope-Itty Mope") 40-60 60

BOSTELS

Singles: 7-inch

FUN (1092 "Oriental Goddess") 50-75 66
(Identification number shown since no selection number is used.)

BOSTIC, Earl — R&B '48

Singles: 78 rpm

GOTHAM 5-15 46-51
KING 5-15 47-58
MAJESTIC 5-10 46
QUALITY/KING 8-12 54
(Canadian.)

Singles: 7-inch

GOTHAM (7154 "845 Stomp") 25-35 51
KING (500 series) 4-6 77
KING (4000 series, except 4491) 10-20 50-57
(Black vinyl.)
KING (4491 "I Got Loaded") 25-40 52
KING (4000 series) 25-50 52-56
(Colored vinyl.)
KING (5000 series) 5-15 57-65
KING (6000 series) 5-10 65-69
KING (15000 series) 4-6 72
QUALITY/KING (4289 "These Foolish Things") 15-25 54
(Canadian.)
20TH FOX (5017 "Hot Sauce! Boss") 10-20

EPs: 7-inch

KING 10-25 52-62

LPs: 10/12-inch

GRAND PRIX (416 "Earl Bostic") .... 15-20 '60s
KING (64 "Earl Bostic & His Alto Sax") ... 50-100 51
(Black vinyl. 10-inch LP.)
KING (64 "Earl Bostic & His Alto Sax"). 100-200 51
(Colored vinyl. 10-inch LP.)
KING (72 "Earl Bostic & His Alto Sax") ... 50-100 52
(10-inch LP.)
KING (76 "Earl Bostic & His Alto Sax") ... 50-100 52
(10-inch LP.)
KING (77 "Earl Bostic & His Alto Sax") ... 50-100 52
(10-inch LP.)
KING (78 "Earl Bostic & His Alto Sax") ... 50-100 52
(10-inch LP.)
KING (79 "Earl Bostic & His Alto Sax") ... 50-100 52
(10-inch LP.)
KING (95 "Earl Bostic Plays Old Standards") 50-100 54
(10-inch LP.)
KING (103 "Earl Bostic & His Alto Sax"). 50-100 54
(10-inch LP.)
KING (119 "Earl Bostic & His Alto Sax"). 50-100 54
(10-inch LP.)
KING (500 series) 20-50 55-58
KING (600 thru 1000 series) 8-18 59-70
KING (5000 series) 10-15 77
Also see HAMPTON, Lionel
Also see PAGE, Hot Lips

BOSTIC, Earl, & Bill Doggett

Singles: 78 rpm

KING 6-12 56

Singles: 7-inch

KING 10-15 56
Also see DOGGETT, Bill

BOSTIC, Earl / Jimmie Lunceford

LP: 10/12-inch

ALLEGRO 8-12
Also see BOSTIC, Earl

BOSTICK, Calvin

Singles: 78 rpm

CHESS (1530 "Four Eleven Boogie") 30-40 52
CHESS (1572 "Bang Bang Blues") 10-20 53

Singles: 7-inch

CHESS (1530 "Four Eleven Boogie") ... 100-150 52
CHESS (1572 "Bang Bang Blues") 25-35 53

BOSTON — P&R/LP '76

Singles: 12-inch

EPIC (491 "Don't Look Back") 5-8 78
(Promotional issue only.)

Singles: 7-inch

EPIC 4-6 76-79
MCA 3-5 85-87

Picture Sleeves

MCA 3-5 85-87

LPs: 10/12-inch

EPIC (E99-34188 "Boston") 15-25 78
(Picture disc. Without cover.)
EPIC (E99-34188 "Boston") 30-40 78
(Picture disc. With cover.)
EPIC (HE-34188 "Boston") 12-15 80
(Half-speed mastered.)
EPIC (34188 "Boston") 15-25 76
(With "JE" or "PE" prefix.)
EPIC (35000 series, except 35050) 10-12 78
EPIC (35050 "Don't Look Back") 10-20 78
(Promotional black vinyl issue.)
EPIC (35050 "Don't Look Back") 50-60 80
(Picture disc.)
EPIC (35050 "Don't Look Back") 65-75 80
(Promotional picture disc.)
EPIC (HE-45000 series) 12-15 81
(Half-speed mastered.)
MCA 5-10 85-87
MFSL (249 "Boston") 25-35
Members: Brad Delp; Barry Goudreau; Sib Hashian; Tom Scholz; Fran Sheehan.
Also see ORION THE HUNTER

BOSTON, Bobby

Singles: 7-inch

STAR-WIN (7001 "Lazy Daisy") 50-100

BOSTON POPS ORCHESTRA — P&R '38
(Conducted by Arthur Fiedler)

Singles: 78 rpm

RCA 3-5 49-57
VICTOR 3-6 38

Singles: 7-inch

POLYDOR 4-6 70
RCA 4-8 50-65
RCA RED SEAL (Colored vinyl) .... 5-10 '50s

Picture Sleeves

RCA (8378 "I Want to Hold Your Hand") .. 10-15 64

EPs: 7-inch

RCA 4-8 50-61
RCA RED SEAL (Colored vinyl) .... 8-12 '50s

LPs: 10/12-inch

CAMDEN 4-8
DEUTSCHE GRAMMOPHON 4-8 78
FLEETWOOD 4-8 72
MIDSONG INT'L 4-8 79
PICKWICK/CAMDEN 4-8
POLYDOR 5-10 71-72
QUINTESSENCE 4-8
RCA 5-20 50-69
RCA/READER'S DIGEST (48 "Boston Pops Orchestra") 25-50 67
(Boxed, 10-disc set.)
Also see ATKINS, Chet, & Boston Pops
Also see ELLINGTON, Duke, & Boston Pops
Also see GETZ, Stan, & Boston Pops Orchestra
Also see SHERMAN, Allan

BOSTON TEA PARTY

Singles: 7-inch

BIG BOSS (1002 "Words") 30-40 67
CHALLENGE (59368 "Words") 20-30 67
FLICK-DISC (900 "Free Service") 15-25 68
FONA (311 "Is It Love") 20-30 67
VOGUE INT'L (101 "My Daze") 20-30 67

LPs: 10/12-inch

FLICK DISC (45,000 "The Boston Tea Party") 50-75 68
Members: Travis Fields; Mike Stevens; Richard De Perna; Robert De Perna; Dave Novogroski.

BOSWELL, JoAnn, & ElTones / ElTones

Singles: 78 rpm

CHIEF 100-150 55

Singles: 7-inch

CHIEF (8 00 "You Were Meant for Me"/"I Won't Be Your Fool") 300-400 55

BOTTLE COMPANY

Singles: 7-inch

HIDEOUT (1230 "Lives for No One") ... 100-150 '60s

BOTTOMS, Custer
(With the Bill Woods Band)

Singles: 7-inch

BAKERSFIELD (108 "Stood Up Blues") 400-600

BOULEVARDS

Singles: 7-inch

EVEREST (19316 "Delores") 20-30 59

BOUNTY, Rick, & Rockits

Singles: 7-inch

BOW (6144 "It'll Be Me") 100-150 58
MASSABESIC (102 "Folsom Prison Blues") 5-10 86
(600 made.)

Picture Sleeves

MASSABESIC (102 "Folsom Prison Blues") 3-5 86
(Pictures Bounty with guitar and credits Rockits. 100 made.)
MASSABESIC (102 "Folsom Prison Blues") 3-5 86
(Pictures Bounty without guitar and does not credit Rockits. 100 made.)

BOUQUETS

Singles: 7-inch

BLUE CAT (115 "Welcome to My Heart") 15-25 65
MALA (472 "I Love Him So") 5-10 64
VEST (8000 "Yeah Babe") 10-20 63

BOURBONS

Singles: 7-inch

ROYAL FAMILY (267 "A Dark Corner") ... 20-30 67

BOURELL, Ray

Singles: 7-inch

REVA (103 "Bad News") 100-200

BOW STREET RUNNERS

LPs: 10/12-inch

B.T. PUPPY (1026 "Bow Street Runners") 800-1000 70

BOWDEN, Don

Singles: 7-inch

JAN (104 "My Heaven") 10-20 58
LAGREE ("TV Commercials") 50-75
(Selection number not known.)

BOWEN, Bill, & Rockets

Singles: 78 rpm

METEOR 200-300 56

Singles: 7-inch

METEOR (5033 "Don't Shoot Me Baby") 1000-2000 56

BOWEN, Billy
(With the Butterball Four; with Butterball Five)

Singles: 78 rpm

MGM 10-20 52

Singles: 7-inch

MGM (11271 "You Broke My Heart") 30-40 52
X-TRA (101 "Butterball") .... 75-100 '50s
Also see CHANELLS / Butterballs

BOWEN, Jimmy — P&R/R&B '57

Singles: 78 rpm

ROULETTE 25-50 57

Singles: 7-inch

CAPEHART (5005 "Teenage Dreamworld") 10-15 61
CREST (1085 "Don't Drop It") 10-15 61
REPRISE 5-10 64-66
ROULETTE (4001 "I'm Stickin' with You") 30-40 57
(With roulette wheel circling label. Label may be either red/orange or maroon.)
ROULETTE (4001 "I'm Stickin' with You") 15-25 57
(With roulette wheel on top half of label.)
ROULETTE (4001 "I'm Stickin' with You") 10-20 57
(No roulette wheel on label.)
ROULETTE (4002 "Party Doll") 30-40 57
(Credited to "Jimmy Bowen with the Rhythm Orchids" though actually by Buddy Knox.)
ROULETTE (4010 thru 4224) 10-20 57-60

Picture Sleeves

CAPEHART (5005 "Teenage Dreamworld") 30-40 61

EPs: 7-inch

ROULETTE (302 "Jimmy Bowen")........... 50-75 57

LPs: 10/12-inch

REPRISE (6210 "Sunday Morning with the Comics").......... 20-25 66
ROULETTE (25004 "Jimmy Bowen") 75-100 57
(Black label.)
ROULETTE (25004 "Jimmy Bowen") .. 100-150 57
(White label. Promotional issue only.)
ROULETTE (25004 "Jimmy Bowen") 5-10
(Reissue for the Outlet Book Co. and Publishers Central Bureau, and labeled as such.)
Members (Rhythm Orchids): Buddy Knox; Jimmy Bowen; Dave Alldred; Don Lanier.
Also see KNOX, Buddy / Jimmy Bowen

BOWENS, James

Singles: 7-inch

ROOSEVELT LEE (21831 "This Boy and Girl") 20-30

BOWENS, Pvt. Charles

Singles: 7-inch

ROJAC (111 "Christmas in Viet Nam").... 15-20 66

BOWER, Chuck, & Stardusters

Singles: 78 rpm

BLUE RIBBON (101 "Cy Boogie") 10-20 55

Singles: 7-inch

BLUE RIBBON (101 "Cy Boogie") 25-35 55

BOWERS, Chuck
(With the Anita Kerr Singers)

Singles: 78 rpm

CHOICE.......... 15-25 56
DECCA.......... 5-10 57

Singles: 7-inch

CHOICE (841 "Pinball Boogie") 50-75 56
DECCA (30356 "Till My Baby Comes Home")........... 10-20 57
DECCA (30578 "Blabber Mouth") 10-20 58
Also see KERR, Anita

BOWIE, David — P&R/LP '72

Singles: 12-inch

EMI AMERICA.......... 5-10 82-87
RCA.......... 10-15 79-80

Promotional 12-inch Singles

EMI AMERICA.......... 8-15 82-87
RCA.......... 15-25 79-80

Singles: 7-inch

BACKSTREET 3-5 82
DERAM (85009 "Rubber Band")............. 20-40 67
DERAM (85016 "Did You Ever Have a Dream")........... 20-40 67
EMI AMERICA.......... 3-5 83-87
(Black vinyl.)
EMI AMERICA (8231 "Blue Jean") 5-8 84
(Colored vinyl.)
EMI AMERICA (8246 "Tonight")..................6-10 84
(Limited edition with poster sleeve.)
LONDON (20079 "The Laughing Gnome")........... 15-25 73
MCA/BACKSTREET ("Cat People") 50-65 82
(Promotional only picture disc. No selection number used.)
MCA/BACKSTREET ("Cat People") 75-90 82
(Promotional only picture disc. No selection number used. B-side says: "Filmex" promo.)
MERCURY (72949 "Space Oddity") 30-50 69
MERCURY (73075 "Memory of a Free Festival")........... 35-50 70
MERCURY (73173 "All the Madmen")..... 40-60 71
RCA.......... 3-6 71-84
W.B. (5815 "Can't Help Thinking About Me")........... 50-75 66

Picture Sleeves

BACKSTREET (1767 "Cat People") 4-8 82
EMI AMERICA.......... 3-5 83-87
RCA (0001 "Time") 200-400 73
RCA (0719 "Starman").......... 15-20 72
RCA (0876 "Space Oddity").......... 10-15 73
RCA (12078 "Ashes to Ashes").......... 10-15 80
RCA (12134 "Fashion").......... 5-10 80
RCA (13660 "White Light White Heat").........3-5 83
RCA (13769 "1984")..........3-5 80

Promotional Singles

BACKSTREET.......... 5-10 82
DERAM (85009 "Rubber Band")............. 30-40 67
EMI AMERICA (8158 thru 8190)..............4-8 83-84
EMI AMERICA (8231 "Blue Jean") 4-8 84
EMI AMERICA (8246 thru 8308)..................4-8 83-86
EMI AMERICA (8380 "Day in Day Out") 4-8 87
EMI AMERICA (8380 "Day in Day Out") ..15-20 87
(Colored vinyl. Boxed edition.)
EMI AMERICA (43000 series) 4-8 87
LONDON (20079 "The Laughing Gnome").......... 15-25 73
MERCURY (311 "All the Madmen").........40-60 70
MERCURY (72949 "Space Oddity").........30-50 69
MERCURY (73075 "Memory of a Free Festival")..........40-60 70
RCA.......... 5-12 71-84
W.B. (5815 "Can't Help Thinking About Me")..........50-75 66
WHAT'S IT ALL ABOUT .... 10-20 '70s

EPs: 7-inch

RCA.......... 20-25 '70s
(Promotional issues only.)

LPs: 10/12-inch

DERAM (16003 "David Bowie")...........100-200 67
(Monaural.)
DERAM (18003 "David Bowie")...........100-200 67
(Stereo.)
EMI AMERICA.......... 5-10 83-87
LONDON.......... 10-20 73-85
MFSL (064 "Rise and Fall of Ziggy Stardust")..........50-75 82
MFSL (083 "Let's Dance")..........40-60 82
MERCURY (61246 "Man of Words/Man of Music")..........75-125 69
MERCURY (61246 "Space Oddity")..........10-20 72
MERCURY (61325 "The Man Who Sold the World")..........50-75 71
(Front cover pictures Bowie wearing a dress.)
MERCURY (61325 "The Man Who Sold the World")..........20-30 '70s
(Front and back covers have cartoon drawings.)
MERCURY (61325 "The Man Who Sold the World")..........10-15
(Front cover pictures Bowie in concert.)
PRECISION (1 "Don't Be Fooled By the Name")..........20-25 81
(10-inch LP.)
RCA (0291 "Bowie Pin Ups")..........10-15 73
RCA (0576 "Diamond Dogs")........... 2000-3000 74
(With "Dog Genitals" cover.)
RCA (0576 "Diamond Dogs")..........10-15 74
(With dog's genitals covered.)
RCA (0700 thru 1300 series)..........10-15 74-76
RCA (1732 "Changesone Bowie")........100-200 76
(With alternate take of *John, I'm Only Dancing.* Lyrics are: Annie's kind of sweet, she always eats her meat. But Joey comes on strong. Bet your life he's putting us on.)
RCA (1732 "Changesone Bowie")...........10-20 76
(With the commonly issued take of *John, I'm Only Dancing.* Lyrics are: Annie's pretty neat, she always eats her meat. But Joe is awful strong. Bet your life he's putting us on.)
RCA (2000 thru 2500)..........10-15 77
RCA (2743 "Peter and the Wolf")..........10-15 78
(Black vinyl. With Eugene Ormandy & Philadelphia Orchestra.)
RCA (2743 "Peter and the Wolf")..........40-60 78
(Colored vinyl. With Eugene Ormandy & Philadelphia Orchestra.)
RCA (2900 thru 4200 series)..........5-10 79-82
RCA (4600 thru 4800 series)..........10-20 71-73
(With "LSP" prefix.)
RCA (4700 thru 4900 series, except 4862)..........5-10 83-84
(With "AFL," "AYL" or "CPL" prefix.)
RCA 4862 "Ziggy Stardust")..........5-10 83
(Black vinyl.)
RCA 4862 "Ziggy Stardust")..........60-80 83
(Clear vinyl.)
RYKODISC (Except 0120/2)..........8-12 87-90
RYKODISC (0120/2 "Sound and Vision").50-75 89
(Boxed, six-disc set.)

Promotional LPs

DERAM (18003 "David Bowie")...........250-350 67
EMI AMERICA (9960 "Let's Talk")..........50-75 83
MERCURY (61246 "Man of Words/Man of Music")..........75-125 69
MERCURY (61325 "The Man Who Sold the World")..........75-125 71
RCA (0200 thru 4800 series)..........20-40 71-73
(With programmer's strip on front cover.)
RCA (2697 "Bowie Now")..........30-50 78
RCA (3016 "An Evening with David Bowie")..........150-200 78
RCA (3545 "Bowie 1980")..........50-75 80
RCA (3829 "RCA Special Radio Series").30-50 80
RCA (3840 "Interview")..........35-50 80
RCA (11306 "Peter and the Wolf") 30-40 78
Also see HOUSTON, Cissy
Also see QUEEN & DAVID BOWIE
Also see TURNER, Tina

BOWIE, David / Joe Cocker / Youngbloods

LPs: 10/12-inch

MERCURY (SRD-2-29 "Zig Zag Festival")..........50-75 70
(Promotional issue only.)
Also see COCKER, Joe
Also see YOUNGBLOODS

BOWIE, David, & Bing Crosby

Singles: 7-inch

RCA (13400 "Peace on Earth")..........8-12 77
(Promotional issue only.)
RCA..........3-6 83

Picture Sleeves

RCA (13400 "Peace on Earth")..........8-12 77
(Promotional issue only.)
RCA..........4-8 83
Also see CROSBY, Bing

BOWIE, David, & Mick Jagger — P&R/D&D '85

Singles: 12-inch

EMI AMERICA (19200 "Dancing in the Streets")..........8-12 85

Singles: 7-inch

EMI AMERICA (8288 "Dancing in the Streets")..........3-5 85

Picture Sleeves

EMI AMERICA (8288 "Dancing in the Streets")..........3-5 85
Also see JAGGER, Mick

BOWIE, David, & Pat Metheny Group — P&R/D&D '85

Singles: 12-inch

EMI AMERICA..........4-8 85

Singles: 7-inch

EMI AMERICA..........3-5 85

Picture Sleeves

EMI AMERICA..........3-5 85

LPs: 10/12-inch

EMI AMERICA..........5-10 85

BOWIE, David / Iggy Pop

Singles: 12-inch

RCA (10956 "Sound and Vision")..........30-50 77
(Promotional issue only.)
Also see BOWIE, David
Also see POP, Iggy

BOWLES, Doug, & Rubarbs

Singles: 7-inch

TUNE (206 "Cadillac Cutie")..........75-125 59

BOWMAN, Bob

Singles: 7-inch

REVELLO (1001 "Betty Lou")..........75-125 59

BOWMAN, Cecil

Singles: 7-inch

D (1048 "Man a Waitin' ")..........50-75 59
STARDAY (336 "Blues Around My Door ")..........150-250 57

BOWMAN, Jane

Singles: 7-inch

SAPIEN (1002 "Dearest Little Angel")....75-125 61
SAPIEN (1005 "Eternally")..........75-125 61
(Yellow vinyl.)

BOWMAN, Leon

EPs: 7-inch

REED (903 "Rockin' the Blues")..........250-350

BOWMAN, Leroy

Singles: 7-inch

REGIS (1002 "Graveyard")..........75-100

BOWMAN, Priscilla

Singles: 7-inch

ABNER (1018 "A Rockin' Good Way").....10-20 58
ABNER (1033 "Like a Baby")..........10-20 60
FALCON (1004 "Yes I'm Glad")..........15-25 57
FALCON (1008 "Sugar Daddy")..........15-25 57
Also see MC SHANN, Jay, & Priscilla Bowman

BOWMAN, Ralph / Ray Lunsford

Singles: 7-inch

EXCELLENT (400 "Tragedy of School Bus 27"/"Sheila")..........10-20 58

BOWMAN BROTHERS & NORMAN PETTY TRIO

Singles: 7-inch

COLUMBIA (41176 "Hey Pumpkin") 15-25 58
Also see CRAWFORD, Fred
Also see HUDDLE, Jack

BOWSER, Donnie — C&W '89
(Little Donnie Bowshier & Radio Ranch Boys; Donnie Bowshier)

Singles: 7-inch

BAMBOO (508 "Talk to Me")..........150-200 61
CHOICE..........10-15
DESS (7002 "Rock and Roll Joys")......150-200 57
DESS (7004 "I Love You Baby")..........50-75 57
ERA (3029 "I Love You Baby")..........15-25 60
FRATERNITY (801 "I Love You Baby")...30-40 58
J.D. (379 "Move It Over")..........50-75
RIDGEWOOD..........3-5 89
ROBBINS (1001 "I Love You Baby")....100-150 58
ROBBINS (1009 "I Love You Baby")........50-80 59
ROME..........4-8
SAGE (265 "Stone Heart")..........30-50 58
SAGE (276 "Got the Best of Me")..........50-75 58
STOP (406 "Pretty Things")..........4-8 71

BOWTIES
(Cirino & Bowties)

Singles: 78 rpm

ROYAL ROOST..........10-15 55-56

Singles: 7-inch

ROYAL ROOST..........15-25 55-56
Members: Cirino Colocrai (a.k.a. Del Serino); Jimmy Piro; John Granada; Vince Sepaldo.
Also see SERINO

BOX, David
(With Bob Moore's Orchestra & Chorus)

Singles: 7-inch

CANDIX (339 "If You Can't Say Something Nice")..........10-20 62
JOED (114 "If You Can't Say Something Nice")..........8-12 63
JOED (116 "Little Lonesome Summer Girl")..........10-20 64
Also see CRICKETS
Also see MOORE, Bob

BOX TOPS — P&R/R&B/LP '67

Singles: 7-inch

BELL (865 thru 981)..........5-8 70-71
FLASHBACK (9488 "Neon Rainbow") 3-5 86
GUSTO (2112 "The Letter")..........3-6 84
HI (2228 thru 2242)..........5-8 72-73
MALA..........5-10 67-69
PHILCO (27 "The Letter") 25-30 67
("Hip-Pocket" flexi-disc.)
SPHERE SOUND (77001 "The Letter").....5-10 67
SPHERE SOUND (77002 "Cry Like a Baby")..........5-8 70
STAX (0199 "It's Gonna Be Okay")..........4-6 74

LPs: 10/12-inch

BELL (6011 "The Letter/Neon Rainbow") 20-25 67
(Monaural.)
BELL (S-6011 "The Letter/Neon Rainbow")..........15-20 67
(Stereo.)
BELL (6017 "Cry Like a Baby")..........15-20 68
BELL (6023 "Non-Stop")..........15-20 68
BELL (6025 "Super Hits")..........15-20 68
BELL (6032 "Dimensions")..........15-20 69
COTILLION (057 "A Lifetime Believing")..10-20 71
KORY (3007 "Best of the Box Tops")........8-12 76
RHINO (161 "Greatest Hits")..........8-12 82
Members: Alex Chilton; Rick Allen; Tom Boggs; Harold Cloud; Bill Cunningham; John Evans; Swain Scharfar; Gary Talley; Danny Smythe; Rick Stevens.
Also see BIG STAR

BOXX, Freda, & Rockin' Aces

Singles: 7-inch

MARLO (1513 "Havin' a Ball")..........50-75 '50s

BOY BLUES

Singles: 7-inch

FRANTIC (2131 "Coming Down to You").20-30 67

BOYCE, Tommy *P&R '62*
Singles: 7-inch
A&M (Except 826)....................5-10 66
A&M (826 "In Case the Wind Should Blow")....................10-12 66
CAPITOL (3136 "Alice My Sweet")....................4-6 71
COLPIX (794 "Let's Go Where the Action Is")....................8-12 66
DOT (16117 "Give Me the Clue")....................15-25 60
MGM (13400 "Pretty Thing")....................8-12 65
MGM (13429 "Little Suzie Somethin' ")....................8-12 65
RCA (7975 "Along Came Linda")....................15-25 61
RCA (8025 thru 8208)....................10-15 62-63
R-DELL (111 "Betty Jean")....................20-30 58
WOW (345 "Little One")....................10-20 61
LPs: 10/12-inch
CAMDEN (2202 "Twofold Talent")....................15-25 68

BOYCE, Tommy, & Bobby Hart *P&R/LP '67*
(Boyce & Hart)
Singles: 7-inch
A&M....................5-10 67-69
AQUARIAN (380 "Smilin' ")....................5-10 68
Picture Sleeves
A&M....................8-12 67-69
AQUARIAN....................8-12 68
LPs: 10/12-inch
A&M....................10-20 67-69
Also see BOYCE, Tommy
Also see DOLENZ, JONES, BOYCE & HART
Also see HART, Bobby

BOYD, Barry, & Frantiks
Singles: 7-inch
DART (155 "Walk with Me")....................25-50 61
DONNA (1363 "Wishing")....................10-20 62

BOYD, Bill, & His Cowboy Ramblers
(With Jim Boyd) *C&W '45*
Singles: 78 rpm
BLUEBIRD (Except 33-0530)....................10-15 34-45
BLUEBIRD (33-0530 "Shame On You")..20-30 45
RCA (Except 20-1907)....................5-10 46-50
RCA (20-1907 "New Steel Guitar Rag")..10-20 46
TNT (1019 "Definition of Love")....................5-10 56
Singles: 7-inch
RCA (48-0067 thru 48-0375)....................10-20 49-50
(Green vinyl.)
RCA GOLD STANDARD....................5-10 '50s
TNT (1019 "Definition of Love")....................10-20 56
LPs: 10/12-inch
BLUEBIRD....................20-30
TEXAS ROSE....................10-20
Members [Cowboy Ramblers]: Jim Boyd; Ken Pitts; Knocky Parker; Marvin "Smoky" Montgomery.

BOYD, Billy
LPs: 10/12-inch
CROWN (196 "Twangy Guitars")....................15-20 63
(Stereo. Black vinyl.)
CROWN (196 "Twangy Guitars")....................50-75 63
(Stereo. Colored vinyl.)
CROWN (5170 "Twangy Guitars")....................15-20 63
(Monaural.)
Also see DAILEY, Don

BOYD, Bobby
(Bobby Boyd's Jazz Bombers)
Singles: 78 rpm
20TH CENTURY....................5-10 55
Singles: 7-inch
20TH CENTURY (75034 "Rockin' and Rollin' the Blues")....................15-25 55

BOYD, Donnie
(With the 4 D's)
Singles: 7-inch
DART (1003 "Martha")....................50-75 58
DART (1004 "With All My Heart")....................20-30 58
DART (1005 "Waggle")....................15-25 58
DART (1012 "I Love the Ground You Walk On")....................8-12 59
GALLIANT (1005 "I Love the Ground You Walk On")....................15-25 59
LAUREL (1022 "Brahm's Lullabye # 9")..15-25 59
STAR ANGEL (1020 "With All My Heart")....................75-125 59
(Blue vinyl.)
TWIN STAR (1012 "I Love the Ground You Walk On")....................15-25 60
Also see SULTANS

BOYD, Eddie *R&B '52*
(With His Chess Men; with Daylighters; Eddie Boyd Blues Combo; Little Eddie Boyd & His Boogie Band; "Eddie Boyd Sings and Plays")
Singles: 78 rpm
CHESS....................15-25 52-56
HERALD....................50-75 52
J.O.B.....................25-75 52-57
RCA....................15-25 47-50
Singles: 7-inch
ART TONE (832 "I'm Comin' Home")....................10-15 62
BEA & BABY....................20-30 59
CHESS (1523 thru 1573, except 1541)....40-60 52-54
CHESS (1541 "Third Degree")....................40-60 53
(Black vinyl.)
CHESS (1541 "Third Degree")....................100-200 53
(Red vinyl.)
CHESS (1576 thru 1674)....................20-40 54-57
CHESS (Colored vinyl)....................150-200 54
(We are unable at this time to specify exactly which Chess numbers were pressed on colored vinyl.)
HERALD (406 "I'm Goin' Downtown")....75-125 53
J.O.B. (1007 "Five Long Years")....................75-125 52
(Black vinyl.)
J.O.B. (1007 "Five Long Years")....................200-300 52
(Red vinyl.)
J.O.B. (1009 "It's Miserable to Be Alone")....................40-60 53
J.O.B. (1114 "I Love You")....................150-250 57
KEYHOLE (107 "Come On Home")....................15-20 59
KEYHOLE (114 "All the Way")....................15-20 59
LA SALLE (503 "I Cry")....................10-20 61
MOJO (2167 "It's Too Bad")....................8-12 '60s
ORIOLE (1316 "Five Long Years")....................20-30 58
PALOS (1206 "Empty Arms")....................8-12 63
PUSH (1050 "Ten to One")....................8-12 62
RCA (50-0006 "What Makes These Things Happen to Me")....................35-50 50
(Cherry red vinyl.)
EPs: 7-inch
ESQUIRE (247 "Eddie Boyd Blues Combo")....................25-50 60
LPs: 10/12-inch
EPIC (26409 "7936 South Rhodes")....................15-25 69
LONDON (554 "I'll Dust My Broom")....................15-20 69
Session: Willie Dixon; Howard Dixon; J.T. Brown; James Clark; Lonnie Graham; Sax Mallard; Bill Casimir; Willie Lacey.
Also see BOYD, Ernie
Also see DIXON, Willie

BOYD, Ernie
(Eddie Boyd)
Singles: 78 rpm
REGAL (3305 "Why Don't You Be Wise, Baby")....................35-50 50
Also see BOYD, Eddie

BOYD, Idalia
Singles: 7-inch
DIMENSION (1007 "Hula Hoppin' ")....................15-25 63
Session: Little Eva; Cookies.
Also see COOKIES
Also see LITTLE EVA

BOYD, Jim
Singles: 7-inch
RCA (48-0301 "Mule Boogie")....................15-25 50
(Green vinyl.)

BOYD, Jimmy *P&R/C&W '52*
(Little Jimmy Boyd)
Singles: 78 rpm
COLUMBIA (Except 21571)....................5-10 52-56
COLUMBIA (21571 "Rockin' Down the Mississippi")....................10-15 56
Singles: 7-inch
CAPITOL (4967 "Day Dreamer")....................5-10 63
COLUMBIA (152 "I Saw Mommy Kissing Santa Claus")....................10-20 52
COLUMBIA (21571 "Rockin' Down the Mississippi")....................30-40 56
COLUMBIA (39000 & 40000 series)....................10-20 52-56
IMPERIAL....................5-10 66-67
MGM (12788 "Cream Puff")....................40-50 59
TAKE TEN (1502 "Vicki, This Is Susie")...20-30 63
VEE-JAY (686 "My Hometown")....................5-10 65
Picture Sleeves
COLUMBIA (152 "I Saw Mommy Kissing Santa Claus")....................15-25 52
(With die-cut center hole.)
EPs: 7-inch
COLUMBIA (1913 "Jimmy Boyd")....................10-20 '50s
LPs: 10/12-inch
COLUMBIA (6270 "Christmas with Jimmy Boyd")....................20-40 53
(10-inch LP.)
Also see LAINE, Frankie, & Jimmy Boyd

BOYD, Jimmy, & Rosemary Clooney *P&R '53*
Singles: 78 rpm
COLUMBIA....................5-10 53
Singles: 7-inch
COLUMBIA (39000 series)....................10-20 53
COLUMBIA (41000 series)....................8-12 60
Also see BOYD, Jimmy
Also see CLOONEY, Rosemary

BOYD, Melvin
Singles: 7-inch
ERA (3167 "Exit Loneliness, Enter Love")....................15-25 66

BOYD, Mickey, & Plain Viewers
(Keith McCormick)
Singles: 7-inch
7 ARTS (700 "Tell the World")....................20-30 61
Also see STRING-A-LONGS

BOYD, Reggie
(Reggie "Guitar" Boyd)
Singles: 7-inch
AGE (29110 "Nothing But Good")....................10-20 62
LIBERTY (55621 "Cotton Picker")....................10-20 63

BOYD, Robert
Singles: 78 rpm
WASCO (201 "East St. Louis Baby")....350-450 50
Also see PROFESSOR LONGHAIR

BOYD, Tim, & Esquires
(With the Bill Gibbs Combo)
Singles: 7-inch
ODESSA (101 "My Dearest, My Darling")....................400-500 59
Also see ESQUIRES
Also see GIBBS, Bill

BOYER, Jim
(With the Chocolate Pickles; with Newports)
Singles: 7-inch
A.D.A.V.....................10-15 64
DARN (10 "Hey You")....................50-100

BOYFRIENDS
(With Mort Garson Orchestra)
Singles: 7-inch
KAPP (569 "Let's Fall in Love")....................100-150 64
(Black label.)
KAPP (569 "Let's Fall in Love")....................100-150 64
(White label. Title at top, artist credits at bottom. Promotional issue only.)
KAPP (569 "Let's Fall in Love")....................75-125 64
(White label. Top is blank. Title and artist credits at bottom. Promotional issue only.)
Members: Steve Bray; Pat Collier; Mark Henry; Chris Skornia; Chris Smith.
Also see FIVE DISCS

BOYKIN, Burl
Singles: 7-inch
CLOVER ("Come My Way")....................100-200
(Selection number not known.)

BOYLAN, Terence *LP '77*
Singles: 7-inch
ASYLUM....................3-5 77-80
LPs: 10/12-inch
ASYLUM....................5-10 77-80
VERVE FORECAST....................12-15 69
Session: Darius Davenport.
Also see APPLETREE THEATRE CO.

BOYLES, Tommy
Singles: 7-inch
MURCO (1014 "We're Buggin' Out")......75-125

BOYS
Singles: 7-inch
DOT (15794 "Cobra")....................10-20 58
LIL-TEE (1003 "Shake It Up")....................10-20
#1 (0001 "Cobra")....................20-30 58
(First issue.)

BOYS
Singles: 7-inch
CAMEO (351 "I Want You")....................10-15 65
KAMA SUTRA (203 "Every Morning")......15-25 65
SVR (1001 "Angel of Mine")....................20-30 64
SVR (1002 "It's Hopeless")....................25-35 64

BOYS
Singles: 7-inch
EMCEE (15 "You Deceived Me")....................25-35 66

BOYS NEXT DOOR
Singles: 78 rpm
RAINBOW....................10-15 55
VIK....................5-10 56
Singles: 7-inch
RAINBOW (349 "We Belong Together")..30-40 55
VIK (0207 "Sweet Love of Mine")....................10-15 56

BOYS NEXT DOOR
Singles: 7-inch
ATCO....................8-12 66-67
BAD....................15-18 67
CAMEO (394 "There Is No Greater Sin").15-18 65
SOMA (Except 1428)....................15-18 65
SOMA (1428 "Central High Playmate")....20-25 65
Also see FOUR WHEELS

BOZE, Calvin *R&B '50*
(With His All-Stars; with Maxwell Davis & His All-Stars)
Singles: 78 rpm
ALADDIN....................35-75 50-52
G&G (1029 "Safronia B.")....................30-60 46
SCORE (4003 "Satisfied")....................15-25 48
Singles: 7-inch
ALADDIN (3045 "Waitin' & Drinkin' ")...100-150 50
ALADDIN (3055 "Safronia B.")....................100-150 50
ALADDIN (3065 thru 3147)....................50-100 50-52
ASTRA....................5-10
IMPERIAL....................10-15 62
Also see JOHNSON, Marvin, & His Orchestra

BOZEMAN, Helen
Singles: 7-inch
SANDY (1011 "Sugar Baby")....................40-50 58

BOZEMAN, Johnny
Singles: 7-inch
SANDY (1001 "Blues and I")....................75-100 57
SANDY (1035 "Gardenias")....................10-20 61

BOZMAN, Virgil
Singles: 7-inch
O.T. ("Blues for Oklahoma")....................50-75
(Selection number not known.)

BRACY, Lorenza
Singles: 7-inch
SANDY (1038 "Miss You")....................50-100 61

BRAD & JERRY
Singles: 7-inch
SHAD (5009 "I've Got It Bad for You Baby")....................10-15 59

BRADBURY, Ray
LP: 10/12-inch
TOWER....................10-20 '60s

BRADEN, Frank
Singles: 7-inch
DOT (15640 "At Peace with the World")..10-15 57

BRADEN, Tommy
(Tommy "Mary Jo" Braden; with His Flames)
Singles: 78 rpm
UNITED (177 "Do the Do")....................10-15 54
Singles: 7-inch
UNITED (177 "Do the Do")....................15-25 54
Also see BLASERS
Also see FOUR BLAZES

BRADFORD, Aubrey
Singles: 7-inch
SHELBY (294 "Get Your Feet on the Floor")....................100-200

BRADFORD, Don
Singles: 7-inch
SPOT (101 "Someone's Gotta Go")......75-125 59

BRADFORD, Scott
LPs: 10/12-inch
PROBE (4509 "Rock Slides")....................10-15 69

BRADFORD, Willie
Singles: 7-inch
FIRE (500 "Wanna Be Loved")....................15-25 61

BRADFORD BOYS
Singles: 78 rpm
RAINBOW (307 "That Feeling") 50-75 55
Singles: 7-inch
RAINBOW (307 "That Feeling") 100-125 55

BRADIX, Big Charley
Singles: 78 rpm
ARISTOCRAT (418 "Numbered Days") 100-125 48
BLUE BONNET (153 "Boogie Like You Wanna") 100-125 48
COLONIAL (108 "Boogie Like You Wanna") 300-500 48

BRADLEY, Allen, Quintet
Singles: 7-inch
OKEH (7100 "Space Race") 15-25 57

BRADLEY, Burt
Singles: 7-inch
BRADLEY (1000 "Girl in the Tight Blue Jeans") 50-75

BRADLEY, James R&B '79
(With the Bill Smith Combo)
Singles: 7-inch
MALACO 3-5 79-84
MANCO (1022 "Lonesome for You") 15-25 61
LPs: 10/12-inch
MALACO 5-10 84

BRADLEY, Jan P&R/R&B '63
Singles: 7-inch
ADANTI (1050 "Back in Circulation") 8-12 65
CHESS 6-12 62-68
DOYLEN 4-8 70
ERIC 4-6 73
FORMAL (1014 "Curfew Blues") 10-20 62
FORMAL (1044 "Mama Didn't Lie") 35-50 62
HOOTENANNY 5-10 62
NIGHT OWL (1055 "Behind the Curtains") 10-20 63
SOUND SPECTRUM (36002 "Back in Circulation") 8-12 65
Session: Impressions.
Also see IMPRESSIONS

BRADLEY, Mamie
Singles: 7-inch
CHESS (1686 "I Feel Like a Million") 10-15 58
SUE (702 "I Feel Like a Million") 25-30 58
(First issue.)
SUE (718 "Bye Bye") 15-20 59

BRADLEY, Owen C&W/P&R '49
(Owen Bradley Quintet)
Singles: 78 rpm
CORAL 4-8 49-50
DECCA 5-10 54-57
Singles: 7-inch
CORAL 8-15 50
DECCA 8-15 54-61
EPs: 7-inch
CORAL 10-20 54
DECCA 10-20 58
LPs: 10/12-inch
CORAL 20-30 53-55
DECCA 20-30 58-60
VOCALION ....5-15 '60s
Also see SHANNON, Pat

BRADLEY, Patrick
Singles: 7-inch
DECCA (32148 "Just One More Chance") 100-150 67
(Multi-color label.)
DECCA (32148 "Just One More Chance") 50-75 67
(Pink label. Promotional issue only.)

BRADLEY, Will
(With Ray McKinley; with His Boogie-Woogie Boys; with Will Bradley Jr.)
Singles: 78 rpm
ATLANTIC 10-20 50
BEACON 5-15 44
COLUMBIA 5-15 42
FABOR 5-10 56
SIGNATURE 5-15 47
Singles: 7-inch
FABOR 10-20 56
EPs: 7-inch
EPIC 15-30 54-56
LPs: 10/12-inch
EPIC (1005 "Boogie Woogie") 75-100 54
(10-inch LP.)
EPIC (1127 "Will Bradley") 50-75 56
EPIC (3115 "Boogie Woogie") 40-50 56
EPIC (3199 "The House of Bradley") 40-50 56
Also see BROWN, Ruth

BRADLEY, Will, & Johnny Guarnieri Band
LPs: 10/12-inch
RCA (2098 "Live Echoes") 20-30 60
Also see BRADLEY, Will

BRADLEY BOYS
Singles: 7-inch
POWER (11 "Evil Train") 50-75

BRADSHAW, Carolyn C&W '53
Singles: 78 rpm
ABBOTT 5-10 53-54
Singles: 7-inch
ABBOTT (141 "Marriage of Mexican Joe") 20-30 53
ABBOTT (151 "Say No, No, No") 8-12 54
ABBOTT (153 "Man on the Loose") 8-12 54
CHESS (4861 "This Is the Night") 15-25 54

BRADSHAW, Jack
Singles: 78 rpm
MAR-VEL 15-25 54-55
Singles: 7-inch
GLENN (754 "No No") 10-20 59
GLENN (755 You Hurt Me") 10-20 59
MAR-VEL (750 "Don't Tease Me") 50-75 54
MAR-VEL (751 "Searchin' ") 20-30 55
MAR-VEL (752 "It Just Ain't Right") 20-30 58
MAR-VEL (753 "Joe Joe") 50-75 58
MAR-VEL (756 "Saturday Night Special") 15-25 59

BRADSHAW, Jimmy
Singles: 7-inch
McBRAD (1000 "When School's Out") 50-75

BRADSHAW, Tiny R&B '50
Singles: 78 rpm
KING (4357 "Well Oh Well") 15-25 50
KING (4397 "I'm Going to Have Myself a Ball") 15-25 50
KING (4427 "Walk That Mess") 15-25 50
KING (4457 "Walkin' the Chalk Line") 15-25 50
KING (4467 "I'm a Hi-Ballin' Daddy") 25-50 51
KING (4487 "T-99") 25-50 52
KING (4497 "The Train Kept A-Rollin' ") ...25-50 52
KING (4547 "Rippin' & Runnin' ") 25-50 52
KING (4577 thru 4787) 10-20 52-55
MANOR (1147 "I Found Out Too Late") ...10-20 48
MANOR (1181 "Six Shooter") 10-20 49
REGIS (1010 "Bradshaw Bounce") 10-20 44
REGIS (1011 "After You've Gone") 10-20 44
SAVOY (650 "These Things Are Love") ...10-20 47
SAVOY (655 "If I Had a Million Dollars") ..10-20 47
Singles: 7-inch
GUSTO 3-5 80-83
KING (4357 "Well Oh Well") 25-50 50
KING (4397 "I'm Going to Have Myself a Ball") 25-50 50
KING (4457 "Walkin' the Chalk Line") 25-50 50
KING (4467 "I'm a Hi-Ballin' Daddy") 75-125 51
KING (4487 "T-99") 75-125 52
KING (4497 "The Train Kept A-Rollin' ") .75-125 52
KING (4547 "Rippin' & Runnin' ") 75-125 52
KING (4577 thru 4787) 20-40 52-55
(For King 4000 series colored vinyl singles, the price range will double or triple.)
EPs: 7-inch
KING (208 thru 360) 25-50 52-56
LPs: 10/12-inch
KING (74 "Off and On") 150-250 52
(10-inch LP.)
KING (501 "Tiny Bradshaw") 100-200 55
KING (653 "Great Composer") 50-75 59
KING (953 "24 Great Songs") 20-30 66

BRADY, Dave, & Stars
Singles: 7-inch
DARBY (8189 "Ridin' High") 20-25 67

BRADY, Howard
Singles: 7-inch
FLAGSHIP (914 "Hot Rod Boogie") 75-125 57

BRADY, Pal
Singles: 7-inch
KING (5758 "Who Cries the Most") 10-20 63
LUCKY (0013 "Love Is Just That Way") ...50-75 60

BRADY, Pete, & Blazers
LPs: 10/12-inch
ABC-PAR (310 "Murder Ballads") 15-25 59

BRADY BUNCH
Singles: 7-inch
PARAMOUNT 5-10 70-73
Picture Sleeves
PARAMOUNT 10-20 72-73
LPs: 10/12-inch
PARAMOUNT (5026 "Merry Christmas from the Brady Bunch") 30-60 70
PARAMOUNT (6032 "Meet the Brady Bunch") 20-50 72
PARAMOUNT (6037 "Kids from the Brady Bunch") 20-50 72
PARAMOUNT (6058 "Brady Bunch Phonographic Album") 20-50 73
Members: Barry Williams; Maureen McCormick, Mike Lookinland, Chris Knight; Susan Olsen; Eve Plumb.
Also see KNIGHT, Chris, & Maureen McCormick

BRADY BUNCH KIDS
Singles: 7-inch
PARAMOUNT 5-10 73
Also see BRADY BUNCH

BRAGG, Doug
Singles: 78 rpm
CORAL (61364 "Daydreamin' ") 50-75 55
Singles: 7-inch
CORAL (61364 "Daydreamin' ") 100-150 55
D (1018 "Daydreaming Again") 75-125 58
D (1045 "Calling Me Back") 10-20 59
D (1087 "When the Blues Came Walking In") 10-20 59
DIXIE (2002 "Red Rover") 50-75 58
DIXIE (2004 "Jerry") 100-150 58

BRAGG, Doug, & Cheri Robbins
Singles: 7-inch
SKIPPY (106 "Teenage Feeling") 15-20 59
Also see BRAGG, Doug

BRAGG, Joe
Singles: 7-inch
ARLISS (1013 "Pretty Please") 10-15 62
ATLAS (1208 "If I Had a Lover Like You") 10-20 60
BOCART (101 "I've Got to Make It") 50-75 63

BRAGG, Johnny
(With the Marigolds)
Singles: 78 rpm
EXCELLO 15-25 56
Singles: 7-inch
DECCA 15-25 59
ELBEJAY 8-12 69
EXCELLO 30-40 56
HOLLYWOOD (1130 "Freedom Marches") 8-12 68
Also see MARIGOLDS
Also see PRISONAIRES

BRAGGS, Al "TNT"
Singles: 7-inch
PEACOCK (1693 "Chase 'Em Tom Cat").10-15 60
PEACOCK (1698 "There") 10-15 60
PEACOCK (1699 "I Don't Think I Can Make It") 15-20 61
PEACOCK (1907 thru 1967) 10-15 61-68
Also see FIVE NOTES

BRAM RIGG SET
Singles: 7-inch
KAYDEN (400 "I Can Only Give You Everything") 15-20 66
Members: Pete Neri; Rich Bednarzyck; Jerry Poulton; Benet Segal; Bobby Schlosser.
Also see PULSE

BRAMAN, Bobbi, Trio
Singles: 78 rpm
VITA (122 "Kisses") 10-15 56
Singles: 7-inch
VITA (122 "Kisses") 20-30 56

BRANAM, Ronnie
Singles: 7-inch
PEP (111 "Puppy Dog Love") 150-250 57

BRANCH, Phyllis, & Twilights
Singles: 78 rpm
TUXEDO (919 "Calypso Fever") 10-15 56
Singles: 7-inch
TUXEDO (919 "Calypso Fever") 40-50 56

BRAND, Oscar
Singles: 7-inch
DOUGLAS (3 "The Gooney Bird") 8-12 61
(Promotional issue made by Elektra for the Douglas Aircraft Company, Inc.)
LPs:10/12-inch
ABC-PAR 10-20 61
AUDIO FIDELITY (1884 "Old Time Bawdy Sea Shanties, Vol. 2") 10-15 59
(Monaural.)
AUDIO FIDELITY (5884 "Old Time Bawdy Sea Shanties, Vol. 2") 20-25 59
(Stereo.)
AUDIO FIDELITY 15-25 60-64
ELEKTRA 15-25 60-63
FOLKWAYS 10-15
IMPULSE (25 "Morality") 10-15 62
KAPP 10-15
OFFBEAT (4021 "Drinking Man's Songbook") 10-20 61
RIVERSIDE 20-25 59-61
TRADITION 10-20 67

BRAND, Oscar, & Jean Ritchie
LPs: 10/12-inch
ARCHIVE OF FOLK MUSIC (107 "Oscar Brand and Jean Ritchie") 10-15 67
(Monaural.)
ARCHIVE OF FOLK MUSIC (207 "Oscar Brand and Jean Ritchie") 15-20 67
(Stereo.)
WASHINGTON (706 "Courting and Riddle Songs") 15-25 61

BRAND, Oscar, & Tarriers
LPs: 10/12-inch
DECCA (4275 "Folk Songs for Fun") 10-15 62
Also see BRAND, Oscar
Also see TARRIERS

BRANDON, Bill R&B '72
Singles: 7-inch
MOONSONG 10-20 72-73
PIEDMONT 4-6 76
PRELUDE 4-6 77-78
QUINVY (7007 "Strange Feeling") 50-75
SOUTH CAMP 5-10 67
TOWER (430 "Rainbow Road") 20-30 68

BRANDON, Don
Singles: 7-inch
CHALLENGE (9183 "Here Comes Trouble") 10-15 64
CHALLENGE (59224 "It's Wonderful Being Young") 10-15 64
DOT (16600 "Doin' the Swim") 10-15 64
DOT (16644 "Party Last Night") 10-15 64
LANCELOT (5 "Our Love Is Here to Stay") 20-30 62
Also see COMPETITORS

BRANDON, Luther
Singles: 7-inch
FRATERNITY (852 "Tuff-E-Nuff") 15-25 59

BRANDY, Charles
Singles: 7-inch
BLUE CAT (126 "I Can't Get Enough of You") 150-250 66

BRANNON, Linda
Singles: 7-inch
CHESS (1720 "Wherever You Are") 10-15 59
EPIC (9612 "Funny Face") 6-12 63
EPIC (9640 "Don't Cross Over") 6-12 64
PHILIPS (40016 "Deep Inside of Me") 6-12 62
RAM 10-20 59

BRANT, Bobby
Singles: 7-inch
EAST WEST (124 "Piano Nellie") 50-75 59
WHITE ROCK (1114 "Piano Nellie") 100-150 59

BRANTLEY, Charles
(Charlie Brantley)
Singles: 78 rpm
KING 10-20 53

Singles: 7-inch
JAX (301 "Beggin' Blues") 75-125 53
(Red vinyl.)
KING 30-50 53

BRANTLEY, Johnny
(Johnny Brantley's All Stars)
Singles: 7-inch
CARLTON (453 "The Place") 15-25 58

BRASSETTES
Singles: 7-inch
EBB (107 "Brassette Rock") 15-25 57

BRASSEUR, Andre
(With the Burners)
Singles: 7-inch
CONGRESS (271 "The Kid") 10-20 66
4 CORNERS (130 "Early Bird Satellite").. 10-15 65

BRASWELL, Jimmy
Singles: 7-inch
KING (6374 "I Can't Give You My
Heart") 30-50 71
QUINVY (7004 "Home for the Summer"). 20-30

BRAVE NEW WORLD
Singles: 7-inch
EPIC (10123 "It's Tomorrow") 10-15 66
PICCADILLY (225 "It's Tomorrow") 20-30 66
LP: 10/12-inch
PANORAMA .... 15-25 '60s

BRAVES
Singles: 7-inch
VANTAGE (701 "Mo-Combo") 10-15 62

BRAVES
("Vocal, Nat Couty")
Singles: 7-inch
FOX (101 "Woodpecker Rock") 500-600
Member: Nat Couty.

BRAZELL, Nicky, & Satellites
Singles: 7-inch
SPARR (2259 "Betty Jo") 75-125

BRAZIANO, Jerry
Singles: 7-inch
DAVIS (460 "Give Me Your Love") 10-20 58

BRAZIL, Johnny
Singles: 7-inch
PURE GOLD (306 "Twisted Sue") 30-40

BREAD LP '69
(David Gates & Bread)
Singles: 7-inch
ASYLUM (45054 "Make It with You") .... 4-6 '70s
(Label misprint; Asylum should be Elektra.)
ELEKTRA (Except 45666 & 45668) 4-6 70-77
ELEKTRA (45666 "Dismal Day") 5-10 69
ELEKTRA (45668 "Could I") 5-10 69
Picture Sleeves
ELEKTRA 4-8 70-72
LPs: 10/12-inch
ELEKTRA (100 & 1000 series) 8-12 73-77
ELEKTRA (5000 series) 15-25 72-73
(Quadraphonic series.)
ELEKTRA (74000 & 75000 series, except 75015 &
75056) 10-15 69-73
ELEKTRA (75015 "Baby I'm a Want
You") 15-25 72
(With die-cut cover.)
ELEKTRA (75015 "Baby I'm a Want
You") 10-15 72
(Standard cover.)
ELEKTRA (75056 "Best of Bread") 25-35 73
K-TEL 5-10 82
Members: David Gates; James Griffin; Mike Botts; Larry Knechtel; Robb Royer.
Also see CEYLEIB PEOPLE
Also see GATES, David
Also see GRIFFIN, James
Also see JOSHUA FOX
Also see PLEASURE FAIR

BREAKAWAYS
Singles: 7-inch
ROY (7799 "Red Skin Rock") 100-150

BREAKERS
Singles: 7-inch
BRANA (1001 "Kami-Kaze") 20-30 63
DJB (116 "Jet Stream") 15-25 64
DJB (116 "Super Jet Rumble") 15-25 64
(Same number is used twice.)
IMPACT (14 "Surfin' Tragedy") 15-25 63
(Black vinyl.)
IMPACT (14 "Surfin' Tragedy") 30-50 63
(Colored vinyl.)
MARSH (206 "Balboa Memories") 40-50 63
Also see WALLER, Jim, & Deltas

BREAKERS
(Wailers)
Singles: 7-inch
JERDEN (789 "All My Nights") 15-20 66
RIVERTON (102 "All My Nights") 25-35 66
Also see WAILERS

BREEDLOVE, Jimmy
Singles: 7-inch
ATCO 10-20 57
DIAMOND (144 "Jealous Fool") 5-10 63
EPIC (Except 9289) 10-15 58-60
EPIC (9289 "Ooh-Wee Good Gosh
A-Mighty") 15-25 58
JUBILEE (5551 "Jealous Fool") 5-10 66
OKEH 8-12 62
ROULETTE (7010 "I Can't Help Lovin'
You") 5-10 68
EPs: 7-inch
CAMDEN (447 "Rock 'N' Roll Music") 25-40 58
LPs: 10/12-inch
CAMDEN (430 "Rock 'N' Roll Hits") 40-60 58
Also see CUES

BREEN, Bobby
Singles: 7-inch
CHIC (1003 "If the Night Could Tell
You") 10-20 56
CHIC (1013 "Rainbow") 10-15 57
LYRIC (105 "It's a Sin") 10-15 59
MOTOWN (1053 "How Can We Tell
Him") 10-20 64
MOTOWN (1059 "You're Just Like You"). 10-20 64
NRC (055 "Hawaii Calls") 8-12 60
Picture Sleeves
MOTOWN (1059 "You're Just Like
You") 50-100 64

BRELYN, Bobby
Singles: 7-inch
JOREL (5396 "Hanna") .... 25-35 '60s

BRENDA & TABULATIONS P&R/R&B/LP '67
Singles: 12-inch
CHOCOLATE CITY 4-6 77
Singles: 7-inch
CHOCOLATE CITY 3-5 76-78
DIONN 5-10 67-69
EPIC 4-6 72-75
TOP & BOTTOM 4-8 69-71
LPs: 10/12-inch
CHOCOLATE CITY 5-10 77
DIONN (2000 "Dry Your Eyes") 20-30 67
TOP & BOTTOM 15-20 70
Members: Brenda Payton; Jerry Joures; Eddie Jackson; Maurice Coates; Deborah Martin; Pat Mercer; Dennis Dozier; Lee Smith; Kenneth Wright; Donald Ford.

BRENNAN, Cody
(With the Temptations)
Singles: 7-inch
SWAN (4089 "Am I the One") 25-35 61
SWAN (4103 "Shake the Hand of a
Fool") 10-15 62

BRENNAN, Walter P&R '60
(With Billy Vaughn's Orchestra & Chorus; with Patriots; with Johnny Mann Singers)
Singles: 7-inch
DOT (142 "Dutchman's Gold") 5-10 66
DOT (16066 "Dutchman's Gold") 10-15 60
DOT (16136 "Space Mice") 10-15 60
EVEREST (19365 "Noah's Ark") 5-10 60
KAPP 4-6 71
LIBERTY 6-12 62-63
RPC (502 "Knight in Bright Armor") 8-10 61
Picture Sleeves
DOT (16066 "Dutchman's Gold") 10-20 60
DOT (16136 "Space Mice") 10-20 60
LIBERTY (55477 "Houdini") 8-12 62
LIBERTY (55518 "White Christmas") 8-12 62
LPs: 10/12-inch
DOT 20-30 60
EVEREST 20-30 60
HAMILTON 15-25 65
LIBERTY 20-30 62
LONDON 15-20 70
RPC (106 "By the Fireside") 20-30 62
SUNSET 8-12 66
U.A. 5-10 75
Also see GOLDWATER, Barry
Also see VAUGHN, Billy

BRENSTON, Jackie R&B '51
(With His Delta Cats)
Singles: 78 rpm
CHESS (Except 1458) 15-30 51-53
CHESS (1458 "Rocket 88") 250-350 51
(See note below regarding 45 rpms.)
FEDERAL 15-40 56-57
Singles: 7-inch
CHESS (1458 "Rocket 88") 3000-5000 51
(With Ike Turner on guitar. Original 45s from 1951 are not known to exist. There are legit reissue 45s, made circa 1954. These have a delta symbol [Δ] and the number stamped in the trail-off. Fakes, without the delta mark, also exist.)
CHESS (1469 "In My Real Gone
Rocket") 150-250 51
CHESS (1472 "Juiced") 150-250 52
CHESS (1496 "Leo the Louse") 100-150 52
CHESS (1532 "The Blues Got Me
Again") 50-100 53
FEDERAL (12291 "Much Later") 25-50 56
FEDERAL (12283 "Gonna Wait for My
Chance") 25-50 57
MEL-LON (1000 "Down in My Heart") 30-40 63
SUE (736 "You Ain't the One") 8-12 61
Session: Elites.
Also see TURNER, Ike

BRENSTON, Jackie / Muddy Waters
Singles: 7-inch
CHESS (113 "Rocket 88") 4-6
Also see WATERS, Muddy

BRENSTON, Jackie / Joe Thomas
Singles: 7-inch
PLAYBACK (2321 "Independent
Woman") 20-30
Also see BRENSTON, Jackie
Also see THOMAS, Joe

BRENT, Bryan, & Cut Outs
Singles: 7-inch
PENNY (2201 "Vacation Time") 200-300 62

BRENT, Frankie
(With the Counts; Frankie Brent Revue Featuring Little Linda Lou)
Singles: 7-inch
CALVERT (201 "No Rock & Rollin'
Here") 50-75 57
CAMEO (181 thru 196) 8-12 60-61
CUTTY ("All I Have to Do Is Dream") 5-10
(Selection number not known.)
EPIC 5-10 64
PALETTE 8-12 59
STRAND (25014 "No Rock & Rollin'
Here") 15-25 60
VIK 10-20 58
Picture Sleeves
EPIC 8-12 64

BRENT, Randy
Singles: 7-inch
CUPID (1 "Run Like the Wind") 10-20 59

BRENT, Ronnie
Singles: 7-inch
COLT-45 ("Cowboys & Indians") 20-30 59
(Selection number not known.)
U.A. (108 "My Sweet Verlene") 30-50 58

BRENT, Royal
Singles: 78 rpm
ROCKIN' (521 "Sugar Bun") 15-25 53

BRENT & SPECTRAS
Singles: 7-inch
SPECTRA ("Oh Darling") 30-40
(Selection number not known.)

BRENTWOODS
Singles: 7-inch
DORE (559 "Midnight Star") 40-50 60
TALENT (1003 "Gee, But I Miss Him") 10-20 63

BRENTWOODS
Singles: 7-inch
OUR (101 "Yeah Yeah, No, No") 20-30 67

BRET & TERRY
Singles: 7-inch
PRESTIGE (313 "Beatle Hop") 10-15 64

BREWER, Betty
Singles: 7-inch
LINCOLN (707 "You're Breaking My
Heart") 15-25 61

BREWER, Deanna
Singles: 7-inch
LEMCO (885 "I've Gotta Know") .... 10-20 '60s

BREWER, Teresa P&R '50
(With the Lancers; with Dixieland Band; with Bobby Wayne)
Singles: 78 rpm
CORAL 5-15 52-57
LONDON 5-15 50-52
Singles: 7-inch
ABC 4-6 67
AMSTERDAM 4-6 72-73
CORAL (60591 thru 61067) 15-25 52-53
CORAL (61152 thru 61636) 10-20 54-56
CORAL (61700 "I Love Mickey") 25-35 56
(With Mickey Mantle.)
CORAL (61737 thru 62428) 8-15 56-64
CORAL (65000 series) 5-10 61-65
DOCTOR JAZZ 3-5 83
FLYING DUTCHMAN 4-6 72
LONDON 10-20 50-52
PHILIPS 5-10 63-67
PROJECT 3 .... 3-5 82
RCA (11882 "Merry Christmas") 4-6 79
(With picture label. Special products issue.)
SSS INT'L 4-6 68
SIGNATURE 3-6 74-83
Picture Sleeves
CORAL 10-20 58-60
SIGNATURE 3-5 80
EPs: 7-inch
CORAL 10-20 55-60
LONDON (6039 "Teresa Brewer") 20-30 51
LONDON (6041 "Teresa Brewer") 20-30 51
LPs: 10/12-inch
AMSTERDAM 6-10 73-74
COLUMBIA 5-10 81
CORAL (7 "Best of Teresa Brewer") 15-25 65
CORAL (56072 "A Bouquet of Hits from Teresa
Brewer") 50-75 52
(10-inch LP.)
CORAL (56093 "Till I Waltz Again with
You") 50-75 53
(10-inch LP.)
CORAL (57027 thru 57297) 25-50 55-59
(Monaural. Stereo numbers in the 57000 series are preceded by a "7.")
CORAL (57315 thru 57414) 15-30 60-65
(Monaural. Stereo numbers in the 57000 series are preceded by a "7.")
DOCTOR JAZZ 5-10 79-83
FLYING DUTCHMAN 6-10 73-74
IMAGE 5-10 78
LONDON (1006 "Teresa Brewer") 50-100 51
(10-inch LP.)
MCA 5-10 83
PHILIPS 10-20 63-67
PROJECT 3 .... 5-10 82
RCA 5-10 75
SIGNATURE 5-10 74-75
VOCALION 8-15 69
WING 8-10 66
Also see CORNELL, Don, & Teresa Brewer
Also see McGUIRE SISTERS / Lancers / Dorothy Collins / Teresa Brewer

BREWER, Teresa / Eileen Barton
Singles: 78 rpm
CORAL .... 5-10 '50s
Also see BARTON, Eileen

BREWER, Teresa, & Count Basie
LPs: 10/12-inch
DOCTOR JAZZ 5-10 84
Also see BASIE, Count

BREWER, Teresa, & Duke Ellington
LPs: 10/12-inch
COLUMBIA 5-10 81
FLYING DUTCHMAN 6-10 74

Also see BREWER, Teresa
Also see ELLINGTON, Duke

BRIAN, Neil
Singles: 7-inch
JAMIE (1216 "Lucky Coin") 5-10 62
PARKWAY....5-10 63-64
PHILTOWN (107 "I Just Sat Down")....10-15 63
PHILTOWN (108 "1000 Years")....10-15 64
PHILTOWN (40000 " Tough Guy")....20-30 '60s
20TH FOX (6686 "Barefoot Girl")....5-10 67

BRIAN, Russ
Singles: 7-inch
HORIZON (1001 "Hillbilly Rock")....300-400

BRIANS, Robin Hood
(Robin Hood Brians Quintet)
Singles: 7-inch
FRATERNITY (803 "Dis a Itty Bit")....75-125 58
FRATERNITY (1012 "Papago Yo")....15-25 69
(B-side is Harry Carlson & Bandoleros.)
RBE (101 "Only One Heart")....10-15 '60s
UNI (55226 "Miami")....10-15 70

BRIDGES, Curly
Singles: 78 rpm
HOLLYWOOD (1066 "Don't Go")....10-15 56
Singles: 7-inch
HOLLYWOOD (1066 "Don't Go")....40-50 56

BRIDGES, Curly, & Frank Motley
Singles: 78 rpm
GEM....8-12 53
Singles: 7-inch
DC (0435 "What Can I Do")....10-15 62
DC (0436 "Prayer of Love")....10-15 62
GEM (216 "Curly's Lament")....15-25 53
GEM (217 "Curly's Lament")....15-25 53
(Sung in Spanish.)
Also see MOTLEY, Frank

BRIDGES, Fred
Singles: 7-inch
VERSATILE (111 "It Must Be Love")....15-25 62

BRIGADE
LPs: 10/12-inch
BAND 'N' VOCAL (1066 "Last Laugh")....1000-2000 70
Members: Peter Belknap; Bob Anderson; Ed Wallo; Mark Hartman; Eric Anderson; Tim Vetter; Dennis Steindal.

BRIGGS, Freddie
(Fred Briggs)
Singles: 7-inch
CONGRESS (228 "Train Song")....5-10 64
GROOVE CITY ("I'm So Sorry")....50-75 '60s
(Selection number not known.)

BRIGHT, Jerry, & Embers
Singles: 7-inch
YUCCA (139 "Jim's Jive")....20-30 61
YUCCA (143 "Be Mine")....20-30 62

BRIGHT, Larry *P&R '60*
(Pete Roberts)
Singles: 7-inch
BRIGHT (0014 "She Belongs to Me")....5-10 65
DEL-FI (4204 "Surfin' Queen")....10-20 63
DEL-FI (4209 thru 4241)....8-12 63-64
DIPLOMAT....5-10 '60s
DOT (16923 "Money")....5-10 66
EDIT (2001 "It Ain't Right")....8-12 62
HIGHLAND (1052 "Should I")....10-20 61
JOJO....4-6 76
ORIGINAL SOUND....4-6 72
RENDEZVOUS (124 "Hold Me")....8-10 60
(Reissued as by Pete Roberts.)
TIDE (006 thru 1083)....10-20 59-61
Also see GREASERS
Also see HUMDINGERS
Also see ROBERTS, Pete

BRIGMAN, George
(With Split)
EPs: 7-inch
BONA FIDE....5-10 85
LPs: 10/12-inch
SOLID (001 "Jungle Rot")....75-125 75

BRIKS
Singles: 7-inch
BISMARK (1013 "Can You See Me")....25-35 66
BISMARK (1020 "From a Small Room")..10-15 66
DOT (16878 "Can You See Me")....15-20 66

BRIKTA, Danny
Singles: 7-inch
NITRO (998 "Sweet Little Angel")....50-100 63

BRILLIANT, Ashleigh
LPs: 10/12-inch
DORASH (1001 "Ashleigh Brilliant in the Haight Ashbury")....40-60 67

BRILLIANT KORNERS
Singles: 7-inch
MODERN (1059 "Three Lonely Guys")....10-20 68

BRILLIANTS
Singles: 7-inch
FRISCO (3221 "Slow Lovin' ")....30-40

BRIM, Grace
Singles: 78 rpm
J.O.B. (117 "Man Around My Door")....75-100 52
Also see BRIM, John
Also see BRIM, Mrs. John

BRIM, John
(With His Combo; Trio; with His Gary Kings; with His Stompers.)
Singles: 78 rpm
FORTUNE (801 "Strange Man")....75-125 50
J.O.B. (110 "Trouble in the Morning")....50-75 52
J.O.B. (1011 "Drinking Woman")....50-75 53
(Though not credited, the flip of J.O.B. 1011, *Woman Trouble*, is by Sunnyland Slim & His Boys.)
RANDOM (201 "Dark Clouds")....75-125 51
Singles: 7-inch
CHESS (1588 "Go Away")....75-125 55
CHESS (1624 "I Would Hate to See You Go")....75-125 56
PARROT (799 "Tough Times")....100-150 54
(Black vinyl.)
PARROT (799 "Tough Times")....150-250 54
(Red vinyl.)
Members: Little Walter; Robert Lockwood Jr.; Big Maceo; James Watkins.
Also see BIG MACEO
Also see BRIM, Grace
Also see JAMES, Elmore, & John Brim
Also see LITTLE WALTER
Also see SUNNYLAND SLIM

BRIM, Mrs. John
(Grace Brim)
Singles: 78 rpm
RANDOM (202 "Going Down the Line").75-125 51
Also see BRIM, Grace

BRIMSTONE
Singles: 7-inch
FIREBIRD ("Blowin' in the Wind")....8-12 69
(Selection number not known.)
LANGCO (3122 "Home Cooking")....10-15
LPs: 10/12-inch
BRIMSTONE ("Paper Winged Dreams")....150-250 '60s
(No selection number used.)
Members: Gregg Andrews; Chris Wintrip; Ken Miller; Bernie Nau; Jim Papatoukakis.

BRIMSTONES
Singles: 7-inch
MGM (13653 "It's All Over But the Crying")....10-20 66

BRIMSTONES
Singles: 7-inch
WORLD PACIFIC (77834 "Cold Hearted Woman")....15-25 66

BRINK, James
Singles: 7-inch
ROTARY (101 "It's Rough")....75-125

BRINKLEY, Jay
Singles: 78 rpm
DOT (15371 "Forces of Evil")....5-10 55
Singles: 7-inch
DOT (15371 "Forces of Evil")....10-15 55
KLIFF (100 "Guitar Smoke")....10-20 58
ROULETTE (4117 "The Creep")....15-25 58

BRINKLEY, Larry
Singles: 7-inch
HOLIDAY INN (2210 "Guitar Pickin' DJ")...5-10 68
MAGIC (3004 "Right String But Wrong Yo-Yo")....100-150
ROCK IT (101 "Jackson Dog")....4-8 78
WESTWOOD (206 "Jackson Dog")....100-150 59

BRISCOE, Joey
Singles: 78 rpm
DECCA (30414 "Eternal Love")....15-25 57
Singles: 7-inch
DECCA (30414 "Eternal Love")....15-25 57
GREENWICH (413 "Pretty Kisses")....10-20 59
Also see DEL-VIKINGS

BRISTOL, Bobby
(Bob Bristol)
Singles: 7-inch
PARIS (519 "School's Out")....15-25 58
RIDER (105 "Humpty Dumpty")....10-15 61

BRITISH WALKERS
Singles: 7-inch
CAMEO (466 "Shake")....8-10 67
CHARGER (108 "The Girl Can't Help It").10-20 65
MANCHESTER (651120 "Watch Yourself")....15-25 65
TRY (502 "I Found You")....10-20 64
Members: Bobby Howard; Roy Buchanan.

BRITT, Darryl
Singles: 7-inch
BLUE (1199 "Lover, Lover")....400-600

BRITT, Elton *C&W '45*
(With the Skytoppers with Zeke Manners Band)
Singles: 78 rpm
BLUEBIRD....10-15 40-45
RCA....5-10 49-56
VICTOR....8-12 46-48
Singles: 7-inch
ABC-PAR....5-8 60-66
RCA (48-0044 thru 48-0408)....10-20 49-51
(Green vinyl.)
RCA (0006 thru 6429)....10-20 49-56
RCA (9000 series)....4-6 68-69
EPs: 7-inch
RCA....10-20 55-56
LPs: 10/12-inch
ABC-PAR (293 thru 521)....20-30 59
ABC-PAR (322 thru 521)....15-25 60-66
ABC-PAR (744 "16 Great Country Performances")....10-15 71
CAMDEN....10-20 69
CERTRON....8-12 70
KOALA....8-10 79
PREMIER....5-10 '60s
RCA (1288" Yodel Songs")....30-50 56
RCA (2669 "Best of Elton Britt")....20-30 63
RCA (3222" Yodel Songs")....50-100 54
(10-inch LP.)
RCA (4822 "Best of Elton Britt, Vol. 2")....5-10 73
SPIN-O-RAMA....8-15 '60s

BRITT, Elton, Rosalie Allen & Skytoppers
(Elton Britt / Rosalie Allen) *C&W '50*
Singles: 78 rpm
RCA....5-10 50
Singles: 7-inch
RCA (48-0168 thru 48-0405)....10-20 50-51
(Green vinyl.)
EPs: 7-inch
RCA....15-25 55
LPs: 10/12-inch
GRAND AWARD (262 "Starring Elton Britt & Rosalie Allen")....15-25 66
WALDORF (1206 "Rosalie Allen & Elton Britt")....20-30 57
Also see ALLEN, Rosalie
Also see BRITT, Elton

BRITT, Lynn
Singles: 7-inch
DOT (16203 "Too Long")....8-12 61
MIKI (1117 "Too Long")....20-30 61
(First issue.)

BRITT, Mel
Singles: 7-inch
FESTIVAL INT'L (650 "She'll Come Running Back")....150-250 '60s

BROADWAY JAZZ ORCHESTRA
LPs: 10/12-inch
HALO (50252 "Ain't Misbehavin' – Fats Waller Hits")....75-125 '50s
(Cover pictures Betty Page, although she is not heard on the disc.)

BROCK, Norma, & Keynoters
(With the Jack Hale Orchestra)
Singles: 7-inch
PEPPER (896 "Evergood")....10-15 59

BRODIE, Henry, & Red Toppers
Singles: 7-inch
DAN (3214 "All Night Jump")....10-20 61

BROGUES
Singles: 7-inch
CHALLENGE (59311 "But Now I Find")...20-25 65
CHALLENGE (59316 "Don't Shoot Me Down")....20-25 65
TWILIGHT (408 "But Now I Find")....40-50 65
Members: Eddie Rodrigues; Rick Campbell; Gary Duncan; Greg Elmore.
Also see QUICKSILVER

BROKEN HEARTS
Singles: 7-inch
ROSINA (147 "Crying Over You")....15-25

BRONZVILLE, Lewis
(Lewis Bronzville Five)
Singles: 78 rpm
BLUEBIRD....40-60 40
MONTGOMERY WARD....20-40

BROOKE, Stormy, & Escapades
Singles: 7-inch
ASTRONAUT (115 "Doris")....100-150 61

BROOKES, Bobby
Singles: 7-inch
CAPITOL (4780 "Someone Like You")....10-15 62
CARLTON (515 "Looka, Looka, Looka")..10-15 59
TWIST (601 "Confession of Love")....40-50 62

BROOKLYN BOYS
Singles: 78 rpm
DYNAMIC....100-200 56
FERRIS....8-12 56
Singles: 7-inch
DYNAMIC (107 "If She Should Call")...600-800 56
(First issue.)
FERRIS (902 "If She Should Call")....10-20 56

BROOKLYN BRIDGE *P&R '68*
(Johnny Maestro & Brooklyn Bridge)
Singles: 7-inch
BROOKLYN BRIDGE (881 "Christmas Is")....10-15 88
BUDDAH....5-10 68-72
COLLECTABLES....3-5 84
ERIC....3-5 78
FLASHBACK....4-6 '70s
HARVEY (500 "Worst That Could Happen")....5-10 81
(Colored vinyl.)
RADIO ACTIVE GOLD....3-5
LPs: 10/12-inch
BUDDAH (5034 "Brooklyn Bridge")....20-25 69
BUDDAH (5042 "Second Brooklyn Bridge")....20-25 69
BUDDAH (5065 "Brooklyn Bridge")....20-25 70
BUDDAH (5107 "Bridge in Blue")....20-25 72
BUDDAH (69000 series)....5-10 84
COLLECTABLES....5-10 82
Members: Johnny Maestro; Fred Ferrara; Les Cauchi; Mike Gregorio; Tom Sullivan; Carolyn Wood; Jimmy Rosica; Richie Macioce; Artie Cantanzarita; Shelly Davis; Joe Ruvio.
Also see DEL SATINS
Also see ISLEY BROTHERS / Brooklyn Bridge
Also see MAESTRO, Johnny

BROOKS, Billy
(With the Red Saunders Band)
Singles: 78 rpm
DUKE....10-20 55-56
PEACOCK....15-25 53
Singles: 7-inch
DUKE (142 "Song of the Dreamer")....20-30 55
DUKE (149 "I Want Your Love Tonight").20-30 56
PEACOCK (1629 "I Called My Baby")....25-50 53

BROOKS, Billy
LPs: 10/12-inch
CROSSOVER (9003 "Windows of the Mind")....100-200 75

BROOKS, Bobby
Singles: 78 rpm
RAINBOW....5-10 56

Singles: 7-inch
HIT (109 "My Heart Belongs to Only You") 5-10
HIT (120 "World Without Love") 10-15
RAINBOW 10-15 56
EPs: 7-inch
RCA (1/2-1598 "This Is the Night") 20-40 58
(Price is for either of two volumes.)
RCA (4273 "Teenagers Dance to Bobby Brooks") 20-40 58
LPs: 10/12-inch
RCA (1598 "This Is the Night") 50-75 58
Also see JALOPY FIVE

BROOKS, Chuck, & Sharpies
Singles: 7-inch
DUB (2844 "Spinning My Wheels") 200-300 58

BROOKS, Clinton, & B's
Singles: 7-inch
APACHE (1828 "Tom Dooley Rock") ... 100-150 59

BROOKS, Dale
Singles: 7-inch
BISHOP (1006 "Ambridge Boogie") 15-25
COZY (499 "Ambridge Boogie") 50-75
DOLPHIN (1 "Army Green") 5-10 65
TWIRL (2028 "My Foolish Pride") 5-10 66

BROOKS, David
Singles: 78 rpm
CHART (618 "Bus Ride") 10-15 56
Singles: 7-inch
CHART (618 "Bus Ride") 15-25 56

BROOKS, Donnie P&R '60
Singles: 7-inch
CALICO (108 "Everytime We Kiss") 10-15 59
CHALLENGE 5-10 66
COLLECTABLES 3-5 81
DJ (669 "Pink Carousel") 5-10 65
ERA (3004 thru 3014) 15-20 59-60
ERA (3018 thru 3063) 10-15 60-61
ERA (3071 thru 3077) 8-12 62
ERA (3095 "It's Not That Easy") 10-15 62
ERA (3194 "Blue Soldier") 5-10 68
HAPPY TIGER 4-8 70-71
MIDSONG 3-5 79
OAK (1019 "This Song That I Sing") 4-6 71
REPRISE (261 thru 363) 5-10 64-65
USA .... 10-15 '60s
YARDBIRD 5-10 68-69
Picture Sleeves
ERA (3028 "Doll House") 15-25 60
ERA (3042 "Memphis") 10-20 61
ERA (3049 "All I Can Give") 10-20 61
REPRISE (261 "Gone") 15-25 64
Promotional Singles
ERA ("Mission Bell"/"Doll House") 50-75 60
(Distributed during a personal appearance.)
LPs: 10/12-inch
ERA (105 "The Happiest") 30-40 61
OAK 8-10 71
WISHBONE 5-10 75
Also see BUSH, Dick
Also see FAIRE, Johnny
Also see JORDAN, Johnny

BROOKS, Dusty
(With the Four Tones; with Tones)
Singles: 78 rpm
COLUMBIA 15-25 50-51
DOOTONE 10-20 52
LAMARR STAR (101 "I'll Follow You") 15-25 46
LAMARR STAR (102 "Seclusion") 15-25 46
LAMARR STAR (103 "Little Chum") 15-25 46
MAJESTIC (123 "Ole' Man River") 15-25 50
MAJESTIC (127 "Shuffle Board Boogie") 15-25 50
MEMO (1001 "Play Jackpot") 15-25 46-48
MEMO (1002 "Little Chum") 15-25 46-48
MEMO (1003 "Please Don't Rush Me") ... 15-25 46-48
MEMO (1005 "Put Your Cards on the Table") 15-25 46-48
MEMO (7001 "Please Don't Rush Me") ... 15-25 48
PREVIEW (666 "Someone Over Here Loves Someone Over There") 20-30 45
PREVIEW (668 "Two Tears Met") 20-30 45
SUN (182 "Heaven Or Fire") 200-300 53
SUPREME 10-20 49
Singles: 7-inch
SUN (182 "Heaven Or Fire") 1000-1500 53
Members: Dusty Brooks; Juanita Brown; Joe Alexander.
Also see ALEXANDER, Joe
Also see BROWN, Juanita

BROOKS, Elouise, & Dreamers
Singles: 78 rpm
ALADDIN (3303 "My Plea") 50-100 55
Singles: 7-inch
ALADDIN (3303 "My Plea") 250-350 55
Also see DREAMERS

BROOKS, Hadda R&B '47
(Hadda Brooks Trio; Hedda Brooks)
Singles: 78 rpm
LONDON 15-25 50
MODERN 15-30 45-56
MODERN MUSIC 15-25 47
OKEH 10-20 54
Singles: 7-inch
ALWIN 5-10 69
ARWIN (1001 "Careless Years") 8-12 59
KENT (321 "The Thrill Is Gone") 8-12 59
LONDON (684 "I Hadn't Anyone Till You") 25-50 50
LONDON (45895 "Vanity") ....20-30 '50s
MODERN (100 series) 15-25 52
MODERN (804 "Let's Be Sweethearts Again") 50-100 51
MODERN (825 "When a Woman Cries") 50-100 51
MODERN (841 "I Feel So Good") 50-100 51
MODERN (861 "Romance in the Dark") .50-100 52
MODERN (1008 "Close Your Eyes") 25-50 56
MODERN MUSIC (Colored vinyl) 4-6 86
OKEH (7031 "He's Coming Home") 20-40 54
EPs: 7-inch
LONDON (6149 "Presenting Hadda Brooks") 50-75 54
MODERN (114 "Boogie") 50-100 52
LPs: 10/12-inch
CROWN (5010 "Femme Fatale") 40-60 57
CROWN (5374 "Hadda Brooks Sings and Swings") 15-25 63
MODERN (1210 "Femme Fatale") 100-200 56
Members: Hadda Brooks; Al Wichard; Basie Day; Jim Black.

BROOKS, Hadda / Pete Johnson
LPs: 10/12-inch
CROWN (5058 "Boogie") 35-45 58
Also see BROOKS, Hadda
Also see JOHNSON, Pete

BROOKS, Joey
Singles: 7-inch
AURORA (151 "Little Bit of Rain") 5-10 65
(Has two different flip sides.)
CANADIAN AMERICAN 15-25 59-60
COLUMBIA (42392 "I'll Bring a Ring for You") 5-10 61
MUSICOR (1037 "Cry Cry Cry") 5-10 64

BROOKS, Junior
Singles: 78 rpm
RPM (320 "Whiskey Head Woman") 25-50 51
RPM (343 "Lone Town Blues") 40-60 52

BROOKS, Lillian
(With the Moroccos)
Singles: 78 rpm
EPIC 8-12 56
KING 8-15 56
MGM 5-10 57
Singles: 7-inch
B&F (1321 thru 1335) 5-10 59-60
B&F (1345 "Lead On Mr. President") 8-12 60
EPIC (9190 "Mean Words") 15-25 56
KING (4934 "For Only You") 20-30 56
KING (4956 "Sweet Sweet William") 30-40 56
MGM 10-20 57-58
NEWPORT 8-12 61-63
ORIOLE (1318 "You Ought to Get to Know Me Better") 8-12 59
Picture Sleeves
B&F (1345 "Lead On Mr. President"/"First Lady of America") 10-20 60
(Die-cut sleeve pictures John and Jackie Kennedy.)
Also see MOROCCOS

BROOKS, Louis R&B '55
(With His Hi-Toppers)
Singles: 78 rpm
EXCELLO 15-25 54-57
Singles: 7-inch
EXCELLO (2030 "Bus Station Blues") 40-50 54
EXCELLO (2042 "Double Shot") 40-50 54
EXCELLO (2056 "It's Love Baby") 40-50 55
EXCELLO (2063 "Can't Keep from Cryin'") 40-50 55
EXCELLO (2100 "X-Cello Rock") 15-25 57
EXCELLO (2119 "Don't You Know") 15-25 57
EXCELLO (2141 "Frisco") 10-20 58
EXCELLO (2159 "Ridin' Home") 10-20 59
Also see BIRDSONG, Larry

BROOKS, Nat
Singles: 7-inch
RAINBOW (220 "No No Baby") 25-50 53
(Red vinyl.)

BROOKS, Orville, & Ink Spots
EPs: 7-inch
BROOKS (1 "Singalong with Orville Brooks and His Ink Sports") 30-50
(Red vinyl. Compact 33. Issued with a paper sleeve.)
Members: Orville Brooks; Frank Houston; Pete Hatch; Bill Hosey.

BROOKS, Rosa Lee
Singles: 7-inch
REVIS (1013 "My Diary") 30-40 63
Also see HENDRIX, Jimi

BROOKS, Skippy, Combo
Singles: 7-inch
EXCELLO (2188 "Doin' the Horse") 10-20 60

BROOKS, Sonny
(With the Savoys)
Singles: 78 rpm
GROOVE 8-12 54
TIP TOP 50-75 56
Singles: 7-inch
GROOVE (0027 "Champ Ale") 15-25 54
TIP TOP (1007 "Here I Am") 150-200 56
TIP TOP (1008 "Sweetheart Darling") ..200-250 56

BROOKS, Tommy
Singles: 7-inch
CAPITOL 4-8 70
IN ARTS (106 "Foolish Pride") 5-10 68
INSIGNIA (101 "Lovesick") 25-35

BROOKS, Wayne, & Cyclones
Singles: 7-inch
TOP RANK (2099 "Runaway") 10-20 61
(First issue; by about four or five months.)
WARWICK (629 "Runaway") 10-15 61

BROOKS & BROWN
Singles: 78 rpm
DUKE (172 "They Call Her Rosalie") 10-15 57
Singles: 7-inch
DUKE (172 "They Call Her Rosalie") 15-25 57
Members: Billy Brooks; Piney Brown.

BROOKS BOND FOOD
Singles: 7-inch
GINK (9612 "Red Rose Tea") 35-45

BROOKS BROTHERS
Singles: 78 rpm
DECCA 15-25 47-48
DIAMOND 15-25 46

BROOKS FOUR
Singles: 7-inch
SINCLAIR (1007 "I'll Be Faithful") 50-100 62

BROONZY, Big Bill
(With His Fat Four; Little Sam; Big Bill & His Rhythm Band; Chicago Bill)
Singles: 78 rpm
CHESS (1546 "Little City Woman") 75-125 53
COLUMBIA 15-25 45-47
HUB 15-25 45
MELODISC 15-25 51
MERCURY 25-50 49-51
OKEH ....15-25 '40s
VOCALION ....20-50 '40s
VOGUE 10-20 49-51
Singles: 7-inch
CHESS (1546 "Little City Woman") 250-350 53
MERCURY 25-50 51
EPs: 7-inch
MERCURY 15-20 63
LPs: 10/12-inch
ARCHIVE OF FOLK MUSIC 10-12 67
BIOGRAPH 8-10 73
COLUMBIA (111 "Big Bill's Blues") 50-100 57
DISC 12-20 65
EMARCY (26034 "Folk Blues") 50-75 54
(10-inch LP.)
EMARCY (26137 "Blues by Broonzy") 50-75 55
(10-inch LP.)
EPIC 10-12 69
FOLKWAYS 15-30 57-58
GNP 8-10 74-75
MERCURY 20-30 63-64
PERIOD (1114 "Big Bill Broonzy Sings") 50-100 55
(10-inch LP.)
ROOTS N' BLUES 5-8 90
TRIP 8-10 75
VERVE (3000-5 "The Big Bill Broonzy Story") 50-100 61
(Boxed, five-disc set.)
VERVE (3001 "Last Session, Vol. 1") 15-25 61
VERVE (3001 "Last Session, Vol. 2") 15-25 61
VERVE (3001 "Last Session, Vol. 3") 15-25 61
YAZOO 8-12 69-70
Also see CHICAGO BILL
Also see GILLUM, Jazz
Also see LITTLE SAM
Also see McGHEE, Brownie, & Sonny Terry
Also see WHITE, Josh & Big Bill Broonzy
Also see WHITE, Josh / Leadbelly / Bill Broonzy

BROONZY, Big Bill, & Pete Seeger
LPs: 10/12-inch
VERVE FOLKWAYS (9008 "In Concert") 10-15 65
Also see SEEGER, Pete

BROONZY, Big Bill, & Washboard Sam
LPs: 10/12-inch
CHESS (1468 "Big Bill Broonzy & Washboard Sam") 35-45 62
Also see BROONZY, Big Bill
Also see WASHBOARD SAM

BROTHER BLUES & BACK ROOM BOYS
(Champion Jack Dupree)
Singles: 78 rpm
ABBEY (3015 "Featherweight Mama") ...75-100 50
Also see DUPREE, Champion Jack

BROTHER BONES R&B '49
(With His Shadows; World Famous Harlem Globetrotters Featuring Brother Bones)
Singles: 78 rpm
TEMPO (652 "Sweet Georgia Brown") 15-25 48
TEMPO (4566 "Bubber's Boogie") 10-15 50
Singles: 7-inch
GLOBETROTTERS (300 "Sweet Georgia Brown") ....10-15 '60s
(Reissue of Tempo 652.)
TEMPO (4564 "Sweet Georgia Brown") ...40-60 50
(Red vinyl.)
TEMPO (4566 "Bubber's Boogie") 15-25 50
THEME (4564 "Sweet Georgia Brown") ...15-25 51
Picture Sleeves
GLOBETROTTERS (300 "Sweet Georgia Brown") ....10-20 '60
Member: Joe Darensbourg.

BROTHER L. CONGREGATION
Singles: 7-inch
KUMQUAT (1 "Bringing Me Down") 20-30 68

BROTHER SOUL
Singles: 7-inch
JANION (101 "Train Song") 200-250

BROTHER ZEE & DECADES
Singles: 7-inch
RAMCO (3725 "Sha Boom Bang") 30-40 63
Also see REVERE, Paul, & Raiders
Also see WOMACK, Bobby

BROTHERLY LOVE R&B '72
Singles: 7-inch
MUSIC MERCHANT 5-10 72
LPs: 10/12-inch
MUSIC MERCHANT (104 "Brotherly Love") 25-50 72

BROTHERS
Singles: 7-inch
ARGO (5318 "Lazy Susan") 10-20 58
ARGO (5329 "Sioux City Sue") 10-15 59
CHECKER (995 "My True Love") 8-15 61
Members: Dean Mathis; Marc Mathis.

Also see DEAN & MARC

BROTHERS & SISTERS

Singles: 7-inch

SOFT (979 "And I Know")... 20-30 66
TOWER (262 "And I Know")... 15-25 66

BROTHERS CAIN

Singles: 7-inch

ACTA (810 "Better Times")... 10-20 67
ACTA (820 "Anyway You Like It")... 10-20 68
MERCURY... 10-20 65

BROTHERS FOUR — P&R/LP '60

Singles: 7-inch

AURAVISION (6725 "San Francisco Bay Blues")... 10-15 64
(Cardboard flexi-disc, one of six by six different artists. Columbia Record Club "Enrollment Premium." Set came in a special paper sleeve.)
COLUMBIA (Except 43547)...5-10 59-69
COLUMBIA (43547 "Ratman & Bobbin in the Clipper Caper")...8-12 69
FANTASY...4-6 70

Picture Sleeves

COLUMBIA... 10-15 60-63

LPs: 10/12-inch

COLUMBIA... 10-20 59-69
FANTASY...8-12 70
FIRST AMERICAN...5-10 81
GRT... 10-12 77
HARMONY...6-10 69-72
Members: Bob Flick; Dick Foley; John Paine; Mike Kirkland.

BROTHERS OF HOPE

Singles: 7-inch

GAMBLE (224 "Nickol, Nickol")... 20-30 69
GAMBLE (4003 "Spring Fever")...5-10 69

BROTHERS OF SOUL — R&B '68

Singles: 7-inch

BOO (111 "You Better Believe It")... 15-25 70
BOO (112 "Love Is Fever")... 15-25 70
BOO (1004 "I Guess That Don't Make Me a Loser")... 15-25 68
BOO (1005 "Come On Back")... 15-25 68
BOO (1006 "I'd Be Grateful")... 50-100 69
CRISS-CROSS (1001 "Can't Get You Out of My Mind")... 25-50 '60s
SHOCK (1314 "Candy")... 15-25 '60s
Members: Richard Knight; Robert Eaton; Fred Bridges.

BROUGHTON, Edna

Singles: 78 rpm

MODERN (773)... 40-60 50
(Exact title not known.)

BROUSSARD, Van

(With Grace Broussard; Van Broussard / Bobby Loveless)

Singles: 7-inch

BAYOU BOOGIE (106 thru 160)...4-8 77-79
CSP (1003 "Your Picture")...3-6 90
CHAMPAGNE...4-6 79-80
HARTCO (1010 "Yak Yak")...5-10 65
JIN...3-5 81
MALA (12021 "Nothing Sweet As You")...5-10 68
MICHELLE (924 thru 937)...5-10 64-65
MONTEL (917 thru 924)...5-10 63-64
RED STICK (1001 "Feel the Flame")...5-10 68
REX (1016 "I Can't Complain")... 10-15 61
SSS INT'L (445 "Set Me Free")...4-8 77

LPs: 10/12-inch

BAYOU BOOGIE (105 "More Bayou Boogie")... 15-25 78
BAYOU BOOGIE (148 "King of the Bayou Boogie")... 15-25 77
CHAMPAGNE (150 "Van Broussard & Bayou Boogie Band")... 10-15 80
JIN (9025 "More Bayou Boogie")... 10-15 81
JIN (9029 "King of Bayou Boogie")... 10-15 81
WAGON WHEEL (202 "Live")... 15-20 79
Also see DALE & GRACE

BROWN, Al, & His Tunetoppers

(Featuring Cookie Brown) — P&R/R&B '60

Singles: 7-inch

AMY (804 "The Madison")... 15-20 60
AMY (806 thru 829)... 10-20 60-61

EPs: 7-inch

AMY (1 "Madison Dance Party")... 40-60 60

LPs: 10/12-inch

AMY (1 "Madison Dance Party")... 50-75 60

BROWN, B., & His McVouts

Singles: 78 rpm

FLASH (102 "Good Woman Blues")...300-400 55

BROWN, B., & Rockin' McVouts

(Buster Brown)

Singles: 7-inch

EVERLAST (5014 "Chewing Gum")...20-30 62
VEST (827 "My Baby Left Me")...20-30 59
VEST (830 "Fannie Mae Is Back")...20-30 60
Despite incredible name similarities, there seems to be no connection between this artist and the previous one, who recorded for Flash.
Also see BROWN, Buster

BROWN, Barbara

Singles: 7-inch

ATCO (6549 "Can't Find No Happiness")...5-10 68
CARNIVAL (503 "Send Him to Me")...10-20 64
CARNIVAL (508 "So in Love")...10-20 65
SOUNDS OF MEMPHIS...4-6 72
TOWER (429 "There's a Look on Your Face")...5-10 68
Also see BARBARA & BROWNS

BROWN, Benny

Singles: 78 rpm

GOTHAM...15-25 53

Singles: 7-inch

GOTHAM (293 "Slick Baby")...30-40 53
(Black vinyl.)
GOTHAM (293 "Slick Baby")...75-100 53
(Colored vinyl.)

BROWN, Bep

(J.T. Brown)

Singles: 78 rpm

METEOR...40-60 52

Singles: 7-inch

METEOR (5001 "Kickin' the Blues Around")...100-120 52
Also see BROWN, J.T.

BROWN, Betty

Singles: 7-inch

BETHLEHEM (3001 "I'm Gonna Tell My Mama")...10-15 61
BETHLEHEM (3003 "Can't You Just Feel It")...10-15 62

BROWN, Bill

Singles: 7-inch

CUSTOM SOUND (164 "Tight Levis and Boots")...35-50 57

BROWN, Billie, & Ballards

Singles: 7-inch

ELTONE (439 "Why Baby Why")...500-750 63

BROWN, Billy

Singles: 78 rpm

DECCA (29559 "High Heels But No Soul")...5-10 55

Singles: 7-inch

CHALLENGE...5-10 69
COLUMBIA (41029 "Did We Have a Party")...15-25 57
COLUMBIA (41100 thru 41380)...10-20 58-59
DECCA (29559 "High Heels But No Soul")...15-20 55
REPUBLIC...10-20 60
STARS (552 "Did We Have a Party")...50-75 57

BROWN, Bobby

(With the Curios)

Singles: 7-inch

CURIO (100 "Falling from Paradise")...15-25 63
(Yellow vinyl.)
KING (5214 "I'm Beggin' You Baby")...10-15 59
KING (S-5214 "I'm Beggin' You Baby")...20-40 59
KING (5246 "Pleading")...10-15 59
PAK (1313 "Falling from Paradise")...40-50 62
VADEN (100 "Down at Mary's House")...100-200 59
VADEN (109 "Please, Please Baby")...200-300 59
(With Larry Donn.)
VERVE (10594 "Why")...5-10 68

EPs: 7-inch

VADEN (107 "Bobby Brown")...100-200 59
Also see DONN, Larry

BROWN, Bobby

LPs: 10/12-inch

DESTINY (4001 "Live")...75-100 72
DESTINY (4002 "The Enlightening Beam of Axonda")...100-150 72

BROWN, Boots — P&R '58

(With Blockbusters; with Pelugelpipers; with Dan Drew; Shorty Rogers)

Singles: 78 rpm

RCA...5-15 53-57

Singles: 7-inch

DOT...4-6 67-68
RCA...8-15 53-60

EPs: 7-inch

GROOVE (1000 "Rock That Beat")...25-50 55

LPs: 10/12-inch

GROOVE (1000 "Rock That Beat")...50-100 55
Also see COOL, Calvin
Also see ROGERS, Shorty

BROWN, Bucky, & Curios

Singles: 7-inch

XYZ (610 "Dream Date")...20-30 60

BROWN, Buster — P&R/R&B '60

(With Chas. Lucas & Thrillers)

Singles: 78 rpm

FIRE (1008 "Fannie Mae")...300-400 59

Singles: 7-inch

ABC...4-6 73
CHECKER (1099 "Crawling King Snake".10-20 63
FIRE (507 "Sugar Babe")...10-15 62
FIRE (516 "Raise a Ruckus Tonight")...10-15 62
FIRE (1008 "Fannie Mae")...15-25 59
FIRE (1020 "John Henry")...10-20 60
FIRE (1023 "Is You Is or Is You Ain't My Baby")...15-25 60
FIRE (1032 "Doctor Brown")...10-20 61
FIRE (1040 "I Get the Blues When It Rains")...10-20 61
FIRE (2021 "Sugar Babe")...8-10 68
GWENN (600 "Slow Drag Blues")...15-25 62
GWENN (601 "Trying to Learn How to Love You")...15-25 62
NOCTURN (1000 "I Love You for Sentimental Reasons")...10-15 64
OLDIES 45...4-6
RCA...4-6 74
ROULETTE...4-6 72
SEROCK (2005 "My Blue Heaven")...10-15 63
TURBO (008 "I Love You for Sentimental Reasons")...5-10 70
WHITE WHALE (316 "I've Got It Made")...5-10 69

LPs: 10/12-inch

COLLECTABLES...6-10 88
FIRE (101/102 "The New King of the Blues")...300-400 60
(Blue cover. Track listing includes *Blueberry Hill* and *When Things Go Wrong*. Disc number is 101 though cover indicates 102.)
FIRE (101/102 "The New King of the Blues")...150-300 60
(White cover. With *Blueberry Hill* and *When Things Go Wrong* replaced by *Going on a Picnic* and *Corena*. Disc number is 101 though cover indicates 102.)
KOALA...8-12
SOUFFLE...10-20 73
Also see BROWN, B., & Rockin' McVouts

BROWN, Camille, & Angelenos

Singles: 7-inch

PEEPERS (2825 "Angels in Heaven")...30-40 61
Also see ANGELENOS

BROWN, Charles — R&B '49

(With Johnny Moore's Three Blazers; "Vocal Quartet – The Song Stylists"; "Charles Brown singing and accompanying himself on piano;" with His Smarties)

Singles: 78 rpm

ALADDIN...25-50 49-57
CASH...15-25 57
HOLLYWOOD...15-25 53-54
SWING TIME...25-50 52

Singles: 7-inch

ACE (599 "Boys Will Be Boys")...10-20 60
ALADDIN (3076 "Black Night")...100-125 51
ALADDIN (3091 "I'll Always Be in Love with You")...50-100 51
ALADDIN (3092 "Seven Long Days")...50-100 52
ALADDIN (3116 "Hard Times")...50-100 52
ALADDIN (3120 "My Last Affair")...50-100 52
ALADDIN (3138 "Without Your Love")...50-100 52
ALADDIN (3157 "Rollin' Like a Pebble in the Sand")...50-100 52
ALADDIN (3163 "Evening Shadows")...40-60 53
ALADDIN (3176 "Take Me")...40-60 53
ALADDIN (3191 "Lonesome Feeling")...40-60 53
ALADDIN (3200 "All My Life")...30-50 53
ALADDIN (3220 "Everybody's Got Troubles")...30-50 54
ALADDIN (3235 "Let's Walk")...30-50 54
ALADDIN (3254 "Foolish")...30-50 54
ALADDIN (3272 "Honey Sipper")...30-50 55
ALADDIN (3284 "Walk with Me")...30-50 55
ALADDIN (3290 "Fool's Paradise")...30-50 55
ALADDIN (3296 "My Heart Is Mended")..30-50 55
ALADDIN (3316 "One Minute to One")...20-40 56
ALADDIN (3339 "Soothe Me")...20-40 56
ALADDIN (3342 "Confidential")...20-40 56
ALADDIN (3348 "Merry Christmas Baby")...20-40 56
ALADDIN (3366 "It's a Sin to Tell a Lie") .20-40 57
CENCO (123 "I Want to Go Home")...5-10
EAST WEST (106 "When Did You Leave Heaven")...10-20 58
GALAXY (762 "Cry No More")...5-10 68
GALAXY (766 "Abraham, Martin and John")...5-10 69
HOLLYWOOD (1006 "Pleading for Your Love")...25-50 53
IMPERIAL (018 "Black Night")...5-10 62
IMPERIAL (5830 "Fool's Paradise")...5-10 62
IMPERIAL (5902 "Merry Christmas Baby")...5-10 62
IMPERIAL (5905 "Black Night")...5-10 63
IMPERIAL (5961 "I'm Savin' My Love for You")...5-10 63
JEWEL...4-6 70-75
KENT (501 "Merry Christmas Baby")...5-10 68
KING (5439 "Angel Baby")...10-15 61
KING (5523 "Butterfly")...8-10 61
KING (5530 "Christmas in Heaven")...8-10 61
KING (5570 "Without a Friend")...8-10 61
KING (5722 "I'm Just a Drifter")...8-10 62
KING (5726 "It's Christmas Time")...8-10 62
KING (5731 "Wrap Yourself in a Christmas Package")...8-10 62
KING (5802 "I Wanna Be Close")...5-10 63
KING (5825 "Lucky Dreamer")...5-10 63
KING (5852 "Come Home")...5-10 64
KING (5946 "Christmas Blues")...5-10 64
KING (5947 "Christmas")...5-10 64
KING (6192 "Black Night")...5-10 68
KING (6194 "Let's Make Every Day a Christmas Day")...5-10 68
LIBERTY...3-5 84
LILLY (506 "Bon Voyage")...8-10 62
MAINSTREAM (607 "Pledging My Love")..5-10 65
NOLA (702 "I'll Love You")...5-10 63
STARDAY...5-10 69
SWING TIME (253 "I'll Miss You")...100-150 52
SWING TIME (259 "Be Fair with Me")..100-150 52

LPs: 10/12-inch

ALADDIN (702 "Mood Music")...500-1000 52
(10-inch LP. Black vinyl.)
ALADDIN (702 "Mood Music")...2000-3000 52
(10-inch LP. Red vinyl.)
ALADDIN (809 "Mood Music")...100-200 57
BIG TOWN...8-10 77-78
BLUES SPECTRUM...4-6
BLUESWAY (6039 "Legend!")...8-10 70
IMPERIAL (9178 "Million Sellers")...50-75 62
JEWEL...8-15 72
KING (775 "Christmas Songs")...75-125 61
KING (878 "The Great Charles Brown")...40-60 63
KING (5000 series)...8-10
MAINSTREAM (300 series)...8-12 72
MAINSTREAM (6035 "Ballads My Way") 10-20 65
(Monaural.)
MAINSTREAM (56035 "Ballads My Way")...15-25 65
(Stereo.)
SCORE (4011 "Driftin' Blues")...150-200 57
Also see CHARLES, Ray / Charles Brown
Also see 5 EMBERS
Also see McCRACKLIN, Jimmy / T-Bone Walker / Charles Brown
Also see MOORE, Johnny
Also see SCOTT, Mabel

BROWN, Charles / Basin Street Boys

Singles: 78 rpm

CASH...10-20 57

Singles: 7-inch

CASH (1052 "Lost in the Night")...15-25 57
Also see BASIN STREET BOYS

BROWN, Charles / Lloyd Glenn
(With Johnny Moore's 3 Blazers)
Singles: 78 rpm
HOLLYWOOD.......10-20 54
Singles: 7-inch
HOLLYWOOD (1021 "Merry Christmas Baby")......20-30 54
Also see GLENN, Lloyd

BROWN, Charles, & Jimmy McCracklin
LPs: 10/12-inch
IMPERIAL (9257 "Best of the Blues")......25-50 64
Also see McCRACKLIN, Jimmy

BROWN, Charles, & Amos Milburn
(Charles Brown / Amos Milburn)
Singles: 7-inch
ACE (561 "Educated Fool")......10-20 59
KING (5464 "My Little Baby")......8-10 61
KING (6000 series)......4-6 75
LPs: 10/12-inch
GRAND PRIX (421 "Original Blues Sound")......10-15 64
(With Jackie Shane and Bob Marshall & Crystals.)
Also see BROWN, Charles
Also see MILBURN, Amos

BROWN, Charlie
Singles: 78 rpm
ROSE......25-50 55
Singles: 7-inch
ROSE (101 "Mean Mama")......100-150 55
ROSE (102 "Have You Heard the Gossip")......75-125 55

BROWN, Clarence "Gatemouth" *R&B '49*
Singles: 78 rpm
ALADDIN......15-25 47
PEACOCK......10-20 49-54
Singles: 7-inch
CINDERELLA......10-20 65
CUE (1050 "Leftover Blues")......8-10 64
PEACOCK (1600 "Baby Take It Easy")......50-100 52
PEACOCK (1607 thru 1637)......25-50 52-54
PEACOCK (1692 "Just Before Dawn")......15-25 60
PEACOCK (1696 "Slop Time")......15-25 60
LPs: 10/12-inch
BLUE STAR......30-40
MUSIC IS MEDICINE......8-12 78
ROUNDER......5-10 82
Also see McVEA, Jack

BROWN, Clarence "Gatemouth"/ Camille Howard / Bill Johnson Quartet / Van "Piano Man" Walls
EPs: 7-inch
BIG TOWN (150 "Without Me Baby")......25-50 '50s
(Probably not issued with cover. For reference, title shown is of Brown track, not EP overall.)
Also see BROWN, Clarence "Gatemouth"
Also see HOWARD, Camille
Also see WALLS, Van

BROWN, Dennis, & Atomics
Singles: 7-inch
ATOMIC (101 "Show Me the Rose")......500-1000 57

BROWN, Doug
(With the Omens)
Singles: 7-inch
CHECKER (1001 "Swingin' Sue")......10-20 61
PUNCH (1008 "T.G.I.F.")......25-50 65
(Reportedly 500 made.)
Session: Bob Seger; Lenny Drake.
Also see BEACH BUMS
Also see LENNY & THUNDERTONES
Also see SEGER, Bob
Also see THUNDERTONES

BROWN, Dusty
Singles: 78 rpm
PARROT......40-60 55
Singles: 7-inch
BANDARA (2503 "Please Don't Go")......15-25 59
PARROT (820 "Yes, She's Gone")......150-200 55

BROWN, Earl
(Earl Brown Singers)
Singles: 78 rpm
CHECKER......15-25 54
SWING TIME......20-40 52
Singles: 7-inch
CHECKER (802 "The Cat's Wiggle")......30-40 54
CHECKER (926 "Courtin' in the Rain")......10-15 59
KAPPA (207 "Tambourine")......15-25 58
SWING TIME (307 "Dust My Broom")......50-100 52
Also see FULSON, Lowell
Also see KAYE, Danny

BROWN, Gabriel
Singles: 78 rpm
BEACON......15-25 45-46
CORAL......10-20 49
GENNETT......15-25 45-46
JAY-DEE (779 "Hold Me Baby")......10-15 53
JOE DAVIS......15-25 45-46
MGM......10-20 53
Singles: 7-inch
JAY-DEE (779 "Hold Me Baby")......20-25 53

BROWN, Gary
(With the Chants)
Singles: 7-inch
BROWNIE (103 "Would You Laugh at Me")......35-45 '60s
DYNAMIC SOUND (2005 "Would You Laugh at Me")......8-12 67
USA (821 "Cold Day in June")......6-10 66
VENUS (101 "Cold Day in June")......10-15 66

BROWN, Gene
Singles: 7-inch
B&E ("Wild Cat Boogie")......50-100
(Selection number not known.)
DOT (15709 "Big Door")......40-60 58
GENE BROWN (28 "Big Door")......75-100 58

BROWN, George, & High Notes
Singles: 7-inch
DE'BESTH (1125 "Who Said Fred Was Dead")......50-75 59

BROWN, Gloria
Singles: 7-inch
CHECKER (1050 "Happy Birthday")......15-25 63

BROWN, Hank
Singles: 7-inch
ROYALTY (123 "Operation Stomp")......50-75

BROWN, Harry C.
Singles: 78 rpm
COLUMBIA (1999 "Nigger Love a Watermelon Ha Ha Ha")......50-100 1909

BROWN, Hiawatha
Singles: 7-inch
MR. PEACOCK (105 "My Imagination")......75-125 62

BROWN, Honey
(With Lefty Bates' Combo)
Singles: 78 rpm
CLUB "51"......25-50 55
Singles: 7-inch
CLUB "51" (107 "No Good Daddy")......75-100 55

BROWN, Hubert
Singles: 7-inch
PEACH (717 "Unfaithful")......50-100 59

BROWN, J.T.
(Sax Man Brown; with the Broomdusters)
Singles: 78 rpm
HARLEM......20-30 49-50
JOB (1103 "Boogie Baby")......75-100 54
METEOR......25-50 54
Singles: 7-inch
JOB (1103 "Boogie Baby")......75-100 54
METEOR (5016 "Dumb Woman Blues")......50-100 54
METEOR (5024 "Flaming Blues")......50-100 54
LPs: 10/12-inch
PEARL......5-10 78
Session: Elmore James.
Also see BROWN, Bep
Also see BROWN, Nature Boy
Also see JAMES, Elmore
Also see ROGERS, Jimmy

BROWN, James *R&B '56*
(With His Famous Flames; with the J.B.s; "James Brown Band")
Singles: 12-inch
CHURCHILL......4-6 83
POLYDOR......4-6 78
Singles: 78 rpm
FEDERAL (Except 12337, 12348 & 12364)......30-50 56-59
FEDERAL (12337 "Try Me")......75-125 58
FEDERAL (12348 "I Want You So Bad")......75-125 59
FEDERAL (12364 "Got to Cry")......100-150 59
Singles: 7-inch
AUGUSTA......3-5 83
BACKSTREET......3-5 83
BETHLEHEM (3089 "I Loves You Porgy")......10-15 65
BETHLEHEM (3098 "The Drunk")......8-12 70
CHURCHILL......3-5 83
FEDERAL (12258 "Please Please Please")......50-100 56
FEDERAL (12258 "Please Please Please")......15-25 '60s
(Audience noises are added to give a live concert effect.)
FEDERAL (12277 "No No No No")......50-75 56
FEDERAL (12289 "Just Won't Do Right")......50-75 57
FEDERAL (12290 "I Won't Plead No More")......50-75 57
FEDERAL (12300 "I Walked Alone")......50-75 57
FEDERAL (12311 "Baby Cries Over the Ocean")......50-75 57
FEDERAL (12337 "Try Me")......40-60 58
(Unsweetened.)
FEDERAL (12337 "Try Me")......15-25 '60s
(Has added strings and instrumentation.)
FEDERAL (12348 "I Want You So Bad")......30-50 59
FEDERAL (12352 "I've Got to Change")......25-35 59
(Monaural.)
FEDERAL (S-12352 "I've Got to Change")......50-75 59
(Stereo.)
FEDERAL (12361 "Good, Good Lovin'")......25-35 59
(Monaural.)
FEDERAL (S-12361 "Good, Good Lovin'")......50-75 59
(Stereo.)
FEDERAL (12364 "Got to Cry")......20-30 59
FEDERAL (12369 "I'll Go Crazy")......20-30 60
FEDERAL (12370 "Think")......20-30 60
FEDERAL (12378 "This Old Heart")......20-30 60
KING (5423 "The Bells")......20-30 60
KING (5438 "Hold It")......15-25 61
KING (5442 thru 5968, except 5739)......10-20 61-64
KING (5739 "Prisoner of Love")......10-20 63
KING (5739 "Prisoner of Love")......25-35 63
("Special Programming Side. Has Intro by James Brown." Flip side is regular version. Promotional issue only.)
KING (5995 thru 6065)......10-15 65-66
KING (6071 thru 6363)......8-12 67-71
KING (11221 "Mashed Potatoes '66")......10-20 66
(Promotional issue only. Identification number shown since no selection number is used.)
PEOPLE......4-6 71-76
POLYDOR (Except 14304)......3-6 71-84
POLYDOR (14304 "For Sentimental Reasons")......5-10 76
RIPETE......3-5 '80s
SCOTTI BROTHERS......3-5 85-88
SMASH (1898 "Caledonia")......10-15 64
SMASH (1908 "The Things That I Used to Do")......10-15 64
SMASH (1919 "Out of Sight")......10-15 64
SMASH (1975 thru 2093)......8-12 65-67
T.K.......3-5 80-81
Picture Sleeves
KING (5842 "Oh Baby Don't You Weep")......10-20 64
POLYDOR (14116 "King Heroin")......10-15 72
(A drawing of the "King Heroin" ghost and tombstone.)
POLYDOR (14116 "King Heroin")......4-8 72
(Omits ghost and tombstone drawing.)
POLYDOR (14223 "The Payback")......4-8 74
SCOTTI BROTHERS......3-5 85-88
SMASH (1898 "Caledonia")......10-15 64
SMASH (1908 "The Things That I Used to Do")......10-15 64
SMASH (1919 "Out of Sight")......10-15 64
EPs: 7-inch
KING ("Month of Soul")......35-50
(Promotional issue only. No selection number used.)
KING (430 "Please Please Please")......30-50 59
KING (826 "Live at the Apollo")......20-40 63
SMASH (703 "Grits & Soul")......15-25 65
(Juke box issue only. Includes title strips.)
SMASH (707 "James Brown Plays the New Breed")......15-25 66
(Juke box issue only. Includes title strips.)
LPs: 10/12-inch
AGUSTA SOUND......5-8
AUDIO FIDELITY (326 "James Brown")......10-15 83
(Picture disc.)
CHURCHILL......5-10 83
HRB......8-10 73
KING (610 "Please, Please, Please")......100-200 59
(Cover pictures a woman's legs.)
KING (635 "Try Me")......100-200 59
(Cover pictures a woman with a smoking gun.)
KING (683 "James Brown & His Famous Flames *Think*")......400-600 60
(Cover pictures a baby.)
KING (683 "James Brown & His Famous Flames *Think*")......25-40 61
(Cover has pictures of James Brown.)
KING (743 "The Always Amazing James Brown and the Famous Flames")......50-75 61
(Cover is pink and blue.)
KING (771 "Jump Around")......50-75 62
KING (780 "Good Good Twistin' with James Brown")......50-75 62
KING (804 "James Brown and the Famous Flames Tour the U.S.A.")......50-75 62
KING (826 "Apollo Theatre Presents, in Person, the James Brown Show")......40-60 63
KING (851 "Prisoner of Love")......30-50 63
KING (883 "Pure Dynamite")......25-50 64
KING (883 "Pure Dynamite")......500-750 64
(Banded edition. Promotional issue only.)
KING (900 series)......15-25 65-66
KING (1000 & 1100 series, except 1024 and 1038)......10-15 67-71
KING (1024 "Show of Tomorrow")......100-150 67
KING (1038 "Thinking About Little Willie John")......30-35 68
POLYDOR......5-10 71-84
SCOTTI BROTHERS......5-8 86-88
SMASH......10-20 64-68
SOLID SMOKE......5-10 80-81
T.K.......5-10 80
Also see BYRD, Bobby, & James Brown
Also see FRANKLIN, Aretha, & James Brown
Also see J.B.s
Also see KENDRICK, Nat, & Swans
Also see POETS

BROWN, James, & Vicki Anderson *P&R '67*
Singles: 7-inch
KING......8-12 67-70
POLYDOR......4-6 73

BROWN, James, & Lyn Collins *P&R/R&B '72*
Singles: 7-inch
POLYDOR (14157 "What My Baby Needs Now Is a Little More Lovin' ")......4-8 72
Also see COLLINS, Lyn

BROWN, James / Martha & Vandellas
Singles: 7-inch
A&M (3022 "I Got You")......3-5 88
Picture Sleeves
A&M (3022 "I Got You")......3-5 88
Also see MARTHA & VANDELLAS

BROWN, James, & Marva Whitney
Singles: 7-inch
KING (6206 "In the Middle")......5-10 69
KING (6218 "I'm Tired, I'm Tired, I'm Tired")......5-10 69
Also see BROWN, James
Also see WHITNEY, Marva

BROWN, James "Widemouth"
(With Henry Hayes)
Singles: 7-inch
JAX (306 "A Weary Silent Night")......100-200 51
(Red vinyl.)
Also see HAYES, Henry

BROWN, Jay
(With the Jets)
Singles: 7-inch
ATCO (6394 "Don't Push Me Around")......5-10 65
PEACH (736 "Rockin' the Guitar")......10-20 60

BROWN, Jericho
(Jericho Browne)
Singles: 7-inch
CHANCELLOR (1104 "Bluebird")......8-12 62
DEL-FI (4103 "I Need You")......15-25 58
MERCURY (72392 "Gabrielle")......5-10 65
RKO UNIQUE (412 "Little Neva")......20-30 57
W.B. (5161 thru 5458)......10-15 60-64

BROWN, Jimmy
Singles: 7-inch
A-BET 5-10 67-68
BIG LEAGUE (564 "My Little Girl") 30-40
KENO (1001 "Hootchi Koo") 10-20 61

BROWN, John, L.
Singles: 7-inch
LIKE IT IS (690 "I'm Losing You") 15-25 '60s

BROWN, John, Trio
Singles: 7-inch
FENTON 15-25 68

BROWN, Johnny "Scat"
(Johnny Powers)
Singles: 7-inch
LEEDON (514 "Indeed I Do") 75-125
Also see POWERS, Johnny

BROWN, Juanita
Singles: 78 rpm
ALADDIN (3022 "Key to My Door") 15-25 49
Also see BROOKS, Dusty

BROWN, Judy
Singles: 7-inch
FIFO (104 "Heaven & Paradise") 25-35 61
SKYLA (1121 "First Day of School") 20-30 61
SKYLA (1122 "Dear Santa") 30-40 61

BROWN, Kay
Singles: 78 rpm
CROWN (127 "Oop-Shoop") 5-10 54
Singles: 7-inch
CROWN (127 "Oop-Shoop") 10-20 54
METRO (20004 "If I Had You") 8-12 58
MGM (12694 "If I Had You") 8-12 58

BROWN, Kenny
Singles: 78 rpm
PEP 20-30 55-56
Singles: 7-inch
PEP (100 "Baby Baby Baby") 75-125 55
PEP (102 "Throw a Little Wood on the Fire") 50-75 56
SUNDOWN (127 "Let's Love Again") 8-12 60
TOPPA (1040 "Standing By") 8-12 61

BROWN, Lattimore
(Sir Lattimore Brown)
Singles: 7-inch
ACE (3012 "Warm & Tender Love") 4-6 75
DUCHESS (1002 "Night Time Is the Right Time") 15-20 61
DUCHESS (1007 "What Have I Done Wrong") 10-15 61
DUCHESS (1015 "Say What") 10-15 62
EXCELLO (2196 "Somebody's Gonna Miss Me") 8-12 61
RENEGADE (101 "I Wish I Felt This Way at Home") 10-15 '60s
RENEGADE (1201 "I Will") 10-15 69
SEVENTY 7 5-10 '60s
SOUND STAGE 7 5-10 65-68
ZIL (9005 "It Hurts Me So") 10-20 60
ZIL (9006 "Chick Chick Chicky") 10-20 60

BROWN, Leadell
Singles: 7-inch
MASON (1101 "My Destiny") 20-30 66

BROWN, Lee, & His Barbeton Boogie Woogie Cats
(Lee Brown "The Heartbreaker")
Singles: 78 rpm
CHICAGO 20-30 46
QUEEN 20-30 46

BROWN, Leon
Singles: 7-inch
ARGO (5320 "He's in My Corner") 10-15 58

BROWN, Little Willie
Singles: 78 rpm
SUNTAN 15-25 56
Singles: 7-inch
DO-RA-ME (1404 "Cut It Out") 20-30 61
SUNTAN (1112 "Going Back to the Country") 50-75 56
TOPIC 25-35

BROWN, Louise *P&R '61*
Singles: 7-inch
WITCH (101 "Son-in-Law") 30-50 61

BROWN, Lover Boy
Singles: 78 rpm
REGENT (1007 "Just the Blues") 10-20 49

BROWN, Marcus
Singles: 7-inch
KHOURY'S (734 "Lover Lee") 10-15 60

BROWN, Maxine *P&R '60*
(With the Leroy Glover Orchestra)
Singles: 7-inch
ABC 4-6 75
ABC-PAR (10235 thru 10388) 8-12 61-62
AVCO EMBASSY 4-6 71
COLLECTABLES 3-5 81
COMMONWEALTH UNITED 4-8 69-70
EPIC 5-10 69
ERIC 3-5 83
MUSICTONE (1118 "All in My Mind") 8-12 63
NOMAR (103 "All in My Mind") 10-20 60
NOMAR (106 "Funny") 10-20 61
NOMAR (107 "Heaven in Your Arms") 20-30 61
WAND 5-15 63-67
WHAM 4-8
Picture Sleeves
WAND (135 "Ask Me") 10-15 63
WHAM (7036 "All in My Mind") 10-15
EPs: 7-inch
COMMONWEALTH UNITED (1001 "Maxine Brown") 5-10 69
(Promotional issue only.)
LPs: 10/12-inch
COLLECTABLES 6-8 88
COMMONWEALTH UNITED 10-12 69
GUEST STAR 10-12 64
WAND 15-25 63-67
Also see ADAMS, Faye / Little Esther / Maxine Brown
Also see JACKSON, Chuck, & Maxine Brown

BROWN, Maxine / Irma Thomas
LPs: 10/12-inch
GRAND PRIX 12-15 64
Also see BROWN, Maxine
Also see THOMAS, Irma

BROWN, Milan
Singles: 7-inch
BATON (204 "I'm Goin' Back") 15-25 54

BROWN, Nappy *P&R/R&B '55*
(With the Gibralters; with Southern Sisters; with Zippers)
Singles: 78 rpm
REO (8033 "Piddily Patter") 10-15 55
(Canadian.)
SAVOY 10-20 55-57
Singles: 7-inch
REO (8033 "Piddily Patter") 25-35 55
(Canadian.)
SAVOY (1129 thru 1196) 15-20 54-56
SAVOY (1506 thru 1555, except 1525) 10-15 57-58
SAVOY (1525 "The Right Time") 25-35 57
(Dionne Warwick's first appearance on record, as a backup vocalist.)
SAVOY (1562 thru 1592) 8-12 59-60
SAVOY (1594 thru 1621) 5-10 61-63
LPs: 10/12-inch
ICHIBAN 5-10
LANDSLIDE 5-10
SAVOY (14002 "Nappy Brown Sings") 150-250 57
SAVOY (14025 "The Right Time") 50-100 60
SAVOY (14427 "Nappy Brown") 8-15 77
Session: Gospelaires (featuring Dionne Warwick).
Also see GIBRALTERS
Also see WARWICK, Dionne

BROWN, Nature Boy, & His Blues Ramblers
(J.T. Brown)
Singles: 78 rpm
UNITED 10-20 51-52
Singles: 7-inch
B&F (1341 "House Party Groove") 8-10 60
UNITED (103 "Windy City Boogie") 50-75 51
UNITED (106 "Rock 'Em") 50-75 52
UNITED (121 "Strictly Gone") 50-75 52
(Black vinyl.)
UNITED (121 "Strictly Gone") 75-125 52
(Colored vinyl.)
Also see BROWN, J.T.

BROWN, Neal
Singles: 7-inch
CHART SOUND (129 "If By Chance") 15-20 '60s

BROWN, Oscar, Jr. *P&R/R&B '74*
(With Luis Henrique)
Singles: 7-inch
ATLANTIC 4-6 74
COLUMBIA 10-15 60-62
FONTANA 5-10 65-66
MAD 15-25 59
LPs: 10/12-inch
ATLANTIC 5-10
COLUMBIA 15-25 61-63
FONTANA 10-15 66

BROWN, Otis
(With the Haywood Singers)
Singles: 7-inch
EX SPECT MORE (10655 "You Girl") 10-20 '60s
EX SPECT MORE (66551 "I Don't Wanna Cry") 10-20 '60s
EXPECT MORE (106551 "I Don't Wonn'a Cry") 5-10 '60s
(Note slight label name variation.)
LUJUNA (10655 "Will You Wait") 10-20 '60s
OLÉ (100 "South Side Chicago") 15-25 '60s
OLÉ (102 "What Would You Do") 15-25 '60s

BROWN, Pat
Singles: 7-inch
SEVEN B (7009 "He's a Wonderful Guy") 5-10 67
WEDGE (1001 "Forbidden Fruit") 100-150

BROWN, Piney
Singles: 78 rpm
JUBILEE 10-15 54
KING 10-15 53
Singles: 7-inch
CIMARRON 5-10 63
DEEP GROOVE (23931 "Everything But You") 5-10
(Identification number shown since no selection number is used.)
JUBILEE 20-25 54
KING 20-25 53
MAD (1295 "My Love") 10-15 59
SOUND STAGE 7 4-6 69-70
Also see BROOKS & BROWN

BROWN, Richard (Rabbit)
Singles: 78 rpm
VICTOR (35840 "Sinking of the Titanic") 500-750 27
(12-inch 78 rpm.)

BROWN, Richard
Singles: 7-inch
STEELTOWN (686 "Sweet & Kind") 10-15 69

BROWN, Rocky
Singles: 7-inch
MELRON (Except 5001) 8-12 '60s
MELRON (5001 "Den of Love") 50-75 64
Also see STUDENTS

BROWN, Romaine, & Romaines
Singles: 78 rpm
DECCA 10-20 56-57
Singles: 7-inch
DECCA (30054 thru 30399) 15-25 56-57

BROWN, Roy *R&B/C&W '48*
(With His Mighty-Mighty Men)
Singles: 78 rpm
DELUXE 25-50 47-51
GOLD STAR (636 "Deep Sea Diver") 50-75 48
IMPERIAL 15-25 57
KING 15-25 52-57
Singles: 7-inch
ATLANTIC (2026 "I Can't Hear a Word You Say") 5-10 59
BLUESWAY (61002 "New Orleans Women") 5-10 67
DELUXE (3318 "Big Town") 400-500 51
DELUXE (3319 "Bar Room Blues") 250-350 51
(Black vinyl.)
DELUXE (3319 "Bar Room Blues") 350-450 51
(Blue vinyl.)
DELUXE (3323 "I've Got the Last Laugh Now") 75-100 51
(Black vinyl.)
DELUXE (3323 "I've Got the Last Laugh Now") 500-750 51
(Blue vinyl.)
FRIENDSHIP 5-10
GERT (11123 "Baby, It's Love") 5-10 68
GUSTO 3-5 83
HOME OF THE BLUES (107 thru 122) 15-25 60-61
IMPERIAL (5422 thru 5489) 20-30 57-58
IMPERIAL (5510 "Hip Shakin' Baby") 150-200 58
KING (4602 "Travelin' Man") 30-60 53
(Black vinyl.)
KING (4602 "Travelin' Man") 100-150 53
(Colored vinyl.)
KING (4609 thru 4834) 50-75 53-55
KING (5178 thru 5333) 15-25 59-60
MERCURY 4-6 71
MOBILE FIDELITY 4-6 72
SUMMIT (1001 "Let the Four Winds Blow") 8-12
TRU-LOVE (449 "I'm Making Love") 4-6
EPs: 7-inch
KING (254 "Roy Brown") 400-600 53
LPs: 10/12-inch
BLUESWAY (6056 "Hard Times") 10-20 68-73
EPIC 10-15 71
GUSTO 8-12
INTERMEDIA 5-10 84
KING (956 "24 Hits") 35-45 66
KING (1100 series) 10-15 71
KING (5000 series) 8-10 79
Session: Johnny Burnette; Dorsey Burnette.
Also see BURNETTE, Johnny & Dorsey
Also see HARRIS, Wynonie / Roy Brown
Also see HARRIS, Wynonie / Roy Brown / Eddie Vinson

BROWN, Ruth *R&B '49*
(With the Rhythmakers)
Singles: 78 rpm
ATLANTIC 20-40 49-57
Singles: 7-inch
ATLANTIC (919 "Teardrops from My Eyes") 200-250 50
ATLANTIC (930 "I'll Wait for You") 50-100 51
ATLANTIC (941 "I Know") 50-100 51
ATLANTIC (948 "Shine On") 50-100 51
ATLANTIC (962 thru 1005) 30-50 52-53
ATLANTIC (1018 thru 1113) 25-35 54-56
ATLANTIC (1125 thru 1166) 20-30 57
ATLANTIC (1177 thru 2008) 15-25 58
ATLANTIC (2015 thru 2052) 15-20 59-60
ATLANTIC (2064 thru 2104) 10-20 60-61
DECCA (31598 "What Happened to You") 5-10 64
DECCA (31640 "Come a Little Closer") 5-10 64
LG (102 "Time After Time") 5-10
NOSLEN (102 "Secret Love") 5-10 64
PHILIPS (40028 thru 40119) 8-12 62-63
SKYE (21 "Yesterday") 5-10 69
EPs: 7-inch
ATLANTIC (505 "Ruth Brown Sings") 50-75 53
ATLANTIC (535 "Ruth Brown Sings") 50-75 53
ATLANTIC (585 "Ruth Brown") 35-60 57
PHILIPS (028 "Jim Dandy") 15-25 62
(Juke box issue.)
PHILIPS (623 "Along Comes Ruth") 15-25 62
(Juke box issue.)
LPs: 10/12-inch
ATLANTIC (1308 "Last Date with Ruth Brown") 100-200 59
ATLANTIC (SD-1308 "Last Date with Ruth Brown") 150-250 59
(Stereo.)
ATLANTIC (8004 "Ruth Brown") 75-100 57
(Black label.)
ATLANTIC (8004 "Ruth Brown") 50-75 60
(Red label.)
ATLANTIC (8026 "Miss Rhythm") 40-60 59
(Black label.)
ATLANTIC (8026 "Miss Rhythm") 75-125 59
(Multi-color label.)
ATLANTIC (8026 "Miss Rhythm") 40-60 59
(White label.)
ATLANTIC (8026 "Miss Rhythm") 20-30 60
(Red label.)
ATLANTIC (8080 "Best of Ruth Brown") 20-30 63
COBBLESTONE (9007 "The Real Ruth Brown") 8-12 72
DOBRE (1041 "You Don't Know Me") 5-10 78
FLAIR (8201 "The Soul Survivors") 5-10 82
MAINSTREAM (369 "Softly") 8-10 72
MAINSTREAM (6034 "Ruth Brown '65") 10-20 65
(Stereo.)
MAINSTREAM (56034 "Ruth Brown '65") 10-20 65
(Monaural.)
PHILIPS (20028 "Along Comes Ruth") 15-25 62
(Monaural.)

PHILIPS (20055 "Gospel Time") 15-25 62
(Monaural.)
PHILIPS (60028 "Along Comes Ruth") 20-30 62
(Stereo.)
PHILIPS (60055 "Gospel Time") 20-30 62
(Stereo.)
SKYE (13 "Black Is Brown and Brown Is Beautiful") 10-12 70
Session: James Quintet.
Also see BRADLEY, Will, & Ray McKinley
Also see JACKSON, Willis
Also see JAMES QUINTET
Also see JOHNSON, Buddy

BROWN, Ruth, & Delta Rhythm Boys

Singles: 7-inch

ATLANTIC (1023 "Sentimental Journey") 30-40 54
Also see DELTA RHYTHM BOYS

BROWN, Ruth, & Clyde McPhatter R&B '55

Singles: 78 rpm

ATLANTIC 15-25 55

Singles: 7-inch

ATLANTIC (1077 "Love Has Joined Us Together") 25-35 55
Also see BROWN, Ruth
Also see McPHATTER, Clyde

BROWN, Skip, & Shantons

Singles: 7-inch

PAM (112 "Why Don't You Believe Me") . 30-40 61
Also see JACKSON, Skip
Also see SHANTONS

BROWN, Skippy

Singles: 78 rpm

CHANCE (1129 "So Many Days") 50-75 53

Singles: 7-inch

CHANCE (1129 "So Many Days") 100-200 53

BROWN, Texas Johnny

Singles: 78 rpm

ATLANTIC (876 "The Blues Rock") 50-75 49

BROWN, Tom, & Tom Toms
(Tommy & Tom Toms)

Singles: 7-inch

JARO INT'L (77023 "Tomahawk") 40-60 60
Also see MR. SAKS & BLUE STRINGS
Also see SMITH, Bill

BROWN, Tommy
(With his Combo; Little Tommy Brown)

Singles: 78 rpm

ACORN 30-40 51
GROOVE 10-20 55
IMPERIAL 15-25 57
KING 15-25 53
SAVOY 10-20 52
UNITED (183 "Remember Me") 20-40 54

Singles: 7-inch

ABC-PAR 5-10 65
GROOVE (0132 "Don't Leave Me") 15-25 55
GROOVE (0143 "The Thrill Is Gone") 40-50 56
IMPERIAL (5476 "Rock My Blues Away") 20-40 57
KING (4658 "How Much Do You Think I Can Stand") 75-125 53
KING (4679 "Goodbye I'm Gone") 25-50 53
SAVOY (838 "Never Trust a Woman") 25-50 52
UNITED (183 "Remember Me") 75-125 54
(Black vinyl.)
UNITED (183 "Remember Me") 150-250 54
(Red vinyl.)

BROWN, Tommy

Singles: 7-inch

K&B (101 "That Cat") 100-200

BROWN, Walter
(With Ben Webster; with His Band)

Singles: 78 rpm

CAPITOL (806 "Nasty Attitude") 15-25 50

Singles: 7-inch

CAPITOL (806 "Nasty Attitude") 40-50 50
LUNNAR #2 (006 "Alley Cat") 4-6 78
ZIP (4686 "Alley Cat") 300-400 57
(Dark blue label.)
ZIP (4686 "Alley Cat") 25-50 58
(Light blue label.)
Also see McSHANN, Jay

BROWN, Waymon

Singles: 78 rpm

DECCA (48264 "Barefoot Susie") 15-25 51

Singles: 7-inch

DECCA (48264 "Barefoot Susie") 30-40 51

BROWN, Willie, & Cameos

Singles: 7-inch

DO-RA-ME (1404 "Cut It Out") 15-25 59

BROWN, Wini R&B '52
(With the Boyfriends)

Singles: 78 rpm

COLUMBIA 10-20 51
MERCURY 25-35 52

Singles: 7-inch

COLUMBIA (872 "A Good Man Is Hard to Find") 25-35 51
JARO (77018 "Gone Again") 10-15 60
MERCURY (5870 "Here in My Heart") 50-75 52
MERCURY (8270 "Be Anything") 75-125 52
MERCURY (70062 "Tear Down the Sky") 50-75 52
RCA (6970 "Available Lover") 15-25 57
(With Larry Dale.)
Members: Wini Brown; Joe Van Loan; Warren Suttles; Percy Green; Fred Francis.
Also see DALE, Larry
Also see DOGGETT, Bill
Also see DREAMERS
Also see HAMPTON, Lionel
Also see VAN LOAN, Joe
Also see WILLIAMS, Cootie, & Wini Brown

BROWN & GREENE

Singles: 7-inch

FLASH (119 "Kiss Me Baby") 10-20 57

BROWN DOTS
(Deek Watson & Brown Dots)

Singles: 78 rpm

CASTLE 15-25 48
MAJESTIC 10-20 48
MANOR 10-20 45-49
VARSITY 15-25 42
Members: Deek Watson; Jimmy Gordon; Jimmie Nabbie; Pat Best.
Also see BELL, Gwenn, & Brown Dots
Also see INK SPOTS
Also see FOUR DOTS
Also see FOUR TUNES
Also see NABBIE, Jimmie

BROWN PAPER BAG

Singles: 7-inch

JOX (065 "Something Tells Me") 15-25 67

BROWNE, Al
(Al Browne & His Band; Al Brown)

Singles: 7-inch

BM (2835 "The Whip") .... 10-20 '60s
GENEVA 5-10 65
LAKE 5-10
PROVIDENCE (408 "Soul") 5-10 65
RIC (409 "Buggy Boo") .... 10-20 '60s
XAVIER ("Hot Dog Twist") 10-20 60
(No selection number used.)
Also see CRESTS
Also see CONCEPTS
Also see DEL COUNTS
Also see EDDIE & STARLITES
Also see JIMMY & CRESTONES
Also see ROULETTES
Also see STARLITES
Also see STYLISTS
Also see TWINKLES
Also see VELTONES
Also see VERDICTS
Also see VIOLINS

BROWNE, Doris
(With the Capris)

Singles: 78 rpm

GOTHAM 20-40 53-54

Singles: 7-inch

COLLECTABLES 3-5 81
GOTHAM (290 "Please Believe Me") 50-75 53
(Blue label.)
GOTHAM (290 "Please Believe Me") 20-30 53
(Red or yellow label.)
GOTHAM (296 "Until the End of Time") ... 50-75 53
GOTHAM (298 "The Game of Love") 50-75 53
GOTHAM (303 "Am I Asking Too Much") . 40-60 54
Also see CAPRIS

BROWNE, Jackson P&R/LP '72

Singles: 12-inch

ASYLUM 4-6 81-82
ELEKTRA 4-8 89
(Promotional only.)

Singles: 7-inch

ASYLUM 3-6 72-86
COLUMBIA 3-5 86
ELEKTRA 3-5 80-89

Picture Sleeves

ASYLUM 3-5 80-86
ELEKTRA 4-8 80

LPs: 10/12-inch

ASYLUM (Except 5051) 8-10 72-86
ASYLUM (5051 "Jackson Browne") 10-15 72
(With burlap cover.)
ASYLUM (5051 "Jackson Browne") 8-10 72
(Without burlap.)
ELEKTRA ("Jackson Browne's First Album") 25-35 67
(Promotional issue only.)
ELEKTRA (60830 "World in Motion") 5-8 89
MFSL (055 "Pretender") 40-60 81
Also see SPRINGSTEEN, Bruce / Jackson Browne

BROWNER, Duke, & Kaddo Strings

Singles: 7-inch

IMPACT (1008 "Cryin' Over You") 50-75 66
Also see KADDO STRINGS

BROWNETTES

Singles: 7-inch

KING (6153 "Never Find a Love Like Mine") 10-15 68

BROWNING, Bill

Singles: 7-inch

ISLAND (4 "Hula Rock") 25-50 59
ISLAND (7 "Born with the Blues") 75-100 59
ISLAND (10 "Breaking Hearts") 20-40 60
ISLAND (11 "Sinful Woman") 50-75 60
LUCKY (1 "I'll Pay You Back") 100-150 59
STARDAY (432 "Don't Push, Don't Shove") 100-125 59
STARDAY (488 "Down in the Hollow") 50-75 60
Also see BROWNING, Zeke

BROWNING, Zeke
(With the Dynamics)

Singles: 7-inch

LUCKY (5 "Bad Case of the Blues") 50-75 59
LUCKY (11 "Spinning Wheel Rock") 50-75 61
RUBY (220 "It's Too Late Now") 15-25 57
Also see BROWNING, Bill

BROWNS C&W '54
(Jim Edward & Maxine Brown; Jim Edward, Maxine & Bonnie Brown; with the Louisiana Hayride Band; Browns featuring Jim Edward Brown)

Singles: 78 rpm

FABOR 5-15 54-55
RCA 5-15 56-57

Singles: 7-inch

COLUMBIA 5-10 62
FABOR 10-20 54-55
RCA (6480 thru 7427) 10-15 56-58
RCA (47-7555 "The Three Bells") 5-10 59
(Monaural.)
RCA (61-7555 "The Three Bells") 10-15 59
(Stereo.)
RCA (47-7614 "Scarlet Ribbons") 5-10 59
(Monaural.)
RCA (61-7614 "Scarlet Ribbons") 10-15 59
(Stereo.)
RCA (47-7700 "Old Lamplighter") 5-10 60
(Monaural.)
RCA (61-7700 "Old Lamplighter") 10-15 60
(Stereo.)
RCA (47-7755 "Lonely Little Robin") 5-10 60
(Monaural.)
RCA (61-7755 "Lonely Little Robin") 10-15 60
(Stereo.)
RCA (47-7780 "Whiffenpoof Song") 5-10 60
(Monaural.)
RCA (61-7780 "Whiffenpoof Song") 10-15 60
(Stereo.)
RCA (47-7820 "Send Me the Pillow You Dream On") 5-10 60
(Monaural.)
RCA (61-7820 "Send Me the Pillow You Dream On") 10-15 60
(Monaural.)
RCA (7820 "Blue Christmas") 5-10 60
RCA (37-7866 "Angel's Dolly") 10-15 61
(Compact 33 single.)
RCA (47-7866 "Angel's Dolly") 5-10 61
RCA (37-7917 "My Baby's Gone") 10-15 61
(Compact 33 single.)
RCA (47-7917 "My Baby's Gone") 5-10 61
RCA (37-7969 "Foolish Pride") 10-15 61
(Compact 33 single.)
RCA (47-7969 "Foolish Pride") 5-10 61
RCA (37-7997 "Remember Me") 10-15 62
(Compact 33 single.)
RCA (47-7997 "Remember Me") 5-10 62
RCA (8066 thru 9364) 5-10 62-67

Picture Sleeves

RCA (7700 "The Old Lamplighter") 10-15 60
RCA (7755 "Lonely Little Robin") 10-15 60
RCA (7780 "Whiffenpoof Song") 10-15 60

EPs: 7-inch

RCA 10-20 57-60

LPs: 10/12-inch

CAMDEN 8-12 65-68
CANDLELITE (0422 "Beautiful Country Music of the Browns") 5-10 80
(Mail order offer.)
MCA/DOT 5-8 86
RCA (524 "20 of the Best") 5-8 85
RCA (1000 thru 3000 series) 5-10 75-81
(With "ANL1" or "AYL1" prefix.)
RCA (1438 Jim Edward, Maxine & Bonnie Brown") 35-55 57
(With "LPM" prefix.)
RCA (2000 series) 15-30 59-65
(With "LPM" or "LSP" prefix.)
RCA (3000 series) 12-20 65-67
(With "LPM" or "LSP" prefix.)
Members: Jim Edward Brown; Maxine Brown; Bonnie Brown.
Also see COOKE, Sam / Rod Lauren / Neil Sedaka / Browns
Also see SEDAKA, Neil / Ann-Margret / Browns / Sam Cooke

BRUBECK, Dave, Quartet LP '55
(Dave Brubeck Trio; Octet; with Paul Desmond)

Singles: 78 rpm

COLUMBIA 4-8 55-57
FANTASY 4-8 52-55

Singles: 7-inch

COLUMBIA (Except 40000 & 41000 series) 4-6 62-65
COLUMBIA (40000 & 41000 series) 5-10 55-61
FANTASY (500 series) 5-10 52-55

Picture Sleeves

COLUMBIA 5-10 61-63

EPs: 7-inch

COLUMBIA 10-25 55-59
FANTASY 15-30 51-57

LPs: 10/12-inch

ATLANTIC (79 "Fantasy Years") 8-12 74
COLUMBIA (566 "Jazz Goes to College") 50-75 54
COLUMBIA (590 "Dave Brubeck at Storyville") 50-75 54
COLUMBIA (622 "Brubeck Time") 40-60 55
COLUMBIA (699 "Jazz: Red Hot and Cool") 40-60 55
COLUMBIA (826 "Dave Brubeck Quintet at Carnegie Hall 20-30 63
COLUMBIA (878 "Brubeck Plays Brubeck") 30-50 56
COLUMBIA (932 "Brubeck, Jay & Kai at Newport") 30-50 57
COLUMBIA (984 "Jazz Impressions of the U.S.A.") 30-50 57
COLUMBIA (1000 thru 1200 series) 20-35 57-59
(Monaural.)
COLUMBIA (1300 thru 2300 series) 12-25 59-65
(Monaural.)
COLUMBIA (6321 "Jazz Goes to College") 50-100 54
(10-inch LP.)
COLUMBIA (6322 "Jazz Goes to College") 50-75 54
(10-inch LP.)
COLUMBIA (6330 "Dave Brubeck at Storyville") 50-75 54
(10-inch LP.)
COLUMBIA (6331 "Dave Brubeck at Storyville") 50-75 54
(10-inch LP.)

COLUMBIA (8000 series)........................ 20-45 57-59
(Stereo.)
COLUMBIA (8100 thru 9300 series)........ 15-30 59-66
(Stereo.)
COLUMBIA (30625 "Adventures in Time")... 10-15 71
(Two discs in gatefold cover.)
CROWN... 10-15 62-64
FANTASY (1 "Dave Brubeck Trio")...... 100-150 51
(10-inch LP. Colored vinyl.)
FANTASY (2 "Dave Brubeck Trio")...... 100-150 51
(10-inch LP. Colored vinyl.)
FANTASY (3 "Dave Brubeck Octet") ... 100-150 52
(10-inch LP. Colored vinyl.)
FANTASY (5 "Dave Brubeck Quartet with Paul Desmond").. 100-150 52
(10-inch LP. Colored vinyl.)
FANTASY (7 "Dave Brubeck Quartet with Paul Desmond").. 100-150 53
(10-inch LP. Colored vinyl.)
FANTASY (8 "At Storyville")................ 100-150 53
(10-inch LP. Colored vinyl.)
FANTASY (10 "Jazz at the Black Hawk").. 100-150 53
(10-inch LP. Colored vinyl.)
FANTASY (11 "Jazz at Oberlin")......... 100-150 53
(10-inch LP. Colored vinyl.)
FANTASY (13 "Jazz at the College of the Pacific")... 100-150 54
(10-inch LP. Colored vinyl.)
FANTASY (16 "Old Sounds from San Francisco")..................................... 100-150 55
(10-inch LP. Colored vinyl.)
FANTASY (204 "Dave Brubeck Trio").... 75-125 56
(Colored vinyl.)
FANTASY (205 "Dave Brubeck Trio").... 50-100 56
FANTASY (210 "Jazz at the Black Hawk").. 50-100 56
FANTASY (223 "Jazz at the College of the Pacific")... 50-100 56
FANTASY (229 "Dave Brubeck Quartet with Paul Desmond").. 50-100 56
FANTASY (230 "Dave Brubeck Quartet with Paul Desmond").. 50-100 56
FANTASY (239 "Dave Brubeck Octet") . 50-100 56
FANTASY (240 "At Storyville").............. 50-100 57
FANTASY (245 "Jazz at Oberlin").......... 50-100 57
FANTASY (3249 "Jazz at Wilshire-Ebell")... 50-100 57
(Monaural.)
FANTASY (3259 "Dave Brubeck Plays Solo").. 30-40 62
FANTASY (3268 "Reunion")................... 30-40 62
(Monaural.)
FANTASY (3301 "Brubeck a La Mode") .. 30-40 62
(Monaural.)
FANTASY (3319 "Near Myth") 30-40 62
(Monaural.)
FANTASY (3331 "Brubeck-Tjader")......... 30-40 62
(Monaural.)
FANTASY (3332 "Brubeck-Tjader, Vol. 2")... 30-40 62
(Monaural.)
FANTASY (8007 "Reunion")................... 30-40 62
(Stereo.)
FANTASY (8047 "Brubeck a La Mode") 50-100 62
(Blue vinyl. Stereo.)
FANTASY (8063 "Near Myth") 30-40 62
(Stereo.)
FANTASY (8073 "Brubeck-Tjader")......... 30-40 62
(Stereo.)
FANTASY (8074 "Brubeck-Tjader, Vol. 2")... 30-40 62
(Stereo.)
FANTASY (8095 "Jazz at Wilshire-Ebell")... 30-40 62
(Stereo.)
HORIZON...5-10 76
JAZZTONE (1272 "Dave Brubeck")......... 25-50 57
Session: Dave Brubeck; Paul Desmond; Cal Tjader; David Van Kriedt; Joe Morello; Eugene Wright; Dick Collins.
Also see ARMSTRONG, Louis
Also see BEE GEES / Dave Brubeck
Also see BERNSTEIN, Leonard, & Dave Brubeck
Also see RUSHING, Jimmy
Also see TJADER, Cal

BRUBECK, Dave, & Paul Desmond — LP '76

Singles: 7-inch

A&M...4-6 76
HORIZON...4-6 75

LPs: 10/12-inch

HORIZON...6-10 74-75
As a member of Dave Brubeck's group, Paul Desmond was often credited prominently on releases which, for consistency, appear in the Brubeck section.
Also see DESMOND, Paul

BRUBECK, Dave, & Gerry Mulligan

Singles: 7-inch

COLUMBIA..4-8 68

LPs: 10/12-inch

COLUMBIA...8-15 68-73
VERVE 8-12 73

BRUBECK, Dave, Gerry Mulligan, & Paul Desmond

LP: 10/12-inch

MFSL (216 "We're All Together Again for the First Time")..30-50 '90s
Also see BRUBECK, Dave
Also see DESMOND, Paul
Also see MULLIGAN, Gerry

BRUCE, Alan

Singles: 7-inch

GAIT (1443 "I Feel Better") 15-25 65

BRUCE, Donn, & Little Beats

Singles: 78 rpm

TUXEDO 30-40 56

Singles: 7-inch

TUXEDO (914 "Love Leads a Fool") 100-200 56

BRUCE, Ed — C&W '67

(Edwin Bruce)

Singles: 78 rpm

SUN (276 "Rock Boppin' Baby") 50-100 57

Singles: 7-inch

APT (25095 "Ebb Tide")..........................5-10 65
EPIC 4-6 77-78
GOOD BUDDY 4-6 76
MCA...3-5 80-85
MONUMENT..4-8 68-69
RCA (5000 series) 3-5 86
RCA (47-7842 "Flight 303").....................5-10 61
(Monaural.)
RCA (61-7842 "Flight 303").....................10-20 61
(Stereo Compact 33.)
RCA (9000 series) 5-8 66-68
RCA (13000 & 14000 series) 3-5 84-86
SUN (276 "Rock Boppin' Baby") 25-50 57
SUN (292 "Sweet Woman") 20-40 58
TRANS-SONIC ....10-20 '60s
U.A. 4-6 73-76
WAND (136 "It's Coming to Me") 8-12 63
WAND (140 "See the Big Man Cry")..........10-20 63
WAND (148 "Don't Let It Happen")...........8-12 64
WAND (156 "I'm Gonna Have a Party") 8-12 64

Promotional Singles

MCA (52109 "Ever Never Lovin' You") 3-5 82
(5-inch disc with LP-size hole and label. Packaged in a special sleeve that unfolds as a 1983 calendar.)

LPs: 10/12-inch

EPIC 6-10 77-78
MCA...5-10 80-83
MONUMENT..10-15 69
RCA (3948 "If I Could Just Go Home").....20-30 68
RCA (5000 series) 5-10 84-85
U.A. 8-10 76
Session: Willie Nelson.
Also see NELSON, Willie

BRUCE, James, & Del Catos

Singles: 7-inch

PALOS (1203 "Brand New Baby")...........50-75

BRUCE, Lenny — LP '75

Singles: 7-inch

FANTASY (Black vinyl).............................5-10
FANTASY (Colored vinyl).........................10-15

Picture Sleeves

W.B. (598 "The Law, Language and Lenny Bruce") 20-30 74

EPs: 7-inch

FANTASY (2 "Curran Theater Concert") ..10-20
(Promotional issue only.)

LPs: 10/12-inch

CAPITOL (2630 "Why Did Lenny Bruce Die")..15-20 66
DOUGLAS...15-25 68-71
FANTASY (1 "Lenny Bruce")....................50-75
(Promotional issue only.)
FANTASY (7001 "Lenny Bruce's Interviews of Our Times") 30-40 58
(THICK red vinyl.)
FANTASY (7001 "Lenny Bruce's Interviews of Our Times") 15-25
(Black vinyl.)
FANTASY (7001 "Lenny Bruce's Interviews of Our Times") 8-12
(THIN red vinyl.)
FANTASY (7003 "The Sick Humor of Lenny Bruce")..30-40 58
(THICK red vinyl.)
FANTASY (7003 "The Sick Humor of Lenny Bruce")..15-20
(Black vinyl.)
FANTASY (7003 "The Sick Humor of Lenny Bruce")..8-12
(THIN red vinyl.)
FANTASY (7007 "I Am Not a Nut, Elect Me")..30-40 59
(THICK red vinyl.)
FANTASY (7007 "I Am Not a Nut, Elect Me")..15-20
(Black vinyl.)
FANTASY (7007 "I Am Not a Nut, Elect Me")..8-12
(THIN red vinyl.)
FANTASY (7011 "Lenny Bruce, American")..30-40 62
(THICK red vinyl.)
FANTASY (7011 "Lenny Bruce, American")..15-20
(Black vinyl.)
FANTASY (7011 "Lenny Bruce, American")..8-12
(THIN red vinyl.)
FANTASY (7012 "Best of Lenny Bruce") .25-30 63
(THICK red vinyl.)
FANTASY (7012 "Best of Lenny Bruce") .15-20
(Black vinyl.)
FANTASY (7012 "Best of Lenny Bruce") ...8-12
(THIN red vinyl.)
FANTASY (7017 "Thank You Masked Man")...10-15 72
FANTASY (34201 "Lenny Bruce Live at the Curran Theatre")..10-15 72
FANTASY (79003 "Real Lenny Bruce") 8-12 75
LENNY BRUCE RECORDS ("Recordings Submitted As Evidence in the San Francisco Obscenity Trial in March, 1962")...75-100 62
PHILLES (4010 "Lenny Bruce Is Out Again")..50-75 66
REPRISE (6329 "Berkeley Concert") 15-20 69
U.A. (3580 "Midnight Concert")................15-20 67
U.A. (9800 "At Carnegie Hall")..................15-25 71
(3 LPs.)
W.B. (9101 "The Law, Language and Lenny Bruce")..10-20 74
(Promotional issue only.)

BRUCE & JERRY

Singles: 7-inch

ARWIN (1003 "I Saw Her First")...............30-50 59

BRUCE & TERRY — P&R '64

Singles: 7-inch

COLUMBIA (11 "Spinning Wheel Rock") .10-20 64
COLUMBIA (42956 "Custom Machine")...15-25 64
COLUMBIA (43055 thru 43582)...............10-20 64-66
Members: Bruce Johnston; Terry Melcher.
Also see BOONE, Pat
Also see HONDELLS
Also see JOHNSTON, Bruce
Also see MELCHER, Terry, & Bruce Johnston
Also see NEWTON, Wayne
Also see RIP CHORDS
Also see ROGUES
Also see SAGITTARIUS

BRUDICK, Doni

Singles: 7-inch

SOUND IMPRESSION (6808 "I Have Faith in You")...50-100 '60s

BRUINS

Singles: 7-inch

COMET 15-20 64
GENERAL AMERICAN (721 "Go on and Cry")..25-30 65
ROULETTE (4566 "Believe Me")..............10-15 64

BRUNO, Bruce

Singles: 7-inch

ROULETTE (4386 "Hey Little One")..........15-25 61
ROULETTE (4427 "Dear Joanne")...........40-50 62
Session: Del Satins.
Also see DEL SATINS

BRUNO & GLADIATORS

Singles: 7-inch

VAULT (901 "Warm Is the Sun") 10-20 63

BRUNSON, Frankie

(Frank Brunson; "Little" Frankie Brunson; "Big Daddy")

Singles: 78 rpm

GROOVE 8-12 56
RCA...8-12 57

Singles: 7-inch

FAIRMOUNT (613 "Move Baby Move") ...10-15 63
GEE (1058 "You'll Never Get Away").......10-15 60
GEE (1063 "Give Me Something to Live For")..10-15 60
GROOVE (0173 "Charmaine") 15-25 56
RCA (7039 "Love Is Bloom")....................10-20 57
Also see BIG DADDY
Also see FASHIONS
Also see PEOPLE'S CHOICE

BRUNZELL, Jim

LP: 10/12-inch

MATLAND (14622 "Matlands")..................25-30
(Picture disc.)

BRUTES

Singles: 7-inch

NOVA (7401 "Make Me Happy, Girl") 20-30 66

BRUTHERS

Singles: 7-inch

RCA (8920 "Bad Way to Go")...................10-20 66

BRYAN, Billy

(Gene Pitney)

Singles: 7-inch

BLAZE (351 "Going Back to My Love")....30-40 59
Also see PITNEY, Gene

BRYAN, Dave

(With the Choraltones; with Hollywood Quintet)

Singles: 78 rpm

SPECK (102 "Right Time for Love").........10-15 56
SPECK (103 "Please Forgive Me") 50-75 56

Singles: 7-inch

SPECK (102 "Right Time for Love").........50-75 56
SPECK (103 "Please Forgive Me") 200-300 56

BRYAN, Donnie, & Raging Storms

Singles: 7-inch

KELDON (321 "Hold Me").........................15-25 60

BRYAN, Eddie

Singles: 7-inch

ARLEN (733 "Your Lips")..........................10-15 63

BRYAN, George

(With the Ding Dongs)

Singles: 7-inch

SILVER (101 "On Bended Knees") ....10-20 '50s
TODD (1015 "I Love Only You")...............40-50 59

BRYAN, Jamie

Singles: 7-inch

DEBBIE (1019 "Summer Love") 50-100

BRYAN, Larry

Singles: 7-inch

VISCOUNT (103 "Set Me Free") 10-20 62

BRYAN, Wes

Singles: 7-inch

CLOCK (1013 "Honey Baby")....................15-20 59
ROULETTE (4289 "Melodie D'Amour")....10-15 60
U.A. (102 "Tiny Spacemen")....................15-25 57
U.A. (122 "Wait For Me Baby")................15-25 58

Picture Sleeves

U.A. (102 "Tiny Spacemen")....................30-40 57

BRYANT, Anita — P&R '59

Singles: 78 rpm

DAVIS (443 "Somebody Sees")..................5-10 56

Singles: 7-inch

CARLTON (512 thru 523) 10-15 58-59
CARLTON (528 "Paper Roses")...............10-15 60
(Monaural.)
CARLTON (S-528 "Paper Roses")...........20-30 60
(Stereo.)
CARLTON (530 thru 553) 8-12 61

COLUMBIA....4-8 61-67
DAVIS (443 "Somebody Sees")....10-20 56
DISNEYLAND (560 "The Orange Bird")....5-10 71
DISNEYLAND (823 "The Orange Bird")..10-15 71
("Little Gem" series.)
TRIP....4-6

Picture Sleeves

COLUMBIA....5-10 61-67
DISNEYLAND (560 "The Orange Bird")..10-15 71

EPs: 7-inch

ACSP (1779 "See America with AC")....5-10
(Promotional issue for AC Spark Plugs.)

LPs: 10/12-inch

CARLTON....10-20 59-61
COLUMBIA....8-15 62-67
DISNEYLAND (3991 "The Orange Bird") 15-20 71
(With the Mike Sammes Singers.)
HARMONY....8-12

BRYANT, Anita / Jo Stafford & Gordon MacRae

Singles: 7-inch

COLUMBIA....5-10 60
Also see MacRAE, Gordon, & Jo Stafford

BRYANT, Ardie

Singles: 7-inch

AD&A (101 "What's It All About")....15-25 '60s

BRYANT, Audrey

Singles: 7-inch

DO-RA-ME (1405 "Someone Like You").15-25 59

BRYANT, Ben

Singles: 78 rpm

SABRE (101 "Blue Midnight")....10-15 53

Singles: 7-inch

SABRE (101 "Blue Midnight")....15-25 53

BRYANT, Beulah
(Big Beulah Bryant)

Singles: 78 rpm

EXCELLO....50-75 54

Singles: 7-inch

DO-KAY-LO....5-10 63
EXCELLO (2049 "Prize Fighting Papa")....100-150 54

BRYANT, Carl

Singles: 7-inch

RIDGECREST ("She's a Peach of a Girl")....250-350 59
(Selection number not known.)

BRYANT, Charles

Singles: 7-inch

PEACH (741 "Don't Take My Woman Away")....10-20 60

BRYANT, Elmer

Singles: 7-inch

DIXIE (906 "Gertie's Garter Broke")....50-100

BRYANT, Helen

Singles: 7-inch

FURY (1042 "That's a Promise")....10-15 61

BRYANT, Jay Dee
(With the Kiddie-O's; J.D. Bryant & USA)

Singles: 7-inch

ALFA (201 "Don't Stop Now")....10-20
CEE=JAY (577 "Searching for Tomorrow")....40-50 60
ENJOY (2017 "Get It")....10-15 65
GRASSROOTS....4-6 73
HERALD (570 "Come Summer")....15-20 62
JOSIE (984 thru 998)....5-10 68
SHRINE (108 "I Won't Be Coming Back")....4000-5000 66
STOP (103 "Come Summer")....8-12 64

BRYANT, Jimmy

Singles: 7-inch

IMPERIAL (66176 "Julie's Gone")....5-10 66

EPs: 7-inch

CAPITOL (1314 "Country Cabin Jazz")...10-15 60

LPs: 10/12-inch

CAPITOL (1314 "Country Cabin Jazz")...30-50 60
DOLTON (16505 "Play Country Guitar").10-15 66
(Monaural.)
DOLTON (17505 "Play Country Guitar").10-15 66
(Stereo.)
IMPERIAL (9310 "Bryant's Back in Town")....10-15 66
(Monaural.)
IMPERIAL (9315 "Laughing Guitar, Crying Guitar")....10-15 66
(Monaural.)
IMPERIAL (9338 "We Are Young")....10-15 67
(Monaural.)
IMPERIAL (9360 "Fastest Guitar in the Country")....10-15 67
(Monaural.)
IMPERIAL (12310 "Bryant's Back in Town")....10-20 66
(Stereo.)
IMPERIAL (12315 "Laughing Guitar, Crying Guitar")....10-20 66
(Stereo.)
IMPERIAL (12338 "We Are Young")....10-20 67
(Stereo.)
IMPERIAL (12360 "Fastest Guitar in the Country")....10-20 67
(Stereo.)
Session: Speedy West
Also see WEST, Speedy, & Jimmy Bryant

BRYANT, Lillie

Singles: 7-inch

CAMEO (122 "Good Good Morning, Baby")....15-25 57
SWAN (4029 "I'll Never Be Free")....10-20 59
TAY-STER (6016 "Meet Me Half Way")....200-300 67
Also see BILLY & LILLIE

BRYANT, Paul

Singles: 7-inch

FANTASY (576 "Sister Lovie")....10-20 64

BRYANT, Lil' Phil, & Bridgettes
("Music By Big Sam Mason")

Singles: 7-inch

ALTHEA (002 "Down on My Knees")....15-25 '50s

BRYANT, Ray P&R/R&B '60
(Ray Bryant Combo; Ray Bryant Quintet; Ray Bryant Trio)

Singles: 7-inch

ATLANTIC....5-10
CADET....4-8 66-69
COLUMBIA....5-10 60-64
SIGNATURE....5-10 60
SUE....5-10 63-65

Picture Sleeves

CADET....5-10 67
COLUMBIA....10-15 60

LPs: 10/12-inch

CADET....10-20 66-67
COLUMBIA....15-30 60-62
EPIC (3279 "Ray Bryant Trio")....40-60 56
NEW JAZZ (8213 "Alone with the Blues")....15-25 59
SIGNATURE....15-25 60
SUE....15-30 60-64
Also see CARTER, Betty, & Ray Bryant
Also see JONES, Jo

BRYANT, Rusty
(With the Carolyn Club Band)

Singles: 78 rpm

CAROLYN (333 "Castle Rock")....10-15 53
DOT (Except 15449)....5-10 54-59
DOT (15449 "I Need Somebody")....10-20 56

Singles: 7-inch

CAROLYN (333 "Castle Rock")....20-30 53
DOT (Except 15449)....10-20 54-59
DOT (15449 "I Need Somebody")....20-30 56
PRESTIGE....4-6 71

EPs: 7-inch

DOT (1023 "All Night Long")....25-35 55
DOT (1047 "Rusty Bryant and the Carolyn Club Band")....20-30 56

LPs: 10/12-inch

DOT (3006 "All Night Long")....50-100 55
PRESTIGE....10-12 70-74

BRYSON, Eldon

Singles: 78 rpm

STELLA (1043 "Rock & Roll Daddy")....20-30 55

Singles: 7-inch

STELLA (1043 "Rock & Roll Daddy")....35-50 55

BUA, Gene

Singles: 7-inch

ABC-PAR (9928 "Golly Gee")....10-15 58
HERITAGE (816 "When Love Slips Away")....5-10 69
RUST (5124 "And So It Goes")....5-10 68
SAFARI (1007 "Golly Gee")....20-30 58
(First issue.)
W.B. (5037 "Unchained Melody")....10-20 59
W.B. (5098 "Danny")....10-15 59
WARWICK (602 "I Dream of You")....10-20 60

Picture Sleeves

HERITAGE (816 "When Love Slips Away")....8-12 69
Also see ANDERSON, Candy, & Gene Bua

BUBBLE PUPPY P&R/LP '69

Singles: 7-inch

INT'L ARTISTS (128 thru 138)....15-25 68-69

Promotional Singles

INT'L ARTISTS (Black vinyl)....20-30 69-70
INT'L ARTISTS (Colored vinyl)....25-50 70

LPs: 10/12-inch

INT'L ARTISTS (10 "A Gathering of Promises")....100-200 69
(Green label)
INT'L ARTISTS (10 "A Gathering of Promises")....150-250 69
(White label. Promotional issue only.)
Members: Rod Prince; Todd Potter; Roy Cox; M. Taylor; Dave Fore.
Also see DEMIAN
Also see MUSIC MACHINE / Bubble Puppy

BUCCANEERS
(With the Matthew Child & His Drifters)

Singles: 78 rpm

RAINBOW (211 " Dear Ruth")....100-200 53
RAMA (21 "The Stars Will Remember")....400-500 53
RAMA (24 "In the Mission of St. Augustine")....250-350 53
SOUTHERN (100/101 "Dear Ruth")....200-300 53

Singles: 7-inch

RAINBOW (211 "Fine Brown Frame")..500-750 53
RAMA (21 "The Stars Will Remember")....4000-5000 53
RAMA (24 "In the Mission of St. Augustine")....2500-3500 53
SOUTHERN (100/101 "Dear Ruth").1000-2000 53
(Red vinyl.)
Members: Ernest Smith; Julius Robinson; Richard Gregory; Sam Johnson; Don Marshall.
Also see METRONOMES

BUCCANEERS

Singles: 78 rpm

TIFFANY....10-20 54

Singles: 7-inch

TIFFANY....20-30 54

BUCCANEERS

Singles: 7-inch

CRYSTALETTE (718 "Blonde Hair, Blue Eyes and Ruby Lips"....10-15 58

BUCCANEERS

Singles: 7-inch

CUPID (5006 "Bye Bye Baby")....100-150 58
Members: Robert Mansfield; Donald Emilian; Robert Wentworth; Lee de Felice.
Also see DUSTERS

BUCHANAN, Art
(With the Pioneers)

Singles: 7-inch

DIXIE (823 "Queen from Bowling Green")....250-350 '50s
LOST GOLD ("Little Elf Jed")....5-10 92
(Red vinyl.)
LOST GOLD (41193 "Easter Parade")....5-10 93
(White vinyl.)
Also see ONTARIO, Art

BUCHANAN, Roy LP '72

Singles: 7-inch

ALLIGATOR....3-5 85-86
ATLANTIC....4-6 76-78
BOMARC....10-15 61
POLYDOR....4-6 72-75
SWAN (4088 "Mule Train Stomp")....5-10 61

LPs: 10/12-inch

ALLIGATOR....5-10 85
ATLANTIC....5-10 76-77
BIOYA....30-40 71
POLYDOR....8-15 72-75
WATERHOUSE....10-15 81
Also see CANNON, Freddy
Also see GREGG, Bobby
Also see HAWKINS, Dale
Also see MOORE, Bob, & Temps
Also see ROCK, Jimmy

BUCHANAN, Wayne

Singles: 7-inch

KIM (921 "The Boy and the Guitar Twist")....150-250

BUCHANAN, Wes C&W '68

Singles: 7-inch

COLUMBIA....4-6 68
PEP (114 "Give Some Love My Way")....50-75 58

BUCHANAN & ANCELL P&R '57

Singles: 78 rpm

FLYING SAUCER....20-30 57

Singles: 7-inch

FLYING SAUCER (501 "The Creature")..20-30 57
Members: Bill Buchanan; Bob Ancell.

BUCHANAN & CELLA

Singles: 7-inch

ABC-PAR (10033 "String Along with Pal-O-Mine")....10-20 59
Member: Bill Buchanan.

BUCHANAN & GOODMAN P&R/R&B '56

Singles: 78 rpm

LUNIVERSE (101 "The Flying Saucer")...25-35 56
(Label is printed "Universe," with a handwritten "L," making "Luniverse.")
LUNIVERSE (101 "The Flying Saucer")...15-25 56
(Label is "Luniverse.")
LUNIVERSE (101X "Back to Earth")....50-100 56
LUNIVERSE (102 thru 108)....15-25 56-58
RADIO-ACTIVE....20-30 56

Singles: 7-inch

COMIC (500 "Flying Saucer the 3rd")....15-25 59
LUNIVERSE (101 "The Flying Saucer")...50-75 56
(Label is printed "Universe," with a handwritten "L," making "Luniverse.")
LUNIVERSE (101 "The Flying Saucer")...30-40 56
(Label is "Luniverse.")
LUNIVERSE (101X "Back to Earth")....150-200 56
LUNIVERSE (102 "Buchanan & Goodman on Trial")....30-40 56
LUNIVERSE (103 "The Banana Boat Story")....30-40 56
LUNIVERSE (105 "Flying Saucer the 2nd")....30-40 57
LUNIVERSE (107 "Santa and the Satellite")....30-40 57
LUNIVERSE (108 "Flying Saucer Goes West")....30-40 57
NOVELTY (301 "Frankenstein '59")....15-25 59
RADIO-ACTIVE (101 "The Flying Saucer")....75-100 56
(No artist credit shown. Unauthorized issue.)
Members: Bill Buchanan; Dickie Goodman.
Session: Paul Sharman.
Also see GOODMAN, Dickie
Also see INVADERS

BUCHANAN & GREENFIELD

Singles: 7-inch

NOVEL (711 "The Invasion")....15-20 64
(Red label.)
NOVEL (711 "The Invasion")....4-6 72
(Red and white label.)
Members: Bill Buchanan; Howard Greenfield.

BUCHANAN BROTHERS P&R '69

Singles: 7-inch

EVENT....4-6 69-71

LPs: 10/12-inch

EVENT (101 "Medicine Man")....20-25 69
Members: Terry Cashman; Gene Pistilli; Tommy West.

BUCK ROGERS MOVEMENT

Singles: 7-inch

21ST CENTURY (601 "Baby Come On")....25-50 67
21ST CENTURY (603 "Take It from Me Girl")....10-20 67

BUCKAROOS C&W '67
(Featuring Don Rich)

Singles: 7-inch

CAPITOL....5-8 67-69

LPs: 10/12-inch

CAPITOL (322 "Roll Your Own")....15-25 69
CAPITOL (440 "Rompin & Stompin'")....15-25 70
CAPITOL (550 "Boot Hill")....15-25 70

CAPITOL (767 "The Buckaroos Play the Hits")............ 15-25 70
CAPITOL (2436 "The Buck Owens Songbook")............ 20-30 66
CAPITOL (2828 "Again")............ 20-30 67
CAPITOL (2973 "Meanwhile, Back at the Ranch")............ 15-25 68
Members: Don Rich; Doyle Holly; Tom Brumley; Willie Cantu.
Also see ALAN, Buddy
Also see HOLLY, Doyle
Also see OWENS, Buck
Also see RICH, Don

BUCKET CITY DISTORTION RACKETT

Singles: 7-inch

SPLIT SOUND............ 15-25 67
Member: Stephen E. Lewis.

BUCKETT, Johnny

EPs: 7-inch

FORTUNE (1330 "Let Me Play with Your Poodle")............ 100-150

BUCKEYES

("Vocal by the Buckeyes with Orchestra")

Singles: 78 rpm

DELUXE (6110 "Since I Fell for You")............ 50-75 57
DELUXE (6126 "Dottie Baby")............ 75-125 57

Singles: 7-inch

DELUXE (6110 "Since I Fell for You")............ 100-200 57
DELUXE (6126 "Dottie Baby")............ 250-350 57
Also see STEREOS

BUCKINGHAM NICKS

Singles: 7-inch

POLYDOR (14335 "Down Let Me Down Again")............ 20-30 76
POLYDOR (14428 "Crying in the Night")............ 20-30 77

Picture Sleeves

POLYDOR (14428 "Crying in the Night")............ 40-60 77

LPs: 10/12-inch

POLYDOR (5058 "Buckingham Nicks")............ 30-40 73
Members: Lindsey Buckingham; Stevie Nicks.
Also see NICKS, Stevie

BUCKINGHAMS *P&R '66*

Singles: 7-inch

COLUMBIA............ 4-8 67-70
PHILCO (14 "Kind of a Drag"/"Lawdy Miss Clawdy")............ 10-20 67
("Hip Pocket" flexi-disc.)
RED LABEL............ 3-5 85
ROWE/AMI............ 10-20 66
(Red vinyl. "Play Me" Sales Stimulator promotional issue.)
SPECTRA-SOUND (003 "Sweets for My Sweet")............ 10-20 65
USA............ 10-15 66-67

Picture Sleeves

COLUMBIA............ 8-15 67-68
RED LABEL............ 3-5 85

LPs: 10/12-inch

COLUMBIA............ 15-25 67-75
RED LABEL............ 5-10 85
USA (107 "Kind of a Drag")............ 75-125 67
(With 13 tracks. Includes *I'm a Man*, which is not listed on either cover or label.)
USA (107 "Kind of a Drag")............ 30-40 67
(With 12 tracks. Omits *I'm a Man*.)
Members: Dennis Tufano; Carl Giammarese; Nick Fortune; Martin Grebb; Dennis Miccoli; Jon-Jon Poulos.
Also see CENTURIES
Also see EXCEPTIONS
Also see FALLING PEBBLES
Also see TUFANO & GIAMMARESE

BUCKINGHAMS / Byrds / Aretha Franklin / Paul Revere & Raiders

EPs: 7-inch

COLUMBIA (566 "Great Shakes: Shake-Out 2")............ 10-20 67
(Special products, limited edition made for General Foods Corp.)
Also see BUCKINGHAMS
Also see BYRDS
Also see FRANKLIN, Aretha
Also see REVERE, Paul, & Raiders

BUCKLE

Singles: 7-inch

LPI (1001 "Woman")............ 15-25 67

BUCKLEY, Lord

(With Lyle Griffin's All Star Jazz Band; Lord Richard Buckley, Professor of Hipology)

Singles: 7-inch

HIP (270 "Flight of the Saucer")............ 75-100 56
(With "Space Correspondent" Lyle Griffin.)

EPs: 7-inch

HIP (301 "The Gettysburg Address [Narration and Hip Translation]")............ 20-40 56
(Colored vinyl. Autographed copies—which were available in 1956 for $1.50 via mail order—may be valued at double this price range. Issued in a brown paper sleeve.)
HIP (302 "James Dean's [Message to Teenagers]")............ 75-100 56
(Issued in a brown paper sleeve.)
RCA (3246 "Hipsters, Flipsters, and Finger-Poppin' Daddies, Knock Me Your Lobes")............ 75-125 54
(Two EPs in double-pocket cover.)

LPs: 10/12-inch

BIZARRE/REPRISE (6389 "A Most Immaculately Hip Aristocrat")............ 10-20 70
CRESTVIEW (CRV-801 "The Best of Lord Buckley")............ 25-40 63
(Monaural.)
CRESTVIEW (CRV-801 "The Best of Lord Buckley")............ 25-40 63
(Promotional issue only. Monaural.)
CRESTVIEW (CRV7-801 "The Best of Lord Buckley")............ 40-60 63
(Stereo.)
ELEKTRA (74047 "The Best of Lord Buckley")............ 15-25 69
(Repackage of the 1963 Crestview LP.)
RCA (3246 "Hipsters, Flipsters, & Finger Poppin' Daddies")............ 150-175 54
(10-inch LP. With the Royal Court Orchestra.)
REPRISE (6389 "A Most Immaculately Hip Aristocrat")............ 12-25 70
STRAIGHT (1054 "A Most Immaculately Hip Aristocrat")............ 15-30 70
STRAIGHT (1054 "A Most Immaculately Hip Aristocrat")............ 25-35 70
(White label. Promotional issue only.)
VAYA (1715 "Euphoria")............ 150-200 51
(10-inch LP. Colored vinyl.)
VAYA (101 "Euphoria, Vol. 1")............ 75-125 55
VAYA (107 "Euphoria, Vol. 2")............ 125-175 56
WORLD PACIFIC (1279 "Way Out Humor")............ 100-150 59
(Back cover may read "Far Out Humor" instead of "Way Out Humor.")
WORLD PACIFIC (1815 "Lord Buckley in Concert")............ 20-40 64
(Repackage of *Way Out Humor*.)
WORLD PACIFIC (1849 "Blowing His Mind [And Your's Too]")............ 30-50 66
WORLD PACIFIC (21879 "Buckley's Best")............ 25-40 68
WORLD PACIFIC (21889 "Bad Rapping of the Marquis De Sade")............ 20-30 69
Session: Dodo Marmarosa; Lucky Thompson.

BUCKLEY, Tim *LP '67*

Singles: 7-inch

DISC REET............ 4-6 73-74
ELEKTRA............ 5-10 66-67

LPs: 10/12-inch

DISC REET............ 8-10 73-74
ELEKTRA (Except 74004)............ 15-20 67-70
ELEKTRA (74004 "Tim Buckley")............ 25-35 66
RHINO............ 5-10 83
STRAIGHT (Except 1060)............ 15-25 70
STRAIGHT (1060 "Blue Afternoon")............ 25-35 69
W.B.............. 10-15 70-72

BUCKNER, Milt

Singles: 7-inch

ARGO (5356 "Organ Grinder's Swing")............ 10-15 60
ARGO (5361 "Two Flights Up")............ 10-15 60
BETHLEHEM............ 5-10 63
CAPITOL............ 15-25 57-59
SAVOY............ 10-20 52

BUCKY & PREMIERS

Singles: 7-inch

NU-PHI (365 "Cruisin' ")............ 100-200

BUD & KATHY

Singles: 7-inch

DOWNEY (136 "Hang It Out to Dry")............ 15-25 66

BUDD, Landon, & "Grunion"

Singles: 7-inch

ALERT (1002 "Killer Reef")............ 20-35 62

BUDDIES

Singles: 78 rpm

GLORY............ 100-150 55

Singles: 7-inch

GLORY (230 "I Stole Your Heart")............ 400-500 55
Members: Leon Harrison; Luther Dixon; Roger Wainwright; Danny Ferguson.
Also see BARONS

BUDDIES

Singles: 7-inch

OKEH (7123 "Castle of Love")............ 40-60 59
TIARA (6121 "She's a Loser")............ 10-20 59

BUDDIES

Singles: 7-inch

COMET (2143 "Hully Gully Mama")............ 10-20 61

BUDDIES

Singles: 7-inch

SWAN (4073 "Spooky Spider")............ 5-10 61
SWAN (4170 "The Beatle")............ 10-20 64
Members: John Mahoney; Dave Zelinski; Dave Marsciak; Bob Horbette.

BUDDIES

Singles: 7-inch

SWING (102 "On the Go")............ 10-20 64
Members: Jay Siegel; Henry Medress; Mitch Margo; Phil Margo.
Also see TOKENS

BUDDIES

LPs: 10/12-inch

WING (12306 "Go Go with the Buddies")............ 20-30 65
(Monaural.)
WING (16306 "Go Go with the Buddies")............ 25-35 65
(Stereo.)

BUDDIES / Compacts

LPs: 10/12-inch

WING (12293 "The Buddies and the Compacts")............ 25-35 65
(Monaural.)
WING (16293 "The Buddies and the Compacts")............ 30-40 65
(Stereo.)
Also see BUDDIES

BUDDY

Singles: 7-inch

K-NUZ (LH-1786/1787 "Buddy in Britain [A Chat with the Beatles]"/"Buddy in Britain [A Chat with Cilla Black]")............ 450-500 64
(Identification number shown since no selection number is used.)
Also see BEATLES
Also see BLACK, Cilla

BUDDY & CITATIONS

Singles: 7-inch

BODDIE (3264 "A-E-I-O-U")............ 20-30
IRC (6918 "Don't Let Her Have Her Way")............ 100-125 64
Member: Bob Penney.
Also see SECOND COMING

BUDDY & CLAUDIA *R&B '55*

Singles: 78 rpm

CHESS............ 8-12 54-55

Singles: 7-inch

CHESS (1586 "I Wanna Hug Ya, Kiss Ya, Squeeze Ya")............ 30-40 54
CHESS (1597 "You Keep Me Guessin' ")............ 15-25 55
Members: Buddy Griffin; Claudia Swann.

BUDDY & EDNA

Singles: 7-inch

SAVOY (1543 "No Change")............ 15-25 58
Members: Buddy Lucas; Edna McGriff.
Also see LUCAS, Buddy
Also see McGRIFF, Edna

BUDDY & FADS

Singles: 7-inch

MOROCCO (1001 "Is It Just a Game")............ 100-200 58

BUDDY & HEARTS

Singles: 7-inch

LANDA (701 "Let It Rock")............ 50-75 64

Member: Kirby St. Romain.
Also see ST. ROMAIN, Kirby

BUDGIE

Singles: 7-inch

KAPP............ 4-8 72
MCA............ 4-6 75

LPs: 10/12-inch

A&M............ 8-15 76-78
ACTIVE............ 12-15 80
KAPP (3656 "Budgie")............ 30-40 71
KAPP (3669 "Squawk")............ 30-40 71
MCA............ 10-12 74
Members: Pete Boot; Tony Bourge; Burke Shelley; Ray Phillips; Steve Williams.

BUENA VISTAS *P&R '66*

Singles: 7-inch

BB (4001 "Sunset")............ 10-20 '60s
MARQUEE (443 "Here Come Da Judge")............ 5-10 68
SWAN (4255 thru 4277)............ 10-15 66-67
Members: Kathleen Keppen; Nick Ameno.

BUFFALO, Cecil, & Prophets

Singles: 7-inch

SHO BOAT (102 "Big Red")............ 10-20 '60s
Also see FIVE SOUNDS / Cecil Buffalo

BUFFALO HIGHLITES

Singles: 7-inch

COLLEGIATE (1001 "Spyder")............ 15-25 63

BUFFALO NICKEL JUGBAND

LPs: 10/12-inch

HAPPY TIGER............ 15-25 71

BUFFALO REBELS

Singles: 7-inch

MARLEE (0095 "Buffalo Blues")............ 15-20 60
Also see REBELS
Also see ROCKIN' REBELS

BUFFALO SPRINGFIELD *P&R/LP '67*

Singles: 7-inch

ATCO (Except 6459)............ 8-12 66-68
ATCO (6459 "For What It's Worth")............ 10-15 67

LPs: 10/12-inch

ATCO (105 "Retrospective")............ 8-10 75
ATCO (200 "Buffalo Springfield")............ 30-50 66
(Contains *Baby Don't Scold Me*.)
ATCO (200 "Buffalo Springfield")............ 15-25 67
(*Baby Don't Scold Me* replaced by *For What It's Worth*.)
ATCO (226 thru 283)............ 20-30 67-69
ATCO (806 "Buffalo Springfield")............ 15-20 73
Members: Stephen Stills; Neil Young; Dewey Martin; Jim Messina; Richie Furay; Jim Fielder; Doug Hastings; Bruce Palmer.
Also see MARTIN, Dewey, & Medicine Ball
Also see MESSINA, Jim
Also see POCO
Also see STILLS, Stephen
Also see YOUNG, Neil

BUFFALOS

Singles: 7-inch

GMC (10000 "She Wants Me")............ 10-20 '60s

BUFFETT, Jimmy *C&W '73*

Singles: 7-inch

ABC............ 4-6 75-78
ASYLUM (47073 "Hello Texas")............ 3-5 80
BARNABY (2013 thru 2023)............ 20-30 70
DUNHILL............ 4-8 73-75
FULL MOON............ 3-5 80
MCA (Black vinyl)............ 3-6 79-86
MCA (Colored vinyl)............ 4-6 85

Picture Sleeves

ABC............ 4-8 '70s
MCA............ 3-6

LPs: 10/12-inch

ABC (914 "Havana Daydreamin' ")............ 100-150 76
(Instead of *Defying Gravity*, mistakenly plays a track about "Please Take Your Drunken 15-Year-Old Girlfriend Home." Also track 1 on side A is a variation of *Second Wind*, instead of *Woman Goin' Crazy on Caroline Street*, as shown on cover and label. The only way to know which you have is to play it.)
ABC (914 "Havana Daydreamin' ")............ 10-20 76
(Mistakes noted above are corrected on this issue.)
ABC (990 "Changes in Latitudes, Changes in Attitudes")............ 10-20 77
ABC (1008 "You Had to Be There")............ 15-20 78
(Two discs.)

ABC (1046 "Son of a Son of a Sailor")..... 10-20 78
BARNABY (6014 "High Cumberland Jubilee") 50-100 76
BARNABY (30093 "Down to Earth").... 150-250 70
DUNHILL (50132 "Living and Dying in 3/4 Time")........ 15-25 74
DUNHILL (50183 "A1A")........ 15-25 75
MCA........ 5-10 79-90
U.A. 8-10 75
Also see FREDDIE & FISHSTICKS

BUFORD, Mojo
(George Buford)

Singles: 7-inch

ADELL (103 "Mojo Woman")........ 20-25 '60s
BANGAR (622 "Whole Lot a Woman").... 20-25 64
GARRETT........ 20-25 65
INDIGO (139 "Something on My Mind").. 25-35 62
TWIN TOWN........ 20-25 '60s

Picture Sleeves

ADELL (103 "Mojo Woman")........ 25-35 '60s
Also see JOHNSON, Luther / Mojo Buford
Also see LITTLE MOJO
Also see MOJO

BUG MEN

Singles: 7-inch

DOT (16592 "Beatles, You Bug Me")....... 15-25 64

BUGGS

Singles: 7-inch

SOMA (1413 "She Loves You")........ 20-25 64

Picture Sleeves

SOMA (1413 "She Loves You")........ 40-60 64
Also see ANDY & LIVE WIRES
Also see ANDY & MANHATTANS
Also see ANDY & PLAYBOYS

BUGGS

LPs: 10/12-inch

CORONET (212 "Beetle Beat")........ 25-30 64
Also see 4 SEASONS / Connie Francis / Barbara Brown & Buggs
Also see RASCALS / Buggs / Four Seasons / Johnny Rivers

BUGGS

Singles: 7-inch

BITTNER'S (16024 "It's All Right")........ 30-50

BUGS

Singles: 7-inch

ASTOR (002 "Pretty Girl")........ 20-30 66
(First issue.)
POLARIS (001 "Pretty Girl")........ 10-20 66
Also see DESALVO, Albert / Bugs

BULLARD, John
(John Bullard Quartet; with Bobby Sands)

Singles: 78 rpm

DELUXE........ 25-50 52
INDEX (300 "Don't Talk Dem Trash")...... 50-75 50

Singles: 7-inch

DELUXE (6019 "Western Union Blues") 75-100 52
DELUXE (6035 "Mary Lou")........ 75-100 52

BULLDOGS

Singles: 7-inch

MERCURY (72262 "John, Paul, George and Ringo")........ 10-15 64

BULLOCK, Norman

Singles: 7-inch

M&J (2 "Lies, Lies, Lies")........ 75-125

BUMBLE BEE SLIM
(Amos Easton)

Singles: 78 rpm

FIDELITY (3004 "Lonesome Old Feeling")........ 25-50 51

LPs: 10/12-inch

PACIFIC JAZZ (54 "Back in Town")....... 75-125 62
Also see EASTON, Amos, & His Orchestra

BUMBLE BEES

Singles: 7-inch

JOEY (6220 "A Girl Called Love")........ 30-40 63

BUMP

Singles: 7-inch

PIONEER (2147 "Winston Built That Bridge")........ 20-40 70

LPs: 10/12-inch

PIONEER (2150 "Bump")........ 350-550 70

BUMPS

Singles: 7-inch

PICCADILLY (238 thru 251)........ 10-20 67
SIN-A-WAY (301 "You Don't Love Me Anymore") 10-15
WALRUS (001/002 "Shining")........ 10-15 69

BUMPY & JAGUARS

Singles: 7-inch

DEPRI (226 "Here I Go Again")........ 25-35

BUNN, Allen
(Alden Bunn)

Singles: 78 rpm

APOLLO........ 35-50 52
RED ROBIN........ 50-75 54

Singles: 7-inch

APOLLO (436 "She'll Be Sorry")........ 75-100 52
APOLLO (439 "Discouraged")........ 75-100 52
RED ROBIN (124 "My Kinda Woman")........ 200-300 54
Also see BAUM, Allen
Also see LARKS
Also see TARHEEL SLIM & LITTLE ANN
Also see WHEELS

BUNN, Bennie
(With the Cadets; with Inspirations)

Singles: 7-inch

EASTMAN (790 "If I Were King")........ 15-25 59
EASTMAN (793 "Rock and Roll Luau").... 15-25 59
SHERWOOD (211 "You Must Be an Angel")........ 75-100 60
Also see CADETS

BUNN, Bennie, & Martine Dalton

Singles: 7-inch

TCF (10 "No Matter What the People Say")........ 10-20 64

BUNN, Billy, & His Buddies

Singles: 78 rpm

RCA........ 50-75 51-52

Singles: 7-inch

RCA (4483 "I Need a Shoulder to Cry On")........ 100-200 51
RCA (4657 "That's When Your Heartaches Begin")........ 100-200 52

BUNNIES

Singles: 7-inch

ROOMATE (007 "You've Got It Made").... 15-25 65

BUNNY, Bobby, & Jackrabbits

Singles: 7-inch

ARROW (714 "Scatty Cat")........ 15-25 57

BURCH, Woody

Singles: 7-inch

KAY BAR DANE ("Aquagel Blues")...... 100-200
(Selection number not known.)

BURCHAM, Barney

Singles: 7-inch

METEOR (5023 "Can't Steal My Way Around")........ 150-250 55

BURCHETTE, Wilburn

LPs: 10/12-inch

AMOS (7014 "Occult Concert")........ 75-100 71
BURCHETTE BROS (1 "Guitar Grimore")........ 40-60 73
BURCHETTE BROS (2 "Psychic Meditation")........ 40-60 74
BURCHETTE BROS (3 "The Godhead") .40-60 74
BURCHETTE BROS (4 "Transcendental Music for Meditation")........ 40-60 76
BURCHETTE BROS (7 "Mind Storm")..... 40-60 77
EBOS (0001 "Seven Gates of Transcendental Consciousness")........ 50-100 72

BURD & BOMBSHELLS Featuring the Waverlys

Singles: 7-inch

RONDACK (9781 "Shake, Rattle and Roll")........ 50-60

BURDEN, Ray

Singles: 7-inch

ADONIS (112 "Hot Rodder's Dream")...... 50-75 61
CULLMAN (6403 "That Kind of Carryin' On")........ 50-75 58

BURDETTE, Lew

Singles: 7-inch

DOT (15672 "Three Strikes and You're Out")........ 10-20 58

BURDON, Eric, & War *P&R/LP '70*
(With Sharon Scott)

Singles: 7-inch

ABC........ 4-6 76
CAPITOL........ 5-10 74-75
LIBERTY........ 4-6
MGM........ 5-10 70

Picture Sleeves

MGM........ 4-6 70

LPs: 10/12-inch

ABC........ 8-10 77
MGM (Except 4710)........ 10-15 70
MGM (4710 "Black Man's Burdon")........ 20-30 70
(Promotional issue only.)
Also see WAR

BURDON, Eric, & Jimmy Witherspoon

Singles: 7-inch

MGM........ 4-6 71

LPs: 10/12-inch

MGM........ 10-15 71
Also see BURDON, Eric
Also see WITHERSPOON, Jimmy

BURGANDY RUNN

Singles: 7-inch

LAVETTE (5014 "Stop")........ 15-25 66

BURGANDYS

Singles: 7-inch

EXCLUSIVE (2281 "Ridin' Shotgun")....... 10-20 64

BURGESS, Dave
(With Chimes; with Buddy Cole Quartet; with Toppers)

Singles: 78 rpm

CHALLENGE........ 10-20 57
GILMAR........ 10-15 56
OKEH........ 10-15 53-55
TAMPA........ 10-15 55

Singles: 7-inch

CHALLENGE........ 10-20 57-59
GILMAR........ 10-20 56
OKEH........ 15-20 53-55
TAMPA........ 15-20 55

EPs: 7-inch

TOPS........ 10-20 56
(Not issued with cover. May have tracks by Neil Hunt, Norma Zimmer, Jerry Case, and the Lew Raymond Orchestra.)

LPs: 10/12-inch

TOPS........ 20-30 57
Also see CHAMPS
Also see FLEAS
Also see NELSON, Rick
Also see TROPHIES
Also see WILLIAMS, Ken / Dave Burgess / "Scat Man" Crothers / Johnny James

BURGESS, Dave / Lew Raymond Orchestra / Ralph Brewster / "Scat Man" Crothers
(With the Toppers; with Lew Raymond Orchestra)

EPs: 7-inch

TOPS (408 "4 Hits")........ 15-25 57
(Not issued with cover.)
Also see BURGESS, Dave
Also see CROTHERS, Scatman

BURGESS, Dewayne
(With the Rhythm Group)

Singles: 7-inch

BRAMLEY (103 "Moments to Recall").. 100-200 '50s

BURGESS, Sonny
(With the Pacers; with King IV)

Singles: 78 rpm

SUN........ 50-100 56-57

Singles: 7-inch

ARA (222 "Fraulein")........ 5-10 65
NORTON (852 "Thunderbird")........ 4-6 2001
PHILLIPS INT'L (3551 "Sadie's Back in Town")........ 20-30 60
RAZORBACK (120 thru 136)........ 5-10 65-66
ROLANDO........ 10-15 68
SUN (247 "We Wanna Boogie")........ 75-100 56
SUN (263 "Ain't Got a Thing")........ 40-60 57
SUN (285 "My Bucket's Got a Hole in It").35-45 58
SUN (304 "Thunderbird")........ 50-75 58
TSBS........ 4-8 70

Members: Sonny Burgess; Johnny Hubbard; Bobby Crafford; Kern Kennedy.
Also see PACERS
Also see PERKINS, Carl / Sonny Burgess
Also see TRAMMELL, Bobby Lee

BURGESS, Sonny, & Larry Donn

Singles: 7-inch

AD-BUR (100 "The Girl Next Door")..... 100-150 61

LPs: 10/12-inch

WHITE........ 8-12 80
Also see BURGESS, Sonny
Also see DONN, Larry

BURGETT, Jim
(With the Make Believers)

Singles: 7-inch

COLUMBIA (41962 "Living Dead")........ 10-20 61
COLUMBIA (41962 "Living Dead")........ 20-30 61
(Compact 33.)
GO (6565 "Pick Up a Coupl'a of Records")........ 75-100
LAMA (7784 "Sugaree")........ 10-15 62
LAMA (7792 "Fire's On")........ 10-15 62
MGM (14032 "Now I Taste the Tears")...... 5-10 69
ORO (1502 "Live It Up")........ 75-100 60
ORO (1505 "Scene of the Crime")........ 20-30 60
ORO (1506 "This Is the Night")........ 20-30 60

LPs: 10/12-inch

WOLFGANG ("For the Swim Set")........ 30-40
(Selection number not known.)

BURK, Tommy
(With the Counts; Counts with "Vocal By Tommy Burk")

Singles: 7-inch

ATCO (6340 "You Better Move On")....... 10-20 65
HIP (101 "Rainy Day Lovin'")........ 20-30 66
NAT (100 "You'll Feel It Too")........ 15-25 62
NAT (101 "Stormy Weather")........ 15-25 63
(First issue.)
RICH-ROSE (1001 "Cute")........ 30-40 64
RICH-ROSE (1002 "You Took My Heart")........ 40-50 64
SMASH (1821 "Stormy Weather")........ 10-15 63
SOUTHERN ARTISTS (2026 "Without Me")........ 20-30 65
Also see COUNTS

BURKE, Buddy, & Canadian Meteors

Singles: 7-inch

BULLSEYE (1002 "That Big Old Moon")........ 75-125 59
REGENCY (686 "That Big Old Moon")... 75-125 59

BURKE, Jimmy
(With the Sequins & Rhythm Kings)

Singles: 7-inch

FORTUNE (537 "Forbidden Love")........ 50-75 59

BURKE, Solomon *P&R/R&B '61*

Singles: 12-inch

SAVOY........ 4-6 84

Singles: 78 rpm

APOLLO........ 15-25 56-57

Singles: 7-inch

ABC/DUNHILL........ 4-6 74
AMHERST........ 4-6 78
APOLLO (500 "No Man Walks Alone").... 15-25 56
APOLLO (505 "A Picture of You")........ 20-30 56
APOLLO (511 "This Is It")........ 15-25 57
APOLLO (527 "My Heart Is a Chapel").... 15-25 58
ATLANTIC (2089 thru 2131)........ 10-15 61
ATLANTIC (2147 thru 2276)........ 8-12 62-65
ATLANTIC (2288 thru 2566)........ 5-10 65-68
BELL (759 thru 891)........ 5-10 69-70
CHESS........ 4-6 75-77
DUNHILL........ 4-6 74
INFINITY (50046 "Boo Hoo Hoo")........ 4-6 79
MALA (420 "I'm Not Afraid")........ 5-10 60
MGM........ 4-8 70-73
ODEON........ 4-6
PRIDE........ 4-8 72-73
SINGULAR (1314 "It's All Right")........ 10-20 60
SOULTOWN (3001 "Bettin' on America").... 3-6 81

EPs: 7-inch

ATLANTIC (SD-8109 "The Best of Solomon Burke")........ 10-20 65
(Stereo. Juke box issue only. Includes title strips.)

LPs: 10/12-inch

ABC/DUNHILL........ 10-12 74
APOLLO (498 "Solomon Burke")........ 150-250 62
ATLANTIC (8067 "Greatest Hits")........ 40-60 62
ATLANTIC (8085 "If You Need Me")........ 35-50 63

ATLANTIC (8096 "Rock 'N' Soul).......... 35-50 64
ATLANTIC (8109 "Best of Solomon Burke").......... 20-30 65
(No W.B. logo on label.)
ATLANTIC (8158 "King Solomon").......... 15-25 68
(No W.B. logo on label.)
ATLANTIC (8185 "I Wish I Knew").......... 15-25 68
(No W.B. logo on label.)
ATLANTIC (8100 series).......... 5-10 '80s
(Has Warner Bros. logo on label.)
BELL (6033 "Proud Mary").......... 15-20 69
CHESS.......... 8-10 75-76
CLARION (607 "I Almost Lost My Mind") 15-20 64
INFINITY.......... 5-10 79
KENWOOD (498 "Solomon Burke").......... 20-30 64
MGM.......... 10-15 71-72
PRIDE.......... 8-12 73
ROUNDER.......... 5-10 84
SAVOY.......... 5-10 81-83
Session: Ray Charles Singers.
Also see CHARLES, Ray / Solomon Burke
Also see SOUL CLAN

BURKE, Solomon, & Lady Lee
Singles: 7-inch
PRIDE (1038 "Sentimental Journey").......... 4-6 73
Also see BURKE, Solomon

BURKS, Gene
Singles: 7-inch
AROCK (1001 "Monkey Man").......... 10-20 63
AROCK (1006 "Shirley Jean").......... 10-20 64
CALLA (138 "You Got It").......... 8-12 67

BURLINGTON EXPRESS
Singles: 7-inch
CAVERN (2207 "Memories").......... 20-30 '60s

BURNADETTES
Singles: 7-inch
DIVINITY (99007 "I'm Going Home").......... 15-25 '60s

BURNAM, Buzz
(Buzz Burham)
Singles: 78 rpm
VIV (4000 "Mama Lou").......... 50-75 56
Singles: 7-inch
VIV (4000 "Mama Lou").......... 100-150 56

BURNETT, Carl, & Hustlers
Singles: 7-inch
CARMAX (102 "Sweet Memories").......... 15-25 65
Session: Barry White.
Also see LITTLE CAESAR & ROMANS
Also see WHITE, Barry

BURNETT, Frances
(With Dick Jacobs & Orchestra)
Singles: 7-inch
CORAL (62016 "Walkin' Into Love").......... 25-50 58
CORAL (62092 "Come to Me").......... 25-50 59
CORAL (62127 "How I Miss You").......... 25-50 59
CORAL (62164 "Too Proud ").......... 25-50 60
CORAL (62214 "She Was Taking My Baby").......... 25-50 60
Also see JACOBS, Dick, & His Orchestra

BURNETT, Geraldine
Singles: 7-inch
RENO (171 "Poor Girl's Dream").......... 20-30 62

BURNETTE, Al
Singles: 7-inch
FORTUNE (231 "Lookie Here, Baby").......... 50-75
HAPPY HEARTS (147 "Lookie Here, Baby").......... 50-75

BURNETTE, Dorsey *P&R '60*
Singles: 78 rpm
ABBOTT.......... 15-25 56-57
Singles: 7-inch
ABBOTT (188 "Devil's Queen").......... 25-50 56
ABBOTT (190 "At a Distance").......... 25-50 57
CALLIOPE.......... 4-6 77
CAPITOL.......... 4-6 71-74
CEE-JAM (16 "Bertha-Lou").......... 50-100 57
COLLECTABLES.......... 3-5 81
CONDOR (1005 "Magnificent Sanctuary Band").......... 4-6 70
DOT (16230 thru 16305).......... 10-15 61
ELEKTRA.......... 4-6 79-80
ERA.......... 8-15 60-69
HAPPY TIGER.......... 4-6 70
HICKORY (1458 "Ain't That Fine").......... 5-10 67
IMPERIAL (5561 thru 5756).......... 15-25 59-61
IMPERIAL (5987 "Circle Rock").......... 10-15 63
LAMA (7791 "Rolling Restless Stones").......... 15-25 62
LIBERTY (56087 "The Greatest Love").......... 5-10 69
MC.......... 4-6 77
MEL-O-DY (113 thru 118).......... 10-15 64
MELODYLAND.......... 4-6 75-76
MERCURY (72546 "In the Morning").......... 5-10 66
MERRI (206 "Lucy Darling").......... 8-12 60
MOVIE STAR.......... 4-8
MUSIC FACTORY (417 "Son, You've Got to Make It Alone").......... 5-10 68
REPRISE.......... 10-20 62-63
SMASH.......... 5-10 66
SURF (5019 "Bertha Lou").......... 150-200 57
(Same number used on a Johnny Faire release.)
U.S. NAVY ("Be a Navy Man").......... 10-20 '60s
(U.S. Navy recruiting promotional issue.)
Picture Sleeves
ERA (3033 "The River and the Mountain").......... 15-25 61
REPRISE (246 "4 for Texas").......... 25-50 63
U.S. NAVY ("Be a Navy Man").......... 15-25 '60s
(U.S. Navy recruiting promotional issue.)
LPs: 10/12-inch
BUCKBOARD (1024 "Dorsey").......... 8-10 73
CALLIOPE.......... 8-10 77
CAPITOL.......... 10-12 72-73
DOT (3456 "Dorsey Burnette Sings").......... 20-40 63
(Monaural.)
DOT (25456 "Dorsey Burnette Sings").......... 25-50 63
(Stereo.)
ERA (EL-102 "Tall Oak Tree").......... 40-80 60
(Monaural.)
ERA (ES-102 "Tall Oak Tree").......... 100-150 60
(Stereo.)
ERA (800 series).......... 15-20 69
GUSTO.......... 5-10 79
TRIP.......... 8-12 74
Also see BURNETTE, Johnny & Dorsey

BURNETTE, Johnny *P&R '60*
(With the Rock'n Roll Trio; Johnny Burnette Trio)
Singles: 78 rpm
CORAL.......... 150-250 56-57
VON (106 "Go Mule Go").......... 100-150 54
Singles: 7-inch
CAPITOL (5023 thru 5176).......... 10-15 63-64
CHANCELLOR (1116 "I Wanna Thank You Folks").......... 10-20 62
CHANCELLOR (1123 "Tag-Along").......... 15-25 62
CHANCELLOR (1129 "Remember Me").......... 10-20 62
CORAL (61651 "Tear It Up").......... 150-250 56
CORAL (61675 "Midnight Train").......... 150-250 56
CORAL (61719 "Honey Hush").......... 150-250 56
CORAL (61758 "Lonesome Train").......... 150-250 56
CORAL (61829 "Eager Beaver Baby").......... 150-250 57
CORAL (61869 "Drinkin' Wine Spo-Dee-O-Dee").......... 150-250 57
CORAL (61918 "Rock Billy Boogie").......... 150-250 57
FREEDOM (44001 "I'm Restless").......... 30-50 58
FREEDOM (44011 "Gumbo").......... 30-50 59
FREEDOM (44017 "Sweet Baby Doll").......... 30-50 59
LIBERTY (55222 "Settin' the Woods on Fire").......... 20-30 59
LIBERTY (55243 "Don't Do It").......... 15-25 60
LIBERTY (55258 "Dreamin' ").......... 10-20 60
(Green and silver label.)
LIBERTY (55258 "Dreamin' ").......... 8-12 61
(Multi-color label.)
LIBERTY (55285 thru 55489).......... 10-20 60-62
LIBERTY ALL-TIME HITS.......... 3-5
MAGIC LAMP (515 "Bigger Man").......... 20-30 64
SAHARA (512 "Fountain of Love").......... 8-12 64
U.A.......... 3-5 84
VON (106 "Go Mule Go").......... 500-750 54
(At least one source shows this number as 1006. We don't know yet which is correct.)
Picture Sleeves
LIBERTY (55258 "Dreamin' ").......... 5-10 '90s
LIBERTY (55285 "You're Sixteen").......... 15-25 60
LIBERTY (55298 "Little Boy Sad").......... 15-25 61
LIBERTY (55318 "Big, Big World").......... 15-25 61
MAGIC LAMP (515 "Bigger Man").......... 75-100 64
EPs: 7-inch
LIBERTY (1004 "Dreamin' ").......... 75-100 60
LIBERTY (1011 "Johnny Burnette's Hits").......... 50-75 61
LPs: 10/12-inch
CORAL (57080 "Johnny Burnette and the Rock'n Roll Trio").......... 3000-4000 56
(Counterfeits can be identified by their lack of printing on the spine and hand-etched identification numbers in the trail-off. Originals have the numbers mechanically stamped. Canadian issues are worth at least as much as U.S. issues.)
LIBERTY (3179 "Dreamin' ").......... 30-40 60
(Monaural.)
LIBERTY (3183 "Johnny Burnette").......... 30-40 61
(Monaural.)
LIBERTY (3190 "Johnny Burnette Sings").......... 30-40 61
(Monaural.)
LIBERTY (3206 "Johnny Burnette's Hits and Other Favorites").......... 30-40 62
(Monaural.)
LIBERTY (3255 "Roses Are Red").......... 30-40 62
(Monaural.)
LIBERTY (3389 "The Johnny Burnette Story").......... 40-50 64
(Monaural.)
LIBERTY (7179 "Dreamin' ").......... 40-60 60
(Stereo.)
LIBERTY (7183 "Johnny Burnette").......... 40-50 61
(Stereo.)
LIBERTY (7190 "Johnny Burnette Sings").......... 40-50 61
(Stereo.)
LIBERTY (7206 "Johnny Burnette's Hits and Other Favorites").......... 40-50 62
(Stereo. Black & rainbow colored label with gold & white logo.)
LIBERTY (7206 "Johnny Burnette's Hits and Other Favorites").......... 15-25 66
(Stereo. Black & rainbow label with box style logo.)
LIBERTY (7206 "Johnny Burnette's Hits and Other Favorites").......... 5-10 91
(Stereo. Peach and coral colored label.)
LIBERTY (7255 "Roses Are Red").......... 40-50 62
(Stereo.)
LIBERTY (7389 "The Johnny Burnette Story").......... 50-60 64
(Stereo.)
LIBERTY (7300 series).......... 25-30 63
LIBERTY (10000 series).......... 5-10 81
MCA.......... 5-10 82
SOLID SMOKE (Black vinyl).......... 5-10 78-80
SOLID SMOKE (Colored vinyl).......... 10-15 78
SUNSET.......... 15-25 67
U.A.......... 10-15 75
Members (Trio): Johnny Burnette; Dorsey Burnette; Paul Burlison.
Also see BURNETTE, Dorsey
Also see BURNETTE, Johnny
Also see VEE, Bobby / Johnny Burnette / Ventures / Fleetwoods

BURNETTE, Johnny & Dorsey
(Burnette Brothers)
Singles: 7-inch
CORAL (62190 "Blues Stay Away from Me").......... 50-75 60
IMPERIAL (5509 "Warm Love").......... 50-75 58
REPRISE (20153 "Hey Sue").......... 10-20 63
Also see BROWN, Roy
Also see BURNETTE, Dorsey
Also see BURNETTE, Johnny
Also see SHAMROCKS
Also see TEXANS

BURNETTE, Linda
Singles: 7-inch
PERRY (5 "Rattle Bones Rock").......... 100-150 58

BURNING BUSH
Singles: 7-inch
MERCURY (72657 "Keep on Burning").......... 10-15 67

BURNING SLICKS
Singles: 7-inch
BATTLE (45926 "Hard Drivin' Man").......... 10-15 64
RIVERSIDE (4571 "Hard Drivin' Man").......... 15-25 63
Picture Sleeves
BATTLE (45926 "Midnight Drag").......... 35-50 64

BURNS, Bink
Singles: 7-inch
ROSE ("Muddy River").......... 50-75
(Selection number not known.)

BURNS, Eddie
Singles: 78 rpm
CHESS.......... 15-25 57
DELUXE (6024 "Hello Miss Jessie Lee").......... 100-150 52
JVB.......... 25-50 57
Singles: 7-inch
CHESS (1672 "Treat Me Like I Treat You").......... 20-30 57
DELUXE (6024 "Hello Miss Jessie Lee").......... 350-450 52
HARVEY (111 "Orange Driver").......... 50-75 62
HARVEY (115 "The Thing to Do").......... 20-30 62
HARVEY (118 "Orange Driver").......... 20-30 62
JVB (82 "Treat Me Like I Treat You").......... 50-75 57
RED BIRD.......... 3-5 83
VON (728 "You Better Cut That Out").......... 50-100 65
Also see BIG ED & HIS COMBO
Also see GAYE, Marvin
Also see HOOKER, John Lee / Eddie Kirkland / Eddie Burns / Sylvester Cotton
Also see PICKENS, Slim
Also see SWING BROTHERS

BURNS, Jackie
(With the Bo-Bells)
Singles: 7-inch
CROSBY (21 "Queen of Fools").......... 5-10 62
DEL-FI (4102 "Hey Then, There Now").......... 25-35 59
MGM (13182 "He's My Guy").......... 5-10 63

BURNS, Jimmy
Singles: 78 rpm
COMBO (28 "Nervous").......... 15-25 53
Singles: 7-inch
COMBO (28 "Nervous").......... 35-50 53

BURNS, Jimmy
(Jimmy & Fantastic Epics; with La Casics)
Singles: 7-inch
ERICA (02 "I Really Love You").......... 200-300
MINIT (32085 "I Tried").......... 4-6 70
TIP TOP (2012 thru 2014).......... 15-25 65

BURNS, Linda
Singles: 7-inch
TY-TEX (121 "The Reason Why").......... 10-20 66

BURNS, Norm
Singles: 7-inch
STERLING (550 "Red Hot Mama").......... 50-75

BURNS, Ronnie
Singles: 7-inch
VERVE (10125 "Kinda Cute").......... 10-15 58

BURNS, Sonny
Singles: 78 rpm
STARDAY (118 "Too Hot to Handle").......... 15-25 53
STARDAY (209 "Real Cool Cat").......... 30-40 54
Singles: 7-inch
STARDAY (118 "Too Hot to Handle").......... 50-75 53
STARDAY (209 "Real Cool Cat").......... 200-300 54
TNT (171 "Bottom of the Bottle").......... 10-15 59
U.A. (395 "Patches on My Heart").......... 5-10 61

BURNT SUITE
LPs: 10/12-inch
BJW (9 "Burnt Suite").......... 100-150 68

BURR, Francis
Singles: 7-inch
SALEM (191 "I'll Make a New World").......... 15-25 64

BURRAGE, Harold *R&B '65*
(Harold Barrage)
Singles: 78 rpm
ALADDIN.......... 15-25 52
COBRA.......... 15-25 56-57
DECCA.......... 15-25 50
STATES.......... 25-50 55
Singles: 7-inch
ALADDIN (3194 "Sweet Brown Gal").......... 40-60 52
COBRA (5004 thru 5026).......... 30-40 56-58
DECCA (48175 "Hi-Yo").......... 40-60 50
FOXY.......... 10-20 62
M-PAC (7201 "Faith").......... 8-12 62
M-PAC (7204 "I'll Take One").......... 8-12 63
M-PAC (7210 thru 7234).......... 5-10 64-67
PASO (102 "Fool").......... 10-20 61
STATES (144 "Feel So Fine").......... 50-100 55
(Black vinyl.)
STATES (144 "Feel So Fine").......... 100-200 55
(Red vinyl.)
VEE-JAY (318 "Crying for My Baby").......... 15-25 59
VEE-JAY (318 "356 "Great Day in the Morning").......... 15-25 60
VIVID (101 "Heart").......... 8-12 64

VIVID (102 "Betty Jean")..........8-12 64

BURRELL, Kenny LP '63

Singles: 7-inch

BLUE NOTE (1884 thru 1886)..........5-10 63
CADET (5548 thru 5597)..........5-10 66-68
PRESTIGE (238 thru 367)..........5-10 63-65
VERVE (10375 thru 10618)..........5-10 66-68

LPs: 10/12-inch

ARGO (655 "A Night at the Vanguard")... 20-30 60
BLUE NOTE (4021 "At the Five Spot Café")..........20-30 60
CADET (772 "Tender Gender")..........10-20 66
CADET (798 "Ode to 52nd Street")..........10-20 68
COLUMBIA (1703 "Weaver of Dreams"). 20-30 60
(Monaural.)
COLUMBIA (8503 "Weaver of Dreams"). 25-35 60
(Stereo.)
KAPP (1326 "Lotsa Bossa Nova")..........15-25 63
PRESTIGE (7277 "All Day Long")..........10-20 64
PRESTIGE (7448 "Best of Kenny Burrell")..........10-20 67
VERVE (8612 "Guitar Forms")..........10-20 65
VERVE (8656 "Generation Ago Today"). 10-20 67
VERVE (8746 "Blues – The Common Ground")..........10-20 68

BURRELL, Kenny, & John Coltrane

LPs: 10/12-inch

NEW JAZZ (8276 "Kenny Burrell and John Coltrane")..........15-25 63
PRESTIGE (7532 "Kenny Burrell and John Coltrane")..........10-20 68

BURRELL, Kenny, Richard Davis & Roy Haynes

LPs: 10/12-inch

CADET (769 "Man at Work")..........10-20 66

BURRELL, Kenny, & Brother Jack McDuff

LPs: 10/12-inch

PRESTIGE (7265 "Somethin' Slick").......20-30 63
Also see McDUFF, Brother Jack

BURRELL, Kenny, Billie Poole & Junior Mance Trio

LPs: 10/12-inch

RIVERSIDE (458 "Confessin' the Blues") 15-25 63

BURRELL, Kenny, & Jimmy Smith LP '63

Singles: 7-inch

BLUE NOTE (1769 "Motorin' Along")....... 20-30 61

LPs: 10/12-inch

PRESTIGE (8553 "Blue Bash")..........20-30 63
VERVE..........15-25 66-68
Also see BURRELL, Kenny
Also see SMITH, Jimmy

BURRIS, Daisy

Singles: 7-inch

DEE-SU (303 "In Love to Stay")..........5-10 66
PORT (3007 "Take the Same Thing")...... 15-25 65

BURT, Wanda
(With the Creschendos)

Singles: 7-inch

MUSIC CITY (840 "Scheming")..........100-150 61
(Black vinyl.)
MUSIC CITY (840 "Scheming")..........250-300 61
(Yellow vinyl.)
Also see CRESCHENDOS

BURT & BACKBEATS

Singles: 7-inch

BIG TOP (3087 "Move It on the Backbeat")..........10-15 61

BURTON, Ben

Singles: 78 rpm

MODERN..........10-20 54

Singles: 7-inch

MODERN..........20-30 54

BURTON, Bob

Singles: 78 rpm

MAR-VEL..........20-50 53

Singles: 7-inch

MAR-VEL (951 "Boogie Woogie Baby of Mine")..........75-125 53
MAR-VEL (952 "Don't Cry Little Girl")...... 40-60 55
MAR-VEL (953 "Tired of Rocking")........75-125 56

BURTON, Bob, & Ginny Carter

Singles: 78 rpm

MAR-VEL..........20-40 53

Singles: 7-inch

MAR-VEL (950 "40 Acres of My Heart")...35-50 53
(Black vinyl.)
MAR-VEL (950 "40 Acres of My Heart").75-100 53
(Colored vinyl.)
Also see BURTON, Bob

BURTON, Dorian

Singles: 7-inch

NEIL (106 "One Little Kiss")..........10-15 57
PRESIDENT (1008 "Flyin' Home to My Baby")..........10-15 58

BURTON, Earl

Singles: 78 rpm

MONEY (210 "Sleep, Drink & Play")..........5-10 55

Singles: 7-inch

MONEY (210 "Sleep, Drink & Play")..........10-20 55

BURTON, Harold

Singles: 7-inch

LA (12 "Yellow Gal")..........20-30 58

BURTON, James
(Jimmy Burton)

Singles: 7-inch

GUYDEN (6004 "If I'm a Fool")..........4-6 72
GUYDEN (6006 "You Done Me Wrong")......4-6 72
MIRAMAR (108 "Jimmy's Blues")..........20-30 65
ROMAN (101 "Christmas Party")..........20-30 65
(Colored vinyl. Music is *Jimmy's Blues* [Miramar 108] reworked.)
TNT (187 "Wild River")..........50-100 61

LPs: 10/12-inch

A&M (4293 "James Burton")..........15-20 71
Also see ANDERSON, Bill / Jimmie Burton
Also see BURTON, James, & Ralph Mooney
Also see DENVER, John
Also see DOBRO, Jimmie
Also see EDDY, Duane
Also see HAGGARD, Merle
Also see HARRIS, Emmylou
Also see HAWKINS, Dale
Also see JENNINGS, Waylon
Also see JIM & JOE
Also see LONGBRANCH PENNYWHISTLE
Also see NELSON, Ricky
Also see ORBISON, Roy
Also see PRESLEY, Elvis

BURTON, James, & Ralph Mooney

Singles: 7-inch

CAPITOL (2140 "Cornpickin'")..........10-15 68

LPs: 10/12-inch

CAPITOL (2822 "Corn Pickin' and Slick Slidin'")..........50-100 68
Also see BURTON, James
Also see MOONEY, Ralph

BURTON, June

Singles: 7-inch

RED FOX (28 "My Confession of Love")..........500-600 62
Session: Famous Dukes Of Rhythm.

BURTON, Ronnie

Singles: 7-inch

M&M (2916 "No Place to Run to Anymore")..........5-10 68
NUGGET (259 "Let Me Down Easy")..........5-10 67
TAM (102 "Somebody's Been Babyin' My Baby")..........75-125

BURTON, Scott

Singles: 7-inch

BIG TOP (3084 "Nashville Express")........10-20 61

BURTON, Ward, & Music Men Inc.

Singles: 7-inch

PANTHER (1 "Salty Dog")..........15-25 '60s
Also see BURTON, Willard

BURTON, Willard
(Willard Burton & Funky Four; Ward Burton)

Singles: 7-inch

CAPITOL..........4-6 71
PANTHER (5 "Sweet Temptation")..........10-20 '60s
PARADISE (1018 "The Freeze")..........10-20 '60s
PEACOCK (1903 "Teardrops of Love")....10-20 61
PEACOCK (1917 "Twistin' Twist")..........8-12 62
MONEY..........4-6 76
Also see BURTON, Ward, & Music Men Inc.
Also see PIANO SLIM

BUSBEE, Buford
(With the Epitomes)

Singles: 7-inch

DEE DEE (101 "This Is All I Ask")..........20-25 59
DORE (551 "This Is All I Ask"/"It Can't Be Wrong")..........15-20 60
DORE (584 "This Is All I Ask"/"Don't Drop It")..........10-15 61

BUSBY, Buzz

Singles: 7-inch

EMPIRE (507 "Pretty Polly")..........10-20 58
STARDAY (425 "Going Home")..........10-20 59
STARDAY (452 "Reno Bound")..........10-20 59
Also see HARRIS, Ray, / Buzz Busby

BUSBY, Jay

Singles: 7-inch

BETHLEHEM (3086 "Apple Cider")..........10-20 64

BUSBY, Jim

Singles: 7-inch

DALE (104 "Our Wife")..........10-20 57

BUSBY, Johnny

Singles: 7-inch

TALENT (108 "Cadillac Mama")..........10-20 60

BUSBY, Wayne

Singles: 7-inch

EMPIRE (506 "Goin' Back to Dixie").....100-125 58
OTT (201 "Goin' Back to Dixie")..........50-100 58

BUSCHER, Dick, & Cliches
(Dick Busher)

Singles: 7-inch

CUCA (1040 thru 1168)..........15-20 61-64
CUCA (1235 "Don't Say You're Sorry")....10-15 65
Members: Nick White; Ton Weig; Harry Bluett; Benny Bryson; Denny Tranel; Terry William; Joe Huseman.
Also see CLICHES

BUSH

Singles: 7-inch

HIBACK (102 thru 110)..........10-20 65-66

Picture Sleeves

HIBACK (102 "Got Love if You Want It")..20-30 65

BUSH, Dick
(Donnie Brooks)

Singles: 7-inch

ERA (1067 "Hollywood Party")..........50-75 58
Also see BROOKS, Donnie

BUSH, Eddie

Singles: 7-inch

JAXON (503 "Little Darling")..........50-75 57
PHILLIPS INT'L (3558 "Baby, I Don't Care")..........15-20 60
ROCK IT (106 "I've Got Grass on My Back")..........4-8 79

BUSH, Johnny C&W '67
(With Bill Freeman & His Texas Plainsmen)

Singles: 7-inch

ALLSTAR (7166 "In My World All Alone")..........100-125 57
ALLSTAR (7172 "Your Kind of Love")....75-100 57
DELTA..........3-5 81-82
GUSTO..........4-6 78
MILLION..........4-6 72
NEW STAR..........4-6 '60s
RCA..........4-6 72-74
STOP..........4-8 67-71
WHISKEY RIVER..........4-6 79

LPs: 10/12-inch

BUCKBOARD..........5-10
DELTA..........10-15 80-83
MILLION..........15-25 72
PICKWICK..........5-10 '70s
PICKWICK/HILLTOP..........10-15
POWER PAK..........5-10 74
RCA..........10-15 73
STOP..........10-20 68-72
WHISKEY RIVER..........15-20
Session: Fiddlin' Frenchie Burke.
Also see NELSON, Willie
Also see PRICE, Ray

BUSH, Kate P&R '79

Singles: 12-inch

EMI AMERICA..........4-6 85-86

Singles: 7-inch

COLUMBIA..........3-5 89
EMI AMERICA (8000 series)..........3-8 78-86
EMI AMERICA (9605 "Hounds of Love")...8-10 85
(Long version/Short version. Promotional issue only.)
EMI AMERICA (EMR-20490 "Them Heavy People")..........25-50
(Promotional issue only.)
GEFFEN..........3-5 87
HARVEST..........5-8 78-79

Picture Sleeves

EMI AMERICA (8003 "Kite")..........4-6 78
EMI AMERICA (8285 "Running Up That Hill")..........4-6 85
EMI AMERICA (8302 "Hounds of Love")..... 4-6 85
EMI AMERICA (EMR-20490 "Them Heavy People")..........25-50
(Promotional issue only.)
GEFFEN..........3-5 87
HARVEST..........10-15 78

LPs: 10/12-inch

COLUMBIA..........5-10 89
EMI AMERICA..........6-12 78-86
HARVEST..........10-15 78
Also see SUN FERRY AID

BUSH, Little David
(David Ruffin)

Singles: 7-inch

VEGA (1002 "You and I")..........150-200 59
Also see RUFFIN, David

BUSH, Tommy

Singles: 7-inch

RIKA (108 "I Like It")..........50-75
SPECIALTY..........4-6 71-72

BUSHKIN, Joe LP '56

LPs: 10/12-inch

CAPITOL..........20-30 56-59
REPRISE..........10-20 63
Also see COLLINS, Al

BUSHKIN, Joe, & Teddy Wilson

LPs: 10/12-inch

RONDO (845 "Jazz – Joe Bushkin and Teddy Wilson")..........10-20 59

BUSHMEN

Singles: 7-inch

DIMENSION (1049 "Baby")..........20-30 65
MUSTANG (3002 "You're the One")..........8-12 65
SMASH (2054 "Friends and Lovers Forever")..........5-10 66

BUSKIRK, Kenny

Singles: 7-inch

COWTOWN (819 "Bartender's Place")....50-75
COWTOWN (832 "Get with It")..........50-75

BUSKIRK, Paul, & His Little Men (Featuring Hugh Nelson)

Singles: 7-inch

BELLAIRE (106 "Memories of You")........10-15 63
R (502 "Nite Life")..........50-100 64
STONEWAY..........4-6 '70s
Members: Willie Hugh Nelson; Paul Buskirk; Dick Shannon.
Also see NELSON, Willie

BUSSY, Terry

Singles: 7-inch

JAZZMAR (103 "How Could You").......400-500 57

BUSTER, Bob

Singles: 7-inch

DARSA (129 "Swamp Hop")..........50-75

BUSTER & EDDIE

Singles: 7-inch

CLASS (1518 "Can't Be Still")..........50-75 66

BUSTERS P&R '63

Singles: 7-inch

ARLEN (735 thru 745)..........10-20 63-64
Members: Jack Baker; Fran Parda; Richard Eriksen; Rick LaFrenier; Tink Hermanson.
Also see COLE, Fred E.
Also see TROPHIES

BUTALA, Tony

Singles: 7-inch

CAPITOL..........4-6 73
TOPIC (8001 "Long Black Stockings").....10-20 59
TOPIC (8002 "My First Real Romance")..10-20 59
Also see LETTERMEN

BUTANES *P&R '61*
(With Teddy McRae's Orchestra)
Singles: 7-inch
ENRICA (1007 "Don't Forget I Love You") 15-25 61
Also see McRAE, Teddy

BUTCH GREASER & HOODS
Singles: 7-inch
TOILET (7135 "Teenager with V.D.") .... 20-25 '60s

BUTERA, Sam
(With the Witnesses)
Singles: 78 rpm
CADENCE 5-10 55
GROOVE 5-10 54-55
PREP (105 "10 Little Women") 10-15 57
RCA 5-10 53
Singles: 7-inch
CADENCE (1281 "Goin' In") 10-20 55
CAPITOL (Except 4862) 5-10 58-62
CAPITOL (4862 "Later Baby, Later") 15-20 62
COLISEUM (2710 "Love Bandit") 5-10 68
DOT 8-12 59-62
GROOVE 10-15 54
PREP (102 "Equator") 10-15 57
PREP (105 "10 Little Women") 20-40 57
PREP (134 "Good Gracious Baby") 10-15 58
PRIMA 5-10 63
RCA 10-20 53
EPs: 7-inch
CAPITOL 10-20 58
"X" 15-25 54
LPs: 10/12-inch
CAPITOL 20-30 58-62
DOT 15-25 60-62
PREP 5-10 84
PRIMA 15-20 64
Also see PRIMA, Louis
Also see DAVIS, Sammy, Jr., & Sam Butera

BUTLER, Andy
Singles: 7-inch
TANGERINE (985 "Sunshine Love") 10-20 68
TANGERINE (988 "Coming Apart at the Seams") 10-20 68

BUTLER, Billy *P&R/R&B '65*
(With the Chanters; with Infinity; with Enchanters)
Singles: 7-inch
BRUNSWICK 8-12 66-68
CURTOM (0120 "Feel the Magic") 4-6 76
MEMPHIS (103 "I Don't Want to Lose You") 4-6 71
MGM (14589 "Storm") 4-6 73
OKEH (Except 7207) 10-15 63-66
OKEH (7207 "My Sweet Woman") 15-25 64
PRIDE 4-6 72-73
LPs: 10/12-inch
EDSEL 5-10 86
OKEH (12115 "The Right Track") 50-100 66
(Monaural.)
OKEH (14115 "The Right Track") 50-100 66
(Stereo.)
PRESTIGE 10-15 69-70
PRIDE 10-12 73
Members: Billy Butler; Earl Batts; Jess Tillman; Larry Wade; Phyllis Know.

BUTLER, Carl *C&W '61*
Singles: 78 rpm
CAPITOL 5-10 51-52
OKEH 4-8 54-55
Singles: 7-inch
CAPITOL 10-20 51-52
COLUMBIA 8-12 59-63
OKEH 10-20 54-55
LPs: 10/12-inch
COLUMBIA 10-20 63
HARMONY 10-15 66-71

BUTLER, Carl & Pearl *C&W '62*
Singles: 7-inch
CHART 4-6 71-73
COLUMBIA 5-10 62-69
LPs: 10/12-inch
CHART 8-12 72
CMH 5-10 80
COLUMBIA 10-20 64-70
HARMONY 8-12 72
PEDACA 5-10
Also see BUTLER, Carl

BUTLER, Champ *P&R '51*
Singles: 78 rpm
COLUMBIA 3-8 50-54
CORAL 3-8 55-56
Singles: 7-inch
CII (500 "Gonne Get Some Lovin' ") .... 10-15 '50s
COLUMBIA 10-20 50-54
CORAL 10-20 55-56
GILLETTE 5-10 62
KEEN (2001 "Mississippi Mud") 10-15 58
KEEN (2019 "Mourning in the Morning") 10-15 59
VISCOUNT (1001 "This Can't Be Love") 10-15 59
ZEPHYR (019 "This Is Love") 10-15 57
EPs: 7-inch
COLUMBIA 10-15 53
LPs: 10/12-inch
CLARITY (810 "16 Top Western Hits") 10-20
GILLETTE 10-20 62

BUTLER, Cliff
(With the Singing Doves; with Lovers; with His Band; with Blue Boys)
Singles: 78 rpm
KIT (885 "Rent's Too High") 10-20 55
STATES (112 "Adam's Rib") 25-50 53
STATES (123 "People Will Talk") 50-75 53
STATES (148 "Jealous Hearted Woman") 25-50 55
Singles: 7-inch
EXCELLO (2126 "Lover's Plea") 15-25 58
FAVORITE (600) 50-100
(Title not known.)
FRANTIC (801 "I Can't Believe") .... 100-150 '50s
KIT (885 "Rent's Too High") 30-50 55
NASCO (6003 "My Mood") 10-15 57
NASCO (6010 "That's How I Go for You") 10-15 58
NASCO (6014 "Love One Another") 10-15 58
STATES (112 "Adam's Rib") 50-100 53
STATES (123 "People Will Talk") 100-200 53
(Black vinyl.)
STATES (123 "People Will Talk") 400-500 53
(Red vinyl.)
STATES (148 "Jealous Hearted Woman") 100-200 55
Also see ECKSTINE, Billy / Arthur Prysock / Cliff Butler

BUTLER, Davy
Singles: 7-inch
JCP (1032 "If I Had a Girl") 10-20 64
JCP (1044 "She's a Baby") 10-20 65

BUTLER, Daws
(As Huckleberry Hound; with Ernie Freeman Orchestra)
Singles: 7-inch
MERRI (6011 "Bingo Ringo") 10-15 64
Picture Sleeves
MERRI (6011 "Bingo Ringo") 15-25 64
Also see BACKUS, Jim, & Daws Butler
Also see FREEMAN, Ernie

BUTLER, Daws, & Don Messick
LPs: 10/12-inch
COLPIX (202 "Huckleberry Hound") 25-45 59
COLPIX (205 "Yogi Bear and Boo Boo") 25-45 61
COLPIX (207 Here Comes Huckleberry Hound") 25-45 61
COLPIX (208 "Mr. Jinks, Pixie & Dixie") 25-45 61
Also see BUTLER, Daws

BUTLER, Daws, Don Messick & Doug Young
LPs: 10/12-inch
COLPIX (203 "Quick Draw McGraw") 25-50 66

BUTLER, Dee Dee
Singles: 7-inch
SMC (110 "I Can't Stand Another Hurt") .... 40-60 '60s

BUTLER, Freddy
Singles: 7-inch
KAPP (819 "This Thing") 5-10 67
STAR MAKER (1930 "This Road") 15-20 62
LPs: 10/12-inch
KAPP (1519 "With a Dab of Soul") 10-20 67
(Monaural.)
KAPP (3519 "With a Dab of Soul") 10-20 67
(Stereo.)

BUTLER, Gene
Singles: 7-inch
ZODIAC (333 "L.C.") 10-20 63

BUTLER, Howie, & Reflections
Singles: 7-inch
GAITY (6017 "Treasure of Love") 30-50 60

BUTLER, Jerry *P&R/R&B '58*
(With the Impressions; with Riley Hampton's Orchestra)
Singles: 78 rpm
ABNER (1013 "For Your Precious Love") 75-125 58
ABNER (1024 "Lost") 75-125 59
FALCON (1013 "For Your Precious Love") 75-125 58
Singles: 7-inch
ABC 4-6 73
ABNER (1013 "For Your Precious Love") 40-50 58
ABNER (1024 thru 1035) 15-25 59-60
COLLECTABLES 3-5 81
ERIC 4-6 73
FALCON (1013 "For Your Precious Love") 50-60 58
FOUNTAIN 3-5 82
ICHIBAN 3-5 92-93
MCA 3-5 83
MERCURY 4-8 67-74
MISTLETOE (803 "O Holy Night") 4-6 75
MOTOWN 4-6 76-77
OLDIES 45 3-5
PHILA. INT'L 3-6 78-81
TRIP 4-6
VEE-JAY (280 "For Your Precious Love") 5000-6000 58
(First issue.)
VEE-JAY (354 thru 396) 15-20 60-61
VEE-JAY (405 thru 567) 10-15 62-63
VEE-JAY (588 thru 715) 8-12 64-65
VEE-JAY (1971 "Aware of Love") 20-30 63
(Stereo compact 33 single.)
Picture Sleeves
MOTOWN (1403 "Devil in Mrs. Jones") 5-8 76
VEE-JAY (475 "Theme from *Taras Bulba*") 10-20 62
VEE-JAY (598 "I Stand Accused") 10-20 64
LPs: 10/12-inch
ABNER (2001 "Jerry Butler Esquire") 250-350 59
BUDDAH (4001 "Very Best of Jerry Butler") 10-20 69
EXODUS 5-10
FOUNTAIN (282-1 "Ice 'N' Hot") 5-10 82
DYNASTY (7302 "Just For You") 10-20
KENT (536 "Just Beautiful") 10-15 68
LOST NITE (22 "Jerry Butler and the Impressions") 10-20 81
(10-inch LP. Red vinyl. 1000 made.)
MERCURY (006 "Sweet Sixteen") 8-12 74
MERCURY (689 "Power of Love") 8-12 73
MERCURY (1171 "The Soul Goes On") 10-15 68
MERCURY (7502 "Spice of Life") 15-20 72
(Two discs.)
MERCURY (61005 "Soul Artistry") 10-15 67
MERCURY (61146 "Mr. Dream Merchant") 10-15 67
MERCURY (61151 "Golden Hits") 10-15 68
MERCURY (61198 "The Ice Man Cometh") 8-12 69
MERCURY (61234 "Ice on Ice") 8-12 69
MERCURY (61269 "You and Me") 8-12 70
MERCURY (61281 "Best of Jerry Butler") 8-12 70
MERCURY (61320 "Assorted Songs") 8-12 71
MERCURY (61347 "Sagittarius Movement") 8-12 71
MOTOWN (850 "Love's on the Menu") 5-10 75
MOTOWN (878 "Suite for the Single Girl") 5-10 77
MOTOWN (892 "It All Comes Out in My Song") 5-10 77
PHILA. INT'L (35510 "Nothing Says I Love You Like I Love You") 5-10 78
PHILA. INT'L (36413 "Best Love I Ever Had") 5-10 81
POST (7000 "Jerry Butler Sings") 5-10
PRIDE (0006 "Melinda") 8-10 72
SCEPTER (18009 "Best of Jerry Butler") 8-10
SUNSET (5216 "Gift of Love") 10-15 68
TRADITION (2068 "Starring Jerry Butler") 5-10 82
TRIP (16-45 "16 Greatest Hits") 10-15 78
TRIP (8011 "All Time Hits") 10-15 71
(Two discs.)
TRIP (9516 "Infinite Style") 10-12 71-78
U.A. (498 "Very Best of Jerry Butler") 8-10 75
UPFRONT (100 "Souled Out") 8-10
UPFRONT (107 "Great Soul Hits") 8-10
UPFRONT (124 "All Time Hits") 8-10
VEE-JAY (1003 "Jerry Butler Gold") 20-30
(Two discs.)
VEE-JAY (1027 "Jerry Butler Esquire") 40-60 61
VEE-JAY (1029 "He Will Break Your Heart") 40-60 60
VEE-JAY (1034 "Love Me") 25-35 61
(Repackage of Vee-Jay 1027.)
VEE-JAY (1038 "Aware of Love") 40-60 61
VEE-JAY (1046 "Moon River") 25-35 62
VEE-JAY (1048 "Best of Jerry Butler") 25-35 62
VEE-JAY (1057 "Folk Songs") 25-35 63
VEE-JAY (1075 "For Your Precious Love") 25-35 63
VEE-JAY (1076 "Giving Up On Love/Need to Belong") 25-35 63
VEE-JAY (1119 "More of the Best of Jerry Butler") 20-30 65
Members (Impressions): Jerry Butler; Arthur Brooks; Sam Gooden; Richard Brooks; Curtis Mayfield.
Also see AUSTIN, Patti, & Jerry Butler
Also see CHANDLER, Gene, & Jerry Butler
Also see McPHATTER, Clyde / Little Richard / Jerry Butler
Also see RIVERS, Johnny / 4 Seasons / Jerry Butler / Jimmy Soul

BUTLER, Jerry, & Brenda Lee Eager *P&R/R&B '72*
Singles: 7-inch
MERCURY (73255 thru 73422) 4-6 71-73
LPs: 10/12-inch
MERCURY (660 "Love We Have, Love We Had") 8-12 73

BUTLER, Jerry, & Betty Everett *P&R/R&B '64*
Singles: 7-inch
ABC (2444 "Let It Be Me") 4-6 73
VEE-JAY (613 thru 691) 8-12 64-65
LPs: 10/12-inch
BUDDAH (7505 "Together") 10-15 69
VEE-JAY (1099 "Delicious Together") 20-30 64
Also see DELLS
Also see EVERETT, Betty

BUTLER, Jerry, & Debra Henry *R&B '80*
("Jerry 'The Iceman' Butler featuring Debra Henry of Silk")
Singles: 7-inch
PHILA. INT'L (3113 "Don't Be an Island") 3-5 80

BUTLER, Jerry, & Thelma Houston *R&B '77*
Singles: 7-inch
MOTOWN (1422 "It's a Lifetime Thing") 4-6 77
LPs: 10/12-inch
MOTOWN (887 "Thelma & Jerry") 8-10 77
Also see BUTLER, Jerry
Also see HOUSTON, Thelma

BUTLER, Pat
Singles: 7-inch
BARGAIN (5005 "Consider Me, Darling") 15-25 62

BUTLER, Rod
Singles: 7-inch
ARTEEN (1005 "Yellow Moon") 10-20 60

BUTLER, Tommy
Singles: 7-inch
CHATTAHOOCHEE (688 "Ask Miss Rose") 10-20 65
CHATTAHOOCHEE (704 "Move On Stay Gone") 10-20 66
ROULETTE (4399 "Turn Around Look At Me") 10-20 61
ROULETTE (4405 "I Will Get Along Somehow") 10-20 62

BUTLERS
Singles: 7-inch
GAMBLE (233 "She's Gone") 5-10 69
GUYDEN (2081 "Lovable Girl") 50-75 63
(White label. Promotional issue only.)
GUYDEN (2081 "Lovable Girl") 50-60 63
(Purple and silver label.)
GUYDEN (2081 "Lovable Girl") 10-20 63
(Purple and blue label.)
LIBERTY BELL (1024 "She Tried to Kiss Me") 15-25 64
PARKWAY (148 "Shop Around") 10-15 67
Members: Frankie Beverly; John Finch; Sonny Nicholson; T. Conway; Joe Collins.
Also see BEVERLY, Frankie

BUTTER REBELLION
Singles: 7-inch
MAUDZ (002 "Aftermath") .... 15-20 '60s

BUTTERFIELD, Erskine
(With His Blue Boys)
Singles: 78 rpm
CORAL 8-12 49
Singles: 7-inch
CORAL 20-25 49
DAVIS (458 "I'm the One") 10-15 58

BUTTERFLYS P&R '64
(Ellie Greenwich)
Singles: 7-inch
RED BIRD (009 "Good Night Baby") 15-25 64
RED BIRD (016 "I Wonder") 10-20 64
Also see GREENWICH, Ellie

BUTTONS
Singles: 7-inch
ARLEN (719 "You Set My Soul on Fire") 8-12 63
CAPITOL (4223 "Jerry") 8-12 59
COLUMBIA (42618 thru 42834) 5-10 62-63
DOT (15988 "Calendar of Love") 10-15 59
EMBER (1100 "Absence Makes the Heart Grow Fonder") 10-15 64

BUTTONS & BEAUS
Singles: 7-inch
ZEN (104 "Never Leave Your Sugar") 10-20 63

BUTTRAM, Pat
Singles: 7-inch
FILMWAYS (104 "Get Up Early in the Morning") 5-10 66
LPs: 10/12-inch
DORE (102 "As I Look into Your Faces") 15-25 61
Also see MOONBILLIES

BUZON, John, Trio
Singles: 7-inch
LIBERTY (55189 "Lizette") 15-25 59
LPs: 10/12-inch
LIBERTY (3108 "Inferno") 20-40 59
(Monaural.)
LIBERTY (7108 "Inferno") 25-45 59
(Stereo.)
LIBERTY (3124 "Cha Cha on the Rocks") 20-40 59
(Monaural.)
LIBERTY (7124 "Cha Cha on the Rocks") 25-45 59
(Stereo.)

BUZZ & BUCKY
Singles: 7-inch
AMY (924 "Tiger a Go-Go") 15-20 65
Members: Buzz Cason; Bucky Wilkin.
Also see RONNY & DAYTONAS

BY THE MORRISON
Singles: 7-inch
VIKING (376 "Gonna Have That Girl") 15-20

BYAS, Don, Quartet R&B '48
Singles: 78 rpm
SAVOY (626 "September Song") 10-20 48
SAVOY (668 "London Donnie") 10-20 48
Also see LITTLE SAM

BYE BYES
Singles: 7-inch
MERCURY (71530 "Blond Hair, Blue Eyes, Ruby Lips") 10-15 59

BYERS, Ann
Singles: 7-inch
ACADEMY (109 "Dead End") 10-20 64
ACADEMY (111 "Here I Am") 10-20 65
ACADEMY (124 "Happy Without You") ... 30-50 67

BYERS, Bernard
(Bernard Byars)
Singles: 7-inch
END (1078 "I Love You") 10-20 60
END (1087 "Sitting by the River") 10-20 61
V-TONE (225 "No Time to Cry") 10-15 61
V-TONE (234 "Please Be True") 10-15 62

BYNUM, Beth
Singles: 7-inch
STAR MAKER (1927 "I'll Set You Free"). 10-20 61

BYRD, Bobby
(Robert Byrd & His Birdies; Bobby Day)
Singles: 78 rpm
CASH 20-30 56
JAMIE 15-25 57
SAGE & SAND 10-20 55
SPARK 15-25 57
Singles: 7-inch
BROWNSTONE 8-10 71-72
CASH (1031 "The Truth Hurts") 50-60 56
JAMIE (1039 "Bippin' and Boppin' Over You") 10-15 57
SAGE & SAND (203 "Please Don't Hurt Me") 20-30 55
SPARK (501 "Bippin' and Boppin' Over You") 20-35 57
STRAWBERRY 4-6
Also see BOB & EARL
Also see DAY, Bobby
Also see HOLLYWOOD FLAMES
Also see IMPALAS
Also see LAURELS
Also see NUNN, Bobby
Also see SOUNDS
Also see VOICES

BYRD, Bobby R&B '65
(With the Byrds; with James Brown Band)
Singles: 7-inch
BANG (562 "If She's There") 5-10 68
BROWNSTONE 4-6 71-72
FEDERAL (12486 "I Found Out") 10-15 63
INTERNATIONAL BROTHERS 4-6 75
KING 5-10 67-71
KWANZA 4-6 73
SMASH (1868 thru 2052) 8-12 64-66
ZEPHYR (018 "If We Should Meet Again") 15-25 57
LPs: 10/12-inch
KING (1118 "I Need Help") 10-15 70

BYRD, Bobby, & James Brown R&B '68
Singles: 7-inch
KING (6151 "You've Got to Change Your Mind") 8-12 68
Also see BROWN, James
Also see BYRD, Bobby

BYRD, Charlie P&R '62
(Charlie Byrd Trio)
Singles: 7-inch
COLUMBIA (44473 "The Look of Love") 5-10 68
COLUMBIA (44782 "Wichita Lineman") 5-10 69
EVEREST (2021 "Bamba Samba") 5-10 63
RIVERSIDE 5-10 62-63
LPs: 10/12-inch
COLUMBIA 15-25 65-69
FANTASY (9429 "Chrystal Silence") 10-15 73
MFSL (515 "At the Village Gate") .... 40-60 '80s
OFFBEAT 25-35 59-60
RIVERSIDE 15-25 62-82
SAVOY 30-50 58
Also see ALMEIDA, Laurindo
Also see GETZ, Stan, & Charlie Byrd

BYRD, Charlie, & Woody Herman
LPs: 10/12-inch
EVEREST 10-20 63
PICKWICK 8-12 66
Also see BYRD, Charlie
Also see HERMAN, Woody

BYRD, Curtis
Singles: 7-inch
CANDIX (340 "Pretty Woman") 15-20 62
JOED (714 "Pretty Woman") 30-40 61

BYRD, Donald LP '64
Singles: 7-inch
BLUE NOTE 4-6 73-77
ELEKTRA 4-6 78-82
WARWICK (650 "Mr. Lucky Theme") 5-10 61
(With Pepper Adams Quintet.)
Picture Sleeves
BLUE NOTE (965 "Dancing in the Street") ... 4-6 77
LPs: 10/12-inch
BLUE NOTE 15-25 59-65
(Label reads "Blue Note Records Inc. - New York, U.S.A.")
BLUE NOTE 10-20 66-77
(Label reads "Blue Note Records - a Division of Liberty Records Inc.")
COLUMBIA (998 "Jazz Lab") 40-60 57
(With Gigi Gryce.)
COLUMBIA (1058 "Jazz Lab, Vol. 2, Modern Jazz Perspective") 40-60 57
(With Gigi Gryce.)
ELEKTRA 5-10 78-82
JAZZLAND (6 "Hard Bop") 30-40
JUBILEE (1059 "Jazz Lab") 40-60 57
(With Gigi Gryce.)
PRESTIGE (7062 "Two Trumpets") 75-100 56
(Yellow label. With Art Farmer.)
PRESTIGE (7080 "Youngbloods") 60-80 57
(Yellow label. With Phil Woods.)
PRESTIGE (7092 "Three Trumpets") 60-80 57
(Yellow label. With Art Farmer & Idrees Sulieman.)
REGENT (6056 "Jazz Eyes") 40-60 57
SAVOY (12032 "Byrd's Word") 40-60 56
(With Frank Foster.)
TRANSITION (4 "Byrd's Eye View") 50-80 55
(With Hank Mobley.)
TRANSITION (5 "Byrd Jazz") 50-80 55
(With Yusef Lateef.)
TRANSITION (17 "Byrd Blows on Beacon Hill") 50-80 56
VERVE 20-30 58
Also see ADAMS, Pepper

BYRD, Jerry P&R '50
Singles: 78 rpm
MERCURY 4-6 53-55
Singles: 7-inch
MERCURY 4-8 53-55
MONUMENT 4-6 59-67
EPs: 7-inch
DECCA 8-12 58
MERCURY 10-20 53-55
RCA 8-12 58
LPs: 10/12-inch
DECCA 20-35 58
LEHUA 8-10
MERCURY (Except 25000 series) 10-20 58-64
MERCURY (25000 series) 20-40 53-54
(10-inch LPs.)
MONUMENT 12-25 61-63
RCA (1687 "Hawaiian Beach Party") 30-40 59
SESAC 40-60 59
WING 10-15 60-66
Also see ALLEN, Rex
Also see KIRK, Red

BYRD, Joe, & Field Hippies
Singles: 7-inch
COLUMBIA 10-20 70
LPs: 10/12-inch
COLUMBIA (7317 "American Metaphysical Circus") 35-55 69
Members: Joe Byrd; John Clauder; Gregg Kovner; Ted Greene; Dana Chalberg; Fred Selden; Tom Scott; Meyer Hirsch.
Also see UNITED STATES OF AMERICA

BYRD, Roy R&B '50
(With His Blues Jumpers; Roy "Bald Head" Byrd; with His New Orleans Rhythm; Roland Byrd)
Singles: 78 rpm
ATLANTIC (947 "Hey Little Girl") 150-250 50
FEDERAL (12061 "K.C. Blues") 150-250 52
(All Federal 45s known to exist are bootlegs.)
FEDERAL (12073 "Rockin' with Fess") .. 75-125 52
MERCURY (8175 "Bald Head") 50-100 50
MERCURY (8184 "Her Mind Is Gone") .. 50-100 50
Also see PROFESSOR LONGHAIR

BYRDS
Singles: 7-inch
RAYNARD (10038 "Your Lies") 50-100 65

BYRDS P&R/LP '65
Singles: 7-inch
ASYLUM 4-6 73
COLUMBIA (1600 series) 4-6 73
COLUMBIA (43271 "Mr. Tambourine Man") 8-10 65
(Black vinyl.)
COLUMBIA (43271 "Mr. Tambourine Man") 50-75 65
(Colored vinyl. Promotional issue only.)
COLUMBIA (43332 "I'll Feel a Whole Lot Better") 8-10 65
(Black vinyl.)
COLUMBIA (43332 "I'll Feel a Whole Lot Better") 50-75 65
(Colored vinyl. Promotional issue only.)
COLUMBIA (43332 "All I Really Want to Do") 8-10 65
(Black vinyl.)
COLUMBIA (43332 "All I Really Want to Do") 50-75 65
(Colored vinyl. Promotional issue only.)
COLUMBIA (43424 "Turn, Turn, Turn") 8-10 65
(Black vinyl.)
COLUMBIA (43424 "Turn, Turn, Turn") ... 50-75 65
(Colored vinyl. Promotional issue only.)
COLUMBIA (43501 thru 45761) 6-12 66-72
COLUMBIA PICTURES ("Ballad of Easy Rider") 150-250 69
(No actual label name. Issued by movie studio. Labeled "Promotion Record for Radio Airplay Only.")
Picture Sleeves
COLUMBIA (43271 "Mr. Tambourine Man") 150-250 65
(Promotional issue only.)
COLUMBIA (43578 "Eight Miles High") 30-40 65
COLUMBIA (44157 "Have You Seen Her Face") 25-35 65
EPs: 7-inch
COLUMBIA (10287 "The Byrds") 300-500 66
(Columbia Special Products issue for the Scholastic Book Services.)
COLUMBIA (116003/4 "Fifth Dimension Open-End Interview") 50-100 66
(Promotional issue only.)
LPs: 10/12-inch
ASYLUM (5058 "Byrds") 8-12 73
COLUMBIA (2372 "Mr. Tambourine Man") 25-50 65
(Monaural.)
COLUMBIA (2454 "Turn, Turn, Turn") 20-40 65
(Monaural.)
COLUMBIA (2549 "Fifth Dimension") 20-40 66
(Monaural.)
COLUMBIA (2642 "Younger Than Yesterday") 20-40 67
(Monaural.)
COLUMBIA (2716 "Greatest Hits") 20-40 67
(Monaural.)
COLUMBIA (2775 "Notorious Byrd Brothers") 20-40 68
(Monaural.)
COLUMBIA (9172 "Mr. Tambourine Man") 20-30 65
(Stereo.)
COLUMBIA (9254 "Turn, Turn, Turn") 20-30 65
(Stereo.)
COLUMBIA (9349 "Fifth Dimension") 20-30 66
(Stereo.)
COLUMBIA (9442 "Younger Than Yesterday") 20-30 67
(Stereo.)
COLUMBIA (9516 "Greatest Hits") 20-30 67
(Stereo.)
COLUMBIA (9575 "Notorious Byrd Brothers") 20-30 68
(Stereo.)
COLUMBIA (9670 "Sweetheart of the Rodeo") 20-30 68
(Stereo.)
COLUMBIA (9755 "Dr. Byrds & My Hyde") 20-30 69
(Stereo.)
COLUMBIA (9942 "The Ballad of Easy Rider") 20-30 69
(Stereo.)
COLUMBIA (30127 "The Byrds") 10-20 70
COLUMBIA (30640 "Byrdmaniax") 8-15 71
COLUMBIA (31050 "Farther Along") 8-15 71
COLUMBIA (31795 "Best of the Byrds") 8-15 72
COLUMBIA (32183 "Preflyte") 8-15 73
COLUMBIA (34000 thru 37000 series) 6-12 75-81
COLUMBIA (46773 "The Byrds") 30-50 90
(Four-disc set. Includes 55-page booklet.)
MURRAY HILL 5-10 87
PAIR 10-12 83
REALM 8-12 76
RHINO 5-10 88
TOGETHER (1001 "Preflyte") 15-25 69
Promotional LPs
BROADCAST ("Byrds Live") 35-50 81
COLUMBIA (2000 series) 50-100 65-67
(White label.)

COLUMBIA (9000 series) 35-55 65-69
(White label.)
COLUMBIA (116003/4 "*Fifth Dimension* Interview Album") 100-200 66
Members: Jim (Roger) McGuinn; Gene Clark; David Crosby; Chris Hillman; Michael Clarke; Gram Parsons; Clarence White; Gene Parsons; John York; Skip Battin. Session: Jay Dee Maness; Bayard Jones; Jim Wessely; Frank Laurie; John Jamnick; Frank Inman; Robert Stanley. Session: Van Dyke Parks.
Also see BATTIN, Skip
Also see BEEFEATERS
Also see BUCKINGHAMS / Byrds / Aretha Franklin / Paul Revere & Raiders
Also see CLARK, Gene
Also see McGUINN, Roger
Also see PARKS, Van Dyke
Also see PARSONS, Gram
Also see REVERE, Paul, & Raiders / Simon & Garfunkel / Byrds / Aretha Franklin

BYRNE, Jerry
Singles: 7-inch
SPECIALTY (635 "Lights Out") 20-30 58
SPECIALTY (651 "Why Did I Ever Say Goodbye") 20-30 58
SPECIALTY (662 "Carry On") 20-30 59

BYRNES, Edd "Kookie," with Joanie Sommers & Mary Kaye Trio
Singles: 7-inch
W.B. (5114 "Kookie's Love Song") 10-15 59
Picture Sleeves
W.B. (5114 "Kookie's Love Song") 20-30 59
Also see KAYE, Mary
Also see SOMMERS, Joanie

BYRNES, Edward — P&R '59
(Edd "Kookie" Byrnes; with Connie Stevens & Don Ralke's Orchestra; with Friend; with Mary Kaye Trio; with Warren Barker & His Orchestra.)
Singles: 7-inch
W.B. (5047 "Kookie Kookie") 10-15 59
W.B. (S-5047 "Kookie Kookie") 20-30 59
(Stereo.)
W.B. (5087 "Like I Love You") 10-15 59
W.B. (S-5087 "Like I Love You") 20-30 59
(Stereo.)
W.B. (5121 "Yulesville") 10-15 59
Picture Sleeves
W.B. (5047 "Kookie Kookie") 20-30 59
W.B. (5087 "Like I Love You") 20-30 59
W.B. (5121 "Yulesville") 20-30 59
EPs: 7-inch
W.B. (1309 "Edd 'Kookie' Byrnes") 25-35 59
LPs: 10/12-inch
W.B. (1309 "Kookie") 35-50 59
Also see BYRNES, Edd "Kookie," with Joanie Sommers & Mary Kaye Trio
Also see RALKE, Don
Also see STEVENS, Connie

BYRON, April
Singles: 7-inch
INTERPHON (7705 "He's My Bobby") 10-20 64

BYRON, Jimmy
(Jimmie Byron)
Singles: 7-inch
EVEREST (19335 "Another") 8-12 60
EVEREST (19368 "Oo La La") 8-12 60
TEEN (113 "Sidewalk Rock") 20-30 57

BYRON, Lord Douglas
Singles: 7-inch
DOT (16685 "Surfin' Santa") 15-25 65

BYRON, Lord Douglas / Continentals
Singles: 7-inch
UNION (505 "Big Bad Ho-Dad") 20-30 62
Also see BYRON, Lord Douglas
Also see CONTINENTALS

BYRON & MORTALS
Singles: 7-inch
X-PRESHUN (2 "Do You Believe Me") 25-35 66

BYSTANDERS
Singles: 7-inch
CHESS (2007 "Royal Blue Summer Sunshine Day") 5-10 67
ON TAP (1001 "Girls Are Made to Love") 30-40 64

C

C & C BOYS
Singles: 7-inch
DUKE (358 "Hey Marvin") 10-20 62
DUKE (379 "It's All Over Now") 10-20 64

C.A. QUINTET
Singles: 7-inch
CANDY FLOSS (102 "Smooth As Silk") .75-125 68
FALCON (70 "Mickey's Monkey") 50-100 67
FALCON (71 "Blow to My Soul") 50-100 67
LPs: 10/12-inch
CANDY FLOSS (7764 "A Trip Through Hell") 1500-2500 68
Members: Jim Erwin; Ken Erwin; Donnie Chapin; Doug Reynolds; Tom Pohling; Paul Samuels; Rick Johnson; Rick Patron; Tony Wright.

C.L. & PICTURES
(C.L. Weldon & Pictures)
Singles: 7-inch
CADETTE (8005 "Love Will Find a Way") 10-15 62
DUNES (2010 "I'm Asking Forgiveness") . 10-15 62
DUNES (2017 "Afraid") 10-15 62
DUNES (2023 "I'm Sorry") 15-20 63
JAMIE (1398 "You Really Slipped One by Me") 10-15 71
MONUMENT (854 thru 958) 5-10 64-65
SABRA 4-6 79
SILVER BULLET 3-5 84-86
Member: Charlie Broyles.

C-MINORS
Singles: 7-inch
IMPRESSION (106 "Don't Go") 20-30 66

C-NOTES
Singles: 78 rpm
EVERLAST 30-50 57
Singles: 7-inch
ARC (4447 Last Saturday Night") 15-25 59
EVERLAST (5005 "From Now On") 15-25 57
NOTE-WORTHY (200,684 "My Coloring Book") 20-30

C.O.D.s — P&R '65
Singles: 7-inch
KELLMAC (1003 thru 1007) 8-12 65-66
KELLMAC (1012 "Coming Back Girl") 50-100 66
Members: Larry Brownlee; Robert Lewis; Carl Washington. Session: Ruby Andrews.

C - QUENTS
Singles: 7-inch
CAPTOWN (4027 "Merry Christmas Baby") 200-300 68
CAPTOWN (4028 "Dearest One") 50-150 68
ESSICA (004 "Dearest One") 10-15 68
QUEST (262 "I've Got to Love You") 10-20 65

C-QUINS
Singles: 7-inch
CHESS (1815 "My Only Love") 5-10 62
DITTO (501 "My Only Love") 10-20 62
(First issue.)

CABARETS
Singles: 7-inch
SAXONY (1002 "There Must Be a Way"). 20-30 62
SAXONY (2006 "There Must Be a Way") 4-6 97
Member: Tommy Liss.
Also see LISS, Tommy, & Matadors

CABBOT, Johnny
Singles: 7-inch
COLUMBIA (3-42283 "Night and Day") .. 75-100 62
(Compact 33 Single.)
COLUMBIA (4-42283 "Night and Day") 50-75 62
Also see 4 SEASONS

CABINEERS
Singles: 78 rpm
ABBEY (72 "Whirlpool") 200-300 49
ABBEY (3001 "Tell Me Now") 75-150 49
ABBEY (3003 "Whirlpool") 75-150 49
PRESTIGE (902 "My, My, My") 50-100 51
PRESTIGE (904 "Each Time") 50-100 52
PRESTIGE (917 "Baby Mine") 50-100 55
Singles: 7-inch
ABBEY (902 "My, My, My") 4-6 76
PRESTIGE (904 "Each Time") 500-600 52

CADDELL, Freddie, & Twirls
Singles: 7-inch
ARDENT (12 "At the Rockhouse") 100-125

CADDELL, Shirley
Singles: 78 rpm
ABC 8-12 56
Singles: 7-inch
ABC (9704 "Where Did the Sunshine Go") 10-15 56
COLUMBIA (40939 "Part Time Gal") 10-15 57
LESLEY (1927 "Big Bounce") 10-20 63
Session: Aristocrats.

CADETS — P&R/R&B '56
Singles: 78 rpm
MODERN (Except 971) 10-20 55-57
MODERN (971 "If It Is Wrong") 50-75 55
Singles: 7-inch
COLLECTABLES 3-5 81
MODERN (Except 971 & 1019) 15-25 55-57
MODERN (971 "If It Is Wrong") 75-125 55
MODERN (1019 "Rum Jamaica Rum") 50-75 57
LPs: 10/12-inch
CROWN (370 "The Cadets") 50-75 63
(Stereo.)
CROWN (5015 "Rockin' 'N' Reelin'") 100-200 57
(Monaural.)
CROWN (5370 "The Cadets") 50-75 63
(Monaural.)
RELIC 10-15
Members: Ted Taylor; Aaron Collins; Willie Davis; Will "Dub" Jones; Lloyd McGraw; Tom Fox; Prentice Moreland; Randolph Jones.
Also see CLASS-NOTES
Also see FLARES
Also see JACKS
Also see JESSIE, Young
Also see JONES, Will, & Cadets
Also see PEPPERS
Also see ROCKETEERS
Also see THOR-ABLES
Also see TAYLOR, Ted

CADETS
Singles: 7-inch
FIREFLY (328 "Don't") 3-5 74
JAN LAR (102 "Don't") 75-125 60
Members: Willie Davis; Aaron Collins; George Hollis; Tom Miller; Robbie Robinson; Beverley Harris.
Also see BUNN, Bennie
Also see PEPPERS

CADILLACS — P&R '55
(With the Jesse Powell Orchestra)
Singles: 78 rpm
JOSIE (765 "Gloria") 75-125 54
JOSIE (769 "Wishing Well") 50-75 54
JOSIE (773 thru 820) 25-50 55-57
JUBILEE (846 "Peek-a-Boo") 30-50 58
(Canadian.)
REO 25-75 55-57
(Canadian.)
Singles: 7-inch
ABC 4-6 73
ARCTIC (101 "Fool") 75-100 64
CAPITOL (4825 "White Gardenia") 10-20 62
JOSIE (765 "Gloria") 250-350 54
JOSIE (769 "Wishing Well") 250-350 54
JOSIE (773 "No Chance") 75-100 55
JOSIE (778 "Down the Road") 75-100 55
JOSIE (785 "Speedoo") 50-75 55
JOSIE (792 "Zoom") 100-200 56
(Brownish vinyl.)
JOSIE (792 "Zoom") 50-75 56
(Black vinyl.)
JOSIE (798 "Betty My Love") 20-30 56
JOSIE (805 "The Girl I Love) 40-50 56
JOSIE (807 "Shock-a-Doo) 15-25 56
JOSIE (812 "Sugar Sugar") 15-25 57
JOSIE (820 "My Girl Friend") 30-40 57
JOSIE (836 "Speedoo Is Back") 10-20 58
JOSIE (842 "I Want to Know") 15-25 58
JOSIE (846 "Peek-a-Boo") 30-40 58
JOSIE (857 "Copy Cat") 10-15 59
JOSIE (861 "Please Mr. Johnson") 10-15 59
JOSIE (866 "Romeo") 15-25 59
JOSIE (870 "Big Dan McGoon") 10-15 59
JOSIE (883 "That's Why") 10-20 60
JUBILEE (846 "Peek-a-Boo") 20-30 58
(Canadian.)
JUBILEE (9010 "Romeo") 40-60 59
(Stereo.)
LANA (118 "Baby It's All Right") 4-6 64
MERCURY (71738 "I'm Willing") 50-100 60
REO (8002 "No Chance") 75-125 55
(Canadian.)
REO (8071 "Speedoo") 50-100 55
(Canadian.)
REO (8100 "Zoom") 50-100 55
(Canadian.)
REO (8139 "Shock-a-Doo") 50-100 56
(Canadian.)
REO (8150 "Sugar Sugar") 50-100 57
(Canadian.)
REO (8163 "My Girl Friend") 50-100 57
(Canadian.)
ROULETTE (4654 "Let's Get Together") ... 5-10 65
SMASH (1712 "You Are to Blame") 15-20 61
VIRGO 4-6 72-73
LPs: 10/12-inch
CADAVER 5-10
HARLEM HITPARADE .... 10-15 '70s
JUBILEE (1045 "Fabulous Cadillacs") . 300-400 57
(Blue label.)
JUBILEE (1045 "Fabulous Cadillacs") . 200-250 59
(Flat black label.)
JUBILEE (1045 "Fabulous Cadillacs") . 100-150 60
(Glossy black label.)
JUBILEE (1089 "Crazy Cadillacs") 150-250 58
(Flat black label.)
JUBILEE (1089 "Crazy Cadillacs") 100-150 60
(Glossy black label.)
JUBILEE (5009 "Twistin' with the Cadillacs") 50-100 62
(Monaural.)
JUBILEE (5009 "Twistin' with the Cadillacs") 100-150 62
(Stereo.)
MURRAY HILL (1195 "Very Best of the Cadillacs") 5-10 88
MURRAY HILL (1285 "The Cadillacs") .... 30-45 '80s
(Boxed, five-disc set.)
MURRAY HILL (61250 "Best of the Cadillacs, Vol. 1") 6-10 83
Members: Earl "Speedoo" Carroll; Jim "Papa" Clark; Gus Willingham; Bobby Phillips; James Bailey; Laverne Drake; Charles Brooks; Earl Wade.
Also see CARROLL, Earl, & Original Cadillacs
Also see CRICKETS
Also see CRYSTALS
Also see FIVE CROWNS
Also see HOWARD, Gregory
Also see MISSLES
Also see NEW YORK CITY
Also see OPALS
Also see ORIGINAL CADILLACS
Also see PEARLS
Also see POWELL, Jesse
Also see RAY, Bobby, & Cadillacs
Also see SCHOOLBOYS
Also see SOLITAIRES
Also see SPEEDO & CADILLACS

CADILLACS / Orioles
LPs: 10/12-inch
JUBILEE (1117 "The Cadillacs Meet the Orioles") 75-100 61
Also see CADILLACS
Also see ORIOLES

CAESAR, Pearline
Singles: 7-inch
AMY (880 "Be Mine Tonight") 10-15 63

CAESAR & CLEO — P&R '65
Singles: 7-inch
REPRISE (0308 "Love Is Strange") 15-25 64
REPRISE (0419 "Love Is Strange") 10-20 65
VAULT (909 "The Letter"/"String Fever") . 15-25 64
(Reissued in 1965 [Vault 916] as by Sonny & Cher. On that issue "String" is correctly shown as "Spring.")
Picture Sleeves
REPRISE (0419 "Love Is Strange") 35-50 65
Members: Salvatore "Sonny" Bono; Cher La Piere.
Also see SONNY & CHER

CAESARS R&B '67
Singles: 7-inch
LANIE (2001 "Get Yourself Together") 40-50 67
LANIE (2002 "Girl I Miss You") 15-25 67

CAFFERY, Robert
Singles: 78 rpm
CHESS (1470 "Ida Bee") 50-75 51

CAGER, Willie
Singles: 7-inch
CONTACT (504 "He's a Player") 10-20 66

CAGLE, Aubrey
Singles: 7-inch
GLEE (1000 "Be-Bop Blues") 100-150 60
GLEE (1001 "Come Along Little Girl") ... 75-125 60
HOUSE OF SOUND (504 "Real Cool") 700-800 59

CAGLE, Danny
Singles: 7-inch
MARLO (1503 "Hi Yo Silver") 100-200

CAGLE, Wade, & Escorts
Singles: 7-inch
SUN (360 "Highland Rock") 10-15 61

CAHILL, Graig, & Off-Beats
Singles: 7-inch
MERRITT (0001 "Landslide") 15-25 63
MERRITT (0002 "Grind") 15-25 63
MERRITT (0003 "Surfin' Elephant") 15-25 64
Also see OFF-BEATS

CAHILL, Mike
Singles: 7-inch
FORD (112 "Lady Love") 10-15 62
FOXIE (7001 "Angel") 15-25 61

CAHPERONES
(Chaperones)
Singles: 7-inch
JOSIE (880 "Cruise to the Moon") 50-75 60
(Repressed to show group as the Chaperones.)
Also see CHAPERONES

CAIN, Bobby
(Bob Cain)
Singles: 7-inch
BIG TOP (3109 "I Don't See Me in Your Eyes Anymore") 10-15 62
MINARET (117 "Everything") 5-10 64
VULCAN (1011 "Chance of a Lifetime") .. 10-15
20TH FOX (118 "Spider") 15-25 58

CAIN, Jackie, & Roy Kral
(Jackie & Roy)
Singles: 78 rpm
ABC-PAR 5-10 56
Singles: 7-inch
ABC-PAR (9711 "Glory of Love") 10-20 56
(Black vinyl.)
ABC-PAR (9711 "Glory of Love") 30-40 56
(Gold vinyl. Promotional issue only.)
ROULETTE (4585 "I Got Rhythm") 5-10 64
ROULETTE (4600 "Star Sounds") 5-10 65
VERVE (10438 "Changes") 5-10 66
LPs: 10/12-inch
ABC-PAR (120 "Glory of Love") 40-60 56

CAIN, Mike
Singles: 7-inch
REECO (1001 "Shake a Hand") 50-75

CAINE, Gladys
Singles: 7-inch
TO GO (602 "Please Mr. DJ") 50-75 63
(Blue vinyl.)
Also see KANE, Gladys

CAIOLA, Al P&R '60
Singles: 78 rpm
CORAL 5-10 57
RCA 4-8 53-55
REGENCY 4-8 56
Singles: 7-inch
AVLANCHE 4-6 73
CORAL (61855 "Honky Tonk Parade") 5-10 57
CORAL (61890 "Blue Angel Blues") 5-10 58
PREFERRED (601 "Aegean Love Song") .. 5-10 59
PREFERRED (602 "Evening Tide") 5-10 60
RCA 5-10 53-55
REGENCY 5-10 56
SUNBEAM 5-10 58
U.A. 4-8 60-68
EPs: 7-inch
RCA (551 "Latin Beat") 10-15 53
RCA (555 "Guitar Sketches") 10-15 53
SESAC (85 "Boffola Caiola") 10-15 60
LPs: 10/12-inch
ATCO (117 "Music for Space Squirrels") .. 10-15 60
BAINBRIDGE 5-8 80
CAMDEN (710 "Guitar Style of Al Caiola") . 8-12 62
CHANCELLOR (5008 "Great Pickin' ") 10-15 60
(With Don Arnone.)
RCA (2031 "High Strung") 10-15 59
ROULETTE (25108 "Salute Italia") 10-15 60
SAVOY 15-25 56
TIME 10-20 60-61
TWO WORLDS 8-10 72
UNART 8-12 67
U.A. 10-15 60-69
Also see JUVENILES
Also see TONES

CAIOLA, Al, & Riz Ortolani
LPs: 10/12-inch
U.A. (3617 "Sound of Christmas") 10-15 67
(Monaural.)
U.A. (6617 "Sound of Christmas") 10-15 67
(Stereo.)
Also see CAIOLA, Al

CAIRO, Tino, & Earthquakes
Singles: 7-inch
HI-Q (5020 "Love in Portofino") 20-30 61

CAIROS
Singles: 7-inch
SHRINE (111 "Don't Fight It") 150-250 66
Members: Keni Lewis; Famon Johnson; Tommy Montier; Gerald Richardson; Wilford Ruffin.

CAITON, Richard
Singles: 7-inch
GNP (327 "Listen to the Drums") 15-25 64
(Blue label.)
GNP (327 "Listen to the Drums") 5-10 64
(Yellow label.)

CAJUNS
Singles: 7-inch
FRATERNITY (836 "Cajun Blues") 15-25 58
SAGE (321 "One, One, One") 10-20 60
Member: Rusty York.
Also see YORK, Rusty

CAKE
Singles: 7-inch
DECCA 5-10 67-68
Picture Sleeves
DECCA 5-10 68
LPs: 10/12-inch
DECCA (74927 "The Cake") 50-70 67
DECCA (75039 "A Slice of the Cake") 50-70 68
Members: Jeanette Jacobs; Barbara Morillo.

CALAMITY JANE C&W '81
Singles: 7-inch
COLUMBIA 3-5 81-82
LPs: 10/12-inch
COLUMBIA 5-10 82
LYLE (9183 "Calamity Jane") 30-40 82
(Picture disc. Promotional issue only.)
Members: Pam Rose; Mary Fiedler; Linda Moore; Mary Ann Kennedy.

CAL-CONS
Singles: 7-inch
ALLRITE (621 "Daddy Cool") 15-25 62

CALDWELL, Andy
Singles: 7-inch
LIBERTY (55142 "Tell Me") 10-20 58

CALDWELL, Joe
(With the Majestics)
Singles: 7-inch
BIM (1 "How Long Will It Last") 100-150
ESTA (100 "Rollin' Tears") 250-300 59
(Esta 100 is also used for an Escos release.)
M.C. (1 "Guess I'm the Lonely One") . 750-1000 59
(Reportedly 100 made.)
Also see ESCOS
Also see FOUR PHARAOHS

CALDWELL, Louise Harrison
("Sister of George Harrison")
LPs: 10/12-inch
RECAR (2012 "All About the Beatles Answered By Louise Harrison Caldwell") 75-125 64
(Includes fan club insert.)

CALE, Johnny
Singles: 7-inch
CHAN (101 "Ain't That Lovin' You Baby") 20-30 61
MERCURY 8-12

CALEB & PLAYBOYS
(With the Emporers [sic]; with Gary K. Pepper & Orchestra)
Singles: 7-inch
OLIMPIC (4575 "I'm Yours") 200-300 63
(Identification number shown since no selection number is used.)
Member: Caleb Talbert.

CALEN, Frankie P&R '61
Singles: 7-inch
BEAR (5002 "Portrait of a Lady") 5-10 62
EPIC (9628 thru 9742) 5-10 63-64
KIP (1517 "Pretty Dimple") 8-12
NRC (029 "Angel Face") 10-20 59
NRC (5008 "Angel Face") 10-20 59
(Same number used for a Jerry Reed issue.)
SPARK (902 "Joanie") 35-45 61
U.A. (521 "Little Cry Baby") 10-20 62
Picture Sleeves
NRC (5008 "Angel Face") 10-20 59

CALENDARS
Singles: 7-inch
CYCLONE (5012 "If I Could Hold Your Hand") 2000-3000 58

CALENDARS
Singles: 7-inch
CHATTAHOOCHEE (722 "You Don't Fall in Love") 200-300 62
COED (564 "I'm Gonna Laugh at You") 200-300 62
PALACE (104 "Weekend") 10-20 61

CALENDARS / Milestones
Singles: 7-inch
SWINGIN' (649 "One Week Romance"/"Roasted Peanuts") 30-40 63

CALHOUN, Charles, & Four Students
Singles: 78 rpm
GROOVE (0149 "Jamboree") 10-20 56
Singles: 7-inch
GROOVE (0149 "Jamboree") 30-40 56
Also see CALHOUN, Charlie
Also see FOUR STUDENTS

CALHOUN, Charlie
(With His Orchestra & Chorus)
Singles: 78 rpm
MGM 10-15 55
Singles: 7-inch
MGM (11989 "Smack Dab in the Middle") 20-30 55
Also see CALHOUN, Charles, & Four Students

CALHOUN, Chuck
Singles: 7-inch
ATLANTIC (1120 "Hey Tiger") 10-15 57

CALHOUN, Lena
(With the Emotions)
Singles: 7-inch
FLIP (357 "First Love Baby") 15-25 61
FLIP (358 "I Can Tell") 10-20 62
HTE (6068 "Been Lookin' Your Way") 15-25 61
Also see EMOTIONS

CALHOUN, Millie
Singles: 7-inch
LO LACE (708 "This Love Will Last Forever") 15-25 65
(First issue.)
MYTIME (643 "This Love Will Last Forever") 5-10 65

CALHOUN, Nate
Singles: 7-inch
GLADES (1760 "Jazz-Freak") 10-20 80

CALHOUN, Rory
Singles: 78 rpm
MGM 5-10 56
Singles: 7-inch
MGM (12359 "Flight to Hong Kong") 5-10 56
Picture Sleeves
MGM (12359 "Flight to Hong Kong") 15-25 56

CALIA, Billy
Singles: 7-inch
HULL (734 "I Still Need You") 10-20 60

CALICO WALL
Singles: 7-inch
DOVE ("Flight Reaction") 5-10
(Colored vinyl. Number not known.)
TURTLE (1107 "Flight Reaction") 150-250 67
(Reissued in '87, but we do not yet have the details as to how to identify originals.)

CALIFORNIANS
Singles: 78 rpm
FEDERAL (12231 "My Angel") 50-100 55
Singles: 7-inch
FEDERAL (12231 "My Angel") 200-300 55

CALIFORNIANS
Singles: 7-inch
CRAFT (1001 "Please Don't Tell Me") .... 15-25 '50s
(Colored vinyl.)
CRAZY HORSE (1318 "Glass Disguise") .. 5-10 69

CALIPHS
Singles: 7-inch
SCATT (111 "Mother Dear") 400-500 58
VINTAGE (1008 "I Need You") 10-15 73
(Blue vinyl.)

CALIPHS
Singles: 7-inch
SARA (6772 "Today, Tomorrow") 15-25 67

CALL, Bob
Singles: 78 rpm
CORAL 20-40 49

CALLAHAN, Mike
Singles: 7-inch
PRO-TONE (204 "I Can't Help It") 50-75

CALLAWAY, Bob
(With the Spiro Hep Cats; with Chicks)
Singles: 7-inch
BIG RED (102 "Tick Tock") 300-500 58
RCA (7593 "Native") 20-30 59
UBC (1013 "Wake Up, Little Boy Blue") 100-150

CALLENDER, Bobby P&R '63
(Bob Callender)
Singles: 7-inch
CORAL (62528 "Sweet Song of Life") 10-15 67
GOLD (102 "Baby, I'm Ready") 30-40 61
ROULETTE (4471 "Little Star") 15-25 63
LPs: 10/12-inch
MGM (4557 "Rainbow") 75-125 68
(Includes lyrics insert.)
Session: Accents
Also see ACCENTS

CALLENDER, Red
(Red Callender Sextet; Red Callender Trio; with Buddy Collette)
Singles: 78 rpm
BAYOU 5-10 53
BLACK & WHITE (781 "Red Light") 10-15 46
BLACK & WHITE (782 "Red Boogie") 10-15 46
EXCLUSIVE (201 "How Come") 10-20 44
EXCLUSIVE (201 "I Wonder") 10-20 44
FEDERAL 5-10 51
HOLLYWOOD (1008 "Voodoo") 10-20 54
(With J.D. Nicholson)
RCA 10-15 51-52
RECORDED IN HOLLYWOOD (139 "Basin Street Blues") 10-20 51
RECORDED IN HOLLYWOOD (140 "C Jam Blues") 10-20 51
RECORDED IN HOLLYWOOD (141 "Dolphin Street Boogie") 10-20 51
RECORDED IN HOLLYWOOD (142 "Till I Waltz Again with You") 10-20 51
(With Scatman Crothers)
RECORDED IN HOLLYWOOD (166 "September in the Rain") 10-20 51
RECORDED IN HOLLYWOOD (168 "I'd Rather Stay in the House with the Mouse") 10-20 51

RECORDED IN HOLLYWOOD (237 "You're Part of Me") 10-20 52
(With Little Caesar)
SUNSET (10056 "These Foolish Things") 10-15 45
SWING (394 "I Cover the Waterfront") 10-15 45
SWING (395 "These Foolish Things") 10-15 45

Singles: 7-inch

BAYOU (001 "The Honey Jump") 25-50 53
BAYOU (002 "Soldiers Blues") 25-50 53
FEDERAL (12045 "Dolphin Street Boogie") 20-30 51
(Reissue of Recorded In Hollywood tracks.)
FEDERAL (12049 "September in the Rain") 25-50 51

LPs: 10/12-inch

CROWN (5012 "Speaks Low") 40-60 57
CROWN (5025 "Swingin' Suite") 40-60 57
METROJAZZ (1007 "The Lowest") 20-30 59
MODERN (1201 "Swingin' Suite") 60-80 56
Also see COLLETTE, Buddy
Also see CRAYTON, Pee Wee
Also see CROTHERS, Scatman
Also see EWING, John, & Streamliners
Also see GRISSOM, Jimmy
Also see HOLLYWOOD ARIST-O-KATS
Also see KAY, Carol
Also see LEE, Julia
Also see LITTLE CAESAR
Also see NICHOLSON, J.D.
Also see SUMMERS, Gene
Also see TJADER, Cal
Also see YOUNG, Lester

CALLICUTT, Dudley
(With the Go Boys)

Singles: 7-inch

DC (412 "Get Ready Baby") 50-100 59

CALLIER, J.J.

Singles: 7-inch

MAISON ("Just You and Me") 15-25
(Selection number not known.)

CALLIER, Terry *R&B '79*

Singles: 12-inch

ERECT 4-6 82

Singles: 7-inch

CADET (5623 "Look at Me Now") 50-75 68
CADET (5692 "Ordinary Joe") 5-10 72
CADET (5697 "I Just Can't Help Myself") ... 5-10 73
ELEKTRA 4-6 78-79

LPs: 10/12-inch

CADET 10-12 72-73
CHESS 10-15 71
ELEKTRA 8-10 78-79

CALLIOPE

Singles: 7-inch

AUDIO SEVEN (151 "Everybody's High") 30-40 67
AUDIO SEVEN (152 "Streets of Boston") 25-35 67

CALLOWAY, Al

Singles: 7-inch

CASH (1048 "Uncle John") 50-75 57

CALLOWAY, Baby

Singles: 7-inch

BAY-TONE (106 "Midnight Blues") 15-25 59

CALLOWAY, Bob

Singles: 7-inch

UBC (1014 "Wake Up Little Boy Blue") 250-350 59

CALLOWAY, Cab *P&R '30*
(With Cab Jivers; with Caballiers)

Singles: 78 rpm

ABC-PAR 5-10 56
BANNER 8-12 31-32
BELL 4-8 53-55
BLUEBIRD 5-10 49
BRUNSWICK 5-15 30-36
CAMEO 6-12
COLUMBIA 5-10 42-49
CONQUEROR 6-12 38-41
DOMINO 10-15 30
FILMOPHONE 8-12
HI-TONE 5-10 49
JEWEL 8-12 31
MEL-O-DEE 10-15 31
MELOTONE 8-12 32-33
OKEH 5-10 40-42
ORIOLE 8-12 32-33
PERFECT 8-12 32
RCA 4-8 49
REGAL 6-12 31-51
ROMEO 8-12 32-33
SIGNATURE 5-8 49
VARIETY 8-12 33-37
VICTOR 5-15 33-34
VOCALION 5-10 38-40

Singles: 7-inch

ABC-PAR 5-10 56
BOOM (60006 "After Taxes") 4-6 66
CORAL 4-8 61-62
GONE (5018 "Tomorrow Night") 8-15 57
OKEH (6896 "Willow Weep for Me") 20-30 52
RCA (007 "Rooming House Boogie") 50-75 49
RCA (8000 series) 4-6 62
RCA (11000 series) 3-5 78

EPs: 7-inch

EPIC (7016 "Cab Calloway & His Orchestra") 15-25 53

LPs: 10/12-inch

BRUNSWICK (58010 "Cab Calloway") 40-60 52
COLUMBIA 10-20 73
CORAL (57408 "Blues Make Me Happy") 15-20 62
(Monaural.)
CORAL (757408 "Blues Make Me Happy") 20-30 62
(Stereo.)
EPIC (3265 "Cab Calloway") 30-50 57
GONE (101 "Cotton Club Revue") 30-50 58
GUEST STAR .... 10-15 '60s
MARK 56 .... 15-25 '60s
RCA (LPM-2021 "Hi De Hi De Ho") 15-25 60
(Monaural.)
RCA (LSP-2021 "Hi De Hi De Ho") 25-35 60
(Stereo.)
VOCALION (73820 "Sings the Blues") 10-20 68

CALLOWAY, Janet, & Chuck Paulin

Singles: 7-inch

ENJOY (1003 "Lover's Prayer") 10-15 62

CALS

Singles: 7-inch

LOADSTONE (1500 "Country Woman") 50-100
LOADSTONE (1600 "Amazon Bossa Nova") 25-50
LOADSTONE (1604 "Stand Tall") 25-50 64

CALVAES

Singles: 78 rpm

COBRA 75-125 56

Singles: 7-inch

COBRA (5003 "Fine Girl") 400-500 56
COBRA (5014 "Born with Rhythm") 200-300 57
Member: Oscar Boyd.

CALVANES
(With the Val Anthony Combo)

Singles: 78 rpm

DOOTONE 50-75 55

Singles: 7-inch

CLASSIC ARTISTS (127 "Take Me Back") .. 4-6 92
(Red vinyl. 1000 made.)
DECK (579 "Dreamworld") 100-150 58
DECK (580 "My Love Song") 100-150 58
DOOTONE (356 "They Call Me Fool") 4-6
DOOTONE (371 "Crazy Over You") 75-125 55
DOOTONE (380 "Florabelle") 75-125 56

EPs: 7-inch

DOOTO (205 "Voices for Lovers") 50-100 60
DOOTONE (205 "Voices for Lovers") ... 500-750 56
Members: Stewart Crunk; Joe Hampton; Jack Harris; Lorenzo Adams; Herman Pruitt.
Also see NUGGETS
Also see YOUNGSTERS

CALVERT, Duane

Singles: 7-inch

DMD (102 "Somewhere Somehow") 100-150 64
DMD (105 "Do You Live for Me") 15-25 64
Session: Kittens.

CALVERTS

Singles: 7-inch

SALEM (1302 "Listen for the Raindrops") .... 15-25 '60s

CALVEYS Featuring Gino Romano

Singles: 7-inch

COMMA (445 "The Wind") 10-20 61

CALVIN, Tony

Singles: 7-inch

RADAR (2622 "Danger") 10-20 62

CALVIN & TWILITES

Singles: 7-inch

HAR-LOW (705 "Moments Like This") 30-40 65

CAMACHO, Ray, & Teardrops

Singles: 7-inch

COPPER STATE ("I Told You So") 10-20
(Selection number not known.)

CAMARATA
(Camarata Orchestra; Camarata Strings; Tutti's Trumpets; Tutti's Trombones)

Singles: 7-inch

BUENA VISTA 10-25 58-67
COLISEUM 5-10 65-68
Also see STYLE SISTERS

CAMARIONOS, George J.

Singles: 7-inch

BUZZ (111 "Tip Tip Toe") 30-40 61

CAMBELL, Ray

EPs: 7-inch

REB-BEL ("Ray Cambell") 100-200
(Selection number not known.)

CAMBRIDGE FIVE

Singles: 7-inch

USA (850 "Floatin'") 10-15 66

CAMELOTS
(With Al Browne & the Cordials)

Singles: 7-inch

AANKO (1001 "Your Way") 30-40 63
AANKO (1004 "Sunday Kind of Love") 50-60 63
COMET (2150 "Chase") 8-12 62
COMET (2158 "Scratch") 8-12 63
CRIMSON (1001 "The Letter") 5-10 63
DREAM (1001 "I Wonder") 4-6 73
EMBER (1108 "Pocahontas") 5-10 64
INVICTA (9005 "Bad Girl") 10-15 63
NIX (101 "Lulu") 10-15 61
PORTRAIT (108 "Thirsty") 10-15 62
Also see EBONAIRES / Camelots

CAMELOTS / Bootleggers

Singles: 7-inch

RELIC (530 "Chain of Broken Hearts"/"Rat Race") 8-12 65
(Black vinyl.)
RELIC (530 "Chain of Broken Hearts"/"Rat Race") 10-20 65
(Red vinyl.)

CAMELOTS / Suns

Singles: 7-inch

RELIC (541 "Dance Girl"/"That's My Baby") 5-10 65
TIMES SQUARE (32 "Dance Girl"/"That's My Baby") 10-15 64
Also see CAMELOTS

CAMEOS

Singles: 78 rpm

DOOTONE (365 "Craving") 75-125 55

Singles: 7-inch

DOOTONE (365 "Craving") 300-400 55

CAMEOS
(With the Emeralds; with Shipmates)

Singles: 78 rpm

CAMEO 25-50 57

Singles: 7-inch

ADELPHI (604 "I'll Keep Your Heart Forever") 100-200
ASTRA (5002 "I Remember When") 3-5 85
CAMEO (123 "Merry Christmas") 75-125 57
CAMEO (176 "Best of Can Can") 15-25 60
COLLECTABLES 3-5 81
FLAGSHIP (115 "Please Love Me") 30-40 59
GIGI (100 "Can You Remember") 8-12 63
MATADOR (1808 "I Remember When") .. 40-50 60
(Orange label.)
MATADOR (1808 "I Remember When") .. 20-30 60
(Maroon or blue label.)
MATADOR (1813 "Never Before") 10-15 60
SOUNDCRAFT ("Can You Remember") .. 15-25
(Selection number not known.)

Picture Sleeves

CAMEO (176 "Best of the Can Can") 10-20 58
Members: Earl Wortham; John Christian; Tony Lewis; Reg Price; James Williams.
Also see DEAN, Tiny, & Cameos

CAMEOS

Singles: 7-inch

DEAN (504 "Wait Up") 50-75 60
JOHNSON (108 "Wait Up") 20-30 61

CAMEOS Featuring Billy Rome

Singles: 7-inch

ALL (501 "Pretty Penny") 15-25 58
Also see ROME, Billy

CAMERON, Barbara
(With Dan Belloc & His Orchestra)

Singles: 78 rpm

FRATERNITY 5-10 56

Singles: 7-inch

FRATERNITY (748 "Goodbye My Love") 10-20 56

CAMERON, Jimmy & Vella

Singles: 7-inch

REPRISE (483 "I Know a Place") 15-25 66
UNLIMITED GOLD 3-5 80-81

LPs: 10/12-inch

UNLIMITED GOLD 5-10 81

CAMERON, Johnny
(With the Camerons)

Singles: 7-inch

ATLANTIC 4-8 70
RCA (8065 "The Crying I'm Doing Alone") 10-20 62
20TH FOX (179 "Fantastic") 10-15 60

Picture Sleeves

20TH FOX (179 "Fantastic") 20-30 60

CAMERON, Ken

Singles: 7-inch

HILLTOP (91961 "Hello Mary Lee") 50-75
ZYNN (500 "Prisoner's Song") 15-25 58

CAMERONS

Singles: 7-inch

COUSINS (1-2 "Cheryl") 75-100 60
CRYSTAL BALL (112 "Laura") 4-8 78
(Black vinyl. 500 made.)
CRYSTAL BALL (112 "Laura") 8-12 78
(Red vinyl. 25 made.)
Also see TAYLOR, Mike

CAMERONS

Singles: 7-inch

COUSINS (1003 "Guardian Angel") 150-200 61
(This is a different group than the one above who recorded *Cheryl*, though both recorded for Cousins.)
FELSTED (8638 "Guardian Angel") 20-30 61
Also see DEMILLES

CAMILLE, Bob
(With the Lollipops; "Lil" Bob Camille)

Singles: 7-inch

LA LOUISIANNE (8122 "Soul Woman") ... 10-15
SOUL UNLIMITED (102 "Brother Brown") 30-50 72
WHIT (6906 "Got to Get Away") 10-15 70
Also see LITTLE BOB

CAMILLE & CREATIONS

Singles: 7-inch

GEDINSON'S (100 "Johnny") 50-100 62

CAMP

Singles: 7-inch

SCEPTER (12159 "Marching") 50-75 66

CAMP, Georgie

Singles: 7-inch

ATCO (6228 "Wonderful") 15-25 62
ATLANTIC (2139 "Jimmie Told a Lie") 5-10 62

CAMPANELLA, David, & Dellchords

Singles: 7-inch

CANDLELITE (415 "Over the Rainbow") ... 5-10 63
(Black vinyl.)
CANDLELITE (415 "Over the Rainbow") ... 8-12 63
(Red vinyl.)
KANE (25593 "Somewhere Over the Rainbow") 50-75 59
KANE (25593 "Over the Rainbow") 15-25 59
(Note shorter title.)

CAMPANIONS
Singles: 7-inch
DEE-DEE (1047 "I Want a Yul Brynner Haircut") 30-40 61
Also see DEL SATINS

CAMPBELL, Archie C&W '60
Singles: 7-inch
ELEKTRA 4-6 76-77
RCA (0147 thru 0766) 4-6 72-73
RCA (7660 thru 9987) 4-8 60-71
STARDAY 4-8 61-64
LPs: 10/12-inch
ELEKTRA 5-10 76
NASHVILLE 10-15 68
RCA 10-15 66-71
STARDAY (167 "Bedtime Stories for Adults") 20-25 62
STARDAY (223 "The Joker Is Wild") 15-20 63
STARDAY (377 "Grand Ole Opry's Good Humor Man") 10-20 66

CAMPBELL, Bernie
(With the Four Ekkos Vocal Quartet)
Singles: 7-inch
FINE (26571 "When I Find My Baby") . 400-500 61
Also see FOUR EKKOS

CAMPBELL, Carl
(With Henry Hayes' 4 Kings.)
Singles: 78 rpm
FREEDOM 15-25 49
PEACOCK 15-25 50
Also see HAYES, Henry

CAMPBELL, Cecil C&W '49
(With the Tennessee Ramblers)
Singles: 78 rpm
MGM (12118 "Steel Guitar Waltz") 5-10 55
MGM (12245 "Dixieland Rock") 10-20 56
MGM (12482 "Rock & Roll Fever") 25-50
MGM (12605 "On the Prado") 10-15 57
RCA 5-8 49
Singles: 7-inch
MGM (12118 "Steel Guitar Waltz") 10-15 55
MGM (12245 "Dixieland Rock") 25-50 56
MGM (12482 "Rock & Roll Fever") 75-100 57
MGM (12605 "On the Prado") 15-25 57
RCA (48-0076 thru 48-0219) 10-20 49-50
(Green vinyl.)
LPs: 10/12-inch
STARDAY (254 "Steel Guitar Jamboree") 30-40 63

CAMPBELL, Choker
(With Horace Williams; Walter Campbell)
Singles: 78 rpm
ATLANTIC 15-25 53-54
FORTUNE 25-35 53
Singles: 7-inch
APT (25011 "Walk Awhile") 40-60 58
ATLANTIC (1014 "Last Call for Whiskey") 20-30 53
ATLANTIC (1038 "Have You Seen My Baby") 20-30 54
CANDY APPLE (740 "Carioca") 5-8
EVERLAST (5007 "Walk Awhile") 20-30 57
FORTUNE (808 "Rocking and Jumping") 40-60 53
MAGIC CITY (002 "Going Christmas Shopping") .... 20-30 '60s
MOTOWN (1072 "Come See About Me") 10-20 65
EPs: 7-inch
MOTOWN (60620 "Hits of the '60s") 25-35 64
LPs: 10/12-inch
MOTOWN (620 "Hits of the '60s") 50-75 64
Also see FULSON, Lowell

CAMPBELL, Dick
Singles: 7-inch
CUCA (6962 "Train to Hollywood") 10-20 69
GREAT (4703 "She's My Girl") 30-60 63
MERCURY (72511 "Blues Peddlers") 15-25 65
LP: 10/12-inch
MERCURY 15-25 65
Also see STOKER, Billy

CAMPBELL, Don
Singles: 7-inch
STANSON (509 "Campbell Lock") 10-20 65

CAMPBELL, George, & Kool 5
Singles: 7-inch
WITCH'S BREW (121 "Sugar") 15-25

CAMPBELL, Glen P&R '61/C&W '62
(With the Glen-Aires; with Green River Boys; with Bandits)
Singles: 7-inch
ATLANTIC AMERICA 3-5 82-86
CAPEHART (5008 "Death Valley") 10-20 61
CAPITOL (2000 & 3000 series) 4-8 68-74
CAPITOL (4000 series) 4-6 75-81
(Orange or purple labels.)
CAPITOL (4783 thru 5360) 10-15 61-65
(Orange/yellow swirl labels.)
CAPITOL (5441 "Guess I'm Dumb") 30-40 65
(With Brian Wilson.)
CAPITOL (5504 thru 5939, except 5927) ... 5-10 65-67
CAPITOL (5927 "My Baby's Gone"/"Kelli Hoedown") 8-12 67
(Has alternative takes. Promotional issue only.)
CAPITOL STARLINE 4-8
CENECO (1324 "Dreams for Sale") 150-200 59
CENECO (1356 "You, You, You") .... 20-30 '60s
CREST (1087 "Turn Around Look at Me") 20-30 61
(Mistakenly credits "Glen Cambpbell" on some Crest labels.)
CREST (1096 "Miracle of Love") 15-25 62
EVEREST 4-8 69
STARDAY 4-8 68
MCA 3-5 84-89
MIRAGE 3-5 81
UNIVERSAL 3-5 89
W.B. 3-5 80
Picture Sleeves
ATLANTIC AMERICA 3-5 85-86
CAPITOL (2076 "Hey Little One") 5-10 68
CAPITOL (4856 "Long Black Limousine") 15-20 62
CAPITOL (5279 "Summer, Winter, Spring and Fall") 10-15 64
EPs: 7-inch
CAPITOL 5-10 68-69
(Juke box issues.)
CAPITOL/CHEVROLET (55 "The Glen Campbell Good Time Hour") .... 5-10 '60s
CAPITOL CREATIVE PRODUCTS .... 5-10 '60s
LPs: 10/12-inch
ATLANTIC AMERICA 5-10 82-86
BUCKBOARD 8-10
CAPITOL (103 thru 752) 8-15 68-71
CAPITOL (1810 "Big Bluegrass Special") 25-75 62
(Credits the "Green River Boys Featuring Glen Campbell.")
CAPITOL (1881 thru 2392) 10-20 63-65
(With "T" or "ST" prefix.)
CAPITOL (2809 thru 2978) 8-15 67-69
(With "T" or "ST" prefix.)
CAPITOL (SM-300 series) 5-10 82
CAPITOL (SM-2000 series) 5-10 78
CAPITOL (4000 series) 5-10 73
CAPITOL (11000 thru 16000 series) 5-10 72-85
CAPITOL (11722 "Basic") 50-100 78
(Picture disc. Promotional issue only. One of a four-artist, four-LP set. 250 made.)
CAPITOL (80000 series) 5-10
CAPITOL (94000 series) 8-15 72
(Capitol Record Club issues.)
CAPITOL (120000 series) 5-10
(Capitol Record Club issues.)
CAPITOL CREATIVE PRODUCTS 8-12
CAPITOL SPECIAL PRODUCTS 5-8 84
CUSTOM TONE 15-20
LONGINES (5408 "Gentle on My Mind") 5-10 69
LONGINES ("Glen Campbell's Golden Favorites") 20-30 72
(Boxed, six-disc set.)
PAIR 5-8 84
PICKWICK 8-10 64-79
SEARS 8-12
STARDAY 15-20 68-69
Session: Jerry Puckett.
Also see BEACH BOYS
Also see BILLS, Dick
Also see CAPEHART, Jerry
Also see CHAMPS
Also see DOLTON, Billy
Also see FABARES, Shelley
Also see FLEAS
Also see FOLKSWINGERS
Also see FORD, Tennessee Ernie, & Glen Campbell
Also see GEE CEES
Also see HONDELLS
Also see IN-GROUP
Also see JAN & DEAN
Also see KNIGHTS
Also see LEGENDARY MASKED SURFERS
Also see MARTIN, Dean / Glen Campbell
Also see MR. TWELVE STRING
Also see NELSON, Rick
Also see NELSON, Willie
Also see RIP CHORDS
Also see ROGERS, Weldon
Also see SAGITTARIUS
Also see STEWART, Wynn
Also see SWEET SOULS
Also see TILLIS, Mel, & Glen Campbell
Also see TROPHIES
Also see WILSON, Brian
Also see YORK, Dave, & Beachcombers

CAMPBELL, Glen, & Rita Coolidge C&W/P&R '80
Singles: 7-inch
CAPITOL 3-5 80

CAMPBELL, Glen, & Bobbie Gentry C&W/LP '68
Singles: 7-inch
CAPITOL 4-6 68-70
EPs: 7-inch
CAPITOL 8-10 68
(Juke box issue only.)
LPs: 10/12-inch
CAPITOL 8-10 68

CAMPBELL, Glen / Lettermen / Ella Fitzgerald / Sandler & Young
LPs: 10/12-inch
CAPITOL (56 "B.F. Goodrich Presents Christmas 1969") 10-15 69
(Promotional, special products issue.)
Also see FITZGERALD, Ella
Also see LETTERMEN
Also see SANDLER & YOUNG

CAMPBELL, Glen, & Anne Murray C&W/P&R/LP '71
Singles: 7-inch
CAPITOL 4-6 71-72
LPs: 10/12-inch
CAPITOL 5-10 71-80

CAMPBELL, Glen / Anne Murray / Kenny Rogers / Crystal Gayle
LPs: 10/12-inch
CAPITOL/U.A. (11743-F-19 "Glen/Anne/Kenny/Crystal") 300-500 78
(Four framed picture disc set. Promotional issue only. 250 made)
Also see GAYLE, Crystal
Also see MURRAY, Anne
Also see ROGERS, Kenny

CAMPBELL, Glen, & Leon Russell
LPs: 10/12-inch
KOALA (14169 "Way Back When") 20-30 79
Also see CAMPBELL, Glen
Also see RUSSELL, Leon

CAMPBELL, Glen, & Billy Strange
LPs: 10/12-inch
SURREY 12-20 65
Also see STRANGE, Billy

CAMPBELL, Glen / Texas Opera Company
Singles: 7-inch
W.B./VIVA 3-5 80

CAMPBELL, Glen, & Steve Wariner C&W '87
Singles: 7-inch
MCA 3-5 87

CAMPBELL, Glen / Dionne Warwick / Burt Bacharach
LPs: 10/12-inch
CHEVROLET (6658 "On the Move") 5-10 70
(Chevrolet promotional issue.)
Also see CAMPBELL, Glen

CAMPBELL, Jo Ann P&R '60
Singles: 78 rpm
ELDORADO 25-50 57
POINT 10-20 56
Singles: 7-inch
ABC-PAR (10134 "Kookie Little Paradise") 20-30 60
ABC-PAR (10172 thru 10335) 10-20 60-62
CAMEO (223 thru 249) 15-25 62-63
ELDORADO (504 "Forever Young") 15-25 57
ELDORADO (509 "Funny Thing") 20-30 57
GONE (5014 "Wait a Minute"/"It's True") . 20-30 57
GONE (5014 "Wait a Minute"/"I'm in Love with You") 15-25 57
GONE (5021 thru 5068) 15-25 58-59
POINT (4 "Where Ever You Go") 20-30 56
RORI (711 "Five Minutes More") 10-15 62
LPs: 10/12-inch
ABC-PAR (393 "Twistin' and Listenin'") ... 50-75 62
(Monaural.)
ABC-PAR (393 "Twistin' and Listenin'") ... 60-80 62
(Stereo.)
CAMEO (1026 "All the Hits of Jo Ann Campbell") 30-40 62
CORONET (199 "Starring Jo Ann Campbell") 10-20 62
END (306 "I'm Nobody's Baby") 75-100 59
Also see JO ANN & TROY

CAMPBELL, Little Miss Charlotte
Singles: 7-inch
WANGER (194 "True Lover") 40-60 59

CAMPBELL, Louis
Singles: 78 rpm
EXCELLO 30-50 54
Singles: 7-inch
EXCELLO (2035 "Gotta Have You Baby") 75-100 54
Also see LEAP FROGS

CAMPBELL, Rev. Anthony, Hank Davis, & Calvin Morris
EPs: 7-inch
FOLKART (5002 "How Long Have You Been a Negro") 15-25 64
LPs: 10/12-inch
FOLKART (5002 "God Made the Blues") . 25-50 64
Also see DAVIS, Hank

CAMPERS
Singles: 7-inch
PARKWAY (974 "Ballad of Batman") 20-25 66
(Previously issued as by the Camps.)
Members: Sonny Curtis & Crickets.
Also see CAMPS
Also see CRICKETS
Also see CURTIS, Sonny

CAMPI, Ray
Singles: 78 rpm
DOT 25-50 57
Singles: 7-inch
COLPIX (166 "French Fries") 15-25 60
D (1047 "Ballad of Donna and Peggy Sue" 30-40 59
DOMINO (700 "My Screamin' Mimi") 75-100 59
DOT (15617 "Give That Love to Me") 75-100 57
ROLLIN' ROCK 4-8 78-83
WINSOR (001 "Billie Jean") 15-25 64
Picture Sleeves
DOMINO (700 "My Screamin' Mimi") ... 100-200 59
LPs: 10/12-inch
ROLLIN' ROCK (001 "Rockabilly") .... 8-12 '70s
ROLLIN' ROCK (006 "Rockabilly Rebel") .. 8-12 '70s
ROLLIN' ROCK (008 "The Eager Beaver Boy") .... 8-12 '70s
ROLLIN' ROCK (011 "Born to Rock") 8-12 77
ROLLIN' ROCK (013 "Rockabilly Rocket") . 8-12
ROLLIN' ROCK (023 "Rockabilly Music") .. 8-12
ROLLIN' ROCK (104 "Rockabilly Lives") ... 8-12
ROLLIN' ROCK (6901 "Rockabilly Rebellion") 8-12
ROLLIN' ROCK (6902 "Ray Campi") 8-12
ROUNDER 5-10
Also see McCOY BOYS

CAMPI, Ray / Jerry Dove
EPs: 7-inch
TNT (145 "Catapillar"/"Play It Cool") 250-350 57
(Not issued with cover.)
Also see DOVE, Jerry

CAMPI, Ray, & Merle Travis
EPs: 7-inch
ROLLIN' ROCK (031 "Ray Campi & Merle Travis") 5-8
Also see CAMPI, Ray
Also see TRAVIS, Merle

CAMPO, Lucy

Singles: 7-inch

RCA (8121 "Silly Boy")............10-15 62

RCA (8172 "Evil Eye")............10-15 63

CAMPS

Singles: 7-inch

PARKWAY (974 "Ballad of Batman").......25-30 65

(Later issued as by the Campers.)

Members: Sonny Curtis & Crickets.

Also see CAMPERS

Also see CRICKETS

Also see CURTIS, Sonny

CAMPUS SINGERS

Singles: 7-inch

ARGO (5475 "Another Man")............5-10 64

LPs: 10/12-inch

ARGO (4023 "Campus Singers at the Fickle Pickle")............15-25 63

CAMS

Singles: 7-inch

INDIE (1303 "Smashin'")............15-25 58

CANADA, Jane

Singles: 7-inch

CRUSADER (215 "Am I Dreaming")..........5-10 66

MAGIC LAMP (616 "Am I Dreaming")......15-25 65

CANADIAN BEADLES

Singles: 7-inch

TIDE (2003 "Think I'm Gonna Cry")........10-15 64

TIDE (2006 "I'm Coming Home")............10-15 64

LPs: 10/12-inch

TIDE (2005 "Three Faces North")..........35-50 65

Members: Vic Blunt; Paul Case; Bruce Pollard.

Also see MOJO MEN

CANADIAN CLASSICS

Singles: 7-inch

VALIANT (723 "Gone Away")............25-35 65

Also see CLASSICS

Also see COLLECTORS

CANADIAN DOWNBEATS

Singles: 7-inch

SOUNDAROUN (1265 "Surf Party")......75-125

CANADIAN ROGUES

Singles: 7-inch

CHARAY (19 "Keep in Touch")............20-30 66

FULLER ("You Better Stop")............15-25 66

PALMER (5017 "Keep in Touch")............20-30 67

PARIS TOWER (112 "Run and Hide").....15-25 67

ROGUE (1967 "Do You Love Me")............15-20 67

CANADIAN SWEETHEARTS C&W '64

Singles: 7-inch

A&M (713 "Out for Fun")............5-10 63

A&M (727 "Hootenanny Express")............5-10 64

EPIC............4-8 67-68

SOMA (1156 "No Help Wanted")............40-60 61

LPs: 10/12-inch

A&M (106 "Introducing the Canadian Sweethearts")............20-30 64

EPIC............15-25 72

Members: Bob Regan; Lucille Starr.

Also see BOB & LUCILLE

Also see STARR, Lucille

CANADIAN V.I.P's

Singles: 7-inch

ARAGON (401 "Lucille")............50-75

CANALES, Johnny

Singles: 7-inch

PENCO (116 "Johnny B. Goode")............50-75

CANARIES

Singles: 7-inch

DIMENSION (1047 "I'm Sorry Baby")......10-15 65

CANARIES

Singles: 7-inch

B.T. PUPPY (557 "I'll Cry Again")............4-8 70

LPs: 10/12-inch

B.T. PUPPY (1007 "Flying High with the Canaries")............20-30 70

CANDIDA, Carl

Singles: 7-inch

CREOLE (1740 "Party Date")............150-250

CANDIDATES

Singles: 7-inch

CONCORD (2003 "Hypnotize")............30-40 '60s

CANDIES

Singles: 7-inch

EMBER (1092 "Yes I Love You")............10-15 63

FLEETWOOD (7003 "Stop")............20-30 63

(Green vinyl.)

CANDLELIGHTERS

Singles: 7-inch

DELTA (203 "Would You Do the Same for Me")............750-1000 58

CANDLELIGHTS

Singles: 7-inch

ARIES (1262 "I'm Without a Boyfriend").75-125

CANDLES

(Blenders)

Singles: 7-inch

NIKE (1016 "Down on My Knees")..........15-20 63

Session: Johnny Pate.

Also see BLENDERS

Also see PATE, Johnny

CANDLETTES

Singles: 7-inch

RONDA (1001 "Moments to Remember")............40-50 61

CANDLETTS

Singles: 7-inch

VITA (179 "Angel Love")............20-30 58

VITA (182 "My Only Love")............20-30 59

Members: Ruth Christie; Cathy Saunders.

Also see CHRISTIE, Ruth

CANDOLI BROTHERS

(Pete & Conte Candoli)

Singles: 7-inch

DOT (15614 "Rockin' Boogie")............15-25 57

LPs: 10/12-inch

W.B. (1462 "There Is Nothing Like a Dame")............10-15 62

CANDY, Penny

Singles: 7-inch

DWAIN (816 "Come on Over")............10-15 60

FLIPPIN' (201 "Rockin' Lady")............25-35 59

CANDY & KISSES P&R/R&B '64

Singles: 7-inch

CAMEO (336 "The 81")............10-20 64

CAMEO (355 "Shakin' Time")............8-12 65

COLLECTABLES............3-5 81

DECCA (32415 "Chains of Love")............5-10 68

R&L (500 "A Good Cry")............15-25 63

SCEPTER (12106 thru 12136)............8-12 65-66

Members: Candy Nelson; Suzanne Nelson; Jeanette Johnson.

CANDY & SUGARTONES

Singles: 7-inch

JACKPOT (46008 "Hurtin' All Over")........10-15 58

CANDY GIRLS

Singles: 7-inch

ROTATE (5001 "Tomorrow My Love").....10-15 63

Also see LORIN, Tempi, & Candy Girls

CANDYMEN

Singles: 7-inch

PROMENADE (24 "Spearmint Twist")........5-10 62

EPs: 7-inch

PREMIUM (8 "Twist Party")............10-20 61

LPs: 10/12-inch

DIPLOMAT (100 "The Twist")............10-20 62

CANDYMEN P&R/LP '67

Singles: 7-inch

ABC............4-8 67-69

LIBERTY (56172 "Happy Tonight")............4-6 70

LPs: 10/12-inch

ABC............15-25 67-68

Members: Rodney Justo; Barry Bailey; Dean Daughtry; Billy Gilmore; Paul Goddard; John Adkins; Bob Nix.

Also see ATLANTA RHYTHM SECTION

Also see CLASSICS IV

Also see ORBISON, Roy

CANE, Gary P&R '60

(With His Friends)

Singles: 7-inch

SHELL (303 "After Midnight")............10-20 61

SHELL (717 "The Fight")............10-20 60

SHELL (719 "The Yen Yet Song")............10-20 60

CANE, Stacey

Singles: 7-inch

JUBILEE (5500 "Funny Face")............10-15 65

CANECUTTERS

Singles: 78 rpm

CHECKER............75-125 54

Singles: 7-inch

CHECKER (795 "No More Heartaches")............300-400 54

CANES

Singles: 7-inch

STAX (123 "I'll Never Give Her Up").........15-25 62

CANJOES

Singles: 7-inch

DAPT (208 "Speaking of Love")............10-15 61

CANN, Dupree

Singles: 7-inch

DUEL (603 "Mean Ole Daddy")..........100-150

CANNED HEAT LP '67

(Heat Brothers)

Singles: 7-inch

ALA............3-5 84

ATLANTIC............4-6 74

LIBERTY............5-10 67-70

U.A............4-6 71-73

Picture Sleeves

LIBERTY (75979 "Bullfrog Blues")............5-10 67

LIBERTY (76077 "Going Up the Country").5-10 68

LPs: 10/12-inch

ACCORD............5-10 81

ALA............8-10 84

ATLANTIC............10-12 73-74

DESTINY (10007 "Kings of the Boogie")....8-10 81

HAPPY BIRD (90135 "Dog House Blues")............10-20 83

(Picture disc.)

JANUS (3009 "Vintage")............10-15 69

LIBERTY (1000 series)............5-10 80

LIBERTY (3526 "Canned Heat")............25-40 67

(Monaural.)

LIBERTY (7526 "Canned Heat")............15-25 67

(Stereo.)

LIBERTY (7541 "Boogie")............15-25 68

LIBERTY (7618 "Hallelujah")............15-20 69

LIBERTY (10000 series)............5-10 81

LIBERTY (11000 "Cook Book")............10-15 69

LIBERTY (11002 "Future Blues")............10-15 70

LIBERTY (27200 "Living the Blues")........10-20 68

PICKWICK............5-10 '70s

SCEPTER............10-15

SPRINGBOARD............5-10

SUNSET............10-15 71

TAKOMA (7066 "Human Condition")..........8-10 79

U.A............10-15 71-75

WAND............15-20 70

Members: Bob Hite; Joel Scott Hill; Ed Bayer; Harvey Mandel; Mark Andes; James Shane; Frank Cook; Richard Hite; Chris Morgan; Gene Taylor; Larry Taylor; Henry Vestine; Adolfo "Fito" de la Parra; Alan Wilson.

Also see GAMBLERS

Also see HILL, Joel

Also see HOOKER, John Lee, & Canned Heat

Also see LITTLE RICHARD

Also see MANDEL, Harvey

Also see SMOKE

CANNED HEAT & CHIPMUNKS

Singles: 7-inch

LIBERTY (56079 "The Chipmunk Song").20-30 68

Also see CANNED HEAT

Also see CHIPMUNKS

CANNIBAL & HEADHUNTERS P&R/LP '65

Singles: 7-inch

AIRES............5-10 68

CAPITOL............5-10 69

COLLECTABLES............3-5 81

DATE............5-10 66

ERA............4-6 73

RAMPART............10-15 65-66

LPs: 10/12-inch

DATE (3001 "Land of 1000 Dances").......20-30 66

RAMPART (3302 "Land of 1000 Dances")............40-60 65

Members: Frankie "Cannibal" Garcia; Robert Jaramillo; Joe Jaramillo; Richard Lopez.

CANNON, Ace P&R '61

(Johnny "Ace" Cannon)

Singles: 7-inch

FERNWOOD (135 "Hoe Down Rock").......8-12 63

FERNWOOD (137 "Big Shot")............8-12 64

(First issued as by Johnny Cannon.)

HI (2000 series)............8-12 61-65

HI (2100 thru 2300 series)............4-8 66-78

LOUIS (2001 "Tuff")............30-40 61

MOTOWN............3-5 82

SANTO............8-12 62

Picture Sleeves

HI............8-12 62-63

EPs: 7-inch

HI (1133 "In the Spotlight")............8-12 68

(Juke box issue.)

LPs: 10/12-inch

ALLEGIANCE............5-10 84

GUSTO............5-10 80

HI (007 thru 040)............10-20 62-67

(Numbers in this series are preceeded by a "12" for mono or a "32" for stereo issues.)

HI (043 thru 090)............8-15 68-75

(Numbers in this series are preceded by a "32," indicating stereo.)

HI (6000 & 8000 series)............8-10 77-79

MOTOWN............5-10 83

Also see BLACK, Bill

Also see CANNON, Johnny

Also see TRAMMELL, Bobby Lee

CANNON, Dyan

LP: 10/12-inch

HMF (001 "Having It All")............60-80 83

(Picture disc. Promotional issue only.)

CANNON, Freddy P&R/R&B '59

(Freddie Cannon; Freddie Cannon / Cannon's Express)

Singles: 78 rpm

QUALITY (1897 "Tallahassee Lassie")..50-100 59

(Canadian.)

Singles: 7-inch

AMHERST............3-5 88

ANDEE............4-6 75

BUDDAH............4-6 71

CLARIDGE............4-6 74-76

ERIC............4-6 78

HQ ("Kennywood Park")............4-6 87

(KDKA promotional issue only. No selection number used.)

MCA............4-6 74

METROMEDIA............4-6 72

QUALITY (1897 "Tallahassee Lassie")....20-30 59

(Canadian.)

ROYAL AMERICAN............4-6 69-70

SIRE............4-6 69

SWAN (4031 thru 4078)............10-20 59-61

SWAN (4083 thru 4178)............8-15 61-64

W.B............6-12 64-67

WE MAKE ROCK & ROLL RECORDS............4-8 68

Picture Sleeves

HQ ("Kennywood Park")............5-8 87

(KDKA promotional issue only. No selection number used.)

SWAN (4043 "Way Down Yonder in New Orleans")............15-25 59

SWAN (4050 "Chattanooga Shoe Shine Boy")............15-25 60

SWAN (4053 "Jump Over")............15-25 60

SWAN (4057 "Happy Shades of Blue")....15-25 60

SWAN (4061 "Humdinger")............15-25 60

SWAN (4066 "Muskrat Ramble")............15-25 61

SWAN (4071 "Buzz Buzz A-Diddle-It")....15-25 61

SWAN (4078 "Transistor Sister")............15-25 61

W.B. (5616 "In the Night")............10-20 64

LPs: 10/12-inch

RHINO............5-10 82

SWAN (502 "The Explosive Freddy Cannon")............50-100 60

(Monaural.)

SWAN (502 "The Explosive Freddy Cannon")............75-125 60

(Stereo.)

SWAN (504 "Happy Shades of Blue")....50-75 62

SWAN (505 "Solid Gold Hits")............100-200 61

SWAN (507 "Palisades Park")............50-75 62

SWAN (511 "Freddy Cannon Steps Out")............50-75 62

W.B. (1544 "Freddie Cannon") ... 30-40 64
W.B. (1612 "Action") ... 30-40 64
W.B. (1628 "Greatest Hits") ... 30-40 64
Also see BUCHANAN, Roy
Also see DANNY & JUNIORS
Also see G-CLEFS
Also see SLAY, Frank, & His Orchestra
Also see SPINDRIFTS

CANNON, Freddy, & Belmonts
Singles: 7-inch
MIA SOUND ... 4-6 81
Also see BELMONTS, Freddy Cannon & Bo Diddley
Also see CANNON, Freddy

CANNON, Gus
LPs: 10/12-inch
STAX (702 "Walk Right In") ... 300-500 62
(Stax appears to have recalled this LP shortly after release, as the number 702 was also used for a various artists collection, *Hit Sounds of the South.*)

CANNON, Jackie
Singles: 7-inch
CHAN (103 "Proof of Your Love") ... 30-40 61
CHESS (1807 "Proof of Your Love") ... 40-60 61
RADAR (2617 "Who Is It, It's Me") ... 10-20 62

CANNON, Johnny
(Ace Cannon)
Singles: 7-inch
FERNWOOD (117 "Big Shot") ... 15-25 60
Also see CANNON, Ace

CANNON, Lonzine
Singles: 7-inch
PHILIPS (40128 "One at a Time") ... 15-25 63
PHILIPS (40190 "You Still Love Her") ... 10-15 64
PHILIPS (40240 "Quit While You're Ahead") ... 50-100 64
CADET (5623 "Look at Me Now") ... 25-50 68-73

CANNON, Maureen
Singles: 7-inch
BARTONE (100 "I Want to Know") ... 10-15
DERBY (809 "Did I Speak Out of Turn") 75-100 52

CANNON BROTHERS
Singles: 7-inch
RIC (107 "Surfin' in Bermuda") ... 15-25 64

CANNON SISTERS
Singles: 7-inch
REAL FINE (833 "Johnny") ... 50-100 62
VALIANT (6020 "I Don't Want to Be the One") ... 10-20 62
VALIANT (6024 "I'm Sorry I Went") ... 10-20 62

CANNONBALLS
Singles: 7-inch
BOBBY (222 "Johnny B. Goode") ... 50-75

CANO, Eddie *LP '62*
Singles: 7-inch
DUNHILL ... 4-6 66-67
GNP ... 4-6 62
REPRISE ... 4-8 62-65
Picture Sleeves
REPRISE (20113 "Greenfields") ... 5-10 62
LPs: 10/12-inch
DUNHILL ... 10-15 67
GNP ... 10-20 61-62
RCA ... 10-20 62
REPRISE ... 10-20 62-65

CANO, Eddie, & Nino Tempo
Singles: 7-inch
ATCO (6397 "On Broadway") ... 5-10 66
LP: 10/12-inch
ATCO (184 "On Broadway") ... 10-15 66
Also see CANO, Eddie
Also see TEMPO, Nino

CANOISE
Singles: 7-inch
IGL (120 "Born in Chicago") ... 15-20 66
SONIC (141 "Oh No, Not My Baby") ... 15-20 67
SONIC (153 "Right Track") ... 15-20 67
TRIM (1972 "Look Inside") ... 8-12 66

CANTELON, Willard
LPs: 10/12-inch
SUPREME (113 "LSD Battle for the Mind") ... 25-30 66

CANYON, Laurel
Singles: 7-inch
NAME (5 "High School Hero") ... 15-20 60
NAME (6 "Stood Up") ... 15-20 62

CAPEHART, Jerry
(Jerry Neal)
Singles: 7-inch
CASH (1021 "Rollin' ") ... 25-40 56
(With the Cochran Brothers.)
CREST (1101 "Song of New Orleans") ... 20-30 62
(With Eddie Cochran and Glen Campbell.)
Also see CAMPBELL, Glen
Also see COCHRAN, Eddie
Also see COCHRAN BROTHERS
Also see NEAL, Jerry

CAPELLO, Lenny
(With the Dots)
Singles: 7-inch
RIC (960 "Cotton Candy") ... 15-25 59
RIC (965 "She Moves") ... 15-25 60
RIC (991 "Genevieve") ... 15-25 62

CAPERS
Singles: 7-inch
VEE-JAY (297 "Miss You My Dear") ... 10-20 58
VEE-JAY (315 "High School Diploma") ... 15-25 59

CAPERS, Valerie
LPs: 10/12-inch
ATLANTIC (3003 "Portrait in Soul") ... 15-20 66

CAPES
Singles: 78 rpm
CHAT (5005 "The Vow") ... 250-450 '50s
Singles: 7-inch
CHAT (5005 "The Vow") ... 1500-2000 '50s

CAPES & MASKS
Singles: 7-inch
MAINSTREAM (639 "Man from T.A.N.T.A.") ... 5-10 66
LPs: 10/12-inch
MAINSTREAM (56069 "Comic Book Heroes") ... 15-20 66
(Monaural.)
MAINSTREAM (6069 "Comic Book Heroes") ... 20-25 66
(Stereo.)

CAPES OF GOOD HOPE
Singles: 7-inch
ROUND (1001 "Shades") ... 30-50 66
ROUND (1002 "Winter's Children") ... 30-50 66

CAPITALS
Singles: 7-inch
TRIUMPH (601 "Write Me a Love Letter") ... 10-15 59

CAPITOLS
Singles: 7-inch
CARLTON (461 "I Let Her Go") ... 500-750 58

CAPITOLS *P&R/R&B/LP '66*
Singles: 7-inch
COLLECTABLES ... 3-5 81
KAREN ... 5-10 66-68
LPs: 10/12-inch
ATCO ... 15-20 66
COLLECTABLES ... 6-8 88
SOLID SMOKE ... 5-10 85
Members: Sam George; Don Storball; Richard McDougall.

CAPITOLS
Singles: 7-inch
PET (807 "Angel of Love") ... 300-400 58

CAPITOLS
Singles: 7-inch
PORTRAIT (109 "I'll Drink a Toast") ... 30-40 62

CAPITOLS
Singles: 7-inch
KORAN (1526 "In the Groove") ... 20-30

CAPITOLS
(Capitol's)
Singles: 7-inch
GATEWAY (721 "Little Things") ... 150-200 64
(Beige label.)
GATEWAY (721 "Little Things") ... 100-150 64
(White label. Promotional issue only.)
Also see TOLIVER, Mickey, & Capitols

CAPONE, Susan
(With the Four Esquires)
Singles: 78 rpm
PILGRIM ... 10-15 56
Singles: 7-inch
EVENT (4288 "I Understand") ... 8-12 58
PILGRIM (704 "I'll be Dancing") ... 10-15 56
Also see FOUR ESQUIRES

CAPP, Howard
Singles: 7-inch
CHRISTY (102 "Berna Doll") ... 50-75 60

CAPP, Joe,
(With the Count Downs; with Starfires)
Singles: 7-inch
ROULETTE (4436 "Comic Strip Wobble") ... 10-15 62
ROULETTE (4458 "Groovy Movie") ... 10-15 62
Member: Bill Ramal.
Also see RAMAL, Bill

CAPPS, Judy
Singles: 7-inch
CHERRY (1008 "Are You Really My Friend") ... 50-75 59
CHERRY (1009 "You Can Have My Love") ... 150-200 60

CAPREES
Singles: 7-inch
BUCCANEER (502 "If I Should Lose You") ... 400-500 62

CAPREES / Dawns
Singles: 7-inch
STOOP SOUNDS (503 "If I Should Lose You") ... 100-150 96
(Limited edition. Estimates range from less than 10 to a few dozen made.)
Also see CAPREES

CAPREEZ
(Capris)
Singles: 7-inch
SOUND (126 "Rosanna") ... 10-15 66
SOUND (126 "Roseanna") ... 15-25 66
(Credits "Capris." Also, note spelling error in title.)
SOUND (149 "It's Good to Be Home Again") ... 25-50 67
SOUND (171 "Time") ... 10-20 67
TOWER (370 "Time") ... 5-10 67

CAPRI, Bobby
(With the Velvet Satins)
Singles: 7-inch
ARTISTE (101 "One Sided Love") ... 100-200 62
CLIFTON (14 "The Night") ... 4-6 76
JASON SCOTT (17 "One Sided Love") ... 3-5 81
(500 made.)
JOHNSON (124 "You and I") ... 40-60 63
JOHNSON (126 "The Night") ... 75-100 63
Also see VELVET SATINS

CAPRI, Jimmy
Singles: 7-inch
GONE (5115 "The Girl for Me") ... 10-20 61

CAPRI, John
(With the Fabulous Fours)
Singles: 7-inch
BOMARC (306 "When I'm Lonely") ... 50-75 59

CAPRI, Johnnie
Singles: 7-inch
MASTER (13 "Mine Alone") ... 15-25 61

CAPRI, Mike
Singles: 7-inch
CECIL (4450 "She's My Baby") ... 30-40

CAPRI, Tony
Singles: 7-inch
LIBAN (1001 "Sandy, Come Back to Me") ... 75-125 59
LIBAN (1003 "You Thrill Me") ... 15-25 60
LIBAN (1005 "That's the Way") ... 10-20 60

CAPRIES
Singles: 7-inch
RAINBOW ("Hey Girl") ... 10-20
(No selection number used.)

CAPRIS
("With Rhythm Accompaniment")
Singles: 78 rpm
GOTHAM ... 50-75 54-56
RAGE ... 50-75 54
Singles: 7-inch
CANDLELITE (422 "Oh, My Darling") ... 5-10 64
GOTHAM (304 "God Only Knows") ... 100-150 54
(Blue label.)
GOTHAM (304 "God Only Knows") ... 50-100 54
(Red label.)
GOTHAM (304 "God Only Knows") ... 30-40 56
(Yellow label.)
GOTHAM (306 "It Was Moonglow") ... 100-150 55
GOTHAM (308 "It's a Miracle") ... 100-150 56
LIFETIME (1001 "Oh, My Darling") ... 50-100 61
RAGE (101 "Fools Fall in Love") ... 150-200 54
(Also issued as by Mel Williams & Montclairs.)
TWENTIETH CENTURY (1201 "My Weakness") ... 30-40 60
TWENTIETH CENTURY (7304 "That's What You're Doing to Me") ... 10-15
LPs: 10/12-inch
COLLECTABLES ... 8-10 80
Members: Erina Hinton; Bobby Smart; Herb Johnson; Larry Scott; Rubin Wright.
Also see BELLTONES
Also see BROWNE, Doris

CAPRIS
(Capri's)
Singles: 7-inch
FABLE (665 "This Is Goodbye") ... 200-300 59
SABRE (201 "My Promise to You") ... 400-500 59

CAPRIS
Singles: 7-inch
TENDER (518 "Endless Love"/ "Beware") ... 75-125 59
(*Beware* is by Jesse Belvin, and was issued in 1956 on Cash by him. Same number used on a Shields release.)
Member: Jesse Belvin.
Also see BELVIN, Jesse

CAPRIS *P&R '60*
Singles: 7-inch
AMBIENT SOUND (02697 "Morse Code of Love"/ "There's a Moon Out Again") ... 5-10 82
JANUS (714 "Why Did I Cry") ... 4-6 77
COLLECTABLES ... 3-5 81
DELTA (3118 "There's a Moon Out Tonight") ... 10-20 61
(Canadian.)
LOST NITE (101 "There's a Moon Out Tonight") ... 20-30 60
(Pink label. Black vinyl.)
LOST NITE (101 "There's a Moon Out Tonight") ... 40-50 60
(Pink label. Red vinyl.)
LOST NITE (101 "There's a Moon Out Tonight") ... 5-10 '60s
(Yellow label.)
LOST NITE (148 "When") ... 10-20
MR. PEEKE (118 "Limbo") ... 10-15 62
OLD TOWN (1094 "There's a Moon Out Tonight") ... 20-30 60
OLD TOWN (1099 "Where I Fell in Love") ... 30-40 61
OLD TOWN (1103 "Why Do I Cry") ... 20-30 61
OLD TOWN (1107 "Girl in My Dreams") .. 40-50 61
PLANET (1010 "There's a Moon Out Tonight") ... 750-1000 59
TROMMERS (101 "There's a Moon Out Tonight") ... 15-25 65
LPs: 10/12-inch
AMBIENT SOUND ... 8-12 82
COLLECTABLES ... 5-10 84
Members: Nick "Santos" Santamaria; Mike Mitchell; Vince Narcardo; John Apostol; Frank Reina.
Also see COLE, Clay

CAPRISIANS
Singles: 7-inch
INDIGO (109 "Lovely Way to Spend an Evening") ... 15-25 60
LAVENDER (004 "Oh What a Nite") ... 10-20 61

CAPS
Singles: 7-inch
LEO ... 20-40 57
WHITE STAR (102 "Red Headed Flea") .. 30-40 59
WHITE STAR (103 "Daddy Dean Part Two") ... 30-40 59

CAPTAIN & TENNILLE *P&R/LP '75*

Singles: 7-inch

A&M 4-6 75-78
BUTTERSCOTCH CASTLE (001 "The Way I Want to Touch You") 50-75 73
JOYCE (101 "The Way I Want to Touch You") 20-40 74
CASABLANCA 3-6 79-80

Picture Sleeves

A&M 4-6 75-78

LPs: 10/12-inch

A&M 8-10 75-79
CASABLANCA 5-10 79
Members: Daryl Dragon; Toni Tennille.
Also see BEACH BOYS
Also see YELLOW BALLOON

CAPTAIN BEEFHEART *LP '72*
(With His Magic Band)

Singles: 7-inch

A&M (794 "Diddy Wah Diddy") 50-75 66
A&M (818 "Moonchild") 40-60 66
BUDDAH 5-8 67-69
EPIC 3-5 82
MCA (40897 "Hard Workin' Man") 4-8 '70s
MERCURY 4-6 74
REPRISE 4-6 72
VIRGIN 3-5 82

Promotional Singles

REPRISE (434 "Lick My Decals Off, Baby") 40-50 70
REPRISE (447 "Talking About") 40-50 71
REPRISE (514 "Click Clack") 50-75 71
REPRISE (547 "Low Yo Yo Stuff") 40-50 72
(Issued with gatefold, EP-like, cover.)
REPRISE (1068 "Click Clack") 25-35 72

LPs: 10/12-inch

A&M 5-10 84
ACCORD 5-10 83
BIZARRE 10-12 72
BLUE THUMB (1 "Strictly Personal") 20-30 68
(Black label.)
BLUE THUMB (1 "Strictly Personal") 10-15 69
(Tan label.)
BUDDAH (1001 "Safe As Milk") 25-35 67
(Monaural. Add $10 to $15 if accompanied by 4" x 15" *Safe As Milk* bumper sticker.)
BUDDAH (5001 "Safe As Milk") 25-30 67
(Stereo. Add $10 to $15 if accompanied by 4" x 15" *Safe As Milk* bumper sticker.)
BUDDAH (5077 "Mirror Man") 10-15 71
BUDDAH (5063 "Safe As Milk") 8-12 70
D.I.R. (57 "Direct News, Week of 12-18-78") 35-45 78
(Five, 5-minute radio programs, one of which has an interview with Don Van Vliet. Promotional issue only.)
EPIC 5-10 82
MERCURY (709 "Unconditionally Guaranteed") 8-12 74
MERCURY (1018 "Bluejeans and Moonbeams") 8-12 74
REPRISE (2027 "Trout Mask Replica") 8-12 77
REPRISE (2050 "Spotlight Kid") 10-15 72
REPRISE (2115 "Clear Spot") 10-20 72
(With embossed "Clear Spot" plastic bag.)
REPRISE (2115 "Clear Spot") 15-20 72
(White label. Has printed inserts instead of standard cover. Promotional issue only.)
STRAIGHT (1053 "Trout Mask Replica"). 30-40 68
(With lyrics sleeve.)
STRAIGHT (1053 "Trout Mask Replica"). 20-25 68
(Without lyrics sleeve.)
STRAIGHT (6420 "Lick My Decals Off, Baby") 10-15 70
VIRGIN 5-10 80-82
W.B. 5-15 78
Members: Don "Captain Beefheart" Van Vliet; Doug Moon; Paul Blakely; Alex St. Claire; Jerry Handley; Ry Cooder; Jeff Cotton; John French; Bill "Zoot Horn Rollo" Harkleroad; Rockette Morton; Jimmy Semens; Jerry Handsley; Ty Grimes.
Also see COODER, Ry
Also see MOTHERS OF INVENTION
Also see MU
Also see TRIANGLE

CAPTAIN BEYOND *LP '72*

Singles: 7-inch

CAPRICORN 4-6 72-73

LPs: 10/12-inch

CAPRICORN (Except 0105) 8-12 72-73
CAPRICORN (0105 "Captain Beyond") 45-55 72
(With 3-D cover.)
CAPRICORN (0105 "Captain Beyond") 15-25 72
(With standard cover.)
W.B. 8-10 77
Members: Bobby Caldwell; Rod Evans; Willie Daffern; Lee Dorman; Larry Reinhardt.
Also see DEEP PURPLE
Also see IRON BUTTERFLY

CAPTAIN ZAP & MOTORTOWN CUT-UPS

Singles: 7-inch

MOTOWN (1151 "Luney Landing") 10-20 69

CAP-TANS

Singles: 78 rpm

CORAL 50-75 51
DOT 25-50 50-53

Singles: 7-inch

ANNA (1122 "I'm Afraid") 20-30 60
CORAL (65071 "Asking") 200-300 51
DOT (15114 "I'm So Crazy for Love") 100-150 53
(First issued in 1950 on 78 rpm as Dot 1009.)
GOTHAM (233 "My, My, Ain't She Pretty") 100-200 50
GOTHAM (268 "Yes, I Thought I Could Forget") 100-200 51
Members: Harmon Bethea; Buddy Slaughter; Les Fountain; Floyd Bennett.
Also see BETHEA, Harmon
Also see BETHEA & CAP-TANS
Also see L'CAP-TANS

CAPTIONS

Singles: 7-inch

KAYHAM (8 "Turn Out the Lights") 50-75 60

CAPTIVATIONS

Singles: 7-inch

GARPAX (44179 "Red Hot Scrambler-Go") 10-20 64
(Reissue: note slightly different title.)
PENTACLE (1635 "Red Hot Scramblers-Go") 20-35 64

CARADINE, Mike

Singles: 7-inch

HILLCREST (200 "Don't Ever Take Your Love") 50-75

CARAMAN, Art "Turk"

Singles: 7-inch

DASA (101 "Falling For You") 40-50 62

CARAVAN, Jimmy

LPs: 10/12-inch

TOWER 15-20 68
VAULT 15-20 69

CARAVANS

Singles: 7-inch

T.J. (1123 "Baby Drives Me Crazy") 8-12 65
TORNADO (106 "Twistin' Rockin' Baby") 50-75 '60s

CARAVELLES
(Caravelle's)

Singles: 7-inch

KEY (301 "Teardrops") 150-200

CARAVELLES

Singles: 7-inch

STAR MAKER (1925 "Angry Angel") 10-20 61

CARAVELLES

Singles: 7-inch

JOEY (301 "Fallin' for You") 75-100 63
JOEY (6208 "One Little Kiss") 40-50 62

CARAVELLES

Singles: 7-inch

ONACREST (502 "Lovin' Just My Style") 15-25 66

CARAVELLES *P&R '63*

Singles: 7-inch

SMASH 5-10 63-65

LPs: 10/12-inch

SMASH (27044 "You Don't Have to Be a Baby to Cry") 20-40 63
(Monaural.)
SMASH (67044 "You Don't Have to Be a Baby to Cry") 20-40 63
(Stereo.)
Members: Lois Wilkinson; Andrea Simpson.

CARAWAY, Bobby & Terry

Singles: 7-inch

CREST (1065 "Ballin' Keen") 65-85 59
Also see CARAWAY, Bobby

CARBO, Chick
(Chic Carbo; Leonard Carbo)

Singles: 7-inch

INSTANT (3245 In the Night") 10-15 62
INSTANT (3254 "Two Tables Away") 10-15 62
REVUE (11019 "Touch Me") 5-10 68
Also see CARBO, Leonard
Also see SPIDERS

CARBO, Chuck

Singles: 78 rpm

IMPERIAL 20-40 57

Singles: 7-inch

ACE (631 "I Shouldn't But I Do") 10-15 61
ACE (666 "Cutting Out") 10-15 62
"504" 5-10
IMPERIAL (5452 "Poor Boy") 15-25 57
IMPERIAL (5479 "I Miss You") 15-25 57
REX (1003 "Promises") 10-20 59
REX (1011 "Picture of You") 10-15 60
REX (1012 "Black Velvet") 10-15 60
Session: Spiders.
Also see SPIDERS

CARBO, Leonard

Singles: 78 rpm

ATLANTIC 10-15 56

Singles: 7-inch

ATLANTIC (1119 "Sentimental Journey Blues") 20-30 56
VEE-JAY (291 "Pigtails and Bluejeans") 15-25 58
Session: Spiders.
Also see CARBO, Chick
Also see SPIDERS

CARBONE, Jackie
(With the Concords; with Eddie Bartel & Orchestra)

Singles: 7-inch

CIRO'S (3317 "Let Me Go Daddy") 15-25 60
FOX (103 "Sugar Eyes") 15-25 59
STAR-X (503 "Just Foolin'") 50-75 57

CARBONE, Raymond

Singles: 7-inch

STAR-X (502 "Rockin' on My Rockin' Horse") 15-25 57

CARDBOARD ZEPPELIN

Singles: 7-inch

LAURIE (3433 "City Lights") 15-25 68
Also see REGENTS

CARDELL, Johnny, & Three Pals

Singles: 78 rpm

RAMA 30-50 57

Singles: 7-inch

RAMA (227 "Rock-A-Billy Yodeler") 50-75 57
Also see LA RUE, Roc, & Three Pals

CARDELL, Nick

Singles: 7-inch

AMCAN (405 "Everybody Jump") 10-15 64
(Flip is **not** *I Stand Alone*, though we do not yet know its title.)
AMCAN (405 "I Stand Alone") 100-150 64
(Flip is *Everybody Jump*.)
LIBERTY (55556 "Arlene") 15-20 63

CARDELLS
("Featuring Wm. Gardner")

Singles: 78 rpm

MIDDLE-TONE (011 "Helen") 200-300 56

Singles: 7-inch

MIDDLE-TONE (011 "Helen") 750-1000 56
Members: William Gardner; Sonny Mayberry; Robert Carey; Charles Bearden.

CARDIGANS

Singles: 78 rpm

MERCURY 25-35 57

Singles: 7-inch

MERCURY (71251 "Your Graduation Means Goodbye") 10-15 57
MERCURY (71349 "It's Better That You Love") 10-15 58
MERCURY (71367 "Poor Boy") 8-12 58
SPANN (431 "Make Up Your Mind") 20-30 59

CARDINALS *R&B '51*

Singles: 78 rpm

ATLANTIC (938 "Shouldn't I Know") 50-75 51
ATLANTIC (958 thru 1126) 25-75 51-57

Singles: 7-inch

ATLANTIC (938 "Shouldn't I Know") 3-4 '70s
ATLANTIC (952 "I'll Always Love You") 150-250 51
ATLANTIC (958 "Wheel of Fortune") 200-300 52
ATLANTIC (972 "The Bump") 50-100 52
ATLANTIC (995 "You Are My Only Love") 100-200 53
ATLANTIC (1025 "Under a Blanket of Blue") 150-250 54
ATLANTIC (1054 "The Door Is Still Open") 75-100 55
ATLANTIC (1067 "Two Things I Love") 50-75 55
ATLANTIC (1079 "Here Goes My Heart to You") 50-75 55
ATLANTIC (1090 "Off Shore") 30-40 56
ATLANTIC (1103 "The End of the Story") 15-25 56
ATLANTIC (1126 "Near You") 25-35 57

EPs: 7-inch

BIM BAM BOOM (1000 "The Cardinals") 6-12 '70s
(Black vinyl.)
BIM BAM BOOM (1000 "The Cardinals") 5-10 '70s
(Blue vinyl.)
Members: Ernie Warren; Meredith Brothers; Leon Hardy; Donald Johnson; Jack "Sam" Aydelotte; Luther MacArthur; James Brown; Lee Tarver.

CARDINALS

Singles: 7-inch

ROSE (835 "Why Don't You Write Me") 1000-1500 63
Members: Al Turner; Reginald Grant; Oscar Drummand; Lynn Thomas; Gary Evans; R. Foreman.
Also see EQUADORS

CARDINALS

Singles: 7-inch

CHA CHA (740 "I Want You") 20-30 66
CHA CHA (748 "I'm Gonna Tell on You") 20-30 66
CHA CHA (1441 "Hatchet Face") 20-30 '60s

CARDWELL, Jack *C&W '53*

Singles: 78 rpm

KING 5-15 53-55

Singles: 7-inch

KING 15-25 53-55
SANDY (1023 "All Alone") 10-20 59
STARDAY (310 "Hey Hey Baby") 50-100

CAREFREES *P&R '64*

Singles: 7-inch

LONDON INT'L (10614 "We Love You Beatles") 15-25 64
LONDON INT'L (10615 "Paddy Wack") 5-8 64

Picture Sleeves

LONDON INT'L (10614 "We Love You Beatles") 20-30 64

LPs: 10/12-inch

LONDON (379 "We Love You All") 35-45 64
Members: Lyn Cornell; Betty Prescott; Barbara Kay.
Also see VERNON GIRLS

CARELESS FIVE

Singles: 7-inch

CAREFUL (1010 "I'm So Lonely") 30-40 62
VI-TOSE (101 "Summertime") 5-10

CARESSORS

Singles: 7-inch

RU-JAC (0020 "Who Can It Be") 25-50

CARETAKERS OF DECEPTION

Singles: 7-inch

SANCTUS (11 "Cuttin' Grass") 20-30 67

CAREW, Bennie

Singles: 7-inch

FENTON 10-20 66

CAREY, Bill
(With the Hugo Winterhalter Orchestra & Chorus)

Singles: 78 rpm

CORAL (61540 "Poor Me") 5-10 55
DOT (15618 "Single") 5-10 57
RCA (5785 "Juba") 5-10 54

Singles: 7-inch

CORAL (61540 "Poor Me") 10-15 55
DOT (15618 "Single") 10-15 57
DOT (16755 "I Am") 5-10 65

RCA (5785 "Juba").. 10-15 54
WARWICK (527 "Won't You Let Go")...... 10-20 60
Also see WINTERHALTER, Hugo, & His Orchestra

CAREY, Charlie
Singles: 7-inch
LE CAM (712 "Wear My Ring")................. 15-25 61
SULTAN (22 "Little Red Wagon")............ 50-75

CAREY, Vince
Singles: 7-inch
TURNTABLE (712 "Don't Worry")............ 10-15 65
TURNTABLE (717 "Love Letters")........... 10-15 65

CARI, Claudia
Singles: 7-inch
RICKARBY (102 "A Boy Like You")......... 10-20

CARI, Eddie
Singles: 7-inch
MERMAID (104 "This Love of Mine")...... 20-30 63

CARIANS
Singles: 7-inch
INDIGO (136 "She's Gone").................... 50-60 61
MAGENTA (04 "Only a Dream")............. 30-40 61
Also see CORDIALS

CARIBBEANS
Singles: 7-inch
20TH FOX (112 "Keep Her By My Side") 25-35 58

CARL, Danny
Singles: 7-inch
SKYROCKET (1009 "Long Tall Sally")..... 50-75

CARL, Donnie, & Donnells
Singles: 7-inch
TY-TEX (113 "It Happened to Me")......... 15-25 65

CARL, Eddie
(With the Emblems)
Singles: 7-inch
MERMAID (104 "Wishing Time")............ 40-50 61
OH MY (1000 "Every Little Dream Comes True").. 40-50 62

CARL, Johnny
Singles: 7-inch
GONE (5139 "How Will It End")............... 20-30 62
NELBER (101 "The Wrong Gal")............ 10-20 63
UA (589 "The Wrong Gal")..................... 10-20 63

CARL, Steve, & Jags
Singles: 7-inch
METEOR (5046 "Curfew").................... 300-400 58

CARL & COMMANDERS
("Vocal Marco King")
Singles: 7-inch
CAMEO (197 "Farmer John")................. 10-20 61
JADCO (161 "I Need Your Love")........... 50-75 64

CARL & SPINDLE TOPPERS
Singles: 7-inch
ABC-PAR (10346 "Hey Moon")................ 10-15 62

CARL JUNIOR
Singles: 7-inch
MILLS (0489 "Look Who's Lonely")......... 15-25

CARLE, Bobby, & Blendaires
(With Jack Pleis & His Orchestra)
Singles: 7-inch
DECCA (30605 "Walk with Me")............. 10-20 58
DECCA (30699 "I Couldn't Stand It")...... 10-20 58
DECCA (30938 "I Got It Bad and That Ain't Good").. 10-20 59

CARLINO, Tony
Singles: 7-inch
MILO (117 "Again")................................ 15-25 61

CARLISLE, Bill C&W '48
(With the Carlisles; Bill Carlisle's Kentucky Boys)
Singles: 78 rpm
BLUEBIRD (Except 6478)...................... 10-15
BLUEBIRD (6478 "Rattlin' Daddy")......... 25-40
DECCA.. 10-20 '30s
FEDERAL.. 5-10
KING... 5-10 48
MERCURY.. 4-8 53
VOCALION (02520 "Rattle Snake Daddy")... 20-40
VOCALION (02946 "I'm Gonna Kill Myself")... 20-40
Singles: 7-inch
COLUMBIA.. 4-8 62
HICKORY.. 4-8 65
MERCURY.. 10-20 53
VANGUARD.. 4-6 72
EPs: 7-inch
MERCURY.. 10-20 56
LPs: 10/12-inch
BRYLEN.. 5-10 83
HICKORY.. 10-20 66
Also see CARLISLES
Also see SEA, Johnny / Bill Carlisle

CARLISLE, Jim
Singles: 7-inch
MONEY (103 "Sweet Baby").................... 10-15 64

CARLISLE, Ken, & Martells
Singles: 7-inch
JUNGLE (502 "I'm Just Walkin' in the Rain").. 40-50 60

CARLISLES C&W '46
(Carlisle Brothers; Carlisle Family)
Singles: 78 rpm
DECCA.. 10-15 40-41
KING... 8-12 46
MERCURY.. 5-10 53-56
Singles: 7-inch
MERCURY.. 10-20 51-54
EPs: 7-inch
MERCURY.. 10-20 55
LPs: 10/12-inch
GUEST STAR... 10-15 '60s
KING (643 "Fresh from the Country")....... 15-25 59
MERCURY (20359 "On Stage")................ 30-40 58
OLD HOMESTEAD...................................... 5-8 '80s
Members: Bill Carlisle; Cliff Carlisle.
Also see CARLISLE, Bill

CARLO
(With the Glen Stuart Orchestra; Carlo Mastrangelo)
Singles: 7-inch
LAURIE (3151 thru 3175)...................... 10-20 62-63
LAURIE (3227 "Ring-A-Ling").................. 50-60 64
RAFTIS (110 "Fever")................................ 8-12 70
RAFTIS (112 "Let There Be Love")............ 8-12 70
Also see BELMONTS
Also see CARLO & JIMMY
Also see CARLO'S CROWN JEWEL
Also see DEMILLES
Also see STUART, Glen

CARLO & CUPIDS
Singles: 7-inch
JUDD (1007 "Crazy Rock")...................... 10-15 59
PARKER (501 "Crazy Rock").................... 15-25 58

CARLO & JIMMY
Singles: 7-inch
LAURIE (3063 "Happy Tune")................... 10-20 60
Also see CARLO

CARLO & SECRETS
Singles: 7-inch
THRONE (801 "Pony Party").................... 25-35 62

CARLO'S CROWN JEWEL
Singles: 7-inch
TOWER (497 "It's Alright")....................... 10-20 69
Also see CARLO

CARLOS, Randy
Singles: 78 rpm
GEE (6 "Mambo Va")................................. 5-10 54
Singles: 7-inch
FIESTA (099 "Satellite USA")..................... 8-12 59
(Monaural.)
FIESTA (1001 "Satellite USA").................. 15-25 59
(Stereo.)
GEE (6 "Mambo Va")................................ 15-25 54
LPs: 10/12-inch
FIESTA (1245 "Hot Cha Cha").................. 15-20 59
FIESTA (1252 "Swingin' with Randy")...... 15-20 59

CARLOS BROTHERS
Singles: 7-inch
DEL-FI (4112 "Tonight")............................ 10-20 59
DEL-FI (4118 "Little Cupid")..................... 10-20 59
DEL-FI (4145 "La Bamba")........................ 10-20 60
ZEN (106 "I Realize").................................. 5-10 64

CARLSON, Dave
Singles: 7-inch
HIFI (590 "Dave's Blues")......................... 10-20 60

CARLTON
(Carlton Beck)
Singles: 7-inch
PENNEY (1306 "The Girl I Left Behind")... 1000-1500 62
(Reissued as by Carlton Beck.)
Also see BECK, Carlton

CARLTON, Carl P&R/R&B '68
(Little Carl Carlton)
Singles: 12-inch
20TH FOX.. 4-6 80
Singles: 7-inch
ABC.. 4-6 73-76
BACK BEAT.. 6-12 68-75
CASABLANCA.. 3-5 86
GOLDEN WORLD (23 "Nothin' No Sweeter Than Love")... 10-20 65
LANDO (3046 "Don't You Need a Boy Like Me")... 15-25 65
LANDO (8527 "So What")......................... 10-20 65
MCA.. 3-5 84
MERCURY.. 4-6 77
RCA.. 3-5 82
20TH FOX.. 3-6 81-82
LPs: 10/12-inch
ABC.. 10-12 74
BACK BEAT.. 10-15 73
CASABLANCA.. 5-10 86
RCA.. 5-10 82
20TH FOX.. 5-10 81

CARLTON, Chick
(With the Majestics)
Singles: 7-inch
ATCO (6763 "Preach Love")........................ 5-8 70
DEMON (1504 "You Enchanted Me")....... 10-15 58
FARO (592 "So You Want to Rock")........ 15-25 59
FARO (611 "Turkey Time")...................... 10-15 61
IMPERIAL (5873 "Tomorrow Never Comes").. 10-15 62
IMPERIAL (5925 "Beyond Belief")............ 15-20 62

CARLTON, Eddie
Singles: 7-inch
CRACKERJACK (4009 "Wait")................ 15-20 64
SWAN (4218 "Misery")............................. 20-30 65

CARLTON, Kenny
Singles: 7-inch
BLUE ROCK (4054 "Lost and Found")...50-100 68
VALLI (305 "You're 16")........................... 10-15 64

CARLTON, Richard
Singles: 7-inch
UPTIGHT ("I Like to Get Near You")........ 10-20 '60s
(No selection number used.)

CARLYLE
Singles: 7-inch
STEVENSON'S (680068 "Is It")............... 10-20 '60s

CARMACKS
Singles: 7-inch
AUTOGRAPH (205 "With All My Heart")..10-15 60

CARMEL COVERED POPCORN
Singles: 7-inch
VISTONE (2055 "Suzie Q")....................... 10-15 68

CARMEL SISTERS
Singles: 7-inch
JUBILEE (5464 "Joey's Comin' Home")...10-15 63
Members: Carol Carmel (Carol Connors); Cheryl Carmel (Cheryl Connors).
Also see CAROL & CHERYL

CARMELETTES
Singles: 7-inch
ALPINE (53 "My Foolish Heart")............... 10-20 59
ALPINE (61 "Aching for You")................... 10-20 60

CARMEN
(Carmen Menna)
Singles: 7-inch
INFERNO (100 "Isle of Love")................... 25-35 59
JODAY (1003 "False Hearted Love").....50-150 63

CARMEN
LPs: 10/12-inch
DUNHILL... 10-15 74
EPIC... 15-20 69
MERCURY.. 8-12 75
PRIORITY.. 5-10 82-83
Members: Angela Allen; David Allen; Roberto Amaral; Paul Fenton; John Glascock.

CARMEN, Jerry
Singles: 7-inch
BARRISH (500 "Cherry Pie").................... 50-75 62

CARMEN, Thaddeus
Singles: 7-inch
MILESTONE (2016 "Thinking Back")....... 10-15 62

CARMEN, Tony, & Spitfires
Singles: 7-inch
ABEL (224 "Don't Run to Me")................. 20-30 59
Also see TONY & DAYDREAMS

CARMICHAEL, Lucky
Singles: 7-inch
DILLIE (7750 "1109")............................... 15-25 60
LOMA (2006 "Hey Girl")............................. 8-12 64
SHAR (4 "I'm Comin' Home").................... 50-75 60

CARNABY STREET SET
Singles: 7-inch
COLUMBIA (44092 "Tender Savage")..... 10-15 67

CARNATIONS
Singles: 78 rpm
DERBY..50-100 52
SAVOY... 10-20 55
Singles: 7-inch
DERBY (789 "Tree in the Meadow").....250-350 52
SAVOY (1172 "The Angels Sent You to Me").. 30-40 55
Members: Bill Reid; Horace Holmes.

CARNATIONS
(With the Eddie Wilcox Orchestra)
Singles: 7-inch
ENRICA (1001 "Love Open Up My Heart").. 10-15 59

CARNATIONS
Singles: 7-inch
JODI (4103 "Angels Rock")....................... 50-75 59

CARNATIONS
Singles: 7-inch
ACE (130 "A Fool in Love")...................... 60-80 60
TERRY-TONE (199 "Barbary Coast")...... 15-25 60

CARNATIONS
(With the Joe René Orchestra)
Singles: 7-inch
LESCAY (3002 "Long Tall Girl")............... 50-75 61
(Black vinyl.)
LESCAY (3002 "Long Tall Girl")............ 75-125 61
(Brown vinyl.)
LOST NITE... 10-20 '60s
Members: Matt Morales; Harvey Arrington; Carl Hatton; Ed Kennedy; Tommy Blackwell.
Also see STARTONES

CARNATIONS
Singles: 7-inch
LAURIE (3163 "Funny Time").................... 10-15 63
TILT (780 "Scorpion")................................. 5-10 61
Also see COSMO

CARNES, Kim P&R '79
Singles: 12-inch
EMI AMERICA.. 4-6 80-85
Singles: 7-inch
A&M.. 3-5 75-82
AMOS (165 "I Won't Call You Back")........... 4-6 71
AMOS (166 "To Love Somebody")............... 4-6 71
EMI AMERICA.. 3-6 79-86
ELEKTRA... 3-5 84
Picture Sleeves
EMI AMERICA.. 3-5 80-86
LPs: 10/12-inch
A&M (3000 series)....................................... 5-10 82
A&M (4000 series)....................................... 8-10 75-77
AMOS.. 12-18 71
EMI AMERICA.. 5-10 79-86
MCA.. 5-10 84
MFSL (073 "Mistaken Identity")................ 35-50 82
Session: Lyle Lovett.
Also see LOVETT, Lyle
Also see ROGERS, Kenny, & Kim Carnes
Also see STREISAND, Barbra, & Kim Carnes
Also see SUGAR BEARS

CARNES, Kim, & Dave Ellingson

Singles: 7-inch

AMOS (167 "It's Love That Keeps It All Together") 4-6 71

Also see CARNES, Kim

CARNES, Paul

Singles: 7-inch

P.R.C. (4481 "I'm a Mean, Mean Daddy") 300-500

CARNEY, Art

Singles: 78 rpm

COLUMBIA....5-10 54-56

Singles: 7-inch

COLUMBIA....10-20 54-56

Picture Sleeves

COLUMBIA....20-30 54-56

EPs: 7-inch

COLUMBIA (2034 "Art Carney") 25-45 55

CARNIVAL OF SOUND

Singles: 7-inch

USA (892 "I Can't Remember")....15-20 67

Also see TROLLS

CAROL, Benae

Singles: 7-inch

FRESH (2105 "The Werewolf")....10-20 61

CAROL, Cammy
(Cammy Carol & Halos)

Singles: 7-inch

ELMOR (302 "Until the Day I Die") 40-50 61

WARWICK (574 "Hand Me Down Heart") 10-15 60

CAROL, Ce Cee

Singles: 7-inch

TRANS-WORLD (6907 "Tag-A-Long") 15-20 60

CAROL, Joni

Singles: 7-inch

COUNSEL (1010 "No Love")....10-15 62

CAROL, Lily Ann

Singles: 78 rpm

BRUCE (2000 "If I Can't Have You All") 5-10 55

RCA (4736 "I'm Sorry")....5-10 52

Singles: 7-inch

BRUCE (2000 "If I Can't Have You All") .. 10-20 55

RCA (4736 "I'm Sorry")....10-20 52

CAROL, Lily Ann, & Jimmy Saunders
(With Chris Griffin's Cornball Serenaders)

Singles: 78 rpm

SIGNATURE (15289 "Walkin' with the Blues")....15-25 51

CAROL & CHERYL

Singles: 7-inch

COLPIX (767 "Go Go GTO")....75-125 65

Members: Carol Carmel (Carol Connors); Cheryl Carmel (Cheryl Connors).

Also see CARMEL SISTERS

Also see CONNORS, Carol

CAROL & GERRI

Singles: 7-inch

MGM (13568 "How Can I Ever Find the Way")....20-30 66

CAROL ANN

Singles: 7-inch

PJ (1351 "Let Me Be Yours")....10-15 63

CAROL, LINDA & CATHY

Singles: 7-inch

UNITED (216 "I Don't Want to Be the Last on Santa's List")....15-25 57

CAROLE, Nancy

Singles: 7-inch

COOL (181 "Tell Him Goodbye")....40-50 '60s

LUXOR (1028/1029 "My Joey"/"The Memories We Share")....30-40 64

UNITED INT'L (500 "Polar Bear")....10-15 63

CAROLINA SLIM
(Ed Harris)

Singles: 78 rpm

ACORN (319 "Come Back, Baby")....30-50 51

ACORN (323 "Blues Knocking at My Door")....30-50 52

ACORN (324 "Rag Mama")....30-50 52

ACORN (3015 "Mama's Boogie")....30-50 51

LPs: 10/12-inch

SHARP (2002 "Blues from the Cottonfields")....50-100 59

Also see COUNTRY PAUL

Also see JAMMIN' JIM

Also see LAZY SLIM JIM

CAROLINA TIKIS

Singles: 7-inch

CHARAY (1010 "Four Season Girl")....10-20 '60s

CAROLONS

Singles: 7-inch

MELLOMOOD (1003 "Let It Please Be You")....10-15 64

CAROLS

Singles: 78 rpm

COLUMBIA....15-25 50

SAVOY....25-50 53

Singles: 7-inch

SAVOY (896 "Fifty Million Women") 100-150 53

SAVOY (989 "Call for Me if You Want") 4-8

(Previously unreleased.)

Members: Tommy Evans; Richard Coleman; Wilbert Tindle; William Davis; James Worthy; Ken Duncan.

CAROLS

Singles: 7-inch

LAMP (2001 "My Search Is Over")....30-40 57

CARONATORS

Singles: 7-inch

CLOCK (1045 "Long Hot Summer")....15-25 60

CLOCK (1047 "Lonely Street")....15-25 61

CLOCK (1049 "This Is the Time")....15-25 61

CAROUSEL

Singles: 7-inch

TEEN TOWN (108 "I've Been with You") .10-15 68

TEEN TOWN (116 "I Get Along Indefinitely")....10-15 69

CAROUSELS

Singles: 7-inch

G.C. (601 "Fading Away")....400-500 60

JAGUAR (3029 "Rendezvous")....75-125 59

SPRY (116 "I've Cried Enough")....100-200 59

SPRY (121 "Rendezvous")....200-300 59

CAROUSELS

Singles: 7-inch

GONE (5118 "You Can Come If You Want To")....30-40 61

GONE (5118 "If You Want To")....10-15 61

(Note shorter title.)

GONE (5131 "Never Let Him Go")....15-20 62

ROULETTE....4-6 71

CAROUSELS

Singles: 7-inch

VINTAGE (1012 "Just for Your Love") 10-15 73

(Red vinyl.)

CARPENTER, Chris
(Preston Carnes)

Singles: 7-inch

OCEAN-SIDE (100 "This World")....10-20 68

(First issue.)

U.A. (50266 "This World")....5-10 68

Also see LENNY & THUNDERTONES

Also see PRESTON

CARPENTER, Everett

Singles: 7-inch

SQUARE DEAL (501 "Let Your Hair Down Baby")....125-150

CARPENTER, Freddie

Singles: 7-inch

ATHENS (705 "Money Money Money") 50-75 58

EAST WEST (112 "Money Money Money")....15-25 58

CARPENTER, Ike
(With the Merry Macs)

Singles: 78 rpm

ALADDIN....10-20 53

DECCA....10-15 52

INTRO....10-15 52

DISCOVERY....5-10 50

MODERN....15-25 47-48

RCA....5-10 49

Singles: 7-inch

ALADDIN....15-25 53

DECCA....15-25 53

INTRO....15-25 52

MODERN (116 "Yesterdays")....30-50 51

MODERN (117 "Day Dream")....30-50 51

LPs: 10/12-inch

ALADDIN (811 "Light's Out")....75-125 57

INTRO (950 "Lights Out")....100-200 52

(10-inch LP.)

SCORE (4010 "Light's Out")....50-75 57

Members: Ike Carpenter; Nick Fatool; Stan Black; John Kitzmiller.

Also see FERGUSON, Maynard

Also see SMITH, Effie

Also see ZENTNER, Si

CARPENTER, Karen

Singles: 7-inch

MAGIC LAMP (704 "Looking for Love")....2500-3000 66

Members: Karen Carpenter; Richard Carpenter; Wes Jacobs.

Also see CARPENTERS

CARPENTER, Steve

Singles: 7-inch

BRUNSWICK (55322 "You're Putting Me On")....20-30 63

SAW DEE (1004 "The Big Hit")....50-100

CARPENTER, Thelma *P&R '60*

Singles: 78 rpm

COLUMBIA (30212 "Melody")....5-10 50

MAJESTIC....5-10 45-46

Singles: 7-inch

CORAL (62241 "Yes, I'm Lonesome Tonight")....8-12 60

CORAL (62255 thru 62287)....10-20 61

CORAL (62303 thru 62332)....8-12 62

LPs: 10/12-inch

CORAL (57433 "Thinking of You Tonight")....15-25 63

(Monaural.)

CORAL (7-57433 "Thinking of You Tonight")....25-35 63

(Stereo.)

CARPENTER, Thelma, With Orchestra / Russell Bennett & His Orchestra

EPs: 7-inch

ROYALE (111 "Show Boat")....10-20 '50s

Also see CARPENTER, Thelma

CARPENTER BROTHERS

Singles: 7-inch

KASH (1023 "I Had a Date")....5-10 65

RIDGECREST (1211 "Don't Cry Little Darling")....500-750

CARPENTERS *P&R/LP '70*

Singles: 7-inch

A&M (Except 2735)....3-6 69-85

A&M (2735 "Yesterday Once More")....10-15 85

(Promotional issue only.)

Picture Sleeves

A&M (Except 2735)....5-12 70-81

A&M (2735 "Yesterday Once More")....10-15 85

(Promotional issue only. With paper sleeve.)

EPs: 7-inch

A&M....10-15 72-85

LPs: 10/12-inch

A&M (3000 series)....8-15 71-85

A&M (4000 series, except 4205)....8-15 70-83

A&M (4205 "Offering")....50-100 69

A&M (4205 "Ticket to Ride")....10-20 71

(Repackage of "Offering.")

A&M (5100 series)....5-8 90

A&M (50000 series)....15-25 74-75

(Quadraphonic series.)

A&M (6000 series)....8-12 85

MFP (50431 "Ticket to Ride")....10-15 70

Members: Karen Carpenter; Richard Carpenter; Tony Peluso.

Also see CARPENTER, Karen

CARPER, Jack

Singles: 78 rpm

TNT (140 "Big Texas")....8-12 56

Singles: 7-inch

TNT (140 "Big Texas")....10-20 56

CARPETBAGGERS

Singles: 7-inch

LTD (407 "Let Yourself Go")....20-30 66

CARPETS

Singles: 78 rpm

FEDERAL....50-75 56

Singles: 7-inch

FEDERAL (12257 "Why Do I")....100-150 56

FEDERAL (12269 "Lonely Me")....100-150 56

Also see CHANDELIERS

CARR, Cathy *P&R '56*
(With Dan Belloc)

Singles: 78 rpm

CORAL....5-10 53-56

FRATERNITY....5-15 55-56

Singles: 7-inch

ABC....4-6 73

COLLECTABLES....3-5 81

CORAL (61092 "I'll Cry At Your Wedding")....15-20 53

CORAL (61646 "I'll Cry At Your Wedding")....10-15 56

FRATERNITY (712 thru 793)....10-20 55-58

LAURIE (3133 thru 3206)....8-12 62-63

LAURIE (3378 "The Ghost of a Broken Heart")....5-10 67

ROULETTE (4107 thru 4383, except 4152)....10-20 58-61

ROULETTE (4152 "I'm Gonna Change Him")....10-20 59

(Monaural.)

ROULETTE (SSR-4152 "I'm Gonna Change Him")....30-40 59

(Stereo.)

SMASH (1726 "Footprints in the Snow") 8-12 61

EPs: 7-inch

BRUNSWICK (71033 "Cathy Carr")....10-20 57

LPs: 10/12-inch

DOT (3674 "Ivory Tower")....15-25 66

(Monaural.)

DOT (25674 "Ivory Tower")....15-25 66

(Stereo.)

FRATERNITY (1005 "Ivory Tower")....50-100 57

ROULETTE (R-25077 "Shy")....30-40 59

(Monaural.)

ROULETTE (SR-25077 "Shy")....40-60 59

(Stereo.)

CARR, Craig

Singles: 7-inch

DOT (16926 "What's Your Game")....15-20 66

CARR, Danny

Singles: 7-inch

A (102 "Too Shy")....10-15 59

ARC (4448 "Too Shy")....15-20 59

(First issue.)

PRINCESS (109 "Ponytail Princess")....10-20 60

CARR, Georgia

Singles: 78 rpm

BIG (602 "Sitting Alone")....5-10 55

Singles: 7-inch

BIG (602 "Sitting Alone")....20-30 55

RENDEZVOUS (121 "Don't Go")....15-20 60

VEE-JAY (667 "Softly")....10-15 65

LPs: 10/12-inch

ROULETTE....10-20

TOPS....10-20

VEE-JAY (1105 "Rocks in My Bed")....15-25 64

CARR, Gunter Lee
(Cecil Gant)

Singles: 78 rpm

DECCA....10-20 50

Singles: 7-inch

DECCA (48167 "Goodnight Irene")....30-40 50

DECCA (48170 "We're Gonna Rock")....30-40 50

Also see GANT, Cecil

CARR, James *P&R/R&B '66*

Singles: 7-inch

ATLANTIC....4-8 71

GOLDWAX....10-20 65-69

LPs: 10/12-inch

GOLDWAX (3001 "You Got My Mind Messed Up")....50-100 67

GOLDWAX (3002 "A Man Needs a Woman")....100-200 68

Also see SOUL STIRRERS

CARR, Joe "Fingers" *P&R '50*
(Lou Busch)

Singles: 78 rpm

CAPITOL....5-10 50-57

Singles: 7-inch
CAPITOL 10-20 50-59
CORAL 5-10 63
DOT 4-8 66
W.B. 5-10 60-62
EPs: 7-inch
CAPITOL 5-15 51-57
LPs: 10/12-inch
CAPITOL (Except 2000 series) 20-40 51-61
CAPITOL (2000 series) 10-15 64
CORAL 10-15 63
DOT 10-15 66
W.B. 10-20 60-62
Also see BUSCH, Lou
Also see CANDIDO, Candy
Also see FORD, Tennessee Ernie, & Joe "Fingers" Carr
Also see YOUNG, Vicki, & Joe Carr

CARR, Leroy
LPs: 10/12-inch
BIOGRAPH 8-12 73
COLUMBIA (1911 "Blues Before Sunrise") 20-30 62
(Monaural.)
COLUMBIA (8511 "Blues Before Sunrise") 25-35 62
(Stereo.)
COLUMBIA (30000 series) 8-10 71

CARR, Linda
(With the Impossibles; with Love Squad)
Singles: 7-inch
BELL (654 "Give Him One More Try") 5-10 66
BELL (658 "Everytime") 5-10 67
DCP (1138 "Baby, Are You Puttin' Me On") 8-12 65
DCP (1151 "Heart Without Love") 10-20 66
RANWOOD 5-10 68
RAY STAR (779 "Shy One") 200-300 61
(White label. Promotional issue only.)
RAY STAR (779 "Shy One") 100-200 61
ROMAR 4-6 72
ROXBURY 4-6 75
SAR (153 "Sweet Talk") 5-10 64
SKYLA (1111 "Happy Teenager") 10-15 61
LPs: 10/12-inch
ROXBURY 8-12 74

CARR, Timmy, & Persianettes
Singles: 7-inch
GUYDEN (2104 "I Could Never Stop Crying") 15-25 64
Also see PERSIANETTES
Also see TIMMY & PERSIANETTES

CARR, Valerie P&R '58
Singles: 7-inch
ATLAS (1258 "Rockin' Bed") 5-10 64
ROULETTE (4038 thru 4365) 10-20 57-61
LPs: 10/12-inch
ROULETTE (25094 "Ev'ry Hour, Ev'ry Day") 30-40 59

CARR, Wynona R&B '57
(Sister Wynona Carr)
Singles: 78 rpm
SPECIALTY 5-15 52-57
Singles: 7-inch
REPRISE (20033 thru 20201) 5-10 61-63
SPECIALTY (575 "Nursery Rhyme Rock") 20-30 56
SPECIALTY (580 "Hurt Me") 25-35 56
SPECIALTY (589 "Should I Ever Love Again") 20-30 56
SPECIALTY (600 "What Do You Know About Love") 25-35 57
SPECIALTY (628 thru 683) 15-25 57-60
SPECIALTY (826 "Did He Die in Vain") 15-25 52
SPECIALTY (834 "A Letter to Heaven") 15-25 52
SPECIALTY (855 "The Ballgame") 15-25 52
LPs: 10/12-inch
REPRISE (6023 "Wild, Wonderful Wynona") 15-25 62
SPECIALTY 8-10 88
Session: Turks.
Also see TURKS

CARRIBEANS
Singles: 7-inch
AMY (871 "Wonderful Girl") 30-40 62
CARRIE 10-15 60

CARRIBIANS
(Coleman Brooks Anderson)
Singles: 7-inch
BROOKS (2000 "Baby") 2000-3000 59
CLIFTON (07 "Baby") 4-6 74

CARRILLO, Martin
Singles: 7-inch
WEST COAST (10001 "Don't Take My Girl") 100-200

CARRINGTON, Curtis
Singles: 7-inch
FURY (1018 "I'm Gonna Catch You") 100-200 58
GEE (1057 "Don't Be a Meanie") 15-25 60

CARRINGTON, Sunny
Singles: 7-inch
DEEP (004 "The Girl That Every Guy Should Know") 10-15

CARROLL, Andrea P&R '63
Singles: 7-inch
BIG TOP (515 "The Doolang") 30-40 64
BIG TOP (3156 "It Hurts to Be Sixteen") 10-20 63
EPIC (9438 "Young and Lonely") 50-100 61
(Yellow label.)
EPIC (9438 "Young and Lonely") 50-75 61
(White label. Promotional issue.)
EPIC (9450 "Please Don't Talk to the Lifeguard") 10-15 61
EPIC (9471 "Gee Dad") 15-20 61
EPIC (9523 "Fifteen Shades of Pink") 15-20 62
RCA (8618 "Sally Fool") 10-20 65
Picture Sleeves
EPIC (9471 "Gee Dad") 25-35 61
RCA (8618 "Sally Fool") 15-25 65
U.A. (982 "The World Isn't Big Enough") 8-15 66
U.A. (50039 "Hey Beach Boy") 8-15 66

CARROLL, Andrea / Beverly Warren
LPs: 10/12-inch
B.T. PUPPY (1017 "Andrea Carroll and Beverly Warren – Side by Side") 50-75 63
Also see CARROLL, Andrea
Also see WARREN, Beverly

CARROLL, Barbara
Singles: 7-inch
KAPP (297 "North By Northwest") 5-10 59
Picture Sleeves
KAPP (297 "North By Northwest") 20-30 59

CARROLL, Bernadette P&R '64
Singles: 7-inch
CLEOPATRA (5 "Heavenly") 4-8
COLLECTABLES 3-5 81
JULIA 10-15 62
LAURIE (3217 "All the Way Home I Cried") 10-15 64
LAURIE (3238 "Party Girl") 10-15 64
LAURIE (3268 thru 3320) 8-12 64-65
Session: 4 Seasons.
Also see 4 SEASONS

CARROLL, Bill
Singles: 7-inch
DIXIE (2010 "Feel So Good") 300-400 58

CARROLL, Bob P&R '53
(With Alvy West & His Orchestra)
Singles: 78 rpm
BALLY 5-10 56-57
CAMDEN 5-10 55
DERBY 5-10 53
MGM 5-10 55
Singles: 7-inch
BALLY 10-20 56-57
CAMDEN (7-19 "Suddenly There's a Valley") 10-20 55
DERBY 10-20 53
DOT 5-10 66
MGM 10-20 55
MURBO 4-8 67
UNART (2012 "I Can't Get You Out of My Heart") 8-12 59
U.A. (129 "Hi Ho Silver") 8-12 58
U.A. (184 "Love in Bloom") 8-12 59
Picture Sleeves
U.A. (129 "Hi Ho Silver") 10-20 58
Also see JENKINS, Gordon, & His Orchestra

CARROLL, Cathy P&R '62
Singles: 7-inch
CHEER (1004 "Deep in a Young Boys Heart") 10-15 63
CHEER (1005 "I'll Be Hurt") 10-15 64
DOT (16908 "I Wish You Were a Girl") 5-10 66
MUSICOR (1056 "Here's to Our Love") 5-10 64
PHILIPS (40134 "I Don't Wanna Give You Up") 5-10 63
TRIODEX (110 "Jimmy Love") 10-15 61
W.B. (5263 thru 5354) 8-12 62-63

CARROLL, Chuck
Singles: 7-inch
HAPPY HEARTS (133 "Mean Ole Blues") 50-75

CARROLL, Diahann
Singles: 78 rpm
RCA 4-8 56
Singles: 7-inch
COLUMBIA 4-6 66-68
DISQUE D-OR 4-6 65
RCA (6391 "Help Yourself") 5-10 56
RCA (6576 "Rebel in Town") 5-10 56
RCA (6767 "Don't Cry Baby") 5-10 56
U.A. 4-8 59-60
EPs: 7-inch
RCA (1-1467 "Sings Harold Arlen") 10-20 57
LPs: 10/12-inch
ATLANTIC 15-25 61
CAMDEN 10-15 62
COLUMBIA 10-15 67
DISQUE D-OR 10-15 65
MOTOWN 5-8 74
RCA (1467 "Dianne Carroll Sings Harold Arlen") 30-40 57
SUNSET 10-15 69
U.A. 10-20 62
VIK (1131 "Best Beat Forward") 20-30 58

CARROLL, Diahann, & Duke Ellington Orchestra
(Conducted by Mercer Ellington)
LPs: 10/12-inch
ORINDA (133 "Tribute to Ethel Waters") 10-20 78
Also see ELLINGTON, Duke

CARROLL, Diahann, & Andre Previn
Singles: 7-inch
U.A. 4-8 60
LPs: 10/12-inch
U.A. 15-25 59-60
Also see CARROLL, Diahann
Also see PREVIN, Andre

CARROLL, Dolores, & Four Tops
(With Maurice King & His Wolverines)
Singles: 78 rpm
CHATEAU (2002 "Everybody Knows") 40-50 56
Singles: 7-inch
CHATEAU (2002 "Everybody Knows") 75-125 56
Also see FOUR TOPS
Also see HAYES, Carolyn, & Four Tops

CARROLL, Don
(With the Sharpies)
Singles: 78 rpm
BATON (230 "Where Do I Stand") 8-12 56
Singles: 7-inch
BATON (230 "Where Do I Stand") 10-20 56
CADENCE (1405 "Seven-Up and Ice Cream Soda") 8-12 61
NRC (039 "Silver Bracelet") 10-15 59
NRC (5005 "Teardrops on Your Letter") 10-20 59
STARS (540 "My Heart") 10-20

CARROLL, Earl, & Original Cadillacs
Singles: 7-inch
JOSIE (829 "Buzz-Buzz-Buzz") 15-25 57
REO (8195 "Buzz-Buzz-Buzz") 15-25 57
(Canadian. One source gives this number as 8199. We're not sure yet which is correct.)
Also see CADILLACS
Also see COASTERS
Also see ORIGINAL CADILLACS
Also see SPEEDO & CADILLACS

CARROLL, Eddie
Singles: 7-inch
FERNWOOD (138 "Golden Door Night Club") 10-15 64
GUYDEN (2046 "Rules of Love") 10-15 61
RU LU (6098 "Where Are You") 20-30 58
SANTO (504 "Wait Eternally") 15-20 62

CARROLL, Evan, & Tempos
Singles: 7-inch
BANGAR (615 "Come Back Baby") 50-75 64

CARROLL, Gregory
Singles: 7-inch
EPIC (9416 "Stand By Me") 10-20 60
OKEH (7129 "Twinkle") 15-25 60

CARROLL, Jack
(With the Joe Leahy Orchestra & Chorus; Jack Carroll & Eliot Glen's Orchestra)
Singles: 78 rpm
UNIQUE (Except 354) 5-10 55-56
UNIQUE (354 "The Story of James Dean") 10-15 56
Singles: 7-inch
CLEF (505 "Pity Me") 10-15
LAURIE (3039 "Goodnight Little Girl of My Dreams") 8-12 59
LAURIE (3046 "Sandy Harbor") 8-12 60
LAURIE (3064 "Sally Come Back") 8-12 60
LAURIE (3273 "Goodnight Little Girl of My Dreams") 5-8 64
LAURIE (3566 "Crazy Over You") 4-6 71
LAURIE (3584 "Wa Wa Time") 4-6 72
TALENT (1002 "In the Still of the Night") 8-12 62
UNIQUE (314 "Sweet Kentucky Rose") 10-20 55
UNIQUE (329 "Why Don't You Call Me") 10-20 56
UNIQUE (354 "The Story of James Dean") 20-30 56
UNIQUE (369 "My Last Night in Rome") 10-20 56
UNIQUE (401 "Don't Look at Me") 10-20 57
VRC (101 "Stop, Listen and Love") 5-10 63

CARROLL, Jack, & Dolly Houston
Singles: 78 rpm
UNIQUE 5-10 56
Singles: 7-inch
UNIQUE (333 "I've Grown Accustomed to Her Face") 10-15 56
Also see CARROLL, Jack

CARROLL, Jimmy
Singles: 7-inch
CAROUSEL (44 "Angelina") 10-15 59
(Monaural.)
CAROUSEL (44 "Angelina") 25-35 59
(Stereo.)
FASCINATION (2000 "Big Green Car") 50-100 58
Picture Sleeves
CAROUSEL (44 "Angelina") 15-25 59
Also see KING, Peggy

CARROLL, Johnny
(With His Hot Rocks)
Singles: 78 rpm
DECCA 25-50 56
PHILLIPS INT'L 50-75 57
SARG 25-50 56
Singles: 7-inch
DECCA (29940 "Rock and Roll Ruby") 50-75 56
DECCA (29941 "Wild, Wild Women") 60-80 56
DECCA (30013 "Hot Rock") 50-75 56
DUCHESS (1018 "The Sally Ann") 10-20 62
PHILLIPS INT'L (3520 "That's the Way I Love") 50-75 57
SARG (144 "I'll Think of You") 40-60 56
W.B. (5042 "Bandstand Doll") 15-25 59
W.B. (5080 "Sugar") 15-25 59
LPs: 10/12-inch
ROLLIN' ROCK 8-12 78

CARROLL, Jona
Singles: 7-inch
SEECO (6065 "I Am in Love") 10-15 60

CARROLL, Linda
Singles: 7-inch
CAMELOT (113 "I Wanna Go Home") 10-20 '60s

CARROLL, Lisa
Singles: 7-inch
KEYMAN (701 "Diamonds and Pearls") 10-15 63

CARROLL, Ruth
Singles: 78 rpm
KING (4873 "Partners for Life") 5-10 56
Singles: 7-inch
KING (4873 "Partners for Life") 20-30 56

CARROLL, Scotty
(With the Metropolitans)

Singles: 7-inch

DUEL (524 "Tell Me More")....5-10 63
GONE (5023 "Heartstrings")....10-15 58
RKO UNIQUE (408 "Two Young Lovers")....10-15 57
VIM (506 "Perfidia")....10-15 60

CARROLL, Toni

Singles: 7-inch

MGM (12808 "My Lover Boy")....10-15 59
MGM (12834 "All Smart Girls")....10-20 59
MGM (12893 "I Wanna Be Loved")....10-20 60
MGM (13184 "Lonely")....5-10 63
MGM (13329 "Welcome Home Baby")....5-10 65

LPs: 10/12-inch

MGM (4063 "Hits of the Roaring '20s")....10-20 62

CARROLL, Wayne

Singles: 78 rpm

KING....50-75 57

Singles: 7-inch

KING (5123 "Chicken Out")....50-75 57
KING (5134 "Rocking Chair Mama")....50-75 57
KING (5146 "He Created")....50-75 57

CARROLL, Yvonne
(Yvonne Caroll)

Singles: 7-inch

CHALLENGE (59275 "A Little Bit of Soap")....15-25 65
CHALLENGE (59297 "Mister Loveman")....15-25 65
DOMAIN (1018 "Gee What a Guy")....10-15 63
DOMAIN (1020 "Earth Angel")....15-20 63
VEE-JAY (592 "There He Goes")....5-10 64

CARROLL BROTHERS — P&R '62

Singles: 7-inch

CAMEO (140 "Red Hot")....50-75 58
CAMEO (213 "Bo Diddley")....8-12 62
CAMEO (221 "Sweet Georgia Brown")....8-12 62
FELSTED (8550 "I Found You")....10-15 59

LPs: 10/12-inch

CAMEO (C-1015 "College Twist Party")....30-40 62
(Monaural.)
CAMEO (SC-1015 "College Twist Party")....40-50 62
(Stereo.)
Members: Pete Carroll; Dick Noble; Kenneth Dorn; Bill McGraw; Jimmy Chick.

CARROLL COUNTY BOYS

Singles: 78 rpm

FLAIR....15-25 53-55

Singles: 7-inch

FLAIR (1001 "Carroll County Blues")....75-100 53
FLAIR (1023 "Carroll County Boogie")....75-100 54
FLAIR (1046 "Eyes of Texas")....75-100 54
Also see CRAYTON, Pee Wee

CARS — P&R/LP '78

Singles: 12-inch

ELEKTRA....5-10 86
(Promotional issues only.)

Singles: 7-inch

ELEKTRA....3-6 78-88

Picture Sleeves

ELEKTRA....3-6 78-88

LPs: 10/12-inch

ELEKTRA (Except 5E-567)....5-10 78-87
ELEKTRA (5E-567 "Shake It Up")....125-150 81
(Picture disc with blank B-side. Promotional issue only. 500 made.)
ELEKTRA (5E-567 "Shake It Up")....150-175 81
(Picture disc with KMET radio logo on B-side. Promotional issue only. 50 made.)
NAUTILUS (14 "The Cars")....20-40 82
(Half-speed mastered.)
NAUTILUS (49 "Candy-O")....20-40 82
(Half-speed mastered.)
Members: Ric Ocasek; Elliot Easton; Benjamin Orr; Greg Hawkes; Dave Robinson.
Also see MILKWOOD
Also see MODERN LOVERS

CARSON, Chuck

Singles: 7-inch

HEP (2142 "Moonlight Rock")....75-125

CARSON, Colleen

Singles: 7-inch

ABBEY (202 "Going, Going, Going")....75-125

CARSON, Don
(With the Whirlaways; with Casuals)

Singles: 7-inch

CREST (1051 "Smoke, Smoke, Smoke")....10-20 58
BERTRAM INT'L (209 "Jungle Bungalow")....20-30 59

CARSON, Eddie
(With Buddy Lucas Orchestra; Big Blues Carson)

Singles: 78 rpm

JOSIE (776 "Jailbird Blues")....10-15 55

Singles: 7-inch

FORTUNE....5-10 63
JOSIE (776 "Jailbird Blues")....20-30 55
M.R.C. (1203 "The Devastating Bombs")....40-60 '60s

CARSON, Joe — C&W '63

Singles: 7-inch

LIBERTY (55547 thru 55664)....5-10 63-64

LPs: 10/12-inch

LIBERTY (3360 "In Memoriam")....20-30 64
(Monaural.)
LIBERTY (7360 "In Memoriam")....30-40 64
(Stereo.)

CARSON, Johnny

LPs: 10/12-inch

COLUMBIA (2199 "Introduction to New York and the World's Fair")....20-30 62

CARSON, Kit — P&R '55

Singles: 78 rpm

CAPITOL (3283 "Band of Gold")....8-10 55

Singles: 7-inch

CAPITOL (3283 "Band of Gold")....10-20 55

CARSON, Martha
(With the Gospel Singers)

Singles: 78 rpm

CAPITOL....5-10 52
RCA....5-10 55-57

Singles: 7-inch

CADENCE (1356 "That Ain't Right")....10-20 59
CAPITOL (2145 "I'm Gonna Walk and Talk with My Lord")....10-20 52
RCA....10-20 55-57
SIMS....4-8 63

LPs: 10/12-inch

CAMDEN....5-10 65
Also see PRESLEY, Elvis / Martha Carson / Lou Monte / Herb Jeffries

CARSON, Vince

Singles: 78 rpm

ESSEX....5-10 56
X (0033 "Mary Lou")....5-10 54

Singles: 7-inch

BLUE BELL (105 "Boulevard of Broken Dreams")....30-40
CHANCELLOR....5-10 62
ESSEX (326 "You Are Mine")....10-20 53
ESSEX (410 "Homesick")....10-20 56
X (0033 "Mary Lou")....10-20 54

CARTER, Anita — C&W '51

Singles: 78 rpm

COLUMBIA....4-8 53-54
RCA....4-8 51-56

Singles: 7-inch

CADENCE (1333 "Blue Doll")....40-60 57
CAPITOL....4-6 71
COLUMBIA....5-10 53-54
JAMIE (1154 "Moon Girl")....4-8 60
JAMIE (1167 "That's All I Want from You")....4-8 60
MERCURY....4-8 63-64
RCA (0426 thru 0493)....10-20 51-53
RCA (6000 series)....8-15 55-56
RCA (8000 & 9000 series)....4-8 66-67
U.A.....4-6 68-69

LPs: 10/12-inch

CAPITOL....8-10 72
MERCURY....15-25 63-64
Also see CARTER FAMILY
Also see CARTER SISTERS
Also see DARRELL, Johnny, & Anita Carter
Also see JENNINGS, Waylon, & Anita Carter
Also see SNOW, Hank, & Anita Carter

CARTER, Ann

Singles: 78 rpm

BLUE LAKE (103 "Lovin' Daddy Blues")....50-100 54

Singles: 7-inch

BLUE LAKE (103 "Lovin' Daddy Blues")....150-300 54

CARTER, Betty
(With Richard Wess & Orchestra)

Singles: 7-inch

ABC-PAR (10184 "My Reverie")....5-10 61
ATCO (6239 "One Note Samba")....5-10 62
ATCO (6254 "The Good Life")....5-10 63

LPs: 10/12-inch

ABC-PAR (363 "Modern Sound of Betty Carter")....15-25 61
ATCO (152 "'Round Midnight")....15-25 63
BET-CAR....10-12 80
COLUMBIA....5-10 80
IMPULSE....8-10 76
ROULETTE....8-10 76
Also see CHARLES, Ray, & Betty Carter
Also see HAMPTON, Lionel

CARTER, Betty, & Ray Bryant

LPs: 10/12-inch

EPIC (3202 "Meet Betty Carter and Ray Bryant")....50-75 56
Also see BRYANT, Ray
Also see CARTER, Betty

CARTER, Bill
(Billy Carter)

Singles: 78 rpm

REPUBLIC....5-10 56

Singles: 7-inch

CHALLENGE (59067 "Latin Lover")....10-20 60
HONEE B (104 "Jailer Man")....10-20 59
OZARK (1234 "Cool Tom Cat")....50-100 59
REPUBLIC (7126 "By the Sweat of My Brow")....15-25 56
SHOWBOAT (1504 "Pony Express")....15-25 60
TALLY (111 "I Wanna Feel Good")....20-30 57
TALLY (115 "I Used to Love You")....20-30 57
Session: A.V. Looper.

CARTER, Bob

Singles: 7-inch

DEN (11229 "Downtown Twist")....50-75 62
DEN (25731 "Every Night")....50-100 61

Picture Sleeves

DEN (11229 "Downtown Twist")....100-150 62
(Fold-out, promotional only sleeve.)

CARTER, Bobby

Singles: 7-inch

CAROLL ("Run Run Run")....50-75
(Selection number not known.)

CARTER, Calvin
(Cal Carter; Cal Carter Singers)

Singles: 7-inch

VEE-JAY (419 thru 439)....5-10 62

LPs: 10/12-inch

VEE-JAY (1041 "Twist Along")....20-30 62
Also see CHANDLER, Gene

CARTER, Cecil "Count"

Singles: 78 rpm

FEDERAL....10-20 53

Singles: 7-inch

FEDERAL (12130 "What's Wrong with Me")....20-30 53
FEDERAL (12135 "I Know, I Know")....20-30 53

CARTER, Clarence — P&R/R&B '67

Singles: 12-inch

ICHIBAN....4-6 88

Singles: 7-inch

ABC....4-6 75-76
ATLANTIC (2461 thru 2660)....5-10 68-69
ATLANTIC (2702 thru 2842)....4-8 70-72
ATLANTIC (13000 series)....3-5
FAME (179 "Put On Your Shoes and Walk")....4-8 73
FAME (250 "Sixty Minute Man")....5-10 73
FAME (330 "I'm the Midnight Special")....4-8 73
FAME (1010 "Tell Daddy")....10-15 67
FAME (1013 "Thread the Needle")....10-15 67
FAME (1016 "Road of Love")....10-15 67
FAME (91006 "Holdin' Out")....4-8 72
FUTURE STARS....3-5
ICHIBAN....3-5 86-92
RONN....4-6 77
VENTURE....3-5 80-81

LPs: 10/12-inch

ABC....8-10 74-76
ATLANTIC....10-20 68-71
BIG C....5-10 83
BRYLEN....5-10 84
FAME....10-12 73
ICHIBAN....5-10 86-88
VENTURE....5-10 80-81

CARTER, Clarence & Candi

Singles: 7-inch

ATLANTIC (2875 "If You Can't Beat 'Em")....4-8 72
Also see CARTER, Clarence

CARTER, Dean
(Dean Carter Sound; Arlie Neaville)

Singles: 7-inch

LIMELIGHT (3019 "Sixteen Tons")....10-15 64
(With Arlie Miller.)
MILKY WAY (003 "Number-One Girl")....250-350 65
(With Arlie Miller, Dave Marten & Kookie.)
MILKY WAY (004 "The Rockin' Bandit")....5-10 65
MILKYWAY (010 "Run Rabbit Run")....40-60 66
(Has Milky Way as "Milkyway" [one word].)
MILKY WAY (011 "Rebel Woman")....40-50 67
TELL INT'L (369 "Mary Sue")....20-40 68
(With Jerry Merritt.)
TELL INT'L (373 "Good Side of My Mind")....75-100 69

Picture Sleeves

TELL INT'L (373 "Good Side of My Mind")....100-125 69
Also see KOOKIE
Also see MARTEN, Dave
Also see MERRITT, Jerry
Also see MILLER, Arlie, & Bullets
Also see NEAVILLE, Arlie

CARTER, Ed
(With the Carterays; Eddie Carter Quartet)

Singles: 78 rpm

GRAND (107 "Take Everything But You")....200-300 54
MGM (11405 "Don't Turn Your Back on Me")....20-30 53
SOUND (105 "Oh Baby")....40-50 54

Singles: 7-inch

GRAND (107 "Take Everything But You")....2000-3000 54
(Reissued as by the Carter Rays.)
MGM (11405 "Don't Turn Your Back on Me")....50-75 53
SOUND (105 "Oh Baby")....75-125 54
Also see CARTER RAYS

CARTER, Fred

Singles: 7-inch

HICKORY (1230 "Take Me As I Am")....20-30 63
LODE (2001 "Freeloader")....50-75 58
MAY (143 "Anna, I Love You")....10-20 63

CARTER, Goree
(With His Hep Cats; Gory Carter)

Singles: 78 rpm

CORAL....20-40 50
FREEDOM....20-40 49-50
MODERN....15-25 51
SITTIN' IN WITH....15-25 50
Also see LITTLEFIELD, Little Willie / Goree Carter
Also see THOMPSON, Rocky

CARTER, Goree / Clarence Samuels

Singles: 78 rpm

BAYOU (010 "Drunk Or Sober")....10-20 53

Singles: 7-inch

BAYOU (010 "Drunk Or Sober")....50-75 53
Also see CARTER, Goree
Also see SAMUELS, Clarence

CARTER, Harold, & Dixie Rhythmaires
(Harry Carter)

Singles: 7-inch

MAR-VEL (1300 "Jump Baby Jump")....300-500 57
MAR-VEL (1301 "You Made Me Love You")....50-75 57
ZAP (1001 "Jump Baby Jump")....50-75

CARTER, James
(With the Sentimentals; with Twilights; with Tuxedo Sleepers)

Singles: 7-inch

TUXEDO (922 "I Know")....100-150 57
(Title shown in large print.)
TUXEDO (922 "I Know")....15-25 '60s
TUXEDO (938 "I Want to Love You")....50-75 60
Also see NICHOLS, Ann, & Sentimentals
Also see SENTIMENTALS

CARTER, James "Sweet Lucy," & His Orchestra

Singles: 78 rpm

20TH CENTURY (20-51 "Mean Red Spider")....500-1000 47
Session: Muddy Waters.
Also see WATERS, Muddy

CARTER, Jean

Singles: 7-inch

DECCA (31965 "Like One")....35-55 66
SUNFLOWER (101 "I Bet You")....25-50

CARTER, Jimmy

Singles: 7-inch

HANOVER (4508 "Let Me Know")....10-15 58

CARTER, Jimmy, & Dollettes

Singles: 7-inch

CAYCE (2002 "I'll Never Let You Go")....20-30

CARTER, Joe L.
(With Johnnie M. Matthews)

Singles: 7-inch

AUDREY (112 "My Life Story")....10-20

CARTER, Kenny
(With Barbara Webb Singers)

Singles: 7-inch

JOLA....8-10
RCA (8791 "I've Gotta Find Her")....15-25 66
RCA (8841 "I've Got to Get Myself Together")....15-25 66
RCA (8970 "Don't Go")....10-20 66
RENEE (3001 "Why Do You Have to Go")...4-6
U.A. (308 "Hey Lover")....15-25 61

CARTER, Lynda

Singles: 7-inch

EPIC....3-5 78

LPs: 10/12-inch

EPIC (KE-35308 "Portrait")....8-12 78
EPIC (JE-35308 "Portrait")....75-100 78
(Picture disc. 1000 made.)

CARTER, Martha

Singles: 7-inch

RON (336 "Nobody Knows")....10-15 60
RON (339 "One Man's Woman")....10-15 61
RON (346 "You Shall Not Be Moved")....10-15 62
Also see NELSON, Martha

CARTER, Mel *P&R/R&B '63*

Singles: 7-inch

ABKCO....3-5 84
AMOS (120 "San Francisco Is a Lonesome Town")....5-8 69
AMOS (132 "This Is My Life")....4-8 70
AMOS (139 "Kiss Tomorrow Goodbye")....4-8 70
ARWIN (23 "I'm Coming Home")....10-20 60
BELL (743 "Didn't We")....5-8 68
BELL (775 "Another Saturday Night")....5-8 69
CREAM (8041 "You Changed My Life Again")....3-5 81
CREAM (8143 "Who's Right, Who's Wrong")....3-5 81
DERBY (1003 thru 1008)....10-15 63-64
EMI (83 "Hold Me, Thrill Me, Kiss Me")....3-5 '80s
IMPERIAL (045 "Hold Me, Thrill Me, Kiss Me")....5-8 67
IMPERIAL (66052 thru 66208)....5-10 64-66
LIBERTY (1 "The Star Spangled Banner").8-12 67
(Promotional issue only.)
LIBERTY (55970 thru 56015)....4-8 67-68
MERCURY (71893 "I Need You So")....5-10 62
MERCURY (71998 "What Will I Tell My Heart")....5-10 62
PRIVATE STOCK....4-6 75-76
ROMAR (711 "Do Me Wrong")....4-6 73
ROMAR (716 "Treasure of Love")....4-6 74
TRI-STATE....15-20 59

LPs: 10/12-inch

AMOS (7010 "This Is My Life")....10-15 70
DERBY (702 "When a Boy Falls in Love")....50-100 63
IMPERIAL (9289 "Hold Me, Thrill Me, Kiss Me")....15-25 65
(Monaural.)
IMPERIAL (9300 "My Heart Sings")....15-25 65
(Monaural.)
IMPERIAL (9319 "Easy Listening")....15-25 66
(Monaural.)
IMPERIAL (12289 "Hold Me, Thrill Me, Kiss Me")....15-25 65
(Stereo.)
IMPERIAL (12300 "My Heart Sings")....15-25 65
(Stereo.)
IMPERIAL (12319 "Easy Listening")....15-25 66
(Stereo.)
LIBERTY (3530 "Be My Love")....10-20 67
(Monaural.)
LIBERTY (7530 "Be My Love")....10-20 67
(Stereo.)
SUNSET (5227 "Mel Carter")....10-15 68

CARTER, Mel / Vic Dana

EPs: 7-inch

ROWE/AMI....5-10 '60s
(Colored vinyl. Juke box issue.)
Also see DANA, Vic

CARTER, Mel, & Clydie King

Singles: 7-inch

PHILIPS (40049 "Who Do You Love")....5-10 62
Also see CARTER, Mel
Also see KING, Clydie, & Sweet Things

CARTER, Melvin

Singles: 7-inch

PEACOCK (1956 "I'll Be True to You")....10-20 67

CARTER, Nelson
(With His Guitar)

Singles: 78 rpm

SITTIN' IN WITH (557 "My Baby Left Me")....20-30 50

CARTER, Pat

Singles: 7-inch

LIBERTY (55471 "Lover Doll")....8-12 62
MIRA (201 "Lost and Lonely")....5-10 65
7 ARTS (702 "What Should I Do")....10-20 61

CARTER, Prince
(Sonny Bono)

Singles: 7-inch

GO (711 "Mr. Pawnshop")....10-20 61
Also see SONNY

CARTER, Sonny

Singles: 78 rpm

KING....15-25 54

Singles: 7-inch

CARLTON (481 "Crying, Crying Over You"....15-25 58
DOT (15921 "Crying, Crying Over You")..10-15 59
KING (4739 "There Is No Greater Love").20-30 54
KING (4756 "It's Strange But True")....20-30 54

CARTER, Tal

Singles: 78 rpm

COMBO (29 "Echo Blues")....10-15 54

Singles: 7-inch

COMBO (29 "Echo Blues")....20-25 54

CARTER, Tom, & Ramrods

Singles: 7-inch

CARRAM (106 "El Cumbanchero")....10-20 '60s
NORTHWAY SOUND (1005 "Flyin' Saucer Twist")....10-20 62

CARTER, Tommy

Singles: 7-inch

GAYNOTE (106 "Please Find My Love")....400-500 61

CARTER, Woody, & Hoedown Boys *C&W '49*

Singles: 78 rpm

LUCKY....10-15 52
MACY'S (101 "Only You")....10-15 49

Singles: 7-inch

MACY'S (101 "Only You")....20-25 49

CARTER FAMILY *P&R '28/C&W '72*

Singles: 78 rpm

BANNER....15-25 35
BLUEBIRD....15-25 '30s
DECCA....10-20 '30s
ELEKTRADISK....25-50 32-33
(Made for sale through Woolworth Stores.)
MONTEGOMERY WARD....15-25 '30s
VICTOR (20000 series)....50-150 28
VICTOR (40000 series)....25-75 28
VOCALION....25-35

Singles: 7-inch

COLUMBIA....4-8 66-67
LIBERTY (55501 "Fourteen Carat Nothing")....5-10 62

EPs: 7-inch

ACME....25-50 '50s
DECCA....10-20 65

LPs: 10/12-inch

ACME (1 "All Time Favorites")....100-200 '50s
ACME (2 "In Memory of A.P. Carter: Keep On the Sunny Side")....100-200 '50s
ANTHOLOGY OF COUNTRY MUSIC....10-15
COLUMBIA ("CL" & "CS" series)....10-20 64-67
DECCA (4404 "Carter Family")....20-30 63
DECCA (4557 "More Favorites")....20-30 65
CAMDEN (586 "Original and Great Carter Family")....15-20 62
CAMDEN (2473 thru 0501)....5-10 71-74
COLUMBIA ("KC" & "PC" series)....5-10 72-82
HARMONY (7280 "Famous Carter Family")....15-25 61
HARMONY (7300 "Carter Family")....15-25 63
HARMONY (7344 "Home Among the Hills")....15-25 65
HARMONY (7396 "Sacred Songs")....10-15 66
HARMONY (7422 "Country Sounds")....10-20 67
HARMONY (11000 series)....10-15 69-70
J.E.M.F.....10-15
LIBERTY (3230 "Carter Family Album")....15-25 62
(Monaural.)
LIBERTY (7230 "Carter Family Album")....25-35 62
(Stereo.)
OLD HOMESTEAD....5-8
OLD TIME CLASSICS....5-10
PICKWICK....5-10 75
PINE MOUNTAIN....8-10
RCA (Except 2772)....5-15 75-78
RCA (2772 "Mid the Green Fields of Virginia")....15-25 63
STARDAY (248 "Echoes")....15-25 63
SUNSET....10-15 67
Members: A.P.; Sara; Maybelle; Anita; June; Helen; Joe; Janette; Carlene.
Session: Johnny Cash.
Also see CARTER, Anita
Also see CARTER SISTERS
Also see CASH, Johnny, & Carter Family
Also see HAGGARD, Merle

CARTER KIDS

Singles: 7-inch

GAMBLER (1638 "Gotta Rock")....75-125

CARTER RAYS

Singles: 78 rpm

GONE....100-200 57
GRAND....50-100 54
LYRIC....200-300 57

Singles: 7-inch

COLLECTABLES....3-5 81
GONE (5006 "My Secret Love")....200-300 57
(First issue.)
GRAND (107 "Take Everything But You")....200-300 54
(Previously issued as by the Ed Carter Quartet.)
LYRIC (2001 "My Secret Love")....500-750 57
MALA (433 "Keep Listening to Your Heart")....30-40 61
Also see CARTER, Ed
Also see MANN, Gloria, & Carter Rays

CARTER SISTERS
(With Mother Maybelle)

Singles: 78 rpm

COLUMBIA....5-10 52-53
RCA....5-10 50-51

Singles: 7-inch

COLUMBIA....10-15 52-53
RCA....10-15 50-51
Members: Anita; June; Helen.
Also see CARTER, Anita
Also see CARTER FAMILY

CARTEY, Ric

Singles: 78 rpm

RCA....50-100 56-57
STARS (539 "Oooh-Eee")....50-75 56

Singles: 7-inch

ABC-PAR....4-8 63
NRC (503 "Scratching on My Screen").150-200 58
RCA (6751 "Oooh-Eee")....50-75 56
RCA (6828 "Heart Throb")....50-75 57
RCA (6920 "Born to Love One Woman")....75-100 57
RCA (7011 "My Babe ")....75-100 57
STARS (539 "Oooh-Eee")....75-100 56

CARTEY, Ric / Paul Evans

EPs: 7-inch

RCA (DJ-73 "Heart Throb")....100-150 57
(Promotional issue only. Not issued with cover.)
Also see CARTEY, Ric
Also see EVANS, Paul

CARTHAYS

Singles: 7-inch

TAG (446 "So Bad")....10-15 61
(Blue label.)
TAG (446 "So Bad")....15-20 61
(Red label.)

CARUSO, Dick

Singles: 7-inch

MGM (12811 thru 13052, except 12852).10-15 59-61
MGM (12852 "If I")....40-50 59

CARVELLS

Singles: 7-inch

LU PINE (104 "He's So Fine")....10-15 62

CARVELS

Singles: 7-inch

TWIRL (2002 "Don't Let Him Go")....10-15 63
TWIRL (2022 "Seventeen")....5-10 66

CARVER SMITH HIGH COMBO

Singles: 7-inch

VARSITY (79 "Cry for Love")....75-100

CARVETTES

Singles: 7-inch

COPA (200-1 "Lover's Prayer")....600-800 59

CARYL, Naomi

Singles: 78 rpm

EMBER....10-15 56

Singles: 7-inch

EMBER (1006 "If You Want to Be My Baby")....20-30 56
Session: Five Satins
Also see FIVE SATINS

CASAL, Carlos, Jr.

Singles: 7-inch

EMGE (1005 "Don't Meet Mr. Frankenstein")....10-15 58

CASANOVA, Jimmy

Singles: 7-inch

FELSTED (8572 "If It Wasn't for the Kids")....10-15 59

CASANOVA, Tony

Singles: 7-inch

AMERICAN INT'L (533 "Diary of a Highschool Bride")....10-15 59
CHARIOT (1001 "My Little Nancy")....20-30
CREST (1053 "Yea! Yea! Come Another Day")....30-50 58
DORE (535 "Boogie Woogie Feeling")...50-100 59

CASANOVA JR.

Singles: 78 rpm

PORT (7001 "Sally Mae")....40-60 57

Singles: 7-inch

PORT (7001 "Sally Mae")....50-75 57

CASANOVA II

Singles: 7-inch

EARLY BIRD (49658 "We've Got to Keep On")....10-20 '60s

CASANOVAS

Singles: 78 rpm

APOLLO....50-75 55-57

Singles: 7-inch

APOLLO (471 "That's All")....100-150 55
APOLLO (474 "It's Been a Long Time")....100-150 55
APOLLO (477 "I Don't Want You to Go")....150-250 55
APOLLO (483 "My Baby's Love")....100-150 55
APOLLO (519 "Please Be Mine")....150-200 57
APOLLO (523 "Good Lookin' Baby")....150-200 57

CASANOVAS

Singles: 7-inch

PLANET (1027 "In the Land of Dreams")....250-350 62

CASASSA, Tommy
Singles: 7-inch
VALLI (103 "Three Rows Over") .... 10-20 '60s

CASCADES *P&R/R&B/LP '63*
Singles: 7-inch
ABC 3-6 73
ARWIN (132 "Cheryl's Goin' Home") 5-10 66
ARWIN (134 "Midnight Lace") 5-10 66
C-R-C (1018 "She Was Never Mine") 8-12 64
CANBASE (714 "Sweet America") 4-8 72
CHARTER (1018 "She Was Really Never Mine") 8-12 64
CHARTER (1018 "She Was Never Mine") .5-10 64
(Note shorter title.)
COLLECTABLES 3-5 81
GOLDIES 45 .... 3-6 73
LIBERTY (55822 "She'll Love Again") 5-10 65
LONDON (177 "Two Sided Man") 4-8 72
McCORMICK (105 "Pains in My Heart") .. 10-15 64
PROBE (453 "Two Sided Man") 8-10 68
RCA (8206 "Cinderella") 5-10 63
RCA (8268 "For Your Sweet Love") 5-10 63
RCA (8321 "Those Were the Good Old Days") 5-10 64
RCA (8402 "I Dare You to Try") 5-10 64
RENEE (105 "Pains in My Heart") 5-10 64
SMASH (2083 "Hey Little Girl of Mine") 5-8 67
SMASH (2101 "Flying on the Ground") 5-8 67
UNI (55152 "Maybe the Rain Will Fall") 5-8 69
UNI (55169 "Indian River"/"Big City Country Boy") 5-8 69
UNI (55169 "Indian River"/"Floatin' Down the River") 4-8 69
(Note different flip side.)
VALIANT (702 "Rhythm of the Rain") 5-8 65
VALIANT (6021 "There's a Reason") 10-15 62
VALIANT (6026 "Rhythm of the Rain") 5-10 62
VALIANT (6028 "Shy Girl") 5-10 63
VALIANT (6032 "My First Day Alone") 8-12 63
W.B. 3-6
Picture Sleeves
PROBE (453 "Two Sided Man") 10-15 68
RCA (8206 "Cinderella") 15-25 63
LPs: 10/12-inch
BLOSSOM 10-15
CASCADES (6820 "What Goes on Inside the Cascades") 20-35
UNI (73069 "Maybe the Rain Will Fall") ... 15-20 69
VALIANT (W-405 "Rhythm of the Rain") . 40-60 63
(Monaural.)
VALIANT (WS-405 "Rhythm of the Rain") 50-100 63
(Stereo.)
Members: John Gummoe; David Stevens; David Zabo; Eddie Snyder; David Wilson.
Also see VON GAYELS
Also see YOUNG, Neil

CASCADES / Sir Douglas Quintet
Singles: 7-inch
TRIP .... 4-6 '70s
Also see CASCADES
Also see SIR DOUGLAS QUINTET

CASE, Allen
(With Ray Conniff & His Orchestra)
Singles: 78 rpm
COLUMBIA (40585 "Watch Out") 5-10 55
Singles: 7-inch
COLUMBIA (40585 "Watch Out") 15-25 55
COLUMBIA (40872 "Me Too") 10-15 57
COLUMBIA (40977 "A New Town Is a Blue Town") 10-15 57
GOTHIC (002 "She's My Love") 5-10 61
LPs: 10/12-inch
COLUMBIA (1406 "Deputy Sings") 15-20 59
(Monaural.)
COLUMBIA (8202 "Deputy Sings") 20-25 59
(Stereo.)
Also see CONNIFF, Ray

CASE, Jimmy
Singles: 7-inch
WILCO (114 "High School Hall of Fame") 50-100

CASEY, Al *P&R/R&B '62*
(Al Casey Combo; with the K-C Ettes; with His Sextet)
Singles: 78 rpm
DOT 20-30 56-57
MCI 10-20 55
Singles: 7-inch
BLUE HORIZON (925 "Cookin'") 20-30 62
(First issue.)
DOT (15524 "A Fool's Blues") 10-20 56
DOT (15563 "Guitar Man") 15-25 57
HIGHLAND (1002 "Got the Teenage Blues") 50-75 59
HIGHLAND (1004 "Night Beat") 15-25 60
LIBERTY (55117 "Willa Mae") 30-50 58
MCI (1004 "Pink Panther") 15-25 55
STACY (925 thru 971, except 962) 10-20 61-64
STACY (962 "Surfin' Hootenanny") 10-20 63
(Black vinyl.)
STACY (962 "Surfin' Hootenanny") 25-50 63
(Colored vinyl.)
U.A. (158 "Stinger") 10-20 59
U.A./STACY (494 "Jivin' Around") 10-20 62
LPs: 10/12-inch
STACY (100 "Surfin' Hootenanny") 40-60 63
(Black vinyl.)
STACY (100 "Surfin' Hootenanny") 150-200 63
(Green vinyl.)
Also see CLARK, Sanford
Also see COLE, Don, & Al Casey
Also see CRITERIONS
Also see EDDY, Duane
Also see HONEYS
Also see PRICE, Sam
Also see RAINTREE COUNTY SINGERS
Also see REYNOLDS, Jody
Also see ROGERS, Frantic Johnny
Also see ROLLER, Lonesome Long John / Ned Mullan
Also see SHARPE, Ray
Also see STORMS

CASEY, Al / Benny Goodman & His Orchestra
Singles: 78 rpm
CAPITOL 5-10 51
Singles: 7-inch
CAPITOL 10-15 51
Also see CASEY, Al
Also see GOODMAN, Benny, Orchestra

CASEY, Patti
Singles: 78 rpm
VITA (136 "Unkind Heart") 10-15 56
Singles: 7-inch
HOLLYWOOD (503 Crossroads of Life") ... 8-12 60
VITA (136 "Unkind Heart") 20-30 56

CASH, Alvin *P&R '65*
(With Crawlers; with Registers)
Singles: 7-inch
CHESS 4-8 70
COLLECTABLES 3-5 81
DAKAR 4-6 76
ERIC 3-6 73
MAR-V-LUS 8-12 64-67
SEVENTY SEVEN 4-6 72
SOUND STAGE 7 .... 8-12 73
TODDLIN' TOWN 5-10 68-69
TRIP 4-6
WESTBOUND 4-6 70
XL ("Twine Time") 20-30 65
(Selection number not known.)
LPs: 10/12-inch
MAR-V-LUS 15-20 65
SOUND STAGE 7 .... 10-15 73

CASH, Bobby
Singles: 7-inch
KING (5844 "Teen Love") 10-20 64
KING (5864 "It's Only Make Believe") 10-20 64
KING (5894 "Answer to My Dreams") 10-20 64
EPs: 7-inch
KING (25327 "Bobby Cash") 10-15 80
(Bonus EP, packaged with the various artists, Elvis sound-alikes LP, *The Other Kings*, [Revival 002]. Not issued with special cover.)

CASH, Eddie
(With the Cashiers)
Singles: 7-inch
PEAK (1001 "Doing All Right") 100-125 58
PEAK (1010 "Come On Home") 50-100 60
ROULETTE (4380 "Lonely Island") 10-20 61
TODD (1057 "Livin' Lovin' Temptation") ... 15-25 60

CASH, Johnny *C&W '55*
(With the Tennessee Two; with Tennessee Three; with Gene Lowery Singers; with Rosey Nix)
Singles: 78 rpm
SUN (221 thru 302) 20-40 55-58
SUN (309 "It's Just About Time") 30-50 58
SUN (316 "Luther Played the Boogie") .. 50-100 59
Singles: 7-inch
CACHET (4506 "Wings in the Morning") 3-5 80
COLUMBIA (02189 thru 05896) 3-5 81-86
COLUMBIA (10011 thru 11424) 3-6 74-81
COLUMBIA (30427 "Five Feet High and Rising") 15-25 59
(Stereo Seven single.)
COLUMBIA (30843 "Loading Coal") 15-25 60
(Stereo Seven single.)
COLUMBIA (30844 "Lumberjack") 15-25 60
(Stereo Seven single.)
COLUMBIA (30846 "Boss Jack") 15-25 60
(Stereo Seven single.)
COLUMBIA (30847 "Run Softly, Blue River") 15-25 60
(Stereo Seven single.)
COLUMBIA (4-41251 "All Over Again") 10-15 58
COLUMBIA (4-41313 "Don't Take Your Guns to Town") 10-15 59
COLUMBIA (4-41371 "Frankie's Man, Johnny") 10-15 59
COLUMBIA (4-41427 "Five Feet High and Rising") 10-15 59
COLUMBIA (4-41481 "The Little Drummer Boy") 10-15 59
COLUMBIA (4-41618 "Seasons of My Heart") 10-15 60
COLUMBIA (4-41707 "Second Honeymoon") 10-15 60
COLUMBIA (3-41804 "Loading Coal") 15-25 60
(Compact 33 single.)
COLUMBIA (4-41804 "Loading Coal") 10-15 60
COLUMBIA (4-41920 "Girl in Saskatoon") 10-15 61
COLUMBIA (3-41995 "The Rebel – Johnny Yuma") 15-25 61
(Compact 33 single.)
COLUMBIA (4-41995 "The Rebel – Johnny Yuma") 8-12 61
COLUMBIA (3-42147 "Tennessee Flat-Top Box") 15-25 61
(Compact 33 single.)
COLUMBIA (4-42147 "Tennessee Flat-Top Box") 10-15 61
COLUMBIA (3-42301 "The Big Battle") 15-25 62
(Compact 33 single.)
COLUMBIA (4-42301 "The Big Battle") 8-12 62
COLUMBIA (3-42425 "In the Jailhouse Now") 15-25 62
(Compact 33 single.)
COLUMBIA (4-42425 "In the Jailhouse Now") 8-12 62
COLUMBIA (3-42512 "Bonanza") 15-25 62
(Compact 33 single.)
COLUMBIA (4-42512 "Bonanza") 8-12 62
COLUMBIA (3-42615 "Were You There") 15-25 62
(Compact 33 single.)
COLUMBIA (4-42615 "Were You There") .. 8-12 62
COLUMBIA (42665 "Busted") 5-10 63
COLUMBIA (42788 "Ring of Fire") 5-10 63
COLUMBIA (42880 "The Matador") 5-10 63
COLUMBIA (42964 "Understand Your Man") 5-10 64
(Black vinyl.)
COLUMBIA (42964 "Understand Your Man") 15-25 64
(Green vinyl. Promotional issue only.)
COLUMBIA (43058 "Ballad of Ira Hayes") . 5-10 64
(Black vinyl.)
COLUMBIA (43058 "Ballad of Ira Hayes") 15-25 64
(Red vinyl. Promotional issue only.)
COLUMBIA (43145 "It Ain't Me Babe") 5-10 64
(Black vinyl.)
COLUMBIA (43145 "It Ain't Me Babe") 15-25 64
(Red vinyl. Promotional issue only.)
COLUMBIA (43206 thru 46028) 4-8 65-74
COLUMBIA (60516 "The Baron") 3-5 81
COLUMBIA BOOK/RECORD LIBRARY ("The Bug That Tried to Crawl Around the World") ...... 4-8 '60s
COLUMBIA HALL OF FAME 4-8 59-64
SSS/SUN (1103 "Get Rhythm") 5-10 69
(Black vinyl.)
SSS/SUN (1103 "Get Rhythm") 10-15 69
(Gold vinyl. Promotional issue.)
SSS/SUN (1111 "Rock Island Line") 5-10 70
(Black vinyl.)
SSS/SUN (1111 "Rock Island Line") 10-15 70
(Gold vinyl. Promotional issue.)
SSS/SUN (1121 "Big River") 5-10 70
(Black vinyl.)
SSS/SUN (1121 "Big River") 10-15 70
(Gold vinyl. Promotional issue.)
SCOTTI BROS 3-5 82
SUN (221 "Cry! Cry! Cry!") 30-40 55
SUN (232 "So Doggone Lonesome") 30-40 55
SUN (241 "I Walk the Line") 30-40 56
SUN (258 "There You Go") 30-40 56
SUN (266 "Next in Line") 30-40 57
SUN (279 "Home of the Blues") 30-40 57
SUN (283 "Ballad of a Teenage Queen") . 30-40 57
SUN (295 "Guess Things Happen That Way") 30-40 58
SUN (302 "The Ways of a Woman in Love") 15-25 58
SUN (309 "It's Just About Time") 15-25 58
SUN (316 "Luther Played the Boogie") 15-25 59
SUN (321 "Katy Too") 15-25 59
SUN (331 "Goodbye Little Darlin' ") 15-25 59
SUN (334 "Straight A's in Love") 15-25 60
SUN (343 "The Story of a Broken Heart") 15-25 60
SUN (347 "Mean Eyed Cat") 15-25 60
SUN (355 "Oh Lonesome Me") 15-25 61
SUN (363 "Sugartime") 15-25 61
SUN (376 "Blue Train") 15-25 62
SUN (392 "Wide Open Road") 15-25 64
Picture Sleeves
CACHET (4506 "Wings in the Morning") 3-5 80
COLUMBIA (10000 series) 4-6 79
COLUMBIA (41000 series) 10-20 58-61
COLUMBIA (42000 series) 5-15 61-64
COLUMBIA (44000 series) 5-10 68
SUN (295 "Guess Things Happen That Way") 15-25 58
EPs: 7-inch
COLUMBIA (2155 "Johnny Cash Sings The Rebel – Johnny Yuma") 20-30 59
COLUMBIA (12531/2/3 "Fabulous Johnny Cash") 20-30 58
(Price is for any of three volumes.)
COLUMBIA (12841 /2/3 "Hymns By Johnny Cash") 15-25 59
(Price is for any of three volumes.)
COLUMBIA (13391/2/3 "Songs of Our Soul") 20-30 59
(Price is for any of three volumes.)
COLUMBIA (14631/2/3 "Now There Was a Song") 20-30 60
(Price is for any of three volumes.)
COLUMBIA (12531 "Fabulous") 20-30 58
SUN (111 "Johnny Cash Sings Hank Williams") 25-35 58
SUN (112 "Johnny Cash") 25-35 58
SUN (113 "Johnny Cash") 25-35 58
SUN (114 "Johnny Cash with the Tennessee Two") 25-35 58
SUN (116 "Johnny Cash") 25-35 58
SUN (117 "Johnny Cash") 25-35 58
LPs: 10/12-inch
AMERICAN .... 8-10 '90s
BLAINE HOUSE 6-12
(Mail order offer.)
BUCKBOARD 5-10
CBS 5-10 82
CACHET 5-10
COLUMBIA (29 "The World of Johnny Cash") 8-12 70
COLUMBIA (363 "Legends and Love Songs") 10-15 68
(Columbia Record Club issue.)
COLUMBIA (1200 thru 1799) 15-30 58-61
(With "CL" prefix. Monaural.)
COLUMBIA (8100 thru 8599) 20-40 58-61
(With "CS" prefix. Stereo.)
COLUMBIA (1800 thru 2650) 10-20 62-68
(With "CL" prefix. Monaural.)
COLUMBIA (2004 "The Heart of Johnny Cash") .... 15-25 '60s
(Columbia Star Series.)

COLUMBIA (8600 thru 9478) 10-20 62-68
(With "CS" prefix. Stereo.)
COLUMBIA (9726 "Holy Land") 35-50 69
(With 3-D cover.)
COLUMBIA (9726 "Holy Land") 10-20 69
(Standard cover.)
COLUMBIA (9827 thru 9943) 8-12 69-70
COLUMBIA (10000 series) 5-10 73
COLUMBIA (30000 thru 38000 series) 5-15 70-82
COLUMBIA SPECIAL PRODUCTS 5-10 75
COLUMBIA/SUFFOLK 8-10 79
DESIGN 5-8
DORAL 20-40
(Promotional mail-order LP from Doral cigarettes.)
HARMONY 8-12 69
IMPERIAL HOUSE 5-10
(Mail order offer.)
LONGINES 5-8
(Mail order offer.)
MERCURY 5-10 87
OUT OF TOWN DIST 5-10 82
PICKWICK .... 5-10 '70s
POWER PAK 5-10
PRIORITY 5-10 81-82
SSS/SUN 5-15 69-84
(Some may be colored vinyl.)
SHARE 5-10
STACK-O-HITS 5-8
SUN (1220 "Johnny Cash and His Hot and Blue Guitar") 20-40 56
SUN (1235 "Songs That Made Him Famous") 20-40 58
SUN (1240 "Greatest") 20-30 59
SUN (1245 "Johnny Cash Sings Hank Williams and Other Favorite Tunes") 15-25 60
SUN (1255 "Now Here's Johnny Cash") .. 15-25 61
SUN (1270 "All Aboard the Blue Train") .. 15-25 63
SUN (1275 "Original Sun Sound of Johnny Cash") 15-25 64
SUN/CAPITOL (90000 series) .... 15-20 '60s
(Record club issues.)
SUNRISE MEDIA 5-10 81
SUNNYVALE 5-8
TIME-LIFE ("Johnny Cash") 10-15 82
(Three-disc set.)
TRIP 8-10 74
U.A. 10-12 68
Session: George Jones; Marty Robbins; Waylon Jennings.
Also see HARRIS, Emmylou
Also see JONES, George
Also see KILGORE, Merle
Also see RICH, Charlie
Also see ROBBINS, Marty / Johnny Cash / Ray Price
Also see STATLER BROTHERS
Also see TUBB, Ernest

CASH, Johnny, & June Carter
(Johnny Cash & June Carter Cash) *C&W '64*
Singles: 7-inch
COLUMBIA (10000 series) 4-6 76
COLUMBIA (43145 thru 45929) 4-8 64-73
LPs: 10/12-inch
COLUMBIA (9500 series) 10-20 64-67
COLUMBIA (32000 series) 5-10 73
HARMONY 6-10 72
Also see JENNINGS, Waylon, Willie Nelson, Johnny Cash, & Kris Kristofferson

CASH, Johnny, & Carter Family
(Carter Family with Johnny Cash) *C&W '63*
Singles: 7-inch
COLUMBIA 4-8 63-72

CASH, Johnny, Carter Family & Oak Ridge Boys *C&W '73*
Singles: 7-inch
COLUMBIA 4-6 73
Also see CARTER FAMILY
Also see OAK RIDGE BOYS

CASH, Johnny, & Mother Maybelle Carter *C&W '73*
Singles: 7-inch
COLUMBIA 4-6 73
Also see CARTER FAMILY

CASH, Johnny, Rosanne Cash & Everly Brothers *C&W '89*
Singles: 7-inch
MERCURY (872 420-7 "Ballad of a Teenage Queen") 3-5 89
Also see EVERLY BROTHERS

CASH, Johnny / Roy Clark / Linda Ronstadt
LPs: 10/12-inch
POINTED STAR (10178 "Concert Behind Prison Walls") 10-15 78
(NAPA special products TV soundtrack.)
Also see CASH, Rosanne
Also see CLARK, Roy
Also see RONSTADT, Linda

CASH, Johnny / Billy Grammer / Wilburn Brothers
LPs: 10/12-inch
PICKWICK/HILLTOP 10-15 65
Also see GRAMMER, Billy

CASH, Johnny, & Waylon Jennings *C&W '86*
Singles: 7-inch
COLUMBIA 3-6 78-86
EPIC 3-5 80
Also see JENNINGS, Waylon

CASH, Johnny / Jerry Lee Lewis / Jeanie C. Riley
LPs: 10/12-inch
PICKWICK .... 5-10 '70s

CASH, Johnny, Carl Perkins & Jerry Lee Lewis
LPs: 10/12-inch
COLUMBIA 5-10 82
Also see PERKINS, Carl, Jerry Lee Lewis, Roy Orbison & Johnny Cash

CASH, Johnny / Jeanie C. Riley
LPs: 10/12-inch
LONGINES (5283-5287 "Born to Sing") ... 20-30 '70s
(Boxed, 5-disc set.)
LONGINES (5288 "Rock Island Line") .... 5-8 '70s
(Mail order offer.)
Also see RILEY, Jeanie C.

CASH, Johnny, & Hank Williams Jr. *C&W '88*
Singles: 7-inch
MERCURY 3-5 88
Also see WILLIAMS, Hank, Jr.

CASH, Johnny / Tammy Wynette
LPs: 10/12-inch
COLUMBIA (5418 "King & Queen") 10-15
(Columbia Musical Treasury issue.)
Also see CASH, Johnny
Also see WYNETTE, Tammy

CASHER, Billy
Singles: 7-inch
EPIC (9478 "Give Her Back") 20-30 61

CASHMERES
Singles: 78 rpm
HERALD 30-50 56
MERCURY 30-50 54-55
Singles: 7-inch
ACA (1216 "Stairsteps to Heaven") 75-150 59
HERALD (474 "Little Dream Girl") 50-75 56
(Black vinyl.)
HERALD (474 "Little Dream Girl") 75-150 56
(Brown vinyl. Promotional issue only.)
MERCURY (70501 "My Sentimental Heart") 50-75 54
MERCURY (70617 "Don't Let It Happen Again") 50-75 55
MERCURY (70679 "There's a Rumor") 50-75 55
Members: Glover Mitchell; Henry Boyd; Romeo Schuler; Ralph Riley; Mark Allan.

CASHMERES
Singles: 7-inch
JOSIE (894 "Where Have You Been") 15-25 62
LAKE (703 "Four Lonely Nights") 20-30 60
LAKE (705 "Satisfied") 8-12 60
LAURIE (3078 "A Very Special Birthday") 15-25 61
LAURIE (3088 "I Gotta Go") 10-20 61
LAURIE (3105 "Poppa Said") 10-20 61
RELIC (1005 "Satisfied") 5-10 65
Members: Windsor King; Bill Jordan; Robert Bowers; Jean Reeves; Neta Arnold.
Also see ROYAL SONS QUINTET
Also see KING & SHARPETTES

CASHMERES
Singles: 7-inch
HEM (1000 "Show Stopper") 400-500 65

CASHMERES
Singles: 7-inch
HUBBA HUBBA (100 "Back to School Again") 400-500 65

CASINOS
Singles: 7-inch
CASINO (111 "My Love for You") 50-150 60
DEL VAL (1002 "Everybody Can't Be Pretty") 15-20
MASKE (803 "I'm Falling") 200-300 59

CASINOS
Singles: 7-inch
ALTO (2002 "I Like It Like That") 10-15 61
S&G (301 "Please Let Her") 75-125 62

CASINOS *P&R/LP '67*
(Gene Hughes & Casinos; with Saturns; Casino's)
Singles: 7-inch
ABC 4-6 73
AIRTOWN (002 "That's the Way") 10-15 67
BUCCANEER (3000 "Then You Can Tell Me Goodbye") 30-40 66
(First issue.)
CAROL (201 "Wisdom of a Fool") 4-6 80
CAROL (1001 "You Belong to Me") 4-6 80
CERTRON (10015 "Coal River") 5-8 70
COLLECTABLES 3-5 81
FRATERNITY 6-12 65-71
ITZY (2 "Do You Recall") 10-20 66
MILLION (13 "Angels Are All Asleep") 5-8 72
NAME (001 "Do You Recall") 200-300 62
OLIMPIC (251 "Do You Recall") 50-75 65
(Re-recording of Name release.)
TERRY (115 "Gee Whiz") 30-40 64
TERRY (116 "Too Good to Be True") 10-20 64
TRIP 4-6
U.A. (50255 "Here I Am") 5-10 68
LPs: 10/12-inch
FRATERNITY (1019 "Then You Can Tell Me Goodbye") 20-30 67
Members: J.T. Sears; Pete Bolton; Mickey Denton; Gene Hughes; Pete Bolton; Denny Frecke; Joe Patterson; Ray White; Tommy Matthews; Bob Armstrong; Bill Hawkins.
Also see DENTON, Mickey

CASLONS *P&R '61*
Singles: 7-inch
AMY (836 "For All We Know") 10-20 62
SEECO (6078 "Anniversary of Love") 30-40 61
Also see ZEE, Lani

CASPER, Bobby
Singles: 7-inch
ARGO (5342 "Lovin' Honey") 10-15 59

CASRI, Marty
Singles: 7-inch
SPOTLIGHT ("So Long Sandy") 50-75
(No selection number used.)

CASS, Aubrey
Singles: 7-inch
HELTON ("Corn Fed Gal") 50-75
(Selection number not known.)

CASS, Bob
Singles: 7-inch
RBC (100 "Corvette Baby") 50-75

CASSELL, Tommy
Singles: 7-inch
CASSELL (1343 "Go On Ahead") 200-300
CASSELL (58-3 "Rockin' Rollin' Stone") 250-350

CASSELLE, Mai, & Spaceriders
Singles: 7-inch
HALF-PEACH (500 "Don't Deceive Me") . 50-75

CASSIDY, David *P&R '71*
Singles: 7-inch
BELL 5-10 71-74
FLASHBACK 4-6 73
MCA (41101 "Hurt So Bad") 4-6 79
RCA 4-6 75-77
Picture Sleeves
BELL (45150 "Cherish") 6-12 71
BELL (45187 "Could It Be Forever") 6-12 72
MCA (41101 "Hurt So Bad") 6-10 79
LPs: 10/12-inch
BELL 10-15 72-74
RCA 8-12 74-76
Also see PARTRIDGE FAMILY

CASSIDY, Ted
("Ted Cassidy as Lurch [of TV's Addams Family] with the Music of Gary Paxton")
Singles: 7-inch
CAPITOL (5503 "The Lurch") 10-15 65
Picture Sleeves
CAPITOL (5503 "The Lurch") 15-25 65
Also see PAXTON, Gary

CASSIDY SISTERS
(With the Titanics)
Singles: 7-inch
HOP (505 "Stardust Waltz") 15-25 58

CAST OF THOUSANDS
Singles: 7-inch
AMY (11040 "Long Way to Go") 10-20 68
AMY (11056 "Country Gardens") 10-20 69
SOFT (1002 "Have It Your Way") 20-30 67
TOWER (276 "Girl") 15-25 66
Member: Stevie Ray Vaughan
Also see VAUGHAN, Stevie Ray

CASTALEERS
("With Rhythm Accompaniment"; "Solo - Richard A. Jones")
Singles: 7-inch
DONNA (1349 "That's Why I Cry") 15-25 61
FELSTED (8504 "Come Back") 50-75 58
FELSTED (8512 "Lonely Boy") 40-60 58
FELSTED (8585 "You're My Dream") 40-60 59
PLANET (44 "That's Why I Cry") 30-50 60
Member: Richard A. Jones.

CASTANETS
Singles: 7-inch
TCF (1 "I Love Him") 15-25 64

CASTAWAYS
Singles: 78 rpm
EXCELLO (2038 "I Wish") 10-15 54
Singles: 7-inch
EXCELLO (2038 "I Wish") 15-25 54

CASTAWAYS
Singles: 7-inch
ASSAULT (1869 "I Found You") 15-25 63

CASTAWAYS
Singles: 7-inch
WITCH (124 "Don't You Just Know It") 20-25 64

CASTAWAYS *P&R '65*
Singles: 7-inch
APEX 12-18 65
BEAR (2000 "Feel So Fine") 25-35 67
COLLECTABLES 3-5 81
ERA 4-6 72
ERIC 3-5 78
FONTANA 12-18 68
LANA 4-6 64
SOMA (Except 1461) 8-12 65
SOMA (1461 "Girl in Love") 15-25 67
TAUNAH (7745 "I Feel So Fine") 15-25 67
TERRIFIC 4-8
EPs: 7-inch
SOMA (03 "Liar Liar") 10-20
(Reportedly 500 made.)
Members: Merlin Dean; Richard Robey; Robert Folschon; Ron Hensley; James Donna; Dennis Craswell.
Also see BLACKWOOD APOLOGY
Also see CROW

CASTAWAYS
Singles: 7-inch
HEARTBEAT (0010 "The Girl Next Door") 10-20
PIT (100,001 "If Our Love Is Strong") 15-25
SMOKE (215 "Love Me Baby") 25-35
TORNADO 15-20

CASTAWAYS FIVE
Singles: 7-inch
RAOL (001 "Revenge") 15-20

CASTELLES
(George Grant & Castelles)
Singles: 78 rpm
ATCO (6069 "Happy and Gay") 25-35 56
GRAND (Blue label).......................... 200-400 54
GRAND (Yellow label) 100-200 54
Singles: 7-inch
ATCO (6069 "Happy and Gay") 50-75 56
CLASSIC ARTISTS (114 "One Little Teardrop") 40-50 89
(Black vinyl. Has CAR-1035 in vinyl trailoff. 40 made.)
CLASSIC ARTISTS (114 "One Little Teardrop") 5-8 89
(Black vinyl. Remastered version. Has CAR-1035-RE in vinyl trailoff. 1000 made.)
CLASSIC ARTISTS (114 "One Little Teardrop")...8-10 89
(Red vinyl. 1000 made.)
CLASSIC ARTISTS (126 "Surrender to Love")..5-8 91
(Red vinyl. 1000 made.)
CLASSIC ARTISTS (128 "Heaven's for Real") 4-6 91
(Red vinyl. 1000 made.)
COLLECTABLES 3-5 81
GRAND (101 "My Girl Awaits Me") .. 1500-2000 53
(Glossy blue label. Reportedly 600 made.)
GRAND (101 "My Girl Awaits Me") 750-1000 53
(Flat blue label.)
GRAND (101 "My Girl Awaits Me") 150-250 53
(Yellow label. Rigid disc. No company address shown.)
GRAND (101 "My Girl Awaits Me") 30-40 61
(Yellow label. Flexible disc. No company address shown.)
GRAND (101 "My Girl Awaits Me") .... 15-25 '60s
(Yellow label. Company address is shown.)
GRAND (103 "This Silver Ring") 750-1000 54
(Glossy yellow label. Rigid disc. No company address shown.)
GRAND (103 "This Silver Ring") 40-50 61
(Yellow label. Flexible disc. No company address shown.)
GRAND (103 "This Silver Ring") .... 15-25 '60s
(Yellow label. Company address is shown.)
GRAND (105 "Do You Remember") 500-750 54
(Glossy yellow label. Rigid disc. No company address shown.)
GRAND (105 "Do You Remember") 40-50 61
(Yellow label. Flexible disc. No company address shown.)
GRAND (105 "Do You Remember") .... 15-25 '60s
(Yellow label. Company address is shown.)
GRAND (109 "Over a Cup of Coffee").. 1000-1500 54
(Blue label.)
GRAND (109 "Over a Cup of Coffee"). 250-500 '50s
(Glossy yellow label. Rigid disc. No company address shown.)
GRAND (109 "Over a Cup of Coffee")... 50-100 61
(Yellow label. Flexible disc. No company address shown.)
GRAND (109 "Over a Cup of Coffee")..... 15-25 '60s
(Yellow label. Company address is shown.)
GRAND (114 "Marcella") 2000-2500 54
(Cream color label. Rigid disc. No company address shown.)
GRAND (114 "Marcella") 50-100 61
(Yellow label. Flexible disc. No company address shown.)
GRAND (114 "Marcella") .... 15-25 '60s
(Yellow label. Company address is shown.)
GRAND (122 "Heavenly Father")..... 1000-2000 55
(Cream color label. Rigid disc. No company address shown.)
GRAND (122 "Heavenly Father")........... 50-100 61
(Yellow label. Flexible disc. No company address shown.)
GRAND (122 "Heavenly Father")............ 15-25 '60s
(Yellow label. Company address is shown.)
LOST NITE...4-6 '70s
Note: Not all of the Grand variations may exist with all of their titles; however, they are listed in case they do exist.
Members: George Grant; Frank Vance; William Taylor; Ron Everett; Octavius Anthony; Walt Miller; Clarence Scott.

CASTELLS *P&R '61*
Singles: 7-inch
COLLECTABLES ("Castells") 5-10 81
(Selection number not known.)
COLLECTABLES ("Castells") 10-15 82
(Picture disc.)
DECCA...5-10 65-66
ERA (3038 "Little Sad Eyes")...................15-25 61
ERA (3048 thru 3107)...............................10-20 61-63
LAURIE (3444 "Rocky Ridges")................15-20 68
U.A. (50324 "Two Lovers")..........................5-10 68
W.B. (5421 "I Do")......................................40-60 64
W.B. (5445 "Could This Be Magic")............8-12 64
W.B. (5486 "Love Finds a Way")................8-12 64
LPs: 10/12-inch
ERA (EL-109 "So This Is Love") 50-100 62
(Monaural.)
ERA (ES-109 "So This Is Love")...........100-150 62
(Stereo.)
Members: Chuck Girard; Bob Ussery; Joe Kelly; Tom Hicks.
Also see WILSON, Brian

CASTELS
Singles: 7-inch
BLACK GOLD (306 "Save a Chance") 20-40
SOLOMON (1351 "In a Letter to Me") 10-20 67
WILDFIRE ("Save a Chance") 20-40
(Selection number not known. Different version than on Black Gold.)

CASTINOS
(Castino's)
Singles: 7-inch
C&M (440 "Loapin") 10-20 58

CASTLE, Ann
Singles: 7-inch
X-POWER (1001 "Just a Line")................50-75 59
X-POWER (1002 "Go Get the Shotgun, Grandpa") 50-75 59

CASTLE, Birdie
(Birdie Castle Quartet; with Stardusters)
Singles: 7-inch
JET (101 "Play the Fool")........................50-75 57
MUSIC CENTER (6001 "Goodbye, So Long, I'm Gone")..5-8 65
PORT (70005 "Crazy Beat")......................15-25 58

CASTLE, Joey
(With the Daddy-O's)
Singles: 7-inch
HEADLINE (1008 "Rock n' Roll Daddy-O")...150-200 59
RCA (7283 "That Ain't Nothin' But Right") 50-75 58
Also see RIVERS, Cliff

CASTLE, Roy
Singles: 7-inch
PHILIPS (40065 "Lonesome Cup of Coffee")..5-10 62
LPs: 10/12-inch
PHILIPS (200057 "Newcomer") 10-20 63
(Monaural.)
PHILIPS (600057 "Newcomer") 15-25 63
(Stereo.)
REPRISE (6107 "Garry Moore Presents Roy Castle")..10-20 64

CASTLE, Tony
(With the Raiders)
Singles: 7-inch
EAST WEST (107 "Terry") 15-25 58
GONE (5099 thru 5107)............................10-15 61
TREY (3002 "The Fool")...........................10-15 60

CASTLE SISTERS *P&R '62*
(With the Billy Mure Orchestra)
Singles: 7-inch
ROULETTE (4157 thru 4274) 8-12 59-60
TERRACE (7506 thru 7517).......................8-12 62-63
TRIODEX (108 thru 111) 8-12 61
Picture Sleeves
TERRACE (7506 "Wishing Star")..............15-25 62
Also see MURE, Billy

CASTLEBERRY, Leo
Singles: 7-inch
UNITED SOUTHERN ARTISTS (101 "Teenage Blues") 30-40 61

CASTLES
Singles: 7-inch
TRIBUTE (100 "I Was a Fool")...............75-125 61

CASTLE-TONES
(With Jimmy Johnson's Band; Castlestones)
Singles: 7-inch
FIREFLY (321 "We Met at a Dance") 4-6 74
(Black vinyl.)
FIREFLY (321 "We Met at a Dance") 5-10 74
(Red vinyl.)
RIFT (103 "Goodnight")..............................50-75 61
(Blue label. Selection number is in vinyl trail-off.)
RIFT (502 "Goodnight")..........................100-125 59
(Pink label.)
RIFT (504 "We Met at a Dance") 75-125 59

CASTON, Bobbe
Singles: 7-inch
ATLAS (1103 "Call Me Darling")..............40-60 58

CASTON, Willie
(With the Ever Ready Gospel Singers)
Singles: 78 rpm
ABBOTT (149 "I Claim Jesus") 10-15 53
Singles: 7-inch
ABBOTT (149 "I Claim Jesus")..................15-25 53

CASTOR, Jimmy *P&R/R&B '66*
(Jimmy Castor Bunch; Jimmy Caster Quintet)
Singles: 12-inch
SALSOUL (403 "It's Just Begun")...............4-6 83
Singles: 7-inch
ATLANTIC..4-6 74-78
CAPITOL..4-8 68-69
CATAWBA (05676 "Godzilla") 3-5 85
CLOWN..5-10 62
COMPASS (7019 "Sister Soul")...................4-8 68
COTILLION 3-5 79
DECCA..5-10 66
DREAM 3-5 84-85
DRIVE 3-5 78
HULL (758 "Poor Loser")..........................10-20 63
JET SET..5-10 65
KINETIC 4-6 70
LM (542 "Don't Cry Out Loud") 5-8 81
LONG DISTANCE 3-5 80
RCA...4-6 71-73
SALSOUL...3-5 82-83
SLEEPING BAG 3-5 88
SMASH..5-10 66-67
LPs: 10/12-inch
ATLANTIC..8-10 74-77
COTILLION 5-10 79
DREAM (6001 "Return of Leroy")..............5-10 83
DRIVE 5-10 78
LONG DISTANCE (1201 "C") 5-10 80
PAUL WINLEY...5-15
RCA...10-15 72-75
SMASH..15-20 67
Members: Jimmy Castor; Gerry Thomas; Doug Gibson; Lenny Fridie Jr.; Harry Jensen; Bobby Manigault.
Also see CLINTONIAN CUBS
Also see JOEY & TEENAGERS
Also see LYMON, Lewis, & Teenchords

CASTOR, Jimmy / Joey & Teenagers / Sherman Garnes
LPs: 10/12-inch
CRYSTAL BALL (104 "Jimmy Castor Remembers Yesterday")..10-15 82
(Black vinyl. 1000 made.)
CRYSTAL BALL (104 "Jimmy Castor Remembers Yesterday")..25-35 82
(Colored vinyl. 25 made.)
CRYSTAL BALL (104 "Jimmy Castor Remembers Yesterday")..55-65 82
(Picture disc. No cover. 25 made.)

CASTOR, Jimmy, & Juniors
Singles: 78 rpm
ATOMIC 75-150 57
WING...50-75 56
Singles: 7-inch
ATOMIC (100 "This Girl of Mine")........400-600 57
WING (90078 "I Promise to Remember")..75-150 56
Also see CASTOR, Jimmy

CASTRO, Bernadette
Singles: 7-inch
COLPIX (747 "Sports Car Sally").............10-20 64
(Previous editions showed this as first being issued as Colpix 163. We have since learned that number is for a Del Marino release.)
COLPIX (759 "Get Rid of Him") 10-20 64
Also see BERNADETTE
Also see MARINO, Del

CASTRO, Frankie
Singles: 78 rpm
MERCURY (70873 "Too Much")................8-12 56
WING 5-10 55-56
Singles: 7-inch
MERCURY (70873 "Too Much").............15-25 56
RKO UNIQUE (396 "Is There Someone for Me")..10-20 57
WHITEHALL (30001 "That's the Way Love Goes")..10-15 59
WING 10-20 55-56

CASTRO, Vince
Singles: 7-inch
APT (25007 "Bong Bong") 10-15 58
APT (25025 "Cause I Love You")............15-25 59
APT (25047 "You're My Girl") 8-12 60
DOE (102 "Bong Bong"/"You're My Girl")...75-100 58
(First issue.)
ORCHID (660 "I Feel So Grand") 10-20 60
Session: Tonettes.
Also see TONETTES

CASTROES
Singles: 7-inch
COLLECTABLES 3-5 81
GRAND (2002 "Dearest Darling").........200-300 59

CASTROS
Singles: 7-inch
LASSO (501 "Lucky Me")......................500-750 59
(Reportedly 100 made.)
LASSO (502 "In My Dreams") 1000-1500 59
(Reportedly 100 made.)

CASUAL CRESCENDOS
Singles: 7-inch
MRC (12001 "Wish That You Were Here")..400-500 63
Also see CRESCHENDOS

CASUAL THREE
Singles: 7-inch
LUNIVERSE (109 "Invisible Thing") 20-30 58
MARK-X (7009 "Candy Store Blues") 30-40 58
Also see GOODMAN, Dickie

CASUALAIRS
Singles: 7-inch
AUTUMN (21 "Just for You") 15-25 65
MONA-LEE (136 "At the Dance")............30-40 59

CASUAL-AIRES
Singles: 7-inch
BRUNSWICK (55064 "Thunderbird") 10-15 58
C.B. (5001 "Cruising") 10-15 63
CRAIG (5001 "Cruising")...........................30-40 62
ENTERPRISE (1000 "The Millionaire") 40-50 63

CASUALS
Singles: 78 rpm
DOT..5-10 57
Singles: 7-inch
BLACK HAWK 3-5
DOT..10-15 57
NU-SOUND (801 "My Love Song for You")..30-40 57

CASUALS
Singles: 7-inch
KEM (2755 "Beautiful Friendship")...........15-25 57

CASUALS
Singles: 7-inch
SCOTTY (628 "Darling, Do You Love Me") 150-250 59

CASUALS
("Vocal Joe Hoffman")
Singles: 7-inch
MOONBEAM (71613 "Some Day") 25-35 63

CASUALTONES
Singles: 7-inch
SUCCESS (102 "The Very End") 10-15 63

CASWELL, Johnny *P&R '63*
Singles: 7-inch
DECCA (32017 "I.O.U.") 50-75 66
LUV (250 "Faces")......................................8-12 67
SMASH 5-10 63-64

CAT MOTHER P&R/LP '69
(With the All Night News Boys)
Singles: 7-inch
POLYDOR....4-6 69-72
LPs: 10/12-inch
POLYDOR....20-30 69-73
Members: Steve Davidson; Michael Equine; Roy Michaels; Charlie Prichard; Bob Smith.

CATALANAS
Singles: 7-inch
WONDER (14 "Why Oh Why")....200-300

CATALANO, Vinny
Singles: 7-inch
HAMMER (6312 "Rags to Riches")....30-40 63
Also see ALLEN, Ray
Also see KENNY & WHALERS
Also see LOVE NOTES
Also see MASCOTS
Also see ROYAL JACKS

CATALINA SIX
Singles: 7-inch
FLAGSHIP (126 "Moon 2000")....20-30 62
FLAGSHIP (127 "It Had to Rain")....20-30 62

CATALINAS
Singles: 7-inch
JAYNE....4-8 73
LITTLE (811 "Give Me Your Love")....100-200 58
Members: Jimmy Colwell; Johnny Luth; Johnny Kunz; Artie DeNicholas; Tom Juliano.
Also see VAN DYKES

CATALINAS
Singles: 7-inch
GLORY (285 "Marlene")....20-30 58

CATALINAS
Singles: 7-inch
BACK BEAT (513 "Speechless")....75-100 58
CRYSTAL BALL (135 "That Lucky Old Sun")....4-8 80
(500 made.)

CATALINAS
Singles: 7-inch
FORTUNE (535 "Long Walk")....10-15 60

CATALINAS
("Featuring Bob Meyer")
Singles: 7-inch
CATALINAS (16560 "Hey Little Girl")....10-20 82
DOMINANT....8-15
RITA (1006 "Ring of Stars")....15-25 60
S.E.I. (16535 "Tick Tock")....20-30 64
SCEPTER (12188 "Tick Tock")....8-15 67
SUGARBUSH....4-6 75
SUMMERTIME SOUNDS (15 "Tick Tock")....15-25 '60s
ZEBRA (101 "Hey Little Girl")....75-125 61
LPs: 10/12-inch
CATALINAS....5-10 82
Members: Bob Meyer; Tommy Black; Reggie Smith; Buddy Emmerke; Johnny Wyatt; Jack Stallings; O.C. Gravitte; Johnny Edwards; Tom Plyler; Sidney Smith; Rob Thorne; Bobby Pace; Gary Barker; Ken Carriker; Mike Hewat; Mike Suddreth; Earl Dawkins; Mark Goins; Bobby Nantz; Rex Cole.

CATALINAS
Singles: 7-inch
20TH FOX (286 "Sweetheart")....10-20 61
20TH FOX (299 "Safari")....10-20 62

CATALINAS
(Golden Catalinas)
Singles: 7-inch
CUCA (1094 "War Party")....10-20 62
KNIGHT (101 "Come to Me")....15-25 65
MEAN MT. (1422 "Dee Dee")....3-5 82
MUNDO (1000 "Hey Little Girl")....75-125 63
SARA (6392 "By My Window")....15-20 63
TARGET (101/102 "Varsity Club Song"/"Can Your Monkey Do the Dog")....15-25 66
TEE PEE (117/118 "Dee Dee"/"Mojo Workin' ")....15-25 67
Picture Sleeves
MUNDO (1000 "Hey Little Girl")....8-12 63
Members: Al Posniak; Harry Wheelock; Bob Dix; Jim Kelly; Roger Loos; Pete Sorce; Judy Lee Reeths; Denny Noie.
Also see NOIE, Denny
Also see SOURCE, Pete

CATALINAS
Singles: 7-inch
DEE JAY (1010 "Bail Out")....40-60 63
RIC (113 "Banzai Washout")....20-30 64
RIC (164 "Surfer Boy")....20-30 65
SIMS (134 "Bail Out")....15-25 63
LPs: 10/12-inch
RIC (1006 "Fun, Fun, Fun")....30-50 64
Members: Tommy Tedesco; Steve Douglas; Hal Blaine; Leon Russell; Billy Strange; Jerry Cole; Bruce Johnston.

CATALINAS
Singles: 7-inch
DIAL (3008 "Echo One")....5-10 63
MILLION (77 "Stormy Weather")....30-40 63
(Yellow vinyl.)
ORIGINAL SOUND (48 "Your Tender Lips")....15-20 64
PAGODA....5-10 68

CATALINAS
Singles: 7-inch
FOOTNOTE (707 "The Wonder of Love")....20-30

CATALINAS
Singles: 7-inch
NOVART (25 "My Misery")....75-125

CATALINAS
Singles: 7-inch
SOUNDCRAFT ("My Darling")....15-25
(Selection number not known.)

CATAMORANDS
Singles: 7-inch
DGMR (101 "Over You")....20-30

CATES, Ronnie
Singles: 7-inch
TERRACE (7501 "Long Time"/"Ol' Man River")....75-125 61
(Black label.)
TERRACE (7508 "Long Time"/"For My Very Own")....100-150 62
(White label.)
Session: Travellers.
Also see TRAVELLERS

CATHEY, Bob
Singles: 7-inch
CLEF (11078 "Johnny B. Goode")....50-75

CATHEY, Frank
Singles: 7-inch
CATHEY (201 "My Rock and Roll Daddy")....100-200

CATHY JEAN P&R '61
(With the Roomates; Cathy Jean / Roomates)
Singles: 7-inch
ERIC....4-6 73
PHILIPS (40014 thru 40143)....10-15 62
QUALITY (1251 "Please Love Me Forever")....10-20 61
(Canadian.)
VALMOR (007 "Please Love Me Forever")....15-25 60
VALMOR (009 thru 016)....10-20 61-62
Picture Sleeves
VALMOR (007 "Please Love Me Forever")....100-150 60
(Title sleeve. Promotional issue only.)
LPs: 10/12-inch
VALMOR (78 "Great Oldies")....400-600 61
(Repackage of 789.)
VALMOR (789 "At the Hop")....400-600 61
(Repackaged as *Great Oldies.*)
Also see ROOMATES

CATS
Singles: 78 rpm
FEDERAL....10-20 55
Singles: 7-inch
FEDERAL (12238 "I Don't Care No More")....50-75 55
FEDERAL (12248 "You're So Nice")....30-40 55
Members: Gene Ford; Bill Boyd.

CATS & FIDDLE
Singles: 78 rpm
BLUEBIRD....20-30 39-42
DECCA....10-20 50
GOTHAM....15-25 49-50
MANOR....15-25 45-48
MONTGOMERY WARD....15-25
RCA....10-20 46-50
REGIS....15-25 45
Singles: 7-inch
DECCA (48151 "Wine Drinker")....100-200 50
LPs: 10/12-inch
RCA....10-12 76
Members: Austin Powell; Jim Henderson; Ernie Price; Chuck Barksdale; Tiny Grimes; Shirley Moore; Herb Miles; Johnny Davis.
Also see POWELL, Austin

CATS & FIDDLE / Four Clefs
Singles: 78 rpm
RCA....50-100 50
Singles: 7-inch
RCA (0077 "I Miss You So"/"Dig These Blues")....300-500 50
(Cherry red vinyl.)
RCA (4393 "I Miss You So")....100-150 50
(Black vinyl.)
Also see CATS & FIDDLE
Also see FOUR CLEFS

CATTIVA, Savina / Marvels
Singles: 7-inch
PYRAMID (6210/6211 "Hallelulu-la"/"Guiding Angel")....200-300 62
(The only copy of this we've seen is a promotional only issue that combines two "A-sides." We do not yet know the B-side titles of the two commercial issues, 6210 and 6211, being promoted.)
Also see SEDAKA, Neil / Marvels

CAULSTON, Jerry
Singles: 7-inch
CHRISTY (131 "Bon Bon Baby")....10-15 60

CAUSEY, Sam
(With the Southlanders)
Singles: 7-inch
DEB (1007 "Janie")....10-20 59
SCOTTIE (1308 "I Ran All the Way Home")....10-20 59

CAUTIONS
Singles: 7-inch
IKON (113 "Groovin' ")....15-25 63
SHRINE (104 "Watch Your Step")....150-250 65
SHRINE (115 "No Other Way")....400-500 66
TORÉ (1010 "On Our Way to School")....75-125 59
Member: Joe Clyburn.

CAVA, Jim
Singles: 7-inch
ROYALTY (1011 "Humpty Dumpty Heart")....30-40 '60s

CAVALIER, Johnny
Singles: 7-inch
HI CLASS (105 "Rockin' Chair Roll")....30-45 59
Picture Sleeves
HI CLASS (105 "Rockin' Chair Roll")....40-50 59

CAVALIERS
Singles: 7-inch
APT (25004 "Dance, Dance, Dance")....15-25 58
Also see STEVENS, Scott

CAVALIERS
Singles: 7-inch
MUSIC WORLD (101 "Magic Age of Sixteen")....30-40 63
NRC (028 "Charm Bracelet")....20-30 59

CAVALIERS
Singles: 7-inch
TEL (1006 "I Wanna Dance")....25-35 59

CAVALIERS
Singles: 7-inch
CORAL (62245 "Teen Fever")....8-12 61
GALENA....10-20 60
Also see NASH, Lloyd, & Cavaliers

CAVALIERS
Singles: 7-inch
ASKEL (12 "Crazy Guitar")....10-20 '60s
GUM (1002 "I Wanna Know")....10-15 62
GUM (1004 "The Right Time")....10-15 62

CAVALIERS
Singles: 7-inch
RCA (9054 "Hold on to My Baby")....20-30 66
RCA (9321 "I Really Love You")....10-20 67

CAVALIERS
Singles: 7-inch
CUCA (1437 "Cavalier's Twist")....10-20 68

CAVALIERS QUARTET
Singles: 78 rpm
ATLAS (1031 "You Thrill Me")....250-350 53
Members: Lester Gardner; Cecil Holmes; Ron Anderson; Lowe Murray.
Also see CHANCES
Also see FI-TONES

CAVALLARO, Carmen P&R '45
Singles: 78 rpm
DECCA....3-6 45-57
Singles: 7-inch
DECCA....4-8 50-61
EPs: 7-inch
DECCA (Except 844)....5-10 50-59
DECCA (844 "The Eddy Duchin Story")....20-30 56
(Boxed three-disc set.)
LPs: 10/12-inch
DECCA (Except "Eddy Duchin Story")....10-20 50-61
DECCA (DL-8289 "Eddy Duchin Story")....25-35 56
(Soundtrack. Monaural.)
DECCA (DL7-8289 "Eddy Duchin Story") 25-30 59
(Soundtrack. Stereo.)
DECCA (8396 "Eddy Duchin Story")....60-75 56
(Soundtrack. Also has music from three other shows.)
DECCA (DL-9121 "Eddy Duchin Story")....10-15 65
(Soundtrack. Monaural.)
DECCA (DL7-9121 "Eddy Duchin Story") 10-15 65
(Soundtrack. Stereo.)
VOCALION....10-15 59
Also see CROSBY, Bing

CAVALLARO, Carmen, Featuring Al Cernick
Singles: 78 rpm
DECCA (24330 "Dream Girl")....15-25 48
DECCA (24410 "Evelyn")....15-25 48
DECCA (24488 "Ah, But It Happens")....15-25 48
Also see CAVALLARO, Carmen
Also see MITCHELL, Guy

CAVALLO, Jimmy
(With His House Rockers; with His Quintet; Jimmy Cavello)
Singles: 78 rpm
BSD....50-100 51
CORAL....10-20 56-57
Singles: 7-inch
BSD (1004 "I Got Eyes for You")....400-500 51
BSD (1005 "Rock the Joint")....200-300 51
CORAL (61689 thru 61919)....20-30 56-57
DARCY (5001 "Fanny Brown")....50-75 61
LITTLE STAR (129 "Fanny Brown")....10-15 63
ROMAR (4035/4036 "Hold Me in Your Arms")....8-12 '60s
SUNNYSIDE (3105 "Don't Move Me No More")....10-20 59
Also see FREED, Alan

CAVANAUGH, Page
(Page Cavanaugh Trio)
Singles: 78 rpm
HUB OF HOLLYWOOD....25-35 54
Singles: 7-inch
HUB OF HOLLYWOOD (1107 "The Tropicana")....35-45 54
LPs: 10/12-inch
TIME (2121 "Softly")....10-15 64
(Monaural.)
TIME (52121 "Softly")....15-20 64
(Stereo.)
TOPS (1523 "Page Cavanaugh")....30-40 56
Members: Dave Parazzo; Jack Smolley.

CAVAZOS, Buddy, & Epics
Singles: 7-inch
DANTE (3005 "Answer Me")....40-50 60

CAVE DWELLERS
Singles: 7-inch
JIM-KO (41085 "Run Around")....15-25 65

CAVE DWELLERS
Singles: 7-inch
ABC-PAR (10735 "Sinking Feeling")....10-20 65
BAY TOWN (003 "Meditation")....10-20 68

CAVE MEN

Singles: 7-inch

CHELLE (148 "It's Trash") 25-35 66

CAVELL, Marc
(With the Classmates)

Singles: 7-inch

CANDIX (322 "That's All I Want") 10-20 61
CANDIX (329 "I Didn't Lie") 30-40 62
WESBURN (1000 "School Day Romance") 15-25 60

CAVEMEN

Singles: 7-inch

CAPITOL STAR ARTIST (18285 "All About Love") 15-25 66
(Identification number shown since no selection number is used.)
Members: Al Cretacci Jr.; Jim Crouse; Skip Maciezewski; Ron Gorski; Joey Calato.

CAVEMEN

Singles: 7-inch

20TH FOX (6643 "Small World") 10-20 66
Members: Vic Rose; Hector Sorano; Eddie Reyes; Willy Reyes; Len Szczesny.

CAVEMEN

LPs: 10/12-inch

ART (7594 "Looking for a Break") .... 15-25 '70s
(Includes insert.)

CAVER, Bobby

Singles: 7-inch

CORAL (62337 "Roller Coaster") 20-30 62

CAY, Phil
(With the Blue Notes; with the Chantels)

Singles: 7-inch

HART (1001 "Meet Me in the Barnyard") 100-150 59
(Blue label.)
HART (1003 "Take My Everything") 50-75 59
RON (338 "Blue Eyes") 40-60 59
TIFCO (832 "The T-Bird") 20-30 62

CAZZ, Lue

Singles: 7-inch

ART TONE (830 "Daddy Long Legs") 10-15 62
CLOCK (1044 "Forgive and Forget") 10-15 61
VEE-JAY (483 "Dreaming") 8-12 63

CECIL & EMMITT
(Cecil - Emmitt)

Singles: 7-inch

REVOLVO (27 "Don't Let My Dream Come True") 10-15 59
Members: Cecil Null; Emmitt Luttrell.

CEE, Richie

Singles: 7-inch

CONCEPT (923 "Games Too Cold Blues") 10-20

CEE JAYS

Singles: 7-inch

MOSAIC (1010 "Tequila and Lemon") 20-30 63

CEE VEE

Singles: 7-inch

CARROLLTON (800 "I'm Yours") 100-150 59

CEEDS

Singles: 7-inch

EMLAR (1001 "You Won't Do That") 10-20 66

CELEBRATED RENAISSANCE BAND

Singles: 7-inch

LION (1001) 10-20 68
(Exact title not known.)

Picture Sleeves

LION (1001) 25-35 68

CELEBRITIES

Singles: 7-inch

MUSIC MAKERS (101 "I Want You") 15-20 61
ROUND (1003 "My Obsession") 15-20 59
ROUND (1010 "Different School Now") 15-20 59

CELEBRITIES

Singles: 7-inch

BOSS (502 "Good Night") 50-100 59

CELEBRITYS

Singles: 78 rpm

CAROLINE 300-400 56

Singles: 7-inch

CAROLINE (2301 "Juanita") 3000-4000 56
Also see HAMMOND, Clay, with Johnnie Young & Celebritys

CELESTINE

Singles: 7-inch

ADORE (900 "One More Chance") 15-25 64

CELESTRALS

Singles: 7-inch

ALPHA (008 "Man's Best Friend") 10-15 64
DON-EL (125 "Alone") 20-30 63
DON-EL (126 "Checkerboard Lover") 40-50 63
RCA (9016 "Chain Reaction") 15-25 66

CELLAR DWELLERS

Singles: 7-inch

CENTURY (24501 "Child of the Devil") .... 10-20 '60s
LANCE (111 "Love Is a Beautiful Thing") 15-20 67

CELLOS P&R '57

Singles: 78 rpm

APOLLO (Except 510) 25-50 57
APOLLO (510 "Rang Tang Ding Dong") 40-50 57
(No subtitle used.)
APOLLO (510 "Rang Tang Ding Dong [I Am the Japanese Sandman]") 20-30 57
(With subtitle.)

Singles: 7-inch

APOLLO (510 "Rang Tang Ding Dong") 50-75 57
(No subtitle used.)
APOLLO (510 "Rang Tang Ding Dong [I Am the Japanese Sandman]") 30-40 57
(With subtitle.)
APOLLO (515 "Under Your Spell") 20-30 57
APOLLO (516 "The Be-Bop Mouse") 40-50 57
APOLLO (524 "I Beg for Your Love") 100-150 58
APOLLO (543 "Adele") 3-5
(Previously unreleased.)
Members: Cliff Williams; Ken Levinson; Alvin Campbell; Bill Montgomery; Alton Thomas.

CELTICS

Singles: 7-inch

AL-JACK'S (0002 "Can You Remember") 3000-4000 62
(Approximately 200 made.)
WAR CONN (2216 "Darline Darling") 150-250 62

CELTICS

Singles: 7-inch

CORONADO (133 "Wondering Why") 20-30 65
LINJO (106 "And She'll Cry") 15-25 66

CELTS, Bonnie, & Continentals

Singles: 7-inch

VALMON (067 "Chicken") 25-35 65

CENTAURS

Singles: 7-inch

ROCKET (65219 "Weird Turtle") 10-20 65

CENTAURUS

LP: 10/12-inch

AZRA (002 "Centaurus") 15-20 78
(Numbered edition picture disc. 1000 made. Promotional issue only.)

CENTENNIALS

Singles: 7-inch

DOT (16180 "My Dear One") 15-25 61
RANK (271 "Don't Go") .... 30-50 '50s

CENTER, Sandy, & Rainbow Rhythmaires

Singles: 7-inch

RUBY (260 "Come On Baby, It's Christmas") 40-60 57

CENTURIANS

Singles: 7-inch

TIGER (1001 "We Mean More to Each Other") 40-50 60

CENTURIES

Singles: 7-inch

DOOTO (469 "Geraldine") 10-15 62
LIFE (501 "In This Whole World") 40-50 61

CENTURIES

Singles: 7-inch

CLEOPATRA (2 "Outer Limits") 25-35 63
(Black vinyl.)
CLEOPATRA (2 "Outer Limits") 75-125 63
(Red vinyl. Promotional issue only.)
CLEOPATRA (3 "Jack 23") 20-30 64
Member: Tom Falcone

CENTURIES

Singles: 7-inch

RICH (102 "I'd Cry for You") 20-30

CENTURIES

Singles: 7-inch

SPECTRA-SOUND (641 "I Love You No More") 15-25 65
Also see BUCKINGHAMS

CENTURIES / Jaytones

Singles: 7-inch

TIMES SQUARE (5 "Crying for You"/"Oh, Darling") 15-25 63
(Blue or green vinyl.)
Also see CENTURIES / Revlons

CENTURIES / Revlons

Singles: 7-inch

TIMES SQUARE (15 "Betty"/"Rideaway") 15-25 63
Also see CENTURIES / Jaytones

CENTURY FIVE

Singles: 7-inch

BELMONT (4003 "La Moomba Kasa Boo Boo Cha Cha") 25-50 61

CENTURYS
(With the Walter Hamilton Combo)

Singles: 7-inch

FORTUNE (533 "Take My Hand") 75-125 59
Members: John Stevenson; Bernie Dupree; Melvin Cornelious; James Jefferson; Stanley Reed.
Also see HAMILTON, Walter, Combo

CENTURYS

Singles: 7-inch

VELTONE (104 "Strollin' Time") 10-20 60

CENTURYS

Singles: 7-inch

MICRO (6344 "Her Love") 50-75 63

LP: 10/12-inch

MARKUS (1003 "Centurys Live") 10-15 72
Members: Phil Cornelisen; Jim Morrison; Paul Willems; Donne Cornell; David K. Pilz; Eddie Farah; Dave Parpovich; Mark Helniak; James Copeland (Scovell).

CENTURYS

Singles: 7-inch

MARK C (101 "Whole Lot of Shakin' Going On") 10-20 64
Members: Wink; Bill Bellamy Jr.; Jim "Tex" Taylor Jr.

CENTURYS
(With Carson Sisters)

Singles: 7-inch

BANGAR (638 "Lonely Heart") 10-15 65
STUDIO CITY (1027 "Falling") .... 8-12 '60s

CENTURYS

Singles: 7-inch

B-B (4002 "Catch Me Fast") 25-35 67
RENCO (115 "The 83") 20-30 65
RENCO (116 "Don't Bother") 20-30 65
SWAN (4265 "Hard Times") 15-25 66

EPs: 7-inch

BONA FIDE (7001 "The Centurys") 8-10 84
(Repackage of the four Renco tracks.)
Members: Bob Koch; Billy Beard; Bernie Orner; Larry McKinney; John Iacovone.

CEPTORS

Singles: 7-inch

PANORAMA (1001 "I Can't Make It") 20-30

CERF, Christopher
(Chris Cerf)

Singles: 7-inch

AMY (954 "Sweet Music") 20-40 66
AMY (977 "Watch Your Step") 15-25 67
CUB (9116 "Cheerleader") 15-25 62
(First issue.)
MGM (13103 "Cheerleader") 10-15 62
VANITAS (928 "The Penguin") 10-15 61

CESANA

Singles: 7-inch

MODERN (2000 "My Only Love") 5-10 64

LPs: 10/12-inch

MODERN (1000 "Tender Emotions") 15-20 64

CEYLEIB PEOPLE

Singles: 7-inch

VAULT (940 "Changes") 10-15 68

LPs: 10/12-inch

VAULT (117 "Tanyet") 60-100 68
Members: Larry Knechtel; Ry Cooder; Mike Deasy; Joe Osborn; Sean Deasy.
Also see BREAD
Also see COODER, Ry
Also see DILLARDS

CEZANNES
("Featuring Ceressa")

Singles: 7-inch

MARKAY (108 "Pardon Me") 1000-1500 63

CHACKSFIELD, Frank, Orchestra P&R '53

Singles: 78 rpm

LONDON 5-10 53-57

Singles: 7-inch

LONDON (1342 thru 1901) 10-15 53-59
LONDON (1945 thru 20043) 5-10 60-69

EPs: 7-inch

LONDON 5-10 53-61

LPs: 10/12-inch

LONDON 10-15 53-61
MASTERSEAL 10-20 57
PARIS 10-20 57
REMINGTON 15-20 52
RICHMOND 8-12 59-62

CHAD & JEREMY P&R/LP '64

Singles: 7-inch

COLLECTABLES 3-5 81
COLUMBIA (Except 43277) 4-8 65-68
COLUMBIA (43277 "Before & After") 4-8 65
(Black vinyl.)
COLUMBIA (43277 "Before & After") 10-15 65
(Colored vinyl. Promotional issues only.)
ERIC 4-6 73
LANA .... 4-6 '60s
ROCSHIRE 3-5 84
TEEN SCOOP ("Interview") .... 20-30 '60s
(Square cardboard picture disc still bound in *Teen Scoop* magazine.)
TEEN SCOOP ("Interview") .... 15-20 '60s
(Square cardboard picture disc by itself)
TRIP .... 4-6 '70s
WORLD ARTISTS 5-10 64-65

Picture Sleeves

COLUMBIA 5-10 65-66
WORLD ARTISTS 8-12 64-65

LPs: 10/12-inch

CBS ("The Ark") .... 15-20 '60s
(Selection number not known.)
CAPITOL (2000 series) 15-20 66
CAPITOL (12000 & 16000 series) 5-10 80
COLUMBIA 20-25 65-68
FIDU 10-12
HARMONY 12-15 69
MDA (6000 "Olde English Gold") 10-20
ROCSHIRE 5-10 84
SIDEWALK 12-20 69
TRADITION REST 10-12
WORLD ARTISTS (2002 "Yesterday's Gone") 20-40 64
(Monaural.)
WORLD ARTISTS (2005 "Chad & Jeremy Sing for You") 20-40 65
(Monaural.)
WORLD ARTISTS (3002 "Yesterday's Gone") 30-50 64
(Stereo.)
WORLD ARTISTS (3005 "Chad & Jeremy Sing for You") 30-50 65
(Stereo.)
Members: Chad Stuart; Jeremy Clyde.
Also see STUART, Chad

CHAFFIN, Dickie
(Little Dickie Chaffin)

Singles: 7-inch

HILLTOP (1869 "Crying Heart") 10-20 61
KARL (230 "Princess Whitefoot") 10-20 59

CHAFFIN, Ernie

Singles: 78 rpm

FINE 20-30 56
SUN 25-50 57

Singles: 7-inch

FINE (1010 "Stop Look & Listen") 35-50 56
RKP 10-15

SUN (262 "Feelin' Low")........................ 15-25 57
SUN (275 "I'm Lonesome")...................... 15-25 57
SUN (307 "My Love for You")................. 10-20 58
SUN (320 "Don't Ever Leave Me")......... 10-20 59
VILLAGE.. 10-20

CHAIN REACTION
Singles: 7-inch
DATE (1538 "When I Needed You")........ 15-25 66
Member: Steve Tallarico (a.k.a. Steve Tyler).
Also see AEROSMITH

CHAIN REACTION
Singles: 7-inch
EARL (1003 "Chain Reaction") 35-45

CHAINO
(With Kirby Allan & Orchestra)
Singles: 7-inch
ORB (1002/1003 "Gone Ape"/"Ubangi Stomp") 30-50 58
(We suspect this issue of *Ubangi Stomp* precedes the Tampa one; however, we are not certain they are the exact same track.)
TAMPA (142 "The Slide")......................... 20-30 58
TAMPA (144 "Ubangi Rock") 20-30 58
Also see ALLAN, Kirby

CHAINS
Singles: 7-inch
HBR (460 "Carol's Got a Cobra")............ 15-20 66
PINPOINT (6902 "You're in Love") 20-30 67
PINPOINT (6903 "It's a Shame") 20-30 68

CHAISSON, Billy Don
Singles: 7-inch
TAB (1011 "Soul Walk")......................... 15-25 66

CHALETS
Singles: 7-inch
CHANEL (101 "Angel by My Side")..............4-6
COLLECTABLES...3-5 81
DART (1026 "Who's Laughing Who's Crying").. 10-15 61
LAURIE (3348 "She's Not the Marrying Type")..5-10 66
MUSICTONE (1115 "Who's Laughing Who's Crying") 8-12 63
TRU-LITE (1001 "Who's Laughing Who's Crying") 40-50 61
(101A in dead wax.)
TRU-LITE (1001 "Who's Laughing Who's Crying")...8-12 61

CHALLENGERS
Singles: 7-inch
DEBONAIR (105 "Troubles At an End") 50-100 '50s

CHALLENGERS
Singles: 7-inch
TRIODEX (102 "Goofus")........................ 10-20 60
TRIODEX (107 "Deadline") 10-20 61

CHALLENGERS
Singles: 7-inch
TRI-PHI (1012 "Stay with Me")................ 15-25 62
Also see CHALLENGERS III

CHALLENGERS
Singles: 7-inch
EXPLOSIVE (3621 "Why") 400-500 63
(First issued on Revenge as by the Executives.)
Also see EXECUTIVES

CHALLENGERS
Singles: 7-inch
GNP (362 "Theme from the Man from U.N.C.L.E.")..5-10 65
GNP (368 thru 412).................................5-10 66-68
PRINCESS (53 "Mr. Moto '65") 10-20 65
PRINCESS (55 "Pipeline") 10-20 65
TRIUMPH (64 "Dating Game").................. 15-25 65
TRIUMPH (112 "Pipeline") 15-25 66
VAULT (900 thru 918)............................. 10-15 63-65
EPs: 7-inch
TRIUMPH (1 "Club Audition")................. 25-50 65
LPs: 10/12-inch
FANTASY (9443 "Where Were You in the Summer of '62")...8-12 73
GNP (609 "25 Great Instrumental Hits") .. 25-40 67
(Two discs.)
GNP (2010 "At the Teenage Fair")........... 20-30 65
GNP (2018 "The Man from U.N.C.L.E.").. 20-30 65
GNP (2025 "California Kicks")................ 20-30 66
GNP (2031 "Wipe Out") 20-30 66
GNP (2045 "Light My Fire with Classical Gas")..20-30 68
GNP (2056 "Vanilla Funk").......................20-30 70
GNP (2093 "Sidewalk Surfing")................15-25 77
RHINO (053 "Best of the Challengers")......5-10 82
TRIUMPH (100 "The Challengers Go Sidewalk Surfing") 30-50 65
VAULT (100 "Surfbeat") 30-50 63
(Black vinyl.)
VAULT (100 "Surfbeat") 50-100 63
(Colored vinyl.)
VAULT (101 "Lloyd Thaxton Goes Surfin' with the Challengers")..50-75 63
(Black vinyl.)
VAULT (101 "Lloyd Thaxton Goes Surfin' with the Challengers")..75-125 63
(Orange vinyl.)
VAULT (101 "Surfing with the Challengers")..30-50 63
(Black vinyl.)
VAULT (101 "Surfing with the Challengers")..50-100 63
(Blue vinyl.)
VAULT (102 "The Challengers on the Move Surfing Around the World")..............................30-50 63
VAULT (107 "K-39")..................................30-50 64
VAULT (109 "Surf's Up! The Challengers on TV")...30-50 65
VAULT (110 "Challengers A Go Go") 30-50 66
VAULT (111 "Greatest Hits")....................30-50 67
Members: Richard Delvy; Jim Roberts; Glen Grey; Randy Nauert; Nick Hefner; Ed Fornier; Art Fisher; Phil Pruden; Phil Miles.
Also see BELAIRS
Also see DELVY, Richard
Also see EDDIE & SHOWMEN
Also see JOURNEYMEN
Also see STRANGE, Billy, & Challengers
Also see SURFARIS / Challengers
Also see SURFRIDERS
Also see THAXTON, Lloyd

CHALLENGERS
Singles: 7-inch
KIX INT'L (2263 "Moon, Send My Baby") .25-35 66

CHALLENGERS
(Challengers of Who)
Singles: 7-inch
AGE OF AQUARIUS (1500 "Hear My Message")...10-15 70
NIGHT OWL (1457 "Leave Me Be") 15-25 69
NIGHT OWL (6794 "Challengers Take a Ride on the Jefferson Airplane")..................................15-25 67
Members: John McCurdy; Mike Hoolihan; Keith Pentler; David Wayne; John Beaster; Chris Connors; Pat Clark.
Also see UNDERGROUND SUNSHINE

CHALLENGERS III
(Featuring Ann Bogan; Challengers)
Singles: 7-inch
TRI-PHI (1020 "Every Day")....................15-25 63
Also see CHALLENGERS

CHALONS
Singles: 7-inch
DICE (89 "Oh You") 200-300 58
(Pictures a hand throwing dice, with "Dice Records, New York, N.Y." below.)

CHAMAELEON CHURCH
Singles: 7-inch
MGM 5-10 68
LPs: 10/12-inch
MGM (4574 "Chamaeleon Church") 15-20 68
Members: Chevy Chase; Ted Myers; Tony Scheuren; Kyle Garrahan.
Also see ULTIMATE SPINACH

CHAMBERLAIN, Bruce, & Rondells
Singles: 7-inch
HIT (668 "No Love Have I")......................15-25 63

CHAMBERLAIN, Richard — P&R '62
Singles: 7-inch
MCA..3-5 77
MGM 5-10 62-65
Picture Sleeves
MGM 8-12 62-65
LPs: 10/12-inch
MGM (4088 "Richard Chamberlain Sings") 15-25 63
MGM (4287 "Joy in the Morning")............15-25 65
METRO (564 "Richard Chamberlain Sings") 8-12 66

CHAMBERLAIN, Wilt "The Stilt"
Singles: 7-inch
END (1066 "That's Easy to Say") 20-30 60

CHAMBERLIN BROTHERS
Singles: 7-inch
COLUMBIA (41227 "Debbie Jean")..........20-30 58
PORTER (1001/1002 "Cry Blue Baby"/"My Baby Walked Out On Me")..........................100-200 57

CHAMBERS, Cliff
Singles: 7-inch
CYCLONE (120 "Contract On Love").......50-75 61
GARDENA (104 "Time Has Made Her Change")..10-15 60
KENT (4523 "Just for You") 4-6 70
TOWER (442 "Uh Huh Oh Yea")...............5-10 68
Also see VERNON & CLIFF

CHAMBERS, Don
Singles: 7-inch
SWASTIKA (1000 "I Overlooked an Orchid")...15-25 59

CHAMBERS BROTHERS — P&R/LP '68
(Chambers Brothers Quartet)
Singles: 7-inch
AVCO 4-6 74-75
COLUMBIA..10-15 66-73
PROVERB (1021 "I Trust in God") ....10-20 '60s
ROXBURY 4-6 76
S B W (101 "I Trust in God") ....20-30 '60s
(First issue.)
TEAR DROP...4-6 74
VAULT...8-15 65-70
Picture Sleeves
COLUMBIA..6-12 68-69
LPs: 10/12-inch
AVCO 8-12 74-75
CHELSEA..8-10 77
COLUMBIA (20 "Love, Peace and Happiness")...20-30 69
(Two LPs, the second being *The Chambers Brothers Live at Bill Graham's Fillmore East.*)
COLUMBIA (2000 & 9000 series).............15-20 67-68
COLUMBIA (30000 series, except 31158)..10-20 71-75
COLUMBIA (31158 "Oh My God")............40-60 72
FANTASY..10-15 74
RIVERSIDE..10-15 68
ROXBURY 8-10 76
VAULT (100 series)....................................15-20 67-70
VAULT (9003 "People Get Ready")...........20-30 65
Members: Joe Chambers; Willie Chambers; Lester Chambers; George Chambers; Brian Keenan.
Also see AXTON, Hoyt, & Chambers Brothers
Also see DANE, Barbara, & Chambers Brothers
Also see PEANUT BUTTER CONSPIRACY / Ashes / Chambers Brothers
Also see WINTER, Johnny / Argent / Chambers Brothers / John Hammond

CHAMBLEE, Eddie — R&B '49
(With "Friend Martha"; with His Orchestra)
Singles: 78 rpm
CORAL...10-20 52
FEDERAL..15-25 51
MERCURY..15-25 57
UNITED 15-25 54
MIRACLE 10-20 47-51
UNITED..10-15 53
Singles: 7-inch
CORAL (65080 "Southern Comfort").........20-40 52
FEDERAL..20-40 51
MERCURY...10-20 57
TRAVIS (036 "My Funny Valentine")........10-20 '50s
UNITED (160 "Walkin' Home")..................15-25 53
UNITED (181 "Come On In") 15-25 54
LPs: 10/12-inch
EMARCY (36124 "Chamblee Music") 30-60 58
EMARCY (36131 "Doodin' ") 30-60 58
(Monaural.)
EMARCY (80007 "Doodin' ") 50-100 59
(Stereo.)
MERCURY (60127 "Chamblee Music")....30-40 59
PRESTIGE (7321 "Eddie Chamblee")......25-35 64
(Yellow label.)
PRESTIGE (7321 "Eddie Chamblee")......20-30 64
(Blue label.)
Also see WASHINGTON, Dinah

CHAMP, Billy
Singles: 7-inch
ABC-PAR (10518 "Believe Me") 20-30 64

CHAMPAGNE, Charles
Singles: 7-inch
HITT ("Last Night") 50-75
(Selection number not known.)

CHAMPAGNES
Singles: 7-inch
LAURIE (3189 "Crazy").................................5-10 63
SKYMAC (1002 "Crazy")..........................15-25 63
(First issue.)

CHAMPION, Hollis
Singles: 7-inch
LINCO (1317 "Old Red Devil")..................50-75
STRIPE (501 "Long Gone Lonesome Blues") 200-300 64

CHAMPION, Johnny
Singles: 7-inch
NATURAL SOUND (2004 "Beer Drinking Daddy")...100-150

CHAMPION, Mickey
(Mickie Champion)
Singles: 78 rpm
ALADDIN (3137 "Don't Say You Love Me") 10-20 52
ALADDIN (3152 "What Have You Got")... 10-20 52
MODERN (778 "I've Got It Bad")............. 10-20 50
MODERN (855 "He's a Mean Man") 10-20 52
RPM (321 "Good for Nothin' Man")........... 10-20 51
Singles: 7-inch
LILLY (505 "Bam-A-Lam")......................... 10-20 62
LILLY (509 "Wait for Me") 10-20 62
MUSETTE (9115 "What Good Am I").......20-40 '60s
Also see MILTON, Roy
Also see NIC NACS

CHAMPIONS
Singles: 78 rpm
CHART..15-25 55-56
SCOTT...25-45 55
Singles: 7-inch
ACE (541 "I'm So Blue") 15-25 58
CHART (602 thru 631)...............................30-50 55-56
SCOTT ("Annie Met Henry")....................50-100 55
(Selection number not known.)
SCOTT (1201 "It's Love It's Love")........... 10-15 61

CHAMPLAINS
Singles: 7-inch
U.A. (346 "Ding Dong") 40-50 61
Also see FIVE SATINS

CHAMPS
Singles: 7-inch
CHATAM (350 "Teenage Sweetheart")..750-1000 59
(Previously issued as by the Mystics.)
Also see MYSTICS

CHAMPS — P&R/R&B '58
Singles: 78 rpm
CHALLENGE (1016 "Tequila") 50-75 58
Singles: 7-inch
CHALLENGE... 10-20 58-65
ERIC..3-5 78
HI OLDIES 3-5 77
LANA..4-6 64
REPUBLIC (246 "Tequila '76") 3-5 76
Picture Sleeves
CHALLENGE (1016 "Tequila") ....5-10 '90s
CHALLENGE (59143 "I've Just Seen Her") 20-30 61
REPUBLIC (246 "Tequila '76") 4-6 76
EPs: 7-inch
CHALLENGE (7100 "Tequila")...................40-60 58
CHALLENGE (7101 "Caramba") 40-60 58
LPs: 10/12-inch
CHALLENGE (601 "Go Champs Go!")...50-100 58
(Black vinyl.)
CHALLENGE (601 "Go Champs Go!").250-350 58
(Colored vinyl.)
CHALLENGE (605 "Everybody's Rockin' with the Champs")..50-75 58
CHALLENGE (613 "Go Champs Go!").....40-60 62

CHALLENGE (614 "The Champs Play *All American*") 40-60 62
(Monaural.)
CHALLENGE (2514 "The Champs Play *All American*") 50-75 62
(Stereo.)
DESIGN SPOTLIGHT SERIES .... 10-20 '60s
INTERNATIONAL AWARD .... 10-20 '60s
POINT .... 10-20 '60s
SPECTRUM .... 10-20 '60s
Members: Dave Burgess; Danny "Chuck Rio" Flores; Gene Alden; Dale Norris; Joe Burness; Van Norman; Jim Seals; Dash Crofts; Dean Beard; Bob Morris; Glen Campbell; Jerry Cole; Keith MacKendrick; Rich Grissom; Johnny Meeks; Chuck Downs; Keith MacKendrick; Mo Marshall; Dean McDaniel; Gary Nieland; Curtis Paul; Jerry Puckett; Leon Sanders; Dave Smith; John Trombatore.
Also see APOLLOS
Also see BEARD, Dean
Also see BURGESS, Dave
Also see CAMPBELL, Glen
Also see COLE, Jerry
Also see DEMONS
Also see RIO, Chuck
Also see ROXSTERS
Also see SEALS & CROFTS
Also see SHADOWS FIVE
Also see THINGS TO COME
Also see TROPHIES
Also see VINCENT, Gene

CHAMPS / Fabulous Cyclones

LPs: 10/12-inch
INTERNATIONAL AWARD SERIES (223 "Champs & Fabulous Cyclones") 10-20 63
Also see CHAMPS

CHAN, Joie

Singles: 7-inch
CHATTAHOOCHEE (642 "Who'll Be the Boy This Summer") 10-15 64

CHANACLAIRS

Singles: 78 rpm
COLEMAN (1056 "Yuletide Love") 30-50 49

CHANCE, Larry
(With the Earls Today)

Singles: 7-inch
BARRY (110 "Promise Her Anything") 30-40 64
CHANCE 10-15 83
Also see BARONS
Also see EARLS

CHANCE, Nolan
(Charles Davis)

Singles: 7-inch
BUNKY (161 "Just Like the Weather") 150-250 65
CONSTELLATION (144 "She's Gone") 10-20 65
CONSTELLATION (161 "Just Like the Weather") 50-100 65
SCEPTER (12353 "Sara Lee") 4-6 72
THOMAS (802 "I'll Never Forget You") 10-20 69
Also see DUKAYS
Also see TRINIDADS

CHANCE, Tony

Singles: 7-inch
SWEETHEART (301 "Maybe Now") 50-100 59

CHANCE, Wayne

Singles: 7-inch
WHIRLYBIRD (2006 "Send Her to Me") 15-25 64

CHANCELLORS

Singles: 78 rpm
UNIQUE 15-25 56
XYZ 25-50 57
Singles: 7-inch
PORT (5000 "Tell Me You Love Me") 50-75 58
(Also issued as by the Five Chancellors.)
STORM (503 "My Thoughts of You") 150-200 59
UNIQUE (341 "Too Many Memories") 10-20 56
XYZ (104 "I'm Coming Home") 15-20 57
XYZ (105 "Seaport at Sunrise") 10-15 58

CHANCELLORS

Singles: 7-inch
BRENT (7031 "Straightaway") 10-20 62
CAP CITY (107 "All the Way from Heaven") 10-20 69
CAP CITY (112 "Girls Do Wonderful Things for Boys") 10-20 69
CORBY (200 "Jam") 10-20 62
EL CID .... 5-10 '60s
USA (783 "My Girl") 10-20 64

CHANCELLORS

Singles: 7-inch
APEX .... 10-20 '60s
SOMA (1421 "Little Latin Lupe Lu") 10-15 65
SOMA (1435 "So Fine") 10-15 65
Picture Sleeves
SOMA (1421 "Little Latin Lupe Lu") 100-125 65

CHANCELLORS

Singles: 7-inch
FENTON (2066 "Once in a Million") 25-40 66
FENTON (2072 "Dear John") 25-40 66

CHANCELLORS LTD.

Singles: 7-inch
DENE (101 "You Be the Judge") 20-30

CHANCERS

Singles: 7-inch
DOT (15870 "Shirley Ann") 40-50 58

CHANCES
(With Cecil Holmes Jr. & Orchestra)

Singles: 7-inch
ROULETTE (4549 "Through a Long and Sleepless Night") 50-75 64
Members: Milton Love; Bob Baylor; Reggie Barnes; Fred Barksdale; Cecil Holmes; Monte Owens.
Also see CAVALIERS QUARTET

CHANCES

Singles: 7-inch
DOT (16634 "Blackgrass") 10-15 64

CHANCES R

Singles: 7-inch
QUILL (105 "I'll Have You Cryin'") 10-20 65

CHANCETEERS
(With Clyde Wright)

Singles: 78 rpm
CHANCE 10-20 51-52
Singles: 7-inch
CHANCE (1107 "The Flame") 20-30 51
CHANCE (1112 ("I May Be Down") 20-30 52
Also see PORTER, Johnny

CHANDELIERS
(Chandeliers Quintet)

Singles: 7-inch
ANGLE TONE (520 "Tender Love") 4-6 73
(Previously unreleased from 1957.)
ANGLE TONE (521 "Blueberry Sweet") 300-400 58
(Credits "Chandeliers Quintet." Black vinyl.)
ANGLE TONE (521 "Blueberry Sweet") 100-200 58
(Credits "Chandeliers." Black vinyl.)
ANGLE TONE (521 "Blueberry Sweet") 250-350 58
(Red vinyl.)
ANGLE TONE (529 "Dolly") 75-125 58
Also see CARPETS

CHANDELIERS

Singles: 7-inch
DU-WELL (102 "Once More") 30-40 62
SUE (761 "She's a Heartbreaker") 15-25 62

CHANDELLES

Singles: 7-inch
DOT (16553 "El Gato") 10-20 63

CHAN-DELLS

Singles: 7-inch
ARC (8101 "Sand Surfer") 15-25 63

CHANDLER, Bobby
(With His Stardusters; with Escorts)

Singles: 7-inch
ATLAS (1090 "Just You and Me") 50-100 58
HI (2012 "By-O") 15-25 58
OJ (1000 "I'm Serious") 25-35 57
OJ (1005 "Shadows of Love") 30-40 57
OJ (1010 "Misty Eyes") 15-25 58
OJ (1012 "Winter Time") 15-25 59

CHANDLER, Chuckie

Singles: 7-inch
DEL-FI (4153 "Rockin' Monday") 10-15 61

CHANDLER, Deniece
(Denise Chandler)

Singles: 7-inch
LOCK (752 "Love Is Tears") 10-20 68
(First issue.)
LOCK (753 "Yes I'm Ready") 10-20 68
TODDLIN' TOWN (107 "Love Is Tears") 8-10 68
TODDLIN' TOWN (118 "I Don't Wanna Cry") 8-10 69
TODDLIN' TOWN (127 "Come On Home to Me Baby") 4-6 71

CHANDLER, Dub

Singles: 7-inch
SUNDOWN (120 "Blues in Your Brown Eyes") 10-15 59

CHANDLER, Gene — P&R/R&B/LP '62
(Eugene Dixon)

Singles: 12-inch
20TH FOX 4-8 79
Singles: 7-inch
BRUNSWICK (55312 "Girl Don't Care") 8-12 67
BRUNSWICK (55339 "There Goes the Lover") 8-12 67
BRUNSWICK (55383 "There Was a Time") 8-12 67
CHECKER (1155 "I Fooled You This Time") 10-15 66
CHECKER (1165 "To Be a Lover") 8-12 67
CHECKER (1199 "River of Tears") 8-12 68
CHI-SOUND (Except 2411) 4-6 79-82
CHI-SOUND (2411 "When You're #1") 8-10 79
COLLECTABLES 3-5 81
CONSTELLATION (112 thru 172) 8-12 63-67
CURTOM 4-8 72-73
ERIC 4-6 73
FASTFIRE 3-6 85
MCA 3-5 84
MARSEL 4-6 76
MERCURY (73083 thru 73258) 4-8 70-71
OLDIES 45 (21 "Duke of Earl") .... 5-10 '60s
SOLID SMOKE 3-5 84
TRIP (54 "Rainbow") 4-8
20TH FOX (2411 "When You're #1") 4-6 79
VEE-JAY (416 "Duke of Earl") 15-25 61
VEE-JAY (450 thru 536) 10-20 62-63
U.A. 4-6 78
LPs: 10/12-inch
BRUNSWICK (54124 "The Girl Don't Care") 15-20 67
(Monaural.)
BRUNSWICK (754124 "The Girl Don't Care") 10-15 67
(Stereo.)
BRUNSWICK (754131 "There Was a Time") 10-15 68
BRUNSWICK (754149 "Two Sides of Gene Chandler") 10-15 69
CHECKER (3003 "Duke of Soul") 15-20 67
CHI-SOUND/20TH-FOX (578 "Get Down") 5-10 78
CHI-SOUND/20TH-FOX (598 "When You're #1") 5-10 79
CONSTELLATION (1421 "Greatest Hits") 15-25 65
CONSTELLATION (1423 "Just Be True") 15-25 65
CONSTELLATION (1425 "Gene Chandler") 15-25 65
KENT 5-10 86
MERCURY (61304 "The Gene Chandler Situation") 10-15 70
SOLID SMOKE 5-10 84
20TH FOX (605 "Gene Chandler '80") 5-10 80
20TH FOX (625 "Ear Candy") 5-10 80
20TH FOX (629 "Here's to Love") 5-10 80
UPFRONT (105 "Duke of Earl") 8-12
VEE-JAY (1040 "Duke of Earl") 50-100 62
(Monaural.)
VEE-JAY (1040 "Duke of Earl") 100-150 62
(Stereo.)
Note: At least six early Vee-Jay tracks, including *Duke of Earl*, are actually by the Dukays, not just Gene Chandler.
Session: Calvin Carter.
Also see CARTER, Calvin
Also see DUKAYS
Also see DUKE OF EARL

CHANDLER, Gene, & Barbara Acklin — P&R/R&B '68

Singles: 7-inch
BRUNSWICK (55366 thru 55405) 8-12 68
Also see ACKLIN, Barbara

CHANDLER, Gene, & Jerry Butler — P&R/R&B/LP '71
(Gene & Jerry)

Singles: 7-inch
MERCURY (73163 thru 73195) 4-8 70-71
LPs: 10/12-inch
MERCURY (61330 "One & One") 10-15 71
Also see BUTLER, Jerry

CHANDLER, Gene, & Jamie Lynn — R&B '83

Singles: 7-inch
SALSOUL (7051 "You're the One") 3-5 83
Also see CHANDLER, Gene

CHANDLER, Howard

Singles: 78 rpm
WAMPUS (100 "Wampus Cat") 50-100 56
Singles: 7-inch
WAMPUS (100 "Wampus Cat") 300-400 56

CHANDLER, Jeff — P&R '54
(With Ralph Brewster)

Singles: 78 rpm
DECCA 5-10 54-55
Singles: 7-inch
DECCA 10-20 54-55
LIBERTY (55092 "Half of My Heart") 10-15 58
LPs: 10/12-inch
LIBERTY (3067 "Sings to You") 15-25 57
LIBERTY (3074 "Warm & Easy") 15-25 57

CHANDLER, Karen — P&R '52
(With the Jacks; Eve Young)

Singles: 78 rpm
CORAL 5-10 52-55
DECCA 5-10 56
Singles: 7-inch
CARLTON (534 "Irma La Douce") 8-12 60
CORAL 10-20 52-58
DECCA (29881 "Love Is the $64,000 Question") 10-15 56
DECCA (29945 "Free Little Bird") 10-15 56
DOT 5-10 67-68
MOHAWK (131 "G.I. Johnny Don't Go Home") 5-10 62
STRAND (25035 "My Own True Love") 8-12 61
SUNBEAM (117 "Till the End of Time") 10-15 58
SUNBEAM (131 "Faraway Places") 10-15 59
TIVOLI (999 "Kiss in the Night") 5-8 65
TIVOLI (1702 "Hold Me, Thrill Me, Kiss Me") 5-8 65
EPs: 7-inch
CORAL (81075 "Hold Me, Thrill Me, Kiss Me") 15-20 52
LPs: 10/12-inch
STRAND (1028 "Dear Mr. Gable") 15-25 61
Also see FONTAINE, Eddie, & Karen Chandler

CHANDLER, Karen, & Jimmy Wakely

Singles: 78 rpm
DECCA (30040 "Crazy Arms") 5-10 56
Singles: 7-inch
DECCA (30040 "Crazy Arms") 10-15 56
Also see CHANDLER, Karen
Also see WAKELY, Jimmy

CHANDLER, Kenny — P&R '63
(Kenny Bolognese)

Singles: 7-inch
AMY (890 "Happy to Be Unhappy") 5-10 63
COLLECTABLES 3-5 81
CORAL (62309 "It Might Have Been") 8-12 62
EPIC (9758 thru 10009) 5-10 65-66
LAURIE (3140 thru 3181, except 3158) 8-12 62-63
LAURIE (3158 "Heart") 10-15 63
LAURIE (3577 "Leave Me if You Want To") 4-6 71
TOWER (354 "Sleep") 5-10 68
TOWER (405 "Beyond Love") 5-10 68
U.A. (342 "Drums") 10-20 61
U.A. (384 "What Kind of Love Is Yours") 10-15 61
Also see BEAU, Kenny
Also see KENNY, FRANK & RAY
Also see TREE SWINGERS

CHANDLER, Lee, & Blue Rhythms

Singles: 7-inch
BAND BOX (224 "Consideration") 15-25 58

CHANDLER, Lorraine

Singles: 7-inch

GIANT (703 "What Can I Do")................. 25-50 66
RCA (8810 "What Can I Do")................. 15-25 66
RCA (8980 "I Can't Hold On")................. 15-25 66
RCA (9349 "I Can't Change")................. 35-45 67

CHANDLER, Ronnie

Singles: 7-inch

VEEDA (4003 "Shirley")........................... 10-20 59

CHANDLERS

Singles: 7-inch

BLEU ROSE (100 "Your Love Keeps Drawing Me Closer").. 15-25 68

CHANELS

Singles: 78 rpm

DEB (500 "The Reason")........................ 20-40 58

Singles: 7-inch

DEB (500 "The Reason")........................ 50-60 58
(Reissued as by the 5 Chanels.)
Also see 5 CHANELS
Also see VIRGIL & 4 CHANELS

CHANELLS / Butterballs

Singles: 7-inch

TIMES SQUARE (24 "Give Me a Chance"/"Butterball").. 10-20 63
Also see BOWEN, Billy
Also see PHAROTONES

CHANELS

Singles: 7-inch

MAG (4063 "Four Walls")...................... 50-100

CHANEY, Al

Singles: 7-inch

CHART (1270 "Be My Girl")......................5-10 65
CHART (1365 "If This Is Love")..................5-10 66
SABER (106 "Return to Sandra")............ 30-40 64
(First issue.)
SOUND STAGE 7 (2524 "Return to Sandra").. 10-15 64

CHANFER, Linda

Singles: 7-inch

GLASER (1000 "My Own Angel Love")... 25-35 62
(First issue.)
ROSE (3342 "My Own Angel Love")........ 15-25 62

CHANG LE & DU BARRYS

Singles: 7-inch

JAMISON (864 "Tell Me").................... 400-500 '50s

CHANGE OF PACE

Singles: 7-inch

STONE LADY (006 "Bring My Buddies Back").. 10-15 '60s
TABOO (100 "You Can Depend on Me")....8-12 '60s

CHANGING TIMES

Singles: 7-inch

MARK VII (1013 "I'm Alone").................. 20-30 67
Members: Dale Hastings; Rick Laymon; Sandy Charles; Garry Ford; Joe Reynolds; Rick Davidson.

CHANGING TIMES

Singles: 7-inch

VIBRA ("Free As the Wind").................... 30-40 '60s
(Selection number not known.)

CHANGING TYMES

Singles: 7-inch

R.D. (1 "You Make It Hard").................... 15-25 66

CHANGING TYMES

Singles: 7-inch

HARD TYMES (5811 "You Had It Made").. 10-15 '60s

CHANIER, Cliston
("King of the South"; Clifton Chenier)

Singles: 78 rpm

ELKO.. 50-75 54
IMPERIAL.. 30-40 54
POST.. 35-45 55

Singles: 7-inch

ELKO (920 "Louisiana Stomp")........... 150-200 54
IMPERIAL (5352 "Louisiana Stomp")...... 50-75 54
POST (2010 "Country Bred").................. 50-75 55
POST (2016 "Rockin' Hop").................. 50-75 55
Also see CHENIER, Clifton

CHANNEL 3

Singles: 7-inch

DAKAR (4520 "The Sweetest Thing")......10-15

CHANNEL, Bruce *P&R/R&B/LP '62*
(With the Straitjackets)

Singles: 7-inch

BROWNFIELD (29 "Don't Let Go")............8-12 65
CHARAY..4-8 68
COLLECTABLES..3-5 81
ELEKTRA..3-5 80
JADE..5-10 '60s
JAMIE (1412 "Going Back to Louisiana").....4-6 73
KING (5294 "Slow Down Baby")..............25-50 59
KING (5331 "Now Or Never")....................15-20 60
KING (5620 "Now Or Never")....................10-15 62
LE CAM (122 "Going Back to Louisiana")..5-10 64
LE CAM (125 "Blue Monday")....................8-12 64
LE CAM (953 "Hey Baby")........................30-40 61
LE CAM (963 "Number One Man")...........10-20 62
LE CAM (983 "Stand Tough")....................5-10 '60s
LE CAM (1100 series)..............................3-5 77
LE CAM (7277 "The King Is Free")..............5-8 77
MALA (579 thru 12041)............................5-10 67-68
MANCO (1035 "Run Romance, Run")......10-20 62
MEL-O-DY (112 "Satisfied Mind")............10-15 64
MEL-O-DY (114 "You Never Looked Better")..10-15 64
NAP..3-5
SHAH (304 "Court of Love")......................8-12 64
SMASH (1731 thru 1838)........................8-12 62-63
SOFT..5-10 '60s
TEEN AGER (601 "Run Romance, Run")..30-40 59
SHALIMAR..5-10
ZUMA..3-5 77

Picture Sleeves

SMASH..10-15 62-63

LPs: 10/12-inch

SMASH (27008 "Hey! Baby")...................30-50 62
(Monaural.)
SMASH (67008 "Hey! Baby")...................25-40 62
(Stereo.)
Session: Delbert McClinton.
Also see McCLINTON, Delbert
Also see STRAITJACKETS

CHANNEL, Bruce / Paul & Paula

Singles: 7-inch

ERA ("Hey Baby"/"Hey Paula")....................4-6 '70s
(Selection number not known. *Hey Paula* is a re-recorded version.)
Also see CHANNEL, Bruce
Also see LUKE, Jimmy, & Bruce Channel
Also see PAUL & PAULA

CHANNELLS

Singles: 7-inch

CHANNEL (1004 "In My Arms to Stay").....8-10 74
HIT RECORD (700 "In My Arms to Stay")..20-30 63
Members: Tony Williams; Gene Williams; Larry Hampden; Revo Hodge.

CHANNELS
(Earl Lewis & Channels)

Singles: 78 rpm

FURY..50-100 58
GONE..50-75 57
WHIRLIN' DISC..50-75 56-57

Singles: 7-inch

ABC..4-6 73
CHANNEL (Black vinyl)..............................4-6 71-74
CHANNEL (Colored vinyl)..........................5-10 '70s
CLASSIC ARTISTS (124 "You Promised Me Love")..8-10 91
(Red vinyl. 1000 made.)
COLLECTABLES..3-5
FIRE (1001 "My Heart Is Sad")................15-25 59
FLASHBACK..5-10 65
FURY (1021 "Bye Bye Baby")..................40-50 59
(Label name in small print.)
FURY (1021 "Bye Bye Baby")..................15-25 59
(Label name in larger print.)
FURY (1021 "Bye Bye Baby")....................5-10
(Has horse head on label.)
FURY (1071 "Bye Bye Baby")..................10-15 63
GONE (5012 "That's My Desire").............50-60 57
(Black label.)
GONE (5012 "That's My Desire").............10-15 60
(Multi-color label.)
GONE (5019 "Altar of Love")...................50-60 57
(Black label.)
GONE (5019 "Altar of Love")...................10-15 58
(Multi-color label.)
KING TUT (173 "Tell Me Why")....................4-8 78
LANA (122 "The Closer You Are")...............4-6 64
PORT (70014 thru 70023)........................10-15 59-61
RARE BIRD (5017 "Breaking Up Is Hard to Do")..4-6 71
ROULETTE..4-6 71
VIRGO..4-6 72-73
WHIRLIN' DISC (100 "The Closer You Are")..150-250 56
(Label name is in a sans serif – or block – typestyle. Label stock is glossy. Publisher credited is "Bob-Dan Music.")
WHIRLIN' DISC (100 "The Closer You Are")..100-200 56
(Label name is in a sans serif – or block – typestyle. Publisher credited is "Spinning Wheel Music.")
WHIRLIN' DISC (100 "The Closer You Are")..100-200 56
(Label name is in a serif style type.)
WHIRLIN' DISC (102 "The Gleam in Your Eyes")..100-200 56
WHIRLIN' DISC (107 "I Really Love You")..100-200 57
WHIRLIN' DISC (109 "Flames in My Heart")..100-200 57
WHIRLIN' DISC (1035 "The Closer You Are")..15-25 '60s
(Actually shows *Now You Know* as the A-side.)

LPs: 10/12-inch

CHANNEL..10-20 73-80
COLLECTABLES (5012 "Earl Lewis & the Channels")..10-15 82
(Picture disc.)
LOST NITE ("The Channels")..................10-20 81
(10-inch LP. Red vinyl. 1000 made.)
RELIC..5-10 90
Members: Earl Lewis; Larry Hampden; Cliff Wright; Bill Morris; Ed Dolphin; John Felix; Alton Thomas.

CHANO
(With the Rialtos)

Singles: 7-inch

CUE (751 "Love Party")..........................50-75
JIN (154 "Guardian Angel")......................40-50 62

CHANSONAIRES

Singles: 7-inch

HAMILTON (50012 "Love Always Finds a Way")..10-20 58

CHANTAYS *P&R/R&B/LP '63*

Singles: 7-inch

ABC (2704 "Pipeline")..............................4-6 74
COLLECTABLES (1171 "Pipeline")............3-5 81
DOT (145 "Pipeline")...............................5-10 63
DOT (16440 "Pipeline")...........................10-20 63
DOT (16492 "Monsoon")..........................10-20 63
DOWNEY (104 "Pipeline").......................25-35 63
DOWNEY (108 "Monsoon").......................20-30 63
DOWNEY (116 "Space Probe")...............15-25 64
DOWNEY (126 "Beyond").........................15-25 64
DOWNEY (130 "Three Coins in the Fountain")..15-25 65
MCA (2704 "Pipeline")..............................3-5 84

LPs: 10/12-inch

DOT (3516 "Pipeline")............................30-40 63
(Monaural.)
DOT (25516 "Pipeline")..........................40-50 63
(Stereo.)
DOT (3771 "Two Sides of the Chantays")..30-40 63
(Monaural.)
DOT (25771 "Two Sides of the Chantays")..40-50 63
(Stereo.)
DOWNEY (1002 "Pipeline")...................150-200 63
Members: Bob Marshall; Bob Welch; Brian Carman; Bob Spickard; Steve Cahn; Warren Waters
Also see LEAPING FERNS

CHANTECLAIRS

Singles: 78 rpm

DOT..15-25 54-55

Singles: 7-inch

DOT (1227 "Someday My Love Will Come My Way")..40-50 54
DOT (15404 "Believe Me, Beloved")........40-50 55
Member: Prentice Moore.
Also see MORELAND, Prentice

CHANTEERS

Singles: 7-inch

MERCURY (71979 "She's Coming Home")..10-15 61
MERCURY (72037 "Just a Little Boy").....30-40 62

CHANTEL, Dale

Singles: 7-inch

JIN (147 "Fools Must Cry")......................10-15 60

CHANTELS *P&R '57*

Singles: 78 rpm

END..25-35 57-58

Singles: 7-inch

ABC..4-6 73
CARLTON (555 thru 569)........................10-20 61
END (1001 "He's Gone")..........................30-40 57
(Black label.)
END (1005 "Maybe")...............................30-40 57
(Black label.)
END (1005 "Maybe")...............................15-25 '50s
(White or gray label.)
END (1005 "Maybe")...............................10-15 '60s
(Multi-color label.)
END (1015 "Every Night")........................15-25 58
(White label.)
END (1015 "Every Night")........................10-15 '60s
(Multi-color label.)
END (1020 "I Love You So")....................15-25 58
END (1026 "Sure of Love")......................15-25 58
END (1030 "Congratulations")................15-25 58
END (1037 "I Can't Take It")..................15-20 59
END (1048 "I'm Confessin'")..................15-20 59
END (1069 "Whoever You Are")..............10-15 60
END (1103 "Believe Me")........................10-15 61
END (1105 "I'm the Girl")........................15-25 61
ERIC..3-6 73
LANA..4-6 64
LUDIX (101 "Eternally")..........................20-30 63
LUDIX (106 "That's Why You're Happy")...5-10 63
MEM-O-REE (002 "Look in My Eyes").........3-5
RCA..4-6 70
ROULETTE..4-6 69-71
STOOP SOUNDS (113 "So Real"/"My Memories of You")..100-150 97
TCF (123 "Take Me As I Am")....................5-10 65
VERVE..5-10 66

EPs: 7-inch

END (201 "I Love You So")..................300-400 58
END (202 "I Love You So")..................300-400 58

LPs: 10/12-inch

CARLTON (LP-144 "The Chantels on Tour – Look in My Eyes")..50-100 62
(Monaural.)
CARLTON (STLP-144 "The Chantels on Tour – Look in My Eyes")..75-150 62
(Stereo.)
END (301 "We Are the Chantels").....1000-2000 58
(Pictures the group on front cover.)
END (301 "The Chantels")....................150-300 59
(Pictures a juke box on front cover.)
END (312 "There's Our Song Again").....50-100 62
FORUM CIRCLE (9104 "The Chantels Sing Their Favorites")..25-50 64
MURRAY HILL (000385 "Arlene Smith & the Chantels")..20-30 87
(Three discs. Includes booklet.)
ROULETTE..5-10
Members: Arlene Smith; Lois Harris; Rene Minus; Sonia Gorring; Jackie Landry; Annette Smith; Sandra Dawn. Session: Richard Barrett; Buddy Lucas Orchestra.
Also see BARRETT, Richard
Also see PEMBERTON, Jimmy
Also see RHYTHM ACES / Chantels
Also see SMITH, Arlene
Also see VENEERS

CHANTELS

Singles: 7-inch

BRYAN (100 "Time Slips Out the Window")..10-15 64
Members: Wes Jerving; Tom Frank; Bob Kampmann; Joel Grollmus; Chuck Hertini.

CHANTELS

Singles: 7-inch

FANTASTIC (3662 "Tu N'Avais Pas Besoin de Moi")..10-20
MW (1001 "Shaggy Baggy Joe")..............20-30

CHANTELS & AQUA LADS
Singles: 7-inch
AQUA (8755 "I'll Never Know") 15-20

CHANTERS
(Featuring Ethel Brown & Brother Woodman's Combo)
Singles: 78 rpm
COMBO (78 "Why") 50-75 55
COMBO (92 "I Love You") 50-75 55
KEM (2740 "Lonesome Me") 15-25 55
RPM (415 "Tell Me, Thrill Me") 75-100 54
Singles: 7-inch
COMBO (78 "Why") 150-200 55
COMBO (92 "I Love You") 100-150 55
KEM (2740 "Lonesome Me") 50-75 55
RPM (415 "Tell Me, Thrill Me") 300-350 54
Members: Ethel Brown; Gene Ford; Billy Boyd; Alan Boyd.
Also see WOODMAN, Brother

CHANTERS P&R/R&B '61
(Bud Johnson & Chanters)
Singles: 7-inch
DE LUXE (6162 "My My Darling") 50-75 58
DE LUXE (6166 "Row Your Boat") 40-50 58
(Black label.)
DE LUXE (6166 "Row Your Boat") .... 10-15 '60s
(Yellow label.)
DE LUXE (6172 "Five Little Kisses") 75-100 58
DE LUXE (6177 "No, No, No") 50-75 61
DE LUXE (6191 "No, No, No") 40-50 61
DE LUXE (6194 "My My Darling") 15-25 61
DE LUXE (6200 "Row Your Boat") 8-12 63
GUSTO (2169 "Over the Rainbow") 4-6 83
SSP (1001 "Heavenly You") 15-20
Members: Bud Johnson Jr; Larry Pendergrass; Fred Paige; Bobby Thompson; Elliot Green.

CHANTEURS
(With King Kolax & His Band)
Singles: 7-inch
LA SALLE (501 "Wishin' Well") 50-100 57
RENEE ("You've Got a Great Love") 20-30
(Selection number not known.)
VEE-JAY (519 "You've Got a Great Love") 10-15 63
Members: Eugene Record; Sollie McElroy; Robert Lester; Clarence Johnson.
Also see CHI-LITES
Also see McELROY, Sollie
Also see MOROCCOS

CHANTICLEERS
Singles: 7-inch
ARC (4452 "My Little Baby Doll") 15-25 59
LYRIC (103 "To Keep Your Love") 25-35 58
OLD TOWN (1137 "Green Satin") 10-15 63

CHANTIERS
Singles: 7-inch
DCP (1005 "Dear Mr. Clock") 5-10 64
DJB (112 "Dear Mr. Clock") 10-15 64
(First issue.)

CHANTONES
Singles: 7-inch
TNT (167 "Dear Diary") 150-200 59

CHANTONES
Singles: 7-inch
CAPITOL (4661 "Stormy Weather") 8-12 61
CARLTON (485 "It's Just a Summer Love") 10-15 58
TOP RANK (2066 "Tangerock") 10-15 60
Also see SCOTT, Jack

CHANTS
Singles: 7-inch
CAPITOL (3949 "Lost & Found") 15-25 58
MGM (13008 "Respectable") 10-15 61
TRU EKO (3567 "Respectable") 15-25 61
(First issue.)
UWR (4243 "Respectable") 8-12 62
VERVE (10244 "Dick Tracy") 10-15 61
Picture Sleeves
CAPITOL (3949 "Lost & Found") 30-40 58
Also see SOUL, Jimmy

CHANTS
(With the Joymakers Orchestra)
Singles: 7-inch
BIG MOMENT (102 "A Thousand Miles in My Path") 500-750 59

CHANTS
Singles: 7-inch
NITE-OWL (40 "Heaven & Paradise") 200-300 60
(Maroon label.)
NITE-OWL (40 "Heaven & Paradise") 50-100 60
(Black label. Colored vinyl.)
NITE-OWL (40 "Heaven & Paradise") 25-50 60
(Black label. Black vinyl.)

CHANTS
Singles: 7-inch
B. WARE (869 "Hypnotized") 15-25

CHAPARRALS
(Featuring Tooter Boatman)
Singles: 7-inch
REBEL (108 "Poor Gal") 500-750 58
Also see BOATMAN, Tooter

CHAPEL, Jean
Singles: 78 rpm
SUN 15-25 56
RCA 10-20 56
Singles: 7-inch
CHALLENGE 4-8 66-68
KAPP 4-6 69
SMASH (1829 "Don't Let Go") 5-10 63
SUN (244 "I Won't Be Rockin' Tonight") 70-80 56
RCA (6892 "I Had a Dream") 20-30 56
Also see PRESLEY, Elvis / Jean Chapel

CHAPELAIRES
(With Lenny Martin Orchestra)
Singles: 7-inch
GATEWAY (746 "Vacation Time") 20-25 64
HAC (101 "Not Good Enough") 50-100 61
HAC (102 "Gloria") 10-20 61
Also see JACKSON, Chuck, & Chapelaires
Also see KAYE, Joni, & Chapelaires

CHAPELLES
(Billy & the Kids)
Singles: 7-inch
ADARA (101 "Nightrider") 25-35 61
(Reissued as by Billy & Kids.)
Also see BILLY & KIDS

CHAPELLS
Singles: 7-inch
DOUBLE CHECK (4001 "Are You Ready") .... 10-20 '60s

CHAPERONES
Singles: 7-inch
JOSIE (880 "Cruise to the Moon") 20-30 60
(First issued crediting the Cahperones.)
JOSIE (885 "Shining Star") 15-25 60
JOSIE (891 "Blueberry Sweet") 50-75 61
Also see CAHPERONES
Also see JORDAN, Lou

CHAPINS
(With Will Jordan & Friends)
Singles: 7-inch
EPIC 4-6 71
ROCK-LAND 5-10 67
Picture Sleeves
ROCK-LAND 10-15 67
LPs: 10/12-inch
ROCK LAND (66 "Chapin Music") 20-30 67
Members: Tom Chapin; Steve Chapin; Phil Forbes; Doug Walkers.

CHAPLAIN, Paul P&R '60
(With His Emeralds; Paul Chaplin)
Singles: 7-inch
ELGIN 5-10
HARPER (100 "Shortnin' Bread") 20-30 60
HARPER (101 "So All Alone") 10-20 61
PAT (101 "Caledonia") 60-80

CHAPMAN, Gene
Singles: 7-inch
WESTPORT (145 "Oklahoma Blues") 50-75 60

CHAPMAN, Grady
(With the Suedes; with Don Ralke's Orchestra)
Singles: 78 rpm
MONEY 50-100 55
Singles: 7-inch
IMPERIAL (5591 "Garden of Memories") 10-15 59
IMPERIAL (5611 "Come Away") 10-15 59
KNIGHT (2003 "Star Light, Star Bright") 20-30 58
MERCURY (71632 "Sweet Thing") 10-20 60
MERCURY (71698 "Ambush") 30-50 60
MERCURY (71771 "I'll Never Question Your Love") 10-20 61
MONEY (204 "I Need You So") 300-400 55
(Bootleg shows only the Suedes as artist.)
ZEPHYR (016 "My Love Will Never Change") 20-30 57
Also see RALKE, Don
Also see ROBINS

CHAPMAN, Monroe
Singles: 7-inch
AJAR (101 "Come Dance with Rudy") 50-75 59

CHAPMAN, Ronnie
Singles: 7-inch
COLUMBIA (41469 "Annie B. Is Gone") 20-30 59

CHAPPELL, Bill
Singles: 7-inch
YUCCA (121 "Lovey Dovey") 10-20 60
YUCCA (145 "Big Mama Twist") 10-20 62
YUCCA (156 "Saddest World") 50-75 63
YUCCA (171 "Lonely Train") 10-20 65
YUCCA (186 "Rodeo") 10-20 66
YUCCA (219 "Lovey Dovey") 5-10 67

CHAPPIES
Singles: 7-inch
CHELTON (750 "Suddenly There Were Tears") ... 75-125 '60s

CHAPS
Singles: 7-inch
BRENT (7016 "Perfect Night for Love") 10-15 60
DELTA (16891 "There'll Never Be") 3-5
MATADOR (1814 "There'll Never Be") 50-75 61

CHAPTER V
Singles: 7-inch
VERVE FOLKWAYS (5046 "The Sun Is Green") 10-20 67
VERVE FORECAST (5057 "Headshrinker") 10-20 67

CHAPTERS
("With Band")
Singles: 78 rpm
REPUBLIC 100-150 53
Singles: 7-inch
REPUBLIC (7038 "Goodbye, My Love") 400-500 53
Also see FOSTER, Helen

CHARACTERS
Singles: 7-inch
PIP (100 "Columbus, You Big Bag of Steam") .. 10-15 59
VIRTRON 5-10
LPs: 10/12-inch
PIP (1900 "Smash Flops") 30-50 59

CHARADES
Singles: 7-inch
LANCER (101 "Last Goodbye") 15-25 58

CHARADES
Singles: 7-inch
U.A. (132 "Make Me Happy") 20-30 58
U.A. (183 "Let Me Love You") 400-500 59
Member: Billy Storm.
Also see STORM, Billy

CHARADES
(Charades Band; "Featuring Syl Grigsby")
Singles: 7-inch
ÄVA (154 "Please Be My Love Tonight") 30-40 64
(Has Anthony Music Corp. under center hole.)
ÄVA (154 "Please Be My Love Tonight") 5-10 64
(Has "Produced by Tony Hilder" under center hole.)
CHARADE 3-6 75-82
IMPACT (32 "Christina") 15-25 64
NORTHRIDGE (1002 "For You") 150-200 62
ORIGINAL SOUND (47 "Close to Me") 10-15 64
LPs: 10/12-inch
CHARADE 10-15 82
Members: Syl Grisby; Raymond A. Baradat; Tom Johnston; Ed Cuellar.
Also see EL TRIO DEL PUEBLO
Also see GAYE, Marvin
Also see MASERANG
Also see RHYTHM KINGS

CHARADES
Singles: 7-inch
MGM (13540 "Weeping Cup") 25-35 66
MGM (13584 "Never Set Me Free") 25-35 66
MERCURY (72414 "You're with Me All the Way") 15-25 65
OKEH (7195 "Can't Make It without You") 5-10 64
SKYLARK (502 "Flamingo") 10-15 64
W.B. (5415 "Hey, Operator") 5-10 64

CHARGE, Gary
(With Paul Sawtell & Orchestra)
Singles: 7-inch
BLUE DIAMOND (3215 "Peaches & Cream") 10-20 61

CHARGERS P&R '58
Singles: 7-inch
RCA (7301 "Old MacDonald") 25-30 58
RCA (7417 "Here in My Heart") 25-30 58
Members: Jesse Belvin; James Scott; Dunbar White; Ben Easley; Johnny White; Mitchell Alexander; Jimmy Norman.
Also see BELVIN, Jesse
Also see FEATHERS
Also see NORMAN, Jimmy

CHARGERS
Singles: 7-inch
B.E.A.T. (1006 "Large Charge") 10-20 58

CHARGERS
Singles: 7-inch
HOLLYWOOD (1104 "Speedway") 15-20 62

CHARIOT
LPs: 10/12-inch
NAT'L GENERAL (2003 "Chariot") 50-75 71
Members: Mike Koplan; Pug Baker; Larry Gould.

CHARIOTEERS P&R '40
Singles: 78 rpm
BRUNSWICK 25-50 38-39
COLUMBIA 25-50 39-49
DECCA 20-30 35
JOSIE 10-20 55
KEYSTONE 10-20 52
LANG-WORTH .... 10-20 '40s
(16-inch transcriptions.)
MGM 20-30 57
OKEH 15-25 40-42
TUXEDO 15-25 55
VOCALION 15-25 38-39
Singles: 7-inch
COLUMBIA (168 "A Kiss and a Rose") 250-350 50
(Microgroove 33 single.)
COLUMBIA (363 "This Side of Heaven") 250-350 50
(Microgroove 33 single.)
JOSIE (787 "I've Got My Heart on My Sleeve") 30-40 55
MGM (12569 "The Candle") 25-35 57
LPs: 10/12-inch
COLUMBIA (6014 "Sweet and Low") 150-200 49
(10-inch LP.)
HARMONY (7089 "The Charioteers and Billy Williams") 50-100 57
Members: Billy Williams; Eddie Jackson; Ira Williams; Howard Daniel; James Sherman.
Also see BAILEY, Mildred, & Charioteers
Also see PATRICK, Gladys
Also see SINATRA, Frank, & Charioteers
Also see WILLIAMS, Billy

CHARIOTS
Singles: 7-inch
GALLANT (3003 "Problem Girl") 30-40 62
RSVP (1105 "Tiger in the Park") 15-25 64
TIME (1006 "Gloria") 30-40 59
(Blue label. First pressing.)
TIME (1006 "Gloria") 15-25 59
(Red label.)

CHARLATANS
Singles: 7-inch
KAPP (779 "The Shadow Knows") 50-75 66
PHILIPS (40610 "High Coin") 50-75 69
PHILIPS (44824 "Date: May 19, 1969") 40-60 69
(Promotional issue only.)
LPs: 10/12-inch
PHILIPS (600309 "The Charlatans") 75-125 69
Members: Dan Hicks; George Hunter; Michael Ferguson; Richard Olson; Mike Wilhelm; Terry Wilson; Patrick Bogert; Sam Linde.
Also see WILHELM

CHARLENA & ROCKETTES
Singles: 7-inch
MORGAN (9018 "Ramrod") ... 10-20 65

CHARLES, Andy, & Blues Kings
Singles: 7-inch
D (1061 "Baby Don't Go") ... 30-40 59
(Yellow label.)
D (1061 "Baby Don't Go") ... 8-12 59
(Tan label.)

CHARLES, Bobby *R&B '56*
Singles: 78 rpm
CHESS (1609 thru 1638) ... 15-30 55-56
CHESS (1647 thru 1670) ... 25-50 57
Singles: 7-inch
BEARSVILLE (0010 "Small Town Talk") ... 4-6 73
CHESS (1609 thru 1638) ... 30-50 55-56
CHESS (1647 thru 1670) ... 20-30 57
HUB CITY ... 8-12 63
IMPERIAL (5579 thru 5691) ... 10-15 59-60
JEWEL (728 thru 740) ... 5-10 64
PAULA (226 "Worrying Over You") ... 5-10 65
RICE & GRAVY ... 3-5 86-90
LPs: 10/12-inch
BEARSVILLE ... 10-15 72
CHESS ... 8-12 76

CHARLES, Buddy
(With Richard Phillips & Orchestra)
Singles: 7-inch
CHARMAN (0001 "Be a Man") ... 15-25
MERCURY (5793 "Purple Reverie") ... 20-30 52
WARWICK (516 "A Soldier's Prayer") ... 20-30 59

CHARLES, Claire, & Terrytones
Singles: 7-inch
WYE (1002 "You're My Ideal") ... 10-20 60

CHARLES, Dick
Singles: 7-inch
TOWN (1961 "Do You Love Me") ... 20-30

CHARLES, Elaine
Singles: 7-inch
ACAMA (130 "I'm Not Too Young") ... 15-25 62
OCTIVE (102 "I'm Not Too Young") ... 30-40 62
(First issue.)

CHARLES, Jimmy *P&R/R&B '60*
(With the Revelletts or Revellettes)
Singles: 7-inch
ABC ... 3-6 73
COLLECTABLES ... 3-5 81
ERIC ... 3-5 79
GLENVILLE (1002 "A Million to One") ... 40-60 60
(First issue.)
MCA ... 3-5 84
PROMO (1002 thru 1006) ... 10-20 60-61
Love") ... 10-20 61
ROULETTE ... 4-6 71
Picture Sleeves
PROMO (1003 "The Age for Love") ... 10-20 60
PROMO (1004 "I Saw Mommy Kissing Santa Claus") ... 10-20 60
PROMO (1005 "Christmasville U.S.A.") ... 10-20 61
Also see JOHNNIE & JOE / Jimmy Charles

CHARLES, Morris
Singles: 7-inch
FELSTED (8523 "Dream of Love") ... 10-15 59

CHARLES, Nick
Singles: 7-inch
FERNWOOD (118 "Don't Take Your Love from Me") ... 10-15 60
GUYDEN (2049 "For You") ... 10-15 61
SATELLITE (109 "Ain't That Love") ... 10-15 61
STAX (119 "Sunday Jealous") ... 10-20 62
STAX (122 "The Three Dogwoods") ... 10-20 62

CHARLES, Norman
Singles: 7-inch
COLUMBIA (44039 "In These Uncertain Times") ... 5-10 67
COLUMBIA (44223 "She's a Woman") ... 5-10 67
GATEWAY (715 "Over and Gone") ... 10-15 63
TRY ME (28010 "Over and Gone") ... 10-15 63
VEE-JAY (445 "Climb Every Mountain") ... 5-10 62

CHARLES, Owen
Singles: 7-inch
GUYDEN (2025 "Stagecoach") ... 10-15 59

CHARLES, Pete
Singles: 7-inch
BUZZ (107 "Susan, Susan") ... 15-25 60

CHARLES, Ray *R&B '51*
(With the Cookies; with Raelettes or Raelets)
Singles: 78 rpm
ATLANTIC (900 & 1000 series) ... 15-25 52-57
ATLANTIC (2006 "Rockhouse") ... 50-100 58
ATLANTIC (2010 "Night Time Is the Right Time") ... 100-150 58
ATLANTIC (2022 "That's Enough") ... 150-200 59
ATLANTIC (2031 "What'd I Say") ... 300-400 59
JAX (641 "Baby Let Me Hear You Call My Name") ... 100-200 52
ROCKIN' ... 15-25 52
SWING BEAT ... 20-40 49
SWING TIME ... 20-40 50-53
Singles: 12-inch
W.B. (5978 "I'll Be There") ... 5-8 93
Singles: 7-inch
ABC-PAR (335-5 "Deep in the Heart of Texas") ... 15-25 60
(Stereo.)
ABC-PAR (10081 thru 10785) ... 8-12 60-66
ABC/TRC (10808 thru 11351) ... 3-8 66-73
ATLANTIC (976 "Roll with Me Baby") ... 50-75 52
ATLANTIC (984 "The Sun's Gonna Shine Again") ... 50-75 53
ATLANTIC (999 "Mess Around") ... 30-60 53
ATLANTIC (1021 thru 2118) ... 30-50 54-61
ATLANTIC (2174 thru 2470) ... 5-15 63-64
ATLANTIC (3000 series) ... 3-6 77-80
ATLANTIC (5005 "Doodlin' ") ... 10-20 60
BARONET (7111 "See See Rider") ... 8-12 62
COLUMBIA ... 3-5 82-87
CROSSOVER ... 4-6 73-78
DUNHILL GOLDIES ... 3-6 73
HURRAH ... 8-12
IMPULSE (200 "One Mint Julep") ... 8-12 61
IMPULSE (202 "I've Got News for You") ... 8-12 61
JAX (641 "Baby Let Me Hear You Call My Name") ... 300-500 52
MAYFAIR (121 "Pony Boy") ... 4-8
(With "Uncle Stu.")
RCA ... 4-6 76
ROCKIN' (504 "Walkin' and Talkin' to Myself") ... 100-200 52
SITTIN' IN WITH (641 "Baby Let Me Hear You Call My Name") ... 75-150 52
SWING TIME (250 "Baby Let Me Hold Your Hand") ... 75-100 51
SWING TIME (274 "Kiss Me Baby") ... 75-100 52
SWING TIME (297 "Hey Now") ... 800-1200 52
SWING TIME (300 "Baby Let Me Hear You Call My Name") ... 75-100 52
SWING TIME (326 "The Snow Is Falling") ... 500-750 53
TANGERINE ... 4-6 71
TIME (1026 "I Found My Baby") ... 10-15 60
TIME (1054 "Why Did You Go") ... 10-15 62
Picture Sleeves
ABC (11045 "That's a Lie") ... 4-8 68
BARONET (7111 "See See Rider") ... 10-15 62
EPs: 7-inch
ABC-PAR (119 "The Genius Hits the Road") ... 15-25 61
ABC-PAR (335 "Basin St. Blues") ... 15-25 60
(Stereo. Juke box issue only.)
ABC-PAR (410 "Modern Sounds in Country and Western Music") ... 25-35 62
ABC-PAR (415 "Greatest Hits") ... 15-25 62
(Stereo. Juke box issue only.)
ABC-PAR (465 "Ingredients in a Recipe for Soul") ... 15-25 63
(Stereo. Juke box issue only.)
ATLANTIC (567 "Ray Charles") ... 25-45 56
ATLANTIC (587 "Ray Charles") ... 25-45 57
ATLANTIC (597 "Great Ray Charles") ... 25-45 57
ATLANTIC (607 "Rock with Ray Charles") ... 25-45 58
ATLANTIC (614 "Soul Brothers") ... 25-45 58
(With Milt Jackson.)
ATLANTIC (619 "The Genius of Ray Charles") ... 25-45 59
ATLANTIC (8029 "What'd I Say") ... 25-45 59
U.A. (1004 "In the Heat of the Night") ... 10-20 67
(Promotional issue only.)
LPs: 10/12-inch
ABC (Except 590) ... 10-12 66-73
ABC (590 "A Man and His Soul") ... 20-25 67
ABC-PAR (300 series) ... 15-25 60-61
ABC-PAR (400 & 500 series) ... 10-20 62-66
AHED ... 8-12
(TV mail-order offer.)
ARCHIVES ... 8-12
ATLANTIC (500 series) ... 10-15 73
ATLANTIC (900 "The Ray Charles Story, Vols. 1 & 2") ... 30-40 62
(Combines Atlantic 8063 and 8064.)
ATLANTIC (1259 "The Great Ray Charles") ... 50-75 57
ATLANTIC (1279 "Soul Brothers") ... 40-60 58
(With Milt Jackson.)
ATLANTIC (1289 "Ray Charles at Newport") ... 40-60 58
ATLANTIC (1312 "The Genius of Ray Charles") ... 30-50 59
ATLANTIC (1360 "Soul Meeting") ... 25-35 62
(With Milt Jackson. Number indicates a '61 release, but not actually issued until 1962.)
ATLANTIC (1369 "Genius After Hours") ... 25-35 61
ATLANTIC (1500 series) ... 10-20 70
ATLANTIC (3700 series) ... 20-25 82
ATLANTIC (7000 series) ... 15-20 64
ATLANTIC (8006 "Ray Charles") ... 50-100 57
(Black label.)
ATLANTIC (8006 "Ray Charles") ... 25-45 59
(Red label.)
ATLANTIC (8025 "Yes Indeed") ... 40-60 59
(Black label.)
ATLANTIC (8025 "Yes Indeed") ... 25-45 60
(Red label.)
ATLANTIC (8029 "What'd I Say") ... 40-50 59
(Black label.)
ATLANTIC (8029 "What'd I Say") ... 25-45 60
(Red label.)
ATLANTIC (8039 "Ray Charles in Person") ... 40-50 60
(Black label.)
ATLANTIC (8039 "Ray Charles in Person") ... 25-35 60
(Red label.)
ATLANTIC (8052 "The Genius Sings the Blues") ... 30-40 61
ATLANTIC (8054 "Do the Twist") ... 30-40 61
ATLANTIC (8063 "The Ray Charles Story, Vol. 1") ... 25-35 62
ATLANTIC (8064 "The Ray Charles Story, Vol. 2") ... 25-35 62
ATLANTIC (8083 "The Ray Charles Story, Vol. 3") ... 25-35 63
ATLANTIC (8094 "The Ray Charles Story, Vol. 4") ... 25-35 64
ATLANTIC (19000 series) ... 5-12 77-80
BARONET ... 15-20 62
BLUESWAY ... 8-10 73
BULLDOG ... 5-10 84
COLUMBIA ... 5-10 83-86
CORONET ... 8-12 '60s
CROSSOVER ... 8-15 73-76
DESIGN ... 10-20 62
EVEREST ... 8-10 70-82
GRAND PRIX ... 10-20 '60s
GUEST STAR ... 10-20 64
HOLLYWOOD (504 "The Original Ray Charles") ... 100-150 59
HOLLYWOOD 505: see CHARLES, Ray / Charles Brown)
HURRAH ... 8-15
IMPULSE (2 "Genius Plus Soul Equals Jazz") ... 20-30 61
INTERMEDIA ... 5-10 84
JAZZ INT'L ... 15-25
KING ... 8-10 77
PALACE ... 5-10
PREMIER ... 8-10
SCEPTER ... 8-12
SPIN-O-RAMA ... 10-15 '60s
STRAND ... 10-15 '60s
TANGERINE ... 10-12 70-73
UPFRONT ... 8-10 '70s
Also see COOKIES
Also see GUITAR SLIM
Also see FULSON, Lowell
Also see JOEL, Billy, & Ray Charles
Also see JONES, Quincy, Ray Charles & Chaka Khan
Also see MAXIM TRIO
Also see RAELETTES

CHARLES, Ray / Charles Brown
LPs: 10/12-inch
HOLLYWOOD (505 "The Fabulous Artistry of Ray Charles") ... 100-150 59
(Brown, barely credited, provides four tracks.)
Also see BROWN, Charles

CHARLES, Ray / Solomon Burke
LPs: 10/12-inch
GRAND PRIX ... 10-20 64
Also see BURKE, Solomon

CHARLES, Ray, & Betty Carter *LP '61*
Singles: 7-inch
ABC-PAR ... 5-10 61-62
LPs: 10/12-inch
ABC-PAR (ABC-385 "Ray Charles & Betty Carter") ... 50-75 61
(Monaural.)
ABC-PAR (ABCS-385 "Ray Charles & Betty Carter") ... 75-100 61
(Stereo.)
DCC (2005 "Ray Charles & Betty Carter") ... 10-15 95
(Audiophile issue.)
Also see CARTER, Betty

CHARLES, Ray, & Clint Eastwood *C&W '80*
Singles: 7-inch
W.B. (49608 "Beers to You") ... 3-5 80
Also see EASTWOOD, Clint

CHARLES, Ray / Phil Flowers
Singles: 7-inch
BONUS (7019 "Walkin' & Talkin' ") ... 5-10 62
Picture Sleeves
BONUS (7019 "Walkin' & Talkin' ") ... 8-12 62

CHARLES, Ray, & Mickey Gilley *C&W '85*
Singles: 7-inch
COLUMBIA (04860 "It Ain't Gonna Worry My Mind") ... 3-5 85
Also see GILLEY, Mickey

CHARLES, Ray / Ivory Joe Hunter / Jimmy Rushing
LPs: 10/12-inch
DESIGN (909 "Three of a Kind") ... 15-20 '60s
(Black label, silver print.)
DESIGN (909 "Three of a Kind") ... 10-15 '60s
(Black, red, blue and yellow label.)
Also see HUNTER, Ivory Joe
Also see RUSHING, Jimmy

CHARLES, Ray, George Jones & Chet Atkins *C&W '83*
Singles: 7-inch
COLUMBIA (04297 "We Didn't See a Thing") ... 3-5 83
Also see ATKINS, Chet
Also see JONES, George

CHARLES, Ray, & Cleo Laine *LP '76*
LPs: 10/12-inch
RCA (1831 "Porgy & Bess") ... 10-15 76
(Two discs.)
Also see LAINE, Cleo

CHARLES, Ray & Jimmy Lewis *P&R/R&B '69*
Singles: 7-inch
ABC (11170 "If It Wasn't for Bad Luck") ... 4-8 69
Also see LEWIS, Jimmy

CHARLES, Ray / Little Richard / Sam Cooke
LPs: 10/12-inch
ALMOR (102 "Soul Blues") ... 10-20
Also see COOKE, Sam
Also see LITTLE RICHARD

CHARLES, Ray / Mo Jo & Mo Jo Chi Fours
LPs: 10/12-inch
VERNON (519 "Onstage at the Palladium") ... 10-20 '60s

CHARLES, Ray, & Willie Nelson *C&W '84*
Singles: 7-inch
COLUMBIA (04715 "Seven Spanish Angels") ... 3-5 84
Also see NELSON, Willie

CHARLES, Ray / Arbee Stidham / Li'l Son Jackson / James Wayne
LPs: 10/12-inch
MAINSTREAM ... 8-12 71
Also see JACKSON, Li'l Son

Also see STIDHAM, Arbee
Also see WAYNE, James

CHARLES, Ray, & B.J. Thomas — *C&W '84*
Singles: 7-inch
COLUMBIA (04531 "Rock and Roll Shoes") ... 3-5 — 85
Also see THOMAS, B.J.

CHARLES, Ray, & Hank Williams Jr. — *C&W '85*
Singles: 7-inch
COLUMBIA (05575 "Two Old Cats Like Us") ... 3-5 — 85
Also see WILLIAMS, Hank, Jr.

CHARLES, Ray, & Jimmy Witherspoon
LPs: 10/12-inch
CROWN (418 "Mr. Ray Charles") ... 15-25 — 65
(Stereo.)
CROWN (5418 "Mr. Ray Charles") ... 15-25 — 65
(Monaural.)
Also see CHARLES, Ray
Also see WITHERSPOON, Jimmy

CHARLES, Ray, Singers — *P&R '55*
(Ray Charles Chorus)
Singles: 78 rpm
JUBILEE ... 4-6 — 54
MGM ... 4-6 — 51-56
Singles: 7-inch
COMMAND ... 4-6 — 64-70
DECCA ... 10-15 — 58-59
JUBILEE ... 10-20 — 54
MGM ... 10-20 — 51-56
EPs: 7-inch
CADENCE ... 8-15 — '50s
DECCA ... 8-15 — 59
ESSEX ... 8-15 — '50s
JAMESTOWN ... 8-15 — 57
MGM ... 8-15 — 55-57
LPs: 10/12-inch
ABC ... 5-10 — 73
ALSHIRE ... 5-10 — 70
ATCO ... 8-15 — 68
CAMDEN ... 5-10 — 67
COMMAND ... 10-20 — 62-71
DECCA ... 10-20 — 58-60
ESSEX (110 "Far Away Places") ... 15-25 — 54
(10-inch LP.)
MCA ... 4-6 — 82
MGM (100 series) ... 5-10 — 71
MGM (3000 series) ... 15-25 — 55-60
MGM (4000 series) ... 10-20 — 63-66
METRO ... 6-10 — 65
SOMERSET ... 5-10 — 64
VOCALION ... 8-10 — 66
Also see BARRY, Jack
Also see COMO, Perry
Also see DEAN, Libby
Also see JAMES, Joni
Also see KNIGHT, Evelyn
Also see LASSIES

CHARLES, Roosevelt
LPs: 10/12-inch
VANGUARD (9136 "Blues, Prayer, Work and Trouble Songs") ... 10-20 — 64

CHARLES, Tommy — *P&R '56*
Singles: 78 rpm
DECCA ... 10-20 — 56
WILLETT (111 "Hey There Baby") ... 50-100 — 57
Singles: 7-inch
DECCA ... 10-20 — 56
WILLETT (111 "Hey There Baby") ... 40-60 — 57
Session: Anita Kerr Singers.
Also see KERR, Anita

CHARLES, Vince, & Sonics
Singles: 7-inch
LORI (9553 "Let's Fall in Love") ... 20-30 — 63

CHARLES & CARL
Singles: 78 rpm
RED ROBIN (137 "One More Chance") ... 40-60 — 55
Singles: 7-inch
RED ROBIN (137 "One More Chance") ... 100-150 — 55
Members: Charles Sampson; Carl Hazan.

CHARLES & ESQUIRES
Singles: 7-inch
SALEM (22064 "Sometime Beats No Time") ... 10-20 — '60s

CHARLES K
Singles: 7-inch
TUPELO (2984 "Right Bird Baby") ... 150-250

CHARLEY & JR.
Singles: 7-inch
MGM (12615 "Cuddle Lovin' Baby") ... 20-40 — 58

CHARLIE & CHAN
Singles: 7-inch
KAPP (582 "Rickshaw Drag Race") ... 10-15 — 64

CHARLIE & DON
Singles: 7-inch
DUEL (513 "Hush Little Baby") ... 30-40 — 62

CHARLIE & JIVES
Singles: 7-inch
HOUR (104 "The Coffee Grind") ... 10-15 — 62
Also see EASELY, Benny
Also see JIVES
Also see ROYAL JESTERS
Also see TAYLOR, Bobby

CHARLIE & RAY
Singles: 78 rpm
HERALD ... 15-30 — 54-57
Singles: 7-inch
FLASHBACK (006 "I Love You Madly") ... 4-8 — 65
HERALD (438 "I Love You Madly") ... 30-50 — 54
HERALD (447 "My Lovin' Baby") ... 30-50 — 55
HERALD (454 thru 487) ... 20-40 — 55-56
HERALD (503 "I Love You Madly") ... 15-25 — 57
HERALD (515 "Dearest One") ... 20-25 — 58
HI (436 "I Love You Madly") ... 4-6
JANUS (727 "I Love You Madly") ... 4-6
JOSIE (989 "Alright, Okay, You Win") ... 8-10 — 68
TEL (1005 "This Is Love") ... 15-25 — 59

CHARM KINGS
Singles: 7-inch
MARK (146 "Tell Me a Tale") ... 800-1200 — 60

CHARMAINE
Singles: 7-inch
SEROCK (2000 "Young Girl") ... 10-20 — 62
20TH FOX (497 "Till the End") ... 8-12 — 64

CHARMERS
("With Rhythm Acc.")
Singles: 78 rpm
CENTRAL ... 200-300 — 54
TIMELY (1009 "I Was Wrong") ... 300-400 — 54
TIMELY (1011 "Church on the Hill") ... 200-300 — 54
Singles: 7-inch
CENTRAL (1002 "The Beating of My Heart") ... 500-750 — 54
CENTRAL (1006 "Tony, My Darling") ... 1500-2000 — 54
TIMELY (1009 "I Was Wrong") ... 500-1000 — 54
Member: Vicki Burgess.
Also see JOYTONES

CHARMERS
Singles: 78 rpm
ALADDIN ... 15-25 — 56
Singles: 7-inch
ALADDIN (3337 "All Alone") ... 40-50 — 56
ALADDIN (3341 "He's Gone") ... 40-50 — 56
IMPERIAL (5957 "All Alone") ... 8-12 — 63

CHARMERS
Singles: 7-inch
SILHOUETTE (521 "Rock Rhythm and Blues") ... 40-50 — 57
(This same number was used for *Sent Up*, by the Falcons.)
Also see FALCONS

CHARMERS
Singles: 7-inch
JAF (2021 "Little Fool") ... 20-30 — 61

CHARMERS
Singles: 7-inch
CO-REC (101 "Watch What You Do") ... 15-25 — 63
SURE PLAY (104 "Lesson from the Stars") ... 300-400 — 62

CHARMERS
Singles: 7-inch
LAURIE (3142 "Johnny") ... 10-15 — 62
LAURIE (3173 "I Cried") ... 15-25 — 63
LAURIE (3203 "Sweet Talk") ... 10-15 — 63
LOUIS (6806 "Where's the Boy") ... 10-20 — 65
P.I.P. (8000 "After You Walk Me Home") ... 15-25 — 64
STUYVESANT ... 8-10

CHARMETTES — *P&R/R&B '63*
(Charmetts)
Singles: 7-inch
FEDERAL (12345 "Johnny Johnny") ... 30-40 — 59
HI (2003 "My Love with All My Heart") ... 15-25 — 58
KAPP (547 "Please Don't Kiss Me Again") ... 15-25 — 63
KAPP (570 "He's a Wise Guy") ... 10-15 — 64
MALA (491 "Mailbox") ... 5-10 — 64
MARKAY (101 "Donnie") ... 75-100 — 62
MARLIN (16001 "One More Time") ... 20-30 — 62
MELOMEGA ... 5-10 — 62
MONA (553 "The Deeds to My Heart") ... 40-50 — 60
TRI DISC (103 "Why Oh Why") ... 25-35 — 62
WORLD ARTISTS (1053 "Sugar Boy") ... 10-20 — 65
Also see MARGARET & CHARMETTES

CHARMS — *P&R/R&B '54*
(Otis Williams & the Charms; Otis Williams & His New Group; Otis Williams)
Singles: 78 rpm
CHART ... 15-25 — 55-56
DELUXE ... 25-75 — 54-57
QUALITY/KING ... 40-60 — 54
(Canadian.)
ROCKIN' ... 200-300 — 53
Singles: 7-inch
CHART (608 "Love's Our Inspiration") ... 30-40 — 55
(Has "Vocal Group The Charms" between the horizontal line patterns.)
CHART (608 "Love's Our Inspiration") ... 15-25 — 55
(Has "Vocal Group The Charms" below horizontal rope-like lines.)
CHART (613 "Heart of a Rose") ... 40-60 — 56
CHART (623 "I'll Be True") ... 50-75 — 56
DELUXE (6000 "Heaven Only Knows") ... 100-200 — 53
DELUXE (6014 "Happy Are We") ... 75-150 — 53
DELUXE (6034 "Bye-Bye Baby") ... 75-150 — 54
DELUXE (6050 "Quiet Please") ... 50-125 — 54
DELUXE (6056 "My Baby Dearest Darling") ... 100-200 — 54
DELUXE (6062 "Hearts of Stone") ... 50-75 — 54
DELUXE (6065 "Two Hearts") ... 20-30 — 54
DELUXE (6072 "Crazy, Crazy Love") ... 20-30 — 54
DELUXE (6076 "Ling, Ting, Tong") ... 50-75 — 54
DELUXE (6080 thru 6097) ... 20-30 — 55-56
DELUXE (6098 "I'll Remember You") ... 15-25 — 56
DELUXE (6105 "Blues Stay Away from Me") ... 15-25 — 56
(Monaural.)
DELUXE (6105 "Blues Stay Away from Me") ... 30-40 — 56
(Stereo.)
DELUXE (6115 thru 6183, except 6160) ... 15-25 — 57-59
DELUXE (6160 "Baby-O") ... 20-30 — 57
DELUXE (6185 "Tears of Happiness") ... 15-25 — 59
(Monaural.)
DELUXE (6185 "Tears of Happiness") ... 30-40 — 59
(Stereo.)
DELUXE (6186 "Who Knows") ... 15-25 — 59
DELUXE (6187 "Blues Stay Away from Me") ... 15-25 — 59
GUSTO ... 4-6 — 77
KING (5323 thru 5558, except 5372) ... 10-20 — 60-61
KING (5372 "Image of a Girl") ... 30-40 — 60
KING (5682 thru 5880) ... 8-12 — 62-63
OKEH (7225 thru 7261) ... 5-10 — 65-66
QUALITY/KING (4302 "Hearts of Stone") ... 50-100 — 54
(Canadian.)
QUALITY/KING (4323 "Two Hearts") ... 50-100 — 54
(Canadian.)
ROCKIN' (516 "Heaven Only Knows") ... 400-500 — 53
STOP ... 5-8 — 69
EPs: 7-inch
DELUXE (357 "Hits By the Charms") ... 200-300 — 55
DELUXE (364 "Hits By the Charms") ... 200-300 — 55
DELUXE (385 "Otis Williams and the Charms") ... 200-300 — 56
KING (357 "Hits By the Charms") ... 50-100 — 58
KING (364 "Hits By the Charms, Vol. 2") ... 50-100 — 58
KING (385 "Otis Williams and His Charms") ... 50-100 — 58
LPs: 10/12-inch
DELUXE (570 "All Their Hits") ... 800-1200 — 58
(With color photo of the group on cover.)
KING (614 "This Is Otis Williams and the Charms") ... 100-200 — 59
KING/GUSTO ... 8-10 — 78
POWER PAK ... 8-10 — 74
Members: Otis Williams; Ron Bradley; Don Peark; Joe Penn; Richard Parker; Rollie Willis.
Also see ESCOS
Also see REDELL, Teddy
Also see TINY TOPSY
Also see WILLIAMS, Otis
Also see WILLIS, Rollie, & Contenders

CHARMS
Singles: 7-inch
CANADIAN-AMERICAN (193 "Ram-Bunk-Shush") ... 10-15 — 66
EMERSON (101 "Ram-Bunk-Shush") ... 12-18 — 64
JAY-DEE (2766 "Oh Mercy") ... 25-35 — 62
JAY-DEE (2949 "I Wouldn't Be So Sure") ... 25-35 — 62
MAURY (3929 "Night Train to Memphis") ... 25-35 — 63
STUDIO CITY (1009 "Night Train to Memphis") ... 25-35 — 64
Member: Gary Ray Emerson.

CHARMS
(Charms Ltd.)
Singles: 7-inch
EMBLEM (104 "If You Got the Notion") ... 20-25
EMBLEM (109 "What Goes Up") ... 20-25

CHARTERS
(With the Wanderers)
Singles: 7-inch
ALVA (1001 "I Lost You") ... 75-100 — 63
MEL-O-DY (104 "Trouble Lover") ... 1000-1500 — 62
MERRY GO ROUND (103 "Lost in a Dream") ... 30-40 — 64
TARX (1003 "My Rose") ... 50-75 — 62

CHARTS — *P&R '57*
Singles: 78 rpm
EVERLAST (5001 "Deserie") ... 100-150 — 57
Singles: 7-inch
ABC ... 4-6 — 73
COLLECTABLES ... 3-5 — '80s
ENJOY (1002 "Deserie") ... 75-125 — 62
EVERLAST (5001 "Deserie") ... 75-100 — 57
("Vocal Quintet" in upper and lower case.)
EVERLAST (5001 "Deserie") ... 20-30 — 57
("Vocal Quintet" in all upper case letters.)
EVERLAST (5001 "Deserie") ... 10-20 — 57
(Reads: "Distributed by Enjoy Record Corp.")
EVERLAST (5002 "Dance Girl") ... 25-35 — 57
EVERLAST (5006 "You're the Reason") ... 25-35 — 57
EVERLAST (5008 "All Because of Love") ... 25-35 — 57
EVERLAST (5010 "My Diane") ... 40-50 — 57
EVERLAST (5026 "Deserie") ... 8-12 — 63
GUYDEN (2021 "For the Birds") ... 10-15 — 59
LOST NITE ... 4-8
VEL-V-TONE (102 "Keep Dancing with Me") ... 50-100 — '60s
WAND (1112 "Deserie") ... 15-25 — 66
WAND (1124 "Livin' the Nightlife") ... 25-50 — 66
LPs: 10/12-inch
COLLECTABLES ... 8-10 — 86
LOST NITE (10 "The Charts") ... 10-20 — 81
(10-inch LP. Red vinyl. 1000 made.)
Members: Joe Grier; Glen Jackson; Steve Brown; Ross Buford; Leroy Binns.
Also see COOPER, Les

CHARTS / Bop-Chords / Ladders / Harmonaires
LPs: 10/12-inch
EVERLAST (201 "Our Best to You") ... 100-200 — 60
Also see BOP-CHORDS
Also see LADDERS
Also see HARMONAIRES

CHASE, Al, & Midnighters
Singles: 7-inch
JIN (118 "Lubby Lou") ... 20-30 — 60

CHASE, Allan
Singles: 7-inch
CINEMA (102 "I Live Each Day") ... 15-25 — 62
CINEMA (108 "I'm in Love with Miss Connie Francis") ... 25-35 — 62
COLUMBIA (41446 thru 41693) ... 10-20 — 59-60

CHASE, Bobby

Singles: 7-inch

ASCOT (2195 "Missing Someone") 10-20 65
SOUTHERN ARTISTS (2027 "Missing Someone") 40-50 65

CHASE, Buddy

Singles: 7-inch

20TH FOX (205 "Look for a Star") 10-15 60

CHASE, Eddie

Singles: 7-inch

VISCOUNT (529 "If You Only Knew") 15-25 59

CHASE, Lincoln
(With the Sandmen)

Singles: 78 rpm

COLUMBIA 5-10 55
DAWN 8-12 56-57
DECCA 8-12 53
RCA 8-12 53

Singles: 7-inch

COLUMBIA (40475 "That's All I Need") ... 10-15 55
COLUMBIA (41914 "MissOrangutang") ... 25-35 60
COLUMBIA (42051 "Do I Worry") 5-10 61
DAWN 10-15 56-57
DECCA 10-15 53
LIBERTY (55074 "You're Driving Me Crazy") 10-15 57
LIBERTY (55080 "Save the Last Dance for Me") 10-15 57
RCA 10-15 53
SPLASH (802 "Deep in the Jungle") 8-12 59
SWAN (4120 "Sweet Torture") 5-10 62

LPs: 10/12-inch

LIBERTY (3076 "The Explosive Lincoln Chase") 30-50 57
PARAMOUNT 8-12 74

CHASE & GENE

Singles: 7-inch

HALLWAY (1911 "I'm Through Foolin' ") 5-10 63
SUGAR (1001 "You Are Everything to Me") 30-40

CHASE & JEAN

Singles: 7-inch

DART (146 "Good Loving") 10-15 61

CHASTAIN, Jody

Singles: 7-inch

KAY (1002 "My My") 50-100 58

CHATEAUS

Singles: 78 rpm

EPIC (9163 "Let Me Tell You Baby") 20-30 56

Singles: 7-inch

EPIC (9163 "Let Me Tell You Baby") 50-75 56

CHATEAUS
(With Leroy Kirkland & Orchestra)

Singles: 7-inch

W.B. (5023 "Satisfied") 40-60 58
W.B. (5043 "If I Didn't Care") 50-75 59
W.B. (5071 "Ladder of Love") 25-50 59

CHATEAUS

Singles: 7-inch

CORAL (62364 "Honest I Will") 25-35 63

CHATEAUS

Singles: 7-inch

BOSS (9912 "I'm the One") 75-150 65
JAM (114 "Count On Me") 10-20 65
SMASH (2021 "I'm the One") 8-12 66
SOUND STAGE 7 (2536 "Seven Come Eleven") 10-15 65

CHATEAUX

Singles: 7-inch

EYE (100 "Reference Man") 40-60 68
Member: Tommy Bolin
Also see SHATTOES

CHATEAUX, Nicky C.

Singles: 7-inch

BAY-SOUND (67012 "Those Good Times") 10-20

CHATMAN, Christine
(With Mabel Smith)

Singles: 78 rpm

DECCA (8660 "Hurry Hurry") 10-15 44
MILLION (1002 "Wind's Lament") 10-15
Also see BIG MAYBELLE
Also see PRINCE, Peppy

CHATMAN, Earl

Singles: 7-inch

FORTUNE (844 "Love Me Baby") 100-200 58

CHATMAN, Sam

Singles: 7-inch

ARHOOLIE (1005 "Nigger Be a Nigger") . 10-20 60
ARHOOLIE (1006 "God Don't Like Ugly") 10-20 60
Also see SAMPSON, Phil

CHATMAN, Sam, & Sparks

Singles: 7-inch

BOSS (2121 "Nobody But Me") 40-50 63
Also see CHATMAN, Sam
Also see SINGING SAM & SPARKS

CHATTERS

Singles: 7-inch

VIKING (1001 "Teenage Love Affair") 10-20 59

CHAUMONTS

Singles: 7-inch

BAY SOUND (2740 "I Need Your Love") . 30-50 67
BAY SOUND (2750 "All of My Life") 20-30 69
CARAVELLE (2470 "I Need Your Love") 50-100 67

CHAUNTES

Singles: 7-inch

TONIX (15 "Bohemian Love") 10-20

CHAVELLES

Singles: 78 rpm

VITA (127 "Valley of Love") 50-75 56

Singles: 7-inch

VITA (127 "Valley of Love") 100-125 56
Members: Billy Storm; Sheridan Spencer; Gary Pipkins; Bruce Corfield.
Also see STORM, Billy
Also see UNTOUCHABLES
Also see VALIANTS

CHAVELLS

Singles: 7-inch

BUTANE (777 "It's Goodbye") 10-15 63

CHAVEZ, Freddie

Singles: 7-inch

LOOK (5010 "They'll Never Know Why") 50-100 68

CHAVIS, Boozoo
(Wilson Chavis)

Singles: 78 rpm

FOLK STAR 30-50 55
IMPERIAL 15-25 56

Singles: 7-inch

FOLK STAR (1197 "Boozoo Stomp") 50-75 55
FOLK STAR (1201 "Forty-One Days") 50-75 55
GOLDBAND 5-10 63
IMPERIAL (5374 "Boozoo Stomp") 25-35 56

CHAVIS BROTHERS
(Five Chavis Brothers)

Singles: 7-inch

ASCOT (2177 "Torture Me") 8-12 65
BIG TOP (3027 "Love Me Baby") 100-200 59
CLOCK (1025 "So Tired") 150-200 60
CORAL (62270 "Baby, Don't Leave Me") . 50-75 61
HEADLINE (1015 "Walk with Me Baby") .. 10-20 62
PARKWAY (851 "Slippin' & Slidin' ") 15-25 62

LPs: 10/12-inch

HOW (410 "Dedicated to You") 100-150 63
Member: Danny Chavis.

CHAYNS
(Chaynes)

Singles: 7-inch

CHAYN REACTION ("Night Time") 25-35 67
(No selection number used.)
CHAYN REACTION (002 "Run and Hide") 20-30 68
INT'L ARTISTS (114 "Night Time") 15-25 67
INT'L ARTISTS (119 "There's Something Wrong") 15-25 67

CHEAP TRICK — LP '77

Singles: 12-inch

EPIC 8-12 83
PASHA (1827 "Up the Creek") 8-12 84
(Promotional issue only.)

Singles: 7-inch

ASYLUM 3-5 81
COLUMBIA 3-5 86
EPIC 3-6 77-91
PASHA 3-5 84
W.B. 3-5 83

Picture Sleeves

EPIC (Except 50814) 3-6 79-88
EPIC (50814 "Voices") 5-10 79
(Promotional issue only.)

EPs: 7-inch

CSP 5-10 81
(Promotional issue only. Made for Nestle's.)

LPs: 10/12-inch

EPIC (Except 35773) 5-10 76-90
EPIC (35773 "Dream Police") 35-40 80
(Picture disc. Promotional issue only.)
EPIC/NU-DISC 10-15 80
(Includes bonus single.)
PASHA 5-10 84
Members: Robin Zander; Tom Petersson; Rick Nielson; Bun E. Carlos; Jon Brant.
Also see FUSE
Also see GRIM REAPERS
Also see PAEGENS

CHEAP TRICK / Aldo Nova / Saxon

Singles

CBS ("Southwest Tour") 8-12 82
(Square cardboard picture disc. Selection number not known.)
Also see CHEAP TRICK
Also see NOVA, Aldo

CHEATERS
(Vic Pitts & Cheaters)

Singles: 7-inch

BREWTOWN (9 "Astrology Child") 4-8 72
JEWEL (846 "Loose Boodie") 4-6 74
RAYNARD (10056 "You're Mine") 15-25 66
Members: Beverly Pitts; Vic Pitts; Sharon Pitts; Omar Dupree; Lee Brown; Van Patterson; E.C. Reynolds; Ray Maxwell; Bertha Downs; Rollo Armstead; Al Vance; Greg Browder.
Also see PITTS, Beverly, & Cheaters

CHEATERS

Singles: 7-inch

WAX (213 "Suzanne") 25-50 65

CHECKER, Chubby — P&R '59
(With Dee Dee Sharp)

Singles: 7-inch

ABKCO 4-6 72
AMHERST 4-6 76
BUDDAH 4-6 69
MCA 3-5 82
PARKWAY (006 "The Jet") 10-15 62
PARKWAY (70E-1 "Blueberry Hill") .... 8-12 '60s
(Orange label.)
PARKWAY (70E-1 "Blueberry Hill") .... 10-20 '60s
(White label. Promotional issue only.)
PARKWAY (105 "Looking at Tomorrow") 5-10 66
PARKWAY (112 "Karate Monkey") 5-10 66
PARKWAY (804 "The Class") 10-20 59
PARKWAY (808 "Whole Lotta Laughin' ") 10-20 59
PARKWAY (810 "Dancing Dinosaur") 10-20 60
PARKWAY (811 "The Twist"/"Toot") 15-25 60
(White label.)
PARKWAY (811 "The Twist"/"Toot") 10-15 60
(Orange label.)
PARKWAY (811 "The Twist"/"Twistin' U.S.A.") 5-10 61
(Yellow/orange or orange label.)
PARKWAY (811 "The Twist") 20-30 61
(Colored vinyl.)
PARKWAY (813 thru 959, except 824) 5-10 60-65
PARKWAY (824 "Let's Twist Again") 5-10 61
(Black vinyl.)
PARKWAY (824 "Let's Twist Again") 20-30 61
(Colored vinyl.)
PARKWAY (965 "You Just Don't Know") 100-200 66
PARKWAY (989 "Hey You! Little Boo-Ga-Loo") 5-10 66
PRACTICE RECORD (333 "Twister") 20-30 62
(No actual label name shown. Promotional issue only.)
20TH FOX 4-6 73-74

Picture Sleeves

PARKWAY 15-20 61-65

EPs: 7-inch

PARKWAY 15-20 61
(Includes Compact 33 Doubles.)

LPs: 10/12-inch

ABKCO 8-12 72
D.C.M. 5-10
EVEREST 5-10 81
51 WEST 5-10 84
MCA 8-10 82
PARKWAY (5001 "Chubby Checker") 20-30 62
PARKWAY (7001 "Twist with Chubby Checker") 20-30 60
PARKWAY (7002 "For Twisters Only") 20-30 60
PARKWAY (7002 "For Teen Twisters Only") 20-30 61
(Monaural.)
PARKWAY (SP-7002 "For Teen Twisters Only") 30-40 61
(Stereo.)
PARKWAY (7003 "It's Pony Time") 20-30 61
PARKWAY (7004 "Let's Twist Again") 20-30 61
PARKWAY (7007 "Your Twist Party with the King of the Twist") 20-30 61
PARKWAY (7008 "Twistin' 'Round the World") 20-30 62
(Monaural.)
PARKWAY (SP-7008 "Twistin' 'Round the World") 30-40 62
(Stereo.)
PARKWAY (7009 "For Teen Twisters Only") 25-35 62
PARKWAY (SP-7009 "For Teen Twisters Only") 30-40 62
PARKWAY (7014 "All the Hits") 20-30 62
(Monaural.)
PARKWAY (SP-7014 "All the Hits") 25-35 62
(Stereo.)
PARKWAY (7020 "Limbo Party") 20-30 62
(Monaural.)
PARKWAY (SP-7020 "Limbo Party") 25-35 62
(Stereo.)
PARKWAY (7022 "Biggest Hits") 20-30 62
(Monaural.)
PARKWAY (SP-7022 "Biggest Hits") 25-35 62
(Stereo.)
PARKWAY (7026 "In Person") 20-30 63
(Monaural.)
PARKWAY (SP-7026 "In Person") 25-35 63
(Stereo.)
PARKWAY (7027 "Let's Limbo Some More") 20-30 63
(Monaural.)
PARKWAY (SP-7027 "Let's Limbo Some More") 25-35 63
(Stereo.)
PARKWAY (7030 "Beach Party") 20-30 63
(Monaural.)
PARKWAY (SP-7030 "Beach Party") 25-35 63
(Stereo.)
PARKWAY (7036 "Chubby Checker") 20-30 63
(Monaural.)
PARKWAY (SP-7036 "Chubby Checker") 25-35 63
(Stereo.)
PARKWAY (7040 "Folk Album") 20-30 63
(Monaural.)
PARKWAY (SP-7040 "Folk Album") 25-35 63
(Stereo.)
PARKWAY (7045 "Discoteque") 15-25 65
(Monaural.)
PARKWAY (SP-7045 "Discoteque") 20-30 65
(Stereo.)
PARKWAY (7048 "18 Golden Hits") 15-25 66
(Monaural.)
PARKWAY (SP-7048 "18 Golden Hits") ... 20-30 66
(Stereo.)
Also see DREAMLOVERS
Also see LITTLE SISTERS

CHECKER, Chubby / Gary U.S. Bonds

LPs: 10/12-inch

EXACT 5-10 80
Also see BONDS, Gary "U.S."

CHECKER, Chubby, & Bobby Rydell — LP '61

Singles: 7-inch

CAMEO (12 "Your Hits & Mine") 10-20 61
(Promotional issue only.)
CAMEO (205 "Jingle Bell Rock") 8-15 61
CAMEO (214 "Teach Me to Twist") 8-15 62

Picture Sleeves

CAMEO (205 "Jingle Bell Rock") 10-20 61
CAMEO (214 "Teach Me to Twist") 10-20 62

LPs: 10/12-inch
CAMEO (1013 "Chubby Checker & Bobby Rydell")....................... 20-30 61
CAMEO (1063 "Chubby Checker & Bobby Rydell")....................... 20-30 63
Also see RYDELL, Bobby

CHECKER, Chubby, & Dee Dee Sharp *LP '62*
Singles: 7-inch
PARKWAY (835 "Slow Twistin' ")................5-10 62
PARKWAY (7041 "The Twist")................ 10-15 63
(Promotional issue only. Bonus single, packaged with *Oldies By the Dozen, Vol. 2*)
LPs: 10/12-inch
CAMEO (1029 "Down to Earth")............ 20-30 62
Also see CHECKER, Chubby
Also see SHARP, Dee Dee

CHECKER BOARD SQUARE
Singles: 7-inch
VILLA (705 "Double Cooking")............ 100-200

CHECKER COAT BOYS
Singles: 7-inch
BELL (51 "Whispering Bells").................. 10-15 57

CHECKER DOTS
Singles: 7-inch
PEACOCK (1688 "Alpha Omega")........... 15-25 59

CHECKERLADS
Singles: 7-inch
RCA (8986 "Shake Yourself Down")........ 10-20 66

CHECKERS
Singles: 78 rpm
KING (4558 "Flame in My Heart")........ 100-200 52
KING (4581 "Night's Curtains")............ 200-300 52
KING (4596 "My Prayer Tonight")........... 100-200 53
KING (4626 "I Wanna Know")............... 100-200 53
KING (4673 "I Promise You")............... 50-100 53
KING (4675 "White Cliffs of Dover")....... 50-100 53
KING (4710 "House with No Windows") 50-100 54
KING (4719 "Over the Rainbow").......... 50-100 54
KING (4751 "I Wasn't Thinkin', I Was Drinkin' ").. 50-100 54
KING (4764 "Trying to Hold My Girl") 50-100 54
Singles: 7-inch
FEDERAL (12355 "Sentimental Heart") .. 10-20 59
FEDERAL (12375 "White Cliffs of Dover").. 10-20 60
GUSTO..3-5 80
KING (4558 "Flame in My Heart")........ 600-800 52
KING (4581 "Night's Curtains")............ 600-800 52
KING (4596 "My Prayer Tonight")......... 500-750 53
KING (4626 "I Wanna Know")............ 300-400 53
KING (4673 "I Promise You")............... 150-250 53
KING (4675 "White Cliffs of Dover")....... 50-150 53
KING (4710 "House with No Windows") 50-150 54
KING (4719 "Over the Rainbow")......... 50-150 54
KING (4751 "I Wasn't Thinkin', I Was Drinkin' ").. 50-150 54
KING (4764 "Trying to Hold My Girl") ... 50-150 54
KING (5156 "Heaven Only Knows")......... 60-80 58
Members: Charlie White; Bill Brown.
Also see DOMINOES
Also see ORIGINAL CHECKERS

CHECKERS
Singles: 7-inch
KING (5199 "Teardrops Are Falling")....... 30-40 59
(Previously issued as by the Five Wings.)
Also see FIVE WINGS

CHECKERS
Singles: 7-inch
ARVEE (5035 "Skooby Doo")................. 10-20 61
JERDEN (710 "Black Cat")................... 10-20 63
PATRICE (8720 "Double Jump")............ 10-20 60

CHECKERS
Singles: 7-inch
SKYLA (1120 "Cascade")..................... 10-20 61

CHECKERS
Singles: 7-inch
MICKAY'S (3008 "Applesauce").............. 10-20 65

CHECK-MATES
Singles: 7-inch
BLACK DOG (1001 "Scrappy").............. 15-25 59
(Reissued as by the Shamrocks.)
Member: Jim Ford.
Also see FORD, Jim
Also see SHAMROCKS

CHECK-MATES
Singles: 7-inch
ARVEE (500 "Hey Mrs. Jones")...............20-30 58
ARVEE (5030 "Hey Mrs. Jones")............10-20 61

CHECKMATES
Singles: 7-inch
CHAMP...15-20
LONDON (10520 "Checkmate Twist")........5-10 62
RUFF (1003 "Hey Girl").........................8-12 65
RUFF (1006 "So Hard to Find")..............8-12 65
(Shown as by the Charming Checkmates.)

CHECK-MATES
Singles: 7-inch
REGENCY (26 "What Do You Do")..........10-15 62

CHECKMATES
LPs: 10/12-inch
JUSTICE (149 "Checkmate")...............350-500 68
Members: Billy Carden; Baron Conklin; Dave Mack; John McCurdy; Jon Mueller; George Outlaw; Roddy Porter; Sammy Winston.

CHECKMATES LTD. *P&R/LP '69*
(Featuring Sonny Charles)
Singles: 7-inch
A&M..4-6 69
CAPITOL (5603 thru 5922, except 5753).10-20 66-67
CAPITOL (5753 "Kissin' Her and Cryin' for You")...20-30 66
FANTASY...4-6 77-78
GREEDY...4-6 77
POLYDOR (14313 "All Alone by the Telephone")..4-6 76
RUSTIC...4-6 74
LPs: 10/12-inch
A&M (4183 "Love Is All We Have to Give")...15-25 69
CAPITOL (2840 "Live")........................25-35 67
FANTASY...8-10 77
IKON..5-10
POLYDOR..8-10 76
RUSTIC...8-10 74
Members: Sonny Charles; Bill Van Buskirk; Marvin Smith; Bobby Stevens; Harvey Trees.
Also see STEVENS, Bobby, & Checkmates Ltd.

CHEECH & CHONG *LP '71*
Singles: 12-inch
MCA..4-6 85
Singles: 7-inch
A&M..4-6
EPIC/ODE...4-6 77
MCA..3-5 85
ODE..4-6 71-77
W.B...4-6 78
Picture Sleeves
A&M..4-6
MCA..3-5 85
ODE..8-12 73-77
W.B...4-6 78
EPs: 7-inch
ODE (8 "Cheech & Chong")....................5-8 71
LPs: 10/12-inch
("Cheech & Chong") 40-50 83
(No label name or selection number used. Promotional only, unplayable picture disc.)
EPIC/ODE...8-10 77
MCA..5-8 85
ODE..8-12 71-76
W.B...8-10 78-80
Members: Richard Marin; Thomas Chong.
Also see TAYLOR, Bobby

CHEEK-O-VASS & SOLA-TEARS
Singles: 7-inch
TWY-LITE (752 "Bo-Peep Rock").........200-250
Also see VANCE, Chico

CHEERIOS
Singles: 7-inch
GOLDEN OLDIES (1 "Ding Dong Honeymoon")..15-25
INFINITY (011 "Ding Dong Honeymoon").......................................200-300 61

CHEERS *P&R '54*
(With Les Baxter's Orchestra & Chorus; with Buddy Bregman)
Singles: 78 rpm
CAPITOL..15-20 54-56
MERCURY...10-15 57
Singles: 7-inch
CAPITOL (2921 thru 3353).................20-30 54-56
MERCURY (71083 "Big Feet")................15-25 57
EPs: 7-inch
CAPITOL (584 "Bazoom")......................50-100 55
Members: Bert Convy; Gil Garfield; Susan Allen.
Also see BAXTER, Les
Also see CONVY, Bert

CHEKKERS
Singles: 7-inch
LOOK (5007 "Please Don't Go")................5-10 67
RED FEATHER (8122 "I Love You for Sentimental Reasons")...20-30
(Black vinyl.)
RED FEATHER (8122 "I Love You for Sentimental Reasons")...40-50
(Blue vinyl.)

CHELL-MARS
Singles: 7-inch
HI MAR (505/506 "Roamin' Heart"/"Feel Alright")...15-25 63
JAMIE (1266 "Roamin' Heart")...............10-15 63
Members: Buddy Swords; Tony Mann; Jimmy Hoar; Mike Wickenheiser.
Session: Gwen Speller; Donza Rae.

CHELLOWS
Singles: 7-inch
PONCELLO (713 "Be My Baby")............30-40 61

CHENIER, Clifton
(With the Red Hot Louisiana Band)
Singles: 78 rpm
ARGO..15-25 57
CHECKER...75-100 60
SPECIALTY...20-30 55
Singles: 7-inch
ARGO (5262 "Where Can My Baby Be") .40-60 57
ARHOOLIE (506 thru 518).......................5-10 64-66
BAYOU (701 thru 719)............................5-10 '60s
BELL (811 "Frog Legs")..........................4-8 69
CHECKER (939 "Bayou Drive")................30-40 60
CRAZY CAJUN (520 "Say Too Koreck")....5-10 66
SPECIALTY (552 "Boppin' the Rock")......25-50 55
SPECIALTY (556 "Think It Over")...........40-60 55
SPECIALTY (568 "The Cat's Dreaming").40-60 55
ZYNN (506 "It Happened So Fast")..........15-25 58
ZYNN (1004 "Worried Life Blues")...........15-25 59
ZYNN (1011 "Night and Day My Love") ...15-25 61
LPs: 10/12-inch
ALLIGATOR (4729 "I'm Here")..................5-10 82
ARHOOLIE (1024 "Louisiana Blues and Zydeco")..10-15 69
ARHOOLIE (1031 "Bon Ton Roulet").......10-15 70
ARHOOLIE (1059 "Clifton Chenier Live") ..8-12 73
ARHOOLIE (1086 "King of Zydeco")..........5-10 83
BLUE THUMB (8815 "Very Best")............15-25 70
GNP (2119 "New Orleans")......................8-12 78
PROPHESY (1004 "Cajun Blues")............10-15 70
SPECIALTY (2139 "Bayou Blues").........10-15 70
UTOPIA...10-12 76
Session: Elmore Nixon; Robert Pete; Lonesome Sundown; James Jones; Little Brother Griffin; Philip Walker; Bob Murphy.
Also see BERNARD, Rod / Clifton Chenier
Also see BIG CHENIER
Also see CHANIER, Cliston
Also see LONESOME SUNDOWN
Also see NIXON, Elmore
Also see PERSIANS / Clifton Chenier
Also see WALKER, Philip

CHENIER, Rosco
Singles: 7-inch
REYNAUD (1018 "I Broke the Yo Yo").....15-25 63

CHENTELLES
Singles: 7-inch
FENTON (2032 "Be My Queen")..............50-75 67

CHER *P&R/LP '65*
(Cher Bono; Cher Allman)
Singles: 12-inch
CASABLANCA..8-10 79-82
Singles: 7-inch
ATCO...4-6 69-72
ATLANTIC...4-6 69
CASABLANCA..3-5 79
COLUMBIA..3-5 82
GEFFEN..3-5 87-91
IMPERIAL...5-10 64-68
KAPP...4-6 71-72
LIBERTY...3-5 82
MCA..4-6 73-75
U.A...4-6 71-72
W.B...4-6 75-77
W.B./SPECTOR..4-6 74
Picture Sleeves
COLUMBIA..3-5 82
GEFFEN..3-5 87-89
LPs: 10/12-inch
ATCO...15-20 69
CASABLANCA (Except NBPIX-7133)........8-12 79
CASABLANCA (NBPIX-7133 "Take Me Home")..50-75 79
(Picture disc.)
COLUMBIA..5-10 82
GEFFEN..5-12 87-91
IMPERIAL...15-25 65-68
KAPP...12-15 71-72
LIBERTY...5-10 81
MCA..10-15 73-74
SPRINGBOARD...8-10 72
SUNSET..8-10 70
U.A...8-10 71-75
W.B...8-15 75-77
Also see CHERILYN / Cherilyn's Group
Also see MASON, Bonnie Jo
Also see SONNY & CHER

CHER & PETER CETERA *P&R '89*
Singles: 7-inch
GEFFEN..3-5 89
Picture Sleeves
GEFFEN..3-5 89
Also see CETERA, Peter

CHER & NILSSON
Singles: 7-inch
SPECTOR..4-6 75
Members: Cher; Harry Nilsson.
Also see CHER
Also see NILSSON, Harry

CHERILYN / Cherilyn's Group
(Cher Bono)
Singles: 7-inch
IMPERIAL (66081 "Dream Baby")...........20-30 64
Also see CHER

CHERLOS
Singles: 78 rpm
ULTRA D'OR..75-100 56
Singles: 7-inch
ULTRA D'OR (8 "99 ½ Won't Do") 300-400 56

CHEROKEES
Singles: 78 rpm
GRAND...200-300 54
PEACOCK...25-35 55
Singles: 7-inch
COLLECTABLES..3-5 84
GRAND (106 "Rainbow of Love").........400-600 54
(Yellow label. Rigid disc.)
GRAND (110 "Please Tell Me So") ..2000-3000 54
(Yellow label. Rigid disc.)
GRAND (111 "Brenda")..........................5-10 78
(Black vinyl.)
GRAND (111 "Brenda")..........................15-25 78
(Red vinyl.)
PEACOCK (1656 "Is She Real")...............50-75 55
Member: Russell Carter; Melvin Story; Karl English; George Pounds.

CHEROKEES
Singles: 7-inch
GUYDEN (2044 "Cherokee").....................5-10 60
Picture Sleeves
GUYDEN (2044 "Cherokee")...................10-20 60

CHEROKEES
Singles: 7-inch
U.A. (367 "My Heavenly Angel")..............50-75 61

CHEROKEES
Singles: 7-inch
GARY (1001 "It's Gonna Work Out Fine")..20-30

CHERRY, Carl
Singles: 7-inch
TENE (1023 "The Itch")........................400-500 59

CHERRY, Don P&R '54

Singles: 78 rpm

COLUMBIA....5-10 55-57
DECCA....5-10 50-56

Singles: 7-inch

COLUMBIA....5-10 55-59
DECCA....8-12 50-56
MONUMENT....4-6 65-78
ROULETTE (4364 "Gettysburg")....5-10 61
7 ARTS (701 "Tennessee Babe")....4-8 61
STRAND....4-8 59
VERVE....4-8 62
WARWICK....4-8 60

EPs: 7-inch

COLUMBIA....8-15 56

LPs: 10/12-inch

COLUMBIA....15-25 56
HARMONY....10-15 59
MONUMENT....8-12 66-73
Also see DAY, Doris, & Don Cherry
Also see TUNESMITHS WITH ROSEMARY CLOONEY & DON CHERRY

CHERRY SLUSH

Singles: 7-inch

COCONUT GROOVE (2032 "I Cannot Stop You")....20-30 68
USA (895 "I Cannot Stop You")....10-20 68
USA (904 "Gotta Take It Easy")....10-20 68
CAPITOL (4979 "Fluff")....5-10 63

CHERVAL, Frank
(With Cinnamon Calliope)

Singles: 7-inch

ACE (647 "Mama Loves Papa")....10-15 62
ACE (648 "Red-Headed Stranger")....10-15 62
BIG B....20-25
CONGRESS (242 "Initials on the Wall")....5-10 65
LAURIE (3184 "Carnival Girl")....10-20 63
MERCURY (72260 "Baby Be Good to Me")....5-10 64
MGM (13095 "Tag Along")....5-10 62
NOLA (725 "To Make a Big Man Cry")....5-10 66
WIZDOM....4-8 70

CHERYL ANN

Singles: 7-inch

PARSAY (2001 "Here Comes Another Teardrop")....25-35
PATTY (52 "Goodbye Baby")....40-50

CHESS, Hank

Singles: 7-inch

FAME (819 "I Love Ya Baby")....50-75

CHESSMAN, The
("Featuring Bobby")

Singles: 7-inch

RAZORBACK (119 "She's the One For Me")....15-25 65
RIOT-CHOUS (877 "Lucille")....50-75
SAFARI (1011 "Keeper of My Love")....300-400 58
(Original must be on thick wax.)

CHESSMAN SQUARE

Singles: 7-inch

LION (1002 "Circles")....15-25 69

Picture Sleeves

LION (1002 "Circles")....25-50 69

CHESSMEN
(With the Karol-Thorn Orchestra)

Singles: 7-inch

MIRASONIC (1002 "I Live for You")....100-150 59

CHESSMEN

Singles: 7-inch

GOLDEN CREST (2661 "Bells Bells")....500-1000 59

CHESSMEN

Singles: 7-inch

PAC (100 "Lola")....100-200 61
(Blue label.)
PAC (100 "Lola")....150-250 61
(White label. Promotional issue.)

CHESSMEN

Singles: 7-inch

AMC (101 "Mr. Cupid")....10-20 62
AMY (841 "Stormy Dreams")....20-30 62
DON-DEE (101 "Mr. Cupid")....10-20 63

CHESSMEN

LPs: 10/12-inch

CHESSMEN (12918 "Live")....15-25 64
Members: Tom Van Atla; Mike Catalano; Danny Midgett; Gary Barrington; Michael Holloway.

CHESSMEN

Singles: 7-inch

COULEE (106 "Dark Eyes")....10-15 64

CHESSMEN

Singles: 7-inch

GMA (12 "Touchdown")....20-30 '60s
(Canadian.)
JERDEN (743 "Mustang")....10-15 64
LONDON (17334 "Mustang")....15-25 64
(First issue. Canadian.)
Also see BEDIENT, Jack, & Chessmen

CHESSMEN
("Featuring Tom Salem")

Singles: 7-inch

G-CLEF (707 "Sorry")....20-30 64
Member: Tom Salem.

CHESSMEN

Singles: 7-inch

SALEM (001 "It'll Be Me")....50-150 65

CHESSMEN

Singles: 7-inch

PHALANX (1018 "You Can't Catch Me")....40-50 66

CHESSMEN

Singles: 7-inch

BISMARK (1010 "Dreams and Wishes")....10-20 66
BISMARK (1012 "I Need You There")....15-25 66
BISMARK (1015 "No More")....15-25 66

CHESTER, Gary

LPs: 10/12-inch

DCP (3803 "Yeah, Yeah, Yeah")....10-20 64
(Monaural.)
DCP (6803 "Yeah, Yeah, Yeah")....15-25 64
(Stereo.)
Also see COLE, Cozy

CHESTERFIELDS

Singles: 78 rpm

CHESS (1559 "I'm in Heaven")....50-100 54

Singles: 7-inch

CHESS (1559 "I'm in Heaven")....200-300 54

CHESTERFIELDS

Singles: 7-inch

CUB (9008 "I Got Fired")....15-25 58
Member: Al Reno.
Also see RENO, Al

CHESTERFIELDS

Singles: 7-inch

PHILIPS (40060 "A Dream Is But a Dream")....200-300 62

CHESTERS

Singles: 78 rpm

APOLLO (521 "Fires Burn No More")....15-25 57

Singles: 7-inch

APOLLO (521 "Fires Burn No More")....30-40 57
Members: "Little Anthony" Gourdine; Tracy Lord; Ernest Wright; Nat Rogers; Clarence Collins; Keith Williams.
Also see LITTLE ANTHONY & IMPERIALS

CHESTNUT, Morris

Singles: 7-inch

AMY (981 "Too Darn Soulful")....100-200 67

CHESTNUTS

Singles: 78 rpm

MERCURY (70489 "Don't Go")....15-25 54

Singles: 7-inch

MERCURY (70489 "Don't Go")....40-50 54
Member: Louis Heyward.

CHESTNUTS
(Lyman Hopkins & Chestnuts; Ruby Whitaker & Chestnuts; "Featuring Ruby Whitaker")

Singles: 78 rpm

DAVIS....35-50 57
ELDORADO....15-25 57
STANDORD....100-200 57

Singles: 7-inch

DAVIS (447 "Love Is True")....50-100 57
(Copies on Crescent [45-201] are boots.)
DAVIS (452 "Forever I Vow")....100-200 57
ELDORADO (511 "Who Knows Better Than I"/"I'm So Blue")....30-50 57
NIGHTRAIN (906 "I'm So Blue")....4-6 73
STANDORD (100 "Who Knows Better Than I")....150-250 57
(Same selection number previously used for a Five Satins issue.)
Members: Ruby Whitaker; Lyman Hopkins; Bill Baker; Franklin Hopkins; Reuben White; Jimmy Curtis; Sylvester Hopkins;
Also see BAKER, Bill, & Chestnuts
Also see FIVE SATINS

CHESTNUTS

Singles: 7-inch

ALADDIN (3444 "This Is My Love")....25-35 58

CHEVALIER, Jay

Singles: 7-inch

CAJUN (101 "Rock n' Roll Angel")....100-200
CREST (1097 "Check Out Time")....15-25 62
GOLDBAND (1105 "Castro Rock")....15-25 60
MINARET (120 "Big Wheels")....10-15 64
PEL (201 "High School Days")....100-200 58
RECCO (1002 "Ballad of Earl K. Long")....10-15 60

CHEVELLE V

Singles: 7-inch

ASKEL (7 "Come Back Bird")....20-30 66
TITAN (1737 "Dangling Little Friends")....10-20 67
UMI (100 "Come Back Bird")....10-20 66

Picture Sleeves

TITAN (1737 "Dangling Little Friends")....20-25 67

CHEVELLES

Singles: 7-inch

CHEVELLE (101 "Riptide")....25-35 63
FLAMING ARROW....5-10 68
SD....15-25

CHEVELLES

Singles: 7-inch

BANGAR (603 "Blue Chevelle")....25-35 64
BANGAR (603 "Chevelle Stomp")....20-30 64

Picture Sleeves

BANGAR (603 "Blue Chevelle")....60-80 64
Also see DEE JAY & RUNAWAYS
Also see STOREY, Denny

CHEVELLES

Singles: 7-inch

GOLDEN (101 "One Kiss")....30-40 64

CHEVELLES

Singles: 7-inch

INFINITY (029 "I'm Sorry")....100-150 64
Also see TURNER, Betty

CHEVELLS

Singles: 7-inch

JUSTICE (1004 "Pretty Little Girl")....75-100

CHEVELS

Singles: 7-inch

GASS (1001 "Hendersonville")....10-15 63
MUSICLAND USA (20010 "Play Me a Sad Song")....10-15 66

CHEVIES
("Wayne Johnson – Vocal Orchestration")

Singles: 7-inch

DOVE (1033 "I Love That Girl")....100-200 59

CHEVRONS

Singles: 7-inch

BRENT (7000 "That Comes with Love")....10-15 59
BRENT (7007 "Lullabye")....20-30 59
(White label. Promotional issue.)
BRENT (7007 "Lullabye")....10-20 59
BRENT (7015 "Little Star")....10-15 60
TIME (1 "Come Go with Me")....15-25 60

LPs: 10/12-inch

TIME (10008 "Sing-A-Long Rock and Roll")....100-200 61

CHEVRONS

Singles: 7-inch

SARA (6381 "Good Good Lovin' ")....10-15 63
SARA (6462 "Please Don't Make Me Cry")....40-50 64
Members: Dave Zadra; Fred Herrmann; Tom Olivas; Ken Vanslett; Tom Louchbaum; Jim Woelfel.

CHEVRONS

Singles: 7-inch

KISKI (2065 "Who Does He Cry To")....100-200 64

CHEVRONS

Singles: 7-inch

FENTON (2092 "Hey Little Teaser")....15-25 66

CHEVRONS

Singles: 7-inch

INDEPENDENCE (88 "Dreams")....10-15 68
INDEPENDENCE (94 "Mine Forever More")....10-15 69
MMC (016 "Dreams")....15-25 68
(First issue.)

CHEV-RONS

Singles: 7-inch

GAIT (100 "The Defense Rest")....50-100 61
(Also issued on the same label, by Lee Ward.)
Also see WARD, Lee

CHIC P&R/R&B/LP '77

Singles: 12-inch 33/45

ATLANTIC (Except 131)....4-8 78-83
ATLANTIC (131 "Le Freak")....20-25 78
(Picture disc. Promotional issue only.)

Singles: 7-inch

ATLANTIC....3-6 77-83
MIRAGE....3-5 82

Picture Sleeves

ATLANTIC....3-6 78-80

LPs: 10/12-inch

ATLANTIC....5-10 77-82
Also see NORMA JEAN

CHIC / Leif Garrett / Roberta Flack / Genesis

EPs: 7-inch

W.B. SPECIAL PRODUCTS....8-12 78
(Coca-Cola/Burger King promoticnal issue. Issued with paper sleeve.)
Also see CHIC
Also see GENESIS

CHICAGO P&R/LP '69

Singles: 12-inch

COLUMBIA....4-8 80

Singles: 7-inch

COLUMBIA (10049 thru 11345)....4-6 74-80
COLUMBIA (44909 "Questions 67 and 78")....10-15 69
COLUMBIA (45127 thru 46062)....4-8 69-74
FULL MOON....3-6 82-86
REPRISE....3-5 88-91
W.B.....3-5 87

Picture Sleeves

COLUMBIA (44909 "Questions 67 and 78")....10-15 69
COLUMBIA (45127 thru 45717)....5-8 69-72
FULL MOON....3-6 84-86
REPRISE....3-5 88-89
W.B.....3-5 87

EPs: 7-inch

COLUMBIA....10-15 70-73
(Juke box issues only.)

LPs: 10/12-inch

ACCORD....5-10 81
COLUMBIA ("Chicago")....200-250 76
(No selection number used. Boxed set of first 10 LPs [17 discs]. Promotional issue only.)
COLUMBIA (8 "Chicago Transit Authority")....25-35 69
COLUMBIA (24 "Chicago II")....20-30 70
COLUMBIA (C2-30110 "Chicago III")....10-20 70
COLUMBIA (C2Q-30110 "Chicago III")....20-25 74
(Quadraphonic.)
COLUMBIA (30863 "Chicago IV")....15-20 71
COLUMBIA (C4X-30865 "Chicago IV")....20-30 71
(Boxed, four-disc set. Includes three posters, booklet and card.)
COLUMBIA (CQ-30865 "Chicago IV")....20-30 74
(Quadraphonic.)
COLUMBIA (31102 thru 38590)....8-15 72-82
(With "C2," "FC," "HC," "KC," "JC," or "PC" prefix.)
COLUMBIA (31102 thru 34200)....15-25 74-76
(Quadraphonic. With "CQ," "C2Q," "GQ," or "PCQ" prefix.)
COLUMBIA (43000 & 44000 series)....15-25 82
(Half-speed mastered.)
FULL MOON....5-10 82-86
MFSL (2-128 "Chicago Transit Authority")....40-60 85

REPRISE....5-8 88-89
SHOWCASE (121 "Chicago Live")....8-10 85
MAGNUM....10-12 78
W.B....5-8 86
Members: Peter Cetera; Terry Kath; Robert Lamm; James Pankow; Lee Loughnane; Bill Champlin; Daniel Seraphine; Jason Scheff; Walter Parazaider; Donnie Dacus. Session: Beach Boys.
Also see BEACH BOYS

CHICAGO, Artie
(Artie Chicago from the Bronx)
Singles: 7-inch
LAURIE (3424 "The Wanderer"/"Please Don't Play Me a 7")....8-12 68
LAURIE (3424 "Keep the Boy Happy"/"Please Don't Play Me a 7")....8-12 68
Session: Tremonts.
Also see MARESCA, Ernie
Also see TREMONTS

CHICAGO ALL STARS
Singles: 78 rpm
COLUMBIA (37928 "No No Baby")....15-25 47
Members: Eddie "Sugarman" Penigar; Sax Mallard; Johnny Morton; Jump Jackson; Bail Beach; Bill "Doc" Owens; Elmer Ewing.
Also see MALLARD, Sax
Also see PENIGAR, Eddie

CHICAGO BILL
(Bill Broonzy)
Singles: 78 rpm
MELODISC....10-20 51
Also see BROONZY, Big Bill

CHICAGO SUNNY BOY
(Joe Hill Louis)
Singles: 78 rpm
METEOR (5004 "Western Union Man")....200-300 53
METEOR (5008 "Love You Baby")....200-300 53
Singles: 7-inch
METEOR (5004 "Western Union Man")....500-750 53
(Though a higher number than *Western Union Man* original 45s of 5008 are not known to exist.)
Also see LOUIS, Joe Hill

CHICK, Tony
Singles: 7-inch
HY-JOY (1001 "A Car")....100-150

CHICK & NOBLES
Singles: 7-inch
USA (772 "Island for Two")....15-25 65
Also see NOBLES

CHICKLETS
Singles: 7-inch
LESCAY (3007 "I Believe in Love")....10-15 62

CHIC-LETS
Singles: 7-inch
JOSIE (919 "I Want You to Be My Boyfriend")....15-25 64

CHIEFS
Singles: 7-inch
GREENWICH (408 "Apache")....10-20 58
GREENWICH (410 "Enchiladas")....10-20 58
VALIANT (6038 "The Tom Tom")....10-15 63

CHIEFTONES
Singles: 7-inch
CLAREMONT (5592 "Big Fat Woman")....5-10
CUCA (1287 "Do Lord")....10-15 66
SCEPTER (12234 "Don't Dare")....8-12 68
Also see THUNDERKLOUD, Billy, & Chieftones

CHIFFONS P&R '60
Singles: 7-inch
B.T. PUPPY (558 "My Secret Love")....4-8 70
BIG DEAL (6003 "Tonight's the Night")....50-75 60
BUDDAH (171 "So Much in Love")....4-8 71
LAURIE (3152 "He's So Fine")....15-20 63
LAURIE (3166 "Lucky Me")....15-20 63
LAURIE (3179 "One Fine Day")....15-20 63
LAURIE (3195 thru 3357)....10-15 63-66
LAURIE (3364 thru 3497)....8-12 66-69
LAURIE....4-6 75-76
REPRISE (20103 "Doctor of Hearts")....15-25 62
WILDCAT (601 "Never Never")....20-30 61
LPs: 10/12-inch
B.T. PUPPY (1011 "My Secret Love")....35-45 70
COLLECTABLES....5-10 87
LAURIE (2018 "He's So Fine")....35-50 63
LAURIE (2020 "One Fine Day")....40-60 63
LAURIE (LLP-2036 "Sweet Talkin' Guy")....35-45 66
(Monaural.)
LAURIE (SLP-2036 "Sweet Talkin' Guy")....40-50 66
(Stereo.)
LAURIE (4001 "Everything You Always Wanted to Hear")....10-20 74
Members: Judy Craig; Barbara Lee; Patricia Bennett; Sylvia Peterson.
Also see CHRISTIE, Lou, & Classics / Isley Brothers / Chiffons
Also see FOUR PENNIES

CHILD
Singles: 7-inch
JUBILEE (5673 "You'll Never Walk Alone")....10-15 69
(Black vinyl.)
JUBILEE (5673 "You'll Never Walk Alone")....20-30 69
(Red vinyl.)
LPs: 10/12-inch
JUBILEE (8029 "Child")....25-35 68

CHILD'S GARDEN OF GRASS
LPs: 10/12-inch
ELEKTRA (75012 "A Pre-Legalization Comedy")....20-30 70
Members: Anton Greene; Carl Esser; Michael Gwynne; Ron Jacobs; Jack S. Margolis; Cyrus Faryar; Anna-Lee Austin; Dorina May; Marly Stone; Oz Knox; Dr. Franklin D. Wacco; Mary Howard; George Savage; Tom Rounds; John Horton; Renais Faryar; Peter Gallway; Murray Roman; Alex Hassilev.
Also see RON & JON

CHILDREN
Singles: 7-inch
ATCO (6633 "Maypole")....10-15 68
CINEMA (025 "Pills")....15-25 68
DRAGONET....5-10
LARAMIE (666 "Picture Me")....20-30 67
MAP CITY (304 "Evil Woman")....4-8 70
ODE (66005 "From the Very Start")....10-15 70
ODE (66013 "Fire Ring")....10-15 71
SWEET SMOKE (2 "Jumping Jack Flash")....10-15 68
LPs: 10/12-inch
ATCO (271 "Rebirth")....15-25 68
CINEMA (0001 "Rebirth")....100-200 67
Members: Stephen Perron; Cassell Webb; Ken Corday; William Ash; Andrew Szuch Jr.; Louis Cabaza.
Also see MIND'S EYE
Also see STOICS

CHILDREN OF DARKNESS
Singles: 7-inch
ROYCE (5140 "She's Mine")....15-25 66

CHILDREN OF ONE
LPs: 10/12-inch
REAL (101 "Children of One")....100-200 70

CHILDREN OF THE MUSHROOM
Singles: 7-inch
SOHO (101 "You Can't Erase a Mirror")....10-20 68

CHILDREN OF THE NIGHT
Singles: 7-inch
BELLA (101 "World of Tears")....75-100 67
MOON ROCK (100 "Dinner with Drac")....5-10
P.I.P. (6530 "Dinner with Drac")....4-8 76
LPs: 10/12-inch
P.I.P....15-20 76
Member: John DiBella

CHILDRESS, Buddy
Singles: 7-inch
DUB (2838 "Two Young True Hearts")....40-60 57
SCOTTIE (1324 "Once Your Girl Was Mine")....10-15 60

CHILDS, Billy
Singles: 7-inch
REKA (113 "Call Me Shorty")....150-200 60
REKA (297 "Call Me Shorty")....100-150 62

CHILDS, Leon
Singles: 7-inch
VIN (1018 "Jet Stream")....10-15 60

CHILDS, Lillian
(With Johnny "Mr. Blues" Bird Orchestra)
Singles: 78 rpm
GROOVE (0155 "Twenty-Two Minutes")....8-12 56
Singles: 7-inch
GROOVE (0155 "Twenty-Two Minutes")....20-30 56
Session: Twi-Lighters.
Also see TWI-LIGHTERS

CHILDS, Matthew
Singles: 7-inch
RAE COX (1002 "Funky Onions")....10-20 63

CHILES, Buddy
Singles: 78 rpm
GOLD STAR (660 "Mistreated Blues")....25-50 49

CHI-LITES P&R/R&B/LP '69
Singles: 12-inch
LARC....4-8 83
PRIVATE 1....4-6 84
Singles: 7-inch
BLUE ROCK (4007 "I'm So Jealous")....10-20 65
BLUE ROCK (4020 "The Monkey")....10-20 65
BLUE ROCK (4037 "She's Mine")....20-30 65
BRUNSWICK....4-8 69-78
CHI-SOUND....3-5 80-82
EPIC....3-5 83
INPHASION....3-5 79
LARC....3-5 83
MERCURY....3-5 76-77
O'RETTA....4-8 70
PRIVATE I....3-5 84
REVUE....5-10 67-68
20TH FOX....3-5 81
LPs: 10/12-inch
BRUNSWICK....10-15 69-74
CHI-SOUND....5-8 80-82
EPIC....5-10 83-84
LARC....5-10 83
MERCURY....5-10 77
PICKWICK....5-10 '70s
20TH FOX....5-10 80-81
Members: Eugene Record; Creadel Jones; Robert Lester; Marshall Thompson; Danny Johnson.
Also see ACKLIN, Barbara
Also see CHANTEURS
Also see HI-LITES
Also see MARSHALL & CHI-LITES
Also see WILSON, Jackie, & Chi-Lites

CHILLY CHARLIE
Singles: 7-inch
BAND BOX (329 "Crisis at Ole Miss")....10-20 63
Picture Sleeves
BAND BOX (329 "Crisis at Ole Miss")....30-40 63

CHIMES
Singles: 78 rpm
FLAIR....50-75 54
Singles: 7-inch
FLAIR (1051 "My Heart's Crying for You")....400-500 54
(Red label.)
FLAIR (1051 "My Heart's Crying for You")....100-150 54
(Black label.)
Members: Cornell Gunter; Young Jessie; Tom Fox; Richard Berry; Beverly Thompson.
Also see FLAIRS

CHIMES
Singles: 78 rpm
ROYAL ROOST (577 "Dearest Darling")....1000-1500 53
Also see FIVE CHIMES

CHIMES
(With the Bumps Blackwell Band)
Singles: 78 rpm
SPECIALTY....10-15 55-56
Singles: 7-inch
JAY TEE (1000 "Losing You Baby")....100-200 '50s
SPECIALTY (555 "Tears on My Pillow")....50-75 55
(Rigid disc.)
SPECIALTY (555 "Tears on My Pillow")....40-60 55
(Flexible disc.)
SPECIALTY (574 "Pretty Little Girl")....20-30 56
Also see ALLEN, Tony
Also see STARR, Bobby

CHIMES
Singles: 7-inch
ARROW (724 "Please Call")....20-30 58
ARROW (726 "Lovin' Baby")....15-25 58
Member: Freddie Scott.
Also see SCOTT, Freddie

CHIMES P&R '60
Singles: 7-inch
ABC....4-6 75
COLLECTABLES....3-5 81
ERIC....4-6 '70s
LAURIE (3211 "Who's Heart Are You Breaking Now")....5-10 63
LOST NITE....4-8 '70s
METRO INT'L (1 "Who's Heart Are You Breaking Now")....15-20 63
MUSICNOTE (1103 "I'm in the Mood for Love")....20-30 61
MUSICTONE (1101 "Once in Awhile")....15-25 61
RESERVE (120 "When School Starts Again")....30-40 57
TAG (444 "Once in Awhile"/"Summer Night")....50-75 60
(Maroon label. "Tag" in normal letters.)
TAG (444 "Once in Awhile"/"Summer Night")....100-150 60
(Blue label. "Tag" in normal letters.)
TAG (444 "Once in Awhile"/"Summer Night")....15-25 60
(Green label. Has "Tag" in a triangle.)
TAG (444 "Once in Awhile"/"Oh How I Love You So")....15-25 60
(Though shown as by the Chimes, *Oh How I Love You So* is by the BiTones.)
TAG (445 "I'm in the Mood for Love")....15-25 61
TAG (447 "Let's Fall in Love")....15-25 61
TRIP....4-6 '70s
LPs: 10/12-inch
CHIMES....10-15 83
Members: Lenny Cocco; Joe Croce; Pat De Prisco; Pat McGuire; Rich Mercado.
Also see BI-TONES
Also see LENNY & CHIMES
Also see RIFFS
Also see THREE CHIMES

CHIMES
Singles: 7-inch
HOUSE OF BEAUTY (3 "Tears from an Angel's Eyes")....40-50 60

CHIMES
Singles: 7-inch
LIMELIGHT (3000 "Cry Baby, Cry")....10-15 63
LIMELIGHT (3002 "Du Wap")....10-15 63

CHIOTA, Bazil Blavis
Singles: 7-inch
UA (531 "Jailhouse Rock")....10-15 66

CHIP & QUARTERTONES
Singles: 7-inch
CARLTON (604 "Simple Simon")....50-100 64
Members: Chip Kopaczewski; Tony Galantino; Jim Murkens; Dick Curry.
Also see INTENTIONS

CHIPMUNKS P&R/R&B '58
(Starring Alvin, Theodore, & Simon; Featuring David Seville; David Seville & Chipmunks)
Singles: 7-inch
AMERICAN TELECARD....10-15 64
(Cardboard flexi-disc.)
DOT (16997 "Sorry About That Herb")....5-10 67
LIBERTY (55168 thru 55832)....5-10 58-65
LIBERTY (77200 "Ragtime Cowboy Joe")....15-25 59
(Stereo.)
LIBERTY (77250 "Chipmunk Song")....15-25 59
(Stereo.)
MISTLETOE....4-6 75
SUNSET....4-6 68
U.A....4-6 74
Picture Sleeves
LIBERTY....10-20 59-65
EPs: 7-inch
LIBERTY....10-25 59-64
LPs: 10/12-inch
LIBERTY (3132 "Let's All Sing with the Chipmunks")....25-40 59
(Monaural. Black vinyl. Cover shows Chipmunks as

animals. If Chipmunks are drawn as cartoon characters, deduct 50%.)
LIBERTY (3132 "Let's All Sing with the Chipmunks") 50-75 59
(Monaural. Red vinyl. Cover shows Chipmunks as animals. If Chipmunks are drawn as cartoon characters, deduct 50%.)
LIBERTY (3159 "Sing Again with the Chipmunks") 25-40 60
(Monaural. Cover shows Chipmunks as animals. If Chipmunks are drawn as cartoon characters, deduct 50%.)
LIBERTY (3170 "Around the World with the Chipmunks") 25-40 60
(Monaural. Cover shows Chipmunks as animals. If Chipmunks are drawn as cartoon characters, deduct 50%.)
LIBERTY (3200 thru 3400 series) 15-25 61-65
(Monaural.)
LIBERTY (7132 "Let's All Sing with the Chipmunks") 35-45 59
(Stereo. Black vinyl. Cover shows Chipmunks as animals. If Chipmunks are drawn as cartoon characters, deduct 50%.)
LIBERTY (7132 "Let's All Sing with the Chipmunks") 75-85 59
(Stereo. Red vinyl. Cover shows Chipmunks as animals. If Chipmunks are drawn as cartoon characters, deduct 50%.)
LIBERTY (7159 "Sing Again with the Chipmunks") 35-45 60
(Stereo. Cover shows Chipmunks as animals. If Chipmunks are drawn as cartoon characters, deduct 50%.)
LIBERTY (7170 "Around the World with the Chipmunks") 35-45 60
(Stereo. Cover shows Chipmunks as animals. If Chipmunks are drawn as cartoon characters, deduct 50%.)
LIBERTY (7200 thru 7400 series) 15-30 61-65
(Stereo.)
LIBERTY (10000 series) 5-10 82
PICKWICK 5-10 80
SUNSET 8-15 68-69
U.A. 5-10 74-76
Also see BEDBUGS
Also see CANNED HEAT & CHIPMUNKS
Also see SEVILLE, David

CHIPPER & HIS PLAYMATES

LPs: 10/12-inch

U.A. (11032 "Sing Along With") 10-15 64

CHIPS

Singles: 78 rpm

JOSIE (803 "Rubber Biscuit") 20-30 56

Singles: 7-inch

JOSIE (803 "Rubber Biscuit") 50-75 56
(With "Joz" logo.)
JOSIE (803 "Rubber Biscuit") 25-35 58
(With "Josie" logo.)
VIRGO 4-8 73
Members: Kinrod Johnson; Bubbie Lincoln; Nathaniel "Lil John" Epps; Paul Fulton; Sam Strain; Charles Johnson.
Also see LITTLE ANTHONY & IMPERIALS
Also see O'JAYS

CHIPS

Singles: 7-inch

SATELLITE (105 "As You Can See") 50-100 61
Members: Curtis Johnson; Richard Harris; Eddie Stanbeck; Sam Byrnes.
Also see ASTORS

CHIPS

Singles: 7-inch

STRAND (25027 "Darling") 15-25 61
VENICE (101 "Darling") 40-60 60

CHIPS

Singles: 7-inch

EMBER (1077 "Bye Bye My Love") 15-25 61
TOLLIE (9042 "Party People") 8-10 65
Also see SOUTH, Joe

CHIPS

Singles: 7-inch

PHILIPS (40520 "Break It Gently") 5-10 68

Picture Sleeves

PHILIPS (40520 "Break It Gently") 10-20 68
Members: Daren Pasterik; Sheri Hartman; Aleat Maciejewski; Klayre Hartmann; Charlotte O'Neill.

CHIPS & CO.

(Chips)

Singles: 7-inch

ABC (11157 "When You Hold Me Baby") 5-10 68
ABC-PAR (10749 "Every Night") 8-12 65
ABC-PAR (10769 "Walk Tall") 8-12 66
M5 (191 "Let the Winds Blow") 20-30 66

CHIRCO

Singles: 7-inch

CRESTED BUTTE 4-8 72

LPs: 10/12-inch

CRESTED BUTTE ("Visitation") 30-45 72
(Selection number not known.)
Members: Alvin Roth; John Naylor.

CHOB

(Choäb)

Singles: 7-inch

LAVETTE (5016 "Ain't Gonna Eat Out My Heart Anymore") 20-30 66
Q.Q. (224 "Why Am I Alone") 20-30 66

CHOCOLATE MILK — R&B/LP '75

Singles: 12-inch

RCA 5-10 83

Singles: 7-inch

RCA 4-8 75-83

LPs: 10/12-inch

RCA (2331 "We're All in This Together") 20-30 77
RCA (3081 "Milky Way") 20-30 79
RCA (3569 "Hipnotism") 20-30 80
RCA (3896 "Blue Jeans") 20-30 81
RCA (4412 "Friction") 20-30 82
Members: Frank Richard; Amadee Castanell; Robert Doban; Joe Foxx; Mario Tio; Dwight Richards.

CHOCOLATE MOOSE

Singles: 7-inch

SPOTLIGHT (1012 "Take a Ride") 20-30 66
SPOTLIGHT (1015 "Rosie") 20-30 66

CHOCOLATE WATCH BAND

Singles: 7-inch

TOWER (373 "No Way Out") 30-40 67
UPTOWN (740 "Baby Blue") 30-40 67
UPTOWN (749 "Misty Lane") 30-40 67

LPs: 10/12-inch

RHINO 5-10 83
TOWER (5096 "No Way Out") 150-200 67
TOWER (5106 "Inner Mystique") 150-200 68
TOWER (5153 "One Step Beyond") 125-150 69
Also see HOGS

CHOCOLATEERS

Singles: 78 rpm

PARROT 30-50 53

Singles: 7-inch

PARROT (781 "Bartender Blues") 75-100 53

CHOICE OF COLOUR

Singles: 7-inch

APT (26011 "Your Love") 10-15 72

CHOIR — P&R '67

Singles: 7-inch

CANADIAN AMERICAN (203 "It's Cold Outside") 25-35 67
INTREPID (75020 "So Much Love") 4-6 70
ROULETTE 10-15 67-68

EPs: 7-inch

BOMP 8-10 76
Members: Wally Bryson; David Smalley; Jim Bonfanti.
Also see RASPBERRIES

CHOLLI MAYE

(Shirley Alston)

Singles: 7-inch

GOLD (212 "You Will Never Get Away") 20-30 63
Also see ALSTON, Shirley

CHORALETTES

Singles: 7-inch

FARGO (1063 "Won't You Call on Me") 15-25 64

CHORALS

Singles: 78 rpm

DECCA (29914 "In My Dreams") 15-25 56

Singles: 7-inch

DECCA (29914 "In My Dreams") 40-50 56

CHORDCATS

Singles: 78 rpm

CAT (109 "Zippety Zum") 10-15 54
CAT (112 "Hold Me, Baby") 20-25 54

Singles: 7-inch

CAT (109 "Zippety Zum") 15-25 54
(Second issue. First issued as by the Chords.)
CAT (112 "Hold Me, Baby") 30-40 54
Members: Carl Feaster; Claude Feaster; Jimmy Keys; Floyd McRae; William Edwards.
Also see CHORDS

CHORDELLS

Singles: 78 rpm

ONYX 150-250 56

Singles: 7-inch

ONYX (504 "Here's a Heart for You") 600-800 56
RELIC (523 "Here's a Heart for You") 5-10 64

CHORDELLS

Singles: 7-inch

JARO (77005 "At Last") 15-25 59

CHORDELLS

Singles: 7-inch

TIGRE (601 "Quit While You're Ahead") 20-30 63

CHORDETTES — P&R '54

(With Archie Bleyer; with Jeff Kron & Jackie Ertel)

Singles: 78 rpm

CADENCE (1200 series) 10-20 54-57
CADENCE (1300 series) 20-40 57-58
COLUMBIA 10-15 50

Singles: 7-inch

BARNABY 4-6 70-76
CADENCE (1239 thru 1299) 15-25 54-56
CADENCE (1319 thru 1442) 10-20 57-63
COLUMBIA (38949 "Oh Joe") 15-25 50
ERIC 4-6 78

Picture Sleeves

CADENCE (1349 "Zorro") 10-20 58
CADENCE (1366 "No Wheels") 15-25 59
(Promotional issue only. Pictures Jeff and Jackie. Sleeve and disc has *No Wheels* on both sides.)
CADENCE (1366 "No Wheels"/"A Girl's Work Is Never Done") 10-15 59
(Pictures Jeff and Jackie on the *No Wheels* side and Jackie only on the other side.)

EPs: 7-inch

CADENCE 10-20 57-61
COLUMBIA (Except 201 thru 401) 10-25 54-57
COLUMBIA (201 "Harmony Time") 30-40 50
(Boxed, four-disc set.)
COLUMBIA (241 "Harmony Time, Vol. 2") 30-40 51
(Boxed, four-disc set.)
COLUMBIA (309 "Harmony Encores") 30-40 52
(Boxed, four-disc set.)
COLUMBIA (401 "Your Requests") 30-40 53
(Boxed, four-disc set.)

LPs: 10/12-inch

BACK-TRAC 5-10
BARNABY 8-10 76
CADENCE (1002 "Close Harmony") 35-50 55
CADENCE (3001 "Chordettes") 25-40 57
CADENCE (3020 "Barbershop Harmonies") 25-40 58
CADENCE (3062 "Never on Sunday") 20-30 62
(Monaural.)
CADENCE (25062 "Never on Sunday") 30-40 62
(Stereo.)
COLUMBIA (956 "Listen") 25-40 57
COLUMBIA (2519 "Chordettes") 25-35 56
(10-inch LP.)
COLUMBIA (6111 "Harmony Time") 35-45 50
(10-inch LP.)
COLUMBIA (6170 "Harmony Time, Vol. 2") 35-45 51
(10-inch LP.)
COLUMBIA (6218 "Harmony Encores") 35-45 52
(10-inch LP.)
COLUMBIA (6285 "Your Requests") 35-45 53
(10-inch LP.)
EVEREST 5-10 82
HARMONY 12-15 59
Members: Margie Needham; Janet Ertel (Bleyer); Carol Bushman; Lynn Evans.
Also see BLEYER, Archie

CHORD'R NOTES

Singles: 7-inch

FARGO (1061 "How Still the Night") 20-30 64

CHORDS

Singles: 78 rpm

GEM (211 "In the Woods") 25-50 53

CHORDS — P&R/R&B '54

Singles: 78 rpm

CAT (104 "Sh-Boom"/"Cross Over the Bridge") 40-50 54
CAT (104 "Sh-Boom"/"Little Maiden") 20-30 54
CAT (109 "Zippety Zum") 10-20 54
QUALITY (1268 "Sh-Boom") 35-50 54
(Canadian.)
QUALITY (1293 "Zippety Zum") 10-20 54
(Canadian.)

Singles: 7-inch

CAT (104 "Sh-Boom"/"Cross Over the Bridge") 50-100 54
CAT (104 "Sh-Boom"/"Little Maiden") 40-50 54
CAT (109 "Zippety Zum") 30-40 54
(First issue. Also issued as by the Chordcats.)
LOST NITE 4-8
QUALITY (1268 "Sh-Boom") 150-200 54
(Canadian.)
QUALITY (1293 "Zippety Zum") 15-25 54
(Canadian.)
Members: Carl Feaster; Claude Feaster; Jimmy Keys; Floyd McRae; William Edwards.
Also see CHORDCATS
Also see SH-BOOMS
Also see THORPE, Lionel

CHORDS

Singles: 7-inch

METRO (20015 "Pretty Face") 15-20 59

CHORDS

Singles: 7-inch

CASINO (451 "Tears in Your Eyes") 30-40 58

CHOSEN FEW

Singles: 7-inch

MARSH (201 "Jump Down") 20-30 62
Members: Scott Engel; John Stewart.
Also see ENGEL, Scott, & John Stewart

CHOSEN FEW

Singles: 7-inch

CANYON .... 8-12 '60s
CRYSTAL .... 8-12 '60s
DART (1080 "We Walk Together") 8-12 67
LIBERTY (55919 "Last Man Alive") 10-20 66
LIBERTY (55962 "Asian Chrome") 10-20 67
MAPLE 4-6 71
PLAYBOY (106 "I've Had It") 8-12 65
POWER INT'L (872 "Forget About the Past") 25-35 66
ROULETTE (7015 "Footsee") 5-10 68

LPs: 10/12-inch

MAPLE 10-20

CHOSEN FEW

Singles: 7-inch

DENIM (1092 "Pink Clouds and Lemonade") 25-35 66
Members: Warren Mittlestadt; Gary Huboldt; Des Smith; Dave Huegel; John Baker.

CHOSEN FEW

Singles: 7-inch

B.F.D. (6948 "Feel Alright") 10-20 66

CHOSEN FEW

Singles: 7-inch

CANUSA 5-10 68
CO-OP 25-35 66-67
Members: Bobby White; Billy Paul; Jimmie O'Connor; Harry Jeroleman; Mike Helske; Richard Zwick.
Also see BARRIES
Also see SONICS

CHRIS & CYTATIONS

Singles: 7-inch

CATAMOUNT (100 "Glory of Love") 10-20 63
(Yellow vinyl.)

CHRIS & KATHY

(Chris Montez & Kathy Young)

Singles: 7-inch

MONOGRAM (517 "All You Had to Do") 10-15 64
MONOGRAM (520 "Shoot That Curl") 10-15 64
Members: Chris Montez; Kathy Young.
Also see MONTEZ, Chris
Also see YOUNG, Kathy

CHRISTENSEN, John

LPs: 10/12-inch

ROBBINS (5001 "The Spirit: Every Little Thing") 30-40 87

(Picture disc.)

CHRISTIAN, Bobby

Singles: 78 rpm

BALLY.......... 10-15 57
FORMAL.......... 5-10 56

Singles: 7-inch

AUDIO FIDELITY (083 "Rock and Roll Symphony").......... 5-10 61
BALLY (1023 "Skip-It-Ty Beat").......... 10-15 56
FORMAL (1002 "Grasshopper Jump").......... 10-20 56
FORMAL (1003 "White Christmas").......... 10-20 56
SALEM.......... 5-10
STEPHENY (1833 "Caravan").......... 15-25 59
STEPHENY (1835 "Frankie and Johnny Cha Cha").......... 15-25 59
STEPHENY (1839 "Jumpin' Jack").......... 15-25 59
TOP RANK (2004 "Bobby's Tune").......... 15-25 59

EPs: 7-inch

MERCURY (6008 "Bobby Christian").......... 15-25 59

LPs: 10/12-inch

AUDIO FIDELITY (3005 "Percussive Big Band Jazz").......... 25-35 60
(Monaural.)
AUDIO FIDELITY (5959 "Strings for a Space Age").......... 25-35 62
AUDIO FIDELITY (7005 "Percussive Big Band Jazz").......... 35-45 60
(Stereo.)
STEPHENY (4012 "Smooth Man").......... 25-35 59
WESTMINSTER (6116 "Percussion in Velvet").......... 25-35 59
(Monaural.)
WESTMINSTER (6131 "Nothing But Percussion").......... 25-35 61
(Monaural.)
WESTMINSTER (15046 "Percussion in Velvet").......... 35-45 59
(Stereo.)
WESTMINSTER (15065 "Nothing But Percussion").......... 35-45 61
(Stereo.)

CHRISTIAN, Charlie

LPs: 10/12-inch

BLUE NOTE (5026 "Memorable Sessions").......... 75-125 53
(10-inch LP.)
COLUMBIA (652 "Charlie Christian with the Benny Goodman Sextet and Orchestra").......... 50-100 55
(Label has three black Columbia logo boxes on each side. No number shown in lower right corner of back cover.)
COLUMBIA (652 "Charlie Christian with the Benny Goodman Sextet and Orchestra").......... 20-30 '60s
(Label has one white Columbia logo box on each side. Has number [i.e. "3"] in lower right corner of back cover.)
COUNTERPOINT (548 "Jazz Immortal 1941").......... 50-75 56
ESOTERIC (1 "Jazz Immortal").......... 75-125 53
ESOTERIC (548 "Jazz Immortal").......... 40-60 56
Also see GOODMAN, Benny, Orchestra

CHRISTIAN, Chris

Singles: 7-inch

TESTA (104 "Lover Boy").......... 10-20 59

CHRISTIAN, Diane

Singles: 7-inch

BELL (610 "Wonderful Guy").......... 5-10 65
BELL (617 "Little Boy").......... 5-10 65
SMASH (1862 "There's So Much About My Baby That I Love").......... 10-15 63

CHRISTIAN, Janice / Johnny & Charmers

Singles: 7-inch

SWAN (4174 "Just a Bad Thing"/"Promises").......... 10-15 64

CHRISTIAN, Roger

Singles: 7-inch

NBI (100 "Big Bad Ho-Dad").......... 25-35 63
RENDEZVOUS (195 "Little Mary Christmas").......... 10-15 62
Also see BEACH BOYS
Also see SUPER STOCKS / Hot Rod Rog / Shutdown Douglas

CHRISTIE, Dean *P&R '62*
(Dean Christy)

Singles: 7-inch

CONGRESS (240 "Vacation Time").......... 5-10 65
MERCURY (72140 "Mona").......... 10-15 63
MERCURY (72228 "Get With It").......... 10-15 63
MERCURY (72296 "She's Got It").......... 8-12 64
SWL (1607 "Heart Breaker").......... 15-25 62
(First issue.)
SELECT (715 "Heart Breaker").......... 10-20 62
SELECT (718 "Teenage Jezebel").......... 5-10 63
TOP FLIGHT (113 "Oh What a Love").......... 20-30 61
Session: Hi-Flyers.

CHRISTIE, Gaylon
(Gaylon Christy & Downbeats Featuring Roy Robinson)

Singles: 7-inch

BID (503 "Too Late").......... 5-10 63
CAPRI.......... 4-8 '60s
FAME (503 "Hootchie Cootchie Man").......... 10-20 58

CHRISTIE, Lou *P&R/R&B/LP '63*
(With the Classics; Lou Christy)

Singles: 12-inch

PLATEAU (101 "Guardian Angels").......... 40-50 81
(Promotional issue only.)
PLATEAU (4551 "Guardian Angels").......... 40-50 81

Singles: 7-inch

ABC.......... 4-6 73
ALCAR (207 "Close Your Eyes").......... 15-25 63
ALCAR (208 "You're with It").......... 15-25 63
AMERICAN MUSIC MAKERS (006 "The Jury").......... 8-12 67
BUDDAH.......... 5-15 68-72
C AND C (102 "The Gypsy Cried").......... 75-100 62
CO & CE (235 "Outside the Gates of Heaven").......... 5-10 66
COLPIX.......... 10-15 64-66
COLUMBIA.......... 10-15 67
EPIC.......... 10-15 76
MGM (Except 13473).......... 5-10 65-66
MGM (13473 "Rhapsody in the Rain").......... 10-15 66
(With "making out in the rain" lyrics.)
MGM (13473 "Rhapsody in the Rain").......... 5-10 66
(With "fell in love in the rain" lyrics.)
MIDLAND INT'L.......... 10-15 76-77
MIDSONG.......... 10-12 77
PLATEAU (4551 "Guardian Angels").......... 40-50 81
POLYDOR (519 "Rhapsody in the Rain").......... 3-5
RHINO.......... 3-5 '90s
ROULETTE (4457 "The Gypsy Cried").......... 15-20 62
(White label with color spokes.)
ROULETTE (4457 "The Gypsy Cried").......... 5-10 63
(Pink label.)
ROULETTE (4481 "Two Faces Have I").......... 15-25 63
(White label with color spokes.)
ROULETTE (4481 "Two Faces Have I").......... 5-10 63
(Pink label.)
ROULETTE (4504 "How Many Teardrops").......... 10-15 63
ROULETTE (4527 "Shy Boy").......... 10-15 63
ROULETTE (4545 "Stay").......... 10-15 64
ROULETTE (4554 "When You Dance").......... 20-25 64
SLIPPED DISC.......... 10-15 75
THREE BROTHERS.......... 5-15 73-75
WORLD ARTISTS (1002 "The Jury").......... 25-30 63

Picture Sleeves

COLPIX (799 "Big Time").......... 10-20 66
MGM (13473 "Rhapsody in the Rain").......... 8-12 66
MGM (13533 "Painter").......... 8-12 66
MGM (13576 "If My Car Could Only Talk").......... 20-25 66

LPs: 10/12-inch

BUDDAH (5052 "I'm Gonna Make You Mine").......... 10-15 69
BUDDAH (5073 "Paint America Love").......... 15-20 71
CO & CE (1231 "Lou Christie Strikes Back").......... 30-50 66
(Label may read: "Lou Christie Strikes Again.")
COLPIX (4001 "Lou Christie Strikes Again").......... 20-25 66
(Gold label.)
COLPIX (4001 "Lou Christie Strikes Again").......... 10-20 66
(Blue label.)
CSP (18260 "Lou Christie Does Detroit").......... 5-8
51 WEST ("Lou Christie Does Detroit").......... 10-15 83
MGM (4360 "Lightnin' Strikes").......... 12-18 66
MGM (4394 "Painter of Hits").......... 15-20 66
RHINO.......... 5-8 88
ROULETTE (25208 "Lou Christie").......... 50-60 63
(Cover has a blue background.)
ROULETTE (25208 "Lou Christie").......... 30-40 63
(Cover has white wall background.)
ROULETTE (25332 "Lou Christie Strikes Again").......... 20-30 63
(Repackage of Co & Ce 1231, *Lou Christie Strikes Back.*)
UNDERGROUND (50002 "Self Expression").......... 8-10 83
(Canadian.)
THREE BROTHERS (2000 "Lou Christie").......... 15-20 74
Session: Angels; Tammys.
Also see CHRISTY, Chic
Also see CLASSICS
Also see CRITTERS / Young Rascals / Lou Christie
Also see GORE, Leslie, & Lou Christie
Also see JACK, Johnny
Also see LUGEE & LIONS
Also see MARCY JOE
Also see RICHIE & RUNAROUNDS
Also see SACCO
Also see ZADORA, Pia, & Lou Christie

CHRISTIE, Lou / Len Barry & Dovells / Bobby Rydell / Tokens

LPs: 10/12-inch

WYNCOTE.......... 10-20 '60s
Also see DOVELLS
Also see RYDELL, Bobby
Also see TOKENS

CHRISTIE, Lou, & Classics / Isley Brothers / Chiffons

LPs: 10/12-inch

SPIN-O-RAMA (173 "Lou Christie and the Classics").......... 20-30 66
Also see CHIFFONS
Also see ISLEY BROTHERS

CHRISTIE, Lynn, & Deckers

Singles: 7-inch

NAR (225 "What Did I Do").......... 15-25 57

CHRISTIE, Ruth
(Ruth Christy)

Singles: 7-inch

LIBERTY (55225 "Let Me Love You").......... 10-20 59
TIDE (0018 thru 1087).......... 10-20 61-62
TIDE (2008 thru 2014).......... 8-12 65-67
UPTOWN (726 "Dancing Feet").......... 5-10 66
Also see CANDLETTS

CHRISTLAND SINGERS

Singles: 7-inch

CHECKER (1000 "God Has Done So Much").......... 10-20 61

CHRISTMAS, Connie

Singles: 7-inch

CHECKER (1015 "What a Night, What a Morning").......... 10-15 62

CHRISTMAS, Johnny, & Dynamics

Singles: 7-inch

P.D.Q. (5002 "Soft Lips").......... 50-75 59
WHIRLYBIRD (80 "Soft Lips").......... 15-25 61

CHRISTMAS SPIRIT

Singles: 7-inch

WHITE WHALE (290 "Christmas Is My Time of Year").......... 50-75 68
Members: Mark Volman; Howard Kaylan; Linda Ronstadt.
Also see RONSTADT, Linda
Also see TURTLES

CHRISTMON, John

Singles: 78 rpm

EXCELLO (2031 "My Baby's Gone").......... 15-25 54

Singles: 7-inch

EXCELLO (2031 "My Baby's Gone").......... 25-35 54

CHRISTOPHER

LPs: 10/12-inch

METROMEDIA (1024 "Christopher").......... 50-100 70
Members: Ron Cramer; Terry Hand; Richard Avitts; John Simpson; Doug Walden; Doug Tull.

CHRISTOPHER

LPs: 10/12-inch

CHRIS-TEE (12411 "What'cha Gonna Do").......... 1500-2000 70
(Reportedly 100 made.)
Members: Frank Smoak; Gary Lucas; Steve Nagle; Bill McKee.

CHRISTOPHER, Jordan

Singles: 7-inch

JUBILEE (5440 "Goodbye My Love").......... 5-10 62
U.A. (954 "The Knack").......... 10-15 65

Picture Sleeves

JUBILEE (5440 "Goodbye My Love").......... 10-20 62

CHRISTOPHER, Rod

Singles: 7-inch

TRU LITE (111 "Daybreak").......... 10-20 62

CHRISTOPHER, Ron

Singles: 7-inch

PYRO (54 "Debra").......... 10-15 66

CHRISTOPHER & SOULS

Singles: 7-inch

PHARAOH (151 "Diamonds, Rats and Gum").......... 20-30 66

CHRISTY, Charles
(With the Crystals; Charles Christie)

Singles: 7-inch

HBR (455 "Cherry Pie").......... 10-15 65
HBR (473 "In the Arms of a Girl").......... 10-15 66

Picture Sleeves

HBR (473 "In the Arms of a Girl").......... 15-25 66

CHRISTY, Chic
(Lou Christie)

Singles: 7-inch

HAC (103 "With This Kiss").......... 10-15 62
Session: Kay Chick; Susan Christie.
Also see CHRISTIE, Lou

CHRISTY, Don
(Sonny Bono)

Singles: 7-inch

FIDELITY (3020 "Wearing Black").......... 15-20 60
GO (1001/1002 "As Long As You Love Me").......... 20-25 60
NAME (3 "As Long As You Love Me").......... 15-20 60
SPECIALTY (672 "One Little Answer").......... 15-25 59
Also see SONNY

CHRISTY, June *P&R '53*

Singles: 78 rpm

CAPITOL.......... 4-8 51-57

Singles: 7-inch

CAPITOL (1800 thru 3900 series).......... 10-20 51-58
CAPITOL (4000 thru 4800 series).......... 5-10 59-62

EPs: 7-inch 33/4rpm

CAPITOL.......... 5-15 53-55

LPs: 10/12-inch

CAPITOL (H-516 "Something Cool").......... 35-50 54
(10-inch LP.)
CAPITOL (T-516 "Something Cool").......... 25-35 55
(Green label.)
CAPITOL (T-516 "Something Cool").......... 15-25 60
(Monaural. Black label.)
CAPITOL (ST-516 "Something Cool").......... 20-30 60
(Stereo. Black label.)
CAPITOL (SM-516 "Something Cool").......... 5-10 75
CAPITOL (600 thru 900 series).......... 15-25 55-57
(Green label.)
CAPITOL (600 thru 900 series).......... 10-20 60
(Black label.)
CAPITOL (1000 thru 2400 series).......... 10-20 60-65
CAPITOL (11000 series).......... 5-10 79
DISCOVERY.......... 5-10 82
SEABREEZE.......... 5-10 80

CHRISTY, June, with Stan Kenton

EPs: 7-inch

CAPITOL.......... 5-10 56

LPs: 10/12-inch

CAPITOL (656 "Duet").......... 20-35 56
(10-inch LP.)
Also see JONES, Jonah
Also see KENTON, Stan, & His Orchestra

CHROMATICS
(With the Ernie Freeman Orchestra)

Singles: 78 rpm

BLEND.......... 25-50 55
CREST.......... 10-15 55
MILLION.......... 25-50 55-56

Singles: 7-inch

BLEND (1005 "Believe Me").......... 75-125 55
BLEND (1006 "I'll Never Change").......... 150-200 55
CREST (1011 "Wild Man, Wild").......... 15-25 55
DUCKY (716 "My Conscience").......... 75-100 59
MILLION (2010 "Here in the Darkness").......... 50-75 55
MILLION (2014 "Here in the Darkness").......... 50-75 56

Also see SINGLETON, Eddie
Also see WASHINGTON, Sherry, & Chromatics
Also see WYNN, Lee, & Chromatics

CHRYSALIS

LPs: 10/12-inch

MGM (4547 "Definition")........................ 10-15 68

CHUBBY & TURNPIKES

Singles: 7-inch

CAPITOL (5840 "I Didn't Try")................. 30-40 67

CHUCK & BILL

Singles: 7-inch

BRUNSWICK (55011 "Way Out There") . 50-75 57
BRUNSWICK (55034 "Tears")................ 20-30 57

CHUCK & CHUCKLES

Singles: 7-inch

SHAD (5015 "One Hundred Baby") 10-20 59

CHUCK & EDDIE

Singles: 7-inch

S.I.G.N. (127 "Good Thing Going")......... 15-25

CHUCK & SENTRIES

Singles: 7-inch

RENDEZVOUS (207 "Sentinal Walk")..... 10-20 63

CHUCK-A-LUCKS

Singles: 7-inch

BOW (305 "Heaven Knows").................. 40-60 58
CANDLELITE (424 "Heaven Knows").........5-10 64
JUBILEE (5415 "Tarzan's Date") 10-20 61
LIN (5010 "Who Am I")........................... 25-35 58
LIN (5014 "Disc Jockey Fever") 40-50 58
MEL-O-DY (106 "Sugar Cane Curtain")... 25-35 63
W.B. (5198 "Long John")........................ 10-20 61
W.B. (5234 "Cotton Pickin' Love")........ 10-20 61
Members: Charles Dickerson; Adrian McLish; Ruben Noel.

CHUCKIE D

Singles: 7-inch

PARLIAMENT (11-4 "Way Later Baby") 100-200
PARLIAMENT (97701 "Patty Ann")......... 10-15

CHUCKLES

Singles: 7-inch

WEST SIDE (1019 "On the Street Where You Live").. 20-30 63
Also see CONSORTS

CHUG & DOUG

Singles: 7-inch

CHARGER (101 "My Girl") 10-20 64

CHURCH, Eugene P&R/R&B '58
(With the Fellows)

Singles: 78 rpm

CLASS (235 "Pretty Girls Everywhere") 100-150 58
CLASS (254 "Miami")............................ 100-200 59

Singles: 7-inch

CLASS (235 "Pretty Girls Everywhere") .. 15-25 58
CLASS (254 thru 266) 10-20 59-60
COLLECTABLES...3-5 81
KING (5545 thru 5715) 10-15 61-62
RENDEZVOUS (132 "Good News") 10-20 60
SPECIALTY (604 "Open Up Your Heart")... 20-30 57
WORLD PACIFIC (77866 "Dollar Bill").... 10-15 67
Session: Jesse Belvin; Gaynel Hodge; Alex Hodge; Bobby Day; David Ford; Earl Nelson; Buster Williams.
Also see CLIQUES
Also see DAY, Bobby
Also see FORD, David, & Ebbtides
Also see NELSON, Earl

CHURCH, Jimmy
(Jimmy Church Orchestra)

Singles: 7-inch

OKEH (7186 "The Hurt")......................... 15-25 63
PEACHTREE (101 "Thinkin' About the Good Times").. 50-100 '60s
SOUND STAGE 7 (2559 "I Don't Care Who Knows")...5-10 66
SOUND STAGE 7 (2580 "You've Got Me")..5-10 67
VERVE (10126 "Corrido Rock").............. 15-25 58

CHURCH MICE

Singles: 7-inch

HOUSE OF GUITARS (43 "Baby, We're Not Part of Society").. 20-30 '60s

Picture Sleeves

HOUSE OF GUITARS (43 "Baby, We're Not Part of Society").......................................40-60 '60s

CHURCH STREET FIVE
("Featuring Gene 'Daddy G' Barge")

Singles: 7-inch

LEGRAND (1004 "A Night with Daddy G")...10-20 61
LEGRAND (1010 "Fallen Arches")...........10-20 61
LEGRAND (1014 "Church Street Walk")..10-20 61
LEGRAND (1021 "Daddy G Rides Again")..10-20 62
Members: Gene Barge; Earl Swanson; Leonard Barks; Willie Burnell; Ron Fairley.
Also see BARGE, Gene
Also see BONDS, Gary "U.S."
Also see DADDY G

CHURCHILL, Kenneth, & Lyrics

Singles: 7-inch

JOYCE (304 "Fate of Rock and Roll") ..400-500 58

CHURCHILL, Savannah R&B '45
(With Her All Star Seven; with the Five Kings; with Four Tunes; with Al Killian & His Orchestra)

Singles: 78 rpm

ARCO (1202 "I'll Never Be Free")............10-15 50
ARCO (1253 "Foolishly Yours")...............10-15 50
ARCO (1259 "The Devil Sat Down and Cried")...10-15 50
ARCO (1263 "Ain't 'Cha Glad I Love You")...10-15 50
ARGO...10-15 56
COLUMBIA (30146 "The Best of Friends") 10-15 50
DECCA...10-15 53-55
KAY-RON...10-15 54
MANOR 10-15 44-48
RCA..10-15 51-52

Singles: 7-inch

ARGO (5251 "Let Me Be the First to Know") 20-30 56
DECCA (28836 thru 29262) 15-25 53-54
(Price range of 28000 and 29000 series is for black or pink label originals. Pink are promo only. Any Decca multi-color labels in that series are $5 to $10 reissues.)
JAMIE (1172 "Time Out for Tears") 10-15 60
KAY-RON (1000 "I Want to Be Loved")....20-30 54
KAY-RON (1005 "Just in Case You Change Your Mind")..20-30 54
RCA (4280 "Sin") 15-25 51
RCA (4448 "In Spite of Everything You Do")..30-40 52
RCA (4583 "I'm So Lonesome I Could Cry")..25-35 52
RCA (4773 "Don't Worry 'Bout Me") 25-35 52
RCA (5031 "Walkin' By the River") 25-35 52

EPs: 7-inch

CAMDEN (270 "Love and Sin")................40-60 55
CAMDEN (282 "Savannah Churchill Sings") 40-60 55
Session: King Odom Four.
Also see FIVE KINGS
Also see FOUR TUNES
Also see ODOM, King

CHURCHILL, Savannah, & Striders

Singles: 78 rpm

REGAL (3309 "When You Come Back to Me")..25-50 50
REGAL (3313 "And So I Cry")...................10-20 50

Singles: 7-inch

REGAL (468 "When You Come Back to Me")..300-400 51
(Reissue of Regal 3309, a 78 rpm only.)
REGAL (3313 "And So I Cry")..............100-200 50
Also see CHURCHILL, Savannah
Also see STRIDERS

CHYLDS

Singles: 7-inch

GIANT (101 "Hay Girl")............................20-30 67
W.B. (7058 "Hay Girl")..............................10-15 67
W.B. (7095 "Psychedelic Soul")...............10-15 67

CHYMES
(Four Chymes)

Singles: 7-inch

CHATTAHOOCHEE (715 "He's Not There Anymore")..5-10 66
DOWN TO EARTH 5-10
MUSICNOTE (121 "The Gypsy") 15-25 64
MUSICTONE (6125 "On the Street Where You Live")..10-15 64
Members: Pat Gerlardi; Ronnie Gerlardi; Gil Pabon; Billy Reid.
Also see PRECISIONS

CINCINNATIANS

Singles: 7-inch

EMERALD (16116 "Magic Genie") 20-30 63
ROOSEVELT LEE (16116 "Magic Genie")..200-300 63
(First issue.)

CINDERELLAS

Singles: 7-inch

BLUE ROCK (4004 "Fairy Tale")..............10-15 64
COLUMBIA (41540 "Puppy Dog") 10-15 59
DECCA (30830 "Yum Yum Yum") 8-12 59
DECCA (30925 "I Was Only 15")................8-12 59
ESCAPADE (100 "Boy Like That") 5-10 63
LIMELIGHT (3039 "Fairy Tale")................10-15 64
MERCURY (72394 "Fairy Tale")..................5-10 65
TAMARA (763 "More Than Yesterday")...15-25 64

CINDERELLAS

Singles: 7-inch

DIMENSION (1026 "Baby Baby") 20-30 64
Member: Margaret Ross.
Also see COOKIES

CINDERMEN

Singles: 7-inch

MOONGLOW...15-25 65-67

CINDERS

Singles: 7-inch

RICK (156 "Poison Ivy") 10-15 65
Member: John David Souther
Also see JOHN DAVID & CINDERS

CINDY LYNN & IN-SOUNDS

Singles: 7-inch

IN-SOUND (402 "Meet Me at Midnight") ..40-60 67

CINEEMAS

Singles: 7-inch

DAVE (911 "Never Gonna Cry") 10-15 64

CINERAMAS

Singles: 7-inch

CANDLELITE (433 "Crying Over You")........4-6
CHAMP (103 "It Must Be Love") 15-25 59
CLIFTON (04 "Crying Over You")................4-6 73
RHAPSODY (71964 "Crying Over You")..40-60 60
Members: Frankie Palmer; Joey Bennett.
Also see ROWLAND, Roc

CIOLINO, Pete

Singles: 7-inch

RECORTE (401 "Daddy Joe") 75-100 58

CIRCUS

Singles: 7-inch

REMBRANDT ("Games We Play") 10-20 66
(Selection number not known.)
USA (903 "Sink Or Swim")..........................8-12 68

CIRCUS

Singles: 7-inch

OFFE (101 "Bad Seed") 15-25 67

CIRCUS P&R '73

Singles: 7-inch

METROMEDIA...5-8 72-73

LPs: 10/12-inch

HEMISPHERE...10-15 74
METROMEDIA...15-25 73
Members: Tom Dobeck; Frank Salle; Craig Balzer; Phil Alexander; Mick Sabol; Bruce Balzer.
Also see STANLEY, Michael, Band

CIRCUS MAXIMUS

LPs: 10/12-inch

VANGUARD..15-25 67-68
Members: Jerry Jeff Walker; Bob Bruno; David Scherstrom; Peter Troutner; Gary White.
Also see WALKER, Jerry Jeff

CIRELL, Terri
(With the Backbeats)

Singles: 7-inch

VEKO (528 "Hallelujah, I Love Him So") ..10-20 61
VEKO (529 "Let's Go") 8-12 61

CIRKYT

Singles: 7-inch

JODY (6701 "That's the Way Life Is") 20-30 67

Picture Sleeves

JODY (6701 "That's the Way Life Is") 20-30 67

CIRO, Vic

Singles: 7-inch

AGON (1001 "Sentimental Rock and Roll")..15-25 61
DRAGON (4405 "I'm Lonesome") 5-10 64

CITADELS

Singles: 7-inch

MONOGRAM (501 "Let's Fall in Love") 2500-3500 62
Also see PHAROTONES / Citadels

CITATIONS

Singles: 7-inch

SWAN (4062 "Fire Ritual")........................15-20 60

CITATIONS

Singles: 7-inch

CLIFTON (23 "It Hurts Me")..........................4-6 77
DON-EL (113 "It Hurts Me")......................20-30 62

CITATIONS

Singles: 7-inch

JUST (101 "That Is You")..........................10-15 62

CITATIONS

Singles: 7-inch

EPIC (9603 "Moon Race") 10-20 63
SARA (3301 "Moon Race")........................20-30 63
Members: Brad Meyers; Ted Kasper; David Gustin; Bob Sanderson; Joe Halser; Kenny Stupek; Tom Lamanchek; Plamen Sisters.
Also see MEYERS, Brad, & Citations

CITATIONS

Singles: 7-inch

FRATERNITY (910 "The Girl Next Door")..20-30 63
FRATERNITY (992 "The Girl Next Door")..10-15 67
VANGEE (301 "The Girl Next Door")........25-35 63

CITATIONS

Singles: 7-inch

MAJESTIC (1001 "Panda Bear")..............10-20 60
MGM (13373 "That Girl of Mine") 10-15 65
MERCURY (77286 "Chicago") 5-10 64
PRINCESS..5-10 66
ROME (196 "Chartreuse")............................8-12
ROULETTE (4623 "Everybody Philly")........5-10 65
UNIVERSITY ("Phantom Freighter") 8-12
(Selection number not known.)
Also see ALMA-KEYS

CITATIONS

Singles: 7-inch

BALLAD (101 "I Will Stand by You") 50-75 67

CI-TATIONS

Singles: 7-inch

SEA SEVEN (24 "Justine") 50-75

CITIES SERVICE BAND
(Cities Service Green & White Quartet)

Singles: 78 rpm

RCA...3-5 '50s

Singles: 7-inch

RCA (4154 thru 4157)....................................4-8 51
RCA (4615 "The Trumpet Polka") 4-8 52
RCA (5123 "Guadalcanal March")................4-8 53

EPs: 7-inch

RCA (3014 "Sousa Marches") 10-20 52
(Two-discs.)
RCA (3020 "Just a Song at Twilight").......10-20 52
(Two-discs.)
RCA (3120 "Cities Service Band")............10-20 53
(Two-discs.)
Member: Paul Lavalle.

CITY

Singles: 7-inch

ODE (113 "Paradise Alley") 8-12 68
ODE (119 "That Old Sweet Roll")...............8-12 69

LPs: 10/12-inch

ODE (44012 "Now That Everything's Been Said")..75-100 69
(Color photo on front cover.)

ODE (44012 "Now That Everything's Been Said")....8-12 71
(Black and white photo on front cover.)
Members: Carole King; Danny Kortchmar; Jim Gordon; Charles Larkey.
Also see KING, Carole

CITY FOLK

LPs: 10/12-inch

20TH FOX (3153 "Here Come the City Folk")....10-20 64
(Monaural.)
20TH FOX (4153 "Here Come the City Folk")....10-20 64
(Stereo.)

CITY LIMITS

Singles: 7-inch

CAMELIA (100 "There She Goes")....20-30 '60s
UPTOWN (728 "Stagger Lee")....5-10 66
Member: Rocky Rhoades.
Also see IMPERIALS

CITY SURFERS

Singles: 7-inch

CAPITOL....15-20 63-64

CITY ZU

Singles: 7-inch

COLUMBIA (44342 "Give a Little Bit")....10-15 67
DOT....5-10 68-69

CIULO, Jerry

Singles: 7-inch

JEREE (114 "Don't Cry")....15-25 65

CLAIR-TONES

Singles: 7-inch

ANNOUNCING (1000 "Lost in a Dream World")....50-100

CLANCY BROTHERS & TOMMY MAKEM LP '63

Singles: 7-inch

COLUMBIA....4-6 62-69

LPs: 10/12-inch

COLUMBIA....10-20 62-69
GWP....10-15
HARMONY....6-10 71-72
SHANACHIE....5-10
TRADITION....20-40 59-61
Also see CLANCY BROTHERS
Also see MAKEM, Tommy

CLANN

Singles: 7-inch

G.A.R. (103 "Stubborn Kind of Fellow")....20-30 66
G.A.R. (109 "Tall Towers")....15-25 67
Members: Ross Dickerson; Dave Dister; Terry Kolkmann; Bill Stone; Jeff Gorman.

CLANTON, Bobby, & Cyclones

Singles: 7-inch

CYCLONE (500 "Angel")....50-100
KOOL (1010 "Beat Back Baby")....100-200 61
KOOL (1018 "Sincerely")....20-30 63

CLANTON, Ike P&R '60

Singles: 7-inch

ACE (569 "Land of Dreams")....10-15 59
ACE (583 "I'm Sorry")....15-25 60
ACE (604 "When Did You Leave Heaven")....10-15 60
ARLEN (503 "She's Different")....10-20 59
MERCURY (71975 "Sugar Plum")....10-15 62
MERCURY (72035 "Champ")....8-12 62
MERCURY (72084 "Judy's in Love")....5-10 63
Also see EDDY, Duane

CLANTON, Jimmy P&R/R&B '58
(With His Rockets; Jimmie Clanton)

Singles: 78 rpm

ACE....25-50 57

Singles: 7-inch

ABC....4-6 73
ACE (Except 567)....10-25 57-62
ACE (567 "My Own True Love")....10-20 59
(Monaural.)
ACE (567 "My Own True Love")....35-50 59
(Stereo.)
COLLECTABLES....3-5 81
ERIC....4-6 73
IMPERIAL....5-10 67-68
LAURIE (3508 "The Girl Who Cried Love")....5-10 69
LAURIE (3534 "Tell Me")....5-10 69
MALA (500 "Hurting Each Other")....5-10 65
MALA (516 "That Special Way")....5-10 65
OLDIES 45....3-5
PHILIPS....5-10 63-64
SPIRAL....4-6 71
STARCREST....4-6 76
STARFIRE (104 "I Wanna Go Home")....8-10 78
(Orange vinyl.)
STARFIRE ("I Wanna Go Home")....15-20 81
(Picture disc. Selection number not known.)
VIN (1028 "Wedding Bells")....8-12 61

Promotional Singles

ACE (664 "Venus in Blue Jeans")....15-25 62
ACE (51860 "The Slave")....10-20 60
(Promotional, bonus disc with the *Jimmy's Happy/Jimmy's Blue* LP.)
U.A. ("Teenage Millionaire")....10-20 62
(Cardboard 6-inch flexi-disc.)

Picture Sleeves

ACE (546 "Just a Dream")....5-10 '90s
ACE (567 thru 8007)....8-15 59-63
ACE (51860 "The Slave")....15-25 60
(Promotional only, mail-order bonus offer to buyers of the *Jimmy's Happy/Jimmy's Blue* LP. All copies of this sleeve were autographed by Clanton.)
PHILIPS (40181 "I'll Step Aside")....5-10 64
STARCREST....4-6 76

EPs: 7-inch

ACE ("Jimmy's Happy/Jimmy's Blue")....25-50 60
(Colored vinyl. Exact title and selection number not known.)
ACE (101 "Just a Dream")....20-40 59
ACE (102 "Thinking of You")....20-40 59
ACE (103 "I'm Always Chasing Rainbows")....20-30 59
ACE (642 "Teenage Millionaire")....15-25 61

LPs: 10/12-inch

ACE (100 "Jimmy's Happy/Jimmy's Blue")....50-75 60
(Black vinyl.)
ACE (100 "Jimmy's Happy/Jimmy's Blue")....75-125 60
(Colored vinyl.)
ACE (1001 "Just a Dream")....50-75 59
ACE (1007 "Jimmy's Happy")....40-50 60
ACE (1008 "Jimmy's Blue")....40-50 60
ACE (1011 "My Best to You")....50-75 61
ACE (1014 "Teenage Millionaire")....50-75 61
ACE (1026 "Venus in Blue Jeans")....40-60 61
MONTAGNE....10-15 81
PHILIPS....15-25 64
Also see DALE, Jimmy

CLANTON, Jimmy / Frankie Ford / Jerry Lee Lewis / Patsy Cline

EPs: 7-inch

MEMORY LANE....3-5 92
(Promotional issue only. Not issued with cover.)
Also see CLINE, Patsy
Also see FORD, Frankie
Also see LEWIS, Jerry Lee

CLANTON, Jimmy / Bristow Hopper

LPs: 10/12-inch

DESIGN....15-20 '60s

CLANTON, Jimmy, & Mary Ann Mobley

Singles: 7-inch

ACE (616 "Down the Aisle")....8-10 61

Picture Sleeves

ACE (616 "Down the Aisle")....10-15 61
Also see CLANTON, Jimmy

CLAN-TONES

Singles: 7-inch

EMONY (1021 "May I Never Love Again")....75-125 59

CLAPTON, Eric P&R/LP '70

Singles: 12-inch

W.B. (2248 "Forever Man")....5-10 85
(Promotional issue only.)
W.B. (2683 "Miss You")....5-10 85
(Promotional issue only.)

Singles: 7-inch

ATCO (6784 "After Midnight")....4-8 70
DUCK....3-5 83-86
POLYDOR....4-6 72-73
RSO....3-6 74-82
W.B.....3-5 86

Picture Sleeves

DUCK....3-5 85-89
POLYDOR....3-6
RSO....3-5 80-81
W.B.....3-5 86

LPs: 10/12-inch

ATCO (329 "Eric Clapton")....20-30 70
ATCO (803 "History of Eric Clapton")....20-30 72
DUCK....5-10 83-89
MFSL (030 "Slowhand")....100-125 79
MFSL (183 "Bluesbreakers")....40-60 87
MFSL (220 "Eric Clapton")....30-50 94
NAUTILUS (32 "Just One Night")....75-100 80
(Half-speed mastered.)
POLYDOR (Except 835261)....8-15 72-73
POLYDOR (835261 "Crossroads")....30-40 88
(Boxed, six-disc set.)
RSO (Except 035, 1009 & 4801)....8-20 73-82
RSO (035 "Slowhand")....20-25 77
(Colored vinyl. Promotional issue only.)
RSO (1009 "Limited Backless)....40-50 78
(Colored vinyl. Promotional issue only.)
RSO (4801 "461 Ocean Blvd.")....8-12 74
(With *Give Me Strength*.)
RSO (4801 "461 Ocean Blvd.")....5-10 74
(*Give Me Strength* is replaced with *Better Make It Through the Day*.)
Also see BLIND FAITH
Also see CREAM
Also see CURTIS, Sonny
Also see DELANEY & BONNIE
Also see DEREK & DOMINOES
Also see GUY, Buddy, with Dr. John & Eric Clapton / Buddy Guy & J. Geils Band
Also see HARRISON, George
Also see LOMAX, Jackie
Also see MAYALL, John
Also see RUSSELL, Leon
Also see SPANN, Otis
Also see STARR, Ringo
Also see TOWNSHEND, Pete, & Ronnie Lane
Also see WATERS, Muddy, & Howlin' Wolf
Also see YARDBIRDS

CLAPTON, Eric, Jeff Beck & Jimmy Page

LPs: 10/12-inch

RCA (4624 "Guitar Boogie")....10-15 71
Also see BECK, Jeff
Also see PAGE, Jimmy

CLAPTON, Eric, & Tina Turner

Singles: 7-inch

DUCK....3-5 87

Picture Sleeves

DUCK....3-5 87
Also see CLAPTON, Eric
Also see TURNER, Tina

CLARE SISTERS

Singles: 7-inch

VAN (1922 "Cool, Cool, Cool")....15-25

CLAREMONTS

Singles: 78 rpm

APOLLO....30-40 57

Singles: 7-inch

APOLLO (517 "Why Keep Me Dreaming")....40-50 57
APOLLO (751 "Why Keep Me Dreaming").8-12 61

CLARK, Alice

Singles: 7-inch

MAINSTREAM (5520 "I Keep It Hid")....4-6 72
RAINY DAY (8004 "You Got a Deal")....5-10 68
W.B. (7270 "You Hit Me")....20-40 69

LPs: 10/12-inch

MAINSTREAM....10-12 72

CLARK, Ann

Singles: 78 rpm

ACE (512 "I Had a Dream")....10-15 56
TRUMPET....10-15 55

Singles: 7-inch

ACE (512 "I Had a Dream")....15-25 56
TRUMPET (241 "Infatuation")....20-30 55
TRUMPET (242 "I Had a Dream")....30-50 55

CLARK, Ann & George

Singles: 78 rpm

TRUMPET (237 "Jole Blon")....10-20 55

Singles: 7-inch

TRUMPET (237 "Jole Blon")....20-30 55

CLARK, Billy
(Bill Clark)

Singles: 7-inch

ORANGE (1002 "I Know Why")....50-100 59
PEACH (727 "Love for You")....20-30 59

CLARK, Bobby, & Rhythm Knights

Singles: 7-inch

SOMA (1168 "Little Ragged Dolly")....15-20 60

CLARK, Bruce, & Qs

Singles: 7-inch

HULL (762 "Penny for Your Thoughts")....25-35 64

CLARK, Charles

Singles: 7-inch

ARGO (5332 "Another Chance")....10-15 59
ARTISTIC....15-25 58

CLARK, Chris R&B '66

Singles: 7-inch

MOTOWN (1114 "From Head to Toe")....10-15 67
MOTOWN (1121 "Whisper You Love Me, Boy")....10-15 68
V.I.P. (25031 "Do Right Baby Do Right")....10-15 66
V.I.P. (25038 "Love's Gone Mad")....50-60 66
(Title incorrect on label.)
V.I.P. (25038 "Love's Gone Bad")....10-15 66
(Title corrected.)
V.I.P. (25041 " I Love You")....10-15 67

LPs: 10/12-inch

MOTOWN (664 "Soul Sounds")....50-75 67
WEED (801 "CC Rides Again")....50-75 '60s
Session: Lewis Sisters.
Also see LEWIS SISTERS

CLARK, Claudine P&R/R&B '62
(With the Spinners)

Singles: 7-inch

CHANCELLOR (1113 "Party Lights")....15-20 62
CHANCELLOR (1124 "Walkin' Through a Cemetery")....8-12 62
CHANCELLOR (1130 "Walk Me Home")....8-12 63
COLLECTABLES....3-5 81
ERIC....4-6 73
HERALD (521 "Teenage Blues")....20-30 58
JAMIE (1279 "Moon Madness")....5-10 64
JAMIE (1291 "Buttered Popcorn")....5-10 64
TCF (18 "Standin' on Tip Toe")....5-10 64

LPs: 10/12-inch

CHANCELLOR (5029 "Party Lights")....40-60 62

CLARK, Connie

Singles: 7-inch

JOKER (716 "My Sugar Baby")....75-125 '60s

CLARK, Cortelia

LPs: 10/12-inch

RCA (3568 "Blues in the Street")....10-20 66

CLARK, Dave, Five P&R/LP '64
(With Friends)

Singles: 7-inch

CONGRESS (212 "I Knew It All the Time")....10-15 64
EPIC (2000 series)....4-6 72
EPIC (9656 thru 10265)....10-15 64-67
EPIC (10325 thru 10894)....5-10 68-72
EPIC MEMORY LANE....3-5
HOLLYWOOD....3-5 93
JUBILEE (5476 "Chaquita")....10-20 64
LAURIE (3188 "I Walk the Line")....25-35 63
RUST (5078 "I Walk the Line")....20-30 64

Promotional Singles

EPIC (9656 thru 9833)....10-20 64-65
EPIC (9863 "Over & Over")....10-20 65
(Black vinyl.)
EPIC (9863 "Over & Over")....25-35 65
(Red vinyl.)
EPIC (9882 thru 10894)....10-20 65-72

Picture Sleeves

CONGRESS (212 "I Knew It All the Time")....20-30 64
EPIC (2000 series)....5-8 72
EPIC (9656 "Glad All Over")....10-20 64
EPIC (9671 "Bits and Pieces")....10-20 64
EPIC (9692 "Can't You See That She's Mine")....10-20 64
EPIC (9704 "Because")....10-20 64
EPIC (9722 "Everybody Knows")....10-20 64
EPIC (9763 "Come Home")....10-20 65
EPIC (9811 "I Like It Like That")....10-20 65
EPIC (9833 "Catch Us If You Can")....10-20 65
EPIC (9863 "Over and Over")....10-20 65

EPIC (9882 "At the Scene") 10-20 66
EPIC (10004 "Try Too Hard") 10-20 66
EPIC (10031 "Please Tell Me Why") 10-20 66
EPIC (10053 "Satisfied with You") 10-20 66
EPIC (10076 "Nineteen Days") 10-20 66
EPIC (10114 "I've Got to Have a Reason") 10-20 66
EPIC (10144 "You Got What It Takes") 10-20 67
EPIC (10179 "You Must Have Been a Beautiful Baby") 10-20 67
EPIC (10209 "A Little Bit Now") 10-20 67
EPIC (10265 "Everybody Knows") 10-20 67
EPIC (10375 thru 10684) 15-25 68-72
HOLLYWOOD (65909 "Over and Over") 4-6 93
HOLLYWOOD (65912 "Do You Love Me") 4-6 93

EPs: 7-inch

COLUMBIA/AURAVISION ("Catch Us If You Can") 125-150 65
(Promotional issue made for Ponds. Single-sided, square, cardboard picture disc.)
EPIC 15-25 66
(Juke box issues only. Includes title strips.)

LPs: 10/12-inch

CAPITOL (6162 "Instrumental Album") 100-150 66
(Canadian.)
EPIC (24093 "Glad All Over") 75-125 64
(Instruments are not pictured on cover.)
EPIC (24093 "Glad All Over") 20-30 64
(Instruments are pictured on cover.)
EPIC (24104 "The Dave Clark Five Return") 20-30 64
EPIC (24117 "American Tour") 20-30 64
EPIC (24128 "Coast to Coast") 20-30 64
EPIC (24139 "A Weekend in London") 20-30 65
EPIC (24162 "Having a Wild Weekend") 20-30 65
EPIC (24178 "I Like It Like That") 20-30 65
EPIC (24185 "Greatest Hits") 20-30 66
EPIC (24198 "Try Too Hard") 20-30 66
EPIC (24212 "Satisfied with You") 20-30 66
EPIC (24221 "More Greatest Hits") 20-30 66
EPIC (24236 "5 by 5") 20-30 67
EPIC (24312 "You Got What It Takes") 20-30 67
EPIC (24354 "Everybody Knows") 20-30 68
EPIC (26000 series) 15-25 64-68
(Reprocessed stereo issues.)
EPIC (30434 "Dave Clark Five") 35-50 71
EPIC (33459 "Glad All Over Again") 20-25 75

Promotional LPs

EPIC (77238 "The Dave Clark Interviews") 40-45 65
I-N-S RADIO NEWS (1006 "It's Here Luv") 75-100 64
Members: Dave Clark; Denny Payton; Mike Smith; Lenny Davidson; Rick Huxley.

CLARK, Dave, Five / Rick Astor & Switchers

LPs: 10/12-inch

CORTLEIGH (1073 "Dave Clark Five") 15-25 66
(Has only two Dave Clark Five tracks.)

CLARK, Dave, Five / Lulu

Singles: 7-inch

EPIC (10260/65 "Everybody Knows"/"Best of Both Worlds") 10-20 67
(Promotional issue only.)
Also see LULU

CLARK, Dave, Five / Roy Meriwether Trio / Bobby Vinton / Bob Dylan

EPs: 7-inch

COLUMBIA SPECIAL PRODUCTS (319 "Step Lively") 75-100 66
(Promotional issue only for Hot Potatoes by Keds.)
Also see DYLAN, Bob
Also see MERIWETHER, Roy, Trio
Also see VINTON, Bobby

CLARK, Dave, Five / New Christy Minstrels / Bobby Vinton / Jerry Vale

EPs: 7-inch

COLUMBIA SPECIAL PRODUCTS (223 "Limited Edition") 10-15 65
Also see NEW CHRISTY MINSTRELS
Also see VALE, Jerry
Also see VINTON, Bobby

CLARK, Dave, Five / Playbacks

LPs: 10/12-inch

CROWN (400 "Playbacks") 20-25 64
(Stereo.)
CROWN (473 "Original Recordings from London England") 20-25 65
(Stereo.)
CROWN (5400 "Playbacks") 20-25 64
(Monaural.)
CROWN (5473 "Original Recordings from London England") 20-25 65
(Monaural.)
CUSTOM (1098 "It's Happening") 15-20 65
Note: Each Crown and Custom LP has only two Dave Clark Five tracks – *Chaquita* and *In Your Heart.*

CLARK, Dave, Five / Simon & Garfunkel / Yardbirds / New Christy Minstrels

EPs: 7-inch

COLUMBIA SPECIAL PRODUCTS (468 "Great Shakes Shake-Out") 20-30 65
(Mail-order promotional offer from General Foods.)
Also see CLARK, Dave, Five
Also see NEW CHRISTY MINSTRELS
Also see SIMON & GARFUNKEL
Also see YARDBIRDS

CLARK, Dee — P&R/R&B '58

(With the Riley Hampton Orchestra)

Singles: 78 rpm

ABNER (1019 "Nobody But You") 50-75 59
ABNER (1026 "Just Keep It Up") 75-100 59
ABNER (1029 "Hey Little Girl") 75-125 59
FALCON (1002 "Gloria") 15-25 57

Singles: 7-inch

ABC 4-6 73
ABNER (1019 "Nobody But You") 10-20 58
ABNER (1026 "Just Keep It Up") 10-20 59
(Monaural.)
ABNER (1029 "Hey Little Girl") 10-20 59
ABNER (1032 "How About That") 10-20 59
ABNER (1037 "At My Front Door") 10-20 60
ABNER (51026 "Just Keep It Up") 50-75 59
(Stereo.)
CHELSEA 4-6 75
COLLECTABLES 3-5 83
COLUMBIA (44200 "So You Say You Lost Your Baby") 5-10 67
CONSTELLATION (108 thru 165) 8-12 63-65
ERIC 4-6 73
FALCON (1002 "Gloria") 15-25 57
FALCON (1005 "24 Boyfriends") 40-50 57
FALCON (1009 "Oh Little Girl") 50-100 57
LIBERTY (56152 "24 Hours of Loneliness") 8-15 70
MCA 3-5 84
ROCKY 4-6 73
VEE-JAY (DC-1 "Lucky Me") 15-25 61
(Stereo.)
VEE-JAY (DC-2 "Your Friends") 15-25 61
(Stereo.)
VEE-JAY (DC-3 "Hold On") 15-25 61
(Stereo.)
VEE-JAY (355 thru 548) 10-15 60-63
U.A. 4-6 71
WAND (1177 "Nobody But You") 5-10 68
W.B. 4-8 73

Picture Sleeves

ABNER (1029 "Hey Little Girl") 20-30 59

EPs: 7-inch

ABNER (900 "Dee Clark") 50-75 61
VEE-JAY (900 "Dee Clark") 35-50 61

LPs: 10/12-inch

ABNER (LP-2000 "Dee Clark") 50-100 59
(Monaural.)
ABNER (SR-2000 "Dee Clark") 75-125 59
(Stereo.)
ABNER (LP-2002 "How About That") 50-100 59
(Monaural.)
ABNER (SR-2002 "How About That") 75-125 59
(Stereo.)
SOLID SMOKE (8026 "Dee Clark") 8-12 84
SUNSET (5217 "Wondering") 10-15 68
VEE-JAY (1019 "You're Looking Good") 30-40 60
VEE-JAY (1028 "Dee Clark") 30-40 61
VEE-JAY (1037 "Hold On, It's Dee Clark") 30-40 61
(Monaural.)
VEE-JAY (S-1037 "Hold On, It's Dee Clark") 40-50 61
(Stereo.)
VEE-JAY (1047 "Best of Dee Clark") 30-40 62
VEE-JAY (S-1047 "Best of Dee Clark") 40-50 62
Session: Delegates; Dells; Upsetters.
Also see DELEGATES
Also see DELLS
Also see KOOL GENTS
Also see SAUNDERS, Red
Also see UPCHURCH, Phil

CLARK, Delores

(Delores Clarke)

Singles: 7-inch

ANTARAS (101 "He's Gone") 5-10 66
ROMULUS (3002 "Praying Time") 10-20 63

CLARK, Denver Bill

Singles: 7-inch

PROCESS (105 "My Bird Dog") 50-75

CLARK, Dorisetta

Singles: 7-inch

LIBRA (217 "My Baby's Gone") 50-100
MERCURY (71253 "You Love Me") 75-125 58

CLARK, Dottie

(Dotty Clark)

Singles: 7-inch

BIG TOP (3081 "It's Been a Long, Long Time") 8-12 61
BIG TOP (3120 "Cradle in the Wind") 8-12 62
HOLLYWOOD (1138 "All Woman") 5-8 68

LPs: 10/12-inch

TIME (2126 "Dottie Clark") 10-20 64
(Monaural.)
TIME (52126 "Dottie Clark") 10-20 64
(Stereo.)

CLARK, Doug

(With the Nuts; with the Hot Nuts)

Singles: 7-inch

JUBILEE (5536 "Baby Let Me Bang Your Box") 10-15 66
JUBILEE (5546 "Go Doug, Go") 10-15 66
PORT (70043 "Peanuts") 8-12 65

EPs: 7-inch

GROSS (1000 "Excerpts") 15-20
(Excerpts from Gross LPs, 102, 103 & 105.)
GROSS (2065 "Burlesque") 15-20

LPs: 10/12-inch

GROSS (101 "Nuts to You") 20-30
GROSS (102 "On Campus") 20-30
GROSS (103 "Homecoming") 20-30
GROSS (104 "Rush Week") 20-30
GROSS (105 "Panty Raid") 20-30
GROSS (106 "Summer Session") 20-30
GROSS (107 "Hell Night") 20-30
GROSS (108 "Freak Out") 20-30
GROSS (109 "With a Hat On") 20-30

CLARK, Fred

Singles: 78 rpm

FEDERAL 10-20 53

Singles: 7-inch

FEDERAL (12136 "Walkin' and Wonderin'") 20-30 53
Also see JACKSON, Jump / Fred Clark

CLARK, Freddie

Singles: 78 rpm

X-TRA (105 "Ward 13") 15-25 57

Singles: 7-inch

X-TRA (105 "Ward 13") 15-25 57

CLARK, Gene — LP '74

(With the Gosdin Brothers)

Singles: 7-inch

ASYLUM 4-6 74
COLUMBIA (43000 series) 5-8 66
RSO (876 "Home Run King") 3-5 77

LPs: 10/12-inch

A&M 10-15 71
ASYLUM 8-10 74
COLUMBIA (2618 "Gene Clark") 20-30 67
(Monaural.)
COLUMBIA (9418 "Gene Clark") 25-35 67
(Stereo.)
COLUMBIA (31123 "Early L.A. Sessions") 10-15 72
RSO 5-10 77
TAKOMA 5-10 84
Also see BYRDS
Also see DILLARD & CLARK
Also see NEW CHRISTY MINSTRELS

CLARK, Jackie

Singles: 7-inch

UNART (2005 "Walkie Talkie") 25-35 58
XYZ (2005 "Walkie Talkie") 15-25 59

CLARK, James "Beale Street"

Singles: 78 rpm

COLUMBIA 10-20 46
Also see MEMPHIS JIMMY

CLARK, Jimmy

(Jimmy "Soul" Clark; with Benny & Sportsmen)

Singles: 7-inch

KAREN (101 "I Blew a Good Thing") 10-15 '60s
KAREN (1539 "Do It Right Now") 10-15 68
MOIRA (104 "Tell Her") 8-12 69
SOULHAWK (001 "Come On and Be My Sweet Darlin'") 10-20 67
SOULHAWK (003 "I'll Be Your Winner") 25-50 67
TEEK (4824 "Shook Up Over You") 20-30 63
TEEK (4829 "Nothing Like a Mother") 20-30 63

CLARK, Jimmy, Trio

Singles: 7-inch

ROUND (1001 "The Cat") 15-25 59

CLARK, Lee

Singles: 7-inch

ATCO (6266 "As Long As You're in Love with Me") 5-10 63
GALLO (103 "Warm Lips and Cold Cold Kisses") 20-30 57
REJO (100/101 "As Long As You're in Love with Me") 15-25 63
(First issue.)

CLARK, Leonard

Singles: 7-inch

KLUB (3108 "Come Home to Your Tommy Now") 300-500

CLARK, Lewis

Singles: 7-inch

BRENT (7071 "I Need You Baby") 5-10 67
FULLER 5-10 68
RED RAM (13672 "I Got My Eyes on You") 10-20 '60s
TIGERTOWN (004 "If You Ever, Ever Leave Me") 15-25 '60s

CLARK, Louis

Singles: 7-inch

DIXIE (1116 "Lonesome Truck Driver") 50-100 60

CLARK, Lucky

Singles: 7-inch

CHESS (1782 "So Sick") 10-15 61
CHESS (1806 "Feeling of Love") 10-15 61

CLARK, Michael

Singles: 7-inch

EDMAR (1031 "Never Never Say Goodbye") 8-12 64
IMPERIAL (5893 "None of These Girls") 10-15 62
IMPERIAL (5927 "Dreaming of You") 10-15 63

CLARK, Patsy

Singles: 7-inch

SAGE (264 "Whatcha Do to Me") 100-150 58

CLARK, Petula — P&R '64

(Pet Clark)

Singles: 78 rpm

CORAL 5-15 53-54
KING 5-15 54
MGM 5-15 55

Singles: 7-inch

CORAL (60971 "Tell Me Truly") 10-20 53
CORAL (61077 "Three Little Kittens") 10-20 54
DUNHILL 4-8 74
ERIC 3-5 83
IMPERIAL (5582 "Baby Lover") 10-15 59
IMPERIAL (5655 "Now That I Need You") 10-15 59
JANUS 4-6 76
KING (1371 "Little Shoemaker") 10-20 54
LAURIE (3143 "The Road") 8-12 62
LAURIE (3156 thru 3316) 5-10 63-65
LAURIE (3573 "The Road") 4-6 71
LONDON (10504 "With All My Love") 8-12 62
LONDON (10516 "Tender Love") 8-12 62
MGM (12049 "Romance in Rome") 10-20 55
MGM (14392 "Little Bit of Lovin'") 15-25 72
MGM (14431 "The Wedding Song") 4-6 72
ROWE/AMI 5-10 66
("Play Me" Sales Stimulator promotional issue.)
SCOTTI BROTHERS 3-5 82
W.B. 5-10 64-69
WARWICK (652 "Romeo") 8-12 61

EPs: 7-inch
W.B. 5-10 65-66
(Juke box issues only.)
LPs: 10/12-inch
GNP 5-8 73
IMPERIAL (9079 "Pet Clark") 20-40 59
(Monaural.)
IMPERIAL (9281 "Uptown") 15-25 65
IMPERIAL (12027 "Pet Clark") 20-30 65
(Stereo.)
LAURIE (2032 "In Love") 20-25 65
(Monaural.)
LAURIE (S-2032 "In Love") 25-35 65
(Stereo.)
LAURIE (2043 "Petula Clark Sings for Everybody") 15-20 65
(Monaural.)
LAURIE (2043 "Petula Clark Sings for Everybody") 20-25 65
(Stereo.)
MGM 8-12 72
PREMIER 15-25 64
SUNSET 10-20 66
W.B. 10-20 65-71
Also see FELICIANO, Jose / Petula Clark

CLARK, Ray

Singles: 7-inch
CRYSTAL (962 "Little Betty Twist") 75-125 '60s

CLARK, Roy — C&W/P&R '63

(With Buck Trent)
Singles: 78 rpm
4 STAR 15-25 54
Singles: 7-inch
ABC 4-6 74-79
ABC/DOT 4-6 75-77
CAPITOL 5-10 61-66
CHURCHILL 3-5 82-84
DEBBIE (103 "Please Mr. Mayor") 150-250 58
DOT 4-6 68-74
4 STAR (1659 "Mysteries of Life") 25-50 54
HALLMARK 3-5 89
MCA 3-5 79-84
SILVER DOLLAR 3-5 86
SONGBIRD 3-5 81
TOWER 4-6 67
LPs: 10/12-inch
ABC 5-10 77-79
ABC/DOT 6-12 74-77
ABC SPECIAL PRODUCTS (1002 "Roy Clark") 10-15 78
(Promotional issue, made for Pringles.)
CAPITOL (300 series) 10-12 69
CAPITOL (1700 thru 2500 series) 15-25 62-66
(With "T" or "ST" prefix.)
CAPITOL (2400 series) 5-10 81
(With "SM" prefix.)
CAPITOL (11000 series) 8-12 74-75
CAPITOL (12000 thru16000 series) 5-10 80-81
CHURCHILL 5-10 82
DOT 8-12 68-74
GUEST STAR 8-12 '60s
MCA 5-8 79-84
PICKWICK 5-10 '70s
PICKWICK/HILLTOP (6046 "Roy Clark") 8-15 66
SONGBIRD 5-10 81
TOWER 10-15 67-68
WORD 5-10 75
Also see CASH, Johnny / Roy Clark / Linda Ronstadt

CLARK, Royce

Singles: 7-inch
AIRWAYS (1001 "Losing Side of Town") 4-6 81
MINARET (204 "Oh Boy") 25-50 81
VEEDA ("They'll Never Know") 100-150 '60s
(Selection number not known.)
VEEDA (4011 "Like a Man") 100-150 '60s

CLARK, Sanford — P&R/R&B/C&W '56

Singles: 78 rpm
DOT 20-30 56
MCI (1003 "The Fool") 25-50 55
REO 35-55 57
(Canadian.)
Singles: 7-inch
ABC 4-6 74
DESERT SUN (15481 "Now I Know I'm Not in Kansas") 25-50 82
DOT (243 "The Fool") 5-10 65
DOT (15481 "The Fool") 30-40 56
(Maroon label.)
DOT (15481 "The Fool") 15-25 57
(Black label.)
DOT (15516 "A Cheat") 20-30 56
(Maroon label.)
DOT (15516 "A Cheat") 15-25 57
(Black label.)
DOT (15534 "9 Lb. Hammer") 20-30 57
DOT (15556 "Darling Dear") 25-35 57
DOT (15585 "Loo Be Doo") 20-30 57
DOT (15646 "Swanee River Rock") 20-30 57
DOT (15738 "Modern Romance") 75-100 58
JAMIE (1107 thru 1153) 15-25 58-60
LHI (9 "Footprints in Her Yard") 5-10 68
LHI (1203 "Son of Hickory Holler's Tramp") 5-10 68
LHI (1213 "Farm Labor Camp #9") 5-10 68
MCI (1003 "The Fool") 75-125 55
PROJECT (5004 "Tennessee Walk") 50-75 '60s
RAMCO (1972 thru 1992) 5-10 66-67
REO (8143 "9 Lb. Hammer") 20-30 57
(Canadian.)
TREY (3016 "It Hurts Me Too") 10-15 61
W.B. (5473 "She Taught Me") 8-12 64
W.B. (5624 "Hard Feelings") 8-12 65
LPs: 10/12-inch
LHI (12003 "Return of the Fool") 30-40 68
Session: Al Casey.
Also see CASEY, Al
Also see REYNOLDS, Jody

CLARK, Sanford, & Duane Eddy

Singles: 7-inch
JAMIE (1107 "Sing 'Em Some Blues") 15-25 58
Also see CLARK, Sanford
Also see EDDY, Duane

CLARK, Vern

Singles: 7-inch
S&R (301 "Bull Moose") 150-200 59

CLARK, W.C., & Cobras

Singles: 7-inch
HOLE (1520 "My Song") 125-175 79
Members: W.C. Clark; Stevie Ray Vaughan.
Also see COBRAS
Also see VAUGHAN, Stevie Ray

CLARK, Wilbur

Singles: 7-inch
JOB (1124 "I'll Give My Whole Life") 150-250 58

CLARK SISTERS

Singles: 7-inch
DOT (15896 "Hot Toddy") 5-10 59
LPs: 10/12-inch
CORAL 10-20 60-62
DOT (3137 "Swing Again") 10-20 59
(Monaural.)
DOT (25137 "Swing Again") 15-25 59
(Stereo.)

CLARKE, Gary

Singles: 7-inch
DECCA (31511 "The Virginian") 5-10 63
RCA (7870 "Green Finger") 5-10 61
Picture Sleeves
DECCA (31511 "The Virginian") 15-25 63

CLARKE, Jimmy

Singles: 7-inch
DIAMOND (157 "Everything's Fine") 10-20 64

CLARKE, Tony — P&R/R&B '64

Singles: 7-inch
CHESS (1880 "Woman, Love and a Man") 8-12 64
CHESS (1924 "The Entertainer") 8-12 65
CHESS (1935 "Poor Boy") 8-12 65
CHICORY (409 "Love Power") 4-8 70
ERIC 3-5 78
M-S (206 "A Wrong Man") 50-100 68

CLASH — LP '79

Singles: 12-inch
EPIC (617 "Gates of the West") 15-20 79
(Promotional issue only.)
EPIC (723 "Clampdown") 15-20 79
(Promotional issue only.)
EPIC (905 "Magnificent Seven") 15-20 80
(Promotional issue only.)
EPIC (2036 "Call Up") 8-12 81
(Blue label. Promotional issue only.)
EPIC (2036 "Call Up") 8-12 81
(Roulette wheel label. Promotional issue only.)
EPIC (2230 "This Is England") 8-12 85
(Promotional issue only.)
EPIC (2277 "Fingerpoppin' ") 8-12 85
(Blue label. Promotional issue only.)
EPIC (2662 "This Is Radio Clash") 15-20 81
(Promotional issue only.)
EPIC (3144 "Rock the Casbah") 8-12 82
EPIC (6899 "Radio Clash") 5-10 87
EPIC (7829 "Rock the Casbah") 5-10 89
(Mixed masters issue.)
Singles: 7-inch
CBS (2479 "Rock the Casbah") 4-6 82
EPIC (1178 "Gates of the West") 4-6 79
(Promotional issue only. Issued with promo edition of *The Clash*.)
EPIC (3006 "Should I Stay") 8-10 82
(Promotional issue only.)
EPIC (3088 "London Calling") 5-8 80
(Hall of Fame series.)
EPIC (3245 "Rock the Casbah") 8-10 82
(Promotional issue only.)
EPIC (3547 "Should I Stay") 3-5 82
EPIC (3571 "Should I Stay") 15-20 82
(Single-sided disc. Promotional issue only.)
EPIC (5749 "Train in Vain") 15-20 79
(10-inch single. Promotional issue only.)
EPIC (5788 "Clampdown") 15-20 79
(10-inch single. Promotional issue only.)
EPIC (8470 "Should I Stay") 5-8 82
(Hall of Fame series.)
EPIC (20000 series) 3-5 82
EPIC (30000 series) 3-5 82
EPIC (50000 series, except 50738, 50851 & 51013) 3-5 79-81
EPIC (50738 "White Man in Hammersmith Palais") 5-10 79
EPIC (50851 "Train in Vain") 10-15 79
(Promotional issue only.)
EPIC (51013 "Hitsville UK") 10-15 80
(Promotional issue only.)
Picture Sleeves
EPIC (3061 "Should I Stay") 10-15 82
(Shown as "Special Limited Edition.")
EPIC (3547 "Should I Stay") 5-10 82
(Lists B-side, *Cool Confusion*.)
EPIC (3547 "Should I Stay") 10-15 82
(No B-side shown. Promotional issue only.)
LPs: 10/12-inch
EPIC (913 "Sandinista Now") 15-20 80
(Promotional issue only.)
EPIC (952 "If Music Could Talk") 15-20 81
(Promotional issue only.)
EPIC (1574 "World According to Clash") 30-35 82
(Black cover, with printing.)
EPIC (1574 "World According to Clash") 25-30 82
(Black cover, with no printing.)
EPIC (1592 "Combat Rock") 40-50 82
(Logo picture disc, with "Face the Future" sticker. Promotional issue only.)
EPIC (35543 "Give 'Em Enough Rope") 8-12 78
(Orange label.)
EPIC (35543 "Give 'Em Enough Rope") 5-10 78
(Blue label.)
EPIC (35543 "Give 'Em Enough Rope") 10-15 78
(White label. Promotional issue only. With insert.)
EPIC (36060 "The Clash") 5-10 79
EPIC (36060 "The Clash") 15-20 79
(White label. Promotional issue only. With lyric insert and bonus single, #1178 *Gates of the West*)
EPIC (36328 "London Calling") 10-15 79
EPIC (36328 "London Calling") 15-20 79
(White label. Promotional issue only. With lyric sleeve.)
EPIC (37037 "Sandinista") 15-20 80
(Promotional issue only. With *Armagideon Times #3*)
EPIC (37037 "Sandinista") 10-15 80
(With *Armagideon Times #3.*)
EPIC (37689 "Combat Rock") 8-10 82
(Black label.)
EPIC (37689 "Combat Rock") 5-8 82
(Blue label.)
EPIC (37689 "Combat Rock") 10-15 82
(Promotional issue only. With lyric sleeve.)
EPIC (37689 "Combat Rock") 40-50 82
(Limited edition, camouflage vinyl. Promotional issue only. With "Face the Future" sticker.)
EPIC (38540 "Black Market Clash") 5-10 80
EPIC (40017 "Cut the Crap") 5-10 85
EPIC (40017 "Cut the Crap") 10-15 85
(Promotional issue only.)
EPIC (44035 "Story of the Clash") 10-15 88
EPIC (53191 "Super Black Market Clash") 30-40 93
(Limited edition, three 10-inch LPs.)
EPIC/NU-DISC (36846 "Black Market Clash") 10-15 80
(10-inch LP.)
Members: Joe Strummer; Mick Jones; Nick Sheppard; Pete Howard; Terry Chimes; Paul Simonon; Topper Headon; Vince White.

CLASS MATES

Singles: 7-inch
MARQUEE (101 "Don't Make Me Cry") 15-25 60
SEG-WAY (104 "Homework") 15-25 61

CLASS-AIRS

Singles: 7-inch
HONEY BEE (81631 "Too Old to Cry") 750-1000
(Identification number shown since no selection number is used.)
JASON SCOTT (16 "Too Old to Cry") 4-8 82
(500 made.)

CLASSIC FOUR

(Classic IV)
Singles: 7-inch
ALGONQUIN (1650 "Early Christmas") 50-75 61
ALGONQUIN (1651 "What Will I Do") 75-125 61
TWIST (1001 "What Will I Do") 50-75 62
(Twist credits "Classics IV," and shows title with subtitle: *What Will I Do (Without You)*, whereas on Algonquin they're the "Classics Four" and there is no subtitle.)
TWIST (1004 "Heavenly Bliss") 800-1200 62

CLASSIC SULLIVANS — R&B '73

Singles: 7-inch
KWANZA 4-6 73
MASTER KEY (03 "Shame, Shame, Shame") 15-25
Members: Eddie Sullivan; Lorraine; Barbara Sullivan.

CLASSICAL HEADS

LPs: 10/12-inch
PROBE (4516 "Classical Heads") 10-12 70

CLASSICALS

Singles: 7-inch
KENT (379 "One More River") 30-40 62
PRUDENTIAL (1002 "Help Me") 10-15 61

CLASSICS

Singles: 7-inch
CLASS (219 "If Only the Sky Was a Mirror") 75-125 58

CLASSICS

Singles: 7-inch
RO-ANN (1002 "Je Vous Aime") 1000-1500 59

CLASSICS

Singles: 7-inch
ABEL (231 "To Live My Life") 20-30 60

CLASSICS

Singles: 7-inch
CREST (1063 "Let Me Dream") 20-30 59

CLASSICS

Singles: 7-inch
MV (1000 "Christmas Is Here") 30-40 60

CLASSICS

Singles: 7-inch
STARR (508 "Close Your Eyes") 75-125 60
(Reissued on Alcar 207, credited to Lou Christie & Classics.)
Members: Lou Christie; Kay Chick; Shirley Herbert; Ken Krease.
Also see CHRISTIE, Lou
Also see LUGEE & LIONS

CLASSICS

Singles: 7-inch
TOP RANK (2061 "Burning Love") 15-25 60

CLASSICS — R&B '61

Singles: 7-inch
BED-STUY (222 "Again") 5-10 72
COLLECTABLES (1275 "P.S. I Love You") 3-5 83
(Colored vinyl.)
DART (1015 "Cinderella") 30-40 60
(Address shows Fairlawn, NJ.)
DART (1015 "Cinderella") 10-15
(Address shows Nutley, NJ.)

DART (1015 "Cinderella")....4-8
(Address shows New York.)
DART (1024 "Life Is But a Dream")...... 300-400 61
DART (1032 "Angel Angela") 20-30 61
DART (1038 "That's the Way")........ 15-25 61
ERIC.......3-5 82
MERCURY (71829 "Life Is But a Dream Sweetheart")........ 25-35 61
MUSICNOTE (118 "P.S. I Love You") 15-20 63
(White label.)
MUSICNOTE (118 "P.S. I Love You") 10-15 63
(Blue label.)
MUSICNOTE (1116 "Till Then")........ 10-20 63
(Black vinyl.)
MUSICNOTE (1116 "Till Then")........ 75-125 63
(Colored vinyl.)
MUSICTONE (6131 "Too Young")........ 15-25 64
PICCOLO (500 "I Apologize") 15-25 65
STORK (2 "You'll Never Know")........ 10-15 64
STREAMLINE (1028 "Life's But a Dream")........ 15-25 61
TRIP.......3-5

LPs: 10/12-inch

CRYSTAL BALL (114 "Classics Greatest Hits")........ 15-20 84
(Black vinyl. 1000 made.)
Members: Emil Stuccio; Tony Victor; John Gamble; Jamie Troy.

CLASSICS

Singles: 7-inch

JERDEN (742 "Till I Met You") 20-30 64
Also see CANADIAN CLASSICS

CLASSICS

Singles: 7-inch

JOSIE (939 "Over the Weekend")........ 10-20 65

CLASSICS

Singles: 7-inch

WIDE WORLD (62767 "Looking for a Love")........ 50-100 '60s

CLASSICS

Singles: 7-inch

DAN GUY (592 "I'm in Love")........ 15-25

CLASSICS

Singles: 7-inch

KAREN (316 "The Wheel of Love")...... 200-300

CLASSICS 4
("Vocal By Bobby Osborn")

Singles: 7-inch

GAYLO (2484 "My Heart's Been Broken")........ 100-200 64
Also see OSBURN, Bob

CLASSICS IV

Singles: 7-inch

ARLEN (746 "It's Too Late")........ 10-20 64
TWIST (1001 "Island of Paradise") 50-75 62
TWIST (1003 "Heavenly Bliss")........ 150-250 62
Member: Andrew Petruzelli.

CLASSICS IV P&R '67
(Dennis Yost & Classics IV; Classics)

Singles: 7-inch

AMERICAN PIE.......3-5 '90s
CAPITOL (5710 "Pollyana") 10-15 66
CAPITOL (5816 "Little Darlin' ") 10-15 66
GUSTO.......3-5
IMPERIAL (Except 66328)........ 4-8 67-70
IMPERIAL (66328 "Stormy"/"Ladies Man")........ 10-20 68
IMPERIAL (66328 "Stormy"/"24 Hours of Loneliness")........ 5-8 68
(Note different flip.)
LIBERTY (56182 "God Knows I Loved Her")........ 4-6 70
LIBERTY (56200 "Where Did All the Good Times Go")........ 4-6 70
LIBERTY (SP-36 "Song")........ 15-25 70
(Radio spots. Promotional issue only.)
MGM.......4-6 75
MGM/SOUTH.......4-6 72-73
PLAYBACK.......3-5 90
SILVER SPOTLIGHT SERIES.......3-5
U.A. 4-6 71

LPs: 10/12-inch

IMPERIAL.......12-20 68-69
KOALA (14258 "Greatest Hits of the Classic IV")........ 8-10 79
(Mistakenly credits group as the "Classic IV.")
LIBERTY (10000 series)........ 5-10 81-85
LIBERTY (11000 series)........ 10-12 70
MGM/SOUNDS OF THE SOUTH........ 8-10 73
SUNSET.......10-12 70
U.A. 8-10 75
Members: Dennis Yost; James Cobb; Dean Daughtry; Wally Eaton; Auburn Burrell; Kim Venable; Joe Wilson; Mike Sharpe.
Also see ATLANTA RHYTHM SECTION
Also see CANDYMEN
Also see YOST, Dennis

CLASSINETTES

Singles: 7-inch

MARKAY (107 "Little Boy") 200-300 62

CLASSMATES

Singles: 78 rpm

SILHOUETTE.......5-10 56

Singles: 7-inch

SILHOUETTE (509 "Gotta Go and See My Baby")........ 20-30 56

CLASSMATES

Singles: 78 rpm

DOT.......8-12 56-57
KING.......8-12 55

Singles: 7-inch

DOT (15460 thru 15589) 10-15 56-57
FELSTED (8673 "Cotton Pickin', Pickle Packin', Fish Strippin', Claw Hoppin' Hands")........ 5-10 63
KING (1487 "A Kiss Is Not a Kiss")........ 10-15 55
STACY (935 "Did You Ever")........ 10-15 62

CLASSMATES
(With Henry J. Beau Orchestra; with Heini Beau Orchestra)

Singles: 7-inch

MARQUEE (101 "High School")........ 20-30 60
MARQUEE (102 "Pretty Little Pet") 25-35 60
(Letters in "Marquee" are almost touching each other at the bottom.)
MARQUEE (102 "Pretty Little Pet") 20-30 60
(Letters in "Marquee" have extra space between each character.)

CLASSMATES
("Vocal: David London - Music: Al Greiner")

Singles: 7-inch

RADAR (2624 "Graduation")........ 10-15 62
RADAR (3962 "All I Want Is to Love You")........ 10-15 62

Picture Sleeves

RADAR (3962 "All I Want Is to Love You")........ 15-20 62
Member: David London.

CLASSMATES / Johnny Mastrio & Classmates

Singles: 7-inch

FRANKIE.......15-25 57
Members: John DeLisa; Pete DeLisa.
Also see MASTRIO, Johnny

CLASSMEN

Singles: 78 rpm

CORAL (61534 "Wonder Why")........ 5-10 56

Singles: 7-inch

CORAL (61534 "Wonder Why")........ 10-15 56

CLASSMEN

Singles: 7-inch

C-M (8464 "I Won't Cry")........ 50-75 63
GATEWAY (712 "True Love")........ 10-15 63
IMPACT (1012 "Susie Jones")........ 20-30 66
JR (5006 "Why Did You Put Me On") 10-15 64
JR (5008 "Look Out World")........ 10-15 64
JR (5009 "Ping Pong")........ 10-15 64
LIMELIGHT (3012 "Love Is Gone")........ 5-10 63
LIMELIGHT (3016 "All Time Fool")........ 5-10 63
PEARCE (5806 "Julie")........ 10-20 67
PEARCE (5913 "Yang Yang")........ 10-20 67
VOLKANO (5002 "Susie Jones")........ 75-100 66

CLASS-NOTES

Singles: 7-inch

DOT (15786 "You Inspire Me")........ 75-100 58
HAMILTON (50011 "Take It Back") 25-35 58
Also see CADETS
Also see ROCKETEERS

CLAUD, Vernon

Singles: 78 rpm

DECCA.......15-25 56

Singles: 7-inch

DECCA (30174 "Jungle of Cement and Stone")........ 20-40 56

CLAUDE & HIGHTONES

Singles: 7-inch

BAY-TONE (113 "Bucket Head")........ 15-25 59
PAM-MAR.......8-12 64

CLAUDIA & BUDDY

Singles: 78 rpm

CHESS.......15-25 55

Singles: 7-inch

CHESS (1586 "Please Come Back to Me")........ 25-35 55

CLAUDIA & CARDINALS

Singles: 7-inch

TELTONE ("Much too Much too Soon")... 50-75
(Selection number not known.)

CLAUDIA & CRYSTALS

Singles: 7-inch

DORE (601 "Little Love of Mine")........ 15-25 61

CLAY, Cassius LP '63
(Cassius Marcellus Clay Jr; Muhammed Ali)

Singles: 7-inch

COLUMBIA (43007 "Stand By Me")........ 10-20 64
COLUMBIA (75716/75717 "I Am the Greatest"/"Will the Real Sonny Liston Please Fall Down") 25-50 64
(Promotional issue only. Identification numbers shown since no selection numbers are used.)

Picture Sleeves

COLUMBIA (43007 "Stand By Me")........ 25-35 64

LPs: 10/12-inch

COLUMBIA (2093 "I Am the Greatest")....30-40 63
(Monaural.)
COLUMBIA (8893 "I Am the Greatest")....35-45 63
(Stereo.)
Also see ALI, Muhammad, & Frank Sinatra

CLAY, Chris

Singles: 7-inch

VELTONE (111 "Santa Under Analysis"). 10-20 60

CLAY, Clarence, & William Scott

LPs: 10/12-inch

PRESTIGE BLUESVILLE........ 15-20 63

CLAY, Jeffrey
(With the Diggers)

Singles: 78 rpm

CORAL.......5-10 55

Singles: 7-inch

CORAL.......10-15 55
LAMAR (2809 "It's Hard to Stand Tall").... 40-50
MGM.......5-10 65

CLAY, Joe

Singles: 78 rpm

VIK.......40-60 56

Singles: 7-inch

VIK (0211 "Duck Tail")........ 75-125 56
VIK (0218 "Cracker Jack") 150-200 56

CLAY, Judy R&B '70

Singles: 7-inch

ATLANTIC (2669 "Get Together")........ 5-10 69
ATLANTIC (2697 "Greatest Love")........ 5-10 70
EMBER (1080 "More Than You Know")... 10-15 61
EMBER (1085 "Stormy Weather")........ 10-20 62
LA VETTE (1004 "Let It Be Me")........ 5-10
SCEPTER (1273 thru 12157) 8-12 64-66
STAX (0026 "It Ain't Long Enough")........ 5-10 69
STAX (230 "You Can't Run Away from Your Heart")........ 5-10 67
Also see VERA, Billy, & Judy Clay

CLAY, Judy, & William Bell P&R/R&B '68
(William Bell & Judy Clay)

Singles: 7-inch

STAX (0005 "Private Number")........ 5-10 68
STAX (0017 "My Baby Specializes")........ 5-10 68
Also see CLAY, Judy

CLAY, Rayna

Singles: 7-inch

ATHENA (102 "I Can Pretend") 10-15 60

CLAY, Tom P&R/R&B/LP '71
(With the Blackberries; with Raybor Voices)

Singles: 7-inch

BIG TOP (3055 "That's All")........ 10-20 60
CHANT (103 "Marry Me")........ 30-50 59
MOTOWN.......3-5 81
MOWEST.......4-6 71
OFFICIAL IBBB INTERVIEW (45629 "We Don't Like Them, We Love Them")........ 125-150 65
(Tom Clay interviews the Beatles. Promotional issue only. Identification number shown since no selection number is used.)
OFFICIAL IBBB INTERVIEW (97436 "Remember, We Don't Like Them, We Love Them")........ 50-75 64
(Tom Clay interviews the Beatles. Promotional issue only. Identification number shown since no selection number is used.)

Picture Sleeves

MOWEST (5002 "What the World Needs Now - Abraham Martin and John")........ 4-6 71
(Promotional issue only.)
OFFICIAL IBBB INTERVIEW (97436 "Remember, We Don't Like Them, We Love Them")...... 100-150 64

LPs: 10/12-inch

MOWEST.......10-15 71
Also see BEATLES

CLAY, Verna Rae

Singles: 7-inch

SURE SHOT (5001 "He Loves Me, He Loves Me Not")........ 10-15 63

CLAYBURNS

Singles: 7-inch

PYRO (51 "What Did He Mean")........ 10-20 66

CLAYTON, BOB
(Gene Autry)

Singles: 78 rpm

BROADWAY (4004 "Dallas County Jail Blues")........ 25-75
BROADWAY (4062 "In the Jailhouse Now, No. 2")........ 25-75
BROADWAY (4067 "Jailhouse Blues")... 25-75
BROADWAY (4073 "Silver Haired Daddy of Mine")........ 25-75
BROADWAY (4093 "Crimes I Didn't Do")........ 25-75
BROADWAY (4094 "Back to Old Smokey Mountain")........ 25-75
BROADWAY (4095 "My Carolina Mountain Home")........ 25-75

Singles: 7-inch

SIMS (116 "Heart She Broke") 10-15 60
Also see AUTRY, Gene
Also see CLAYTON & BREEN

CLAYTON, Doctor
(Peter Clayton)

Singles: 78 rpm

BLUEBIRD.......10-20 41-42
GROOVE (5006 "Hold That Train, Conductor")........ 15-25 56
OKEH.......15-25 39
RCA.......10-20 46

Singles: 7-inch

GROOVE (5006 "Hold That Train, Conductor")........ 30-50 54

CLAYTON, Doug

Singles: 7-inch

PURE GOLD (501 "Sally Ann") 150-250

CLAYTON, Jerry

Singles: 7-inch

BIG I (302 "Metal Monster")........ 50-75

CLAYTON, Johnny

Singles: 7-inch

DIXIE (838 "Never Again")........ 200-300 '50s

CLAYTON, Merry P&R '70

Singles: 7-inch

CAPITOL (4984 thru 5243)........ 8-12 63-64
MCA.......3-6 80-88
ODE (66007 thru 66116)........ 4-8 70-75
TELDISC (501 "The Doorbell Rings") 10-15 62

LPs: 10/12-inch

MCA.......5-10 80
ODE (34948 "Merry Clayton")........ 5-10 77
ODE (34957 "Keep Your Eye On the Sparrow")........ 5-10 77
ODE (77000 series)........ 10-12 71-75
Also see BEACH BOYS / Merry Clayton
Also see RAELETTES

CLAYTON, Paul

Singles: 7-inch

MONUMENT.......5-10 60-64

LPs: 10/12-inch

ELEKTRA (147 "Unholy Matrimony") 20-30 57
ELEKTRA (155 "Bobby Burns' Merry Muses") 20-30 58
FOLKWAYS (2007 "Cumberland Mountain Folk Songs") 10-20
(10-inch LP.)
FOLKWAYS (47 "Folk Songs and Ballads of Virginia") 10-20
(10-inch LP.)
FOLKWAYS (2310 "Folk Ballads") 10-20
MONUMENT (8017 "Folk Singer") 10-20 65
(Monaural.)
MONUMENT (18017 "Folk Singer") 10-20 65
(Stereo.)
RIVERSIDE (615 "Bloody Ballads") 30-40 57
RIVERSIDE (640 "Wanted for Murder") ... 30-40 58
RIVERSIDE (648 "Timber") 30-40 58
STINSON (69 "Whaling Songs and Ballads") 20-30 58
STINSON (70 "Waters of Tyne") 20-30 58
TRADITION 10-20
WASHINGTON 10-20

CLAYTON, Rich, & Rumbles

Singles: 7-inch

DAWN CORY (1003 "Flip Side") 40-60 63
Also see FABULOUS RUMBLES
Also see RUMBLES LTD.

CLAYTON, Steve

Singles: 78 rpm

CORAL 5-10 56

Singles: 7-inch

CORAL 10-15 56-57
DECCA (31516 "He Will Call") 5-10 63
EPIC (59695 "My Summer Love") 5-10 64
JAMIE 5-10 67
MEDALLION 10-15 59
ROULETTE (4112 "Somebody Else Took Her Home") 20-30 58
SPIRAL 4-8 65-71
T-BIRD (2918 "Make Her Smile") 5-10 63

CLAYTON, Von

Singles: 7-inch

SURE PLAY (1003 "Bandstand") 10-15 62

CLAYTON & BREEN

Singles: 78 rpm

BROADWAY (4095 "Alone with My Sorrows") 25-75
Member: Gene Autry.
Also see AUTRY, Gene
Also see CLAYTON, Bob

CLEANLINESS & GODLINESS SKIFFLE BAND

LPs: 10/12-inch

VANGUARD (79285 "Greatest Hits") 10-20 68
Also see MASKED MARAUDERS

CLEAR BLUE SKY

Singles: 7-inch

ROMAT (1005 "Morning of Creation") ..... 20-30 '60s

CLEAR LIGHT *LP '67*

Singles: 7-inch

ELEKTRA 5-10 67

LPs: 10/12-inch

ELEKTRA (4011 "Clear Light") 15-25 67
Members: Cliff DeYoung; Bob Seal; Douglas Lubahn; Michael Ney; Ralph Schuckett; Dallas Taylor.

CLEARY, Eddie

Singles: 7-inch

KAWANA (101/102 "I Don't Care"/"Think It Over Baby") 500-700 59

CLEARY, Mark, with Bill German & His Bop Cats

Singles: 7-inch

BOP CAT (101/102 "Two Drops of Water"/"Bop Cat Rock") 10-15

CLEE-SHAYS

Singles: 7-inch

TRIUMPH (65 "Man from U.N.C.L.E.") 10-15 66

LPs: 10/12-inch

TRIUMPH (101 "Super Spy Themes") 15-25 66

CLEE-SHAYS

Singles: 7-inch

ZOOMA (101 "My Dream") 200-400

CLEFFTONES

Singles: 78 rpm

OLD TOWN 300-400 55

Singles: 7-inch

OLD TOWN (1011 "My Dearest Darling") 2000-3000 55
Member: Cas Bridges.
Also see FOUR FELLOWS
Also see VICTORIANS

CLEFMEN

Singles: 7-inch

CHERRY (7889 "Shimmer") 10-20 64

CLEFS

Singles: 78 rpm

CHESS (1521 "We Three") 50-100 52
PEACOCK (1643 "I'll Be Waiting") 25-50 54

Singles: 7-inch

PEACOCK (1643 "I'll Be Waiting") 50-75 54
Members: Scotty Mann; Frank Newman; Pav Bess; Leroy Flack; Fred Council; Leo Carter.
Also see MANN, Scotty, & Masters

CLEFS

("Vocal: Lonnie Hathaway Jr.")

Singles: 7-inch

RED BIRD (1210 "Don't Cry") ..... 100-150 '50s

CLEFS OF LAVENDER HILL *P&R '66*

Singles: 7-inch

DATE (1510 thru 1567) 10-20 66-67
THAMES (100 "Stop! Get a Ticket") 25-35 66
Members: Travis Fairchild; Coventry; Bill Moss; Fred Moss.

CLEFTONES *P&R/R&B '56*

(Herb Cox & Cleftones)

Singles: 78 rpm

GEE 20-30 56-57
ROULETTE 30-40 58

Singles: 7-inch

ABC 4-6 73
CLASSIC ARTISTS (121 "My Angel Lover") 5-8 90
(Black vinyl. 1000 made.)
GEE (1000 "You Baby You") 50-75 55
GEE (1011 "Little Girl of Mine") 40-60 56
(Red and black label.)
GEE (1011 "Little Girl of Mine") 8-12 60
(Gray label.)
GEE (1016 "Can't We Be Sweethearts") .. 15-25 56
(Red and black label.)
GEE (1016 "Can't We Be Sweethearts") 8-12 60
(Gary label.)
GEE (1025 "String Around My Heart") 15-25 56
GEE (1031 "Why Do You Do Me Like You Do") 15-25 57
(Red and black label.)
GEE (1031 "Why Do You Do Me Like You Do") 8-12 61
GEE (1038 "See You Next Year") 15-25 57
(Red and black label.)
GEE (1038 "See You Next Year") 8-12 61
(Gray label.)
GEE (1041 "Hey Babe") 15-25 57
GEE (1048 "Lover Boy") 15-25 58
(Red and black label.)
GEE (1048 "Lover Boy") 8-12 60
(Gray label.)
GEE (1064 "Heart & Soul") 20-30 61
GEE (1067 "For Sentimental Reasons") .. 20-30 61
GEE (1074 "Earth Angel") 10-15 61
GEE (1077 "Again") 10-15 61
GEE (1079 "Lover Come Back to Me") 20-30 61
GEE (1080 "How Deep Is the Ocean") 10-15 62
ROBIN HOOD (133 "Please Say You Want Me") 10-20 76
(Red vinyl. Promotional issue only.)
ROULETTE (4094 "She's So Fine") 15-20 58
ROULETTE (4161 "Mish-Mash Baby") 10-15 59
ROULETTE (4302 "She's Gone") 10-15 60
ROULETTE GOLDEN GOODIES ..... 4-6 '70s
WARE (6001 "He's Forgotten You") 10-20 64

LPs: 10/12-inch

EMUS 5-10 79
GEE (GLP-705 "Heart & Soul") 100-200 61
(Monaural.)
GEE (SGLP-705 "Heart & Soul") 200-300 61
(Stereo.)
GEE (GLP-707 "For Sentimental Reasons") 150-250 62
(Monaural.)
GEE (SGLP-707 "For Sentimental Reasons") 250-350 62
(Stereo.)
Members: Herbie Cox; Berman Patterson; Bill McClain; Charles James; Warren Corbin; Pat Span; Eugene Pearson.
Also see COX, Herbie
Also see DRIFTERS

CLEFTS

Singles: 7-inch

V-TONE (213 "Come On") 10-20 60

CLEMAN, Bob

Singles: 7-inch

MANCO (1063 "Teentown U.S.A.") 10-15 65

CLEMENT, Henry

(With the Trojans; with Dewdrops; Little Henry Clement)

Singles: 7-inch

SPOT 10-15 62
ZYNN (503 "I'm So in Love with You") 50-75 58
(Artist shown as Henry Clement & Dewdrops.)
ZYNN (503 "I'm So in Love with You") 20-30 58
(Artist shown as Henry Clement.)
ZYNN (513 "What Have I Done Wrong") 75-100 58
ZYNN (1006 "I'll Be Waiting") 20-30 61

CLEMENT, Jack *C&W '78*

Singles: 78 rpm

SUN 15-25 57

Singles: 7-inch

ELEKTRA (45474 "We Must Believe in Magic") 3-5 78
ELEKTRA (45518 "All I Want to Do in Life") 3-5 78
HALLWAY (1205 "Ruby, Are You Mad") 5-10 65
HALLWAY (1796 "Time After Time After Time") 5-8 63
HALLWAY (1912 "Time After Time After Time") 8-10 62
JMI (10 "The One On the Right Is On the Left") 4-6 72
MALA (514 "What Made the Babies Cry, Mama") 5-10 65
RCA (7602 "Whole Lotta Lookin'") 10-20 59
SUN (291 "Ten Years") 20-30 57
SUN (311 "Wrong") 15-25 57

LPs: 10/12-inch

ELEKTRA (122 "All I Want to Do in Life") ... 5-10 78

CLEMENT, Jack, & Dale Stevens

Singles: 7-inch

FRATERNITY (911 "Dog Doctor") 5-10 63

LPs: 10/12-inch

FRATERNITY (1012 "Weird and the Beard") 20-30 61
Also see CLEMENT, Jack

CLEMENT, Terry

(With the Tune Tones)

Singles: 7-inch

ROCKO (517 "Teenage Rock") 10-15 61
ZYNN (1007 "Jacqueline") 20-30 61

CLEMENTINO, Clairette

Singles: 7-inch

CAPITOL (5003 thru 5276) 8-12 63-64
ENCORE (1201 "You've Been Telling Our Secrets") 10-15 61
ENCORE (1204 "Teenage Fair") 10-15 62

CLEMENTS, Sonny

Singles: 7-inch

DRAGON (411 "Sleepy Guitar") 10-20 61

CLEMENTS, T.

Singles: 7-inch

HOT (107 "Kick That Tiger") 10-20 64

CLEMENTS, Zeke

EPs: 7-inch

JANET (303 "Zeke Clements") 100-150

CLEMONS, T.L., & Sir Nites

(With the Dr. Yack Combo)

Singles: 7-inch

COMBO (168 "I Love You So") 100-150 60

CLEO & RAMONE

Singles: 7-inch

ARVEE (5041 "Soul Mate") 10-20 61

CLEOPATRA

Singles: 7-inch

SHERYL (335 "Heaven Only Knows") . 200-300 61

CLEO-PATRETTES

Singles: 78 rpm

J-V-B (23 "Say You Would, Babe") 200-300 53

CLERMONT, Eddy

Singles: 7-inch

DIANNA (1000 "Love By the Numbers") 100-150

CLERVERS

(Clerver's)

Singles: 7-inch

REEL (114 "Tears") 50-100

CLE-SHAYS

Singles: 7-inch

MONEX (5232 "Spend All My Money") 15-25 68

CLETRO, Eddie

Singles: 78 rpm

IMPERIAL (3002 "Sittin' and Rockin'") 20-40 56

Singles: 7-inch

IMPERIAL (3002 "Sittin' and Rockin'") ... 50-100 56
LARIAT (45 "Flyin' Saucer Boogie") ..... 200-300 '50s

CLICHES

Singles: 7-inch

CUCA (1040 "Outlaw") 10-20 61
Also see BUSCHER, Dick, & Cliches

CLICHES

(Cliché's)

Singles: 7-inch

MAARC (1530 "What's Your Name") 15-25 66
WES MAR (1020 "Save it for Me") 20-30

CLICK-CLACKS

Singles: 7-inch

ALGONQUIN (715 "A Kiss Goodbye") . 100-150 58
APT (25010 "Pretty Little Pearly") 20-30 58
APT (25032 "Rocket Roll") 10-20 59

CLICKETTES

(Click-Ettes; Clicketts)

Singles: 7-inch

CHECKER (1060 "I Just Can't Help It") 5-10 63
COLLECTABLES 3-5 82
DICE (83/84 "A Teenager's First Love"/"Jive Time Turkey") 50-75 58
DICE (92/93 "To Be a Part of You"/"Because of My Best Friend") 50-75 59
(Pictures a hand throwing dice, with "Dice Records, New York, N.Y." below.)
DICE (92/93 "To Be a Part of You"/"Because of My Best Friend") 10-20
(No hand on label.)
DICE (94/95 "Warm, Soft and Lovely"/"Why Oh Why") 40-60 59
(Pictures a hand throwing dice, with "Dice Records, New York, N.Y." below.)
DICE (96/97 "Lover's Prayer"/"Grateful") . 50-75 59
(Pictures a hand throwing dice, with "Distributed Exclusively by Memo Record Corp." below.)
DICE (96 "Lover's Prayer") 15-25 59
(Reads: "Nationally Distributed by Jubilee Records" at bottom.)
DICE (100 "But Not for Me") 150-200 60
GUYDEN (2043 "Where Is He") 15-25 60
LOST NITE 4-6
TUFF (373 "I Understand Him") 10-15 63

CLICKS

Singles: 78 rpm

JOSIE 25-35 55

Singles: 7-inch

JOSIE (780 "Come Back to Me") 75-125 55

CLICKS

Singles: 7-inch

RUSH (2004 "You Ran Away from My Heart") 15-25 63

CLIENTELLES

Singles: 7-inch

M.B.S. (07 "Church Bells May Ring") ... 100-200 61

CLIFF, Benny
(With the Benny Cliff Trio)

Singles: 7-inch

DRIFT (1441 "Shake Em Up Rock") 1500-2000 59

CLIFF, Zelma

Singles: 7-inch

BATTLE (45916 "I Don't Believe")..............8-10 63
SPINO (1011 "I Don't Believe")............... 15-20

CLIFF & SUN-RAYS

Singles: 7-inch

ZIL (9002 "No Treason In My Heart") 10-20

CLIFFORD, Buzz — P&R/C&W/R&B '61
(With the Teenagers; with Blenders)

Singles: 7-inch

BOW (300 "14 Karat")...................... 200-300 58
BOW (308 "Padiddle")............................ 50-75 59
CAPITOL...4-8 67
COLUMBIA (41774 "Hello Mr. Moonlight")................................ 10-15 60
COLUMBIA (41876 "Baby Sitter Boogie")................................ 20-30 60
(Note slightly different title.)
COLUMBIA (41876 "Baby Sittin' Boogie").................................. 30-50 60
(With "3" prefix. Compact 33 Single.)
COLUMBIA (41876 "Baby Sittin' Boogie")................................. 10-15 61
COLUMBIA (41979 "Simply Because") ... 30-50 61
(With "3" prefix. Compact 33 Single.)
COLUMBIA (41979 "Simply Because") ... 15-25 61
COLUMBIA (42019 "I'll Never Forget").... 30-50 61
(With "3" prefix. Compact 33 Single.)
COLUMBIA (42019 "I'll Never Forget").... 15-25 61
COLUMBIA (42290 "Forever")................ 30-50 62
(With "3" prefix. Compact 33 Single.)
COLUMBIA (42290 "Forever")................ 15-25 62
COLUMBIA (42177 "Moving Day")............5-10 61
DOT..4-6 69-70
ERIC...3-5 83
RCA..4-8 66
ROULETTE (4451 "No One Loves Me Like You Do")..5-10 62

Picture Sleeves

COLUMBIA (41774 "Hello Mr. Moonlight")................................ 15-25 60
COLUMBIA (41876 "Baby Sittin' Boogie")................................ 15-25 60
COLUMBIA (41979 "Simply Because") ... 15-25 61
COLUMBIA (42019 "I'll Never Forget").... 15-25 61
COLUMBIA (42177 "Moving Day") 15-25 61
COLUMBIA (42290 "Forever")................ 15-25 62

LPs: 10/12-inch

COLUMBIA (1616 "Baby Sittin' Boogie"). 50-75 61
(Monaural.)
COLUMBIA (8416 "Baby Sittin' Boogie")................................ 50-100 61
(Monaural.)
DOT (25965 "See Your Way Clear")........ 15-20 69
Also see DAVE & MARKSMEN
Also see MARVELS / Buzz Clifford

CLIFFORD, Marty

Singles: 7-inch

BELLE (107 "Sweet Little You") 100-150

CLIFFORD, Mike — P&R '62
(With the Alan Lorber Orchestra)

Singles: 7-inch

AIR (171 "It's a Dream Away")....................4-6 71
AMERICAN INT'L (138 "Broken-Hearted Man")..8-12 70
AMERICAN INT'L (158 "Do Your Own Thing")..4-8 70
CAMEO (381 "Before I Loved Her")...........5-10 65
CAMEO (395 "Out in the Country")............5-10 66
COLUMBIA (41964 "Look in Any Window")..5-10 61
COLUMBIA (42029 "At Last")....................5-10 61
COLUMBIA (42226 "Bombay")...................5-10 61
COLUMBIA (42335 "Joanna")....................5-10 62
LIBERTY (55219 "I Don't Know Why").......5-10 59
SIDEWALK (917 "Send Her Flowers").......5-10 67
SIDEWALK (939 "Mary Jane")...................5-10 68
U.A. (489 thru 823).................................8-12 62-65

Picture Sleeves

COLUMBIA (42226 "Bombay") 10-15 61

LPs: 10/12-inch

U.A. (3409 "For the Love of Mike") 15-25 65
(Monaural.)
U.A. (6409 "For the Love of Mike")..........25-35 65
(Stereo.)
Also see LORBER, Alan

CLIFFORD, Mike, with Patience & Prudence

Singles: 7-inch

LIBERTY (55207 "Should I"/"Whisper Whisper")..10-15 59
Also see CLIFFORD, Mike
Also see PATIENCE & PRUDENCE

CLIFTON, Bill

Singles: 7-inch

LONDON (9638 "Beatle Crazy")..............10-20 64

LPs: 10/12-inch

STARDAY (271 "Code of the Mountains")..10-20 64

CLIFTON, Johnny, & His String Band
(Bill Haley)

Singles: 78 rpm

CENTER (102 "Stand Up and Be Counted")................................. 1000-1500 50
Also see HALEY, Bill

CLIFTON, Paul

Singles: 7-inch

CLASS (210 "I Need You")......................10-20 57
FLASH (127 "Are You Alright") 15-25 58
TEEN POST (1100 "No Pains in Your Heart")..8-12
Also see TAYLOR, Little Johnny

CLIMATES

Singles: 7-inch

HOLIDAY INN (2206 "Don't Be Cruel") 8-12 68
SUN (404 "Breaking Up Again")...............15-20 67

CLIMATICS
(With Clark Darie & His Combo)

Singles: 7-inch

RE-NO (1000 "My Gift from Heaven")..150-200 62
REQUEST (3008 "All Alone")...............200-250 59

CLIMBERS
("With Orchestra")

Singles: 7-inch

J&S (1652 "My Darlin' Dear").......... 2000-3000 57
(With straight horizontal lines.)
J&S (1652 "My Darlin' Dear")...................40-50 '60s
(With wavy horizontal lines.)
J&S (1658 "I Love You")................. 2000-3000 57
Member: Joe Rivers.
Also see JOHNNIE & JOE

CLINE, Cecil
(With the Sons Of The West)

Singles: 7-inch

BLUE HEN (555 "Blue Shadows")...........30-40 60
BLUE HEN ("Do Drop In")......................30-40 62
(Selection number not known.)

CLINE, Patsy — C&W/P&R '57

Singles: 78 rpm

CORAL..20-30 55-56
DECCA (29963 thru 30542)....................25-75 56-57
DECCA (30659 "Come On In")................50-75 58
DECCA (30706 "Never No More")............60-80 58
DECCA (30746 "Just Out of Reach") 75-100 58

Singles: 7-inch

CORAL (61464 "Honky Tonk Merry Go Round")..30-50 55
CORAL (61523 "Turn the Cards Slowly").30-50 55
CORAL (61583 "I Love You Honey")........30-50 56
(First issue.)
DECCA (25673 thru 25747)......................5-10 65-69
DECCA (29963 thru 30846)....................20-30 56-59
DECCA (30929 "Gotta Lot of Rhythm in My Soul")..25-35 59
DECCA (31061 thru 31754)......................8-12 60-65
DECCA (74282 "Decca Artist of the Week: Patsy Cline")...125-175 62
(Envelope/sleeve with five singles from LP *Sentimentally Yours*. A "7" Stereo 33 1/3 rpm Pop Pre-Pak." Includes five juke box title strips and color photo of LP. Promotional issue only.)
EVEREST (2011 thru 2045)......................8-12 63-64
EVEREST (2052 "Gotta Lot of Rhythm in My Soul")..10-15 64
EVEREST (20005 "I Can't Forget") 10-15 62
4 STAR (11 "I Love You Honey")..............20-30 56
4 STAR (1033 "Life's Railway to Heaven")...3-5 78
KAPP (659 "Just a Closer Walk with Thee")..4-8 65
MCA..3-6 73-80
STARDAY (7030 "Lovesick Blues").............4-8 65
STARDAY (8024 "Lovesick Blues").............4-6 71

Picture Sleeves

DECCA (30221 "Walkin After Midnight")..25-50 57
DECCA (31377 "When I Get Through with You")..15-25 62
DECCA (31455 "Leavin' on Your Mind")..15-25 63
EVEREST (2011 "Hungry for Love") 10-15 63
(With die-cut center hole. Read's "Patsy Cline's on Everest.")

EPs: 7-inch

CORAL (81159 "Songs By Patsy Cline") .50-75 58
DECCA (Except 2542) 15-25 61-65
DECCA (2542 "Patsy Cline")....................35-50 57
EVEREST (196200 "Golden Hits")...........15-25 62
(Stereo.)
4 STAR ("Patsy Cline")............................25-35 57
(Reissue of *Patsy Cline* [Decca 2542]. Issued with paper sleeve. Number not known. Promotional issue only.)
PATSY CLINE...25-35 57

LPs: 10/12-inch

ACCORD (7153 "Let the Teardrops Fall")..5-10 81
ALBUM GLOBE (8206 "Still Singing")........5-10
ALLEGIANCE (5021 "Stop, Look and Listen")..5-10 84
AUDIO FIDELITY (204 "Patsy Cline")......10-15 84
(Picture disc.)
AUDIO FIDELITY (205 "Crazy Dreams") .25-50 84
(Picture disc.)
BREAKAWAY 5-10
BULLDOG..5-10
COLUMBIA (5280 "Portrait of Patsy") 12-15 69
(2-LP. Columbia Musical Treasury issue.)
COUNTRY FIDELITY (202 "Patsy Cline – Her Greatest") 5-10 82
DECCA (176 "Patsy Cline Story")............25-40 63
(Monaural. Includes booklet.)
DECCA (7-176 "Patsy Cline Story") 30-50 63
(Stereo. Includes booklet.)
DECCA (4202 "Showcase")......................20-30 61
(Monaural.)
DECCA (7-4202 "Showcase")...................25-35 61
(Stereo.)
DECCA (4282 "Sentimentally Yours")......15-25 62
(Monaural.)
DECCA (7-4282 "Sentimentally Yours")...20-30 62
(Stereo.)
DECCA (4508 "Portrait")..........................15-25 64
(Monaural.)
DECCA (7-4508 "Portrait").......................20-30 64
(Stereo.)
DECCA (4586 "That's How a Heartache Begins")..30-50 64
(Monaural.)
DECCA (7-4586 "That's How a Heartache Begins")..40-60 64
(Stereo.)
DECCA (4854 "Greatest Hits") 10-15 67
(Monaural.)
DECCA (7-4854 "Greatest Hits") 25-30 67
(Stereo.)
DECCA (8611 "Patsy Cline") 30-50 57
EVEREST (300 series)..............................5-10 75
EVEREST (1200 "Golden Hits") 15-20 62
(Stereo.)
EVEREST (1204 "Encores") 15-20 63
(Stereo.)
EVEREST (1217 "In Memoriam") 15-20 63
(Stereo.)
EVEREST (1223 "Patsy Cline – A Legend")..15-20 63
(Stereo.)
EVEREST (1229 "Reflections") 15-20 64
(Stereo.)
EVEREST (5200 "Golden Hits") 15-20 62
(Monaural.)
EVEREST (5204 "Encores") 15-20 63
(Monaural.)
EVEREST (5217 "In Memoriam") 15-20 63
(Monaural.)
EVEREST (5223 "Patsy Cline – A Legend")..15-20 63
(Monaural.)
EVEREST (5229 "Reflections") 15-20 64
(Monaural.)
EVEREST (90000 series)..........................8-12
51 WEST (16263 "Today, Tomorrow, Forever")..5-10 82
51 WEST (16282 "Loved and Lost Again")...5-10 82
H.S.R.D. (1615 "Patsy Cline") 8-10 84
HOLLYWOOD (462 "At Her Best")..............4-8 92
LONGINES 8-12
MCA...8-12 80-97
METRO (540 "Gotta Lot of Rhythm in My Soul")..10-20 65
MUSIC MASTERS....................................5-10
PICCADILLY...5-10 80
PICKWICK...5-12 '70s
PICKWICK/HILLTOP (6001 "Today, Tomorrow, Forever")...10-20 '60s
PICKWICK/HILLTOP (6016 "I Can't Forget You")..10-20 65
PICKWICK/HILLTOP (6039 "Stop the World and Let Me Off") 10-20 66
PICKWICK/HILLTOP (6054 "Miss Country Music")..10-20 67
PICKWICK/HILLTOP (6072 "In Care of the Blues") 10-20 68
ROLLER SKATE......................................5-10 82
SEARS (127 "Patsy Cline in Care of the Blues")..10-20 '60s
VOCALION (7-3753 "Here's Patsy Cline")..10-20 65
VOCALION (7-3872 "Country Great")......10-20 69
Session: Jordanaires; Anita Kerr Singers.
Also see HAGGARD, Merle / Patsy Cline
Also see JORDANAIRES
Also see KERR, Anita
Also see PIERCE, Webb / Patsy Cline / T. Texas Tyler
Also see REEVES, Jim, & Patsy Cline
Also see TUBB, Ernest

CLINE, Patsy / Cowboy Copas / Hawkshaw Hawkins

LPs: 10/12-inch

STARDAY...15-20 65
Also see HAWKINS, Hawkshaw

CLINE, Patsy / Cowboy Copas / Johnny Horton

LPs: 10/12-inch

HILLTOP ....10-15 '60s
Also see COPAS, Cowboy
Also see HORTON, Johnny

CLINE, Patsy / Hank Locklin / Miller Brothers / Eddie Marvin

EPs: 7-inch

4 STAR (136 "Hidin' Out")........................25-50 56
(Promotional 10-inch, 45 rpm. Not issued with cover.)
Also see LOCKLIN, Hank

CLINE, Patsy / Pete Pike / Jack Bradshaw / Miller Brothers

EPs: 7-inch

4 STAR (137 "Come On In") 25-50 56
(Promotional 10-inch, 45 rpm. Not issued with cover.)

CLINE, Patsy / T. Texas Tyler / Bill Taylor / Eddie Marvin

EPs: 7-inch

4 STAR (139 "Dear God").........................25-50 56
(Promotional 10-inch, 45 rpm. Not issued with cover.)
Also see CLINE, Patsy
Also see TYLER, T. Texas

CLINGMAN, Loy
(L.C.)

Singles: 7-inch

CAPITOL (2209 "Guy Who Told You So")...5-8 68
ELKO (15 "Blue Black Hair")....................10-20 63
LIBERTY BELL (9012 "It's Nothing to Me")..15-25 57
RIMROCK...5-10
VIV (2000 "Uranium Blues")......................20-30
VIV (3401 "Rockin' Down Mexico Way")..150-250

EPs: 7-inch

VIV (2002 "Loy Clingman") 15-25
Also see HAWKS

CLINGMAN CLAN

Singles: 7-inch

4 CORNERS (110 "Cause I'm Tired") 5-10 64
TREY (3010 "Man About Time")..................8-12 60
VIV..5-10 82

LPs:10/12-inch

TREY (900 "At the Baboquivari")..............25-35 '60s
Member: Loy Clingman.

Also see CLINGMAN, Loy

CLINTON, Buddy

Singles: 7-inch

MADISON (144 "Joanie's Forever")......... 10-15 60
TIME (1016 "Across the Street from Your House").. 15-25 59
Session: Belmonts.
Also see BELMONTS

CLINTON, Larry
(With His Orchestra)

Singles: 78 rpm

JUBILEE.. 10-15 57
RCA..5-10 49

Singles: 7-inch

DYNAMO (300 "She's Wanted in Three States").. 100-200
JUBILEE.. 10-15 57
LAWN (247 "Walkin' with Willie")..................4-8 64
RCA..5-10 49

EPs: 7-inch

TOPS..5-10

CLINTON, Mac, & Straitjackets

Singles: 7-inch

LE CAM (714 "Wake Up Baby").............. 35-50 60
Members: Delbert McClinton; Robert Harwell; Ralph Dixon; Billy Cox; Ray Clark.
Also see McCLINTON, Delbert
Also see STRAITJACKETS

CLINTON, Terry, & Berry Cups

Singles: 7-inch

KHOURY'S (710 "Hurt by a Letter")......... 30-40 59
Also see COOKIE & CUPCAKES

CLINTONIAN CUBS

Singles: 7-inch

MY BROTHER'S (508 "She's Just My Size").. 1000-2000 60
Member: Jimmy Castor.
Also see CASTOR, Jimmy

CLIPS
(With Jimmy Beck & His Band)

Singles: 78 rpm

CALVERT.. 50-100 56
REPUBLIC.. 100-150 54

Singles: 7-inch

CALVERT (105 "Kiss Away")............. 125-150 56
REPUBLIC (7102 "Wish I Didn't Love You So").. 300-400 54

CLIQUE P&R '69

Singles: 7-inch

ABC..4-6 73
CINEMA (001 "Splash One")............... 25-35 67
LAURIE (3365 "Drifters Medley")...............8-12 66
SCEPTER (12202 "Splash One")........... 10-20 67
WHITE WHALE......................................8-15 69-71

LPs: 10/12-inch

WHITE WHALE (7126 "The Clique")....... 10-20 69
Also see LAVENDER HOUR

CLIQUES P&R '56

Singles: 78 rpm

MODERN.. 10-15 56

Singles: 7-inch

KENT (20 "Girl in My Dreams")...................5-10
MODERN (987 "Girl in My Dreams")....... 10-20 56
(Black label.)
MODERN (987 "Girl in My Dreams")....... 40-50 56
(Blue label.)
MODERN (995 "My Desire").................. 15-25 56
Members: Jesse Belvin; Eugene Church.
Also see BELVIN, Jesse
Also see CHURCH, Eugene

CLOCK, Thomas

Singles: 7-inch

COOKING (109 "Where You Go")........... 10-20 62

CLOCKS & CLASSMEN

Singles: 7-inch

MAIL CALL (1011 "It's Written")........... 150-250 62

CLOCKWATCHERS

Singles: 7-inch

DOT (17026 "Hey It's Summertime")....... 10-15 67

CLOCK-WORK ORANGE

Singles: 7-inch

CREOLE (1002 "Your Golden Touch").... 10-20 67
RUST (5119 "Help Me")...................... 10-20 67
RUST (5126 "What Am I Without You")....10-20 68

CLOONEY, Rosemary P&R '51
(Clooney Sisters; with Percy Faith Orchestra)

Singles: 78 rpm

COLUMBIA..4-8 50-57

Singles: 7-inch

APCO..4-6 75
COLUMBIA (Except 4-112)....................10-15 50-57
COLUMBIA (4-112 "Alice in Wonderland Songs")..20-30
(Two discs.)
CORAL..5-10 59
DOT..4-6 68
GIBSON/COLUMBIA..............................10-20 55
("Musicards," with fold-out covers.)
MGM..5-15 59-65
RCA..5-10 60-61
REPRISE..5-10 63-64
SATURDAY EVENING POST (1055 "Hollywood's Favorite Songbird")..............................15-25 54
(Promotional issue only. Includes interview script.)

Picture Sleeves

RCA..10-15 60

EPs: 7-inch

COLUMBIA..15-25 51-56
EPIC (7139/7140/7141 "Clooney Sisters")..10-20 56
(Price is for any of three volumes.)
MGM..8-15 58-60

LPs: 10/12-inch

COLUMBIA (500 thru 1200 series)...........15-25 54-58
COLUMBIA (2500 series)........................20-30 '50s
(10-inch LPs.)
COLUMBIA (6297 "While We're Young").25-35 51
(10-inch LP.)
CONCORD JAZZ....................................5-10 78-83
CORAL..15-25 59
EPIC (3160 "Clooney Sisters")................20-30 56
HARMONY..8-15 59-68
MGM (Except 1000 series)....................10-15 59-62
MGM (1000 series)................................8-12 67
RCA..15-25 60-63
REPRISE..10-25 63-64
Also see BOYD, Jimmy, & Rosemary Clooney
Also see CROSBY, Bing, Louis Armstrong, Rosemary Clooney & Hi-Los
Also see FAITH, Percy, Orchestra
Also see GOODMAN, Benny, Trio, & Rosemary Clooney
Also see HERMAN, Woody
Also see TUNESMITHS WITH ROSEMARY CLOONEY & DON CHERRY

CLOONEY, Rosemary, & Bing Crosby

Singles: 7-inch

RCA..4-8 59

LPs: 10/12-inch

CAMDEN..6-10 69
CAPITOL (2300 series)..........................8-12 65
CAPITOL (11000 series)........................5-10 77
Also see CROSBY, Bing

CLOONEY, Rosemary, & Marlene Dietrich

Singles: 78 rpm

COLUMBIA..4-8 52

Singles: 7-inch

COLUMBIA..5-10 52

EPs: 7-inch

COLUMBIA (1699 "Rosie and Marlene")..15-20 52
Also see DIETRICH, Marlene

CLOONEY, Rosemary, & Duke Ellington

LPs: 10/12-inch

COLUMBIA (872 "Blue Rose")..................15-25 56
Also see ELLINGTON, Duke

CLOONEY, Rosemary, & Jose Ferrer

Singles: 78 rpm

COLUMBIA..5-10 53-54

Singles: 7-inch

COLUMBIA..10-15 53-54

EPs: 7-inch

MGM..10-20 58

CLOONEY, Rosemary, & Hi-Los LP '57

EPs: 7-inch

COLUMBIA..5-10 57

LPs: 10/12-inch

COLUMBIA (1006 "Ring Around Rosie")..20-25 57
Also see HI-LOs

CLOONEY, Rosemary, & Dick Haymes

LPs: 10/12-inch

EXACT..5-10 80
Also see HAYMES, Dick

CLOONEY, Rosemary, & Harry James

LPs: 10/12-inch

COLUMBIA (6224 "Hollywood's Best").....20-40 52
(10-inch LP.)

CLOONEY, Rosemary, & Guy Mitchell
(With Joanne Gilbert) P&R '51

EPs: 7-inch

COLUMBIA (377 "Red Garters")..............15-20 54
(Soundtrack.)

LPs: 10/12-inch

COLUMBIA (6282 "Red Garters")............40-50 54
(10-inch LP. Soundtrack.)
Also see MITCHELL, Guy

CLOONEY, Rosemary, & Perez Prado

Singles: 7-inch

RCA..4-8 60

LPs: 10/12-inch

RCA..10-12 60
Also see CLOONEY, Rosemary
Also see PRADO, Perez

CLOUD, Bruce

Singles: 7-inch

ERA (3087 "Lucky Is My Name")..............20-40 63
ERA (3101 "Little Spark of Fire")..............5-10 63
MOTIF (015 "Let Me Come Back Home")..50-75 63

LPs: 10/12-inch

CAPITOL (343 "California Soul")..............10-20 69

CLOUDS

Singles: 78 rpm

COBRA (5001 "I Do")..........................200-250 56

Singles: 7-inch

COBRA (5001 "I Do")........................2000-2500 56
Members: Sharard (Sherrard) Jones; Al Butler; William English; Bobby Walker.
Also see MAPLES

CLOUDS

Singles: 7-inch

GALA (100 "Baby")..............................300-400 59

CLOUDS

Singles: 7-inch

SKYLARK (116 "Baby It's Me")...............150-200 61

CLOUDS

Singles: 7-inch

ROUND (1008 "Darling I Love You")......75-125 59

CLOUDS

Singles: 7-inch

MEDLEY (1001 "Night Owl")....................20-30 64
VOUS (1000 "Say Hey Hey")..................75-100 64
Member: Bill Medley.
Also see MEDLEY, Bill

CLOUDS

Singles: 7-inch

INDEPENDENCE (82 "Visions"/"Migada Bus")..10-20 67
Also see LOOKING GLASSES

CLOUDS

Singles: 7-inch

VOUS (1000 "A Lovely Way to Spend an Evening")..100-150 '60s

CLOUR, Deral, & Charley Drake

Singles: 7-inch

HU-SE-CO (1056 "Sundown Boogie").......50-75

CLOVERS R&B '51
("Featuring Buddy Bailey")

Singles: 78 rpm

ATLANTIC..20-50 51-57
RAINBOW (122 "Yes Sir, That's My Baby")..200-400 51

Singles: 7-inch

ATLANTIC (934 "Don't You Know I Love You")..600-800 51
ATLANTIC (944 "Fool, Fool, Fool").......150-250 51
ATLANTIC (963 "One Mint Julep").......100-200 52
ATLANTIC (969 "Ting-A-Ling")............100-200 52
ATLANTIC (977 "I Played the Fool").....100-200 52
ATLANTIC (989 "Crawlin'")....................75-150 53
ATLANTIC (1000 "Good Lovin'")............75-150 53
ATLANTIC (1010 "Comin' On")...............75-150 53
ATLANTIC (1022 "Lovey Dovey")............50-75 54
ATLANTIC (1035 "Your Cash Ain't Nothin' But Trash")..50-75 54
ATLANTIC (1046 "I Confess")..................50-75 54
ATLANTIC (1052 "Blue Velvet")..............50-75 54
ATLANTIC (1060 "Love Bug")..................50-75 55
ATLANTIC (1073 "Nip Sip")....................50-75 55
ATLANTIC (1083 "Devil Or Angel")..........50-75 56
ATLANTIC (1094 "Your Tender Lips").......50-75 56
ATLANTIC (1107 "From the Bottom of My Heart")..20-30 56
ATLANTIC (1118 "A Lonely Fool")...........30-40 56
ATLANTIC (1129 "You Good Looking Woman")..20-30 57
ATLANTIC (1139 "So Young")..................10-20 57
ATLANTIC (1152 "Down in the Alley").......10-20 57
ATLANTIC (1175 "Wishing for Your Love")..10-20 58
ATLANTIC (2129 "Drive It Home")............8-12 61
BRUNSWICK (55249 "Love Love Love")...8-12 63
JETT (3019 "Darbytown")........................5-10 75
JOSIE (992 "Too Long Without Some Loving")..5-10 68
JOSIE (997 "Try My Lovin' on You")..........5-10 68
POPLAR (110 "The Gossip Wheel")........10-15 58
POPLAR (111 "The Good Old Summertime")..10-15 58
(This same number was also used for a Zack Norman release.)
PORT (3004 "Poor Baby")........................5-10 65
PORWIN (1001 "Stop Pretending")..........10-15 63
(Has sans-serif logo and straight horizontal lines.)
PORWIN (1002 "Stop Pretending")............5-10 63
(Has serif logo and wavy horizontal lines.)
PORWIN (1004 "It's All in the Game").........8-12 63
RIPETE..3-5 88
U.A. (174 "Rock and Roll Tango")...........15-25 59
U.A. (180 thru 307)..............................10-20 59-61
WINLEY (255 "Wrapped Up in a Dream")..20-30 61
WINLEY (265 "Gotta Quit Now")..............20-30 62
(Same number used on a Fabulous Clovers release.)

Picture Sleeves

ATLANTIC (1052 "Blue Velvet")..................5-10 '90s

EPs: 7-inch

ATLANTIC (504 "The Clovers Sing")....100-200 56
ATLANTIC (537 "The Clovers Sing")....100-200 56
ATLANTIC (590 "The Clovers")............100-150 57

LPs: 10/12-inch

ATCO (374 "Greatest Recordings")..........10-15 71
ATLANTIC (1248 "The Clovers")...........300-400 56
ATLANTIC (8009 "The Clovers").........200-300 57
(Black label.)
ATLANTIC (8009 "The Clovers")...........50-100 59
(Red label.)
ATLANTIC (8034 "The Clovers' Dance Party")..50-100 59
GRAND PRIX (428 "The Original Love Potion No. 9")..15-25 64
POPLAR (1001 "Clovers in Clover").....100-150 58
TRIP..8-10 72
U.A. (3033 "Clovers in Clover")...........50-100 59
(Monaural.)
U.A. (6033 "Clovers in Clover")..........100-125 59
(Stereo.)
U.A. (3099 "Love Potion Number Nine")..50-100 60
(Monaural.)
U.A. (6099 "Love Potion Number Nine")..100-125 60
(Stereo.)
Members: John "Buddy" Bailey; Harold Winley; Hal Lucas; Bill Harris; Matthew McQuater; Charlie White; Billy Mitchell. Session: King Curtis.
Also see FABULOUS CLOVERS
Also see HARPTONES / Paragons / Jesters / Clovers
Also see JACKSON, Willis
Also see KING CURTIS
Also see MITCHELL, Billy
Also see NORMAN, Zack
Also see TIPPIE & CLOVERMEN
Also see WHITE, Charlie

CLOVERS / Deltones

Singles: 7-inch

LANA (113 "Love Potion No. 9"/"Hey Little Girl")..5-10 65
LANA (114 "Devil Or Angel"/"Since I Met You")..5-10 65
Also see DELTONES

CLOWER, Jerry
Singles: 7-inch
MCA 4-6 '70s
LPs: 10/12-inch
DECCA (75286 "Mississippi Talkin'") 10-20 71
DECCA (75342 "Mouth of the Mississippi") 10-15 72
MCA 5-10 73-83

CLOWNEY, David, Band
(David Cortez Clowney; with Duponts)
Singles: 78 rpm
EMBER (1010 "Soft Lights") 10-15 56
Singles: 7-inch
EMBER (1010 "Soft Lights") 15-25 56
PARIS (513 "Shakin'") 15-25 58
Also see CORTEZ, Dave, "Baby"
Also see JESTERS

CLUE
Singles: 7-inch
BYRON (101 "Bad Times") 20-25 67

CLUSTERS
Singles: 7-inch
END (1115 "Darling Can't You Tell") 10-15 62
EPIC (9330 "Forecast of Our Love") 200-300 59
TEE GEE (102 " Darling Can't You Tell") 200-300 58
(Publisher shown as "Emkay Music." No mention of distribution by Gone.)
TEE GEE (102 " Darling Can't You Tell") 200-300 58
(Publisher shown as "Emkay Music." Reads: "Nat Dist. Gone Records.")
TEE GEE (102 " Darling Can't You Tell") 75-125 58
(Publisher shown as "RealGone Music." No mention of distribution by Gone.)
Also see RAIN DROPS / Jay & Americans / Empires / Clusters

CLYDE
(Dick Hyman)
Singles: 7-inch
COLUMBIA (413332 "Clyde's Blast") 10-20 59
Also see HYMAN, Dick

COACHMEN
Singles: 78 rpm
"X" (0044 "Fame & Fortune") 5-10 54
Singles: 7-inch
"X" (0044 "Fame & Fortune") 10-20 54

COACHMEN
Singles: 7-inch
HI-FI (560 "Soldier's Joy") 10-15 59
HI-FI (561 "Marry in the Fall") 10-15 59
ORBIT (544 "Those Brown Eyes") 10-15 59

COACHMEN
("Vocal by Ricky Mann")
Singles: 7-inch
IONA (1004 "Teen Bride") 20-30 60

COACHMEN
Singles: 7-inch
PICO (522"Gonna Take a Chance") 100-200 61

COACHMEN
Singles: 7-inch
AUSTIN (65120 "El Dorado") 10-20 65
SPOTLITE (5025/6 "Splash Day") 10-20 '60s
TYPE (3580 "Movin'") 10-20 63
WORLD ARTISTS (1011 "I'm Going Home Now") 8-12 63

COACHMEN
Singles: 7-inch
BEAR (819 "Mr. Moon") 10-15 65
BEAR (1976 "Linda Lou") 10-15 66
MMC (010 "Mr. Moon") 10-20 65
(Black vinyl.)
MMC (010 "Mr. Moon") 35-50 65
(Blue vinyl.)
MMC (013 "My Generation") 10-15 66
MMC (014 "Tyme Won't Change") 10-15 67
Members: Jeff Travis; Craig Perkins, Kelly Kotera, Frank Elia; Bruce Watson.
Also see ALEXANDER'S ROCK TIME BAND
Also see PROFESSOR MORRISON'S LOLLIPOP

COACHMEN FIVE Featuring Ray Davis
Singles: 7-inch
JANSON (100 "Oh Joan") 50-75
Member: Ray Davis.

COASTERS P&R/R&B '56
Singles: 78 rpm
ATCO (6064 thru 6126) 40-50 56-58
ATCO (6132 "Charlie Brown") 50-100 59
ATCO (6141 "Along Came Jones") 75-125 59
ATCO (6146 "Poison Ivy") 175-200 59
ATCO (6153 "What About Us") 100-150 59
Singles: 7-inch
ATCO (6064 "Down in Mexico") 50-60 56
(Maroon label.)
ATCO (6073 "One Kiss Led to Another") 50-60 56
(Maroon label.)
ATCO (6087 "Searchin'") 30-40 57
(Maroon label.)
ATCO (6087 "Searchin'") 20-30 57
(Yellow and white label.)
ATCO (6098 "Idol with the Golden Head) 15-25 57
ATCO (6104 "Sweet Georgia Brown") 15-25 57
ATCO (6111 "Dance") 15-25 58
ATCO (6116 "Yakety Yak") 15-25 58
ATCO (6126 "The Shadow Knows") 15-25 58
ATCO (6132 "Charlie Brown") 15-25 59
(Monaural.)
ATCO (6132 "Charlie Brown") 50-100 59
(Stereo. Blue label. With "SD" prefix.)
ATCO (6141 "Along Came Jones") 15-25 59
ATCO (6146 "Poison Ivy") 15-25 59
ATCO (6153 thru 6210) 10-20 59-61
ATCO (6219 thru 6407, except 6287 & 6379) 8-12 62-66
ATCO (6287 "T'ain't Nothin' to Me") 10-15 64
ATCO (6379 "Crazy Baby") 20-30 65
DATE (1552 thru 1617) 8-12 67-68
KING (6385 thru 6404) 4-8 71-73
KING/GUSTO 3-5 79
SALWA (1001 "You Move Me") 4-8 75
TURNTABLE (504 "Act Right") 5-10 69
EPs: 7-inch
ATCO (4501 "Rock and Roll with the Coasters") 50-70 58
ATCO (4503 "Keep Rockin'") 50-70 58
ATCO (4506 "The Coasters") 30-50 59
ATCO (4507 "Top Hits") 30-50 59
LPs: 10/12-inch
ARCHIVES 8-12
ATCO (101 "The Coasters") 75-100 58
(Yellow label.)
ATCO (101 "The Coasters") 25-50 59
(Yellow and white label.)
ATCO (111 "Greatest Hits") 50-75 59
ATCO (123 "One by One") 40-50 60
(Monaural.)
ATCO (SD-123 "One By One") 50-60 60
(Stereo.)
ATCO (135 "Coast Along") 30-40 59
(Monaural.)
ATCO (SD-135 "Coast Along") 40-50 59
(Stereo.)
ATCO (371 "Their Greatest Recordings") 10-20 71
ATLANTIC (4003 "Young Blood") 10-20 82
(Two discs.)
CLARION (605 "That's Rock & Roll") 10-20 64
GUSTO 5-10
KING (1146 "On Broadway") 10-15 71
PHOENIX 20 5-8
POWER PAK 5-10 83
TRIP (8028 "It Ain't Sanitary") 8-10 72
WEST-ONE 8-15
Members: Bobby Nunn; Leon Hughes; Billy Guy; Carl Gardner; Adolph Jacobs; Ronnie Bright; Cornel Gunter; Will Jones; Earl Carroll; Jimmy Norman.
Session: King Curtis.
Also see CARROLL, Earl, & Original Cadillacs
Also see DRIFTERS / Coasters
Also see HENDRICKS, Bobby
Also see KING CURTIS
Also see NORMAN, Jimmy
Also see NUNN, Bobby
Also see ROBINS

COASTLINERS
Singles: 7-inch
ASTRO (109 "Lonely Sea") 15-25 65
BACK BEAT (554 "Alright") 10-15 65
BACK BEAT (566 "She's My Girl") 15-20 66
BACK BEAT (577 "I See You") 15-20 67
D.E.A.R. (1300 "I See Me") 8-12 67
INT'L ARTISTS (101 "Alright") 15-25 65
Also see U.S. MALES

COATES, Jesse
Singles: 78 rpm
HEADLINE 50-75 55
Singles: 7-inch
HEADLINE (101 "Nobody Can Take My Baby") 100-200 55

COATS, Don
(Don Coates)
Singles: 7-inch
ROUND (1006 "Spinnin' My Wheels") 100-150 59
ROUND (1011 "You Are My Sunshine") 15-25 59

COBB, Arnett
(With His Orchestra & Suttle's Dreamers)
Singles: 78 rpm
APOLLO 5-15 47-49
ATLANTIC 15-25 54-55
COLUMBIA 5-10 50-51
HAMP-TONE (102 "Down Home") 5-15 46
HAMP-TONE (107 "Jenny") 5-15 46
MERCURY 5-10 53
OKEH (Except 6912 and 6928) 5-10 51-52
OKEH (6912 "The Shy One") 25-35 52
(With the Ravens.)
OKEH (6928 "Linger Awhile") 25-35 52
(With the Ravens.)
Singles: 7-inch
ATLANTIC (1031 "Night") 30-50 54
ATLANTIC (1042 "Horse Laff") 30-50 54
ATLANTIC (1056 "Flying Home Mambo") 30-50 55
ATLANTIC (5031 "Night") 10-15 60
COLUMBIA (39040 "Smooth Sailing") 15-25 50
COLUMBIA (39139 "That's All, Brother") 15-25 50
COLUMBIA (39247 "Willow Weep for Me") 10-20 51
COLUMBIA (39369 "Holy Smoke") 10-20 51
MERCURY (70101 "Congratulations to Someone") 10-20 53
OKEH (6823 "Cocktails for Two") 10-20 51
OKEH (6830 "Smooth Sailing") 10-20 51
OKEH (6851 "Charmaine") 10-20 52
OKEH (6872 "Jumpin' the Blues") 10-20 52
OKEH (6887 "Whispering") 10-20 52
OKEH (6912 "The Shy One") 50-75 52
(With the Ravens.)
OKEH (6928 "Linger Awhile") 50-75 52
(With the Dreamers.)
PRESTIGE (113 thru 185) 8-12 59-61
LPs: 10/12-inch
APOLLO (105 "Swingin' with Arnett Cobb") 100-200 52
(10-inch LP.)
PRESTIGE (7165 "Party Time") 50-75 59
(Yellow label.)
PRESTIGE (7165 "Party Time") 25-35 64
(Blue label.)
PRESTIGE (7175 "More Party Time") 50-75 60
(Yellow label.)
PRESTIGE (7175 "More Party Time") 25-35 64
(Blue label.)
PRESTIGE (7184 "Smooth Sailing") 50-75 61
(Yellow label.)
PRESTIGE (7184 "Smooth Sailing") 25-35 64
(Blue label.)
PRESTIGE (7216 "Movin' Right Along") 40-60 61
(Yellow label.)
PRESTIGE (7216 "Movin' Right Along") 20-30 64
(Blue label.)
PRESTIGE (7227 "Sizzlin'") 40-60 61
(Yellow label.)
PRESTIGE (7227 "Sizzlin'") 20-30 64
(Blue label.)
PRESTIGE (7711 "Best Of") 8-12 69
PRESTIGE/MOODSVILLE (14 "Ballads by Cobb") 30-40 61
Also see DREAMERS
Also see RAVENS
Also see VAN LOAN, Joe

COBB, Arnett, & Eddie "Lockjaw" Davis
LPs: 10/12-inch
PRESTIGE (7151 "Blow, Arnett, Blow") 50-75 59
(Yellow label.)
PRESTIGE (7151 "Blow, Arnett, Blow") 25-35 64
(Blue label.)
Also see COBB, Arnett
Also see DAVIS, Eddie "Lockjaw"

COBB, Danny
(Danny Boy Cobb)
Singles: 78 rpm
ACORN (309 "Please Don't Leave Me") 20-30 49
JUBILEE (5206 "A Brand New Deal") 5-10 55
SAVOY (754 "Danny Boy") 15-25 49
SAVOY (869 "Farewell Baby") 8-12 52
Singles: 7-inch
DELUXE (6106 "Hey Mr. Warden") 10-20 57
DELUXE (6120 "What Could I Do") 10-20 57
JUBILEE (5206 "A Brand New Deal") 10-20 55
SAVOY (869 "Farewell Baby") 15-25 52
Session: Noble Watts; Paul Williams.
Also see WATTS, Noble
Also see WILLIAMS, Paul

COBB, Johnny
(With the Attractions; with Mellow Souls)
Singles: 7-inch
CRISS COBB (100 "Yes I Do") 10-20 '60s
JAGUAR (468 "Love Doesn't Pay") 10-20 '60s

COBB, Julius
Singles: 7-inch
BETHLEHEM (3024 "Oh Baby, I Want You Back Home") 15-20 62

COBB, Wayne (Red)
Singles: 7-inch
REJECT (1001 "Shopping Around") 50-75

COBBLERS
Singles: 7-inch
STUDIO CITY (1060 Smokin' at the Half Note") 50-75 66
Members: Ron Spanbauer; Pat Nugent; Mike Meidl; Bob Weisapple; Nick Christas; Bob Misky.
Also see SYNDICATE

COBBLESTONES
Singles: 7-inch
MOBIE (3425 "Flower People") 20-30 67

COBBS, Willie
(Willie Cobb)
Singles: 7-inch
ASCOT (2113 "Five Long Years") 8-12 62
BRACOB ("C.C. Rider") 10-20 '60s
(Selection number not known.)
C&F 10-20 62
CHIMNEYVILLE 4-6 77
HOME OF THE BLUES (230 "You Don't Love Me") 15-25 61
(First issue.)
JOB (1127 "Too Sad") 15-20 63
MINARET (147 "Don't Worry About Me") 8-10 69
MOJO 15-25 61
PHILWOOD (254 "Why Did You Change Your Mind") 4-6 76
PURE GOLD (313 "Come On Home") 5-10 65
RICE BELT 8-12 63
RICELAND (111 "I'll Love Only You") 10-20 '60s
RULER (1131 "Slowdown") 10-20 63
RULER (5000 "We'll All Be There") 10-20 63
SHIELD 5-10
SOUL BEAT (113 "Worst Feeling") 10-20 66
VEE-JAY (411 "You Don't Love Me") 10-20 61
WHIRL-A-WAY 5-10
Also see WILLIE C.

COBRA BROTHERS
Singles: 7-inch
MAGNET (701 "My Baby Doll") 10-15 60

COBRA KINGS
Singles: 7-inch
BLACK GOLD (200 "Night Walk") 15-25
BLACK GOLD (300 "Tragedy") 15-25

COBRAS
Singles: 78 rpm
MODERN (964 "Sindy") 50-100 55
MODERN (964 "Cindy") 25-50 55
Singles: 7-inch
MODERN (964 "Sindy") 150-200 55
MODERN (964 "Cindy") 50-100 55
(Note different spellings.)

COBRAS
Singles: 7-inch
BIG BEAT (1002 "Instant Heartache") 20-25 66

COBRAS
Singles: 7-inch
MILKY WAY (006 "Try") 15-20 66

COBRAS
(Featuring Stevie Ray Vaughan)
Singles: 7-inch
ARMADILLO (79-1 "Blow Joe, Blow").. 100-125 80
VIPER (30372 "Other Days") 150-200 75
Picture Sleeves
VIPER (30372 "Other Days") 150-200 75
Also see CLARK, W.C., & Cobras
Also see VAUGHAN, Stevie Ray

COBURN, Kimball
(With the Six O'Clock Boys; with Sy Rose Orchestra)
Singles: 7-inch
CHALLENGE (59009 "Cute") 15-25 58
CHAN (106 "No Reason Why") 30-40 62
COVER (6061 "What a Day") 30-40 60
HI (2010 "Teenage Love") 30-40 58
HI (2016 "Darlin' ") 15-25 59
PHILIPS (40191 "Spring Rain") 8-12 64
PHILIPS (40299 "Evil Eye") 8-12 65
RCA (7592 "I'm My Own Grandpaw") 10-15 59
RIVERMONT (1159 "Cute") 50-75 58

COCHRAN, Alane
Singles: 7-inch
CONCO (149 "Gone Twistin' ") .... 200-300 '60s

COCHRAN, Don
Singles: 7-inch
BIG-K (40064 "Pig Pen Boogie") 10-20 64

COCHRAN, Eddie P&R/R&B '57
Singles: 78 rpm
CREST (1026 "Skinny Jim") 75-125 56
LIBERTY 100-150 57-58
Singles: 7-inch
CAPEHART (5003 "Rough Stuff") 50-100 60
(Same number used for an Eddie Donno release.)
CREST (1026 "Skinny Jim") 500-600 56
LIBERTY (54502 "Sittin' in the Balcony"). 20-40 62
LIBERTY (54503 "Summertime Blues").. 20-40 62
LIBERTY (54504 "C'mon Everybody") 20-40 62
LIBERTY (55056 "Sittin' in the Balcony"). 35-50 57
LIBERTY (55070 "Mean When I'm Mad") 35-50 57
LIBERTY (55087 "Drive-in Show") 35-50 57
LIBERTY (55112 "Twenty Flight Rock") 200-300 57
LIBERTY (55123 "Jeannie Jeannie Jeannie") 35-50 58
LIBERTY (55138 "Pretty Girl") 25-40 58
LIBERTY (55144 "Summertime Blues")... 40-60 58
(Spoken lines with reverb. Identification number is 45-LB-859.)
LIBERTY (55144 "Summertime Blues")... 40-60 58
(Spoken lines without reverb. Identification number is 45-LB-859-2.)
LIBERTY (55166 "C'mon Everybody") 35-50 58
(Green label.)
LIBERTY (55166 "C'mon Everybody") 25-35 58
(Black label.)
LIBERTY (55177 "Teenage Heaven") 20-30 59
LIBERTY (55203 "Somethin' Else") 35-50 59
(With horizontal silver lines.)
LIBERTY (55203 "Somethin' Else") 25-35 59
(Without horizontal silver lines.)
LIBERTY (55217 "Hallelujah, I Love Her So") 20-30 59
LIBERTY (55242 "Cut Across Shorty") 35-50 59
(Green label.)
LIBERTY (55242 "Cut Across Shorty") 25-35 61
(Black label.)
LIBERTY (55278 "Sweetie Pie") 20-30 60
LIBERTY (55389 "Weekend") 20-30 60
Picture Sleeves
CAPEHART (5003 "Rough Stuff") 100-200 60
LIBERTY (55070 "Mean When I'm Mad") 1000-1500 57
EPs: 7-inch
LIBERTY (3061-1/2/3 "Singin' to My Baby") 150-250 58
(Price is for any of three volumes.)
LPs: 10/12-inch
LIBERTY (3061 "Singin' to My Baby") . 300-400 58
(Green label.)
LIBERTY (3061 "Singin' to My Baby") ... 75-125 60
(Black label.)
LIBERTY (3172 "Memorial Album") 50-100 60
LIBERTY (3220 "Never to Be Forgotten") 50-75 62
(Black label.)
LIBERTY (3220 "Never to Be Forgotten") 75-100 62
(Yellow label. Promotional issue only.)
LIBERTY (10000 series) 5-10 81-83
SUNSET (1123 "Summertime Blues") 30-40 66
U.A. (428 "Very Best of Eddie Cochran") .15-25 75
U.A. (9959 "Legendary Masters") 15-25 71
Also see CAPEHART, Jerry
Also see COCHRAN BROTHERS
Also see DAVIS, Bo
Also see DENSON, Lee
Also see GALAXIES
Also see GEE CEES
Also see HOLLY TWINS
Also see KELLY FOUR
Also see KEY, Troyce
Also see NEAL, Jerry
Also see STANLEY, Ray
Also see STEWART, Wynn

COCHRAN, Hank C&W '62
Singles: 7-inch
CAPITOL (4585 "Willie") 3-5 78
DOT (17361 "One Night for Willie") 4-6 70
ELEKTRA (47062 "A Little Bitty Tear") 3-5 80
GAYLORD (6426 "When You Gotta Go") ...5-10 63
GAYLORD (6431 "A Good Country Song") 5-10 63
GAYLORD (6432 "Just for the Record") 5-10 63
LIBERTY (55402 thru 55644) 8-12 62-63
MONUMENT (994 thru 1051) 4-8 67-68
RCA (8329 thru 8955) 5-10 64-66
LPs: 10/12-inch
CAPITOL (11807 "Hank Cochran") 10-20 78
ELEKTRA (277 "Make the World Go Away") 5-10 80
MONUMENT (18089 "The Heart of Hank Cochran") 10-15 68
RCA (3303 "Hits from the Heart") 10-20 65
RCA (3431 "Going in Training") 10-20 65
Session: Jack Greene; Merle Haggard; Willie Nelson; Jeannie Seely; Rafe Van Hoy.
Also see COCHRAN BROTHERS
Also see HAGGARD, Merle
Also see SEELY, Jeannie

COCHRAN, Hank, & Willie Nelson
Singles: 7-inch
CAPITOL (4635 "Ain't Life Hell") 3-5 78
Also see COCHRAN, Hank
Also see NELSON, Willie

COCHRAN, Jackie Lee
(Jack Cochran; Jackie Cochran)
Singles: 78 rpm
DECCA (30206 "Mama Don't You Think I Know") 100-150 57
SIMS (107 "Riverside Jump") 75-125 56
Singles: 7-inch
ABC-PAR (9930 "Buy a Car") 50-100 58
AVALON (102 "Buy a Car") 200-300 58
(First issue.)
DECCA (30206 "Mama Don't You Think I Know") 100-150 57
JAGUAR (3031 "I Want to See You") ...100-200 59
JAGUAR (3032 "Pity Me") 25-50 59
SIMS (107 "Riverside Jump") 100-200 56
SPRY (120 "Endless Love") 400-600 59
VIV (988 "Buy a Car") 100-150 58
LPs: 10/12-inch
ROLLIN' ROCK ....10-20 '70s

COCHRAN, Wayne LP '68
(With the C.C. Riders; with Fabulous C.C. Riders; with Rockin' Capris)
Singles: 7-inch
AIRE ("Cindy Marie") 100-150
(Selection number not known.)
BETHLEHEM (3097 "Hey Jude") 4-8 69
BOBLO (101 "Hey Baby") 5-10 68
CHESS (2020 "Some-A Your Sweet Love") 5-10 67
CHESS (2029 "Get Ready") 5-10 67
CHESS (2054 "You Can't Judge a Book By the Cover") 5-10 68
CONFEDERATE (155 "Linda Lu") 15-25 63
DECK (151 "Monkey Monkey") 15-25 63
DRIVE (6249 "Sea Cruise") 4-6 76
EPIC (10859 "Do You Like the Sound of Music") 4-6 72
EPIC (10893 "Long Long Day") 4-6 72
ERA (18 "Last Kiss") 3-5 78
(Credits Cochran but track is by J. Frank Wilson.)
GALA (117 "Last Kiss") 20-30 62
GALICO (105 "Last Kiss") 15-25 61
KING (5832 thru 5994) 5-15 63-65
KING (6253 thru 6358) 4-8 69-71
KING GOLD (517 "Last Kiss"/"C.C. Rider") ...4-6 72
MERCURY (72507 thru 72623) 4-8 65-66
SCOTTIE (1303 "The Coo") 25-50 59
SOFT (779 "Harlem Shuffle") 10-15 65
SOFT (1009 "Hang on Sloopy") 5-10 68
SOFT (1010 "Hey Baby") 5-10 68
Picture Sleeves
CHESS (2020 "Some-A Your Sweet Love") 5-10 67
MERCURY (72507 "Harlem Shuffle") 8-12 65
EPs: 7-inch
PLAYBACK (32 "Long Long Day") 8-12 72
(Also has tracks by other artists.)
LPs: 10/12-inch
BETHLEHEM (10002 "High & Ridin' ") 10-20 70
CHESS (1519 "Wayne Cochran") 20-30 68
EPIC (30989 "Cochran") 8-12 72
KING (1116 "Alive & Well") 15-25 70
KING (16001 "Old King Gold") 5-10 75
Also see GREAT SEBASTIAN
Also see REDDING, Otis
Also see ROCKIN' CAPRIS
Also see WILSON, J. Frank

COCHRAN BROTHERS
Singles: 78 rpm
CASH (1021 "Walkin' Stick Boogie") 150-250
EKKO (1003 "Two Blue Singing Stars") 350-450 55
EKKO (1005 "Guilty Conscience") 50-100 55
EKKO (3001 "Tired & Sleepy") 75-125 56
Singles: 7-inch
CASH (1021 "Walkin' Stick Boogie") 500-700
EKKO (1003 "Two Blue Singing Stars") 500-700 55
EKKO (1005 "Guilty Conscience") 700-900 55
EKKO (3001 "Tired & Sleepy") 700-900 56
Members: Eddie Cochran; Hank Cochran. (Eddie and Hank were not really brothers).
Also see CAPEHART, Jerry
Also see COCHRAN, Eddie
Also see COCHRAN, Hank

COCHRANE TWINS
Singles: 7-inch
GARPAX (44084 "Cherry Pie") 20-30 64
Members: Lani Cochrane; Boni Cochrane.

COCKER, Joe P&R '68
(With the Chris Stainton Band)
Singles: 7-inch
A&M 4-8 68-78
ASYLUM 3-5 78-79
CAPITOL 3-5 84-88
ISLAND 3-5 83
PHILIPS (40255 "I'll Cry Instead") 10-20 65
Picture Sleeves
A&M 4-8 69-74
CAPITOL 3-5 84
ISLAND 3-5
LPs: 10/12-inch
A&M (Except 3100 series) 8-15 69-77
A&M (3100 series) 5-10 82
ASYLUM (Except 145) 5-10 78-79
ASYLUM (145 "Luxury You Can Afford") ...5-10 79
ASYLUM (145 "Luxury You Can Afford") .15-25 79
(Picture disc. Promotional issue only.)
CAPITOL 5-10 84-90
ISLAND 5-8 82
MFSL (223 "Sheffield Steel") 30-50 94
Also see ARNOLD, Vance, & Avengers
Also see BOWIE, David / Joe Cocker / Youngbloods
Also see RUSSELL, Leon

COCKER, Joe, & Jennifer Warnes P&R '82
Singles: 7-inch
ISLAND (99996 "Up Where We Belong") 3-5 82
Picture Sleeves
ISLAND (99996 "Up Where We Belong") 3-5 82
Also see COCKER, Joe
Also see WARNES, Jennifer

COCKERHAM, Chuck
Singles: 7-inch
MALA (12036 "Have I Got a Right") 10-20 69

COCKRELL, Charles
Singles: 7-inch
HI (2015 "Little Girl") 10-15 59

COCKRELL, Mat
Singles: 78 rpm
FLAIR (1037 "Baby Please") 15-25 54
Singles: 7-inch
FLAIR (1037 "Baby Please") 25-50 54

COCOAS
Singles: 78 rpm
CHESTERFIELD 50-75 55
Singles: 7-inch
CHESTERFIELD (364 "Flip Your Daddy") 100-150 55
(Label name in script typeface. Has clef and staff above name.)
CHESTERFIELD (364 "Flip Your Daddy") 50-75 55
(Label name in normal – not script – typeface. No clef and staff shown.)

CODAS
Singles: 7-inch
BELL (122 "Sleepwalk") 15-25 59

CODAY, Bill R&B '71
Singles: 7-inch
CRAJON (48202 "Sixty Minute Teaser") .. 10-15 69
CRAJON (48203 "Right On Baby") 50-75 70
CRAJON (48204 "Get Your Lie Straight") 4-8 71
CRAJON (48208 "I'm Back to Collect") 4-8 72
EPIC 4-8 73-75
GALAXY (777 "Get Your Lie Straight") 4-6 71
GALAXY (779 "When You Find a Fool, Bump His Head") 4-8 71
GALAXY (781 "I Got a Thing") 4-8 71

CODY, Skip
Singles: 7-inch
JET (503 "Feets Too Big") 20-30

CODY SISTERS
Singles: 7-inch
ARCH (1608 "Join the Society for the Prevention of Cruelty to Girls in Love") 10-15 59

COE, David Allan C&W '74
Singles: 7-inch
COLUMBIA 3-6 74-87
PLANTATION 4-6 73
SSS INT'L (Black vinyl) 4-6 71-72
SSS INT'L (Colored vinyl) 8-10 71-72
(Promotional issues only.)
Picture Sleeves
COLUMBIA 3-5
LPs: 10/12-inch
COLUMBIA 5-10 72-86
D.A.C. (0003 "Underground") 20-30
(Reportedly sold only at concerts.)
SSS INT'L (9 "Penitentiary Blues") 50-75 70
Session: Lacy J. Dalton; Dianne Sherrill; Eve Shapiro; Bill Anderson; George Jones; Dickey Betts; Kris Kristofferson; Guy Clark; Larry Jon Wilson; Waylon Jennings.
Also see JENNINGS, Waylon
Also see JONES, George
Also see JONES, George, & David Allan Coe
Also see KRISTOFFERSON, Kris

COE, David Allan, & Bill Anderson
Singles: 7-inch
COLUMBIA 3-5 80
Also see ANDERSON, Bill

COE, David Allan, & Willie Nelson C&W '86
Singles: 7-inch
COLUMBIA 3-5 86
Also see COE, David Allan
Also see NELSON, Willie
Also see NELSON, Willie / Jerry Lee Lewis / Carl Perkins / David Allan Coe

COE, Jamie
(Jamie Coe & Gigolos)
Singles: 7-inch
ABC-PAR (10120 "There's Never Been a Night") 10-15 60
ABC-PAR (10149 "Say You") 10-15 60
ABC-PAR (10267 "How Low Is Low") 10-15 61
ADDISON (15001 "There's Gonna Be a Day") 10-15 59
ADDISON (15003 "School Day Blues") 10-15 59

BIG TOP (3107 "Cleopatra") 10-20 62
BIG TOP (3139 "The Fool") 10-20 63
CAMEO (424 "Greenback Dollar") 10-15 66
ENTERPRISE (5005 "Dealer") 10-15 64
ENTERPRISE (5050 "My Girl") 10-15 65
REPRISE (0295 "Dealer") 10-15 64
Also see GIGOLOS

COE, Jimmy, & His Gay Cats of Rhythm
(Jimmy Coe & His Cohorts)

Singles: 78 rpm

STATES 15-25 53-56

Singles: 7-inch

INTRO (002 "Cold Jam for Breakfast") 10-20 66
NOTE (10013 "Wazoo") 15-25 58
STATES (118 "After Hours Joint") 20-40 53
(Black vinyl.)
STATES (118 "After Hours Joint") 50-100 53
(Red vinyl.)
STATES (129 "Raid on the After Hour Joint") 20-40 54
(Black vinyl.)
STATES (129 "Raid on the After Hour Joint") 50-100 54
(Red vinyl.)
STATES (155 "Run Jody, Run") 20-40 56
Also see COHORTS

COE, Tommy

Singles: 78 rpm

PEP (110 "Teenage Heart") 5-10 56

Singles: 7-inch

PEP (110 "Teenage Heart") 10-15 56

CO-EDS
(Featuring Gwen Edwards)

Singles: 78 rpm

OLD TOWN 25-35 56

Singles: 7-inch

OLD TOWN (1027 "Love You Baby All the Time") 50-75 56
OLD TOWN (1033 " I Love an Angel") ... 75-100 57

COEDS
(Co-Eds)

Singles: 7-inch

CAMEO (129 "Big Chief") 30-50 58
CAMEO (134 "La La") 20-30 58
CHA CHA (715 "Annabelle Lee") 15-25 61
CHECKER (996 "Annabelle Lee") 8-12 61
DWAIN (802 "With All My Heart") 20-30 59
SHERYL (330 "Time After Time") 10-20 61

CO-EDS

Singles: 7-inch

USA (724 "The Magic of Your Love") 25-35 62

COEDS
(With the Tokens)

Singles: 7-inch

SWING (101 "Mark My Words") 10-20 64
Also see TOKENS

COEFIELD, Brice
(With the Untouchables; with Wooden Nickels)

Singles: 7-inch

MADISON (137 "Cha Cha Twist") 15-25 60
OMEN (10 "Ain't That Right") 10-15 66
Also see UNTOUCHABLES
Also see WOODEN NICKELS

COETTES

Singles: 7-inch

POP-SIDE (6 "Friends") 10-15 61

COFFEE HOUSE

LPs: 10/12-inch

DORIAN (1001 "Coffee House") 20-30 59
Members: Judy Henske; Paul Sykes.
Also see HENSKE, Judy

COFIELD, Peter

Singles: 7-inch

CORAL (62563 "Gone") 5-10 70

LPs: 10/12-inch

CORAL (757508 "Peter Cofield") 10-15 69

COGAN, Alma

Singles: 78 rpm

RCA 10-15 55-56

Singles: 7-inch

AMERICAN ARTS (4 "I Love You Much Too Much") 5-10 64
CAPITOL (4547 "Just Couldn't Resist Her with Her Pocket Transistor") 15-25 61
RCA (6063 "Blue Again") 15-25 55
RCA (6236 "Got'n Idea") 20-30 55
RCA (6573 "Pickin' a Chicken") 15-25 56

COGAN, Don

Singles: 7-inch

MGM (12632 "Playboy") 10-15 58
MGM (12676 "The Singing Hills") 10-15 58

COGAN, Shaye

Singles: 7-inch

GEE (1034 "Stay Away Nearer") 10-20 57
MGM (12771 "Half As Much") 8-12 59
MGM (12866 "Mean to Me") 8-12 60
ROULETTE (4013 "Pathway to Sin") 10-20 57
ROULETTE (4027 "Doodle Doodle Doo") 10-20 57
ROULETTE (4052 "Satisfaction Guaranteed") 10-15 58
ROULETTE (4095 "Little Ring") 10-15 58
Also see MORROW, Buddy, & Orchestra

COGNACS

Singles: 7-inch

ROULETTE (4340 "Charlena") 30-40 61

CO-HEARTS

Singles: 7-inch

VEE-JAY (289 "My Love") 50-75 58

CO-HIERS

Singles: 7-inch

JCP (1009 "She Cried") 10-20 64

COHORTS

Singles: 7-inch

NOTE (20001 "Country Blues") 20-30 57
Also see COE, Jimmy, and His Gay Cats of Rhythm

COINS
("Vocal Don Trotter & Al Perry")

Singles: 78 rpm

GEE 200-400 54
MODEL (2001 "Loretta") 300-400 56

Singles: 7-inch

GEE (10 "Cheatin' Baby") 1000-2000 54
(Black vinyl.)
GEE (10 "Cheatin' Baby") 4000-5000 54
(Red vinyl.)
GEE (11 "Look at Me Girl") 750-1000 54
MODEL (2001 "Loretta") 3000-4000 55
Members: Don Trotter; Al Perry.
Also see CURTIS, Eddie

COINS / Colonials

Singles: 78 rpm

GEE 20-30 56

Singles: 7-inch

GEE (1007 "Look at Me Girl"/"Two Loves Have I") 75-125 56
Also see COINS
Also see GORDON, Bill "Bass," & Colonials

COKER, Al
(Alvadean Coker)

Singles: 78 rpm

ABBOTT 15-25 54-55
DECCA 20-30 57

Singles: 7-inch

ABBOTT (163 "Sugar Doll") 20-30 54
ABBOTT (167 "Funny Little Things") 20-30 54
ABBOTT (169 "Crying Heart") 20-30 54
ABBOTT (176 "We're Gonna Bop") 50-75 55
DECCA (30053 "Don't Go Baby") 20-30 57
DECCA (30490 "One More Chance") 20-30 57
Also see REEVES, Jim / Alvadean Coker

COKER, Sandy

Singles: 78 rpm

ABBOTT (171 "Toss Over") 10-15 54
DECCA .... 10-15 '50s

Singles: 7-inch

ABBOTT (171 "Toss Over") 15-25 54
DECCA (30051 "Rock Island Ride") 15-25 56
DECCA (30534 "Under Cover") 15-25 58

COKIE & TY RONES

Singles: 7-inch

AL-FANG (16790 "Let's Start Anew") ... 200-300 66

COLAVITA, Don

Singles: 7-inch

PLAID (1001 "Babee") 15-25 60

COLBERT, Chuck

Singles: 7-inch

BEE (10829 "Don't Cry Baby") 10-15 67

COLBERT, Phil

Singles: 7-inch

KC (105 "Deep Down Inside") 10-20 62
PHILIPS (40313 "Who's Got the Action") . 10-20 65
PHILIPS (40361 "Edge of Heaven") 10-20 66

COLBERT, Tiny

Singles: 78 rpm

MODERN (580 "Bumble Bee Baby") 10-20 48

COLBURN, Lou

Singles: 7-inch

MAYAN (366 "Cowboy Twist") 40-60 62

COLBY, Wendy, & Bonnevilles

Singles: 7-inch

DRUM BOY (101 "Don't You Dare Let Me Down") 40-60 63

Picture Sleeves

DRUM BOY (101 "Don't You Dare Let Me Down") 50-70 63
Also see BONNEVILLES

COLDER, Ben — C&W/P&R '62
(Sheb Wooley)

Singles: 7-inch

MGM 4-8 62-73
PORTLAND 4-6 78
SCORPION 3-5 79-80
SUNBIRD 3-5 80
TPL 3-5 87

LPs: 10/12-inch

LAKESHORE (621 "Ben Colder & Sheb Wooley") 10-20
(Mail order offer.)
LAKESHORE/GUSTO (110 "Greatest Hits of Sheb Wooley & Ben Colder") 8-12 79
(Mail order offer.)
MGM (139 "Ben Colder") 8-12 70
MGM (4421 thru 4876) 10-20 66-73
MGM (4173 "Spoofing the Big Ones") 15-25 63
Also see WOOLEY, Sheb

COLE, Ann — R&B '56
(With the Suburbans; with Cole-Miners)

Singles: 78 rpm

BATON 8-12 55-57
TIMELY 10-20 54

Singles: 7-inch

BATON (218 thru 232) 15-20 55-56
BATON (237 thru 258) 10-15 57-58
MGM (12954 "In the Chapel") 10-15 60
ROULETTE (4452 "Have Fun") 10-15 62
SIR (272 "That's Enough") 10-15 59
SIR (275 "A Love of My Own") 20-30 60
TIMELY (1006 "Danny Boy") 30-40 54
TIMELY (1007 "I'll Find a Way") 20-30 54
TIMELY (1010 "So Proud of You") 20-30 54
Also see SUBURBANS

COLE, Billy

Singles: 7-inch

E&M (1609 "Dancing Little Judy") 50-100

COLE, Bob

Singles: 7-inch

JAY (623 "You Lied") 50-60

COLE, Carmen

Singles: 7-inch

GROOVE (0045 "I'll Never Stand in Your Way") 10-15 64
GROOVE (0057 "I Just Don't Understand") 8-12 65

COLE, Clay

Singles: 7-inch

IMPERIAL (5771 "Happy Times") 10-15 61
IMPERIAL (5804 "Twist Around the Clock") 15-25 61
ROULETTE (4280 "Skip Skip") 10-15 60
Session: Capris.
Also see CAPRIS

COLE, Cozy — R&B '44
(With His All Stars; with Gary Chester; with Pete Johnson; with Red Norvo; with Alan Hartwell & Orchestra; Cozy Cole Septet; "Vocal Intro by 'Miss Whether' ")

Singles: 78 rpm

CANDY (3002 "Stardust") 5-10 49
GUILD 5-10 45
KEYNOTE (656 "They Didn't Believe Me") 10-15 45
KEYNOTE (1300 "Blue Moon") 10-15 44
MGM 5-10 54

Singles: 7-inch

ARTISTIQUE (6124 "Charleston") 5-10 61
BETHLEHEM (3067 "Big Boss") 5-10 63
CHARLIE PARKER (202 "Cozy's Groove") 5-10 62
COLUMBIA (43657 "Whole Lotta Shakin' Goin' On") 5-10 66
CORAL 5-10 62-67
FELSTED (8546 "Caravan") 10-15 59
GRAND AWARD (1023 "Caravan") 10-20 58
KING 10-15 59-60
LOVE (5004 "Topsy") 15-25 58
LOVE (5014 "Turvy") 15-25 58
(Monaural.)
LOVE (5014 "Turvy") 30-40 58
(Stereo.)
LOVE (5016 "Everything Is Topsy Turvy") 15-25 59
LOVE (5024 "Charleston") 10-20 59
MGM (11794 "Hound Dog Special") 10-15 54
MERCURY (25013 "Blue Moon") 10-15 58
RANDOM (602 "Ala Topsy 3") 10-15 60

Picture Sleeves

RANDOM (602 "Ala Topsy 3") 15-25 60

EPs: 7-inch

GRAND AWARD (2035 "After Hours") 20-30 55
MGM 15-20 54
WALDORF .... 10-15 '50s

LPs: 10/12-inch

CHARLIE PARKER (403 "A Cozy Conaption of Carmen") 30-40 62
COLUMBIA (2553 "It's a Rocking Thing") 10-15 66
(Monaural.)
COLUMBIA (9353 "It's a Rocking Thing") 10-20 66
(Stereo.)
CORAL (57423 "Drum Beat Dancing Feet") 15-20 62
(Monaural.)
CORAL (57457 "It's a Cozy World") 15-20 62
(Monaural.)
CORAL (757423 "Drum Beat Dancing Feet") 15-20 62
(Stereo.)
CORAL (757457 "It's a Cozy World") 15-20 62
(Stereo.)
EVEREST 8-10 74
FELSTED (7002 "Cozy's Caravan") 50-75 59
GRAND AWARD (334 "After Hours") 50-75 55
KING (673 "Cozy Cole") 20-25 59
LOVE (500 "Cozy Cole Hits") 50-75 59
PARIS (112 "Cozy Cole & His All Stars") . 50-75 58
SAVOY 8-12 72-77
TRIP 8-10 74
Session: Rex Stewart; Tyree Glenn; Claude Hopkins; Billy Bauer; Arvell Shaw.
Also see HAMPTON, Lionel
Also see HOPKINS, Claude, Quartet
Also see PAGE, Hot Lips, & Cozy Cole
Also see SHEARING, George, Quintet
Also see STEWART, Rex, & Vernon Story

COLE, Cozy, & Illinois Jacquet

LPs: 10/12-inch

AUDITION (5943 "Cozy Cole") 50-100 55
Also see COLE, Cozy
Also see JACQUET, Illinois

COLE, Diana

Singles: 78 rpm

JOSIE 10-20 56

Singles: 7-inch

ALLISON (919 "Alone Again") 8-12 62
JOSIE (808 "So Much Rockin' to Do") 10-20 56
STRAND (25002 "Picture on My Wall") 10-20 59
STRAND (25012 "I Created a Scene") 8-12 60

COLE, Don

Singles: 7-inch

COED (548 "Squad Car") 10-15 61
GUYDEN (2059 "Born to Be with You") ... 10-15 61
KENT (305 "Sweet Lovin' Honey") 50-75 58
Also see GIGOLOS
Also see HAWKS
Also see RIO ROCKERS
Also see TIARAS

COLE, Don & Alleyne
Singles: 7-inch
SON-RAY ... 5-10 65
TOLLIE (9015 "Something's Got a Hold on Me") ... 10-15 64
TOLLIE (9036 "Leave Me Alone") ... 10-15 64
LPs: 10/12-inch
TOLLIE (56001 "Live at the Whiskey A-Go-Go") ... 20-30 64

COLE, Don, & Al Casey
Singles: 78 rpm
RPM (502 "Snake Eyed Mama") ... 40-60 57
Singles: 7-inch
RPM (502 "Snake Eyed Mama") ... 50-100 57
Also see CASEY, Al
Also see COLE, Don

COLE, Eddie
(Eddie Cole's Solid Swingers)
Singles: 78 rpm
DECCA (7210 "Honey Hush") ... 30-50 36
DECCA (7215 "Stompin' at the Panama") ... 30-50 36
Members: Eddie Cole; Nat "King" Cole; Bill Wright; Tom Thompson; Ken Roane.
Also see COLE, Nat "King"

COLE, Ernie
Singles: 7-inch
DOR-COLE (101 "Whatever You Do") ... 75-125

COLE, Fred E.
(With the Northern Lights; with Northsiders; Freddie Cole)
Singles: 7-inch
BAND BOX (284 "Don't Be Mad") ... 50-75 61
DELITE (508 "Soulful Woman") ... 5-10 68
DELITE (515 "Wrong For Me") ... 5-10 68
DOT (16110 "Black Coffee") ... 10-15 60
LOIS (101 "Hey Little Lover") ... 10-15 61
PATT (058 "All Alone") ... 15-25 59
PATT (059 "Please Love Me Now") ... 15-25 60
SUE (775 "Right Now") ... 5-10 62
TRU GLO TOWN ... 5-10
WINLEY (222 "One More Nite") ... 20-30 58
LPs: 10/12-inch
DOT (3316 "Waiter, Ask the Man to Play the Blues") ... 20-30 60
(Monaural.)
DOT (25316 "Waiter, Ask the Man to Play the Blues") ... 30-50 60
(Stereo.)
PATT (101 "College Hop") ... 75-100 60
Members: Jack Baker; John Kowecki; Freddie Cole; John Kosic; John Chappel; Fran Parda; Alan Orkins; Don Gates Jr.
Also see BUSTERS

COLE, Freddy
Singles: 7-inch
TITANIC (100 "Don't Be Mad") ... 20-30 63

COLE, Gene
Singles: 7-inch
REED (400 "Coal Miner's Blues") ... 150-250

COLE, Ike
(With Lew Douglas & His Orchestra)
Singles: 7-inch
BALLY (1047 "Hear Me Good") ... 15-25 57
DEE GEE (3009 "My Blue Heaven") ... 5-10 66
DEE GEE (3015 "Don't Blame Me") ... 5-10 66
PERSONALITY ... 10-15
TODD (1052 "Cloud Nine") ... 8-12 60
U.A. (50103 "Same Old You") ... 5-10 66
LPs: 10/12-inch
DEE GEE (4001 "Ike Cole's Tribute to His Brother Nat") ... 10-20 66
Also see DOUGLAS, Lew

COLE, Jack
Singles: 7-inch
BRYTE (15571 "Night Train to Memphis") ... 75-125

COLE, Jerry
(With the Spacemen; with Trinity; with Stingers: Jerry Kole)
Singles: 7-inch
CAPITOL (5056 thru 5394) ... 8-12 63-65
HAPPY TIGER ... 4-6 70
MIDGET ... 4-6 75
W.B. ... 4-6 75
Promotional Singles
CAPITOL ("Movin' Surf"/"Racing Waves") .. 5-10 64
(Bonus single, packaged with the *Summer Surf* LP by Dick Dale & His Del-Tones.)
LPs: 10/12-inch
CAPITOL (T-2044 "Outer Limits") ... 20-30 63
(Monaural.)
CAPITOL (ST-2044 "Outer Limits") ... 30-40 63
(Stereo.)
CAPITOL (T-2061 "Hot Rod Dance Party") ... 20-30 63
(Monaural.)
CAPITOL (ST-2061 "Hot Rod Dance Party") ... 30-40 63
(Stereo.)
CAPITOL (T-2112 "Surf Age") ... 25-35 63
(Monaural. With *Thunder Wave*, a bonus single by Dick Dale & His Del-Tones.)
CAPITOL (T-2112 "Surf Age") ... 20-30 63
(Monaural. Without bonus single.)
CAPITOL (ST-2112 "Surf Age") ... 35-45 63
(Stereo. With *Thunder Wave*, a bonus single by Dick Dale & His Del-Tones.)
CAPITOL (ST-2112 "Surf Age") ... 30-40 63
(Stereo. Without bonus single.)
CROWN (539 "A Go Go Guitars") ... 15-25 65
CROWN (553 "Guitars A Go Go, Vol. 2") .15-25 66
CUSTOM ... 15-20
VOGUE ... 15-25 63
Also see CATALINAS
Also see CHAMPS
Also see DALE, Dick
Also see ID
Also see KICKSTANDS
Also see KNIGHTS
Also see RIVERS, Johnny / Jerry Cole
Also see SUPER STOCKS
Also see VALENS, Ritchie / Jerry Kole

COLE, Johnny
(With the Reptiles)
Singles: 7-inch
DORE (605 "How the Time Flies") ... 5-10 61
ORIGINAL SOUND (24 "War, No More") .10-20 62
PARADE (202 "Stop the Rain") ... 8-12 64
RADIANT (1503 "Wrap My Heart in Velvet") ... 75-125 61
(Orange label.)
RADIANT (1503 "Wrap My Heart in Velvet") ... 40-60 61
(Black label.)

COLE, Junior
(Jr. Cole & Crescents; with Johnny Winter's Band)
Singles: 7-inch
FROLIC (506 "Go On") ... 10-15 64
JIN (163 "I Won't Cry") ... 30-50 62
Also see WINTER, Johnny

COLE, Lee
Singles: 7-inch
MIST (1010 "Cool Baby") ... 75-100 59

COLE, Les
Singles: 7-inch
D (1010 "Bee Boppin' Daddy") ... 150-250 58
MIST (1010 "Cool Baby") ... 100-150 58

COLE, Maria
(Mrs. Nat Cole)
Singles: 78 rpm
CAPITOL ... 5-10 56
Singles: 7-inch
CAPITOL (3351 "No School Tomorrow") .10-20 56
CAPITOL (3446 "Somebody's Gotta Lose") ... 10-20 56
LPs: 10/12-inch
CAPITOL (2612 "Love Is a Special Feeling") ... 10-15 66

COLE, Nat "King" *R&B '42*
(King Cole Trio; Quintet; Quartet)
Singles: 78 rpm
AMMOR ... 15-25 42
ATLAS ... 10-20 43-45
CAPITOL ... 5-15 43-49
DAVIS & SCHWEGLER ... 20-40 39-40
DECCA ... 10-20 42-47
DISC ... 15-25 42
EXCELSIOR ... 10-20 42-45
PREMIER ... 10-20 44
SAVOY ... 10-15 46
VARSITY ... 15-25 40
Singles: 7-inch
CAPITOL (Red/orange labels) ... 4-6
(Label color is a reddish orange.)
CAPITOL (889 thru 3619) ... 10-20 50-57
(Purple labels.)
CAPITOL (3702 "When Rock & Roll Came to Trinidad") ... 15-25 57
CAPITOL (3737 thru 4623) ... 8-15 57-61
(Purple labels.)
CAPITOL (4804 thru 5683) ... 5-10 62-66
(Orange/yellow labels.)
CAPITOL (90036 "Christmas Song") ... 20-30 49
CAPITOL STARLINE ... 4-6 '60s
EXCELSIOR (1 "I'm Lost") ... 20-40 50
TAMPA (134 "Vom-Vim-Veedle") ... 10-15 57
Picture Sleeves
CAPITOL ... 10-20 59-66
TAMPA (134 "Vom-Vim-Veedle") ... 15-25 57
EPs: 7-inch
CAPITOL ... 10-25 50-60
DECCA ... 15-20 56
LPs: 10/12-inch
CAMAY ... 8-12
CAPITOL ... 5-10
(With "SM" prefix.)
CAPITOL (H-156 "Nat 'King' Cole at the Piano") ... 50-100 49
(10-inch LP.)
CAPITOL (H-177 "Nat 'King' Cole Trio") ... 50-75 49
(10-inch LP.)
CAPITOL (H-220 "The King Cole Trio") ... 50-75 50
(10-inch LP.)
CAPITOL (252 "Close Up") ... 6-12 69
(Two discs.)
CAPITOL (H-332 "Penthouse Serenade") ... 50-75 52
(10-inch LP.)
CAPITOL (H-357 "Unforgettable") ... 50-75 52
(10-inch LP.)
CAPITOL (332 thru 993) ... 20-40 55-58
(With "T" or "W" prefix.)
CAPITOL (420 thru 1031) ... 10-15 63
(With "DT" prefix.)
CAPITOL (1031 thru 1574) ... 15-25 58-61
(With "T," "ST" or "W" prefix.)
CAPITOL (1613 "Nat 'King' Cole Story") .. 40-60 61
(Boxed, three-disc set. Includes 24-page booklet.)
CAPITOL (1713 thru 2944) ... 10-20 58-68
(With "T," "DT," "ST," "W" or "SW" prefix.)
CAPITOL (4903 "Nat 'King' Cole") ... 10-20 65
(Commemorative, promotional issue only. Signed by Cole's widow.)
CROWN ... 10-15 64
DECCA (8260 "In the Beginning") ... 35-50 56
DYNAMIC HOUSE ... 5-10 72
EVEREST (290 "Nat King Cole") ... 5-10 74
MCA ... 5-10 73
MARK 56 ... 5-10 76
MONARCH ("Nat 'King' Cole") ... 75-100 53
(Colored vinyl.)
PICKWICK ... 5-10 '70s
SCORE (4019 "King Cole Trio") ... 20-40 58
SEARS (426 "Nat 'King' Cole") ... 15-25 '60s
(Promotional issue for Sears dept. stores.)
SPINORAMA ... 10-15 '60s
VSP ... 10-15 66
WYNCOTE ... 10-15 63
Members (King Cole Trio): Harry Edison; Willie Smith; Juan Tizol.
Also see COLE, Eddie
Also see COLE, Maria
Also see FOUR KNIGHTS
Also see KENTON, Stan
Also see LUTCHER, Nellie, & Nat "King" Cole
Also see MARTIN, Dean, & Nat "King" Cole
Also see NELSON, Willie / Nat "King" Cole / Johnny Mathis / Shirley Bassey
Also see PRESLEY, Elvis / Frank Sinatra / Nat "King" Cole
Also see SINATRA, Frank / Nat "King" Cole
Also see YOUNG, Lester, & Nat "King" Cole

COLE, Nat "King" / Phil Flowers
LPs: 10/12-inch
EXCELSIOR ... 5-10
Also see FLOWERS, Phil

COLE, Nat "King," & Stubby Kaye
Singles: 7-inch
CAPITOL ... 4-6 65
Picture Sleeves
CAPITOL ... 4-8 65

COLE, Nat "King," & His Trio / George Kingston
LPs: 10/12-inch
WYNCOTE ... 10-15 '60s

COLE, Nat "King," & George Shearing
LPs: 10/12-inch
CAPITOL ... 20-30 61
Also see COLE, Nat "King"
Also see SHEARING, George, Quintet

COLE, Natalie *P&R/R&B/LP '75*
(With George Shearing)
Singles: 12-inch
EMI ... 4-6 88
EPIC ... 4-6 83
MODERN ... 4-6 85
Singles: 7-inch
CAPITOL ... 3-6 75-80
EMI ... 3-5 88-89
EPIC ... 3-5 83
MANHATTAN ... 3-5 87
MODERN ... 3-5 85
Picture Sleeves
EMI ... 3-5 88-89
MANHATTAN ... 3-5 87
MODERN ... 3-5 85
LPs: 10/12-inch
CAPITOL (Except 11928) ... 8-12 75-82
CAPITOL (11928 "I Love You So") ... 20-25 79
(Promotional only picture disc.)
EMI ... 5-8 89
ELEKTRA ... 5-8 91
EPIC ... 5-10 83
MANHATTAN ... 5-10 87
MFSL (032 "Thankful") ... 40-60 79
MFSL (081 "Natalie Cole Sings, George Shearing Plays") ... 35-50 82
MODERN ... 5-10 85
Also see SHEARING, George, Quintet

COLE, Natalie, & Peabo Bryson *R&B/LP '79*
Singles: 7-inch
CAPITOL ... 3-5 79
LPs: 10/12-inch
CAPITOL ... 5-10 79

COLE, Natalie, & Beth Norman
("Vocal By Natalie Cole, Narration By Beth Norman"; with Billy May Orchestra)
Singles: 78 rpm
CAPITOL (3246 "Good Will") ... 10-15 57
Singles: 7-inch
CAPITOL (3246 "Good Will") ... 10-20 57
Picture Sleeves
CAPITOL (3246 "Good Will") ... 25-35 57
Also see COLE, Natalie

COLE, Sammie
Singles: 7-inch
NATIONAL (1001 "I'm Sorry About That") ... 100-200

COLE, Sonny, & Rhythm Roamers
Singles: 78 rpm
EXCELL ... 20-30 56
Singles: 7-inch
EXCELL (123 "I Dreamt I Was Elvis") .. 100-200 56
EXCELL (124 "Robinson Crusoe Bop") ... 200-300 56
ROLLIN' ROCK ... 5-10 69

COLE BROTHERS
Singles: 7-inch
JAMIE ... 5-10 68-69
MILLMONT (101 "Betty Betty Betty") ... 50-75 '60s

COLE & EMBERS
Singles: 7-inch
STAR-TREK (1220 "Hey Girl") ... 15-25 68

COLE & GRANDURES
Singles: 7-inch
CHI-SOUND (3066 "I Need You") ... 200-300

COLE & LES FEMMES
Singles: 7-inch
VARBEE (5001 "Love Is No Stranger") ... 15-25

COLEMAN, Cy
(Cy Coleman Co-Op)
Singles: 7-inch
AVA (168 "Jack's Theme") 5-10 64
CAPITOL 5-10 63-66
INDIGO (123 "Tall Hopes") 5-10 61
LONDON 4-6 72
MGM 5-8 68
NOTABLE 4-8 69-70
PLAYBOY (1001 "Playboy's Theme") 8-12 60
RCA 4-6 75-76
EPs: 7-inch
JUBILEE (5062 "Jamaica") 10-15 58
LPs: 10/12-inch
AVA (49 "Troublemaker") 10-20 64
BAINBRIDGE (6247 "Barnum") 8-10 83
CAPITOL (Except 11985) 10-20 62-65
CAPITOL (11985 "Piano Witchcraft") 8-12 79
COLUMBIA (2578 "If My Friends Could See Me Now") 10-15 67
(Monaural.)
COLUMBIA (9378 "If My Friends Could See Me Now") 15-20 67
(Stereo.)
COLUMBIA (32804 "Broadway Tunesmith") 8-12 74
(Reissue of 9378.)
EVEREST 10-20 60
GRYPHON (918 "Barnum") 8-12
INDIGO (502 "Wildcat") 10-20 61
JUBILEE (1062 "Jamaica") 15-25 58
MGM (4502 "Plastic Classics") 10-15 67
RCA (1252 "Party's On Me") 8-12 76
WESTMINSTER 10-20 59

COLEMAN, David
Singles: 7-inch
BARRY (1013 "My Foolish Heart") 10-20 67
Also see LADDINS

COLEMAN, Diane
Singles: 7-inch
COED (578 "He's the Only Boy For Me") 10-20 63

COLEMAN, Honey
Singles: 78 rpm
COMBO 20-40 52
Singles: 7-inch
COMBO (3 "Talk About a Girl Child Being Down") 50-75 52

COLEMAN, Joe
Singles: 7-inch
REM (304 "Rock All Night") 50-75 60

COLEMAN, King
(Carlton "King" Coleman)
Singles: 7-inch
ATLANTIC (2125 "Do the Hully Gully") 8-12 61
COLUMBIA (41927 "Bulldog") 8-12 61
DADE (1807 "Loo-Key Doo-Key") 10-15 60
FAIRMOUNT (1014 "Freedom") 5-10 66
KAREN (1008 "Holiday Season") 10-15 59
KENCO (5017 "Alley Rat") 8-12 61
KING 4-6 67-71
PORT (3015 "Do the Booga Lou") 5-10 66
PORT (3017 "Get On Board") 5-10 66
SYLVIA 5-10 65
SYMBOL (909 "Let's Shimmy") 10-15 60
TOGO (600 "Crazy Feeling") 5-10 63
Picture Sleeves
KING (6365 "The Boo Boo Song") 4-8 71

COLEMAN, Lenny
(With Nino & the Ebb Tides)
Singles: 7-inch
LAURIE (3290 "Four Seasons") 10-20 65
Also see NINO & EBB TIDES

COLEMAN, Ray
Singles: 7-inch
ARCADE (147 "Juke box Rock and Roll") 100-150 58
SALIANO (111 "My Rock & Roll Baby") 75-100 '50s
SKYROCKET (1002 "Toodle Oo-Bamboo") 50-75 59

COLEMAN, Richard
Singles: 7-inch
PRIMA (712 "Summer Job") 10-20 59

COLEMAN, Woody
Singles: 7-inch
JEDCO (5007 "Linda Darling") 20-30

COLEMANAIRES
Singles: 78 rpm
APOLLO 5-10 56
TIMELY 8-12 53-54
Singles: 7-inch
APOLLO (308 "This May Be My Last Time") 10-20 56
TIMELY (102 "Somebody Save Me") 20-30 53
TIMELY (103 "When the Pearly Gates Unfold") 20-30 54
TIMELY (105 "Be Ready When He Comes") 20-30 54

COLEMANS
(Coleman Brothers)
Singles: 78 rpm
ARCO (1208 "Plenty of Room in the Kingdom") 5-10 49
CORAL (65003 "His Eye Is on the Sparrow") 5-10 49
DECCA (8662 "His Eye Is on the Sparrow") 5-10 44
DECCA (8673 "Get Away Mr. Satan") 10-15 46
DECCA (48041 "Where Shall I Be") 10-15 47
DECCA (48051 "Seek") 10-15 47
MANOR (100 "It's My Desire") 10-15 45
MANOR (101 "Will Understand") 10-15 45
MANOR (102 "Plenty of Room in the Kingdom") 10-15 45
MANOR (1003 "Plenty of Room in the Kingdom") 10-15 45
MANOR (1055 "New What a Time") 10-15 47
MANOR (1065 "Noah") 10-15 47
REGAL (3281 "Ooh La La") 10-20 50
REGAL (3297 "You Know I Love You, Baby") 10-20 50
REGAL (3308 "I Ain't Got Nobody") 10-20 50

COLLAGE
Singles: 7-inch
BELL (920 "My Kind of Music") 4-8 70
SMASH (2135 "Lookin' at a Baby") 5-10 67
SMASH (2150 "Driftin' ") 5-10 68
SMASH (2170 "Story of Rock and Roll") 5-10 68
LPs: 10/12-inch
CREAM (9008 "Collage") 8-12 71
SMASH (27101 "Collage") 15-25 68
(Monaural.)
SMASH (67101 "Collage") 10-20 68
(Stereo.)

COLLAY, Allan
Singles: 7-inch
ACE (633 "One More Time") 10-20 61
INSTANT (3241 "Bye Bye Blackbird") 10-20 62
INSTANT (3248 "Not Old Enough") 10-20 62

COLLAY & SATELLITES P&R '60
Singles: 7-inch
SHO-BIZ (1002 "Last Chance") 15-25 60

COLLEAGUES
Singles: 7-inch
GLODUS (1651 "A Tear Fell") 10-20 61

COLLECTORS
Singles: 7-inch
LONDON 8-12 70
VALIANT (760 "Old Man") 20-30 67
W.B. (7059 "Listen to the Words") 10-20 67
W.B. (7159 "Fat Bird") 10-20 68
W.B. (7194 "Lydia Purple") 10-15 68
W.B. (7300 "Easy Morning") 10-15 69
LPs: 10/12-inch
W.B. (1746 "The Collectors") 20-35 68
W.B. (1774 "Grass & Wild Strawberries") 20-30 69
Also see CANADIAN CLASSICS

COL-LEE-JETS
Singles: 7-inch
NORTHWESTERN (2477 "Jam & Jelly") 10-20 60
SHADOW (7711 "Jo Ann") 10-15
SHADOW (7712 "Cynthia") 10-15
Member: Vance Barrett.

COLLEGIANS
Singles: 78 rpm
CAT (110 "Rickety Tickety Melody") 8-12 54
GROOVE(0163 "Blue Solitude") 8-12 56
Singles: 7-inch
CAT (110 "Rickety Tickety Melody") 10-20 54
GROOVE (0163 "Blue Solitude") 10-20 56

COLLEGIANS
Singles: 78 rpm
WINLEY 30-50 57
Singles: 7-inch
LOST NITE 4-8
TIMES SQUARE (11 "Heavenly Night") 10-20 63
WINLEY (224 "Zoom Zoom Zoom") 50-75 57
(Rigid disc.)
WINLEY (224 "Zoom Zoom Zoom") 15-25 57
(Flexible disc.)
WINLEY (261 "Oh, I Need Your Love") 15-25 62
WINLEY (263 "Right Around the Corner") 15-25 62
X-TRA (108 "Heavenly Night") 600-800 57
(Titles and artists shown on label in print approximately 1/8-inch letters. Label also has double horizontal lines.)
X-TRA (108 "Heavenly Night") 30-50
(Titles and artists shown in print approximately 1/4-inch letters.)
LPs: 10/12-inch
LOST NITE ("Collegians") 10-20 81
(10-inch LP. Red vinyl. 1000 made.)
WINLEY (6004 "Sing Along with the Collegians") 200-300 62
Members: Roger Hayes; Vernon Riley; Henry Brown; William Tarkenton; Holland Jackson.

COLLEGIANS
Singles: 7-inch
HILLTOP (1867 "The Saints") 10-20 60
HILLTOP (1868 "Cookin' ") 10-20 60
POST (10002 "I'm Ready") 15-25 62

COLLEGIATES
Singles: 7-inch
CAPO (001 "Brief Romance") 10-15 59

COLLEGIATES
Singles: 7-inch
RD GLOBE (009 "Teenage Plea") 10-15 60

COLLEGIATES
(With the Classmates)
Singles: 7-inch
CAMPUS (10 "Say Hello to My Angel") 30-40 60
HERITAGE (105 "I Had a Dream") 15-25 62

COLLETT, Jimmy
Singles: 78 rpm
ARCADE 20-30 52-53
Singles: 7-inch
ARCADE (101 "Beside the Alamo") 20-30 52
ARCADE (106 "Four Alarm Boogie") 75-125 52
ARCADE (109 "I Don't Want to Be Alone for Christmas") 15-25 52
ARCADE (120 "Beetle Bug Boogie") 25-50 54
ARCADE (138 "Shackled") 10-20 55
ARCADE (182 "It Just Takes One") 5-10 64

COLLETT, Vic
Singles: 7-inch
BLUE JAY (101 "To Stop My Missing You") 75-125

COLLETTE, Buddy
LPs: 10/12-inch
CROWN (5019 "Bongo Madness") 25-35 57
Also see CALLENDER, Red
Also see GRAYSON, Larry
Also see MOORE, Mel, & Marc Shaw

COLLETTI, Gus, & Clusters
Singles: 7-inch
TIN PAN ALLEY (206 "Hold My Hand") 150-250 58
TIN PAN ALLEY (207 "My Darling, Wait for Me") 150-250 58
TIN PAN ALLEY (214 "At the Rock and Roll Party") 150-250 59

COLLEY, Keith P&R '63
Singles: 7-inch
CHALLENGE (504 "Sugaree") 5-10 70
CHALLENGE (59334 "Tonight I'm Telling You") 5-10 66
COLUMBIA (44410 "Enamorado") 5-10 68
ERA (3054 "Zing Went the Strings of My Heart") 10-20 61
ERA (3067 "Scarlet") 10-20 62
ERA (3078 "The Number") 10-20 62
JAF 5-10 '60s
UNICAL (3006 "Enamorado") 10-20 63
UNICAL (3011 "Queridita Mia") 10-20 63
VEE-JAY (682 "Billy Girl") 5-10 65
WHITE WHALE (311 "Enamorado") 5-10 69

COLLEY, Steve
Singles: 7-inch
EXCELLO (2148 "Pack Your Bags") 10-20 59

COLLIE, Shirley C&W '61
Singles: 7-inch
LIBERTY (55291 "I' Rather Hear Lies") 10-15 60
LIBERTY (55268 "My Charlie") 10-15 60
LIBERTY (55324 "Dime a Dozen") 10-15 61
LIBERTY (55391 "If I Live Long Enough") 10-15 61
LIBERTY (55472 "No Wonder I Sing") 10-15 62
Also see NELSON, Willie, & Shirley Collie
Also see SMITH, Warren, & Shirley Collie

COLLIER, Mitty R&B '63
Singles: 7-inch
CHESS (1791 thru 2050) 8-12 61-68
ENTRANCE 4-8 72
ERIC 3-5 78
PEACHTREE 5-10 69-70
LPs: 10/12-inch
CHESS (1492 "Shades of a Genius") 15-25 65
GOSPEL ROOTS (5020 "Hold the Light") 5-10 79

COLLIER, Ralph
Singles: 7-inch
BLAZON (105 "You'll Come Running") 50-75
SIMS (168 "Leaving the Heartaches") 5-10 64

COLLINS, Al
Singles: 78 rpm
ACE (500 "I Got the Blues for You") 15-25 54
Singles: 7-inch
ACE (500 "I Got the Blues for You") 75-100 54

COLLINS, Al P&R '53
(With the Men From Mars; with Pablo Savedra; with Joe Bushkin; Al "Jazzbo" Collins)
Singles: 78 rpm
CORAL (61589 "Sam") 5-10 56
Singles: 7-inch
CORAL (61589 "Sam") 10-15 56
IDONGOTOSHOWYOUNOSTINKINBADGES (1225 "Hip Nite B-4 Xmas") 10-15
(Label name is correct—as in "I Don't Got to Show You No Stinkin' Badges" and is not the result of a typist gone berserk.)
SINCERELY YOURS (3491 "A Lullaby") 5-10
Picture Sleeves
BRUNSWICK (86001 "Little Red Riding Hood") 20-30 53
LPs: 10/12-inch
CORAL (57035 "East Coast Jazz Scene") 50-100 56
Also see BUSHKIN, Joe
Also see FREED, Alan, Steve Allen, Al "Jazzbo" Collins & Modernaires

COLLINS, Al "Jazzbo," & Lou Stein
Singles: 78 rpm
BRUNSWICK 5-10 53
CAPITOL 5-10 53
Singles: 7-inch
BRUNSWICK (86001 "Little Red Riding Hood") 10-20 53
BRUNSWICK (80226 "Three Little Pigs") 10-20 53
CAPITOL (2580 "Snow White and the Seven Dwarfs") 10-20 53
CAPITOL (2624 "The Invention of the Airplane") 10-20 53
Also see COLLINS, Al

COLLINS, Albert R&B/LP '72
(With the Ice Breakers; with His Rhythm Rockers)
Singles: 12-inch
ALLIGATOR (5 "Cold Snap") 5-10 86
(Promotional issue only.)
Singles: 7-inch
GREAT SCOTT (007 "Albert's Alley") 15-25 59
HALL/HALLWAY 8-12 63-65
IMPERIAL 4-8 69
KANGAROO (103 "Freeze") 30-50 58
LIBERTY (56184 "Coon 'n' Collards") 4-6 70
TCF/HALL 5-10 65
TRACIE (2003 "I Don't Know") 10-20 62
TUMBLEWEED 4-6 72-73
20TH FOX 5-10 68
LPs: 10/12-inch
ALLIGATOR 6-10 79-87
BLUE THUMB 10-15 69

BRYLEN 5-10 84
IMPERIAL 12-25 69-70
MFSL (226 "Cold Snap") 30-50
TCF/HALL (8002 "Cool Sound of Albert Collins") 30-35 65
TUMBLEWEED (103 "There's Gotta Be a Change") 10-15 71

COLLINS, Albert, Robert Cray & Johnny Copeland *LP '86*

Singles: 12-inch

ALLIGATOR (5 "T-Bone Shuffle") 5-10 86
(Promotional issue only.)

LPs: 10/12-inch

ALLIGATOR (4743 "Showdown") 10-15 86
MFSL (217 "Showdown") ....30-50 '90s
Also see COLLINS, Albert
Also see COPELAND, Johnny

COLLINS, Big Tom
(Brownie McGhee)

Singles: 78 rpm

KING 50-75 51-52

Singles: 7-inch

KING (4483 "Heartache Blues") 75-100 51
KING (4568 "Heart Breaking Woman") ..75-100 52
Also see McGHEE, Brownie

COLLINS, Carol

Singles: 7-inch

DUNES (2005 "Dear One") 10-15 61
Also see CONNORS, Carol

COLLINS, Cecil / Fretts

Singles: 7-inch

BLUE MOON (414 "Rockin' Baby"/"Full Moon Above") 50-75 59

COLLINS, Choo Choo

Singles: 7-inch

TORNADO (1007 "My Competition") 10-20

COLLINS, Crystal, & Cellarmen

Singles: 7-inch

JODY (4001 "When You Grow Tired of Her") 20-30

COLLINS, Dave, & Scrubs

Singles: 78 rpm

IMPERIAL (5294 "Don't Break-a-My Heart") 75-125 54

Singles: 7-inch

IMPERIAL (5294 "Don't Break-a-My Heart") 400-500 54

COLLINS, Dorothy *P&R '55*

Singles: 78 rpm

AUDIOVOX 5-10 54-55
CORAL 5-10 55-56
DECCA 5-10 52
MGM 5-10 50-51

Singles: 7-inch

AUDIOVOX (107 thru 117) 10-20 54-55
CORAL (61510 thru 61669) 10-20 55-56
DECCA (28251 thru 28574) 10-20 52-53
GOLD EAGLE (1806 "I'm Just a Girl") 8-12 61
GOLD EAGLE (1809 "Lover") 8-12 61
MGM (10753 "I'm Playing with Fire") 10-20 50
MGM (11020 "How Many Times") 10-20 51
MGM (11038 "Yesterday's Ice Cubes") 10-20 51
ROULETTE (4479 "Sweeter Than Honey") 5-10 63
TOP RANK (2013 "Everything I Have Is Yours") 10-15 59
TOP RANK (2024 "Baciare Baciare") 10-15 59
TOP RANK (2052 "Banjo Boy") 10-15 60

EPs: 7-inch

AUDIOVOX (11000 "Dorothy Collins") 10-20 55
CORAL (81129 "Parade of Hits") 10-20 55
MGM (11137 "Dorothy Collins") 10-20 55

LPs: 10/12-inch

CORAL (57105 "At Home with Dorothy") 15-25 57
CORAL (57106 "Dorothy Collins") 15-25 57
MOTIVATION (0316 "Experiment Songs") 10-15 62
TOP RANK (340 "New Way to Travel") 10-20 60
(Monaural.)
TOP RANK (640 "New Way toTravel") 15-25 60
(Stereo.)
VOCALION (3724 "Dorothy Collins") 8-12 65
Also see McGUIRE SISTERS / Lancers / Dorothy Collins / Teresa Brewer

COLLINS, Eddie

Singles: 7-inch

FERNWOOD (104 "Patience Baby") 50-75 58

COLLINS, Jimmy

Singles: 7-inch

J&S (101 "You're By My Side") 10-20 60
ORBIT 10-20 59

COLLINS, Judy *LP '64*

Singles: 7-inch

ELEKTRA (Except 45008 thru 45680) 3-5 69-84
ELEKTRA (45008 thru 45680) 4-8 64-69
ELEKTRA (47437 "Drink a Round to Ireland") 10-20 82
(Green vinyl.)

Picture Sleeves

ELEKTRA (Except "The Hostage") 3-5 69-84
ELEKTRA ("The Hostage") 4-8 73
(Promotional issue only.)

LPs: 10/12-inch

ELEKTRA (Except 200 & 300 series) 10-15 67-84
ELEKTRA (209 "Maid of Constant Sorrow") 30-40 61
ELEKTRA (222 "Golden Apples of the Sun") 25-35 62
ELEKTRA (243 "Judy Collins No. 3") 20-30 63
(Monaural.)
ELEKTRA (7-243 "Judy Collins No. 3") 25-35 63
(Stereo.)
ELEKTRA (253 "Running for My Life") 5-8 80
ELEKTRA (300 series) 15-20 65-68
(Monaural.)
ELEKTRA (7-300 series) 15-20 65-72
(Stereo.)
ELEKTRA (6002 "So Early in the Spring") .8-12 77
(Two discs.)
ELEKTRA (60001 "Times of Our Lives") 5-8 82
Session: Van Dyke Parks.
Also see PARKS, Van Dyke

COLLINS, Judy, & T.G. Sheppard *C&W '84*

Singles: 7-inch

ELEKTRA 3-5 84
Also see COLLINS, Judy

COLLINS, Lee, & Orbits

Singles: 7-inch

DOOTO (601 "Tell Me Baby") 10-20 64

COLLINS, Linda

Singles: 7-inch

TIME (1039 "I'm Crying") 15-25 61

COLLINS, Lyle

Singles: 7-inch

HARVEST (104 "Left My Lover") 50-100
NASHVILLE (5113 "Johnnycake Mountain") 75-125 63

COLLINS, Lyn *P&R/R&B '72*
(With the Famous Flames)

Singles: 7-inch

PEOPLE (Except 608) 4-6 72-76
PEOPLE (608 "Think") 15-25 72

LPs: 10/12-inch

PEOPLE (5602 "Think") 40-60 72
PEOPLE (6605 "Check Me Out") 30-50 75
Also see BROWN, James, & Lyn Collins

COLLINS, Pat

Singles: 7-inch

QUALITY (3000 "Blue Teardrops") 15-25 62

COLLINS, Pat

LPs: 10/12-inch

GNP (93 "Sleep with Pat Collins, the Hip Hypnotist") 15-25 63

COLLINS, Ramona

Singles: 7-inch

CLARK'S (346 "You've Been Cheating") 300-400

COLLINS, Teddy

Singles: 7-inch

CRAZY CAJUN (500 "Two Kinds of Love") 50-75

COLLINS, Tom, & Mixers

Singles: 7-inch

("Mixer's Rock") 250-500 59
(Label name and selection number not known.)
Members: Laurie Collins; Pete Glystein; Bob Merkt; Gene Stoiber; Tony Kolp.

COLLINS, Tommy *C&W '54*
(With Wanda Collins)

Singles: 78 rpm

CAPITOL 10-20 54-56

Singles: 7-inch

CAPITOL (2701 thru 4421) 15-25 54-60
CAPITOL (4495 "Black Cat") 20-30 61
CAPITOL (4962 thru 5345) 5-10 63-65
COLUMBIA 5-10 66-68

EPs: 7-inch

CAPITOL (607 "Tommy Collins") 30-50 54
CAPITOL (776 "Words and Music Country Style") 25-40 56
(Price is for any of three volumes in this series.)
CAPITOL (1125 "Light of the Lord") 10-20 59
(Price is for any of three volumes in this series.)
CAPITOL (1196 "This Is Tommy Collins") 10-20 59
(Price is for any of three volumes in this series.)

LPs: 10/12-inch

CAPITOL (776 "Words and Music Country Style") 50-75 56
CAPITOL (1125 "Light of the Lord") 50-60 59
CAPITOL (1196 "This Is Tommy Collins") 40-60 59
CAPITOL (1436 "Songs I Love to Sing") ..30-50 61
COLUMBIA (2510 "The Dynamic Tommy Collins") 15-25 66
(Monaural.)
COLUMBIA (9310 "The Dynamic Tommy Collins") 15-25 66
(Stereo.)
COLUMBIA (9578 "On Tour") 15-25 68
GOLDEN COUNTRY 5-8 83
STARDAY 10-15 72
TOWER (5021 "Let's Live a Little") 15-25 66
TOWER (5107 "Shindig") 15-25 68
VERVE (10565 "I Wanna Thank You") 10-20 67
Session: Buck Owens.
Also see OWENS, Buck
Also see SIPES, Leonard, & Rhythm Oakies
Also see STEWART, Wynn

COLLINS, Tommy, & Paragons

Singles: 7-inch

WINLEY (236 "Darling, I Love You") 100-200 59
Also see PARAGONS

COLLINS, Vivian

Singles: 7-inch

SEROCK (2002 "Answer Me") 10-20 62

COLLINS KIDS

Singles: 78 rpm

COLUMBIA 20-50 55-57

Singles: 7-inch

COLUMBIA (21470 "Hush Money") 15-25 55
COLUMBIA (21514 "Rockaway Rock") 15-25 56
COLUMBIA (21543 "I'm in My Teens") 15-25 56
COLUMBIA (21560 "Rock & Roll Polka") .15-25 56
COLUMBIA (40824 "Move a Little Closer") 20-30 57
COLUMBIA (40921 "Hop, Skip & Jump") .20-30 57
COLUMBIA (41012 "Party") 50-75 57
(Black vinyl.)
COLUMBIA (41012 "Party") 100-200 57
(Purple vinyl. Promotional issue only.)
COLUMBIA (41087 "Hoy Hoy") 30-45 58
COLUMBIA (41149 "Mercy") 30-45 58
COLUMBIA (41225 "Whistle Bait") 35-55 58
COLUMBIA (41329 "Sugar Plum") 20-30 59

LPs: 10/12-inch

COLUMBIA 8-12 83
Members: Larry Collins; Lawrencine "Lorrie" Collins.

COLOGNES
(With the Chuck Hamilton Combo)

Singles: 7-inch

LUMMTONE (102 "A River Flows") 200-300 59

COLOMBO, Joe
(Joe Columbo)

Singles: 7-inch

AMP 3 (130 "Please Come Back Darling") 20-30 57
DOMINO (1000 "Cha-Rock") 8-12 61
STYLE 8-10
TAURUS (359 "I Need You") 20-30 63
Session: Donnie & Delchords.
Also see DONNIE & DELCHORDS

COLOMBO, Peter

Singles: 7-inch

ORCHID (226 "Mighty John Glenn") 100-150

COLON, Johnny

Singles: 7-inch

COTIQUE (108 "Boogaloo Blues") 10-15 67
COTIQUE (302 "What You Mean") 10-15

COLONAIRS

Singles: 78 rpm

EMBER (1017 "Can't Stand to Lose You") 40-60 57

Singles: 7-inch

EMBER (1017 "Can't Stand to Lose You") 50-75 57
TRU-LITE (127 "Do-Pop-Si") 50-75 63

COLONEL JOYE
(With the Joy Boys; Col Joye)

Singles: 7-inch

DECCA (30933 "Rockin' Rollin' Clementine") 75-125 59
FONO GRAF (1241 "Please Give It a Chance") 200-300 62

COLONIALS

Singles: 7-inch

FABOR (131 "Lazy Mississippi") 8-12 64
SENATE (1003 "Where Is My Love") 15-25
TRU-LITE (127 "Little Miss Muffet") 50-75 64

COLONY

Singles: 7-inch

SUNDERLAND (2293 "Pseudo-Psycho Institution") 30-50

COLORING BOOK

Singles: 7-inch

PACIFIC CHALLENGE (117 "Smokestack Lightning") 30-50

COLQUITT, Bobby
(With the Renaults)

Singles: 7-inch

CJ (621 "Searching") 10-20 61
COLT (620 "I'm Gone") 15-25 61
COLTON (101 "I'm Not a Know It All") 25-50

COLT, Steve
(With the Mustangs; with Blue Knights; with 45s; with Fabulous Counts; Steve Colt's Paradox)

Singles: 7-inch

AMOS (114 "If You Gotta Make a Fool of Somebody") 5-10 69
BIG BEAT (1001 "I've Been Loving You") ..5-10 66
BIG BEAT (1006 "Dynamite") 5-10 67
FLEETWOOD (4550 "Gloria") 75-125 62
(Credits "Steve Colt and The Mustangs.")
FLEETWOOD (4550 "Gloria") 30-40 62
(Credits "Steve Colt and The Blue Knights.")
MIRANDA (265 "In the Still of the Night") .30-40 '60s
RCA 5-10 66
VANGUARD 4-6 71

LPs: 10/12-inch

VANGUARD 10-12 71

COLTER, Jessi *C&W/P&R '75*
(Mirriam Johnson; Mirriam Eddy)

Singles: 7-inch

CAPITOL 3-6 75-82
RCA 4-6 69-72

LPs: 10/12-inch

CAPITOL 5-10 75-81
RCA (4333 "A Country Star Is Born") 15-25 70
Session: Waylon Jennings; Gary Scruggs.
Also see EDDY, Duane & Mirriam
Also see JENNINGS, Waylon, & Jessi Colter
Also see JOHNSON, Mirriam

COLTON, Tony
(With the Concords)

Singles: 7-inch

ABC-PAR (10705 "I Stand Accused") 10-15 65
ROULETTE (4475 "Goodbye Cindy, Goodbye") 15-25 63
Also see CONCORDS

COLTRANE, John *LP '67*

Singles: 78 rpm

PRESTIGE 10-20 57

Singles: 7-inch

ATLANTIC 5-10 60-61
PRESTIGE 5-10 57-64

LPs: 10/12-inch
ATLANTIC (1300 & 1400 series) 20-40 59-66
BLUE NOTE (1577 "Blue Train") 100-150 51
(Label gives New York street address for Blue Note Records.)
BLUE NOTE (1577 "Blue Train") 35-55 59
(Label reads "Blue Note Records Inc. - New York, U.S.A.")
COLTRANE (4950 "Cosmic Music") 150-200 66
COLTRANE (5000 "Cosmic Music") 150-200 66
IMPULSE (Except 6 thru 77) 10-25 66-71
IMPULSE (6 thru 77)................................ 25-45 61-65
JAZZLAND 20-40 61
PRESTIGE (7043 "Two Tenors") 50-100 56
(Yellow label.)
PRESTIGE (7043 "Two Tenors") 25-35 64
(Blue label.)
PRESTIGE (7105 "Coltrane")................ 50-100 57
(Yellow label.)
PRESTIGE (7105 "Coltrane")................... 25-35 57
(Blue label.)
PRESTIGE (7123 "John Coltrane & Red Garland Trio").. 50-75 57
(Yellow label.)
PRESTIGE (7123 "Traneing In")............. 25-35 64
(Blue label, logo on right. Reissue of *John Coltrane & Red Garland Trio.*)
PRESTIGE (7123 "Traneing In")............. 15-25 69
(Blue label, logo at top.)
PRESTIGE (7142 "Soultrane")................ 40-70 58
(Yellow label.)
PRESTIGE (7158 "Cattin' ")..................... 40-70 59
(Yellow label.)
PRESTIGE (7158 "Cattin' ")..................... 25-35 64
(Blue label.)
PRESTIGE (7131 "Wheelin' & Dealin' ") .. 40-70 59
(Yellow label.)
PRESTIGE (7188 "Lush Life")................. 40-70 60
(Yellow label.)
PRESTIGE (7188 "Lush Life")................. 25-35 64
(Blue label.)
PRESTIGE (7200 series) 20-40 61-64
(Yellow label.)
PRESTIGE (7200 series) 15-25 64
(Blue label.)
PRESTIGE (7300 series) 15-25 65
U.A. 25-35 62
Also see ADDERLEY, Julian "Cannonball," & John Coltrane
Also see BURRELL, Kenny, & John Coltrane
Also see ELLINGTON, Duke, & John Coltrane

COLTRANE, John, & Miles Davis
LPs: 10/12-inch
PRESTIGE 10-20 64
Also see DAVIS, Miles

COLTRANE, John, & Thelonious Monk
LPs: 10/12-inch
JAZZLAND 20-30 61
MILESTONE.. 8-12 73
RIVERSIDE (Except 039) 10-20 65-68
RIVERSIDE (039 "Thelonious Monk & John Coltrane")..5-10 82
Also see COLTRANE, John
Also see MONK, Thelonious

COLTS — R&B '55
("Featuring Joe Grundy")
Singles: 78 rpm
ANTLER (4003 "Never No More")........... 10-15 57
ANTLER (4007 "Guiding Angel") 50-75 57
MAMBO (112 "Adorable")..................... 100-150 55
VITA (112 "Adorable")........................... 25-35 55
VITA (121 "Sweet Sixteen")..................... 15-25 56
VITA (130 "Never No More") 15-25 56
Singles: 7-inch
ANTLER (4003 "Never No More") 20-30 57
ANTLER (4007 "Guiding Angel") 100-150 57
DELCO (4002 "I Never Knew") 10-15 59
(First issued as by the Red Coats.)
MAMBO (112 "Adorable")....................... 250-300 55
PLAZA (505 "Sweet Sixteen") 5-10 62
VITA (112 "Adorable") 75-100 55
VITA (121 "Sweet Sixteen")..................... 30-40 56
VITA (130 "Never No More") 30-40 56
Members: Eddie Williams; Joe Grundy; Rubin Grundy; Leroy Smith; Carl Moland; Don Wyatt.
Also see FORTUNES
Also see KELSO, Jackie
Also see RED COATS

COLUMBO, Chris — P&R '63
(Chris Colombo Quintet)
Singles: 7-inch
BATTLE (45904 "You Can't Sit Down") 5-10 62
MAXX (327 "Mr. Wonderful")........................5-10 64
STRAND (25056 "Summertime")..................5-10 63
LPs: 10/12-inch
MERCURY 5-10 75
STRAND (1044 "Jazz") 15-25 63

COLUMBUS, Ray
(With the Invaders; with Art Collection)
Singles: 7-inch
COLSTAR (1001 "Kick Me").....................15-25 67
COLSTAR (1003 "In the Morning of Today") 15-25 67
MEMORY 8-10 67
PHILIPS (40189 "I Wanna Be Your Man") .8-12 64
PHILIPS (40326 "Where Have You Been") 5-10 65
PHILIPS (40340 "She's a Mod") 5-10 65

COLUMBUS PHARAOHS
(With the Tommy Wills Orchestra; 4 Pharaohs)
Singles: 7-inch
ESTA (290 "Give Me Your Love").........400-600 58
Members: Morris Wade; Bobby Taylor; Ron Wilson; Bernard Wilson.
Also see EGYPTIAN KINGS
Also see 4 PHARAOHS
Also see TAYLOR, Bobby

COLWELL-WINFIELD BLUES BAND
Singles: 7-inch
VERVE FORECAST.....................................5-10 68
LPs: 10/12-inch
VERVE FORECAST (3056 "Cold Wind Blues") 10-20 68
ZA-ZOO (1 "Live Bust") 20-30 71
Members: Bill Colwell; Mike Winfield; Chuck Purro; Jack Schroer; Charles "Moose" Sorrento; Collin Tilton.

COMBENASHUNS
Singles: 7-inch
LEO (3801 "What'cha Gonna Do") 5-10 66
Picture Sleeves
LEO (3801 "What'cha Gonna Do") 10-20 66
(Plain white sleeve with "Introducing the Combinashuns" printed at the bottom.)

COMBINATIONS
Singles: 7-inch
COMBO (167 "Back Home Again").........50-100 60

COMBINATIONS
Singles: 7-inch
CARRIE (010 "Voo Doo")...............................4-8 70
CARRIE (1514 "Just One More Chance")...100-150 62
KIM-TONE (1001 "Goddess of Love") ......15-25 '60s
MASTER (1020 "Pretty Boy")..................75-100 63

COMBONAIRES
Singles: 7-inch
DART (1010 "Wicked")...............................15-25 59
RESCUE (31044 "Topaz") ....10-15 '60s

COMBONETTES
Singles: 78 rpm
COMBO (74 "If I Had My Wish")..............10-20 55
Singles: 7-inch
COMBO (74 "If I Had My Wish")..............25-35 55

COMBS, Lefty
Singles: 7-inch
ALVIC (20316 "We Split the Blanket) ...300-500 '50s

COMBS, Shirley
Singles: 7-inch
LISA (101 "Why Should We Stop Now") ..15-25 64

COMER, Chuck
Singles: 7-inch
VADEN (302 "Little More Lovin' ") 200-300 60

COMFORTABLE CHAIR
Singles: 7-inch
ODE (109 "Be Me")..5-10 68
ODE (112 "I'll See You")..............................5-10 68
LPs: 10/12-inch
ODE (44005 "Comfortable Chair") 15-25 68
Members: Barbara Wallace; Bernie Schwartz; Greg Leroy; Tad Baczec; Gary Davis.
Also see ATELLO, Don

COMIC BOOKS
("""Comic Books""")
Singles: 7-inch
CITATION (5001 "Manuel").........................40-50 62
DYNAMIC SOUND (2005 "The First Time in My Life")..15-25 67
MAGIC TOUCH (2004 "Bat-Mo")...............10-20 62
NEW PHOENIX (6199 "Manuel")..............20-30 62
Members: Bob Barian; Bob Casper; Ronnie Premier; Floyd Dorsey; James Pike; Bill Dorsey; Lloyd Johnson; Greg Browder.
Also see PREMIER, Ronnie

COMMANCHES
Singles: 7-inch
HICKORY (1264 "Tomorrow") 15-25 64

COMMANDERS
Singles: 78 rpm
DECCA...5-10 53
MODERN (567 "Lonesome Road") 10-20 48
Singles: 7-inch
DECCA...8-12 53
MODERN (567 "Lonesome Road") 10-20 48
(Flexidisc.)

COMMANDERS
Singles: 7-inch
EMBASSY (1004 "Trouble in the Jungle")..15-25

COMMANDS
(With the Dell Tones)
Singles: 7-inch
DYNAMIC (104 "No Time for You")..........25-35 64
(Black vinyl.)
DYNAMIC (104 "No Time for You")..........40-50 64
(Red vinyl.)
DYNAMIC (111 "Don't Be Afraid to Love Me")..15-25 65
(Yellow or red vinyl.)

COMMANDS
Singles: 7-inch
BACK BEAT (570 "Hey It's Love")............10-20 66

COMMERCIALS
Singles: 7-inch
DAYHILL (2012 "Power in Your Love") ....20-30 '60s
STAR MAKER (5001 "Lover's Train").......10-20 '60s

COMMODORES
Singles: 78 rpm
DOT 8-12 55-56
Singles: 7-inch
DOT (15372 "Riding on a Train") 10-15 55
DOT (15439 "Speedo") 10-15 55
DOT (15461 "Two Loves Have I") 10-15 56

COMMODORES
Singles: 78 rpm
CHALLENGE 10-20 57
Singles: 7-inch
CHALLENGE (1004 "Sweet Angel").........10-15 57
CHALLENGE (1007 "Faith") 10-15 57

COMMODORES
Singles: 7-inch
BRUNSWICK (55126 "Who Dat")..............10-15 59

COMMON BUG COMBO
("Vocal By Jeanne Turnbow")
Singles: 7-inch
BEN-RON ("Beatle Bug") 10-15 64
(Selection number not known.)
Picture Sleeves
BEN-RON ("Beatle Bug") 15-25 64
DATE (1657 "Peddler's Blues")....................5-10 69

COMMON PEOPLE
LPs: 10/12-inch
CAPITOL (266 "Of the People/By the People/For the People")..50-75 69

COMMONS LTD.
Singles: 7-inch
MOD (1005 "Change the World") 25-35 67

COMO, Amos, & His Tune Toppers
Singles: 78 rpm
STARDAY (257 "Hole in the Wall").........75-100 56
Singles: 7-inch
STARDAY (257 "Hole in the Wall").......350-450 56

COMO, Chuck
Singles: 7-inch
FOXY (1001 "Teardrops on My Pillow")... 15-25 64
(First issue.)
GUYDEN (2107 "Teardrops on My Pillow")..10-15 64

COMO, Nicky
(With the Glen Stuart Orchestra)
Singles: 7-inch
LAURIE (3061 "Look for a Star") 10-15 60
LAURIE (3087 "Honey, Honey")...............10-15 61
TANG (1231 "Your Guardian Angel").......50-75 60
Session: Del Satins.
Also see DEL SATINS
Also see STUART, Glen

COMO, Perry — P&R '43
(With Hugo Winterhalter's Orchestra; with Ramblers; with Ray Charles Singers; with Anita Kerr Quartet)
Singles: 78 rpm
BLUEBIRD 5-10 50
RCA...5-10 43-58
Singles: 7-inch
BLUEBIRD 10-20 50
(May also be shown as RCA Victor "Bluebird Children's Records.")
RCA (157 "Here Comes My Baby")..............5-8 67
(Promotional issue only.)
RCA (237 "Supper Club Favorites") 15-25 49
(Three disc set.)
RCA (0071 "Ave Maria") 10-15 49
(Black vinyl.)
RCA (0071 "Ave Maria") 15-25 49
(Colored vinyl.)
RCA (0100 thru 0900 series) 4-6 69-73
RCA (VP-2000 series).................................8-12 59
(Stereo.)
RCA (2700 thru 7400 series) 8-20 48-59
RCA (61-7000 series)...................................8-12 58-60
(Stereo.)
RCA (7500 thru 9700 series) 4-10 59-69
RCA (10000 thru 13000 series).....................3-6 74-83
Picture Sleeves
RCA (157 "Here Comes My Baby")..............8-10 67
(Promotional issue only.)
RCA (3800 thru 7100 series) 10-20 50-58
RCA (7200 thru 9700 series) 5-15 58-69
EPs: 7-inch
CAMDEN ....5-10 '50s
RCA (Except SPD series) 10-25 52-70
RCA (SPD-27 "Perry Como")....................40-60 56
(Boxed 10-EP set. Includes inserts and biography booklet.)
RCA (SPD-28 "Perry Como Highlighter").20-30 56
(Sampler from Kleenex Tissues. Includes picture cover.)
LPs: 10/12-inch
CAMDEN 5-15 57-74
RCA (0100 thru 4000 series)......................5-15 73-83
(With "AFL1," "ANL1," "APL1," "AQL1," "AYL1," "CPL1," or "DVL2" prefix.)
RCA (1004 "Saturday Night with Mr. C")..20-30 58
RCA (1007 "Golden Records") 20-30 58
RCA (LPM-1085 "So Smooth")..................20-40 55
RCA (LPM-1172 "I Believe")......................20-40 56
RCA (LPM-1176 "Relaxing with Perry Como")...20-40 56
RCA (LPM-1177 "Sentimental Date with Perry Como")...20-40 56
RCA (LPM-1191 "Perry Como Sings Hits from Broadway Shows")......................................20-40 56
RCA (LPM-1243 Perry Sings Christmas Music")..20-40 56
RCA (LPM-1463 We Get Letters")............20-30 57
RCA (LPM-1800 thru LPM-2900 series) .. 15-25 58-63
RCA (LSP-1085 thru LSP-1463)..............10-20 62-68
(Electronic stereo reissues.)
RCA (LSP-1800 thru LSP-2900 series).... 15-30 58-63
(Stereo.)
RCA (3013 "TV Favorites") 25-50 52
(10-inch LP.)
RCA (3035 "A Sentimental Date") 25-50 52
(10-inch LP.)
RCA (3044 "Supper Club Favorites") 25-50 52
(10-inch LP.)
RCA (3124 "Broadway")............................25-50 53
(10-inch LP.)
RCA (3133 "Christmas") 25-50 53
(10-inch LP.)

RCA (3188 "I Believe") ... 25-50 53
(10-inch LP.)
RCA (3224 "Golden Records") ... 25-50 54
(10-inch LP.)
RCA (3300 thru 4500 series) ... 8-15 64-71
(With "LPM" or "LSP" prefix.)
READER'S DIGEST ... 8-15 75
Also see CHARLES, Ray, Singers

COMO, Perry / Ames Brothers / Harry Belafonte / Radio City Music Hall Orchestra

EPs: 7-inch

RCA (SP-35 "Merry Christmas") ... 10-20 56
(Record dealer giveaway. Issued with paper sleeve.)
Also see AMES BROTHERS
Also see BELAFONTE, Harry
Also see WINTERHALTER, Hugo, & His Orchestra

COMO, Perry, & Eddie Fisher P&R '52

Singles: 78 rpm

RCA ... 4-8 52

Singles: 7-inch

RCA ... 5-10 52
Also see FISHER, Eddie

COMO, Perry, & Fontane Sisters P&R '50

Singles: 78 rpm

RCA ... 4-8 50-51

Singles: 7-inch

RCA ... 8-15 50-51
Also see FONTANE SISTERS

COMO, Perry, & Betty Hutton P&R '50

Singles: 78 rpm

RCA ... 4-8 50

Singles: 7-inch

RCA ... 8-15 50
Also see HUTTON, Betty

COMO, Perry, & Jaye P. Morgan

Singles: 78 rpm

RCA ... 4-8 55

Singles: 7-inch

RCA ... 5-10 55
Also see COMO, Perry
Also see MORGAN, Jaye P.

COMPACTS

Singles: 7-inch

CARLA (718 "Why Can't It Be") ... 10-20 68

COMPANIONS
(With Bob Mersey & Orchestra)

Singles: 7-inch

DOVE (240 "Falling") ... 100-150 58

COMPANIONS
(With Able Baker & Orchestra)

Singles: 7-inch

AMY (852 "No Fool Am I") ... 50-100 62
ARLEN (722 "It's Too Late") ... 20-30 63
BROOK'S (100 "I Didn't Know") ... 50-75 59
COLLECTABLES ... 3-5 81
FEDERAL (12397 "I Didn't Know") ... 15-25 61
GENERAL AMERICAN (711 "Be Yourself") ... 5-10 64
GINA (722 "It's Too Late") ... 15-25 63

COMPANIONS

Singles: 7-inch

COLUMBIA (42279 "I'll Always Love You") ... 10-20 62

COMPETITORS

Singles: 7-inch

DOT (16560 "Power Shift") ... 10-20 63

LPs: 10/12-inch

DOT (3542 "Hits of the Street and Strip") ... 75-100 63
(Monaural.)
DOT (25542 "Hits of the Street and Strip") ... 100-125 63
(Stereo.)
Members: Don Brandon; Larry Brown.
Also see BRANDON, Don

COMPLIMENTS

Singles: 7-inch

CONGRESS (243 "Shake It Up, Shake It Down") ... 10-15 65
CONGRESS (252 "The Time of Her Life") ... 15-25 65
MIDAS (304 "Beware, Beware") ... 30-40 68

COMPOSERS

Singles: 7-inch

ERA (3118 "I Had a Dream") ... 15-25 63

COMPOSERS

Singles: 7-inch

AMPEN (221 "Woe Is Me") ... 300-400 63
Session: Johnny Moore
Also see MOORE, Johnny

COMSATS

Singles: 7-inch

FELSTED (8705 "Astronaut") ... 10-20 64

COMSTOCK, Bobby P&R '59
(With the Counts)

Singles: 7-inch

ASCOT (2164 thru 2216) ... 10-15 64-66
ATLANTIC (2051 "Jambalaya") ... 10-20 60
BLAZE (349 "Tennessee Waltz") ... 10-20 59
ERIC ... 4-6 73
FESTIVAL (25000 "Garden of Eden") ... 10-20 61
JUBILEE (5392 "Bony Moronie") ... 10-20 60
JUBILEE (5396 "Jezebel") ... 50-75 60
LAWN (202 thru 255. Except 219) ... 10-20 63-65
LAWN (219 "Your Boyfriend's Back") ... 20-25 63
MOHAWK (124 "Everyday Blues") ... 10-20 61
TRIUMPH (602 "Jealous Fool") ... 10-20 59

LPs: 10/12-inch

ASCOT (13026 "Out of Sight") ... 40-50 66
(Monaural.)
ASCOT (16026 "Out of Sight") ... 50-60 66
(Stereo.)
BLAZE ("Tennessee Waltz") ... 100-150
(Selection number not known.)
Members: Bobby Comstock; Wally Richardson; Everett Barksdale; Henry Jones; Oslo Jones; Danny Small.
Session: King Curtis.
Also see BOBBY & COUNTS
Also see KING CURTIS

CONCEPTION

Singles: 7-inch

PERFECTION (1001 "Babylon") ... 15-25 68

CONCEPTS

Singles: 7-inch

TOPS ("Heaven Help Me") ... 150-200 '50s
(Selection number not known.)

CONCEPTS
(With Al Browne's Orchestra)

Singles: 7-inch

APACHE (1515 "Whisper") ... 400-500 57
MUSICTONE (1109 "Whisper") ... 10-15 61
Member: Johnnie James.
Also see BROWNE, Al

CONCEPTS / Tokens

Singles: 7-inch

STOOP SOUNDS (119 "Heaven Sent You"/"Every Breath I Take") ... 75-100 98
Also see TOKENS

CONCEPTS & EMANONS

Singles: 7-inch

J&J (3000 "Cry") ... 40-60
Also see EMANONS

CONCORDS

Singles: 78 rpm

EMBER ... 15-25 56
HARLEM ... 250-350 54

Singles: 7-inch

EMBER (1007 "Satisfied with Rock 'n Roll") ... 40-50 56
HARLEM (2328 "Candlelight") ... 1000-1500 54
Members: Milton Love; Joe Willis; Jimmy Hunter; Bob Thompson.
Also see REAVES, Pearl, & Concords

CONCORDS

Singles: 7-inch

BOOM (60021 "Down the Aisle of Love") ... 10-20 66
EPIC (9697 "Should I Cry") ... 50-75 64
GRAMERCY (304 "Cross My Heart") ... 100-150 61
(Special Christmas issue, with two candy canes on each side of label.)
GRAMERCY (304 "Cross My Heart") ... 40-50 62
(No candy canes on label.)
GRAMERCY (305 "My Dreams") ... 15-25 62
HERALD (576 "Marlene") ... 10-15 62
HERALD (578 "Cold & Frosty Morning") ... 15-25 63
POLYDOR (14036 "Down the Aisle of Love") ... 4-6 70
RCA (7911 "Again") ... 10-15 61
RUST (5048 "One Step from Heaven") ... 15-25 62

LPs: 10/12-inch

CRYSTAL BALL (136 "Best of the Concords") ... 10-15 91
(Black vinyl. 1000 made.)
Also see COLTON, Tony
Also see KENNY, Sue
Also see LISA & LULLABIES
Also see SCOTT, Neal
Also see SHERWOODS
Also see SNOWMEN

CONCORDS SUPREME

Singles: 7-inch

VIRTUE (8505 "Everything and More") ... 75-100

CONDELLO
(Michael Condello; Commodore Condello's Salt River Navy Band)

Singles: 7-inch

RAMCO (2003 "Ho Ho Ha Ha Hee Hee") ... 5-10 68
SCEPTER (12233 "Crystal Clear") ... 5-10 68
SCEPTER (12261 "Goodnight") ... 5-10 69

EPs: 7-inch 33/45

BLOSSOM KIDS REVUE ... 8-12

LPs: 10/12-inch

SCEPTER ... 15-25 66
Also see HUB KAPP & WHEELS

CONDOLI, Conti

Singles: 78 rpm

CHANCE (1153 "Flamingo") ... 15-25 54

Singles: 7-inch

CHANCE (1153 "Flamingo") ... 35-50 54
Members: Chubby Jackson; Ira Sullivan; R. Winn; T. Papa; G. Esposito.

CON-DONS

Singles: 7-inch

CARLTON (587 "Centennial March") ... 10-15 63

CONDORS

Singles: 7-inch

HUNTER (2504 "Sweetest Angel") ... 1000-2000 60

CONDUCTORS

Singles: 7-inch

DATER (1304 "She Said So") ... 10-15 67
Members: Mike Ranck; Frank Angello; Donny Sammarko; Rick Lorman.

CONE, Jimmy

Singles: 7-inch

BELL (65 "The Joker") ... 15-25 57
BELL (70 "I Beg of You") ... 15-25 58

CONEY, King, & Hot Dogs

Singles: 7-inch

LEGRAND (1038 "Ba-Pa-Da") ... 10-20 65

CONEY ISLAND KIDS

Singles: 78 rpm

JOSIE ... 5-10 56
JUBILEE ... 5-10 55

Singles: 7-inch

JOSIE (791 "I Love It") ... 10-20 56
JOSIE (802 "We Want a Rock and Roll President") ... 10-20 56
JOSIE (809 "Popcorn and Candy") ... 10-15 57
JUBILEE (5215 "Moonlight Beach") ... 10-15 55

CONFEDERACY

Singles: 7-inch

UA (1139 "Feelin' Free") ... 10-15 64

CONFESSIONS

Singles: 7-inch

EPIC (9474 "Be Bop Baby") ... 20-30 61

CONFIDENTIAL FOUR

Singles: 7-inch

BOSS (001 "Please Be My Girl Friend") ... 200-300 66

CONFINERS OF MISSISSIPPI STATE PENITENTIARY
("Under Direction of Windell Cannon")

Singles: 7-inch

ELECTRO (261 "Harmonica Boogie") ... 150-200 61

CONGO RHYTHM BOYS

Singles: 78 rpm

INTERNATIONAL (607 "Week End Blues") ... 25-50 50
INTERNATIONAL (611 "Please Don't Cry") ... 25-50 50

CONLEY, Arthur P&R/R&B/LP '67

Singles: 7-inch

ATCO ... 4-8 67-70
CAPRICORN ... 4-6 71-74
FAME (1007 "In The Same Old Way") ... 8-12 66
FAME (1009 "Take Me") ... 8-12 66
JOTIS (472 "Who's Fooling Who") ... 5-10 66
PHILCO (15 "Sweet Soul Music"/"You Don't Have to See Me") ... 10-20 67
("Hip Pocket" flexi-disc.)

LPs: 10/12-inch

ATCO ... 15-25 67-69
Also see ARTHUR & CORVETS
Also see CORVETTS
Also see SOUL CLAN

CONLEY, Patricia, & Royal Robins

Singles: 7-inch

ALDO (504 "Mama What'll I Do") ... 10-20 62

CONLON, Jud
(Jud Conlon's Rhythmaires)

Singles: 7-inch

ZEPHYR (015 "Bridge of Sighs") ... 10-20 57
Also see ARMSTRONG, Louis, & Gary Crosby

CONLON & CRAWLERS

Singles: 7-inch

MARLIN (16006 "I Won't Tell") ... 15-20 67
Member: Chuck Conlon.
Also see NIGHTCRAWLERS

CONN, Billy

Singles: 7-inch

FEDERAL (12500 "I Promise You") ... 15-20 63

CONN, Tony

Singles: 7-inch

DECCA (30813 "Like Wow") ... 20-35 59
DECCA (30865 "Run Rabbit Run") ... 10-20 59

CONNELL, Doug, & Hot Rods

Singles: 7-inch

ALTON (600 "On Our Way from School") ... 20-30 59

CONNELL, Harvey
(With the Efics)

Singles: 7-inch

FRATERNITY (891 "Autumn Heart") ... 10-15 61
TRI-CITY (17637 "Autumn Heart") ... 20-30 61
(First issue.)
VERNON (100 "A Million Hearts") ... 15-25 62

CONNELLY, Chris

Singles: 7-inch

PHILIPS (40274 "Theme from Peyton Place") ... 5-10 65

Picture Sleeves

PHILIPS (40274 "Theme from Peyton Place") ... 8-12 65

LPs: 10/12-inch

PHILIPS (200173 "Boy from Peyton Place") ... 10-20 65
(Monaural.)
PHILIPS (600173 "Boy from Peyton Place") ... 10-20 65
(Stereo.)

CONNELLY, Earl

Singles: 7-inch

ALTO (2003 "Just to Hold My Hand") ... 20-30 61
ALTO (2005 "Since You've Been Gone") ... 20-30 61
MASTER (120 "Tell Me Why") ... 20-30
MAYCON (Except 100) ... 15-25
MAYCON (100 "I Don't Know Why") ... 40-60

CONNER, Buddy

Singles: 7-inch

BREAKTHROUGH ("When You're Alone") ... 100-200
(Selection number not known.)

CONNER, Harold

Singles: 78 rpm

PEACOCK ... 10-20 54-55

Singles: 7-inch
PEACOCK (1635 "Come Back, Come Back") ... 20-30 54
PEACOCK (1652 "Don't Be No Fool") ... 20-30 55
RECONA (3504 "I'll Be There") ... 15-25 64

CONNER, Lynn
Singles: 7-inch
MONUMENT (808 "Forgive Me") ... 10-15 63

CONNIE & CONES
Singles: 7-inch
NRC (5006 "Let Us Pretend") ... 10-20 59
ROULETTE (4223 "I Love My Teddy Bear") ... 10-15 60
ROULETTE (4313 "No Time for Tears").. 15-25 60

CONNIE & LEE
Singles: 7-inch
GONE (5035 "Cool Cool Baby") ... 10-15 58
LOOK ... 10-20 58

CONNIE'S COMBO
(Connie's Combo)
Singles: 78 rpm
EDDIE'S (1203 "Why Don't You Come Back") ... 15-25 48
FREEDOM (1508 "Ugly Mae") ... 15-25 48
Members: Conrad Johnson; L.C. Williams.
Also see JOHNSON, Conrad
Also see WILLIAMS, L.C.

CONNIFF, Ray P&R/LP '57
(With the Rockin' Rhythm Boys; Ray Conniff Orchestra & Chorus)
Singles: 78 rpm
BRUNSWICK ... 4-8 53-57
COLUMBIA ... 4-8 56-57
CORAL ... 4-8 55
Singles: 7-inch
BRUNSWICK ... 10-15 53-57
COLUMBIA (02987 thru 03165) ... 3-5 82
COLUMBIA (10002 thru 11177) ... 3-6 74-80
COLUMBIA (30447 "Please") ... 8-12 59
(Compact 33.)
COLUMBIA (30582 "None But the Lonely Heart") ... 8-12 60
(Compact 33.)
COLUMBIA (40660 thru 41484) ... 8-12 56-59
COLUMBIA (41582 thru 45002) ... 4-8 60-69
COLUMBIA (45137 thru 45996) ... 3-6 70-74
CORAL (61371 "B.R. Boogie") ... 10-15 55
Picture Sleeves
COLUMBIA (41484 "Christmas Bride").... 10-15 60
EPs: 7-inch
COLUMBIA (Except 10041/2/3) ... 5-10 56-59
COLUMBIA (10041/2/3 "Dance the Bop") ..8-12 57
(Price is for either volume.)
LPs: 10/12-inch
COLUMBIA (Except 925 & 1004) ... 5-15 58-82
COLUMBIA (925 "S'Wonderful") ... 10-20 56
COLUMBIA (1004 "Dance the Bop") ... 15-25 57
HARMONY ... 4-8 69
Also see CASE, Allen
Also see MATHIS, Johnny
Also see MATHIS, Johnny / Tony Bennett / North Carolina Ramblers / Ray Conniff & Jerry Vale with Eugene Ormandy
Also see RAY, Johnnie
Also see ROBBINS, Marty

CONNOR, Chris P&R '56
Singles: 78 rpm
ATLANTIC ... 5-15 56-57
BETHLEHEM ... 5-10 54-55
Singles: 7-inch
ATLANTIC (1097 thru 2017) ... 15-20 56-59
ATLANTIC (2037 thru 5014) ... 10-15 59-61
BETHLEHEM (1200 & 1300 series) ... 10-20 54-55
BETHLEHEM (1291 thru 3081) ... 5-10 64
BETHLEHEM (11000 series) ... 8-12 58
FM (3002 "I Concentrate On You") ... 8-12 63
EPs: 7-inch
ATLANTIC (593/4/5/6 "Chris Connor Sings the George Gershwin Almanac") ... 30-40 57
(Price is for any of four volumes.)
ATLANTIC (580 "I Miss You So") ... 30-40 57
ATLANTIC (615 "Jazz Date") ... 30-40 58
BETHLEHEM ... 20-40 54-56
LPs: 10/12-inch
ABC-PAR ... 10-20 65-66
ATLANTIC (601 "Chris Connor Sings the George Gershwin Almanac") ... 50-100 57
ATLANTIC (1228 "Chris Connor") ... 50-100 57
ATLANTIC (1240 "He Loves Me He Loves Me Not") ... 50-100 57
ATLANTIC (1286 "Jazz Date") ... 50-75 58
ATLANTIC (1290 "Chris Craft") ... 50-75 58
ATLANTIC (1307 "Sad Cafe") ... 50-75 59
(Monaural.)
ATLANTIC (SD-1307 "Sad Cafe") ... 60-80 59
(Stereo.)
ATLANTIC (8014 "I Miss You So") ... 50-75 58
ATLANTIC (8032 "Witchcraft") ... 50-75 59
(Monaural.)
ATLANTIC (SD-8032 "Witchcraft") ... 60-80 59
(Stereo.)
ATLANTIC (8040 "In Person") ... 40-60 59
(Monaural.)
ATLANTIC (SD-8040 "In Person") ... 50-75 59
(Stereo.)
ATLANTIC (8046 "A Portrait") ... 30-50 60
(Monaural.)
ATLANTIC (SD-8046 "A Portrait") ... 40-60 60
(Stereo.)
ATLANTIC (8061 "Free Spirits") ... 25-50 62
(Monaural.)
ATLANTIC (SD-8061 "Free Spirits") ... 30-60 62
(Stereo.)
BETHLEHEM (20 "This Is Chris") ... 50-100 55
(Maroon label.)
BETHLEHEM (56 "Chris") ... 50-100 56
(Maroon label.)
BETHLEHEM (1001 Lullabys of Birdland") ... 100-200 54
(10-inch LP.)
BETHLEHEM (1002 Lullabys for Lovers") ... 100-200 54
(10-inch LP.)
BETHLEHEM (6000 series) ... 10-12 78
(Gray label.)
BETHLEHEM (6004 "Lullabys of Birdland") ... 50-100 56
(Maroon label.)
BETHLEHEM (6005 "Lullabys for Lovers") ... 50-100 56
(Maroon label.)
FM ... 10-15 63
Also see BON BONS
Also see FERGUSON, Maynard, & Chris Connor

CONNOR, Chris / Julie London / Carmen McRae
LPs: 10/12-inch
BETHLEHEM (6006 "Bethlehem Girlfriends") ... 50-100 56
(Maroon label.)
Also see CONNOR, Chris
Also see LONDON, Julie
Also see McRAE, Carmen

CONNORS, Carol
(With Hank Levine & His Orchestra; Annette Kleinbard)
Singles: 7-inch
CAPITOL (5152 "Never") ... 10-20 64
COLUMBIA (3-41976 "You Are My Answer") ... 40-50 61
(Compact 33.)
COLUMBIA (4-41976 "You Are My Answer") ... 15-25 61
COLUMBIA (3-42155 "Listen to the Beat") ... 40-50 61
(Compact 33.)
COLUMBIA (4-42155 "Listen to the Beat") ... 15-25 61
COLUMBIA (3-42337 "What Do You See in Him") ... 40-50 62
(Compact 33.)
COLUMBIA (4-42337 "What Do You See in Him") ... 15-25 62
ERA (3084 "Two Rivers") ... 10-20 62
ERA (3096 "I Wanna Know") ... 10-20 62
MIRA (219 "My Baby Looks, But He Don't Touch") ... 10-20 66
N.T.C. (3131 "Yum-Yum Yamaha") ... 20-25 64
(Single-sided pressing.)
Picture Sleeves
MIRA (219 "My Baby Looks, But He Don't Touch") ... 15-25 66
N.T.C. (3131 "Yum-Yum Yamaha") ... 25-50 64
Also see BARD, Annette
Also see CAROL & CHERYL
Also see COLLINS, Carol
Also see STORYTELLERS
Also see SURFETTES
Also see TEDDY BEARS

CONNORS, Greg
Singles: 7-inch
GUYDEN (2017 "Till the End") ... 10-15 59
TREY (3003 "Your Love Tears Me Up")... 15-25 60

CONNOTATIONS
Singles: 7-inch
CLIFTON (25 "Two Hearts Fall in Love") ... 4-6 78
CLIFTON (51 "When You Wish Upon a Star") ... 3-5 80
GRECO (611 "No More") ... 4-8 '70s
TECHNICHORD (1000 "Two Hearts Fall in Love") ... 75-125 62
(Black vinyl.)
TECHNICHORD (1000 "Two Hearts Fall in Love") ... 200-300 62
(Red vinyl.)

CONNY
Singles: 7-inch
CAPITOL (4526 "This Little Girl's Gone Rockin' ") ... 8-12 61
LPs: 10/12-inch
CAPITOL (10253 "Conny of Germany")... 20-25 60

CONNY & BELLHOPS
Singles: 7-inch
DAMON (12315 "Shot Rod") ... 20-30 60
R (OUR) (505 "Shot Rod") ... 15-25 61
(Rerecorded version.)
R (511 "Fafine") ... 150-200 61

CONQUEROO
Singles: 7-inch
SONOBEAT (103 "I've Got Time") ... 15-25 68
Picture Sleeves
SONOBEAT (103 "I've Got Time") ... 25-50 68
LPs: 10/12-inch
FIVE HOURS (8 "From the Vulcan Gas Co.") ... 10-15 87
Members: Bob Brown; Ed Guinn; Gerry Storm; Charles Pritchard.

CONQUERORS
Singles: 7-inch
LU PINE (108 "Bill Is My Boyfriend") ... 50-60 62

CONQUEST
Singles: 7-inch
GAIL (114 "Is It Right") ... 15-25 67

CONQUISTADORS
Singles: 7-inch
ACT (4 "Just Can't Stop Lovin' You") ... 50-100

CONRAD, Bob
Singles: 7-inch
W.B. (5211 thru 5317) ... 5-10 61-62
Picture Sleeves
W.B. (5211 "I Want You Pretty Baby") ... 10-20 61
W.B. (5242 "Bye Bye Baby") ... 10-20 61

CONRAD, Charlie
Singles: 7-inch
SPEC (125 "Night Club Blues") ... 200-300

CONRAD, Jess
Singles: 7-inch
LONDON (1967 "Mystery Girl") ... 10-15 61
LONDON (2005 "Little Ship") ... 10-15 61

CONRAD & HURRICANE STRINGS
Singles: 7-inch
DAYTONE (6401 "Hurricane") ... 15-25 64
ERA (3130 "Hurricane") ... 8-12 64
Members: Conrad Couwenberg; Pat Couwenberg; Ed Sigarlaki; Don Sigarlaki.

CONRAD & VAN-DELLS
Singles: 7-inch
BMC (1001 "Dead End") ... 15-25 '60s

CONROY, Bert, & Misfits
Singles: 7-inch
DEB-CO (1000 "Debbie") ... 50-75 63

CONSERVATIVES
Singles: 7-inch
EBONIC (6569 "That's All") ... 10-15 '60s
ON TIME (100 "Happiness") ... 10-20 '60s
TRIBE (8326 "One Too Many Mornings") .. 5-10 68
TRIBE (8327 "Miami") ... 5-10 68

CONSIDINE, Tim
Singles: 78 rpm
DISNEYLAND ("Triple-R Song") ... 10-20 57
(Selection number not known.)
Singles: 7-inch
DEL-FI (4212 "What Do Little Girls Dream Of") ... 8-12 63
DISNEYLAND ("Triple-R Song") ... 10-20 57
(Selection number not known.)
Picture Sleeves
DISNEYLAND ("Triple-R Song") ... 20-30 57
(Selection number not known.)

CONSORTS
Singles: 7-inch
APT (25066 "Please Be Mine") ... 75-125 62
COUSINS (1004 "Please Be Mine") ... 75-125 61
(Same number used on a Guy Villari release.)
CRYSTAL BALL (111 "Star Above") ... 4-8 78
(Black vinyl. 500 made.)
CRYSTAL BALL (111 "Star Above") ... 8-12 78
(Red vinyl. 25 made.)
Members: Bruce Laurent; Sal Donnarumma; William Abbatte.
Also see CHUCKLES

CONSTELLATIONS
Singles: 7-inch
GEMINI STAR (30005 "Pop Daddy") ... 10-20 68
GEMINI STAR (30008 "Easy to Be Hard") ... 75-100 68
PROCESS (127 "Quoidas") ... 15-25 65
SMASH (1923 "Tear It Up Baby") ... 15-20 64
VIOLET (1053 "My Dear") ... 25-35 63

CONSTRUCTION
Singles: 7-inch
SYNC (6 "Hey Little Way Out Girl") ... 50-75

CONSULS
Singles: 7-inch
ABEL (222 "Runaway") ... 40-50 59

CONTE, Johnny
Singles: 7-inch
CHATTAHOOCHEE ... 10-20 61-64

CONTELS
Singles: 7-inch
WARWICK (103/104 "Hey You"/"Lovers Dream") ... 50-75 59

CONTEMPORARIES
Singles: 7-inch
RICHIE (672 "Fool for Temptation") ... 15-25 66

CONTENDERS
Singles: 7-inch
JACKPOT (48002 "Tequila") ... 10-20 58
Member: Chuck "Tequila" Rio.
Also see RIO, Chuck

CONTENDERS
Singles: 7-inch
BLUE SKY (105 "Mr. Dee Jay") ... 100-200 59

CONTENDERS
Singles: 7-inch
CHATTAHOOCHEE (644 "Dune Buggy") ... 10-20 64
CHATTAHOOCHEE (656 "Johnny B Goode") ... 10-20 64

CONTENDERS
Singles: 7-inch
EDGE (506 "Do What You Gotta Do") ... 15-25 65

CONTENDERS
(With the Rogues)
Singles: 7-inch
JAVA (101 "The Clock") ... 40-50 66
(Red label. LW in dead wax.)
JAVA (101 "The Clock") ... 10-20 66
(Red label. FW in dead wax.)
JAVA (101 "The Clock") ... 4-6 '70s
(Gold label.)
JAVA (102 "Surprise") ... 20-30 66
JAVA (103 "I Like It Like That") ... 15-25 66
JAVA (104 "Hetta Hetta") ... 50-100 66
WHITNEY (1929 "Gunga Din") ... 30-40 66
Members: Jack Strong; Lou Tavani; Frank Torpey; Frank DiSantis.

CONTENTS ARE:
Singles: 7-inch
ROK (6707 "Future Days") ... 25-35 67
ROK (6709 "I Don't Know") ... 25-35 67

CONTESSAS
Singles: 7-inch
E ... 10-15
WITCH (113 "Boy of My Heart") ... 10-15 63

CONTINDERS
(Featuring Clifford Curry)
Singles: 7-inch
BLUE SKY (105 "Mr. Dee Jay") ... 500-1000 59
Also see CURRY, Clifford

CONTINENTAL CO-ETS
Singles: 7-inch
IGL (105 "I Don't Love You No More") ... 40-60 66

CONTINENTAL FIVE
(With the Lil Walters Band)
Singles: 7-inch
NU KAT (105 "My Lonely Friend") ... 75-100 59
NU KAT (10132 "Perdelia") ... 50-75 59
(Identification number shown since no selection number is used.)
Also see VELVATONES / Continentals

CONTINENTAL V
Singles: 7-inch
CONTINENTAL (101 "Wake Me Up Girl") ... 30-50 67
RADEL (107 "Wake Me Up Girl") ... 15-25 67

CONTINENTAL 5
Singles: 7-inch
LIFETIME (1038 "Yours") ... 10-20 68

CONTINENTAL GEMS
Singles: 7-inch
GUYDEN (2091 "My Love Will Follow You") ... 500-750 63

CONTINENTALS
Singles: 78 rpm
WHIRLIN' DISC ... 50-75 56-57
Singles: 7-inch
DAVIS (466 "Tongue Twister") ... 50-60 59
PORT ... 10-15 60-61
VIRGO ... 4-6 72
WHIRLIN' DISC (101 "Dear Lord") ... 75-125 56
WHIRLIN' DISC (105 "Picture of Love") 50-100 57
Member: Daniel Hicks.

CONTINENTALS
Singles: 78 rpm
KEY ... 10-15 56
Singles: 7-inch
HUNTER (3503 "It Doesn't Matter") ... 400-500 60
KEY (517 "Take a Gamble on Me") ... 30-40 56

CONTINENTALS
Singles: 78 rpm
RAMA (190 "You're an Angel") ... 200-300 56
(Blue label.)
RAMA (190 "You're an Angel") ... 25-35 56
(Red label.)
Singles: 7-inch
OWL (331 "Goodbye") ... 4-6 74
RAMA (190 "You're an Angel") ... 750-1000 56
(Blue label.)
RAMA (190 "You're an Angel") ... 50-75 56
(Red label.)
ROULETTE ... 4-6 70
Members: James Gooden; Sidney Gray; Bill Davis; Demetrius Cleare.

CONTINENTALS
Singles: 7-inch
RIVIERA (101 "Music Shop Hop") ... 15-25 58

CONTINENTALS
Singles: 7-inch
ERA (3003 "Cool Penguin") ... 10-15 59
PENGUIN (1002 "Cool Penguin") ... 15-25 59

CONTINENTALS
Singles: 7-inch
RED TOP (121 "Sad Love Affair") ... 40-50 59

CONTINENTALS
Singles: 7-inch
BOLO (720 "I'm Coming Home") ... 15-25 60
Member: Don Stevenson.

CONTINENTALS
Singles: 7-inch
CUCA (1063 "Tic-Toc") ... 15-25 61
Members: Vince Megna; Rusty Harding; Roger Roessler; Ron Evans; Dennis Madigan; Lee Breest.
Also see BONNEVILLES

CONTINENTALS
Singles: 7-inch
UNION (505 "Big Bad Ho-Dad") ... 10-20 62
Also see BYRON, Lord Douglas / Continentals

CONTINENTALS
Singles: 7-inch
M (500 "Saxy Twist") ... 100-150 62

CONTINENTALS
Singles: 7-inch
A-OK (1025 "Take Me") ... 10-20 66
GAYLO (124 "I'm Gone") ... 20-30 '60s

CONTINENTALS
Singles: 7-inch
YALE (1614 "High School Days Are Almost Over") ... 30-40

CONTINENTALS & COUNTS OF RHYTHM
Singles: 7-inch
(CC-2 "Don't Leave Me") ... 1500-2000 58
(No actual label name shown although "Muncie" has been mentioned. 100 made.)
Members: (Continentals – vocals) Theotis Barnes; Phil Butts; Ralph Kersey; Elsworth Williams; Ray Jimerson. (Counts of Rhythm) Roy Alexander; Gerald (Bud) Cole; James Cox.

CONTINETTES
Singles: 7-inch
RICHIE (452 "Billy the Kidder") ... 30-40 61
RICHIE (4300 "Billy the Kidder") ... 15-25 63

CONTOURS
Singles: 7-inch
FINCH (360 "The Mission") ... 50-75 58

CONTOURS P&R/R&B '62
(With Jack Surrell)
Singles: 12-inch
MOTOWN ... 4-8 88
Singles: 7-inch
GORDY ... 8-15 62-67
HOB (116 "I'm So Glad") ... 75-100 61
MOTOWN (400 series) ... 3-5 82-88
MOTOWN (1008 "Whole Lotta Woman") ... 125-150 61
MOTOWN (1012 "Funny") ... 300-400 61
TAMLA (7012 "Shake Sherry") ... 75-125 62
(Tamla label with Gordy selection number.)
ROCKET ... 3-5 80
Picture Sleeves
GORDY (7005 "Do You Love Me") ... 5-10 '90s
MOTOWN ... 3-5 88
EPs: 7-inch
MOTOWN (2002 "The Contours") ... 15-25 '60s
LPs: 10/12-inch
GORDY (901 "Do You Love Me") ... 200-300 62
MOTOWN ... 5-10 82
Members: Dennis Edwards; Bill Gordon; Billy Hoggs; Sylvester Potts; Joe Billingslea; Huey Davis; Joe Stubbs; Hubert Johnson.
Also see HANKS, Mike
Also see HI-FIDELITIES
Also see ORIGINALS
Also see STUBBS, Joe

CONTRAILS
("Vocal By Dick and Jack")
Singles: 7-inch
DIAMOND (213 "Someone") ... 5-10 66
REUBEN (711 "Someone") ... 40-50 64

CONTRASTS
("Vocalist: Colin Hopkins")
Singles: 7-inch
RHAPSODY (71965 "Steady") ... 100-150 60
Member: Colin Hopkins.

CONVERTERS
Singles: 7-inch
STAR HI (10560 "Dave's Place") ... 10-15 60

CONVERTS
Singles: 7-inch
RAMPRO (117 "Don't Leave Me") ... 15-25 66

CONVINCERS
(With Al Clark's Band)
Singles: 7-inch
MOVIN (100 "Rejected Love") ... 400-500 62
Also see APPEGGIOS
Also see ARROWS

CONVY, Bert
(With the Cheers)
Singles: 78 rpm
CAPITOL ... 10-20 56
MERCURY ... 10-20 57
Singles: 7-inch
CAPITOL (3409 "Heaven On Earth") ... 20-30 56
CONTENDER ... 10-20 58
ERA (112 "Just Give Me a Chance") ... 4-6 70
MERCURY (71100 "Two Hearts") ... 10-20 57
MOONGLOW (212 "Nee No Nah Nee") ... 10-15 62
STORM ... 5-10
Also see CHEERS

CONWAY, Connie
Singles: 7-inch
DOT (15590 "I Sure Need You") ... 15-25 57
JAMIE (1113 "Can It Be") ... 10-20 58
JAMIE (1124 "Call It a Stormy Monday") . 10-20 59
LPs: 10/12-inch
JAMIE (3005 "33 Minutes and 20 Seconds with Connie Conway") ... 20-30 59

CONWAY, Dave C&W '77
Singles: 7-inch
TEDDY BEAR (17505 "Jingle Bears") ... 20-30 85
(Picture disc.)
TRUE (105 "If You're Gonna Love") ... 4-6 77

CONWAY, Inez
Singles: 7-inch
EMERSON (2106 "The Twirl") ... 15-25

CONWAY, Russ
(With Michael Collins & His Concert Orchestra)
Singles: 7-inch
CUB (9038 "Song from *North By Northwest*") ... 8-12 59
POLARIS (200 "I'm Still Missing You") ... 75-100

CONWELL, James
Singles: 7-inch
4J (511 "The Trouble with Girls") ... 10-15 64
MIRWOOD (5530 "Second Hand Happiness") ... 5-10 67

COODER, Ry LP '72
Singles: 7-inch
MUSICOR (1148 "Life Game") ... 10-20 66
REPRISE ... 5-10 69-72
W.B. ... 4-6 77-82
LPs: 10/12-inch
MFSL/W.B. (085 "Jazz") ... 300-400 82
REPRISE ... 10-15 72-76
W.B. ... 5-10 77-87
Session: Van Dyke Parks.
Also see CAPTAIN BEEFHEART
Also see CEYLEIB PEOPLE
Also see LITTLE FEAT
Also see LONGBRANCH PENNYWHISTLE
Also see PARKS, Van Dyke
Also see RISING SONS

COOK, Bill, & Marshalls
Singles: 78 rpm
SAVOY (828 "Just Because") ... 50-75 51
Also see MARSHALL BROTHERS

COOK, Billy
Singles: 7-inch
LAWN (204 "Mystery Girl") ... 10-15 63

COOK, Ira, & Mellowmen
Singles: 7-inch
IMPERIAL (5627 "What Is a Girl") ... 10-15 59

COOK, J. Lawrence
LPs: 10/12-inch
MERCURY (20407 "Piano Rock 'N Roll") ... 20-30 59
(Monaural.)
MERCURY (60083 "Piano Rock 'N Roll") ... 30-50 59
(Stereo.)

COOK, Jack
Singles: 7-inch
RAMCO (1739 "Run Boy, Run Boy") ... 10-20 62
RAMCO (1771 "I Stepped In") ... 10-15 62
RUBY (1 "My Evil Mind") ... 8-12 63

COOK, Jerry
Singles: 7-inch
APPLAUSE (1248 "I'm Gonna Lock My Heart") ... 8-12 68
CAPITOL (5981 "Take What I've Got") ... 20-30 67

COOK, Jimmy
("Of Don, Dick 'N Jimmy")
Singles: 78 rpm
CROWN (139 "Melody of Love") ... 8-12 55
CROWN (160 "Lazy River") ... 8-12 56
Singles: 7-inch
CROWN (139 "Melody of Love") ... 15-25 55
CROWN (160 "Lazy River") ... 15-25 56
JOPZ (201 "Two Black Eyes") ... 75-100 56
Also see DON, DICK 'N JIMMY

COOK, Johnnie
Singles: 7-inch
FIDELITY (4052 "Blues Comin' On") ... 10-15 62

COOK, Johnny
Singles: 7-inch
LAMP (2006 "It's All in Your Mind") ... 30-40 57
TUNE (235 "Don't Knock No More") ... 50-75

COOK, Ken
(With Roy Orbison)
Singles: 7-inch
PHILLIPS INT'L (3534 "I Was a Fool") ... 50-75 58
Also see ORBISON, Roy

COOK, Little Becky
(With the Mad Lads; with Rag Mops; "Music By The Intruders")
Singles: 7-inch
CBM (314 "The Itchy Scratchy") ... 40-50 61
CBM (504 "Let's Dance") ... 30-40 61

COOK, Little Joe
(Joe Cook)
Singles: 7-inch
FURY (1060 "These Lonely Tears") ... 15-25 62
GAMBLE (4011 "America, Don't Turn Your Back") ... 4-6 70
HOT (1003 "I'm Falling in Love") ... 50-100
J.J. ... 10-20
JOYETTE (101 "Just in Time") ... 10-20 59
LOMA (2026 "Don't Have Feelings") ... 8-12 66
LOVE TOWN (770 "Please Don't Go") ... 15-25 '60s
OKEH (7211 "Meet Me Down in Soulville") ... 8-12 64
TOP-TOP (1001 "Please Don't Go") ... 40-50 '60s
(Same sides as Love Town 770. We're not sure which came first.)
20TH FOX (420 "I'll Never Go to a Party Again") ... 8-12 63
Also see DE-LOS
Also see IVY TONES
Also see LITTLE JOE & THRILLERS

COOK, Roland
Singles: 7-inch
ACE (525 "I've Got a Girl") ... 15-25 57
Also see COOKIE

COOK, Ronnie
(With the Gaylords; with Gaylads; Ronnie Cooke)
Singles: 7-inch
ASTRA (1013 "The Scotch") ... 8-12 65
AUDAN (122 "The Scotch") ... 10-20 62
DORE (565 "My Angel") ... 10-15 60
DORE (600 "If I May") ... 10-15 61
DORE (721 "Only the Lonely") ... 10-15 64
TRI DISC (105 "Such a Night") ... 10-15 62
(Same selection number also used for an Olympics release.)

COOK, Vic, & Esquires
Singles: 7-inch
TYME (106 "Teenage Heartbreak") ... 50-75

COOK BROTHERS
Singles: 7-inch
ARCADE (158 "Always Together") ... 10-20 60
EMPEROR (300 "Jingle Jingle") ... 10-20 59
Session: Bill Haley's Comets.
Also see HALEY, Bill

COOK E. JARR
(With His Crums)
Singles: 7-inch
EPIC (10735 "Who Wears Hot Pants") ... 4-8 71

RCA (0119 "Pledging My Love")...5-10 69
RCA (0182 "Reason to Believe")...5-10 69
RCA (9708 "Darling Be Home Soon")...5-10 69
REAL GEORGE (1001 "Now That You're Mine")...5-10
ROULETTE (7170 "Ain't No Use")...4-6 75

LPs: 10/12-inch

RCA (4159 "Pledging My Love")...10-15 69

COOKE, Dale
(Sam Cooke)

Singles: 78 rpm

SPECIALTY (596 "Lovable")...15-25 57

Singles: 7-inch

SPECIALTY (596 "Lovable")...25-35 57
Also see COOKE, Sam

COOKE, James Curley

LPs: 10/12-inch

FIRST AMERICAN (7767 "Curley Cooke")...20-30 80

COOKE, Joe

Singles: 78 rpm

APOLLO (1202 "Dish Rag")...5-10 55

Singles: 7-inch

APOLLO (1202 "Dish Rag")...10-20 55

COOKE, L.C.
(L.C. Cook)

Singles: 78 rpm

CHECKER (903 "Do You Remember")...50-75 58

Singles: 7-inch

BLUE ROCK (4030 "Wonderful World")...8-12 65
CHECKER (903 "Do You Remember")...10-20 58
CHECKER (925 "Please Think of Me")...10-20 59
CHECKER (935 "If I Could Only Hear")...10-20 59
DESTINATION (601 "I'll Wait for You")...8-12 65
SAR (109 "Teach Me")...10-15 60
SAR (112 "Lover")...10-15 61
SAR (134 thru 148)...8-12 62-64
WAND (1171 "Half a Man")...5-10 68

LPs: 10/12-inch

BLUE ROCK (24001 "L.C. Cooke")...15-25 65
(Monaural.)
BLUE ROCK (64001 "L.C. Cooke")...20-30 65
(Stereo.)

COOKE, Pete
(With the Baby Dolls)

Singles: 7-inch

DIMENSION (1037 "Little Darlin' ")...10-15 64
LOGO (503 "Take It and Git")...8-12 '60s

COOKE, Sam — P&R/R&B '57
(With the Soul Stirrers; with Bumps Blackwell Orchestra; with René Hall Orchestra; with Don Ralke Orchestra)

Singles: 78 rpm

KEEN (2005 "Stealing Kisses")...50-75 58
KEEN (2006 "Win Your Love for Me")...50-75 58
KEEN (2008 "Love You Most of All")...50-75 58
KEEN (2018 "Everybody Likes to Cha Cha Cha")...50-100 59
KEEN (2022 "Only Sixteen")...75-125 59
KEEN (4002 "For Sentimental Reasons")...50-75 58
KEEN (4009 "Lonely Island")...50-75 58
KEEN (4013 "You Send Me")...40-60 57
SPECIALTY (619 "I'll Come Running Back to You")...30-50 57
SPECIALTY (627 "I Don't Want to Cry")...35-55 58

Singles: 7-inch

CHERIE...4-6 71
COLLECTABLES...3-5 81
KEEN (2005 "Stealing Kisses")...20-30 58
KEEN (2006 "Win Your Love for Me")...15-25 58
KEEN (5-2006 "Win Your Love for Me") 50-100 58
(Stereo. Blue vinyl.)
KEEN (2008 "Love You Most of All")...20-30 58
KEEN (2018 "Everybody Likes to Cha Cha Cha")...15-25 59
(Monaural.)
KEEN (5-2018 "Everybody Likes to Cha Cha Cha")...35-50 59
(Stereo.)
KEEN (2022 "Only Sixteen")...15-25 59
(Monaural.)
KEEN (5-2022 "Only Sixteen")...35-50 59
(Stereo.)
KEEN (2101 "Summertime")...15-25 59
KEEN (2105 "There I've Said It Again")...15-25 59
KEEN (2111 "No One")...15-25 60
KEEN (2112 "Wonderful World")...15-25 60
KEEN (2117 "With You")...15-25 60
KEEN (2118 "So Glamorous")...15-25 60
KEEN (2122 "Mary, Mary Lou")...15-25 61
KEEN (4002 "For Sentimental Reasons")...20-30 57
KEEN (4009 "Lonely Island")...20-30 58
KEEN (4013 "You Send Me")...25-35 57
Note: Some Keen numbers in the 2000 and 4000 series have either a "3" or an "8" preceding the 2000 or 4000 series number.
RCA (47-7701 "Teenage Sonata")...10-20 60
(Monaural.)
RCA (61-7701 "Teenage Sonata")...35-50 60
(Stereo.)
RCA (47-7730 "I Belong to Your Heart")..15-25 60
(Monaural.)
RCA (61-7730 "I Belong to Your Heart")..40-60 60
(Stereo.)
RCA (47-7783 "Chain Gang")...10-20 60
(Monaural.)
RCA (61-7783 "Chain Gang")...35-50 60
(Stereo.)
RCA (47-7816 "Sad Mood")...10-20 60
(Monaural.)
RCA (61-7816 "Sad Mood")...35-50 60
(Stereo.)
RCA (37-7853 "That's It – I Quit, I'm Movin' On")...35-50 61
(Compact 33 Single.)
RCA (47-7853 "That's It – I Quit, I'm Movin' On")...10-20 61
RCA (37-7883 "Cupid")...30-40 61
(Compact 33 Single.)
RCA (47-7883 "Cupid")...10-15 61
RCA (37-7927 "Feel It")...30-40 61
(Compact 33 Single.)
RCA (47-7927 "Feel It")...10-15 61
RCA (37-7983 "Twistin' the Night Away").30-40 62
(Compact 33 Single.)
RCA (47-7983 "Twistin' the Night Away")...6-12 62
RCA (8036 thru 8934)...5-15 62-66
RCA GOLD STANDARD...4-8
(With "447" prefix.)
SAR (122 "Just for You")...10-20 61
SPECIALTY (SPBX series)...15-20 87
(Boxed set of six colored vinyl singles.)
SPECIALTY (619 "I'll Come Running Back to You")...15-25 57
SPECIALTY (627 "I Don't Want to Cry")...15-25 58
SPECIALTY (667 "Happy in Love")...15-25 59
SPECIALTY (900 series)...4-6 70-72

Picture Sleeves

KEEN (4013 "You Send Me")...5-10 '90s
RCA (7730 "I Belong to Your Heart")...20-30 60
RCA (7783 "Chain Gang")...10-20 60
RCA (7883 "Cupid")...10-20 60
RCA (7927 "Feel It")...10-20 61
RCA (8088 "Nothing Can Change This Love")...10-20 62
RCA (8129 "Send Me Some Lovin' ")...10-20 63
RCA (8164 "Another Saturday Night")...10-20 63
RCA (8215 "Frankie & Johnny")...10-20 63
RCA (8247 "Little Red Rooster")...10-20 63
RCA (8631 "Sugar Dumpling")...10-20 65

EPs: 7-inch

KEEN (2001/2002/2003 "Songs by Sam Cooke")...50-75 57
(Price is for any of three volumes.)
KEEN (2012/2013/2014 "Tribute to the Lady")...40-60 59
(Price is for any of three volumes.)
KEEN (2006 "Encore")...25-50 58
KEEN (2008 "Encore, Vol. 2")...25-50 58
KEEN (2010 "Houseboat")...25-50 58
RCA (126 "Sam Cooke Sings")...25-50 61
(Compact 33.)
RCA (2555 "Sam Cooke")...15-25
(Stereo compact 33.)
RCA (3373 "Sam Cooke")...15-25 64
(Juke box issue only. Includes title strips.)
RCA (4375 "Another Saturday Night")...15-25 63

LPs: 10/12-inch

CAMDEN (0445 "You Send Me")...5-10 74
CAMDEN (2264 "One & Only")...8-12 68
CAMDEN (2433 "Sam Cooke")...8-12 70
CAMDEN (2610 "Unforgettable")...8-12 73
CANDLELITE...15-20 74
(Mail-order offer.)
CHERIE (1001 "Right On")...8-10 71
FAMOUS (502 "Sam's Songs")...10-20 69
FAMOUS (505 "Only Sixteen")...10-20 69
FAMOUS (508 "So Wonderful")...10-20 69
FAMOUS (509 "You Send Me")...10-20 69
FAMOUS (512 "Cha-Cha-Cha")...10-20 69
KEEN (2001 "Sam Cooke")...60-100 58
KEEN (2003 "Encore")...50-75 58
KEEN (2004 "Tribute to the Lady")...30-50 59
KEEN (86101 "Hit Kit")...100-200 59
KEEN (86103 "I Thank God")...100-200 60
KEEN (86106 "The Wonderful World of Sam Cooke")...50-100 60
PHOENIX 10...5-10 81
PICKWICK...5-10 76
RCA (2221 "Cooke's Tour")...20-30 60
RCA (2236 "Hits of the '50s")...20-30 60
RCA (2293 "Sam Cooke")...15-25 61
RCA (2392 "My Kind of Blues")...15-25 61
RCA (2555 "Twistin' the Night Away")...15-25 62
RCA (2625 "Best of Sam Cooke")...15-25 62
RCA (2658 "At the Copa")...5-10 78
RCA (2673 "Mr. Soul")...15-25 63
RCA (2709 "Night Beat")...15-25 63
RCA (2899 "Ain't That Good News")...15-25 64
RCA (2970 "At the Copa")...15-25 64
RCA (3367 "Shake")...15-25 65
RCA (3373 "Best of Sam Cooke, Vol. 2").15-25 65
RCA (3435 "Try a Little Love")...15-20 65
RCA (3466 "Best of Sam Cooke")...8-10 79
RCA (3517 "Unforgettable")...15-20 66
RCA (3863 "Best of Sam Cooke")...5-8 81
RCA (3991 "The Man Who Invented Soul")...10-20 68
RCA (5000 series)...5-10 78-85
(With "AFL1," "ANL1" or "AYL1" prefix.)
RCA (7000 series)...8-12 86
SOUFFLE...5-10
SPECIALTY (2119 "Two Sides of Sam Cooke")...6-12 69
TRIP (8030 "Golden Sounds")...8-10 72
UPFRONT (160 "The Billie Holiday Story")...8-10 73
Also see ANKA, Paul / Sam Cooke / Neil Sedaka
Also see BLACKWELL, Bumps, Orchestra
Also see CHARLES, Ray / Little Richard / Sam Cooke
Also see COOKE, Dale
Also see HALL, René
Also see RALKE, Don
Also see RAWLS, Lou
Also see SEDAKA, Neil / Ann-Margret / Browns / Sam Cooke
Also see SOUL STIRRERS

COOKE, Sam / Rod Lauren / Neil Sedaka / Browns

EPs: 7-inch

RCA (33-99 "Compact 33 Double")...15-20 60
(Has the same four songs on each side, mono on one side, stereo on the reverse.)
Also see BROWNS
Also see LAUREN, Rod
Also see SEDAKA, Neil

COOKE, Sam / Johnny Morisette

Singles: 7-inch

CAPITOL (6069 "You Send Me"/"Never")..5-10 65
("Starline" series.)
Also see MORISETTE, Johnnie

COOKE, Sam / Lloyd Price / Larry Williams / Little Richard

LPs: 10/12-inch

SPECIALTY (2112 "Our Significant Hits")...35-45 60
(Black and gold label.)
Also see COOKE, Sam
Also see LITTLE RICHARD
Also see PRICE, Lloyd
Also see WILLIAMS, Larry

COOKE, Sarah

Singles: 7-inch

BIG TOP (519 "Please Don't Go")...30-50 64

COOKER, John Lee
(John Lee Hooker)

Singles: 7-inch

KING (4504 "Moaning Blues")...50-100 52
Also see HOOKER, John Lee

COOKIE
(Roland Cook)

Singles: 7-inch

RCA (7305 "That's What You Do to Me").15-25 58
Also see COOK, Roland
Also see STEVE / Cookie

COOKIE & CHARLIE

Singles: 7-inch

CAL (1001/1002 "Dede-Dum"/"Bye Bye Baby, Don't Cry")...40-60 57
JEFF (1212 "Let's Go Rock & Roll")...15-20

COOKIE & HIS CUPCAKES — P&R '59
(Cookie & His Berry Cups)

Singles: 7-inch

CHESS (1848 "Got You on My Mind")...10-15 63
GOLDBAND (1260 "Matilda Has Finally Come Home")...10-15 '60s
JUDD (1002 "Mathilda")...20-30 58
(Incorrect title spelling.)
JUDD (1002 "Matilda")...15-25 58
(Correct title spelling.)
JUDD (1015 "Until Then")...15-25 59
KHOURY'S (703 "Matilda")...30-40 58
LYRIC (1003 thru 1020, except 1004)...10-15 63-65
LYRIC (1004 "Got You on My Mind")...15-20 63
(First issue.)
MERCURY (71748 "Matilda Has Finally Come Back")...8-10 61
PAULA (221 "Matilda")...5-10 65
PAULA (230 "Belinda")...10-15 65
PAULA (312 "Breaking Up Is Hard to Do") 5-10 68
Members: Terry "Cookie" Clinton; Lil' Alfred; Shelton Dunaway.
Also see BOOGIE RAMBLERS
Also see CLINTON, Terry, & Berry Cups

COOKIE & HIS CUPCAKES / Little Alfred

Singles: 7-inch

LYRIC (1016 "Even Though")...8-12 64
Also see COOKIE & HIS CUPCAKES
Also see LITTLE ALFRED

COOKIES — R&B '56

Singles: 78 rpm

ATLANTIC...10-25 55-57
JOSIE (822 "King of Hearts")...15-25 57
LAMP (8008 "Don't Let Go")...10-20 54

Singles: 7-inch

ATLANTIC (1061 "Precious Love")...25-35 55
ATLANTIC (1084 "In Paradise")...20-30 56
ATLANTIC (1110 "My Lover")...15-25 56
ATLANTIC (2079 "In Paradise")...8-12 60
JOSIE (822 "King of Hearts")...15-25 57
LAMP (8008 "Don't Let Go")...15-25 54
Members: Earl-Jean McCree; Margie Hendrix; Pat Lyles.
Also see CHARLES, Ray
Also see COOKIES (Group that follows)
Also see DILLARD, Varetta
Also see TORME, Mel
Also see WILLIS, Chuck

COOKIES — P&R/R&B '62

Singles: 7-inch

ABC...4-6 74
DIMENSION (1002 thru 1020)...10-20 62-63
DIMENSION (1032 "The Old Crowd")...15-25 64
ERIC...4-6 73
MCA...3-5 83
Members: Earl-Jean McCree; Margaret Ross; Dorothy Jones.
Also see BOYD, Idalia
Also see CINDERELLAS
Also see EARL-JEAN
Also see SEDAKA, Neil

COOKIES / Little Eva / Carole King

LPs: 10/12-inch

DIMENSION (6001 "The Dimension Dolls, Vol. 1")...150-250 63
(12 tracks.)
EMUS (12044 "Carole King Plus")...10-15 79
(10-track repackage of *Dimension Dolls*.)
Also see COOKIES
Also see KING, Carole
Also see LITTLE EVA

COOKS, Donald

Singles: 78 rpm

JADE (202 "Trouble-Making Woman")...15-25 51
Also see COOKS, Silver, & Gondoliers

COOKS, Silver, & Gondoliers
(Donald Cooks)

Singles: 78 rpm

PEACOCK (1510 "Mr. Ticket Man")...50-75 49

Also see COOKS, Donald

COOL, Calvin
(With the Surf-Knobs; Shorty Rogers)
Singles: 7-inch
CHARTER (7 "Beach Bash")................... 15-25 63
LPs: 10/12-inch
CHARTER (CL-103 "Surfer's Beat")........ 50-75 63
(Monaural.)
CHARTER (CLS-103 "Surfer's Beat").... 75-125 63
(Stereo.)
Also see BROWN, Boots
Also see ROGERS, Shorty

COOL, Harry / Frances Langford
Singles: 78 rpm
MERCURY/SAV-WAY (3066 "Ragtime Cowboy Joe").. 100-150 47
(Picture disc. Promotional issue only.)

COOL, Oliver
Singles: 7-inch
BRAND (6789 "Nobody Can Like Joanne").. 100-150 62
ROULETTE (4292 "Oliver Cool")............ 10-20 60
ROULETTE (4330 "Give Me the Summertime")....................................... 10-20 61

COOL BREEZE & HIS BAND WITH THE LITTLE COOL BREEZES
(With Jimmy Petty, Rupert Jones & the Senders)
Singles: 7-inch
EBONY (1014 "Won't You Come In").. 1000-2000 59

COOL SOUNDS
Singles: 7-inch
PULSAR (2421 "Comin' Home")............ 35-45 69
W.B. (7538 "I'll Take You Back")............ 10-20 71
W.B. (7575 "Love Like Ours Could Last a Million Years Or More").. 15-25 71
W.B. (7615 "Free")................................. 15-25 71

COOL TONES
Singles: 7-inch
RADIANT (1510 "Dixie Blues")...................5-10 62
WARWICK (505 "Ginchy")..................... 10-15 59
Also see COOLTONES (one word)

COOLBREEZERS
(With the Don Costa Orchestra; with Al White & Band)
Singles: 78 rpm
ABC-PAR... 50-75 57
Singles: 7-inch
ABC-PAR (9865 "My Brother")............... 75-100 57
BALE (100 "Eda Weda Bug")................ 40-60 58
BALE (102 "Hello Mr. New Year")....... 200-300 58
Also see COSTA, Don, Orchestra

COOLEY, Eddie P&R '56
(With the Dimples)
Singles: 78 rpm
ROYAL ROOST................................ 20-40 56-57
Singles: 7-inch
ABC..4-6 73
ROULETTE (4272 "Priscilla"/"A Spark Met a Flame")...5-10 60
ROYAL ROOST (621 "Priscilla")............ 10-15 56
ROYAL ROOST (626 "A Spark Met a Flame").. 15-20 57
ROYAL ROOST (628 "Hey You!")........... 15-20 57
TRIUMPH (609 "Be My Steady")...............8-12 59

COOLEY, Jack
Singles: 7-inch
STATES (125 "Could, But I Ain't")........... 50-75 53
(Colored vinyl.)
Also see AMMONS, Albert / Jack Cooley

COOLEY, Spade, & His Orchestra C&W '45
(With the Buckle Busters; with Tex Williams)
Singles: 78 rpm
BLUEBIRD..5-10
COLUMBIA.......................................5-10 46-47
DECCA..4-8 51-55
OKEH..5-10 45-46
RCA..5-10 47-48
Singles: 7-inch
DECCA..8-10 51-52
RCA (48-0027 thru 48-0157)............. 10-20 49-50
(Green vinyl.)
EPs: 7-inch
DECCA (2225/2226 "Dance-O Rama")... 10-20 55
(Price is for either volume.)
LPs: 10/12-inch
CLUB of SPADE......................................8-15
COLUMBIA (9007 "Sagebrush Swing")....40-80 '50s
(10-inch LP.)
COLUMBIA (37000 series)........................5-10
DECCA (5563 "Dance-O-Rama")............30-50 55
RAYNOTE (RN-5007 "Fidoodlin'")..........20-30 59
(Monaural.)
RAYNOTE (RS-5007 "Fidoodlin'")..........30-40 59
(Stereo.)
ROULETTE (R-25145 "Fidoodlin'")..........15-20 61
(Monaural.)
ROULETTE (S-25145 "Fidoodlin'")..........20-25 61
(Stereo.)
Also see CRUDUP, Big Boy / Spade Cooley / Dick Leibert / Saul Meisels / Al Goodman & His Orchestra
Also see ROGERS, Roy, with Spade Cooley's Buckle Busters

COOLTONES
Singles: 7-inch
DICE (750 "Cry All Night").........................40-60
Also see COOL TONES (two words)

COOPER, Al, & Savoy Sultans
LPs: 10/12-inch
DECCA (4444 "Jumpin' at the Savoy").....15-25 64

COOPER, Alice LP '69
(Alice Cooper Group)
Promotional Singles: 12-inch
EPIC (1347 "I Got a Line on You")..............5-8
EPIC (1663 "Poison")..................................5-8 89
EPIC (1686 "Trash")....................................5-8 89
EPIC (1890 "I'm Your Gun")..........................5-8 89
MCA (17177 "He's Back")..............................5-8 86
MCA (17205 "Give It Up")..............................5-8 86
W.B. (864 "Clones")................................10-15 80
W.B. (1059 "I Like Girls")...........................5-8
Singles: 7-inch
ATLANTIC...4-6 75
EPIC...3-5 89-90
MCA...3-5 86-87
STRAIGHT (101 "Reflected")..................15-25 69
STRAIGHT (7398 "Shoe Salesman").......15-20 70
W.B...3-6 70-82
Promotional Singles
ATLANTIC..5-10 75
MCA..3-6 86-87
W.B..8-12 70-80
Picture Sleeves
MCA..3-5 87
W.B...4-8 72-80
EPs: 7-inch
W.B..15-25 73
(Juke box issues only.)
LPs: 10/12-inch
ATLANTIC..5-10 75-78
EPIC...5-8 89
MFSL (063 "Welcome to My Nightmare")..50-75 82
MCA...5-10 86-87
STRAIGHT (1051 "Pretties for You").......30-40 69
(Cover has a drawing of a woman raising her dress, with a yellow sticker covering her crotch area. Price is for cover with sticker still intact.)
STRAIGHT (1051 "Pretties for You").......20-30 69
(Cover shows the woman with the sticker removed and panties showing.)
W.B. (Except 1883, 2567 & 2623)..............8-12 73-84
W.B. (1883 "Love It to Death")................25-30 71
(Black cover has Cooper's right thumb showing through his wrap. Does NOT have white block reading "Including Their Hit *I'm Eighteen.*")
W.B. (1883 "Love It to Death")................15-20 71
(Black cover has Cooper's right thumb showing through his wrap. Has white block reading "Including Their Hit *I'm Eighteen.*" Also includes issue with huge white stripes at top and bottom of cover.)
W.B. (1883 "Love It to Death")..................5-10 71
(Black cover does NOT have Cooper's right thumb showing through his wrap. Has the white block reading "Including Their Hit *I'm Eighteen.*")
W.B. (2567 "Killer")...............................15-18 71
(With poster and 1972 calendar.)
W.B. (2567 "Killer")..................................5-10 72
(Without poster and calendar.)
W.B. (2623 "School's Out")......................30-40 72
(With panties attached. Panties came in four different colors: pink, white, yellow, and blue. Back cover does not list titles.)
W.B. (2623 "School's Out").......................15-20 72
(With panties attached. Back cover lists titles.)
W.B. (2623 "School's Out")........................5-10 72
(With no paper panties. Back cover lists titles.)
W.B. (2685 "Billion Dollar Babies")............5-10 73
W.B. (BS4-2685 "Billion Dollar Babies")...20-25 73
(Quadraphonic.)
W.B. (2748 "Muscle of Love")......................5-10 73
W.B. (BBS4-2748 "Muscle of Love")........20-25 73
(Quadraphonic.)
W.B. (2803 thru 3581).............................5-10 74-81
W.B./STRAIGHT (1051 "Pretties for You")..15-18 69
W.B./STRAIGHT (1845 "Easy Action").....30-35 70
(With the name "Alice Cooper" in black letters on front cover.)
W.B./STRAIGHT (1845 "Easy Action").......5-10 70
(With "Alice Cooper" in white letters on front.)
Promotional LPs
CHELSEA PROD ("Allison's Tea House")..25-30 74
STRAIGHT (1051 "Pretties for You").........45-55 69
(Cover has drawing of a woman raising her dress, with a yellow sticker covering her crotch area. Price is for cover with sticker still intact.)
STRAIGHT (1051 "Pretties for You")........30-40 69
(Cover shows the woman with the sticker removed and panties showing.)
STRAIGHT (1845 "Easy Action")..............25-30 70
STRAIGHT (1883 "Love It to Death")........20-25 71
W.B..20-40 71-78
(Includes all white label promo labels.)
W.B./STRAIGHT ("Pretties for You")........25-30 69
Members: Alice Cooper; Dennis Dunaway; Ken K. Mary; Glen Buxton; Neal Smith; Michael Bruce; Kane Roberts.
Also see NAZZ
Also see SPIDERS

COOPER, Babs
Singles: 7-inch
INDIGO (144 "Honest I Do")....................10-20 62

COOPER, Christine
Singles: 7-inch
PARKWAY (122 "Good Looks")...............15-25 66
PARKWAY (971 "S.O.S.")........................20-30 66
PARKWAY (983 "Heartaches Away My Boy")...30-50 66

COOPER, Dave, & Continentals
Singles: 7-inch
WESTCO (7 "Church Key")......................15-20 '60s

COOPER, Dolly
(With the Four Buddies)
Singles: 78 rpm
DOT..8-12 56
EBB..8-12 57
MODERN...10-15 55
SAVOY...10-15 53-54
Singles: 7-inch
DOT (15495 "I'm Looking Through Your Window")..10-15 56
DOT (15535 "Tell Me, Tell Me")..............10-15 56
EBB (109 "Wild Love")............................15-25 57
MODERN (965 "My Man")........................15-25 55
MODERN (977 "Teenage Prayer")............15-25 55
MODERN (986 "Teenage Wedding Bells")...15-25 55
SAVOY (891 "I'd Climb the Highest Mountain")..50-75 53
SAVOY (1121 "Love Can't Be Blind").......30-40 54
Also see FOUR BUDDIES
Also see WANDERERS

COOPER, Ed
Singles: 7-inch
NIMROD (904 "Just Like a Hero")............15-25

COOPER, Gary
Singles: 7-inch
QUALITY (1275 "Come On Pretty Baby")..50-75

COOPER, Gene
Singles: 7-inch
HI-Q (5037 "Kind of Man I Am")...............10-15 64

COOPER, Glenn
Singles: 7-inch
MECCA (1113 "Sugar Mama")............200-300

COOPER, Herb
Singles: 78 rpm
OKEH (7037 "Ready, Miss Betty")...........10-15 54
Singles: 7-inch
GLORY (274 "Corey Corey").......................8-12 58
OKEH (7037 "Ready, Miss Betty")..........20-30 54
Also see SEARS, Al

COOPER, Jackie
Singles: 7-inch
DOT (15793 "Midnight Train")..................15-25 58
DOT (15834 "A Doodlin' Song")..............15-25 58

COOPER, John Lee
Singles: 78 rpm
KING (4504 "Stomp Boogie")...................10-15 52
Singles: 7-inch
KING (4504 "Stomp Boogie")...................20-30 52

COOPER, Johnnie
Singles: 7-inch
RU LU (6754 "My Heart Is Chained").......50-75 58

COOPER, Johnny
Singles: 7-inch
BARRINGTON..5-10
CHALLENGE (59356 "Must You Be So Good")...5-10 67
ERMINE (37 thru 42)..........................10-15 61-62
ERMINE (44 "Oreo")...............................40-60 63
PLANTATION (41 "Don't Let It Trouble Your Mind")...4-6 69
TODDLIN' TOWN (8200 "Her Mother Read Her Diary")..5-10 65

COOPER, Les, & Soul Rockers P&R/R&B '62
Singles: 7-inch
ABC...4-6 73
ARRAWAK (1008 "I Can Do the Soul Jerk")..5-10 65
ATCO (6644 "Gonna Have a Lotta Fun").....4-8 69
DIMENSION (1023 "Motor City")..............10-15 64
ENJOY (2024 "Let's Do the Boston Monkey")...5-10 65
EVERLAST (5016 thru 5023)..............10-15 62-63
FURY (5054 "The Thang")..........................5-10 63
SAMAR (114 "Wahoo")..............................5-10 66
LPs: 10/12-inch
EVERLAST (202 "Wiggle Wobble")..........50-75 63
Members: Les Cooper; Joe Grier.
Also see CHARTS
Also see EMPIRES
Also see WHIRLERS

COOPER, Marty
(Marty Cooper Clan)
Singles: 7-inch
BARNABY...4-8 72-73
CAPITOL (5832 "Dearborn, Michigan").......5-10 67
CREST (1043 "You Bet Your Little Life").15-25 57
DOPPLER (7501 "American Farming Man")..5-10 '60s
(Asgrow Seed Special products issue.)
HOLIDAY (1212 "Gonna Move Away").......5-10 64
RCA (8185 "Raunchy")..............................8-12 63
UNLIMITED GOLD...............................3-5 80-81
Picture Sleeves
DOPPLER (7501 "American Farming Man")..5-10 '60s
(Asgrow Seed Special products issue.)
LPs: 10/12-inch
RCA (2694 "New Sounds - Old Goodies")...15-25 63

COOPER, Prince
Singles: 78 rpm
CLUB 51 (101 "The Wiggler")..................15-25 55
Singles: 7-inch
CLUB 51 (101 "The Wiggler")..................25-35 55
Members: Prince Cooper; H. Wynne; J. Cosby; J. Slaughter; H. Ashby.

COOPER, Rattlesnake
Singles: 78 rpm
TALENT (804 "Rattlesnake Blues")...... 150-250 49

COOPER, Tommy
Singles: 7-inch
HIGHLAND (1166 "Sweet Words of Love")..5-10 66

PHIL TONE (1101 "Sweet Words of Love")....15-20 60
W.B. (5262 "Ginger")....8-12 62

COOPER, Wade

Singles: 7-inch

EMBER (1059 "Oh Me Oh My")....10-15 60
HERALD (551 "Look Around")....10-20 60

COOPER, Willie, & Webs

Singles: 7-inch

DYNAMIC (105 "You Don't Love Nobody")....20-30 64

COOPER, Wilma Lee & Stoney
(With the Clinch Mountain Clan; with Carolee & Clinch Mountain Clan) C&W '56

Singles: 78 rpm

COLUMBIA....5-10 54-55
HICKORY....5-10 56-57

Singles: 7-inch

COLUMBIA....10-15 54-55
HICKORY....10-15 56-64

EPs: 7-inch

COLUMBIA....10-15 59

LPs: 10/12-inch

COUNTY....5-10
DECCA....15-20 66
HARMONY....15-25 60-66
HICKORY....10-20 60-62
POWER PAK....6-10
ROUNDER....5-10
SKYLIGHT COUNTRY....8-12
STARDAY....8-12 77
Also see WILMA LEE

COOPERETTES

Singles: 7-inch

ABC (11156 "Trouble")....5-10 68
BRUNSWICK (55296 "Goodbye School")..8-15 66
BRUNSWICK (55307 "Don't Trust Him")....8-15 66
BRUNSWICK (55329 "Shing-a-ling")....15-25 67

COPAS, Cowboy C&W '46
(Cowboy "Poppy" Copas; Lloyd Copas; with Kathy Copas)

Singles: 78 rpm

KING....5-15 44-57

Singles: 7-inch

DOT....10-20 57-58
KING (951 thru 1507)....15-25 50-55
KING (4865 thru 5270)....10-20 55-59
KING (5392 thru 5734)....6-12 60-63
STARDAY (476 thru 750)....6-12 60-66
STARDAY (7000 series)....4-8 64
STARDAY (8000 series)....4-6 71

EPs: 7-inch

KING....15-25 52-53
STARDAY....10-20 60

LPs: 10/12-inch

BUCKBOARD....5-10
GUEST STAR....10-15
KING (553 "All-Time Hits")....45-55 57
KING (556 "Favorite Sacred Songs")....40-50 57
KING (619 thru 835)....25-40 59-64
KING (894 thru 1049)....10-20 64-69
MONTGOMERY WARD....10-15 '60s
NASHVILLE....8-12 68-70
PICKWICK/HILLTOP....10-20 66
STARDAY (113 "All Time Country Music Great")....20-30 60
STARDAY (133 "Inspirational Songs")....20-30 61
STARDAY (144 "Songs That Made Him Famous")....20-30 62
STARDAY (157 "Opry Star Spotlight")....20-30 63
STARDAY (175 "Mr. Country Music")....20-30 64
STARDAY (200 series)....12-25 64-67
STARDAY (300 series)....10-20 65-67
STARDAY (400 series)....8-12 68-70
TRIO CLUB....5-10 82
Also see COPAS, Lloyd
Also see MULLICAN, Moon / Cowboy Copas / Red Sovine
Also see ROCKING MARTIN

COPAS, Cowboy / Hawkshaw Hawkins

LPs: 10/12-inch

KING....12-25 63-66
Also see CLINE, Patsy / Cowboy Copas / Hawkshaw Hawkins
Also see COPAS, Cowboy
Also see HAWKINS, Hawkshaw

COPAS, Lloyd

Singles: 7-inch

DOT (15735 "Circle Rock")....60-80 58
Also see COPAS, Cowboy

COPELAND, Allan, & Hotrodders
(With Frank Comstock's Orchestra)

Singles: 7-inch

ARWIN (105 "Crack the Whip")....20-30 58

COPELAND, Jimmy

Singles: 7-inch

ALLSTAR....10-20 60-62
B&K ("Satellite Rock")....250-350
(Selection number not known.)
BOONE (1071 "Kiss and Make Up")....4-8 68
(With Mary McCoy.)

COPELAND, Johnny
(With the Soul Agents)

Singles: 7-inch

ALL BOY (8500 "Please Let Me Know")...10-15 62
ATLANTIC (2474 thru 2618)....5-10 68-69
BRAGG (102 "Ain't Nobody's Business")...5-10 64
CRAZY CAJUN....4-8 77
EVENT....5-10
GHETTO CHILD....5-10
GOLDEN EAGLE (101 "Just One More Time")....10-15 63
GOLDEN EAGLE (107 "Mama Told Me")....10-15 64
JET STREAM (712 thru 718)....8-12 63-64
JET STREAM (802 "Sufferin' City")....10-15 67
KENT....5-10 70-71
MERCURY (71280 "Rock and Roll Lilly").50-75 58
MR. R&B....3-6 83
PARADISE (1013 "I Need You Now")....8-12 65
RESCO....4-8 75
SUAVE (712 "That's All Right Mama")....10-15 64
SUAVE (717 "All These Things")....10-15 64
TTC (1001/1002 "Do Better Somewhere Else")....5-10
WAND (1114 thru 1130)....5-10 66
WET SOUL....4-8

LPs: 10/12-inch

ROUNDER....5-10 81-83
Also see COLLINS, Albert, Robert Cray & Johnny Copeland
Also see MEYERS, Augie

COPELAND, Ken

Singles: 78 rpm

IMPERIAL....10-20 57

Singles: 7-inch

DOT (15686 "Where the Rio De Rosa Flows")....15-25 58
IMPERIAL (5453 "Teenage")....10-20 57
IMPERIAL (5466 "I Want to Go Steady")..10-20 57
KAI (5352 "Hey! Little Girl")....8-12 '60s
LIN (5013 "Love Only Me")....30-50 58
LIN (5017 "Fanny Brown")....50-75 58

COPELAND, Ken / Mints P&R '57

Singles: 78 rpm

IMPERIAL....10-15 57
LIN....10-20 57

Singles: 7-inch

IMPERIAL (5432 "Pledge of Love")....10-15 57
(Maroon label.)
IMPERIAL (5432 "Pledge of Love")....8-12 57
(Black label.)
LIN (5007 "Pledge of Love"/"Night Air")....40-50 57
Also see COPELAND, Ken
Also see FOUR MINTS
Also see MINTS

COPELAND, Vivian R&B '69

Singles: 7-inch

D'ORO (1003/1004 "He Knows My Key"/"So Nice, I Had to Kiss You Twice")....5-10 69
D'ORO (1006/1007 "I Don't Care"/"Oh No Not My Baby")....5-10 69
D'ORO (3500 "He Knows My Key"/"So Nice, I Had to Kiss You Twice")....4-8 69
MALA (577 "I Don't Care What He's Done"/"So Nice, I Had to Kiss You Twice")....10-15 67

COPESETICS

Singles: 78 rpm

PREMIUM (409 "Collegian")....50-75 56

Singles: 7-inch

PREMIUM (409 "Collegian")....125-150 56

COPNEY, Bobby

Singles: 7-inch

TUFF (414 "Ain't No Good")....10-15 66

COPS 'N ROBBERS

Singles: 7-inch

CORAL (62462 "Just Keep Right On")....8-12 65
CORAL (62473 "I Found Out")....8-12 65
PARROT (9716 "There's Got to Be a Reason")....10-15 64

CORALAIRS
(With T. Renaldi)

Singles: 7-inch

BEE (1543 "Baby Blue Eyes")....75-125 58
NRC (036 "Gimme a Little Kiss")....10-15 59

CORALITES

Singles: 7-inch

CARIB (1008 "True Love")....15-25 62

CORALS

Singles: 7-inch

CHEER (1001 "Tell Me Yes")....15-25 62
KRAM (1001 "My Best Friend")....20-30 62
RAYNA (5010 "My Best Friend")....10-15 62

CORALS

Singles: 7-inch

BIG SOUND (308 "Blue Moon")....10-20 66
BIG SOUND (311 "Baby My Heart")....10-20 67
Members: Ray Kannon; James Curley Cooke.
Also see KANNON, Ray, & Corals

CORBIN, Harold

LPs: 10/12-inch

ROULETTE (52079 "Soul Brother")....15-25 61

CORBY, Chuck
(With the Chances; with Entrees)

Singles: 7-inch

CHESS (2077 "Soul Brother")....5-10 69
FEE BEE (219 "Honey Let Me Stay")....30-40 58
SONIC (118 "City of Strangers")....15-25
SOUND (717 "Happy Go Lucky")....15-25 66
VEEP (1235 "Happy Go Lucky")....10-20 66

CORBY, Doug

Singles: 7-inch

JC (121 "Heartbreak Train")....50-75 61
VAULT (922 "Let's Get Together")....8-12 66

CORBY, Ron

Singles: 78 rpm

VIK (0262 "Destiny Is a Woman")....10-15 57

Singles: 7-inch

VIK (0262 "Destiny Is a Woman")....10-20 57
Also see FORD, Billy, & Thunderbirds / Ron Corby

CORCORAN, Noreen
(With Nino Tempo)

Singles: 7-inch

VEE-JAY (555 "Love Kitten")....10-20 63
VEE-JAY (590 "Love of Mike")....10-20 64
Also see TEMPO, Nino

CORDEL, Pat
(With the Crescents "Later Known As the Elegants"; with Cherokee & Band; with Elegants)

Singles: 7-inch

CLUB (1011 "Darling Come Back")..1000-1500 56
MICHELE (503 "Darling Come Back")....40-50 59
VICTORY (1001 "Darling Come Back")....20-30 63
Members: Pat "Cordel" Croccitto; Vito Picone; Carman Romano; Ronnie Jones.
Also see ELEGANTS
Also see PICONE, Vito

CORDELL, Jeff

Singles: 7-inch

BIG TOP (3158 "Marching Orders")....10-15 63
RADIANT (1513 "The Touch of His Hand")....8-12 62

CORDELL, Richie

Singles: 7-inch

AMY (882 "Georgiana")....10-15 63
RORI (707 "Tick Tock")....50-60 62
STREETCAR (101 "Raindrops")....8-12 65
STREETCAR (400 "I Wish It Could Be Me")....8-12 65
Session: Paul Simon; Les Levine.
Also see BASEMAN, M.R., & Symbols / Marty & Symbols
Also see SIMON, Paul

CORDELLS

Singles: 7-inch

ADOR (6402 "Happy Time")....15-25 64
BARGAIN (5004 "Beat of My Heart")....20-30 62
BULLSEYE (1017 "Please Don't Go")....75-125 58
CASKET....5-10

CORDIALS

Singles: 7-inch

BETHLEHEM (3019 "I'm Not Crying Anymore")....15-25 62
PANIC (1000 "Blue Moon")....10-20 62

CORDIALS

Singles: 7-inch

FELSTED (8653 "Once in a Lifetime")....10-15 62
7 ARTS (707 "Dawn Is Almost Here")....75-125 61
(White label. Promotional issue only.)
7 ARTS (707 "Dawn Is Almost Here")....50-100 61
Members: Bobby Pickett; Leonard Capizzi; Bill Capizzi; Ron Deltorto; Lou Toscano.
Also see PICKETT, Bobby
Also see STOMPERS

CORDIALS
(With the Cutups)

Singles: 7-inch

CORDIAL (1001 "I'm Ashamed")....75-125 60
(Reportedly 500 made.)
REVEILLE (106 "Eternal Love")....200-300 62
Also see CARIANS

CORDIALS
("Vocal by Lee Dorian")

Singles: 7-inch

STAN (111 "A Fool in Love")....30-50 61

CORDIALS

Singles: 7-inch

WHIP (276 "Listen My Heart")....250-350 61

CORDIALS

Singles: 7-inch

LIBERTY (55784 "Oh, How I Love Her")..10-15 65

LPs: 10/12-inch

CATAMOUNT (902 "Blue Eyed Soul")....10-20 67

CORDING, Henry
(With Big Mike & His Parisian Rockets)

Singles: 78 rpm

COLUMBIA....20-30 56

Singles: 7-inch

COLUMBIA (40762 "Hiccough Rock")....40-60 56

COR-DONS
(Cor-Don's; with Ron Butko & Orchestra)

Singles: 7-inch

ROWE (010 "Some Kinda Wonderful") 400-500 62

CORDOVANS

Singles: 7-inch

COLLECTABLES....3-5 81
JOHNSON (731 "My Heart")....50-75 58
(Title in small print.)
JOHNSON (731 "My Heart")....15-25 60
(Title in large print.)

CORDS

Singles: 7-inch

ATCO (6687 "Ain't That Love")....10-20 69
RAKKI (101 "Termites")....10-20 63
Member: Billy Stull.

CORDS

Singles: 7-inch

CUCA (1512 "Cords Inc.")....20-30 66
CUCA (1513 "Ghost Power")....15-25 70
Member: Jim Bertler.

CORDUROYS

Singles: 7-inch

HALE (100 "Forever Yours")....75-100 61

COREY, Don, & Montereys

Singles: 7-inch

MONTEREY (106 "I Wish You Love")....75-100

COREY, Herb

Singles: 7-inch

TOP RANK (2018 "This Could Be the Night")....10-15 59

COREY, Jill P&R '54
(With Percy Faith and Orchestra)

Singles: 78 rpm

COLUMBIA....5-10 54-57
RCA (5934 "Song from Desiree")....5-10 54

Singles: 7-inch
AMERICAN MUSIC MAKERS (0014 "The Other Side of Me")....5-10 68
COLUMBIA (40188 thru 41202)....10-20 54-58
MERCURY (71913 "I Miss You Already")...8-12 62
RCA (5934 "Song from Desiree")....10-20 54
20TH FOX (532 "Easy to Remember")....5-10 64
EPs: 7-inch
COLUMBIA (10951/10952 "Sometimes I'm Happy Sometimes Blue")....10-15 57
LPs: 10/12-inch
COLUMBIA (1095 "Sometimes I'm Happy Sometimes Blue")....30-40 57
Also see FAITH, Percy, Orchestra

COREY, Jill, & Four Lads
Singles: 78 rpm
COLUMBIA (40177 "Cleo & Meo")....5-10 54
Singles: 7-inch
COLUMBIA (40177 "Cleo & Meo")....10-20 54
Also see COREY, Jill
Also see FOUR LADS

COREY, John
(Jon Corey)
Singles: 7-inch
20TH FOX (446 "Have You Heard")....10-15 63
VEE-JAY (466 "I'll Forget")....20-30 62
VEE-JAY (514 "Hey Little Runaround")....15-25 63
Session: 4 Seasons.
Also see 4 SEASONS

COREY, Will
Singles: 7-inch
ENRICA (1016 "Memories")....10-15 62

CORI, Troy
(With the Jackson Brothers Orchestra)
Singles: 7-inch
BINGO (1002 "Torture")....10-15 59
COAST (101 "Junior Flip")....25-35 56
Also see CORY, Troy

CORIN, Terry
(With Her Boy Friends)
Singles: 7-inch
COLONY (110 "Dream Date")....20-30 60
MOHAWK (127 "My Ding Dong Heart")....10-20 62
RIDER (108 "Truly, I Love You, Truly")....15-25 61
Also see TERRY & MELLOS

CORKY & CONTINENTALS
Singles: 7-inch
HAP (100 "Bring My Baby Back")....50-75

CORLETTES
Singles: 7-inch
KANSOMA (02 "I Love You")....20-30 62
NITA (711 "Tears on My Pillow")....50-75 '60s

CORLEY, Bob — P&R '55
Singles: 78 rpm
RCA....5-10 56
STARS....10-20 55
Singles: 7-inch
RCA (6438 "Bermuda Bound")....10-15 56
RCA (6587 "Mr. Chairman")....10-15 56
RCA (6946 "Number One Street")....10-20 57
STARS (4773 "Number One Street")....40-50 55

CORLEY, Cozy
Singles: 7-inch
BO-BO (8669 "I Need True Love")....10-15 64

CORNBREAD & BISCUITS — P&R/R&B '60
(With Lea Landon & Orchestra)
Singles: 7-inch
ANNA (102 "The Big Time Spender")....25-50 59
(This is the Maske disc with an Anna label sticker applied to each side, covering "Maske.")
MASKE (102 "The Big Time Spender")....15-25 60

CORNBREAD & JERRY
Singles: 7-inch
LIBERTY (55322 "Lil' Ole Me")....10-15 61
Member: Jerry Smith.
Also see SMITH, Jerry

CORNELIUS BROTHERS & SISTER ROSE — P&R/R&B '71
Singles: 7-inch
PLATINUM....10-15 70
U.A.....4-6 70-74
LPs: 10/12-inch
PICKWICK....5-10 76
U.A.....10-15 72-76
Members: Ed Cornelius; Carter Cornelius; Rose Cornelius.

CORNELL, Don — P&R '50
Singles: 78 rpm
CORAL....5-10 52-57
RCA....5-10
Singles: 7-inch
ABC-PAR....4-6 65
CORAL....10-20 52-57
DOT....5-10 59-60
JAYBEE....4-6 69
JUBILEE....4-8 62
RCA (4043 "That Old Feeling")....10-20 51
ROULETTE (4355 "Flying Trapeze")....4-8 61
SIGNATURE....5-10 59-60
20TH FOX....4-8 64
EPs: 7-inch
CORAL....5-10 54-56
LPs: 10/12-inch
ABC-PAR....8-12 66
CORAL....15-25 54-57
DOT....10-15 59
MOVIETONE....5-10 66
SIGNATURE....10-15 59
RCA (3116 "Don Cornell Sings")....15-25 52
(10-inch LP.)
VOCALION....8-15 59
Also see KAYE, Sammy

CORNELL, Don, & Teresa Brewer
(With Jack Pleis Orchestra)
Singles: 78 rpm
CORAL....4-6 52
Singles: 7-inch
CORAL (60829 "You'll Never Get Away")....8-12 52
Also see BREWER, Teresa

CORNELL, Don, Johnny Desmond & Alan Dale — P&R '53
Singles: 78 rpm
CORAL....3-6 53
Singles: 7-inch
CORAL....5-10 53
EPs: 7-inch
CORAL....5-10 54
Also see CORNELL, Don
Also see DALE, Alan
Also see DESMOND, Johnny

CORNELL, Doug
(With the Hot Rods; Douglas Cornell)
Singles: 7-inch
BRUNSWICK (55088 "Hey! Cool")....10-15 58
DEB (1000 "Hong Kong Rock")....15-25 59

CORNELL SISTERS
Singles: 7-inch
LABEL (2021 "Walking Along")....10-20 59

CORNELLS
Singles: 7-inch
GAREX....20-30 62-63
LPs: 10/12-inch
GAREX (100 "Beach Bound")....100-125 63
Members: Bob Linkletter; Peter Young; James O'Keefe; Charles Cornell; Tom Crumpler.

CORNER, Eddie, & Discords
Singles: 7-inch
SMOKE (101 "Bad Habit")....30-50 59
(Also issued as by Willie Loftin & Discords.)

CORNERS FOUR
Singles: 7-inch
PHILIPS (40488 "It's So Right")....10-20 67

CORNERSTONES
Singles: 7-inch
METROBEAT (4447 "You Rule Me")....20-30 67
METROBEAT (4455 "When Will My Day Come")....30-40 67

CORNISH, Gene
(With the Unbeatables)
Singles: 7-inch
DAWN (550 "Do the Capri")....20-30 64
DAWN (551 "I Wanna to Be a Beetle")....75-100 64
VASSAR (319 "Since I Lost You")....75-100 62
Also see RASCALS
Also see UNBEATABLES

CORONA, Larry
Singles: 78 rpm
FORTUNE (523 "Jane")....5-10 56
Singles: 7-inch
FORTUNE (523 "Jane")....15-25 56

CORONADOS
Singles: 78 rpm
VIK (0217 "Let's Get Acquainted")....5-10 56
Singles: 7-inch
VIK (0217 "Let's Get Acquainted")....10-15 56

CORONADOS / Jackie Jocko
(With George Sirabo & His Orchestra & Chorus)
EPs: 7-inch
VIK (7 "My Beautiful Dream")....10-20 57
(Promotional issue.)

CORONADOS
Singles: 7-inch
PEERLESS (5134 "Why")....20-30 61
RIC (979 "Lying")....15-20 61

CORONADOS
Singles: 7-inch
ARLINGWOOD (6467 "Florida Sun")....20-30

CORONATORS
Singles: 7-inch
CLOCK (1045 "Senorita")....15-25 61
CLOCK (1047 "Lonely Street")....15-25 61
CLOCK (1049 "This Is the Time")....15-25 61

CORONETS — R&B '53
(With Sax Mallard & Combo)
Singles: 78 rpm
CHESS....25-50 53
GROOVE....25-50 55
Singles: 7-inch
CHESS (1549 "Nadine")....100-200 53
(Silver top label with chess pieces.)
CHESS (1549 "Nadine")....10-15
(Blue label.)
CHESS (1553 "It Would Be Heavenly")....400-500 53
(Black vinyl. Silver top label with chess pieces.)
CHESS (1553 "It Would Be Heavenly")....10-20 53
(Black vinyl. Blue label.)
CHESS (1553 "It Would Be Heavenly")....1500-2000 53
(Red vinyl. Silver top label.)
GOLDEN GOODIES (1549 "Nadine")....3-6
GROOVE (0114 "I Love You More")....100-150 55
GROOVE (0116 "Hush")....100-150 55
Members: Charles Carothers; Lester Russaw; George Lewis; William Griggs; Sam Griggs; Babby Ward.
Also see MALLARD, Sax

CORPORATE BODY
Singles: 7-inch
MGM (14045 "Wait and See")....5-10 69
MUSIC FACTORY (416 "Mr. Nickels and Dimes")....5-10 68
LPs: 10/12-inch
MGM (4624 "Prospectus '69")....10-15 69

CORPORATION — LP '69
Singles: 7-inch
AGE OF AQUARIUS (1496 "You Make Me Feel So Good")....10-20 69
CAPITOL (2467 "Highway")....10-15 69
LPs: 10/12-inch
AGE OF AQUARIUS (4150 "The Corporation")....30-50 70
AGE OF AQUARIUS (4250 "Hassels in My Mind")....20-30 69
CAPITOL (175 "The Corporation")....20-30 69
Members: Danny Peil; Ken Berdoll; Gerald Smith; John Kondos; Nicholas Kondos; Pat McCarthy.
Also see PEIL, Danny

CORPUS
LPs: 10/12-inch
ACORN (1001 "Creation of a Child")....100-150 71
Members: William Grate; James Castilla; Gilbert Pena; Richard Deleon.

CORRENTE, Sal
Singles: 7-inch
ROULETTE (4673 "Love Me")....10-20 66
Session: Regents.
Also see DIALS
Also see LAW, Johnny, Four
Also see LITTLE DAVID
Also see 1929 DEPRESSION
Also see TRACES

CORRIDORS
(Corridor's)
Singles: 7-inch
WILDCAT (57 "Dear One")....15-25 63
ZONE (2160 "Dear One")....50-75 59

CORSAIRS
Singles: 7-inch
HY-TONE (110 "Goodbye Darling")....2500-3500 57
(Reportedly 500 made.)

CORSAIRS — P&R '61
(Featuring Jay "Bird" Uzzell)
Singles: 7-inch
CHESS (1808 "Smokey Places")....8-12 61
CHESS (1818 "I'll Take You Home")....8-12 62
ERIC....3-5 78
SMASH (1715 "Time Waits")....10-15 61
TUFF (375 "Save a Little Monkey")....8-12 64
TUFF (1808 "Smokey Places")....10-20 61
TUFF (1818 "I'll Take You Home")....10-20 62
(First issue.)
TUFF (1830 "While")....15-25 62
TUFF (1840 "At the Stroke of Midnight")....10-20 62
TUFF (1847 "Stormy")....10-20 63
TUFF (3027 "Time Waits")....10-20 '60s
Members: Jay "Bird" Uzzell; "King" Moe Uzzell; James Uzzell; George Wooten.
Also see McNEIL, Landy

CORSELLS
Singles: 7-inch
HUDSON (8104 "Party Time")....20-30 64

CORT, Bob, Skiffle Group
Singles: 7-inch
LONDON (1713 "Don't You Rock Me Daddy-O")....10-15 57
LONDON (1742 "Freight Train")....10-15 57
LONDON (1748 "Maggie May")....10-15 57
(With Liz Winters.)

CORTEZ, Alberto, Orchestra
LPs: 10/12-inch
TOLLIE (56002 "Welcome to Le Discotheque")....15-20 64

CORTEZ, Dave "Baby" — P&R/R&B '59
(With the Moon People; Baby Cortez; with Blazers)
Singles: 78 rpm
CLOCK (1006 "You're the Girl")....15-25 58
CLOCK (1009 "The Happy Organ")....50-75 59
WINLEY (213 "Saturday Night Rock")....8-12 56
Singles: 7-inch
ABC....4-6 74
ALL PLATINUM....4-6 72
ARGO (5462 "Let It Be You")....5-10 64
CHESS....5-10 61-63
CLOCK....15-25 58-62
COLLECTABLES....3-5 81
EMIT (301 "Fiesta")....8-12 62
ERIC....4-6 73
HI OLDIES....4-6 77
JULIA (1829 "Rinky Dink")....20-30 62
OKEH (7102 "Honey Baby")....50-75 58
OKEH (7208 "Popping Popcorn")....10-15 64
ROULETTE (4628 thru 4759)....5-10 65-67
SOUND....4-6 71
SPEED....3-5
TETRAGRAMMATON....5-10 69
T-NECK....5-10 69
WINLEY (213 "Saturday Night Rock")....15-20 56
WINLEY (259 thru 267)....10-15 61-62
EPs: 7-inch
CLOCK (4039 " Dave 'Baby' Cortez and His Happy Organ")....20-30 61
RCA (EPA-4342 "Dave 'Baby' Cortez and His Happy Organ")....20-30 59
(Monaural.)
RCA (ESP-4342 "Dave 'Baby' Cortez and His Happy Organ")....35-50 59
(Stereo.)
LPs: 10/12-inch
CHESS (1473 "Rinky Dink")....25-30 62
CLOCK....25-35 60-63
CORONET....10-15 '60s
CROWN....15-20 63
DESIGN....10-15 '60s
METRO (550 "Fabulous Organ")....10-20 65

RCA (LPM-2099 "Dave 'Baby' Cortez and His Happy Organ") 25-35 59
(Monaural.)
RCA (LSP-2099 "Dave 'Baby' Cortez and His Happy Organ") 35-50 59
(Stereo.)
ROULETTE (25298 "Organ Shindig") 15-20 65
ROULETTE (25328 "In Orbit") 15-20 66
Also see CLOWNEY, David, Band
Also see ISLEY BROTHERS & DAVE "BABY" CORTEZ
Also see JESTERS
Also see PARAGONS
Also see PEARLS
Also see VALENTINES

CORTEZ, Dave "Baby" / Jerry's House Rockers
LPs: 10/12-inch
CROWN 10-20 63
Also see CORTEZ, Dave "Baby"

CORTEZ & ENTERTAINERS
Singles: 7-inch
YOUR TOWN (711 "Life") ..... 15-25 '60s

CORVAIRS
(With Little Joe Williams; with Ross Aldrich & Orchestra)
Singles: 7-inch
CLOCK (1037 "Love Her So") 75-100 61
COLLECTABLES 3-5 81
CROWN (004 "Darlin' ") 50-100 61
CUB (9065 "Yeah Yeah") 10-20 60
TWIN (779 "Black Diamonds") ..... 50-75 '60s
(Red label.)
TWIN (1001 "Gee Whiz") 150-250 62
(Red label. Reads "Twin Records" at top.)
TWIN (1001 "Gee Whiz") 50-75 62
(Blue label. Reads only "TWIN" at top.)
Also see JIVE FIVE
Also see STITH, Bill

CORVAIRS
Singles: 7-inch
COLUMBIA (43603 "Swinging Little Government") 10-15 66
COLUMBIA (43861 "Ain't No Soul") 10-20 66
COMET (2145 "True True Love") 25-35 62
(Black label.)
COMET (2145 "True True Love") 10-15 62
(Yellow label.)
LEOPARD (5005 "Don't Wanna Be Without You") 50-75 63
SYLVIA (5003 "Victim of Her Charms") ... 20-30 64
Members: Edward Alston; Nelson Shields; Joe Shepard; Ronald Judge; Prince McKnight; Bill Fiason; Edgar Brown
Also see LEADERS

CORVAIRS / Valroys
EPs: 7-inch
MAGIC CARPET (501 "Corvairs-Valroys") 10-15
(Black vinyl. Issued with paper sleeve. 500 made.)
MAGIC CARPET (501 "Corvairs-Valroys") 20-25
(Blue vinyl. Issued with paper sleeve. 25 made.)
MAGIC CARPET (501 "Corvairs-Valroys") 50-55
(Multi-colored vinyl. Issued with paper sleeve. Three made.)

CORVANS
("Vocal By Bobby Arsena")
Singles: 7-inch
CABOT (131 "Sleepless Nights") 40-50 59

CORVELLS
(With the Royalteens)
Singles: 7-inch
ABC-PAR (10324 "Take My Love") 75-125 62
ABC-PAR (10324 "Take My Love") 50-75 62
(West Coast. Styrene.)
BLAST (203 "The Bells") 250-350 61
CUB (9122 "The Joke's on Me") 8-12 63
LIDO (509 "We Made a Vow") 100-200 57
LU PINE (104 "He's So Fine") 15-25 62

CORVELLS
Singles: 7-inch
CENTURY (19805 "Dune Buggy Ride") .. 15-20
Picture Sleeves
CENTURY (19805 "Dune Buggy Ride") .. 20-30

CORVETS
Singles: 7-inch
ABC-PAR (9891 "String Band Hop") 10-20 58

CORVETS
(With Vince Catalano & Orchestra)
Singles: 7-inch
LAUREL (1012 "So Long") 50-75 60
(Writer shown as V. Zellola.)
LAUREL (1012 "So Long") 20-30 60
(Writer shown as V. Zeccola.)
20TH FOX (223 "Only Last Night") 20-30 60
WAY-OUT (101 "My Darling") 75-125 58
Members: Vince Zeccola; George DeAlfonso; Jules Hahn; Joe Lento; Vance Hallup Hank Shuh.
Also see LYNN, Sandy

CORVETS
Singles: 7-inch
SURE (1003 "I'm Pleadin' ") 50-75 59

CORVETS
Singles: 7-inch
RE-CAR (9013 "Can It Be") 8-12 64
SOMA (1164 "Wailin' Wailin' Party") 150-200 61
SOMA (1425 "You Don't Want Me") 30-40 65

CORVETS
(Johnny Acey & Corvets)
Singles: 7-inch
RUN BACK (9777 "Please Don't Go") ..... 30-40 '60s
(Red vinyl.)

CORVETS
Singles: 7-inch
TONE CRAFT (1009 "Voodoo Baby") .. 100-150 '60s

CORVETTES
Singles: 7-inch
CORVETTE (1000 "Corvette") 40-60 60

CORVETTES
Singles: 7-inch
MEGAPHONE (707 "So Long") 1500-2500 64

CORVETTES
Singles: 7-inch
BEE DEE (102 "Tears Are Free") ..... 25-35 '60s
BITCHEN (100 "Surf Don't Walk") ..... 10-20 '60s

CORVETTES
(With Bill Duzan)
Singles: 7-inch
DUNCAN (401 "Janice") ..... 20-30 '60s

CORVETTES
Singles: 7-inch
VALUE ("When You're in Love") 200-300
(Selection number not known.)

CORVETTES & TODDETTES
Singles: 7-inch
DUTCH (1061 "Today") 15-25 61
FAN JR. (1000 "Jeri") 50-75 61
Members: Shane Todd; Tom Van Maren; Bob Gugel; Gene Clifford; Jim Bisbee; George Moll; Bruce Benson.
Also see TODD, Shane

CORVETTS
Singles: 7-inch
SHERATON (201 "In the Chapel") 100-150 61

CORVETTS
Singles: 7-inch
MOON (100 "I'm Going to Cry") 500-750 64
Member: Arthur Conley.
Also see ARTHUR & CORVETS
Also see CONLEY, Arthur

CORWIN, Roy
Singles: 7-inch
HOB (111 "The World Is a Better Place") .25-35 61

CORWIN, Vic, Orchestra
Singles: 7-inch
GILMAR (222 "Little Star") 10-20 57
Also see MARKS, Steve / Jack Richards / Vic Corwin Orchestra

CORY, Troy
Singles: 78 rpm
SPECIALTY (620 "Yearning") 20-30 58
Singles: 7-inch
HIGHLAND (1030 "Teeny Weeny Wiggle") 8-12 62
MERCURY (71548 "Little Pink Toe") 10-15 59
SPECIALTY (620 "Yearning") 15-25 58

SQUARE BLOCK 4-6 72
Picture Sleeves
SQUARE BLOCK 4-6 72
Also see CORI, Troy

COSBY, Bill *LP '64*
Singles: 12-inch
MOTOWN (110 "Super Special for Radio") 5-10 82
(Promotional issue only.)
Singles: 7-inch
CAPITOL 3-6 76-78
UNI 4-8 69-70
W.B. (5499 "When I Marry You") 5-10 65
W.B. (7072 "Little Ole Man"/"Hush Hush") . 8-12 67
W.B. (7072 "Little Ole Man"/"Don't Cha Know") 5-8 68
W.B. (7096 "Hooray for the Salvation Army Band") 5-10 67
W.B. (7171 "Funky North Philly") 5-10 68
EPs: 7-inch
W.B. (274 "A Taste of Cosby") 5-10
(Promotional issue only.)
LPs: 10/12-inch
CAPITOL 5-10 76-78
COLUMBIA (40270 "Music from the Bill Cosby Show") 5-10 86
(Featuring Grover Washington Jr.)
GEFFEN 5-10 86
MCA (8005 "Bill") 5-10 73
MOTOWN 5-10 82
PARTEE 5-10
TETRAGRAMMATON (5100 "8:15 12:15") 10-15 69
(Two discs.)
UNI 5-10 69-72
W.B. (249 "Best of Bill Cosby") 15-25 69
(Promotional issue only.)
W.B. (1518 thru 1836) 10-20 64-70
Also see ROSS, Diana, & Bill Cosby / Diana Ross & Jackson Five
Also see WASHINGTON, Grover, Jr.

COSBY, Bill, & Ozzie Davis
LPs: 10/12-inch
BLACK FORUM 8-12 72
Also see COSBY, Bill

COSBY, Bill, & Stu Gardner
Singles: 7-inch
PARAMOUNT (0261 "Bird's Foot") 4-6 73

COSENTINO, Joe, & Nevermores
Singles: 7-inch
MICKEY (10 "Now and Forever") 15-25

COSEY, Cleve, & Riders
Singles: 7-inch
FREELANCE (1001 "Good Lovin' Baby") . 50-75 60

COSGREN, Wally
Singles: 7-inch
WABR (21784 "Blues, Stay Away From My Door") 50-100

COSHART, Terry
(Tiny Coshart)
Singles: 7-inch
COULEE (105 "Why") 15-25 64
COULEE (125 "Double Life") 10-20 68

COSMIC RAYS
(With Le Sun Ra & Arkestra; with Sun Ra & Arkestra)
Singles: 7-inch
SATURN (222 "Bye Bye") 2500-3500 60
SATURN (401 "Dreaming") 1000-2000 60

COSMIC ROCK SHOW
Singles: 7-inch
BLITZ (464 "Psiship") 50-75 68

COSMO
(With the Carnations; with Counts)
Singles: 7-inch
JAM (105 "Small Town Gossip") 15-25 63
SOUND STAGE 7 (2504 "Small Town Gossip") 8-12 63
SOUND STAGE 7 (2520 "You Gotta Dance") 8-12 64
TILT (787 "You Can't Get Kissed") 20-30 62
TILT (789 "Just Words") 20-30 62
Also see CARNATIONS

COSMO, Tony
Singles: 7-inch
FLING (716 "Wise to You") 15-20 60
ROULETTE (4265 "Teenager for President") 10-15 60
VANN (100 "Big Party") 10-15 61
Picture Sleeves
FLING (716 "Wise to You") 15-25 60

COSMOS
Singles: 7-inch
BIG "L" (502 "Angel, Angel") 75-100 62

COSSEN, Ray, Jr.
Singles: 7-inch
MUSICOR (1246 "Try Some Soul") 10-20 67

COSTA, Don, Orchestra *P&R '59*
(With the Mello-Larks)
Singles: 78 rpm
ABC-PAR 4-8 56-57
EPIC 4-8 55
ESSEX 4-8 55
Singles: 7-inch
ABC-PAR 10-20 56-57
COLUMBIA 5-10 62-63
DCP 4-8 64-65
EPIC 10-15 55
ESSEX (405 "Safe in the Harbor") 10-15 55
JAMIE (1123 "I'm in Heaven") 10-15 59
MGM 4-8 66-72
MERCURY 4-8 68
U.A. 10-20 59-62
VERVE 4-8 67
Picture Sleeves
U.A. (221 "The Unforgiven") 15-25 60
(Pictures film's stars Burt Lancaster and Audrey Hepburn, as well as Don Costa.)
U.A. (234 "Never on Sunday") 15-25 60
U.A. (286 "The Misfits") 25-35 61
(Pictures film's stars Clark Gable, Marilyn Monroe and Montgomery Clift.)
VERVE (10511 "Illya Darling") 5-10 67
LPs: 10/12-inch
ABC-PAR 15-30 56-61
COLUMBIA 10-20 62-63
DCP 5-10 64-65
HARMONY 5-10 65
MERCURY 5-10 68-69
U.A. 10-20 59-62
VERVE 5-10 67
Also see ANKA, Paul
Also see BARTEL, Lou
Also see BATES, Judy
Also see COOLBREEZERS
Also see DE CASTRO SISTERS
Also see GALLOP, Frank
Also see HAWKINS, Dolores
Also see LEE BROTHERS
Also see MANN, Gloria
Also see MARTIN, Dean
Also see SCOTT, Bobby
Also see WHITNEY, Jill
Also see WILLIAMS, Danny

COSTANZO, Jack
Singles: 7-inch
GNP (124 "Just One of Those Days") 10-20 57
GNP (454 "Guantanamera") 4-8 72
LIBERTY (55194 "Barracuda") 5-10 59
LIBERTY (55333 "Route 66 Theme") 5-10 61
LPs: 10/12-inch
GNP (19 "Mr. Bongo") 20-30 56
LIBERTY (3093 "Latin Fever") 15-25 58
(Monaural.)
LIBERTY (3137 "Afro Can-Can") 10-20 60
(Monaural.)
LIBERTY (3177 "Learn – Play Bongos") .. 10-20 60
LIBERTY (7020 "Latin Fever") 30-40 58
(Stereo.)
LIBERTY (7137 "Afro Can-Can") 15-25 60
(Stereo.)
VERVE (8157 "Afro Cubano") 15-25 58
ZEPHYR (12003 "Mr. Banjo Has Brass") . 15-25 56

COSTELLO, Danny
Singles: 7-inch
CORAL (62082 "Don't Forget") 10-15 59
CORAL (62114 "Paper Doll") 10-15 59
CORAL (62205 "Love Is Wonderful Ev'rywhere") 10-15 60

ESCAPADE (101 "Bella, Bella Facha Bella")....5-10 63

COSTELLO, Elvis *LP '77*
(With the Attractions; Costello Show)

Singles: 12-inch

COLUMBIA....5-15 83-85

Singles: 7-inch

CBS (Black vinyl)....4-6 79
CBS (Red vinyl)....15-25 79
COLUMBIA....3-6 77-86
W.B. 3-5 89

Promotional Singles

COLUMBIA....5-15 77-86

Picture Sleeves

COLUMBIA (04502 "Everyday I Write the Book")....3-6 83
COLUMBIA (10919 "Accidents Will Happen")....15-20 78
(Promotional issue only.)
COLUMBIA (60519 "Watching Your Step")..4-6 81
W.B. (22981 "Veronica")....3-5 89

EPs: 7-inch

COLUMBIA (529 "Live at Hollywood High")....10-20 78
(Bonus EP. Included with the LP *Armed Forces*.)
COLUMBIA (1171 "Elvis Costello and the Attractions")....25-35 78
(Promotional issue only.)
COLUMBIA (11251 "I Can't Stand Up for Falling Down")....10-20 80
COLUMBIA (11251 "I Can't Stand Up for Falling Down")....20-30 80
(White label. Promotional issue only.)

LPs: 10/12-inch

COLUMBIA (30000 series, except 35709) .8-12 77-86
COLUMBIA (35709 "Armed Forces")....15-25 79
(Includes the bonus EP *Live at Hollywood High*.)
COLUMBIA (35709 "Armed Forces")....8-12 79
(Without *Live at Hollywood High* EP.)
COLUMBIA (35709 "Armed Forces")....30-40 79
(Colored vinyl.)
COLUMBIA/COSTELLO (35331 "This Year's Model")....20-30 78
COLUMBIA (40000 series, except 48157) ...5-8 85-86
COLUMBIA (48157 "Imperial Bedroom"). 30-40 82
(Half-speed mastered.)
W.B. 5-10 89-91

Promotional LPs

COLUMBIA ("My Aim Is True"/"This Year's Model")....125-150 79
(Picture disc. No number given.)
COLUMBIA (529 "Live at Hollywood High")....30-45 79
COLUMBIA (958 "Tom Snyder Interview")....25-35 81
COLUMBIA (1318 "Almost Blue")....25-35 81
COLUMBIA (35709 "Armed Forces")....20-25 79
(With programming sticker on cover.)
COLUMBIA/COSTELLO (847 "Taking Liberties")....30-35 80
KING BISCUIT FLOWER HOUR (For July 13, 1980)....75-125
WESTWOOD ONE ("Off the Record")....40-60
Session: Daryl Hall; Paul McCartney.
Also see McCARTNEY, Paul
Also see ORBISON, Roy

COSTELLO SISTERS
(With "Harpsichord Lou Stein")

Singles: 78 rpm

SOUND (117 "Whas a Malle U")....5-10 55

Singles: 7-inch

SOUND (117 "Whas a Malle U")....10-15 55

COSYTONES

Singles: 78 rpm

MELBA....25-35 56

Singles: 7-inch

MELBA ("Speak to Me of Love")....25-50 56
(Selection number not known.)
WILLOW (1001 "I'm Alone")....20-40 58
Members: Windsor King; Kathy King; Ralph King; Eloise King; Mitch McPhee.
Also see ROYAL SONS QUINTET

COTILLIONS

Singles: 7-inch

ALLEY (1003 "Surf Twist")....10-15 63
Member: Larry Donn.
Also see DONN, Larry

COTILLIONS

Singles: 7-inch

ASCOT (2105 "This Road")....10-15 62

COTTON, James *LP '67*
(James Cotton Blues Band; with Matt "Guitar" Murphy & Luther Tucker)

Singles: 12-inch

ERECT....4-6 82

Singles: 78 rpm

SUN (199 "My Baby")....300-400 54
SUN (206 "Cotton Crop Blues")....350-450 54

Singles: 7-inch

BACKROOM....4-6
BUDDAH....4-6 75
LOMA (2042 "Complete This Order")....10-15 66
SUN (199 "My Baby")....700-900 54
SUN (206 "Cotton Crop Blues")....900-1100 54
VERVE FOLKWAYS....4-8 67
VERVE FORECAST....4-8 67-69

LPs: 10/12-inch

ACCORD (7223 "Red Hot 'N' Blues")....5-10 83
ALLIGATOR....5-10 84
ANTONE'S....5-10 88
BUDDAH (5620 "100% Cotton")....10-15 74
BUDDAH (5650 "High Energy")....10-15 75
BUDDAH (5661 "Live and on the Move") .20-25 76
CAPITOL (814 "Taking Care of Business")....10-15 71
ERECT....5-10 82
INTERMEDIA....5-10 84
VANGUARD (79283 "Cut You Loose")....10-15 68
VERVE FOLKWAYS (3023 "The James Cotton Blues Band")....10-20 67
VERVE FOLKWAYS (3038 "Pure Cotton")....10-20 68
VERVE FORECAST (3060 "Cotton in Your Ears")....10-15 69
Also see HOWLIN' WOLF
Also see WATERS, Muddy

COTTON, James, Carey Bell, Junior Wells, & Billy Branch

LPs: 10/12-inch

ALLIGATOR (4790 "Harp Attack")....5-10 90
Also see BELL, Carey
Also see WELLS, Junior

COTTON, Little Willie

Singles: 78 rpm

SWING TIME (319 "Gonna Shake It Up and Go")....20-30 52

Singles: 7-inch

OKEH (7014 "You're the Kind of Woman")....15-25 53
OKEH (7034 "I Live the Life I Love")....15-25 54
SAVOY (1608 "Nobody")....10-15 61

COTTON, Sylvester

Singles: 78 rpm

MODERN (655 "Ugly Woman Blues")....20-40 49
SENSATION (7000 "Ugly Woman Blues")....75-100 49
Also see HOOKER, John Lee

COUCH, Orville *C&W '62*

Singles: 7-inch

ACTION (108 "Wild Girl")....100-150
CUSTOM....8-12 62
DIXIE (2007 "Easy Does It")....150-200 58
MERCURY (71718 "Downtown")....10-15 60
MONUMENT (915 thru 949)....4-8 66
STARDAY (305 "You're Dreamin' ")....10-20 57
TOWER (469 "Won't It Feel Good")....4-8 69
VEE-JAY (470 thru 631)....5-10 62-64

LPs: 10/12-inch

VEE-JAY (1087 "Hello Trouble")....15-25 64

COULSTON, Jerry

Singles: 7-inch

CHRISTY (112 "Cave Man Hop")....150-250 59
CHRISTY (119 "Go Ask Your Mama")....25-35 59
CHRISTY (131 "Bon-Bon Baby")....25-35 60

COUNT & COLONY

Singles: 7-inch

PA-GO-GO (121 "Can't You See")....15-25 66
PA-GO-GO (201 "Symptoms of Love")....15-25 67
(First issue.)
SSS INT'L (711 "Symptoms of Love")....8-12 67

COUNT FIVE *P&R/LP '66*

Singles: 7-inch

APEX (77019 "Psychotic Reaction")....10-20 66
(Canadian.)
DOUBLE SHOT (104 "Psychotic Reaction")....10-15 66
(Label name at top.)
DOUBLE SHOT (104 "Psychotic Reaction")....5-10 66
(Label name on left side.)
DOUBLE SHOT (106 thru 141)....5-15 66-69

LPs: 10/12-inch

DOUBLE SHOT (1001 "Psychotic Reaction")....25-35 66
(Monaural.)
DOUBLE SHOT (5001 "Psychotic Reaction")....30-40 66
(Stereo.)
PERFORMANCE (398 "Psychotic Reaction")....8-10

COUNT 5

Singles: 7-inch

LES COUNTS (3447 "Count 5")....20-30 '60s

COUNTDOWN 5
(Countdown Five)

Singles: 7-inch

CINEMA (1310 "Uncle Kirby")....10-20 67
CINEMA (1326 "Maybe I'll Love You")....10-20 67
COBBLESTONE (745 "Money Man")....10-20 69
PIC 1 (123 "Shout")....15-25 65
PIC 1 (131 "My Own Style")....15-25 66
TOUCAN (1 "Uncle Kirby")....30-40 67

Picture Sleeves

TOUCAN (1 "Uncle Kirby")....50-75 67

COUNTDOWNS

Singles: 7-inch

IMAGE (5002 "Watermelons")....8-12 61
RORI (706 "Satellite Dan")....10-15 62
SUMIT (0004 "Lost Horizon")....20-30 63

COUNTDOWNS

Singles: 7-inch

BEAR (1968 "You Know I Do")....50-75 66
FIJI (691 "You Know I Do")....50-75 66

COUNTDOWNS

Singles: 7-inch

LINK (101 "I Can't Explain")....20-30 66
LINK (102 "Don't Take My Dreams")....10-15 66

Picture Sleeves

LINK (101 "I Can't Explain")....35-50 66

COUNTDOWNS

Singles: 7-inch

ANDERSON (110 "Do It")....10-20 66

COUNTDOWNS

Singles: 7-inch

APOLLO (71669 "Creative Soul")....10-15 '60s
WG (1 "She Works All Night")....10-15 67

COUNTDOWNS
(Ron Gray & Countdowns)

Singles: 7-inch

N-JOY (1013 "No More")....20-30 66
N-JOY (1015 "Cover of Night")....15-25 66
Member: Ron Gray.

COUNTRY BOY EDDIE

Singles: 7-inch

REED (1031 "Hang in There Like a Rusty Fish Hook")....300-400

COUNTRY BOYS

Singles: 7-inch

DEL-FI (4245 "Oakie Surfer")....25-35 64
Member: David Gates.
Also see GATES, David

COUNTRY FOUR

Singles: 7-inch

JEWEL (881 "Up, Up, Up and Down, Down, Down")....50-75

COUNTRY G-J's

Singles: 7-inch

VALLEY (250 "Go Girl Go")....750-1000 '50s
Member: Alvin Starns; Gene Wells; Joseph Staggs.

COUNTRY GENTLEMEN *C&W '65*

Singles: 78 rpm

RCA....5-8 56

Singles: 7-inch

BRENT (7058 "For You")....15-25 66
RCA (6673 "Why Did You Go")....10-15 56
RCA (6764 "My Heart's Desire")....15-20 56
REBEL (250 "Bringing Mary Home")....10-15 65

EPs: 7-inch

STARDAY....5-10

LPs: 10/12-inch

CIMARRON (2001 "Songs of the Pioneers")....25-35 62
CROWN....10-15 '60s
DESIGN....5-10 63
FOLKWAYS (2409 "Country Gentlemen, Vol. 1")....15-25 60
(Includes booklet.)
FOLKWAYS (2410 "Country Gentlemen, Vol. 2")....15-25 60
(Includes booklet.)
FOLKWAYS (2411 "Country Gentlemen, Vol. 3")....15-25 60
(Includes booklet.)
FOLKWAYS (31031 "Going Back to the Blue Ridge Mountains")....10-15
GUSTO....5-10
MERCURY....10-20 63
PICKWICK/HILLTOP....10-15 '60s
REBEL....5-10 '70s
SUGAR HILL....5-10 83
STARDAY (109 "Traveling Dobro Blues")....25-50 59
STARDAY (174 "Bluegrass at Carnegie Hall")....15-25 62
STARDAY (311 "Songs of the Pioneers")....15-20 65
VANGUARD (40021 "The Country Gentlemen")....15-25 73
(Quadraphonic.)
VANGUARD (79331 "The Country Gentlemen")....10-15 73
(Stereo.)
ZAP....10-15
Members: Charlie Waller; John Duffey; Eddie Adcock; Ed McGlothlin; Ricky Skaggs.
Also see SKAGGS, Ricky

COUNTRY HAMS

Singles: 7-inch

EMI (3977 "Walking in the Park with Eloise")....10-20 74

Picture Sleeves

EMI (3977 "Walking in the Park with Eloise")....50-60 74

Promotional Singles

EMI (3977 "Walking in the Park with Eloise")....25-35 74
Members: Paul McCartney & Wings; Chet Atkins; Floyd Cramer.
Also see ATKINS, Chet
Also see CRAMER, Floyd
Also see McCARTNEY, Paul

COUNTRY JIM
(James Bledsoe)

Singles: 78 rpm

IMPERIAL....35-50 49-50

LPs: 10/12-inch

IMPERIAL....15-20 70
Also see HOT ROD HAPPY

COUNTRY JOE & FISH *P&R/LP '67*

Singles: 7-inch

VANGUARD....5-10 67-69

Picture Sleeves

VANGUARD....8-15 68

EPs: 7-inch

RAG BABY (1001 "Rag Baby")....30-40 66
RAG BABY (1002 "Rag Baby")....30-40 66
RAG BABY (1003 "Rag Baby")....30-40 66

LPs: 10/12-inch

FANTASY....8-10 75-77
VANGUARD (Except 9266)....10-20 67-71
VANGUARD (9266 "I Feel Like I'm Fixin' to Die")....20-30 67
(With cut-out pictures and poster game.)
VANGUARD (9266 "I Feel Like I'm Fixin' to Die")....10-20 67
(Without pictures and poster.)
Members: Country Joe McDonald; Richard Saunders; David Cohen; Mark Kapner; Barry Melton; Bob Steele; Mark Ryan.
Also see McDONALD, Country Joe

Also see MELTON, Barry
Also see REBECCA & SUNNY BROOK FARMERS

COUNTRY LADS
EPs: 7-inch
RUBY-TONE (436 "Country Lads")........ 50-100

COUNTRY PAUL
("Country Paul on His Guitar"; Edward Harris)
Singles: 78 rpm
KING 50-100 51-52
Singles: 7-inch
KING (4517 "Your Picture Done Faded") 300-500 51
KING (4532 "One More Time")............ 200-400 52
KING (4560 "I'll Never Walk in Your Door").. 200-400 52
KING (4573 "Sidewalk Boogie").......... 200-400 52
Also see CAROLINA SLIM
Also see JAMMIN' JIM
Also see LAZY SLIM JIM

COUNTRY SLIM / Miss Country Slim
(Ernest Lewis)
Singles: 78 rpm
HOLLYWOOD (1005 "What Wrong Have I Done").. 50-100 53
Singles: 7-inch
HOLLYWOOD (1005 "What Wrong Have I Done").. 100-200 53
Also see LEWIS, Ernest

COUNTRYMAN, Freddy
Singles: 7-inch
VALTONE (410 "Shimmy")........................5-10 63
W.E.D. (23 "Raven")................................ 30-40 62
Also see FREDDY & LONNIE

COUNTS R&B '54
Singles: 78 rpm
DOT 15-25 53-56
NOTE (20000 "Sweet Names")............... 50-75 56
Singles: 7-inch
DOT (1188 "Darling Dear")...................... 50-75 53
DOT (1199 "Hot Tamales")...................... 40-50 54
DOT (1210 "My Dear My Darling").......... 40-50 54
DOT (1226 "Baby, I Want You")............. 30-40 54
DOT (1235 "Let Me Go Lover")............... 40-50 54
DOT (1243 "From This Day On")............ 30-40 55
DOT (1265 "Sally Walker")...................... 30-40 55
DOT (1275 "Heartbreaker").................... 50-60 56
DOT (16105 "Darling Dear")................... 10-15 60
NOTE (20000 "Sweet Names")........... 100-150 56

COUNTS
Singles: 7-inch
MERCURY (71318 "Teenage Guy and Gal")... 10-15 58

COUNTS
Singles: 7-inch
SUN-SET (502 "Touch Me").................... 25-35 61

COUNTS
Singles: 7-inch
MANCO (1060 "Surfer's Paradise")......... 15-25 64
COUNT (5 "The Beat")........................... 10-20

COUNTS
Singles: 7-inch
PANORAMA (9 "Chitlins, Etc.")..............6-12 65
PANORAMA (33 "Since I Fell for You")......6-12 66
SEA CREST (6003 "Turn On Song")....... 10-20 64
SEA CREST (6004 "Doggin'")................ 10-15 64

COUNTS
Singles: 7-inch
SHRINE (117 "My Only Love")............ 200-300 66

COUNTS
Singles: 7-inch
KEY (15131 "All Night")......................... 10-20 '60s

COUNTS
Singles: 7-inch
RICH-ROSE (102 "Georgi's Theme")...... 10-15 '60s
RICH-ROSE (711 "Just a Little Bit")......... 15-25 64
Also see BURK, Tommy

COUNTS LP '72
Singles: 7-inch
AWARE..4-6 74
WESTBOUND...4-6 72
TCB...4-8
YES (103 "Ask the Lonely")......................8-10
LPs: 10/12-inch
AWARE (2006 "Funk Pump")...................10-15 75
AWARE/GRC (2002 "Love Sign")............15-20 73
GRC..10-15 73
WESTBOUND (2011 "It's What's Up Front That Counts")..20-25 72

COUNTS
Singles: 7-inch
DYNAMO (50 "Someday I'm Gonna Get You")..15-25

COUNTS
Singles: 7-inch
SPIRAL (1002 "My Babe").......................15-20

COUNTS IV
Singles: 7-inch
DATE (1526 "Where Are You")................10-15 66
JCP (1006 "Listen to Me").......................15-25 67

COURCY, Joanne
(Jo Ann Courcy)
Singles: 7-inch
TWIRL (2020 "Silly Girl")..........................15-25 66
TWIRL (2026 "I Got the Power")..........100-200 66

COURIERS
Singles: 7-inch
C.V. (500 "Stomping Time Again")...........50-75 66
TEE PEE (113/114 "Would You Still Be Loving Me"/"You Honey Baby")..................................10-15 67
Members: Steve Kurtz; Carl Beyer; Harry "Hoagie" Strother; Dick Dunkel; Neil "Butch" Schuck; Dave Johnson.
Also see JAY & TECHNIQUES

COURT JESTERS
Singles: 7-inch
BLAST (201 "Roaches")...........................30-40 61
BLAST (208 "Roaches")...........................10-20 63
COLLECTABLES...3-5 81
LIBERTY (55294 "I'm Just a Country Boy")..8-12 61
ROULETTE (4718 "Baby Come Home")....5-10 67
ROULETTE (4746 "Dance for Me")...........5-10 67

COURT JESTERS
Singles: 7-inch
JESTER (2034 "Drive Me Crazy")...........15-25

COURTIERS
Singles: 7-inch
CASE (107 "I've Been Mistreated")......200-300 59

COURTNEY, Bill
Singles: 7-inch
RCA (7558 "Without Her Love")...............10-15 59
RCA (7658 "I'd Like Her to Be")...............10-15 59
ROULETTE (4269 "Blanket on the Beach")...10-15 60
VERSATILE (109 "Two-Timin' Lover")......10-15 62

COURTNEY, Dean
Singles: 7-inch
MGM (13776 "You Just Can't Walk Away")...75-125 67
PARAMOUNT (0214 "It Makes Me Nervous")..10-15 73
RCA (8919 "We Have a Good Thing")......10-15 66
RCA (9049 "I'll Always Need You")..........15-25 66

COURTNEY, Del
Singles: 78 rpm
MERCURY/SAV-WAY (5054 "Hawaiian War Chant")...100-150 47
(Picture disc. Promotional issue only.)

COURTNEY, Lou P&R/R&B '67
(Lew Courtney)
Singles: 7-inch
BUDDAH (121 "Let Me Turn You On").....10-15 69
EPIC (11062 thru 50070)...........................5-10 73-75
HURDY GURDY...3-5
IMPERIAL (66006 "Come On Home")..........5-10 63
IMPERIAL (66043 "Professional Lover")...5-10 64
PHILIPS (40287 "I Watched You Slowly Slip Away")...50-100 65
POP SIDE (4594 "Hey Joyce")...................5-10 67
RAGS (100 "What Do You Want Me to Do")...10-20 73
(First issue.)
RIVERSIDE (4588 thru 4591)....................5-10 66-67
VERVE (10602 "Rubberneckin'")..............5-10 68
VERVE (10631 "Please Stay")...................5-10 68
LPs: 10/12-inch
EPIC..8-10 74
RCA...8-10 76
RIVERSIDE (2000 "Skate Now")..............15-20 67

COURVALE, Keith
Singles: 7-inch
DOT (15844 "Trapped Love")...................50-75 58
VAL (7578 "Trapped Love")..................300-400 58
(First issue.)

COUSIN ARNOLD
Singles: 7-inch
STARDAY (569 "Be My Baby Doll").....200-300
STARDAY (578 "Sweet Talkin' Daddy")..100-200

COUSIN LEROY
(Leroy Rozier)
Singles: 78 rpm
EMBER..25-50 57
GROOVE..20-40 55
Singles: 7-inch
EMBER (1016 "Will a Matchbox Hold My Clothes")..25-40 57
EMBER (1023 "I'm Lonesome")...............25-35 57
GROOVE (0123 "Goin' Back Home").......40-60 55
HERALD (546 "Waiting at the Station")....20-30 60

COUSINS
Singles: 7-inch
NAR (224 "Mademoiselle").......................20-30 57

COUSINS
Singles: 7-inch
FIDELITY (3010 "Love Is Blind")................8-12 59
DECCA (30609 "Be Nice to Me")..............10-15 58

COUSINS
(With Teacho Wiltshire & Orchestra)
Singles: 7-inch
VERSATILE (105 "Lonely Road")............50-75 60
Also see WILTSHIRE, Teacho

COUSINS
Singles: 7-inch
SWIRL (102 "Little Girl")...........................25-35 61

COUSINS
Singles: 7-inch
PARKWAY...10-15 61-63
WYNNE (132 "Guilty")............................250-500 61
LPs: 10/12-inch
PARKWAY (7005 "Music of the Strip").....20-25 61

COVAY, Don P&R '62
(With the Goodtimers; with Jefferson Lemon Blues Band; with Stan Applebaum Orchestra; Don "Pretty Boy" Covay)
Singles: 7-inch
ARNOLD (1002 "Pony Time")...................20-30 61
ATLANTIC...5-10 65-70
BIG TOP (3033 "Beauty and the Beast").15-25 60
BIG TOP (3060 "I'm Coming Down with the Blues")..15-25 60
BLAZE (350 "Standing in the Doorway")..30-40 58
CAMEO (239 "Popeye Waddle")................8-12 62
CAMEO (251 "Do the Bug").......................8-12 63
COLUMBIA (41981 "Shake").....................5-10 61
COLUMBIA (42058 "See About Me").........5-10 61
COLUMBIA (42197 "Now That I Need You")..75-100 61
FLEETWOOD (2001 "Pony Time Twist").15-25
LANDA (704 "You're Good for Me")..........5-10 65
MERCURY (73311 "Overtime Man")...........4-6 72
MERCURY (73385 "Money")......................4-6 73
MERCURY (73430 "Bad Mouthing")...........4-6 73
MERCURY (73469 "Leave Him")...............5-10 74
MERCURY (73648 "Rumble in the Jungle")...5-10 75
NEWMAN (500 "Badd Boy").......................3-5 80
PARKWAY (894 "Ain't That Silly")............10-20 64
PARKWAY (910 "One Little Boy Had Money")..10-20 64
PHILA. INT'L (3594 "No Tell Motel")............4-6 76
PHILA. INT'L (3602 "Once You Have It").....4-6 76
ROSEMART (801 "Mercy, Mercy")............8-10 64
ROSEMART (802 "Please Don't Let Me Know")..8-10 64
SUE (709 "Believe It Or Not")..................30-40 58
U-VON...5-10 77
EPs: 7-inch
BRAVO (205 "Twist Songs")....................25-50 62
(No artist credited, though many feel the singer is Don Covay.)
LPs: 10/12-inch
ATLANTIC (8104 "Mercy")........................15-25 65
ATLANTIC (8120 "See Saw")....................15-25 65
ATLANTIC (8237 "House of Blue Lights")..15-25 69
JANUS (3038 "Different Strokes from Different Folks")..8-12 72
MERCURY (1020 "Hot Blood")..................8-10 74
PHILA. INT'L..8-10 76
VERSATILE..8-10 78
Also see GOODTIMERS
Also see PRETTY BOY
Also see RAINBOWS
Also see SAM & DAVE / Don Covay
Also see SOLDIER BOYS
Also see SOUL CLAN

COVELLE, Buddy
(Veline Hackert)
Singles: 7-inch
CORAL (62181 "Lorraine").............1000-1500 60
(Orange label. Commercial issue.)
CORAL (62181 "Lorraine")..................300-400 60
(Blue label. Promotional issue.)
Also see HACKERT, Veline

COVES
Singles: 7-inch
RAYNARD (1058 "A Love Like That")...... 10-20 66

COVERDALE, Larry, & Four Horsemen
Singles: 7-inch
ROULETTE (4712 "Long Cold Winter")... 10-20 66

COVINAS
(With the Dayna Tones)
Singles: 7-inch
HILTON (3752 "Five Minutes More")........ 15-25 65
Session: Tommy Dee.
Also see DEE, Tommy

COVINGTON, Sonny
Singles: 7-inch
BAND BOX (228 "Hey-Hey Hey-Hey").....35-50 61

COWARD, Noel LP '56
(With Leo Reisman Orchestra)
EPs: 7-inch
COLUMBIA...5-10 55
LPs: 12-inch 78 rpm
COLUMBIA (5063 "Noel Coward at Las Vegas")...20-30 55
RCA VICTOR (39002 "RCA Presents Noel Coward")..300-400 '30s
(Picture disc.)

COWSILLS P&R/LP '67
Singles: 7-inch
JODA (103 "All I Really Want to Be Is Me")..10-20 65
LONDON..4-6 71-72
MGM...4-6 67-71
PHILIPS...4-8 66-67
Picture Sleeves
MGM...4-8 67-69
PHILIPS...5-10 66
EPs: 7-inch
MGM (1 "The Cowsills")...........................15-25 68
(Promotional issue from the American Dairy Association.)
LPs: 10/12-inch
LONDON...8-10 71
MGM..10-12 67-71
Members: Bill; Barry; John; Susan; Bob; Paul; Barbara.

COWSILLS & LINCOLN PARK ZOO
LPs: 10/12-inch
MERCURY (16354 "The Cowsills Plus the Lincoln Park Zoo")..10-12 68
Also see COWSILLS

COX, Billy
Singles: 7-inch
JAN (121159 "I Can't Wait 'Til Saturday Night")...100-200

COX, Herbie
Singles: 7-inch
RAMA (233 "Leave My Woman Alone")...20-30 61
Also see CLEFTONES

COX, Jerry
(With the Cavaliers)

Singles: 7-inch

BUZ (100 "Lover Man") ... 75-85 58
FRANTIC (751 "Sherry") ... 150-200 59

COX, Wally *P&R '53*

Singles: 78 rpm

RCA ... 5-10 53
WALDORF ... 5-10 55

Singles: 7-inch

ARVEE (5008 "Heebee Jeebees") ... 8-12 60
GEORGE (7779 "Love Me with Soul") ... 10-15 61
LAMA (8881 "Love Me with Soul") ... 10-15 61
RCA (5278 "What a Crazy Guy") ... 10-20 53
WALDORF (218 "Pushcart Serenade") ... 10-20 55
WAND (11233 "This Man") ... 4-8 69

Picture Sleeves

RCA (5278 "What a Crazy Guy") ... 25-35 53

COXON'S ARMY

LPs: 10/12-inch

TRACE ("Coxson's Army") ... 300-500 75
(No selection number used.)
Members: Phil Coxson; Pat Benatar.
Also see BENATAR, Pat

COYNE, Ricky, & His Guitar Rockers
(Rick Coyne)

Singles: 7-inch

EVENT (4289 "Rollin' Pin Mim") ... 100-150 59
EVENT (4290 "Little Darleen") ... 100-150 59
EVENT (4294 "An Angel from Heaven") .. 50-75 59
FENWICK (1011 "Rollin' Pin Mim") ... 150-200 58
MGM (13707 "Hush Pretty Baby") ... 10-15 67
MGM (13799 "Little Dreamer") ... 10-15 67
Also see RICKOCHETS

C-QUENTS

Singles: 7-inch

CAPTOWN (4027 "Merry Christmas Baby") ... 150-250
CAPTOWN (4028 "Dearest One") ... 250-350
ESSICA (004 "Dearest One") ... 15-25

C-QUINS

Singles: 7-inch

CHESS (1815 "My Only Love") ... 5-10 62
DITTO (501 "My Only Love") ... 10-20 62

CRABB, Gene

Singles: 78 rpm

RURAL RHYTHM ... 10-20 55

Singles: 7-inch

RURAL RHYTHM (229 "Gotta Have a Woman") ... 50-75 55

CRABTREE, Riley

Singles: 78 rpm

EKKO (1019 "Meet Me at Joe's") ... 5-10 55

Singles: 7-inch

EKKO (1019 "Meet Me at Joe's") ... 10-20 55

CRACKERJACKS

Singles: 78 rpm

KAPP ... 5-10 54

Singles: 7-inch

KAPP (106 "Paper Valentine") ... 10-20 54
KAPP (109 "Whispering Wind") ... 10-20 54

CRADDOCK, Billy "Crash" *P&R '59/C&W '71*
(Billy Craddock; "Crash" Craddock; Billy Graddock)

Singles: 7-inch

ABC ... 4-6 72-78
ABC/DOT ... 4-6 75-77
ATLANTIC ... 3-5 89
CAPITOL ... 3-6 78-82
CARTWHEEL ... 4-6 71-72
CEE CEE ... 3-5 83
CHART ... 4-8 67-73
COLONIAL (721 "Bird Doggin' ") ... 20-30 58
COLUMBIA (41316 thru 41822) ... 10-15 59-60
DATE (1007 "Lulu Lee") ... 30-40 58
KING (5912 "Betty Betty") ... 15-25 64
KING (5924 "My Baby's Got Flat Feet") ... 8-12 64
MERCURY (71811 "Truly True") ... 8-12 61
MERCURY (71862 "A Diamond Is Forever") ... 8-12 61
SKY CASTLE ("Smacky Mouth") ... 20-30
(No selection number used. Shows Columbia identification numbers, 26671/26672.)

Picture Sleeves

COLUMBIA (41470 "Don't Destroy Me") . 15-25 59
COLUMBIA (41619 "Letter of Love") ... 15-25 60

EPs: 7-inch

ABC ... 5-10 74
(Juke box issue only.)

LPs: 10/12-inch

ABC ... 6-10 72-78
ABC/AT EASE ... 10-12 78
(Special issue for the Armed Forces.)
ABC/DOT ... 8-10 76-77
CAPITOL ... 5-10 78-83
CARTWHEEL ... 10-12 71-72
CHART ... 8-12 73
HARMONY ... 10-12 73
KING (912 "I'm Tore Up") ... 45-55 64
PICKWICK ... 5-10 79
POWER PAK ... 5-10 75
STARDAY ... 8-10
MCA ... 5-10 82

CRAFFORD, Bobby
(With the Pacers)

Singles: 7-inch

RAZORBACK (114 "Red Headed Woman") ... 50-60 63
RAZORBACK (122 "Short Squashed Texan") ... 10-15 65
RAZORBACK (128 thru 135) ... 5-15 65-66
Also see PACERS

CRAFT, Morty

Singles: 7-inch

MGM (12648 thru 12741 ... 8-12 58
SMASH (2087 "Music to Think By") ... 5-10 67
TOD (122 "All Mixed Up") ... 15-25 57
WARWICK ... 8-12 59-61
Also see BARRETT, Richard
Also see CRAFTSMEN

CRAFTSMEN

Singles: 78 rpm

ESSEX (343 "The End") ... 8-12 54

Singles: 7-inch

ESSEX (343 "The End") ... 15-25 54

CRAFTSMEN

Singles: 7-inch

SCOUT (435 "Baseball Song") ... 5-10 61
WARWICK ... 10-20 60-62
Also see CRAFT, Morty
Also see JOHNNY & HURRICANES

CRAFTYS
(With the Candysticks)

Singles: 7-inch

ELMOR (310 "I Went to a Party") ... 30-40 62
LOIS (5000 "L-O-V-E") ... 50-75 61
(First issue.)
7 ARTS (708 "L-O-V-E") ... 15-25 61

CRAIG, The

Singles: 7-inch

FONTANA (1579 "I Must Be Mad") ... 20-25 67

CRAIG, Anna

Singles: 7-inch

DECCA (31803 "Life of the Party") ... 5-10 65
20TH FOX (540 "Can't Beat Love") ... 10-20 64

CRAIG, Earl, & Downbeats

Singles: 7-inch

DOMINION ("Craig's Crazy Boogie") ... 15-25 58
(No selection number used.)
DOMINION (1003 "Saki") ... 10-20 60

CRAIG, Jimmy
(Jimmie Craig)

Singles: 7-inch

BRILL (1 "Gonna Love My Baby") ... 50-75 59
IMPERIAL (5592 "Oh Little Girl") ... 15-20 59
WARWICK (542 "Drifter") ... 15-20 60

CRAIG, Jonathan / Colby Wolf Combo

Singles: 7-inch

FLIP (1001 "Rock a Billy Gal") ... 20-30 57

CRAIG, Ken

Singles: 7-inch

BERTRAM INT'L (216 "Silver Coin") ... 10-15 59

CRAIG, Ken & Karol

Singles: 7-inch

BERTRAM INT'L (219 "That Will Be the Day") ... 10-15 61
Also see CRAIG, Ken

CRAIG, Vilas
(With the Viscounts)

Singles: 7-inch

CUCA (1011 "Don't You Just Know It") ... 10-20 60
FAN JR. (1706 "Poor Loser") ... 10-20 62
FAN JR. (4792 "Don't Sweetheart Me") ... 400-500 62
INT'L ARTISTS (2120 "Little Miss Mary") ... 50-75 60
INT'L ARTISTS (2122 thru 6337) ... 20-25 60-63
RIFF (1148 "Spring Fever") ... 300-500 59
RIFF (2119 "If I May") ... 25-40 60
SIMS (259 "Unlucky Am I") ... 10-20 65
Members: Ronnie McDonald; Dick Faith; Gary Kirschner; Bob Smitke; Jack Goodwiler; Gene Moller; Hal Block; Pete Steele; George Cash; Roger Hessling; Al Sugden; Steve Prestigard; Carl Gillingham; Jim Chitwood; Tom Levarda; Bobby Greenwood; Bill McCorkle.

CRAIG, Vilas & Royal Lancers / Badgers

Singles: 7-inch

CUCA (1072 "Skinny Minnie Twist") ... 10-15 62
Also see CRAIG, Vilas
Also see ROYAL LANCERS

CRAIG, Wick, & Autochords

Singles: 7-inch

COOL (6354 "Auto Hop") ... 10-20 60

CRAMER, Floyd *P&R '54/C&W '60*
(With the Louisiana Hayride Band; with Keyboard Kick Band)

Singles: 78 rpm

ABBOTT ... 4-8 53-54
MGM ... 4-8 55-57

Singles: 7-inch

ABBOTT (142 thru 181) ... 10-20 53-54
MGM ... 10-20 55-57
RCA (0152 thru 2014) ... 3-8 69-74
RCA (7775 thru 9396) ... 6-12 60-67
RCA (10000 & 11000 series) ... 3-6 74-81
SIMS (121 "Fancy Pants") ... 8-12 61

Picture Sleeves

RCA (7840 "On the Rebound") ... 6-12 61
RCA (7907 "Your Last Goodbye") ... 5-10 61
RCA (8084 "Losers Weepers") ... 5-10 62
RCA (8171 "The Young Years") ... 5-10 63
RCA (8217 "How High the Moon") ... 5-10 63
RCA (11916 "Dallas") ... 4-6 80

EPs: 7-inch

MGM ... 8-12 57
RCA ... 8-12 61-63

LPs: 10/12-inch

ALSHIRE ... 8-12 68
CAMDEN ... 6-12 65-74
MGM (3500 series) ... 15-25 57
MGM (4200 series) ... 10-15 64
MGM (4600 series) ... 8-12 70
RCA (0100 thru 4000 series) ... 6-12 73-81
(With "AHL1," ANL1," "APD1," "APL1," or "AYL1" prefix.)
RCA (2000 thru 4000 series) ... 10-20 60-73
(With "LPM" or "LSP" prefix.)
Also see ANN-MARGRET
Also see ATKINS, Chet, Floyd Cramer & Danny Davis
Also see ATKINS, Chet, Floyd Cramer & Boots Randolph
Also see BARE, Bobby
Also see COUNTRY HAMS
Also see FRANCIS, Connie
Also see NASHVILLE ALL-STARS
Also see PRESLEY, Elvis
Also see REEVES, Jim
Also see STARR, Frank, & His Rock-Away Boys

CRAMER, Floyd / Peter Nero / Frankie Carle

LPs: 10/12-inch

RCA (2721 "Three Great Pianos") ... 10-15 63
Also see CRAMER, Floyd

CRAMPS
("Cramps with Bryan & Miriam")

Singles: 12-inch

BIG BEAT (6 "Smell of Female") ... 15-25 83
(Black vinyl. With paper sleeve.)
BIG BEAT (6 "Smell of Female") ... 15-25 83
(Colored vinyl. With paper sleeve.)
BIG BEAT (110 "Can Your Pussy Do the Dog") ... 15-20 85
(10-inch 45 rpm.)
BIG BEAT (110 "Can Your Pussy Do the Dog") ... 15-20 85
(12-inch 45 rpm.)
BIG BEAT (115 "What's Inside a Girl") ... 15-20 86
(With paper sleeve.)
BIG BEAT (135 "Eyeball in My Martini") ... 8-12 91
(With paper sleeve.)
ENIGMA (19 "All Women Are Bad") ... 15-20 90
(With paper sleeve.)
I.R.S. (1008 "The Crusher") ... 30-40 81
(With paper sleeve.)
POW WOW (02 "What's Inside a Girl") ... 200-300 82
(Colored vinyl. Interview with Cramps' Poison Ivy and Lux Interior. No music on disc.)

Singles: 7-inch

CRAMPS/NEW ROSE (1 "Smell of Female – Special Limited Edition") ... 80-100 84
(Seven colored vinyl discs. Includes one track, *Psychotic Reaction*, not on LP. Numbered edition of approximately 10,000.)
CREATION (196 "Naked Girl Falling Down the Stairs") ... 5-8 95
("Limited Colored Vinyl Edition.")
ENIGMA (17 "Bikini Girls with Machine Guns"/"Jackyard Backoff") ... 50-75 90
(Die-cut picture disc. Has 12-inch sleeve.)
EPITAPH (6527-7 "I Walked All Night") .75-125 97
(Red vinyl. Reportedly 500 made.)
I.R.S. (9021 "Goo Goo Muck") ... 4-8 81
I.R.S. (9021 "Goo Goo Muck") ... 35-50 81
(Colored vinyl.)
ILLEGAL/I.R.S. (9014 "Garbageman") ... 5-10 80
LUX (102 "Hurricane Fighter Plane") ... 15-25 77
MEDICINE (18045 "Let's Get F*cked Up"). 5-10 94
VENGEANCE ("Human Fly") ... 50-75 78
(Demo version. Colored vinyl. No number used.)
VENGEANCE (666 "Surfin' Bird") ... 75-100 77
(Counterfeits exist but are easily identified. Their labels are all orange, whereas originals are orange and black.)
VENGEANCE (668 "Human Fly") ... 50-75 78
(Counterfeits exist but are easily identified. Their labels are all orange, whereas originals are orange and black.)

Picture Sleeves

CREATION (196 "Naked Girl Falling Down the Stairs") ... 5-8 95
("Limited Edition.")
EPITAPH (6527-7 "I Walked All Night") ... 100-150 97
I.R.S. (9014 "Garbage Man") ... 10-20 80
I.R.S. (9021 "Goo Goo Muck") ... 10-20 81
ILLEGAL/I.R.S. (9014 "Garbageman") ... 10-15 80
LUX (102 "Hurricane Fighter Plane") ... 15-25 77
(Sleeve is also titled *The Cramps in Dance of the Cannibals of Sex*)
VENGEANCE (666 "Surfin' Bird") ... 75-100 77
(Counterfeits exist but are easily identified. They lack color and their photos are enlarged. Originals have color and smaller photos.)
VENGEANCE (668 "Human Fly") ... 50-75 78
(Fold-out, comic book cover.)
VENGEANCE (668 "Human Fly") ... 25-35 78
(Counterfeits exist but are easily identified. They lack color and their photos are enlarged. Originals have color and smaller photos.)

LPs: 10/12-inch

BIG BEAT (46 "A Date with Elvis") ... 15-25 86
BIG BEAT (101 "Look Mom, No Head") ... 15-25 91
CAVE (001 "Tales from the Cramps") .. 300-400 77
CREATION (170 "Flame Job") ... 50-75 94
(Black vinyl.)
CREATION (170 "Flame Job") ... 100-150 94
(Red vinyl.)
ENIGMA (1001 "Stay Sick") ... 30-50 90
(Limited edition vinyl pressing.)
EPITAPH (86516-2 "Big Beat from Badsville") ... 50-75 97
GIANT (24592 "Flame Job") ... 12-18 94
I.R.S. (70042 "Bad Music for Bad People") ... 20-30 84
ILLEGAL/I.R.S. (007 "Songs the Lord Taught Us") ... 10-15 79
(Tracks on disc are different than those shown on the cover, and in a different sequence than shown on label.)
ILLEGAL/I.R.S. (012 "Off the Bone") ... 15-20 83
(With 3-D cover and glasses.)

ILLEGAL/I.R.S. (012 "Off the Bone") 5-10 83
(With standard cover.)
ILLEGAL/I.R.S. (012 "Off the Bone") 50-80 85
(Picture disc. Includes one extra track.)
ILLEGAL (501 "Gravest Hits") 10-20 79
ILLEGAL/I.R.S. (70016 "Psychedelic Jungle") 8-10 81
LAST RECORD (2022 "Transylvania Tapes") 100-150 78
MIDNIGHT 15-20 78
NST 5-10 85
PRAIRIE DOG ("Totally Destroy Seattle") 300-500
(Colored vinyl. Reportedly 100 made.)
W.B. (86449 "Flame Job") ....8-10 '90s
(Colored vinyl.)
Members: Lux Interior; Congo Powers; Bryan Gregory; Ivy "Poison Ivy" Rorschach; Nick Knox.

CRAMPTON SISTERS *P&R '64*
Singles: 7-inch
ABC (10853 "Baby, Baby") 5-10 66
DCP (1001 "I Didn't Know What Time It Was") 10-15 64

CRANE, Ernie & Margie
Singles: 7-inch
GUIDE (110 "Sugar Daddy") 100-150

CRANE, Jimmy
(Jimmy Crain)
Singles: 78 rpm
TNT (131 "Love Bandit") 15-25 56
Singles: 7-inch
MERLENE (95611 "Break a Heart Each Night") .... 10-15 '60s
PRISM (1001 "Rock-a-Sock Hop") 50-75
SPANGLE (2009 "Shing a Shag") 50-75 58
TNT (131 "Love Bandit") 40-60 56
VINCENT (5048 "Why Worry") 100-150 59
Picture Sleeves
SPANGLE (2009 "Shing a Shag") 75-125 59
LPs: 10/12-inch
RAY-O (2005 "Miles to Go") 40-60 60

CRANE, Lor
Singles: 7-inch
BOARDWALK 5-10 60-65
RADIANT (1512 "Hey, Cleopatera") 30-40 62
STRIPE (301 "Hey, Cleopatera") 40-50 61

CRANE, Sherry
Singles: 7-inch
SUN (328 "Willie Willie") 10-15 59

CRAVERS
Singles: 7-inch
CHOCK FULL O' HITS (109 "Flavor Craver") .... 15-25 '60s
Also see GARVIN, Rex, & Mighty Cravers

CRAWFORD, Blackie
(With the Western Cherokees)
Singles: 78 rpm
CORAL 5-10 52
STARDAY (Except 116) 5-10 53-54
STARDAY (116 "Stop Boogie") 20-30 54
Singles: 7-inch
STARDAY (Except 105 & 116) 10-20 53-54
STARDAY (105 "Huckleberry Pie") 40-60 54
STARDAY (116 "Stop Boogie") 75-100 54

CRAWFORD, Carolyn *R&B '65*
(Caroline Crawford)
Singles: 7-inch
MERCURY 3-5 78-79
MOTOWN (1050 "Forget About Me") 20-40 63
MOTOWN (1064 "My Smile Is Just a Frown Turned Upside Down") 75-100 64
MOTOWN (1064 "My Smile Is Just a Frown [Turned Upside Down]") 25-50 64
(Repressing with title variation.)
MOTOWN (1070 "My Heart") 30-40 64
PHILA. INT'L 4-6 74-75
LPs: 10/12-inch
MERCURY 6-12 78-79

CRAWFORD, Cathy
Singles: 78 rpm
CRYSTALETTE (702 "Te Amo") 10-15 56
Singles: 7-inch
CRYSTALETTE (702 "Te Amo") 15-25 56

CRAWFORD, Don
(With the Escorts)
Singles: 7-inch
BLUE RIVER (228 "Someone To Turn To") .4-8 67
CAPITOL 4-6 70
CHALLENGE 4-6 68-69
CONDOR (101 "Four Leaf Clover") 15-25 61
GONE (5066 "Sleeping Beauty") 5-10 59
LOMA (2063 "If You Need Me") 4-8 66
MIKE (200 "You're Gone") 5-10 62
ROULETTE (7108 "If It Feels Good – Do It") 4-6 71
SCEPTER (1201 "Why Why Why") 30-40 58
VALIANT 4-8 65-66
VERVE FOLKWAYS 4-8 66
W.B. 4-8 67
LPs: 10/12-inch
VERVE FOLKWAYS 10-12 66

CRAWFORD, Faye
Singles: 7-inch
RCA ((8555 "So Many Lies") 10-20 65

CRAWFORD, Fred
Singles: 78 rpm
STARDAY (170 thru 243) 20-30 55-56
STARDAY (314 "By the Mission Wall") 50-75 57
Singles: 7-inch
STARDAY (170 "I Just Need Some Loving") 50-75 55
STARDAY (199 "Can't Live with 'Em") 50-75 55
STARDAY (218 "Me and My New Baby") 50-75 55
STARDAY (243 "Rock Candy Rock") ...100-200 56
STARDAY (314 "By the Mission Wall") ..50-100 57
Session: Buddy Holly; Bowman Brothers.

CRAWFORD, Hank *LP '64*
Singles: 7-inch
ATLANTIC 4-8 61-70
KUDU 4-6 72-78
LPs: 10/12-inchs
ATLANTIC 10-20 61-73
KUDU 10-12 72-76
MFSL (224 "Soul of the Ballad") 30-50 94
Also see KING, B.B.
Also see SCOTT, Shirley

CRAWFORD, James
(James "Sugar Boy" Crawford; Sugar Boy)
Singles: 78 rpm
IMPERIAL 10-20 57
Singles: 7-inch
ACE (625 "Have a Little Mercy") 15-25 61
BLUE ROCK (4033 "Got No Excuse") 5-10 65
IMPERIAL (5424 "She's Gotta Wobble") ..20-30 57
IMPERIAL (5513 "I Need Your Love") 20-30 58
KING (6103 "Hold It") 5-10 67
KING (6130 "I'll Work It Out") 5-10 67
MERCURY (72282 thru 72441) 10-20 64-65
MONTELL (1003 "Danny Boy") 10-20 59
OMEN (12 "Honest I Do") 5-10 66
LPs: 10/12-inch
CHESS (209 "Sugar Boy Crawford") 15-25 76
(Two discs.)
Also see SMITH, Huey
Also see SUGAR BOY & HIS CANE CUTTERS

CRAWFORD, Jesse
Singles: 7-inch
RU-JAC (45001 "I Love You So") 8-12 69
SYMBOL (925 "I Love You So") 15-25 63

CRAWFORD, Jimmy, Frank Motley & His Crew
Singles: 78 rpm
GEM (215 "That Ain't Right") 25-45 53
Singles: 7-inch
GEM (215 "That Ain't Right") 60-75 53
(Also issued as by Frank Motley.)
Also see MOTLEY, Frank

CRAWFORD, Johnny *P&R '61*
Singles: 7-inch
ABC 4-6 73
CINDY 4-6
COLLECTABLES 3-5 81
DEL-FI 10-15 61-65
END (1009 "Undecided Lover") 15-20 58
SIDEWALK (932 "Angelica") 5-10 68
SIDEWALK (941 "Good Guys Finish Last") 5-10 68
WYNNE (124 "Dance with the Dolly") 10-15 60
Picture Sleeves
DEL-FI 10-15 61-63
SIDEWALK 5-8 68
EPs: 7-inch
GRASON (6515 "The Restless Ones") 10-15 66
LPs: 10/12-inch
DEL-FI (1220 "The Captivating Johnny Crawford") 20-30 62
DEL-FI (1223 "A Young Man's Fancy") 20-30 62
DEL-FI (1224 "Rumors") 20-30 63
DEL-FI (1229 "His Greatest Hits") 20-30 63
DEL-FI (1248 "Greatest Hits Vol. 2") 20-30 63
GUEST STAR 15-20 63
RHINO 5-10 82
SUPREME (110 "Songs from *The Restless Ones*") 15-20 66
(Soundtrack. Monaural.)
SUPREME (210 "Songs from *The Restless Ones*") 20-30 66
(Soundtrack. Stereo.)
Also see CRAWFORD BROTHERS
Also see MOUSEKETEERS

CRAWFORD, Johnny, with Johnny Smoke & His Firemen
Singles: 7-inch
SCOTT (113 "No, No, Devil") 15-25 58

CRAWFORD, Paul, & Earls
Singles: 78 rpm
DC (0400 "Let Me Back in There Again") ...5-10 56
Singles: 7-inch
DC (0400 "Let Me Back in There Again") .10-20 56

CRAWFORD, Peter
Singles: 7-inch
SANDY (1039 "Dancing with My Lover") 500-1000 61

CRAWFORD, Sonny
Singles: 7-inch
CRAWFORD (103 "On the Prowl") 75-125

CRAWFORD BROTHERS
Singles: 7-inch
ALADDIN (3375 "Midnight Mover Groover") 15-25 57

CRAWFORD BROTHERS
Singles: 7-inch
DEL-FI (4191 "Good Buddies") 8-12 62
Picture Sleeves
DEL-FI (4191 "Good Buddies") 15-25 62
Members: Johnny; Bobby.
Also see CRAWFORD, Johnny

CRAY, Jackie
Singles: 7-inch
LIMELIGHT (3001 "Maybelle") 50-75 58

CRAYNE, Chuck
Singles: 7-inch
GUYDEN (1043 "Suppressed Desire") 40-50 57
JAMIE (1043 "Suppressed Desire") 8-12 57

CRAYONS
(Cray-Ons)
Singles: 7-inch
COUNSEL (121 "Teach Me Mama") 10-15 63
COUNSEL (122 "Love at First Sight") 10-15 63
Also see RONNIE & CRAYONS

CRAYSELL, Rudy, & T-Birds
Singles: 7-inch
AWARD (130 "You'll Be Mine") 25-35 59

CRAYTON, Maxine
Singles: 7-inch
STEELTOWN (670 "Don't Take Your Love") 10-15 69

CRAYTON, Pee Wee *R&B '48*
(With Red Callender Sextette)
Singles: 78 rpm
ALADDIN 40-60 51
FLAIR 15-25 55
4 STAR (1304 "After Hours Boogie") 30-50 47
IMPERIAL 30-50 54-55
MODERN 30-50 49-51
POST (2007 "Don't Go") 30-50 55
RECORDED IN HOLLYWOOD 40-60 53
VEE-JAY 15-25 56-57
Singles: 7-inch
ALADDIN (3112 "When It Rains It Pours") 100-200 51
BLACK DIAMOND 15-25
BLUES SPECTRUM (15 "Texas Bop") 10-20
EDCO (1009 "Little Bitty Things") 20-30
EDCO (1010 "Money Tree") 25-50
FLAIR (1061 "Central Avenue Blues") ...75-100 55
(Actually by Pee Wee Crayton though shown as by the Carroll County Boys. The flip, *Dizzy*, is by the Carroll County Boys.)
FOX (10069 "Give Me One More Chance") 15-25
GUYDEN (2048 "I'm Still in Love with You") 10-20 61
IMPERIAL (5288 "Do Unto Others") 50-75 54
IMPERIAL (5297 "Win-o") 50-75 54
IMPERIAL (5321 "I Need Your Love") 50-75 54
IMPERIAL (5338 "My Idea About You") ...50-75 55
IMPERIAL (5345 "Eyes Full of Tears") 50-75 55
IMPERIAL (5353 "Yours Truly") 30-40 55
JAMIE (1190 "Little Bitty Things") 10-15 61
MODERN (892 "Cool Evening") 50-75 51
MODERN (892 "Cool Evening") 50-75 51
POST (2007 "I Must Go On") 20-40 55
RECORDED IN HOLLYWOOD (408 "Crying and Walking") 100-200 53
RECORDED IN HOLLYWOOD (426 "Baby Pat the Floor") 75-125 53
SMASH (1774 "Hillbilly Blues") 10-15 62
VEE-JAY (214 "Frosty Night") 30-50 56
VEE-JAY (252 "I Found My Peace of Mind") 30-50 57
VEE-JAY (266 "Fiddle De Dee") 30-50 57
LPs: 10/12-inch
CROWN (5175 "Pee Wee Crayton") 50-100 60
(Back cover has text about Crayton and lists other Crown LPs. No photos used. Company address shown is in Culver City, Calif. Black label.)
CROWN (5175 "Pee Wee Crayton") 10-20 69
(Generic back cover makes no mention of Crayton and pictures other Crown LPs. Company address shown is in Los Angeles, Calif. Gray label.)
MURRAY BROTHERS 5-10 83
VANGUARD 8-12 71
Session: El Dorados.
Also see CALLENDER, Red
Also see CARROLL COUNTY BOYS
Also see EL DORADOS
Also see HOMER THE GREAT

CRAZY CRICKETS
Singles: 7-inch
BAND BOX (290 "Honey Walk") 10-20 61

CRAZY ELEPHANT *P&R '69*
Singles: 7-inch
BELL 5-10 69-70
SPHERE SOUND 5-10 69
LPs: 10/12-inch
BELL 15-20 69
Member: Robert Spencer.

CRAZY TEENS
Singles: 7-inch
SCOTT (6867 "Crazy Date") 50-75

CREAM *LP '67*
Singles: 7-inch
ATCO 8-15 67-69
EPs: 7-inch
ATCO ("Goodbye Cream") 10-15 69
(Promotional issue only.)
LPs: 10/12-inch
ATCO (206 "Fresh Cream") 25-35 67
(With *I Feel Free*. On RSO reissues, this track is replaced with *Spoonful*.)
ATCO (206 "Fresh Cream") 10-20 67
(Without *I Feel Free*.)
ATCO (232 "Disraeli Gears") 20-30 67
ATCO (291 "The Best of Cream") 20-30 69
ATCO (328 "Live Cream") 20-30 70
ATCO (700 "Wheels of Fire") 20-30 68
ATCO (7001 "Goodbye Cream") 20-30 69
ATCO (7005 "Live Cream, Vol. 2") 20-30 72
MFSL (066 "Wheels of Fire") 50-75 82
POLYDOR 10-12 72-73
RSO (Except 015) 5-10 72-83
RSO (015 "Classic Cuts") 35-45 75
(Promotional issue only.)
SPRINGBOARD 10-12
Members: Eric Clapton; Jack Bruce; Ginger Baker.
Also see CLAPTON, Eric

CREAM / Vanilla Fudge

LPs: 10/12-inch

ATCO (7001/278 "Promotional LP for Record Department-in-Store Play") 25-35 68
(Promotional issue only.)
Also see CREAM
Also see VANILLA FUDGE

CREASH, Bob, Quintet

Singles: 78 rpm

UNIQUE (356 "Ain't She Sweet") 5-10 56

Singles: 7-inch

UNIQUE (356 "Ain't She Sweet") 10-15 56

CREATION

Singles: 7-inch

DECCA (32155 "Nightmares") 5-10 67
DECCA (32227 "Life Is Just Beginning") 5-10 67
PLANET (116 "Making Time") 10-15 66
PLANET (119 "Painter Man") 10-15 66

CREATION OF SUNLIGHT

LPs: 10/12-inch

WINDI (1001 "Creation of Sunlight") 400-600 68
Members: G.C. Prophet; J. Griffin.
Also see SUNLIGHT'S SEVEN

CREATION'S DISCIPLE

Singles: 7-inch

DAWN (309 "Psychedelic Retraction") 50-75 66
(Red vinyl.)

CREATIONS

Singles: 78 rpm

LIDO (501 "There Goes the Girl I Love") 50-100 56
TIP TOP (400 "Every Night I Pray") 50-100 56

Singles: 7-inch

LIDO (501 "There Goes the Girl I Love") 200-300 56
TIP TOP (400 "Every Night I Pray") 100-200 56

CREATIONS

Singles: 7-inch

PATTI-JO (1703 "You'll Always Be Mine") 400-600 62

CREATIONS

Singles: 7-inch

MEL-O-DY (101 "This Is Our Night") 75-100 62
MERIDIAN (7552/7553 "I've Got a Feeling"/"The Wedding") 75-100 62
(Identification numbers shown since no selection number is used.)
PINE CREST (101 "Woke Up in the Morning") 250-350 61
RADIANT (103 "Don't Listen to What Others Say") 15-25 64

CREATIONS

Singles: 7-inch

GLOBE (102 "Just Remember Me") 10-15 62
GLOBE (103 "I've Got to Find Her") 10-15 62
GLOBE (1000 "Oh Baby!") 10-15 61
JAMIE (1197 "The Bells") 10-15 61
LIBERTY BELL (013 "Peek-A-Boo") .... 15-20 '60s
VIRTUE 4-6 71-73
ZODIAC (1005 "Dream") 5-10 67

CREATIONS

Singles: 7-inch

PENNY (9022 "Let the We're in Love") ... 50-75 62
TAKE TEN (1501 "We're in Love") 20-25 63
(Note title change to something that makes sense.)

CREATIONS

Singles: 7-inch

TOP HAT (1003 "Crash") 15-25 64
TOP HAT (1004 "Don't Be Mean") 25-35 65

Picture Sleeves

TOP HAT (1003 "Crash") 25-35 64
TOP HAT (1004 "Don't Be Mean") 50-75 65
Members: Chuck Delaney; James Burnham; Howard Plant; Danny Gomes.

CREATIONS IV

Singles: 7-inch

HBR (440 "Little Girl") 10-20 65

CREATORS

Singles: 7-inch

DOOTO (463 "I've Had You") 10-15 61
DORE (635 "Too Far to Turn Around") 40-60 62
Members: Gentry Bradley; Charles Perry; Gerald Middleton; Donald Neal; Thomas Harris; Hillary Connody.
Also see HAMILTON, Little Johnny, & Creators

CREATORS

Singles: 7-inch

EPIC (9605 "Crazy Love") 30-40 63
HI-Q (5021 "Wear My Ring") 50-60 61
(Label print is normal.)
HI-Q (5021 "Wear My Ring") .... 10-15 '60s
(Label print is bold, or thick.)
TIME (1038 "Do You Remember") 10-20 61

CREATORS

Singles: 7-inch

PHILIPS (40058 "Boy, He's Got It") 10-15 62
PHILIPS (40083 "I'll Stay Home") 400-500 62
T-KAY (110 "Boy, He's Got It") 15-25 62
(First issue.)
Members: Johnny Allen; Chris Coles; Danny Austin; Hugh Harris; Jimmy Wright; J.T. Taylor.
Also see AD LIBS

CREATURES

LPs: 10/12-inch

RCA (LPM-1923 "Monster Rally") 25-35 58
(Monaural.)
RCA (LSP-1923 "Monster Rally") 35-45 58
(Stereo.)

CREDIBILITY GAP

Singles: 7-inch

CAPITOL (2246 "Comin' Into My Own") 5-10 68

EPs: 7-inch

W.B. (517 "Credibility Gap") 5-10 73
(Promotional issue only.)

LPs: 10/12-inch

CAPITOL 20-25 71
REPRISE 10-12 73
Members: David L. Lander; Michael McKean.

CREEDENCE CLEARWATER REVIVAL — P&R/LP '68

Singles: 12-inch

FANTASY (238 "Creedence Medley") 10-15 85
FANTASY (759 "I Heard It Through the Grapevine") 15-20 76
(Promotional issue only.)

Singles: 7-inch

FANTASY (616 thru 676) 5-10 68-72
FANTASY (759 thru 971) 4-8 76-81
FANTASY (2832 "45 Revolutions Per Minute") 40-60 70
LIBERTY 4-6 70
SCORPIO (412 "Porterville") 15-25 68

Picture Sleeves

FANTASY (634 "Down on the Corner") 8-12 69
FANTASY (637 "Travelin' Band") 8-12 70
FANTASY (641 "Up Around the Bend") 8-12 70
FANTASY (645 "Lookin' Out My Back Door") 8-12 70
FANTASY (665 "Sweet Hitch-Hiker") 8-12 71
FANTASY (759 "I Heard It Through the Grapevine") 5-10 76
FANTASY (2832 "45 Revolutions Per Minute") 20-25 70

LPs: 10/12-inch

BEVERLY ("Willie and the Poor Boys") .. 75-100
(Half-speed mastered. Number not known.)
FANTASY (1 "Live in Europe") 10-15 73
(Two discs.)
FANTASY (2 "Chronicle") 10-15 76
(Two discs.)
FANTASY (68 "1968/1969") 8-12 78
FANTASY (69 "1969") 8-12 78
FANTASY (70 "1970") 8-12 78
FANTASY (4500 series) 5-10 80-85
(Includes reissues of 8382 through 9404.)
FANTASY (8382 "Creedence Clearwater Revival") 10-20
FANTASY (8387 "Bayou Country") 10-20 69
FANTASY (8393 "Green River") 10-20 69
FANTASY (8397 "Willie and the Poor Boys") 10-20 69
FANTASY (8402 "Cosmo's Factory") 10-20 70
FANTASY (8410 "Pendulum") 10-20 70
FANTASY (9404 "Mardi Gras") 10-20 72
FANTASY (9418 "Creedence Gold") 8-12 72
FANTASY (9430 "More Creedence Gold") . 8-12 73
FANTASY (9621 "Chooglin' ") 5-10 82
K-TEL (9360 "20 Super Hits") 8-12 78
MFSL (037 "Cosmo's Factory") 100-125 79
SWEET THUNDER (13 "Green River") .. 75-100 75
(Half-speed mastered.)
W.B. SPECIAL PRODUCTS (3514 "Greatest Hits") 10-15 85
(TV mail-order offer.)
Members: John Fogerty; Tom Fogerty; Doug Clifford; Stuart Cook.
Also see FOGERTY, John
Also see FOGERTY, Tom
Also see GOLLIWOGS

CREEL SISTERS

Singles: 78 rpm

ABBOTT (3015 "I Do What I Do") 5-10 56

Singles: 7-inch

ABBOTT (3015 "I Do What I Do") 10-15 56

CREEL SISTERS & TOM TALL

Singles: 78 rpm

ABBOTT (3022 "Stop the Clock Rock") 10-15 56

Singles: 7-inch

ABBOTT (3022 "Stop the Clock Rock") 15-25 56
Also see TALL, Tom

CREELS

Singles: 7-inch

JUDD (1005 "Do You Wanna Jump") 10-15 59

CREEPER / Vi-Dells

Singles: 7-inch

VDC (605 "A Fool in Love"/"California") ... 50-75

CREEPERS

Singles: 7-inch

RENE (502 "Jammin' Granny") 500-750

CREEPS

Singles: 7-inch

GINCHEE (1002 "The Whip") 15-25 59

CREME SODA

Singles: 7-inch

KIDERIAN (45121 "Keep It Heavy") 10-20 74
KIDERIAN (45122 "I'm Chewin' Gum") 10-20 74
TRINITY (112 "Keep It Heavy") 25-35 75
TRINITY (45121 "Keep It Heavy") 15-25 75
TRINITY (45122 "Chewin' Gum") 15-25 75

LPs: 10/12-inch

TRINITY (11 "Tricky Fingers") 300-500 75

CRENSHAWS

Singles: 7-inch

W.B. (5254 "Moonlight in Vermont") 10-20 61
W.B. (5505 "Wishing Star") 10-20 62

EPs: 7-inch

W.B. (5505 "Crenshaws") 25-50 61
(Promotional only. Issued without cover.)
Members: Al Frazier; Carl White; Sonny Harris; Turner Wilson; Matthew Nelson; Joe Green.
Also see RIVINGTONS
Also see SHARPS

CRESCENDOS

Singles: 78 rpm

ATLANTIC (1109 "Sweet Dreams") 30-40 56

Singles: 7-inch

ATLANTIC (1109 "Sweet Dreams") 20-30 56
ATLANTIC (2014 "Sweet Dreams") 10-15 59

CRESCENDOS — P&R/R&B '58

Singles: 78 rpm

NASCO (6005 "Oh Julie") 50-75 57
SPARTON (525 "Oh Julie") 25-35 57
(Canadian.)

Singles: 7-inch

ABC 4-6 73
MCA 3-5 84
NASCO (6005 "Oh Julie") 15-25 57
NASCO (6009 "School Girl") 10-15 58
NASCO (6021 "Young and in Love") 10-15 58
SCARLET (4007 "Strange Love") 15-25 60
SCARLET (4009 "Angel Face") 30-40 61
SPARTON (525 "Oh Julie") 25-35 57
(Canadian.)
TAP (7027 "Oh Julie") 5-10 62

Picture Sleeves

NASCO (6009 "School Girl") 20-30 58
NASCO (6021 "Young and in Love") 20-30 58
TAP (7027 "Oh Julie") 10-15 62

LPs: 10/12-inch

GUEST STAR (1453 "Oh Julie") 20-30 62
Members: George Lanuis; Ken Brigham; James Hall; Tommy Fortner.
Also see 4 SEASONS
Also see GREEN, Janice

CRESCENDOS

Singles: 7-inch

DOMAIN (1025 "A Fellow Needs a Girl") . 50-75 63
IMPRO (5006 "Tidal Wave") 20-30 62
NU-SOUND (1007 "Count Down") 15-25 61
NU-SOUND (1014 "Movin' Wild") 15-25 61

CRESCENT SIX

Singles: 7-inch

RUST (5102 "Nightmare") 10-20 66

CRESCENTS

Singles: 78 rpm

RESERVE (105 "Julie") 100-200 56

Singles: 7-inch

RESERVE (105 "Julie") 300-500 56

CRESCENTS

Singles: 7-inch

ARLEN (743 "Smoke Gets in Your Eyes") . 5-10 63
DE-LITE (524 "Smoke Gets in Your Eyes") 8-12 63
(First issue.)
DOT (16447 "Hey There") 10-20 63
HAMILTON (50033 "Hey There") 30-40 63

CRESCENTS — P&R '63

(Chiyo & Crescents)

Singles: 7-inch

BREAK OUT (4 "Pink Dominos") 20-30 63
(With straight horizontal lines.)
BREAK OUT (4 "Pink Dominos") 20-25 63
(With jagged horizontal lines.)
ERA (3116 "Pink Dominos") 10-15 63

CRESCENTS

Singles: 7-inch

BLUE RIVER (225 "So Long Happy Heart") 5-10 66
SEVEN B (2159 "I'll Make a Vow") 25-35 65

CRESCHENDOES

Singles: 7-inch

SATURN (404 "Surfin' Strip") 15-25 63
Member: Chuck Rio.
Also see CRUCHENDOES
Also see RIO, Chuck

CRESCHENDOS

("Lead Voice Wanda Burt")

Singles: 7-inch

GONE (5100 "My Heart's Desire") 15-25 61
MUSIC CITY (831 "My Heart's Desire") 200-300 60
(Green label. "Music City" on two lines.)
MUSIC CITY (831 "My Heart's Desire") 100-150 60
(Maroon label. "Music City" on one line.)
MUSIC CITY (831 "My Heart's Desire") ... 30-40 60
(Black vinyl. Black label with multi-color print.)
MUSIC CITY (831 "My Heart's Desire") 100-200 61
(Blue vinyl.)
MUSIC CITY (839 "Teenage Prayer") .. 250-300 61
Member: Wanda Burt.
Also see BURT, Wanda
Also see CASUAL CRESCENDOS

CRESENTS

Singles: 7-inch

JOYCE (102 "Everybody Knew But Me") 75-125 57
JOYCE (108 "Dolores") 5-10 87
(Black vinyl. 400 made. Credits "Crescents.")
JOYCE (108 "Dolores") 15-20 87
(Red vinyl. 100 made. Credits "Crescents.")

CRESHENDALS

Singles: 7-inch

FORTUNE (566 "Oh My Love") 15-25 64

CRESLYNS

Singles: 7-inch

BELTONE (2036 "Boom Chip-a-Boom") .. 10-20 63

CRESTONES

Singles: 7-inch

MARKIE (117 "She's a BadMotorcycle") .. 10-15 64
MARKIE (123 "I've Had It") 20-30 65
USA (835 "My Girl") 5-10 65

CRESTRIDERS

Singles: 7-inch

CRYSTALETTE (756 "Surf Stomp") ... 10-15 63
(Previously issued as *Boomerang*, by the Spinners and as *The Lion*, by Duke Mitchell.)
Also see MITCHELL, Duke
Also see SPINNERS

CRESTS *P&R '57*
(With Johnny Maestro; with Johnny Mastro; Original Crests; with Al Browne & His Orchestra; Crest's)

Singles: 78 rpm

COED (501 "Pretty Little Angel") ... 150-250 58
COED (506 "16 Candles") ... 350-450 58
JOYCE 103 ("Sweetest One") ... 75-125 57
JOYCE 105 ("No One to Love") ... 75-125 57

Singles: 7-inch

ABC ... 4-6 73
CAMEO (256 "I'll Be True") ... 25-35 64
CAMEO (305 "Lean on Me") ... 8-12 64
COED (501 "Pretty Little Angel") ... 100-150 58
COED (506 "16 Candles") ... 40-50 58
(Red label.)
COED (506 "16 Candles") ... 10-15 61
(Black label.)
COED (509 "Six Nights a Week") ... 30-40 59
COED (511 "Flower of Love") ... 30-40 59
COED (515 "The Angels Listened In") ... 30-40 59
COED (521 "A Year Ago Tonight") ... 30-40 59
COED (525 "Step By Step") ... 25-35 60
COED (531 "Trouble in Paradise") ... 25-35 60
COED (535 "Journey of Love") ... 20-30 60
COED (537 "Isn't It Amazing") ... 20-30 60
COED (543 "In the Still of the Night") ... 15-25 61
COED (561 "Little Miracles") ... 15-25 61
COLLECTABLES ... 3-5 81-83
ERIC ... 3-6 73
GOLDIES 45 ... 3-6 73
HARVEY (501 "16 Candles") ... 5-10 81
(Colored vinyl.)
JOYCE (103 "Sweetest One") ... 100-150 57
(With the oversize letter "Y" in the Joyce logo.)
JOYCE (103 "Sweetest One") ... 20-30
(With all of the letters the same size in the Joyce logo.)
JOYCE (105 "No One to Love") ... 200-300 57
KING TUT (172 "Earth Angel") ... 4-8 78
LANA (102 "Trouble in Paradise") ... 4-6 64
LOST NITE ... 4-8
MCA ... 4-6 73
MUSICTONE (1106 "Sweetest One") ... 10-15 62
ORIGINAL SOUND ... 3-5 87
QUALITY ... 15-30
(Canadian.)
RED HOOK (501 "It Must Be Love") ... 3-5
SELMA (311 "Guilty") ... 100-150 62
(Intro has "judge" bringing court to order.)
SELMA (311 "Guilty") ... 15-25 62
(No talking intro.)
SELMA (4000 "Did I Remember") ... 20-30 63
TIMES SQUARE (2 "No One to Love") ... 20-30 62
(Blue or green vinyl.)
TIMES SQUARE (6 "Baby") ... 10-20 64
(Black vinyl. Selection number on both sides is 6.)
TIMES SQUARE (6 "Baby") ... 20-30 64
(Yellow vinyl.)
TIMES SQUARE (97 "Baby") ... 20-30 64
(Selection number on B-side is 6.)
TRANS ATLAS (696 "The Actor") ... 25-35 62
TRIP ... 4-6 '70s

Picture Sleeves

COED (506 "16 Candles") ... 5-10 '90s

EPs: 7-inch

COED (101 "The Angels Listened In") . 400-500 59

LPs: 10/12-inch

COED (901 "The Crests Sing All Biggies") ... 300-500 60
COED (901 "The Crests Sing All Biggies") ... 500-750 60
("Advance Pressing." Promotional issue only.)
COED (904 "Best of the Crests Featuring Johnny Mastro") ... 300-400 60
COLLECTABLES (5009 "Greatest Hits") ... 8-10 82
COLLECTABLES (P-5009 "Greatest Hits") ... 10-15 82
(Picture disc.)
POST ... 8-12 '70s
RHINO ... 5-10 90
Members: Johnny Maestro; Tom Gough; James Ancrum; Harold Torres; Jay Carter.
Also see BROWNE, Al
Also see MAESTRO, Johnny

CRESTS

Singles: 7-inch

CORAL (62403 "You Blew Out the Candles") ... 30-40 64
POPULAR REQUEST (108 "You Blew Out the Candles") ... 3-5 94

CRESTWOODS

Singles: 7-inch

IMPACT (6 "Angel of Love") ... 15-25 61
(Yellow vinyl.)

CREW

Singles: 7-inch

BRASS (194 "Big Junk") ... 15-25 63
(No London distribution noted.)
BRASS (2900 "Big Junk") ... 10-20 63
(Reads: "Dist. by London Records, Inc.")
YUCCA (713 "Flight 889") ... 15-25 59

CREW-CUTS *P&R '54*

Singles: 78 rpm

MERCURY ... 8-15 54-57

Singles: 7-inch

ABC-PAR (10450 "Hip-Huggers") ... 5-10 63
CHESS (1892 "Ain't That Nice") ... 5-10 64
FIREBIRD ... 4-6 70
4 CORNERS (120 "Earth Angel") ... 5-10 65
MERCURY ... 10-15 54-57
RCA ... 8-12 58-60
VEE-JAY (569 "Three Bells") ... 5-10 63
WARWICK ... 5-10 60-61
WHALE ... 5-10 62

EPs: 7-inch

MERCURY ... 10-20 54-57

LPs: 10/12-inch

CAMAY (3002 "Folk") ... 10-15
MERCURY (20067 "Crew-Cuts Go Long Hair") ... 30-40 55
MERCURY (20140 "On the Campus") ... 30-40 56
MERCURY (20143 "Crew-Cut Capers") ... 30-40 56
MERCURY (20144 "Rock & Roll Bash") ... 35-50 56
MERCURY (20199 "Music A La Carte") ... 30-40 57
MERCURY (25200 "On the Campus") ... 40-60 55
(10-inch LP.)
PICCADILLY ... 8-10 80
RCA (1933 "Surprise Package") ... 20-30 58
RCA (2037 "Crew-Cuts Sing") ... 20-30 59
RCA (2067 "You Must Have Been a Beautiful Baby") ... 20-30 60
WING (12125 "Rock & Roll Bash") ... 15-25 59
WING (12180 "High School Favorites") ... 15-25 60
WING (12195 "Swing the Masters") ... 15-25 60
Members: Ray Perkins; John Perkins; Rudi Maugeri; Pat Barrett.

CREW-CUTS / Junior Powell & Charlotte Grubic

LPs: 10/12-inch

RCA CUSTOM ("The Crew-Cuts Have a Ball") ... 20-30 59
(Special products issue for Ebonite Co. One side has "Bowling Tips By Top Stars.")
Also see CREW-CUTS

CREWE, Bob *P&R '60*
(Bob Crewe Orchestra; Bob Crewe Generation; B.C.G.; with Rays)

Singles: 78 rpm

CORAL ... 5-10 56
SPOTLIGHT (393 "Penny, Nickel, Dime, Quarter on a Teenage Date") ... 10-15 56

Singles: 7-inch

ABC-PAR ... 10-15 61
DYNO VOICE ... 5-10 66-68
CORAL (61688 "Melody for Lovers") ... 10-20 56
CREWE (605 "Dandylion") ... 4-6 71
ELEKTRA ... 3-5 76-77
ERIC ... 3-6 73
GAMBLE (228 "Heartaches") ... 4-6 69
JUBILEE (5148 "Change of Heart") ... 10-20 54
JUBILEE (5164 "It's All Over") ... 10-20 54
MELBA (119 "Guessin' Games") ... 10-20 57
METROMEDIA (229 "Mammy Blue") ... 4-6 72
METROMEDIA (243 "Takin' Care of Each Other") ... 4-6 72
PHILIPS (40241 "Rag Doll") ... 5-10 64
SPOTLIGHT ... 15-25 56
20TH FOX (2271 "Street Talk") ... 4-6 76
U.T. (4000 "Sweetie Pie") ... 10-15 59
VIK (0337 "Charm Bracelet") ... 20-30 57
WARWICK ... 10-15 59-61

Picture Sleeves

DYNO VOICE (233 "Miniskirts") ... 4-8 67
PHILIPS (40241 "Rag Doll") ... 15-25 64
(Sleeve pictures the 4 Seasons.)

LPs: 10/12-inch

CGC ... 10-12 70
CREWE ... 10-15
DYNO VOICE ... 10-12 67-68
ELEKTRA ... 8-10 76-77
GAMBLE ... 4-6 69
PHILIPS (200150 "All the Song Hits of the 4 Seasons") ... 15-20 64
(Monaural. Includes lyrics sheet.)
PHILIPS (200238 "The 4 Seasons Hits") . 10-15 67
(Monaural.)
PHILIPS (600150 "All the Song Hits of the 4 Seasons") ... 15-20 64
(Stereo. Includes lyrics sheet.)
PHILIPS (600238 "The 4 Seasons Hits") . 10-15 67
(Stereo.)
WARWICK (2009 "Kicks") ... 25-35 60
WARWICK (2034 "Crazy in the Heart") ... 25-35 61
Also see LA ROSA, Julius, & Bob Crewe Generation

CREWE, Tom

Singles: 7-inch

BELL (602 "Mighty Fine Girl") ... 10-15 64

CREWNECKS
(With the Khakis)

Singles: 7-inch

RHAPSODY (71959/60 "I'll Never Forget You") ... 50-75 59
RHAPSODY (71961 "Rockin' Zombie") ... 50-75 60
Members: Bob Martin; Boyd "Porky" Hoats; Larry Choper; Jerry Pauley; Bruce Miles.

CRICKETS *R&B '53*
("Featuring Dean Barlow")

Singles: 78 rpm

BEACON ... 30-50 54
JAY-DEE ... 50-75 53
MGM ... 50-75 53

Singles: 7-inch

BEACON (104 "Be Faithful"/"Sleepy Little Cowboy") ... 50-75 54
BEACON (555 "Be Faithful"/"I'm Not the One You Love") ... 10-20 63
DAVIS (459 "I'm Going to Live My Life Alone") ... 40-50 58
JAY-DEE (691 "For You I Have Eyes") ... 4-8 73
JAY-DEE (692 "You're Mine") ... 4-8 73
JAY-DEE (777 "Dreams and Wishes") . 200-300 53
JAY-DEE (781 "I'm Not the One You Love") ... 200-300 53
MGM (11428 "You're Mine") ... 100-150 53
MGM (11507 "For You I Have Eyes") ... 150-200 53

LPs: 10/12-inch

RELIC ... 8-12
Members: Harold Johnson; Leon Carter; J.R. Bailey; Eugene Stapleton; Rodney Jackson; Grover "Dean" Barlow; Robert Spencer; Joe Dias; Freddy Barksdale; William Lindsay; Robert Bynum.
Also see BARLOW, Dean
Also see BARLOW, Dean, & Crickets / Deep River Boys
Also see CADILLACS

CRICKETS / Mellows / Deep River Boys

EPs: 7-inch

DAVIS (211 "Rock & Roll Special") .. 2500-3000 '50s
Also see DEEP RIVER BOYS
Also see MELLOWS

CRICKETS

Singles: 7-inch

BARNABY (2061 "Rockin' '50s Rock and Roll") ... 15-25 72
BRUNSWICK (55124 "Love's Made a Fool of You") ... 15-25 59
BRUNSWICK (55153 "When You Ask About Love") ... 15-25 59
CORAL (62198 "More Than I Can Say") .. 15-25 60
EPIC (08028 "T-Shirt") ... 3-5 88
LIBERTY (55392 thru 55696) ... 15-25 61-64
MGM (14541 "Hayride") ... 10-15 73
MUSIC FACTORY (415 "A Million Miles Away") ... 15-20 68
Note: Records by Buddy Holly & Crickets, even if credited only to the Crickets, are listed in the BUDDY HOLLY section.

Promotional Singles

BRUNSWICK (55124 "Love's Made a Fool of You") ... 20-30 59
BRUNSWICK (55153 "When You Ask About Love") ... 20-30 59
CORAL (62198 "More Than I Can Say") .. 20-30 60
EPIC (08028 "T-Shirt") ... 3-5 88

EPs: 7-inch

B.H.M.S. ... 4-6 78
CORAL (81192 "The Crickets") ... 75-100 63
(With Buddy Holly on one track, *It's Too Late.*)

LPs: 10/12-inch

BARNABY (30268 "Rockin' '50s Rock and Roll") ... 15-25 70
CORAL (57320 "In Style") ... 40-60 60
KOALA ... 8-10
LIBERTY (3272 "Something Old, Something New, Something Blue, Somethin' Else") ... 30-40 64
(Monaural.)
LIBERTY (3351 "California Sun") ... 30-40 64
(Monaural.)
LIBERTY (7272 "Something Old, Something New, Something Blue, Somethin' Else") ... 40-50 64
(Stereo.)
LIBERTY (7351 "California Sun") ... 40-50 64
(Stereo.)
VERTIGO ... 10-20 73
Note: Records by Buddy Holly & Crickets, even if credited only to the Crickets, are listed in the BUDDY HOLLY section.
Members: Sonny Curtis; Jerry Naylor; Glen D. Hardin; Jerry Allison; Joe Mauldin; Earl Sinks; David Box.
Also see ALLISON, Jerry, & Crickets
Also see BOX, David
Also see CAMPERS
Also see CURTIS, Sonny
Also see HOLLY, Buddy
Also see IVAN
Also see JENNINGS, Waylon
Also see NAYLOR, Jerry
Also see ORBISON, Roy
Also see PRESLEY, Elvis
Also see SULLIVAN, Niki
Also see VEE, Bobby, & Crickets

CRIDER, Tommy

Singles: 7-inch

TOKEN (1001 "Sandy") ... 15-25 63

CRIMSON SHADES

Singles: 7-inch

CINEMASOUND (8134 "I Wrote My Love a Letter") ... 100-150 64

CRISS, Gary

Singles: 12-inch

SALSOUL (2059 "Rio de Janeiro") ... 4-8 78

Singles: 7-inch

DIAMOND (except 228) ... 5-10 62-67
DIAMOND (228 "Welcome Home to My Heart") ... 10-20 67
SALSOUL (2082 "Amazon Queen") ... 3-5 79
STRAND (25044 "Good Golly, Miss Molly") ... 10-20 61

CRISS, Gene

Singles: 7-inch

RHYTHM (102 "Hep Cat Baby") ... 1500-2000 57

CRISS, Peter *LP '78*

Singles: 7-inch

CASABLANCA ... 3-5 79-80

LPs: 10/12-inch

CASABLANCA (7122 "Peter Criss") ... 15-25 78
(With poster.)
CASABLANCA (7122 "Peter Criss") ... 8-12 78
(Without poster.)
CASABLANCA (PIX-7122 "Peter Criss") . 50-60 79
(Picture disc.)
CASABLANCA (7240 "Out of Control") ... 25-50 80
Note: We have yet to learn of a U.S. release of the European-issued *Let Me Rock You.*
Also see KISS

CRISS, Sonny

Singles: 7-inch

IMPERIAL (5694 "West Coast Blues") ... 5-10 60
PEACOCK (802 "Sweet Lorraine") ... 5-10 61

LPs: 10/12-inch

IMPERIAL ... 20-25 63

CRITERIONS
Singles: 7-inch
CANADIAN AMERICAN (213 "Don't Say Goodbye")....3-5 99
(Gold vinyl.)
CECILIA (1208 "I Remain Truly Yours").. 20-30 59
CECILIA (1210 "Don't Say Goodbye")..... 10-15 59
(Blue label.)
CECILIA (1210 "Don't Say Goodbye")..... 20-30 59
(Orange label.)
LAURIE (3305 "I Remain Truly Yours")......5-10 65
PRINCE (1210 "Island Fever")....5-10 61
ROULETTE (4076 "Choo Choo Rock") ... 15-25 58
Members: Tommy West; Tim Hauser; Mickey "Guitar" Baker; John Mangi; Jim Ruf; Joe Ernst; Steve Casagrande. Session: Al Casey; "Sticks" Evans; Teddy Charles.
Also see BAKER, Mickey
Also see CASEY, Al
Also see MANHATTAN TRANSFER

CRITTERS *P&R/LP '66*
Singles: 7-inch
KAPP....5-10 65-69
MCA....3-6 73-84
MUSICOR (1044 "Georgianna").... 10-20 65
PRANCER....4-8 68
PROJECT 3....4-8 67-69
Picture Sleeves
KAPP (769 "Mr. Dieingly Sad")....8-12 66
PROJECT 3....4-8 67-69
LPs: 10/12-inch
BACK-TRAC....5-10 85
KAPP (1485 "Younger Girl").... 20-30 66
(Monaural.)
KAPP (3485 "Younger Girl").... 25-35 66
(Stereo.)
PROJECT 3.... 15-20 68
Members: Don Ciccone; Chris Darway.

CRITTERS / Young Rascals / Lou Christie
LPs: 10/12-inch
BOTIQUE.... 10-20 66
(Tracks shown as by the Young Rascals are actually by Felix & Escorts.)
Also see CHRISTIE, Lou
Also see CRITTERS
Also see FELIX & ESCORTS

CROCE, Jim *P&R/LP '72*
Singles: 7-inch
ABC....4-6 72-74
LIFESONG (45001 "Stone Walls")....4-6 75
LIFESONG (45005 "Mississippi Lady")......4-6 76
LIFESONG (45018 "It Doesn't Have to Be That Way")....4-6 77
Picture Sleeves
ABC (11413 "Time in a Bottle")....4-8 73
EPs: 7-inch
ABC (769 "Life and Times").... 10-12 73
(Juke box issue only.)
LPs: 10/12-inch
ABC (100 "A Jim Croce Christmas Programming Sampler").... 15-20 73
(Promotional issue only.)
ABC (756 thru 835)....8-12 72-74
ABC/COMMAND (40006 "You Don't Mess Around with Jim").... 15-25 74
(Quadraphonic.)
ABC/COMMAND (40007 "Life & Times") 15-25 74
(Quadraphonic.)
ABC/COMMAND (40008 "I Got a Name").... 15-25 74
(Quadraphonic.)
ABC/COMMAND (40020 "Photographs and Memories").... 15-25 74
(Quadraphonic.)
BURNS MEDIA (1-2 "The Faces I've Been").... 40-60 75
(Two discs. Promotional issue only.)
CASHWEST (77024 "The Jim Croce Collection")....8-10 77
LIFESONG.... 10-15 75-78
MFSL (079 "You Don't Mess Around with Jim").... 40-60 82
Session: Maury Muehleisen; Tommy West; Joe Macho; Gary Chester; Ellie Greenwich; Marty Nelson; Terry Cashman; David Spinozza.
Also see GREENWICH, Ellie

CROCE, Jim & Ingrid
(Jim & Ingrid)
Singles: 7-inch
CAPITOL....10-15 69
LPs: 10/12-inch
CAPITOL (315 "Croce")....30-35 69
PICKWICK (3332 "Another Day, Another Town")....8-12 '70s
Also see CROCE, Jim

CROCHET, Cleveland *P&R '60*
(With the Sugar Bees; with His Hillbilly Ramblers; with Shorty LeBlanc)
Singles: 7-inch
GOLDBAND (1106 "Sugar Bee").... 10-20 60
GOLDBAND (1114 thru 1156)....5-10 61-64
LYRIC....5-10
LPs: 10/12-inch
GOLDBAND (7749 "Cleveland Crochet and All the Sugar Bees")....50-75 61

CROCKER, Frankie "Loveman"
Singles: 7-inch
TURBO (1 "Ton of Dynamite")....30-50

CROCKETT, G.L. *P&R/R&B '65*
(G. Davy Crockett)
Singles: 78 rpm
CHIEF (7010 "Look Out Mabel")....50-75 57
Singles: 7-inch
CHECKER (1121 "Look Out Mabel")......30-40 65
CHIEF (7010 "Look Out Mabel")....100-150 58
4 BROTHERS (445 "It's a Man Down There")....10-15 65
4 BROTHERS (448 "Every Good-bye Ain't Gone")....8-10 65
4 BROTHERS (451 "Think Twice Before You Go")....8-10 66

CROCKETT, Howard *C&W '73*
Singles: 78 rpm
DOT (15593 "If You'll Let Me")....35-50 57
Singles: 7-inch
DOT (15593 "If You'll Let Me")....40-60 57
DOT (15701 "Branded")....20-30 58
DOT (17000 series)....4-6 73
HAMILTON (50024 "Seven Cards from Now")....10-20 59
MANCO (1002 thru 1023)....8-12 60-61
MEL-O-DY....10-20 63-65
SMASH (1721 thru 1782)....8-12 61-62
SOLAR (500 "Trudy Brown")....200-250
STOP (172 "Big Day")....4-6 68

CROCKETT BROTHERS
Singles: 7-inch
DEL-FI (4213 "Mother, Mother, Can I Go Surfin'")....10-20 63
DONNA (1389 "Fastest Car in Town")......10-20 63
Members: Joel; Jeremy; Chris.

CROFFORD, Cliff
Singles: 78 rpm
TALLY....15-30 56-57
Singles: 7-inch
CHIC (1011 "Teenage Tears")....10-15 57
TALLY (104 "Ain't Nothin' Happenin' to Me")....50-75 56
TALLY (109 "A Night for Love")....25-50 57
Also see BILLY & CLIFF

CROMAGNON
LPs: 10/12-inch
ESP (2001 "Cromagnon")....20-30 69

CROME SYRCUS
Singles: 7-inch
COMMAND (4511 "Take It Like a Man")....5-10 68
JERDEN (921 "Lord in Black")....4-8 69
MERRILYN (5303 "White Korte Feather")..8-12 '60s
PICCADILLY (256 "Lord in Black")....5-10 67
LPs: 10/12-inch
COMMAND (925 "Love Cycle")....15-25 68

CROMWELL, George
(With Larry Love Orchestra)
Singles: 7-inch
BRUNSWICK (55131 "Oh Darling Mine")...8-12 59
GLORY (284 "I'll Be There")....10-20 58

CRONIN, Jerry, & Flashes
Singles: 7-inch
FLAME (113 "Rock-A-Me Baby")....100-200 59

CROOK, Ed
Singles: 7-inch
TRI SOUND (601 "That's Alright")....15-25

CROOK, Tom
(With the Rock'n Roll Four)
Singles: 7-inch
DIXIE (624 "Weekend Boogie")....600-1000

CROOM BROTHERS
Singles: 7-inch
VEE-JAY (283 "It's You I Love")....40-50 58
Member: Dillard Croom Jr.

CROSBY, Bing *P&R '31*
(With the Andrews Sisters)
Singles: 78 rpm
BRUNSWICK....10-20 32-34
DECCA....5-15 34-57
GOLDEN (371 "How Lovely Is Christmas")....10-15 57
(Yellow vinyl. 6-inch disc.)
VICTOR....10-20 31
Singles: 7-inch
AMOS (111 "Hey Jude")....4-6 69
AMOS (116 "More and More")....4-6 69
CAPITOL....5-10 63
COLUMBIA....6-12 59
CROWLEY'S/CROSBY ("How Lovely Is Christmas")....10-20
(Promotional issue made for Crowley's Milk Co.)
DAYBREAK....4-6 71
DECCA (23281 thru 30828)....10-20 51-59
DECCA (31000 series)....5-10 61-65
KAPP (196 "How Lovely Is Christmas")....8-12 57
LONDON....3-6 77
MGM (12946 "Second Time Around")....8-12 60
P.I.P. (8903 "Where the Rainbow Ends")...5-10 71
POLYDOR....3-6 78
RCA (7685 "It's a Good Day")....8-12 60
RCA (7695 "It's a Good Day")....8-12 60
REPRISE....5-10 64-67
U.A....4-6 75
VERVE....4-8
Picture Sleeves
DECCA....10-20 53-63
DAYBREAK....4-8 71
KAPP (196 "How Lovely Is Christmas")...10-15 57
EPs: 7-inch
BRUNSWICK....5-15 50-55
COLUMBIA....8-12 50-57
DECCA ("Old Masters")....20-30
(Boxed EP set. No number shown.)
DECCA (Except 1700)....10-20 50-59
DECCA (1700 "Deluxe Box Set")....75-100 54
(Boxed, 17-disc set. "25th Anniversary Musical Autobiography.")
GOLDEN (408 "Bing Crosby Sings Mother Goose")....15-25 57
RCA....5-10 57
THREE ON ONE (407 "Bing Crosby Sings 2 New Christmas Songs")....5-10 '50s
(Though labeled "45 Extended Play," actually has only one song on each side. May not have been issued with cover.)
W.B. (146 "I Wish You a Merry Christmas")....5-10 62
(Promotional issue only.)
LPs: 10/12-inch
AMOS....8-10 69
ARGO....10-15 76
BIOGRAPH....5-10 73
BRUNSWICK (54000 series)....15-25 55
BRUNSWICK (58000 series)....25-40 52
(10-inch LPs.)
CAPITOL (2300 series)....8-12 65
CAPITOL (11000 series)....5-10 77-78
CITADEL....5-10 78
COLUMBIA (43 "Bing in Hollywood")....10-15 67
COLUMBIA (2502 "Der Bingle")....20-30 56
(10-inch LP.)
COLUMBIA (6027 "Classics")....20-40 49
(10-inch LP.)
COLUMBIA (6105 "Classics, Vol. 2")......20-40 50
(10-inch LP.)
COLUMBIA (35000 series)....5-10 78-79
COLUMBIA SPECIAL PRODUCTS....5-8 77
DECCA (152 "Old Masters")....40-60 55
(Boxed, three-disc set. Includes booklet.)
DECCA (154 "Bing")....50-100 55
(Boxed, five-disc set. Includes booklet.)
DECCA (184 "Best of Bing Crosby")....10-20 65
DECCA (4000 series)....20-50 61-64
DECCA (5000 series)....15-25 49-55
(10-inch LPs.)
DECCA (6000 series)....25-50 55-56
(10-inch LPs.)
DECCA (8000 series)....15-25 54-59
(Black label with silver print.)
DECCA (8000 series)....10-20 60-72
(Black label with horizontal rainbow stripe.)
DECCA (8700 series)....10-15 64
DECCA (9000 series)....10-20 61-62
(Decca LP numbers in this series preceded by a "7" or a "DL-7" are stereo issues.)
DECCA CUSTOM (34461 "Bing Crosby")....10-20
(Promotional issue, made for La-Z-Boy.)
ENCORE....8-10 68
GOLDEN....10-15 57-59
HARMONY (7000 series)....10-15 57
HARMONY (11000 series)....5-10 69
LONDON....5-10 77
MCA....5-10 73-82
MGM....10-15 61-64
METRO....5-10 65
P.I.P.....5-10 71
POLYDOR....5-10 77
RCA (500 series)....6-10 72
RCA (1400 thru 2000 series)....15-25 57-59
(With "LPM" or "LSP" prefix.)
RCA (2000 series)....5-10 77
(With "CPL1" prefix.)
REPRISE....10-15 64
20TH FOX....5-10 79
U.A....5-10 76
VOCALION (3600 series)....10-20 57
VOCALION (3769 "Bing Sings for Children")....5-10 66
W.B.....10-20 60-62
"X" (1000 "Young Bing Crosby")....30-40 54
Session: Gary Crosby; Victor Young Orchestra; Grady Martin & His Slew Foot Five; Les Paul Trio; Jimmy Dorsey Orchestra; Bob Crosby; Woody Herman Orchestra; Eddie Heywood; Carmen Cavallaro; John Scott Trotter; Johnny Mercer.
Also see ANDREWS SISTERS
Also see BOWIE, David, & Bing Crosby
Also see CAVALLARO, Carmen
Also see CROSBY, Gary, & Friend
Also see CROSBY, Gary, Phillip, Dennis, Lindsay & Bing
Also see DORSEY, Jimmy
Also see HERMAN, Woody, Orchestra
Also see MARTIN, Grady
Also see PAUL, Les
Also see SINATRA, Frank, Bing Crosby & Dean Martin
Also see YOUNG, Victor

CROSBY, Bing & Gary *P&R '50*
Singles: 78 rpm
DECCA....5-10 50-54
Singles: 7-inch
DECCA....10-20 50-54

CROSBY, Bing, & Louis Armstrong *P&R '51*
Singles: 78 rpm
CAPITOL....5-10 56
DECCA....5-10 51
Singles: 7-inch
CAPITOL (3506 "Now You Has Jazz")..... 10-20 56
DECCA (27623 "Gone Fishin'")....10-20 51
MGM (12961 "Muskrat Ramble")....8-12 60
LPs: 10/12-inch
MGM (137 "Bing & Satchmo")....5-10 70
MGM (3882 "Bing & Satchmo")....15-25 60
SOUNDS RARE....5-10 83

CROSBY, Bing, Louis Armstrong, Rosemary Clooney & Hi-Los
Singles: 7-inch
COLUMBIA (6277 "Music to Shave By").. 10-20 '50s
(Special products flexi-disc from Remington.)
Also see ARMSTRONG, Louis
Also see CLOONEY, Rosemary
Also see CROSBY, Bing, & Louis Armstrong

CROSBY, Bing, & Fred Astaire
LPs: 10/12-inch
U.A....5-10 77
Also see ASTAIRE, Fred

CROSBY, Bing, & Count Basie
LPs: 10/12-inch
DAYBREAK 8-12 72
Also see BASIE, Count

CROSBY, Bing, & Connee Boswell P&R '37
Singles: 78 rpm
DECCA 4-8 37-40
LPs: 10/12-inch
DECCA 20-30 52

CROSBY, Bing, & Buddy Bregman
EPs: 7-inch
VERVE (5022 "Bing Sings While Bregman Swings") 10-15 59
(With envelope/sleeve.)
LPs: 10/12-inch
VERVE/MGM (2030 "Bing Sings While Bregman Swings") 40-60 56

CROSBY, Bing, & Judy Garland P&R '45
(With the Joseph Lilley Orchestra)
Singles: 78 rpm
DECCA (23410 "Yah-Ta-Ta, Yah-Ta-Ta") 5-10 45
Also see GARLAND, Judy

CROSBY, Bing, Dick Haymes & Andrews Sisters P&R '47
Singles: 78 rpm
DECCA (40039 "There's No Business Like Show Business") 5-10 47
Also see ANDREWS SISTERS
Also see HAYMES, Dick

CROSBY, Bing, & Bob Hope P&R '45
Singles: 78 rpm
DECCA (40000 "Road to Morocco") 5-10 45
EPs: 7-inch
CAPITOL CUSTOM (2263 "Vacation Road to Minnesota") 5-10
(Issued to promote Minnesota tourism.)
Also see BAXTER, Les
Also see HOPE, Bob

CROSBY, Bing, & Louis Jordan P&R '45
(With Louis' Tympany Five")
Singles: 78 rpm
DECCA (23417 "My Baby Said Yes") 5-10 45
Also see JORDAN, Louis

CROSBY, Bing, & Grace Kelly / Bing Crosby & Frank Sinatra P&R '56
(With Johnny Green's Orchestra)
Singles: 78 rpm
CAPITOL (3507 "True Love") 5-10 56
Singles: 7-inch
CAPITOL (3507 "True Love") 10-20 56

CROSBY, Bing / Grace Kelly / Frank Sinatra / Celeste Holm
Singles: 7-inch
CAPITOL (281 "Interviews for use with Capitol Soundtrack LP, *High Society*") 50-100 56
(Promotional issue only.)
Also see SINATRA, Frank

CROSBY, Bing, & Peggy Lee P&R '52
Singles: 78 rpm
DECCA (28238 "Watermelon Weather") 4-8 52
Singles: 7-inch
DECCA (28238 "Watermelon Weather") 10-20 52
Also see LEE, Peggy

CROSBY, Bing, & Johnny Mercer P&R '38
Singles: 78 rpm
DECCA (1960 "Mr. Gallagher and Mr. Shean") 5-10 38
DECCA (3182 "Mister Meadowlark") 5-10 40
Also see MERCER, Johnny

CROSBY, Bing, & Mills Brothers P&R '31
(With Connee Boswell & Victor Young's Orchestra)
Singles: 78 rpm
BRUNSWICK (6276 "Shine") 5-10 32
BRUNSWICK (20102 "Gems from *George White's Scandals*") 5-10 31
Also see MILLS BROTHERS

CROSBY, Bing, & Mel Torme P&R '46
(With the Mel-Tones)
Singles: 78 rpm
DECCA (18746 "Day By Day") 5-10 46
Also see TORME, Mel

CROSBY, Bing, & Orson Welles
LPs: 10/12-inch
DECCA (6000 "The Small One, the Happy Prince") 10-25 50
(10-inch LP.)
Also see CROSBY, Bing
Also see WELLES, Orson

CROSBY, Bob, & Bob Cats
(With the Bob-O-Links; with Eddie Miller; with Nappy Lamare)
Singles: 78 rpm
CORAL 5-10 56
DECCA 5-10 35-42
Singles: 7-inch
CORAL (61714 "Milk Cow Blues") 10-15 56
DOT 8-15 59-60
LPs: 10/12-inch
CAPITOL 10-20 62
DOT 15-25 59-61
Also see CROSBY, Bing

CROSBY, Chris P&R '64
Singles: 7-inch
ATLANTIC (2455 "Hippy Lullaby") 4-8 67
CHALLENGE 5-10 64-65
COLUMBIA 4-8 69
DORE (608 "Teenage Dream") 5-10 61
MGM (13191 thru 13258) 5-10 63-64
W.B. (5338 "Something Special") 5-10 63
Picture Sleeves
MGM (13234 "All I Have to Do Is Dream") 10-15 64
LPs: 10/12-inch
MGM (4226 "Meet Chris Crosby") 15-25 64

CROSBY, Eddie C&W '49
Singles: 78 rpm
DECCA (46180 "Blues Stay Away from Me") 10-20 49

CROSBY, Gary
(With the Cheer Leaders)
Singles: 78 rpm
DECCA 5-10 54-55
Singles: 7-inch
DECCA 10-15 54-55
GREGMARK (11 "That's Alright Baby") 20-25 62
HICKORY (1448 "Town Girl") 5-10 66
Also see ARMSTRONG, Louis, & Gary Crosby
Also see DAVIS, Sammy, Jr., & Gary Crosby

CROSBY, Gary, & Friend (Bing Crosby)
Singles: 78 rpm
DECCA 5-10 50
Singles: 7-inch
DECCA (27112 "Play a Simple Melody") 10-15 50
EPs: 7-inch
DECCA (2001 "Gary Crosby & Friend") 10-15 54

CROSBY, Gary, Phillip, Dennis, Lindsay & Bing P&R '50
Singles: 78 rpm
DECCA 5-8 50
Singles: 7-inch
DECCA (40181 "A Crosby Christmas") 10-15 50
Picture Sleeves
DECCA (1-134 "A CrosbyChristmas") 20-40 50
(Sleeve for 45.)
DECCA (796 "A Crosby Christmas") 10-20 50
(Sleeve for 78.)
Also see CROSBY, Bing
Also see CROSBY, Gary

CROSBY, Harold
(With the Pine Tree Boys)
Singles: 7-inch
LORIDA ("Hire a Mockingbird") 50-75
(No selection number used.)
TOP 50 (104 "Crazy Old Dream") 300-400

CROSBY, STILLS & NASH P&R/LP '69
Singles: 7-inch
ATLANTIC (2652 "Marrakesh Express") 5-8 69
ATLANTIC (2676 "Suite: Judy Blue Eyes") 5-8 69
ATLANTIC (3401 "Just a Song Before I Go") 4-6 77
ATLANTIC (3432 "Fair Game") 4-6 77
ATLANTIC (4058 thru 89969) 3-5 82-83
Picture Sleeves
ATLANTIC (3401 "Just a Song Before I Go") 4-8 77
ATLANTIC (4058 "Wasted On the Way") 3-6 82
ATLANTIC (89812 "War Games") 3-6 83
ATLANTIC (89969 "Southern Cross") 3-6 82
LPs: 10/12-inch
ATLANTIC (902 "4 Way Street") 15-20 71
(Two discs.)
ATLANTIC (8229 "Crosby, Stills & Nash") 15-20 69
ATLANTIC (16026 "Replay") 8-12 81
ATLANTIC (19104 "CSN") 8-12 77
ATLANTIC (19117 "Crosby, Stills & Nash") 5-10 81
ATLANTIC (19360 "Daylight Again") 8-12 82
ATLANTIC (80075 "Allies") 8-12 83
ATLANTIC (82107 "Live It Up") 5-10 90
ATLANTIC (82319 "CSN") 30-40 91
(Boxed, four discs.)
Members: David Crosby; Stephen Stills; Graham Nash.

CROSBY, STILLS, NASH & YOUNG P&R/LP '70
Singles: 7-inch
ATLANTIC (2723 thru 2760) 4-6 70
ATLANTIC (88966 "Got It Made") 3-5 89
Picture Sleeves
ATLANTIC (2740 "Ohio") 4-8 70
EPs: 7-inch
ATLANTIC (7200 "Deja Vu") 10-15 70
(Juke box issue only.)
LPs: 10/12-inch
ATLANTIC (165 "Celebration Copy") 25-35 '70s
(Promotional issue only.)
ATLANTIC (902 "4-Way Street") 12-20 71
(With photo applied to cover.)
ATLANTIC (7200 "Deja Vu") 15-20 70
(With photo applied to cover.)
ATLANTIC (7200 "Deja Vu") 8-12 72
(With photo *printed* on cover.)
ATLANTIC (18100 "So Far") 8-12 74
ATLANTIC (19118 "Deja Vu") 5-10 81
ATLANTIC (19119 "So Far") 5-10 81
ATLANTIC (81888 "American Dream") 5-10 88
MFSL (088 "Deja Vu") 50-75 82
Promotional LPs
ATLANTIC (2575 "In Sync") 10-20 88
(Interview LP for film, *American Dream.* Includes cue sheet, letter and family tree.)
Members: David Crosby; Stephen Stills; Graham Nash; Neil Young. Session: Jerry Garcia.
Also see CROSBY, STILLS & NASH
Also see GARCIA, Jerry
Also see NASH, Graham
Also see STILLS, Stephen
Also see YOUNG, Neil

CROSS, Gay, & Good Humor Six
Singles: 78 rpm
REPUBLIC (7027 "G.C. Rock") 10-15 53
Singles: 7-inch
REPUBLIC (7027 "G.C. Rock") 20-30 53

CROSS, Jimmy P&R '65
Singles: 7-inch
CHICKEN (101 "Hey Little Girl") 5-10 65
RECORDO (502 "Suntan Sally") 8-12 61
RED BIRD (042 "Hey Little Girl") 5-10 65
REO 8-12 64
(Canadian.)
TOLLIE 10-20 64-65

CROSSE, Gay
(Gay Crosse & His Good Humor Six)
Singles: 78 rpm
GOTHAM 10-15 51
MERCURY 10-20 47
QUEEN 10-20 46
RCA 10-20 49-50
REPUBLIC (7027 "G.C. Rock") 5-10 53
Singles: 7-inch
RCA (0033 "Saturday Night Fish Fry") 30-50 49
(Colored vinyl.)
RCA (0050 "It Ain't Gonna Be That Way") 30-50 50
(Colored vinyl.)
REPUBLIC (7027 "G.C. Rock") 15-20 53

CROSSEN, Ray, Jr.
Singles: 7-inch
MUSICOR (1246 "Try Some Soul") 10-20 67

CROSSFIRES
Singles: 7-inch
TOWER (278 "Who'll Be the One") 10-20 66
Also see FOUNTAIN OF YOUTH

CROSSFIRES
LPs: 10/12-inch
STRAND (1083 "Limbo Rock") 30-40 63
Members: Les Philbrick; Dennis Day; David Kent.

CROSSFIRES
Singles: 7-inch
CAPCO (104 "Dr. Jekyll & Mr. Hyde") 20-30 63
LUCKY TOKEN (112 "One Potato, Two Potato") 25-35 65
LPs: 10/12-inch
RHINO 5-10 81
Members: Howard Kaylan; Mark Volman; Don Murray; Chuck Portz; Al Nichol; Dale Walton.
Also see TURTLES

CROSSTONES
Singles: 78 rpm
JAGUAR (3014 "Lies") 50-75 56
Singles: 7-inch
JAGUAR (3014 "Lies") 100-150 56

CROSSTOWN BUS
Singles: 7-inch
MCA 4-8 70
WILDCAT (99999 "I Crave Your Love") 20-30

CROTHERS, Scatman
(Scat Man; Scat Man Carothers; Scatman Crothers Mellow Men; with Riff Charles & His Friends; with Red Callender's Sextet)
Singles: 78 rpm
CAPITOL (15076 "The Thing") 10-20 48
CAPITOL (15220 "Riff's Blues") 10-20 48
CAPITOL (15383 "Pretty Little Blue-Eyed Sally") 10-20 48
CAPITOL (15431 "Have You Got the Gumption") 10-20 49
CENTURY 10-15 55
DECCA 10-15 54
INTRO (6016 "Free Samples") 10-20 51
INTRO (6017 "King Berman's Stomp") 10-20 51
LONDON 10-20 50
MGM 10-15 56
RECORDED IN HOLLYWOOD (152 "Man Have I Got Troubles") 15-25 51
RECORDED IN HOLLYWOOD (401 "Waiting for My Baby") 15-25 53
Singles: 7-inch
CENTURY (710 "Dearest One") 25-35 55
CENTURY (712 "Where Or When") 15-25 55
CHALLENGE (59028 "Take Your Time") 5-10 59
CHALLENGE (59065 "Good Times Will Come") 5-10 60
DECCA (28895 "Honeysuckle Rose") 15-25 54
DECCA (29097 "On the Sunnyside of the Street") 15-25 54
HBR (476 "What's a Nice Kid Like You Doing in a Place Like This") 5-10 66
LONDON (30081 "Television Blues") 40-60 50
MGM (12199 "Sweet Lips") 15-25 56
EPs: 7-inch
DOOTO 5-15 61
LPs: 10/12-inch
CRAFTSMAN 15-25 60
DOOTO 10-15 61
MOTOWN 10-12 73
TOPS (1511 "Rock and Roll with Scat Man") 50-100 56
Also see CALLENDER, Red
Also see WILLIAMS, Ken / Dave Burgess / "Scat Man" Crothers / Johnny James

CROTHERS, Scatman / Gene Merlino / Bud Roman
(With the Toppers)
EPs: 7-inch
TOPS (286 "4 Hits") 15-25 56
(Not issued with cover.)
Also see CROTHERS, Scatman

CROW P&R/LP '69
(David Waggoner)
Singles: 7-inch
AMARET 4-6 69-73
INNER EAR (427 "Autumn of Tomorrow") 30-50
PEAK (1005 "Someone") 8-12 83
(Yellow vinyl.)
LPs: 10/12-inch
AMARET 15-20 69-73
PEAK (15002 "On the Run") 5-10 83

Members: David Waggoner (aka David Wagner); Dennis Craswell; Dick Wiegand; Larry Wiegand; Kink Middlemist.
Also see AARDVARKS
Also see CASTAWAYS
Also see SOUTH 40

CROWD, The
Singles: 7-inch
BATTY (1041 "I Have Nothing At All") ... 50-100 64

CROWE BROTHERS
Singles: 7-inch
FRIDDELL (106 "Jane") ... 75-125

CROWLEY, Sheryl
Singles: 78 rpm
FLASH (112 "It Ain't to Play With") ... 15-25 56
Singles: 7-inch
FLASH (112 "It Ain't to Play With") ... 40-60 56
Also see CURRY, James / Sheryl Crowley

CROWN, Bobby, & Capers
(Bobby Lumpkin)
Singles: 7-inch
FELCO (102 "One Way Ticket") ... 500-750 57
MANCO (1005 "Wait a Minute") ... 25-35 60
Also see LUMPKIN, Bobby

CROWNS
Singles: 7-inch
R n B (6901 "Kiss and Make Up") ... 40-50 58
Members: Ben E. King; James Clark; Charlie Thomas; Dock Green; Elsbeary Hobbs.
Also see DRIFTERS
Also see DUVALS
Also see FIVE CROWNS
Also see KING, Ben E.
Also see MOONGLOWS

CROWNS
Singles: 7-inch
WHEEL (1001 "Heart Breaking Train") .. 75-150 59

CROWNS
Singles: 7-inch
OLD TOWN (1171 "Watch Out") ... 15-25 64

CROWNS
Singles: 7-inch
LIMELIGHT (3031 "It's Still Love") ... 10-15 64

CROWNS
Singles: 7-inch
NU=DISC (8002 "I'll Forget About You") .. 10-20 '60s
(Blue vinyl.)

CROWNS featuring Phillip Harris
Singles: 7-inch
VEE-JAY (546 "I Wonder Why") ... 10-15 63

CROWS *P&R/R&B '54*
(With Melino & His Orchestra)
Singles: 78 rpm
QUALITY (1236 "Gee") ... 50-75 53
(Canadian.)
RAMA (3 "Seven Lonely Days") ... 100-200 53
RAMA (5 "Gee") ... 50-100 53
RAMA (10 "Heartbreaker") ... 50-100 53
RAMA (29 "Baby") ... 75-125 54
RAMA (30 "Miss You") ... 100-200 54
RAMA (50 "Baby Doll") ... 50-100 54
TICO (1082 "Mambo Shevitz") ... 50-100 51
Singles: 7-inch
QUALITY (1236 "Gee") ... 100-150 53
(Canadian.)
RAMA (3 "Seven Lonely Days") ... 600-800 53
RAMA (5 "Gee") ... 50-100 53
(Black vinyl. Blue label. No clouds or lines around "Rama" logo.)
RAMA (5 "Gee") ... 40-60 53
(Black vinyl. Blue label. With clouds and lines around "Rama" logo.)
RAMA (5 "Gee") ... 300-500 53
(Red vinyl.)
RAMA (5 "Gee") ... 20-40 56
(Red label.)
RAMA (10 "Heartbreaker") ... 300-500 53
(Black vinyl.)
RAMA (10 "Heartbreaker") ... 1000-2000 53
(Red vinyl.)
RAMA (29 "Baby") ... 200-300 54
RAMA (30 "Miss You") ... 250-350 54
(Black vinyl.)
RAMA (30 "Miss You") ... 1000-2000 54
(Red vinyl.)
RAMA (50 "Baby Doll") ... 250-350 54
TICO (1082 "Mambo Shevitz") ... 200-300 51
(Black vinyl.)
TICO (1082 "Mambo Shevitz") ... 500-750 51
(Red vinyl.)
LPs: 10/12-inch
MURRAY HILL ... 5-8 88
Members: Daniel "Sonny" Norton; Bill Davis; Harold Major; Jerry Hamilton; Mark Jackson.
Also see ELLIS, Lorraine
Also see HARPTONES / Crows
Also see HUMPHRIES, Fat Man, & Four Notes
Also see JEWELS
Also see WATKINS, Viola

CRUCIBLES
Singles: 7-inch
MAD TOWN (401 "You Know I Do") ... 40-60 66
Members: Ed Erickson; Greg Kimmerly; Treble Lysenko; Bruce Hull; Tom Fisher; John Edland; Dave Brownley; Rod Butler; Fred Elwakil.
Also see KIRIAE CRUCIBLE

CRUDUP, Big Boy *R&B '45*
(Arthur "Big Boy" Crudup)
Singles: 78 rpm
ACE (503 "I Wonder") ... 200-300 53
BLUEBIRD ... 20-50 41-46
CHAMPION (108 "I Wonder") ... 200-300 52
GROOVE ... 20-30 53-54
RCA ... 20-50 47-53
Singles: 7-inch
FIRE (1501 "Mean Ol' Frisco") ... 10-20 62
FIRE (1502 "Katie Mae") ... 10-20 62
GROOVE (0011 "I Love My Baby") ... 30-50 54
GROOVE (0026 "She's Got No Hair") ... 30-50 54
GROOVE (5005 "Mean Ol' Frisco") ... 30-50 56
RCA (50-0000 "That's All Right") ... 400-500 49
(Cherry red vinyl.)
RCA (50-0001 "Boy Friend Blues") ... 250-350 49
(Cherry red vinyl.)
RCA (50-0013 "Shout Sister Shout") ... 150-250 49
(Cherry red vinyl.)
RCA (50-0032 "Hoodoo Lady Blues") ... 150-250 50
(Cherry red vinyl.)
RCA (50-0046 "Come Back Baby") ... 150-250 49
(Cherry red vinyl.)
RCA (50-0074 "Dust My Broom") ... 150-250 50
(Cherry red vinyl.)
RCA (50-0092 "Mean Old Santa Fe") ... 150-250 50
(Cherry red vinyl.)
RCA (50-0100 "Lonesome World to Me") ... 150-250 50
(Cherry red vinyl.)
RCA (50-0105 "She's Just Like Caldonia") ... 150-250 50
(Cherry red vinyl.)
RCA (50-0109 "My Baby Left Me") ... 100-200 50
RCA (50-0117 "Nobody Wants Me") ... 100-200 50
RCA (50-0126 "Roberta Blues") ... 100-200 50
RCA (50-0141 "Too Much Competition") ... 150-250 50
RCA (4367 "Love Me Mama") ... 100-200 51
RCA (4572 "Goin' Back to Georgia") ... 75-125 52
RCA (4753 "Worried About You Baby") .. 75-125 52
RCA (4933 "Second Man Blues") ... 75-125 52
RCA (5070 "Pearly Lee") ... 75-125 52
RCA (5167 "Keep on Drinkin'") ... 75-125 53
RCA (5563 "My Wife and Women") ... 100-150 53
EPs: 7-inch
CAMDEN (415 "Arthur 'Big Boy' Crudup") ... 100-125 57
LPs: 10/12-inch
COLLECTABLES ... 6-8 88
DELMARK ... 15-25 69
FIRE (103 "Mean Ol' Frisco") ... 150-200 62
RCA ... 10-20 71
TRIP (7501 "Mean Ol' Frisco") ... 8-12 75
Also see CRUDUP, Percy Lee
Also see CRUMP, Arthur
Also see JAMES, Elmore
Also see LITTLE RICHARD / Arthur Crudup / Red Callender Sextet

CRUDUP, Big Boy / Spade Cooley / Dick Leibert / Saul Meisels / Al Goodman & His Orchestra
Singles: 7-inch
RCA ("The New RCA Victor 45 R.P.M. Record Line") ... 500-750 49
(Seven discs packaged in a "This Is Your Preview" envelope. Promotional issue only.)
Note: Each of the seven is a different color vinyl, representing seven different musical styles: cerise [cherry] for Blues & Rhythm (*That's All Right*, Big Boy Crudup, 50-0000); green for Country & Western (*Spanish Fandango*, Spade Cooley, 48-0027); sky-blue for International (*A Klein Melamedl*, Saul Meisels, 51-0000); midnight blue for Popular Classics (*The French Marching Song*, Al Goodman & His Orchestra, 52-0006); black for Popular (*Because*, Dick Leibert, 47-2857). The other two in the series, the artists and titles of which we do not yet know, are: red for Red Seal and yellow for Children's Entertainment.
As the industry's first 45s, preview envelope reads: "Use these seven records as samples between now and March 31st, and for use with the forthcoming window and counter displays. You may wish to hold them as collector's items – the first production run of a record that will set the pace for the entire industry!"
Also see COOLEY, Spade
Also see CRUDUP, Big Boy

CRUDUP, Percy Lee
(Arthur Crudup)
Singles: 78 rpm
CHECKER (754 "Open Your Book") ... 25-50 52
Also see CRUDUP, Big Boy

CRUISERS
("Featuring Leroy Jones")
Singles: 7-inch
FINCH (353 "The Moon Is Yours") ... 250-300 57

CRUISERS
("Vocal by E. Thornberry")
Singles: 7-inch
ARCH (1611 "I Want Your Love") ... 30-40 59
CODA (3005 "Betty Ann") ... 750-1000 59
COLLECTABLES ... 3-5 83
DORE (500 "Buoys & Gulls") ... 10-20 58
DORE (2003 "Lighthouse Rock") ... 10-20 58
(Promotional issue only.)
ERA (1052 "Buoys & Gulls") ... 15-25 57
JASON SCOTT (15 "Foolish Me") ... 3-5 82
(500 made.)
WINSTON (1033 "My Mary Lou") ... 40-50 59
ZEBRA (119 "There's a Girl") ... 200-300 58

CRUISERS
Singles: 7-inch
GAMBLE (207 "I Need You So") ... 5-10 67
GAMBLE (4000 "Picture Us") ... 5-10 69
GUYDEN (2069 "Cryin' Over You") ... 10-15 62
V-TONE (207 "Miss Fine") ... 30-40 60
(Black label. Block print.)
V-TONE (207 "Miss Fine") ... 10-20 60
(Blue label.)
V-TONE (207 "Miss Fine") ... 8-12 60
(Orange label.)
V-TONE (213 "Cryin' Over You") ... 15-25 60
(Blue label.)

CRUISERS
Singles: 7-inch
PHARAOH (125 "An Angel Like You") ... 50-75 61
PHARAOH (128 "Another Lonely Night") . 30-40 61

CRUM, Simon *C&W '55*
(Ferlin Husky)
Singles: 78 rpm
CAPITOL ... 5-15 55-57
Singles: 7-inch
ABC ... 4-6 74
CAPITOL ... 5-15 55-63
LPs: 10/12-inch
CAPITOL (1880 "The Unpredictable Simon Crum") ... 75-100 63
Also see HUSKY, Ferlin

CRUM, Tom
Singles: 7-inch
MR. CRUM (801 "Dance Baby Dance") ... 50-75
UNIVERSAL SOUND ... 4-6 71

CRUMB, Robert, & His Cheapsuit Serenaders
LPs: 10/12-inch
BLUE GOOSE ... 10-15 74

CRUMP, Arthur
(Arthur Crudup)
Singles: 78 rpm
CHAMPION ("I Wonder") ... 75-100
Also see CRUDUP, Big Boy

CRUMPETS
Singles: 7-inch
TECHNIQUE (101 "Mama Baby") ... 20-30 65

CRUSADE
Singles: 7-inch
GOLDEN NORTH (103 "Psychedelic Woman") ... 20-35 '60s

CRUSADERS
Singles: 7-inch
D.K.R. (12565 "Seminole") ... 20-30 62
(No selection number shown. "12565" is the identification number.)
CAMEO (285 "Boogie Woogie") ... 5-10 63
DOOTO (472 "I Found Someone") ... 10-15 63

CRUSADERS *LP '71*
Singles: 7-inch
ABC ... 4-6 78
BLUE THUMB ... 4-6 72-77
CHISA (8013 "Pass the Plate") ... 4-6 71
MCA (8783 "Street Life") ... 20-30 79
(Picture disc. Promotional issue only. Reportedly 125 made.)
MCA ... 3-5 80-84
MOWEST (5028 "Spanish Harlem") ... 4-6 72
LPs: 10/12-inch
BLUE THUMB ... 10-12 73-77
CHISA (807 "Pass the Plate") ... 10-15 71
GRP ... 5-8 91
MASTERTONE (4453 "I've Fought a Good Fight") ... 10-15 71
MCA ... 8-10 79-86
MFSL (010 "Chain Reaction") ... 40-60 78
(Half-speed mastered.)
MOTOWN ... 10-12 73
MOWEST ... 10-12 72
Members: Wilton Felder; Stix Hooper; Wayne Henderson; Joe Sample; Larry Carlton; Pops Popwell.
Also see JAZZ CRUSADERS

CRYAN' SHAMES *P&R '66*
Singles: 7-inch
COLUMBIA ... 4-8 66-70
DESTINATION (624 "Sugar and Spice") .. 10-15 66
Picture Sleeves
COLUMBIA ... 8-12 67
LPs: 10/12-inch
BACK-TRAC ... 5-10 85
COLUMBIA (2589 "Sugar and Spice") ... 20-25 66
(Monaural.)
COLUMBIA (2786 "A Scratch in the Sky") ... 20-25 67
(Monaural.)
COLUMBIA (9389 "Sugar and Spice") ... 15-20 66
(Stereo.)
COLUMBIA (9586 "A Scratch in the Sky") ... 15-20 67
(Stereo.)
COLUMBIA (9719 "Synthesis") ... 15-20 69
Also see GUILLORY, Isaac

CRYSTAL, Lou
Singles: 7-inch
SFAZ (1001 "Sheila Baby") ... 15-25 62
Session: Elites.
Also see ELITES

CRYSTAL BALL
Singles: 7-inch
SMASH (2092 "You're a Big Girl Now") ... 10-15 67

CRYSTAL CHANDELIER
Singles: 7-inch
COBBLESTONE (730 "Suicidal Flowers") ... 30-40 69
U.A. (50284 "Setting of Despair") ... 10-20 68

CRYSTAL TONES
(Crystaltones)
Singles: 7-inch
M.Z. (110 "A Girl I Love") ... 250-350 59

MZ (174 "I Apologize")....................4-8 '80s
Also see JAMES, Billy, & Crystaltones

CRYSTALAIRES OF LANCASTER, PA.
Singles: 7-inch
SOUND SOUVENIR (1 "Nobody Nowhere")....................100-200 63
(Record store [Stan's Record Bar] promotional issue only.)

CRYSTALETTES
Singles: 7-inch
CRYSTALETTE....................10-15 62-63

CRYSTALIERS
(Cleo & Crystaliers)
Singles: 7-inch
ARCADE (1001 "Please Be My Guy")........5-10 76
CINDY (3003 "Please Be My Guy")..... 400-500 57
JOHNSON (103 "Please Be My Guy")....................1000-1500 57
(First issue.)

CRYSTALS
("Vocal by the Crystals with Orchestra")
Singles: 78 rpm
LUNA....................50-75 54
Singles: 7-inch
LUNA (101 "Come to Me Darling")....... 300-350 54
(Reads "Recorded at Mastertone Studios, New York, N.Y." at bottom.)
LUNA (101 "Come to Me Darling")....... 100-150 54
(No mention of Mastertone Studios.)
LUNA (5001 "Come to Me Darling")....... 75-100 54
Also see OPALS

CRYSTALS
("Vocal by the Crystals with Orchestra")
Singles: 78 rpm
DE LUXE (6013 "My Dear")............ 400-500 53
DE LUXE (6037 "Have Faith in Me").... 400-500 54
DE LUXE (6077 "My Girl")....................50-75 55
ROCKIN' (518 "My Girl")....................300-400 53
Singles: 7-inch
DE LUXE (6013 "My Dear").............2000-3000 53
DE LUXE (6037 "Have Faith in Me")....................1500-2500 54
DE LUXE (6077 "My Girl")....................100-200 55
(No High Fidelity on label.)
Members: Earl Wade; Johnny Hopson; Martin Brown; Ted Williams.
Also see CADILLACS

CRYSTALS
Singles: 78 rpm
ALADDIN (3355 "I Love My Baby")......... 50-75 57
Singles: 7-inch
ALADDIN (3355 "I Love My Baby")......... 50-75 57

CRYSTALS
Singles: 7-inch
SPECIALTY (657 "In the Deep")............ 30-40 58

CRYSTALS
Singles: 7-inch
FELSTED (8566 "Blind Date").................. 10-20 59

CRYSTALS
(With Ray Ellis & Orchestra)
Singles: 7-inch
METRO (20026 "Better Come Back to Me")....................15-20 59
Also see ELLIS, Ray, Orchestra

CRYSTALS
Singles: 7-inch
BRENT (7011 "Gypsy Ribbon")............... 10-20 60
CUB (9064 "Watchin' You")................... 30-40 60
INDIGO (114 "Dreams & Wishes")........... 15-25 61
IONA (1009 "Laughing On the Outside"). 15-25 61
REGALIA (17 "Pony in Dixie")....................8-10 61

CRYSTALS — P&R/R&B '61
Singles: 7-inch
GUSTO....................3-5 '80s
MICHELLE (4113 "Should I Keep On Waiting")....................50-100 67
PAVILLION....................4-6 82
PHILLES (100 "There's No Other")......... 30-40 61
PHILLES (102 "Uptown")................... 30-40 62
PHILLES (105 "He Hit Me")................... 50-100 62
(Orange label.)
PHILLES (105 "He Hit Me")................... 10-20 68
(Blue label.)
PHILLES (106 "He's a Rebel")................ 20-30 62
PHILLES (109 "He's Sure the Boy I Love")....................20-30 62
PHILLES (111 "Let's Dance the Screw")....................5000-7500 63
(Blue label. Beware, counterfeits exist.)
PHILLES (111 "Let's Dance the Screw")....................5000-5500 63
(White label. Promotional Issue Only.)
PHILLES (112 "Da Doo Ron Ron")...........20-30 63
PHILLES (115 "Then He Kissed Me") 20-30 63
(Blue label.)
PHILLES (115 "Then He Kissed Me") 10-15 63
(Yellow label.)
PHILLES (118 "I Wonder")....................200-300 63
(Same selection number used for a Ronettes release.)
PHILLES (119 "Little Boy")....................20-30 64
(Same selection number used for a Darlene Love release.)
PHILLES (119X "Little Boy")................200-300 64
(Single-sided disc.)
PHILLES (122 "All Grown Up")................20-30 64
U.A. (927 "My Place")....................5-10 65
U.A. (994 "I Got a Man")....................5-10 66
LPs: 10/12-inch
PHILLES (4000 "The Crystals Twist Uptown")....................200-300 62
(Monaural. Blue label.)
PHILLES (4000 "The Crystals Twist Uptown")....................550-750 62
(Monaural. White label. Promotional issue only.)
PHILLES (4000 "The Crystals Twist Uptown")....................500-650 62
(Stereo.)
PHILLES (4001 "He's a Rebel")...........200-300 63
(Monaural. Blue label.)
PHILLES (4001 "He's a Rebel")...........500-750 63
(White label. Promotional issue only.)
PHILLES (4003 "Crystals")....................150-250 63
(Monaural. Blue label.)
PHILLES (4003 "Crystals")....................500-750 63
(White label. Promotional issue only.)
PHILLES (90722 "The Crystals Twist Uptown")....................750-1000 62
(Capitol Record Club issue.)
Members: Barbara Alston; Lala Brooks; Mary Thomas; Dee Dee Kennibrew; Patricia Wright.
Also see ALSTON, Shirley
Also see LOVE, Darlene
Also see RONETTES / Crystals / Darlene Love / Bob B. Soxx & Blue Jeans

CUBANS
Singles: 7-inch
FLASH (133 "Tell Me")....................100-150 58

CUBS
Singles: 78 rpm
SAVOY (1502 "I Hear Wedding Bells").....15-25 56
Singles: 7-inch
SAVOY (1502 "I Hear Wedding Bells").....30-40 56

CUCUMBER
Singles: 7-inch
COBBLESTONE (715 "Under")................15-25 68

CUES — P&R '55
Singles: 78 rpm
CAPITOL....................10-15 55-56
JUBILEE....................10-15 55
LAMP....................10-15 54
PREP....................10-20 57
Singles: 7-inch
CAPITOL (3245 thru 3582)....................25-35 55-56
JUBILEE (5201 "Only You")....................15-20 55
LAMP (8007 "Scoochie Scoochie")..........15-25 54
PREP (104 "Crazy, Crazy Party")............15-25 57
Members: Ollie Jones; Jimmy Breedlove; Abe DeCosta; Robey Kirk; Eddie Barnes.
Also see BREEDLOVE, Jimmy
Also see NUGGETS
Also see RAVENS
Also see TUCKER, Anita

CUFF LINKS
Singles: 78 rpm
DOOTO....................30-50 57
DOOTONE....................30-50 56
Singles: 7-inch
DOOTO (409 "Guided Missiles")..............15-25 57
(Second issue.)
DOOTO (413 "How You Lied")....................30-40 57
DOOTO (414 "Twinkle")....................30-40 57
DOOTO (422 "It's Too Late Now")............50-75 57
DOOTO (474 "Chancing My Love")..........10-15 63
DOOTONE (409 "Guided Missiles") 50-75 56
(First issue.)
GAIT (1445 "Only One Love")..............100-150 65
Members: Robert Truesdale; Everett Tyson; John Anderson; Al Gaitwood; Marshall Lamb; Henry Huston.
Also see CUFFLINX
Also see HANK & SUGAR PIE

CUFFLINX
Singles: 7-inch
DOOTO (433 "So tough")....................30-40 58
DOOTO (434 "A Fool's Fortune") 40-50 58
DOOTO (438 "Lawful Wedding")..............30-40 58
Members: Robert Truesdale; Henry Houston; Moses Walker; Ray Dierdan; Johnny Simmons.
Also see CUFF LINKS

CUGAT, Xavier — P&R '35
Singles: 78 rpm
COLUMBIA....................4-8 41-55
RCA....................3-6 50-57
VICTOR....................4-8 35-41
Singles: 7-inch
COLUMBIA....................5-10 50-55
DECCA....................4-6 65
MERCURY....................4-6 62-64
RCA....................5-10 50-62
EPs: 7-inch
COLUMBIA....................5-15 55-59
MERCURY....................5-15 53-54
LPs: 10/12-inch
CAMDEN....................10-15 59
COLUMBIA....................10-20 62
DECCA....................10-20 65-69
HARMONY....................10-15 60
MERCURY....................10-30 53-67
MUSICO....................10-15 69
RCA (Except 3021)....................15-25 58-60
RCA (3021 "Siboney")....................25-40 53
(10-inch LP.)

CUGAT, Xavier, & Dinah Shore
LPs: 10/12-inch
RCA (3022 "Tangos")....................25-40 53

CULLEY, Frank — R&B '49
(Frank "Floorshow" Culley; with the Buddy Tate Orchestra)
Singles: 78 rpm
ATLANTIC....................20-40 49-51
BATON....................10-20 56
LENOX....................15-25 49
Singles: 7-inch
BATON (226 "After Hours Express") 15-25 56
EPs: 7-inch
BATON (7001/2 "Rock & Roll")..............50-100 56
(Price is for either volume.)
LPs: 10/12-inch
BATON (1201 "Rock & Roll")...............150-250 56
Also see RUSHING, Jimmy

CULLENS, Tommy
Singles: 7-inch
CORINA (2002 "Need Your Love").......100-200 60
(Credits Cullens, but may be by the Five Chances. We have yet to learn if copies credited to the Five Chances exist.)

CULMER, Little Iris
(With the Majestics)
Singles: 78 rpm
MARLIN....................300-400 56
Singles: 7-inch
MARLIN (803 "Frankie, My Eyes Are On You")....................2500-3500 56
Also see MAJESTICS

CULVER, Bruce
Singles: 7-inch
M.M.I. (1235 "Square Record")................20-30 58

CUMBERLAND THREE
Singles: 7-inch
ROULETTE (4247 thru 4357)....................5-10 60-61
LPs: 10/12-inch
ROULETTE (25121 "Folk Scene, U.S.A.")....................25-40 60
ROULETTE (25132 "Civil War Almanac – Yankee Songs")....................30-50 60
ROULETTE (25133 "Civil War Almanac – Rebel Songs")....................30-50 60
Members: John Stewart; John Montgomery; Gil Robbins.
Also see STEWART, John

CUMMINGS, Carol
Singles: 7-inch
CHECKER (983 "Just to Make You Mine")....................50-100 61

CUMMINGS, Larry
Singles: 7-inch
ARGO (5343 "When Autumn Calls")........10-15 59
CHESS (1755 "Long Lonely Nights")........10-15 60
MOCKINGBIRD (1006 "Marine")................5-10 '60s

CUMMINGS, William
Singles: 7-inch
BANG BANG ("Make My Love a Hurtin' Thing")....................20-30 '60s
(No selection number used.)

CUMMINS, Christy
Singles: 7-inch
ELECT (100 "Vote Yes On Proposition Love")....................5-10 64
PRO (504 "Sweet Summer Memories")...10-15 61
ROULETTE (4319 "Till Then")................10-15 61
VENETT (103 "Get Together") 10-15 63

CUMMINS, Pete
Singles: 7-inch
RAELEX (50 "In the Middle of the Night")....................100-200

CUNNINGHAM, Buddy
Singles: 78 rpm
SUN (208 "Right Or Wrong") 200-300 54
Singles: 7-inch
SUN (208 "Right Or Wrong") 400-600 54

CUNNINGHAM, Dale
Singles: 7-inch
CASH (1066 "Rockin' Blues")...................20-30 58
CASH (1067 "Trust Me")..........................40-50 58

CUNNINGHAM, Jim
Singles: 7-inch
STARDAY (519 "A Pain a Pill Won't Reach")....................50-75

CUNNINGHAM, Parker
Singles: 7-inch
REBEL (700 "Dry Run")....................2000-2500

CUNNINGHAM, Skip
Singles: 7-inch
CORAL (62406 "Paradise")........................5-10 64
CORAL (62433 "Like Anything")................5-10 64
KAPP (455 "The Best Man Cried")...........10-15 62
KAPP (480 "River's Run Dry")..................10-15 62
20TH FOX (588 "Have We Met Before")....5-10 65

CUNO, Fred & Jesse
Singles: 7-inch
KAY (1 "Mine All Mine")..........................75-125

CUPCAKES
Singles: 7-inch
DIAMOND (177 "Pied Piper") 10-15 65
(Brown vinyl.)
TIME (1011 "It's Willy")....................8-12 59

CUPIDS
Singles: 78 rpm
DECCA (30279 "Answer to Your Prayer")....................15-25 57
Singles: 7-inch
DECCA (30279 "Answer to Your Prayer")....................15-25 57

CUPIDS
Singles: 7-inch
ALADDIN (3404 "Now You Tell Me")........30-40 58
(Brown label.)
ALADDIN (3404 "Now You Tell Me")........15-25 58
(Black label.)

CUPIDS
Singles: 7-inch
CHAN (107 "Troubles Not at End") 40-50 62
UWR (4241 "True Love True Love").........25-35 62

CUPIDS — P&R '63
Singles: 7-inch
AANKO (1002 "Brenda")........................100-200 63
(First issue.)
KC (115 "Brenda")....................40-50 63

CUPIDS
Singles: 7-inch
MUSICNOTE (119 "Lorraine")................. 15-25 63

CUPIDS
Singles: 7-inch
TIMES SQUARE (1 "Pretty Baby") 10-20 64
(Red vinyl.)

CUPIDS
Singles: 7-inch
GALAXY (734 "For You") 10-20 66

CUPIT, Earl
Singles: 7-inch
MYRL (401 "Don't Touch Me").................. 50-75 61

CUPP, Pat
(With the Flying Saucers)
Singles: 78 rpm
RPM.. 20-30 56
Singles: 7-inch
RPM (461 "Do Me No Wrong")................ 40-60 56
RPM (473 "To Be the One")..................... 40-60 56
Also see SMITH, Ray / Pat Cupp

CURB, Mike *P&R/LP '70*
(Mike Curb Congregation; with Sidewalk Sounds; with Curbstones; with Rebelaires; with Waterfall)
Singles: 7-inch
BUENA VISTA...4-6 75
FORWARD..4-6 69
MGM...4-6 70
REPRISE (0287 "Hot Dawg")..................... 10-20 64
SMASH (1938 "The Rebel")...................... 10-15 64
TOWER 10-15 66
W.B. 3-5 77
Picture Sleeves
BUENA VISTA..5-10 75
FORWARD..4-8 69
LPs: 10/12-inch
BUENA VISTA...8-12
COBURT 8-12 70
FORWARD (1023 "Hot Wheels")................5-10 69
(Soundtrack of TV show.)
MGM...5-10 71
Also see ALLAN, Davie
Also see DAVIS, Sammy, Jr.
Also see HANDS OF TIME
Also see HEYBURNERS
Also see OSMONDS
Also see OWENS, Gary
Also see SIDEWALK SOUNDS
Also see WILLIAMS, Hank, Jr.

CURFEWS
Singles: 7-inch
MONTGOMERY (008 "Look at Me")........ 10-20 '60s

CURINGTON, Harold
Singles: 7-inch
TAD (100 "One Day Girl")........................ 10-15 '60s

CURIOSITIES
Singles: 7-inch
SEEBURG (3011 "Walkin' the Dog") 20-35 65
SEEBURG (3013 "Money")....................... 20-35 65
SEEBURG (3014 "Twist & Shout") 20-35 65
SEEBURG (3015 "Johnny B. Goode")..... 20-35 65

CURLESS, Dick *C&W '65*
Singles: 7-inch
ALLAGASH (101 "A Tombstone Every Mile")... 15-25 65
CAPITOL...4-8 70-73
TOWER 5-10 65-68
LPs: 10/12-inch
BELMONT 6-10 78-80
CAPITOL.. 10-20 70-73
INTERSTATE..8-12 76
PICKWICK/HILLTOP ....8-15 '70s
TIFFANY (1016 "Songs of the Open Country")... 50-75 58
TIFFANY (1028 "Singin' Just for Fun") 50-75 59
TIFFANY (1033 "I Love to Tell a Story") 75-100 60
TOWER 15-25 65-68

CURLEY JIM
(With Billy Rocks)
Singles: 7-inch
METRO (100 "Rock & Roll Itch").......... 200-250 58
MIDA (100 "Rock & Roll Itch").............. 75-125 58
MIDA (108 "Sloppy, Sloopy Susie") 75-125 58

CURLEY & JADES
Singles: 7-inch
MUSIC MAKERS (109 "Boom Stix").........20-30 61
REPRISE (20046 "Boom Stix")..................10-15 62

CURRENTS
Singles: 7-inch
LAURIE (3205 "Night Run") 10-20 63

CURRIE, Bob
Singles: 7-inch
STRAND (25032 "Count 7 Stars") 10-20 61

CURRY, Clifford *P&R/R&B '67*
(Cliff Curry)
Singles: 7-inch
ABBOTT 4-6 72
BUDDAH (520 "Body Shop")........................4-6 76
C.C...5-10
CAPRICE (1003 "Delta Dawn").....................4-6 72
ELF...10-20 67-69
RIDGECREST (1202 "Kiss Kiss Kiss").100-150 59
SSS INT'L (812 "Soul Ranger") 10-15 70
LP: 10/12-inch
WOODSHED..8-12
Session: Bergen White.
Also see ACCENTS
Also see CONTINDERS
Also see FIVE PENNIES
Also see NOTATIONS
Also see WHITE, Bergen

CURRY, Dalyce, & Roulettes
Singles: 7-inch
ANGLE (1001 "Surfer's Charge").............10-15 63

CURRY, Dan
Singles: 7-inch
CRIMSON (1 "She's My Girl")..................20-30

CURRY, Earl
(With the Blenders)
Singles: 78 rpm
POST...30-40 55
R&B...100-150 54-55
RPM..50-75 54
Singles: 7-inch
POST (2001 "Special Girl").......................50-75 55
POST (2011 "Love Somebody")..................50-75 55
R&B (1304 "I Want to Be with You").....200-300 54
R&B (1313 "Try and Get Me")..............200-300 55
RPM (402 "One Whole Year Baby") 100-200 54

CURRY, Ed
Singles: 78 rpm
ARCADE (110 "What Do You Think My Heart Is Made Of")..5-10 52
Singles: 7-inch
ARCADE (110 "What Do You Think My Heart Is Made Of")..10-20 52
BRUNSWICK...10-15 58
DOL (101 "Don't Be Long") 10-15 57

CURRY, James "King"
Singles: 78 rpm
FLASH (110 "Please Baby")......................15-25 56
RECORDED IN HOLLYWOOD (210 "The Right Train") 20-30 52
Singles: 7-inch
FLASH (110 "Please Baby").......................30-40 56
MOVIN' (100-19 "Saturday Night Shakin' ")..15-25 57
Also see JAYHAWKS

CURRY, James / Sheryl Crowley
Singles: 78 rpm
FLASH 10-15 56
Singles: 7-inch
FLASH (107 "Still Longing for You") 15-25 56
Also see CROWLEY, Sheryl

CURRY, Kenneth
Singles: 7-inch
SCATT (114/115 "Loneliness"/"I Am").......30-40 59

CURTIN, Lee
Singles: 7-inch
END (1118 "Gee, I'm Sorry").......................8-12 63
GIZMO (003 "Gee, I'm Sorry") 10-20 61

CURTIS, Benny
(With the Millionaires)
Singles: 7-inch
BRIDGES (1102 "I Wonder")...................75-125 61
BRIDGES (1104 "Make It Now") 40-50 61

DYNAMITE (1115 "Ain't That Tuff")............5-10 63
RESIST (502 "Dirty Hearts") ....25-35 '60s

CURTIS, Bill
Singles: 7-inch
ARC (4443 "Panic Stricken")..................75-125 58

CURTIS, Cry Baby
Singles: 7-inch
CASH (1062 "Did You Think I Care") 50-75 58
JULET (1005 "There Will Be Some Changes Made")..5-10
ROMARK (110 "There Will Be Some Changes Made")..25-35
TREVOR (103 "Don't Just Stand There ...25-35

CURTIS, Don
(Butch McClary)
Singles: 7-inch
KLIFF (104 "Rough Tough Man") 100-150 58
Also see McCLARY, Butch

CURTIS, Don Day
Singles: 7-inch
ABC-PAR (10416 "Don't Sit Under the Apple Tree")...10-15 63
ABC-PAR (10459 "Bumble Bee") 10-15 63

CURTIS, Eddie
(With the Bear Cats; Eddie "Tex"Curtis)
Singles: 78 rpm
DOT (15505 "Don't Cry")...........................10-20 56
GEE (7 thru 9)..15-25 54
OKEH (7063 "Sweet Stuff").......................10-20 55
Singles: 7-inch
ABC-PAR 5-10 62-63
BEAR CAT (717 "Love You All the Time")..15-25 60
DECCA..5-10 61-62
DOT (15505 "Don't Cry")..........................15-25 56
GEE (7 "The Girl I Left Behind") 20-30 54
GEE (8 "Brown")......................................20-30 54
GEE (9 "Prayer to the Moon")..................20-30 54
JELL (501 "Ham Hocks")............................5-10 65
JOSIE (957 "Those Foxes & Pussycats") ..5-10 66
OKEH (7063 "Sweet Stuff") 15-25 55
PARKWAY (825 "Let it Live").....................5-10 61
TODD (1039 "Torero Serenade") 5-10 59
Session: Coins.
Also see COINS

CURTIS, Eddie & Jewel
Singles: 78 rpm
ATCO (6063 "Rich Lady from Sugarhill") .10-15 56
Singles: 7-inch
ATCO (6063 "Rich Lady from Sugarhill") .15-25 56
Also see CURTIS, Eddie

CURTIS, George
Singles: 7-inch
BERKLEY (903 "Vacation")....................75-125

CURTIS, Ken
Singles: 78 rpm
BULLET (666 "It's in the Cards") 8-12 48
LIBERTY (55014 "Wedding Day") 5-10 56
Singles: 7-inch
DECCA (30676 "Sugar Lips") 15-20 58
LIBERTY (55014 "Wedding Day") 15-25 56
R-DELL (105 "Five Years")........................10-15 58
LPs: 10/12-inch
CAPITOL (2418 "Gunsmoke's Festus") ...30-40 66
DOT (25859 "Gunsmoke's Festus Haggen")...25-35 68
PICKWICK 10-20

CURTIS, Ken / Rex Allen & Arizona Wranglers
Singles: 78 rpm
MERCURY/SAV-WAY (6045 "Lemme Outa Here")...100-150 47
(Picture disc. Promotional issue only.)
Also see ALLEN, Rex
Also see CURTIS, Ken
Also see SONS OF THE PIONEERS

CURTIS, Lance
(With the Uniques)
Singles: 7-inch
'TEEN (507 "Bye Bye Baby") 50-75 59
'TEEN (509 "Sympathy")......................150-250 60

CURTIS, Lennie
Singles: 7-inch
END (1127 "Who You Gonna Run To")..50-100 64

CURTIS, Mac *C&W '68*
Singles: 78 rpm
KING...25-75 56-57
Singles: 7-inch
DOT..5-10 62
EPIC..4-8 68-70
FELSTED (8592 "Come Back Baby") 10-15 59
GRT..4-6 70
KING (4927 "If I Had Me a Woman").....75-125 56
(Blue label.)
KING (4927 "If I Had Me a Woman")....100-150 56
(White bio label. Promotional issue only.)
KING (4949 "Grandaddy's Rockin'")...100-200 56
KING (4965 "You Ain't Treatin' Me Right")..100-200 56
KING (4995 "That Ain't Nothin' But Right")..100-200 56
KING (5059 "Say So")..............................25-50 57
KING (5107 "What You Want")................40-60 57
KING (5121 "Little Miss Linda") 40-60 58
LIMELIGHT (3010 "Lie and Get By")..........4-6 63
SHAH (982 "Singing the Blues")..............10-15 61
SHALIMAR (103 "Come On Back")............5-10 63
TOWER (319 "Ties That Bind") 4-8 67
LPs: 10/12-inch
EPIC 12-20 68
GRT..10-15 71
ROLLIN' ROCK...8-10
Session: Ron-dells.

CURTIS, Mac / Ron-Dels
Singles: 7-inch
MARIDENE (111 "100 Pounds of Honey")...10-15 63
Also see CURTIS, Mac
Also see RON-DELS

CURTIS, Rita
Singles: 7-inch
WOLFF (102 "This Little Girl") 50-100
(Canadian.)

CURTIS, Sonny
Singles: 78 rpm
CORAL...5-10 53
Singles: 7-inch
CORAL (61023 "The Best Way to Hold a Girl")..10-15 53
CORAL (62207 "Red Headed Stranger"). 10-15 60

CURTIS, Sonny *C&W '66*
Singles: 7-inch
A&M (1359 "The Lights of L.A.")..............20-30 72
CAPITOL..8-12 75-76
DIMENSION (1017 "Last Song I'm Ever Gonna Sing")..8-12 63
DIMENSION (1024 "I Want to Be a Beatle")..8-12 63
DOT (15754 "Wrong Again").....................15-25 58
DOT (15799 "A Pretty Girl") 15-25 58
ELEKTRA..3-5 79-81
LIBERTY (55710 "Bo Diddley Bach").......10-15 64
MERCURY (73438 "Rock 'n Roll") 8-12 73
OVATION (1006 "Here, There and Everywhere")...10-15 70
'STEEM 3-5 85
VIVA..10-15 66-69
LPs: 10/12-inch
ELEKTRA..8-15 79-81
IMPERIAL (9276 "Beatle Hits")................25-35 64
(Monaural.)
IMPERIAL (12276 "Beatle Hits")..............30-40 64
(Stereo.)
VIVA (36012 "1st of Sonny Curtis") 20-30 68
VIVA (36021 "The Sonny Curtis Style") ...20-30 69
Also see CAMPERS
Also see CAMPS
Also see CLAPTON, Eric
Also see CRICKETS
Also see HOLLY, Buddy
Also see PEWTER, Jim

CURTIS & BOYS
Singles: 7-inch
DERBY (1011 "Somewhere There's a Girl")..30-40 64

CURTIS & GALAXIES
Singles: 7-inch
GAITY (6014 "Laura Lee") 25-35 60

CURTIS & JOE
Singles: 7-inch
BELLAIRE (108 "Rock-a-Bayou Baby") 150-250

CURTIS & MELODY COWBOYS
Singles: 7-inch
MURCORD (5443 "Mr. Blues") 50-75

CURTIS & SHOWSTOPPERS
Singles: 7-inch
VICTAN (14880 "Sad Girl") 30-40

CURTISS, C.C.
Singles: 7-inch
AUDICON (109 "Aunt Minnie") 40-60 60
WINK (1001 "Please Let Me Know") 20-30 60

CURTISS, Jimmy
Singles: 7-inch
LAURIE (3312 "You're What's Happening Baby") 8-12 65
LAURIE (3315 "Let's Dance Close") 20-30 65
LAURIE (3383 "Psychedelic Situation")... 15-20 67
U.A. (215 "Without You") 15-25 60
U.A. (312 "Miss Untrue") 15-25 61
W.B. (5257 "Five Smooth Stones") 10-15 62
Session: Regents.
Also see HOBBITS
Also see TREMONTS

CURTOLA, Bobby *P&R '62*
(With the Martells)
Singles: 7-inch
DEL-FI 10-20 61-63
KING 5-10 67
TARTAN-AMERICAN 8-12 63-66
Picture Sleeves
DEL-FI (4182 "I Cry and Cry") 10-20 61
DEL-FI (4185 "Aladdin") 10-20 61

CUSHMAN, Mike
EPs: 7-inch
LEO'S ("Mike Cushman") 100-150
(Selection number not known.)

CUSTOMS
Singles: 7-inch
REGANO (1062 "Steppin' Out") 25-35 62
(Reissued as *Surfin' '63*, as by the Original Sufaris.)
Also see QUADS / Grand Prix / Customs
Also see SURFARIS (Original Surfaris)

CUSTOMS FIVE
Singles: 7-inch
TASK (108 "Let's Go") 15-25 68

CUTCHINS, Bobby
Singles: 7-inch
LASSO (503 "I Did It Again") .... 10-20 '60s

CUTE TEENS
Singles: 7-inch
ALADDIN (3458 "When My Teenage Days Are Over") 100-150 59
Member: Raynoma Gordy.

CUTUPS
Singles: 7-inch
JIM (852 "She Has Gone") 10-15 59
MUSIC MAKERS (301 "Romeo") 5-10 62

CWAZY WABBITS – ROCK STONE & AL MOORE
Singles: 7-inch
CHECKER (950 "The Bunny's Easter Song") 8-12 60
Picture Sleeves
CHECKER (950 "The Bunny's Easter Song") 10-20 60

CYCLONE III
Singles: 7-inch
PHILIPS (40258 "You've Got a Bomb") ... 15-25 65

CYCLONES
Singles: 78 rpm
FLIP (324 "My Dear") 100-200 57
Singles: 7-inch
FLIP (324 "My Dear") 150-250 57

CYCLONES *P&R '58*
Singles: 7-inch
QUALITY (1796 "Bullwhip Rock") 20-30 58
TROPHY (500 "Bullwhip Rock") 20-30 58
TROPHY (503 "Aftermath") 20-30 58
Member: Bill Taylor.

CYCLONES
Singles: 7-inch
FORWARD (313 "Good Goodnight")....150-250 59

CYCLONES
Singles: 7-inch
FESTIVAL (25003 "Say What?")..............15-25 61

CYCLONES
Singles: 7-inch
LEE (5467 "She's No Good") ....10-20 '60s

CYKLE
Singles: 7-inch
LABEL (101 "If You Can") 15-25 69
Picture Sleeves
LABEL (101 "If You Can") 25-50 69
LPs: 10/12-inch
LABEL (101 "Cykle")..............................400-600 69
Also see YOUNG ONES

CYMBAL, Johnny *P&R '63*
Singles: 7-inch
AMARET..4-8 69
COLUMBIA (43842 "Jessica") 5-10 66
DCP (1135 "Go V.W. Go")..........................10-15 65
DCP (1146 "My Last Day")........................10-15 65
KAPP (Except 503)...................................10-15 63-64
KAPP (503 "Mr. Bass Man").......................15-20 63
KEDLEN (20018 "Bachelor Man") 10-15 63
MCA..3-6 73-84
MGM...10-15 60-61
MUSICOR (1261 "It Looks Like Love").......5-10 67
MUSICOR (1272 "Breaking Your Balloon") 5-10 67
VEE-JAY (495 "Bachelor Man") 8-10 63
Picture Sleeves
DCP (1135 "Go V.W. Go")..........................15-25 65
LPs: 10/12-inch
KAPP (1324 "Mr. Bass Man") 25-40 63
(Monaural.)
KAPP (3324 "Mr. Bass Man") 35-50 63
(Stereo.)
Also see MILK
Also see TAURUS

CYMBALS
Singles: 7-inch
AMAZON (709 "One Step Too Far").........15-25 62
DOT (16472 "Voice of a Fool")..................15-25 63

CYNARA
LPs: 10/12-inch
CAPITOL (547 "Cynara")...........................20-30 70

CYNEMAN VYNE
Singles: 7-inch
COCONUT GROVE (2042 "Changes") ..50-100

CYPRESS, Buddy
Singles: 78 rpm
JAB (102 "Don't Forsake Me") 10-15 56
Singles: 7-inch
FLASH (118 "Don't Forsake Me") 15-25 57
JAB (102 "Don't Forsake Me") 40-50 56

CYR, Joe
Singles: 7-inch
ALLEY (1005 "Too Wild to Tame") 15-20 63

CYRESS, Buddy
Singles: 78 rpm
FLASH (118 "I'm in Love with You") 25-35 57
Singles: 7-inch
FLASH (118 "I'm in Love with You") 25-35 57

CYRKLE *P&R/LP '66*
Singles: 7-inch
COLUMBIA (Except picture discs and 43589)...5-10 65-68
COLUMBIA ("Interview") 15-20 66
(Square-shaped cardboard picture disc.)
COLUMBIA ("Interview") 20-30 66
(Square-shaped cardboard picture disc. Still bound in *Teen Scoop* magazine.)
COLUMBIA (43589 "Red Rubber Ball")......5-10 65
(Black vinyl.)
COLUMBIA (43589 "Red Rubber Ball")....10-15 65
(Colored vinyl. Promotional issue only.)
Picture Sleeves
COLUMBIA...20-30 66-68
LPs: 10/12-inch
COLUMBIA (2544 "Red Rubber Ball")......20-25 66
COLUMBIA (9344 "Red Rubber Ball") 25-30 66
COLUMBIA (2632 "Neon")........................20-25 67
(Monaural.)
COLUMBIA (9432 "Neon")........................20-30 67
(Stereo.)
FLYING DUTCHMAN/AMSTERDAM (12007 "The Minx") 20-25 70
(Soundtrack.)

CYRKLE / Paul Revere & Raiders
Singles: 7-inch
COLUMBIA (466 "Camaro"/"SS 396")......10-15 66
(Special Products Chevrolet "Swingin' Chevy Circle" promotional issue only.)
Picture Sleeves
COLUMBIA (466 "Camaro"/"SS 396")......15-25 66
(Special Products Chevrolet "Swingin' Chevy Circle" promotional issue only.)
COLUMBIA (43000 series) 5-10 66-67
Members: Don Danneman; Marty Fried; Tom Dawes; John Simon; Michael Losekamp.
Also see CYRKLE
Also see REVERE, Paul, & Raiders
Also see SIMON, Paul

CZARS
("Vocal By Kent Kauffman")
Singles: 7-inch
SPLASH (300 "What's the Matter Baby").10-20 66
Members: Kent Kauffman; Dave Gruenberger; Boyd Abbott; Pat Abel; Jim Vinelli.

CZARS OF RHYTHM
Singles: 7-inch
DE'VOICE (782 "You Show Me the Way") 150-250 65

Summit
Records, Inc.
Travis Music
(BMI)
1001
Time: 2:08
LET THE FOUR WINDS BLOW
(Bartholomew-Domino)
ROY BROWN
Arranged & Conducted by
Ray Shanklin
SUMMIT RECORDS, INC., LOS ANGELES, CALIF.

The California Raisins
Sing:
I Heard It Through The Grapevine
Lead Vocals by Buddy Miles

Cannons
Solid Gold
Hits!

PRESIDENT
UNBREAKABLE
45 R.P.M.
RECORD NO.
1008
(P 116)
Wemar Music Corp.
Time 2:22 (BMI)
FLYIN HOME TO MY BABY
(Burton, Randolph, Upshore)
DORIAN BURTON

D

D., Ronnie, & Valiants

Singles: 7-inch

SEA LOCK (27 "Hound Dog Guitar")....... 10-20

D MEN

Singles: 7-inch

KAPP (691 "So Little Time")........................8-12 65
VEEP (1206 "Don't You Know")............ 10-15 65
VEEP (1209 "Just Don't Care")............... 10-15 65
Members: Wayne Wadhams; Rick Engler; Doug Ferrara; Bill Shute; Ken Evans.
Also see FIFTH ESTATE

D.A.

Singles: 7-inch

RASCAL (102 "Ready 'N Steady")......... 75-125 79

LPs: 10/12-inch

FRONTLINE...5-10 85-86

D.C. BLOSSOMS

Singles: 7-inch

SHRINE (107 "I Know About Her")...... 200-300 66

D.C. DRIFTERS

Singles: 7-inch

REACTION (1008 "I Know")..................... 40-60 '60s

D.C. MAGNATONES

Singles: 7-inch

D.C. MAGNATONES (216 "Does She Love Me")... 350-450 63

D.D.T. & REPELLENTS

Singles: 7-inch

RCA (8064 "Fly Swatter")........................ 10-15 62

D.J. & CATS

Singles: 7-inch

HEP (2100 "Jeanie 16")............................ 40-60 59
HEP (2101 "Lightning Strikes")............... 40-60 59

D-Y & MOTIVATORS

Singles: 7-inch

LINJO.. 10-20 65-66

DAARTS

Singles: 7-inch

DYNA (109 "Cut Me Up")........................ 15-25 61

DABETTES

Singles: 7-inch

ADVANCE (3933 "Why Do You Care").... 10-20 62
Member: Karen Caple.

D'ACCORDS

Singles: 7-inch

DON-EL (110 "Runnin' Around")............. 15-20 61

DACHE, Bertell

Singles: 7-inch

DIAMOND (201 "Don't Stop the World for Me").. 35-50 66
U.A. (260 "You Gotta Have Chicks")........ 25-30 60
U.A. (290 "Not Just Tomorrow, But Always").. 25-30 61
Members: Tony Orlando; Carole King.
Also see KING, Carole
Also see ORLANDO, Tony

DA COSTA, Rita

Singles: 7-inch

MOHAWK (703 "Don't Bring Me Down") . 15-25 69
PANDORA (7049 "Don't Bring Me Down") 100-200
TOWER (168 "Am I Ever Gonna Learn")...8-12 65

DADDY CLEANHEAD
(Fred Higgins)

Singles: 78 rpm

SPECIALTY(541 "Let Me Come Back Home")... 10-15 55

Singles: 7-inch

SPECIALTY (541 "Let Me Come Back Home")... 20-30 55

DADDY COOL

Singles: 78 rpm

REPRISE (522 "Teenage Heaven")......... 15-25 72
(Promotional issue only.)

Singles: 7-inch

BLUE SKY (107 "Story of Daddy Cool"/ "Wedding Bells Are Ringing in My Ears") ..8-10 73
(B-side by the Blue Sky Boys.)
REPRISE...4-8 71-72
SPARMAC (019 "I'll Never Smile Again").50-75 72

LPs: 10/12-inch

REPRISE (2088 "Teenage Heaven") 15-25 72
REPRISE (6471 "Daddy Who? Daddy Cool")..20-25 71

DADDY "G"
("Daddy;" Gene Barge)

Singles: 7-inch

LEGRAND (1026 "Moonlight in Vermont")...10-20 63
LEGRAND (1028 "Look Alive") 20-30 63
Also see BARGE, Gene
Also see CHURCH STREET FIVE

DADDY O's P&R '58

Singles: 7-inch

CABOT (122 "Got a Match") 10-20 58

DAE, Danny, & Defiants

Singles: 7-inch

ARLEN (521 "Beatle Mania") 15-20 64

DAE, Sonny

Singles: 78 rpm

ARCADE (123 "Movin' Guitar") 10-15 54

Singles: 7-inch

ARCADE (123 "Movin' Guitar") 15-25 54

DAE, Tommy
(With the High Tensions; with Tensionettes; Tom Dae)

Singles: 7-inch

DIAMOND (226 "Summertime Girl")...........5-10 67
GLO (5245 "Candy Heart")..........................5-10 '60s
GOLDISC (G-12 "Janie")............................10-15 63
HITT (01 "Vibrations").................................4-6 78
HITT (03 "So Dedicated")...........................4-6 78
HITT (591 "Tampico Rage").......................20-30 64
HITT (6401 "Watch Out").............................4-8
HITT (7002 "I Shall Walk") 15-25
Also see HIGH TENSIONS & TOMMY DAE

DAFFODILS & CARL JONES / Phyllis Smiley
(With Ike Perkins Band)

Singles: 7-inch

C.J. (100 "Wine"/"These Kissable Lips")..75-100 57

D'AGOSTIN, Dick
(With the Swingers)

Singles: 7-inch

ACCENT (1046 "I'm Your Daddy-O") 15-25
ACCENT (1049 "Mean Mean Woman")....10-15
DOT (15773 "Nancy Lynne")......................35-50 58
DOT (15867 "Night Walk") 15-25 58
LIBERTY (55218 "I Let You Go")...............5-10 59

DAHL, Tiny, & Robyns

Singles: 7-inch

U.A. (582 "Sailin' Home") 10-15 63

DAHLIAS
(With the Big Records Orchestra)

Singles: 7-inch

BIG (612 "Go Away")..................................50-75 57

DAIGLE, Ted

Singles: 7-inch

RODEO (219 "Mary Lou") 400-600

DAILEY, Don

LPs: 10/12-inch

CROWN (5314 "Surf Stompin' ") 30-40 63
Also see BOYD, Billy

DAIRD, Jay, & Four Storms

Singles: 78 rpm

ARCADE (133 "Dear Father in Heaven") ...5-10 54

Singles: 7-inch

ARCADE (133 "Dear Father in Heaven") .10-15 54
Also see FOUR STORMS

DAISIES

Singles: 7-inch

CAPITOL (5667 "Cold Wave") 15-25 66
ROULETTE (4571 "I Wanna Swim with Him")...5-10 64

DAISY MAE & HER HEPCATS

Singles: 78 rpm

GOTHAM (7-317 "Lonesome Playgirl") 10-20 56
RICHLOY (102 "Want Me a Man")............15-25 56

20TH CENTURY (1204 "Hop Scotch!")....15-25 57

Singles: 7-inch

GOTHAM (7-317 "Lonesome Playgirl") 15-25 56
RICHLOY (102 "Want Me a Man") 25-35 56
20TH CENTURY (1204 "Hop Scotch!")....25-35 57

DAKIL, Floyd, Combo

Singles: 7-inch

EARTH (402 "Bad Boy")............................30-40 65
EARTH (403 "Kitty Kitty")...........................25-35 65
EARTH (404 "Stronger Than Dirt")...........25-35 65
GUYDEN (2111 "Dance Franny Dance") .10-15 64
JETSTAR (103 "Dance Franny Dance")...30-50 64
POMPEII (66687 "One Girl").......................10-20 68

DAKUS, Wes
(With the Rebels; with Barry Allen; with Dennis Paul; with Club 93 Rebels)

Singles: 7-inch

CAPITOL...8-12 64-67
GALLIO (102 "Dog Food") 15-25 63
KAPP (815 "Seesaw")..................................5-10 67
QUALITY...10-20 60
(Canadian.)
SWAN (4206 "Las Vegas Scene").............8-12 65
U.A. (Except 722).......................................5-10 64
U.A. (722 "Sidewinder")............................15-25 64

LPs: 10/12-inch

CAPITOL (6120 "The Wes Dakus Album") ....25-35 '60s
(Canadian.)
KAPP (3536 "Wes Dakus' Rebels")..........25-35 67
Also see PAUL, Dennis

DALE, Alan P&R '48
(With Connie Haines)

Singles: 78 rpm

COLUMBIA...4-6 50-51
CORAL...3-6 52-56
DECCA..3-5 52

Singles: 7-inch

ABC-PAR...5-10 64
ADVANCE..4-6
COLUMBIA..5-15 50-51
CORAL (60000 & 61000 series) 5-15 52-56
CORAL (62000 series)..................................5-8 63
DECCA..8-12 52
EMKAY..5-10 62
FTP...5-10 61
JUBILEE..4-6 67
MGM..5-8 59
SINCLAIR (1003 "That's a Teenage Girl")..30-40 61

EPs: 7-inch

CORAL..5-15 52-56

LPs: 10/12-inch

CORAL..15-25 55-56
FORD...10-15 63
U.A. 10-15 60
Also see CORNELL, Don, Johnny Desmond & Alan Dale

DALE, B., & Pedal Pushers

Singles: 7-inch

KO KO (8803 "Love You Lovely Stranger") 30-40

DALE, Billy, Quartet

Singles: 78 rpm

KING..5-10 55

Singles: 7-inch

KING (1420 "So Darlin' Go") 30-40 55
KING (1453 "Cold at Heart") 15-25 55

DALE, Bobby

Singles: 7-inch

DE ROSE (8469 "Love Me More")............15-25 61

DALE, Dick P&R '61
(With His Del-tones)

Singles: 7-inch

CAPITOL (4939 thru 5389) 15-20 62-64
COLUMBIA...3-5 87
CONCERT ROOM (371 "We'll Never Hear the End of It")..5-10 63
COUGAR (711 "You're Hurtin' Now").......10-15 67
COUGAR (712 "Taco Wagon")................10-15 67
CUPID (106 "We'll Never Hear the End of It")...20-30 60
(Yellow vinyl.)
DELTONE (4939 "Misirlou")......................30-40 58
DELTONE (4940 "Peppermint Man") 30-40 58
DELTONE (5012 "Oh Wee Marie")...........30-40 58
DELTONE (5013 "Without Your Love")....20-30 59
DELTONE (5014 "Jessie Pearl") 15-25 60
DELTONE (5017 "Let's Go Trippen [sic]")..25-35 61
(Reads: "Distributed by Rendezvous Records." White label. Promotional issue only.)
DELTONE (5017 "Let's Go Trippin' ") 15-25 61
(No mention of Rendezvous Records. Title corrected.)
DELTONE (5018 "Shake and Stomp").....10-15 62
DELTONE (5019 "Miserlou") 10-15 62
(Reissue of 4939. Note slight spelling change.)
DELTONE (5020 "Peppermint Man").......10-15 62
DELTONE (5028 "Run for Life") 10-15 63
GNP (804 "Let's Go Trippin' ")......................4-8 75
RENDEZVOUS (204 "Reincarnation Parts 1 & 2")..10-20 62
SATURN (401 "We'll Never Hear the End of It") 10-20 63
YES (7014 "We'll Never Hear the End of It") 10-20 63

Promotional Singles

CAPITOL ("Thunder Wave"/"Spanish Kiss")..10-20 64
(Bonus single, packaged with the *Surf Age* LP by Jerry Cole and His Spacemen.)
CAPITOL (2320 "Peppermint Man").........35-50 63
(Compact 33 Single)

Picture Sleeves

CAPITOL (2320 "Peppermint Man").........35-55 63
(Promotional Compact 33 Single sleeve.)
CAPITOL (4963 "King of the Surf Guitar") 20-30 63
COLUMBIA...4-6 87

LPs: 10/12-inch

BALBOA...5-10 83
CAPITOL (T-1930 "King of the Surf Guitar") 50-100 63
(Monaural.)
CAPITOL (ST-1930 "King of the Surf Guitar") 75-125 63
(Stereo.)
CAPITOL (T-2002 "Checkered Flag") 50-100 63
(Monaural.)
CAPITOL (ST-2002 "Checkered Flag")..75-125 63
(Stereo.)
CAPITOL (T-2053 "Mr. Eliminator").......50-100 64
(Monaural.)
CAPITOL (ST-2053 "Mr. Eliminator") 75-125 64
(Stereo.)
CAPITOL (T-2111 "Summer Surf")......125-150 64
(Monaural. With *Movin' Surf*, a bonus single by Jerry Cole & His Spacemen.)
CAPITOL (T-2111 "Summer Surf")..........50-75 64
(Monaural. Without bonus single.)
CAPITOL (ST-2111 "Summer Surf") 150-175 64
(Stereo. With *Movin' Surf*, a bonus single by Jerry Cole & His Spacemen.)
CAPITOL (ST-2111 "Summer Surf") 60-80 64
(Stereo. Without bonus single.)
CAPITOL (T-2293 "Rock Out with Dick Dale Live at Ciro's")...50-100 65
(Monaural.)
CAPITOL (2293 "Rock Out with Dick Dale Live at Ciro's") 75-125 65
(Stereo.)
DELTONE (1001 "Surfer's Choice") 150-200 61
DELTONE (1886 "Surfer's Choice") 100-150 63
(Distributed by Capitol.)
GNP (2095 "Greatest Hits") 8-12 75
Also see ALLAN, Davie
Also see BEACH BOYS / Dick Dale / Surfaris / Surf Kings
Also see HOLLYWOOD SURFERS / Dick Dale
Also see STOMPERS / Dick Dale
Also see TROY, Bo, & His Hot Rods / Dick Dale
Also see VAUGHAN, Stevie Ray, & Dick Dale

DALE, Dick / Jerry Cole / Super Stocks / Mr. Gasser & Weirdos

EPs: 7-inch

CAPITOL (2663 "The Big Surfing Sounds")..35-50 64
(Promotional issue only.)
Also see COLE, Jerry
Also see MR. GASSER & WEIRDOS
Also see SUPER STOCKS

DALE, Dick / Surfaris / Fireballs

LPs: 10/12-inch

ALMOR (108 "World of Surfin' ") 25-35 64
ALMOR (109 "Hot Rod Drag Races") 25-35 64
Also see FIREBALLS

DALE, Dick / Surfaris / Surf Kings (Beach Boys)

LPs: 10/12-inch

GUEST STAR (1433 "Surf Kings")........... 25-35 63
(Credits the Beach Boys, though there are no tracks by the Beach Boys. Also, tracks credited to the Surfaris are by the Original Surfaris.)

GUEST STAR (1433 "Surf Kings")........... 15-25 63
(Does not credit the Beach Boys.)

Also see SURFARIS (Original Surfaris)

DALE, Dick, His Del-Tones, & Francine York / Craig Adams & His Country Cousins

(With the Overland Swingin' Top Brass)

Singles: 7-inch

UNITED STATES ARMY (1301 "Enlistment Twist") 10-20 62
(Colored vinyl. Promotional issue only.)

Picture Sleeves

UNITED STATES ARMY (1301 "Enlistment Twist") 10-20 62

Also see DALE, Dick

DALE, Dick

Singles: 7-inch

ACCENT (1243 "Just a'Waitin' ")................5-10 68

LPs: 10/12-inch

ACCENT (5033 "Coast to Coast")........... 10-15 67

DALE, Eddie

Singles: 78 rpm

IMPERIAL (8283 "Okefenokee")................5-10 55

Singles: 7-inch

IMPERIAL (8283 "Okefenokee")............. 10-20 55

DALE, Gary

Singles: 7-inch

GONE (5007 "Pretty Baby") 15-25 57

DALE, Jeff

Singles: 7-inch

ATCO (6332 "Language of Love")........... 10-15 65
ATCO (6352 "Where Did I Go").............. 10-15 65
ATCO (6405 "Our Love Will Grow Stronger").. 10-15 66

DALE, Jim

Singles: 7-inch

BOONE (1062 "Point of No Return") 5-10 67
CAPITOL (3886 "Be My Girl") 15-25 58
CAPITOL (3981 "Crazy for You")............ 15-25 58
JAMIE (1191 "If You Come Back")..............5-10 61
MONUMENT (890 "Little Boy Blue")...........5-10 65

DALE, Jim, & Comancheroes

Singles: 7-inch

TEEN (1052 "TP")..................................... 10-15 64

Also see DALE, Jim

DALE, Jimmie

Singles: 7-inch

PALOMINO...8-12
SABRE (708 "Baby Doll") 450-550

DALE, Jimmy

(Jimmy Clanton)

Singles: 7-inch

DREW-BLAN (1003 "My Pride and Joy") 15-25 61

Also see CLANTON, Jimmy

DALE, Jimmy

Singles: 7-inch

ORIGINAL (501 "Tennessee Ghost Train") 100-200

DALE, Kenny

Singles: 7-inch

PICTURE (310 "Cindy Lee")................... 50-75

DALE, Larry

Singles: 78 rpm

GROOVE (0029 "You Better Heed My Warning")... 15-25 54
HERALD (463 "Feelin' All Right")............ 15-25 55

Singles: 7-inch

ATLANTIC (2133 "Drinkin' Wine Spo-Dee-O-Dee")..8-12 62
CRYSTAL (107 "Beautiful Delilah")............8-12 59
ELBRIDGE (12762 "Crying Over You") 100-150
EMBER...8-12 56
FIRE (2022 "Rock a While")......................5-10 68
GLOVER (203 "Big Muddy")..................... 10-20 60
GLOVER (208 "Let the Doorbell Ring") ... 10-20 60
GROOVE (0029 "You Better Heed My Warning")...30-40 54
HERALD (463 "Feelin' All Right")...............30-40 55
RAM...4-6 68

Also see BROWN, Wini
Also see DUPREE, Jack, & Mr. Bear
Also see McHOUSTON, Big Red
Also see WILLIAMS, Paul

DALE, Robin

Singles: 7-inch

LIBERTY (55297 "Cry, Cry, Cry") 5-10 61
RAGE ("Big Steel Bucket")...................100-150
(Selection number not known.)

DALE & DEL-HEARTS

Singles: 7-inch

HERALD (564 "Always & Ever") 15-25 61

DALE & GRACE *P&R/R&B '63*

Singles: 7-inch

COLLECTABLES..4-6 '70s
ERIC..4-6 '70s
GUYDEN...4-6 72
HBR (472 "Let Them Talk")........................5-10 66
MICHELLE..8-12 63-64
MONTEL...5-10 63-67
MONTEL MICHELLE (942 "What Am I Living For")..5-10 64
(Shows both label names.)
TRIP..4-6 '70s

LPs: 10/12-inch

MONTEL (100 "I'm Leaving It Up to You")..35-50 64

Members: Dale Houston; Grace Broussard.
Also see BROUSSARD, Van

DALES

Singles: 78 rpm

ONYX (509 "If You Are Meant to Be") 30-40 57

Singles: 7-inch

ONYX (509 "If You Are Meant to Be") 30-40 57

DALES

(Dale's Boys)

Singles: 7-inch

CREST (1045 "The Big Jump")..................15-20 58
CREST (1069 "Rockin' Nellie")..................10-15 60

DALEY, Jimmy, & Ding-A-Lings

("Vocal by Hal Dickinson and the Ding-A-Lings"; "Vocal by Rod McKuen")

Singles: 78 rpm

DECCA...20-30 56-57

Singles: 7-inch

DECCA (30163 "Rock Pretty Baby").........20-30 56
DECCA (30532 "Hole in the Wall") 20-30 57

EPs: 7-inch

DECCA (2480/81/82 "Rock Pretty Baby") 50-75 56
(Soundtrack. Price is for any of these volumes.)

LPs: 10/12-inch

DECCA (8429 "Rock Pretty Baby").......100-150 56
(Black or pink label.)
DECCA (8429 "Rock Pretty Baby")............30-40 '60s
(Rainbow label. Soundtrack. With Rod McKuen, Alan Copeland, & Hal Dickinson.)

DALHART, Vernon *P&R '17*

(With Gladys Rice; with Al Bernard)

Singles: 78 rpm

BANNER...15-25 '20s
BLACK PATTI..75-125
BRUNSWICK...10-20 '20s
BUDDY..50-100
CAMEO..15-25 '20s
CHAMPION..15-25 '20s
CLARION...10-20
COLUMBIA..5-15 22-35
DOMINO...15-25 '20s
EDISON..20-50 17-25
EDISON AMBEROL......................................15-25 '20s
GENNETT...15-25 '20s
HARMONY..15-25 '20s
HERSCHEL..25-50
HERWIN..25-50
OKEH..10-20 24
PATH...15-25 '20s
PERFECT..15-25 20s
RCA...5-10 49
REGAL...15-25 '20s
SILVERTONE..15-25
VICTOR..10-20 21-35
VOCALION..15-25 '20s

Singles: 7-inch

RCA (0016 "Prisoner's Song") 15-25 49

LPs: 10/12-inch

DAVIS UNLIMITED...10-20
GOLDEN OLDEN COUNTRY...........................8-10
MARK 56...8-10
OLD HOMESTEAD...8-10

DALHART, Vernon, & Carson Robison *P&R '28*

Singles: 78 rpm

VICTOR..10-20 27-28

Also see DALHART, Vernon
Also see ROBISON, Carson

DALKAPS

Singles: 7-inch

CORVETTE (1003 "Who Is the One")......10-15 58

DALLAIRE, Art, & Watchmen

Singles: 7-inch

FLIP (202 "A Cryin' Shame")....................20-30

DALLAS, Jackie

(With the Tiaras)

Singles: 7-inch

ALLIANCE (1690 "All I Want") ....10-20 '60s
FAWN (6002 "Lorraine")............................25-35

Also see TIARAS

DALLAS, Jimmy

Singles: 78 rpm

WESTPORT...5-10 55-57

Singles: 7-inch

GLORY (257 "If You Care") 10-15 57
WESTPORT...10-15 55-57

DALLAS, Larry

Singles: 7-inch

MAJESTIC (1001 "Cheatin' Woman") 50-75

DALLAS, Leroy

Singles: 78 rpm

JADE (707 "Your Sweet Man's Blues") 15-25 49
SITTIN' IN WITH (522 "I'm Down Now, But I Won't Be Always")..20-30 49
SITTIN' IN WITH (526 "Good Morning Blues")...20-30 49
SITTIN' IN WITH (537 "Your Sweet Man's Blues")...20-30 49

DALLIS, Chuck

Singles: 7-inch

GLENN (2201 "Come on Let's Go") 40-60 61
GLENN (2202 "Moon Twist") 20-40 62
GLENN (2203 "Good Show, But No Go")..20-40 62
KC (102 "Come on Let's Go") 30-50 62

DALLMAN, Jerry, & Knightcaps

Singles: 7-inch

PUNCH (6000 "The Bug")..........................40-60 63

DALLTIN, Dusty

Singles: 7-inch

UNIQUE (100 "Shotgun")...........................50-75 62
(At least one source shows this artist's name as Dusty Dalton. We don't know yet which is correct.)

DALTON, Danny

Singles: 7-inch

TEEN (505 "Who's Gonna Hold Your Hand")..30-50 59

DALTON, Jimmy

Singles: 7-inch

DON-MAR (101 "Make Up Your Mind")....15-25 '50s

DALTON BOYS

(With Henry Jerome & His Orchestra)

Singles: 7-inch

CAROL (101 "Can't Help Myself") 5-8 65
CORAL (62353 "Billy Don't Play the Banjo Anymore")..10-20 63
CORAL (62387 "Silver Dollar")..................10-20 63
PORT CITY (355 "Anyone Who Had a Heart")...10-20 63
SKYLA (1124 "Much Stronger")................20-30 62
V.I.P. (25025 "Take My Hand")...............75-125 65
V.I.P. (25025 "Something's Bothering You")..30-50 65

Member: Danny Dalton.
Also see DALTON, Danny

DALTON BROTHERS

Singles: 7-inch

MARTAY (2001 "I Only Came to Dance with You")..20-30 63

Members: Scott Engel; John Stewart.
Also see ENGEL, Scott, & John Stewart

DALY, Durwood

Singles: 7-inch

CAPROCK (108 "That's the Way It Goes")..30-40 58

DALY, Sandra

Singles: 7-inch

T.J. (101 "My Only Cure Is You")............75-100 61

DALY, Terry, & Nu-Tones

Singles: 7-inch

MARK (122 "You Don't Bug Me") 200-300 58

DALYS

Singles: 7-inch

BIG TOP (520 "Without You")..................10-15 64
FONTANA (1647 "Early Mornin' Rain")......8-12 69

DAMASCANS

Singles: 7-inch

PYRAMID (6372 "Go 'Way Girl") 10-15 66

D'AMBRA, Joe, & Embers

Singles: 7-inch

MERCURY (71725 "Don't Forget to Write")...10-15 60

DAME, Freddy

(With Bobby's Trailers; with Fables)

Singles: 7-inch

HERITAGE (813 "Sometimes I Don't Like Me") 5-10 71
NIC NAC (331 "Love Is a Game") 40-50 62

Also see FREDDY & CLAIRE / Freddy Dame

DAMERON, Donna

(With the Big Bopper)

Singles: 7-inch

DART (113 "Bopper 486609") 75-125 59
(With "The Story Behind the Record" photo-insert.)
DART (113 "Bopper 486609") 40-60 59
(Without insert.)

Also see BIG BOPPER

D'AMICO, Guido

Singles: 7-inch

QUALITY (1823 "Jimmy Boy")............200-300
(Canadian.)

D'AMICO, Ted

Singles: 7-inch

CAVALIER (902 "Mr. Switchman") 30-50 61

DAMITA JO *P&R '53*

(Damita Joe; with Fred Norman & Orchestra)

Singles: 78 rpm

RECORDED IN HOLLYWOOD 5-10 51
RCA...5-10 53

Singles: 7-inch

BANG BANG...4-8
EPIC (2258 "Yellow Days")..........................5-10 67
EPIC (9766 "Tomorrow Night")......................5-8 65
(Black vinyl.)
EPIC (9766 "Tomorrow Night")..................15-20 65
(Purple vinyl. Promotional issue only.)
EPIC (9797 thru 10235) 5-10 65-67
JODY (2001 "Love Is So Sweet")...............5-10 '60s
RECORDED IN HOLLYWOOD (180 "You Took My Heart") 10-20 51
RECORDED IN HOLLYWOOD (182 "Way Up High")..10-20 51
MELIC...4-6 64
MERCURY...5-10 60-64
RCA...10-20 53
RANWOOD...4-6 68-71
VEE-JAY...5-8 65

Picture Sleeves

EPIC (9766 "Tomorrow Night")...................10-15 65
(Promotional issue only.)
MERCURY..8-12 61-63

EPs: 7-inch

MERCURY..5-10 60-61

LPs: 10/12-inch

CAMDEN...8-12 65
EPIC...10-15 65-67
MERCURY...15-30 61-63
RANWOOD..5-10 68
VEE-JAY...10-20 65

Also see BENTON, Brook, & Damita Jo

DAMITA JO with STEVE GIBSON & RED CAPS
Singles: 78 rpm
RCA (6281 "Always")....8-12 55
Singles: 7-inch
ABC-PAR....5-10 61
RCA (6281 "Always")....10-20 55
LPs: 10/12-inch
ABC-PAR (378 "Big 15")....40-60 61
Also see DAMITA JO
Also see GIBSON, Steve

DAMON
Singles: 7-inch
ANKH ("Song of a Gypsy")....25-50 70
(No selection number used.)
LPs: 10/12-inch
ANKH ("Song of a Gypsy")....2000-2500 70
(No selection number used.)

DAMON, Dennis
Singles: 7-inch
CAMPO (953 "Satisfy You")....15-20
U.A. (984 "Shout Bama Lama")....8-12 66

DAMON, Liz *P&R '70*
(Liz Damon's Orient Express)
Singles: 7-inch
ABC....4-6 73
ANTHEM....5-10 71-72
DONCY....5-8 78
MAKAHA....5-10 70
WHITE WHALE....4-6 70
LPs: 10/12-inch
ANTHEM (5900 "Liz Damon's Orient Express, Vol. 2")....15-25 71
DELILAH....8-12
MAKAHA....10-20 70
WHITE WHALE (5003 "Liz Damon's Orient Express")....8-12 71
Also see ORIENT EXPRESS

DAMON, Mark, & Jordanaires
Singles: 7-inch
WYNNE....8-10 59-60
Picture Sleeves
WYNNE....10-20 59-60
Also see JORDANAIRES

DAMON, Sterling
Singles: 7-inch
INT'L ARTISTS (108 "Rejected")....5-10 66
1A (108 "Rejected")....10-20 66

DAMONE, Vic *P&R '47*
Singles: 78 rpm
COLUMBIA....3-6 56-57
MERCURY....3-6 48-55
MERCURY/SAV-WAY (5053 "Ivy")....100-150 47
(Picture disc. Promotional issue only.)
Singles: 7-inch
CAPITOL....4-6 61-64
COLUMBIA....5-10 56-61
MGM....4-6 72-73
MERCURY....5-10 50-55
RCA....4-6 66-69
REBECCA....4-6 77
UNITED TALENT....4-6 70
W.B.....4-6 65-66
EPs: 7-inch
CAPITOL CUSTOM ("Vic Damone Swings with A&W")....10-15 62
(Special products issue for A&W Root Beer.)
COLUMBIA....5-10 56-58
MERCURY....8-12 50-56
LPs: 10/12-inch
CAPITOL....10-20 61-64
COLUMBIA (900 thru 1500 series)....15-25 56-61
COLUMBIA (1900 series)....10-20 62
COLUMBIA (8000 thru 8300 series)....20-30 58-61
COLUMBIA (8700 series)....10-15 62
HARMONY....5-10 66-67
HOLLYWOOD....5-10
MERCURY (Except 25000 series)....8-12 69
MERCURY (25000 series)....15-30 50-56
RCA....8-12 66-68
UNITED TALENT....5-10
W.B.....10-15 65
WING....10-15 59-63
Also see ANDREWS, Julie & Andre Previn / Vic Damone / Jack Jones / Marian Anderson
Also see FISHER, Eddie / Vic Damone / Dick Haymes

DAMONE, Vic / Dick "Two Ton" Baker
Singles: 78 rpm
MERCURY/SAV-WAY (5056/5055 "You Do")....100-150 47
(Picture disc. Promotional issue only.)

DAMONE, Vic / Johnny Desmond / Stradivari Strings
LPs: 10/12-inch
PREMIER (9013 "Vic Damone with Special Guests")....5-10 '60s
Also see DAMONE, Vic
Also see DESMOND, Johnny

DAMRON, Dick
(Dickie Damron)
Singles: 7-inch
LAUREL (792 "Gonna Have a Party")....1500-2000 '50s
(Canadian.)
QUALITY (1213 "Julie")....50-75
(Canadian.)
RCA (8162 "Strangers Again")....10-15 63

DAN & CLEAN-CUTS
(Dan & the Clean Cut-Guys; Dan & Clean Cut Clan)
Singles: 7-inch
ACCENT (1116 "Perfect Example")....10-20 64
SCEPTER....10-20 65-66
Picture Sleeves
ACCENT (1116 "Perfect Example")....20-30 64

DAN & DALE
Singles: 7-inch
NEWARK (229 "Love Is Blue")....5-10 68
TIFTON (125 "Batman Theme")....5-10 66
Picture Sleeves
TIFTON (125 "Batman Theme")....10-20 66
LPs: 10/12-inch
DIPLOMAT....10-20 '60s
TIFTON (78002 "Batman and Robin")....20-30 66
(Includes color Batman & Robin inner sleeve.)

DANA, Bill *LP '60*
(Jose Jimenez; Bill Dana & Friends)
Singles: 7-inch
A&M....4-8 65-66
KAPP (443 "Jose Jimenez in Orbit")....5-15 62
KAPP (443 "Jose Jimenez in Orbit")....5-15 63
SIGNATURE (12046 "Bob Sled Racer")....5-10 60
Picture Sleeves
KAPP....10-20 61-62
EPs: 7-inch
KAPP....10-20 61
LPs: 10/12-inch
A&M....8-12 68
CAPITOL....6-10 70
HBR (2053 "Time Machine")....8-10 66
KAPP (1215 "More Jose Jimenez")....15-25 60
KAPP (1257 Bill Dana in Orbit")....15-25 60
KAPP (1320 "Jose Jimenez Our Secret Weapon")....15-25 63
(Monaural.)
KAPP (1402 "In Las Vegas")....15-25 64
(Monaural.)
KAPP (3320 "Jose Jimenez Our Secret Weapon")....20-30 63
(Stereo.)
KAPP (3402 "In Las Vegas")....20-30 64
(Stereo.)
ROULETTE (25161 "My Name Jose Jimenez")....15-25 61
SIGNATURE (1013 "My Name Jose Jimenez")....25-30 60

DANA, Jeff
Singles: 7-inch
FLEETWOOD (1011 "Oh Gina")....10-15 60

DANA, Vic *P&R '61*
Singles: 7-inch
CASINO....4-6 76
COLUMBIA....4-6 71
DOLTON....4-8 61-66
LIBERTY....4-6 67-70
MGM....4-6 75
Picture Sleeves
DOLTON (51 "I Will")....5-10 62
DOLTON (73 "Danger")....5-10 63
DOLTON (95 "Love Is All We Need")....5-10 64
DOLTON (99 "Garden in the Rain")....5-10 64
DOLTON (305 "Bring a Little Sunshine")....5-10 65
LPs: 10/12-inch
DOLTON (Except 2013/8013)....15-25 62-65
DOLTON (2013 "This Is Vic Dana")....15-25 61
(Monaural.)
DOLTON (8013 "This Is Vic Dana")....20-30 61
(Stereo.)
LIBERTY....8-15 67-70
SUNSET (1182 "On the Country Side")....10-15 67
(Monaural.)
SUNSET (5182 "On the Country Side")....10-15 67
(Stereo.)
Also see CARTER, Mel / Vic Dana

DANCEY, Mel
Singles: 7-inch
DUCKY (712 "High School Romance")....10-15 59

DANDERLIERS *R&B '55*
("James Campbell & Dallas Taylor Vocalists")
Singles: 78 rpm
STATES (147 "Chop Chop Boom")....75-125 55
STATES (150 "Shu-Wop")....50-75 55
STATES (152 "May God Be with You")....50-75 56
STATES (160 "My Love")....75-125 56
Singles: 7-inch
B&F (150 "Shu-Wop")....10-15 60
B&F (160 "My Love")....10-15 60
B&F (1344 "Shu-Wop")....8-12 61
B&F (1346 "My Love")....8-12 61
MIDAS (9004 "All the Way")....10-20 67
STATES (147 "Chop Chop Boom")....100-150 55
(Black vinyl.)
STATES (147 "Chop Chop Boom")....3000-4000 55
(Red vinyl.)
STATES (150 "Shu-Wop")....200-300 55
(White label. Promotional issue only.)
STATES (150 "Shu-Wop")....75-125 55
STATES (152 "May God Be with You")....150-200 55
STATES (160 "My Love")....100-150 56
Members: Dallas Taylor; James Campbell; Richard Thomas; Walter Stephenson; Bernard Dixon; Louis Johnson.

DANDEVILLES
Singles: 7-inch
FORTÉ (314 "Heavenly Angel")....100-200 59

DANDEVILLES
Singles: 7-inch
GUYDEN (2014 "There's a Reason")....10-15 59
Also see GUIDES
Also see UPTONES

DANDIE, Professor Jim, & Kampus Kids
Singles: 7-inch
BULLSEYE (1006 "Teacher's Comin'")....10-20 58

DANDIES
Singles: 7-inch
PEACH (726 "Have I Lost Your Love")....50-75 59

D'ANDREA, Ann
Singles: 7-inch
JAMIE (1325 "Take Me for a Little While")....10-15 66
JAMIE (1352 "Don't Stop Lookin'")....10-15 68
PHILIPS (40182 "He's the Boy")....10-15 64
PHILIPS (40235 "Baby Be Good to Me")....10-15 64

D'ANDREA, Dick, & Melody Kings with 5 Teens
Singles: 7-inch
BALD EAGLE (1002 "Git Outta the House")....15-20

DANDRIDGE, Ruby, & Her Rhythmanians
Singles: 7-inch
SAND (245 "Hot Tamale Blues")....10-20 57

DANE, Barbara
(With the Earl Hines Orchestra)
Singles: 7-inch
TREY (3012 "I'm On My Way")....10-15 60
LPs: 10/12-inch
CAPITOL (1758 "On My Way")....15-25 62
DOT (3177 "Livin' with the Blues")....15-25 59
(Monaural.)
DOT (25177 "Livin' with the Blues")....20-30 59
(Stereo.)
FOLKWAYS (2471 "The Blues")....10-20 64
HORIZON (1602 "When I Was a Young Girl")....15-25 62
(Black vinyl.)
HORIZON (1602 "When I Was a Young Girl")....30-40 62
(Colored vinyl.)

DANE, Barbara, & Chambers Brothers
LPs: 10/12-inch
FOLKWAYS (2468 "Barbara Dane and the Chambers Brothers")....20-30 64
Also see CHAMBERS BROTHERS
Also see DANE, Barbara

DANE, Bill, & Hot Dogs
(Bill "Great" Dane)
Singles: 78 rpm
CREST....10-20 55-56
Singles: 7-inch
CREST (1002 thru 1021)....15-25 55-56

DANE, Chris
Singles: 78 rpm
CADENCE....5-10 54-55
Singles: 7-inch
CADENCE....10-20 54-55

DANE, Jimmy, & His Great Danes
Singles: 7-inch
MARV (815 "Tattle Tale")....750-1000 '50s

DANE, Johnny
(With the Discorders)
Singles: 7-inch
STEPHENY (1801 "Why Did You Leave Me")....10-15 57
STEPHENY (1806 "My Hula Hula Lulu")....15-25 57
VEE-JAY (312 "Hey Little Girl")....10-15 59

DANE, Shelly
Singles: 7-inch
BAMBOO (502 "Cold in the Nose")....10-15 61

DANES
(With the Marvino Four)
Singles: 7-inch
CHARAY (301 "Come Back Home to Me")....30-40 '60s
CHARAY (303 "Just a Dream")....10-20 '60s
LE CAM (718 "Most of All")....300-400 61
(Reissued as by the Team Mates.)
SMASH (1962 "High on a Hill")....8-10 65
SOFT (103 "Hey Little Girl")....20-30 62
TOWER (247 "Lost Love")....8-10 66
Also see TEAM MATES

DANETTA & STARLETS
(With Carl H. Davis & Orchestra)
Singles: 7-inch
OKEH (7155 "You Belong to Me")....50-75 62

DANFAIR, Billy
Singles: 7-inch
NIKE (1018 "Trouble Trouble Trouble")....10-20 62

DANIELS, Billy
Singles: 78 rpm
MERCURY (5822 "That's How It Goes")....5-10 52
Singles: 7-inch
MERCURY (5822 "That's How It Goes")....10-20 52
EPs: 7-inch
MERCURY (3035 "Billy Daniels")....10-20 53

DANIELS, Charlie *C&W/P&R/LP '73*
(Charlie Daniels Band; with Jaguars)
Singles: 7-inch
CAPITOL....3-5 '90s
EPIC....3-6 76-86
HANOVER (4541 "Robot Romp")....10-20 60
KAMA SUTRA....4-6 71-76
PAULA (246 "Skip It")....5-10 66
PAULA (418 "Skip It")....4-6 76
Picture Sleeves
EPIC....3-6
EPs: 7-inch
KAMA SUTRA (10 "Volunteer Jam")....5-8 74
(Bonus EP packaged with *Fire on the Mountain* LP.)
LPs: 10/12-inch
CAPITOL (11000 series)....8-10 75
CAPITOL (16000 series)....5-10 80
EPIC (Except 273)....5-10 76-91
EPIC (273 "Everything You Always Wanted to Hear")....10-15 77
(Promotional issue only.)
EPIC/CBS (35751 "Million Mile Reflection")....35-45 79

(Picture disc. Six variations, each with a different logo on back side. 250 made of each of the six. Promotional issue only.)
KAMA SUTRA 10-15 73-76
MFSL (176 "Million Mile Reflections") 30-50 85
Members: Tom Crain; Taz DiGregorio; Fred Edwards; Charles Hayward.
Also see BARE, Bobby
Also see TUBB, Ernest

DANIELS, Chuck
Singles: 7-inch
WILCO (104 "Glass Pak") 50-100

DANIELS, Dotty
Singles: 7-inch
AMY (885 "I Wrote You a Letter") 20-30 63
AMY (891 "A Casual Look") 10-15 63

DANIELS, Duke
Singles: 7-inch
EASTERN (002 "Backfire") .... 15-25 '60s

DANIELS, Eddie
(With His Daniels Nine)
Singles: 7-inch
EBB (108 "Playin' Hide & Seek") 40-60 57
EBB (133 "I Wanna Know") 65-75 58
EDDIE MAE'S (501 "Little Ishana Man") .. 10-15
STARLA (9 "Hurry Baby") 40-60 58
Also see JEWEL & EDDIE

DANIELS, J.N.
Singles: 7-inch
WEB ("Falling in Love") 75-125
(Selection number not known.)

DANIELS, Jeff
(Luke McDaniels)
Singles: 7-inch
ASTRO (108 "Foxy Dan") 75-125 64
BIG B (555 "Uh-Huh-Huh") 50-75 58
BIG HOWDY (777 "Switch Blade Sam") 75-100 59
BIG HOWDY (8120 "Uh-Huh Huh") 40-60 59
BIG HOWDY (8121 "Foxy Dan") 50-75 59
DUELL 4-6 79
MELADEE (117 "Daddy-O Rock") 200-300 58
(Orange label.)
MELADEE (117 "Daddy-O Rock") 100-200 58
(Black label.)
Also see McDANIELS, Luke

DANIELS, Little Chuck
Singles: 7-inch
DIXIE (1153 "Night Shift") 50-60

DANIELS, Sloppy
(With Kathy Cooper; with Skillet")
LPs: 10/12-inch
DOOTO (266 "Sloppy's House Party") 10-15 59

DANIELS, Tex
Singles: 78 rpm
BLUE HEN (212 "Blue Hen Boogie") 8-12 56
DIXIE 10-20
Singles: 7-inch
BLUE HEN (212 "Blue Hen Boogie") 30-40 56

DANKWORTH, Johnny P&R '56
(Johnnie Dankworth)
Singles: 78 rpm
CAPITOL 4-8 55-56
Singles: 7-inch
CAPITOL 4-8 55-56
FONTANA 4-6 63-67
ROULETTE (4353 "Afrikaan Waltz") 4-8 61
20TH FOX 4-6 66
LPs: 10/12-inch
FONTANA (Except 7559) 6-12 64-69
FONTANA (27559 "The Idol") 15-20 66
(Soundtrack. Monaural.)
FONTANA (67559 "The Idol") 20-25 66
(Soundtrack. Stereo.)
ROULETTE 10-15 60-61
TOP RANK 10-15 60

DANLEERS P&R/R&B '58
(Dandleers)
Singles: 7-inch
ABC 4-6 75
AMP 3 (1005 " One Summer Night") 20-30 58
(Credits Danleers.)
AMP 3 (2115 " One Summer Night") 100-150 58
(Credits "Dandleers.")
COLLECTABLES .... 3-5 '80s
EPIC (9367 "Half a Block from an Angel") 15-25 60
EPIC (9421 "Little Lover") 50-75 60
EVEREST (19412 "Foolish") 40-50 61
LE-MANS (005 "The Truth Hurts") 10-15 64
LE-MANS (008 "I'm Sorry") 10-15 64
MERCURY (71322 "One Summer Night") 10-15 58
MERCURY (71356 "I Really Love You") .. 15-20 58
(Blue label.)
MERCURY (71356 "I Really Love You") .. 10-15 58
(Black label.)
MERCURY (71401 "Picture of You") 15-20 58
MERCURY (71441 "Your Love") 25-30 59
SMASH (1872 "If") 15-25 64
SMASH (1895 "Where Is My Love") 15-25 64
STONE HARBOR (5805 "You're Everything") 3-5
Members: Jimmy Weston; Johnny Lee; Nat McCune; Willie Ephriam; Roosevelt Mays; Doug Ebron; Louis Williams; Terry Wilson; Frank Clemens; Bill Carey.
Also see FOUR FELLOWS
Also see WEBTONES

DANNY & COUNTS
Singles: 7-inch
CORONADO (136 "You Need Love") 20-30 65

DANNY & CROWNS
Singles: 7-inch
MERCURY (72096 "The Story of Jack and Jill") 15-20 63

DANNY & DEBONAIRS
Singles: 7-inch
DEBONAIR (2250 "I Guess I'm Through with Love") 100-200 61
(Identification number shown since no selection number is used.)

DANNY & DEL-AIRES
Singles: 7-inch
STRIPE (2242 "Rock-a Rhumba") 100-200

DANNY & DIAMONDS / No Names
Singles: 7-inch
STOOP SOUNDS (512 "Possibility"/"Love") 75-125 98
Also see NO NAMES

DANNY & DREAMERS
Singles: 7-inch
DREAM (7 "Forgive Me") 40-50 62

DANNY & FAT BOYS
LPs: 10/12-inch
ALADDIN (102 "American Music") 75-100 76
Member: Danny Gatton.

DANNY & JUNIORS P&R/R&B '57
(With Joe Terry)
Singles: 78 rpm
ABC-PAR 50-100 57-58
SPARTON 50-75 58
(Canadian.)
Singles: 7-inch
ABC 4-6 73
ABC-PAR (9871 "At the Hop") 20-30 57
ABC-PAR (9888 "Rock & Roll Is Here to Stay") 20-30 58
ABC-PAR (9926 "Dottie") 20-30 58
ABC-PAR (9953 thru 10052) 10-20 58-59
CRUNCH 4-6 73
DOWNTOWN 3-5 93
GOLDIES 45 .... 3-6 73
GUSTO 3-5 79
GUYDEN (2076 "Now and Then") 10-15 62
LUV 5-10 68
MCA (2411 "At the Hop") 3-6 79
MERCURY (72240 "Sad Girl") 10-15 64
ROULETTE (121 "At the Hop") 3-6 73
SINGULAR (711 "At the Hop") 600-700 57
(Blue label.)
SINGULAR (711 "At the Hop") 10-15
(Black label.)
SPARTON (582 "Dottie") 40-60 58
(Canadian.)
SWAN (4060 "Twistin' USA") 15-25 60
(With Freddy Cannon.)
SWAN (4064 "Candy Cane Sugar Plum") 15-25 60
SWAN (4068 "Pony Express") 10-20 61
SWAN (4072 "Mister Whisper") 15-25 61
SWAN (4082 "Back to the Hop") 10-20 61
SWAN (4084 "Just Because") 15-25 61
SWAN (4092 "Twistin' All Night Long") 15-20 62
(With Freddy Cannon.)
SWAN (4100 "Mashed Potatoes") 10-15 62
SWAN (4113 "Funny") 10-15 62
TOPAZ 3-6 87
Picture Sleeves
SWAN (4064 "Candy Cane Sugar Plum") 50-75 60
EPs: 7-inch
ABC-PAR (11 "At the Hop") 500-750 58
SWAN (4084 "Just Because") 100-200 62
(Not issued with cover. Promotional issue only.)
LPs: 10/12-inch
MCA (1555 "Rockin' with Danny and the Juniors") 5-10 83
Members: Danny Rapp; Frank Maffei; Joe Terry; Dave White.
Also see ALSTON, Shirley
Also see CANNON, Freddy
Also see WHITE, Dave

DANNY & MEMORIES
Singles: 7-inch
VALIANT (705 "Can't Help Lovin' That Girl of Mine") 10-20 65
VALIANT (6049 "Can't Help Lovin' That Girl of Mine") 25-50 64
Member: Neil Young.
Also see YOUNG, Neil

DANNY & NITROS
Singles: 7-inch
NITRO (100 "International Whirl") 50-75

DANNY & SAINTS
Singles: 7-inch
FANELLE (101 "Long, Long Ago") 40-50
W.B. (5134 No One Has Eyes for Me") 25-35 59

DANNY & SENIORS
Singles: 7-inch
PANORAMA (26 "Oh Devil") 10-15 66

DANNY & VELAIRES
Singles: 7-inch
BRENT (7072 "What Am I Livin' For") 20-30 67
RAMCO (1983 "I Found a Love") 30-40 67

DANNY & ZELLTONES
Singles: 7-inch
BIG TOP (3074 "Steel Guitar Rag") 10-20 61
MR. PEACOCK (116 "Summertime") 5-10 62
Member: Danny Zella.
Also see ZELLA, Danny

DANNY BOY
Singles: 7-inch
DOT (16140 "Send Me Some Lovin' ") 20-30 60
KENT (300 "Don't Go, Pretty Baby") 30-40 58

DANNY'S REASONS
Singles: 7-inch
CARNABY (101 "Under My Thumb") 60-80 67
GREAT HALL (30297 "Vision of Love") 5-10
HAND (420 "With One Eye Closed") 10-15 69
IRC (6935 "Little Diane") 40-60 66
UNCLE SAM (19361 "Young Emotion") 5-10 72

DANO, Eddie
Singles: 78 rpm
VIK (0293 "While Our Hearts Are Young") . 8-12 57
Singles: 7-inch
RED TOP (114 "Lonely") 20-30 59
VIK (0293 "While Our Hearts Are Young") 10-15 57

DANO, Tony
Singles: 7-inch
LORNETTE (782 "I Cry Alone") 30-40

DAN-RAYS
Singles: 7-inch
REGENCY (105 "Surfin' Granny") 20-30 63

DANTE
Singles: 7-inch
DARROW (515 "How Much I Care") 20-30 60
DECCA 10-15 60-61
MERCURY (71621 "How Much I Care") ... 10-15 60
TIDE (003 "My Aching Heart") 10-15 60

DANTE P&R '60
(With the Evergreens; with His Friends)
Singles: 7-inch
A&M (788 "Sweet Lover") 8-10 66
IMPERIAL (5798 thru 5867) 15-25 61-62
MADISON (130 thru 143) 15-25 60
MADISON (154 "Da Doo") 100-150 61
LPs: 10/12-inch
MADISON (1002 "Dante and the Evergreens") 150-200 61
Members: Don "Dante" Drowty; Bill Young; Frank Rosenthal; Tony Moon.
Also see EMERALD CITY BANDITS

DANTE'S INFERNO
Singles: 78 rpm
LIDO (507 "My First True Love") 10-20 57
Singles: 7-inch
LIDO (507 "My First True Love") 10-20 57

DANTÉS
Singles: 7-inch
COURTNEY (713 "Zebra Shoot") 15-25 64
ROTATE (5008 "Top Down Time") 30-40 65

DANTES
Singles: 7-inch
CAMEO (431 "Under My Thumb") 10-20 66
JAMIE (1314 "80-96") 10-20 66
MAIN LINE (1366 "Satisfied") 5-10 67

DANTON, Tommy
(With the Echoes)
Singles: 7-inch
DOT (15650 "Oh Yeah") 30-40 57
KAREN (60549 "Twenty-One") 75-100 59
PAR (235 "Oh Yeah") 50-75 57

DAPPER DANS
Singles: 7-inch
EMBER (1065 "Bird Brain") 10-15 60

DAPPERS
Singles: 78 rpm
PEACOCK (1651 "Come Back to Me") 15-25 55
RAINBOW (373 "Bop Bop Bu") 10-15 56
Singles: 7-inch
EPIC (9423 "My Love Is Real") 10-20 60
PEACOCK (1651 "Come Back to Me") 100-200 55
RAINBOW (373 "Bop Bop Bu") 20-30 56

DAPPERS
Singles: 78 rpm
GROOVE (0156 "Unwanted Love") 75-125 56
Singles: 7-inch
GROOVE (0156 "Unwanted Love") 250-300 56

DAPPERS
Singles: 7-inch
STAR-X (505 "We're in Love") 30-50 58

DAPPERS
Singles: 7-inch
FOXIE (7005 "Lonely Street") 20-30 61

DAPPS
Singles: 7-inch
NORTHERN (3727 "Dreamer") 40-60 59
Also see MATTHEWS, Joannie Mae, & Dapps

DA-PREES
Singles: 7-inch
TWIST (70914 "Payday") 100-200 63

DAPS
Singles: 78 rpm
MARTERRY (5249 "When You're Alone") 10-15 56
Singles: 7-inch
MARTERRY (5249 "When You're Alone") 20-30 56

DAP-TONES
Singles: 7-inch
GEE GEE CEE (8165 "Wonderful Girl") 750-1000 59

DARBY, Ward, & Ravens
Singles: 7-inch
DOT (15952 "Wham-O") 5-10 59
PETITE (501 "Wham-O") 15-25 59
(First issue.)
STAR (511 "Kentucky Blue Grass") 10-20 62

DARCELLS
Singles: 7-inch
TOP TEN (251 "Prancin' Time")............... 10-15 62

DARCY, Johnny
Singles: 7-inch
SYCAMORE (103 "Rockin' the Arc") 15-25 58

DARDENELLES
("Featuring Little Bo")
Singles: 7-inch
CAMEO (271 "Baby, Do the Froog")........ 15-25 63
ENTRE (102 "Now You're Gone")........... 20-30 63
PENNINGTON (108 "A Thing Worth Remembering")........................ 20-30 60
PLAYGIRL (501 "My Baby")..................... 15-25 '60s
(Black vinyl.)
PLAYGIRL (501 "My Baby")..................... 40-50 '60s
(Red vinyl.)

DARE, Timothy
Singles
NFSD (005 "Russian Roulette")............... 15-20 89
(Picture disc, shaped like cigarette pack. 100 made with small picture.)
NFSD (005 "Russian Roulette")..................8-12 89
(Picture disc, shaped like cigarette pack. 500 made with large picture.)

DARELYCKS
Singles: 7-inch
FINE (111 "Bad Trip")............................. 25-35 66
FINE (57027 "Bad Trip")......................... 10-15

DARET, Darla
(With Johnny Mann & Orchestra)
Singles: 7-inch
SILVER (2001 "Don'tcha Wanna")........... 10-15 57
Also see JAMES, Sonny
Also see MANN, Johnny, Singers

DARIAN, Fred — P&R '61
(Freddy Darian)
Singles: 78 rpm
ALLIED (5021 "I Need You")..................... 10-15 54
Singles: 7-inch
ALLIED (5021 "I Need You").................... 15-20 54
DEL-FI (4140 "You Must Believe")............8-12 60
GARDENA (122 "Rib-Bone")........................8-12 61
JAF (62 "North to Durango").........................8-12 63
(First issue.)
JAF (2020 thru 2503).................................8-12 61-62
MAHALO (1006 "Beyond the Reef")...........5-10 63
OKEH (7113 "Now and Then")....................8-12 59
RCA (7610 "And I Believed You")..............8-12 59
U.A. (650 "North to Durango")..................5-10 63
Also see BALLADEERS

DARIANS
Singles: 7-inch
CARLSON INT'L (3670027 "Tell Me Love").. 100-200

DARIN, Bobby — P&R/R&B/C&W '58
(With the Jaybirds; with Rinky Dinks; Bob Darin)
Singles: 78 rpm
ATCO (6092 "Million Dollar Baby") 25-35 57
ATCO (6103 "Pretty Betty")...................... 25-35 57
ATCO (6109 "Just in Case You Change Your Mind").. 25-35 58
ATCO (6117 "Splish Splash").................. 50-75 58
ATCO (6121 "Early in the Morning") 40-60 58
ATCO (6127 "Queen of the Hop")............ 40-60 58
ATCO (6128 "Mighty Mighty Man")........... 50-75 58
DECCA.. 50-100 56-57
Singles: 7-inch
ATCO ("She's Tanfastic")........................ 25-35
(Promotional issue only. No selection number used.)
ATCO (6092 "Million Dollar Baby") 15-25 57
ATCO (6103 "Pretty Betty")...................... 25-35 57
ATCO (6109 "Just in Case You Change Your Mind").. 25-35 58
ATCO (6117 "Splish Splash")................. 15-25 58
ATCO (6121 "Early in the Morning")......... 20-30 58
(This same track was previously issued as by "The Rinky Dinks on Atco and by the Ding Dongs on Brunswick.")
ATCO (6127 "Queen of the Hop")............ 15-25 58
ATCO (6128 "Mighty Mighty Man")........... 25-35 58
ATCO (6133 "Plain Jane")....................... 15-25 59
(Monaural.)
ATCO (SD-45-6133 "Plain Jane")............ 35-50 59
(Stereo.)
ATCO (6140 thru 6183).......................... 10-15 59-60
ATCO (6188 thru 6334, except 6211).........8-15 61-65
ATCO (6211 "Ave Maria") 10-20 61
ATLANTIC...5-8 65-67
CAPITOL (2263 "18 Yellow Roses")........20-30 63
(Promotional issue only.)
CAPITOL 5-8 62-65
DECCA (29883 "Rock Island Line")..........20-30 56
DECCA (29922 "Blue Eyed Mermaid")......30-50 56
DECCA (30031 "The Greatest Builder")...20-30 56
DECCA (30225 "Dealer in Dreams") 25-40 57
DECCA (30737 "Dealer in Dreams") 10-20 59
DIMENSION 4-6 70
DIRECTION 4-6 68-70
MOTOWN...4-6 71-73
Picture Sleeves
ATCO (6133 "Plain Jane")........................30-40 59
ATCO (6140 "Dream Lover").....................30-40 59
ATCO (6147 "Mack the Knife") 30-40 59
ATCO (6158 "Beyond the Sea")................20-30 60
ATCO (6161 "Clementine") 20-30 60
ATCO (6167 "Won't You Come Home Bill Bailey")...15-25 60
ATCO (6173 "Beachcomber") 15-25 60
ATCO (6179 "Artificial Flowers")..............15-25 60
ATCO (6183 "Christmas Auld Lang Syne") 15-25 60
ATCO (6188 "Lazy River").........................15-25 61
ATCO (6196 "Nature Boy") 15-25 61
ATCO (6206 "You Must Have Been a Beautiful Baby")..15-25 61
ATCO (6211 "Ave Maria").......................75-125 61
ATCO (6214 "Multiplication")....................10-20 61
ATCO (6221 "What'd I Say")....................10-20 61
CAPITOL (2263 "18 Yellow Roses").........25-50 63
(Promotional issue only.)
CAPITOL (4837 thru 5443) 10-20 62-65
EPs: 7-inch
ATCO (115 "This Is Darin") 50-100 59
(Promotional issue only. Issued with paper sleeve.)
ATCO (1001 "Bobby Darin for Teenagers Only")..50-100 60
(Promotional issue only. Issued with paper sleeve.)
ATCO (4502 "Bobby Darin").....................35-50 58
ATCO (4504 "That's All") 25-40 59
ATCO (4505 "Queen of the Hop")..............30-50 59
ATCO (4508 "This Is Darin") 20-40 59
ATCO (4512 "Darin at the Copa")..............20-40 60
ATCO (4513 "For Teenagers Only")..30-50 60
CAPITOL (1791 "Look at Me Now")..........25-50 62
(Juke box issue only.)
CAPITOL CUSTOM ("Scripto Presents Bobby Darin")..25-50 63
(Promotional issue only. Made with two different color paper sleeves, each offered in conjunction with a different pen: One with light blue sleeve came with Scripto Wordmaster ball point pen; one with yellow sleeve came with ink cartridge fountain pen. Picture of Bobby Darin is the same on both sleeves.)
CAPITOL CUSTOM/ARTISTIC (2262 "Bobby Darin")..25-50 63
(Promotional issue only. Issued with paper sleeve.)
DECCA (2676 "Here Them Bells")............50-75 60
MOTOWN (4 "Bobby Darin")....................10-20 72
(Promotional issue only.)
LPs: 10/12-inch
ATCO (102 "Bobby Darin").......................50-75 58
ATCO (104 "That's All")...........................25-45 58
(Monaural. Yellow label.)
ATCO (SD-104 "That's All")......................35-55 58
(Stereo. Yellow label.)
ATCO (115 "This Is Darin")......................15-25 60
(Monaural. Yellow label.)
ATCO (SD-115 "This Is Darin")................20-30 60
(Stereo. Yellow label.)
ATCO (122 "Darin at the Copa") 15-25 60
(Monaural. Yellow label.)
ATCO (SD-122 "Darin at the Copa").........20-30 60
(Stereo. Yellow label.)
ATCO (124 "It's You Or No One")..............15-25 63
(Monaural. Yellow label.)
ATCO (SD-124 "It's You Or No One") 20-30 63
(Stereo. Yellow label.)
ATCO (125 "25th Day of December").......25-35 60
(Monaural. Yellow label.)
ATCO (SD-125 "25th Day of December") 35-50 60
(Stereo. Yellow label.)
ATCO (131 "Bobby Darin Story")..............35-45 61
(Monaural. Yellow label. White cover.)
ATCO (SD-131 "Bobby Darin Story").......45-55 61
(Stereo. Yellow label. White cover.)
ATCO (131 "Bobby Darin Story").............10-15 72
(Yellow label. Black cover.)
ATCO (134 "Love Swings")......................15-25 61
(Monaural. Yellow label.)
ATCO (SD-134 "Love Swings")................20-30 61
(Stereo. Yellow label.)
ATCO (138 "Twist with Bobby Darin")......15-25 61
(Monaural. Yellow label. Cover sticker promotes "Bobby's Latest Hit Single *Irresistible You* and *Multiplication*.")
ATCO (SD-138 "Twist with Bobby Darin")..20-30 61
(Stereo. Yellow label. Cover sticker promotes "Bobby's Latest Hit Single *Irresistible You* and *Multiplication*.")
ATCO (138 "Twist with Bobby Darin")......10-20 62
(Monaural. Gold, white, and blue label.)
ATCO (SD-138 "Twist with Bobby Darin")..15-25 62
(Stereo. Gold, white, and blue label.)
ATCO (140 "Bobby Darin Sings Ray Charles")..15-25 62
(Monaural.)
ATCO (SD-140 "Bobby Darin Sings Ray Charles")..20-30 62
ATCO (146 "Things")...............................15-25 61
(Monaural.)
ATCO (SD-146 "Things") 20-30 61
(Stereo.)
ATCO (167 "Winners") 15-25 64
(Monaural.)
ATCO (SD-167 "Winners")......................20-30 64
(Stereo.)
ATCO (1001 "Bobby Darin for Teenagers Only")..100-150 60
(With color foldout photo.)
ATLANTIC..15-25 66-67
BAINBRIDGE...5-10 81
CANDLELITE...15-20 76
CAPITOL (1791 "Oh! Look at Me Now") ..20-25 62
CAPITOL (1826 "Earthy")........................20-25 63
CAPITOL (1866 "You're the Reason I'm Living")..20-25 63
CAPITOL (1942 "18 Yellow Roses")........20-25 63
CAPITOL (2007 "Golden Folk Hits").........20-25 63
CAPITOL (2194 "From *Hello Dolly* to *Goodbye Charlie*")..20-25 64
CAPITOL (2322 "Venice Blue") 50-100 65
CAPITOL (2571 "Best of Bobby Darin") ...20-25 66
CLARION (603 "Clementine")..................15-20 64
DIRECTION..12-20 68-70
IMPERIAL HOUSE...................................12-15 76
MOTOWN (100 series).............................5-10 82
MOTOWN (738 "Finally")......................250-300 72
(Promotional issue only.)
MOTOWN (753 "Bobby Darin") 10-20 72
MOTOWN (813 "Darin: 1936-1973")........10-20 74
W.B. (3501 "Original Bobby Darin").........20-30 76
(Three-disc, mail-order offer.)
Session: King Curtis.
Also see BEHRKE, Richard, Trio
Also see DING DONGS
Also see KING CURTIS
Also see MOGAMBOS
Also see RINKY DINKS

DARIN, Bobby, & Johnny Mercer
LPs: 10/12-inch
ATCO (126 "Two of a Kind") 15-25 61
(Monaural.)
ATCO (SD-126 "Two of a Kind")..............25-40 61
(Stereo.)
Also see DARIN, Bobby
Also see MERCER, Johnny

DARIUS
LPs: 10/12-inch
CHARTMAKER (1102 "Darius") 100-150 68
Session: Jerry Scheff; Toxie French; Ben Benay.
Also see GOLDENROD

DARK, Johnny
Singles: 7-inch
BIG BEN (1004 "Land of a Thousand Dances")..10-20 65

DARK AGE
LPs: 10/12-inch
GARNLY/GREENWOOD (1001 "Dark Age")..20-25 85
(Picture disc.)

DARK ANGEL — LP '89
Singles: 7-inch
COMBAT...3-5 89
METAL STORM (8602 "Merciless Death")..15-25 87
(Saw blade-shaped picture disc. 25 made.)
METAL STORM (8602 "Merciless Death") 10-20 87
(Rectangular picture disc. 50 made.)
METAL STORM (8602 "Merciless Death") ..5-8 87
(Skull or torture wheel shape picture disc. 500 made of each.)
METAL STORM (8817 "We Have Arrived")..10-20 88
(Cross shaped picture disc. 25 made. Promotional issue only.)
METAL STORM (8817 "We Have Arrived") . 5-8 88
(Square picture disc. 500 made.)
LPs: 10/12-inch
COMBAT...5-8 89
METALSTORM (8501 "We Have Arrived")..10-15 87
(Picture disc. 500 made for USA. 500 made for Europe.)

DARKE, Ronny
Singles: 7-inch
LOND ("My Dream Girl")......................200-300 59
(No selection number used.)

DARLENE & JOKERS
Singles: 7-inch
DANCO (115 "Frankie")...........................10-15 60
Also see JOKERS

DARLENE & MELODEERS
Singles: 7-inch
JET (205 "Always Forever").....................20-30

DARLENES
Singles: 7-inch
STACY (965 "I Still Like Rock and Roll").. 10-15 63

DARLETTES
Singles: 7-inch
DUNES (2026 "Here She Comes") 5-10 63
MIRA (203 "Lost")......................................5-10 65
TAFFI (100 "Love Will Make You Cry").....25-35
Also see DIANE & DARLETTES

DAR-LETTS
Singles: 7-inch
SHELL (101 "Til I Fell in Love") 10-15 64

DARLIN, Chris
Singles: 7-inch
DORE (578 "A Casual Look")...................15-25 61

DARLING, Johnny
Singles: 7-inch
DELUXE (6167 "I Don't Want to Wind Up in Love")..50-75 58

DARLINGS
(With the Snub Mosley Quintet)
Singles: 7-inch
PENGUIN (06-98 "In the Evening") 15-25 59

DARLINGS
Singles: 7-inch
DORE (663 "To Know Him Is to Love Him")..75-85 63
DORE (677 "My Pillow")............................30-50 63
KAY•KO (1002 "Two Time Loser") 20-30 63
(First issue.)
MERCURY (72185 "Two Time Loser") 10-15 63

DARLTON, Joe
Singles: 7-inch
TRU-LITE (120 "Don't Say Goodbye Anymore")..10-20 63

DARNEL, Bill
(With the Heathertones)
Singles: 78 rpm
CORAL...3-5 50-51
DECCA...3-5 52-53
Singles: 7-inch
CORAL...5-10 50-51
DECCA...5-10 52-53
JUBILEE...5-10 56-59
LONDON (Except 1665)...........................5-10 56
LONDON (1665 "Rock-a-Boogie Baby").. 10-15 56
PARIS...10-15 59-60
"X"..5-10 54-55

EPs: 7-inch

"X".. 10-20 55

LPs: 10/12-inch

"X".. 20-30 55

DARNELL, Dick

Singles: 7-inch

CLIFF (7003 "The One for Me") 20-30

DARNELL, Gracie

Singles: 7-inch

RUTH (101 "So Long Lover") 20-30

DARNELL, Larry *R&B '49*

(With the Fortunes)

Singles: 78 rpm

DELUXE 8-12 57

OKEH.. 10-20 51-53

REGAL.. 10-20 49-51

SAVOY 10-15 55

Singles: 7-inch

ANNA (1109 (With Tears in My Eyes") 200-300 60

ARGO (5364 "Look at Me") 10-15 60

ARGO (5372 "With Tears in My Eyes") ... 10-15 60

DELUXE (6136 "If You Go") 10-15 57

DELUXE (6141 "It Must Be Love") 15-20 57

INSTANT (3296 "Stomp Down Soul")........4-6 68

MAP (501 "Flame of Love") 75-100 58

MISTY...4-6

OKEH.. 10-20 51-53

REGAL.. 10-20 51

SAVOY (1151 "That's All I Want from You") 10-20 55

WARWICK (506 "If I Had You")..................8-12 59

EPs: 7-inch

EPIC (7072 "For You My Love")............ 50-100 61

Session: Mickey Baker.

Also see BAKER, Mickey

DARNELL, Lucia

Singles: 7-inch

BEDFORD (505 "Teenage Quarrel") 15-25 61

DARNELL, Mike

Singles: 7-inch

FAMTABULOUS (1003 "All I Want Is You") 30-40

DARNELL, Paul

Singles: 7-inch

CREST (1110 "Be My Lovin' Baby") 5-10 62

DELTONE (5021 "Sherry") 10-15 64

DARNELL, Ravon

(With Earl Hyde & His Orchestra; with Voices)

Singles: 78 rpm

MILLION (2015 "I'll Be Back") 20-30 56

MILLION (2017 "Don't Want You Maybelline") 20-30 56

TAMPA (119 "Chicken Little") 15-25 56

Singles: 7-inch

MILLION (2015 "I'll Be Back") 50-75 56

MILLION (2017 "Don't Want You Maybelline") 50-75 56

TAMPA (119 "Chicken Little") 40-60 56

DARNELL & DREAMS

Singles: 7-inch

WEST SIDE (1020 "I Had a Love")........... 20-30 64

DARNELLS

(Marvelettes)

Singles: 7-inch

GORDY (7024 "Too Hurt to Cry, Too Much in Love to Say Goodbye") 30-40 63

Also see MARVELETTES

DARNELLS

Singles: 7-inch

SARA (1055 "She, She, Little Sheila")..... 15-20 61

TIDE (1090 "Spooner") 5-10 63

Members: Tom Fabares; Bruce Welch; Jerry Saworski; Tommy Hahn; Denny King; Gary Myers.

Also see MAD LADS

Also see MOJO MEN

Also see MYERS, Gary

Also see PORTRAITS

DARNELS

Singles: 7-inch

BANA (525 "My Little Homin' Pigeon") 25-35 57

DARRELL & OXFORDS

(Tokens)

Singles: 7-inch

ROULETTE (4174 "Picture in My Wallet") 10-15 59

ROULETTE (4230 "Can't You Tell") 20-30 60

Also see TOKENS

DARRELLS

Singles: 7-inch

LYCO (1003 "So Tenderly") 15-25 61

DARREN, Danny

Singles: 7-inch

ALAN DALE (3063 "Loneliness")..............10-20 67

COULEE (141 "Medals for Mother") 5-10 72

DRAEGER (360 "Road Side Rag")...........20-30 66

DRAEGER (4561 "Fool About You") 100-200 66

KL (KS10 "Love Make the World Go Round") 5-10 72

PYRAMID (15 "No Reason to Quit") 5-10 73

PYRAMID (18 "Take These Charms")........5-10 73

RAINBOW (201 "Go Menasi") 5-10 72

SILVER STAR (1039 "Nothing to Write Home About") 5-10 70

DARREN, James *P&R '59*

(Jimmy Darren)

Singles: 7-inch

ABC 4-6 74

BUDDAH (177 "That's My World") 4-6 70

COLPIX (102 "There's No Such Thing")...10-20 58

COLPIX (113 "Gidget") 10-20 59

COLPIX (119 "Angel Face") 10-20 59

(Monaural.)

COLPIX (SCP-119 "Angel Face") 25-35 59

(Stereo.)

COLPIX (128 thru 708).............................10-20 59-63

COLPIX (758 "Punch and Judy") 15-25 64

COLPIX (765 "Married Man") 8-12 64

ERIC...4-6

JIMMY DARREN FAN CLUB (144 "Message: *Because They're Young*")...................................30-40 60

(Promotional, fan club issue only.)

KIRSHNER...4-6 69-72

MCA..3-5

MGM...4-6 73

PRIVATE STOCK 4-6 75-77

RCA..4-6 78

W.B. 5-10 65-68

Picture Sleeves

COLPIX (102 "There's No Such Thing")...15-25 58

COLPIX (609 "Goodbye Cruel World") 15-25 61

EPs: 7-inch

RMR JUNIORS ("James Darren") 10-15

(Promotional issue, with fashion spots.)

LPs: 10/12-inch

COLPIX (406 "Album No. 1") 25-35 60

COLPIX (418 "Gidget Goes Hawaiian")....25-35 61

COLPIX (424 "For All Sizes")..................25-35 62

COLPIX (428 "Love Among the Young")..25-35 62

(Monaural.)

COLPIX (SCP-428 "Love Among the Young") 35-45 62

(Stereo.)

KIRSHNER..10-20 71-72

W.B. 15-20 67

DARREN, James / Shelley Fabares / Paul Petersen *LP '63*

LPs: 10/12-inch

COLPIX (444 "Teenage Triangle")............25-35 63

COLPIX (468 "More Teenage Triangle") ..25-35 64

Also see DARREN, James

Also see FABARES, Shelley

Also see PETERSEN, Paul

DARRIS, Frank

Singles: 7-inch

ADVANCE (1000 "Ruby Ann").................50-75

THUNDER (101 "Ruby Ann")...................50-75 59

(At least one source shows this artist's name as Frank Darries. We don't know yet which is correct.)

DARRO, George

Singles: 7-inch

NATIONWIDE (100 "Eye'n You Up")..........30-45 59

NATIONWIDE ("Southern Twist") 50-60

(Selection number not known.)

DARRO, Tony

Singles: 7-inch

CROSLEY (217 "Tender Age") 10-20 59

CROSLEY (226 "Young Hearts")..............10-20 60

DARROW, Danny

Singles: 12-inch

MIGHTY 4-6 83

Singles: 7-inch

ALMONT...5-10 63

MIGHTY (Except 101).................................3-5 83

MIGHTY (101 "Handsome Man") 5-10 60

STRAND (25031 "Impulse").....................20-40 61

LPs: 10/12-inch

MIGHTY 5-10

DARROW, Jay

Singles: 7-inch

KEEN (82124 "Girl in My Dreams") 25-35 61

ORIGINAL SOUND (19 "Ballad of a Teenage Prayer") 5-10 62

DARROW, Ken

Singles: 7-inch

GARY (1007 "Everytime") 40-60 57

DART

Singles: 7-inch

GARLAND..10-15 68

LPs: 10/12-inch

GARLAND (4567 "Presenting Dart") 30-40 68

GARLAND (4578 "Dart") 25-35 70

HOOT (4568 "Sound of Dart") 25-35 70

DART, Jimmy

Singles: 7-inch

HITT (185 "You Won't Care")....................40-50 59

DARTELLS *P&R/R&B/LP '63*

Singles: 7-inch

ARLEN (509 "Hot Pastrami") 10-15 62

(Black vinyl.)

ARLEN (509 "Hot Pastrami") 20-30 62

(Colored vinyl.)

ARLEN (513 "Dance Everybody, Dance")...10-15 62

DOT..8-12 63-64

HBR (457 "Clap Your Hands") 5-10 65

LPs: 10/12-inch

DOT (3522 "Hot Pastrami")......................50-75 63

(Monaural.)

DOT (25522 "Hot Pastrami")....................50-75 63

(Stereo.)

Member: Doug Phillips.

Also see RAIN

DARTS

Singles: 7-inch

APT (25023 "On My Mind").......................15-25 58

DARTS

Singles: 7-inch

DOT (15752 "Sweet Little Baby").............10-15 58

DARTS

LPs: 10/12-inch

DEL-FI (DLF-1231 "Hollywood Drag")......10-12 98

("Thick, hard wax" reissue.)

DEL-FI (DFLP-1244 "Hollywood Drag") ...25-35 63

(Monaural.)

DEL-FI (DFST-1244 "Hollywood Drag") ...35-45 63

(Stereo.)

DARTS

Singles: 7-inch

B&S (001 "Square Town").......................75-125

DARTY, Chuck

Singles: 7-inch

CHART (649 "My Steady Girl")..................15-25 57

RAMA (229 "My Steady Girl") 8-12 57

ROULETTE (4159 "Lumberjack")................5-10 59

DARVELL, Barry

(With Hash Brown & His Orchestra)

Singles: 7-inch

ATLANTIC (2128 "Lost Love")....................8-12 61

ATLANTIC (2138 "Adam & Eve")..................8-12 62

COLT 45 (107 "Geronimo Stomp")...........40-60 59

COLT 45 (301 "Run Little Billy")..............10-15 63

COLUMBIA (44197 "My World of Make Believe") 5-10 67

CUB (9088 "Fountain of Love")...............10-20 61

PROVIDENCE (404 "When You're Alone") 8-12 64

WORLD ARTISTS (1042 "I'll Remember").5-10 65

WORLD ARTISTS (1058 "I Found a Daisy") 5-10 65

Also see DEMOLYRS

DARVELS

Singles: 7-inch

EDDIES (69 "I Lost My Baby")..................15-25 63

(Black vinyl.)

EDDIES (69 "I Lost My Baby")................75-125 63

(Blue vinyl.)

Member: Warren Gradis.

DARWIN, Ricky

(With the Bobby Smith Orchestra & Chorus)

Singles: 7-inch

BUZZ (103 "The Great Great Thinker")....10-20 59

DARWIN & CUPIDS

Singles: 7-inch

JERDEN (1 "How Long")..........................10-20 60

JERDEN (9 "Goodnight My Love") 10-20 60

Member: Darwin Lamm.

DARWIN & JUANITA

(With the Melvin Glass Combo)

Singles: 7-inch

COCO (11 "Because It's You") 10-20

COMBO (158 "Baby Baby") 8-12 60

Members: Darwin Jackson; Juanita Manley.

DARWYN, Jane

Singles: 7-inch

RONKO (6995 "Ready to Go Steady")....10-15 62

VEE-JAY (503 "Half a Woman") 5-10 63

DASH, Frankie

Singles: 7-inch

COOL (106 "Rock to the Moon") 100-150 58

DASH, Julian

(With His Sextet; Julian Dash Orchestra)

Singles: 78 rpm

SITTIN' IN WITH (600 "Hot Rod")............15-25 51

VEE-JAY (144 "Zero")..............................15-25 54

Singles: 7-inch

VEE-JAY (144 "Zero")..............................30-40 54

Also see HAWKINS, Erskine

DASHIEL, Bud, & Kinsmen

Singles: 7-inch

W.B. (5231 "I Talk to the Trees")...............5-10 61

LPs: 10/12-inch

W.B. (1429 "Bud Dashiel & Kinsmen").....10-20 61

DATE WITH SOUL

Singles: 7-inch

YORK (408 "Yes Sir That's My Baby").....15-25 67

(Previously issued as by Hale & Hushabyes. See that listing for members)

Also see HALE & HUSHABYES

DAUGHTRY, George, & Shoeless Joe Jackson

Singles: 78 rpm

("Those Wild and Wicked Ways")..........50-100

(No label name nor selection number used.)

DAUN, Bobby

Singles: 7-inch

TWIN STAR (1013 "Come Back to Me")..15-25 60

DAUPHIN TRIO

Singles: 7-inch

EPIC (9432 "Moonlit Sea").......................10-20 61

DAVE & BOB

Singles: 7-inch

M&F (169 "Two Old Sparrows")...............25-30 59

DAVE & CARDIGANS

Singles: 7-inch

BAY (216 "My Falling Star")......................30-40 63

DAVE & CUSTOMS

Singles: 7-inch

DAC (500 "Shortnin' Bread").....................25-35 65

DAC (501 "You Should Be Glad") 25-35 65

DAC (502 "Bony Maronie").......................25-35 66

Members: Dave Zdunich; Mark Zdunich; Ken Cook.

DAVE & LEE

Singles: 7-inch

LONDON (197 "Sad September") 150-175 73

Members: David Gates; Leon Russell.

Also see DAVID & LEE

Also see GATES, David

Also see RUSSELL, Leon

DAVE & MARKSMEN
(David Marks)
Singles: 7-inch
A&M (730 "Cruisin'")...................... 15-25 64
W.B. (5485 "I Wanna Cry")...................... 40-50 64
Also see BEACH BOYS
Also see CLIFFORD, Buzz
Also see HONEYS
Also see MOON

DAVE & ORBITS
Singles: 7-inch
AMERICAN ARTS (14 "Chili Beans") 30-40 65

DAVE & PONCHO
Singles: 7-inch
CUCA (6661 "Riders in the Sky")............ 10-15 66

DAVE & RON
Singles: 7-inch
BAY (5211 "Sharon")............................. 10-15 '50s

DAVE & SAINTS
Singles: 7-inch
BAND BOX (341 "Leavin' Surf City") 10-20 63

DAVE & SHADOWS
Singles: 7-inch
CHECK MATE (1011 "Hereafter")............ 25-50 62
CHECK MATE (1016 "Cheek to Cheek") 35-55 62
FENTON (942 "Playboy")........................ 40-60 64

DAVE & STEREOS
Singles: 7-inch
PENNANT (1001 "Roamin' Romeo") 40-50 61

DAVE C & HIS SHARPTONES
Singles: 7-inch
DOLLEE (2615 "Dolly Waddle").................5-10 '60s
WHIRL (13157 "Hi Spy")......................... 10-15 '60s
Member: Dave Cox.

DAVE T & DEL-RAYS
("Dave T [Del-Rays]")
Singles: 7-inch
CAROUSEL (213 "Girl in My Heart") 75-150 64

DAVENPORT, Bill, & His Circle D Ranch Hands
Singles: 7-inch
WAYNE (1010 "Rock and Roll")............ 50-100

DAVENPORT, Cow Cow
(Charles "Cow Cow" Davenport)
Singles: 78 rpm
BRUNSWICK (80022 "Cow Cow Blues") 10-20 49
COMET.. 10-20 45

DAVENPORT SISTERS
Singles: 7-inch
TRI-PHI (1008 "You've Got Me Crying Again") 30-50 62
VIDA (0109 "I Was Teasin' ") 50-75 63

DAVEY & BADMEN
LPs: 10/12-inch
KRW (054 "Wanted")................................ 60-75

DAVEY & DOLPHINS
Singles: 7-inch
20TH FOX (529 "She Likes Older Boys") 20-30 64
Member: David Liska.

DAVEY & DOO RAYS
Singles: 7-inch
GUYDEN (2002 "It's the Beat")............... 10-15 58

DAVI
Singles: 7-inch
STARK (110 "Reason for Love").......... 300-400 62

DAVID
(The David)
Singles: 12-inch
AZRA (100 "Mother's Warning").............. 10-15 85
(Picture disc. 500 made.)
Singles: 7-inch
20TH FOX (6663 "40 Miles")................... 15-25 66
VMC (716 "I'm Not Alone")...................... 10-20 68
LPs: 10/12-inch
VMC (124 "Another Day, Another Lifetime")... 50-100 68
Members: Tim Harrison; Warren Hansen; Mark Bird; Charles Spieth.

DAVID, Clifford
Singles: 7-inch
OKEH (7184 "Keep It Light").....................10-15 63

DAVID, Johnny
Singles: 7-inch
DOT (16078 "Race with the Devil")..........10-15 60
GIL (104 "Race with the Devil")................30-40 60
(First issue.)

DAVID, Kal, & Exceptions
Singles: 7-inch
TOLLIE (9007 "Searchin' ").......................10-15 64
TOLLIE (9043 "Come On Home")............10-15 65
Also see EXCEPTIONS

DAVID & BOYS NEXT DOOR
Singles: 7-inch
SKIPPER (1240 "Land O' Love").............15-25

DAVID & FREDDIE
Singles: 7-inch
BULLSEYE (1010 "Oy Vay")....................10-20 58
Member: David Ellin.

DAVID & GIANTS
Singles: 7-inch
AMY (983 "On Bended Knees")..................8-12 67
CAPITOL (2893 "Don't Say No")................5-10 70
CRAZY HORSE..10-20 68-69
FAME (1467 "Letter to Josephine") 15-25 67
LPs: 10/12-inch
PRIORITY 5-10 82
Members: David Huff; Rayburn Huff; Clayburn Huff; Keith Thibodeaux.

DAVID & GOLIATH
Singles: 7-inch
AMY (983 "On Bended Knees")..................5-10 67
TOMARO (101 "Like Strangers") 15-20 65
Members: Bill Baker; Roger Koob.
Also see BAKER, Bill

DAVID & JONATHAN *P&R '66*
Singles: 7-inch
AMY (11012 "Something's Gotten Hold of My Heart")..5-10 68
CAPITOL..5-10 66-67
20TH FOX (6641 "Modesty").......................5-10 66
Picture Sleeves
CAPITOL..5-10 66
LPs: 10/12-inch
CAPITOL (2473 "Michelle").......................20-30 66
Members: Roger Greenaway; Roger Cook.
Also see PHILWIT & PEGASUS

DAVID & LEE
Singles: 7-inch
G.S.P. (1 "Sad September").....................20-30 62
Members: David Gates; Leon Russell.
Also see DAVE & LEE
Also see GATES, David
Also see RUSSELL, Leon

DAVID & RUBEN
Singles: 7-inch
RAMPART (662 "Girl in My Dreams") 50-100 69
W.B. (7316 "Girl in My Dreams")..............30-50 69

DAVIDS, Janie
(With Bob Bain & Four Lettermen)
Singles: 7-inch
KEY (576 "Gonna Get Even") 50-100 58
Picture Sleeves
KEY (576 "Gonna Get Even") 50-100 58
(Artist bio sleeve with die-cut center hole.)

DAVIE, Hutch *P&R '58*
(With His Honky-Tonkers; Hutch Davie Convention)
Singles: 7-inch
ATCO...10-15 58-59
CANADIAN AMERICAN (126 "Glow Worm")...5-10 61
CLARIDGE (311 "East Is East")..................5-10 66
CONGRESS (102 "But I Do").....................5-10 62
DYNO VOICE...5-10 68
NEW VOICE (823 "Swingin' Shepherd Blues") 5-10 67
LPs: 10/12-inch
ATCO (105 "Much Hutch") 30-40 59
CONGRESS (3004 "Piano Memories") 25-35 62
Also see ANGELS
Also see RAY, James
Also see RAY, Ricardo

DAVIS, Al
(With the Blackouts)
Singles: 7-inch
MANCO (1052 "Ricky Tic") 25-50 64
MANCO (1067 "Go Baby, Go")............200-300 65

DAVIS, Alec
Singles: 7-inch
CHART (646 "Stand By Baby")................15-25 57

DAVIS, Andrea
(Minnie Riperton)
Singles: 7-inch
CHESS (1980 "Lonely Girl").....................10-20 67

DAVIS, Artie
Singles: 7-inch
COOL (123 "Book of Love").....................30-50 60

DAVIS, Bette, & Debbie Burton
Singles: 7-inch
MGM (13107 "What Ever Happened to Baby Jane")..5-10 62
Picture Sleeves
MGM (13107 "What Ever Happened to Baby Jane")..15-25 62
Also see DAVIS, Bette

DAVIS, Bill
Singles: 7-inch
SARA (1449 "Tell Me")............................15-25 '60s
SARA (1450 "I'll Say Yes").......................15-25 '60s

DAVIS, Bill, Trio
(Billy Davis)
Singles: 78 rpm
OKEH (7013 "Joe Louis Story")..................8-12 53
Singles: 7-inch
OKEH (7013 "Joe Louis Story")..............15-25 53
Also see GAYTEN, Paul

DAVIS, Billy
Singles: 7-inch
R-DELL (118 "Small Fry") 10-15 60

DAVIS, Billy
Singles: 7-inch
"54" (5401 "Knock Kneed Rooster") 50-100

DAVIS, Billy Guitar
Singles: 78 rpm
GOTHAM (322 "Warm and Cooler").........10-15 56
Singles: 7-inch
GOTHAM (322 "Warm and Cooler").........15-25 56

DAVIS, Blind Gary
(Reverend Gary Davis)
Singles: 78 rpm
LENOX 10-20 48
Singles: 7-inch
PRESTIGE..5-10 62
LPs: 10/12-inch
BIOGRAPH 8-10 71
CONTINENTAL 20-40
FANTASY..10-15 72
FOLK LYRIC...10-15
KICKING MULE 8-10 74
PRESTIGE BLUESVILLE (1015 "Harlem Street Singer")..50-100 61
PRESTIGE BLUESVILLE (1032 "A Little More Faith")..50-100 61
VANGUARD...15-20

DAVIS, Blind Gary, & Sonny Terry
LPs: 10/12-inch
STINSON (56 "The Singing Reverend")...50-75 53
(10-inch LP.)
Also see DAVIS, Blind Gary
Also see TERRY, Sonny

DAVIS, Blind John
(Blind Johnny Davis & Blind Johnny Davis Trio)
Singles: 78 rpm
MGM...15-30 49-51
Singles: 7-inch
MGM (10919 "Telegram to My Baby")......50-75 51
MGM (10976 "The Day Will Come").........25-50 51
LPs: 10/12-inch
ALLIGATOR...8-10 77

DAVIS, Bo
Singles: 78 rpm
CREST...20-40 56
Singles: 7-inch
CREST (1027 "Let's Coast Awhile").........50-75 56
Also see COCHRAN, Eddie

DAVIS, Bob
Singles: 78 rpm
ABBOTT (114 "My Gal Comes from Heaven")..10-15 53
Singles: 7-inch
ABBOTT (114 "My Gal Comes from Heaven")..15-25 53

DAVIS, Bob
(With the Rhythm Jesters; Bob Davies)
Singles: 78 rpm
RAMA (224 "Never Anymore") 20-30 57
Singles: 7-inch
APEX (76135 "Never Anymore") 10-20 57
(Canadian.)
BROADLAND 4-8 71
(Canadian.)
CLICK...4-8 63-64
(Canadian.)
RAMA (224 "Never Anymore") 20-30 57
ZIRCON (1003 "That's How Young Love Should Be")..10-20 59
(Canadian.)
LP: 10/12-inch
CELINA 5-10 78
(Canadian.)
RUSTICANA..25-25 63
(Canadian.)
Session: Joyce Germain.
Also see BIG BOB & DOLLARS
Also see MASON, Little Billie
Also see RHYTHM JESTERS

DAVIS, Bob, Quartet
Singles: 78 rpm
BALLY (1004 "Moon Pearls")....................5-10 56
Singles: 7-inch
BALLY (1004 "Moon Pearls")..................10-15 56
DOOTO (414 "Off Day Blues") 15-25 57

DAVIS, Bobby
(With the Rhythm Rockers)
Singles: 7-inch
BANDERA (2505 "I Was Wrong") 10-20 60
BANDERA (2508 "She's a Problem")......40-60 61
M-PAC (7200 "A Human's Prayer")............8-12 62
VEST (8003 "Get with It").........................8-12 64
VEST (8007 "Tell Me Baby").....................8-12 65

DAVIS, Bonnie, & Piccadilly Pipers
Singles: 78 rpm
GROOVE (0032 "How Could You")............8-12 54
MELMAR (101 "If You Only Knew") 5-10 54
"X" (0086 "I Wanna")..................................5-10 54
Singles: 7-inch
GROOVE (0032 "How Could You")..........30-40 54
MELMAR (101 "If You Only Knew") 15-25 54
"X" (0086 "I Wanna")...............................15-25 54

DAVIS, Charlie
Singles: 78 rpm
COLONY (112 "Gorgeous Gal") 10-15 52
Singles: 78 rpm
COLONY (112 "Gorgeous Gal") 15-25 52
IMPERIAL (5011 "Rainin' Blues")..............25-35 47

DAVIS, Chuck
Singles: 7-inch
TILT (1101 "Teaser")................................15-25 58

DAVIS, Cliff
(With Kentucky Play Boys; Cliff Davis Sextet)
Singles: 7-inch
BANANA (501 "Hard Hearted Girl")......100-200 57
CATHAY (1151 "Get That Cargo") 5-10 66
FEDERAL (12359 "Let It Roll")..................10-20 59
FEDERAL (12366 "Rock & Reel")..............10-20 59
JAY JAY (161 "Rocky Road Blues").....150-200 56
LPs: 10/12-inch
EPIC (24173 "Discotheque A Go Go").....15-20 65
EPIC (26173 "Discotheque A Go Go").....15-25 65

DAVIS, Dale, & His Tomcats
Singles: 78 rpm
STARDALE...40-80 56
Singles: 7-inch
STARDALE (100 "Gotta Rock")...........100-150 56
STARDALE (104 "Crazy, Batty and Gone")..100-150 56
STARDALE (333 "Gotta Rock")..............75-125 56

DAVIS, Danny *LP '69/C&W '70*
(With the Nashville Brass; with Arlene Baird; with Titans; with Nashville Strings; Danny Davis Orchestra;)

Singles: 78 rpm

BLUE JAY....4-8 54
HICKORY....4-8 54
MGM....4-8 51-53
UNIQUE....4-8 56-57

Singles: 7-inch

BLUE JAY....10-15 54
CABOT (128 "Trumpet Conga")....10-15 59
CABOT (129 "Harlem Nocturne")....10-15 59
HICKORY (1005 "Can't You Feel It in Your Heart")....10-15 54
LIBERTY (55213 "Glory Bugle")....10-15 59
MGM (11000 series)....10-20 51-53
MGM (13000 series)....5-10 62-65
RCA....3-8 69-84
THUNDER (102 "Glory Bugle")....15-25 59
(First issue.)
UNIQUE....10-15 56-57
VERVE (10233 "Stardust")....5-10 61

LPs: 10/12-inch

MGM....10-25 61-65
RCA SPECIAL PRODUCTS (0176 "America 200 Years Young")....10-15 76
(Special Products issue for the Amana Corp.)
RCA....5-15 69-84
Also see ATKINS, Chet, Floyd Cramer & Danny Davis
Also see LOCKLIN, Hank, with Danny Davis & Nashville Brass
Also see TITANS

DAVIS, Dean

Singles: 7-inch

PACE (1009 "Don't Be Surprised")....75-125

DAVIS, Denny, & Glades

Singles: 7-inch

AGE (29121 "I Love You")....10-15 64

DAVIS, Don, & His Groovers

Singles: 7-inch

NORTHERN (3735 "Let's Do It")....75-100 61
SANDY (1040 "The Bull Twist")....10-20 61
Also see MAGNIFICENT SEVEN

DAVIS, Doreen, & Bobby Lyons

Singles: 7-inch

BIG TOP (3057 "Punch Line")....10-15 60

DAVIS, Earl, & Arabian Knights

Singles: 7-inch

LARO (1301 "Night in Arabia")....40-60

DAVIS, Eddie

Singles: 78 rpm

MODERN....10-20 48
VITA (170 "To Be Or Not to Be")....25-35 57

Singles: 7-inch

VITA (170 "To Be Or Not to Be")....25-35 57

DAVIS, Eddie "Lockjaw"
(Featuring Henry Glover)

Singles: 78 rpm

APOLLO....10-15 47
BIRDLAND....5-10 50
HAVEN....10-15 46
KING (Except 4321)....5-10 55-59
KING (4321 "Mountain Oysters")....75-125 49
LENNOX....8-10 48
PRESTIGE....5-10 59-63
REGENT....5-10 50
ROOST....4-8 52-53
SAVOY....6-12 47-48
SIGNATURE....8-12 47
SITTIN' IN WITH....5-10 49

Singles: 7-inch

JAZZLAND....5-10 60-61
KING....10-15 55-59
PRESTIGE....8-12 58-63
RCA....4-6 66

EPs: 7-inch

KING....10-20 56-59

LPs: 10/12-inch

BETHLEHEM....20-30 60
CONTINENTAL (5140 "Kickin' and Wailin")....25-35
JAZZLAND....20-30 60-62
KING (500 & 600 series)....25-50 56-59
MOODSVILLE....20-30 63
PRESTIGE....20-40 58-65
RCA....10-20 66-68
RIVERSIDE....20-30 61-62
ROULETTE....20-30 58-60
Also see COBB, Arnett, & Eddie "Lockjaw" Davis
Also see DOGGETT, Bill
Also see GLOVER, Henry

DAVIS, Eddie

Singles: 7-inch

FABLE ("Tick Tock Rock")....75-125
(Selection number not known.)

DAVIS, Emmett

Singles: 7-inch

BELTONE (1008 "As Sweet As You")....10-15 61
CRAIG (102 "You're Walking on Me")....5-10 63
END (1101 "Thanks")....10-15 61
FLING (717 "You")....10-15 60
FLING (721 "Here Comes My Baby")....15-20 61
M&B (101 "How About It Baby")....50-75 59
RED TOP (112 "So Fine")....20-30 58
Also see PARKER, Jack "The Bear"

DAVIS, Eunice
(With Freddie Mitchell Orchestra)

Singles: 78 rpm

ATLANTIC....15-25 53
CORAL....5-15 52
DELUXE....10-15 54
DERBY....8-12 51
GRAND....5-15 55

Singles: 7-inch

ATLANTIC (992 "Go to Work Pretty Daddy")....40-60 53
CORAL....15-20 52
DELUXE (6068 "Get Your Enjoys")....10-20 54
DERBY (752 "Rock Little Daddy")....30-40 51
GRAND....10-15 55

DAVIS, Freddy, & Counts

Singles: 7-inch

COUNT (405 "I Hope You're Happy")....20-30 58

DAVIS, Frank

Singles: 7-inch

ROY (1020 "Ruby Ann")....35-50

DAVIS, Gale

Singles: 7-inch

DOC HOLIDAY (102 "Rock to the Moon")....50-100

DAVIS, Garland

Singles: 7-inch

WILDCAT (001 "I've Got a Girl")....50-100 59

DAVIS, Gene

Singles: 7-inch

CHALLENGE (59091 "My Only Prayer")....10-15 60
LIBERTY (55562 "Take a Good Look")....8-12 63
LIBERTY (55658 "I'm in the Book")....8-12 64
ROSCO (407 "I've Had It, I'm Through")....200-300
SUPER-SONIC (1001 "Little Boy Cried")....10-20 61

EPs: 7-inch

BOOGIE BOY....8-12

DAVIS, Gene / Chuck & Gene

Singles: 7-inch

R-DELL (107 "Curfew"/"No Rock and Rollin' ")....50-75 58
Also see DAVIS, Gene
Also see MILLS, Chuck

DAVIS, George

Singles: 7-inch

PHILIPS (40082 "Out of a Million Girls")....200-250 62

DAVIS, Ginger

Singles: 7-inch

SWAN (4090 "I'm No Runaround")....15-25 61

DAVIS, Hal
(With Brenda Holloway; Hal "Sonny" Davis)

Singles: 7-inch

ALDEN (1301 "Sweet & Lovely")....20-30 59
ALDEN (1302 "Time After Time")....20-30 59
ALDEN (1303 "King of Lovers")....20-30 59
AMAZON (1004 "Let's Get Married")....10-20 61
DEL-FI (4146 "You're Playing with Me")....15-25 60
DYNAMITE (1010 "Why Did You Go Away")....150-200 62
FEDERAL (12429 "My Only Flower")....10-20 61
G.S.P. (2 "I Don't Know")....15-25 63
GARDENA (125 "Show Me")....15-25 62
KELLEY (105 "Way to My Heart")....20-30 59
(Black vinyl.)
KELLEY (105 "Way to My Heart")....50-75 59
(Red vinyl.)
KENT (375 "Without You")....10-15 62
M.J.C. (104 "You'll Find Love")....40-50 60
(Black vinyl.)
M.J.C. (104 "You'll Find Love")....75-125 60
(Red vinyl.)
MARIE (100 "Why Did You Go Away")....4-8 76
MINASA (6714 "It's You")....15-25 63
WIZARD (101 "What Do You Mean to Me")....50-75 61
(Black label.)
WIZARD (101 "What Do You Mean to Me")....30-50 61
(Yellow label.)
WIZARD (102 "I Need Someone")....30-50 61
VEE-JAY (387 " What Do You Mean to Me")....15-25 61
Also see HOLLOWAY, Brenda

DAVIS, Hal, & Ercelle Tisby

Singles: 7-inch

EDSEL (785 "You, You, You")....15-25 60
Also see DAVIS, Hal

DAVIS, Hank
(Hank & the Elektras)

Singles: 7-inch

STACY (919 "One-Way Track")....40-60 59
WIZZ (716 "I Want You to Be My Baby")....30-40 59

LPs: 10/12-inch

DUCKTAIL....10-15
RR....10-15
REDITA....10-15
Also see CAMPBELL, Rev. Anthony, Hank Davis, & Calvin Morris
Also see HANK & CAROLEE
Also see HANK & ELECTRAS
Also see RADLEY, Raunch

DAVIS, Harvey

Singles: 7-inch

CINDY (3011 "Calling All Cats")....150-250 58

DAVIS, Hayward

Singles: 7-inch

CHRISTY (103 "Bubble Gum Rock")....10-20 60
CHRISTY (103 "Showdown")....10-20 60
(Retitled reissue of *Bubble Gum Rock*.)

DAVIS, Jan
(With the Routers; with Ricco-Shays; "The Jan Davis Guitar")

Singles: 7-inch

A&M....8-12 64
ALJO (104 "Surfing Matador")....15-25 64
BEAR....4-6 69
BIG BIRD....5-10 67
COLUMBIA....5-10 65
DIRECT HIT....4-8
1ST PRESIDENT....5-10 60
GUILD (1900 "Destination Love")....150-250 58
HOLIDAY....5-10 64
QUAD-ETT (10039 "Hot Sauce")....4-8 74
RCA....5-10 66
RANWOOD....4-6 75
RENDEZVOUS (131 thru 218, except 214)....5-10 60-63
RENDEZVOUS (214 "You're Not Welcome")....75-125 63
SHAMLEY....4-6 69
SMASH (1863 "Surfing Matador")....10-15 64
SOAP....3-5 82
UNI....5-10 67
WHITE WHALE (226 "Lost in Space")....5-10 66
Also see HOLLYWOOD PRODUCERS

DAVIS, Jess
(With Freddie Flynn & Flashes)

Singles: 7-inch

BOB-O-LINK (100 "With All My Heart and Soul")....10-20 59
BOB-O-LINK (102 "Do You Love Me")....10-20 60

DAVIS, Jesse

Singles: 7-inch

ERA (3189 "Gonna Hang in There Girl")....50-100 66
ERA (3192 "Something to Think About")....40-60 66

DAVIS, Jimmie *C&W '44*
(With the Jimmie Davis Singers; with Anita Kerr Singers)

Singles: 78 rpm

BLUEBIRD....25-75 '30s
DECCA (1500 thru 6100 series)....20-40 35-45
DECCA (20000 & 30000 series)....8-15 43-57
ELECTRADISK....100-200 '30s
(Made for sale through Woolworth Stores.)
SUNRISE (3128 "Bear Cat Mama from Horner Corners")....100-200 33
SUNRISE (3237 "It's All Coming Home to You")....100-200 33
SUNRISE (3267 "I Wonder If She's Blue")....100-200 33
SUNRISE (3400 "There's Evil in Ye Children Gather 'Round")....100-200 33
SUNRISE (3440 "I Want Her Tailor Made")....100-200 33
VICTOR (23000 series)....75-150 '30s

Singles: 7-inch

PAULA....6-10 74-76

EPs: 7-inch

DECCA....5-15 55-65

LPs: 10/12-inch

CANAAN....4-8 74-81
CORAL....4-8 73
DECCA....8-20 55-72
MCA....4-10 75
PAULA....6-10 74-75
PLANTATION....6-12 78-81
RIVERSONG....5-8
VOCALION....5-15 60-69
Also see KERR, Anita

DAVIS, Jimmy

Singles: 7-inch

NEADMORE ("Eenie Meanie Miney Mo")....50-100
(Selection number not known.)

DAVIS, Judge

Singles: 7-inch

FLASH (120 "Sawmill Section")....10-15 57

DAVIS, Ken
(With Honey Bees)

Singles: 7-inch

BADGER (250 "Shook Shake")....100-200 59
BADGER (251 "Oh So Blue")....15-25 59
KAY DEE (031 "Play Ginger Play")....5-10 67
MEAN MT. (1419 "Shook Shake")....3-5 82
PFAU (3057 "Sittin' Pretty")....40-60 58
SINGING BLUE ("Next Little Town")....15-25 62
(No selection number used.)
STAR-LIGHT (1002 "Uh Huh, That's Right")....50-75 58
STAR-LIGHT (1006 "Shook Shake")....100-150 58

Picture Sleeves

MEAN MT. (1419 "Shook Shake")....3-5 82

DAVIS, Ken

Singles: 7-inch

DOT (16654 "Drop Out")....25-35 64

DAVIS, King

Singles: 78 rpm

RECORDED IN HOLLYWOOD....20-30 54

Singles: 7-inch

RECORDED IN HOLLYWOOD (422 "Someday You'll Understand")....40-50 54
Also see KING DAVIS HOUSE ROCKERS

DAVIS, Larry

Singles: 7-inch

DUKE (192 "Texas Flood")....25-35 58
DUKE (313 "My Little Girl")....15-25 59
HUB CITY (629-73 "Same Thing They Did to Me")....5-10
KENT (507 "Sweet Little Angel")....10-15 69
KENT (4519 "For Five Long Years")....10-15 70
KENT (4532 "Rock Me Baby")....10-15 70
ROOSTER BLUES (47 "Since I Been Loving You")....4-6 82
VIRGO (100 "As the Years Go Passing By")....5-10
Session: Oliver Sain.

DAVIS, Larry & Dixie

Singles: 7-inch

KANGAROO (13 "Gonna Live It Up")....30-40 58
KANGAROO (13 "Gonna Live It Up")....100-150 58
(Thick red vinyl. Promotional issue.)

DAVIS, Lee, & Naturals

Singles: 7-inch

CUB (9026 "Three Young Men") ... 10-20 59

DAVIS, Lem

Singles: 7-inch

PATTERN (103 "Hot Chocolate") ... 15-25 58

DAVIS, Lenny

(Lennie Davis)

Singles: 7-inch

DO-RA-ME ... 15-25 61
PRISM (8006 "The Beginning") ... 30-40
SHEEN (103 "Someone") ... 5-10 59

EPs: 7-inch

DE VAY (8900 "Lenny Davis") ... 5-10

DAVIS, Link

Singles: 78 rpm

COLUMBIA ... 10-20 55
NU-CRAFT ... 25-35 55
SARG ... 25-40 56
STARDAY (Except 235) ... 15-25 56
STARDAY (235 "16 Chicks") ... 40-60 56

Singles: 7-inch

Al'S (1503 "Johnny B. Goode") ... 75-125
ALL BOY (8505 "Forget-Me-Nots") ... 15-25 62
ALL BOY (8508 "Jole Blonde") ... 15-25 63
ALLSTAR (7203 "Little People") ... 15-25 60
COLUMBIA (21350 "Kajalena") ... 20-30 55
COLUMBIA (21431 "Cajun Love") ... 20-30 55
KOOL (1026 "Beatle Bug") ... 10-15 64
NU-CRAFT (2026 "Grasshopper Rock") ... 75-125 55
PRINCESS (4057 "Face in the Glass") ... 10-20 66
SARG (136 "Cockroach") ... 50-100 56
STARDAY (235 "16 Chicks") ... 50-100 56
STARDAY (242 "Grasshopper Rock") ... 50-100 56
STARDAY (255 "Trucker from Tennessee") ... 50-100 56
STARDAY (275 "Bayou Buffalo") ... 50-100 56
STARDAY (293 "Slippin' and Slidin' ") .. 100-150 57
STARDAY (331 "Big Connie") ... 25-50 57
TANKER (715 "Airliner") ... 200-300 59

DAVIS, Little Sam

Singles: 78 rpm

DELUXE ... 30-50 53
ROCKIN' ... 40-60 53

Singles: 7-inch

DELUXE (6025 "She's So Good to Me") ... 50-75 53
ROCKIN' (512 "Goin' Home to Mother") .. 60-80 53
ROCKIN' (519 "She's So Good to Me") . 75-100 53

DAVIS, Mac C&W/P&R '70

Singles: 7-inch

CAPITOL ... 5-10 65
COLUMBIA ... 4-6 70-78
CASABLANCA ... 3-5 80-84
JAMIE (1227 "I'm a Poor Loser") ... 10-20 62
MCA ... 3-5 85-86
NITE-TIME (Our First "Pick Hit of the Week") ... 15-25 62
VEE-JAY (492 "Lookin' at Linda") ... 10-15 63
VEE-JAY (565 "Honey Love") ... 10-15 63

Picture Sleeves

COLUMBIA ... 4-6 70-75

LPs: 10/12-inch

ACCORD ... 5-10 82
BUCKBOARD ... 5-10
CASABLANCA ... 5-10 81-85
COLUMBIA ... 8-10 70-83
MCA ... 5-10 86
SPRINGBOARD ... 6-10
TRIP ... 8-10 73

DAVIS, Martha R&B '48

Singles: 78 rpm

CORAL ... 5-10 51-52
DECCA ... 5-10 48
JEWEL ... 5-15 48
URBAN ... 5-15 46

Singles: 7-inch

CORAL ... 10-20 51-52

LPs: 10/12-inch

ABC-PAR (213 "Tribute to Fats Waller") . 40-50 57
Also see JORDAN, Louis

DAVIS, Maxwell

(With His Blenders; with Harlem Brass)

Singles: 78 rpm

ALADDIN ... 10-15 56
GOTHAM ... 10-15 51
RPM ... 10-15 56
MILTONE ... 10-20 47
RPM ... 10-20 53-56
SWING BEAT ... 10-20 49

Singles: 7-inch

ALADDIN (3143 "Blue Shuffle") ... 15-25 56
KENT (454 "Green Hornet") ... 5-10 67
RPM (449 "Thunderbird") ... 15-25 55
RPM (482 "Tempo Rock") ... 15-25 56

EPs: 7-inch

ALADDIN ("Maxwell Davis") ... 20-30 56
(Selection number not known.)

LPs: 10/12-inch

ALADDIN (709 "Maxwell Davis") ... 40-60 56
(10-inch LP. Black vinyl.)
ALADDIN (709 "Maxwell Davis") ... 50-100 56
(10-inch LP. Colored vinyl.)
ALADDIN (804 "Maxwell Davis") ... 25-50 56
SCORE (4016 "Blue Tango") ... 20-35 57
Also see FABULOUS FOUR
Also see HIGHTOWER, Donna
Also see LITTLE CAESAR
Also see LITTLE MISS CORNSHUCKS
Also see MARY ELLEN

DAVIS, Melvin

(With the Nite Sounds)

Singles: 7-inch

FORTUNE (551 "Playboy") ... 15-25 63
GROOVESVILLE (1003 "I Must Love You") ... 100-150 '60s
INVICTUS (1259 "You Made Me Over") ... 5-8 74
INVICTUS (9115 "Just As Long") ... 5-8 72
KE-KE (1815 "It's No News") ... 200-300
MALA (590 "Save It") ... 20-30 67
MALA (12009 "Faith") ... 10-15 68
WHEEL CITY (1003 "Find a Quiet Place") ... 300-400 '60s
Also see NITE SOUNDS

DAVIS, Meyer

Singles: 7-inch

CAMEO (210 "Let's Twist Again") ... 5-10 62
WARWICK (617 "Jacqueline") ... 5-10 61

LPs: 10/12-inch

CAMEO (C-1014 "The Twist") ... 10-20 61
(Monaural.)
CAMEO (SC-1014 "The Twist") ... 15-25 61
(Stereo.)

DAVIS, Miles LP '61

(Miles Davis All Stars; Miles Davis Sextet; with Gil Evans & His Orchestra)

Singles: 78 rpm

BLUE NOTE ... 5-10 54-56
PRESTIGE ... 5-10 52-57

Singles: 7-inch

BLUE NOTE (1600 series) ... 10-20 54-56
COLUMBIA (02000 thru 03000 series) ... 3-5 81-83
COLUMBIA (10000 series) ... 4-6 75
COLUMBIA (41000 thru 46000 series) ... 5-10 61-74
PRESTIGE (100 thru 400 series) ... 8-15 57-66
PRESTIGE (700 thru 900 series) ... 15-25 52-55
W.B. (28501 "Tutu") ... 3-5 87

EPs: 7-inch

BLUE NOTE ... 15-25 52
CAPITOL (459 "Jeru") ... 50-100 53
COLUMBIA ... 10-20 59
PRESTIGE ... 15-25 52-53

LPs: 10/12-inch

BLUE NOTE (100 series) ... 8-12 73
BLUE NOTE (1500 series) ... 30-60 56-58
(Label gives New York street address for Blue Note Records.)
BLUE NOTE (1500 series) ... 25-35 58
(Label reads "Blue Note Records Inc. - New York, U.S.A.")
BLUE NOTE (1500 series) ... 15-25 66
(Label shows Blue Note Records as a division of either Liberty or United Artists.)
BLUE NOTE (5013 "Miles Davis") ... 100-200 52
(10-inch LP.)
BLUE NOTE (5022 "Tempus Fugit") ... 100-200 53
(10-inch LP.)
BLUE NOTE (5044 "Miles Davis") ... 100-200 54
(10-inch LP.)
CAPITOL (H-459 "Jeru") ... 100-200 53
(10-inch LP.)
CAPITOL (T-459 "Jeru") ... 50-75 53
CAPITOL (762 "Birth of Cool") ... 75-125 56
CAPITOL (1900 series) ... 15-25 63
CAPITOL (11000 series) ... 8-12 72
CAPITOL (16000 series) ... 5-10 81
COLUMBIA (20 "Friday and Saturday Nights in Person") ... 30-40 61
(Monaural.)
COLUMBIA (26 "Bitches Brew") ... 8-12 70
COLUMBIA (820 "Friday and Saturday Nights in Person") ... 40-50 61
(Stereo.)
COLUMBIA (900 thru 1600 series) ... 25-50 57-61
(With six black Columbia "eye" logos on red label.)
COLUMBIA (1800 thru 2300 series) ... 25-35 61-65
COLUMBIA (8000 thru 8400 series) ... 40-60 58-62
(With six black Columbia "eye" logos on red label.)
COLUMBIA (8600 thru 9800 series) ... 12-25 61-69
COLUMBIA (10000 series) ... 8-12 73
COLUMBIA (30000 series, except 36976) . 6-12 70-85
COLUMBIA (36976 "The Miles Davis Collection") ... 30-40 80
(Boxed, six-disc set.)
COLUMBIA (40000 series) ... 8-12 81-85
DEBUT (043 "Blue Moods") ... 5-8 83
DEBUT (120 "Blue Moods") ... 100-200 55
FANTASY (6001 "Blue Moods") ... 20-30 62
FONTANA ... 15-25 65
MFSL (177 "Someday My Prince Will Come") ... 30-50 85
MOODSVILLE ... 15-25 63
MOSAIC (158 "Complete Plugged Nickel Sessions") ... 125-150 '90s
(Boxed 10-LP audiophile set. 5000 made.)
MOSAIC (164 "Complete Columbia Studio Recordings") ... 135-160 '90s
(Boxed 11-LP audiophile set. 5000 made. With Gil Evans.)
PRESTIGE (004 thru 093) ... 5-8 80-85
PRESTIGE (100 series) ... 100-200 52-54
(10-inch LPs.)
PRESTIGE (7007 thru 7166) ... 50-75 55-59
(Yellow label.)
PRESTIGE (7168 thru 7281) ... 20-30 60-64
(Yellow label.)
PRESTIGE (7000 thru 7600 series) ... 10-15 64-69
(Blue label.)
PRESTIGE (7700 thru 7800 series) ... 6-12 70-71
PRESTIGE (24000 series) ... 8-12 72-78
SAVOY ... 20-30 61
TRIP ... 5-10 73
U.A. ... 8-12 71
W.B. ... 5-10 86-90
Session: J.J. Johnson; Lucky Thompson; Horace Silver.
Also see COLTRANE, John, & Miles Davis
Also see FORREST, Jimmy
Also see SILVER, Horace, Quintet
Also see THOMPSON, Lucky

DAVIS, Miles, Dizzy Gillespie & Fats Navarro

LPs: 10/12-inch

NEW JAZZ (8296 "Trumpet Giants") ... 15-25 64
Also see GILLESPIE, Dizzy

DAVIS, Miles, & Thelonious Monk

LPs: 10/12-inch

COLUMBIA (2178 "Miles and Monk at Newport") ... 10-20 64
(Monaural.)
COLUMBIA (8978 "Miles and Monk at Newport") ... 15-25 64
(Stereo.)
Also see DAVIS, Miles
Also see JACQUET, Illinois, & Miles Davis
Also see MONK, Thelonious

DAVIS, Pat

Singles: 7-inch

ACTS (4501 "Spinner Hub Caps") ... 50-75 60

DAVIS, Paul C&W '60

Singles: 7-inch

DOKE (107 "One of Her Fools") ... 10-20 60

DAVIS, Rocky, & Sky Rockets

("Background Voices by the Contenders")

Singles: 7-inch

BLUE SKY (101 "You're a Doll") ... 400-600 59
BLUE SKY (102 "Hot Rod Baby") ... 400-600 59

DAVIS, Ronny

Singles: 7-inch

SHERIDAN (573 "Let's Beetle in the Rocket") ... 10-20 64

Picture Sleeves

SHERIDAN (573 "Let's Beetle in the Rocket") ... 30-40 64

DAVIS, Sammy, Jr. P&R '54

(With Morton Stevens Orchestra; Sammy Davis)

Singles: 78 rpm

DECCA ... 5-10 54-57

Singles: 7-inch

A.L.B.B. (38032 "The House I Live In") ... 3-5
(Promotional issue only.)
APPLAUSE ... 3-5 82
D.D.R. (101 "Who Needs Spring") ... 5-10
(Red vinyl.)
DECCA (25500 series) ... 4-6 62
DECCA (29000 thru 31000 series) ... 8-15 54-60
DECCA (32000 series) ... 4-6 69
ECOLOGY ... 4-6 71
MGM ... 4-6 71-79
VERVE ... 5-8 60
REPRISE ... 4-8 61-71
20TH FOX ... 4-6 75-76
W.B. ... 3-5 77

Picture Sleeves

A.L.B.B. (38032 "The House I Live In") ... 5-10
(Promotional issue only.)

EPs: 7-inch

CAPITOL (555 "Sammy Davis Jr.") ... 10-20 54
DECCA ... 10-20 54-55

LPs: 10/12-inch

DECCA (100 series) ... 10-20 66
DECCA (4000 series) ... 10-20 61-65
DECCA (8100 thru 8700 series) ... 20-30 54-58
DECCA (8900 series) ... 10-20 59
DECCA (9032 "Mr. Wonderful") ... 60-70 56
(Soundtrack.)
HARMONY ... 5-10 69-71
MCA ... 5-10 77
MGM ... 5-10 72-73
MOTOWN ... 6-10 70
RCA (1086 "Three Penny Opera") ... 15-25 64
REPRISE ... 10-20 61-69
20TH FOX (Except 5014) ... 5-10 76
20TH FOX (FXG-5014 "Of Love and Desire") ... 25-30 64
(Soundtrack. Monaural.)
20TH FOX (SXG-5014 "Of Love and Desire") ... 35-40 64
(Soundtrack. Stereo.)
W.B. ... 5-10 77
U.A. (5187 "Salt and Pepper") ... 15-20 68
(Soundtrack.)
VOCALION ... 5-10 68
Also see CURB, Mike
Also see SINATRA, Frank, Sammy Davis Jr. & Dean Martin

DAVIS, Sammy, Jr., & Laurindo Almeida

LPs: 10/12-inch

REPRISE ... 10-15 67
Also see ALMEIDA, Laurindo

DAVIS, Sammy, Jr., & Count Basie LP '65

Singles: 7-inch

VERVE ... 5-10 65

LPs: 10/12-inch

MGM ... 8-12 73
VERVE ... 10-15 65
Also see BASIE, Count

DAVIS, Sammy, Jr., & Sam Butera

LPs: 10/12-inch

REPRISE ... 10-15 64
Also see BUTERA, Sam

DAVIS, Sammy, Jr., & Gary Crosby

Singles: 78 rpm

DECCA ... 5-10 55

Singles: 7-inch

DECCA (29737 "Ac-cent-tchu-ate the Positive") ... 10-15 55
Also see CROSBY, Gary

DAVIS, Sammy, Jr., & Carmen McRae

Singles: 7-inch

DECCA ... 5-10 55

EPs: 7-inch

DECCA ... 8-12 59

LPs: 10/12-inch

DECCA ... 10-20 59
Also see McRAE, Carmen

DAVIS, Sammy, Jr., & Buddy Rich
LPs: 10/12-inch
REPRISE.......... 10-20 66
Also see RICH, Buddy

DAVIS, Sammy, Jr. / Joya Sherril
LPs: 10/12-inch
DESIGN.......... 5-10 '60s
Also see DAVIS, Sammy, Jr.

DAVIS, Sherry
(With Buddy Holly)
Singles: 78 rpm
CREST (1005 "God Speaks").......... 5-10 55
Singles: 7-inch
CREST (1005 "God Speaks").......... 10-15 55
FASHION (1001 "Humble Heart").......... 50-75 57
Also see HOLLY, Buddy

DAVIS, Skeeter *C&W '58*
Singles: 7-inch
MERCURY.......... 3-5 76-77
PART TWO.......... 3-5 80
RCA (Except 7000 thru 9600 series).......... 4-6 69-74
RCA (7000 thru 8300 series).......... 6-15 58-64
RCA (8400 thru 9600 series).......... 5-10 64-68
Picture Sleeves
RCA.......... 5-10 63
EPs: 7-inch
RCA.......... 5-10 63
LPs: 10/12-inch
CAMDEN.......... 5-10 65-74
GUSTO.......... 5-10 78
RCA (2179 thru 4818, except 3790).......... 10-20 60-73
RCA (3790 "Skeeter Davis Sings Buddy Holly").......... 20-30 67
TUDOR.......... 5-10 84
Also see BARE, Bobby, & Skeeter Davis
Also see DAVIS SISTERS
Also see HAMILTON, George, IV, & Skeeter Davis
Also see JENNINGS, Waylon
Also see WAGONER, Porter, & Skeeter Davis

DAVIS, Skeeter, & Don Bowman *C&W '68*
Singles: 7-inch
RCA (9415 "For Loving You").......... 4-8 68

DAVIS, Skeeter, & George Hamilton IV *C&W '70*
Singles: 7-inch
RCA.......... 4-6 70
LPs: 10/12-inch
RCA.......... 10-12 70
Also see HAMILTON, George, IV

DAVIS, Skeeter, & NRBQ
Singles: 7-inch
ROUNDER.......... 3-5 85
Also see DAVIS, Skeeter
Also see NRBQ

DAVIS, Sonny Boy
Singles: 78 rpm
TALENT (802 "Rhythm Blues").......... 50-100 49

DAVIS, Spencer *P&R '66*
(Spencer Davis Group; with Peter Jameson)
Singles: 7-inch
ALLEGIANCE.......... 3-5 84
ATCO (6400 "Keep On Running").......... 10-15 66
ATCO (6416 "Stevie's Blues").......... 10-15 66
FONTANA (1960 "I Can't Stand It").......... 8-12 65
U.A. 5-10 66-72
VERTIGO.......... 4-6 73-74
Picture Sleeves
U.A. 8-12 66-67
LPs: 10/12-inch
ALLEGIANCE.......... 5-10 84
DATE.......... 10-12 70
FONTANA.......... 20-30 66
ISLAND.......... 5-10 83
MEDIARTS.......... 10-12 71
RHINO.......... 5-10 84
U.A. 15-30 67-75
VERTIGO.......... 10-12 73-74
WING.......... 10-15
Members: Spencer Davis; Steve Winwood; Pete York; Brian Dexter; Ray Fenwick; Ken Salmon; Muff Winwood.
Also see WINWOOD, Steve

DAVIS, Tim *P&R '72*
(With the Chordairs)
Singles: 7-inch
LEAF (6467 "Wine Wine Wine").......... 10-20 64
METROMEDIA.......... 4-6 72-73
LPs: 10/12-inch
METROMEDIA.......... 8-10 72-73
Members: Jim Marcotte; David Chaffee; Curley Cooke; Jim Peterman; Dick Personett; Denny Geyer.
Also see MILLER, Steve

DAVIS, Walter
Singles: 78 rpm
BLUEBIRD.......... 25-50 33-42
BULLET.......... 15-25 49-50
RCA.......... 15-25 46-52
Singles: 7-inch
RCA (5012 "You Made My World So Bright").......... 75-100 52
RCA (5168 "So Long Baby").......... 75-100 52

DAVIS, "Wild" Bill
(With Orchestra)
Singles: 7-inch
CORAL
EVEREST.......... 5-10 60-61
RCA VICTOR.......... 4-8 65
LPs: 10/12-inch
BEAT (10002 "Swingin' Dixie").......... 15-20 62
CORAL.......... 15-20 62-63
EVEREST.......... 15-20 59-61
IMPERIAL.......... 15-20 63
JAZZOLOGY.......... 10-15 66
RCA VICTOR.......... 10-15 65-67
Also see HODGES, Johnny, & "Wild" Bill Davis

DAVIS, "Wild" Bill, & Charlie Shavers
Singles: 7-inch
EVEREST.......... 5-10 61
LPs: 10/12-inch
EVEREST.......... 15-20 61

DAVIS SISTERS *C&W '53*
Singles: 78 rpm
FORTUNE (174 "Kaw-Liga").......... 10-20 52
RCA.......... 10-15 53-56
TNT (1008 "Ricochet").......... 10-20 53
Singles: 7-inch
FORTUNE (174 "Kaw-Liga").......... 15-25 52
FORTUNE (3000 series).......... 4-8
RCA (5000 & 6000 series).......... 10-20 53-56
TNT (1008 "Ricochet").......... 20-30 53
Members: Skeeter Davis; Betty J. "Bee Jay" Davis.
Also see DAVIS, Skeeter
Also see RED RIVER DAVE / Davis Sisters

DAVIS SISTERS / Chuck Hatfield & the Treble-Aires
Singles: 7-inch
FORTUNE.......... 10-15 52
Singles: 7-inch
FORTUNE (175 "Heartbreak Ahead").......... 15-25 52

DAVIS SISTERS / Roy Hall & His Cahutta Mountain Boys
Singles: 78 rpm
FORTUNE (170 "Jealous Love").......... 10-20 53
Singles: 7-inch
FORTUNE (170 "Jealous Love").......... 20-40 53
Also see DAVIS SISTERS
Also see HALL, Roy

DAWN
(The Dawn; Five Discs)
Singles: 7-inch
GAMBLE (4002 "In Love Again").......... 5-10 69
LAURIE (3388 "I'm Afraid They're All Talking About Me").......... 5-10 67
LAURIE (3417 "For the Love of Money").......... 5-10 68
RUST (5128 "Baby I Love You").......... 10-15 68
Also see FIVE DISCS

DAWN, Billy
(With the Madison Mashers; Billy Dawn Smith)
Singles: 78 rpm
HULL (715 "This Way to Love").......... 10-15 56
Singles: 7-inch
ABC-PAR (10227 "Look What I've Found").......... 10-15 61
COED (504 "This Is Real").......... 15-25 58
COED (516 "Gotta Find My Baby").......... 10-15 59
COLUMBIA (42605 "The Madison's Back in Town").......... 10-15 62
HULL (715 "This Way to Love").......... 20-30 56
Also see RONNIE & SCHOOLMATES

DAWN, Billy, Quartet
(With Connie Frederick & Orchestra)
Singles: 78 rpm
DECATUR.......... 100-150 52
Singles: 7-inch
DECATUR (3001 "This Is the Real Thing Now").......... 2000-3000 52
(Maroon label.)
DECATUR (3001 "This Is the Real Thing Now").......... 10-15
(Red label. Red vinyl.)
FIREFLY.......... 4-6 74
VINTAGE (1010 "Miracle of Love").......... 10-15 73
(Purple vinyl.)
Members: Billy Dawn Smith; Sonny Benton; Donny Sheested; Tommy Smith.
Also see DAWN, Billy
Also see HERALDS
Also see MIGHTY DUKES

DAWN, Diana
Singles: 7-inch
ED-NEL (66-3 "Wonder Boy").......... 15-25 66
Picture Sleeves
ED-NEL (66-3 "Wonder Boy").......... 30-40 66

DAWN, Johnny
Singles: 7-inch
SWIRL (110 "Walking down the Avenue").......... 100-150 62

DAWN, Sunny
Singles: 78 rpm
ESSEX (342 "Girlfriend's Prayers").......... 8-12 54
Singles: 7-inch
ESSEX (342 "Girlfriend's Prayers").......... 15-25 54

DAWN, Tommy, & Sunsets
Singles: 7-inch
WHITE CLIFFS (246 "Wanted: $10,000 Reward").......... 15-25 66

DAWN BREAKERS
Singles: 7-inch
CORAL (61619 "Things I Love").......... 20-30 57

DAWNBEATS
Singles: 7-inch
AMP (792 "Midnight Express").......... 10-20 59

DAWNBREAKERS
Singles: 7-inch
RALDO (7363 "She'll Meet Her Match").......... 50-75 64

DAWNELLS
Singles: 7-inch
BOGAN ("Scorpion").......... 20-30 65
(No selection number used.)

DAWNS
Singles: 7-inch
BELL (121 "Three Bells").......... 10-15 59

DAWNS
Singles: 7-inch
CATALINA (1000 "Trav'lin'").......... 400-500 59

DAWNS
(With Sid Feller Orchestra)
Singles: 7-inch
CLIMAX (104 "Why Did You Let Me Love You").......... 25-35 59

DAWNS
Singles: 7-inch
ATCO (6296 "It Seems Like Yesterday").......... 10-15 64

DAWSON, Dandee, & Ginger Snaps
Singles: 7-inch
DUNHILL (4003 "Sh-Down-Down Song").......... 10-15 65

DAWSON, Jimmy
Singles: 7-inch
BANNER (711 "Cricket in Your Ear").......... 50-75
COUNTY FAIR (711 "Big Black Bug Boogie").......... 10-15 67
(Includes photo insert.)
FAN JR. (1992 "Playboy").......... 10-15 '60s
K-ARK (774 "Big Black Bug Boogie").......... 10-15 67
RUSTIC (808 "It Took An Older Woman").......... 75-125

DAWSON, Leah
Singles: 7-inch
MAGIC CITY (001 "My Mechanical Man").......... 10-20 '60s
OKEH (7316 "Good Man").......... 5-10 68

DAWSON, Ronnie
(Commonwealth Jones)
Singles: 7-inch
BANNER.......... 5-10
LEVEE.......... 4-6 70
MAVERICK (101 "My Big Desire").......... 100-150 61
ROCKIN' (1 "Rockin' Bones").......... 200-250 59
SWAN (4047 "Hazel").......... 10-15 60
SWAN (4054 "Summer's Comin' ").......... 20-30 60
Session: Ron-Dels.
Also see DEE, Ronnie
Also see JONES, Commonwealth
Also see RON-DELS
Also see SUMMERS, Gene

DAY, Bing
Singles: 7-inch
FEDERAL (12320 "Pony Tail Partner").......... 15-25 58
MERCURY (71446 "I Can't Help It").......... 15-25 59
MERCURY (71494 "How Do I Do It").......... 5-10 59

DAY, Bobby *P&R '57*
(With the Satellites; with Blossoms; Bobby Byrd)
Singles: 78 rpm
CLASS.......... 50-100 57-58
Singles: 7-inch
CLASS (207 "So Long Baby").......... 20-30 57
CLASS (211 "Little Bitty Pretty One").......... 20-30 57
CLASS (215 "Beep Beep Beep").......... 15-25 57
CLASS (220 thru 263).......... 15-25 58-59
CLASS (705 "When I Started Dancin' ").......... 5-8 65
HIGHLAND (1100 "Little Turtle Dove").......... 8-10 64
RCA (8133 "Another Country, Another World").......... 15-25 63
RCA (8196 thru 8316).......... 8-12 63-64
RENDEZVOUS (130 thru 146).......... 10-15 60-61
RENDEZVOUS (158 thru 175).......... 8-12 61-62
SURE SHOT (5036 "So Lonely").......... 5-10 67
LPs: 10/12-inch
CLASS (5002 "Rockin' with Robin").......... 225-275 59
RHINO.......... 5-10 84
Also see BYRD, Bobby
Also see CHURCH, Eugene
Also see SATELLITES

DAY, Cora Lee
LPs: 10/12-inch
ROULETTE (52048 "My Crying Hour").......... 15-20 60

DAY, Danny
Singles: 7-inch
FRONT (122 "Look at Me Now").......... 25-35 '60s
V.I.P. (25019 "This Time Last Summer").......... 10-20 65

DAY, Darlene
Singles: 7-inch
MUSIC MAKERS (106 "I Love You So").......... 50-100 61
Session: Imaginations.
Also see IMAGINATIONS

DAY, Dave
(With the Red Coats; Dave Diddle Day)
Singles: 7-inch
CASA BLANCA (5529 "Calypso Rock").......... 15-25 59
(First issue.)
FEE BEE (212 "Blue Moon Baby").......... 15-25 57
(First issue.)
FEE BEE (215 "Jelly Billy").......... 15-25 57
FEE BEE (219 "Motorcycle Mike").......... 15-25 58
KAPP (163 "Calypso Rock").......... 10-15 59
MERCURY (71114 "Blue Moon Baby").......... 10-15 57
Session: Bill Haley's Comets.
Also see HALEY, Bill

DAY, DAWN & DUSK
("Featuring Charlie Laverne & His Guitars"; with "Chas. Laverne Orch."; Day Dawn, Dusk Trio)
Singles: 78 rpm
APOLLO.......... 10-20 55
DENT.......... 8-12 55
HERALD.......... 8-12 54
JOSIE.......... 10-20 56
Singles: 7-inch
APOLLO (476 "Miss Petunia").......... 20-30 55
DENT (519 "Let the Tears Fall").......... 20-30 55
HERALD (5000 "All Through the Years").......... 15-20 54

JOSIE (794 "Anytime, Anyplace, Anywhere") 15-25 56

DAY, Doris P&R '47
(With the Mellomen; with Norman Luboff Choir; with Buddy Clark)

Singles: 78 rpm
COLUMBIA 5-15 47-57

Singles: 7-inch
ARWIN (250 "Everlasting Arms") .... 5-15 '50s
COLUMBIA (38000 & 39000 series) 5-15 50-53
COLUMBIA (40000 thru 44000 series) 4-8 54-67

Picture Sleeves
COLUMBIA 10-20 57-61

EPs: 7-inch
COLUMBIA 10-30 50-59

LPs: 10/12-inch
COLUMBIA (1 "Listen to Day") 20-30 60
COLUMBIA (600 thru 1300 series) 15-30 55-59
COLUMBIA (1400 thru 2100 series) 10-20 60-64
COLUMBIA (2500 series) 20-35 56
(10-inch LPs.)
COLUMBIA (6000 series) 25-50 49-55
(10-inch LPs.)
COLUMBIA (8000 thru 8900 series) 15-30 58-64
COLUMBIA (2200 thru 2300 series) 10-25 64-65
(Monaural.)
COLUMBIA (9000 thru 9100 series) 15-35 64-65
(Stereo.)
HARMONY 8-12 66-72
Also see STREISAND, Barbra / Doris Day / Jim Nabors / Andre Kostelanetz

DAY, Doris, & Don Cherry

EPs: 7-inch
COLUMBIA 10-20 56
Also see CHERRY, Don

DAY, Doris, & Frankie Laine P&R '52

Singles: 78 rpm
COLUMBIA 5-10 52

Singles: 7-inch
COLUMBIA 5-15 52
Also see LAINE, Frankie

DAY, Doris, & Andre Previn

LPs: 10/12-inch
COLUMBIA 10-20 62
Also see PREVIN, Andre

DAY, Doris, & Johnnie Ray P&R '53

Singles: 78 rpm
COLUMBIA 5-10 52-53

Singles: 7-inch
COLUMBIA 5-15 52-53
Also see RAY, Johnnie

DAY, Doris, & Dinah Shore

Singles: 78 rpm
COLUMBIA (1377 "It's Better to Conceal than Reveal") 5-10 47
Also see SHORE, Dinah

DAY, Doris, & Frank Sinatra P&R '49

Singles: 78 rpm
COLUMBIA 5-10 49

Singles: 7-inch
COLUMBIA 5-15 49

DAY, Doris / Frank Sinatra LP '55

EPs: 7-inch
COLUMBIA (571 "Young at Heart") 10-20 55
COLUMBIA (34178 "Young at Heart") 30-50 54
(Promotional issue only.)

LPs: 10/12-inch
COLUMBIA (6339 "Young at Heart") 40-60 55
(Soundtrack. 10-inch LP.)
Also see DAY, Doris, & Frank Sinatra
Also see SINATRA, Frank

DAY, Doris, & Danny Thomas

EPs: 7-inch
COLUMBIA (289 "I'll See You in My Dreams") 10-15
Also see DAY, Doris
Also see THOMAS, Danny

DAY, Eddie, & Night Timers

Singles: 7-inch
BB (4005 "How to Be a Musician") 15-25 66

DAY, Gene

Singles: 7-inch
BERGEN (530 "Those Teenage Years") . 30-40

DAY, Greg

Singles: 7-inch
HI-HAT (218 "Away") 50-100 64

DAY, Jack

Singles: 7-inch
ARCADE (155 "Rattle Bone Boogie") 30-50 59
VALIANT (514 "Little Joe") 2000-3000
Session: Bill Haley's Comets.
Also see HALEY, Bill

DAY, Jackie

Singles: 7-inch
MODERN (1028 thru 1037) 10-20 67
PAULA (338 "I Can't Wait") 4-6 70
PHELECTRON (382 "Naughty Boy") 200-300
SUGAR HILL 4-8 69
SPECIALTY 4-8 69

DAY, Jimmy

Singles: 78 rpm
ABBOTT (175 "Rippin' Out") 10-15 55

Singles: 7-inch
ABBOTT (175 "Rippin' Out") 15-25 55

DAY, Joey, & Nite Tymes

Singles: 7-inch
BEAVER (8662 "Good Times") 20-30
RUST (5114 "The Chase") 5-10 67

DAY, Johnny

Singles: 7-inch
CAMEO (371 "Something Little") 5-10 65
DORE (582 "Lights Out") 10-20 60

DAY, Little Sunny, & Clouds

Singles: 7-inch
TANDEM (7001 "Lou Ann") 700-800 61

DAY, Margie R&B '50
(With the Griffin Brothers Orchestra)

Singles: 78 rpm
CAT (118 "Ho-Ho") 10-20 55
DECCA 5-10 54
DELUXE 8-12 56-57
DOT (1010 thru 1042) 15-25 50-51
DOT (1153 thru 1190) 10-15 54

Singles: 7-inch
CAT (118 "Ho-Ho") 20-30 55
COED (544 "It Started All Over Again") 8-10 61
COED (554 "Let Me Know") 8-10 61
DECCA (28872 thru 48330) 25-35 53-54
DELUXE (6096 "Dumplin Dumplin") 15-25 56
DELUXE (6131 "That's the Way Love Goes") 15-25 57
DOT (1010 "Street Walkin' Daddy") 40-60 50
DOT (1019 "Little Red Rooster") 40-60 50
DOT (1024 "Hot Pepper") 40-60 51
DOT (1041 "Sadie Green") 40-60 51
DOT (1042 "Your Best Friend") 40-60 51
DOT (1094 thru 1190) 25-35 52-54
LEGRAND (1017 "Crazy Over You") 10-20 62
MARTHAY .... 10-20 '60s
Also see GRIFFIN BROTHERS

DAY, Nancy

Singles: 7-inch
JAY WING (5804 "Teenage Hop") 50-75 59

DAY, Reginald

Singles: 7-inch
MIDAS (9005 "Lost Love") 10-20 67

DAY, Rusty

Singles: 7-inch
MALTESE (104 "I Gotta Move") 15-25 66
MALTESE (110 "I Gotta Move") 15-25 66
Also see AMBOY DUKES

DAY, Sonny
(With the Versatiles; with Rare Breed; Little Sunny Day & the Clouds)

Singles: 78 rpm
STAR 15-25 56

Singles: 7-inch
ABC-PAR (9950 "Beyond the Shadow of a Doubt") 15-20 58
CHECKER (886 "Speedillac") 40-60 58
JUBILEE (5543 "Tarzan") 5-10 66
MALA (461 "37 Men") 15-25 63
POWER 5-8
STAR (226 "Creature from Outer Space") 40-60 56
TANDEM (7001 "Lou Ann") 600-700 61

DAY, Terry
(Terry Melcher)

Singles: 7-inch
COLUMBIA (3-42427 "I Waited Too Long") 30-40 62
(Compact 33 Single.)
COLUMBIA (3-42678 "Be a Soldier") 40-50 63
(Compact 33 Single.)
COLUMBIA (4-42427 "I Waited Too Long") 8-12 62
COLUMBIA (4-42678 "Be a Soldier") 10-15 63

Picture Sleeves
COLUMBIA (42678 "Be a Soldier") 30-40 63
Also see MELCHER, Terry

DAY BIRDS

Singles: 7-inch
JAMA (502 "I'm Just the Postman") 40-60 62
Member: Bobby Day.

DAY BLINDNESS

Singles: 7-inch
STUDIO 10 (2494 "Horse & Dog") 10-15 70

LPs: 10/12-inch
STUDIO 10 (101 "Day Blindness") 40-60 69

DAY BROTHERS

Singles: 7-inch
CHANCELLOR (1059 "A Thousand Miles Away") 5-10 60
COLUMBIA (43006 "Make Up Your Mind") 5-10 64
FIREBIRD (103 "Wait for Me") 15-25 63

DAYBREAK

Singles: 7-inch
PAP (003 "I Need Love") 10-20

DAYBREAKERS

Singles: 7-inch
ALADDIN (3434 "I Wonder Why") 50-75 58
LAMP (2016 "I Wonder Why") 75-100 58
(First issue.)

DAYBREAKERS

Singles: 7-inch
DIAL (4066 "Psychedelic Siren") 10-20 67

DAYCHORDS

Singles: 7-inch
DON-EL (120 "One More Time") 10-15 62
Also see ROXY & DAYCHORDS

DAYE, Billie

Singles: 7-inch
BLISS (1002 "When a Girl Gives Her Heart to a Boy") 20-30 61

DAYE, Eddie
(With the Four Bars; Eddie Daye's 4 Bars with Soul Bandits)

Singles: 7-inch
DAYCO (2500 "Stay on the Job") 30-50 62
SHRINE (112 "Guess Who Loves You") 300-400 66
Also see FOUR BARS

DAYE, Frankie, & His Knights

Singles: 7-inch
CADDY (109 "I Don't Care") 15-20 57
DA-MAR (2001 "Dance Party Rock") 10-15 61
STUDIO (9904 "Drag It") 10-20 59

DAYE, Joey, & Dares

Singles: 7-inch
FORTUNE (868 "True True Love") 20-30 65

DAYE, Roberta

Singles: 7-inch
ABNER (7002 "Every Day") 20-30 62

DAYE, Sonny
(With the Muffins)

Singles: 7-inch
C-FLAT 10-20
POWER (203 "Come Back Sandy") .... 15-25 '60s
POWER (208 "Long Long Road") .... 15-25 '60s
RING-O (305 "I Can't Keep Score") 10-15 65
ST. CLARK (104 "Skinny Minnie") 5-10 65

DAYJOBBERS

Singles: 7-inch
TMP-TING (116 "Hootchie Koochie Man") 20-30

DAYLIGHTERS
(Chuck & Daylighters; with Al Perkins Band; "Strings by Johnny Pate)

Singles: 7-inch
ASTRA (1001 "This Heart of Mine") 5-10 65
BEA & BABY (103 "Mad House Jump") 15-25 59
C.J. (614 "Tough Love") 10-20 60
CHECKER (1051 "No One's Gonna Help You") 5-10 63
DOMINO (904 "I'll Never Let You Go") 15-25 61
DOT (16326 "Oh What a Way to Be Loved") 10-20 62
NIKE (1011 "This Heart of Mine") 50-75 61
NIKE (10011 "Why Do You Do Me Wrong") 100-150 61
SMASH (2040 "Tell Me") 8-10 66
TIP TOP (2001 "Oh What a Way to Be Loved") 40-60 62
TIP TOP (2002 "Cool Breeze") 30-40 62
TIP TOP (2006 "Bottomless Pit") 25-35 63
TIP TOP (2007 thru 2010) 10-20 63-64
TOLLIE (9028 "Whisper of the Wind") 8-12 64
Members: Tony Gideon; Levi Moreland; Eddie Thomas; George Wood; Dorsey Wood; Gerald Sims; Curtis Burrell; Ulysses McDonald; Gary & Knight Lites.
Also see DONALD & DELIGHTERS
Also see EVERETT, Bettie, & Daylighters
Also see GARY & NITE LITES
Also see PATE, Johnny
Also see SIMS, Gerald
Also see PERKINS, Al

DAYLIGHTS

Singles: 7-inch
PROPULSION (601 "A Tear Fell from My Eyes") 10-15 63

DAYTON, David, & Colos

Singles: 7-inch
LOMAR (704 "I Gotta Have Love") 15-25 64

DAYTONAS

Singles: 7-inch
AMY (961 "Hey Little Girl") 10-20 66

DAYTONS

Singles: 7-inch
NORGOLDE (101 "King of Broken Hearts") 400-500 59

DAYTRIPPERS

Singles: 7-inch
AMERICAN MUSIC MAKERS (005 "You Cheated") 20-30 66
KARATE (524 "You Cheated") 5-10 66

DAYWINS

Singles: 7-inch
ARWIN (22 "Heartbeat") 10-20 60
D-F (1000 "Thump Thump") .... 10-20 '60s

DAZZLERS

Singles: 7-inch
KNICK 8-12
LEE (100 "Somethin' Baby") 300-400 58
LEE (102 "Gee Whiz") 100-150 58

DEACON & ROCK & ROLLERS

Singles: 7-inch
NAU-VOO (804 "Rockin' on the Moon") 2000-3000 59
Member: Deacon Gilliland.

DEACONS

Singles: 7-inch
RE-CAR (9004 "Baldie Stomp") 25-35 64
SOMA (1452 "Empty Room") 40-60 65

DEACONS R&B '68

Singles: 7-inch
CAMELOT 8-10
SHAMA (100 "Sock It to Me") 10-20 68
Also see JOHNSON, Syl

DEAD BEATS

Singles: 7-inch
CUE WEST (002 "Can't Go On This Way") 15-25 67

DEAD BOLTS

Singles: 7-inch
COFFIN (9009 "Torture Chamber") 15-25 84
(500 made.)

Picture Sleeves
COFFIN (9009 "Torture Chamber") 15-25 84
(500 made.)
Members: Russ Bell; Dave Wall; Rob Hislop; Stefanie Cassandra Bell.

DEAD KENNEDYS
Singles: 7-inch
ALTERNATIVE TENTACLES 4-8 83-86
I.R.S. 4-8 80-81
OPTIONAL (2 "California Uber Alles") 10-15 79
SUBTERRANEAN (24 "Nazi Punks") 10-15 81
(Includes armband.)
LPs: 10/12-inch
ALTERNATIVE TENTACLES (27 "Plastic Surgery Disasters") 10-20 83
ALTERNATIVE TENTACLES (45 "Frankenchrist") 30-40 86
(With Geiger poster.)
I.R.S. (70014 "Fresh Fruit for Rotting Vegetables") 10-12 81
Members: Jello Biafra; East Bay Ray; Deron Peligro; Klaus Flouride.

DEAD SEA FRUIT
Singles: 7-inch
ATCO (6489 "Kensington High Street") ... 10-15 67

DEAD WUNZ
Singles: 7-inch
ORLYN (5123 "Drums") 10-20 66

DEADBEATS
Singles: 7-inch
CROQUETTE (201066 "Hungry Monday") 10-15 66

DEADLY ONES
LPs: 10/12-inch
VEE-JAY (1090 "It's Monster Surfing Time") 40-50 64

DEAL, Bill *P&R '69*
(With the Rhondels; with Pleasers; with Big Deals)
Singles: 7-inch
BEACH (1601 "May I") .... 25-35 '60s
BUDDAH 4-6 72
CHESLICK 4-8
COLLECTABLES .... 3-5 '80s
ERIC .... 4-6 '70s
HERITAGE 5-10 68-70
LEGRAND (1054 "Big Toe in the Wind") . 10-15 67
MALA (502 "Don't Put Me Down") 15-25 65
POLYDOR 4-6 70-73
RED LION 3-5 79
ROLL CALL ("Lucious") 15-20
(No selection number used.)
Picture Sleeves
HERITAGE (812 "I've Been Hurt") 10-15 69
HERITAGE (818 "Swingin' Tight") 10-15 70
LPs: 10/12-inch
HERITAGE (35003 "Vintage Rock") 15-20 69
HERITAGE (35006 "Best of Bill Deal & the Rondells") 15-20 69
RHINO 5-10 86
Members: Bill Deal; Jeff Pollard; Mike Kerwin; Ken Dawson; Ronny Rosenbaum; Bob Fisher; Don Quisenburry; Ammon Tharp.
Also see SOUL, Jimmy

DEAL, Don *C&W '79*
(With the Moonstars)
Singles: 78 rpm
CASH (1028 "Cryin' in One Eye") 10-15 56
Singles: 7-inch
CAPITOL 5-10 63
CASH (1028 "Cryin' in One Eye") 20-30 56
CHALLENGE 4-8 68
DONJIM (1008 "Second Best") 5-7 79
ERA (Except 1070) 10-15 57-58
ERA (1070 "Sweet Love") 15-25 58
MGM (13235 "Lyin' Again") 5-10 64
SAND 5-8 69

DEAL, Mike
Singles: 7-inch
ERWIN (506 "One Heartbeat Away") .... 25-35 '50s

DEALERS
Singles: 7-inch
BIG BUNNY 5-10 66
DEAL (999 "This Rock Is Rollin'") 40-60

DEAN, Al
(Al Dean & All Stars)
Singles: 7-inch
BOP-TEX 5-10
KIK-R 10-15 67
MANCO (1043 "Blue Sky Waltz") 15-25 63
WARRIOR (506 "Fragile Heart") 50-100 59

DEAN, Anthony
Singles: 7-inch
CORAL (62499 "What Is Right") 10-20 66

DEAN, Bob
Singles: 7-inch
ARCADE (195 "Hot Rod Daddy") 10-15 68
SUMMIT 10-15 64

DEAN, Bobby
Singles: 7-inch
CHESS (1673 "Wild Over Rock & Roll") ... 30-50 57
CHESS (1710 "Go Mr. Dillon") 20-30 58
PROFILE (4006 "It's a Fad") 20-30 59
SCARLET TARGET (100 "Amazon Dance") 200-300

DEAN, Buddy
Singles: 7-inch
DJ (1961 "Say Mama") 200-300

DEAN, Carl
Singles: 7-inch
DONNA & RUSSELL (100 "Wait Til the Sun Come Down") 50-75

DEAN, Charles, & Rondells
Singles: 7-inch
BENTON (103 "Itchy") 1000-2000 58

DEAN, David
Singles: 78 rpm
PEACOCK (1645 "To Fine to Be Mine") ... 10-15 54
Singles: 7-inch
PEACOCK (1645 "To Fine to Be Mine") ... 20-25 54
Also see ROBINSON, Fention / David Dean's Combo

DEAN, Debbie *P&R '61*
(With the Petites; with Paulette Singers)
Singles: 7-inch
MOTOWN (1007 "Don't Let Him Shop Around") 50-75 61
MOTOWN (1014 "Itsy Bity Pity Love") 15-25 62
MOTOWN (1025 "Everybody's Talking About My Baby") 50-75 62
SUE (103 "Don't Bug Me Baby") 15-20 64
TREVA (223 "Take My Hand") 10-15 66
V.I.P. (25044 "Why Am I Lovin' You") ... 100-200 68
Picture Sleeves
MOTOWN (1025 "Everybody's Talking About My Baby") 75-125 62

DEAN, Dizzy
Singles: 78 rpm
COLONIAL (4 "Wabash Cannon Ball") ... 75-100 54

DEAN, Donnie
Singles: 7-inch
APT (25082 "Movie Star") 20-30 65
DRIFT (1451 "Frankie and Johnnie") 100-200

DEAN, Eddie *C&W '48*
(With the Frontiersmen; with Cort Johnson; with Biblical-Aires)
Singles: 78 rpm
CAPITOL 4-8 51-52
CORAL 4-8 52
CRYSTAL 5-10 48
SAGE & SAND 4-8 54-55
Singles: 7-inch
CAPITOL 8-12 51-52
CORAL 8-12 52
MISS (619 "Holy Place") 4-8
SAGE & SAND 8-12 54-55
LPs: 10/12-inch
CRICKET 5-10
CROWN ("Eddie Dean Sings") 10-15 65
(Selection number not known.)
DESIGN .... 10-15 '60s
KING (686 "Favorites of Eddie Dean") 30-40 60
SAGE (1 "Greatest Westerns") 25-50 56
SAGE (5 "Hi-Country") 25-50 57
SAGE (16 "Hillbilly Heaven") 20-30 61
SHASTA 8-12 74
SOUND (603 "Greatest Westerns") 25-50 56
SUTTON 10-20
TIARA 5-10

WFC 5-10 76
Also see RIDERS OF THE PURPLE SAGE
Also see WILLING, Foy, Eddie Dean & His Riders of the Purple Sage

DEAN, Frank
Singles: 7-inch
TREND (30008 "Bubblin' ") 10-15 58

DEAN, Gabe
Singles: 7-inch
GOLDBAND (1108 "Slop and Stroll") 75-100 60

DEAN, Gary
Singles: 7-inch
LIBERTY (55455 "The Right Kind of Love") 8-12 62
NITE STAR (009 "Leavin' You") 50-75

DEAN, Hannah
Singles: 7-inch
COLUMBIA (41768 "Itty Bitty Love") 10-15 60

DEAN, James
(With Bob Romeo)
Singles: 7-inch
ROMEO (129 "Ad-Lib Jam Session") 15-25 57
Picture Sleeves
ROMEO (129 "Ad-Lib Jam Session") 50-75 57
LPs: 10/12-inch
SANDY HOOK (2103 "Rare Broadcast Recordings") 15-20 84
(Picture disc.)
Also see MANTOVANI
Also see MOONEY, Art
Also see PERKINS, Tony / James Dean

DEAN, Jerry
Singles: 7-inch
CREOLE (1002 "Walking in My Sleep") .50-100

DEAN, Jimmy *C&W '53*
(Jimmie Dean)
Singles: 78 rpm
COLUMBIA 5-10 57
4 STAR 5-10 53
MERCURY 5-10 56
Singles: 7-inch
CASINO (052 "I.O.U.") 4-6 76
CASINO (074 "To a Sleeping Beauty") 4-6 76
CHURCHILL (94024 "I.O.U.") 3-5 83
COLUMBIA (33051 "Big Bad John"/"Little Black Book") 8-12 64
COLUMBIA (33064 "Cajun Queen"/"Steel Men") 8-12 64
COLUMBIA (40995 thru 41956) 8-12 57-61
COLUMBIA (42175 "Big Bad John") 15-20 61
(Dean says: "At the bottom of this mine lies one hell of a man.")
COLUMBIA (42175 "Big Bad John") 5-10 61
(Dean says: "At the bottom of this mine lies a big, big man." Note slight title change.)
COLUMBIA (42248 thru 43754) 5-10 61-66
COLUMBIA (45000 & 46000 series) 4-6 73-74
4 STAR (1613 "Bumming Around") 15-25 53
4 STAR (1732 "Bumming Around") 8-12 59
KING (5862 "Bumming Around") 5-10 64
MERCURY (70786 "Glad Rags") 10-20 56
MERCURY (70855 "I Found Out") 10-20 56
RCA 4-8 66-71
Picture Sleeves
CHURCHILL (94024 "I.O.U.") 3-5 83
COLUMBIA (41025 "Little Sandy Sleighfoot") 15-25 57
COLUMBIA (42175 "Big Bad John") 5-10 61
COLUMBIA (42259 "Dear Ivan") 5-10 61
COLUMBIA (42282 "Cajun Queen") 5-10 61
COLUMBIA (42338 "P.T. 109") 5-10 62
COLUMBIA (42483 "Steel Men") 5-10 62
COLUMBIA (42529 "Little Black Book") 5-10 62
COLUMBIA (42600 "Gonna Raise a Ruckus Tonight") 5-10 62
COLUMBIA (42934 "Mind Your Own Business") 5-10 63
EPs: 7-inch
COLUMBIA (10251/52/53 "Hour of Prayer") 10-20 57
(Price is for any of three volumes.)
LPs: 10/12-inch
ACCORD (7906 "Straight From the Heart") 5-10 82
BRYLEN (4431 "For You") 5-10

CASINO (8014 "I.O.U.") 8-10 76
(Black and gray cover.)
CASINO (8014 "I.O.U.") 5-8 76
(Rust cover.)
COLUMBIA (1025 "Hour of Prayer") 20-30 57
(Monaural.)
COLUMBIA (1735 "Big Bad John") 30-40 61
(Monaural. Dean says: "At the bottom of this mine lies one hell of a man." Identification number, in the vinyl trail-off, is XLP54925-2A.)
COLUMBIA (1735 "Big Bad John") 20-30 61
(Monaural. Dean says: "At the bottom of this mine lies a big, big man.")
COLUMBIA (1894 "Portrait of Jimmy Dean") 10-20 62
(Monaural.)
COLUMBIA (2027 "Everybody's Favorite") 10-20 63
(Monaural.)
COLUMBIA (2188 "Songs We All Love Best") 10-20 64
(Monaural.)
COLUMBIA (2401 "First Thing Ev'ry Morning") 10-20 65
(Monaural.)
COLUMBIA (2404 "Christmas Card") 10-20 65
(Monaural.)
COLUMBIA (2485 "Greatest Hits") 10-20 66
(Monaural.)
COLUMBIA (2538 "The Big Ones") 10-20 66
(Monaural.)
COLUMBIA (8535 "Big Bad John") 20-30 61
(Stereo.)
COLUMBIA (8694 "Portrait of Jimmy Dean") 15-25 62
(Stereo.)
COLUMBIA (8827 "Everybody's Favorite") 15-25 63
(Stereo.)
COLUMBIA (8988 "Songs We All Love Best") 15-25 64
(Stereo.)
COLUMBIA (9201 "First Thing Ev'ry Morning") 10-20 65
(Stereo.)
COLUMBIA (9204 "Christmas Card") 10-20 65
(Stereo.)
COLUMBIA (CS-9285 "Greatest Hits") 10-20 66
(Stereo.)
COLUMBIA (PC-9285 "Greatest Hits") .... 5-8 '80s
COLUMBIA (9338 "The Big Ones") 10-20 66
(Stereo.)
COLUMBIA (9424 "Hour of Prayer") 10-20 67
(Stereo.)
COLUMBIA (9677 "Dean's List") 10-20 68
COLUMBIA (10036 "Everybody's Favorite") 8-12 73
CROWN .... 10-15 '60s
CUSTOM 5-10
GRT (8014 "I.O.U.") 5-8 77
GUEST STAR (1437 "Jimmy Dean and the Town & Country Men") .... 8-12 '60s
HARMONY (7268 "Hymns") 10-15 60
(Monaural.)
HARMONY (7408 "Mr. Country Music") 8-12 67
HARMONY (7470 "Country's Favorite Son") 8-12 68
HARMONY (11042 "Hymns") 15-20 60
(Stereo.)
HARMONY (11208 "Mr. Country Music") ... 8-12 67
HARMONY (11270 "Country's Favorite Son") 8-12 68
HARMONY (11356 "Gotta Travel On") 8-12 69
KING (686 "Favorites of Jimmy Dean") 25-35 60
LA BREA (8014 "Bummin' Around with Jimmy Dean") 20-30
MERCURY (20319 "Jimmy Dean Sings His Television Favorites") 15-25 57
PICKWICK .... 5-10 '70s
PICKWICK/HILLTOP (6004 "Golden Favorites") 10-12 65
RCA (3727 "Jimmy Dean Is Here") 10-20 67
RCA (3824 "Most Richly Blessed") 10-20 67
RCA (3890 "The Jimmy Dean Show") 10-20 68
RCA (3999 "A Thing Called Love") 10-20 68
RCA (4035 "Speaker of the House") 10-20 68
RCA (4511 "Everybody Knows") 8-12 71
RCA (4618 "These Hands") 8-12 71
SPIN-O-RAMA .... 8-12 '60s

WING (12292 "Jimmy Dean Sings His Television Favorites") ... 10-15 64
(Monaural.)
WING (16292 "Jimmy Dean Sings His Television Favorites") ... 10-15 64
(Stereo.)

DEAN, Jimmy / Luke Gordon
LPs: 10/12-inch
PREMIER ... 10-15 '60s
SPIN-O-RAMA (108 "Featuring the Country Singing of Jimmy Dean") ... 10-15 '60s

DEAN, Jimmy / Johnny Horton
LPs: 10/12-inch
STARDAY (325 "Bummin' Around") ... 15-20 65
Also see HORTON, Johnny

DEAN, Jimmy / David Houston / Warner Mack / Autry Inman
LPs: 10/12-inch
DIPLOMAT (2436 "Great Stars of Country and Western") ... 10-15 '60s
Also see HOUSTON, David
Also see INMAN, Autry
Also see MACK, Warner

DEAN, Junior
Singles: 7-inch
MIKE (7328 "Chick Chick") ... 450-550 58

DEAN, Lenny, & Rockin' Chairs
Singles: 7-inch
RECORTE (412 "Girl of Mine") ... 30-40 59
Also see ROCKIN' CHAIRS

DEAN, Libby
(With the Ray Charles Singers & Billy Ver Planck Orchestra)
Singles: 7-inch
SAVOY (1518 "Ding Dong Rock-A-Billy Wedding") ... 10-15 57
Also see CHARLES, Ray, Singers

DEAN, Lonnie
Singles: 7-inch
KING (6234 "Navajo") ... 10-20 68

DEAN, Nick, & Sports
Singles: 78 rpm
DEB (1001 "High School Baby") ... 5-10 56
Singles: 7-inch
DEB (1001 "High School Baby") ... 20-30 56

DEAN, Ricky
Singles: 7-inch
DEL-FI ... 5-10 62-63
EMMY (1013 "Blue Tears") ... 30-40 62
ORIGINAL SOUND (84 "I'll Never Love Another") ... 5-8 68

DEAN, Terri
Singles: 7-inch
LAUREL (1003 "I Blew Out the Flame") ... 15-25 59
LAURIE (3032 "Adonis") ... 10-15 59
LAURIE (3049 "Friendship Ring") ... 10-15 60
MADISON (167 "Your Heart's Not Made of Wood") ... 10-15 61

DEAN, Tex
Singles: 78 rpm
TRUMPET ... 10-20 53-55
Singles: 7-inch
TRUMPET (202 "Naponee") ... 20-30 53
TRUMPET (203 "Dreamy Georginna Moon") ... 20-30 53
TRUMPET (235 "Jealous Teardrops") ... 15-25 55

DEAN, Tiny, & Cameos
Singles: 7-inch
FLAGSHIP (118 "Now That Summer Is Over") ... 30-40 60
Also see CAMEOS

DEAN, Wally
(Wally Deane)
Singles: 7-inch
ARTIC (102 "Rockin' with Rosie") ... 50-75 59
ARTIC (103 "Saddle Up a Satellite") ... 50-75 59
ARTIC (65221 "Drinkin' Wine Spo-Dee-O-Dee") ... 10-15 60
GLOBE (238 "Cool, Cool Daddy") ... 35-50 59

DEAN & DEL-TONES
Singles: 7-inch
PYRAMID (6571 "Mystery") ... 10-20 66

DEAN & JEAN P&R '63
Singles: 78 rpm
EMBER (1048 "We're Gonna Get Married") ... 50-75 58
Singles: 7-inch
BUCKEYE (1001 "Oh Yeah") ... 100-150
EMBER (1048 "We're Gonna Get Married") ... 20-30 58
EMBER (1054 "Turn It Off") ... 15-25 60
EMBER (1086 "Cross My Heart") ... 10-15 62
RUST ... 10-15 62-66
Members: Welton Young; Brenda Lee Jones.

DEAN & MARC P&R '59
(Dean & Mark)
Singles: 7-inch
BULLSEYE (1025 "Tell Him No") ... 15-25 59
BULLSEYE (1026 "Beginning of Love") ... 10-20 59
CHECK MATE (1008 "Boogie-Woogie Twist") ... 15-25 62
HICKORY ... 5-10 63-65
MAY (135 "Pins and Needles") ... 5-10 63
Members: Dean Mathis; Marc Mathis.
Also see BROTHERS
Also see NEWBEATS

DEANE, Christopher
Singles: 7-inch
SIDEWALK (906 "Angel's Last Trip") ... 10-15 66

DEANE, Janet
(With the Skyliners)
Singles: 7-inch
GATEWAY (719 "Another Night Alone") ... 20-30 64
MASTODON (101 "Another Night Alone") ... 5-10
(Colored vinyl.)
Also see SKYLINERS

DEANE, Jeril
(With Hub Atwood & Choraleers Orchestra)
Singles: 7-inch
RRC (103 "Run Darlin', Don't Walk") ... 10-15 '50s

DEANS
Singles: 7-inch
LAURIE (3114 "I Don't Want to Wait") ... 10-15 61
MOHAWK (114 "My Heart Is Low") ... 15-20 60
MOHAWK (119 "Humpty Dumpty") ... 10-15 60
MOHAWK (126 "I Don't Want to Wait") ... 30-40 61
STAR MAKER (1928 "Oh Little Star") ... 200-300 62
STAR MAKER (1931 "Chills, Chills, Chills") ... 50-75 62
TIN PAN ALLEY (316 "I'm Gonna Love You") ... 100-150
TIN PAN ALLEY (319 "Pretty Nola") ... 30-50
Also see LONNIE & CAROLLONS / Deans

DEARLY BELOVEDS
Singles: 7-inch
COLUMBIA ... 5-10 66-67
SPLITSOUND (5 "Flight 13") ... 10-20 67
Also see BELOVED ONES
Also see INTRUDERS

DEATON, Billy
Singles: 7-inch
SHANNON (777 "Is It Really Over") ... 5-10 63
SMASH (1714 thru 1783) ... 5-10 61-62
TNT (176 thru 188) ... 5-10 60-61

DEATON, Frank
(Franklin Deaton; with the Mad Lads)
Singles: 7-inch
ALTA (2000 "I Was Framed") ... 15-25
BALLY (1042 "Just a Little Bit More") ... 50-75 57
BANNER (5941 "I Was Framed") ... 40-60 60
TARGET (862 "Don't Let Go") ... 50-75 60

DEAUVILLE, Ronnie LP '57
Singles: 7-inch
ERA (1056 "Laura") ... 10-15 58
HOLLYWOOD (1053 "I Keep Telling My Heart") ... 15-25 56
IMPERIAL (5559 "King of Fools") ... 8-12 59
Picture Sleeves
ERA (1056 "Laura") ... 20-40 58
LPs: 10/12-inch
ERA (20002 "Smoke Dreams") ... 30-50 57

DEBELAIRES
Singles: 7-inch
LECTRA (502 "So Long My Sailor") ... 10-20 62

DE BERRY, Jimmy
Singles: 78 rpm
SUN (185 "Take a Little Chance") ... 100-200 53
Singles: 7-inch
SUN (185 "Take a Little Chance") ... 450-650 53
Also see JIMMY & WALTER

DEBB JOHNSON
Singles: 7-inch
MONOLITH (7026 "Dancing in the Ruins") ... 5-10 71
LPs:10/12-inch
MONOLITH (7025 "Debb Johnson") ... 15-25 71

DEBBIE & DARNELS
Singles: 7-inch
COLUMBIA (42530 "Daddy") ... 8-12 62
Members: Dorothy Yutenkas; Joan Yutenkas; Marie Broncotti.
Also see TEEN DREAMS

DEBBIE & DIPLOMATS
Singles: 7-inch
STEPHENY (1826 "Unchangeable Heart") ... 15-25 58

DEBERONS
Singles: 7-inch
BOND (1480 "It Only Takes One") ... 50-75 60

DE 'BONAIRS
Singles: 78 rpm
PING ... 100-200 56
Singles: 7-inch
PING (1000 "Lanky Linda") ... 400-500 56
PING (1001 "Say a Prayer for Me") ... 300-400 56
Also see DEBONAIRS (on B and F)

DEBONAIRES
Singles: 7-inch
MASKE (804 "Every Other Day") ... 25-35 59

DEBONAIRES
(Debonairs)
Singles: 78 rpm
GEE (1008 "Won't You Tell Me") ... 20-30 56
HERALD (509 "Darlin' ") ... 40-50 57
Singles: 7-inch
DORE (526 "Every Once in a While") ... 150-200 59
DORE (592 "Every Once in a While") ... 15-25 61
DORE (654 "Mama Don't Care") ... 40-50 62
DORE (702 "Every Once in a While") ... 10-20 64
DORE (712 "Mama Don't Care") ... 8-10 64
GEE (1008 "Won't You Tell Me") ... 40-50 56
GEE (1054 "We'll Wait") ... 20-30 60
HERALD (509 "Darlin' ") ... 50-60 57
(White label. Promotional issue only.)
HERALD (509 "Darlin' ") ... 40-50 57
(Previously issued as by the Five Debonaires.)
Also see FIVE DEBONAIRES

DEBONAIRES
Singles: 7-inch
ELMONT (1004 "This Must Be Paradise") ... 75-125 58

DEBONAIRES
Singles: 7-inch
HOLIDAY (61001 "Lonely Little Room") ... 25-35 61

DEBONAIRES
Singles: 7-inch
RON-CRIS (1008 "No Tears-No Sighs") ... 40-50 61

DEBONAIRES
(Debonairs)
Singles: 7-inch
GOLDEN WORLD (17 thru 44) ... 10-15 64-66
REVILOT (202 "Loving You Takes All My Time") ... 10-20 66
SOLID HIT (102 "Loving You Takes All My Time") ... 250-350 67
Members: Joyce Vincent; Telma Hopkins.
Also see DAWN

DEBONAIRES
Singles: 7-inch
PYRAMID (501 "True Love Has Come") ... 200-300

DEBONAIRS
Singles: 78 rpm
COMBO (129 "Bill Collector") ... 200-300 57
Singles: 7-inch
COMBO (129 "Bill Collector") ... 750-1500 57
COMBO (149 "Cause of a Bad Romance") ... 50-75 58

DEBONAIRS
(With Billy Emmerson & Orch.)
Singles: 7-inch
B&F (1353 "Fools Love") ... 50-100 61
Also see DE 'BONAIRS

DEBONAIRS
Singles: 7-inch
CAROL ANN (1001 "Going to Town") ... 15-20 62
SOUTHSIDE (1004 "Steel Men") ... 8-10 62

DE BREE, Peter, & Wanderers
Singles: 7-inch
FORTUNE (193 "My Bucket's Got a Hole in It") ... 50-75 58
FORTUNE (200 "Hey, Mr. Presley") ... 100-150 58

DEBRIS
LPs: 10/12-inch
STATIC DISPOSAL (0000 "Debris") ... 50-100 76
Members: John Gregg; Richard Davis; Charles Ivy.

DEBS
Singles: 78 rpm
BRUCE (129 "Shoo Doo-Be Doo") ... 30-40 55
CROWN (153 "If You Were Here Tonight") ... 10-15 55
Singles: 7-inch
BRUCE (129 "Shoo Doo-Be Doo") ... 75-100 55
CROWN (153 "If You Were Here Tonight") ... 20-30 55

DEBS
Singles: 78 rpm
KEEN (34003 "Johnny Darling") ... 15-25 57
Singles: 7-inch
KEEN (34003 "Johnny Darling") ... 15-25 57

DEBS
Singles: 7-inch
DOUBLE L (727 "Danger Ahead") ... 10-20 64
ECHO (1008 "If Wishes Were Kisses") ... 20-30 61
INFINITY (035 "The Mask") ... 10-20 64

DEBS
Singles: 7-inch
SQUALOR (1314 "Stars in the Sky") ... 200-300 58

DEBTEENS
Singles: 7-inch
BOSS (403 "Darling") ... 30-40 59

DEBUTANTES
Singles: 78 rpm
SAVOY (1191 "Just Leave It to Me") ... 10-15 56
Singles: 7-inch
SAVOY (1191 "Just Leave It to Me") ... 15-20 56

DEBUTANTES
Singles: 7-inch
KAYO (928 "Going Steady") ... 100-200 58
(Same number used on a Splashers release.)

DEBUTANTES
Singles: 7-inch
GAIL & RICE (101 "Little Latin Lupe Lu"). 10-15
LUCKY ELEVEN (237 "Love Is Strange") .. 8-12
STANDOUT (601 "Shake a Tail Feather") ... 10-15

DEBUTS
Singles: 7-inch
ATCO (6591 "If I Cry") ... 10-15 68
SCUDDER (101 "Gettin' Mellow") ... 20-30 68

DECADES
Singles: 7-inch
DAYTONE (1306 "Dance Forever") ... 15-25 63
DAYTONE (6403 "Lonely Drummer") ... 15-20 64
ERA (3174 "I'm Gonna Dance") ... 10-15 67
LADY LUCK ("On Sunset") ... 50-75 66
(Selection number not known.)
LADY LUCK (101 "I'm Gonna Dance") ... 50-75 66

DECADES
Singles: 7-inch
JANIE (10646 "Strange World") ... 15-25 64

DECADES
Singles: 7-inch
AVENUE D (1 "Please Say It Isn't So") ... 10-15 80
(Black vinyl. 350 made.)
AVENUE D (1 "Please Say It Isn't So") ... 25-35 80
(Orange vinyl. 20 made.)

AVENUE D (1 "Please Say It Isn't So").... 30-50 80
(Clear or gray vinyl. 10 of each made.)
AVENUE D (2 "Teenage Rose") 10-15 81
(Black vinyl. 500 made.)
AVENUE D (3 "To Make a Long Story Short") 15-25 82
(Black vinyl. 353 made.)
AVENUE D (3 "To Make a Long Story Short") 15-25 82
(Orange vinyl. 60 made.)
DAYTONE 5-10
GREAT SCOTT (1002 "Pledging My Love") 15-25
Members: Tom Jones; Dennis Nagel; Bobby Cannizzaro; Jeff Beckman; Chris Mahoney; Marc Scott.
Also see SUBWAY SERENADERS

DE CARLO, Don
Singles: 7-inch
HONEY BEE (292 "Let's Go to the Beach") 30-40
LITTLE TOWN (290 "Sweet Cora Lee") 8-12 62
Also see DINO

DE CARLO, Yvonne
Singles: 7-inch
IMPERIAL (5532 "Rockin' in Orbit") 50-75 58

DE CARO BROTHERS
Singles: 7-inch
LIBERTY (55708 "Candy Coated Lies") .. 15-25 64

DE CASTRO, Gregory
Singles: 12-inch
AZRA (210 "Island's Embrace") 10-15 83
(Picture disc. 500 made.)
Singles
ERIKA (109 "Love Letter to Malvinas")......8-12 83
(8-inch picture disc.)
ERIKA (109 "Love Letter to Malvinas").... 15-25 83
(Heart-shaped picture disc. 150 made.)
ERIKA (109 "Love Letter to Malvinas").... 10-15 83
(Square picture disc. 500 made.)

DE CASTRO SISTERS — P&R '54
(With Don Costa's Orchestra; with Joe Reisman's Orchestra & Chorus)
Singles: 78 rpm
ABBOTT 5-10 54-56
RCA 5-10 56
TICO 5-10 52
Singles: 7-inch
ABC-PAR 5-10 58
ABBOTT 10-20 54-56
CAPITOL 5-10 60-61
RCA 10-15 56-58
TICO 10-15 52
ZODIAC 4-6 77
LPs: 10/12-inch
ABBOTT (5002 "DeCastro Sisters")......... 40-60 56
CAPITOL 15-25 60-61
20TH FOX 8-15 65
Members: Peggy; Babette; Cherie.
Also see COSTA, Don, Orchestra
Also see RAVENSCROFT, Thurl

DE CASTRO SISTERS / Hugo Winterhalter & His Orchestra
EPs: 7-inch
RCA (DJ-51 "I Never Meant to Hurt You") 10-20 56
(Promotional issue only. Not issued with cover.)
Also see DE CASTRO SISTERS
Also see WINTERHALTER, Hugo, & His Orchestra

DECEMBER, Bobby
Singles: 7-inch
ORCHESTRA (100 "Bye Bye Baby") .... 20-30 '60s
ORCHESTRA (209 "Invasion") .... 10-20 '60s

DECEMBER'S CHILDREN
Singles: 7-inch
MAINSTREAM (728 "Sweet Talking Woman") 8-12 70
LPs: 10/12-inch
MAINSTREAM (6128 "December's Children") 20-30 70
Members: Bill Petti; Craig Balzer; Bruce Balzer.

DECEMBER'S CHILDREN LTD.
Singles: 7-inch
DOMESTIC SOUND (123 "Signed D.C.") 40-50 67

DECISIONS
Singles: 7-inch
TOPPER (1013 "Tears, Tears") 15-25 66

DECKER, Jodie
Singles: 7-inch
FABLE (607 "Teenage Blues")..................50-75

DECKERS
Singles: 7-inch
YEADON (101 "Sincerely with All My Heart") 75-125 58
YEADON (1041 "Sincerely with All My Heart") 15-25
Members: Sam Connors; John Williams; Larry Williams; Ben Hart.

DECKLEMAN, Bud
Singles: 78 rpm
METEOR (5014 "Daydreamin' ") 15-25 54
Singles: 7-inch
METEOR (5014 "Daydreamin' ") 30-50 54

DECKLEMAN, Sonny
Singles: 7-inch
VAN DECK (750 "Just One More Time") 75-125

DE COSTA, Barbara
Singles: 7-inch
RIC-TIC (103 "The One in Your Arms")....15-25 62

DECOU, Art
(Art Decoy)
Singles: 7-inch
FORM (100 "Where Are You") 5-10 59
STARLA (4 "Only You for Me") 20-30 57
STARLA (5 "I'm Glad for Your Sake").......20-30 57
SUTTER 8-12

DECOYS
(With Al Browne and His Orchestra)
Singles: 7-inch
AANKO (1005 "I Want Only You") 400-500 63
TIMES SQUARE (9 "I Want Only You") ...15-25 64
VELVET (1001 "Listen to Me").............100-200 64

DECOYS / Bel-Airs
Singles: 7-inch
TIMES SQUARE (8 "It's Going to Be Alright"/"Oh Baby") 15-25 63
(Blue and green vinyl.)
Also see DECOYS

DECOYS / Four Fellows
Singles: 7-inch
ALJON (1261 "Memories"/"Happy Honeymoon") 15-25 72
Also see DECOYS

DEDICATIONS
Singles: 7-inch
AVENUE D (8 "Why Don't You Write Me").8-15 83
(Black vinyl. 350 made.)
AVENUE D (8 "Why Don't You Write Me") 10-20 83
(Red vinyl. 150 made.)
AVENUE D (9 "Crazy for You")..................5-10 83
(Black vinyl. 782 made.)
AVENUE D (9 "Crazy for You")................10-20 83
(Blue vinyl. 200 made.)
BELL (611 "Toy Boy") 5-10 65
C&A (506 "Shining Star")......................150-200 63
CARD (2001 "Why Don't You Write Me") .15-25 62
CLIFTON (86 "Flower of Love") 3-5 90
CLIFTON (92 "For Your Love") 3-5 91
(Colored vinyl.)
JASON SCOTT (10 "Shining Star") 3-5 81
(Black vinyl. 500 made.)
JASON SCOTT (10 "Shining Star") 5-10 81
(Blue vinyl. 20 made.)
RAMARCA (602 "Someone to Love")......10-15 63
WHITE WHALE (340 "Teardrops") 20-30 70
Picture Sleeves
CARD (2001 "Why Don't You Write Me") .20-30 62
Members: Freddie; Charlie; Tony; Marty; Lou; Mike Paquette; Joe Burke; John Mallon; Ronni Petri; Steve Petri.
Also see ADMIRATIONS
Also see SHEPHERD, Johnnie

DEDMON, Danny
Singles: 78 rpm
FLAIR (1005 "Sally Anne") 8-12 53
Singles: 7-inch
FLAIR (1005 "Sally Anne") 10-20 53

DEDRICK, Martin
Singles: 7-inch
SPRY (106 "Don't Lead Me On") 50-75 57

DEE, Billy
Singles: 78 rpm
FABOR 10-15 54
Singles: 7-inch
FABOR (104 "Drinking Tequila") 15-20 54
FABOR (111 "Puppy Love") 15-20 54

DEE, Billy
(With the Superchargers)
Singles: 7-inch
LE CAM (127 "Moon Maid") 10-20 64
WESTFORD (101 "Curb Service") 10-20 63

DEE, Charlie
Singles: 7-inch
USA (101 "World on the Moon") 75-125

DEE, Dave, Dozy, Beaky, Mick & Tich — LP '67
Singles: 7-inch
ATLANTIC 3-5 83
FONTANA 5-10 65-67
IMPERIAL 5-10 67-68
LPs: 10/12-inch
FONTANA (27567 "Greatest Hits")...........20-30 67
(Monaural.)
FONTANA (67567 "Greatest Hits")...........25-30 67
(Stereo.)
IMPERIAL (12402 "Time to Take Off") 20-25 68

DEE, Davey, & Mudcats
Singles: 7-inch
EMBER (1055 "Puddle Jumper") 10-20 59

DEE, Davey, & Redcoats
Singles: 78 rpm
KAPP (163 "Calypso") 10-15 56
Singles: 7-inch
KAPP (163 "Calypso") 15-25 56

DEE, David
Singles: 7-inch
DOT (16085 "Mr. D") 10-20 60
EDGE (003 "I Wanna Get into You") 3-5 87
VANESSA 4-8

DEE, Dixie
Singles: 7-inch
TEROCK (1000 "Bright Lights") 50-75

DEE, Donna
(With the Clouds; with Penetrators)
Singles: 7-inch
ABC-PAR (10296 "Television") 10-15 62
KC (120 "Mirror on the Wall") 10-20 63
(Brown vinyl.)
RAMADA (501 "The More I See Him") 20-30 61

DEE, Eddie, & Sputniks
Singles: 7-inch
DIXIE (2027 "Journey to the Moon")..........10-15 59

DEE, Earl, & Three Naturals
Singles: 7-inch
JERRLEN (112 "So High") 20-30 64

DEE, Errol
Singles: 7-inch
INSTANT (3240 "I Love You") 10-15 62

DEE, Fern
("Orch. Directed by Bob Creash")
Singles: 7-inch
EMBER (1035 "Hello Mr. Dream Man")....10-15 58
JUBILEE (5344 "Grown Up") 10-20 58

DEE, Frankie
(With the Mastertones; Frank Detrano)
Singles: 7-inch
ABCO (1002 "Walking in the Rain")..........10-20
FUTURE (1001 "I Made a Boo Boo") 8-12 58
FUTURE (1003 "Let's Go Steady")...........40-60 57
RCA (7276 "Shake It Up Baby") 10-20 58
TEE JAY (333 "Darling Arlene")............200-300 61
20TH FOX (146 "Swinging in a Hammock") 15-25 59

DEE, Georgie, & Ladds
Singles: 7-inch
KON-TI-KI ("I Can't Go on Like This") 75-125
(No selection number used.)

DEE, Gina
Singles: 7-inch
HOME OF THE BLUES (236 "Six Feet Below") 10-15 62

DEE, Harrill
Singles: 7-inch
TOPIC (504 "Just Pass Me By") 75-125

DEE, Jackie
(Jackie De Shannon)
Singles: 78 rpm
GONE (5008 "I'll Be True") 30-40 57
Singles: 7-inch
GONE (5008 "I'll Be True") 50-75 57
LIBERTY (55148 "Buddy").........................50-75 58
Also see DE SHANNON, Jackie

DEE, James, & A Piece of the Action
(With the Primettes)
Singles: 7-inch
ENRICA (1020 "Jealous Over Love")....... 15-25 62

DEE, Jimmy — P&R '58
(With the Offbeats; with Universals)
Singles: 78 rpm
DOT (15664 "Henrietta") 50-75 57
TNT (148 "Henrietta")...........................75-125 57
Singles: 7-inch
ACE (627 "Wanda") 15-25 61
CANARY (6418 "Two Pillows")..................10-15 66
CUTIE (1400 "I've Got a Secret") 10-20 63
DOT (15664 "Henrietta") 30-40 57
DOT (15721 "You're Late Miss Kate")......50-75 58
HEAR ME 5-10
INNER-GLO (105 "Guitar Pickin' Man") .75-100 57
SCOPE (103 "I Ain't Givin' Up Nothin' ") 150-250 59
SHURFINE (015 "I Don't Know What's Troubling Me") 8-12 66
TNT (148 "Henrietta")...........................75-100 57
TNT (152 "You're Late Miss Kate")........75-100 58
TNT (161 "I Feel Like Rockin' ")...........300-400 59
TAPER (101 "I Ain't Givin' Up Nothin' ") ...30-50 59

DEE, Joe, & Top Hands
Singles: 7-inch
PAT RICCIO (1105 "Blind Heart") 10-15 62
Also see TREMONTS

DEE, Joey — P&R/R&B/LP '61
(With the Starliters; with Starlites; with New Starliters; with the Hawk)
Singles: 7-inch
ABC 4-6 73
BONUS (7009 "Lorraine") 20-30 63
CANEIL 4-6
JANUS ....4-8 '70s
JUBILEE 5-10 66-67
LITTLE (813 "Lorraine") 800-1000 58
ROULETTE 10-20 61-65
ROULETTE GOLDEN GOODIES...............3-6 '70s
SCEPTER (1210 "Face of an Angel") 15-25 60
(Red label. Must have "Scepter" in script.)
SCEPTER (1210 "Face of an Angel") 5-10 60
(Multi-color label.)
SCEPTER (1225 "Bulldog") 8-12 61
SUNBURST 4-6 73
TONSIL RECORDS 4-8 70
VASELINE HAIR TONIC (12 "Learn to Dance the Peppermint Twist") 15-25 62
(Special products issue from Chesebrough-Ponds.)
Picture Sleeves
BONUS (7009 "Lorraine") 30-40 63
ROULETTE 15-25 62
LPs: 10/12-inch
ACCORD 5-10 82
JUBILEE (8000 "Hitsville") 15-25 66
ROULETTE 15-25 61-63
SCEPTER (503 "The Peppermint Twisters") 15-25 62
Members: Joey Dee; Tony Scuito; John Yanic; Vinnie Correo; Ralph Fazio; Roger Freeman; David Brigati; Joe Pesci; Willie Davis; Carlton Latimore.
Session: Ronettes.
Also see HI-FIVES
Also see RASCALS
Also see RONETTES

DEE, Joey, & Starliters / Dion
Singles: 7-inch
MONUMENT ("YaYa Twist")......................8-12 61
(No selection number used. Promotional issue only.)
Also see DION

DEE, Joey, & Starliters / Randy Andy & Candymen

EPs: 7-inch

DIPLOMAT (66-2 "The Girl I Walk to School")....10-20 62

LPs: 10/12-inch

DIPLOMAT (66-2 "Come Twist with Me")....15-25 62

Also see ANDY, Randy, & Candymen
Also see DEE, Joey

DEE, Joey, & Lois Lee

Singles: 7-inch

STEADY (37004 "Storybook Children")........4-8 '70s

Also see DEE, Joey
Also see LEE, Lois

DEE, Joey, & Top Hands

Singles: 7-inch

PAT RICCIO (1105 "Honky Tonk Guitar")....10-20 62

DEE, Johnny *P&R '57*

(John D. Loudermilk; "Featuring Joe Tanner on Guitar")

Singles: 78 rpm

COLONIAL (430 "Sittin' in the Balcony"). 25-50 57

Singles: 7-inch

COLONIAL (430 "Sittin' in the Balcony"). 30-40 57
(Has "45 RPM" on left side of label.)
COLONIAL (430 "Sittin' in the Balcony"). 10-15 57
(Has "45 RPM" on right side of label.)
COLONIAL (430 "Sittin' in the Balcony")....8-12 57
(No "45 RPM" on label. Reads "Dist. by AM-PAR Record Corp.")
COLONIAL (435 "1000 Concrete Blocks")....15-20 57
DOT....5-10 58

Picture Sleeves

COLONIAL (430 "Sittin in the Balcony") 50-100 57

Also see LOUDERMILK, John D.
Also see TANNER, Joe

DEE, Johnny, Trio

Singles: 78 rpm

JUBILEE (6001 "Sincere")....5-10 52

Singles: 7-inch

JUBILEE (6001 "Sincere")....10-20 52
(Same number used on a later release by the Orioles.)

DEE, Kathy *C&W '63*

Singles: 7-inch

B-W (611 "Ways of a Heart")....8-12 61
B-W (619 "If I Never Get to Heaven")....8-12 62
CARLTON (563 "Livin' on Love")....8-12 61
U.A. (562 thru 687)....5-8 63-64

Picture Sleeves

B-W (619 "If I Never Get to Heaven")....15-20 63

LPs: 10/12-inch

B-W....15-25 63
GUEST STAR....10-20 64

DEE, Kitty

Singles: 7-inch

JUBILEE (5326 "I Went to the Dance")....10-15 58
SEECO (6029 "Flat Top")....8-12 59

DEE, Lola *P&R '54*

(With Stubby & the Buccaneers; with Carl Stevens & His Orchestra)

Singles: 78 rpm

BALLY (1046 "A Little More Love")....5-10 57
MERCURY....5-10 54-56
WING....5-10 55

Singles: 7-inch

BALLY (1046 "A Little More Love")....5-10 57
MERCURY....15-25 54-56
WING (90004 thru 90035)....10-20 55

DEE, Lola, & Rusty Draper

Singles: 78 rpm

MERCURY....5-10 56

Singles: 7-inch

MERCURY....10-15 56

Also see DEE, Lola
Also see DRAPER,Rusty

DEE, Lou

(With Jim Flaherty's Caravan)

Singles: 7-inch

FRANKIE (12 "My Darling Rosie")....20-30 58
OLD TOWN (305 "King of the Hill")....100-150 57

DEE, Lynn, & Pagans

Singles: 7-inch

MUSIC CITY (835 "Fool That I Am")....200-300 60

DEE, Lynn, & Statics

Singles: 7-inch

MANTIS (101 "Little Girl's Dream")....50-75

Also see STATICS

DEE, Margie

Singles: 7-inch

DOAK (371 "Waitress")....50-75

DEE, Ronnie

(Ronnie Dawson)

Singles: 7-inch

BACK BEAT (522 "Action Packed")....75-100 59
WYE (1008 "Little Boy")....10-15 61

Also see DAWSON, Ronnie

DEE, Ronny, with Benny King & Royal Jesters

Singles: 7-inch

WRH (1001 "One Two Three")....10-20

DEE, Sandra

Singles: 7-inch

DECCA (31042 "Dear Johnny")....10-15 60
DECCA (31063 "Questions")....10-15 60
DECCA (31265 "Tammy, Tell Me True")..10-15 61

Picture Sleeves

DECCA (31042 "Dear Johnny")....25-35 60

DEE, Sonny

Singles: 7-inch

KAPP (421 "Here I Stand")....15-25 61

Session: Regents.
Also see REGENTS

DEE, Tommy *P&R '59*

(With the Mellotones)

Singles: 7-inch

A&M....3-5 80
CHALLENGE (59083 "The Hobo and the Puppy")....8-10 60
CHALLENGE (59087 "Ballad of a Drag Race")....8-10 60
CREST (1061 "Hello Someone")....8-12 59
CREST (1067 "Angel of Love")....8-12 59
K-ARK....4-6 70
PIKE (5906 "Loving You")....5-10 61
PIKE (5909 "A Little Dog Cried")....5-10 61
SIMS (308 "Goodbye High School")....10-15 66

Also see COVINAS

DEE, Tommy, with Teen Tones & Orchestra / Teen Tones *P&R '59*

Singles: 7-inch

CREST (1057 "Three Stars")....15-25 59
(Flip, *I'll Never Change*, is also credited to Teen Tones here and to Carol Kay and the Teen-Aires on copies below. The track is exactly the same on both discs.)

DEE, Tommy, with Carol Kay & Teen-Aires / Carol Kay & Teen-Aires *P&R '59*

Singles: 7-inch

CREST (1057 "Three Stars")....15-25 59
(Monaural.)
CREST (1057 "Three Stars")....35-50 59
(Stereo.)

Also see DEE, Tommy

DEE, Toni

Singles: 7-inch

BRUNSWICK (55262 "My Babe")....8-10 64
RINGO (007 "Billy Is the Boy for Me")....10-15 65

DEE, Tony

(With the Pageants; Tony I. Dee)

Singles: 7-inch

ARLEN (731 "Saturday Romance")....20-30 63
KAYSAL (103 "Good Lovin'")....10-20 '60s
DU-WELL (101 "Saturday Romance")..100-150 61

Also see PAGEANTS

DEE, Tonya

Singles: 7-inch

UBC (1032 "Shake This Town")....50-75

DEE & DI

Singles: 7-inch

KEEN (82119 "Goodbye")....10-15 60
KEEN (82121 "Just You")....10-15 60
SIMS (153 "Just You")....5-10 63

DEE & DON

Singles: 7-inch

A-BET (9429 "I Can't Stand It")....10-15 68
ARGO (5399 "Then I'll Be Happy")....5-10 61

DEE & JOE

Singles: 7-inch

JUBILEE (5670 "I Found a Love")....10-15 69

DEE & PATTY

Singles: 78 rpm

MERCURY....20-30 57

Singles: 7-inch

D (1020 "Sweet Lovin' Baby")....25-35 58
MERCURY (71252 "First Date")....25-35 57

DEE & TEE

Singles: 7-inch

CORAL (62507 "Something's Comin'")....10-15 66

DEE & YEOMEN

Singles: 7-inch

BELL (633 "Why Why Why")....10-15 65
WOLFF (101 "Say Baby")....20-30

DEE CALS

Singles: 7-inch

CO ED (1960 "Stars in the Blue What Should I Do")....50-60 59
MAYHAMS (1960 "Stars in the Blue What Should I Do")....40-50 61
(Yellow label.)
MAYHAMS (1960 "Stars in the Blue What Should I Do")....5-10
(Red label.)

DEE JAY & RUNAWAYS *P&R '66*

Singles: 7-inch

COULEE (109 "Love Bug Crawl")....25-35 64
DEE JAY (101 "Love Tender Love")....3-6 82
IGL (100 "Jenny Jenny")....100-150 65
IGL (103 "Peter Rabbit")....20-40 66
(First issue.)
SMASH (2034 "Peter Rabbit")....8-12 66
SONIC (132 "Don't You Ever")....10-20 66
STONE (45 "Don't You Ever")....10-20 66

Picture Sleeves

DEE JA Y (101 "Love Tender Love")....4-8 82
(With insert)

Members: Denny Storey; John Senn; Terry Klein; Gary Lind; Bob; Tom.
Also see CHEVELLES
Also see STOREY, Denny
Also see TEMPTORS

DEE JAYES

Singles: 7-inch

HIGHLAND (1031 "Bongo Beach Party").15-20 62

DEE-JAYS

(Dee-Jay's)

Singles: 7-inch

SONATA (1100 "You Took Your Love from Me")....200-300 62

DEEP, The

LPs: 10/12-inch

PARKWAY (7051 "Psychedelic Moods")....200-400 66

Members: David Bromberg; Rusty Evans; Mark Barkan.
Also see FREAK SCENE

DEEP PURPLE *P&R/LP '68*

Singles: 12-inch

MERCURY....4-8 87

Singles: 7-inch

GRP....4-6 73
MERCURY....3-5 84-87
TETRAGRAMMATON....5-10 68-69
W.B.....4-6 70-73
W.B./PURPLE....4-6 74-75

Picture Sleeves

MERCURY....3-5 85
TETRAGRAMMATON....8-15 68
W.B./PURPLE....4-6 74-75

EPs: 7-inch

W.B./PURPLE....10-20 74
(Juke box issue.)

LPs: 10/12-inch

MERCURY....6-12 84-88
PASSPORT....5-10 88
PORTRAIT....5-10 82
RCA....5-8 90
SCEPTER/CITATION....8-10 72
TETRAGRAMMATON (102 "Shades of Deep Purple")....20-30 68
TETRAGRAMMATON (107 "Book of Taliesyn")....20-30 69
TETRAGRAMMATON (119 "Deep Purple")....20-30 69
W.B. (Except 3000 series)....15-25 70-74
W.B. (3000 series)....5-10 77
W.B./PURPLE....10-15 74-80

Members: Ritchie Blackmore; Jon Lord; Roger Glover; Ian Paice; Rod Evans; Nick Simper; Ian Gillan; David Coverdale; Tommy Bolin.
Also see CAPTAIN BEYOND
Also see TRAPEZE

DEEP RIVER BOYS *P&R '48*

Singles: 78 rpm

BEACON....20-30 52-54
BLUEBIRD (10676 "I Was a Fool to Let You Go")....20-40 40
BLUEBIRD (10847 "Bird in the Hand")....20-40 40
BLUEBIRD (11178 "My Heart at Thy Sweet Voice")....20-40 41
BLUEBIRD (11217 "I Wish I Had Died in My Cradle")....20-40 41
JAY-DEE....15-25 54
LANG-WORTH....10-25
(16-inch transcriptions, made in the '40s.)
PILOTONE (118 "Spirituals & Jubilees")..10-25 46
(Four-disc set.)
RCA....10-25 40-53
VICTOR....15-25 40
VIK....10-15 56

Singles: 7-inch

BEACON (104 "Sleepy Little Cowboy")....40-60 54
BEACON (9143 "Truthfully")....40-60 52
BEACON (9146 "All I Need Is You")....40-60 52
GALLANT (101 "Nola")....15-20 59
GALLANT (2001 "I Don't Know Why")....10-15 59
JAY-DEE (788 "Truthfully")....40-50 54
MICHELLE (1001 "Clouds Before the Storm")....15-25 65
RCA (0078 "Free Grace")....30-40 50
(Cherry red vinyl.)
RCA (5268 "Biggest Fool")....15-25 53
SEECO (6046 "I Don't Know Why")....10-15 60
VIK (0205 "All My Love Belongs to You"). 15-20 56
VIK (0224 "You're Not too Old")....15-20 56
WAND (117 "Are You Certain")....5-10 61

Picture Sleeves

GALLANT (2001 "I Don't Know Why")....15-25 59

EPs: 7-inch

CAMDEN (341 "Presenting the Deep River Boys")....40-50 56
WALDORF MUSIC HALL (113 "Songs of Jubilee")....50-75 56
(May also be shown as *Spirituals and Jubilees.*)
WALDORF MUSIC HALL (114 "Songs of Jubilee")....50-75 56
(Black vinyl. Has picture of group on cover.
WALDORF MUSIC HALL (114 "Spirituals & Jubilees")....75-100 56
(Colored vinyl. No picture of group on cover.)

LPs: 10/12-inch

CAMDEN (303 "Presenting the Deep River Boys")....40-60 56
CAPITOL (6050 "Presenting Harry Douglas and the Deep River Boys")....20-40
(Canadian.)
QUE (104 "Midnight Magic")....50-75 57
WALDORF MUSIC HALL (108" Songs of Jubilee")....75-125 56
(10-inch LP. Label gives title as *Spirituals and Jubilees.*)
"X" (1019 "Deep River Boys")....60-80 56

Members: Harry Douglas; Vernon Gardner; Ed Ware; George Lawson; Carter Wilson.
Also see BARLOW, Dean, & Crickets / Deep River Boys

DEEP SIX

Singles: 7-inch

LIBERTY (55838 thru 55926)....5-10 65-66
SAW-MAN....5-10 65
SOFT (960 "Last Time Around")....5-10 65

LPs: 10/12-inch

LIBERTY (3475 "Deep Six")....15-25 66
(Monaural.)
LIBERTY (7475 "Deep Six")....15-25 66
(Stereo.)

DEEP TONES
Singles: 78 rpm
CORAL (65062 "The Night You Said Goodbye")..........50-100 51

DEEPEST BLUE
Singles: 7-inch
BLUE-FIN (102 "Somebody's Girl")..........10-20 66

DEEPS
Singles: 7-inch
QUE (1000 "Calypso Rock & Roll")..........15-25 57
QUE (1001 "Deep Purple")..........10-15 57

DEERFIELD
LPs: 10/12-inch
FLAT ROCK ("Nil Desperandum")..........75-125 71
(Selection number not known.)

DEE-VINES
(With Quentin Solano Orchestra)
Singles: 7-inch
LANO (2001 "I Believe")..........20-30 60
(White label.)
LANO (2001 "I Believe")..........10-20 60
(Red label.)
RELIC (514 "I Believe")..........5-10 64

DEF LEPPARD LP '80
Singles: 12-inch
MERCURY..........4-8 80-87
(Promotional only.)
Singles: 7-inch
MERCURY..........3-5 80-89
EPs: 7-inch
BLUDGEON RIFFOLA..........10-15 78
Picture Sleeves
MERCURY (Except 811-215-7)..........3-5 80-89
MERCURY (811-215-7 "Photograph")..........4-6 83
LPs: 10/12-inch
MERCURY (Except 832-962)..........5-10 80-88
MERCURY (832-962 "Hysteria")..........25-35 87
(Picture disc.)
Members: Joe Elliott; Pete Willis; Rick Allen; Steve Clark; Phil Collen; Rick Savage; Vivian Campbell.
Also see DIO, Ronnie

DE-FENDERS
Singles: 7-inch
WORLD PACIFIC (382 "Wild One")..........10-20 63
LPs: 10/12-inch
DEL-FI (DFLP-1242 "Drag Beat")..........40-50 63
(Monaural.)
DEL-FI (DFST-1242 "Drag Beat")..........50-60 63
(Stereo.)
DEL-FI (DLF-1231 "Drag Beat")..........10-12 98
("Thick, hard wax" reissue.)
WORLD PACIFIC (1810 "The De-Fenders Play the Big Ones")..........50-60 63
(Black vinyl.)
WORLD PACIFIC (1810 "The De-Fenders Play the Big Ones")..........75-125 63
(Red vinyl.)

DE-FENDERS / Deuce Coupes
Singles: 7-inch
DEL-FI (4226 "Little Deuce Coupe")..........10-20 63
Also see DE-FENDERS
Also see DEUCE COUPES

DEFENDERS
Singles: 7-inch
CARLTON (598 "I'm Going Home")..........10-20 63
PARKWAY (926 "Island of Love")..........15-25 64
REALM..........8-10 64

DEFIANT 4
Singles: 7-inch
DELTA (2195 "Away from Home")..........25-30

DEFIANT ONES
Singles: 7-inch
ESSAR (1000 "Deep Six")..........20-30 61
ESSAR (1002 "Defiant Drums")..........20-30 61
REAL FINE (834 "Defiant Drums No. 2")..........15-25 62

DEFIANTS
Singles: 7-inch
BARONET (5 "Surfer's Twist")..........15-25 62

DEFIANTS
Singles: 7-inch
STUDIO CITY (10442 "Bye Bye Johnny")..........20-25 66

DE GRINDA, Joe
Singles: 7-inch
BOFUZ (19694 "Smokestack Lightning")..........25-35 69

DE-ICERS
Singles: 7-inch
DE-ICER (100 "Callin' My Love")..........40-50 57

DE JAN & ELGINS
Singles: 7-inch
LESSIE (0099 "That's My Girl")..........4000-5000 60

DE JOHN SISTERS P&R '54
Singles: 78 rpm
COLUMBIA..........8-12 57
EPIC..........5-10 54-56
OKEH..........5-10 53
Singles: 7-inch
COLUMBIA..........10-20 57
EPIC..........10-20 54-56
OKEH..........10-20 53
SUNBEAM..........10-20 58-59
U.A. (213 "Yes Indeed")..........8-12 60
LPs: 10/12-inch
U.A. (3103 "Yes Indeed")..........15-25 60
(Monaural.)
U.A. (6103 "Yes Indeed")..........25-35 60
(Stereo.)
Members: Julie De Giovanni; Dux De Giovanni.
Also see McGUIRE SISTERS & DE JOHN SISTERS

DEKKER, Desmond, & Aces P&R/LP '69
Singles: 7-inch
UNI..........4-8 69-70
LPs: 10/12-inch
UNI (73059 "Israelites")..........20-30 69

DEL, Mary
(With Archie Bleyer and Orchestra)
Singles: 78 rpm
CADENCE (1250 "Hurts Me to My Heart")..........10-15 54
CADENCE (1257 "Leave My Heart")..........5-10 55
Singles: 7-inch
CADENCE (1250 "Hurts Me to My Heart")..........20-30 54
CADENCE (1257 "Leave My Heart")..........10-20 55

DEL & ESCORTS
(Dell & Escorts)
Singles: 7-inch
ROME (103 "Baby Doll")..........75-125 61
(Reissued as by Jo-Ann.)
SYMBOL (913 "You Don't Love Me")..........300-400 60
TAURUS (350/351 "You're for Me")..........200-300 61
Also see EARLS
Also see JO-ANN

DEL & PEARL
Singles: 7-inch
COCO (152 "I, I Wonder Why")..........10-20 58

DEL & RIC
Singles: 7-inch
LOOK (5001 "I'm Looking for Someone")..........20-30 64
Members: Del Trolinder; Ric Matlock.

DELACARDOS P&R '61
Singles: 7-inch
CANDLELITE (423 "Letter to a School Girl")..........5-10 64
ELGEY (1001 "Letter to a School Girl")..........30-40 59
IMPERIAL (5992 "On the Beach")..........5-10 63
Q-CITY (1001 "She's the One I Love")..........20-30
SHELL (308 "Dream Girl")..........10-15 61
SHELL (311 "Love Is the Greatest Thing")..........10-15 62
U.A. (276 "I Got It")..........15-20 60
U.A. (310 "Hold Back the Tears")..........15-20 61

DEL-AIRES
Singles: 7-inch
CORAL (62370 "Elaine")..........15-25 63
CORAL (62404 "My Funny Valentine")..........15-25 63
CORAL (62419 "Arlene")..........75-100 64
DELSEY (302 "It Took a Long Time")..........15-25 65
Also see RONNIE & DELAIRES

DEL-AIRS
Singles: 7-inch
M.B.S. (001 "While Walking")..........20-30 60

DEL-AIRS
Singles: 7-inch
ARRAWAK (1003 "I'm Lonely")..........15-20 62

DEL AMOS
Singles: 7-inch
NIKKO (703 "She's So Wonderful")..........30-40 59

DELANCEYS
Singles: 7-inch
ABC-PAR (10353 "High Voltage")..........10-20 62

DELANEY & BONNIE LP '69
(Delaney & Bonnie and Friends)
Singles: 7-inch
ATCO..........4-8 69-72
COLUMBIA..........4-6 72-73
ELEKTRA..........5-10 69
INDEPENDENCE..........5-10 67
STAX..........5-10 68-69
LPs: 10/12-inch
ATCO..........15-25 70-72
COLUMBIA..........15-25 72
ELEKTRA..........15-25 69
GNP..........15-25 70
STAX..........15-25 69
Members: Delaney Bramlett; Bonnie Bramlett.
Also see CLAPTON, Eric
Also see MASON, Dave
Also see SHINDOGS
Also see WHITLOCK, Bobby

DELATONES
Singles: 7-inch
TNT (9027 "Little Jeanie")..........100-200 60
TNT (9028 "Teenagers Love")..........300-400 60

DEL-BROOKS
Singles: 7-inch
KID (101 "Darling Barbara")..........75-125 58

DEL CADES
Singles: 7-inch
UNITED SOUND ASSOCIATES (175 "Two to Fall in Love")..........15-25 64
Picture Sleeves
UNITED SOUND ASSOCIATES (175 "Two to Fall in Love")..........25-35 64

DEL CAPRIS
(Del-Capris)
Singles: 7-inch
AMBER (304 "Speak to Me of Love")..........30-40 63
AMBER (854 "Up on the Roof")..........5-10 66
CATAMOUNT (115 "Teardrops Follow Me")..........5-10 66
(Black vinyl.)
CATAMOUNT (115 "Teardrops Follow Me")..........8-12 66
(Gold or blue vinyl.)

DEL CAPRIS
Singles: 7-inch
KAMA SUTRA (235 "Hey Little Girl")..........5-10 67
RONJERDON (39 "Hey Little Girl")..........10-15 67

DEL CAPRIS
Singles: 7-inch
ALMONT (304 "Teresa")..........30-50 63

DEL CHONTAYS
Singles: 7-inch
STEELTOWN (2467 "Baby I Need You")..........20-30
Session: Emmett Smith.
Also see EXCITING INVICTAS

DEL-CHORDS
Singles: 7-inch
COOL (5816 "Marsha-Mellow")..........200-300 58

DEL-CHORDS
Singles: 7-inch
JIN (126 "Help Me")..........50-75 60
(Has tiny bubbles in the vinyl.)
JIN (126 "Help Me")..........10-20 60
(No bubbles in vinyl.)

DEL-CHORDS
Singles: 7-inch
IMPALA (215 "Everybody's Gotta Lose Someday")..........10-15 63
MR. GENIUS (401 "Everybody's Gotta Lose Someday")..........25-35 62
MR. GENIUS (1028 "Your Mommy Lied to Your Daddy")..........40-60 '60s
Members: Dave Bupp; Buddy King.
Also see MAGNIFICENT MEN

DEL CONTE, Dave
Singles: 7-inch
DELCON (1 "Face in the Crowd")..........10-15 '60s
MERRI (6003 "Lonely Surfer")..........15-25 63

DELCOS
(With Buddy Kay's Band; Delco's)
Singles: 7-inch
EBONY (01 "Arabia")..........50-75 62
SHOWCASE (2501 "Arabia")..........25-35 62
(White label. Promotional issue only.)
SHOWCASE (2501 "Arabia")..........20-30 62
(Blue label.)
SHOWCASE (2501 "Arabia")..........10-15 62
(Red label.)
SHOWCASE (2515 "Still Miss You So")..........20-30 64
SOUND STAGE 7 (2501 "Arabia")..........10-15 63
SOUND STAGE 7 (2515 "Still Miss You So")..........10-15 63
Members: Glenn Madison; Ralph Woods; Otis Smith; Richard Greene; Pete Woodard.
Also see MADISON, Glenn

DEL COUNTS
(With Al Browne's Orchestra)
Singles: 7-inch
ARCADE (1002 "Lone Stranger")..........4-6 76
ROSE (22 "Lone Stranger")..........100-150 60
Also see BROWNE, Al

DEL COUNTS
Singles: 7-inch
APA..........8-12 73
APEX (77058 "What Is the Reason")..........20-30 67
(First issue.)
HAND..........8-12 72
MAPLE LEAF..........8-12 74
MAR-BIL (109 "Ain't Got the Time")..........10-20 68
MOON SOUND..........8-12 74
SOMA (1430 "Bird Dog")..........15-25 66
SOMA (1465 "What Is the Reason")..........15-25 67
Picture Sleeves
MOON SOUND..........8-12 74

DELEGATES
(Kool Gents)
Singles: 78 rpm
VEE-JAY (243 "Mother's Son")..........25-35 57
Singles: 7-inch
VEE-JAY (243 "Mother's Son")..........25-35 57
Members: Dee Clark; Johnny Carter; John McCall; Ted Long; Doug Brown.
Also see CLARK, Dee
Also see EL DORADOS
Also see KOOL GENTS

DELEGATES / Big Jay McNeely
Singles: 78 rpm
VEE-JAY..........20-30 57
Singles: 7-inch
VEE-JAY (212 "The Convention"/"Jay's Rock")..........20-30 57
Also see DELEGATES
Also see McNEELY, Big Jay

DELEGATES
Singles: 7-inch
AURA (88120 "Peeper")..........5-10 65
WORLD PACIFIC..........5-10 65-66
LPs: 10/12-inch
AURA (3002 "The Delegates")..........15-20 65
WORLD PACIFIC..........15-20 65-66
Member: Billy Larkin.

DELEGATES OF SOUL
Singles: 7-inch
UPLOOK (51470 "I'll Come Running Back")..........15-25 '60s

DEL-FIS
("Del-Fi's Combo - Vocal By Pete Bosquez")
Singles: 7-inch
CADETTE (8010 "The Magic of Your Love")..........15-25 65
CRYSTAL BALL (117 "My Darling")..........4-8 78
(Black vinyl. 500 made.)
CRYSTAL BALL (117 "My Darling")..........8-12 78
(Red vinyl. 25 made.)
1001 (101 "Let's Start All Over")..........50-75 63
Also see DEL-PHIS
Also see HANKS, Mike

DELFONICS
Singles: 7-inch
DEE-SU (308 "Come On Down")...............5-10 65
FLING (727 "There They Go")................ 15-25 62
Member: Carlton Lee.

DELI-CADOS
Singles: 7-inch
PMP (4979 "Now I've Confessed") .. 2000-2500 60
(Identification number shown since no selection number is used.)

DELICADOS
Singles: 7-inch
HEIGH-HO (640 "I Can Tell")................. 50-75 67

DELICATES
Singles: 7-inch
CELESTE (676 "My Pillow")................... 15-25 59
CHALLENGE...5-10 64-65
DEE DEE (677 "My Pillow")..................... 10-20 61
ROULETTE (4321 thru 4387).....................5-10 61
SOUL TOWN..8-12
U.A. 5-10 60-61
UNART (2017 "Black and White Thunderbird")..8-12 59
UNART (2024 "Ringa Ding")......................8-12 59
Also see ANGELS
Also see SOUL SURFERS / Delicates

DELIGHTS
Singles: 7-inch
NITE (1034 "My One Desire")................. 15-25 61
(Shows distributor – Discmaker.)
NITE (1034 "My One Desire")................. 50-75 61
(No distributor shown.)

DELIGHTS
Singles: 7-inch
GOLDEN CREST (574 "Lucky Old Sun") 10-20 62

DELIGHTS
Singles: 7-inch
ARLEN (753 "I Cry")............................... 10-15 64
DELAWARE... 10-20 65

DE-LIGHTS
Singles: 7-inch
AD-LIB (346 "I'm Comin' Home")............ 15-25 62
(Previously issued as by the Del Knights.)
Also see DEL KNIGHTS

DEL KNIGHTS
Singles: 7-inch
UNART (2008 "Everything")..................... 10-15 59

DEL KNIGHTS
Singles: 7-inch
SHERYL (339 "I'm Comin' Home")......... 25-35 61
(Reissued as by the De-Lights.)
Also see DE-LIGHTS

DEL KNIGHTS
(Del-Knights)
Singles: 7-inch
BRONKO (502 "Speedy Gonzales")..........8-12 62
CHANCELLOR (1075 "Wherever You Are").. 10-15 61

DELL, Danny
(With the Trends)
Singles: 7-inch
GUARANTEED (220 "I'll Wait")............... 15-25 61
ROCKIN' (160 "Froggy Went a-Courtin' ")... 150-250 60
(First issue.)
WORLD PACIFIC (824 "Froggy Went a-Courtin' ")....................................... 100-150 60

DELL, Dicky, & Bing Bongs
(With Sonny Dale Orchestra)
Singles: 7-inch
DRAGON (10205 "Ding-A-Ling-A-Ling-Ding Dong").. 100-150 58
Also see TROYS

DELL, Don
(With the Up Starts; with Montereys; with Dominants)
Singles: 7-inch
EAST COAST (102 "Time").................... 40-50 61
EAST COAST (106 "A Special Love") . 150-200 61
(With cardboard picture sleeve.)
EAST COAST (106 "A Special Love") ... 75-125 61
(Without cardboard picture sleeve.)
ROMAN (2963 "Make Believe Love")...... 20-30 64

DELL, Evelyn, & Vibrations
Singles: 7-inch
ABC-PAR (10218 "Sincerely")..................10-20 61

DELL, Frank
Singles: 7-inch
VALISE (6900 "He Broke Your Game Wide Open")..10-20
VALISE (6901 "Baby, You've Got It") 10-20

DELL, Jeanie
(With Johnny M. & Rock-A-Bops)
Singles: 7-inch
JOSIE (878 "Kiss You a Thousand Times")..100-150 60
RITZ...15-25

DELL, Jimmy
(Jimmy Delbridge)
Singles: 7-inch
PHILIPS (40080 "Skippin' ")........................5-10 63
RCA (7355 "I've Got a Dollar")..................10-15 58
Also see JIMMY & DUANE

DELL, Joey
Singles: 7-inch
ROULETTE (4422 "Only Last Night").......20-30 62

DELL, Jovan
Singles: 7-inch
BALLY (1038 "Love Me Forever")............10-15 57

DELL, Richie
Singles: 7-inch
KING (5888 "King Lover")........................10-15 64

DELL, Roy
Singles: 7-inch
ESCO (300 "Classroom")..........................10-20 59

DELL, Sly
Singles: 7-inch
FLAME (10148 "Let Me Tell You Bout It")..100-150

DELL, Tony
Singles: 7-inch
KING (5766 "My Girl")..............................30-40 63

DELL, Wailin' Bill
Singles: 7-inch
OJ (1003 "You Gotta Be Loose")..........100-200 57

DEL-LARKS
Singles: 7-inch
EAST WEST (116 "Remember the Night")..40-50 58
(White label. Promotional issue only.)
EAST WEST (116 "Remember the Night")..30-40 58
(Green label.)
PARK AVENUE (08 "Remember the Night")..4-6 92
(Dark maroon vinyl. 500 made.)

DEL-LARKS
Singles: 7-inch
QUEEN CITY (2004 "Job Opening") 1500-2000

DELL-COEDS
Singles: 7-inch
DOT (16314 "Love in Return")...................5-10 62
ENITH INT'L (712 "Love in Return").........10-15 62
(First issue.)

DELL KINGS
Singles: 7-inch
RENCO (3002 "Just Remember")............10-15 62

DELLORDS
Singles: 7-inch
MIDAS (09 "In Togetherness")..................50-75 62

DEL-LOURDS & SHADES
Singles: 7-inch
SOLAR (1001 "Alone")..............................15-25 63
SOLAR (1003 "Gloria")..............................15-25 63

DELL-RAYS
Singles: 7-inch
BOPTOWN (102 "Pauline").......................25-35 '70s

DELL RAYS
(With Joe Panama & Orchestra)
Singles: 7-inch
LAVETTE (1007 "The Way You Look Tonight")..50-100 65

DELL RAYS & SPADES
Singles: 7-inch
DICE (479 "DiDi")....................................50-100 58

DELL REYES
Singles: 7-inch
CAVALIER (888 "Birth of an Angel")........40-50 61
(Red vinyl.)

DELLS *R&B '56*
Singles: 78 rpm
VEE-JAY (166 "Dreams of Contentment")...50-75 55
VEE-JAY (204 thru 292)........................40-60 56-57
Singles: 12-inch
ABC...4-6 79
Singles: 7-inch
ABC...4-6 73-78
ARGO (5415 "God Bless the Child")........10-15 62
(Black label.)
ARGO (5415 "God Bless the Child").........5-10 62
(Tan label.)
ARGO (5428 "Eternally")............................5-10 62
ARGO (5442 "If It Ain't One Thing It's Another")...5-10 63
ARGO (5456 "After You").........................10-15 63
CADET...4-8 66-74
CHESS...4-6 73
COLLECTABLES...3-5 '80s
MCA...3-5 79
MERCURY...4-6 75-77
OLDIES 45..4-8 '60s
PRIVATE I...3-5 84
SKYLARK...4-6 79
20TH FOX..3-5 80-82
VEE-JAY (166 "Dreams of Contentment").......................................100-150 55
Note: Vee-Jay 134, *Tell the World*, is listed in the following section for DELLS / Count Morris.
VEE-JAY (204 "Oh, What a Nite")...........50-75 56
VEE-JAY (230 "Movin' On")......................30-40 56
VEE-JAY (236 "Why Do You Have to Go")...30-40 57
VEE-JAY (251 "Distant Love")..................30-40 57
VEE-JAY (258 "Pain in My Heart")...........30-40 57
VEE-JAY (274 "The Springer")..................20-30 58
VEE-JAY (292 "I'm Calling")......................20-30 58
VEE-JAY (300 "Wedding Day")..................50-75 58
VEE-JAY (324 "Dry Your Eyes")...............20-40 58
VEE-JAY (338 thru 712)...........................10-20 59-65
W.B. (8606 "Love Island")..........................4-6 78
LPs: 10/12-inch
ABC...8-10 78
BUDDAH..10-15 69
CADET...10-20 68-75
LOST NITE (21 "The Dells").....................10-20 81
(10-inch LP. Red vinyl. 1000 made.)
MERCURY..10-15 75-77
PRIVATE I...5-10 84
TRIP...10-12 73
20TH FOX..5-10 80-81
UPFRONT...10-15 68
VEE-JAY (1010 "Oh What a Nite").......400-500 59
(Maroon label, with thin circular ring.)
VEE-JAY (1010 "Oh What a Nite").......300-400 59
(Maroon label, with thick circular ring.)
VEE-JAY (1010 "Oh What a Nite").......100-200 61
(Black label. Monaural.)
VEE-JAY (1010 "Oh What a Nite").......100-200 61
(Black label. Stereo.)
VEE-JAY (1141 "It's Not Unusual")......100-200 65
Members: Johnny Funches; Mike McGill; Marvin Junior; Vern Allison; Johnny Carter.
Also see BUTLER, Jerry, & Betty Everett
Also see CLARK, Dee
Also see EL RAYS
Also see GINO
Also see GREENE, Barbara
Also see LEWIS, Barbara
Also see SOUTH, Joe / Dells

DELLS / Count Morris
Singles: 78 rpm
VEE-JAY (134 "Tell the World")............100-200 55
Singles: 7-inch
VEE-JAY (134 "Tell the World")............400-500 55
(Black vinyl.)
VEE-JAY (134 "Tell the World")........3000-5000 55
(Red vinyl.)
Also see DELLS

DELLTONES
(Dell-Tones; with Kelly Owens Orchestra)
Singles: 78 rpm
BATON...10-20 55-56
BRUNSWICK...50-75 53
RAINBOW...50-75 54
Singles: 7-inch
BATON (212 "Don't Be Long")..................20-30 55
BATON (223 "My Special Love")..............15-25 56
BRUNSWICK (84015 "My Heart's on Fire")..75-125 53
MAESTRO (1919 "No Darling, No").........15-25
RAINBOW (244 "I'm Not in Love with You")..75-125 54

DELLWOODS
Singles: 7-inch
BIG TOP (3137 "Don't Put Onions on Your Hamburger")...10-20 63
EPs: 7-inch
MAD ("She Got a Nose Job")...................40-50 62
(Cardboard cutout picture disc, attached to *The Worst of Mad* magazine. Pictures Alfred E. Neuman. No selection number used.)

DELLWOODS / Mike Russo / Jeanne Hayes
LPs: 10/12-inch
BIG TOP (1305 "Mad Twists Rock 'N' Roll")..50-75 63
Also see DELLWOODS
Also see RUSSO, Mike

DELMAR
Singles: 7-inch
FURY (1038 "Lizzie Mae").......................20-30 60

DELMAR, Eddie
Singles: 7-inch
MADISON (168 "Love Bells")..................50-100 61
VEGAS (628 "Garden in the Rain")..........30-40 65
Session: Bob Knight Four.
Also see KNIGHT, Bob, Four

DELMAR & SYDNEY
Singles: 7-inch
ANCHOR (140 "You Are My Queen")......10-15 57

DEL-MARS
Singles: 7-inch
ABC-PAR (10426 "That's My Desire")......10-20 63
MERCURY (72244 "Snacky Poo")............8-12 64

DEL-MINGOS
Singles: 7-inch
LOMAR (702 "Goodnite My Love")...........10-20 63

DELMIRAS
Singles: 7-inch
DADE (1821 "Dry Your Eyes")...........750-1000 61
Session: Steve Alaimo.
Also see ALAIMO, Steve

DELMIRAS / Sof-Tones
Singles: 7-inch
STOOP SOUNDS (500 "Dry Your Eyes")..100-150 96
(Limited edition. Estimates range from less than 10 to a few dozen made.)
Also see DELMIRAS

DEL MONACOS
(With Jay Brower & Orchestra)
Singles: 78 rpm
DOUBLE AA (111 "Teardrops")...............10-20 55
HOLIDAY (152 "Since We Met")..............10-15 '50s
Singles: 7-inch
DOUBLE AA (111 "Teardrops")...............25-35 55
HOLIDAY (152 "Since We Met")..............15-25 '50s

DELMONICOS
Singles: 7-inch
AKU (6318 "There They Go")..................30-50 63
MUSICTONE (6122 "Until You")..............15-25 64
Also see GERMAINE, Denise

DELMORE, Alton
Singles: 7-inch
LINCO (1315 "Good Times in Memphis")...100-150 59

DELMORE BROTHERS *C&W '46*
(Delmores)
Singles: 78 rpm
BLUEBIRD..20-40 35-41
COLUMBIA (15724 "Alabama Lullaby")...25-50 '30s
DECCA...10-20 40-48

KING....................5-15 43-57
Singles: 7-inch
KING (769 thru 5407)....................10-25 51-60
(Black vinyl.)
KING (1023 "I'll Be There")....................30-50 51
(Colored vinyl.)
EPs: 7-inch
KING....................10-20
LPs: 10/12-inch
COUNTY....................5-10
KING (589 thru 785)....................30-60 58-62
KING (910 thru 1090)....................10-30 64-70
OLD HOMESTEAD....................5-8
STARDAY....................5-10
Members: Alton Delmore; Rabon Delmore.

DE-LOS
Singles: 7-inch
CEDAR (302 "Lullabye Serenade")....................40-50 62
Session: Joe Cook.
Also see COOK, Little Joe

DEL-PHIS
Singles: 7-inch
CHECK MATE (1005 "It Takes Two")....................50-150 61
Members: Gloria Williamson; Martha Reeves; Annette Beard; Rosalind Ashford.
Also see DEL-FIS
Also see HANKS, Mike
Also see MARTHA & VANDELLAS
Also see VELLS

DELPHS, Jimmy *P&R/R&B '68*
Singles: 7-inch
CARLA (1904 "Dancing a Hole in the World")....................100-200 68
CARLA (2535 "Almost")....................10-20 67
KAREN (1538 "Don't Sign the Paper Baby")....................5-10 68

DEL-PRADOS
Singles: 7-inch
LUCKY FOUR (1021 "Oh, Baby")....................50-60 62

DEL PRIS
("By Baby Washington")
Singles: 7-inch
VARBEE (2003 "The Time")....................200-300 61
Members: Harold Shields; Bill Cyrus; Wilson Rue; Jack Derbish; Dan Carr.
Also see WASHINGTON, Baby

DELRAYES
(With Rockin' Roland)
Singles: 7-inch
CENTRAL (4S-27 "In This Whole Wide World")....................150-200 61

DELRAYS
Singles: 7-inch
BOPTOWN (102 "Darling I Pray")....................30-50 58
JASON SCOTT (08 "Lorraine")....................4-6 81
(500 made.)

DEL RAYS
Singles: 7-inch
FUTURE (2203 "When We're Alone")....................40-50 58

DELRAYS
(Del Rays)
Singles: 7-inch
CORD (1001 "Our Love Is True")....................2000-3000 58
MOON (110 "Have a Heart")....................150-250 59
W.B. (5022 "My Darling")....................50-75 58

DEL-RAYS
Singles: 7-inch
PLANET (52 "Lorraine")....................400-500 64

DEL-RAYS
Singles: 7-inch
TAMMY (1020 "Run-Around-Lou")....................40-60 61

DEL-RAYS
Singles: 7-inch
SWINGLINE (1800 "Freeze")....................10-20 62

DEL RAYS
Singles: 7-inch
TEISLO/DEL RAY (6142 "Wipe Out")....................20-30 63

DEL-RAYS
Singles: 7-inch
ATCO (6348 "Fortune Teller")....................5-10 65
STAX (162 "I Want to Do It")....................10-15 65

DEL RAYS
Singles: 7-inch
R&H (1002 "Night Prowl")....................10-20 65

DEL RAYS
Singles: 7-inch
CUCA (68121 "I Feel a Whole Lot Better")....................10-20 68

DELREE & ENCORES
Singles: 7-inch
WGW (3002 "Gerry Gerry")....................50-75

DEL-REYS
Singles: 7-inch
DELRECO (500 Should I Ever Love Again")....................20-30 60

DEL-RHYTHMETTES
Singles: 7-inch
JVB (5000 "I Need Your Love")....................40-50 59

DEL-RICOS
Singles: 7-inch
620 (1008 "Beatle Crawl")....................10-20 64
GAITY ("Buggin' The Boogie")....................40-60 '60s
(Selection number not known.)

DEL RIOS
(With the Bearcats)
Singles: 78 rpm
METEOR (5038 "Lizzie")....................100-150 56
Singles: 7-inch
METEOR (5038 "Lizzie")....................450-650 56

DEL RIOS
(Del Rio's)
Singles: 7-inch
BET..T (7001 "Heavenly Angel")....................1500-2000 62
BIG H (613 "The Vines of Love")....................750-1000 57
RUST (5066 "Valerie")....................15-25 63

DEL-RIOS
Singles: 7-inch
NEPTUNE (108 "I'm Crying")....................15-25 59
STAX (125 "There's a Love")....................25-35 62
Members: William Bell; David Brown; Melvin Jones; Harrison Austin.
Also see OVATIONS

DEL-RONS
Singles: 7-inch
LAURIE (3252 "Your Big Mistake")....................10-20 64
Members: Mary Aiese; Sheila Reillie; Carol Drobnicki.
Also see REPARATA

DELRONS
Singles: 7-inch
FORUM (700 "This Love of Ours")....................600-800 61

DEL ROYALS
Singles: 7-inch
MINIT (610 "She's Gone")....................10-20 60
MINIT (620 "Close to You")....................10-15 61
MINIT (637 "I Fell in Love with You")....................10-15 61
Also see TEMPLET, Doyle

DEL ROYS
Singles: 7-inch
CAROL (4113 "Love Me Tenderly")....................20-30 61
(Rigid disc.)
CAROL (4113 "Love Me Tenderly")....................10-15 61
(Flexible disc.)
Members: Ronald Coleman; Ray Pain; Norman Baquie; Cliff Davis.
Also see DELROYS

DELROYS
(Milton Sparks with the Delroys; with Larry Greenwich & Orchestra; Delroy's)
Singles: 78 rpm
APOLLO (514 "Bermuda Shorts")....................15-25 57
Singles: 7-inch
APOLLO (514 "Bermuda Shorts")....................10-20 57
SPARKELL (102 "Wise Old Owl")....................400-500 59
Members: Reggie Walker; John Blunt; Ronald Coleman; Bobby Taylor; Junior Talbot; Robert Coleman.
Also see DEL ROYS
Also see SPARKS, Milton

DEL SATINS
(Del-Satins; Dell Satins)
Singles: 7-inch
B.T. PUPPY (506 "My Candy Apple Vette")....................5-10 65
B.T. PUPPY (509 "A Girl Named Arlene")....................10-15 65
B.T. PUPPY (509 "A Girl Named Arlene")....................15-20 65
(White label. Promotional issue only.)
B.T. PUPPY (514 "Relief")....................5-10 65
B.T. PUPPY (514 "Relief")....................10-15 65
(White label. Promotional issue only.)
COLLECTABLES....................3-5 '80s
COLUMBIA (42802 "Who Cares")....................15-25 63
DIAMOND (216 "Love, Hate, Revenge")....................10-15 67
(Black vinyl.)
DIAMOND (216 "Love, Hate, Revenge")....................15-25 67
(Brown vinyl when held to light.)
END (1096 "I'll Pray for You")....................250-300 61
GENIE (31865 "I'll Never Know")....................4-6 95
(Red vinyl. 500 made.)
LAURIE (3132 "Teardrops Follow Me")....................10-15 62
LAURIE (3149 "Does My Love Stand a Chance")....................10-15 62
MALA (475 "Two Broken Hearts")....................30-40 64
PARK AVENUE (11 "I'll Never Know")....................4-6 95
(Red vinyl. 500 made.)
WIN (702 "Counting Tear Drops")....................100-150 61
(Black label. Reads "Record No. 702," but also shows "102.")
WIN (702 "Counting Tear Drops")....................30-40 61
(Orange label. Also shows "102" on label.)
Picture Sleeves
COLUMBIA (42802 "Who Cares")....................30-40 63
(Pictures Dion, producer of this release, and has a note from him to dee jays. Promotional issue only.)
LPs: 10/12-inch
B.T. PUPPY (1019 "Out to Lunch")....................100-150 72
Members: Stan Sommers; Rich Green; Fred Ferrara; Tom Ferrara; Les Cauchi.
Also see BAKER, Bill
Also see BROOKLYN BRIDGE
Also see BRUNO, Bruce
Also see CAMPANIONS
Also see COMO, Nicky
Also see DION
Also see LAURIE, Linda
Also see MAESTRO, Johnny
Also see MARESCA, Ernie
Also see SUNDOWNERS
Also see VINCENT, Stan, & Del Satins

DEL SHAYS
Singles: 7-inch
CHARGER (102 "I'll Love You Forever")....................200-300 64
CHARGER (102 "[Love You] Forever")....................250-350 64
(Note slight variation of title.)

DEL-STARS
Singles: 7-inch
MELLOMOOD (1001 "For Your Love")....................10-15 64
MELLOMOOD (1004 "Why Do You Have to Go")....................15-20 64
RELIC (1014 "Why Do You Have to Go")....................5-10 65

DELTA JOE
(Albert Luandrew)
Singles: 78 rpm
CHANCE (1115 "4 O'Clock Blues")....................40-50 52
OPERA (5 "Roll, Tumble & Slip")....................50-60 53
Singles: 7-inch
CHANCE (1115 "4 O'Clock Blues")....................50-60 52
Also see SUNNYLAND SLIM

DELTA JOHN
(John Lee Hooker)
Singles: 78 rpm
REGENT (1001 "Helpless Blues")....................40-60 49
Also see HOOKER, John Lee

DELTA RHYTHM BOYS *P&R/R&B '46*
Singles: 78 rpm
ATLANTIC (889 "The Laugh's On Me")....................50-75 49
ATLANTIC (900 "Nobody Knows")....................40-60 50
DECCA....................20-30 42-55
MUSICRAFT....................15-25 49
RCA....................15-25 47-48
Singles: 7-inch
DECCA (29000 series)....................20-30 54-55
DECCA (48140 "You Are Closer to My Heart")....................50-75 50
DECCA (48148 "It's All in Your Mind")....................50-75 50
GENERAL (3270 "Here's to Your Wedding")....................15-25 63
GENERAL (3272 "You Will Wear My Ring")....................15-25 63
LONDON (1145 "Blow Out the Candle")....................15-25 52
MERCURY (1407 "I've Got You Under My Skin")....................30-40 52
MERCURY (1408 "They Didn't Believe Me")....................30-40 52
MERCURY (1409 "All the Things You Are")....................30-40 52
RCA (WP-193 "Dry Bones")....................75-100 50
(Boxed, three-disc set. Disc numbers are 47-2826, 47-2827 and 47-2828.)
RCA (5094 "I'll Never Get Out of This World Alive")....................20-25 53
RCA (5217 "Long Gone Baby")....................20-25 53
SIGNATURE (12045 "My Sunday Baby")....................10-15 '60s
EPs: 7-inch
RCA (3085 "Dry Bones")....................75-100 50
(Double EP.)
LPs: 10/12-inch
CAMDEN (313 "Delta Rhythm Boys")....................40-50 56
CORAL (57358 "Swingin' Spirituals")....................20-30 60
(Monaural.)
CORAL (757358 "Swingin' Spirituals")....................25-40 60
(Stereo.)
ELEKTRA (138 "Delta Rhythm Boys")....................25-35 57
JUBILEE (1022 "Delta Rhythm Boys in Sweden")....................25-50 57
(Black vinyl.)
JUBILEE (1022 "Delta Rhythm Boys in Sweden")....................75-100 57
(Colored vinyl.)
MERCURY (25153 "Delta Rhythm Boys")....................75-100 53
(10-inch LP.)
RCA (3085 "Dry Bones")....................100-150 50
(10-inch LP.)
Members: Traverse Crawford; Karl Jones; Kell Pharr; Lee Gaines.
Also see BAILEY, Mildred, & Delta Rhythm Boys
Also see BROWN, Ruth, & Delta Rhythm Boys
Also see FITZGERALD, Ella, & Delta Rhythm Boys
Also see FOUR SHARPS

DELTAIRS
Singles: 7-inch
IVY (101 "Lullaby of the Bells")....................75-150 57
(Yellow label.)
IVY (101 "Lullaby of the Bells")....................15-25 58
IVY (105 "Standing at the Altar")....................40-50 58
IVY ("Lullaby of the Bells")....................5-10 64
(No selection number used.)
RAY-BORN (132 "Whoever You Are")....................10-15
VINTAGE (1005 "Whoever You Are")....................10-15 73
(Orange vinyl.)
Also see MALDONEERS

DELTAIRS
Singles: 7-inch
FELSTED (8525 "Who Would Have Thought It")....................10-20 59

DELTAS
Singles: 7-inch
GONE (5010 "Let Me Share Your Dream")....................2000-3000 57
(Black label.)
GONE (5010 "Let Me Share Your Dream")....................100-150 61
(Multi-color label.)
SOLD (504 "Let Me Share Your Dream")....................4-6 73
Also see PREMIERS

DELTAS
Singles: 7-inch
CAMBRIDGE (124 "Goodnight My Love")....................15-20 62
PHILIPS (40023 "My Own True Love")....................10-15 62

DELTAS
Singles: 7-inch
CENTURY (1028 "In the Shade")....................8-12 '60s
EMP (10001 "She's My Girl")....................15-25

DELTEENS
(With the Orbits and Devora Brown Orchestra)
Singles: 7-inch
FORTUNE (541 "Listen to the Rain")....................150-200 61
(Purple label.)
FORTUNE (541 "Listen to the Rain")....................15-25
(Blue label.)

DEL-TINOS
Singles: 7-inch
DEL-TINO (100 "Go! Go! Go!") 20-30 63
DEL-TINO (200 "Ramblin' On My Mind"). 10-20 66
NORTON (074 "Go! Go! Go!") 3-5 98
SONIC (1451 "Night Life") 15-25 65
Members: Cub Koda; Doug Hankes; Rusty Creech.

DEL TONES
Singles: 78 rpm
BRUNSWICK (85015 "Your's Alone")...... 15-25 48

DEL TONES
(The Beau-Marks)
Singles: 7-inch
QUALITY (1881 "Moonlight Party"/"Rockin' Blues").. 75-125 58
(Canadian. Both sides later issued as by the Beau-Marks.)
Also see BEAU-MARKS

DELTONES
Singles: 7-inch
VEE-JAY (288 "I'm Coming Home") 20-30 58
VEE-JAY (303 "A Lovers Prayer") 50-75 58

DEL-TONES
Singles: 7-inch
RO-ANN (1001 "Best Wishes") 500-750 59

DEL-TONES
Singles: 7-inch
JUBILEE (5374 "Bow-Legged Annie") 40-60 59
PEACH (714 "Could I") 50-75 59

DELTONES
(With the Tony Bruno Orchestra)
Singles: 7-inch
DAYHILL (1002 "Since I Met You") 50-75 61
Also see CLOVERS / Deltones

DEL TONES
(With Sal & Side Man)
Singles: 7-inch
USA (711 "Please Talk to Me") 400-500 61

DEL-TONES
Singles: 7-inch
STORM (982 "Taboo") 10-15 61

DEL-TONES
Singles: 7-inch
COUNT (1000 "You're the One") .... 20-30 '60s

DE LUGG, Milton
(Milton De Lugg & His Orchestra)
Singles: 7-inch
DOT (15898 "Ain't She Sweet") 4-8 59
DOT (15933 "Swingin' Gypsys") 4-8 59
EPIC (9728 "Munster's Theme") 4-8 64
4 CORNERS (114 "Hooray for Santa Claus") 4-8 64
MAINSTREAM (649 "Space Walk") 4-6 66
MAINSTREAM (654 "Think Tall") 4-6 66
RCA (9052 "Spy with a Cold Nose") 4-6 66
RCA (9172 "Penny Lane") 4-6 67
ROULETTE (4368 "Untouchables") 4-8 61
SIGNATURE (12006 "Ain't She Sweet") 4-8 59
SIGNATURE (12028 "Dog of Flanders") 4-8 60
20TH FOX (489 "Walking Down Church Street") 4-8 64
20TH FOX (6611 "Barnaby Jones") 4-8 64
Picture Sleeves
EPIC (9728 "Munster's Theme") 5-10 64
LPs: 10/12-inch
DOT (3145 "Louella's Favorites") 8-12 59
EPIC (24125 "Music for Monsters, Munsters, Mummies, and Other TV Fiends") 40-60 64
(Monaural.)
EPIC (26125 "Music for Monsters, Munsters, Mummies, and Other TV Fiends") 75-85 64
(Stereo.)
METRO (544 "Man from U.N.C.L.E.") 10-15 65
MUSICOR (2010 "51 Greatest Broadway Favorites") 8-12 64
(Monaural. Two discs.)
MUSICOR (3010 "51 Greatest Broadway Favorites") 10-15 64
(Stereo. Two discs.)
RCA 8-12 66-67
Also see McNAIR, Barbara

DELVETTS
Singles: 7-inch
END (1106 "I Want a Boy for Christmas"/ "Repeat After Me") 20-30 62
END (1107 "Will You Love Me in Heaven"/ "Repeat After Me") 15-25 62

DEL-VETTS
Singles: 7-inch
DUNWICH (125 "Last Time Around") 10-20 66
DUNWICH (142 "I Call My Baby STP") 10-20 66
SEEBURG (3018 "Ram Charger") 20-35 65
(Monaural.)
SEEBURG (3018 "Ram Charger") 25-40 65
(Stereo.)
Picture Sleeves
DUNWICH (142 "I Call My Baby STP") 20-30 66
(Includes bonus decal.)
Members: Jim Lauer; Bob Good; Paul Wade; Les Goldboss.

DEL-VIKINGS ***P&R/R&B '57***
(Featuring Krips Johnson; with Joey Biscoe; Original Dell Vikings; Del Vikings; Dell-Vikings)
Singles: 78 rpm
DOT 40-60 57
FEE BEE 25-50 56-57
MERCURY 30-40 57
Singles: 7-inch
ABC 4-6 75
ABC-PAR (10208 "I'll Never Stop Crying") 10-20 61
ABC-PAR (10248 "I Hear Bells") 40-50 61
ABC-PAR (10278 "Kiss Me") 10-20 62
ABC-PAR (10304 "One More River to Cross") 10-20 62
ABC-PAR (10341 "Confession of Love") ..10-20 62
ABC-PAR (10385 "An Angel Up in Heaven") 50-75 63
(Vinyl pressing.)
ABC-PAR (10385 "An Angel Up in Heaven") 40-50 63
(Polystyrene pressing.)
ABC-PAR (10425 "Too Many Miles") 8-12 63
ALPINE (66 "The Sun") 50-100 60
BVM 3-5 91
BIM BAM BOOM (111 "Cold Feet") 4-6 72
(Black vinyl.)
BIM BAM BOOM (111 "Cold Feet") 5-8 72
(Red vinyl.)
BIM BAM BOOM (113 "Watching the Moon") 4-8 73
BIM BAM BOOM (115 "I'm Spinning") 4-8 73
BLUE SKY (104 "Over the Rainbow") 4-6 73
BROADCAST 3-5
COLLECTABLES 3-5 80
CRUISIN' 3-5
DRC (101 "Can't You See") ....10-20 '60s
DOT (15538 "Come Go with Me") 20-30 57
DOT (15571 "What Made Maggie Run") ..20-30 57
DOT (15592 "Whispering Bells") 20-30 57
DOT (15636 "I'm Spinning") 15-20 57
DOT (16092 "Come Go with Me") 8-12 60
DOT (16236 "Come Go with Me") 8-12 61
FEE BEE (173 "Welfare Blues") 5-8 77
FEE BEE (205 "Come Go with Me") 250-300 56
(Has "45 RPM" on each side at top of label. With two sets of thin, horizontal, double parallel lines.)
FEE BEE (205 "Come Go with Me") 15-25 61
(Does not have "45 RPM." With one set of lines, one thick, one thin.)
FEE BEE (206 "Down in Bermuda") 15-25 61
FEE BEE (210 "What Made Maggie Run"/"Down by the Stream") 40-60 58
FEE BEE (210 "What Made Maggie Run"/"Uh Uh Baby") 50-75 58
FEE BEE (210 "What Made Maggie Run"/"When I Come Home") 75-125 58
FEE BEE (214 "Whispering Bells") 100-150 58
FEE BEE (218 "I'm Spinning") 50-75 58
(First issued, on 218-A, as by the "Del Viking Kripp Johnson." See his section for that listing.)
FEE BEE (221 "Willette") 50-75 59
(First issued as by the "Dell Viking Kripp Johnson and Charles Jackson." See their section for that listing.)
FEE BEE (227 "Tell Me") 20-30 59
FEE BEE (902 "True Love") 20-30 61
GATEWAY (743 "We Three") 15-25 64
GOLDIES 45 ....3-6 73
JOJO 4-6 76
LIGHTNING (9013 "Come Go with Me") 3-5
LUNIVERSE (106 "Somewhere Over the Rainbow") 40-60 57
LUNIVERSE (110 "Heaven and Paradise") . 4-8 73
LUNIVERSE (113 "White Cliffs of Dover") ... 4-8 73
LUNIVERSE (114 "There I Go") 4-8 73
MCA ....4-6 '70s
MERCURY (30112 "Come Along with Me") 15-25 63
MERCURY (71132 "Cool Shake") 10-15 57
MERCURY (71180 "Come Along with Me") 10-15 57
MERCURY (71198 "I'm Spinning") 15-20 57
MERCURY (71241 "Your Book of Life") ...10-15 57
MERCURY (71266 "Voodoo Man") 15-20 58
MERCURY (71345 "You Cheated") 15-20 58
(Blue label.)
MERCURY (71345 "You Cheated") 10-15 58
(Black label.)
MERCURY (71390 "How Could You") 15-20 58
SCEPTER (12367 "Come Go with Me") 4-6 73
SHIP (214 "Over the Rainbow") 4-6
SPARTON/ABC-PAR (1104 "Confession of Love") 15-25 62
(Canadian.)
Picture Sleeves
ALPINE (66 "The Sun") 75-125 60
EPs: 7-inch
DEL (5191 "Del-Vikings") 3-5
DOT (1058 "Come Go with Us") 200-300 57
MERCURY (3359 "They Sing, They Swing") 50-100 57
MERCURY (3362 "They Sing, They Swing") 75-100 57
MERCURY (3363 "They Sing, They Swing") 75-100 57
LPs: 10/12-inch
BVM 5-10 91
COLLECTABLES (Except picture discs) 5-10 80-83
COLLECTABLES 10-15 82
(Picture disc.)
DOT (3695 "Come Go with Me") 200-400 66
JANGO (778 "Greatest Hits") 15-20
LUNIVERSE (1000 "Come Go with the Del Vikings") 500-750 57
MERCURY (20314 "They Sing, They Swing") 100-200 57
MERCURY (20353 "Del Vikings' Record Session") 100-200 58
Members: Kripp Johnson; Norman Wright; Don Jackson; Clarence Quick; Gus Backus; David Lerchey; Joey Briscoe; Bill Blakely; Ritzi Lee; Billy Woodruff.
Also see BACKUS, Gus
Also see BRISCOE, Joey
Also see JOHNSON, Kripp
Also see JOHNSON, Kripp, and Chuck Jackson
Also see KING, Ben E.

DEL-VIKINGS / Diamonds / Big Bopper / Gaylords
Singles: 7-inch
MERCURY (53 "60 Second Spots") 20-40 58
(Promotional issue only.)
Also see BIG BOPPER
Also see DIAMONDS
Also see GAYLORDS

DEL-VIKINGS / Sonnets
LPs: 10/12-inch
CROWN (5368 "The Del-Vikings and the Sonnets") 20-30 63
(Tracks shown by the Sonnets are actually by either the Meadowlarks or the Sounds.)
Also see DEL-VIKINGS
Also see JULIAN, Don, & Meadowlarks
Also see SONNETS
Also see SOUNDS

DEL-VONS
Singles: 7-inch
WELLS (1001 "Gone Forever") 10-15 66

DELVONS
Singles: 7-inch
J.D.F. (760 "Stay Clear of Love") 5-10 67
(Black vinyl.)
J.D.F. (760 "Stay Clear of Love") 10-15 67
(Gold or blue vinyl.)

DEL VICTORS
Singles: 7-inch
HI-Q (5028 "Oh Lover"/"Acting Up") 40-50 63
HI-Q (5028 "Oh Lover"/"Baby Sitter I Love You") ....15-25 '60s

DEL VUES
("Featuring W. Voss")
Singles: 7-inch
U TOWN (8008 "My Confession") 1000-1500 61

DELVY, Richard
Singles: 7-inch
TRIUMPH (55 "Atlantis") 10-20 63
Also see BELAIRS
Also see CHALLENGERS

DE LYON, Leo
(With the Musclemen)
Singles: 7-inch
MUSICOR (1001 "Sick Manny's Gym") 10-20 60
LPs: 10/12-inch
LONDON (5551 "Leo's Here") 15-25 60

DEMANDS
Singles: 7-inch
CLIM ("Say It Again") 15-25 62
(Selection number not known.)

DEMAR, Jerry
Singles: 7-inch
FORD (1003 "Cross-eyed Alley Cat") .. 175-225

DE MARCO, Arlene
(With Ray Ellis Orchestra & Chorus)
Singles: 78 rpm
CAMEO 10-20 57
Singles: 7-inch
CAMEO (100 "Old Enough to Know") 15-25 57
EMBER (1044 "Don't Love Me") 10-15 58
Also see DE MARCO SISTERS
Also see ELLIS, Ray, Orchestra

DE MARCO, Billy
(With the Renditions)
Singles: 7-inch
KEEFO 15-20
UP (113 "Goodby Mister Blues") 50-75 60

DE MARCO, Gloria
Singles: 7-inch
ARROW (731 "I Forgive") 15-25 58

DEMARCO, Lou
("With Vocal Quartet & Orchestra [Rock & Roll]")
Singles: 78 rpm
FERRIS (903 "Careless Love") 8-12 56
Singles: 7-inch
FERRIS (903 "Careless Love") 10-20 56

DE MARCO, Phil, & Valiants
Singles: 7-inch
DEBBY (065 "Lonely Guy") 300-400 64

DE MARCO, Ralph ***P&R '59***
(With Billy Mure & Orchestra)
Singles: 7-inch
GUARANTEED (202 "Old Shep") 10-15 59
SHELLEY (1011 "Donna") 40-60 60
20TH FOX (309 "Lonely for a Girl") 5-10 62
Picture Sleeves
GUARANTEED (202 "Old Shep") 20-30 59
Also see MURE, Billy
Also see PARAMOUNTS

DE MARCO SISTERS
(Five DeMarco Sisters)
Singles: 78 rpm
DECCA 5-10 54-56
MGM 5-10 54
Singles: 7-inch
DECCA 10-15 54-56
MGM 10-15 54
Members: Gloria; Jean; Arlene; Terri; Ann.
Also see DE MARCO, Arlene

DE MARINO, Ronnie, & Rockin' Kings
Singles: 7-inch
JUBILEE (5377 "Ding Dong Daddy Wants to Rock") 40-55 59

DE MATTEO, Nicky ***P&R '60***
(With the Sorrows)
Singles: 7-inch
ABC-PAR (10186 "Right Now") 5-10 61
ACE (110 "Please Don't Go Away") 20-30 57
CAMEO (407 "I Want to Be Lonely") 5-10 66
DIAMOND (138 "Baby That's All") 5-15 63
END (1021 "School House Rock") 30-40 58
GUYDEN (2024 "Suddenly") 10-20 59

GUYDEN (2042 "As Big As My Love") 5-10 60
KELSO (101 "I Have But One Heart")........5-10 61
PARIS (529 "Story of Love")........................8-12 59
TORE (1007 "Make Her Mine")..................8-12 59

DEMENS

Singles: 7-inch

TEENAGE (1006 "Take Me As I Am") . 250-350 58
TEENAGE (1007 "I'm Not in Love with You") 200-250 58
TEENAGE (1008 "The Greatest of Them All")........................... 400-500 58
(Company address shown as on Eighth Avenue.)
TEENAGE (1008 "The Greatest of Them All")........................... 650-750 58
(Company address shown as on 127th Street.)
Members: Eddie Jones; Tom Cook; Frank Cook; Joe Caines.
Also see EMERSONS

DEMENSIONS P&R '60
(Dimensions; Lenny Dell & Demensions; with Irv Spice & Orchestra)

Singles: 7-inch

COLLECTABLES..................................3-5 '80s
CORAL (62277 thru 65559, except 62344)........................ 10-20 61-62
CORAL (62344 "My Foolish Heart")......... 20-30 63
CORAL (65611 "As Time Goes By")...........5-10 67
MOHAWK (116 "Over the Rainbow")....... 30-40 60
(Maroon label.)
MOHAWK (116 "Over the Rainbow")....... 15-25 60
(Brown label.)
MOHAWK (116 "Over the Rainbow")....... 10-20 61
(Red label.)
MOHAWK (120 "Zing Went the Strings of My Heart")........................ 20-30 60
MOHAWK (121 "God's Christmas")......... 40-50 61
MOHAWK (123 "A Tear Fell")............. 40-50 61
MOHAWK (123 "A Tear Fell")...................4-6 95
(Black vinyl. 500 made.)
OLD HIT 3-5

Picture Sleeves

CORAL (62344 "My Foolish Heart")......... 50-75 63

LPs: 10/12-inch

CORAL (57430 "My Foolish Heart")..... 100-150 63
(Monaural.)
CORAL (7-57430 "My Foolish Heart") . 150-200 63
(Stereo.)
CRYSTAL BALL (108 "The Demensions Featuring Lenny Dell") 10-15 82
(Black vinyl. 1000 made.)
CRYSTAL BALL (108 "The Demensions Featuring Lenny Dell") 25-35 82
(Colored vinyl. 25 made.)
CRYSTAL BALL (108 "The Demensions Featuring Lenny Dell") 55-65 82
(Picture disc. No cover. 25 made.)
MCA...5-10
Members: Lenny Dell; Phil Del Giudice; Howard Margolin; Marisa Martelli.

DEMERITTE, Kenny, & Swinging Vibrations

Singles: 7-inch

GRAND BAHAMA (3305 "Sitting and Thinking Alone") 100-200

DEMIAN

Singles: 7-inch

ABC (11297 "Face the World")..................5-10 70

LPs: 10/12-inch

ABC (718 "Demian") 25-30 70
Members: Rod Prince; Todd Potter; Roy Cox; Dave Fore.
Also see BUBBLE PUPPY

DEMILLES

Singles: 7-inch

LAURIE (3230 "Donna Lee").............. 30-40 64
(Promotional issue only.)
LAURIE (3230 "Donna Lee").....................5-10 64
LAURIE (3247 "Cry and Be On Your Way")............................... 200-300 64
Also see CAMERONS
Also see CARLO

DE MILO, Cordella

Singles: 78 rpm

MODERN (954 "Lonely Girl") 15-25 55

Singles: 7-inch

MODERN (954 "Lonely Girl").................. 50-75 55

DEMIRES

Singles: 7-inch

LUNAR (519 "Wheels of Love") 25-35 59

DEMOLYRS
(With Hash Brown & His Orchestra)

Singles: 7-inch

JASON SCOTT (07 "Rain")..........................3-5 80
(500 made.)
UWR (900 "Rain")........................... 1000-1500 64
UWR (901 "Shang").......................................4-6 92
(Red vinyl. 500 made.)
Also see DARVELL, Barry

DEMOLYRS / Mystics / Five Discs / Fascinators

EPs: 7-inch

THEY SANG IN BROOKLYN (2 "Demolyrs / Mystics / Five Discs / Fascinators") 8-10 92
(Black vinyl. 500 made.)

DEMONS

Singles: 7-inch

UNART (2002 "Doo Doo Dah")................15-25 58

DEMONS

Singles: 7-inch

GEMCO (1001 "El Lobo").........................10-20 '60s
KEET (1000 "Big D Blues")......................10-20 63
KEET (1001 "Night Train") 10-20 63

DEMONS

Singles: 7-inch

CLOVER (338 "Island of Romance")........20-30 66
Members: Johnny Manasia; Dave Smith.
Also see CHAMPS

DEMONS

Singles: 7-inch

NATIONAL G.R.C. (1321 "Do You Really Care").......................................200-300

DEMOTRONS

Singles: 7-inch

ATLANTIC (2589 "I Want a Home in the Country")..5-8 68
CAMEO (456 "Midnight in New York")..........5-8 67
DORSET 5-10 61
ENRICA..10-20 61
RADAR (2615 thru 2621) 5-10 62
RUST (5025 "Home on the Pad")............10-15 60
SCEPTER (12148 thru 12174)....................5-10 66

DEMPSEY, Little Jimmy

Singles: 7-inch

ABC (10955 thru 11020)............................5-10 67
DOT (16913 "We Gotta Stick Together")....8-12 66
FOX (5 "Bop Hop") 150-200 58
LINK (500 "She Done Moved") 200-300
STARDAY (451 "Honky Tonk World") 25-35 59
TANNER (9310 "Turn Around") 15-25 62
TREND (662 "Be-Bop-a-Lulu")..................10-20 66

LPs: 10/12-inch

ABC (619 "Guitar Country of Little Jimmy Dempsey") 15-20 67

DEMURES

Singles: 7-inch

BRUNSWICK (55284 "Raining Teardrops")...30-40 65

DENBY, Junior

Singles: 78 rpm

KING...20-30 54

Singles: 7-inch

KING (4717 "With This Ring")................40-60 54
KING (4725 "This Fool Has Learned")......40-60 54
Also see SWALLOWS

DENELS

Singles: 7-inch

BAMBOO (517 "Here Come the Ho-Dads")...20-30 62
UNION (502 "Here Come the Ho-Dads") .15-25 62

DENET, Mike
(Mike De Net)

Singles: 7-inch

RAYNARD (1015 "Ghost of Your Love")..10-15 62
STACY (955 "Ghost of Your Love")...........5-10 63

DENHAMS

Singles: 7-inch

NOTE (10009 "I'm So Lonely")..................50-75 57

DENIMS

Singles: 7-inch

CAVORT ("Salty Dog")...........................10-20 63
(No selection number used. Promotional issue, made for Salty Dog Scrub Denim/Canton Textile Mills.)
COLUMBIA (43312 "I'm Your Man")..........8-12 65
COLUMBIA (43367 "Everybody, Let's Dance")...8-12 65
COLUMBIA SPECIAL PRODUCTS (1 "The Adler Sock")...15-25 65
(Special product for the Adler Sock Co.)
MERCURY (72572 "I Do Love You Baby") ..5-8 66
MERCURY (72613 "Salty Dog Man")...........5-8 66

Picture Sleeves

CAVORT ("Salty Dog")............................15-25 63
(No selection number used. Promotional issue, made for Salty Dog Scrub Denim/Canton Textile Mills.)

DENISON, Homer
(Homer Denison Jr.)

Singles: 7-inch

BRUNSWICK (55150 "Chickie Run") 15-20 59
MADISON (104 "Fire Island")...................10-15 58
TIME (1042 "Endless Tide").......................5-10 61

DENNEY, Dave

Singles: 7-inch

RCA (48-0110 "For a Lifetime") 10-20 49
(Green vinyl.)
RCA (48-0151 "I Have My Baby Back") ...10-20 50
(Green vinyl.)

DENNIS, Beverlee
(With the Ben Bennett Orchestra)

Singles: 7-inch

PLAZA (5006 "Keep Talkin' ")..................10-20 57

DENNIS, Bill

Singles: 7-inch

SHRINE (113 "I'll Never Let You Get Away")...300-400 66

DENNIS, Bradford

Singles: 7-inch

CANADIAN (1600 "The Wings of an Angel")...10-20 60

DENNIS, Marv
(Marv Dennis IV)

Singles: 7-inch

BAGDAD (1962 "The Girl with the Lollipop")..15-25 62
BEAR (1975 "Honeycomb").....................10-15 65
COULEE (143 "The Great Drinkin' Bout") ..5-10 72
FILM (1020 "Love Is Something")............10-15 65
SPARTON (1238 "Love Is Something") 10-15 65

LP: 10/12-inch

COULEE (1002 "Caught in the Act") 10-15 72
GARPAX ("Marv Dennis' Greatest Hits – We Hope")...20-30 65
(Selection number not known.)
Members: Marv Dennis Blihovde; Ed Cree; Leo Breidel; Terry Meale.
Also see BLIHOVDE, Marv
Also see MINNESOTA MARV

DENNIS, Marv, & Ed Cree

LP: 10/12-inch

D&C ("The Nashville Sounds of Dennis and Cree")..15-25 62
(Selection number not known.)
Also see DENNIS, Marv
Also see MINNESOTA MARV & ED CREE

DENNIS, Richie

Singles: 7-inch

CAMEO (417 "Dear Judy").........................5-10 66
JULIA (1101 "I Am Alone")......................20-30 60

DENNIS & EXPLORERS

Singles: 7-inch

CORAL (62295 "Remember")..................40-50 61
Also see EXPLORERS

DENNIS & MENACES

Singles: 7-inch

DOT (16143 "Pigeon-Toed")....................10-20 60

DENNIS BROTHERS

Singles: 7-inch

HEP (2145 "Hush, Hush Little Baby")......50-100

DENNY, Galen

Singles: 7-inch

LIBERTY (55164 "Gonna Build a Rocket")...25-35 58

DENNY, Martin P&R/R&B/LP '59
(Exotic Sounds of Martin Denny)

Singles: 7-inch

LIBERTY (55162 thru 55928) 5-10 57-66
LIBERTY (56126 "Midnight Cowboy")..........4-8 69
LIBERTY 5-15 59-60
(Stereo.)

Picture Sleeves

LIBERTY 5-15 59-63

EPs: 7-inch

LIBERTY 5-15 59

LPs: 10/12-inch

FIRST AMERICAN 5-10 81
LIBERTY (3034 thru 3328) 12-25 57-63
(Monaural.)
LIBERTY (3378 thru 3513) 10-20 64-67
(Monaural.)
LIBERTY (7034 thru 7328) 15-30 59-63
(Stereo.)
LIBERTY (7378 thru 3513) 10-20 64-67
(Stereo.)
(Albums with bird calls and animal sounds, and those with covers picturing model Sandy Warner, are at the higher end of the ranges.)
LIBERTY (7550 thru 7621) 8-15 68-69
SUNSET..5-10 66-68
U.A. 5-10 74-80
Also see ZENTNER, Si

DENNY & DEDICATIONS

Singles: 7-inch

SUSAN (1111 "Lost Love").......................10-20 65

DENNY & LP's
(B.B. Butler & Band)

Singles: 7-inch

ROCK-IT (001 "Why Not Give Me Your Heart") 200-300 58

DENNY & LENNY
(With the Hollywood Ghouls)

Singles: 7-inch

CHANCE (569 "Ghoul Love") 50-75 63
RADAR (2613 "Yo Yo Twist")...................20-30 62
RADAR (2619 "Image").............................10-15 62

DE NOIA, Paul

Singles: 7-inch

KENCO (5020 "Dear Abby") 40-50 62

DENOTATIONS

Singles: 7-inch

LAWN (253 "Lone Stranger")................150-200 65

DENSON, Denny

Singles: 7-inch

RAYNA (5003 "Too Long") 10-15 61

DENSON, Lee

Singles: 78 rpm

VIK...15-25 56

Singles: 7-inch

ENTERPRISE (9086 "A Mom and Dad for Christmas")..4-6 73
KENT (306 "High School Hop") 40-60 58
VIK (0251 "Heart of a Fool") 20-40 56
VIK (0281 "New Shoes")...........................40-60 56
Also see COCHRAN, Eddie

DENTON, Johnny

Singles: 7-inch

MEL-O-TONE (1147 "Hey Babe") 450-500 57

DENTON, Mickey
(With the New York Express)

Singles: 7-inch

AMY (902 "Top 10").....................................8-12 64
BIG TOP (3078 "Steady Kind")..................15-25 61
BIG TOP (3094 thru 3142).......................10-20 62-63
IMPACT (1002 "Ain't Love Grand") 15-25 65
IMPACT (1011 "Heartache Is My Name")...15-20 66
WORLD ARTISTS (1043 "One More Time")..8-12 65

LPs: 10/12-inch

CHERIE...8-12 82
Also see CASINOS
Also see PATTI & MICKEY

DENVER, John *LP '69*

Singles: 12-inch

RCA (11189 "Bet on the Blues") 5-10 77
(Promotional issue only.)

Singles: 7-inch

ALLEGIANCE..3-5
CBS..3-5 '90s
CHERRY MOUNTAIN (02 "Flying Or Me")...3-5 86
RCA (Except 0067 thru 0955)......................3-6 74-86
RCA (0067 thru 0955)..............................5-10 70-74

Promotional Singles

EVA-TONE (106026 "Trees for America")....3-5 86
RCA (2008 "Rocky Mountain High") 5-10 72

Picture Sleeves

ALLEGIANCE..3-5
CBS..3-5 '90s
CHERRY MOUNTAIN (02 "Flying Or Me")...3-5 86
RCA (Except 2008)..................................3-6 74-86
RCA (2008 "Rocky Mountain High") 5-10 72
(Promotional issue only.)

LPs: 10/12-inch

HJD (66 "John Denver Sings")............ 200-300 66
(Promotional issue only. Less than 300 copies made as Christmas gifts for friends.)
MOS ("Something to Sing About") 50-100 66
(Promotional issue only. No actual label name is used. Various artists LP with three Denver tracks not available elsewhere.)
MERCURY (704 "Beginnings") 10-15 72
(Pictures John Denver on cover.)
MERCURY (704 "Beginnings") 8-10 74
(With mountain scene photo on cover.)
RCA (0101 thru 3449)...............................5-10 73-80
RCA (0075 "The John Denver Radio Show").. 20-30 74
(Single-sided LP. Promotional issue only.)
RCA (0683 "The Second John Denver Radio Show").. 20-30 74
RCA (4000 series) 10-20 69-72
(Orange labels.)
RCA (4000 & 5000 series)..........................5-10 81-85
(Black labels.)
RCA (5398 "The John Denver Holiday Radio Show").. 10-20 84
(Promotional issue only.)
WINDSTAR 5-8 90
Session: Hal Blaine; John Sommers; Steve Weisberg; Dick Kniss; Lee Holdridge; James Burton.
Also see BLAINE, Hal
Also see BURTON, James
Also see FAT CITY
Also see MITCHELL, Chad, Trio
Also see TRAVERS, Mary
Also see WONDER, Stevie / John Denver

DENVER, John, & Placido Domingo *P&R '82*

Singles: 7-inch

COLUMBIA...3-5 82

DENVER, John, & Emmylou Harris *C&W '83*

Singles: 7-inch

RCA (13562 "Wild Montana Skies")............3-5 83
Also see HARRIS, Emmylou

DENVER, John, & Muppets *LP '79*

Singles: 7-inch

RCA 3-5 79

LPs: 10/12-inch

RCA...5-10 79-83

DENVER, John, & Olivia Newton-John *P&R '75*

Singles: 7-inch

RCA 4-6 75
Also see NEWTON-JOHN, Olivia

DENVER, John, & Nitty Gritty Dirt Band *C&W '89*

Singles: 7-inch

UNIVERSAL..3-5 89
Also see NITTY GRITTY DIRT BAND

DENVER, John / Diana Ross

Singles: 7-inch

WHAT'S IT ALL ABOUT 4-8 81
(Public service, radio station issue.)
Also see ROSS, Diana

DENVER MINT LTD.

Singles: 7-inch

SMALL TOWN (106 "I've Got to Find Myself") 25-35

DEONE, Larry

Singles: 7-inch

PEPPER (904 "Heart and Soul")..............10-15 59

DE PARIS, Wilbur

Singles: 7-inch

ATLANTIC (2030 "Majorca") 15-25 59

DEPECHE MODE *LP '81*

Singles: 12-inch

SIRE (Except 2271 & 2952) 4-6 81-87
SIRE (2271 "Blasphemous Rumors").......40-50 '80s
(Promotional issue only.)
SIRE (2952 "Behind the Wheel") 20-30 87
(Promotional issue only.)

Singles: 7-inch

REPRISE..3-5 97
SIRE 3-5 81-90

Picture Sleeves

SIRE 3-5 85-88

LPs: 10/12-inch

SIRE 5-10 81-90
Members: Vince Clarke; David Gahan; Martin Gore; Andy Fletcher; Alan Wilder.

DEPRESSIONS

Singles: 7-inch

MADD (123167 "Can't Tell You") 50-75 67

DERAN, Richie

Singles: 7-inch

PONTIAC (63229 "Girl and a Hot Rod") 200-300

DERBY-HATVILLE

Singles: 7-inch

SEA ELL (102 "You'll Forget Me") 30-40 67

DERBYS

Singles: 7-inch

KC (111 "Any Old Way")...........................5-10 63
MERCURY (71437 "Night After Night") ..75-125 59
SAVOY (1609 "Travelin' Man") 10-15 62

DEREK, Tommy

Singles: 7-inch

FLAG (120 "Meet Me at the Hop")........150-200 62

DEREK & DOMINOS *LP '70*

Singles: 7-inch

ATCO (6780 "Tell the Truth") 5-10 70
ATCO (6803 "Bell Bottom Blues")..............5-10 71
ATCO (6809 "Layla") 5-10 71
(2:43 version.)
ATCO (6809 "Layla") 5-10 71
(7:05 version.)
RSO (400 "Why Does Love Got to Be So Sad") 4-6 73

LPs: 10/12-inch

ATCO (704 "Layla") 20-30 70
ATCO (704 "Layla") 50-60 70
(Promotional issue only.)
MFSL (2-239 "In Concert") ....40-60 '90s
POLYDOR (3501 "Layla") 10-15 74
RSO (3801 "In Concert") 10-15 77
RSO (8800 "In Concert") 15-25 72
Members: Eric Clapton; Jim Gordon; Bobby Whitlock; Carl Radle; Duane Allman.
Also see CLAPTON, Eric
Also see WHITLOCK, Bobby

DEREK & RAY

Singles: 7-inch

MERCURY (72744 "To Sir with Love").......5-10 67
MERCURY (72763 "Thoroughly Modern Millie") 5-10 68
RCA (9111 "Interplay") 10-20 67

DE RIEUX, Larry

Singles: 7-inch

ARCO (102 "Chicken Session")..............75-100

DERKSEN, Arnie

Singles: 7-inch

DECCA (30906 "She Wanna Rock") 20-30 59

DERONS

Singles: 7-inch

JEWL (1001 "It's Okay") 10-20

DE ROSA, Frank

Singles: 7-inch

BIG TOP (3019 "Hubcaps").......................15-25 59
DOT (15696 "Big Guitar").........................10-15 58
KEN (25 "Big Guitar") 25-35 57

DE ROSE, Marty

Singles: 7-inch

LANE...15-25 58

DERRICK, Vernon

Singles: 7-inch

FOREST (2007 "Let Go of Your Love")..150-250

DERRIS, Daneal

Singles: 7-inch

J GEMS (417 "Why Am I Crying") 20-30

DESALVO, Albert / Bugs

Singles: 7-inch

ASTOR (001 "Strangler in the Night"/"Albert Albert") 20-30 66
Also see BUGS

DESANTO, Sugar Pie *R&B '60*
("Sugar Pie" De Santo; Sugarpie Di Santo; Umpeylia Balinton; with Pee Wee Kingsley Band; with LaFemmes)

Singles: 7-inch

BRUNSWICK...5-10 67-68
CHECK (103 "I Want to Know")...............10-20 60
CHECKER..10-15 61-66
GEDINSON (100 "Little Taste of Soul")....10-15 62
JASMAN 4-6 74
SOUL CLOCK..5-10 69
VELTONE (103 "I Want to Know")...........10-20 60
VELTONE (108 "Wish You Were Mine")..10-20 60
WAX (103 "Little Taste of Soul")................8-12 64

EPs: 7-inch

CHECKER (2979 "Sugar Pie")..................30-50 61
(Stereo. Juke box issue only.)

LPs: 10/12-inch

CHECKER (2979 "Sugar Pie")................50-100 61
Also see HANK & SUGAR PIE
Also see KINGSLEY, Pee Wee
Also see SUGAR PIE & PEE WEE

DE SANTOS, Paliya

Singles: 7-inch

JODY (11 "If I Had a Wishing Well"/"Darling Be Mine")..250-350 57
(B-side by Paliya & Alvin.)

DESCENDANTS

Singles: 7-inch

MTA (112 "Lela") 20-30 66

DESCIPLES OF SOUL

Singles: 7-inch

DINK (02 "Living in a Glass House") 10-20 73
G.V. (001 "Peek-A-Boo")..........................10-20 72
PHANTOM (2755 "Together")...................10-20 74
Members: Benny Williams; Charles Hills.
Also see ROYAL KNIGHTS

DE SHANNON, Jackie *P&R '63*

Singles: 7-inch

AMHERST..6-12 78
ATLANTIC...5-10 72-74
CAPITOL...5-10 71
COLUMBIA (Except 10221) 5-10 75
COLUMBIA (10221 "Boat to Sail")...........10-15 76
(With Brian Wilson.)
EDISON INT'L (416 "I Wanna Go Home")..50-100 60
EDISON INT'L (418 "Put My Baby Down") 50-100 60
IMPERIAL 5-10 65-70
LIBERTY (55288 thru 55735, except 55602)...15-25 60-64
LIBERTY (55602 "Little Yellow Roses") ... 15-25 63
(Black vinyl.)
LIBERTY (55602 "Little Yellow Roses") ...40-60 63
(Yellow vinyl. Promotional issue only.)
LIBERTY (56187 "It's So Nice")..................5-10 70
RCA (11902 "I Don't Need You Anymore") .. 3-6 80

Picture Sleeves

LIBERTY (55526 "Faded Love")............75-100 63

LPs: 10/12-inch

AMHERST (1010 "You're the Only Dancer")..15-25 77
ATLANTIC..10-15 72-74
CAPITOL 15-20 71
COLUMBIA 10-15 75
IMPERIAL (9286 "This Is Jackie De Shannon")......................................25-50 65
(Monaural.)
IMPERIAL (9294 "You Won't Forget Me") 25-50 65
(Monaural.)
IMPERIAL (9296 "In the Wind")...............25-50 65
(Monaural.)
IMPERIAL (9328 "Are You Ready for This") 25-50 66
(Monaural.)
IMPERIAL (9344 "New Image")...............25-50 67
(Monaural.)
IMPERIAL (9352 "For You") 25-50 67
(Monaural.)
IMPERIAL (12286 "This Is Jackie De Shannon").......................................25-50 65
(Stereo.)
IMPERIAL (12294 "You Won't Forget Me") 25-50 65
(Stereo.)
IMPERIAL (12296 "In the Wind").............25-50 65
(Stereo.)
IMPERIAL (12328 "Are You Ready for This") 25-50 66
(Stereo.)
IMPERIAL (12344 "New Image").............25-50 67
(Stereo.)
IMPERIAL (12352 "For You") 25-50 67
(Stereo.)
IMPERIAL (12386 "Me About You").........25-50 68
IMPERIAL (12404 "What the World Needs Now Is Love")...25-50 68
IMPERIAL (12415 "Laurel Canyon") 25-50 68
IMPERIAL (12442 "Put a Little Love in Your Heart")..25-50 69
IMPERIAL (12453 "To Be Free")..............25-50 70
LIBERTY (3320 "Jackie De Shannon")..50-100 63
(Monaural.)
LIBERTY (3390 "Breakin' It Up On the Beatles Tour")..50-100 64
(Monaural.)
LIBERTY (7320 "Jackie De Shannon") ..75-100 63
(Stereo.)
LIBERTY (7390 "Breakin' It Up on the Beatles Tour")..75-100 64
(Stereo.)
LIBERTY (10000 series) 5-10 82
SUNSET..10-15 68-71
U.A. 8-10 75
Also see DEE, Jackie
Also see HALE & HUSHABYES
Also see SHERRY LEE
Also see SHANNON, Jackie
Also see WILSON, Brian

DE SHANNON, Jackie / Bobby Vee / Eddie Hodges

LPs: 10/12-inch

LIBERTY (3430 "C'mon Let's Live a Little")..15-20 66
(Monaural. Soundtrack)
LIBERTY (7430 "C'mon Let's Live a Little")..20-25 66
(Stereo. Soundtrack)
Also see DE SHANNON, Jackie
Also see HODGES, Eddie
Also see VEE, Bobby

DESIDEROS

Singles: 7-inch

RENEE (1040 "I Pledge My Love") 10-15 63

DESIRES

Singles: 7-inch

HERALD (532 "Bobby You")....................20-30 58

DESIRES

Singles: 7-inch

HULL (730 "Let It Please Be You").........75-100 59
(Red label.)
HULL (730 "Let It Please Be You")..........10-15
(Tan label.)
HULL (733 "Set Me Free") 50-75 60
ROULETTE..4-6 73
Members: Robert White; Charles Hurston; George Smith; Charles Powell; James Whittier.
Also see JIVE TONES

DESIRES

Singles: 7-inch

DEE IMPULSE ("Need Someone") 200-300 62
(Selection number not known.)
MONEYTOWN (602 "Need Someone") 100-200 62

SMASH (1763 "I Never Loved Like This Before")........ 15-25 62
20TH FOX (195 "I Don't Know Why")...... 15-25 60

Picture Sleeves

20TH FOX (195 "I Don't Know Why")...... 20-35 60

DESIRES

Singles: 7-inch

DASA (102 "The Girl for Me").................. 30-40 62

DESIRES
(With Billy Mure & Orchestra)

Singles: 7-inch

SEVILLE (118 "Story of Love")................ 25-35 62
Also see REGENTS
Also see MARESCA, Ernie
Also see MURE, Billy

DESIRES

Singles: 7-inch

STARVILLE (1206 "Oh What a Lonely Night")........ 20-30

DESMOND, Johnny P&R '46

Singles: 78 rpm

CORAL........3-5 52-56
MGM........3-6 50-51

Singles: 7-inch

ARTISTS OF AMERICA........4-6 76
ATCO........4-6 66
COLUMBIA........5-10 59-60
CORAL........10-20 52-56
DIAMOND........4-8 62
EDGEWOOD........4-8 62
MGM........10-20 50-51
MUSICANZA........3-5
RCA........4-8 63
RED LITE........5-10
20TH FOX........4-6 64
VIGOR........4-6 73

Picture Sleeves

CORAL........10-20 55

EPs: 7-inch

CORAL........10-20 54-56
MGM........10-20 52
P.R.I. (11 "So Nice")........5-10

LPs: 10/12-inch

CAMDEN........10-20 53-54
COLUMBIA........5-10 59-60
CORAL........15-25 55-56
EVON........10-15 '50s
LION........10-15 56
MGM........10-20 55
MAYFAIR........10-15 58
MOVIETONE........5-10 66
P.R.I. (98 "90th Anniversary Album")...... 10-20
(Colored vinyl. Promotional issue for Montgomery Ward stores.)
TOPS........5-10 '60s
VOCALION........5-10 66
Also see CORNELL, Don, Johnny Desmond & Alan Dale

DESMOND, Johnny, Eileen Barton & McGuire Sisters P&R '54

Singles: 78 rpm

CORAL........5-10 54
Also see BARTON, Eileen
Also see McGUIRE SISTERS

DESMOND, Johnny / John Gary / Gordon MacRae

LPs: 10/12-inch

INT'L AWARD........8-15 '60s
Also see DESMOND, Johnny
Also see GARY, John
Also see MacRAE, Gordon

DESMOND, Paul LP '63
(Paul Desmond Quartet)

Singles: 7-inch

A&M........4-6 69-70
RCA VICTOR........4-8 62-63

LPs: 10/12-inch

A&M........5-15 69-76
CTI........8-12 75
CAMDEN........8-12 73
DISCOVERY........5-8 81
FANTASY (21 "Paul Desmond")........ 50-100 54
(10-inch LP.)
FANTASY (220 "Paul Desmond")........ 40-60 56
RCA (2400 & 2500 series)........ 15-25 62-63
RCA (2800 series)........5-10 78
RCA (3300 & 3400 series)........10-20 65-66
W.B.........20-30 60
Also see BRUBECK, Dave, & Paul Desmond
Also see MULLIGAN, Gerry, & Paul Desmond

DE SOTO, Bobby

Singles: 7-inch

CLARO (5914 "The Cheater")........15-25 59

DESTINAIRES

Singles: 7-inch

OLD TIMER (609 "Teardrops")........10-15 65
OLD TIMER (610 "Chapel Bells")........15-20 65
(Red vinyl.)
OLD TIMER (613 "Diamonds and Pearls").8-12 65
SIAMESE (409 "Diamonds and Pearls")....5-10 66
Also see ZIRCONS / Destinaires

DESTINAIRES / Lancers

Singles: 7-inch

OLD TIMER (614 "You're Cheating On Me"/"The Sky")........5-10 65
Also see DESTINAIRES
Also see LANCERS

DESTINATION SOUL

Singles: 7-inch

UPTOWN (753 "Ease My Mind")........8-15 67

DESTINATIONS

Singles: 7-inch

FORTUNE (864 "Valley of Tears")........300-400 64
(Reportedly 200 made.)

DESTINATIONS

Singles: 7-inch

CAMEO (422 "Tell Her")........15-25 66

DESTINATIONS

Singles: 7-inch

ANDO (114 "I Can't Leave You")........75-125 68

DESTINY'S CHILDREN

Singles: 7-inch

PYRO (52 "For Me")........15-25 66
VENTURAL (730 "Your First Time")........35-45 '60s

DESTINYS

Singles: 7-inch

ALTA (102 "What's Up")........10-20 61
(First issue.)
DIAMOND (105 "What's Up")........5-10 61

DETERGENTS P&R '64

Singles: 7-inch

KAPP........5-10 66
ROULETTE........5-10 64-65

Picture Sleeves

ROULETTE (4590 "Leader of the Laundromat")........15-25 64

LPs: 10/12-inch

ROULETTE (25308 "The Many Faces of the Detergents")........25-35 65
Members: Ron Dante; Tommy Wynn; Danny Jordan.

DETERMINATIONS

Singles: 7-inch

SPACE (304 "O My Love, Sweet Love")..20-30 59

DETERMINATIONS

Singles: 7-inch

KING (6297 "Girl, Girl, Girl")........10-15 70
IMPORTANT (1010 "You Can't Hold on to Love")........35-50 67

DETOURS

Singles: 7-inch

ATCO (6448 "Peace of Mind")........10-20 66
MCA (40626 "Try to Hold On")........4-6 76
McSHERRY (1285 "Bring Back My Beatles")........10-20 64

DETROIT & INTRUDERS
(Detroit & Invaders)

Singles: 7-inch

DELLWOOD (778 "Let Me Love You")......30-50 '60s
DELLWOOD (10677 "There She Goes")..30-50 '60s

DETROIT COUNT
(The Detroit Count)

Singles: 78 rpm

JVB (75830 "Hastings Street Opera, Part 1")........40-80 48
JVB (75831 "Crazy About You")........40-80 48
KING (4264 "Hastings Street Opera, Part 1")........20-40 48
KING (4265 "Crazy About You")........20-40 48
KING (4279 "Little Tille Willie")........20-40 48

DETROIT EMERALDS P&R/R&B '68

Singles: 7-inch

RIC-TIC........10-15 68
WESTBOUND........4-6 70-78

LPs: 10/12-inch

WESTBOUND........10-15 71-78
Members: Abrim Tilmon; Ivory Tilmon; James Mitchell; Cleophus Tilmon; Raymond Tilmon; Paul Riser; Maurice King; Johnny Allen.

DETROIT JR.
(With the Delrays)

Singles: 7-inch

BEA & BABY (111 "Money Tree")........10-15 60
C.J. (636 "Zig Zag")........10-15 64
C.J. (638 "Mother-In-Law")........10-15 64
CHESS (1772 "Too Poor")........5-10 60
FOXY (002 "Christmas Day")........15-25 61
TIP TOP (2015 "Young Love")........5-10 67
USA (807 "Talk Fast")........10-15 65

DETROIT SOUL

Singles: 7-inch

MUSIC TOWN (208 "Love Without Meaning")........10-20 '60s
MUSIC TOWN (502 "Mr. Hip")........10-20 67

DETROIT WHEELS

Singles: 7-inch

INFERNO (5002 "Tally Ho")........10-20 68
Also see RYDER, Mitch, & Detroit Wheels

DEUCE COUPES

LPs: 10/12-inch

DEL-FI (DFLP-1243 "Hotrodder's Choice")........40-50 63
(Monaural.)
DEL-FI (DFST-1243 "Hotrodder's Choice")........50-75 63
(Stereo.)
DEL-FI (DLF-1243 "Hotrodder's Choice") 10-15 98
("Thick, hard wax" reissue.)
Also see DE-FENDERS / Deuce Coupes

DEUCE COUPES

LPs: 10/12-inch

CROWN (393 "Shut Downs")........40-60 64
(Stereo.)
CROWN (5393 "Shut Downs")........40-60 64
(Monaural.)

DEUCES WILD
(With Don Ralke's Orchestra)

Singles: 7-inch

FARO (623 "Summer's End")........5-10 66
SHEEN (108 "Just the Boy Next Door")...10-15 60
SPECIALTY (654 "The Meaning of Love")........15-25 59
VAULT (927 "Keep On")........5-10 66
Also see RALKE, Don

DEVAL, Buddy

Singles: 78 rpm

ABBOTT (183 "Guilty")........10-15 55

Singles: 7-inch

ABBOTT (183 "Guilty")........15-25 55
Also see LORRIE, Myrna, & Buddy DeVal

DEVANEY, Yvonne

Singles: 7-inch

CHART (661 "I'll Go Back to Him")........15-25 57

DE-VAURS
(With Cliff Driver & His Orchestra; De Vaurs)

Singles: 7-inch

D-TONE (3 "Baby Doll")........200-300 58
MOON (105 "Where Are You")........75-125 59
RED FOX (104 "Where Are You")........8-12 65

DEVERONS

Singles: 7-inch

REO (8892 "Blue Is the Night")........150-250 65
(Canadian.)
REO (8916 "Lost Love")........100-200 65
(Canadian.)
Members: Burton Cummings; Edd Smith; Ronn Savoie; Derek Blake.

DEVIANTS

LPs: 10/12-inch

SIRE (97001 "Ptooff")........30-40 68
SIRE (97005 "Disposable")........30-40 69
SIRE (97016 "Deviants, No. 3")........30-40 69
Members: Mick Farren; Russ Hunter; Duncan Sanderson; Steve Sparks; Jon Weber.

DEVIL'S OWN

Singles: 7-inch

EXIT (1907 "I Just Wanna Make Love")...20-30 66

DEVILED HAM

LPs: 10/12-inch

SUPER K (6003 "I Had too Much to Dream Last Night")........15-25 68

DEVILLE SISTERS
(With Reuben Grundy)

Singles: 7-inch

IMPERIAL (5539 "Hula Hoop")........8-12 58
SPRY (110 "Every Word")........75-125 58
SPRY (111 "Love and Desire")........8-12 58

DE VILLES

Singles: 7-inch

ALADDIN (3423 "Kiss Me Again and Again")........50-75 58

DE VILLES

Singles: 7-inch

NAU-VOO (806 "I Didn't Do It")........40-50 59

DEVILLES

Singles: 7-inch

DIXIE (1108 "Without Warning")........20-30 60
Also see JOHNS, Sammy, & DeVilles

DEVILLES

Singles: 7-inch

ACCLAIM (1002 "Give Your Love to Me")........15-25 61
ARRAWAK (1001 "I Do Believe")........30-40 62
(Green label.)
ARRAWAK (1001 "I Do Believe")........10-15 63
(Yellow label. Although 201 is more prominent on the label, 1001 follows series numbering.)
ORBIT (540 "Joan of Love")........25-35 59
SPARTON (752 "Joan of Love")........15-25 61
(Canadian.)
TALENT (103 "Goddess of Angels")......100-125 60

DEVILLES

Singles: 7-inch

KERRY (1109 "Baby Blue")........60-80 66
KERRY (1110 "Denise")........150-175 66
STUDIO CITY (1045 "Cry Baby")........40-60 66
Also see SECOND THOUGHT

DEVILS

Singles: 7-inch

SARA (1449 "Tell Me")........15-25 67
SARA (1450 "I'll Be There When You Come")........15-25 67

DE VITO, Buddy, & Fabulous Storms

Singles: 7-inch

KM (721 "I Only Need to Think of You").75-100

DEVLIN, Johnny

Singles: 7-inch

CORAL (62335 "Angel of Love")........15-20 62

EPs: 7-inch

COCA COLA (1 "Johnny Devlin")........50-75

DEVO LP '78

Singles: 12-inch

ENIGMA........4-6 88
W.B (Except 2006)........4-8 80-85
W.B. (2006 "That's Good")........15-20 83
(Picture disc. Promotional issue only.)

Singles: 7-inch

ASYLUM........3-5 81
BOOJI BOY........4-8 78
ENIGMA........3-5 88
FULL MOON........3-5 81
W.B. (Except 49826)........3-6 78-85
W.B. (49826 "Beautiful World")........10-15 81
(Space helmet shaped picture disc.)
W.B. (49826 Beautiful World")........40-80 81
(Space helmet shaped colored vinyl. Experimental pressing only. 20 made.)

Picture Sleeves

FULL MOON........3-5 81
W.B.........3-5 79-85

LPs: 10/12-inch

ENIGMA........5-10 88
W.B. (Except 3595)........5-10 78-88

W.B. (3595 "New Traditionalists") 10-12 81
(With poster and bonus single, *Working in the Coal Mine*.)
W.B. (3595 "New Traditionalists") 5-10 81
(Without poster and bonus single.)
Members: Mark Mothersbaugh; Bob Casale; Bob Mothersbaugh; David Kendrick; Gerald Casale.

DE VOL, Frank, Orchestra *P&R '50*
(With the Rainbow Strings; with Earl Wrightson & Lois Hunt; "Music By DeVol")

Singles: 78 rpm
CAPITOL 3-5 50-56
KEM 3-5 55

Singles: 7-inch
ABC-PAR 4-8 64-65
CAPITOL 5-15 50-56
COLGEMS (1015 "Guess Who's Coming to Dinner") 4-8 68
COLUMBIA 5-10 59-62
KEM 5-10 55

Picture Sleeves
COLGEMS (1615 "Guess Who's Coming to Dinner") 5-10 68
COLUMBIA (41987 "Theme from *David and Goliath*") 10-20 61

LPs: 10/12-inch
ABC-PAR 5-10 65-66
COLGEMS (COM-108 "Guess Who's Coming to Dinner") 20-25 68
(Soundtrack. Monaural.)
COLGEMS (COS-108 "Guess Who's Coming to Dinner") 25-30 68
(Soundtrack. Stereo.)
COLGEMS (COMO-5006 "The Happening") 15-20 67
(Soundtrack. Monaural.)
COLGEMS (COSO-5006 "The Happening") 20-25 67
(Soundtrack. Stereo.)
COLUMBIA 8-10 59-63
HARMONY 5-10 65
Also see ANDERSON, Herb Oscar
Also see MORGAN, Jaye P. & Frank De Vol Orchestra

DEVONAIRES

Singles: 7-inch
DEVON (112 "Letters from You") 10-15 60

DEVONS

Singles: 7-inch
DECCA (31777 "Free Fall") 25-35 65
DECCA (31899 "Come On") 25-35 66
Members: Chuck Girard; Gary Usher.
Also see USHER, Gary

DEVONS
(Sir Douglas Quintet)

Singles: 7-inch
PIC-1 (111 "Wine Wine Wine") 10-15 65
Also see SIR DOUGLAS QUINTET

DEVORE, Florence

Singles: 7-inch
PHI-DAN (5000 "Kiss Me Now") 10-20 65
YEW (1009 "He Doesn't Love You") 8-12 70

DEVOTIONS

Singles: 7-inch
CUB (9020 "Worried About You Baby")... 10-15 58

DEVOTIONS *P&R '64*

Singles: 7-inch
DELTA (1001 "Rip Van Winkle") 100-125 61
KAPE (701 "Teardrops Follow Me") 4-8 72
ROULETTE (4406 "Rip Van Winkle") 15-25 63
(White label.)
ROULETTE (4541 "Rip Van Winkle") 8-12 64
(Orange label.)
ROULETTE (4556 "Sunday Kind of Love") 20-30 64
ROULETTE (4580 "Snow White") 25-35 64
Members: Joe Pardo; Frank Pardo; Louis DeCarlo; Bob Weisbrod; Ray Sanchez; Bob Havorka; Larry Frank.

DEVOTIONS

Singles: 7-inch
NATION ("It's Alright") 100-200
(Selection number not known.)

DEVROE, Billy & Devilaires
(Billy Dev-roe; Devroe's Devilaires)

Singles: 78 rpm
TAMPA 10-25 55-57

Singles: 7-inch
TAMPA (107 thru 127) 10-15 55-57
TAMPA (133 "I'm Packin' ") 20-40 58

Picture Sleeves
TAMPA (127 "Buttercup") 50-75 57

LPs: 10/12-inch
TAMPA (31 "Billy Devroe and the Devilaires, Vol. 1") 25-35 58
TAMPA (39 "Billy Devroe and the Devilaires, Vol. 2") 25-35 58

DEW DROPS

Singles: 7-inch
JEFF (1963 "No Other Guy") 20-30 63

DEWEY, George & Jack

Singles: 7-inch
RAVEN (700 "Flying Saucers Have Landed") 20-25

DeWITT, Bobby

Singles: 7-inch
RIDGECREST (1204 "Annie Mae") 150-250 59

DE WOLF, Dean

Singles: 7-inch
ARGO (5457 "Little Drummer Boy") 5-10 63

LPs: 10/12-inch
ARGO (4035 "High Tide") 15-20 65

DEXTER, Al, & Troopers *P&R/R&B '43*

Singles: 78 rpm
COLUMBIA 5-10 46
EKKO 5-10 55
OKEH 8-12 43-44
VOCALION 10-20

Singles: 7-inch
EKKO (1020 "Pistol Packin' Mama") 10-20 55

LPs: 10/12-inch
AUDIO LAB 8-12
CAPITOL (1701 "Greatest Hits") 20-30 62
COLUMBIA (9005 "Songs of the Southwest") 30-40
(10-inch LP.)
HARMONY 8-10
HILLTOP 8-10

DEY, Tracey *P&R '63*

Singles: 7-inch
AMY (894 thru 928) 10-15 63-65
COLUMBIA (43889 "Teddy's the Boy I Love") 5-10 66
LIBERTY (55604 "Teenage Cleopatra")...10-20 63
VEE-JAY (467 "Jerry") 10-20 62
VEE-JAY (506 "Jealous Eyes") 10-20 63

DIABLOS *R&B '56*
(Featuring Nolan Strong; with Maurice King Orchestra)

Singles: 78 rpm
FORTUNE 10-25 54-57

Singles: 7-inch
FORTUNE (509 thru 522) 20-30 54-56
FORTUNE (525 thru 563) 12-25 57-64
FORTUNE (574 "The Way You Dog Me Around") 4-6 78
(Black vinyl.)
FORTUNE (574 "The Way You Dog Me Around") 10-15 78
(Colored vinyl.)
FORTUNE (841 "Come Home, Little Girl") 30-40 58

Picture Sleeves
FORTUNE (563 "Village of Love") 20-30 64

LPs: 10/12-inch
FORTUNE (8010 "Fortune of Hits") 50-75 61
FORTUNE (8012 "Fortune of Hits, Vol. 2") 40-60 62
FORTUNE (8015 "Mind Over Matter") 40-60 63
FORTUNE (80810 "Fortune of Hits") 10-15
Members: Nolan Strong; Bob "Chico" Edwards; Juan Guiterriec; Willie Hunter, George Scott; Jim Strong; Quentin Eubanks; J.W. Johnson.
Also see STRONG, Nolan

DIABLOS / Five Dollars

Singles: 7-inch
FORTUNE (511 "The Wind"/"So Strange") 10-20
(Gray vinyl.)
Also see DIABLOS
Also see FIVE DOLLARS

DIABLOS

Singles: 7-inch
JUBILEE (5553 "Hombre") 10-20 66

DIABOLIQUES

Singles: 7-inch
MERRI (6005 "Bubbles") 10-20 63

Picture Sleeves
MERRI (6005 "Bubbles") 10-20 63

DIACO, Al

Singles: 7-inch
FOUR SEASONS ("Lover's Hideaway")...40-50 65
(No selection number used.)

DIADEMS
(With Buddy Sharpe & the Shakers)

Singles: 7-inch
GOLDIE (715 "I'll Do Anything") 10-20 61
LAVERE (187 "What More Is There to Say") 10-20 61
STAR (514 "Why Don't You Believe Me") 25-35 63
Also see HILTON, Jerry, & Diadems

DIAL TONES
(Dynamic Dial Tones)

Singles: 7-inch
HORIZON (1596 "Boss") 10-15 61

DIALOGUE

Singles: 7-inch
JAMIE (1420 "Aslon, the Lion") 4-6 74

LPs: 10/12-inch
COLD ("Dialogue") 300-400 68
(Selection number not known.)

DIALS

Singles: 7-inch
HILLTOP (219 "No Hard Feelings") 50-100 61
HILLTOP (2009 "Ring-Ting-a-Ling") 400-500 60
HILLTOP (2010 "Wondering About Your Love") 150-250 60
NORGOLDE (105 "Ring Ting-a-Ling") 30-40 59

DIALS

Singles: 7-inch
PHILIPS (40040 "These Foolish Things") 50-75 62
Member: Sal Corrente.
Also see CORRENTE, Sal

DIALS

Singles: 7-inch
TIME (1068 "Monkey Dance") 5-10 63

LPs: 10/12-inch
TIME (2100 "It's Monkey Time") 15-25 64

DIALTONES
(Dial-Tones)

Singles: 7-inch
DANDY DAN (1 "Cherry Pie") 20-30 63
LAWN (203 "So Young") 15-25 63

DIALTONES

Singles: 7-inch
GOLDISC (3005 "Johnny") 20-30 60
GOLDISC (3020 "Johnny") 5-10 61
Also see RANDY & RAINBOWS

DIALTONES

Singles: 7-inch
DIAL (4054 "Don't Let the Sun Shine on Me") 10-20 67

DIAMOND, Danny, & Rubies

Singles: 7-inch
IRVANNE (115 "Rhythm in My Bones") .50-100 59

DIAMOND, Dave
(With the Higher Elevation)

Singles: 7-inch
CHICORY (408 "Diamond Mine") 15-25 66
CLARIDGE 5-10 75-76
VISION (1003 "Dr. Darekil") 10-20 62
Also see SOOTHSAYERS

DIAMOND, Hank & Carol

Singles: 7-inch
WORKSHOP JAZZ (2001 "I Remember You") ....25-35 '60s

DIAMOND, Jerry, & Sparkles

Singles: 7-inch
RCA (7257 "Lindy Lou") 15-20 58

DIAMOND, Joe

Singles: 7-inch
STAR ARTISTS (102 "Three Sheets to the Wind") 75-125

DIAMOND, Larry

Singles: 7-inch
ARGO (5330 "Bye Bye Doll") 20-30 59
DIMAX 8-12 60

DIAMOND, Lee

Singles: 7-inch
GARDENA (112 "Betty Booper") 30-45 60
LIKE YOUNG (101 "Now That You're Gone") 5-10 65
MINIT (617 "Please Don't Leave") 10-15 60
MINIT (635 "Let Me Know") 10-15 61
VEE-JAY (272 "Mama Loochie") 20-25 58
Also see HILL, Jessie / Aaron Neville / Lee Diamond / Ernie K-Doe

DIAMOND, Leo *P&R '53*
(With Van Alexander & Orchestra)

Singles: 78 rpm
AMBASSADOR 5-10 51-53
RCA 5-10 55
ROULETTE 5-10 57

Singles: 7-inch
AMBASSADOR 10-20 53
RCA 10-20 55
ROULETTE (4025 "Till") 10-20 57
ROULETTE (4047 "Flunky") 10-20 58

DIAMOND, Neil *P&R/LP '66*

Singles: 12-inch
COLUMBIA (99-1586 "Heartlight") 30-40 83
(Picture disc. Promotional issue only.)
CONTINUUM II (001 "We Wrote a Song Together") 1500-2000 76
(Made exclusively for Neil's son Jesse's grade school class. Has Neil and a band composing and recording, with children, in a studio. Includes an alternative version of *Beautiful Noise*. Neil made and autographed a copy for each child in attendence – estimated to be 30 to 40 copies.)

Singles: 7-inch
BANG (100 series) 3-5
("Best Hits" reissue series.)
BANG (500 & 700 series) 5-10 66-73
CAPITOL 3-5 80-81
COLUMBIA (02600 thru 06100 series) 3-5 81-86
COLUMBIA (10000 & 11000 series) 4-6 74-80
COLUMBIA (33000 series) 3-5
("Hall of Fame" series.)
COLUMBIA (42809 "Clown Town") 400-600 63
COLUMBIA (42809 "Clown Town") 100-200 63
(Promotional issue only.)
COLUMBIA (45000 series) 4-6 73-74
MCA (40000 series) 4-6 73
MCA (60000 series) 4-6 73
PHILCO (5 "Girl, You'll Be a Woman Soon"/"Cherry Cherry") 25-30 67
PHILCO (17 "You Got to Me"/"Solitary Man") 25-30 67
(Above two are "Hip-Pocket" flexi-discs.)
SOLID ROCK 5-8
UNI 4-8 68-72

Promotional Singles
BANG (Except 55075) 10-15 66-73
UNI (55075 "Two-Bit Manchild") 40-50 68
(Colored vinyl.)
CAPITOL 3-5 80-81
COLUMBIA (1115 "Song Sung Blue") 4-8 77
COLUMBIA (1193 "September Morn") 4-8 79
(Alternative version.)
COLUMBIA (02600 thru 11000) 3-8 74-86
COLUMBIA (42809 "Clown Town") 300-400 63
COLUMBIA (45000 series) 4-8 73-74
MCA 4-6 73
UNI 8-12 68-72
WHAT'S IT ALL ABOUT ....20-30 '70s
(Public service disc, made for radio stations.)

Picture Sleeves
CAPITOL 3-6 80-81
COLUMBIA 3-6 73-86
UNI 5-10 68-70

EPs: 7-inch
COLUMBIA (32919 "Serenade") 35-40 74
(Juke box issue only. Includes title strips.)
MCA (34989 "12 Greatest Hits") 25-30 74
(Juke box issue only. Includes title strips.)

UNI (34818 "Neil Diamond Gold")........... 25-30 71
(Juke box issue only. Includes title strips.)
UNI (34871 "Stones")........................... 45-50 71
(Juke box issue only. Includes title strips.)

LPs: 10/12-inch

BANG (214 "The Feel of Neil Diamond")........................... 125-150 66
BANG (217 "Just For You")..................... 25-50 67
BANG (219 "Greatest Hits")..................... 25-50 68
BANG (221 "Shilo")................................ 40-50 70
BANG (224 "Do It")................................ 40-50 71
BANG (227 "Double Gold")....................... 25-30 73
CAPITOL...5-10 80
COLUMBIA (30000 series, except 39915) .8-12 73-86
COLUMBIA (39915 "Primitive")............... 35-40 84
(Picture disc.)
COLUMBIA (40000 series)........................8-10 86-89
COLUMBIA (42550 "Jonathan Livingston Seagull")................................ 25-30 81
(Half-speed mastered.)
COLUMBIA (45025 "Best Years of Our Lives")...5-8 89
COLUMBIA (46525 "You Don't Bring Me Flowers")... 30-35 80
(Half-speed mastered.)
COLUMBIA (47628 "On the Way to the Sky").. 45-50 82
(Half-speed mastered.)
DIRECT-TO-DISK................................... 25-30
FROG KING (1 "Early Classics")............ 65-75 78
(Includes music and lyrics songbook. Columbia Record Club issue.)
HARMONY (30023 "Chartbusters")....... 75-100 70
(Various artists LP, containing the 1963 Columbia tracks, and the otherwise unavailable *I've Never Been the Same.*)
MCA...6-15 72-81
MFSL (2-024 "Hot August Night")........... 50-75 79
MFSL (071 "Jazz Singer")...................... 40-60 82
UNI (11 "Neil Diamond Sampler")........ 150-200 71
(With paper envelope cover. Has sticker promoting a special event. Promotional souvenir "Hits" pakage for those attending.)
UNI (11 "Neil Diamond D.J. Sampler") 100-125 71
(With paper envelope cover. Does not have sticker promoting the event. Promotional issue for dee jays only.)
UNI (1913 "Open-End Interview with Neil Diamond")...................................... 75-100 72
(Promotional issue only.)
UNI (73030 "Velvet Gloves and Spit") 50-60 68
(Gatefold cover pictures Neil and some female mannequins. Does not contain *Shilo.*)
UNI (73030 "Velvet Gloves and Spit") 40-50 68
(Gatefold cover pictures Neil and some female mannequins. Contains *Shilo.*)
UNI (73030 "Velvet Gloves and Spit") 15-25 70
(Standard cover – no mannequins. Contains *Shilo.*)
UNI (73047 "Brother Love's Traveling Salvation Show")... 40-50 69
(Gatefold cover pictures Neil on a wagon on front side and a game board on the back. Known as "Purple Wagon" cover.)
UNI (73047 "Sweet Caroline – Brother Love's Traveling Salvation Show")......................... 15-25 69
(Standard cover – reworked, including revised title. No game board.)
UNI (73071 "Touching You, Touching Me").. 15-25 69
UNI (73084 "Gold")................................ 15-25 70
UNI (73092 "Tap Root Manuscript")......... 15-25 70
(Some 70000 series LPs were reissued in the 90000 series, with the only change being the first digit.)
UNI (93106 "Stones").............................. 15-25 71
UNI (93136 "Moods")............................... 15-25 72
UNI (93501 "Tap Root Manuscript")......... 15-25 70
(Capitol Record Club issue.)
Also see JUDAS PRIEST
Also see NEIL & JACK
Also see STREISAND, Barbra, & Neil Diamond
Also see TEN BROKEN HEARTS

DIAMOND, Neil / Diana Ross & Supremes

LPs: 10/12-inch

MCA (734727 "It's Happening") 30-40 72
(One side of LP devoted to each artist.)
Also see DIAMOND, Neil
Also see SUPREMES

DIAMOND, Ronnie

Singles: 7-inch

IMPERIAL (5554 "Zig Zag")......................20-30 58
IMPERIAL (5570 "Candy Store")..............20-30 59
IMPERIAL (5588 "Life Begins at 4 O'Clock")..50-75 59
IMPERIAL (5605 "Please Please")...........10-15 59

DIAMOND, Tony

Singles: 7-inch

BLUE ROCK (4019 "Don't Turn Away")...10-15 65

DIAMONDS

Singles: 78 rpm

ATLANTIC (981 "A Beggar for Your Kisses")..150-250 52
ATLANTIC (1003 "Two Loves Have I").100-200 53
ATLANTIC (1017 "Cherry")...................100-200 53

Singles: 7-inch

ATLANTIC (981 "A Beggar for Your Kisses").. 750-1000 52
ATLANTIC (1003 "Two Loves Have I").400-600 53
ATLANTIC (1017 "Cherry")..................300-500 53
(Thick vinyl.)
ATLANTIC (1017 "Cherry").......................50-75
(Thin vinyl.)
Members: Harold Wright; Ernest Ward; Myles Hardy; Dan Stevens.
Also see METRONOMES

DIAMONDS *P&R/R&B '56*
(With Dick Jacobs & Orchestra)

Singles: 78 rpm

CORAL...5-10 55-56
MERCURY (Except 71060 & 71242)........15-25 56-57
MERCURY (71060 "Little Darlin'")..........75-125 57
MERCURY (71242 "The Stroll")...............50-75 57
MERCURY/STARDAY (71242 "The Stroll")...25-35 57
(We have yet to confirm any 45s of this with the Starday logo.)

Singles: 7-inch

CHURCHILL (94101 "Just a Little Bit")........4-6 87
CHURCHILL (94102 "Two Kinds of Woman")...4-6 87
CORAL (61502 "Black Denim Trousers and Motorcycle Boots")..10-15 55
CORAL (61577 "Smooch Me")..................10-15 56
MERCURY (70790 thru 71021) 15-20 56
MERCURY (71060 "Little Darlin' ")...........20-25 57
MERCURY (71128 thru 71404, except 71242)..15-20 57-58
MERCURY (71242 "The Stroll")...............20-25 57
MERCURY (71449 thru 71956, except 71831)..10-15 59-62
MERCURY (71831 "One Summer Night")..15-20 61

Picture Sleeves

MERCURY (71291 "High Sign")...............20-30 58

EPs: 7-inch

BRUNSWICK (70131 "Diamonds").......175-225 57
MERCURY (4038 "Golden Hits")............75-125 56
MERCURY (1-3390 "Stroll with the Diamonds")..75-125 57

LPs: 10/12-inch

MERCURY (20213 "Golden Hits")............50-75 56
MERCURY (20309 "Diamonds")...............50-75 57
MERCURY (20480 "Songs from the Old West")...30-50 60
(Monaural.)
MERCURY (60159 "Songs from the Old West") 30-50 60
(Stereo.)
SOUND (4644 "Diamonds").......................10-20 71
WING (12114 "America's Famous Song Stylists")...30-50 58
WING (12178 "Pop Hits")........................25-35 59
Members: David Somerville; Phil Leavitt; Bill Reed; Ted Kowalski; Bob Duncan; Gary Cech; Gary Owens; Steve Smith.
Also see DEL-VIKINGS / Diamonds / Big Bopper / Gaylords
Also see JACOBS, Dick, & Orchestra
Also see VEE, Bobby / Diamonds / Drifters

DIAMONDS / Georgia Gibbs / Sarah Vaughan / Florian Zabach

EPs: 7-inch

MERCURY (4026 "Tops in Pops")...........15-20 56
Also see GIBBS, Georgia
Also see VAUGHAN, Sarah
Also see ZABACH, Florian

DIAMONDS & PETE RUGOLO

LPs: 10/12-inch

MERCURY (20368 "The Diamonds Meet Pete Rugolo")...30-50 58
(Monaural.)
MERCURY (60076 "The Diamonds Meet Pete Rugolo")...50-75 59
(Stereo.)
Also see DIAMONDS
Also see RUGOLO, Pete, & His Orchestra

DIAMONDS IV

Singles: 7-inch

JAMAKA (8346 "Panic Beat")...................10-15 59

DIANE & DARLETTES

Singles: 7-inch

DUNES (2016 "Just You").........................10-15 62
Also see DARLETTES

DIANTE, Denny

Singles: 7-inch

HOLIDAY (1210 "Little Lover")...................40-50 64
HOLIDAY (1211 "What Makes Little Girls Cry")..10-15 64

DIATONES

Singles: 7-inch

BANDERA (2509 "Oh, Baby Come Dance with Me") 30-40 61

DIAZ, Carlos, & Royal Tones

Singles: 7-inch

TRIANGLE (001 "Sugaree")................450-650

DIAZ, Vic
(Vickie Diaz)

Singles: 7-inch

DEL-FI (4149 "For Eternity")....................50-75 60
DONNA (1351 "Mr. Moon").......................10-15 61

DICK & DEEDEE *P&R '61*
(With the Don Ralke Orchestra; Dick & Dee Dee)

Singles: 7-inch

DOT...4-8 68-69
LAMA (7778 "The Mountain's High")........15-25 61
LAMA (7780 "Goodbye to Love")..............15-25 61
LAMA (7783 "Tell Me").............................15-25 61
LIBERTY (54528 "The Mountain's High"/"Tell Me") ....4-6 '70s
LIBERTY (55350 thru 55478) 8-12 61-62
U.A. 4-6
W.B. 5-10 62-69

Picture Sleeves

W.B. (5320 "The River Took My Baby")...15-25 62
W.B. (5482 "Thou Shalt Not Steal")..........15-25 63
(Promotional sleeve, made for Triumph Motorcycle company.)

LPs: 10/12-inch

LIBERTY (3236 "Tell Me"/"The Mountain's High")...40-50 62
(Monaural.)
LIBERTY (7236 "Tell Me"/"The Mountain's High")...40-50 62
W.B. (1500 "Young and in Love")............20-30 63
W.B. (1538 "Turn Around") 20-30 64
W.B. (1586 "Thou Shalt Not Steal")..........25-35 65
W.B. (1623 "Songs We've Sung on Shindig")...20-30 65
Members: Dick St. John; Dee Dee Sperling.
Also see RALKE, Don
Also see ST. JOHN, Dick

DICK & GEES

Singles: 7-inch

ARGO (5288 "Foolish Tears").................10-15 58

DICK & LIBBY
(With the Dick Halleman Orchestra)

Singles: 7-inch

SUMMIT (189-11 "Why Do They Call It Puppy Love")...10-20 61
Members: Dick Halleman; Libby Page.
Also see HALLEMAN, Dick

DICK & TEENBEATS

Singles: 7-inch

BIGTOP (3144 "Strawberries") 10-20 63
Also see FIVE TEENBEATS

DICKENS, Doles, Quintet
(Doles Dickens Band; with DeCosta Choir)

Singles: 78 rpm

CONTINENTAL 15-25 47
DECCA (Except 48110) 15-25 49-55
DECCA (48110 "Rock and Roll")............50-100 49
GOTHAM 15-25 49
SUPERDISC..15-25 47

Singles: 7-inch

DECCA (29490 "Gonna Rock This Morning")..20-30 55
DECCA (48199 "Blues in the Back Room")...50-100 51
DECCA (48229 "Gonna Rock This Morning")..50-100 51
DECCA (48242 "Blues in the Evening").50-100 51
LINCOLN (1000 "Piakukaungcung") ....10-20 '50s

DICKENS, Doug

Singles: 7-inch

VULCO (1506 "Raw Deal")..................200-300 59

DICKENS, Jimmy *C&W '49*
(Little Jimmy Dickens; Jimmie Dickens)

Singles: 78 rpm

COLUMBIA...5-10 49-57

Singles: 7-inch

COLUMBIA (10000 series) 4-6 76
COLUMBIA (20000 & 21000 series) 10-20 50-56
COLUMBIA (40000 series) 8-12 56
COLUMBIA (41000 series, except 41173). 8-12 57-60
COLUMBIA (41173 "I Got a Hole in My Pocket")...30-45 57
COLUMBIA (42000 thru 44000 series) 4-8 60-67
DECCA...4-6 67-69
LITTLE GEM..4-6 75
PARTRIDGE...3-5 80
STARDAY...4-6 73
U.A. 4-6 70-72

EPs: 7-inch

COLUMBIA (Except 2800 series)............15-20 52-57
COLUMBIA (2800 series) 10-15 57-58

LPs: 10/12-inch

COLUMBIA (1047 "Raisin' the Dickens").40-50 57
COLUMBIA (1500 thru 2500 series) 10-20 60-66
(Monaural.)
COLUMBIA (8300 thru 9600 series, except 9025) 15-25 60-68
(Stereo.)
COLUMBIA (9025 "The Old Country Church")...50-100 54
(10-inch LP.)
COLUMBIA (10000 & 11000 series) 6-10 70-73
COLUMBIA (38000 series) 5-10 84
DECCA...10-15 68-69
GUSTO...5-10
HARMONY (7000 series)..........................15-25 64-65
HARMONY (11000 series)..........................8-12 67
QCA...5-10 75

DICKERSON, Dub

Singles: 78 rpm

SIMS (106 "Shotgun Wedding") 15-25 56

Singles: 7-inch

SIMS (106 "Shotgun Wedding") 50-75 56
SIMS (127 "Name Your Price")....................5-10 62
TODD (1053 "The Bottle")..........................10-15 60

DICKERSON, Herb

Singles: 7-inch

MARLENE (661 "I Want a Girl") 600-800
(Black vinyl.)
MARLENE (661 "I Want a Girl") 1000-1200
(Red vinyl.)

DICKEY, Milt
("With String Band")

Singles: 78 rpm

SHOME (528 "Neon Love") ....10-15 '50s
WESTPORT...5-10 55-56

Singles: 7-inch

SHOME (528 "Neon Love") ....25-35 '50s
WESTPORT...10-15 55-56

DICKIE & DEBONAIRES

Singles: 7-inch

ASTA (101 "Stomp")...................................15-25 61
JASON SCOTT (19 "Yo Yo Girl") 4-8 82
(500 made.)
VALLI (302 "Yo Yo Girl")........................200-300 60

DICKIE & EBB TIDES

Singles: 7-inch

FLEETWOOD (4561 "One Girl, One Boy")...175-225 66
GOLDEN WORLD (45 "One Girl, One Boy")...15-25 66

THUNDER (501 "I Don't Want Your Love")...10-20

DICKY DOO & DON'TS *P&R/R&B '58*
(With the West Texas Marching Band)
Singles: 7-inch
ASCOT (2178 "Click Clack '65")...5-10 65
CASINO (106 "Click-Clack")...4-6
CASINO (107 "Flip Top Box")...4-6
COLLECTABLES...3-5 '80s
DANNA (4001 "Doo Plus Two")...5-10 67
SWAN (4001 "Click-Clack")...15-25 57
SWAN (4006 "Nee Nee Na Na Na Na Nu Nu")...15-25 58
SWAN (4014 thru 4046)...10-20 58-60
U.A. (238 thru 362)...10-20 60-61
EPs: 7-inch
U.A. (10,008 "Madison")...40-60 60
LPs: 10/12-inch
DANNA (1566 "Recorded in Stereo Before a Live, Live, Live, Live Audience")...40-60 67
(Recorded at Eagle Rock Ski and Golf Club, Hazleton, Pa.)
U.A. (3094 "Madison & Other Dances")...40-60 60
(Monaural.)
U.A. (3097 "Teen Scene")...40-60 60
U.A. (6094 "Madison & Other Dances"). 50-100 60
(Stereo.)
U.A. (6097 "Teen Scene")...50-100 60
(Stereo.)
Members: Gerry Granahan; Harvey Davis; Ray Gangi; Jerry Grant; Joey Paige.
Also see GRANAHAN, Gerry

DICKSON, Duke
Singles: 7-inch
GLOBAL (716 "My Baby Doll")...40-60 58
GLOBAL (720 "Is You Is Or Is You Ain't")...30-40 59

DICKSON, Richie, & Rosebuds
Singles: 7-inch
CLASS (308 "Moonlight & Roses")...25-35 63

DIDDLEY, Bo *R&B '55*
Singles: 78 rpm
CHECKER (814 thru 907)...50-75 55-58
CHECKER (914 "I'm Sorry")...50-100 59
CHECKER (924 "Crackin' Up")...75-125 59
CHECKER (931 "Say Man")...100-200 59
REO (8022 "Bo Diddley")...50-75 55
(Canadian.)
Singles: 7-inch
ABC...4-6 74
CHECKER (814 "Bo Diddley")...30-40 55
CHECKER (819 "Diddley Daddy")...40-50 55
CHECKER (827 thru 907)...30-40 55-58
CHECKER (914 thru 931)...20-30 59
CHECKER (936 thru 997)...15-25 59-61
CHECKER (1019 "Book By the Cover You Can't Judge")...20-30 62
CHECKER (1019 "You Can't Judge a Book By Its Cover")...15-25 62
CHECKER (1045 thru 1083)...10-20 63-64
CHECKER (1098 thru 1158)...10-15 65-66
CHECKER (1168 thru 1213)...5-12 67-69
CHECKER (1238 "The Shape I'm In")...4-8 71
CHESS (2117 "I Said Shutup, Woman")...4-8 71
CHESS (2129 "Infatuation")...4-8 72
GOLDEN GOODIES...4-6
RCA...4-6 76
REO (8022 "Bo Diddley")...50-100 55
(Canadian.)
EPs: 7-inch
CHESS (5125 "Bo Diddley")...250-300 58
(With cardboard cover.)
CHESS (5125 "Bo Diddley")...50-75 58
(With paper cover.)
LPs: 10/12-inch
ACCORD (7182 "Toronto Rock 'N' Roll Revival")...5-10 82
CHECKER (1436 "Go Bo Diddley")...150-250 59
CHECKER (2974 "Have Guitar Will Travel")...100-150 59
CHECKER (2976 "Bo Diddley in the Spotlight")...75-125 60
CHECKER (2977 "Bo Diddley Is a Gunslinger")...50-100 61
CHECKER (2980 "Bo Diddley Is a Lover")...50-100 61
CHECKER (2982 "Bo Diddley's a Twister")...50-75 62
CHECKER (2984 "Bo Diddley")...50-75 62
CHECKER (2985 "Bo Diddley and Company")...50-75 63
CHECKER (2987 "Surfin' with Bo Diddley")...60-80 63
(Most of the tracks on this LP are by the Megatons.)
CHECKER (2988 "Bo Diddley's Beach Party")...35-55 63
CHECKER (2989 "Bo Diddley's 16 All-Time Greatest Hits")...25-50 63
CHECKER (2992 "Hey Good Lookin'")...25-50 64
CHECKER (2996 "500% More Man")...25-50 64
CHECKER (3001 "The Originator")...25-45 66
CHECKER (3006 "Go Bo Diddley")...25-45 67
CHECKER (3007 "Boss Man")...40-60 67
CHECKER (3013 "The Black Gladiator") .25-35 69
CHESS (1431 "Bo Diddley")...150-200 58
CHESS (8204 "Greatest Sides")...8-12 83
CHESS (50001 "Another Dimension")...10-15 71
CHESS (50016 "Where It All Began")...10-15 72
CHESS (50029 "The London Bo Diddley Sessions")...10-15 73
CHESS (50047 "Big Bad Bo")...10-15 74
CHESS (60005 "Got My Own Bag of Tricks")...15-25 72
(Two discs.)
MCA/CHESS...5-8 88
RCA (1229 "20th Anniversary of Rock 'N Roll")...10-20 76
(With numerous guest stars.)
Session: Jody Williams; Cliff James; Frank Kirkland; Jerome Green. Session: Willie Dixon; Otis Spann; Moonglows.
Also see BELMONTS, Freddy Cannon & Bo Diddley
Also see DIXON, Willie
Also see McCAIN, Jerry
Also see MOONGLOWS
Also see SPANN, Otis

DIDDLEY, Bo, & Chuck Berry
Singles: 7-inch
CHECKER (13370 "Bo's Beat")...5-10 64
LPs: 10/12-inch
CHECKER (2991 "Two Great Guitars")...20-25 64
Also see BERRY, Chuck

DIDDLEY, Bo, Howlin' Wolf & Muddy Waters
LPs: 10/12-inch
CHECKER (3008 "Super Blues")...15-20 67
CHECKER (3010 "Super Super Blues Band")...15-20 68
Also see DIDDLEY, Bo
Also see HOWLIN' WOLF
Also see WATERS, Muddy

DIETRICH, Marlene
Singles: 78 rpm
COLUMBIA...5-10 55
Singles: 7-inch
COLUMBIA (40497 "Peter")...10-20 55
COLUMBIA (44326 "Where Have All the Flowers Gone"...4-8 68
DECCA (32076 "This World of Ours")...4-8 67
INDEPENDENCE (91 "Where Have All the Flowers Gone")...5-8 68
LIBERTY (55690 "Where Have All the Flowers Gone")...8-12 64
Picture Sleeves
COLUMBIA (49778 "An Open End Interview with Marlene Dietrich")...10-20 59
(Promotes *Dietrich in Rio* LP. Identification number shown since no selection number is used. Promotional issue only.)
LPs: 10/12-inch
CAPITOL (10282 "Wiedersehen Mit Marlene")...20-30 63
(Monaural.)
CAPITOL (10282 "Wiedersehen Mit Marlene")...10-20 67
(Stereo.)
CAPITOL (10397 "Marlene")...20-30 65
CAPITOL (10443 "Marlena Dietrich's Berlin")...20-30 66
COLUMBIA (105 "Marlena Dietrich Overseas")...40-60 52
(10-inch LP.)
COLUMBIA (164 "Dietrich in Rio")...25-35 59
(Monaural.)
COLUMBIA (316 "Dietrich in Rio")...35-40 59
(Stereo.)
COLUMBIA (2615 "Marlena Dietrich Overseas")...30-50 56
(10-inch LP.)
COLUMBIA (2830 "Dietrich in London")...15-25 65
(Stereo.)
COLUMBIA (4975 "At the Cafe de Paris")...30-50 55
COLUMBIA (6430 "Dietrich in London")...10-20 65
(Monaural.)
DECCA (5100 "Souvenir Album")...40-60 49
(10-inch LP.)
DECCA (7021 "Curtain Call")...30-40 51
DECCA (8465 "Marlene Dietrich")...25-35 57
DECCA (78465 "Marlene Dietrich")...10-20 68
MCA (1501 "Her Complete Recordings")...5-10 82
VOX (3040 "Dietrich Sings")...50-75 50
Also see CLOONEY, Rosemary, & Marlene Dietrich

DIETZEL, Elroy, & Rhythm Bandits
Singles: 7-inch
BO-KAY (101 "Teenage Ball")...250-300 57
BO-KAY (103 "Rock-N-Bones")...300-500 58
(Counterfeits exist of this release.)

DIFFERENT PARTS
Singles: 7-inch
AMS (101 "Why")...25-35

DIKES
Singles: 78 rpm
FEDERAL (12249 "Light Me Up")...20-30 56
Singles: 7-inch
FEDERAL (12249 "Light Me Up")...50-150 56

DILL, Danny
Singles: 78 rpm
ABC-PAR (9681 "My Girl and His Girl")...8-12 56
ABC-PAR (9734 "Hungry for Your Lovin'")...15-25 56
Singles: 7-inch
ABC-PAR (9681 "My Girl and His Girl")...15-25 56
ABC-PAR (9734 "Hungry for Your Lovin'")...50-75 56
CUB (9045 "He Ain't Gonna Study War No More")...10-15 59
LPs: 10/12-inch
LIBERTY (3301 "Folk Songs from the Country")...20-30 63
(Monaural.)
LIBERTY (7301 "Folk Songs from the Country")...25-35 63
(Stereo.)
MGM...25-35 58

DILLARD, Bill
Singles: 78 rpm
UNIQUE (318 "Enchantment")...5-10 55
Singles: 7-inch
UNIQUE (318 "Enchantment")...10-15 55

DILLARD, Bobby
Singles: 7-inch
CHI (110 "Spider")...10-20 61

DILLARD, Moses, & Dynamic Showmen
Singles: 7-inch
MARK V (26 "Pretty As a Picture")...20-30 '60s
Also see MOSES & JOSHUA

DILLARD, Varetta *R&B '52*
(With the Roamers; with Four Students; with El Venos; with Nitecaps; with Buddy Tate & Orchestra)
Singles: 78 rpm
GROOVE...15-35 55-56
RCA...10-20 57
SAVOY (Except 1153)...10-15 51-55
SAVOY (1153 "Johnny [Ace] Has Gone")...20-30 55
Singles: 7-inch
CUB (9073 thru 9091)...10-15 60-61
GROOVE (0139 "Darling, Listen to the Words of This Song")...30-40 56
GROOVE (0152 "Cherry Blossom")...10-20 56
GROOVE (0159 "Got You on My Mind")..15-25 56
GROOVE (0167 "I Miss You Jimmy")...15-25 56
GROOVE (0177 "One More Time")...15-25 56
RCA (6869 thru 7285)...10-20 57-58
SAVOY (822 thru 1118)...30-40 52-53
SAVOY (1137 thru 1166, except 1153)...20-30 54-55
SAVOY (1153 "Johnny [Ace] Has Gone")...75-100 55
TRIUMPH (608 "Scorched")...15-25 59
Also see COOKIES
Also see FERGUSON, H-Bomb, & Varetta Dillard
Also see FOUR STUDENTS
Also see NITECAPS
Also see ROAMERS
Also see TATE, Buddy

DILLARD, Varetta / T.J. Fowler
Singles: 78 rpm
SAVOY (884 "Three Lies")...10-20 53
Singles: 7-inch
SAVOY (884 "Three Lies")...30-40 53
Also see DILLARD, Varetta
Also see FOWLER, T.J.

DILLARD & CLARK
LPs: 10/12-inch
A&M...10-15 68-69
Members: Doug Dillard; Gene Clark.
Also see CLARK, Gene
Also see DILLARDS

DILLARDS *P&R '71*
Singles: 7-inch
ANTHEM...4-6 71-72
CAPITOL...4-6 65
ELEKTRA...4-8 63-69
POPPY...4-6 74
U.A...4-6 75
WHITE WHALE...4-6 70
LPs: 10/12-inch
ANTHEM...6-10 72
ELEKTRA (200 series)...20-30 63-65
(Gold label.)
ELEKTRA (7-200 series)...20-30 63-65
(Gold label.)
ELEKTRA (7-200 series)...10-15
(Brown label.)
ELEKTRA (74000 series)...8-12 68
FLYING FISH...5-10 77-81
POPPY...8-12 73
20TH FOX...8-12 73
Members: Doug Dillard; Rodney Dillard; Dean Webb; Mitch Jayne; Joe Osborn.
Also see CEYLEIB PEOPLE
Also see DILLARD & CLARK
Also see NELSON, Rick

DILLON, Zig
Singles: 7-inch
R (501 "On Down the Line")...15-25 64
R (512 "Bird Song Boogie")...10-20 62

DILLY SISTERS
Singles: 7-inch
GORDO (691 "Sometimes Good Guys Don't Wear White")...10-20 69

DIMENSIONS
Singles: 7-inch
HBR (477 "She's Boss")...5-10 66
PANORAMA (25 "She's Boss")...20-30 66
PANORAMA (41 "Baby What Do You Say")...20-30 66

DIMENSIONS
LPs: 10/12-inch
EVA (10218 "From All Dimensions")...10-15 '80s
SAHARA ("From All Dimensions")...300-500 66
(Selection number not known.)
Members: Barry Probst; Jim Sebastian; Steve Purnell; Jack Brunsfield.

DIMENSIONS
Singles: 7-inch
CARRAM (105 "Surfside")...15-25 '60s
WASHINGTON SQUARE...4-8

DIMPLES
Singles: 7-inch
CAMEO (325 "Dreaming of You")...5-10 64
DORE (517 "My Sister's Beau")...10-15 59
ERA (1079 "Gimme Jimmy")...10-15 58
ERA (3079 "Gimme Jimmy")...5-10 62

DINATONES
Singles: 7-inch
LINDA (105 "Promise")...15-25 61

DING-A-LINGS
Singles: 7-inch
CAPITOL (4467 "C. Percy Mercy")...10-15 60

DING DONG DADDIES
Singles: 7-inch
TOMLAN (1000 "Shortnin' Bread")...50-75

DING DONGS
(Bobby Darin)
Singles: 7-inch
BRUNSWICK (55073 "Early in the Morning") ... 50-100 58
(This same track was reissued as by "The Rinky Dinks" and later by "Bobby Darin & the Rinky Dinks.")
Also see DARIN, Bobby

DING DONGS
Singles: 7-inch
TODD (1043 "Lassie Came Home") ... 10-15 60

DING DONGS
Singles: 7-inch
ELDO (109 "Ding Dong") ... 15-20 60

DINGOES
(With Joe Johnson's Combo)
Singles: 7-inch
DALLAS (2001 "What Would You Do") ... 400-500 57

DINGUS, Bob
Singles: 7-inch
FLORENTINE (100 "Step It Up and Go") ... 150-250

DINKINS, Curlee
(With Travis Warren's Orchestra)
Singles: 7-inch
JAY-TONE (802 "King in the Sky") ... 15-25 58
JAY-TONE (806 "Love 'N in Me") ... 15-25 58

DINKINS, Tim
Singles: 7-inch
FABLE (595 "Cattin' Tonight") ... 150-250

DINNING, Jean
Singles: 78 rpm
ESSEX ... 8-12 55
Singles: 7-inch
ESSEX (395 "Bo Diddley") ... 15-25 55
ESSEX (401 "Lonesome Road") ... 15-25 55

DINNING, Mark P&R '59
Singles: 78 rpm
MGM ... 10-20 57
Singles: 7-inch
CAMEO (299 "January") ... 5-10 64
CAMEO (313 "Should We Do It") ... 5-10 64
HICKORY ... 5-10 65-66
MGM (12553 "School Fool") ... 15-20 57
MGM (12691 "You Thrill Me") ... 10-15 58
MGM (12732 "Secretly in Love with You") ... 10-15 58
MGM (12775 "Cutie Cutie") ... 20-25 59
MGM (12845 "Teen Angel") ... 15-20 59
MGM (12888 thru 13150, except 12980). 10-15 60-63
MGM (12980 "Top 40, News, Weather and Sports") ... 20-30 61
(With mention of Patrice Lumumba in lyrics.)
MGM (12980 "Top 40, News, Weather and Sports") ... 10-15 61
(No mention of Patrice Lumumba in lyrics.)
MGM GOLDEN CIRCLE ... 3-5
U.A. ... 4-6 67-68
Picture Sleeves
MGM (12888 "A Star Was Born") ... 15-20 60
MGM (12929 "The Lovin' Touch") ... 15-20 60
LPs: 10/12-inch
MGM (E-3828 "Teen Angel") ... 40-60 60
(Monaural.)
MGM (SE-3828 "Teen Angel") ... 50-75 60
(Stereo.)
MGM (E-3855 "Wanderin'") ... 40-60 60
(Monaural.)
MGM (SE-3855 "Wanderin'") ... 50-75 60
(Stereo.)

DINO
Singles: 7-inch
GLOVER (200 "Together, You and Me"). 15-25 59
REGALIA (14 "Old Dan Tucker") ... 8-12 60
Session: Barney Zarzana (of Bay Bops).
Also see BAY BOPS

DINO
(With the Ex-Teens; Don De Carlo)
Singles: 7-inch
DINO (79920 "Cathy") ... 10-15 '60s
HONEY BEE (101 "Tearing My Heart Out") ... 10-15 61
Also see DE CARLO, Don

DINO, Bobby
Singles: 7-inch
RIDGECREST (1203 "You Rock Me, Jean") ... 20-30 59

DINO, Kenny P&R '61
Singles: 12-inch
KDK PRODUCTIONS ("Love Songs for Seka") ... 15-25 80
(Picture disc. Has photo of adult-film star, Seka.)
Singles: 7-inch
COLUMBIA (43062 "Betty Jean") ... 5-10 64
DOT (16207 "Just a Little Bit") ... 8-12 61
MUSICOR (1013 "Your Ma Said You Cried in Your Sleep Last Night") ... 10-15 61
MUSICOR (1015 "Rosie, Why Do You Wear My Ring") ... 8-12 62
MUSICOR (1021 "What Good Are Dreams") ... 8-12 62
RADNOR (311 "Sha La La") ... 5-10 '60s
SMASH (1827 "I Wanna Know") ... 5-10 63
SMASH (1861 "DanhoffsTheme") ... 5-10 63

DINO, Paul P&R '61
Singles: 7-inch
ENTRE (101 "Your Candy Kisses") ... 15-25 63
PROMO (2180 "Ginnie Bell") ... 10-15 60

DINO & DIPLOMATS
Singles: 7-inch
DIVA (0103 "Such a Fool for You") ... 20-30 62
(Diva label pasted over original Vida label.)
LAURIE (3103 "I Can't Believe") ... 25-35 61
VIDA (101 "Hush-a-Bye My Love") ... 15-25 61
VIDA (102 "Such a Fool for You") ... 10-20 62

DINO, DESI & BILLY P&R/LP '65
Singles: 7-inch
COLUMBIA (44975 "Let's Talk It Over") ... 5-8 69
UNI (55127 "Someday") ... 5-8 69
REPRISE (0324 "Since You Broke My Heart") ... 10-15 65
REPRISE (0367 thru 0698) ... 5-10 65-68
REPRISE (0965 "Lady Love") ... 10-15 70
Picture Sleeves
REPRISE (0367 "I'm a Fool") ... 8-12 65
REPRISE (0401 "Not the Lovin' Kind") ... 8-12 65
REPRISE (0426 "Please Don't Fight It") ... 8-12 65
REPRISE (0653 "My What a Shame") ... 10-15 67
LPs: 10/12-inch
REPRISE (6176 "I'm a Fool") ... 15-25 65
REPRISE (6194 "Our Time's Coming") ... 15-25 66
REPRISE (6198 "Memories Are Made of This") ... 15-25 65
REPRISE (6224 "Souvenir") ... 25-40 66
(With bonus wallet-sized photos.)
REPRISE (6224 "Souvenir") ... 15-25 66
(Without bonus photos.)
UNI (73056 "Follow Me") ... 15-20 69
Members: Dino Martin; Desi Arnaz Jr.; Billy Hinsche.

DINOS
Singles: 7-inch
FOX (105 "Lover's Holiday") ... 15-25 59
FOX (1010 "So Hard to Tell") ... 100-150 62
FOX (3000 "Darling Oh Darling") ... 75-125

DINOS
(With the Kounts)
Singles: 7-inch
FINE (001 "It's So Good to Know") ... 100-200 '60s
FUN (101 "Our Love's About Over") ... 100-200 64
Member: Abraham Quintanilla.

DINWIDDIE COLORED QUARTET
Singles: 78 rpm
MONARCH (1714 "Down on the Old Camp Ground") ... 300-500 1902
MONARCH (1715 "Poor Mourner") ... 400-600 1902
MONARCH (1716 "Steal Away") ... 400-600 1902
MONARCH (1724 "My Way Is Cloudy") ... 400-600 1902
MONARCH (1725 "Gabriel's Trumpet") ... 300-500 1902
MONARCH (1726 "We'll Anchor Bye-and-Bye") ... 300-500 1902
VICTOR (1714 "Down the Old Camp Ground") ... 200-300 1905
VICTOR (1715 "Poor Mourner") ... 300-400 1905
VICTOR (1716 "Steal Away") ... 300-400 1905
VICTOR (1724 "My Way Is Cloudy") ... 300-400 1905
VICTOR (1725 "Gabriel's Trumpet") ... 300-400 1905
VICTOR (1726 "We'll Anchor Bye-and-Bye") ... 300-400 1905
These are thick, single-sided discs which actually played at about 75 revolutions per minute. They are believed to be the earliest black vocal group recordings.
Members: Sterling Rex; Clarence Meredith; James Thomas; Harry Cruder.

DIO, Andy
(With the Hi-Ways)
Singles: 7-inch
CRUSADE (1023 "Bonnie Jean") ... 20-40 61
GONE (5038 "Daisy Belle") ... 35-50 58
JOHNSON (096 "Daisy Belle") ... 4-6 73
JOHNSON (114 "Satellite") ... 10-20 62
JOY (283 "Daisy Belle") ... 25-40 64
MUSICOR (1118 "Shout") ... 5-8 65
THOR (104 "Rough and Bold") ... 50-75 59

DIO, Ronnie LP '83
(With the Red Caps; with Prophets; Ronnie James Dio; Dio)
Singles: 7-inch
ATLANTIC (2145 "The Ooh-Poo-Pah-Doo") ... 50-75 62
KAPP (697 "Say You're Mine Again") ... 50-75 65
KAPP (725 "Smiling By Day") ... 30-50 65
KAPP (770 "Walking Alone") ... 30-50 66
LAWN (218 "Swingin' Street") ... 30-50 63
PARKWAY (143 "Walking in Different Circles") ... 25-50 67
SENECA (178-102 "An Angel Is Missing") ... 200-300 59
(Reportedly 100 made.)
SWAN (4165 "Mr. Misery") ... 30-50 63
VALEX ("Love Potion No. 9") ... 30-50 64
(No selection number used.)
W.B. ... 3-5 83-86
LPs: 10/12-inch
JOVE (108 "Dio at Domino's") ... 150-250 63
(Reportedly fewer than 1000 made.)
W.B. ... 5-10 83-87
Members: Ronnie James Dio; Dick Bottoff; Nick Pantas; Tom Rogers; Vinny Appice; Jimmy Bain; Vivian Campbell; Claude Schell; Craig Goldie; Jen Johansson; Simon Wright; Rowan Robertson; Terry Cook.
Also see AC/DC
Also see BLACK SABBATH
Also see ELECTRIC ELVES
Also see ELVES
Also see RONNIE & RED CAPS

DIOBOLICS
Singles: 7-inch
TOGETHERNESS (1001 "I Bet That You Never Knew I Followed You") ... 15-25

DION P&R '60
(Dion DiMucci)
Singles: 7-inch
ARISTA ... 3-5 89
BIG TREE/SPECTOR ... 4-6 76
COLUMBIA (3-42662 "Ruby Baby") ... 25-35 62
(Compact 33 single.)
COLUMBIA (4-42662 "Ruby Baby") ... 5-10 62
COLUMBIA (42776 "This Little Girl") ... 5-10 63
COLUMBIA (42810 "Be Careful of Stones You Throw") ... 5-10 63
(Black vinyl.)
COLUMBIA (42810 "Be Careful of Stones You Throw") ... 15-25 63
(Colored vinyl. Promotional issue only.)
COLUMBIA (42852 "Donna the Prima Donna") ... 5-10 63
(Black vinyl.)
COLUMBIA (42852 "Donna the Prima Donna") ... 15-25 63
(Red vinyl. Promotional issue only.)
COLUMBIA (42917 thru 44719) ... 5-10 63-68
DAY SPRING (642 "Hearts Made of Stone") ... 3-5 81
LAURIE (100 series) ... 3-5
LAURIE (3070 thru 3303) ... 10-20 60-65
LAURIE (3464 thru 3504) ... 5-10 68-69
LIFESONG (1765 thru 45082) ... 3-5 78-80
MYRRH ... 3-5 85
SPECTOR ... 4-6 75
STOOP SOUNDS (118 "If I Should Fall Behind") ... 75-125 98
W.B. (Except 814) ... 4-6 69-79
W.B. (814 "The Wanderer") ... 5-10 79
(Promotional issue only.)
W.B./SPECTOR ... 4-6 75
Picture Sleeves
ARISTA ... 3-5 89
COLUMBIA (Except 42662 & 42852) ... 10-20 63-66
COLUMBIA (42662 "Ruby Baby") ... 30-50 62
(Promotional sleeve for *Ruby Baby*, but does not show title or number. Simply reads, "Dion Is Now on Columbia Records.")
COLUMBIA (42662 "Ruby Baby") ... 10-15 62
(Commercially issued sleeve.)
COLUMBIA (42852 "Donna the Prima Donna") ... 20-30 63
(Promotional sleeve for *Donna the Prima Donna*, but does not show title or number. Simply reads, "Dion Over the Top." Issued with red vinyl promo 45.)
LAURIE ... 15-25 60-62
W.B. (7537 "Sanctuary") ... 10-15 71
LPs: 10/12-inch
ARISTA ... 6-12 77-89
COLLECTABLES ... 6-8 83-87
COLUMBIA ... 15-25 63-73
DAY SPRING ... 5-10 80-86
LAURIE (2004 "Alone with Dion") ... 25-35 61
LAURIE (2009 "Runaround Sue") ... 20-30 61
(Black vinyl.)
LAURIE (2009 "Runaround Sue") ... 75-100 61
(Colored vinyl.)
LAURIE (2012 "Lovers Who Wander") ... 25-35 62
LAURIE (2015 "Love Came to Me") ... 25-35 63
LAURIE (2017 "Dion Sings to Sandy and All Other Girls") ... 25-35 63
LAURIE (2019 "15 Million Sellers") ... 25-35 63
LAURIE (2022 "More of Dion's Greatest Hits") ... 25-35 63
LAURIE (2047 "Dion") ... 15-20 68
LAURIE (4000 series) ... 8-15 '70s
LIFESONG ... 5-10 78
PAIR ... 10-12 86
REALM ... 5-10
W.B. ... 10-15 69-76
Also see ADAMS, Bryan
Also see DEE, Joey, & Starliters / Dion
Also see DION & BELMONTS
Also see EDMUNDS, Dave
Also see NEWTON-JOHN, Olivia / Dion
Also see REED, Lou
Also see SIMON, Paul

DION, Jerry
Singles: 7-inch
ZONE (1063 "River of Love") ... 50-75

DION & BELMONTS P&R/R&B '58
(Featuring Dion DiMucci)
Singles: 7-inch
ABC (10868 "My Girl the Month of May") ... 5-10 66
ABC (10896 "For Bobbie") ... 5-10 67
COLLECTABLES ... 3-5 '80s
LAURIE (609 "A Teenager in Love") ... 75-100 59
(Stereo compact 33.)
LAURIE (607 "In the Still of the Night") .. 75-100 59
(Stereo compact 33.)
LAURIE (610 "I've Cried Before") ... 75-100 59
(Stereo compact 33.)
LAURIE (611 "When You Wish Upon a Star") ... 75-100 59
(Stereo compact 33.)
LAURIE (3013 "I Wonder Why") ... 40-60 58
(Gray label.)
LAURIE (3013 "I Wonder Why") ... 20-30 58
(Blue label.)
LAURIE (3013 "I Wonder Why") ... 15-25 59
(Red and white label.)
LAURIE (3015 "No One Knows") ... 30-40 58
(Blue label.)
LAURIE (3015 "No One Knows") ... 15-25 58
(Red and white label.)
LAURIE (3021 "Don't Pity Me") ... 20-30 58
LAURIE (3027 "A Teenager in Love") ... 15-25 59
(Monaural.)
LAURIE (3027S "A Teenager in Love") ... 40-60 59
(Stereo.)
LAURIE (3035 thru 3059) ... 15-25 59-60
LAURIE ("Teen Angel") ... 4-8 95
(Red vinyl. 500 made. Selection number not known.)
LAURIE DOUBLE GOLD ... 3-5 78
MOHAWK (107 "Tag Along") ... 30-40 57

REO (8363 "A Teenager in Love") 15-25 59
(Canadian.)
ROCK'N MANIA 3-5
Picture Sleeves
LAURIE (3027 "A Teenager in Love") .... 5-10 '90s
LAURIE (3035 "Every Little Thing I Do") .. 25-35 59
LAURIE (3044 "Where Or When") 25-35 59
LAURIE (3052 "Wonderful Girl") 25-35 60
LAURIE (3059 "In the Still of the Night") .. 25-35 60
EPs: 7-inch
LAURIE (301 "Their Hits") 100-200 59
LAURIE (302 "Where Or When") 50-75 59
LPs: 10/12-inch
ABC (599 "Together Again") 15-25 67
ARISTA 8-12 84
COLLECTABLES 5-10 83
GRT 8-10 75
JUKE BOX (95140 "A Teenager in Love") .... 20-30 '70s
(Boxed, four-disc set. Also includes Dion solo tracks.)
LAURIE (1002 "Presenting Dion and the Belmonts") 100-200 59
LAURIE (2002 "Presenting Dion and the Belmonts") 100-200 60
(Monaural.)
LAURIE (2002 "Presenting Dion and the Belmonts") 300-500 60
(Stereo.)
LAURIE (2006 "Wish Upon a Star") 50-75 60
LAURIE (2013 "Dion Sings His Greatest Hits - with the Belmonts") 50-75 62
LAURIE (2016 "By Special Request") 30-50 62
LAURIE (4002 "Everything You Always Wanted to Hear") 10-15 76
LAURIE (6000 "60 Greatest") 15-20 71
(Standard cover.)
LAURIE (6000 "60 Greatest") 20-30 71
(Boxed edition.)
PICKWICK 8-10 75
RHINO 5-10 87
W.B. 10-15 73
Also see BELMONTS
Also see DION

DION & BELMONTS / Belmonts
LPs: 10/12-inch
MIASOUND (001 "Half & Half") 15-20 81

DION & TIMBERLANES
(Featuring Dion DiMucci)
Singles: 7-inch
JUBILEE (5294 "Chosen Few") 10-15 57
MOHAWK (105 "Chosen Few") 30-35 57
VIRGO 4-6 73
Also see DION

DIPLOMATS — P&R/R&B '64
Singles: 7-inch
AROCK (1004 "Here's a Heart") 10-20 64
AROCK (1008 "Help Me") 10-20 64
DYNAMO (Except 122) 5-10 68-69
DYNAMO (122 "I Can Give You Love") ... 15-20 68
HOLIDAY (106 "Point of No Return") 10-20 61
MAY (105 "Let's Be in Love") 15-25 61
MINIT (32006 "Don't Bug Me") 8-12 66
WAND (174 "So Far Away") 8-12 65
WAND (195 "I've Got Feelings") 8-12 65

DIPPERS
Singles: 7-inch
DIPLOMACY (4 "Goin' Ape") 10-20 64

DIPPERS QUINTET
(With Van Perry's Combo)
Singles: 7-inch
FLAYR (500 "It's Almost Christmas") 3500-5000 55

DIRTE FOUR
Singles: 7-inch
CHARAY (34 "On the Move") 10-20 65
MERCURY (72885 "On the Move") 8-12 68
SOFT (1027 "I Want to Give You All My Love") 15-25 69
Also see HOBBS, Willie

DIRTY FILTHY MUD
Singles: 7-inch
WOREX (2340 "Forest of Black") 20-30 67
EPs: 7-inch
WOREX ("Dirty Filthy Mud") 250-350 67
(Selection number not known.)

DIRTY RED
(Nelson Wilborn)
Singles: 78 rpm
ALADDIN (194 "Mother Flyer") 75-125 47
ALADDIN (207 "Hotel Boogie") 40-60 48

DIRTY SHAMES
Singles: 7-inch
IMPRESSION (112 "I Don't Care") 10-20 66
PHILIPS (40436 "Coconut Grove") 8-12 67
PHILIPS (40474 "Blow Your Mind") 8-12 67

DIRTY WURDS
Singles: 7-inch
CHESS (1983 "Midnight Hour") 8-12 67
MARINA (502 "Why") 100-125 65

DISCHORDS
Singles: 7-inch
BONNEVILLE (205 "Wipe Out") 25-35 63

DISCIPLES
Singles: 7-inch
FORTUNE (573 "I Found Out") 10-15 65

DISCIPLES
Singles: 7-inch
FEATURE (9427 "It's Over") 25-35 67

DISCIPLES
Singles: 7-inch
FOUNDATION (709 "Darlin' ") 15-20

DI SENTRI, Turner
(Bob Gaudio)
Singles: 7-inch
TOPIX (6001 "10,000,000 Tears") 25-35 61
Also see 4 SEASONS
Also see ROYAL TEENS

DISHAW, Tommy
Singles: 7-inch
D&C (500 "We're Gonna Rock") 30-50 59
GLORY (299 "Angela") 10-15 59

DISSENSION
Singles: 7-inch
METALSTORM (8815 "We the Fooled") .. 10-20 89
(Picture disc, packaged in a metal can. 500 made.)

DISSONAIRES
Singles: 7-inch
ALTAIR (101 "One Love") 30-50 59
(Reissued as by the Penetrators.)
Also see PENETRATORS

DISTANT SOUNDS
Singles: 7-inch
CITATION ("It Reminds Me") 10-20 66
(Selection number not known.)

DISTANTS
("Vocal By Richard Strick")
Singles: 7-inch
NORTHERN (3732 "Come On") 100-150 60
WARWICK (546 "Come On") 75-125 60
WARWICK (577 "Always") 100-150 60
Members: Richard Street [Strick]; Otis Williams; Melvin Franklin; Eldridge Bryant.
Also see STREET, Richard, & Distants
Also see TEMPTATIONS

DISTORTERS
Singles: 7-inch
CLARK (364 "Distortion") 10-20 64

DIVINE — D&D '83
Singles: 12-inch
O (722 "Shoot Your Shot") 5-10 83
PROTO (127 "Twistin' the Night Away") ... 20-40 84
(Includes bonus disc, *Native Love '84*, which is single-sided.)

DIVISION
Singles: 7-inch
TRANSACTION (710 "Not Fade Away") .. 15-25 69

DIVITO, Buddy, & Meadowlarks
Singles: 78 rpm
CHANCE 10-15 54
Singles: 7-inch
CHANCE (Black vinyl) 10-15 54
CHANCE (Colored vinyl) 15-25 54

DIXIE BLUES BOYS
(With Vocal by Dee Dee)
Singles: 78 rpm
FLAIR (1072 "Monte Carlo") 25-50 55
Singles: 7-inch
FLAIR (1072 "Monte Carlo") 75-100 55

DIXIE CUPS — P&R/R&B/LP '64
Singles: 7-inch
ABC-PAR (10692 thru 10855) 8-12 65-66
ANTILLES 3-5 87
LANA .... 4-6 '60s
RED BIRD (001 "Chapel of Love") 8-12 64
RED BIRD (006 "People Say") 8-12 64
RED BIRD (012 "You Should Have Seen the Way He Looked at Me") 8-12 64
RED BIRD (017 "Little Bell") 10-20 65
RED BIRD (024 "Iko Iko"/"Gee Baby, Gee") 10-15 65
RED BIRD (024 "Iko Iko"/"I'm Gonna Get You Yet") 8-10 65
RED BIRD (032 "Gee the Moon Is Shining Bright") 8-12 65
TRIP .... 4-6 '70s
Picture Sleeves
ANTILLES 3-5 87
EPs: 7-inch
ABC-PAR (525 "Riding High") 15-25 65
(Juke box issue only. Includes title strips. Stereo.)
LPs: 10/12-inch
ABC-PAR (ABC-525 "Riding High") 25-30 65
(Monaural.)
ABC-PAR (ABCS-525 "Riding High") 30-40 65
(Stereo.)
BACK-TRAC (1001 "Best of the Dixie Cups") 8-12 85
(Red vinyl.)
RED BIRD (RB-100 "Chapel of Love") 35-45 64
(Monaural.)
RED BIRD (RBS-100 "Chapel of Love") ... 50-75 64
(Stereo.)
RED BIRD (RB-103 "Iko Iko") 35-55 65
(Monaural.)
RED BIRD (RBS-103 "Iko Iko") 60-80 65
(Stereo.)
Members: Barbara Hawkins; Rosa Hawkins; Joan Johnson.

DIXIE FLIERS
Singles: 7-inch
GUYDEN (2055 "Nail It") 10-20 61
LARK (452 "Yellow Dog Blues") 5-10

DIXIE GUITARS
Singles: 7-inch
SHELLEY (1004 "Dixieland Guitars") 10-20 59

DIXIE HARMONAIRES
Singles: 7-inch
DIXIE (1008 "Honey Hush") 200-300 58

DIXIEAIRES — R&B '48
(Dixie-Aires)
Singles: 78 rpm
EXCLUSIVE 15-25 48-49
GOTHAM 15-25 48
HARLEM 25-75 54
LENOX 15-25 49
SITTIN' IN WITH 15-25 50
Singles: 7-inch
HARLEM (2326 "Traveling All Alone") .. 400-500 54
Members: Joe Van Loan; Clyde Reddick; Henry Owens; Conrad Frederick; Arlandus Wilson; Willie Ray; Joe Floyd; John Hines; Bob Kornegay; J.C. Giuyard.
Also see BELLS
Also see DU DROPPERS
Also see GOLDEN GATE QUARTET
Also see VALIANTS
Also see VAN LOAN, Joe

DIXIEBELLES — P&R/R&B '63
Singles: 7-inch
MONUMENT 4-6 72
SOUND STAGE 7 .... 5-10 63-64
EPs: 7-inch
SOUND STAGE 7 .... 15-20 63
LPs: 10/12-inch
SOUND STAGE 7 .... 20-30 63
MONUMENT 15-20 65
Also see SMITH, Jerry

DIXIELAND DRIFTERS
Singles: 7-inch
B.B. (222 "The Trot") 50-75
B.B. (223 "Don't You Be Still") 75-100
HAP (1005 "You Won't Fall in Love") 75-100

DIXIELANDERS
Singles: 7-inch
DO-RE-ME 15-25 59-60

DIXON, Billy, & Topics
Singles: 7-inch
TOPIX (6002 "I Am All Alone") 40-50 61
TOPIX (6008 "Lost Lullabye") 50-75 62
Also see 4 SEASONS
Also see TOPICS

DIXON, Danny
Singles: 78 rpm
ABBOTT (112 "Sweater Girl") 10-15 52
Singles: 7-inch
ABBOTT (112 "Sweater Girl") 15-25 52

DIXON, Dave
Singles: 78 rpm
ACE (519 "I'm Not Satisfied") 15-25 56
SAVOY 8-12 54
Singles: 7-inch
ACE (519 "I'm Not Satisfied") 20-30 56
HOME OF THE BLUES (108 "You Don't Love Me No More") 10-15 60
HOME OF THE BLUES (120 "Hey Hey Pretty Baby") 10-15 61
PZAZZ (043 "Hitchhiking Hippie") 4-8 70
SAVOY (1126 "My Plea") 20-30 54

DIXON, Dick, & Roommates
Singles: 7-inch
KAPP (292 "Caterpillar Crawl") 10-20 59

DIXON, Dizzy
Singles: 78 rpm
VEE-JAY (174 "Soup Line") 10-15 56
Singles: 7-inch
SPARKLE 15-25
VEE-JAY (174 "Soup Line") 20-25 56
(With Al Smith's Orchestra.)
Also see SMITH, Al

DIXON, Floyd — R&B '49
(Floyd Dixon's Trio)
Singles: 78 rpm
ALADDIN (3073 "She's Understanding") . 20-30 50
ALADDIN (3074 "San Francisco Blues") .. 20-30 50
ALADDIN (3078 "Let's Dance") 20-30 51
ALADDIN (3083 "Rockin' at Home") 20-30 51
ALADDIN (3084 "Don't Cry Now Baby") .. 20-30 51
ALADDIN (3101 "Time & Place") 20-30 51
ALADDIN (3111 "Too Much Jelly Roll") ... 20-30 51
ALADDIN (3135 thru 3151) 20-30 52
CASH (1057 "Oh Baby") 15-25 57
CAT (106 "Moonshine") 15-25 54
CAT (114 "Hey Bartender") 15-25 55
MODERN (653 "Dallas Blues") 15-25 49
MODERN (664 "That'll Get It") 15-25 49
MODERN (700 "Drafting Blues") 15-25 49
MODERN (724 "Milky White Way") 15-25 49
MODERN (725 "Cow Town") 15-25 49
MODERN (727 "Gloomy Baby") 15-25 50
MODERN (744 "People Like Me") 15-25 50
MODERN (761 "It's Gettin' Foggy") 15-25 50
MODERN (776 "Playboy Blues") 15-25 50
MODERN (797 "You Made a Fool Out of Me") 15-25 51
PEACOCK (1528 "Let's Dance") 15-25 50
PEACOCK (1544 "She's Understanding") 15-25 50
QUALITY (1288 "Moonshine") 15-25 54
(Canadian.)
SUPREME (1528 "Houston Jump") 20-30 49
SUPREME (1535 "Broken Hearted") 20-30 49
SUPREME (1546 "You Need Me Now") .. 20-30 49
SUPREME (1547 "Worries") 20-30 50
SWING TIME (261 "Houston Jump") 15-25 51
SWING TIME (287 "You Need Me Now") 15-25 51
Singles: 7-inch
ALADDIN (3135 "Wine Wine Wine") 200-300 52
ALADDIN (3144 "Red Cherries") 300-400 52
(Black vinyl.)
ALADDIN (3144 "Red Cherries") 500-700 52
(Red vinyl.)

ALADDIN (3151 "Tired, Broke and Busted") 200-300 52
BOXER (101 "I Been Waiting") 15-25
CASH (1057 "Oh Baby") 20-30 57
CAT (106 "Moonshine") 50-75 54
CAT (114 "Hey Bartender") 50-75 55
CHATTAHOOCHEE (652 "There Goes My Heart") 8-12 64
CHATTAHOOCHEE (697 "Don't Leave Me Baby") 8-12 66
CHECKER (857 "Alarm Clock Blues") 20-30 58
DODGE (807 "Daisy") 10-15 61
DUCHESS (1004 "Girl Down in New Orleans") 5-10 61
EBB (105 "Ooh Little Girl") 20-30 57
IMPERIAL (5849 "Tired, Broke and Busted") 8-12 62
INCULCATION (47192 "I Think of You Babe") 4-8
JELLO 10-15 60
KENT (311 "Change Your Mind") 10-20 58
PEARL (25 "For Mother") 10-15
QUALITY (1288 "Moonshine") 50-75 54
(Canadian.)
REVA (7 "Late Freight") 10-15 62
SPECIALTY (468 "Hard Living Alone") 50-75 53
(Black vinyl.)
SPECIALTY (468 "Hard Living Alone") 100-200 53
(Red vinyl.)
SPECIALTY (477 "Hole in the Wall") 50-75 53
(Black vinyl.)
SPECIALTY (477 "Hole in the Wall") ... 100-200 53
(Red vinyl.)
SPECIALTY (486 "Ooh-Eee Ooh-Eee") .. 50-75 54
(Black vinyl.)
SPECIALTY (486 "Ooh-Eee Ooh-Eee") 100-200 54
(Red vinyl.)
SWINGIN' (626 "Tight Skirts") 10-15 60

LPs: 10/12-inch

INCULCATION 8-10
Session: Roy Hayes; Eddie Williams; Nat McFay; Willie Dixon; Fred Below; Robert Lockwood Jr.
Also see DIXON, Willie
Also see LOCKWOOD, Robert, Jr.
Also see WILLIAMS, Eddie

DIXON, Floyd, & Johnny Moore's Three Blazers

Singles: 78 rpm

ALADDIN (3069 "Girl Fifteen") 20-30 50
ALADDIN (3074 "Empty Stocking Blues") 20-30 50
ALADDIN (3075 "Real Lovin' Mama") 20-30 50
ALADDIN (3083 "Unlucky Girl") 20-30 51
ALADDIN (3101 "Do I Love You") 20-30 51
ALADDIN (3121 "Blues for Cuba") 20-30 52
ALADDIN (3166 thru 3230) 20-30 52-54

Singles: 7-inch

ALADDIN (3101 "Do I Love You") 50-100 51
ALADDIN (3166 "Broken Hearted Traveller") 50-100 53
ALADDIN (3196 "Married Woman") 50-100 53
ALADDIN (3221 "Bad Neighborhood") .. 50-100 54
ALADDIN (3230 "You Need Me Now") .. 50-100 54
Also see DIXON, Floyd
Also see MOORE, Johnny

DIXON, Helene
(Helen Dixon)

Singles: 78 rpm

EPIC 6-12 54-55
OKEH 10-15 53
VIK 6-12 56

Singles: 7-inch

EPIC (9078 "I'm Too Busy Crying") 8-12 54
EPIC (9113 "Heaven Came Down to Earth") 10-20 55
EPIC (9121 "Por Favor") 8-12 55
OKEH (6964 "Don't Call My Name") 15-25 53
PEACH (753 "I Can't Stop My Heart") 5-10 62
VIK (0212 "Roll Over Beethoven") 15-25 56
VIK (0228 "The Opposite Sex") 10-20 56

DIXON, Jim, & Regence

Singles: 7-inch

GOLDEN ARROW (718 "Natural Beauty") .... 10-20 '60s

DIXON, Mason, & Redskins

Singles: 78 rpm

METEOR 25-35 56

Singles: 7-inch

METEOR (5028 "Don't Worry 'Bout Nuthin'" 100-150 56
REED (1045 "I Want My Baby Back") 50-75 60
REED (1051 "Cold, Cold Heart") 15-25 60
REED (1064 "Hello Memphis") 100-150 61

DIXON, Richie

Singles: 7-inch

DORSET (5008 "Lesson in Love") 10-20 61

DIXON, Ted

Singles: 7-inch

STOMPER TIME (1158 "I Had to Let You Go") 50-75

DIXON, Walter

Singles: 7-inch

ERWIN (211 "Goodbye, She's Gone") 20-30 57

DIXON, Webb

Singles: 7-inch

ASTRO (101 "Rock Awhile") 50-70 59
ASTRO (102 "Rock and Roll Angel") 50-70 59

DIXON, Willie R&B '55

Singles: 78 rpm

CHECKER 10-20 55-56

Singles: 7-inch

CHECKER (822 "Walking the Blues") 30-40 55
CHECKER (828 "Crazy for My Baby") 30-40 55
CHECKER (851 "Twenty-Nine Ways") 30-40 56

LPs: 10/12-inch

BLUE HORIZON 10-15 70
COLUMBIA (9987 "I Am the Blues") 10-15 70
OVATION (14-33 "Catalyst") 8-12 74
ROOTS N' BLUES 5-8 90
SPIVEY 8-10
YAMBO 8-10
Session: Lafayette Leake; Ollie Crawford; Harold Ashby; Fred Below; Al Duncan.
Also see BOYD, Eddie
Also see DIDDLEY, Bo
Also see DIXON, Floyd
Also see GUY, Buddy
Also see LITTLE WALTER
Also see EMERSON, Billy
Also see FIVE BREEZES
Also see HOWLIN' WOLF
Also see NIGHTHAWKS
Also see REED, Jimmy
Also see ROGERS, Jimmy
Also see RUSH, Otis
Also see TAYLOR, Koko
Also see WASHBOARD SAM
Also see WATERS, Muddy
Also see WELLS, Junior
Also see WILLIAMSON, Sonny Boy
Also see WITHERSPOON, Jimmy

DIXON, Willie, & Memphis Slim

Singles: 7-inch

PRESTIGE BLUESVILLE 5-10 62

LPs: 10/12-inch

BATTLE (6122 "Memphis Slim and Willie Dixon in Paris") 20-30 63
FOLKWAYS 8-12
PRESTIGE BLUESVILLE (1003 "Willie's Blues") 25-35 60
VERVE (3007 "Blues Every Which Way") 25-35 61
Also see BIG THREE TRIO
Also see MEMPHIS SLIM
Also see SELLERS, Johnny

DIXON, Wylie, & Wheels
(Willie Dixon & the Big Wheels)

Singles: 7-inch

ACE 4-6 75
CCHY-TOWN (101 "Sweet Pea") 10-15 65
CHECKER (1164 "How Long Must I Wait") 5-10 67
CONDUC (103 "Sweet Pea") 15-25 65
FEDERAL (12524 "Our Kind of Love") 8-12 64
JERMA (104 "Sweet Pea") 15-25
TODDLIN' TOWN (105 "Gotta Hold On") ... 5-10 68
Also see MARCHAN, Bobby, & Willie Dixon
Also see SIMMONS, Simtec, & Wylie Dixon

D'MATICS

Singles: 7-inch

DRAHCIR (1126 "The Love of Ours") 20-30

DO's & DONT's

Singles: 7-inch

RED BIRD (072 "I Wonder If She Loves Me") 5-10 66
ZORCH (103 "Be Sure") 10-15 66
ZORCH (104 "Cherry Lane") .... 10-15 '60s
ZORCH (105 "The Scrogg") .... 10-15 '60s
ZORCH (106 "Woman") .... 10-15 '60s
ZORCH (107 "Let the Sun Shine Free") ... 10-15 '60s
ZORCH (108 "Hot Rock and Roll to Go") . 10-15 '60s
Also see ESCORTS

DOBBIN, Joseph, & Four Cruisers / Four Cruisers

Singles: 78 rpm

CHESS 100-150 53

Singles: 7-inch

CHESS (1547 "On Account of You") 250-300 53

DOBKINS, Carl, Jr. P&R/R&B '59
(With the Seniors; with the Orbits)

Singles: 7-inch

ATCO (6283 "If Teardrops Were Diamonds") 5-10 64
CHALET 4-8 69
COLPIX (762 "His Loss Is My Gain") 5-10 65
DECCA 10-20 59-62
FRATERNITY (794 "That's Why I'm Asking") 8-12 58
MCA 4-6 73

Picture Sleeves

DECCA (31020 "Lucky Devil") 5-10 59
DECCA (31088 "Exclusively Yours") 5-10 60

EPs: 7-inch

DECCA (2664 "My Heart Is an Open Book") 50-75 59

LPs: 10/12-inch

DECCA (8938 "Carl Dobkins Jr.") 40-50 59
(Monaural.)
DECCA (7-8938 "Carl Dobkins Jr.") 50-65 59
(Stereo.)
Also see LEE, Brenda / Carl Dobkins Jr.

DOBRO, Jimmie
(James Burton)

Singles: 7-inch

PHILIPS (40137 "Swamp Surfer") 30-40 63
Also see BURTON, James

DOBRO, Lon
(Lon Dobro Combo; with Leonel Dobro & Orchestra)

Singles: 7-inch

4 STAR (1754 "All the Time") 30-40 61
MILESTONE (2017 "All the Time") 10-20 63
TROY (1003 "Undercurrent") 15-25 63

DOBSON, Dobby
(With the Deltas)

Singles: 7-inch

GAYDISC (10 "Diamonds and Pearls") 40-50 61
TRANQUILITY (30 "What Love Has Joined Together") 10-15

DOBSON, Leroy

Singles: 7-inch

LUDWIG (1006 "I Wanna Make Love") 100-150

DOC & DOLPHINS

Singles: 7-inch

DINO (2 "Something About You Darling") 400-500

DOC & PROBIHITION

Singles: 7-inch

LAURIE (3619 "Superman") 10-20 74

DOC & ROUNDY

Singles: 7-inch

CUCA (6759 "Not Your Kind") 15-25 67

DOC SAUSAGE & HIS MAD LADS R&B '50

Singles: 78 rpm

REGAL (3251 "Rag Mop") 10-20 49
REGAL (3256 "Sausage Rock") 10-20 50

DOCKERY, Chuck

Singles: 7-inch

NEW SONG (123 "Baby Let's Dance") .. 75-100 59
(At least one source shows this number as 117. We don't know yet which is correct.)
NEW SONG (129 "Rock While We Ride") 40-60 59
(At least one source shows this number as 123. We don't know yet which is correct.)

DR. BOP & HEADLINERS

LPs: 10/12-inch

CHICKEN (1001 "Live") 35-50

DOCTOR FEELGOOD P&R '62
(Doctor Feelgood & Interns)

Singles: 7-inch

COLUMBIA (43236 "Good Guys") 5-10 65
COLUMBIA (43372 "Doctor of Love") 5-10 65
COLUMBIA (43615 "Where Did You Go") . 5-10 66
EPIC .... 4-6 '70s
MASTER SOUND (1115 "I'm Sticking with You Baby") 5-10 67
OKEH (7144 thru 7185) 10-15 62-63
1-2-3 (1701 "Sugar Bee") 5-10 68

LPs: 10/12-inch

OKEH (12101 "Doctor Feelgood") 25-35 62
(Monaural.)
OKEH (14101 "Doctor Feelgood") 35-45 62
(Stereo.)
NUMBER ONE 15-20
Also see JOHNSON, Roy Lee
Also see PIANO RED

DR. HEP CAT
(Lavada Durst)

Singles: 78 rpm

UPTOWN ("Hattie Green") 75-100 48
Also see DURST, L.

DOCTOR ROCK

Singles: 78 rpm

CARAVAN 15-25 56

Singles: 7-inch

CARAVAN (15610 "One Way of Livin'") .. 35-50 56

DOCTOR SOUL

Singles: 7-inch

NATURAL SOUL (17,000 "Soul Is the Answer") 100-150
Member: Lloyd Brown.

DR. SPEC'S OPTICAL ILLUSION

Singles: 7-inch

FLAMBEAU (103 "She's the One") 20-30 67

DR. T. & UNDERTAKERS

Singles: 7-inch

TARGET (101 "Undertaker's Theme") .... 15-25 '60s
TARGET (4610 "Times Have Changed") . 15-25 '60s

DR. WEST'S MEDICINE SHOW & JUNK BAND P&R '66

Singles: 7-inch

GO GO (100 thru 106) 5-10 66-68
ROWE/AMI 5-10 66
("Play Me" Sales Stimulator promotional issue.)

Picture Sleeves

GO GO (102 "Playboys & Bums") 10-20 67

LPs: 10/12-inch

GO GO (002 "The Eggplant That Ate Chicago") 20-30 67
GREGAR .... 15-20 '60s

DOCTOR WHO

LPs: 10/12-inch

GEMCOM (22002 "Doctor Who") 20-25 85
(Picture disc.)
GEMCOM (22004 "Doctor Who") 20-25 85
(Picture disc.)

DODD, Dick

Singles: 7-inch

ATTARACK .... 8-10 '60s
TOWER (447 Little Sister") 8-10 68

LPs: 10/12-inch

TOWER (5142 "First Evolution of Dick Dodd") 30-40 68
Also see STANDELLS

DODD, Jimmy

Singles: 78 rpm

ABC-PAR 5-10 55-56

Singles: 7-inch

ABC-PAR 15-25 55-56

LPs: 10/12-inch

DISNEYLAND (1235 "Sing Along with Jimmy Dodd") 20-30 63
WORD (3241 "Children's Bible Story Time") 10-15 63
Also see ANNETTE
Also see MOUSEKETEERS

DODDS, Billy

Singles: 7-inch

PRIME (2601 "Praying for You")............. 15-25 61

DODDS, Johnny
(Gene Autry)

Singles: 78 rpm

OKEH (45317 "Railroad Boomer")........... 25-75 '30s
OKEH (45417 "Frankie and Johnny")...... 25-75 '30s
OKEH (45462 "No One to Call Me Darling").. 25-75 '30s
OKEH (45472 "Slu Foot Lou").................. 25-75 '30s
OKEH (45560 "Cowboy Yodel")............... 25-75 '30s
Also see AUTRY, Gene

DODDS, Malcolm
(With the Tunedrops)

Singles: 7-inch

AMY (861 "All My Wildest Dreams")...........5-10 62
AURORA (1997 "Now I Have Someone") ..5-10 62
DECCA (30653 thru 30970).................... 10-20 58-59
END (1000 "It Took a Long Time")........... 20-30 57
END (1004 "Can't You See").................... 20-30 57
END (1010 "Unspoken Love").................. 30-40 58
MGM (12975 thru 13029)...........................5-10 61
PARAMOUNT 4-6 73
RAMROD (3 "Every Time We Say Goodbye")...5-10 60

LPs: 10/12-inch

CAMDEN (831 "Try a Little Tenderness").. 10-20 64
Also see LUBRANO, Bill
Also see TUNEDROPS

DODDS, Nella P&R/R&B '64

Singles: 7-inch

WAND (167 "Come See About Me")...........8-12 64
WAND (171 thru 187).................................5-10 64
WAND (1111 "Gee Whiz")........................ 10-15 65
WAND (1136 "Honey Boy")...................... 50-75 65

DODDS, Troy

Singles: 7-inch

BAYTOWN (4001 "Earthquake")..................5-10 64
DAYTONA (2101 "Count of Love") .... 20-30 '60s
EL CAMINO (701 "Try My Love")........... 75-150 66
PENT HOUSE (002 "Down in Tennessee")... 10-20 62
W.B. (5309 "Down in Tennessee").............8-12 62

DODGER & JOHNNY ANGEL

Singles: 7-inch

SKYWAY (117 "Boogie Man")............. 100-125 58

DODGERS

Singles: 78 rpm

ALADDIN (3259 "Let's Make a Whole Lot of Love")... 30-40 54
ALADDIN (3271 "Drip Drop") 50-100 54

Singles: 7-inch

ALADDIN (3259 "Let's Make a Whole Lot of Love")... 100-150 54
(Maroon label.)
ALADDIN (3259 "Let's Make a Whole Lot of Love")... 40-50 54
(Blue label.)
ALADDIN (3271 "Drip Drop") 150-250 54
Member: Thomas Fox.

DODGERS

Singles: 7-inch

TOP RANK (2021 "Upturn") 10-15 59

DODGERS & JOHNNY ANGEL

Singles: 7-inch

SKYWAY (117 "Pretty Baby") 25-35 58

DODO, Joe, & Groovers

Singles: 7-inch

RCA (7207 "Goin' Steady") 15-25 58

DOGGETT, Bill P&R/R&B '56
(With "Vocal By the Combo")

Singles: 78 rpm

KING 5-10 53-57

Singles: 7-inch

ABC-PAR...5-10 64
CHUMLEY...4-6 74
COLUMBIA...5-10 62-63
GUSTO..3-5 '80s
KING (4000 series) 10-20 53-56
(Black vinyl.)
KING (4000 series)....................................25-50 '50s
(Colored vinyl. We're not yet sure how many different releases came on colored plastic.)
KING (5000 series).......................................6-15 56-65
KING (6000 series)...4-8 66-71
ROULETTE (4732 "Sapphire")......................5-8 67
ROULETTE (4749 "Lovin' Mood")................5-8 67
SUE (2 "Fat Back").......................................4-8 68
SUE (10-002 "Fat Back")............................5-10 64
W.B. 5-10 60-61

Picture Sleeves

COLUMBIA...5-10 62

EPs: 7-inch 33/45

KING...10-20 53-59
W.B. ("Bill Doggett & His Combo")...........10-15 60
(Promotional issue only. No selection number used.)

LPs: 10/12-inch

ABC-PAR 10-20 65
COLUMBIA..10-20 62-63
HARMONY..10-15 67
KING (82 thru 118) 20-40 52-55
(10-inch LPs.)
KING (500 thru 900 series) 15-35 56-66
ROULETTE..10-15 66
STARDAY 5-10
W.B. 15-25 61-62
Session: Howard Tate; Bill Butler; Clifford Scott.
Also see BOSTIC, Earl, & Bill Doggett
Also see BROWN, Wini
Also see DAVIS, Eddie "Lockjaw"
Also see FITZGERALD, Ella, & Bill Doggett
Also see HARLEMAIRES
Also see HUMES, Helen
Also see JACQUET, Illinois
Also see PAGE, Hot Lips
Also see SCOTT, Clifford
Also see TATE, Howard

DOGGETT, Ray

Singles: 78 rpm

DECCA..25-35 57
SPADE 50-75 56

Singles: 7-inch

DECCA (30295 "It Hurts the One Who Loves You")..25-50 57
KEN-LEE (101 "Beach Party") 15-25
PEARL (716 "No Doubt About It").........100-125 58
SPADE (1926 "Go Go Heart")................75-100 56
SPADE (1932 "It Hurts the One Who Loves You")..75-100 56
TNT (159 "Whirlpool of Love") 30-50 58
TOP RANK (2025 "Can I Be the One")......15-25 59

LPs: 10/12-inch

ROCK IT (1001 "The Personal Side of Ray Doggett")..8-12 79

DOJO

LPs: 10/12-inch

ECLIPSE (7309 "Down for the Last Time")..20-30 71

DOLAN, Don

Singles: 7-inch

REECO (1003 "Alabama Girl")..................50-75

DOLAN, Jimmie C&W '51
(Ramblin' Jimmie Dolan; with Texas Ramblers)

Singles: 78 rpm

CAPITOL...5-10 51-54
MODERN...10-15 47-49

Singles: 7-inch

CAPITOL...10-20 51-54

DOLENZ, Micky P&R '67
(Mickey Dolenz)

Singles: 7-inch

CHALLENGE (59353 "Don't Do It") 10-20 66
CHALLENGE (59372 "Huff Puff") 10-20 67
MGM...8-12 71-72
ROMAR...8-10 73-74

Picture Sleeves

CHALLENGE (59353 "Don't Do It") 10-20 66
CHALLENGE (59372 "Huff Puff") 20-30 67

LPs: 10/12-inch

CHRYSALIS...8-10 79
Also see MONKEES
Also see NILSSON

DOLENZ, Micky, Davy Jones & Peter Tork

Singles: 7-inch

CHRISTMAS RECORDS 8-12 76
(Fan club, mail-order issue. Issued with special poster.)
Members: Micky Dolenz; David Jones; Peter Tork.
Also see MONKEES

DOLENZ, JONES, BOYCE & HART

Singles: 7-inch

CAPITOL (4180 "I Remember the Feeling") 10-15 75
CAPITOL (4271 "I Love You") 10-15 75

LPs: 10/12-inch

CAPITOL...10-15 76
Members: Micky Dolenz; David Jones; Tommy Boyce; Bobby Hart.
Also see BOYCE, Tommy, & Bobby Hart
Also see DOLENZ, Micky
Also see JONES, Davy, & Micky Dolenz

DOLL, Andy

Singles: 7-inch

AD (101 "Hey Baba Re Bop") 50-75 59
AD (3408 thru 4783)...................................10-20 59-61
CUCA (1259 "Little Jessie") 5-10 66
JAY JAY (300 "Hot Chicken") 5-10 64
MASTERTONE (1014 "Muskrat Ramble")...15-25 '50s
STARDAY (345 "That's Life")......................50-75 57

LPs: 10/12-inch

AUDIO (1001 "On Stage").........................20-30

DOLL BABY

Singles: 7-inch

RIDGECREST (1207 "Hammy in the Holee")..300-400 59

DOLLAR BILL

Singles: 7-inch

TAHOE (2539 "Mr. Cool") 20-30

DOLLS

Singles: 7-inch

OKEH (7122 "In Love") 15-25 59
TEENAGE (1010 "Just Before You Leave") 2000-2500 58

DOLLS
(With the Henry Hayes Orchestra)

Singles: 7-inch

KANGAROO (101 "Tell Me Now") 15-25 64
MALTESE (100 "This Is Our Day")...........20-30 65
MALTESE (107 "Airplane Song") 200-300 65
Member: Norma Jenkins.

DOLLY
(With the Fashions)

Singles: 7-inch

IVANHOE (5019 "Just Another Fool") 10-15 65
TRI DISC (111 "Waiting for My Man") 10-15 64

DOLLY & DEANS
(With the Karol-Thorn Orchestra)

Singles: 7-inch

THORNETT (1008 "The Happiest Years")..50-75 '50s

DOLPHINS P&R '64

Singles: 7-inch

EMPRESS (102 "Rainbow's End") 10-15 61
FRATERNITY (937 "Hey-Da-Da-Dow")....10-15 64
FRATERNITY (940 "Little Donna") 8-12 65
GEMINI (501 "Pony Race").......................10-15 62
(First issue.)
LAURIE (3202 "Hang On")..........................5-10 63
SHAD (5020 "Tell-Tale Kisses") 30-40 60
TIP TOP (2003 "Pony Race")....................10-15 62
TIP TOP (2005 "It Might Break Your Heart")..5-10 62
Members: Carl Edmonson; Paul Singleton; Marvin Lockhard.

DOLPHINS

Singles: 7-inch

YORKSHIRE (125 "Surfing East Coast") .15-20 66

DOLTON, Billy
(Glen Campbell)

Singles: 7-inch

KAYBO (617 "Winkie Doll").......................30-40 61
Also see CAMPBELL, Glen

DOMESTIC HELP

Singles: 7-inch

ACTA (805 "A Woman Owns the Biggest Part of Man") 35-50 67
(With four-page bio-lyrics insert.)
ACTA (805 "A Woman Owns the Biggest Part of Man") 15-25 67
(Without insert.)
ACTA (814 "Try to Forgive") 5-10 67
Members: Hal Ross; Jim Barnaby; Bill Adems; Johnny Bravata Jr.

DOMINEERS

Singles: 7-inch

ROULETTE (4245 "Nothing Can Go Wrong") 20-30 60

DOMINICO, Michael
(With the Three Chicks & Orchestra)

Singles: 7-inch

BELL (661 "To Have and to Hold")............5-10 67
GONE (5123 "Now Is the Time") 5-10 62
P&L (1028 "Write Me Baby Please")........10-15 60
PER-SONA (11-61 "Lover Boy")...............10-20 60

DOMINO

Singles: 7-inch

20TH FOX (2198 "Have You Had a Little Happiness Lately") 15-25 75
Member: Tony Burrows.

DOMINO, Bobby

Singles: 7-inch

DONNA (1339 "Marilyn")...........................30-40 61

DOMINO, Fats R&B '50

Singles: 78 rpm

IMPERIAL (5058 "The Fat Man")............50-100 50
IMPERIAL (5065 "Boogie Woogie Baby")..50-100 50
IMPERIAL (5085 "Brand New Baby").....50-100 50
IMPERIAL (5099 thru 5340).......................25-50 52-54
IMPERIAL (5348 thru 5477).......................15-25 55-57
IMPERIAL (5492 "Yes, My Darling") 50-75 58
IMPERIAL (5515 "Sick & Tired")...............50-75 58
IMPERIAL (5526 "Little Mary") 50-75 58
IMPERIAL (5553 "Whole Lotta Lovin' ").75-125 59

Singles: 7-inch

ABC 4-6 73
ABC-PAR (455-1 thru 455-5)....................15-25 63
(Stereo Compact 33.)
ABC-PAR (10444 thru 10902) 8-12 63-67
BROADMOOR (104 "Lady in Black")...........5-8 67
IMPERIAL (001 thru 028).............................5-8 '60s
(Back-to-Back Hits series.)
IMPERIAL (5099 "Every Night About This Time")..500-1000 52
IMPERIAL (5167 "You Know I Miss You")..300-400 52
IMPERIAL (5180 "Goin' Home") 200-300 52
IMPERIAL (5197 "Poor Poor Me")........100-200 52
IMPERIAL (5209 "How Long")................50-100 52
(Black vinyl.)
IMPERIAL (5209 "How Long")..............150-250 52
(Red vinyl.)
IMPERIAL (5220 "Nobody Loves Me")...50-100 53
(Black vinyl.)
IMPERIAL (5220 "Nobody Loves Me").250-350 53
(Red vinyl.)
IMPERIAL (5231 "Going to the River")...50-100 53
(Black vinyl.)
IMPERIAL (5231 "Going to the River").300-400 53
(Red vinyl.)
IMPERIAL (5240 "Please Don't Leave Me") 40-80 53
(Black vinyl.)
IMPERIAL (5240 "Please Don't Leave Me") 150-250 53
(Red vinyl.)
IMPERIAL (5251 "You Said You Love Me") 40-80 53
IMPERIAL (5262 "Something's Wrong") ..25-50 53
(Black vinyl.)
IMPERIAL (5262 "Something's Wrong") 100-200 53
(Red vinyl.)
IMPERIAL (5272 "Little School Girl").......20-50 54
IMPERIAL (5283 "Baby, Please")............20-50 54
IMPERIAL (5301 "You Can Pack Your Suitcase")..20-50 54
IMPERIAL (5313 "Love Me") 20-50 54
IMPERIAL (5323 "I Know") 20-50 54
IMPERIAL (5340 "Don't You Know") 20-40 55
IMPERIAL (5348 "Ain't It a Shame").........20-30 55
IMPERIAL (5357 "All By Myself") 15-25 55
IMPERIAL (5369 "Poor Me").....................15-25 55
IMPERIAL (5375 "Bo Weevil") 15-25 56
IMPERIAL (5386 "I'm in Love Again") 15-25 56
IMPERIAL (5396 "So Long").....................15-25 56

IMPERIAL (5407 "Blueberry Hill")........... 15-25 56
(Black vinyl.)
IMPERIAL (5407 "Blueberry Hill")........ 100-200 56
(Colored vinyl.)
IMPERIAL (5417 "What's the Reason I'm Not Pleasing You") 15-25 56
IMPERIAL (5428 "I'm Walkin'") 15-25 57
IMPERIAL (5442 "Valley of Tears") 15-25 57
IMPERIAL (5454 "When I See You") 15-25 57
IMPERIAL (5467 "Wait & See")............... 15-25 57
IMPERIAL (5477 "The Big Beat")............. 15-25 57
IMPERIAL (5492 "Yes, My Darling")........ 15-25 58
(Black vinyl.)
IMPERIAL (5492 "Yes, My Darling").... 100-150 58
(Red vinyl.)
IMPERIAL (5515 "Sick & Tired") 15-25 58
IMPERIAL (5526 "Little Mary") 15-25 58
IMPERIAL (5537 "Young School Girl") 15-25 58
IMPERIAL (5553 "Whole Lotta Loving") .. 15-25 58
IMPERIAL (5569 "Telling Lies") 15-25 59
IMPERIAL (5585 "I'm Ready").................. 15-25 59
IMPERIAL (5606 "I Want to Walk You Home") 15-25 59
IMPERIAL (5629 "Be My Guest").............. 15-25 59
IMPERIAL (5645 "Country Boy").............. 10-20 60
IMPERIAL (5660 "Before I Grow Too Old") 10-20 60
IMPERIAL (5675 "Walking to New Orleans").. 10-20 60
(Monaural.)
IMPERIAL (5675 "Walking to New Orleans").. 30-50 60
(Stereo.)
IMPERIAL (5687 "Three Nights a Week") 10-20 60
IMPERIAL (5704 "Natural Born Lover")... 10-20 60
IMPERIAL (5723 thru 5999) 10-15 61-63
IMPERIAL (54024 "My Blue Heaven").........5-8 '60s
(Back-to-Back Hits series.)
IMPERIAL (66005 "Goin' Home")...............8-12 63
IMPERIAL (66016 "When I Was Young")...8-12 64
IMPERIAL GOLDEN SERIES ....4-6 '70s
MERCURY (72463 "I Left My Heart in San Francisco")..8-12 65
MERCURY (72485 "It's Never Too Late") ..8-12 65
REO (8026 "Ain't That a Shame")........... 40-60 55
(Canadian.)
REO (8117 "Blueberry Hill") 40-60 56
(Canadian. Has the same pitch error found on U.S. issues.)
REPRISE (763 thru 891) 5-10 68-70
RIGHT STUFF (18216 "Please Come Home for Christmas") 5-8 93
(Red vinyl. Juke box issue only.)
TOOT TOOT (001 "My Toot Toot") 3-5 85
(With Doug Kershaw.)
U.A. 4-6 74
W.B. 3-5 80

Picture Sleeves

IMPERIAL (5428 "I'm Walkin'") 25-35 57
IMPERIAL (5477 "The Big Beat")............ 25-35 57
IMPERIAL (5606 "I Want to Walk You Home") 15-25 59
IMPERIAL (5629 "Be My Guest")............ 15-25 59
MERCURY (72485 "It's Never Too Late")... 20-30 65

EPs: 7-inch

ABC-PAR (455 "Here Comes Fats Domino") 15-25 63
(Juke box issue only. Includes title strips.)
ABC-PAR (479 "Fats on Fire") 15-25 64
(Juke box issue only. Includes title strips.)
ABC-PAR (510 "Getaway") 15-25 65
(Juke box issue only. Includes title strips.)
IMPERIAL (127 "Fats Domino – America's Outstanding Piano Stylist").. 75-125 53
(Red, script logo label.)
IMPERIAL (127 "Fats Domino – America's Outstanding Piano Stylist")... 40-60 56
(Maroon label.)
IMPERIAL (138 "Fats Domino") 40-60 56
IMPERIAL (139 "Fats Domino") 40-60 56
IMPERIAL (140 "Fats Domino") 40-60 56
IMPERIAL (141/142/143 "Rock 'n Rollin' with Fats Domino") 40-60 56
(Price for any of three volumes.)
IMPERIAL (144/145/146 "This Is Fats Domino") 40-60 56
(Price for any of three volumes.)
IMPERIAL (147 "Here Comes Fats") 40-60 57
IMPERIAL (148/149/150 "Here Stands Fats Domino")..40-60 57
(Price for any of three volumes.)
IMPERIAL (151 "Cookin' with Fats").........40-60 57
IMPERIAL (152 "Rockin' with Fats").........40-60 57
IMPERIAL (175 "Fats Domino")................10-20 '60s
(Stereo compact 33. Juke box issue only.)
MERCURY (659 "Fats Domino '65")..........20-30 65
(Juke box issue only. Includes title strips.)

LPs: 10/12-inch

ABC-PAR (455 "Here Comes Fats Domino")..20-40 63
ABC-PAR (479 "Fats on Fire")..................20-40 64
ABC-PAR (510 "Getaway") 20-40 65
AUDIO FIDELITY (344 "Fats Domino") 10-15 84
(Picture disc.)
CANDLELITE (13197 "Legendary Music Man")...15-20 76
(Two discs.)
EVEREST 8-10 74-77
GRAND AWARD (267 "Fats Domino") .....10-15 '60s
HARLEM HITPARADE (5005 "Fats' Hits")..10-15 75
HARMONY (11343 "When I'm Walking") .10-15 69
IMPERIAL (9004 "Rock 'n Rollin'") 100-200 56
(Maroon label.)
IMPERIAL (9004 "Rock 'n Rollin'") 50-75 58
(Black label.)
IMPERIAL (9009 "Fats Domino Rock 'n Rollin'") 100-200 56
(Maroon label.)
IMPERIAL (9009 "Fats Domino Rock 'n Rollin'") 50-75 58
(Black label.)
IMPERIAL (9028 "This Is Fats Domino")...100-200 57
(Maroon label.)
IMPERIAL (9028 "This Is Fats Domino")..50-75 58
(Black label.)
IMPERIAL (9038 "Here Stands Fats Domino")..100-200 57
(Maroon label.)
IMPERIAL (9038 "Here Stands Fats Domino")..50-75 58
(Black label.)
IMPERIAL (9040 "This Is Fats")...........100-200 57
(Maroon label.)
IMPERIAL (9040 "This Is Fats")...............50-75 58
(Black label.)
IMPERIAL (9055 "The Fabulous Mr. 'D'")..50-100 58
IMPERIAL (9062 "Fats Domino Swings")..50-100 59
IMPERIAL (9065 "Let's Play Fats Domino")..50-100 59
IMPERIAL (9103 "Million Record Hits")..50-100 60
IMPERIAL (9127 "A Lot of Dominos") 50-75 60
(Monaural.)
IMPERIAL (9138 "I Miss You So") 50-75 61
IMPERIAL (9153 "Let the Four Winds Blow")..40-60 61
(Monaural.)
IMPERIAL (9164 "What a Party") 40-60 61
IMPERIAL (9170 "Twistin' the Stomp")......30-50 62
IMPERIAL (9195 "Million Sellers")............30-50 62
IMPERIAL (9208 "Just Domino")...............30-50 62
IMPERIAL (9227 "Walkin' to New Orleans")..30-50 63
IMPERIAL (9239 "Let's Dance") 30-50 63
IMPERIAL (9248 "Here He Comes Again") 30-50 63
IMPERIAL (12066 "A Lot of Dominos") 40-60 60
(Stereo.)
IMPERIAL (12073 "Let the Four Winds Blow")..40-60 61
(Stereo.)
IMPERIAL (12091 "Fats Domino Swings")..20-40 64
IMPERIAL (12103 "Fats Domino")...........20-40 64
LIBERTY...5-10 80-81
MERCURY (21039 "Fats Domino '65") 15-25 65
(Monaural.)
MERCURY (61039 "Fats Domino '65") 15-25 65
(Stereo.)
PICKWICK...8-12 '70s
REPRISE (6304 "Fats Is Back")...............20-30 68
REPRISE (6439 "Fats").........................300-500 71
SILVER EAGLE 5-8 86
SUNSET (5103 "Fats Domino")................10-15 66
SUNSET (5158 "Stompin'") 10-15 66
SUNSET (5200 "Trouble in Mind") 10-15 68
SUNSET (5299 "Ain't That a Shame")......10-15 70
TOMATO..10-20 89
U.A. (104 "Legendary Masters") 15-25 73
(Edited tracks. Promotional issue only.)
U.A. (233 "Very Best") 8-12 74
U.A. (380 "Very Best") 5-10 75
U.A. (9958 "Legendary Masters") 15-25 71
Members (Band): Dave Bartholomew; Ernest McLean; Herbert Hardesty; Clarence Hall; Joe Harris; Alvin "Red" Tyler; Salvador Doucette; Lee Allen.
Also see ALLEN, Lee
Also see BARTHOLOMEW, Dave
Also see PRICE, Lloyd
Also see WILLS, Oscar

DOMINO, Renaldo

Singles: 7-inch

BLUE ROCK (4061 "Just Say the Word") 20-30 68
SMASH (2127 "I'm Getting Nearer to Love")...10-20 67
SMASH (2160 "You Don't Love Me No More")..10-20 68
TWINIGHT 5-10

DOMINOES R&B/P&R '51

Singles: 78 rpm

DELUXE (309 "Sixty Minute Man"/"Chicken Blues") 300-500 51
(Canadian. Note different flip than U.S. issue.)
FEDERAL (12001 "Do Something for Me")..100-150 50
FEDERAL (12010 "Harbor Lights").......250-350 51
(Original 45s of #12010 are not known to exist.)
FEDERAL (12022 "Sixty Minute Man") 100-150 51
FEDERAL (12039 "I Am with You") 50-100 51
FEDERAL (12059 "When the Swallows Come Back to Capistrano")..50-100 52
FEDERAL (12068 "Have Mercy Baby")..50-100 52
FEDERAL (12072 "Love, Love, Love")...50-100 52

Singles: 7-inch

FEDERAL (12001 "Do Something for Me")..750-1000 50
FEDERAL (12022 "Sixty Minute Man") 300-500 51
FEDERAL (12039 "I Am with You") 400-600 51
FEDERAL (12059 "When the Swallows Come Back to Capistrano")..400-600 52
FEDERAL (12068 "Have Mercy Baby") 200-300 52
FEDERAL (12072 "Love, Love, Love").200-300 52
For later Federal singles — as well all EPs and LPs — see the Billy Ward & Dominoes section.
GUSTO..3-5 '80s
Members: Billy Ward; Clyde McPhatter; Charlie White; William Lamont; Bill Brown; James Van Loan; David McNeil.
Also see CHECKERS
Also see GREENWOOD, Lil, & Dominoes
Also see LITTLE ESTHER & EARLE WARREN ORCHESTRA
Also see McPHATTER, Clyde
Also see WARD, Billy, & Dominoes

DON'S ROCKERS

Singles: 7-inch

DONROC (245 "Moonlight Stroll") 200-300

DON & BOB

Singles: 7-inch

ARGO (5373 "Little Red Schoolhouse")...15-25 60
ARGO (5400 "Good Morning Little School Girl")...15-25 60
SPEEDWAY (1000 "The Only Girl") 35-55 64

DON & CHEVELLS

Singles: 7-inch

SPEEDWAY (1000 "Inner Limits")...........10-20 64
Member: Don Ciccone.

DON & DAVE

Singles: 7-inch

PEARCE (5808 "If I Were the Wind") ....10-20 '60s

DON & DEWEY

(With the Titans)

Singles: 78 rpm

SHADE (1000 "Miss Sue")........................15-25 56
SPECIALTY (599 thru 631).......................10-15 57-58
SPECIALTY (639 "The Letter")..................20-25 58
SPECIALTY (659 "Farmer John")............25-50 59
SPOT (101 "Fiddlin' the Blues")................10-15 56

Singles: 7-inch

FIDELITY (3018 "Little Sally Walker")......10-20 60
HIGHLAND (1050 "Don't Ever Leave Me") 15-25 62
RUSH (1002 "Soul Motion")......................10-15 62
RUSH (1003 "Don't Ever Leave Me").......10-15 62
(First issue.)
SHADE (1000 "Miss Sue").......................60-80 56
SPECIALTY (SPBX series).......................15-25 86
(Boxed set of six colored vinyl 45s.)
SPECIALTY (599 "Jungle Hop")...............15-25 57
SPECIALTY (610 "I'm Leaving It All Up to You")..15-25 57
(Label makes no mention of Don & Dewey LP.)
SPECIALTY (610 "I'm Leaving It All Up to You")..4-6 '80s
(On A-side only, reads "From the Specialty LP *Don and Dewey*.")
SPECIALTY (617 thru 691).......................10-20 57-61
SPOT (101 "Fiddlin' the Blues")...............15-25 56

LPs: 10/12-inch

SPECIALTY (2131 "They're Rockin' Till Midnight")...10-15 70
(Black and gold label.)
SPECIALTY (2131 "They're Rockin' Till Midnight")..5-10 88
(Black and white label.)
Members: Don Harris (a.k.a. Don Bowman); Dewey Terry. Session: Blossoms.
Also see BLUEJAYS
Also see BLOSSOMS
Also see SHARPS
Also see SQUIRES
Also see TERRY, Dewey
Also see TITANS

DON & DEWEY / H.B. Barnum

Singles: 7-inch

FIDELITY (3017 "Jump Awhile"/"H.B. Boogie")...10-20 60
Also see BARNUM, H.B.
Also see DON & DEWEY

DON & DOMINOS

Singles: 7-inch

CUCA (1088 "Just Let Me Be")................40-60 62
CUCA (1109 "Weary Blues") 10-20 62
CUCA (1143 "Domino Theme") 10-20 63
Also see DON & HARRY

DON & DOVES

Singles: 7-inch

DYNAMIC (107 "I Need You") ....15-25 '60s

DON & EDDIE

Singles: 7-inch

DECCA (31245 "Hey") 50-60 61

DON & GALAXIES

Singles: 7-inch

FOX-FIDEL (2 "Avalanche") 8-12 60

Picture Sleeves

FOX-FIDEL (2 "Avalanche") 15-25 60

DON & GOODTIMES P&R/LP '67

(Don Gallucci)

Singles: 7-inch

BURDETTE (3 "Colors of Life") 10-20 68
DUNHILL (4008 thru 4022)........................8-10 65
EPIC..5-10 67-68
JERDEN (805 "I'm Real")............................8-12 66
JERDEN (808 "I Hate to Hate You")...........8-12 66
PICCADILLY (223 "I Hate to Hate You")....5-10 66
WAND (165 "Turn On") 10-12 64
WAND (184 "There's Something on Your Mind") 8-10 65

Picture Sleeves

EPIC (10199 "Happy & Me").....................20-30 67

LPs: 10/12-inch

BURDETTE (300 "Greatest Hits") 40-50 66
EPIC (24311 "So Good").........................15-20 67
(Monaural.)
EPIC (26311 "So Good")..........................15-20 67
(Stereo.)
PANORAMA (104 "Harpo").......................30-40
PICCADILLY (3394 "Goodtime Music") 5-10 82
WAND (679 "Where the Action Is") 25-35 67
Members: Don Gallucci; Joe Newman; Jeff Hawks.
Also see KINGSMEN
Also see TOUCH
Also see VALLEY, Jim

DON & HARRY
Singles: 7-inch
CUCA (1062 "Wabash Cannonball") 10-20 61
Also see DON & DOMINOS

DON & HIS ROSES
(Don Lanier)
Singles: 7-inch
DOT (15755 "Right Now") 25-50 58
DOT (15784 "Leave Those Cats Alone") 125-150 58
Also see HOLLY, Buddy
Also see LANIER, Don
Also see ROSES

DON & JERRY
(With the Fugitives)
Singles: 7-inch
FABOR (140 "In the Cover of the Night") 10-15 65
N-JOY (1018 "Better Run and Hide")..........5-10 66

DON & JUAN P&R '62
Singles: 7-inch
BIG TOP (3079 "What's Your Name") 15-25 61
BIG TOP (3106 "Two Fools Are We") 10-20 62
BIG TOP (3121 "Magic Wand")............... 20-30 62
BIG TOP (3145 "True Love Never Runs Smooth") 10-20 63
COLLECTABLES (3855 "Magic Wand").......3-5 '80s
ERIC ....4-6 '70s
LANA (150 "What's Your Name")..................4-8 '60s
LOST NITE (219 "What's Your Name") 4-8
MALA (469 thru 494).................................8-12 63-64
MALA (509 "Heartbreaking Truth") 15-25 65
TERRIFIC...4-6 '70s
TWIRL (2021 "Because I Love You")....... 15-25 66
Members: Roland Trone; Claude Johnson.
Also see GENIES

DON & LEE
Singles: 78 rpm
ROYAL ROOST (631 "Turn Out the Lights") 10-15 57
Singles: 7-inch
ROYAL ROOST (631 "Turn Out the Lights") 15-25 57

DON & MARTY
Singles: 7-inch
CANDIX (309 "Mandolin Rock")............... 10-20 60

DON CLAIRS
Singles: 7-inch
AMP 3 (1001 "I Lost My Job") 20-30 58

DON, DICK 'N JIMMY P&R '55
(Don, Dick N' Jimmy; Don, Dick & Jimmy)
Singles: 78 rpm
CROWN..5-10 54-56
Singles: 7-inch
CROWN (104 thru 162)........................ 10-20 54-56
VERVE (1010 "Ya Gotta Have Eyes") 10-20 57
LPs: 10/12-inch
CROWN (5005 "Spring Fever")............... 30-40 57
DOT (3152 "Don, Dick 'N Jimmy") 20-30 59
MODERN (1205 "Spring Fever")............... 40-60 56
VERVE (2107 "Songs for the Hearth")..... 15-25 59
Members: Don Ralke; Dick Crowe; Jimmy Cook.
Also see COOK, Jimmy
Also see RALKE, Don

DON JUANS
Singles: 7-inch
JAGUAR (3020 "Yum Yum") 15-25 57

DON JUANS
Singles: 7-inch
ONEZY (101 "The Girl of My Dreams") 1000-2000 59

DON Q
(Don Q's Band Featuring Clenest Gant)
Singles: 78 rpm
BULLET..5-10 '40s
KIT (884 "Jump-Jump-Hi Ho")................. 10-15 56
Singles: 7-inch
KIT (884 "Jump-Jump-Hi Ho").................. 15-25 56
Also see GANT, Clentt

DON THE DRIFTER
Singles: 7-inch
TEE PEE (21/22 "Christine"/"Three Steps") 10-15 67

DONALD & DELIGHTERS P&R '63
(Donald Jenkins & Delighters; Donald & Daylighters)
Singles: 7-inch
BLACK BEAUTY (302 "Elephant Walk") 8-10 72
CHEST (2001/2002 "Elephant Walk"/"Cool Breeze")............................10-20 '60s
(*Cool Breeze* is by the Daylighters.)
CORTLAND (109 "Elephant Walk")..........20-25 63
(Credits: "Donald Jenkins & the Delighters.")
CORTLAND (109 "Elephant Walk")..........10-15 63
(Credits: "Donald & the Delighters.")
CORTLAND (112 "Adios")..........................8-12 64
CORTLAND (116 "I've Settled Down") 8-12 64
DUCHESS (104 "Happy Days") 10-20 65
THOMAS (806 "Fighting for My Baby") 20-30 70
Members: Donald Jenkins; Walter Granger; Daylighters.
Also see DAYLIGHTERS

DONALDS, Joe
Singles: 7-inch
DART (111 "Honey Babe").........................30-50 59

DONALDSON, Lou LP '63
(Lou Donaldson Quintet)
Singles: 78 rpm
BLUE NOTE...3-8 52-57
Singles: 7-inch
ARGO...4-6 63-65
BLUE NOTE (100 thru 300 series) 4-6 73-74
BLUE NOTE (1500 & 1600 series) 5-10 52-58
BLUE NOTE (1700 thru 1900 series) 4-8 58-72
CADET (5521 "Musty Rusty") 4-6 66
LPs: 10/12-inch
ARGO..15-25 63-65
BLUE NOTE..8-15 64-80
(Label shows Blue Note Records as a division of either Liberty or United Artists.)
BLUE NOTE (1500 series)........................50-75 57-58
(Label gives New York street address for Blue Note Records.)
BLUE NOTE (1500 series)........................30-40 58
(Label reads "Blue Note Records Inc. - New York, USA.")
BLUE NOTE (1500 series)........................15-20 66
(Label shows Blue Note Records as a division of either Liberty or United Artists.)
BLUE NOTE (4000 & 84000 series).........15-25 58-63
(Label reads "Blue Note Records Inc. - New York, U.S.A.")
BLUE NOTE (5000 series).....................50-100 52-54
(10-inch LPs.)
BLUE NOTE (5000 series).....................50-100 52-54
(10-inch LPs.)
CADET 8-12 65-71
COTILLION 5-10 76-77
SUNSET...5-10 69-71
TRIP...5-10 79

DONATO, Mike
(With the Tridels)
Singles: 7-inch
PM (0101 "Summertime Love")..................40-50

DONAYS
Singles: 7-inch
BRENT (7033 "Devil in His Heart") 20-25 62

DONEGAN, Lonnie P&R '56
(With His Skiffle Group)
Singles: 78 rpm
LONDON 5-10 56
MERCURY 5-10 56
Singles: 7-inch
ABC 4-6 76
APT (25067 "Ramblin' Around")................10-15 62
ATLANTIC (2058 "My Old Man's a Dustman")..15-25 60
ATLANTIC (2081 "Junco Partner") 10-20 61
ATLANTIC (2108 "Have a Drink on Me")..10-20 61
DOT (15873 "Sally Don't You Grieve") 10-20 58
DOT (15911 "Does Your Chewing Gum Lose Its Flavor") 10-20 59
(Charted in 1961 when reissued.)
DOT (15953 "Whoa Back, Buck") 10-20 59
DOT (16263 "Light from the Lighthouse") ..8-12 61
FELSTED (8630 "Rock Island Line") 8-12 61
HICKORY..5-10 64-65
LONDON (1650 "Rock Island Line").........10-20 56
MCA..3-5
MERCURY (70872 thru 71248) 10-20 56-57
PYE (5256 "My Old Man's a Dustman") ...10-20 60
(Canadian.)
LPs: 10/12-inch
ABC-PAR (433 "Lonnie Donegan Sings Hallelujah") 15-20 63
ATLANTIC (8038 "Skiffle Folk Music") 20-30 60
DOT (3159 "Lonnie Donegan") 25-40 59
DOT (3394 "Lonnie Donegan") 20-30 61
MERCURY..25-40 57
U.A. 10-12 77

DONLEY, Jimmy
Singles: 7-inch
CHESS (1843 "Think It Over") 8-12 62
DECCA (30392 thru 31005, except 30308)..10-20 57-59
DECCA (30308 "Come Along")..................30-40 59
DECCA (31116 "My Baby's Gone")..........15-25 60
TEAR DROP (3005 Honey, Stop Twistin' ")...8-12 62
LPs: 10/12-inch
CRAZY CAJUN...10-15 '70s
STARFLITE (2002 "Born to Be a Loser") .20-35 '70s

DONN, Larry
(With the Killer Possum Band)
Singles: 7-inch
AD BUR (100 "Girl Next Door")............100-200
ALLEY 10-15 62
RIMROCK 4-6 72
SHELBY..3-5 79
THREE SUNS (1 "The Great American Superstar") 3-5 89
VADEN (113 "Honey Bun")..............2000-2500 59
LPs: 10/12-inch
SHELBY 5-10 72-78
Also see BROWN, Bobby
Also see BURGESS, Sonny, & Larry Donn
Also see COTILLIONS
Also see LEE, Joe
Also see OWENS, Kenny, & Travelers
Also see RILEY, Billy Lee

DONNA
(Donna Ludwig)
Singles: 7-inch
POP (1103 "Lost Without You") 15-25 59

DONNA, Vic
(With the Parakeets)
Singles: 78 rpm
ATLAS 20-30 57
Singles: 7-inch
ABC-PAR (10382 "Everytime") 5-10 62
ANGLE TONE (1071 "Teenage Rose")........4-8
ANGLE TONE (1075 "Love Was a Stranger to Me") 4-8
ATLAS (1071 "Teenage Rose") 40-60 57
(Atlas man logo at 9:00 on label. Reads "Atlas Records.")
ATLAS (1071 "Teenage Rose") 10-20 57
(Atlas man logo at 11:00 on label. Reads "Atlas Angletone Records" at bottom.")
ATLAS (1075 "Love Was a Stranger to Me") 50-150 57
CARLTON (488 "Dream Girl") 20-30 59
LIDO (601 "Young Princess") 10-20 59
TIGER (106 "Dance Marie").......................5-10 64
Also see PARAKEETS QUINTET

DONNA LOU
Singles: 7-inch
LOMAR (703 "White Cadillac") 10-20 63

DONNELS
Singles: 7-inch
ALPHA (001 "Here Comes the Bride") 10-15 63

DONNER, Ral P&R '61
(With the Starfires; with Scotty Moore, D.J. Fontana & Jordanaires)
Singles: 7-inch
ABC (2490 "So Close to Heaven") 4-8 73
CHICAGO FIRE (7402 "The Wedding Song")..8-12 74
COLLECTABLES (128 "Girl of My Best Friend")..4-6 '90s
COLLECTABLES (129 "You' Don't Know What You've Got")...4-6 '90s
END (19 "You Don't Know What You've Got")..10-20 63
FONTANA (1502 "Poison Ivy League")....10-20 65
FONTANA (1515 "Good Lovin' ") 10-20 65
GONE (5102 "Girl of My Best Friend") 20-30 61
(Black label.)
GONE (5102 "Girl of My Best Friend") 10-20 61
(Multi-color label.)
GONE (5108 "To Love"/"And Then")........30-40 61
(Shortly after this release, *You Don't Know What You've Got* was issued using the same selection number.)
GONE (5108 "You Don't Know What You've Got") 15-25 61
GONE (5114 "Please Don't Go") 15-25 61
GONE (5119 "School of Heartbreakers") .30-40 61
GONE (5121 "She's Everything"/"Because We're Young")...10-20 61
GONE (5121 "She's Everything"/"Will You Love Me in Heaven")..30-40 61
(Though credited to "Ral Donner," *Will You Love Me in Heaven* is by a thus far unidentified girl group.)
GONE (5121 "She's Everything"/"To Love Someone") 15-25 61
GONE (5125 "To Love Someone"/"Will You Love Me in Heaven")...15-25 62
(*Will You Love Me in Heaven* is credited to and sung by Ral Donner.)
GONE (5129 "Loveless Life") 15-25 62
GONE (5133 "To Love")...........................15-25 61
MJ (222 "My Heart Sings")........................5-10 70
MID-EAGLE (101 "Life to Live Over") 8-12 68
MID-EAGLE (275 "The Wedding Song")....5-10 76
RED BIRD (057 "Love Isn't Like That") 100-150 66
REPRISE (20135 "Christmas Day") 20-30 62
REPRISE (20141 "I Got Burned") 20-30 63
REPRISE (20176 "I Wish This Night Would Never End")..40-50 63
REPRISE (20192 "Run Little Linda")........15-25 63
RISING SONS (714 "If I Promise")............5-10 68
ROULETTE (19 "You Don't Know What You've Got") ....5-10 '60s
ROULETTE (97 "Girl of My Best Friend") ..5-10 '60s
SCOTTIE (1310 "Tell Me Why") 200-300 59
SMASH (34774 "Good Lovin' ") 50-75 65
(Promotional issue only.)
STARFIRE (100 "Wait a Minute Now") 5-10 78
STARFIRE (103 "Christmas Day") 5-10 78
STARFIRE (114 "Rip It Up") 5-10 79
(Black vinyl.)
STARFIRE (114 "Rip It Up") 10-25 79
(Picture disc.)
SUNLIGHT (1006 "Don't Let It Slip Away") 8-10 72
TAU (105 "Loneliness of a Star")............50-75 63
(Blue label. First issue—1,000 made.)
TAU (105 "Loneliness of a Star") 30-50 63
(Yellow label. 2,000 made.)
THUNDER (7801 "The Day the Beat Stopped")...4-6 78
(Clear vinyl.)
Picture Sleeves
MJ (222 "My Heart Sings")........................5-10 70
REPRISE (20141 "I Got Burned") 50-100 63
STARFIRE 10-15 78-79
LPs: 10/12-inch
AUDIO RESEARCH 12-15 80
GONE (5012 "Takin' Care of Business") 100-200 61
GONE (5033 "Elvis Scrapbook") 10-15
GYPSY...8-12 79
MID-EAGLE (7902 "1935-1977 - Been Away for a While Now")..40-60 79
(Two discs. 5000 made.)
MURRAY HILL (393 "She's Everything") ... 8-12 88
SESSIONS (1014 "1935-1977 - Been Away for a While Now") 20-30 80
(Two discs.)
STARFIRE (1004 "An Evening with Ral Donner") 10-20 82
(Multi-color vinyl.)
STARFIRE (1004 "An Evening with Ral Donner") 15-25 82
(Picture disc.)
Session: Scotty Moore; Jordanaires.
Also see JORDANAIRES
Also see MOORE, Scotty
Also see PRESLEY, Elvis

DONNER, Ral / Mickey & Larry
Singles: 7-inch
CHI-TOWN (4 "Maria Forever"/"A Message to Ayatullah Khomeini")............................100-200 80

DONNER, Ral / Ray Smith / Bobby Dale
LPs: 10/12-inch
CROWN (5335 "Ral Donner, Ray Smith & Bobby Dale") 25-35 63
Also see SMITH, Ray

DONNIE & DARLINGTONS
Singles: 7-inch
ABC-PAR (10633 "Poppin' My Clutch") ... 10-20 65

DONNIE & DELCHORDS
(Donnie & Delcords; Donnie Huffman)
Singles: 7-inch
EPIC (9495 "So Lonely") 10-15 62
TAURUS (352 "So Lonely") 25-35 62
TAURUS (357 "I Don't Care") 20-30 63
TAURUS (361 "That Old Feeling") 15-25 63
TAURUS (363 "I Found Heaven") 20-30 63
TAURUS (364 "I'm in the Mood for Love") 30-40 64
LPs: 10/12-inch
TAURUS (1000 "Donnie and the Delchords") 200-300 63
Also see COLOMBO, Joe
Also see HUFFMAN, Donnie

DONNIE & DIANE
Singles: 7-inch
DJB (115 "Hotrod Weekend") 10-20 64

DONNIE & DREAMERS P&R '61
Singles: 7-inch
DECCA (31312 "Carole") 40-50 61
(Multi-color label.)
DECCA (31312 "Carole") 50-75 61
(Pink label. Promotional issue only.)
WHALE (500 "Count Every Star") 20-30 61
WHALE (505 "My Memories of You") 30-40 61
Members: Louis "Donnie" Burgio; Andy Catalano; Frank Furstaci; Pete Vecchiarelli.
Also see KENNY & WHALERS

DONNIE & STYLES
Singles: 7-inch
TIMES SQUARE (106 "Chapel of Love") 30-40 64
(Colored vinyl.)

DONNO, Eddie
Singles: 7-inch
CAPEHART (5003 "Rough Stuff") 50-75 60
(Same number used for an Eddie Cochran release.)
ERBURY (505 "Always Getting Hurt") 5-10 67

DONNY & BI-LANGOS
Singles: 7-inch
COLTON (101 "I'm Not a Know It All") 20-30

DONNY & DUKE
Singles: 7-inch
MGM (12641 "Rock Baby") 15-25 58

DONOMAN
Singles: 7-inch
TROCADERO (100 "You've Been Gone Too Long") 15-25 64

DONOMAN & SKYLARKS
Singles: 7-inch
THUNDERBIRD (102 "Do You Know") 10-15 63

DONOVAN P&R/LP '65
(Donovan P. Leitch)
Singles: 12-inch
ALLEGIANCE (1437 "Donovan") 5-10 83
Singles: 7-inch
ALLEGIANCE 3-5 83
ARISTA 3-5 77
EPIC 4-8 66-76
(Black vinyl.)
EPIC (10045 "Sunshine Superman") 10-15 66
(Colored vinyl. Promotional issue only.)
EPIC MEMORY LANE 3-5
HICKORY 8-15 65-68
Picture Sleeves
EPIC 5-10 66-71
LPs: 10/12-inch
ALLEGIANCE 5-10 83
ARISTA 8-10 77
BELL 10-12 73
COLUMBIA 5-10 73
EPIC (Except 26439) 10-20 66-76
EPIC (BXN-26439 "Greatest Hits") 15-20 69
(Gatefold cover. Includes booklet.)
EPIC (PE-26439 "Greatest Hits") 5-10 77
(Standard cover. No booklet.)
HICKORY (123 "Catch the Wind") 20-40 65
HICKORY (127 "Fairy Tale") 20-40 65
HICKORY (135 "The Real Donovan") 20-40 66
HICKORY (143 "Like It Is") 20-40 68
HICKORY (149 "The Best of Donovan") 20-40 69
JANUS 10-12 70-71
KORY 5-10 77
PYE 8-10 76

DONOVAN & JEFF BECK GROUP P&R '69
Singles: 7-inch
EPIC 4-8 69
Picture Sleeves
EPIC (10510 "Goo Goo Barabajagal") 5-10 69
Also see BECK, Jeff
Also see DONOVAN

DONTELS
Singles: 7-inch
BELTONE (2040 "Lovers Reunion") 400-500 63
(Black vinyl.)
BELTONE (2040 "Lovers Reunion") 500-600 63
(Brown vinyl.)

DOOBIE BROTHERS P&R/LP '72
Singles: 12-inch
W.B. 4-8 79
Singles: 7-inch
ASYLUM 3-5 80
CAPITOL 3-5 89
SESAME STREET 3-5 81
W.B. 3-6 71-83
Picture Sleeves
CAPITOL 3-5 89
SESAME STREET 4-6 81
W.B. 4-6 79-83
EPs: 7-inch
W.B. 10-20 74
(Juke box issue.)
LPs: 10/12-inch
CAPITOL 5-10 89-91
MFSL (122 "Takin' It to the Streets") 30-50 84
NAUTILUS (5 "Captain and Me") 25-35 80
(Half-speed mastered.)
NAUTILUS (18 "Minute By Minute") 15-20 81
(Half-speed mastered.)
PICKWICK 6-10 80
W.B. (2634 "Toulouse Street") 8-12 72
W.B. (4-2634 "Toulouse Street") 15-25 74
(Quadraphonic.)
W.B. (2694 "The Captain and Me") 8-12 73
W.B. (4-2694 "The Captain and Me") 15-25 74
(Quadraphonic.)
W.B. (2750 "What Were Once Vices Are Now Habits") 8-12 74
W.B. (4-2750 "What Were Once Vices Are Now Habits") 15-25 74
(Quadraphonic.)
W.B. (2835 "Stampede") 8-12 75
W.B. (4-2835 "Stampede") 15-25 75
(Quadraphonic.)
W.B. (2899 thru 3612) 5-10 76-81
W.B. (23772 "Farewell Tour") 10-12 83
(Two discs.)
Members: Tom Johnston; Patrick Simmons; John Hartman; Tiran Porter; Jeff "Skunk" Baxter; Michael McDonald; John McFee; Chet McCracken;
Also see HELP
Also see McDONALD, Michael

DOOBIE BROTHERS, JAMES HALL & JAMES TAYLOR
Singles: 7-inch
ASYLUM 3-5 80
Also see TAYLOR, James

DOOBIE BROTHERS / Kate Taylor & Simon-Taylor Family
Singles: 7-inch
W.B. 3-5 80
Picture Sleeves
W.B. 3-5 80
Also see DOOBIE BROTHERS
Also see SIMON SISTERS
Also see TAYLOR, James
Also see TAYLOR, Livingston

DOODLERS
Singles: 78 rpm
RCA (6074 "Two Hearts") 5-10 55
Singles: 7-inch
JONES (1001 "Solitude") 15-20
JONES (1002 "The Dangerous Dangeroo") 10-15
LIBERTY (55116 "Sugar Plum") 8-12 57
RCA (6074 "Two Hearts") 10-15 55

DOODY WOO
Singles: 7-inch
AURA (110 "Certainly I Do") 50-75

DOOLEY, Dottie
Singles: 7-inch
MONITOR (1244 "I'll Always Have Memories of You") 40-60

DOOLEY SISTERS
Singles: 78 rpm
TAMPA 8-10 55
Singles: 7-inch
R-DELL ("Spider in the Web") 20-30 58
(Selection number not known.)
TAMPA 10-15 55

DOONE, Lorna
Singles: 7-inch
RCA (8532 "Dangerous Town") 15-25

DOOR NOBS
Singles: 7-inch
VIV (10 "Hi Fi Baby") 50-75

DOORS P&R/LP '67
Singles: 7-inch
ELEKTRA (12400 "The End") 5-10 80
ELEKTRA (45611 "Break on Through") 20-30 67
(Yellow label with Elektra Girl logo.)
ELEKTRA (45611 "Break on Through") 10-20 67
(Standard Elektra logo – no girl pictured.)
ELEKTRA (45615 "Light My Fire") 15-25 67
(Yellow label with Elektra Girl logo. Canadian copies with this label have been verified. First pressings credit Allied Records; second, Kinney Music, and third, WEA. Confirmation of U.S. issues is pending.)
ELEKTRA (45615 "Light My Fire") 5-10 67
(Standard Elektra logo – no girl pictured.)
ELEKTRA (45621 thru 45757) 5-10 67-71
ELEKTRA (45768 "Ships with Sails") 10-20 72
ELEKTRA (45793 "Get Up and Dance") 10-20 72
ELEKTRA (45807 "The Mosquito") 5-10 72
ELEKTRA (45825 "Good Rockin' ") 10-20 72
ELEKTRA (69770 "Gloria") 5-10 83
PHILCO (9 "Light My Fire"/"Break on Through") 10-20 67
("Hip-Pocket" flexi-disc.)
Promotional Singles
ELEKTRA (45611 "Break on Through") 15-20 67
ELEKTRA (45615 thru 45757) 10-15 67-71
ELEKTRA (45768 "Ships with Sails") 15-25 72
ELEKTRA (45793 "Get Up and Dance") 15-25 72
ELEKTRA (45807 "The Mosquito") 10-15 72
ELEKTRA (45825 "Good Rockin' ") 15-25 72
ELEKTRA (69770 "Gloria") 8-12 83
Picture Sleeves
ELEKTRA (45611 "Break on Through") 75-125 67
ELEKTRA (45621 "People Are Strange") 15-25 67
ELEKTRA (45628 "The Unknown Soldier") 30-40 68
ELEKTRA (45663 "Tell All the People") 30-40 69
LPs: 10/12-inch
ELEKTRA (502 "American Prayer") 8-10 78
ELEKTRA (515 "Greatest Hits") 8-10 80
ELEKTRA (4007 "The Doors") 200-300 67
(Monaural.)
ELEKTRA (4014 "Strange Days") 100-150 67
(Monaural.)
ELEKTRA (4024 "Waiting for the Sun") 150-250 68
(Monaural.)
ELEKTRA (4024 "Waiting for the Sun") 20-30 68
(Stereo.)
ELEKTRA (5035 "Best of the Doors") 15-20 73
ELEKTRA (EKS-6001 "Weird Scenes Inside the Gold Mine") 12-15 72
ELEKTRA (8E-6001 "Weird Scenes Inside the Gold Mine") 8-12 73
ELEKTRA (9002 "Absolutely Live") 15-20 70
(Red label.)
ELEKTRA (60269 "Alive, She Cried") 8-10 83
ELEKTRA (60269 "Alive, She Cried") 10-15 83
(Promotional issue.)
ELEKTRA (60345 "Best of the Doors") 10-12 87
(Two discs.)
ELEKTRA (60417 "Classics") 8-10 85
ELEKTRA (60741 "Live at the Hollywood Bowl") 8-10 87
ELEKTRA (61047 "The Doors") 8-10 91
(Two discs.)
ELEKTRA (74007 "The Doors") 20-25 67
(Gold label.)
ELEKTRA (74007 "The Doors") 15-20 67
(Red label.)
ELEKTRA (74014 "Strange Days") 15-25 67
(Gold label.)
ELEKTRA (74024 "Waiting for the Sun") 15-25 68
(Gold label.)
ELEKTRA (74024 "Waiting for the Sun") 15-20 68
(Red label.)
ELEKTRA (75005 "Soft Parade") 10-20 69
(Red label.)
ELEKTRA (75007 "Morrison Hotel"/"Hard Rock Cafe") 12-15 70
(Red label.)
ELEKTRA (74079 "Doors 13") 10-20 70
(Includes poster.)
ELEKTRA (75011 "L.A. Woman") 25-35 71
(With die-cut cover.)
ELEKTRA (75011 "L.A. Woman") .... 5-10 Re
(With standard cover.)
ELEKTRA (75017 "Other Voices") 8-12 71
ELEKTRA (75038 "Full Circle") 8-12 72
MFSL (051 "The Doors") 75-100 81
Members: Jim Morrison; Robbie Krieger; Ray Manzarek; John Densmore.
Also see MANZAREK, Ray

DOOTONES
Singles: 78 rpm
DOOTONE (366 "Teller of Fortune") 50-75 55
Singles: 7-inch
DOOTONE (366 "Teller of Fortune") 100-150 55
DOOTONE (470 "Strange Love Affair") 10-15 62
DOOTONE (471 "Sailor Boy") 10-15 62
Member: Ronald Barrett.
Also see JULIAN, Don, & Meadowlarks
Also see PENGUINS / Meadowlarks / Medallions / Dootones

DOR & CONFEDERATES
(With the Jack Hansen Orchestra & Chorus)
Singles: 7-inch
BRUNSWICK (55159 "4-D Man") 10-15 59
Session: Rod McKuen.
Also see McFADDEN, Bob
Also see McKUEN, Rod

DORAY, Johnny
Singles: 7-inch
PROFILE (4001 "One of These Days") 8-12 58
PROFILE (4003 "Judgement") 20-30 59

DO-RAY-ME TRIO R&B '48
(Do-Re-Mi-Trio; "Featuring Buddy Hawkins"; Do Ray & Me)
Singles: 78 rpm
BRUNSWICK 20-30 53
COMMODORE 15-25 47-48
CORAL 20-30 54
IVORY 15-25 49-50
RAINBOW 10-15 52
VARIETY 8-12 57
Singles: 7-inch
BRUNSWICK (80218 "I'm Only Human") 150-250 53
CORAL (61184 "I'll Never Fail You") 75-100 54
IVORY (001 "Let's Go Down Town") 50-75 50
RAINBOW (181 "She Would Not Yield") 50-75 52
REET (001 "Wrapped Up in a Dream") .... 15-25 '50s
REET (101 "Holding Hands") .... 15-25 '50s
STERE-O-CRAFT (112 "Saturday Night Fish Fry") 10-15 59
STERE-O-CRAFT (115 "Oo-Wee") 10-15 59
VARIETY (1002 "Oo-Wee") 20-30 57
LPs: 10/12-inch
STERE-O-CRAFT (508 "That Wonderfully Musically Do Ray Mi Trio") 30-45 59
Also see HAWKINS, Buddy, & Do Re Me Trio
Also see RUSSELL, Al

DORELLS
Singles: 7-inch
ATLANTIC (2244 "Beating of My Heart") 8-12 64
BRONE (102 "I Need Someone to Love") 15-25
GEL (4401 "Beating of My Heart") 10-20 64

DOREMUS, John
(Doremus)
Singles: 7-inch
CUCA (1303 "What Is a Boy") 10-15 66

DOREN, Van
Singles: 7-inch
HICKORY (1262 "Surfin' Lisa") 10-20 64

DORETY, Dee Dee
Singles: 7-inch
FREEDOM (44021 "Billy Billy") 10-20 59
MAGNET (703 "Tommy Green") 5-10 60

DO-REYS
Singles: 78 rpm
JOY (2401 "A New World") 40-50 56
Singles: 7-inch
JOY (2401 "A New World") 400-500 56

DORIES
Singles: 7-inch
DORE (528 "I Loved Him So") 15-25 59
DORE (556 "Don't Jum") 10-15 60
DORE (629 "Stompin' Sh-Boom") 20-30 62

D'ORLEANS, Barbara, & Marquees
Singles: 7-inch
D-TONE (1001 "Summertime") 50-75

DORMAN, Harold P&R/R&B '60
Singles: 7-inch
ABC 4-6 73
COLLECTABLES 4-6
RITA (1003 "Mountain of Love") 30-50 60
(No mention of NRC. String section not yet added.)
RITA (1003 "Mountain of Love") 10-20 60
(Label indicates NRC distribution. With string section added.)
RITA (1008 "River of Tears") 10-20 60
RITA (1012 "Take a Chance On Me") 10-20 60
SANTO (9051 "What Comes Next") 8-12 63
SUN (362 thru 377) 20-30 61-62
TINCE 10-15 60
TOP RANK (2092 "Take a Chance On Me") 10-15 60
Also see SMITH, Ray / Harold Dorman

DORN, Georgie
(Little Georgie Dorn)
Singles: 7-inch
KING (5540 "Angel in the Sky") 10-20 61
SSS INT'L (722 "Be My Love") 5-10 67

DORN, Jerry
Singles: 7-inch
ARWIN (122 "Brother Can You Spare a Dime") 10-15 59
FLING (711 "Rockin' Chair Rock") 75-125 59
KING (Except 4932) 15-25 56-57
KING (4932 "Wishing Well") 40-50 56
(With the Hurricanes.)
Also see HURRICANES

DORN, Lee
Singles: 7-inch
RANGER (8051 "Rockin' Daddy") 200-300

DORR, Lillian
Singles: 7-inch
CORREC-TONE (3810 "The Thrill Is Gone") 15-25 63

DORS, Diana
Singles: 7-inch
FONTANA (1943 "So Little Time") 5-10 64
LPs: 10/12-inch
COLUMBIA (1436 "Swinging Dors") 25-35 60
(Monaural.)
COLUMBIA (8232 "Swinging Dors") 35-45 60
(Stereo.)

DORSALS & GATORMEN
Singles: 7-inch
CAMELOT (120 "Namu") 10-15 66
Also see GATORMEN

DORSAM, Tom
Singles: 7-inch
LOREN (45001 "Baby of Mine") 200-300 64

DORSEY, Jimmy, Orchestra & Chorus
(With Bob Eberly) P&R '35
Singles: 78 rpm
BELL 3-5 54
COLUMBIA 3-5 50-52
CORAL ("60M" Series) 10-15 50
(Boxed, four-disc sets.)
DECCA 3-8 35-57
FRATERNITY 3-5 57
MGM 3-5 54
OKEH 10-15 29
Singles: 7-inch
ABC 3-5 73
BELL 5-10 54
COLUMBIA 5-10 50-52
DECCA 5-10 51-67
DOT 4-6 63
EPIC 5-10 59
FRATERNITY (Except 735) 8-12 57-60
FRATERNITY (735 "So Rare") 10-20 58
MGM 5-10 54
EPs: 7-inch
COLUMBIA 5-10 52-56
LPs: 10/12-inch
COLUMBIA 15-25 55-56
CORAL 15-25 54
DECCA 15-25 57-66
EPIC 10-20 59
FRATERNITY (1008 "The Fabulous Jimmy Dorsey") 20-30 57
HINDSIGHT 5-10 81
LION 15-25 56
MCA 5-10 75
Also see CROSBY, Bing, & Jimmy Dorsey
Also see MARTIN, Dean / Bob Eberly / Gordon MacRae

DORSEY, Lee P&R/R&B '61
(With the Ya Ya Band)
Singles: 7-inch
ABC 4-6 78
ABC-PAR (10192 "Lotti Mo") 8-12 61
ACE (640 "Lonely Evening") 10-20 61
AMY 5-10 65-69
BELL (908 "What You Want") 5-8 70
CONSTELLATION (115 "Organ Grinder's Swing") 10-20 64
CONSTELLATION (135 "You're Breaking Me Up") 10-20 64
FLASHBACK 4-8 65
FURY 10-15 61-63
GUSTO .... 3-5 '80s
POLYDOR 4-6 70-72
REX (1005 "Rock") 15-25 59
SANSU 5-10 67
SMASH (1842 "Someday") 5-10 63
SPRING 4-6 71
VALIANT (1001 "Lotti Mo") 20-30 58
LPs: 10/12-inch
ABC (1048 "Night People") 8-12 78
AMY (8010 "Ride Your Pony") 20-30 66
AMY (8011 "New Lee Dorsey") 20-30 66
ARISTA 5-10 85
FURY (1002 "Ya Ya") 100-200 62
POLYDOR 10-12 70
SPHERE SOUND (7003 "Ya Ya") 15-25 67
Also see JAMES, Tommy & Shondells / Lee Dorsey

DORSEY, Lee, & Betty Harris
Singles: 7-inch
SANSU (474 "Love Lots of Lovin' ") 8-12 67
Also see DORSEY, Lee

DORSEY, Mel
Singles: 78 rpm
ORBIT (106 "I Ain't Gonna Take It No More") 20-30 56
Singles: 7-inch
BLACK JACK (103 "Little Lil") 100-150 59
BLACK JACK (4051 "Annie Miss Fannie") 50-75
ORBIT (106 "I Ain't Gonna Take It No More") 50-75 56

DORSEY, Mel, & Vince Wallace
Singles: 7-inch
BLACK JACK (4051 "Funky") 50-75 59
Also see DORSEY, Mel

DORSEY, Tommy, Orchestra P&R '35
(Starring Warren Covington)
Singles: 78 rpm
BELL 4-8 54
(7-inch disc.)
BLUEBIRD 4-8 40
DECCA 4-8 52-56
OKEH 10-15 29
RCA 4-8 41-57
VICTOR 4-8 35-48
Singles: 7-inch
DECCA 5-10 52-64
MCA 3-5 73
RCA 5-10 50-57
EPs: 7-inch
COLUMBIA 5-10 52-56
DECCA 5-10 52-63
RCA 5-10 51-61
WALDORF .... 5-10 '50s
LPs: 10/12-inch
ACCORD 5-10 82
BRIGHT ORANGE 5-10 73
CAMDEN (Except 200 series) 5-10 61-73
CAMDEN (200 series) 15-25 53-55
COLPIX 15-25 58-63
COLUMBIA 10-20 58
CORAL 5-10 73
CORONET (186 "Tommy Dorsey Featuring Sinatra") 5-10 63
DECCA 15-25 52-60
GOLDEN MUSIC SOCIETY 15-25 56
HARMONY 5-15 65-72
MCA 5-10 75-81
MOVIETOWN 8-10 67
RCA 5-25 51-82
SPIN-O-RAMA .... 5-10 '60s
SPRINGBORAD 5-10 77
20TH FOX 5-20 59-73
Also see GARLAND, Judy / Tommy Dorsey
Also see GOODMAN, Benny / Tex Beneke / Tommy Dorsey / Charlie Barnet
Also see SINATRA, Frank

DORTCH, Slim
Singles: 7-inch
EUGENIA (1001 "Big Boy Rock") .... 600-800 '50s

DOSS, Bob
(Bobby Doss)
Singles: 78 rpm
STARDAY 25-35 56
Singles: 7-inch
LYNN (505 "I've Got You") 50-100 60
STARDAY (265 "Don't Be Gone Long") 150-250 56
Session: Hal Harris.

DOSWELL, Kittie "Miss Soul"
(With the Ray Johnson Combo)
Singles: 7-inch
DONNA (1347 "Need Your Love So Bad") 15-25 61
Also see JOHNSON, Ray

DOTS
Singles: 7-inch
CADDY (101 "I Confess") 50-100 57
CADDY (107 "I Lost You") 50-100 57
CADDY (111 "Good Luck to You") 200-300 57
REV (3512 "Ring Chimes") 750-1000 57
Member: Jeanette Baker.
Also see BAKER, Jeanette

DOTSON, "Big Bill," & His Guitar
Singles: 78 rpm
BLUES & RHYTHM (7004 "Dark Old World") 50-100 50
(There are no original 45s of this, other than bootlegs.)

DOTSON, James
Singles: 7-inch
RED WING ("Hi Lift") 50-100
(Selection number not known.)

DOTSON, Jimmy
(With the Blues Dots)
Singles: 7-inch
HOME OF THE BLUES (244 "Feel Alright") 8-12 62
MERCURY (72801 "Heartbreak Avenue") 20-30 68
ROCKO (516 "I Need Your Love") 10-20 61
VOLT (4013 "I Used to Be a Loser") 40-60 69
ZYNN (511 "I Wanna Know") 10-20 59

DOTSON BROTHERS
Singles: 7-inch
JANET (204 "My Baby") 50-75
LORAN (1027 "Orbit") 15-25
Also see ROCKETTS

DOTTIE & RAY R&B '65
Singles: 7-inch
LE SAGE (701 "I Love You Baby") 10-15 65

DOUBLE DATERS
Singles: 7-inch
CARLTON (457 "Hey! Blondie Girl") 10-15 58

DOUBLE DATES
Singles: 7-inch
LUCK (103 "I Love You, Girl") 15-25 61

DOUBLE FEATURE
Singles: 7-inch
DERAM (85004 "Come On Baby") 10-20 67
DERAM (85025 "Handbags and Glad Rags") 10-20 68

DOUBLE SIX
Singles: 7-inch
PHILIPS (40192 "Hallelujah, I Love Her So") 10-20 64
PHILIPS (40220 "Lonely Avenue") 10-20 64

DOUBLE SOUL
Singles: 7-inch
MINARET (133 "Blue Diamonds") 10-15 67

DOUG & FREDDY
(With the Pyramids)
Singles: 7-inch
FINER ARTS (1001 "Take a Chance on Love") 150-250 61
(Red label. Company has a Hollywood address.)
FINER ARTS (1001 "Take a Chance on Love") 200-300 61
(White label. Promotional issue only. Company has a Hollywood address.)
FINER ARTS (1001 "Take a Chance on Love") 75-125
(Gray label. Company has a Denver address.)
K&G (100 "Need Your Love") 25-35 61
RENDEZVOUS (111 " A Lover's Plea") 10-20 59
Members: Doug Salma; Freddy Ruiz.

DOUG & JOSIE
(With the Joe Scott Orchestra)
Singles: 7-inch
BACK BEAT (500 "I'll Give Love to You") 20-40 57

DOUG & MARKAYS
Singles: 7-inch
SWINGIN' (625 "Why Why Why") 25-35 61

DOUG E. FRESH & GET FRESH CREW R&B/D&D '85
Singles: 12-inch
REALITY 4-6 85
Singles: 7-inch
REALITY 3-5 85-88
LPs: 10/12-inch
REALITY (9649 "Oh My God") 25-50 88
REALITY (9658 "The World's Greatest Entertainer") 4-8 88

DOUGHBOYS
Singles: 7-inch
BELL (662 "Rhoda Mendelbaum") 10-15 67
BELL (678 "Candy Candy") 10-15 67
SUE (780 "Copy Cat") 10-15 63

DOUGHERTY, Big Bob
(Bob Dougherty)
Singles: 78 rpm
COSMOPOLITAN 25-50
DECCA 10-15 53
Singles: 7-inch
DECCA (48276 "Big Bob's Boogie") 15-25 53
GOLDEN CREST (517 "Honky") 15-25 59
WESTPORT (137 "Movin' ") 15-25 57
WESTPORT (139 "Teen-age Flip") 15-25 58

DOUGIE & DOLPHINS
Singles: 7-inch
ANGLE TONE (542 "Yesterday's Dream") 25-35 62

DOUGIE THE DUDE
Singles: 7-inch
AMY (869 "Cowboy Joy") 10-15 62
KEITH (6500 "Fire") 10-20 61
Also see DOUGLAS, Freddy

DOUGLAS, Barry, Trio
Singles: 78 rpm
ATLANTIC (1068 "Titena") 8-12 55

Singles: 7-inch
ATLANTIC (1068 "Titena") 10-20 55

DOUGLAS, Bethe
Singles: 7-inch
FRATERNITY (758 "Dancing in the Streets") 10-15 57

DOUGLAS, Bob
(With the Rhythm Aces)
Singles: 78 rpm
ACE (518 "Rock & Roll March") 6-12 56
Singles: 7-inch
ACE (518 "Rock & Roll March") 10-20 56

DOUGLAS, Freddy
Singles: 7-inch
KEITH (6501 "Who Would Have Thought") 10-15 61
Also see DOUGIE THE DUDE

DOUGLAS, Glenn
Singles: 7-inch
DECCA (29815 "Let It Roll") 15-25 56
DECCA (30311 "I Can Love Enough") 10-15 57

DOUGLAS, Joe
Singles: 7-inch
PLAYHOUSE (1000 "Crazy Things") .... 25-35 '60s
(At least one source reports this number as 1008. We're not sure yet which is correct, or if there are two different issues.)

DOUGLAS, K.C.
Singles: 78 rpm
DOWN TOWN (2004 "Mercury Boogie") 25-50 48
GILT EDGE (5042 "Mercury Boogie") 20-30 48
HOLLYWOOD 25-50 55
RHYTHM 50-75 54
Singles: 7-inch
ARHOOLIE (504 "I Know You Didn't Want Me") 10-15 63
GALAXY (753 "Little Green House") 5-10 67
HOLLYWOOD (1040 "Lonely Blues") 75-125 55
RHYTHM (1780 "Lonely Blues") 150-250 54
LPs: 10/12-inch
ARHOOLIE 8-12
COOK ROAD RECORDINGS ("5002 "A Dead-Beat Guitar and the Mississippi Blues – Street Corner Blues 'Bout Women and Automobiles") 750-1000 56
PRESTIGE BLUESVILLE (1023 "K.C.'s Blues") 75-100 61
PRESTIGE BLUESVILLE (1050 "Big Road Blues") 50-75 63

DOUGLAS, Kirk
(With the Mellomen)
Singles: 78 rpm
DECCA (29355 "The Moon Grew Brighter and Brighter") 5-10 54
Singles: 7-inch
DECCA (29355 "The Moon Grew Brighter and Brighter") 10-20 54

DOUGLAS, Lew
(Lew Douglas & His Orchestra; Featuring Allan 'Blackie' Shackner; Lou Douglas)
Singles: 78 rpm
BALLY (1025 "Levi Lullaby") 10-15 57
WING (90007 "How Can You Say") 5-10 55
Singles: 7-inch
B&F (1329 "Mary Ann's Rock") 10-20 59
B&F (1331 "Heavenly") 10-20 60
(First issue.)
BALLY (1002 "10,000 Years") 15-20 56
BALLY (1014 "High Society") 15-20 56
BALLY (1025 "Levi Lullaby") 15-20 57
BALLY (1043 "Night Bird") 15-20 57
CARLTON (533 "*From the Terrace* Love Theme") 10-15 60
DOT (15918 "Rhoom Ba-Cha") 20-30 59
FRATERNITY 10-15 57-58
MERCURY (71593 "Heavenly") 8-10 60
NEWPORT (107 "Gadabout") 8-10 64
NEWPORT (113 "Lonely Nights") 8-10 64
TODD (1029 "After Hours") 10-15 59
VASSAR 5-10
WING (90007 "How Can You Say") 10-20 55
LPs: 10/12-inch
CARLTON (126 "Themes from Motion Pictures & TV") 15-25 60
Also see BOONE, Pat
Also see COLE, Ike
Also see EDGE, Bobby
Also see HIGHLIGHTS
Also see JAMES, Joni
Also see MASTRO, Andy
Also see PEPPER & RED HOTS
Also see PIZANI, Frank
Also see WRIGHT, Dale

DOUGLAS, Mel
Singles: 7-inch
SAN (1506 "Cadillac Boogie") 100-150 59

DOUGLAS, Ron
Singles: 7-inch
SMASH (2206 "Never You Mind") 10-20 69

DOUGLAS, Ronny — P&R '61
Singles: 7-inch
DECCA (31512 "Big Walk") 5-10 63
EPIC (9843 "Worth Waiting For") 5-10 65
EVEREST (19413 "Run, Run, Run") 10-15 61

DOUGLAS, Scott
Singles: 7-inch
APOGEE (105 "Beatles Barber") 10-15 64
TOLLIE (9048 "Miss You") 5-10 65

DOUGLAS, Shy Guy
(Thomas Douglas)
Singles: 78 rpm
CHANE 10-15 54
EXCELLO 10-20 53
Singles: 7-inch
CHANE (517 "Yankee Doodle") 20-30 54
EXCELLO (2008 "Detroit Arrow") 50-75 53
EXCELLO (2024 "I'm Your Country Man") 50-75 54
EXCELLO (2032 "No Place Like Home") 50-75 54
EXCELLO (2200 series) 4-8 66
SUR-SPEED 4-8
TODD (1092 "What's This I Hear") 5-10 63

DOUGLAS, Steve
(With the Snowplows; with Rebel Rousers)
Singles: 7-inch
CAPITOL (5527 "Yesterday") 5-10 65
GRAPEVINE (601 "Rockin' Green Sleeves") 10-15 61
MGM (13218 "Schussing") 5-10 64
PHILLES (104 "Yes Sir, That's My Baby") 10-20 62
TANDEM (7000 "Magic Sound") 10-15 61
LPs: 10/12-inch
CROWN 15-25 62
Also see CATALINAS
Also see EDDY, Duane
Also see FOGERTY, John
Also see GOOD GUYS
Also see KICKSTANDS
Also see KNIGHTS
Also see KUSTOM KINGS
Also see PETERSEN, Paul
Also see SUPER STOCKS / Hot Rod Rog / Shutdown Douglas
Also see TYLER, Kip
Also see VETTES
Also see YORK, Dave, & Beachcombers

DOUGLAS, Tony — C&W '63
(With His Shrimpers)
Singles: 7-inch
COCHISE (113 "Meridian") 3-5 77
COCHISE (115 "Walking Over Yonder") 3-5 77
CUSTOM (102 "Gabby Abby") 10-15 62
D (Except 1005) 10-15 58-61
D (1005 "World in My Arms") 50-75 58
DOT 4-6 73-74
PAULA 4-8 67-74
SIMS 5-10 64-66
20TH CENTURY (2257 "Honky Tonk Man") 4-6 75
U.A. (387 "Skrimpin' ") 10-15 61
U.A. (432 "Battle Cry ") 10-15 62
VEE-JAY (481 "Gabby Abby") 5-10 63
LPs: 10/12-inch
DOT (26009 "Thank You For Touching My Life") 8-12 73
PAULA (2198 "Heart") 10-15 67
PAULA (2206 "Versatile Tony Douglas") 10-15 69
SIMS (131 "Mr. Nice Guy") 15-25 66
Also see SHRIMPERS

DOUGLAS FIR
LPs: 10/12-inch
QUAD (5002 "Hard Heart Singin' ") 15-20

DOUZER
Singles: 7-inch
DORE (844 "The Sneak") 25-35 70

DOVAL, Jim
(With the Gauchos)
Singles: 7-inch
ABC-PAR 8-12 65
DIPLOMACY 10-20 64-65
DOT 8-12 63-64
LPs: 10/12-inch
ABC-PAR (ABC-506 "The Gauchos Featuring Jim Doval") 25-35 65
(Monaural.)
ABC-PAR (ABCS-506 "The Gauchos Featuring Jim Doval") 35-45 65
(Stereo.)
Members: Jim Doval; Joe Silva; Marty Murilly; Al Lopez; Al Hernandez; Kelly Smith.
Also see SANDOVAL, Jimmy, & Gauchos

DOVALE, Debbie — P&R '63
Singles: 7-inch
ROULETTE (4521 "Hey Lover") 10-15 63
ROULETTE (4543 "Come Home") 10-15 64

DOVE, Diana
Singles: 7-inch
NRC (018 "To Prove My Love") 10-15 58

DOVE, Jerry
(With the Stringmasters; "Vocal by Bob Martin")
Singles: 78 rpm
TNT (Except 141) 15-25 54-56
TNT (141 "Pink Bow Tie") 50-100 56
Singles: 7-inch
TNT (118 "I Just Want You") 30-50 54
TNT (122 "Stand Still") 30-50 55
TNT (132 "Restless Falls") 30-50 56
TNT (141 "Pink Bow Tie") 200-300 56
TNT (144 thru 173) 15-25 57-59
Also see CAMPI, Ray / Jerry Dove

DOVE, Johnny
Singles: 7-inch
DOVE (983 "I Gotta Go") 100-200
DOVE (1260 "Lookin' for Money") 200-300

DOVE, Ronnie — P&R '64
(With the Beltones)
Singles: 7-inch
ABC 4-6 74
DECCA (31288 "Party Doll"/"Yes Darling, I'll Be Around") 15-25 61
(B-side is a re-recorded version of the B-side of Dove 1021. Only tracks with the Beltones.)
DECCA (32000 & 33000 series) 4-6 71-73
DIAMOND (100 & 200 series) 5-10 64-70
DIAMOND (300 series) 3-5 87
DOVE (1021 "Lover Boy"/"I'll Be Around") 2000-3000 58
(Black vinyl. 500 made.)
DOVE (1021 "Lover Boy"/"I'll Be Around") .... 20-25 '90s
(Green vinyl. 500 made. Reportedly made in Europe, listed here for identification purposes.)
ERIC .... 4-8 '70s
HITSVILLE 4-6 76
JALO (1406 "Saddest Song") 25-35 62
MC 4-6 78
MCA 4-6 73
MELODYLAND 4-6 75-76
MOTION 3-5 81
MOON SHINE 3-5 83
WRAYCO 4-6 71
Picture Sleeves
DIAMOND 8-10 66
DOVE (1021 "Lover Boy") .... 20-25 '90s
LPs: 10/12-inch
CERTRON 10-12 70
DESIGN (186 "Swingin' Teen Sounds") 10-15 64
(Four tracks by Dove; six by Terry Phillips.)
DIAMOND 15-25 65-70
MCA 8-10 72-73
POWER PAK 8-12 75

DOVELLS — P&R/R&B '61
Singles: 7-inch
ABKCO (4029 "Baby Work Out") 4-6 83
COLLECTABLES .... 3-5 '80s
DECCA (32919 "Kiss the Hurt Away") 4-6 70
EVENT (216 "Dancing in the Street") 4-6 74
EVENT (3310 "Roll Over Beethoven") 4-8 70
JAMIE (1369 "Our Winter Love") 4-6 69
KING (2064 "Bristol Stomp") 3-6 79
MGM (13628 "There's a Girl") 5-10 66
MGM (14568 "Mary's Magic Show") 4-6 73
PARKWAY (819 "No No No") 15-25 61
PARKWAY (827 "Bristol Stomp"/"Out in the Cold") 20-25 61
PARKWAY (827 "Bristol Stomp"/"Letters of Love") 15-20 61
(Orange label with black print. Note different flip.)
PARKWAY (827 "Bristol Stomp"/"Letters of Love") 10-15 61
(Orange and yellow label with black and white print. Note different flip.)
PARKWAY (833 thru 925, except 867) 10-15 62-64
PARKWAY (867 "You Can't Sit Down"/ "Wildwood Days") 10-20 63
PARKWAY (867 "You Can't Sit Down"/ "Stompin' Everywhere") 10-15 63
SWAN (4231 "Happy") 10-15 65
VERVE (10701 "Sometimes") 4-8 73
Picture Sleeves
PARKWAY (833 "Do the New Continental") 10-20 62
PARKWAY (838 "Bristol Twistin' Annie") 10-20 62
PARKWAY (845 Hully Gully Baby") 10-20 62
PARKWAY (855 "The Jitterbug") 10-20 62
PARKWAY (861 "You Can't Run Away from Yourself") 20-30 63
PARKWAY (867 "You Can't Sit Down") 10-20 63
PARKWAY (882 "Betty in Bermudas") 10-20 63
PARKWAY (889 "Stop Monkeyin' Aroun' ") 10-20 63
PARKWAY (925 "Watusi with Lucy") 15-25 64
LPs: 10/12-inch
DOVCO (84710 "Live On Stage") 5-10 76
PARKWAY (7006 "The Bristol Stomp") 30-50 61
PARKWAY (7010 "All the Hits of the Teen Groups") 40-60 62
PARKWAY (7021 "For Your Hully Gully Party") 50-75 63
PARKWAY (7025 "You Can't Sit Down") 30-50 63
WYNCOTE (9052 "Discotheque") 10-20 65
WYNCOTE (9114 "Biggest Hits") 10-20 65
Members: Len Barry; Arnie Silver; Mike Dennis; Jerry Summers; Danny Brooks.
Also see BARRY, Len
Also see CHRISTIE, Lou / Len Barry & Dovells / Bobby Rydell / Tokens
Also see MAGISTRATES
Also see ORLONS / Dovells

DOVER, Arnold
Singles: 7-inch
YALE (247 "You Can't Play Tag with My Heart") 50-75 61

DOVERS
Singles: 7-inch
DAVIS (465 "Sweet As a Flower") 30-40 59
NEW HORIZON (501 "Devil You May Be") 15-25 61
Members: Miriam Grate; Eddie Quiñones; Wyndon Porter; James Sneed.
Also see GRATE, Miriam, & Dovers
Also see VOCALTONES

DOVERS
(With Billy Mure & Orchestra)
Singles: 7-inch
VALENTINE (1000 "A Lonely Heart") 350-450 62
Also see MURE, Billy

DOVERS
Singles: 7-inch
MIRAMAR (118 "She's Gone") 35-45 65
MIRAMAR (121 "I Could Be Happy") 40-60 66
MIRAMAR (123 "Third Eye") 35-45 66
MIRAMAR (124 "She's Not Just Anybody") 35-45 66
REPRISE (0439 "I Could Be Happy") 10-20 66

DOVES
Singles: 7-inch
BIG TOP (3046 "Let's Make Up") 10-15 60

DOW, Johnny
(With the Spydels)
Singles: 7-inch
ASSAULT (1839 "Johnny Playboy") 8-12 62
ASSAULT (1865/1866 "You Were an Angel to Me"/ "Talk to Me") 15-25 63
Also see SPYDELS

DOWD, Larry, & Rockatones
Singles: 7-inch
SPINNING (6004 "Why, Oh, Why")..........50-75 58
SPINNING (6009 "Blue Swingin' Mama")..........100-200 59
Members: Loren Dowd; Ivan Reaseu; Mick Montgomery; Don Archer; Ron Fiscle.
Also see FIRST GARRISON

DOWN BEATS
Singles: 7-inch
ENTENTE (001 "Again")..........75-100 61

DOWN 5
Singles: 7-inch
PARROT (320 "Show Me")..........15-20 67

DOWN HOMERS C&W '49
(Kenny Roberts & the Downhomers; Wowo Down Homers)
Singles: 78 rpm
CORAL..........4-8 49-50
VOGUE (736 "Who's Gonna Kiss You When I'm Gone")..........200-300 46
(Picture disc.)
VOGUE (786 "Boogie Woogie Yodel")..........300-500 47
(Picture disc.)
LPs: 10/12-inch
SOMERSET (22400 "The Downhomers")..........15-20 '60s
Members: Bob Mason; Bill Haley; Shorty Cook; Guy Campbell; Lloyd Cornell.
Also see HALEY, Bill
Also see ROBERTS, Kenny

DOWN TOWN TRIO
Singles: 78 rpm
DOWN TOWN (2017 "Make Love to Me Baby")..........50-75 48

DOWNBEATS
(Down Beats)
Singles: 7-inch
GEE (1019 "My Girl")..........750-1000 56
(Red and black label.)
GEE (1019 "My Girl")..........10-15 60
(Gray label.)
PEACOCK (1679 "So Many Tears")..........40-50 57
PEACOCK (1689 "You're So Fine")..........20-30 59
SAFARI (1010 "Here")..........50-75 58
SAFARI (1014 "Jelly Bean")..........25-50 58
Session: Sonny Woods.
Also see WOODS, Sonny

DOWNBEATS
("Vocal by Charles Lighteard & Chorus")
Singles: 7-inch
SARG (168 "Darling of Mine")..........40-50 59
SARG (173 "I Need Your Love")..........40-50 59
SARG (186 "Oh Please")..........40-50 61
SARG (223 thru 233)..........10-20 66-69
Member: O.S. Grant.
Also see GRANT, O.S., & Downbeats

DOWNBEATS
Singles: 7-inch
ARDENT (101 "The Hucklebuck")..........10-20 60

DOWNBEATS
Singles: 7-inch
DIAMOND..........5-10 '60s
DYNAMITE (1011 "Rug Cuttin' ")..........10-20 62
WILCO (16 "One at a Time")..........10-15 60

DOWNBEATS
Singles: 7-inch
HAMPSHIRE (1002 "Growing Love")..........10-15 61

DOWNBEATS
Singles: 7-inch
TAMLA (54056 "Request of a Fool")..........30-50 62
(Tamla logo in circular letters at top.)
TAMLA (54056 "Request of a Fool")..........20-30 62
(Tamla logo in straight letters at top.)
V.I.P. (25029 "Put Yourself in My Place")..........100-150 65
Members: Cleo Miller; Robert Flemming; John Dawson.
Also see ELGINS
Also see FIVE EMERALDS

DOWNBEATS
Singles: 7-inch
DOWNBEAT (1029 "Dedicated to the One I Love")..........10-20 65

DOWNBEATS
Singles: 7-inch
DOMINION ("The Loneliest Night")..........50-75
(Selection number not known.)

DOWNEN, Bob
Singles: 7-inch
REBEL ACE (732 "Blue Yodel No.1")..........50-75

DOWNES, Jack E., & His Friends
Singles: 7-inch
JEDCO (5001 "Surfin' Way Out")..........15-25 63
JEDCO (5002 "Strictly Drums")..........15-20 63
(Retitled reissue of *Surfin' Way Out*.)

DOWNES, Vinnie
Singles: 7-inch
TRANSCONTINENTAL (1011 "Foolish Pride")..........40-60 59

DOWNEY, Morton, Jr.
(With the Terrytones)
Singles: 7-inch
ARTISTS OF AMERICA..........4-6 76
CADENCE (1407 "Ballad of Billy Brown")..5-10 61
LAKE ERIE..........4-8 '60s
IMPERIAL..........4-8 '60s
MAGIC LAMP (517 "Ballad of Billy Brown").5-8 64
PERSONALITY (3506 "Little Miss U.S.A.")..........5-10 63
PRIVATE STOCK..........4-6 77
WYE (1010 "I Beg Your Pardon")..........5-10 61

DOWNING, Al P&R '63
("Big" Al Downing; with Poe Kats)
Singles: 7-inch
CARLTON (489 "Miss Lucy")..........30-50 58
CARLTON (507 "It Must Be Love")..........20-40 59
CHALLENGE (59006 "Down on the Farm")..........20-40 58
CHESS (1817 "Story of My Life")..........8-12 62
CHESS (2000 series)..........4-6 75
COLUMBIA (43028 "I'm Just Nobody")..........5-10 64
COLUMBIA (43185 "I Feel Good")..........5-10 64
DOOR KNOB..........3-5 89
HOUSE OF THE FOX..........4-6 71
JANUS..........4-6 74
KANSOMA (01 "Story of My Life")..........30-40 62
KANSOMA (0004 "Saints")..........10-15 62
LENOX (5572 "Mr. Hurt Walked In")..........8-12 63
POLYDOR..........4-6 76
SILVER FOX (3 "The Saints")..........5-10 69
SILVER FOX (11 "These Arms You Push Away")..........5-10 69
TEAM..........3-5 82-84
V-TONE (220 "Word of Love")..........10-15 61
V-TONE (230 "So Many Memories")..........10-15 61
VINE ST...........3-5 87
W.B...........3-6 78-80
WHITE ROCK (1111 "Down on the Farm")..........100-200 58
WHITE ROCK (1113 "Miss Lucy")..........100-200 58
LPs: 10/12-inch
TEAM..........5-10 83-85
Also see LITTLE ESTHER & BIG AL DOWNING

DOWNS, Bobbie
Singles: 7-inch
CORREC-TONE (3807 "It Won't Be Long")..........30-40 63

DOWNS, Laverne C&W '60
Singles: 7-inch
PEACH (735 "But You Used To")..........15-20 60

DOYLE, Bobby
(Bobby Doyle Three)
Singles: 7-inch
BACK BEAT (528 "Pauline")..........15-20 59
BACK BEAT (531 "Unloved")..........25-35 60
BELL (45294 "Sail Away")..........4-6 72
BELL (45329 "Hey Buddy")..........4-6 73
TOWNHOUSE..........4-6
Picture Sleeves
BACK BEAT (531 "Unloved")..........50-100 60
LPs: 10/12-inch
COLUMBIA (1858 "In a Most Unusual Way")..........20-35 62
(Monaural.)
COLUMBIA (8658 "In a Most Unusual Way")..........25-40 62
(Stereo.)
Members: Bobby Doyle; Kenny Rogers.
Also see BLOOD, SWEAT & TEARS
Also see ROGERS, Kenny

DOYLE, Dicky
Singles: 7-inch
VIKING (4226 "Little Baby Lee")..........30-40 59
WYE (1009 "My Little Darlin' ")..........100-150 61

DOYLE, Mike
LPs: 10/12-inch
FLEETWOOD (3018 "Secrets of Surfing")..........20-30 63

DOYLE, Richard
Singles: 7-inch
PERSPECTIVE (6002 "Santa's Little Helper, Dingo")..........25-50 73
(Some have shown this as by Shamus M'Cool. We're not yet certain which is correct, or if it came out both ways. For now, we will list both.)
Also see M'COOL, Shamus

DOYLE BROTHERS
Singles: 78 rpm
TNT (113 "TNT Baby")..........10-15 54
Singles: 7-inch
TNT (113 "TNT Baby")..........15-25 54

DOZIER, Billy
Singles: 7-inch
SUWANEE (10500 "A Thing Called Love")..........200-300

DOZIER, Lamont P&R/R&B '72
(Holland-Dozier featuring Lamont Dozier)
Singles: 12-inch
M&M..........4-6 82
W.B...........4-8 79
Singles: 7-inch
ABC..........4-6 73-76
COLUMBIA..........3-5 81
INVICTUS..........4-6 72-73
M&M..........3-5 82
MEL-O-DY (102 "Dearest One")..........75-100 62
LPs: 10/12-inch
ABC..........8-10 73-74
COLUMBIA..........5-10 81
INVICTUS..........8-12 74
M&M..........5-10 82
W.B...........8-10 76-79
Also see ANTHONY, Lamont
Also see ROMEOS
Also see VOICE MASTERS

DOZIER, Rudy
Singles: 7-inch
TEEN TIME (108 "Wicked")..........40-60 62

DOZIER BOYS
Singles: 78 rpm
ARISTOCRAT (409 "She's Gone")..........30-50 50
ARISTOCRAT (3001 "She Only Fools with Me")..........30-50 49
ARISTOCRAT (3002 "Big Time Baby")..........30-50 49
CHESS (1436 "You Got to Get It")..........30-50 50
FRATERNITY..........10-15 57
UNITED..........50-100 53
Singles: 7-inch
APT (25014 "My Heart Is Yours")..........30-40 58
FRATERNITY (767 "Special Kind of Lovin' ")..........10-15 57
JANIE (457 "Special Kind of Lovin' ")..........30-50 57
UNITED (143 "I Keep Thinking of You").50-100 53
(Black vinyl.)
UNITED (143 "I Keep Thinking of You")..........100-200 53
(Red vinyl.)
UNITED (163 "Early Morning Blues")..........50-100 53
(Black vinyl.)
UNITED (163 "Early Morning Blues")..........150-250 53
(Red vinyl.)
Also see TIBBS, Andrew, & Dozier Boys

DRAFT, Morty, & Jay White
Singles: 78 rpm
ESSEX (323 "Laura")..........8-12 53
Singles: 7-inch
ESSEX (323 "Laura")..........15-25 53

DRAG KINGS
(Sonny & Demons)
Singles: 7-inch
U.A. (676 "Nitro")..........10-15 64
WAYNE WAY (105 "Midnight Drag of Paul Revere")..........35-45 '60s
Also see SONNY & DEMONS

DRAGON, Carmen LP '62
LPs: 10/12-inch
CAPITOL (8575 "Nightfall")..........10-20 62

DRAGON, Paul
(With the Jordanaires)
Singles: 7-inch
BELLE MEADE..........5-10 77
STARFIRE (109 "Mean Woman Blues")..........4-6 79
(Colored vinyl.)
STARFIRE (117 "Memphis Blue Streak")..........4-6 79
(Colored vinyl.)
Picture Sleeves
STARFIRE (109 "Mean Woman Blues")..........4-6 79
STARFIRE (117 "Memphis Blue Streak")..........4-8 79
LPs: 10/12-inch
BELLE MEADE (1002 "Golden Memories")..........20-30 77
Session: Scotty Moore; D.J. Fontana; Bob Moore; Dale Sellars; Little Willie Rainsford; Jordanaires.
Also see JORDANAIRES
Also see MOORE, Bob
Also see MOORE, Scotty

DRAGONFLY
LPs: 10/12-inch
MEGAPHONE (1202 "Dragonfly")..........200-300 68
Also see LEGEND

DRAGSTERS
LPs: 10/12-inch
WING (12269 "Hey Little Cobra – Drag City")..........35-45 64
(Monaural.)
WING (16269 "Hey Little Cobra – Drag City")..........50-75 64
(Stereo.)

DRAKE, Charlie P&R '62
Singles: 7-inch
CAPITOL (72015 "My Boomerang Won't Come Back")..........15-25 61
(Canadian. Longer version than on U.A. With "Practiced till I was BLACK in the face" lyrics.)
U.A. (Except 398)..........5-10 61-62
U.A. (398 "My Boomerang Won't Come Back")..........15-25 61
(With "Practiced till I was BLACK in the face" lyrics.)
U.A. (398 "My Boomerang Won't Come Back")..........5-10 61
(With "Practiced till I was BLUE in the face" lyrics.)

DRAKE, Eddie
Singles: 7-inch
GAR (320 "Duck Soup")..........10-15 67
JUKE (2024 "Guitar")..........5-10 73
TOWER (241 "Your Cute's A-Showin' ")..........5-10 66
TOWER (339 "After Loving You")..........5-10 67

DRAKE, Galen
LPs: 10/12-inch
RCA (3204 "A Cure for Loneliness")..........20-30 54
(10-inch LP.)

DRAKE, Larry, & His Vagabonds
("Vocal by Jesse Hodges & the Spotlighters")
Singles: 78 rpm
FABLE (575/576 "Tears"/"Boppin' Baby")..........35-50 57
Singles: 7-inch
FABLE (575/576 "Tears"/"Boppin' Baby")..........40-60 57
Also see HODGES, Jesse

DRAKE, Lenny
Singles: 7-inch
RATED X (6970 "Love Eyes")..........40-60

DRAKE, Marty
Singles: 78 rpm
ESSEX (301 "The Uh Uh Song")..........8-12 52
Singles: 7-inch
ESSEX (301 "The Uh Uh Song")..........15-25 52

DRAKE, Shari, & Veronairs
Singles: 7-inch
HILLTOP (1877 "Why Did You Do This").10-20 62

DRAKE & EN SOLIDS
Singles: 7-inch
ALTEEN (8652 "I'll Always Be There")..........10-20

DRAKES
("Featuring K.L. Jett - Accom. Skip Chavis;" with Nick Kurlas & Buddy Cahn & Orchestra)
Singles: 7-inch
OLIMPIC (252 "I Made a Wish")........... 100-150 65

DRAKES with J.J. Macambo / J.J. Macambo
Singles: 7-inch
CONQUEST (1001 "Oo Wee So Good"/ "Kitty") 400-500 58

DRAMATICS R&B '67
(Ron Banks & Dramatics)
Singles: 7-inch
ABC...4-6 75-78
BELL (5 "Toy Soldier")......................... 20-30 '60s
CADET (5704 "Door to Your Heart")............4-6 74
CADET (5706 "Tune Up")............................4-6 74
CAPITOL..3-5 82
CRACKERJACK (4015 "Toy Soldier")..... 50-75 63
FANTASY...3-5 86
MAINSTREAM 4-6 75
MCA...3-6 79-80
SPORT (101 "All Because of You") 40-60 67
VOLT...5-10 69-74
WINGATE (018 "Bingo")........................... 25-35 66
WINGATE (022 "Baby I Need You")........ 25-35 66
LPs: 10/12-inch
ABC.. 10-15 75-78
CADET...8-12 74
CAPITOL..5-10 82
FANTASY 5-10 86
MCA...5-10 80
STAX..8-12 77-78
VOLT.. 15-25 72-74
Members: Ron Banks; Elbert Wilkins; L.J. Reynolds; William Howard; Larry Demps; Lenny Mayes; Carl Smalls; Willie Ford.
Also see DYNAMICS
Also see SWEAT BAND
Also see UNDISPUTED TRUTH

DRAPELS
Singles: 7-inch
VOLT (114 "Please Don't Leave")........... 10-20 64
VOLT (119 "Young Man")............................8-12 64

DRAPER, Joseph
Singles: 7-inch
OXCART ("Learning How to Live") 50-75
(Selection number not known.)

DRAPER, Robert
Singles: 7-inch
BERMA (1312 "Joannie & Me").............. 50-75 61
ENSIGN (4019 "Joannie & Me").......... 100-200 58

DRAPER, Rusty C&W/P&R '53
Singles: 78 rpm
MERCURY (Except 70921).........................5-10 52-57
MERCURY (70921 "Pink Cadillac") 10-15 56
Singles: 7-inch
KL..3-5 80
MERCURY (Except 70921).........................5-15 52-62
MERCURY (70921 "Pink Cadillac") 15-25 56
MONUMENT..4-8 63-70
EPs: 7-inch
MERCURY 10-15 54-56
MONUMENT (005 "Greatest Hits")..............5-10 63
(Juke box issue. Issued in paper sleeve.)
LPs: 10/12-inch
GOLDEN CREST..5-10 73
HARMONY...5-10 72
MERCURY 15-30 54-62
MONUMENT..8-15 64-75
WING..8-15 63-64
Also see DEE, Lola, & Rusty Draper
Also see PLATTERS / Nick Noble / Rusty Draper / Ralph Marterie

DRAPERS
Singles: 7-inch
UNICAL (3001 "Merry-Go-Round")......... 20-30 60
VEST (831 "Best Love") 30-40 61
Members: Wilbur Paul; Richard Lewis; Dock Green; Leroy Brown; Jesse Facing.
Also see DUVALS

DRAPERS
Singles: 7-inch
GEE (1081 "You Got to Look Up").......... 15-25 62
Members: Johnny Moore; Charles Hughes; Dock Green; Tommy Evans.
Also see DRIFTERS

DREAM GIRLS
Singles: 7-inch
BIG TOP (3059 "Don't Break My Heart")..20-30 60
CAMEO (165 "Don't Break My Heart") 20-30 59
METRO (20029 "Crying in the Night") 10-15 59
METRO (20034 "Heartaches")..................10-15 60
TWIRL (1002 "Don't Break My Heart") .100-150 59
(First issue.)
Also see SMITH, Bobbie, & Dream Girls

DREAM KINGS
Singles: 78 rpm
CHECKER (858 "M.T.Y.L.T.T.")................50-75 57
Singles: 7-inch
CHECKER (858 "M.T.Y.L.T.T.")..............75-100 57

DREAM MERCHANTS
Singles: 7-inch
LONDON (1015 "Rattler") 5-10 67
Also see MERCHANTS OF DREAM

DREAM WEAVERS P&R '55
(Featuring Wade Buff)
Singles: 78 rpm
DECCA...10-15 55-56
Singles: 7-inch
DECCA...15-25 55-56
EPs: 7-inch
DECCA...20-40 56
Member: Wade Buff.

DREAMERS
Singles: 78 rpm
JUBILEE (5053 "These Things I Miss")..75-125 51
MERCURY..50-75 52
Singles: 7-inch
JUBILEE (5053 "These Things I Miss")..200-300 51
MERCURY (5843 "I'm Gonna Hate Myself in the Morning") 75-100 52
MERCURY (70019 "Walkin' My Blues Away")..75-100 52
Members: Warren Suttles; Harriet Callendar; Freddy Francis; Percy Green.
Also see BROOKS, Elouise, & Dreamers
Also see BROWN, Wini
Also see COBB, Arnett
Also see RAVENS

DREAMERS
Singles: 78 rpm
DREAM (101 "Seconds").........................75-125 53
GRAND (131 "Tears in My Eyes") 100-150 55
ROLLIN' (1001 "No Man Is an Island") .100-150 55
Singles: 7-inch
DREAM (101 "Seconds").......................200-300 53
GRAND (131 "Tears in My Eyes") 200-300 55
(Glossy yellow label. Rigid disc. No company address shown.)
GRAND (131 "Tears in My Eyes") 25-35 61
(Yellow label. Flexible disc. No company address shown.)
GRAND (131 "Tears in My Eyes") ....15-25 '60s
(Yellow label. Company address is shown.)
ROLLIN' (1001 "No Man Is an Island")... 1000-2000 55
(Outer edge of disc is fairly sharp.)
ROLLIN' (1001 "No Man Is an Island") ...50-100
(Outer edge of disc is blunt, or squared off.)
Members: Mitch Stevens; Harry Palter; Leroy Sproul; Kent Peeler; Robert Mott; Buddy Nolan.

DREAMERS
Singles: 78 rpm
FLIP (319 "Do Not Forget").......................10-20 56
Singles: 7-inch
FLIP (319 "Do Not Forget") 25-35 56
FLIP (354 "Do Not Forget") 10-15 61
Also see BERRY, Richard

DREAMERS
Singles: 78 rpm
MANHATTAN (503 "Lips Were Meant for Kissing")...50-100 56
Singles: 7-inch
MANHATTAN (503 "Lips Were Meant for Kissing")..200-300 56

DREAMERS
Singles: 7-inch
BULLSEYE (1013 "Only Your Love") 30-40 58

DREAMERS
Singles: 7-inch
EVENT (4270 "Ding Dong") 100-150 58

DREAMERS
Singles: 7-inch
NUGGET (1000 "Don't Cry")....................50-75 59

DREAMERS
Singles: 7-inch
APT (25053 "I Sing This Song")...............10-15 60
COUSINS (1005 "Because of You")......75-100 61
(Same number used on an Elegant 4 release.)
DREAM (1223 "This I Swear")......................3-5 87
GOLDISC (3015 "Teenage Vows of Love")..15-25 61
GUARANTEED (219 "Canadian Sunset")...10-15 61
MAY (133 "Because of You") 15-25 62
LPs: 10/12-inch
DREAM 8-12 87
Members: Frank Cammarata; Bruce Goldie; John Trancynger; Tony Frederico; Frank Nicholas.

DREAMERS
Singles: 7-inch
BLUE STAR (8001 "I Really Love You") ..20-30 60

DREAMERS
Singles: 7-inch
FAIRMOUNT (612 "Daydreamin' of You")..10-15 63

DREAMETTES
Singles: 7-inch
U.A. (921 "Gonna Make That Little Boy Mine")..10-15 65

DREAMLINERS
Singles: 7-inch
COBRA (013 "Just Me and You") 10-15 63
JOX (037 "Best Things in Life") 5-10 65
JOX (042 "Lonely Fool")..............................5-10 65

DREAMLINES
Singles: 78 rpm
SIESTA (6311 "Easy Rockin'") 10-15 55
Singles: 7-inch
SIESTA (6311 "Easy Rockin'") 20-30 55

DREAMLOVERS P&R '61
(Dream Lovers)
Singles: 7-inch
CAMEO (326 "Oh Baby Mine")..................5-10 64
CASINO (1308 "Amazons and Coyotes") 10-15 64
COLLECTABLES...3-5 82
COLUMBIA (42698 "Sad Sad Boy").........10-15 63
COLUMBIA (42752 "Sad Sad Boy")............5-10 63
COLUMBIA (42842 "Pretty Little Girl") 20-30 63
(Promotional issue only.)
COLUMBIA (42842 "Pretty Little Girl") 10-20 63
(Orange label.)
COLUMBIA (42842 "Pretty Little Girl") 5-10 63
(Red label.)
DOWN (2004 "If I Should Lose You")...100-200 61
END (1114 "If I Should Lose You")..........15-25 62
HERITAGE (102 "When We Get Married")..15-25 61
HERITAGE (104 "Welcome Home").........10-15 61
HERITAGE (107 "Zoom Zoom Zoom").....15-25 62
LEN (1006 "For the First Time")...........400-500 60
LOST NITE...4-8
MERCURY (72595 "Bless Your Soul").....5-10 66
MERCURY (72630 "Calling Jo Ann") 10-15 66
STOOP SOUNDS (510 "Take It from a Fool")..100-125 98
SWAN (4167 "Amazons and Coyotes")....15-20 63
(White label.)
SWAN (4167 "Amazons and Coyotes")....10-15 63
(Black label.)
V-TONE (211 "Annabelle Lee") 10-15 60
V-TONE (229 "May I Kiss the Bride").......10-15 61
W.B. (5619 "You Gave Me Somebody to Love")..5-10 65
LPs: 10/12-inch
COLLECTABLES ("Dreamlovers") 5-10 82
(Selection number not known.)
COLLECTABLES (5005 "Volume Two") 5-10 82
COLLECTABLES (5005 "Volume Two") .. 10-15 82
(Picture disc.)
COLUMBIA (2020 "The Bird")...................20-40 63
(Monaural.)
COLUMBIA (8820 "The Bird") 25-50 63
(Stereo.)
HERITAGE..8-12 79
Members: Tommy Ricks; Cleveland Hammock; Cliff Dunn; Morris Gardner; Ray Dunn.
Also see CHECKER, Chubby
Also see SHARP, Dee Dee

DREAMS
Singles: 78 rpm
SAVOY..50-75 54-55
Singles: 7-inch
SAVOY (1130 "Darlene") 100-150 54
(Black vinyl. Maroon label.)
SAVOY (1130 "Darlene") 150-200 54
(White label. Promotional issue only.)
SAVOY (1130 "Darlene") ....10-20 '60s
(Black vinyl. Purple label.)
SAVOY (1130 "Darlene") ....25-35 '60s
(Red vinyl.)
SAVOY (1140 "Under the Willow") 100-150 54
(Black vinyl. Maroon label.)
SAVOY (1140 "Under the Willow")...........25-35 '60s
(Yellow vinyl.)
SAVOY (1157 "I'll Be Faithful") 50-100 55
Members: George Tindley; Bernard Harris; Wes Hayes; Bobby Henderson; Steve Pressbury.
Also see STARLITES
Also see TINDLEY, George

DREAMS
(With the Frank Perry & Orchestra)
Singles: 7-inch
SMASH (1748 "Too Late")...................... 15-25 62
TALENT (1 "I Love You") 125-175 58
(Same number used on a Lee Williams & Cupids release.)

DREAMTEAM
Singles: 7-inch
EPIC (9701 "I'm Not Afraid")......................20-30 64

DREAM-TIMERS
(With the Flippin' Teens Orchestra)
Singles: 7-inch
FLIPPIN' (107 "An Invitation")................. 10-15 61
Also see HENRY, Stacy, & Flip-Jacks Orch.

DREAMTONES
Singles: 7-inch
MERCURY (71222 "Was I Dreaming") 10-15 57

DREAMTONES
(With the Tommy Wilson Orchestra)
Singles: 7-inch
ASTRA (551 "A Lover's Answer")...........75-125 59
(White label. Promotional issue.)
ASTRA (551 "A Lover's Answer")...........50-100 59
EARLY BIRD (005 "Stand Beside Me")........3-5 96
(Purple vinyl.)
EXPRESS (501 "Praying for a Miracle")...100-200 59
KLIK (8505 "Stand Beside Me")............400-500 58
SOLD (501 "Stand Beside Me")..................4-6 72
Member: Major Branch.
Also see MITLO SISTERS

DRESSLER, Jon
Singles: 7-inch
BULLSEYE (1016 "Brigitte") 10-15 58

DRESSER, Lee C&W '78
(With the Krazy Kats)
Singles: 7-inch
AIR INT'L..3-5 83
AMOS (118 "Camino Real")........................4-6
BELL (45352 "Once in a Lifetime Thing")..... 4-6 73
CAPITOL...4-6 78
DAMON (12350 "Beat Out My Love For You")..100-200
ROBIN (102 "Ooh Poo Pah Doo")............20-30 64
Also see KRAZY KATS

DREW, Patti P&R/R&B '67
(With the Drew-Vels)
Singles: 7-inch
CAPITOL...5-8 67-69
INNOVATION 4-6 75
QUILL..5-10 65
LPs: 10/12-inch
CAPITOL (Except 408) 10-20 69-70
CAPITOL (408 "Wild Is Love")..................60-90 79
(Picture disc. Promotional issue only. With plastic cover.)
CAPITOL (408 "Wild Is Love")................80-100 79

(Picture disc. Promotional issue only. With cardboard album jacket.)
Also see DREW-VELS

DREW-VELS P&R '63
("Featuring Patti Drew")
Singles: 7-inch
CAPITOL (5055 "Tell Him") ... 10-15 63
CAPITOL (5145 "It's My Time") ... 15-20 64
CAPITOL (5244 "I've Known") ... 8-12 64
LPs: 10/12-inch
CAPITOL (2804 "Tell Him") ... 20-30 67
Members: Patti Drew; Erma Drew; Lorraine Drew; Carlton Black.
Also see DREW, Patti
Also see DUVALS

DREXEL, Steve, & Cut-Ups
Singles: 7-inch
RIP (131 "Baby Blue") ... 15-25 58

DRIFTER
Singles: 7-inch
TARGET (105/106 "Show Me the Road to Heaven"/"Why Didn't You Wait") ... 50-75 66

DRIFTERS
Singles: 78 rpm
CORAL ... 100-200 50
EXCELSIOR (1314 "Honey Chile") ... 150-250 51
Singles: 7-inch
CORAL (65037 "I'm the Caring Kind") . 300-400 50
CORAL (65040 "I Had to Find Out for Myself") ... 300-400 50

DRIFTERS
Singles: 78 rpm
RAMA (22 "Summertime") ... 10-20 53
Singles: 7-inch
RAMA (22 "Summertime") ... 25-35 53

DRIFTERS
Singles: 7-inch
CLASS (500 "Three Lies") ... 20-30 53

DRIFTERS R&B '53
(Clyde McPhatter & the Drifters)
Singles: 78 rpm
ATLANTIC (1006 thru 1161) ... 25-50 53-57
ATLANTIC (1187 "Drip Drop") ... 50-100 58
ATLANTIC (2025 "There Goes My Baby") ... 100-200 59
CROWN ... 50-75 54
Singles: 7-inch
ANDEE (0014 "Black Silk") ... 10-15 '60s
ATLANTIC (1006 "Money Honey") ... 50-75 53
(Black and yellow label.)
ATLANTIC (1006 "Money Honey") ... 100-200 53
(Black and white label. Promotional issue only.)
ATLANTIC (1019 "Such a Night") ... 50-75 54
ATLANTIC (1029 "Honey Love") ... 30-50 54
ATLANTIC (1043 "Bip Bam") ... 30-50 54
ATLANTIC (1048 "White Christmas") ... 30-50 54
ATLANTIC (1055 "What'cha Gonna Do") 30-50 55
ATLANTIC (1078 "Adorable") ... 30-50 55
ATLANTIC (1089 "Ruby Baby") ... 20-40 56
ATLANTIC (1101 "I Got to Get Myself a Woman") ... 20-40 56
ATLANTIC (1123 "Fools Fall in Love") ... 20-30 57
ATLANTIC (1141 "Hypnotized") ... 20-30 57
ATLANTIC (1161 "I Know") ... 20-30 57
ATLANTIC (1187 "Drip Drop") ... 15-25 58
ATLANTIC (2025 "There Goes My Baby") ... 15-25 59
ATLANTIC (2040 thru 2127) ... 10-20 59-61
ATLANTIC (2134 thru 2786) ... 5-15 62-71
(Black vinyl.)
ATLANTIC (2201 "I'll Take You Home") ... 1000-1200 63
(Yellow and purple splash vinyl.)
ATLANTIC OLDIES SERIES ... 4-6 '70s
BELL (45320 "You've Got Your Troubles") ... 4-6 73
BELL (45387 "Like Sister & Brother") ... 4-6 73
BELL (45600 "I'm Feeling Sad") ... 4-6 74
CROWN (108 "The World Is Changing") ... 300-400 54
Picture Sleeves
ATLANTIC (2260 "Saturday Night at the Movies") ... 25-35 64
ATLANTIC (2261 "Christmas Song") ... 15-25 64
EPs: 7-inch
ATLANTIC (534 "The Drifters Featuring Clyde McPhatter") ... 75-100 55
ATLANTIC (592 "The Drifters") ... 40-60 58
LPs: 10/12-inch
ARISTA ... 8-12 76
ATCO (375 "Their Greatest Recordings") 10-15 71
ATLANTIC (8003 "Clyde McPhatter and the Drifters") ... 150-250 57
(Black label.)
ATLANTIC (8003 "Clyde McPhatter and the Drifters") ... 40-60 59
(Red label.)
ATLANTIC (8022 "Rockin' & Driftin' ") ... 100-200 59
(Black label.)
ATLANTIC (8022 "Rockin' & Driftin' ") ... 100-200 59
(White label.)
ATLANTIC (8022 "Rockin' & Driftin' ") ... 30-50 59
(Red label.)
ATLANTIC (8041 "The Drifters' Greatest Hits") ... 50-75 60
ATLANTIC (8059 "Save the Last Dance for Me") ... 50-75 62
(Monaural.)
ATLANTIC (SD-8059 "Save the Last Dance for Me") ... 60-80 62
(Stereo.)
ATLANTIC (8073 "Up on the Roof") ... 30-50 63
(Monaural.)
ATLANTIC (SD-8073 "Up on the Roof") ... 40-50 63
(Stereo.)
ATLANTIC (8093 "Biggest Hits") ... 30-40 64
(Monaural.)
ATLANTIC (SD-8093 "Biggest Hits") ... 40-50 64
(Stereo.)
ATLANTIC (8099 "Under the Boardwalk") ... 40-60 64
(Monaural. With black and white group photo.)
ATLANTIC (8099 "Under the Boardwalk") ... 20-30 64
(Monaural. With color group photo.)
ATLANTIC (SD-8099 "Under the Boardwalk") ... 50-70 64
(Stereo. With black and white group photo.)
ATLANTIC (SD-8099 "Under the Boardwalk") ... 25-35 64
(Stereo. With color group photo.)
ATLANTIC (8100 series) ... 20-30 65-68
CANDLELITE ... 10-15 '70s
CLARION ... 15-20 64
51 WEST ... 5-10
GUSTO ... 5-10 80
MUSICOR ... 5-10 74
TRIP ... 5-10 76
Members: Clyde McPhatter; Johnny Moore; Ben E. King; Rudy Lewis; Bobby Hendricks; Johnny Williams; Elsbeary Hobbs; William Anderson; David Baldwin; James Johnson; Charlie Hughes; Charlie Thomas; Bill Pinckney; Andrew Thrasher; Gerhart Thrasher; Willie Ferbie; Walter Adams; Jimmy Milner; Reggie Kimber; Jimmy Oliver; David Baughn; Tommy Evans; Eugene Pearson; Billy Davis (Abdul Samad); Tommy Evans; Dock Green; Johnny Terry; Butch Leak; Grant Kitchings; Bill Fredericks; Butch Mann.
Also see ALSTON, Shirley
Also see CLEFTONES
Also see CROWNS
Also see DRAPERS
Also see DUVALS
Also see FLOATERS
Also see HARMONY GRITS
Also see HENDRICKS, Bobby
Also see HORNETS
Also see KING, Ben E.
Also see LITTLE DAVID & HARPS
Also see McPHATTER, Clyde
Also see MOONGLOWS
Also see ORIGINAL DRIFTERS
Also see PINKNEY, Bill
Also see SPRITES
Also see VEE, Bobby / Diamonds / Drifters

DRIFTERS / Coasters
LPs: 10/12-inch
TVP (1002 "The Drifters Meet the Coasters") ... 10-15
(TV mail-order offer.)
Also see COASTERS

DRIFTERS / Lesley Gore / Roy Orbison / Los Bravos
EPs: 7-inch
SWINGERS FOR COKE ("Swing the Jingle") ... 100-125 66
(No selection number used. Promotional issue only. Each artist sings a song about Coca Cola. Has paper cover.)
Also see GORE, Lesley
Also see LOS BRAVOS
Also see ORBISON, Roy

DRIFTERS
Singles: 7-inch
CAPITOL (4220 "Don't Be a Fool") ... 20-25

DRIFTERS / Grady K. & Kuhfuss Band
Singles: 7-inch
QUALITY CHEKD (82592 "Cherry Chocolate Twist") ... 25-35 62
(Promotional issue only.)

DRIFTIN' SLIM
(Elmon Mickle; Driftin' Smith)
Singles: 78 rpm
MODERN (849 "My Little Machine") ... 150-250 51
RPM (370 "Good Morning Baby") ... 50-75 52
LPs: 10/12-inch
MILESTONE (93004 "Driftin' Slim and His Blues Band") ... 20-25 68
Also see MICKLE, Elmon

DRIFTWOOD, Jimmy C&W '59
Singles: 7-inch
CD ... 8-12
RCA ... 5-10 59-60
EPs: 7-inch
RCA ... 10-20 59
LPs: 10/12-inch
MONUMENT ... 10-20 63-76
RCA (1635 "Newly Discovered Early American Folk Songs") ... 45-65 58
RCA (1994 thru 2443) ... 20-50 59-62
RACKENSACK ... 8-12
RIMROCK ... 8-12
Also see MEMPHIS SLIM / Muddy Waters / Jimmy Driftwood & Stoney Mountain Boys

DRIFTWOODS
Singles: 7-inch
FAN JR. (5080 "Have You Ever Had the Blues") ... 15-25 64
LEAF (8973 "Have You Ever Had the Blues") ... 15-25 62
Members: Pete Sorce; Al Babicky; Nick Fera; Dick Aulbaencher; Mike Tezaloff; Steve Olson; Wayne Walters.
Also see SOURCE, Pete

DRIFTWOODS
Singles: 7-inch
LAURIE (3198 "Ferndoc Street") ... 10-20 63

DRIFTWOODS
Singles: 7-inch
DBS (163 "Wobble Willie") ... 30-40

DRISCOLL, Julie
LPs: 10/12-inch
MARMALADE (608002 "Open") ... 10-15 68

DRIVERS
Singles: 78 rpm
DELUXE (6094 "Smooth, Slow & Easy") . 20-30 56
DELUXE (6104 "My Lonely Prayer") ... 50-75 56
DELUXE (6117 "Oh, Miss Nellie") ... 20-30 57
RCA (7023 "Blue Moon") ... 30-40 57
Singles: 7-inch
DELUXE (6094 "Smooth, Slow & Easy") . 30-40 56
DELUXE (6104 "My Lonely Prayer") ... 75-125 56
(Black label.)
DELUXE (6104 "My Lonely Prayer") ... 200-225 56
(White label with bio. Promotional issue only.)
DELUXE (6117 "Oh, Miss Nellie") ... 30-40 57
RCA (7023 "Blue Moon") ... 20-30 57
Members: Charlie Harris; Leroy Harmshaw; Carl Rogers; Leroy Smith; Willie Price.

DRIVERS
Singles: 7-inch
COMET (2142 "High Gear") ... 15-25 61
LIN (1002 "A Man's Glory") ... 150-200 58

DRIVERS
Singles: 7-inch
DRIVE (101 "No One for Me") ... 100-150 '50s

DRIVERS & SPACEMEN
Singles: 7-inch
ALTON (252 "Doe Doe") ... 15-25 59

DRIVING STUPID
Singles: 7-inch
KR (116 "Horror Asparagus Stories") ... 25-35 66

DRIVING WHEELS
Singles: 7-inch
PAN AM (4001 "One Year Ago Today") ... 15-25 66

DRNWYN
LPs: 10/12-inch
WILDERLAND (31778 "Gypsies in the Mist") ... 50-75 78

DROPOUTS
Singles: 7-inch
ACME (1936 "I'm Leaving") ... 100-200

DRUIDS
Singles: 7-inch
COLUMBIA (43450 "It's a Day") ... 10-15 65
COLUMBIA (43639 "Old Willow") ... 10-15 66
SELECT (743 "I Can't Leave You") ... 10-15 65
THUNDERBIRD (505 "She's Got a Secret") ... 15-20 66

DRUIDS
Singles: 7-inch
MNO (101 "Sorry's Not Enough") ... 15-25 66
SELECT (743 "I Can't Leave You") ... 5-10 64

DRUIDS OF STONEHENGE
Singles: 7-inch
UNI (55021 "Painted Woman") ... 10-15 67
LPs: 10/12-inch
UNI (3004 "Creation") ... 40-60 67
(Monaural.)
UNI (73004 "Creation") ... 50-75 67
(Stereo.)
Members: Carl Hauser; Dave Budge; Tom Workman; Bill Tracy; Steve Tindall.

DRUMMOND, Dee
Singles: 7-inch
MIRASONIC (1003 "Like This") ... 20-30 59

DRUMMOND, Mike
Singles: 7-inch
BIG TOP (3042 "Love Affair") ... 10-15 60

DRYSDALE, Don
Singles: 7-inch
REPRISE (20162 "Give Her Love") ... 5-10 63
Picture Sleeves
REPRISE (20162 "Give Her Love") ... 15-25 63
Also see BASEBALL ("HOW TO" SERIES)

DUAL TONES
Singles: 7-inch
SABRE (104 "I'll Belong to You") ... 20-30 60

DUALS
Singles: 7-inch
FURY (1013 "Wait Up Baby") ... 30-40 58

DUALS
Singles: 7-inch
ARC (4446 "Bye-Bye") ... 10-15 59

DUALS P&R '61
Singles: 7-inch
COLLECTABLES ... 3-5 '80s
INFINITY (032 "Big Race") ... 20-30 64
JUGGY (321 "Big Race") ... 15-25 62
STAR REVUE (1031 "Stick Shift") ... 50-75 61
SUE (745 "Stick Shift") ... 10-15 61
SUE (758 "Travelin' Guitar") ... 10-15 62
LPs: 10/12-inch
SUE (2002 "Stick Shift") ... 175-200 61
Members: John Lagemann; Henry Bellinger.
Also see BARRETT, Ron

DU'AMBRA, Joey
Singles: 7-inch
ABC-PAR (9917 "Baby Sue") ... 15-25 58

DUBOIS, Morey
Singles: 7-inch
MELL (121 "If You Can Spare the Time") ... 100-150

DU BOY, Jess
(With the Hitchhikers; Jess Dubois & Hitch-Hikers)
Singles: 78 rpm
ABC-PAR ... 10-20 57
Singles: 7-inch
ABC-PAR (9848 "Beautiful Love") ... 15-25 57

BROOKE (121 "Achin' Breakin' Heart")......5-10 60
BRUNSWICK (55270 "Silhouettes") 5-10 64
COLONIAL (7002 "Puppy Love")............ 10-15 59

DUBS P&R '57
(Richard Blandon & Dubs)

Singles: 78 rpm

GONE (5002 "Don't Ask Me")................ 50-100 57
GONE (5011 "Could This Be Magic") .. 100-150 57
GONE (5020 "Beside My Love") 50-100 58
GONE (5034 "Be Sure")....................... 75-125 58

Singles: 7-inch

ABC-PAR (10056 "Early in the Morning") 15-25 59
ABC-PAR (10100 "Don't Laugh at Me")... 40-50 60
ABC-PAR (10150 "For the First Time").... 15-25 60
ABC-PAR (10198 "If I Only Had Magic") . 25-35 61
ABC-PAR (10269 "Lullaby")................... 30-40 61
CLASSIC ARTISTS (120 "Wherever You Are")..5-8 90
(Black vinyl. 1000 made.)
CLASSIC ARTISTS (120 "Wherever You Are")..8-10 90
(Red vinyl. 1000 made.)
CLIFTON 4-8 72-73
END (1108 "This to Me Is Love")........... 30-40 62
END (5020 "Beside My Love") 10-15 60
GONE (5002 "Don't Ask Me")................ 75-125 57
(Black label. With double image, shadow-like lettering.)
GONE (5002 "Don't Ask Me")................ 30-40 57
(Black label. With normal lettering.)
GONE (5002 "Don't Ask Me")................ 10-15 '60s
(Multi-color label.)
GONE (5011 "Could This Be Magic") 75-125 57
(Black label.)
GONE (5011 "Could This Be Magic")...... 15-25 '60s
(Multi-color label.)
GONE (5020 "Beside My Love")............ 20-30 57
GONE (5034 "Be Sure")........................ 20-30 58
(Black label.)
GONE (5034 "Be Sure")........................ 10-15 61
(Multi-color label.)
GONE (5046 "Chapel of Dreams").......... 50-60 58
GONE (5069 "Chapel of Dreams")........... 20-30 59
(Black label.)
GONE (5069 "Chapel of Dreams").......... 10-15 60
(Multi-color label.)
GONE (5138 "Is There a Love for Me") ... 20-30 62
(Black label.)
JOHNSON (097 "Connie")..........................4-8 73
JOHNSON (098 "Somebody Goofed") 4-8 73
JOHNSON (102 "Don't Ask Me to Be Lonely")... 750-1000 57
(First issue.)
JOSIE (911 "This I Swear")..................... 15-25 63
LANA (115 "Could This Be Magic").............4-8 64
LANA (116 "Don't Ask Me to Be Lonely")....4-8 64
MARK-X (8008 "Be Sure My Love")......... 10-15 60
MUSICTONE (1141 "Could This Be Magic")..5-10 64
MUSICTONE (1142 "Don't Ask Me to Be Lonely") 5-10 64
OLDIES 45...4-8 64
RECORD'S (437 "We Three")....................4-8 70
REO (8186 "Could This Be Magic") 50-75 57
(Canadian.)
ROULETTE...4-6 '70s
SCM (901 "I Love You")..............................3-5
TRIP OLDIES (96 "Could This Be Magic"/"Don't Ask Me to Be Lonely")..4-6
VICKI (229 "Lost in the Wilderness")....... 10-20 62
WILSHIRE (201 "Just You").................... 25-40 63
ZIRKON (5002 "Chapel of Dreams") 5-10

Picture Sleeves

GONE (5011 "Could This Be Magic") ....5-10 '90s

LPs: 10/12-inch

CANDLELITE... 10-15 73
MURRAY HILL...5-10 88

Members: Richard Blandon; Billy Carlisle; Cleveland Still; James Miller; Tom Gardner; Tom Grate; Cordell Brown; Dave Shelley.
Also see BOPCHORDS
Also see 5 WINGS
Also see MARVELS
Also see SCALE-TONES

DUBS / Actuals

Singles: 78 rpm

CANDLELITE (438 "We Three") 5-10 72
Also see VOCALAIRES / Actuals

DUBS / Shells

LPs: 10/12-inch

CANDLELITE..10-15 '70s
JOSIE (4001 "The Dubs Meet the Shells")..200-300 62
Also see DUBS
Also see SHELLS

DUCANES

Singles: 7-inch

GOLDISC (3024 "I'm So Happy") 20-35 61
LOST NITE (245 "I'm So Happy") ....5-10 '60s
Members: Jeff Breny; Eddie Brian; Dennis Buckley; Louie Biscardi; Rick Scrofani; Ron Nagel.

DUCANES / Temptations

Singles: 7-inch

GOLDISC (3030 "I'm So Happy"/"Barbara")...10-20
Also see DUCANES
Also see TEMPTATIONS

DUCATS

Singles: 7-inch

ROCK IT (200 "Hey Woman")..............100-150

DUCES OF RHYTHM & TEMPO TOPPERS
(Featuring Little Richard)

Singles: 78 rpm

PEACOCK...25-50 53-54

Singles: 7-inch

PEACOCK (1616 "Fool at the Wheel").....50-75 53
PEACOCK (1628 "Always")......................50-75 54
Also see LITTLE RICHARD
Also see TEMPO TOPPERS

DUCHESS / Jake Porter

Singles: 7-inch

COMBO (2 "The Monkey"/"The Whang") .50-75 53
Also see PORTER, Jake

DUCHESSES

Singles: 7-inch

CHIEF (7019 "Why")...............................20-30 60
CHIEF (7023 "Will I Ever Make It") 20-30 60
Also see FOUR DUCHESSES

DUCHOW, Lawrence, & His Red Raven Orchestra
(With His Red Ravens)

Singles: 7-inch

POTTER (1004 "I Get a Kick Out of Corn")...5-10
RCA (51-1178 "Holka Polka") 10-20 50
(Blue vinyl.)

DUD, Bo, & Johnny Twist

Singles: 7-inch

T.D.S. (4715 "Honky Tonk")....................10-20 62

DUDADS

Singles: 78 rpm

DELUXE (6083 "I Heard You Call Me Dear")...25-50 55

Singles: 7-inch

DELUXE (6083 "I Heard You Call Me Dear")...50-75 55

DUDES

Singles: 7-inch

GAIETY (12 "Let's Not Pretend") 15-25 66

DUDLEY, Bo

Singles: 7-inch

F-M (4981 "Shotgun Rider")......................50-75

DUDLEY, Dave C&W '61
(With Charlie Douglas)

Singles: 78 rpm

KING...5-10 55-56

Singles: 7-inch

CIRCLE DOT (101 "Picture of My Heart")..10-20 60
COLUMBIA (10851 "Changin' of the Guards")...4-6 78
CURIO...5-8
GOLDEN RING (3030 "Cowboy Boots") 8-12 63
GOLDEN WING (3020 "Six Days on the Road")..8-12 63
(Black vinyl.)
GOLDEN WING (3020 "Six Days on the Road")..30-40 63
(Red vinyl.)
JUBILEE (5436 "Please Let Me Prove").....5-10 62
KING (1508 "Cry Baby Cry") 10-20 55
KING (4866 "Ink Dries Quicker Than Tears")..10-20 55
KING (4933 "Rock & Roll Nursery Rhyme")..20-30 56
KING (5792 "Ink Dries Quicker Than Tears")..5-10 63
MERCURY...4-8 63-73
NRC (024 "I Won't Be Just Your Friend")...8-12 59
NEW STAR (6420 "Please Let Me Prove")..10-15 62
(First issue.)
PELHAM...5-10 63
RICE...4-6 73-78
STARDAY (Except 364)............................10-15 58-60
STARDAY (364 "Cry Baby") 50-75
SUN (Black vinyl)..3-6 79-80
SUN (Gold vinyl)...5-10 79-80
U.A. 4-6 75-76
VEE (7003 "Maybe I Do")..........................20-30 61

LPs: 10/12-inch

CORONET/PREMIER ....8-12 '60s
CROWN ....8-12 '60s
DESIGN..8-12 '60s
GOLDEN RING (110 "Six Days on the Road")...25-35 63
GUEST STAR...8-12
HILLTOP...8-12
MERCURY...10-15 64-73
MOUNTAIN DEW 8-12 69
NASHVILLE...8-12 68
PICKWICK ....5-10 '70s
PLANTATION 5-10 81
RICE (711 "Greatest Hits")............................5-8 78
SPIN-O-RAMA...5-10 '60s
SUN...5-10 80
U.A. 8-12 75-76
WING...8-12 68
Also see JAMES, Sonny / Dave Dudley / Sunny Williams

DUDLEY, Dave / Link Wray

LPs: 10/12-inch

GUEST STAR..15-25 63
Also see DUDLEY, Dave
Also see WRAY, Link

DU DROPPERS R&B '53
(Du-Droppers; with Ben Smith's Quintet)

Singles: 78 rpm

GROOVE 25-35 53-55
RCA...15-25 53
RED ROBIN...50-100 52-53

Singles: 7-inch

GROOVE (0001 "Dead Broke") 40-50 54
GROOVE (0013 "Just Whisper") 50-100 54
GROOVE (0036 "Let Nature Take It's Course")...30-40 55
GROOVE (0104 "Talk That Talk")...............40-50 55
GROOVE (0120 "You're Mine Already") ..40-50 55
RCA (5229 "I Wanna Know") 30-40 53
RCA (5321 "I Found Out")...........................30-40 53
RCA (5425 "Whatever You're Doin' ") 30-40 53
RCA (5504 "Don't Pass Me By")..................30-40 53
RCA (5543 "The Note in the Bottle") 30-40 53
RED ROBIN (108 "Can't Do Sixty No More")...100-150 52
(Black vinyl.)
RED ROBIN (108 "Can't Do Sixty No More")...250-300 52
(Red vinyl.)
RED ROBIN (116 "Come On and Love Me Baby")..75-125 53

EPs: 7-inch

GROOVE (2 "Talk That Talk") 100-200 55
GROOVE (5 "Tops in Rhythm & Blues")..100-200 55
Members: Julius Ginyard; Willie Ray; Eddie Hashaw; Harvey Ray; Bob Kornegay; Prentice Moreland; Joe Van Loan; Charlie Hughes.
Also see BELLS
Also see DIXIEAIRES
Also see GALE, Sunny, & Du Droppers
Also see VAN LOAN, Joe
Also see WATTS, Maymie

DU-ETTES

Singles: 7-inch

LOST NITE (1003 "Lonely Days")................5-10 65
MAR-V-LUS (6003 "Every Beat of My Heart")..5-10 64
M-PAC (7203 thru 7214)............................5-10 63-64
MECCA (2422 "Donny")..............................10-20 59
ONE-DERFUL (4827 "Lonely Days") 5-10 64
Members: Barbara Livsey; Mary Francis Hayes.

DUFFETT, Johnny

Singles: 7-inch

BRUNSWICK (55145 "Baby, Oh Baby") .. 10-12 59

DUFFILL, Tamson
(Tam Duffill)

Singles: 7-inch

GROOVE (0004 "Cooly Dooly")...............30-40 62

DUFFY

Singles: 7-inch

DIAL (4097 "Come Back, Come Back") ... 10-15 67

DUGAN, Johnny, & Shamrocks

Singles: 7-inch

FORD (103 "School Bells, Wedding Bells")...50-75 59

DUGAS, Jay, & Four Kings

Singles: 7-inch

QQ (302 "Fireball Mail")..............................10-20 63

DUGOSH, Eddie

Singles: 78 rpm

SARG (135 "Strange Kind of Feeling")..... 15-25 56

Singles: 7-inch

AWARD (116 "One Mile")..........................50-75 58
SARG (135 "Strange Kind of Feeling").....50-75 56

DU-KANES

Singles: 7-inch

HSH (501 "Our Star")................................15-25 64

DUKAYS P&R '61

Singles: 7-inch

JERRY-O (105 "Jerk")...............................10-15 64
JERRY-O (106 "Mellow-Fezneckey").......10-15 64
NAT (4001 "The Girl's a Devil") 15-20 61
NAT (4002 "Nite Owl")...............................15-20 61
OLDIES 45..4-6 '60s
VEE-JAY (430 thru 491)...........................10-20 62-63
Members: Eugene "Gene Chandler" Dixon; James Lowe; Earl Edwards; Ben Broyles; Shirley Jones; Charles Davis; Claude McRae.
Also see ARTISTICS
Also see CHANCE, Nolan
Also see CHANDLER, Gene

DUKE, Billy
(Billy Duke & His Dukes; Bill Duke)

Singles: 78 rpm

CASINO (138 "Flip, Flop & Fly") 15-25 56
CORAL (61203 "I Cried")............................8-12 54
SOUND (130 "This Is What I Ask")...........15-25 56
TEEN..10-15 56

Singles: 7-inch

CAPITOL (4784 thru 4907).........................5-10 62-63
CAPITOL (5012 "Echoes")..........................8-12 63
CASINO (138 "Flip, Flop & Fly")..............40-60 56
CORAL (61203 "I Cried") 15-25 54
DATE (1005 "What You Told Me") 10-15 58
PEAK (104 "Chalypso").............................15-25 57
SEVILLE (132 thru 136)...............................5-10 64-65
SOUND (130 "This Is What I Ask")...........40-50 56
TEEN (110 "Paradise Princess")..............20-30 56
TEEN (112 "Rocky Piano")........................15-25 56
20TH FOX (242 thrru 301)..........................5-10 61-62

DUKE, Denver

Singles: 78 rpm

MERCURY ("Rock & Roll Blues")..............15-25 56

Singles: 7-inch

MERCURY (70970 "Rock & Roll Blues") .25-50 56

DUKE, Patty P&R/LP '65

Singles: 7-inch

U.A. 5-10 65-68

Picture Sleeves

U.A. (875 "Don't Just Stand There").........10-20 65
U.A. (915 "Say Something Funny") 10-20 65

LPs: 10/12-inch

U.A. 15-25 65-68

DUKE, Roy

Singles: 78 rpm

DECCA...8-12 56-57
REJECT (1002 "Behave")..........................10-20 56

Singles: 7-inch

DECCA..10-20 56-57
REJECT (1002 "Behave")...........................20-30 56

DUKE & AMBERS
Singles: 7-inch
STROLL (109 "Joanie")............................ 10-15 60

DUKE & LEONARD
Singles: 7-inch
CALLA ("Just Do the Best You Can")..........8-12 '60s
(Selection number not known.)
STOMP TOWN (101 "Just Do the Best You Can").. 15-25 '60s

DUKE & NULL
Singles: 7-inch
GUITAR (777 "Blue, Blue, Blue")............. 50-75

DUKE BAYOU
(Champion Jack Dupree)
Singles: 78 rpm
APOLLO (442 "Two Time Loser")........... 30-50 50
Also see DUPREE, Champion Jack

DUKE OF EARL P&R '62
(Gene Chandler)
Singles: 7-inch
VEE-JAY (440 "Walk On with the Duke") 10-20 62
VEE-JAY (450 "Daddy's Home")............. 10-20 62
Also see CHANDLER, Gene

DUKE OF IRON
LPs: 10/12-inch
PRESTIGE (13068 "Limbo")..................... 15-20 63

DUKES
Singles: 78 rpm
IMPERIAL.. 50-75 56
SPECIALTY (543 "Ooh Bop She Bop")... 30-50 54
Singles: 7-inch
FLIP (343 "Looking for You")................. 50-100 59
FLIP (345 "I Love You")..................... 100-150 59
IMPERIAL (5344 "I Found a Love")..............4-8
IMPERIAL (5385 "Tell Me Why")..................4-8
IMPERIAL (5399 "I Was a Fool")..................4-8
(Above three Imperial sides previously unreleased.)
IMPERIAL (5401 "Teardrop Eyes")........ 75-125 56
IMPERIAL (5415 "Wini Brown").............. 30-40 56
SPECIALTY (543 "Ooh Bop She Bop")... 50-75 54
Also see MIGHTY DUKES
Also see PRICE, Lloyd

DUKES
Singles: 7-inch
SIGNETT (326 "First Time I Saw Her").... 10-15 66

DUKES
Singles: 7-inch
DUKES (68003 "Meet Me at Mary's Place")... 10-15

DUKES
Singles: 7-inch
APAX (76682 "Little Woman").................. 50-75

DUKES, Aggie
(Agnes Dukes)
Singles: 78 rpm
ALADDIN (3388 "John John").................. 30-50 57
Singles: 7-inch
ALADDIN (3388 "John John").................. 35-55 57

DUMANE, Steve
Singles: 7-inch
GENIE (105 "Teenage Rose").................. 50-75 66

DU MAURIERS
Singles: 78 rpm
FURY (1011 "Baby, I Love You")............. 50-75 58
Singles: 7-inch
FURY (1011 "Baby, I Love You")........... 75-125 58
(Lighter maroon with record time on left.)
FURY (1011 "Baby, I Love You")............. 50-60 58
(Darker maroon label.)
FURY (1011 "Baby, I Love You")............. 15-25 62
(Yellow label. Black wax.)
FURY (1011 "Baby, I Love You")............. 40-50 62
(Yellow label. Red wax.)

DUMONTS
Singles: 7-inch
KING (5552 "But Only with You")............. 10-15 61
PROMOTIONAL (3 "She's My Love")...... 40-50 62

DUNAVAN, Terry
Singles: 7-inch
DEVCO (101 "Rock It on Mars")........... 350-450
FANFARE (727 "Rock It on Mars")....... 250-350

DUNCAN, Bill
Singles: 7-inch
BETHLEHEM (3077 "Country Home")........8-12 62
DBC (1232 "Whirlin' Twirlin' Rock")......100-200

DUNCAN, Cleve
Singles: 7-inch
DOOTO (451 "To Keep Our Love")..........20-30 59
(With the Radiants.)
DOOTO (456 "You're an Angel")..............10-20 59
(With the Penguins.)
Also see PENGUINS

DUNCAN, Don
Singles: 7-inch
VENTURE (111 "Something Special")....75-100 59

DUNCAN, Dusty
Singles: 7-inch
SAN JOAQUIN (1002 "Milk Cow Blues")..50-100

DUNCAN, Ferrell
Singles: 7-inch
KIM (100 "Little Susie")..........................400-600 58

DUNCAN, Herbie
Singles: 7-inch
GLENN (1401 "Escape")..........................75-125 59
GLENN (1402 "That's All")........................50-75 60
MAR-VEL (1400 "Hot Lips Baby").........300-400 58
MAR-VEL (1401 "Roll Along")...................50-75 58
MAR-VEL (1402 "That's All")....................50-75 58
RIC (176 "Serenade You").........................10-20 65

DUNCAN, James
(With the Duncan Trio)
Singles: 7-inch
FEDERAL (928 "My Baby Is Back")..............4-6 76
FEDERAL (12549 "Money Can't Buy True Love")...5-10 69
FEDERAL (12552 "I've Got It Made")..........5-10 69
KING (5587 thru 6052)...........................10-20 64-66

DUNCAN, Jimmy
Singles: 78 rpm
CUE (7929 "Here I Am")..............................5-10 56
KING (5028 "I'm on the Outside")............10-20 57
UNIQUE (353 "Hurricane")...........................5-10 56
Singles: 7-inch
BACK BEAT (527 "Doll House")................10-20 59
BRUNSWICK (55077 "I Close the Door").15-25 58
CUE (7929 "Here I Am")............................10-20 56
DECCA (30455 "Run Little Joey")...............8-12 58
KING (5028 "I'm on the Outside")............15-25 57
ROULETTE (4394 "Eighth Wonder of the World")..15-25 61
UNIQUE (353 "Hurricane")........................10-15 56

DUNCAN, Johnny C&W '67
Singles: 7-inch
COLUMBIA...3-6 67-81
LEADER (807 "Bring Your Heart")...........20-30 60
LEADER (812 "Freddy & His Go-Cart").....10-20 60
LEADER (814 "Raindrops")......................10-15 61
PHAROAH...3-5 86
LPs: 10/12-inch
COLUMBIA...5-10 69-80
HARMONY..5-10 73
PHAROAH...5-10 86
Session: Janie Fricke.

DUNCAN, Johnny, & Janie Fricke C&W '77
Singles: 7-inch
COLUMBIA...3-5 77
LPs: 10/12-inch
COLUMBIA...5-10 80
Also see DUNCAN, Johnny
Also see FRICKE, Janie

DUNCAN, Lanny
Singles: 7-inch
CANDIX (304 "Romeo's Teacher")...........50-75 60
CANDIX (316 "Tummy Tickles")..................8-12 61
CANDIX (328 "Don't Be Afraid to Cry")......8-12 62
GOLDEN STATE (654 "Hold Me, Thrill Me, Kiss Me")..8-12 65

DUNCAN, Tommy
Singles: 78 rpm
FIRE (101 "Daddy Loves Mommy-O")......20-30 56
Singles: 7-inch
FALEW (104 "Dance Dance Dance").......10-15 64
FALEW (107 "Too Much Time")...............10-15 64
FIRE (101 "Daddy Loves Mommy-O")..150-250 56

MOON (115 "Darling")............................75-125 60
SMASH (2073 "Let Me Take You Out")....15-25 66

DUNCAN BROTHERS
Singles: 7-inch
CAPITOL (5711 "Make Me What You Want Me to Be")..10-20 66

DUNDEES
("Featuring Carlyle Dundee")
Singles: 78 rpm
SPACE (201 "Never")............................75-125 54
Singles: 7-inch
SPACE (201 "Never").........................200-300 54
Also see WONDERS

DUNES
Singles: 7-inch
MADISON (156 "Lonely Sands")..............10-20 61

DUNGAREE DARLINGS
(With the Al Sears Orchestra; Dungaree Dolls)
Singles: 7-inch
KAREN (1005 "Boy of My Dreams").......75-100 59
Also see DUNGAREE DOLLS
Also see SEARS, Al

DUNGAREE DOLLS
(With the Al Sears Orchestra)
Singles: 7-inch
REGO (1003 "Boy of My Dreams").......250-300 58
(Reissued as by the Dungaree Darlings.)
Also see DUNGAREE DARLINGS
Also see SEARS, Al

DUNGEON OF FUSION
Singles
AZRA (36 "Digital Darkness")..................25-35 89
(Woman shaped, also square car shaped picture disc. 25 made of each shape.)
AZRA (36 "Digital Darkness")..................10-20 89
(Square shaped picture disc. 500 made.)

DUNHAM, Andrew
Singles: 78 rpm
SENSATION (23 "Sweet Lucy")................40-60 49

DUNHAM, Jackie
(Jack Dunham)
Singles: 7-inch
DIXIE (900 "Lonely Girl").........................15-25 59
DONDEE (1934 "Something on Your Mind")..10-20 60
IMPERIAL (5768 "I Think of You")............20-30 61
IMPERIAL (5797 "My Yearbook")............10-15 61
TOWER (60251 "Rebound to Tulsa").........5-10 66

DUNHILLS
Singles: 7-inch
ROYAL (110 "Sound of the Wind")..........25-35 61

DUNIVEN, Bill
Singles: 7-inch
VADEN (306 "Knockin' on the Backside")..100-200 60

DUNKIRK, Dick, & Strangers
Singles: 7-inch
BANGAR (652 "Don't You Believe Them")..10-20 64
SOMA (1424 "Don't You Believe Them")...8-12 65
Also see VEE, Bobby

DUNLAP, Gene
Singles: 7-inch
HITT (182 "Made in the Shade")..............50-75 58

DUNLAP, Norman, & Melodettes
Singles: 78 rpm
ALADDIN (3213 "A Dream and a Prayer")..50-75 53
Singles: 7-inch
ALADDIN (3213 "A Dream and a Prayer")..150-250 53

DUNN, Bobby
Singles: 7-inch
HOLIDAY (2613 "Laughing")....................10-15 57
LOGO (500 "Darlin' ")................................5-10 63
ORDELL (501 "Am I Too Late")...............10-15 62
U.A. (435 "Slow Drag")..............................5-10 62
WARWICK (631 "Nobody But You")...........5-10 61

DUNN, Bobby, & Les Cooper
LPs: 10/12-inch
PALACE...10-15
Also see COOPER, Les
Also see DUNN, Bobby

DUNN, David
Singles: 7-inch
GOLDEN EAGLE (109 "Rock Me")..........50-75
LORI (9541 "I'll Never Let You Go").........25-35 62
LORI (9545 "Say It Isn't So")....................25-35 63

DUNN, Elaine
Singles: 7-inch
RCA (7450 "Just for Once").......................10-15 59
RCA (7552 "Touch Me")............................10-15 59

DUNN, Fred
(With His Barrelhouse Rhythm)
Singles: 78 rpm
JIFFY (100 "Fred's Boogie Woogie")....200-300 47
SIGNATURE (1026 "Fred's Boogie Woogie")..25-50 47
SIGNATURE (32010 "Railroad Blues")....25-50 48

DUNN, Joanie
Singles: 78 rpm
ELDORADO (501 "To Johnny B from Joanie D")..8-12 56
Singles: 7-inch
ELDORADO (501 "To Johnny B from Joanie D")..15-25 56

DUNN, Joyce
Singles: 7-inch
BLUE ROCK (4081 "The Push I Need")...10-20 69

DUNN, Leona
Singles: 7-inch
HALLMARK (500 "Our Songs of Love")...10-15 65

DUNN, Webster
Singles: 7-inch
DUNMAR (101 "Black & White Shoes").75-100

DUOTONES
Singles: 7-inch
HARLEQUIN (611026 "And My Heart Came Tumblin' Down")...15-25 61

DUPIN, Sunny
(Sunny Joe Dupin; with Moonmen)
Singles: 7-inch
GOLDBAND (Except 1107).........................8-12 57-67
GOLDBAND (1107 "Why Should I")...30-40 60
PAULA (237 "This Oak Tree")....................5-8 66
TEK (102 "Looney and Goon")..............15-25

DU PONT, Shelley, & Calendars
Singles: 7-inch
TRIBUNE (1001 "Share My Love")...........20-30 65

DUPONTS
(Little Anthony Gourdine & Duponts)
Singles: 78 rpm
ROYAL ROOST (627 "Prove It Tonight").20-40 57
WINLEY (212 "Must Be Falling in Love").20-40 56
Singles: 7-inch
ROYAL ROOST (627 "Prove It Tonight").40-50 57
SAVOY (1552 "Must Be Falling in Love") 10-15 58
WINLEY (212 "Must Be Falling in Love").50-75 56
Members: Anthony Gourdine; Bill Dokery; Bill Delk; Bill Bracey.
Also see LITTLE ANTHONY & IMPERIALS

DUPONTS
Singles: 7-inch
ROULETTE (4060 "Screamin' Ball")........ 15-25 58

DUPREE, Champion Jack R&B '55
Singles: 78 rpm
ALERT...15-25 46
APOLLO...15-25 49-50
CELEBRITY..15-25 46
CONTINENTAL...15-25 45
JOE DAVIS...15-25 46
KING..10-20 53-56
RED ROBIN..25-75 52-54
VIK..25-35 57
Singles: 7-inch
ATLANTIC..5-10 61
EVERLAST (5032 "Highway Blues")...........4-8 65
FEDERAL..5-10 61
GUSTO..3-5 '80s
KING (4633 "The Blues Got Me Rockin' ")..15-25 53
KING (4695 "Walkin' Upside Your Head")...15-25 53
KING (4706 "Rub a Little Boogie")...........15-25 53
KING (4812 "Walking the Blues")............15-25

KING (4938 "Big Leg Emma's") 15-25 56
RED ROBIN (109 "Stumblin' Block Blues") 150-200 52
RED ROBIN (112 "Highway Blues") 150-200 52
RED ROBIN (130 "Drunk Again") 150-200 54
VIK (260 "Dirty Woman") 20-30 57
VIK (279 "Old Time Rock & Roll") 20-30 57

LPs: 10/12-inch

ARCHIVE OF FOLK MUSIC..................... 10-15 68
ATLANTIC (8019 "Blues from the Gutter") 75-100 59
(Green label.)
ATLANTIC (8019 "Blues from the Gutter") 40-60 59
(Black label.)
ATLANTIC (8019 "Blues from the Gutter") 40-60 59
(White label.)
ATLANTIC (8019 "Blues from the Gutter") 20-30 59
(Red label.)
ATLANTIC (8045 "Natural and Soulful Blues") 30-40 61
(Monaural.)
ATLANTIC (SD-8045 "Natural and Soulful Blues") 40-50 61
(Stereo.)
ATLANTIC (8056 "Champion of the Blues") 30-40 61
(Monaural.)
ATLANTIC (SD-8056 "Champion of the Blues") 40-50 61
(Stereo.)
ATLANTIC (8255 "Blues from the Gutter") 8-10 70
BLUE HORIZON 10-15 69
EVEREST... 8-12
FOLKWAYS (3825 "Women Blues of Champion Jack Dupree") 20-30 61
GNP... 8-12 74
JAZZMAN... 5-10 82
KING (735 "Champion Jack Dupree Sings the Blues") 50-60 61
KING (1084 "Walking the Blues") 10-15 70
LONDON 10-15 69
OKEH (12103 "Cabbage Greens") 50-75 63
STORYVILLE 5-10 82
Members: Jack Dupree; Larry Dale; Al Lucas; Gene Moore; Stick McGhee; Willie Jones; Pete Brown.
Also see BROTHER BLUES & BACK ROOM BOYS
Also see DUKE BAYOU
Also see DUPREE, Jack, & Mr. Bear
Also see FIVE SATINS / Champion Jack Dupree
Also see JOHNSON, Blind Boy, & His Rhythms
Also see JOHNSON, Meat Head
Also see JORDAN, Willie, & His Swinging Five
Also see LIGHTNIN' JR. & EMPIRES
Also see McGHEE, Brownie
Also see McGHEE, Stick
Also see RUSHING, Jimmy, & Jack Dupree

DUPREE, Champion Jack, & Mickey Baker

LPs: 10/12-inch

SIRE... 10-15 69
Also see BAKER, Mickey

DUPREE, Champion Jack, & His Combo / Lucy Roberts with Neal Hefti & His Orchestra

EPs: 7-inch

VIK (3 "Champion Jack Dupree / Lucy Roberts") 30-50 57
(Promotional issue only. Not issued with cover.)
Also see DUPREE, Champion Jack
Also see HEFTI, Neal
Also see ROBERTS, Lucy

DU PREE, Florence
(With the Elliot Carpenter Orchestra)

Singles: 7-inch

SKYWAY (130 "Shakin' Hands") .... 10-15 '60s

DUPREE, Jack, & Mr. Bear

Singles: 78 rpm

GROOVE (0171 "Lonely Road Blues") 10-15 56
KING (4812 "Walking the Blues") 10-20 55

Singles: 7-inch

GROOVE (0171 "Lonely Road Blues") 20-30 56
KING (4812 "Walking the Blues") 25-35 55
Members: Jack Dupree; Teddy "Mr. Bear" McRae; Larry Dale; Al Lucas; Gene Moore.
Also see DALE, Larry
Also see DUPREE, Champion Jack
Also see MR. BEAR

DUPREE, Lebron

Singles: 7-inch

SPANN (411 "Yea Yea Yea") 20-30 59

DUPREE, Lillian

Singles: 7-inch

D-TOWN (1051 "Hide & Seek") 40-60 66

DUPREE, Nelson

Singles: 7-inch

PALM (201 "Lost") 10-15 59
V-TONE (204 "Iceberg Heart") 15-25 59

DUPREE, Simon, & Big Sound

Singles: 7-inch

TOWER (427 "Daytime, Night Time") 5-10 68

LPs: 10/12-inch

TOWER (5097 "Without Reservations") ... 15-25 68

DUPREES P&R/LP '62

Singles: 7-inch

COED (569 thru 580) 10-20 62-63
COED (584 "Why Don't You Believe Me"/"The Things I Love") 15-20 63
COED (584 "Why Don't You Believe Me"/"My Dearest One") 10-15 63
(Note different flip.)
COED (585 thru 596) 10-15 63-65
COLLECTABLES 3-5 80
COLUMBIA 8-12 65-67
ERIC .... 4-6 '70s
1ST CHOICE ("It's Christmas Once Again") 3-5 89
(No selection number used.)
HERITAGE 4-8 68-70
LOST NITE (black vinyl) .... 4-6 '70s
LOST NITE (colored vinyl) 10-15
RCA (10407 "The Sky's the Limit") 4-6 75

Picture Sleeves

COLUMBIA (43577 "Let Them Talk") 35-45 66
HERITAGE (805 'Goodnight My Love") 5-10 68

LPs: 10/12-inch

COED (905 "You Belong to Me") 75-125 62
COED (906 "Have You Heard") 75-125 63
COLLECTABLES 5-10 80
(Black vinyl.)
COLLECTABLES 10-15 82
(Picture disc.)
1ST CHOICE 10-15 87
HERITAGE (35002 "Total Recall") 20-30 68
PICCADILLY 8-12 80
POST (1000 "The Duprees Sing") 15-25
POST (11000 "The Duprees Sing, Vol. 2") 15-20
Members: Joey "Vann" Canzano; Mike Arnone; Tom Bialaglow; John Salvato; Joe Santollo; Richie Rosato.
Also see VANN, Joey

DUPREES / Rivieras

LPs: 10/12-inch

LOST NITE (122 Jerry Blavat Presents Drive-In Sounds") .... 10-15 '70s
Also see DUPREES
Also see RIVIERAS

DUPRIES

Singles: 7-inch

TEST (100 "Baby Doll") 25-35 65
THUNDER (106 "Baby Doll") 25-35 65
Members: Dick Schulz; Annie Duprey Schulz; Joanie Duprey Rousseau; Carol Duprey; Dave Pilz; Dave Parpovich.
Also see CANDY & CORALS

DU PUY, Helda & Ike Perkins Orchestra

Singles: 78 rpm

UNITED (157 "Riding with the Blues") 5-10 53

Singles: 7-inch

UNITED (157 "Riding with the Blues") 15-20 53

DURAIN, Johnny, & Cytones

Singles: 7-inch

BIG CITY (300 "About to Lose My Mind") .. 8-12 '60s
BIG CITY (301 "I'll Show You") .... 8-12 '60s
DORE (624 "My Last Love") 15-25 62

DURAN, Lucy

Singles: 7-inch

FIFO (109 "I Tried to Make You Understand") 10-15 62

DURAN DURAN P&R/LP '82
(Duranduran)

Singles: 12-inch

CAPITOL (Except 12352) 4-8 82-87
CAPITOL (12352 "The Reflex") 10-20 84
(Picture disc.)

Singles: 7-inch

CAPITOL (Black vinyl) 3-5 82-90
CAPITOL (Colored vinyl) 5-10 86-87
(Promotional issues only.)
HARVEST 3-5 81-82

Picture Sleeves

CAPITOL (Except 5345) 3-5 83-89
CAPITOL (5345 "The Reflex") 4-8 84
(Poster sleeve.)
CAPITOL (5438 "Save a Prayer") 5-10 82
(Promotional issue only.)
HARVEST 3-5 82

EPs: 7-inch

HARVEST 15-20 82

LPs: 10/12-inch

CAPITOL 5-10 82-90
HARVEST (12158 "Duran Duran") 8-12 81
MFSL (110 "Rio") 40-60 84
MFSL (182 "Seven and the Ragged Tiger") 40-60 87
Members: Nick Rhodes; Roger Taylor; John Taylor, Andy Taylor; Simon LeBon; Warren Cuccurullo; Mark Kennedy.
Also see HAIG, Ronnie

DURAND, Al

Singles: 7-inch

AMP (103 "I Live Again") 15-25 59

DURAND, Ruth

Singles: 78 rpm

POST (2012 "I'm Wise") 10-15 55

Singles: 7-inch

POST (2012 "I'm Wise") 25-35 55

DURANTE, Jimmy P&R '34
(With Helen Traubel; with Roy Bargy & Orchestra)

Singles: 78 rpm

BRUNSWICK 5-10 34
DECCA 4-8 44-57
RCA (3229 "The Song's Gotta Come from the Heart") 5-10 48

Singles: 7-inch

DECCA 4-8 51-59
W.B. 4-6 63-70
RCA (49-3229 "The Song's Gotta Come from the Heart") 25-35 49
(Red vinyl.)

EPs: 7-inch

DECCA 5-10 54-56
MGM 5-10 53-55
VARSITY 5-10 55

LPs: 10/12-inch

DECCA (9000 series) 15-25 54-56
DECCA (78000 series) 8-12 70
HARMONY 8-12 68
LIGHT 5-10 71
LION 15-20 56
MGM (3200 series) 15-25 55
MGM (4200 series) 10-15 64
ROULETTE (25123 "At the Copacabana") 15-20 61
W.B. 10-15 63-67
Also see GOLDSBORO, Bobby / Jimmy Durante
Also see KAYE, Danny, Jimmy Durante, Jane Wyman & Groucho Marx
Also see MARTIN, Dean
Also see PRESLEY, Elvis

DURELL, Lee, & Tamaras

Singles: 7-inch

MUSIC CITY (836 "Party Time") 200-300 60

DURETTES / Perfections

Singles: 7-inch

SVR (1006 "Sweet, Sweet Love"/"I Love You My Love") 40-50 64
Also see PERFECTIONS

DURHAM, Charles

Singles: 7-inch

JAMBOREE (900 "Teenage Beat") 100-150

DURHAM, Judith

LPs: 10/12-inch

A&M 10-12 75

DURHAM, Paul

Singles: 7-inch

McDOWELL (507 "Mean Woman") 50-75
SANDSPUR (15302 "She Lied") 35-50

DURST, L.
(Lavada Durst)

Singles: 78 rpm

PEACOCK (1509 "Hattie Green") 20-30 49
Also see DR. HEP CAT

DUSHON, Jean
(Jean Du Shon)

Singles: 7-inch

ABC-PAR (10092 "Together") 5-10 60
ARGO (5497 thru 5518) 5-8 65
ATCO (6198 "Talk to Me") 25-35 61
CADET (5530 thru 5550) 5-8 66
LENOX (5568 "Look the Other Way") 5-10 63
OKEH (7151 "Plaything") 5-10 62

LPs: 10/12-inch

ARGO (4039 "Make Way For") 10-20 64
CADET (4048 "Feeling Good") 10-20 66

DUSTERS
(With Jimmy Binkley's Orchestra)

Singles: 78 rpm

ARC (3000 "Give Me Time") 75-125 56
HUDSON (4 "Don't Leave Me to Cry") 50-75 55

Singles: 7-inch

ARC (3000 "Give Me Time") 150-250 56
HUDSON (4 "Don't Leave Me to Cry") . 150-250 55
(First released as by the Belvaderes.)
Member: Tommy Tucker.
Also see BELVADERES
Also see TUCKER, Tommy

DUSTERS

Singles: 7-inch

ABC-PAR (9887 "Pretty Girl") 10-20 58
CUPID (5003 "Rock at the Hop") 100-125 58
GLORY (287 "Darling Love") 50-75 58
Members: Robert Mansfield; Donald Emilian; Lee de Felice; Robert Wentworth.
Also see BUCCANEERS

DUVALL, Huelyn P&R '59

Singles: 78 rpm

CHALLENGE 25-50 58

Singles: 7-inch

CHALLENGE (1012 "Comin' Or Goin'") ... 40-60 58
(Blue label.)
CHALLENGE (1012 "Comin' Or Goin'") ... 20-30 58
(Maroon label.)
CHALLENGE (59002 "Humdinger") 20-30 58
CHALLENGE (59014 "Little Boy Blue") 20-40 58
CHALLENGE (59025 "Juliette") 10-20 58
CHALLENGE (59069 "Pucker Paint") 50-75 59
STARFIRE (600 "It's No Wonder") 50-75 59
TWINKLE (506 "Beautiful Dreamer") .... 50-75 '50s

DUVALS

Singles: 78 rpm

CLUB (1013 "Wanna Be Free") 20-30 56

Singles: 7-inch

CLUB (1013 "Wanna Be Free") 100-200 56
LA SALLE (502 "Wanna Be Free") 50-75 57

DUVALS
(Five Crowns)

Singles: 7-inch

LOST NITE .... 4-6 '70s
RAINBOW (335 "You Came to Me") 100-200 57
(Yellow label.)
RAINBOW (335 "You Came to Me") 30-40 62
(Blue label.)
Members: Wilbur Paul; Jesse Facing; Richard Lewis; Dock Green; William Bailey.
Also see DRAPERS
Also see DRIFTERS
Also see FIVE CROWNS

DUVALS

Singles: 78 rpm

GEE (1003 "Guide Me") 25-35 56

Singles: 7-inch

GEE (1003 "Guide Me") 50-75 56

DUVALS

Singles: 7-inch

PRELUDE (110 "The Last Surf") 20-30 63

DUVALS

Singles: 7-inch

BOSS (2117 "What Am I")........................ 20-30 63
(First issue.)
RED ROCKET (471 "What Am I")..............5-10 63
Members: Carlton Black; Charles Perry; Andy Thomas; Charles Woolridge; Arthur Cox.
Also see DREW-VELS
Also see NATURALS

DUVELLS

Singles: 7-inch

RUST (5045 "How Come")...................... 15-25 62

DWELLERS

(With the Jap Curry Blazers)

Singles: 7-inch

CONROSE (101 "Lonely Guy")........... 100-200 60
HOWARD (503 "Tell Me Why")........... 100-200 59
OASIS (101 "Oh Sweetie")................... 75-125 59

DWIGHT, Susan, & Minks

(With the Darrell Balasty Orchestra)

Singles: 7-inch

ERMINE (31 "Lotsa' Luck")...................... 10-15 61
(Previously issued as by the Minks.)
Also see MINKS

DYCUS, Connie

Singles: 7-inch

DIXIE (886 "I Could Shoot Myself")...... 100-200 '50s
MERCURY (71376 "Rock-a-bye Baby Rock")................................ 100-200 58
POOR BOY (108 "Same Old Thing")....... 50-75

DYKE, Jerry

(With the Ventells)

Singles: 7-inch

CASINO (1001 "Deep in My Heart")..........5-10
HOLIDAY INN (2203 thru 2211)................5-10 68
SATURN (5010 "Mean Woman Blues").. 100-150

DYKE & BLAZERS P&R/R&B/LP '67

Singles: 7-inch

ARTCO...8-10 67
ORIGINAL SOUND....................................4-8 66-71

LPs: 10/12-inch

ORIGINAL SOUND (8876 "Funky Broadway") 30-35 67
ORIGINAL SOUND (8877 "Dyke's Greatest Hits").. 20-30 67
Member: Arlester "Dyke" Christian.

DYLAN, Bob LP '63

(With the Band)

Singles: 7-inch

ASYLUM (11033 "On a Night Like This") 4-6 74
ASYLUM (11043 "Most Likely You Go Your Way")...4-6 74
ASYLUM (45000 series)...............................3-5 74
COLUMBIA (04301 "Sweetheart Like You").3-5 83
COLUMBIA (04425 "Joker Man")..................3-5 84
COLUMBIA (04933 "Tight Connection to My Heart")..3-5 85
COLUMBIA (05697 "Emotionally Yours").....3-5 85
COLUMBIA (10106 "Tangled Up in Blue") .8-12 75
COLUMBIA (10217 "Million Dollar Bash") ..8-12 75
COLUMBIA (10245 "Hurricane")..................4-6 75
COLUMBIA (10298 "Mozambique")..............4-6 75
COLUMBIA (10454 "Rita Mae")..................8-12 77
COLUMBIA (10805 "Baby Stop Crying")......4-8 78
COLUMBIA (10851 "Changing of the Guards")..8-12 78
COLUMBIA (11072 "Gotta Serve Somebody")..4-6 79
COLUMBIA (11235 "Slow Train") 4-6 80
COLUMBIA (11318 "Solid Rock") 4-6 80
COLUMBIA (11370 "Saved") 4-6 80
COLUMBIA (13-0000 series) 3-5
COLUMBIA (18-02510 "Heart of Mine").......3-5 81
COLUMBIA (42656 "Mixed Up Confusion")...................................... 750-1000 63
COLUMBIA (42856 "Blowin' in the Wind") 250-350 63
COLUMBIA (43242 "Subterranean Homesick Blues").. 10-20 65
(Gray label.)
COLUMBIA (43242 "Subterranean Homesick Blues")...4-8 65
(Red label.)
COLUMBIA (43346 "Like a Rolling Stone") ..4-8 65
COLUMBIA (43389 "Positively 4th Street")..10-20 65
(Gray label.)
COLUMBIA (43389 "Positively 4th Street")..4-8 65
(Red label.)
COLUMBIA (43477 "Can You Please Crawl Out Your Window")...10-12 65
COLUMBIA (43683 "I Want You") 4-8 66
COLUMBIA (43541 "One of Us Must Know") 8-12 66
COLUMBIA (43592 "Rainy Day Women #12 and 35")...50-100 66
(Red vinyl. Promotional issue.)
COLUMBIA (43592 "Rainy Day Women #12 and 35")..4-8 66
COLUMBIA (43792 "Just Like a Woman") ...4-8 66
COLUMBIA (44069 "Leopard-Skin Pill-Box Hat")..8-12 67
COLUMBIA (44826 "I Threw It All Away") ..8-10 69
COLUMBIA (44926 "Lay Lady Lay")............4-8 69
COLUMBIA (45004 "Tonight I'll Be Staying Here with You)...8-10 69
COLUMBIA (45199 "Wigwam")....................5-10 69
COLUMBIA (45409 "Watching the River Flow")..5-10 71
COLUMBIA (45516 "George Jackson")......8-10 71
COLUMBIA (45913 "Knockin' on Heaven's Door")..4-6 73
COLUMBIA (45982 "A Fool Such As I") 4-6 73
MCA (52811 "Band of the Hand")................4-6 86

Picture Sleeves

COLUMBIA (02510 "Heart of Mine").............4-8 81
COLUMBIA (04301 "Sweetheart Like You")...4-6 84
COLUMBIA (04933 "Tight Connection to My Heart")..4-6 85
COLUMBIA (10245 "Hurricane")...............25-50 75
COLUMBIA (11235 "Slow Train") 5-10 80
COLUMBIA (43242 "Subterranean Homesick Blues")..300-500 65
(Promotional issue only.)
COLUMBIA (43242 "Subterranean Homesick Blues") 40-60 65
(Columbia "Hit Pack" picture sleeve.)
COLUMBIA (43389 "Positively 4th Street")...25-35 65
COLUMBIA (43683 "I Want You") 20-25 66
MCA (52811 "Band of the Hand")................4-6 86

Promotional Singles

ASYLUM (11033 "On a Night Like This") ...8-12 74
ASYLUM (11043 "Most Likely You Go Your Way") 8-12 74
COLUMBIA (25 "All the Tired Horses") 30-40 70
COLUMBIA (1039 "If Not for You")..........30-40 71
COLUMBIA (04301 "Sweetheart Like You") 4-8 83
COLUMBIA (04425 "Joker Man") 4-8 84
COLUMBIA (04933 "Tight Connection to My Heart")..4-8 85
COLUMBIA (05697 "Emotionally Yours").....4-8 85
COLUMBIA (10106 "Tangled Up in Blue") 10-20 75
COLUMBIA (10245 "Hurricane")..............15-20 75
COLUMBIA (10245 "Hurricane")..............20-30 75
(Compact 33 Single.)
COLUMBIA (10298 "Mozambique")...........8-10 75
COLUMBIA (10454 "Rita Mae") 10-20 77
COLUMBIA (10805 "Baby Stop Crying") ..10-20 78
COLUMBIA (11072 "Gotta Serve Somebody")..5-10 79
COLUMBIA (11235 "Slow Train") 5-10 80
COLUMBIA (11318 "Solid Rock") 5-10 80
COLUMBIA (11370 "Saved") 5-10 80
COLUMBIA (18-0000 series) 3-6 81
COLUMBIA (42656 "Mixed Up Confusion") 500-750 63
COLUMBIA (42856 "Blowin' in the Wind")..200-300 63
(Add $100 to $200 if accompanied by "Rebel with a Cause" letter-insert, which introduces Bob Dylan.)
COLUMBIA (43242 "Subterranean Homesick Blues")...40-60 65
(Black vinyl.)
COLUMBIA (43242 "Subterranean Homesick Blues")..100-150 65
(Red vinyl.)
COLUMBIA (43346 "Like a Rolling Stone")..40-60 65
(Black vinyl. Labels may show identification numbers "JZSP-110939/110940," but not selection number, 43346.)
COLUMBIA (43346 "Like a Rolling Stone") 100-150 65
(Red vinyl.)
COLUMBIA (43389 "Positively 4th Street")..30-40 65
(Black vinyl.)
COLUMBIA (43389 "Positively 4th Street")..100-150 65
(Colored vinyl.)
COLUMBIA (43389 "Positively 4th Street")..100-150 65
(Outtake promo. Has an alternate take of *Can You Please Crawl Out Your Window.*)
COLUMBIA (43477 "Can You Please Crawl Out Your Window") 40-60 65
COLUMBIA (43683 "I Want You")............30-45 66
(Black vinyl.)
COLUMBIA (43683 "I Want You") 100-150 66
(Red vinyl.)
COLUMBIA (43541 "One of Us Must Know") 40-55 66
COLUMBIA (43592 "Rainy Day Women #12 and 35") 30-40 66
COLUMBIA (43792 "Just Like a Woman")..30-40 66
(Black vinyl.)
COLUMBIA (43792 "Just Like a Woman")..100-150 66
(Red vinyl.)
COLUMBIA (44069 "Leopard-Skin Pill-Box Hat") 30-40 67
COLUMBIA (44826 "I Threw It All Away")..15-25 69
COLUMBIA (44926 "Lay Lady Lay").........15-25 69
COLUMBIA (45004 "Tonight I'll Be Staying Here with You") 15-25 69
COLUMBIA (45199 "Wigwam") 15-25 69
COLUMBIA (45409 "Watching the River Flow")...15-25 71
COLUMBIA (45516 "George Jackson")....15-25 71
COLUMBIA (45913 "Knockin' on Heaven's Door")..10-20 73
COLUMBIA (45982 "A Fool Such As I") ...10-20 73
COLUMBIA (75606 "Blowin' in the Wind") 250-400 63
("Special Album Excerpt.")

EPs: 7-inch

COLUMBIA (319 "Step Lively")............200-300 65
COLUMBIA (9128 "Bringing It All Back Home")...200-300 65
(Juke box issue only. Includes title strips.)
COLUMBIA/PLAYBACK.........................75-100 73
(Promotional issue only. Contains four tracks by four different artists.)

LPs: 10/12-inch

ASYLUM (201 "Before the Flood") 10-15 74
ASYLUM (1003 "Planet Waves")..............15-20 74
(Without cut corner.)
ASYLUM (1003 "Planet Waves")...............8-10 74
(With cut corner.)
ASYLUM (EQ-1003 "Planet Waves") 15-20 74
(Quadraphonic.)
COLUMBIA (C2L-41 "Blonde on Blonde")..50-100 66
(Monaural. With "female photos" on inside of jacket.)
COLUMBIA (C2L-41 "Blonde on Blonde")..40-60 66
(Monaural. With Dylan photo replacing female photos.)
COLUMBIA (C2S-841 "Blonde on Blonde")..50-100 66
(Stereo "360 Sound" label. With "female photos" on inside of jacket.)
COLUMBIA (C2S-841 "Blonde on Blonde")..40-60 66
(Stereo "360 Sound" label. With Dylan photo replacing female photos.)
COLUMBIA (CL-1779 "Bob Dylan")......600-800 62
(Monaural. Red and black label with six Columbia "eye" boxes.)
COLUMBIA (CL-1779 "Bob Dylan")........50-100 62
(Monaural. Red "360 Sound" label.)
COLUMBIA (CL-1986 "The Freewheelin' Bob Dylan") 10000-15000 63
(Monaural. With *Let Me Die in My Footsteps, Talkin' John Birch Society Blues, Gamblin' Willie's Dead Man's Hand,* and *Rocks and Gravel,* which may also be shown as *Solid Gravel.* We suggest verification of the above tracks by listening to the LP, rather than accepting the information printed on the label. In fact, some copies of the rare pressing have reissue labels. Identification numbers of this press are XLP-58717-1A and XLP-58718-1A.)
COLUMBIA (CL-1986 "The Freewheelin' Bob Dylan")..50-100 63
(Monaural. With the above tracks replaced by four others.)
COLUMBIA (CL-2105 "The Times They Are A-Changin' ")..50-100 64
(Monaural.)
COLUMBIA (CL-2193 "Another Side of Bob Dylan")..50-100 64
(Monaural.)
COLUMBIA (CL-2328 "Bringin' It All Back Home") 50-100 65
(Monaural.)
COLUMBIA (CL-2389 "Highway 61 Revisited") 300-400 65
(Monaural. With alternate take of *From a Buick 6.* The alternate take begins with a harmonica riff. This pressing has a "-1" at the end of the identification number, stamped in the vinyl trailoff.)
COLUMBIA (CL-2389 "Highway 61 Revisited") 50-75 65
(Monaural.)
COLUMBIA (KCL-2663 "Bob Dylan's Greatest Hits")..50-75 67
(Monaural.)
COLUMBIA (CL-2804 "John Wesley Harding") 100-200 68
(Monaural.)
COLUMBIA (CS-8579 "Bob Dylan")......200-300 62
(Stereo. Red and black label with six Columbia "eye" boxes.)
COLUMBIA (CS-8579 "Bob Dylan").......50-100 62
(Stereo. Red "360 Sound" label. Some, if not all, Canadian pressings fail to list *Don't Think Twice, It's Alright* on the back cover, though the song is on the disc – Side 2, Track 1.)
COLUMBIA (PC-8579 "Bob Dylan")...........5-10
COLUMBIA (CS-8786 "The Freewheelin' Bob Dylan")..15000-20000 63
(Stereo. With *Let Me Die in My Footsteps, Talkin' John Birch Society Blues, Gamblin' Willie's Dead Man's Hand,* and *Rocks and Gravel,* which may also be shown as *Solid Gravel.* We suggest verification of the above tracks by listening to the LP, rather than accepting the information printed on the label. In fact, some copies of the rare pressing have reissue labels.
COLUMBIA (CS-8786 "The Freewheelin' Bob Dylan")..50-100 63
(Stereo. With the above tracks replaced by four others. Red "360 Sound" label. Black print at bottom.)
COLUMBIA (CS-8786 "The Freewheelin' Bob Dylan")..25-50 '60s
(Stereo. Red "360 Sound" label. White print at bottom.)
COLUMBIA (PC-8786 "The Freewheelin' Bob Dylan")..5-10
COLUMBIA (CS-87686 "The Freewheelin' Bob Dylan")..300-400 63
(Stereo. Canadian. Cover lists *Let Me Die in My Footsteps, Talkin' John Birch Society Blues, Gamblin' Willie's Dead Man's Hand,* and *Solid Road.* Instead of these four songs, LP actually plays *Bob Dylan's Dream, Girl from the North Country, Masters of War* and *Talking World War III Blues.* We have yet to verify a monaural version of this issue.)
COLUMBIA (CS-8905 "The Times They Are A-Changin' ")..50-100 64
(Stereo. Red "360 Sound" label. Black print at bottom.)
COLUMBIA (CS-8905 "The Times They Are A-Changin' ")..25-50 '60s
(Stereo. Red "360 Sound" label. White print at bottom.)
COLUMBIA (CS-8993 "Another Side of Bob Dylan")..50-100 64
(Stereo. Red "360 Sound" label. Black print at bottom.)
COLUMBIA (CS-8993 "Another Side of Bob Dylan")..25-50 '60s
(Stereo. Red "360 Sound" label. White print at bottom.)
COLUMBIA (CS-9128 "Bringin' It All Back Home")..50-100 65
(Stereo. Red "360 Sound" label. Black print at bottom.)
COLUMBIA (CS-9128 "Bringin' It All Back Home")..25-50 '60s
(Stereo. Red "360 Sound" label. White print at bottom.)
COLUMBIA (PC-9128 "Bringin' It All Back Home")..5-10 '70s
COLUMBIA (CS-9189 "Highway 61 Revisited")..100-150 65

(Stereo. With alternate take of *From a Buick 6*. The alternate take begins with a harmonica riff. This pressing has a "-1" at the end of the identification number, stamped in the vinyl trailoff.)

COLUMBIA (CS-9189 "Highway 61 Revisited") ... 20-30 65
(Stereo.)
COLUMBIA (KCS-9463 "Bob Dylan's Greatest Hits") ... 35-50 67
(Stereo. Red "360 Sound" label. With bonus poster.)
COLUMBIA (KCS-9463 "Bob Dylan's Greatest Hits") ... 25-40 67
(Stereo. Red "360 Sound" label. Without poster.)
COLUMBIA (CS-9604 "John Wesley Harding") ... 20-30 68
(Stereo. Red "360 Sound" label.)
COLUMBIA (KCS-9825 "Nashville Skyline") ... 10-15 69
(Two discs. With "360 Sound" at bottom of label.)
COLUMBIA (C2X-30050 "Self Portrait") .. 50-75 70
(Two discs. With "360 Sound" at bottom of label.)
COLUMBIA (C2X-30050 "Self Portrait") .. 10-15 70
(Without "360 Sound" at bottom of label.)
COLUMBIA (KC-30290 "New Morning") ... 8-10 70
COLUMBIA (KC-31120 "Greatest Hits, Vol. 2") ... 10-12 71
COLUMBIA (KC-32460 "Pat Garrett and Billy the Kid") ... 8-12 73
(Soundtrack.)
COLUMBIA (KC-32747 "Dylan") ... 8-12 73
COLUMBIA (CQ-32872 "Nashville Skyline") ... 50-100 74
(Quadraphonic.)
COLUMBIA (PC-33235 "Blood on the Tracks") ... 30-50 75
(With mural pictured on the back cover.)
COLUMBIA (PC-33235 "Blood on the Tracks") ... 10-15 75
(With liner notes on the back cover.)
COLUMBIA (PC2-33682 "The Basement Tapes") ... 10-12 75
COLUMBIA (PC-33893 "Desire") ... 8-10 76
COLUMBIA (PCQ-33893 "Desire") ... 40-50 76
(Quadraphonic.)
COLUMBIA (PC-34349 "Hard Rain") ... 8-10 76
COLUMBIA (JC-35453 "Street Legal") ... 8-10 78
COLUMBIA (PC2-36067 "Bob Dylan at Budokan") ... 8-10 79
COLUMBIA (FC-36120 "Slow Train Comin'") ... 8-10 79
COLUMBIA (FC-36553 "Saved") ... 8-10 80
COLUMBIA (FC-37496 "Shot of Love") ... 8-10 81
COLUMBIA (PC-38819 "Infidels") ... 8-10 83
COLUMBIA (C5X-38830 "Biograph") ... 20-30 85
(Boxed, five-disc set. Includes 36-page booklet.)
COLUMBIA (FC-39944 "Real Live") ... 5-10 84
COLUMBIA (FC-40110 "Empire Burlesque") ... 5-10 85
COLUMBIA (OC-40439 "Knocked Out Loaded") ... 5-10 86
COLUMBIA (OC-40957 "Down in the Groove") ... 5-10 88
COLUMBIA (HC-43235 "Blood on the Tracks") ... 20-30 83
(Half-speed mastered.)
COLUMBIA (45281 "Oh Mercy") ... 5-10 89
COLUMBIA (46794 "Under the Red Sky") ... 5-10 90
COLUMBIA (47382 "The Bootleg Series Volumes 1 - 3") ... 15-20 89
COLUMBIA (HC-49825 "Nashville Skyline") ... 20-30 81
(Half-speed mastered.)
FOLKWAYS (5322 "Bob Dylan Vs. A.J. Weberman") ... 100-175
ISLAND (1 "Before the Flood") ... 25-30 74
MFSL (114 "The Times They Are A-Changing") ... 20-30

Promotional LPs

ASYLUM (201 "Before the Flood") ... 25-40 74
ASYLUM (1003 "Planet Waves") ... 25-40 74
COLUMBIA (422 "Renaldo and Clara") ... 25-35 76
(Soundtrack.)
COLUMBIA (798 "Saved") ... 25-35 80
COLUMBIA (1259 "Dylan London Interview") ... 25-35 80
COLUMBIA (1263 "Shot of Love") ... 25-35 81
COLUMBIA (1471 "Electric Lunch") ... 15-25 83
COLUMBIA (1770 "Infidels") ... 10-20 83
COLUMBIA (C2L-41 "Blonde on Blonde") ... 60-75 66
(Monaural. With "female photos" on inside of jacket.)
COLUMBIA (C2S-841 "Blonde on Blonde") ... 60-75 66
(Stereo. With "female photos" on inside of jacket.)
COLUMBIA (CL-1779 "Bob Dylan") ... 200-300 62
(Monaural.)
COLUMBIA (CL-1986 "The Freewheelin' Bob Dylan") ... 10000-15000 63
(Monaural. With *Let Me Die in My Footsteps, Talkin' John Birch Society Blues, Gamblin' Willie's Dead Man's Hand,* and *Rocks and Gravel*, which may also be shown as *Solid Gravel*. We suggest verification of the above tracks by listening to the LP, rather than accepting the information printed on the label. In fact, some copies of the rare pressing have reissue labels. Identification numbers of this press are XLP-58717-1A and XLP-58718-1A.)
COLUMBIA (CL-1986 "The Freewheelin' Bob Dylan") ... 75-100 63
(Monaural. With the above tracks replaced by four others.)
COLUMBIA (CL-2105 "The Times They Are A-Changin'") ... 75-100 64
COLUMBIA (CL-2193 "Another Side of Bob Dylan") ... 60-75 64
(Monaural.)
COLUMBIA (CL-2328 "Bringin' It All Back Home") ... 60-75 65
(Monaural.)
COLUMBIA (CL-2389 "Highway 61 Revisited") ... 60-75 65
(Monaural.)
COLUMBIA (KCL-2663 "Bob Dylan's Greatest Hits") ... 60-75 67
(Monaural.)
COLUMBIA (CL-2804 "John Wesley Harding") ... 50-60 68
(Monaural.)
COLUMBIA (CS-8579 "Bob Dylan") ... 200-300 62
(Stereo.)
COLUMBIA (CS-8786 "The Freewheelin' Bob Dylan") ... 75-100 63
(Stereo.)
COLUMBIA (CS-8905 "The Times They Are A-Changin'") ... 75-100 64
(Stereo.)
COLUMBIA (CS-8993 "Another Side of Bob Dylan") ... 60-75 64
(Stereo.)
COLUMBIA (CS-9128 "Bringin' It All Back Home") ... 60-75 65
(Stereo.)
COLUMBIA (CS-9189 "Highway 61 Revisited") ... 60-75 65
(Stereo.)
COLUMBIA (KCS-9463 "Bob Dylan's Greatest Hits") ... 60-75 67
(Stereo.)
COLUMBIA (KCS-9825 "Nashville Skyline") ... 50-60 69
COLUMBIA (30050 "Self Portrait") ... 50-60 70
COLUMBIA (31120 "Greatest Hits Vol. 2") ... 10-20 71
COLUMBIA (32460 "Pat Garrett and Billy the Kid") ... 15-25 73
(Soundtrack.)
COLUMBIA (32747 "Dylan") ... 10-15 73
COLUMBIA (33235 "Blood on the Tracks") ... 20-25 75
COLUMBIA (33682 "The Basement Tapes") ... 10-15 75
COLUMBIA (33893 "Desire") ... 10-15 76
COLUMBIA (34349 "Hard Rain") ... 10-15 76
COLUMBIA (35453 "Street Legal") ... 10-15 78
(With programmer's timing strip.)
COLUMBIA (36067 "Bob Dylan at Budokan") ... 10-20 79
COLUMBIA (36120 "Slow Train Comin'") ... 10-15 79
COLUMBIA (36553 "Saved") ... 10-15 80
COLUMBIA (37496 "Shot of Love") ... 10-15 81
COLUMBIA (38819 "Infidels") ... 10-15 83
COLUMBIA (39944 "Real Live") ... 10-15 84
COLUMBIA (40110 "Empire Burlesque") ... 10-15 85
COLUMBIA (40439 "Knocked Out Loaded") ... 10-15 86
COLUMBIA (43235 "Blood on the Tracks") ... 25-50 83
(Half-speed mastered.)
COLUMBIA (49825 "Nashville Skyline") ... 25-35 81
(Half-speed mastered.)
COLUMBIA (67000 "Unplugged") ... 10-15 '90s
FOLKWAYS (5322 "Bob Dylan Vs. A.J. Weberman") ... 75-100
ISLAND (1 "Before the Flood") ... 25-35 74
MFSL (114 "The Times They Are A-Changin'") ... 30-50 '80s

Session: Michael Bloomfield; Al Kooper; Paul Griffin; Bobby Gregg; Charlie McCoy; Frank Owens; Russ Savakus; Harvey Goldstein.

Also see BAND
Also see BELAFONTE, Harry
Also see BLOOMFIELD, Mike
Also see CLARK, Dave, Five / Roy Meriwether Trio / Bobby Vinton / Bob Dylan
Also see GREGG, Bobby
Also see HARRISON, George
Also see HESTER, Carolyn
Also see McCOY, Charlie
Also see SAHM, Doug
Also see SWEATHOG / Free Movement / Bob Dylan / Edgar Winter's White Trash
Also see THREE KINGS & A QUEEN
Also see TRAVELING WILBURYS

DYLAN, Bob, & Grateful Dead — LP '89

LPs: 10/12-inch

COLUMBIA (45056 "Dylan and the Dead") ... 5-10 89
Also see GRATEFUL DEAD

DYLAN, Bob, & Heartbreakers / Michael Rubini

Singles: 7-inch

MCA ... 3-5 86
Also see DYLAN, Bob
Also see PETTY, Tom, & Heartbreakers

DYNAMIC DISCHORDS

Singles: 7-inch

IGL (150 "Passageway to Your Heart") ... 40-60 67

DYNAMIC DRIFTERS

Singles: 7-inch

BANGAR (636 "Let's Have a Party") ... 50-75 65

Picture Sleeves

BANGAR (636 "Let's Have a Party") ... 75-125 65

DYNAMIC HEARTBEATS

Singles: 7-inch

P.S. (1781 "Danger") ... 10-20 '60s

DYNAMIC HURSMEN

Singles: 7-inch

IGL (135 "Love Is a Beautiful Thing") ... 10-20 67

DYNAMIC NUTONES

Singles: 7-inch

SIMS (314 "Sick and Tired") ... 15-20 67

DYNAMIC TINTS

Singles: 7-inch

TWINIGHT (123 "Package of Love") ... 15-25 69
TWINIGHT (145 "Falling in Love") ... 15-25 71

DYNAMICS

Singles: 7-inch

CINDY (3005 "Gone Is My Love") ... 50-100 57

DYNAMICS
(With the Hutch Davie Orchestra)

Singles: 7-inch

DYNAMIC SOUND (504 "The Girl I Met Last Night") ... 50-75 62

DYNAMICS
(Dynamics with Jimmy Hanna)

Singles: 7-inch

BOLO ... 8-15 62-65
GUARANTEED (201 "Aces Up") ... 10-15 59
JERDEN ... 5-10 66
PENGUIN (1005 "Aces Up") ... 30-50 59
(First issue.)
PANORAMA ... 5-10 67
SEAFAIR ... 10-20 60-62

LPs: 10/12-inch

BOLO (8001 "The Dynamics with Jimmy Hanna") ... 25-35 64

Members (1959-'60): Terry Afdem; Dave Williams; Larry Smith; Tom Larson; Jeff Afdem; Pete Borg. (1961-'64): Terry Afdem; Ron Woods; Mark Doubleday; Harry Wilson; Pete Borg; Larry Coryell; Gary Snyder; Jimmy Hanna; Randi Green.

Also see GALLAHADS
Also see SPRINGFIELD RIFLE

DYNAMICS
(Dynamic's)

Singles: 7-inch

ARC (4450 "Enchanted Love") ... 40-50 59
CAPRI (104 "No One But You") ... 400-500 59
DELTA (1002 "Blue Moon") ... 30-40 59
IMPALA (501 "Moonlight") ... 50-75 58
LAVERE (186 "Wrap Your Troubles in Dreams") ... 10-20 61
LIBAN (1006 "Blind Date") ... 30-40 62
LIBERTY (55628 "Chapel on a Hill") ... 15-25 63
SEECO (6008 "Moonlight") ... 25-35 59
WARNER RECORDS (1016 "A Hundred Million Lies") ... 50-75 59
Also see MILO, Skip

DYNAMICS
(Zerben R. Hicks & the Dynamics; with Royal Playboys)

Singles: 7-inch

DYNAMIC ("Darling") ... 100-150 62
(No selection number used. Reissued as by the "Dynamo's.")
DYNAMIC (109 "Don't Be Late") ... 15-25 59
(We're not sure if 109 is the selection number or an identification number.)
DYNAMIC (579 "Dream Girl") ... 30-40 62
(Identification number shown since no selection number is used.)
DYNAMIC (1001 "Don't Leave Me") ... 40-50 59
DYNAMIC (1002 "Delsinia") ... 15-25 59
RCA (9084 "Love Me") ... 30-40 67
RCA (9278 "You Make Me Feel Good") ... 25-50 67
REPRISE (20183 "Delsinia") ... 5-10 63
TOP TEN (100 "Yes I Love You Baby") ... 25-35 '60s
TOP TEN (9409 "Love to a Guy") ... 15-25 '60s
Also see DYNAMOS

DYNAMICS

Singles: 7-inch

DECCA (31046 "How Should I Feel") ... 10-20 60
DECCA (31450 "How Should I Feel") ... 5-10 62

DYNAMICS

Singles: 7-inch

DOUGLAS (200 "I Love to Be Loved") ... 20-30 61
FARRALL (694 "Later On") ... 15-25 60

DYNAMICS

Singles: 7-inch

CUCA (1081 "Come Go with Me") ... 15-25 62

Members: Bobby Price; Don Anderson; Dick Ford; John Thompson; Jack Rygg; Dennis Murphy; John Murray.

Also see NEW DYNAMICS
Also see PRICE, Bobby, & Dynamics

DYNAMICS

Singles: 7-inch

DO-KAY-LO (101 "Oh, Night of Nights") .. 15-25 63
(Brown vinyl.)

DYNAMICS — P&R/R&B '63

Singles: 7-inch

BIG TOP (516 "I Wanna Know") ... 8-12 64
BIG TOP (3161 "Misery") ... 10-15 63
BLACK GOLD ... 4-8 73-74
COTILLION ... 5-10 68-69

LPs: 10/12-inch

BLACK GOLD ... 8-10 73
COTILLION ... 12-15 69

Members: Sam Stevenson; Zeke Harris; Fred Baker; George White.

DYNAMICS

Singles: 7-inch

USA (769 "Summertime in the U.S.A.") ... 15-20 64

Members: Norman Welch; Danny Michel; Roger Maltz; Peter Logan.

DYNAMICS

Singles: 7-inch

WINGATE (18 "Bingo") ... 35-50 66
Also see DRAMATICS

DYNAMICS Featuring Tony Maresco
(Anthony & the Sophmores)

Singles: 7-inch

HERALD (569 "Forever") ... 400-500 62
Also see ANTHONY & SOPHMORES
Also see TONY & TWILIGHTS

DYNAMITES

Singles: 7-inch

ELBRIDGE (92261 "Easy Pickin") 10-20 61

DYNAMITES

Singles: 7-inch

PAY (209 "Let's Try") .... 15-25 '60s
PAY (210 "Don't Leave Me This Way").... 15-25 '60s

DYNAMO, Skinny

Singles: 78 rpm

EXCELLO (2097 "So Long, So Long")..... 10-15 56

Singles: 7-inch

EXCELLO (2097 "So Long, So Long")..... 15-25 56

DYNAMOS
(Dynamo's)

Singles: 7-inch

AZUZA (1002 "Darling")............................ 50-75 64
(First issued as by the Dynamics.)
Also see DYNAMICS

DYNAMOS

Singles: 7-inch

CUB (9096 "Manhunt") 10-15 61
PRESS (101 "Teen Blues") 10-20 61

DYNA-SORES P&R '60

Singles: 7-inch

RENDEZVOUS (120 "Alley-Oop") 15-25 60
Members: Jimmy Norman; H.B. Barnum.
Also see BARNUM, H.B.
Also see NORMAN, Jimmy

DYNASTY

Singles: 7-inch

ROYAL COURT (262 "I've Gotta Shout") 100-125 66
WESTCHESTER (1155 "Flying on the Ground Is Wrong") 15-20 68
Members: Jack Casper; Mark Casper; Ken Clark; Fred Anderson; Dan Egnash; Mike Polaski.

DYNASTYS
(Dynasty's)

Singles: 7-inch

COULEE (108 "Go Gorilla")..................... 25-35 64
(Black vinyl.)
COULEE (108 "Go Gorilla")..................... 30-40 64
(Colored vinyl.)
FAN JR (9347 "I'll Be Forever Loving You") 30-40 64
(Identification number shown since no selection number is used.)
JERDEN (783 "It's Been a Long Long Time") 10-20 66

DYNATONES

Singles: 7-inch

BOMARC (300 "The Girl I'm Searching For") 15-25 58
BOMARC (303 "Steel Guitar Rag")......... 10-20 59
BOMARC (305 "Moon Shot") 10-20 59
QUALITY ("Steel Guitar Rag") 10-20 59
(Selection number not known.)

DYNATONES P&R/R&B '66

Singles: 7-inch

HBR (494 "Fife Piper")..................................5-10 66
ST. CLAIR (117 "Fife Piper")................. 10-15 66
(First issue.)

LPs: 10/12-inch

HBR (8509 "Fife Piper")........................ 20-25 66
(Monaural.)
HBR (9509 "Fife Piper")........................ 20-25 66
(Stereo.)
Members: Ray Figlar; Gary Van Scyoc; Eddie Evans; Jack Wolfe; Pat Wallace.

DYNELS
(Dynells)

Singles: 7-inch

ATCO (6638 "Call On Me")...................... 10-15 68
BLUEBERRY...5-10 68
DOT (16382 "Boy Friend")...................... 10-15 62
NATURAL (7001 "Just a Face in the Crowd") 20-30 64

DYSFUNCTION

LPs: 10/12-inch

METALSTORM (8816 "The $235,000 Demo") 10-20 88
(Picture disc. 500 made.)

DYSON, Joe, & His Orchestra
(With Luther Hill)

Singles: 78 rpm

ACE (531 "Marie")....................................10-15 57
CHAMPION (102 "Merc-O-Matic Boogie") 15-25 49

Singles: 7-inch

ACE (531 "Marie")....................................10-15 57

E

E.G., Rob

Singles: 7-inch

BIG TOP (3154 "Jezebel") 10-20 63

E.J. & ECHOES

Singles: 7-inch

DIAMOND JIM (8787 "Put a Smile on Your Face")..15-25 67
DIAMOND JIM (8789 "If You Just Love Me")..15-25 67
RANGER (410 "Say You're Mine") 15-25 59

ESB

Singles: 7-inch

IN ARTS (102 "Mushroom People")..........30-40 67
Members: George Caldwell; Pat Burke; Steve Lagana; Richard Fortunato.

EADY, Ernestine

Singles: 7-inch

JUNIOR...10-15 63-65

EAGER, Clay

Singles: 7-inch

KARL (560 "T.V. Boogie") 75-125

EPs: 7-inch

KARL (22 "Clay Eager") 100-200

EAGER, Jimmy, & His Trio
(Tampa Red)

Singles: 78 rpm

SABRE (100 "Please Mr. Doctor")...........50-75 53

Singles: 7-inch

SABRE (100 "Please Mr. Doctor") 100-150 53
Also see TAMPA RED

EAGER, Johnny

Singles: 7-inch

DESIGN (818 "Join Me Baby")..................35-50 58
END (1054 "Stay By Me") 10-20 59
END (1061 "I Understand") 8-12 59

EAGLEAIRES

Singles: 78 rpm

J.O.B. (1104 "Cloudy Weather") 30-40 54

Singles: 7-inch

J.O.B. (1104 "Cloudy Weather") 300-400 54

EAGLES

Singles: 78 rpm

MERCURY 8-12 54
PREP (118 "Kiss Them for Me") 5-10 57

Singles: 7-inch

MERCURY (70391 "Trying to Get to You") 15-25 54
MERCURY (70464 "Such a Fool")............15-25 54
MERCURY (70524 "What a Crazy Feeling")..15-25 54
PREP (118 "Kiss Them for Me") 10-15 57

EAGLES P&R/LP '72

Singles: 12-inch

ASYLUM (11402 "Please Come Home for Christmas & Funky New Year") 5-10 78
(Promotional issue only.)

Singles: 7-inch

ASYLUM..4-8 72-80
FULL MOON 3-5 81

Picture Sleeves

ASYLUM (45555 "Please Come Home for Christmas") 4-8 78

LPs: 10/12-inch

ASYLUM...8-12 72-82
MFSL (126 "Hotel California") 40-60 84
Members: Don Felder; Don Henley; Glenn Frey; Randy Meisner; Timothy B. Schmidt; Joe Walsh; Bernie Leadon.
Also see NEWMAN, Randy
Also see POCO
Also see RONSTADT, Linda
Also see WALSH, Joe

EAGLIN, Snooks
(Ford Eaglin; Blind Snooks Eaglin)

LPs: 10/12-inch

FANTASY..10-12 73
FOLKWAYS (2476 "Snooks Eaglin")........20-25 59
GNP..5-10 79
PRESTIGE BLUESVILLE (1046 "That's All Right") 75-100 62
Also see WILLIAMS, Robert Pete, & Snooks Eaglin

EANES, Jim

Singles: 7-inch

BLUE RIDGE (510 "Lady of Spain") 10-20 60
D (1232 "Crazy Dream")...........................10-20 62
DECCA (29112 "Wiggle Worm Wiggle") ..25-35 54
K-ARK (761 "My Paper Sack")....................5-10 67
SALEM (512 "Wide, Wide Road")..............5-10 64
STARDAY (Except 504) 15-30 53-61
STARDAY (504 "I Gotta Know") 75-125 60
TOWER (129 "These Memories")..............5-10 65

EPs: 7-inch

STARDAY (108 "Jim Eanes") 40-60 59

EARGAZM

LPs: 10/12-inch

EARRESISTIBLE.......................................15-20 81
Members: Peter Parkhurst; Roger Anderson; David Thomas Stanton; K. Paul Wichterman-West; Mark Killion; Randal Nelson.

EARL, Johnny

Singles: 7-inch

GYRO (102 "Pull It Man")......................150-250 60

EARL, Little Billy

Singles: 7-inch

GOLDBAND (1075 "Couple in the Car") ..15-25 58

EARL, Robert

Singles: 7-inch

CAROL (103 "Say You'll Be Mine") 10-20

EARLES

Singles: 7-inch

TEE TI (802 "What Would Your Daddy Say") 20-25

EARLINGTON, Lyn

Singles: 7-inch

JAMIE...5-10 63-64
LE MONDE (1501 "Love Drops").............10-15 62
SOUTHERN SOUND (104 "D.D.T. and Boll Weevil"/ "Rags")..10-15 61
(Other side is by T.J. Timber.)

EARL-JEAN P&R '64
(Earl Jean McCree)

Singles: 7-inch

COLPIX (729 "I'm into Somethin' Good") .10-15 64
COLPIX (748 "Randy")............................10-15 64
Also see COOKIES
Also see KING, Ben E.
Also see RAELETTES

EARLS

Singles: 78 rpm

GEM (221 "Believe Me My Love") 40-60 54

Singles: 7-inch

GEM (221 "Believe Me My Love") 1000-2000 54
GEM (227 "My Marie") 5-10 75
(Recorded in 1954. Previously unreleased.)

EARLS P&R '62
(Larry Chance & the Earls)

Singles: 12-inch

WOODBURY 10-15 76-77

Singles: 7-inch

ABC (11109 "It's Been a Long Time Coming")..5-10 68
ATLANTIC..4-6
BARRY (1021 "I Believe") 30-40 68
CLIFTON...3-5 79-80
COLLECTABLES...3-5 '80s
COLUMBIA (10225 "Goin' Uptown") 4-6 75
COTILLION (44114 "Remember Then").......4-6 71
GONE (5117 "I'll Never Cry") 5-10 61
HARVEY (100 "Teenager's Dream") 4-6 75
MEMORIES..3-5
MR. G (801 "If I Could Do It Over Again")...15-20 67
OLD TOWN (1130 "Remember Then") 40-50 62
(Blue label. Publisher credit is "January Music." Artist credit is in serif style typeface [i.e. THE EARLS], title is sans-serif [REMEMBER THEN.)
OLD TOWN (1130 "Remember Then") 25-35 62
(Blue label. Publisher credit is "Maureen Music." Both title & artist credit is sans-serif.)
OLD TOWN (1130 "Remember Then") 15-25 63
(Multi-color label.)
OLD TOWN (1133 "Never") 25-35 63
(Blue label.)
OLD TOWN (1133 "Never") 15-20 63
(Multi-color label.)
OLD TOWN (1141 "Look My Way") 15-20 63
OLD TOWN (1145 "Kissin'") 15-25 63
OLD TOWN (1149 "I Believe")..................25-35 63
(Blue label.)
OLD TOWN (1149 "I Believe")..................15-20 63
(Multi-color label.)
OLD TOWN (1169 "Ask Anybody") 20-30 64
OLD TOWN (1181 "Remember Me Baby")..30-40 65
(Promotional issue only.)
OLD TOWN (1182 "Remember Me Baby")..15-25 65
ROADHOUSE (1021 "I'm All Alone") 4-6
(Colored vinyl.)
ROME (101 "Life Is But a Dream"/"It's You")...50-100 61
(Shiny red label.)
ROME (101 "Life Is But a Dream"/"It's You")..30-40 61
(Maroon label.)
ROME (101 "Life Is But a Dream"/"Without You")..15-25 61
(Maroon label. Note different flip side title.)
ROME (102 "Lookin' for My Baby") 15-25 61
ROME (111 "Stormy Weather")....................4-8 76
ROME (112 "Little Boy and Girl")................4-8 76
ROME (114 "All Through Our Teens") 5-10 76
(Black vinyl.)
ROME (114 "All Through Our Teens") 10-15 76
(Colored vinyl.)
ROME (5117 "My Heart's Desire") 30-40 62
(Pink label.)
WOODBURY (101 "Tonight") 8-10 77
Note: Rome 111, 112 and 114 were recorded in 1961 but not released.

EPs: 7-inch

CRYSTAL BALL (131 "Remember When")..10-20 80
(Red vinyl.)

LPs: 10/12-inch

CHANCE (1001 "Today")............................8-12 83
CRYSTAL BALL (103 "Remember Rome") 10-15 82
(Black vinyl. 3000 made.)
CRYSTAL BALL (103 "Remember Rome") 25-35 82
(Colored vinyl. 25 made.)
CRYSTAL BALL (103 "Remember Rome") 55-65 82
(Picture disc. No cover. 25 made.)
OLD TOWN (104 "Remember Me Baby")..200-400 63
(Counterfeits exist but can be identified by their 1/2-inch vinyl trail-off and poor fidelity. Originals have a 3/4-inch trail-off and excellent fidelity.)
RAINBOW (1001 "Live") 8-12 87
WOODBURY (104 "Remember Me Baby")..15-20 76
(Red label.)
WOODBURY (104 "Remember Me Baby")..10-15 77
(Green and brown label.)
Members: Larry Chance; Robert Del Din; Jack Wray; Ed Harder; Larry Polumbo.
Also see CHANCE, Larry
Also see DEL & ESCORTS

EARLS / Pretenders

Singles: 7-inch

ROME/POWER MARTIN (111/1005 "Stormy Weather"/ "Could This Be Magic")...........................10-15 76
Also see EARLS
Also see PRETENDERS

EARLS, Jack, & Jimbos

Singles: 78 rpm

SUN (240 "Slow Down")...........................30-50 56

Singles: 7-inch

SUN (240 "Slow Down")...........................50-75 56

EARLS, Jay
Singles: 7-inch
REDWING (1046 "Baby, I'm Lonesome")....75-125

EARLY, Bernie
Singles: 7-inch
MGM (12640 "Rock Doll")....20-30 58
RODEO (220 "I've Got a Date with Evalina")....50-75

EARLY, Sam
Singles: 7-inch
APT (25041 "Do You Love Me")....10-20 60

EARLY, Sammy
Singles: 7-inch
MARLIN (6066 "I'm Gonna Find Me a Girl")....15-25 59

EARLY AMERICANS
Singles: 7-inch
PARIS TOWER (106 "Night After Night") 15-25 67

EARLY TIMES
Singles: 7-inch
ROLLEM (102 "Don't Laugh at Me")....10-20

EARTH BORN
Singles: 7-inch
L.C.R. (10104 "Universe of Love")....15-25 '60s

EARTH, WIND & FIRE *P&R/R&B/LP '71*
Singles: 12-inch
COLUMBIA....4-8 75-83
Singles: 7-inch
ARC....3-6 78-82
COLUMBIA....3-8 73-90
W.B.....4-8 71-72
Picture Sleeves
ARC (11366 "Let Me Talk")....4-6 80
COLUMBIA (03375 thru 07695)....3-6 80-88
COLUMBIA (10090 "Shining Star")....4-8 75
COLUMBIA (10373 "Getaway")....4-8 76
COLUMBIA (46007 "Mighty Mighty")....4-8 74
LPs: 10/12-inch
ARC (35647 "Best of Earth, Wind & Fire")....8-10 79
ARC (35647 "Best of Earth, Wind & Fire")....15-20 79
(Picture disc. Promotional issue only.)
ARC (35730 "I Am")....8-10 79
ARC (36795 "Faces")....10-12 80
(Two discs.)
ARC (37548 "Raise!")....8-10 81
COLUMBIA (31702 thru 33280)....10-20 71-75
COLUMBIA (33694 "Gratitude")....10-15 75
(Two discs.)
COLUMBIA (34241 thru 45268)....6-12 76-90
COLUMBIA (45647 "Best of Earth, Wind & Fire")....15-25 81
(Half-speed mastered.)
COLUMBIA (47548 "Raise!")....15-25 82
(Half-speed mastered.)
MFSL (159 "That's the Way of the World")....30-50 85
W.B. (1905 "Earth, Wind & Fire")....10-20 71
W.B. (1958 "The Need of Love")....10-20 72
W.B. (2798 "Another Time")....10-20 74
(Two discs. Repackage of 1905 and 1958.)
Members: Philip Bailey; Maurice White; Verdine White; Ronnie Laws; Fred White; Andy Woolfolk; Larry Dunn; Ralph Johnson; Al McKay; Johnny Graham; Wade Flemons.
Also see FLEMONS, Wade
Also see LEWIS, Ramsey
Also see SALTY PEPPERS

EARTH, WIND & FIRE & THE EMOTIONS *P&R/R&B '79*
Singles: 12-inch
ARC (10950 "Boogie Wonderland")....5-8 79
Singles: 7-inch
ARC (10956 "Boogie Wonderland")....4-6 79
COLUMBIA (10956 "Boogie Wonderland")..4-6 79

EARTH, WIND & FIRE & RAMSEY LEWIS *R&B '74*
Singles: 7-inch
COLUMBIA....4-6 74-75
Also see EARTH, WIND & FIRE
Also see LEWIS, Ramsey

EARTHMEN
Singles: 7-inch
RIM (2025 "Space Mood")....10-20 67
TROPICAL (123 "She's Mine")....20-30

EARTHQUAKES
(With the Rhythm Kings; with Armando King)
Singles: 7-inch
FORTUNE (534 "Darling Be Mine")....100-150 59
(Orange label.)
FORTUNE (534 "Darling Be Mine")....15-25 59
(Blue label.)
FORTUNE (538 "This Is Really Real")...75-100 60
FORTUNE (549 "Baby, Only You")....30-40 62

EASELY, Benny
(With Charlie & the Jives)
Singles: 7-inch
WORLD'S (123 "You Say You Love Me")....20-25 63
Also see CHARLIE & JIVES

EAST OAKLAND
Singles: 7-inch
TRACK (5709 "Run Away Streaker")....100-200 71

EAST RIVER BOYS
Singles: 7-inch
TOWER (123 "High School Letter")....10-15 65

EAST SIDE KIDS
Singles: 7-inch
ORANGE-EMPIRE ("Close Your Mind")....5-10 67
(Selection number not known.)
UNI (55105 "Taking the Time")....5-10 69
VALHALLA (672 "Little Bird")....5-10 67
W.B. (5821 "Night Mist Blue")....5-10 66
LPs: 10/12-inch
UNI (73032 "Tiger & Lamb")....15-25 68
Member: Joe Madrid.

EASTER, Jim
(With the Artistics)
Singles: 7-inch
CHA CHA (720 "Here I Go Again")....20-30 60
CHA CHA (721 "Stroll & Boogie")....15-25 60
Also see ARTISTICS

EASTERLING, James, & Blue Notes
Singles: 7-inch
RENO (133 "Angel of Mine")....40-50

EASTERN ALLIANCE
Singles: 7-inch
WRIGA (124 "Love Fades Away")....10-20 66

EASTMAN BLUES BAND
Singles: 7-inch
CUCA (6766 "I Found a New World")....15-25 67
Members: Gerry Smith; John Kondos; James Hanns Walner; Tom Jones; Nick Kondos; Curt Vandenhuevel.

EASTMEN
Singles: 7-inch
MERCURY (71434 "Lover Come Home")....50-60 59

EASTON, Amos, & His Orchestra
Singles: 78 rpm
SPECIALTY (410 "Strange Angel")....20-30 51
Also see BUMBLE BEE SLIM
Also see KING BUMBLE BEE SLIM & HIS PACIFIC COAST SENDERS

EASTSIDE KIDS
Singles: 7-inch
PHILIPS (40295 "Subway Train")....10-20 65

EASTWOOD, Clint
Singles: 7-inch
CAMEO (240 "Rowdy")....10-20 63
CERTRON (10010 "Burning Bridges")....4-8 70
GNP (177 "Get Yourself Another Fool")...15-25 65
GOTHIC (005 "Unknown Girl")....15-25 61
PARAMOUNT....5-10 69
W.B.....3-5 81
Picture Sleeves
CAMEO (240 "Rowdy")....30-50 63
CERTRON (10010 "Burning Bridges")....5-8 70
GNP (177 "Get Yourself Another Fool")...50-75 65
GOTHIC (005 "Unknown Girl")....30-50 61
LPs: 10/12-inch
CAMEO (1056 "Cowboy Favorites")....75-125 63
Also see CHARLES, Ray, & Clint Eastwood
Also see HAGGARD, Merle, & Clint Eastwood
Also see MARVIN, Lee / Lee Marvin & Clint Eastwood

EASY PAPA JOE
Singles: 78 rpm
BLUE LAKE (116 "Easy Loving")....15-20 55
Singles: 7-inch
BLUE LAKE (116 "Easy Loving")....20-25 55

EASY RIDERS
(With Terry Gilkyson)
Singles: 78 rpm
COLUMBIA....5-10 57
Singles: 7-inch
COLUMBIA....10-15 57
LPs: 10/12-inch
COLUMBIA....20-30 59
EPIC....15-25 60-63
Also see GILKYSON, Terry

EASYBEATS *P&R/LP '67*
Singles: 7-inch
ASCOT (2214 "Make You Feel Alright")....8-12 66
RARE EARTH (5009 "St. Louis")....10-15 69
U.A. (Except 50106)....5-10 67-69
U.A. (50106 "Friday on My Mind")....10-15 67
Picture Sleeves
ASCOT (2214 "Make You Feel Alright")...20-25 66
LPs: 10/12-inch
RARE EARTH (517 "Easy Ridin'")....10-20 70
RHINO....5-10 85
U.A. (3588 "Friday on My Mind")....30-40 67
(Monaural.)
U.A. (6588 "Friday on My Mind")....30-40 67
(Stereo.)
U.A. (6667 "Falling off the Edge of the World")....30-40 68
Members: Steve Wright; Harry Vanda; George Young; Dick Diamonde.

EAY, Eddie
Singles: 7-inch
ECHO (5911 "Dancin' Girl")....100-200

EBB TIDES
Singles: 7-inch
ACME (720 "Darling, I'll Love Only You")....100-150 57

EBB TIDES
Singles: 7-inch
R&R (303 "Low Tide")....15-25 63

EBB TIDES
Singles: 7-inch
MALA (480 "Automatic Reaction")....10-20 64
Members: Nino Aiello; Vince Drago; Tony DeLesio.
Also see EBBS
Also see NINO & EBB TIDES

EBB TIDES
Singles: 7-inch
MONUMENTAL (520 "Come on and Cry")....50-75 66

EBB TIDES
Singles: 7-inch
ARCO (107 "My Baby's Gone")....15-25 66
Also see TANGERINE ZOO

EBB TONES
Singles: 7-inch
BEE (301 "Boogie Woogie")....10-15 61

EBBS
Singles: 7-inch
DORE (521 "Vickie Sue")....20-30 59
Also see EBB TIDES
Also see NINO & EBB TIDES

EBBTIDES
(With the Butch Ballard Orchestra)
Singles: 7-inch
TEEN (121 "What is Your Name Dear")....2000-3000 58

EBBTIDES
Singles: 7-inch
FIREFLY (329 "Love Doctor")....3-5 74
JAN LAR (101 "Love Doctor")....250-300 59
Members: Carl White; Al Frazier; Sonny Harris; Turner Wilson.
Also see RIVINGTONS

EBBTIDES
Singles: 7-inch
DUANE (1022 "Star of Love")....2500-3500 64

EBB-TONES
Singles: 78 rpm
CREST....15-35 56-57
Singles: 7-inch
CREST (1016 "I Want You Only")....40-50 56
CREST (1024 "Baby")....15-25 56
(Black vinyl.)
CREST (1024 "Baby")....40-50 56
(Red vinyl.)
CREST (1032 "Dust off the Bible")....10-15 57

EBBTONES
("Featuring Freddie Romaine")
Singles: 7-inch
EBB (100 "I've Got a Feeling")....75-100 57

EBBTONES
Singles: 7-inch
PORT (70026 "Ram Induction")....10-20 61

EBBTONES
Singles: 7-inch
EVA'S (1001 "We're Wobbling")....30-50

EBERT, Lee
Singles: 7-inch
ROCKET (801 "Let's Jive It")....200-300 58

EBLING, Barry, & Invaders
Singles: 7-inch
NORMAN (581 "I Can Make It Without You")....20-30 67

EBONAIRES
Singles: 78 rpm
COLONIAL (117 "We're in Love")....50-75 50
MODERN (656 "Song of the Wanderer")..35-55 49
MODERN (711 "That Lucky Old Sun")....35-55 49

EBONAIRES
Singles: 78 rpm
ALADDIN....100-150 54
HOLLYWOOD....100-150 55
MGM (1036 "Come in Mr. Blues")....50-75 49
MONEY (220 "Very Best Luck in the World")....10-15 56
Singles: 7-inch
ALADDIN (3211 "Three O'Clock in the Morning")....250-350 53
ALADDIN (3212 "You're Nobody Till Somebody Loves You")....250-350 54
HOLLYWOOD (1046 "Love for Christmas")....200-300 55
HOLLYWOOD (1062 "Let's Kiss and Say Hello Again")....200-300 55
LENA (1001 "Love Call")....75-125 59
LOST NITE (118 "Love Call")....5-10 '60s
MONEY (220 "Very Best Luck in the World")....15-25 56

EBONAIRES / Camelots
Singles: 7-inch
CAMEO (334 "Love Call"/"Don't Leave Me Baby")....10-15 64
Also see CAMELOTS
Also see EBONAIRES

EBONETTES
Singles: 7-inch
EBB (147 "All Alone")....15-25 58

EBONIERS
Singles: 7-inch
PORT (70013 "Hand in Hand")....30-40 59

EBON-KNIGHTS
Singles: 7-inch
STEPHENY (1817 "The Way the Ball Bounces")....20-30 58
STEPHENY (1822 "First Date")....20-30 58
LPs: 10/12-inch
STEPHENY (4001 "First Date")....600-800 59

EBONY MOODS
Singles: 78 rpm
THERON (108 "I've Got News for You") 75-100 55

EBONY MOUNTAIN MAN
LPs: 10/12-inch
DURHAM (6487 "Tribute to the World's Grand Champions")....15-20 81
(Picture disc.)

EBONY THREE
Singles: 78 rpm
DECCA....30-50 38

EBSEN, Buddy

Singles: 7-inch

MGM (13210 "Mail Order Bride") 5-10 64
REPRISE (389 "Howdy") 5-10 65

Picture Sleeves

MGM (13210 "Mail Order Bride") 10-20 64

LPs: 10/12-inch

REPRISE (6174 "Howdy") 15-25 65
Also see PARKER, Fess

ECCENTRICS

Singles: 7-inch

APPLAUSE (1008 "Share Me") 15-25 64
APPLAUSE (1013 "I Still Love You") 10-20 65

Picture Sleeves

APPLAUSE (1008 "Share Me") 10-15 64
Members: Rick Evans; Denny Zager.
Also see ZAGER & EVANS

ECCENTRICS

Singles: 7-inch

SHANE (60 "Baby, I Need You") 20-30 66

ECHO VALLEY BOYS

Singles: 7-inch

ISLAND (1 "Wash Machine Boogie") ... 200-300 57

ECHOES

Singles: 78 rpm

ROCKIN' (523 "All That Wine Is Gone") .. 30-50 53
(The Echoes on Deluxe 6001, *Please Come Back*, is a bootleg.)

ECHOES

Singles: 78 rpm

GEE (1028 "Ding Dong") 30-50 57
SPECIALTY (601 "Rainbow") 15-25 57

Singles: 7-inch

GEE (1028 "Ding Dong") 50-75 57
(Red and black label.)
GEE (1028 "Ding Dong") 10-20 60
(Gray label.)
SPECIALTY (601 "Rainbow") 15-25 57

ECHOES

Singles: 78 rpm

COMBO (128 "My Little Honey") 30-40 57

Singles: 7-inch

COMBO (128 "My Little Honey") 100-200 57

ECHOES

Singles: 7-inch

EDCO (510 "Teenage Love") 75-125 58

ECHOES

Singles: 7-inch

SWAN (4013 "Little Green Man") 10-15 58
Members: Dominick "Chubby" Salvatore; Joe "Gig" Giglio; Fiore "Cookie Deli" Delbuono; Bobby "Bobby Pal" Palese.

ECHOES

Singles: 7-inch

ANDEX (22101 "Time") 30-50 59
(First issue.)
KEEN (2102 "Time") 20-30 59
Members: Darron Stankey; Al Candaleria; Jim West.
Also see INNOCENTS

ECHOES

Singles: 7-inch

COLUMBIA (41549 "Do I Love You") 10-20 59
COLUMBIA (41709 "Ecstasy") 10-20 60
Members: Eddie Sulik; George Kiriakis. Session: Buddy Harman; Hank Garland; Anita Kerr Singers; Grady Martin.
Also see GARLAND, Hank
Also see KERR, Anita
Also see MARTIN, Grady
Also see SULIK, Eddie

ECHOES

Singles: 7-inch

DOLTON (18 "Born to Be with You") 10-20 60
Members: Bonnie Guitar; Don Robertson.
Also see GUITAR, Bonnie
Also see ROBERTSON, Don

ECHOES

Singles: 7-inch

OAK (203 "My Baby") 100-150 60

ECHOES P&R '61

Singles: 7-inch

ASCOT (2188 "I Love Candy") 20-30 65
SRG (101 "Baby Blue") 150-200 60
SEG-WAY (103 "Baby Blue") 15-25 61
SEG-WAY (106 "Sad Eyes") 15-25 61
SEG-WAY (1002 "Angel of My Heart") 10-15 62
ZIRCON (1044 "Baby Blue") 30-40 60
(Canadian.)

LPs: 10/12-inch

CRYSTAL BALL (118 "Echoes Greatest Hits") 15-20 84
(Black vinyl. 1000 made.)
Members: Harry Doyle; Tom Morrissey; Tom Duffy.

ECHOES

Singles: 7-inch

ACE (657 "Restless") 10-20 62

ECHOES

Singles: 7-inch

U.S.A. (1215 "Sleep Beauty Sleep") 75-125 59

ECHOES

Singles: 7-inch

PULSE (2071 "Million Dollar Bill") 30-40

ECHOES OF CARNABY STREET

Singles: 7-inch

THAMES (105 "No Place") 15-25 67

ECHOMEN

Singles: 7-inch

SOMA (1197 "My Maria") 25-35 62

ECHOMEN

Singles: 7-inch

FOX (1 "Long Green") 50-75 66
Also see BEDLAM FOUR

ECHOMORES
(Featuring Lee Wagoner)

Singles: 7-inch

ROCKET (1042 "Cute Chick") 75-100 59
ROCKET (1048 "How Does It Feel to Be Lonely") 40-60 59

ECHOS
(Echo's)

Singles: 7-inch

FELSTED (8614 "Angel of Love") 40-50 61
HI-TIDE (106 "Angel of Love") 250-500 61
(Black vinyl.)
HI-TIDE (106 "Angel of Love") 750-1000 61
(Green vinyl.)

ECHOTONES

Singles: 7-inch

DART (1009 "So in Love") 10-20 59

ECKSTINE, Billy R&B '44
(Billy Eckstein; with the Billy May Orchestra; with Deluxe All Star Band)

Singles: 78 rpm

DELUXE 15-20 44
EMARCY 5-10 54
MGM 5-10 47-56
NATIONAL 10-15 45-48
RCA 5-10 56

Singles: 7-inch

A&M 4-6 76
EMARCY 10-15 54
ENTERPRISE 4-6 70-74
MGM 10-15 51-56
MGM GOLDEN CIRCLE (100 series)...........4-8 60
MERCURY 5-10 59-64
MOTOWN 8-15 65-68
RCA 10-15 56
ROULETTE 5-10 59-60

Picture Sleeves

A&M (1858 "The Best Thing") 3-5 76
MERCURY 5-10 62

EPs: 7-inch

EMARCY 10-20 54-55
KING 10-20 53
MGM 10-20 50-56
MOTOWN (60632 "Prime of My Life") 15-25 65
RENDITION 15-25 50

LPs: 10/12-inch

AUDIO LAB (1549 "Mr. B") 30-40 60
EMARCY (26025 "Blues for Sale") 50-100 54
(10-inch LP.)
EMARCY (26027 "Love Songs of Mr. B") 50-100 54
EMARCY (36010 "I Surrender Dear") 30-60 55
EMARCY (36029 "Blues for Sale") 25-50 55
EMARCY (36030 "Love Songs of Mr. B") 50-100 55
EMARCY (36129 "Eckstine's Imagination") 25-50 58
ENTERPRISE 5-10 71-74
FORUM CIRCLE (9027 "Once More with Feeling") 10-15 62
KING (12 "The Great Mr. B") 75-125 52
(10-inch LP.)
MGM (219 "Tenderly") 30-50 53
(10 Inch LP.)
MGM (257 "I Let a Song Go Out of My Heart") 40-60 55
(10 Inch LP.)
MGM (548 "Favorites") 40-60 51
(10 Inch LP.)
MGM (3176 "Mr. B with a Beat") 15-25 55
MGM (3209 "Rendezvous") 15-25 55
MGM (3275 "That Old Feeling") 15-25 55
MERCURY 15-25 57-64
METRO 10-15 65
MOTOWN (632 "Prime of My Life") 15-25 65
MOTOWN (646 "My Way") 15-25 66
MOTOWN (677 "For Love of Ivy") 10-20 69
NATIONAL (2001 "Billy Eckstine Sings") 75-125 50
(10-inch LP.)
REGENT 20-40 56-57
ROULETTE (25104 "Once More with Feeling") 15-25 60
ROULETTE (52052 "No Cover, No Minimum") 15-25 60
SAVOY 8-10 76-79
TRIP 5-10 75
WING 8-12 67
Also see BASIE, Count, & Billy Eckstine
Also see FOUR BLUES

ECKSTINE, Billy, & Woody Herman

Singles: 78 rpm

MGM 5-10 51

Singles: 7-inch

MGM 10-15 51
Also see HERMAN, Woody, & Orch.

ECKSTINE, Billy, & Quincy Jones

Singles: 7-inch

A&M (1858 "The Best Thing") 4-6 76

Picture Sleeves

A&M (1858 "The Best Thing") 4-6 76

LPs: 10/12-inch

MERCURY (20674 "At Basin Street East") 15-25 62
(Monaural.)
MERCURY (60674 "At Basin Street East") 25-35 62
(Stereo.)
Also see JONES, Quincy

ECKSTINE, Billy / Arthur Prysock / Cliff Butler

LPs: 10/12-inch

GUEST STAR (1903 "Billy Eckstine, Arthur Prysock and Cliff Butler") 8-12 64
Also see BUTLER, Cliff
Also see PRYSOCK, Arthur

ECKSTINE, Billy, & Sarah Vaughan

Singles: 78 rpm

MGM 5-10 52

Singles: 7-inch

MGM 8-12 52
MERCURY (71122 "Passing Strangers") ...5-10 57
MERCURY (71393 "Alexander's Ragtime Band") 5-10 59

EPs: 7-inch

MGM (1002 "Dedicated to You") 10-15 52

LPs: 10/12-inch

GUEST STAR 8-12 64
LION (70088 "Billy and Sarah") 15-25 59
MERCURY (20316 "Best of Irving Berlin") 20-30 57
Also see ECKSTINE, Billy
Also see VAUGHAN, Sarah

ECMORE, Roy

Singles: 7-inch

CAT ("Let Me Be Your Man") 50-75
(Selection number not known.)

ECSTASIES

Singles: 7-inch

AMY (853 "That Lucky Old Sun") 20-25 62

ECUADORS

Singles: 7-inch

ARGO (5353 "Say You'll Be Mine") 15-25 59

ED & TWILIGHTERS

Singles: 7-inch

FUTURA (11615 "Skippin' Home") 25-30 63
(Identification number shown since no selection number is used.)
LAURIE (3270 "Skippin' Home") 5-10 64

EDDIE & BETTY P&R '59

Singles: 7-inch

LARK (4512 "Sweet Someone") 10-15 59
SIX THOUSAND (601 "Sweet Someone") 15-25 57
W.B. (5054 "Sweet Someone") 8-12 59

LPs: 10/12-inch

W.B. 20-30 59
Members: Eddie Cole; Betty Cole.

EDDIE & CHUCK

Singles: 7-inch

CHANCE (107 "Boogie the Blues") 100-200

EDDIE & EMPIRES

Singles: 7-inch

COLPIX (112 "Tears in My Eyes") 75-125 59

EDDIE & ERNIE R&B '65
(Ernie & Eddie)

Singles: 7-inch

CHECKER (1057 "Who's That Knocking at My Door") 10-20 63
CHECKER (1086 "Time Waits for No One") 10-20 64
CHESS (1984 "I Believe She Will") 5-10 67
COLUMBIA (44276 "Doggone It") 5-10 67
EASTERN (602 thru 609) 5-10 65-66
REVUE (11049 thru 11063) 5-10 69
Members: Eddie Campbell; Ernie Johnson.

EDDIE & JIMMIE

Singles: 7-inch

DELUXE (6179 "Hold that Kiss") 30-50 58

EDDIE & SHOWMEN

Singles: 7-inch

LIBERTY (55566 "Toes on the Nose") 10-20 63
LIBERTY (55608 "Squad Car") 10-20 63
LIBERTY (55659 "Mr. Rebel") 10-20 64
LIBERTY (55695 "Far Away Places") 10-20 64
LIBERTY (55720 "Young and Lonely") 10-20 64

EPs: 7-inch

MOXIE 5-10 80
Members: Eddie Bertrand; Phil Pruden; Dick Dodd; Fred Buxton; Robert Edwards; Bob Knight.
Also see BELAIRS
Also see CHALLENGERS

EDDIE & STARLITES
(With Al Browne Orchestra)

Singles: 7-inch

ALJON (1260 "Come On Home") 75-125 63
BIM BAM BOOM (102 "Three Steps to Go") 4-6 72
SCEPTER (1202 "To Make a Long Story Short") 50-75 59
(White label.)
SCEPTER (1202 "To Make a Long Story Short") 20-25 59
(Red label.)
VINTAGE (1004 "I Can Dream") 10-15 73
(Purple vinyl.)
Also see STARLITES

EDDIE & TROPICS

Singles: 7-inch

JOSIE (930 "Don't Monkey with Another Monkey's Monkey") 10-15 65

EDDIE & UPSETS

Singles: 7-inch

DEKTR (41666 "El Mosquito") 10-20 66
DEKTR (41668 "Cry Cry Cry") 30-40 66

EDDY, Don, & Donettes

Singles: 7-inch

RONA (1002 "Sugar Coated Candy Kisses") 20-30 60

EDDY, Duane *P&R/C&W/R&B '58*
(With the Rebels; with Rebelettes; with His Rock-a-billies; with His Twangy Guitar)

Singles: 78 rpm

FORD (500 "Ramrod") 75-125 57
JAMIE (1101 "Moovin' N' Groovin' ") 50-75 58
(Pink label.)
JAMIE (1101 "Moovin' N' Groovin' ") 30-50 58
(Yellow label.)
JAMIE (1104 " Rebel-'Rouser ") 30-50 58
JAMIE (1109 "Ramrod") 30-50 58
JAMIE (1111 "Cannon Ball") 30-50 58
JAMIE (1117 "The Lonely One") 50-75 59
JAMIE (1122 "Yep!") 50-100 59

Singles: 7-inch

BIG TREE 5-10 72
CAPITOL 3-5 87
COLPIX 10-15 65-66
CONGRESS (6010 "Freight Train") 4-8 70
CHRYSALIS (42986 "Art of Noise") 3-5 86
ELEKTRA 4-6 77
FORD (500 "Ramrod") 150-250 57
(Credits Duane Eddy, but is by Al Casey.)
GREGMARK (5 "Caravan") 10-20 61
(Credits Duane Eddy, but is by Al Casey.)
JAMIE (73 "Peter Gunn") 35-50 61
(Compact 33 stereo single.)
JAMIE (74 "Hard Times") 35-50 61
(Compact 33 stereo single.)
JAMIE (75 "The Battle") 35-50 61
(Compact 33 stereo single.)
JAMIE (1101 "Movin' & Groovin' ") 20-30 58
JAMIE (1104 "Rebel-'Rouser") 25-35 58
(Reads "From the Production Rebel-'Rouser Starring John Buck." Both the production and film star are fictitious.)
JAMIE (1104 "Rebel-'Rouser") 15-25 58
(No mention of Rebel-'Rouser Production.)
JAMIE (1109 thru 1195) 10-20 58-61
(Monaural.)
JAMIE (1100 series) 30-40 59-60
(Stereo.)
JAMIE (1200 series) 10-20 61-62
JAMIE (1303 " Rebel-'Rouser ") 5-10 65
RCA (Except 8507) 15-20 61-65
RCA (8507 "Moon Shot") 25-35 65
REPRISE 8-15 66-68
UNI 4-8 70

Picture Sleeves

CAPITOL 4-6 87
COLPIX (788 "House of the Rising Sun") 30-40 66
JAMIE 15-25 59-61
RCA 10-20 62-64

EPs: 7-inch

JAMIE (100 "Movin' & Groovin' ") 50-75 59
JAMIE (301 "Detour") 50-75 59
JAMIE (302 "Yep!") 40-60 59
JAMIE (303 "Shazam") 40-60 60
JAMIE (304 "Because They're Young") 40-60 60
RCA/WURLITZER DISCOTHEQUE MUSIC 15-25 64

LPs: 10/12-inch

CAMDEN 8-15
CAPITOL 8-10 87
COLPIX (490 "Duane A-Go-Go") 25-30 65
COLPIX (494 "Duane Eddy Does Bob Dylan") 25-30 65
JAMIE (3000 "Have Twangy Guitar Will Travel") 50-80 58
(White cover.)
JAMIE (3000 "Have Twangy Guitar Will Travel") 25-50 58
(Red cover.)
JAMIE (3006 "For You") 40-60 59
JAMIE (3009 "The 'Twang's' the Thing") . 40-60 59
JAMIE (3011 "Songs of Our Heritage") 100-200 60
(Red vinyl.)
JAMIE (3011 "Songs of Our Heritage") 40-60 60
(Gatefold cover. Black vinyl.)
JAMIE (3011 "Songs of Our Heritage") 20-40 61
(Standard cover. Black vinyl.)
JAMIE (3014 "$1,000,000 Worth of Twang") 40-60 61
JAMIE (3019 "Girls! Girls! Girls!") 20-30 61
JAMIE (3021 "$1,000,000 Worth of Twang, Vol. 2") 40-60 62
JAMIE (3022 "Twistin' with Duane Eddy") 30-50 62
JAMIE (3024 "Surfin' with Duane Eddy"). 30-50 63
JAMIE (3025 "In Person") 20-30 63
JAMIE (3026 "16 Greatest Hits") 20-30 64
RCA (2525 thru 2648) 25-50 62
RCA (2671 "Pure Gold") 5-10 78
RCA (2681 thru 3477) 20-40 63-66
REPRISE 15-20 66-67
SIRE 10-15 75

Session: Duane Eddy; Al Casey; Corki Casey; Donnie Owens; Plas Johnson; Steve Douglas; Ike Clanton; Mike Bermani; Waylon Jennings; Willie Nelson; Kin Vassy.
Also see BLOSSOMS
Also see BURTON, James
Also see CASEY, Al
Also see CLANTON, Ike
Also see CLARK, Sanford, & Duane Eddy
Also see DOUGLAS, Steve
Also see FOGERTY, John
Also see JENNINGS, Waylon
Also see JIMMY & DUANE
Also see JOHNSON, Plas
Also see NELSON, Willie
Also see OWENS, Donnie
Also see ROBINSON, Mark
Also see SHARPE, Ray
Also see SHARPS
Also see THOMAS, B.J.

EDDY, Duane & Mirriam

Singles: 7-inch

REPRISE (0622 "Guitar on My Mind") 10-15 67
Also see EDDY, Duane
Also see JOHNSON, Mirriam

EDDY, Jim
(With Carl Stevens & Orchestra)

Singles: 78 rpm

MERCURY (71171 "I Have No Sweetheart") 8-12 57

Singles: 7-inch

DORE (537 "Teen Age Angel") 10-20 59
MERCURY (71171 "I Have No Sweetheart") 10-15 57
SOMA (1091 "Livin' Doll") 15-25 58
SPINNING (6002 "Bells of Love") 8-15 58

EDDY, Jim, & Highlights

Singles: 7-inch

PLAY (1001 "With a Prayer in Your Heart") 20-25 58
Also see HIGHLIGHTS

EDDY, Sam, & Revels

Singles: 7-inch

ACCENT (1085 "Skip to My Lou") 8-12 62
DACO (702 "Skip to My Lou") 10-20 62
(First issue.)
Also see REVELS

EDE, Dave, & Rabin Band

Singles: 7-inch

LAURIE (3056 "Easy On") 10-20 60
RUST (5047 "Twistin' Those Meeces to Pieces") 10-15 62

EDEN, Barbara

Singles: 7-inch

DOT (16999 "Bend It") 5-10 67
DOT (17022 "Heartaches") 5-10 67
DOT (17032 "Pledge of Love") 5-10 67
PLANTATION 4-8 78
(Colored vinyl.)

Picture Sleeves

DOT 10-15 67

LPs: 10/12-inch

DOT (3795 "Miss Barbara Eden") 25-30 67
(Monaural.)
DOT (25795 "Miss Barbara Eden") 30-40 67
(Stereo.)

EDEN, Jack, & Dimensions

Singles: 7-inch

CORSAIR (513 "Betty Lou") 40-50
JULENE (1000 "Betty Lou") 40-50

EDEN, Jack, & Sundowners

Singles: 7-inch

T.J. (600 "Come Back Baby") 25-35 66

EDEN, Jimmie, & Revelers

Singles: 7-inch

HARAL (779 "Goddess of Love") 100-200 64

EDEN'S CHILDREN *LP '68*

Singles: 7-inch

ABC 11053 "Goodbye Girl") 5-10 68

LPs: 10/12-inch

ABC (624 "Eden's Children") 20-30 68
ABC (652 "Sure Looks Real") 15-25 68

EDGAR, Jim
(With the Roadrunners)

Singles: 7-inch

BISMARK (1011 "What Is One to Do") 10-15 66
DISCOVERY (1001 "The Place") 8-12 66
HAMA (1002 "Hey Little Girl") 10-15 66
POMPEII (66684 "Artificial Army") 8-12 69
SCEPTER (12147 "Tennessee Stud") 5-10 66

EDGE

Singles: 7-inch

ENITH (1011 "Something New") 20-30 65

EDGE

Singles: 7-inch

CASABLANCA 3-5 80

LPs: 10/12-inch

NOSE (48003 "Edge") 20-30 70
Members: Dave Novogroski; John Keith; Richard Barcellona; Gallen Murphy.
Also see AMERICAN REVOLUTION
Also see BOSTON TEA PARTY

EDGE, Bobby
(With Lew Douglas & Orchestra)

Singles: 7-inch

B&F (1330 "Gambler's Guitar") 8-12 59
CENTAUR (850 "Twelve O'clock") 10-20 59
FELSTED (8573 "Helping Hand") 8-12 59
Also see DOUGLAS, Lew

EDGE OF DARKNESS

Singles: 7-inch

JAMIE (1363 "So Many Years") 10-20 68

EDGEWOODS

Singles: 7-inch

EPIC (10275 "Those Golden Oldies") 20-30 68

EDIE & CHANNELS

Singles: 7-inch

HERALD (584 "Love's Burning Fire") 15-25 63

EDISON, Harry "Sweets"

Singles: 7-inch

SUE (101 "I Wish You Love") 5-10 64
SUE (117 "Blues for Christmas") 5-10 65

LPs: 10/12-inch

LIBERTY (3484 "When Lights Are Low") . 10-15 66
(Monaural.)
LIBERTY (7484 "When Lights Are Low") . 15-20 66
(Stereo.)
PACIFIC JAZZ (11 "Inventive Mr. Edison") 15-20 60
ROULETTE (52041 "Patented by Edison") 15-20 60
SUE (1030 "Sweets for the Sweet") 10-15 64
VEE-JAY (1104 "Sweets for the Sweet Taste of Love") 10-15 64
VERVE (6118 "Mr. Swing") 15-20 60
(Monaural.)
VERVE (8353 "Mr. Swing") 20-25 60
(Stereo.)

EDMINSTER, Corky

Singles: 7-inch

RAYNOR (10820 "Chilli Dippin' Baby") 50-75

EDMONDSON, Travis

Singles: 7-inch

REPRISE (20071 "The Web") 5-10 62

LPs: 10/12-inch

HORIZON (1606 "Travis On Cue") 10-15 62
REPRISE (6035 "Travis On His Own") 10-15 62
Also see GATEWAY SINGERS

EDMUND, Lada, Jr.

Singles: 7-inch

CORAL (6??34 "Trouble") .... 5-10 '60s
(Complete selection number not yet known.)
DECCA (31937 "Once Upon a Time") 10-20 66
DECCA (32007 "Soul A-Go-Go") 50-75 66
ROULETTE (4449 "I Want a Man") 5-10 62

EDMUNDS, Dave *P&R '70*

Singles: 12-inch

COLUMBIA (Except 1725) 4-8 85-87
(Promotional issue only.)
COLUMBIA (1725 "Information") 15-20 84
(Picture disc. Promotional issue only.)

Singles: 7-inch

ARISTA (522 "Slipping Away") 3-5 83
(Clear vinyl.)
COLUMBIA 3-5 80-85
MAM (3601 "I Hear You Knocking") 5-8 70
(Black label.)
MAM (3601 "I Hear You Knocking") 4-6 70
(Blue label.)
MAM (3608 "I'm Coming Home") 4-6 71
MAM (3611 "Blue Monday") 4-6 71
RCA 4-6 73-74
SWAN SONG 3-6 77-81

Promotional Singles

COLUMBIA (1576 "Run Rudolph Run") 4-6 82
(Compact 33 single.)
COLUMBIA (03428 "Run Rudolph Run") 3-5 82

Picture Sleeves

COLUMBIA 3-5 85
SWAN SONG 3-5 81

LPs: 10/12-inch

ATLANTIC (320 "College Network") 35-45
(Promotional issue only.)
CAPITOL 5-8 90
COLUMBIA (Except 1725) 5-10 80-87
COLUMBIA (1725 "Information") 15-25 83
(Picture disc. Promotional issue only.)
MAM (3 "Rockpile") 30-40 72
RCA (4238 "Subtle As a Flying Mallet") 5-10 82
RCA (5003 "Subtle As a Flying Mallet") ... 10-12
SWAN SONG 8-10 77-81
Also see DION
Also see HARRISON, George / Jeff Beck / Dave Edmunds
Also see HARRISON, George / Dave Edmunds
Also see LEWIS, Huey, & News
Also see LOVE SCULPTURE

EDSELS *P&R '61*

Singles: 7-inch

ABC 4-6 75
CAPITOL (4588 "My Jealous One") 8-12 61
CAPITOL (4675 "Shake Shake Sherry") ... 8-12 62
CAPITOL (4836 "Don't You Feel") 10-15 62
DOT (16311 "My Whispering Heart") ... 100-150 62
DUB (2843 "Lama Rama Ding Dong") 50-75 58
(Black and gold label. Copies with black and silver labels are counterfeits. Humorously, fakes have the 1961 Twin label track, which is noticeably different than the Dub one.)
DUB (2843 "Rama Lama Ding Dong") 40-50 58
(Note title correction.)
EMBER (1078 "Three Precious Words") .. 10-20 61
LOST NITE .... 4-6 '70s
MUSICTONE (1144 "Rama Lama Ding Dong") 5-10 64
REGENCY ("Rama Lama Ding Dong") 10-20 61
(Canadian. Has the Twin track.)
ROULETTE (4151 "Do You Love Me") 20-30 59
TAMMY (1010 "What Brought Us Together") 40-50 60
(No reference to distribution by Ember.)
TAMMY (1010 "What Brought Us Together") 15-25 60
(Has "Distributed by Ember" on label.)
TAMMY (1014 "Three Precious Words") .. 25-35 61
TAMMY (1023 "The Girl I Love") 20-30 61
TAMMY (1027 "Count the Tears") 20-30 61
TWIN (700 "Rama Lama Ding Dong") 15-25 61
(This track is noticeably different than the one previously issued on Dub.)
Members: George Jones Jr; Larry Green; James Reynolds; Marshall Sewell; Harry Green.

EDWARD BROTHERS

Singles: 7-inch

MUSIC WORLD (106 "Keep On Knockin' ") 10-20 65

EDWARD SISTERS

Singles: 7-inch

KAISER (388 "Don't Make Me Cry Again") 20-30 58

EDWARDS, Alvis

Singles: 7-inch

ENALL (80 "Real Gone Baby") 150-200

EDWARDS, Bobby *P&R/C&W '61*
(Bobby Edwards Combo)
Singles: 7-inch
ASCOT (2104 "Groovy") 10-15 62
BLUEBONNET (710 "Stranger to Me") 15-20 59
CAPITOL (4726 thru 5006) 5-10 62-63
CHART (1045 "Just Ain't My Day") 5-10 68
CREST (1075 "I'm a Fool for Loving You") 10-15 60
MANCO (1026 "Jealous Heart") 5-10 62
MUSICOR (1101 "Within Your Arms") 5-10 65
OZARK (1241 "I'm a Long Gone Daddy") 50-100
POLARIS 3-5

EDWARDS, Chuck
(With the Five Crowns)
Singles: 78 rpm
APOLLO (495 "Just for a Day") 8-12 56
DUKE 10-20 56-57
Singles: 7-inch
ALANNA (557 "If I Were King") 15-25 60
APOLLO (495 "Just for a Day") 15-25 56
DUKE (159 "If You Love Me") 15-25 56
DUKE (163 "I'm Wondering") 15-25 57
DUKE (174 "Morning Train") 10-20 57
RENE (7001 "Bullfight") 10-20 66
(First issue.)
RENE (20013 "Bullfight #2") 10-15
ROULETTE (4705 "Bullfight") 8-12 66

EDWARDS, Dee *R&B '79*
Singles: 12-inch
COTILLION 4-6 79
Singles: 7-inch
COTILLION 3-6 78-80
D-TOWN (1024 "He Told Me Lies") 50-75 65
D-TOWN (1031 "What a Party") 10-20 66
D-TOWN (1048 "His Majesty My Love") 15-25 66
D-TOWN (1063 "All the Way Home") 20-40 66
RCA 5-10 72
TUBA 10-20 62
LPs: 10/12-inch
COTILLION 5-10 80

EDWARDS, Dewey
Singles: 7-inch
CAMEO (364 "Come On Over to My Place") 10-15 65

EDWARDS, Don
Singles: 7-inch
SINGULAR (1001 "Fancy Nancy") 50-75

EDWARDS, Gary, & Abominable Snow-Men
Singles: 7-inch
GENUINE (154 "I Can't Believe") 30-40

EDWARDS, Honeyboy
(David Edwards)
Singles: 78 rpm
ARTIST (102 "Build a Cave") 75-125 51

EDWARDS, J.D.
Singles: 78 rpm
IMPERIAL (5245 "Cryin' ") 25-50 53
Singles: 7-inch
IMPERIAL (5245 "Cryin' ") 50-100 53

EDWARDS, Jack
Singles: 7-inch
MICHELE (508 "All Night Long") 15-20 61

EDWARDS, Jimmy *C&W '57*
(Jimmie Edwards; Jim Bullington)
Singles: 78 rpm
MERCURY 10-20 57
Singles: 7-inch
MERCURY (71209 "Love Bug Crawl") 25-35 57
MERCURY (71272 "My Honey") 20-30 57
RCA (7597 "Your Love Is a Good Love") 15-25 59
RCA (7717 "Rosie Lee") 10-20 60
RCA (7773 "What Do You Want from Me") 10-20 60
WEDNESDAY (0977 "Love Bug Crawl") 300-400 57
(First issue. Identification number shown since no selection number is used.)

EDWARDS, Joey
Singles: 7-inch
COLUMBIA (43620 "Trapped") 8-10 66
LILLY (501 "Shirley, Shirley") 50-75 61
Picture Sleeves
COLUMBIA (43620 "Trapped") 10-15 66

EDWARDS, John *R&B '73*
Singles: 7-inch
AWARE 4-8 73-74
BELL (45205 "Look on Your Face") 30-50 72
COTILLION 4-6 76-77
LPs: 10/12-inch
AWARE 5-10 74
CREED 5-10 75
GENERAL/GRC 5-10 74

EDWARDS, Johnny, & White Caps
Singles: 7-inch
NORTHLAND (7002 "Rock and Roll Saddle") 200-300 57
(White label. Shown as by the White Caps.)
NORTHLAND (7002 "Rock and Roll Saddle") 100-200 57
(Maroon label. Credits Johnny Edwards & the White Caps.)
NORTHLAND (7002 "Rock and Roll Saddle") 75-125 57
(Maroon label. Shown as by the White Caps.)
Members: Ricky Lee Smolinski; Jerry Stengl; Jack Gardner; Duke Wright; Denny Noie.

EDWARDS, Jonathan & Darlene
(Paul Weston & Jo Stafford)
LPs: 10/12-inch
COLUMBIA (1024 "Piano Artistry") 25-40 57
COLUMBIA (1513 "In Paris") 20-30 60
(Monaural.)
COLUMBIA (8313 "In Paris") 25-35 60
(Stereo.)
CORINTHIAN 5-10
RCA (LPM-2495 "Sing Along") 15-25 61
(Monaural.)
RCA (LSP-2495 "Sing Along") 20-30 61
(Stereo.)
Also see STAFFORD, Jo
Also see WESTON, Paul, Orchestra

EDWARDS, Mary, & Saxons
Singles: 78 rpm
METEOR (5031 "Chilly Winds") 10-15 56
Singles: 7-inch
METEOR (5031 "Chilly Winds") 20-30 56

EDWARDS, Millard
(Mill Edwards)
Singles: 7-inch
BUNKY (7761 "Use What You Got") 10-20 68
CONSTELLATION (170 "Things Won't Be the Same") 10-20 66
CUTLASS 5-10 72
Also see ESQUIRES

EDWARDS, Monte
(With Bob Ross & His Orchestra)
Singles: 7-inch
ROSCO (409 "Oh! I Never Knew") 50-75

EDWARDS, Shirley
Singles: 7-inch
SHRINE (110 "It's Your Love") 100-150 66

EDWARDS, Slim, & His Western Wildcats
Singles: 7-inch
JEREE (6652 "Nite Beat") 100-200

EDWARDS, Sonny
Singles: 7-inch
CEVETONE (508 "Toy Balloon") 30-40 63
CEVETONE (516 "I Love You Tenderly") 50-60 63

EDWARDS, Tibby
Singles: 7-inch
TODD (1065 "Teenage Troubles") 10-20 61

EDWARDS, Tom *P&R '57*
(With Mort Garson & Orchestra)
Singles: 7-inch
CORAL (61773 "What Is a Teenage Girl") 10-15 57
CORAL (61938 "Goodnight Rock and Roll") 15-20 58

EDWARDS, Tommy *P&R/R&B '51*
Singles: 78 rpm
MGM (10000 & 11000 series) 5-15 51-55
MGM (12000 series) 15-25 58
TOP 10-20 49-50
Singles: 7-inch
MGM (10000 & 11000 series) 15-20 51-55
MGM (12000 & 13000 series) 8-15 55-65
MGM (50112 "Please Mr. Sun") 25-35 59
(Stereo.)
POLYDOR (871-850-7 "It's All in the Game"/ "Please Mr. Sun") 4-6
Picture Sleeves
MGM (12890 "I Really Don't Want to Know") 10-20 60
EPs: 7-inch
MGM (1003 "It's All In the Game") 30-40 52
MGM (1614 "It's All in the Game") 15-25 58
MGM (1666/1667/1668 "For Young Lovers") 10-20 59
(Monaural. Price is for any of three volumes.)
MGM (SX-1666/1667/1668 "For Young Lovers") 15-25 59
(Stereo. Price is for any of three volumes.)
LPs: 10/12-inch
LION (70120 "Tommy Edwards") 15-25 59
MGM 20-40 58-63
METRO (511 "Tommy Edwards") 8-12 65
REGENT (6096 "Tommy Edwards Sings") 20-30 58

EDWARDS, Vern
Singles: 7-inch
PROBE (100 "Cool Baby Cool") 150-175 59

EDWARDS, Vincent *P&R/LP '62*
(Vince Edwards)
Singles: 7-inch
CAPITOL (4789 "Here's My Heart") 5-10 62
CAPITOL (4819 "Lollipop") 5-10 62
COLPIX (771 "See That Girl") 5-10 65
DECCA (31413 thru 31563) 5-10 62-63
DECCA (34039 "Open End Interview") 8-12 62
(Promotional issue only.)
DECCA (34074 "Unchained Melody") 5-10 62
(Compact 33 stereo.)
KAMA SUTRA (221 "To Be with You") 5-10 67
REMEMBER (7773 "I've Got the World to Hold Me Up") 5-10
RUSS-FI (1 "Oh Babe") 5-10 59
RUSS-FI (7001 "Why Did You Leave Me") 15-25 62
Picture Sleeves
COLPIX (771 "See That Girl") 5-10 65
DECCA (31413 "Don't Worry 'Bout Me") 5-10 62
DECCA (31426 "Say It Isn't So") 5-10 62
EPs: 7-inch
DECCA (2731 "Vincent Edwards Sings") 8-10 62
LPs: 10/12-inch
DECCA (4311 "Vincent Edwards Sings") 10-20 62
(Monaural.)
DECCA (7-4311 "Vincent Edwards Sings") 15-25 62
(Stereo.)
DECCA (4336 "Sometimes I'm Happy... Sometimes I'm Blue") 10-20 62
(Monaural.)
DECCA (7-4336 "Sometimes I'm Happy...Sometimes I'm Blue") 15-25 62
(Stereo.)
DECCA (4399 "In Person At the Riviera") 10-20 63
(Monaural.)
DECCA (7-4399 "In Person At the Riviera") 15-25 63
(Stereo.)

EDWARDS, Winni
Singles: 7-inch
FLAME ("More Than Words Can Say") 100-200
(Selection number not known.)

EDWARDS' GENERATION
(Chuck Edwards)
Singles: 7-inch
TIGHT (302 "I Want You Girl") 10-15
LPs: 10/12-inch
TIGHT (401 "In San Francisco – The Street Thang") 10-20

EEE, Don
Singles: 7-inch
CMI (102 "Stop at the Hop") 100-200

EGANS, Willie
(Little Willie Egans)
Singles: 78 rpm
MAMBO (102 "What a Shame") 30-40 55
MAMBO (106 "Sad Sad Feeling") 20-30 55
MAMBO (111 "Oh, Baby") 20-30 55
SPRY (107 "Treat Me Right") 30-40 55
VITA (119 "Willie's Blues") 20-30 56
VITA (125 "Wear Your Black Dress") 30-40 56
Singles: 7-inch
DASH (55001 "Rock and Roll Fever") 100-200 57
MAMBO (102 "What a Shame") 100-200 55
MAMBO (106 "Sad Sad Feeling") 50-75 55
MAMBO (111 "Oh, Baby") 50-75 55
SPRY (107 "Treat Me Right") 75-100 55
VITA (119 "Willie's Blues") 50-75 56
VITA (125 "Wear Your Black Dress") 100-200 56
Also see LLOYD & WILLIE
Also see WILLIE & RUTH

EGGINS, Willie, & Orchestra
(Willie Eagins)
Singles: 78 rpm
MAMBO (102 "What a Shame") 10-20 55
Singles: 7-inch
MAMBO (102 "What a Shame") 40-60 55

EGGLESTON, Cozy
Singles: 78 rpm
STATES (133 "Big Heavy") 10-15 55
Singles: 7-inch
CO-EGG (3621 "Joker's Wild") 10-20
STATES (133 "Big Heavy") 40-60 55
(Black vinyl.)
STATES (133 "Big Heavy") 100-150 55
(Colored vinyl.)

EGYPTIAN COMBO
Singles: 7-inch
MGM (13518 "Norma's Theme") 5-10 66
NORMAN (549 "Gale Winds") 5-10 64
NORMAN (555 "St. Louis Blues") 5-10 65
Picture Sleeves
NORMAN (555 "St. Louis Blues") 15-25 65

EGYPTIAN KINGS
Singles: 7-inch
NANC (1120 "Give Me Your Love") 15-25 61
(Has company address under label name.)
NANC (1120 "Give Me Your Love") 10-15 61
(Has "Dist. By Swingin' Records" under name.)
Members: Morris Wade; Leo Blakely; Pete Oden; Paul Moore; Sylvester Moore.
Also see COLUMBUS PHARAOHS
Also see 4 PHARAOHS
Also see KING PHARAOH & EGYPTIANS

EGYPTIANS
Singles: 7-inch
BIG TOP (3099 "The Wiggle") 10-20 62
DANAE (1002 "That's Alright") 10-15
MAH'S (0001 "The Party Stomp") 20-40 60
PRIME TIME (202 "Turn Around") 35-55

EGYPTIANS
Singles: 7-inch
CHANCE (100 "My Little Girl") 15-25 65

EHRET, Bob
Singles: 7-inch
ALADDIN (3377 "Stop the Clock") 75-125 57
HAMILTON (50009 "Too Soon") 15-25 58

EIGHT BELLS
(With Jimmy Carroll & Orchestra)
Singles: 78 rpm
BELL (1060 "Dream") 10-15 54
Singles: 7-inch
BELL (1060 "Dream") 15-25 54

EIGHT MINUTES
Singles: 7-inch
JAY PEE (130 "Will You Be Mine") 10-15 '60s
JAY PEE (200 "Let's Sign a Peace Treaty") 10-15 '60s
PERCEPTION (533 "Looking for a Brand New Game") 4-6 73

18TH CENTURY CONCEPTS
Singles: 7-inch
SIDEWALK (934 "Happy Together") 5-10 68
LPs: 10/12-inch
SIDEWALK (5900 "In the 20th Century Bag") 10-15 67
SIDEWALK (5909 "Off On a 20th Century Cycle") 10-15 67

88s
Singles: 7-inch
MONUMENT (417 "Chasing a Dream") 10-20 60

EIH, Damin, A.L.K. & Brother Clark

LPs: 10/12-inch

DEMELOT (7310 "Never Mind")........... 100-150 73

Members: Damin Eih; A.L. Katzner; Brother Clark Dircz.

EIRE APPARENT

Singles: 7-inch

BUDDAH (67 "Let Me Stay")..................... 10-15 68

LPs: 10/12-inch

BUDDAH (5031 "Sunrise")........................ 25-35 69

Members: Michael Charles Cox; Ernest Harold Graham; William David Lutton; Eric Christopher Stewart.

EISENHOWER, General Dwight

Singles: 7-inch 78 rpm

PICTUREPLAS ("I Like Ike")..................... 40-50 52

(Promotional issue for Presidential campaign. Words and music by Irving Berlin. Includes envelope mailer.)

ELASTIC PRISM

Singles: 7-inch

KUSTOM (101 "In the Garden").............. 35-50 69
JANA (6969 "Red Purple & Blue")........... 10-20 70
JANA (7235 "Going Down")..................... 10-20 71

Members: Terry Atwell; Donnie Atwell.

ELASTIK BAND

Singles: 7-inch

ATCO (6537 "Paper Mache")................... 10-15 67
KAPP (965 "I Would Still Love You")....... 10-15 68

ELBERT, Donnie *P&R/R&B '57*

Singles: 78 rpm

DELUXE.. 15-25 57

Singles: 7-inch

A-O... 4-6 75
ALL PLATINUM.. 4-8 71-77
ATCO (6550 "Too Far Gone")..................... 5-10 68
AVCO.. 4-8 72
CHECKER (1062 "Everything to Me")...... 10-15 63
COMMAND PERFORMANCE...................... 3-5
CUB (9125 "Don't Cry My Love").............. 5-10 63
DELUXE (01 "What Can I Do"/"Have I Sinned")... 8-12 '60s
DELUXE (133 "Have I Sinned")................. 4-8 71
DELUXE (958 "Have I Sinned")................. 8-12 '60s
DELUXE (6125 "What Can I Do")............ 15-25 57
DELUXE (6143 thru 6168)...................... 10-20 57-58
ELBERT... 4-6
GATEWAY.. 5-10 64-65
GUSTO.. 3-5 '80s
JALYNNE (107 "Mommies' [sic] Gone").. 30-40 60
JALYNNE (110 "Lucille")........................... 5-10 62
PARKWAY (844 "Baby Cakes")............... 10-15 62
RARE BULLET... 4-8 70
RED TOP (122 "Hey Baby")..................... 15-25 60
RED TOP (130 "Someday")...................... 15-25 62
TRIP.. 4-6
UP STATE... 5-8
VEE-JAY (336 "Hey Baby")...................... 10-20 60
VEE-JAY (353 "Half As Old").................... 10-20 60
VEE-JAY (370 "I Beg of You")................. 10-20 60

LPs: 10/12-inch

ALL PLATINUM... 10-15 71
DELUXE... 10-15 71
KING (629 "The Sensational Donnie Elbert Sings")... 100-200 59
SUGARHILL... 5-10 81
TRIP.. 8-10 72

Also see VIBRAHARPS

ELBOW BENDERS & KUKIE KATS

Singles: 7-inch

HANOVER (4524 "Kukie")....................... 10-15 59

EL BOY

(With the Ralph Sayho Calypso Singers)

Singles: 78 rpm

RAMA (220 "Jack, Jack, Jack")................... 5-10 57

Singles: 7-inch

RAMA (220 "Jack, Jack, Jack")............... 10-20 57

EL CAPRIS

("Featuring Sam Crumby")

Singles: 78 rpm

BULLSEYE (102 "Ooh But She Did")...... 30-50 56

Singles: 7-inch

ARGYLE (1010 "Oh But She Did").......... 10-15 61
BIG CITY (1502 "Oh But She Did")............ 5-10 64
BULLSEYE (102 "Ooh But She Did").. 100-150 56
BULLSEYE (102 "Oh But She Did")......... 50-75 56
FEE BEE (216 "Your Star").................. 200-300 57

(Has all thin lines.)

FEE BEE (216 "Your Star")........................ 15-25 61

(Has thin and thick lines.)

HI-Q (5006 "Girl of Mine")........................ 50-75 58

(Blue label.)

HI-Q (5006 "Girl of Mine")........................ 10-15 58

(Yellow label.)

PARIS (525 "They're Always Laughing At Me").. 15-20 58
RING-O (308 "Quit Pulling My Woman").. 15-25 65

Member: Sam Crunby.

ELCHORDS

("Featuring Butchy Saunders")

Singles: 78 rpm

GOOD (544 "Peppermint Stick")............. 50-100 58

Singles: 7-inch

GOOD (544 "Peppermint Stick").............. 50-75 58

(Has straight horizontal lines on label. Shows publisher as "Don Music" on both sides of label.)

GOOD (544 "Peppermint Stick")............... 20-30 62

(Red vinyl.)

GOOD (544 "Peppermint Stick")............... 10-20 62

(Has sawtooth horizontal lines on label.)

GOOD (544 "Peppermint Stick")................. 8-12 62

(No lines on label. Shows publisher as "Dan Publishers.")

MUSICTONE (1107 "Peppermint Stick").... 8-12 61

Members: Butchy Saunders; Ron Talbert; David Ballot.

Also see SAUNDERS, Little Butchie

EL DAMONTS

Singles: 7-inch

SCOTTY (640 "Over Easy")..................... 10-20 65

ELDAROS

(With Ray Parratore & Rhythm Rockaways)

Singles: 7-inch

VESTA (102 "Please Surrender")...... 750-1000 58

Members: Jimmy Singleton; James Crawford; Robert Green; Kenny Tucker; Levy Hall.

EL DEENS

Singles: 7-inch

FEDERAL (12347 "My Love for You").... 30-40 59
FEDERAL (12356 "Where Are You")....... 15-25 59

ELDER, Eddie, & Harmonaires

Singles: 7-inch

VITA (176 "With a Tear in My Heart")...... 20-30 58

ELDER, Nelvin

Singles: 7-inch

BRENT (7027 "I Dream").......................... 20-30 61

ELDERBERRY JAK

LPs: 10/12-inch

ELECTRIC FOX ("Long Overdue").......... 15-25 75

(Selection number not known.)

FOREST ("Elderberry Jak")....................... 50-75 69

(Selection number not known.)

EL-DEROCKS

Singles: 7-inch

SAPPHIRE (1005 "Hound Dog Blues").... 50-75

EL DOMINGOES

Singles: 7-inch

KAPPA (206 "I'm Not Kidding You").. 800-1000 58

EL DOMINGOS

Singles: 7-inch

CANDLELITE (418 "Made in Heaven")...... 5-10 64

(Black vinyl.)

CANDLELITE (418 "Made in Heaven")...... 8-12 64

(Red vinyl.)

CHELSEA (1009 "Made in Heaven").... 100-150 62

(White label. Promotional issue only.)

CHELSEA (1009 "Made in Heaven")........ 50-75 62

(Shiny black label.)

KARMIN (1001 "Are You Ready")......... 500-750 64

Also see WILDE, Jimmy

EL DORADOS *P&R/R&B '55*

Singles: 78 rpm

VEE-JAY (115 "Baby I Need You")........... 30-50 54
VEE-JAY (118 "Annie's Answer")............. 30-50 54

(With Hazel McCollum & Al Smith's Orchestra.)

VEE-JAY (127 "One More Chance")...... 50-100 54
VEE-JAY (147 thru 302)........................ 35-65 56-57

Singles: 7-inch

COLLECTABLES.. 3-5
OLDIES 45 (171 "A Fallen Tear")............... 4-6
VEE-JAY (115 "Baby I Need You")......... 50-100 54

(Black vinyl.)

VEE-JAY (115 "Baby I Need You")....... 550-650 54

(Red vinyl.)

VEE-JAY (118 "Annie's Answer")........... 50-100 54

(Black vinyl. With Hazel McCollum & Al Smith's Orchestra.)

VEE-JAY (118 "Annie's Answer")......... 400-500 54

(Red vinyl.)

VEE-JAY (127 "One More Chance").... 150-250 54
VEE-JAY (147 "At My Front Door")......... 50-75 55
VEE-JAY (165 "I'll Be Forever Lovin' You").. 50-75 55
VEE-JAY (180 "Now That You've Gone")... 50-75 56
VEE-JAY (197 "A Fallen Tear")................ 50-75 56
VEE-JAY (211 "Bim Bam Boom").............. 50-75 56
VEE-JAY (250 "Tears on My Pillow")....... 25-50 57
VEE-JAY (263 "Three Reasons Why")... 75-125 58
VEE-JAY (302 "Lights Are Low")............ 75-125 58

LPs: 10/12-inch

COLLECTABLES (20 "Best of the El Dorados").. 8-10 '80s

(10-inch LP.)

LOST NITE (20 "El Dorados")................... 10-20 81

(10-inch LP. Red vinyl. 1000 made.)

SOLID SMOKE.. 5-10 82
VEE-JAY (1001 "Crazy Little Mama")... 300-500 58

(Maroon label.)

VEE-JAY (1001 "Crazy Little Mama")... 200-300 58

(Black label.)

Note: Vee-Jay 1001 also contains two tracks by the Magnificents.

Members: Pirkle Lee Moses Jr; Arthur Bassett; Louis Bradley; James Maddox; Jewel Jones; Richard Nickens; Johnny Carter; Ted Long; John McCall; Douglas Brown.

Also see CRAYTON, Pee Wee
Also see DELEGATES
Also see KOOL GENTS
Also see MAGNIFICENTS
Also see SMITH, Al
Also see TEMPOS
Also see THOSE FOUR ELDORADOS

EL DORADOS

Singles: 7-inch

ROCK-HIGHLAND (109 "Linda Lee")... 200-300 60

Members: Robert Henderson; John Westling; Johnny Dee; Bob Henderson.

ELDORAYS

Singles: 7-inch

BUD (114 "Nights of Ecstasy")................. 15-25 61

ELDRIDGE, Billy

(With the Fire Balls)

Singles: 7-inch

UNART (2011 "Let's Go Baby")............. 75-100 59
VULCO (1501 "Let's Go Baby")........... 100-200 59

(First issue.)

VULCO (1507 "Half a Heart").............. 100-200 59
VULCO (1580 "It's Over")................... 100-200 '60s

ELDRIDGE, Roy, Quintet

Singles: 78 rpm

DAWN (201 "Ain't No Flies on You")........ 10-15 54

Singles: 7-inch

DAWN (201 "Ain't No Flies on You")........ 15-25 54

ELECTRAS

Singles: 7-inch

CHALLENGE (59243 "Can't You See It in My Eyes"/"Boo Babe").. 5-10 64
INFINITY (012 "You Lied")........................ 30-40 61
INFINITY (016 "The Stomp"/"Boo Babe"). 10-15 63
LOLA (100 "Can't You See It in My Eyes"/"You Know")... 20-30 62

Member: Billy Storm.

Also see STORM, Billy

ELECTRAS / Surgeons

Singles: 7-inch

CEE JAM (100 "You Know"/"Don't Tell Me").. 10-15 63

Also see ELECTRAS

ELECTRAS

("Vocal: Tim")

Singles: 7-inch

RUBY DOO (2 "Little Girl of Mine")............ 5-10 66
SCOTTY (11A "'Bout My Love")............... 30-40 65

(Second issue. Improved quality pressing.)

SCOTTY (6194 "'Bout My Love")........... 75-125 65
SCOTTY (6351 "Dirty Old Man"/"Courage To Cry").. 50-75 66
SCOTTY (6511 "'Bout My Love")............. 25-35 65

(First release. Fidelity is poor.)

SCOTTY (6613 "Soul Searchin")............ 75-125 66
SCOTTY (6621 "Dirty Old Man")............. 20-30 66
SCOTTY (6720 "Action Woman")......... 750-850 67
SCOTTY (6720 "I'm Not Talkin'")........... 75-125 67

(Same selection number used twice.)

Members: Earl Bulinski; Bill Bulinski; Jerry Fink; Gary Omerza; Tim Elving.

Also see TWAS BRILLIG

ELECTRATONES

Singles: 7-inch

GONE (7005 "Guitar Bossa Nova")......... 30-40

ELECTRIC ELVES

Singles: 7-inch

MGM (13839 "It Pays to Advertise")......... 20-30 67

Also see DIO, Ronnie
Also see ELVES

ELECTRIC EXPRESS *P&R/R&B '71*

Singles: 7-inch

AVCO (4607 "I Can't Believe We Do")......... 4-8 '70s
KEY-VAC (2930 "Hearsay")...................... 40-60
LINCO (1001 "It's the Real Thing")............... 4-8 71

ELECTRIC INDIAN *P&R/R&B/LP '69*

Singles: 7-inch

MARMADUKE (4001 "Keem-O-Sabe").... 10-15 69
U.A. (50563 "Keem-O-Sabe").................... 5-10 69
U.A. (50613 "Land of 1000 Dances")......... 5-10 69

LPs: 10/12-inch

U.A. (6728 "Keem-O-Sabe")..................... 10-15 69

ELECTRIC LIGHT ORCHESTRA *LP '72*

(ELO)

Singles: 12-inch

JET (Black vinyl).. 10-15 76-78
JET (137 "Livin' Thing").............................. 20-30 76

(Blue vinyl. Promotional issue only.)

JET (164392 "Mr. Blue Sky")..................... 15-20 78

(Promotional issue only.)

Singles: 7-inch

CBS (05766 "Calling America").................... 3-5 86
JET (1099 "Turn to Stone")........................... 4-6 76
JET (1145 "Sweet Talkin' Woman")............. 4-8 77

(Purple vinyl. Promotional issue only.)

JET (02408 thru 04130)................................ 3-6 81-83
JET (5050 thru 5067).................................... 3-6 78-79
MCA (41246 "I'm Alive")............................... 3-6 80
MCA (41289 "All Over the World")............... 3-6 80
U.A. (173 thru 939)...................................... 5-10 73-76
U.A. (1000 "Telephone Line").................... 10-15 77

(Green vinyl. Promotional issue only.)

U.A. (50914 "10538 Overture")................... 5-10 72

Picture Sleeves

CBS (05766 "Calling America").................... 3-5 86
JET (1099 "Turn to Stone")........................... 4-6 76
JET (1145 "Sweet Talkin' Woman")............. 4-8 77
JET (5057 "Shine a Little Love").................... 4-6 79
MCA (41246 "I'm Alive")............................... 3-6 80
MCA (41289 "All Over the World")............... 3-6 80
U.A. (573 "Can't Get It Out of My Head")... 5-10 74
U.A. (770 "Strange Magic")......................... 5-10 75
U.A. (1000 "Telephone Line")...................... 5-10 77

LPs: 10/12-inch

CBS (40048 "Balance of Power")................ 5-10 86
JET (JZ-35524 "No Answer")...................... 6-10 78
JET (PZ-35524 "No Answer")....................... 5-8 81
JET (JZ-35525 "On the Third Day").............. 6-10 78
JET (JZ-35526 "Eldorado")........................... 6-10 78
JET (JZ-35527 "Face the Music")................ 6-10 78
JET (PZ-35527 "Face the Music")................. 5-8 81
JET (JZ-35528 "Olé ELO")........................... 6-10 78
JET (PZ-35528 "Olé ELO")............................ 5-8 81
JET (JZ-35529 "New World Record")......... 6-10 78
JET (PZ-35529 "New World Record").......... 5-8 81
JET (KZ2-35530 "Out of the Blue").......... 10-15 78

(Two discs.)

JET (JZ-35533 "Electric Light Orchestra II").. 6-10 78
JET (FZ-35769 "Discovery")........................ 6-10 79
JET (FZ-36310 "ELO's Greatest Hits")....... 6-10 79
JET (Z4X-36966 "Box of Their Best")....... 20-30 80

(Boxed, three-LP set. Includes *Out of the Blue*, *A New World Record*, and *Discovery*, plus a bonus single, *Doin' That Crazy Thing.*)

JET (FZ-37371 "Time")................................ 6-10 81

JET (HZ-46310 "ELO's Greatest Hits").... 25-35 81
(Half-speed mastered.)
JET (HZ-45769 "Discovery") 25-35 80
(Half-speed mastered.)
U.A. (040 "Electric Light Orchestra II")..... 10-15 73
U.A. (123 "Olé ELO") 25-35 76
(Colored vinyl. May be gold, red, white, or blue. Promotional issues only.)
U.A. (188 "On the Third Day") 10-15 73
U.A. (339 "Eldorado")............................. 10-15 74
U.A. (546 "Face the Music") 10-15 75
U.A. (546 "Face the Music") 25-30 75
(Banded for airplay. Promotional issue only.)
U.A. (630 " Olé ELO")................................8-12 76
U.A. (679 "A New World Record")..............8-12 76
U.A./JET (823 "Out of the Blue") 10-20 77
(Two discs. Black vinyl. Add $5 if accompanied by a poster.)
U.A./JET (823 "Out of the Blue") 30-40 77
(Two discs. Blue vinyl. Promotional issue only.)
U.A. (5573 "No Answer") 10-15 72
Also see LYNNE, Jeff
Also see NEWTON-JOHN, Olivia, & Electric Light Orchestra

ELECTRIC LOVE

Singles: 7-inch

CHARAY (40 "This Seat Is Saved")......... 15-20 68

ELECTRIC PRUNES — P&R '66

Singles: 7-inch

REPRISE (PRO-277 "Sanctus").............. 35-45 67
(Promotional issue only.)
REPRISE (PRO-0305 "Help Us") 25-35 68
(Promotional issue only.)
REPRISE (0473 "Little Olive")................. 25-35 66
REPRISE (0532 "I Had Too Much to Dream") 10-15 66
REPRISE (0564 "Get Me to the World on Time").. 10-20 67
REPRISE (0594 "Dr. Do Good") 10-20 67
REPRISE (0607 "The Great Banana Hoax") 10-20 67
REPRISE (0652 "You Never Had It Better") 20-30 68
REPRISE (0805 "Hey Mr. President") 10-20 69
REPRISE (0833 "Violet Rose") 25-35 69
REPRISE (0858 "Love Grows") 15-20 69

LPs: 10/12-inch

REPRISE (6248 "I Had Too Much to Dream").. 20-30 67
REPRISE (6262 "Underground") 30-40 67
REPRISE (6275 "Mass in F Minor")......... 20-30 67
REPRISE (6262 "Release of an Oath")... 15-25 68
REPRISE (6342 "Just Good Rock 'N' Roll").. 15-25 69

ELECTRIC RUBAYYAT

Singles: 7-inch

INT'L ARTISTS (124 "If I Was a Carpenter") 15-25 67

ELECTRIC TOILET

Singles: 7-inch

NASCO ("In the Hands of Karma"/"Revelations") 150-250 70
(No selection number used. Promotional issue only.)

LPs: 10/12-inch

NASCO (9004 "In the Hands of Karma").. 250-300 70
Member: Dave Hall.

ELECTRIC UNDERGROUND

LPs: 10/12-inch

PREMIER (9060 "Guitar Explosion") 50-75 67

ELECTRIFIED PEOPLE

Singles: 7-inch

RED LITE (113 "One Thousand Dimension in Blue").. 10-15 66
Member: Jimmy Peterson.

ELECTRIFYING CASHMERES

Singles: 7-inch

SOUND STAGE 7 (1500 "What Does It Take") 10-20 71
SOUND STAGE 7 (2666 "You Send Me")....4-6 70

ELECTRONAIRES

Singles: 7-inch

COUNT (505 "One Lonely Night")............ 40-50 59
Also see RANADO, Chuck

ELECTRONS

Singles: 7-inch

DATE (1575 "It Ain't No Big Thing")..........10-20 67
LAGUNA (103 "For Sale") 25-35 64
(First issued as by the Wright Sounds.)
SHOCK (289 "It Ain't No Big Thing") ....30-40 '60s
SHOCK (290 "Turn on Your Lovelight")....20-30 '60s
Also see WRIGHT SOUNDS

ELECTROSONIKS

LPs: 10/12-inch

PHILIPS (200047 "Electronic Music")........50-75 62
PHILIPS (600047 "Electronic Music").....75-100 62

ELEGANT 4

Singles: 7-inch

COUSINS (1005 "Time to Say Goodbye") 20-30 65
(Same number used on a Dreamers release.)
MERCURY (72516 "Time to Say Goodbye") 15-25 65

ELEGANTS — P&R/R&B '58

(Vito & Elegants)

Singles: 78 rpm

APT (25005 "Little Star") 75-125 58
SPARTON/ABC-PAR (620 "Little Star") .50-100 58
(Canadian.)

Singles: 7-inch

ABC (2404 "Little Star") 4-6 73
ABC-PAR (10219 "Tiny Cloud")................30-40 61
APT (25005 "Little Star") 30-40 58
(Silver print on black label. No mention of ABC-Paramount on label.)
APT (25005 "Little Star") 20-30 58
(Silver print on black label. Reads: "A Product of AM-PAR Record Corp.")
APT (25005 "Little Star") 10-20 58
(White or multi-colored label.)
APT (25017 "Goodnight") 10-20 58
APT (25029 "Payday")...............................10-20 59
BIM BAM BOOM (121 "Lonesome Weekend") 4-6 74
(Black vinyl.)
BIM BAM BOOM (121 "Lonesome Weekend") 5-8 74
(Green vinyl.)
CRYSTAL BALL (139 "Maybe")....................4-8 81
(Black vinyl. 500 made.)
CRYSTAL BALL (139 "Maybe")...............30-40 81
(Multi-colored vinyl. Five made.)
HULL (732 "Little Boy Blue") 50-75 60
LAURIE (3283 "A Letter from Viet Nam") .15-25 65
LAURIE (3298 "Wake Up")........................25-35 65
LAURIE (3324 "Belinda")..........................10-15 65
MCA..3-5
PHOTO (2662 "A Dream Can Come True") 30-50 63
PLANET (2727 "Human Angel") 4-6 95
(Red vinyl. 500 made.)
SPARTON/ABC-PAR (620 "Little Star") ...25-50 58
(Canadian.)
U.A. (230 "Speak Low")............................20-30 60
U.A. (295 "Happiness")............................15-25 61

Picture Sleeves

APT (25005 "Little Star") ....5-10 '90s
CRYSTAL BALL (139 "Maybe") 15-20 81
PHOTO (2662 "A Dream Can Come True") 75-100 63
(Add $10 to $20 if accompanied by printed insert.)

LPs: 10/12-inch

CRYSTAL BALL (101 "A Knight with the Elegants") 10-15 81
(Black vinyl. 2000 made.)
CRYSTAL BALL (101 "A Knight with the Elegants") 25-35 81
(Colored vinyl. 25 made.)
CRYSTAL BALL (101 "A Knight with the Elegants") 55-65 81
(Picture disc. No cover. 25 made.)
CRYSTAL BALL (132 "Back in Time")........8-12 90
(Black vinyl. 1000 made.)
MURRAY HILL (210 "Little Star")...............8-10 86
Members: Vito Picone; Frank Tardagno; Carman Romano; Jimmy Moschella; Artie Venosa.
Also see BARBARIANS
Also see CORDELL, Pat
Also see PICONE, Vito

ELEGANTS

Singles: 7-inch

BANGAR (613 "Minor Chaos")..................20-30 64

ELEMENTS

Singles: 7-inch

TITAN (1708 "Lonely Hearts Club")......100-200 60
Member: Kenneth Sinclair.
Also see SIX TEENS

ELEMENTS

Singles: 7-inch

SARU (1224 "Just to Be with You")..........20-40

ELENA MARIE

Singles: 7-inch

GEEBEE (1 "Soldier Boy") 30-40 61

ELEPHANTS MEMORY — LP '69

Singles: 7-inch

APPLE (1854 "Liberation Special"/"Madness") 8-12 72
APPLE (1854 "Liberation Special"/"Power Boogie") 300-400 72
(Note different flip side.)
BUDDAH...5-10 69
METROMEDIA..4-8 70-71
RCA...4-6 74

Promotional Singles

APPLE (1854 "Liberation Special")..........20-25 72

Picture Sleeves

APPLE (1854 "Liberation Special")............8-10 72
METROMEDIA...4-8 70

LPs: 10/12-inch

APPLE..10-15 72
BUDDAH...10-15 69-74
METROMEDIA...10-12 70
MUSE...8-10 '70s
RCA..8-10 74
Also see BERRY, Chuck
Also see LENNON, John

ELGART, Larry — P&R/LP '82

(With His Manhattan Swing Orchestra)

Singles: 78 rpm

DECCA...3-5 54-55

Singles: 7-inch

DECCA...10-15 54-55
MGM...5-10 61-62
RCA (7461 thru 8517) 5-10 59
RCA (13000 series) 3-5 83

EPs: 7-inch

BRUNSWICK (72003 "Impressions of Outer Space")..5-10 54
DECCA (637 "Until the Real Thing Comes Along") 5-10 54
DECCA (712 "Music for Barefoot Ballerinas and Others") 5-10 55

LPs: 10/12-inch

BRUNSWICK (58054 "Impressions of Outer Space")..15-25 54
(10-inch LPs.)
CAMDEN...5-15 60-73
DECCA (5526 "Until the Real Thing Comes Along") 15-25 54
(10-inch LP.)
DECCA (8034 "Music for Barefoot Ballerinas and Others") 15-25 55
MGM..10-20 60-62
RCA (1961 thru 2166) 10-20 59
RCA (4000 series) 5-8 82-83

ELGART, Les, Orchestra — P&R/LP '56

Singles: 78 rpm

COLUMBIA 4-8 53-57

Singles: 7-inch

COLUMBIA (40137 thru 40179)...............10-15 53-54
COLUMBIA (40180 "Bandstand Boogie") 15-20 54
COLUMBIA (40202 thru 42622).................8-15 54-62
COLUMBIA (56767 "Bandstand Twist").....5-10 62
(Promotional issue only.)
GOLD-MOR 4-6 73

EPs: 7-inch

COLUMBIA 5-10 53-59

LPs: 10/12-inch

COLUMBIA 15-30 53-62
HARMONY 5-10 66

ELGART, Les & Larry — LP '64

Singles: 7-inch

COLUMBIA 5-10 64-68
SWAMPFIRE 4-8 69

Picture Sleeves

COLUMBIA 5-10 65

LPs: 10/12-inch

COLUMBIA (Except 38000 series)..........10-25 57-68
COLUMBIA (38000 series) 5-10 82

HARMONY...8-12 68-73
SWAMPFIRE..5-10 70
Also see ELGART, Larry
Also see ELGART, Les

ELGINS

(With Stanley Applebaum Orchestra)

Singles: 7-inch

MGM (12670 "Mademoiselle")................75-100 58

ELGINS

Singles: 7-inch

FLIP (353 "Uncle Sam's Man") 50-60 61
(Blue label.)
FLIP (353 "Uncle Sam's Man") 75-100 61
(White label. Promotional issue only.)

ELGINS

("Vocal by Allan Sheafer")

Singles: 7-inch

A-B-S (113 "Pretending") 400-500 61

ELGINS

Singles: 7-inch

JOED (716 "Once Upon a Time").........400-500 62

ELGINS

Singles: 7-inch

LUMMTONE (109 "A Winner Never Quits"/"Finally")..30-40 62
LUMMTONE (109 "A Winner Never Quits"/"Johnny I'm Sorry")..20-30 62
LUMMTONE (110 "Johnny, I'm Sorry")....40-50 62
LUMMTONE (112 "Finally")......................15-25 63
LUMMTONE (113 "Your Lovely Ways")...20-30 64
TITAN (1724 "My Illness")......................150-200 62
TITAN (1724 "Heartache Heartbreak").....50-75 62
(No. 1724 issued twice, but with same flip.)
Members: Kenneth Sinclair; Jimmy Smith.
Also see LITTLE TOMMY & ELGINS
Also see SIX TEENS

ELGINS

Singles: 7-inch

DOT (16563 "Cheryl") 75-125 63

ELGINS

Singles: 7-inch

CONGRESS (214 "The Times We've Wasted")..8-12 64
CONGRESS (225 "Here in Your Arms") .. 15-25 64
VALIANT (712 "Street Scene") 15-25 65

ELGINS — P&R/R&B '66

Singles: 7-inch

V.I.P. 10-20 66-71

LPs: 10/12-inch

V.I.P. (400 "Darling Baby")......................50-100 66
Members: Saundra Mallet; Cleo Miller; Robert Flemming; John Dawson; Norbert McClean.
Also see DOWNBEATS
Also see FIVE EMERALDS
Also see MALLET, Saundra

ELIGIBLES

(With Al Capp)

Singles: 7-inch

CAPITOL...8-12 59-60
COURTNEY (712 "Walkin' with My Baby")..5-10 63
MERCURY (72000 "Come Back, Music") ..5-10 62
W.B. (5344 "See What You Can Do for Me") 5-10 63

EPs: 7-inch

CAPITOL...10-15 60

LPs: 10/12-inch

CAPITOL (1310 "Along the Trail") 20-35 60
CAPITOL (1411 "Love Is a Gamble")........20-35 60
MERCURY (20710 "Live at Vegas").........15-20 62

ELIMINATORS

Singles: 7-inch

TE...10-20 '60s

LPs: 10/12-inch

LIBERTY (3365 "Liverpool, Dragsters, Cycles and Surfing")..20-30 64
(Monaural.)
LIBERTY (3365 "Liverpool, Dragsters, Cycles and Surfing")..25-30 64
(Stereo.)

ELITE

Singles: 7-inch

CHARAY (17 "One Potato, Two Potato")...5-10 65
CHARAY (31 "My Confusion")..................15-25 66

CHARAY (56 "Bye Bye Baby")....................5-10 67

ELITES

Singles: 7-inch

ABEL (225 "In the Little Chapel")............ 40-50 59
Also see CRYSTAL, Lou

ELITES

Singles: 7-inch

HI-LITE (106 "You Mean So Much to Me").. 40-50 60

ELITES

Singles: 7-inch

CHIEF (7028 "Dapper Dan")................... 40-50 61
CHIEF (7032 "Jack the Ripper").............. 15-25 61
CHIEF (7040 "The Blues")...................... 20-30 61

E'LITES

Singles: 7-inch

EGS (001 "Restless")............................ 10-20 62

ELITES

Singles: 7-inch

ABC-PAR (10460 "Tree of Love")........... 10-15 63

ELIZABETH

Singles: 7-inch

VANGUARD (35070 "Mary Anne")............8-12 68
PARAMOUNT (0197 "Oh Girl")....................4-6 73

Picture Sleeves

VANGUARD..8-12 68

LPs: 10/12-inch

VANGUARD (6501 "Elizabeth").............. 50-75 68
Members: Bob Patterson; Steve Weingart; Steve Bruno; Hank Ransome; Jim Dahme.

ELJAYS

Singles: 7-inch

CB (5008 "I Wonder")........................... 50-100 62

EL JUANS

Singles: 7-inch

SUNDOWN (208 "Golden Teardrops") 300-400

ELKINS, Bill

Singles: 7-inch

BLANK (103 "You Made Me Mad")...... 200-300 60

ELL, Carl, & Buddies

Singles: 7-inch

COMBO (154 "Bobby My Love")............. 50-75 59
(Purple label. Small print.)
COMBO (154 "Bobby My Love")............. 10-15
(Purple label. Large print.)
Also see LAMPLIGHTERS
Also see RIVINGTONS
Also see SHARPS

ELLEDGE, Jimmy P&R '61

Singles: 7-inch

4 STAR...4-6 75
HICKORY..5-10 65-67
LITTLE DARLIN' (0047 "Florence Jean") ...5-10 68
RCA (Except 7910 & 8012).....................8-12 61-64
RCA (7910 "Swanee River Rocket")........ 25-35 61
RCA (8012 "Can't You See It in My Eyes").. 10-20 62
SIMS (204 "I Gotta Live Here")..................5-10 64

Picture Sleeves

RCA.. 10-15 62-63

LPs: 10/12-inch

LITTLE DARLIN'.......................................8-12 68

ELLEN & SHANDELS

Singles: 7-inch

LA SALLE (25 "Gypsy")........................... 10-20

ELLIE POP

Singles: 7-inch

MAINSTREAM (686 "Can't Be Love")...... 10-15 68

LPs: 10/12-inch

MAINSTREAM (6115 "Ellie Pop")........... 30-50 68

ELLINGTON, Duke P&R '27

Singles: 78 rpm

BRUNSWICK...5-15 27-39
CAPITOL..3-8 53-56
COLUMBIA...3-8 50-53
RCA..3-8 51-55

Singles: 7-inch

BETHLEHEM...5-10 58-60
CAPITOL (2000 series)..............................5-15 53-56
COLUMBIA (33000 series)...........................4-6 76
COLUMBIA (39000 series).........................8-15 50-53
COLUMBIA (40000 thru 42000 series).......5-10 58-61
COLUMBIA PRICELESS EDITION 5-10
RCA (0300 series).......................................4-6 74
RCA (4000 thru 6000 series).....................8-15 51-55
REPRISE..5-10 67

EPs: 7-inch

BRUNSWICK...10-20 54
CAPITOL...10-20 53-56
COLUMBIA..10-20 50-56
RCA..10-20 52-60
ROYALE..10-20 '50s

LPs: 10/12-inch

ALLEGIANCE...5-8 84
ALLEGRO...25-50 54
(10-inch LPs.)
ATLANTIC...5-10 71-82
BASF..5-10 73
BETHLEHEM...15-30 56-57
BRIGHT ORANGE.......................................5-10 73
BRUNSWICK (54000 series)....................15-30 56
BRUNSWICK (58000 series)....................30-50 54
(10-inch LPs.)
CAMDEN (400 series)...............................15-25 58
CAPITOL (400 series)...............................25-50 53
(With "H" prefix. 10-inch LPs.)
CAPITOL (400 thru 600 series)................25-40 55-57
CAPITOL (1600 series).............................10-20 61
(With "T" prefix.)
CAPITOL (11000 series)..............................5-10 72-77
CAPITOL (16000 series)................................4-6 81
COLUMBIA (27 "The Ellington Era, Volume 1")..25-40 63
COLUMBIA (39 "The Ellington Era, Volume 2, 1927-1940")...25-40 66
COLUMBIA (500 thru 900 series).............20-30 54-57
COLUMBIA (1085 thru 2029, except 1360)..15-30 57-63
(Monaural.)
COLUMBIA (1360 "Anatomy of a Murder")..35-50 59
(Soundtrack. Monaural.)
COLUMBIA (4000 series)..........................25-50 55
COLUMBIA (6000 series)..........................30-60 50
(10-inch LPs.)
COLUMBIA (8053 thru 9600, except 8166)..10-20 57-68
(Stereo.)
COLUMBIA (8166 "Anatomy of a Murder")..45-60 59
(Soundtrack. Stereo.)
COLUMBIA (14000 series)..........................5-10 79
(Columbia Special Products series.)
COLUMBIA (32000 thru 38000 series).......5-10 73-82
COLUMBIA SPECIAL PRODUCTS...............5-8 82
DECCA...8-15 67-70
DOCTOR JAZZ..5-8 84
EVEREST...5-10 70-73
FANTASY...6-12 71-75
FLYING DUTCHMAN.....................................5-10 69
HARMONY..5-10 67-71
IMPULSE (Except 9200 series)................15-20 62
IMPULSE (9200 series)...............................8-12 73
MOSAIC (160 "Complete Capitol Recordings of Duke Ellington")...100-120 '90s
(Boxed, eight-disc set. 5000 made.)
ODYSSEY..8-12 68
PABLO..5-10 76-80
PRESTIGE...6-12 73-77
RCA (500 series)...10-20 64-69
RCA (0700 thru 2000 series).......................5-8 75-78
(With "ANL1" or "APL1" prefix.)
RCA (1000 series)......................................25-40 54
(With "LJM" or "LPT" prefix.)
RCA (1300 thru 2800 series)....................10-30 57-66
(With "LPM" or "LSP" prefix.)
RCA (3000 series)......................................25-50 52-53
(10-inch LPs.)
RCA (3500 thru 3900 series).......................8-15 66-68
RCA (4000 series)...8-10 81
RCA (6009 "The Indispensible Duke Ellington")...20-30 61
RCA (6042 "This Is Duke Ellington")........10-15 71
REPRISE...10-20 63-68
RIVERSIDE (Except 100 series)...............10-20 62-64
RIVERSIDE (100 series)............................15-30 56-59
RON-LETTE...15-30 58
SOLID STATE..5-10 70
SUNSET...5-10 69
TOPS..10-20 56
TRIP...5-10 75-76
U.A. (Except 14000 & 15000 series)..........5-10 72
U.A. (14000 & 15000 series)......................15-25 62
VERVE..10-15 67
"X" (3037 "Duke Ellington").......................25-50 55
(10-inch LP.)
Session: Jimmy Grissom.
Also see ANDERSON, Ivie
Also see ARMSTRONG, Louis, & Duke Ellington
Also see BASIE, Count, & Duke Ellington
Also see BREWER, Teresa, & Duke Ellington
Also see CARROLL, Diahann, & Duke Ellington Orchestra
Also see CLOONEY, Rosemary, & Duke Ellington
Also see FITZGERALD, Ella, & Duke Ellington
Also see GRISSOM, Jimmy
Also see HIBBLER, Al, & Duke Ellington
Also see JACKSON, Mahalia, & Duke Ellington
Also see SINATRA, Frank, & Duke Ellington
Also see VAN LOAN, Joe

ELLINGTON, Duke, & Boston Pops Orchestra LP '66

LPs: 10/12-inch

RCA (2857 "Duke at Tanglewood").........15-20 66
Also see BOSTON POPS ORCHESTRA

ELLINGTON, Duke, & John Coltrane

LPs: 10/12-inch

IMPULSE...15-25 63
Also see COLTRANE, John

ELLINGTON, Duke, & Johnny Hodges

Singles: 7-inch

BETHLEHEM (11067 "Ko-Ko")..................5-10 60

LPs: 10/12-inch

PRESTIGE...8-10 81
VERVE (Except 8800 series)...................15-30 59-60
VERVE (8800 series)...................................8-12 73
Also see ELLINGTON, Duke
Also see HODGES, Johnny

ELLINGTON, Harvey

LPs: 10/12-inch

STEPHENY (4010 "I Can't Hide the Blues")..25-30 59

ELLINGTON, Ron

Singles: 7-inch

ERA (3110 "Ballad of Billy Strong")...........5-10 63
LOCKET (102 "This Is the Last Time").....20-30

ELLINGTONS

Singles: 7-inch

G-CLEF (708 "Hurry Home")......................20-30 64

ELLIOT, Bill, & Elastic Oz Band / Elastic Oz Band
(With John Lennon)

Singles: 7-inch

APPLE (1835 "God Save Us")....................5-10 71

Promotional Singles

APPLE (1835 "God Save Us")..................20-25 71

Picture Sleeves

APPLE (1835 "God Save Us")....................8-12 71
Also see LENNON, John

ELLIOT, Cass P&R/LP '68
(Mama Cass)

Singles: 7-inch

DUNHILL..5-10 68-70
RCA...4-6 71-73

LPs: 10/12-inch

DUNHILL...10-20 68-72
PICKWICK..8-12
RCA...10-15 72-73
Also see BIG THREE
Also see MAMAS & PAPAS
Also see MASON, Dave, & Mama Cass
Also see MUGWUMPS

ELLIOT, Linda

Singles: 7-inch

JOSIE (958 "Little Girl Grew Up a Little Last Night")..15-25 66

ELLIOTT, Shawn
(Shawn Eliott)

Singles: 7-inch

DOUBLE L (721 "I Found a New Baby")..10-20 63
ROULETTE...5-10 64-67

LPs: 10/12-inch

ROULETTE..15-25 65

ELLIS, Alton, & Flames

Singles: 7-inch

TREASURE ISLE (7010 "Duke of Earl")..15-25

ELLIS, Anita / Albert Ammons

Singles: 78 rpm

MERCURY/SAV-WAY (3059 "Ask Anyone Who Knows")...100-150 47
(Picture disc. Promotional issue only.)

ELLIS, Anita / Glen Gray & His Orchestra

Singles: 78 rpm

MERCURY/SAV-WAY (3059 "Ask Anyone Who Knows")...100-150 47
(Picture disc. Promotional issue only.)
Also see ELLIS, Anita / Albert Ammons

ELLIS, Big Boy
(Wilbert Ellis)

Singles: 78 rpm

LENOX (521 "Dices Dices")......................15-25 49
Also see BIG CHIEF TRIO

ELLIS, Bobby
(With Gary Sherman & Orchestra)

Singles: 7-inch

CAMEO (354 "It's the Talk of the Town").40-60 65
CHELTENHAM (1007 "It's the Talk of the Town")..75-150 65
(First issue.)

ELLIS, Buzz

Singles: 7-inch

ARTISTS INT'L (155 "Be Mine")..............20-30

ELLIS, Cindy

Singles: 7-inch

LAURIE (3043 "Do You Think of Me")........8-12 59

Picture Sleeves

LAURIE (3043 "Do You Think of Me")......15-25 59

ELLIS, Dolan

Singles: 7-inch

CAPQ..4-6 72

EPs: 7-inch

WESTERN SAVINGS ("Arizona's Balladeer")...10-15 67

LPs: 10/12-inch

ARLIS (1387 "Man from the Big Country")...15-25 65
CAPQ..8-15 72-78
COMMENTARY...15-20 61
REPRISE...10-20 62

ELLIS, Don, & Royal Dukes

Singles: 7-inch

BEE (201 "Party Doll")..............................15-25 61
BEE (1110 "Blue Diamonds")....................25-35 58
BEE (1111 "Come in World")....................75-100 59
BEE (1114 "Half of Me")..........................100-125 59
Also see SIGLER, Bunny

ELLIS, Dorothy

Singles: 78 rpm

FEDERAL..20-30 52

Singles: 7-inch

FEDERAL (12062 "He's Gone")................40-60 52
FEDERAL (12070 "Drill Daddy Drill").....50-100 52

ELLIS, Herb, & Vince Megna

Singles: 7-inch

EMP (1001 "Poinciana")............................10-20 65
Also see CONTINENTALS

ELLIS, Jimmy

Singles: 7-inch

BLANK LABEL (1142 "That's All Right")..10-15 79
(Gold vinyl. Label has no printing. Identification number – from vinyl trail-off – shown since no selection number is used. Promotional issue only. Includes insert letter from Shelby Singleton.)
BOBLO...8-12 77-78
CENTURY CITY (511 "Looking Through the Eyes of Love")..10-20 '60s
CHALLENGER...4-6 73
DRADCO (905 "Don't Count Your Chickens")..50-100 64
GOLDBAND...8-12 '60s
KRISTAL..3-5 85
MCA...4-6 73
SSS/SUN (Black vinyl).................................5-10 72-77
SSS/SUN (Gold vinyl)................................10-20 '70s
(Promotional issues only.)
SOUTHERN TRACKS.......................................3-5 86-87
TONY LAWRENCE...4-6 83-84

Picture Sleeves

BOBLO (536 "I'm Not Trying to Be Like Elvis")...10-20 78

EPs: 7-inch
JIMMY ELLIS FAN CLUB ("Merry Christmas") 5-10 81
(No selection number used. Promotional issue only.)
LPs: 10/12-inch
BOBLO (829 "By Request, Ellis Sings Elvis") 75-125 77
ROLLER SKATE 8-10 82
Also see LEWIS, Jerry Lee, Carl Perkins & Charlie Rich
Also see ORION

ELLIS, Lloyd
Singles: 78 rpm
MERCURY 10-15 54
Singles: 7-inch
MERCURY (70463 "Yo-Yo Boogie") 15-25 54
MERCURY (70520 "Boogie Blues") 15-25 54

ELLIS, Lorraine
(With the Crows; with Ray Barrow & His Orchestra)
Singles: 78 rpm
BULLSEYE (100 "Perfidia") 10-15 55
GEE (1 "Perfidia") 40-50 54
Singles: 7-inch
BULLSEYE (100 "Perfidia") 40-50 55
GEE (1 "Perfidia") 400-500 54
Also see CROWS

ELLIS, Ray, Orchestra *P&R '60*
Singles: 78 rpm
COLUMBIA 4-8 57
Singles: 7-inch
ASCOT (2203 "1000 Clowns") 4-8 66
ATCO 4-8 65-66
COLUMBIA 5-10 57
MGM 5-10 59-60
RCA (7888 "La Dolce Vita") 4-8 61
RCA (7953 "Portofino") 4-8 61
RCA (8023 "Dumpy") 4-8 62
RCA (8150 "Rubia") 4-8 62
EPs: 7-inch
COLUMBIA 5-10 57
LPs: 10/12-inch
COLUMBIA 10-20 57
HARMONY (7183 "Gigi") 10-15 59
(Monaural.)
HARMONY (10003 "Gigi") 10-15 59
(Stereo.)
MGM (3779 "I'm in the Mood for Strings") 10-15 59
MGM 10-15 59-60
RCA (2400 "Ray Ellis Plays the Top 20") 10-15 61
RCA (2410 "La Dolce Vita") 10-15 61
RCA (2493 "How to Succeed in Business Without Really Trying (selections)" 10-15 61
RCA (2615 "Our Man on Broadway") 10-15 63
Also see BAKER, LaVern
Also see CRYSTALS
Also see DE MARCO, Arlene
Also see HANLEY, Pete
Also see MADHATTANS
Also see RUSSELL, Nathan

ELLIS, Rex
Singles: 7-inch
RIVERMONT (1160 "Bog Hop Jamboree") 500-750 59

ELLIS, Ronnie
Singles: 7-inch
VAN (01864 "Honey Blonde") 50-75

ELLIS, Shirley *P&R/R&B '63*
Singles: 7-inch
COLUMBIA (43829 thru 44137) 5-10 66-67
CONGRESS (202 thru 260) 5-10 63-65
MCA 4-6 73
Picture Sleeves
CONGRESS (230 "Name Game") 10-20 64
CONGRESS (234 "Clapping Song") 10-20 65
CONGRESS (246 "I Told You So") 10-20 65
LPs: 10/12-inch
COLUMBIA (2679 "Sugar, Let's Shing-A Ling") 15-25 67
(Monaural.)
COLUMBIA (9479 "Sugar, Let's Shing-A Ling") 15-25 67
(Stereo.)
CONGRESS (3002 "In Action") 20-30 64
CONGRESS (3003 "Name Game") 20-30 65
Also see ELLISTON, Shirley
Also see METRONOMES
Also see SHIRLEE MAY

ELLIS, Steve, & Starfires
Singles: 7-inch
DECIMA (2001 "Walking Around") 25-35 65
LPs: 10/12-inch
IGL (105 "Steve Ellis Songbook") 500-700 67
Members: Steve Ellis; Jimmy Groth; Clem Hatting; Dean Sefner; Barry Hanson.

ELLIS BROTHERS
Singles: 7-inch
ABC-PAR (9954 "Sneaky Alligator") 10-15 58

ELLISON, Lorraine *R&B '65*
Singles: 7-inch
LOMA (2074 thru 2094) 5-10 67
MERCURY 5-10 65-66
SHARP (635 "Open Up Your Heart") 10-15 63
W.B. 4-6 66-69
LPs: 10/12-inch
W.B. (1000 series) 15-20 67-69
W.B. (2000 series) 8-10 74

ELLISTON, Shirley
Singles: 7-inch
SHELL (307 "Beautiful Love") 10-15 61
Also see ELLIS, Shirley

ELLSWORTH, Ray
Singles: 7-inch
ELLSWORTH (101 "Rock n' Roll Show") 200-300

ELLUSIONS
Singles: 7-inch
LAMON (2004 "You Didn't Have to Leave") ....20-30 '60s

ELMER GANTRY'S VELVET OPERA
LPs: 10/12-inch
EPIC (26415 "Elmer Gantry's Velvet Opera") 25-30 68

ELMO, Sunnie, & Minor Chords
Singles: 7-inch
FLICK (009 "Let Me") 30-40 60
Also see MINOR CHORDS

ELMORE, Johnny, & Silver-Tones
Singles: 7-inch
JAR (105 "War Chant Boogie") 100-150

ELMORE, Russ & Russanne
Singles: 7-inch
DOLTON (14 "Big Words") 10-15 59

EL PAULING
(El Pauling & Royalton; El Pauling & Royal Abbit)
Singles: 7-inch
FEDERAL (12383 thru 12464, except 12396) 10-20 60-62
FEDERAL (12396 "Now Baby, Don't Do It") 15-25 61
Session: Loman Pauling Jr.; Royal J. Abbit.
Also see 5 ROYALES

EL POLLOS
Singles: 7-inch
NEPTUNE (1001 "School Girl") 150-200 58
STUDIO (999 "High School Dance") 600-800 58

EL POOKS
Singles: 7-inch
ORIVIOUS (11129 "Trisha") 25-35

ELQUIN'S
Singles: 7-inch
ROGO (1026 "Up's And Downs") 10-20 61

EL RAYS
(With Willie Dixon & Orchestra)
Singles: 78 rpm
CHECKER (794 "Darling I Know") 200-300 54
Singles: 7-inch
CHECKER (794 "Darling I Know") ... 1000-1500 54
GOLDEN GOODIES (794 "Darling I Know") 5-10
Members: Marvin Junior; Vern Allison; Mike McGill; Charles Barksdale.
Also see DELLS
Also see DIXON, Willie

EL RAYS
Singles: 7-inch
M.M. (104 "Till the End of Time") 15-25 63

EL REY & NIGHT BEATS
Singles: 7-inch
REVIVE (103 "My Secret") 40-50 63
Member: Raymond Ojeda; Dick Whitstone; Ron Kurtz; Gerald Bartelmas; Bruce Rudan; Tom Montez; Jack Staumbeil; Terry Thuemling; Jack Gebhardt.
Also see LANE, Tommy
Also see NIGHT BEATS

EL REYES
Singles: 7-inch
JADE (501 "Mr. Moonglow") 750-1000 58

EL REYS
Singles: 7-inch
IDEAL (94706 "Diamonds and Pearls") 10-15 64
(Identification number shown since no selection number is used.)
IDEAL (95388 "Angalie") 15-20 65
(Identification number shown since no selection number is used.)

EL-RICH TRIO & COMBO
Singles: 7-inch
ELCO (1 "This I Swear") 10-15 66

ELROY & EXCITEMENTS
Singles: 7-inch
ALANNA (565 "My Love Will Never Die") 150-200 61
(Same number used in a Chuck Osborne release.)

EL SIERROS
Singles: 7-inch
RELIC (534 "Love You So") 5-10 65
TIMES SQUARE (29 "Love You So") 15-25 64
TIMES SQUARE (101 "Life Is But a Dream") 10-20 64
YUSSELS (7702 "Sunday Kind of Love") .15-25 63
Also see YOUNG ONES / El Sierros

ELTON & ROCKIN' ELTRADORS
Singles: 7-inch
LANOR (501 "I Love My Baby") 15-25 58
Also see ELTRADORS

EL TONES
Singles: 78 rpm
CHIEF (800 "I Won't Be Your Fool") 20-30 55
Singles: 7-inch
CHIEF (800 "I Won't Be Your Fool") 200-300 55
CUB (9011 "Like Mattie") 15-25 58
CUB (9012 "Honest I Do") 3-5
(Previously unissued.)

EL TORRO & BANLONS
Singles: 7-inch
TRIANGLE (60-30 "I Love You Baby") .100-150 63

EL TORROS
Singles: 78 rpm
DUKE (175 "Dance with Me") 10-15 57
Singles: 7-inch
DUKE (175 "Dance with Me") 15-25 57
DUKE (194 "You Look Good to Me") 50-60 58
DUKE (321 "What's the Matter") 20-30 60
DUKE (333 "Two Lips") 15-20 61
DUKE (353 "Mama's Cookin'") 10-15 62

EL TORROS
Singles: 7-inch
FRATERNITY (811 "Love Is Love") 50-75 58

ELTRADORS
Singles: 7-inch
LANOR (523 "All These Things") 10-15
Also see ELTON & ROCKIN' ELTRADORS

EL VENOS
(El Vinos)
Singles: 78 rpm
GROOVE (0170 "Now We're Together") ..20-30 56
VIK (0305 "My Heart Beats Faster") 40-60 57
Singles: 7-inch
GROOVE (0170 "Now We're Together") 75-100 56
PARK AVENUE (01 "Are You an Angel") ...5-10 90
(Green vinyl. 500 made.)
RCA (8303 "My Heart Beats Faster") 10-15 64
VIK (0305 "My Heart Beats Faster") 50-75 57
Also see DILLARD, Varetta
Also see KEITH, Anne

ELVES
(Electric Elves)
Singles: 7-inch
DECCA (32507 "Walking in Different Circles") 50-75 69
DECCA (32617 "Amber Velvet") 100-125 70
Also see DIO, Ronnie
Also see ELECTRIC ELVES

EL VIREOS
Singles: 7-inch
REVELLO (1002 "First Kiss") 75-125 59

ELY, Dick
Singles: 7-inch
MARLEE (102 "Keep A'Rollin' ") 200-300

ELY, Jack, & Courtmen
(Jack Eely)
Singles: 7-inch
BANG (520 "Louie Louie '66") 10-15 66
BANG (534 "Louie Go Home") 8-12 66
Members: Jack Ely; Charlie Coe; Leon Ettinger; Mike McGrath; Bill Truitt.
Also see EMERGENCY EXIT
Also see KINGSMEN

EMANON FOUR
Singles: 78 rpm
FLASH (106 "Oh! That Girl") 20-30 56
Singles: 7-inch
FLASH (106 "Oh! That Girl") 75-100 56

EMANONS
Singles: 78 rpm
GEE (1005 "Change of Time") 75-125 56
JOSIE (801 "Blue Moon") 20-30 56
Singles: 7-inch
GGS (443 "You Know I Miss You") 500-750
GEE (1005 "Change of Time") 750-1000 56
JOSIE (801 "Blue Moon") 40-60 56
Members: Robert Coleman; Carl White; James Hill; Jim Dukes; Ralph Steeley.
Also see CONCEPTS & EMANONS

EMANONS
Singles: 7-inch
ABC-PAR (9913 "Dear One") 8-12 58
WINLEY (226 "Dear One") 15-25 58
Members: Jim Danella; Phil DeVito; Mike Buono; Joe Buono.
Also see 3 FRIENDS

EMANONS
Singles: 7-inch
DELBERT (5290 "Emanons Rock") 200-300 59
DOLL ("Stomper") 15-25 59
(Selection number not known.)

EMBERGLOWS
Singles: 7-inch
AMAZON (1005 "Make Up Your Mind") ... 10-20 62
DORE (591 "Have You Found Someone New") 20-30 61

EMBERMEN FIVE
(Embermen)
Singles: 7-inch
BANGAR (0628 "I'm Gonna Marry Mary") 20-25 65
CENTURY (30851 "Do You Have to Be So Cruel") ....10-20 '60s
SOMA (1429 "Karen") 25-35 65
STUDIO CITY (1053 "Fire In My Heart") ..25-35 66
STUDIO CITY (1062 "That's Why I Need You") 20-25 67
STUDIO CITY ("My Love for You Won't Die") 25-35 67
(No selection number used.)
Picture Sleeves
CENTURY (30851 "Do You Have to Be So Cruel") ....25-35 '60s
Members: Herb Parker Jr.; Ron Boen; Bob Johnson; Paul Unwin; Larry Tanner.

EMBERS
(With Vi Hamilton Trio)
Singles: 78 rpm
COLUMBIA (40287 "Sweet Lips") 8-12 54
EMBER (101 "Paradise Hill") 200-300 53
HERALD (410 "Paradise Hill") 25-50 53
Singles: 7-inch
COLUMBIA (40287 "Sweet Lips") 15-25 54
EMBER (101 "Paradise Hill") 1000-1500 53

HERALD (410 "Paradise Hill")............. 200-300 53
(Black label.)
HERALD (410 "Paradise Hill")............... 50-100 53
(Yellow label.)
HERALD (410 "Paradise Hill")............. 100-200 53
(Red vinyl.)
Member: Eugene Pearson.
Also see DRIFTERS
Also see RIVILEERS

EMBERS

Singles: 7-inch

DOT (16101 "Wait for Me")...................... 20-30 60
DOT (16162 "Please Mr. Sun")............... 15-25 60
Also see SANDERS, Willis

EMBERS

Singles: 7-inch

COLLECTABLES...3-5 '80s
EMPRESS (101 "Solitaire")..................... 15-25 61
EMPRESS (101 "Solitaire")..................... 25-50 61
(Single-sided. Promotional issue only.)
EMPRESS (104 "I Won't Cry Anymore") . 20-30 61
EMPRESS (104 "I Won't Cry Anymore") . 50-75 61
(Single-sided. Promotional issue only.)
EMPRESS (107 "Abigail")....................... 15-25 62
EMPRESS (107 "Abigail")....................... 25-50 62
(Single-sided. Promotional issue only.)
EMPRESS (108 "What a Surprise")......... 50-75 62

Picture Sleeves

EMPRESS (101 "Solitaire").................. 75-100 61
(Promotional issue only.)
Also see BOB & EARL / Embers

EMBERS

Singles: 7-inch

ATLANTIC 10-15 69
BELL (664 "It Ain't Necessary")............... 15-20 67
EEE.. 10-20
JCP (1008 "In My Lonely Room") 15-25 64
JCP (1028 "A Fool in Love").................. 50-100 64
JCP (1034 "First Time")........................... 40-60 64
JCP (1054 "It Ain't Necessary")................ 20-30 65
LIBERTY (55944 "Evelyn")........................5-10 67
MGM (14167 "Watch Out Girl")................ 15-25 70

LPs: 10/12-inch

EEE... 10-15 80-82
JCP (2006 "Rock & Roll")................... 100-150 65
RIPETE...5-10 82
Members: Jackie Hamilton Gore; Johnny Hopkins; Bobby Tomlison; Craig Woolard; Gerald Davis; Doug Strange; Johnny Barker.
Also see SWINGING EMBERS

EMBERS

Singles: 7-inch

ACT IV (94147 "Forever").................... 100-150 65
(Identification number shown since no selection number is used. Reissued as by the Seminoles.)
Also see SEMINOLES

EMBERTONES
(With Tony Agbay & Continentals)

Singles: 7-inch

BAY (203 "I Remember")..................... 200-300 62

EMBLEMS

Singles: 7-inch

BAYFRONT (107 "Would You Still Be Mine").. 40-50 62
(Has straight, parallel horizontal lines.)
BAYFRONT (107 "Would You Still Be Mine").. 10-20 62
(With wavy, parallel horizontal lines.)
BAYFRONT (108 "Too Young") 30-40 62
(Black vinyl.)
BAYFRONT (108 "Too Young") 150-200 62
(Green vinyl.)

EMBRACEABLES
("Featuring Herman Bracey")

Singles: 7-inch

CY (1004 "My Foolish Pride")................. 10-20 62
DOVER (4100 "A Wall Between Us") 15-25 62
DOVER (4101 "Come Back") 15-25 62
SANDY (1025 "From Someone Who Loves You").. 75-125 59

EMBRACERS

Singles: 7-inch

LUCKY LABEL (1000 "Mr. Sunrise") 50-100

EMBRY, Jerry

Singles: 7-inch

EBONY (03 "Jackie's Goodbye") 40-60 63

EMBRY, Ted

Singles: 7-inch

ACCENT (1057 "New Shoes")..................40-60 58

EMCEES
(Tommy McCleland & Emcees)

Singles: 7-inch

CIMARRON (4041 "Ific")..........................20-30 60
CIMARRON (4044 "Hot Rock")..................20-30 60

EMERALD CITY BANDITS

Singles: 7-inch

PHILIPS (40197 "Full Blown Caddy")...100-150 64
Member: Donald Drowty.
Also see DANTE

EMERALD ENTERTAINMENT

Singles

EMERALD (36 "Dungeon of Fusion").......15-20 89
(Diamond-shaped picture disc. 100 made.)

EMERALDS

Singles: 78 rpm

KICKS (3 "Why Must I Wonder")..........100-200 54

Singles: 7-inch

ALLIED (10002 "Sally Lou").......................30-40 58
KICKS (3 "Why Must I Wonder")...... 1500-2000 54
Members: Bobby Parker; Billy Mann.

EMERALDS

Singles: 78 rpm

FEDERAL (12279 "I Cry") 10-20 56

Singles: 7-inch

FEDERAL (12279 "I Cry") 30-40 56
Also see BOND, Luther

EMERALDS

Singles: 7-inch

ABC-PAR (9889 "You Belong to My Heart")...10-15 58
ABC-PAR (9948 "I'm Dreaming")..............10-15 58
TOY (7734 "Roadrunner")..........................8-12 61
YALE (232 "Trapped") 8-12 60

EMERALDS

Singles: 7-inch

BOBBIN' (107 "That's the Way It's Got to Be")...100-150 59
BOBBIN' (121 "Lover's Cry")................100-150 60
Member: Billy Davis.

EMERALDS

Singles: 7-inch

REX (1004 "All the Time") 15-25 59
REX (1013 "I Kneel At Your Throne").......10-15 60
VENUS (1002 "Mademoiselle")............100-200 59
VENUS (1003 "Marsha") 200-300 59

EMERALDS

Singles: 7-inch

PEL (3836 "You're a Fallen Angel")..........30-40 62

EMERALDS

Singles: 7-inch

JUBILEE (5474 "Dancing Alone")............20-30 63
JUBILEE (5489 "Did You Ever Love a Guy")..10-15 64

EMERALDS

Singles: 7-inch

DC (179 "Emerald Surf") 15-25 64
MOONGLOW (228 "Sittin' Bull") 15-25 64
MOONGLOW (230 "Ooh Poo Pah Doo") .15-25 64
MOONGLOW (232 "Moonlight Surf") 15-25 64
(Black vinyl.)
MOONGLOW (232 "Moonlight Surf") 40-50 64
(Green vinyl.)
RIVIERA (714 "Search for Love") 15-25 64

EMERALDS

Singles: 7-inch

KING (6078 "Promises")..........................10-15 67

EMERALDS

Singles: 7-inch

DEE-JAY SPECIAL (18108 "Earthquake")...30-40
(Colored vinyl.)

Picture Sleeves

DEE-JAY SPECIAL...................................10-20

EMERALS

Singles: 7-inch

TIMES SQUARE (111 "Please Don't Crush My Dreams")..15-25 67
TRIPLE X (100 "Please Don't Crush My Dreams")..400-500 58
Member: Tony Pabon.

EMERGENCY EXIT

Singles: 7-inch

DUNHILL (4060 "Maybe Too Late") 10-15 67
DUNHILL (4082 "It's Too Late Baby") 10-15 67
RU-RO (412 "Maybe Too Late") 20-30 66
RCA...10-15 '60s
(Canadian.)
Members: Paul Goldsmith; Luther Rabb; Jim Walters; Bill Leyritz; Mike McGrath; Al Malosky.
Also see ELY, Jack, & Courtmen
Also see NITE SOUNDS

EMERSON, Billy
(Billy "The Kid" Emerson; Bill Emerson; with Willie Dixon's Band)

Singles: 78 rpm

SUN (195 "No Teasin' Around")............150-250 54
SUN (203 "The Woodchuck")................100-200 54
SUN (214 "When It Rains It Pours").......50-100 55
SUN (219 "Red Hot")..............................50-100 55
SUN (233 "Little Fine Healthy Thing") 25-50 55
VEE-JAY 20-30 56-57

Singles: 7-inch

CHESS (1728 "Believe Me")....................10-20 59
CHESS (1740 "I'll Get to You") 10-20 59
CONSTELLATION (148 "Aunt Molly")........8-12 65
MAD..10-20 60-61
M-PAC (7207 "The Whip") 5-10 63
SUN (195 "No Teasin' Around")...........300-400 54
SUN (203 "The Woodchuck")................250-350 54
SUN (214 "When It Rains It Pours") 100-150 55
SUN (219 "Red Hot")............................100-150 55
SUN (233 "Little Fine Healthy Thing") 50-100 55
TARPON (6606 "When It Rains It Pours")...10-20 60
TOPIC (8009 "Judge Her Gently")...........50-75 65
TOPIC (8013 "Going Out to Hollywood") .50-75 65
USA (751 "I Get That Feeling")..................5-10 63
USA (777 "When It Rains It Pours") 5-10 64
VEE-JAY (219 "Tomorrow Never Comes")...20-30 56
VEE-JAY (247 "Somebody Show Me") 20-30 57
VEE-JAY (261 "You Never Miss the Water")...20-30 57
Also see DIXON, Willie
Also see TURNER, Ike

EMERSON, Billy "The Kid" / Smokey Joe

Singles: 7-inch

SSS/SUN 5-10 80
Also see EMERSON, Billy
Also see SMOKEY JOE

EMERSON, Lee, & Marty Robbins

Singles: 78 rpm

COLUMBIA 8-12 56

Singles: 7-inch

COLUMBIA (40868 "Where D'ja Go") 10-20 56
Also see ROBBINS, Marty

EMERSON, LAKE & PALMER P&R/LP '71

Singles: 7-inch

ATLANTIC..3-6 77-80
COTILLION..4-6 71-72
MANTICORE (2003 "Brain Salad Surgery").4-6 74
MANTICORE (2003 "Brain Salad Surgery")...5-10 74
(Promotional issue only.)
POLYDOR (885101 "Touch & Go").............3-5 86

Picture Sleeves

MANTICORE (2003 "Brain Salad Surgery")..10-20 78
(Promotional issue only.)
POLYDOR (885101 "Touch & Go").............3-5 86

LPs: 10/12-inch

ATLANTIC (Except 281)............................8-10 77-80
ATLANTIC (281 "Emerson, Lake & Palmer")...12-15 77
(With the London Philharmonic Orchestra. Also contains interviews with the three members. Promotional issue only.)
COTILLION..12-15 71-72
MFSL (031 "Pictures at an Exhibition") 30-50 79
MFSL (203 "Tarkus")...............................20-30 94
MFSL (218 "Trilogy")...............................20-30 94
MANTICORE (200 "Ladies and Gentlemen")...10-20 74
(Three discs.)
Members: Keith Emerson; Greg Lake; Carl Palmer.

EMERSONS

Singles: 7-inch

CUB (9027 "Hokey Pokey") 8-12 59
NEWPORT (7004 "Joannie, Joannie").....40-50 58
U.A. (379 "Loneliness") 15-25 61
Members: Eddie Jones; Thomas Cook; Frank Cook; Joe Caines. Session: King Curtis.
Also see DEMENS
Also see KING CURTIS

EMERY, Ross
(Ross Emery Band)

LPs: 10/12-inch

CJ (101 "Lonely Too Long")......................30-40 78
ODESSA (00002 "The Jogger")...............15-25 76
Members: Ross Emery; Pat Maguire; Les Harmeyer; Tom Svanoe.

EMILY

Singles: 7-inch

CHALLENGE (59064 "Hoppin' with Emily") 10-15 60

EMJAYS

Singles: 7-inch

GREENWICH (411 "Waitin' ")....................10-15 58
GREENWICH (412 "Cross My Heart").....10-15 59
PARIS (538 "Over the Rainbow") 10-15 59
Members: Jimmy Curtis; Mike Fox; Judy Lloyd.

EMMETT, Ray, & Superiors

Singles: 7-inch

JOY (293 "I'll Always Love You")..............15-25 65

EMMETT & JADES

Singles: 7-inch

RUSTONE (1404 "They Tell Me") 20-30 60
RUSTONE (1405 "No One") 10-20 61

EMMONS, Bobby

Singles: 7-inch

ATLANTIC (2124 "This Is What's Happening") 10-20 61
HI (2090 "Blue Organ") 10-20 65

LPs: 10/12-inch

HI (024 "Blues with a Beat")....................20-30 65

EMMY LOU

Singles: 7-inch

LUTE (6018 "I Wanna Know") 75-125 61

EMORY & DYNAMICS

Singles: 7-inch

PEACHTREE (120 "A Love That Is Real")..50-75 69

EMOTIONALS

Singles: 7-inch

ROBIN (189 "Out of Sight, Out of Mind") .25-35 67
Members: Mike Polaski; Jim Van Puymbrouck; Bob Davern; Rick Davern; Skip Anderson; Dick Shaul.

EMOTIONS

Singles: 7-inch

FLIP (356 "I Ran to You").........................20-30 61
Also see CALHOUN, Lena

EMOTIONS

Singles: 7-inch

CARD (600 "Silvery Moon")..................100-150 62
FURY (1010 "It's Love") 40-50 58

EMOTIONS P&R '62
(With the Billy Mure Orchestra)

Singles: 7-inch

BRAINSTORM...5-10 68
CALLA (122 "She's My Baby")....................5-10 66
CRYSTAL BALL (155 "Echo 90") 3-5 90
(Black vinyl. 500 made.)
JASON SCOTT (12 "Silvery Moon")............3-5 81
(500 made.)
KAPP (490 "Echo")...................................15-25 62
KAPP (513 "L-o-v-e")...............................15-25 63
KARATE (506 "Hey Baby")..........................5-10 65
LAURIE (3167 "Starlit Night") 10-15 63
20TH FOX (430 thru 478)........................10-15 63-64
20TH FOX (6623 "Everytime")...................5-10 66
VARDAN (201 "Love of a Girl") 20-40 65

LPs: 10/12-inch
CRYSTAL BALL (133 "Doo Wopp on Your Dial")...8-12 90
(Black vinyl. 1000 made.)
MAGIC CARPET (1006 "Fond Memories")...8-12 91
(Black vinyl. 2000 made.)
MAGIC CARPET (1006 "Fond Memories")...25-30 91
(Red vinyl. 10 made.)
MAGIC CARPET (1006 "Fond Memories")...40-50 91
(Picture disc. No cover. 25 made.)
Members: Joe Favale; Tony Maltese; Don Colluri; Larry Cusamanno; Joe Nigro; Sal Covais.
Also see HI TONES
Also see MOTIONS
Also see MURE, Billy
Also see RUNAROUNDS
Also see SHY-TONES

EMOTIONS
Singles: 7-inch
CENTURY (24742 "Sometimes")...15-20

EMPALA SIX
Singles: 7-inch
BLUE MOON (417 "Double Time")...15-25 60
BLUE MOON (419 "Sweet and Sour")...15-25 60

EMPALAS
Singles: 7-inch
MARK V (501 "It's Been a Long Time")...100-150 58

EMPALLOS
Singles: 7-inch
DRUM (009 "Hi-Cups")...50-75 59

EMPEROR
Singles: 78 rpm
ARGO (5264 "Tough De Times")...10-15 57
Singles: 7-inch
ARGO (5264 "Tough De Times")...10-15 57

EMPERORS
Singles: 7-inch
3-J (121 "No Regrets")...50-75 58

EMPERORS
Singles: 7-inch
OLIMPIC (245 "In the Moonlight")...20-30 64
WICKWIRE...5-10 64
Picture Sleeves
OLIMPIC (245 "In the Moonlight")...30-40 64
Also see STEVE & EMPERORS

EMPERORS
Singles: 7-inch
SABRA (5555 "I Want My Woman")...25-35 '60s
TWO PLUS TWO (102 "Love Till")...5-10 66

EMPERORS P&R/R&B '66
Singles: 7-inch
BRUNSWICK (55333 "Karate Boogaloo")..5-10 67
MALA (543 "I've Got to Have Her")...10-20 66
MALA (554 "You Got Me Where You Want Me")...5-10 67
MALA (561 "Looking for My Baby")...5-10 67

EMPERORS WITH RHYTHM
Singles: 78 rpm
HAVEN...250-350 54
Singles: 7-inch
HAVEN (511 "I May Be Wrong")...500-750 54
(Black vinyl.)
HAVEN (511 "I May Be Wrong")...2000-3000 54
(Red vinyl.)

EMPIRES
("Featuring Johnny Ace Jr.")
Singles: 78 rpm
AMP 3...75-100 57
HARLEM...50-100 54
WHIRLIN' DISC (104 "Linda")...100-125 57
WING...15-25 55-56
Singles: 7-inch
AMP 3 (132 "If I'm a Fool")...100-150 57
HARLEM (2325 "Corn Wiskey")...400-500 54
HARLEM (2333 "Make Me or Break Me")...400-500 55
WHIRLIN' DISC (104 "Linda")...50-75 57
WING (90023 "I Want to Know")...35-50 55
WING (90050 "Tell Me, Pretty Baby")...25-40 56
WING (90080 "My First Discovery")...20-30 56
Members: Johnny Barnes; Les Cooper; Bobby Dunn; William Goodman.
Also see COOPER, Les
Also see LIGHTNIN' JR. & EMPIRES
Also see PRESTOS
Also see WHIRLERS

EMPIRES
Singles: 7-inch
CALICO (121 "Only in My Dreams")...15-25 61
CANDI (1026 "Love You So Bad")...30-40 62
(First issue.)
CANDI (1033 "You're on Top Girl")...150-250 63
CHAVIS (1026 "Love You So Bad")...8-12 62
COLPIX (680 "Everyone Knew But Me")..10-15 63
DCP (1116 "Have Mercy")...5-10 64
LAKE (711 "Over the Summer Vacation")...15-25 62
OLYMPIC (245 "Darling, in the Moonlight")...30-40 64
Also see FRIEND, Eddie, & Empires

EMPIRES
Singles: 7-inch
EPIC (9527 "Time and a Place")...15-25 62
Member: Jay Black.
Also see BLACK, Jay
Also see RAIN DROPS / Jay & Americans / Empires / Clusters

EMPIRES
Singles: 7-inch
PHOTO DISC ("Ride On")...30-40
(Selection number not known.)

ENALOUISE & HEARTS
Singles: 7-inch
ARGYLE (1635 "From a Cap and a Gown")...100-200

ENCHANTED FIVE
Singles: 7-inch
CVS (1002 "Try a Little Love")...10-20 61

ENCHANTERS
Singles: 78 rpm
JUBILEE...75-125 52
Singles: 7-inch
JUBILEE (5072 "Today Is Your Birthday")...500-600 52
JUBILEE (5080 "I've Lost")...200-250 52
Also see SUGAR-TONES

ENCHANTERS
(With Maurice King & Orchestra)
Singles: 78 rpm
CORAL...20-40 56-57
MERCER (1674 "True Love Gone")...100-150 56
Singles: 7-inch
CORAL (61756 "True Love Gone")...40-50 56
CORAL (61832 "There Goes a Pretty Girl")...50-75 57
(Complete version. Identification number is 100974.)
CORAL (61832 "There Goes a Pretty Girl")...15-25 57
(Edited version. Identification number is 102966.)
CORAL (61916 "Bottle Up & Go")...40-50 57
CORAL (62373 "True Love Gone")...15-25 63
CORAL (65610 "True Love Gone")...5-10 67
MERCER (1674 "True Love Gone") 2000-3000 56

ENCHANTERS P&R '61
(With the Dave McRae Orchestra)
Singles: 7-inch
BALD EAGLE (3001 "Come On Baby, Let's Do the Stroll")...10-15 58
BAMBOO (513 "Touch of Love")...10-15 61
CANDLELITE (432 "Oh Rosemarie")...4-6
EP-SOM (1003 "I Need Your Love")...500-600 62
J.J.&M. (1562 "Oh Rosemarie")...50-100 62
MUSITRON (1072 "I Lied to My Heart")...40-50 61
(Blue or gold label.)
ORBIT (532 "Touch of Love")...25-35 59
SHARP (105 "We Make Mistakes")...20-30 60
STARDUST (102 "Spellbound By the Moon")...1000-1500 58
TOM TOM (301 "Surf Blast")...25-35 63

ENCHANTERS
Singles: 7-inch
GOLDEN EAR (100 "A Fool Like Me")...10-20
TURFSIDE (401 "Like a Love I Never Had")...10-20

ENCHANTERS
Singles: 7-inch
CONFEDERATE ("Everybody Rock")..250-300
(Selection number not known.)

ENCHANTMENTS
Singles: 7-inch
DOYLE ("Why Can't We Fall in Love")...30-50 '70s
(No selection number used.)
FARO (620 "I'm in Love with Your Daughter")...50-75 65
GONE (5130 "Sherry")...20-30 62
RITZ (17003 "I Love My Baby")...150-250 63
ROULETTE (4751 "Sherry")...5-10 67

ENCHANTMENTS Featuring Leroy
(With Jim Drake Orchestra)
Singles: 7-inch
ROMAC (1001 "Lonely Heart")...50-75 62

ENCHANTONES
Singles: 7-inch
POPLAR (116 "My Picture of You")...50-75 62

ENCHORDS
Singles: 7-inch
LAURIE (3089 "Zoom Zoom Zoom")...40-50 61

ENCORES
Singles: 78 rpm
CHECKER (760 "When I Look at You")...250-500 52
Singles: 7-inch
CHECKER (760 "When I Look at You")...3000-4000 52

ENCORES
Singles: 78 rpm
HOLLYWOOD (1034 "Time Is Moving On")...10-20 55
LOOK (105 "Time Is Moving On")...50-75 55
RONNEX (1003 "Time Is Moving On")...15-25 55
Singles: 7-inch
HOLLYWOOD (1034 "Time Is Moving On")...30-40 55
LOOK (105 "Time Is Moving On")...100-150 55
(First issue.)
RONNEX (1003 "Time Is Moving On")...40-50 55

ENCORES
Singles: 7-inch
BOW (302 "Barbara")...30-40 58

ENCORS
Singles: 7-inch
VAVRAY (1005 "No One")...10-15 62

ENCOUNTERS
Singles: 7-inch
LOST NITE (235 "Don't Stop")...10-15
SWAN (4205 "Don't Stop")...50-75 65

END, The
Singles: 7-inch
LONDON (1016 "Loving, Sacred Loving") .5-10 68
PHILIPS (40323 "Hey Little Girl")...5-10 65
LPs: 10/12-inch
LONDON (560 "Introspection")...20-25 69

END, The
Singles: 7-inch
CAROL (218 "Yeah I'm Comin' ")...30-50 61
Picture Sleeves
CAROL (218 "Yeah I'm Comin' ")...75-100 61

END, The
Singles: 7-inch
CHA CHA (746 "Not Fade Away")...25-35

END GAME
Singles: 7-inch
ROUNDTABLE (151 "Piccadilly Circus Clown")...25-35

ENDD
Singles: 7-inch
SEASCAPE (500 "So Sad")...20-30 65
SEASCAPE (501 "Out of My Mind")...20-30 66
SEASCAPE (504 "Come On in to My World")...20-30 67

ENDEAVORS
Singles: 7-inch
J&S (254 "Suffering with My Heart")...750-1000 60

ENDELLS
Singles: 7-inch
HEIGH-HO (605 "Vicky")...15-25 63

ENDLESS
Singles: 7-inch
CARDINAL (521 "Prevailing Darkness")..25-35 66

ENDORSERS
Singles: 7-inch
MOON (109 "Crying")...750-1000 59

ENDSLEY, Melvin
Singles: 78 rpm
RCA...30-50 57-58
Singles: 7-inch
HICKORY...5-10
MELARK (2002 "Everlovin' Never Changing Mind")...5-10 68
RCA...10-20 57-58

ENDSLEY, Melvin / Doree Post
Singles: 7-inch
RCA (DJ-58 "Dealer Prevue")...15-25 57
(Promotional issue only.)

ENERGY PACKAGE
Singles: 7-inch
LAURIE (3392 "This Is the 12th Night")...10-20 67

ENFIELDS
Singles: 7-inch
RICHIE (669 "Eyes of the World")...15-25 66
RICHIE (670 "She Already Has Somebody")...15-25 66
RICHIE (671 "Face to Face")...15-25 66
RICHIE (675 "Time Card")...15-25 66
Members: Mac Morgan; Ted Munda; Robin Eaton; John Bernard; Bill Gallery; John Rhodes.

ENGEL, Gary
(With the Top Hatters)
Singles: 7-inch
KP (1010 "Kimmy Lee")...75-100 60
PEE BEE (1001 "Money Honey")...150-250

ENGEL, Joanne
Singles: 7-inch
AMY (904 thru 926)...5-10 64-65
DANCE ALONG (6051 "The Parachute Jump")...5-10
SABINA (508 thru 516)...8-12 62-63
SUITE 16 (101 "Hurry Back")...30-50 61

ENGEL, Scott
(Scotty Engel)
Singles: 78 rpm
RKO UNIQUE...15-25 57
Singles: 7-inch
CHALLENGE (2004 "Devil Surfer")...15-25 63
LIBERTY (55312 "Mr. Jones")...10-15 62
LIBERTY (55428 "Forever More")...10-15 62
MARTAY (2004 "Devil Surfer")...25-35 63
ORBIT (506 "The Livin' End")...50-75 58
ORBIT (511 "Charley Bop"/"All I Do Is Dream of You")...20-30 58
(B-side selection is No. 512.)
ORBIT (512 "Blue Bell"/"Paper Doll")...20-30 58
(B-side selection is No. 511.)
ORBIT (537 "Golden Rule of Love")...15-25 59
ORBIT (545 "Comin' Home")...15-25 59
RKO UNIQUE (386 "Steady As a Rock").20-30 57
Picture Sleeves
ORBIT (506 "The Livin' End")...25-35 58
ORBIT (511 "Charley Bop")...25-35 58
ORBIT (512 "Blue Bell/"Paper Doll")...25-35 58
ORBIT (537 "Golden Rule of Love")...25-35 59
ORBIT (545 "Comin' Home")...25-35 59
Also see WALKER, Scott

ENGEL, Scott, & John Stewart
Singles: 7-inch
TOWER (218 "I Only Came to Dance with You")...10-15 66
(Shown as by "John Stewart & Scott Engel, Now Known As the Walker Brothers.")
LPs: 10/12-inch
TOWER (5026 "I Only Came to Dance with You")...30-50 66
Also see CHOSEN FEW
Also see DALTON BROTHERS
Also see ENGEL, Scott
Also see NEWPORTERS
Also see MOONGOONERS

Also see WALKER BROTHERS

ENGELBERG, Fred
LPs:10/12-inch
CRESTVIEW (802 "Smoke Dreams of Fred Engelberg") 15-25 63

ENGLAND, Benny
Singles: 7-inch
SNAP (400 "Elopin' ") 200-300 59
ZENITH (103 "Elopin' ") 100-150

ENGLAND, Hank
Singles: 7-inch
KELLY (600 "My Little Kangaroo") 100-200

ENGLE, Butch, & Styx
Singles: 7-inch
LOMA (2065 "I Like Her") 10-20 66
MEA .... 10-15 '60s
ONYX (2200 "Hey I'm Lost") 20-30 67
Also see STYX

ENGLER, Jerry, & Four Ekkos
Singles: 78 rpm
BRUNSWICK (55037 "Sputnik") 40-50 57
Singles: 7-inch
BRUNSWICK (55037 "Sputnik") 60-80 57
CLASSIC EDITION (55037 "What a You Gonna Do") 3-5 92
Picture Sleeves
CLASSIC EDITION (55037 "What a You Gonna Do") 3-5 92
(Sleeve pictures Buddy Holly and Jerry Engler.)
Members: Jerry Engler; Buddy Holly; Harvey Possamato; Dale Masters; Stew Love; Bryan Williams; Jimmy Symonds.
Also see FOUR EKKOS
Also see HOLLY, Buddy

ENGLISH, Anna
Singles: 7-inch
FELSTED (8524 "My Favorite Record") .. 15-20 58

ENGLISH, Barbara *R&B '73*
(Barbara Jean English; with Fashions)
Singles: 7-inch
ALITHIA 4-6 73-74
AURORA (155 "Sittin' in the Corner") 50-75 65
MALA (488 "Easy Come Easy Go") 10-20 64
REPRISE (290 "I've Got a Date") 10-20 65
REPRISE (349 "Small Town Girl") 10-20 65
ROULETTE (4428 "We Need Them") 20-30 62
ROULETTE (4450 "Fever") 20-30 62
W.B. (5685 "All Because I Love Somebody") 10-15 65
LPs: 10/12-inch
ALITHIA 8-10 73
Also see FASHIONS

ENGLISH, Scott *P&R '64*
(With the Accents; with Dedications)
Singles: 7-inch
DOT (16099 "White Cliffs of Dover") 10-15 60
JANUS (171 "Brandy") 8-12 71
JANUS (192 "Woman in My Life") 4-6 72
JOKER (777 "Ugly Pills") 40-50 62
SPOKANE (4003 "High on a Hill") 15-25 64
SPOKANE (4007 "Here Comes the Pain") 15-25 64
SULTAN (4003 "High on a Hill") 10-20 63
Also see ACCENTS

ENGLISH MUFFINS
Singles: 7-inch
B.T. PUPPY (511 "Why Am I So Shy") 5-10 65
GAMA (702 "Leave Or Stay") 20-30 67

ENGLISH SETTERS
Singles: 7-inch
GLAD-HAMP (2029 "Tragedy") 15-25 66
GLAD-HAMP (2033 "Someday You'll See") 15-25 66
JUBILEE (5560 "Wake Up") 5-10 66

ENGLISHMEN
Singles: 7-inch
BRITISH LION (415 "Long Ago") .... 15-25 '60s

ENGLUND, Ernie
Singles: 78 rpm
CADENCE 5-10 55-56
Singles: 7-inch
CADENCE 10-15 55-56
LEADER (809 "Willie's Theme") 5-10 60

ENJOYABLES
Singles: 7-inch
CAPITOL (5321 "Push a Little Harder") 10-20 64
SHRINE (118 "Shame") 250-350 66
Members: James Johnson; Carl Kidd; William Britton; Gerald Richardson.

ENOIS, Lucky, Quintet
(Vocal by Jimmy Waters)
Singles: 78 rpm
MODERN 10-15 53
Singles: 7-inch
MODERN (905 "Crazy Man Crazy") 20-30 53
MODERN (912 "K.C. Limited") 20-30 53

ENSENATORS
Singles: 7-inch
TARX (1001 "Just Like Before") 300-400 62
(Original must be on thick wax.)
TARX (1001 "Just Like Before") 15-25 97
(Gray vinyl.)

ENSENADAS
(Ensenators)
Singles: 7-inch
TARX (1005 "Love I Beg of You") 500-600 63
(Original must be on thick wax.)
TARX (1005 "Love I Beg of You") .... 75-100 '80s
TARX (1005 "Love I Beg of You") 15-25 97
(Yellow vinyl.)

ENTERTAINERS
Singles: 7-inch
DEMAND (2932 "Danny Boy") 10-20 63

ENTERTAINERS
Singles: 7-inch
JCP (1033 "Mr. Pitiful") 15-25 64

ENTERTAINERS IV *R&B '66*
Singles: 7-inch
DORE (749 "Temptation Walk") 10-15 66
DORE (759 "My Garden of Eden") 15-20 66
DORE (770 "When You're Young and in Love") 10-15 66
DORE (788 "Hey Lady") 10-15 67
DORE (802 thru 819) 5-10 67-69
Members: Kennard Gardner; Frank Monroe; Charlie Davis; Bobby Swayne.

EPAE, Jay
Singles: 7-inch
CAPITOL (5029 "Surfin' on Waikiki") 10-20 63
MERCURY 5-10 62

EPIC FIVE
Singles: 7-inch
LOVE ("Humpty Dumpty") 20-30 66
(Selection number not known.)

EPICS
Singles: 7-inch
LIFETIME (1004 "Lonely") 50-75 61

EPICS
Singles: 7-inch
BANDERA (2512 "Summer's Coming In") 400-500 62
ERIC (7001 "Wishing You Were Mine") 30-40 62
LYNN (510 "Girl By the Wayside") 20-30 61
LYNN (513 "The Magic Kiss"/"The Very Same Coin") 75-100 61
LYNN (516 "The Magic Kiss") 40-50 61
LYNN (516 "Most of All") 40-50 61
(Same Lynn selection number used twice. Both have the same flip: *Last Night I Dreamed.*)
SABRA (516 "The Magic Kiss") 20-30 62
(Reissue uses same Lynn number.)
Also see INDIGOS

EPICS
Singles: 7-inch
KIM (101 "Wild One") 75-100 62
(500 made.)
Members: Walter Smith; Everett Norris; Mike Mathis; Ed Thacker; Tommy.

EPICS
Singles: 7-inch
ATHENS (202 "On the Rocks") 10-20 62

EPICS
Singles: 7-inch
FULLER (2680 "Cruel World") 5-10 65
JONI 15-25 63-64
MERCURY (72283 "Bells Are Ringing") 30-40 64
ZEN (202 "Louie Come Home") 5-10 65

EPICS
Singles: 7-inch
BRIDGE TOWN (100 "We Are Made As One") 25-35 69

EPICS Featuring Jeannie
Singles: 7-inch
DANTE (3004 "So Many Times") 50-100 60

EPICUREANS
Singles: 7-inch
IGL (113 "Baby Be Mine") 20-25 66
UA (551 "Break Out and Run") 8-12 69
Also see HIGHWAY

EPISODE SIX
Singles: 7-inch
CHAPTER ONE (2902 "Lucky Sunday") .... 20-30 '60s
COMPASS (7007 "Morning Dew") 5-10 67
ELEKTRA (45617 "Baby, Baby, Baby") 5-10 67
W.B. (5851 "Here, There & Everywhere") 5-10 66

EPISODES
Singles: 7-inch
FOUR SEASONS (1014 "Where Is My Love") 100-200 60
(Identification number shown since no selection number is used.)

EPITOME
(Epitome of Sound)
Singles: 7-inch
KAMA SUTRA (265 "Sleep") 5-10 69
MONA LEE (219 "Flower Power") 5-10 68
SANDBAG (101 "You Don't Love Me") .... 25-35 '60s

EPP, Al
Singles: 7-inch
WILDCAT (0018 "Breakin' My Heart") 40-60 59

EPPERSON, Don
Singles: 7-inch
AMARET (116 "Butch Cassidy and the Sundance Kid") 4-6 70
EXCEL (132 "You're Gone Again") 75-125
SIDEWALK (933 "Please Mrs. Peckingpaw") 10-20 68

EPPS, Charles
Singles: 7-inch
BROSH (800 "Rock with the Boogie") 15-25 62
HILLTOP (913 "Rock with the Boogie") 50-100

EPPS, Earl
Singles: 7-inch
MINOR (103 "Be-Bop Blues") 700-900 57

EPPS, Preston *P&R '59*
("Lord Preston Epps")
Singles: 7-inch
ADMIRAL (901 "Bongo Express") 5-10 65
DONNA (1367 "Mister Bongos") 5-10 62
EMBASSY (203 "Rockin' in the Congo") 8-12 62
JO JO (107 "Afro Mania") 5-10 69
MAGNET (801 "Bongo Shout") 5-10 65
MAJESTY (1300 "Bongo Boogie") 8-12 60
ORIGINAL SOUND (4 "Bongo Rock") 10-20 59
(Monaural.)
ORIGINAL SOUND (4 "Bongo Rock") 30-40 59
(Stereo.)
ORIGINAL SOUND (9 "Bongo Bongo Bongo") 10-15 60
ORIGINAL SOUND (14 "Bongo in the Congo") 10-15 60
ORIGINAL SOUND (17 "Bongo Rocket") 10-15 61
POLO (214 "Say Yeah!!") 5-10 65
POLO (218 "Bongo Rock 1965") 5-10 65
TOP RANK (2067 "Blue Bongo") 10-15 60
TOP RANK (2091 "Bongo Hop") 10-15 60
EPs: 7-inch
ORIGINAL SOUND (1001 "Bongo Rock") 15-25 60
LPs: 10/12-inch
CROWN .... 10-20 '60s
ORIGINAL SOUND (5002 "Bongo Bongo Bongo") 30-40 60
(Monaural.)
ORIGINAL SOUND (5009 "Surfin' Bongos") 25-40 63
(Monaural.)
ORIGINAL SOUND (8851 "Bongo Bongo Bongo") 30-50 60
(Stereo.)
ORIGINAL SOUND (8872 "Surfin' Bongos") 25-50 63
(Stereo.)
TOP RANK (349 "Bongola") 30-50 61
Also see SKYLINERS / Preston Epps

EPSILONS
Singles: 7-inch
HEM (1003 "Mind in a Bind") .... 35-50 '60s
SHRINE (106 "Mad At the World") 150-250 66
STAX (0021 "The Echo") 5-10 69
Members: Lloyd Parkes; Gene McFadden; John Whitehead.
Also see MELVIN, Harold
Also see McFADDEN & WHITEHEAD
Also see TALK OF THE TOWN

EQUADORS
Singles: 7-inch
RCA (4286 "Equadors") 30-40 58
(Single has same number as EP below.)
EPs: 7-inch
RCA (4286 "Equadors") 40-50 58
(Issued with paper sleeve.)
Members: Al Turner; Reginald Grant; Oscar Drummand; Lynn Thomas; R. Foreman.
Also see CARDINALS
Also see MODERN INK SPOTS

EQUADORS
Singles: 7-inch
MIRACLE (7 "You're My Desire") 75-100 61

EQUALLOS
("Featuring Willie Logan")
Singles: 7-inch
M&M (30 "Beneath the Sun") 2000-3000 62

EQUALOS
Singles: 7-inch
MAD (1296 "Patty Patty") 30-40 59

EQUALS *P&R '68*
Singles: 7-inch
BANG (582 "Ain't Got Nothing to Give You") 5-10 71
PRESIDENT 5-10 67-69
RCA (9583 "Baby, Come Back") 5-10 68
LPs: 10/12-inch
LAURIE (2045 "Unequalled") 20-25 67
PRESIDENT 15-25 68-69
RCA (4078 "Baby, Come Back") 10-15 68
Members: Eddy Grant; Derv Gordon.

EQUIPE 84
Singles: 7-inch
IMPERIAL (66266 "29th September") 10-15 67

ERA OF SOUND
Singles: 7-inch
DELTA (2255 "Girl in the Mini Skirt") 15-25 67

ERADICATORS
Singles: 7-inch
PYRAMID (7232 "Reputation") 30-50 66

ERHARDT, Dian
Singles: 7-inch
RCA (7136 "I'll Wait") 10-20 57

ERI, Chiemi
Singles: 78 rpm
FEDERAL (12140 "Pretty Eyed Baby") 8-12 53
Singles: 7-inch
FEDERAL (12140 "Pretty Eyed Baby") 20-30 53

ERIC
(With the Plazas & Ralph Casals Trio)
Singles: 7-inch
PRODUCTION (612 "I Wish...") 400-600 63
(Black label. Black vinyl. Promotional issue.)
PRODUCTION (612 "I Wish...") 500-750 63
(Purple label.)
PRODUCTION (612 "I Wish...") 4-6 91
(Purple vinyl.)

ERIC & CHESSMEN
Singles: 7-inch
KAMA (777 "You Don't Want My Loving") 10-20 65

ERIC & NORSEMEN
Singles: 7-inch
CHROME (103 "Get It On") 15-25 67

ERIC & VIKINGS
Singles: 7-inch
SOULHAWK (10 "Vibrations") .... 10-20 '60s

ERICA
LPs: 10/12-inch
ESP (1099 "You Used to Think") 100-200 68

ERICKSON, Roky
(With the Aliens; with Bleibalien; with Explosives; with Resurrectionists; Roky Erickson Band)
Singles: 7-inch
DYNAMIC 3-5 85
MARS (1000 "Red Temple Prayer")......... 50-75 75
RHINO 3-5 77
SFTRI 3-5 99
TRANCE 3-5 94
Picture Sleeves
RHINO 3-5 77
LPs: 10/12-inch
415 RECORDS 5-10 81
PINK DUST 5-10 86-87
SKYCLAD 5-10 90
Also see 13TH FLOOR ELEVATORS

ERIK
(With the Vikings)
Singles: 7-inch
AMOS (123 "Midnight Rider") 5-10 69
COLISEUM 4-6
EDEN 4-6 73
GAMBIT 4-8
GENERAL INT'L 5-10 65-66
GORDY 4-6 72-73
KARATE (503 "Heaven and Paradise") ... 10-15 65
LPs: 10/12-inch
KARATE (1401 "Sing Along Rock 'N' Roll") 15-20 65
VANGUARD (9267 "Look Where I Am").. 25-35 67
(Monaural.)
VANGUARD (79267 "Look Where I Am") 30-40 67
(Stereo.)

ERIK & SMOKE PONIES
Singles: 7-inch
KAMA SUTRA (227 "I'll Give You More") 10-15 67

ERIKA
LPs: 10/12-inch
ESP (1099 "You Used to Think") 50-100 68
Members: Erica Pomerance; Ron Price; Tom Moore; D. Cooper Smith; Bill Mitchell; Richard Heisler; Michael Ephraim; Lanny Brooks; Dion Brody; Gail Pollard; Trevor Koehler; Craig Justin.

ERLENE & HER GIRLFRIENDS
Singles: 7-inch
OLD TOWN (1150 "Guy Is a Guy") 20-30 63
OLD TOWN (1152 "Casanova") 25-35 63

ERNESTINA
Singles: 78 rpm
JAY-DEE (800 "Special Delivery") 20-30 55
Singles: 7-inch
JAY-DEE (800 "Special Delivery") 40-60 55

ERNIE & CHARLES
LPs: 10/12-inch
("A Cid Symphony") 550-650 69
(Three discs. Colored vinyl: one green, one yellow, one purple. No selection number used. Label name unknown.)
Members: Ernie Fischbach; Charles Ewing; Tom Harris; John Goeckermann; David Goines.

ERNIE & HALOS
Singles: 7-inch
BURG (5801 "Girl from Across the Sea") ...5-10
GUYDEN (2085 "The Girl from Across the Sea") 40-50 63
Also see FOUR DATES

ERNIE'S NUTTY GUITAR
Singles: 7-inch
HEARTBEAT (54 "Don't Fence Me In") ... 10-20 63

ERRICO, Ray
Singles: 78 rpm
MASQUERADE (56003 "Humpty Dumpty Rock") 10-15 56
Singles: 7-inch
MASQUERADE (56003 "Humpty Dumpty Rock") 40-50 56
Session: Honeytones.

ERSKINE, Joe
Singles: 7-inch
ARROW (728 "I Love You So, Oh") 15-25 58
GLOW-HILL (506 "Weak for You Baby") ..15-25 59
Also see LONG, Bobby

ERVIN, Dee
(Big Dee Ervin & Pastels)
Singles: 7-inch
ASTRA (1024 "I Can't Help It") 5-10 66
HULL (738 "I Can't Help It") 10-20 60
SIGNPOST (70009 "Darling, Please Take Me Back") 4-6 72

ERVIN, Frankie
(With the Spears; "Lead Singer of the Shields")
Singles: 7-inch
BLAZE (103 "Hot Rod") 10-15 59
CONTENDER (1316 Wilhelmina") 40-60 59
DON (202 "Why Did It End") 150-200 61
GUYDEN (2010 "Believe Me") 10-15 59
HART (1691 "Some Other Guy") 100-200 60
INDIGO (138 "Detour") 10-20 62
RENDEZVOUS (112 "The Story") 30-50 59
RENDEZVOUS (126 "You Hurt Me") 50-75 60
Also see SHIELDS

ERVIN, Leroy
Singles: 78 rpm
GOLD STAR (628 "Rock Island Blues") ...20-35 47
SWING (415 "Rock Island Blues") 40-60 47

ERVIN, Odie
Singles: 78 rpm
BIG TOWN (111 "She's a Bad Bad Woman") 15-25 54
Singles: 7-inch
BIG TOWN (111 "She's a Bad Bad Woman") 25-50 54

ERVIN, Sid
(Sid King)
Singles: 78 rpm
STARDAY (147 "Who Put the Turtle in Myrtle's Girdle") 15-25 54
Singles: 7-inch
STARDAY (147 "Who Put the Turtle in Myrtle's Girdle") 30-40 54

ERVIN, Tom
Singles: 7-inch
EL RIO (2558 "Down Boy") 50-75

ERVIN SISTERS
Singles: 7-inch
TRI-PHI (1014 "Do It Right") 30-50 62
TRI-PHI (1022 "Every Day's a Holiday") ...40-60 63

ERWIN, Bill
(With the 4 Jacks)
Singles: 7-inch
FAIRLANE (21020 "High School Days") 8-12 62
PEL (501 "High School Days") 20-25 60

ERWIN, Dee
(Difosco Erwin; Big Dee Erwin)
Singles: 7-inch
CUB (9155 "Wrong Direction") 5-10 68
HULL 15-25 59-61
PHIL-L.A. OF SOUL (303 "Linda") 10-15 67
ROULETTE (4596 "Discotheque") 5-10 65
Also see DIFOSCO
Also see ERVIN, Dee
Also see IRWIN, Big Dee

ERWIN, Durward, & Mile'Tones
Singles: 7-inch
CANARY 8-12 65-67
LPs: 10/12-inch
CANARY (6710/6711 "Mod-N-Country") ..15-25 67

ESCAPADES
Singles: 7-inch
POPPY (1002 "Rockin' the Blues") 10-15 59

ESCAPADES
Singles: 7-inch
ARBET (1010 "She's the Kind") 20-30 66
VERVE (10415 "Mad Mad Mad") 10-20 66
XL (356 "She's the Kind") 20-30 66

ESCAPADES
("Escapade's")
Singles: 7-inch
GLOW (87895 "No Body Know's") 50-75
(Identification number shown since no selection number is used.)

ESCHELONS
(Echelons)
Singles: 7-inch
SET=CO (110 "Tears of Life") 40-50
SET=CO ("This Broken Heart") 100-150
(No selection number used.)

ESCORTS
("With Kay")
Singles: 78 rpm
ESSEX (372 "Oh, Honey") 8-12 54
Singles: 7-inch
ESSEX (360 "Yes Indeed") 10-15 54
ESSEX (372 "Oh, Honey") 10-15 54
ESSEX (383 "Paradise Hill") 10-15 55

ESCORTS
Singles: 78 rpm
PREMIUM (407 "Sorry") 50-75 56
Singles: 7-inch
PREMIUM (407 "Sorry") 150-200 56

ESCORTS
Singles: 78 rpm
RCA 10-20 57
Singles: 7-inch
JUDD (1014 "My First Year") 10-15 59
RCA (6834 "Bad Boy") 10-15 57
RCA (6963 "Lonely Man") 10-15 57
RCA (8228 "You Can't Even Be My Friend") 15-25 63
RCA (8327 "Hurt") 8-12 64
SCARLET (4005 "I Will Be Home Again") 15-25 60
WELLS (102 "One More Kiss Good Night") 25-35 59

ESCORTS
(Featuring Roger Booth)
Singles: 7-inch
FREDLO (6311 "I Found Love") 50-75 63
FREDLO (6403 "Wobble Drum") 75-100 64
FREDLO (6416 "Heart of Mine") 15-25 64
SOMA (1144 "The Main Drag") 15-25 60
ZORCH (101 "Space Walk") 30-50 66
ZORCH (102 "I Wonder") 30-50 66
Also see DO's & DON'Ts

ESCORTS
Singles: 7-inch
CORAL (62302 "Gloria") 40-60 62
(Blue label.)
CORAL (62302 "Gloria") 30-50 62
(Orange Label.)
CORAL (62317 "Gaudeamus") 50-75 62
(Blue label.)
CORAL (62317 "Gaudeamus") 20-30 62
(Orange label.)
CORAL (62336 "Somewhere") 10-15 62
CORAL (62385 "My Heart Cries for You") 10-15 63
Also see GOLDIE & ESCORTS

ESCORTS
Singles: 7-inch
BOOMERANG (621 "Little Big Horn") 15-25 62

ESCORTS
Singles: 7-inch
DATE (1609 "S.O.S.") 5-10 68
TEO (105 "Big Boy Pete") 10-15 66
SOUL-O ....5-10 '60s
LPs: 10/12-inch
TEO (5000 "Bring Down the House") 40-60 66
(Shown on cover as also being issued in stereo [LPS-5000], but no stereo copies have been verified.)

ESCORTS
Singles: 7-inch
DE'VOICE 5-10
LONE WOLF (6302 "Cajun Queen") 100-200
Members: Bill Roberts.

ESCOS
("Vocal By Lonnie Carter. Background: George Carter, Wilbert Bell and Winfred Gerald. Music By the Swingin' Rocks")
Singles: 7-inch
ESTA (100 "I'm Lonesome for You") 650-750 59
(Same number also used for a Joe Caldwell release.)
FEDERAL (12380 "Diamonds & Pearls"). 15-25 60
FEDERAL (12430 "Golden Rule of Love") 15-25 61
FEDERAL (12445 "Yes I Need Someone") 15-25 62
FEDERAL (12493 "That's Life") 15-25 63
Members: Lonnie Carter; Don Peark; Richard Parker; Joe Renn; Roland Bradley. Session: George Carter; Wilbert Bell; Winfred Gerald; Swingin' Rocks.
Also see CALDWELL, Joe
Also see CHARMS
Also see FERGUSON, H-Bomb / Escos / Mascots

ESKRIDGE, Murrie
Singles: 7-inch
APEX (7764 "So in Need for Love") 15-25 60

ESQUERITA
Singles: 7-inch
CAPITOL (1075 "Hey Miss Lucy") 50-75 58
(Promotional issue only.)
CAPITOL (4007 "Oh Baby") 50-75 58
CAPITOL (4058 "Rockin' the Joint") 50-75 58
CAPITOL (4145 "Laid Off") 50-75 59
Picture Sleeves
CAPITOL (1075 "Hey Miss Lucy 750-1000 58
(Promotional issue only.)
LPs: 10/12-inch
CAPITOL (1186 "Esquerita") 300-500 59
Also see REEDER, Eskew

ESQUIRE, Kenny, & Starlites
(George Tindley)
Singles: 78 rpm
EMBER 15-25 56
Singles: 7-inch
EMBER (1011 "They Call Me a Dreamer") 50-100 56
EMBER (1021 "Tears Are Just for Fools") 30-50 56
Also see STARLITES
Also see TINDLEY, George

ESQUIRE BOYS *P&R '53*
(With Kay Karol)
Singles: 78 rpm
DOT 8-10 55
GUYDEN 8-10 54
MEDIA 8-12 55
NICKELODEON 8-10 53
RAINBOW 10-15 52-53
TOP TUNE 5-10 51
Singles: 7-inch
DOT (15380 "Guitar Mambo") 10-20 55
DOT (15433 "Dance with a Rock") 10-20 55
FRANSIL (16 "Frantic Franny") 10-15 61
GUYDEN (601 "St. Louis Blues Walk") 10-20 54
GUYDEN (705 "Rock-a-Beatin' Boogie") . 10-20 54
MEDIA (1004 "Play Me Boogie") 10-20 55
NICKELODEON (102 "Guitar Boogie Shuffle") 10-15 53
(Black vinyl.)
NICKELODEON (102 "Guitar Boogie Shuffle") 25-35 53
(Red vinyl.)
RAINBOW (100 & 200 series) 10-20 52-53
(Black vinyl.)
RAINBOW (100 & 200 series) 30-40 52-53
(Colored vinyl.)
TOP TUNE (447 "Forgetting You") 10-20 51
20TH FOX (110 "Taboo") 10-15 58
Members: Danny Cedrone; Bob Scaltrito.
Also see HALEY, Bill
Also see SQUIRES

ESQUIRE TRIO
Singles: 7-inch
COAST (9005 "They Were Doin' the Mambo") 10-15 55
Members: Bob; Dick; Joe.

ESQUIRERS
Singles: 7-inch
INTERNATIONALE (276 "The Girl in Chinatown") 750-1000 63

ESQUIRES
(Five Tinos)
Singles: 78 rpm
EPIC (9024 "If You Only Knew What a Three Cent Stamp Could Do")........200-300 54
HI-PO (1003 "Only the Angels Know")........300-400 55
Singles: 7-inch
HI-PO (1003 "Only the Angels Know")........3000-4000 55
Also see FIVE TINOS

ESQUIRES
Singles: 7-inch
CAPITOL (72126 "Atlantis")........10-20 63
(Canadian.)
CAPITOL (72137 "Man from Adano")......10-20 63
(Canadian.)

ESQUIRES
Singles: 7-inch
DURCO (1001 "Flashin' Red")........20-30 64
Members: Rick Clingman; Durby Wheeler; Marv Gillum; Jim Thompson.
Also see LAUGHING GRAVY

ESQUIRES
Singles: 7-inch
ALLEY (1023 "Sadie's Ways")........20-30 65
(We have also seen this number as 650 and as 996. We don't yet know which is right.)

ESQUIRES
Singles: 7-inch
CFP (2 "Heartaches Stay the Night")......10-20 65
TOWER (174 "Summertime")........5-10 65

ESQUIRES
Singles: 7-inch
GLENVALLEY (103 "Come On")........20-30 66
GLENVALLEY (104 "Time Don't Mean So Much")........20-30 66
GLENVALLEY (105 "These Are the Tender Years")........20-30 66

ESQUIRES *P&R/R&B '67*
Singles: 7-inch
B&G (7751 "Ain't No Reason")........5-10 69
BUNKY........8-12 67-68
CAPITOL (2650 "Reach Out")........5-10 69
HOT LINE (103 "Henry Ralph")........4-6 72
JU-PAR (104 "Get On Up '76")........4-6 76
LAMARR (1001 "Girls in the City")........5-10 71
LASCO (1101 "The Fish")........4-8 79
NEW WORLD (101 "Stay")........5-10 74
ROCKY RIDGE (403 "Ain't No Reason")......4-6 71
WAND........8-12 68-69
LPs: 10/12-inch
BUNKY (300 "Get on Up & Get Away")....20-25 68
Members: Millard Evans; Gilbert Alvis; Betty Moorer; Sam Pace; Harvey Scales; Gilbert Moorer; Sean Taylor; Alvis Moorer; Danny Reed; Sam Davidson; John Bursey; Ortez Guzman; Clint Mosley.
Also see BOYD, Tim, & Esquires
Also see EDWARDS, Millard
Also see SCALES, Harvey
Also see MOORE, Betty
Also see MOORER, Betty
Also see SHEPPARDS
Also see TAYLOR, Sean

ESQUIRES / Mike St. Shaw & Prophets / Thunder Frog Ensemble
LPs: 10/12-inch
AUDIO FIDELITY (2168 "Where It's At: Live at the Cheetah")........30-50 66
(Monaural.)
AUDIO FIDELITY (6168 "Where It's At: Live at the Cheetah")........40-60 66
(Stereo.)
Members: (Esquires) Jeff Ginman; Dante Renzi; Jay Savino; Danny Mahony; Mike Rubin. (Mike St. Shaw & Prophets) Mike St. Shaw; Ray Garcia; Harold Logan; Danny Taylor; Chuck Hatfield. (Thunder Frog Ensemble) Nichael Orrell; John Porsche; Jack Van Osten; Mark Gauche; Glen Wayne.
Also see ST. SHAW, Mike

ESQUIRES
Singles: 7-inch
COLUMBIA (43815 "It's a Dirty Shame"). 10-20 66

ESQUIRES
Singles: 7-inch
DOT (16954 "She's My Woman")........10-15 66

ESQUIRES
Singles: 7-inch
RAVEN (3 "What Made You Change Your Mind")........15-25 66
ROCKY RIDGE (403 "Dancin' a Hole in the World")........10-20 '60s

ESQUIRES
Singles: 7-inch
CIGAR MAN (79880 "The Show Ain't Over")........5-8 80
PHALANX (1002 "Crazy Horse")........15-25 '60s
SCRATCH........10-20 '60s

ESQUIRES
Singles: 7-inch
STOOP SOUNDS (105 "Why Must I Love You")........125-150 97

ESSENTIALS
Singles: 7-inch
TVR (6201 "Moonlight Rock a Bop")......75-100

ESSEX
Singles: 7-inch
BEST (101 "Cemetery Stomp")........20-30 63

ESSEX *P&R/R&B/LP '63*
Singles: 7-inch
BANG (537 "The Eagle")........5-10 66
ROULETTE........5-10 63-64
LPs: 10/12-inch
ROULETTE (25234 "Easier Said Than Done")........25-35 63
ROULETTE (25235 "A Walkin' Miracle")..25-35 63
ROULETTE (25246 "Young and Lively")..25-35 64
Members: Anita Humes; Walter Vickers; Rodney Taylor; Billie Hill; Rudolph Johnson.
Also see HUMES, Anita

ESSEX, David *P&R '73*
Singles: 7-inch
COLUMBIA........4-6 73-76
RSO (1006 "Oh What a Circus")........3-5 79
UNI (55020 "She's Leaving Home")........5-10 67
Picture Sleeves
COLUMBIA........4-6 73-75
UNI (55020 "She's Leaving Home")........8-12 67
LPs: 10/12-inch
COLUMBIA (CQ-32560 "Rock On")........15-25 74
(Quadraphonic)
COLUMBIA (KC-32560 "Rock On")........15-20 73
COLUMBIA (33289 "David Essex")........8-15 74
COLUMBIA (33813 "All the Fun of the Fair")........8-15 75
MERCURY........5-10 83

ESSEX, Herb, & Walters Sisters
Singles: 7-inch
JO-REE (502 "Come My Little Baby")......20-30 62

ESSQUIRES
Singles: 7-inch
MERIDIAN (6282 "Mission Bells")........50-75 63
(Identification number shown since no selection number is used.)

ESTELLE
(Estelle Bennett)
Singles: 7-inch
LAURIE (3449 "In the Year 2000")........75-100 68
Also see RONETTES

ESTER, Sidney
(With the Dreamers)
Singles: 7-inch
DART (114 "Reach and Get It")........15-25 59
GOLDBAND (1087 "After You've Gone").10-15 59
(Same number used on a Johnny Jano release.)

ESTES, Lindy
Singles: 7-inch
FRATERNITY (872 "Where Will I Go")......20-30 60

ETERNALS *P&R '59*
Singles: 7-inch
COLLECTABLES........3-5
HOLLYWOOD (68 "Rockin' in the Jungle")........40-50 59
(White label.)
HOLLYWOOD (68 "Rockin' in the Jungle")........30-40 59
(Blue label. Has label name at bottom.)
HOLLYWOOD (68 "Rockin' in the Jungle")........20-30 '60s
(Blue label. Has label name at top.)
HOLLYWOOD (68 "Rockin' in the Jungle")........10-20 '60s
(Yellow label. Label name is changed slightly to "Transphonic Hollywood Productions.")
HOLLYWOOD (70 "Babalu's Wedding Day")........15-25 59
(Red or label.)
HOLLYWOOD (70 "Babalu's Wedding Day")........10-15 59
(Blue label.)
LOST NITE........3-5
MUSICTONE (1110 "Babalu's Wedding Day")........8-12 62
MUSICTONE (1111 "Rockin' in the Jungle")........8-12 62
WARWICK (611 "Blind Date")........15-25 61
Members: Charles Girona; Alex Miranda; Fred Hodge; Ernie Sierra; Arnold Torres; George Villanueva.

ETERNALS
Singles: 7-inch
QUALITY (1922 "Hideaway")........15-25 59
(Canadian.)

ETERNITY'S CHILDREN *P&R '68*
Singles: 7-inch
A&M (866 "Wait and See")........5-10 67
LIBERTY (56162 "Alone Again")........4-8 70
TOWER (416 thru 498)........5-10 68-69
Picture Sleeves
TOWER (416 "Mr. Bluebird")........8-12 68
LPs: 10/12-inch
TOWER (5123 "Eternity's Children")........20-25 68
TOWER (5144 "Timeless")........20-25 68
Member: Bruce Blackman.
Also see ALLAN, Davie / Eternity's Children / Main Attraction / Sunrays

ETHICS
Singles: 7-inch
DYNAMIC SOUND (2001 "A Whole Lot of Confusion")........15-25 66
Members: Don Gruender; Mark Miller; Mike Jablonski; Gene Peranich.

ETRIS, Barry
Singles: 7-inch
LEO'S (20012 "I've Met My One and Only")........100-200
SIMS (141 "The Young Ones")........5-10 63
Picture Sleeves
SIMS (141 "The Young Ones")........10-15 63

ETTA & AMELIA
Singles: 7-inch
JO ANN (129 "Teenage Boy")........10-20 61

ETTA & HARVEY *P&R/R&B '60*
Singles: 7-inch
CHESS (1760 "If I Can't Have You")........15-25 60
CHESS (1771 "Spoonful")........15-25 60
COLLECTABLES (3448 "If I Can't Have You")........3-5 '80s
Members: Etta James; Harvey Fuqua.
Also see HARVEY
Also see JAMES, Etta

E-TYPES
Singles: 7-inch
DOT (16864 "I Can't Do It")........5-10 66
LINK (1 "I Can't Do It")........20-25 66
SUNBURST (001 "Love of the Love")......15-20 66
TOWER (325 "Put the Clock Back on the Wall")........10-20 67
UPTOWN (754 "Big City")........10-20 67

ETZEL, Jack
Singles: 7-inch
MONUMENT........10-20 62-64
RAT (45 "Meanwhile at the Convention"). 10-15 64

EUGENE & CYCLONES
Singles: 7-inch
BRYTE (308 "Thunderbird Twist")........10-20 62

EUGGENIO, Sam
Singles: 7-inch
BOFUZ ("Got Caught")........200-300
(Selection number not known.)

EUNIQUES
Singles: 7-inch
JASON SCOTT (06 "Cry, Cry, Cry")........4-8 80
(500 made.)
620 (1006 "Cry Cry Cry")........150-200 63
Also see UNIQUES

EUPHONIOUS WAIL
LPs: 10/12-inch
KAPP (3668 "Euphonius Wail")........35-45 73
Members: Susie Rey; Doug Hoffman; Bart Libby; Gary Violetti; Steve Tracey.

EUPHORIA
Singles: 7-inch
BAND BOX (393 "Somebody Listen")......20-25 '60s
MAINSTREAM (655 "Hungry Women")...10-15 68
Also see WILDFLOWER / Harbinger Complex / Euphoria / Other Side

EUPHORIA
Singles: 7-inch
HERITAGE (831 "You Must Forget")........10-15 71
LPs: 10/12-inch
HERITAGE (35005 "Euphoria")........30-40 71
Member: Tom Pacheco.

EUPHORIA
LPs: 10/12-inch
CAPITOL (363 "A Gift from Euphoria")....40-60 69
Members: William Lincoln; Hamilton Watt.

EUPHORIA
LPs: 10/12-inch
RAINBOW (1003 "Lost in a Trance")....200-300 73

EUPHORIA'S ID
Singles: 7-inch
EADIT (201,365 "Hey Joe")........25-35 67

EUSTICE, Jimmie
Singles: 7-inch
PATRICE (203 "Jennie Lou")........50-75

EUSTIS, Bill
Singles: 7-inch
PARAMOUNT (0032 "Let It Be Known")......4-8 70
R (506 "I'm Sorry You're Gone")........15-25 61

EUSTIS, Sister Elizabeth
Singles: 78 rpm
BATTLE (007 "A Sinner's Plea")........5-10 53
Singles: 7-inch
BATTLE (007 "A Sinner's Plea")........10-15 53

EVANS, Barbara
Singles: 7-inch
PIONEER (7002 "Charlie Wasn't There")..5-10
PIONEER (71874 "Flashlight of Love")......5-10 61
SMASH (1736 "Good Old Days")........5-10 62
RCA (7519 "Souvenirs")........10-15 59
RCA (7634 "Beatnik Daddy")........10-15 59

EVANS, Dale
Singles: 7-inch
RCA (48-0360 "Two-Seated Saddle on a One-Gaited Horse")........10-20 50
RCA (48-0395 "San Angelo")........10-20 50
LPs: 10/12-inch
ALLEGRO (4116)........15-25 '50s
(10-inch LP.)
CAPITOL (2772 "It's Real")........8-15 67
EVON........10-15 '50s
WORD........5-8
Also see ROGERS, Roy

EVANS, Donna
Singles: 7-inch
CHEER (1003 "Foolish Me")........10-20 62
COMET (1050 "Foolish Me")........30-40 63

EVANS, Frank
Singles: 7-inch
NUGGET (1001 "Got to Get Some Money")........100-200 59
STARDAY (645 "Pull Down the Shades Ma")........75-125 63
STARDAY (674 "I've Got a Patent")......50-100 64
STARDAY (719 "Ain't Got Blues")........75-125 65

EVANS, Jackie

Singles: 7-inch

VIDA (0119 "Teasin' Her Hair") 10-15 63

EVANS, Jerry

(With the Off Keys & Deans; with Rhythmairs; with Rhythmaires)

Singles: 7-inch

BUBBLE (1333 "Knock on Wood") 10-20 62
DREAM (5533 "Still In Love with You") 50-75 65
PENNY (201 "Green, Green Grass of Home") 5-10
ROWE (001 "Oh Little Girl") 150-200 62
ROWE (002 "Oh Little Girl") 100-150 62
(Reissue, re-recorded faster version.)
STARFIRE (102 "Knock on Wood") 10-15 62
Also see OFF KEYS

EVANS, Jimmy

(With the Jesters)

Singles: 7-inch

CAVEMAN (502 "The Joint's Really Jumpin'") 500-750 55
CLEARMONT (502 "The Joint's Really Jumpin'") 300-500 55
REBEL ACE 5-10 65
RIVER 5-10 65
RIVERTOWN 4-8 79
SHIMMY (1054 "Messy Bessy") 50-100 60

EVANS, Joey

Singles: 7-inch

DOLA (5091 "I'm in Love with Mary Ann") 10-15 62

EVANS, Larry

(James Wayne)

Singles: 78 rpm

FABOR 10-20 54-56

Singles: 7-inch

FABOR (4001 "Patricia") 25-50 54
FABOR (4008 "Henpecked") 25-50 56
FABOR (4009 "Junco Returns") 25-50 56
Also see WAYNE, James

EVANS, Leon

Singles: 7-inch

DE'BESTH (1111 "Satellite Beep Bop") ... 10-20 '60s

EVANS, Marion

Singles: 7-inch

BULLSEYE (1018 "Bandit") 10-15 58

EVANS, Mark

Singles: 7-inch

TAB (28 "Gang's House") 500-750
(Pink label. At least one source shows this number as 401. Also issued as by Tommy Beckham.)
TAB (101 "It's Love") 100-200
Also see BECKHAM, Tommy

EVANS, Mickey

Singles: 78 rpm

ARCADE (141 "Crazy in Love") 5-10 56

Singles: 7-inch

ARCADE (141 "Crazy in Love") 10-20 56
FINE (2657 "You're No Good") 50-75 57

EVANS, Mill

Singles: 7-inch

CONSTELLATION (170 "Things Won't Be the Same") 10-15 66
SHARP (6041 "Don't Forget About Me") . 10-20 '60s

EVANS, Paul *P&R '59*

(With the Curls)

Singles: 7-inch

ATCO (6138 "Beat Generation") 10-20 59
ATCO (6170 "Long Gone") 10-20 60
BIG TREE 4-6 75
CARLTON (539 thru 558) 10-20 61
CINNAMON INT'L 3-5 80
COLLECTABLES .... 3-5 '80s
COLUMBIA 4-8 68
DECCA (30680 "I Think About You All the Time") 10-20 58
DOT 4-6 73
EPIC 5-10 64-65
GUARANTEED (200 thru 213) 10-20 59-60
KAPP 8-12 62-63
LAURIE (3571 "Think Summer") 4-6 71
LAURIE (3581 "The Man in a Row Boat") 4-6 71
MERCURY 4-6 74-75
MUSICOR 3-5 77
RCA (6806 "What Do You Know") 10-20 57
RANWOOD 4-6 72
SPRING 4-6 78-79

EPs: 7-inch

KAPP (1346 "21 Years in a Tennessee Jail") 10-15 64
(Promotional issue only.)

LPs: 10/12-inch

CARLTON (129 "Hear Paul Evans in Your Home Tonight") 25-40 61
(Monaural.)
CARLTON (129 "Hear Paul Evans in Your Home Tonight") 30-50 61
(Stereo.)
CARLTON (130 "Folk Songs of Many Lands") 25-40 61
(Monaural.)
CARLTON (130 "Folk Songs of Many Lands") 30-50 61
(Stereo.)
GUARANTEED (1000 "Fabulous Teens") 25-40 60
(Monaural.)
GUARANTEED (1000 "Fabulous Teens") 30-50 60
(Stereo.)
KAPP (1346 "21 Years in a Tennessee Jail") 15-25 64
(Monaural.)
KAPP (1475 "Another Town, Another Jail") 15-25 66
(Monaural.)
KAPP (3346 "21 Years in a Tennessee Jail") 20-30 64
(Stereo.)
KAPP (3475 "Another Town, Another Jail") 20-30 66
Members (Curls): Sue Singleton; Sue Terry.
Also see CARTEY, Ric / Paul Evans

EVANS, Shelly

Singles: 7-inch

SILVER LEAF (2100 "Ain't It the Truth") ... 15-25 60

EVANS, Skip

Singles: 7-inch

QUALITY (1765 "Dusty Road") 10-20 64
QUALITY (1824 "Lemon Merengue") 10-20 64
(Canadian.)
TWIRL (2019 "Dusty Road") 10-20 64
(U.S. release.)

EVANS, Sticks, & House Rockets

Singles: 7-inch

HAMILTON (50032 "Mad Dog") 8-12 59
ZEBRA (118 "Zulu's Court") 15-25 57
Also see HALEY, Bill

EVANS, Sue

(With the Solitaires; with Richard Wess & Orchestra)

Singles: 7-inch

CADILLAC (137 "Try Baby") 20-30 54
CADILLAC (2001 "Hey Shorty") 20-30 60
MADISON (148 "I Returned the Ring") 10-20 61
20TH FOX (199 "Rumble at Joe's") 10-20 60

Picture Sleeves

20TH FOX (199 "Rumble at Joe's") 25-35 60

EVANS, Terry

(With Maxwell Davis & Orchestra)

Singles: 7-inch

KAYO (5102 "Just 'Cause") 50-100 61

EVANS, Tony

Singles: 7-inch

CAMERON (1 "I'm Looking Over") 100-150

EVELS

Singles: 7-inch

TRA=X (14 "The Magic of Love") 30-40

EVENTUALS

Singles: 7-inch

OKEH (7142 "Charlie Chan") 15-25 61

Picture Sleeves

OKEH (7142 "Charlie Chan") 30-40 61

EVER-READY SINGERS

Singles: 78 rpm

CAPITOL 10-15 54

Singles: 7-inch

CAPITOL (2763 "One Day When I Was Walking") 15-25 54
CAPITOL (2867 "This Heart of Mine") 15-25 54
CAPITOL (2984 "I Don't Care What the World May Do") 20-30 54

EVERETT, Bettie, & Daylighters

("Al Perkins Band, Mickey on Sax"; Betty Everett)

Singles: 7-inch

C.J. (611 Please Come Back") 20-30 61
Also see DAYLIGHTERS
Also see EVERETT, Betty

EVERETT, Betty *P&R/R&B '63*

Singles: 7-inch

ABC (10829 thru 10978) 5-10 66-67
C.J. (619 "Your Lovin' Arms") 15-25 61
(Credits Earl Hooker, Al Perkins & Betty Everett.)
C.J. (619 "Happy I Long to Be") 8-12 64
(Credits Betty Everett.)
C.J. (674 "Days Are Gone") .... 5-10 '60s
COBRA (5019 "My Love") 30-40 57
COBRA (5024 "Ain't Gonna Cry") 20-30 58
COBRA (5031 "Weep No More") 20-30 59
COLLECTABLES .... 3-5 '80s
DOTTIE (1126 "Tell Me Darling") 15-25 64
ERIC .... 4-6 '70s
FANTASY 4-8 70-74
OLDIES 45 .... 4-8 '60s
ONE-DERFUL (4806 "Your Love Is Important to Me") 10-15 62
ONE-DERFUL (4823 "I'll Be There") 10-15 63
SOUND STAGE 7 (1520 "My Love to Lean On") 4-6 76
U.A. (1200 "True Love") 3-6 78
UNI 5-10 68-69
VEE-JAY (513 thru 628) 10-15 63-64
VEE-JAY (683 thru 716) 8-12 65-66

LPs: 10/12-inch

FANTASY (9447 "Love Rhymes") 8-10 74
FANTASY (9484 "Happy Endings") 8-10 75
SUNSET (5220 "I Need You So") 10-15 68
UNI (73048 "There'll Come a Time") 10-15 69
VEE-JAY (1077 "It's in His Kiss") 35-50 63
VEE-JAY (1122 "The Very Best of Betty Everett") 25-35 65
Session: Blossoms; Earl Hooker All Stars.
Also see BLOSSOMS
Also see BUTLER, Jerry, & Betty Everett
Also see EVERETT, Bettie, & Daylighters
Also see HOOKER, Earl
Also see MORRIS & BETTY

EVERETT, Betty / Ketty Lester

LPs: 10/12-inch

GRAND PRIX (125 "Betty Everett and Ketty Lester") 10-15 64
Also see LESTER, Ketty

EVERETT, Betty / Impressions

LPs: 10/12-inch

CUSTOM (1031 "Betty Everett and the Impressions") 10-15 64
Also see EVERETT, Betty
Also see IMPRESSIONS

EVERETT, Bracy

Singles: 7-inch

ATLANTIC (2013 "I Want Your Love") 10-15 59
Session: King Curtis.
Also see KING CURTIS

EVERETT, Keith

Singles: 7-inch

MERCURY (72854 "The Chant") 8-12 68
TMP-TING (118 "Don't You Know") 10-20 66
TMP-TING (121 "Lookin' So Fine") 10-20 66

EVERETT, Vince

(Marvin Benefield)

Singles: 7-inch

ABC-PAR (10313 "Such a Night") 30-50 62
ABC-PAR (10360 "I Ain't Gonna Be Your Low Down Dog No More") 30-40 62
ABC-PAR (10472 "Baby Let's Play House") 30-40 63
ABC-PAR (10624 "To Have, to Hold and Let Go") 20-30 64
SAGA (1002 "Don't Worry") 25-50 58
TOWN (1964 "Buttercup") 10-20 60

EPs: 7-inch

ROCKIN' (005 "The Presley Sound of Vince Everett") 10-20
Also see BENEFIELD, Marvin

EVERETTE, Dewell

Singles: 7-inch

JED INT'L (0001 "Janie Mae") 40-60 62

EVERETTE, Leon *C&W '77*

Singles: 7-inch

ORLANDO 3-5 79-86
RCA 3-5 80-84
TRUE 5-10 77

LPs: 10/12-inch

ORLANDO 5-10 86
RCA 5-10 81-84
TRUE (1002 "Goodbye King of Rock & Roll") 15-25 77
(With 18" x 23" bonus poster of Elvis Presley.)
TRUE (1002 "Goodbye King of Rock & Roll") 10-15 77
(Without poster.)

EVERGLADES

Singles: 7-inch

BVP (112577 "While Sitting in the Chapel") 75-150 63
SYMBOL (920 "Limbo Lucky") 20-30 62
Also see HAYWARD, Jerry, & Everglades

EVERGREEN BLUE SHOES

Singles: 7-inch

AMOS (115 "Johnny B. Goode") 5-10 69

LPs: 10/12-inch

AMOS 10-20 69
MUSIC FACTORY (12004 "Ballad of Evergreen Blue Shoes") 10-20 68
Member: Chet McCracken.
Also see HELP

EVERGREENS

Singles: 78 rpm

CHART (605 "Very Truly Yours") 20-30 55

Singles: 7-inch

CHART (605 "Very Truly Yours") 100-150 55

EVERHART, Bobby

Singles: 7-inch

MONUMENTAL (515 "Boney Maronie") ... 30-50 65

EVERLY BROTHERS *P&R/R&B/C&W '57*

Singles: 78 rpm

CADENCE (1315 thru 1355) 40-80 57-58
CADENCE (1364 "Take a Message to Mary") 150-200 59
COLUMBIA (21496 "The Sun Keeps Shining") 50-100 56

Singles: 7-inch

BARNABY 5-10 70-76
CADENCE (1315 "Bye Bye Love") 15-25 57
CADENCE (1337 "Wake Up Little Susie") 15-25 57
CADENCE (1342 "This Little Girl of Mine") 15-25 58
CADENCE (1348 "All I Have to Do Is Dream") 15-25 58
(Silver and maroon label.)
CADENCE (1348 "All I Have to Do Is Dream") 10-20 61
(Red label with black print.)
CADENCE (1348 "All I Have to Do Is Dream") 50-75 61
(Colored vinyl.)
CADENCE (1350 "Bird Dog") 15-25 58
CADENCE (1355 "Problems") 15-25 58
CADENCE (1364 "Take a Message to Mary") 15-25 59
CADENCE (1369 "('Til) I Kissed You") 15-25 59
CADENCE (1376 "Let It Be Me") 15-25 60
CADENCE (1380 "When Will I Be Loved") 15-25 60
CADENCE (1388 "Like Strangers") 15-25 60
CADENCE (1429 "I'm Here to Get My Baby Out of Jail") 15-25 62
COLUMBIA (21496 "The Sun Keeps Shining") 400-500 56
(Red label.)
COLUMBIA (21496 "The Sun Keeps Shining") 150-250 56
(White label. Promotional issue only.)
ERIC .... 4-6 '70s
MERCURY 3-5 84-86
RCA 4-8 72-73
W.B. (5151 "Cathy's Clown") 10-20 60
(Monaural.)

W.B. (S-5151 "Cathy's Clown") ... 20-30 60
(Stereo.)
W.B. (5151 "Cathy's Clown") ... 50-100 60
(Gold vinyl. Promotional issue only.)
W.B. (5163 "So Sad") ... 10-20 60
(Black vinyl.)
W.B. (5163 "So Sad") ... 50-100 60
(Gold vinyl.)
W.B. (5199 "Ebony Eyes") ... 10-20 61
(Black vinyl.)
W.B. (5199 "Ebony Eyes") ... 50-100 61
(Gold vinyl. Promotional issue only.)
W.B. (5220 thru 5833) ... 10-20 61-66
W.B. (5857 "Fifi the Flea") ... 20-25 67
(Credits "Don Everly Brother" on one side, and "Phil Everly Brother" on the flip.)
W.B. (5901 thru 7425) ... 8-12 67-70

Picture Sleeves

CADENCE (1337 "Wake Up Little Susie") ... 75-125 57
CADENCE (1355 "Problems") ... 25-50 58
CADENCE (1369 "(Til') I Kissed You") ... 25-50 59
CADENCE (1376 "Let It Be Me") ... 25-50 60
W.B. (5151 "Cathy's Clown") ... 40-60 60
W.B. (5163 "So Sad") ... 40-60 60
W.B. (5199 "Ebony Eyes") ... 40-60 61
W.B. (5220 "Temptation") ... 15-25 61
W.B. (5250 "Crying in the Rain") ... 15-25 62
W.B. (5273 "That's Old Fashioned") ... 15-25 62
W.B. (5297 "Don't Ask Me to Be Friends") ... 15-25 62
W.B. (5649 "Love Is Strange") ... 100-150 65
MERCURY ... 3-6 84

EPs: 7-inch

CADENCE (3 "Rockin' with the Everly Brothers") ... 25-35 61
(Has single sheet cardboard insert/cover. Compact 33.)
CADENCE (4 "Dream with the Everly Brothers") ... 25-35 61
(Has single sheet cardboard insert/cover. Compact 33.)
CADENCE (104 "Everly Bros., Vol. 1") ... 30-50 57
CADENCE (105 "Everly Bros., Vol. 2") ... 30-50 57
CADENCE (107 "The Everly Brothers") ... 30-50 58
CADENCE ("Songs Our Daddy Taught Us") ... 100-150 58
(White, typewritten label. No selection number shown, only identification numbers "K80H-1719/20." Labeled "Cadence Disc Jockey Pressing." Promotional issue only.)
CADENCE (108/109/110 "Songs Our Daddy Taught Us") ... 30-50 58
(Price is for any of three volumes.)
CADENCE (111 "The Everly Brothers") ... 25-50 59
CADENCE (118 "The Everly Brothers") ... 25-35 59
CADENCE (121 "Very Best of The Everly Brothers") ... 25-35 60
W.B. (120 "Everly Brothers Show") ... 15-25 70
(Juke box issue only. Includes title strips.)
W.B. (135 "Souvenir Sampler") ... 100-125 61
(Don and Phil discussing *The Everly Brothers - Both Sides of an Evening*. Has an LP discount coupon on sleeve. Promotional issue only.)
W.B. (1381-1 "Foreverly Yours") ... 15-25 60
(Black vinyl.)
W.B. (1381-1 "Foreverly Yours") ... 35-50 60
(Colored vinyl. Promotional issue only.)
W.B. (1381-2 "Especially for You") ... 15-25 60
W.B. (1471 "Golden Hits") ... 15-25 62
(Juke box issue only. Includes title strips.)
W.B. (5501 "The Everly Brothers Plus Two Oldies") ... 15-25 61

LPs: 10/12-inch

ARISTA ... 8-12 84
BARNABY (350 "Original Greatest Hits") 10-15 70
BARNABY (15008 "History of the Everly Brothers") ... 15-20 73
(Two discs.)
BARNABY (30260 "End of an Era") ... 10-15 71
BARNABY (4000 series) ... 6-10 77
BARNABY (6006 "Greatest Hits") ... 8-12
CADENCE (3003 "The Everly Brothers") ... 75-125 58
CADENCE (3016 "Songs Our Daddy Taught Us") ... 50-75 58
CADENCE (3025 "The Everly Brothers' Best") ... 75-100 59
(Blue cover.)
CADENCE (3040 "The Fabulous Style of the Everly Brothers") ... 50-75 60
CADENCE (3059 "Folk Songs") ... 35-40 63
CADENCE (3062 "15 Everly Hits") ... 45-65 63
CADENCE (25040 "The Fabulous Style of the Everly Brothers") ... 75-100 60
(Stereo.)
CADENCE (25059 "Folk Songs") ... 35-40 63
(Stereo.)
CADENCE (25062 "15 Everly Hits") ... 45-65 63
(Stereo.)
CANDLELITE ... 10-15 76
EXCELSIOR ... 5-10
HARMONY ... 10-12 68-70
HAPPY DAYS ... 5-10
MERCURY ... 5-10 84-86
PAIR ... 8-12 84
PASSPORT ... 5-12 84-86
RCA ... 8-12 72
RHINO (214 "All They Had to Do Was Dream") ... 5-10 85
RHINO (258 "Heartache 'n Harmonies") ... 8-10 85
(Picture disc.)
RONCO ... 8-10
TIME-LIFE ... 10-15 86
W.B. (1381 "It's Everly Time") ... 30-50 60
W.B. (1395 "A Date with the Everly Brothers") ... 50-100 60
(With gatefold cover and eight "wallet pix" cut-out photos.)
W.B. (1395 "A Date with the Everly Brothers") ... 20-40 61
(With standard cover.)
W.B. (1418 "Songs for Both Sides of an Evening") ... 20-40 61
W.B. (1430 "Instant Party") ... 20-40 62
W.B. (1471 "Golden Hits") ... 20-40 62
W.B. (1483 "Christmas with the Everly Brothers") ... 20-40 61
W.B. (1513 "Great Country Hits") ... 20-40 63
W.B. (1554 "Very Best of the Everly Brothers") ... 20-40 64
(Yellow cover. Gray label.)
W.B. (1554 "Very Best of the Everly Brothers") ... 10-15 70
(Blue cover. Gray label.)
W.B. (1554 "Very Best of the Everly Brothers") ... 8-12 72
(Blue cover. "Skyline" label.)
W.B. (1578 "Rock 'N Soul") ... 20-35 65
W.B. (1585 "Gone Gone Gone") ... 20-35 65
W.B. (1605 "Beat and Soul") ... 15-25 65
W.B. (1620 "In Our Image") ... 35-45 66
W.B. (1646 "Two Yanks in London") ... 15-25 66
(With the Hollies.)
W.B. (1676 "The Hit Sound of the Everly Brothers") ... 15-20 67
W.B. (1708 "Everly Brothers Sing") ... 15-25 67
W.B. (1752 "Roots") ... 15-25 68
W.B. (1858 "The Everly Brothers Show") . 12-15 70

Promotional LPs

W.B. (134 "The Everly Brothers") ... 300-500 61
(Single-sided, 10-inch LP with five tracks from *The Everly Brothers - Both Sides of an Evening* [WB 1418]. Promotional issue only.)
W.B. (1381 "It's Everly Time") ... 50-100 60
W.B. (1395 "A Date with the Everly Brothers") ... 75-100 60
(With gatefold cover and eight "wallet pix" cut-out photos.)
W.B. (1418 "Both Sides of an Evening") .. 50-75 61
W.B. (1430 "Instant Party") ... 50-75 62
W.B. (1471 "Golden Hits") ... 50-75 62
W.B. (1483 "Christmas with the Everly Brothers") ... 50-75 61
W.B. (1513 "Great Country Hits") ... 40-60 63
W.B. (1554 "Very Best of the Everly Brothers") ... 40-60 64
(Yellow cover.)
W.B. (1578 "Rock 'N Soul") ... 40-60 65
W.B. (1585 "Gone Gone Gone") ... 40-60 65
W.B. (1605 "Beat 'N Soul") ... 35-50 65
W.B. (1620 "In Our Image") ... 35-50 66
W.B. (1646 "Two Yanks in London") ... 35-50 66
W.B. (1676 "The Hit Sound of the Everly Brothers") ... 35-50 67
W.B. (1708 "The Everly Brothers Sing") ... 35-50 67
W.B. (1752 "Roots") ... 25-40 68
W.B. (1858 "The Everly Brothers Show") . 25-35 70

Members: Don Everly; Phil Everly. Session: Chet Atkins.
Also see ATKINS, Chet
Also see CASH, Johnny, Rosanne Cash & Everly Brothers
Also see EVERLY, Don
Also see EVERLY, Phil
Also see HOLLIES

EVERLY BROTHERS & BEACH BOYS

Singles: 7-inch

CAPITOL (44297 "Don't Worry Baby") ... 3-5 88

Picture Sleeves

CAPITOL (44297 "Don't Worry Baby") ... 3-5 88
Also see BEACH BOYS

EVERPRESENT FULLNESS

Singles: 7-inch

WHITE WHALE ... 5-10 66-67

LPs: 10/12-inch

WHITE WHALE (7132 "Everpresent Fullness") ... 20-30 70
Member: Paul Johnson.
Also see BELAIRS

EVERYTHING IS EVERYTHING — P&R '69

Singles: 7-inch

VANGUARD APOSTOLIC (35082 "Witchi Tai To") ... 4-8 69

LPs: 10/12-inch

VANGUARD ... 15-20 69
Members: Chris Hill; Danny Weiss.

EVIL

Singles: 7-inch

BRIDGE SOCIETY ... 10-15
CAPITOL (2038 "Whatcha Gonna Do") ... 10-20 67
LIVING LEGEND (108 "Whatcha Gonna Do") ... 20-40 67
Members: John Doyle; Stan Kinchen; Al Banyai; Doug Romanella; Larry O'Connell; George Hall; Mike Hughes.

EVIL ENCORPORATED

Singles: 7-inch

SCENE (101 "Hey You") ... 15-25 67
SCENE (102 "Baby It's You") ... 15-25 67

EVIL "I"

Singles: 7-inch

BRIDGE SOCIETY (25-66 "Can't Live Without You") ... 15-25 '60s

EVOLUTION

Singles: 7-inch

LAURIE (3579 "Sing Me a Song") ... 75-125 71

EWING, John, & Streamliners

Singles: 7-inch

LARK (459 "Tavern in the Town") ... 10-15 58
Session: John Ewing; Joe Graves; Mel Moore; Buddy Collette; Bill Green; René Hall; Eddie Beal; Red Callender; Bill Douglass.
Also see CALLENDER, Red
Also see COLLETTE, Buddy
Also see EWING, Streamline
Also see GRAVES, Joe

EWING, Streamline

Singles: 7-inch

EDSEL (784 "Soul Time") ... 10-15 60
Also see EWING, John, & Streamliners

EWING SISTERS

Singles: 78 rpm

CROWN (146 "Tica-ti Tica-Tay") ... 8-12 55

Singles: 7-inch

CROWN (146 "Tica-ti Tica-Tay") ... 15-20 55

EX SAVEYONS

Singles: 7-inch

SMOKE (600 "I Don't Love You No More") ... 15-25 '60s
SMOKE (609 "Where Do I Go from Here") ... 15-25 '60s

EXCALIBURS

Singles: 7-inch

TRENT TOWN (1010 "Xmas Dreaming") ... 150-200
TRENT TOWN (1017 "Christmas Dreaming") ... 75-100

EXCELLENTS — P&R '62

Singles: 7-inch

BLAST (205 "Coney Island Baby") ... 40-50 62
(Red label.)
BLAST (205 "Coney Island Baby") ... 10-20 62
(Red and white label.)
BLAST (205 "Coney Island Baby") ... 50-75 62
(White label. Promotional issue only.)
BLAST (205 "Coney Island Baby") ... 15-25 65
(Purple label.)
COLLECTABLES ... 3-5
MERMAID (106 "Love No One But You") ... 150-200 61
(Label pictures a mermaid.)
MERMAID (106 "Love No One But You") 25-50 64
(Mermaid not pictured.)

LPs: 10/12-inch

ON THE CORNER (135 "Excellents Go Bob Bob Bobbin' Along") ... 10-15 90
(Black vinyl. 1000 made.)
Also see EXCELLONS

EXCELLENTS
(Ultimates)

Singles: 7-inch

BLAST (207 "I Hear a Rhapsody") ... 35-55 63
(Not the same artist as on the preceding Blast issues. This group is really the Ultimates.)
Also see ULTIMATES

EXCELLONS
(Excellents)

Singles: 7-inch

BOBBY (601 "Helene") ... 20-30 64
(First issue.)
OLD TIMER (601 "Helene") ... 8-12 64
(Black vinyl.)
OLD TIMER (601 "Helene") ... 10-15 64
(Blue vinyl.)
Also see EXCELLENTS

EXCELS

Singles: 78 rpm

CENTRAL ... 40-50 57

Singles: 7-inch

CENTRAL (2601 "Baby Doll") ... 40-50 57
RELIC (1007 "Baby Doll") ... 5-10 65

EXCELS — P&R '61

Singles: 7-inch

GONE (5094 "My Foolish Heart") ... 15-25 60
RSVP (111 "Can't Help Lovin' That Girl of Mine") ... 50-75 61

EXCELS

Singles: 7-inch

GIBSON (210 "Let's Dance") ... 100-150 65

EXCELSIOR NORFOLK QUARTETTE

Singles: 78 rpm

BLACK SWAN (2060 "Jelly Roll Blues") 50-100 1922
PARAMOUNT (12131 "Jelly Roll Blues") ... 50-100 1922
Member: James C. Brown.
Also see EXCELSIOR QUARTETTE

EXCELSIOR QUARTETTE

Singles: 78 rpm

GENNETT (4881 "Jelly Roll Blues") ... 50-100 1922
OKEH (8033 "Roll Them Bones") ... 50-75 1922
OKEH (8035 "Over the Green Hill") ... 50-75 1922
OKEH (8038 "If Hearts Win") ... 50-75 1922
OKEY (Except 4881) ... 15-25
OKEY (4881 "Jelly Roll Blues") ... 25-50
STARR (9250 "Jelly Roll Blues") ... 25-50
Member: James C. Brown.
Also see EXCELSIOR NORFOLK QUARTETTE

EXCEPTIONS

Singles: 7-inch

CAMEO (378 "Down by the Ocean") ... 5-10 65
PRO (1 "Down by the Ocean") ... 40-50 63
Member: Jimmy Ellis.
Also see MOODS

EXCEPTIONS

Singles: 7-inch

CAPITOL (2046 thru 5982) ... 8-12 67
MERCURY (72562 "Ask Me if I Care") ... 8-12 66
QUILL (114 "Girl from New York") ... 15-25 67
Members: Peter Cetera; Marty Grebb; Kal David; Jimmy Vincent; Billy Herman.
Also see BUCKINGHAMS
Also see DAVID, Kal, & Exceptions

EXCEPTIONS

EPs: 7-inch

FLAIR (6444 "Rock & Roll Mass")........... 20-30 67

EXCEPTIONS

Singles: 7-inch

NIGHT OWL (67123 "Candy").................. 10-20 67

EXCEPTIONS

Singles: 7-inch

TRUMP (354 "Still on the Run") 15-25

EXCHEQUERS

Singles: 7-inch

BOOM (115 "Is There Some Girl") 20-40 65
(Green vinyl.)
Members: Arnie Bacon; Tom Hake; Rick Blomquist; Dan Woodard.

EXCITERS *P&R/R&B '62*

Singles: 7-inch

BANG (515 "A Little Bit of Soap") 5-10 65
BANG (518 "Weddings Make Me Cry") ... 15-25 66
ROULETTE (4591 thru 4632).....................5-10 65
RCA (9633 "If You Want My Love") 15-25 68
RCA (9723 "Blowing Up My Mind")......... 15-25 68
SHOUT (205 thru 214)............................5-10 66-67
TODAY (1002 "Life, Love & Peace") 4-8 70
U.A. (544 thru 830) 5-10 62-65

Picture Sleeves

ROULETTE (4591 "I Want You to Be My Boy")... 10-20 65

LPs: 10/12-inch

RCA (4211 "Caviar & Chitlins") 20-30 69
ROULETTE (25326 "The Exciters")......... 15-25 66
SUNSET... 10-12 70
TODAY (1001 "Black Beauty")................ 10-15 71
U.A. (3264 "Tell Him")............................ 30-40 63
(Monaural.)
U.A. (6264 "Tell Him").............................. 40-50 63
(Stereo.)
Members: Brenda Reid; Herb Rooney; Carol Johnson; Lillian Walker.
Also see MASTERETTES

EXCITING AVIANTES

Singles: 7-inch

SCOTTY (645 "My Plea") 100-200 65

EXCITING INVICTAS
(Exciting Invicta's)

Singles: 7-inch

KINGSTON (427 "I Don't Care") 300-400 60
(Black vinyl.)
KINGSTON (427 "I Don't Care") 500-750 60
(Red vinyl.)
STOOP SOUNDS (505 "I Don't Care").. 75-125 97
Members: Jimmy Noon; Ron Brennan; Jim Baumbauch; Don Humble; Emmett Smith.
Also see DEL CHONTAYS
Also see INTENTIONS

EXCLUSIVES
(With the Arcs)

Singles: 7-inch

K&C (103 "My Girl Friend").................. 100-150 58

EXECS

Singles: 7-inch

FARGO (1055 "Walking in the Rain") .. 200-300 64

EXECUTIONERS

Singles: 7-inch

ACTION (500 "Don't Put Me On") 20-30 65
ACTION (502 "Dead End") 10-20 65
SUNBURST (108 "Guillotine")................... 10-20 65
SWAN (4259 "I Want the Rain")..................5-10 66

EXECUTIVE FOUR
(With the Jesse Powell Orchestra)

Singles: 7-inch

LU MAR (202 "You Are")....................... 75-125 '60s
Also see POWELL, Jesse

EXECUTIVES

Singles: 7-inch

BLACK HOLE (1981 "A Girl Like You") ... 25-45 '60s
EXPLOSIVE (3621-8 "River of Tears") 150-200 63
(Reissued as by the Challengers.)
REVENGE (5003 "Why")................. 1000-1500 63
(First issue.)
Also see CHALLENGERS

EXILES

Singles: 7-inch

REM (358 "Stay with Me")........................25-35 65

EXITS *R&B '67*

Singles: 7-inch

GEMINI (1004 "Under the Street Lamp") .10-15 67
KAPP (2028 "I'm So Glad") 15-25 69

EXODUS
(Four Epics)

Singles: 7-inch

WAND (11248 "M&M") 100-125 72
(Black and white label. Promotional issue only.)
WAND (11248 "M&M") 30-50 72
(Multi-color label.)
Also see FOUR EPICS

EXOTICS

Singles: 7-inch

BOLO (722 "Oasis")......................................5-10 61
JERDEN (106 "Four Banger")...................15-20 60
SEAFAIR 5-10 62-65

EXOTICS

Singles: 7-inch

CORAL (62268 "That's My Desire")...........25-35 61
CORAL (62289 "The Gang That Sang Heart of My Heart")...15-20 61
CORAL (62310 thru 62439) 10-15 62-64
Also see ROSE, Andy

EXOTICS

Singles: 7-inch

SPRINGBOARD (101 "Lorraine") 20-30 63

Picture Sleeves

SPRINGBOARD (101 "Lorraine") 50-60 63

EXOTICS

Singles: 7-inch

MONUMENT (984 "Fire Engine Red")........5-10 67
NUNSUCH ("Hey Little Girl").......................5-10 66
(No selection number used.)
TAD (2410 "Come with Me") 15-25 66
TAD (6701 "Queen of Shadows") 15-25 67

EXPERTS

Singles: 7-inch

TAG LTD. (101 "Shing-A-Loo and Boog-A-Ling Big Mama") 10-15 66

EXPLORERS

Singles: 7-inch

CORAL (62147 "Vision of Love")..............20-30 59
CORAL (62175 "Don't Be a Fool") 20-30 60
CORAL (65575 "Don't Be a Fool") 10-20 63
POPULAR REQUEST (101 "Don't Be a Fool"/"Vision of Love")..3-5 94
Also see DENNIS & EXPLORERS

EXPORTS

Singles: 7-inch

KING (5917 "Car Hop") 20-30 64
KING (5985 "Always It's You") 20-30 65

EXPRESS

Singles: 7-inch

MGM (13851 "Hurry Love") 5-10 67
PICCADILLY (226 "Long Green") 10-15 66

EXPRESSIONS

Singles: 7-inch

TEEN (101 "Now That You're Gone")...100-200 59

EXPRESSIONS

Singles: 7-inch

WOW! (2621 "Daydream") 10-20 61

EXPRESSIONS

Singles: 7-inch

ARLISS (1012 "My Love, My Love") 40-50 62
FEDERAL (12533 "Out of My Life")...........5-10 64
PARKWAY (892 "On the Corner") 5-10 63
REPRISE (360 "Playboy")...........................8-10 65
SMASH (1848 "Karen") 5-10 63
Members: Bobby Bloom; Phil Agtuca; Richie Le Causi.
Also see IMAGINATIONS

EXPRESSIONS

Singles: 7-inch

EXP (1002 "Temptation") 20-30

EXPRESSMEN

Singles: 7-inch

WESTCHESTER (274 "It's About Time") .20-25 '60s

EXPRESSOS
(Expresso's)

Singles: 7-inch

CHAMP (2 "Straightaways")...................15-25 62
TRANS AMERICAN (600 "Teenage Express") 40-60 60
Member: Aki Aleong.
Also see ALEONG, Aki
Also see SURFMEN

EXTENSIONS

Singles: 7-inch

NICKEL (111 "This Love of Mine") ....10-20 '60s
SUCCESS (109 "I Want to Know") 10-15 63

EXTERMINATORS

Singles: 7-inch

CHANCELLOR (1148 "Beatle Bomb") 10-20 64
GOLDEN WEST (1002 "Beatle Wig Party")..10-20 64
Members: Del Katcher; Jimmie Maddin.
Also see KACHER, Del
Also see MADDIN, Jimmy

EXTREMES

Singles: 7-inch

EVERLAST (5013 "Come Next Spring")..100-150 62
PARO (733 "The Bells") 250-350 62
Member: Bobby Sanders.
Also see BOBBY & VELVETS

EXZELS

Singles: 7-inch

CROSS FIRE (228 "Canadian Sunset") .75-125 62
(Promotional issue only.)
CROSS FIRE (228 "Canadian Sunset")...50-75

EYE ZOOMS

Singles: 7-inch

ATILA (213 "She's Gone")........................10-15 66

EZBA, Denny
(With the Goldens; Ezba)

Singles: 7-inch

C.A. ("Go Somewhere and Cry") 25-50 58
(Selection number not known.)
DOME...4-6 71
JAMIE (1377 "Queen Mary") 10-15 69
JOX (059 thru 068)..................................10-20 66-68
QUANTA (271 "Sunnyside of My Life") ......8-12 '60s
RENNER (Except 225)..............................5-10 61-65
RENNER (225 "Dirty Dirty Feeling").........50-75 '60s
TEXAS RE-CORD CO. 3-5 77
Members: Denny Ezba; Augie Meyers; Keith Allison; Harvey Kagan; Marty Kagan. Session: Michael Nesmith.
Also see ALLISON, Keith
Also see GOLDENS
Also see MEYERS, Augie
Also see SAHM, Doug

F

FSQ

Singles: 7-inch

RAYNARD (10079 "A Girl Named Mae") .15-25 66

FAB FOUR

Singles: 7-inch

PEARCE (5842 "River Days")..................15-25 '60s

FABARES, Shelley *P&R/LP '62*
(With the Blossoms)

Singles: 7-inch

COLPIX (621 thru 705).........................10-20 62-63
COLPIX (721 "Football Season's Over")..50-100 64
DUNHILL (4001 "My Prayer") 15-25 65
DUNHILL (4041 "See Ya 'Round on the Rebound") 15-25 65
ERIC...3-5
VEE-JAY (632 "Lost Summer Love") 15-25 64

Picture Sleeves

COLPIX (621 "Johnny Angel").............500-750 62
COLPIX (636 "Johnny Loves Me") 50-75 62

LPs: 10/12-inch

COLPIX (426 "Shelley") 45-55 62
(Monaural.)
COLPIX (426 "Shelley")..........................55-65 62
(Stereo.)
COLPIX (431 "The Things We Did Last Summer") 35-45 62
(Monaural.)
COLPIX (431 "The Things We Did Last Summer") 45-55 62
(Stereo.)
Session: Sally Stevens.
Also see BLOSSOMS
Also see DARREN, James / Shelley Fabares / Paul Petersen
Also see PETERSEN, Paul, & Shelley Fabares

FABIAN *P&R/R&B/LP '59*
(With the Fabulous Four)

Singles: 7-inch

ABC...4-6 74
CHANCELLOR (1020 "I'm in Love")......... 15-25 58
CHANCELLOR (1024 "Be My Steady Date")... 15-25 58
CHANCELLOR (1029 "I'm a Man") 15-25 58
(Monaural.)
CHANCELLOR (S-1029 "I'm a Man").......25-50 58
(Stereo.)
CHANCELLOR (1033 "Turn Me Loose").. 15-25 59
(Monaural.)
CHANCELLOR (S-1033 "Turn Me Loose") 25-50 59
(Stereo.)
CHANCELLOR (1037 "Tiger") 15-20 59
(Monaural.)
CHANCELLOR (S-1037 "Tiger") 25-50 59
(Stereo.)
CHANCELLOR (1041 "Come On and Get Me") 10-20 59
(Monaural.)
CHANCELLOR (S-1041 "Come On and Get Me") 25-50 59
(Stereo.)
CHANCELLOR (1044 "Hound Dog Man") 10-20 59
(Monaural.)
CHANCELLOR (S-1044 "Hound Dog Man")..25-50 59
(Stereo.)
CHANCELLOR (1047 "String Along") 10-20 60
(Monaural.)
CHANCELLOR (S-1047 "String Along")...25-50 60
(Stereo.)
CHANCELLOR (1051 thru 1067) 10-20 60
CHANCELLOR (1072 thru 1092) 10-15 61
COLLECTABLES ....3-5 '80s
CREAM..4-6 77
DOT (16413 "Break Down and Cry")...........8-12 62
ERIC..4-6 '70s

Picture Sleeves

CHANCELLOR (1029 "I'm a Man") 20-30 58
CHANCELLOR (1033 "Turn Me Loose")..20-30 59
CHANCELLOR (1037 "Tiger")..................20-30 59
CHANCELLOR (1041 "Come On and Get Me") 15-25 59
CHANCELLOR (1044 "Hound Dog Man")...15-25 59
CHANCELLOR (1047 "String Along") 15-25 60
CHANCELLOR (1051 "Strollin' in the Springtime")..15-25 60
CHANCELLOR (1055 "King of Love")...... 15-25 60
CHANCELLOR (1061 "Kissin' and Twistin' ")...15-25 60
CHANCELLOR (1067 "Hold On")............. 15-25 61
CHANCELLOR (1079 "You're Only Young Once")..15-25 61
CHANCELLOR (1084 "A Girl Like You").. 15-25 61
CHANCELLOR (1092 "Wild Party")..........30-40 61
CREAM..4-6 77

EPs: 7-inch

CHANCELLOR (301 "Hound Dog Man")..20-40 60
CHANCELLOR (5003 "Hold That Tiger!")..20-40 59
(Black label. Price for any of three volumes.)
CHANCELLOR (5003 "Excerpts from *Hold That Tiger!*") 30-50 59
(With paper sleeve. White label. Promotional issue only.)
CHANCELLOR (5005 "The Fabulous Fabian")..20-40 60
CHANCELLOR (5012 "The Good Old Summertime") 20-40 60
(Black label. Price is for any of three volumes.)

CHANCELLOR (9802 "Young and Wonderful") 20-40 60

LPs: 10/12-inch

ABC.......... 10-12 73
CHANCELLOR (5003 "Hold That Tiger") 50-75 59
(Monaural.)
CHANCELLOR (5003 "Hold That Tiger") 50-100 59
(Stereo.)
CHANCELLOR (5005 "The Fabulous Fabian") 40-60 59
(Monaural.)
CHANCELLOR (5005 "The Fabulous Fabian") 50-75 59
(Stereo.)
CHANCELLOR (5012 "The Good Old Summertime") 40-60 60
(Monaural.)
CHANCELLOR (5012 "The Good Old Summertime") 50-75 60
(Stereo.)
CHANCELLOR (5019 "Rockin' Hot") 50-75 61
CHANCELLOR (5024 "16 Fabulous Hits") 50-75 62
CHANCELLOR (69802 "Young and Wonderful") 40-60 60
EVEREST.......... 5-10 83
MCA.......... 5-10 85
TRIP.......... 8-10 77
U.A. 10-15 75
Also see FABULOUS FOUR
Also see 4 DATES

FABIAN / Frankie Avalon

Singles: 7-inch

CHANCELLOR/WIBG 99 ("When the Saints Go Marchin' In") 25-50 61
(Colored vinyl. Radio station special products issue. No selection number used. Flip is by the Live Five, who were the WIBG dee jays.)

LPs: 10/12-inch

CHANCELLOR (5009 "Hit Makers") 75-100 60
MCA.......... 5-10 85
Also see AVALON, Frankie
Also see FABIAN

FABIANS

Singles: 7-inch

BLUE ROCKET (315 "Confidential") 15-25

FABLES

Singles: 7-inch

ELGO (3001 "Cleopatra") 40-50 62

FABRIC, Bent — P&R/LP '62

Singles: 7-inch

ATCO.......... 4-8 62-66

Picture Sleeves

ATCO (6226 "Alley Cat") 10-15 62

EPs: 7-inch

ATCO (164 "Organ Grinder's Swing") .... 8-12 '60s
(Stereo. Juke box issue. Includes title strips.)

LPs: 10/12-inch

ATCO (148 "Alley Cat") 10-20 62
ATCO (155 "Happy Puppy") 10-20 63

FABS

Singles: 7-inch

COTTON BALL (1005 "That's the Bag I'm In") 20-30 66

FABULAIRES

Singles: 78 rpm

EAST WEST.......... 50-75 57

Singles: 7-inch

EAST WEST (103 "While Walking") 50-75 57
(White label. Promotional issue only.)
EAST WEST (103 "While Walking") 30-50 57
(Green label.)
MAIN LINE (103 "While Walking") 100-150 58

FABULAIRES

Singles: 7-inch

CHELSEA (103 "Wedding Song") 50-75 63
(White label. Promotional issue.)
CHELSEA (103 "Wedding Song") 15-25 63
(Black label. Distributed by Red Fox.)

FABULEERS
(With the Joe Shaw Orchestra)

Singles: 7-inch

KENCO (5002 "If I Had Another Chance") 40-50 59

FABULONS

Singles: 7-inch

BENSON (100 "Connie") 10-20 63
BENSON-RITCO (100 "Connie") 15-25 63
(First issue.)
EMBER (1069 "Smoke from Your Cigarette") 25-35 60
(White label.)
EMBER (1069 "Smoke from Your Cigarette") 15-25 60
(Black label.)
JO-DEE (1001 "Trying") 20-30 63

FABULOUS APOLLOS

Singles: 7-inch

VALTONE (105 "Some Good in Everything Bad") 10-20

FABULOUS BROTHERS

Singles: 7-inch

VOSS (1010 "What'd You Say") 10-15 59

FABULOUS CAPRICES

Singles: 7-inch

CAMARO (3442 "My Love") .... 15-25 '60s

FABULOUS CAROUSELS

Singles: 7-inch

TOWN HOUSE (108 "Would You Love Me") 20-30

FABULOUS CHANCELLORS

Singles: 7-inch

CHANDEL (101 "Pharaoh") 25-35 63
CHANDEL (102 "Blackout") 25-35 63
(First issue.)
DOT (16535 "Blackout") 10-15 63
ECCO (1000 "Gotta Leave This Town") ... 20-30 64
ECCO (1002 "Hey Girl") 20-30 65
(Reissued as by the Affections.)
Members: Rich Crowley; Terry Call; Dale Rich; Tom Lowe; Monty Saxton; Dennis Swindle.
Also see AFFECTIONS

FABULOUS CHIMES
("With Bobby Bell & Satalites Inst. Accomp.")

Singles: 7-inch

INVINCIBLE ("Faithful to Me") 25-35 64
(No selection number used.)

FABULOUS CLOVERS

Singles: 7-inch

WINLEY (265 "They're Rockin' Down the Street") 15-25 62
(Same number used on a Clovers release.)
Members: Buddy Bailey; Harold Winley.
Also see CLOVERS

FABULOUS COBRAS

Singles: 7-inch

JCP (1051 "I Was a Fool") 10-20 65

FABULOUS CONTINENTALS

Singles: 7-inch

CB (5003 "Undertow") 15-25 63
CB (5007 "Let's Get Goin'") 10-20 64
RORI (709 "Venus") 10-20 62
SIOUX (42061 "Rockinental") 10-20 61

FABULOUS COUNTS — R&B '69

Singles: 7-inch

HIGHLAND (1171 "So Far Away") 25-50 66
KIM (811 "Money") .... 8-12 '60s
MOIRA.......... 5-10 68-70

LPs: 10/12-inch

COTILLION (9011 "Jan Jan") 10-15 69

FABULOUS CRYS-TELS

Singles: 7-inch

DELANO (11032 "Left Front Row") 500-750 62

FABULOUS DENOS

Singles: 7-inch

KING (5908 "Bad Girl") 10-15 64
KING (5971 "Hard to Hold Back the Tears") 10-15 65

FABULOUS DIALS

Singles: 7-inch

D n B (1000 "Forget Me Not") 100-200 63
(First issue.)
JOY (276 "Forget Me Not") 30-40 63

FABULOUS DINOS

Singles: 7-inch

MUSICOR (1025 "Where Have You Been") 10-15 62
SABER (105 "Retreat") .... 10-15 '60s
SABER (1009 "Instant Love") 10-15 64

FABULOUS ECHOES

Singles: 7-inch

LIBERTY (55755 "Please Leave Her to Me") 10-15 64
LIBERTY (55769 "Keep Your Love Strong") 10-15 65
LIBERTY (55801 "Candy") 10-15 65

FABULOUS EGYPTIANS

Singles: 7-inch

CINDY (96749 "End of Time") 10-15 65
(Identification number shown since no selection number is used.)

FABULOUS ENCHANTERS

Singles: 7-inch

FINER ARTS (1007 "Why Are You Crying") 40-50 61

FABULOUS FABULIERS

Singles: 7-inch

ANGLE TONE (539 "She's the Girl for Me") 40-50 59

FABULOUS FANATICS

Singles: 7-inch

T-BIRD (201 "Givin' Up On Love") 30-40 61

FABULOUS FIDELS

Singles: 7-inch

JAA DEE (106 "Westside Boy Meets Eastside Girl") .... 30-40 '60s

FABULOUS FIVE

Singles: 7-inch

KING (5220 "Gettin' Old") 15-20 59

FABULOUS FIVE FLAMES

Singles: 7-inch

TIME (1023 "Lonely Lover") 20-30 60

FABULOUS FLAMES
(With the Original Sunglows)

Singles: 7-inch

BAY-TONE (102 "Do You Remember") .75-125 60
(White label. Credits "B Flat" Publishing.)
BAY-TONE (102 "Do You Remember") ... 50-75 60
(Yellow label. Credits "Bay Tone" Publishing.)
BAY-TONE (105 "Lover") 30-50 60
HARLEM (114 "I'm Gonna Try to Live My Life All Over") 500-600 60
REX (3000 "Josephine") 50-75 58
SUNGLOW (102 "I'm Gonna Try to Live My Life All Over") 100-150
Also see FLAMES
Also see WILLIS, Robert

FABULOUS FLARES

Singles: 7-inch

HIT (102 "You Love Her More Than I") 10-20 64

FABULOUS FLIPPERS

Singles: 7-inch

CAMEO (439 "Harlem Shuffle") 10-20 66
CAMEO (454 "Shout") 10-20 67
FONA (307 "Don't Fight It") 15-20 66
FONA (312 "Dry My Eyes") 15-20 66
LARIM ASSOCIATON (204 "Harlem Shuffle") 8-12 73
QUILL (110 "Dry My Eyes") 10-20 66
QUILL (111 "Harlem Shuffle") 10-20 66

LPs: 10/12-inch

VERITAS (2570 "Something Tangible") ... 15-25 70
Also see SANCTUARY
Also see TERRY & FLIPPERS

FABULOUS FOUR
(With Jerry Ragavoy Orchestra)

Singles: 7-inch

CHANCELLOR (1062 "In the Chapel in the Moonlight") 20-30 60
CHANCELLOR (1068 "Let's Try Again") .. 15-25 60
CHANCELLOR (1078 "Why Do Fools Fall in Love") 20-30 61
CHANCELLOR (1085 "Betty Ann") 50-75 61
CHANCELLOR (1090 "I'm Coming Home") 10-20 61
CHANCELLOR (1098 "Everybody Knows") 8-12 61
CHANCELLOR (1102 "Forever") 10-15 62

EPs: 7-inch

AGL (1869 "Fabulous Four") 15-25

LPs: 10/12-inch

CRYSTAL BALL (115 "Fabulous Four Fabulous Hits") 10-15 84
(Black vinyl. 2000 made.)
Members: Joe Prolia; Joe Mollera; Jimmy Finzino; James Testa.
Also see FABIAN
Also see FOUR Js

FABULOUS FOUR
(With the Maxwell Davis Orchestra)

Singles: 7-inch

MELIC (4114 "Welcome Me Home") 15-25 62
Also see DAVIS, Maxwell

FABULOUS FREMONTS

Singles: 7-inch

VALERIE (2003 "Gee Whiz") 25-35 63

FABULOUS GARDENIAS

Singles: 7-inch

LIZ (1004 "It's You, You, You") 30-40 62
Also see GARDENIAS

FABULOUS IDOLS

Singles: 7-inch

KENCO (5011 "Baby") 100-200 60

FABULOUS IMPACS

Singles: 7-inch

BOMB (3017 "I'll Be Crying") 50-100

FABULOUS IMPACTS

Singles: 7-inch

DAD (8001 "Tell Me") 10-15 67
DAD (8002 "Cry Cry") 10-15 67

Picture Sleeves

DAD (8001 "Tell Me") 20-30 67
DAD (8002 "Cry Cry") 20-30 67

FABULOUS IMPERIALS

Singles: 7-inch

IMPRA ("Weird") 300-400 58
(First issue. No selection number used.)
MGM (12687 "Weird") 30-50 58
SUE (109 "Hold My Hand") 5-10 64

FABULOUS JADES

Singles: 7-inch

RIKA ("Come On and Live") .... 20-30 '60s
(Selection number not known.)

FABULOUS JETS

Singles: 7-inch

KIM (809 "Ball & Chain of Love") 10-20

FABULOUS JOKERS

Singles: 7-inch

LINCOLN (708 "Little Rain Drops") 50-75 61

FABULOUS JOKERS

LPs: 10/12-inch

MONUMENT (8059 "Guitars Extraordinary") 50-100 66
(Monaural.)
MONUMENT (18059 "Guitars Extraordinary") 50-100 66
(Stereo.)

FABULOUS KING PINS

Singles: 7-inch

BIG "G" (501 "For What It's Worth") 15-25 60
IGL (151 "What Kind of Love Is That") 10-20 67

FABULOUS MAJESTICS

Singles: 7-inch

TEE VEE (2508 "Early Bird") 10-20 67

FABULOUS McCLEVERTYS

Singles: 78 rpm

VERVE (10029 "Don't Blame It on Elvis") 15-25 57

Singles: 7-inch

VERVE (10029 "Don't Blame It on Elvis") 20-30 57

LPs: 10/12-inch

VERVE (2034 "Calypso!") 50-75 57
Members: Carl McCleverty; Johnny McCleverty; Gus McCleverty; David McCleverty; Cornelius McCleverty.

FABULOUS MINKS

LPs: 10/12-inch

PLAYGIRL ("The Fabulous Minks") 50-100
(Red vinyl. Selection number not known.)

FABULOUS MUSTANGS

Singles: 7-inch

STANG (2001 "I Won't Let You Go") 25-35 65

FABULOUS NU-TONES

Singles: 7-inch

WHITEHOUSE (5002 "I'm Not Worthy of Your Love") .... 50-75 '60s

Picture Sleeves

WHITEHOUSE (5002 "I'm Not Worthy of Your Love") .... 75-125 '60s

FABULOUS PEARL DEVINES

Singles: 7-inch

ALCO (1016631 "You've Been Gone") 300-400 63
(Identification number shown since no selection number is used.)

FABULOUS PEARLS

Singles: 7-inch

COLLECTABLES 3-5
DOOTO (448 "My Heart's Desire") 40-50 59

FABULOUS PEPS

Singles: 7-inch

D-TOWN (1065 "My Love Looks Good on You") 30-50 66
GE GE (503 "She's Going to Leave You") 25-35 65
PREMIUM STUFF (1 thru 7) .... 20-30 '60s
WEE 3 (1001 "With These Eyes") 15-25 67
WHEELSVILLE 8-10
Also see OHIO UNTOUCHABLES
Also see PEPS
Also see STORM, Tom, & Peps

FABULOUS PHARAOHS

Singles: 7-inch

REPRIZE (36-22-36 "Hold Me Tight") ...... 15-20 '60s
REPRIZE (38-22-38 "Talking About You") .... 15-20 '60s
THREE STAR (2668 "Route 66") 35-45 68
Member: Eddie Stevenson.
Also see MOUZAKIS

FABULOUS PLAIDS

Singles: 7-inch

DIXIE (1110 "I'm Coming Home to You") 10-15 65

Picture Sleeves

DIXIE (1110 "I'm Coming Home to You") 15-25 65

FABULOUS PLATEAUS

Singles: 7-inch

SHOUT (5001 "Rear Back") .... 10-20 '60s

FABULOUS PLAYBOYS

Singles: 7-inch

APOLLO (758 "Forget the Past") 10-15 61
APOLLO (760 "Tears Tears Tears") 10-15 61
CONTOUR (004 "I Fooled You") 15-20 59
DACO (1001 "Forget the Past") 25-35 61
Also see FALCONS

FABULOUS PLAYBOYS

Singles: 7-inch

CATALINA (1069 "Cheater Stomp") 10-20 62

FABULOUS RAIDERS

Singles: 7-inch

DOLLY (21694 "Harmonica Rock") 10-20 60
DOLLY (21703 "Bootblack Blues") 10-20 60
WYE (1007 "C.C. Rider") 10-20 61

FABULOUS RUMBLES

Singles: 7-inch

SOMA (1448 "Echoing Past") 15-25 65
Members: Richard Clayton; Bud Phillips.
Also see CLAYTON, Rich, & Rumbles
Also see RUMBLES LTD.

FABULOUS 7 DIMENSIONS

Singles: 7-inch

EMM (63267 "But It's Alright") 8-12 67

Picture Sleeves

EMM (63267 "But It's Alright") 10-20 67

FABULOUS SILVER TONES

Singles: 7-inch

WEST COAST ("Hey Sally Mae") .... 20-30 '60s
(Selection number not known.)
Also see SILVERTONES

FABULOUS SPLENDORS
("Music By Howard Biggs")

Singles: 7-inch

O-GEE (105 "Your Change of Heart") 40-50 60

FABULOUS TABLE TOPPERS

Singles: 7-inch

REM (309 "My Wild Irish") 10-20 61

FABULOUS TERRIFICS

Singles: 7-inch

TBWCD (100 "The Keeper of My Heart") .50-75

FABULOUS 3 + 1

Singles: 7-inch

T&L (1039 "Bad Girl") 40-50

FABULOUS THUNDERBOLTS

Singles: 7-inch

POVERTY (1072 "My Girl Sue") .... 50-75 '60s

FABULOUS TONES
("George Garabedian Presents the Fabulous Tones")

Singles: 7-inch

MARK 56 (819 "I'll Never Cry Again") 30-40 59
RUSHMORE (103 "You've Broken My Heart") 100-150
Also see GARABEDIAN, George

FABULOUS TRAITS

Singles: 7-inch

TELE-PHONIC (1001 "Lonely Man") 10-20

FABULOUS TYNSIONS 5

Singles: 7-inch

NATCHEZ-JOE (101 "Lone Ranger Man") 20-30

FABULOUS UPTOWNS

Singles: 7-inch

TULIP (100 "New Love I Have Found") 400-500 62

FABULOUS VALIENTS
(With the Del Reys)

Singles: 7-inch

HOLIDAY (61005 "Your Golden Teardrops") 250-350 61

FABULOUS VERBS

Singles: 7-inch

CAMARO (3384 "Let Me Be the Man") ..... 15-25 '60s

FABULOUS WANDERERS

Singles: 7-inch

MIDESSA (1002 "I'm a Road Runner") 50-75

FABULOUS WUNZ

Singles: 7-inch

PYRAMID (6934 "I Cry") 10-20 66

FABUS, Ray, & Strikes

Singles: 7-inch

SOMA (1158 "Camel Walk") 15-25 61
SOMA (1191 "Please") 30-40 62

FABUTONES

Singles: 7-inch

BIM BAM BOOM (100 "Baby") 20-30 72
(White label. Promotional issue only.)

FACENDA, Tommy *P&R/R&B '59*

Singles: 7-inch

ATLANTIC (51 "High School U.S.A. [Virginia]") 25-40 59
ATLANTIC (52 "High School U.S.A. [New York City Area]") 25-40 59
ATLANTIC (53 "High School U.S.A. [North Carolina – South Carolina]") 25-40 59
ATLANTIC (54 "High School U.S.A. [Washington D.C. Area]") 25-40 59
ATLANTIC (55 "High School U.S.A. [Philadelphia Area]") 25-40 59
ATLANTIC (56 "High School U.S.A. [Detroit Area]") 25-40 59
ATLANTIC (57 "High School U.S.A. [Pittsburgh Area]") 25-40 59
ATLANTIC (58 "High School U.S.A. [Minneapolis – St. Paul Area]") 25-40 59
ATLANTIC (59 "High School U.S.A. [Florida]") 25-40 59
ATLANTIC (60 "High School U.S.A. [Newark Area]") 25-40 59
ATLANTIC (61 "High School U.S.A. [Boston Area]") 25-40 59
ATLANTIC (62 "High School U.S.A. [Cleveland Area]") 25-40 59
ATLANTIC (63 "High School U.S.A. [Buffalo Area]") 25-40 59
ATLANTIC (64 "High School U.S.A. [Hartford Area]") 25-40 59
ATLANTIC (65 "High School U.S.A. [Nashville Area]") 25-40 59
ATLANTIC (66 "High School U.S.A. [Indiana]") 25-40 59
ATLANTIC (67 "High School U.S.A. [Chicago Area]") 25-40 59
ATLANTIC (68 "High School U.S.A. [New Orleans Area]") 25-40 59
ATLANTIC (69 "High School U.S.A. [St. Louis – Kansas City Area]") 25-40 59
ATLANTIC (70 "High School U.S.A. [Alabama – Georgia]") 25-40 59
ATLANTIC (71 "High School U.S.A. [Cincinnati Area]") 25-40 59
ATLANTIC (72 "High School U.S.A. [Memphis Area]") 25-40 59
ATLANTIC (73 "High School U.S.A. [Los Angeles Area]") 25-40 59
ATLANTIC (74 "High School U.S.A. [San Francisco Area]") 25-40 59
ATLANTIC (75 "High School U.S.A. [Texas]") 25-40 59
ATLANTIC (76 "High School U.S.A. [Seattle – Portland Area]") 25-40 59
ATLANTIC (77 "High School U.S.A. [Denver Area]") 25-40 59
ATLANTIC (78 "High School U.S.A. Oklahoma]") 25-40 59
ATLANTIC (2057 "Bubba Ditty") 15-20 59
LEGRAND (1001 "High School U.S.A. Virginia]") 30-40 59
(We have yet to learn how to positively identify original pressings, since many reissues exist.)
NASCO (6018 "Little Baby") 15-25 58
Session: King Curtis.
Also see KING CURTIS
Also see VINCENT, Gene

FACES

Singles: 7-inch

IGUANA (601/602 "Christmas") 100-200 65
REGINA (1326 "What Is This Dream") 15-20 65
REGINA (1328 "I'll Walk Alone") 15-20 65

FACINATORS

Singles: 7-inch

QUEEN BEE (1001 "Love Will Conquer All") 75-125

FACTORY

Singles: 7-inch

USA (922 "High Blood Pressure") 10-20 68

FACTS OF LIFE

Singles: 7-inch

FRANA (59 "I've Seen Darker Nights") 10-15 67

FADS

Singles: 7-inch

MERCURY (72542 "Just Like a Woman") 20-40 66

FAGAN, Dick

Singles: 7-inch

SARG (155 "Love Like the Sun") 40-60 58

FAGEN, Donald *P&R/R&B/LP '82*

Singles: 12-inch

W.B. 4-6 82

Singles: 7-inch

W.B. 3-5 82-88

Picture Sleeves

W.B. 3-5 82-88

LPs: 10/12-inch

MFSL (120 "Nightfly") 30-50 84
W.B. 5-10 82-88
Also see STEELY DAN

FAHEY, John

Singles: 7-inch

VANGUARD (35076 "March for Martin Luther King") 5-10 68

LPs: 10/12-inch

REPRISE 8-10 72-73
RIVERBOAT 10-12
TAKOMA 10-15 59-81
VANGUARD 10-15 67-74
Also see KOTTKE, Leo, John Fahey & Peter Lang

FAINE JADE

Singles: 7-inch

PROVIDENCE (420 "It Ain't True") 15-25 66
RSVP (1130 "Introspection") 10-20 66

LPs: 10/12-inch

PSYCHO (13 "Introspection") 10-15 83
RSVP (8002 "Introspection") 300-500 68
Also see RUSTILS

FAIR, Carlo

Singles: 7-inch

EXPRESS (801 "Beetle Bounce") 10-15 64

FAIR, Yvonne *R&B '74*

Singles: 7-inch

DADE (5006 "Say Yeah Yeah") 5-10 63
KING (5594 "I Found You") 5-10 62
KING (5654 "Tell Me Why") 10-15 62
KING (5687 "You Can Make It If You Try") 5-10 62
MOTOWN 4-6 74-76
SMASH (2030 "Baby, Baby, Baby") 5-10 66
SOUL (Black vinyl) 4-6 70
SOUL (Colored vinyl) 5-10 70
(Promotional issue only.)

Picture Sleeves

MOTOWN (1323 "Walk Out the Door If You Wanna") 5-10 74

LPs: 10/12-inch

MOTOWN 5-10 76

FAIRBURN, Werly
("The Delta Balladeer;" with the Delta Boys; with Whirlybirds)

Singles: 78 rpm

CAPITOL 5-10 54-55
COLUMBIA (Except 21528) 5-15 56
COLUMBIA (21528 "Everybody's Rockin'") 20-30 56
DIAMOND 15-25 53
SAVOY 5-10 56-57
TRUMPET 15-25 53

Singles: 7-inch

CAPITOL 15-25 54-55
COLUMBIA (21432 "I Guess I'm Crazy") . 15-25 56
COLUMBIA (21483 "Stay Close to Me") .. 15-25 56
COLUMBIA (21528 "Everybody's Rockin'") 50-75 56
FAIR-LEW 5-10 65
MILESTONE (2013 "Doggone That Moon") 5-10 62
PAULA (295 "My Crazy World") 4-8 68
SAVOY (1503 "All the Time") 15-25 56
SAVOY (1509 "Speak to Me Baby") 15-25 57
SAVOY (1521 "Telephone Baby") 15-25 57
TRUMPET (195 "Let's Live It Over") 20-30 53

FAIRCHILD, Johnny

Singles: 7-inch

ACE (565 "I Was a Fool") 15-25 59
ACE (586 "A Fool or a Wise Man") 15-25 60

FAIRE, Johnny
(John Faircloth)

Singles: 7-inch

FABLE (601 "If I'm a Fool"/"You Gotta Walk That Line") 40-60 57
FABLE (601 "If I'm a Fool"/"Make Up Your Mind Baby") 40-60 57
(Note different flip.)
SURF (5019 "Bertha Lou") 40-60 58
(Same number used on a Dorsey Burnette release.)
SURF (5024 "Betcha I Getcha") 25-35 58
Also see BROOKS, Donnie

FAIRFIELD FOUR
(Fairfield 4)

Singles: 78 rpm

DOT 5-10 50-52

Singles: 7-inch

DOT 10-15 50-52
OLD TOWN (1081 "Memories") 15-25 60

FAIRLANES

Singles: 7-inch

ARGO (5357 "Little Girl") 10-15 60
DART (109 "Just for Me") 40-50 59
LUCKY SEVEN (102 "Seventeen Steps") 30-40 59
MINARET (103 "I'm Not That Kind of Guy") 10-15 62
RADIANT (101 "Baby Baby") 200-300 64
RADIANT (104 "The New York Sound") .. 10-15 64

FAIRLANES

Singles: 7-inch

CONTINENTAL (1001 "Writing This Letter") 200-300 61

FAIRLANES

Singles: 7-inch

REPRISE (20213 "Surf Train") 10-20 63

FAIRMOUNT SINGERS

Singles: 7-inch

DOT (16340 "The Man Who Shot Liberty Valance") 5-10 62
DOT (16422 "A-Wanderin' ") 5-10 62

LPs: 10/12-inch

DOT (3439 "Jimmie Rodgers Presents the Fairmount Singers") 10-15 62
(Monaural.)
DOT (25439 "Jimmie Rodgers Presents the Fairmount Singers") 15-20 62
(Stereo.)

FAIRMOUNTS

Singles: 7-inch

PLANET (53 "Times & Places") 40-50 64

FAIRVIEWS

Singles: 7-inch

SPIN IT (120 "Twinkle Lee") 50-75

FAITH, Adam *P&R '65*

Singles: 7-inch

AMY 10-15 64-65
CAPITOL 5-10 65-66
CUB 5-10 60
DOT 5-10 62
LAURIE 5-10 68

LPs: 10/12-inch

AMY (8005 "Adam Faith") 20-30 65
MGM (3951 "England's Top Singer") 25-30 61
W.B. 8-12 74

FAITH, Percy, Orchestra *P&R '50*
(With the Paulette Sisters; with Burt Taylor)

Singles: 78 rpm

COLUMBIA 3-5 50-57
RCA 3-5 51

Singles: 7-inch

COLUMBIA 5-15 50-76
RCA 10-20 51

Picture Sleeves

COLUMBIA 5-10 60

EPs: 7-inch

COLUMBIA 5-10 50-59
ROYALE .... 5-10 '50s

LPs: 10/12-inch

COLUMBIA 5-15 51-82
HARMONY 5-10 68-72
Also see CLOONEY, Rosemary
Also see COREY, Jill
Also see KING, Peggy
Also see RAY, Johnnie
Also see SANDERS, Felicia
Also see TAYLOR, Burt

FAITH, Percy, Orchestra / Johnny Mathis

Singles: 7-inch

COLUMBIA (7 "Theme from a Summer Place"/"The Best of Everything") 5-10
Also see FAITH, Percy, Orchestra
Also see MATHIS, Johnny

FAITHFULL, Marianne *P&R '64*

Singles: 12-inch

ISLAND 5-8 83

Singles: 7-inch

ISLAND (49121 "Broken English"/"Brain Drain") 4-6 79
ISLAND (49121 "Broken English"/"Broken English") 5-8 79
(Mono/Stereo. Promotional issue only.)
ISLAND (94997 "Why D'Ya Do It"/"Broken English") 12-25 79
(Full-length [6:35] track. Promotional issue only.)
LONDON (1022 "Sister Morphine") 75-100 69
(With the Rolling Stones.)
LONDON (9697 thru 9802) 6-12 64-65
LONDON (20000 series) 5-10 66-67
LONDON (Except 1022) 5-10 67-72

Picture Sleeves

LONDON (9802 "Go Away from My World") 5-10 65

LPs: 10/12-inch

ISLAND 5-10 79-90
LONDON 15-25 65-69
Also see ROLLING STONES

FALANA, Fluffy

Singles: 7-inch

ALPHA (007 "Hangover from Love") 30-50 67

FALCON, Max

Singles: 7-inch

BOONE (1039 "Saturday and Sunday") 5-10 66
FRATERNITY (903 "Money Back Guarantee") 15-25 60

FALCONE, Tommy, & Centuries

Singles: 7-inch

DESIGN (841 "Like Weird") 10-15 61
Also see CENTURIES
Also see MONTGOMERYS, The

FALCONS

Singles: 78 rpm

CASH (1002 "Tell Me Why") 150-250 55
FLIP (301 "Stay Mine") 50-100 54
SAVOY (893 "It's You I Miss") 100-200 53

Singles: 7-inch

CASH (1002 "Tell Me Why") 500-600 55
FLIP (301 "Stay Mine") 300-400 54
SAVOY (893 "It's You I Miss") 400-500 53
Also see RIVERS, Candy, & Falcons

FALCONS *P&R/R&B '59*
(With Al Smith's Orchestra; "Musical Direction Sax Kari")

Singles: 78 rpm

SILHOUETTE (522 "Can This Be Christmas") 200-300 57
UNART (2013 "You're So Fine") 500-750 59

Singles: 7-inch

ANNA (1110 "This Heart of Mine") 75-125 60
ATLANTIC (2153 "Darling") 8-12 62
ATLANTIC (2175 "Take This Love") 8-12 63
ATLANTIC (2207 "Oh Baby") 8-12 63
BIG WHEEL (1967 "I Can't Help It") 5-10 66
CHESS (1743 "This Heart of Mine") 10-15 59
FALCON (1006 "Now That It's Over") 125-150 57
FLICK (001 "You're So Fine") 100-150 59
FLICK (008 "You Must Know I Love You") 30-40 60
KUDO (661 "This Heart of Mine") 200-300 58
LIBERTY 3-5
LU PINE (103 "I Found a Love") 15-25 62
LU PINE (124 "Lonely Nights") 10-20 62
LU PINE (1003 "I Found a Love") 5-10 62
LU PINE (1024 "Lonely Nights") 30-40 62
MERCURY (70940 "Baby That's It") 15-25 56
QUALITY (1721 "Now That It's Over") 20-30 61
(Canadian.)
SILHOUETTE (522 "Can This Be Christmas") 250-350 57
(Flip, *Sent Up*, is Silhouette 521, a number also used for a Charmers release.)
UNART (2013 "You're So Fine") 10-15 59
UNART (2013-S "You're So Fine") 50-100 59
(Reprocessed stereo.)
UNART (2022 "Country Shack") 15-20 59
U.A. (229 "The Teacher") 15-25 60
U.A. (255 "Wonderful Love") 15-25 60
U.A. (289 "Working Man's Song") 15-25 60
U.A. (420 "You're So Fine") 10-15 62

EPs: 7-inch

U.A. (10010 "The Falcons") 300-400 59
Members: Wilson Pickett; Joe Stubbs; Eddie Floyd; Arnet Robinson; Lance Finnie; Sonny Monroe; Ben Rice.
Also see CHARMERS
Also see FIVE SCALDERS
Also see FLOYD, Eddie
Also see KARI, Sax
Also see KIRKLAND, Eddie
Also see OHIO UNTOUCHABLES
Also see 100 PROOF Aged in Soul
Also see PICKETT, Wilson
Also see RICE, Mack
Also see SMITH, Al
Also see STUBBS, Joe

FALKONS

Singles: 7-inch

FUJIMO (2521 "Why Marianne") 100-200

FALL GUYS

Singles: 7-inch

ROSEMONT (9161 "Teen Age Fool") 10-20 60

FALLEN ANGELS

Singles: 7-inch

TOLLIE (9049 "Up on the Mountain") 30-40 65

FALLEN ANGELS

Singles: 7-inch

LAURIE (3343 "Everytime I Fall in Love") 5-10 66
LAURIE (3369 "Have You Ever Lost a Love") 5-10 66
PHILCO (23 "Room at the Top"/"Most Children Do") 10-20 67
("Hip Pocket" flexi-disc.)
ROULETTE (4770 "Room at the Top") 5-10 67
ROULETTE (4785 "Hello Girl") 5-10 67
SUN DREAM (704 "Everything Would Be Fine") .... 10-15 '60s

LPs: 10/12-inch

ROULETTE (25358 "The Fallen Angels") 50-100 68
ROULETTE (42011 "It's a Long Way Down") 30-60 68
Members: Jack Bryant; Jack Lauritsen; Wally Cook; Richard Kumer; Howart Danchik.
Also see MAD HATTERS

FALLEN ANGELS

Singles: 7-inch

ECEIP (1003 "Bad Woman") 40-60 70

FALLIN, Johnny
(John Fallin)

Singles: 7-inch

CAPITOL (4216 "Creation of Love") 10-20 59
CAPITOL (4283 "If I Could Write a Love Song") 10-20 59
DART (144 "Why the Town Is Asleep") 5-10 61

FALLING PEBBLES
(Buckinghams)

Singles: 7-inch

ALLEY CAT (201 "Lawdy Miss Clawdy") 12-18 66
Also see BUCKINGHAMS

FALLON, Phillipa

Singles: 7-inch

MGM (12661 "High School Drag") 10-15 58

FALLOWS, Scott, & Ebbtones

Singles: 7-inch

DOT (16577 "Surfing Boop-Boop-A-Do") 15-20 64

FAMEN

Singles: 7-inch

DELTA (157 "If You Want Me") 35-50 65
X-POSE ("Crackin' Up") 35-50 66
(No selection number used.)

FAMES

Singles: 7-inch

PYRAMID (6897 "Drinkin' Wine Spo-Dee-O-Dee") .... 15-25 '60s

FAMILY

Singles: 7-inch

USA (886 "Face the Autumn") 10-20 67
USA (894 "Without You") 10-20 68

FAMILY CIRCLE

Singles: 7-inch

CALLA (5001 "Haven't Seen Nothin' ") 5-8
SKY DISC (642 "Change") 8-10 72
SKY DISC (644 "I Hope You Really Love Me") 8-10 72

LPs: 10/12-inch

SKY DISC (301 "Family Circle") 100-200 72

FAMILY JEWELS

Singles: 7-inch

BANG (565 "You Baby You") 5-10 69
HARBOUR (306 "You Baby You") 15-25

FAMILY OF APOSTOLIC

LPs: 10/12-inch

VANGUARD (79301 "Family of Apostolic") 20-30 69
Members: John Townley; Gil Townley; Lyn Hardy.
Also see TOWNLEY, John, & Apostolic Family

FAMILY PLOT

Singles: 7-inch

DMC (102 "Love Show") 15-25 68

FAMILY TREE

Singles: 7-inch

MIRA (228 "Prince of Dreams") 10-20 66
PAULA (329 "Electric Kangaroo") 4-8 70
RCA (9184 thru 9671) 5-10 67-68

LPs: 10/12-inch

RCA (3955 "Miss Butters") 15-20 68

FAMOUS CHROMES

Singles: 7-inch

DRIVE (6225 "Teach Me") .... 10-20 '60s

FAMOUS HEARTS

Singles: 7-inch

GUYDEN (2073 "Isle of Love") 250-300 62
Also see ANDREWS, Lee
Also see HEARTS

FANANDOS
(With Emmet Carter Combo; Fanando's)

Singles: 7-inch

CARTER (2050 "The One I Love") 1500-2000 57
Also see ROCKERS

FANATICS

Singles: 7-inch

BACK BEAT (553 "You're Moving too Fast") 5-10 65
SKYWAY (127 "Is There Still a Chance") 20-30 61

FANATICS

Singles: 7-inch

GINA (1118 "Be Mine") 20-30 65
Also see FORD, Neal, & Fanatics

FANELLI, Frankie
(Frank Fanelli)

Singles: 7-inch

ABC (10966 "Loneliness") 5-10 67
BEVERLY HILLS (9355 "Saturdays Only") .. 5-8 71
RCA 5-10 64-66

LPs: 10/12-inch

BEVERLY HILLS (28 "Saturdays Only") 8-12 71
RCA 10-15 64-66

FANKHAUSER, Merrell
(With H.M.S. Bounty; with Maui Band; Murl Fankhauser)

Singles: 7-inch

D-TOWN 3-5 85
FREE SPIRIT 4-6 79
SHAMLEY (44006 "Things") 8-12 68
SHAMLEY (44008 "I'm Flying Home") 8-12 69

Picture Sleeves

FREE SPIRIT 4-6 79

LPs: 10/12-inch

CHERRY RED 8-10 85
D-TOWN 8-10 86
DISC MELOCOTON (001 "Back This Way Again") 15-25 90
MAUI (101 "Merrell Fankhauser") 40-50 76
OCEAN 5-10 88
SHAMLEY (701 "Things Going Round in My Mind") 50-75 68
SOURCE (2 "A Day in Paradise") 8-10 85
UIP (2250 "Fapardokly") 350-450 67
(Only title is shown on cover—no artist credited. Has tracks recorded by Merrell & Exiles. *Fapardockly* combines portions of each band member's name: FAnkhauser-PARrish-DOdd-dicK LEe.)
Session: Merrell Fankhauser; Dan Parrish; Bill Dodd; Dick Lee; Peter Noone; Mary Lee; Jimmy Dillon; Bill Berg; Ben Benay; Colin Cameron; Bill Cuomo; Gary Malabar; John Cipollina; Jim Murray; John "Drumbo" French.
Also see IMPACTS
Also see MERRELL & EXILES
Also see MU
Also see QUICKSILVER
Also see SENTINELS
Also see ZAPPA, Frank

FANNIE & VARCELLS

Singles: 7-inch

LASH (1326 "The Guy") 200-300

FANNING, Jay

Singles: 7-inch

ACME (100 "Baby Baby") 8-12 61
ACME (2030 "Dreamer") 8-12 60
ACME (2031 "This Green Earth") 8-12 61
ACME (2032 "Be My Sweetheart") 10-15 61
ACME (2033 "Baby Baby") 8-12 61
ACME (2034 "Baby Baby") 8-12 61
(Issued with two different numbers.)

ACME (2035 "Church Bells")................... 15-25 61
ACME (2035 "Church Bells")................... 20-30 61
(White label. Promotional issue only.)

Picture Sleeves

ACME (2032 "Be My Sweetheart") 15-25 61

FANNOM, Patrick, & Footnotes

Singles: 7-inch

PEE JAY (300 "So Easy for You") 100-150

FANTASTIC BAGGYS

Singles: 7-inch

IMPERIAL (66047 "Tell 'Em I'm Surfin' "). 15-25 64
IMPERIAL (66072 "Anywhere the Girls Are") 15-25 64
IMPERIAL (66092 "Alone on the Beach") 15-25 65

LPs: 10/12-inch

IMPERIAL (9270 "Tell 'Em I'm Surfin' "). 75-125 64
(Black label with five stars under logo. Monaural.)
IMPERIAL (9270 "Tell 'Em I'm Surfin' ")... 50-75 64
(Multi-color label. Monaural.)
IMPERIAL (9270 "Tell 'Em I'm Surfin' "). 75-125 64
(White label. Promotional issue only.)
IMPERIAL (12270 "Tell 'Em I'm Surfin' ")... 100-150 64
(Black label with five stars under logo. Stereo.)
IMPERIAL (12270 "Tell 'Em I'm Surfin' "). 60-85 64
(Multi-color label. Stereo.)
LIBERTY..5-10 82
Members: Phil Sloan; Steve Barri.
Also see BARRI, Steve
Also see INNER CIRCLE
Also see LIFEGUARDS
Also see PHILIP & STEPHEN
Also see RALLY PACKS
Also see RINCON SURFSIDE BAND
Also see RIP CHORDS
Also see SLOAN, P.F.
Also see STREET CLEANERS
Also see THEMES, INC.

FANTASTIC DEE-JAYS

Singles: 7-inch

FLEETWOOD (1096 "Love Is So Tuff")... 20-30 65
RED FOX (102 "You're the One") 15-25 65
SHERRY (309 "Apache") 20-30 65
TRI-POWER (421 "Fight Fire")................ 15-25 66
STONE (044 "Love Is So Tuff")................ 15-20 66

LPs: 10/12-inch

STONE (4003 "The Fantastic Dee Jays") 400-600 66
Members: Dick Newton; Denny Nicholson; Bob Hocko.
Also see SWAMP RATS

FANTASTIC FOUR ***P&R/R&B '67***

Singles: 7-inch

EASTBOUND.......................................4-6 73-74
RIC-TIC (Except 113 & 121).................... 10-20 66-68
RIC-TIC (113 "Can't Stop Looking for My Baby") 100-200 66
RIC-TIC (121 "Can't Stop Looking for My Baby") 50-75 67
SOUL 8-15 68-70
WESTBOUND.......................................4-6 75-79

LPs: 10/12-inch

SOUL (717 "Best of the Fantastic Four"). 25-40 69
20TH FOX/WESTBOUND (201 "Alvin Stone")..8-10 75
WESTBOUND.......................................8-10 75-78
Members: Joe Pruitt; James Epps; Robert Pruitt; Toby Childs; Ernest Newsome; Cleveland Horn.

FANTASTIC FOUR / Wingate's Love-in Strings

Singles: 7-inch

RIC-TIC (129 "Let's Have a Love-In"/"Let's Have a Love-In")..5-10 67
RIC-TIC (131 "She's a Real Live Wire"/"Let's Have a Love-In")..5-10 67
Also see FANTASTIC FOUR
Also see FLAMING EMBERS / Wingate's Love-in Strings

FANTASTIC JOHNNY C. ***P&R/R&B '67***
(Johnny Corley)

Singles: 7-inch

BRANDING IRON (170 "Let's Do It Together") 10-20
KAMA SUTRA..4-6 70
PHIL-L.A. OF SOUL..................................4-8 67-73

LPs: 10/12-inch

PHIL-L.A. OF SOUL................................ 15-20 68

FANTASTIC RHYTHMS

Singles: 7-inch

B&B (1435 "The Girl in Lace")..................20-25 67

FANTASTIC VONTASTICS

Singles: 7-inch

TUFF (406 "Gee What a Boy")..................10-15 65
Also see VONTASTICS

FANTASTIC ZOO

Singles: 7-inch

DOUBLE SHOT (105 "This Calls for a Celebration")...10-20 66
DOUBLE SHOT (109 "Light Show") 10-20 67
Members: Don Cameron; Erik Karl.

FANTASTICS

Singles: 7-inch

PARK AVENUE (02 "Angie Lee") 4-6 90
(Red vinyl. 500 made.)
PARK AVENUE (02 "Angie Lee") ....4-6 '90s
(Yellow vinyl. 500 made.)
PARK AVENUE (03 "My Girls") ....4-6 '90s
(Black vinyl. 300 made.)
PARK AVENUE (03 "My Girls") ....4-6 '90s
(Yellow vinyl. 500 made.)
PARK AVENUE (04 "Dancing Doll")............5-7 '90s
(500 made.)
POPULAR REQUEST (102 "I Got a Zero")..3-5 94
RCA (7572 "There Goes My Love").........20-30 59
(RCA dog at top of label.)
RCA (7572 "There Goes My Love").........10-15 65
(RCA dog at left side of label.)
RCA (7572 "There Goes My Love").........15-25 65
(Orange label. No dog.)
RCA (7664 "I Got a Zero").......................25-50 59
U.A. (309 "Dancing Doll").......................75-125 61
Members: Bill Forrest; Bill Sutton; Sam Strain; Fred Warner; Larry Lawrence.

FANTASTICS

Singles: 7-inch

DONNA (1313 "Blabbermouth")...............30-40 59
IMPRESARIO (124 "In Times Like These") 75-125 61

FANTASTICS

Singles: 7-inch

DMD (103 "Goodbye to Love")..................40-50 64

FANTASTICS

Singles: 7-inch

COPA (8005 "High Note") 15-25
SCORPIO (407 "Malaguena")....................5-10 66
SOUND STAGE 7 (2548 "High Note")........5-10 65
SOUND STAGE 7 (2565 "Have a Little Faith")..5-10 66

FANTASYS

Singles: 7-inch

GUYDEN (2029 "Why Oh Why")...............40-60 60
Members: Rich Schmidt; Arum Oornazian; Ben Asero; Charles Berberian.

FANTASYS

Singles: 7-inch

SHIRLE (4 "Surfs Up")............................20-30 '60s
Member: Scott Hicks.

FANTOM

Singles: 7-inch

SULLY (911 "Baby Come Home") 15-25 65

FANTOMES

LPs: 10/12-inch

KAPP (1410 "Discotheque a Go-Go") 10-15 64
(Monaural.)
KAPP (3410 "Discotheque a Go-Go") 15-20 64
(Stereo.)

FAR CRY

Singles: 7-inch

VANGUARD (35085 "Shapes")..................5-10 69

LPs: 10/12-inch

VANGUARD (6510 "Far Cry")...................20-30 69
Members: Dave Perry; Paul Lenart; Dick Martin; Sean Hutchinson.

FARDON, Don ***P&R '68***

Singles: 7-inch

CHELSEA (0115 "Delta Queen") 4-6 73
GNP (405 "Indian Reservation") 5-8 68
GNP (418 "Take a Heart")............................5-8 68

LPs: 10/12-inch

DECCA...10-12 70
GNP (2044 "Lament of the Cherokee Indian") 15-20 68

FARLEY, Dave

Singles: 7-inch

BONANZA (11 "Flat Top Boogie")...........20-30 '50s
BONANZA (806 "Walking 'Round in Circles") ....10-20 '50s

FARLEYS

Singles: 7-inch

JODY (902 "Summertime Blues")............40-50 '60s

FARLOWE, Chris
(Chris Farlow; with the Thunderbirds)

Singles: 7-inch

GENERAL AMERICAN (718 "Just a Dream") ....10-20 '60s
IMMEDIATE...5-10 67-68
MGM (13567 "Out of Time")........................8-12 66
POLYDOR...4-8 70

LPs: 10/12-inch

COLUMBIA...15-20 67
IMMEDIATE...15-20 68
POLYDOR...10-12 70

FARMER, Donny

Singles: 7-inch

ROULETTE (4193 "My Bride")..................10-15 59
SPECTRUM (1001 "Friendship Ring")......10-15 60

FARMER, Ernie

Singles: 7-inch

YOUNG (101 "Things to Remember")..100-200 59

FARMER, Jimmy

Singles: 7-inch

SARG (201 "Long Black Train")...............50-75

FARMER BOYS

Singles: 78 rpm

CAPITOL...5-10 56

Singles: 7-inch

CAPITOL (3322 "Flip Flop").....................10-20 56
CAPITOL (3476 "My Baby Done Left Me")..10-20 56
CAPITOL (3569 "Cool Down Mame").......10-20 56

FARNER, Mark
(Mark Farner Band)

Singles: 7-inch

ATLANTIC..4-6 77-78
LUCKY ELEVEN (352 "Down in the Valley") 10-20 67

LPs: 10/12-inch

ATLANTIC..5-10 77-78

FARNER, Mark, & Don Brewer

Singles: 7-inch

LUCKY ELEVEN (366 "Does It Matter to You Girl")..10-20 67

Picture Sleeves

LUCKY ELEVEN (366 "Does It Matter to You Girl")..20-30 67

LPs: 10/12-inch

QUADICO (7401 "Monumental Funk").......5-10 79
QUADICO (7401 "Monumental Funk")....20-25 79
(Limited edition, numbered picture disc.)
Also see FARNER, Mark
Also see GRAND FUNK RAILROAD

FAROS

Singles: 7-inch

TARGET (103/104 "I'm Calling You Back"/"I'm Crying")...20-40 66
Members: Gary Daily; Steve Berg; Chris Wyman; Dan Meredith.

FARR, Lance, & Beltones

Singles: 7-inch

N-JOY (1001 "Mona Lisa").......................10-15 64

FARR, Little Joey
(Joey Farr)

Singles: 7-inch

BAND BOX (286 "Rock n' Roll Santa") 40-50 61
(Different recording than on Kangaroo 112.)
EAGLE (1002 "Movin' on Down") 30-40 58
KANGAROO (112 "Rock n' Roll Santa")...150-250 60

FARRAH, Fred

Singles: 7-inch

SABRE (5506 "Settle Down")...............100-200

FARRAR, Lucien
(With the Lifesavers; with Don Abney Orchestra; "Cham-Ber Huang, Harmonica")

Singles: 7-inch

HANOVER (4504 "When First We Met")..10-20 58
JUPITER (1 "Didn't You Know")..........250-350 57
JUPITER (2 "Tomorrow Night")...........300-400 57
ROULETTE (4242 "I Want the World to Know")..15-25 60
ROULETTE (4331 "My Dream")..............15-25 61

FARRAR, Tony

Singles: 7-inch

TRANS ATLAS (001 "A Blast from the Past")..15-25 61
(Opens with *In the Still of the Nite*, by the Five Satins.)
Also see FIVE SATINS

FARREL, Lee

LPs: 10/12-inch

TMS (101 "Hard Times")..........................40-50 78
(Boxed picture disc set. Includes bonus autographed photo.)
TMS (101 "Hard Times")..........................30-40 78
(Picture disc.)

FARREL & FLAMES

Singles: 7-inch

FRANSIL (14 "Dreams & Memories") ..400-500 61
(Reportedly 500 made.)

FARRELL, Billy ***R&B '49***
(With the Quartones; with Russ Case & Orchestra; Bill Farrell)

Singles: 78 rpm

EPIC...15-25 57
IMPERIAL...8-12 54
MGM...10-15 49-51
MERCURY..8-12 55-56

Singles: 7-inch

CUB (90915 "My Heart and My Hands")..10-20 58
DATE (1002 "Yeah Yeah").......................15-25 58
EPIC (9211 "Still in Love with You").........15-25 57
IMPERIAL..20-30 54
JARO (77026 "East of the Sun")................8-12 60
MGM (10900 "In the Land of Make Believe") 10-20 51
MERCURY..15-25 55-56
TEL (1000 "You Were Only Fooling").......15-25 58

FARRELL, Leon

Singles: 7-inch

NATION (92767 "Pure Unadulterated Love") 10-20

FARRELL, Mickey, & Dynamics

Singles: 7-inch

BETHLEHEM (3069 "We Did the Bossa Nova")..15-25 63
BETHLEHEM (3080 "Baby Mine")............15-25 64

FARRELL, Pat, & Believers

Singles: 7-inch

DIAMOND (236 "War Baby")....................10-20 68
DIAMOND (239 "All My Love") 10-20 68
Also see RAZOR'S EDGE
Also see TRIUMPHS

FARRELL, Tony

Singles: 7-inch

TIME (1000 "Flame in My Heart").............10-15 58

FARRELL, Wes
(With the Art Paris Orchestra)

Singles: 7-inch

F.T.P. (405 "What Is Life") ....5-10 '60s
HANOVER (4547 "Mama's Baby")...........10-15 60

FASCINATES

Singles: 7-inch

PORT (70010 "Pizza Train")....................10-15 59

FASCINATIONS

Singles: 7-inch

ABC-PAR (10387 "Mama Didn't Lie").........5-10 62
ABC-PAR (10443 "You're Gonna Be Sorry")...5-10 63
DORE (593 "If I Had Your Love") 40-50 61
PAXLEY (750 "If I Had Your Love")......200-300 61
SURE (106 "It's Midnight")....................150-250 60
SURE (106 "Midnight")............................50-100 60
(Note slight title change.)

FASCINATIONS R&B '66
Singles: 7-inch
A&G (101 "Since You Went Away")......... 15-25 72
(Previously unreleased from 1962 master.)
MAYFIELD.. 10-15 66-67
Members: Shirley Walker; Joanne Levell; Bernadine Boswell Smith; Fern Bledsoe.
Also see FASINATIONS

FASCINATORS
("Music by the Baseliners")
Singles: 78 rpm
YOUR COPY.. 75-125 54-55
Singles: 7-inch
YOUR COPY (1135 "The Bells of My Heart").. 500-750 54
(Black vinyl.)
YOUR COPY (1135 "The Bells of My Heart").. 1000-2000 54
(Red vinyl.)
YOUR COPY (1136 "My Beauty, My Own").. 700-1200 55
Members: Jerry Potter; Donald Blackshear; Bob Rivers; Clarence Smith; Earl Richardson.

FASCINATORS
Singles: 78 rpm
BLUE LAKE (112 "Can't Stop")........... 500-600 55
Singles: 7-inch
BLUE LAKE (112 "Can't Stop")........3000-4000 55
Member: Andrew Smith.
Also see MAPLES

FASCINATORS
Singles: 7-inch
DOOTO (441 "Teardrop Eyes")............... 50-75 58
KING (5119 "Cuddle Up with Carolyn") ... 50-75 58

FASCINATORS
(With Sid Bass & His Orchestra)
Singles: 7-inch
BIM BAM BOOM (110 "Oh Rose Marie") 4-6 72
(Black vinyl.)
BIM BAM BOOM (110 "Oh Rose Marie") ...5-10 72
(Red vinyl.)
CAPITOL (4053 "Chapel Bells")............ 75-100 58
(Purple label.)
CAPITOL (4053 "Chapel Bells")............. 50-75 58
(Yellow label. Promotional issue only.)
CAPITOL (4053 "Chapel Bells")............ 75-125 58
(White label. Promotional issue only.)
CAPITOL (4137 "Come to Paradise")........ 50-75 59
(Purple label. Has N 1 in dead wax.)
CAPITOL (4137 "Come to Paradise")...... 10-20 '60s
(Purple label. Has UB-2539-F1 in dead wax.)
CAPITOL (4137 "Come to Paradise").... 75-100 59
(White label. Promotional issue only.)
CAPITOL (4247 "Oh Rose Marie")....... 200-250 59
(Purple label.)
CAPITOL (4247 "Oh Rose Marie")....... 250-300 59
(Blue label. Promotional issue only.)
CAPITOL (4544 "Chapel Bells")............. 20-30 61
SPOT HITS (11 "Oh Rose Marie")........... 10-15 63
Members: Tony Passalaqua; Ed Wheeler; Nick Trivatto; Angelo LaGrecca; George Cernaeck.
Also see ARCHIES
Also see DEMOLYRS / Mystics / Five Discs / Fascinators

FASCINATORS
Singles: 7-inch
TRANS ATLAS (688 "You're to Blame").. 10-20 62
Members: Paul Tesluk; Dave Yorko; Lionel "Butch" Mattice; Bill Savitch; Eddie Fields.
Also see JOHNNY & HURRICANES

FASHIONS
Singles: 7-inch
CAMEO (331 "Baby That's Me") 5-10 64
COLLECTABLES..3-5 '80s
ELMOR (301 "Please Let It Be Me")........ 20-30 61
EMBER (1084 "Try My Love")................ 10-15 62
V-TONE (202 "I'm Dreaming of You")...... 20-30 59
(Blue label. First issue.)
V-TONE (202 "I'm Dreaming of You"/"I Love You So").. 15-20 59
(Orange label.)
V-TONE (202 "I'm Dreaming of You"/"Lonesome Road").. 10-15 59
(Orange label.)
WARWICK (646 "Dearest One")............. 10-15 61
Members: Barbara English; Frankie Brunson; Jackie La Vant; Herb Williams.
Also see ENGLISH, Barbara
Also see PEOPLE'S CHOICE

FASHIONS
Singles: 7-inch
AMY (884 "I Set a Trap for You").............10-20 63

FASHIONS
Singles: 7-inch
FELSTED (8689 "Surfers Memories")......15-25 64
GREYBAR (201 "Surfers Memories").......40-60 63
(First issue.)

FASHIONS
Singles: 7-inch
IPG (1001 "Trampoline") 10-20 63

FAST BACKS
Singles: 7-inch
ARA (201 "Fast Back Coupe") 10-20 64

FASTELLS
Singles: 7-inch
NIGHT OWL (6781 "So Much")................15-25 67

FASTEST GROUP ALIVE
Singles: 7-inch
TEEN (100 "The Bears") 20-30 67
VALIANT (754 "The Bears")......................10-20 66
VALIANT (759 "Lullabye 5:15 Sports").....10-20 67
Member: Davie Allan.
Also see ALLAN, Davie

FAT CITY
Singles: 7-inch
PARAMOUNT (0162 "Morning Go Away")...4-6 72
PARAMOUNT (0176 "Workingman's Day") .4-6 72
PROBE (469 "City Cat")............................5-10 69
LPs: 10/12-inch
PROBE (4508 "Reincarnation") 15-20 69
PARAMOUNT..12-15 72
Members: Bill Danoff; Taffy Nivert.
Also see DENVER, John

FAT MAN
Singles: 78 rpm
J.O.B. (103 "You've Got to Stop This Mess")..100-125 50
NASHBORO (516 "You've Got to Stop This Mess")..75-100 50

FAT WATER
Singles: 7-inch
MGM (14101 "Santa Anna Speed Queen")..5-8 69
LPs: 10/12-inch
MGM..10-15 69
Also see ONE EYED JACKS

FATS JR.
(Fats, Jr.)
Singles: 7-inch
D&H (4021 "Little Mary") ....20-30 '60s

FATS JR. & SKYSCRAPERS
Singles: 7-inch
ALTON (256 "Flying Low") 20-30 59
Also see FATS JR.
Also see SKYSCRAPERS

FATSO & FLAIRS
(Fatso Theus)
Singles: 78 rpm
ALADDIN..75-125 56
Singles: 7-inch
ALADDIN (3324 "Be Cool, My Heart")..300-400 56

FAULK, Roland
Singles: 7-inch
BIG STATE (592 "My Baby's Gone")........50-75

FAULKCON, Lawrence, & Sounds
Singles: 7-inch
CHECK MATE (1004 "My Girl and My Friend")..30-40 61
MAH'S (0007 "My Girl and My Friend") ..50-100 61

FAULKNER, Freddy
Singles: 7-inch
SWAN (4134 "Little Driftin' Amy") 15-20 63

FAULKNER, Gary
Singles: 7-inch
RENDEZVOUS (119 "Everybody Wants to Know") 15-25 60

FAUN
Singles: 7-inch
GREGAR (7000 "I Asked My Mother").....10-20 69
GREGAR (7001 "Son of a Literate Man") 10-20 69
LPs: 10/12-inch
GREGAR (7000 "Faun")..........................50-75 69
Members: Ross Vallory; James Trumbo; Lynn Chatwin; George Tickner.
Also see FRUMIOUS BANDERSNATCH

FAUTHEREE, Jimmy
Singles: 7-inch
PAULA (239 "Box Full of Git")..................10-20 66
PAULA (249 "Bells of Monterey") 10-20 66
PAULA (279 "Overdue")............................10-20 67

FAWCETT, Ed
Singles: 7-inch
BIG RED (101 "Love Me Love Me Love Me") 100-200

FAWNS
Singles: 7-inch
APT (25015 "Until I Die")..........................10-15 58
CAPCITY (105 "Wish You Were Here with Me")..10-15 67
RCA (0521 "Problem Child")........................4-8 71
TEC (3015 "Girl in Trouble") 8-12 65
Picture Sleeves
RCA (0521 "Problem Child")........................5-8 71

FAX
(With Alex Campbell)
Singles: 7-inch
TRANSACTION (701 "Her Love") 20-30 66
TRANSACTION (702 "Just Walking in the Rain")..20-30 66
Members: Mike Palmer; Greg Fritsch; Steve Noffke; Greg Haskell.
Also see LADDS

FAX / Lost & Found
Singles: 7-inch
TRANSACTION (704 "I'll Go Crazy"/"If I Needed Someone")..20-30 67
Picture Sleeves
TRANSACTION (704 "I'll Go Crazy"/"If I Needed Someone")..25-35 67
Members [Lost & Found]: Larry Leach; Mark Heller; Eric Severson; Jeff Cozy.
Also see FAX

FAX, Tony R&B '68
Singles: 7-inch
CALLA (151 "Lean on Me")......................10-15 68

FAY, Flo
Singles: 7-inch
LAWN (206 "I Promise")...........................10-20 63

FAY, Johnny, & Blazers
Singles: 7-inch
DANI (1539 "Cindy")...............................100-150

FAYNE, Chuck
Singles: 7-inch
CREST (1094 "Tokyo Stomp")..................10-20 62
CREST (1108 "If My Heart Had Wings") ..10-20 62

FAYNE, Wally
Singles: 7-inch
HI-FIRE (1001 "Lonely")..........................20-30 59

FAYROS
Singles: 7-inch
RCA (37-7914 "Skokiaan").......................15-25 61
(Compact 33 Single.)
RCA (47-7914 "Skokiaan")..........................8-12 61

FEAGANS, Jimmy, & Jap Curry Blazers
Singles: 7-inch
HOWARD (501 "Saturday Night")............15-25 59

FEARSOME FOURSOME
Singles: 7-inch
CAPITOL (5482 "Stranded in the Jungle").8-12 65
Picture Sleeves
CAPITOL (5482 "Stranded in the Jungle")..15-25 65
Members: Merlin Olson; Roosevelt Greer; Deacon Jones; Lamar Lundy.

FEATHERBED
(Barry Manilow)
Singles: 7-inch
BELL (971 "Amy")......................................50-75 71
BELL (45133 "Could It Be Magic") 50-100 71
Also see MANILOW, Barry

FEATHERS
(Johnny Staton & Feathers; with Johnny Moore's Blazers)
Singles: 78 rpm
ALADDIN 50-75 54-55
HOLLYWOOD 150-200 56
SHOW TIME..50-75 54-55
Singles: 7-inch
ALADDIN (3267 "Johnny Darling").......100-200 54
ALADDIN (3277 "I Need a Girl")...........200-300 55
(Maroon label.)
ALADDIN (3277 "I Need a Girl")...........300-400 55
(Orange label.)
CLASSIC ARTISTS (109 "Irene")...............5-8 88
(Black vinyl. 1000 made.)
CLASSIC ARTISTS (109 "Irene")............. 10-20 88
(Blue vinyl. 250 made.)
CLASSIC ARTISTS (125 "At the Altar")....... 4-6 91
(Black vinyl. 1000 made.)
HOLLYWOOD (1051 "Dear One")....1000-1200 56
SHOW TIME (1104 "Nona")..................100-150 54
SHOW TIME (1105 "Why Don't You Write Me"/"Busy As a Bee")..150-200 55
SHOW TIME (1105 "Why Don't You Write Me"/"Where Did Caledonia Go")..................................50-75 55
(Flip by Five Stars.)
SHOW TIME (1106 "Love Only You")..200-250 55
Members: Johnny Staton; Mitchell Alexander; Louis Staton.
Also see BELVIN, Jesse, & Five Keys / Feathers
Also see CHARGERS
Also see FIVE STARS
Also see MOORE, Johnny
Also see MOY, June
Also see STATON, Johnny, & Feathers / Jaguars

FEATHERS, Charlie
(With Jody & Jerry)
Singles: 78 rpm
FLIP (503 "I've Been Deceived") 200-300 55
KING...50-100 56
METEOR..100-200 56
SUN (231 "Defrost Your Heart") 100-200 56
SUN (503 "I've Been Deceived") 200-300 55
Singles: 7-inch
FEATHERS..3-5 80
FLIP (503 "I've Been Deceived") 500-600 55
HOLIDAY INN (114 "Deep Elm Blues")..100-200 63
KAY (1001 "Jungle Fever") 100-200 58
KING (4971 "Everybody's Lovin' My Baby")..200-400 56
KING (4971 "Everybody's Lovin' My Baby")..500-600 56
(White bio label. Promotional issue only.)
KING (4997 "One Hand Loose")...........300-500 56
(Blue label.)
KING (4997 "One Hand Loose")...........600-750 56
(White bio label. Promotional issue only.)
KING (5022 "Nobody's Woman")..........200-300 56
KING (5043 "Too Much Alike") 200-300 56
MEMPHIS (103 "Wild Wild Party") 150-250 62
METEOR (5032 "Tongue Tied Jill")....800-1200 56
(Maroon label.)
METEOR (5032 "Tongue Tied Jill")......400-600 56
(Black label.)
PHILWOOD (223 "Tear It Up") 25-35
POMPADOUR 4-6 74
ROLLIN' ROCK..3-5 78
SUN (231 "Defrost Your Heart") 600-700 56
SUN (503 "I've Been Deceived") 500-600 55
LPs: 10/12-inch
BARRELHOUSE 8-10 78
Session: Jody Chastain; Jerry Huffman.
Also see MORGAN, Charlie
Also see SELF, Mack, & Charlie Feathers

FEDERAL DUCK
LPs: 10/12-inch
MUSICOR (3162 "Federal Duck") 15-20 68

FEDERALS
Singles: 78 rpm
DELUXE (6112 "Come Go with Me").......20-30 57
FURY 30-40 57-58

Singles: 7-inch
DELUXE (6112 "Come Go with Me")....... 30-40 57
FURY (1005 "While Our Hearts Are Young")........ 50-75 57
FURY (1009 "Dear Lorraine")................ 75-100 58
Members: Rudy Anderson; James Pender; Ken Fox; Lorenzo Cook.
Also see WHEELS

FE-FI FOUR + TWO
Singles: 7-inch
LANCE (101 "I Wanna Come Back [From the World of LSD]")........ 100-150 66
ODEX (1042 "Mr. Sweet Stuff")............... 10-15 67

FEGER, Don, & Embers
Singles: 7-inch
EBONY (102 "Don't Be Mad")............... 75-100 58
EBONY (103 "Look Out Baby")............. 75-100 58

FELDMAN, Victor P&R '62
(Victor Feldman All Stars; Trio; Quartet; Vic Feldman)
Singles: 7-inch
AVA (123 "David and Lisa Theme")............4-8 63
INFINITY (020 "Valerie")..........................4-8 63
INFINITY (025 "New Dell High")..................4-8 63
INFINITY (030 "Moon River").......................4-8 64
PACIFIC JAZZ (88127 "Do the Jake")..........4-8 66
VEE-JAY (630 "Hard to Find").......................4-8 64
LPs: 10/12-inch
AVA.................... 10-20 63
CONTEMPORARY.................... 15-25 58-60
INTERLUDE.................... 15-20 59
MODE.................... 20-30 58
NAUTILUS.................... 10-20 82
(Half-speed mastered.)
PACIFIC JAZZ.................... 10-15 67-68
PALTO ALTO....................5-10 83-84
RIVERSIDE.................... 15-20 61
VEE-JAY.................... 15-25 59-65
WORLD PACIFIC.................... 15-25 62

FELICIANO, Jose P&R/R&B/LP '68
Singles: 7-inch
ALA....................3-5 80
MOTOWN....................3-5 81-83
PRIVATE STOCK....................4-6 75-77
RCA (0206 thru 0341)....................3-6 70-74
RCA (8004 "Tu Me Haces Falla")...............3-5 70
RCA (8425 "Everybody Do the Click").......8-12 64
RCA (8683 thru 9085)....................5-10 65-67
RCA (9550 thru 9807)....................4-8 68-70
RCA (10000 series)....................3-6 74-75
LPs: 10/12-inch
CAMDEN....................8-10 72
MOTOWN....................5-10 81
PRIVATE STOCK....................6-10 76-77
RCA (Except 183 & 3000 series)...............8-15 68-76
RCA (183 "Sombres, Una Vox, Una Guitarra")........ 10-15 67
RCA (3358 "The Voice and Guitar of Jose Feliciano")........ 10-20 65
RCA (3503 "Bag Full of Soul")................ 10-15 66
RCA (3581 "Fantastic Feliciano")............ 10-15 66
RCA (3957 "Feliciano")................ 10-15 68

FELICIANO, Jose / Petula Clark
EPs: 7-inch
TK (334 "Mackenna's Gold")................... 10-20 69
Also see CLARK, Petula

FELICIANO, Jose, & Quincy Jones
LPs: 10/12-inch
RCA (4096 "Mackenna's Gold").............. 15-25 69
(Soundtrack.)
Also see FELICIANO, Jose
Also see JONES, Quincy

FELICITY
Singles: 7-inch
WILSON (101 "Hurtin' ")........................ 20-30 67

FELIX & ESCORTS
Singles: 7-inch
JAG (685 "The Syracuse")...................... 30-40 62
Members: Felix Cavaliere; Mike Esposito.
Also see BLUES MAGOOS
Also see CAVALIERE, Felix
Also see CRITTERS / Young Rascals / Lou Christie

FELIX & FABULOUS CATS
("With His Fabulous Guitar")
Singles: 7-inch
AUL (1 "Puerto Rican Riot")................... 15-25 59

ENITH (1272 "Savage Girl")......................10-20 65
Also see GARCIA, Felix

FELLER, Herman, Jr.
Singles: 7-inch
CUCA (1007 "Swiss Teen Song")............15-25 60

FELT
LPs: 10/12-inch
NASCO (9006 "Felt")............................150-250 71
Members: Mike Neel; Mike Jackson; Stan Lee; Tom Gilstrap; Al Dalrymple.

FELTS, Derrell
Singles: 7-inch
DIXIE (2008 "Playmates")......................200-250 58
OKEH (7118 "Great Big Day")..............100-200 59

FELTS, Narvel P&R '60/C&W '73
Singles: 78 rpm
MERCURY....................10-20 57
Singles: 7-inch
ABC....................3-5 78
ABC/DOT....................4-6 75-77
ACTION....................4-8 70
ARA....................5-10 64-65
CELEBRITY CIRCLE....................4-8 65
CINNAMON....................4-6 73-74
COLLAGE....................3-5 79
COMPLEAT....................3-5 82-83
CONE....................3-5 92
DOT....................4-6 75-77
EVERGREEN....................3-5 82-91
GMC....................3-5 81
GROOVE....................5-10 63
HI (2100 series)....................4-8 66-68
HI (2305 "I Had to Cry Again")....................4-6 76
HI COUNTRY (8000 series)....................4-6 72-73
KARI....................3-5 80
LOBO....................3-5 82
MCA....................3-5 79
MERCURY (71140 "Kiss a Me Baby").....20-30 57
MERCURY (71190 "Cry Baby Cry")........20-30 57
MERCURY (71249 "Rocket Ride")..........20-30 57
MERCURY (71275 "Rocket Ride Stroll")..20-30 57
MERCURY (71347 "Little Girl Step This Way")....................20-30 58
PINK....................15-25 59-60
RENAY....................5-10 62-65
RENEGADE....................3-5 91
STARLINE....................8-12 62
Picture Sleeves
CONE....................3-5 92
LPs: 10/12-inch
ABC....................5-10 78-79
ABC/DOT....................8-10 75-77
ACTION....................30-40 70
CINNAMON....................8-10 73-74
MCA....................5-8 '80s
HI....................8-10 76

FELTS, Narvel / Red Sovine / Mel Tillis
LPs: 10/12-inch
POWER PAK....................5-10 77
Also see SOVINE, Red
Also see TILLIS, Mel

FELTS, Narvel, & Sharon Vaughn C&W '74
Singles: 7-inch
CINNAMON (793 "Until the End of Time")...4-6 74
Also see FELTS, Narvel

FEMALE BEATLES
Singles: 7-inch
20TH FOX (531 "I Want You")................10-20 64

FEMININE COMPLEX
Singles: 7-inch
ATHENA (5006 "I Won't Run")....................5-10 69
LPs: 10/12-inch
ATHENA....................15-20 69

FENCEMEN
Singles: 7-inch
LIBERTY (55509 "Bach N' Roll").............10-20 62
LIBERTY (55535 "Sunday Stranger").......10-20 63
Member: David Gates.
Also see GATES, David

FENDER, Freddy C&W/P&R/LP '75
(Baldemar Huerta)
Singles: 78 rpm
FALCON....................5-10 56

Singles: 7-inch
ABC....................4-6 76-79
ABC/DOT....................4-6 75-77
ARV INT'L....................4-8 75
ARGO (5375 "A Man Can Cry")...............10-15 60
DISCOS DOMINANTE....................5-10
DUNCAN (1000 "Mean Woman")............30-40 59
DUNCAN (1001 "Wasted Days, Wasted Nights")....................20-30 59
GRT....................4-8 75-76
GOLDBAND....................5-10 '60s
GOLDIES 45....................3-6 74
IDEAL....................10-20 '60s
IMPERIAL (5659 "Mean Woman")............8-12 60
IMPERIAL (5670 "Wasted Days, Wasted Nights")....................10-20 60
INSTANT (3332 "Some People Say").........4-8 72
MCA....................3-5 82
NORCO....................5-10 63-65
STARFLITE....................3-6 79-80
TALENT SCOUT (1013 "Wasted Days, Wasted Nights")....................20-30 60
W.B.....................3-5 83
LPs: 10/12-inch
ABC....................5-10 78-79
ABC/DOT....................8-10 75-77
ACCORD....................5-10 81
BIRCHMONT....................5-10 '80s
BRYLEN....................5-10 82
51 WEST....................5-10 79
GRT....................8-10 75
PICCADILLY....................5-10 81
PICKWICK....................5-10 '70s
POWER PAK....................5-10 75-80
STARFLITE....................5-10 80
SUFFOLK MARKETING....................5-10 76
Also see HUERTA, Baldemar
Also see WAYNE, Scotty

FENDER, Freddy, & Tommy McLain
LPs: 10/12-inch
CRAZY CAJUN....................5-10 78
Also see FENDER, Freddy
Also see McLAIN, Tommy

FENDER, Freddy, & Sir Douglas
LPs: 10/12-inch
CRAZY CAJUN....................5-10 78
Also see SAHM, Doug

FENDER, Freddy, & Noel Vill
Singles: 7-inch
NORCO (107 "The Magic of Love")...........5-10 65
SOCK-O (101 "The Magic of Love").........10-20 65
(First issue.)
Also see FENDER, Freddy

FENDER, Jerry, & Secrets
Singles: 7-inch
ROYALTY (99005 "Come On Little Angel")....................40-50

FENDERBENDERS
(Sherwin Linton & Fenderbenders)
Singles: 7-inch
AGAR (5407 "Six Days on the Road #2")....................8-12 '60s
RAKO (6201 "Twist a Hole in the Ground")....................10-20 62
LPs:10/12-inch
RISE (5-5745 "One Night At the Frontier Club")....................5-10 65
SMIGER (6-6374 "Sherwin Linton and the Fenderbenders")....................10-15 66
Also see LINTON, Sherwin
Also see TREBUS, Bob, & Fender Benders

FENDER IV
Singles: 7-inch
IMPERIAL (Except 66061)......................10-20 64-66
IMPERIAL (66061 "Mar Gaya")...............75-100 64
Member: Randy Holden.
Also see HOLDEN, Randy

FENDER "GUITAR" SLIM
Singles: 7-inch
ENRICA (1006 "Atomic Blues")...............10-15 60

FENDERMEN
Singles: 7-inch
DAB (102 "Rain Drop")...........................15-25 59
Also see STEWART, Don, & Fendermen

FENDERMEN P&R/C&W '60
Singles: 78 rpm
APEX (76683 "Mule Skinner Blues")....100-150 60
(Canadian.)
Singles: 7-inch
APEX (21802 "Mule Skinner Blues")........10-15 '60s
(Canadian. Reissue)
APEX (76683 "Mule Skinner Blues")........20-30 60
(Canadian.)
COLLECTABLES....................3-5 '80s
CUCA (1003 "Mule Skinner Blues").....100-150 60
(Reportedly 500 made.)
ERA....................4-6 72
ERIC....................4-6 '70s
KOALA....................3-5
SOMA (1137 "Mule Skinner Blues").........10-20 60
SOMA (1142 "Don't You Just Know It")....10-20 60
(Has "KB 1969A" etched in vinyl trail-off.)
SOMA (1142 "Don't You Just Know It")....25-50 60
(Alternative take. Has "KB 1969A R-5" etched in vinyl trail-off.)
SOMA (1155 "Heartbreakin' Special")......10-20 60
LPs: 10/12-inch
POINT (213 "Mule Skinner Blues").......250-350 61
(Canadian.)
SOMA (1240 "Mule Skinner Blues")...800-1200 60
(Solid black vinyl. The cover stock on at least one known counterfeit is soft and flimsy – not of rigid cardboard like originals.)
SOMA (1240 "Mule Skinner Blues").1000-1500 60
(Vinyl is clearer and appears to be blue when held to a light.)
Members: Phil Humphrey; Jimmy Sundquist; John Hauer; Denny Dale Gudin.
Also see HUMPHREY, Phil
Also see MULESKINNERS
Also see SUN, Jimmy, & Radiants

FENDERS
Singles: 7-inch
QQ (245 "Honky Tonk Hardwood Floor").50-75

FENWAYS
Singles: 7-inch
BEV MAR (401 "Nothing to Offer You")...10-15 64
BEV MAR (402 "Be Careful Little Girl")....10-15 64
BLUE CAT (116 "Hard Road Ahead")......10-15 65
CHESS (1901 "Nothing to Offer You").......5-10 64
CO & CE....................5-10 66-67
IMPERIAL (66082 "The Walk")..................8-12 64
RICKY "C" (106 "Nothing to Offer You") 75-125 64
ROULETTE (4573 "Be Careful Little Girl").5-10 64
Members: Sonny DiNuzio; Joey Covington.
Also see JEFFERSON AIRPLANE
Also see RACKET SQUAD
Also see VIBRA-SONICS

FENWYCK
Singles: 7-inch
CHALLENGE (59369 "I'm Spinning").......15-25 67
PROGRESSIVE SOUNDS (103 "Lye").....15-25 67
Also see RAYE, Jerry / Fenwyck

FERGERSON, Charlie (Little Jazz)
Singles: 78 rpm
TIMELY (1008 "Low Lights")....................8-12 54
Singles: 7-inch
TIMELY (1008 "Low Lights")....................15-25 54

FERGERSON, Dottie
(With Five Stars; Dottie Ferguson)
Singles: 78 rpm
KERNEL (003 "Slow Burn")....................25-50 57
MERCURY....................15-25 57
Singles: 7-inch
KERNEL (003 "Slow Burn")....................25-50 57
MERCURY (71129 "Slow Burn")..............15-25 57
MERCURY (71182 "Darling It's Wonderful")....................10-15 57

FERGUSON, H-Bomb
(With His Mad Lads; Robert Ferguson)
Singles: 78 rpm
ARC (9001 "Little Tiger")....................50-75 57
SAVOY....................20-30 52
Singles: 7-inch
ARC (9001 "Little Tiger")....................50-75 57
ATLAS (1250 "I Love My Baby")..............10-20 61
BIG BANG (103 "No-Sackie Sack")..........50-75 58
FEDERAL (12399 "Boo Hoo")..................15-25 61
FEDERAL (12411 "I'm So Lonely")...........15-25 61
FINCH (354 "She Don't Want Me").......100-200
SAVOY (830 "Slowly Goin' Crazy")..........40-60 52

SAVOY (836 "Bookie's Blues") 40-60 52
SAVOY (848 "Preachin' the Blues") 40-60 52
Also see PARKER, Jack "The Bear"

FERGUSON, H-Bomb / Escos / Mascots
LPs: 10/12-inch
AUDIO LAB (1567 "A Little Rock and Roll for Everybody") 800-1200 61
Also see ESCOS
Also see MASCOTS

FERGUSON, H-Bomb, & Varetta Dillard
Singles: 78 rpm
SAVOY (865 "Tortured Love") 15-25 52
Singles: 7-inch
SAVOY (865 "Tortured Love") 35-45 52
Also see DILLARD, Varetta
Also see FERGUSON, H-Bomb

FERGUSON, Johnny *P&R '60*
Singles: 7-inch
DECCA (30731 "Last Date") 10-20 58
MGM (12789 "Afterglow") 10-20 59
MGM (12855 "Angela Jones") 10-20 60
MGM (12905 "I Understand") 10-20 60
MGM (12960 "Valley of Love") 10-20 60

FERGUSON, Leon
Singles: 7-inch
GALAXY (737 "Stokin' ") 10-20 65

FERGUSON, Maynard *LP '73*
(Maynard Ferguson Sextet; with His Octet)
Singles: 78 rpm
CAPITOL 4-8 50-51
EMARCY 4-8 54
MERCURY 4-8 55
Singles: 12-inch
COLUMBIA 5-8 79
Singles: 7-inch
CAMEO (261 "Theme from Naked City") 5-10 63
CAMEO (275 "Groove") 5-10 63
CAPITOL 10-20 50-51
COLUMBIA 3-6 71-82
EMARCY 10-20 54
MAINSTREAM 4-6 71-72
MERCURY (70686 "Finger Snappin' ") 10-20 55
ROULETTE 8-12 58-62
Picture Sleeves
CAPITOL (1713 "Hot Canary") 20-30 51
EPs: 7-inch
EMARCY 10-20 54-57
LPs: 10/12-inch
BETHLEHEM 5-10 78
CAMEO 20-30 63
COLUMBIA 5-10 71-82
EMARCY (400 series) 5-10 76
EMARCY (1000 series) 5-10 81
EMARCY (26017 "Hollywood Party") ... 100-200 54
(10-inch LP.)
EMARCY (26024 "Dimensions") 100-200 54
(10-inch LP.)
EMARCY (36000 series) 25-50 55-57
ENTERPRISE 8-12 68
MAINSTREAM (300 series) 6-12 71-72
MAINSTREAM (6000 series) 15-25 64-65
(Stereo.)
MAINSTREAM (56000 series) 10-20 64-65
(Monaural.)
MERCURY 20-30 60
MOSAIC (156 "Complete Roulette Recordings of Maynard Ferguson") .... 200-225 '90s
(Boxed 14 audiophile LP set. 5000 made.)
PALTO ALTO 5-10 83
PRESTIGE 8-12 69
ROULETTE (Except 52027 thru 52110) 8-12 68-72
ROULETTE (52027 thru 52110) 20-40 58-64
SKYLARK (17 "Great Jazz Solos") 50-75 53
TRIP 5-10 74
WYNCOTE .... 10-15 '60s
Also see AXIDENTALS
Also see BASIE, Count, & Maynard Ferguson
Also see CARPENTER, Ike
Also see KENTON, Stan
Also see MANN, Herbie / Maynard Ferguson

FERGUSON, Maynard, & Chris Connor
Singles: 7-inch
ATLANTIC (5014 "Through the Teenage Years") 8-12 61
EPs: 7-inch
ROULETTE (1-333 "Two's Company") 10-20 58
LPs: 10/12-inch
ATLANTIC (8049 "Double Exposure") 25-35 61
(Monaural.)
ATLANTIC (SD-8049 "Double Exposure") 35-45 61
(Stereo.)
ROULETTE (52068 "Two's Company") 40-60 58
Also see CONNOR, Chris
Also see FERGUSON, Maynard

FERGUSON, Pat
Singles: 7-inch
STOMPER TIME (13 "Fool That I Am") 50-75

FERGUSON, Rudy
(With Teacho Wiltshire & His Band)
Singles: 78 rpm
CHART (604 "Together") 10-15 55
PRESTIGE (798 "Cool Goofin' ") 15-25 52
Singles: 7-inch
CHART (604 "Together") 15-25 55
PRESTIGE (798 "Cool Goofin' ") 25-45 52
Also see WILTSHIRE, Teacho

FERGUSON, Sheila
Singles: 7-inch
LANDA (706 "How Did That Happen") 15-25 65
SWAN (4217 "Don't") 20-30 65
SWAN (4225 "And in Return") 15-25 65
SWAN (4234 "Heartbroken Memories") ...20-30 65

FERGUSON, Tommy, Trio
Singles: 78 rpm
ARCADE (119 "Just an Old Fashioned Christmas") 5-10 54
Singles: 7-inch
ARCADE (119 "Just an Old Fashioned Christmas") 10-20 54
CAMEO (104 "Mary Anne") 10-15 57

FERGUSON, Troy
Singles: 7-inch
FLAME (101 "At the Jamboree") 400-500
SHARP (107 "Should I Get Wise") 5-10 60
SHARP (114 "How Many Hearts") 5-10 61

FERGUSON, DAVIS & JONES
Singles: 7-inch
EPIC (10592 "I Think I'm Gonna Cry") 10-15 70

FERGUSON, DAVIS & LEE
Singles: 7-inch
CHESS (2138 "She's Gone") 5-10 73
GRT (51 "Please Don'tcha Mention") 10-15 72

FERIS WHEEL
Singles: 7-inch
MAGENDA (5653 "Best Part of Breaking Up") 10-15 65

FERN, Mike
(Mike Fernandez)
Singles: 7-inch
DEMO (4 "A-Bomb Bop") 100-150

FERNANDEZ, Mike
Singles: 7-inch
RAYMOND'S (735 "A-Bomb Bop") 200-300
Also see FERN, Mike

FERRANTE & TEICHER *P&R/R&B '60*
Singles: 78 rpm
COLUMBIA 3-5 53
ENTRE 3-6 53
Singles: 7-inch
ABC-PAR 8-12 58-62
COLUMBIA 8-12 53
DAVIS (451 "Boogie Express") 8-12 57
ENTRE 8-12 53
MGM 8-12 54
U.A. (196 thru 373) 8-12 59-61
U.A. (431 thru 50963) 3-8 62-72
WESTMINSTER 5-10 55-58
Picture Sleeves
U.A. (231 "Theme from *The Apartment*") ..10-20 60
U.A. (274 "Theme from *Exodus*") 10-15 60
U.A. (300 "Love Theme from *One Eyed Jacks*") 10-15 61
(Pictures film's star, Marlon Brando.)
U.A. (537 "The Wishing Star") 8-12 63
U.A. (735 "The 7th Dawn") 8-12 64
U.A. (816 "Greatest Story Ever Told") 8-12 65
U.A. (50038 "Khartoum") 5-10 67
EPs: 7-inch
COLUMBIA (418 "Continental Holiday") 5-10 55
COLUMBIA (1719/1720 "Me and Juliet") ...5-10 55
(Price is for either volume.)
MGM (209 "Piano Playhouse") 8-12 54
LPs: 10/12-inch
ABC 5-10 73-76
ABC-PAR 12-25 58-66
AVANT GARDE 5-10
COLUMBIA (1607 "Broadway to Hollywood") 10-20 61
(Monaural.)
COLUMBIA (6264 "Me and Juliet") 20-40 55
COLUMBIA (6291 "Continental Holiday") 20-40 55
COLUMBIA (8407 "Broadway to Hollywood") 10-20 61
(Stereo.)
COLUMBIA (10073 "Broadway to Hollywood") 5-10 73
DORAL 10-20
(Promotional mail-order issue, from Doral cigarettes.)
GUEST STAR 5-10 64
HARMONY 5-10 64-70
LIBERTY 5-10 81-84
MGM (209 "Piano Playhouse") 20-40 54
METRO 8-12 66
MISTLETOE 4-8 75
SUNSET 5-10 70-71
WESTMINSTER 20-30 55-58
UNART 5-10 67
U.A. (70 "Golden Piano Hits") 10-15 70
(Two discs.)
U.A. (73 "Best of Ferrante and Teicher") ..10-15 71
(Two discs.)
U.A. (77 "Ferrante and Teicher") 10-15 71
(Two discs.)
U.A. (072 thru 1016) 5-10 73-80
U.A. (3121 thru 3636) 10-20 60-68
U.A. (5000 series) 5-10 71-72
U.A. (6121 thru 6659) 12-25 60-68
U.A. (6677 thru 6792) 5-10 69-71
URANIA 4-8
Members: Arthur Ferrante; Louis Teicher.
Also see BELL, Vincent

FERRARI'S OF CANADA
Singles: 7-inch
DCP (1110 "Girls") 15-25 64
DCP (1140 "Tennessee Waltz") 15-25 65

FERRARIS
Singles: 7-inch
WELHAVEN (1001 "Can't Explain") ....20-30 '60s

FERREL BROTHERS
Singles: 7-inch
FLASH (101 "Oh Moon") 50-75

FERRELL, Eddie
Singles: 7-inch
ASTA (100 "Teach Me How to Rock") 50-70 61

FERRIER, Al
(With His Boppin' Billies)
Singles: 78 rpm
EXCELLO (2105 "Hey! Baby!") 30-50 57
GOLDBAND 15-25 56-57
Singles: 7-inch
EXCELLO (2105 "Hey! Baby!") 50-100 57
(Counterfeits have "Issued in 1973" etched in the vinyl trail-off.)
GOLDBAND (1031 "No No Baby") 100-200 56
GOLDBAND (1035 "My Baby Done Gone Away") 100-200 56
GOLDBAND (1072 "Let's Go Boppin' Tonight") 150-250 58
GOLDBAND (1212 thru 1295) ....8-12 '60s
ROCKO (502 "Kiss Me Baby") 35-45 60
ZYNN (510 "Chisholm Trail Rock") 15-25 58
ZYNN (1013 "She Left Me") 10-15 59
LPs: 10/12-inch
JIN 5-10 90

FERRIS & WHEELS
Singles: 7-inch
BAMBI (801 "Chop Chop") 10-20 61
U.A. (458 "Moments Like This") 50-100 62
U.A. (458 "Moments Like This") 100-150 62
(White label. Promotional issue only.)

FERROS
Singles: 7-inch
HI-Q (5008 "Come Home My Love") 40-50 58

FEUER, Ron
LPs: 10/12-inch
DEL-FI (1209 "Vital Organ") 30-50 59
(Stereo.)

FEVER TREE *P&R/LP '68*
Singles: 7-inch
AMPEX (11013 "She Comes in Colors") ..10-20 71
MAINSTREAM (661 "Hey Mister") 5-10 67
MAINSTREAM (665 "Girl, Oh Girl") 5-10 67
UNI (Except 55060) 10-20 68-69
UNI (55060 "San Francisco Girls") 8-12 68
(Black vinyl.)
UNI (55060 "San Francisco Girls") 20-40 68
(Colored vinyl. Promotional issue only.)
LPs: 10/12-inch
AMPEX (10113 "For Sale") 15-25 71
MCA 8-10 76
UNI (73024 "Fever Tree") 20-30 68
UNI (73040 "Another Time, Another Place") 15-25 68
UNI (73067 "Creation") 15-25 70
Members: Dennis Keller; Rob Landes; E.E. Wolfe; John Tuttle. Session: Frank Davis.
Also see TRAVEL AGENCY

FEW
Singles: 7-inch
MAESTRO (4977 "Escape") 10-20 67

FIATS
Singles: 7-inch
UNIVERSAL (5003 "Speak Words of Love") 30-40 64

FIDELITONES
Singles: 7-inch
ALADDIN (3442 "The Game of Love") .100-150 58

FIDELITONES
Singles: 7-inch
MARLO (1518 "Playboy") 25-35 61

FIDELITYS *P&R '58*
(With Sammy Lowe & Orchestra)
Singles: 7-inch
BATON (252 "The Things I Love") 20-30 58
BATON (256 "Memories of You") 10-15 58
BATON (261 "My Greatest Thrill") 10-15 58
SIR (271 thru 276) 10-15 59-60
SIR (277 "Wishing Star") 15-20 60
Member: Buddy Miles.
Also see LOWE, Sammy, Orchestra
Also see MILES, Buddy

FI-DELLS
Singles: 7-inch
IMPERIAL (5780 "What Is Love") 10-20 61

FI-DELLS
Singles: 7-inch
WARNER RECORDS (1014 "No Other Love") 30-40 58
LPs: 10/12-inch
JU-PAR 8-10 77

FI DELLS QUARTET
("With Rhythm Accompaniment")
Singles: 7-inch
INDIA (2663 "Hey Senorita") 150-250 61

FI-DELS
Singles: 7-inch
BARDO (529 "Why Do I Love You") 500-750 58

FIDELS
Singles: 7-inch
MUSIC CITY (806 "Love Me Tender") .200-300 57

FIDELS
Singles: 7-inch
DORE (761 "I'm Givin' You Notice") 15-25 66
MAVERICK (1008 "Boys Will Be Boys") 5-10 69

FI-DELS
Singles: 7-inch
KEYMEN (106 "Try a Little Harder") ....25-50 '60s

FIDELTONES
Singles: 7-inch
ALADDIN (3442 "Game of Love") 100-150 58
POOP DECK (101 "For Your Love") 40-50 60

FIELD, Jerry
(With the Lawyers; with Philadelphia Lawyers; with Winners)
Singles: 7-inch
PARKWAY (801 "The Trial") 15-25 58
STRAND (25003 "Celery Stalks at Midnight") 10-15 59

FIELD, Sally P&R/LP '67
(With Marge Redmond; with Madeleine Sherwood)
Singles: 7-inch
COLGEMS 5-10 67-68
Picture Sleeves
COLGEMS (1008 "Felicidad") 10-15 67
LPs: 10/12-inch
COLGEMS (106 "Sally Field, Star of The Flying Nun") 15-20 67

FIELD BROTHERS
Singles: 7-inch
CARLTON (475 "Time and Time Again") 30-40 58

FIELDS, Bobby
Singles: 78 rpm
ACE (504 "Pity Poor Me") 15-25 55
Singles: 7-inch
ACE (504 "Pity Poor Me") 35-50 55

FIELDS, Ernie P&R/R&B '59
(With His Orchestra)
Singles: 78 rpm
FRISCO (3 "Thursday Evening Blues") ... 15-20 47
GOTHAM (273 "Butch's Blues") 10-20 52
Singles: 7-inch
CAPITOL (5161 "St. Louis Blues") 5-10 64
CAPITOL (5326 "Chloe") 5-10 64
GOTHAM (273 "Butch's Blues") 20-30 52
HIGHLAND .... 8-12 '60s
JAMIE (1102 "Annie's Rock") 10-15 58
RENDEZVOUS 10-15 59-62
LPs: 10/12-inch
RENDEZVOUS (1309 "In the Mood") 40-60 60
Also see WALLS, Ann, & Ernie Fields

FIELDS, Herbie, Orchestra
Singles: 78 rpm
PARROT 10-15 53-54
Singles: 7-inch
PARROT (775 "Harlem Nocturne") 20-25 53
PARROT (806 "I Love You") 20-25 54

FIELDS, Irving, Orchestra
(Irving Fields Trio)
Singles: 78 rpm
ABC-PAR 3-5 56
FALCON 3-5 55
FIESTA 3-5 55
RCA 3-5 49
TICO 3-5 56
Singles: 7-inch
ABC-PAR 5-10 56
ATCO 5-10 58
FALCON 5-10 55
FIESTA 5-10 55
LAURIE 4-8 64
POCKET 5-10
RCA 10-15 49
TICO 8-12 56
EPs: 7-inch
KING 10-15
LPs: 10/12-inch
ABC-PAR 15-25 56
CAMDEN 15-25 57
EVEREST 10-20 61
RCA (38 "Fields Favorites") 25-40 50
(10-inch LP.)
TOPS (1562 "Irving Fields Plays Irving Berlin") 20-30 57

FIELDS, Richard
Singles: 7-inch
CORDON (101 "Devoted") 20-30 61

FIELDS, W.C. LP '69
Albums: 78 rpm
VARIETY (101 "W.C. Fields") 10-20 49
(Three discs.)
EPs: 7-inch
DECCA (34576 "W.C. Fields Excerpts") 5-10 68
(Promotional issue only.)
LPs: 10/12-inch
AMERICAN 5-10 75
BLUE THUMB 8-12
COLUMBIA 8-15 69-77
DECCA (79164 "Original Voice Tracks from His Greatest Movies") 8-12 68
(Includes poster.)
HUDSON (2002 "Tribute to W.C. Fields") 15-25 60
JAY (2001 "Temperance Lecture") .... 15-25 '50s
(10-inch LP.)
MARK '56 (571 "Original Radio Broadcasts") 10-15 73
MARK '56 (571 "Nostalgia") 70-90 78
(Picture disc. Two variations made, one with full photo of Fields standing, other shows only his upper body. Original Radio Broadcasts.)
SUTTON .... 10-20 '60s
Also see WEST, Mae, & W.C. Fields

FIESTAS P&R/R&B '59
Singles: 78 rpm
OLD TOWN (1062 "So Fine") 100-200 59
OLD TOWN (1069 "Our Anniversary") . 100-200 59
Singles: 7-inch
CHIMNEYVILLE (10216 "Tina, the Disco Queen") 10-15 77
CHIMNEYVILLE (10221 "Is That Long Enough for You") 10-15 78
COLLECTABLES .... 3-5 '80s
OLD TOWN (1062 "So Fine") 40-50 59
(With piano intro. Identification number is "ZTSP 29364.")
OLD TOWN (1062 "So Fine") 20-30 58
(No piano intro. Identification number is "920.")
OLD TOWN (1067 thru 1104) 20-30 59-61
OLD TOWN (1111 "Hobo's Prayer") 40-50 61
OLD TOWN (1122 "Broken Heart") 15-25 62
OLD TOWN (1127 "I Feel Good All Over") 15-25 62
OLD TOWN (1134 thru 1166) 10-20 63-64
OLD TOWN (1178 "Think Smart") 30-40 65
OLD TOWN (1187 "Love Is Good to Me") 10-15 65
OLD TOWN (1189 "Ain't She Sweet") 20-30 65
RESPECT 4-6 75
STRAND (25046 "Julie") 30-40 61
VIGOR (712 "So Fine") 4-6 74
Members: Tom Bullock; Eddie Morris; Sam Ingalls; Preston Lane.
Also see ROBERT & JOHNNY / Fiestas

5TH AVENUE BUSSES
Singles: 7-inch
20TH FOX (6652 "Green Hornet") 5-10 66
20TH FOX (6653 "Fantastic Voyage") 5-10 66
LPs: 10/12-inch
MOVIETONE (71029 "Trip to Gotham City") 15-20 67
(Monaural.)
MOVIETONE (72029 "Trip to Gotham City") 20-25 67
(Stereo.)

FIFTH DIMENSION P&R/LP '67
(5th Dimension)
Singles: 7-inch
ABC 4-6 75-76
ARISTA (101 "No Love in the Room") 4-6 75
BELL 4-6 70-74
FLASHBACK (9406 "Wedding Bell Blues") .. 3-5 85
FLASHBACK (9489 "Up-Up and Away") 3-5 86
MOTOWN 4-6 78-79
SOUL CITY (752 "I'll Be Lovin' You Forever") 50-75 66
SOUL CITY (753 thru 780) 4-8 66-70
SUTRA 3-5 83
Picture Sleeves
BELL (880 "Puppet Man") 4-6 70
SOUL CITY (753 "Go Where You Wanna Go") 5-10 66
SOUL CITY (755 "Another Day, Another Heartache") 5-10 67
SOUL CITY (766 "Stoned Soul Picnic") 5-10 68
SOUL CITY (768 "Sweet Blindness") 5-10 68
SOUL CITY (772 "Aquarius/Let the Sunshine In") 5-10 69
LPs: 10/12-inch
ABC (897 "Earthbound") 8-10 75
ARISTA 8-10 75
BELL 8-12 70-74
KORY 8-10 77
MOTOWN 5-10 78-79
RHINO 5-10 86
SOUL CITY 10-15 67-70
Members: Marilyn McCoo; Billy Davis Jr; Lamonte McLemore; Florence LaRue; Ron Townson; Danny Miller Beard; Terri Bryant; Michel Bell.
Also see GOLDENROD
Also see HI-FIs
Also see INTERVALS
Also see MAMAS & PAPAS / Association / Fifth Dimension

FIFTH ESTATE P&R '67
Singles: 7-inch
JUBILEE 5-10 67-69
RED BIRD (064 "Love Is All a Game") 10-15 66
LPs: 10/12-inch
JUBILEE (JGM-8005 "Ding Dong the Witch Is Dead") 20-30 67
(Monaural.)
JUBILEE (JGS-8005 "Ding Dong the Witch Is Dead") 25-35 67
(Stereo.)
Members: Wayne Wadhams; Rick Engler; Doug Ferrara; Bill Shute; Ken Evans.
Also see D MEN

FIFTH GENERATION
Singles: 7-inch
FONE BOOTH (1001 "If I See Her") 5-10
IGL (155 "Carolyn") 15-25 68

FIFTH ORDER
Singles: 7-inch
COUNTERPART (2571 "Goin' Too Far") . 15-25 66
COUNTERPART (2595 "Today I Got a Letter") 15-25 67
DIAMOND (212 "Goin' Too Far") 10-15 66
LAURIE (3404 "Today I Got a Letter") 5-10 67

FIFTY FOOT HOSE
(50 Foot Hose)
Singles: 7-inch
GET HIP 3-5 90
Picture Sleeves
GET HIP 3-5 90
LPs: 10/12-inch
LIMELIGHT (86062 "Cauldron") 50-100 68
Members: Nancy Blossom; Larry Evans; David Blossom.

FIG LEAF FIVE
Singles: 7-inch
DELTONE (5027 "Always Be Mine") 10-15 63

FILET OF SOUL
Singles: 7-inch
DYNAMIC SOUND (1002 "Sweet Lovin' ") 10-20 69
ZAP (002 "Moving to the Country") 8-12 70
LP: 10/12-inch
MONOQUID SOUND (4857 "Freedom") .. 10-15 68
Also see ATTILA & HUNS
Also see PEACE, Mike

FILETS OF SOUL
Singles: 7-inch
SAVOY (1630 "C'mon Let's Dance") 10-20 68
LPs: 10/12-inch
SQUID (4857 "Freedom") 75-100 68

FILLER, Marty
Singles: 7-inch
TAURUS (358 "Lucky Dreamer") 15-25 62
TAURUS (360 "Pretty Little Joanie") 8-12 62

FILMORE, Ted
Singles: 78 rpm
TNT (112 "I'm Going Home") 10-15 54
Singles: 7-inch
TNT (112 "I'm Going Home") 15-25 54

FINA, Jack
Singles: 78 rpm
MGM (10085 thru 11477) 5-8 47-53
MERCURY/SAV-WAY (5047 "Rhapsody in Blue") 100-150 47
(Picture disc. Promotional issue only.)
Singles: 7-inch
MGM 8-12 50-53
MERCURY 10-15 55
LPs: 10/12-inch
MERCURY (20084 "Jack Fina") 20-40 55
(10-inch LP.)

FINAL SECONDS
Singles: 7-inch
BOO-KOU (422/423 "Society"/"Lost on a Highway") 40-60 73

FINCH
Singles: 7-inch
MONTAGE .... 30-50 '70s
LPs: 10/12-inch
ATCO (124 "Glory of the Inner Force") 8-12 75

FINCHLEY BOYS
LPs: 10/12-inch
GOLDEN THROAT (200-19 "Everlasting Tribute") 150-200 72
Members: George Faver; J. Michael Powers.

FINDERS KEEPERS
Singles: 7-inch
CHALLENGE (59338 "Lavender Blue") ... 10-15 66
CHALLENGE (59364 "Don't Give In to Him") 10-15 67
FONTANA (1609 "On the Beach") 8-12 68

FINGER LICKIN' GOOD
Singles: 7-inch
SOUND PATTERNS (90 "Bless You") ..... 10-20 '60s

FINGERS, Rollie
Singles
AMERICAN AUDIOGRAPHICS ("Milwaukee Spells Relief") .... 10-15 '80s
(Square postcard picture disc. No selection number used.)

FINN, Gar, & Spydels
Singles: 7-inch
ASSAULT (1854 "Lonesome") 10-20 62
Also see SPYDELS

FINN, Lee
Singles: 7-inch
WESTPORT (141 "Pour Me a Glass of Wine") 15-25 59

FINN & SHARKS
Singles: 12-inch
PARK PLACE (1001 "Finn and the Sharks") 40-50 81
REBEL 15-20 81
Singles: 7-inch
HME 4-8 85
Picture Sleeves
HME 4-8 85

FINNEGAN, Mike
(With the Serfs)
Singles: 7-inch
COLUMBIA (10741 "Just One More Minute") 4-6 78
PARKWAY (113 "Bread and Water") 15-20 66
RHYTHM & SOUL (101 "Bread and Water") 15-20 66
W.B. (8264 "Misery Loves Company") 4-6 76
LPs: 10/12-inch
COLUMBIA (35258 "Black and White") 8-10 78
W.B. (2944 "Mike Finnegan") 8-10 76

FINNEY – MO
Singles: 7-inch
JELLO-JIM (102 "My Baby's Gone") 15-25 63
ROULETTE (4518 "My Baby's Gone") 8-12 63

FINNICUM
Singles: 7-inch
RUFF (1011 "Come On Over") 10-20 66

FIRE ESCAPE
Singles: 7-inch
GNP (384 "Blood Beat") 5-10 67
LPs: 10/12-inch
GNP (2034 "Psychotic Reaction") 25-35 67

FIRE OVER GIBRALTAR
Singles: 7-inch
KIM (103 "Epitaph of Tomorrow") 75-100 65
(500 made.)

FIREBALLS P&R '59
Singles: 7-inch
ASTRA (1021 "Torquay") 5-10 66
ATCO 4-8 67-69
DOT 8-12 63-67
HAMILTON (50036 "Tuff-A-Nuff") 10-20 63
KAPP (248 "Fireball") 75-100 59

QUALITY (048 "Quite a Party") 10-15 61
(Canadian.)
TOP RANK (2008 "Torquay") 10-15 59
TOP RANK (2026 "Bulldog") 10-15 59
(Monaural.)
TOP RANK (2026-ST "Bulldog") 15-25 59
(Stereo.)
TOP RANK (2038 "Foot Patter") 10-15 60
(Monaural.)
TOP RANK (2038-ST "Foot Patter") 15-25 60
(Stereo.)
TOP RANK (2054 "Vaquero") 10-15 60
TOP RANK (2081 "Sweet Talk") 10-15 60
TOP RANK (3003 "Rik-A-Tik") 10-15 61
WARWICK (630 "Rik-A-Tik") 8-10 61
WARWICK (644 "Quite a Party") 8-10 61

EPs: 7-inch

TOP RANK (1000 "The Fireballs") 50-75 60

LPs: 10/12-inch

ATCO 10-20 68-69
TOP RANK (324 "The Fireballs") 50-75 60
TOP RANK (343 "Vaquero") 50-75 60
(Monaural.)
TOP RANK (643 "Vaquero") 75-125 60
(Stereo.)
WARWICK (2042 "Here Are the Fireballs") 50-75 61
Members: Chuck Tharp; George Tomsco; Dan Trammell; Eric Budd; Stan Lark; Doug Roberts; Jimmy Gilmer; Keith McCormick.
Also see DALE, Dick / Surfaris / Fireballs
Also see GILMER, Jimmy
Also see GUITARS INC.
Also see STRING-A-LONGS
Also see THARP, Chuck
Also see TOMSCO, George

FIREFLIES — P&R '59

Singles: 7-inch

CANADIAN AMERICAN (117 "Give All Your Love to Me") 15-25 60
ERIC .... 4-6 '70s
RIBBON (6901 "You Were Mine") 15-25 59
RIBBON (6904 "I Can't Say Goodbye") ... 15-25 59
RIBBON (6906 "My Girl") 15-25 60
TAURUS (355 thru 380) 10-15 62-65

LPs: 10/12-inch

TAURUS (1002 "You Were Mine") 100-150 61
(Monaural.)
TAURUS (1002 "You Were Mine") 250-350 61
(Stereo.)
Members: Ritchie Adams; Lee Reynolds; John Viscelli; Paul Giacolone.

FIREFLYS

Singles: 7-inch

ROULETTE (4098 "The Crawl") 10-15 58

FIREMEN

Singles: 7-inch

LE CAM (13 "Jaywalk") .... 10-20 '60s
LE CAM (951 "Louie's Theme") 10-20 62

FIRESIDE SINGERS

Singles: 7-inch

HERALD (582 "Darlin' Come Home") 10-20 63

FIRESIDERS

Singles: 7-inch

SWAN (4074 "One and All") 20-30 61

FIRESTONE, Johnny

Singles: 7-inch

D&M (001 "It Happens Every Night") 3-5 85
ELMONT (1003 "Is It Love") 75-100 58

FIRST, Carl, & Showmen

Singles: 7-inch

LAWN (223 "I'm Still in Love with You") ... 10-20 63
Member: Carl "First" Falso (a.k.a. Kal Dee).
Also see SIR MEN

FIRST CROW TO THE MOON

Singles: 7-inch

ROULETTE (4774 "The Sun Lights Up Shadows of Your Mind") 15-25 67

FIRST EDITION — P&R/LP '68

Singles: 7-inch

REPRISE (0655 "Just Dropped In") 5-10 67
REPRISE (0799 "But You Know I Love You") 5-10 68

LPs: 10/12-inch

INTERMEDIA/QUICKSILVER (5056 "The First Edition") 10-15 84
(Picture disc.)
REPRISE 15-25 67-68
Members: Kenny Rogers; Mike Settle; Thelma Lou Camacho; Terry Williams; Mickey Jones.
Also see NEW CHRISTY MINSTRELS
Also see ROGERS, Kenny, & First Edition

FIRST GARRISON

Singles: 7-inch

DAMION (6532 "Tell Me No Lies") 15-25 65
Also see DOWD, Larry, & Rockatones

FIRST GRADE

Singles: 7-inch

FROG (767 "Please Come Back") .... 15-25 '60s

FIRST NATIONAL BAND

Singles: 7-inch

TENER (1018 "My Generation") 15-25 67

FIRST PLATOON

Singles: 7-inch

S.P.Q.R. (3303 "Ten Ways") 40-60 62

FIRST THEREMIN ERA

Singles: 7-inch

EPIC (10440 "Barnabas Theme from *Dark Shadows*") 5-8 69

Picture Sleeves

EPIC (10440 "Barnabas Theme from *Dark Shadows*") 10-20 69

FISCHER, Wild Man

Singles: 7-inch

REPRISE (781 "Circle") 5-10 68

LPs: 10/12-inch

BIZARRE (6332 "An Evening with Wild Man Fischer") 20-30 69
(With Frank Zappa & Mothers of Invention.)
RHINO 5-10 81
Also see MOTHERS OF INVENTION

FISHER, Al, & Lou Marks

LPs: 10/12-inch

CAMEO (1081 "Rome on the Range") 12-15 64
MARKAL (1081 "Rome on the Range") 5-10
SWAN (514 "It's a Beatle World") 15-25 64

FISHER, Brian

Singles: 7-inch

U.A. (115 "It's Up to You") 40-60 58

FISHER, Chip

Singles: 7-inch

ADDISON (16002 "No One") 15-25 59
ESCO (200 "Just As You Are") 10-20 59
RCA (7308 "Sugar Bowl Rock") 15-25 58
20TH FOX (202 "Junior High") 10-20 60

LPs: 10/12-inch

RCA (LPM-1797 "Chipper at the Sugar Bowl") 20-30 58
(Monaural.)
RCA (LSP-1797 "Chipper at the Sugar Bowl") 30-40 58
(Stereo.)

FISHER, Eddie — P&R '50

Singles: 78 rpm

RCA 5-10 50-57

Singles: 7-inch

ABC-PAR 5-10 61
DOT 4-8 65-66
MUSICOR 4-6 69
RCA (47-3000 thru 47-6000 series) 10-20 50-57
RCA (WP-3025 "Eddie Fisher Sings") ...... 25-50 '50s
(Boxed, four-disc set.)
RCA (7000 thru 9000 series) 5-15 57-68
RAMROD 5-10 60-63
7 ARTS (719 "Tonight") 5-10 62
TRANS ATLAS (698 "Till There Was You") 5-10 62

Picture Sleeves

RCA (5000 series) 15-25 53-55
RCA (6000 series) 10-15 55-57
RAMROD 8-12 60

EPs: 7-inch

RCA 10-20 51-58
RCA/COCA-COLA .... 10-20 '50s

LPs: 10/12-inch

CAMDEN 6-10 63
CROWN 8-12
DOT 10-15 65-67
FAMOUS TWINSETS 8-12 74
HAMILTON 6-10 66
RCA (1024 thru 2504) 15-30 55-62
RCA (3025 thru 3231) 20-35 52-54
(10-inch LPs.)
RCA (3375 "Best of Eddie Fisher") 10-15 65
RCA (3700 & 3800 series) 10-20 66-67
RAMROD (1 "At the Winter Garden") 10-20 63
RAMROD (6001 "Scent of Mystery") 50-60 60
(Soundtrack. Monaural.)
RAMROD (6001 "Scent of Mystery") 75-85 60
(Soundtrack Stereo.)
Also see COMO, Perry, & Eddie Fisher

FISHER, Eddie / Vic Damone / Dick Haymes

LPs: 10/12-inch

ALMOR 10-15
Also see DAMONE, Vic
Also see HAYMES, Dick

FISHER, Eddie, & Debbie Reynolds

EPs: 7-inch

RCA (4018 "Bundle of Joy") 15-25 56
(Soundtrack.)

LPs: 10/12-inch

RCA (1399 "Bundle of Joy") 40-50 56
(Soundtrack.)
Also see FISHER, Eddie
Also see REYNOLDS, Debbie

FISHER, Gene, & Mystics

Singles: 7-inch

PLATEAU (101 "Remember, You're My Girl") 75-100 62
(Same number used on a Four Pages release.)

FISHER, Johnny

Singles: 7-inch

EMMY (1003 "Tell Me Yes") .... 10-20 '60s
PARK AVENUE (125 "Tan Dan") 15-20 63

FISHER, Mary Ann — P&R '61

Singles: 7-inch

FIRE (1002 "Put On My Shoes") 5-10 59
FIRE (1010 "Only Yesterday") 5-10 60
(Another Fire 1010 exists, by the Variatones, but it is a different company.)
IMPERIAL (5853 "I Keep Comin' Back for More") 5-10 62
SEG-WAY (1001 "I Can't Take It") 10-15 61
Also see VARIATONES

FISHER, O'Brien

Singles: 7-inch

SPANGLE (502 "Monkey Love") .... 10-20 '60s
SPANGLE (2001 "Fingertips") 50-100 57

FISHER, Randy

Singles: 7-inch

SALINO (112 "I've Got the Feeling") 50-75

FISHER, Sonny

Singles: 78 rpm

STARDAY 50-75 55-56

Singles: 7-inch

PEACOCK (1947 "Hurtin' ") 5-10 66
STARDAY (179 "Rockin' Daddy") 100-200 55
STARDAY (190 "Sneaky Pete") 100-200 55
STARDAY (207 "Rockin' and a Rollin' ") 100-200 55
STARDAY (244 "Pink & Black") 100-200 56

FISHER, Toni — P&R '59

(Miss Toni Fisher)

Singles: 7-inch

BIG TOP (3097 "West of the Wall") 10-15 62
BIG TOP (3124 "Music from the House Next Door") 10-15 62
CAPITOL (5901 "Train of Love") 5-10 67
COLLECTABLES .... 3-5 '80s
COLUMBIA (42066 "Love Big") 5-10 61
ERA 4-6 72
SIGNET 5-10 59-64
SMASH 5-10 63

LPs: 10/12-inch

SIGNET (509 "The Big Hurt") 30-50 60

FITCH, Wally

Singles: 7-inch

CHART (614 "Misbelievin' Baby") 15-25 56
CHART (632 "She Loves Me So") 15-25 56
CHART (640 "Little Girl") 15-25 57
CHART (644 "I Cried All the Way Home") 15-25 57

FI-TONES

(Fi-Tones Quintette; Fi-Tone Featuring Lloyd Davis)

Singles: 78 rpm

ATLAS 25-50 55-56
OLD TOWN (1042 "My Heart") 100-200 57

Singles: 7-inch

ANGLE TONE (525 "You'll Be the Last") 75-100 58
ANGLE TONE (530 "What Am I Gonna Do") 30-40 58
ANGLE TONE (536 "Deep in My Heart") . 50-75 59
ANGLE TONE (1050 thru 1056) 3-5
ATLAS (1050 "Foolish Dreams") 200-300 55
(Atlas man logo at 11:00 on label. Reads "Atlas Record Company.")
ATLAS (1050 "Foolish Dreams") 40-60 55
(Atlas man logo at 9:00 on label. Reads "Atlas Records.")
ATLAS (1051 "It Wasn't a Lie") 50-100 55
(Large Atlas on label.)
ATLAS (1051 "It Wasn't a Lie") 20-30 55
(Small Atlas on label.)
ATLAS (1052 "I Call to You") 50-75 56
ATLAS (1055 "I Belong to You") 75-125 56
ATLAS (1056 "Waiting for Your Call") .. 100-150 56
OLD TOWN (1042 "My Heart") 300-400 57

LPs: 10/12-inch

RELIC 8-10
Members: Lloyd Davis; Gene Redd; Lowe Murray; Cecil Holmes; Ron Anderson.
Also see CAVALIERS QUARTET
Also see FIVE CHIMES

FITONES

Singles: 7-inch

STROLL (102 "Mr. Faith") 400-500 59
Also see THOMAS, Carl

FITZGERALD, Ella — P&R '36

(With the Andy Love Quintet)

Singles: 78 rpm

DECCA (800 thru 3000 series) 10-15 36-41
DECCA (18000 thru 29000 series) 5-10 42-54
VERVE 3-5 54-57

Singles: 7-inch

CAPITOL 4-8 67-68
DECCA (27000 & 28000 series) 15-25 50-53
DECCA (29000 series) 10-20 54-56
DECCA (30000 series, except 30405) 5-15 56-67
DECCA (30405 "Goody Goody") 15-25 57
PABLO 4-6 75
PRESTIGE 4-6 69
REPRISE 4-6 69-71
SALLE 4-6 68
VERVE (10000 series) 8-12 56-59
VERVE (10100 thru 10300 series, except 10340) 4-8 60-65
VERVE (10340 "Ringo Beat") 8-12 64

Picture Sleeves

VERVE 10-20 59-60

EPs: 7-inch

DECCA 15-30 50-58
VERVE 10-25 56-61

LPs: 10/12-inch

ATLANTIC 5-10 72
BAINBRIDGE 5-10 81
CAPITOL (2000 series) 8-15 67-68
CAPITOL (11000 series) 5-10 78
CAPITOL (16000 series) 4-6 82
COLUMBIA 5-12 73
CORAL 4-8 73
DECCA (156 "The Best of Ella Fitzgerald") 25-45 58
(Black label with silver print.)
DECCA (156 "The Best of Ella Fitzgerald") 15-20 65
(Black label with horizontal rainbow band.)
DECCA (4000 series) 10-20 61-67
DECCA (5084 "Souvenir Album") 75-125 49
(10-inch LP.)
DECCA (5300 "Gershwin Songs") 75-125 51
(10-inch LP.)
DECCA (8000 series) 20-40 55-59
EVEREST 5-10 73
MCA 5-10 76-82
MGM 5-10 70
MPS 5-10 72
METRO 10-15 65-66
OLYMPIC 5-10 74

PABLO....5-10 75-83
REPRISE....8-12 69-71
VERVE (29 "Ella Fitzgerald Sings the George & Ira Gershwin Songbook")....30-50 64
(Boxed, five-disc reissue of Verve 4029.)
VERVE (2500 & 2600 series)....5-10 76-82
(Reads "Manufactured By MGM Record Corp.," or mentions either Polydor or Polygram at bottom of label.)
VERVE (4001 thru 4009)....50-75 56
(Reads "Verve Records, Inc." at bottom of label.)
VERVE (4010 "Ella Fitzgerald Sings the Duke Ellington Song Book")....100-125 56
(Boxed, four-disc set.)
VERVE (4013 thru 4015)....30-50 57
(Reads "Verve Records, Inc." at bottom of label.)
VERVE (4019 "Ella Fitzgerald Sings the Irving Berlin Songbook")....30-50 58
VERVE (4020 thru 4028)....25-50 58-59
(Reads "Verve Records, Inc." at bottom of label.)
VERVE (4029 "Ella Fitzgerald Sings the George & Ira Gershwin Songbook")....50-100 59
(Boxed, five-disc set, containing individual LPs 4024 thru 4028.)
VERVE (4036 thru 4071)....10-20 59-66
VERVE (6000 series)....25-50 57-59
(Reads "Verve Records, Inc." at bottom of label.)
VERVE (6100 series)....15-25 60
(Reads "Verve Records, Inc." at bottom of label.)
VERVE (8200 series)....20-40 58
(Reads "Verve Records, Inc." at bottom of label.)
VERVE (64036 thru 64071)....15-30 59-66
VERVE (67000 & 68000 series)....8-15 67-73
VERVE (2610000 series)....20-30 83
VOCALION....6-10 67
Also see CAMPBELL, Glen / Lettermen / Ella Fitzgerald / Sandler & Young

FITZGERALD, Ella, & Louis Armstrong R&B '46

Singles: 78 rpm

DECCA....3-6 53

Singles: 7-inch

DECCA....5-8 53

EPs: 7-inch

VERVE....15-30 56

LPs: 10/12-inch

MFSL (248 "Ella & Louie Again")....35-50
METRO (601 "Louis and Ella")....5-10 67
VERVE (4003 "Ella & Louis")....50-100 56
VERVE (4006 "Ella & Louis Again")....50-100 56
VERVE (4011 "Porgy & Bess")....40-60 57
(Monaural.)
VERVE (4018 "Ella & Louis Again, Volume 2")....40-60 57
VERVE (6040 "Porgy & Bess")....50-100 59
(Stereo.)
VERVE (8811 "Ella & Louis")....5-10 72
Also see ARMSTRONG, Louis

FITZGERALD, Ella, & Count Basie LP '63

LPs: 10/12-inch

PABLO....5-10 79
VERVE....15-20 63
Also see BASIE, Count

FITZGERALD, Ella, & Delta Rhythm Boys

Singles: 78 rpm

DECCA....5-10 54

Singles: 7-inch

DECCA (29136 "For Sentimental Reasons")....10-20 54
Also see DELTA RHYTHM BOYS

FITZGERALD, Ella / Bill Doggett

Singles: 78 rpm

DECCA....4-6 53

Singles: 7-inch

DECCA....8-12 53

LPs: 10/12-inch

VERVE....15-25 62
Also see DOGGETT, Bill

FITZGERALD, Ella, & Duke Ellington

Singles: 7-inch

VERVE....4-6 66

LPs: 10/12-inch

VERVE....10-20 65-67
Also see ELLINGTON, Duke

FITZGERALD, Ella / Billie Holiday

LPs: 10/12-inch

MCA....5-10 76
VERVE (6022 "At Newport")....40-60 58
(Stereo.)
VERVE (8234 "At Newport")....30-50 58
(Monaural.)

FITZGERALD, Ella / Billie Holiday / Lena Horne

EPs: 7-inch

COLUMBIA (2531 "Ella, Lena & Billie")....25-45 56

LPs: 10/12-inch

COLUMBIA (2531 "Ella, Lena & Billie")..75-100 56
(10-inch LP.)
Also see HOLIDAY, Billie
Also see HORNE, Lena

FITZGERALD, Ella, & Ink Spots

Singles: 78 rpm

DECCA (18000 series)....4-8 44-45
DECCA (27419 "Little Small Town Girl")..10-15 51

Singles: 7-inch

DECCA (27419 "Little Small Town Girl")..15-25 51

EPs: 7-inch

DECCA (2040 "Ella Fitzgerald and the Ink Spots")....10-20 53
Also see INK SPOTS

FITZGERALD, Ella, & Antonio Carlos Jobim

LPs: 10/12-inch

PABLO....5-10 81
Also see JOBIM, Antonio Carlos

FITZGERALD, Ella, & Louis Jordan R&B '46

Singles: 78 rpm

DECCA (23546 "Petootie Pie"/"Stone Cold Dead in the Market")....5-10 46
DECCA (24644 "Baby, It's Cold Outside").5-10 49
DECCA (27200 "I'll Never Be Free")....5-10 50

Singles: 7-inch

DECCA (27200 "I'll Never Be Free")....15-25 50
DECCA (30222 "Stone Cold Dead in the Market")....8-12 57
Also see JORDAN, Louis

FITZGERALD, Ella, & Peggy Lee LP '55

LPs: 10/12-inch

DECCA (8166 "Pete Kelly's Blues")....40-60 55
Also see LEE, Peggy

FITZGERALD, Ella, & Mills Brothers P&R '37

Singles: 78 rpm

DECCA (1148 "Dedicated to You")....5-10 37
Also see MILLS BROTHERS

FITZGERALD, Ella, & Oscar Peterson

LPs: 10/12-inch

PABLO....5-10 76
Also see PETERSON, Oscar

FITZGERALD, Ella / Teddy Wilson / Lena Horne

EPs: 7-inch

COLUMBIA (1672 "Floor Show")....10-20 56
Also see FITZGERALD, Ella
Also see HORNE, Lena
Also see WILSON, Teddy

FITZHUGH, Sammy

Singles: 7-inch

ATCO (6181 "Lover's Plea")....10-20 60
POPLAR (115 "Sadie Mae")....50-75 59

FIVE, The

EPs: 7-inch

RCA (EPC-1121 "The Five")....10-20 55
(Two discs.)

LPs: 10/12-inch

RCA (LPM-1121 "The Five")....30-50 55

FIVE AMERICANS P&R/LP '66

Singles: 7-inch

ABC-PAR (10686 "Love Love Love")....5-10 65
ABNAK (Except 109)....10-15 65-69
(Black vinyl.)
ABNAK (Except 109)....15-25 67-69
(Colored vinyl.)
ABNAK (109 "I See the Light")....15-25 65
(Black vinyl.)
ABNAK (109 "I See the Light")....25-30 65
(Colored vinyl.)
HBR (454 "I See the Light")....5-10 65
HBR (468 "Evol-Not Love")....5-10 66
HBR (483 "Good Times")....5-10 66
JETSTAR (104 "It's You Girl")....10-15 65
JETSTAR (105 "Slippin' & Slidin' ")....15-20 65
PHILCO (10 "Western Union"/"Sounds of Love")....10-20 67
("Hip-Pocket" flexi-disc.)

Picture Sleeves

ABNAK (125 "Stop Light")....10-15 67
ABNAK (126 "Guided Tour")....10-15 68
HBR (468 "Evol-Not Love")....10-20 66

LPs: 10/12-inch

ABNAK....20-30 67-68
HBR (8503 "I See the Light")....30-35 66
(Monaural.)
HBR (9503 "I See the Light")....35-40 66
(Stereo.)
Members: Michael Rabon; Jimmy Wright; John Durrill.
Also see PEDESTRIANS / Association / Five Americans / Soulblenders

5 ARCADES

Singles: 7-inch

ANTRELL (103 "Heaven's Own Desire")....8-12 85
(Red vinyl.)
ANTRELL (104 "Ruby Lee")....8-12 85
(Red vinyl.)
SACTO (101 "Ruby Lee")....30-40 73
(Original must have glossy blue label.)
SACTO (103 "Heaven's Own Desire")....30-40 73
(Original must have glossy blue label.)

FIVE BARS

Singles: 78 rpm

MONEY (224 "Stormy Weather")....40-50 57

Singles: 7-inch

MONEY (224 "Stormy Weather")....50-60 57

5 BARS

Singles: 7-inch

BUBBLE (1010 "Deep in My Heart")....10-20 63

FIVE BELLS

Singles: 7-inch

CLOCK (1017 "It's You")....20-30 60

FIVE BELLS

Singles: 7-inch

STOLPER (100 "Please Remember My Heart")....10-15 '70s
(Previously unreleased.)

FIVE BILLS
(With Orchestra)

Singles: 78 rpm

BRUNSWICK (84002 "Can't Wait for Tomorrow")....100-200 53
BRUNSWICK (84004 "Till Dawn and Tomorrow")....200-300 53

Singles: 7-inch

BRUNSWICK (84002 "Can't Wait for Tomorrow")....400-600 53

FIVE BLACKS

Singles: 7-inch

B&C (100 "Forever in Love")....15-25 61
(Previously issued as by Herman Willis.)
Also see WILLIS, Herman

FIVE BLAZES

Singles: 78 rpm

ARISTOCRAT (201 "Dedicated to You")..15-25 47
ARISTOCRAT (202 "All My Geets Are Gone")....15-25 47

FIVE BLIND BOYS OF MONTANA / Sparktones

Singles: 7-inch

VINTAGE (1000 "Brother Bill"/"Well Done Baby")....10-15 72
(Red vinyl.)

FIVE BLOBS P&R '58

Singles: 7-inch

COLUMBIA (41250 "The Blob")....15-20 58
JOY (226 "Rockin' Pow Wow")....10-15 59
JOY (230 "Young and Wild")....10-15 59
Member: Bernie Nee (only member).

FIVE BLUE FLAMES

Singles: 78 rpm

COLUMBIA (39407 "My Love Has Gone")....100-200 51
OKEH (6818 "The Masquerade Is Over")....50-100 51
OKEH (6875 "Ida Red")....25-50 52
OKEH (6900 "Blue Boy")....25-50 52

Singles: 7-inch

COLUMBIA (39407 "My Love Has Gone")....350-400 51
OKEH (6818 "The Masquerade Is Over")....150-250 51
OKEH (6875 "Ida Red")....50-75 52
OKEH (6900 "Blue Boy")....50-75 52

FIVE BLUE NOTES
(Five Blue Notes/Jammers featuring Sonny Stevenson)

Singles: 78 rpm

SABRE (103 "My Gal Is Gone")....150-200 54
SABRE (108 "The Beat of Our Hearts")....150-200 54

Singles: 7-inch

ONDA (108 "My Special Prayer"/"The Thunderbird")....25-35 59
ONDA (888 "My Special Prayer"/"Somethin' Awful")....50-75 58
(First issue.)
SABRE (103 "My Gal Is Gone")....500-750 53
(Black vinyl.)
SABRE (103 "My Gal Is Gone")....1000-1500 53
(Red vinyl.)
SABRE (108 "The Beat of Our Hearts")....1000-2000 54
(White label.)
Members: Fleming Briscoe; Andy Magruder; Jackie Shedrick; Bob Stroud; Moise Vaughan; Louis Smalls.

FIVE BOB-O-LINKS

Singles: 78 rpm

OKEH ("Trying")....150-250 53
(Selection number not known. May have been a promotional only issue.)
Members: Gerald Fields; Charles Perry; Len Henry; Charles Johnston.
Also see RIVIERAS

FIVE BOPS

Singles: 7-inch

HAMILTON (50023 "Unforgotten Love")..15-25 59

FIVE BOROUGHS

Singles: 7-inch

AVENUE D (15 "Sunday Kind of Love")....5-8 89
(Black vinyl. 900 made.)
AVENUE D (15 "Sunday Kind of Love")...10-15 89
(Red vinyl. 100 made.)
CLASSIC ARTISTS (119 "One Too Many Lies")....55-65 90
(Black vinyl. Excessive hiss apparent. Has "RE-1" in vinyl trail-off. 25 made.)
CLASSIC ARTISTS (119 "One Too Many Lies")....5-8 90
(Black vinyl. Hiss problem resolved. No "RE-1" in vinyl trail-off.)
CLASSIC ARTISTS (119 "One Too Many Lies")....5-10 90
(Red vinyl.)
CLASSIC ARTISTS (122 "Heaven and Cindy")....5-8 90
(Black vinyl.)
CLASSIC ARTISTS (122 "Heaven and Cindy")....5-10 90
(Red vinyl.)
CLASSIC ARTISTS (135 "Like a Kid at Christmas")....4-6 92
(Red vinyl only.)
CRESCENT (500 "Secret Love")....4-6 '90s
MONA (31866 "Recess in Heaven")....4-6 91
(Colored vinyl.)

Picture Sleeves

CRESCENT (500 "Secret Love")....4-8 '90s

EPs: 7-inch

TELE-MEDIA ("Don't Say Goodnight")....5-10
(No selection number used.)
Members: Frank Iovino; Dave Strum; Geno Radicello; Charlie Notobartolo; Bruce Goldie.

FIVE BOSSES

Singles: 7-inch

UNITY (1313 "You're Gonna Need My Love")....75-125 63

FIVE BREEZES

Singles: 78 rpm

BLUEBIRD (8590 "Sweet Louise")....40-50 40
BLUEBIRD (8614 "Return Gal O' Mine")..40-50 41
BLUEBIRD (8679 "What's the Matter with Love")....40-50 41
BLUEBIRD (8710 "Laundry Man")....40-50 41
Member: Willie Dixon.

Also see DIXON, Willie

FIVE BUCKS

Singles: 7-inch

AFTON (1701 "No Use in Trying") 15-25 66
USA (882 "Breath of Time") 5-10 67

FIVE BUDDS

(With Bert Keys Orchestra)

Singles: 78 rpm

RAMA 100-200 53

Singles: 7-inch

RAMA (1 "I Was Such a Fool") 400-500 53
RAMA (2 "I Guess It's All Over Now") .. 400-500 53

FIVE Cs

(Five C's)

Singles: 78 rpm

UNITED 75-100 54

Singles: 7-inch

UNITED (172 "Tell Me") 100-200 54
(Black vinyl.)
UNITED (172 "Tell Me") 400-500 54
(Red vinyl.)
UNITED (180 "My Heart's Got the Blues") 100-200 54
(Black vinyl.)
UNITED (180 "My Heart's Got the Blues") 650-750 54
(Red vinyl.)

5 CAMPBELLS

Singles: 78 rpm

MUSIC CITY (794 "Hey Baby") 100-200 56

Singles: 7-inch

MUSIC CITY (794 "Hey Baby") 400-500 56

FIVE CANADIANS

Singles: 7-inch

DOMAR (1120 "Goodnight") 30-40 66
DOMAR (1121 "Never Alone") 30-40 66
DOMAR (1123 "Don't Tell Me") 30-40 66

FIVE CARDS STUD

(Five Card Stud)

Singles: 7-inch

RED BIRD (082 "Be-Bop-a-Lula") 10-15 66
SMASH (2080 "Beg Me") 10-15 67

FIVE CASHMERES

(V Cashmeres)

Singles: 7-inch

GOLDEN LEAF (108 "Walkin' Through the Jungle") 20-30 62

FIVE CATS

Singles: 78 rpm

RCA 5-10 54-55

Singles: 7-inch

RCA (5885 "Santa Lucia") 10-15 54
RCA (6012 "Rockin' Chair") 10-15 55
RCA (6081 "I Was Wrong") 10-15 55

FIVE CHANCELLORS

Singles: 7-inch

PORT (5000 "Tell Me You Love Me") .. 100-150 58
(Also issued as by the Chancellors.)

FIVE CHANCES

(Featuring Johnny Jones; "Music by Julius Cain")

Singles: 78 rpm

BLUE LAKE (115 "All I Want") 500-600 55
CHANCE (1157 "I May Be Small") 300-400 54
FEDERAL (12303 "My Days Are Blue") 150-250 57
STATES (156 "Gloria") 200-300 56

Singles: 7-inch

ATOMIC (2494 "Make Love to Me") 5-10 77
BLUE LAKE (115 "All I Want") 2000-3000 55
(Black vinyl.)
BLUE LAKE (115 "All I Want") 2500-3500 55
(Colored vinyl.)
CHANCE (1157 "I May Be Small") ... 1500-2000 54
FEDERAL (12303 "My Days Are Blue") 300-400 57
PS (1510 "Is This Love") 200-300 61
STATES (156 "Gloria") 400-600 56
(Black vinyl.)
STATES (156 "Gloria") 2000-3000 56
(Red vinyl.)
Members: Johnny Jones; John Austell; Darnell Austell; Reggie Smith; Howard Pitman; Harold Jones.
Also see BLENDERS
Also see BLUENOTES / Five Echoes / Five Chances
Also see CULLENS, Tommy
Also see MAPLES

5 CHANELS

P&R '58

(Chanels)

Singles: 7-inch

DEB (500 "The Reason") 30-40 58
(Previously issued as by the Chanels.)
Also see CHANELS

FIVE CHESTNUTS

Singles: 7-inch

ELGIN (003 "My Kind of Baby") 200-300 59
Also see BASKERVILLE, Hayes, & Five Chestnuts / Norven Baskerville & Five Chestnuts

FIVE CHIMES

Singles: 78 rpm

BETTA (2011 "Rosemarie") 200-300 53
Members: Gene Redd; Gary Morrison; Pat Gaston; John Murray; Arthur Crier.
Also see CHIMES
Also see FI-TONES
Also see PRE-HISTORICS

FIVE CHORDS

("Featuring Johnny Jones")

Singles: 78 rpm

JAMIE (1110 "Don't Just Stand There") ... 30-40 58

Singles: 7-inch

JAMIE (1110 "Don't Just Stand There") ... 20-30 58

FIVE CHORDS

(5 Chords)

Singles: 7-inch

CUCA (1031 "Red Wine") 10-20 61
MACON (104 "Sally") 15-25
SOMA (1151 "I Need Your Lovin' ") 75-100 60

LP: 10/12-inch

BOOM (4949 "Wild Are the Five Chords") .... 50-75 '60s

FIVE CHUMS

Singles: 7-inch

BLENDA ("Give Me a Chance") 100-200
(Selection number not known.)
EXCELLO (2123 "High School Affair") 50-75 57

FIVE CLASSICS

("5 Classic's")

Singles: 7-inch

A (317 "My Imagination") 10-20 61
ARC (4454 "My Imagination") 20-30 60
(First issue.)
MEDIEVAL (204 "Magic Star") 8-12 64
POVA (6142 "Love Me") 10-20 61
(First issued as by the Suburbans.)
RODE (101 "Magic Star") 200-300 63
Also see SUBURBANS

FIVE CROWNS

(5 Crowns; with Orchestra)

Singles: 78 rpm

CARAVAN 15-25 55
OLD TOWN (790 "You Could Be My Love") 75-125 52
OLD TOWN (792 "Lullaby of the Bells") 300-400 52
RAINBOW 100-200 52-56
RIVIERA (990 "You Came to Me") 200-300 55
TRANS-WORLD 25-50 55

Singles: 7-inch

CARAVAN (15609 "I Can't Pretend") 75-125 55
OLD TOWN (790 "You Could Be My Love") 100-200 52
(Black vinyl.)
OLD TOWN (790 "You Could Be My Love") 1000-2000 52
(Red vinyl.)
RAINBOW (179 "A Star") 300-400 52
(Black vinyl.)
RAINBOW (179 "A Star") 500-1000 52
(Red vinyl.)
RAINBOW (179 "A Star") 40-50
(Yellow label. Black vinyl.)
RAINBOW (202 "Keep It a Secret") . 3000-4000 53
(Red vinyl.)
RAINBOW (281 "I Was Wrong") 350-550 53
RAINBOW (335 "You Came to Me") 150-250 56
(Reissued the following year but credited to the Duvals.)
RIVIERA (990 "You Came to Me") ... 2000-3000 55
TRANS-WORLD (717 "I Can't Pretend") 200-300 55
(First issue.)
Members: Wilbur "Yonkie" Paul; Claude "Nicky" Clark; John "Sonny Boy" Clark; James "Poppa" Clark; Dock Green; Jesse Facing; Ben E. King; William Bailey; Bernard Ward; Elsberry Hobbs.
Also see CADILLACS
Also see CROWNS
Also see DUVALS

FIVE CROWNS

(With Jimmy Wright & His Orchestra)

Singles: 78 rpm

GEE (1001 "God Bless You") 50-100 55
(Vocal.)
GEE (1001 "God Bless You") 20-40 55
(Instrumental.)

Singles: 7-inch

GEE (1001 "God Bless You") 250-300 55
(Vocal.)
GEE (1001 "God Bless You") 75-100 55
(Instrumental.)
Also see WRIGHT, Jimmy

FIVE CROWNS

(With the Chuck Danzie Orchestra)

Singles: 7-inch

DE'BESTH (1122 "Memories of Yesterday") 100-200 59
(Flip side number is 1121.)
DE'BESTH (1124 "I Want You") 4000-5000 59
Also see LYNN, Laura

FIVE CROWNS

Singles: 7-inch

FIVE-O (503 "Just a Part of Life") .... 20-30 '60s

FIVE CRYSTALS

Singles: 7-inch

KANE (25592 "Hey, Landlord") 30-40 59
RELIC (1003 "Hey, Landlord") 5-10 65

5 CRYSTELS

Singles: 7-inch

DELCRO (827 "Path of Broken Hearts") 300-400 59
MUSIC CITY (821 "Path of Broken Hearts") 150-250 59

FIVE DAPPS

(With the Band of Joe Hunter)

Singles: 7-inch

BRAX (208 "Doo Whop a Do") 300-400 58

FIVE DEBONAIRES

Singles: 78 rpm

HERALD (509 "Darlin' ") 150-200 57

Singles: 7-inch

HERALD (509 "Darlin' ") 150-200 57
Also see DEBONAIRES

FIVE DELIGHTS

Singles: 7-inch

ABEL (228 "The Thought of Losing You") 400-500 59
ABEL (228 "The Thought of Losing You") 4-6 92
(Red vinyl. 500 made.)
NEWPORT (7002 "There'll Be No Goodbye") 100-150 58
UNART (2003 "There'll Be No Goodbye") 30-40 58

EPs: 7-inch

ABEL 228 "Five Delights") 8-12
(Red vinyl.)

FIVE DIAMONDS

(With the Hen Gates Orch.)

Singles: 78 rpm

TREAT 100-150 55

Singles: 7-inch

LOST NITE 5-10
TREAT (501 "The Ten Commandments of Love") 800-1000 55
Also see GATES, Hen, & Orchestra

FIVE DIPPS

Singles: 78 rpm

ORIGINAL 100-150 54

Singles: 7-inch

ORIGINAL (1005 "Teach Me Tonight") 300-400 54

FIVE DISCS

(Mario & the Five Discs)

Singles: 7-inch

CALO (202 "Adios") 75-125 61
(Green label. Has double lines above and below hole.)
CALO (202 "Adios") 50-100 61
(Green label. Has single lines above and below hole.)
CALO (202 "Adios") 75-125 61
(White label.)
CANDLELITE (429 "Come On Baby") .... 5-10 '60s
CHEER (1000 "Never Let You Go") 40-60 63
(White label. Promotional issue.)
CHEER (1000 "Never Let You Go") 30-40 63
(Black label.)
CHEER (1000 "Never Let You Go") 15-25 63
(Red label.)
CHEER (1000 "Never Let You Go") 75-125
(Released as by "The Five Dics.")
CHEER (4002 "Never Let You Go") 100-150 62
(White label. Promotional issue.)
CHEER (4002 "Never Let You Go") 75-125 62
(Black label.)
COLLECTABLES .... 3-5 '80s
CRYSTAL BALL (114 "Mirror Mirror") 5-10 78
(Black vinyl. 500 made.)
CRYSTAL BALL (114 "Mirror Mirror") 10-15 78
(Red vinyl. 25 made.)
CRYSTAL BALL (120 "Unchained Melody") 5-10 78
(Black vinyl. 500 made.)
CRYSTAL BALL (120 "Unchained Melody") 10-15 78
(Red vinyl. 25 made.)
CRYSTAL BALL (136 "Playing the Game of Love") 4-8 80
(Black vinyl. 500 made.)
CRYSTAL BALL (136 "Playing the Game of Love") 8-12 80
(Red vinyl. 25 made.)
CRYSTAL BALL (141 "This Love of Ours") . 4-8 81
(Black vinyl. 500 made.)
CRYSTAL BALL (141 "This Love of Ours") 8-12 81
(Red vinyl. 25 made.)
CRYSTAL BALL (141 "This Love of Ours") 30-40 81
(Multi-colored vinyl. Five made.)
DOWNSTAIRS (1001 "Roses") 4-6 73
DWAIN (803 "Roses") 300-400 59
(Credits: "Mario & the Five Discs.")
DWAIN (803 "Roses") 100-200 59
(Credits: "Five Discs.")
DWAIN (6072 "Roses") 2000-3000 59
EMGE (1004 "I Remember") 200-300 58
LAURIE (3601 "Rock and Roll Revival") ... 5-10 73
MELLOMOOD (1002 "Roses") 5-10 64
OUR OWN (001 "Zu Zu") 3-5 91
(Colored vinyl.)
PYRAMID (166 "Let's Fall in Love") 4-6
RUST (5027 "I Remember") 10-15 61
VIK (0327 "I Remember") 25-35 58
YALE (244 "Come On Baby") 100-200 60

Picture Sleeves

CRYSTAL BALL (136 "Playing the Game of Love") 20-25 80
(200 made.)
OUR OWN (001 "Zu Zu") 3-5 91

LPs: 10/12-inch

CRYSTAL BALL (119 "Unchained Thru the Years") 15-18 84
(Black vinyl. 1000 made.)
MAGIC CARPET (1002 "The Five Discs Sing Again") 15-20 91
(1st cover, dark blue.)
MAGIC CARPET (1002 "The Five Discs Sing Again") 25-35 91
(1st cover, dark blue. Red vinyl. 10 made.)
MAGIC CARPET (1002 "The Five Discs Sing Again") 10-15 91
(2nd cover, light blue.)
MAGIC CARPET (1002 "The Five Discs Sing Again") 40-50 91
(Picture disc. No cover. 25 made.)
Members: Mario deAndrade; Andy Jackson; Paul Albano; Joe Barsalona; Charles DiBella; Frank Arnone; Ed Pardocchi; Tony Basil; Bobby Stewart.
Also see ALLEN, Adrienne
Also see BOYFRIENDS
Also see DAWN
Also see DEMOLYRS / Mystics / Five Discs / Fascinators
Also see GEE, Frankie
Also see LEE, Davey
Also see MARTIN, Steve

FIVE DOLLARS

Singles: 78 rpm

FORTUNE 15-25 55-57

Singles: 7-inch

FORTUNE (821 "Harmony of Love") 30-50 55
FORTUNE (826 "So Strange") 30-50 56
FORTUNE (830 "I Will Wait") 75-125 56
FORTUNE (833 "You Fool") 50-75 57
FORTUNE (854 "That's the Way It Goes") 75-125 60
SKYLARK (561 "The Bells") 4-6 79
(Black or red vinyl.)
Members: Eddie Hurt; Lonnie Heard; James Drayton; Charles Evens; Richard Lawrence.
Also see DIABLOS / Five Dollars
Also see LITTLE EDDIE & FIVE DOLLARS
Also see WILLIAMS, Andre

FIVE DOTS

Singles: 78 rpm

DOT (1204 "The Other Night") 50-75 54
NOTE (10003 "I Just Love the Things She Do") 50-75 57

Singles: 7-inch

DOT (1204 "The Other Night") 150-250 54
NOTE (10003 "I Just Love the Things She Do") 200-300 57

FIVE DREAMERS

Singles: 78 rpm

PORT (5001 "Beverly") 50-60 57

Singles: 7-inch

PORT (5001 "Beverly") 50-60 57

FIVE DREAMS

Singles: 78 rpm

MERCURY (71150 "You Are My Only Love") 40-50 57

Singles: 7-inch

MERCURY (71150 "You Are My Only Love") 40-50 57

FIVE DUKES OF RHYTHM
(With Gene Moore & His Combo)

Singles: 78 rpm

FORTUNE (812 "Soft, Sweet and Really Fine") 50-75 54
RENDEZVOUS (812 "Soft, Sweet and Really Fine") 200-300 54

Singles: 7-inch

FORTUNE (812 "Soft, Sweet and Really Fine") 100-200 54
RENDEZVOUS (812 "Soft, Sweet and Really Fine") 1000-1500 54

FIVE ECHOES
(With Fats Coles' Band; Five Echos)

Singles: 78 rpm

SABRE 300-400 53-54
VEE-JAY 100-150 54-55

Singles: 7-inch

OLDIES 45 (419 "Lonely Mood") 4-6
SABRE (102 "Lonely Mood") 400-600 53
(Black vinyl.)
SABRE (102 "Lonely Mood") 1000-1500 53
(Red vinyl.)
SABRE (105 "So Lonesome") 400-600 54
(Black vinyl.)
SABRE (105 "So Lonesome") 1000-1500 54
(Red vinyl.)
VEE-JAY (129 "Tell Me Baby") 750-1000 54
VEE-JAY (156 "Fool's Prayer") 750-1000 55
Members: Johnny Taylor; Count Sims; Earl Lewis; Herbert Lewis; Jimmy Marshall.
Also see BLUENOTES / Five Echoes / Chances
Also see HUNT, Tommy
Also see SPRIGGS, Walter
Also see TAYLOR, Johnny

5 EMBERS

Singles: 78 rpm

GEM (224 "Please Come Home") 100-200 54

Singles: 7-inch

GEM (224 "Please Come Home") 500-600 54

5 EMBERS
(Featuring Richard Brown; featuring Charles Brown)

Singles: 7-inch

ROYCE (0006 "I'm Free") 400-600 60
X-BAT (1006 "I'm Free") 4-8 95
(Colored vinyl.)

Picture Sleeves

X-BAT (1006 "I'm Free") 4-8 95
Members: Richard Brown; Charles Brown; Raymond Johnson; Melvin Smith; Sonny Rates.
Also see BROWN, Charles

5 EMERALDS
(Five Emeralds)

Singles: 78 rpm

S-R-C (106 "I'll Beg") 200-300 54
S-R-C (107 "Darling") 200-300 54

Singles: 7-inch

S.R.C. (106 "I'll Beg") 800-1200 53
(Credits "5 Emeralds." Blue label. Logo has periods between letters.)
S-R-C (106 "I'll Beg") 800-1200 53
(Credits "Five Emeralds." Maroon label. Has hyphens between letters.)
S.R.C. (107 "Darling") 800-1200 54
(Credits "Five Emeralds." Blue label. Logo has periods between letters.)
S-R-C (107 "Darling") 800-1200 54
Also see DOWNBEATS
Also see ELGINS

FIVE EMPREES P&R '65
(Five Empressions)

Singles: 7-inch

FREEPORT 10-15 65-66
GOLD STANDARD (262 "Little Miss Sad") .... 10-20 '60s
(Colored vinyl.)
SMASH (2065 "Gone from My Mind") 4-8 66

LPs: 10/12-inch

FREEPORT (3001 "The Five Emprees [Little Miss Sad]") 35-45 65
(Monaural.)
FREEPORT (3001 "Little Miss Sad") 20-30 66
(Reissue.)
FREEPORT (4001 "The Five Emprees [Little Miss Sad]") 30-40 65
(Stereo.)
FREEPORT (4001 "Little Miss Sad") 25-35 66
(Reissue.)
Also see FIVE EMPRESSIONS

FIVE EMPRESSIONS
(Five Emprees)

Singles: 7-inch

FREEPORT (1001 "Little Miss Sad") 10-20 65
Also see FIVE EMPREES

FIVE ENCHANTERS

Singles: 7-inch

RPM (1009 "RnR ers Never Gather Moss") 10-20 60
RPM (1010 "Who's Breaking Whose Heart Now") 10-20 60

FIVE ENCORES

Singles: 78 rpm

RAMA 5-10 55-56

Singles: 7-inch

RAMA (180 "Double Date") 10-20 55
RAMA (185 "Quaker Ben") 10-20 55
RAMA (187 "Dance with the Rock") 10-20 56

FIVE FABULOUS DEMONS

Singles: 7-inch

KING (5761 "You'd Better Come Home") . 10-15 63

FIVE FINKS

Singles: 7-inch

BERTRAM INT'L (226 "Crying Guitar") 30-50 64
Also see LAWRENCE, Bill, & Five Finks

FIVE FLEETS

Singles: 7-inch

FELSTED (8513 "I Been Crying") 20-30 58
FELSTED (8522 "Slight Case of Love") 20-30 59
SEVILLE (112 "Cheer Up") 10-15 61

FIVE FLYS

Singles: 7-inch

SAMRON (104 "Dance Her by Me") 15-25 62

5 FORTUNES

Singles: 7-inch

RANSOM (103 "You Are My Love"). 1000-1500 58

FIVE G's

Singles: 7-inch

WASHINGTONIAN (200,042 "Forget Her") 100-200 59

5 "GENTS"

Singles: 7-inch

CREST (51657 "I Never Told You") 500-750 58

FIVE GENTS
("Soprano")

Singles: 7-inch

VEIKING (101 "Baby Doll") 200-300

5 GLOW TONES

Singles: 7-inch

JAX (101 "At a Dance") 10-20 58

FIVE GRANDS

Singles: 7-inch

BRUNSWICK (55059 "Kiss Me") 15-25 58

FIVE HEARTS

Singles: 78 rpm

FLAIR (1026 "Please, Please Baby") ... 100-200 54

Singles: 7-inch

FLAIR (1026 "Please, Please Baby") ... 300-400 54
Members: Cornell Gunter; Richard Berry; Young Jessie; Beverly Thompson; Tom Fox.
Also see FIVE HOLLYWOOD BLUEJAYS
Also see FLAIRS

FIVE HEARTS

Singles: 7-inch

ARCADE (107 "Unbelievable") 150-250 59
Also see ANDREWS, Lee

FIVE HEARTS / Lord Luther & Esquires

Singles: 7-inch

MUSIC CITY (833 "Tell Ya What"/ "Tremble") 400-500 60

FIVE HOLLYWOOD BLUEJAYS

Singles: 78 rpm

RECORDED IN HOLLYWOOD 200-300 52

Singles: 7-inch

RECORDED IN HOLLYWOOD (162 "Put a Nickle in the Juke box") 500-600 52
Members: Cornell Gunter; Richard Berry; Young Jessie; Beverly Thompson; Tom Fox.
Also see FIVE HEARTS
Also see HOLLYWOOD BLUEJAYS

FIVE Js

Singles: 7-inch

FULTON (2454 "My Darling") 75-100 58

FIVE JADES

Singles: 7-inch

DUKE (188 "Without Your Love") 30-50 58

FIVE JETS

Singles: 78 rpm

DELUXE 10-20 53-54

Singles: 7-inch

DELUXE (6018 "I Am in Love") 30-40 53
DELUXE (6053 "I'm Stuck") 30-40 54
DELUXE (6058 "Tell Me You're Mine") 200-300 54
DELUXE (6064 "Crazy Chickens") 15-25 54
DELUXE (6071 "Down Slow") 200-300 54
Members: Billy Davis; Joe Murphy; John Dorsey; Carl Stewart.
Also see VERNITA / Five Jets
Also see THRILLERS

FIVE JETS

Singles: 7-inch

JEWEL (739 "Sugaree") 10-15 64

FIVE JINKS

Singles: 78 rpm

BLUEBIRD (6857 "I'm Moaning All Day For You") 40-60 37
BLUEBIRD (6905 "Cushion Foot") 40-60 37
BLUEBIRD (6951 "Dirt-Dishing Daisy") 40-60 37

5 JOHNSON BROTHERS

Singles: 7-inch

CARRIE ("Sleep with a Dream") 30-40
(Selection number not known.)
FULTON (2455 "Sleep with a Dream") 40-50 58
(First issue.)

FIVE KEEYS

Singles: 7-inch

BANGAR (661 "Run Around") 25-35 67
Also see RAVONS

FIVE KEYS R&B '51
(Rudy West & the Five Keys; "Featuring Rudy West"; 5 Keys)

Singles: 78 rpm

ALADDIN (3085 "With a Broken Heart") 100-200 51
ALADDIN (3099 "The Glory of Love") .. 100-200 51
ALADDIN (3113 "It's Christmas Time") 100-200 51
ALADDIN (3118 "Yes Sir, That's My Baby") 100-200 52
ALADDIN (3127 "Red Sails in the Sunset") 100-200 52
ALADDIN (3131 "Mistakes") 100-200 52
ALADDIN (3136 "I Hadn't Anyone 'Til You") 100-200 52
ALADDIN (3158 "I Cried for You") 100-200 52
ALADDIN (3167 "Can't Keep from Crying") 100-200 53
ALADDIN (3175 "There Ought to Be a Law") 100-200 53
ALADDIN (3190 "These Foolish Things") 100-200 53
ALADDIN (3204 "Teardrops in Your Eyes") 100-200 53
ALADDIN (3214 "My Saddest Hour") ... 100-200 53
ALADDIN (3228 "Someday Sweetheart") 100-200 54
ALADDIN (3245 "Deep in My Heart") ... 100-200 54
ALADDIN (3263 "My Love") 100-200 55
ALADDIN (3312 "Story of Love") 75-100 56
CAPITOL 25-50 54-57
GROOVE (0031 "I'll Follow You") 1000-2000 54

Singles: 7-inch

ALADDIN (3099 "The Glory of Love") .. 500-750 51
ALADDIN (3113 "It's Christmas Time") 1000-1500 51
ALADDIN (3118 "Yes Sir, That's My Baby") 1500-2000 52
ALADDIN (3127 "Red Sails in the Sunset") 1500-2000 52
ALADDIN (3131 "Mistakes") 750-1000 52
ALADDIN (3136 "I Hadn't Anyone 'Til You") 1000-1500 52
ALADDIN (3158 "I Cried for You") 750-1000 52
ALADDIN (3167 "Can't Keep from Crying") 750-1000 53
ALADDIN (3175 "There Ought to Be a Law") 1500-2000 53
ALADDIN (3190 "These Foolish Things") 2000-3000 53
ALADDIN (3204 "Teardrops in Your Eyes") 500-750 53
ALADDIN (3214 "My Saddest Hour") ... 600-800 53
(Flat blue label.)
ALADDIN (3214 "My Saddest Hour") ... 500-750 53
(Glossy blue label.)
ALADDIN (3228 "Someday Sweetheart") 500-750 54
ALADDIN (3245 "Deep in My Heart") ... 500-750 54
ALADDIN (3263 "My Love") 150-250 54
ALADDIN (3312 "Story of Love") 100-150 56
BIM BAM BOOM (116 "Out of Sight, Out of Mind") 4-6 73
(Black vinyl.)
BIM BAM BOOM (116 "Out of Sight, Out of Mind") 5-8 73
(Red vinyl.)
CAPITOL (828 "Just for a Thrill") 50-75 57
(Promotional issue only.)
CAPITOL (2945 "Ling Ting Tong") 40-60 54
CAPITOL (3032 "Close Your Eyes") 30-50 55
CAPITOL (3127 "The Verdict") 30-50 55
CAPITOL (3185 "I Wish I'd Never Learned to Read") 30-50 55
CAPITOL (3267 "'Cause You're My Lover") 30-50 55
CAPITOL (3318 "What Goes On") 30-50 56
CAPITOL (3392 "I Dreamt I Dwelt in Heaven") 30-50 56
(Standard 45 rpm hole.)
CAPITOL (3392 "I Dreamt I Dwelt in Heaven") 50-75 56
(LP-size, 1/4-inch hole. Purple label.)
CAPITOL (3392 "I Dreamt I Dwelt in Heaven") 50-75 56
(LP-size, 1/4-inch hole. White label. Promotional issue only.)
CAPITOL (3455 "Peace and Love") 30-50 56
CAPITOL (3502 "Out of Sight, Out of Mind") 30-50 56

CAPITOL (3597 "Wisdom of a Fool")....... 30-50 56
CAPITOL (3660 "Let There Be You") 20-40 57
CAPITOL (3710 "Four Walls")................. 20-40 57
CAPITOL (3738 "This I Promise You") 20-40 57
CAPITOL (3786 "Face of an Angel") 20-40 57
CAPITOL (3830 "Do Anything") 20-40 57
CAPITOL (3861 "From Me to You")......... 15-30 58
CAPITOL (3948 "With All My Heart")....... 15-30 58
CAPITOL (4009 "Handy Andy")............... 15-30 58
CAPITOL (4092 "Our Great Love").......... 15-30 58
CAPITOL (6000 series) 8-12 64
CLASSIC ARTISTS (112 "Miracle Moment of Love")..5-8 89
(Black vinyl. 1000 made.)
CLASSIC ARTISTS (112 "Miracle Moment of Love")..8-10 89
(Red vinyl. 1000 made.)
CLASSIC ARTISTS (115 "I Want You for Christmas") 5-8 89
(Black vinyl. 1000 made.)
CLASSIC ARTISTS (115 "I Want You for Christmas") 8-10 89
(Red vinyl. 1000 made.)
GUSTO...3-5
IMPERIAL (016 "The Glory of Love")..........5-10 62
INFERNO (4500 "No Matter") 5-10 67
KEY (62 "Wisdom of a Fool") 5-10
KEY (63 "The Verdict") 5-10
KING (5221 "I Took Your Love for aToy")... 20-30 59
KING (5273 "Dream On") 15-20 59
KING (5302 "How Can I Forget You")...... 15-20 59
KING (5330 "Rosetta")............................ 10-15 60
KING (5358 "I Didn't Know")..................... 10-15 60
KING (5398 "Valley of Love") 10-15 60
KING (5446 "You Broke the Only Heart") 10-15 61
KING (5496 "Stop Your Crying") 15-25 61
KING (5877 "I Can't Escape from You") 5-10 64
LANDMARK (101 "Goddess of Love").......5-10 73
(Black vinyl.)
LANDMARK (101 "Goddess of Love")..... 20-30 73
(Multi-colored vinyl.)
OWL (321 "A Dreamer") 4-6 73
POPULAR REQUEST 3-5
SEG-WAY (1008 "Out of Sight, Out of Mind")... 10-20 62
U.A. (0150 "Glory of Love").........................5-10 '60s

Picture Sleeves

CAPITOL (3502 "Out of Sight, Out of Mind")... 400-500 56
(Die-cut sleeve with photo insert. Promotional issue only.)

EPs: 7-inch

CAPITOL (572 "The Five Keys").......... 100-200 55
CAPITOL (828 "The Five Keys on Stage") 250-400 57
(In cover photo, group member on left is holding his right hand in a phallic-like position.)
CAPITOL (828 "The Five Keys on Stage") 100-200 57
(Reworked cover, with offending hand removed from picture.)
CRYSTAL (101 "Five Keys").................... 10-15

LPs: 10/12-inch

ALADDIN (806 "Best of the 5 Keys").. 2000-4000 56
(Maroon label. Bootlegs have the Score reissue cover art but using the Aladdin name and number. There is no original Aladdin LPs titled *On the Town.*)
CAPITOL (828 "The Five Keys on Stage") 500-750 57
(In cover photo, group member on left is holding his right hand in a phallic-like position.)
CAPITOL (828 "The Five Keys on Stage") 700-900 57
(Black label, reads "Sample Album for Radio-TV Program Use." Cover has white sticker reading "For Promotional Use Only – Not for Sale." In cover photo, group member on left is holding his right hand in a phallic-like position.)
CAPITOL (828 "The Five Keys on Stage") 100-200 57
(Reworked cover, with offending hand removed from the picture.)
CAPITOL (1769 "The Fantastic Five Keys").. 100-200 62
(With "T" prefix.)
CAPITOL (1769 "The Fantastic Five Keys")..8-12 77
(With "M" prefix.)
GREAT GROUP CLASSICS.......................8-12 '70s
HARLEM HITPARADE 10-15 72
KING (688 "The Five Keys")..................200-400 60
KING (692 "Rhythm & Blues Hits: Past and Present")......................................200-300 60
KING (5013 "14 Hits")................................8-12 78
SCORE (4003 "On the Town").............500-750 57
(Repackage of *Best of the 5 Keys,* Aladdin 806. See that listing for bootleg information.)
Members: Rudy West; Ripley Ingram; Maryland Pierce; Dickie Smith; Ray Loper; Bernie West; Ulysses Hicks; Thomas Threat.
Also see BELVIN, Jesse, & Five Keys / Feathers
Also see TEAGARDEN, Jack
Also see SMITH, Dickie
Also see WEST, Rudy

FIVE KEYS / Ferlin Husky

EPs: 7-inch

CAPITOL (503 "Five Keys/Ferlin Husky") 60-80 57
Also see FIVE KEYS
Also see HUSKY, Ferlin

FIVE KIDS

Singles: 78 rpm

MAXWELL (101 "Carolyn") 400-500 55

Singles: 7-inch

MAXWELL (101 "Carolyn") 4000-5000 55

FIVE KINGS

Singles: 78 rpm

MANOR (1061 "I Can't Get Up the Nerve to Miss You") 30-50 47
MANOR (1062 "Meet Me at No Special Place") 30-50 47
MANOR (1066 "Sincerely Yours") 30-50 47
Also see CHURCHILL, Savannah

FIVE KINGS

(With Band of Purvis Henson)

Singles: 7-inch

YVETTE (101 "Here Comes My Baby")....30-50 60

FIVE KINGS

Singles: 7-inch

COLUMBIA (43060 "Light Bulb") 30-40 64
(Red label.)
COLUMBIA (43060 "Light Bulb") 15-25 64
(Promotional issue only.)

FIVE KNIGHTS

(With the Dukes)

Singles: 7-inch

TAU (104 "Take Me in Your Arms")........50-100 59

FIVE KNIGHTS

(With John Johnson's Invaders)

Singles: 7-inch

BUMP'S (1504 "Dark Was the Night")......15-25 61
MINIT (626 "Let Me In")............................10-20 61
SPECIALTY (675 "Miracle").....................50-75 59
Also see TAYLOR, Tommy, & Five Knights

FIVE LARKS

(Larks)

Singles: 78 rpm

APOLLO (1177 "My Heart Cries for You")..50-100 51
Also see LARKS

FIVE LETTERS

Singles: 7-inch

IVY (102 "Your First Love") 400-500 57

FIVE LORDS

Singles: 7-inch

D&S (2078 "Oo-La-La").......................200-300 60

5 LYRICS

Singles: 78 rpm

MUSIC CITY..250-350 56

Singles: 7-inch

MUSIC CITY (799 "I'm Traveling Light").. 3000-4000 56
Members: Robert Rose; Ike Perry.
Also see PERRY, Ike, & His Lyrics

FIVE MASKS

(Five Stars)

Singles: 7-inch

JAN (101 "Forever and a Day")................15-25 58
(Time is on left side of hole.)
JAN (101 "Forever and a Day")................10-20 58
(Time is on right side of hole.)
Members: Al "TNT" Braggs; Cal Valentine; Robert Valentine; Billy Fred Thomas; Jesse Lee Floyd.
Also see BRAGGS, Al "TNT"
Also see 5 NOTES
Also see SUMMERS, Gene

FIVE MASTERS & ORCHESTRA

Singles: 7-inch

BUMBLE BEE (502 "We Are Like One") ..50-75 59
Also see SATINTONES

FIVE MOORE

Singles: 7-inch

PARROT (323 "Whole Lotta Soul") 10-20 67

5 NOTES

(With the Hamil-Tones; Five Notes)

Singles: 78 rpm

CHESS...25-35 55
JEN D...100-200 55
JOSIE...10-15 55
SPECIALTY 50-100 53

Singles: 7-inch

CHESS (1614 "Show Me the Way") 50-100 55
JEN D (4185 "You Are So Beautiful") ...500-750 55
(Identification number shown since no selection number is used.)
JOSIE (784 "You Are So Beautiful") 30-40 55
SPECIALTY (461 "Thrill Me, Baby") 150-200 53
(Black vinyl.)
SPECIALTY (461 "Thrill Me, Baby") 300-500 53
(Red vinyl.)
Members: Al Braggs; Cal Valentine.
Also see BRAGGS, Al "TNT"
Also see FIVE MASKS

FIVE OF A KIND

Singles: 7-inch

SIDRA (9003 "The Other Side")...............35-55 65
VANDAN (3668 "Never Again") 15-25 65

FIVE OF US

Singles: 7-inch

CURRENT (110 "Hey You")......................10-15 66

FIVE OWLS

(With the Vulcan Orchestra)

Singles: 7-inch

OWL (327 "The Thrill Is Gone")...................4-6 74
VULCAN (1025 "Pleading to You").......200-300 55

FIVE PALMS

Singles: 78 rpm

STATES 20-30 57

Singles: 7-inch

STATES (163 "Little Girl of Mine")...........25-50 57
(Same number used for a Strollers release.)
Also see WILKINS, Artie, & Palms

FIVE PASTELS

Singles: 7-inch

DOME (249 "You're Just an Angel").....250-350 59

FIVE PEARLS

Singles: 78 rpm

ALADDIN (3265 "Please Let Me Know") ..50-75 54

Singles: 7-inch

ALADDIN (3265 "Please Let Me Know") 100-150 54
(Maroon label.)
ALADDIN (3265 "Please Let Me Know") 200-300 54
(Orange label.)
Members: Howard Guyton; Derek Martin.
Also see GUY, Bobby
Also see MARTIN, Derek
Also see PEARLS

FIVE PENNIES

Singles: 78 rpm

SAVOY 10-15 56

Singles: 7-inch

SAVOY (1182 "Mr. Moon").......................20-30 56
SAVOY (1190 "Mr. Heart Trembles") 15-25 56
Members: Benjamin Washington; James Myers; Herb Myers; Clifford Curry; Charles Holloway.
Also see CURRY, Clifford
Also see MILLER, Big

FIVE PLAYBOYS

(5 Playboys)

Singles: 78 rpm

DOT (15605 "When We Were Young") 10-20 57
FEE BEE (213 "Pages of My Scrapbook") 25-35 57

Singles: 7-inch

DOT (15605 "When We Were Young") 10-20 57
FEE BEE (213 "Pages of My Scrapbook"/"Love Me Right")...30-40 57
FEE BEE (213 "Pages of My Scrapbook"/"When We Were Young")...50-60 57
FEE BEE (232 "Angel Mine")....................40-50 58
MERCURY (71269 "Why Be a Fool").......10-20 58
PETITE (504 "Mr. Echo") 30-40 58

FIVE QUAILS

Singles: 78 rpm

MERCURY (71154 "Jungle Baby")...........30-40 57

Singles: 7-inch

MERCURY (71154 "Jungle Baby")...........30-40 57

FIVE QUAILS

Singles: 7-inch

HARVEY (114 "Been a Long Time") 15-25 61
Member: Harvey Fuqua.
Also see HARVEY
Also see QUAILS

5 RAMBLERS

Singles: 7-inch

LUMMTONE (111 "I Want You to Know")...100-200 63

FIVE REASONS

Singles: 7-inch

CUB (9006 "Go to School").......................40-50 58

FIVE RED CAPS — P&R/R&B/C&W '44

(5 Red Caps)

Singles: 78 rpm

BEACON..15-25 43-45
GANNETT..15-25 43-45
JOE DAVIS 15-25 43-45
DAVIS..10-20 46
MGM...10-20 48
Members: Steve Gibson; Jim Springs; Romaine Brown; Dave Patillo; Emmett Matthews.
Also see GIBSON, Steve

FIVE ROGUES

Singles: 7-inch

RAZORBACK (127 "Tab Top") 10-20 65

FIVE ROSES

(With the Lil Walters Band)

Singles: 7-inch

CLIFTON (11 "Romance in the Spring") 4-6 75
NU KAT (101 "Romance in the Spring")...100-200 59

5 ROVERS

Singles: 78 rpm

MUSIC CITY...50-75 56

Singles: 7-inch

MUSIC CITY (798 "Down to the Sea") .200-300 56
Also see ROVERS

FIVE ROYALES — R&B '53

("5" Royales; 5 Royals)

Singles: 78 rpm

APOLLO...50-75 51-55
KING..25-75 54-57

Singles: 7-inch

ABC-PAR (10348 "Catch That Teardrop") . 8-12 62
ABC-PAR (10368 "I Want It Like That") 8-12 62
APOLLO (441 "Courage to Love")..........50-100 52
(Black vinyl.)
APOLLO (441 "Courage to Love")........200-300 52
(Red vinyl.)
APOLLO (443 "Baby Don't Do It") 50-100 52
(Black vinyl.)
APOLLO (443 "Baby Don't Do It") 150-250 52
(Red vinyl.)
APOLLO (446 "Help Me, Somebody") ...50-100 53
APOLLO (448 "Laundromat Blues").........50-75 53
APOLLO (449 "I Want to Thank You") 40-50 53
APOLLO (452 "I Do") 40-50 54
APOLLO (454 "Cry Some More") 50-75 54
APOLLO (458 "What's That") 50-75 54
APOLLO (467 "With All Your Heart").........50-75 55
GUSTO ....3-5 '80s
HOME OF THE BLUES (112 "Please, Please, Please")...10-20 60
HOME OF THE BLUES (218 "If You Need Me") 10-20 61
HOME OF THE BLUES (232 "Not Going to Cry")..10-20 61
HOME OF THE BLUES (234 "They Don't Know") 10-20 61
HOME OF THE BLUES (257 "Catch That Teardrop") 10-20 62

KING (4740 "I'm Gonna Run It Down")....50-75 54
KING (4744 "Monkey Hips and Rice").....50-75 54
KING (4762 "One Mistake")..........50-75 54
KING (4770 "You Didn't Learn It At Home")..........50-75 55
KING (4785 "Mohawk Squaw")..........50-75 55
KING (4806 "When I Get Like This")........40-60 55
KING (4819 "Do Unto You")..........40-60 55
KING (4830 "Someone Made You for Me")..........40-60 55
KING (4869 "Right Around the Corner")..40-60 56
KING (4901 "I Could Love You")..........40-60 56
KING (4952 "Come on and Save Me")....40-60 56
KING (4973 "Just As I Am")..........40-60 56
KING (5032 "Tears of Joy")..........30-50 57
KING (5053 "Think")..........30-50 57
KING (5082 "Messin' Up")..........30-50 57
KING (5098 "Dedicated to the One I Love")..........30-50 57
KING (5131 "The Feeling Is Real")..........20-30 58
KING (5141 "Double Or Nothing")..........20-30 58
KING (5153 "Don't Let It Be in Vain").......20-30 58
KING (5162 "The Real Thing")..........20-30 59
KING (5191 "Miracle of Love")..........20-30 59
KING (5237 "Tell Me You Care")..........20-30 59
KING (5266 "It Hurts Inside")..........20-30 59
KING (5329 "I'm with You")..........15-25 60
KING (5357 "Why")..........15-25 60
KING (5453 "Dedicated to the One I Love")..........15-25 61
KING (5756 "Dedicated to the One I Love")..........10-20 63
KING (5892 "I Need You Lovin' Baby")....10-20 64
SMASH (1936 "I Like It Like That")..........10-20 64
SMASH (1963 "Faith")..........10-20 65
TODD (1086 "Doin' Everything")..........10-20 63
TODD (1088 "Baby Don't Do It")..........10-20 63
VEE-JAY (412 "Much in Need")..........10-20 61
VEE-JAY (431 "Talk About My Woman") 10-20 61
WHITE CLIFFS (224 "I'm on the Right Road Now")..........15-25 64

LPs: 10/12-inch

APOLLO (488 "The Rockin' 5 Royales")..........1500-2000 59
(Green label.)
APOLLO (488 "The Rockin' 5 Royales")..........800-1200 59
(Yellow label.)
KING (580 "Dedicated to You")..........350-500 58
KING (616 "The 5 Royales Sing for You")..........200-300 59
KING (678 "The 5 Royales")..........300-400 60
KING (955 "24 All Time Hits")..........50-75 66
Members: Johnny Tanner; Eugene Tanner; Lowman Pauling; Clarence Pauling; Jim Moore; Otto Jeffries; Obadiah "Scoop" Carter; Eudell Graham; Bobby Burris.
Also see EL PAULING
Also see JOHN, Little Willie / 5 Royales / Earl (Connelly) King / Midnighters
Also see PAUL, Clarence
Also see ROYAL SONS QUINTET
Also see WILSON, Jimmy

FIVE SATANS

Singles: 7-inch

JCP (1014 "Here's to You")..........10-20 64

FIVE SATINS — P&R/R&B '56

(5 Satins; Featuring Fred Parris; "Featuring Dick Arnold"; Bill Baker & Five Satins)

Singles: 78 rpm

EMBER..........50-100 56-57
REGENCY (532 "In the Still of the Nite")..........75-125 '50s
(Canadian.)
REO (8463 "In the Still of the Nite")..........50-75 56
(Canadian.)
STANDORD (100 "All Mine")..........200-300 57
STANDORD (200 "In the Still of the Nite")..........300-500 56

Singles: 7-inch

ABC..........4-6 73
ANOTHER FIRST (104 "When Your Love Comes Along")..........30-50 59
(First issue. Reissued on "First" label.)
CANDLELITE (411 "She's Gone")..........10-15 63
(Black vinyl.)
CANDLELITE (411 "She's Gone")..........15-25 63
(Red vinyl.)
CHANCELLOR (1110 "The Masquerade Is Over")..........10-20 62
CHANCELLOR (1121 "Do You Remember")..........10-20 62
COLLECTABLES..........3-5 '80s
CUB (9071 "Your Memory")..........15-25 60
CUB (9077 "These Foolish Things")..........15-25 60
CUB (9090 "Can I Come Over Tonight")..15-25 61
EMBER (1005 "In the Still of the Nite").200-300 56
(Has Ember label pasted over Standord label. Can be identified by the identification number 6106 in the vinyl trail-off.)
EMBER (1005 "In the Still of the Nite").....40-60 56
(Black vinyl.)
EMBER (1005 "In the Still of the Nite").100-200 56
(Brown vinyl.)
EMBER (1005 "[I'll Remember] in the Still of the Nite")..........100-200 56
(White label. Promotional issue.)
EMBER (1005 "[I'll Remember] in the Still of the Nite")..........50-75 59
(Red label. Reads "Special Demand Release.")
EMBER (1005 "In the Still of the Nite")....25-35 60
(Multi-color "burning logs" label. May also have full title, with "I'll Remember.")
EMBER (1005 "[I'll Remember] in the Still of the Nite")..........15-25 61
(Black label.)
Note: Some Ember pressings read In the Still of the NIGHT, instead of NITE.
EMBER (1008 "Wonderful Girl")..........25-50 56
EMBER (1014 "Oh, Happy Day")..........25-50 57
EMBER (1019 "To the Aisle")..........25-50 57
(Red label.)
EMBER (1019 "To the Aisle")..........20-30 59
("Burning logs" label.)
EMBER (1025 "Our Anniversary")..........25-50 57
(Red label.)
EMBER (1025 "Our Anniversary")..........20-25 57
(Black label.)
EMBER (1028 "A Million to One")..........25-50 57
EMBER (1038 "A Night to Remember")...25-35 58
EMBER (1056 "Shadows")..........25-35 59
EMBER (1061 "I'll Be Seeing You")..........25-35 60
EMBER (1066 "Candlelight")..........25-35 60
EMBER (1070 "Wishing Ring")..........25-35 61
ELEKTRA (47411 "Memories of Days Gone By")..........15-25 82
FIRST (104 "When Your Love Comes Along")..........40-50 59
(Orange label. First issued on "Another First.")
FIRST (104 "When Your Love Comes Along")..........10-15
(Light green label.)
FLASHBACK (1 "In the Still of the Night"/"Jones Girl")..........4-8 65
GW (562 "Again"/"To the Aisle")..........8-12
GLENVILLE (106 "In the Still of the Night")..4-6
KIRSHNER..........5-10 73
KLIK (1020 "I Love You So")..........4-8 73
(Previously unissued.)
LANA (106 "In the Still of the Night")..........4-8 64
LOST NITE..........4-8
MUSICTONE (1108 "To the Aisle")..........10-15 61
(Some sources show this as by Bill Baker, others as by the 5 Satins.)
MUSICTONE (1125 "In the Still of the Night")..........10-15 63
NIGHTRAIN (901 "All Mine")..........4-6 73
RCA..........4-8 71-87
REGENCY (532 "In the Still of the Nite")..15-25 '50s
(Canadian.)
REO (8463 "In the Still of the Nite")..........75-125 56
(Canadian.)
ROULETTE (4563 "You Can Count on Me")..........8-12 64
SAMMY (103 "No One Knows")..........15-25 65
S.G. (001 "Everybody's Got a Home but Me")..........3-5 90
STANDORD (100 "All Mine")..........500-550 56
(Red label. Copies on a maroon-brown label are unauthorized reissues. Same selection number used for a Chestnuts issue.)
STANDORD (200 "In the Still of the Nite")..........1000-2000 56
(Red label. Reads "Produced By Martin Kuegull.")
STANDORD (200 "In the Still of the Nite")..........500-750 56
(Red label.)
STANDORD (5051 "All Mine")..........250-500 57
STANDORD (7107 "The Time")..........4-6 89
(Blue vinyl. 500 made.)
TIME MACHINE..........4-8 74
TIMES SQUARE (4 "All Mine")..........20-30 63
(Blue vinyl.)
TRIP..........4-8 '70s
U.A. (368 "Til the End")..........15-20 61
W.B. (5367 "Remember Me")..........8-12 63

Picture Sleeves

EMBER (1005 "In the Still of the Nite").......5-10 '90s

EPs: 7-inch

EMBER (100 "The Five Satins Sing")...100-200 60
(Red label.)
EMBER (100 "The Five Satins Sing")......25-50 61
(Black or multi-color label.)
EMBER (101 "The Five Satins Sing, Vol. 2")..........100-200 60
(Red label.)
EMBER (101 "The Five Satins Sing, Vol. 2")..........25-50 61
(Black or multi-color label.)
EMBER (102 "The Five Satins Sing, Vol. 3")..........100-200 60
(Red label.)
EMBER (102 "The Five Satins Sing, Vol. 3")..........25-50 61
(Black or multi-color label.)
EMBER (104 "In the Still of the Night").250-350 61

LPs: 10/12-inch

CELEBRITY SHOWCASE..........10-12 70
COLLECTABLES..........5-10 83
EMBER (100 "The Five Satins Sing")...250-500 57
(Red label. Group is pictured on front cover.)
EMBER (100 "The Five Satins Sing")...100-200 58
(Multi-color label. Black vinyl.)
EMBER (100 "The Five Satins Sing")..........3000-3500 58
(Blue vinyl.)
EMBER (100 "The Five Satins Sing").....50-100 60
(Black label.)
EMBER (401 "The Five Satins Encore")..........50-100 60
(Black label.)
EMBER (401 "The Five Satins Encore")..40-60 61
(Multi-color label.)
LOST NITE (8 "The Best of the Five Satins, Pt.1")..........10-20 81
(10-inch LP. Red vinyl. 1000 made.)
LOST NITE (9 "The Best of the Five Satins, Pt.2")..........10-20 81
(10-inch LP. Red vinyl. 1000 made.)
MT. VERNON (108 "The Five Satins Sing")..........20-30
RELIC..........8-10
Members: Fred Parris; Louis Peebles; Stan Dortch; Jim Freeman; Nate Moseley; Bill Baker; Jimmy Curtis; Nate Marshall; Ed Martin; John Brown; Tom Killebrew; Al Denby; Jessy Murphy; Wes Forbes; Richard Freeman; Dick Arnold.
Also see ALSTON, Shirley
Also see BAKER, Bill
Also see BLACK SATIN
Also see CARYL, Naomi
Also see CHAMPLAINS
Also see CHESTNUTS
Also see FARRAR, Tony
Also see FREDDIE & LOU
Also see HIGGINS, Ben
Also see NEW YORK CITY
Also see NEW YORKERS
Also see PARRIS, Fred
Also see ROMANS
Also see SCARLETS
Also see STARLARKS
Also see WILDWOODS

FIVE SATINS / Champion Jack Dupree

Singles: 7-inch

CUB (3007/8 "Can I Come Over Tonight"/"Nasty Boogie Woogie")..........4-6
(Red vinyl.)
Also see DUPREE, Champion Jack

FIVE SATINS / Gerry Granahan & Five Satins

Singles: 7-inch

X-BAT (1000 "When the Swallows Come Back to Capistrano")..........3-5 95
(Red vinyl. 500 made.)

Picture Sleeves

X-BAT (1000 "When the Swallows Come Back to Capistrano")..........3-5 95
(500 made.)
Also see GRANAHAN, Gerry
Also see WILDWOODS

FIVE SATINS / Pharotones

Singles: 7-inch

TIMES SQUARE (21 "Paradise on Earth"/"Monkey Business")..........15-25 63
TIMES SQUARE (94 "Paradise on Earth"/"Monkey Business")..........10-20 64
Also see PHAROTONES

FIVE SATINS / Youngtones / Youngsters / Shells

EPs: 7-inch

NEW YORK CITY (1002 "Gus Gossert Presents")..........10-15 71
Also see FIVE SATINS
Also see SHELLS
Also see YOUNGSTERS
Also see YOUNGTONES

FIVE SCALDERS

(With "Bill Moore Tenor Sax")

Singles: 78 rpm

DRUMMOND..........300-400 56
SUGAR HILL..........300-400 56

Singles: 7-inch

DRUMMOND (3000 "If Only You Were Mine")..........800-1000 56
DRUMMOND (3001 "Girl Friend")....1000-1500 56
(Green label.)
DRUMMOND (3001 "Girl Friend")....1000-1500 56
(Maroon label.)
SUGAR HILL (3000 "If Only You Were Mine")..........2000-2500 56
Members: Mack Rice; Johnny Mayfield; James Bryant; Sol Tilman; Gerald Young.
Also see FALCONS
Also see RICE, Mack

FIVE SCAMPS

Singles: 78 rpm

COLUMBIA (30157 "Chicken Shack Boogie")..........40-50 49
OKEH (7049 "With All My Heart")..........40-50 54

Singles: 7-inch

OKEH (7049 "With All My Heart")..........150-200 54

FIVE SCRIPTS

(5 Scripts)

Singles: 7-inch

LONGFIBER (201 "The Clock")..........15-25 66
SCRIPT (102 "You Left My Heart")..........15-25 65
SCRIPT (103 "My Friends Tell Me")..........10-15 65

FIVE SECRETS

Singles: 78 rpm

DECCA..........20-30 57

Singles: 7-inch

DECCA (30350 "See You Next Year").....50-75 57
Also see LOUNGERS
Also see SECRETS

FIVE SHADES

Singles: 7-inch

EMBER (1074 "Mary Had a Little Man")..10-20 61
MGM (13035 "One Hot Dog")..........5-10 61

FIVE SHADES

Singles: 7-inch

VEEP (1208 "Vickie")..........10-15 65

5 SHADOWS

Singles: 7-inch

FROSTY (1 "Blue Moon")..........100-150 60

FIVE SHADOWS

Singles: 7-inch

MELLOMOOD (011 "Don't Say Goodnight")..........20-30 65

FIVE SHARKS

Singles: 7-inch

AMBER (852 "The Lion Sleeps Tonight")..8-12 66
(Red vinyl.)
FELLATIO (104 "Fine Fine Frame")..........5-10 66
OLD TIMER (604 "Gloria")..........10-15 64
OLD TIMER (605 "Stand By Me")..........5-10 64
(Black vinyl.)
OLD TIMER (605 "Stand By Me")..........10-15 64
(Red or gold vinyl.)
OLD TIMER (611 "Gloria")..........5-10 65
(Black vinyl.)
OLD TIMER (611 "Gloria")..........10-15 65
(Red vinyl.)

RELIC (525 "Stormy Weather")..................5-10 65
SIAMESE (404 "Gloria")............................5-10 65
SIAMESE (405 "I'll Never Let You Go")......5-10 65
TIMES SQUARE (35 "Stormy Weather"). 30-40 64
(Black vinyl.)
TIMES SQUARE (35 "Stormy Weather"). 50-75 64
(Multi-colored vinyl.)

EPs: 7-inch

SIAMESE (410 "Five Sharks")................ 10-15 66
Also see GOLD BUGS

FIVE SHARPS

Singles: 78 rpm

JUBILEE (5104 "Stormy Weather")...............................14000-16000 52
(No original 45s of this have been verified. Bootleg 45s are common, but can be identified by their lighter shade of blue paper than was used by Jubilee in the '50s. They also have thicker horizontal lines than originals.)

Singles: 7-inch

BIM BAM BOOM (103 "Stormy Weather")....4-6 72
(Black vinyl.)
BIM BAM BOOM (103 "Stormy Weather")..5-10 72
(Red vinyl.)
Members: Ron Cuffey; Clarence Bassett; Mickey Owens; Robert Ward; Tom Ducket.
Also see VIDEOS

FIVE SHILLINGS

Singles: 7-inch

DECCA (30722 "Letter to an Angel")....... 40-50 58

FIVE SMOOTH STONES

Singles: 7-inch

CHISA (8006 "I Will Never Love Another").. 50-75 69
(Black vinyl.)
CHISA (8006 "I Will Never Love Another").. 20-30 69
(Red vinyl.)

FIVE SOUNDS
(With the Julius Dixon Orchestra)

Singles: 7-inch

DEB (1006 "Greatest Gift of All")......... 400-500 58

5 SOUNDS

Singles: 7-inch

BARITONE (0940 "That's When I Fell in Love")... 20-30 60

FIVE SOUNDS

Singles: 7-inch

EPIC (9856 "Loadin' Coal")..................... 10-20 65
EPIC (10016 "Peanut Butter").................. 10-20 66

FIVE SOUNDS / Cecil Buffalo & Prophets

Singles: 7-inch

LAKESIDE (2001 "Clumsy Dragon")........ 10-15 60
Also see BUFFALO, Cecil, & Prophets

FIVE SPARKS

Singles: 7-inch

JIMBO (1 "A Million Tears")................... 75-100 59

5 SPEEDS
("Narr. By Ducky DeCoy")

Singles: 7-inch

WIGGIE (131 "Tell Me")........................ 50-100 59

5 SPENDERS

Singles: 7-inch

VERSATILE (113 "No Hard Feelings").... 15-25 62
Also see REGENTS

FIVE SPIRITS OF RHYTHM

Singles: 78 rpm

BRUNSWICK (6728 "My Old Man")......... 30-50 33

FIVE SPLENDORS

Singles: 7-inch

STROLL (106 "Your Dog Hates Me")...... 10-20 60

FIVE SPOTS

Singles: 7-inch

APEX (76732 "Black Rock")..................... 20-25 '60s
FUTURE (2201 "Get with It")............... 100-200 59
SOMA (1147 "Black Rock")...................... 15-25 60
Member: Don Glenn.

FIVE STARS

Singles: 78 rpm

SHOW TIME (1102 "Where Did Caledonia Go").. 50-100 54

Singles: 7-inch

SHOW TIME (1102 "Where Did Caledonia Go")..200-300 54
Also see FEATHERS

FIVE STARS

Singles: 78 rpm

TREAT (505 "Let's Fall in Love")..........100-200 55

Singles: 7-inch

TREAT (505 "Let's Fall in Love")..... 1500-2000 55

FIVE STARS

Singles: 78 rpm

ATCO (6065 "Take Five")........................10-20 56

Singles: 7-inch

ABC-PAR (9911 "Dreaming")..................10-15 58
ATCO (6065 "Take Five")........................15-25 56

FIVE STARS
(With Milliard Lee & Orchestra)

Singles: 7-inch

BLUES BOYS KINGDOM (106 "So Lonely, Baby")..50-100 57
(Previously issued as by Milliard Lee.)
Also see LEE, Milliard

FIVE STARS

Singles: 7-inch

COLUMBIA (3-42056 "Baby, Baby").......40-60 61
(Compact 33 single.)
COLUMBIA (4-42056 "Baby, Baby")........15-25 61
DOT (15579 "Atom Bomb Baby")............10-15 57
END (1028 "Baby Baby").......................75-100 58
KERNEL (002 "Atom Bomb Baby")..........50-75 57
(First issue.)
MARK-X (7006 "Dead Wrong")................20-30 57
Members: Walter Gaines; C.P. Spencer.
Also see ORIGINALS
Also see THRILLERS

FIVE STARS

Singles: 7-inch

HUNT (318 "Dreaming")............................8-12 58
NOTE (10011 "Dreaming").......................15-25 58
(First issue.)
NOTE (10016 "My Paradise")..................20-30 59
NOTE (10031 "Am I Wasting My Time")...20-30 60

FIVE STEPS

Singles: 7-inch

DADE (2001 "These Boots Are Made for Walkin' ")..10-15 65

FIVE SUPERIORS

Singles: 7-inch

GARPAX (3 "There's a Fool Born Every Day")..100-150 62
(Orange label.)
GARPAX (44170 "There's a Fool Born Every Day")..50-75 62
Session: Gary Paxton.
Also see PAXTON, Gary

5 SWANS

Singles: 78 rpm

MUSIC CITY (795 "Lil Girl of My Dreams")...50-100 56

Singles: 7-inch

MUSIC CITY (795 "Lil Girl of My Dreams")...300-400 56

FIVE TECHNIQUES

Singles: 7-inch

IMPERIAL (5742 "Heaven Above").........10-20 61

FIVE TEENBEATS

Singles: 7-inch

BIG TOP (3062 "Time to Rock")..............10-20 61
Also see DICK & TEENBEATS

FIVE THRILLS

Singles: 78 rpm

PARROT (796 "My Baby's Gone")........300-500 54
PARROT (800 "Gloria").........................300-500 54

Singles: 7-inch

LOST NITE...4-8
PARROT (796 "My Baby's Gone")... 1000-1500 54
(Title cut off by center hole.)
PARROT (796 "My Baby's Gone")........400-600 54
(Title not cut off.)
PARROT (800 "Gloria")................... 1000-2000 54
(Black vinyl.)
PARROT (800 "Gloria")................... 2500-3500 54
(Red vinyl.)

Members: Levi Jenkins; Gilbert Warren; Oscar Robinson; Leon Pace; Fred Washington; Obie Washington.

FIVE TINOS

Singles: 78 rpm

SUN (222 "Sitting by My Window").......300-500 55

Singles: 7-inch

SUN (222 "Sitting by My Window")...1000-1500 55
(Counterfeits exist of this release.)
SUN (514 "Gonna Let You Go")................5-10 76
Members: Melvin Walker; Marvin Walker; Melvin Jones; Haywood Hebron; Luchrie Jordan.
Also see ESQUIRES

5 TROJANS

Singles: 7-inch

TENDER (516 "Don't Ask Me to Be Lonely")..100-200 58
(Reissued as by the Trojans.)
Also see TROJANS

FIVE TROJANS

Singles: 7-inch

EDISON INT'L (412 "Little Doll")..............25-35 59
Also see ST. CLAIR, Nicky, & Five Trojans

FIVE TRUMPETS

Singles: 78 rpm

GOTHAM 15-25 51-52
RCA...15-25 49
SAVOY 5-10 55-56

Singles: 7-inch

GOTHAM (681 "Stand by Me")................20-40 51
GOTHAM (693 "My Chains Fell Off").......20-40 52
GOTHAM (696 "No Not One")..................20-40 52
RCA (0014 "O Lord")...............................25-45 49
(Colored vinyl.)
RCA (0034 "Swing Low Sweet Chariot")..25-45 49
(Colored vinyl.)
RCA (0064 "Preach My Word")................25-45 49
(Colored vinyl.)
RCA (0080 "When the Saints Go Marchin' In")..25-45 50
(Colored vinyl.)
SAVOY (4060 "Amazing Grace")................8-12 55
SAVOY (4072 "I've Got Jesus")..................8-12 56

FIVE VETS

Singles: 78 rpm

ALLSTAR (713 "You're in Love")...........75-100 56

Singles: 7-inch

ALLSTAR (713 "You're in Love")..........250-350 56

FIVE WAGERS
(V Wagers)

Singles: 7-inch

NATION TIME (1013 "You're My World"). 15-25 '60s
SALEM (1013 "Lucky I Found You")......... 15-25 '60s
TIARA...10-15

FIVE WHISPERS

Singles: 7-inch

DOLTON (61 "Midnight Sun")..................10-15 62
DOLTON (69 "Awake Or Asleep")...........10-15 63
DOLTON (90 "Sleep Walk").....................10-15 64

5 WILLOWS
(With Don Archer & Orchestra; with Le Roy Kirkland Orchestra)

Singles: 78 rpm

ALLEN (1000 "My Dear, Dearest Darling")...50-75 53
ALLEN (1002 "Delores")........................200-300 53
ALLEN (1003 "White Cliffs of Dover")..400-500 53
HERALD...50-75 54
PEE DEE (290 "Love Bells")................100-200 53

Singles: 7-inch

ALLEN (1000 "My Dear, Dearest Darling")..400-500 53
(Original issued with block print.)
ALLEN (1000 "My Dear, Dearest Darling")..100-200 53
ALLEN (1002 "Delores")........................600-700 53
ALLEN (1003 "White Cliffs of Dover")..1500-2000 53
HERALD (433 "Baby, Come a Little Closer")...100-150 54
HERALD (442 "Look Me in the Eyes") .200-300 54
LOST NITE...5-10
PEE DEE (290 "Love Bells")..................650-750 53
Members: Tony Middleton; Richard Davis; Joe Martin; John Steele; Ralph Martin.
Also see MIDDLETON, Tony

Also see WILLOWS

5 WINGS

Singles: 78 rpm

KING..50-75 55

Singles: 7-inch

KING (4778 "Johnny Has Gone").........100-200 55
KING (4781 "Teardrops Are Falling")...200-300 55
(Reissued in 1959 as by the Checkers.)
Members: Jackie Rue; Frank Edwards; Billy Carlisle; Melvin Flood; Tom Grate; Kenny "Butch" Hamilton; Richard Blandon.
Also see BOP CHORDS
Also see CHECKERS
Also see DUBS
Also see JACKIE & STARLIGHTS
Also see SCALE-TONES
Also see SONICS
Also see VOCALTONES

FIVE WINGS
(Billy Nelson & Five Wings)

Singles: 78 rpm

SAVOY (1183 "Walk Along")....................10-20 56

Singles: 7-inch

SAVOY (999 "Hurry Up Honey")..................4-8
(Previously unreleased.)
SAVOY (1183 "Walk Along")....................30-40 56

FLAGG, Bill
(With His Rockabillies)

Singles: 78 rpm

TETRA..50-100 56

Singles: 7-inch

MGM (12637 "Doin' My Time")................50-75 58
TETRA (4445 "Go Cat, Go")..................75-125 56
TETRA (4448 "Guitar Rock")..................75-125 57

EPs: 7-inch

FLUKE (1002 "Bill Flagg & His Rockabillies")..?
(Since we do not know the year of this EP, we cannot yet price it. Also, having seen only the disc, we are not certain it came with a cover.)

FLAGG, Fannie *LP '67*
(Patricia Neal)

LPs: 10/12-inch

RCA (3856 "Rally 'Round the Flagg")....... 10-20 66

FLAGMEN

Singles: 7-inch

LIMELIGHT (3104 "Drag Strip USA").......10-20 64
Members: Lloyd Hugo; Jimmy Lenten; Greg Coby; Jay Milhelich.

FLAHARTY, Sonny
(With the Mark V)

Singles: 7-inch

COUNTERPART (2592 "You Bring These Tears to Me")..5-8 67
DECCA (31419 "C'mon Little Mary")..........5-10 62
EPIC (9394 "Heartbreak Station")..............5-10 60
FALCON (1001 "Jo Ann")...........................5-10 63
FRATERNITY (3366 "Wrong Side of the Road")..4-6 '70s
HURON (22004 ("Teenage War Chant").. 15-25 61
PHILIPS (40479 "You Bring These Tears to Me")..10-15 67
SPANGLE (2011 "My Baby's Casual").....30-50 58

FLAIRS

Singles: 78 rpm

ABC (9740 "Aladdin's Lamp")..................10-15 56
FLAIR...50-100 53-55

Singles: 7-inch

ABC-PAR (9740 "Aladdin's Lamp")......... 15-25 56
ANTLER (4005 "I'd Climb the Hills and Mountains")..50-75 57
FLAIR (1012 "I Had a Love")................250-350 53
FLAIR (1019 "Tell Me You Love Me")..400-500 53
FLAIR (1028 "Love Me, Girl")..............100-200 54
FLAIR (1041 "You Were Untrue").........100-200 54
FLAIR (1044 "This Is the Night for Love")..200-300 54
(Shiny red label.)
FLAIR (1044 "This Is the Night for Love") 50-75
(Black and silver label.)
FLAIR (1056 "I'll Never Let You Go") ...250-350 55
FLAIR (1067 "My Darling, My Sweet") .100-200 55

LPs: 10/12-inch

CROWN (356 "The Flairs")........................40-60 63
(Reprocessed Stereo.)
CROWN (5356 "The Flairs")....................50-100 63
(Monaural.)

Members: Cornell Gunter; Richard Berry; Young Jessie; Beverly Thompson; Tom Fox; George Hollis; Patience Valentine.
Also see BERRY, Richard
Also see CHIMES
Also see FIVE HEARTS
Also see GUNTER, Cornell, & Flairs
Also see GUNTER, Shirley, & Flairs
Also see HAYES, Linda
Also see HOLLYWOOD BLUEJAYS
Also see HUNTERS
Also see JAMES, Etta
Also see JESSIE, Young
Also see RAMS
Also see VALENTINE, Patience
Also see WHIPS

FLAIRS
(Redwoods)
Singles: 7-inch
EPIC (9447 "Shake Shake Sherry")........ 10-20 61
(Also issued as by the Redwoods.)
Also see REDWOODS

FLAIRS
Singles: 7-inch
PALMS (726 "Roll Over Beethoven")....... 30-50 61
(Reissued as by the Velaires.)
Also see VELAIRES

FLAIRS
Singles: 7-inch
RAP (007 "You Got to Steal It")............... 15-25 '60s

FLAMBEAUS
Singles: 7-inch
OLD TOWN (2001 "Darling, I'm with You") 10-20 66

FLAME, The P&R '70
Singles: 7-inch
BROTHER (3500 "See the Light") 10-15 70
BROTHER (3501 "Another Day Like Heaven") 10-15 71
LPs: 10/12-inch
BROTHER (2500 "The Flame")............... 20-30 71
(Includes bonus poster.)
Members: Rick Fataar; Steve Fataar; Terry "Blondie" Chaplin; Brother Fataar. Session: Carl Wilson.
Also see RUTLES

FLAMES
Singles: 78 rpm
SELECTIVE (113 "Young Girl").............. 50-75 50
7-11 (2106 "Keep on Smiling")............ 100-200 53
7-11 (2107 "Together") 500-750 53
SPIN (101 "Cryin' for My Baby").......... 100-150 52
Singles: 7-inch
7-11 (2106 "Keep on Smiling")............ 400-600 53
7-11 (2107 "Together") 750-1000 53
Members: Bobby Byrd; Willie Rockwell; David Ford; Curley Dinkins; Curtis Williams; Leon Hughes.
Also see BYRD, Bobby
Also see HOLLYWOOD FLAMES
Also see PATTI ANNE & FLAMES

FLAMES
Singles: 7-inch
BERTRAM INT'L (203 "Crazy")............... 30-40 57

FLAMES
(Fabulous Flames)
Singles: 7-inch
DOT (15813 "The Scramble") 15-25 58
FARGO (1019 "Making Time") 10-15 61
GAITY (168 "Rockin' with the Blues") 10-15 59
HARLEM (114 "So Long My Darling") . 450-550 60

FLAMES
Singles: 7-inch
VENTURAL (727 "Going Home")............ 10-20 62

FLAMES
Singles: 7-inch
CUCA (64111 "The Bird")........................ 15-25 64

FLAMES
Singles: 7-inch
HOT SPOT (101 "Scorched Earth")......... 10-20 65
HOT SPOT (103 "Williams Estate") 10-20 65

FLAMETTES
Singles: 7-inch
LAURIE (3109 "You You You")............... 10-20 61

FLAMIN' GROOVIES LP '76
Singles: 7-inch
BOMP (101 "You Tore Me Down") 4-6 75
EPIC (10507 "First One's Free") 4-6 69
EPIC (10564 "Somethin' Else") 4-6 70
KAMA SUTRA (527 "Have You Seen My Baby") 4-6 71
SIRE (731 "I Can't Hide") 4-6 76
Picture Sleeves
BOMP (101 "You Tore Me Down") 4-8 75
EPs: 7-inch
SKYDOG 5-10
LPs: 10/12-inch
BUDDAH 10-12 77
EPIC (26487 "Supernazz")...................... 35-45 69
KAMA SUTRA (2021 "Flamingo")............ 15-25 70
(Pink label.)
KAMA SUTRA (2021 "Flamingo")............ 10-15 '70s
(Blue label.)
KAMA SUTRA (2031 "Teenage Head")....15-25 71
(Pink label.)
KAMA SUTRA (2031 "Teenage Head")....10-15 '70s
(Blue label.)
SIRE 10-12 76-79
SNAZZ (2371 "Sneakers") 60-80 68
(10-inch LP.)
VOXX... 5-10
Members: Roy Loney; Cyril Jordan; George Alexander; Tim Lynch; Danny Mihm; Chris Wilson; James Farrell; David Wright.
Also see GROUP "B"

FLAMING EMBER P&R '69
Singles: 7-inch
HOT WAX... 4-8 69-71
RADIO ACTIVE GOLD (115 "Stop the World and Let Me Off") 4-6 71
LPs: 10/12-inch
HOT WAX... 10-15 70-71
Members: Joe Sladich; Jerry Plunk; Bill Ellis; Jim Bugnel.
Also see FLAMING EMBERS

FLAMING EMBERS
Singles: 7-inch
FORTUNE (869 "Gone Gone Gone") 30-50 65
FORTUNE (870 "Rain Go Away")............30-50 65

FLAMING EMBERS / Al Kent
Singles: 7-inch
RIC-TIC (140 "Bless You")....................10-15 68

FLAMING EMBERS / Wingate's Love-in Strings
Singles: 7-inch
RIC-TIC 10-15 67-68
Also see FANTASTIC FOUR / Wingate's Love-in Strings
Also see FLAMING EMBERS

FLAMING HEARTS
(With the Tornadoes)
Singles: 7-inch
VULCO (1 "Baby") 1000-1500 58

FLAMING KINGS
Singles: 7-inch
BRU-CLA (2706 "So Wild About You").....15-25 '60s

FLAMING RED LIGHTNING BOLTS
Singles: 7-inch
DMC (101 "Wine Wine Wine") 10-20 65

FLAMING YOUTH
LPs: 10/12-inch
UNI (73075 "Ark 2") 30-50 69
Member: Phil Collins.

FLAMINGO, Chuck
(Chuck Jackson)
Singles: 7-inch
BELTONE (1004 "Tonight Is Gone") 20-30 61
ROJAC (1002 "Little Bit of This") 10-20 64
Also see JACKSON, Chuck

FLAMINGO, Johnny
(Johnny Flamingo Orchestra)
Singles: 78 rpm
ALADDIN (3385 "When I Lost You").........10-15 56
Singles: 7-inch
ALADDIN (3385 "When I Lost You").........30-50 57
CADDY (112 "Make Me a Present of You") 30-40 57
CADDY (4175 "You're Mine")................. 75-125 61
CANTON (1785 "I") 20-30 60
DIADON (103 "This Was Really Love")....10-15 61
DONNA (1357 "You're Mine")..................20-30 62
DUB-TONE (2580 "I Just Cry")................30-40 59
MALYNN (101 "United") 20-30 59
PICO (2800 "I") 15-25 60
SPECIALTY (640 "Will She Think of Me") 15-20 58

FLAMINGO, Johnny / Chuck Higgins
Singles: 78 rpm
CADDY (105 "So Long"/"Roller Coaster").. 25-35 57
Singles: 7-inch
CADDY (105 "So Long"/"Roller Coaster").. 30-50 57
Also see FLAMINGO, Johnny
Also see HIGGINS, Chuck

FLAMINGOS R&B '56
(With Red Holloway's Orchestra; with King Kolax Orchestra)
Singles: 78 rpm
CHANCE (1133 " If I Can't Have You") 100-200 53
CHANCE (1140 "That's My Desire")..... 100-200 53
CHANCE (1145 "Golden Teardrops") ..250-350 53
CHANCE (1149 "Plan for Love").......... 100-200 53
CHANCE (1154 "Cross Over the Bridge") 100-200 54
CHANCE (1162 "Blues in the Letter") .. 100-150 54
CHECKER 20-40 55-57
DECCA... 15-25 57
END (1035 "Lovers Never Say Goodbye") 500-750 58
END (1046 "I Only Have Eyes for You"/ "Goodnight Sweetheart") 500-750 59
END (1046 "I Only Have Eyes for You"/"At the Prom") 500-750 59
(Note different flip.)
Note: Though possibly made but not yet confirmed on 78 are End 1035 (*Please Wait for Me*), End 1040 and End 1044.
PARROT (808 "Dream of a Lifetime") ..200-300 54
(Black vinyl.)
PARROT (808 "Dream of a Lifetime") 800-1200 54
(Red vinyl.)
PARROT (811 "I Really Don't Want to Know") 3000-4000 55
PARROT (812 "I'm Yours") 500-600 55
(Black vinyl.)
PARROT (812 "I'm Yours") 1000-1500 55
(Red vinyl.)
REO ("Lovers Never Say Goodbye")....400-600 58
(Canadian. Selection number not known.)
REO (8377 "I Only Have Eyes for You"/ "Goodnight Sweetheart") 400-600 59
(Canadian.)
Singles: 7-inch
ABC 4-6 73
BELLVILLE (101 "Lover Come Back to Me") 15-25 64
CHANCE (1133 "If I Can't Have You") .500-750 53
(Black vinyl.)
CHANCE (1133 "If I Can't Have You") 750-1500 53
(Red vinyl.)
CHANCE (1140 "That's My Desire").....400-600 53
(Black vinyl.)
CHANCE (1140 "That's My Desire")...500-1000 53
(Red vinyl.)
CHANCE (1145 "Golden Teardrops") ..500-750 53
(Black vinyl.)
CHANCE (1145 "Golden Teardrops") 1500-2500 53
(Red vinyl.)
CHANCE (1149 "Plan for Love").........750-1200 53
(Yellow and black label.)
CHANCE (1149 "Plan for Love")..........500-750 53
(Blue and silver label.)
CHANCE (1154 "Cross Over the Bridge") 500-750 54
CHANCE (1162 "Blues in the Letter") ..400-600 54
CHECKER (815 "When") 50-75 55
(Maroon label, checkerboard design at top.)
CHECKER (815 "When") 10-20 57
(Maroon label, "Checker" logo vertical on left.)
CHECKER (821 "Please Come Back Home") 50-75 55
(Maroon label, checkerboard design at top.)
CHECKER (821 "Please Come Back Home") 10-20 57
(Maroon label, "Checker" logo vertical on left.)
CHECKER (830 "I'll Be Home")................ 60-80 56
(Maroon label, checkerboard design at top.)
CHECKER (830 "I'll Be Home")................ 10-20 57
(Maroon label, "Checker" logo vertical on left.)
CHECKER (830 "I'll Be Home")..................... 4-8 '60s
(Blue label.)
CHECKER (837 "A Kiss from Your Lips") 60-80 56
(Maroon label, checkerboard design at top.)
CHECKER (837 "A Kiss from Your Lips") 10-20 57
(Maroon label, "Checker" logo vertical on left.)
CHECKER (846 "The Vow") 30-40 56
(Maroon label, checkerboard design at top.)
CHECKER (846 "The Vow") 10-20 57
(Maroon label, "Checker" logo vertical on left.)
CHECKER (853 "Would I Be Crying")...... 30-40 56
(Maroon label, checkerboard design at top.)
CHECKER (853 "Would I Be Crying")...... 10-20 57
(Maroon label, "Checker" logo vertical on left.)
CHECKER (915 "Dream of a Lifetime") ... 20-30 59
CHECKER (1084 "Lover Come Back to Me") 5-10 64
CHECKER (1091 "Goodnight Sweetheart") 5-10 64
CHESS.. 4-6 73
COLLECTABLES .... 3-5 '80s
DECCA (30335 "The Ladder of Love")..... 10-15 57
DECCA (30454 "Helpless")...................... 10-15 57
DECCA (30687 "Rock & Roll March") 10-15 58
DECCA (30880 "Kiss-A-Me") 10-15 58
DECCA (30948 "Hey Now") 10-15 59
END (1035 "Please Wait for Me") 50-60 58
(Gray label. Title later changed to *Lovers Never Say Goodbye.*)
END (1035 "Please Wait for Me") 8-12 58
(Multi-color label.)
END (1035 "Lovers Never Say Goodbye") 30-40 58
END (1040 "I Shed a Tear at Your Wedding") 15-25 59
END (1044 "At the Prom") 15-25 59
END (1046 "I Only Have Eyes for You"/ "Goodnight Sweetheart") 15-25 59
(Gray label.)
END (1046 "I Only Have Eyes for You"/ "Goodnight Sweetheart") 8-12 59
(Multi-color label.)
END (1046 "I Only Have Eyes for You"/"At the Prom") 8-12 59
(Note different flip.)
END (1046 "I Only Have Eyes for You"/"At the Prom") 30-40 59
(Stereo.)
END (1046 "I Only Have Eyes for You"/"Love Walked In") 8-12
(Note different flip.)
END (1055 "Love Walked In") 10-15 59
(Monaural.)
END (1055 "Love Walked In") 20-30 59
(Stereo.)
END (1062 "I Was Such a Fool") 15-20 59
END (1065 thru 1124) 10-15 60-62
JULMAR (506 "Dealin' ") 4-8 69
LOST NITE 4-8
OLDIES 45 .... 4-8 64
OWL (322 "If I Can't Have You") 4-6 73
PARROT (808 "Dream of a Lifetime") 500-1000 54
(Black vinyl.)
PARROT (808 "Dream of a Lifetime") 2500-3500 54
(Red vinyl.)
PARROT (811 "I Really Don't Want to Know") 3000-4000 55
(Black vinyl.)
PARROT (811 "I Really Don't Want to Know") 5000-7000 55
(Red vinyl.)
PARROT (812 "I'm Yours") 250-300 55
(Black vinyl.)
PARROT (812 "I'm Yours") 750-1000 55
(Red vinyl.)
PHILIPS (40308 "Temptation") 5-10 65
PHILIPS (40347 "Boogaloo Party") 5-10 66
PHILIPS (40452 "It Keeps the Doctor Away") 5-10 67
PHILIPS (40496 "Oh Mary, Don't You Worry") 5-10 67

POLYDOR (14019 "Buffalo Soldier"/"Buffalo Soldier") 4-6 70
POLYDOR (14019 "Buffalo Soldier, Part 1"/ Buffalo Soldier, Part 2") 4-6 72
POLYDOR (14044 "Lover Come Back to Me") 4-6 74
REO (8377 "I Only Have Eyes for You"/"Goodnight Sweetheart") 15-25 59
(Canadian.)
RONZE (111 "Welcome Home") 4-8 74
RONZE (115 "Heavy Hips") 4-6 75
RONZE (116 "Love Keeps the Doctor Away") 4-6 75
ROULETTE (4524 "Ol' Man River") 5-10 63
SKYLARK (541 "If I Could Love You") 4-6 78
(Black or red vinyl.)
STOOP SOUNDS (114 "My Foolish Heart") 100-150 97
TIMES SQUARE (102 "A Lovely Way to Spend an Evening") 10-20 64
VEE-JAY (384 "Golden Teardrops") 10-15 61
WORLDS (103 "Think About Me") 4-6 75

EPs: 7-inch

END (205 "Goodnight Sweetheart") 100-200 59
(Monaural.)
END (205 "Goodnight Sweetheart") 200-300 59
(Stereo.)

LPs: 10/12-inch

CHECKER (1433 "Flamingos") 75-125 59
(Monaural.)
CHECKER (3005 "Flamingos") 25-50 66
(Stereo.)
CHESS 6-12 76-84
CONSTELLATION (3 "Collectors Showcase") 15-20 64
EMUS 5-10 79
END (304 "Flamingo Serenade") 50-100 59
(Monaural.)
END (304 "Flamingo Serenade") 75-125 59
(Stereo.)
END (307 "Flamingo Favorites") 40-60 60
(Monaural.)
END (307 "Flamingo Favorites") 50-75 60
(Stereo.)
END (308 "Requestfully Yours") 40-60 60
(Monaural.)
END (308 "Requestfully Yours") 50-75 60
(Stereo.)
END (316 "The Sound of the Flamingos") 40-60 62
(Monaural.)
END (316 "The Sound of the Flamingos") 50-75 62
(Stereo.)
LOST NITE (7 "Flamingos") 10-20 81
(10-inch LP. Red vinyl. 1000 made.)
MEKA (1001 "Greatest Hits") 10-15
PHILIPS (200206 "Their Hits Then and Now") 15-25 66
(Monaural.)
PHILIPS (600206 "Their Hits Then and Now") 15-25 66
(Stereo.)
RONZE (1001 "Flamingos Today") 10-15 72
ROULETTE 8-10 81-84
SOLID SMOKE 5-10 82
Members: Sollie McElroy; John Carter; Zeke Carey; Jake Carey; Paul Wilson; Nate Nelson; Tommy Hunt; Terry Johnson.
Also see ALSTON, Shirley
Also see HUNT, Tommy
Also see McELROY, Sollie
Also see NELSON, Nate
Also see STARGLOWS

FLAMINGOS / Moonglows

Singles: 7-inch

TRIP 3-5

LPs: 10/12-inch

VEE-JAY (1052 "The Flamingos Meet the Moonglows") 30-50 62
(Canadian.)
Also see FLAMINGOS
Also see MOONGLOWS

FLANAGAN BROTHERS

Singles: 7-inch

BRUNSWICK (55078 "Salton City") 75-125 58

FLANNELS

Singles: 78 rpm

TAMPA (121 "So Shy") 25-35 56

Singles: 7-inch

TAMPA (121 "So Shy") 50-75 56

FLANNIGAN, Dick

Singles: 7-inch

ALPINE ("Rough and Tough") 50-75
(Selection number not known.)

FLARES P&R/R&B '61

Singles: 7-inch

COLLECTABLES ....3-5 '80s
FELSTED (8604 "Loving You") 8-12 60
FELSTED (8607 "Jump & Bump") 8-12 60
LANDA (708 "I Found Out") 4-8 65
PRESS (2800 thru 2810) 5-10 62-63

Picture Sleeves

FELSTED (8607 "Jump & Bump") 30-50 60

LPs: 10/12-inch

PRESS (73001 "Encore of Foot Stompin' Hits") 40-60 61
(Monaural.)
PRESS (83001 "Encore of Foot Stompin' Hits") 50-75 61
(Stereo.)
Members: Aaron Collins; Willie Davis; Tom Miller; Randy Jones.
Also see CADETS
Also see JACKSON, Cookie
Also see PEPPERS

FLARES / Ramrocks

Singles: 7-inch

FELSTED (8624 "Foot Stompin'") 10-15 61
Also see FLARES

FLASH & MEMPHIS CASUALS

Singles: 7-inch

BLOCK (1001 "I Promise to Remember") 100-150

FLASHER BROTHERS

Singles: 78 rp

ALADDIN (3156 "Love Gave Me You") 50-75 52
ALADDIN (3186 "It's the Last Thing I Do") 50-75 52

Singles: 7-inch

ALADDIN (3156 "Love Gave Me You") 250-350 52
ALADDIN (3186 "It's the Last Thing I Do") 150-250 52

FLAT EARTH SOCIETY

LPs: 10/12-inch

FLEETWOOD (3027 "Waleeco") 800-1200 68
Members: Jack Kerivan; Paul Carter; Phil Dubuque; Curt Girard.

FLATT, Allen

Singles: 78 rpm

MERCURY (70372 "Counterfeit Baby") 8-12 54
REPUBLIC (7029 "Close Your Eyes") 5-10 53

Singles: 7-inch

MERCURY (70372 "Counterfeit Baby") 20-30 54
REPUBLIC (7029 "Close Your Eyes") 10-20 53

FLATT, Lester, & Earl Scruggs C&W '52

(With the Foggy Mountain Boys; Flatt & Scruggs)

Singles: 78 rpm

COLUMBIA 5-15 51-57
MERCURY 5-10 49-53

Singles: 7-inch

COLUMBIA (20000 & 21000 series) 8-15 51-56
COLUMBIA (40000 thru 42000 series) 5-10 56-63
COLUMBIA (43000 thru 45000 series) 4-8 64-67
MERCURY 10-15 50-53

Picture Sleeves

COLUMBIA 4-8 62-68
MERCURY 4-6 68

EPs: 7-inch

COLUMBIA 10-20 57-60

LPs: 10/12-inch

CBS 5-10
COLUMBIA (30 "Flatt & Scruggs") 8-12 75
COLUMBIA (400 series) 10-15 69
COLUMBIA (1000 & 2000 series, except 1019) 10-25 60-68
COLUMBIA (1019 "Foggy Mountain Jamboree") 30-50 57
COLUMBIA (8000 & 9000 series) 10-25 60-70
(With "CS" prefix.)
COLUMBIA (8000 & 9000 series) 5-10
(With "PC" prefix.)
COLUMBIA (10000 series) 6-12 73
COLUMBIA (30000 thru 37000 series) 5-12 70-82
COPPER CREEK 5-10
COUNTY 5-10
EVEREST 5-10 71-82
51 WEST ....5-10 '80s
HARMONY 8-15 60-71
MERCURY (20000 series) 20-40 58-63
(Monaural.)
MERCURY (60000 series) 20-30 63
(Stereo.)
MERCURY (61000 series) 10-15 68
NASHVILLE 8-10 70
PICKWICK/HILLTOP 8-12 68
POWER PAK 5-10
ROUNDER 5-8
WING 8-12 68
Members: Lester Flatt; Earl Scruggs; Mac Wiseman; Jim Shoemate; Cedric Rainwater.

FLATT, Lester, Earl Scruggs & Jim & Jesse

LPs: 10/12-inch

STARDAY (365 "Stars of the Grand Ole Opry") 15-20 66

FLATT, Lester, Earl Scruggs, & Doc Watson

LPs: 10/12-inch

COLUMBIA (2643 "Strictly Instrumental") 10-15 67
(Monaural.)
COLUMBIA (9443 "Strictly Instrumental") 10-15 67
(Stereo.)
Also see FLATT, Lester, & Earl Scruggs
Also see WATSON, Doc

FLEAS

Singles: 7-inch

CHALLENGE (9115 "Scratchin'") 15-25 61
Members: Dave Burgess; Glen Campbell; Jerry Fuller; Ricky Nelson.
Also see BURGESS, Dave
Also see CAMPBELL, Glen
Also see FULLER, Jerry
Also see NELSON, Rick
Also see TROPHIES

FLEET & FREDDY

Singles: 7-inch

ARLEN (1002 "Sunset Till Dawn") 10-15 61
PROTONE 10-20 59

FLEETONES

Singles: 7-inch

BANDERA (2511 "Please Tell Me") 30-40 61

FLEETS

Singles: 7-inch

HIP (100 "Disillusioned") 5-10 66
VOLT (120 "Please Return to Me") 10-20 64

FLEETWOOD, Jimmy

(Jimmy Johnson)

Singles: 78 rpm

JAB 10-20 54

Singles: 7-inch

JAB 35-50 54
(Title and selection number not known.)
Also see JOHNSON, Jimmy

FLEETWOOD MAC LP '68

Singles: 12-inch

W.B. (652 "Go Your Own Way") 15-25 76
(Promotional issue only.)
W.B. (2688 "Big Love") 15-25 87
(Promotional issue only.)
W.B. (2728 "Tango in the Night") 15-25 87
(Promotional issue only.)
W.B. (20842 "Family Man") 8-12 87

Singles: 7-inch

EPIC (10351 "Black Magic Woman") 5-10 68
EPIC (10368 "Stop Messin' Around") 5-10 68
EPIC (10436 "Albatross") 4-6 69
EPIC (11029 "Albatross") 4-6 73
EPIC (139609 "Albatross") 5-8
(Promotional issue only.)
REPRISE (0108 "Green Manalishi"/"Oh Well") 5-10 73
REPRISE (0860 "Coming Your Way") 10-15 70
REPRISE (0883 "Oh Well") 10-15 70
REPRISE (0925 thru 1317) 8-12 70-74
REPRISE (1339 thru 1359) 5-10 75-76
W.B. (8304 "Go Your Own Way") 8-12 76
W.B. (8371 thru 8483) 3-6 77
W.B. (19866 thru 29966) 3-6 82-90
W.B. (49000 series) 3-6 79-81

Picture Sleeves

W.B. 4-8 77-88

LPs: 10/12-inch

BLUE HORIZON (3801 "Fleetwood Mac in Chicago") 20-25 70
BLUE HORIZON (4803 "Blues Jam in Chicago, Vol. 1") 20-25 70
BLUE HORIZON (4805 "Blues Jam in Chicago, Vol. 2") 20-25 70
BLUE HORIZON (66227 "Blues Jam at Chess") 20-25 69
BLUE HORIZON (83110 "Mr. Wonderful") 20-25
COLUMBIA SPECIAL PROD. 8-12 73
EPIC (26402 "Peter Green's Fleetwood Mac") 20-30 68
EPIC (26446 "English Rose") 50-60 69
EPIC (30632 "Black Magic Woman") 15-25 71
(Repackage of *Fleetwood Mac* and *English Rose.*)
EPIC (33740 "English Rose") 10-15 73
EPIC (33740 "Fleetwood Mac/English Rose") 10-15 74
(Repackage of *Black Magic Woman.*)
MFSL (012 "Fleetwood Mac") 75-100 78
MFSL (119 "Mirage") 40-60 84
NAUTILUS (8 "Rumours") 25-35 80
(Half-speed mastered.)
REPRISE (Except 6368) 8-15 70-77
REPRISE (6368 "Then Play On") 15-25 69
(Without *Oh Well.*)
REPRISE (6368 "Then Play On") 10-15 69
(With *Oh Well.*)
SIRE 8-10 75-77
VARRICK 5-10 85
W.B. 8-12 77-90
Members: Mick Fleetwood; John McVie; Peter Green; Jeremy Spencer; Christine McVie; Bob Welch; Danny Kirwan; Dave Walker; Lindsay Buckingham; Bob Weston; Stevie Nicks; Rick Vito; Billy Burnette.
Also see KIRWAN, Danny
Also see MAYALL, John
Also see NICKS, Stevie
Also see SPANN, Otis, & Fleetwood Mac
Also see WELCH, Bob

FLEETWOOD MAC / Gun

Singles: 7-inch

EPIC (139609 "Albatross"/"Race with the Devil") 8-10 69
("Special Back-to-Back Reservice." Promotional issue only.)

Picture Sleeves

EPIC (139609 "Albatross"/"Race with the Devil") 10-20 69
(Promotional issue only.)

FLEETWOODS P&R/R&B '59

Singles: 7-inch

DOLPHIN (1 "Come Softly to Me") 15-25 59
(No mention of distribution by Liberty.)
DOLPHIN (1 "Come Softly to Me") 10-20 59
(Reads: "Distributed by Liberty Record Sales Co.")
DOLTON (1 "Come Softly to Me") 30-40 59
DOLTON (3 "Graduation's Here") 5-10 59
(Monaural.)
DOLTON (S3 "Graduation's Here") 15-25 59
(Stereo.)
DOLTON (5 thru 315) 10-15 59-65
LIBERTY (55188 "Come Softly to Me") 8-12 59
(Monaural.)
LIBERTY (77188 "Come Softly to Me") 10-20 59
(Stereo.)
QUALITY 10-20
(Canadian.)
U.A. 4-6 74

Picture Sleeves

DOLTON (5 "Mr. Blue") ....5-10 '90s
DOLTON (22 "Runaround") 10-15 60

EPs: 7-inch

DOLTON (502 "The Fleetwoods") 20-30 60

LPs: 10/12-inch

DOLTON (2001 "Mr. Blue") 25-35 59
(Monaural.)
DOLTON (8001 "Mr. Blue") 30-40 59
(Stereo.)

DOLTON (2002 thru 2039) 20-30 60-65
(Monaural.)
DOLTON (8002 thru 8039) 20-35 60-65
(Stereo.)
LIBERTY 5-10 82-83
SUNSET 10-15 66
U.A. 8-10 75
Members: Gary Troxel; Barbara Ellis; Gretchen Christopher.
Also see VEE, Bobby / Johnny Burnette / Ventures / Fleetwoods

FLEMING, Ann
Singles: 7-inch
COOKIN' (605 "Beside You") 20-30
WINLEY (241 "If I Can't Do You No Good") 8-12 59
WINLEY (247 "Jive Time Baby") 8-12 61
WINLEY (249 "They're Rockin' on the Hill") 8-12 61
(With J. McMichael & Mac Paul.)
WINLEY (253 "You're Just One Man") 8-12 61

FLEMING, Dorothea
Singles: 78 rpm
JAGUAR (3009 "I'm Glad You're Leaving Me") 10-15 55
Singles: 7-inch
JAGUAR (3009 "I'm Glad You're Leaving Me") 15-20 55

FLEMING, Frank
(Frankie Fleming, Jr.)
Singles: 7-inch
AMY (879 "All By Myself Alone") 15-25 63
LAURIE (3131 "All By Myself Alone") 15-25 62

FLEMING, George
Singles: 7-inch
FLEMING (501 "The Shake") 200-300

FLEMING, Jim, & Casuals
Singles: 78 rpm
MCI (1020 "Don't You Just Know It") 50-75 56
Singles: 7-inch
MCI (1020 "Don't You Just Know It") 100-200 56

FLEMING, King
(King Fleming's Quintet)
Singles: 78 rpm
BLUE LAKE (104 "One O'Clock Jump") 15-25 54
CHESS (1633 "Please Come Back") 10-20 56
Singles: 7-inch
ARGO (5410 "Lonely One") 5-10 62
BLUE LAKE (104 "One O'Clock Jump") 25-35 54
(Black vinyl.)
BLUE LAKE (104 "One O'Clock Jump") 75-100 54
(Red vinyl.)
CHESS (1633 "Please Come Back") 20-30 56

FLEMING, Ray
Singles: 7-inch
CUB (9119 "Humpty Dumpty") 8-12 63
GAMBIT (1105 "Something in the Wind") 15-25 63

FLEMING, Rhonda
LPs: 10/12-inch
COLUMBIA (1080 "Rhonda") 30-50 57

FLEMONS, Wade *P&R/R&B '58*
(With the Newcomers; Wade Flemmons)
Singles: 7-inch
RAMSEL (1001 "Jeannette") 10-20
VEE-JAY (295 "Here I Stand") 20-25 58
VEE-JAY (309 "Hold Me Close") 15-25 59
VEE-JAY (321 "Slow Motion") 15-25 59
VEE-JAY (335 "What's Happening") 15-25 59
VEE-JAY (344 "Easy Lovin' ") 10-20 60
VEE-JAY (368 "I'll Come Running") 20-30 60
VEE-JAY (377 "At the Party") 10-15 61
VEE-JAY (389 "Please Send Me Someone to Love") 10-15 61
VEE-JAY (427 "Half a Love") 8-12 61
VEE-JAY (471 "Ain't These Tears") 8-12 62
VEE-JAY (578 "When It Rains It Pours") 8-12 63
VEE-JAY (614 "I Knew You When") 5-10 64
VEE-JAY (668 "Empty Balcony") 5-10 65
LPs: 10/12-inch
VEE-JAY (1011 "Wade Flemons") 75-125 59
(Maroon label.)
VEE-JAY (1011 "Wade Flemons") 25-50 61
(Black label.)
Also see EARTH, WIND & FIRE
Also see SALTY PEPPERS
Also see SKYLINERS / Wade Flemons
Also see VELVETS / Wade Flemmons

FLENER, Charlie
Singles: 7-inch
TEMPWOOD (1034 "Moon in My Window") 50-75 62
TEMPWOOD (1040 "So in Love with Him") 25-35 63

FLETCHER, Dusty *R&B '47*
Singles: 78 rpm
NATIONAL (4012 "Open the Door, Richard") 10-20 47
NATIONAL (4013 "Mad Hour") 10-20 47
NATIONAL (4014 "I'm Going Back in There") 10-20 47
NATIONAL (4018 "Put the Last Clean Shirt on Bill") 10-20 48
Singles: 7-inch
SAVOY (1585 "Open the Door, Richard") 10-20 60

FLETCHER, Jimmie
Singles: 7-inch
WINSTON (1031 "What's Wrong with You") 100-150 59

FLETCHER, Maria Beale
Singles: 7-inch
MONUMENT (812 "Nickels & Pennies") 5-10 62
Picture Sleeves
MONUMENT (812 "Nickels & Pennies") 10-15 62

FLETCHER, Sam
Singles: 7-inch
CUB (9032 "No Such Luck") 10-15 59
CUB (9048 "Only Heaven Knows") 10-15 59
METRO (20013 "Torn Between Two Loves") 10-20 59
METRO (20022 "If You Love Me") 10-20 59
RCA (7676 thru 8076) 15-25 60-62
TOLLIE (9012 "I'd Think It Over") 25-50 64
VAULT (934 "Look of Love") 8-12 67
VEE-JAY (623 "Guess Who") 5-10 64
W.B. (5384 "As Time Goes By") 10-15 63
LPs: 10/12-inch
VAULT (116 "The Look of Love, the Sound of Soul") 15-25 67
VEE-JAY (1094 "Sam Fletcher Sings") 25-35 64

FLINT, Jimmy, & Stones
Singles: 7-inch
W.B. (5236 "Have You Been There") 10-20 61

FLINT, Shelby *P&R '60*
Singles: 7-inch
CADENCE (1352 "I Will Love Him") 5-10 58
QUANTUM 4-8
VALIANT 5-10 60-66
LPs: 10/12-inch
MCA 8-12 73
VALIANT (W-401 "Shelby Flint") 25-35 61
(Monaural.)
VALIANT (WS-401 "Shelby Flint") 35-50 61
(Stereo.)
VALIANT (W-403 "Shelby Flint Sings Folk") 25-35 61
(Monaural.)
VALIANT (WS-403 "Shelby Flint Sings Folk") 35-50 61
(Stereo.)
VALIANT (5003 "Cast Your Fate to the Wind") 15-25 66
(Monaural.)
VALIANT (25003 "Cast Your Fate to the Wind") 20-30 66
(Stereo.)

FLINTONES
Singles: 7-inch
CAREER (1601 "Unforgettable You") 75-125

FLINTS
(Flint's)
Singles: 7-inch
HEART (100 "Why Did You Go") 250-350 62
OKEH (7126 "People Say") 50-75 59
PETITE (101 "Over the Ocean") 75-100 58

FLINTSTONE, Fred
(Fred Flintstone & His Orchestra; Freddy Flintstone)
Singles: 7-inch
B-H (001 "Quarry Stone Rock") 10-20 62
EPIC (9475 "Stone Age Rock") 10-20 61
Picture Sleeves
B-H (001 "Quarry Stone Rock") 25-35 62
LPs: 10/12-inch
HBR (2035 "Songs from Mary Poppins") 30-40 65

FLIPPERS
Singles: 78 rpm
FLIP (305 "My Aching Heart") 50-100 55
Singles: 7-inch
FLIP (305 "My Aching Heart") 250-350 55

FLIPPO, Lawrence
Singles: 7-inch
VAN (00162 "Cry Cry Cry") 50-75

FLIPS
(With Russell & Band)
Singles: 78 rpm
SAPPHIRE (1052 "Why Should I") 10-15 55
Singles: 7-inch
SAPPHIRE (1052 "Why Should I") 75-125 55

FLIPS
Singles: 7-inch
MERCURY (71426 "Gone Away") 15-20 59

FLIPTEENS
Singles: 7-inch
CALYORK ("Anxiously Awaiting") 100-200
(No selection number used.)

FLIRTATIONS
Singles: 7-inch
FESTIVAL (705 "Stronger Than Her Love") 30-50 67
JOSIE (956 "Natural Born Lover") 8-12 66

FLOATERS
Singles: 7-inch
B.E.B. (1001 "Walkin' on a Rainbow") 10-15 66
Members: Tommy Evans; Dock Green; Wilbur Paul.
Also see DRIFTERS

FLOATING BRIDGE
Singles: 7-inch
VAULT (947 "Watch Your Step") 5-10 69
VAULT (953 "Don't Mean a Thing") 5-10 69
LPs: 10/12-inch
VAULT (124 "The Floating Bridge") 20-30 69
Members: Rick Dangel; Jo Johansen.

FLOCK-ROCKER
("The Crown Prince of the Blues")
Singles: 78 rpm
PLANET (100 "Political Prayer Blues") 20-40 57
Singles: 7-inch
PLANET (100 "Political Prayer Blues") 20-40 57

FLOOR ROCKERS
Singles: 7-inch
PACIFIC (365 "Summer Time Beat") 10-15 65

FLOOR TRADERS
Singles: 7-inch
MTA (136 "Live a Little") 20-30 67

FLORE, Mike
Singles: 7-inch
RON-CRIS (1005 "Dream Girl") 50-100 61

FLORES, Bobby
Singles: 7-inch
WHIZ MASTERS (604 "Everyday I Have to Cry") 10-20 68

FLORES, Danny
Singles: 7-inch
RPM (491 "Trying to Forget") 15-25 57
Also see ATWOOD, Eddie, & His Goodies
Also see RIO, Chuck

FLORES, Ree
(With the Duprells)
Singles: 7-inch
CHELAN (556 "Never Let Me Go") 400-500
M&H (9343 "Look into My Heart") 40-60

FLORESCENTS
Singles: 7-inch
ABC-PAR (10317 "Twist Beat") 10-20 62
BETHLEHEM (3079 "What Are You Doing Tonight") 15-25 63

FLORIDIANS
Singles: 7-inch
ABC-PAR (10185 "I Love Marie") 50-75 61

FLOWER COMPANY
Singles: 7-inch
COCONUT GROOVE (2033 "Did You Love Me from the Start") 40-50 68

FLOWER POWER
Singles: 7-inch
TENER (1010 "I Can Feel It") .... 15-25 '60s
TUNE-KEL (608 "You Make Me Fly") 15-25 68
TUNE-KEL (611 "Bye Bye Baby") 15-25 69
TUNE-KEL (612 "Trivialities") 15-25 69
TUNE-KEL (613 "Don't Burn My Wings") 15-25 69
TUNE-KEL (614 "Stop!") 15-25 69

FLOWERPOT MEN
(Flower Pots)
Singles: 7-inch
DERAM (7513 "Let's Go to San Francisco") 10-15 67
DERAM (7516 "Walk in the Sky") 10-15 67
DERAM (85051 "In a Moment of Madness") .... 8-12 '60s
Members: Tony Burrows; Pete Nelson; Roger Greenaway; Roger Cook.
Also see IVY LEAGUE
Also see WHITE PLAINS

FLOWERS, Pat
Singles: 7-inch
DOT (15469 "Rock, Sock the Boogie") 15-25 56

FLOWERS, Phil
(With the Flower Shop; with the Bat Men)
Singles: 78 rpm
EMPIRE 15-25 51
HOLLYWOOD 15-25 56
Singles: 7-inch
A&M (1122 "Like a Rolling Stone") 4-8 69
A&M (1168 "Every Day I Have to Cry") 4-8 70
ALMANAC (803 "C'mon Dance with Me") 10-20 64
BELL (928 "Nothing Lasts Forever") 4-8 70
BELL (993 "I Just Walked Away") 4-8 71
COLUMBIA (43397 "Comin' Home to You") 5-10 65
DOMINO (500 "Twistin' Beat") 8-12 62
DOT 5-10 67-69
EMPIRE 30-50 51
HOLLYWOOD (1070 "I'm a Lover Man") 30-50 56
HOLLYWOOD (1089 "You Stole My Heart") 30-50 58
JOSIE (909 "Cleopatra") 8-12 63
U.A. (257 "Bingo") 8-12 60
WING (2100 "No Kissin' at the Hop") 50-75 58
LPs: 10/12-inch
DOT 10-20 68
GUEST STAR (1456 "I Am the Greatest!") 25-35 64
GUEST STAR (1457 "Phil Flowers Sings a Tribute") 25-35 64
MOUNT VERNON (154 "Rhythm 'N' Blues") 15-25
Also see CHARLES, Ray / Phil Flowers
Also see COLE, Nat "King" / Phil Flowers
Also see HALEY, Bill / Phil Flowers

FLOWERS, Phil, / Joe Lyons & Arrows
Singles: 78 rpm
HOLLYWOOD 20-30 56
Singles: 7-inch
HOLLYWOOD (1065 "Honey Chile"/"What's New with You") 100-150 56
Also see LYONS, Joe, & Arrows

FLOWERS, Vancie
Singles: 7-inch
CREST (1073 "You Taught Me to Love You") 8-12 59
PIKE (5901 "What a Man") 10-20 60

FLOWERZ
Singles: 7-inch
KINGSTON (1967 "I Need Your Love Now") 10-20 67
(Selection number seems incompete, since other Kingston issues have one or two digits following the year – "1967" in this case.)
KINGSTON (19684 "Flyte") 10-20 68

FLOYD, Bill
Singles: 7-inch
STARDAY (663 "Hey Boy") 100-200
TOPIC (8017 "This Time She's Gone") 5-10 66

TOPIC (8028 "I Cut the Apron String Last Night")....................5-10 67
WAYSIDE (1025 "I'm Gonna Make You Throw Rocks")....................5-10 68

FLOYD, Billy

Singles: 7-inch

ARCTIC (145 "My Oh My")....................5-10 68
20TH FOX (6678 "Sweeter Than Candy")....................10-15 67

FLOYD, Bobby

Singles: 7-inch

MUSIC HALL (100 "It Gives Me Chills")..15-25

FLOYD, Eddie *P&R/R&B '66*

Singles: 7-inch

ATLANTIC (2275 "Drive On")....................8-12 65
LU PINE (115 "Set My Soul on Fire")......15-25 64
LU PINE (122 "I'll Be Home")....................15-25 65
MALACO....................4-6 77
MERCURY....................4-6 78
SAFICE (334 "Never Get Enough of Your Love")....................10-15 64
STAX....................4-8 66-75

LPs: 10/12-inch

ATCO....................8-10 74
MALACO....................5-10 77
STAX....................10-20 67-79
Also see FALCONS
Also see REDDING, Otis / Carla Thomas / Sam & Dave / Eddie Floyd

FLOYD, Eddie, & Mavis Staples

Singles: 7-inch

STAX (0041 "Never Never Let You Go")....5-10 69
Also see FLOYD, Eddie

FLOYD, Frank

Singles: 7-inch

F&L (100 "Monkey Love")....................1500-2000 57
Also see HARMONICA FRANK

FLOYD, Jessie

Singles: 7-inch

DIXIE (1063 "Hangover Blues")..........300-400

FLOYD, Merdell

Singles: 7-inch

ERWIN (100 "Juke Box Mama")..........200-300

FLUORESCENTS

Singles: 7-inch

CANDLELITE (420 "Facts of Love")..........5-10 64
HANOVER (4520 "Facts of Love")........50-100 59

FLY BI NIGHTS

Singles: 7-inch

TIFFANY (564 "Found Love")....................20-40 67

FLYERS

Singles: 78 rpm

ATCO (6088 "On Bended Knee")............20-30 57

Singles: 7-inch

ATCO (6088 "On Bended Knee")............30-40 57
Members: Bobby Hendricks; Bill Pinckney; Dee Bailey; Bill Kennedy.
Also see HENDRICKS, Bobby
Also see PINKNEY, Bill

FLYERS
(With Dave McRae Orch.)

Singles: 7-inch

TAB (501 "A Sign That You're Mine")..500-550 '50s

FLYING CIRCUS

Singles: 7-inch

CAPITOL (3521 "Train Ride")....................4-6 73
CAPITOL (3694 "Gypsy Road")....................4-6 73
GNP (426 "Hayride")....................5-10 69
MTA (117 "Midnight Highway")............15-25 67
MTA (130 "Got to Learn to Love")............15-25 67

LPs: 10/12-inch

CAPITOL (11147 "Flying Circus")............10-15 73-74
CAPITOL (11240 "Last Laugh")............10-15 73-74

FLYING MACHINE

Singles: 7-inch

NIGHT OWL (1493 "I'll Find You Anyway")....................15-25 69

FLYNN, Freddy, & Flashes

Singles: 7-inch

LYRIC (107 "Hazel")....................40-60 59

FLYS

Singles: 7-inch

MYSKATONIC (100 "Reality Composition")....................15-25 66
MYSKATONIC (101 "Be What You Is")....15-25 66

FOAMY BRINE

Singles: 7-inch

BRINE (101 "Tell Her")....................40-50 67

FOGCUTTERS

Singles: 7-inch

CARTHAY (777 "Cry Cry Cry")....................25-30 65
CHARTER (1217 "Casting My Spell")......10-20 65
CHARTER (1218 "It's My World")............15-20 66
LIBERTY (55793 "Cry Cry Cry")..............10-15 65

FOGERTY, John *P&R '72*

Promotional Singles: 12-inch

W.B. (2234 thru 2514)....................5-10 84-86

Singles: 7-inch

ASYLUM....................4-6 75-76
FANTASY....................4-6 73
W.B....................3-5 84-86

Picture Sleeves

W.B. (Except 291007)....................3-5 84-87
W.B. (291007 "The Old Man Down the Road")....................3-5 84
(With blue pictures.)
W.B. (291007 "The Old Man Down the Road")....................5-8 84
(With black pictures.)

LPs: 10/12-inch

ASYLUM (1046 "John Fogerty")..........5-10 75
W.B. (25203 "Centerfield")....................10-15 84
(Last track is mistitled, *Zanz Kant Danz.*)
W.B. (25203 "Centerfield")....................5-8 85
(Last track is *Vanz Kant Danz.*)
W.B. (25449 "Eye of the Zombie")..............5-8 85
Also see CREEDENCE CLEARWATER REVIVAL
Also see EDDY, Duane

FOGERTY, Tom *LP '72*
(With the Blue Velvets; with Blue Violets)

Singles: 7-inch

FANTASY....................4-8 71-82
ORCHESTRA ("Now You're Not Mine")...35-50 62
(Selection number not known.)
ORCHESTRA (1010 "Have You Ever Been Lonely")....................35-50 61
ORCHESTRA (6177 "Come on Baby")...35-50 61
(Despite the higher number, this is the first Orchestra single.)

Picture Sleeves

FANTASY (661 "Goodbye Media Man").....5-10 71

LPs: 10/12-inch

FANTASY....................8-15 72-81
Members: Tom Fogerty; John Fogerty; Doug Clifford; Stuart Cook.
Also see CREEDENCE CLEARWATER REVIVAL

FOGGY NOTIONS

Singles: 7-inch

GINNY (904 "Need a Little Lovin'")..........20-30 66

FOLAND, Bill, & Surfs

Singles: 7-inch

TISHMAN (903 "Surfin' Trumpets")..........25-35 63

FOLEY, Jim
(With the Big Beats)

Singles: 7-inch

BLUE ORCHID (8642 "My Isle of Golden Dreams")....................200-300 68
BLUE ORCHID (306012 "My Isle of Golden Dreams")....................4-6 81
LUCKY (1001 "Goodbye Train")......1500-2000 60
(Lucky also used the number 1001 on a release by Ronny & Johnny.)
Also see RONNY & JOHNNY

FOLEY, Red *C&W '44*
(With the Cumberland Valley Boys; with His Log Cabin Quartet; with Betty Foley; with Roberta Lee; with Anita Kerr Singers; with Grady Martin & His Slew Foot Five)

Singles: 78 rpm

BANNER....................10-15
DECCA (Except 30067 & 30674)..........4-10 42-57
DECCA (30067 "Rock 'N Reelin'")..........10-20 56
DECCA (30674 "Crazy Little Guitar Man")....................10-20 58
MELOTONE....................10-15
ORIOLE....................10-15

Singles: 7-inch

DECCA (25000 series)....................4-8 61-67
DECCA (27000 thru 29000 series)..........15-30 50-56
DECCA (30000 series, except 30067 & 30674)....................10-20 56-59
DECCA (30067 "Rock 'N Reelin'")..........25-35 56
DECCA (30674 "Crazy Little Guitar Man")....................25-35 58
DECCA (31000 thru 32000 series)..........4-8 60-67
DECCA (46411 "Lonely Mile")....................4-6 68
MCA....................4-6 73

EPs: 7-inch

DECCA....................10-25 53-59

LPs: 10/12-inch

CORAL....................5-8 73
COUNTRY MUSIC....................6-10 76
DECCA (100 series)....................15-25 64
DECCA (4000 series, except 4140)..........10-25 61-67
DECCA (4140 "Company's Comin'")..........10-20 61
DECCA (5303 "The Red Foley Souvenir Album")....................40-60 51
(10-inch LP.)
DECCA (5338 "Lift Up Your Voice")..........40-60 51
(10-inch LP.)
DECCA (7100 series)....................15-25 64
DECCA (8294 "The Red Foley Souvenir Album")....................20-30 56
DECCA (8296 "Beyond the Sunset")........15-25 56
DECCA (8767 "He Walks with Thee")......10-20 58
DECCA (8806 "My Keepsake Album").....20-30 58
DECCA (8847 "Let's All Sing with Red Foley")....................15-25 59
DECCA (8903 "Let's All Sing to Him")......10-20 59
DECCA (74000 & 75000 series)..........8-12 68-69
DECCA/DICKIES ("Red Foley's Dickies Souvenir Album")....................50-100 58
(Special Products issue for the Dickies company.)
MCA....................5-8 '80s
PICKWICK/HILLTOP....................8-12 66
VOCALION....................6-12 65-71
Also see KERR, Anita
Also see KNIGHT, Evelyn, & Red Foley
Also see MARTIN, Grady
Also see WELK, Lawrence, & His Orchestra
Also see WELLS, Kitty, & Red Foley

FOLEY, Red, & Ernest Tubb

EPs: 7-inch

DECCA....................10-20 52-56

LPs: 10/12-inch

DECCA (8298 "Red & Ernie")..................30-50 56

FOLEY, Webb
(With the Jordanaires)

Singles: 78 rpm

EMERALD (2013 "Bee Bop Baby")........50-100 56

Singles: 7-inch

EMERALD (2013 "Bee Bop Baby")......350-450 56
M (668 "Marlene")....................200-300 '60s

EPs: 7-inch

EMERALD (750 "Webb Foley")...........250-350 56
Also see JORDANAIRES

FOLKLORDS

LPs: 10/12-inch

ALLIED (11 "Release the Sunshine")...100-200
(Canadian.)

FOLKSWINGERS *LP '63*

Singles: 7-inch

WORLD PACIFIC....................5-10 66

LPs: 10/12-inch

WORLD PACIFIC....................10-20 63-66
Members: Glen Campbell; Tut Taylor; Harihar Rao.
Also see CAMPBELL, Glen
Also see SHANK, Bud

FONTAIN, Maurice

Singles: 7-inch

DECCA (30713 "I'm Frantic")....................30-50 58

FONTAINE, Eddie *P&R '58*
(With the Excels; Eddie Reardon)

Singles: 78 rpm

DECCA....................10-20 56-57
JALO (102 "Where Is Da Woman")..........25-50 56
VIK....................10-15 55-56
"X"....................10-20 54

Singles: 7-inch

ARGO (5309 "Nothin' Shakin'")..............15-25 58
ARGO (5309 "Nothin' Shakin'")..............25-35 58
(White label. Promotional issue.)
CHANCELLOR (1018 "Middle of the Road")....................15-25 58
DECCA....................15-25 56-57
JALO (102 "Where Is Da Woman")..........50-75 56
LIBERTY (55776 "Blue Roses")................8-10 65
LIBERTY (55823 "I Need You")................8-10 65
SUNBEAM (105 "Nothin' Shakin'")..........40-50 58
SUNBEAM (118 "Love Eyes")..........10-15 58
VIK....................15-25 55-56
W.B....................10-15 62-63
"X" (0096 "Rock Love")....................30-50 54
"X" (0108 "On Bended Knee")................30-50 54
Also see REARDON, Eddie

FONTAINE, Eddie, & Karen Chandler

Singles: 78 rpm

DECCA....................5-10 57

Singles: 7-inch

DECCA....................10-15 57
Also see CHANDLER, Karen

FONTAINE, Eddie, & Gerry Granahan

Singles: 7-inch

SUNBEAM....................10-15 58
Also see FONTAINE, Eddie
Also see GRANAHAN, Gerry

FONTAINE, Frank

Singles: 78 rpm

MGM (12129 "Everybody Rocks")..........15-25 55

Singles: 7-inch

MGM (12129 "Everybody Rocks")..........25-50 55

FONTAINE, Jacki
(With the Starlighters; with Lloyd Shafer & Orchestra)

Singles: 78 rpm

CRYSTALETTE....................10-15 52
FORECAST....................5-10 54

Singles: 7-inch

CRYSTALETTE (656 "Are You Lonesome Tonight")....................15-25 52
CRYSTALETTE (663 "Fortune Teller")....15-25 52
FORECAST (102 "Jack O' Diamonds")....10-20 54

FONTAINE, Vic

Singles: 7-inch

FUTURE (102 "One Love")....................10-20 60
Also see PAT THE CAT & HIS KITTENS featuring VIC FONTAINE

FONTANA, Wayne, & Mindbenders *P&R/LP '65*

Singles: 7-inch

BRUT (812 "Sweet America")....................4-6 74
FONTANA (1503 "Game of Love")..........10-15 64
FONTANA (1509 "Game of Love")............8-12 65
FONTANA (1514 "It's Just a Little Bit Too Late")....................8-12 65

LPs: 10/12-inch

FONTANA (27542 "The Game of Love").30-35 65
(Monaural.)
FONTANA (67542 "The Game of Love").35-40 65
(Stereo.)
Members: Wayne Fontana; Bob Land; Graham Gouldman; Paul Hancox; Eric Stewart; James O'Neil; Rick Rothwell.
Also see FONTANA, Wayne
Also see GOULDMAN, Graham
Also see MINDBENDERS

FONTANE SISTERS *P&R '51*
(With Billy Vaughn's Orchestra)

Singles: 78 rpm

DOT....................5-15 54-57
RCA....................5-10 51-54

Singles: 7-inch

DOT....................10-20 54-60
RCA....................15-25 51-54

Picture Sleeves

RCA (5524 "Kissing Bridge")....................25-35 54

EPs: 7-inch

DOT (1019/1020 "Fontane Sisters")........15-25 56
(Price is for either volume.)

LPs: 10/12-inch

DOT (108 "Fontane Sisters")..................40-60 55
(10-inch LP.)
DOT (3004 "Fontane Sisters Sing")..........30-40 56
DOT (3042 "Visit with the Fontane Sisters")....................30-40 57
DOT (3294 "Sweet Hour of Prayer")........15-25 60
(Monaural.)
DOT (3531 "Tip of My Fingers")..............15-25 63
(Monaural.)

DOT (25294 "Sweet Hour of Prayer")...... 20-30 60
(Stereo.)
DOT (25531 "Tip of My Fingers")............ 20-30 63
(Stereo.)
EVON.. 20-30 '50s
Members: Bea Fontane; Marge Fontane; Geri Fontane.
Also see BOONE, Pat
Also see COMO, Perry, & Fontane Sisters
Also see SINATRA, Frank / Fontaine (sic) Sisters / Glenn Miller & His Orchestra
Also see VAUGHN, Billy, Orchestra

FOOD

LPs: 10/12-inch
CAPITOL (304 "Forever Is a Dream")...... 20-30 69
Member: Steve White.

FOOL, The

Singles: 7-inch
MERCURY.......................................5-10 68-69
EPs: 7-inch
MERCURY (91 "The Fool")..................... 10-20 68
(Promotional issue only.)
LPs: 10/12-inch
MERCURY (61178 "The Fool")................ 20-30 68
Members: Barry Finch; M. Koker; J. Leeger.

FOOTE, Chuck

Singles: 7-inch
ROULETTE (4474 "I've Got an Empty House Tonight")..............................5-10 63
SONCRAFT (401 "Come On Back")....... 10-15 61
20TH FOX (302 "I Stopped Asking")..........5-10 62

FOOTE, Dick

Singles: 7-inch
CORVETTE (1005 "A Blonde Can Be a Dangerous Weapon")...................................... 20-30 58

FORBES, Dorothy
(With David Clowney Orchestra; Dottie Forbes)

Singles: 78 rpm
RAINBOW (340 "My Love Is Just for You")...................................... 10-15 56
Singles: 7-inch
RAINBOW (340 "My Love Is Just for You")...................................... 30-40 56
WINLEY (217 "I Still Want You")............. 10-20 57

FORBES, Graham, & Trio

LPs: 10/12-inch
PHILLIPS INT'L (1955 "The Martini Set")...................................... 500-750 59

FORBIDDEN FIVE

Singles: 7-inch
CAPITOL (4205 "Enchanted Farm")........ 15-25 59

FORD, Ann
(Ann Alford)

Singles: 7-inch
APOLLO (532 "The Fool")...................... 10-20 59
HY SIGN (2111 "If It Ain't One Thing")..... 20-40 '60s
MOHAWK (128 "Mister Humpty Dumpty")..5-10 62
Also see ALFORD, Annie

FORD, Art

Singles: 78 rpm
ESSEX (302 "Rock Island Line")................8-12 52
Singles: 7-inch
ESSEX (302 "Rock Island Line")............. 15-25 52

FORD, Billy
(With the Thunderbirds; Billy Ford Combo; with Night Riders; with Harmonaires)

Singles: 78 rpm
JOSIE.. 10-20 55
UNITED.. 10-20 53-54
VIK.. 10-20 57
Singles: 7-inch
JOSIE (775 "Stop Lying on Me")............. 20-30 55
REPRISE (265 "My Girl")..........................5-10 64
SLATE (3065 "Put Yourself in My Place")...................................... 20-30 61
UNITED (142 "Smooth Rockin'")............ 15-25 53
UNITED (167 "Old Age")........................ 15-25 53
VIK (0263 "How Can I Be Sure")............. 25-35 57
Note: Billy Ford & the Thunderbirds tracks may be found on the flip of Swan releases by Billy & Lillie. See that section for those.
Also see AUGUST, Joseph
Also see BILLY & LILLIE
Also see SHAW, Joan, & Billy Ford

FORD, Billy, & Thunderbirds / Ron Corby

EPs: 7-inch
VIK (5 "Billy Ford & the Thunderbirds")....30-50 57
(Promotional issue only. Not issued with cover.)
Also see CORBY, Ron
Also see FORD, Billy

FORD, Bobby, & Blazers

Singles: 7-inch
LUCK (105 "Grasshopper")......................10-20 61

FORD, Bubba

Singles: 7-inch
MCM (202 "Wigglin' Blond")..................200-300
MCM (777 "Lindy Lou")........................300-400 59

FORD, David, & Ebbtides

Singles: 78 rpm
SPECIALTY (588 "My Confession").........10-15 56
Singles: 7-inch
SPECIALTY (588 "My Confession").........40-50 56
Also see CHURCH, Eugene

FORD, Dee Dee
(D.D. "Foots" Ford; D.D. Ford)

Singles: 7-inch
ABC-PAR (10503 "Just Like a Fool")........8-10 63
BRIAR (142 "Good Morning Blues")...........5-10 63
CHATTAHOOCHEE (707 "You Know")........4-8 66
GLOW HILL (500 "D.D.'s Bounce")..........10-15 61
POTOMAC (902 "D.D.'s Madison")..........10-20 60
TODD (1049 "Good Morning Blues")..........5-10 59
Also see GARDNER, Don, & Dee Dee Ford

FORD, Eddie

Singles: 7-inch
SABRINA (103 "The Drag").....................20-30 59
SABRINA (332 "The Drag").....................15-25 59
(Reissued as by the Mar-Villes, then again as by Rick & Rick-A-Shays.)
Also see MAR-VILLES
Also see RICK & RICK-A-SHAYS

FORD, Frankie — P&R/R&B '59
(With Huey "Piano" Smith's Orchestra)

Singles: 78 rpm
ACE (549 "Cheatin' Woman")..................25-50 58
ACE (554 "Sea Cruise").......................200-300 59
Singles: 7-inch
ABC..4-6 73-74
ACE (549 "Cheatin' Woman")..................10-20 58
ACE (554 "Sea Cruise")..........................20-30 59
ACE (566 "Alimony")................................10-20 59
ACE (580 "Time After Time")...................10-20 60
ACE (592 "Chinatown")...........................10-20 60
ACE (8009 "Ocean Full of Tears")..............8-15 63
BRIARMEADE..3-5
CINNAMON...4-6 73
COLLECTABLES...3-5 81
CONSTELLATION (101 "Chinatown")........5-10 63
DOUBLOON (101 "Half a Crown")...............5-8 67
IMPERIAL..5-10 60-62
PAULA (351 "Peace of Mind").....................4-6 71
SYC...3-5 82
20TH FOX (510 "Hello Dolly")....................5-10 64
Picture Sleeves
ACE (592 "Chinatown")...........................15-25 60
EPs: 7-inch
ACE (105 "Best of Frankie Ford").........100-150 59
LPs: 10/12-inch
ACE (1005 "Let's Take a Sea Cruise")...75-125 59
BRIARMEADE...8-10 76
Also see CLANTON, Jimmy / Frankie Ford / Jerry Lee Lewis / Patsy Cline
Also see MARVIN & JOHNNY / Frankie Ford
Also see SMITH, Huey

FORD, Gloria

Singles: 7-inch
ARRAWAK (1009 "Jive Daddy")..............10-15 65

FORD, Jack

Singles: 78 rpm
CHESS (4858 "That's All You Gotta Do")...10-15 54
Singles: 7-inch
CHESS (4858 "That's All You Gotta Do")...20-30 54

FORD, Jim

Singles: 7-inch
DRUMFIRE (2 "The Story of Elvis Presley")...10-20 60
PARAMOUNT (0258 "Big Mouth U.S.A.")....4-6 73

SUNDOWN (116 "To Make My Life Beautiful")..5-10 59
Also see CHECK-MATES
Also see MANHATTANS
Also see MOHAWKS
Also see STARFIRES
Also see SHAMROCKS

FORD, Jimmy
(Jimmy Forde)

Singles: 7-inch
ESTHER (101 "Got a Gal")....................75-100
FLICK CITY...8-12
MUSTANG (3025 "Sing with Linda")..........5-10 67
MUSTANG (3027 "Ramona").....................5-10 67
STYLO (2102 "You're Gonna Be Sorry")..50-75 59
STYLO (2105 "We Belong Together")......50-75 59

FORD, Johnny

Singles: 7-inch
COLONIAL (51 "I'm Gonna Keep On Loving You")...10-20 '50s

FORD, Kenney
(With the Jubilaires and Bill Ward & His Band)

Singles: 7-inch
HEART (5001 "A Thousand Lives")..........10-20 '50s

FORD, Neal, & Fanatics
(Neal Ford Factory)

Singles: 7-inch
ABC (11184 "You Made Me a Man")..........5-10 69
HICKORY..5-15 67-68
TANTARA (1101 "Don't Tie Me Down")...15-25 66
TANTARA (1104 "Searchin'")..................15-25 66
TANTARA (1107 "I Will if You Want").......15-25 66
LPs: 10/12-inch
HICKORY (141 "Neal Ford and the Fanatics")...20-30 68
Also see FANATICS

FORD, Rocky Bill
(With His Rocky Road Ramblers)

Singles: 78 rpm
4 STAR (1655 "In All My Dreams")..........10-15 54
GILT EDGE (5023 "Aggravatin' Woman")..15-25 51
GILT EDGE (5031 "I'm a Henpecked Man")..15-25 51
GILT EDGE (5039 "Was I Dreaming")......15-25 51
GILT EDGE (5058 "Blowing Suds off My Beer")...15-25 52
GILT EDGE (5067 "Darling, Why Do You Pretend")..15-25 52
STARDAY (253 "Have You Seen Mabel")..25-40 56
Singles: 7-inch
4 STAR (1655 "In All My Dreams")..........25-35 54
STARDAY (253 "Have You Seen Mabel")..200-250 56

FORD, Sandy

Singles: 78 rpm
TNT (137 "Cat Man Boogie")....................25-40 56
Singles: 7-inch
TNT (137 "Cat Man Boogie")..................75-125 56

FORD, Ted

Singles: 7-inch
GAYE (34 "You Don't Love Me")...............8-10
SOUND STAGE 7 (2594 "Pretty Girls Everywhere")...10-20 67
SOUND STAGE 7 (2604 "You're Gonna Need Me")..10-20 68

FORD, Tennessee Ernie — C&W/P&R '49
(With the Green Valley Singers & Orchestra; Tennessee Ernie; with Billy May & Orchestra; with Cliffie Stone's Orchestra; with Jack Fascinato & Orchestra)

Singles: 78 rpm
CAPITOL (1 "Sixteen Tons")....................5-10 69
(Promotional "Special Commemorative Pressing" for Ford's 20th year on Capitol.)
CAPITOL (1200 thru 2900 series).............5-15 50-57
CAPITOL (40000 series)...........................5-10 49-50
Singles: 7-inch
CAPITOL (1275 thru 2900 series)...........10-30 50-54
(Purple labels. Ford's many "Boogie" titles represent the higher end of this price range.)
CAPITOL (2000 thru 4100 series)................4-6 70-75
(Orange labels.)
CAPITOL (3000 thru 4400 series, except 3343)..5-15 54-60
CAPITOL (3343 "Bright Lights and Blond-Haired Women")...15-25 56
CAPITOL (4500 thru 5700 series)................4-6 61-67
CAPITOL (40000 series)...........................10-15 50
Picture Sleeves
CAPITOL..10-20 55-60
EPs: 7-inch
CAPITOL (Except 413)................................5-10 55-61
CAPITOL (413 "Backwoods Boogie and Blues")...20-30 53
GREEN GIANT (2566 "When Pea-Pickers Get Together")..10-15
(Mail order offer. Add $3 to $5 if accompanied by special mailer/sleeve. Promotional issue made for the Green Giant Co.)
LPs: 10/12-inch
CAPITOL (Except 888)...............................5-15 56-80
CAPITOL (888 "Ol' Rockin' Ern")..............25-50 57
EVEREST..5-10 '70s
LONGINES...5-10
PICKWICK..5-10 '70s
READER'S DIGEST (241 "Tennessee Ernie Ford")..20-40
(Boxed, eight-disc set. With booklet.)
SEARS (458 "Jealous Heart")..................10-20
Session: Jordanaires.
Also see HUTTON, Betty, & Tennessee Ernie Ford
Also see JORDANAIRES
Also see LAWRENCE, Steve / Tennessee Ernie Ford
Also see LEE, Brenda / Tennessee Ernie Ford
Also see OWENS, Buck / Tennessee Ernie Ford
Also see STARR, Kay, & Tennessee Ernie Ford
Also see STONE, Cliffie, & His Orchestra

FORD, Tennessee Ernie, & Glen Campbell

LPs: 10/12-inch
CAPITOL..10-12 75
Also see CAMPBELL, Glen

FORD, Tennessee Ernie, & Joe "Fingers" Carr — C&W '51

Singles: 78 rpm
CAPITOL...5-10 51
Singles: 7-inch
CAPITOL (1349 "Tailor Made Woman")...15-25 51
Also see CARR, Joe "Fingers"

FORD, Tennessee Ernie, & Dinning Sisters

Singles: 78 rpm
CAPITOL...5-10 '50s
Singles: 7-inch
CAPITOL..10-15 '50s

FORD, Tennessee Ernie, & Ella Mae Morse
(With Cliffie Stone's Orchestra)

Singles: 78 rpm
CAPITOL..4-8 52
Singles: 7-inch
CAPITOL (2215 "I'm Hog-Tied Over You")..8-12 52
Also see MORSE, Ella Mae

FORD THEATRE

Singles: 7-inch
ABC (11118 "From a Back Door Window")..5-10 68
ABC (11192 "Time Changes")...................5-10 69
ABC (11227 "I've Got the Fever")..............5-10 69
LPs: 10/12-inch
ABC (658 "Trilogy")..................................20-30 68
ABC (681 "Time Changes")......................15-25 69
Members: Joey Scott; John Mazzarelli.

FOREIGNER — P&R/LP '77

Singles: 7-inch
ATLANTIC...3-6 77-90
ATLANTIC (3543 "Blue Morning, Blue Day")..4-8 78
(Black vinyl.)
ATLANTIC (3543 "Blue Morning, Blue Day")..6-12 78
(Colored vinyl. Promotional issue only.)
ATLANTIC/W.B. 3-5 79
Picture Sleeves
ATLANTIC...3-6 78-88
LPs: 10/12-inch
ATLANTIC...5-10 77-91
GEFFEN..5-10 85
MFSL (052 "Double Vision")....................30-50 81
Members: Lou Gramm; Rick Wills; Mick Jones; Dennis Elliott; Ian McDonald; Al Greenwood.
Also see FRASER, Andy
Also see WALKER, Junior

FORERUNNERS
Singles: 7-inch
LIBERTY (55852 "Magic of a Girl") 15-25 65

FOREST, Danny
Singles: 7-inch
BIG TOP (102 "Little Girl") 10-15 66

FOREST, Jimmy R&B '52
(Jimmy Forrest; with All Star Combo)
Singles: 78 rpm
DOT (15340 "Night Train Mambo") 5-10 55
UNITED 5-15 52-54
Singles: 7-inch
DOT (15340 "Night Train Mambo") 10-15 55
PRESTIGE 5-10 61-62
TRIUMPH (607 "Night Flight") 8-12 59
UNITED (Except 110) 10-20 52-54
UNITED (110 "Night Train") 15-25 52
(Black vinyl.)
UNITED (110 "Night Train") 35-50 52
(Colored vinyl.)
LPs: 10/12-inch
NEW JAZZ (8250 "Forrest Fire") 25-50 61
NEW JAZZ (8293 "Soul Street") 25-50 64
PRESTIGE 20-30 61-62
(Yellow label.)
PRESTIGE 10-20 64
(Blue label.)
UNITED (002 "Night Train") 75-100 57
(10-inch LP.)
Also see DAVIS, Miles
Also see JONES, Jo

FOREST CITY JOE
(Joe Pugh)
Singles: 78 rpm
ARISTOCRAT (3110 "Memory of Sonny Boy") 50-75 49

FOREVERS
Singles: 7-inch
APT (25022 "Baby") 10-15 58

FORMATIONS P&R '68
Singles: 7-inch
BANK (1007 "At the Top of the Stairs") ... 20-30 67
MGM (13899 "At the Top of the Stairs") 5-8 68
MGM (13963 "Love's Not Only for the Heart") 10-20 68
MGM (14009 "Don't Get Close") 8-12 68
Members: Victor Drayton; Jerry Akines; Ernie Brooks; Reginald Turner; Johnny Bellman.

FORREST, Andrea / Plastic Ice Cube
Singles: 7-inch
WARICK (6750 "Sooner or Later") 15-25 67

FORREST, Earl R&B '53
("Earl "Whoopin' & Hollerin'" Forrest; Earl Forest)
Singles: 78 rpm
DUKE (Except 103) 15-25 52
DUKE (103 "Rock the Bottle") 40-60 52
METEOR 50-75 53
Singles: 7-inch
DUKE (108 "Whoopin' and Hollerin'") 25-35 52
DUKE (113 "Last Night's Dream") 20-30 53
DUKE (121 "Out on a Party") 20-30 54
DUKE (130 "Your Kind of Love") 20-30 54
DUKE (349 "Memphis Twist") 10-20 62
DUKE (363 "The Duck") 10-20 63
METEOR (5005 "I Wronged a Woman") 50-100 53
Also see ACE, Johnny / Earl Forrest
Also see KING, B.B.

FORREST, Gene, & Four Feathers
(With Chuck Higgins & His Orchestra)
Singles: 78 rpm
ALADDIN (3224 "Wiggle") 15-25 54
RPM (376 "Aching & Crying") 10-20 53
Singles: 7-inch
ALADDIN (3224 "Wiggle") 30-40 54
Also see GENE & EUNICE
Also see HIGGINS, Chuck

FORREST, Jackie
Singles: 7-inch
HITSVILLE (1138 "Breakin' Your Heart for Fun") 30-40 62

FORREST, Nick
Singles: 78 rpm
FORTUNE (513 "I Can't Fall in Love") 20-30 55
Singles: 7-inch
FORTUNE (513 "I Can't Fall in Love") 30-40 55
TEEN LIFE ("Let Me Be") 50-100
(No selection number used.)

FORREST, Sonny
Singles: 7-inch
ATCO (6157 "Diddy Bop") 10-15 60
RED TOP (128 "Mama, Keep My Wife at Home") 15-25 60

FORSE, Beanon
Singles: 7-inch
RODNEY (514 "You Better Go Now") .. 300-400

FORSE, Truitt
Singles: 7-inch
STARDAY (596 "Chicken Bop") 500-600

FORT, Ruben
(Rubien Fort)
Singles: 7-inch
ANNA (1117 "So Good") 10-20 60
CHECK MATE (1007 "Nobody") 20-30 61

FORT MUDGE MEMORIAL DUMP
LPs: 10/12-inch
MERCURY (61256 "The Fort Mudge Memorial Dump") 20-30 70

FORT WORTH DOUGHBOYS
Singles: 78 rpm
BLUEBIRD (5257 "Nancy Jane") .... 150-250 '30s
Also see WILLS, Bob

FORTE, Joe, & Originals
Singles: 7-inch
HI MAR (105/106 "Heaven Right Here"/"Rockin' Queen") 10-20 62

FORTE, Nicky
Singles: 7-inch
HARRISON (100 "Rockin' Guitar") 15-25 57

FORTES
Singles: 7-inch
CURRENT (103 "Waiting for My Baby") ... 30-40 64

FORTUNE, Billy
Singles: 78 rpm
EXCELLO (2114 "I'm Waiting") 10-20 57
Singles: 7-inch
DICE (478 "Listen to Your Heart") 400-500 58
(Reissued as by Billy Jones & Squires.)
EXCELLO (2114 "I'm Waiting") 20-30 57
Also see JONES, Billy, & Squires

FORTUNE, Gayle, & Terrytones
Singles: 7-inch
WYE (1003 "I Cry the Blues") 10-20 61

FORTUNE, Jimmy
Singles: 7-inch
CHANCELLOR (1097 "I Feel a Heartache Comin' On") 10-15 61
DECCA (31032 "Don't Tell Me Not to Love You") 10-15 59

FORTUNE, Johnny
Singles: 7-inch
ARENA (102 "Gee But I Miss You") 10-15 63
ARHAVEN (1001 "Gee But I Miss You") .. 15-25 62
BEAVER (111 "Stay Just One More Day") .5-10 66
CRUSADER (104 "Gee But I Miss You") 8-12 64
CURRENT (101 "Say You Will") 8-12 64
CURRENT (104 "Dan Stole My Girl") 10-20 65
EMMY (1001 "Alone & Crying") 150-250 60
EMMY (1002 "Gee But I Miss You") 30-50 60
PARK AVENUE (104 thru 4905) 15-25 63-65
U.A. (720 "Juarez") 8-12 64
U.A. (780 "Don't You Lie to Me") 8-12 64
VAULT (954 "Your True Love") 4-8 69
LPs: 10/12-inch
PARK AVENUE (401 "Soul Surfer") 30-50 63
(Monaural.)
PARK AVENUE (401 "Soul Surfer") 40-60 63
(Stereo.)
Session: Johnny Fortune; Joe Sudetta; Jim O'Keith.
Also see SWEET SOULS

FORTUNE, Lance
Singles: 7-inch
SIGNATURE (12030 "Be Mine") 10-15 60

FORTUNE, Mickey
Singles: 7-inch
LOGAN (3110 "It's Gonna Hurt Me More") 50-100 59

FORTUNE, Terry
Singles: 7-inch
PINK (704 "Daddy Rabbit") 15-25 60

FORTUNE BROTHERS
Singles: 7-inch
ACCENT (1166 "Malibu Run") 10-20 65

FORTUNE SEEKERS
Singles: 7-inch
TRIDENT (9966 "Why I Cry") 20-40 66

FORTUNE TELLERS
Singles: 7-inch
MUSIC MAKERS (105 "Song of the Nairobi Trio") 5-10 61
SHERYL (340 "School Prom") 10-15 61

FORTUNE TELLERS
Singles: 7-inch
FESTIVAL (3702 "Gypsy Rock") 10-20 67

FORTUNEERS
Singles: 7-inch
SKYTONE (1000 "Look A' There") 10-15 63
Session: Teacho Wiltshire; Prince Eddie McDowell.
Also see WILTSHIRE, Teacho

FORTUNES
Singles: 78 rpm
CHECKER (818 "Believe in Me") 20-30 55
Singles: 7-inch
CHECKER (818 "Believe in Me") 50-75 55

FORTUNES
(With the Eddie Beale Orchestra)
Singles: 7-inch
DECCA (30541 "Tarnished Angel") 50-75 58
DECCA (30688 "How Clever of You") 30-40 58
Member: Don Wyatt.
Also see COLTS

FORTUNES
Singles: 7-inch
ARGO (5364 "Congratulations") 20-30 60
QUEEN (24010 "Nothing Matters Anymore") 10-15 61
TOP RANK (2019 "Steady Vows") 40-50 59
YUCCA (168 "The Laugh of the Town") ... 20-30 64
YUCCA (170 "This Is Love") 30-40 64

FORTUNES
Singles: 7-inch
LAKE (704 "Runnin") 10-20 61

FORTUNES
(Fortune's; with the Max Davis Orchestra)
Singles: 7-inch
DRA (320 "Tell Me") 250-350 62

FORTUNES
Singles: 7-inch
HARMON (1016 "Little Egypt") 15-25 63

FORTUNES
Singles: 7-inch
CUCA (1173 "You Got the Right") 15-25 64

FORTUNES P&R '65
Singles: 7-inch
CAPITOL 4-6 71-74
COLLECTABLES .... 3-5 '80s
LONDON 3-5
PRESS (9773 "You've Got Your Troubles") 10-15 65
(White label, commercial issue.)
PRESS (9773 "You've Got Your Troubles") 5-10 65
(Color label.)
PRESS (9798 "Here It Comes Again") 10-15 65
(White label, commercial issue.)
PRESS (9798 "Here It Comes Again") 10-15 65
(Red or orange labels.)
PRESS (9811 "This Golden Ring") 5-10 66
U.A. (50211 "His Smile Was a Lie") 5-10 67
U.A. (50280 "Painting a Shadow") 5-10 68
WORLD PACIFIC (77937 "That Same Old Feeling") 4-8 70
LPs: 10/12-inch
CAPITOL 8-10 71-73
COCA-COLA (21904 "It's the Real Thing") .... 30-40 '60s
(Special products issue.)
PRESS (73002 "The Fortunes") 20-25 65
(Monaural.)
PRESS (83002 "The Fortunes") 25-30 65
(Stereo.)
WORLD PACIFIC (21904 "That Same Old Feeling") 8-10 70
Members: Glen Dale; Barry Pritchard; Shel MacRae; Rod Allen.

FORTY-SEVEN TIMES ITS OWN WEIGHT
Singles: 7-inch
FABLE (101 "Cumulo Nimbus") 30-50

49TH PARALLEL
Singles: 7-inch
BARRY (3518 "I Need You") .... 15-25 '60s
(Canadian.)
MAVERICK (1004 thru 1011) 15-20 68-69
RCA (3447 "She Says") .... 8-12 '60s
(Canadian.)
RCA (9293 "You Do Things") 8-12 67
VENTURE (612 "Blue Bonnie Blue") .... 15-25 '60s
(Canadian.)
VENTURE (1004 "Twilight Woman") .... 15-25 '60s
(Canadian.)
LPs: 10/12-inch
MAVERICK (7001 "49th Parallel") 150-250 69

FORUM P&R '67
Singles: 7-inch
MIRA (232 thru 248) 10-15 66-68
PENTHOUSE (504 "River Is Wide") 10-20 66
LPs: 10/12-inch
MIRA 15-20 67
Members: Phil Campos; Rene Nole; Riselle Vaine.

FORUMS
Singles: 7-inch
PRISM (1235 "Bring It on Back") 15-25

FORWOOD, Shirley
Singles: 78 rpm
DOT (15487 "Two Hearts") 8-12 56
Singles: 7-inch
DOT (15487 "Two Hearts") 10-15 56
SALEM (1003 "Johnny Please Come Back") 10-15 57

FOSTER, Alan
Singles: 78 rpm
ESSEX (365 "All Along the N.J. Shore") 5-10 54
Singles: 7-inch
ESSEX (365 "All Along the N.J. Shore") .. 10-20 54

FOSTER, Art
Singles: 7-inch
STAR (527 "Houston, Texas") 150-250

FOSTER, Cell, & Audios
Singles: 78 rpm
ULTRA (105 "Honest I Do") 50-100 55
Singles: 7-inch
ULTRA (105 "Honest I Do") 200-300 55
(Yellow label. First issue.)
ULTRA (105 "Honest I Do") 100-150 55
(Maroon label.)

FOSTER, Chuck
LPs: 10/12-inch
PHILLIPS INT'L (1965 "Chuck Foster at the Hotel Peabody") 100-200 60

FOSTER, Dell
(With the Sanford Hertz Combo)
Singles: 78 rpm
CANON (513 "Somebody Else Is Taking My Place") 5-10 55
Singles: 7-inch
CANON (513 "Somebody Else Is Taking My Place") 10-15 55

FOSTER, Eddie
(With the Blazers)
Singles: 7-inch
IN (6311 "I Never Knew") 15-25
LYONS (108 "You Are the Only One") . 100-150 61
(Yellow vinyl.)
Also see HOLLIDAYS

FOSTER, Helen
(With the Chapters; with Rovers)
Singles: 78 rpm
REPUBLIC...50-100 52-53
Singles: 7-inch
REPUBLIC (7013 "You Belong to Me")...100-150 52
REPUBLIC (7037 "Somebody, Somewhere")...150-200 53
Also see CHAPTERS

FOSTER, Jamie
Singles: 7-inch
WUFF (1201 "Yeah, Pretty Baby")...40-60

FOSTER, John, & Sons Ltd.
(Black Dyke Mills Band)
Singles: 7-inch
APPLE (1800 "Yellow Submarine")...100-125 68

FOSTER, Leroy, & Muddy Waters
Singles: 78 rpm
ARISTOCRAT (12334 "Locked Out Boogie")...50-75 49
Also see BABY FACE
Also see WATERS, Muddy

FOSTER, Little Willie
Singles: 78 rpm
BLUE LAKE (113 "Falling Rain Blues")...50-75 55
COBRA (5011 "Crying the Blues")...50-75 57
PARROT (813 "Falling Rain Blues")...50-75 55
Singles: 7-inch
BLUE LAKE (113 "Falling Rain Blues")...100-150 55
(Black vinyl.)
BLUE LAKE (113 "Falling Rain Blues")...150-250 55
(Colored vinyl.)
COBRA (5011 "Crying the Blues")...50-75 57
PARROT (813 "Falling Rain Blues")...75-125 55

FOSTER, Millie
Singles: 7-inch
PRESIDENT (826 "Love Wheel")...10-15 62
PRESIDENT (829 "What a Thrill")...10-15 63
TCF (4 "Ole Father Time")...5-10 64

FOSTER, Pat
LPs:10/12-inch
RIVERSIDE (654 "Gold Rush Songs")...35-45
Session: Dick Weissman.

FOSTER, Pat, & Quintones
Singles: 7-inch
LEE (1114 "In the Doorway Crying")...15-25 60
Also see QUINTONES

FOSTER, Phil
Singles: 7-inch
CORAL (61200 "A Brooklyn Baseball Fan")...10-20 54
EPs: 7-inch
CORAL...15-25 54
LPs: 10/12-inch
CORAL...20-30 54
Also see ALLEN, Steve

FOSTER BROTHERS
(With Lefty Guitar Bates & His Band; Foster Bros.)
Singles: 7-inch
B&F (1333 "Revenge")...10-20 60
DILLIE (101 "Land of Love")...10-20 60
EL BEE (161 "Tell Me Who")...15-25 57
HI MI (3005 "Never Again")...15-25
MERCURY (71360 "Show Me")...15-20 58
PROFILE (4004 "Trust in Me")...10-15 59
Members: Laverne Gayles; George Lattimore; Lindsay Langston; Donald Clay; Ray Pettis.
Also see BATES, Lefty Guitar

FOTO-FI-FOUR
Singles: 7-inch
FOTO-FI (107 "Stand Up and Holler")...10-15 64
Picture Sleeves
FOTO-FI (107 "Stand Up and Holler")...20-30 64
Member: Harry Nilsson.
Also see NILSSON

FOUCHA, Jerry
Singles: 7-inch
NOLA (728 "Come On Baby")...10-20 67
TRAJON (101 "If It's Better")...10-20 '60s

FOUL DOGS
LPs: 10/12-inch
RHYTHM SOUND (481 "No. 1")...250-350 66

FOUNTAIN, Morris
Singles: 78 rpm
SAVOY (1139 "Cryin' My Heart Out")...10-15 54
Singles: 7-inch
SAVOY (1139 "Cryin' My Heart Out")...30-40 54

FOUNTAIN, Pete P&R/LP '60
(With the Village Scramblers)
Singles: 7-inch
CORAL...6-12 58-62
LPs: 10/12-inch
CORAL...10-25 59-69
CROWN ("Jazz")...5-10 66
(Selection number not known.)
FIRST AMERICAN...4-8 78
GUEST STAR...5-10 64
SOUTHLAND (215 "New Orleans to L.A.")...25-40 56
Also see LEE, Brenda, & Pete Fountain

FOUNTAIN, Roosevelt, & Pens of Rhythm P&R '63
Singles: 7-inch
PRINCE-ADAMS (447 "Red Pepper")...10-20 62

FOUNTAIN OF YOUTH
Singles: 7-inch
COLGEMS...10-20 67-69
SUR-SPEED (223 "Hard Woman")...8-12
Also see CROSSFIRES

FOUR
(The Four)
Singles: 7-inch
CLARK (225 "Lonely Surfer Boy")...20-30 65

FOUR ACES
Singles: 78 rpm
TRILON (143 "I Wonder, I Wonder, I Wonder")...15-25 46
TRILON (145 "There's a Rumor Going Around")...15-25 47
TRILON (153 "Richard Ain't Gonna Open That Door")...15-25 47
TRILON (178 "I'll Never Let You Go Again")...15-25 47
TRILON (179 "I'm Crying All the Time")...15-25 47
TRILON (180 "Ain't It a Crying Shame")...15-25 47
Also see ORIGINAL FOUR ACES

FOUR ACES P&R '51
Singles: 78 rpm
DECCA...5-15 51-57
FLASH (102 "Who's to Blame")...15-25 55
MERION (104 "Wanted")...15-25 52
VICTORIA...10-15 51
(Black Plastic.)
VICTORIA (101 "Sin")...20-30 51
(Colored Plastic.)
Singles: 7-inch
ABC-PAR...5-10 60
DECCA (25000 series)...4-8 61-64
DECCA (27000 & 28000 series)...10-15 51-53
DECCA (29000 thru 31000 series)...5-10 54-60
FLASH (102 "Who's to Blame")...15-25 55
MERION (104 "Wanted")...10-20 52
VICTORIA (101 "Sin")...15-25 51
(Black vinyl.)
VICTORIA (101 "Sin")...40-60 51
(Colored vinyl.)
VICTORIA (102 "There's a Christmas Tree in Heaven")...15-25 51
Picture Sleeves
ABC-PAR...5-10 60
EPs: 7-inch
DECCA...10-20 52-59
LPs: 10/12-inch
ACCORD...5-10 81-82
CRANE NOTTIS...8-10 77
DECCA (4013 "The Golden Hits")...15-25 60
DECCA (5429 "The Four Aces")...20-40 52
(10-inch LP.)
DECCA (8122 thru 8693)...15-30 55-58
DECCA (8766 "Swingin' Aces")...15-25 58
(Monaural.)
DECCA (8766 "Swingin' Aces")...20-30 58
(Stereo. With "DL-7" prefix.)
DECCA (8855 "Hits from Broadway")...15-25 59
(Monaural.)
DECCA (8855 "Hits from Broadway")...20-30 59
(Stereo. With "DL-7" prefix.)
DECCA (8944 "Beyond the Blue Horizon")...10-20 59
(Monaural.)
DECCA (8944 "Beyond the Blue Horizon")...15-25 59
(Stereo.)
MCA...5-10 74
U.A....10-15 61
VOCALION...5-10 69
WESTOWN...5-8
Members: Al Alberts; Dave Mahoney; Sol Vocarro; Louis Silvestri.
Also see ALBERTS, Al
Also see LEE, Brenda / Bill Haley & Comets / Kalin Twins / Four Aces

4 AFTER 5s
Singles: 7-inch
ALL TIME (9076 "Hello, Schoolteacher")...30-40 61
Members: Carl White; Al Frazier; Sonny Harris; Turner Wilson.
Also see RIVINGTONS

FOUR AIMS
Singles: 78 rpm
GRADY...200-250 56
Singles: 7-inch
GRADY (012 "If Only I Had Known")...400-500 56
Also see FOUR TOPS

FOUR AMIGOS
Singles: 7-inch
CAPITOL (4614 "Mr. Sandman")...5-10 59
CAPITOL (4680 "El Cid")...5-10 60
CAPITOL (5750 "High Flying Love")...5-10 66
RIC (159 "The Clock")...5-10 65
LPs: 10/12-inch
CAPITOL (1617 "Four Amigos")...15-20 59
CAPITOL (2626 "Goes Latin")...10-15 66
CAPITOL (2860 "Live at the Ilikai Hotel, Hawaii")...10-15 68
RIC (1007 "Live at the Hungry i")...10-15 64

FOUR ANDANTES
Singles: 7-inch
MO DO (107 "The End of Love")...75-100 64

FOUR ARCS
Singles: 78 rpm
BOULEVARD...100-150 54
Singles: 7-inch
BOULEVARD (102 "Life of Ease")...300-400 54
(This exact same track was also issued by the Imperials.)
Also see IMPERIALS

FOUR ARTS
Singles: 7-inch
SHEE (100 "Just One Night")...30-40

FOUR AVALONS
Singles: 7-inch
OVIDE...25-35 '60s

FOUR Bs
Singles: 7-inch
D (1013 "Love Eternal")...15-25 58

FOUR BARONS
Singles: 78 rpm
REGENT (1026 "Lemon Squeezer")...30-50 50
Also see LARKS

FOUR BARONS
Singles: 7-inch
ROMAN (235 "Old Enough to Know")...30-40 57

FOUR BARS
(With Billy Mure's Orch.)
Singles: 78 rpm
BULLET (1009 "I'm All Dressed Up with a Broken Heart")...30-50 47
BULLET (1010 "Deep in My Heart")...30-50 47
JOSIE (762 "Grief By Day, Grief By Night")...50-100 54
JOSIE (768 "If I Give My Heart to You")...50-100 54
JOSIE (783 "Let Me Live")...100-150 55
REPUBLIC (7101 "Memories of You")...100-200 54
Singles: 7-inch
CADILLAC (2006 "Love Me Forever More")...200-300 60
DAYCO (101 "Try Me One More Time")...30-40 62
(First issue.)
DAYCO (4564 "Lean On Me When Heartaches Get Rough")...15-25 62
JOSIE (762 "Grief By Day, Grief By Night")...250-350 54
JOSIE (768 "If I Give My Heart to You")...250-350 54
JOSIE (783 "Let Me Live")...500-600 55
LEN (1014 "Just Bid Me Farewell")...100-125 61
REPUBLIC (7101 "Memories of You")...400-500 54
SHELLEY (180 "Try Me One More Time")...150-250 62
SHELLEY (183 "Let the Wedding Bells Ring")...40-50 62
TIME (4 "Why Did You Do It")...50-75 60
Picture Sleeves
SHELLEY (180 "Try Me One More Time")...250-350 62
Member: Jimmy Sweeney.
Also see DAYE, Eddie
Also see HUNTER, Shane, & Four Bars
Also see SWEENEY, Jimmy
Also see WILSON, Betty, & Four Bars

FOUR BARS
("Featuring Betty Wilson")
Singles: 7-inch
FALEW! (108 "I've Got to Move")...25-35 64
Also see WILSON, Betty, & Four Bars

FOUR BARS
Singles: 7-inch
FLYING HAWK (1501 "We Are Together")...20-30 64

FOUR BARS & A MELODY
Singles: 78 rpm
SAVOY (657 "Near You")...30-50 48

FOUR BARS / Kimble Kadettes
Singles: 7-inch
WOW (1003 "When We Met"/"Everybody Loves You, Barry")...10-15 64

FOUR BEAUS
Singles: 7-inch
TODD (1028 "Tight Shoes")...10-20 59

FOUR BEL'AIRES
Singles: 7-inch
KING TUT (169 "Where Are You")...4-6 76
M.Z. (006 "Can I Be in Love")...300-400 59
(Reissued as *Stolen Love* and credited to Larry Lee.)
X-TRA (113 "Where Are You")...800-1200 58
Also see LEE, Larry

FOUR BELLS
(With Fred Norman & Orchestra)
Singles: 78 rpm
GEM...200-300 53-54
Singles: 7-inch
GEM (207 "Please Tell It to Me")...600-800 53
GEM (220 "Only a Miracle")...600-800 54

FOUR BELOW ZERO
Singles: 7-inch
DOUBLE SHOT (108 "Don't Send Me Away")...10-20 67
JERDEN (903 "Getting Thru to You")...8-12 68
ROULETTE (7186 "My Baby's Got E.S.P.")...4-6 76

FOUR BLACKAMOORS
Singles: 78 rpm
DECCA...15-25 41

FOUR BLADES
Singles: 78 rpm
GATEWAY PARADE OF HITS...8-12 56
Singles: 7-inch
GATEWAY PARADE OF HITS...15-20 56

FOUR BLADES
Singles: 7-inch
ALERT (522 "You Didn't Sign Your Letter")...25-35 63

FOUR BLAZERS
Singles: 7-inch
BUDDY (143 "Girl")...15-25

FOUR BLAZES R&B '52
Singles: 78 rpm
UNITED...10-20 52-55
Singles: 7-inch
UNITED (114 "Mary Jo")...30-50 52
(Black vinyl.)

UNITED (114 "Mary Jo")........................ 75-100 52
(Red vinyl.)
UNITED (125 "Night Train")...................... 15-25 52
UNITED (127 "Stop Boogie Woogie")...... 15-25 52
(Black vinyl.)
UNITED (127 "Stop Boogie Woogie")...... 50-75 52
(Red vinyl.)
UNITED (146 "Not Any More Tears") 15-25 53
UNITED (158 "Ella Louise")..................... 15-25 53
(Black vinyl.)
UNITED (158 "Ella Louise").................. 75-125 53
(Red vinyl.)
UNITED (168 "My Great Love Affair")...... 15-25 53
UNITED (191 "She Needs to Be Loved") 15-25 55
(Reissued as by the Blasers.)
Members: Tommy Braden; Lindsley Holt; Floyd McDaniels; William Hill.
Also see BLASERS
Also see BRADEN, Tommy, & His Flames
Also see HOLLYWOOD'S FOUR BLAZES

FOUR BLUEBIRDS / Johnny Otis & His Orchestra

Singles: 78 rpm
EXCELSIOR (540 "My Baby Done Told Me").. 50-100 49
Member: Bobby Nunn.
Also see NUNN, Bobby
Also see OTIS, Johnny

FOUR BLUEJACKETS

Singles: 78 rpm
MERCURY 15-25 46-47

FOUR BLUES

Singles: 78 rpm
APOLLO (398 "It Takes a Long Tall Brownskinned Gal") 30-50 48
APOLLO (1145 "Re Bop De Boom")........ 30-50 50
APOLLO (1160 "Missing You") 30-50 50
DECCA (8517 "Easy Does It") 30-50 41
DECCA (8637 "Bluer Than Bluer Than Blue")... 30-50 42
DELUXE (1000 "I'm Gone")..................... 30-50 45
DELUXE (1001 "Chittlins & Pigs Feet") ... 30-50 48
DELUXE (1002 "Things You Want Most of All")... 30-50 45
DELUXE (1003 "I Got a Date with Rhythm") 30-50 45
DELUXE (1004 "When the Old Gang's Back on the Corner")..30-50 45
DELUXE (1005 "Study War No Mo") 30-50 45
DELUXE (3195 "Am I Asking Too Much")... 30-50 48
Member: Carroll Jones.
Also see ECKSTINE, Billy

FOUR BROTHERS & A COUSIN

(With Jimmy Cannady's Quartet)
Singles: 78 rpm
JAGUAR 100-200 54
Singles: 7-inch
JAGUAR (3003 "Trust in Me")............. 400-500 54
JAGUAR (3005 "Whispering Winds") .. 400-500 54

FOUR BUDDIES R&B '51

(With Lefty Bates Orchestra)
Singles: 78 rpm
SAVOY 50-75 50-53
Singles: 7-inch
CORAL (62217 "Hurt")........................... 10-15 60
CORAL (62325 "The Light").................... 10-15 62
SAVOY (769 "I Will Wait") 300-400 50
SAVOY (779 "Don't Leave Me Now") .. 300-400 51
SAVOY (779 "Don't Leave Me Now") 15-25 61
(Blue vinyl.)
SAVOY (789 "My Summer's Gone").... 150-350 51
SAVOY (817 "Heart & Soul").............. 150-350 51
SAVOY (817 "Heart & Soul")................... 15-25 61
(Blue vinyl.)
SAVOY (845 "You're Part of Me") 100-200 52
SAVOY (866 "What's the Matter with Me")... 100-150 52
SAVOY (888 "My Mother's Eyes") 75-125 53
Members: Leon Harrison; Greg Carroll; Bert Palmer; Tommy Smith.
Also see BARONS
Also see COOPER, Dolly
Also see FOUR BUDS
Also see GREENE, Rudy, & Four Buddies

FOUR BUDDIES

Singles: 78 rpm
CLUB 51 (105 "Delores")......................100-150 56
Singles: 7-inch
CLUB 51 (105 "Delores")......................300-400 56
(Black vinyl.)
CLUB 51 (105 "Delores")................ 2000-3000 56
(Red vinyl.)
Also see JAMES, Bobbie, & Four Buddies

FOUR BUDDIES

Singles: 7-inch
IMPERIAL (66018 "I Want to Be the Boy You Love")...75-125 64
IMPERIAL (66018 "I Want to Be the Boy You Love")...50-100 64
(White label. Promotional issue only.)
PHILIPS (40122 "Lonely Summer") 20-40 63

FOUR BUDS

Singles: 78 rpm
SAVOY (769 "I Will Wait") 100-200 50
Singles: 7-inch
SAVOY (769 "I Will Wait") 400-500 50
(Second pressings shown as by the Four Buddies.)
Also see FOUR BUDDIES

FOUR C's

Singles: 7-inch
CHRISTY (141 "Scottish Rock") 10-20 61

FOUR C's featuring Gallupin' Cliff Gallup

LPs: 10/12-inch
PUSSY CAT (701 "Straight Down the Middle")...50-100 '60s
Also see VINCENT, Gene

FOUR CAL-QUETTES

Singles: 7-inch
CAPITOL (4574 "Starbright") 10-15 61
CAPITOL (4657 "Most of All") 5-10 61
CAPITOL (4725 "Again")...........................5-10 62
LIBERTY (55549 "I Cried").........................5-10 63
Also see FOUR COQUETTES

FOUR CANDIDATES / Jim Faraday

Singles: 7-inch
BUDDY (1004 "Attention Convention"/"Dance of the Martians")...25-35 56

FOUR CASTS

Singles: 7-inch
ATLANTIC (2228 "Stormy Weather") 10-20 64

FOUR CHAPS

Singles: 78 rpm
SHERATON (51 "Night Train")................30-50 55
Singles: 7-inch
SHERATON (51 "Night Train")................50-75 55
(Later issued as by the Owens Brothers.)
Members: John Owens; Bob Owens; Bill Owens; D.J. Owens.

FOUR CHAPS

Singles: 78 rpm
RAMA 5-10 56
Singles: 7-inch
RAMA (195 "Completely Yours") 10-20 56
RAMA (199 "Roll Over Beethoven") 10-20 56

FOUR CHECKERS

Singles: 7-inch
ACE (129 "Broken Heart").........................25-35 59

FOUR CHECKS

Singles: 7-inch
TRI DISC (101 "I'll Be Around") 15-25 61

FOUR CHEERS

(4 Cheers)
Singles: 7-inch
END (1034 "Fatal Charms of Love").....150-200 58

FOUR CHEVELLES

Singles: 7-inch
BAND BOX (357 "This Is Our Wedding Day")...30-40 64
(Publishing company shown as "Valjean.")
BAND BOX (357 "This Is Our Wedding Day")...8-12 '60s
(Publishing company shown as "Band Box.")
BAND BOX (358 "I Can't Believe") 50-75 64
DELFT (6408 "This Is Our Wedding Day")...500-750 64
(Identification number shown since no selection number is used.)
GATEWAY (358 "I Can't Believe")..............5-10 64

FOUR CHICADEES

Singles: 78 rpm
CHECKER (849 "Ding Dong") 10-15 56
Singles: 7-inch
CHECKER (849 "Ding Dong") 20-30 56

FOUR CHICKS

Singles: 7-inch
TRI DISC (101 "I'll Be Around") 10-15 61

FOUR CHORDS

Singles: 78 rpm
SITTIN' IN WITH (516 "Again")................20-30 49

FOUR CLEFS

Singles: 78 rpm
BLUEBIRD 10-20 39-42
BULLET (268 "Am I Still Your Baby") 10-15 48
RCA...15-25 45-52
Singles: 7-inch
RCA (4507 "Dig These Blues")..................25-35 52
Also see CATS & FIDDLE

FOUR CLIPPERS

(With the Band of Lucky Lee)
Singles: 78 rpm
FOX (961 "You Can't Trust a Woman")...200-250 57
Singles: 7-inch
FOX (961 "You Can't Trust a Woman")...200-250 57
Members: Bobby Martin; Hershel Hunter.

FOUR CLOSURES

Singles: 7-inch
SPECIALTY (643 "Maybe").........................10-20 58

FOUR COACHMEN

(With "Chorus & Orchestra")
Singles: 7-inch
ADONIS (102 "Wintertime") 10-20 59
ADONIS (106 "Swamp Legend") 10-20 60
CASTLE (507 "If You Believe")..................10-20 59
DOT (16297 "Swamp Legend") 5-10 61
STELLAR (712 "Swamp Legend")...............10-20 61

FOUR COINS P&R '54

(With Joe Sherman & Orchestra; with Marion Evans Orchestra)
Singles: 78 rpm
EPIC...5-10 54-57
Singles: 7-inch
COLUMBIA (44006 "If You Love Me")..........5-8 67
EPIC...10-15 54-60
EPIC (2212 "Shangri-La") 4-8 64
JOY...5-10 64
JUBILEE...8-12 61-62
LAURIE 5-10 66
MGM...8-12 60-61
VEE-JAY 8-12 62-63
Picture Sleeves
EPIC (9258 "My Baby Loves Me")...........10-15 57
EPs: 7-inch
EPIC 10-20 55-58
LPs: 10/12-inch
EPIC (1104 "The Four Coins")..................20-30 55
(10-inch LP.)
EPIC (3445 "In Shangri-La") 15-25 58
MGM (3944 "Greek Songs") 10-20 61
ROULETTE (25288 "Greek Songs Mama Never Taught Me")...10-15 65
Members: George Mahramas; Michael Mahramas; George Mantalis; Jim Gregorakis.

FOUR COQUETTES

Singles: 7-inch
CAPITOL (4534 "Sparkle and Shine")......10-15 61
Also see FOUR CAL-QUETTES

4 CORNERS

(With the Blake Brothers)
Singles: 7-inch
GLORY (268 "Winter in Wisconsin").........10-20 57

FOUR CORNERS

Singles: 7-inch
PHILIPS (40488 "It's So Right")...............10-20 67

FOUR COUNTS

Singles: 7-inch
CHAM (003 "I Love You with All My Heart")...15-25 58
JOSIE (840 "Cuckoo")..............................10-15 58

FOUR COUNTS

Singles: 7-inch
ACE (597 "Heavenly")...............................15-25 60

FOUR COUNTS

("Vocal Phil Trunzo with the Tomlinson Sisters")
Singles: 7-inch
FINE (2562 "Graduation") 50-100 62

FOUR DADDYOS

(Four Daddyo's)
Singles: 7-inch
LOGAN (3108 "Pink Camel Walk")...........50-75 59

FOUR DARLINGS

Singles: 7-inch
FORTE (1105 "Give Me Love") ....20-30 '60s

FOUR DATES P&R '58

Singles: 7-inch
CHANCELLOR (1014 "I'm Happy").........10-20 58
CHANCELLOR (1019 "I Say Babe") 20-30 58
CHANCELLOR (1027 "Teenage Neighbor") 20-30 58
Members: Johnny October; Ernie Spano; Ed Gentile; Pat Marioni
Also see ERNIE & HALOS
Also see FABIAN
Also see OCTOBER, Johnny

FOUR DEALS

Singles: 78 rpm
CAPITOL (1313 "It's Too Late Now").......25-35 50
Singles: 7-inch
CAPITOL (1313 "It's Too Late Now").....75-125 50
EPs: 7-inch
TOPS (240 "Sh-Boom") 20-30 55

FOUR DEEP TONES

Singles: 78 rpm
CORAL (65061 "Just in Case You Change Your Mind") 100-150 51
CORAL (65062 "The Night You Said Goodbye")...100-150 51

FOUR DEUCES

(4 Deuces)
Singles: 78 rpm
MUSIC CITY (796 "Down It Went") 15-25 56
Singles: 7-inch
EVEREST (19311 "Polly").........................10-15 59
MUSIC CITY (796 "Down It Went") 40-50 56

FOUR DEUCES / Kary Maeson

Singles: 7-inch
MUSIC CITY (790 "W-P-L-J"/"Spingle Spangle")...15-25 '60s
(Black vinyl. Multi-color print.)

FOUR DEUCES / Mr. Undertaker

Singles: 78 rpm
MUSIC CITY (790 "W-P-L-J"/"Here Lies My Love") 40-50 55
(Maroon label.)
MUSIC CITY (790 "W-P-L-J"/"Here Lies My Love")...30-40 55
(Black label.)
Singles: 7-inch
MUSIC CITY (790 "W-P-L-J"/"Here Lies My Love") 100-150 55
(Maroon label.)
MUSIC CITY (790 "W-P-L-J"/"Here Lies My Love") 50-75 55
(Black label. Silver print.)
MUSIC CITY (790 "W-P-L-J"/"Here Lies My Love") 75-100 57
(Red vinyl.)
Members: Jim Dunbar; Luther McDaniels; Orvis Lee Teamer; Henry Shufford.
Also see FOUR DEUCES

FOUR DIMENSIONS

Singles: 7-inch
GOLDUST (5013 "Sand Surfin'") 20-30 64
KISKI (2069 "Moe's Cast")......................10-20 65
RAMCO (1980 "What Are They Doing Now")...5-10 67

IV DIMENSIONS

Singles: 7-inch
SARA (6644 "My Babe") 15-25 66

4 DIRECTIONS
Singles: 7-inch
CORAL (62456 "Tonight We Love")......... 30-40 65
FRAN & CHUCK ("Tonight We Love")... 75-125 65
(Blue vinyl. No selection number used.)

FOUR DIRECTIONS
Singles: 7-inch
DIRECTIONS! LTD. (73003 "Lovely Way").. 40-50 '60s

FOUR DOLLS
Singles: 78 rpm
CAPITOL...8-12 57
Singles: 7-inch
CAPITOL (3766 "Proud of You")............ 10-15 57
CAPITOL (3895 "I'm Following You")...... 10-15 58

FOUR DOTS
Singles: 78 rpm
DOT (1043 "My Dear")............................ 40-60 51
Member: George Davis.
Also see HEARTBREAKERS

FOUR DOTS
("Featuring Fletcher Williams")
Singles: 78 rpm
BULLSEYE.. 15-30 56
Singles: 7-inch
BULLSEYE (103 "Rita").................... 100-150 56
BULLSEYE (104 "Peace of Mind"/"Kiss Me, Sugar Plum")... 50-75 56
BULLSEYE (104 "Peace of Mind"/"My Dear").. 40-50 56
FREEDOM (44002 "It's Heaven")........... 30-40 58
FREEDOM (44005 "Pleading for Your Love")... 30-40 59
Members: Fletcher Williams; Jerry Stone; Jewel Akens; Eddie Cochran.
Also see AKENS, Jewel
Also see COCHRAN, Eddie

FOUR DOTS
("Featuring Deek Watson formerly of the Ink Spots")
Singles: 78 rpm
CASTLE (2006 "Strange As It Seems")... 15-25 52
Singles: 7-inch
CASTLE (2006 "Strange As It Seems"). 50-150 52
(Black vinyl.)
CASTLE (2006 "Strange As It Seems").. 300-400 52
(Red vinyl.)
Also see BROWN DOTS
Also see INK SPOTS

FOUR DUCHESSES
Singles: 7-inch
CHIEF (7014 "Cry For My Baby").......... 40-50 60
Also see DUCHESSES

4 DUKES
(With Al Browne Orchestra)
Singles: 78 rpm
DUKE (116 "Crying in the Chapel")...... 200-300 53
Singles: 7-inch
DUKE (116 "Crying in the Chapel").. 1000-1500 53
Member: Billy Dawn Smith.
Also see DAWN, Billy, Quartet
Also see HERALDS
Also see MIGHTY DUKES

FOUR DUKES
Singles: 7-inch
IMPERIAL (5653 "Baby Won't You Please Come Home").. 10-20 60

FOUR EKKOS
(Four Ekko's)
Singles: 7-inch
LABEL (2022 "Hand in Hand").............. 75-100 59
RIP (12558 "My Love I Give")............. 10-20 58
Also see ENGLER, Jerry, & Four Ekkos
Also see CAMPBELL, Bernie

FOUR 'EM
Singles: 7-inch
ROLLO (5905 "While I'm Away")............ 10-20 65

FOUR EMBERS
Singles: 7-inch
SMASH (1846 "But Beautiful")................ 10-15 63

FOUR EPICS
Singles: 7-inch
COLLECTABLES...3-5 '80s
HERITAGE (109 "I'm on My Way to Love")...75-125 62
LAURIE (3155 "Again")...............................10-15 63
LAURIE (3183 "How I Wish I Was Single Again")...5-10 63
LPs: 10/12-inch
CRYSTAL BALL (107 "Getting High on the Four Epics")...10-15 82
(Black vinyl. 1000 made.)
CRYSTAL BALL (107 "Getting High on the Four Epics")...25-35 82
(Colored vinyl. 25 made.)
CRYSTAL BALL (107 "Getting High on the Four Epics")...55-65 82
(Picture disc. No cover. 25 made.)
Members: Mickey Neil; Jack McNight; Jim Mullin; Rich Lally.
Also see EXODUS
Also see VESPERS

FOUR ESCORTS
Singles: 78 rpm
RCA (5886 "Love Me")...............................5-10 54
Singles: 7-inch
RCA (5886 "Love Me")...............................10-15 54
SKYLA (1113 "My Special Girl")..................5-10 61

FOUR ESQUIRES **P&R '56**
(With Rosemary June; with Ben Bennett Orchestra & Chorus)
Singles: 78 rpm
CADENCE...5-10 55
EPIC (9063 "Little Girl, Little Girl")...............5-10 54
LONDON (1652 "Look Homeward Angel").5-10 56
PARIS...10-20 57
PILGRIM..5-10 56
Singles: 7-inch
CADENCE (1242 "Ev'rything")..................10-20 54
(With Jack Gold.)
CADENCE (1260 "Three Things")............10-20 55
CADENCE (1277 "Adorable")...................10-20 55
EPIC (9063 "Little Girl, Little Girl")...........10-20 54
LONDON (1652 "Look Homeward Angel")...10-20 56
PARIS (501 thru 520)..............................10-20 57-58
PARIS (526 thru 544)..............................10-15 58-60
PARIS (549 "Sweet Sixteen She'll Never Be")..10-20 60
PILGRIM (717 "Follow Me")......................10-15 56
PILGRIM (718 "Maybe Someday")...........10-15 56
TERRACE (7502 "Can't Help Falling in Love")..5-10 61
TERRACE (7516 "Summer Vacation").......5-10 63
Members: Frank Mahoney; Bill Courtney; Bob Golden; Wally Gold.
Also see CAPONE, Susan
Also see JUNE, Rosemary

FOUR EXCEPTIONS
Singles: 7-inch
PARKWAY (986 "You Got the Power").....20-40 66

FOUR FELLAS
Singles: 7-inch
CORAL (62248 "It's Nice").........................20-30 61

FOUR FELLOWS
Singles: 78 rpm
TRI-BORO (101 "Stop Crying")................40-60 53
Members: Cas Bridges; Bill Carey.
Also see CLEFTONES
Also see DANLEERS

FOUR FELLOWS **R&B '55**
(With the Abie Baker Orchestra; with Toni Banks)
Singles: 78 rpm
DERBY...50-75 54
GLORY...20-40 55-57
Singles: 7-inch
DERBY (862 "I Tried")..........................100-200 54
GLORY (231 "I Wish I Didn't Know You")..65-75 55
GLORY (234 "Soldier Boy").....................50-60 55
GLORY (236 "Angels Say").....................15-25 55
GLORY (238 "Fallen Angel")....................15-25 56
GLORY (242 "Darling You").....................50-60 56
GLORY (244 "I Sit in My Window")...........15-25 56
GLORY (248 "You Don't Know Me").........30-40 56
GLORY (250 "Give Me Back My Broken Heart")..50-60 57
GLORY (263 "You're Still in My Heart")....40-50 57
(Released as by Toni Banks & Four Fellows.)
NESTOR (27 "Remember")...................400-500 58
Members: David Jones; Ted Williams; Larry Banks; Jim McGowan.
Also see DECOYS / Four Fellows
Also see McLAURIN, Bette
Also see RYAN, Cathy

FOUR FELLOWS
Singles: 7-inch
AD-LIB/POP LINE (0208 "That's Why I Pray")...10-15 62

FOUR FIFTHS
Singles: 7-inch
HUDSON (8101 "Come on Girl")..............50-75 63
(Black vinyl.)
HUDSON (8101 "Come on Girl")..........400-500 63
(Blue vinyl.)

FOUR FIFTHS
Singles: 7-inch
COLUMBIA (43913 "If You Still Want Me")..10-15 66
LP: 10/12-inch
VICTORY (2258 "Clap Your Hands").......15-25 67

FOUR FINKS
Singles: 7-inch
ANTLER (4024 "Wiki Wiki Woo")...............5-10 61
KERNEL (107 "Ka-Bongin").......................15-25 63

FOUR FLARES
Singles: 7-inch
EDISON INT'L (402 "Jump Back Honey Ride")..10-15 58

FOUR FLAMES
(Hollywood Flames)
Singles: 78 rpm
FIDELITY (3001 "Tabarin")..................150-250 51
(First issued as by the Hollywood Four Flames.)
SPECIALTY (423 "Wheel of Fortune").200-300 52
Also see HOLLYWOOD FLAMES
Also see HOLLYWOOD FOUR FLAMES

FOUR FLAMES / Sherman Williams Orchestra
Singles: 78 rpm
FIDELITY (3002 "Bounce")..................100-150 51
Also see FOUR FLAMES
Also see WILLIAMS, Sherman

FOUR FLICKERS
(With Perry Wilson Orchestra)
Singles: 7-inch
LEE (1002 "Is There a Way")....................15-25 59

FOUR FLIGHTS
Singles: 7-inch
ALMERIA (4002 "All I Want Is You").......50-75 78

440
Singles: 7-inch
SONA (103 "It's Just Your Mind")............20-30 67

FOUR FRESHMEN **P&R '52**
Singles: 78 rpm
CAPITOL..5-10 50-57
Singles: 7-inch
CAPITOL..5-15 50-65
DECCA (32070 "Nowhere to Go")..............5-8 67
LIBERTY (56047 "Cherish – Windy")...........4-8 68
LIBERTY (56099 "It's a Blue World")...........4-8 69
Picture Sleeves
CAPITOL (5007 "Summertime")..................5-10 63
EPs: 7-inch
CAPITOL..10-20 54-59
LPs: 10/12-inch
CAPITOL (With "SM" prefix)......................5-10 75-79
CAPITOL (H-522 "Voices in Modern")......30-40 54
(10-inch LP.)
CAPITOL (522 thru 992)..........................20-40 54-58
(With "T" prefix.)
CAPITOL (1000 & 2000 series)...............10-25 58-64
(With "T" or "ST" prefix.)
CREATIVE WORLD..................................5-10 72
LIBERTY...5-10 68-82
PHONORAMA..5-8 82
SUNSET...5-10 70
Members: Don Barbour; Ross Barbour; Ken Errair; Bob Flanagan; Hal Kratzsch; Bill Comstock; Ken Albers.

FOUR FRESHMEN / Kirby Stone Four / University Four
LPs: 10/12-inch
CORONET..5-10 '60s
Also see FOUR FRESHMEN
Also see STONE, Kirby, Four

FOUR FRIENDS
Singles: 7-inch
FEE BEE (225 "Save This Fallen Heart") 15-25 59

FOUR FROGS
Singles: 7-inch
FROGDEATH (2 "Mr. Big").........................5-10 66
Picture Sleeves
FROGDEATH (2 "Mr. Big").......................20-30 66

FOUR FROLICS
Singles: 7-inch
CHEX (1001 "Frolic")................................10-20 62

FOUR GABRIELS
Singles: 78 rpm
WORLD (2505 "Gloria")............................30-50 48

FOUR GEMS
Singles: 7-inch
SANDERS (106 "Gloria")......................100-150 64
Member: Charlie Bellizzi.

FOUR GEMS
Singles: 7-inch
BROADCAST (4 "Outside of Paradise")..20-30 71
(Red vinyl.)

FOUR GENTS
Singles: 7-inch
PARK (114 "On Bended Knee")...........300-400 57

FOUR GENTS
Singles: 7-inch
NITE OWL (50 "Please Don't Ask Me")....30-40 62
Also see GENTS

4 GENTS
("Featuring Jimmy Mana")
Singles: 7-inch
VIDA (0120 "Far Away at Sea")...........100-200 64
VIDA (0123 "I Refuse to Try")..............400-500 64

FOUR GENTS
Singles: 7-inch
HBR (509 "Soul Sister")............................10-20 66
LIBERTY (56013 "He Got Soul")...............10-20 68

FOUR GENTS
Singles: 7-inch
ONCORE (63 "Young Girls Beware")...400-600

FOUR GIRLS
Singles: 78 rpm
CAPITOL..5-10 56
CORAL..5-10 54-55
Singles: 7-inch
CAPITOL..10-15 56
CORAL..10-15 54-55
EPs: 7-inch
CORAL (81106 "Make a Joyful Noise Unto the Lord")...20-30 57
LPs: 10/12-inch
CORAL (57158 "Make a Joyful Noise Unto the Lord")...40-60 57
Members: Jane Russell; Connie Haines; Della Russell; Beryl Davis.
Also see HAINES, Connie

FOUR GRADUATES
Singles: 7-inch
CRYSTAL BALL (116 "May I Have This Dance")...4-8 78
(Black vinyl. 500 made.)
CRYSTAL BALL (116 "May I Have This Dance")...8-12 78
(Red vinyl. 25 made.)
CRYSTAL BALL (119 "Every Year About This Time")..4-8 78
(Black vinyl. 500 made.)
CRYSTAL BALL (119 "Every Year About This Time")..8-12 78
(Red vinyl. 25 made.)
RUST (5062 "Lovely Way to Spend an Evening")...50-100 63
RUST (5084 "Candy Queen")...............250-350 64
Members: Robert Miranda; Tom Guliano; Dave Libert; Ralph DeVito.
Also see HAPPENINGS

FOUR GUYS
("Featuring Larry Austin")

Singles: 78 rpm

CORAL 5-10 54
KENT (111 "You Don't Have to Tell Me") ...5-10 53
MERCURY 5-10 54-56
WING (90036 "May This Be Your Life")......5-10 55

Singles: 7-inch

CORAL (61160 "Oh How I Love-A-You") 10-15 54
CORAL (61252 "Mine")........ 10-15 54
KENT (111 "You Don't Have to Tell Me") 10-15 53
(Black vinyl.)
KENT (111 "You Don't Have to Tell Me") 15-20 53
(Red vinyl.)
MERCURY....... 10-15 54-56
WING (90036 "May This Be Your Life")... 15-20 55
Member: Larry Austin.

FOUR GUYS

Singles: 7-inch

BARRON (5001 "Tear Drops from My Eyes")....... 15-25 63
STRIDE (5001 "Tear Drops from My Eyes")....... 15-25 63
(Aside from the name and a different publishing company credited, Barron and Stride labels are nearly identical. Both have the same address and phone #. We don't know which came first.)

4 HAVEN KNIGHTS
(Haven Knights)

Singles: 78 rpm

ATLAS (1066 "In My Lonely Room").... 100-150 57
ATLAS (1092 "Why Go on Pretending")....... 100-150 57
JOSIE (824 "In My Lonely Room")........ 40-50 57

Singles: 7-inch

ANGLETONE (1066 "In My Lonely Room") .3-5
ANGLETONE (1092 "Why Go on Pretending").......3-5
ATLAS (1066 "In My Lonely Room").... 150-250 57
ATLAS (1092 "Why Go on Pretending")....... 100-200 58
JOSIE (824 "In My Lonely Room")........ 40-50 57
SOLD (503 "Why Go on Pretending")........4-6 73
Members: LeRoy Gomes; Robert Johnson; Tom Griffin; Everett Johnson; Carl Haley.

FOUR HAVENS

Singles: 7-inch

VEEP (1214 "What Time Is It")....... 30-40 65

FOUR HI'S

Singles: 7-inch

VERVE (10450 "Pretty Little Face")........ 10-15 66

FOUR HITS & A MISS

Singles: 7-inch

FLAMINGO (540 "She Wobbles")........ 10-15 62

FOUR HOLIDAYS

Singles: 7-inch

U.A. (163 "Who Can Say")....... 15-25 59

FOUR HOLLIDAYS

Singles: 7-inch

MARKIE (109 "Grandma Bird")....... 30-40 63
MARKIE (115 "I'll Walk Right Out the Door")....... 40-60 63
MASTER (55196 "Deep Down in My Heart")....... 15-25 63
Member: Jimmy Ruffin.
Also see RUFFIN, Jimmy

FOUR HORSEMEN

Singles: 78 rpm

MGM (12159 "Go On with the Wedding")...5-10 56

Singles: 7-inch

MGM (12159 "Go On with the Wedding") 10-15 56
U.A. (134 "My Heartbeat")....... 200-300 58

FOUR HUES
(With Hal Brooks & Orchestra)

Singles: 78 rpm

CROWN (159 "Rock-A-Bye")....... 10-15 55

Singles: 7-inch

CROWN (159 "Rock-A-Bye")....... 15-25 55

FOUR IMPERIALS

Singles: 7-inch

CHANT (101 "Teen Age Fool")....... 30-50 58
DIAL (101 "Valley of Tears")....... 100-200 59
DOT (15737 "Lazy Bonnie")....... 10-15 58
FOX (102 "Look Up and Live")....... 50-100 58
LORELEI (4444 "Lazy Bonnie")....... 50-100 58
TWIRL (2005 "Seven Lonely Days")........40-50 60

FOUR IMPS

Singles: 7-inch

CIMARRON (4053 "Wabash Blues")........15-25 60

FOUR Js

Singles: 7-inch

CONGRESS (6003 "Dreamin' ")........4-8 69
4J (506 "Will You Be My Love")........10-20 63
HERALD (528 "Dreams Are a Dime a Dozen")........20-25 58
JAMIE (1267 "Here Am I Broken Hearted")........10-20 63
JAMIE (1274 "My Love My Love")........10-20 64
U.A. (125 "Rock and Roll Age")........15-25 58
Members: James Testa; Joseph Prolia; Jimmy Finzino; Joe Mollera.
Also see FABULOUS FOUR

FOUR JACKS
R&B '49

Singles: 78 rpm

ALADDIN (3274 "Tired of Your Sexy Ways")........50-75 55
ALLEN (21000 "I Challenge Your Kiss").75-125 49
FEDERAL (12075 "You Met a Fool")....100-200 52
FEDERAL (12087 "The Last of the Good Rockin' Men")........50-100 52
GOTHAM (219 "Take Me")........25-50 50

Singles: 7-inch

ALADDIN (3274 "Tired of Your Sexy Ways")........200-300 55
FEDERAL (12075 "You Met a Fool")........ 1500-2000 52
FEDERAL (12087 "The Last of the Good Rockin' Men")........300-500 52
Also see HAVEN, Shirley, & Four Jacks
Also see McBURNEY & ORIGINAL FOUR JACKS
Also see SHAY, Janet
Also see WILLIAMS, Cora, & Four Jacks

FOUR JACKS / Allen Trio

Singles: 78 rpm

ALLEN (21001 "Carless Love")........30-50 49
Also see FOUR JACKS

FOUR JACKS

Singles: 78 rpm

MGM (11179 "You're in Love with Someone Else")........5-10 52

Singles: 7-inch

MGM (11179 "You're in Love with Someone Else")........15-25 52

FOUR JACKS
(With Herbie Layne's Orchestra; with Benn Zeppa; with Cathy Landon; with Lou Raymond Orch.)

Singles: 78 rpm

GATEWAY PARADE OF HITS........5-8 56
TOP TUNES........5-8 56

Singles: 7-inch

ARC (5008 "She Say")........15-25 59
GATEWAY PARADE OF HITS........10-15 56-57
TOP TUNES........8-12 56

EPs: 7-inch

GILMAR (119 "6 Hits On Each Record") ..20-30 56
(Issued with paper sleeve.)
TOPS........15-25 56
(Issued with paper sleeve.)

FOUR JACKS

Singles: 7-inch

REBEL (1313 "Becky Ann")........30-40 58

FOUR JACKS

Singles: 7-inch

PEL (601 "I've Waited Long Enough")......15-20 60

FOUR JACKS & A JILL

Singles: 78 rpm

FORTUNE........10-15 54

Singles: 7-inch

FORTUNE........30-50 54

4 JADES

Singles: 7-inch

BLUE BIRD ("Valarie")........75-125
(Selection number not known.)

FOUR JAYS & FABULOUS IMPERIALS

Singles: 7-inch

IMPRA (1268 "Class Ring")........20-30 58
(Identification number, which is nearly identical to MGM number, is shown since no selection number is used.)
MGM (12687 "Class Ring")........10-15 58

FOUR JETS
(Shadows)

Singles: 7-inch

CAPITOL (4270 "Driftin' ")........10-20 59
Also see SHADOWS

FOUR JEWELS

Singles: 7-inch

CHECKER........5-10 61-64
START (638 "Loaded with Goodies")........15-20 63
START (638 "Someone Special")........15-20 63
(The same number is used twice.)
START (641 "All That's Good")........10-15 64
TEC (3007 "Baby It's You")........5-10 64
Members: Sandra Bears; Margie Clark; Carrie Mingo; Martha Harvin; Grace Ruffin.
Also see JEWELS
Also see RUBIES
Also see STEWART, Billy

FOUR JOES

Singles: 78 rpm

MGM........5-10 54-56

Singles: 7-inch

DARL (1005 "Lifetime of Happiness")........8-12 57
MGM (11857 "In Your Loving Care")........10-15 54
MGM (11911 "Oh How I Miss You")........20-30 55
MGM (12147 "Honey, My Little Honey")...10-15 55
MGM (12259 "Sometimes")........10-15 56
MGM (12316 "My Heart Says Thanks to You")........10-15 56

FOUR JOKERS

Singles: 78 rpm

MGM (11815 "Tell Me Now")........8-12 54

Singles: 7-inch

MGM (11815 "Tell Me Now")........15-20 54

FOUR JOKERS

Singles: 78 rpm

DIAMOND (3004 "Transfusion")........5-10 56

Singles: 7-inch

DIAMOND (3004 "Transfusion")........10-20 56

FOUR JOKERS

Singles: 7-inch

SUE (703 "Written in the Stars")........100-125 58
(Promotional issue only.)
SUE (703 "Written in the Stars")........50-75 58

FOUR JOKERS

Singles: 7-inch

AMY (832 "She's a Flirt")........10-15 61

FOUR JUMPS OF JIVE

Singles: 78 rpm

MERCURY (2001 "Satchel Mouth Baby")........20-40 46
MERCURY (2015 "Boo Boo Fine Jelly")..20-40 46

FOUR KINGS
(With the All Stars)

Singles: 78 rpm

FORTUNE (517 "Rose of Tangier")........25-35 55
FORTUNE (811 "You Don't Mean Me Right")........100-200 53

Singles: 7-inch

FORTUNE (517 "Rose of Tangier")........50-100 55
FORTUNE (811 "You Don't Mean Me Right")........400-500 53

FOUR KINGS

Singles: 78 rpm

JAX (323 "You Never Knew")........150-250 54
Also see KINGS

FOUR KINGS

Singles: 78 rpm

FRATERNITY (752 "Willingly")........5-10 56

Singles: 7-inch

FRATERNITY (752 "Willingly")........10-15 56

FOUR KINGS

Singles: 7-inch

CEE=JAY (580 "Guess Who")........30-40 60

FOUR KINGS

Singles: 7-inch

CANADIAN AMERICAN (173 "One Night")........10-15 64
(Single-sided.)
CANADIAN AMERICAN (173 "One Night"/"Lonely Lovers")........20-30 64

FOUR KNIGHTS
P&R '51

Singles: 78 rpm

CAPITOL........10-30 51-57
CORAL........10-20 49
DECCA........15-25 46-47
LANG-WORTH........10-20 '40s
(16-inch transcriptions.)

Singles: 7-inch

CAPITOL (346 "Spotlight Songs")........30-50 52
(Boxed set of three singles.)
CAPITOL (1587 "Sentimental Fool")........40-50 51
CAPITOL (1707 thru 1914)........20-30 51-52
CAPITOL (1930 thru 2517)........15-25 52-53
CAPITOL (2654 "Oh Baby Mine")........20-30 53
CAPITOL (2654 "I Get So Lonely")........8-12 53
(Note title change.)
CAPITOL (2782 thru 3730)........10-15 54-57
CORAL (61936 thru 62110)........5-10 58-59
DECCA (48018 "He'll Understand and Say Well Done")........25-35 52
SOUVENIR (1008 "These Things I Hear")........10-15 62

EPs: 7-inch

CAPITOL (346 "Spotlight Songs")........50-75 52
(Two-disc set.)
CAPITOL (414 "The Four Knights Sing") .40-60 53
CAPITOL (506 "I Get So Lonely")........40-60 54

LPs: 10/12-inch

CAPITOL (H-346 "Spotlight Songs")....100-200 52
(10-inch LP.)
CAPITOL (T-346 "Spotlight Songs").....100-200 55
CORAL (57221 "Four Knights")........50-100 58
CORAL (57309 "Million Dollar Baby")....30-60 60
(Monaural.)
CORAL (757309 "Million Dollar Baby")....50-75 60
(Stereo.)
Members: Gene Alford; Clarence Dixon; Oscar Broadway; John Wallace.
Also see COLE, Nat "King"
Also see HUNT, Pee Wee

FOUR KNIGHTS

Singles: 7-inch

TRI-ODE (104 "La La")........30-40 62

4 KNIGHTS

Singles: 7-inch

FABAR (285-11 "Bye Bye Baby")........15-25 '60s

FOUR LABELS

Singles: 7-inch

GRA LOW (5524 "Susie")........20-30 59

FOUR LADS
P&R '52

Singles: 78 rpm

COLUMBIA........5-10 52-58
EPIC........5-10 56
OKEH........5-10 52

Singles: 7-inch

COLUMBIA (39865 thru 41058)........10-20 52-57
COLUMBIA (41136 thru 41733)........8-12 58-60
DOT........5-10 62
EPIC (9150 "Mocking Bird")........8-12 56
FONA........4-6 77-78
KAPP........5-10 60-61
OKEH (6860 "Turn Back")........10-20 52
OKEH (6885 "Mocking Bird")........10-20 52
U.A.........5-10 63-69

Picture Sleeves

COLUMBIA (40811 "Who Needs You")...10-20 57
COLUMBIA (40974 "The Eyes of God")...10-20 57
COLUMBIA (41194 "Enchanted Island")..10-20 58
COLUMBIA (41497 "Happy Anniversary")........10-20 59
KAPP (359 "Just Young")........10-15 60

EPs: 7-inch

COLUMBIA........10-20 55-59

LPs: 10/12-inch

AC........8-10
COLUMBIA (912 "On the Sunny Side")...30-40 56
COLUMBIA (1045 "The Four Lads Sing Frank Loesser")........25-35 57
COLUMBIA (1111 "Four on the Aisle")....15-25 58
(Monaural.)
COLUMBIA (1223 "Breezin' Along")........15-25 58
(Monaural.)
COLUMBIA (1235 "Greatest Hits")........15-25 58
COLUMBIA (1299 "Swing Along")........15-25 59
(Monaural.)

COLUMBIA (1407 "High Spirits") ... 15-25 60
(Monaural.)
COLUMBIA (1502 "Love Affair") ... 15-25 60
(Monaural.)
COLUMBIA (1550 "Everything Goes") ... 15-25 60
(Monaural.)
COLUMBIA (6329 "Stage Show") ... 30-40 54
(10-inch LP.)
COLUMBIA (8035 "Breezin' Along") ... 20-30 58
(Stereo.)
COLUMBIA (8047 "Four on the Aisle") ... 20-30 58
(Stereo.)
COLUMBIA (8106 "Swing Along") ... 20-30 59
(Stereo.)
COLUMBIA (8203 "High Spirits") ... 20-30 60
(Stereo.)
COLUMBIA (8293 "Love Affair") ... 20-30 60
(Stereo.)
COLUMBIA (8350 "Everything Goes") ... 20-30 60
(Stereo.)
DOT (3438 "Hits of the '60s") ... 10-15 62
(Monaural.)
DOT (25438 "Hits of the '60s") ... 15-20 62
(Stereo.)
ENCORE ... 5-8 86
FONA ... 8-12 76-77
KAPP (1224 "12 Hits") ... 10-15 61
(Monaural.)
KAPP (1254 "Dixieland Doins") ... 10-15 61
(Monaural.)
KAPP (3224 "12 Hits") ... 15-20 61
(Stereo.)
KAPP (3254 "Dixieland Doins") ... 15-20 61
(Stereo.)
HARMONY ... 5-10 69
U.A. (3337 "Record Oldies") ... 10-15 64
(Monaural.)
U.A. (3356 "Top Movie Songs") ... 10-15 64
(Monaural.)
U.A. (3399 "Songs of World War I") ... 10-15 64
(Monaural.)
U.A. (6337 "Record Oldies") ... 10-20 64
(Stereo.)
U.A. (6356 "Top Movie Songs") ... 10-20 64
(Stereo.)
U.A. (6399 "Songs of World War I") ... 10-20 64
(Stereo.)
VIKING ... 5-10
Members: Frankie Busseri; Jimmy Arnold; Connie Coderini; Bernie Toorish.
Also see COREY, Jill
Also see HAWKINS, Delores / Four Lads
Also see LAINE, Frankie, & Four Lads
Also see RAY, Johnnie

FOUR LARKS

Singles: 78 rpm

GUYDEN (707 "Night and Day") ... 5-10 54

Singles: 7-inch

GUYDEN (707 "Night and Day") ... 10-15 54
TOWER (364 "You and Me") ... 15-25 67
TOWER (402 "Groovin' at the Go-Go") ... 30-40 67
TOWER (450 "I've Got Plenty") ... 5-10 67
UPTOWN (748 "You and Me") ... 25-35 67
UPTOWN (761 "Keep Climbing Brothers") ... 25-35 69
Members: Irma McDougal; Weldon McDougal III.

FOUR LETTER WORDS

Singles: 7-inch

PARIS TOWER (107 "Quadruple Feature") ... 25-30 67

FOUR LOVERS — P&R '56

(With Jesse Stone & Orchestra)

Singles: 78 rpm

EPIC (9255 "My Life for Your Love") ... 250-300 57
RCA ... 15-30 56-57

Singles: 7-inch

EPIC (9255 "My Life for Your Love") ... 1000-1200 57
(White label. Promotional issue only.)
EPIC (9255 "My Life for Your Love") . 800-1000 57
MAGIC CARPET (504 "My Life for Your Love") ... 10-15
(Black vinyl. 475 made.)
MAGIC CARPET (504 "My Life for Your Love") ... 25-35
(Colored vinyl. 25 made.)
RCA (6518 "You're the Apple of My Eye") ... 30-40 56
RCA (6519 "Honey Love") ... 15-25 56
RCA (6646 "Jambalaya") ... 10-20 56
RCA (6768 "Happy Am I") ... 15-25 56
RCA (6812 "Shake a Hand") ... 40-50 57
RCA (6819 "Night Train") ... 15-25 57

EPs: 7-inch

RCA (869 "The Four Lovers") ... 150-200 56
RCA (871 "Joyride") ... 400-500 56

LPs: 10/12-inch

RCA (1317 "Joyride") ... 500-750 56
Members: Frankie Valli; Tom Devito; Nick Devito; Hank Majewski.
Also see 4 SEASONS
Also see STONE, Jesse
Also see VALLI, Frankie

FOUR LOVERS / Homer & Jethro

EPs: 7-inch

RCA (47 "The Four Lovers"/"Homer & Jethro") ... 30-50 56
(Promotional only. Not issued with cover.)
Also see HOMER & JETHRO

FOUR LOVERS / Teddi King

EPs: 7-inch

RCA (64 "Four Lovers"/"Teddi King") ... 30-50 56
(Promotional only. Not issued with cover.)
Also see KING, Teddi

FOUR MINTS

Singles: 78 rpm

DECCA (30464 "Ruby Baby") ... 10-15 57
LIN (5001 "Alone") ... 10-15 56

Singles: 7-inch

BRONCO (501 "Wild Streak") ... 5-10 63
DECCA (30464 "Ruby Baby") ... 10-15 57
LIN (5001 "Alone") ... 15-25 56
NRC (003 "Teenage Wonderland") ... 10-15 58
NRC (011 "You Belong to My Heart") ... 10-15 58
NRC (037 "Piña Colada") ... 10-15 59

LPs: 10/12-inch

AZTEC (1002 "The Fabulous Four Mints") ... 200-250 63
Also see COPELAND, Ken / Mints
Also see MINTS

FOUR MINTS

Singles: 7-inch

CHOCTAW (8002 "What 'Cha Gonna Do") ... 30-40 59

FOUR MINTS — R&B '73

Singles: 7-inch

CAPSOUL (27 "Do You Really Love Me") ... 10-20 73
CAPSOUL (28 "You're My Desire") ... 10-20 73
HOLIDAY (175 "You're My Desire") ... 40-50 73

LPs: 10/12-inch

CAPSOUL ... 15-25 73

FOUR MORE

Singles: 7-inch

DEE GEE (3013 "Hold On") ... 10-20 66

FOUR MORE

Singles: 7-inch

FAIRCHILD (1001 "Problem Child") ... 20-30 66

4 MOST

Singles: 78 rpm

DAWN (220 "Ooh Baby, It Scares Me") ... 5-10 56

Singles: 7-inch

DAWN (220 "Ooh Baby, It Scares Me") ... 10-15 56

4 MOST

Singles: 7-inch

MILO (107 "The Breeze and I") ... 50-75 59
(Black vinyl.)
MILO (107 "The Breeze and I") ... 10-20 61
(Blue vinyl.)
RELIC (501 "The Breeze and I") ... 5-10 63

FOUR NATURALS

Singles: 7-inch

ARCADE (1004 "Long, Long Ago") ... 5-10 77
RED TOP (119 "I Hear a Rhapsody") ... 15-25 59
RED TOP (125 "Long, Long Ago") ... 100-150 60
Also see NATURALS

FOUR OF A KIND

(4 Of A Kind)

Singles: 7-inch

BOMARC (302 "I Care for You") ... 8-12 59
CAMEO (154 "You Were Made T'Love") .. 10-15 58
LAURIE (3309 "Prance Around") ... 5-10 65
MELBA (110 "Dedicated to You") ... 10-15 56
MELBA (117 "Dreamy Eyes") ... 10-15 57
REX (104 "Next Fall") ... 15-25 61
TOY ... 5-10 72

FOUR OF US

Singles: 7-inch

ADORE (902 "Loving a Girl Like You") ... 50-75 61

4 OF US

Singles: 7-inch

HIDEOUT (1003 "You Gonna Be Mine"/"Free Fall") ... 25-30 65
HIDEOUT (1003 "You Gonna Be Mine"/ "Batman") ... 20-25 65
(Note different flip.)
HIDEOUT (1012 "I Feel a Whole Lot Better") ... 15-25 66

4 ON THE FLOOR

Singles: 7-inch

FRATERNITY (3490 "I Don't Stand a Chance") ... 15-25 83

Picture Sleeves

FRATERNITY (3490 "I Don't Stand a Chance") ... 25-35 83
(Sleeve mentions no titles.)

IV PACK

Singles: 7-inch

HIPPIE (2019 "Whatzit") ... 10-20 '60s

FOUR PALMS

Singles: 7-inch

ALADDIN (3411 "Consideration") ... 25-35 58
Members: Louis Faison; Hasker Nelson; James Jackson; Nate Thomas.
Also see RAINBEAUS
Also see SARGENT, Don

FOUR PALS

Singles: 78 rpm

ROYAL ROOST ... 10-20 55-56

Singles: 7-inch

ROYAL ROOST (610 "If I Can't Have the One I Love") ... 25-30 55
ROYAL ROOST (616 "No One Ever Loved Me") ... 25-30 56

FOUR PEARLS

Singles: 7-inch

DOLTON (26 "Look at Me") ... 150-200 60

FOUR PENNIES — P&R '63

Singles: 7-inch

RUST (5070 "When the Boy's Happy") ... 15-25 63
RUST (5071 "My Block") ... 15-25 63
Members: Judy Craig; Barbara Lee; Patricia Bennett; Sylvia Peterson.
Also see CHIFFONS
Also see RANDY & RAINBOWS / Four Pennies

FOUR PENNIES

Singles: 7-inch

BRUNSWICK (55304 "You Have No Time to Lose") ... 8-10 66
BRUNSWICK (55324 "Shake a Hand") ... 15-25 67

4 PHARAOHS

("4" Pharaohs)

Singles: 7-inch

PARADISE (109 "Give Me Your Love") .. 75-125 58
RANSOM (101 "Give Me Your Love") .. 200-300 58
RANSON (100 "Pray for Me") ... 200-300 58
(Label name is Ranson on 100 and Ransom on 101.)
Members: Morris Wade; Bobby Taylor; Ron Wilson; Bernard Wilson; Tommy Willis.
Also see CALDWELL, Joe
Also see COLUMBUS PHARAOHS
Also see EGYPTIAN KINGS
Also see KING PHARAOH & EGYPTIANS
Also see SUPREMES
Also see TAYLOR, Bobby
Also see WADE, Morris

FOUR PIPS & POP

("Four Pip's & a Pop Featuring Pop with Orchestra")

Singles: 7-inch

MERCEDES (5001 "For You") ... 75-125 59

FOUR PLAID THROATS

Singles: 78 rpm

MERCURY (70143 "My Inspiration") ... 200-300 53

Singles: 7-inch

MERCURY (70143 "My Inspiration") ... 600-800 53

FOUR PLAYBOYS

Singles: 7-inch

S.R.C. ("Rave On") ... 75-100 59
SOUVENIR (1002 "Stay with Me") ... 30-50 60

FOUR PREPS — P&R '56

(With Lincoln Mayorga & Orchestra)

Singles: 78 rpm

CAPITOL ... 5-10 56-57

Singles: 7-inch

CAPITOL (3576 thru 4312) ... 10-15 56-59
CAPITOL (4362 thru 5074, except 4568) ... 8-12 60-63
CAPITOL (4568 "Dream Boy, Dream") ... 15-25 61
CAPITOL (5143 "Letter to the Beatles") ... 15-25 64
CAPITOL (5178 thru 5921) ... 5-10 64-67

Picture Sleeves

CAPITOL (4599 "More Money for You and Me") ... 8-12 61
CAPITOL (4716 "The Big Draft") ... 8-12 62

EPs: 7-inch

CAPITOL (862 "Dreamy Eyes") ... 10-20 56
CAPITOL (994 "Four Preps") ... 10-20 57
CAPITOL (1015 "26 Miles") ... 10-20 58
CAPITOL (PRO 1149 "Dancing and Dreaming") ... 20-30 59
(Issued with paper sleeve. Promotional issue only.)

LPs: 10/12-inch

CAPITOL (994 thru 1647) ... 20-40 58-62
CAPITOL (1814 thru 2708) ... 15-25 63-67
Members: Bruce Belland; Glen Larson; Marv Ingraham; Ed Cobb; Don Clarke.
Also see KINGSTON TRIO / Four Preps
Also see MAYORGA, Lincoln
Also see NELSON, Rick

FOUR PUZZLES

Singles: 7-inch

FAT BACK (215 "Right Or Wrong") ... 10-15 67
Also see PUZZLES

FOUR QUEENS

Singles: 7-inch

ABC-PAR (10409 "It's Too Late") ... 8-12 63
TERON (782 "Boy Next Door") ... 25-35 64

FOUR REBELS

Singles: 7-inch

REM (319 "Boogie Woogie Sally") ... 200-300

FOUR REPUTATIONS

Singles: 7-inch

MILLAGE (105 "Call on Me") ... 15-25 '60s

FOUR RIVERS

Singles: 7-inch

JOSIE (901 "Sooner Or Later") ... 15-25 62

FOUR ROBINS

(With Sidney Charron Orchestra)

Singles: 78 rpm

PREVUE (1001 "Guess Who") ... 8-10 53

Singles: 7-inch

PREVUE (1001 "Guess Who") ... 15-25 53

FOUR ROCKETS

Singles: 78 rpm

ALADDIN (3007 "Little Red Wagon") ... 20-30 48
ALADDIN (3017 "Little Brown Jug") ... 20-30 48

FOUR ROMANS

Singles: 7-inch

WYNNE (116 "Drag Race") ... 10-20 59

FOUR SAINTS

Singles: 7-inch

W.B. (5327 "Heaven Help a Man") ... 5-10 62
W.B. (5335 "Days of Wine and Roses") ... 5-10 63

Picture Sleeves

W.B. (5335 "Days of Wine and Roses") ... 10-15 63

LPs: 10/12-inch

W.B. (1477 "Four Saints") ... 10-20 62
Members: Doug Evans; John Howell; Bob Erickson; Jerry Duchene.

FOUR SCORES

Singles: 7-inch

BART (21 "Rock a Little Lucy") ... 50-75

FOUR SEASONS

Singles: 7-inch

ALANNA (555 "Don't Sweat It Baby") ... 25-35 59
(Black and white label.)
ALANNA (555 "Don't Sweat It Baby") ... 10-20 59
(Orange and white label.)
ALANNA (555 "I'm Still in Love with You") 8-12 60

ALANNA (558 "Hot Water Bottle") ... 20-30 60
(Black and white label.)
ALANNA (558 "Hot Water Bottle") ... 8-12 60
(Orange and white label.)
ROBBEE (106 "Mirage") ... 200-250 60

4 SEASONS *P&R/R&B/LP '62*
(Four Seasons; Frankie Valli & 4 Seasons)
Singles: 7-inch
AURAVISION (6724 "Big Man's World").. 20-30 64
(Cardboard flexi-disc, one of six by six different artists. Columbia Record Club "Enrollment Premium." Set came in a special paper sleeve.)
BOB CREWE PRESENTS ... 10-15 70
(Promotional issue only.)
COLLECTABLES (Except 9) ... 3-5 81
COLLECTABLES (9 "Greatest Hits") ... 30-40 81
(Boxed, six-disc set. Colored vinyl.)
CREWE (333 "And That Reminds Me") ... 5-10 69
GONE (5122 "Bermuda") ... 20-30 62
MCA/CURB ... 3-5 85-86
MOTOWN (1255 "How Come") ... 5-10 73
MOTOWN (1288 "Hickory") ... 5-10 73
MOWEST (5026 "Walk On, Don't Look Back") ... 5-10 72
OLDIES 45 (18 "Sherry") ... 5-10 62
OLDIES 45 (47 "Big Girls Don't Cry") ... 5-10 62
OLDIES 45 (60 "Walk Like a Man") ... 5-10 63
OLDIES 45 (116 "Candy Girl") ... 5-10 63
PHILIPS (40166 thru 40662) ... 5-10 64-69
PHILIPS (40688 "Lay Me Down") ... 15-25 70
PHILIPS (40694 "Where Are My Dreams") ... 20-25 70
PHILIPS DOUBLE-HIT ... 4-8
SEASONS ... 4-6 75
SEASONS 4-EVER (Black vinyl) ... 4-6 71
SEASONS 4-EVER (Colored vinyl) ... 10-15 71
VEE-JAY (456 "Sherry") ... 10-15 62
VEE-JAY (465 "Big Girls Don't Cry") ... 10-15 62
VEE-JAY (478 "Santa Claus Is Coming to Town") ... 10-20 62
VEE-JAY (485 "Walk Like a Man") ... 10-15 62
VEE-JAY (512 "Ain't That a Shame") ... 10-15 63
VEE-JAY (539 "Candy Girl") ... 10-15 64
VEE-JAY (562 "New Mexican Rose") ... 10-15 64
VEE-JAY (576 "Stay"/"Peanuts") ... 40-50 63
VEE-JAY (582 "Stay"/"Goodnight My Love") ... 10-15 64
VEE-JAY (597 "Alone") ... 10-20 64
(Yellow label.)
VEE-JAY (597 "Alone") ... 8-12 64
(Black label.)
VEE-JAY (597 "Alone") ... 5-10 64
(Multi-color label.)
VEE-JAY (608 thru 719) ... 8-12 64-66
VEE-JAY (901 "Peanuts") ... 100-150 63
(Single-sided. Promotional issue only.)
WABC RADIO (77 "Cousin Brucie Go Go") ... 75-125 64
(Special products custom pressing. Colored vinyl.)
WXYZ-DETROIT (121003 "Joey Reynolds' Theme") ... 50-75 65
(Special products custom pressing.)
W.B. (8122 thru 49597) ... 4-6 75-80
WIBBAGE (WIBG "Joey Reynolds' Theme") ... 50-75 70
(Special products custom pressing.)
Picture Sleeves
CREWE (333 "And That Reminds Me") ... 10-15 69
PHILIPS (40185 "Ronnie") ... 10-20 64
PHILIPS (40211 "Rag Doll") ... 10-20 64
PHILIPS (40238 "Big Man in Town") ... 10-20 64
PHILIPS (40260 "Bye Bye Baby") ... 10-20 64
PHILIPS (40278 "Toy Soldier") ... 10-20 65
PHILIPS (40305 "Girl Come Running") ... 10-20 65
PHILIPS (40370 "Opus 17") ... 10-20 66
PHILIPS (40393 "I've Got You Under My Skin") ... 10-20 66
PHILIPS (40412 "Tell It to the Rain") ... 10-20 67
PHILIPS (40433 "Beggin' ") ... 10-20 67
PHILIPS (40460 "C'mon Marianne") ... 10-20 67
PHILIPS (40490 "Watch the Flowers Grow") ... 10-20 67
PHILIPS (40542 "Saturday's Father") ... 20-30 68
(Fold-out sleeve.)
PHILIPS (40542 "Saturday's Father") ... 10-20 68
(Standard sleeve.)
PHILIPS (40597 "Idaho") ... 10-20 69
PHILIPS (40662 "Patch of Blue") ... 10-20 69
VEE-JAY (456 "Sherry") ... 5-10 '90s
VEE-JAY (597 "Alone") ... 40-60 64
VEE-JAY (626 "I Saw Mommy Kissing Santa Claus") ... 25-35 64
EPs: 7-inch
MAGIC CARPET (502 "Jingles") ... 20-25
(Black vinyl. Issued with paper sleeve. 500 made.)
MAGIC CARPET (502 "Jingles") ... 40-45
(Colored vinyl. Issued with paper sleeve. 100 made.)
PHILIPS (2704 "Genuine Imitation Life Gazette") ... 20-30 68
(Compact 33 juke box issue only. Includes title strips.)
PHILIPS (2705 "Edizione D'Oro") ... 20-30 68
(Compacet 33 juke box issue only. Includes title strips.)
VEE-JAY (901 "Peanuts + 3") ... 20-35 64
VEE-JAY (902 "Alone + 3") ... 20-35 64
LPs: 10/12-inch
ARISTA ... 8-12 84
CANDLELITE (151 "Complete Musical Treasury") ... 35-45 82
(Boxed, five-disc set.)
CANDLELITE (151B "Souvenirs in Gold") ... 10-15 82
(Bonus LP, offered to buyers of the above set.)
ERA ... 5-10 82
FBI ... 10-15 84
GUEST STAR (1481 "Bermuda & Spanish Lace") ... 15-20 64
(Also has tracks by the Barrons, a.k.a. the Crescendos.)
KOALA ... 5-10 80
K-TEL ... 15-20 77
LONGINES (95833 "Greatest Hits of Frankie Valli & 4 Seasons") ... 25-35
(Boxed, four-disc set. TV mail-order offer.)
LONGINES (95833 "Greatest Hits of Frankie Valli & 4 Seasons") ... 20-30
(Gatefold, four-disc set. TV mail-order offer.)
MCA ... 5-10 85
MCA/CURB ... 5-10 88
MOTOWN ... 5-10 80
MOWEST ... 10-15 72
PHILIPS (2-6501 "Edizione D'Oro") ... 20-25 68
PHILIPS (200124 "Dawn and 11 Other Great Hits") ... 15-20 64
(Monaural.)
PHILIPS (200129 "Born to Wander") ... 15-20 64
(Monaural.)
PHILIPS (200146 "Rag Doll") ... 15-20 64
(Monaural.)
PHILIPS (200164 "The 4 Seasons Entertain You") ... 15-20 65
(Monaural.)
PHILIPS (200193 "Big Hits by Burt Bacharach, Hal David & Bob Dylan") ... 50-65 65
(Photos of group on front and back cover. Monaural.)
PHILIPS (200193 "Big Hits by Burt Bacharach, Hal David & Bob Dylan") ... 15-20 65
(No group photos on cover. Monaural.)
PHILIPS (200196 "Gold Vault of Hits") ... 15-20 65
(Monaural.)
PHILIPS (200201 "Working My Way Back to You") ... 15-20 66
(Monaural.)
PHILIPS (200221 "2nd Gold Vault of Hits") ... 15-20 66
(Monaural.)
PHILIPS (200222 "Lookin' Back") ... 15-20 66
(Monaural.)
PHILIPS (200223 "Christmas Album") ... 15-25 66
(Stereo.)
PHILIPS (200243 "New Gold Hits") ... 15-20 67
(Monaural.)
PHILIPS (600124 "Dawn and 11 Other Great Hits") ... 15-20 64
(Stereo.)
PHILIPS (600129 "Born to Wander") ... 15-20 64
(Stereo.)
PHILIPS (600146 "Rag Doll") ... 15-20 64
(Stereo.)
PHILIPS (600164 "The 4 Seasons Entertain You") ... 15-20 65
(Stereo.)
PHILIPS (600193 "Big Hits by Burt Bacharach, Hal David & Bob Dylan") ... 50-65 65
(Photos of group on front and back cover. Stereo.)
PHILIPS (600193 "Big Hits by Burt Bacharach, Hal David & Bob Dylan") ... 15-20 65
(No group photos on cover. Stereo.)
PHILIPS (600196 "Gold Vault of Hits") ... 15-20 65
(Stereo.)
PHILIPS (600201 "Working My Way Back to You") ... 15-20 66
(Stereo.)
PHILIPS (600221 "2nd Gold Vault of Hits") ... 15-20 66
(Stereo.)
PHILIPS (600222 "Lookin' Back") ... 15-20 66
(Stereo.)
PHILIPS (600223 "Christmas Album") ... 15-25 66
(Stereo.)
PHILIPS (600243 "New Gold Hits") ... 15-20 67
(Stereo.)
PHILIPS (600290 "Genuine Imitation Life Gazette") ... 35-45 69
(Yellow cover.)
PHILIPS (600290 "Genuine Imitation Life Gazette") ... 10-15 69
(White cover.)
PHILIPS (600341 "Half and Half") ... 10-15 70
PICKWICK ... 8-10 70
PRIORITY ... 8-10 86
PRIVATE STOCK (7000 "4 Seasons Story") ... 10-12 75
RHINO (Except 72998) ... 6-12
RHINO (72998 "25th Anniversary") ... 15-25 87
(Four-disc set.)
SEARS (609 "Brotherhood of Man") ... 20-30 70
TIME-LIFE (15 "Rock & Roll Era") ... 15-20 87
VEE-JAY (1053 "Sherry") ... 30-40 62
(Monaural.)
VEE-JAY (1053 "Sherry") ... 50-75 62
(Stereo.)
VEE-JAY (1055 "Four Seasons Greetings") ... 30-40 62
VEE-JAY (1056 "Big Girls Don't Cry") ... 30-40 63
VEE-JAY (1059 "Ain't That a Shame") ... 30-40 63
VEE-JAY (1065 "Golden Hits") ... 30-40 63
VEE-JAY (1082 "Folk-Nanny") ... 40-50 64
VEE-JAY (1082 "Stay and Other Great Hits") ... 20-30 64
(Repackage of *Folk-Nanny.*)
VEE-JAY (1088 "More Golden Hits") ... 25-35 64
VEE-JAY (1121 "We Love Girls") ... 25-35 64
VEE-JAY (1154 "Recorded Live on Stage") ... 25-35 65
WCI (502 "Silver Anniversary") ... 15-25 85
(Three-disc set.)
W.B. ... 8-12 75-81
Members: Frankie Valli; Tom Devito; Nick Devito; Hank Majewski; Bob Gaudio; Charlie Calello; Nick Massi; Joe Long; Don Ciccone; Bill Deloach; Paul Wilson; Jerry Corbetta.
Also see BEACH BOYS with FRANKIE VALLI & 4 SEASONS
Also see BEATLES / 4 Seasons
Also see CABBOT, Johnny
Also see CARROLL, Bernadette
Also see COREY, John
Also see CRESCENDOS
Also see CREWE, Bob
Also see DISENTRI, Turner
Also see DIXON, Billy, & Topics
Also see FOUR LOVERS
Also see HALO, Johnny
Also see HAYES, Tommy
Also see JAN & DEAN / Roy Orbison / 4 Seasons / Shirelles
Also see KOKOMOS
Also see LARRY & LEGENDS
Also see MATTHEWS, Shirley
Also see MILLER, Hal
Also see RASCALS / Buggs / Four Seasons / Johnny Rivers
Also see REID, Matthew
Also see REYNOLDS, Joey / Joey & Danny
Also see RIVERS, Johnny / 4 Seasons / Jerry Butler / Jimmy Soul
Also see ROYAL TEENS
Also see SANTOS, Larry
Also see SIMON, Paul
Also see TOPICS
Also see TREVOR, Van
Also see VALLI, Frankie
Also see VILLAGE VOICES
Also see WONDER WHO

4 SEASONS / Charlie Francis / Barbara Brown & Buggs
LPs: 10/12-inch
CORONET (244 "At the Hop") ... 15-25 64
PREMIER (9052 "At the Hop") ... 15-25

4 SEASONS / Little Royal
Singles: 7-inch
GORDA (500 "Rag Doll"/"Jealous") ... 5-10 65
Also see LITTLE ROYAL

4 SEASONS / Scarlets
Singles: 7-inch
OLDIES 45 (115 "Candy Girl"/"Dear One") ... 5-10 63
Also see SCARLETS

4 SEASONS / Neil Sedaka / J Brothers / Johnny Rivers
LP: 10/12-inch
DESIGN ... 10-20 '60s
Also see J BROTHERS
Also see RIVERS, Johnny
Also see SEDAKA, Neil

4 SEASONS / Ray Stevens
Singles: 7-inch
OLDIES 45 ... 5-10 63
Also see 4 SEASONS
Also see STEVENS, Ray

FOUR SENSATIONS
Singles: 78 rpm
RAINBOW ... 5-10 52-53
Singles: 7-inch
RAINBOW (157 "Heaven Knows") ... 10-15 52
(Black vinyl.)
RAINBOW (157 "Heaven Knows") ... 15-25 52
(Red vinyl.)
RAINBOW (217 "Tabu") ... 15-25 53

FOUR SHADES OF RHYTHM
Singles: 78 rpm
CHANCE (1126 "Yesterdays") ... 50-100 53
OLD SWINGMASTER (13 "My Blue Walk") ... 10-20 49
OLD SWINGMASTER (23 "I Can Dream") ... 10-20 49
VITACOUSTIC (1005 "A Hundred Years from Today") ... 10-15 52
Singles: 7-inch
APEX (967 "A Hundred Years from Today") ... 8-12 60
CHANCE (1126 "Yesterdays") ... 300-400 53
MAD (1202 "I Don't Stand a Ghost of a Chance") ... 40-50 60
VITACOUSTIC (1005 "A Hundred Years from Today") ... 15-20 52

FOUR SHARPS
(Delta Rhythm Boys)
Singles: 78 rpm
ATLANTIC (875 "Don't Ask Me Why") ... 30-50 49
Members: Traverse Crawford; Karl Jones; Kelsey Pharr; Lee Gaines.
Also see DELTA RHYTHM BOYS

FOUR SHARPS
Singles: 7-inch
DARROW (512 "Safari") ... 15-25 58
Also see SHARPS

FOUR SHARPS
Singles: 7-inch
DONNA (1330 "Church Key") ... 15-25 61
(Same single also issued as by the Gonzos.)
Also see GONZOS

FOUR SHARPS
Singles: 7-inch
SHARP (5064 "Surf Guitar") ... 15-25 63

FOUR SHOTS
Singles: 78 rpm
CADILLAC (159 "Love Hit Me and I Hollered") ... 50-75 55
Singles: 7-inch
CADILLAC (159 "Love Hit Me and I Hollered") ... 100-200 55

FOUR SINGING AVALONS
Singles: 7-inch
ATCO (6585 "She's My Woman, She's My Girl") ... 10-20 68

FOUR SONICS *P&R/R&B '68*
Singles: 7-inch
SPORT (110 "You Don't Have to Say You Love Me") ... 25-35 68

SPORT (111 "Easier Said Than Done").. 15-25 68
Members: Eddy Daniels; James Johnson; Steve Gaston; Willie Frazier.

FOUR SONS

Singles: 7-inch

LINCO (1316 "Little Rock")... 50-75 60

FOUR SOUNDS
(With the Lawrence Keyes Trio)

Singles: 7-inch

CELESTE (3010 "Afraid")... 300-400 57
CELESTE (3013 "You Stole My Heart")...4-6 74

FOUR SOUNDS

Singles: 7-inch

FEDERAL (12421 "Someone to Show Me the Way")... 15-25 61
RAN-DEE (104 "Nobody Wants Me")...5-10 62
TUFF (1 "The Ring")... 10-15 60

FOUR SOUTHERNERS

Singles: 78 rpm

DECCA (7291 "Dan the Back Door Man")... 50-100 37

FOUR SPARKS

Singles: 7-inch

CLEFF=TONE (151 "Key to My Heart")... 20-30 58

FOUR SPARKS

Singles: 7-inch

ABC-PAR (9906 "Out of This World")... 10-15 58

FOUR SPEEDS

Singles: 78 rpm

DELUXE (6070 "I Need You, Baby")... 20-30 54

Singles: 7-inch

DELUXE (6070 "I Need You, Baby")... 40-50 54

FOUR SPEEDS

Singles: 7-inch

CHALLENGE (9187 "R.P.M.")... 30-50 63
CHALLENGE (9202 "Four on the Floor") 30-50 63
Members: Gary Usher; Chuck Girard; Richard Burns; Dennis Wilson.
Also see HONDELLS
Also see SUNSETS
Also see USHER, Gary
Also see WILSON, Dennis

FOUR SPORTSMEN P&R '61

Singles: 7-inch

SUNNYBROOK (1 "Surrender")... 30-40 60
SUNNYBROOK (2 "Lucille")... 15-25 61
SUNNYBROOK (4 "Pitter-Patter")... 20-30 61
SUNNYBROOK (5 "Sixty Minute Man")... 15-25 61
SUNNYBROOK (6 "If Your Heart Can Take It")... 25-35 61

FOUR STAGS

Singles: 7-inch

TOPAZ (1301 "Confession")... 10-20 60

FOUR STARS

Singles: 78 rpm

LONDON (1327 "The Rumbleseat")...5-10 53

Singles: 7-inch

LONDON (1327 "The Rumbleseat")... 10-20 53

FOUR STARS

Singles: 78 rpm

KING (1382 "Win Or Lose")... 10-15 54

Singles: 7-inch

KING (1382 "Win Or Lose")... 20-30 54

FOUR STARS
("Piano: Milton Harris Jr.")

Singles: 7-inch

KAY-Y (66781 "The Chapel By the Sea")... 250-350 58

FOUR STORMS

Singles: 78 rpm

ARCADE (134 "Mississippi Mud")...5-10 55

Singles: 7-inch

ARCADE (134 "Mississippi Mud")... 10-20 55
Also see DAIRD, Jay, & Four Storms

FOUR STUDENTS

Singles: 78 rpm

GROOVE (0110 "So Near and Yet So Far")... 10-15 55

Singles: 7-inch

GROOVE (0110 "So Near and Yet So Far")... 30-40 55
Also see BLACK, Oscar, & Sue Allen
Also see CALHOUN, Charles, & Four Students
Also see DILLARD, Varetta, & Four Students
Also see GREER, Big John, & Four Students
Also see MAYS, Zilla
Also see McKENZIE, Lil, & Four Students
Also see WRIGHT, Beverly

FOUR TEENS

Singles: 7-inch

CHALLENGE (59021 "Go Little Go-Cat").60-80 58

FOUR TEES

Singles: 7-inch

KENT (4530 "One More Chance")...10-15 70
KENT (4536 "I Could Never Love Another")...10-15 71
VEE-JAY (627 "I Said, She Said")...5-10 64

FOUR TEMPOS

Singles: 7-inch

RAMPART (Except 665)...5-8 67-69
RAMPART (665 "Memories")...30-40 67

FOUR TEMPTATIONS

Singles: 7-inch

ABC-PAR (9920 "Cathy")...30-40 58

FOUR THOUGHTS

Singles: 7-inch

WOMAR (103 "When I'm with You")...50-75 '60s

FOUR TONES

Singles: 78 rpm

PREVIEW...15-25 45

FOUR TOPHATTERS

Singles: 78 rpm

CADENCE...5-10 54-57
VANITY (1609 "You're So Lovely")...5-10 52

Singles: 7-inch

CADENCE (1243 "Dim, Dim the Lights")..10-15 54
CADENCE (1255 "Go Baby Go")...10-15 55
CADENCE (1268 "Wild Rosie")...10-15 55
CADENCE (1311 "The House")...10-15 57
VANITY (1609 "You're So Lovely")...10-20 52
Also see TOPHATTERS

FOUR TOPS P&R/R&B '64

Singles: 12-inch

ABC...4-8 77-78
MOTOWN...4-8 80

Singles: 78 rpm

CHESS (1623 "Could It be You")...25-35 56

Singles: 7-inch

ABC/DUNHILL...4-6 75-79
ARISTA...3-5 88
CASABLANCA...3-5 81-82
CHESS (1623 "Could It be You")...50-150 56
COLUMBIA (41755 "Lonely Summer")...30-40 60
COLUMBIA (43356 "Lonely Summer")...10-15 65
DUNHILL...4-6 72-74
MOTOWN (Colored vinyl)...8-12 70
(Promotional issue only.)
MOTOWN (400 series)...3-5
MOTOWN (1062 thru 1254)...8-12 64-72
MOTOWN (1706 thru 1854)...3-5 83-86
MOTOWN/TOPPS (5 "I Can't Help Myself")...50-75 67
(Topps Chewing Gum promotional item. Single-sided, cardboard flexi, 6-inch picture disc. Issued with generic paper sleeve.)
MOTOWN/TOPPS (9 "Baby I Need Your Loving")...50-75 67
(Topps Chewing Gum promotional item. Single-sided, cardboard flexi, 6-inch picture disc. Issued with generic paper sleeve.)
RSO (1069 "Back to School Again")...3-5 82
RELIANT...3-5 88
RIVERSIDE (4534 "Pennies from Heaven")...40-60 62

Picture Sleeves

ARISTA...3-5 88
MOTOWN (1073 "Ask the Lonely")...50-75 64
MOTOWN (1098 "Reach Out I'll Be There")...20-40 66
MOTOWN (1164 "It's All in the Game")...8-10 70
MOTOWN (1175 "Just Seven Numbers") ..8-10 71
RSO...3-5 82

EPs: 7-inch

ABC (259 "Main Street People")...15-20 74
(Quadraphonic.)
MOTOWN (60647 "On Top")...25-50 66

LPs: 10/12-inch

ABC...8-10 75-78
ARISTA...5-8 88
CASABLANCA...5-10 81-82
COMMAND...10-20 74
DUNHILL...8-10 72-74
GORDY...5-10 85
MOTOWN (100 & 200 series)...5-10 82-84
MOTOWN (622 "Four Tops")...20-30 64
MOTOWN (634 "Second Album")...15-25 65
MOTOWN (647 "On Top")...15-20 66
MOTOWN (654 "Live")...15-25 66
MOTOWN (657 "On Broadway")...15-25 67
MOTOWN (660 "Reach Out")...10-20 67
MOTOWN (662 "Greatest Hits")...10-20 67
MOTOWN (669 "Yesterday's Dream")...10-20 68
MOTOWN (675 thru 748)...10-20 69-72
MOTOWN (764 "Best of the Four Tops").10-15 73
(Two discs.)
MOTOWN (6000 series)...5-8 83-86
MOTOWN (9809 "Anthology")...15-20 74
MOTOWN (M9809 "Anthology")...10-15 86
PICKWICK...5-8 74
NATURAL RESOURCES...8-10 78
WORKSHOP (217 "Breaking Through")...1000-1500 62
WORKSHOP (217 "Jazz Impressions by the Four Tops")...500-1000 62
(Retitled reissue.)
Members: Levi Stubbs; Lawrence Payton; Abdul "Duke" Fakir; Obie Benson.
Also see CARROLL, Delores, & Four Tops
Also see FOUR AIMS
Also see HAYES, Carolyn, & Four Tops
Also see HOLLAND - DOZIER
Also see SUPREMES & FOUR TOPS
Also see TEMPTATIONS & FOUR TOPS

FOUR TOTS

Singles: 7-inch

PS (9010 "Tender Years")...10-20 '60s

FOUR TOWNSMEN

Singles: 7-inch

ART-FLOW (145 "It Wasn't So Long Before")...400-500 60
(Number 10075 must be on label.)

FOUR TROYS

Singles: 7-inch

FREEDOM (44013 "In the Moonlight")...30-40 59

FOUR TRUMPS

Singles: 7-inch

MIRA (2050 "I've Waited All My Life for You")...200-300 58
(Identification number shown since no selection number is used.)

FOUR TUNES P&R/R&B '53
("Featuring Jimmie Nabbie")

Singles: 78 rpm

COLUMBIA...5-15 48
JUBILEE...10-20 53-57
MANOR...10-20 46-49
RCA...10-20 49-53

Singles: 7-inch

CROSBY (3 "Never Look Down")...10-20 60
CROSBY (4 "Twinkle Eyes")...15-25 60
(Black vinyl.)
CROSBY (4 "Twinkle Eyes")...40-50 60
(Blue vinyl.)
GOLDIES 45 (2562 "Marie")...3-6 73
JUBILEE (5128 "Marie")...25-35 53
JUBILEE (5132 "I Understand")...20-30 54
JUBILEE (5135 "My Wild Irish Rose")...10-20 54
JUBILEE (5152 "Lonesome")...10-20 54
JUBILEE (5165 "Don't Cry Darling")...20-30 54
JUBILEE (5174 "I Sold My Heart to the Junkman")...20-30 54
JUBILEE (5183 "I Close My Eyes")...20-30 55
JUBILEE (5200 "Time Out for Tears")...20-30 55
JUBILEE (5212 "Brooklyn Bridge")...10-20 55
JUBILEE (5218 "You Are My Love")...10-20 55
JUBILEE (5232 "Our Love")...10-20 56
JUBILEE (5239 "I Gotta Go")...10-20 56
JUBILEE (5245 "Far Away Places")...10-20 56
JUBILEE (5255 "The Ballad of James Dean")...20-30 56
JUBILEE (5276 "Cool Water")...10-20 57
JUBILEE (6000 "Marie")...5-10 59
KAY-RON (1000 "I Want to Be Loved")...25-50 54
KAY-RON (1005 "I Understand")...25-50 54
RCA (50-0008 "You're Heartless")...150-250 49
(Cherry red vinyl.)
RCA (50-0016 "My Last Affair")...150-250 49
(Cherry red vinyl.)
RCA (50-0042 "I'm Just a Fool in Love")...150-250 49
(Cherry red vinyl.)
RCA (50-0072 "Am I Blue")...100-200 50
(Cherry red vinyl.)
RCA (50-0085 "Old Fashioned Love") .100-200 50
(Cherry red vinyl.)
RCA (50-0131 "May That Day Never Come")...100-150 51
RCA (3881 "Do I Worry")...50-75 50
RCA (3967 "Cool Water")...50-75 50
RCA (4102 "Wishing You Were Here Tonight")...40-50 51
RCA (4241 "I Married an Angel")...40-50 51
RCA (4280 "It's No Sin")...25-35 51
RCA (4305 "Early in the Morning")...25-35 51
RCA (4427 "I'll See You in My Dreams") .25-35 51
RCA (4489 "Come What May")...15-25 52
RCA (4663 "I Wonder")...15-25 52
RCA (4828 "They Don't Understand")...15-25 52
RCA (4968 "I Don't Want to Set the World on Fire")...15-25 52
RCA (5532 "Don't Get Around Much Anymore")...15-25 53
VIRGO ("Marie")...3-6 72
(Selection number not known.)

EPs: 7-inch

RCA (586 "Four Tunes")...100-150 54

LPs: 10/12-inch

JUBILEE (1039 "12 x 4")...100-200 57
Members: Jim Nabbie; Danny Owens; William "Pat" Best; Jimmy Gordon; Deek Watson.
Also see CHURCHILL, Savannah
Also see HALL, Juanita, & Four Tunes
Also see NABBIE, Jimmie
Also see SENTIMENTALISTS

4 UNIQUES
(The "4" Uniques with the Stereos Combo)

Singles: 7-inch

ADAM (9002 "Too Young")...50-100 61
ADAM (9004 "She's the Only Girl")...75-125 62
DEER (3002 "Good Luck Charm")...100-200 62

4 UNIQUES

Singles: 7-inch

USA (753 "Maybe Next Summer")...100-150 63

FOUR UNKNOWNS

Singles: 7-inch

MIDA (112 "Fearless")...15-20 59

FOUR UPSETTERS

Singles: 7-inch

SUN (381 "Midnight Soiree")...10-20 62
SUN (386 "Surfin' Calliope")...10-20 63
Members: George Webb; John Guthrie; Luke Wright; William Felts.

FOUR VAGABONDS P&R/R&B '43

Singles: 78 rpm

APOLLO (1030 "Kentucky Babe")...20-40 47
APOLLO (1039 "Do You Know What It Means to Miss New Orleans")...20-40 47
APOLLO (1055 "Dreams Are a Dime a Dozen")...20-40 47
APOLLO (1057 "P.S. I Love You")...20-40 47
APOLLO (1060 "Ask Anyone Who Knows")...20-40 47
APOLLO (1075 "Choo-Choo")...20-40 47
APOLLO (1076 "The Gang That Sang Heart of My Heart")...20-40 47
ATLAS (111 "I Can't Make Up My Mind").20-40 45
BLUEBIRD (0810 "I Had the Craziest Dream")...30-50 43
BLUEBIRD (0811 "Rose Ann of Charing Cross")...30-50 43
BLUEBIRD (0815 "It Can't Be Wrong")...30-50 43
BLUEBIRD (11519 "Slow & Easy")...30-50 42
LLOYDS (102 "P.S. I Love You")...50-100 53
MERCURY (2050 "Taking My Chance with You")...15-25 46
MIRACLE (141 "My Heart Cries")...15-25 49
RCA (1677 "If I Were You")...20-30 45

Singles: 7-inch

LLOYDS (102 "P.S. I Love You")...400-500 53

EPs: 7-inch
LLOYDS (706 "Four Vagabonds") 400-500 54
Members: Johnny Jordan; Robert O'Neal; Ray Grant; Norval Taborn.
Also see VAGABONDS

FOUR VANNS
Singles: 78 rpm
VIK (0246 "So Young & Pretty") 10-15 56
Singles: 7-inch
VIK (0246 "So Young & Pretty") 15-25 56

FOUR VIBES
Singles: 7-inch
SWA=RAY (1001 "You're All I Live For"). 25-35 64
Session: Jesse Herring.

FOUR VOICES *P&R '56*
Singles: 78 rpm
COLUMBIA 5-10 55-57
Singles: 7-inch
ABC-PAR (10202 "This World We Live In") 8-10 61
COLUMBIA (40516 thru 41076)................ 10-20 55-57
COLUMBIA (41167 thru 41699) 5-10 58-60
MR. PEACOCK (106 "Lovely One")............5-10 62
MR. PEACOCK (114 "Everybody Loves Saturday Night") 5-10 62
VOICE (1112 "Your Love Is Getting Stronger") 20-30
VOICE (1113 "Summer Kind of Love") 20-30

FOUR WHEELS
Singles: 7-inch
DELEWARE (1703 "Ratchet")................. 20-30 64
SOMA (1428 "Central High Playmate") ... 10-20 64
Also see BOYS NEXT DOOR

FOUR WINDS
Singles: 78 rpm
MIDDLETONE 40-60 56
Singles: 7-inch
MIDDLETONE (008 "I Promise") 75-125 56
MIDDLETONE (013 "Living in a Dream") 75-125 56

FOUR WINDS
(With Their Teenage Friends & Eddie Platt's Band)
Singles: 7-inch
CHATTAHOOCHEE (655 "Down and Out") 5-10 64
DECOR (175 "Five Minutes More")......... 10-15 57
DERY (10022 "Jennifer") 40-50 63
DIAL (3006 "Promised Land") 8-12 62
EXPLORER (713 "Five Minutes More")... 15-25 57
(Opinions vary as to whether this label preceded or followed Decor. Readers?)
EXPLORER (713 "Doin' the Stroll") 25-35 57
FELSTED (8703 "Jennifer") 10-15 64
HIDE-A-WAY (101 "Mission By the Sea") 10-20 58
SHERLUCK (1027 "Ol' Man River")..... 100-150
STUDIO CITY (1047 "Take These Chains from My Heart") 5-10 66
VIK (0221 "Find Someone New")............ 10-15 56
WARWICK (633 Daddy's Home") 50-75 61
WESTLAND (15771 "Hear the Sound").......5-10 66

FOUR WINDS
(4 Winds; Tokens)
Singles: 7-inch
B.T. PUPPY (555 "Let It Ride") 5-10 69
CRYSTAL BALL (102 "Dear Judy") 4-8 77
(Black vinyl. 500 made.)
CRYSTAL BALL (102 "Dear Judy") 8-12 77
(Red vinyl. 25 made.)
CRYSTAL BALL (105 "Arlene").....................4-8 77
(Black vinyl. 500 made.)
CRYSTAL BALL (105 "Arlene")..................8-12 77
(Red vinyl. 25 made.)
SWING (100 "Remember Last Summer") 10-20 64
Also see TOKENS

FOUR Xs
Singles: 7-inch
LOST (101 "I'll Remember") 30-40 60

4U & HIM
Singles: 7-inch
FENTON ("Back Door Man") .... 75-100 '60s
(Selection number not known.)

FOUR-EVERS *P&R '64*
(Four Evers)
Singles: 7-inch
CHATTAHOOCHEE (630 "Colors") 5-10 63
COLUMBIA (3-42303 "You Belong to Me") 75-100 62
(Compact 33 Single.)
COLUMBIA (4-42303 "You Belong to Me") 40-50 62
COLUMBIA (43886 "A Lovely Way to Say Goodbye") 10-15 66
CONSTELLATION (151 "Stormy")...........10-15 65
CRYSTAL BALL (121 "Dreamland") 4-8 78
(Black vinyl. 500 made.)
CRYSTAL BALL (121 "Dreamland") 8-12 78
(Red vinyl. 25 made.)
JAMIE (1247 "One More Time") 20-30 63
JASON SCOTT (04 "You Belong to Me") 3-5 80
(1000 made.)
RED BIRD (078 "What a Scene") 10-15 66
SMASH (1853 "It's Love") 10-15 63
SMASH (1887 "Please Be Mine") 15-25 64
SMASH (1887 "Be My Girl") 10-20 64
(Same selection number used on both issues above.)
SMASH (1921 "Doo Be Dum") 10-15 63
LPs: 10/12-inch
MAGIC CARPET (1004 "Our Special Sound") 8-12 91
(Black vinyl. 2000 made.)
MAGIC CARPET (1004 "Our Special Sound") 25-30 91
(Red vinyl. 10 made.)
MAGIC CARPET (1004 "Our Special Sound") 40-50 91
(Picture disc. No cover. 25 made.)
Members: Joe Di Benedetto; John Capriani; Steve Tudanger; Nick Zagami.

FOUR-EVERS / Billy & Essentials
Singles: 7-inch
CRYSTAL BALL (145 "Resolutions"/"You're So Fine") 4-8 81
(Black vinyl. 500 made.)
CRYSTAL BALL (145 "Resolutions"/"You're So Fine") 8-12 81
(Red vinyl. 25 made.)
CRYSTAL BALL (145 "Resolutions"/"You're So Fine") 30-40 81
(Multi-colored vinyl. Five made.)
Picture Sleeves
CRYSTAL BALL (145 "Resolutions"/"You're So Fine") 10-15 81
(200 made.)
Also see BILLY & ESSENTIALS
Also see FOUR-EVERS

FOURMOST
Singles: 7-inch
LU PINE (105 "Twist-A-Taste") 15-20 62

FOURMOST
Singles: 7-inch
ATCO (6280 "Hello Little Girl") 10-20 63
ATCO (6285 "Respectable") 10-15 64
ATCO (6307 "If You Cry") 10-15 64
ATCO (6317 "How Can I Tell Her")...........10-15 64
CAPITOL (5591 "Why Do Fools Fall in Love") 8-12 66
CAPITOL (5738 "Here, There and Everywhere") 15-20 66

4TH AMENDMENT
Singles: 7-inch
CONSTITUTION (5109 "Always Blue") 10-15 67
4 SONS ....10-15 '60s

FOURTH CEKCION
LPs: 10/12-inch
SOLAR (110 "Fourth Cekcion")................25-35 70

FOWLER, Buck
Singles: 7-inch
ECHO (5001 "She's Just That Kind")....450-550

FOWLER, Buddy
Singles: 7-inch
CRYSTALETTE (741 "That's Why") 10-15 60

FOWLER, Don
Singles: 7-inch
OAKRIDGE (121 "Oklahoma Baby") 50-100

FOWLER, Gloria, & Entros
Singles: 7-inch
C.J. (654 "Will You Be My Guy")..............10-20 65

FOWLER, Jimmy
Singles: 7-inch
DART (118 "Let's Rock n' Roll")...........100-200 59

FOWLER, T.J.
Singles: 78 rpm
GOTHAM (254 "Hot Sauce").....................10-20 52
SAVOY 10-20 52-53
SENSATION (28 "Midnight Clipper") 10-20 50
SENSATION (36 "Hot Sauce") 10-20 50
STATES (132 "The Queen") 10-20 54
Singles: 7-inch
BOW (309 "Milk Shake") 15-25 57
GOTHAM (254 "Hot Sauce")......................20-30 52
SAVOY (843 "Night Crawler") 15-25 52
SAVOY (857 "Back Biter") 15-25 52
SAVOY (885 "Camel Walk") 15-25 53
STATES (132 "The Queen") 15-25 54
Also see DILLARD, Varetta / T.J. Fowler
Also see FRASIER, Clavin

FOWLER, Tommy
Singles: 7-inch
REED (1038 "Pretty Baby")...................250-350

FOWLER, Wally *C&W '84*
(With the Tennessee Valley Boys)
Singles: 7-inch
DOVE (100 "A New Star in Heaven") 5-10 77
MERCURY 10-15 47
NASHWOOD 3-5 84
SONGS OF FAITH 3-5
EPs: 7-inch
DECCA...5--10 60
LPs: 10/12-inch
DECCA..12-20 60
DOVE (1000 "Tribute to Elvis Presley")....15-20 77
KING 20-30 60
NASHWOOD 5-10
PICKWICK 6-12
PICKWICK/HILLTOP.....................................8-12 65
STARDAY 15-25 60-64
VOCALION 10-15 67
Session: J.D. Sumner & Stamps; D.J. Fontana; Charlie McCoy; Harold Bradley; Anita Kerr Singers; Oak Ridge Quartet.
Also see KERR, Anita
Also see McCOY, Charlie
Also see OAK RIDGE BOYS
Also see PRESLEY, Elvis
Also see SUMNER, J.D., & Stamps Quartet

FOWLEY, Kim *LP '69*
Singles: 7-inch
CAPITOL 4-8 72-73
CREATIVE FAMILY 15-25
IMPERIAL 5-10 68-69
LIVING LEGEND (721 "Mr. Responsibility") 10-15 65
LOMA (2064 "Lights") 8-10 66
MIRA (209 "American Dream") 10-15 65
ORIGINAL SOUND (81 "Young America – Saturday Night") 5-10 68
ORIGINAL SOUND (98 "Thunder Road") ..5-10 70
REPRISE (569 "Don't Be Cruel") 5-10 67
TOWER (342 "Love Is Alive and Well")......5-10 67
LPs: 10/12-inch
CAPITOL (11075 "I'm Bad") 15-25 72
CAPITOL (11159 "International Heroes"). 10-20 73
CAPITOL (11248 "Automatic") 10-20 74
IMPERIAL (12413 "Born to Be Wild") 15-25 68
IMPERIAL (12423 "Outrageous") 15-25 69
IMPERIAL (12443 "Good Clean Fun") 15-20 69
PVC (7906 "Sunset Boulevard") 8-12 79
TOWER (5080 "Love Is Alive and Well")..25-30 67
Also see BERRY, Richard

FOWLEY, Kim / Paul & Victors
Singles: 7-inch
CORBY (216 "The Trip") 15-25 65
Also see FOWLEY, Kim

FOWLKES, Doug, & Airdales
LPs: 10/12-inch
ATCO (145 "Airdale Walk") 10-12 62

FOX, The
Singles: 78 rpm
RPM (420 "The Dream") 8-12 55
Singles: 7-inch
RPM (420 "The Dream") 15-20 55

FOX
(The Fox—High Priest Smoking Bear)
Singles: 7-inch
RINGS OF SATURN (1000 "The Man, the Man") 200-300

FOX, Damon
Singles: 7-inch
CRIMSON (1013 "Gotta Get My Baby Back") 8-12 68
FAIRMOUNT (1021 "Packin' Up") 10-20 67

FOX, Eugene
(The Fox; Sly Fox)
Singles: 78 rpm
CHECKER (792 "Sinner's Dream") 20-30 54
RPM (421 "The Dream") 30-50 54
SPARK (108 "Hoodoo Say") 30-50 54
SPARK (112 "My Four Women") 30-50 54
Singles: 7-inch
CHECKER (792 "Sinner's Dream") 30-50 54
RPM (421 "The Dream") 50-75 54
SPARK (108 "Hoodoo Say") 50-75 54
SPARK (112 "My Four Women") 50-75 54

FOX, Johnny, & Foxes
Singles: 7-inch
NEWTIME (507 "Mountain Dew") 10-15 62

FOX, Lance, & Bloodhounds
Singles: 7-inch
BANG (523 "You Got Love") 10-20 66

FOX, Norman, & Rob-Roys
("Rob Roys featuring Norman Fox"; with Sid Bass Orchestra)
Singles: 78 rpm
BACK BEAT (501 "Tell Me Why") 50-75 57
BACK BEAT (508 "Dance Girl Dance") 200-300 58
Singles: 7-inch
BACK BEAT (499 "Lover Doll") ....5-10 '80s
BACK BEAT (500 "Rainy Day Bells")..........5-10 88
BACK BEAT (501 "Tell Me Why") 40-50 57
(White label.)
BACK BEAT (501 "Tell Me Why") 10-20 57
(Red label.)
BACK BEAT (508 "Dance Girl Dance")....40-50 58
CAPITOL (4128 "Dream Girl") 300-400 59
(Purple label.)
CAPITOL (4128 "Dream Girl") 200-300 59
(Yellow label. Promotional issue only.)
HAMMER (544 "Pizza Pie") 10-15 58
(Red or green label.)
POPULAR REQUEST (105 "Tell Me Why"/"Dance Girl Dance") 3-5 94
Members: Norman Fox; Robert Thierer; Bobby Trotman; Andre Lilly; Marshall "Buzzy" Helfand.

FOX, Orville
Singles: 7-inch
ELLIS (101 "Honey, You Talk Too Much") 100-125

FOX, Tony
Singles: 7-inch
CALLA (146 "Do It to It") 5-10 68
CALLA (151 "Lean On Me") 5-10 68
EMERALD CITY (7219 "Give It All Up Tonight") 4-6 80
MOONSHOT (6712 "Say What You Mean, Mean What You Say") 5-10 69
TRI-SPIN (003 "I've Been Searchin' ") 25-50 67

FOX & HUNTAHS
Singles: 7-inch
MALCOLM Z (45004 "Love Minus Zero") 20-30 66

FOXALL, Art, Combo
Singles: 7-inch
DOT (15732 "Potato Chips") 10-20 62

FOXES
Singles: 7-inch
ABC-PAR (10446 "I Just Might Fall in Love") 8-12 63
BRIDGEVIEW...5-10
PICKWICK 5-10
TITANIC (101 "Who Loved You") 15-25 63

FOXX, Inez *P&R/R&B '63*
(With Charlie Foxx)
Singles: 7-inch
DYNAMO 4-8 67-70

LANA ... 4-6 '60s
MUSICOR ... 5-8 66-68
SUE ... 5-10 65
SYMBOL ... 5-10 62-66
VOLT ... 4-6 72-74
U.A. ... 4-6 74

LPs: 10/12-inch

DYNAMO ... 10-15 67
SUE (1037 "Inez & Charlie Foxx") ... 20-40 65
(Monaural.)
SUE (1037 "Inez & Charlie Foxx") ... 25-50 65
(Stereo.)
SYMBOL (4400 "Mockingbird") ... 100-150 63
VOLT ... 8-10 73
Also see JOHNSTON, Inez, & Florios
Also see PLATTERS / Inez & Charlie Foxx / Jive Five / Tommy Hunt

FOXX, Redd LP '72
(With Hattie Noel)

Singles: 78 rpm

DOOTO (Except 416) ... 5-10 57
DOOTO (416 "Real Pretty Mama") ... 10-15 57
DOOTONE ... 3-5 56-57
SAVOY ... 5-10 46

Singles: 7-inch

DOOTO (Except 416) ... 5-10 57-61
DOOTO (416 "Real Pretty Mama") ... 15-25 57
DOOTONE ... 8-12 56-57

EPs: 7-inch

DOOTO ... 5-10 57-61
DOOTONE ... 5-10 56-57
LOMA (244 "Redd Foxx") ... 5-8 66
(Promotional issue only.)

LPs: 10/12-inch

ATLANTIC ... 5-10 75
AUTHENTIC ... 15-25 55-56
DOOTO ... 5-15 60-74
DOOTONE ... 10-20 57
KING ... 5-10 69-71
LAFF ... 5-10 79
LOMA ... 8-12 66-68
MF ... 5-8
RCA ... 5-10 72
W.B. ... 8-10 69

FRACTION

Singles: 7-inch

ANGELUS (571 "Sanc Divided") ... 40-60 71

LPs: 10/12-inch

ANGELUS (5005 "Moon Blood") ... 1200-1500 71
Members: Jim Beach; Don Swanson; Vic Hemme; Curt Swanson.

FRALEY, Toad

Singles: 7-inch

ALLIED (10009 "Rock and Roll Music Box") ... 25-40 59

FRAMPTON, Peter LP '72

Singles: 7-inch

A&M (1795 thru 1972) ... 4-6 74-77
A&M (1988 "Tried to Love") ... 4-6 77
(With Mick Jagger.)
A&M (1988 "Tried to Love") ... 10-15 77
(White label. Promotional issue only.)
A&M (2000 series) ... 4-6 78-81
ATLANTIC (89463 "Lying") ... 3-5 86

Picture Sleeves

A&M (1795 "Show Me the Way") ... 4-8 76
A&M (1832 "Baby, I Love Your Way") ... 4-8 76
A&M (1941 "I'm in You") ... 4-6 77
A&M (1972 "Signed, Sealed, & Delivered") .. 4-6 77
A&M (1988 "Tried to Love") ... 4-6 77
A&M (2148 "I Can't Stand It No More") ... 4-6 79
ATLANTIC (89463 "Lying") ... 3-5 86

LPs: 10/12-inch

A&M (3619 "Somethin's Happening") ... 8-12 74
A&M (3703 "Frampton Comes Alive") ... 10-15 76
(Two discs.)
A&M (3703 "Frampton Comes Alive") ... 10-15 79
(Picture disc.)
A&M (3710 "Where I Should Be") ... 8-12 79
A&M (3722 "Breaking All the Rules") ... 5-10 81
A&M (4348 "Wind of Change") ... 8-15 72
A&M (4512 "Frampton") ... 8-12 75
A&M (4704 "I'm in You") ... 8-10 77
A&M (4704 "I'm in You") ... 15-25 77
(Picture disc. Promotional issue only.)
A&M (4905 "The Art of Control") ... 5-10 82
ATLANTIC (848 "Frampton Is Alive") ... 10-15 86
(Promotional issue only.)
ATLANTIC (81290 "Premonition") ... 5-10 86
ATLANTIC (82030 "When All the Pieces Fit") ... 5-10 89
Also see FRAMPTON'S CAMEL
Also see JAGGER, Mick
Also see STARR, Ringo
Also see TAGES

FRAN, Carol

Singles: 7-inch

EXCELLO (2118 "Emmitt Lee") ... 15-20 57
EXCELLO (2133 "I Quit My Knockin' ") ... 10-15 58
EXCELLO (2156 "Knock Knock") ... 10-15 59
EXCELLO (2175 "Hold Me") ... 15-25 60
JOSIE (1016 "I'm Gonna Try") ... 4-8 70
KHOURY'S (735 "So Tired of Crying") ... 8-12 61
PORT (3000 "I'm Gonna Try") ... 5-10 65
PORT (3005 "It's My Turn Now") ... 5-10 65
PORT (3006 "I Know") ... 5-10 65

FRAN & FLO

Singles: 7-inch

JUPITER (211 "I Got the Blues") ... 10-20 57
JUPITER (212 "You Walked Out the Door") ... 40-50 57

FRANCE, Steve, & Varatones

Singles: 7-inch

KAY (101 "Repeto") ... 8-12
RENOWN (110 "Bad Boy") ... 75-125 59

FRANCE, Vicki, & Kings

Singles: 7-inch

SPARKETTE (1002 "Cry on My Shoulder") ... 15-25 59

FRANCETTES
(Fran-Cettes)

Singles: 7-inch

BESCHE (100 "Cradle Love") ... 10-20 63
CHALLENGE (59255 "Nothing to Write Home About") ... 5-10 64
SLEEPER (201 "I'm Leaving You") ... 30-40 63
(First issue.)
VALIANT (718 "I Know Him Well") ... 5-10 65
WOLFIE (104 "I'm Leaving You") ... 15-25 63
Member: Frances Gray.

FRANCIS, Connie P&R/R&B '58

Singles: 78 rpm

MGM (12015 "Freddy") ... 50-100 55
MGM (12056 "Oh, Please Make Him Jealous") ... 50-75 55
MGM (12122 thru 12490) ... 10-20 55-57
MGM (12588 "Who's Sorry Now") ... 30-50 57
MGM (12647 "I'm Sorry I Made You Cry") ... 30-50 58
MGM (12683 "Stupid Cupid") ... 50-100 58
MGM (12713 "Fallin' ") ... 50-100 58

Singles: 7-inch

GSF ... 4-6 73
IVANHOE ... 4-6 '70s
MGM CELEBRITY SCENE (CS6-5 "Connie Francis") ... 30-50 66
(Boxed, five-disc set with bio insert and title strips.)
MGM (9 "Rock-a-Bye Your Baby with a Dixie Melody") ... 20-30 60
(Stereo.)
MGM (10 "I Almost Lost My Mind") ... 20-30 60
(Stereo.)
MGM (100 series) ... 5-10 62-64
(Golden Circle reissue series.)
MGM (3000 series) ... 4-6 71
MGM (12015 "Freddy") ... 75-100 55
MGM (12056 "Oh, Please Make Him Jealous") ... 50-75 55
MGM (12122 "My Treasure") ... 25-35 55
MGM (12191 "My First Real Love") ... 40-50 56
MGM (12251 "Forgetting") ... 25-35 56
MGM (12335 "My Sailor Boy") ... 20-30 56
MGM (12375 "I Never Had a Sweetheart") ... 20-30 56
MGM (12440 "No Other One") ... 20-30 57
MGM (12490 "Eighteen") ... 20-30 57
MGM (12588 "Who's Sorry Now") ... 10-20 57
MGM (12647 "I'm Sorry I Made You Cry") ... 10-20 58
MGM (12683 "Stupid Cupid") ... 10-20 58
MGM (12713 "Fallin' ") ... 10-20 58
MGM (12738 "My Happiness") ... 10-20 58
MGM (12769 "If I Didn't Care") ... 10-20 59
MGM (12793 "Lipstick on Your Collar") ... 10-20 59
(Monaural.)
MGM (12793 "Lipstick on Your Collar") ... 30-40 59
(Stereo. This is very likely in the 50000 series, like Connie's other stereo singles; however, we do not yet have that number. Since we know it exists, it is listed here for now.)
MGM (12824 "You're Gonna Miss Me") ... 10-20 59
MGM (12841 "Among My Souvenirs") ... 10-20 59
MGM (12878 "Mama") ... 10-20 60
MGM (12899 thru 13051, except 13005) . 10-15 60-61
MGM (13005 "Swanee") ... 15-20 61
MGM (13059 thru 13470) ... 8-12 62-66
MGM (13505 "Empty Chapel"/"When You Come Home Again") ... 10-15 66
MGM (13505 "Empty Chapel"/"It's a Different World") ... 8-12 66
(Note different flip side.)
MGM (13545 "Letter from a Soldier") ... 8-12 66
MGM (13550 "A Nurse in the U.S. Army Corp") ... 15-20 66
(Promotional issue only.)
MGM (13578 "So Nice") ... 8-12 66
MGM (13610 "Spanish Nights and You") ... 8-12 66
MGM (13665 "Another Page") ... 8-12 67
MGM (13708 thru 14034) ... 5-10 67-69
MGM (14058 "Gone Like the Wind") ... 10-15 69
MGM (14091 "Mr. Love") ... 10-15 69
MGM (14853 "I'm Me Again") ... 5-10 81
MGM (50117 "My Happiness") ... 30-40 58
(Stereo.)
MGM (50129 "You're Gonna Miss Me") ... 30-40 59
(Stereo.)
MGM (50133 "Among My Souvenirs") ... 30-40 59
(Stereo.)
POLYDOR ... 3-5 83

Picture Sleeves

MGM (12738 "My Happiness") ... 25-50 58
(Pink sleeve.)
MGM (12738 "My Happiness") ... 55-65 58
(Black and white sleeve.)
MGM (12769 "If I Didn't Care") ... 15-25 59
MGM (12899 "Everybody's Somebody's Fool") ... 15-25 60
MGM (12923 "My Heart Has a Mind of Its Own") ... 15-25 60
MGM (12964 "Many Tears Ago") ... 15-25 60
MGM (12971 "Where the Boys Are") ... 10-20 61
MGM (12995 "Breakin' in a Brand New Broken Heart") ... 10-20 61
MGM (13019 "Together") ... 10-20 61
MGM (13039 "Dreamboat") ... 10-20 61
MGM (13051 "When the Boy in Your Arms") ... 10-20 61
MGM (13059 "Don't Break the Heart That Loves You") ... 10-15 62
MGM (13074 "Second Hand Love") ... 10-15 62
MGM (13087 "Vacation") ... 10-15 62
MGM (13096 "I Was Such a Fool") ... 10-15 62
MGM (13116 "I'm Gonna Be Warm This Winter") ... 10-15 62
MGM (13127 "Follow the Boys") ... 10-15 63
MGM (13143 "If My Pillow Could Talk") ... 10-15 63
MGM (13160 "Drownin' My Sorrows") ... 10-15 63
MGM (13176 "Your Other Love") ... 10-15 63
MGM (13203 "In the Summer of His Years") ... 10-15 63
MGM (13214 "Blue Winter") ... 10-15 64
MGM (13237 "Be Anything") ... 10-15 64
MGM (13256 "Looking for Love") ... 10-15 64
MGM (13287 "Don't Ever Leave Me") ... 10-15 64
MGM (13303 "Whose Heart Are You Breaking Tonight") ... 10-15
MGM (13331 "Wishing It Was You") ... 10-15
MGM (13470 "Love Is Me, Love Is You") . 10-20
MGM (13505 "Empty Chapel") ... 10
(Note different flip side.)
MGM (13550 "A Nurse in the U.S. Army Corp") ... 67
(Promotional issue only.) 69
MGM (13610 "Spanish Nights a[illegible] 69
MGM (13773 "My Heart Cries [illegible]
MGM (14058 "Gone Like th[illegible] 58-62
MGM (14091 "Mr. Love") [illegible] 2-15 '60s
[illegible] 40-50 59
MGM ... 10-15 70
... 30-40 58
LEO [illegible]
LION (70126 [illegible]
MGM (100 [illegible]
MGM (F[illegible]
(Yell[illegible]

MGM (SE-3686 "Who's Sorry Now") ... 15-25 60
(Reprocessed stereo.)
MGM (E-3761 "Exciting Connie Francis") 25-35 58
(Yellow label. Monaural.)
MGM (SE-3761 "Exciting Connie Francis") ... 30-40 58
(Yellow label. Stereo.)
MGM (E-3776 thru E-3969) ... 20-35 59-61
(Monaural.)
MGM (SE-3776 thru SE-3969) ... 25-40 59-61
(Stereo.)
MGM (E-4000 series, except E-4023) ... 15-25 62-68
(Monaural.)
MGM (SE-4000 series) ... 15-30 62-69
(Stereo.)
MGM (E-4023 "Fun Songs for Children") . 20-40 62
MGM (5400 series) ... 5-10
MGM (10000 series) ... 8-12 71
MGM (90000 series) ... 10-15 '60s
(Capitol Record Club series.)
MATI-MOR (8002 "Brylcreem Presents Sing Along with Connie Francis") ... 10-20 61
(Promotional issue, made for Brylcreem.)
MATI-MOR (8002 "Silvirkin Shampoo Presents Sing Along with Connie Francis") ... 10-20 61
(Promotional issue, made for Silvirkin Shampoo.)
METRO ... 10-15 65-67
MGM/SESSIONS ... 10-12 75
POLYDOR ... 5-10 83
SUFFOLK ... 8-12
Session: Jordanaires; Boots Randolph.
Also see CRAMER, Floyd
Also see JORDANAIRES
Also see RANDOLPH, Boots
Also see SOUL, Jimmy, & Belmonts / Connie Francis

FRANCIS, Connie, & Marvin Rainwater

Singles: 78 rpm

MGM (12555 "Majesty of Love") ... 35-50 57

Singles: 7-inch

MGM (12555 "Majesty of Love") ... 50-75 57
Also see FRANCIS, Connie
Also see RAINWATER, Marvin

FRANCIS, Connie, & Hank Williams Jr.

LPs: 10/12-inch

MGM (4251 "Great Country Favorites") ... 15-25 64
Also see FRANCIS, Connie
Also see WILLIAMS, Hank, Jr.

FRANCIS, Hubert

Singles: 7-inch

DREW-BLAN (1014 "Here We Go Again") 5-10 62

FRANCIS, Jim

Singles: 7-inch

GULFCO (401 "Travelin' ") ... 150-250

FRANCISCANS

Singles: [illegible]inch

JIMBO (4001 "Mother Ple[illegible] Answer Me") ... 20-30 '60s

FRANCISCO
(Francisco Lupica) [illegible]/12-inch

COSMIC BE[illegible] [illegible]c Beam Experience ... 50-75 76

FRA[illegible]

Singles: 78 rpm

[illegible] "Off to Parts Unknown") ... 10-15 53

Singles: 7-inch

[illegible]25 "Off to Parts Unknown") ... 15-25 53

[illegible], Joe, & Knights

Singles: 7-inch

PAR (10782 "Can't Find a Way") ... 8-12 66
[illegible]AY (100463 "Five Elephants in a [illegible]olkswagon") ... 10-20 64
[illegible]RIM (4109 "Palisades Park") ... 8-12 63

FRANK, Johnny

Singles: 78 rpm

HERALD (453 "Li'l Lover") ... 10-15 55

Singles: 7-inch

HERALD (453 "Li'l Lover") ... 20-30 55

FRANK, Lenny

Singles: 7-inch

A.B.S. (214 "Let's Go Steady for the Summer") ... 10-15 63

FRANK, Stanley
Singles: 7-inch
ATTIC (130 "S'Cool Days")........................ 10-20 76

FRANK & ERNIE
Singles: 7-inch
CREST (1056 "Spotlight") 10-15 58

FRANK & JACK
(With the Monulanes; with Nightwinds)
Singles: 7-inch
BERGEN (100 "Twas the Night Before Christmas").. 25-30 57
EMBLEM (108 "Count On Me")............... 10-20
FELSTED (8539 "Oh My Darling")........... 15-25 59
JOSIE (827 "Twas the Night Before Christmas").. 10-15 57

FRANKIE & C-NOTES
Singles: 7-inch
RICHIE (2 "Forever & Ever")........... 1000-2000 61

FRANKIE & C-NOTES / Montels
Singles: 7-inch
TIMES SQUARE (10 "Forever & Ever"/"Union Hall").. 20-30 63
(Green vinyl.)
Also see FRANKIE & C-NOTES
Also see MONTELS

FRANKIE & DAMONS
Singles: 7-inch
JCP (1031 "Everybody's Time")............. 10-20 67
JCP (1057 "I Hope You Find the Way")... 10-20 67

FRANKIE & ECHOS
Singles: 7-inch
SAVOY (1544 "Come Back Baby")......... 10-15 58

FRANKIE & FASHIONS
Singles: 7-inch
AVENUE D (19 "Linda")...................................4-6 93
(Black vinyl. 900 made.)
AVENUE D (19 "Linda")...................................5-8 93
(Mauve vinyl. 100 made.)
AVENUE D (21 "Blame It on Another Rainy Day") 4-6 94
(Black vinyl. 900 made.)
AVENUE D (21 "Blame It on Another Rainy Day") 5-8 94
(Clear vinyl. 100 made.)
CLASSIC ARTISTS (137 "This Time It's Forever")...4-6 94
(Red vinyl. Reportedly 900 made.)
CRESCENT (501 "Looking for an Echo").....3-5 '90s
CRYSTAL BALL (162 "United in Harmony")..3-5 94
(Black vinyl. 500 made.)
49TH ST. (34159 "...at Do I Have to Do") ..3-5 93
49TH ST. (36391 "Ho...e, Darling")..........3-5 93
STOOP SOUNDS (110 "...nce I Don't Have You") 100-150 97

FRANKIE & FASHIO...S / ...OE
Singl... 7-inch
STOOP SOUNDS (111 "...ton"/"Countdown to Love").................................... 50-100 97
Also see FRANKIE & FASHI...

FRANKIE & FLIPS
Singles: 7-in...
NO MAR (107 "Maxine's Place")...... 61
SAVOY (1602 "Pop Eye Twist")...... 61

FRANKIE & JOHNNY
Singles: 7-inch
BLAST OFF ....
EPIC (10010 "Over the Rainbow") 5
HICKORY (1391 "I'll Hold You")........... 10
LIBERTY (55271 "Do You Love Me") 15-2
LIDO (604 "Together Tonight")................
MERCURY (72955 "Hometown, U.S.A.") ...5-10
SABRINA (101/102 "Do You Love Me"/"My First ... 15-25
Love").. 15-25
SABRINA (331 "Do You Love Me")............
Members: Frankie Sardo; Johnny Sardo.
Also see SARDO, Frankie
Also see SARDO, Johnny

FRANKIE & JOHNNY
Singles: 7-inch
INT'L ARTISTS (112 "Sweet Thang") 10-15 66
INT'L ARTISTS (117 "A Present of the Past").. 10-15 67

FRANKIE & LARRY
Singles: 7-inch
CAPITOL (4415 "A Fool for You")............30-40 60

FRANKIE & MARGIE
Singles: 7-inch
WARWICK (101 "Bop Guitar") 50-60

FRANKIE & MATADORES
Singles: 7-inch
PEERLESS (9012 "With a Girl Like You") 20-30

FRANKIE & TEENTONES
Singles: 7-inch
SONIC (4502 "Told You Little Baby") ...100-200

FRANKLIN, Al
Singles: 7-inch
FINCH (352 "Down on the Farm") 100-125

FRANKLIN, Alan, Explosion
LPs: 10/12-inch
ALADDIN ("Come Home Baby") 50-100 68
(Selection number not known.)
HORNE (888 "The Blues Climax")...........30-50 70

FRANKLIN, Aretha *R&B '60*
(With Rev. C.L. Franklin.)
Singles: 78 rpm
CHECKER...10-20 57
J-V-B (47 "Never Grow Old")..................25-50 56
Singles: 12-inch
ARISTA...4-8 84-86
Singles: 7-inch
ARISTA (Black vinyl) 3-5 80-91
ARISTA (9528 "Jumpin' Jack Flash") 5-8 86
(Colored vinyl.)
ATLANTIC (2000 series) 4-8 67-74
ATLANTIC (3000 series) 4-6 74-79
ATLANTIC (13000 series) 3-6
BATTLE (45000 series) 4-6 62
CHECKER (861 "Never Grow Old")..........15-25 57
CHECKER (941 "Precious Lord") 10-15 60
COLUMBIA (Except 44000 series) 5-10 60-67
COLUMBIA (44000 series) 5-10 67-68
CHESS 4-6 73
J-V-B (47 "Never Grow Old")..................250-350 56
PHILCO (24 "Respect"/"Soul Serenade").10-20 67
("Hip Pocket" flexi-disc.)
Picture Sleeves
ARISTA...3-5 85-87
COLUMBIA (42266 "I Surrender Dear") ...10-20 62
COLUMBIA (42456 "Don't Cry Baby") 10-20 62
COLUMBIA (42796 "Here's Where I Came In")...10-20 63
EPs: 7-inch
ATLANTIC (8176 "Lady Soul")...............10-20 68
(Stereo. Juke box issue only.)
ATLANTIC (33093 "Let It Be")...................10-15 70
(Promotional issue only.)
ATLANTIC (78139 "Aretha Franklin") 10-20 67
(Stereo. Juke box issue only.)
COLUMBIA...10-15 64
(Juke box issues.)
LPs: 10/12-inch
ARISTA..5-10 80-89
ATLANTIC (Except "QD" series)................8-15 67-79
ATLANTIC ("QD" series) 15-20 73
(Quadraphonic.)
BATTLE 5-15
CANDLELITE..8-10 77
CHECKER (10009 "Songs of Faith") 15-25 65
CHESS ("Gospel") 50-100 58
(Selection number not known.)
...OLUMBIA (12 "Aretha Franklin")............10-15 68
...UMBIA (1612 thru 2281).....................12-25 61-64
...ural.)
...BIA (2300 thru 2700 series).........10-20 65-67
...)
... (8402 thru 9081) 15-30 61-64
...fix. Stereo.)
...0 thru 9700 series).........10-20 65-69
...Stereo.)
...series).........................5-10 73
...ries).............................5-10 72-82
....10-12 68-71
....5-10 79
Also ...
Also ...Byrds / Aretha Franklin / ...
...s / Simon & ...
...klin

Also see SANTANA
Also see SIMON, Paul
Also see SWEET INSPIRATIONS

FRANKLIN, Aretha, & George Benson *P&R/R&B '81*
Singles: 7-inch
ARISTA (0624 "Love All the Hurt Away") 3-5 81
Also see BENSON, George

FRANKLIN, Aretha, & James Brown *R&B '89*
Singles: 7-inch
ARISTA (9884 "Gimme Your Love")............3-5 89
Picture Sleeves
ARISTA (9884 "Gimme Your Love").............4-6 89
Also see BROWN, James

FRANKLIN, Aretha, with James Cleveland & Southern California Community Choir
EPs: 7-inch
ATLANTIC (1025 "Amazing Grace")............4-8 72
(Promotional issue only.)
LPs: 10/12-inch
ATLANTIC...6-10 72

FRANKLIN, Aretha, & Larry Graham
Singles: 7-inch
ARISTA (9623 "If You Need My Love Tonight")..3-5 87

FRANKLIN, Aretha, & Whitney Houston *P&R '89*
Singles: 7-inch
ARISTA 3-5 89
Picture Sleeves
ARISTA 3-5 89

FRANKLIN, Aretha, & Elton John *P&R '89*
Singles: 7-inch
ARISTA 3-5 89
Picture Sleeves
ARISTA 3-5 89
Also see JOHN, Elton

FRANKLIN, Aretha, & George Michael *P&R/R&B '87*
Singles: 7-inch
ARISTA 3-5 87
Picture Sleeves
ARISTA 3-5 87

FRANKLIN, Aretha / Union Gap / Blood, Sweat & Tears / Moby Grape
EPs: 7-inch
COLUMBIA (791 "The Tipalet Experience")...25-35 68
(Columbia Special Products issue for Tipalet cigars. Reportedly 500 made.)
Also see BLOOD, SWEAT & TEARS
Also see FRANKLIN, Aretha
Also see MOBY GRAPE
Also see PUCKETT, Gary

FRANKLIN, Doug *P&R '58*
(With the Bluenotes)
Singles: 7-inch
COLONIAL...10-20 58-59
Also see BLUENOTES
Also see FRANKLIN BROTHERS

FRANKLIN, Erma *P&R/R&B '67*
Singles: 7-inch
BRUNSWICK (55403 "Gotta Find Me a Lover")..5-10 69
BRUNSWICK (55415 "Saving My Love")...5-10 69
BRUNSWICK (55424 "It Could Have Been Me")...5-10 69
EPIC (9468 thru 9610).............................10-20 61-63
SHOUT (221 "Piece of My Heart")..............8-12 67
SHOUT (234 "I'm Just Not Ready for Love")..8-12 68
LPs: 10/12-inch
BRUNSWICK (754147 "Soul Sister") 15-25 69
EPIC (619 "Her Name Is Erma")..............30-40 62
(Stereo.)
EPIC (3824 "Her Name Is Erma") 20-30 62
(Monaural.)
Also see PRICE, Lloyd

FRANKLIN, Gene
("Vocal By Texas Ray"; with His House Rockin' Spacemen; with Spacemen)
Singles: 7-inch
ALTON (400 "Hackensack") 15-20 60
(Reissued as by Texas Ray.)
KAYDEE (50001 "Itchin' and Twistin") 15-25 60
Also see TEXAS RAY

FRANKLIN, Joe
(With the Mimosa Boys)
Singles: 78 rpm
MGM (11612 "Hillbilly Boy")......................15-25 53
Singles: 7-inch
MGM (11612 "Hillbilly Boy")......................30-50 53
RENOWN (113 "Who Put the Pop in the Punch")..5-10 60

FRANKLIN, Mike
Singles: 7-inch
DANTE (3009 "All Alone")........................30-40 61

FRANKLIN, Morty
Singles: 7-inch
CADENCE (1321 "Jamaica Farewell").......5-10 57

FRANKLIN, Pete
Singles: 78 rpm
RCA (0012 "Casey Brown Blues")............30-50 47
LPs: 10/12-inch
PRESTIGE BLUESVILLE (1068 "Blues of Pete Franklin") 15-20 63

FRANKLIN, Rev. C.L.
Singles: 78 rpm
CHESS (1631 "The Old Ship of Zion") 5-10 56
Singles: 7-inch
CHESS (1631 "The Old Ship of Zion") 10-20 56
Also see FRANKLIN, Aretha

FRANKLIN, Roy
Singles: 78 rpm
EMPIRE (502 "Joni")...............................10-20 50
Singles: 7-inch
EMPIRE (502 "Joni")...............................20-30 50
HONEY (100 "My Diary")..........................15-25

FRANKLIN, Sammy, Orchestra
Singles: 7-inch
CASH (1049 "Chicken Scratch")..............15-25 57

FRANKLIN, Sonny Boy
Singles: 78 rpm
EDDIE'S 20-30 49

FRANKLIN BROTHERS
Singles: 7-inch
BLUE SKY (735 "Oh, Laura") 200-250 59
COLONIAL (7000 "So Real")..................75-125 59
Also see FRANKLIN, Doug

FRANKS, Jay, Orchestra
Singles: 78 rpm
RPM (357 "Stripped Gears")....................15-25 52
Singles: 7-inch
RPM (357 "Stripped Gears")....................25-50 52
Also see LEE, Jimmy, & Artis

FRANKS, Tillman *C&W '63*
(With the Cedar Grove Three; Tillman Franks Singers)
Singles: 78 rpm
GOTHAM (7412 "Hi-Tone Poppa")..........10-15 51
Singles: 7-inch
GOTHAM (7412 "Hi-Tone Poppa")..........25-35 51
HILLTOP (3000 "Hey Good Lookin' ") 5-10 64
HILLTOP (3003 "Cold Cold Heart") 5-10 64
HILLTOP (3005 "Pretty Rainbow") 5-10 65
PAULA (1210 "Take the Chain off Your Brain")..4-8 69
STARDAY (651 "Tadpole").......................10-15 63
STARDAY (670 "When the World's On Fire")..10-15 64
LPs: 10/12-inch
PICKWICK/HILLTOP (6019 "Tillman Franks Singers")..8-12 65
Session: Faron Young.
Also see YOUNG, Faron

FRANTIC
Singles: 7-inch
LIZARD (20002 "Shady Sam") 8-12 70
LPs: 10/12-inch
LIZARD (20103 "Conception")..................15-25 71
Members: Max Byfuglin; Kim Sherman; Phil Head; Jim Haas; Dennis Devlin.

FRANTICS P&R '59

Singles: 7-inch

BOLO (728 "Pony Maronie")................. 15-20 62
DOLTON (2 "Straight Flush")................. 15-20 59
DOLTON (6 "Fog Cutter")..................... 15-20 59
DOLTON (13 "Werewolf"/ "Checkerboard")..................................... 15-25 59
DOLTON (16 "Werewolf"/"No Werewolf").. 15-25 60
DOLTON (24 "Delilah")........................... 15-25 60
DOLTON (31 "Yankee Doodlin'")............ 10-20 61
DOLTON (33 "San Antonio Rose")......... 10-20 61
REO (8468 "Werewolf")......................... 10-20 61
(Canadian.)
SEAFAIR (111 "San Francisco Swim").......5-10 64
VIBRA-SONIC...5-10 '60s
Members: Ron Petersen; Dick Goodman; Jim Manolides; Chuck Schoning; Bob Hosko.
Also see ACCENTS
Also see MOBY GRAPE

FRANTICS

Singles: 7-inch

SUNCO (1008 "Route 66").................... 75-125

FRANTICS FOUR
("Vocal By Bobby Shane")

Singles: 7-inch

GULFSTREAM (1000 "T.V. Mama").... 100-200

FRASER, Jan

Singles: 7-inch

LONDON (1976 "Night Train")................ 10-20 60

FRASIER, Clavin
(With the T.J. Fowler Orchestra)

Singles: 78 rpm

SAVOY (858 "Little Baby Child")............. 10-15 52

Singles: 7-inch

SAVOY (858 "Little Baby Child")............. 15-25 52
Also see FOWLER, T.J.

FRATERNITY BROTHERS

Singles: 78 rpm

CADENCE (1309 "In the Evening")............5-10 57
VERVE (10081 "Passion Flower")........... 15-20 57

Singles: 7-inch

CADENCE (1309 "In the Evening")......... 10-15 57
VERVE (10081 "Passion Flower")........... 15-20 57

FRATERNITY MEN

Singles: 7-inch

COURIER (114 "Little Star").................... 20-30 64

FRATERNITY OF MAN

Singles: 7-inch

ABC (11106 "Don't Bogart Me")..................5-10 68

LPs: 10/12-inch

ABC (647 "Fraternity of Man")................. 15-25 68
DOT (25955 "Get It On").......................... 10-20 69
Members: Larry Wagner; Martin Kibbee; Warren Klein; Richard Hayward; Elliot Ingber.

FRATS

Singles: 7-inch

COCONUT GROOVE (2030 "Do You Love Me").. 25-35 68
WASHINGTON SQUARE (2030 "Do You Love Me")... 15-25

FRAZE, Ron

Singles: 7-inch

YOLK (103 "Baby Hold Me").................... 40-60 61

FRAZER, Johnny

Singles: 7-inch

STAR-X (504 "Rock with the Mambo").... 50-75

FRAZIER, Beulah

Singles: 78 rpm

ESSEX (705 "Salt Lake City Blues")........ 50-75

FRAZIER, Calvin

Singles: 78 rpm

J-V-B.. 50-75 56
NEW SONG (121 "Got Nobody to Tell My Troubles To").. 400-500
(May be the original label, before Savoy, but we have yet to confirm this.)
SAVOY (858 "Got Nobody to Tell My Troubles To")... 25-50 52

Singles: 7-inch

CHECKER (908 "Have Blues Must Travel").. 50-75 58
J-V-B (49 "Rock House")........................ 75-100 56
J-V-B (86 "Have Blues Must Travel")......75-100 58
SAVOY (858 "Got Nobody to Tell My Troubles To")...50-75 52

FRAZIER, Coleen

Singles: 7-inch

FABLE (614 "Your Mama's Here")............75-85 58

FRAZIER, Dallas P&R '66/C&W '67

Singles: 78 rpm

CAPITOL...5-10 54

Singles: 7-inch

AUDAN...4-8 '60s
CAPITOL (2000 thru 2400 series)...............4-8 67-69
CAPITOL (2800 & 2900 series)...............10-15 54
CAPITOL (5500 series)..............................4-8 65
JAMIE (1135 "Can't Go On")......................8-12 59
MERCURY...5-8 64
MUSIKON..5-10 61
RCA...4-6 71-73
20TH FOX..4-6 75

LPs: 10/12-inch

CAPITOL...10-20 66-67
RCA...8-12 70-71
Also see HOLLYWOOD ARGYLES

FRAZIER, Frank

Singles: 7-inch

OUR (502 "Lovin' One")..........................30-40

FRAZIER, Ray
(With the Lovers; with Moonrays; with Shades of Madness; with Sharps)

Singles: 78 rpm

EXCEL...10-15 55-56

Singles: 7-inch

BARONET (8 "Walkin' with My Baby")......40-50 62
CARRIAGE TRADE.......................................4-8
COMBO (161 "Darling")..........................75-125 59
DYNAMITE (1009 "My Dream Love")...150-200 61
EXCEL (111 "Turn Me On")......................30-40 55
EXCEL (112 "All My Love").......................30-40 56
PLAYBACK (1198 "My Son")..................400-500 58
Also see SHARPS

FREAK SCENE

Singles: 7-inch

COLUMBIA (44056 "A Million Grains of Sand")..10-20 67

LPs: 10/12-inch

COLUMBIA (2656 "Psychedelic Psoul")...50-75 67
(Monaural.)
COLUMBIA (9456 "Psychedelic Psoul").75-100 67
(Stereo.)
Members: David Bromberg; Rusty Evans; David Rubinson.
Also see DEEP, The

FREBERG, Stan P&R '51
(Stan Freberg Show; with Dick Roberts & Red Rountree; with Billy May's Orchestra; with Les Baxter's Orchestra; with Jud Conlon Chorale; with Daws Butler & June Foray; with the Toads; with George Burns Quintet)

Singles: 78 rpm

CAPITOL...20-40 50-57

Singles: 7-inch

BELFAST SPARKLING WATER (1515 "Invisible Bubbles")..50-75
(Product commercials for radio use.)
BUBBLE UP (2227 "Music to Bubble Up By")..20-30 '60s
(Product commercials for radio use.)
BUTTERNUT COFFEE (2000 "Instant Sales for Instant Butternut by Instant Freberg")..................40-50 '60s
(Product commercials for radio use.)
BUTTERNUT COFFEE (2237 "Amazing Butternut Coffee")..25-35 '60s
(Product commercials for radio use.)
CAPITOL (303 "The Do-It-Yourself Dragnet")...50-100 53
(Capitol in-house, record sales promotional issue only.)
CAPITOL (1356 "John & Marsha")...........20-30 51
CAPITOL (1711 "I've Got You Under My Skin")..20-30 51
CAPITOL (1962 "Tele Vee Shun")............20-30 52
CAPITOL (2029 "Try")..............................20-30 52
CAPITOL (2125 "Abe Snake for President")...35-45 52
CAPITOL (2279 "The World Is Waiting for the Sunrise")..20-30 52
CAPITOL (2596 "St. George and the Dragonet")...20-30 53
CAPITOL (2671 "Christmas Dragnet")......20-30 53
CAPITOL (2677 "C'est Si Bon")................20-30 53
CAPITOL (2929 "Sh-Boom")......................20-30 53
CAPITOL (2838 "Point of Order")............10-20 54
CAPITOL (2986 "Yulenet").......................15-25 54
(Reissue of *Christmas Dragnet.*)
CAPITOL (3138 "The Lone Psychiatrist") 30-40 55
CAPITOL (3249 "The Yellow Rose of Texas")...15-25 55
CAPITOL (3280 "Nuttin' for Christmas")...15-25 55
(Add $15 to $25 if accompanied by cartoon insert.)
CAPITOL (3396 "The Great Pretender")..15-25 56
CAPITOL (3480 "Heartbreak Hotel").........25-35 56
CAPITOL (3503 "Green Chritma").........15-25 56
CAPITOL (3687 "Banana Boat")...............15-25 57
(Add $25 to $35 if accompanied by banner insert.)
CAPITOL (3815 "Wun'erful, Wun'erful")...15-25 57
CAPITOL (3892 "Ya Got Trouble")...........10-20 58
CAPITOL (4097 "Green Chritma").........10-20 58
CAPITOL (4239 "The Old Payola Roll Blues")...10-20 60
CAPITOL (4433 "Comments for Our Time")..10-20 60
CAPITOL (5726 "Flackman & Reagan")...10-15 66
COCA COLA BOTTLING CO. (2227 Music to Bubble-Up By")..30-50 '60s
(Product commercials for radio use.)
CONTADINA (2574 "Pizza Anyone").......15-25 '60s
(Product commercials for radio use.)
CONTADINA (4476/4471 "The Whole Peeled Bounce"/ "Little Bitty Ballad")..................................35-50
(Product commercials for radio use. With the Hi Lo's.)
CONTADINA (4476/4477 "The Whole Peeled Bounce"/ "Program Notes")......................................35-50
(Product commercials for radio use. Note different flip.)
MILKY WAY (23300 "Tom Sweet and His Electric Milky Way Machine")...35-50
PITTSBURGH PAINT (1/2 "Four Pittsburgh Paint Commercials")..20-30
(Product commercials for radio use.)
RADIO (2225 "Who Listens to Radio")......25-40
(Promotional spots for advertising with radio.)
SOUTHERN BAPTIST CHURCH (101578 "Southern Baptist Radio and TV Commission")........15-20
(Product commercials for radio use.)
STAINLESS STEEL (1369 "Stainless Steel")...35-50
(Product commercials for radio use.)
STAN FREBERG on COMMERCIALS ("Rubblemeyer Farms")..40-60 '70s
(Promotional issue only. Commercial parodies, comparing right and wrong production of radio spots.)
TERMINIX (3540 "Floor Show, Now Going on at Your House")...30-40
(Product commercials for radio use.)
UNITED PRESBYTERIAN CHURCH (1401 "Three More Radio Messages for Our Time")......10-20
(Product commercials for radio use.)
UNITED PRESBYTERIAN CHURCH (101578 "The Presbyterian Church")..............................15-20
(Product commercials for radio use.)
ZEE (2020 "Zee with Freberg - Hey You Up There")...35-50
(Product commercials for radio use.)
ZEE (4108 "Z-E-E Spells Zee")................30-35
(Product commercials for radio use.)
ZEE (24005 "Zee Spot Commercials")......35-50
(Product commercials for radio use.)

Picture Sleeves

BUBBLE UP (2227 "Music to Bubble Up By")..85-100 '60s
(Gatefold sleeve.)
CAPITOL (415 "Wun'erful Wun'erful")......25-35 57
(Promotional issue only.)
CAPITOL (4097 "Green Chritma)..........15-25 58
CAPITOL (4329 "The Old Payola Roll Blues")...15-25 60
CAPITOL (5726 "Flackman & Reagan")...10-20 66
H.I.S. (122667 "Funny Record by Stan Freberg for H.I.S.")...35-50
(Product commercials for radio use.)
PITTSBURGH PAINT (1/2 "Four Pittsburgh Paint Commercials")..20-30
(Reads: "The Stations Representatives Assn. presents: Some Exciting new commercials for Radio!")
RADIO (2225 "Who Listens to Radio")......25-40
(Promotional spots for using radio advertising.)
SOUTHERN BAPTIST CHURCH (101578 "Southern Baptist Radio & TV Commission")............15-20
(Product commercials for radio use.)
TERMINIX (3540 "Floor Show")...............10-20
(Product commercials for radio use.)
ZEE (2020 "Zee Here, Mr. Freberg")........35-50
(Product commercials for radio use.)

EPs: 7-inch

CAPITOL (415 "Wun'erful Wun'erful")......15-25 57
(Single-sided, two track promotional issue. Add $10 to $20 if accompanied by "Two Sides of Bubbling Hilarity" insert. Issued with generic Capitol paper sleeve.)
CAPITOL (496 "Any Requests")...............20-30 54
CAPITOL (628 "Real St. George")...........15-25 55
CAPITOL (731 "Elderly Man River").........40-50 58
(Promotional issue only.)
CAPITOL (1101 "Omaha").........................15-25 59
CAPITOL (1589 "Stan Freberg")..............25-40 61
(Compact 33.)
CAPITOL (3192 "Ugly Duckling")..............15-25
CAPITOL (4097 "The Meaning of Christmas – Stan Freberg Presents His Favorite Carols")...30-50
(Promotional issue only.)
SWIMSUITSMANSHIP (2080 "Swimsuitsmanship")............................100-125
(Promotional issue only. Cover reads: "Fit Facts and Figures, You and Rose Marie Reid.")
UNITED PRESBYTERIAN CHURCH (1400 "Is God Dead?")...30-45
(Product commercials for radio use.)

LPs: 10/12-inch

BEKINS (27713 "Bekins Presents the Sound of Moving")...35-50
(Product commercials for radio use.)
BIG SOUND (2 "Jockey's Little Helper")..35-50
(Product commercials for radio use.)
BUTTERNUT COFFEE (2000 "Instant Butternut Coffee")..40-60 '60s
(Product commercials for radio use.)
CAPITOL (777 "A Child's Garden of Freberg")..20-40 57
CAPITOL (1035 "The Best of the Stan Freberg Shows")...40-60 58
CAPITOL (1242 "Stan Freberg with the Original Cast")..30-50 59
(With "T" prefix.)
CAPITOL (1242 "Stan Freberg with the Original Cast")..15-25 69
(With "DT" prefix.)
CAPITOL (1242 "Stan Freberg with the Original Cast")..8-12 75
(With "SM" prefix.)
CAPITOL (1573 "Stan Freberg Presents the United States of America, Volume 1 - the Early Years")..25-25 61
(With "W" or "SW" prefix.)
CAPITOL (1694 "Face the Funnies").......25-35 62
CAPITOL (1816 "Madison Avenue Werewolf")...25-35 62
CAPITOL (2020 "Best of Stan Freberg")..15-25 64
CAPITOL (2551 "Freberg Underground") 15-25 66
(With "T" or "ST" prefix.)
CAPITOL (2551 "Freberg Underground")..5-10 75
(With "SM" prefix.)
CAPITOL (3264 "Mickey Mouse's Birthday Party")..15-25 63
CAPITOL (11000 series)...........................5-10 78
CAPITOL (80700 "Uncle Stan Wants You")..60-80 61
(Promotional issue for the LP series, *Stan Freberg Presents the United States of America.*)
COCA COLA (2468 "The Freedle Family Singers")..175-200
COLUMBIA (105947 "Hey, Look Us Over")...60-75
(Label lists shows. Promotional issue only. With booklet.)
COLUMBIA (105948 "Hey, Look Us Over")...60-75
(Label does not list shows. Promotional issue only. With booklet.)
ESSKAY (59-2 "Esskay Commercials")...60-75
(Four one-minute spots.)
ESSKAY (2161 "Second Helping – More Rare Esskay Commercials")..60-75
(Single-sided. Product commercials for radio use.)
ESSKAY (2249 "Still More Expensive Cuts – Esskay Quality Meats")..60-75
(Single-sided. Product commercials for radio use.)
FREBERG LTD. (2343 "Woburn-Salada Tea")..35-50
(Product commercials for radio use.)

KAISER FOIL ("Message to Grocers") 35-50
(10-inch LP. Single-sided.)
KAISER FOIL (22077 "A Kaiser Foil Salesman Faces Life") 125-175
(10-inch LP. Product commercials for radio use.)
GUARDIAN MAINTENANCE (2581 "Spring Commercials") 25-35 64
(Single-sided. Product commercials for radio use.)
MEADOWGOLD (2152 "Meadowgold Dairies") 85-100
(Product commercials for radio use.)
OREGON (2039 "Oregon Soundtrack") 125-150
(Product commercials for radio use. Includes press kit.)
RAB ("More Here Than Meets The Ear") 75-125
(Promotional issue only.)
RADIO (3 "Radio Briefings") 35-50
(Promotional spots for using radio advertising.)
RADIO (1499 "More Here Than Meets the Ear") 30-45
(Promotional spots for using radio advertising.)
RADIO (2226 "Who Listens to Radio") 35-50
(Promotional spots for using radio advertising.)
TV GUIDE (2889 "TV Guide Spots") 60-75
(Product commercials for radio use.)
Note: Advertising agency discs containing commercials for radio station use are listed by product name, since there are no other label names used.
Members: Stan Freberg; Daws Butler; June Foray; George Burns; Jesse White; Peter Leeds; Paul Frees; Billy May.

FRED, John P&R '59
(With His Playboy Band; with Creepers)
Singles: 7-inch
BELL 4-6 73
JEWEL 5-10 64-65
MONTEL 10-20 59-62
N-JOY (1005 "My First Love") 8-12 64
PAULA 4-8 65-68
UNI 4-6 69-70
LPs: 10/12-inch
PAULA 15-25 66-68
UNI 10-15 70

FREDDI & AI
Singles: 78 rpm
CREST (1015 "Love On the Loose") 5-10 56
Singles: 7-inch
CREST (1015 "Love On the Loose") 10-15 56

FREDDIE & DREAMERS P&R/LP '65
Singles: 7-inch
CAPITOL (5053 "I'm Telling You Now") ... 15-20 63
CAPITOL (5137 "You Were Made for Me") 15-20 64
ERIC .... 4-6 '70s
MERCURY (72285 thru 72487) 5-10 64-65
SUPER K 4-8 70
TOWER (125 "I'm Telling You Now") 5-10 65
Picture Sleeves
MERCURY (72487 "I Don't Know") 8-12 65
EPs: 7-inch
MERCURY (74 "Interview with the Dreamers") 20-30 65
(Promotional issue only.)
MERCURY (661 "Fun Loving Freddie and the Dreamers") 20-30 65
(Juke box issue only.)
LPs: 10/12-inch
CAPITOL 8-10 76-79
MERCURY (21017 "Freddie & the Dreamers") 20-30 65
(Monaural.)
MERCURY (21026 "Do the Freddie") 20-30 65
(Monaural.)
MERCURY (21053 "Frantic Freddie") 20-30 65
(Monaural.)
MERCURY (21061 "Fun Lovin' Freddie") 20-30 66
(Monaural.)
MERCURY (61017 "Freddie & the Dreamers") 20-30 65
(Stereo.)
MERCURY (61026 "Do the Freddie") 20-30 65
(Stereo.)
MERCURY (61053 "Frantic Freddie") 20-30 65
(Stereo.)
MERCURY (61061 "Fun Lovin' Freddie") 20-30 66
(Stereo.)
TOWER (5003 "I'm Telling You Now") 20-30 65
(Also contains tracks by Linda Laine & Sinners; Four Just Men; Mike Rabin & Demons; Toggerty Five; and Heinz.)
Members: Freddie Garrity; Derek Quinn; Roy Crewsdon; Peter Birrell; Bernie Dwyer.
Also see JONES, Tom / Freddie & Dreamers / Johnny Rivers

FREDDIE & DREAMERS / Beat Merchants P&R '65
Singles: 7-inch
TOWER (127 "You Were Made for Me"/"So Fine") 10-15 65
Also see FREDDIE & DREAMERS

FREDDIE & DREAMERS / Four Just Men
Singles: 7-inch
TOWER (163 "Send a Letter to Me"/"There's Not One Thing") 5-10 65
Also see FREDDIE & DREAMERS

FREDDIE & FISHSTICKS
(Jimmy Buffett)
Singles: 7-inch
MCA (51224 "Elvis Imitator") 20-25 81
Session: Jordanaires.
Also see BUFFETT, Jimmy
Also see JORDANAIRES

FREDDIE & FLO
EPs: 7-inch
CHESS (5130 "Fun with Freddie & Flo") .. 10-15 62
LPs: 10/12-inch
CHESS (1459 "Fun with Freddie & Flo") .. 15-25 62
Members: Freddie Robinson; Flo Robinson.

FREDDIE & FREELOADERS
(Freddy & Freeloaders)
Singles: 7-inch
CROSSROAD (104 "Octopus Song") 25-35
I & I 10-20 73
LAURIE (3334 "Patty") 20-30 66
REDD HEDD 15-25 72
3 0 9 4-6
Member: Fred Halls.
Also see LITTLE PRINCE & FREELOADERS / Freddie & Freeloaders

FREDDIE & HEARTACHES
Singles: 7-inch
DOT (16247 "Mule Train") 10-15 61
SCOTT (1206 "Womp-Womp") 20-30 61

FREDDIE & HITCHHIKERS
Singles: 7-inch
BAND BOX (251 "Mop Flop") 10-20 60

FREDDIE & LOU
Singles: 7-inch
ASTRA (1003 "You'll Be Mine Tonight") ... 10-15 65
THUNDERHEAD (2150 "You'll Be Mine Tonight") 35-45 61
Members: Fred Parris; Lou Peeples.
Also see FIVE SATINS

FREDDIE & PARLIAMENTS
Singles: 7-inch
TWIRL (1003 "Darlene") 75-100 59
Also see JOHNNY & HURRICANES

FREDDIE & QUANTRILS
Singles: 7-inch
KAREM (1904 "If I Give My Heart to You") 1000-1500 64

FREDDIE & SWINGIN' BACHELORS
Singles: 7-inch
KNOLL ("Snookie Baby") 50-70
(No selection number used.)

FREDDY & CLAIRE / Freddy Dame
Singles: 7-inch
REPRISE (20049 "After School"/"Love Is a Game") 10-15 62
Member: Freddy Dame.
Also see DAME, Freddy

FREDDY & DYNAMICS
Singles: 7-inch
USA (824 "I'll Be Forever Loving You") 100-150 66

FREDDY & FAT BOYS
Singles: 7-inch
FAT MAN (101 "Why Do Fools Fall in Love") 15-20

FREDDY & KINFOLK
Singles: 7-inch
DADE (2016 "Blabbermouth") 10-20 68
DADE (2024 "Last Take") 10-15 69
Also see SCOTT, Freddy

FREDDY & LONNIE
(Freddy & Lonie)
Singles: 7-inch
LA RAE (501 "Hot Doggin'") 20-30 63
WED ("Another Love") 10-20 62
(Selection number not known.)
WESTERN (21 "Allen's Way") 10-20 62
Members: Freddy Countryman; Lonnie Allen.
Also see COUNTRYMAN, Freddy

FREDERICK, Dotty
Singles: 7-inch
20TH FOX (115 "Ricky") 10-15 58

FREDERICK, Tommy, & Hi-Notes
Singles: 7-inch
CARLTON (450 "I'm Not Pretending") 10-15 58
CORAL (62170 "Sundown") 40-50 60

FREDRIC
Singles: 7-inch
EVOLUTION (1001 "5 O'Clock Traffic") ... 15-25 69
FORTE (3001 "5 O'Clock Traffic") 15-25 68
LPs: 10/12-inch
FORTE (80461 "Phases and Faces") .750-1000 68
Members: Joe McCarger; Ron Bera; Steve Thrall.

FREE
Singles: 7-inch
ATCO (6662 "Decision for Lost Soul Blue") 5-10 69
MARQUEE (448 "Decision for Lost Soul Blue") 15-25 69

FREE LP '69
Singles: 7-inch
A&M 4-8 70-71
ISLAND 4-6 72
Picture Sleeves
A&M 4-8 70
LPs: 10/12-inch
A&M 8-15 69-75
ISLAND (Except 7) 8-10 73
ISLAND (7 "The Free Story") 25-30 73
(Includes booklet. Promotional issue only.)
Members: Andy Fraser; Paul Rodgers; Simon Kirke; Paul Kossoff.
Also see BACK STREET CRAWLER

FREE, Billy
Singles: 7-inch
DIANNE (407 "I'll Tear Your Playhouse Down") 50-75

FREE, Stan
Singles: 7-inch
AMY (896 "Gideon's Run") 5-10 64
LPs: 10/12-inch
OLD TOWN (2002 "Piano a la Percussion") 10-20 61

FREE DESIGN
Singles: 7-inch
PROJECT 3 .... 5-10 67-71
LPs: 10/12-inch
PROJECT 3 (4006 "Free Design Sing for Very Important People") 10-20 70
PROJECT 3 (5019 "Kites Are Fun") 10-20 67
PROJECT 3 (5031 "You Could Be Born Again") 10-20 68
PROJECT 3 (5037 "Heaven/Earth") 8-12 69
PROJECT 3 (5045 "Stars/Time/Bubbles Love") 8-12 70
PROJECT 3 (5061 "One By One") 8-12 72

FREE FOR ALL
Singles: 7-inch
CHALLENGE (59339 "Show Me the Way") 10-15 66

FREE SPIRITS
Singles: 7-inch
ABC 5-10 66-67
Picture Sleeves
ABC (10873 "Tattoo Man") 20-30 66
LPs: 10/12-inch
ABC 15-20 67

FREE THINKERS
Singles: 7-inch
MALA (517 "She's Hurt") 10-15 65
MALA (532 "Why, Why, Why") 10-15 66

FREEBEES
Singles: 7-inch
MUSITRON (1061/2 "Seymour The Beatnik Elf") 10-20 60

FREEBEEZ
Singles: 7-inch
STRANGE (2216 "Walk Away") 15-25 66

FREEBORNE
LPs: 10/12-inch
MONITOR (607 "Peak Impression") 75-125 67
Members: Nick Castolin; Bob Margolin; Dave Codd.

FREED, Alan
(With His Rock 'N Roll Band)
Singles: 78 rpm
CORAL 10-30 56-58
Singles: 7-inch
CORAL (61626 "Right Now, Right Now"). 15-25 56
CORAL (61660 "Camel Rock") 15-25 56
CORAL (61749 "Rock & Roll Boogie") 15-25 56
CORAL (61818 "Sentimental Journey") ... 10-20 58
EPs: 7-inch
CORAL (81136 "Rock 'N Roll Dance Party") 30-50 56
LPs: 10/12-inch
BRUNSWICK (54043 "The Alan Freed Rock 'N Roll Show") 75-100 58
(With "Guests" Buddy Holly & Crickets, Jackie Wilson & Terry Noland.)
CORAL (57063 "Rock 'N Roll Dance Party, Vol. 1") 40-60 56
(With the Modernaires.)
CORAL (57115 "Rock 'N Roll Dance Party, Vol. 2") 40-60 56
(With Jimmy Cavallo & His House Rockers.)
CORAL (57177 "TV Record Hop") 40-60 57
CORAL (57213 "Rock Around the Block") 40-60 58
CORAL (57216 "Alan Freed Presents the King's Henchmen") 40-60 58
(With King Curtis, Sam "The Man" Taylor, Count Hastings, Kenny Burrell, Everett Barksdale, Ernie Hayes.)
Also see CAVALLO, Jimmy, & His House Rockers
Also see KING CURTIS
Also see HOLLY, Buddy
Also see NOLAND, Terry
Also see TAYLOR, Sam "The Man
Also see WILSON, Jackie

FREED, Alan, Steve Allen, Al "Jazzbo" Collins & Modernaires
("With George Cates' Out Of Spacers")
Singles: 78 rpm
CORAL (61693 "The Space Man") 8-12 56
Singles: 7-inch
CORAL (61693 "The Space Man") 15-25 56
Also see COLLINS, Al
Also see FREED, Alan

FREEDOM NORTH
Singles: 7-inch
AQUARIUS (5006 "Losing You") 5-10 70
AQUARIUS (5008 "Ordinary Man") 5-10 70
AQUARIUS (5015 "Gone Forever") 5-10 70
GAMMA (611 "Doctor Tom") 5-10 70
(All above are Canadian releases.)
LPs: 10/12-inch
AQUARIUS (501 "Freedom North") 70-90 70
(Canadian.)
Member: Bill Hill.
Also see J.B. & PLAYBOYS

FREEDOM ROAD
Singles: 7-inch
IGL (193 "Hayseed") .... 25-35 '60s

FREEFALL THREE
Singles: 7-inch
CUCA (1174 "616") 15-25 64
Members: Doug Tank; Roy Malvitz; Lee Breest.

FREELANCERS
Singles: 7-inch
FREELANCE (20 "High School Flame") 50-100
(Also issued as by Dan Williams & the Freelancers.)
Member: Dan Williams.
Also see WILLIAMS, Dan, & Freelancers

FREEMAN, Arthur
(Art Freeman)
Singles: 7-inch
DADE (1852 "Shirley")....10-15 62
EXCELLO (2322 "Played Out Playgirl")...10-20 67
FAME (1008 "I Can't Get You Out of My Mind")....20-40 66
FAME (1012 "Piece of My Heart")....10-20 66

FREEMAN, Betty
Singles: 7-inch
BARGAIN (5008 "What Can I Do")....10-15 62

FREEMAN, Bo
Singles: 7-inch
PURL (901 "The Girl for Me")....200-300 '60s

FREEMAN, Bobby P&R/R&B '58
Singles: 78 rpm
JOSIE (835 "Do You Want to Dance"). 100-150 58
JOSIE (841 "Betty Lou Got a New Pair of Shoes")....100-150 58
JUBILEE (835 "Do You Want to Dance")....100-150 58
(Canadian.)
JUBILEE (841 "Betty Lou Got a New Pair of Shoes")....100-150 58
(Canadian.)
Singles: 7-inch
ABC....4-6 73
AUTUMN....8-12 64-65
DOUBLE SHOT....4-8 69-70
GUSTO....3-5 '80s
JOSIE (835 "Do You Want to Dance")....20-30 58
JOSIE (841 "Betty Lou Got a New Pair of Shoes")....20-30 58
JOSIE (844 "Need Your Love")....20-30 58
JOSIE (855 "When You're Smiling")....15-25 59
JOSIE (863 "Mary Ann Thomas")....15-25 59
JOSIE (867 "My Guardian Angel")....15-25 59
JOSIE (872 "Ebb Tide")....15-25 59
JOSIE (879 "I Need Someone")....15-25 60
JOSIE (886 "Miss You So")....10-15 61
JOSIE (887 "Mess Around")....10-15 61
JOSIE (889 "She Wants to Dance")....10-15 61
JOSIE (896 "Love Me")....10-15 62
JOSIE (928 "Mess Around")....5-10 65
KING (5373 "Shimmy Shimmy")....10-15 60
KING (5953 "Fever")....5-10 64
KING (5962 "Be My Little Chickadee")....5-10 64
LOMA (2056 "Shadow of Your Love")....4-8 67
LOMA (2080 "Lies")....4-8 67
PARKWAY (875 "Whip It Up Baby")....5-10 63
RNOR....4-6
TOUCH (101 "Everything's Love")....4-6 73
VIRGO....4-6 72
Picture Sleeves
RNOR....5-10
LPs: 10/12-inch
AUTUMN (102 "C'mon & Swim")....20-30 64
JOSIE (4007 "Get in the Swim")....15-25 65
JUBILEE (1086 "Do You Wanna Dance")....50-100 59
(Monaural.)
JUBILEE (1086 "Do You Wanna Dance")....100-150 59
(Stereo.)
JUBILEE (5010 "Twist with Bobby Freeman")....25-40 62
KING (930 "The Lovable Style of Bobby Freeman")....100-200 65
Also see ROMANCERS

FREEMAN, Bobby, & Chuck Jackson
LPs: 10/12-inch
GRAND PRIX....15-20 64
Also see FREEMAN, Bobby
Also see JACKSON, Chuck

FREEMAN, Eddie
Singles: 7-inch
KEM (2747 "Bullwhip")....15-25 57

FREEMAN, Ernie R&B '56
(Ernie Freeman Combo)
Singles: 78 rpm
CASH....5-10 55
IMPERIAL....8-12 57
MAMBO....8-12 55
Singles: 7-inch
ÄVA (176 "Raunchy '65")....5-10 65
CASH (1017 "Jivin' Around")....8-12 55
IMPERIAL (Except 5752)....8-15 57-62
IMPERIAL (5752 "Theme from Igor")....10-20 61
LIBERTY (55515 "Half As Much")....5-10 62
MAMBO (107 "Poor Fool")....10-20 55
EPs: 7-inch
DOOTONE (209 "Jazz Organ")....10-15 56
LPs: 10/12-inch
DUNHILL....10-15 67
IMPERIAL....20-30 57-62
LIBERTY....10-20 62-63
Members: Ernie Freeman; Irvin Ashby; Joe Comfort; R. Martinez.
Also see ASHBY, Irving
Also see B. BUMBLE & STINGERS
Also see BISHOP, Joey
Also see BUTLER, Daws
Also see JACKS & JILLS
Also see JOINER, ARKANSAS JUNIOR HIGH SCHOOL BAND
Also see MARTIN, Dean
Also see NELSON, Willie
Also see OTIS, Johnny
Also see RAIN DROPS
Also see RELF, Bobby
Also see SCOOBY DOO ALL STARS
Also see SIR CHAUNCEY
Also see VOICES
Also see WITHERSPOON, Jimmy

FREEMAN, Ernie, & Frank Motley
EPs: 7-inch
HOLLYWOOD (1068 "Ernie Freeman and Frank Motley")....10-15 56

FREEMAN, Evelyn
(With the Exciting Voices)
Singles: 7-inch
DOT (15726 "Come to Me My True Love")....15-25 58
IMPERIAL (5967 "Didn't It Rock")....5-10 63
U.A. (406 "Didn't It Rain")....10-15 62
WHITE WHALE (317 "I Heard the Voice")...5-8 69
LPs: 10/12-inch
BEL CANTO....15-25 '60s
(Colored vinyl.)
U.A. (3178 "Didn't It Rain")....15-25 62

FREEMAN, George
Singles: 7-inch
EPIC (10668 "Stop Now")....4-6 71
GARDENA (129 "Sugar Lips")....10-20 62
OKEH (7333 "All Right Now")....8-12 69
SHOUT (201 "Why Are You Doing This to Me")....15-25 66
VALIANT (6035 "Come to Me")....15-25 63
VALIANT (6039 "Down and Out")....50-75 63
VALIANT (6057 "One Last Dance")....15-25 64

FREEMAN, James
Singles: 78 rpm
TNT (8001 "You're Gonna Need Me")....20-30 53
Singles: 7-inch
TNT (8001 "You're Gonna Need Me")....50-100 53

FREEMAN, Roger
Singles: 7-inch
EMERSON (1102 "I Love the Ground You Walk On")....15-25 60
R (1512 "All Shook Up")....15-25 67

FREEMAN, Von
Singles: 7-inch
MARKIE (103 "When You Love Someone")....10-20 63

FREEMAN BROTHERS
Singles: 7-inch
MALA (485 "I'm Counting on You")....15-25 64
MALA (553 "I'm Counting on You")....10-15 67
SOUL (35011 "My Baby")....20-30 65

FREESE, Harrison J.
(Harrison J. Freese Jr.)
Singles: 7-inch
FRESHMEN (302 "Earth Angel")....15-25 64

ROULETTE (4429 "Just Say No")....10-20 62
ROULETTE (4496 "I Am")....5-10 62

FREEWAYS
Singles: 7-inch
HUGO (11723 "My Baby Loves Me")....15-25 65

FREEWAYS
Singles: 7-inch
HIBACK (107 "Goffin Goffin")....20-40 66

FREEZE, Sonny, & Unchained
Singles: 7-inch
ACQUARIUS (1001 "Welcome to My World")....100-200
GUITAR (102 "Cotton' Pickin' Heartache")....450-550
MAGIC TOUCH (2075 "White Snowflake-Blue Christmas")....5-10 69

FREHLEY, Ace P&R/LP '78
Singles: 7-inch
CASABLANCA....4-6 78
MEGAFORCE....3-5 87
Picture Sleeves
MEGAFORCE....3-5 87
LPs: 10/12-inch
CASABLANCA (7121 "Ace Frehley")....15-25 78
(With poster.)
CASABLANCA (7121 "Ace Frehley")....8-12 78
(Without poster.)
CASABLANCA (PIX-7121 "Ace Frehley")....50-60 79
(Picture disc.)
MEGAFORCE....5-10 87-89
Also see KISS

FRENCH, Don P&R '59
Singles: 7-inch
LANCER (104 "Lonely Saturday Night")...15-25 59

FRENCH, Irlton
Singles: 78 rpm
OKEH (6816 "My Run Around Baby")....15-25 51
Singles: 7-inch
OKEH (6816 "My Run Around Baby")....30-50 51

FRENCH, Steve
Singles: 7-inch
G&G (102 "Crying with the Blues")....40-60 59

FRENCH CHURCH
Singles: 7-inch
PRINCETON (101 "Without Crying")....15-25 66

FRENCHY & CHESSMEN
Singles: 7-inch
TEMPLE (2081 "Beetle Bebop")....10-15 64

FRESANDOS
("Fresando's with Eddie Bartell & His Dukes of Rhythm")
Singles: 78 rpm
STAR-X (501 "Your Last Goodbye")....100-200 57
Singles: 7-inch
STAR-X (501 "Your Last Goodbye")....200-300 57

FRETTS
Singles: 7-inch
BLUE MOON (414 "Rock n' Roll Baby").75-100 59

FRIAR, Hugh, & Virginia Vagabonds
Singles: 7-inch
CLIX (805 "I Can't Stay Mad at You")...350-400 57
CLIX (806 "Empty Arms")....350-400 57

FRIAR TUCK
Singles: 7-inch
BANSHEE....8-12 '60s
MERCURY (72684 "Alley Oop")....5-10 67
LPs: 10/12-inch
MERCURY (21111 "Friar Tuck & His Psychedelic Guitar")....15-25 67
(Monaural.)
MERCURY (61111 "Friar Tuck & His Psychedelic Guitar")....20-30 67
(Stereo.)
Members: Curt Boetcher; Jim Bell; Michelle O'Malley; Sandy Salisbury; Dottie Holmberg; Sharon Olson; Dyann King; Alicia Vigil; Bob Turner; Mike Deasy; Ben Benay; Jim Troxel; Mike Henderson; Jerry Scheff; Toxie French; Butch Parker; Jim Healms.
Also see GOLDENROD

FRIARS FOUR
Singles: 7-inch
DECCA (31390 "Wonderful Things")....15-25 62

FRICKE, Janie C&W '77
(Janie Frickie)
Singles: 7-inch
COLUMBIA....3-6 77-89
LPs: 10/12-inch
CBS (99-1535 "On Tour")....50-75 82
(Picture disc. Promotional issue only.)
COLUMBIA....5-10 78-84
Session: Benny Wilson; Larry Gatlin; Steve Gatlin; Ricky Skaggs.
Also see BANDY, Moe
Also see DUNCAN, Johnny, & Janie Fricke
Also see GATLIN, Larry, & Janie Fricke
Also see HAGGARD, Merle, & Janie Fricke
Also see JONES, George, & Johnny Paycheck
Also see MANDRELL, Barbara
Also see RICH, Charlie, & Janie Fricke
Also see SKAGGS, Ricky

FRIDAY & WEEKENDS
Singles: 7-inch
DYNAMIC SOUND (2008 "You Baby")....15-25 67

FRIDAY'S CHILD
Singles: 7-inch
DORE (827 "As I Sit Here")....20-30 69

FRIEDLES
(Fried Brothers)
Singles: 7-inch
BAT (1004 "She Can Go")....15-20 66
SCOPE (4818 "I Lost Her")....15-20 65
HANNA (1001 "I Lost Her")....5-10 65

FRIEL, Bill, & Fabulous Furies
Singles: 7-inch
JOKER (1009 "Ft. Lauderdale U.S.A.")....30-40 62

FRIEND, Eddie, & Empires
(With Phil Medley & Orchestra)
Singles: 7-inch
COLPIX (112 "Tears in My Eyes")....150-200 59
Also see EMPIRES

FRIENDLY ROOM
Singles: 7-inch
DELCREST (1005 "Follow Me Back to Louisville")....10-20 '60s

FRIENDLY TORPEDOS
Singles: 7-inch
ORIGINAL SOUND (95 "Nothing's Too Good for My Car")....10-20 70
Member: Sean Bonniwell.
Also see BONNIWELL'S MUSIC MACHINE

FRIENDSHIP
Singles: 7-inch
(27044 "Chains")....8-12 '70s
(No label name used.)
LPs:10/12-inch
FRIENDSHIP (3 "Friendship")....15-25 '70s
Also see UNBELIEVABLE UGLIES

FRIGO, John
Singles: 7-inch
U.S.A. (1311 "Rock Em Sock Em")....10-20 '60s
LPs: 10/12-inch
CORAL (57088 "Dick Marx & John Frigo")....15-25 56

FRIIS, Jim
Singles: 7-inch
ALLSTAR (3054 "Bop-a-Lena")....100-200

FRIJID PINK P&R/LP '70
Singles: 7-inch
LION....4-8 72
LONDON....4-6
PARROT....5-10 69-71
LPs: 10/12-inch
FANTASY (9464 "All Pink Inside")....10-15 74
LIONEL (1004 "Earth Omen")....10-20 72
PARROT (71033 "Frijid Pink")....15-25 70
PARROT (71041 "Defrosted")....15-25 70

FRITCHIE, Vonnie
Singles: 78 rpm
FABOR (119 "There I Stood")....10-15 55
Singles: 7-inch
FABOR (119 "There I Stood")....15-20 55

FRITZ, Hal, & Playboys
Singles: 7-inch
SOMA (1089 "Three Bad Habits")....100-200 58

FRITZ, Joe — R&B '50
(Joe "Papoose" Fritz)

Singles: 78 rpm

MODERN....5-15 50
PEACOCK....10-20 51-54
SITTIN' IN WITH....15-25 50-51

Singles: 7-inch

JET STREAM (732 "Aw, She's a Stepper")....5-10 68
PEACOCK (1606 "Real Fine Girl")....20-40 52
PEACOCK (1627 "Honey Honey")....20-40 53
PEACOCK (1640 "Cerelle")....20-40 55
SITTIN' IN WITH (559 "I Love You My Darlin' ")....50-75 50

FRITZ & JERRY

Singles: 7-inch

RIP (202 "Pad")....10-20 59

FRIZZELL, Lefty — C&W '50

Singles: 78 rpm

COLUMBIA....5-15 50-57

Singles: 7-inch

ABC....4-6 73-76
COLUMBIA (20000 & 21000 series)....10-20 50-56
COLUMBIA (40000 & 41000 series)....5-15 56-61
COLUMBIA (42000 thru 45000 series, except 42924)....4-8 61-72
COLUMBIA (42924 "Saginaw, Michigan")....4-6 64
(Black vinyl.)
COLUMBIA (42924 "Saginaw, Michigan")....10-15 64
(Colored vinyl. Promotional issue only.)

EPs: 7-inch

COLUMBIA....15-35 51-59

LPs: 10/12-inch

ABC....8-12 73-77
COLUMBIA (1342 "The One and Only Lefty Frizzell")....15-25 59
COLUMBIA (2169 "Saginaw, Michigan")....15-25 64
COLUMBIA (2386 "The Sad Side of Life")....15-25 65
COLUMBIA (2488 "Lefty Frizzell's Greatest Hits")....15-25 66
(Monaural.)
COLUMBIA (2772 "Puttin' On")....15-25 67
COLUMBIA (8969 "Saginaw, Michigan")....15-25 64
COLUMBIA (9019 "Songs of Jimmie Rodgers")....75-100 51
(10-inch LP.)
COLUMBIA (9021 "Listen to Lefty")....75-100 52
(10-inch LP.)
COLUMBIA (9186 "The Sad Side of Life")....20-25 65
COLUMBIA (9288 "Lefty Frizzell's Greatest Hits")....20-25 66
(Stereo. With "CS" prefix.)
COLUMBIA (9288 "Lefty Frizzell's Greatest Hits")....5-10
(With "PC" prefix.)
COLUMBIA (9572 "Puttin' On")....20-25 67
COLUMBIA (10000 series)....5-12 73-83
COLUMBIA (30000 series)....5-12 75-82
HARMONY (7241 "Songs of Jimmie Rodgers")....15-25 60
HARMONY (11000 series)....8-15 66-68
MCA....8-12 82
ROUNDER....5-10 80-83
2X4 (111 "Lefty Frizzell Story")....5-10 80
Also see BOND, Johnny, & Lefty Frizzell
Also see PRICE, Ray / Lefty Frizzell / Carl Smith
Also see SMITH, Carl / Lefty Frizzell / Marty Robbins

FRIZZLE, Billy

Singles: 7-inch

ARLEN (1015 "Oh Foolish Me")....50-75 61

FROG, Shorty

Singles: 7-inch

HI-Q (12 "Sheddin' Tears Over You")....100-200

FROGGIE BEAVER

LPs: 10/12-inch

FROGGIE BEAVER (7301 "From the Pond")....50-75 73
Members: John Troia; John Fischer; Rick Brown; Ed Stazko.

FROGMEN — P&R '61

Singles: 7-inch

ASTRA (1009 "Underwater")....5-10 65
ASTRA (1010 "Beware Below")....5-10 65
CANDIX (314 "Underwater")....15-25 61
CANDIX (326 "Beware Below")....30-40 61
SCOTT (101 "Tioga")....25-50 61
(First issue.)
SCOTT (102 "Underwater")....25-50 61
(First issue.)
TEE JAY (131 "Sea Haunt")....15-25 64
(Black vinyl.)
TEE JAY (131 "Sea Haunt")....25-50 64
(Blue vinyl.)
Also see BEACH BOYS / Marketts / Frogmen

FROLK HEAVEN

LPs: 10/12-inch

LRS (6032 "At the Apex of High")....400-500 '70s
Members: Stewart Copeland; Charles Ostman; Bailey Pendergrass.

FRONT LINE

Singles: 7-inch

TITAN (2001 "Saigon Girl")....15-25 67
YORK (9000 "I Don't Care")....8-12 65

FRONT OFFICE

Singles: 7-inch

MIJJI (3007 "Girl")....15-25 67

FRONT PAGE NEWS

Singles: 7-inch

DIAL (4052 "Thoughts")....10-20 66

FRONTERA, Tommy

Singles: 7-inch

HI-LITE (84952 "Be Mine")....10-20
(Identification number shown since no selection number is used.)
PALMER (5015 "Street of Shame")....15-25 67
REM (103 "After Tonite")....250-350 60
Session: Dennis Coffey.

FRONTIERS
(New Frontiers)

Singles: 7-inch

KING (5481 "Why Pretend")....10-15 61
KING (5534 "Oh Nurse")....10-15 61
KING (5609 "Each Night I Pray")....15-20 62
KING (6007 "Each Night I Pray")....5-10 65

FRONTIERS

Singles: 7-inch

MGM (13722 "When I See You")....5-10 67
PHILIPS (40113 "Don't Come Cryin' ")....10-20 63
PHILIPS (40148 "I Just Want You")....10-20 63
Members: Roger Koob; Andy Smith; Skippy Bianco; Fred Maffeo; Phil Vallie; Jerry Warner.
Also see BETTER DAYS

FROST, Frank — R&B '66
(With the Night Hawks)

Singles: 7-inch

JEWEL (765 "My Back Scratcher")....5-10 66
JEWEL (771 "Things You Do")....5-10 66
JEWEL (778 "Ride with Your Daddy Tonight")....5-10 67
PHILLIPS INT'L (3578 "Jelly Roll King")....10-20 62

LPs: 10/12-inch

JEWEL (5013 "Frank Frost")....10-20 74
PHILLIPS INT'L. (1975 "Hey Boss Man!")....2000-2500 61

FROST, Max, & Troopers — P&R '68

Singles: 7-inch

SIDEWALK (938 "Stomper's Ride")....8-12 68
TOWER....8-12 68-69

Picture Sleeves

TOWER (419 "Shapes of Things to Come")....10-15 68
TOWER (478 "Paxton Quigley's Had the Course")....10-15 68

LPs: 10/12-inch

TOWER (5147 "Shape of Things to Come")....25-35 68
Member: Davie Allan.
Also see ALLAN, Davie

FROSTY & DIAMONDS

Singles: 78 rpm

COMBO (122 "Destination Mars")....10-15 56

Singles: 7-inch

COMBO (122 "Destination Mars")....20-25 56

FRUGE, Lawrence

Singles: 78 rpm

TNT (104 "T-Mamou")....10-15 53

Singles: 7-inch

TNT (104 "T-Mamou")....25-35 53

FRUIT & SKIP / Algers
(Skip & Fruit)

Singles: 7-inch

NORTHERN (3730 "Heavenly Father"/"Oh Baby")....40-50 60

FRUMIOUS BANDERSNATCH

EPs: 7-inch

MUGGLES GRAMOPHONE WORKS ("Frumious Bandersnatch")....400-600 '60s
(No selection number used. Disc shows purple vinyl when held to a light.)
Members: Jimmy Warner; Bob Winkleman; Jackson King; David Denny; Ross Valory; Jack Notestein.
Also see FAUN
Also see JOURNEY
Also see MILLER, Steve

FRY, James

Singles: 7-inch

HI (2142 "Still Around")....10-20 68

FRYE, Gary

Singles: 7-inch

LUXOR (1026 "Spring Fever")....15-25 64

FUGITIVES

Singles: 7-inch

ARVEE (5014 "Freeway")....10-20 60
SIMS (115 "Freeway")....30-50 60

FUGITIVES

Singles: 7-inch

COLUMBIA (43261 "Mean Woman")....10-15 65
MALA (533 "Your Girl's a Woman")....5-10 66

FUGITIVES

Singles: 7-inch

D-TOWN (1034 "A Fugitive")....20-40 65
D-TOWN (1044 "On Trial")....50-100 65
WESTCHESTER (1002 "You Can't Make Me Lonely")....10-20 65

LPs: 10/12-inch

HIDEOUT (1001 "The Fugitives at Dave's Hideout")....750-1000 65
Members: Gary Quackenbush; Glen Quackenbush; Elmer Clawson.
Also see SRC

FUGITIVES / Oxford Five / Lourds / Individuals

LPs: 10/12-inch

WESTCHESTER (1005 "Friday at the Cage A-Go-Go")....1000-1500 65
(Distributed at the Cage A-Go-Go club and other locations. Some copies have a sticker on labels showing title as *Long Hot Summer*. Not issued with a cover.)
Also see FUGITIVES

FUGITIVES

Singles: 7-inch

MIDNIGHT (101 "Easy Come Easy Go")....15-25 65

FUGITIVES

Singles: 7-inch

FENTON (2075 "I'll Hang Around")....50-75 66

FUGITIVES

Singles: 7-inch

TREND (101 "Come On and Clap")....15-25 66
Member: Dick Moulder.

FUGITIVES

Singles: 7-inch

CLEVELAND (128 "This Is It")....15-25 '60s
ROULETTE (4779 "Don't Play That Song")....5-10 67

FUGITIVES

LPs: 10/12-inch

JUSTICE (141 "On the Run")....300-400 67

FUGITIVES

Singles: 7-inch

PATH (251 "I Love You More Than Anything")....15-25 '60s
PATH (252 "I Love You More Than Ever")....15-25 '60s
SANDMAN (701 "Good Lovin' if You Can Get It")....15-25 '60s

FUGS — LP '66
(Village Fugs)

Singles: 7-inch

ESP (4507 "Frenzy")....5-10 66

LPs: 10/12-inch

BROADSIDE (304 "Ballads of Contemporary Protest, Point of Views, and General Dissatisfaction")....300-400 65
(Double slot cover; one for disc and one for quarter-folded insert.
ESP (1018 "Fugs First Album")....30-50 65
(Reissue of Broadside 304.)
ESP (1028 "The Fugs")....25-40 66
ESP (1038 "Virgin Fugs")....25-40 67
ESP (2018 "Fugs Four")....20-25 67
PVC....5-10 82
REPRISE (6280 "Tenderness Junction")....15-25 67
REPRISE (6305 "It Crawled Into My Hand, Honest")....15-25 67
REPRISE (6359 "The Belle of Avenue A")....10-20 69
REPRISE (6396 "Golden Filth")....10-20 70
Members: Ed Saunders; John Anderson; Lee Crabtree; Pete Kearney; Tuli Kupferberg; Ken Weaver; Vinny Leary; Pete Stampfel; Steve Weber.
Also see HOLY MODAL ROUNDERS
Also see SANDERS, Ed, & Hemptones

FULLER, Blind Boy

Singles: 78 rpm

COLUMBIA....20-30 46
CONQUEROR....15-25
DECCA....15-25
OKEH....25-35 39-41
PERFECT....20-30 36
VOCALION....15-25

FULLER, Bobby

Singles: 78 rpm

CAPITOL (3038 "All Night Long")....8-10 55

Singles: 7-inch

CAPITOL (3038 "All Night Long")....10-20 55

FULLER, Bobby — P&R/LP '66
(Bobby Fuller Four; with Jim Reese & Embers; with Fanatics)

Singles: 7-inch

ABC....4-6 73
DONNA (1403 "Our Favorite Martian")....75-125 65
EASTWOOD (0345 "Nervous Breakdown")....400-500 62
(Identification number shown since no selection number is used.)
ERIC....4-6 '70s
EXETER (122 "Wine, Wine, Wine")....150-250 64
EXETER (124 "I Fought the Law")....200-300 64
EXETER (126 "Fool of Love")....150-250 64
LIBERTY (55812 "Let Her Dance")....15-25 65
MUSTANG (3004 thru 3018, except 3014)....15-25 65-66
MUSTANG (3014 "I Fought the Law")....8-12 65
REGENCY (965 "I Fought the Law")....15-25 65
(Canadian.)
TODD (1090 "Saturday Night")....50-100 63
YUCCA (141 "Guess We'll Fall in Love")....50-100 62
(Identification number is N80W-3009. Slow version. No address on label.)
YUCCA (141 "Guess We'll Fall in Love")....50-100 62
(Identification number is 4109. Fast version. Has address on the label.)
YUCCA (144 "My Heart Jumped")....50-100 62

LPs: 10/12-inch

MUSTANG (900 "KRLA King of the Wheels")....50-100 66
(Monaural.)
MUSTANG (900 "KRLA King of the Wheels")....75-125 66
(Stereo.)
MUSTANG (901 "I Fought the Law")....35-55 66
(Monaural.)
MUSTANG (901 "I Fought the Law")....45-65 66
(Stereo.)
RHINO....5-10 81
VOXX....5-10 84
Members: Bobby Fuller; Randy Fuller; Duane Quirico; Jim Reese; Dalton Powell; Johnny Barbata.
Also see BARBATA, Johnny
Also see FULLER, Randy
Also see HORTON, Jay
Also see SHINDIGS
Also see TAYLOR, Bobby

FULLER, Curtis

Singles: 7-inch

WARWICK (655 "Chant of the Congo")....10-20 61

FULLER, Donna

Singles: 7-inch

COLPIX (679 "Only One") 5-10 63
DCP (1131 "Who Am I") 5-10 65
DCP (1137 "Again") 5-10 65
LIBERTY (55051 "Dusky January") 8-12 57

LPs: 10/12-inch

DCP (3807 "Who Is Donna Fuller") 15-20 65
(Monaural.)
DCP (6807 "Who Is Donna Fuller") 20-25 65
(Stereo.)

FULLER, Irving, & Corvettes

Singles: 7-inch

EMERY (121 "I Can't Stop") 30-40 60
RENOWN (106 "Cheer Up Pretty Baby") 40-50 59

FULLER, Jerry P&R '59

Singles: 7-inch

ABC 4-6 78
BELL 4-8 72-74
CHALLENGE (9114 thru 9184) 10-20 61-63
CHALLENGE (59052 "Betty My Angel") .. 20-30 59
CHALLENGE (59057 "Tennessee Waltz") 15-25 59
CHALLENGE (59068 "Two Loves Have I") 10-20 60
CHALLENGE (59085 "Gone for the Summer") 10-20 60
CHALLENGE (59104 "Shy Away") 10-20 61
(Black vinyl.)
CHALLENGE (59104 "Shy Away") 50-100 61
(Green vinyl.)
CHALLENGE (59217 "I Only Came to Dance with You") 10-20 63
CHALLENGE (59235 "Hollywood Star") .. 10-20 64
CHALLENGE (59252 "Don't Let Go") 10-20 64
CHALLENGE (59269 "Killer") 10-20 64
CHALLENGE (59279 "I Got Carried Away") 20-30 65
CHALLENGE (59307 "Don't Look at Me Like That") 5-10 65
CHALLENGE (59315 "Man in Black") 5-10 65
CHALLENGE (59329 "Double Life") 15-25 66
COLUMBIA 4-8 70
LIN (5011 "Blue Memories") 30-50 58
LIN (5012 "Teenage Love") 30-50 58
LIN (5015 "Angel from Above") 30-50 58
LIN (5016 "The Door Is Open") 30-50 58
LIN (5019 "Lipstick and Rouge") 30-50 59
MCA 4-6 79

LPs: 10/12-inch

LIN (100 "Teenage Love") 25-35 60
MCA 5-10 79
Also see FLEAS
Also see NELSON, Rick
Also see TROPHIES

FULLER, Jerry, & Diane Maxwell

Singles: 7-inch

CHALLENGE (59074 "Above and Beyond") 10-20 60
Also see FULLER, Jerry
Also see MAXWELL, Diane

FULLER, Jesse

Singles: 7-inch

GOOD TIME JAZZ (45100 "San Francisco Bay Blues") 5-10 63

LPs: 10/12-inch

CAVALIER (5006 "Frisco Bound") 50-75 55
CAVALIER (6009 "Frisco Bound") 35-50 57
FANTASY 8-12
GOOD TIME JAZZ (10039 "The Lone Cat") 100-150 61
(Stereo.)
GOOD TIME JAZZ (10051 "San Francisco Bay Blues") 50-100 64
(Stereo.)
GOOD TIME JAZZ (12039 "The Lone Cat") 75-125 61
(Monaural.)
GOOD TIME JAZZ (12051 "San Francisco Bay Blues") 40-60 64
(Monaural.)
PRESTIGE (7368 "Jesse Fuller's Favorites") 30-40 65
WORLD SONG (1 "Working on the Railroad") 75-120 54
(10-inch LP.)

FULLER, Johnny

Singles: 78 rpm

ALADDIN 20-40 55
HOLLYWOOD 20-40 55-56
IRMA (110 "First Stage of the Blues") 35-50 58
MONEY (206 "I Walk All Night") 15-25 55
RHYTHM (1767 "Fool's Paradise") 20-40 54
RHYTHM (1773 "Train, Train Blues") 20-40 55
RHYTHM (1777 "Lovin' Lovin' Man") 20-40 56
RHYTHM (1779 "Mean Old World") 20-40 55
SOUND (107 "She's Too Much") 15-25 54

Singles: 7-inch

ALADDIN (3278 "Johnny Ace's Last Letter") 40-60 55
ART TONE (828 "No More") 5-10 62
CHECKER (899 "All Night Long") 20-30 58
FLAIR (1054 "Buddy") 50-100 55
HOLLYWOOD (1043 "Train, Train Blues") 40-60 55
HOLLYWOOD (1057 "Mean Old World") .40-60 56
HOLLYWOOD (1063 "Roughest Place in Town") 75-100 56
HOLLYWOOD (1077 "My Mama Told Me") 40-60 57
HOLLYWOOD (1084 "Sunny Road") 40-60 58
IMPERIAL (5580 "Heavenly One") 20-30 59
IMPERIAL (5697 "Miss You") 20-30 60
IMPERIAL (5850 "My Heart Beats for You") 20-30 62
IRMA (106 "Strange Land") 40-60 57
IRMA (110 "First Stage of the Blues") ..200-300 58
IRMA (112 "All Night Long") 30-50 58
MONEY (206 "I Walk All Night") 30-50 55
SOUND (107 "She's Too Much") 30-40 54
SPECIALTY (655 "Haunted House") 10-20 59
SPECIALTY (671 "Swingin' at the Creek") 10-20 59
VELTONE (107 "She's Too Much") 10-20 60
Also see PRETTY BOY

FULLER, Little Boy

Singles: 78 rpm

SAVOY 15-25 47

FULLER, Playboy
(Iverson Minter)

Singles: 78 rpm

FULLER (171 "Sugar Cane Highway") .200-300 52
Also see FULLER, Rocky

FULLER, Randy

Singles: 7-inch

MUSTANG (3020 "Wolfman") 10-20 66
MUSTANG (3023 "The Things You Do") ..10-20 66
SHOW TOWN (466 "It's Love") 10-20 69
SHOW TOWN (482 "1000 Miles") 10-20 69

Picture Sleeves

SHOW TOWN (466 "It's Love") 15-20 69
Also see FULLER, Bobby
Also see SHINDIGS

FULLER, Rocky
(Iverson Minter)

Singles: 78 rpm

CHECKER (753 "Soon One Morning") 50-75 52
Also see FULLER, Playboy

FULLER, Tiny
(With His Combo)

Singles: 7-inch

MARLIN (6301 "Cat Walk") 10-20 63
TAP (1000 "Cockleur") 10-20 61

FULLER, Tommy

Singles: 7-inch

GIANT (1005 "Soul Twist") 10-20 62

FULLER, Walter
(Walter Fuller's Club Royale Band)

Singles: 78 rpm

KICKS 10-15 54-55

Singles: 7-inch

KICKS (4 "Closer to My Heart") 75-125 54
KICKS (7 "I'm Gonna Mess Around") 50-60 55

FULLER BROTHERS

Singles: 7-inch

MONUMENT (925 "Judge Me with Your Heart") 10-15 66

FULLER BROTHERS

Singles: 7-inch

BELL (734 "Let Me Love You") 20-30 68
SOUL CLOCK (101 "Let Me Love You") ..10-15 69

FULLYLOVE, Leroy
(With the Buffs)

Singles: 7-inch

ELKO (2 "I Want to Know") 400-500 60
JO-REE (503 "Day After Day") 30-40 62
JO-REE (504 "Betrayed") 30-40 62
TANDEM (7002 "I'm So Lonely") 150-250 61

FULSON, Lowell R&B '48
(With the Ful-Tones; with His Trio; with His Guitar; with Jon Blue & Band; Lowell Folsom; Lowel Fulsom)

Singles: 78 rpm

ALADDIN 25-50 51
BIG TOWN (1068 "Crying Blues") 20-40 46
BIG TOWN (1070 "Miss Katie Lee Blues") 20-40 46
BIG TOWN (1072 "San Francisco Blues") 20-40 46
BIG TOWN (1074 "Trouble Blues") 20-40 46
BIG TOWN (1077 "Black Widow Spider Blues") 20-40 46
CASH (1051 "Blue Shadows") 15-25 57
CAVATONE (250 "Stormin' & Rainin' ") 15-25 49
CHECKER (804 "Reconsider Baby") 30-40 54
CHECKER (812 thru 865) 10-25 55-57
CHECKER (882 "I Want to Make Love to You") 20-30 57
CHECKER (937 "It Took a Long Time") ...25-50 59
Note: Checker 937 may be the last 78 with the checkerboard design at top, as opposed to 45s which switched designs beginning with 876. Also, 78s as early as 900 have Checker name vertically on left side.
CHECKER (952 "Have You Changed Your Mind") 150-250 60
COLONIAL (122 "I'm Prison Bound") 20-30 49
DOWN BEAT 20-40 46-49
DOWN TOWN (2002 "Three O'Clock Blues") 20-30 48
DOWN TOWN (2021 "My Baby Left Me") 50-75 48
GILT EDGE (5041 "Miss Katie Lee Blues") 20-30 51
GILT EDGE (5050 "Rambling Blues") 20-30 51
HOLLYWOOD 10-20 54-55
PARROT 25-50 53
RPM (305 "I'm Prison Bound") 20-30 50
SCOTTY'S RADIO (101 "Scotty's Blues") 20-40 46
SWING BEAT 25-50 49-50
SWING TIME 15-30 50-53
TRILON (185 "Jelly Jelly") 20-40 47
TRILON (186 "Thinkin' Blues") 20-40 47
TRILON (192 "Tryin' to Find My Baby") 20-40 48
TRILON (193 "Highway 99") 20-40 48

Singles: 7-inch

ALADDIN (3088 "Double Trouble Blues") 75-125 53
ALADDIN (3104 "Night & Day") 75-125 51
ALADDIN (3104 "Stormin' & Rainin' ") 75-125 53
(Black vinyl.)
ALADDIN (3104 "Stormin' & Rainin' ") 1000-2000 53
(Green vinyl.)
ALADDIN (3217 "Don't Leave Me, Baby") 75-100 53
ALADDIN (3233 "Blues Never Fail") 75-100 53
CASH (1051 "Blue Shadows") 20-40 57
CHECKER (804 "Reconsider Baby") 40-60 54
CHECKER (812 "Loving You") 30-40 55
CHECKER (820 "Lonely Hours") 30-40 55
CHECKER (829 "Trouble Trouble") 30-40 55
CHECKER (841 "It's All Your Fault Baby") 30-40 56
CHECKER (854 "Baby Please Don't Go") 30-40 56
CHECKER (865 "You're Gonna Miss Me") 25-35 57
CHECKER (882 "I Want to Make Love to You") 25-35 57
CHECKER (937 "It Took a Long Time") 15-25 59
CHECKER (952 "Have You Changed Your Mind") 15-25 60
CHECKER (959 "I'm Glad You Reconsidered") 15-25 60
CHECKER (972 "I Want to Know") 10-20 60
CHECKER (992 "So Many Tears") 10-20 61
CHECKER (1027 "Shed No Tears") 10-20 62
CHECKER (1046 "Trouble with the Blues") 10-20 62
GRANITE 4-6 76
HOLLYWOOD (242 "The Original Lonesome Christmas") 35-55 53
(Shiny red label stock.)
HOLLYWOOD (242 "The Original Lonesome Christmas") 15-25 55
(Flat maroon label stock.)
HOLLYWOOD (242 "The Original Lonesome Christmas") ....4-8 '70s
(Black label stock.)
HOLLYWOOD (1029 "Rocking After Midnight") 50-75 55
HOLLYWOOD (1103 "Guitar Shuffle") 10-20 62
JEWEL 4-6 69-72
KENT 4-8 64-70
MOVIN' (128 "Baby") 8-12 64
PARROT (787 "I've Been Mistreated") .250-350 53
(Black vinyl.)
PARROT (787 "I've Been Mistreated") .500-700 53
(Red vinyl.)
PROWLIN' (128 "Baby") 8-12
SWING TIME (196 "Everytime I Have the Blues") 250-350 50
SWING TIME (289 "Let's Live Right") 40-60 51
SWING TIME (295 "Guitar Shuffle") 40-60 51
SWING TIME (301 "The Highway Is My Home") 40-60 51
SWING TIME (308 "Black Widow Spider") 40-60 51
SWING TIME (315 "Raggedy Daddy Blues") 40-60 52
SWING TIME (320 "Ride Until the Sun Goes Down") 40-60 52
SWING TIME (325 "Upstairs") 40-60 52
SWING TIME (330 "I Love My Baby") 40-60 52
SWING TIME (335 "Cash Box Boogie") 40-60 53
SWING TIME (338 "I've Been Mistreated") 40-60 52

Picture Sleeves

KENT (463 "Make a Little Love") 8-10 67

LPs: 10/12-inch

ARHOOLIE (2003 "Lowell Fulson") 10-12 62
BIG TOWN 5-10 78
CHESS (205 "Lowell Fulson") 15-25 76
(Two discs.)
CHESS (408 "Hung Down Head") 10-12 74
JEWEL 8-10 70-73
KENT 10-20 65-71
UNITED 8-12
Session: Lloyd Glenn; Earl Brown; Bob Harvey; Bill Hadnott; David "Fathead" Newman; Phillip Gibeaux; Julian Beasley; Choker Campbell; Fats Morris; Paul Drake; Leroy Cooper; Chick Booth.
Also see BROWN, Earl
Also see CAMPBELL, Choker
Also see CHARLES, Ray
Also see GLENN, Lloyd
Also see JAMES, Ulysses / Lowell Fulson
Also see MEMPHIS SLIM & LOWELL FULSON
Also see TURRENTINE, Stanley

FULTON, Jack

Singles: 7-inch

SCOPE (1956 "Ivory Tower") ....10-15 '60s

FULTON, Sonny
(Sunny Fulton & the Mixmasters)

Singles: 7-inch

BIG DADDY (101 "Sugar Woogah") 10-15 61
CHELSEA (533 "Honest I Do") 40-50 59
(White label.)
CHELSEA (533 "Honest I Do") 30-40 59
(Black label.)
LASH (1127 "Here She Comes Now") 30-40 59
SUNBEAM (125 "Fingerprints") 150-200 59
U.A. (426 "Simple Things") 10-15 62

FUN & GAMES P&R '69

Singles: 7-inch

UNI (55086 "Elephant Candy") 5-10 68
UNI (55098 "The Grooviest Girl in the World") 5-10 68

LPs: 10/12-inch

UNI (73042 "Elephant Candy") 15-25 68
Members: Paul Guille; Joe Romano; Rock Romano; Sam Irwin; Joe Dugan; Carson Graham.
Also see SIXPENTZ

FUN SONS

Singles: 7-inch

CAMEO (478 "Hang Ten") 10-20 67

FUN-ATICS
("Vocal by Billy Lee")
Singles: 7-inch
VERSAILLES (100 "Wise Guy")..........350-450 62

FUNKADELIC P&R/R&B '69
(Featuring George Clinton)
Singles: 7-inch
W.B. 3-6 77-81
WESTBOUND..........4-8 69-76
Picture Sleeves
W.B. 3-6 78-81
EPs: 7-inch
W.B. (3209 "One Nation Under a Groove")..........10-15 78
LPs: 10/12-inch
20TH CENTURY/WESTBOUND..........8-15 75
W.B. 5-10 76-81
WESTBOUND (215 "Let's Take It to the Stage")..........30-50 75
WESTBOUND (227 "Tales of Kidd Funkadelic")..........30-50 76
WESTBOUND (1001 "Standing on the Verge")..........30-50 74
WESTBOUND (1004 "Greatest Hits")..........25-35 75
WESTBOUND (2000 "Funkadelic")..........40-50 70
WESTBOUND (2001 "Free Your Mind")..30-50 70
WESTBOUND (2007 "Maggot Brain")..........40-60 71
WESTBOUND (2020 "America Eats Its Young")..........30-50 72
WESTBOUND (2022 "Cosmic Slop")..........30-50 73
Also see PARLIAMENT
Also see PARLIAMENTS

FURNESS BROTHERS
Singles: 78 rpm
MGM..........10-20 52
Singles: 7-inch
FUTURE (1002 "I Want a Date")..........10-15 60
MGM..........20-30 52
MELMAR (114 "Only Fate")..........10-15 55
MELMAR (116 "Say It Isn't So")..........10-15 55
RAE COX (104 "Duke's Place")..........10-15 60
Also see BERRY, Al, & Furness Bros.

FURNITURE
Singles: 7-inch
STATURE (1105 "Keep On Running")..........10-15 68

FURR, Curt
Singles: 7-inch
CRYSTAL (292 "Candy Store")..........200-300

FURY, Charlie, & Rebel Rockets
Singles: 7-inch
AL-BE (167 "Reptile")..........20-30 61

FURY, Ron
Singles: 7-inch
DART (406 "Baltimore Baby")..........10-20 60
SESSION (701 "Long Long Time")..........50-75 59

FURYS
Singles: 7-inch
CUCA (1010 "This Way Out")..........15-25 60
Members: Wally Henel; Steve Getschou; Dennis Radloff; Joel Jetzer.

FURYS
Singles: 7-inch
DEE JAY (1097 "Run to Him")..........15-25 62
Member: Jimmy Delwood.

FURYS P&R '63
Singles: 7-inch
MACK IV (112 "Zing! Went the Strings of My Heart")..........20-30 62
MACK IV (114 "If There's a Next Time")..20-30 63
Members: Jerome Evans; Jerome Green; Melvin White; Robert Washington; George Taylor.

FURYS
Singles: 7-inch
AURA (395 "Cover Girl")..........5-10 63
FLEETWOOD..........15-25 62
LIBERTY (55692 "Baby You Can Bet Your Boots")..........10-20 64
LIBERTY (55719 "Dream")..........10-20 64
MANOR (51621 "Lost Caravan")..........20-30 63
WORLD PACIFIC (386 "Anything for You")..........10-20 63

FURYS
Singles: 7-inch
D&D (31563 "Furyous")..........10-20 63

FURYS
Singles: 7-inch
LAVENDER (1805 "Parchman Farm")......10-20 62
LAVENDER (1926 "Maryann")..........10-20 63

FURYS
Singles: 7-inch
STUDIO CITY (1026 "Baby What's Wrong")..........20-25 64

FURYS
(With Jerry DeMarr)
Singles: 7-inch
KAY BEE (6006 "Without Your Love")......10-20 '60s

FUSE
Singles: 7-inch
EPIC (10514 "Hound Dog")..........8-12 69
LPs: 10/12-inch
EPIC (26502 "Fuse")..........30-35 70
Members: Rick Neilsen; Robert Antoni; Tom Peterson; Craig Myers; Thom Mooney; Bun .E. Carlos; Randy Hogan.
Also see CHEAP TRICK

FUTURAS
Singles: 7-inch
RAMPRO (119 "Signed, Sealed & Delivered")..........40-50 66
Picture Sleeves
RAMPRO (119 "Signed, Sealed & Delivered")..........50-100 66
Members: Jerry Mallon; Gary Josing; Jack Edwards Strucel; Gary Dee Bareman; Al James.

FUTURAS
Singles: 7-inch
ARJAY (115 "Mile Zero")..........15-25
WARWICK (129/130 "Hurt"/"Sally")..........15-25 '60s

FUTURETONES
Singles: 7-inch
TRESS (2 "I Know")..........800-1000 57
Member: Edwin Starr.
Also see STARR, Edwin

FYDELLS
Singles: 7-inch
CAMELIA (100 "That Certain One")..........15-25 59

FYREBIRDS
Singles: 7-inch
GREAT LAKES (2528 "Can't Get No Ride")..........10-15 67

G

G - CLEFS P&R/R&B '56
(With Jay Raye & Orchestra)
Singles: 78 rpm
PARIS..........10-20 57
PILGRIM..........10-20 56
Singles: 7-inch
DITTO (503 "Ka Ding Dong")..........10-15 62
(Blue vinyl.)
LOMA (2034 "Little Lonely Boy")..........5-10 66
LOMA (2048 "I Can't Stand It")..........5-10 66
PARIS (502 "Symbol of Love")..........20-30 57
PARIS (506 "Zing Zang Zoo")..........20-25 57
PILGRIM (715 "Ka Ding Dong")..........20-30 56
(Purple label, no pilgrims.)
PILGRIM (715 "Ka Ding Dong")..........10-15 56
(Red label with pilgrims.)
PILGRIM (720 "Cause You're Mine")..........15-25 56
REGINA (1314 "I Believe in All I Feel")....10-15 64
REGINA (1319 "Angel, Listen to Me")......10-15 64
ROULETTE GOLDEN GOODIES..........4-6 '70s
TERRACE (7500 "I Understand")..........8-12 61
TERRACE (7503 "A Girl Has to Know")......8-12 62
TERRACE (7507 "They'll Call Me Away")..8-12 62
TERRACE (7510 "A Lover's Prayer")......10-15 62
TERRACE (7514 "All My Trials")..........15-20 63
VEEP (1218 "I Have")..........8-12 65
VEEP (1226 "This Time")..........8-12 66
Also see CANNON, Freddy

G - NOTES
("Linda, 11 yrs; Nancy, 9 yrs")
Singles: 7-inch
GUYDEN (2012 "Johnny Johnny")..........10-15 59
FORM (102 "Say You're Mine")..........20-30 59
JACKPOT (48000 "Ronnie")..........10-15 58
REMEMBER (57 "How Long Does It Take")..........10-20 '50s
TENDER (510 "Ronnie")..........20-30 58
Members: Linda; Nancy.

G - TONES
Singles: 78 rpm
GEE (1013 "Sweet Pea")..........10-15 56
Singles: 7-inch
GEE (1013 "Sweet Pea")..........10-15 56

G's
Singles: 7-inch
YOUNG GENERATIONS (104 "There's a Time")..........15-25 66

G.T.O.
(G.T.O.'s; Girls Together Outrageously)
Singles: 7-inch
STRAIGHT (104 "Circular Circulation")....15-25 69
LPs: 10/12-inch
REPRISE..........10-15 70
REPRISE (6390 "Permanent Damage")...20-30 70
STRAIGHT (1059 "Permanent Damage")..........40-60 69
Members: Rod Stewart; Jeff Beck; Frank Zappa; Nicky Hopkins; Jimmy Carl Black.
Also see BECK, Jeff
Also see STEWART, Rod
Also see ZAPPA, Frank

G.T.O.s
Singles: 7-inch
CLARIDGE (312 "She Rides with Me")....10-15 66
PARKWAY (108 "Girl from New York City")..........5-10 66
Also see JOEY & CONTINENTALS

GABBART & HOLT
Singles: 7-inch
SAGE (287 "Hey Baby")..........100-125 59
Members: Harley Gabbart; Aubrey Holt.

GABREYS
Singles: 7-inch
SOFT (984 "Down at the Go Go")..........10-20 65

GABRIEL P&R '62
(Gabriel & Angels; Gabriel & His Trumpet)
Singles: 7-inch
AMY (802 "Chumba")..........15-25 60
AMY (823 "Zing Went the Strings of My Heart")..........75-100 61
NORMAN (506 "I'm Gabriel")..........50-75 61
NORMAN (510 "Gabriel, Blow Your Horn")..........10-20 61
NORMAN (514 "See See Rider")..........10-20 62
SWAN (4118 "That's Life")..........10-20 62
SWAN (4133 "Peanut Butter Song")..........10-20 63
Member: Rick Kellis.

GABRIEL
Singles: 7-inch
ELEKTRA (45848 "Back on the Road Again")..........4-6 73
ROYAL AMERICAN ("Don't Stay Out All Night")..........50-75 '70s
(Selection number not known.)

GABRIEL BONDAGE
LPs: 10/12-inch
DHARMA (804 "Angel Dust")..........30-40 75
DHARMA (808 "Another Trip to Earth")....10-15 77
(Colored vinyl.)

GADABOUTS P&R '56
Singles: 78 rpm
MERCURY..........5-10 54-56
WING..........5-10 55-56
Singles: 7-inch
JARO (77022 "Caress Me")..........8-12 60
MERCURY (Except 70898)..........10-15 54-56
MERCURY (70898 "Stranded in the Jungle")..........15-25 56
WING..........10-15 55-56

GADDIE, Grover
Singles: 7-inch
BLUE ANGEL (2007 "High Stepping Daddy")..........50-75

GADDIS, Rudy
Singles: 78 rpm
STARDAY (217 "Uranium Fever")..........40-60 55
Singles: 7-inch
LIBERTY (103 "Girl from Mars")..........100-150
STARDAY (217 "Uranium Fever")..........100-200 55

GADDY, Bob
(With His Alley Cats; with His Keys)
Singles: 78 rpm
HARLEM..........25-50 55
JACKSON..........40-60 52
OLD TOWN (1031 "Operator")..........20-30 56
OLD TOWN (1039 "Paper Lady")..........20-30 57
OLD TOWN (1050 "Rip & Run")..........20-30 58
OLD TOWN (1057 "Take My Advice")......30-40 58
OLD TOWN (1064 "Paper Lady")..........40-50 59
OLD TOWN (1070 "Till the Day I Die")...50-100 59
Singles: 7-inch
HARLEM (2330 "Blues Has Walked in My Room")..........75-100 55
JACKSON (2303 "I (Believe You Got a Sidekick)")..........150-250 52
(Colored vinyl.)
JAX (308 "No Help Wanted")..........150-250 52
(Red vinyl.)
OLD TOWN (1031 "Operator")..........20-30 56
OLD TOWN (1039 "Paper Lady")..........20-30 57
OLD TOWN (1050 "Rip & Run")..........20-30 58
OLD TOWN (1057 "Take My Advice")......20-30 58
OLD TOWN (1064 "Paper Lady")..........20-30 59
OLD TOWN (1070 "Till the Day I Die")....20-30 59
OLD TOWN (1077 "Early One Morning").15-25 60
OLD TOWN (1085 "Could I")..........15-25 60
OLD TOWN (1119 "Forgive Me")..........5-10 62
OLD TOWN (1162 "Operator")..........5-10 64
Session: Sonny Terry; Brownie McGhee; Jack Dupree; Joe Ruffin; Jimmy Spruill; Al Hall; Gene Brooks; Willie Jones; Pete Brown.
Also see GADDY, Doctor, & His Orchestra
Also see McGHEE, Brownie, & Sonny Terry

GADDY, Doctor, & His Orchestra
(Bob Gaddy)
Singles: 78 rpm
DOT (1185 "Evil Man Blues")..........20-40 53
Singles: 7-inch
DOT (1185 "Evil Man Blues")..........75-125 53
Also see GADDY, Bob

GADSON, Mel P&R '60
Singles: 7-inch
BIG TOP (3034 "Comin' Down with Love")..........10-20 60
BIG TOP (3048 "Blood Brothers")..........10-20 60

GAIDA, Bill
Singles: 7-inch
ANTHEM (60726 "Yes Baby, I'm Scared")..........50-100

GAIE, Barbie
Singles: 7-inch
DART (1002 "My Boy Lollipop")..........15-25 58

GAIL & SANDRA
Singles: 7-inch
RADIO (103 "Bill")..........40-50 58

GAILLARD, Slim P&R/R&B '46
(Slim Gaillard Trio; with Boogiereeners)
Singles: 78 rpm
ATOMIC..........10-15 46
BEL-TONE..........10-15 45
CADET..........15-20 46
CLEF..........5-10 53-54
COLUMBIA..........5-10 '40s
4 STAR..........5-10 46
KING..........5-10 45-46
MAJESTIC..........10-15 46
OKEH..........5-15 40-42
20TH CENTURY..........10-15 46
VOCALION..........10-20 38-40
Singles: 7-inch
CLEF..........10-20 53-54
DOT (15919 "Down By the Station")..........10-15 59
ELGO (3001 "Angel")..........25-50 62
EPIC (10336 "Blowin' in the Wind")..........5-10 68
EPIC (10410 "On the South Side of Chicago")..........5-10 68
EPs: 7-inch
CLEF..........10-20 53
KING..........10-20 54

NORGRAN ... 10-20 54
ROYALE ... 10-20 '50s

LPs: 10/12-inch

CLEF (126 "Mish Mash") ... 25-50 53
CLEF (138 "Slim Cavorts") ... 25-50 53
DOT (3190 "Slim Gaillard Rides Again") . 20-30 59
(Monaural.)
DOT (25190 "Slim Gaillard Rides Again") ... 25-40 59
(Stereo.)
KING (80 "Boogie") ... 50-75 '50s
(10-inch LP.)
NORGRAN (13 "Slim Gaillard") ... 25-40 54
VERVE (2013 "Smorgasbord") ... 20-40 56
Also see GILLESPIE, Dizzy, & Slim Gaillard

GAILTONES

Singles: 7-inch

DECCA (30726 "Lover Boy") ... 20-30 58

GAINES, Alvin, & Themes

Singles: 7-inch

FIDELITY (420592 "Cross My Heart") . 300-400 59

GAINES, Earl — R&B '66

(Earl Gains)

Singles: 7-inch

ACE (3010 "Drownin' on Dry Land") ... 4-6 75
CHAMPION (1001 "Now Do You Hear") . 15-25 58
CHAMPION (1004 "Love You So") ... 10-20 60
DELUXE ... 5-10 68-69
EXCELLO (2217 "Baby, Baby, What's Wrong") ... 10-20 62
HBR (481 "It's Worth Anything") ... 5-10 66
HBR (510 "I Have Loved and I Have Lived") ... 5-10 66
HOLLYWOOD ... 5-10 67-68
KING (6408 "Don't Deceive Me") ... 4-6 73
SEVENTY SEVEN (131 "Hymn Number 5") ... 4-6 73

LPs: 10/12-inch

DELUXE ... 10-15 69
HBR ... 10-20 66

GAINES, Eddie, & Rockin' Five

Singles: 7-inch

SUMMIT (101 "Be-Bop Battlin' Ball") . 750-1000 58
SUMMIT (104 "Out of the Shadows") ... 15-25 58

GAINES, Fats, Band

("Presents Lou Washington Vocalist")

Singles: 78 rpm

BIG TOWN (108 "Homework Blues") ... 15-25 53
BIG TOWN (124 "Feeling Happy") ... 15-25 56

Singles: 7-inch

AVAMAR (105 "For Your Precious Love") ... 10-15
BIG TOWN (108 "Homework Blues") ... 25-50 53
BIG TOWN (124 "Feeling Happy") ... 25-50 56
Also see GRAHAM, Bonnie, & Fats Gaines
Also see THOMAS, Rita, & Fats Gaines Band
Also see WASHINGTON, Lou

GAINES, Joe

(With the Original Hi-Lites)

Singles: 7-inch

ARCADIA (116 "Voo Doo Lou") ... 10-20 59

GAINES, Roy

("Mr. Guitar")

Singles: 78 rpm

CHART (600 "Loud Mouth Lucy") ... 15-25 55
DELUXE ... 10-20 57
GROOVE ... 8-12 56

Singles: 7-inch

BELL (915 "Lay Lady Lay") ... 4-8 70
CHART (600 "Loud Mouth Lucy") ... 25-50 55
CU-BE-AR (58 "Don't Deceive Me") ... 10-15
DEL-FI (4169 "Lizzie") ... 5-10 61
DELUXE (6119 "Isabella") ... 10-20 57
DELUXE (6132 "Stolen Moments") ... 10-20 57
DELUXE (6147 "Night Beat") ... 10-20 57
GROOVE (0146 "Right Now, Baby") ... 20-25 56
GROOVE (0161 "Worried 'Bout You, Baby") ... 20-25 56
RCA (7243 "Skippy Is a Sissy") ... 40-60 58
UNI (55067 "Ella Speed") ... 5-10 68
Also see ROY & GLORIA

GAINORS

Singles: 7-inch

CAMEO (151 "The Secret") ... 10-15 58
CAMEO (156 "Follow Me") ... 500-600 59
MERCURY (71466 "She's My Lollipop") .. 10-15 59
MERCURY (71569 "She's Gone") ... 20-30 60
MERCURY (71630 "I'm in Love with You") ... 15-20 60
RED TOP (110 "Follow Me") ... 100-150 58
TALLY-HO (102 "This Is a Perfect Moment") ... 10-15 61
TALLY-HO (105 "Tell Him") ... 20-30 61
Members: Garnet Mimms; Sam Bell; Howard Tate; Willie Combo; John Jefferson.
Also see MIMMS, Garnet
Also see TATE, Howard

GAINS, Eddie, & Rockin' Five

Singles: 7-inch

SUMMIT (101 "Be-Bop-Battlin' Ball") ... 200-300 '50s

GAITHERS, Gene

Singles: 7-inch

ASTRO (232 "Cute Little Chickie") ... 50-100

GALABOOCHIES

Singles: 7-inch

STAFF (188 "It'll Never Work Out") ... 20-30 66

GALACTUS

LPs: 10/12-inch

AIRSHIP ("Cosmic Force Field") ... 20-30 71
(Selection number not known.)
Member: Bob Hocko.
Also see SWAMP RATS

GALAHAD, Johnny

Singles: 7-inch

DECCA (31564 "'29 Model-A") ... 10-15 63

GALAHADS

LPs: 10/12-inch

LIBERTY (3371 "Hello Galahads") ... 15-20 64
(Monaural.)
LIBERTY (7371 "Hello Galahads") ... 15-25 64
(Stereo.)

GALAXIES

Singles: 7-inch

DARBO (1595 "If You Want to Be My Baby") ... 150-200 '50s
GUARANTEED (216 "My Tattle Tale") ... 50-75 61
UNITED SOUTHERN ARTISTS (117 "It's All Over Now") ... 75-100 62
Session: Eddie Cochran.

GALAXIES

Singles: 7-inch

CHESS (1757 "This Rock & Roll") ... 10-20 60

GALAXIES

Singles: 7-inch

CAPITOL (4427 "The Big Triangle") ... 8-12 60
RICHIE (458 "Dear Someone") ... 100-200 61

GALAXIES

Singles: 7-inch

ETIQUETTE (17 "I'm a Worker") ... 10-20 65
ETIQUETTE (20 "On the Beach") ... 10-20 65
ETIQUETTE (25 "I") ... 10-20 66
PANORAMA (54 "Along Comes the Man") ... 5-10 66
SEAFAIR (110 "Tacoma") ... 5-10 64
Members: Bob Lowery; Chuck Naubert; Bob Koch; Phil Hanson; Mark Eubanks.
Also see SONICS / Wailers / Galaxies

GALAXIES IV

Singles: 7-inch

MOHAWK (169 "Piccadilly Circus") ... 10-15 66
RCA (9235 "Don't Lose Your Mind") ... 10-15 67
VEEP (1211 "Til Then You'll Cry") ... 10-15 65

GALAXY

LPs: 10/12-inch

SKY QUEEN (1677 "A Day Without the Sun") ... 100-200 76

GALAXYS

Singles: 7-inch

CARTHAY (103 "A Lover's Prayer") 1500-3000 59

GALE, Barbara, & Larks

Singles: 78 rpm

LLOYDS ... 50-75 54

Singles: 7-inch

LLOYDS (111 "When You're Near") ... 100-200 54
LLOYDS (115 "Johnny Darlin'") ... 100-200 54
Also see GALE, Barbara
Also see LARKS

GALE, E., & Ad's

Singles: 7-inch

PHONA (709 "444") ... 10-20 62

GALE, Jim

Singles: 7-inch

KEN (105 "Rockin' Party") ... 250-350

GALE, Jimmy

(Jimmy Gale Quartet)

Singles: 7-inch

SOMA (1431 "School Is Over") ... 40-60 65

GALE, Sunny — P&R '52

(With the Saints & Sinners Dixieland Band; with Ralph Burns Orchestra; Sunny Gail)

Singles: 78 rpm

DECCA ... 4-8 56-57
DERBY ... 4-6 52
RCA ... 4-6 52-56

Singles: 7-inch

BLAINE (4002 "Stay") ... 5-10 65
BLAINE (4003 "March of the Angels") ... 5-10 65
CANADIAN AMERICAN (163 "To Bad for You") ... 5-10 63
CANADIAN AMERICAN (171 "I Wish I Didn't Love You So") ... 5-10 64
CANADIAN AMERICAN (176 "I'm Telling My Heart") ... 5-10 64
DECCA ... 10-15 56-59
DERBY (700 series) ... 15-25 52
(Colored vinyl.)
RCA (4000 thru 6000 series) ... 10-15 52-56
RCA (9000 series) ... 4-8 68
RIVERSIDE (4558 "I Know I Know") ... 5-10 63
STAGE ... 5-10 62
TERRACE (7505 "Love Me Again") ... 5-10 62
THIMBLE ... 4-6 74
WARWICK (526 "Falling Star") ... 5-10 60
WARWICK (540 "My Foolish Heart") ... 5-10 60
WARWICK (578 "It's Your Turn") ... 5-10 60
WARWICK (626 "Sunny") ... 5-10 61
WARWICK (648 "Need You") ... 5-10 61

EPs: 7-inch

KING ... 5-10
RCA ... 5-10 56

LPs: 10/12-inch

CANADIAN AMERICAN (1015 "Goldies by the Girls") ... 15-25 64
RCA (1277 "Sunny and Blue") ... 30-40 56
WARWICK (2018 "Sunny") ... 20-30 60
Also see WILCOX, Eddie, Orchestra

GALE, Sunny, & Du Droppers

Singles: 78 rpm

RCA (5543 "The Note in the Bottle") ... 10-15 53

Singles: 7-inch

RCA (5543 "The Note in the Bottle") ... 25-35 53
Also see DU DROPPERS
Also see GALE, Sunny

GALE, Terry

Singles: 7-inch

LARRY BEE (1107 "Voodoo") ... 15-25 65
LAS VEGAS STRIP (1001 "Betty Jean") .. 15-25 63
PRO-GRESS ... 5-10 74
WATER ST ... 5-10 75

GALES

Singles: 78 rpm

J.O.B. ... 75-125 56
J-V-B. ... 300-400 56

Singles: 7-inch

J.O.B. (3001 "Darling Patricia") ... 800-1000 56
J-V-B. (34 "Don't Let the Sun Catch You Crying") ... 1500-2000 56
J-V-B. (35 "Darling Patricia") ... 2500-3000 56
MEL-O (111 "Guiding Angel") ... 500-1000 58
MEL-O (111 "Guiding Angel") ... 5-10 '90s
(Black vinyl. 485 made.)
MEL-O (111 "Guiding Angel") ... 25-30 '90s
(Blue vinyl. 15 made.)
MEL-O (113 "If I Could Forget") ... 300-500 58
MEL-O (113 "If I Could Forget") ... 5-10 '90s
(Black vinyl. 485 made.)
MEL-O (113 "If I Could Forget") ... 25-30 '90s
(Blue vinyl. 15 made.)
Also see VIOLINAIRES

GALES

Singles: 7-inch

WINN (916 "I Love You") ... 450-500 60

GALES

Singles: 7-inch

DEBRA (1002 "Tommy") ... 15-25 63

GALES, Billy

Singles: 7-inch

SHOCK (200 "Dreaming of You") ... 50-75

GALLA, Tony, & Rising Sons

Singles: 7-inch

SWAN (4275 "In Love") ... 50-75 67

GALLAGHER, James

Singles: 78 rpm

DECCA (29984 "Crazy Chicken") ... 50-75 56

Singles: 7-inch

B&G (222 "Are You the One") ... 200-300
B&G (223 "Crazy About You Baby") ... 100-150
DECCA (29984 "Crazy Chicken") ... 50-75 56

GALLAGHER, Jay

Singles: 7-inch

DIXIE (2023 "Crazy Legs") ... 200-300 59

GALLAHADS — P&R '56

(With Billy Mure & Orchestra)

Singles: 78 rpm

CAPITOL ... 5-10 55
JUBILEE ... 5-10 56

Singles: 7-inch

CAPITOL (3060 "Ooh Ah") ... 10-20 55
CAPITOL (3175 "Do You Believe Me") ... 10-20 55
JUBILEE (5252 "The Fool") ... 15-25 56
JUBILEE (5259 "Take My Love") ... 10-15 56
VIK (0291 "Take Back My Ring") ... 10-20 57

Picture Sleeves

CAPITOL (3060 "Ooh Ah") ... 20-25 55
(Promotional issue only.)
Members: Frank Kreisel; Jackie Vincent; Buddy Raymond; Len Carrie; Bob Alexander; Vincent Bell.
Also see BELL, Vincent
Also see MURE, Billy

GALLAHADS

Singles: 7-inch

BEECH WOOD (3000 "Keeper of Dreams") ... 75-125 60
BEECH WOOD (5000 Once I Had a Love") ... 250-300 61
DEL-FI (4137 "Lonely Guy") ... 20-30 60
(Green label.)
DEL-FI (4137 "Lonely Guy") ... 8-12 60
(Black label.)
DEL-FI (4148 "Be Fair") ... 30-40 60
(Green label.)
DEL-FI (4148 "Be Fair") ... 8-12 60
(Black label.)
DONNA (1322 "Lonely Guy") ... 200-300 60
LOST NITE ... 4-8
NITE OWL (20 "Gone") ... 40-50 60
RENDEZVOUS (153 "Gone") ... 30-40 61
STARLA (15 "Keeper of Dreams") ... 20-30 59
Members: "Tiny" Tony Smith; James Pipkin.
Also see DYNAMICS
Also see PIPKIN, Jimmy, & Gallahads
Also see TINY TONY & STATICS

GALLAHADS

(With the Counts)

Singles: 7-inch

SEA CREST (6005 "Have Love Will Travel") ... 25-35 64

GALLANT, Billy

(With the Roulettes)

Singles: 7-inch

DEE DEE (501 "Thinking, Hoping, Wishing") ... 100-150 61
GOLDISC (G-6 "Thinking, Hoping, Wishing") ... 15-25 63
Also see ROULETTES

GALLANT, Bobby

Singles: 7-inch

LEVEE (706 "Run Boy Run") ... 10-20 61

GALLANT, Rodney

Singles: 7-inch

ELGIN (019 "Scuse Me Baby") ... 40-50 59
(First issue.)
SCOOPO (019 "Scuse Me Baby") ... 30-40 59
Session: Chestnuts.

GALLANT MEN

Singles: 7-inch

FORD (117 "Lost Romance")..................10-20 62

GALLEGOS, Chuck, & Fabulous Cyclones

Singles: 7-inch

CBG (Except 1110)..................8-12 63-64
CBG (1110 "I Love You So")..................40-50 64

GALLEONS

Singles: 7-inch

VITA (184 "I Played the Fool")..................50-75 59

GALLION, Bob C&W '58

Singles: 78 rpm

MGM (Except 12195)..................5-15 56-57
MGM (12195 "My Square Dancin' Mama")..................25-50 56

Singles: 7-inch

HICKORY..................4-8 60-63
MGM (Except 12195 & 12628)..................10-15 55-59
MGM (12195 "My Square Dancin' Mama")..................40-60 56
MGM (12628 "Baby, Love Me")..................15-25 58
U.A...................4-6 68

LPs: 10/12-inch

HICKORY (159 "Bob Gallion")..................8-12 70

GALLIS, Paul Orchestra
(Featuring Tommy Shepard)

Singles: 7-inch

GLEN (5011 "Hoot 'N' Switch")..................5-10 63
HEARTBEAT (5 "Boogie Twist")..................10-20 62

GALLO, Pat

Singles: 7-inch

CHARLIE PARKER (209 "Arabian Camel Walk")..................10-20 62

GALLON, Vic

Singles: 7-inch

GONDOLA ("I'm Gone")..................300-500
(Selection number not known.)

GALLOP, Frank P&R '58
(With Don Costa & His Orchestra; with Lou Jacobi & Betty Walker; Frank Gallup)

Singles: 7-inch

ABC-PAR (9931 "Got a Match")..................10-15 58
KAPP (745 "Ballad of Irving")..................4-8 66
MUSICOR (1191 "Son of Irving")..................4-8 66

Picture Sleeves

MUSICOR (1191 "Son of Irving")..................8-10 66

LPs: 10/12-inch

KAPP (4506 "When You're in Love")..................10-15 66
(Monaural.)
KAPP (5506 "When You're in Love")..................10-15 66
(Stereo.)
MUSICOR (2110 "Frank Gallop Sings")..................10-15 66
(Monaural.)
MUSICOR (3110 "Frank Gallop Sings")..................10-15 66
(Stereo.)
Also see COSTA, Don, Orchestra
Also see JACOBI, Lou

GALLOW'S POLE

LPs: 10/12-inch

AZRA (7886 "Gallow's Pole")..................10-15 87
(Picture disc. Promotional issue only. 500 made.)

GALLOWAY, Pearl

Singles: 7-inch

AMP 3 (2114 "Think It Over Baby")..................20-30 58

GALT, James

Singles: 7-inch

AURORA ("Don't Put Out the Fire")..................15-25 66
(Selection number not known.)
AURORA (158 "With My Baby")..................10-20 66

GAMBLE, Johnny

Singles: 7-inch

SFA ("Wicked Woman")..................100-200
(Selection number not known.)

GAMBLE, Kenny
(With the Romeos; with Tommy Bell)

Singles: 7-inch

ARCTIC (107 "Down By the Seashore")..................100-150 65
ARCTIC (114 "Ain't It Baby, Part 1"/"Ain't It Baby, Part 2")..................100-150 65
ARCTIC (114 "Ain't It Baby")..................40-60 65
(Single-sided. Promotional issue only.)
ARCTIC (123 "The Joke's on You")..................100-150 65
ARCTIC (127 "Chains of Love")..................15-25 67
ATCO (6470 "Hard to Find the Right Girl")..................10-15 67
COLUMBIA (43132 "Our Love")..................100-150 64
EPIC (9636 "Standing in the Shadows")..................10-20 63
HERITAGE (108 "Someday You'll Be My Love")..................50-75 62
Also see ROMEOS

GAMBLERS

Singles: 7-inch

LAST CHANCE (2 "Teen Machine")..................25-35 61
LAST CHANCE (108 "Teen Machine")..................20-30 62
WORLD PACIFIC (815 "Moon Dawg")..................40-60 60
Members: Larry Taylor; Elliot Ingber; Darry Weaver; Bruce Johnston; Sandy Nelson.
Also see ASCOTS
Also see CANNED HEAT
Also see HOLLYWOOD GAMBLERS
Also see JOHNSTON, Bruce
Also see MOTHERS OF INVENTION
Also see NELSON, Sandy
Also see RENEGADES
Also see WEAVER, Darry

GAMBLERS

Singles: 7-inch

GAS-LITE (807 "Ooh-Poo-Pah Doo")..................10-20 66

GAMBRELLS

Singles: 7-inch

CUB (9156 "Love Is in the Air")..................10-15 68

GAMINS

Singles: 7-inch

SOMA (1459 "Ridin' High")..................10-15 65
Member: Gunner Olness.
Also see OLNESS, Gunner

GAMMA GOOCHEE

Singles: 7-inch

COLPIX (786 "Gamma Goochee")..................10-20 65
COLPIX (804 "I'm So Glad")..................10-20 66
MGM (13874 "Everybody's Somebody's Fool")..................8-15 67

Picture Sleeves

COLPIX (786 "Gamma Goochee")..................20-30 65

GANDALF

Singles: 7-inch

CAPITOL (2400 "Golden Earring")..................10-20 69

LPs: 10/12-inch

CAPITOL (121 "Gandalf")..................100-200 69
Members: Peter Sando; Bob Muller; Davy Bauer; Frank Hubach.

GANDALF THE GREY

LPs: 10/12-inch

GWR (7 "Grey Wizard Am I")..................200-400 72

GANDY, Jack, Trio

Singles: 78 rpm

BLUE KEY (1000 "Rock 'n Roll n' Rhythm Doll")..................10-20 52
KING (1388 "Isn't It a Shame")..................8-12 54

Singles: 7-inch

BLUE KEY (1000 "Rock 'n Roll n' Rhythm Doll")..................50-100 52
KING (1388 "Isn't It a Shame")..................10-20 54

GANDY, Little Jimmy

Singles: 7-inch

ROULETTE (7047 "Cool 13")..................10-15 69

GANEY, Jerry
(With the Break of Dawn)

Singles: 7-inch

BI-TRUCKIN' (12345 "Just for Us")..................5-10
MGM (13697 "You Don't Love Me")..................10-20 67
VERVE (10454 "Just a Fool")..................50-75 66

GANN, Don

Singles: 7-inch

HOUSTON (1001 "Have You Ever Been Loved")..................25-35 69
HOUSTON (1002 "Wildcat Willie")..................35-45 70

GANT, Cecil R&B '44
(Pvt. Cecil Gant "The G.I. Sing-Sation"; with His Trio; Cecil Grant)

Singles: 78 rpm

BOP..................15-20
BRONZE..................10-20 44
BULLET..................10-20 46
DECCA..................15-30 50-51
DOT (1000 series)..................15-25 50-51
DOWN BEAT..................15-25 49
4 STAR..................15-25 47-52
GILT-EDGE (500 "Cecil Boogie")..................200-300 45
(Cardboard picture disc. Add $100 to $150 for mailer.)
IMPERIAL..................15-25 50-51
KING..................15-25 47
NATIONAL..................15-25 44
SWING TIME..................15-25 49

Singles: 7-inch

DECCA (30320 "I Wonder")..................35-50 57
DECCA (48171 "Someday You'll Be Sorry")..................50-75 50
DECCA (48185 "It's Christmas Time Again")..................50-75 50
DECCA (48191 "Train Time Blues, No. 2")..................50-75 50
DECCA (48200 "Shot Gun Boogie")..................50-75 51
DECCA (48212 "Don't You Worry")..................50-75 51
DECCA (48231 "Owl Stew")..................50-75 51
DECCA (48249 "God Bless My Daddy")..................50-75 51
DOT (1121 "Train Time Blues")..................40-60 52
GILT-EDGE (5090 "I Wonder")..................30-40 55

LPs: 10/12-inch

KING (671 "The Incomparable Cecil Gant")..................40-50 60
RED MILL ("Piano and Voice")..................300-500
(No selection number used. Colored vinyl.)
SOUND (601 "The Incomparable Cecil Gant")..................75-125 57
Also see CARR, Gunter Lee

GANT, Clentt

Singles: 7-inch

CHANSON (1000 "Certainly")..................10-20 59
CHANSON (1001 "I Need You So")..................10-20 60
CHANSON (1003 "Stormy Weather")..................10-20 60
CHANSON (1004 "Growing Strong")..................10-20 60
CHANSON (1005 "All Mine")..................10-20 61
DUKE (348 "All Mine")..................5-10 62
Also see DON Q

GANTNER, Dennis

Singles: 7-inch

BLUE STAR (001 "Once I Had a Girl")..................30-40

GANTS

Singles: 78 rpm

ALADDIN (3387 "My Unfaithful Love")..................40-50 57

Singles: 7-inch

ALADDIN (3387 "My Unfaithful Love")..................100-200 57

GANTS P&R '65

Singles: 7-inch

LIBERTY (55829 thru 55965)..................10-15 65-67
STATUE (605 "Road Runner")..................30-40 65
(First issue.)

LPs: 10/12-inch

LIBERTY..................15-25 65-66

GANZBERG, Jimmy

Singles: 7-inch

JET (1419 "Rebel Yell")..................25-35 58
JET (5434 "White Saddle Shoes")..................25-35 58
JET (5436 "Jo-Ellen")..................25-35 58

GARABEDIAN, George
(George Garabedian Players; Troubadours)

Singles: 7-inch

LIBERTY (55215 "Artistry in Rhythm")..................8-12 59
MARK 56..................10-15 58-59
Also see FABULOUS TONES

GARCIA, Augie
(Augie Garcia Quintet)

Singles: 7-inch

KIRK (133 "Ivy League Baby")..................75-125 '50s
NO. STAR (2023 "Drinking Wine")..................75-125 58
NO. STAR (2025 "Hi Yo Silver")..................75-125 58
NO. STAR (2065 "Ring-A-Ling")..................75-125 '50s

GARCIA, Felix

Singles: 7-inch

R-DELL (104 "Summer Love")..................10-20 58
Also see FELIX & FABULOUS CATS

GARCIA, Jerry P&R/LP '72
(Jerry Garcia Band)

Singles: 7-inch

DOUGLAS..................8-15 73
ROUND..................8-15 72-74
W.B...................8-15 72

LPs: 10/12-inch

ARISTA..................6-12 78-82
ROUND..................10-20 74-75
U.A...................10-15 76
W.B. (2582 "Garcia")..................40-50 72
Also see CROSBY, STILLS, NASH & YOUNG
Also see DYLAN, Bob, & Grateful Dean
Also see GRATEFUL DEAD
Also see HART, Mickey
Also see IT'S A BEAUTIFUL DAY
Also see JEFFERSON AIRPLANE
Also see OLD AND IN THE WAY
Also see ROWANS
Also see WALES, Howard, & Jerry Garcia

GARCIA, Jerry, & Robert Hunter

Singles: 7-inch

ROUND (102 "Sampler for Dead Heads")..................50-75 74
(Includes letter about the Grateful Dead LP, *The Mars Hotel*, and some miniature LP covers. Promotional fan club issue.)
ROUND (102 "Sampler for Dead Heads")..................25-35 74
(Price for disc without inserts.)
Also see GARCIA, Jerry
Also see GRATEFUL DEAD
Also see HUNTER, Robert

GARDENIAS

Singles: 78 rpm

FEDERAL (12284 "Flaming Love")..................20-30 56

Singles: 7-inch

FEDERAL (12284 "Flaming Love")..................50-75 56
HI-Q (5005 "I'm Laughing at You")..................75-125 58
(Reissued as by the Tempos.)

GARDENIAS

Singles: 7-inch

FAIRLANE (21019 "Darling It's You, You, You")..................15-20 62
Also see FABULOUS GARDENIAS

GARDNER, Dave P&R '57
(Brother Dave Gardner)

Singles: 7-inch

DECCA (30548 "All By Myself")..................10-15 58
DECCA (30627 "Slick Slacks")..................20-30 58
OJ (1002 "White Silver Sands")..................20-30 57
OJ (1006 "Love Is My Business")..................10-15 58
RCA..................8-12 59-61
TOWER (PRO 4393 "Smoking")..................5-10 67
(Promotional issue only.)

EPs: 7-inch

CAPITOL (2610 "It's All in How You Look At 'It'")..................8-12 64

LPs: 10/12-inch

CAMDEN..................5-10 73
CAPITOL (1867 "It Don't Make No Difference")..................15-25 63
CAPITOL (2055 "It's All in How You Look At 'It'")..................15-25 64
RCA..................15-25 60-64
TOWER..................10-20 67

GARDNER, Don
(With His Sonotones; with Alteers)

Singles: 78 rpm

BRUCE..................20-30 54-55
CAMEO..................10-20 57
DELUXE..................10-15 57

Singles: 7-inch

BRUCE (105 "How Do You Speak to an Angel")..................40-60 54
BRUCE (108 "I'll Walk Alone")..................35-55 54
BRUCE (127 "It's a Sin to Tell a Lie")..................30-40 55
CAMEO (102 "Only Love Brings Happiness")..................20-30 57
DELUXE (6133 "A Dagger in My Chest")..................10-20 57
DELUXE (6155 "I Don't Want to Go Home")..................10-20 57
G-CLEF (704 "Let's Get a Thing Goin' ")..................15-25 64
JUNIOR (393 "High School Baby")..................20-30 57
JUNIOR (394 "Dark Alley")..................15-25 57
JUBILEE (5484 "The Bitter with the Sweet")..................5-10 64
JUBILEE (5493 "Little Girl Blue")..................5-10 64
KAISER (399 "Ask Anything")..................10-20 59
MR. G (824 "Your Love Is Driving Me Crazy")..................8-12 69
SEDRICK..................15-25
VAL-UE (214 "Deed I Do")..................15-25 60
VERVE (10582 "You Babe")..................5-10

Also see ALTEERS
Also see SMITH, Dickie
Also see WASHINGTON, Baby, & Don Gardner

GARDNER, Don, & Dee Dee Ford *P&R/R&B '62*
Singles: 7-inch
COLLECTABLES (1626 "I Need Your Lovin' ")...3-5 '80s
FIRE (508 "I Need Your Lovin' ")...15-25 62
(Red label.)
FIRE (508 "I Need Your Lovin' ")...10-15 62
(Multi-color label.)
FIRE (513 "Don't You Worry")...10-15 62
FIRE (517 "Lead Me On")...10-15 62
FLASHBACK (0010 "I Need Your Lovin' ")...5-8 65
KC (106 "Glory of Love")...10-15 62
LUDIX (104 "You Upset My Soul")...8-12 63
M.O.C. (654 "I Love You")...5-10 64
RED TOP (6501 "People Sho' Act Funny")...8-12 63
TRU-GLO-TOWN (501 "My Baby Likes to Boogaloo")...5-10 66
LPs: 10/12-inch
FIRE (105 "Need Your Lovin' ")...75-125 62
SUE (1044 "Don Gardner & Dee Dee Ford in Sweden")...20-30 66
Also see FORD, Dee Dee
Also see GARDNER, Don
Also see WASHINGTON, Baby, & Don Gardner

GARDNER, Leon
Singles: 7-inch
CHATTAHOOCHEE (667 "You're Gonna Cry")...10-20 65
IGLOO (101 "Tell Me Why")...10-20 '60s
IGLOO (316 "Stay Here")...10-20 '60s
VAULT (915 "Can't Stop Now")...8-12 65

GARFUNKEL, Art *P&R/LP '73*
Singles: 7-inch
COLUMBIA (Except SQ-45926)...3-8 73-88
COLUMBIA (SQ-45926 "All I Know")...5-10 73
(Quadraphonic. Promotional issue only.)
Picture Sleeves
COLUMBIA (45926 "All I Know")...4-6 81
LPs: 10/12-inch
COLUMBIA (KC-31474 "Angel Clare")...10-15 73
COLUMBIA (CQ-31474 "Angel Clare")...15-25 73
COLUMBIA (PC-33700 "Breakaway")...8-12 75
COLUMBIA (PCQ-33700 "Breakaway")...15-25 75
COLUMBIA (34975 "Watermark")...8-12 78
COLUMBIA (35780 "Fate for Breakfast")...8-12 79
COLUMBIA (FC-37392 "Scissors Cut")...5-10 81
COLUMBIA (HC-47392 "Scissors Cut")...20-30 81
(Half-speed mastered.)
COLUMBIA (40942 "Lefty")...5-10 88
Also see GARR, Artie
Also see SIMON & GARFUNKEL

GARFUNKEL, Art, James Taylor & Paul Simon *P&R '78*
Singles: 7-inch
COLUMBIA (10676 "Wonderful World")...4-6 78
Also see GARFUNKEL, Art
Also see SIMON, Paul
Also see TAYLOR, James

GARI, Frank *P&R '60*
Singles: 7-inch
ATLANTIC (2171 "Ain't That Fun")...8-10 62
CAPITOL (2101 "April")...5-8 68
CRUSADE (1020 "Utopia")...10-15 60
CRUSADE (1021 "Lullaby of Love")...10-15 61
CRUSADE (1022 "Princess")...10-15 61
CRUSADE (1024 "You Better Keep Runnin' ")...8-12 62
RIBBON (6903 "Your Only Love")...8-12 59
U.A. (297 "Be My Girl")...8-12 61
Picture Sleeves
CRUSADE (1021 "Lullaby of Love")...20-30 61
CRUSADE (1022 "Princess")...20-30 61
CRUSADE (1024 "You Better Keep Runnin' ")...20-30 62

GARLAND, Bill
Singles: 7-inch
PAM (502 "Guitar Blues")...50-75

GARLAND, Dickie
Singles: 7-inch
PIKE (5905 "Shake Bop")...10-20 61
Also see HOWARD, Jim

GARLAND, Gabe
(With His Orchestra, Featuring the Garland-Aires)
Singles: 78 rpm
ONYX (217 "If You Don't Dance")...10-20 55
Singles: 7-inch
ONYX (217 "If You Don't Dance")...20-25 55
WYNNE (109 "Weekend Rock")...10-20 59

GARLAND, Hank
LPs: 10/12-inch
COLUMBIA...15-25 61-62
HARMONY (7231 "Velvet Guitar")...15-20 60
(Monaural.)
HARMONY (11028 "Velvet Guitar")...20-25 60
(Stereo.)
Also see ECHOES
Also see PRESLEY, Elvis
Also see STEWART, Wynn

GARLAND, Judy *P&R '39*
Singles: 78 rpm
CAPITOL...3-8 56-57
COLUMBIA...3-8 53-54
DECCA (Except 2000 through 4000 series)...5-15 42-55
DECCA (2000 thru 4000 series)...10-20 39-42
Singles: 7-inch
ABC...4-8 67
CAPITOL...8-15 56-63
COLUMBIA (40000 series)...10-20 53-54
DECCA (25000 series)...4-8 65
DECCA (29000 series)...10-20 55
MCA...4-6 73-78
MGM (166 "Over the Rainbow")...4-6 64
(Golden Circle reissue series.)
W.B....4-8 63
Promotional Singles
CAPITOL ("After You've Gone"/"When You're Smiling")...10-20 59
(No selection number used.)
Picture Sleeves
CAPITOL ("After You've Gone"/"When You're Smiling")...20-30 59
(Sleeve reads "Two of the Top Tunes from *Garland at the Grove*.")
EPs: 7-inch
CAPITOL (676 "Miss Show Business")...10-20 55
CAPITOL (734 "Judy")...10-20 56
CAPITOL (835 "Alone")...10-20 57
CAPITOL (1569 "Judy at Carnegie Hall")...10-15 62
COLUMBIA (1201 "A Star Is Born")...15-20 54
(Soundtrack.)
COLUMBIA (2598 "Judy Garland")...20-30 57
COLUMBIA (7621 "Born in a Trunk")...25-50 56
DECCA (620 "Judy Garland at the Palace/ Greatest Performances")...10-20 55
DECCA (661 "The Wizard of Oz")...15-25 51
DECCA (2050 "Judy Garland, Vol. 2")...12-20 53
MGM (40 "Easter Parade")...30-50 50
(Gatefold cover.)
MGM (268 "If You Feel Like Singing, Sing")...10-20 54
MGM (1038 "Get Happy")...10-20 55
MGM (1116 "Look for the Silver Lining")...10-20 55
MGM (1122 "Judy Garland")...10-20 55
LPs: 10/12-inch
ABC (620 Judy Garland at Home at the Palace")...10-15 67
ABC (30007 "Judy Garland the ABC Collection")...5-10 76
AEI (3101 "Meet Me in St. Louis"/"The Harvey Girls")...10-15
(Soundtrack. Reissue.)
ACCESSOR...8-15
AUDIOFIDELITY (311 "Judy Garland")...15-20 83
(Picture disc.)
C.I.T....8-12
CAPITOL (W-676 "Miss Show Business")...30-40 55
CAPITOL (SW-676 "Miss Show Business")...10-20 63
CAPITOL (T-734 "Judy")...25-35 56
CAPITOL (DT-734 "Judy")...10-20 63
CAPITOL (T-835 "Alone")...25-35 57
CAPITOL (DT-835 "Alone")...10-20 63
CAPITOL (1036 "Judy in Love")...20-35 58
CAPITOL (1118 "Garland at the Grove")...40-60 59
CAPITOL (1188 "The Letter")...25-35 59
(With John Ireland.)
CAPITOL (1467 "Judy - That's Entertainment")...20-35 60
CAPITOL (1569 "Judy at Carnegie Hall")...20-35 61
CAPITOL (1710 "The Garland Touch")...20-30 62
CAPITOL (W-1861 "I Could Go On Singing")...25-30 63
(Soundtrack.)
CAPITOL (SW-1861 "I Could Go On Singing")...35-40 63
(Soundtrack.)
CAPITOL (1941 "Our Love Letter")...15-20 63
(With John Ireland.)
CAPITOL (1999 "The Hits of Judy Garland")...20-30 64
(With "T" or "ST" prefix.)
CAPITOL (SM-1999 "The Hits of Judy Garland")...5-10 75
CAPITOL (2062 "Just for Openers")...15-25 64
CAPITOL (2988 "Judy Garland Deluxe Set")...20-35 68
CAPITOL (11763 "Alone")...5-10 78
CAPITOL (11876 "Judy - That's Entertainment")...5-10 79
CAPITOL (12034 "Just for Openers")...5-10 80
CAPITOL (16175 "The Hits of Judy Garland")...4-6 81
COLUMBIA (762 "Born in a Trunk")...50-100 56
(10-inch LP.)
COLUMBIA (1101 "A Star Is Born")...20-25 58
(Soundtrack.)
COLUMBIA (1201 "A Star Is Born")...35-45 54
(Soundtrack. Deluxe boxed edition.)
COLUMBIA (8740 "A Star Is Born")...20-30 63
(Soundtrack.)
COLUMBIA (10011 "A Star Is Born")...6-12 73
(Soundtrack.)
COLUMBIA/CSP (8740 "A Star Is Born")...5-10
(Soundtrack.)
COMPUSONIC...8-12
DRG...10-20
DECCA (5 "Collector's Items: 1936-1945")...15-25 70
DECCA (172 "The Best of Judy Garland")...15-20 63
(Monaural.)
DECCA (7-172 "The Best of Judy Garland")...15-20 63
(Stereo.)
DECCA (4199 "The Magic of Judy Garland")...15-20 61
DECCA (5152 "Wizard of Oz")...25-50 52
(Soundtrack. 10-inch LP.)
DECCA (6020 "Judy Garland at the Palace")...35-45 55
DECCA (8190 "Judy Garland - Greatest Performances")...35-45 55
DECCA (8387 "The Wizard of Oz")...20-35 56
(Soundtrack. One side, *The Song Hits from Pinocchio*, does not feature Judy.)
DECCA (8498 "Meet Me in St. Louis"/"The Harvey Girls")...60-70 57
(Soundtrack. Different show on each side.)
DECCA (75150 "Judy Garland's Greatest Hits")...8-12 69
DECCA (78387 "Wizard of Oz")...10-15 67
(Soundtrack.)
51 WEST...5-10
HARMONY (11366 "A Star Is Born")...10-15 69
(Soundtrack.)
JUNO (1000 "Judy–London 1969")...6-12 69
MCA (4003 "The Best of Judy Garland")...10-15 73
MFSL (048 "Live at London Palladium")...40-60 80
MGM (1 "Golden Years at MGM")...15-25 69
MGM (21 "The Pirate")...50-75 51
(Soundtrack. With Gene Kelly. 10-inch LP.)
MGM (82 "Judy Garland Sings")...50-100 51
MGM (113 "Judy Garland")...8-12 70
MGM (3149 "Judy Garland")...35-45 54
MGM (3234 "The Pirate")...25-30 55
(Soundtrack. With Gene Kelly.)
MGM (3464 "The Wizard of Oz")...35-45 61
(Soundtrack.)
MGM (3771 "Words and Music")...15-25 60
MGM (3989 "The Judy Garland Story, Vol. 1")...15-20 61
MGM (3996 "The Wizard of Oz")...15-20 61
(Soundtrack.)
MGM (4005 "The Judy Garland Story, Vol. 2")...15-20 61
MGM (4204 "The Very Best of Judy Garland")...12-20 64
MARK 56 (632 "Live In San Francisco")...125-150 79
(Picture disc.)
METRO (505 "Judy Garland")...10-15 65
METRO (581 "Judy Garland in Song")...10-15 66
PARAGON...5-10
PHOENIX 10...8-12 81
PICKWICK...5-10 '70s
RADIANT...6-12
RADIOLA...5-10
SPRINGBOARD...5-10
STANYAN...5-10 74
STAR TONE...5-10
TRIP (9 "16 Greatest Hits")...5-10 76
TROPHY...5-10
Also see CROSBY, Bing, & Judy Garland
Also see HAYMES, Dick, & Judy Garland
Also see MARTIN, Dean
Also see YOUNG, Victor

GARLAND, Judy / Tommy Dorsey
Singles: 78 rpm
VOGUE ("The Trolley Song")...750-1000 46
(Picture disc.)
Also see DORSEY, Tommy

GARLAND, Judy, & Liza Minnelli *LP '65*
Singles: 7-inch
CAPITOL...5-8 65
LPs: 10/12-inch
CAPITOL (2295 "Live at the London Palladium")...15-20 65
CAPITOL (11191 "Live at the London Palladium")...5-10 73
MFSL (048 "Live at the London Palladium")...30-50 81
TROLLEY CAR...5-10
Also see GARLAND, Judy
Also see MINNELLI, Liza

GARLAND THE GREAT
Singles: 78 rpm
SPARK (121 "Hello Miss Simms")...8-12 55
Singles: 7-inch
SPARK (121 "Hello Miss Simms")...20-25 55

GARLOW, Clarence *R&B '50*
(With the Clarence "Bon Ton" Barlow)
Singles: 78 rpm
ALADDIN...30-50 52
FEATURE...20-30 51-54
FLAIR...30-50 54
FOLK STAR...15-25 54
GOLDBAND...10-20 56-57
LYRIC...10-20 51
MACY'S...10-15 49
Singles: 7-inch
ALADDIN (3179 "New Bon Ton Roulay")...50-75 52
ALADDIN (3225 "You Got Me Crying")...50-75 52
FEATURE (3005 "If I Keep on Worrying")...40-60 54
FLAIR (1021 "Crawfishin' ")...50-75 54
FOLK STAR (1130 "Za Belle")...25-40 54
FOLK STAR (1199 "No No Baby")...25-40 54
GOLDBAND...20-25 56-57

GARMON, Bob
Singles: 7-inch
AMBER (275 "I'm Ready Baby")...50-75

GARMON, Johnny
Singles: 7-inch
MISSILE (1 "You're Wrong")...800-1200

GARNER, Al
(Al Gardner)
Singles: 7-inch
DECCA (31170 "The Stomp")...15-25 60
DELTA...8-12
EXCELLO (2199 "I Wonder")...10-15 61
EXCELLO (2208 "Disgusted")...10-15 61
GROOVESVILLE (777 "I'll Get Along")...30-50 64
LUPINE (121 "I'll Get Along")...20-30 64
SIR-RAH (504 "Watch Yourself")...10-20 '60s

GARNER, Billy
Singles: 7-inch
MOJO (2171 "Little School Girl")...40-60 61

GARNER, Emmett, Jr.
Singles: 7-inch
MAXWELL (802 "Check Out What You've Got")...15-25 '60s

GARNER, Erroll *R&B '49*
(Erroll Garner Trio)
Singles: 78 rpm
BLACK & WHITE (16 "Movin' Around") ... 10-15 45
COLUMBIA ... 5-10 53-54
IMPERIAL (5059 "Movin' Around") ... 5-10 50
IMPERIAL (5078 "White Rose Bounce") ... 5-10 50
MERCURY ... 5-10 54
RECORDED IN HOLLYWOOD (110 "Lotus Blues") ... 5-10 50
RECORDED IN HOLLYWOOD (124 "Garner in Hollywood") ... 5-10 50
RECORDED IN HOLLYWOOD (128 "New York Concerto") ... 5-10 50
SAVOY ... 5-15 45-49
Singles: 7-inch
ABC-PAR ... 5-10 61-62
ATLANTIC (600 series) ... 25-35 50-52
COLUMBIA (40000 & 41000 series) ... 10-20 53-54
MGM ... 4-8 66-69
MERCURY (70000 series) ... 10-20 54
MERCURY (72000 & 73000 series) ... 4-8 63-71
OCTAVE ... 5-10 63
REPRISE ... 5-10 63
SAVOY ... 10-20 '50s
Picture Sleeves
ABC-PAR ... 10-15 61-62
MGM ... 5-10 67
EPs: 7-inch
ATLANTIC ... 10-15 56
BRUNSWICK ... 10-15 53
COLUMBIA ... 10-15 50-59
EMARCY ... 10-15 56
KING ... 10-15 54
MERCURY ... 10-15 54-56
SAVOY ... 10-15 51-55
LPs: 10/12-inch
ABC-PAR (395 "Erroll Garner Close Up in Swing") ... 20-30 61
ATLANTIC (109 "Rhapsody") ... 50-100 49
(10-inch LP.)
ATLANTIC (112 "Piano Solos") ... 50-100 50
(10-inch LP.)
ATLANTIC (128 "Passport to Fame") ... 50-100 51
(10-inch LP.)
ATLANTIC (138 "Piano Solos") ... 50-100 52
(10-inch LP.)
ATLANTIC (1227 "Greatest Garner") ... 30-40 56
BARONET ... 15-25 61
BLUE NOTE (5000 series) ... 20-40 52-53
(10-inch LP.)
COLUMBIA (535 "At the Piano") ... 45-65 53
(Red and gold label.)
COLUMBIA (535 "At the Piano") ... 30-50 56
(Red and black label.)
COLUMBIA (583 "Gems") ... 40-60 54
(Red and gold label.)
COLUMBIA (583 "Gems") ... 30-50 56
(Red and black label.)
COLUMBIA (617 "Gonest") ... 40-60 55
(Red and gold label.)
COLUMBIA (617 "Gonest") ... 30-50 56
(Red and black label.)
COLUMBIA (651 "Music for Tired Lovers") ... 25-50 55
(Red and gold label.)
COLUMBIA (883 "Concert by the Sea") .. 25-50 56
COLUMBIA (939 thru 1587) ... 20-40 57-61
COLUMBIA (2540 "Garnerland") ... 40-60 56
(10-inch LP.)
COLUMBIA (6139 "Piano Moods") ... 50-75 50
(10-inch LP.)
COLUMBIA (6173 "Gems") ... 50-75 51
(10-inch LP.)
COLUMBIA (8000 series) ... 30-40 60
COLUMBIA (9000 series) ... 6-12 70
COLUMBIA SPECIAL PRODUCTS ... 5-8 79
DIAL (205 "Garner Trio") ... 75-100 50
(10-inch LP.)
DIAL (902 "Gaslight Session") ... 75-100 50
(10-inch LP.)
EMARCY (26016 "Garnering") ... 60-80 54
(10-inch LP.)
EMARCY (26042 "Gone with Garner") ... 60-80 54
(10-inch LP.)
EMARCY (36001 "Contrasts") ... 35-50 55
EMARCY (36026 "Garnering") ... 35-50 55
EMARCY (36069 "Erroll") ... 35-50 56
ENRICA (2002 "Garner Plays Garner") ... 15-25 59
EVEREST ... 5-10 70
GRAND AWARD ... 20-35 56
HARMONY ... 8-12 68
JAZZTONE ... 20-35 57
KING (265-17 "Erroll Garner") ... 50-75 54
(10-inch LP.)
KING (540 "Erroll Garner") ... 25-35 58
LONDON ... 8-12 72-73
MGM ... 15-25 65-68
MERCURY (20009 "At the Piano") ... 50-75 50
MERCURY (20055 "Mambo") ... 40-60 54
MERCURY (20063 "Solitaire") ... 40-60 54
MERCURY (20090 "Afternoon of an Elf") ... 40-60 55
MERCURY (20662 thru 20859) ... 15-25 62-63
(Monaural.)
MERCURY (25117 "At the Piano") ... 50-75 51
(10-inch LP.)
MERCURY (25157 "Gone with Garner") .. 50-75 51
(10-inch LP.)
MERCURY (60662 thru 60859) ... 20-30 62-63
(Stereo.)
MERCURY (61000 series) ... 8-12 70
REPRISE (6080 "Erroll Garner One World Concert") ... 12-25 63
RONDO-LETTE ... 25-35 58
ROOST (10 "Piano Magic") ... 50-75 52
(10-inch LP.)
ROOST (2213 "Giants") ... 30-40 56
SAVOY (1100 series) ... 5-10 78
SAVOY (2000 series) ... 5-10 76
SAVOY (12002 "Erroll Garner") ... 40-50 55
SAVOY (12003 "Erroll Garner, Vol. 2") ... 40-50 55
SAVOY (12008 "Erroll Garner") ... 40-50 55
SAVOY (15000 "At the Piano") ... 100-200 49
(10-inch LP.)
SAVOY (15001 "At the Piano, Vol. 2") ... 75-125 50
(10-inch LP.)
SAVOY (15002 "At the Piano, Vol. 3") ... 75-125 50
(10-inch LP.)
SAVOY (15004 "At the Piano, Vol. 4") ... 75-125 50
(10-inch LP.)
SAVOY (15026 "At the Piano, Vol. 5") ... 75-125 50
(10-inch LP.)
TRIP ... 5-10 74
WING (12134 "Moods") ... 15-25 62
(Monaural.)
WING (16134 "Moods") ... 15-25 62
(Stereo.)
Also see STARR, Kay / Erroll Garner

GARNER, Gabby
Singles: 7-inch
EMERALD (2052 "Smokin' Heat") ... 50-100

GARNER, Johnny
Singles: 7-inch
IMPERIAL (5536 "Kiss Me Sweet") ... 25-35 58
IMPERIAL (5548 "Didi Didi") ... 25-35 58

GARNER, Merlene
Singles: 7-inch
DAVCO (102 "You're It") ... 15-25 '60s
DAVCO (106 "Will You Remember Mine") ... 20-30 '60s

GARNER, Trice
Singles: 7-inch
GULF (633 "Lover's Hill") ... 50-75

GARNETT, Gale *P&R/C&W/LP '64*
Singles: 7-inch
RCA GOLD STANDARD ... 5-8 64
(With "447" prefix.)
RCA (8388 thru 8472) ... 5-10 64
RCA (8549 "I'll Cry Alone") ... 25-50 65
RCA (8668 thru 9020) ... 5-10 65-67
Picture Sleeves
RCA (8472 "Lovin' Place") ... 10-15 64
LPs: 10/12-inch
RCA ... 10-20 64-66

GARO, Tony
Singles: 7-inch
PLA-MOR (6425 "Whole Lot of Shakin' ") ... 100-150

GARR, Artie
(Art Garfunkel)
Singles: 7-inch
OCTAVIA (8002 "Private Love") ... 20-30 61
WARWICK (515 "Beat Love") ... 75-125 59
Also see GARFUNKEL, Art

GARRETT, Bobby
(Bobby Byrd; Bobby Relf)
Singles: 7-inch
E&M (1602 "Short Skirts") ... 50-75 63
MIRWOOD (5508 "I Can't Get Away") ... 8-12 65
MIRWOOD (5511 "My Little Girl") ... 8-12 66
Also see BYRD, Bobby
Also see RELF, Bobby

GARRETT, Bobby, & Comanches
Singles: 7-inch
TROPHY (501 "Bobcat") ... 15-25 58

GARRETT, Jo Ann
(With the Rock)
Singles: 7-inch
CHESS (1959 "Whole New Plan") ... 20-30 66
CHESS (1992 "I'm So Afraid") ... 10-15 67
CHESS (2031 "Just Say When") ... 10-15 67
CHESS (2097 "Unforgettable") ... 10-15 70
DUKE (475 "Under Your Control") ... 4-6 73
DUO ... 4-8 69-70
SCORPIO (101 "Your Faithful Love") ... 4-6

GARRETT, Kelly
Singles: 7-inch
AVA (137 "Baby, It Hurts") ... 8-12 63
AVA (156 "This Heart Is Haunted") ... 8-12 64
PALOMAR (2207 "The Boy on the Drums") ... 5-10 65
RCA ... 4-6 76
SMASH (2195 "Knowing When to Leave") ... 50-75 68
SMASH (2216 "Nothing Left to Give") ... 15-20 69
WIZDOM ... 4-6

GARRETT, Scott *P&R '59*
(Scott Garret)
Singles: 7-inch
LAURIE (3023 "House of Love) ... 15-20 59
LAURIE (3029 "Love Story") ... 30-40 59
(With the Mystics.)
LAURIE (3034 "Where Are You) ... 10-15 59
OKEH (7104 "In My Heart") ... 10-15 58
Session: Mystics.
Also see MYSTICS

GARRETT, Vernon *R&B '69*
(With His Cross Road Band)
Singles: 7-inch
GATOR (1201 "Think People") ... 5-10
GLOW HILL ("Johnny Walker Red") ... 10-15
(No selection number used.)
GLOW HILL (517 "I Got to Get Over") ... 10-15
ICA (003 "I'm at the Crossroad") ... 4-6 77
KAPP ... 4-8 70
KENT (459 "Shine It On") ... 10-15 67
KENT (476 "Running Out") ... 10-15 67
L.A. WEST (001 "I Learned My Lesson") ... 5-10
MODERN (1026 "If I Could Turn Back the Hands of Time") ... 20-30 57
OPEN.G (401 "Cave Man") ... 8-12
(Not a typo – label name is correct.)
SAFE (101 "Drowning in the Sea of Love") ... 5-10
VENTURE ... 5-10 69
WATTS U.S.A. (054 "I Made My Own World") ... 5-10
WATTS U.S.A. (0006 "Don't Do What I Do") ... 5-10
Also see BIGGIE RATT
Also see JACQUET, Russell, Orchestra, & Vernon Garrett
Also see VERNON & JEWELL

GARRETT BROTHERS
Singles: 7-inch
GEEBEES (1101 "Mule Skinner Blues") .. 30-50

GARRIGAN, Eddie
Singles: 7-inch
FONTANA (1535 "I Wish I Was") ... 25-35 65
FONTANA (1575 "I Wish I Was") ... 15-25 67

GARRIS, Al
Singles: 7-inch
GLODIS (1005 "That's All") ... 15-25 61

GARRISH, George
Singles: 7-inch
TOWN (2003 "All Night Diner") ... 50-75

GARRISON, Glen *C&W '67*
(With the Note Kings)
Singles: 7-inch
CREST (1047 "Lovin' Lorene") ... 40-60 58
IMPERIAL ... 4-8 67-68
LODE (106 "Pony Tail Girl") ... 75-100 59
LPs: 10/12-inch
IMPERIAL ... 10-15 67-68

GARRITY, Hughie, & Hollywood Playboys
Singles: 7-inch
DUEL (522 "Too Pooped to Popeye") ... 10-15 63

GARRY & LARRY
Singles: 7-inch
GOLIATH (600 "Garlic Bread") ... 10-20 62

GARTELL, Dee Dee
(Delia Gartell; Dee Dee Gartrell; Delia Gartrell)
Singles: 7-inch
BAHITH ... 5-10
MAVERICK (1006 "Would It Break Your Heart") ... 10-20 69
MAVERICK (1010 "If You Got What It Takes") ... 10-20 69
RIGHT ON ... 4-6

GARTIN, Jimmy
Singles: 7-inch
FORTUNE (134 "Honey Won't You Love Me") ... 50-75
HI-Q (14 "Gonna Ride That Satellite") ... 50-75

GARVIN, Rex, & Mighty Cravers
Singles: 7-inch
CHIEFTAIN (4000 "Strange Happening") 10-20 64
EPIC (9437 "Emulsified") ... 15-25 61
LIKE (301 "Sock It to 'Em J.B.") ... 10-20 66
OKEH (7174 "Emulsified") ... 10-20 63
SEATT (103 "Oh Yeah") ... 50-75
TOWER (374 "Queen of the Go-Go") ... 10-20 67
TOWER (437 "By the Time I Get to Phoenix") ... 10-20 68
UPTOWN (760 "Raw Funky") ... 5-10 69
ZORRO (100 "Soul Street") ... 10-15 63
LPs: 10/12-inch
TOWER (5130 "Raw Funky Earth") ... 20-30 68
Also see CRAVERS
Also see HEARTS
Also see MARIE & REX

GARY, Clyde, & His Orchestra
Singles: 7-inch
SHAD (5016 "Tami's Dance") ... 10-20 60
Members: Gary Paxton; Clyde Batton.
Also see GARY & CLYDE

GARY, Ethel
Singles: 7-inch
AL (101 "So Lonely") ... 100-200

GARY, Jeane
Singles: 7-inch
BARCLAY (1308 "Love Is My Lighthouse") ... 30-50

GARY, John *LP '63*
Singles: 7-inch
ACE (661 "First Lady Waltz") ... 5-10 62
BIG B (3615 "Our Last Night Together") ... 5-10 64
FRATERNITY ... 5-10 59-66
RCA ... 4-8 63-71
ST. JAMES (100 "First Lady Waltz") ... 5-10 63
EPs: 7-inch
RCA (2804 "John Gary") ... 8-12 63
(Stereo Compact 33.)
LPs: 10/12-inch
CAMDEN ... 5-10 68
CHURCHILL ... 4-8 77
LA BREA (8010 "John Gary") ... 10-15 64
METRO (522 "John Gary") ... 5-10 65
RCA ... 5-15 63-78
SPIN-O-RAMA ... 5-10 '60s
WYNCOTE ... 5-10 '60s
Also see ANN-MARGRET & JOHN GARY
Also see DESMOND, Johnny / John Gary / Gordon MacRae

GARY, Phil
(With the Catalinas; with Rock & Roll Zoo)
Singles: 7-inch
BRAVO (1303 "Rock and Roll Is Back to Stay") ... 5-10
COUNTERPOINT ... 5-10

TOWER (371 "Rollin' Stone")..........15-20 62
TRIODEX (106 "June 30th")..........10-15 61
Also see PHIL & CATALINAS

GARY, Rickey

Singles: 7-inch

ORCHESTRA (6131 "Cajun Hop")..........10-20 61

GARY & BILLY

Singles: 7-inch

20TH FOX (170 "Lisa")..........10-15 59

GARY & CASUALS

Singles: 7-inch

VANDAN (609 "My One Desire")..........50-75 62

GARY & CHUCK

Singles: 7-inch

ON BEAT (101 "Only Love")..........10-15 59

GARY & CLYDE

Singles: 7-inch

REV (3523 "Why Not Confess")..........20-30 59
(First issue.)
TIME (1007 "Why Not Confess")..........10-15 59
Members: Gary Paxton; Clyde Batton.
Also see GARY, Clyde, & His Orchestra
Also see PAXTON, Gary
Also see PLEDGES
Also see SKIP & FLIP

GARY & DETONATORS

Singles: 7-inch

TNT (1000 "I Wanna Dance")..........75-125

GARY & HORNETS

Singles: 7-inch

SMASH (2061 "Hi Hi Hazel")..........10-15 66
SMASH (2078 "A Kind of Hush")..........8-12 67
SMASH (2090 "Baby It's You")..........8-12 67
SMASH (2145 "Turn the World On")..........8-12 68

Picture Sleeves

SMASH (2061 "Hi Hi Hazel")..........15-25 66
SMASH (2078 "A Kind of Hush")..........10-15 67

GARY & NITE LITES
(Gary & Knight Lites)

Singles: 7-inch

BELL (643 "Lonely Soldier's Pledge")..........10-20 66
NIKE (1020 "I'm Glad She's Mine")..........15-25 63
PRIMA (1016 "Will You Go Steady")..........30-40 59
SEEBURG JUKE BOX (3016 "Sweet Little 16")..........25-35 65
SEEBURG JUKE BOX (3017 "Bony Maronie")..........25-35 65
USA (833 "I Don't Need Your Help")..........10-20 66
Also see AMERICAN BREED
Also see DAYLIGHTERS
Also see LITE NITES

GARY & SUNNY

Singles: 7-inch

CADETTE (8001 "It's All Over")..........10-15 62
CADETTE (8007 "Kiss and Run")..........10-15 63
Members: Gary Smith; Sunny Jones.

GARY & UNIVERSALS

Singles: 7-inch

CSS (669/670 "Fifth Dimensions")..........10-20 64

GAS & FUNK FACTORY

Singles: 7-inch

BRUNSWICK (55434 "Goodnight Song")..........15-25 70

GAS LANTERN

Singles: 7-inch

RISING SONS (717 "Mach 1")..........10-20 68
Member: Charlie McCoy.
Also see MCCOY, Charlie

GASOLINE POWERED CLOCK

Singles: 7-inch

GPC (1001 "Forest Fire on Mail Street")..........30-40 67

GASS, Aubrey

Singles: 7-inch

HELTON ("Corn Fed Gal")..........50-100
(Selection number not known.)

GASSERS
("Gassers & Orchestra")

Singles: 78 rpm

CASH (1035 "Tell Me")..........25-35 56

Singles: 7-inch

CASH (1035 "Tell Me")..........50-75 56
ENCINO (1011 "Dody Mighty")..........30-40 57

GATES
(Golden Gate Quartet)

Singles: 78 rpm

COLUMBIA (30149 "I'm Just a Dreamer")..........15-25 48
Also see GOLDEN GATE QUARTET

GATES Featuring Bobby Ferguson

Singles: 7-inch

PEACH (628 "Letter to Dick Clark")..........200-300 59
PEACH (716 "Wedding Bells Gonna Ring")..........400-500 59

GATES, David *P&R/LP '73*
(With the Accents)

Singles: 7-inch

ARISTA (0615 "Take Me Now")..........4-6 81
DEL-FI (4206 "No One Really Loves a Clown")..........10-20 63
EAST WEST (123 "Walkin' & Talkin'")..........100-150 59
ELEKTRA..........4-8 73-80
MALA (413 "You'll Be My Baby")..........200-300 60
MALA (418 "Happiest Man Alive")..........40-50 60
MALA (427 "Jo-Baby")..........40-50 61
PERSPECTIVE ("Jo-Baby")..........50-100 58
(No selection number used. 1200 made.)
PLANETARY (108 "Once Upon a Time")..........10-20 65
ROBBINS (1008 "Jo-Baby")..........30-40 58

Picture Sleeves

ELEKTRA (45450 "Goodbye Girl")..........5-8 77
ELEKTRA (45857 "Clouds")..........5-8 73

LPs: 10/12-inch

ARISTA (9563 "Take Me Now")..........5-10 81
ELEKTRA (148 "Goodbye Girl")..........8-12 78
ELEKTRA (251 "Falling in Love Again")..........8-12 80
ELEKTRA (1028 "Never Let Her Go")..........8-12 75
ELEKTRA (EKS-75066 "David Gates' First")..........10-15 73
ELEKTRA (EQ-75066 "David Gates' First")..........15-25 73
(Quadraphonic.)
Also see ASHLEY, Del
Also see AVALANCHES
Also see BREAD
Also see COUNTY BOYS
Also see DAVID & LEE
Also see FENCEMEN
Also see JENNIE & JAY
Also see MANCHESTERS
Also see PETERSEN, Paul
Also see PICKETT, Bobby
Also see VIBES

GATES, Ed "Great" *R&B '49*
(Great Gates & Band; Ed [The Great] Gates; Edward White)

Singles: 78 rpm

ALADDIN..........8-12 55
RECORDED IN HOLLYWOOD (199 "Ain't Got No Money")..........15-25 52
SELECTIVE (103 "Late After Hours")..........10-20 49

Singles: 7-inch

ALADDIN (3310 "Jump, Jump, Jump")..........25-35 55
4 STAR (1712 "You Are My Love")..........15-25 57
ROBINS NEXT (103 "Can You Feel It")..........15-20 62
SPECIALTY (674 "There Goes My Love")..........15-20 59

GATES, Everett

Singles: 7-inch

TALLY (6401 "Mean Machine")..........50-75

GATES, Hen, & Orchestra
(With His Gaters)

Singles: 78 rpm

TREAT (503 "Flash")..........15-25 55

Singles: 7-inch

TREAT (503 "Flash")..........25-35 55

LPs: 10/12-inch

MASTERSEAL (700 "Let's Go Dancing to Rock & Roll")..........75-125 56
(Title on label is "Let's All Dance to Rock and Roll." Copies exist with Masterseal labels and Palace covers.)
MASTERSEAL (5005 "Let's Go Dancing to Rock & Roll")..........50-75 57
(Title on label and back cover states "Let's All Dance to Rock and Roll.")
PALACE (P-700 "Let's All Dance to Rock & Roll")..........50-75 58
(Monaural.)
PALACE (PST-700 "Let's All Dance to Rock & Roll")..........75-125 58
(Stereo.)
PALACE ("Rock & Roll")..........20-40 '50s
(Selection number not known.)
PARIS (101 "Rock & Roll Festival")..........20-40 58
PLYMOUTH (144 "Rock & Roll")..........30-50 '50s
PLYMOUTH (149 "Rock & Roll, No. 2")..........30-50 '50s
Also see FIVE DIAMONDS

GATES, Jackie

Singles: 7-inch

SKYWAY (128 "I Want Love")..........40-60 61

GATEWAY SINGERS

Singles: 78 rpm

DECCA..........3-8 56-57

Singles: 7-inch

DECCA..........5-10 56-58
MGM..........4-8 60-63
W.B...........5-8 59

LPs: 10/12-inch

DECCA (8413 "Puttin' on the Style")..........20-30 56
DECCA (8671 "The Gateway Singers at the Hungry i")..........15-25 58
DECCA (8742 "The Gateway Singers in Hi-Fi")..........20-30 58
MGM..........12-20 61-63
W.B...........15-20 59
Members: Travis Edmondson; Jerry Walter; Lou Gottlieb; Elmerlee Thomas.
Also see EDMONDSON, Travis
Also see LIMELITERS

GATLIN, Jimmy

Singles: 7-inch

RBE (105 "Texarkana Baby")..........150-250

GATLIN, June

Singles: 7-inch

REVUE (11021 "Baby Cakes")..........10-20 68

GATLIN, Larry *C&W '73*
(With the Gatlin Brothers Band; with Family & Friends; Gatlin Quartet)

Singles: 7-inch

CAPITOL..........3-5 90
COLUMBIA..........3-6 79-88
MONUMENT..........4-6 73-78
UNIVERSAL..........3-5 89

LPs: 10/12-inch

COLUMBIA..........5-10 79-86
HITSVILLE..........5-10 76
MONUMENT..........5-10 74-78
SWORD & SHIELD (9009 "The Old Country Church")..........25-50 61
(By the Gatlin Quartet, which included sister Donna.)
Members: Larry Gatlin; Steve Gatlin; Rudy Gatlin.
Also see NELSON, Willie

GATLIN, Larry, & Janie Frickie *C&W '87*
(With the Gatlin Brothers)

Singles: 7-inch

COLUMBIA..........3-5 87
Also see FRICKE, Janie

GATORMEN

Singles: 7-inch

CAMELOT (119 "Hey Girl")..........10-15 66
CAMELOT (124 "You See")..........10-15 66
Also see DORSALS & GATORMEN

GATORS
(Chuck Lechner 'N' His Gators)

Singles: 7-inch

GATOR ("Your [sic] a Thousand Miles Away")..........2000-2500 57
(No selection number used.)

GATORS

Singles: 7-inch

DOT (16252 "Sunburst")..........10-20 61

GATORVETTES
("Vocal by Hugh Bowers;" "Vocal by Lawrence Johnson")

Singles: 7-inch

BOCALDUN (1001 "If It's Tonight")..........50-75 59
THUNDER (1001 "If It's Tonight")..........200-300 59
(First issue.)
Members: Hugh Bowers; Lawrence Johnson.

GAUDET, Dee Dee

Singles: 7-inch

DODGE (805 "Where's the Law")..........15-20 63

GAUDET, John, & Laurels

Singles: 7-inch

MARY GLEN (1001 "Your Name Shall Be Remembered")..........30-40 61

GAUFF, Willie
(With the Kind Brothers; with Love Brothers)

Singles: 7-inch

EUREKA..........5-10 69
KENT (459 "Everybody Needs Love")..........5-10 68
WATTS WAY (201 "It Hurt So Bad")..........15-25 '60s

GAUNGA DINS

Singles: 7-inch

BUSY-B (2 "Stick with Her")..........20-30 67
BUSY-B (4 "No One Cares")..........20-30 67

GAVIN, Tony

Singles: 7-inch

SIMS (165 "The Old Timer")..........5-10 64
20TH FOX (228 "Ever Lovin' Baby")..........20-30 61

GAY, Betsy
(With Jack Fascinato & Orchestra)

Singles: 78 rpm

DECCA (29340 "Cool Man")..........5-10 54

Singles: 7-inch

DECCA (29340 "Cool Man")..........10-20 54

GAY, Bobby

Singles: 7-inch

GAYBAR (1005 "It's Too Late")..........30-45
MIDA (104 "Let's Dance")..........40-60 58

GAY, Bud

Singles: 7-inch

NASHVILLE (1003 "I'm a Long Gone Daddy")..........100-200

GAY, Elaine
(With the Five Harmonaires; "With String Band")

Singles: 78 rpm

DELUXE..........10-20 54

Singles: 7-inch

DELUXE (2022 "Am I the One to Blame")..........15-25 54
DELUXE (2029 "Ebony Eyes")..........30-40 54

GAY, Frank, & Gay Blades

Singles: 7-inch

CUCA (1138 "Down Bound Train")..........10-20 '60s

GAY CHARMERS

Singles: 78 rpm

G&M (2021 "Honky Tonk")..........10-15 56

Singles: 7-inch

G&M (2021 "Honky Tonk")..........15-25 56
GRAND (2001 "What Can I Do")..........75-100 58
SAVOY (1549 "Groovey Shoes")..........10-15 58
SAVOY (1561 "Walk Beside Him")..........10-15 59
SWAN (4032 "What Can I Do")..........15-25 59

GAY KNIGHTS
(With the Buddy Lucas Orchestra)

Singles: 7-inch

PET (801 "Angel")..........100-150 58
(Pink label. Promotional issue.)
PET (801 "Angel")..........75-100 58
Also see LUCAS, Buddy

GAY NOTES

Singles: 78 rpm

DREXEL (905 "For Only a Moment")..........100-200 55

Singles: 7-inch

DREXEL (905 "For Only a Moment")..........300-400 55

GAY NOTES

Singles: 78 rpm

POST (2006 "Hear My Plea")..........10-20 55

Singles: 7-inch

POST (2006 "Hear My Plea")..........30-40 55

GAY NOTES

Singles: 7-inch

VIM (501 "Cherie")..........30-50 59

GAY POPPERS

Singles: 7-inch

FIRE (1026 "I Want to Know")..........10-15 60
FIRE (1039 "Please Mr. Cupid")..........15-20 61
SAVOY (1573 "I Need Your Love")..........10-15 59

GAY TUNES

Singles: 78 rpm

TIMELY (1002 "The Thrill of Romance")..........200-400 53

Singles: 7-inch

TIMELY (1002 "The Thrill of Romance")..........2500-3000 53
(Red vinyl.)

Members: Earl Kirton; Wayman Corey; Leroy Williams; Fred Davis; Henry Pinchback.

GAY TUNES
(With Sammy Lowe Orchestra)

Singles: 7-inch

DOME (502 "Don't Go")........................ 300-400 58

GAYDON SISTERS

Singles: 78 rpm

BALLY (1003 "Honestly Honestly")............5-10 56

Singles: 7-inch

BALLY (1003 "Honestly Honestly")......... 10-15 56

GAYE, Barbie

Singles: 7-inch

DARL (1002 "My Boy Lollipop") 25-35 57

GAYE, Ellie
(Ellie Greenwich)

Singles: 7-inch

RCA ("Silly Isn't It") .... 15-25 '50s
(Selection number not known.)
Also see GREENWICH, Ellie

GAYE, Marvin — P&R/R&B '62
(With the Love Tones)

Singles: 12-inch

COLUMBIA (Except 40133)..........................4-6 83-85
COLUMBIA (40133 "Sanctified Lady")..... 10-15 85
(Picture disc.)
MOTOWN..4-8 78

Singles: 7-inch

COLUMBIA...3-5 82-85
DETROIT FREE PRESS ("The Teen Beat Song") 50-100 66
(Promotional issue only.)
JOBETE (1 "Save the Children")............. 20-30
MOTOWN...3-5
MOTOWN/TOPPS (6 "How Sweet It Is to Be Loved by You").. 50-75 67
(Topps Chewing Gum promotional item. Single-sided, cardboard flexi, picture disc. Issued with generic paper sleeve.)
TAMLA ("Witchcraft")......................... 300-500 61
(Promotional issue only. No selection number used. Credited to "Marvin Gay.")
TAMLA ("My Way")............................... 30-50 65
(Promotional issue only. No selection number used.)
TAMLA (1800 series)..................................3-5 86
TAMLA (54041 "Let Your Conscience Be Your Guide")... 50-75 61
TAMLA (54055 "Sandman")................... 45-55 62
TAMLA (54062 "The Masquerade Is Over").. 45-55 62
TAMLA (54063 "Soldier's Plea") 25-35 62
(Credits only Marvin Gaye.)
TAMLA (54063 "Soldier's Plea") 15-25 62
(Credits Marvin Gaye and "Love Tones.")
TAMLA (54068 "Stubborn Kind of Fellow") 15-25 62
TAMLA (54075 thru 54185)..................... 10-15 63-69
TAMLA (54190 "Gonna Give Her All the Love I've Got")..5-10 69
(Black vinyl.)
TAMLA (54190 "Gonna Give Her All the Love I've Got") 10-15 69
(Colored vinyl. Promotional issue only.)
TAMLA (54195 thru 54326)........................3-6 70-81
(Black vinyl.)
TAMLA (54000 series).............................5-10 72-76
(Colored vinyl. Promotional issues only.)

Picture Sleeves

TAMLA (1800 series)..................................3-5 86
TAMLA (54095 "Try It Baby")................. 20-40 64
TAMLA (54101 "Baby, Don't You Do It") . 20-40 64
TAMLA (54138 "Little Darlin I Need You") 30-50 66
TAMLA (54280 "Got to Give It Up") 4-8 77

EPs: 7-inch

MOTOWN (2016 "Marvin Gaye")............ 15-25 '60s
TAMLA (60252 "Greatest Hits") 20-30 66
(Stereo. Juke box issue only. Includes title strips.)

LPs: 10/12-inch

COLUMBIA..5-10 82-85
KORY...8-10 76-77
MOTOWN...8-12 64-83
NATURAL RESOURCES 5-10 78
TAMLA (221 "The Soulful Moods of Marvin Gaye")... 600-800 61
TAMLA (239 "That Stubborn Kind of Fella")... 300-400 63
TAMLA (242 "On Stage")....................... 50-100 63
TAMLA (251 "When I'm Alone I Cry").....50-100 64
TAMLA (252 "Greatest Hits") 20-40 64
TAMLA (258 "How Sweet It Is") 20-40 65
TAMLA (261 "Tribute to the Great Nat King Cole")..20-40 65
TAMLA (266 "Moods")..............................50-75 66
TAMLA (278 thru 299) 15-30 67-69
TAMLA (300 series)...................................8-15 70-81
TAMLA (6100 series)..................................5-10 86
Also see BURNS, Eddie
Also see CHARADES
Also see MARQUEES
Also see MARTHA & VANDELLAS
Also see MARVELETTES / Mary Wells / Miracles / Marvin Gaye
Also see MOONGLOWS

GAYE, Marvin / Gladys Knight & Pips

Singles: 7-inch

MOTOWN (1128 "His Eye Is On the Sparrow")..5-10 68
Also see KNIGHT, Gladys

GAYE, Marvin, & Diana Ross — LP '73

Singles: 7-inch

MOTOWN (1269 "My Mistake") 4-6 74
MOTOWN (1280 "You're a Special Part of Me")..4-6 74
MOTOWN (1296 "Don't Knock My Love")....4-6 74

LPs: 10/12-inch

MOTOWN...8-12 73
Also see ROSS, Diana

GAYE, Marvin, & Tammi Terrell — P&R '67

Singles: 7-inch

TAMLA (Black vinyl) 5-10 67-70
TAMLA (54192 "Onion Song")..................10-15 70
(Colored vinyl. Promotional issue only.)

LPs: 10/12-inch

MOTOWN...5-10 80-82
TAMLA...10-15 67-70
Also see TERRELL, Tammi

GAYE, Marvin, & Mary Wells — P&R/R&B/LP '64

Singles: 7-inch

MOTOWN (1057 "What's the Matter with You Baby")...10-15 64

Picture Sleeves

MOTOWN (1057 "What's the Matter with You Baby") 20-40 64

LPs: 10/12-inch

MOTOWN (613 "Together").....................40-50 64
Also see WELLS, Mary

GAYE, Marvin, & Kim Weston — P&R/R&B '64

Singles: 7-inch

TAMLA (54104 "What Good Am I Without You")...10-15 64
TAMLA (54141 "It Takes Two")................10-15 66

LPs: 10/12-inch

TAMLA (270 "Marvin Gaye and Kim Weston")..20-25 66
Also see GAYE, Marvin
Also see WESTON, Kim

GAYLARKS
(With John Heartsman Band; Gaylarks/Lord Luther)

Singles: 78 rpm

MUSIC CITY...50-75 56-57

Singles: 7-inch

MUSIC CITY (793 "Romantic Memories")..100-200 56
Note: Music City 792, *Tell Me, Darling*, is in the next section: GAYLARKS/Rovers.
MUSIC CITY (805 "My Greatest Sin") 50-150 57
MUSIC CITY (809 "Church on the Hill")...300-400 57
MUSIC CITY (812 "Somewhere in This World")..75-125 57
(No company address shown.)
MUSIC CITY (812 "Somewhere in This World")..40-50 57
(Has company address under logo.)
MUSIC CITY (819 "Ivy League Clothes") .50-60 58
Members: Oliver Stevens; Henry Swan; Jay Payton; Billy Ray Williams; Ralph Helms.
Also see LORD LUTHER

GAYLARKS / Rovers

Singles: 78 rpm

MUSIC CITY (792 "Tell Me, Darling"/"Whole Lot of Love")...30-50 56

Singles: 7-inch

MUSIC CITY (792 "Tell Me, Darling"/"Whole Lot of Love")..50-150 56
Also see GAYLARKS
Also see HEARTSMAN, Johnny
Also see ROVERS

GAYLE, Crystal — C&W '70

Singles: 7-inch

COLUMBIA 3-6 79-82
DECCA...4-6 70-72
ELEKTRA..3-5 82
MCA...4-6 77
U.A. 3-6 74-80
W.B. 3-5 83-90

Picture Sleeves

COLUMBIA 3-6 79-82
U.A. 4-8 77

LPs: 10/12-inch

COLUMBIA 5-10 79-83
ELEKTRA..5-10 82
LIBERTY 5-10 80-82
MCA...5-10 78
MFSL (043 "We Must Believe in Magic") .30-50 80
U.A. (Except "Somebody Loves You" picture disc) 5-10 75-80
U.A. ("Somebody Loves You")...............50-100 78
(Picture disc. Promotional issue only. One of a four-artist, four-LP set. 250 made.)
W.B. 5-10 83-90
Also see CAMPBELL, Glen / Anne Murray / Kenny Rogers / Crystal Gayle
Also see RABBITT, Eddie, & Crystal Gayle

GAYLE, Melvin

Singles: 7-inch

CASTLE (1602 "Some of Your Love")......40-60 62

GAYLES

Singles: 78 rpm

ABC-PAR (9707 "Shortnin' Bread Rock")...8-12 56
KING...8-12 55
MEDIA (1021 "All I Want Is You")..............8-12 56

Singles: 7-inch

ABC-PAR (9707 "Shortnin' Bread Rock").10-15 56
KING (4846 "My Boy Flat-Top")...............10-15 55
KING (4860 "I Had to Love You").............10-15 55
MEDIA (1021 "All I Want Is You")............15-20 56

GAYLES, Billy
(Billy Gale)

Singles: 78 rpm

FEDERAL..10-20 56
FLAIR (1038 "Night Howler") 20-30 54

Singles: 7-inch

FEDERAL (12265 "I'm Tore Up").............20-30 56
FEDERAL (12272 "Take Your Fine Frame Home")...30-40 56
FEDERAL (12282 "Do Right, Baby").......20-30 56
FEDERAL (12287 "Just One More Time")..20-30 57
FLAIR (1038 "Night Howler") 50-75 54
Also see BLUE TONES

GAYLORD, Ronnie — P&R '54

Singles: 78 rpm

MERCURY..5-10 54-55
WING...5-10 55-56

Singles: 7-inch

MERCURY..10-20 54-55
WING...10-20 55-56

EPs: 7-inch

MERCURY..8-12 55

GAYLORDS — P&R '52

Singles: 78 rpm

MERCURY...5-15 52-57
SAVOY (852 "Get Mad Baby")..................10-20 52

Singles: 7-inch

MERCURY..10-20 52-62

EPs: 7-inch

MERCURY..15-25 54-56

LPs: 10/12-inch

MERCURY (Except 25198)......................15-35 55-63
MERCURY (25198 "By Request") 25-50 55
(10-inch LP.)
TIME..10-15 64
WING...10-20 59-64
Members: Ronnie Gaylord; Don Rea; Burt (Holiday) Bonaldi; Billy Christ.
Also see DEL-VIKINGS / Diamonds / Big Bopper / Gaylords

GAYNELS

Singles: 7-inch

OKEH (7114 "Chubby")............................30-40 59

GAYNOR, Mel — R&B '55

Singles: 78 rpm

MODERN (977 "Ebony Rhapsody") 5-10 55

Singles: 7-inch

MODERN (977 "Ebony Rhapsody") 15-20 55

GAYNOR, Mitzi

Singles: 78 rpm

DECCA...3-5 56

Singles: 7-inch

DECCA...5-10 56
LAURIE (3050 "Happy Anniversary").........5-10 60

Picture Sleeves

LAURIE (3050 "Happy Anniversary") 8-12 60

EPs: 7-inch

DECCA...5-15 56

LPs: 10/12-inch

DECCA...20-30 56
VERVE...15-25 59

GAYNOR, Steve

Singles: 78 rpm

GUYDEN (710 "4 Jacks and a Jill")............5-10 54

Singles: 7-inch

GUYDEN (710 "4 Jacks and a Jill")..........10-15 54
MGM (12796 "High School Dance")...........5-10 59

GAYNOTES
(Gay Notes)

Singles: 7-inch

ZYNN (504 "Waiting in the Chapel").......50-100 58
(Credits "Gaynotes." Previously issued as by Little Clem & Dewdrops.)
ZYNN (504 "Waiting in the Chapel").........15-25 60
(Credits "Gay Notes.")
Also see LITTLE CLEM & DEWDROPS

GAYNOTES

Singles: 7-inch

ALADDIN (3424 "Once He Loved Me")....30-40 58

GAYTEN, Paul — R&B '47
(Paul Gayten Trio; Paul Gayten Orchestra)

Singles: 78 rpm

ARGO...15-25 56-57
CHECKER 10-15 55-56
DELUXE...10-15 47-49
OKEH...10-15 52-55
REGAL...10-15 49-51

Singles: 7-inch

ANNA...15-25 59-60
ARGO...15-25 56-58
CHECKER..20-30 55-58
OKEH...20-30 52-55
Session: Lee Allen; Alvin "Red" Tyler; Frank Field; Edgar Blanchard; Earl Palmer; Charles "Hungry" Williams; Edgar "Big Boy" Myles; Ray Abrams; Billy Davis.
Also see ABRAMS, Ray, Band
Also see ALLEN, Lee
Also see BLANCHARD, Edgar
Also see DAVIS, Bill, Trio
Also see HENRY, Clarence
Also see LAURIE, Annie
Also see MYLES, Big Boy
Also see NEWSOM, Chubby, & Her Hip Shakers
Also see PALMER, Earl
Also see TUNE WEAVERS
Also see TYLER, Alvin "Red"
Also see WILLIAMS, Charles
Also see WILLS, Oscar / Paul Gayten

GAYTUNES

Singles: 78 rpm

JOYCE (101 "I Love You").......................50-100 57
TIMELY (1002 "Thrill of Romance") 100-200 53

Singles: 7-inch

JOYCE (101 "I Love You")......................100-150 57
(With the oversize letter "Y" in the Joyce logo.)
JOYCE (106 "Pen Pal")..............................4-6 '90s
(Black vinyl. 400 made.)
JOYCE (106 "Pen Pal")............................8-10 '90s
(Red vinyl. 100 made.)
TIMELY (1002 "Thrill of Romance") 400-500 53
(Red vinyl.)

GAZELLES

Singles: 78 rpm

GOTHAM (315 "Honest")........................30-40 56

Singles: 7-inch
GOTHAM (315 "Honest") 100-150 56

GEAN, Ralph
Singles: 7-inch
LORI (9543 "Weeping Willow") 10-15 62

GEARS / Emeralds / Dedicated Followers / Internal Canitery Sin
EPs: 7-inch
HILLSIDE (1967 "We're Through") 20-30 67
(Since we've seen only the disc, there may not be a special cover. No EP title is given, so we use the Gears' track. Promotional issue only.)

GEATER
Singles: 7-inch
HOUSE OF ORANGE ("Breathtaking Girl") .... 25-35 '60s
(Selection number not known.)

GEDDINS, Bob / Sherman's Trio
(Louis Sherman)
Singles: 78 rpm
CAVA-TONE (5 "Thinkin' and Thinkin' ") .. 40-60 49
(First issue.)
MODERN (685 "Thinkin' and Thinkin' ") ... 20-30 49

GEDDINS, Bob / Turner Willis
(With His Cavaliers; Bob Geddins' Cavaliers)
Singles: 78 rpm
BIG TOWN (1058 "Irma Jean") 15-25 45
TRILON (1058 "Irma Jean") 30-50 45
(First issue.)
Also see GEDDINS, Bob / Sherman's Trio

GEE, Billy
(With Mark Reynolds Orchestra & Chorus)
Singles: 7-inch
CORONET (1303 "King of Hearts") 10-20 59

GEE, Bobby
(With the Celestials)
Singles: 7-inch
NYE (611 "Sealed with a Kiss") 15-25 60
STACY (922 "Julie Is Mine") 30-40 59
XYZ (611 "Sealed with a Kiss") 25-35 60
(First issue.)

GEE, Ellie
(Ellie Greenwich)
Singles: 7-inch
MADISON (160 "Red Corvette") 15-25 61
Also see GREENWICH, Ellie

GEE, Frankie
Singles: 7-inch
CHANNEL (101 "Mixed Up, Shook Up Boy") 10-20 64
CLARIDGE (410 "Ya Ya") 10-15 75
LIPSTICK 5-10
Also see FIVE DISCS

GEE, Jay
Singles: 7-inch
STACY (916 "The Slouch") 10-20 59

GEE, Joey
(With the Bluetones; with Come-Ons)
Singles: 7-inch
SARA (6451 "Don't You Just Know It") 8-12 64
SARA (6599 "She's Mean") 15-20 65
Members: Joe Giannunzio; Craig Sorensen; Billy Morrison; Rickey Bates; Vaughn Ryan.

GEE, Joey
Singles: 7-inch
ABC-PAR (10781 "Don't Blow Your Cool") 10-20 66

GEE, Kenny
Singles: 7-inch
SCOTTIE (1311 "Bluenote") 10-15 60
SCOTTIE (1322 "Give Me Your Love") 10-15 61

GEE, Lenny
Singles: 7-inch
BAYE (577 "I Need Your Love") 40-50 60

GEE, Ray
Singles: 7-inch
PLANET (54 "Hootenanny Baby") 10-15 62

GEE, Ronnie
Singles: 7-inch
HIDDY-B (1234 "When Girls Do It") 10-20

GEE, Shirley
Singles: 7-inch
7 ARTS (711 "Behind the Makeup") 15-25 61

GEE, Sonny, & Standels
Singles: 7-inch
ARLEN (506 "Tidal Wave") 40-60 59

GEE CEES
Singles: 7-inch
CREST (1088 "Buzzsaw"/"Annie Had a Party") 30-40 61
(Glen Campbell plays guitar on *Buzzsaw*. Eddie Cochran plays on *Annie Had a Party*, first issued as *Annie Has a Party*, by the Kelly Four.)
Also see CAMPBELL, Glen
Also see COCHRAN, Eddie
Also see KELLY FOUR

GEE GEE & UPNILONS
Singles: 7-inch
LUMMTONE (117-13 "Do the Movement") 15-25 65
Also see SMITH, Lester, Jr., & Upnilons

GEERS
Singles: 7-inch
SSS INT'L (760 "I Need You") 10-15 69

GEESIN & WATERS
LPs: 10/12-inch
HARVEST/EMI (4008 "Music from the Body") 25-35 73
IMPORT 8-10 77
Members: Ron Geesin; Roger Waters.

GEM, Frankie
Singles: 7-inch
ARDMORE (782 "My Love") 50-75
USA (713 "Crystal Rock") 15-25 61

GEM TONES
Singles: 7-inch
SCARLET (4219 "War Chant") 10-20 60

GEMINI 6
Singles: 7-inch
IGL (142 "Two-Faced Girls") 20-25 67

GEMINILES
Singles: 7-inch
SANDBAG (781 "Thinkin' About My Baby") .... 15-25 '60s

GEMS
Singles: 78 rpm
DREXEL 75-150 54-57
Singles: 7-inch
DREXEL (900 "Ow You're So Fine") 3-5 75
DREXEL (901 "Deed I Do") 250-350 54
(Black vinyl.)
DREXEL (901 "Deed I Do") 2000-3000 54
(Red vinyl.)
DREXEL (903 "I Thought You'd Care") 400-600 55
(Red vinyl.)
DREXEL (904 "You're Tired of Love") .. 400-600 55
(Red vinyl.)
DREXEL (909 "One Woman Man") 350-450 56
DREXEL (915 "Till the Day I Die") 350-450 57
Members: Ray Pettis; Bobby Robinson; Wilson James; Dave Taylor; Rip Reed.
Also see LOGAN, Dorothy, & Gems

GEMS
Singles: 7-inch
RECORTE (407 "Waiting") 75-125 59
WIN (701 "The Night Is Over") 400-500 58
WIN (701 "The Night Is Over") 4-6 95
(Green vinyl. 500 made.)

GEMS
Singles: 7-inch
VALOR ("Shutdown") 15-25 59
(Selection number not known.)

GEMS
Singles: 7-inch
MERCURY (71819 "Crazy Chicken") 10-20 61

GEMS
(With the Ted McCrae Orchestra)
Singles: 7-inch
PAT (101 "School Rock") 20-30 61

GEMS
Singles: 7-inch
UPTOWN (1001 "Slave Girl") 20-30 61

GEMS
Singles: 7-inch
VIRGELLE (711 "Punch Happy") 10-20 61

GENE, Sonny
Singles: 7-inch
RIP (101 "Just Be Good") 10-20 57
RIP (109 "You Tear Me Up") 8-12 57

GENE & BILLY
Singles: 78 rpm
LOMA (702 "Zerlene"/"The Whip") 15-25 55
SPARK (120 "It's Hot"/"Zerlene") 15-25 55
Singles: 7-inch
LOMA (702 "Zerlene"/"The Whip") 30-50 55
(B-side by Billy & Billygoats.)
SPARK (120 "It's Hot"/"Zerlene") 75-125 55
Members: Gene Ford; Billy Boyd.

GENE & DEBBE P&R '67
Singles: 7-inch
HICKORY 4-8 70
SAN (1519 "Go with Me") 10-20 67
TRX 5-10 67-69
LPs: 10/12-inch
TRX (1001 "Here and Now") 15-25 68
Members: Gene Thomas; Debbe Nevills.
Also see THOMAS, Gene

GENE & ESQUIRES
Singles: 7-inch
GNP (345 "Space Race") 10-20 65

GENE & EUNICE R&B '55
Singles: 78 rpm
ALADDIN 10-15 55
COMBO 8-12 55
Singles: 7-inch
ALADDIN (3276 "Ko Ko Mo") 20-30 55
ALADDIN (3282 thru 3351) 15-25 55-56
ALADDIN (3374 thru 3414) 10-20 57-58
CASE (1001 thru 1007) 15-25 59-60
COLLECTABLES 3-5
COMBO (64 "Ko Ko Mo") 20-30 55
ERA 4-6 72
IMPERIAL (015 "Ko Ko Mo"/"This Is My Story") 5-10 64
LILLY (512 "Got a Right to Know") 8-12 62
OLDIES 45 (311 "Ko Ko Mo") 5-10 65
U.A. (0151 "Ko Ko Mo") 4-6
EPs: 7-inch
CASE (100 "Gene & Eunice") 25-50 59
(Issued with paper sleeve.)
Members: Gene Forrest; Eunice Levy.
Also see FORREST, Gene, & Four Feathers

GENE & EUNICE / Shirley & Lee
Singles: 7-inch
TRIP (153 "Ko Ko Mo"/"Let the Good Times Roll") 4-6
Also see GENE & EUNICE
Also see SHIRLEY & LEE

GENE & JEANETTES
Singles: 7-inch
FORTUNE (565 "A Lover") 20-30 64

GENE & STRANGERS
Singles: 7-inch
FIRESIDE ("Miss New Love") 50-75
(No selection number used.)

GENE & TEAM BEATS
Singles: 7-inch
LEATHERWOOD (2096 "Apple Fuzz") 10-20 65

GENE & WENDELL R&B '61
(With the Sweethearts)
Singles: 78 rpm
SPECIALTY (613 "Lula Baby") 30-40 57
Singles: 7-inch
PHILIPS (40066 "Tight Skirts") 5-10 62
PHILIPS (40129 "Honey Chile") 5-10 63
RAY STAR (777 The Roach") 15-25 61
RAY STAR (785 "Roach Stomp") 10-15 62
RAY STAR (888 "Party Time") 10-15 62
SPECIALTY (613 "Lula Baby") 20-30 57
Picture Sleeves
RAY STARR (777 The Roach") 25-35 61
Members: Eugene Washington; Wendell Jones.

GENE THE HAT
Singles: 7-inch
CHECKER (960 "Ram-Bunk-Shush") 10-12 60
DEAUVILLE (1007 "The Bug") 8-10 62
GEE (1078 "Pass the Bug") 8-10 61
PURL (903 "Big Cigar") 10-20 61
WALDEN (101 "Ram-Bunk-Shush") 20-30 60
(First issue.)

GENELLS
Singles: 7-inch
DEWEY (101 "Linda, Please Wait") 30-40 63

GENERAL SOUL ASSEMBLY
Singles: 7-inch
SCARAB (1001 "Happy Song") .... 15-25 '60s

GENERALS
Singles: 7-inch
TAMMY (1009 "Never Too Late") 50-75 60

GENERALS
Singles: 7-inch
PYRAMID (6987 "For What More Could I Ask") 10-20 66

GENERALS
Singles: 7-inch
GENERAL (6167 "Without You") .... 10-20 '60s

GENERATION
Singles: 7-inch
MOCKINGBIRD (1010 "Hold On") 20-30

GENESIS
Singles: 7-inch
RIPCHORD (004 "Window of Sand") 15-25 67

GENESIS
Singles: 7-inch
MERCURY (72806 "Angeline") 5-10 68
MERCURY (72869 "Gloomy Sunday") 5-10 68
LPs: 10/12-inch
MERCURY (61175 "In the Beginning") 15-25 68
Members: Sue Richman; Jack Tanna; Bob Metke; Kent Henry; Fred Rivera.

GENESIS LP '73
Singles: 12-inch
ATLANTIC 4-6 86
Singles: 7-inch
ATCO 4-8 75-77
ATLANTIC 3-6 78-91
CHARISMA (103 "Watcher of the Skies") 30-50 73
PARROT (3018 "Silent Sun") 10-15 68
(Promotional issue only.)
Picture Sleeves
ATLANTIC 3-6 80-87
EPs: 7-inch
ATLANTIC (1800 "Spot the Pigeon") 5-10 77
(Promotional issue only.)
LPs: 10/12-inch
ABC (816 "Trespass") 8-10 74
ATCO 8-15 74-77
ATLANTIC 5-10 78-86
BUDDAH (5659 "Best of Genesis") 10-15 76
CHARISMA 8-12 72-79
IMPULSE (9205 "Genesis") 15-25 70
LONDON (600 series) 10-15 74
LONDON (50000 series) 5-10 77
MCA 5-10 78
MFSL (062 "Trick of the Tail") 50-75 82
Members: Phil Collins; Peter Gabriel; Tony Banks; Steve Hackett; Anthony Phillips; Mike Rutherford; John Mayhew.
Also see AMERICAN CHEESE
Also see CHIC / Roberta Flack / Leif Garrett / Genesis
Also see PHILLIPS, Anthony

GENESIS
Singles: 7-inch
BUDDAH (132 "Journey to the Moon") 5-10 69
LPs: 10/12-inch
BUDDAH ("Journey to the Moon") 10-20 69
(Selection number not known.)

GENEVIEVE
(With Johnny Tillotson)
Singles: 7-inch
CADENCE (1354 "Cherie Cherie") 10-15 58
Also see TILLOTSON, Johnny

GENIES P&R '59
Singles: 7-inch
ERIC .... 3-6 '70s

HOLLYWOOD (69 "No More Knocking ") 20-30 59
SHAD (5002 "Who's That Knocking") 20-30 58
(Pink label.)
SHAD (5002 "Who's That Knocking") 10-15 59
(Blue label.)
WARWICK 8-12 60-61
Members: Eugene Pitt; Roy Charles Hammond; Claude Johnson; Jay Washington; Roland Trone.
Also see DON & JUAN
Also see JIVE FIVE

GENIES

Singles: 7-inch

KING (5541 "I Got It From a Bird") 10-15 61
Also see WILSON, Gene, & Genies

GENO, Bobby (Mr. Big Guitar)

Singles: 7-inch

DORSET (5003 "Nothing") 10-20 60
FIRST (101 "The Shawnee") 10-20 59

GENO, Sonny

Singles: 7-inch

RIP (130 "Rumble Rock") 50-75

GENOS

(With the Blue Rays Orchestra)

Singles: 7-inch

SUNDANCE (202 "Wishful Dreaming") 100-200 59

GENOTONES

Singles: 7-inch

CASINO (52261 "Counting Stars") 250-350 58
WGW (3003 "Midnight Walk") 10-20 62

GENOVA, Tommy

(With the Precisions; with Blue Counts)

Singles: 7-inch

BELLA 10-30 61-64
DEBRA (1007 "The Whole World In My Arms") 15-25 63
DEBRA (2004 "Mama Done Told Me") 15-25 64
WHITE ROCK (361 "I Loved and I Lost") 20-30 61
Also see LANZO, Mike, & Blue Counts

GENT, J.C.

Singles: 7-inch

MARLO (1501 "Bad Girl Blues") 100-150 60

GENTEELS

Singles: 7-inch

CAPITOL (4798 "Take It Off") 10-20 62
STAG (2930 "Take It Off") 20-30 62
(First issue.)
STAG (4949 "Force of Gravity") 20-30 62
Member: Lenny Angelo.

GENTLE MEN

Singles: 7-inch

CAMEO (419 "Only Me") 10-15 66

GENTLE REIGN

LPs: 10/12-inch

VANGUARD ("Gentle Reign") 15-25 68
(Selection number not known.)

GENTLE TOUCH

Singles: 7-inch

KAPP (882 "Be Young, Be Foolish, Be Happy") 10-20 68

GENTLEMAN JIM

(With the Horsemen)

Singles: 7-inch

FOX (2 "Shackled and Bound") 15-25 66
JERDEN (732 "Soul Searchin' ") 10-15 64
TERA (3007 "If You Don't Like My Apples") 30-45
Members: Jim Dunlap; Doug Morrison; Ross Alamang; Chuck Jameson; Herb Hamilton; Bob Edwards; Larry Roberts; Bob Bailee.

GENTLEMEN

Singles: 78 rpm

APOLLO 50-75 54-55

Singles: 7-inch

APOLLO (464 "Something to Remember You By") 150-200 54
APOLLO (470 "Don't Leave Me Baby") 100-150 55

GENTLEMEN

Singles: 7-inch

SPIRIT (5791 "I Really Love You") 15-25 65

Members: Shane Todd; Bob Kenison; Robert Cardwell; David Kenison; Jon St. John; Bruce Shaw; Chuck Scalia.

GENTLEMEN

Singles: 7-inch

VANDAN (8303 "It's a Cry'n Shame") 30-50 66

GENTLEMEN FOUR

Singles: 7-inch

WAND (1184 "It Won't Hurt Baby") 40-60 67

GENTLEMEN WILD

Singles: 7-inch

NWI (2694 "You Gotta Leave") 10-15 65

GENTONES

Singles: 7-inch

CASINO (52261 "City Lights") 300-400 61

GENTRY, Art

Singles: 7-inch

A-BET (9446 "Wonderful Dream") 10-20 71

GENTRY, Beau

Singles: 7-inch

FEATURE (202 "Just in Case") 15-25 67

GENTRY, Bill

Singles: 7-inch

UNIVERSAL ARTIST (1001 "Baby What'Ya Say") 50-75

GENTRY, Donny

Singles: 7-inch

ROMULUS (3000 "From This Day On") ... 30-50 63

GENTRY, Johnny

Singles: 7-inch

STYLE (1923 "Memphis, Rave On") 50-75

GENTRY, Ray

Singles: 7-inch

MAVERICK (614 "Willie Was a Bad Boy") 450-550 58

GENTRY, Steve

Singles: 7-inch

BLAST (213 "I'll Be Waiting") 40-50 64

GENTRYS *P&R/LP '65*

Singles: 7-inch

BELL 5-8 68
CAPITOL 4-6 72
MGM (Except 13690) 5-10 65-67
MGM (13690 "There's a Love") 8-10 67
STAX 4-6 74
SUN (1108 thru 1122) 4-6 70-71
(Black vinyl, whether commercial or promo.)
SUN (1108 thru 1122) 10-15 70-71
(Colored vinyl. Promotional issues only.)
SUN (1126 "God Save Our Country") 10-20 71
YOUNGSTOWN (600 "Little Drops of Water") 15-25 65
YOUNGSTOWN (601 "Keep on Dancing") 15-25 65

Picture Sleeves

MGM 5-10 65

LPs: 10/12-inch

MGM 20-30 65-70
SUN 20-30 70
Members: Larry Raspberry; Jimmy Johnson; Bruce Bowles; Pat Neal; Jimmy Hart.

GENTRYS

Singles: 7-inch

DADO (0074 "Wild") 750-1000

GENTS

Singles: 7-inch

ALL BOY (8501 "It's Too Late to Cry") 15-25 62
EVE (5153 "Surfin' All Day") .... 20-30 '60s
LIBERTY (55332 "Jumpin' the Line") 10-15 61
NITE OWL (10 "Moonlight Surf") 20-25 60
Also see FOUR GENTS

GENTS / Teen 5

Singles: 7-inch

TIMES SQUARE (2 "I'll Never Let You Go") 15-25 64
TIMES SQUARE (4 "Island of Love") 15-25 64
TIMES SQUARE (98 "I'll Never Let You Go") 10-15 67
TIMES SQUARE (99 "Island of Love") 10-15 67

GENTS

Singles: 7-inch

DELAWARE 10-15 64-65
DUANE ("If You Don't Come Back") 10-15 66
(Selection number not known.)
NORMANDY (91067 "I Wonder Why") 10-15 67

GENTS

Singles: 7-inch

MIDNIGHT (102 "Facing This World Without You") .... 15-25 '60s

GENTS

LPs: 10/12-inch

("Dallas, Texas 1962") .... 400-500 '60s
(No label name or selection number used.)

GEORGE, Barbara *P&R/R&B '61*

Singles: 7-inch

A.F.O. (302 "I Know") 8-15 61
A.F.O. (304 "You Talk About Love") 8-15 62
HEP'ME 5-10
SUE 5-10 62-63
U.A. 4-6 74

LPs: 10/12-inch

AFO (5001 "I Know") 50-75 62

GEORGE, Brenda

Singles: 7-inch

GATOR (501 "I'm Not Trying to Make You Pay") .... 10-20 '60s
KENT (4557 "I Can't Stand It") 8-12 71
MESA (101 "I'm Not Trying to Make You Pay") .... 20-30 '60s
RONN (60 "Everybody Don't Know About My Good Thing") 8-12 72

GEORGE, Cassietta

Singles: 7-inch

AUDIO ARTS (60023 "Reach Out and Touch Me') 10-20 69

GEORGE, Johnny, & Pilots

Singles: 7-inch

COED (555 "Flying Blue Angels") 8-12 61
MUSIC CITY (818 "Music City Hop") 10-20 57

GEORGE, Kenny

Singles: 78 rpm

UNIQUE (312 "Heads You Win") 5-10 55

Singles: 7-inch

UNIQUE (312 "Heads You Win") 10-15 55

GEORGE, Lloyd

Singles: 7-inch

IMPERIAL (5837 Lucy Lee") 10-15 62
IMPERIAL (5896 "Frog Hunt") 10-15 62
POST (10006 "Frog Hunt") 10-15 63

GEORGE, Sunny

Singles: 7-inch

MGM (12697 "Tell Me, Tell Me") 15-25 58

GEORGE, Terry

Singles: 7-inch

COMET (2144 "My Love, My Dreamy Eyes") 15-25 62
Also see TERRY, George

GEORGE, Wally

Singles: 7-inch

ACCENT (1060 "Drag Strip") 25-35 58

GEORGE & BABS

Singles: 7-inch

DOT (18667 "You Don't Need Me") 10-15 66
Members: George Tomsco; Babs Tomsco.
Also see TOMSCO, George

GEORGE & EARL

Singles: 78 rpm

MERCURY (70605 "Can I") 10-15 55
MERCURY (70632 "Goin' Steady with the Blues") 10-15 55
MERCURY (70683 "Don't, Don't, Don't") . 10-15 55
MERCURY (70773 "Cry, Baby, Cry") 15-20 55
MERCURY (70852 "Done Gone") 10-20 56
MERCURY (70935 "11 Roses") 10-20 56

Singles: 7-inch

MERCURY (70605 "Can I") 20-30 55
MERCURY (70632 "Goin' Steady with the Blues") 20-30 55
MERCURY (70773 "Cry, Baby, Cry") 40-60 55
MERCURY (70852 "Done Gone") 30-40 56
MERCURY (70935 "11 Roses") 15-25 56

GEORGE & GENE

Singles: 7-inch

BARONET (7 "Teenage Love") 10-15 62

GEORGE & GREER

Singles: 7-inch

GOLDWAX (313 "You Didn't Know It But You Had Me") .... 15-25 '60s
(Also issued as by George Jackson & Dan Greer.)
Also see JACKSON, George, & Dan Greer

GEORGE & LOUIS

(George & Louis / Jerry Lee Lewis)

Singles: 7-inch

SUN (301 "Return of Jerry Lee"/"Lewis Boogie") 15-25 58
(*Lewis Boogie* is by Jerry Lee Lewis.)
SUN (301 "Return of Jerry Lee Part 1"/"Return of Jerry Lee Part 2") 10-20 58
Member: George Klein.
Also see LEWIS, Jerry Lee

GEORGETTES

Singles: 78 rpm

EBB (125 "Oh Tonight") 10-15 57

Singles: 7-inch

CHALLENGE (59012 "Dizzy Over You") 8-12 58
EBB (125 "Oh Tonight") 10-15 57
GOLDISC (3006 "Forget Me Not") 10-15 60
JACKPOT (48001 "Dizzy Over You") 10-15 58
(First issue.)
TROY (1001 "The Story") 10-15 63
U.A. (237 "Pair of Eyes") 10-15 60

GEORGIA CRACKERS

Singles: 7-inch

RCA (48-0033 "Broken Doll") 20-30 49
(Green vinyl.)
RCA (48-0051 "Gone Down the Drain") ... 20-30 49
(Green vinyl.)

GEORGIA PROPHETS

Singles: 7-inch

RIPETE (108 "I Get the Fever") .... 150-200 '80s
Member: Roy Smith.
Also see SMITH, Roy

GERBER, Vince

Singles: 7-inch

JERDEN (726 "Cyclone") 10-20 64
Also see VINCE & VICTORS

GERDSEN, Ray

Singles: 7-inch

TREY (1001 "So What") 10-20 59

GERMAINE, Denise

(With the Delmonicos)

Singles: 7-inch

ABC-PAR (10645 "He's a Strange One") ... 5-10 65
AKU (6139 "Teenage Idol") 75-125 61
U.A. (707 "Playboy") 5-10 64
Also see DELMONICOS

GERMZ

Singles: 7-inch

VERTIGO (8001 "Boy-Girl Love") 10-15 67
Also see KING, Carole

GERNON, Sheila

Singles: 7-inch

COOL (119 "Money Honey") 40-60

GERROIR, Carol

("Featuring Mike Jonas & the Harmoderns, Music by Sandy Stanton's Panics")

Singles: 7-inch

FABLE (700 "My Heart's in a Heaven") 25-30 60
Also see STANTON, Sandy

GERRY & LESLIE

Singles: 7-inch

HUSH (229 "Me Love Am Gone") 20-30 60

GERRY & PACEMAKERS *P&R/LP '64*

Singles: 7-inch

ERIC .... 4-6 '70s
LAURIE (3162 "How Do You Do It") 10-20 62
LAURIE (3196 "I Like It") 10-20 63
LAURIE (3218 "It's All Right") 8-12 64
LAURIE (3233 "I'm the One") 8-12 64
(Released with three different B-sides.)
LAURIE (3251 thru 3370) 5-10 64-67

LPs: 10/12-inch

ACCORD 5-10 81
CAPITOL 5-10 79

LAURIE....15-25 64-66
LAURIE/CAPITOL....8-10 81
(Label reads "Mfd. by Capitol Records." Record club issue.)
U.A....20-25 65
Member: Gerry Marsden.
Also see MARSDEN, Gerry
Also see MARTIN, George, & His Orchestra

GESTICS

Singles: 7-inch

SURFER (106 "Let's Go Trippin'")....20-30 63
SURFER (114 "Rockin' Fury")....20-30 63
Member: Jon Gest.

GESTURES P&R '64

Singles: 7-inch

APEX (76939 "Run Run Run")....10-15 '60s
APEX (76953 "Don't Mess Around")....10-15 '60s
SOMA (1417 "Run Run Run")....10-15 64
(Black vinyl.)
SOMA (1417 "Run Run Run")....25-35 64
(Colored vinyl.)
Member: Dale Menton.
Also see MADHATTERS
Also see MENTEN, Dale

GETTYSBURG ADDRESS

Singles: 7-inch

FRANKLIN (100 "Love Is a Beautiful Thing")....15-25 '60s
FRANKLIN (546 "My Girl")....15-25 '60s
FRANKLIN (601 "You've Got to Let Me Know")....15-25 '60s

GETZ, Stan LP '92

(Stan Getz Quartet; Quintet)

Singles: 78 rpm

CLEF....3-8 53-54
DAWN....3-8 54
MERCURY....3-8 53
NORGRAN....3-8 54-55
PRESTIGE....5-8 50-53
ROOST....5-8 50-53

Singles: 7-inch

CLEF....10-20 53-54
COLUMBIA....3-6 75-80
DAWN....10-20 54
MGM....4-8 65
MERCURY....10-20 53
NORGRAN....10-20 54-55
PRESTIGE....10-20 50-53
ROOST....10-20 50-53
VERVE....5-10 60-72

EPs: 7-inch

CLEF....10-20 53
DALE....15-25 51
NORGRAN (11 thru 155)....20-30 53-55
NORGRAN (2000-6 "At the Shrine")....50-100 55
(Boxed, six-disc set.)
PRESTIGE (1309 "Stan Getz")....20-40 52
ROOST....15-25 50-53

LPs: 10/12-inch

A&M....5-8 90
AMERICAN RECORDING SOCIETY....20-30 57
BARONET....10-20 62
BLUE RIBBON....10-20 61
CLEF (137 "Stan Getz Plays")....75-100 53
(10-inch LP.)
CLEF (143 "Artistry of Stan Getz")....75-100 53
(10-inch LP.)
COLUMBIA....5-10 74-82
CONCORD JAZZ....5-10 81
CROWN (5002 "Groovin' High")....25-50 57
DALE (21 "Retrospect")....100-150 51
(10-inch LP.)
INNER CITY....5-10 78
JAZZ MAN....5-10 82
JAZZTONE (1240 "Saxes of Stan Getz and Charlie Parker")....50-75 57
MGM (Except 4312)....5-10 70
MGM (4312 "Mickey One")....12-20 65
(Soundtrack.)
METRO (501 "Melodic Stan Getz")....10-15 65
MODERN (1202 "Groovin' High")....35-50 56
NEW JAZZ (8214 "Long Island Sound")..15-25 59
NORGRAN (4 "Stan Getz")....100-150 53
(10-inch LP.)
NORGRAN (1000 "Interpretations")....50-100 54
NORGRAN (1008 "Interpretations, Vol. 2")....50-100 54
NORGRAN (1029 "Interpretations, Vol. 3")....50-100 55
NORGRAN (1032 "West Coast Jazz")....40-60 55
NORGRAN (1087 "Stan Getz '57")....40-60 57
NORGRAN (2000-2 "At the Shrine")....100-200 55
(With booklet.)
PICKWICK....8-12 '70s
PRESTIGE (102 "Stan Getz")....100-200 52
(10-inch LP.)
PRESTIGE (7002 thru 7022)....25-50 56
(Yellow label.)
PRESTIGE (7252 thru 7256)....25-50 56
(Yellow label.)
PRESTIGE (7000 series)....8-18 64-68
(Blue label.)
PRESTIGE (24000 series)....8-12 72-79
ROOST (103 "Stan Getz Years")....30-40 64
ROOST (402 "Stan Getz")....100-150 50
(10-inch LP.)
ROOST (404 "Stan Getz and the Swedish All Stars")....100-125 51
(10-inch LP.)
ROOST (407 "Jazz at Storyville")....75-100 53
(10-inch LP.)
ROOST (411 "Jazz at Storyville, Vol. 2")....75-100 54
(10-inch LP.)
ROOST (420 "Jazz at Storyville, Vol. 3")....75-100 54
(10-inch LP.)
ROOST (417 "Chamber Music")....75-100 54
(10-inch LP.)
ROOST (2207 "Sounds of Stan Getz")....25-40 56
ROOST (2249 thru 2258)....20-30 63
ROULETTE....8-12 71-72
SAVOY (1100 series)....5-10 77
SAVOY (9004 "All Star Series")....100-150 51
(10-inch LP.)
SEECO (7 "Highlights in Modern Jazz").75-125 54
(10-inch LP.)
VSP....8-12 66-67
VERVE....30-60 57-60
(Reads "Verve Records, Inc." at bottom of label.)
VERVE....15-30 61-72
(Reads "MGM Records - a Division of Metro-Goldwyn-Mayer, Inc." at bottom of label.)
VERVE....5-10 73-84
(Reads "Manufactured By MGM Record Corp.," or mentions either Polydor or Polygram at bottom of label.)
Also see BENNETT, Tony
Also see GILLESPIE, Dizzy, & Stan Getz
Also see HAMPTON, Lionel, & Stan Getz
Also see HOLIDAY, Billie, & Stan Getz
Also see KIRKLAND, Jimmy
Also see POWERS, Johnny
Also see TJADER, Cal, & Stan Getz

GETZ, Stan, & Laurindo Almeida

Singles: 7-inch

VERVE (10468 "Winter Moon")....5-10 66

LPs: 10/12-inch

VERVE (8665 "Stan Getz and Laurindo Almeida")....10-15 66
Also see ALMEIDA, Laurindo

GETZ, Stan, & Boston Pops Orchestra

LPs: 10/12-inch

RCA....10-20 67
Also see BOSTON POPS ORCHESTRA

GETZ, Stan, & Charlie Byrd P&R/LP '62

Singles: 7-inch

MGM....4-6 78
VERVE....4-8 62

LPs: 10/12-inch

VERVE....15-25 62
Also see BYRD, Charlie

GETZ, Stan, & Oscar Peterson

LPs: 10/12-inch

VERVE....20-40 57-60
(Reads "Verve Records, Inc." at bottom of label.)
VERVE....10-25 61-72
(Reads "MGM Records - a Division of Metro-Goldwyn-Mayer, Inc." at bottom of label.)
Also see PETERSON, Oscar

GETZ & GILBERTO

(With Joao & Astrud Gilberto) P&R/LP '64

Singles: 7-inch

MGM....4-6 78
VERVE....5-8 64-65

LPs: 10/12-inch

MFSL (208 "Getz & Gilberto")....25-35 94
VERVE (8545 "Getz & Gilberto")....30-40 64
Also see GETZ, Stan

GHOST RIDERS

Singles: 7-inch

NEWLAND (1001 "Ghost Riders Theme")....20-30 65

GHOSTERS

Singles: 7-inch

GHOST (102 "Traveling Light")....20-30
GHOST (105 "I Get a Little Bit Lonely")....10-20
GHOST (21518 "Drums and Then Some")....10-20

GHOSTWRITERS

Singles: 7-inch

ARMADA (107 "Sunday School Rock Is Sinking")....10-15 '60s
Members: Sam McCue; Mike Larsheid.

GHOULS

(Super Stocks)

LPs: 10/12-inch

CAPITOL (T-2215 "Dracula's Deuce")....40-60 65
(Monaural.)
CAPITOL (ST-2215 "Dracula's Deuce")...50-75 65
(Stereo.)
Also see SUPER STOCKS

GIAMO, Joey, & Nobelmen

Singles: 7-inch

KLIK....10-20 58

GIANOTTA, Sonny / Phil Cammarata

Singles: 7-inch

ABC-PAR (10308 "Last Blast of the Blasted Bugler"/"Pain Set to Music")....10-20 62

GIANT, Bill

Singles: 7-inch

AVON (5701 "Life of the Party")....15-25 59

GIANT, Ethan

Singles: 7-inch

MARK '56 (141 "Where's My Baby")....100-200 59

GIANT, Jimmy

Singles: 7-inch

VEE-JAY (345 "Everything's Gonna Be Alright")....10-20 59

GIANTS

Singles: 7-inch

SPINDLETOP (101 "Loose Juice")....8-15 61
T-BIRD (103 "Loose Juice")....10-20 61
(First issue.)

GIB & WAYNE

Singles: 7-inch

STARFIRE (100 "World of Dreams")....15-25 65
Members: Floyd "Gib" Guilbeau; Wayne Moore.

GIBB, Barry P&R '80

Singles: 12-inch

MCA (23529 "Fine Line")....4-8 84

Singles: 7-inch

ATCO (6786 "One Bad Thing")....100-150 70
MCA (52443 "Shine Shine")....3-5 84

Picture Sleeves

MCA (52443 "Shine Shine")....3-5 84

LPs: 10/12-inch

MCA (5506 "Now Voyager")....5-10 84
Also see BEE GEES
Also see STREISAND, Barbra, & Barry Gibb
Also see WARWICK, Dionne

GIBBONS, Lloyd

Singles: 78 rpm

GLOBE....15-25 47

GIBBONS, Seymour

LPs: 10/12-inch

TAMERLANE (100 "Seymour Gibbons Plays with Himself")....30-40

GIBBS, Bill

Singles: 7-inch

ODESSA (308 "Rodney's Blues")....10-20 61
Also see BOYD, Tim, & Esquires

GIBBS, Georgia P&R '50

Singles: 78 rpm

CORAL....5-10 50-51
MERCURY....5-10 51-57

Singles: 7-inch

BELL....4-8 65-66
CORAL....10-20 50-51
EPIC (Except 9606)....4-8 63-64
EPIC (9606 "Tater Poon")....10-15 63
IMPERIAL....5-10 60
KAPP....5-10 59
MERCURY....10-20 51-57
RCA (Except 6922, 7047 & 7098)....5-15 57-67
RCA (6922 "I'm Walking the Floor Over You")....15-25 57
RCA (7047 "Fun Lovin' Baby")....15-25 57
RCA (7098 "Great Balls of Fire")....15-25 57
ROULETTE (4106 "The Hula Hoop Song")....5-10 58
ROULETTE (4126 "Hucklebuck")....5-10 59

EPs: 7-inch

MERCURY....10-20 54-56
ROYALE (239 "Georgia Gibbs Sings")....10-20 '50s
(Colored vinyl.)

LPs: 10/12-inch

BELL....10-15 66
CORAL (56037 "Ballin' the Jack")....30-50 51
(10-inch LP.)
CORAL (57183 "Her Nibs")....20-40 57
EMARCY (36103 "Swingin' with Gibbs")..20-40 57
EPIC....10-20 63
GOLDEN TONE (14093 "Her Nibs")....10-15 '50s
IMPERIAL....10-20 60
MERCURY (20071 "Music & Memories") 20-40 55
MERCURY (20114 "Song Favorites of Georgia Gibbs")....20-40 56
MERCURY (20170 "Swingin' with Her Nibs")....20-40 56
MERCURY (25175 "Georgia Gibbs Sings Oldies")....40-60 53
(10-inch LP.)
MERCURY (25199 "The Man That Got Away")....40-60 54
(10-inch LP.)
RONDO....8-12
SUNSET....8-12 66
TOPS....10-20 57
Also see DIAMONDS / Georgia Gibbs / Sarah Vaughan / Florian Zabach

GIBBS, Sheldon

Singles: 78 rpm

SMART (1016 "Houn' Dog Boogie")....25-35 52

GIBBS, Sherri, & Quovans

Singles: 7-inch

PHILLY SOUNDS ("Oh My Baby")....25-35 60
(No selection number used.)

GIBRALTARS

Singles: 7-inch

A&W (100 "Side By Side")....20-30
SAVOY (1581 "Crying Cause I Lost")....15-25 59
Also see BROWN, Nappy

GIBSON, Beverly Ann R&B '59

Singles: 7-inch

DEB (506 "Love's Burning Fire")....10-15 59
IMPERIAL (5505 "The Ways of Love")....10-15 58
JUBILEE (5447 "Do the Monkey")....5-10 63
KING (5244 "Call On Me")....10-15 63
KING (5288 "Wait and See")....5-10 63
KING (5315 "Love We Shared")....5-10 60
LANDA (671 "Love's Burning Fire")....5-10 61

GIBSON, Bob

Singles: 7-inch

DECCA (25612 "Marching to Pretoria")....5-10 63
ELEKTRA (7 "Super Skier")....5-10 59
GIBSON (6003 "B-52")....10-15 59

LPs: 10/12-inch

ELEKTRA (177 "Ski Songs")....15-25 59
(Monaural.)
ELEKTRA (7177 "Ski Songs")....20-30 59
(Stereo.)
ELEKTRA (EKL-239 "Where I'm Bound") 10-20 63
(Monaural.)
ELEKTRA (EKS7-239 "Where I'm Bound")....15-25 63
(Stereo.)
RIVERSIDE (802 "Offbeat Folk Songs")..30-40 56

RIVERSIDE (806 "Folk Songs")...25-40 57
RIVERSIDE (816 "Carnegie Hall Concert")...25-40 57
RIVERSIDE (1111 "There's a Meetin' Here Tonight")...25-35 58
(Stereo.)
RIVERSIDE (7542 "Hootenanny at Carnegie")...15-20 63

GIBSON, Bob, & Bob Camp
LPs: 10/12-inch
ELEKTRA (207 "At the Gate of Horn")...15-25 61
Also see GIBSON, Bob

GIBSON, Bobby, & Voyagers
Singles: 7-inch
GIBSON (6003 "B-52")...25-30 61

GIBSON, Buddy
(With Jesters; with Vanguards)
Singles: 7-inch
SPRY (118 "To Be Or Not to Be")...10-20 59
SWINGIN' (615 "Just a Game")...50-100 59
(Original must be thick vinyl.)
SWINGIN' (615 "Just a Game")...8-12 '70s

GIBSON, Byron
Singles: 7-inch
LAURIE (3108 "Sittin' Here Cryin' ")...10-15 61

GIBSON, Cindy
(With the Tiffanys)
Singles: 7-inch
ARCTIC (104 "Step by Step")...5-10 65
GENERAL AMERICAN (700 "A Lovely Summer Night")...20-30 64

GIBSON, Clarence, & Four Airs
Singles: 7-inch
GIBSON'S (982 "Do You Really Care")...100-150

GIBSON, Curly
(Curly Gibson's Sunshine Playboys)
Singles: 7-inch
LEO (1824 "Hillbilly Hop")...75-100 57

GIBSON, Daddyo
Singles: 7-inch
CHECKER (848 "Night Train")...15-20 58

GIBSON, Dave, & Devonetts
Singles: 7-inch
LEEWELD (210 "Can't Do Nothin' ")...15-25 63

GIBSON, Don *C&W '56*
Singles: 78 rpm
COLUMBIA...5-10 52-54
MGM...15-35 55-56
RCA...8-12 51
Singles: 7-inch
ABC/HICKORY...4-6 75-78
COLUMBIA (20000 series)...8-15 52-54
HICKORY...4-6 70-72
MCA...4-6 79
MGM (12109 "Run Boy")...20-30 55
MGM (12194 "Sweet Dreams")...20-30 56
MGM (12290 "I Ain't Gonna Waste My Time")...30-40 56
MGM (12331 "I Believed in You")...20-30 56
MGM (12393 "I'm Gonna Fool Everybody")...30-40 57
MGM (12494 "I Ain't A-Studying You Baby")...40-60 57
RCA (0400 series)...10-20 51
RCA (4300 & 4400 series)...10-20 51-52
RCA (6000 series)...10-15 57-58
RCA (7000 series, except 7762)...10-15 58-61
RCA (47-7762 "Legend in My Time")...8-10 60
(Monaural.)
RCA (61-7762 "Legend in My Time")...15-25 60
(Stereo.)
RCA (8000 & 9000 series)...5-10 62-70
W.B./CURB...3-6 80
Picture Sleeves
RCA...8-12 63
EPs: 7-inch
COLUMBIA...15-20 57
RCA...10-20 58-59
LPs: 10/12-inch
ABC/HICKORY...6-10 75-78
CAMDEN...10-15 65-74
HARMONY (7300 series)...15-20 65
HARMONY (31000 series)...5-10 72
HICKORY...8-12 70-72
HICKORY/MGM...6-10 73-75
LION (70069 "Songs by Don Gibson")...25-50 58
MGM...8-12 70
METRO...12-18 65
RCA (1743 thru 2878)...15-30 58-63
(With "LPM" prefix. Monaural.)
RCA (1743 thru 2878)...20-40 58-63
(With "LSP" prefix. Stereo.)
RCA (3376 thru 4378)...10-20 63-70
(With "LPM" or "LSP" prefix.)
Session: Jordanaires.
Also see JORDANAIRES
Also see WEST, Dottie, & Don Gibson

GIBSON, Don, & Sue Thompson *C&W '71*
Singles: 7-inch
HICKORY...4-6 71-76
LPs: 10/12-inch
HICKORY (168 "Two of Us Together")...8-12 73
HICKORY/MGM...5-10 75
Also see GIBSON, Don
Also see THOMPSON, Sue

GIBSON, Douglas, with the Sweet & Sours
Singles: 7-inch
TANGERINE (969 "Run for Your Life")...10-20 67

GIBSON, Grandpappy
(Clifford Gibson)
Singles: 7-inch
BOBBIN (124 "It's Best to Know Who You're Talking To")...25-35 60
BOBBIN (127 "The Monkey Likes to Boogie")...25-35 61

GIBSON, Jill
Singles: 7-inch
IMPERIAL (66068 "It's As Easy As 1, 2, 3")...40-50 64
(Black label.)
IMPERIAL (66068 "It's As Easy As 1, 2, 3")...20-30 64
(White label. Promotional issue only.)
Also see MATADORS

GIBSON, Joe D.
Singles: 7-inch
TETRA (4450 "Good Morning Captain")...40-60 59

GIBSON, Johnny *P&R '62*
(Johnny Gibson Trio)
Singles: 7-inch
BIG TOP (3088 "Midnight")...10-20 61
BIG TOP (3118 "After Midnight")...10-20 62
BIG TOP (3149 "Ooh Poo Pah Doo")...10-20 63
LAURIE (3256 "Beachcomber")...8-12 64
TWIRL (1023 "Beachcomber")...10-20 64
(First issue.)
Also see JOHNNY & HURRICANES

GIBSON, Julie, & Anglows
Singles: 7-inch
HERALD (575 "I Got News for You")...10-20 62

GIBSON, Steve *P&R '48*
(With the Red Caps; with Original Red Caps; Red Caps; "Vocal Solo By George Tinley")
Singles: 78 rpm
ABC-PAR...10-25 56-57
BEACON...15-25 44
JAY-DEE...15-25 54
MERCURY...25-50 47-54
RCA...20-30 51-55
Singles: 7-inch
ABC-PAR (9702 "Love Me Tender")...15-25 56
ABC-PAR (9750 "Write to Me")...15-25 56
ABC-PAR (9796 "You May Not Love Me")...15-25 57
ABC-PAR (9856 "Silhouettes")...15-25 57
ABC-PAR (10105 "I Went to Your Wedding")...10-15 61
BAND BOX (325 "No More")...10-15 62
CASA BLANCA (5505 "Where Are You")...75-125 59
(First issue.)
HI LO (101 "I Want to Be Loved")...20-30 58
HI LO (103 "It's Love")...20-30 58
HUNT (326 "Cheryl Lee")...15-25 59
HUNT (330 "Where Are You")...10-20 59
JAY-DEE (796 "It Hurts Me But I Like It")...40-50 54
MERCURY (1253 "I Don't Want to Set the World on Fire")...100-200 49
MERCURY (1255 "Blueberry Hill")...100-200 49
MERCURY (5380 "I'll Never Love Anyone Else")...75-100 50
MERCURY (8038 "San Antonio Rose")...30-40 51
MERCURY (8069 "Wedding Bells")...75-100 51
MERCURY (8146 "Blueberry Hill")...30-40 51
MERCURY (70389 "Wedding Bells")...20-30 54
RCA (0127 "I'm to Blame")...50-100 51
RCA (0138 "Would I Mind")...50-100 51
RCA (3986 "The Thing")...75-125 50
RCA (4076 "Three Dollars and Ninety-Eight Cents")...30-60 51
RCA (4294 "Shame")...30-60 51
RCA (4670 "Two Little Kisses")...30-60 52
RCA (4835 "I Went to Your Wedding")...30-60 52
RCA (5103 "Truthfully")...30-60 52
RCA (5130 "Big Game Hunter")...30-60 53
RCA (6096 "Feelin' Kinda Happy")...15-25 55
RCA (6345 "How I Cry")...15-25 55
ROSE (555 "My Heart Belongs to Only You")...10-15 59
ROSE (5534 "Bless You")...10-15 60
STAGE (3001 "Blueberry Hill")...10-15
EPs: 7-inch
MERCURY (3215 "Blueberry Hill")...200-300 52
LPs: 10/12-inch
MERCURY (25115 "You're Driving Me Crazy")...300-400 52
(10-inch LP. Title on label is *Harmony Time.*)
MERCURY (25116 "Blueberry Hill")...300-400 52
(10-inch LP. Title on label is *Singing & Swinging.*)
Member: George Tinley.
Also see DAMITA JO with STEVE GIBSON & RED CAPS
Also see FIVE RED CAPS
Also see GIBSON, Steve
Also see GREGG, Bobby
Also see JENKINS, Duke, & Roulettes
Also see MODERN RED CAPS
Also see TOPPERS

GIBSON, Steve, & His Red Caps / Damita Jo with Steve Gibson & the Red Caps
Singles: 78 rpm
RCA (5987 "My Tzatskele")...10-15 55
Singles: 7-inch
RCA (5987 "My Tzatskele")...15-25 55
Also see DAMITA JO with STEVE GIBSON & RED CAPS
Also see GIBSON, Steve

GIBSON, Virginia
Singles: 7-inch
CABOT (118 "Teenage Dance")...10-15 58

GIBSON, Willie
(With the Boys)
Singles: 78 rpm
BENIDA (5016 "I Cried for You")...5-10 54
Singles: 7-inch
BENIDA (5016 "I Cried for You")...10-20 54
W.B. (5294 "Cheatin' On Me")...5-10 62

GIDDY SMITTY
Singles: 78 rpm
CHIC (1001 "Dixie Doll")...10-20 56
Singles: 7-inch
CHIC (1001 "Dixie Doll")...20-30 56

GIDEON, Tony
Singles: 7-inch
CHESS (1776 "The Way You Move Me Baby")...15-25 60

GIGOLOS
Singles: 7-inch
CHESS (1715 "Luna Rock")...15-25 59

GIGOLOS
(Gigolo's)
Singles: 7-inch
DAYNITE (1 "Swingin' Saints")...20-30 60
Members: Don Cole; Bob Taylor.

GIGOLOS
Singles: 7-inch
BROADWAY (1000 "Movin' Out")...10-15 61
ENTERPRISE (5000 "Movin' Out")...5-10 64
Also see COE, Jamie

GILBERT, Jewell
(With Mac McCray's Band)
Singles: 78 rpm
HI-PO (1002 "Mad Nervous Woman")...15-25 57
Singles: 7-inch
HI-PO (1002 "Mad Nervous Woman")...20-40 57

GILBERT, Jimmy
Singles: 7-inch
DARN-L (5264 "Believe What I Say")...100-200

GILBERTSON, Leroy
Singles: 7-inch
CUCA (1082 "Russian Rumble")...10-20 62

GILES, GILES & FRIPP
LPs: 10/12-inch
DERAM (18019 "The Cheerful Insanity of Giles, Giles & Fripp")...25-35 68
Members: Mike Giles; Peter Giles; Robert Fripp; Nicky Hopkins.
Also see McDONALD & GILES

GILFORD, Jimmy
(Jimmy Guilford)
Singles: 7-inch
SOLID HIT (103 "I Want to Be Your Baby")...10-15
THELMA (501 "Too Late to Cry")...15-25 65
WHEELSVILLE (101 "I Want to Be Your Baby")...20-40 65

GILKYSON, Terry *P&R '57*
(With the Easy Riders; with South Coasters)
Singles: 78 rpm
COLUMBIA...8-12 54-57
DECCA...8-12 51-52
Singles: 7-inch
COLUMBIA...10-20 54-57
DECCA...10-20 51-52
KAPP...10-15 60
Picture Sleeves
COLUMBIA (40817 "Marianne")...15-25 57
KAPP (355 "Ballad of the Alamo")...20-30 60
(Sleeve pictures John Wayne and the Alamo.)
EPs: 7-inch
COLUMBIA...10-20 57
DECCA...10-20 53
LPs: 10/12-inch
DECCA (5263 "Folk Songs by a Solitary Singer")...30-40 50
DECCA (5305 "Solitary Singer")...40-60 51
(10-inch LP.)
DECCA (5457 "Golden Minutes of Folk Music")...40-60 53
(10-inch LP.)
KAPP (1196 "Rollin' ")...15-25 60
(Monaural.)
KAPP (1216 "Remember the Alamo")...15-25 61
(Monaural.)
KAPP (1327 "Cry of the Wild Goose")...15-25 63
(Monaural.)
KAPP (3196 "Rollin' ")...15-25 60
(Stereo.)
KAPP (3216 "Remember the Alamo")...15-25 61
(Stereo.)
KAPP (3327 "Cry of the Wild Goose")...15-25 63
(Stereo.)
Members: Terry Gilkyson; Rich Dehr.
Also see EASY RIDERS
Also see LAINE, Frankie, & Easy Riders
Also see MARTIN, Dean
Also see WEAVERS & Terry Gilkyson

GILL, Jimmie
Singles: 78 rpm
BATTLE (006 "Gather Round")...5-10 53
Singles: 7-inch
BATTLE (006 "Gather Round")...10-15 53

GILL, Robert
(With Band)
Singles: 78 rpm
REPUBLIC (7076 "Let's Have Some Fun")...10-15 54
Singles: 7-inch
REPUBLIC (7076 "Let's Have Some Fun")...40-60 54
WONDER (109 "Baby, That's Alright")...40-60 58

GILL, Ronnie, & Pastel Keys
Singles: 7-inch
EXPEDITE (2853 "Geraldine")...75-125 58
RIP (108 "Geraldine")...50-75 58
Also see LOVE NOTES

GILL, Scooter, & Accents

Singles: 7-inch

RIVER (1313 "Phantom Wheels")........... 20-30

GILLARD, Joel

Singles: 7-inch

SPHINX (1001 "Why Should I Cry")........ 40-50 60
SPHINX (1003 "What Can I Give") 40-50 60

GILLEN, Jack

Singles: 7-inch

ABCO (1003 "Good Luck Charm")..............5-10 66
PROVENCHER (1001 "Don't Treat Me This Way").. 40-60
S AND S (1 "Early One Morning")........ 250-350

Picture Sleeves

PROVENCHER (1001 "Don't Treat Me This Way")... 100-200

GILLESPIE, Darlene

Singles: 78 rpm

DISNEYLAND (50 "Too Much") 10-20 57
DISNEYLAND (51 "Butterfly") 10-20 57
DISNEYLAND (52 "Rock-A-Billy")........... 10-20 57

Singles: 7-inch

BUENA VISTA (330 "Porcupine") 15-25 58
CORAL (62178 "I Loved, I Laughed, I Cried")...8-12 60
DISNEYLAND (50 "Too Much") 20-30 57
DISNEYLAND (51 "Butterfly") 20-30 57
DISNEYLAND (52 "Rock-A-Billy")........... 20-30 57

LPs: 10/12-inch

DISNEYLAND (3010 "Darlene of the Teens").. 40-50 57
DISNEYLAND/MICKEY MOUSE (32 "Songs from *Sleeping Beauty*")............................ 25-35 59
Also see MOUSEKETEERS

GILLESPIE, Dizzy — P&R '45

(With His All Star Quintet)

Singles: 78 rpm

ATLANTIC 5-10 52-53
CONTEMPORARY 5-10 53
GUILD...5-10 45
NORGRAN 5-10 54-56
PRESTIGE 5-10 51
RCA...5-10 48-52

Singles: 7-inch

ATLANTIC 10-20 52-53
CONTEMPORARY 10-20 53
LIMELIGHT...5-10 65-67
NORGRAN.. 10-20 54-56
PERCEPTION 4-8 69
PHILIPS...5-10 64
SOLID STATE...4-8 69
VERVE...8-15 57-62

EPs: 7-inch

ATLANTIC (514/521 "Dizzy Gillespie").... 25-50 52
CLEF (153 "Dizzy with Strings").............. 25-50 53
CLEF (291/292/293/294 "Roy and Diz").. 20-40 55
(Price is for any volume.)
DEE GEE (4000/4003/4004 "Dizzy Gillespie")... 40-60 51
(Price is for any volume.)
DISCOVERY (13 "Dizzy Plays").............. 25-50 50
GNP (1/2/3 "Dizzy Gillespie") 25-50 50
(Price is for any volume.)
NORGRAN (114/115 "Big Band") 25-50 55
(Price is for either volume.)
RCA (432 "Dizzier and Dizzier")............... 20-40 54

LPs: 10/12-inch

ALLEGRO (3017 "Dizzy Gillespie Plays")... 50-100 52
(10-inch LP.)
ALLEGRO (3083 "Dizzy Gillespie")........ 50-100 52
(10-inch LP.)
ALLEGRO (4023 "Dizzy Gillespie")........ 50-100 53
(10-inch LP.)
AMERICAN RECORDING SOCIETY (405 "Jazz Creations") 75-125 55
AMERICAN RECORDING SOCIETY (423 "Big Band Jazz") 75-125 55
ATLANTIC (138 "Dizzy Gillespie") 200-300 52
(10-inch LP.)
ATLANTIC (142 "Dizzy Gillespie, Vol. 2")... 200-300 52
(10-inch LP.)
ATLANTIC (1257 "Dizzy at Home and Abroad").. 75-100 57
(Black label, silver print.)
BARONET (105 "A Handful of Modern Jazz") 30-40 61
BLUE NOTE (5017 "Horn of Plenty")....150-200 52
(10-inch LP.)
CLEF (136 "Dizzy with Strings")...........125-150 53
(10-inch LP.)
CLEF (641 "Roy & Diz") 75-100 55
(With Roy Eldridge.)
CLEF (671 "Roy & Diz, Vol. 2")..............75-100 55
CLEF (730 "Trumpet Kings")...................75-100 56
CLEF (731 "Trumpet Battle")...................75-100 56
CONTEMPORARY (2504 "Dizzy in Paris") 100-150 53
(10-inch LP.)
DEE GEE (1000 "Dizzy Gillespie") 200-250 51
(10-inch LP.)
DIAL (212 "Modern Trumpets")...............75-125 52
(10-inch LP.)
DISCOVERY (3013 "Dizzy Plays") 150-200 50
(10-inch LP.)
GNP (4 "Dizzy Gillespie")......................100-200 50
(10-inch LP.)
GNP (23 "Dizzy Gillespie").......................50-75 57
IMPULSE (9149 "Swing Low, Sweet Cadillac")...10-20 67
LIMELIGHT (82022 "New Continent") 15-25 65
(Monaural.)
LIMELIGHT (86022 "New Continent") 15-25 65
(Stereo.)
LIMELIGHT (82042 "Melody Lingers On")...15-25 67
(Monaural.)
LIMELIGHT (86042 "Melody Lingers On")...15-25 67
(Stereo.)
NORGRAN (1003 "Afro Dizzy") 75-100 54
NORGRAN (1023 "Big Band") 75-100 55
NORGRAN (1083 "Jazz Recital") 75-100 56
NORGRAN (1084 "World Statesman")...75-100 56
NORGRAN (1090 "Big Band") 60-80 56
PHILIPS...20-30 62-65
RCA (530 "Dizzy Gillespie") 15-25 66
RCA (1009 "Dizzier and Dizzier") 50-75 54
RCA (2398 "The Greatest")......................30-50 61
REGENT (6043 "School Days") 50-75 57
RON-LETTE (11 "Dizzy Gillespie") 25-50 58
ROOST (106 "Diz and Bird")...................75-100 59
(Boxed, two-disc set.)
ROOST (414 "Dizzy Over Paris") 150-200 53
ROOST (2214 "Concert in Paris")............50-75 57
ROOST (2234 "Diz and Bird in Concert").50-75 59
SAVOY (12000 series) 25-50 55-57
SOLID STATE..10-20 68-69
TRIBUTE...10-15 69
VSP (28 "Soul Mates")..............................15-25 66
VERVE (6047 "Have Trumpet, Will Excite")..50-75 59
(Stereo.)
VERVE (6068 "Ebullient")..........................50-75 59
(Stereo.)
VERVE (6117 "Greatest Trumpet")...........50-75 60
(Stereo.)
VERVE (8000 series) 15-30 62-67
(With "MGM Records - a Division of Metro-Goldwyn-Mayer, Inc." at bottom of label.)
VERVE (8017 "Dizzy in Greece") 50-75 57
(Reads "Verve Records, Inc." at bottom of label.)
VERVE (8109 "Trumpet Kings")................50-75 57
(Reads "Verve Records, Inc." at bottom of label.)
VERVE (8110 "Trumpet Battle") 50-75 57
(Reads "Verve Records, Inc." at bottom of label.)
VERVE (8173 "Jazz Recital")....................50-75 57
(Reads "Verve Records, Inc." at bottom of label.)
VERVE (8174 "World Statesman") 50-75 57
(Reads "Verve Records, Inc." at bottom of label.)
VERVE (8178 "Big Band")..........................50-75 57
(Reads "Verve Records, Inc." at bottom of label.)
VERVE (8191 "Afro Dizzy")........................50-75 57
(Reads "Verve Records, Inc." at bottom of label.)
VERVE (8198 "For Musicians Only").........50-75 58
(Reads "Verve Records, Inc." at bottom of label.)
VERVE (8208 "Manteca")...........................50-75 58
(Reads "Verve Records, Inc." at bottom of label.)
VERVE (8214 "Dizzy & Stuff")...................40-60 58
(Reads "Verve Records, Inc." at bottom of label.)
VERVE (8260 "Duets")...............................50-75 58
(Reads "Verve Records, Inc." at bottom of label.)
VERVE (8262 "Sunny Side Up")...............50-75 58
(Reads "Verve Records, Inc." at bottom of label.)
VERVE (8313 "Have Trumpet, Will Excite")..50-75 59
(Monaural. Reads "Verve Records, Inc." at bottom of label.)
VERVE (8328 "Ebullient") 50-75 59
(Monaural. Reads "Verve Records, Inc." at bottom of label.)
VERVE (8352 "Greatest Trumpet") 50-75 60
(Monaural. Reads "Verve Records, Inc." at bottom of label.)
VERVE (8386 "Portrait")............................50-75 60
(Monaural. Reads "Verve Records, Inc." at bottom of label.)
VERVE (8394 "Gillespiana") 50-75 61
(Monaural. Reads "Verve Records, Inc." at bottom of label.)
VERVE (8401 "An Electrifying Evening") .50-75 62
(Monaural. Reads "Verve Records, Inc." at bottom of label.)
VERVE (68386 "Portrait")..........................50-75 60
(Stereo. Reads "Verve Records, Inc." at bottom of label.)
VERVE (68394 "Gillespiana") 50-75 61
(Stereo. Reads "Verve Records, Inc." at bottom of label.)
VERVE (68401 "An Electrifying Evening") 50-75 62
(Stereo. Reads "Verve Records, Inc." at bottom of label.)
WING (12318 "New Wave") 15-25 66
(Monaural.)
WING (16318 "New Wave").......................15-25 66
(Stereo.)
Also see DAVIS, Miles, Dizzy Gillespie & Fats Navarro

GILLESPIE, Dizzy, & Slim Gaillard

LPs: 10/12-inch

ULTRAPHONIC (50273 "Gaillard & Gillespie") 30-50 58
Also see GAILLARD, Slim

GILLESPIE, Dizzy, & Stan Getz

EPs: 7-inch

NORGRAN (3/4 "Dizzy Gillespie & Stan Getz Sextet")..40-60 53
(Price is for either volume.)
NORGRAN (32 "Dizzy Gillespie & Stan Getz Sextet [Vol. 2]")..40-60 53

LPs: 10/12-inch

NORGRAN (2 "Dizzy Gillespie & Stan Getz Sextet")..150-250 53
(10-inch LP.)
NORGRAN (18 "Dizzy Gillespie & Stan Getz Sextet [Vol. 2]")..150-250 53
NORGRAN (1050 "Dizzy Gillespie & Stan Getz Sextet") 75-125 56
VERVE (8141 "Dizzy Gillespie & Stan Getz Sextet")..50-75 57
VERVE (68141 "Diz & Getz")....................15-25 66
Also see GETZ, Stan
Also see GILLESPIE, Dizzy

GILLESPIE, Dizzy / Django Reinhardt

("With Strings")

LPs: 10/12-inch

VERVE (8015 "Jazz from Paris") 50-75 57
("Clef" series. Reads "Verve Records, Inc." at bottom of label.)

GILLESPIE, Gary, & Galaxies

Singles: 7-inch

DELTA (520 "Honest I Do")......................15-25 62

GILLETTE, Bill, & Collegians

Singles: 7-inch

CAPA (114 "In Love with Love") 20-30 63

GILLETTES

Singles: 7-inch

J&S (1391 "24 Hours of the Day") 10-15 64
J&S (1674 "I Just Can't Help Myself") 15-20 60

GILLEY, Mickey — C&W '68

(With the Urban Cowboy Band)

Singles: 7-inch

ACT 1 ....5-10 66
ASYLUM...3-6 80
ASTRO (Except 100 series)...........................4-6 71-73
ASTRO (102 "Down the Line")..................50-75 64
ASTRO (103 thru 112) 10-15 64-65
DARYL (101 "Three's a Crowd")...............10-15 63
DOT (15706 "Call Me Shorty") 50-100 58
EPIC 3-6 78-86
ERIC...3-5
GRT..4-6 70
GOLDBAND...5-10 '60s
KHOURY'S (712 "Drive-In Movie").......200-300 59
LYNN (503 thru 515)...............................15-25 60-61
MINOR (106 "Ooh Wee").......................400-600 57
PAULA (200 & 300 series)..........................6-12 66-68
PAULA (400 series).....................................3-6 74-83
PAULA (1200 series).....................................4-8 68-69
PLAYBOY 4-6 74-78
POTOMAC (901 "Is It Wrong") 15-25 60
PRINCESS (4004 "Drive-in Movie") 10-20 62
RESCO 4-6 74
REX (1007 "Grapevine") 20-25 59
SABRA..10-20 61
SAN 10-20 63
SUPREME 10-20 62
TCF/HALL (126 "Let's Hurt Together").......8-12 65

LPs: 10/12-inch

ASTRO (101 "Lonely Wine")...................75-150 64
EPIC 5-10 79-86
51 WEST..5-10 79
PAULA (Except 2000 series) 5-10 81
PAULA (2195 "Down the Line")...............20-25 67
PAULA (2224 "Mickey Gilley at His Best")..10-12 74
PAULA (2234 "Mickey Gilley")..................8-10 78
PLAYBOY 8-12 74-78
Also see CHARLES, Ray, & Mickey Gilley
Also see HAGGARD, Merle / Mickey Gilley / Willie Knight

GILLEY, Mickey, & Barbi Benton — C&W '75

Singles: 7-inch

PLAYBOY 4-6 75

Picture Sleeves

PLAYBOY 4-6 75

GILLEY, Mickey, & Johnny Lee

Singles: 7-inch

EPIC..3-5 81
Also see NELSON, Willie / Johnny Lee / Mickey Gilley

GILLEY, Mickey, & Charly McClain — C&W '84

(Charly McClain & Mickey Gilley)

Singles: 7-inch

EPIC..3-5 83-84

LPs: 10/12-inch

EPIC..5-8 84
Also see GILLEY, Mickey

GILLHAM, Archie, & His Saint Louis Band

("Vocals by Leon Bryant")

Singles: 78 rpm

GILSPIN (1 "St. Louis Blues")..................20-40

GILLIAM, Earl

Singles: 78 rpm

SARG 5-10 56

Singles: 7-inch

SARG (128 "Nobody's Blues")..................10-15 56
SARG (133 "Wrong Doing Woman").........10-15 56

GILLS, Don

Singles: 7-inch

ACCENT (1199 "Bad Bass Boogie")........10-20 66

GILLUM, Jazz

(William Gillum)

Singles: 78 rpm

BLUEBIRD 10-20 45-46
GROOVE 20-30 54
RCA...10-20 46-49

Singles: 7-inch

GROOVE (5002 "Key to the Highway")....30-50 54
RCA (50-0004 "Signifying Woman").......50-100 49
(Cherry red vinyl.)
RCA (50-0017 "Take One More Chance with Me")...50-100 49
(Cherry red vinyl.)
RCA (50-0035 "Gonna Be Some Shooting")..50-100 49
(Cherry red vinyl.)
Also see BROONZY, Bill
Also see SYKES, Roosevelt

GILMER, Jimmy — P&R/R&B/LP '63

(With the Fireballs)

Singles: 7-inch

ABC...4-6 74
ATCO 5-10 68-69
DECCA (30942 "Look Alive")....................10-20 59
DOT..8-12 63-66
HAMILTON (55037 "It Won't Be Long") ...10-20 63
7 ARTS (714 "Call in the Sheriff")............10-20 61
WARWICK (547 "True Love Ways").........15-25 60

WARWICK (592 "Do You Think") ... 10-15 61
Picture Sleeves
7 ARTS (714 "Call in the Sheriff") ... 30-40 61
LPs: 10/12-inch
ATCO ... 10-15 68-69
CROWN ... 15-20 63
DOT (3512 "Torquay") ... 15-25 63
(Monaural.)
DOT (3545 "Sugar Shack") ... 15-25 63
(Monaural.)
DOT (3577 "Buddy's Buddy") ... 40-50 64
(Monaural.)
DOT (3643 "Lucky 'Leven") ... 15-25 63
(Monaural.)
DOT (3668 "Folkbeat") ... 15-25 63
(Monaural.)
DOT (3709 "Campusology") ... 15-25 63
(Monaural.)
DOT (25512 "Torquay") ... 20-30 63
(Stereo.)
DOT (25545 "Sugar Shack") ... 20-30 63
(Stereo.)
DOT (25577 "Buddy's Buddy") ... 75-100 64
(Stereo.)
DOT (25643 "Lucky 'Leven") ... 20-30 63
(Stereo.)
DOT (25668 "Folkbeat") ... 20-30 63
(Stereo.)
DOT (25709 "Campusology") ... 20-30 63
(Stereo.)
DOT (25856 "Firewater") ... 20-30 63
Also see FIREBALLS
Also see SEDAKA, Neil, & Tokens / Angels / Jimmy Gilmer and the Fireballs

GILMORE, Boyd
Singles: 78 rpm
MODERN ... 50-75 52
Singles: 7-inch
MODERN (860 "Ramblin' on My Mind") ... 100-200 52
MODERN (872 "All in My Dreams") ... 100-200 52

GILMORE, Boyd /Houston Boines / Charlie Booker
LPs: 10/12-inch
UNITED (7786 "Mississippi Blues") ... 8-12
Also see BOINES, Houston
Also see BOOKER, Charlie
Also see GILMORE, Boyd

GILMORE, Dolly
Singles: 7-inch
DOVE (35467 "Sweet, Sweet Baby") ... 15-20

GILMORE, Geoff / Sheiks
Singles: 7-inch
JAMIE (1132 "Trés Chic") ... 10-20 59
Also see SHEIKS

GILREATH, James P&R/R&B '63
(Jimmy Gilreath)
Singles: 7-inch
JOY (274 "Little Band of Gold") ... 10-20 63
JOY (278 "Lollipops, Lace and Lipstick") . 20-30 63
JOY (286 "Blue Is My Color") ... 8-12 64
JOY (302 "Your Day Is Coming") ... 8-12 65
STATUE (600 "Little Band of Gold") ... 200-250 63
(First issue. Approximately 300 made.)
VEE-EIGHT (1002 "Time Hasn't Helped") ... 75-125 62
Session: Johnny Mihalic.
Also see MAHALIC, Johnny

GILSON, Patti
Singles: 7-inch
GOLDEN WORLD (6 "Don't You Tell a Lie") ... 15-25 64

GIMICKS
Singles: 7-inch
ENSIGN (4028 "Naughty Rooster") ... 15-25 58

GIN & GENTS
Singles: 7-inch
ELDORADO (102 "Boy and Girl") ... 10-15
MISS THING ("Dreams for Sale") ... 20-30
(Selection number not known.)

GINA MAREE
Singles: 7-inch
CLOCK (1046 "He Lied") ... 10-20 61

GINGER
(Sandra Glantz)
Singles: 7-inch
TITAN (1717 "Dry Tears") ... 25-35 61
Also see GINGER & SNAPS
Also see HONEYS
Also see USHER, Gary

GINGER & CHIFFONS
Singles: 7-inch
GROOVE (0003 "She") ... 15-25 62

GINGER & JOHNNY
Singles: 7-inch
ARCADE (159 "Butterfly Love") ... 10-20 61
ARCADE (174 "Covered Wagon Caravan") ... 10-20 63
ARCADE (176 "It Takes Two") ... 10-20 63
Session: Bill Haley's Comets.
Also see HALEY, Bill

GINGER & SNAPS
Singles: 7-inch
MGM (13413 "Growing Up Is Hard to Do") . 8-12 65
TORÉ (1008 "Love Me the Way I Love You") ... 20-30 59
Member: Ginger Blake.
Also see GINGER

GINGER VALLEY
Singles: 7-inch
INTERNATIONAL ARTIST (142 "Country Life") ... 15-25
(Colored vinyl.)

GINGERS
Singles: 7-inch
RADIANT (105 "Heaven Heaven Heaven") ... 10-20 64

GINGERSNAPS
Singles: 7-inch
KAPP (226 "Lenny, Lenny") ... 10-15 58

GINGERSNAPS
Singles: 7-inch
JUPITER (305 "Remembering") ... 10-20 '60s
WINDOW (1115 "Bald Headed Papa") ... 10-20 59

GINNY & GALLIONS
Singles: 7-inch
DOWNEY (110 "Hava Nagila") ... 5-10 63
DOWNEY (112 "Wheel of Fortune") ... 5-10 63
LPs: 10/12-inch
DOWNEY (D-1003 "Two Sides") ... 20-30 64
(Monaural.)
DOWNEY (DS-1003 "Two Sides") ... 25-40 64
(Stereo.)

GINO
(With Ted Tyle & Orchestra)
Singles: 7-inch
FURY (1025 "Right from the Start") ... 15-25 59
GOLDEN CREST (567 "Altar of Dreams") ... 150-250 62
GOLDEN CREST (576 "We'll Make It Some Day") ... 15-20 63
GOLDEN CREST (581 "It's Only a Paper Moon") ... 10-15 63
PARNASO (101 thru 103) ... 15-25 63
Picture Sleeves
GOLDEN CREST (576 "We'll Make It Some Day") ... 50-75 63
Session: Dells.
Also see DELLS

GINO, Marty
Singles: 7-inch
AMY (847 "Paper Doll") ... 5-10 62
R&M (616 "That Feelin' ") ... 15-25
TIME (1012 "I'll Tell You a Secret") ... 10-15 59
TIME (1018 "Protect My Love") ... 8-12 59
WINK (103 "Our Love Is Young") ... 5-10 61

GINO & BARONS
(With the Ramblers)
Singles: 7-inch
LARSEN (100 "Peggy") ... 50-75 59

GINO & GINA P&R/R&B '58
Singles: 7-inch
BRUNSWICK (55215 "I Hope You're Satisfied") ... 5-10 61
MERCURY (71283 "Pretty Baby") ... 10-15 58
MERCURY (71346 "She Belongs to Me") ... 10-15 58
WARWICK (554 "I'm Bugged Over You") .. 5-10 60
Members: Aristedes "Gino" Giosasi; Irene Giosasi.

GINSBURG, Arnie
EPs: 7-inch
VELVET VOICE ("Meet Arnie Ginsburg") 40-60 58
(WBOS radio/Mal's clothier promotional issue only. With the Three Ds.)
Also see JAN & ARNIE

GIORDANO, Lou
Singles: 7-inch
BRUNSWICK (55115 "Stay Close to Me") ... 500-600 59
(Maroon label.)
BRUNSWICK (55115 "Stay Close to Me") ... 300-400 59
(Yellow label. Promotional issue.)
Session: Buddy Holly (guitar).
Also see HOLLY, Buddy

GIPSON, Flick, & Sliders
(Byron "Flick" Gipson)
Singles: 78 rpm
SPECIALTY (566 "One I Love") ... 25-50 55
SPECIALTY (587 "Foot Loose and Fancy Free") ... 10-15 56
Singles: 7-inch
SPECIALTY (566 "One I Love") ... 60-80 55
SPECIALTY (587 "Foot Loose and Fancy Free") ... 25-35 56
Also see PHARAOHS

GIPSON, Wild Child
(With Freddie Tieken & Rockers; with the Katz & Jammers)
Singles: 7-inch
ASTRA (1008 "Uncle John") ... 15-25 65
IT'S A HIT (2001 "Uncle John") ... 40-60 58
IT'S A HIT (2004 "Kool") ... 50-100 58
Note: the Katz & Jammers were actually Freddie Tieken & Rockers.
Also see TIEKEN, Freddie, & Rockers

GIRLFRIENDS P&R '63
Singles: 7-inch
COLPIX (712 "My One and Only, Jimmy Boy") ... 15-25 63
COLPIX (744 "Baby Don't Cry") ... 8-12 64
MELIC (4125 "No More Tears") ... 10-15 63
Members: Carolyn Willis; Gloria Goodson; Nannette Jackson.

GIRLS
Singles: 7-inch
ATCO (6349 "Fannie Hill") ... 10-20 65
CAPITOL (5675 "Chico's Girl") ... 10-20 66
20TH FOX (6651 "Modesty Blaise") ... 10-15 66

GIRLS FROM SYRACUSE
Singles: 7-inch
PALMER (5001 "You Could Have Had Me All Along") ... 20-30 65

GIROY, Gil
Singles: 7-inch
DEMO (3 "Laura Lee") ... 50-100

GIST, Bruce
Singles: 7-inch
CONQUEST (1001 "Tarantula") ... 15-25 59

GIUFRE, Jim, & His Orchestra
Singles: 78 rpm
MODERN (875 "Big Boy") ... 10-15 52
Singles: 7-inch
MODERN (875 "Big Boy") ... 25-30 52

GLACIERS
LPs: 10/12-inch
MERCURY (20895 "From Sea to Ski") ... 15-20 64
(Monaural.)
MERCURY (60895 "From Sea to Ski") ... 20-25 64
(Stereo.)

GLAD
Singles: 7-inch
ABC (11163 "Johnny Silver's Ride") ... 5-10 68
EQUINOX (70004 "See What You Mean") ... 10-15 67
EQUINOX (70006 "Pickin' Up the Pieces") ... 10-15 68
LPs: 10/12-inch
ABC (655 "Feelin' Glad") ... 15-25 69
Members: Timothy Schmidt; Tom Phillips; George Hullin; Ron Flogel.
Also see POCO

GLAD RAGS
Singles: 78 rpm
EXCELLO (2121 "My China Doll") ... 50-75 57
Singles: 7-inch
EXCELLO (2121 "My China Doll") ... 50-100 57
O-GEE (517 "So Close") ... 5-10 62

GLAD-A-BOUTS Featuring Henri Aubin
Singles: 7-inch
HURRICANE (102 "If You Love Me") ... 40-50 59

GLADIATORS
(With the Johnny Otis Orchestra)
Singles: 78 rpm
DIG (135 "Girl of My Heart") ... 100-200 57
Singles: 7-inch
DIG (135 "Girl of My Heart") ... 250-350 57
Also see OTIS, Johnny

GLADIATORS
Singles: 7-inch
DONNIE (701 "I Need You") ... 50-150 66

GLADIATORS
Singles: 7-inch
BRITISH LION (525 "I'm Gonna Cry") ... 15-25

GLADIOLAS P&R/R&B '57
Singles: 78 rpm
EXCELLO ... 15-25 57
Singles: 7-inch
EXCELLO (2101 "Little Darlin' ") ... 50-75 57
(Orange and blue label.)
EXCELLO (2101 "Little Darlin' ") ... 4-8 70
(Blue label.)
EXCELLO (2110 "Run, Run Little Joe") ... 25-35 57
EXCELLO (2120 "I Wanta Know") ... 25-35 57
EXCELLO (2136 "Say You'll Be Mine") ... 25-35 58
OWL (326 "Running Around") ... 4-6 74
Members: Maurice Williams; Norman Wade; Bill Massey; Willie Jones; Earl Gainey; Bobby Robinson.
Also see WILLIAMS, Maurice, & Zodiacs

GLADNESS, Marie
Singles: 7-inch
ABNER (7004 "I'm Anxious") ... 20-30 62
BRAND-X ... 15-25 '60s

GLAS MANAGERIE
Singles: 7-inch
ROMAIN (1009 "Natasha") ... 15-25 66

GLASER, Jim C&W '68
(Jim Glaser Singers)
Singles: 7-inch
MCA ... 3-6 76-86
MGM ... 4-6 73-75
NOBLE VISION ... 3-5 82-84
RCA ... 4-8 68-69
LPs: 10/12-inch
MCA ... 5-8 86
NOBEL VISION ... 5-8 84
STARDAY (149 "Old Time Christmas Singing") ... 50-75 60
STARDAY (158 "Just Looking for a Home") ... 40-60 61
WYNCOTE (9069 "Country Spectacular") ... 15-25 64
Also see NEOPHONIC STRING BAND
Also see TOMPALL & GLASER BROS.

GLASER, Ken
Singles
AZRA (101 "Vicious Circles") ... 35-50 84
(Set of nine square picture discs.)
AZRA (101 "Vicious Circles") ... 4-6 84
(Any of the individual discs.)

GLASS CANDLE
Singles: 7-inch
TARGET (1004 "Light the Glass Candle") ... 20-30 69

GLASS FAMILY
Singles: 7-inch
SIDEWALK (920 "Teenage Rebellion") ... 10-20 67
W.B. (309 "Guess I'll Let You Go") ... 10-15 69
(Promotional issue only.)
W.B. (7262 "Guess I'll Let You Go") ... 5-10 69
LPs: 10/12-inch
W.B. (1776 "Electric Band") ... 15-25 69

Members: Ralph Parrett; Gary Green.

GLASS MENAGERIE

LPs: 10/12-inch

UA (2121 "I Love My Music") .... 10-15 '60s

GLASS OPENING

Singles: 7-inch

DONDEE (12563 "All Those Lies") .... 20-25 '60s
NEW WORLD (001 "My Heart Is Heavy") .... 25-35 '60s
Also see MAJOR SIX / Glass Opening

GLASS SUN

Singles: 7-inch

SOUND PATTERNS (139 "Silence of the Morning").. 40-50
SOUND PATTERNS (150 "Stuck Over You") 40-50

GLASSER, Dick

Singles: 78 rpm

RCA...5-10 56
SILVER (103 "Terri")..................................5-10 50

Singles: 7-inch

ARGO (5279 "Love Me") 8-12 58
ARGO (5283 "Go Along Baby")...................8-12 58
COLUMBIA (Except 41472) 5-10 60
COLUMBIA (41472 "Crazy Alligator")...... 20-25 59
RCA... 10-15 56
SILVER (103 "Terri")................................ 15-25 50

GLAZER, Tom P&R/LP '63

(With the Children's Do-Re-Mi Chorus; with Dotty Evans & Robin Morgan)

Singles: 78 rpm

COLUMBIA..5-10 53-55
CORAL 5-10 56

Singles: 7-inch

COLUMBIA..5-10 53-55
CORAL..5-10 56
KAPP 4-8 63-64
U.A. 4-8 66-67

Picture Sleeves

KAPP 5-10 63

LPs: 10/12-inch

CAMDEN..5-10 64-65
KAPP 10-20 63-64
COLUMBIA... 20-30 55
HARMONY... 10-20 59
MERCURY.. 15-25 55
MOTIVATION......................................5-10 62
RIVERSIDE.. 10-20 61
U.A. (3540 "Namu the Killer Whale") 15-25 66
(Monaural.)
U.A. (6540 "Namu the Killer Whale") 35-45 66
(Stereo.)
WASHINGTON 10-20 59
WONDERLAND 10-20 63

GLEAMS

(Four Gleams)

Singles: 7-inch

J-V (101 "Bad Boy")............................ 100-200 60
KAPP (565 "Mr. Magic Moon") 10-20 63
KIP (236 "You Broke My Heart") 15-25 61
Also see PERRY, Berlin, & Gleams

GLEASON, Jackie P&R '53

(Jackie Gleason's Orchestra; with Sammy Spear & His Orchestra)

Singles: 78 rpm

CAPITOL 3-5 52-57
DECCA...3-5 51-54

Singles: 7-inch

CAPITOL 5-10 52-62
DECCA...5-10 51-54

Picture Sleeves

DECCA (275 "What Is a Boy") 10-20 54

EPs: 7-inch

CAPITOL (Except 511) 5-15 53-60
CAPITOL (511 "And Awa-a-ay We Go").. 50-75 54
(Double EP set.)
CAPITOL (511 "And Awa-a-ay We Go").. 75-100 54
(With "EBF" prefix. Boxed, two-disc set.)

LPs: 10/12-inch

CAPITOL (Except 511)..............................5-15 53-69
CAPITOL (511 "And Awa-a-y We Go").. 75-100 54
(10-inch LP. Has songs by Jackie, sung in character by: Joe the Bartender; The Loud Mouth; Ralph Kramden; Fenwick Babbitt; Reggie Van Gleason III, & the Poor Soul.)
Also see MARTIN, Dean / Jackie Gleason

GLEAVES, Cliff

Singles: 7-inch

DORE (623 "Hold Back the Dawn")...........5-10 62
LIBERTY (55263 "Long Black Hearse") ...10-15 60
PARK AVENUE (103 "Little Rosa") 5-10 62
SUMMER (501 "Love Is My Business")....40-60 58

Picture Sleeves

SUMMER (501 "Love Is My Business")..50-100 58
(Sleeve has die-cut hole in center to display label.)

GLEEMS

Singles: 7-inch

PARKWAY (893 "Sandra Baby") 30-40 63
RIOT (002 "Sandra Baby")..........................3-5

GLEN & CHRISTY

Singles: 7-inch

SONIC (3362 "Wombat Twist")................50-75

GLENN, Darrell C&W/P&R '53

(With the Commodores)

Singles: 78 rpm

DOT...4-8 56
RCA...4-8 54
VALLEY..4-8 53

Singles: 7-inch

ARLEN (725 "She Made It All Up")............8-12 63
COLUMBIA...5-8 66-67
DOT...10-20 56
FASHION (008 "Take Time to Be Happy").5-10 60
LONGHORN (546 "The Ways of the World")...5-10 64
NRC (004 "Make Me Smile Again") 15-20 58
NRC (007 "Mr. Moonlight").......................15-20 58
POMPEII...4-8 68-69
RCA...10-20 54
ROBBEE (101 "A Teardrop Falls") 5-10 64
RPM (488 "Hello Baby")..........................15-25 57
TWINKLE (505 "That's Right")................40-60 58
VALLEY..10-20 53

Picture Sleeves

LONGHORN (546 "The Ways of the World") 8-12 64

LPs: 10/12-inch

NRC (5 "Crying in the Chapel")................20-35 59

GLENN, Gary

(With the Jeweltones; Gary Glenn Family)

Singles: 7-inch

COVE (284-12 "I Want to Do It")..............30-40 '60s
JEREE (11 "Always So True") 5-10 65
(Black vinyl.)
JEREE (11 "Always So True") 15-25 65
(Green vinyl.)
STONE (46 "Always So True")..................10-15
STONE ("I Want to Do It") 15-25
(Selection number not known.)

GLENN, Glen

Singles: 7-inch

DORE (523 "Goofin' Around")..................10-20 59
ERA (1061 "Everybody's Movin'") 100-150 57
ERA (1074 "Laurie Ann")........................75-125 58
ERA (1086 "Blue Jeans and a Boys' Shirt") 300-400 58

GLENN, Jerry

Singles: 7-inch

CHECKER (949 "Just Take Me Like I Am") 10-15 60

GLENN, Lloyd R&B '50

(Lloyd Glenn All Stars)

Singles: 78 rpm

ALADDIN...5-10 56-57
COLONY (109 "Hep Cat Shuffle") 5-10 52
HOLLYWOOD...5-10 55
RPM (332 "Jumpin' with Lloyd")..................5-10 51
SWING TIME..5-15 52-54

Singles: 7-inch

ALADDIN...8-12 56-59
HOLLYWOOD (1028 "Chica-Boo")...........10-15 55
IMPERIAL...5-10 62
SWING TIME..20-30 52-54

EPs: 7-inch

HOLLYWOOD (1024 "Chico-Boo, etc.")...15-25 54

LPs: 10/12-inch

ALADDIN (808 "Chica-Boo") 100-150 56
(Black vinyl.)
ALADDIN (808 "Chica-Boo") 250-500 56
(Red vinyl.)
BLACK & BLUE...8-10 77
IMPERIAL (9174 "Chica-Boo") 30-50 62
(Monaural.)
IMPERIAL (12174 "Chica-Boo") 30-50 62
(Stereo.)
SCORE (4006 "Piano Stylings") 100-150 56
SCORE (4020 "After Hours") 100-150 57
SWING TIME (1901 "All Time Favorites") 500-750 54
(10-inch LP.)
Also see BROWN, Charles / Lloyd Glenn
Also see FULSON, Lowell
Also see MILLER, Red, Trio
Also see WALKER, T-Bone

GLENNIE BROTHERS

Singles: 7-inch

FINE (1461 "Merry Twistmas") 15-25 61

GLENNS

Singles: 7-inch

HERMITAGE (777 "Flip-End") 10-20 61
RENDEZVOUS (118 "In the Chapel in the Moonlight") 15-25 60

GLENRAYS

Singles: 7-inch

GAITY (111 "Easy Rhythm")...................25-35 60
PERRY (601 "When You're Smiling").......25-35 60

GLENS

(With Bill Perry)

Singles: 7-inch

LAITINI (6666 "Cherish My Love")............20-30 60
RO-NAN (1002 "Image of Love")..............40-50
SUDDEN (104 "Cherish My Love")...........10-15 61

GLENTELLS

Singles: 7-inch

S&R (302 "Uprisin' ")...............................10-20 62

GLENWOODS

Singles: 7-inch

JUBILEE (5402 "Elaine")..........................30-40 60

GLIDERS

Singles: 7-inch

SOUTHERN SOUND (103 "School Days") 500-600 62

GLIDERS / Uniques

Singles: 7-inch

STOOP SOUNDS (501 "School Days"/"Silvery Moon") 100-150 96
(Limited edition. Estimates range from less than 10 to a few dozen made.)
Also see GLIDERS
Also see UNIQUES

GLIEDEN, Mike

(With the R.K.s; with Rhythm Kings; Mike Gliden Trio)

Singles: 7-inch

BANGAR (0635 "Poison Ivy") 10-20 65
LITTLE CROW (229 "The Fool")................8-12 '60s
LITTLE CROW (706 "Ya Ya") ....8-12 '60s
SOMA (1188 "The Bash") 10-20 63

LPs:10/12-inch

TRIPLE CROWN (4004 "Plain Brown Wrapper") 5-10 74
Also see ONLY ONES

GLITTERS

Singles: 7-inch

JENERO (104 "Fireball")..........................10-20 63

GLITTERS

Singles: 7-inch

RUBÁIYÁT (413 "You Don't Know")..........25-35

GLITTERS

Singles: 7-inch

J&S (1391 "Same Identical Thing") 15-20

GLOBE TROTTERS

Singles: 78 rpm

KING..8-12 53

Singles: 7-inch

KING (1188 "Darktown Strutter's Ball") 10-20 53
KING (1210 "My Gal Sal") 10-20 53

GLOBELITERS

Singles: 7-inch

GUYDEN (2119 "Turn It On")...................10-20 65
PHILTOWN (40003 "The Way You Do")....5-10 66
VAN DYK (601 "I Know")...................800-1000 60

GLORIES P&R/R&B '67

Singles: 7-inch

DATE (1553 "I Stand Accused") 5-10 67
DATE (1571 "Security")..............................5-10 67
DATE (1579 "Sing Me a Love Song") 10-20 67
DATE (1593 "My Sweet Baby")................10-20 68
DATE (1615 "I Worship You Baby") 20-40 68
DATE (1622 "No News")..........................10-20 68
DATE (1636 "There He Is")........................5-10 69
DATE (1647 "Dark End of the Street") 5-10 69

Picture Sleeves

DATE (1593 "My Sweet Baby") 15-25 68
Members: Yvonne Gearing; Betty Stokes; Mildred Vaney.

GLORY

LPs: 10/12-inch

TEXAS REVOLUTION (69 "Meat Music")..75-125 69
Member: Linden Hudson.

GLORYTONES

Singles: 78 rpm

EPIC (9243 "You Only Came Back to Hurt Me") 20-30 57

Singles: 7-inch

EPIC (9243 "You Only Came Back to Hurt Me") 20-30 57

GLOVER, Clay, Combo

Singles: 7-inch

BROWNFIELD (17 "Drivin' On Ice") 10-20 63

GLOVER, Helen

Singles: 7-inch

NELBER (105 "Just Like That")................10-20 '60s

GLOVER, Henry

Singles: 78 rpm

KING...5-10 53

Singles: 7-inch

KING...10-15 53

EPs: 7-inch

KING (278 "Soft")...................................40-50 54
Also see DAVIS, Eddie "Lockjaw"

GLOWTONES

Singles: 7-inch

ATLANTIC (1156 "Girl I Love")................40-50 57
EAST WEST (101 "Girl I Love")...............30-40 57
(White label. Promotional issue only.)
EAST WEST (101 "Girl I Love")...............15-25 57
(Green label.)

GLYNN, Richard

Singles: 7-inch

DOT (15927 "High School Fool")............10-15 59

GO BETWEENS

Singles: 7-inch

CHEER (1011 "Have You for My Own")...10-15 65

GO BOYS

Singles: 7-inch

DC (0418 "Ramble")...............................10-15 59

GO GO JOES

Singles: 78 rpm

JOSIE (770 "Cool Yule")...........................5-10 55

Singles: 7-inch

JOSIE (770 "Cool Yule") 10-20 55

GO ZOO BAND

Singles: 7-inch

GO GO (101 "Oh Baby Mine")....................8-12 66

LPs: 10/12-inch

GO GO (0003 "Sounds That Are Happening") 15-20 67
(Monaural.)
GO GO (0004 "Sounds That Are Happening") 15-20 67
(Stereo.)

GOBER, Capt. Hershel

(Major Hershel Gober)

Singles: 7-inch

BUDDAH (152 "Pictures of a Man") 8-12 69
TEE PEE (33/34 "Pictures of a Man"/"Here Am I")..15-25 67

GODDARD, Chuck

Singles: 7-inch

EVEREST (19389 "I Didn't Answer the Phone")..10-15 61
TNT (163 "A New Heart to Break").......150-250 59

GODFREY

Singles: 7-inch

CEE JAM (3 "Let's Take a Trip")............. 10-20 '60s
WHITTIER (505 "Down Whittier Blvd.")......5-10 67

GODFREY, John, Trio R&B '51

Singles: 78 rpm

CHESS (1478 "Hey Little Girl") 10-15 51
HILLTOP (701 "Hey Little Girl")............... 20-30 51
(First issue.)

GODFREY, Ray C&W '60

Singles: 7-inch

ABC (10999 "I Can't Go On Living Like This")..5-8 67
COLUMBIA 4-8 65-67
EVENT (255 "I'm the Other Half") 4-6
J&J (001 "The Picture") 10-15 60
PEACH (757 "Let's Move to the City") 50-75 62
SIMS (130 "Ten Silver Dollars") 5-10 63
SPRING (104 "I Gotta Get Away") 4-8 70
SPRING (135 "Candy Clown") 4-6 73
TOLLIE (9030 "Count Me Out")....................5-10 64
YONAH (2002 "Sad But True") 8-12 61

GOGGINS, Curby

Singles: 7-inch

CARNIVAL (510 "Come Home to Daddy") 10-20 65

GOGGINS, Delma, & Yo-Yos

Singles: 7-inch

VIBRO (4008 "Leave Me If You Want To")... 10-20 61

GO-GOs
(Go-Go's)

Singles: 7-inch

RCA (8370 "Chicken of the Sea") 10-20 64
RCA (8435 "Saturday's Hero") 10-20 64

LPs: 10/12-inch

RCA (LPM-2930 "Swim with the Go-Gos") 20-30 64
(Monaural.)
RCA (LSP-2930 "Swim with the Go-Gos") 25-35 64
(Stereo.)
Also see ISLEY BROTHERS / Go-Gos

GOINGS, Scotty

Singles: 7-inch

HOLLYWOOD (1093 "Nobody's Darling But Mine") 40-50 58
MADISON (107 "Nobody's Darling But Mine") 10-20 58

GOLAND, Arnie, & Sunbeams

Singles: 7-inch

SUNBEAM (103 "Boo Hoo") 10-20 58
SUNBEAM (130 "Thunder in theSky") 10-20 59
SUNBEAM (132 "Naive") 10-20 59
SUNBEAM (133 "Viva Cuba Libre") 10-20 59

GOLD, Lynn

Singles: 7-inch

W.B. (1405 "Lynn Gold") 10-15 63

GOLD BUGS

Singles: 7-inch

CORAL (62453 "Stop the Wedding") 30-40 65
Also see FIVE SHARKS

GOLD COASTERS

Singles: 7-inch

BLUE RIVER (206 "You're Mighty Mighty Fine") 10-20 64

GOLD NUGGETS

Singles: 7-inch

RHOMA (101 "Gold Dollar") 15-25 58

GOLDBERG, Barry

Singles: 7-inch

ATCO (6946 "Imagination") 4-6 73
BUDDAH (59 "Hole in My Pocket") 5-10 68
EPIC (10007 "Blowing My Mind") 5-10 66
EPIC (10033 "Ginger Man") 5-10 66
TMP-TING (117 "You Got Me Crying") 5-10 66
VERVE FOLKWAYS (5045 "Carry On") 5-10 67

LPs: 10/12-inch

ATCO 8-10 74
BUDDAH 10-12 68-71
EPIC 15-20 66
RECORD MAN 8-12 72

GOLDBERG, Barry / Harvey Mandell / Charlie Musselwhite / Neil Merryweather

LPs: 10/12-inch

CHERRY RED (5104 "Blues from Chicago") 8-12
Also see MERRYWEATHER, Neil
Also see MUSSELWHITE, Charles

GOLDBERG - MILLER BLUES BAND

Singles: 7-inch

EPIC (Except 9865) 5-10 65-66
EPIC (9865 "Mother Song") 15-20 65
(Colored vinyl. Promotional issue only.)

Picture Sleeves

EPIC (9865 "Mother Song") 10-15 65
Members: Barry Goldberg; Steve Miller.
Also see GOLDBERG, Barry
Also see MILLER, Steve

GOLDCOAST SINGERS

LPs:10/12-inch

WORLD PACIFIC (1806 "Here They Are!") 20-25 62
Members: George Cromarty; Ed Rush.

GOLDEN, Artie, & Golden Flames

Singles: 7-inch

SPECIAL EDITION (2486 "The Night Is Young") 100-150

GOLDEN, John
(With the Indexes; Johnny Golden)

Singles: 7-inch

DOUGLAS (101 "Take a Chance") 75-125 61
W.B. (5660 "Angel on Earth") 10-15 65

GOLDEN, Sandy

Singles: 7-inch

MASTERPIECE ("Your Love Is Everything") ....20-30 '60s
(Selection number not known.)

GOLDEN BELLS
(With the Gems of Rhythm Band)

Singles: 7-inch

SURE (1002 "Pretty Girl") 2000-3000 59

GOLDEN BOYS

Singles: 7-inch

MAINSTREAM (628 "I Don't Want You No More") 10-20 65
Also see TOADS / Golden Boys

GOLDEN CRUSADERS

Singles: 7-inch

EPIC (9773 "Hey Good Lookin") 10-20 65

GOLDEN DAWN

LPs: 10/12-inch

INT'L ARTISTS (4 "Power Plant") 100-125 68
Members: George Kinney; Bob Rector; Tom Ramsey; Bill Hallman; Jim Bird.

GOLDEN EARRING P&R/LP '74

Singles: 7-inch

ATLANTIC 4-8 70
DWARF (2000 "Back Home") 10-20 69
MCA 4-6 76-78
POLYDOR (2000 series) 4-6 79
POLYDOR (14000 series) 5-10 69
TRACK 4-6 74-75
21 ....3-5 82-86

Picture Sleeves

DWARF (2000 "Back Home") 15-25 69
21 ....3-5 84

LPs: 10/12-inch

ATLANTIC 15-20 69
CAPITOL (164 "Miracle Mirror") 30-35 69
CAPITOL (2823 "Winter Harvest") 30-35 67
CAPITOL (11315 "Golden Earrings") 10-12 74
DWARF 10-20
MCA 6-10 75-81
POLYDOR 5-10 79-80
TRACK (396 "Moontan") 50-75 73
(With nude showgirl on cover.)
TRACK (396 "Moontan") 10-15 73
(Showgirl not nude on cover.)
TRACK (2139 "Switch") 8-12 75
21 ....5-10 82-86

GOLDEN GATE QUARTET

Singles: 78 rpm

BLUEBIRD 10-20 37-40
CAPITOL 5-10 48
COLUMBIA 5-15 47-49
LANG-WORTH ....10-20 '40s
(16-inch transcriptions.)
MERCURY 5-10 49-51
MONTGOMERY WARD 5-10
OKEH (Except 6897) 5-15 41-52
OKEH (6897 "Rain Is the Teardrops of Angels") 20-30 52
RCA 5-10 41-48
SITTIN' IN WITH 5-10 52

Singles: 7-inch

APOLLO (1204 "Silent Night") 4-6 76
COLUMBIA (39000 series) 10-15 51
MERCURY (5385 "Didn't That Man Believe") 50-75 50
OKEH (6897 "Rain Is the Teardrops of Angels") 50-75 52

LPs: 10/12-inch

CAMDEN (308 "Golden Gate Quartet") 25-35 56
COLUMBIA (6102 "Golden Gate Spirituals") 75-100 50
(10-inch LP.)
HARMONY (7018 "Golden Chariot") 25-35 57
MERCURY (25063 "Spirituals") 50-75 51
(10-inch LP.)
Members: Willie Johnson; Henry Owens; Bill Langford; Clyde Riddick; Orlandus Wilson; Cliff Givens; Alton Bradley; Caleb Ginyard; Orville Brooks
Also see DIXIEAIRES
Also see GATES

GOLDEN GATE STRINGS LP '67
(With Stu Phillips)

Singles: 7-inch

EPIC (9812 "Mr. Tambourine Man") 4-8 65
EPIC (9853 "Baby Love") 4-8 65

EPs: 7-inch

EPIC (24158 "Bob Dylan Song Book") 10-15 65
(Monaural.)
EPIC (24160 "String of Hits") 10-15 65
(Monaural.)
EPIC (24248 "Monkees Song Book") 10-15 67
(Monaural.)
EPIC (26158 "Bob Dylan Song Book") 10-15 65
(Stereo.)
EPIC (26160 "String of Hits") 10-15 65
(Stereo.)
EPIC (26248 "Monkees Song Book") 10-15 67
(Stereo.)
Also see HOLLYRIDGE STRINGS

GOLDEN HARMONEERS

Singles: 7-inch

MOTOWN (1015 "I Am Bound") 20-40 61

GOLDEN HIGHLIGHTERS

Singles: 7-inch

HANOVER (4509 "Wait") 10-15 58

GOLDEN NUGGETS
(With Rocky Rhodes & California Versatones)

Singles: 7-inch

FUTURA (1691 "I Was a Fool") 1500-2000 59
(Black label.)
FUTURA (1691 "I Was a Fool") 2000-2500 59
(White label. Promotional issue only.)

GOLDEN NUGGETS

Singles: 7-inch

HAWK (105 "Everybody Bird") 20-30 63

GOLDEN TOADSTOOL

Singles: 7-inch

MINARET (138 "Silly Savage") 10-15 68

GOLDEN TONES
(With Johnny Guitar & Band)

Singles: 7-inch

HUSH (101 "Little Island Girl") 30-40 59
HUSH (102 "You Left Me Here to Cry Alone") 30-40 59
Member: Joe Simon.
Also see SIMON, Joe

GOLDEN TONES

Singles: 7-inch

JEFF (801 "Swerve") 10-20 59

GOLDENAIRES

Singles: 7-inch

ANGELUS ("What He Said") 10-20
(Selection number not known.)
RON (325 "My Only Girl") 75-125 59
RON (332 "Love Letter") 25-50 60

GOLDENROD

LPs: 10/12-inch

CHARTMAKER (1101 "Goldenrod") 200-250 68
Members: Jerry Scheff; Toxie French; Ben Benay.
Also see DARIUS
Also see FIFTH DIMENSION
Also see FRIAR TUCK
Also see PRESLEY, Elvis

GOLDENRODS

Singles: 78 rpm

VEE-JAY (307 "I Wish I Was Back in School") 600-800 58

Singles: 7-inch

VEE-JAY (307 "I Wish I Was Back in School") 1000-1200 58
Member: Hiawatha Burnett.

GOLDENS
(Denny Ezba & Goldens)

Singles: 7-inch

BIG STAR 30-50 60
Also see EZBA, Denny

GOLDENTONES
(Golden Tones)

Singles: 78 rpm

JAY-DEE (806 "Meaning of Love") 50-75 55
RAINBOW (351 "She's Funny That Way") 25-35 56
SAMSON (107 "I'm Wrong") 25-35 55

Singles: 7-inch

BEACON (560 "Meaning of Love") 20-30 61
JAY-DEE (806 "Meaning of Love") 100-150 55
RAINBOW (351 "She's Funny That Way") 75-125 56
SAMSON (107 "I'm Wrong") 75-125 56
Members: Vernon Harris; Millie Harris; Harold Holman; Lee McCall; Melvin Johnson.

GOLDENTONES

Singles: 7-inch

EDMAR (1011 "Till Death Do Us Part") 50-75 63

GOLDIE & ESCORTS

Singles: 7-inch

CORAL (62349 "One Hand, One Heart") . 10-15 63
CORAL (62372 "Back Home Again") 10-15 63
Also see ESCORTS

GOLDIE & GINGERBREADS

Singles: 7-inch

ATCO (6354 "That's Why I Love You") 10-15 65
ATCO (6427 "Please Please") 10-15 66
ATCO (6475 "Walking in Different Circles") 10-15 67
SPOKANE (4005 "Skinny Vinnie") 15-20 63
Member: Genya Ravan.

GOLDSBORO, Bobby P&R '62

Singles: 7-inch

BUENA VISTA (561 "These Are the Best Times") 15-25 75
(Promotional issue only.)
CURB 3-5 80-82
EPIC 4-6 77
LAURIE (3130 "You Better Go Home") 10-20 62
LAURIE (3148 "Honey Baby") 10-15 62
LAURIE (3159 "The Runaround") 10-15 63
LAURIE (368 "Light the Candles") 10-15 63
U.A. (251 "Summer") 4-6 73
U.A. (371 "Sing Me a Smile") 4-6 73
U.A. (672 thru 980) 8-12 63-66
U.A. (50018 thru 51107) 4-8 66-73

Picture Sleeves

U.A. (251 "Summer") 5-8 73
U.A. (710 "Whenever He Holds You") 10-20 64
U.A. (50018 "I Know You Better Than That") 8-12 66
U.A. (50318 "Autumn of My Life") 5-10 68

LPs: 10/12-inch

CURB 5-10 80-82
DORAL 15-25
(Promotional mail-order issue, from Doral cigarettes.)
EPIC 8-10 77
K-TEL 5-10
LIBERTY 5-10 81
SUNSET 8-12 66
U.A. 10-20 64-76
Also see ORBISON, Roy
Also see REEVES, Del, & Bobby Goldsboro
Also see WEBS

GOLDSBORO, Bobby / Jimmy Durante
Singles: 7-inch
LIGHT (608 "We Gotta Start Lovin' ")..........4-8 71
Also see GOLDSBORO, Bobby
Also see DURANTE, Jimmy

GOLDTONES
Singles: 7-inch
COLONIAL (52 "High Dive into Love"). 100-200 '50s

GOLDTONES
Singles: 7-inch
Y-R-S (1001 "If I Had the Wings of an Angel") 200-300 61
Y-R-S (1002 "Journey Bells") 100-200 62

GOLDTONES
(Randy Seol & Goldtones)
Singles: 7-inch
A&R (714 "Strike") 20-30 63
Picture Sleeves
A&R (714 "Strike") 30-50 63
LPs: 10/12-inch
LA BREA (8011 "The Goldtones Featuring Randy Seol")... 30-50 64
Members: Randy Seol; Cindy Mac; Glenn Campbell; Bill Ewing; Wayne Purvis; Ken Naylor; Al Doss; Mike Peters; Steve Green.
Also see MISUNDERSTOOD
Also see STRAWBERRY ALARM CLOCK

GOLDTONES
Singles: 7-inch
JCP (1015 "I Can't Help Loving You")...... 10-20 64

GOLDWATER, Barry
Singles: 7-inch
IMPACT (1 "Discrimination").................. 10-15 64
(Colored vinyl. Flip has Efrem Zimbalist Jr., Walter Brennan, Ronald Reagan, Robert Stack, and others, speaking on behalf of presidential candidate Goldwater.)
LPs: 10/12-inch
AMERICAN UNITED................................ 10-20 64
Also see BRENNAN, Walter

GOLLIWOGS
Singles: 7-inch
FANTASY (590 "Don't Tell Me No Lies"). 40-60 64
FANTASY (597 "You Came Walking")..... 40-60 65
FANTASY (599 "You Got Nothing on Me")... 30-50 65
SCORPIO (404 "Brown Eyed Girl").......... 30-50 65
SCORPIO (405 "Fragile Child")............... 30-50 66
SCORPIO (408 "Walking On the Water") 30-50 66
SCORPIO (412 "Porterville")................... 40-60 67
LPs: 10/12-inch
FANTASY (9474 "Pre-Creedence")......... 10-15 75
Members: John Fogerty; Tom Fogerty; Doug Clifford; Stuart Cook.
Also see CREEDENCE CLEARWATER REVIVAL

GOMEZ, Johnny Ray, & U-Neeks
Singles: 7-inch
APPLAUSE (1000 "Romp Out")............... 15-25 64
APPLAUSE (1001 "Kick Off")................... 15-25 64

GOMEZ, Yvonne
(With Eddie C. Campbell & His Studio Band)
Singles: 7-inch
HAWAII (127 "Ease the Pain") .... 10-15 '60s
(We have not yet verified this number; however, we are certain about #6333.)
HAWAII (6333 "Ease the Pain") .... 10-15 '60s

GONDOLIERS
Singles: 7-inch
RIC (957 "Knocked Out")........................ 15-25 58
SUPREME (500 "Tamborino") .... 10-20 '50s
Also see ADAMS, Johnny, & Gondoliers

GONE ALL STARS P&R '58
Singles: 7-inch
GONE (5016 "7-11") 20-25 57
ROULETTE GOLDEN GOODIES 4-6 71
EPs: 7-inch
GONE (101 "Dancin' Bandstand")............ 35-55 58
Member: Buddy Lucas.
Also see LUCAS, Buddy

GONN
Singles: 7-inch
EMIR (9217 "Blackout of Gretley")....... 300-500 66
EMIR/MCCM (88-9217 "Blackout of Gretley")...3-5 88
(Black vinyl.)
EMIR/MCCM (88-9217 "Blackout of Gretley")..5-10 88
(Colored vinyl.)
MERRY JAINE (2316 "You're Looking Fine")...100-200 67
Members: Brent Colvin; Rex Garrett; Larry LaMaster; Gary Stepp; Garry Gable; Dave Johnson; Craig Moore.
Also see ILMO SMOKEHOUSE
Also see MOORE, Craig
Also see TIEKEN, Freddie, & Rockers

GONZALES, Babs
(With CBA Ensemble)
Singles: 78 rpm
BRUCE...5-10 54
ESSEX...5-10 54
KING...8-12 55
OKEH 15-25 57
SAVOY (1115 "The Boss Is Back")............5-10 53
Singles: 7-inch
ATLAS (1206 "Teenage Santa Claus").......5-10 59
BRUCE (122 "Manhattan Fable") 15-25 55
BRUCE (126 "Watch Them Resolutions")..15-25 55
CRAZY (0001 "Dem Jive N.Y. People") 5-10 60
END (1008 "Rock & Roll Santa Claus")....10-15 58
ESSEX (377 "Manhattan Fable")..............10-20 54
KING...10-20 55
O'BÉ (13 "Ali Is the Champ for Me")...........8-12
OKEH (7079 "And About This Rock & Roll") 15-25 57
(Promo copies of this have no selection number on the label.)
LPs: 10/12-inch
JARO (5000 "Tales of Manhattan")..........15-20 59

GONZALES, Charlie
Singles: 78 rpm
GOTHAM (234 "Hi Yo Silver")..................30-40 50

GONZALES, Frank, & Palisades
Singles: 7-inch
F-G (1001 "Let's Make Up") 100-150 61

GONZALEZ, Rudy, & Reno Boys
Singles: 7-inch
TEAR DROP (3057 "All I Could Do Is Cry") 10-20 63

GONZOS
Singles: 7-inch
DONNA (1330 "Church Key") 15-25 60
(Same single also issued as by the Four Sharps.)
Also see FOUR SHARPS

GOOBERS
Singles: 7-inch
SURF (1001 "Hawaiian Holiday") 20-30 63

GOOD, Larry
Singles: 7-inch
BRASS (216 "There's the Blues") 50-100

GOOD, Lemme B.
Singles: 7-inch
COLUMBIA (41939 "Dancing Angel").......40-50 61
MERCURY (72361 "Hard Times") 5-10 64
MERCURY (72418 "Good Lovin' ")..............5-10 65
MERCURY (72470 "Mother May I")............5-10 65

GOOD, Tommy
Singles: 7-inch
GORDY (7034 "Baby I Miss You")............20-30 64

GOOD BUDDY & HIS ROCKIN' BAND
(Buddy Lucas)
Singles: 7-inch
TETRA (4451 "Rockin with the Duke") 15-25 59
Also see LUCAS, Buddy

GOOD FEELING
Singles: 7-inch
EAGLE (122 "Tale of Man") 15-25 66

GOOD FEELIN'S
Singles: 7-inch
LIBERTY (55981 "I'm Captured")..............10-15 67
ROCK-IT (1007 "I'm Captured")................20-30 67
ROCK-IT (2000 "I'm Lost") 20-30 67

GOOD GUYS
Singles: 7-inch
COUNSEL (123 "Perry's Theme") 10-20 63
Member: Perry Botkin.
Also see McCOY BOYS

GOOD GUYS
Singles: 7-inch
GNP (326 "Asphalt Wipe-Out") 15-25 64
SAN-DEE (1007 "I Love My Baby")..........30-40 64
LPs: 10/12-inch
GNP (2001 "Sidewalk Surfing") 25-35 64
U.A. (3370 "Good Guys Sing")..................20-25 64
(Monaural.)
U.A. (6370 "Good Guys Sing")..................25-30 64
(Stereo.)
Members: Jim Roberts; Steve Douglas; Hal Blaine; John Anderson; Art Fisher.
Also see BELAIRS
Also see BLAINE, Hal
Also see DOUGLAS, Steve

GOOD IDEA
Singles: 7-inch
GOOD IDEA (2889 "Inside, Outside") ......25-35 '60s

GOOD RATS
Singles: 7-inch
JESTER (22001 "You're All I Need to Get By") 15-25 73
KAPP (946 "The Truth Is Gone") 5-10 68
PASSPORT..4-6 79
RAT CITY...4-8 76
SMK ("Don't Hate the Ones") ....20-30 '60s
(No label name shown. "SMK" is etched in the trail-off. Distributed at the group's concerts.)
LPs: 10/12-inch
GREAT AMERICAN 5-10 81
KAPP (3580 "The Good Rats")..................35-50 69
PASSPORT (Except 20) 5-10 78
PASSPORT (20 "Rats the Way You Like It")..40-60 78
(Promotional issue only.)
RAT CITY...10-12 76-80
W.B. (2813 "Tasty") 20-25 74
Members: Peppi Marchello; John Gatto; Joe Franco; Larry Kotke; Mickey Marchello.

GOOD ROCKIN' BOB
Singles: 7-inch
GOLDBAND (1067 "Take It Easy Katy") ..20-30 58

GOOD ROCKIN' SAM
Singles: 78 rpm
EXCELLO..10-20 55
Singles: 7-inch
EXCELLO (2059 "Baby, I'm Fool Proof") .20-40 55

GOOD TIME SINGERS
Singles: 7-inch
CAPITOL (5157 "Ramblin' Boy") 5-10 64
CAPITOL (5260 "One Step More")..............5-10 64
LPs:10/12-inch
CAPITOL (2041 "Good Time Singers").... 15-25 64
CAPITOL (2170 "One Step More")........... 15-25 64

GOODE, B., & Goodband
Singles: 7-inch
GEM (0100 "Sabotage")........................300-400 61

GOODE, Ronnie
Singles: 7-inch
DEMON (1510 "Rocking Bug") 10-15 58
DEMON (1525 "Hokus Pokus") 10-15 60

GOODE, Roy
Singles: 7-inch
VEL-TONE (25 "Stupid Heart")..............75-125 59

GOODEN, Bernice, & Cues
Singles: 78 rpm
CAPITOL (3306 "When I Go Away") 5-10 56
Singles: 7-inch
CAPITOL (3306 "When I Go Away") 10-15 56

GOODFELLOWS
Singles: 7-inch
SUN-NEL (535 "Another Chance") 200-250 58

GOODIN, Kenny
Singles: 7-inch
ROSE (126 "Cheri Ann") 40-50 57

GOODMAN, Benny, Orchestra P&R '31
(Benny Goodman Sextet; Benny Goodman & His Boys)
Singles: 78 rpm
CAPITOL..3-6 '40s
COLUMBIA (Except 2856) 5-15 33-56
COLUMBIA (2856 "Your Mother's Son-In-Law") 30-50 34
(Colored plastic. Vocal by Billie Holiday.)
MELOTONE..10-20 31
VICTOR (Except 25808) 5-15 36-58
VICTOR (25808 "Popcorn Man")........750-1000 39
Singles: 7-inch
B G (45-1 "How Can You Forget")..............5-10 60
CAPITOL (800 series).............................10-20 49
CHESS (1742 "Mission to Moscow")..........5-10 59
COLUMBIA (Except 250)........................10-20 50-56
COLUMBIA (250 "1938 Carnegie Hall Concert") ....25-45 '50s
(Boxed, two-disc set.)
COMMAND 4-6 67
DECCA...5-10 62
RCA...10-20 50-59
EPs: 7-inch
BRUNSWICK...5-10 54
CAPITOL...5-10 55-56
COLUMBIA..5-10 50-58
DECCA (798 "The Benny Goodman Story")...10-15 56
MGM..4-8 59
RCA (Except 6703) 10-20 50-59
RCA (EPOT-6703 "The Golden Age of Swing") 100-200 56
(Boxed, 15-disc, limited edition set.)
LPs: 10/12-inch
ABC..5-10 76
BRIGHT ORANGE 5-10 73
BRUNSWICK...10-20 54
CAMDEN 5-10 63-65
CAPITOL (Except 343 thru 1514)...............5-15 64-78
CAPITOL (343 thru 1514) 15-30 55-61
CENTURY..5-10 79
CHESS (1440 "Benny Rides Again")..........5-15 59
COLPIX...8-12 62
COLUMBIA (Red or white label, except 160)..20-35 50-55
(Red label has gold print, white promotional label has black print.)
COLUMBIA (160 "The Famous 1938 Carnegie Hall Concert") ....35-45 '50s
(Boxed, two-disc set. Includes cardboard inner sleeves.)
COLUMBIA (Red or white label)..............15-25 55-62
(Has three Columbia "eye" logos on each side of label.)
COLUMBIA (Red or white label)..............10-20 62-67
(Has one Columbia "eye" logo on each side of label.)
COLUMBIA (Red or white label)................5-15 67-78
(Has six Columbia "eye" logos circling the label.)
COMMAND (921 "Benny Goodman in Paris")...10-20 67
DECCA (188 "The Benny Goodman Story, Vols. 1 & 2") 25-50
DECCA (8252 "The Benny Goodman Story, Vol. 1")..25-50 56
DECCA (8253 "The Benny Goodman Story, Vol. 2")..25-50 56
DECCA (7-8252 "The Benny Goodman Story, Vol. 1")..15-25 59
(Reprocessed stereo.)
DECCA (7-8253 "The Benny Goodman Story, Vol. 2")..15-25 59
(Reprocessed stereo.)
EVEREST...5-10 73
HARMONY..10-20 59-60
LONDON..5-10 72-78
LONDON/PHASE 4.....................................5-10 71-72
MCA..5-10 80
MGM..5-15 59
MARK 56..5-10 77
MEGA...5-10 72-74
MUSICMASTERS...5-10
PAUSA..5-10 83
PRESTIGE...5-10 69
QUINTESSENCE 4-8 79
RCA (17 thru 2698) 15-25 53-64
RCA (3000 series).....................................20-40 53-54
(10-inch LPs.)
RCA (LPT-6703 "The Golden Age of Swing") 100-200 56
(Five-disc set with booklet and special gold or silver case.)
Note: RCA reissues after 1964 are in the $5 to $10 range.
SUNBEAM 5-10 73

TIME-LIFE (354 "Into the '70s" 10-20 72
(Boxed, three-disc set. Includes booklet.)
WESTINGHOUSE ("World Favorites") 40-60 58
(No selection number used.)
"X" (3003 "Benny Goodman") 50-75 54
Also see BASIE, Count, & Benny Goodman
Also see CASEY, Al / Benny Goodman & His Orchestra
Also see CHRISTIAN, Charlie
Also see HOLIDAY, Billie
Also see LEE, Peggy

GOODMAN, Benny / Tex Beneke / Tommy Dorsey / Charlie Barnet

EPs: 7-inch

RCA (3 "Swing to the Big Band Sound") . 10-15 56
(Promotional issue, made for General Electric Flash Bulb buyers.)
Also see DORSEY, Tommy, Orchestra

GOODMAN, Benny, Trio, with Rosemary Clooney

Singles: 78 rpm

COLUMBIA..3-5 50-56

Singles: 7-inch

COLUMBIA..5-10 56

LPs: 10/12-inch

COLUMBIA.. 15-25 56
Also see CLOONEY, Rosemary

GOODMAN, Benny / Lionel Hampton

Singles: 78 rpm

RCA VICTOR (1 "Jumpin' Jive") 10-15
(7-inch 78 rpm single. Made for Colgate-Palmolive Co.)
Also see GOODMAN, Benny, Orchestra
Also see HAMPTON, Lionel

GOODMAN, Dickie P&R '61
(With Bill Ramal)

Singles: 7-inch

AUDIO SPECTRUM (75 "Presidential Interview") 10-20 64
CASH (451 "Mr. Jaws") 4-6 75
(Black vinyl.)
CASH (451 "Mr. Jaws") 25-50 75
(Purple vinyl.)
COTIQUE (158 "On Campus")...................5-10 69
COTIQUE (173 "Luna Trip")....................5-10 69
DIAMOND (119 "Ben Crazy").................. 10-15 62
EXTRAN (601 "Hey E.T.")........................5-10 82
(First issue.)
GOODNAME (7100 "Safe Sex Report") 3-5 88
HOTLINE (1017 "Energy Crisis '79") 4-6 79
J.M.D. (001 "Ben Crazy") 20-25 62
(First issue.)
JANUS (271 "Star Warts")...........................4-6 77
M.D. (101 "Shmonanza")......................... 10-20 61
MARK-X (8009 "The Touchables") 10-20 61
MARK-X (8010 "The Touchables in Brooklyn") 10-20 61
MONTAGE (1220 "Hey E.T.")......................3-5 82
PRELUDE (8018 "Election '80")..................3-5 80
RAINY WEDNESDAY (202 "Watergrate")....4-8 73
RAINY WEDNESDAY (204 "Purple People Eater")...4-8 73
RAINY WEDNESDAY (205 "The Constitution") 4-8 74
RAINY WEDNESDAY (206 "Energy Crisis '74") 4-8 74
RAINY WEDNESDAY (207 "Mr. President")..4-8 74
RAINY WEDNESDAY (208 "Gerry Ford – A Special Report")...4-8 75
RAINY WEDNESDAY (209 "Inflation in the Nation") 4-8 75
RAMGO (501 "Speaking of Ecology").........8-12 70
RED BIRD (058 "Batman and His Grandmother") 10-15 66
RHINO (19 "Radio Russia")........................3-5 84
RORI (601 "Horror Movies")................... 10-15 61
RORI (602 "Berlin Top Ten").................... 10-15 61
RORI (701 "Santa and the Touchables"). 10-15 61
SCEPTER (12339 "Speaking of Ecology")...4-6 71
SHARK (1001 "Mrs. Jaws")..........................4-6 79
SHARK (1002 "Super Superman")...............4-6 79
SHELL (711 "Election '84").........................3-5 84
SHOCK (6 "Kong")..4-6 77
20TH FOX (443 "Senate Hearing") 10-15 63
TWIRL (2015 "James Bomb") 10-15 66
WACKO (1001 "Mr. President") 3-5 81
WACKO (1002 "Super Duper Man")............3-5 81
WACKO (1381 "America '81").......................3-5 81
Z-100 (100 "Attack of the Z Monster") 3-5 84

LPs: 10/12-inch

CASH (6000 "Mr. Jaws") 25-30 75
COMET (69 "My Son the Joke") 20-30 64
IX CHAINS 12-15 73
RHINO..5-10 83
RORI (3301 "The Many Heads of Dickie Goodman")..50-75 62
TSURIS (101 "Just Released") ....10-15 '70s
Also see BUCHANAN & GOODMAN
Also see CASUAL THREE
Also see JEKYLL & HYDE
Also see PENNSYLVANIA PLAYERS
Also see RAMAL, Bill
Also see SPENCER & SPENCER

GOODMAN, George, & Headliners

Singles: 7-inch

VAL (1 "Let Me Love You") 20-30 65
(Some reissues credit only the Headliners.)
VAL (3 "I'm So Tired")..............................10-15 66
VAL (5 "Secret Love")...............................10-15 66
VAL (6 "Need You")...................................10-15 66
VAL (1000 "Let Me Love You") 8-12 66
W.B. (5632 "Let Me Love You") 10-15 65

GOODMAN, Jimmy, & Belmonts

Singles: 7-inch

CAMARO (3385 "Loneliness Is a Word") .15-25

GOODNIGHT, Terri

Singles: 7-inch

PHELECTRON (701 "They Didn't Know") ....250-350 '60s

GOODSON, Willie

Singles: 7-inch

HAMMOND (102 "Put a Nickel in the Jukebox")..50-100

GOODSPEED, Skip

Singles: 7-inch

PLEASON (1001 "Only Me and You")......50-75

GOODTIME WASHBOARD THREE

Singles: 7-inch

FANTASY (582 "Don't Blame the P.G. & E., Pal") 5-10 64

LPs:10/12-inch

FANTASY (3361 "Goodtime Washboard Three")...25-35 64

GOODTIMERS P&R '61

Singles: 7-inch

ARNOLD (1002 "Pony Time") 10-20 61
EPIC (9484 "It's Twistin' Time") 10-20 61
Member: Don Covay.
Also see COVAY, Don

GOODWIN, Bill C&W '63

Singles: 7-inch

BAND BOX (287 "Revenuerman")..............5-10 62
BAND BOX (293 "Those Same Old Things")..5-10 62
BAND BOX (309 "Heartaches") 5-10 62
DIXIE (2014 "Your Lying Ways")...........150-250 58
MTA...4-8 67-70
STARDAY (710 "Teenage Blues").......250-350 65
VEE-JAY (501 "It Keeps Right On a-Hurtin' ") 10-15 63
VEE-JAY (564 "Stand In") 5-10 63

GOON, Peter / Bab Boon

Singles: 7-inch

POLEESE (100 "The Whistler") 20-25 75

GOON BONES / Muzzy Marcellino

Singles: 78 rpm

CRYSTALETTE (706 "Ain't She Sweet"/"Mary Lou")..5-10 56

Singles: 7-inch

CRYSTALETTE (706 "Ain't She Sweet"/"Mary Lou")..10-15 56
Also see MARCELLINO, Muzzy
Also see MR. GOON BONES

GORD'S HORDE

Singles: 7-inch

HODAG (0540 "I Don't Care")..................30-50 66
Members: Gordy Gillman; Phil Van Goethen; Dan Nordall; Dale Smith; Tom Price; Cliff Fellows.

GORDEN, Dwight

Singles: 7-inch

K-ARK (604 "Fifty-Fifty")..........................50-75

GORDON, Barry P&R '55
(With Art Mooney & His Orchestra)

Singles: 78 rpm

MGM...5-10 55-56

Singles: 7-inch

ABC 4-6 68
CAPITOL...4-8 65-71
CADENCE...5-10 62
DUNHILL..4-6 68
ERA 5-10 59
MGM...10-20 55-56
MERCURY..5-10 61
U.A. 4-8 64-66

Picture Sleeves

MGM (12092 "Nuttin' for Christmas") 15-25 56
MGM (12367 "I Like Christmas") 15-25 56

LPs: 10/12-inch

U.A. 10-15 66
Also see MOONEY, Art, & His Orchestra

GORDON, Benny
(With the Soul Brothers; Bennie Gordon)

Singles: 7-inch

DELUXE (145 "Sugar Mama") 4-6 73
ENRICA (1015 "Kansas City Woman") 15-25 64
ESTILL (565 "Give a Damn About Your Feller Man") 50-75 69
ESTILL (600 "So Much in Love") 25-50 69
ESTILL (1000 "Sugar Mama") ....75-100 '60s
(Reads: "A Division of Estill and Colonial Records." Shows South Carolina address.)
ESTILL (1000 "Sugar Mama") ....25-50 '60s
(Shows a New York address for company.)
PHIL-L.A. OF SOUL (351 "Give a Damn")...4-8 71
RCA (8953 "Up and Down").........................8-12 66
RCA (9144 "Greyhound Blues")..................8-12 67
RCA (9194 "What Is Soul") 8-12 67
WANT (1188 "Gonna Give Her All the Love I Got")..10-20 68

LPs: 10/12-inch

HOT BISCUIT (9100 "Tighten Up") 25-50 68

GORDON, Big Mike
(Big Mike; with the Clippers)

Singles: 78 rpm

BATON 10-15 56
SAVOY..10-15 55

Singles: 7-inch

BATON (219 "Walkin' Slippin' & Slidin' ") .15-20 56
BATON (233 "The Clipper") 20-30 56
SAVOY (1152 "Down in New Orleans") ...15-20 55

GORDON, Bill "Bass," & Colonials

Singles: 78 rpm

GEE (12 "Two Loves Have I")..............200-300 54

Singles: 7-inch

GEE (12 "Two Loves Have I")..........1000-1500 54
Also see COINS / Colonials

GORDON, Curtis
(Curtis Gordon Band)

Singles: 78 rpm

MERCURY..10-20 56-57
RCA..20-30 53

Singles: 7-inch

DOLLIE (10050 "From Memphis to New Orleans")...50-100 66
DUKE OF COUNTRY.....................................4-6
MERCURY (70791 "Too Young to Know") 20-30 56
MERCURY (70861 "Draggin' ")...............50-75 56
MERCURY (71037 "So Tired of Crying") .20-30 57
MERCURY (71121 "Cry Cry")...................20-30 57
RCA (5356 "Rompin' and Stompin' ") 50-75 53

GORDON, Don

Singles: 7-inch

FREEDOM (44012 "How Come You Don't Love Me") 10-20 59

GORDON, Gary

Singles: 7-inch

FLEETWOOD (1002 "No One")...............20-25 58

GORDON, Gil

Singles: 7-inch

ATLANTIC (2012 "Kissing Tree") 10-15 59

GORDON, Gus
(With the Darnels)

Singles: 7-inch

BANA (525 "My Little Homing Pigeon")....15-20 57
IPS (102 "Empty Room")...............................5-10 60

GORDON, Hal

Singles: 7-inch

HEP CAT (101 "Rock and Roll Talk").......50-75

GORDON, Joni

Singles: 7-inch

MUSICNOTE (125 "I Guess I'll Miss the Prom")...20-30 64

GORDON, Junior
(With Huey "Piano" Smith's Orchestra)

Singles: 78 rpm

ACE (522 "Blow Wind, Blow")..................10-15 56

Singles: 7-inch

ACE (522 "Blow Wind, Blow")..................20-30 56
JAY-O-PEE (1250 "Brighter Day")............10-15 62
Also see SMITH, Huey

GORDON, Justin

LPs: 10/12-inch

DOT (3214 "Justin Gordon Swings")........30-50 59

GORDON, Larry

Singles: 7-inch

MERCURY (72273 "Lefty Louie")............10-20 64

GORDON, Lena / Sax Kari

Singles: 78 rpm

CHECKER (803 "Mama Took the Baby") .. 8-12 54

Singles: 7-inch

CHECKER (803 "Mama Took the Baby") 15-25 54

GORDON, Little Joe

Singles: 7-inch

JIN (131 "Can't Have Your Love") 10-15 60

GORDON, Luke C&W '58

Singles: 7-inch

ISLAND (0640 "Dark Hollow")..................15-25 58
NASHVILLE 4-8
STARDAY (555 "Baby's Gone")..............350-450

LPs: 10/12-inch

L&C 5-10
MOUNT VERNON...5-10

GORDON, Mike, & Agates

Singles: 7-inch

DORE (681 "Rumble at Newport Beach")..15-20 63
DORE (780 "Curfew on the Strip") 10-15 66

GORDON, Mike, & El Tempos

Singles: 78 rpm

CAT (101 "Why Don't You Do Right") 15-25 54

Singles: 7-inch

CAT (101 "Why Don't You Do Right") 30-50 54
Also see BIG MIKE

GORDON, Phil
(With the Page Cavanaugh Trio; with Beales)

Singles: 78 rpm

DECCA..10-20 56
HUB OF HOLLYWOOD 15-25 53

Singles: 7-inch

DECCA (29787 "Down the Road a Piece")..15-25 56
HUB OF HOLLYWOOD (1105 "Good Morning Judge")...25-50 53
HUB OF HOLLYWOOD (1108 "Drunk")...25-50 53

GORDON, Ramsey

Singles: 7-inch

TAHOE (2530 "Down in the Cellar").........20-30 63

GORDON, Robert P&R/LP '77
(With Link Wray)

Singles: 12-inch

PRIVATE STOCK 10-15 78
RCA...8-12 81
(Promotional issue only.)

Singles: 7-inch

PRIVATE STOCK 4-6 77-79
RCA (Black vinyl)...3-6 79-81
RCA (Colored vinyl)....................................8-12 79-81
(Promotional issue only.)

Picture Sleeves

PRIVATE STOCK (45203 "Fire")...............5-10 79
RCA (11471 "It's Only Make Believe") 5-10 79

LPs: 10/12-inch

PRIVATE STOCK..8-10 77-78

RCA (Except 3294)....................6-12 79-82
RCA (3294 "Rockbilly Boogie")....................8-12 79
(Black vinyl.)
RCA (3294 "Rockbilly Boogie")....................20-30 79
(White vinyl.)

Promotional LPs

RCA (3411 "Robert Gordon"/"Live from Paradise in Boston")....................35-45 79
Also see WRAY, Link

GORDON, Roscoe ***R&B '51***
(Rosco Gordon; with His Orchestra)

Singles: 78 rpm

CHESS (1487 "Booted")....................50-100 52
DUKE (101 "Tell Daddy")....................50-75 52
DUKE (106 thru 129)....................20-50 53-54
FLIP (227 "Just Love Me Baby")....................50-100 55
FLIP (237 "The Chicken")....................20-40 56
RPM....................20-50 51-53
SUN (227 "Just Love Me Baby")....................100-200 55
SUN (237 "The Chicken")....................75-125 56
SUN (257 "Shoobie Oobie")....................25-50 56

Singles: 7-inch

ABC-PAR (10351 "Girl to Love")....................8-12 62
ABC-PAR (10407 "I Want Revenge")....................8-12 63
CALLA (145 "Just a Little Bit")....................4-8 68
CHESS (1487 "Booted")....................200-300 52
COLLECTABLES....................3-5 81
DUKE (106 "T-Model Boogie")....................40-60 53
DUKE (109 "Too Many Women")....................25-50 53
DUKE (114 "Ain't No Use")....................25-50 53
DUKE (129 "Three Cent Love")....................25-50 54
DUKE (320 "Dilly Bop")....................10-15 60
FLIP (227 "Just Love Me Baby")....................200-300 55
FLIP (237 "The Chicken")....................20-30 56
OLD TOWN (1167 "Just a Little At a Time")....................5-10 64
RPM (324 "Saddled the Cow")....................250-350 51
RPM (336 "Dime a Dozen")....................100-200 51
RPM (344 "Booted")....................50-100 52
RPM (350 "No More Doggin' ")....................50-75 52
RPM (358 "New Orleans Wimmen")....................50-75 52
RPM (365 "What You Got on Your Mind")....................50-75 52
RPM (369 "Trying")....................40-60 52
RPM (373 "Lucille")....................40-60 52
RPM (379 "Just in from Texas")....................40-60 53
RPM (384 "We're All Loaded")....................40-60 53
RPM (496 "No More Doggin' ")....................15-25 57
RAE COX (1002 "Goin' to a Party")....................5-10 67
SUN (227 "Just Love Me Baby")....................400-500 55
SUN (237 "The Chicken")....................100-200 56
SUN (257 "Shoobie Oobie")....................40-60 56
SUN (305 "Sally Jo")....................25-50 58
VEE-JAY (316 "No More Doggin' ")....................15-25 59
VEE-JAY (332 "Just a Little Bit")....................15-25 59
VEE-JAY (348 "What You Do to Me")....................15-25 60
VEE-JAY (385 "Let 'Em Try")....................15-20 61
Also see ROSCOE & BARBARA

GORDON, Stomp
(With the Hi-Lites)

Singles: 78 rpm

CHESS....................15-25 54
DECCA....................15-25 52
MERCURY....................15-25 53
SAVOY....................10-15 56

Singles: 7-inch

CHESS (1601 "The Grind")....................30-50 54
DECCA (48287 "Damp Rag")....................30-50 52
DECCA (48289 "Ooh Yes")....................30-50 52
DECCA (48290 "Devil's Daughter")....................30-50 52
DECCA (48297 "Pennies from Heaven")....................30-50 52
MERCURY (70223 "Slow Daddy Blues")....................30-50 53
MERCURY (70246 "What's Her Whimsey, Dr. Kinsey")....................30-50 53
SAVOY (1504 "Ride Superman Ride")....................15-20 56

GORDON & STARLINERS

Singles: 7-inch

STAR (200 "Ding Bat")....................10-20 63

GORDON & SUE & ALGONQUINS

Singles: 7-inch

CARLTON (595 "Surfin' Sal & Charmin' Willie")....................15-25 63

GORE, Charlie, & Louis Innis

Singles: 78 rpm

KING (1212 "[You Ain't Nothin' But a Female] Hound Dog")....................10-15 53

Singles: 7-inch

FAN (1001 "Sock Hop")....................50-100
KING (1212 "[You Ain't Nothin' But a Female] Hound Dog")....................20-30 53
Also see GORE, Charlie

GORE, Lesley ***P&R/R&B/LP '63***

Singles: 7-inch

A&M (1710 "Immortality")....................5-10 75
A&M (1829 "Sometimes")....................5-10 76
CREWE (338 "Why Doesn't Love Make Me Happy")....................8-12 70
CREWE (344 "When Yesterday Was Tomorrow")....................8-12 70
CREWE (601 "Back Together")....................20-30 71
MERCURY (72119 "It's My Party")....................10-15 63
MERCURY (72143 "Judy's Turn to Cry")....................10-15 63
MERCURY (72180 "She's a Fool")....................10-15 63
MERCURY (72206 "You Don't Own Me")....................10-15 63
MERCURY (72245 "Je Ne Sais Plus")....................20-30 64
MERCURY (72259 "That's the Way Boys Are")....................10-15 64
MERCURY (72270 "I Don't Want to Be a Loser")....................10-15 64
MERCURY (72309 "Maybe I Know")....................10-15 64
MERCURY (72352 "Hey Now")....................10-15 64
MERCURY (72372 "The Look of Love")....................10-15 64
MERCURY (72412 "All of My Life")....................10-15 65
MERCURY (72433 "Sunshine, Lollipops and Rainbows")....................10-15 65
MERCURY (72475 "My Town, My Guy and Me")....................10-15 65
MERCURY (72513 "I Won't Love You Anymore")....................10-15 65
MERCURY (72530 "We Know We're in Love")....................10-15 66
MERCURY (72553 "Young Love")....................10-15 66
MERCURY (72580 "Off and Running")....................10-20 66
MERCURY (72611 "Treat Me Like a Lady")....................10-20 66
MERCURY (72649 "California Nights")....................10-15 67
MERCURY (72683 "Summer & Sandy")....................10-15 67
MERCURY (72726 "Brink of Disaster")....................10-20 67
MERCURY (72759 "Magic Colors")....................10-20 67
MERCURY (72787 "Small Talk")....................10-20 68
MERCURY (72819 "He Gives Me Love")....................10-15 68
MERCURY (72842 "Where Can I Go")....................10-20 68
MERCURY (72867 "I'll Be Standing By")....................10-20 68
MERCURY (72892 "Take Good Care of My Heart")....................10-20 69
MERCURY (72931 "Summer Symphony")....................10-20 69
MERCURY (72969 "Wedding Bell Blues")....................10-20 69
MOWEST (5029 "The Road I Walk")....................8-12 72
MOWEST (5042 "Give It to Me Sweet Thing")....................? 73
(Announced for issue; however, we have yet to confirm that copies exist.)
PHILCO (21 "You Don't Own Me"/"That's the Way Boys Are")....................10-20 67
("Hip Pocket" flexi-disc.)

Picture Sleeves

A&M (1710 "Immortality")....................10-15 75
MERCURY (72119 "It's My Party")....................10-15 63
MERCURY (72143 "Judy's Turn to Cry")....................10-15 63
MERCURY (72180 "She's a Fool")....................10-15 63
MERCURY (72206 "You Don't Own Me")....................10-15 63
MERCURY (72259 "That's the Way Boys Are")....................10-15 64
MERCURY (72270 "I Don't Want to Be a Loser")....................10-15 64
MERCURY (72309 "Maybe I Know")....................10-15 64
MERCURY (72352 "Hey Now")....................10-15 64
MERCURY (72372 "The Look of Love")....................10-15 64
MERCURY (72412 "All of My Life")....................10-15 65
MERCURY (72433 "Sunshine, Lollipops and Rainbows")....................10-15 65
MERCURY (72475 "My Town, My Guy and Me")....................10-15 65
MERCURY (72513 "I Won't Love You Anymore")....................10-15 65
MERCURY (72683 "Summer & Sandy")....................10-15 67

EPs: 7-inch

MERCURY (648C "Girl Talk")....................10-20 64
(Juke box issue. Includes title strip and pictures.)

LPs: 10/12-inch

A&M....................8-10 75
51 WEST (16261 "The Canvas Can Do Miracles")....................10-15 82
MERCURY (8000 series)....................5-10 80
MERCURY (20000 & 60000 series)....................20-30 63-68
MOWEST....................8-12 72
POLYDOR....................5-10 85
RHINO (71496 "Anthology")....................10-15 86
(Two discs.)
WING....................10-20 67-69
Also see BILLY & SUE
Also see DRIFTERS / Lesley Gore / Roy Orbison / Los Bravos

GORE, Lesley, & Lou Christie

Singles: 7-inch

MANHATTAN (50039 "Since I Don't Have You")....................5-8 86
Also see CHRISTIE, Lou
Also see GORE, Lesley

GORE, Rufus

Singles: 78 rpm

KING (4768 "Rib Tips")....................10-15 55

Singles: 7-inch

KING (4768 "Rib Tips")....................15-20 55

GORGEOUS BILL
(Bill Yates)

Singles: 7-inch

SUN (397 "Carleen")....................10-15 65
Also see YATES, Bill

GORGEOUS GEORGE
(With the Fabulous Three)

Singles: 7-inch

HALE (501 "Cross Every Mountain")....................100-150 62
NEPTUNE (125 "Will You Love Me")....................15-25 61
PEACHTREE (105 "Love's Not a Hurtin' Thing")....................25-50 66
STAX (165 "Sweet Thing")....................10-20 65

GORMAN, Freddie

Singles: 7-inch

L.A. (70061 "Love Has Seen Us Through")....................3-5 81
MIRACLE (11 "The Day Will Come")....................20-30 62
RIC-TIC....................10-20 64-65
Also see ORIGINALS
Also see SATINTONES
Also see VOICE MASTERS

GORMAN SISTERS
(Barbara Gorman & Sister Viv)

Singles: 7-inch

ARROW (715 "8 O'clock Date")....................30-40 57
ARROW (721 "Silent Night")....................10-15 58
JOY (222 "Sock Hop")....................10-15 58
JOY (224 "Chickery Chick")....................10-15 58

GORME, Eydie ***P&R '54***

Singles: 78 rpm

ABC-PAR....................4-8 55-56
CORAL....................4-8 53-55

Singles: 7-inch

ABC-PAR....................8-12 55-62
CALENDAR (1004 "It's You Again")....................4-8 68
COLUMBIA (Except 43082 & 78862)....................5-10 62-68
COLUMBIA (43082 "I Want You to Be My Baby")....................5-10 64
(Black vinyl.)
COLUMBIA (43082 "I Want You to Be My Baby")....................15-20 64
(Colored vinyl.)
COLUMBIA (78862 "Cinnamon Skin")....................15-20 64
(Yellow vinyl.)
CORAL....................10-20 53-55
GALA....................4-6 76
MGM....................4-6 71-73
RCA....................4-8 69-70
U.A. (Except 283 thru 414)....................3-6 '70s
U.A. (283 thru 414)....................5-10 60-62

Picture Sleeves

COLUMBIA (42424 "Yes My Darling Daughter")....................8-12 62
COLUMBIA (42661 "Blame It On the Bossa Nova")....................8-12 63

LPs: 10/12-inch

ABC-PAR....................15-25 57-65
APPLAUSE....................4-6 81
COLUMBIA....................10-25 63-73
GALA....................5-8 76
HARMONY....................5-10 68-71
MGM....................5-10 71
RCA....................5-10 68-70
U.A....................15-25 61-62
VOCALION....................8-15 63
Also see LAWRENCE, Steve, & Eydie Gorme

GORSEN, Irv

Singles: 7-inch

ROCK IT (1001 "Our Teenage Love")....................10-15 63

GORSHIN, Frank

Singles: 78 rpm

LIBERTY....................5-10 56

Singles: 7-inch

A&M (804 "The Riddler")....................5-10 66
BRAND (1001 "That's the Trouble with Love")....................8-10 '60s
KING (6336 "Turn Around, Look At Me")....................4-8 70
LIBERTY (55044 "The True Story of Jesse James")....................10-15 56

Picture Sleeves

A&M (804 "The Riddler")....................10-15 66
BRAND (1001 "That's the Trouble with Love")....................10-20 '60s

GOSDIN BROTHERS ***C&W '67***

Singles: 7-inch

BAKERSFIELD INT'L (1002 "Hangin' On")....................10-15 67
BAKERSFIELD INT'L (1006 "She Still Wishes I Were You")....................10-15 68
CAPITOL (2265 "Sounds of Goodbye")....................8-12 68

LPs: 10/12-inch

CAPITOL (2852 "Sounds of Goodbye")....................15-20 68
Members: Vern Gosdin; Rex Gosdin.

GOSEY, Johnny
(With Alex Jones & Nite Hawks)

Singles: 7-inch

MOA (1001 "Fools Will Take Chances")....................75-125 '50s

GOSNELL, Leo

Singles: 7-inch

MOUNTAIN (299 "Juke Joint Honey")....................100-200

GOSPEL CONSOLATORS

Singles: 78 rpm

BIG TOWN (125 "There's a God in Heaven")....................15-25 56

Singles: 7-inch

BIG TOWN (125 "There's a God in Heaven")....................25-50 56

GOSPEL STARS

Singles: 7-inch

DIVINITY (99006 "Have You Any Time for Jesus")....................15-25 '60s
TAMLA (54037 "He Lifted Me")....................75-100 61
(With horizontal lines.)
TAMLA (54037 "He Lifted Me")....................40-60 61
(With Tamla globe logo.)

LPs: 10/12-inch

TAMLA (222 "Great Gospel Stars")....................500-750 61

GOSS, Zeno

Singles: 7-inch

MPI (1001 "Doll-Doll")....................15-25 58
THUNDER (1085 "Get Ready for Barry")....................10-15 64

GOTCH, Lee, Singers

Singles: 78 rpm

FABOR....................5-10 56

Singles: 7-inch

FABOR (4015 "Bus Stop Song")....................10-15 56
FABOR (4016 "A Man, a Woman")....................10-15 56

GOTHAM CITY CRIME FIGHTERS

Singles: 7-inch

BATWING (1001 "That's Life")....................15-25 66

GOTHAM'S FOUR NOTES

Singles: 78 rpm

GOTHAM (157 "All By Myself")....................25-35 48
GOTHAM (164 "East Side, West Side")....................25-35 48

GOTHICS
(With the Sal Ditrola Orchestra; Gothic's)

Singles: 7-inch

CAROL (4115 "My Dream")....................200-300 61
DYNAMIC (101 "Marilyn")....................400-600 59

EPs: 7-inch

CAROL (4115 "My Dream")....................4-6 95
(Yellow vinyl. 500 made.)

GO-TOGETHERS

Singles: 7-inch

COAST (100 "Time After Time")....................15-25

GOTROE, Jackie
(With the Scamps)
Singles: 7-inch
KEEN (4029 "Golden Spur") ... 15-25 58
RHYTHM (111 "Raised on Rock and Roll") ... 350-450 58
VORTEX (102 "Lobo Jones") ... 2000-3000 57

GOULD, Sandra
Singles: 7-inch
PHILIPS (40138 "My Son the Surfer") ... 15-20 63

GOULDMAN, Graham
Singles: 7-inch
RCA (9453 "Impossible Years") ... 5-10 68
RCA (9584 "Pamela Pamela") ... 5-10 68
LPs: 10/12-inch
RCA (3954 "Thing") ... 25-35 68
Also see FONTANA, Wayne, & Mindbenders
Also see 10CC
Also see WAX

GOVE
Singles: 7-inch
TRX ... 10-15 69-71
UNI (55335 "Carry On") ... 5-10 72
LPs: 10/12-inch
TRX (1002 "Heavy Cowboy") ... 20-30 71

GOWANS, Sammy
Singles: 7-inch
U.A. (114 "Rockin' by Myself") ... 75-125 58

GOZA, Glen, & Damangos
Singles: 7-inch
IMPACT (4292 "Goshomody Whatabody") ... 100-200

GRABEAU, Bobby, & Teenettes
Singles: 7-inch
CREST (1059 "Olita") ... 10-15 59
CREST (1064 "Back to School") ... 10-15 59

GRACIE, Charlie P&R/R&B '57
("Orchestra and Chorus under direction of Bernie Lowe")
Singles: 78 rpm
CADILLAC ... 30-50 53-55
CAMEO ... 20-30 57
20TH CENTURY ... 15-25 55
Singles: 7-inch
ABKCO ... 4-6 75
CADILLAC (141 "Boogie Woogie Blues") ... 75-100 53
CADILLAC (144 "Rockin' and Rollin' ") 100-150 54
CADILLAC (154 "Ain't No Sin in Rhythm") ... 250-350 55
CAMEO (105 "Butterfly") ... 20-30 57
CAMEO (107 "Fabulous") ... 20-30 57
CAMEO (111 "I Love You So Much It Hurts") ... 15-25 57
CAMEO (118 "Cool Baby") ... 15-25 57
CAMEO (127 "Crazy Girl") ... 15-25 58
CAMEO (141 "Love Bird") ... 15-25 58
CORAL (62073 "Doodlebug") ... 15-20 59
CORAL (62115 "Angel of Love") ... 15-20 59
CORAL (62141 "Oh-Well-A") ... 15-20 59
DIAMOND (178 "He'll Never Love You Like I Do") ... 10-20 65
FELSTED (8629 "Makin' Whoopee") ... 5-10 61
PRESIDENT (825 "Pretty Baby") ... 10-20 62
SOCK & SOUL ... 4-8 70
ROULETTE (4255 "The Race") ... 10-20 60
ROULETTE (4312 "Sorry for You") ... 10-20 60
20TH CENTURY (5035 "Honey Honey"). 40-60 55
LPs: 10/12-inch
REVIVAL (0001 "Early Recordings") ... 10-20
Also see LOWE, Bernie

GRADS
Singles: 7-inch
A&M (797 "Stage Door") ... 5-10 66
MGM (13216 "There Hearts Were Full of Spring") ... 5-10 64
MERCURY (72346 "Wild One") ... 10-15 64
VALIANT (6023 "Once Again") ... 5-10 62
Session: Davie Allan.
Also see ALLAN, Davie

GRADUATES P&R '59
Singles: 7-inch
CORSICAN (0058 "What Good Is Graduation") ... 15-25 59
LAWN (208 "Ballad of a Girl and Boy") ... 10-20 63
SHAN-TODD (0055 "Ballad of a Girl and Boy") ... 20-30 59
Picture Sleeves
CORSICAN (0058 "What Good Is Graduation") ... 30-50 59
Members: John Cappello; Bruce Hammond; Fred Mancuso; Jack Scorsone.

GRADUATES
Singles: 7-inch
MALVERN (500 "Wendy Wendy Went Away") ... 10-20 60

GRADUATES
Singles: 7-inch
GNP (404 "Listen to the Music") ... 5-10 68
RISING SONS (712 "If I Ever Get Out of This Mess I'm In") ... 15-25 68

GRADY, Bob
Singles: 7-inch
CHART ("Granny Tops Em at the Hop") ... 500-750
(Selection number not known.)

GRADY, Don
Singles: 7-inch
CANTERBURY (501 "The Children of St. Monica") ... 8-12 66
CANTERBURY (507 "Impressions with Syvonne") ... 8-12 67
CAPITOL (5181 "Broken Heart Knows Best") ... 8-12 64
CAPITOL (5362 "It's Better This Way") ... 8-12 65
CHALLENGE (59328 "Let It Happen") ... 8-12 66
ORANGE-EMPIRE (91647 "Summertime Game") ... 10-15 65
Picture Sleeves
CANTERBURY (501 "The Children of St. Monica") ... 10-15 66
CANTERBURY (507 "Impressions with Syvonne") ... 10-15 67
Also see AGRATI, Don
Also see YELLOW BALLOON

GRADY, Paul
Singles: 7-inch
GLAIZE (109 "Darlin', I Understand") ... 40-50 63

GRADY & BRADY
(Brady & Grady Sneed)
Singles: 7-inch
DOLTON (38 "Leavin' It All Up to You") ... 10-15 61
PLANETARY (104 "Love or Money") ... 5-10 65
PLANETARY (107 "Sad September") ... 5-10 65
Members: Grady Sneed; Brady Sneed.
Also see SNEED, Grady

GRAFFITI
Singles: 7-inch
ABC-PAR (11123 "He's Got the Knack") .. 10-15 68
LPs: 10/12-inch
ABC-PAR (663 "Graffiti") ... 20-30 68

GRAHAM, Billy, & Escalators
Singles: 7-inch
ATLANTIC (2372 "Oop-Poo-Pa-Doo") ... 15-25 66

GRAHAM, Bobby
Singles: 7-inch
FONTANA (1501 "Zoom, Widge and Wag") ... 10-20 65

GRAHAM, Bonnie, & Fats Gaines
Singles: 7-inch
CHRISTY (104 "Who Dat?") ... 100-150 58
Also see GAINES, Fats, Band

GRAHAM, C., Quintet
Singles: 7-inch
JILL-ANN (101 "I Can't Keep from Crying Sometimes") ... 10-20 '60s

GRAHAM, D., & Crackers
Singles: 7-inch
DYMO DY (4263 "False Love") ... 10-20 62

GRAHAM, Joe, & Rubies
Singles: 7-inch
JCP (1023 "So What") ... 10-20 64

GRAHAM, Lou
Singles: 78 rpm
GOTHAM (7416 "Long Gone Daddy") ... 20-30 51
Singles: 7-inch
CLYMAX (318 "Wee Willie Brown") ... 100-150 57
CORAL (61931 "Wee Willie Brown") ... 50-75 58
GOTHAM (7416 "Long Gone Daddy") ... 50-75 51
Session: Bill Haley, His Saddlemen & Comets.
Also see HALEY, Bill

GRAHAM, Tommy
Singles: 7-inch
KOOL (1002 "I Love My Baby") ... 150-250

GRAHAM & WILSON
Singles: 7-inch
LYNN (103 "Just Pretending") ... 10-15 61

GRAINS OF SAND
Singles: 7-inch
GENESIS (101 "Goin' Away Baby") ... 30-50 66
PHILIPS (40469 "Drop Down Sometime") ... 10-15 67
VALIANT (736 "That's When Happiness Begins") ... 15-25 66

GRAMMER, Billy P&R/R&B '58/C&W '59
Singles: 78 rpm
MONUMENT (400 "Gotta Travel On") ... 40-60 59
Singles: 7-inch
DECCA ... 4-8 61-66
EPIC ... 4-6 66-67
EVEREST ... 5-10 60
MERCURY ... 4-6 68-69
MONUMENT (Except 400 series) ... 4-6 75-76
MONUMENT (400 series) ... 5-15 59-63
RICE (5025 "Mabel") ... 5-10 67
STONEWAY (1129 "Blue Jay Rag") ... 4-6 75
STOP ... 4-6 69
EPs: 7-inch
DECCA ... 5-10 64
LPs: 10/12-inch
CLASSIC CHRISTMAS ... 5-10 77
DECCA ... 10-15 62-64
EPIC ... 8-12 67
MONUMENT (4000 "Travelin' On") ... 20-30 59
(With *Lost in a Small Cafe*.)
MONUMENT (8039 "Travelin' On") ... 10-15 66
(*Lost in a Small Cafe* is replaced with *Gotta Travel On*.)
SKYLITE ... 5-8
STONEWAY ... 5-10 75
VOCALION (3826 "Country Favorites") ... 8-12 68
Also see CASH, Johnny / Billy Grammer / Wilburn Brothers
Also see TUBB, Ernest

GRAMMER, Billy / Judy Lynn / Link Wray
LPs: 10/12-inch
GUEST STAR ... 10-15 '60s
Also see GRAMMER, Billy
Also see JUDY LYNN
Also see WRAY, Link

GRAMS, Casey
Singles: 7-inch
COUNT (101 "Countdown") ... 75-125

GRANAHAN, Gerry P&R '58
(With the Hutch Davie Orchestra; Granahan-Quintal Band)
Singles: 12-inch
DOWNTOWN ... 5-8 87
Singles: 7-inch
ATCO (6122 "Sweet Affection") ... 15-25 58
CANADIAN AMERICAN (116 "In My Heart") ... 10-15 60
CANADIAN AMERICAN (119 "You'll Never Walk Alone") ... 10-15 60
CANADIAN AMERICAN (121 "I'm Afraid You'll Never Know") ... 10-15 60
CAPRICE (106 "Dancing Man") ... 10-15 61
CAPRICE (108 "Dance Girl, Dance") ... 50-75 61
(With the Wildwoods, a.k.a. the Five Satins.)
COLLECTABLES ... 4-6
GONE (5065 "Put Me Anywhere") ... 10-20 59
GONE (5081 "Look for Me") ... 10-20 59
MARK (121 "Love's Young Dream") ... 40-50 57
SUNBEAM (102 "No Chemise, Please") .. 20-30 58
SUNBEAM (108 "Baby Wait") ... 15-25 58
SUNBEAM (122 "King Size") ... 15-25 59
SUNBEAM (127 "A Ring, a Bracelet, a Heart") ... 15-25 59
20TH FOX (425 "Too Weak to Win") ... 5-10 63
VEEP (1205 "All the Live Long Day") ... 5-10 64
Picture Sleeves
GONE (5081 "Look for Me") ... 30-50 59
Also see DICKY DOO & DON'TS
Also see FIVE SATINS / Gerry Granahan & Five Satins
Also see FONTAINE, Eddie, & Gerry Granahan
Also see GRANT, Jerry, & Rockabilly Bandits

GRANATA, Rocco P&R '59
(With the International Quintet)
Singles: 7-inch
LAURIE (3041 "Marina") ... 5-10 59
LAURIE (3048 "Lo Bella") ... 5-10 60
MOONGLOW (222 "Buona Notte Bambino") ... 4-8 63
Picture Sleeves
LAURIE (3041 "Marina") ... 10-15 59
LPs: 10/12-inch
LAURIE (3041 "Marina and Other Italian Favorites") ... 15-25 59

GRANBY ST. REDEVELOPMENT
Singles: 7-inch
LEGRAND (1047 "I Can Take It") ... 10-20 67

GRAND, K.C., & SHADES
Singles: 7-inch
MATT (0003 "Lookie Lookie Lookie") ... 100-150 61

GRAND FUNK RAILROAD P&R/LP '69
(Grand Funk)
Singles: 7-inch
CAPITOL (Black vinyl) ... 4-8 69-76
CAPITOL (Colored vinyl) ... 5-10 73
(Promotional issue only.)
FULL MOON ... 4-8 81
MCA ... 4-6 76-77
Picture Sleeves
CAPITOL ... 4-6 71-76
FULL MOON ... 3-5 81
MCA ... 4-6 76
LPs: 10/12-inch
CAPITOL (307 thru 853) ... 10-20 69-71
CAPITOL (6502 "Mark, Don & Mel: 1969-1971") ... 15-25 72
(Promotional issue only.)
CAPITOL (11000 series, except 11207) ... 8-12 72-76
CAPITOL (11207 "We're an American Band") ... 8-10 73
(Black vinyl.)
CAPITOL (11207 "We're an American Band") ... 25-35 73
(Yellow vinyl. With four cover stickers intact.)
CAPITOL (11207 "We're an American Band") ... 20-30 73
(Yellow vinyl. Without cover stickers.)
CAPITOL (12000 & 16000 series) ... 5-10 80-81
FULL MOON ... 5-10 81-83
MCA ... 8-10 76
Members: Mark Farner; Don Brewer; Craig Frost; Mel Schacher.
Also see FARNER, Mark, & Don Brewer
Also see KNIGHT, Terry

GRAND PREES
("Featuring Bernice Marsh")
Singles: 7-inch
CANDI (1020 "Sit and Cry") ... 15-25 61
GO GO (101 "Heartbreak Hotel") ... 50-75 '60s
GOLDEN GROOVE (101 "Sit and Cry") ... 5-10 62
HARAL (780 "Alone") ... 50-100 64
SCOTTY (825 "No Time to Lose") ... 15-25 '60s

GRAND PRIX
Singles: 7-inch
VAULT (906 " '41 Ford") ... 10-15 63
Also see QUADS / Grand Prix / Customs

GRAND PRIXS
Singles: 7-inch
BIG MACK (2942 "I See Her Pretty Face") ... 25-50 '60s
PONCHO (10 "Late Summer Love") 2000-2500 63

GRAND PRIXS
(Grand Prix's)
Singles: 7-inch
SARA (6354 "San Jose") ... 10-20 63
Members: Rick Berkanovic; Kenny Knoll; Don Longhurst; Jeff Hammer; Bruce Cole.

GRANDMA'S ROCKERS
LPs: 10/12-inch
FREDLO ("Homemade Apple Pie & Yankee Ingenuity") ... 1000-1500 67
(Selection number not known. 500 made.)

Members: Larry ?; Jamie Farnum; Dave Lange; Brain Haas.
Also see GUYS WHO CAME UP FROM DOWNSTAIRS

GRANDMOTHERS

LPs: 10/12-inch

PANDA (001 "Grandmothers") 12-18 83
(Picture disc.)
RHINO 8-10 80-82
Members: Jimmy Carl Black; Don Preston; Elliot Ingber; James Sherwood; Buzz Gardner; Bunk Gardner; Tom Fowler; Walt Flower.
Also see MOTHERS OF INVENTION

GRANFALLOON

LPs: 10/12-inch

TAKOMA (9021 "Laser Pace") 25-35 73
Member: Maureen O'Connor.

GRANGER, Gerri
(Jerri Granger)

Singles: 7-inch

ADDIT 5-8
BELL (969 "I Go to Pieces") 15-25 71
BELL (987 "Get It Together") 15-25 71
BIG TOP (3110 "Castle in the Sky") 10-15 62
BIG TOP (3128 "Ain't I Funny") 10-15 62
BIG TOP (3150 "What's Wrong with Me") 10-15 63
BIG TOP (514 "Breakdown") 10-15 64
DOUBLE L (734 "I Cried") 8-12 65
DOUBLE L (737 "C'est Si Bon") 8-12 66

GRANICUS

LPs: 10/12-inch

RCA (0321 "Granicus") 50-75 73

GRANNY & JIM

LPs: 10/12-inch

PHILIPS (200095 "Granny & Jim") 10-12 63
(Monaural.)
PHILIPS (600095 "Granny & Jim") 15-18 63
(Stereo.)

GRANT, Al
(Al Cernick)

Singles: 78 rpm

KING (15004 thru 15045) 10-20 49-50
Also see MITCHELL, Guy

GRANT, Amy P&R/LP '85

Promotional 12-inch Singles

A&M (75161 "Heart in Motion") 5-10 91
A&M (23821 "Good for Me") 6-12 91
A&M (83311 "Lucky One") 5-10 94

Promotional Singles

A&M 4-8 85-91

Singles: 7-inch

A&M 3-5 85-91
COLLECTABLES .... 3-5 '90s
MYRRH 3-5 80-85

Picture Sleeves

A&M 3-5 85-88

EPs: 7-inch

MYRRH (001 "Ageless Medley") 4-8 83

LPs: 10/12-inch

A&M (Black vinyl) 5-10 85-92
A&M ("Home for Christmas") 40-80 92
(Picture disc. Promotional issue only. Selection number not known.)
MYRRH (Except 901644158) 5-10 77-85
MYRRH (901644158 "Collection") 20-30 86
(Picture disc. Promotional issue only.)

GRANT, Carrie, & Grandeurs

Singles: 7-inch

NEW ART (1003 "There'll Come a Time") 10-15 62
NEWTOWN (5011 "Mish Mash") 10-15 63
Session: Bill Haley's Comets.
Also see HALEY, Bill

GRANT, Charlie

Singles: 7-inch

MALA (414 "My Romance") 10-15 60
UNART (2016 "Night and Day") 10-15 59

GRANT, Gogi P&R '55

Singles: 78 rpm

ERA 8-15 55-56
RCA 5-10 52-57

Singles: 7-inch

CHARTER 5-10 63
ERA 10-20 55-56
LIBERTY 8-12 59-61
MONUMENT 4-6 66-67
PETE 4-6 68-69
RCA 10-20 52-58
20TH FOX 5-10 61-62

Picture Sleeves

20TH FOX (284 "The Second Time Around") 10-15 61

EPs: 7-inch

ERA 10-20 56
RCA (Except 4112) 5-10 57-58
RCA (4112 "Helen Morgan Story") 15-25 57
(Soundtrack.)

LPs: 10/12-inch

CHARTER 8-12 64
ERA (106 "The Wayward Wind") .... 10-20 '60s
ERA (20001 "Suddenly There's Gogi Grant") 25-40 56
(Black vinyl.)
ERA (20001 "Suddenly There's Gogi Grant") 50-100 56
(Colored vinyl.)
LIBERTY (3144 "If You Want to Get to Heaven – Shout") 10-20 60
(Monaural.)
LIBERTY (7144 "If You Want to Get to Heaven – Shout") 20-30 60
(Stereo.)
PETE 6-10 68-70
RCA (Except 1030) 15-25 57-59
RCA (1030 "Helen Morgan Story") 60-70 57
(Soundtrack.)
Also see PRESLEY, Elvis / Vaughn Monroe / Gogi Grant / Robert Shaw

GRANT, Jane

Singles: 78 rpm

DOT (15016 "Doodle Dee Do") 10-15 52

Singles: 7-inch

DOT (15016 "Doodle Dee Do") 10-15 52
STEPHENY (1821 "Pinball Machine") 15-25 58

GRANT, Janie P&R '61

Singles: 7-inch

CAPRICE (104 "Triangle") 10-15 61
CAPRICE (109 "Romeo") 10-15 61
CAPRICE (111 "Unhappy") 10-15 61
CAPRICE (113 "Oh Johnny") 10-15 62
CAPRICE (115 "That Greasy Kid Stuff") 10-15 62
CAPRICE (119 "Peggy Got Engaged") 10-15 62
PARKWAY (982 "My Heart, Your Heart") 15-25 66
U.A. (616 thru 843) 5-10 63-65
Session: James Ray.
Also see RAY, James

GRANT, Jerry, & Rockabilly Bandits
(Gerry Granahan)

Singles: 7-inch

ATCO (6100 "Talkin' About Love") 20-30 57
Also see GRANAHAN, Gerry

GRANT, O.S., & Downbeats

Singles: 7-inch

SARG (197 "Falling Stars") 20-35 61
SARG (200 "You Did Me Wrong") 30-40 61
Also see DOWNBEATS

GRANT'S BLUE BOYS

Singles: 7-inch

GARLAND (2014 "If I Were a Carpenter") 20-40 69

GRAPEFRUIT P&R '68

Singles: 7-inch

EQUINOX (70000 "Dear Delilah") 10-15 68
EQUINOX (70005 "Yes") 10-15 68
EQUINOX (70008 "Ain't It Good") 10-15 68

LPs: 10/12-inch

DUNHILL 10-12 68
RCA 10-12 69

GRAPES OF WRATH

Singles: 7-inch

VITA (006 "Cauz It Was Her") .... 10-20 '60s

GRAPPELLI, Stephane

LP: 10/12-inch

ATLANTIC (1391 "Finesse + Feeling = Jazz") 10-20 62
CONCORD JAZZ (139 "At the Winery") 8-10 81
INNER CITY (1104 "Django, Vol. 1") 10-15 81
(Two discs.)

GRAPPELLI, Stephane, & Barney Kessel

LPs: 10/12-inch

MFSL (111 "I Remember Django") 35-45 84
Also see GRAPPELLI, Stephane
Also see KESSEL, Barney / Grant Green / Oscar Moore / Mundell Lowe
Also see NELSON, Rick

GRASS

Singles: 7-inch

GOLDUST (5016 "I'm Gettin' Tired") 15-25 67

GRASS, Dick, & Hoppers

Singles: 7-inch

ARROW (738 "Mr. John Law") 10-15 58

GRASS ROOTS P&R '66
(Rob Grill & the Grass Roots)

Singles: 7-inch

ABC 4-8 70
DUNHILL (4013 "Mr. Jones") 8-12 65
DUNHILL (4029 thru 15006) 5-8 66-74
DUNHILL OLDIES .... 4-6 '70s
HAVEN 4-6 75-76
MCA 3-5 82
OAK 4-6
ROULETTE GOLDEN GOODIES .... 4-6 '70s

Picture Sleeves

DUNHILL (4094 "Things I Should Have Said") 8-12 67
DUNHILL (4237 "Baby Hold On") 5-10 70
DUNHILL (4249 "Come on and Say It") 5-10 70

EPs: 7-inch

DUNHILL (165 "Grass Roots") 8-12 71
(Promotional issue only.)
DUNHILL (50107 "Grass Roots") 10-20 67
(Promotional issue only.)

LPs: 10/12-inch

ABC 8-10 76
ABC/COMMAND (40013 "Their 16 Greatest Hits") 15-25 74
(Quadraphonic.)
DUNHILL 10-20 66-73
GUSTO 5-8 78
HAVEN 8-10 75
MCA 5-10 81-82
PICKWICK 5-10 78
Members: Rob Grill; Warren Entner; Creed Bratton; Erik Coonce. Session: Denny Provisor; Joel Larson; Joe Osborn; P.F. Sloan; Reid Kailing.
Also see JIM & JOE
Also see MERRY-GO-ROUND
Also see PROVISOR, Denny
Also see SLOAN, P.F.

GRASSFIRE

Singles: 7-inch

STEAMBOAT (48250 "Smell of Incense") 10-20 69
Members: Jerry Edwards; Bill Forseth; Gary Lynn; Roger Lynn; Ed Gallagher.

GRASSHOPPERS

Singles: 7-inch

KAPP (376 "Chewing Gum") 10-15 61
SUNBURST (104 "Twin Beat") 10-20 65
SUNBURST (105 "Pink Champagne") 10-20 65
W.B. (5607 "Twin Beat") 10-20 65

GRASSHOPPERS

Singles: 7-inch

FOX (821 "Sugar and Spice") 20-25 67

GRASSHOPPERS Featuring Eddie Maynard

LPs: 10/12-inch

PIROUETTE (56 "Sing Along") 10-20 59

GRASSI, Lucy Ann, & Del-Aires

Singles: 7-inch

VOLCANIC (1002 "Boy Crazy") 2000-3000 64

GRATE, Miriam, & Dovers / Bob Johnson

Singles: 78 rpm

APOLLO (472 "My Angel"/"Please Squeeze") 50-100 55

Singles: 7-inch

APOLLO (472 "My Angel"/"Please Squeeze") 400-500 55
Also see DOVERS

GRATEFUL DEAD LP '67

Singles: 12-inch

ARISTA 5-10 88

Singles: 7-inch

ARISTA (Black vinyl) 3-8 77-88
ARISTA (Colored vinyl) 5-10 87
FLASHBACK 3-5 80
GRATEFUL DEAD 10-15 73-76
SCORPIO (201 "Don't Ease Me In") 75-150 66
W.B. 10-20 67-73

Promotional Singles

ARISTA 5-10 77-87
GRATEFUL DEAD 15-20 73-76
W.B. 15-25 67-73

Picture Sleeves

ARISTA (0519 "Alabama Getaway") 4-8 80
ARISTA (9606 "Touch of Grey") 3-5 87
GRATEFUL DEAD (03 "U.S. Blues") 15-20 74
W.B. (7186 "Dark Star") 45-55 68

EPs: 7-inch

W.B. (226 "American Beauty") 20-30 70
(Juke box issue only.)
W.B. (438 "American Beauty") 100-200 70
(Radio Spots.)
W.B. (544 "Europe 72") 20-30 72
(Juke box issue only.)

LPs: 10/12-inch

ARISTA 6-12 77-90
DIRECT-DISK 10-15 79
GRATEFUL DEAD (01 "Wake of the Flood") 20-25 73
(No mention on cover of distribution by United Artists.)
GRATEFUL DEAD (01 "Wake of the Flood") .... 15-20 '70s
(Reads "Distribution by United Artists" on cover.)
GRATEFUL DEAD (102 "Mars Hotel") 20-25 74
(No mention on cover of distribution by United Artists.)
GRATEFUL DEAD (102 "Mars Hotel") .... 10-15 '70s
(Reads "Distribution by United Artists" on cover.)
GRATEFUL DEAD (494 "Blues for Allah") 20-25 75
GRATEFUL DEAD (620 "Steal Your Face") 25-30 76
GRATEFUL DEAD (40132 "One from the Vault") 5-10 91
MFSL (014 "American Beauty") 75-100 78
MFSL (172 "From the Mars Hotel") 50-75 85
PAIR 6-12 84
PRIDE 10-20 73
SUNFLOWER (5001 "Vintage Dead") 25-35 70
SUNFLOWER (5004 "Historic Dead") 25-35 71
W.B. (W-1689 "Grateful Dead") 40-60 67
(Monaural. Gold label.)
W.B. (WS-1689 "Grateful Dead") 25-35 67
(Stereo. Gold label.)
W.B. (1689 "Grateful Dead") 20-30 67
(With Warner Bros. - Seven Arts "W7" label.)
W.B. (1689 "The Grateful Dead") 10-20 71
(With Warner Bros. "Arrowhead" label. Cover has copyright date on back.)
W.B. (1749 "Anthem of the Sun") 20-30 68
(Background cover color is purple. With Warner Bros. - Seven Arts "W7" label.)
W.B. (1749 "Anthem of the Sun") 10-20 71
(Background cover color is white. With Warner Bros. "Arrowhead" logo on label.)
W.B. (1790 "Aoxomoxoa") 20-30 69
(With Warner Bros. - Seven Arts "W7" label.)
W.B. (1790 "Aoxomoxoa") 10-20 71
(With Warner Bros. "Arrowhead" label. Cover has copyright date on back.)
W.B. (1830 "Live Dead") 25-35 69
(With Warner Bros. - Seven Arts "W7" label. Issued with bonus pamphlet.)
W.B. (1830 "Live Dead") 15-20 71
(With Warner Bros. "Arrowhead" label. Cover has copyright date on back.)
W.B. (1869 "Workingman's Dead") 20-30 70
(With Warner Bros. - Seven Arts "W7" label.)
W.B. (1869 "Workingman's Dead") 10-15 71
(With Warner Bros. "Arrowhead" label. Cover has copyright date on back.)
W.B. (1893 "American Beauty") 15-25 70
(With Warner Bros. - Seven Arts "W7" label.)
W.B. (1893 "American Beauty") 10-15 71
(With Warner Bros. "Arrowhead" label. Cover has copyright date on back.)
W.B. (1893 "American Beauty") 5-10 75
(With Warner Blvd./street and trees label.)
W.B. (1935 "Skull & Roses") 15-25 71
(Title shown is commonly used to describe what is actually an untitled LP. Includes bonus sticker picturing cover art.)

W.B. (2668 "Europe '72")........................ 15-25 72
W.B. (2721 "History of the Grateful Dead, Vol. 1").. 10-15 73
W.B. (2764 "Skeletons from the Closet")....8-12 74
W.B. (3091 "What a Strange Trip It's Been") 8-10 77

Promotional LPs

ARISTA (35 "Grateful Dead Sampler") 40-50 78
ARISTA (7001 "Terrapin Station")............ 20-25 77
(The lengthy *Terrapin Station* track is banded for radio station airplay.)
U.A. (SP-114 "For Dead Heads")............ 25-50 75
Members: Jerry Garcia; Ron McKernan; Bob Weir; Bill Kreutzman; Phil Lesh; Mickey Hart; Tom Constanten; Ned Lagin; Robert Hunter; Keith Godchaux; Donna Godchaux; Brent Mydland.
Also see GARCIA, Jerry
Also see GARCIA, Jerry, & Robert Hunter
Also see HART, Mickey
Also see HENDRICKS, Jon
Also see HUNTER, Robert
Also see KESEY, Ken
Also see NEW RIDERS OF THE PURPLE SAGE
Also see WEIR, Bob

GRATEFUL DEAD / Elvin Bishop Group

Singles: 7-inch

W.B. (7627 "Johnny B. Goode").............. 10-20 72
Also see GRATEFUL DEAD

GRAVELY, Junior, & Rock-A-Tones

Singles: 7-inch

VEL-A-TONE (796 "You Lied to Me Honey")............................... 1500-2000 58

GRAVEN IMAGE

Singles: 7-inch

V.O.L. (134 "Take a Bite of Life") 20-30

LPs: 10/12-inch

AZRA (1 "Graven Image") 8-12 87
(Picture disc.)

GRAVES, Billy P&R '59

Singles: 7-inch

MONUMENT (Except 401)..........................5-10 59-66
MONUMENT (401 "The Shag").............. 15-20 59

GRAVES, Joe

Singles: 7-inch

PARKWAY (103 "Debbie")...................... 10-15 66
PARKWAY (964 "See Saw")................... 10-15 66
RACK (103 " 'Baby' If You Were Gone") . 10-15 '60s
Also see EWING, John, & Streamliners

GRAVES, Skip

Singles: 7-inch

FIRESIDE (7505 "Indian Giver") 100-200

GRAVESTONE FOUR

Singles: 7-inch

DANI (7749 "Ad Lib Beat") 10-20 63

GRAVITY ADJUSTERS EXPANSION BAND

LPs: 10/12-inch

NOCTURNE (302 "One")..................... 200-300 73

GRAVY TRAIN

Singles: 7-inch

BELT (102 "I'm Lonely") .... 20-25 '60s

GRAVEYARD 5

Singles: 7-inch

STANCO (102 "Marble Orchard") 250-300 66

GRAY, Billy
(With His Western Okies)

Singles: 78 rpm

DECCA (29271 "We Just Don't See Things Alike")...5-10 54
DECCA (29800 "Tennessee Toddy")....... 10-20 56

Singles: 7-inch

DECCA (29271 "We Just Don't See Things Alike")... 10-15 54
DECCA (29800 "Tennessee Toddy")....... 25-40 56
LIBERTY (55599 "I Left My Heart in San Francisco")...5-10 63
LIBERTY (55712 "Late Last Night") 5-10 64
Also see JACKSON, Wanda, & Billy Gray

GRAY, Bobby

Singles: 7-inch

BISMARK (1008 "I'm Not Sleeping")...........5-10 65
EVERLAST (5009 "The Girl I Left Behind") 15-25 57

JODY (101 "There's Gonna Be a Party") ....150-250 '50s
OKEH (7097 "I Still Love You") 15-25 58

GRAY, Carol

Singles: 7-inch

RHYTHM (126 "Cha Cha Bop") 50-100 59
(Rhythm also used the number 126 for one side of a Lyrics release.)
Also see LYRICS

GRAY, Charlie

Singles: 7-inch

CLYMAX (2 "Completely Satisfied") 20-40
Session: Bill Haley's Comets.
Also see HALEY, Bill

GRAY, Clyde

Singles: 7-inch

SHAD (5016 "Chestnut Drive") 10-15 60

GRAY, Dave, & Graytones

Singles: 7-inch

EMPIRE STUDIOS (1001 "You're the One")...10-20 61
NIVEK (1001 "You're the One") 75-100 59

GRAY, Dobie P&R '63

Singles: 12-inch

INFINITY...5-8 79

Singles: 7-inch

ARISTA...3-5 83
CAPITOL (5853 "River Deep, Mountain High")...5-10 67
CAPITOL (44126 "Love Letters")..................3-5 87
CAPRICORN..4-6 75-76
CHARGER (105 "The 'In' Crowd") 5-10 64
CHARGER (107 "See You at the Go-Go") .5-10 65
CHARGER (109 "In Hollywood")..................5-10 65
CHARGER (113 "Monkey Jerk")..................5-10 65
CHARGER (115 "Out on the Floor")............5-10 66
COLLECTABLES..3-5 81
CORDAK (1602 "Look at Me") 8-12 62
CORDAK (1605 "Feelin' in My Heart")........8-12 63
CORDAK (1701 "My Shoes Keep Walkin' Back to You")...8-12 64
DECCA...4-6 73
ERIC...4-6 '70s
GUSTO..3-5 85
INFINITY (50003 "You Can Do It") 4-6 78
INFINITY (50010 "Who's Lovin' You") 4-6 79
INFINITY (50020 "Let This Man Take Hold of Your Life")..4-6 79
INFINITY (50043 " The 'In' Crowd") 4-6 79
JAF (2504 "Be a Man")..................................8-12 63
LANA (138 "The 'In' Crowd") ....4-8 '60s
MCA..4-6 73-75
REAL FINE (835 "Tears Keep Falling on My Tears")...8-12 62
ROBOX..3-5 81
STRIPE (827 "To Be Wanted") 10-15 60
STRIPE (828 "Rags to Riches")................10-15 60
STRIPE (829 "Love Has a Way")..............10-15 60
STRIPE (831 "Love Has a Way")...............10-15 61
STRIPE (832 "Kissin' Doll")......................10-15 61
WHITE WHALE (300 "Rose Garden")........5-10 69
WHITE WHALE (330 "Do You Really Have a Heart"/ "What a Way to Go")..............................100-200 69
WHITE WHALE (330 "Do You Really Have a Heart"/"Do You Really Have a Heart") 50-75 69
(Promotional issue only.)
WHITE WHALE (342 "Honey, You Can't Take It Back")...25-50 70

LPs: 10/12-inch

CAPITOL 5-10 86
CAPRICORN...8-10 76
CHARGER 15-20 65
DECCA...8-10 73
INFINITY...6-10 79
MCA..8-10 73-74
ROBOX...5-10 81
STRIPE...10-12

GRAY, Dobie / Reflections

Singles: 7-inch

ERIC (277 "The 'In' Crowd"/"Just Like Romeo and Juliet")..4-6 79
Also see GRAY, Dobie
Also see REFLECTIONS

GRAY, Dori Anne

Singles: 78 rpm

MERCURY (70801 "Heartbreak Alley")......5-10 56

Singles: 7-inch

MERCURY (70801 "Heartbreak Alley")....10-15 56

GRAY, Duane

Singles: 7-inch

MAJESTIC (2196 "Come Home").........200-300

GRAY, Gene, & Stingrays

Singles: 7-inch

DOT (16478 "Surf Bunny")........................10-15 63
LINDA (110 "Surf Bunny") 40-50 63
(First issue.)

GRAY, Jimmy

Singles: 7-inch

GLOBE (006 "Two Timer")............................60-80 59
SHASTA (135 "Chicksville, U.S.A.") 40-60 60

GRAY, Maureen P&R '62

Singles: 7-inch

CHANCELLOR (1082 "Crazy Over You")...10-15 61
CHANCELLOR (1091 "I Don't Want to Cry")...10-15 61
CHANCELLOR (1100 "There Is a Boy")...20-30 62
GUYDEN (2072 "Slop Time")....................10-20 62
LANDA (689 "Dancin' the Strand") 15-25 62
LANDA (692 "People Are Talking") 30-40 62
MERCURY (72131 "Story of My Love") ...30-40 63
MERCURY (72227 "I'm a Happy Girl").....10-15 64

GRAY, Pearlean
(With the Passengers)

Singles: 7-inch

DCP (1125 "For Your Love").......................5-10 65
DCP (1143 "Don't Rush Me Baby") 5-10 65
GREEN-SEA (104 "Love of My Man")......10-20 66

GRAY, Phil

Singles: 7-inch

RHYTHM (101 "Bluest Boy in Town")..2500-3500
ROBBINS (1002 "Somebody's Got My Baby") 50-75 58

GRAY, Rudy
(Rudy Grayzell)

Singles: 78 rpm

CAPITOL...10-20 55

Singles: 7-inch

CAPITOL (2946 "There's Gonna Be a Ball") 20-30 55
CAPITOL (3044 "You Better Believe It") ..20-30 55
CAPITOL (3149 "Please Big Mama")........20-30 55
Also see GRAYZELL, Rudy

GRAY, Wardell, Quintet

Singles: 78 rpm

VEE-JAY (135 "Hey There") 5-10 55

Singles: 7-inch

VEE-JAY (135 "Hey There") 10-20 55

GRAY, Wayne

Singles: 7-inch

GOLD CIRCLE (1002 "Space Man's Guitar") 15-25 58

GRAY, Wilhelmina
(With Teacho Wiltshire & Orchestra)

Singles: 7-inch

MGM (12500 "When the One You Love Loves You")...15-25 57
Also see WILTSHIRE, Teacho

GRAY THINGS

Singles: 7-inch

LAURIE (3367 "Charity")...........................10-15 66

GRAYDON, Joe

Singles: 7-inch

HAMILTON (50027 "Again") 10-15 59

GRAYSON, Ann

Singles: 7-inch

RCA (7598 "I've Just Discovered Boys")..10-15 59

GRAYSON, Bobby, & His Orbits

Singles: 7-inch

JAMCO (105 "Look Over Here Girl") 10-20 63

GRAYSON, Joel

Singles: 7-inch

RIVERSIDE (4557 "My True Story").......75-100 63

GRAYSON, Kathryn

LPs: 10/12-inch

LION (70055 "Kathryn Grayson") 30-50 56

GRAYSON, Larry
(With the Buddy Collette Orchestra; with John Anderson Orchestra)

Singles: 78 rpm

UNIQUE (302 "House of Love")..................5-10 55

Singles: 7-inch

MARCEL (107 "Whistlestop") 10-20 58
UNIQUE (302 "House of Love")...............10-15 55
Also see COLLETTE, Buddy

GRAYSON, Milton
(With Herb Alpert; Milt Grayson)

Singles: 7-inch

ANDEX (22102 "It Ain't Necessarily So") .10-15 59
ARWIN (1005 "Don't Blame Me") 15-25 59
COLPIX (626 "Reward")...........................30-40 62
DERBY (1007 "Your Old Standby")..........15-25 63
KEEN (2007 "Beggar Boy") 10-20 58
KEEN (5-2007 "Beggar Boy") 30-40 58
(Stereo. Colored vinyl.)
KEEN (2010 "No Greater Love") 15-25 58
KEEN (2020 "I Want You to Know")..........10-15 59
KEEN (82102 "It Ain't Necessarily So")....40-50
MGM (13699 "Hurry Sundown") 10-15 67
Also see ALPERT, Herb

GRAYSON, Milton, & Dr. Samuel J. Hoffman / George T. Davis

Singles: 7-inch

ROYALTY (21420 "I Paid the Penalty") ... 10-15 60
(Pertains to the execution of Caryl Chessman.)

Picture Sleeves

ROYALTY (21420 "I Paid the Penalty") ... 15-25 60

GRAYZELL, Rudy
(With His Thunderbirds; with Sparkels; with the Louisiana Hayride Band; Rudy "Tutti" Grayzell;)

Singles: 78 rpm

ABBOTT...10-15 53-54
MERCURY...25-50 57
STARDAY 30-60 56-57

Singles: 7-inch

ABBOTT (145 "Looking at the Moon") 20-30 53
ABBOTT (147 "I'm Gone Again")..............20-30 53
ABBOTT (157 "Ocean Paradise") 20-30 54
AWARD (130 "You'll Be Mine")................15-25 59
MERCURY (71138 "Let's Get Wild") 25-50 57
STARDAY (229 "The Moon Is Up") 50-60 56
STARDAY (241 "Duck Tail") 50-60 56
STARDAY (270 "Jig-Ga-Lee-Ga")............50-60 56
STARDAY (321 "Let's Get Wild") 60-80 57
SUN (290 "Judy") 40-50 58
Also see GRAY, Rudy

GRAZIANO, Rocky

Singles: 78 rpm

RAMA (178 "Back in My Old Neighborhood")..10-15 55

Singles: 7-inch

RAMA (178 "Back in My Old Neighborhood")..15-25 55

GREASE

Singles: 7-inch

USA (921 "Spoonful")..................................15-25 69
Members: Jim Krueger; Junior Olson; Larry Byrne; Jim Denk; Andy Pigeon; Paul Kowalski; Mike Larsheid; Mark La Que.

GREASERS

Singles: 7-inch

JAYE JOSEPH (1002 "Movin' Out") 20-30 63
Member: Larry Bright.
Also see BRIGHT, Larry

GREAT BELIEVERS

Singles: 7-inch

CASCADE (365 "Comin' Up Fast")............40-60 66
Member: Johnny Winter.
Also see WINTER, Johnny

GREAT IMPOSTERS

Singles: 7-inch

DADS (6398 "Who Do Your Love") 20-25 66

Picture Sleeves

DADS (6398 "Who Do Your Love") 25-35 66

GREAT PRETENDER & TENNESSEE TWO & A HALF
(Mitchell Torok)

Singles: 7-inch

COLUMBIA (41358 "You Can't Get There From Here") 10-15 58
Also see TOROK, Mitchell

GREAT SCOTS
(Great Scotts)
Singles: 7-inch
EPIC (9805 "Don't Want Your Love")....... 10-15 65
EPIC (9866 "That's My Girl")................... 20-30 65
LONDON (17348 "Ball & Chain")............ 10-20 66
(Canadian.)
TRIUMPH (66 "Ball & Chain") 15-25 66
TRIUMPH (67 "Light Hurts My Eyes") 15-25 66

GREAT!! SOCIETY!!
Singles: 7-inch
COLUMBIA (9624 "Conspicuous Only in Its Absence") 30-40 68
(Promotional issue. Recorded live at the Matrix in San Francisco.)
COLUMBIA (44583 "Sally Go 'Round the Roses") 10-15 68
NORTHBEACH (1001 "Someone to Love")... 150-200 66
Member: Grace Slick.
Also see JEFFERSON AIRPLANE
Also see SLICK, Grace

GREAT SEBASTIAN
(Wayne Cochran)
Singles: 7-inch
REBEL (1333 1/2 "The Naughty Coo").. 50-100 59
Also see COCHRAN, Wayne

GREATER EXPERIENCE
Singles: 7-inch
COLONY (2572 "Don't Forget to Remember")... 15-25 '60s

GREATER HARVEST BAPTIST CHURCH CHOIR
Singles: 7-inch
SHARP (632 "What a Difference in My Life")..5-10 63
LPs: 10/12-inch
SHARP 15-25 62
Members: Maurice McAlister; Leonard Caston; Barbara Caston; Richard Dickerson; Green McLaurin.
Also see RADIANTS

GREATS
Singles: 7-inch
EBB (145 "Marching Elvis")..................... 20-25 58

GRECCO, Johnny, & Devies
Singles: 7-inch
SONIC (813 "Hogwalk")........................... 10-20 63

GRECO, Johnny
(With the Davies; with Vandells)
Singles: 7-inch
FAR-MEL (1 "Gloria")........................... 200-300 63
PAGEANT (602 "Rocket Ride")............. 50-100 63
SONIC (813 "High School Dance") 50-75 59

GRECO, Juliette
Singles: 7-inch
COLUMBIA (41011 "Si")...............................5-10 57
Picture Sleeves
COLUMBIA (41011 "Si")......................... 10-15 57

GRECO, Tony
(With the Free Fall 3; Tony Grecco)
Singles: 7-inch
BIG BEAT (100 "Something Else") 10-15 62
BIG BEAT (1053 "Say Mama")................ 10-15 61
BUZZ (101 "Lonely Weekend")..................5-10 64

GREEK FOUNTAINS
Singles: 7-inch
BOFUZ.. 10-20 '60s
MONTEL (976 "Experiment in Terror")..... 10-15 66
MONTEL (983 "What Is Right")............... 10-15 66
PACEMAKER (250 "I'm a Boy")............... 10-15 65
PHILIPS (40355 "Blue Jean")................ 10-15 66
LPs: 10/12-inch
MONTEL (110 "Requests") 50-75 66

GREEN, Al *P&R/R&B '67*
(With the Soul Mates; Al Greene)
Singles: 7-inch
A&M 3-5 85-89
BELL 4-6 72-73
FARGO (1004 "Girl I Love") 15-25 58
FLASHBACK...4-6 '70s
HI 4-8 69-78
HOT LINE (15000 "Back Up Train")......... 10-15 67
HOT LINE (15001 "Don't Hurt Me No More") 10-15 67
HOT LINE (15002 "I'll Be Good to You") ..10-15 68
MOTOWN...3-5 82-85
Picture Sleeves
A&M (2919 "Everything's Gonna Be Alright") 3-5 87
HI (77505 "Belle") 4-8 77
HI (78522 "Wait Here") 4-8 78
LPs: 10/12-inch
A&M...5-10 87
BELL...8-10 72
CAPITOL (Black vinyl)...............................5-8 '90s
CAPITOL (Colored vinyl)..........................10-15 '90s
HI (6004 "Belle Album")..............................8-10 77
HI (27121 "Let's Stay Together") 8-10 95
(Colored vinyl.)
HI (27127 "I'm Still in Love with You") 8-10 95
(Colored vinyl.)
HI (32000 series) 10-20 69-78
HOT LINE (1500 "Back Up Train")...........20-40 67
KORY 8-10 77
MELODY 5-10
MOTOWN...5-10 82-85
MYRRH 5-10 80-83
RIGHT STUFF (27121 "Let's Stay Together")..10-12 95
(Colored vinyl.)
RIGHT STUFF (27627 "I'm Still in Love with You") 10-12 95
(Colored vinyl.)

GREEN, Bernie, & Stereo Mad-Men
LPs: 10/12-inch
RCA (1929 "Musically Mad")....................30-50 58

GREEN, Betty
Singles: 7-inch
CRACKERJACK (4018 "He's Down on Me")..10-15 '60s
CLARA (111 "He's Down on Me")..............8-12 '60s

GREEN, Big Charles
Singles: 7-inch
HITT (180 "Rockin' on the Moon Tonight") 100-125 58

GREEN, Bob, & Missiles
Singles: 7-inch
SOMA (1163 "Above & Beyond")..............20-25 61

GREEN, Bobby, & Sportsmen
Singles: 7-inch
OAK (4429 "Little Heart Attacks") 75-100 61

GREEN, Boy
Singles: 78 rpm
REGIS (120 "A & B Blues")....................50-100 44

GREEN, Byrdie
Singles: 7-inch
END (1117 "Tremblin'").................................8-12 62
END (1122 "Memories Are Made of This").8-12 63
HALLMARK (334 "Don't Make It Hurt")......5-10 69
PENDA MUNGU (100 "We Need Christmas Now")..4-6 73
PERRI (1001 "Be Anything")........................5-10 62
PRESTIGE (440 "Goin' Out of My Head")..5-10 67
20TH FOX (422 "Don't Take Your Love from Me")...15-25 63
20TH FOX (511 "I Found My Place")........15-25 64
20TH FOX (567 "I Deserve It")..................15-25 65

GREEN, Cal
Singles: 7-inch
FEDERAL (12318 "The Big Push")...........10-15 58
MUTT-JEFF 8-12

GREEN, Carl, Orchestra
Singles: 78 rpm
METEOR (5002 "My Best Friend") 30-50 53
METEOR (5009 "Boogie Freight") 30-50 53

GREEN, Clarence
(With the High Type Five; with Rhythmaires)
Singles: 78 rpm
EDDIE'S 15-25 48
Singles: 7-inch
ALL BOY (8510 "Red Light")....................10-20 64
AQUARIUS..4-6
BRIGHT STAR..10-20
C&P (102 "Mary, My Darling 10-20 59
CHESS (1732 "Mary, My Darling") 15-25 59
DUKE (399 "Keep a-Workin' ").....................5-10 66
DUKE (410 "I'm Wondering")......................5-10 66
DUKE (424 "Groundhog") 5-10 67
GOLDEN EAGLE (112 "Empty House of Tears") 10-20 64
LYNN (509 "The Slop") 10-20 60
MASTER 10-20 60
SHOMAR 10-15 61

GREEN, DeRoy
(With the Cool Gents)
Singles: 7-inch
CEE=JAY (584 "At the Teen Center") 50-75 61
SOOZEE (111 "At the Teen Center") 15-25 62

GREEN, Fred
Singles: 7-inch
BOBBIN (111 "Wham Slam Bam") 30-50 59
BOBBIN (123 "Don't Make a Fool of Me") 30-50 59

GREEN, Fred, & Mellards
(With Emmett Carter's Combo)
Singles: 78 rpm
BALLAD...50-100 55-56
Singles: 7-inch
BALLAD (1012 "You Can't Keep Love in a Broken Heart")..250-300 55
BALLAD (1016 "Love Me Crazy")........150-200 56
Also see GREEN, Fred

GREEN, George, & Jimmy Binkley Jazz Quintet
Singles: 78 rpm
CHANCE (1135 "Finance Man")..............30-50 53
Singles: 7-inch
CHANCE (1135 "Finance Man")............75-100 53

GREEN, George, & Hamiltones
Singles: 7-inch
HICO (2435 "You Are My Lonely One")..200-300 58

GREEN, George "Stardust"
(Stardust Green)
Singles: 7-inch
GATEWAY (751 "All Alone") 5-10 65
TEMPUS (1509 "Hug My Pillow") 10-15 59

GREEN, Glenda
Singles: 7-inch
NEPTUNE (103 "He's Gone")..................15-20 59

GREEN, Grant *LP '71*
Singles: 7-inch
BLUE NOTE (1811 "Ain't Nobody's Business If I Do")..5-10 61
BLUE NOTE (1812 "Wee Bit O' Green")....5-10 62
BLUE NOTE (1919 "I Want to Hold Your Hand")...4-8 66
VERVE (10361 "Daddy Grapes") 4-8 65
LPs: 10/12-inch
BLUE NOTE..15-25 61-65
(Label reads "Blue Note Records Inc. - New York, U.S.A.")
BLUE NOTE..10-15 66-71
(Label reads "Blue Note Records - a Division of Liberty Records Inc.")
VERVE..10-18 65
VERSATILE 5-10 78
Also see KESSEL, Barney / Grant Green / Oscar Moore / Mundell Lowe

GREEN, Griz
(With the Happy Timers; Griz Green's Arizonians")
Singles: 78 rpm
LIBERTY BELL 5-10 55-56
Singles: 7-inch
LIBERTY BELL (9007 "Step Right Up and Say Howdy")...10-15 55
LIBERTY BELL (9008 "OK Corral")..........10-15 56
TAMPA (161 "Thankful") 5-10 58

GREEN, Guitar Slim
(Norman Green)
Singles: 7-inch
GEENOTE (907 "Rock the Nation")..........15-25 57
LPs: 10/12-inch
UNITED 10-15
Also see GREEN, R., & Turner
Also see GREEN, Slim

GREEN, Hattie
Singles: 7-inch
ANGEL TONE (1081 "Green Light Baby") ....15-25 '50s

GREEN, Hazell
Singles: 7-inch
KIT KAT (712 "Heartless Lover")..............15-25

GREEN, Henry
Singles: 78 rpm
CHANCE (1109 "Strange Things")...........10-15 51
Singles: 7-inch
CHANCE (1109 "Strange Things")...........25-35 51

GREEN, Howard, & Gay Clefs
Singles: 7-inch
SPRY (1009 "Mary Ann")..........................10-15 60

GREEN, Janice
(The "Oh Julie" Girl)
Singles: 7-inch
NASCO (6013 "With All My Heart")..........10-15 58
(Janice was labeled the "Oh Julie" girl for her vocal assist on the Crescendos' *Oh Julie*.)
Also see CRESCENDOS

GREEN, Johnny, Combo
Singles: 7-inch
GEE (1066 "Lonesome Road")..................10-15 61

GREEN, Johnny "Rockhouse"
(Johnny Green Combo)
Singles: 7-inch
DELUXE (6192 "Green Champagne") 15-25 61
GEE (1066 "Lonesome Road")...................15-25 61
ON THE SQUARE (315 "Little Eva")....100-200 59

GREEN, Johnny, & Greenmen
(Greenmen)
Singles: 7-inch
EMERALD (2001 "Something You Got")..15-25 65
KAPP (619 "I've Had It")..........................15-25 64
RANWOOD (838 "Poor Little Fat Girl") 10-20 69
LP: 10/12-inch
AVI ("Seven Over from Mars")..................10-20 67
(Selection number not known.)
EDMAR (1140 "When You're Green You're Clean")..8-12 74
Members: Johnny Green Pavlick; Howard Wales; Joyce Bowers; Tommy Lee; Dorin Miller; John Frost Trombatore; Russ Harding; Denny Lee Sesso; Bobby Van Holten; Marilyn Winters; Dick Person; John Stratford; George Eberdt.
Also see ROSCOE & LITTLE GREEN MEN

GREEN, Joyce
Singles: 7-inch
VADEN (112 "Black Cadillac")..........1000-2000 60
Session: Bobby Brown; Teddy Redell; Larry Donn.

GREEN, L.C.
(With His Guitar)
Singles: 78 rpm
DOT (1103 "When the Sun Is Shining")...40-60 52
DOT (1128 "Little School Girl")................40-60 52
DOT (1147 "Little Machine")....................40-60 52
VON (42 "Going Down to the River Blues")..250-500 52

GREEN, Larry
(With Pete Wade)
Singles: 7-inch
INDIGO (117 "Dinah")................................15-25 61
INDIGO (142 "Be My Love") 15-25 62
LU-GREEN (101 "Watch Your Ship")........50-75
MOVIN' (133 "Movin' the Blues")................5-10 66
PARIS (510 "The Stars Look Down")........15-25 57
PARIS (517 "Look Homeward Angel") 15-25 58
SOUL (22 "Long Black Train")..................50-75 '60s
Also see PARKER, Bobby / Larry Green

GREEN, Lloyd *C&W '73*
Singles: 7-inch
BIG A (102 "Panic a Trip' ")......................10-20 67
CHART (1071 "Bar Hoppin' ")...................10-15 69
HILLTOP (3010 "Skillet Lickin' ") 8-12 66
(First issue.)
LITTLE DARLIN' (007 "Skillet Lickin' ") 5-10 66
LITTLE DARLIN' (0023 "Little Darlin' ").......5-10 67
LITTLE DARLIN' (0050 "Green Strings") 5-10 68
MGM (14132 "Gotta Travel On") 4-8 70
(With Music City Sounds and Pete Wade.)
MONUMENT...4-6 72-75
OCTOBER (1002 "You and Me")..................4-6 76
OCTOBER (1009 "Feelings").......................4-6 77
PRIZE (01 "Midnight Silence")....................4-8 71
PRIZE (09 "Sound Waves") 4-8 71
LPs: 10/12-inch
BOOT (7205 "Lloyd's of Nashville")............5-10 80

CHART 10-15 68-70
GRT (8018 "Feelings") 8-10 77
LITTLE DARLIN' 15-25 66-69
MID-LAND (10009 "Ten Shades of Green") 8-12 76
MGM (4672 "Music City Sounds") 10-15 70
(With Music City Sounds and Pete Wade.)
MONUMENT (32532 "Shades of Steel") 8-10 75
MONUMENT (33368 "Steel Rides") 8-10 75
PRIZE (498-01 "Lloyd Green & His Steel Guitar") 10-12 71
TIME (2152 "Big Steel Guitar") 10-15 64
(Monaural.)
TIME (52152 "Big Steel Guitar") 15-20 64
(Stereo.)
Also see LEE, Bobby
Also see McCOY, Charlie, & Lloyd Green
Also see STEWART, Wynn

GREEN, Nick, & Don Jackson

Singles: 7-inch

SPRY (107 "San Antonio Rock") 15-25 58
SPRY (1007 "San Antonio Rock") 10-20 60
Also see GREEN, Nick

GREEN, R., & Turner

(Norman Green)

Singles: 78 rpm

J&M FULLBRIGHT (123 "Alla Blues") 50-75 48
Also see GREEN, Guitar Slim
Also see GREEN, Slim

GREEN, Rodger

Singles: 7-inch

DEBONAIR (193 "Betty Mae") 50-100

GREEN, Slim

(Norman Green)

Singles: 78 rpm

CANTON (1789 "Shake 'Em Up") 30-50 57
MURRAY (501 "Baby I Love You") 50-75 48

Singles: 7-inch

CANTON (1789 "Shake 'Em Up") 20-40 57
Also see GREEN, Guitar Slim
Also see GREEN, R., & Turner
Also see SIMMONS, Al, & Slim Green

GREEN, Thomas

Singles: 7-inch

HAPPY HEARTS ("I'd Rather Make Love") 50-75
(Selection number not known.)

GREEN, Vernon, & Medallions

(Medallions; Vernon Greene)

Singles: 78 rpm

DOOTO 20-30 57
DOOTONE 25-35 54-56

Singles: 7-inch

CHELAN (2001 "Please, Please, Please") 4-6 75
CLASSIC ARTISTS (103 "So Bad") 5-8 88
(Black vinyl. 1000 made.)
CLASSIC ARTISTS (129 "Drinkin' Wine") 4-6 91
(Black vinyl. 1000 made.)
DOOTO (419 "For Better or for Worse") 30-40 57
DOOTO (425 "Lover's Prayer") 40-50 57
DOOTO (446 "Magic Mountain") 40-50 58
(Shown as by the Medallions.)
DOOTO (446 "Magic Mountain") 10-20 59
(Shown as by Vernon Green and the Medallions.)
DOOTO (454 "Behind the Door") 30-40 59
DOOTONE (347 "The Letter") 40-50 54
(Red label.)
DOOTONE (347 "The Letter") 15-25 54
(Black label.)
DOOTONE (357 "The Telegram") 40-50 54
(Maroon label.)
DOOTONE (357 "The Telegram") 15-25 54
(Blue label.)
DOOTONE (364 "Edna") 40-50 55
DOOTONE (379 "Dear Darling") 50-60 55
DOOTONE (393 "I Want a Love") 40-50 56
DOOTONE (400 "Push Button Automobile") 50-60 56
DOOTONE (407 "Did You Have Fun") 30-40 56
DOOTONE (479 "Can You Talk") 4-6 73
DOOTONE (480 "You're a Super Star") 3-5 81
MINIT (32034 "Look at Me, Look at Me") 10-15 68
PAN WORLD (71 "Dear Ann") 200-300 62
PAN WORLD (10000 "Deep, So Deep") 40-50 62

EPs: 7-inch

DOOTO (202 "Medallions") 75-125 60
DOOTONE (202 "Medallions") 150-250 56

LPs: 10/12-inch

DOOTO (200 series) 5-10
DOOTO (857 "Vernon Green and Medallions") 10-15
(Counterfeits exist of most Dootone releases.)
Also see BEL-AIRES
Also see PENGUINS / Medallions
Also see TWOVOICE, Johnny, & Medallions
Also see VERNON & CLIFF

GREEN, Vernon, & Phantoms

Singles: 78 rpm

SPECIALTY (581 "Sweet Breeze") 15-25 56

Singles: 7-inch

SPECIALTY (581 "Sweet Breeze") 30-40 56
Also see GREEN, Vernon, & Medallions

GREEN BROTHERS

Singles: 7-inch

TORTOISE (11130 "Sweet Lovin' Woman") 15-25 '60s

GREEN BULLFROG

LPs: 10/12-inch

DECCA (75269 "Green Bullfrog") 15-25 71

GREEN GANG

Singles: 7-inch

BRAGG (226 "She Means That Much to Me") 10-20 '60s

GREEN RIVER

Singles: 7-inch

ICP (01 "Together We'll Never") 15-25 86
(Colored vinyl. 800 made.)
ICP (01 "Together We'll Never") 5-10 86
(Black vinyl.)

EPs: 7-inch

SUB POP (11 "Dry As a Bone") 5-10 87
SUB POP (15 "Rehab Doll") 20-30 88
(Colored vinyl. 1000 made.)
SUB POP (15 "Rehab Doll") 10-15 88
(Black vinyl.)

LP: 10/12-inch

HOMESTEAD (031 "Come on Down") 20-30 85
(Colored vinyl.)
HOMESTEAD (031 "Come on Down") 10-15 85
(Black vinyl.)
Members: Bruce Fairweather, Mark Arm, Jeff Ament, Alex Vincent, Stone Gossard.
Also see PEARL JAM

GREENBERG, Steve — P&R '69

Singles: 7-inch

TRIP (3000 "Big Bruce") 20-25 69

GREENE, Barbara — P&R/R&B '68

(Barbara Green & Dells)

Singles: 7-inch

ATCO (6250 "Long Tall Sally") 8-12 63
RENEE (5001 "Young Boy") 10-15 68
VIVID (105 "Young Boy") 15-20 64
VIVID (110 "A Lover's Plea") 5-10 64
Also see DELLS

GREENE, Dodo

Singles: 7-inch

TIME (1014 "Don't Cry Baby") 5-10 59

LPs: 10/12-inch

TIME (70001 "Dodo Greene") 10-15 60

GREENE, Hazel, & Dick Baker

Singles: 7-inch

KIT KAT (712 "Heartless Lover") 50-100
Also see BAKER, Dick, Combo

GREENE, Kellie

Singles: 7-inch

20TH FOX (6637 "Move On") 10-20 66

GREENE, Lil — P&R '40

Singles: 78 rpm

ALADDIN 25-50 50
ATLANTIC (951 "Every Time") 25-50 51
BLUEBIRD 12-25 39-46
GROOVE 8-15 56
RCA 10-20 46-48

Singles: 7-inch

ATLANTIC (951 "Every Time") 50-100 51
GROOVE (5004 "Why Don't You Do Right") 10-20 56

LPs: 10/12-inch

ROSETTA 5-10 86

GREENE, Rudy

(Rudy Green; with King Kolax Orchestra)

Singles: 78 rpm

BULLET 15-25 47
CHANCE 25-50 53-54
EMBER 15-25 57
EXCELLO 10-20 55

Singles: 7-inch

CHANCE (1139 "Love Is a Pain") 50-100 53
CHANCE (1146 "The Letter") 50-100 53
CHANCE (1151 "I Had a Feeling") 50-100 54
(Black vinyl.)
CHANCE (1151 "I Had a Feeling") 200-300 54
(Colored vinyl.)
EMBER (1012 "You're the One for Me") 20-30 57
EMBER (1020 "Lonesome") 20-30 57
EXCELLO (2074 "Good Lovin' Mama") 25-35 55
EXCELLO (2090 "Teeny Weeny Baby") 25-35 55
PONCELLO (715 "Oh Baby") 50-75 61

GREENE, Rudy, & Four Buddies

Singles: 78 rpm

CLUB 51 (103 "You Mean Everything to Me") 100-150 56

Singles: 7-inch

CLUB 51 (103 "You Mean Everything to Me") 300-400 56
Also see FOUR BUDDIES
Also see GREENE, Rudy

GREENFIELD, Allen

Singles: 7-inch

GOLDEN ROD (201 "Juke Box Hula") 150-250

GREENHILL, Mitch

Singles: 7-inch

FONTANA (1636 "Only As Lonely") 5-10 69
FONTANA (1656 "Foggy Tuesday") 5-10 69

LPs: 10/12-inch

PRESTIGE (7438 "Shepherd of the Highways") 10-15 67

GREENSLADE

LPs: 10/12-inch

MERCURY 10-12 74-75
W.B. 10-12 73
Members: Dave Greenslade; Andy McCulloch; Tony Reeves; Martin Briley; Dave Lawson; Jill Mackintosh.

GREENSTREET, Carl

Singles: 7-inch

ACE (594 "Hey Mama") 10-15 60
DUKE (354 "The Way the Wind Blows") 8-12 62

GREENSTREETS

Singles: 7-inch

CORSAIR (400 "Moon Shot") 20-30 64

GREENWICH, Ellie — P&R '67

Singles: 7-inch

BELL (855 "Ain't That Peculiar") 5-10 70
BELL (933 "That Certain Someone") 5-10 70
RED BIRD (034 "Baby") 10-15 65
U.A. (50151 "I Want You to Be My Baby") 10-15 67
VERVE 5-10 70-73

LPs: 10/12-inch

U.A. (6648 "Ellie Greenwich Composes, Produces and Sings") 30-40 68
VERVE 10-15 73
Also see ARCHIES
Also see BONDS, Gary "U.S."
Also see BUTTERFLYS
Also see CROCE, Jim
Also see GAYE, Ellie
Also see GEE, Ellie
Also see MEANTIME
Also see RAINDROPS

GREENWOOD, Johnny, & Islanders

LPs: 10/12-inch

U.A. (3289 "Let's Limbo") 15-25 63

GREENWOOD, Lil, & Dominoes

Singles: 78 rpm

FEDERAL 30-40 52

Singles: 7-inch

FEDERAL (12158 "I'll Go") 100-150 52
FEDERAL (12165 "All Is Forgiven") 50-75 52

GREENWOOD, Lil, & Four Jacks

Singles: 78 rpm

FEDERAL 50-100 52

Singles: 7-inch

FEDERAL (12082 "My Last Hour") 200-400 52
FEDERAL (12093 "Never Again") 200-400 52
Also see DOMINOES
Also see GREENWOOD, Lil, & Dominoes

GREENWOOD, Paul

Singles: 7-inch

ALLENBERRY (1 "Picture of a Girl") 10-15
MUSICOR (1012 "Outside Heaven's Door") 5-10 61

GREER, Amon

Singles: 7-inch

JEWEL (806 "Jo Jo Rock n' Roll") 200-300

GREER, Big John, & Four Students

Singles: 78 rpm

GROOVE 8-12 55
KING (Except 4941) 10-15 56-57
KING (4941 "Come Back Uncle John") 15-25 56

Singles: 7-inch

GROOVE (0131 "A Man and a Woman") 20-30 55
KING (4878 "Record Hop") 20-30 56
KING (4941 "Come Back Uncle John") 50-75 56
KING (5006 "Midnight Ramble") 20-30 56
KING (5057 "Duck Walk") 20-30 57
Also see FOUR STUDENTS
Also see GREER, John

GREER, John — R&B '52

(Big John Greer; with Rhythm Rockers)

Singles: 78 rpm

GROOVE 8-12 55
KING 8-12 55-56
RCA 20-30 49-53

Singles: 7-inch

GROOVE (0002 thru 0119) 20-30 55
KING (4878 thru 4941) 20-30 55-56
MOA (1002 "Honey, Why") 250-300
RCA (0007 "Drinkin' Wine Spo-Dee-O-Dee") 35-50 49
(Colored vinyl.)
RCA (0029 "If I Told You Once") 35-50 49
(Colored vinyl)
RCA (0051 "Rocking Jenny Jones") 35-50 50
(Colored vinyl)
RCA (0076 "I'll Never Do That Again") 35-50 50
(Colored vinyl.)
RCA (0096 "Cheatin' ") 35-50 50
(Colored vinyl.)
RCA (0104 "Red Juice") 35-50 50
(Colored vinyl.)
RCA (0108 thru 5531) 15-25 51-53
Also see ALLEN, Annisteen
Also see GREER, Big John, & Four Students

GREER, Paula

Singles: 7-inch

WORKSHOP JAZZ (2003 "So in Love") 15-25 63
WORKSHOP JAZZ (2007 "Falling in Love with Love") 15-25 63

LPs: 10/12-inch

WORKSHOP JAZZ (203 "Introducing Miss Paula Greer") 100-200 63

GREER, Paula, & Johnny Griffith Trio

LPs: 10/12-inch

WORKSHOP JAZZ (204 "Detroit Jazz") 100-200 63
Also see GREER, Paula
Also see GRIFFITH, Johnny, Trio

GREG & UNKNOWNS

Singles: 7-inch

VICKI ("Red Beats") 10-20 65
(Selection number not known.)

GREGG, Bobby — P&R/R&B '62

(With His Friends; Bobby Grego; with Desert Sounds)

Singles: 7-inch

COTTON (1003 "The Jam") 10-15 62
COTTON (1006 "Potato Peeler") 10-15 62
EPIC (9541 thru 9669) 8-12 62-64
LAURIE (3358 "If You Wanna Be Happy") 5-10 66
VEEP (1207 "Hullabaloo") 5-10 65

LPs: 10/12-inch

EPIC (24051 "Let's Stomp and Wild Weekend") 20-25 63
(Monaural.)
EPIC (26051 "Let's Stomp and Wild Weekend") 25-30 63
(Stereo.)
Also see BUCHANAN, Roy

Also see DYLAN, Bob
Also see GIBSON, Steve
Also see ROCK, Jimmy

GREGG, David

Singles: 7-inch

MCDOWELL (567 "Baby I Don't Care") ... 200-300

GREGG, Julie

Singles: 7-inch

UNI (55014 "Sunshine") ... 15-20 67

GREGORY, Bobby, & Cardinals

Singles: 7-inch

KIP (403 "Precious One") ... 500-750 59
(500 made.)
Also see SHANNON, Bobby

GREGORY, Dale, & Shouters

Singles: 7-inch

B SHARP (271 "I Remember") ... 150-175 66
Also see THOSE OF US

GREGORY, Harrison
(With Paul Simon)

Singles: 7-inch

CORDELLA (047 "Twistin' Raindrops") ... 20-30
Also see SIMON, Paul

GREGORY, Ivan, & Blue Notes

Singles: 78 rpm

G&G (110 "Elvis Presley Blues") ... 50-75 56

Singles: 7-inch

G&G (110 "Elvis Presley Blues") ... 75-125 56

GREGORY, Steve

Singles: 7-inch

KENCO (5008 "You're My Kinda Girl") ... 50-75 60

GREMLINS

Singles: 7-inch

TEEN TOWN (101 "Sometimes I Feel") .. 15-25 67
Members: Fred Regenfuss; Jim Eide; Dale Pax; Tom Marach; Robin Hauber; George Shuput.

GRESHAM, Jimmy

Singles: 7-inch

BARBARY COAST (100 "Be Prepared to Pay") ... 8-12 63
KITTY (005 "Nothing I Can Do About It"). 15-25
KITTY (105 "Now That I Have You") ... 8-12
RIGHT GROOVE ... 8-12
TAYLOR (803 "Mademoiselle") ... 25-35 59

GREY, Al

Singles: 78 rpm

KING (4650 "Goofa Nut") ... 10-15 54
PEACOCK (1609 "Over and Over") ... 10-15 53

Singles: 7-inch

ARGO ... 8-12 60-64
KING (4650 "Goofa Nut") ... 15-25 54
PEACOCK (1609 "Over and Over") ... 15-25 53

GREY, Buddy

Singles: 7-inch

CHESS (1759 "Slop Around") ... 10-20 60

GREY, Chuck

Singles: 7-inch

FABLE (616 "Push the Panic Button") ... 75-100 58
FABLE (618 "Foot Loose and Free") ... 20-30 58

GREY, Gillian

Singles: 7-inch

HAMILTON (50017 "Love Me") ... 10-20 58

GREY, Gloria

Singles: 7-inch

DEMON (1522 "Hold Me, Thrill Me, Kiss Me") ... 5-10 60
W.B. (5287 "Chapel Up in Heaven") ... 20-30 62

GREY, Joel

Singles: 78 rpm

MGM ... 5-10 53

Singles: 7-inch

COLUMBIA (44095 "Willkommen") ... 5-10 67
MGM (11561 "Too Young to Tango") ... 10-15 53
MGM (11646 "Two Faced") ... 10-15 53

LPs: 10/12-inch

CAPITOL (1373 "Songs My Father Taught Me") ... 20-30 60
CAPITOL (2755 "Songs My Father Taught Me") ... 10-15 67
COLUMBIA (2752 "Only the Beginning") .10-15 67
(Monaural.)
COLUMBIA (9552 "Only the Beginning") .10-15 67
(Stereo.)
COLUMBIA (9794 "Black Sheep") ... 8-12 69

GREY, Joel, & Roberto Seto

Singles: 7-inch

BIG TOP (3086 "Brigitte Bardot") ... 10-20 61
Also see GREY, Joel

GRIECO, Frank

Singles: 7-inch

FHG (101 "To Love Again") ... 75-125

GRIER, Frankie, Quartet

Singles: 7-inch

SWAN (4019 "Oh Gloria") ... 350-450 58

GRIER, Roosevelt
(Rosie Grier; Rosy Grier)

Singles: 7-inch

A (105 "Why Don't You Do Right") ... 50-100 59
A (110 "Smokey Mornin' ") ... 10-20 60
A&M (1457 "Beautiful People") ... 4-6 73
A&M (1500 "You're the Violin") ... 4-6 74
ABC (11275 "Rat Race") ... 4-8 70
A.G.P. (109 "Bad News") ... 5-10 69
AMY (11004 "Half Time") ... 5-10 67
AMY (11015 "C'mon Cupid") ... 5-10 68
AMY (11029 "People Make the World") ... 5-10 68
BATTLE (45911 "Why") ... 10-15 63
BELL (45459 "It's All Right to Cry") ... 4-8 74
D-TOWN (1058 "Pizza Pie Man") ... 20-30 66
LIBERTY (55413 "Struttin' and Twistin' ") ... 8-12 62
LIBERTY (55453 "Your Has Been") ... 8-12 62
MGM (13698 "Yesterday") ... 5-10 67
MGM (13840 "Spanish Harlem") ... 5-10 67
RIC (102 "Fool Fool Fool") ... 10-20 64
RIC (112 "Down So Long") ... 10-20 64
SPINDLE TOP (102 "Jinny") ... 10-15 61
20TH FOX ... 4-6 75
U.A. (50893 "Bring Back the Time") ... 4-6 72

LPs: 10/12-inch

RIC (1008 "Soul City") ... 15-25 64

GRIFFIN, Bill

Singles: 7-inch

NAPTOWN (904 "Try to Run a Game on Me") ... 20-30 '60s

GRIFFIN, Buck

Singles: 78 rpm

LIN ... 10-20 54
MGM ... 15-25 56

Singles: 7-inch

HOLIDAY INN (109 "Pretty Lou") ... 15-25 62
LIN (1005 "Meadowlark Boogie") ... 30-50 54
LIN (1007 "Rollin' Tears") ... 50-75 55
LIN (1008 "Going Home All Alone") ... 50-75 55
LIN (1014 "Next to Mine") ... 30-50 55
LIN (1015 "Ballin' and Squallin' ") ... 50-75 55
LIN (1016 "Go, Stop-O") ... 50-75 55
LIN (1018 "Little Dan") ... 30-50 56
LIN (5030 "First Man on the Moon") ... 10-20 63
METRO (20007 "The Party") ... 50-75 58
MGM (12284 "Stutterin' Papa") ... 50-75 56
MGM (12439 "Bow My Back") ... 50-75 57
MGM (12597 "Jessie Lee") ... 50-75 57
ROTARY (460 "I Can't Keep My Wheels on the Ground") ... 50-75

LPs: 10/12-inch

LONDON ... 50-75
(Canadian.)

GRIFFIN, Buddy

Singles: 78 rpm

EKKO (1017 "A Red Rose, A Bouquet") ... 5-10 55

Singles: 7-inch

EKKO (1017 "A Red Rose, A Bouquet") ... 10-20 55
Also see BUDDY & CLAUDIA

GRIFFIN, C.C.

Singles: 7-inch

ALLEGRO ... 10-20 63
JOYCE (1001 "Storm Clouds") ... 10-20 61

GRIFFIN, Curley

Singles: 78 rpm

ATOMIC (303 "You Gotta Play Fair") ... 50-75 56
ATOMIC(305 "Got Rockin' on My Mind") .. 50-75 56

Singles: 7-inch

ATOMIC (303 "You Gotta Play Fair") ... 200-300 56
ATOMIC (305 "Got Rockin' on My Mind") ... 300-350 56

GRIFFIN, George, & Ensembles

Singles: 7-inch

SEAFAIR (102 "I'll Be at Your Side") ... 20-30 61

GRIFFIN, Herman
(With the Mello-Dees; with Rayber Voices; with Gerry Jackson; with Boys in the Band; with Boys)

Singles: 7-inch

ANNA (1115 "Hurry Up and Marry Me") ... 15-25 60
COLUMBIA (41951 "It's You") ... 10-20 61
DOUBLE L (718 "Never Trust Your Girl Friend") ... 20-30 63
HOUSE OF BEAUTY (112 "I Need You") ... 10-20 60
MAGIC TOUCH (007 "Are You for Me Or Against Me") ... 15-25 68
MERCURY (72401 "Dream Girl") ... 35-55 65
MOTOWN (1028 "Sleep") ... 25-40 62
STEPP (237 "Hurry Up and Marry Me") ... 50-75 60
STONE BLUE (101 "The Right Direction") ... 100-200
TAMLA (54032 "It's You") ... 25-40 60
Also see HOLLAND, Eddie
Also see TWENTIE GRANS

GRIFFIN, James
(James Arthur Griffin; Jimmy Griffin)

Singles: 7-inch

IMPERIAL ... 5-10 65-66
POLYDOR ... 4-6 73-75
REPRISE ... 10-15 62-64
SHOE ... 3-5 82
VIVA ... 5-10 67-69

LPs: 10/12-inch

REPRISE (6091 "Summer Holiday") ... 20-25 63
POLYDOR (6018 "James Griffin & Co.") ... 8-12 73
Also see BLACK TIE
Also see BREAD

GRIFFIN, Jimmy

Singles: 78 rpm

ATCO ... 5-10 55-56

Singles: 7-inch

ATCO (6060 "She's a Woman") ... 10-20 55
ATCO (6068 "Little Mary") ... 15-25 56

GRIFFIN, Merv *P&R '51*
(With the Griffin Family Singers; with Percy Faith Orchestra)

Singles: 78 rpm

COLUMBIA ... 3-5 53
RCA ... 3-5 51-52

Singles: 7-inch

CAMEO (266 "Always") ... 5-10 63
CAMEO (298 "I'm Sorry I Made You Cry"). 5-10 64
CARLTON ... 5-10 61
COLUMBIA ... 10-20 53-56
CORAL (62480 "I Keep Running Away From You") ... 4-8 66
DECCA ... 10-20 '50s
DOT ... 4-8 68
GRIFFIN ... 4-6 73
MGM ... 4-8 65-67
MERCURY (71993 "Pretty Girl") ... 5-10 62
MERCURY (72069 "Casanova Bossa Nova") ... 5-10 62
METROMEDIA ... 4-6 70
RCA ... 10-20 51-52

EPs: 7-inch

RCA (3021 "Midnight Music") ... 10-20 52
RCA (3089 "Quiet Man") ... 20-25 52

LPs: 10/12-inch

CAMEO (1060 "My Favorite Songs") ... 10-20 64
CARLTON (134 "Dance Party") ... 10-20 61
MGM (4326 "Tinkling Piano in the Next Apartment") ... 10-20 65
MGM (4387 " 'Alf and 'Alf") ... 10-20 66
(With Arthur Treacher.)
METROMEDIA ... 5-10 69
RCA (3089 "Quiet Man") ... 25-35 52
(10-inch LP.)

GRIFFIN, Paul

Singles: 7-inch

GOLDEN CREST (511 "Ragdoll Baby") ... 50-75 58

Picture Sleeves

GOLDEN CREST (511 "Ragdoll Baby") .75-125 58

GRIFFIN BROTHERS *R&B '50*
(Featuring Tommy Brown; featuring Margie Day)

Singles: 78 rpm

DOT ... 20-30 50-54

Singles: 7-inch

DOT (1070 "Pretty Baby") ... 75-100 51
DOT (1071 "Weepin' & Cryin' ") ... 75-100 51
DOT (1094 "It'd Surprise You") ... 40-50 51
DOT (1095 "The Teaser") ... 40-50 51
DOT (1104 "I'm Gonna Jump in the River") ... 30-40 52
DOT (1105 "Coming Home") ... 30-40 52
DOT (1108 "Ace in the Hole") ... 30-40 52
DOT (1114 "My Story") ... 30-40 53
DOT (1117 "I Wanna Go Back") ... 30-40 53
DOT (1144 "My Story") ... 50-75 53
DOT (1145 "Black Bread") ... 50-60 53
DOT (1152 "Griff's Mambo") ... 40-50 54
DOT (1171 "Move It On Over") ... 30-40 54
DOT (16130 "Weepin' & Cryin' ") ... 10-15 60
Members: Jimmy Griffin; Edward "Buddy" Griffin.
Also see DAY, Margie

GRIFFINS

Singles: 78 rpm

MERCURY ... 20-40 55-56
WING (90067 "Forever More") ... 50-75 56

Singles: 7-inch

MERCURY (70558 "I Swear by All the Stars Above") ... 75-125 55
MERCURY (70650 "Bad Little Girl") ... 75-125 55
(Pink label.)
MERCURY (70650 "Bad Little Girl") ... 50-75 55
(Black label.)
MERCURY (70913 "My Baby's Gone") .. 75-125 56
WING (90067 "Forever More") ... 100-150 56
Members: Bill Ross; Bill Alford; Larry Tate; Josh Bright; Lewis Thompson.
Also see HEARTBREAKERS
Also see KNIGHT, Marie

GRIFFITH, Andy *P&R '54*
(Deacon Andy Griffith)

Singles: 78 rpm

CAPITOL ... 5-15 53-57
COLONIAL (3 "What It Was—Was Football") ... 8-12 53

Singles: 7-inch

CAPITOL (2500 series) ... 4-6 69
CAPITOL (2600 thru 3800 series) ... 12-25 53-58
CAPITOL (4000 & 5000 series) ... 5-10 59-63
(Purple or orange/yellow swirl labels.)
CAPITOL (4000 series) ... 4-6 76
(Orange labels.)
COLONIAL (3 "What It Was—Was Football") ... 15-25 53
COLUMBIA ... 5-10 72

EPs: 7-inch

CAPITOL ... 20-30 54-61

LPs: 10/12-inch

CAPITOL (872 "A Face in the Crowd") ... 35-50 57
(Soundtrack.)
CAPITOL (962 "Just for Laughs") ... 35-45 58
CAPITOL (1100 thru 1600 series) ... 30-40 59-61
CAPITOL (2000 series) ... 15-25 64-67
COLUMBIA ... 5-10 72

GRIFFITH, Bill

Singles: 7-inch

BELFAIR (1007 "Hey Little Judy") ... 10-15 66

GRIFFITH, Emile

Singles: 7-inch

COLUMBIA (43915 "Everybody Needs Love") ... 5-10 66
TRC (983 "Goin' Goin' Gone") ... 15-20 68

GRIFFITH, Gayle
(With the Masters)

Singles: 78 rpm

EMERALD ... 20-40 55

Singles: 7-inch

EMERALD (2003 "Rockin' & Knockin' ") .75-125 55
SAGA (1001 "Rocket Rock & Roll") ... 40-50 58

GRIFFITH, Joe, & His Teen Age Rebels

Singles: 7-inch

REELFOOT (1215 "Annabelle Lee"/"Walk, Spin, Shake and Rock") ... 200-300 58
REELFOOT (1250 "Annabelle Lee"/"Crazy Sack") ... 25-50 58

Picture Sleeves

REELFOOT (1250 "Annabelle Lee"/"Crazy Sack") ... 75-125 58

GRIFFITH, Johnny, Trio
Singles: 7-inch
WORKSHOP JAZZ (2005 "I Did")...10-15 63
LPs: 10/12-inch
WORKSHOP JAZZ (205 "Jazz")...30-50 63
Also see GREER, Paula, & Johnny Griffith Trio

GRIFFITH, Peggi
Singles: 7-inch
DOLTON (35 "Lonely Girl")...10-20 61
NOW (1008 "Rockin the Blues")...100-200 58

GRIFFITH, Wes, & Treys
Singles: 7-inch
BELLA (17 "It Hurts So Bad")...15-25 59

GRIFFITH HARTER UNION
Singles: 7-inch
JIM-KO (41075 "Progress")...10-20 65

GRIFS
Singles: 7-inch
AMG (1002 "In My Life")...20-30 66
5-D (007 "In My Life")...20-30 66
PALMER (5025 "Keep Dreamin'")...20-30 68

GRIGGS, Bobby
Singles: 7-inch
LIBERTY (55642 "Farewell Party")...8-12 63
TOWER (159 "That's Not What He's Got On His Mind")...10-15 65

GRIGGS, Sammy, & Coronets
("Vocal Charles Carothers")
Singles: 7-inch
JOB (100 "Footsteps")...300-500 60

GRIM REAPERS
Singles: 7-inch
SMACK (15 "Cruisin' for Burgers")...8-12 '60s
Picture Sleeves
SMACK (15 "Cruisin' for Burgers")...10-20 '60s
Member: Rick Nielsen.
Also see CHEAP TRICK

GRIM REEPERS
Singles: 7-inch
CHALON (1003 "Two Souls")...15-25 66

GRIMES, Jerry
Singles: 7-inch
CATHEY (201 "My Rock n' Roll Daddy")...100-200

GRIMES, Paula
Singles: 7-inch
GAYE (368 "Zing Went the Strings of My Heart")...100-150 59
TURF (2025 "You Moved Me So")...10-20 58

GRIMES, Sandra
("With Orchestra")
Singles: 78 rpm
RED ROBIN (129 "You Didn't Give Me a Chance")...15-25 54
Singles: 7-inch
RED ROBIN (129 "You Didn't Give Me a Chance")...50-75 54

GRIMES, Tiny *R&B '48*
(Tiny Grimes Quintet; Swingtet; with Highlanders)
Singles: 78 rpm
APOLLO...5-10 53
ATLANTIC...10-25 48-52
BLUE NOTE...5-15 47
GOTHAM...5-10 49-56
RED ROBIN...10-20 54
SAVOY...5-15 46-48
UNITED...5-10 52-53
Singles: 7-inch
APOLLO...10-15 53
ATLANTIC (990 "Begin the Beguine")...20-30 52
B&F...5-10 59
GOTHAM...10-20 50-56
PRESTIGE...8-12 59
RED ROBIN (123 "Juicy Fruit")...15-25 54
UNITED...10-20 52-53
LPs: 10/12-inch
PRESTIGE SWINGSVILLE...15-25 60
U.A....10-20 62
Also see HOLIDAY, Billie
Also see PRYSOCK, Red

GRINER, Linda
Singles: 7-inch
MOTOWN (1037 "Good-by Cruel World")...200-300 63
MOTOWN (1037 "Good-by Cruel Love")...100-200 63
(Note title correction: "Love" not "World.")

GRINGOS
Singles: 7-inch
DOT (16321 "Gringo Guitar")...15-25 62

GRISHAM, Marlon
(Marlon Grisham Combo)
Singles: 7-inch
CLEARPOOL (101 "Jungle Love")...60-80
COVER (4621 "Now It's Your Time")...15-25 62
COVER (5982 "Ain't That a Dilly")...400-600 59
FERNWOOD (140 "Pins and Needles in My Heart")...10-20 64

GRISSOM, Dan
(With the Ebb Tones; with Buddy Harper's Orchestra)
Singles: 78 rpm
JEWEL...10-20 48
MILLION (2011 "Recess in Heaven")...25-50 55
Singles: 7-inch
MILLION (2011 "Recess in Heaven")...50-100 55

GRISSOM, Jimmy *R&B '51*
(With the Red Callender Sextet)
Singles: 78 rpm
CASH...10-15 55
CLASS...10-15 53
FEDERAL...5-10 51
RECORDED IN HOLLYWOOD (143 "Once There Lived a Fool")...20-25 51
RECORDED IN HOLLYWOOD (149 "Once in Love Blues")...20-25 51
RECORDED IN HOLLYWOOD (153 "Walkin' Blues")...20-25 51
RECORDED IN HOLLYWOOD (245 "So Help Me, I Love You")...20-25 52
Singles: 7-inch
ARGO (5460 "World of Trouble")...5-10 64
CASH (1006 "Listen Pretty Baby")...20-30 55
CLASS (504 "When the Swallows Come Back to Capistrano")...15-25 53
FEDERAL (12046 "Once in Love Blues")...15-25 51
LPs: 10/12-inch
ARGO (729 "World of Trouble")...15-20 64
Also see CALLENDER, Red
Also see ELLINGTON, Duke

GRODECK WHIPPERJENNY
LPs: 10/12-inch
PEOPLE (3000 "Grodeck Whipperjenny")...50-100 67
Members: Kenny Poole; Mary Ellen Bell; Dave Matthews; Mike Moore; Jim Madison.

GRODES
Singles: 7-inch
IMPRESSION (114 "What They Say About Love")...15-25 67
RALLY (505 "Love Is a Sad Song")...20-30 66
SPLITSOUND (4 "Give Me Some Time")...15-25 67
TRI-M (1001 "Uh Huh Girl")...10-20 65
TRI-M (1002 "Cry a Little Longer")...10-20 66
Also see TONGUES OF TRUTH / Grodes

GROGAN, Toby
Singles: 7-inch
VEE-JAY (560 "Angel")...10-20 63

GROLL, Ray
Singles: 7-inch
ROULETTE (4356 "S.W.A.K.")...5-10 61

GROOMS, Sherry *C&W '77*
Singles: 7-inch
ABC (10875 "Night Fall")...15-25 67
PARACHUTE (514 "Me")...4-6 78

GROOP
Singles: 7-inch
BELL (800 "Tears and Joy")...10-15 69
BELL (822 "Jet Song")...10-15 69
JAMIE (1349 "Mad Over You")...5-10 68
JAMIE (1371 "Such a Lovely Way")...5-10 69

GROSS SISTERS
Singles: 7-inch
CHECKER (932 "Oom Baby")...20-30 59

GROTESQUE MOMMIES
Singles: 7-inch
PIECE (1002 "One Night Stand")...25-35

GROUND FLOOR PEOPLE
Singles: 7-inch
MERCURY (72719 "Workaday World")...10-20 67

GROUNDHOGS
Singles: 7-inch
INTERPHON (7715 "Rock Me")...5-10 65
LIBERTY (56205 "Ship on the Ocean")...4-8 70
EPs: 7-inch
U.A....10-12 71
LPs: 10/12-inch
CLEVE (82871 "Groundhogs")...35-40 '60s
(With John Lee Hooker & John Mayall.)
IMPERIAL...15-20 69
LIBERTY...8-10 70
U.A....10-12 71-76
WORLD PACIFIC (21892 "Scratchin the Surface")...30-40 68
Session: Bruce Kulick.
Also see HOOKER, John Lee
Also see JOHN LEE
Also see KISS
Also see MAYALL, John

GROUNDSPEED
Singles: 7-inch
DECCA (32344 "In a Dream")...15-20 68

GROUP, The
LPs: 10/12-inch
RCA (2663 "The Group")...12-18 63
U.A. (5198 "Midnight Cowboy")...10-15 69

GROUP, The
Singles: 7-inch
FREAK (9240 "Why Does My Head Go Boom")...15-25 '60s
W.B. (5840 "Baby, Baby It's You")...5-10 66

GROUP AXIS
Singles: 7-inch
ATCO (6642 "Not Fade Away")...10-15 69

GROUP "B"
Singles: 7-inch
SCORPIO (402 "Stop Calling Me")...10-20 66
SCORPIO (406 "I Know Your Name Girl")...10-20 67
Members: Dick Peterson; Jerri Peterson; Danny Mihm.
Also see BLUE CHEER
Also see FLAMIN' GROOVIES

GROUP FROM QUEENS
Singles: 7-inch
VEEP (1238 "Boss Man")...10-15 66

GROUP INC.
Singles: 7-inch
FREEPORT (1008 "Like a Woman")...10-15 66
STAFF (177 "Like a Woman")...15-25 66

GROUP LOVE CORP.
Singles: 7-inch
PRIDE (8450 "Love Corporation")...30-40

GROUP 1
LPs: 10/12-inch
RCA (3524 "Brothers Go to Mothers – and Others")...10-15 66

GROUPIES
Singles: 7-inch
ATCO (6393 "Primitive")...15-25 65

GROVE, Bobby
Singles: 7-inch
KING (5786 "It Was for You")...5-10 63
KING (5838 "Mockingbird")...5-10 64
LPs: 10/12-inch
KING (831 "It Was For You")...20-35 63

GROVES, Big Boy
(Ervin "Big Boy" Groves; with Grovettes)
Singles: 78 rpm
MONEY (217 "The Solid Rock")...15-20 56
SPARK (114 "I Got a New Car")...10-15 55
VITA (120 "Big Boy's Bounce")...10-15 56
Singles: 7-inch
GME (227 "Teenage Party")...10-15 62
GME (229 "A Million Years Ago")...15-25 62
MONEY (217 "The Solid Rock")...20-30 56
SPARK (114 "I Got a New Car")...20-30 55
VITA (120 "Big Boy's Bounce")...20-30 56

GROWING CONCERN
Singles: 7-inch
MAINSTREAM (685 "Tomorrow Has Been Canceled")...10-20 68
LPs: 10/12-inch
MAINSTREAM (6108 "The Growing Concern")...50-100 68
Members: Mary Gartski; Bonnie MacDonald; Pete Guerino; Dan Passaglia.

GROWING SOCIETY
Singles: 7-inch
DUNHILL (4093 "The Red Fuzz")...8-15 67
MR. BONES ("The Big Red Tomato")...10-20 67
(Selection number not known.)

GRUBBS, Jimmy, & His Music Makers
Singles: 7-inch
MAC (468 "Let's Rock To-Night")...1000-1200

GRUNION HUNTERS
Singles: 7-inch
HIGHLAND (1035 "Four-Eyed, Tongue-Tied, Swimmin' Surfer")...20-30 63

GRUNIONS
Singles: 7-inch
JOCKO (505 "Surfin Psycho")...25-30 63

GRUVE
Singles: 7-inch
LIBERTY (56034 "Said I Wasn't Gonna Tell")...20-40 68

GRYPHON
LPs: 10/12-inch
BELL (1316 "Red Queen to Gryphon Three")...15-25 74
NR (12497 "Gryphon")...50-75 '70s
Member: Geoff Gibor.

GUADALAJARA KINGS
Singles: 7-inch
LIBERTY (55878 "Sandpiper Theme")...5-10 66
LIBERTY (55907 "Ciao, Ciao Bambina")...5-10 66
LIBERTY (55918 "Granada")...5-10 66

GUARALDI, Vince *P&R '62*
(Vince Guaraldi Trio)
Singles: 7-inch
FANTASY...4-8 62-66
LPs: 10/12-inch
FANTASY (3200 series)...20-30 56-58
FANTASY (3300 series)...15-25 62-66
FANTASY (8000 series)...15-25 62
FANTASY (8300 series)...10-20 63-66
MFSL (112 "Jazz Impressions of Black Orpheus")...30-50 84
W.B....8-12 68-69
Also see TJADER, Cal
Also see TJADER, Cal, & Stan Getz

GUARD, Dave, & Whiskeyhill Singers
Singles: 7-inch
CAPITOL (4787 "Ride On Railroad Bill")...5-10 62
LPs: 10/12-inch
CAPITOL (1728 "Dave Guard and the Whiskeyhill Singers")...15-20 62
Members: Dave Guard; Cyrus Faryar; Judy Henske; David "Buck" Wheat.
Also see HENSKE, Judy
Also see KINGSTON TRIO
Also see MFQ

GUARDSMEN
Singles: 7-inch
GOLDCREST (163 "The Weasel")...10-20 61

GUARNIERI, Johnny
Singles: 7-inch
MAGNIFIQUE...8-12 64
LPs: 10/12-inch
BET (1000 "Breakthrough in 5/4")...10-15 69
DOT (3647 "Piano Dimensions")...15-20 65
(Monaural.)
DOT (25647 "Piano Dimensions")...20-25 65
(Stereo.)

GUENTHER, Woody, & Cheaters
Singles: 7-inch
SHOUT (229 "Teardrops")...15-25 68

GUERILLAS

Singles: 7-inch

DONNA (1406 "Lonely") 10-15 65

GUERRERO, Lalo

(Lalo "Pancho Lopez" Guerrero; with Irene Brunilda)

Singles: 78 rpm

L&M 10-20 56
REAL 10-20 55

Singles: 7-inch

CAP/LATINO 4-6
DISCOS CLAVE 4-6
L&M (1000 "Pound Dog") 20-30 56
L&M (1001 "Elvis Perez") 20-30 56
L&M (1003 "Pancho Claus") 10-20 56
REAL (1301 "Pancho Lopez") 15-25 55
REAL (1303 "Mickey Mouse Mambo") 10-20 55

GUESS, Don

Singles: 7-inch

BRUNSWICK (55101 "Shir-Lee") 30-50 58
PROFILE (100 "I Fell in Love") 20-30 59
PROFILE (103 "Hold Back the Night") 50-75 59
RORO (5873 "Bony Maronie") 8-12
YUCCA (111 "Imagination") 20-30 59
Also see HOLLY, Buddy
Also see ROSES
Also see TUCKER, Rick

GUESS, Lenis

Singles: 7-inch

D.P.G. (1007 "Thank Goodness") 10-15 65
LEGRAND (1042 "Working for My Baby") 15-20 66
(First issue.)
LEGRAND (1044 "In My Room") 8-12 67
PEANUT COUNTRY (1002 "Thank Goodness Gotta Good Woman") 8-12 66
S.P.Q.R. (1102 "Working for My Baby") 8-12 66
S.P.Q.R. (2000 "Old Mill Road") 8-12

GUESS WHO *P&R '65*

Singles: 7-inch

AMY (967 "And She's Mine") 10-20 66
AMY (976 "It's My Pride") 10-20 67
FONTANA (1597 "There's No Gettin' Away from You") 10-15 69
HILLTAK (7803 "C'mon Little Mama") 4-6 78
HILLTAK (7807 "Sweet Young Thing") 4-6 79
QUALITY 10-20 65-68
(Canadian.)
RCA 4-8 69-76
RCA RECORDING SERVICES (55829 "Two Wheel Freedom") 4-8
SCEPTER (12108 "Goodnight, Goodnight") 10-20 65
SCEPTER (12118 "Hurting Each Other") 10-20 65
SCEPTER (12131 "Believe Me") 10-20 66
SCEPTER (12144 "One Day") 10-20 66

Picture Sleeves

RCA (0388 "Share the Land") 8-12 70
RCA (0414 "Hang On to Your Life") 8-12 71

EPs: 7-inch

RCA (4574 "So Long, Bannatine") 4-6 71

LPs: 10/12-inch

HILLTAK 5-10 79
MGM (4645 "Guess Who") 15-20 69
PICKWICK 8-10 72
PIP 8-10 71
PRIDE 8-10 73
RCA (Except "AYL1" & LSP-4000 series) 8-12 73-80
RCA ("AYL1" series) 5-10 80
RCA (LSP-4141 thru LSP-4830) 15-25 69-72
RCA (1004 "Best of the Guess Who") 10-20 71
(With bonus, black light poster.)
RCA (1004 "Best of the Guess Who") 8-12 71
(Without bonus poster.)
SCEPTER 8-12 73
SPRINGBOARD 8-12 72
WAND 15-20 69
Members: Chad Allen; Burton Cummings; Randy Bachman; Domenic Troiano.
Also see ALLEN, Chad
Also see WOLFMAN JACK

GUESS WHO / Discotays

Singles: 7-inch

SCEPTER (1295 "Shakin' All Over"/"Till We Kissed") 15-20 65
Also see GUESS WHO

GUESS WHO / Staccatos

LPs: 10/12-inch

RCA/COCA-COLA (100 "Wild Pair") 15-25 '60s
(Canadian. Promotional issue for Coca-Cola.)

GUEVARA, Ruben

Singles: 7-inch

BIG 7 INCH (002 "Star Spangled Banner") 40-60 76
Also see APPOLLO BROTHERS
Also see RUBEN & JETS

GUGEL, Les Barney

Singles: 7-inch

CUCA (6551 "My Hog's Gone Wild") 15-25 65
CUCA (6552 "Devil Woman") 15-25 65

GUIDED TOUR

Singles: 7-inch

SOUND 80 (42-1448 "In a World Full of Fright") 25-35 '60s

GUIDES

Singles: 7-inch

GUYDEN (2023 "How Long Must a Fool Go On") 30-40 59
(First pressings mistakenly credit the Swallows.)
Also see DANDEVILLES
Also see SWALLOWS
Also see UPTONES

GUIDRY, Johnny

Singles: 7-inch

LYNN (514 "The Place") 10-15 61
(First issue.)
MERCURY (71877 "The Place") 5-10 61
SCOPE (101 "High School Dance") 15-25 59

GUILBEAU & PARSONS

Singles: 7-inch

BAKERSFIELD INT'L (1001 "Louisiana Rain") 30-40 68
Members: Floyd "Gib" Guilbeau; Gram Parsons.
Also see PARSONS, Gram

GUILES, Johnny Gee

Singles: 7-inch

COOL ("Just Call On Me") 50-75
(Selection number not known.)

GUILLORY, Teola

(Teola)

Singles: 7-inch

HALL WAY (1908 "Don't Believe It") 10-15 62
HALL WAY (1916 "He's Good Enough for Me") 8-12 63

GUILLOTEENS

Singles: 7-inch

COLUMBIA (43852 "Wild Child") 8-12 66
COLUMBIA (44089 "I Love That Girl") 5-10 66
HBR (446 "I Don't Believe") 8-12 65
HBR (451 "For My Own") 8-12 65
HBR (486 "I Sit and Cry") 10-15 66

Picture Sleeves

COLUMBIA (43852 "Wild Child") 20-30 66
(Promotional issue only.)
HBR (451 "For My Own") 10-20 65
Members: Louis Paul Jr.; Loddie Hutcherson; Joe Davis.

GUISE

Singles: 7-inch

ATCO 5-10 68-69
MUSICLAND USA (20011 "Long Haired Music") 10-20 67
MUSICLAND USA (20015 "Half a Man") 10-20 67

GUITAR, Billy, & Night Hawks

Singles: 7-inch

APEX (76185 "Here Comes the Night") 25-30 58
DECCA (30634 "Here Comes the Night") 40-60 58

GUITAR, Bonnie *C&W/P&R '57*

Singles: 78 rpm

DOT 10-15 57
FABOR (Except 4018) 5-10 55-56
FABOR (4018 "Dark Moon") 15-25 57
4 STAR 5-10 56

Singles: 7-inch

ABC 4-6 74
CHARTER (9 "Outside Looking In") 5-10 63
COLUMBIA (45643 "Happy Everything") 4-8 72
DOLTON (10 "Candy Apple Red") 10-15 59
DOLTON (19 "Candy Apple Red") 10-15 60
DOT (134 "Dark Moon") 5-10 63
DOT (15550 "Dark Moon") 15-20 57
DOT (15587 thru 15894) 10-15 57-59
DOT (16000 & 17000 series) 4-8 66-69
FABOR (138 "Ra Ta Ta Ta") 5-8 64
FABOR (4013 "If You See My Love Dancing") 10-20 56
FABOR (4017 "Clinging Vine") 10-20 56
FABOR (4018 "Dark Moon") 30-40 57
(First issue.)
4 STAR (1006 "I Want to Spend My Life with You") 4-6 75
4 STAR (1041 "Honey on the Moon") 3-5 80
JERDEN (707 "There'll Be No Teardrops Tonight") 5-10 63
MCA (40306 "From This Moment On") 4-6 74
PARAMOUNT (0045 "Allegheny") 5-7 70
PLAYBACK 3-5 89
RCA (7951 "Tell Her Bye") 10-20 61
RCA (8063 "Who Is She") 10-20 62
RADIO (101 "Please, My Love") 5-10 58
RADIO (110 "Only the Moon Man Knows") 5-10 58

LPs: 10/12-inch

CAMDEN (2339 "Night Train to Memphis") 8-12 69
DOT (Except 3069 & 3385) 10-15 59-68
DOT (3069 "Moonlight and Shadows") 15-25 57
DOT (3385 "Dark Moon") 15-20 63
HAMILTON (169 "Sings") 8-12 65
(Monaural.)
HAMILTON (12169 "Sings") 10-15 65
(Stereo.)
LEAL (1001 "Bonnie Guitar") 5-10
PARAMOUNT 8-12 70
PICKWICK 6-12 70
PLAYBACK (13012 "What Can I Say") 5-10
TUMBLEWEED (116 "Yesterday") 5-10 85
TUMBLEWEED (117 "Today") 5-10 85
Also see ECHOES

GUITAR, Jeff

Singles: 7-inch

CREOLE (1762 "Wait a Minute Baby") 75-100
ROCKET (502 "Jump & Shout") 100-125

GUITAR, Johnny

Singles: 7-inch

CONTESTE (1 "Track Seven") 15-25 58

GUITAR, Sonny

Singles: 7-inch

YUCCA (136 "Betty Lou") 75-125 61

GUITAR CRUSHER

Singles: 7-inch

BETHLEHEM (3034 "Lift Me Up Angel") 10-20 62
BETHLEHEM (3056 "Monkey") 10-20 62
KING (5743 "Weak for Your Love") 10-20 63
KING (5813 "I Can't Help It") 10-20 63
COLUMBIA (44217 "Goin' Down Slow") 5-10 67
T&S (101 "Cuddle Up") 15-20

GUITAR FRANK

Singles: 7-inch

BRIDGES MUSIC DEN ("Wild Track") 20-25 60
(Selection number not known.)

GUITAR GABLE

Singles: 7-inch

EXCELLO (2082 "Congo Mambo") 10-20 57
EXCELLO (2094 "Irene") 10-20 57
EXCELLO (2108 "It's Hard but It's Fair") 10-20 57
EXCELLO (2140 "Walking in the Park") 10-20 58
EXCELLO (2153 "This Should Go On Forever") 10-20 59

GUITAR MURPHY

Singles: 7-inch

EMERSON (5555 "Sufferin' Soul") 10-20 64

GUITAR NUBBITT

Singles: 7-inch

BLUESTOWN (701 "Evil Hearted Woman") 10-20 62
BLUESTOWN (702 "Hard Road") 10-20 63
BLUESTOWN (705 "I've Got the Blues") 10-20 64
BLUESTOWN (707 "Crying Blues") 10-20 65

GUITAR RAMBLERS

Singles: 7-inch

COLUMBIA 10-15 64

LPs: 10/12-inch

COLUMBIA (2067 "Happy, Youthful New Sounds") 15-25 64
(Monaural.)
COLUMBIA (8867 "Happy, Youthful New Sounds") 25-35 64
(Stereo.)

GUITAR RAY

Singles: 7-inch

SHAGG (711 "You're Gonna Wreck My Life") 20-30

GUITAR RED

(Paul Johnson)

Singles: 7-inch

CHECKER (988 "Old Fashioned Love") 5-10 61
EXCELLO (2085 "Hot Potato") 15-25 57
EXCELLO (2086 "Chili Pot") 20-30 57
FORMAL (1007 "Red Hot Devil") 15-25 58
Also see JOHNSON, Paul

GUITAR SHORTY

Singles: 7-inch

COBRA (5017 "You Don't Treat Me Right") 50-75 57
PULL (301 "Ways of a Man") 200-300 59

GUITAR SLIM *P&R/R&B '54*

(With Lloyd Lambert & His Orchestra; Eddie Jones)

Singles: 78 rpm

ATCO 15-25 56
IMPERIAL 30-40 54
SPECIALTY 30-40 53-56

Singles: 7-inch

ATCO (6072 "Oh Yeah") 25-35 56
ATCO (6097 thru 6120) 15-25 57-58
IMPERIAL (5278 "Woman Troubles") 40-50 54
IMPERIAL (5310 "New Arrival") 40-50 54
SPECIALTY (482 "The Things That I Used to Do") 40-50 53
SPECIALTY (490 "The Story of My Life") 40-50 54
SPECIALTY (527 thru 569) 30-40 54-56

LPs: 10/12-inch

SPECIALTY 8-10 70-88
Also see CHARLES, Ray
Also see JONES, Eddie

GUITAR SLIM

(Johnny Winter)

Singles: 7-inch

DIAMOND JIM (204 "Crying in My Heart") 100-150 62
(Reissued as by Texas "Guitar" Slim.)
Also see TEXAS "GUITAR" SLIM
Also see WINTER, Johnny

GUITARS INC.

Singles: 7-inch

W.B. (5049 "Guy Dad, It's Early") 15-25 59

GUITARS INC.

Singles: 7-inch

HAMILTON (50035 "Little Toy") 15-25 63
Also see FIREBALLS

GULLEY, Charles

Singles: 7-inch

C.J. (641 "Hey Little Baby") 10-15 64
C.J. (650 "Wonderful Thing") 10-15 65

GUNN, Stan

Singles: 7-inch

RON MAR (1002 "Baby Sitter Boogie") 200-300

GUNNER, Bob

Singles: 7-inch

ROBEY ("3rd Straight Hit") 10-20 65
(Single-sided. No selection number used. A promotional announcement by Duke/Peacock's Bob Gunner, who is not credited on label, plugging a Bobby Bland release. Includes a segment of a Bobby Bland track. Promotional issue only.)
Also see BLAND, Bobby

GUNS 'N' ROSES *LP '87*

Singles: 12-inch

GEFFEN 4-8 89

Singles: 7-inch

GEFFEN 3-5 88-92

Picture Sleeves

GEFFEN 3-5 88-89

LPs: 10/12-inch
GEFFEN (Except 24148 & 24617)..............5-10 88-89
GEFFEN (24148 "Appetite for Destruction").. 50-75 87
(With robot/rape painting on cover.)
GEFFEN (24148 "Appetite for Destruction")..5-8 87
(With skulls and cross cover.)
GEFFEN (24617 "Spaghetti Incident")..... 10-15 93
(Colored vinyl.)
UZI SUICIDE (001 "Live Like a Suicide")... 150-200 86
Members: Axl Rose; Slash; Duff McKagan; Saul Hudson; Steve Adler; Izzy Stradlin; Matt Sorum; Dizzy Reed; Gilby Clarke.

GUNTER, Arthur *R&B '55*
Singles: 78 rpm
EXCELLO... 25-50 54-57
Singles: 7-inch
EXCELLO (2047 "Baby Let's Play House").. 75-100 54
EXCELLO (2053 "She's Mine, All Mine"). 50-75 55
EXCELLO (2058 "Honey Babe")............. 40-60 55
EXCELLO (2073 thru 2137)..................... 20-30 56-59
EXCELLO (2147 thru 2204)..................... 15-25 59-61
LPs: 10/12-inch
EXCELLO (8017 "Black & Blues")........... 10-15 71

GUNTER, Cornell
(With the Flairs; with Ermines)
Singles: 78 rpm
ABC-PAR (9689 "She Loves to Rock").... 10-15 56
DOT (15654 "You Send Me").................. 10-20 57
EAGLE (301 "Baby Come Home")........... 15-25 57
LOMA (701 thru 705).............................. 25-50 55-56
Singles: 7-inch
ABC-PAR (9689 "She Loves to Rock").... 15-25 56
CHALLENGE (59281 "Wishful Thinking") 10-15 64
DOT (15654 "You Send Me").................. 15-25 57
EAGLE (301 "Baby Come Home")........... 15-25 57
LIBERTY (55096 "If We Should Meet Again")... 10-20 57
LOMA (701 "True Love")....................... 75-125 55
LOMA (703 "You Broke My Heart")...... 100-150 56
LOMA (704 "Keep Me Alive").............. 150-200 56
LOMA (705 "I'm Sad")......................... 150-200 56
W.B. (5266 "Lift Me Up Angel")............... 10-20 62
W.B. (5292 "In a Dream of Love")........... 10-20 62
Members: Cornell Gunter; Ken Byle; Tommy Miller; George Hollis; Robbie Robinson; Beverley Harris.
Also see COASTERS
Also see FLAIRS
Also see JAC-O-LACS
Also see PENGUINS
Also see PLATTERS

GUNTER, Hardrock
(Hardrock & Rhythm Rockers with the Buddy Durham Singers)
Singles: 78 rpm
BAMA (9 "Birmingham Bounce")............. 20-40 51
DECCA... 10-15 52-53
EMPEROR (112 "Whoo! I Mean Wheel!").. 50-100 57
KING (4858 "Before My Time")............... 10-15 55
SUN (201 "Gonna Dance All Night").... 200-250 54
Singles: 7-inch
DECCA... 10-20 52-53
EMPEROR (112 "Whoo! I Mean Wheel!").. 100-150 57
KING (4858 "Before My Time")............... 10-20 55
MORGUN (273 "Don't Hold No Benefits for Me")..4-6 '70s
SUN (201 "Gonna Dance All Night") 1000-2000 54
Also see RHYTHM ROCKERS

GUNTER, Launa, with Queen City Ramblers
Singles: 7-inch
EXCELLENT (807 "He's My Man")...... 100-150 58

GUNTER, Shirley *R&B '54*
(With the Flairs; with Queens; with Monroe Tucker Orchestra; with Maxwell Davis Orchestra)
Singles: 78 rpm
FLAIR (Except 1076)............................ 10-15 53-55
FLAIR (1076 "How Can I Tell You")......... 20-30 55
MODERN.. 10-15 55-56
Singles: 7-inch
FLAIR (Except 1076)............................ 15-25 53-55
FLAIR (1076 "How Can I Tell You")......... 30-40 55
MODERN.. 15-25 55-56
TANGERINE (949 "Stuck Up")...................5-10 65
Members: Shirley Gunter; Lula Bea Kinney; Lula Mae Suggs; Zola Taylor.
Also see FLAIRS
Also see TAYLOR, Zola

GUNTHER, Gloria
Singles: 7-inch
ARCH (1610 "Move On Out")....................15-25 59

GUTHRIE, Jack *C&W '45*
Singles: 78 rpm
CAPITOL..10-20 45-47
LPs: 10/12-inch
CAPITOL (2456 "Greatest Songs")...........25-35 66

GUY, Art
Singles: 7-inch
VALIANT (762 "Where You Gonna Go")..15-25 67

GUY, Bob
(Frank Zappa)
Singles: 7-inch
DONNA (1380 "Letter from Jeepers").......50-75 63
Also see ZAPPA, Frank

GUY, Bobby
(Howard Guyton; with Sparkletones)
Singles: 7-inch
APT (25052 "A Vow")...............................10-15 60
MIDA (104 "Let's Dance")..........................50-75 58
Also see FIVE PEARLS
Also see GUYTON, Howard
Also see HOWIE & SAPPHIRES
Also see PEARLS
Also see POWELL, Jessie

GUY, Browley, & Skyscrapers
Singles: 78 rpm
CHECKER (779 "Watermelon Man")........50-75 54
MIRACLE (137 "Knock Me a Zombie")......20-30 49
STATES (101 "Marie")...............................50-75 52
STATES (107 "Blues Train")......................50-75 52
Singles: 7-inch
CHECKER (779 "Watermelon Man")....100-200 54
(Black vinyl.)
CHECKER (779 "Watermelon Man")....500-600 54
(Red vinyl.)
Also see SKYSCRAPERS

GUY, Buddy *R&B '62*
Singles: 78 rpm
ARTISTIC (1501 "Sit and Cry")..............75-125 58
Singles: 7-inch
ARTISTIC (1501 "Sit and Cry")................25-35 58
ARTISTIC (1503 "You Sure Can Do").......25-35 58
CHESS (1753 "I Got My Eyes on You")...15-25 60
CHESS (1759 thru 2067)..........................10-20 60-69
VANGUARD (35060 "Sweet Little Angel") .5-10 67
VANGUARD (35080 "Fever").......................5-10 68
LPs: 10/12-inch
BLUE THUMB (20 "Buddy & the Jrs.").......8-10 70
BLUES BALL..15-25
CHESS (1527 "Left My Blues in San Francisco")..10-15 69
VANGUARD (9272 "Man and the Blues")..15-20 68
VANGUARD (9290 "This Is Buddy Guy").15-20 68
Session: Otis Spann; Jerret Gibson; Leonard Caston; Donald Hankins; Jack Meyers; Clifton James; Lafayette Leake; Al Duncan; Willie Dixon; Fred Below; Bob Neely.
Also see DIXON, Willie
Also see SPANN, Otis
Also see TAYLOR, Koko
Also see WELLS, Junior, & Buddy Guy

GUY, Buddy, with Dr. John & Eric Clapton / Buddy Guy with the J. Geils Band
Singles: 7-inch
ATCO (6890 "Man of Many Words"/"Honey Dripper")..4-8 72
Also see CLAPTON, Eric

GUY, Dewey, & Fabulous Six
Singles: 7-inch
RIDGECREST (1201 "Rock a While")..150-250 59

GUY, Vernon
Singles: 7-inch
ELECTRIC LAND (3 "Ooh Vernon")............4-6 80
SONJA (2007 "Anything to Make It with You")..20-30 63
TEENA (1703 "They Ain't Lovin' You").....30-40 63
Also see SHARPEES
Also see TURNER, Ike & Tina

GUYS
Singles: 7-inch
ORIGINAL SOUND (56 "Walkin' by the School")...10-20 65

GUYS & DOLLS
Singles: 7-inch
APOSTROPHE...8-12
KAROL (42670 "Could This Be Love").......8-12
MELLOW (1006 "You Left Me")...............30-40 67
MELLOW (1008 "Strange World")...........10-20 67
TODDLIN' TOWN (132 "Let's Push and Pull")..8-12 70
TODDLIN' TOWN (135 "Heartaches")......10-20 70

GUYS FROM UNCLE
Singles: 7-inch
SWAN (4228 "I Will Love You")..................5-10 65
SWAN (4240 "The Spy")...........................10-15 66

GUYS WHO CAME UP FROM DOWNSTAIRS
Singles: 7-inch
DISC-GUYS (6836 "Growth")................50-100 66
(Reportedly 200 made.)
Also see GRANDMA'S ROCKERS

GUYTON, Howard
Singles: 7-inch
VERVE (10386 "I Watched You Slowly Slip Away")..50-75 66
Also see GUY, Bobby

GUYTONES
Singles: 78 rpm
DELUXE...20-30 57
Singles: 7-inch
DELUXE (6144 "You Won't Let Me Go")..40-60 57
DELUXE (6152 "She's Mine")..................40-60 57
DELUXE (6159 "This Is Love")..................40-60 57
DELUXE (6163 "Baby, I Don't Care").......50-75 58
DELUXE (6169 "Tell Me").........................40-50 58

GYPSIES
Singles: 78 rpm
GROOVE..8-12 55-56
Singles: 7-inch
GROOVE (0117 "I'm Good to You").........20-30 55
GROOVE (0129 "You've Been Away Too Long")..20-30 55
GROOVE (0137 "Rockin' Pretty Baby")...15-25 56

GYPSIES
("Gypsies Vocal Group")
Singles: 7-inch
ANGLE TONE (1073 "Why").........................3-5
ATLAS (1073 "Why")............................300-500 57

GYPSIES *R&B '65*
Singles: 7-inch
CAPRICE (8442 "Oh Girl")..........................8-10 66
OLD TOWN (1168 "Blue Bird")................10-20 64
OLD TOWN (1180 "Jerk It").....................10-20 65
OLD TOWN (1184 "It's a Woman's World")..40-60 65
OLD TOWN (1193 "Oh I Wonder Why")...10-20 66
Members: Betty Pearce; Ernestine Pearce; Shirley Pearce; Lestine Johnson.

GYPSY TRIPS
Singles: 7-inch
WORLD PACIFIC (77809 "Rock & Roll Gypsies")..15-25 65
Members: Roger Tillison; Terry Tillison.
Also see LEATHERCOATED MINDS

Colt 45
Reg. U.S. Pat. Off.
Wash. 7, D.C. U.S.A.
21 & Penn Ave NW
45-107
BARRY DARVELL
TIME - 1:52
R. LYDON
GERONIMO STOMP
POTOMAC PUB. CO., INC. - BMI
ZTSP 62197

JERRY-O
RECORDS
BMI – 2:10
106
EX 45-789-A
MELLOW - FEZNECKEY
(Jimmy Jones - J. Murray)
THE DUKAYS

Dion
DiMuci
DION
SINGS HIS GREATEST HITS
EXTRA ADDED ATTRACTION
THE BELMONTS

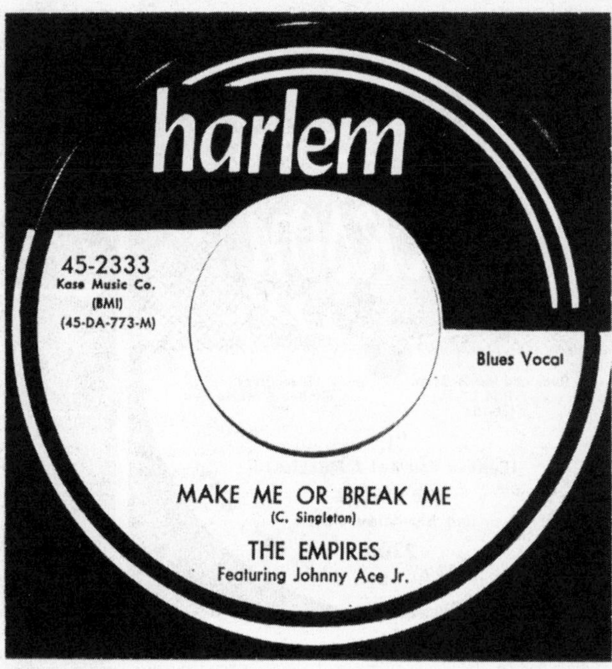
harlem
45-2333
Kase Music Co.
(BMI)
(45-DA-773-M)
Blues Vocal
MAKE ME OR BREAK ME
(C. Singleton)
THE EMPIRES
Featuring Johnny Ace Jr.

GOTTA LEAVE THIS TOWN
(Call, Rich, Crowley)
ECCO
Boise
Music Publishers
BMI
(X-1000)
Time: 2:37
THE
Fabulous
CHANCELLORS
RECORDS
JOHN FOGERTY
PRO-A-2595
PROMOTIONAL COPY.
NOT FOR SALE.
Side 1
33 1/3 RPM
ARRANGED AND PRODUCED BY JOHN FOGERTY
Edited from the John Fogerty album EYE OF THE ZOMBIE
on Warner Bros. Records (1-25449)
CHANGE IN THE WEATHER (Edit) 3:50
(J.C. Fogerty)
Wenaha Music Company ASCAP
℗ 1986 Warner Bros. Records Inc.

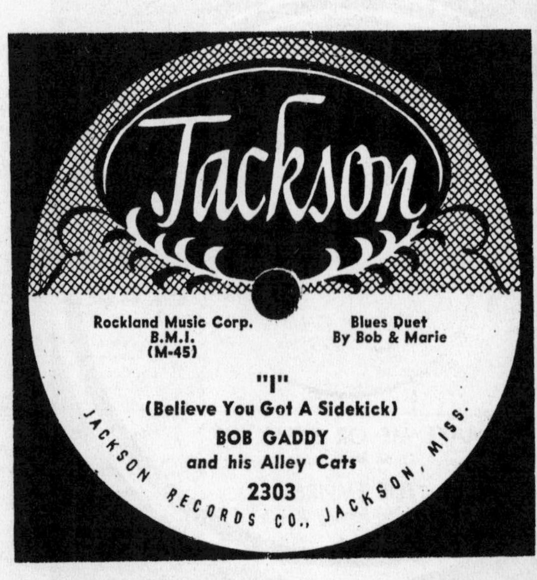
Jackson
Rockland Music Corp.
B.M.I.
(M-45)
Blues Duet
By Bob & Marie
"I"
(Believe You Got A Sidekick)
BOB GADDY
and his Alley Cats
2303
JACKSON RECORDS CO., JACKSON, MISS.

junior
RECORD CO.
K. Williams Music
Inc.
B. M. I.
45-602
HIGH SCHOOL BABY
(D. Gardner)
DON GARDNER
Directed by
K. Williams and D. McRae
393

H

H.B. & CHECKMATES

Singles: 7-inch

LAVENDER (1936 "Summertime") .... 15-25 '60s

H.I. & STORMS

Singles: 7-inch

TREND '63 (107 "Twister") 10-20 63

H.M. ROYALS

Singles: 7-inch

ABC (10957 "Old Town") 15-25 67

H.M. SUBJECTS

Singles: 7-inch

BLUE SAINT (1001 "Don't Put Me Down") 10-20 66
SAINT (1001 "Don't Bring Me Down") 30-40 66
(First issue.)
Also see MONTELLS

H.P. & GRASS ROUTE MOVEMENT

Singles: 7-inch

BBTC ("You Don't Know Like I Know") .... 10-20 '60s
(No selection number used.)
HIDEOUT (1232 "Heavy Music") .... 8-12 '60s

H.P. LOVECRAFT
(Lovecraft)

Singles: 7-inch

MERCURY 5-10 75-76
PHILIPS (40464 "Anyway That You Want Me") 8-12 67
PHILIPS (40491 "Wayfaring Stranger") 8-12 67
PHILIPS (40506 "White Ship") 8-12 68
PHILIPS (40578 "Keeper of the Keys") 8-12 68
REPRISE 5-10 70

Picture Sleeves

PHILIPS (40491 "Wayfaring Stranger") ... 10-20 67

LPs: 10/12-inch

MERCURY (1041 "We Love You") 10-15 76
PHILIPS (200252 "H.P. Lovecraft") 20-30 67
(Monaural.)
PHILIPS (600252 "H.P. Lovecraft") 25-35 67
(Stereo.)
PHILIPS (600279 "Lovecraft II") 20-30 68
REPRISE (6419 "Valley of the Moon") 10-12 70
Also see BLUE CHEER / H.P. Lovecraft / Hello People

H.Y. SLEDGE

LPs: 10/12-inch

SSS INT'L (22 "Bootleg Music") 15-25 71
Members: Jan Pulver; Richard Porter; Mike Ewbank.

HAAS, Wayne

Singles: 7-inch

CHOICE (5607 "Leave Linda Alone") 40-50 57

HACIENDAS

Singles: 7-inch

PACIFIC CHALLENGER (1001 "Sherry Stole My XKE") 20-30 64

HACKERT, Veline
(Buddy Covelle)

Singles: 7-inch

BRUNSWICK (55151 "Billy Boy") 75-100 59
Also see COVELLE, Buddy

HADLEY, Jay

Singles: 7-inch

GLO-LITE (104 "Dance Baby Dance") 50-75

HADLEY, Jim

Singles: 7-inch

BUDDY (117 "Midnight Train") 50-75

HADLEY'S, Red, Wranglers

Singles: 78 rpm

METEOR (5017 "Brother That's All") 40-60 55

Singles: 7-inch

METEOR (5017 "Brother That's All") 75-125 55

HAFF-TONES

Singles: 7-inch

TWILIGHT (001 "I Need You") 75-125 64

HAGAN, Sammy, & Viscounts

Singles: 78 rpm

CAPITOL 15-25 57

Singles: 7-inch

CAPITOL (3772 "Out of Your Heart") 15-25 57
CAPITOL (3818 "Don't Cry") 15-25 57
CAPITOL (3885 "Tail Light") 20-30 58

HAGAR, Ernie

Singles: 7-inch

SAND (400 "Surf 'N Sand") 10-20 63
SAND (402 "Spindrift") 10-20 63

HAGEN, Don

Singles: 7-inch

SEA GULL (103 "Surfin' Son of a Gun") ... 15-25 '60s

HAGER, Don, & Hot Tots

Singles: 7-inch

OAK (357 "Bebop Boogie") 150-200
OAK (358 "Liza Jane Bop") 100-150

HAGGARD, Jay

Singles: 7-inch

DAJA (502 "Want You Now Honey Doll") .50-75 58
DAJA (503 "Tom Cat") 50-75 59

Picture Sleeves

DAJA (503 "Tom Cat") 50-75 59
(Sleeve has die-cut center hole.)

HAGGARD, Merle *C&W '63*
(With the Strangers)

Singles: 7-inch

CAPITOL 4-8 65-77
COLUMBIA 3-5 83
CURB 3-5 90
EPIC 3-5 81-89
MCA 4-6 77-85
MERCURY 3-5 83
TALLY 10-20 63-65

Picture Sleeves

CAPITOL 4-8 67-71
MCA 4-6 77-80

EPs: 7-inch

CAPITOL 8-15 71
(Juke box issues only.)

LPs: 10/12-inch

ALBUM GLOBE (9005 "Melody Ranch Featuring Merle Haggard & Friends") .... 40-50 '80s
CAPITOL (168 thru 735) 8-15 69-71
(With "T," "ST," "STBB" or "SWBB" prefix.)
CAPITOL (168 thru 735) 4-8 69-71
(With "SKAO" or SM" prefix.)
CAPITOL (796 "Merle Haggard's Strangers and Friends Honky Tonkin' ") 20-30 71
CAPITOL (803 "Land of Many Churches") 30-50 71
(With "SWBO" prefix.)
CAPITOL (835 "Someday We'll Look Back") 8-12 71
CAPITOL (882 "Let Me Tell You About a Song") 8-12 72
CAPITOL (2373 thru 2972) 15-25 65-68
(With "T," "ST" or, in the case of 2951, an "SKAO" prefix.)
CAPITOL (2702 thru 2972) .... 5-10 '80s
(With "SM" prefix.)
CAPITOL (11000 thru 16000 series) 5-10 72-82
EPIC 5-10 81-86
MCA 4-8 77-84
MERCURY 5-10 83
PICKWICK/HILLTOP .... 8-12 '60s
RADIANT 5-10 81
RONCO 5-8
SONGBIRD 5-10 81
SPARTON 30-60
(Canadian.)
TEE VEE 5-10 77
Session: Biff Adam; Norm Hamlet; Dennis Hromek; Roy Nichols; Bobby Wayne; Johnny Gimble; Jordanaires; James Burton; Marty Haggard; Ronnie Reno; Bonnie Owens; Carter Family.
Also see BANDY, Moe
Also see BURTON, James
Also see COCHRAN, Hank
Also see JORDANAIRES
Also see MADDOX, Rose
Also see PAYCHECK & HAGGARD
Also see STEWART, Wynn
Also see TUBB, Ernest
Also see WILLS, Bob

HAGGARD, Merle / Patsy Cline

LPs: 10/12-inch

OUT OF TOWN DIST 5-10 82
Also see CLINE, Patsy

HAGGARD, Merle, & Clint Eastwood *C&W '80*

Singles: 7-inch

ELEKTRA 3-5 80

Picture Sleeves

ELEKTRA 3-5 80
Also see EASTWOOD, Clint

HAGGARD, Merle, & Janie Fricke *C&W '84*

Singles: 7-inch

EPIC 3-5 84
Also see FRICKE, Janie

HAGGARD, Merle / Mickey Gilley / Willie Knight

LPs: 10/12-inch

OUT OF TOWN DIST 5-10 82
Also see GILLEY, Mickey

HAGGARD, Merle / Sonny James

LPs: 10/12-inch

CAPITOL .... 10-15 '60s
Also see JAMES, Sonny

HAGGARD, Merle, & George Jones *C&W/LP '82*
(George Jones & Merle Haggard)

Singles: 7-inch

EPIC (03405 "C.C. Waterback") 3-5 82
EPIC (03405 "C.C. Waterback") 40-50 82
(Picture disc. Autographed.)
EPIC (03405 "C.C. Waterback") 10-15 82
(Picture disc. Not signed.)

LPs: 10/12-inch

EPIC 5-10 82
Also see JONES, George

HAGGARD, Merle, & Willie Nelson *C&W/LP '83*
(Willie Nelson & Merle Haggard)

Singles: 7-inch

EPIC 3-5 83-87

LPs: 10/12-inch

EPIC 5-10 83
Also see NELSON, Willie

HAGGARD, Merle, & Bonnie Owens *C&W '64*

Singles: 7-inch

TALLY (181 "Just Between the Two of Us") 10-20 64

LPs: 10/12-inch

CAPITOL (2453 "Just Between the Two of Us") 20-30 66
Also see OWENS, Bonnie

HAGGETT, Jimmy
(With the Daydreamers)

Singles: 78 rpm

METEOR (5043 "Gonna Shut You Off Baby") 100-200 57
SUN (236 "No More") 125-150 56

Singles: 7-inch

CAPROCK (107 "Without You") 10-20 58
METEOR (5043 "Gonna Shut You Off Baby") 250-350 57
SUN (236 "No More") 300-400 56

HAIG, Ronnie
(With the Monograms; Ron Hege)

Singles: 7-inch

ABC-PAR (9912 "Don't You Hear Me Calling, Baby") 20-30 58
ABC-PAR (10209 "Don't You Hear Me Calling, Baby") 10-15 61
ASTRA 5-10
NOTE (10010 "Don't You Hear Me Calling, Baby") 75-100 58
NOTE (10014 "Rocking with Rhythm and Blues") 50-75 58
SILVERBALL (1 "Pork's Chop Boogie") 4-8 93
(Pink vinyl. 200 made.)
SILVERBALL (1 "Pork's Chop Boogie") 4-8 93
(White vinyl. 300 made.)
SILVERBALL (101 "Open House") 4-8 92
(Black vinyl. 900 made.)
SILVERBALL (101 "Open House") 10-15 92
(Colored vinyl. 100 made for promotional use only.)
SILVERBALL (103 "Just One Kiss") 4-6 93
(Colored vinyl.)
SILVERBALL (105 "Mucho Fine ") 3-5 94
(Colored vinyl.)

Picture Sleeves

SILVERBALL (105 "Mucho Fine") 3-5 94

EPs: 7-inch

GET HIP (4 "Ronnie Haig") 4-8 94
(Promotional copies of this 3-track EP are credited to the Hoosier Hotshots.)
Session: Michael Vanhook; Mark Kennedy; John D. Magee.

HAINES, Connie

Singles: 7-inch

MOTOWN (1092 "What's Easy for Two Is Hard for One") 15-25 66

LPs: 10/12-inch

TOPS (1606 "Connie Haines Sings Helen Morgan") 20-40 58
Also see FOUR GIRLS

HAINES, Gary
(With the Five Sequins)

Singles: 7-inch

KAPP (383 "Another Girl Like You") 15-25 61
SOUND (110 "Keep On Going") 25-35

HAIRCUTS

Singles: 7-inch

PARKWAY (899 "She Loves You") 10-20 64

Picture Sleeves:

PARKWAY (899 "She Loves You") 20-30 64

HAIRSTON, Brother Will
("Hurricane of the Motor City)

Singles: 78 rpm

JVB (44 "The Alabama Bus") 50-100 56

Singles: 7-inch

JVB (44 "The Alabama Bus") 100-200 56
KNOWLES 10-20

HAIRSTON, Jackie

Singles: 7-inch

ATCO (6464 "Monkey on My Back") 10-15 67

HAKE, Ron

Singles: 7-inch

BLUE DIAMOND (12972 "Lonely Guitars") 150-250

HAL HOPPERS

Singles: 78 rpm

KEM (2733 "More Love") 50-100 55

Singles: 7-inch

KEM (2733 "More Love") 125-175 55
Member: Hal Hopper.

HALE, Billy Jack

Singles: 7-inch

DECCA (30447 "Your Eyes") 20-25 57

HALE, Kip, & Hearties

Singles: 78 rpm

JUBILEE (5166 "Don't You Care") 5-10 54

Singles: 7-inch

JUBILEE (5166 "Don't You Care") 10-20 54

HALE, Rex, & Rythm Masters

Singles: 78 rpm

RYTHM (303 "Down at Big Mama's House") 100-150 49

Singles: 7-inch

RYTHM (303 "Down at Big Mama's House") 500-750 49

HALE & HUSHABYES

Singles: 7-inch

APOGEE (104 "Yes Sir, That's My Baby") 50-100 65
REPRISE (0299 "Yes Sir, That's My Baby") 20-40 64
(Reissued in 1967 as by Date With Soul.)
Members: Brian Wilson; Sonny & Cher; Jack Nitzsche; Blossoms; Jackie DeShannon; Darlene Love; Edna Wright; Albert Stone.
Also see BLOSSOMS
Also see DATE WITH SOUL
Also see DE SHANNON, Jackie
Also see HONEY CONE
Also see LOVE, Darlene
Also see NITZSCHE, Jack
Also see SONNY & CHER
Also see WILSON, Brian

HALEY, Bill *P&R '53*
(With His Comets; with Saddlemen; with Saddle Men; with Four Aces of Western Swing; with Reno Browne & Her Buckaroos)

Singles: 78 rpm

ATLANTIC (727 "I'm Gonna Dry Ev'ry Tear with a Kiss") 250-350 50

COWBOY (1201 "Too Many Parties Too Many Pals")........300-500 48
COWBOY (1202 "Candy Kisses")........300-500 49
COWBOY (1203 "The Covered Wagon Rolled Right Along")........250-300 49
COWBOY (1204 "Behind the Eight Ball")........250-300 50
COWBOY (1205 "Candy Kisses")........250-350 50
COWBOY (1701 "Candy Kisses")........250-350 49
COWBOY (1701 "My Palomino & I")....250-350 49
(By "Reno Browne & Her Buckaroos featuring Bill Haley." The Cowboy 1701 number is used twice.)
DECCA (29124 "Rock Around the Clock")........50-100 54
(Black label with gold print.)
DECCA (29124 "Rock Around the Clock")........25-50 54
(Black label with silver print. Decca multi-color labels are $4 to $8 reissues.)
DECCA (29204 "Shake, Rattle & Roll")....50-80 54
(Black label with gold print.)
DECCA (29204 "Shake, Rattle & Roll")....25-50 54
(Black label with silver print.)
DECCA (29317 thru 30530)........30-60 54-57
DECCA (30592 thru 30781)........20-40 58
DECCA (30844 "I Got a Woman")........25-50 59
DECCA (30873 "A Fool Such As I")........40-60 59
DECCA (30926 "Caldonia")........50-75 59
DECCA (30956 "Ooh, Look-a-There Ain't She Pretty")........50-100 59
ESSEX........50-75 52-55
HOLIDAY (105 "Rocket 88")........200-300 51
HOLIDAY (108 "Green Tree Boogie")..200-300 51
HOLIDAY (111 "A Year Ago This Christmas")........750-1000 51
HOLIDAY (113 "Juke Box Cannonball")........200-300 52
KEYSTONE (5101 "Deal Me a Hand")........750-1000 50
KEYSTONE (5102 "Susan Van Dusan")........750-1000 50
QUALITY (Except 1082)........30-40 53-54
(Canadian.)
QUALITY (1082 "Rocking Chair on the Moon")........100-200 52
(Canadian. First Haley disc on Quality.)

Singles: 7-inch

APT (25081 "Burn That Candle")........15-20 65
APT (25087 "Haley A-Go-Go")........15-20 65
ARZEE (4677 "Yodel Your Blues Away")...8-12 77
DECCA (29124 "Rock Around the Clock")........20-30 54
DECCA (29204 "Shake, Rattle & Roll")...20-30 54
DECCA (29317 "Dim, Dim the Lights")....20-30 54
DECCA (29418 "Birth of the Boogie")......20-30 55
DECCA (29552 "Razzle-Dazzle")........20-25 55
DECCA (29713 "Burn That Candle")........20-25 55
DECCA (29791 "See You Later, Alligator")........20-25 56
DECCA (29870 "R-O-C-K")........20-25 56
DECCA (29948 "Hot Dog Buddy Buddy")........20-25 56
DECCA (30028 thru 30681)........15-25 56-58
DECCA (30741 thru 31080)........10-20 58-60
DECCA (31650 thru 31677)........8-12 64
ESSEX (102 "Rock Around the Clock")...10-20 '60s
(An unauthorized reissue of the Decca track. Listed because some may confuse it with a 1950s original.)
ESSEX (303 "Rock the Joint")........500-750 52
(Colored vinyl.)
ESSEX (303 "Rock the Joint")........125-150 52
(Black vinyl. Block style logo.)
ESSEX (303 "Rock the Joint")........55-65 52
(Black vinyl. Script style logo.)
ESSEX (305 "Rocking Chair on the Moon")........50-100 52
ESSEX (310 "Real Rock Drive")........50-100 52
ESSEX (321 "Crazy Man Crazy")........50-75 53
ESSEX (327 "Fractured")........50-75 53
ESSEX (332 "Live It Up")........30-40 53
ESSEX (340 "Ten Little Indians")........30-40 53
ESSEX (348 "Chattanooga Choo-Choo") 25-35 54
ESSEX (374 "Juke Box Cannonball")......50-75 54
ESSEX (381 "Rocket 88")........100-125 55
ESSEX (399 "Rock the Joint")........50-75 55
GONE (5111 "Spanish Twist")........15-25 61
GONE (5116 "Riviera")........15-25 61
HOLIDAY (113 "Juke Box Cannonball")........350-450 51
JANUS (162 "Traveling Band")........8-12 71
JUKE BOX........3-5 90
KAMA SUTRA (508 "Rock Around the Clock")........5-10 70
MCA........3-6 73-80
MGM (14688 "Kohoutek")........4-8 74
NEW HITS (5014 "Midnight in Washington")........10-15 63
NEWTOWN (5013 "Tenor Man")........10-15 63
NEWTOWN (5024 "Dance Around the Clock")........10-15 63
NICETOWN (5025 "Tandy")........10-15 63
OLD GOLD........3-5 82
QUALITY (1082 "Rocking Chair on the Moon")........150-250 52
(Canadian. First Haley disc on Quality.)
QUALITY (1120 "Crazy Man, Crazy")......50-100 53
(Canadian.)
QUALITY (1145 "Fractured")........40-60 53
(Canadian.)
QUALITY (1168 "Live It Up")........40-60 53
(Canadian.)
QUALITY (1399 "Rock the Joint")........50-100 54
(Canadian.)
RADIO ACTIVE........4-8 70
TRANSWORLD (381 "Rocket 88")........60-80 54
TRANSWORLD (718 "Real Rock Drive")........100-125 53
U.A. (50483 "That's How I Got to Memphis")........5-10 69
W.B. (5145 "Candy Kisses")........25-35 60
(Yellow vinyl. Promotional issue.)
W.B. (5145 thru 5228)........15-25 60
W.B. (7124 "Rock Around the Clock")......10-15 68

Picture Sleeves

ARZEE (4677 "Yodel Your Blues Away")...8-12 77
DECCA (30314 "Billy Goat")........100-125 57
DECCA (30530 "Mary Mary Lou")........30-40 57

EPs: 7-inch

ARZEE (137 "Bill Haley Sings")........20-30 77
CLAIRE (4779 "Bill Haley and the Comets")........15-20 78
DECCA (2168 "Shake, Rattle & Roll")......40-60 54
DECCA (2209 "Dim, Dim the Lights")......40-60 55
DECCA (2322 "Rock 'N' Roll")........40-60 56
DECCA (2398/2399/2400 "He Digs Rock and Roll")........40-60 56
(Price is for any of three volumes.)
DECCA (2416/2417/2418 "Rock'n Roll Stage Show")........40-60 56
(Price is for any of three volumes.)
DECCA (2532 "Rockin' the Oldies")........40-60 57
DECCA (2533 "Rock 'N' Roll Party")........30-40 57
DECCA (2534 "Rockin' & Rollin' ")........30-40 57
DECCA (2564 "Rockin' Around the World")........30-40 57
DECCA (2576 "Rockin' Around Europe") .30-40 57
DECCA (2577 "Rockin' Around the Americas")........30-40 57
DECCA (2615/2616 "Rockin' the Joint")...30-40 58
(Price is for either of two volumes.)
DECCA (2638 "Bill Haley's Chicks")........30-40 58
DECCA (2670 "Bill Haley and His Comets")........30-40 59
DECCA (2671 "Strictly Instrumental")......30-40 59
DECCA (72638 "Bill Haley's Chicks")......50-75 59
(Stereo.)
DECCA (72670 "Bill Haley and His Comets")........50-75 59
(Stereo.)
DECCA (72671 "Strictly Instrumental")......50-75 59
(Stereo.)
ESSEX (102 "Dance Party")........50-100 54
ESSEX (117/118/119 "Rock with Bill Haley and the Comets")........50-100 54
(Price is for any of three volumes.)
SOMERSET (460 "Rock with Bill Haley and the Comets")........40-60 55
TRANSWORLD (117/118/119 "Rock with Bill Haley and Comets")........50-100 54
(Price is for any of three volumes. May be titled *For Your Dance Party.*)

LPs: 10/12-inch

AEI (3106 "Rock Around the Clock")........8-12 82
ACCORD (7122 "Rockin' & Rollin' ")........5-10 81
ACCORD (7125 "Rockin' & Rollin' ")........5-10 81
ACCORD (7902 "Mr. Rock-n' Roll")........5-10 82
ALSHIRE (5202 "King of Rock 'N Roll")......8-10 70
ALSHIRE (5313 "Bill Haley – King of Rock 'N Roll")........5-8 74
AMBASSADOR (1454 "Bill Haley and the Comets")........5-10
AMBASSADOR........8-15 70-87
BUDDAH........5-10 84
CORAL........8-10 73
DECCA (5560 "Shake, Rattle & Roll")..300-400 54
(10-inch LP.)
DECCA (7211 "Golden Hits")........12-18 72
DECCA (8225 "Rock Around the Clock")........75-125 55
(Black label with silver print.)
DECCA (8225 "Rock Around the Clock") .20-40 60
(Black label with rainbow color stripe. Reads "M'F'D by Decca Records Inc. New York, U.S.A.")
DECCA (8225 "Rock Around the Clock") .15-20 68
(Black label with rainbow color stripe. Reads "Mfr'd by Decca Records, a Div. of MCA Inc. New York, U.S.A.")
DECCA (8315 "He Digs Rock & Roll") .100-200 56
DECCA (8345 "Rock'n Roll Stage Show")........100-200 56
DECCA (8569 "Rockin' the Oldies")......100-200 57
DECCA (8692 "Rockin' Around the World")........50-100 58
DECCA (8775 "Rockin' the Joint")........50-100 58
DECCA (8821 "Bill Haley's Chicks")........50-75 58
DECCA (8964 "Strictly Instrumental")......40-60 60
DECCA (75027 "Greatest Hits")........15-20 68
DECCA (78225 "Rock Around the Clock")........50-100 59
(All black label with silver print.)
DECCA (78225 "Rock Around the Clock")........50-100 59
(Black label with rainbow color stripe.)
DECCA (78692 "Rockin' Around the World")........20-40 62
DECCA (78821 "Bill Haley's Chicks")......50-100 58
DECCA (78964 "Strictly Instrumental")....50-75 60
ESSEX (202 "Rock with Bill Haley and the Comets")........300-500 54
EVEREST (4110 "Bill Haley and the Comets")........5-10 81
EXACT (207 "King of Rock 'N Roll")........5-10 80
51 WEST........5-10 83
GNP (2077 "Rock and Roll")........8-12 74
GREAT NORTHWEST........8-12 81
GUEST STAR (1454 "Billy Haley and the Comets [Live]")........15-20 65
JANUS (3035 "Travelin' Band")........10-15 72
JANUS (7003 "Razzle Dazzle")........15-25 72
(Two discs.)
JOKER........5-10 81
KAMA SUTRA (2014 "Bill Haley's Scrapbook")........20-30 70
KOALA........8-10 79
MCA (161 "Greatest Hits")........8-10
MCA........6-10 73-88
PAIR........5-8 86
PHOENIX........5-10 81
PICKWICK (3256 "Rockin' ")........8-10 71
ROULETTE (25174 "Twistin' Knights at the Round Table")........15-20 62
SILHOUETTE........5-10 81
SOMERSET (1300 "Rock & Roll Dance Party")........300-400 58
(Also contains tracks by the Dinning Sisters; Bunny Paul; Swingers; Ken Carson; Escorts; Aristocrats; and the House Rockers.)
SOMERSET (4600 "Rock with Bill Haley & Comets")........75-125 58
SPRINGBOARD (4066 "Bill Haley and the Comets Greatest Hits")........8-10 77
SUN (143 "R-O-C-K")........10-15 80
TRANSWORLD (202 "Rock with Bill Haley and the Comets")........200-300 56
VOCALION (3696 "Bill Haley and the Comets")........15-25 63
W.B. (W-1378 "Bill Haley and His Comets")........25-35 60
(Monaural.)
W.B. (WS-1378 "Bill Haley and His Comets")........35-45 60
(Stereo.)
W.B. (W-1391 "Haley's Juke Box")........25-35 60
(Monaural.)
WARNER (WS-1391 "Haley's Juke Box")........35-45 60
(Stereo.)
W.B. (1831 "Rock & Roll Revival")........8-12 70

Members: Bill Haley; Rudy Pompilli; Bill Miller; Ray Cawley; Buddy Dee; Cappy Bianco; Franny Beecher; Nick Nastos; Marshall Lytle; Dick Richards; Joey Ambrose; Al Pompilli; Al Rappa; Joe Oliver; Al Rex; Johnny Grande; Billy Williamson; Johnny Kay; Ray Parsons; Jerry Tilley; Geoff Driscoll; Frankie Scott; John Lane; Joey Welz; Bill Nolte; Danny Cedrone; Bob Scaltrito; Panama Francis; Sticks Evans; Art Ryerson; Billy Gussak; Hargus "Pig" Robbins; Bobby Wood; Jimmy Collett; Jimmy Riddle; Lloyd Green; Curley Chawker.

Also see BIANCO, Cappy
Also see BILL & LORETTA & SADDLEMEN
Also see BROWNE, Reno, & Her Buckaroos
Also see CLIFTON, Johnny, & His String Band
Also see COOK BROTHERS
Also see DAY, Dave
Also see DAY, Jack
Also see DOWN HOMERS
Also see ESQUIRE BOYS
Also see EVANS, Sticks, & House Rockets
Also see GINGER & JOHNNY
Also see GRAHAM, Lou
Also see GRANT, Carrie, & Grandeors
Also see GRAY, Charlie
Also see HIGHLIGHTS
Also see JODIMARS
Also see KEEFER, Rusty, & His Greenlights
Also see KINGSMEN
Also see LEE, Brenda / Bill Haley & Comets / Kalin Twins / Four Aces
Also see LIFEGUARDS
Also see LOPEZ, Trini / Scott Gregory
Also see LYTELL, Marshall
Also see MATYS BROS.
Also see MEADE, Freddie, & Calenders
Also see MERRI-MEN
Also see NANTOS, Nick, & Fireballers
Also see RANDOLPH, Boots / Bill Haley
Also see SANDS, Jeri Lynn
Also see SCOTT, Frank, & Scottsmen
Also see WELZ, Joey
Also see ZARIO, Rex

HALEY, Bill / Phil Flowers

Singles: 7-inch

KASEY (7006 "ABC Boogie")........10-15 61

Picture Sleeves

KASEY (7006 "ABC Boogie")........25-35 61

Also see FLOWERS, Phil

HALEY, Bill / Lionel Hampton / Sal Salvador Quartet / Lenny Dee

EPs: 7-inch

DECCA (38088 "Webcor High Fidelity Demonstration Record")........15-25 59
(Special products issue, made for Webcor Phonographs. Not issued with special cover.)

Also see HAMPTON, Lionel

HALEY, Bill / Bunny Paul / Dinning Sisters

EPs: 7-inch

SOMERSET (1300 "Rock and Roll Dance Party")........40-60 55

Also see HALEY, Bill
Also see PAUL, Bunny, & Harptones

HALF BROTHERS

Singles: 7-inch

MERCURY (71299 "My Foolish Fling")....50-75 58

HALL, Alberta

Singles: 78 rpm

SPECIALTY (562 "Oh How I Need Your Love")........15-25 55

Singles: 7-inch

SPECIALTY (562 "Oh How I Need Your Love")........25-35 55

HALL, Arch, Jr.

Singles: 7-inch

FAIRWAY INT'L........5-10 63
SIGNATURE (12014 "Konga Joe")........20-30

HALL, Barbara

Singles: 7-inch

TUSKA (102 "Tell Me, Tell Me, Tell Me")........75-100

HALL, Ben, & Country Drifters

Singles: 7-inch

CORD (101 "Moo Mama")........600-800
FAYETTE........10-15 64

HALL, Betty

Singles: 7-inch

EMBER (1096 "Paradise for Two") 20-30 64

HALL, Bill, & Sonnetts

Singles: 7-inch

CHECKER (884 "Three Wishes") 400-500 58

HALL, Billy

(With the Arabs)

Singles: 7-inch

GLENN (1006 "Good Bye Angel") 25-35 63
GLENN (1007 "I Need Some Lovin' ") 50-75 64
GLENN (1008 "Ooga-Booga Boo Boo") .. 50-75 64
GLENN (1009 "Move Over, Rover") 50-75 64
MAR-VEL (1002 "Move Over, Rover") ... 75-100 57

HALL, Bobby, & Kings

Singles: 78 rpm

HARLEM (2322 "Fire in My Heart") 75-125 54

Singles: 7-inch

HARLEM (2322 "Fire in My Heart") 500-750 54
(Black vinyl.)
HARLEM (2322 "Fire in My Heart") .. 2000-2500 54
(Red vinyl.)
Also see KINGS

HALL, Carl

Singles: 7-inch

COLUMBIA 4-6
LOMA (2086 "You Don't Know Nothing About Love") 30-40 67
LOMA (2098 "The Dam Busted") 5-10 68
MERCURY (72547 "He Gets Everything He Wants") 30-40 66

HALL, Daryl, & John Oates *P&R/LP '74*

(Hall & Oates)

Singles: 12-inch

RCA (Except 13705) 4-8 78-85
RCA (13705 "Jingle Bell Rock") 30-40 83
(Picture disc. Promotional issue only.)

Singles: 7-inch

ARISTA 3-5 88-90
ATLANTIC 4-6 72-77
CHELSEA 4-6 77
RCA 3-6 76-84
SIRE (22967 "Love Train") 3-5 89
RCA GOLD STANDARD 3-5 83-84

Picture Sleeves

ARISTA 3-5 88
RCA 3-6 77-85

Promotional Singles

RCA (Colored vinyl) 5-8 85
(One side by Daryl Hall and one side by John Oates.)

EPs: 7-inch

ATLANTIC (265 "She's Gone") 8-12 73
(Promotional issue only.)

LPs: 10/12-inch

ARISTA (8539 "Ooh Yeah") 5-10 88
ARISTA (8614 "Change of Season") 5-10 90
ATLANTIC (7242 "Whole Oats") 15-20 72
ATLANTIC (7269 "Abandoned Luncheonette") 10-12 74
ATLANTIC (18109 "War Babies") 10-12 74
ATLANTIC (18213 "No Goodbyes") 8-10 77
ATLANTIC (19139 "Abandoned Luncheonette") 5-10 77
CHELSEA (547 "Past Times Behind") 10-15 77
MFSL (069 "Abandoned Luncheonette") . 30-40 82
RCA (1144 "Daryl Hall and John Oates") ... 8-12 75
RCA (1467 "Bigger Than Both of Us") 8-12 76
RCA (2300 "Beauty on a Back Street") 8-12 77
RCA (2802 "Livetime") 8-12 78
RCA (2804 "Along the Red Ledge") 8-12 78
(Black vinyl.)
RCA (2804 "Along the Red Ledge") 15-25 78
(Red vinyl.)
RCA (3463 "Daryl Hall and John Oates") ... 5-10 79
RCA (3494 "X-Static") 5-10 79
RCA (3646 "Voices") 5-10 80
RCA (3836 "Daryl Hall and John Oates") 5-8 80
RCA (3866 "Bigger Than Both of Us") 5-10 81
RCA (4028 "Private Eyes") 5-10 81
RCA (4230 "Beauty on a Back Street") 5-10 82
RCA (4231 "Along the Red Ledge") 5-10 82
RCA (4383 "H_2O") 5-10 82
RCA (4858 "Rock 'N Soul") 5-10 83
RCA (5309 "Big Bam Boom") 5-10 84

Promotional LPs

RCA ("Special Radio Series") 15-25 81

Also see JEFFERSON STARSHIP / Daryl Hall & John Oates / Evelyn "Champagne" King / Minglewood Band

HALL, Daryl, John Oates, David Ruffin & Eddie Kendricks *P&R/R&B/LP '85*

Singles: 7-inch

RCA (14178 "The Way You Do the Things You Do–My Girl") 3-5 85

Picture Sleeves

RCA (14178 "The Way You Do the Things You Do–My Girl") 3-5 85

LPs: 10/12-inch

RCA (7035 "Live at the Apollo") 5-10 85
Also see RUFFIN, David

HALL, Dickson, & Wayfarers

Singles: 7-inch

EPIC (9262 "Cowboy") 5-10 58

Picture Sleeves

EPIC (9262 "Cowboy") 15-25 58

HALL, Erle

Singles: 7-inch

NASCO (6024 "Completely Yours") 10-15 59

HALL, Euel

Singles: 7-inch

TOWN HOUSE ("Stand in Line") 200-300
(Selection number not known.)

HALL, Fox

Singles: 7-inch

LIMELIGHT (3003 "Do the Rock & Roll") . 50-60 63

HALL, Freddie

(With the Night Rockers; with Carl Jones & Orchestra; with Ike Perkins)

Singles: 78 rpm

ABCO (103 "Can This Be Mine") 25-40 56
CHANCE (1159 This Crooked World") 25-50 54

Singles: 7-inch

ABCO (103 "Can This Be Mine") 50-75 56
C.J. (601 "She's an Upsetter") 50-75 59
C.J. (602 "Little Baby's Rock") 50-75 59
C.J. (610 "Love and Affection") 25-35 59
CHANCE (1159 This Crooked World") ... 75-100 54
Members: Freddie Hall; Bill; Ike Perkins; Joe.
Also see PERKINS, Ike

HALL, Jim, & His Radio Pals

Singles: 7-inch

BONEY (204 "Old Fort Smith") 15-20
PROCESS (107 "Hydrogen, Nitrogen, Potassium") 40-60

HALL, Jimmy

Singles: 7-inch

HICKORY (1209 "Cathy's Clown") 10-20 63

HALL, Jimmy, & Hi-Lighters

Singles: 7-inch

CANNON (369 "Jeannie") 15-25 59
Also see HI-LIGHTERS

HALL, Joe

Singles: 7-inch

GLOBAL (721 "Cold Hearted Woman") 40-60 59

HALL, Johnny

Singles: 78 rpm

RECORDED IN HOLLYWOOD 10-20 53

Singles: 7-inch

RECORDED IN HOLLYWOOD (415 "Lover's Lane") 20-30 53
RECORDED IN HOLLYWOOD (416 "Two-Step-Side-Step") 20-30 53

HALL, Juanita

Singles: 7-inch

COUNTERPOINT (008 "You're No Good for Me") 10-15

EPs: 7-inch

VARSITY 10-20 50

LPs: 10/12-inch

COUNTERPOINT (556 "Juanita Hall Sings the Blues") 30-45
VARSITY (8 "Stephen Foster Songs") 20-40 50
(10-inch LP.)

HALL, Juanita / Eric Silver

LPs: 10/12-inch

HALO .... 10-20 '50s

HALL, Juanita, & Four Tunes

Singles: 78 rpm

RCA 15-25 50

Singles: 7-inch

RCA (3149 "I'm in the Mood for Love") 40-50 50
Also see FOUR TUNES
Also see HALL, Juanita

HALL, Larry *P&R '59*

Singles: 7-inch

BARREL (621 "Sandy") 20-30 59
(Canadian.)
EVER GREEN (1001 "Sandy") 25-35 59
GOLD LEAF (212 "I Sit Alone") 8-12 62
HOT (1 "Sandy") 40-50 59
(First issue.)
STRAND (Except 25007 & 25025) 10-15 59-61
STRAND (25007 "Sandy") 15-25 59
STRAND (25025 "Kool Luv") 40-50 61

LPs: 10/12-inch

STRAND (1005 "Sandy") 40-60 60

HALL, Linda

Singles: 7-inch

CUCA (1044 "You Don't Have a Wooden Heart") 10-20 61
CUCA (1070 "Almost Always True") 10-20 62

Picture Sleeves

CUCA (1044 "You Don't Have a Wooden Heart") 20-30 61

HALL, Linda

Singles: 7-inch

ARTCRAFT (007 "Beach Boy") 20-30 65

HALL, Reggie

Singles: 7-inch

RIP/CHESS (1816 "The Joke") 5-10 62
WHITE CLIFFS (255 "Please, Please Phone") 10-15 67

HALL, René

(René Hall Trio; René Hall Sextet)

Singles: 78 rpm

DECCA 10-15 51
JUBILEE (5013 "Chittlin' Switch") 10-20 50
JUBILEE (5020 "Blowing Awhile") 10-20 50
RCA 5-10 53
SPECIALTY 5-10 57

Singles: 7-inch

ALLIED (7779 "O Sole Mio Rock") 10-15 60
ARVEE (580 "South Gate") 10-15 59
CASTILE (101 "Turf") 10-20 59
DECCA (48213 "Old Soldiers Never Die") 25-35 51
DECCA (48217 "My Kind of Rockin' ") 25-35 51
DEL-FI (4135 "The Untouchables") 10-15 60
RCA (5046 "Peace of Mind") 15-25 52
RCA (5274 "Voodoo Moon") 15-25 53
RCA (5407 "Two Guitar Boogie") 15-25 53
RENDEZVOUS (107 "Moritat") 5-10 59
SPECIALTY (618 "Flippin' ") 5-10 57
SPECIALTY (629 "Thunderbird") 5-10 58
SPECIALTY (641 "Frankie and Johnny") ... 5-10 58
Session: Willie Jo.
Also see AUGUST, Joseph
Also see BOB & EARL
Also see COOKE, Sam
Also see HUGHES, Ben
Also see LEWIS, Louise
Also see LIONS
Also see SUGAR & SPICES
Also see TANGENTS
Also see TRONICS

HALL, Roy

(With His Cohutta Mountain Boys)

Singles: 78 rpm

DECCA 15-25 56
FORTUNE 20-45 49-56
HI-Q 25-35 56

Singles: 7-inch

DECCA (29697 "Whole Lotta Shakin' Goin' On") 50-60 55
DECCA (29786 "See You Later Alligator") 50-60 56
DECCA (29880 "Blue Suede Shoes") 50-75 56
DECCA (30060 "Three Alley Cats") 50-75 56
FORTUNE (170 "Going Down That Road") 35-50 53
FORTUNE (521 "Corrine Corrina") 35-50 56
HI-Q (5045 "Three Alley Cats") 10-20 65
HI-Q (5050 "Go Go Little Queenie") 15-25 65
PIERCE (1918 "One Monkey Don't Stop the Show") .... 75-125 '50s
STRATE 8 (1508 "Rockin' the Blues") 20-30 59
Also see DAVIS SISTERS / Roy Hall
Also see HUNT SISTERS

HALL, Royce, & Lucky Four

Singles: 7-inch

NU TRYL 4-6 77-78
RAYNARD (1068 "That's My Life") 10-20 67
Members: Billy Woods; Mark Sands; Richard Kermesey.

HALL, Sam

Singles: 7-inch

LOKS ("Elaine") 75-125
(No selection number used.)

HALL, Sidney

Singles: 7-inch

SHRINE (109 "The Weekend") 250-350 66

HALL, Sonny

(With the Echoes)

Singles: 7-inch

D (1009 "My Big Fat Baby") 50-75 58
D (1035 "Men Do Cry") 10-20 59
INT'L ARTISTS (131 "Poor Planet Earth") 10-20 68

HALL, Vernon, & Casinos

Singles: 78 rpm

BLUE KEY (1003 "So in Love with You") . 10-20 53

Singles: 7-inch

BLUE KEY (1003 "So in Love with You") 75-125 53

HALL BROTHERS

Singles: 7-inch

ARC (4444 "Now You Say We Are Through") 10-15 58
4 STAR (1760 "I'm Still Lonely") 5-10 62

HALLADAY, Chance

Singles: 7-inch

BULLDOG (51 "Lucky Me") 25-50 59
BULLDOG (103 "Home Run") 50-75 59
GENE NORMAN PRESENTS (171 "Thirteen Women") 40-50 62

HALLEMAN, Dick

Singles: 7-inch

SUMMIT (189-10 "Pajama Top") 10-20 61
Also see DICK & LIBBY

HALLEY, Bob

Singles: 7-inch

COLUMBIA (42354 "Doesn't Anybody Make Short Movies Anymore") 5-10 62
COLUMBIA (42524 "That Twistin' Girl of Mine") 5-10 62
REGATTA (2001 "Walking with Joe") 15-20 61

HALLIQUINS

Singles: 7-inch

EARLY BIRD (004 "Confession of Love") 3-5 96
(Orange vinyl.)
JUANITA (102 "Confession of Love") 1000-1500 58

HALLMARKS

Singles: 7-inch

DOT (16418 "Congratulations") 10-15 62
EPIC (9681 "Royal King") 10-20 64

HALLMARKS

Singles: 7-inch

SMASH (2115 "Soul Shakin' Psychedelic Sally") 15-25 67

HALLORAN, Jack, Singers *P&R '62*

Singles: 7-inch

DOT (16275 "Little Drummer Boy") 5-10 61

LPs: 10/12-inch

DOT (3076 "Christmas Is A-Comin' ") 20-30 57
(Includes *Carol of the Drum*, later retitled *Little Drummer Boy*.)
DOT (3233 "Little Drummer Boy") 8-12 59
(Monaural.)
DOT (25233 "Little Drummer Boy") 10-20 59
(Stereo.)
Also see JAMES, Joni
Also see NELSON, Rick
Also see PETERSON, Ray
Also see TAYLOR, Joyce

Also see TYFER, Jerry

HALLOWAY, Larry

Singles: 7-inch

PARKWAY (903 "Beatle Teen Beat") 10-20 64

HALLYDAY, Johnny

Singles: 7-inch

PHILIPS (40014 "Hold Back the Sun") 10-20 62
PHILIPS (40024 "Be Bop a Lula")........... 10-20 62
PHILIPS (40043 "Hey Little Girl")............ 10-20 62

Picture Sleeves

PHILIPS (40024 "Be Bop a Lula")........... 20-30 62

LPs: 10/12-inch

PHILIPS (200019 "America's Rockin' Hits").. 30-40 62
(Monaural.)
PHILIPS (600019 "America's Rockin' Hits").. 35-45 62
(Stereo.)

HALO, Johnny

Singles: 7-inch

ANGLE TONE (538 "Little Annie") 30-40 59
ANGLE TONE (541 "It Hurts Me") 40-50 61
TOPIX (6004 "Betty Jean")...................... 40-50 62
(With the 4 Seasons.)
Also see 4 SEASONS

HALO, Johnny / Cindi Prince

Singles: 7-inch

SOUTHERN SOUND (109 "Errand Boy"/"Baby Sitter") 15-25 62

HALOS — P&R '61

Singles: 7-inch

7 ARTS (709 "Nag")............................ 15-25 61
7 ARTS (720 "Come On")...................... 10-20 62
TRANS ATLAS (690 "Village of Love").... 10-15 62

LPs: 10/12-inch

WARWICK (2046 "The Halos") 200-400 62
Members: Harold Johnson; Al Cleveland; Phil Johnson; Arthur Crier.
Also see KING, Ben E.
Also see LEE, Curtis
Also see LITTLE GUY & GIANTS
Also see MANN, Barry
Also see PRE-HISTORICS

HALOS

Singles: 7-inch

CONGRESS (244 "Do I")...........................5-10 65
CONGRESS (249 "Since I Fell for You")....5-10 65
CONGRESS (253 "Baby What You Want Me to Do")..5-10 65
CONGRESS (262 "Come Softly to Me").....5-10 66

HAMAMURA, Michiko

EPs: 7-inch

RCA (4190 "With a Beat")...................... 40-60 58

HAMBER, Kenny

Singles: 7-inch

ARCTIC (131 "Ain't Gonna Cry").......... 150-250 67
ARCTIC (139 "Looking for a Love")..... 100-150 68
(Single-sided. Promotional issue only.)
ARCTIC (139 "Looking for a Love"/"These Arms of Mine")... 50-100 68
DE JAC (1254 "Show Me Your Monkey") 10-20 64
MEAN (200 "Camel Walk")...................... 15-25 '60s
SPAR (101 "Tears in My Eyes")............. 50-75 60
ZENETTE (101 "Tears in My Eyes")...... 75-150 64
(Different from Spar 101. Reportedly this version has a background group.)

HAMBLEN, Stuart — C&W '49

Singles: 78 rpm

COLUMBIA..4-8 49-57

Singles: 7-inch

BLUEBIRD...5-10 59
COLUMBIA..5-10 50-62
CORAL...4-8 59
ELECTRADISK ....25-50 '30s
(Made for sale through Woolworth Stores.)
KAPP 4-8 66
LAMB & LION..4-6 74
RCA (0500 series) 4-6 71
RCA (5000 & 6000 series).......................5-15 54-56

EPs: 7-inch

COLUMBIA..5-10 58-59
RCA...5-15 54-60

LPs: 10/12-inch

CAMDEN 5-15 59-66
COLUMBIA..5-15 61-62
CORAL...12-25 60
HURRAH..5-10
KAPP...15-20 66
LAMB & LION...5-8 74
RCA...15-30 54-57
SACRED 5-8
VOSS..10-15
WORD...5-8

HAMBLET, Billy

Singles: 7-inch

RIK (5036 "Everyday")............................25-35 '60s

HAMBRIC, Billy

Singles: 7-inch

DRUM (1204 "She Said Goodbye")..........15-25 '60s
FURY (5000 thru 5006)..........................10-20 63
JOVIAL (730 "Someone to Love") 15-25 64
LEE (5001 "New York City Baby") ....8-12 '60s
SOHO (5001 "New York City Baby") ....15-25 '60s

HAMILTON, Chico — LP '64

(Chico Hamilton Trio; Quartet; Quintet; with Players)

Singles: 7-inch

COLUMBIA (42045 "Afternoon of a Breeze")..5-10 61
ENTERPRISE (9102 "Fancy") 4-6 74
IMPULSE..5-8 64-67
PACIFIC JAZZ (600 series)........................8-15 54-55
PACIFIC JAZZ (88134 "Satin Doll").............5-8 66

EPs: 7-inch

DECCA...15-25 57
PACIFIC JAZZ 20-40 55-56

LPs: 10/12-inch

BLUE NOTE 5-10 75
COLUMBIA...15-25 60-62
CROWN 10-20 63
DECCA (8614 "Jazz from Sweet Smell of Success")...25-40 57
DISCOVERY 5-8 81
ELEKTRA..5-8 80
EVEREST..5-8 79
FLYING DUTCHMAN 8-10 71
IMPULSE..10-20 63-71
INSTANT..10-20 64
MERCURY..5-10 77
ODYSSEY 10-20 68
PACIFIC JAZZ (17 "The Chico Hamilton Trio") 75-100 55
(10-inch LP.)
PACIFIC JAZZ (39 "Spectacular Chico Hamilton") 15-25 62
PACIFIC JAZZ (1209 "Chico Hamilton Quintet")..50-75 55
PACIFIC JAZZ (1216 "In Hi Fi") 50-75 56
PACIFIC JAZZ (1220 "Chico Hamilton Trio")..50-75 57
PACIFIC JAZZ (1225 "Chico Hamilton Quintet")..50-75 57
PACIFIC JAZZ (20000 series) 10-20 68
REPRISE...15-25 63
SESAC 35-55 59
SOLID STATE..10-15 68-69
SUNSET..8-15 68
W.B. (1245 "With Strings Attached") 50-75 58
W.B. (1271 "Goings East")........................50-75 58
W.B. (1344 "Three Faces of Chico").........40-60 59
WORLD PACIFIC (1000 & 1200 series)...25-40 58-60
Also see ALMEIDA, Laurindo / Chico Hamilton
Also see MULLIGAN, Gerry

HAMILTON, Chico, & Charles Lloyd

LPs: 10/12-inch

COLUMBIA..10-15 68
Also see HAMILTON, Chico

HAMILTON, Dave

(With His Peppers)

Singles: 7-inch

FORTUNE (861 "Beatle Walk")..................20-30 64
HI-Q (5019 "Donna's Cha-Cha")...............20-30 61
WORKSHOP JAZZ (2004 "Late Freight") 10-20 63

LPs: 10/12-inch

WORKSHOP JAZZ (206 "Blue Vibrations")..40-60 63

HAMILTON, Edward

(With the Arabians; with Fifes; Edw. Hamilton)

Singles: 7-inch

CARRIE (9 "I'm Gonna Love You")...........15-25
JAMECO (2008 "Call Me") 20-30
LANROD (1605 "I Love You So") 50-75 60
MARY JANE (1005 "Baby Don't You Weep")...30-50 '60s
MARY JANE (1006 "My Darling Baby")....30-50 '60s
Also see ARABIANS

HAMILTON, George, & Treys

Singles: 7-inch

BELLA (16 "Come to Me")........................15-25 59

HAMILTON, George, IV — P&R '56/C&W '60

(With the Country Gentlemen; with Arthur Smith)

Singles: 78 rpm

ABC-PAR..10-20 56-57
COLONIAL (420 "A Rose and a Baby Ruth")..30-40 56
COLONIAL (451 "Sam")............................10-20 56

Singles: 7-inch

ABC 4-6 78
ABC/DOT 4-6 77
ABC-PAR (9000 series) 10-20 56-59
ABC-PAR (10000 series) 5-15 59-65
COLONIAL (420 "A Rose and a Baby Ruth")..25-40 56
COLONIAL (451 "Sam")............................20-30 56
GRT (063 "Blue Jeans, Ice Cream, and Saturday Shoes") 4-6 76
MCA..4-6 79-80
RCA..4-8 61-74

EPs: 7-inch

ABC-PAR (220 "On Campus")..................15-25 58

LPs: 10/12-inch

ABC..8-10 72-77
ABC-PAR (ABC-220 "On Campus").........20-40 58
(Monaural.)
ABC-PAR (ABCS-220 "On Campus") 25-50 58
(Stereo.)
ABC-PAR (ABC-251 "Sing Me a Sad Song")..20-40 58
(Monaural.)
ABC-PAR (ABCS-251 "Sing Me a Sad Song")..25-50 58
(Stereo.)
ABC-PAR (ABC-461 "Big 15") 20-30 63
(Monaural.)
ABC-PAR (ABCS-461 "Big 15")................25-35 63
(Stereo.)
CAMDEN...8-10 68-73
GRAND AWARD (266 "Country Style")......5-10 66
HARMONY 8-10 70
MCA...5-10 80
RCA ("APL1" series)...................................8-10 74-76
RCA ("LPM" & "LSP" series)....................10-20 61-73
Also see ANKA, Paul, George Hamilton IV & Johnny Nash
Also see BLUENOTES
Also see DAVIS, Skeeter, & George Hamilton IV

HAMILTON, George, IV / Arthur Smith

LPs: 10/12-inch

LAMB & LION 5-8 74
Also see HAMILTON, George, IV
Also see SMITH, Arthur

HAMILTON, Jimmy

("Mighty Man of the Tenor Sax")

Singles: 78 rpm

STATES (113 "Big Fifty") 5-10 53

Singles: 7-inch

STATES (113 "Big Fifty") 15-25 53

HAMILTON, Joel

Singles: 7-inch

ROULETTE (4462 "Starlight")...................10-15 62
ROULETTE (4484 "Can't Wait") 5-10 63

HAMILTON, Linda, & Tunes

Singles: 7-inch

JERILU ("You Don't Understand") 30-40
(Selection number not known.)

HAMILTON, Little Johnny, & Creators

Singles: 7-inch

DORE (754 "Oh How I Love You") 25-50 66
DORE (760 "Keep on Movin'") 8-12 66
Also see CREATORS

HAMILTON, Peter

Singles: 7-inch

JAMIE (1338 "Hey Girl")...........................15-25 67

HAMILTON, Roy — P&R/R&B '54

Singles: 78 rpm

EPIC 5-10 54-57

Singles: 7-inch

A.G.P. (113 thru 125) 8-12 69
CAPITOL (2057 "Let This World Be Free")..5-8 67
EPIC (9015 thru 9354)..............................10-20 54-59
EPIC (9372 thru 9538) 5-10 60-63
EPIC (70464 "Don't Let Go") 25-50 61
(Stereo.)
EPIC MEMORY LANE 4-6 63-64
MGM (13138 thru 13175)............................5-10 63
MGM (13217 "The Panic Is On").............25-35 64
MGM (13247 "Unchained Melody").............5-10 64
MGM (13291 "You Can Count on Me")....60-80 64
MGM (13315 "Sweet Violet") 5-10 65
RCA (8641 thru 8841).................................5-10 65-66
RCA (8960 "Crackin' Up Over You").........15-25 66
RCA (9061 "I Taught Her Everything She Knows") 8-12 67
RCA (9171 "So High My Love")...............25-45 67

Picture Sleeves

EPIC 10-20 60-62

EPs: 7-inch

EPIC 10-20 54-59

LPs: 10/12-inch

CBS 5-8
EPIC (518 "With All My Love")..................25-35 58
(Stereo.)
EPIC (525 "Why Fight the Feeling") 20-30 59
(Stereo.)
EPIC (530 "Come Out Swingin'") 20-30 59
(Stereo.)
EPIC (535 "Have Blues Must Travel") 20-30 59
(Stereo.)
EPIC (551 "Spirituals") 20-25 60
(Stereo.)
EPIC (578 "Soft 'N Warm") 20-25 60
(Stereo.)
EPIC (595 "You Can Have Her") 20-25 61
(Stereo.)
EPIC (610 "Only You")...............................20-25 61
(Stereo.)
EPIC (632 "You'll Never Walk Alone")......10-20 65
(Stereo.)
EPIC (1023 "You'll Never Walk Alone") .50-100 54
(10-inch LP.)
EPIC (1103 "The Voice of Roy Hamilton")..50-100 55
(10-inch LP.)
EPIC (3176 "Roy Hamilton")......................25-50 57
EPIC (3294 "You'll Never Walk Alone") ...50-75 54
EPIC (3364 "Golden Boy")........................30-40 57
EPIC (3519 "With All My Love")................15-25 58
(Monaural.)
EPIC (3545 "Why Fight the Feeling").......15-25 59
(Monaural.)
EPIC (3561 "Come Out Swingin'") 15-25 59
(Monaural.)
EPIC (3580 "Have Blues Must Travel")....15-25 59
(Monaural.)
EPIC (3628 "At His Best")..........................15-25 60
(Monaural.)
EPIC (3654 "Spirituals")............................15-25 60
(Monaural.)
EPIC (3717 "Soft 'N Warm") 15-25 60
(Monaural.)
EPIC (3775 "You Can Have Her") 15-25 61
(Monaural.)
EPIC (3807 "Only You") 15-25 61
(Monaural.)
EPIC (24000 "Mr. Rock & Soul") 15-25 62
(Monaural.)
EPIC (24009 "Greatest Hits")....................15-25 63
(Monaural.)
EPIC (24316 "Greatest Hits, Vol. 2")........10-20 67
(Monaural.)
EPIC (26000 "Mr. Rock & Soul") 20-25 62
(Stereo.)
EPIC (26009 "Greatest Hits")....................15-25 63
(Stereo.)
EPIC (26316 "Greatest Hits, Vol. 2")........10-20 67
(Stereo.)
MGM (4139 "Warm Soul")..........................15-25 63
MGM (4233 "Sentimental, Lonely and Blue")..15-25 64
RCA (3532 "Impossible Dream") 15-25 66
SEAGULL 8-12

HAMILTON, Russ — P&R/R&B '57

Singles: 78 rpm

KAPP...5-10 57

Singles: 7-inch

KAPP (184 thru 612)...................................5-10 57-64

MGM (12947 "Choir Girl") 5-10 60
LPs: 10/12-inch
KAPP (1076 "Rainbow") 45-55 57

HAMILTON, Walter, Combo
Singles: 7-inch
FORTUNE (849 "Sherry Blues") 20-30 59
HI-Q (5034 "Let Me Be Loved") 10-15 63
HI-Q (5043 "Nobody But Me") 10-15 64
Also see CENTURYS

HAMILTON, Willie
Singles: 7-inch
CONTOUR (500 "I'm So Glad You're Mine") 30-40 60
HRP (001 "Cheer Up") 10-15 '60s

HAMILTON SISTERS
Singles: 78 rpm
COLUMBIA 5-10 54
KING (4892 "You Are the One") 10-15 56
Singles: 7-inch
COLUMBIA 10-15 54
KING (4892 "You Are the One") 50-75 56

HAMILTON STREETCAR
Singles: 7-inch
LHI (17016 "Invisible People") 10-15 67
DOT (17253 "Silver Wings") 5-10 69
W.B. (7285 "No Easy Way Down") 5-10 69
LPs: 10/12-inch
DOT (25939 "Hamilton Streetcar") 15-25 69

HAMLIN, Johnny, Quintet
Singles: 7-inch
FRATERNITY (731 "Don't Do") 15-20 56

HAMM, Mark
Singles: 7-inch
AUDIO ARTISTS (102 "Ruby Baby") 15-25

HAMMAN, Jeff, & Surf Teens
Singles: 7-inch
WESTCO (9 "Moment of Truth") 15-20 63
(Black vinyl.)
WESTCO (9 "Moment of Truth") 30-40 63
(Colored vinyl.)

HAMMEL, Karl, Jr. *P&R '61*
(Carl Hammel)
Singles: 7-inch
ARLISS (1007 "Summer Souvenirs") 15-25 61
ARLISS (1011 "Sittin' Alphabetically") 40-50 61
GONE (5030 "Can It Be") 10-15 58
GONE (5059 "My Broken Heart") 10-15 59
LAURIE (3170 "Drop Me a Line") 5-10 63
20TH FOX (6650 "World of Your Own") 5-8 66

HAMMER, Jack
Singles: 78 rpm
DECCA (30109 "Football Rock") 5-10 56
Singles: 7-inch
DECCA (30109 "Football Rock") 10-20 56
KAPP (274 "We Three") 5-10 59
KAPP (287 "Little Bitty Goose Pimples") 5-10 60
MILESTONE (2001 "Black Widow Spider Woman") 50-75 59
RONNEX (1270 "Melancholy Boy") 5-10 62
RONNEX (1284 "Wiggle") 5-10 62
ROULETTE (4046 "Chant of Love") 5-10 58
SOUL (35088 "Color Combination") 4-6 71

HAMMOND, Clay
Singles: 7-inch
DUO DISC (109 "Dance Little Girl") 5-10 65
EVEJIM 3-5 88
GALAXY (723 "My Baby Left Me Crying") 15-25 63
KENT 5-10 67-69
KEYMEN 8-12 67
LIBERTY (55817 "No One Else Will Do") 5-10 65
MERCURY 4-6 73
RAUSHAN 3-5 82
RONN 4-6 70
TAG 10-20 62
VERSEPTO 3-5 82
Also see HAMMOND BROTHERS

HAMMOND, Clay, with Johnnie Young & Celebritys
Singles: 78 rpm
CAROLINE (2302 "We Made Romance") 200-300 56
Singles: 7-inch
CAROLINE (2302 "We Made Romance") 2000-3000 56
Also see CELEBRITYS
Also see HAMMOND, Clay

HAMMOND, Jay, & Rhythm Kings
(With the Golden Voices)
Singles: 7-inch
HI-Q (5015 "I'll Be Your Fool") 15-25 60

HAMMOND, O'Nita
Singles: 7-inch
BETHLEHEM (3020 "Mighty Fine") 10-15 62

HAMMOND, Roy, & Genies
Singles: 7-inch
FORUM (701 "Mama, Blow Your Top") 40-50 61

HAMMOND, Stick Horse
Singles: 78 rpm
J.O.B. (100 "Gambling Man") 35-55 50
J.O.B. (105 "Highway 51") 35-55 50
GOTHAM (504 "Truck 'Em On Down") 20-30 50
ROYALTY (906 "Highway 51") 35-55 50

HAMMOND, Tommy
Singles: 7-inch
KOOL (1011 "Let's Forget We Ever Met") 75-125 61

HAMMOND, Wayne, & Starfires
Singles: 7-inch
GALA (105 "Carolyn") 100-200 59

HAMPTON, Duke
Singles: 78 rpm
KING (4625 "Please Be Good to Me") 10-20 53
Singles: 7-inch
KING (4625 "Please Be Good to Me") 30-50 53

HAMPTON, John, & Hamptones
Singles: 78 rpm
UNITED (210 "Honey Hush") 50-100 57
Singles: 7-inch
UNITED (210 "Honey Hush") 75-100 57

HAMPTON, Johnny
Singles: 7-inch
DOTTY'S (1001 "Not My Girl") 20-30 '60s
ROSE (003 "Beatle Dance") 10-20 64

HAMPTON, Junior / Brother Jackson
Singles: 78 rpm
MURRAY (500 "J.H. Stomp") 25-50 48
Also see JACKSON, Louis

HAMPTON, Lionel *P&R '37*
(With the Hamptones)
Singles: 78 rpm
CLEF 4-8 55
DECCA 5-10 42-53
MGM 4-8 51-56
NORGREN 4-8 56
VICTOR 5-15 37-41
Singles: 7-inch
CLEF 5-10 55
BRUNSWICK 4-6 74
COLUMBIA 4-6 76
DECCA (Except 140 & 154) 5-10 50-53
DECCA (140 "Moonglow") 15-25 51
(Boxed, four-disc set)
DECCA (154 "Just Jazz") 15-25 53
(Boxed, four-disc set)
GLAD HAMP 5-8 60-67
IMPULSE (234 "Trick or Treat") 4-8 65
LAURIE 4-6 79-80
MGM 5-10 51-61
NORGREN 5-10 56
VERVE (111 "Air Mail Special") 4-8 62
EPs: 7-inch
CAMDEN 10-15 '50s
CLEF 15-30 53-56
COLUMBIA 10-20 56
DECCA 10-20 51-53
EMARCY 10-20 56
EPIC 10-20 56
GLAD HAMP 5-10 62
MGM 10-20 56
MERCURY 10-20 55
NORGREN 10-30 55
RCA 10-20 54-57
LPs: 10/12-inch
AMERICAN RECORDING SOCIETY (403 "Swinging Jazz") 100-150 56
(Includes booklet.)
AUDIO FIDELITY 20-40 57-59
BLUENOTE (5046 "Rockin' and Groovin' ") 100-150 53
(10-inch LP.)
BRUNSWICK 5-10 74
CAMDEN (400 & 500 series) 20-30 58-59
CLEF (142 "Lionel Hampton Quartet") 75-125 53
(10-inch LP.)
CLEF (611 "Lionel Hampton Quartet") 50-100 53
CLEF (628 "Lionel Hampton Quintet") 50-100 54
CLEF (642 "Lionel Hampton Quintet") 50-100 54
CLEF (667 "Quartet/Quintet") 50-100 55
CLEF (670 "Big Band") 50-100 55
CLEF (673 "Big Band") 50-100 55
CLEF (735 "Flying Home") 50-100 56
CLEF (736 "Swingin' with Hamp") 50-100 56
CLEF (744 "Hamp's Big Four") 50-100 56
CLEF (709 "Lionel Hampton Trio") 50-100 56
COLUMBIA (711 "Wailin' at the Trianon") 50-100 56
COLUMBIA (1304 thru 1661) 20-40 59-61
(Monaural.)
COLUMBIA (8110 thru 8461) 25-50 59-61
(Stereo.)
CONTEMPORARY (3502 "Lionel Hampton Swings in Paris") 50-100 55
CORAL 15-25 63
DECCA (4000 series) 20-40 61-63
(Monaural.)
DECCA (7-4000 series) 25-50 61-63
(Stereo.)
DECCA (5230 "Boogie Woogie") 50-100 51
(10-inch LP.)
DECCA (7013 "Just Jazz") 50-100 53
(10-inch LP.)
DECCA (8200 series) 40-60 56
DECCA (9000 series) 25-50 58
DECCA (79000 series) 10-15 69
EMARCY (26037 "In Paris") 50-100 53
(10-inch LP.)
EMARCY (26038 "Crazy Hamp") 50-100 53
(10-inch LP.)
EMARCY (36032 "In Paris") 50-75 53
EMARCY (36034 "Crazy Hamp") 50-75 56
EPIC (3190 "Lionel Hampton Apollo Hall Concert 1954") 50-75 56
EPIC (16027 "Many Splendored Vibes") 20-40 62
(Monaural.)
EPIC (17027 "Many Splendored Vibes") 25-50 62
(Stereo.)
GNP (15 "Lionel Hampton with the Jazz All Stars") 50-100 57
GLAD HAMP (1001 thru 1009) 15-25 61-65
GLAD HAMP (1020 & 1021) 5-10 80
GLAD HAMP (3000 series) 15-25 62
HARMONY (7000 series) 20-35 58-61
HARMONY (32000 series) 5-10 73
LAURIE 5-10 78
MCA 5-8 75-82
MGM (285 "Oh Rock") 75-125 51
(10-inch LP.)
MGM (3386 "Oh Rock") 50-75 56
MUSE 5-8 79
NORGREN (1080 "Lionel Hampton and His Giants") 50-100 55
PERFECT (12002 "Hampton Swings") 40-60 59
RCA (1000 "Hot Mallets") 50-100 54
RCA (1422 "Jazz Flamenco") 50-75 57
RCA (LPM-2318 "Swing Classics") 25-40 61
(Monaural.)
RCA (LSP-2318 "Swing Classics") 35-55 61
(Stereo.)
RCA (3900 series) 10-15 68
RCA (5536 "The Complete Lionel Hampton") 50-75 76
(Boxed, six-disc set.)
SUTRA 5-10 81
VERVE (2018 "Lionel Hampton Plays Love Songs") 50-100 56
VERVE (2500 series) 5-10 82
VERVE (8019 thru 8228) 40-60 57-58
WHO'S WHO IN JAZZ 5-10 78-81
Also see BOSTIC, Earl
Also see BROWN, Wini
Also see CARTER, Betty
Also see COLE, Cozy
Also see GOODMAN, Benny / Lionel Hampton
Also see HALEY, Bill / Lionel Hampton / Sal Salvador Quartet / Lenny Dee
Also see JACQUET, Illinois

HAMPTON, Lionel & Stan Getz
LPs: 10/12-inch
NORGREN (1037 "Hamp and Getz") 75-100 55
VERVE (8128 "Hamp and Getz") 40-60 57
Also see GETZ, Stan

HAMPTON, Lionel & Dinah Washington *R&B '44*
Singles: 78 rpm
DECCA 5-15 44-47
LPs: 10/12-inch
DECCA (8088 "All American Award Concert") 40-60 54
Also see HAMPTON, Lionel
Also see WASHINGTON, Dinah

HAMPTON, Paul
Singles: 7-inch
A&M (831 "Let's Not Take the Lovin' Out of Love") 5-10 67
BATTLE (45919 "Bandera") 5-10 63
CAMEO (204 "Maybe Impossible") 5-10 61
COLUMBIA (41306 "Don't Be Stuck Up") 10-20 58
COLUMBIA (41396 "Write Me") 10-20 59
DECCA (31928 "What Good Am I") 5-10 66
DOT (16084 "Creams") 8-12 60
DOT (16543 "Etiquette") 5-10 63
TOP RANK (2095 "Don't Pretend") 10-20 61
W.B. (5290 "If You Don't Want Me Now") 5-10 62
W.B. (5319 "Empty Feeling") 5-10 62
W.B. (5340 "Chance to Belong") 5-10 63
Picture Sleeves
BATTLE (45919 "Bandera") 10-15 63

HAMPTONS / Brothers Kennedy
Singles: 7-inch
LEGRAND (1007 "Once in a Lifetime"/"I Know Why Dreamers Cry") 15-25 61

HANCHEY, Donald, & Marauders
Singles: 7-inch
MI-TIA (1001 "Hang Loose") 75-125

HANCOCK, Herbie *LP '67*
Singles: 12-inch
COLUMBIA (Except 39913) 4-6 79-85
COLUMBIA (39913 "Rock It") 10-15 84
(Picture disc.)
Singles: 7-inch
BLUE NOTE 5-10 62-65
COLUMBIA 3-6 74-88
W.B. 4-8 69-72
LPs: 10/12-inch
BLUE NOTE 20-30 62-65
(Label reads "Blue Note Records Inc. - New York, U.S.A.")
BLUE NOTE 10-15 66-71
(Label shows Blue Note Records as a division of either Liberty or United Artists.)
COLUMBIA 8-15 67-85
UPFRONT 5-10
W.B. 8-15 70-74
Also see SANTANA

HANDCLAPPERS
Singles: 7-inch
COLLIER (2500 "Three Gassed Rats") 10-20 61

HANDICAPPERS
Singles: 7-inch
ADVANCE (6250 "I Got a Little Girl") 15-25 63

HANDS OF TIME
Singles: 7-inch
SIDEWALK (903 "Got to Get You into My Life") 10-20 66
Members: Mike Curb; Davie Allan.
Also see ALLAN, Davie

HANDY, Cap'n John
(With the New Orleans Stompers)
LPs: 10/12-inch
GHB (41 "All Aboard, Vol. 1") 8-12 67
GHB (42 "All Aboard, Vol. 2") 8-12 67
GHB (43 "All Aboard, Vol. 3") 8-12 67
RCA (3762 "Introducing Cap'n John Handy") 10-15 67
RCA (3929 "New Orleans & the Blues") 10-15 68

Session: Kid Thomas Valentine; Jim Robinson; Sammy Rimmington; Bill Sinclair; Dick Griffith; Dick McCarthy; Sammy Penn.

HANDY, John
(Gene Autry)
Singles: 78 rpm
BENNETT (7290 "Hobo Bill's Last Ride") 25-75
BENNETT (7310 "Dust Pan Blues")........ 25-75
RADIEX........ 25-75
Also see AUTRY, Gene

HANDY, John *P&R/R&B/LP '76*
(John Handy Quartet; Quintet)
Singles: 7-inch
IMPULSE........4-6 76-77
COLUMBIA........4-8 66-69
ROULETTE (4714 "Blues for M.F.")........5-8 66
LPs: 10/12-inch
IMPULSE........5-10 76-77
COLUMBIA........10-15 66-68
ROULETTE (100 series)........5-10 76
ROULETTE (52042 "In the Vernacular") . 15-25 60
ROULETTE (52121 "Jazz")........10-20 66
ROULETTE (52124 "Quote, Unquote") ... 10-20 67
W.B. 5-10 78

HANDY, Mary, & Butterflies
Singles: 7-inch
L&J (50 "Rock and Roll Shuffle")........ 200-300 58

HANDY, Roy
(With the Parlets)
Singles: 7-inch
MARTON (1001 "What Did He Do")........ 20-30
STEPHAYNE (234 "Baby, That's a Groove")........ 20-30

HANDY, Wayne
(With the King Sisters; Wayne C. Handy)
Singles: 7-inch
DIAL (3001 "Conscience Let Me Go") 5-10 61
PARKWAY (812 "So Much to Remember")........5-10 60
RENOWN........10-20 57-59
TREND........10-15 58-59

HANEY, Bill
(With His Dixie Buddies)
Singles: 7-inch
BRIAR (127 "Share Your Love")........ 10-15 62
DOT (16731 "Leavin' Town")........ 10-15 65
JIM DANDY (1013 "Crawdad Song")........ 50-75
RAV (13 "Cause You Were There")........5-10 77
LPs: 10/12-inch
RURAL RHYTHM (2109 "Bill Haney & the Dixie Buddies")........ 10-20
Members: Bob Pierce; Tom Parker; Wilbur Brazzel; Mack Taylor.

HANEY, Bill, & Ken Meggs
Singles: 7-inch
DEE-BEE (69 "Wild Party Twist")........ 10-20 62
Also see HANEY, Bill

HANEY, Jack, & Nikiter Armstrong
Singles: 7-inch
MEL-O-DY (107 "The Interview")........ 10-20 63

HANGMEN
Singles: 7-inch
MONUMENT (910 "What a Girl Can't Do")........ 10-15 65
MONUMENT (951 "Faces")........ 10-15 66
LPs: 10/12-inch
MONUMENT (8077 "Bitter Sweet")........ 20-30 67
(Monaural.)
MONUMENT (18077 "Bitter Sweet")........ 25-35 67
(Stereo.)
Also see REEKERS

HANGMEN OF FAIRFIELD COUNTY
Singles: 7-inch
HIGH CASTLE (401 "Stacey")........ 15-25 66

HANK & CAROLEE
Singles: 7-inch
MALA (424 "Go On and Go")........ 25-30 60
Members: Hank Davis; Kenny Burrell.
Also see DAVIS, Hank

HANK & ELECTRAS
Singles: 7-inch
DAUPHIN (106 "Get Lost Baby")........ 175-225 59
Members: Hank Davis; Barry Kaplan; Mike Kantor; Gerry Greenwald.
Also see DAVIS, Hank

HANK & FRANK
Singles: 78 rpm
COLUMBIA (20675 "I Offer You My Second Hand Heart")........8-15 50
Singles: 7-inch
COLUMBIA (20675 "I Offer You My Second Hand Heart")........15-25 50
(33 single.)
XYZ (101 "Rock-A-Billy"/"Ain'tcha Got Some Room in Your Great Big Heart for Me")........15-25 57
(B-side by Mercy & Justice.)
Members: Johnny Bond; Bert Dodson.

HANK & SUGAR PIE
Singles: 78 rpm
FEDERAL (12217 "I'm So Lonely")........10-15 55
Singles: 7-inch
FEDERAL (12217 "I'm So Lonely")........20-30 55
Members: Hank Huston; Umpeylia Balinton.
Also see CUFF LINKS
Also see DE SANTO, Sugar Pie
Also see LOVE, Preston
Also see LOVE BUGS

HANK THE COWHAND
Singles: 7-inch
COZY (27322 "Would You Care")........25-35

HANK THE DRIFTER
Singles: 7-inch
NEW ENGLAND (7 "Cheaters Never Win")........15-25 61
NEW ENGLAND (70 "I'm Crying My Heart Out for You")........15-25 61
NEW ENGLAND (235 "I'm Gonna Spin My Wheels")........100-200 61
NEW ENGLAND (1540 "Painted Doll")........15-25 63
NEW ENGLAND (1542 "You're Paying for It Now")........15-25 63

HANKINS, Bobby
Singles: 7-inch
AD (104 "Honky Tonk Queen")........100-200
CUCA (1256 thru 6563)........5-10 65-66
WHITE LIGHTNIN' (500 "Root Beer"/"White Lightnin'")........5-10

HANKINS, Esco
Singles: 7-inch
COLUMBIA (42822 thru 43446)........5-10 63-65
SIMS (119 "Oh So Afraid")........8-12 61
(With Jackie Hankins.)
EPs: 7-inch
JEWEL (403 "Esco Hankins and Ted Mullins")........15-25 61
REM (504 "Esco Hankins")........50-75
LPs: 10/12-inch
AUDIO LAB (1547 "Esco Hankins Country Style")........25-50 61

HANKINS, Hank
Singles: 7-inch
REKA (298 "Kentucky Home Rock")........10-20 60

HANKINS, John C.
Singles: 7-inch
LOUIS ("K.C. Twist")........10-20 62
(Selection number not known.)

HANKINS, "Tall" Paul
Singles: 7-inch
BISCAYNE (001 "The Turnpike")........10-20 65
BISCAYNE (003 "Hot Spot")........10-20 65
MALA (585 "The Turnpike")........4-8 68
MISS (622 "Joe's House Party")........4-8

HANKS, Mike
(With the Del-Phis; with Del-Fi's; with Contours)
Singles: 7-inch
AL-JACK'S (0001 "I Cried")........75-125
BRAX (22-1 "Christine")........100-150 59
MAH'S (1003 "The Hawk")........50-75 60
MAH'S (1004 "I Think About You")........50-75 61
MAH'S (1014 "J.F.K.")........15-25 63
SPARTAN (401 "The Hawk")........30-40 61
Also see CONTOURS
Also see DEL-FIS
Also see DEL-PHIS

HANLEY, Pete
(With Ray Ellis & Orchestra; with Leyden Bros.)
Singles: 78 rpm
EPIC (9155 "I Look at You")........5-10 56
OKEH........8-10 53
Singles: 7-inch
EPIC (9155 "I Look at You")........10-20 56
OKEH (6956 "Big Mamou")........15-25 53
OKEH (6980 "Help Me Mend a Broken Heart")........15-25 53
Also see ELLIS, Ray, Orchestra

HANLEY, Tye Tongue
Singles: 7-inch
JVB (88 "You Got My Nose Wide Open") 50-60 57

HANNA, Fletcher, & Red "Joe" Rayner & His Ozark Boys
Singles: 7-inch
VALLEY (101 "Hepcat Boogie")........100-200 '50s

HANNA, Jack
Singles: 7-inch
DIXIE (889 "Brady and Dunky")........75-125

HANNAN, Jimmy
Singles: 7-inch
ATLANTIC (2247 "Beach Ball")........10-15 64

HANNIBAL
(James T. Shaw)
Singles: 7-inch
KING (5706 thru 5837)........10-20 62-64
MEXI (101 "What About You Baby")........40-50 62
MY RECORD KOMPANY........3-5 81
PAN WORLD (517 "Please Take a Chance on Me")........10-20 60
PAN WORLD (521 "Mother Goose Breaks Loose")........10-20 60
SUE (751 "I Need a Woman")........10-20 61
Also see MIGHTY HANNIBAL

HANNS, James, & Soul Entertainers
Singles: 7-inch
RAYNARD (1004 "It's a Fine Thing")........15-25 66
Members: James Hanns Walner; Patrick McCarthy; Tom Jones; Gene Roceb; Curt Vandenhuevel; Doc Mathias; Tom Cody; Dennis Reeves Regowsky.

HANSEN, Doug
(With the Hot Doggers)
Singles: 7-inch
DORE (567 "Sweet Linda Lee")........10-15 60
EVA (104 "Surfin' Movies")........15-25 63

HANSEN, Herbert
Singles: 7-inch
TALLY (120 "Lose My Mind")........100-200

HANSEN, Rudy
Singles: 7-inch
DECCA (30594 "Just As Long")........10-15 58
RUDY HANSEN (1226 "Saturday Jump")........200-300

HANSERD, Kirk
Singles: 7-inch
DOT (1281 "One Night")........50-75 56

HANSLEY, Johnny, & Redhots
Singles: 7-inch
KIP (402 "Shaggin'")........15-25 59

HANSON, Carol
Singles: 7-inch
END (1032 "Knockin' on the Right Front Door")........10-15 58

HANSON, Jerry
Singles: 7-inch
BLUEBONNET (502 "When I Was a Little Boy")........50-75
COLPIX (137 "Cool, Man")........15-25 60
MANCO (1058 "If I Don't Know")........10-20 64
STARDAY (560 "I'm Doing All Right")........1500-2000 61

HANYEL, Arbis
Singles: 7-inch
COUNT (103 "Roadhouse Rock")........100-150

HA'PENNYS
LPs: 10/12-inch
FERSCH (1110 "Love Is Not the Same") .50-75 68

HAPPENINGS *P&R/LP '66*
Singles: 7-inch
ABC........4-6 73
B.T. PUPPY (Except 181)........8-12 66-68
B.T. PUPPY (181 "Have Yourself a Merry Little Christmas")........20-30 67
(Promotional issue only.)
BIG TREE........4-8 72
ERIC........4-6
JUBILEE........4-8 69-71
MIDLAND INT'L........4-6 77
PHILCO (7 "Go Away Little Girl"/"See You in September")........10-20 67
("Hip Pocket" flexi-disc.)
TRIP........4-6
VIRGO........4-6 72
Picture Sleeves
B.T. PUPPY........10-15 67-69
LPs: 10/12-inch
B.T. PUPPY (1001 "Happenings")........15-25 66
B.T. PUPPY (1003 "Psycle")........15-25 67
B.T. PUPPY (1004 "Golden Hits")........25-35 68
JUBILEE (8028 "Piece of Mind")........15-20 69
JUBILEE (8030 "Greatest Hits")........15-20 69
POST........8-12 '70s
Member: Bob Miranda; Tom Guliano; Ralph DeVito; Dave Libert; Bernie Laporte; Mike LaNeue.
Also see 4 GRADUATES
Also see MIRANDA, Bob
Also see TOKENS / Happenings

HAPPY CADAVERS
EPs: 7-inch
UNDEFINED (28109 "I Saw My Baby in the Meat Section")........20-25

HAPPY CATS
Singles: 7-inch
OMACK (803 "My Tune")........20-30 67

HAPPY DRAGON BAND
LPs: 10/12-inch
FIDDLERS ("Happy Dragon Band")........40-60 78
(Selection number not known.)

HAPPY JESTERS
Singles: 78 rpm
ABBOTT (3025 "Just Because")........10-20 56
Singles: 7-inch
ABBOTT (3025 "Just Because")........20-30 56
DOT (15566 "Just Because")........10-20 57

HAPPY PIERRE
Singles: 78 rpm
LIBERTY (55036 "My Man")........5-10 56
Singles: 7-inch
LIBERTY (55036 "My Man")........10-15 56

HAPPY TEENS
Singles: 7-inch
PARADISE (114 "One More Kiss")........20-25 60

HAPPY TIMERS
Singles: 7-inch
CREST (1050 "I'll Never Change")........10-20 58

HARBIN, Tommy
Singles: 7-inch
VALIANT (9/10 "Lover's Lane Blues")..100-200

HARBOR LIGHTS
(Harbor Lites)
Singles: 7-inch
JARO (77020 "What Would I Do Without You")........20-30 60
MALA (422 "Angel of Love")........20-30 60
Members: Kenny Vance; Sandy Deane.
Also see JAY & AMERICANS

HARD, Randy
(With the Hi-Lites)
Singles: 7-inch
NRC (013 "Honey Doll")........15-25 58
NRC (044 "Let Her Go")........10-15 59

HARD TIMES
Singles: 7-inch
GRAY ANT (107 "Can't Wait 'Til Friday"). 10-15 '60s

HARDEN, Doug
Singles: 78 rpm
HUMMINGBIRD ("Dig That Ford")........20-30 56
LIBERTY BELL (9006 "Dig That Ford")....10-20 56
REV (3502 "Foolin' Me")........10-20 57
Singles: 7-inch
HUMMINGBIRD ("Dig That Ford")........75-100 56
(Selection number not known.)
LIBERTY BELL (9006 "Dig That Ford")....40-60 56
REV (3502 "Foolin' Me")........10-20 57

HARDESTY, Herb
Singles: 7-inch
FEDERAL (12410 thru 12460) 10-20 61-62
MUTUAL (1001 "Beatin' and Blowin' ")..... 15-25 60

HARDIN, "Big" George
Singles: 7-inch
RECORTE (403 "Blue")........................... 15-25 58

HARDIN, Bobby
Singles: 7-inch
WESTWOOD (202 "I'm Lovin' You Baby") 200-300 60

HARDIN, Jim, & Musical Erupters
Singles: 7-inch
VOLCANO (100 "High Stepping Woman")... 40-60 58

HARDIN, Pete
Singles: 7-inch
PEACH (743 "Be My Chickadee")........ 300-400 61

HARDIN, Tim *P&R/LP '69*
Singles: 7-inch
COLUMBIA..4-8 69-72
VERVE FOLKWAYS...................................5-10 66-67
VERVE FORECAST....................................4-8 67-71
LPs: 10/12-inch
ANTILLES..5-10 73
ATCO..8-15 67
COLUMBIA (9787 "Suite for Susan Moore and Damian") 20-30 69
COLUMBIA (30551 "Bird on a Wire")...... 15-20 70
COLUMBIA (37164 "Shock of Grace") 5-10 81
MGM...6-10 70-74
POLYDOR..5-10 81
VERVE FORECAST 10-20 67-69
(May show "Verve Folkways" on spine. Some have a silver sticker covering that name with "Verve Forecast.")

HARDIN, Wes, & Roxsters
Singles: 7-inch
AFS (302 "Anyway") 750-1000 58
PERFECT (110 "Honky Tonk Man").... 300-400 57
Also see ROXSTERS

HARDISON, Bernie
(Bernard Hardison; with Band)
Singles: 78 rpm
EXCELLO (2020 "Yeah, It's True") 15-25 53
REPUBLIC (7111 "Too Much") 20-40 55
Singles: 7-inch
EXCELLO (2020 "Yeah, It's True") 40-50 53
REPUBLIC (7111 "Too Much") 50-75 55

HARDLE, Joe, & Orchids
Singles: 7-inch
DERY (10016 "Confusion") 10-20 61

HARDTIMES *P&R '66*
Singles: 7-inch
WORLD PACIFIC.......................................5-10 66-68
LPs: 10/12-inch
WORLD PACIFIC.................................... 15-25 66-68
Members: Lee Kiefer; Bob Morris; Rudy Romero; Bill Richardson.
Also see NEW PHOENIX
Also see STEPPENWOLF
Also see T.I.M.E.

HARDY, Bill
Singles: 7-inch
RITA (1001 "Rockin' at the Zoo") 50-75 59

HARDY, Hal
Singles: 7-inch
HOLLYWOOD (1116 "House of Broken Hearts") 15-25 67

HARDY, Ulyces
Singles: 7-inch
BEVERLY (752 "Fussin' Women")........... 15-25 59

HARGENS, Trilby
Singles: 78 rpm
HERWIN (92012 "Goofer Dust Blues") 100-200 24

HARGETT, Johnnie, & Music Makers
Singles: 7-inch
CHERRY (1016 "Rock the Town Tonight").. 100-200 60

HARGETT, Mackey
Singles: 7-inch
SABLE (100 "So Glad You're Mine") 350-450

HARGO, Charles
(With Bob Fonville Orchestra & Chorus)
Singles: 7-inch
DAB (101 "Baby Oh Baby")....................75-125 59

HARGRAVE, Don
("Big Don" Hargrave)
Singles: 7-inch
SILVER SLIPPER (1003 "Fee-Fi-Fo Fum") 40-50 60

HARGRAVE, Ron
Singles: 78 rpm
MGM (Except 12422) 5-15 56-58
MGM (12422 "Latch on")..........................20-30 57
Singles: 7-inch
CUB...8-12 59
MGM (Except 12422) 10-20 56-58
MGM (12422 "Latch On") 40-60 57

HARGRO, Charles
Singles: 7-inch
DAB (101 "Baby Oh Baby")....................75-100 59

HARINGTON, Jackie
Singles: 7-inch
MUSICTONE (1120 "Reach Out") 10-20 64

HARKEY, Fred
Singles: 7-inch
HILLCREST (1805 "Marooned on an Island")..50-100

HARLAN, Billy
Singles: 7-inch
BRUNSWICK (55066 "I Wanna Bop")....75-100 58

HARLAND BROTHERS
Singles: 7-inch
KUSTOM (4167 "Rockin' at Midnight").....15-20 '60s

HARLEM STARS
Singles: 78 rpm
E&W (100 "All Right, Baby")....................25-50 51
Member: Willie Mae Thornton.
Also see THORNTON, Willie Mae

HARLEMAIRES
Singles: 78 rpm
ATLANTIC (856 "If You Mean What You Say") 40-60 48
Members: Dottie Smith; Chester Slater; Bill Butler; Percy Doell.
Also see BENNET, Connie, Bill Smyth, & Harlem-Aires
Also see DOGGETT, Bill

HARLOWE, Ray, & Gyp Fox
LPs: 10/12-inch
WATER WHEEL (711 "First Rays").........20-30 78

HARMAN, Bobby
Singles: 7-inch
DECCA (29872 "Kingfish Blues")............15-25 56

HARMON, Bob
(With the T Tones; with His Band; with Jack Marshall Orchestra)
Singles: 78 rpm
REPUBLIC (7114 "Shake Rag Shuffle")...15-25 55
Singles: 7-inch
BLUE HEN ("Tombstone, Arizona").........10-20 61
(Selection number not known.)
ORBIT (522 "Mallie Ann")........................15-25 58
REPUBLIC (7114 "Shake Rag Shuffle")...30-40 55
SALEM (523 "Song of Caroline") ....15-25 '50s
Also see WALKER, Lanie

HARMON, Larry
Singles: 7-inch
DORE (570 "Alone and Blue") 40-60 60

HARMON, Lee
(With the Circle C Band)
Singles: 7-inch
CIRCLE C (105 "Ramshackled Shack") 200-300
RENNER (248 "Bad Habit") 15-25 64

HARMONAIRES
Singles: 7-inch
HOLIDAY (2602 "Lorraine") 100-200 57
(Black label.)
HOLIDAY (2602 "Lorraine")......................20-30 60
(Glossy red label. Has double horizontal lines.)
HOLIDAY (2602 "Lorraine") ....10-15 '60s
(Flat red label. Has single horizontal line.)
LOST NITE...4-8
Also see CHARTS / Bop-Chords / Ladders / Harmonaires

HARMONAIRES MALE QUARTET
LPs: 10/12-inch
VARSITY (6915 "Spirituals").....................50-75 '50s
(10-inch LP.)

HARMONICA BLUES KING
Singles: 78 rpm
EBONY (1003 "I Need You Pretty Baby")..50-75 56
Singles: 7-inch
EBONY (1003 "I Need You Pretty Baby")..100-200 56

HARMONICA FATS
Singles: 7-inch
DARCEY (5000 "Tore Up") 15-25 63
DARCEY (5003 "Mama Mama Talk to Your Daughter for Me")..10-20 63
DOT (16978 "Drive Way Blues")..............10-20 66
KRIS (8092 "Mind Your Own Business")..15-25
SKYLARK (600 "Tore Up")..........................5-10

HARMONICA FRANK
(Frank Floyd)
Singles: 78 rpm
CHESS (1475 "Swamp Heat").............150-250 51
CHESS (1494 "Howlin' Tomcat").........150-250 51
SUN (205 "Rockin Chair Daddy") 300-500 54
Singles: 7-inch
SUN (205 "Rockin Chair Daddy") 1500-2000 54
LPs: 10/12-inch
ADELPHI...8-10 76
PURITAN 8-10
Also see FLOYD, Frank

HARMONICA IMPS
Singles: 7-inch
HALIFAX (104 "Steel Guitar Rag") 10-20 64

HARMONICA KING
(George Smith)
Singles: 78 rpm
LAPEL (103 "All Last Night")....................40-60 55
Singles: 7-inch
LAPEL (103 "All Last Night")..................75-100 55
Also see ALLEN, George
Also see LITTLE WALTER JR.
Also see SMITH, George

HARMONICA SLIM
(Travis Blaylock)
Singles: 78 rpm
ALADDIN (3317 "Mary Helen")................10-20 56
SPRY (103 "Thought I Didn't Love You") .10-20 57
VITA...10-20 56
Singles: 7-inch
ALADDIN (3317 "Mary Helen")................20-30 56
CENCO (1001 "I'll Take Love")..................5-10
SPRY (103 "Thought I Didn't Love You") .25-35 57
VITA (138 "My Girl Won't Quit Me")..........25-35 56
VITA (146 "Drop Anchor") 25-35 56
LPs: 10/12-inch
BLUESTIME...10-15

HARMONY BLAZERS
LPs: 10/12-inch
HARMONY (7126 "Rock & Roll Vol. II").....25-35 59
HARMONY (7200 "Big Ten") 25-35 59
Also see BLAZERS

HARMONY BROTHERS
Singles: 7-inch
BOBBIN (109 "Baby, Tonight") 50-75 59
BOBBIN (116 "Saturday Night Bop").........50-75 59
BOBBIN (138 "Remember Me")...............15-25 62

HARMONY GRITS
Singles: 7-inch
END (1051 "Am I to Be the One")............50-75 59
END (1063 "Gee") 15-25 59
Members: Bill Pinkney; Gerhart Thrasher.
Also see DRIFTERS

HARMONY TWIN
Singles: 7-inch
UNITED SOUND (2727 "Barnyard Rock & Roll") ....25-35 '60s

HARNER, Bill
(With the Expressions; Billy Harner)
Singles: 7-inch
ATLANTIC (2351 "A Message to My Babe")..5-10 66
BELL (45366 "What About the Children") 4-6 73
DEBORAH (100 "Pretty Little Girl") 8-12 62
HERITAGE (823 "Homicide Dresser") 4-6 70
KAMA SUTRA 5-10 67-68
KENT (493 "Irresistible You").....................5-10 68
LAWN (239 "Whatcha Gonna Do")...........10-15 64
LAWN (244 "Feel Good")..........................10-15 64
MIDLAND INT'L (10783 "Two Lonely People")...4-6 76
OPEN..8-10 66
OR (1253 "Fool Me")................................10-20 '60s
OR (1255 "Watch Your Step") ....10-20 '60s
PARAMOUNT...4-6 71
PARKWAY (950 "Let's Get in Line")............5-10 65
SOUND GEMS (1007 "I Get It from Heaven")...10-20 '60s
V-TONE (1001 "A Message to My Babe")..15-25 66
(First issue.)
VOLT (1003 "All in My Mind") 5-10 66

HAROLD & BOB
Singles: 7-inch
DELTA (503 "Spitfire")..............................15-25 59

HAROLD & CASUALS
Singles: 7-inch
SCOTTY (628 "Darling Do You Love Me") 200-300 64

HAROLD & CONNIE
Singles: 7-inch
CARNIVAL (519 "Boogaloo Party").........10-20 66

HARP, Lloyd, & His Hoosier Boys
Singles: 7-inch
YORK (102 "Slow Boogie Rock") 100-200 61

HARPER, Ben
(With the Ben & Cincos; with Penetrators; Benny Harper)
Singles: 7-inch
PHIL-L.A. OF SOUL (321 "Don't Let It Happen to You")..5-10 67
SKYLARK (110 "Which-a-Way")..............30-40 61
TALENT (106 "Drive Way Blues") 5-10 60

HARPER, Bud
Singles: 7-inch
PEACOCK (1932 "Wherever You Were") 20-30 64
PEACOCK (1939 "Mr. Soul") 8-12 65
SARG..8-12 '60s

HARPER, Chuck
Singles: 7-inch.
FELSTED (8658 "Call on Me") 10-15 62
Also see REGENTS

HARPER, Jeanette
Singles: 7-inch
20TH FOX (668 "Put Me in Your Pocket")..25-35 66

HARPER, Reed
(With the Three Notes; with Notes; Reed Harper Trio; with Walter Francis Orchestra)
Singles: 7-inch
INTERNATIONAL.......................................10-15
LUCK (105 "Three Charms") 10-20 60
PYRAMID (4012 "Oh Elvis") 25-35 57
TERRY (108 "Mother Please") 5-10 63
RCA (7426 "Shaky Little Baby") 15-25 58
SMART (1001 "I Miss You So") 15-25 58
(First issue.)
VIK (328 "I Miss You So") 8-12 58

HARPER, Ric
Singles: 78 rpm
ABBEY (1028 "I'm a Sixty Minute Rocket Man") 25-50 51

HARPER, Roy
Singles: 7-inch
EPIC (10268 "Zengem")..............................5-10 67
LPs: 10/12-inch
CHRYSALIS (Except 620) 8-10 71-77
CHRYSALIS (620 "Introducing Roy Harper") 15-25 76
(Includes interviews with Paul McCartney, Jimmy Page and others, plus the Led Zeppelin song *Hat's off to Harper*. Promotional issue only.)

HARVEST 8-12 70
SUNSET 15-20 69
WORLD PACIFIC 8-10 72
Also see LED ZEPPELIN
Also see McCARTNEY, Paul

HARPER, Thelma

Singles: 7-inch

JELL (191 "At Last") 15-25 63

HARPO, Slim — P&R/R&B '61

Singles: 78 rpm

EXCELLO 30-50 57

Singles: 7-inch

ABC 4-6 73
EXCELLO (2113 "I'm a King Bee") 50-75 57
(Orange and blue label. Company address at top. Counterfeits have a yellow and blue label.)
EXCELLO (2113 "I'm a King Bee") 50-75 57
(White label. Promotional issue only.)
EXCELLO (2113 "I'm a King Bee") 20-30 60
(Orange and blue label. Company address at bottom.)
EXCELLO (2113 "I'm a King Bee") 30-40 63
(Red, white and blue label.)
EXCELLO (2138 "Wondering and Worrying") 25-50 58
(Orange and blue label. Company address at top.)
EXCELLO (2138 "Wondering and Worrying") 20-40 58
(White label. Promotional issue only.)
EXCELLO (2138 "Wondering and Worrying") 15-25 60
(Orange and blue label. Company address at bottom.)
EXCELLO (2162 "You'll Be Sorry One Day") 25-35 59
(Orange and blue label.)
EXCELLO (2162 "You'll Be Sorry One Day") 25-35 59
(White label. Promotional issue only.)
EXCELLO (2171 "Buzz Me Babe") 25-35 60
(Counterfeits exist, but all we've seen have the hole off-center. Originals do not.)
EXCELLO (2184 "Blues Hang Over") 15-25 60
EXCELLO (2194 "Rainin' in My Heart") 25-35 61
(Counterfeits have "Issued in 1973" etched in the vinyl trail-off.)
EXCELLO (2239 "Buzzin' ") 15-25 63
EXCELLO (2246 "I Need Money") 15-25 64
EXCELLO (2253 "Still Rainin' in My Heart") 15-25 64
EXCELLO (2261 "What's Goin' On Baby") 10-20 64
EXCELLO (2265 "Please Don't Turn Me Down") 20-30 65
EXCELLO (2273 thru 2289) 10-20 65-67
EXCELLO (2294 thru 2309) 8-12 68-69
EXCELLO (2316 "Rainin' in My Heart") 5-10 71
(Remixed, overdubbed version.)
Note: Any Slim Harpo singles with a yellow and blue Excello label are counterfeits.

LPs: 10/12-inch

EXCELLO (Except 8003 & 8005) 10-20 68-70
EXCELLO (8003 "Raining in My Heart") 30-50 61
(Orange and blue label.)
EXCELLO (8003 "Raining in My Heart") 5-10 95
(Blue label. Reprocessed stereo.)
EXCELLO (8005 "Baby, Scratch My Back") 20-30 66
Also see LIGHTNIN' SLIM

HARPS

Singles: 7-inch

LAURIE (3239 "Daddy's Going Away") 10-20 64

HARPTONES — P&R '61

(Harp-Tones; "Featuring Willie Winfield"; with Morty Croft, His Orchestra and Chorus; "Vocal Solo Dicey")

Singles: 78 rpm

ANDREA 20-40 56
BRUCE 25-50 53-55
GEE 20-30 57
PARADISE 25-50 56
RAMA 20-40 56-57
TIP TOP 25-50 56

Singles: 7-inch

AMBIENT SOUND (02807 "Love Needs a Heart"/"It's You") 4-6 82
ANDREA (100 "What Is Your Decision") 40-50 56
(White label. Has rope-like horizontal lines.)
ANDREA (100 "What Is Your Decision") 20-30 56
(Pink label. Has straight horizontal lines.)
BRUCE (101 "A Sunday Kind of Love") 1000-1500 53
(Maroon label. Has "Bruce" in script lettering.)
BRUCE (101 "A Sunday Kind of Love") 75-125 56
(Purple label. Has "Bruce" in block lettering. With straight horizontal lines.)
BRUCE (101 "A Sunday Kind of Love") 50-75 '50s
(Purple label. Has 45-LR-203 in dead wax.)
BRUCE (101 "A Sunday Kind of Love") 20-30 61
(Purple or maroon label. Has "Bruce" in block lettering. With jagged horizontal lines.)
BRUCE (102-X "The Laughs [sic] on You") 50-150 54
(Same as *It Was Just for Laughs*. A-side on all Bruce 102 releases was *My Memories of You*.)
BRUCE (102-X "It Was Just for Laughs") 50-150 54
(Same as *It Was Just for Laughs*.)
BRUCE (102 "It Was Just for Laughs") 40-50 54
(Has LR 207 under selection number.)
BRUCE (102 "It Was Just for Laughs") 15-25
(Has Nuway Pub. under selection number.)
BRUCE (102 "It Was Just for Laughs") 10-15
(Has chains as parallel lines.)
BRUCE (104 "I Depended on You") 75-100 54
(Has N.Y. 19, N.Y. on label.)
BRUCE (104 "I Depended on You") 15-25 61
(Has N.Y.C. on label.)
BRUCE (109 "Forever Mine") 50-75 54
(With the Shytans. Has Nu-Way Pub.)
BRUCE (109 "Forever Mine") 40-50 54
(With the Shytans. Has Rogers Music and N.Y.19, N.Y. on label.)
BRUCE (109 "Forever Mine") 30-40
(With Shytans. Has Nu-Way Enterprises under the label name and Rogers Music on the side.)
BRUCE (109 "Forever Mine") 10-20
(With Shytans. No publisher mentioned.)
BRUCE (113 "Since I Fell for You") 50-75 54
(Has Nu-Way Enterprises, Flair Music and Herman Bradley Orchestra on label.)
BRUCE (113 "Since I Fell for You") 40-50 54
(Has only Nu-Way Enterprises and Herman Bradley Orchestra on label.)
BRUCE (113 "Since I Fell for You") 15-25
(Has only Flair Music on label.)
BRUCE (123 "Loving a Girl Like You") 40-50 61
(Yellow vinyl. Purple label.)
BRUCE (123 "Loving a Girl Like You") 10-20 62
(Maroon label.)
BRUCE (128 "I Almost Lost My Mind") 40-50 55
(Has Nu-Way Enterprises on label.)
BRUCE (128 "I Almost Lost My Mind") 10-20
(No mention of Nu-Way.)
COED (540 "Answer Me My Love") 8-12 60
COMPANION (102 "All in Your Mind") 40-50 61
COMPANION (103 "What Will I Tell My Heart") 100-150 61
CUB (9097 "Devil in Velvet") 10-20 61
GEE (1045 "Cry Like I Cried") 20-30 57
(Red label.)
GEE (1045 "Cry Like I Cried") 8-12 61
(Gray label.)
KT (201 "Sunset") 40-60 63
OLDIES 45 4-8 '60s
PARADISE (101 "Life Is But a Dream") 75-100 56
(Maroon label.)
PARADISE (101 "Life Is But a Dream") 30-40 56
(Purple label.)
PARADISE (103 "My Success [It All Depends on You]") 100-200 56
PARADISE (103 "It All Depends on You") 50-75 56
(Maroon label. Note slight title change.)
PARADISE (103 "It All Depends on You") 25-35 56
(Purple label.)
RAMA (197 "Marie") 4-8 74
(Previously unissued.)
RAMA (203 "Three Wishes") 30-40 56
RAMA (214 "The Masquerade Is Over"/"On Sunday Afternoon") 30-40 56
RAMA (214 "The Masquerade Is Over"/"Can I Come Over On Sunday") 75-125 56
(Same flip with different version of title.)
RAMA (221 "The Shrine of Saint Cecilia") 30-40 57
RAVEN (8001 "A Sunday Kind of Love") 20-30 62
(Has bird at the top of label, over logo.)
RAVEN (8001 "A Sunday Kind of Love") 15-25 62
(No bird on label.)
RELIC (1022 "A Sunday Kind of Love") 3-5 73
RELIC (1023 "My Memories of You") 3-5 73
ROULETTE GOLDEN GOODIES 4-6 71
TIP TOP (401 "My Memories of You") 50-100 56
WARWICK (500 "Laughing on the Outside") 35-45 59
("Warwick" is in sans-serif, or block style type.)
WARWICK (500 "Laughing on the Outside") 25-35 59
("Warwick" is in serif style type.)
WARWICK (512 "Love Me Completely") 25-35 59
WARWICK (551 "No Greater Miracle") 25-35 60

EPs: 7-inch

BRUCE (201 "The Sensational Harptones") 8000-12000 54

LPs: 10/12-inch

AMBIENT SOUND (37718 "Love Needs") 8-12 82
HARLEM HITPARADE (5006 "The Harptones") 10-15 '70s
MURRAY HILL 5-8 88
RARE BIRD 8-10
RELIC 8-10 '70s
Members: Willie Winfield; Nicky Clark; William James; Bill Brown; Bill Dempsey; Bill "Dicey" Galloway; Raoul Cita; Jimmy Beckum; Lynn Daniels; Vicki Burgess; Margaret Moore; Fred Taylor.
Also see BLADES, Carol
Also see JOYTONES
Also see PAUL, Bunny, & Harptones
Also see RAPIDTONES
Also see RHYTHM ACES / Harptones
Also see SOOTHERS
Also see WOODSIDE SISTERS

HARPTONES / Crows

LPs: 10/12-inch

ROULETTE (114 "Echoes of a Rock Era") 15-20 72
(Two LPs, one by each group.)
Also see CROWS

HARPTONES / Paragons / Jesters / Clovers

LPs: 10/12-inch

GRAND PRIX 10-20 '60s
Also see CLOVERS
Also see HARPTONES
Also see JESTERS
Also see PARAGONS

HARRALL, Hank

Singles: 7-inch

CAPROCK 15-25 58-59

HARRELL, Doug

Singles: 7-inch

COLONIAL (501 "Hospitality Blues") 10-15 56
(Mistakenly labeled as an Extended Play.)

Picture Sleeves

COLONIAL (501 "Hospitality Blues") 15-25 56
Members: Jim Crisp; Joe Tanner; Henry Heitman.

HARRELL, Vernon

Singles: 7-inch

ASCOT (2144 "Such a Lonely Guy") 15-25 63
BELTONE (2031 "Little Joe") 10-15 63
CALLA (136 "Can't Take the Hurt") 15-25 67
DECCA (31721 "All That's Good") 15-25 64
SCORE (1009 "Your Love") 10-20 66
Also see LITTLE GIGI

HARRIET, Judy

Singles: 7-inch

AMERICAN INT'L 10-15 59
COLUMBIA 8-10 61
SURF (5023 "Nuff Said") 15-20 58
SURF (5027 "Born Too Late") 15-20 58
SURF (5035 "Just a Guy to Love Me") 15-20 59

HARRIS, Ace

Singles: 78 rpm

STERLING 20-40 48
Also see HAWKINS, Erskine / Ace Harris

HARRIS, Al "Puddler"

Singles: 7-inch

ROCKO (508 "Wait a Minute") 10-15 60

HARRIS, Bill, & Continentals

Singles: 7-inch

EAGLE (1002 "I'm So Glad") 150-200 58

HARRIS, Bob

(Little Bobby Harris)

Singles: 78 rpm

DERBY 10-20 51
JACKSON 100-200 52
PAR 10-20 52

Singles: 7-inch

EAI (101 "Bertha Lou") 50-75
JACKSON (2301 "Friendly Advice") 400-500 52

HARRIS, Bobby — R&B '65

Singles: 7-inch

ATLANTIC (2270 "We Can't Believe You're Gone") 10-15 65

HARRIS, Bobby

Singles: 7-inch

MOON 8-12
SHOUT (203 "Mr. Success") 15-25 66
SHOUT (210 "The Love of My Women") 10-20 67
TURNTABLE (715 "The Password is Love") 15-25 65
TURNTABLE (716 "Lonely Intruder") 15-25 66

HARRIS, Bobby, & Vocaltones

Singles: 78 rpm

WENDEE (1933 "Don't Do It Baby") 10-15 55

Singles: 7-inch

WENDEE (1933 "Don't Do It Baby") 40-60 55

HARRIS, Calvin

(With the Rexettes)

Singles: 7-inch

ZORRO (300 "Foxy Roxy") 25-50 '50s

HARRIS, Dave, & Power House Five

LPs: 10/12-inch

DECCA (4113 "Dinner Music for a Pack of Hungry Cannibals") 15-20 61

HARRIS, Dimples, & Orchestra

Singles: 78 rpm

CREST (1013 "If You'll Be True") 10-15 55

Singles: 7-inch

CREST (1013 "If You'll Be True") 15-25 55

HARRIS, Dinky

Singles: 7-inch

FAD (903 "She Left Me Crying") 100-200 60

HARRIS, Eddie — P&R/R&B/LP '61

Singles: 7-inch

ABC 4-6 73
ATLANTIC 4-6 65-77
COLUMBIA 4-6 64
VEE-JAY 5-8 61-63
W.B. 3-5 81

LPs: 10/12-inch

ANGELACO 5-10 81
ATLANTIC 6-12 65-81
BUDDAH 8-12 69
COLUMBIA 10-20 64-68
CRUSADERS 5-10 82
GNP 5-10 73
HARMONY 5-10 72
RCA 5-10 78
SUNSET 5-10 69
TRIP 5-10 73
VEE-JAY (3016 thru 3028) 20-35 61-62
VEE-JAY (3031 thru 3034) 15-25 63
Also see McCANN, Les, & Eddie Harris
Also see MOORE, Shelly, & Eddie Harris

HARRIS, Edward

(With the Blue Dots)

Singles: 7-inch

JAX (1005 "I Am Sincere") 15-25 59
NRC (504 "All You Gotta Do") 300-400 58

HARRIS, Emmylou — C&W/P&R '75

(With Her Hot Band; with Cheryl White & Sharon White)

Singles: 7-inch

JUBILEE 5-10 69-70
REPRISE (1326 "Too Far Gone") 4-6 75
REPRISE (1332 "If I Could Only Win Your Love") 4-6 75
REPRISE (1341 "Light of the Stable") 4-6 75
REPRISE (1346 thru 1371) 4-6 75-77
W.B. 3-6 77-86

Picture Sleeves

REPRISE (1341 "Light of the Stable") 4-6 75
REPRISE 4-6 75-77
WARNER (49239 "Wayfaring Stranger") 3-5 80

LPs: 10/12-inch

EMUS 10-20 79

JUBILEE (8031 "Gliding Bird") 60-80 69
MFSL (015 "Quarter Moon in a Ten-Cent Town") 35-50 78
REPRISE 8-10 75
W.B. 5-10 77-87
Members: James Burton; Glen D. Hardin; Emory Gordy; Ronnie Tutt. Session: Herb Pedersen.
Also see BURTON, James
Also see CASH, Johnny
Also see CRICKETS
Also see DENVER, John, & Emmylou Harris
Also see JENNINGS, Waylon
Also see LITTLE FEAT
Also see MADDOX, Rose
Also see NELSON, Willie
Also see ORBISON, Roy, & Emmylou Harris / Craig Hundley
Also see OWENS, Buck, & Emmylou Harris
Also see PARSONS, Gram
Also see PARTON, Dolly
Also see PARTON, Dolly, Linda Ronstadt, & Emmylou Harris
Also see PRESLEY, Elvis
Also see RONSTADT, Linda, & Emmylou Harris
Also see WINCHESTER, Jesse
Also see YOUNG, Neil

HARRIS, Emmylou, & Don Williams *C&W '81*
Singles: 7-inch
W.B. (49809 "If I Needed You") 3-5 81
Also see WILLIAMS, Don

HARRIS, Erline
Singles: 78 rpm
DELUXE (3303 "Jump & Shout") 10-15 50
Singles: 7-inch
DELUXE (3303 "Jump & Shout") 20-30 50

HARRIS, Ernie
Singles: 7-inch
DUKE (323 "With You") 10-15 60
OKEH (7196 "Hold On") 5-10 64

HARRIS, Frank
Singles: 7-inch
MAB-JAB (1002 "A Sweet Dream") 100-150 62
NORMAN (543 "I'm Just a Country Boy") 10-20 63

HARRIS, Frosty, & Kool-Tones
(Bruce Harris)
Singles: 7-inch
DON (200 "Big Noise from L.A.") 20-30 60
DOT (16171 "Big Noise from L.A.") 10-15 60

HARRIS, Genee
Singles: 7-inch
ABC-PAR (9900 "Bye Bye Elvis") 15-25 58

HARRIS, Georgia
(With Lyrics; with Hy-Tones; with Steve Samuel's Orchestra)
Singles: 7-inch
HY-TONE (117 "Let's Exchange Hearts for Xmas") 500-600 58
(Reportedly 500 made.)
HY-TONE (121 "Let Me Hold Your Hand") 100-150 59
Also see HY-TONES
Also see LYRICS

HARRIS, Jim, & Sidewinders
Singles: 7-inch
FABAR (15564 "I'm on the Outside Looking In") 10-15 66

HARRIS, Joan
Singles: 7-inch
HUMMINGBIRD (1721 "Crazy Stripes").. 15-20 67

HARRIS, Johnny Ray
Singles: 7-inch
RAY (601 "Cajun Weekend") 50-75 60
RAY (602 "No More Hurtin' ") 50-75 60
RAY (820 "Tired of Crawling") 15-25

HARRIS, Joyce
(With the Slades)
Singles: 7-inch
DOMINO (903 "I Cheated") 15-25 61
DOMINO (905 "No Way Out") 15-25 61
(First issue.)
INFINITY (005 "No Way Out") 8-12 61

HARRIS, Kurt
Singles: 7-inch
DIAMOND (158 "Go On") 10-15 64
JOSIE (898 "Let Her Dance") 8-12 62

HARRIS, Lee
Singles: 7-inch
JACKPOT (48011 "When the One You Love Don't Love You") 10-15 58

HARRIS, Major *P&R/R&B/LP '75*
(Major Harris Boogie Blues Band)
Singles: 7-inch
ATLANTIC 4-6 75-76
OKEH (7314 "Just Love Me") 15-25 68
OKEH (7327 "Like a Rolling Stone") 30-60 69
POP ART 3-5 83
WMOT 3-6 76-81
LPs: 10/12-inch
ATLANTIC 8-10 75
RCA 5-10 78
WMOT 8-10 76

HARRIS, Manzy, Orchestra
(With Harold Young)
Singles: 78 rpm
ROCKIN' (505 "Ain't Gonna Ride No More") 50-75 53
ROCKIN' (506 "You're Gonna Know") 50-75 53
ROCKIN' (507 "Rockin' Mambo") 50-75 53
Also see YOUNG, Harold

HARRIS, Mike
(With the Hi-Tides)
Singles: 7-inch
DORE (678 "Any News About Debbie") 5-10 63
EPIC (9749 "Little Miss Lonely") 5-10 64
KRIMMIE (24 "I'm So Proud") 20-30 63
LIBERTY (55744 "We Never Knew") 10-20 64
SIDEWALK (905 "Dry Bones") 5-10 66
ZUMA .... 5-10 '60s

HARRIS, Nick, & Soundbarriers
Singles: 7-inch
FLEETWOOD (7004 "Freeway Hot Rod") 20-30 63
NORTHWEST SOUND .... 10-15 '60s
TEE PEE 5-10 61

HARRIS, Phil *P&R '33*
Singles: 78 rpm
ARA 4-8 46
COLUMBIA 4-8 33
DECCA 4-6 35
RCA 5-10 47-54
Singles: 7-inch
BUENA VISTA 4-6 67-70
COLISEUM (2711 "This Is All I Ask") 4-8 68
MEGA 4-6 73
MONTCLARE (1450 "How Beautiful It Is Just to Be Alive") 4-6 76
RCA 10-20 50-54
REPRISE 4-8 62
Picture Sleeves
MONTCLARE (1450 "How Beautiful It Is Just to Be Alive") 4-6 76
RCA (87 "The Thing") 30-50 50
EPs: 7-inch
RCA 5-10 53-60
LPs: 10/12-inch
CAMDEN 8-12 63
MEGA 5-10 72-74
RCA (1900 series) 10-20 59
RCA (3000 series) 20-30 53-54
ZODIAC 5-10 77
Also see SHORE, Dinah, Tony Martin, Betty Hutton & Phil Harris

HARRIS, Porky
Singles: 7-inch
CRYSTALETTE (716 "Pig Pen") 10-20 58

HARRIS, Quinn
Singles: 7-inch
MLF ("I'll Always Love You") 15-25
(Selection number not known.)

HARRIS, Ralph
Singles: 7-inch
EXCELLO (2177 "She Might") 10-20 60

HARRIS, Ray
Singles: 78 rpm
SUN 20-50 56-57
Singles: 7-inch
SUN (254 "Come On Little Mama") 75-125 56
SUN (272 "Greenback Dollar, Watch and Chain") 25-50 57
Session: Charlie Rich.
Also see RICH, Charlie

HARRIS, Ray, / Buzz Busby
Singles: 78 rpm
TRUMPET (134 "No One Else"/"I'll Send You Roses") 20-30 51
Also see BUSBY, Buzz

HARRIS, Rene, & Terrans
Singles: 7-inch
GRAHAM (801 "Moonrise"/"Soap Soap") 50-75 63
(Previously issued as by the Terrans.)
GRAHAM (801 "Moonrise"/"Soap n' Water") 20-30 63
Also see TERRANS

HARRIS, Rodney
Singles: 78 rpm
COLONY (104 "Hard Lovin' Papa") 10-15 51

HARRIS, Rolf *P&R/R&B/LP '63*
Singles: 7-inch
EPIC (9567 thru 10037, except 9721) 5-10 63-66
EPIC (9721 "Ringo for President") 15-25 64
MGM (14103 "Two Little Boys") 4-8 70
20TH FOX (207 thru 414) 10-20 60-63
Picture Sleeves
EPIC 8-12 63-64
LPs: 10/12-inch
EPIC (24053 "Sun Arise") 20-30 63
(Monaural.)
EPIC (26053 "Sun Arise") 20-30 63
(Stereo.)
EPIC (24110 "Court of King Caractacus") 20-30 64
(Monaural.)
EPIC (26110 "Court of King Caractacus") 20-30 64
(Stereo.)

HARRIS, Roy, & Magnolia Boys
Singles: 78 rpm
FLAIR (1000 "South of San Antonio") 8-12 53
Singles: 7-inch
FLAIR (1000 "South of San Antonio") 10-20 53

HARRIS, Sammy, Band
Singles: 78 rpm
BATTLE (009 "Fatso") 5-10 53
Singles: 7-inch
BATTLE (009 "Fatso") 10-15 53

HARRIS, Slim, & His Stereophonixs
Singles: 7-inch
FRAN (102 "Frankie and Johnny") 40-60

HARRIS, Thurston *P&R/R&B '57*
(With the Sharps)
Singles: 78 rpm
ALADDIN (3398 "Little Bitty Pretty One") 75-100 57
Singles: 7-inch
ALADDIN (3398 "Little Bitty Pretty One") .30-40 57
(Purple label.)
ALADDIN (3398 "Little Bitty Pretty One") .20-30 57
(Blue label.)
ALADDIN (3398 "Little Bitty Pretty One") .15-25 57
(Maroon label.)
ALADDIN (3399 "Do What You Did") 15-25 57
ALADDIN (3415 "Be Baba Leba") 15-25 58
ALADDIN (3428 "Smokey Joe's") 15-25 58
ALADDIN (3430 "Over and Over") 15-25 58
ALADDIN (3435 "Over Somebody Else's Shoulder") 15-25 58
ALADDIN (3448 "You Don't Know How Much I Love You") 10-20 59
ALADDIN (3450 "Hey Little Girl") 10-20 59
ALADDIN (3452 "Bless Your Heart") 10-20 59
ALADDIN (3456 "Paradise Hill") 10-20 59
CUB (9108 "I'd Like to Start Over Again") .. 8-12 62
DOT (16415 "Goddess of Angels") 8-12 62
DOT (16427 "She's the One") 8-12 63
IMPERIAL (014 "Little Bitty Pretty One") 8-12 62
IMPERIAL (5928 "Got You On My Mind") .. 8-12 63
IMPERIAL (5971 "You're Gonna Need Me") 8-12 63
INTRO (6099 "Little Bitty Pretty One") 30-50 57
REPRISE (0255 "Dancing Silhouettes") ... 15-25 64
U.A. (0512 "Little Bitty Pretty One") .... 4-6 '70s
Also see SHARPS

HARRIS, Tony *P&R '57*
Singles: 78 rpm
EBB (104 "Chicken, Baby, Chicken") 10-15 57
Singles: 7-inch
EBB (104 "Chicken, Baby, Chicken") 15-25 57

HARRIS, Tony, & Woodies
Singles: 7-inch
DEE GEE (3014 "Super Man") 10-15 66
TRIUMPH (60 "Go Go Little Scrambler") . 15-25 64

HARRIS, Wee Willie
Singles: 7-inch
CHARLIE PARKER (217 "I Go Ape") 10-15 63

HARRIS, Willard
Singles: 78 rpm
EKKO (20001 "Straighten Up Baby") 20-30 55
Singles: 7-inch
EKKO (20001 "Straighten Up Baby") 40-60 55

HARRIS, Wynonie *R&B '46*
(With Lucky Millinder; with Todd Rhodes Orchestra)
Singles: 78 rpm
ALADDIN 20-30 46-48
APOLLO 30-40 45-46
ATCO 10-20 56
BULLET 15-25 46
HAMP-TONE 15-25 45
KING 25-50 47-57
PHILO 15-25 45
QUALITY/KING (4074 "Bloodshot Eyes") 200-300 51
(Canadian.)
Singles: 7-inch
ATCO (6081 "Destination Love") 30-40 56
GUSTO (2087 "Drinkin' Wine Spo-Dee-O Dee") 4-6 78
KING (4210 "Good Rockin' Tonight") 50-75 52
KING (4461 "Bloodshot Eyes") 50-75 51
KING (4468 "I'll Never Give Up") 50-75 51
KING (4485 "Lovin' Machine") 50-75 51
(Black vinyl.)
KING (4485 "Lovin' Machine") 200-300 51
(Colored vinyl.)
KING (4507 "My Playful Baby's Gone") ... 50-75 51
KING (4526 "Keep on Churnin' ") 40-50 52
KING (4555 "Night Train") 40-50 52
KING (4565 "Adam, Come and Get Your Rib") 40-50 52
KING (4592 "Greyhound") 40-50 52
KING (4593 "Bad News, Baby") 40-50 52
KING (4620 "Wasn't That Good") 40-50 53
KING (4635 "The Deacon Don't Like It") .. 30-40 53
KING (4662 "Tremblin' ") 30-40 53
KING (4668 "Please, Louise") 30-40 53
KING (4685 "Quiet Whiskey") 30-40 53
KING (4716 "Shake That Thing") 30-40 54
KING (4724 "Don't Take My Whiskey Away from Me") 30-40 54
KING (4763 "Christina") 20-30 54
KING (4774 "Good Mambo Tonight") 20-30 54
KING (4789 "Mr. Dollar") 20-30 54
KING (4814 "Drinkin' Sherry Wine") 20-30 54
KING (4826 "Wine, Wine, Sweet Wine") .. 20-30 54
KING (4839 "Shotgun Wedding") 20-30 54
KING (4900 & 5000 series) 15-25 56-57
KING (5050 "Big Old Country Fool") 10-20 57
KING (5073 "There's No Substitute for Love") 10-20 57
KING (5100 thru 5400 series) 5-10 58-60
KING (6011 "Bloodshot Eyes") 10-15 65
ROULETTE (4291 "Bloodshot Eyes") 10-15 60
EPs: 7-inch
KING (260 "Wynonie 'Mr. Blues' Harris") 400-600 54
LPs: 10/12-inch
KING (1086 "Good Rockin' Blues") 10-15 72
Also see MILBURN, Amos / Wynonie Harris / Crown Prince Waterford
Also see MILLINDER, Lucky, & His Orchestra
Also see RHODES, Todd
Also see ROYALS

HARRIS, Wynonie / Roy Brown
LPs: 10/12-inch
KING (607 "Battle of the Blues") 100-200 58
KING (627 "Battle of the Blues, Vol. 2") 100-200 58

HARRIS, Wynonie / Roy Brown / Eddie Vinson

LPs: 10/12-inch

KING (668 "Battle of the Blues, Vol. 4") 300-600 60
Also see BROWN, Roy
Also see HARRIS, Wynonie
Also see VINSON, Eddie

HARRIS SISTERS

Singles: 78 rpm

CAPITOL (3086 "Kissin' Bug") 5-8 55

Singles: 7-inch

CAPITOL (3086 "Kissin' Bug") 8-12 55
SMASH (2002 "Don't Let Me Fall in Love") 10-20 57

HARRISON, Al

Singles: 78 rpm

BIG TOWN (122 "I'll Forget About You") . 15-25 55

Singles: 7-inch

BIG TOWN (122 "I'll Forget About You") . 25-50 55

HARRISON, Cledus

Singles: 7-inch

NATURAL (502 "Rock and Roll in the Groove") 1000-2000

HARRISON, Danny
(With the Count Victors)

Singles: 7-inch

CORAL 5-10 63-66
DENEBA 4-8 69
EVENT (4273 "Rockabilly Boogie") 40-60 58
(With Audrey Harrison.)
EVENT (4278 "Have You Ever Been Lonely") 5-10 59
MILO (113 "No One to Love Me") 30-40 61
U.A. 4-8 68

LPs: 10/12-inch

DENEBA 10-15 69

HARRISON, Earl

Singles: 7-inch

GARRISON (3001 "Humphrey Stomp") ... 15-25 66

HARRISON, George *LP '69*

Singles: 12-inch

DARK HORSE (949 "All Those Years Ago") 25-30 81
(Promotional issue only. Includes title sleeve.)
DARK HORSE (1075 "Wake Up My Love") 20-30 82
(Promotional issue only. Includes title sleeve.)
DARK HORSE (2845 "Got My Mind Set on You") 20-30 87
(Promotional issue only. Includes picture cover.)
DARK HORSE (2885 "When We Was Fab") 20-30 88
(Promotional issue only.)
DARK HORSE (2889 "Devil's Radio") 20-30 87
(Promotional issue only. Includes picture cover.)

Singles: 7-inch

APPLE (1828 "What Is Life") 10-15 71
(With black star on label.)
APPLE (1828 "What Is Life") 5-8 71
(No black star on label.)
APPLE (1836 "Bangla Desh") 15-25 71
(With black star on label.)
APPLE (1836 "Bangla Desh") 5-8 71
(No black star on label.)
APPLE (1862 "Give Me Love") 5-8 73
APPLE (1877 "Dark Horse") 8-10 74
APPLE (1879 "Ding Dong; Ding Dong") 5-8 74
(Black with *white* tint photo label.)
APPLE (1879 "Ding Dong; Ding Dong") 200-250 74
(Black with *blue* tint photo label.)
APPLE (1884 "You") 5-8 75
APPLE (1885 "This Guitar") 20-25 75
APPLE (2995 "My Sweet Lord") 30-40 70
(With black star on label.)
APPLE (2995 "My Sweet Lord") 5-8 70
(No black star on label. Does not have "All Rights Reserved, etc." print on label.)
APPLE (2995 "My Sweet Lord") 15-25 70
(With "All Rights Reserved, etc." on label.)
CAPITOL (1828 "What Is Life") 25-35 76
(Orange label.)
CAPITOL (1828 "What Is Life") 5-8 78
(Purple label.)
CAPITOL (1828 "What Is Life") 10-15 83
(Black label.)
CAPITOL (1836 "Bangla Desh") 25-35 76
(Orange label.)
CAPITOL (1836 "Bangla Desh") 5-8 78
(Purple label.)
CAPITOL (1836 "Bangla Desh") 10-15 83
(Black label.)
CAPITOL (1862 "Give Me Love") 5-8 78
(Purple label.)
CAPITOL (1879 "Ding Dong; Ding Dong") ... 5-8 78
(Purple label.)
CAPITOL (1879 "Ding Dong; Ding Dong") 10-15 83
(Black label.)
CAPITOL (2295 "My Sweet Lord") 25-35 76
(Orange label.)
CAPITOL (2295 "My Sweet Lord") 5-8 78
(Purple label.)
CAPITOL (2295 "My Sweet Lord") 10-15 83
(Black label.)
CAPITOL (6245 "Dark Horse") 5-8 77
(Tan Starline label, circular Capitol logo.)
CAPITOL (6245 "Dark Horse") 4-6 78
(Tan Starline label, oval Capitol logo.)
CAPITOL (6245 "Dark Horse") 30-40 87
(Black Starline label.)
DARK HORSE (0410 "All Those Years Ago"/"Teardrops") 3-5 88
(Tan label. Back to Back Hits series.)
DARK HORSE (0410 "All Those Years Ago"/"Teardrops") 30-35 91
(White label. Back to Back Hits series.)
DARK HORSE (8294 "This Song") 5-10 76
(Tan or white label)
DARK HORSE (8313 "Crackerbox Palace") 4-6 77
DARK HORSE (8763 "Blow Away") 4-6 79
(Tan label with "Loka Productions" print on label.)
DARK HORSE (8763 "Blow Away") 15-20 79
(Tan label without "Loka Productions" print on label.)
DARK HORSE (8844 "Love Comes to Everyone") 5-10 79
DARK HORSE (27913 "This Is Love") 3-5 88
DARK HORSE (28131 "When We Was Fab") 3-5 88
DARK HORSE (28178 "Got My Mind Set on You") 3-5 87
DARK HORSE (21891 "Got My Mind Set on You"/"When We Was Fab") 3-5 88
(Tan label. Back to Back Hits series.)
DARK HORSE (21891 "Got My Mind Set on You"/"When We Was Fab") 30-35 88
(White label. Back to Back Hits series.)
DARK HORSE (29744 "I Really Love You") 20-25 83
DARK HORSE (29864 "Wake Up My Love") 5-10 82
DARK HORSE (49725 "All Those Years Ago") 4-6 81
(Tan label.)
DARK HORSE (49785 "Teardrops") 5-10 81
W.B. (22807 "Cheer Down") 10-15 89

Picture Sleeves

APPLE (1828 "What Is Life") 30-40 71
APPLE (1836 "Bangla Desh") 15-20 71
APPLE (1877 "Dark Horse") 50-75 74
APPLE (1879 "Ding Dong; Ding Dong") ... 10-15 74
APPLE (1884 "You") 10-15 75
APPLE (2995 "My Sweet Lord") 30-40 70
DARK HORSE (8294 "This Song") 20-30 76
DARK HORSE (8294 "This Song") 60-80 76
(Special promotional sleeve issued with promo single. With insert flyer, "The Story Behind *This Song*.")
DARK HORSE (8294 "This Song") 30-40 76
(Special promotional sleeve issued with promo single. Without insert flyer, "The Story Behind *This Song*.")
DARK HORSE (8763 "Blow Away") 4-6 79
DARK HORSE (8844 "Love Comes to Everyone") 800-900 79
DARK HORSE (27913 "This Is Love") 3-5 88
DARK HORSE (28131 "When We Was Fab") 3-5 88
DARK HORSE (28178 "Got My Mind Set on You") 3-5 87
DARK HORSE (49725 "All Those Years Ago") 3-5 81
W.B. (22807 "Cheer Down") 10-15 89

Promotional Singles

APPLE (1862 "Give Me Love") 35-45 73
APPLE (1877 "Dark Horse") 40-60 74
APPLE (1879 "Ding Dong Ding Dong") 25-35 74
APPLE (1884 "You") 25-35 75
APPLE (1885 "This Guitar") 35-45 75
APPLE/20TH FOX (791 "Concert for Bangla Desh") 700-750 71
(Four radio spots. Sent only to select stations.)
COLUMBIA (2085 "I Don't Want to Do It"/"I Don't Want to Do It") 10-20 85
(Promotional issue only.)
DARK HORSE (8294 "This Song") 15-25 76
DARK HORSE (8313 "Crackerbox Palace") 10-15 77
DARK HORSE (8763 "Blow Away") 10-15 79
DARK HORSE (8844 "Love Comes to Everyone") 10-15 79
DARK HORSE (27913 "This Is Love") 10-15 88
DARK HORSE (28131 "When We Was Fab") 10-15 88
DARK HORSE (28178 "Got My Mind Set on You") 10-15 87
DARK HORSE (29744 "I Really Love You") 10-15 83
DARK HORSE (29864 "Wake Up My Love") 10-15 82
DARK HORSE (49725 "All Those Years Ago") 10-15 81
DARK HORSE (49785 "Teardrops") 10-15 81
W.B. (22807 "Cheer Down") 150-200 89

LPs: 10/12-inch

APPLE (639 "All Things Must Pass") 30-40 70
(Boxed, three-disc set. Includes bonus poster. Disc does not have "S" in trail-off area.)
APPLE (639 "All Things Must Pass") 50-75 88
(Boxed, three-disc set. Includes bonus poster. Disc has "S" – indicating a reissue – in trail-off.)
APPLE (3350 "Wonderwall Music") 20-30 68
(Apple label without Capitol logo.)
APPLE (3350 "Wonderwall Music") 100-125 68
(Apple label with Capitol logo.)
APPLE (3385 "Concert for Bangla Desh") 40-50 71
(Boxed, three-disc set. Includes 64-page booklet. Also has Eric Clapton, Bob Dylan, Ringo Starr, Leon Russell, Ravi Shankar, and others.)
APPLE (3410 "Living in the Material World") 10-15 73
APPLE (3418 "Dark Horse") 15-20 73
APPLE (3420 "Extra Texture") 10-15 75
CAPITOL (639 "All Things Must Pass") 20-30 76-78
(Boxed, three-disc set. Orange or purple labels. Includes bonus poster.)
CAPITOL (639 "All Things Must Pass") 70-90 83
(Black label. Boxed, three-disc set. Includes bonus poster.)
CAPITOL (3410 "Living in the Material World") 10-15 80
CAPITOL (3420 "Extra Texture") 15-25 80
CAPITOL (11578 "The Best of George Harrison") 10-15 76
(Custom label with six photos of Harrison. Also contains tracks by the Beatles that feature George.)
CAPITOL (11578 "The Best of George Harrison") 150-175 77
(Orange label.)
CAPITOL (11578 "The Best of George Harrison") 10-15 78
(Purple label with "Mfd. by Capitol, etc." on perimeter print.)
CAPITOL (11578 "The Best of George Harrison") 15-25 83
(Black label.)
CAPITOL (11578 "The Best of George Harrison") 75-125 89
(Purple label with "Manufactured by Capitol, etc." on perimeter print.)
CAPITOL (12248 "Concert for Bangla Desh") 300-350 82
(Two-disc set. Withdrawn upon release.)
CAPITOL (16055 "Dark Horse") 10-15 80
CAPITOL (16216 "Living in the Material World") 10-15 80
CAPITOL (16217 "Extra Texture") 15-25 80
DARK HORSE (3005 "Thirty-Three and 1/3") 8-12 76
DARK HORSE (3255 "George Harrison") .. 8-10 79
DARK HORSE (3255 "George Harrison") 40-50 79
(Columbia Record Club issue.)
DARK HORSE (3492 "Somewhere in England") 5-10 81
DARK HORSE (23734 "Gone Troppo") 8-12 82
DARK HORSE (25643 "Cloud Nine") 10-15 87
DARK HORSE (25726 "Best of Dark Horse") 15-25 89
ZAPPLE (3358 "Electronic Sound") 20-30 69

Promotional LPs

DARK HORSE ("Dark Horse Radio Special") 250-300 74
(No selection number used.)
DARK HORSE (649 "A Personal Music Dialogue with George Harrison at 33 1/3") 30-40 76
DARK HORSE (23734 "Gone Troppo") ... 20-25 82
(Audiophile Quiex II vinyl pressing.)
Also see BEATLES
Also see CLAPTON, Eric
Also see DYLAN, Bob
Also see RUSSELL, Leon
Also see SHANKAR, Ravi
Also see TRAVELING WILBURYS

HARRISON, George / Jeff Beck / Dave Edmunds

Singles: 12-inch

COLUMBIA (2034 "I Don't Want to Do It"/"Sleepwalk"/"Queen of the Hop") 10-20 85
(One track by each artist. Promotional issue only.)

HARRISON, George / Dave Edmunds

Singles: 7-inch

COLUMBIA (04887 "I Don't Want to Do It"/"Queen of the Hop") 3-5 85
Also see BECK, Jeff
Also see EDMUNDS, Dave
Also see HARRISON, George
Also see HARRISON, George / Jeff Beck / Dave Edmunds

HARRISON, Jim & Bob
(With Jimmy Spruill's Band)

Singles: 7-inch

CLOCK (1035 "Country Boy") 15-25 61
CLOCK (71836 "Country Boy") 15-25 61
CLOCK (71890 "Here Is My Heart") 15-25 61
SMASH (1803 "Little School Girl") 8-12 63
Also see SPRUILL, Wild Jimmy

HARRISON, Jimmy

Singles: 7-inch

ATCO (6144 "Geometry of Love") 10-20 59

HARRISON, John, & Hustlers

Singles: 7-inch

IDEAL (10 "Don't Ask Me Why") 10-15 65

HARRISON, Lee
(With the Kounts)

Singles: 7-inch

JUDD (1003 "So Unimportant") 10-15 58
PEARL (717 "So Unimportant") 20-25 58
(First issue.)

HARRISON, Wes *LP '63*
(With Eddie Gale)

Singles: 78 rpm

LIN (5002 "There Y'Are") 10-15 56

Singles: 7-inch

LIN (5002 "There Y'Are") 15-25 56
PHILIPS 8-12 63

LPs: 10/12-inch

PHILIPS 15-25 63

HARRISON, Wilbert *P&R/R&B '59*
(With the Roamers; with His Kansas City Playboys; "Wilbert Harrison One Man Band"; Wilburt Harrison; Wilbur Harrison)

Singles: 78 rpm

BARREL (604 "Kansas City") 150-200 59
(Canadian.)
CHART (626 "Calypso Man") 10-20 56
DELUXE 20-30 52-53
FURY (1023 "Kansas City") 200-250 59
ROCKIN' 15-25 53
SAVOY 10-20 54

Singles: 7-inch

ABC 4-6 73
BARREL (604 "Kansas City") 10-20 59
(Canadian.)
BELL (869 "Since I Fell for You") 4-6 70
BRUNSWICK 4-6 74
CHART (626 "Calypso Man") 20-30 56
CONSTELLATION (122 "Mama, Mama, Mama") 8-10 64
DEE-SU (301 "Clementine") 5-10 65

DELUXE (6002 "This Woman of Mine")... 40-50 52
DELUXE (6031 "Gin and Coconut Milk") . 40-50 53
DOC (1002 "Off to School Again") 5-10 62
ERIC (161 "Kansas City")..............................4-6 73
FURY (1023 "Kansas City")..................... 10-20 59
FURY (1027 "Cheating Baby") 10-20 59
FURY (1028 "Goodbye Kansas City") 10-20 60
FURY (1031 thru 1063)..............................8-15 60-62
GLADES (603 "Gonna Tell You a Story") 10-15 59
HOT LINE (101 "Get It While You Can") 4-6 72
HOUSE OF SOUND.......................................4-6
JUGGERNAUT (405 "Shoot You Full of Love")..4-6 71
NEPTUNE (123 "After Graduation")...........8-12 61
PORT (3003 "Baby Move On")....................5-10 65
PORT (3009 "Sugar Lump")........................5-10 65
ROCKIN' (526 "This Woman of Mine") .. 75-100 53
ROULETTE (4752 "No One's Love but Yours") 5-8 67
SSS INT'L (830 "My Heart Is") 4-8 71
(Black vinyl.)
SSS INT'L (830 "My Heart Is") 5-10 71
(Blue vinyl. Promotional issue only.)
SAVOY (1138 "Don't Drop It")................. 20-30 54
SAVOY (1149 "Women and Whiskey").... 15-25 55
SAVOY (1164 "Darling, Listen to This Song") 15-25 55
SAVOY (1198 "The Way I Feel") 10-20 56
SAVOY (1517 "My Love Is True")............ 10-20 57
SAVOY (1531 "My Love for You Lingers On")... 10-20 58
SAVOY (1571 "Don't Drop It")................. 10-20 59
SEA HORN (502 "Near to You") 8-10 63
SUE (11 "Let's Work Together")............... 10-20 69
(No company address shown.)
SUE (11 "Let's Work Together")..................5-10 69
(Company address at bottom of label.)
SUE (11 "Let's Work Together")..................4-8 69
(Company address at top or on either side.)
VEST (8006 "Poison Ivy")...............................5-8 65
WET SOUL (4 "My Heart Is Yours").............4-6 70

Picture Sleeves

FURY (1023 "Kansas City")........................5-10 '90s

LPs: 10/12-inch

BUDDAH.. 10-18 71
CHELSEA..8-10 77
FURY...5-8
JUGGERNAUT 15-25 71
RELIC 5-10 90
RES IPSA.. 10-15
SPHERE SOUND 25-40 65
SUE.. 15-25 70
WET SOUL... 10-15 70
Also see ROAMERS

HARROD, Chuck
(With the Anteaters featuring Sammy King)

Singles: 7-inch

CHAMPION (1013 "Sandy")..................... 20-30 59
CHEROKEE (1021 "Crawdad Song") .. 100-200 59

HARSHMAN, Robert Luke
(Bobby Hart)

Singles: 7-inch

GUYDEN (2022 "Is You Is Or Is You Ain't My Baby")... 20-30 59
RADIO (122 "Love Whatcha Doin' to Me")... 20-30 59
Also see HART, Bobby

HART, Bill, & Mountaineers

Singles: 78 rpm

RECORD GUILD OF AMERICA (356 "The Ballad of Davy Crockett")....................................5-10 55

Singles: 7-inch

RECORD GUILD OF AMERICA (356 "The Ballad of Davy Crockett")................................... 10-20 55

Picture Sleeves

RECORD GUILD OF AMERICA (356 "The Ballad of Davy Crockett")....................................... 20-30 55

HART, Billy & Don
(With the Downbeats)

Singles: 7-inch

ROULETTE (4133 "Rock-A Bop-A-Lina") 40-60 59
ROULETTE (4172 "Checkmated and Bingoed") 15-25 59
Also see HART, Don

HART, Bobby

Singles: 7-inch

ARIOLA AMERICAN (809 "Lovers for the Night") 3-5 80
BAMBOO (507 "Girl I Used to Know")......15-25 61
CHELSEA (0026 "California") 4-6 73
DCP...10-20 64-66
ERA (3039 "Girl in the Window")................5-10 61
INFINITY (017 "People Next Door")...........5-10 63
INFINITY (022 "Lovesick Blues") 5-10 63
REEL (100 "Girl in the Window")...............20-30 60
W.B. (8058 "Hard Core Man").......................4-6 74
W.B./CURB (49079 "Sometimes Love").......4-6 79
Also see BOYCE, Tommy, & Bobby Hart
Also see HARSHMAN, Robert Luke

HART, Don
(With the Fyve; with James Shorter)

Singles: 7-inch

COOLSCHOOL (2001 "It's in My Mind")..75-125 '50s
COOLSCHOOL (2002 "Soldier, Come Home")..75-125 '50s
COOLSCHOOL (2003 "I Can Make It")..75-125 '50s
DELIGHTFUL "I'm Not Ready Now")........40-60
RESERVE (118 "Presley on Her Mind")...40-60 57
Also see HART, Billy & Don
Also see HEART, Don

HART, Freddie *C&W '59*
(With the Heartbeats)

Singles: 78 rpm

CAPITOL (2500 thru 3000 series) 5-10 53-55
COLUMBIA (Except 21512) 5-15 56-57
COLUMBIA (21512 "Dig Boy Dig")..........10-20 56

Singles: 7-inch

CAPITOL (2500 thru 3000 series) 10-20 53-55
(Purple labels.)
CAPITOL (2600 thru 4600 series) 4-6 70-79
(Orange labels.)
COLUMBIA (21512 "Dig Boy Dig")...........25-35 56
COLUMBIA (21550 "Snatch It and Grab It")...25-35 56
COLUMBIA (21558 "Blue") 25-35 56
COLUMBIA (40821 thru 42146)................10-20 57-61
COLUMBIA (42285 thru 42768)..................8-15 62-63
KAPP 4-8 65-72
MCA..4-6 73
MONUMENT...4-6 63-64
SUNBIRD 3-5 80-81

Picture Sleeves

KAPP (879 "Togetherness")..........................4-6 68
SUNBIRD (7550 "Sure Thing") 3-5 80

LPs: 10/12-inch

BRYLEN 5-10 84
CAPITOL..5-10 70-79
COLUMBIA (1792 "Spirited") 20-30 62
COLUMBIA (13000 series)........................10-12 72
CORAL..5-8 73
HARMONY...8-12 67-73
KAPP...10-20 65-69
MCA...8-12 75
PICKWICK..5-10 '70s
PICKWICK/HILLTOP ....8-12 '70s
SUNBIRD 5-10 80
VOCALION..5-10 72

HART, Freddie / Sammi Smith / Jerry Reed

LPs: 10/12-inch

HARMONY...5-10 72
Also see HART, Freddie
Also see REED, Jerry

HART, Gloria

Singles: 78 rpm

WING (90024 "Can I Forget") 5-10 55

Singles: 7-inch

WING (90024 "Can I Forget") 10-15 55

HART, Haze, & Gus Jenkins

Singles: 7-inch

SWINGIN' (638 "Last Time")......................10-20 62

HART, Kelly

Singles: 7-inch

OKEH (7109 "Dear Mom & Dad") 10-20 59
SWAN (4172 "There's a Time") 5-10 64
TOP RANK (2078 "Heart Full of Tears") 5-10 60
XYZ (606 "Boy Crazy") 15-25 60

HART, Larry

Singles: 7-inch

OKEH (7077 "If a Dream Could Make You Mine")...15-25 57

HART, Mickey *LP '72*

Singles: 7-inch

W.B. 4-8 71-72

LPs: 10/12-inch

RELIX (Except 2026)...................................5-10 85
RELIX (2026 "Rolling Thunder") 25-30 87
(Picture disc.)
W.B. 10-20 72
Also see GRATEFUL DEAD
Also see RHYTHM DEVILS

HART, Ritchie
(With the Heartbeats; Charles R. Gearheart)

Singles: 7-inch

FELSTED (8593 "The Great Duane")......15-25 59
MCI (1025 "I Want You") 10-20 60
RAMCO ("If You Can't, Don't Worry").........5-10 62
(Selection number not known.)
RAMCO (3707 "Her Singing Idol")..............5-10 61
RAMCO (3709 "Phyllis")..............................5-10 61
RAMCO (3716 "Love Is") 5-10 62

HART, Rocky
(With the Passions)

Singles: 7-inch

BIG TOP (3069 "Crying") 10-15 61
CUB (9052 "Every Day") 15-25 59
GLO (5216 "I Play the Part of a Fool") .200-300 61
GOLDEN WORLD (105 "When a Teenager Gets Blue") 15-25 62
Also see APOLLOS
Also see PASSIONS

HARTFIELD, Pete

Singles: 7-inch

BABY (610 "Mighty Man") 25-50
MIRACLE (8 "Love Me")............................40-60 60

HARTFORD, Ken
(With Frankie Valli)

Singles: 7-inch

SOUTHERN SOUND (119 "Jay Walker") 15-25 63
Also see VALLI, Frankie

HARTLEY, Al
(With the Heartbeats)

Singles: 7-inch

HERMITAGE...10-15
IMPERIAL 10-20 63
LIMELIGHT (3027 "Counterfeit Love") 10-15 64
SCARLET (4000 "Our First Date")...........10-15 59

HARTMAN, Johnny
(With Choir & Norman Leyden Orchestra)

Singles: 78 rpm

RCA (4349 "Wheel of Fortune")..................8-10 51

Singles: 7-inch

BETHLEHEM...8-12 58
HERALD (522 "No Tears Tomorrow") 15-25 58
RCA (4349 "Wheel of Fortune")................15-25 51
(Interestingly, ASCAP files show this song being published in 1952, year of Kay Starr's hit – yet this version came out in November 1951.)

HARVES, Cleo

Singles: 78 rpm

O.T. (105 "Skinny Woman Blues")............20-40 49

HARVEY
("Former Lead of the Moonglows"; "Formerly of the Moonglows; Harvey Fuqua)

Singles: 7-inch

CHESS (1713 "I Want Somebody")..........20-30 59
CHESS (1725 "Twelve Months of the Year")..20-30 59
CHESS (1749 "Blue Skies")......................10-15 60
CHESS (1781 "The First Time") 10-15 61
TRI-PHI (1010 "She Loves Me So"/"Whistling About You") 20-30 62
TRI-PHI (1017 "She Loves Me So"/"Any Way You Wanta")..20-30 62
(Note different flip side.)
TRI-PHI (1024 "Come On and Answer Me") 30-40 63
Also see ETTA & HARVEY
Also see FIVE QUAILS
Also see HARVEY & ANN
Also see HARVEY & MOONGLOWS
Also see HARVEY & SPINNERS
Also see NEW BIRTH

HARVEY, Laurence

Singles: 7-inch

ATLANTIC (5024 "Love Theme from *This Is My Beloved*") 5-10 62
COLUMBIA (42017 "The Long and the Short and the Tall") 5-10 61

LPs: 10/12-inch

ATLANTIC (1367 "This Is My Beloved")...25-50 62

HARVEY, Phil
(Phil Spector)

Singles: 7-inch

IMPERIAL (5583 "Bumbershoot") 125-175 59
Also see HARVEY & DOC & DWELLERS
Also see RONETTES / Crystals / Darlene Love / Bob B. Soxx & Blue Jeans
Also see TEDDY BEARS

HARVEY, Rudy, & Pips

Singles: 7-inch

CAPRI (103 "I Need You So")..................50-75 59

HARVEY & ANN

Singles: 7-inch

HARVEY (121 "What Can You Do Now")..20-30 63
Members: Harvey Fuqua; Ann Bogan.
Also see HARVEY

HARVEY & DOC & DWELLERS

Singles: 7-inch

ANNETTE (1002 "Oh Baby") 50-100 64
Members: Phil Spector; Doc Pomus.
Also see HARVEY, Phil

HARVEY & MOONGLOWS
(Harvey Fuqua)

Singles: 78 rpm

CHESS (1705 "Ten Commandments of Love") 50-100 58

Singles: 7-inch

CHESS (1705 "Ten Commandments of Love") 20-30 58
CHESS (1738 "Mama Loocie")................15-25 59
CHESS/PROTEIN 21 (P 21-01 "Ten Commandments of Love"/"Ten Commandments of Beautiful Hair")..10-20 '70s
(Promotional issue for Protein 21 Shampoo.)
Also see HARVEY
Also see MOONGLOWS

HARVEY & SPINNERS
("Harvey [Former Lead of the Moonglows] & the Spinners")
TRI-PHI (1010 "She Loves Me So") 30-50 62
(Reissued sans credit to the Spinners.)
Also see HARVEY
Also see SPINNERS

HARWELL, George

Singles: 7-inch

DITTO (113 "Pilgrim of Love") 20-30 58

HASKELL, May

Singles: 7-inch

SUNDOWN (102 "Party Line")............200-300 58

HASKINS, Mike, & Valeneers

Singles: 7-inch

SHADOW (105 "Day After Day") 50-75

HASSAN, Ali
(Al Pousan)

Singles: 7-inch

PHILLES (103 "Chop Stick")....................10-20 62

HASSILEV, Alex

Singles: 7-inch

RCA (8630 "Dear Love")..............................6-12 65

LPs: 10/12-inch

RCA (3434 "Affairs of the Heart") 10-15 65
Also see LIMELITERS

HASSLES

Singles: 7-inch

U.A. 8-12 67-69

Picture Sleeves

U.A. 10-12 67-69

LPs: 10/12-inch

LIBERTY...8-10 81
U.A. (6631 "The Hassles") 20-30 68
U.A. (6699 "Hour of the Wolf") 20-30 68
Members: William (Billy) Joel; Howard Blauvelt; Johathan Small; Richard McKenner; John Dizek.
Also see JOEL, Billy

HASTINGS, Count

Singles: 78 rpm

DARL (1006 "The Count")...........................8-10 56

Singles: 7-inch

DARL (1006 "The Count")..........................10-20 56

HATCHER, Roger R&B '76
(Little Roger Hatcher)
Singles: 7-inch
BROWN DOG (9009 "We Gonna Make It")..4-6 76
DOTTY'S 5-10 64
EXCELLO (2297 "Sweetest Girl in the World")....15-25 68
VOLT (4084 "Dedicate My Life to You")......4-6 72

HATCHER, Will
(Willie Hatcher)
Singles: 7-inch
COLUMBIA (44259 "Good Things Come to Those Who Wait")....30-40 67
EXCELLO (2310 "Tell Me So")....10-15 69
KING (6360 "Head Over Heels")....15-25 70
THELMA....15-20 63

HATFIELD, Bobby P&R '69
("Bobby Hatfield of the Righteous Brothers")
Singles: 7-inch
MOONGLOW (220 "I Need a Girl")....15-25 62
(Black vinyl.)
MOONGLOW (220 "I Need a Girl")....40-50 62
(Red vinyl.)
VERVE (10598 thru 10641)....5-10 68-69
W.B. (7566 "Oo Wee Baby, I Love You"/"Rock and Roll Woman")....4-8 72
W.B. (7649 "Stay with Me"/"Rock and Roll Woman")....4-8 73
LPs: 10/12-inch
MGM (4727 "Messin' in Muscle Shoals"). 10-15 70
Also see RIGHTEOUS BROTHERS
Also see SPRINGSTEEN, Bruce

HATFIELD, Chuck
Singles: 7-inch
FORTUNE (175 "Steel Wool")....15-25 58

HATFIELD, Dixie
Singles: 7-inch
MARK E (2511 "Skool Daze")....10-15 63

HATFIELD, Jeanne
Singles: 7-inch
ATCO (6653 "Busy Signal")....10-15 69
CAMEO (386 "Time")....10-20 65
JOX (047 "Time")....15-25 65
PHAROAH....8-12

HATFIELD, Overton
(Gene Autry)
Singles: 78 rpm
Columbia (15987 "A Gangster's Warning")....50-75 '30s
Also see AUTRY, Gene

HATFIELDS
Singles: 7-inch
CHA CHA (754 "Yes I Do")....50-75 67
CHA CHA (760 "The Kid from Cincy")....50-75 67

HATTON SISTERS
(With the Peter Lance Orchestra; with Harry Doran)
Singles: 78 rpm
SKYWAY (114 "Donkey Rock, Elephant Roll")....10-15 56
Singles: 7-inch
SKYWAY (114 "Donkey Rock, Elephant Roll")....15-25 56

HAUNTED
Singles: 7-inch
AMY (959 "1-2-5")....25-35 66
MARK II (7001 "Vapeur Mauve")....15-25 68
QUALITY (1814 "1-2-5")....25-50 66
(Canadian.)
QUALITY (1840 "I Can Only Give You Everything")....25-50 66
(Canadian.)
TRANS-WORLD (1674 "Searching for My Baby")....25-50 67
(Canadian.)
TRANS-WORLD (1682 "Come On Home")....25-50 67
(Canadian.)
TRANS-WORLD (1702 "Land of Make Believe")....25-50 68
(Canadian.)
LPs: 10/12-inch
EVA (12029 "Vapeur Mauve")....10-20 84
TRANSWORLD (6701 "The Haunted")....1200-1500 66
(Canadian.)

VOXX....5-10
Members: Dave Wynne; Bob Burgess.
Also see INFLUENCE
Also see ORIGINAL HAUNTED

HAVEN, Marc, & Aquarians
Singles: 7-inch
VILLA-YORE (201 "Janice")....200-300 61

HAVEN, Shirley, & Four Jacks
Singles: 78 rpm
FEDERAL (12092 "Troubles of My Own")....100-200 52
Singles: 7-inch
FEDERAL (12092 "Troubles of My Own")....500-1000 52
Also see FOUR JACKS
Also see WILLIAMS, Cora, & Four Jacks / Shirley Haven & Four Jacks

HAVENS
Singles: 7-inch
POPLAR (123 "Want You")....15-25 63

HAVENS, Don, & Hi-Fi's
Singles: 7-inch
TONE-CRAFT (205 "Bread and Butter")..10-20 '50s

HAWK, The
(Jerry Lee Lewis)
Singles: 7-inch
PHILLIPS INT'L (3559 "In the Mood")....15-25 60
Also see LEWIS, Jerry Lee

HAWKETTES
Singles: 78 rpm
CHESS (1591 "Mardi Gras Mambo")....20-30 55
Singles: 7-inch
CHESS (1591 "Mardi Gras Mambo")....40-50 55
Also see MOONBEEMS / Hawkettes
Also see NEVILLE BROTHERS

HAWKEYES
Singles: 7-inch
SKY (2636 "Who Is He")....30-40 60

HAWKINS, Bobby
Singles: 7-inch
CUCA (1256 "Root Beer")....15-25 66
CUCA (6533 "White Lightnin'")....10-20 65
CUCA (6563 "Hawaiian War Chant")....15-25 65
CUCA (6681 "Just Between the Two of Us")....10-20 66
WHITE LIGHTNIN' (500 "Root Beer")....15-25 '60s

HAWKINS, Buddy, & Do Re Me Trio
Singles: 7-inch
CARLTON (460 "That's the Way Life Goes")....15-25 58
Also see DO-RE-ME TRIO

HAWKINS, Coleman
Singles: 78 rpm
PARROT (783 "What a Difference a Day Makes")....15-25 53
Singles: 7-inch
PARROT (783 "What a Difference a Day Makes")....50-100 53
(Black vinyl.)
PARROT (783 "What a Difference a Day Makes")....150-250 53
(Red vinyl.)

HAWKINS, Dale P&R/R&B '57
(With the Escapades)
Singles: 78 rpm
CHECKER (843 "See You Soon Baboon")....20-30 56
CHECKER (863 "Suzi-Q")....20-30 57
CHECKER (876 "Baby, Baby")....20-30 57
CHECKER (892 "Little Pig")....25-50 58
CHECKER (900 "La-Do-Dada")....25-50 58
CHECKER (906 "A House, a Car, and a Wedding Ring")....40-60 58
CHECKER (913 "Someday One Day")....50-75 58
CHECKER (923 "Ain't That Lovin' You Baby")....50-100 59
Note: Checker 78s as late as 937 exist with the checkerboard design at top, as opposed to 45s which switched designs beginning with 876. Also, 78s as early as 900 have Checker name vertically on left side.
Singles: 7-inch
ABC-PAR (10668 "La La Song")....8-12 65
ABNAK (110 "The Flag")....5-10 65
ATLANTIC (1022 "Peaches")....10-20 61
ATLANTIC (2126 "Stay at Home Lulu")....10-20 61
ATLANTIC (2150 "What a Feeling")....10-20 62
BELL (807 "Little Rain Cloud")....5-10 69
BELL (827 "Heavy on My Mind")....5-10 69
CHECKER (843 "See You Soon Baboon")....30-40 56
(Maroon label, checkerboard design at top.)
CHECKER (843 "See You Soon Baboon")....15-25 57
(Maroon label, "Checker" logo vertical on left.)
CHECKER (863 "Suzi-Q")....30-40 57
(Maroon label, checkerboard design at top.)
CHECKER (863 "Suzi-Q")....10-20 57
(Maroon label, "Checker" logo vertical on left.)
CHECKER (876 "Baby, Baby")....25-35 57
(Maroon label, checkerboard design at top.)
CHECKER (876 "Baby, Baby")....10-20 57
(Maroon label, "Checker" logo vertical on left.)
CHECKER (892 "Little Pig")....20-30 58
(Maroon label.)
CHECKER (900 "La-Do-Dada")....20-30 58
(Maroon label.)
CHECKER (906 "A House, a Car, and a Wedding Ring")....20-30 58
(Maroon label.)
CHECKER (913 "Someday One Day")....20-30 58
(Maroon label.)
CHECKER (914 "Take My Heart")....15-25 59
(Maroon label.)
CHECKER (916 "Class Cutter")....20-25 59
(Maroon label.)
CHECKER (916 "Yea-Yea [Class Cutter]")....15-25 59
(Maroon label. Note title variation.)
CHECKER (923 "Ain't That Lovin' You Baby")....15-25 59
(Maroon label.)
CHECKER (929 "Our Turn")....15-25 59
(Maroon label.)
CHECKER (934 "Back to School Blues").15-25 59
(Maroon label.)
CHECKER (940 "Hot Dog")....15-25 60
(Maroon label.)
CHECKER (944 "Poor Little Rhode Island")....15-25 60
(Maroon label.)
CHECKER (962 "Linda")....10-20 61
(Maroon label.)
CHECKER (970 "I Want to Love You")....10-20 61
(Maroon label.)
CHECKER (Blue label)....5-10 '60s
(Reissues.)
CHESS (916 "Yea-Yea [Class Cutter]")...25-35 59
(Mistakenly issued on Chess instead of Checker.)
GO GILLIS ("Go Gillis")....25-50
LINCOLN (002 "Baby We Had It")....8-12
PAULA (424 "First Cut Is the Deepest")....4-6 77
TILT (781 "Money Honey")....10-20 61
TILT (783 "Wish I Hadn't Called Home")..10-20 61
ZONK (1002 "Gotta Dance")....10-20 62
Picture Sleeves
CHECKER (944 "Poor Little Rhode Island")....450-650 60
LPs: 10/12-inch
BELL (6036 "L.A., Memphis and Tyler, Texas")....20-30 69
CHESS (1429 "Suzy-Q")....1000-2000 58
(At least one known counterfeit exists with a black and white cover. Original covers are in full color. Between cover and label, the following spellings of the title track are found: "Suzy-Q," "Susie-Q" and "Suzie Q.")
ROULETTE (R-25175 "Let's All Twist at Miami Beach Peppermint Lounge")....50-100 62
(Monaural.)
ROULETTE (SR-25175 "Let's All Twist at Miami Beach Peppermint Lounge")....75-125 62
(Stereo.)
Also see BUCHANAN, Roy
Also see BURTON, James
Also see ORLONS / Dale Hawkins

HAWKINS, Delores
(With Don Costa & Orchestra; with Bill Hayer; with Hector Pellot & Johnny Conquet)
Singles: 78 rpm
CORAL....5-10 52
EPIC....5-10 54-56
MGM....5-10 53
OKEH....5-10 52-53
Singles: 7-inch
CORAL (60832 "Sing You Sinners")....10-20 52
EPIC (9006 thru 9170)....10-20 54-56
MGM (11661 "Prelude to a Kiss")....10-20 53
OKEH (6857 thru 6976)....10-20 52-53
EPs: 7-inch
EPIC (7056 "Hits from Pajama Game")....15-25 54
EPIC (7074 "Mambo Combos")....15-25 55
EPIC (7171 "The Man I Love")....50-75 57
EPIC (7172 "The Nearness of You")....15-25 57
LPs: 10/12-inch
EPIC (1022 "Mambo Combos")....25-50 55
(10-inch LP.)
EPIC (1119 "Meet Delores Hawkins")....25-50 55
(10-inch LP.)
EPIC (3250 "Delores")....20-40 57
Also see COSTA, Don
Also see MELLO-LARKS & DELORES HAWKINS

HAWKINS, Delores / Four Lads
Singles: 78 rpm
OKEH....5-10 52
Singles: 7-inch
OKEH (6880 "Rocks in My Bed"/"Heavenly Father")....20-30 52
OKEH (6903 "Each Time"/"Risin' Sun")...25-25 52
Also see FOUR LADS
Also see HAWKINS, Delores

HAWKINS, Erskine P&R '36
(Erskine Hawkins Quintet)
Singles: 78 rpm
BLUEBIRD....5-15 39-44
DECCA....5-10 56
CORAL....5-10 50-52
KING....5-10 51-52
VICTOR/RCA....5-10 45-52
VOCALION....5-15 36-37
Singles: 7-inch
DECCA (29864 "Waltz in Blue")....15-25 56
CORAL (60313 thru 60750)....15-25 50-52
KING (4514 "Steel Guitar Rag")....15-25 52
(Black vinyl.)
KING (4514 "Steel Guitar Rag")....40-60 52
(Colored vinyl.)
KING (4522 "Down Home Jump")....15-25 52
(Black vinyl.)
KING (4522 "Down Home Jump")....40-60 52
(Colored vinyl.)
KING (4574 "New Gin Mill Special")....15-25 52
KING (4597 "The Way You Look Tonight")....15-25 52
RCA (0029 "After Hours")....15-25 56
RCA (0169 "After Hours")....15-25 56
("Collector's Series" numbers 27-0029 and 420-0169 appear to have been issued simultaneously. We have yet to determine any difference between the two.)
RCA (3835 "Opportunity")....30-40 50
RCA (5059 "Weary Blues")....15-25 53
EPs: 7-inch
CORAL (56061 "Erskine Hawkins")....20-30 52
RCA (5095 "After Hours")....15-25 59
(Gold Standard Series.)
LPs: 10/12-inch
CORAL (56051 "After Hours")....50-100 54
DECCA (4081 "Hawk Blows at Midnight")....20-30 61
IMPERIAL (9191 "25 Golden Years of Jazz")....20-30 62
(Monaural.)
IMPERIAL (9197 "25 Golden Years of Jazz, Vol. 2")....20-30 62
(Monaural.)
IMPERIAL (12191 "25 Golden Years of Jazz")....25-35 62
(Stereo.)
IMPERIAL (12197 "25 Golden Years of Jazz, Vol. 2")....25-35 62
(Stereo.)
RCA (2227 "After Hours")....30-40 60
Also see DASH, Julian

HAWKINS, Erskine, & Four Hawks
Singles: 78 rpm
KING (4671 "My Baby, Please")....40-60 53
KING (4686 "Double Shot")....15-25 53
Singles: 7-inch
KING (4671 "My Baby, Please")....100-150 53
KING (4686 "Double Shot")....50-75 53
Also see HAWKINS, Erskine

HAWKINS, Erskine / Ace Harris

Singles: 78 rpm

BRUNSWICK (84020 "Please Don't Put Me Down"/"At Your Beck and Call") 5-10 53

Singles: 7-inch

BRUNSWICK (84020 "Please Don't Put Me Down"/"At Your Beck and Call") 15-25 53

Also see HARRIS, Ace
Also see HAWKINS, Erskine

HAWKINS, Hawkshaw *C&W '48*

Singles: 78 rpm

KING 4-8 46-53
RCA 4-8 55-57

Singles: 7-inch

COLUMBIA 4-8 59-62
KING (900 thru 1100 series) 5-10 50-53
KING (5000 series) 4-8 60-64
RCA 5-10 55-59
STARDAY 4-6 71

EPs: 7-inch

KING 8-12 53

LPs: 10/12-inch

CAMDEN 10-15 64-66
HARMONY 10-15 63
KING (587 "Hawkshaw Hawkins, Vol. 1") 40-60 58
KING (592 "Hawkshaw Hawkins Sings Grand Ole Opry Favorites, Vol. 2") 40-60 58
KING (599 "Hawkshaw Hawkins") 40-60 59
KING (808 "All New Hawkshaw Hawkins") 20-40 63
KING (858 "Taken From Our Vaults, Vol. 1") 15-20 63
KING (858 "Taken From Our Vaults, Vol. 2") 15-20 63
KING (858 "Taken From Our Vaults, Vol. 3") 15-20 64
KING (1043 "Lonesome 7-7203") 8-12 69
LA BREA (8020 "Hawkshaw Hawkins") ... 25-50 '60s
NASHVILLE 8-12 69
STARDAY 5-10 77

Also see CLINE, Patsy / Cowboy Copas / Hawkshaw Hawkins
Also see COPAS, Cowboy / Hawkshaw Hawkins

HAWKINS, Hillary Nixon

Singles: 7-inch

STONEWAY (1081 "Honky Tonk Hardwood Floor") 10-15
WIDE WORLD 4-8 70-71

HAWKINS, Hugh

Singles: 7-inch

REESE (7001 "Bring It Down Front") 30-40

HAWKINS, Jalacy
(Jay Hawkins)

Singles: 78 rpm

MERCURY (70549 "This Is All") 20-30 55
WING 10-15 55-56

Singles: 7-inch

MERCURY (70549 "This Is All") 50-75 55
WING (90005 "Well, I Tried") 20-30 55
WING (90055 "Even Though") 20-30 56

Also see HAWKINS, Screamin' Jay

HAWKINS, Jennell *R&B '61*

Singles: 7-inch

AMAZON 8-12 61-63
DYNAMIC 8-12 61
DYNAMITE 8-12 61
OLDIES 45 4-6

LPs: 10/12-inch

AMAZON (AM-1001 "Many Moods of Jenny") 25-50 61
(Monaural.)
AMAZON (AS-1001 "Many Moods of Jenny") 40-60 61
(Stereo.)
AMAZON (AM-1002 "Moments to Remember") 25-50 62
(Monaural.)
AMAZON (AS-1002 "Moments to Remember") 40-60 62

Also see RICKIE & JENNELL

HAWKINS, Jerry

Singles: 7-inch

EBB (152 "Swing Daddy Swing") 40-60 58
EBB (157 "Lucky Johnny") 40-60 59

HAWKINS, Jimmy

Singles: 7-inch

KEM (2751 "Sure Do") 10-15 57
(Colored vinyl.)

Picture Sleeves

KEM (2751 "Sure Do") 10-20 57

HAWKINS, Lafay

Singles: 7-inch

CAESAR (101 "Just for Tonight") 50-75

EPs: 7-inch

SPA (1016 "Lafay Hawkins") 150-200

HAWKINS, Nippy, & Nip-Tones
("The Nation's Most Promising Group")

Singles: 7-inch

LORRAINE (1001 "Angie") 15-25 65

HAWKINS, Ronnie *P&R/R&B '59*
(With the Hawks)

Singles: 7-inch

COTILLION (44067 "Forty Days") 4-8 70
COTILLION (44076 "One More Night") 4-8 71
HAWK 5-10
MONUMENT (8548 "Cora Mae") 4-8 72
MONUMENT (8561 "Lonesome Town") 4-8 72
QUALITY (1827 "Hey Bo Diddley") 100-200 63
(Canadian.)
ROULETTE (4154 "Forty Days") 15-25 59
ROULETTE (SSR-4154 "Forty Days") 25-50 59
(Stereo.)
ROULETTE (4177 "Mary Lou") 15-25 59
ROULETTE (SSR-4177 "Mary Lou") 25-50 59
(Stereo.)
ROULETTE (4209 "Southern Love") 15-25 59
ROULETTE (4228 thru 4502) 10-20 60-63
YORKVILLE 8-12

LPs: 10/12-inch

ACCORD (7213 "Premonition") 10-15 83
COTILLION (9019 "Ronnie Hawkins") 10-20 70
COTILLION (9039 "The Hawk") 10-20 71
MONUMENT (31330 "Rock and Roll Resurrection") 8-12 72
MONUMENT (32940 "Giant of Rock and Roll") 8-12 74
ROULETTE (25078 "Ronnie Hawkins") 100-150 59
(Black vinyl. Monaural.)
ROULETTE (SR-25078 "Ronnie Hawkins") 150-250 59
(Black vinyl. Stereo.)
ROULETTE (25078 "Ronnie Hawkins") 400-600 59
(Red vinyl.)
ROULETTE (25102 "Mr. Dynamo") 100-150 60
(Black vinyl. Monaural.)
ROULETTE (SR-25102 "Mr. Dynamo") 150-250 60
(Black vinyl. Stereo.)
ROULETTE (25102 "Mr. Dynamo") 400-600 60
(Red vinyl.)
ROULETTE (25120 "Folk Ballads") 50-100 60
(Monaural.)
ROULETTE (SR-25120 "Folk Ballads") 100-200 60
(Stereo.)
ROULETTE (25137 "Songs of Hank Williams") 50-100 60
(Monaural.)
ROULETTE (SR-25137 "Songs of Hank Williams") 100-200 60
(Stereo.)
ROULETTE (25255 "Ronnie Hawkins") .. 75-125
(Canadian.)
ROULETTE (25390 "Mojo Man") 50-100
(Canadian.)
ROULETTE (42045 "Best of Ronnie Hawkins") 25-35 70
U.A. (968 "The Hawk") 5-10 79

Also see BAND
Also see LENNON, John
Also see LEVON & HAWKS
Also see ROCKIN' RONALD & REBELS

HAWKINS, Roy *R&B '50*

Singles: 78 rpm

DOWN TOWN (2018 "Christmas Blues") . 15-25 48
DOWN TOWN (2020 "It's Too Late to Change") 15-25 48
DOWN TOWN (2024 "Forty Jim") 15-25 48
DOWN TOWN (2025 "Quarter to One") ... 15-25 48
MODERN 15-25 48-54
RPM (440 "If I Had Listened") 15-25 55

Singles: 7-inch

KENT (376 "Trouble in Mind") 5-10 62
MODERN (826 "The Thrill Is Gone") 40-60 51
MODERN (852 "Gloom and Misery All Around") 40-60 51
MODERN (853 "I Don't Know Just What to Do") 40-60 51
MODERN (859 "Highway 59") 25-40 52
MODERN (869 "Doin' All Right") 25-40 52
MODERN (898 "Bad Luck Is Falling") 25-40 54
RPM (440 "If I Had Listened") 75-100 55
RHYTHM (120 "I Hate to Be Alone") 30-50 58

Also see ROYAL HAWK

HAWKINS, Sam *R&B '65*
(Sammy Hawkins)

Singles: 7-inch

ARNOLD (1010 "Goodbye Darling") 5-10 63
BLUE CAT (112 "Hold on Baby") 10-15 65
BLUE CAT (121 "It Hurts So Bad") 5-10 65
DECCA 10-15 59-61
END (1102 "Landlord") 10-15 61
EPIC (10520 "Dream Lover") 4-8 69
GONE (5042 "King of Fools") 20-30 58
GONE (5054 "When Nobody Loves You") 15-25 59
MAY (128 "Standing on the Sidelines") 5-10 62
MAY (140 "Are These Really Mine") 5-10 63
SHELL (1003 "Run to Me") 4-8

Session: Ronnie Bright; J.R. Bailey; Freddie Barksdale.
Also see HO-DADS

HAWKINS, Screamin' Jay
(Jalacy Hawkins; with Leroy Kirkland Orchestra & O.B. Masingill)

Singles: 78 rpm

APOLLO 10-20 56-57
GRAND 10-20 57
OKEH 10-20 56-57
TIMELY 20-30 54

Singles: 7-inch

APOLLO (506 "Please Try to Understand") 25-35 57
APOLLO (528 "Baptize Me in Wine") 25-35 58
DECCA (32019 "I'm Not Made of Clay") .. 10-20 66
DECCA (32100 "I Put a Spell on You") 25-35 67
ENRICA (1010 "Just Don't Care") 8-12 62
EPIC (2209 "I Put a Spell on You") 5-10 63
EPIC MEMORY LANE 3-5
GRAND (135 "Take Me Back") 25-35 57
OKEH (7072 "I Put a Spell on You") 10-20 56
OKEH (7084 "Darling Please Forgive Me") 10-20 57
OKEH (7087 "Person to Person") 10-20 57
OKEH (7101 "Alligator Wine") 10-20 58
PHILIPS (40668 "Do You Really Love Me") . 4-8 70
PHILIPS (40674 "Our Love Is Not for Three") 4-8 70
PROVIDENCE (411 "My Kind of Love") 5-10 65
QUEEN BEE (1001 "Monkberry Moon Delight") 4-8 73
RCA (10127 "You Put the Spell on Me") 4-8 74
ROULETTE (4579 "The Whammy") 5-10 64
TIMELY (1004 "Baptize Me in Wine") ... 200-300 54
TIMELY (1005 "Please Try to Understand") 200-300 54

LPs: 10/12-inch

EPIC (3448 "At Home with Screamin' Jay Hawkins") 900-1100 56
EPIC (3457 "I Put a Spell on You") 100-200 57
EPIC (26457 "I Put a Spell on You") 15-25 69
HOT LINE (10024 "Portrait of a Man and His Woman") 15-25
MIDNIGHT 5-10 88
PHILIPS (600-319 "What That Is") 20-30 69
PHILIPS (600-336 "Screamin' Jay Hawkins") 20-30 70
SOUNDS OF HAWAII (5015 "A Night at Forbidden City") 20-30
VERSATILE 8-10 78

Also see HAWKINS, Jalacy

HAWKINS, Screamin' Jay / Lillian Briggs

LPs: 10/12-inch

CORONET .... 15-25 '60s

HAWKS

Singles: 78 rpm

IMPERIAL 25-50 54-55
MODERN (990 "It's All Over") 40-60 56
POST (2004 "Why Oh Why") 75-100 55

Singles: 7-inch

IMPERIAL (5266 "Joe the Grinder") 100-200 54
IMPERIAL (5281 "She's All Right") 75-125 54
IMPERIAL (5292 "It Ain't That Way") 40-60 54
IMPERIAL (5306 "Nobody But You") 30-50 54
IMPERIAL (5317 "All Women Are the Same") 20-40 54
IMPERIAL (5332 "It's too Late Now") 20-40 55
MODERN (990 "It's All Over") 75-100 56
POST (2004 "Why Oh Why") 150-250 55

HAWKS

Singles: 7-inch

DEL-FI (4108 "Fussy") 50-75 58

Members: Don Cole; Loy Clingman.
Also see CLINGMAN, Loy
Also see COLE, Don

HAWKS

Singles: 7-inch

MALA (401 "Cupcake") 15-25 59

HAWKS

Singles: 7-inch

ABC-PAR (10116 "Grissle") 20-30 60

HAWKS, Mickey *C&W '89*
(With Moon Mullins & His Night Raiders; "Night Raiders Featuring Mickey Hanks")

Singles: 7-inch

C-HORSE 3-5 89
HUNCH (347 "Hidi Hidi Hidi") 25-50 61
PROFILE (4002 "Bip Bop Boom") 75-125 58
PROFILE (4007 "Hidi Hidi Hidi") 75-125 59
(Some copies mistakenly credit "Mickey Hanks.")
PROFILE (4010 "Screamin' Mimi Jeanie") 50-75 59

Also see MULLINS, Moon

HAWLEY, Deane *P&R '60*
(With the Crystals)

Singles: 7-inch

DORE (524 "Pretty Little Mary") 8-12 59
DORE (536 "Boss Man") 8-12 59
DORE (543 "Where Is My Angel") 8-12 60
DORE (554 "Look for a Star") 10-20 60
DORE (569 "Like a Fool") 10-15 60
DORE (577 "Hey There") 10-15 60
LIBERTY (55359 "Pocketful of Rainbows") 10-20 61
LIBERTY (55446 "Queen of the Angels") 10-15 62
SUNDOWN (111 "I Hate to See Me Go"). 10-15 58
SUNDOWN (113 "That's the Name of the Game") 10-15 58
VALOR (2003 "Don't Keep Me Guessin' ") 25-35 59
W.B. (5484 "I Know She'll Be There") 5-10 64

HAYDEN, Rudy

Singles: 7-inch

ARAGON (279 "Want Me a Woman") .. 100-200

HAYDEN SISTERS

Singles: 7-inch

ROYCE (0007 "Silent Tears") 30-40 60
(First issue.)
SMASH (1703 "Silent Tears") 5-10 61
TILT (784 "Silent Tears") 10-15 61
(Second issue.)

Member: Martha Hayden.

HAYDOCK, Ron, & Boppers

Singles: 7-inch

CHA CHA (701 "Be-Bop-a Jean") 100-200 59
(Red label. First issued as by the Boppers.)
CHA CHA (704 "Baby Say Bye-Bye") .. 200-300 60
CHA CHA (785 "Be-Bop-A Jean") 150-250 59
(White label.)
CHA CHA (1002 "In the Mood") 25-35 59

Also see BOPPERS

HAYES, Bill
(Henry Hayes)

Singles: 78 rpm

JADE (211 "Just") 10-20 50
SITTIN' IN WITH (551 "I Want to Cry") 15-25 50
SITTIN' IN WITH (560 "I'm Sorry I Was Reckless") 15-25 50

Also see HAYES, Henry

HAYES, Bill *P&R '55*
(With the Archie Bleyer's Orchestra)

Singles: 78 rpm

ABC-PAR 8-12 57
CADENCE 5-8 54-56

MGM 3-6 55
Singles: 7-inch
ABC-PAR (Except 9895) 10-15 57
ABC-PAR (9895 "Bop Boy") 40-60 58
ABLE 4-8
BARNABY 4-6 76
CADENCE 10-20 54-56
DAYBREAK 4-6 74
KAPP 5-10 59
MGM 5-10 55
SHAW 4-6 65
Picture Sleeves
ABC-PAR 8-12 57
CADENCE (1/1256 "Ballad of Davy Crockett") 20-30 55
(Sleeve is numbered CCS-1 ["Cadence Children's Series], disc is 1256.)
EPs: 7-inch
MGM (312 "Bill Hayes") 10-20 55
LPs: 10/12-inch
ABC-PAR (194 "Bill Hayes Sings the Best of Walt Disney") 25-50 57
DAYBREAK 5-10 74
KAPP 10-20 60
Session: Dick Hyman.
Also see BLEYER, Archie
Also see HYMAN, Dick

HAYES, Carolyn, & Four Tops
Singles: 78 rpm
CHATEAU (2001 "Baby Say You Love Me") 40-50 55
Singles: 7-inch
CHATEAU (2001 "Baby Say You Love Me") 75-125 55
Also see CARROLL, Delores, & Four Tops
Also see FOUR TOPS

HAYES, Clancy
(With Yank Lawson & His Yankee Clippers)
Singles: 7-inch
ABC-PAR (10666 "Don't Forget 127th Street") 5-8 65
LPs: 10/12-inch
ABC-PAR (519 "Happy Melodies") 10-15 65
DELMARK (210 "Oh, By Jingo") 10-15 65

HAYES, Edgar, & Stardusters
Singles: 78 rpm
EXCLUSIVE 10-20 49

HAYES, Gabby
Singles: 78 rpm
CORAL (1312 "Tall Tales") 5-10 54
Singles: 7-inch
CORAL (1312 "Tall Tales") 10-15 54
Picture Sleeves
CORAL (1312 "Tall Tales") 10-20 54

HAYES, Henry
(Henry Hayes' Four Kings)
Singles: 78 rpm
ALADDIN (157 "All Alone Blues") 15-25 46
ALADDIN (158 "Angel Child Blues") 15-25 46
GOLD STAR (633 "Bowlegged Angeline") 15-25 48
SWING (414 "Bowlegged Angeline") 15-25 48
Singles: 7-inch
KANGAROO (109 "Stop Smacking That Wax") 75-125 60
ZEBRA (700 Hog Grunt") 15-25 59
Also see BROWN, James "Widemouth"
Also see CAMPBELL, Carl
Also see HAYES, Bill
Also see KING TUT
Also see NIXON, Elmore

HAYES, Isaac P&R/R&B/LP '69
(Isaac Hayes Movement)
Singles: 12-inch
COLUMBIA 4-6 85-86
Singles: 7-inch
ABC 4-6 77
BRUNSWICK (55258 "Laura") 5-10 64
COLUMBIA 3-5 85-87
ENTERPRISE 4-6 69-74
HBS 4-6 75-76
POLYDOR 3-6 78-80
SAN AMERICAN 4-6 70
STAX 4-6 78
YOUNGSTOWN 15-25 '60s
(Title and selection number not known.)
Picture Sleeves
COLUMBIA (06363 "Ike's Rap") 3-5 86
LPs: 10/12-inch
ABC-PAR 8-10 75-77
ATLANTIC 8-10 72
COLUMBIA 5-10 86
ENTERPRISE 10-12 68-75
HBS 8-12 75-77
POLYDOR 5-10 77-81
STAX 5-10 77-82
Also see REDDING, Otis

HAYES, Isaac, & Millie Jackson R&B/LP '79
Singles: 7-inch
SPRING (2036 "Do You Wanna Make Love") 3-6 79
SPRING (2063 "You Never Cross My Mind") 3-6 80
LPs: 10/12-inch
POLYDOR (6229 "Royal Rappin's") 5-10 79

HAYES, Isaac, & David Porter R&B '72
Singles: 7-inch
ENTERPRISE (9049 "Ain't That Loving You") 4-6 72

HAYES, Isaac, & Dionne Warwick R&B/LP '77
Singles: 7-inch
ABC (12253 "By the Time I Get to Phoenix" – "Say a Little Prayer") 4-6 77
LPs: 10/12-inch
ABC 10-15 77
Also see HAYES, Isaac
Also see WARWICK, Dionne

HAYES, Jay
Singles: 7-inch
SOLID GOLD (715 "Tellin' Lies") 40-60
SPINNING (6006 "Suzy") 8-12 58

HAYES, Jimmy
Singles: 7-inch
HAPPY HEARTS (141 "Tom Cat Boogie") 40-60 62

HAYES, Jimmy, & Soul Surfers
Singles: 7-inch
IMPERIAL (5986 "Summer Surfin' ") 10-15 63

HAYES, Linda R&B '53
(With the Platters; with Tony Williams; with Flairs; with Red Callender Sextet; with Twigs; with Monroe Tucker)
Singles: 78 rpm
ANTLER (4000 "I Had a Dream") 8-12 56
DECCA (29644 "Our Love's Forever Blessed") 5-10 55
HOLLYWOOD (Except 1032) 10-20 53-55
HOLLYWOOD (1032 "Our Love Is Forever Blessed") 20-30 55
KING 10-20 55
RECORDED IN HOLLYWOOD 10-20 52-53
Singles: 7-inch
ANTLER (4000 "I Had a Dream") 15-25 56
DECCA (29644 "Our Love's Forever Blessed") 10-15 55
HOLLYWOOD (1003 "Take Me Back") 20-30 53
HOLLYWOOD (1009 "No Next Time") 20-30 54
HOLLYWOOD (1016 "Play It Right") 20-30 54
HOLLYWOOD (1019 "Non Cooperation") 20-30 54
HOLLYWOOD (1027 "Darling Angel") 20-30 55
HOLLYWOOD (1032 "Our Love's Forever Blessed") 40-50 55
KING (4752 "My Name Ain't Annie") 40-50 54
KING (4773 "Please Have Mercy") 30-40 55
RECORDED IN HOLLYWOOD (200 "I've Tried So Hard") 50-75 52
RECORDED IN HOLLYWOOD (244 "Yes I Know") 30-50 52
RECORDED IN HOLLYWOOD (246 "Big City") 30-50 52
RECORDED IN HOLLYWOOD (407 "What's It to You, Jack") 20-30 53
Also see CALLENDER, Red
Also see FLAIRS
Also see HUGHES, Ben
Also see MOORE, Johnny, & Linda Hayes
Also see PLATTERS
Also see TUCKER, Monroe
Also see WOODS, Sonny

HAYES, Malcolm
Singles: 7-inch
CHATTAHOOCHEE (686 "Searchin' for My Baby") 50-75 65
FILMWAYS (101 "I Gotta Be with You") 10-15 66
LIBERTY (55943 "It's Not Easy") 10-15 67
OKEH (7299 "Baby Please Don't Leave Me") 10-15 67

HAYES, Richard P&R '49
Singles: 78 rpm
MERCURY 5-10 49-55
Singles: 7-inch
ABC-PAR 15-25 56
COLUMBIA 10-20 60-61
CONTEMPO 4-6 64
DECCA 4-6 61
MERCURY 10-20 50-55
EPs: 7-inch
MERCURY 15-25 54
LPs: 10/12-inch
MERCURY 20-30 55

HAYES, Richard, & Kitty Kallen P&R '51
Singles: 78 rpm
MERCURY 4-8 50-51
Singles: 7-inch
MERCURY 5-10 50-51
Also see HAYES, Richard
Also see KALLEN, Kitty

HAYES, Tommy
(With the 4 Seasons)
Singles: 7-inch
PHILIPS (40259 "Trance") 30-40 65
Also see 4 SEASONS

HAYMARKET RIOT
Singles: 7-inch
STATURE (1104 "Footsteps") 10-20 67

HAYMARKET RIOT
Singles: 7-inch
CLB (691 "Leaving") 10-15 69
COCONUT GROOVE (2040 "Nine O'Clock") 20-30 68

HAYMARKET RIOT
Singles: 7-inch
RIOT (101 "Trip On Out") 10-20 '60s

HAYMARKET SQUARE
LPs: 10/12-inch
CHAPARRAL (201 "Magic Lantern") 500-1000 68
Members: Gloria Lambert; Marc Swenson; Robert Homa; John Kowslowski.

HAYMES, Dick P&R/R&B '43
Singles: 78 rpm
CAPITOL 4-8 56
DECCA 5-10 43-54
Singles: 7-inch
CAPITOL 10-20 56
CONGRESS (105 "Down the Road") 5-10 62
DECCA 10-20 50-54
GNP 4-6 75
SUNBEAM 8-12 58
WARWICK (568 "Blue Champagne") 8-12 60
EPs: 7-inch
CAPITOL 5-10 56
DECCA 5-10 50-54
LPs: 10/12-inch
AUDIOPHILE 5-10 78
CAPITOL 10-20 56
CORAL 4-6 73
DAYBREAK 5-10 74
DECCA 10-20 50-54
GLENDALE 5-10 84
MCA 5-10 76-83
WARWICK 10-15 60
Also see CLOONEY, Rosemary, & Dick Haymes
Also see CROSBY, Bing, Dick Haymes & Andrews Sisters
Also see FISHER, Eddie / Vic Damone / Dick Haymes
Also see SINATRA, Frank

HAYMES, Dick, & Andrews Sisters P&R '48
Singles: 78 rpm
DECCA (24320 "Teresa") 4-8 48
Also see ANDREWS SISTERS

HAYMES, Dick, & Judy Garland P&R '47
Singles: 78 rpm
DECCA (23687 "For You, for Me, Forevermore") 4-8 47
Also see GARLAND, Judy
Also see HAYMES, Dick

HAYNES, Henry "Homer"
Singles: 7-inch
RCA (48-0086 "Waltz with Me") 10-20 49
(Green vinyl.)
Also see HOMER & JETHRO

HAYNES, Walter
Singles: 7-inch
JACK O' DIAMONDS (1008 "Tear Time") 10-20 67

HAYS, Red
Singles: 7-inch
STARDAY (164 "Doggone Woman") 50-75 54

HAYWARD, Jerry, & Everglades
Singles: 7-inch
SYMBOL (916 "You Stole My Heart Away") 25-35 62
Also see EVERGLADES

HAYWARD, Justin P&R '75
Singles: 7-inch
COLUMBIA 3-5 78
DERAM (7541 "Lay It on Me") 4-6 77
DERAM (7542 "Country Girl") 4-6 77
LPs: 10/12-inch
DERAM (4801 "Night Flight") 8-12 80
DERAM (18073 "Songwriter") 10-20 77
TOWER BELL (15 "Moving Mountains") 50-75 98

HAYWARD, Justin, & John Lodge P&R/LP '75
Singles: 7-inch
THRESHOLD 4-6 75
Picture Sleeves
THRESHOLD 4-6 75
LPs: 10/12-inch
THRESHOLD (14 "Blue Jays") 10-20 75
THRESHOLD (101 "Blue Jays") 15-25 75
(Promotional issue only. Interview with script.)
Also see HAYWARD, Justin
Also see MOODY BLUES

HAYWOOD, Frank
Singles: 78 rpm
RECORDED IN HOLLYWOOD (181 "Rock-A-Bye Baby") 10-20 51

HAYWOOD, Joe
(With Larry Lucie & Orchestra)
Singles: 7-inch
DEE-SU (313 "Sadie Mae") 10-15 66
DEE-SU (316 "Play a Cornbread Song for Me and My Baby") 10-15 66
ENJOY (2013 "Warm and Tender Love") 15-25 65
ENJOY (2016 "When You Look in the Mirror") 15-25 65
FRONT PAGE (1003 "In Your Heart You Know I Love You") 5-10
FURY (5052 "Debt of Love") 10-15 68
KENT (490 "I Wanna Love You") 10-15 68
WHITE CLIFFS (248 "Let's Make It") 10-20 66

HAZARDS
Singles: 7-inch
GROOVE (502 "Hey Joe") 15-25 66
UNICORN ("Tinted Green") 15-25
(Selection number not known.)

HAZELWOOD, Eddie
Singles: 78 rpm
IMPERIAL (8056 "Back in Texas") 10-15 49
IMPERIAL (8062 "A Package of Lies Tied in Blue") 10-15 49
INTRO (Except 6057 & 6069) 5-10 51-54
INTRO (6069 "Hound Dog") 10-15 53
Singles: 7-inch
INTRO (Except 6057 & 6069) 10-20 51-54
INTRO (6057 "Holdin' My Baby Tight") 30-40 52
INTRO (6069 "Hound Dog") 25-35 53

HEAD, Don
Singles: 7-inch
DUB (2840 "Goin' Strong") 40-60 58

HEAD, Jim, & His Del Rays
LPs: 10/12-inch
H.P. (22893 "Hayden Proffitt Presents Jim Head & His Del Rays") 200-300 63
(Monaural.)
H.P. (22893 "Hayden Proffitt Presents Jim Head & His Del Rays") 350-550 63
(Stereo.)

HEAD, Roy P&R/R&B/LP '65
(With the Traits)
Singles: 7-inch
ABC 4-6 73-79
ABC/DOT 4-6 76-77
AVION 3-5 83
BACK BEAT 8-12 65-67
CHURCHILL 3-5 81
DUNHILL 4-6 70
ELEKTRA 3-6 79-80
MEGA (1219 "Baby's Not Home") 4-6 74
MERCURY 5-10 68
NSD 3-5 82
SCEPTER 5-10 65-66
SHANNON 4-6 75
SUAVE 10-20
TMI 4-6 71-73
TNT (194 "Don't Be Blue") 10-15 65
(First issued in 1959, credited to the Traits.)
TEXAS CRUDE 3-5 85
LPs: 10/12-inch
ABC 5-10 73-78
CRAZY CAJUN 5-10 77
DUNHILL 8-12 70
ELEKTRA 5-10 79-80
SCEPTER (532 "Treat Me Right") 15-25 65
(Monaural.)
SCEPTER (532 "Treat Me Right") 20-30 65
(Stereo. With an "SS" prefix.)
TMI (1000 "Dismal Prisoner") 8-10 72
TNT (101 "Roy Head and the Traits") 100-150 65
(Counterfeits can be identified by their content. They include *Treat Her Right*, as well as other later Head tracks on side two. Originals do not have these.)
TEXAS CRUDE 5-10 85
Also see ROY - SARAH & TRAITS
Also see TRAITS

HEAD & HARES
Singles: 7-inch
H&H PRODUCTIONS (200,891 "I Won't Come Back") 20-30 65

HEAD LYTERS
(Headlyters)
Singles: 7-inch
PHALANX (1010 "The Girl Down the Street") 25-35 '60s
WAND (199 "Better Come Home") 15-25 65

HEAD SHOP
LPs: 10/12-inch
EPIC (26476 "Head Shop") 30-40 69

HEADEN, Willie
(With the Five Birds; Willie Hayden)
Singles: 78 rpm
AUTHENTIC (410 "Let Me Cry") 8-12 56
AUTHENTIC (703 "I Wanna Know") 8-12 56
DOOTONE (410 "Let Me Cry") 8-12 56
Singles: 7-inch
AUTHENTIC (410 "Let Me Cry") 30-40 56
AUTHENTIC (703 "I Wanna Know") 20-30 56
DOOTO (410 "Let Me Cry") 10-15 59
DOOTO (417 "Everybody Has a Fool") 10-20 57
DOOTO (427 "Cool Cat") 10-20 57
DOOTO (437 "Real Fine Daddy") 10-20 58
DOOTO (703 "Back Home Again") 10-20 58
DOOTONE (410 "Let Me Cry") 50-75 57
KENT 4-8 67-68
EPs: 7-inch
DOOTO (457 "Willie Headen") 20-30 60
LPs: 10/12-inch
DOOTO (293 "Willie Headen") 50-100 60

HEADHUNTERS
Singles: 7-inch
FENTON (2518 "Times We Share") 15-25 69

HEADHUNTERS LP '75
LPs: 10/12-inch
ARISTA (4038 "Survival of the Fittest") 25-50 75
ARISTA (4146 "Straight from the Gate") 10-20 78

HEADLEY, Gilbert
Singles: 7-inch
HI-LITE (736 "I Tried to Be Fair") 100-150

HEADLINERS
Singles: 7-inch
BELTONE (2020 "Comin' On Down with Love") 40-50 62
(Brown vinyl.)
KENO (1002 "Back to School Again") 20-30 61
V.I.P. (25011 "You're Bad News") 20-30 64
V.I.P. (25026 "We Call It Fun") 15-20 65

HEADSTONE
LPs: 10/12-inch
STARR (1056 "Still Looking") 75-125 71
Members: Dave Applegate; Tom Applegate; Barry Applegate; Bruce Flynn.

HEADSTONES
Singles: 7-inch
PHARAOH (147 "Wish She Were Mine") 15-25 66
PHARAOH (152 "Bad Day Blues") 15-25 66
Members: Dave Williams; Paul Veale; Winston Logan.

HEAPE, Abe
Singles: 7-inch
ROSE (116 "Short Fellow Blues") 100-200

HEAP, Jimmy P&R/C&W '56
(With the Melody Masters & Perk Williams; "Featuring Ken Ida")
Singles: 78 rpm
CAPITOL 5-15 53-55
IMPERIAL 8-12 50-52
Singles: 7-inch
CAPITOL 10-20 53-55
D (1050 "Born to Love You") 10-20 59
DART (119 "Meanwhile") 5-10 60
FAME (502 "Little Jewel") 200-250 58
FAME (509 "Night Cap") 8-15 61
FAME (510 "Go Get Em") 8-15 61
FAME (511 "Flint Rock") 8-15 61
IMPERIAL (8325 "When They Operated on Papa They Opened Mama's Male") 10-15 60
LPs: 10/12-inch
FAME (1005 "Laff-A-Rammer") 25-40 61

HEARD
Singles: 7-inch
AUDITION (6107 "Stop It Baby") 15-25 66

HEARD
Singles: 7-inch
FEATURE (203 "Stop It Girl") 10-20 67
Also see WYLDE HEARD

HEARD
Singles: 7-inch
ONE WAY (01 "Exit 9") 15-25 67

HEARD, Buddy
Singles: 7-inch
RED TOP (501 "Rock with Me") 40-60

HEARD, Lonnie
Singles: 7-inch
ARLISS (1006 "A Sunday Kind of Love") 20-30 61

HEARD, Oma
Singles: 7-inch
V.I.P. (25008 "Mr. Lonely Heart") 75-150 64
Also see UTMOSTS

HEARNS, Mitch
Singles: 7-inch
DOT (16438 "Miss You So") 10-20 62

HEART P&R/LP '76
Singles: 12-inch
CAPITOL 4-6 85
MUSHROOM 4-8 76
PORTRAIT 4-8 77-79
Promotional 12-inch Singles
MUSHROOM (7023 "Dreamboat Annie") 8-10 76
PORTRAIT (16445 "Straight On") 8-10 78
Singles: 7-inch
CAPITOL 3-5 85-90
EPIC 3-5 81-83
MUSHROOM 4-6 76-79
PORTRAIT 4-6 77-79
Picture Sleeves
CAPITOL 3-5 85-90
EPIC (Except 04047) 3-5 82-83
EPIC (04047 "How Can I Refuse") 3-5 83
EPIC (04047 "How Can I Refuse") 8-10 83
(Promotional sleeve. Labeled: "Demonstration Only—Not for Sale.)
LPs: 10/12-inch
CAPITOL 5-10 85-90
CAPITOL RADIO STAR ("Audio Cue Card") 10-15 87
(Radio interview. Promotional issue only.)
EPIC 5-10 80-83
MUSHROOM (MRS-5005 "Dreamboat Annie") 8-12 76
MUSHROOM (MRS-5008 "Magazine") 50-75 77
(First issue. Last track on Side One is *Magazine*.)
MUSHROOM (MRS-5008 "Magazine") 5-10 77
(Second issue. First track on Side Two is *Magazine*. There are also other differences in song order.)
MUSHROOM (MRS-5008 "Magazine") 50-75 78
(Promotional only picture disc.)
MUSHROOM (MRS-1-SP "Magazine") 15-25 78
(Picture Disc.)
MUSHROOM (MRS-2-SP "Dreamboat Annie") 20-30 79
(Picture Disc.)
NAUTILUS 20-25 80
(Half-speed mastered.)
PORTRAIT (30000 series) 5-10 77-81
PORTRAIT (40000 series) 12-15 81
(Half-speed mastered.)
Members: Nancy Wilson; Ann Wilson; Howard Leese; Steve Fossen; Roger Fisher; Denny Carmassi; Mike Derosier; Mark Andes.
Also see BORDERSONG
Also see SPIRIT
Also see WILSON, Ann & Daybreaks
Also see WILSON, Nancy / Red Hot Chili Peppers

HEART, Don
(Don Hart)
Singles: 7-inch
D-TOWN (1022 "A Telegram with Love") 15-25 64
D-TOWN (1030 "I'm Gonna Make a Comeback") 15-25 64
MAH'S (11 "Just Say You Care") 20-30 63
TUBA (1705 "Lover's Hideaway") 8-12
Also see HART, Don

HEART BEATS QUINTET
("Russell Jacquet & His Orch. - The Heart Beats Quintet")
Singles: 78 rpm
NETWORK (1200 "Tormented") 150-200 55
Singles: 10-inch
CANDLELITE (437 "Tormented") 20-30 72
(Gold vinyl 45 rpm.)
CANDLELITE (437 "Tormented") 10-20 72
(Black vinyl 45 rpm.)
Singles: 7-inch
CANDLELITE (1135 "Tormented") 4-6 76
NETWORK (71200 "Tormented") 200-300 55
(Black vinyl. Pastel yellow label.)
NETWORK (71200 "Tormented") 40-50 55
(Black vinyl. Bright yellow label.)
NETWORK (71200 "Tormented") 5-10 61
(Black vinyl.)
NETWORK (71200 "Tormented") 10-20 61
(Red vinyl.)
Members: James Sheppard; Albert Crump; Vernon Walker; Wally Roker; Rob Adams.
Also see HEARTBEATS
Also see JACQUET, Russell

HEART BREAKERS
Singles: 7-inch
COS-DE (1001 "Boddely Bump") 10-15 59

HEART BREAKERS
("Vocal By Lisa Tomasulo")
Singles: 7-inch
P&M (402 "Who Do You Love") 40-50 65

HEARTBEATS
Singles: 78 rpm
JUBILEE (5202 "Finally") 8-12 55
Singles: 7-inch
JUBILEE (5202 "Finally") 10-15 55
Members: Frank Starro; Al Rosenberg; Flo Guida; Joe Sucamente; Tony Grochowski.
Also see 3 FRIENDS

HEARTBEATS P&R/R&B '56
Singles: 78 rpm
GEE 25-50 57
HULL 25-75 55-56
RAMA 25-50 56-57
ROULETTE (4054 "Down on My Knees") 40-60 58
Singles: 7-inch
COLLECTABLES 3-5
GEE (1043 "When I Found You") 20-30 57
GEE (1047 "After New Year's Eve") 20-30 57
(Red label.)
GEE (1047 "After New Year's Eve") 10-15 60
(Gray label.)
GEE (1061 "People Are Talking") 10-15 60
GEE (1062 "Darling, How Long") 10-15 60
GUYDEN (2011 "One Million Years") 40-50 59
(Yellow label.)
GUYDEN (2011 "One Million Years") 30-40 59
(Purple label.)
HULL (709 "It's Alright with Me") 4-8 74
HULL (711 "Crazy for You") 400-500 55
(White label. Promotional issue only.)
HULL (711 "Crazy for You") 100-200 55
(Pink label. Credits Shane Sheppard.)
HULL (711 "Crazy for You") 50-75 55
(Pink label. Credits Sheppard-Miller.)
HULL (711 "Crazy for You") 20-30 55
(Black label.)
HULL (713 "Darling How Long") 75-125 56
HULL (716 "People Are Talking") 50-150 56
HULL (720 "A Thousand Miles Away") 75-125 56
(Black label.)
HULL (720 "A Thousand Miles Away") 20-30 56
(Red label.)
RAMA (216 "A Thousand Miles Away") 50-75 56
(Black vinyl.)
RAMA (216 "A Thousand Miles Away") 500-750 56
(Red vinyl.)
RAMA (216 "A Thousand Miles Away") 30-40 60
(45 RPM appears only on right side of label.)
RAMA (222 "I Won't Be the Fool Anymore") 40-60 57
RAMA (231 "Everybody's Somebody's Fool") 50-75 57
(Red label. "Rama" in 3-D type, with clouds in background.)
RAMA (231 "Everybody's Somebody's Fool") 35-50 '60s
(Maroon label. "Rama" in normal block-style type. No clouds.)
ROULETTE (4054 "Down on My Knees") 10-15 58
ROULETTE (4091 "One Day Next Year") 10-15 58
ROULETTE (4194 "Crazy for You") 8-12 59
LPs: 10/12-inch
EMUS 8-12 79
ROULETTE (25107 "A Thousand Miles Away") 100-200 60
ROULETTE (59019 "A Thousand Miles Away") 8-12 81
Members: James Sheppard; Albert Crump; Vernon Walker; Wally Roker; Rob Adams.
Also see HEART BEATS QUINTET
Also see SHEP & LIMELIGHTS

HEARTBEATS / Shep & Limelights
LPs: 10/12-inch
ROULETTE (115 "Echoes of a Rock Era") 40-60 72
Also see HEARTBEATS
Also see SHEP & LIMELIGHTS

HEARTBEATS
Singles: 7-inch
BROADCAST (1122 "Lonely Lover") 15-25 75
BROADCAST (1125 "Have Rock Will Roll") 4-8 75

HEARTBREAKERS
Singles: 78 rpm
RCA 75-150 51-52
Singles: 7-inch
RCA (4327 "Heartbreaker") 500-600 51
RCA (4508 "I'm Only Fooling My Heart") 400-500 52
RCA (4662 "Why Don't I") 300-400 52
RCA (4849 "There Is Time") 200-300 52
Members: Robert Evans; Lawrence Green; Jim Rose; Junior Davis; Larry Tate.
Also see FOUR DOTS
Also see GRIFFINS

HEARTBREAKERS
("Vocal Lead: Paul Himmelstein")
Singles: 78 rpm
VIK 50-75 57
Singles: 7-inch
VIK (0261 "Without a Cause") 75-100 57
VIK (0299 "My Love") 100-200 57
Member: Paul Himmelstein.

HEARTBREAKERS
Singles: 7-inch
DONNA (1381 "Every Time I See You").. 40-50 63
Member: Frank Zappa (guitar).
Also see ZAPPA, Frank

HEARTBREAKERS
Singles: 7-inch
ATCO (6258 "The Willow Wept") 10-15 63
BRENT (7037 "I'm Leaving It All Up to You") 15-25 62
DERBY CITY (101 "I've Got to Face It") .. 15-25 '60s
LINDA (114 "Please Answer") 30-40 64
MARKAY (106 "Since You Been Gone") 500-750 62
MIRACLE (101 "I'm Falling in Love Again") 75-100 65

HEARTBREAKERS
Singles: 7-inch
MGM (13129 "It's Hard Being a Girl") 10-15 63

HEARTBREAKERS
Singles: 7-inch
SWAN (4242 "I Told You So") 15-20 66
TOMI .... 5-10 '60s

HEARTBREAKERS / Keynoters
Singles: 7-inch
VANGUARD (9093 "Come Back My Love"/"Who Does She Think She Is") 15-25 75

HEARTBREAKERS / Students
Singles: 7-inch
FORDHAM (109 "Come Back My Love"/"Jennie Lee") 20-30 64

HEARTS R&B '55
Singles: 78 rpm
BATON 8-12 54-56
Singles: 7-inch
BATON (208 "Lonely Nights") 15-25 54
(Has "Record No. 45-208" on left side.)
BATON (208 "Lonely Nights") 10-15 54
(Has "Record No. 45-208" on right side.)
BATON (211 "All My Love Belongs to You") 15-25 55
BATON (215 "Gone Gone Gone") 15-25 55
BATON (222 "Going Home to Stay") 10-15 56
BATON (228 "I Had a Guy") 10-15 56
J&S (425 "My Love Has Gone") 75-125
J&S (995 "A Thousand Years from Today") 20-30 56
J&S (1002 "If I Had Known") 20-30 57
J&S (1180 "You Weren't Home") 20-30 57
J&S (1626 "I Want Your Love Tonight") .. 30-40 58
J&S (1657 "Dancing in a Dream World") . 20-30 57
J&S (1660 "So Long Baby") 20-30 57
J&S (4571 "Goodbye Baby") 30-40
LAVENDER (1008 "Lonely Nights") 8-12 62
TUFF (370 "Dear Abby") 8-12 63
ZELLS (3377 "I Feel Good") 15-20 63
LPs: 10/12-inch
ZELLS (337 "I Feel Good") 200-300 63
Members: Justine "Baby" Washington; Joyce Peterson; Rex Garvin; Pat Ford; Zell Sanders.
Also see GARVIN, Rex, & Mighty Cravers
Also see JAYNETTS
Also see WASHINGTON, Baby

HEARTS
Singles: 7-inch
CHANCELLOR (1057 "On My Honor") 15-25 60
GOTHAM (323 thru 325) 4-6 81
Also see ANDREWS, Lee, & Hearts
Also see FAMOUS HEARTS

HEARTS & FLOWERS
Singles: 7-inch
CAPITOL 5-10 67-68
LPs: 10/12-inch
CAPITOL 15-25 67-68
Members: Rick Cunha; Larry Murray; Dave Lawson; Bernie Leadon; David Jackson.

HEARTSMAN, Johnny R&B '57
(With the Gaylarks; Johnny Hartsman Band)
Singles: 78 rpm
MUSIC CITY 10-15 57
RHYTHM 10-15 53
Singles: 7-inch
BIG J (101 "Syrup Sopping") 15-25
MUSIC CITY (807 "Johnny's House Party") 15-25 57
MUSIC CITY (811 "Johnny's Thunderbird") 15-25 57
TRIAD (501 "One More Time") 8-12 64
WORLD PACIFIC (372 "Sizzlin") 10-20 63
LPs: 10/12-inch
CAT 'N HAT 10-15
Also see SIMON, Joe

HEARTSPINNERS
Singles: 7-inch
X-TRA (109 "I've Searched") 800-1000 58

HEARTSPINNERS / Admirations
Singles: 7-inch
RELIC (537 "I've Searched"/"Mixture of Love") 5-10 65
TIMES SQUARE (20 "I've Searched"/"Mixture of Love") 15-25 63

HEART-THROBS
Singles: 78 rpm
ALADDIN (3394 "So Glad") 20-30 57
LAMP (2010 "So Glad") 20-30 57
Singles: 7-inch
ALADDIN (3394 "So Glad") 30-40 57
LAMP (2010 "So Glad") 30-40 57
Member: Shirley Goodman.
Also see SHIRLEY & LEE

HEATH, Boyd C&W '45
Singles: 78 rpm
BLUEBIRD (33-0522 "Smoke on the Water") 20-30 45

HEATH, Jimmy
Singles: 7-inch
MEGA (2261 "Little Darlin'") 100-150

HEATH, Joyce
(Joyce Heath & Priviteers)
Singles: 7-inch
AGON (1003 "Honor Roll of Love") 30-40 62
(Also issued as by Joyce & Priviteers.)
DRAGON (415 "I Wouldn't Dream of It") .. 10-20 61
DRAGON (4401 "Too Many Walls") .... 10-20 '60s
LAURIE (3062 "Johnny Fair") 5-10 60
MAY (107 "A Lover Wanted") 5-10 61
RCA (7536 "Promise Me, Sweetheart") 5-10 59
ROULETTE (7018 "I Wouldn't Dream of It") . 4-8 68
Also see JOYCE & PRIVITEERS

HEATH BROTHERS R&B '81
Singles: 7-inch
COLUMBIA 3-6 79-81
LPs: 10/12-inch
COLUMBIA 5-10 79-81
STRATA EAST ("Marchin' On") 75-125 76
(Selection number not known.)

HEATHENS
Singles: 7-inch
VIBRA (104 "The Other Way Around") 15-25 67

HEATHERTON, Joey P&R/LP '72
Singles: 7-inch
CORAL (62422 "That's How It Goes") 10-20 64
CORAL (62451 "Hullabaloo") 10-20 65
CORAL (62459 "But He's Not Mine") 10-20 65
DECCA (31962 "When You Call Me Baby") 25-50 66
MGM 5-10 72-73
Picture Sleeves
CORAL (62422 "That's How It Goes") 15-25 64
DECCA (31962 "When You Call Me Baby") 25-50 66
MGM (14387 "Gone") 8-10 72
LPs: 10/12-inch
MGM (4858 "Joey Heatherton Album") 10-15 72

HEAVENLY ECHOES
Singles: 7-inch
BATON (216 "Didn't It Rain") 15-25 55

HEAVY BALLOON
LPs: 10/12-inch
ELEPHANT (104 "16 Ton") 50-75 69

HEBB, Bobby P&R/R&B/LP '66
Singles: 7-inch
BOOM (60017 "Betty Jo from Ohio") 5-8 66
CADET (5690 "I Was a Boy When You Needed a Man") 4-6 72
FM (516 "I Found Somebody") 5-10 61
LAURIE (3632 "Proud Soul Heritage") 4-6 75
LAURIE (3638 "Sunny '76") 4-6 75
PHILIPS 5-10 66-67
RICH (0001 "You Gotta Go") 10-20 60
RICH (1006 "Feel So Good") 10-20 61
SCEPTER (12166 "I Love Mary") 5-8 66
SMASH (1740 "Just a Little Bit More") 5-10 62
Picture Sleeves
PHILIPS (40400 "A Satisfied Mind") 5-10 66
LPs: 10/12-inch
EPIC 10-12 70
PHILIPS 15-20 66

HECK, Tommy, Quintet
Singles: 7-inch
CHARIOT (513 "Lost World") 15-25

HEDGES, Hal, & Dreamers
Singles: 7-inch
ABC-PAR (10406 "On My Knees") 5-10 63
DOT (16406 "On My Knees") 10-20 62
SHOWCASE (1007 "On My Knees") 30-40

HEFTI, Neal LP '55
(With His Orchestra; Neal Hefti Quintet; with Mello-Larks)
Singles: 78 rpm
CORAL 3-5 51-57
EPIC 3-5 55-56
Singles: 7-inch
COLUMBIA 4-8 65
CORAL 10-20 51-59
DOT 4-8 67-68
EPIC 10-15 55-56
RCA 4-8 66-67
RCA GOLD STANDARD SERIES 3-5 89
REPRISE 5-10 62-64
U.A. 4-8 65-66
Picture Sleeves
RCA (8755 "Batman Theme") 10-15 66
RCA GOLD STANDARD SERIES (9011 "Batman Theme") 3-5 89
EPs: 7-inch
CORAL 5-10 52-56
EPIC 5-10 56
"X" 5-10 55
LPs: 10/12-inch
COLUMBIA (1516 "Light & Right") 10-20 60
(Monaural.)
COLUMBIA (8316 "Light & Right") 15-25 60
(Stereo.)
CORAL 15-25 52-60
EPIC (3113 "Singing Instrumentals") 15-25 56
EPIC (3187 "Hot 'N Hearty") 15-25 56
RCA (3621 "Hefti in Gotham City") 10-20 66
RCA (3750 "Oh Dad, Poor Dad") 10-20 67
REPRISE (6018 "Themes from TV's Top 12") 8-15 62
REPRISE (6039 "Jazz Pops") 8-15 62
20TH FOX (3139 "Li'l Darlin' ") 8-12 64
(Monaural.)
20TH FOX (4139 "Li'l Darlin' ") 10-15 64
(Stereo.)
U.A. (573 "Definitely Hefti") 8-15 67
"X" (1039 "Presenting Neal Hefti") 10-20 55
Also see DUPREE, Champion Jack, & His Combo / Lucy Roberts with Neal Hefti & His Orchestra
Also see MARTIN, Dean
Also see SHANNON SISTERS

HEFTI, Neal / Tom Glazer
Singles: 7-inch
WONDERLAND (2101 "Batman Theme"/"Superman Song") .... 10-20 '60s
Also see GLAZER, Tom
Also see HEFTI, Neal

HEIGHT, Donald R&B '66
Singles: 7-inch
BELL 4-6 72
DAKAR 4-6 76
JUBILEE 5-10 63-69
KING (54 08 "How Lonely Can You Be") . 10-20 60
OLD TOWN 10-20 64-65
RCA (8570 "Girl Do You Love Me") 5-10 65
ROULETTE (4644 "Bow 'N' Arrow") 5-10 65
ROULETTE (4658 "Song of the Street") 5-10 65

SHOUT 5-10 66-68
SOOZEE (110 "Don't Cry") 10-15 62
Also see HOLLYWOOD FLAMES

HEIGHT, Ronnie P&R '59
Singles: 7-inch
BAMBOO (500 "I'm Confessin' ") 5-10 61
DORE (516 "Come Softly to Me") 15-20 59
ERA 5-10 59-61

HEINDORF, Ray
(With the Warner Bros. Orchestra)
Singles: 78 rpm
COLUMBIA (Except 40754) 3-5 55-56
COLUMBIA (40754 "Theme from *East of Eden* and *Rebel Without a Cause* – Tribute to James Dean") 5-10 56
Singles: 7-inch
COLUMBIA (Except 40574) 8-12 55-56
COLUMBIA (40574 "Theme from *East of Eden* and *Rebel Without a Cause* – Tribute to James Dean") 10-15 56
Picture Sleeves
COLUMBIA (40574 "Theme from *East of Eden* and *Rebel Without a Cause* - Tribute to James Dean") 30-50 56
EPs: 7-inch
COLUMBIA 5-10 55-56
LPs: 10/12-inch
COLUMBIA (Except 940) 10-20 55-57
COLUMBIA (940 "Tribute to James Dean") 30-50 56

HEIRS
Singles: 7-inch
PANORAMA (39 "Do You Want Me") 10-15 66

HELLER, Jackie / Glenn Miller
Singles: 78 rpm
PHILCO/VOGUE ("Rum and Coca-Cola") 500-700 45
(Picture disc. Promotional issue only. No selection number used.)

HELLERS
LPs: 10/12-inch
COMMAND (934 "Singers, Talkers, Players, Swingers & Doers") 25-50 68
Member: Hugh Heller.

HELLO PEOPLE LP '74
Singles: 7-inch
ABC (12160 "Book of Love") 5-10 76
DUNHILL (15023 "Future Shock") 5-10 75
PHILIPS (40522 "A Stranger at Her Door") 10-15 68
PHILIPS (40531 "It's a Monday Kind of Tuesday") 10-15 68
Picture Sleeves
PHILIPS (40522 "A Stranger at Her Door") 10-20 68
LPs: 10/12-inch
ABC (882 "Bricks") 8-10 75
DUNHILL (50184 "Handsome Devils") 8-10 74
MEDIARTS (41-8 "Have You Seen the Light") 12-15 70
PHILIPS (600265 "The Hello People") 15-20 68
PHILIPS (600276 "Fusion") 15-20 68
Also see BLUE CHEER / H.P. Lovecraft / Hello People

HELMS, Bobby C&W/P&R/R&B '57
Singles: 78 rpm
DECCA (29947 "Tennessee Rock and Roll") 25-75 56
DECCA (30194 "Fraulein") 25-75 57
DECCA (30423 "My Special Angel") 125-175 57
DECCA (30513 "Jingle Bell Rock") 30-50 57
DECCA (30557 "Love My Lady") 40-60 58
DECCA (30619 "Jacqueline") 50-75 58
Singles: 7-inch
BLACK ROSE 3-5 83-84
CAPITOL 5-8 70
CERTRON 4-6 70-71
COLUMBIA 5-10 64
DECCA (29947 "Tennessee Rock and Roll") 35-45 56
DECCA (30194 thru 30749) 15-25 57-58
DECCA (30831 thru 31148) 10-20 59-60
DECCA (31230 thru 31403) 8-12 61-62
GUSTO 4-6 74
KAPP 5-10 65-67
LARRICK 4-6 75
LITTLE DARLIN' 4-6 67-79

MCA....3-5
MILLION....4-6 72
MISTLETOE....4-6 74
PLAYBACK....4-6
PRETTY WORLD (005 "I Feel You, I Love You So Much")....4-6

Picture Sleeves

CERTRON....4-6 70
DECCA ("New Singing Sensation")....10-20 57
(Pictures Helms, but no number or title is shown. Has die-cut center hole.)
DECCA (30194 "Fraulein")....15-20 57
DECCA (30513 "Jingle Bell Rock")....50-75 57

EPs: 7-inch

DECCA (2555 "Bobby Helms Sings to My Special Angel")....15-25 57
DECCA (2586 "Tonight's the Night")....10-20 58
DECCA (2629 "Bobby Helms")....10-20 59

LPs: 10/12-inch

CERTRON....8-10 70
COLUMBIA....12-15 63
DECCA (8638 "Bobby Helms Sings to My Special Angel")....30-50 57
HARMONY....10-12 67
HOLIDAY....5-10 80
KAPP....10-15 66
LITTLE DARLIN'....10-12 68
MCA....5-10 83
MISTLETOE....5-10 74
VOCALION....10-12 65
Session: Anita Kerr Singers.
Also see KERR, Anita

HELMS, Don

Singles: 7-inch

SMASH (1781 "Fire Ball Mail")....10-20 62

LPs: 10/12-inch

SMASH (27001 "Steel Guitar Sound of Hank Williams")....10-20 62
(Monaural.)
SMASH (27019 "Steel Guitar")....10-20 62
(Monaural.)
SMASH (67001 "Steel Guitar Sound of Hank Williams")....15-25 62
(Stereo.)
SMASH (67019 "Steel Guitar")....15-25 62
(Stereo.)

HELMS, Jimmie
(Jimmy Helms)

Singles: 78 rpm

CAPITOL....5-10 55

Singles: 7-inch

CAPITOL....10-15 55
EAST WEST (114 "Senior Class Ring")....15-25 58
FOREST (045 "Fairytale Princess")....5-10 63
SCOTTIE (1301 "My Love for You Is Real")....10-15 59
SCOTTIE (1315 "Lost Lover")....10-15 60
SYMBOL (923 "Suzie's Gone")....5-10 63
Session: Markees.

HELP

Singles: 7-inch

DECCA (32879 "Good Time Music")....5-10 71

LPs: 10/12-inch

DECCA (75257 "Help")....20-30 71
DECCA (75304 "Second Coming")....20-30 71
Members: Chet McCracken; Jack Merrill; Rob Rochan.
Also see DOOBIE BROTHERS
Also see EVERGREEN BLUE SHOES

HEMPHILL, Neal

Singles: 7-inch

HEMPHILL (1003 "Little Booga from Chattanooga")....10-20 '60s

HENCHMEN

Singles: 7-inch

GUILLOTINE....10-20 65-66
LEAF (6684 "Love Till the End of Time")....15-25 67
MONUMENT....5-10 '60s
SWAN (4249 "Baby, What's Wrong")....10-15 66
SWAN (4264 "James Brown")....8-12 66
TOUCHE (2007 "She's a Big Girl Now")....10-20 '60s

HENCHMEN

Singles: 7-inch

PUNCH (1009 "Please Tell Me")....20-30 66

HENCHMEN VI

Singles: 7-inch

CUCA (6731 "All of the Day")....15-25 67
Members: Scott Keinski; Joe DeHut; Bob Durant; Jay Jackson; Art Moinlenen.

HENDERSON, Al

Singles: 7-inch

EAST WEST (113 "Ding Dong Daddy")....75-125 58
KING (5612 "Lemon Twist")....8-12 62

Picture Sleeves

KING (5612 "Lemon Twist")....15-20 62

HENDERSON, Big Bertha, & Al Smith Orchestra

Singles: 78 rpm

CHANCE (1143 "Rock Daddy, Rock")....75-125 53
SAVOY (1119 "Little Daddy")....10-20 54

Singles: 7-inch

CHANCE (1143 "Rock Daddy, Rock")....200-300 53
SAVOY (1119 "Little Daddy")....25-40 54
Also see SMITH, Al

HENDERSON, Bill, & Oscar Peterson Trio

Singles: 7-inch

MGM (13155 "Gravy Waltz")....5-10 63

LPs: 10/12-inch

MGM (4128 "Bill Henderson with the Oscar Peterson Trio")....20-30 63
Also see HENDERSON, Bill
Also see PETERSON, Oscar

HENDERSON, Bugs
(Bugs Henderson Group)

Singles: 7-inch

PLANET EARTH (8505 "Dance Till the Moon Go Down")....4-6
PLANET EARTH (8506 "Rocket in My Pocket")....4-6

LPs: 10/12-inch

ARMADILLO (1 "At Last")....30-50 78
Also see NITZINGER

HENDERSON, Chuck

Singles: 7-inch

OZARK (959 "Rock and Roll Baby")....150-200 58

HENDERSON, Floyd

Singles: 7-inch

TRIANGLE (51315 "Tenderly")....40-60 59
TRIANGLE (51319 "Darling")....8-12 60

HENDERSON, Jesse

Singles: 7-inch

GOLD DUST (001 "The Gator")....15-25

HENDERSON, Joe — P&R/R&B/LP '62
("Fantastic" Joe Henderson; with the Cliff Parman Orchestra)

Singles: 7-inch

ABC....4-6 73
FONTANA (1638 "Help Yourself")....5-10 69
KAPP....5-10 64
RIC....5-10 64-66
SIGNATURE (12,001 "Hey Chick")....10-15 59
TODD....6-12 61-64
VIRGO....4-6 72

LPs: 10/12-inch

FONTANA (27590 "Hits Hits Hits")....20-30 67
(Monaural.)
FONTANA (67590 "Hits Hits Hits")....25-35 67
(Stereo.)
TODD (2701 "Snap Your Fingers")....30-40 62

HENDERSON, Joe "Piano"

Singles: 78 rpm

ATCO (6054 "Sing It with Joe")....5-10 55

Singles: 7-inch

ATCO (6054 "Sing It with Joe")....10-15 55

HENDERSON, Sam "High Pockets"

Singles: 78 rpm

GROOVE (0021 "Go Mother, Go")....5-10 54

Singles: 7-inch

GROOVE (0021 "Go Mother, Go")....10-20 54

HENDERSON, Wayne

Singles: 7-inch

CIRCLE (101 "You're an Angel")....15-25 59
CIRCLE ("Walking in Circles")....50-75
(Selection number not known.)

HENDLEY, John

Singles: 7-inch

MUTT-JEFF (2401 "My Baby Came from Out of Nowhere")....15-25

HENDON, R.D.

Singles: 78 rpm

4 STAR (1644 "Blues Boogie")....10-15 53

Singles: 7-inch

4 STAR (1644 "Blues Boogie")....20-30 53
STARDAY (167 "Return My Broken Heart")....20-30 54
STARDAY (194 "Big Black Cat")....150-250 55
STARDAY (228 "Don't Push Me")....20-30 56

HENDRICKS, Belford

Singles: 7-inch

CAPITOL (5021 "Crazy 'Bout My Baby")....10-20 63
MERCURY....15-25 58-59

LPs: 10/12-inch

WING....10-15 '60s

HENDRICKS, Bobby — P&R/R&B '58

Singles: 7-inch

CUB (9127 "Love in My Heart")....15-25 63
(First issue.)
MGM (13179 "Love in My Heart")....10-20 63
MERCURY (71788 thru 71881)....5-10 61
SUE....15-30 58-60
Also see COASTERS
Also see DRIFTERS
Also see FLYERS
Also see VELVIT, Jimmy

HENDRICKS, Jon

Singles: 7-inch

VERVE (10512 "Sons & Daughters")....200-300 67
Session: Grateful Dead.
Also see GRATEFUL DEAD

HENDRICKS, Lloyd

Singles: 7-inch

MALA (12007 "Your Cold Cold Heart Just Burns Me Up")....10-20 68
STATUE ("Your Cold Cold Heart Just Burns Me Up")....25-50 68
(First issue. Selection number not known.)

HENDRIX, Al
(With Jolly Jody & His Go Daddies)

Singles: 78 rpm

ABC-PAR (9901 "Rhonda Lee")....15-25 57
TALLY (119 "Rhonda Lee")....50-75 57

Singles: 7-inch

ABC-PAR (9901 "Rhonda Lee")....25-35 57
LEGREE (701 "Young and Wild")....75-100 60
PIKE (5912 "Monkey Bite")....10-15 61
TALLY (119 "Rhonda Lee")....50-75 58

HENDRIX, Jimi — P&R/LP '67
(Jimi Hendrix Experience)

Singles: 12-inch

REPRISE (840 "Jimi Hendrix")....50-100 79
(Brown label. Includes cover. Promotional issue only.)

Singles: 7-inch

AUDIO FIDELITY (167 "No Such Animal")....10-20
REPRISE (0572 "Hey Joe")....50-75 67
REPRISE (0597 "Purple Haze")....10-15 67
REPRISE (0641 "Foxey Lady")....10-15 67
REPRISE (0665 "Up from the Skies")....15-25 68
REPRISE (0767 "All Along the Watchtower")....10-15 68
REPRISE (0792 "Crosstown Traffic")....10-15 68
REPRISE (0853 "Stone Free")....15-25 69
REPRISE (0905 "Stepping Stone")....75-125 70
REPRISE (1000 "Freedom")....10-15 71
REPRISE (1044 "Dolly Dagger")....10-15 71
REPRISE (1082 "Johnny B. Goode")....15-25 72
REPRISE (1118 "The Wind Cries Mary")....15-25 72
REPRISE BACK-TO-BACK....4-6 '70s
TRIP (3002 "Suspicious")....5-10 72

Promotional Singles

REPRISE (0572 "Hey Joe")....50-75 67
REPRISE (0597 "Purple Haze")....10-20 67
REPRISE (0641 "Foxey Lady")....10-20 67
REPRISE (0665 "Up from the Skies")....20-30 68
REPRISE (0767 "All Along the Watchtower")....10-20 68
REPRISE (0792 "Crosstown Traffic")....10-20 68
REPRISE (0853 "Stone Free")....20-30 69
REPRISE (0905 "Stepping Stone")....75-100 70
REPRISE (1000 "Freedom")....15-25 71
REPRISE (1044 "Dolly Dagger")....15-25 71
REPRISE (1082 "Johnny B. Goode")....15-25 72
REPRISE (1118 "The Wind Cries Mary")....15-25 72

Picture Sleeves

AUDIO FIDELITY (167 "No Such Animal")....15-25
REPRISE (0572 "Hey Joe")....400-800 67

EPs: 7-inch

REPRISE (595 "And a Happy New Year")....100-200 74
(Promotional issue only. Issued with paper sleeve.)

LPs: 10/12-inch

ACCORD (7101 "Before London")....8-10 81
ACCORD (7112 "Free Sprit")....8-10 81
ACCORD (7139 "Cosmic Feeling")....8-10 81
AUDIO FIDELITY (320 "Jimi Hendrix")....10-20 84
(Picture disc.)
CRAWDADDY (5-1975 "Jimi Hendrix Interview LP")....200-300 75
MCA (112316-1 "Jimi Hendrix Experience")....75-125 2000
(Boxed, 8-disc set with 40-page booklet.)
PHOENIX 10 (320 "Rare Hendrix")....8-10 '80s
PICKWICK (3528 "Jimi")....10-15 75
NUTMEG (1001 "High, Live 'N Dirty")....15-20 78
(Colored vinyl.)
RCA (68233 "Storm")....10-15 '90s
(Picture disc.)
REPRISE (2025 "Smash Hits")....20-30 69
(Orange and brown label. Add $20 to $30 if accompanied by 28" x 20" bonus poster.)
REPRISE (2025 "Smash Hits")....50-100 71
(White label. Promotional issue only. Add $20 to $30 if accompanied by 28" x 20" bonus poster.)
REPRISE (2025 "Smash Hits")....10-15 71
(Brown label.)
REPRISE (2029 "Historic Performances")....10-15 70
REPRISE (2029 "Historic Performances")....15-25 70
(White label. Promotional issue only.)
REPRISE (2034 "The Cry of Love")....10-15 70
(Brown label.)
REPRISE (2034 "The Cry of Love")....300-400 70
(Orange label.)
REPRISE (2034 "The Cry of Love")....50-75 70
(White label. Promotional issue only.)
REPRISE (2040 "Rainbow Bridge")....10-15 71
REPRISE (2040 "Rainbow Bridge")....15-25 71
(White label. Gatefold cover has titles/timing sticker. Promotional issue only.)
REPRISE (2049 "In the West")....10-15 72
REPRISE (2049 "In the West")....15-25 72
(White label. Promotional issue only.)
REPRISE (2103 "War Heroes")....10-15 72
REPRISE (2103 "War Heroes")....15-25 72
(Promotional issue only.)
REPRISE (2204 "Crash Landing")....10-15 75
REPRISE (2204 "Crash Landing")....15-25 75
(White label. Promotional issue only.)
REPRISE (2229 "Midnight Lightning")....10-15 75
REPRISE (2229 "Midnight Lightning")....15-25 75
(White label. Promotional issue only.)
REPRISE (2245 "Essential Jimi Hendrix")....10-15 78
(Two discs.)
REPRISE (2245 "Essential Jimi Hendrix")....15-25 78
(Two discs. White label. Promotional issue only.)
REPRISE (2276 "Smash Hits")....8-12 77
REPRISE (2293 "Essential Jimi Hendrix, Vol. 2")....20-50 79
(Includes the bonus *Gloria*, extended version. Prices vary even more widely than the range shown here – from less than $10 to nearly $100. Egad!)
REPRISE (2293 "Essential Jimi Hendrix, Vol. 2")....30-60 79
(White label. Promotional issue only.)
REPRISE (2293 "Essential Jimi Hendrix, Vol. 2")....8-15 79
(Without the bonus single.)
REPRISE (2299 "Nine to the Universe")....8-12 80
REPRISE (2299 "Nine to the Universe")....15-20 80
(White label. Promotional issue only.)
REPRISE (R-6261 "Are You Experienced")....50-75 67
(Monaural. Green, pink and yellow label.)
REPRISE (R-6261 "Are You Experienced")....200-400 67
(White label. Promotional issue only.)
REPRISE (RS-6261 "Are You Experienced")....50-75 67
(Stereo. Green, pink and yellow label.)

REPRISE (6261 "Are You Experienced") 15-25 68
(Orange and brown label.)
REPRISE (6261 "Are You Experienced") ...8-12 71
(Brown label.)
REPRISE (R-6281 "Axis: Bold As Love") 1000-2000 68
(Monaural. Orange and brown label.)
REPRISE (R-6281 "Axis: Bold As Love") 1000-1500 68
(White label. Promotional issue only.)
REPRISE (RS-6281 "Axis: Bold As Love") 20-30 68
(Stereo. Green, pink and yellow label.)
REPRISE (RS-6281 "Axis: Bold As Love") 10-20 69
(Stereo.Orange and brown label.)
REPRISE (RS-6281 "Axis: Bold As Love").8-12 71
(Brown label.)
REPRISE (6307 "Electric Ladyland") 15-25 68
(Two discs. Orange and brown label.)
REPRISE (6307 "Electric Ladyland") ... 100-150 68
(Two discs. White label. Promotional issue only. Cover has "Promotion – Not for Sale" sticker. Stereo. Mono is not known to exist.)
REPRISE (6307 "Electric Ladyland") 8-12 71
(Brown label.)
REPRISE (6481 "Sound Track Recordings from the film *Jimi Hendrix*") 15-20 73
(Two discs. Soundtrack.)
REPRISE (6481 "Sound Track Recordings from the film *Jimi Hendrix*") 20-30 73
(Two discs. White label. Pink "Not for Sale" sticker on cover. Promotional issue only.)
REPRISE (22306 "Jimi Hendrix Concerts") 8-12 82
(Two discs.)
REPRISE (22306 "Jimi Hendrix Concerts") 15-20 82
(Two discs. White label. Promotional issue only.)
REPRISE (25119 "Kiss the Sky") 8-10 84
REPRISE (25119 "Kiss the Sky") 15-20 84
(White label. Promotional issue only.)
REPRISE (25358 "Jimi Plays Monterey")...8-10 86
REPRISE (25358 "Jimi Plays Monterey") 15-20 86
(White label. Promotional issue only.)
RHINO (254 "Interview") 15-20 82
(Picture disc.)
RYKO 10-15 87-88
SHOUT (502 "In the Beginning") 10-15 72
(White label with red and blue printing.)
SHOUT (502 "In the Beginning") 8-10
(Yellow label.)
SPRINGBOARD (4031 "In Concert") 8-10 72
TRIP (3505 "Superpak") 15-25 74
TRIP (3509 "Superpak") 15-25 74
(Same title but different tracks than Trip 3505.)
TRIP (9500 "Rare Hendrix") 15-25 72
(Gatefold cover. Includes Hendrix poster.)
TRIP (9500 "Rare Hendrix") 10-15 72
(Standard cover.)
TRIP (9501 "Roots of Hendrix") 10-15 72
TRIP (9523 "Genius of Jimi Hendrix") 10-15 74
U.A. (505 "Very Best of the World of Jimi Hendrix") 8-12 75
Session: Al Kooper; Buddy Miles; Freddie Smith; Mike Finnigan; Larry Faucette; Stevie Winwood; Jack Cassidy; Chris Wood.
Also see BROOKS, Rosa Lee
Also see REDDING, Otis / Jimi Hendrix

HENDRIX, Jimi, & Isley Bros.
LPs: 10/12-inch
T-NECK (3007 "In the Beginning") 10-20 71
Also see ISLEY BROTHERS

HENDRIX, Jimi, & Curtis Knight
LPs: 10/12-inch
CAPITOL (659 "Flashing") 8-10 70
CAPITOL (2856 "Get That Feeling") 10-15 67
CAPITOL (2894 "Flashing") 10-15 68
51 WEST 5-10 82
Also see KNIGHT, Curtis

HENDRIX, Jimi, & Lightnin' Rod
Singles: 12-inch
CELLULOID (166 "Doriella Du Fontaine")..5-10 84

HENDRIX, Jimi, & Little Richard
(Little Richard - Jimi Hendrix)
Singles: 7-inch
ALA (1175 "Goodnight Irene") 5-10 72
LPs: 10/12-inch
ALA (1972 "Friends from the Beginning").10-15 72
EVEREST (296 "Roots of Rock") 8-10 74
PICKWICK (3347 "Together") 8-10 73
Also see LITTLE RICHARD

HENDRIX, Jimi, & Buddy Miles
(With Billy Cox)
LPs: 10/12-inch
CAPITOL (472 "Band of Gypsys") 10-20 70
CAPITOL (12416 "Band of Gypsys 2") 5-10 86
(Mini-LP. Shows three tracks correctly on Side 2.)
CAPITOL (12416 "Band of Gypsys 2") ...75-125 86
(Has four tracks on Side 2 – all different than the three listed on label.)
CAPITOL (16319 "Band of Gypsys") 8-10 86
CAPITOL (96414 "Band of Gypsys") 10-15 95
(Limited numbered edition.)
Also see MILES, Buddy

HENDRIX, Jimi, & Lonnie Youngblood LP '71
(Lonnie Youngblood with Jimi Hendrix)
Singles: 7-inch
FAIRMOUNT 10-20 65
LPs: 10/12-inch
MAPLE (6004 "Two Great Experiences Together") 20-25 71
Also see HENDRIX, Jimi
Also see YOUNGBLOOD, Lonnie

HENNESSEE, Jorris
Singles: 7-inch
REO (940 "Jorris Boogie") 75-125

HENRIETTA
(With the Hairdooz)
Singles: 7-inch
LIBERTY (55545 "Slow Motion") 8-12 63
LIBERTY (55572 "It Might As Well Be Me") 8-12 63
LIBERTY (55606 "I Love Him") 20-25 63

HENRY, Andrea
Singles: 7-inch
MGM (13893 "I Need You Like a Baby")..10-20 68

HENRY, Clarence P&R/R&B '56
(Clarence "Frogman" Henry)
Singles: 78 rpm
ARGO 15-25 56-57
Singles: 7-inch
ARGO (5200 series) 15-20 56-58
ARGO (5300 & 5400 series) 8-15 58-64
DIAL (4057 "This Time") 5-10 67
DIAL (4072 "Shake Your Money Maker")...5-10 68
PARROT (309 "Think It Over") 5-10 66
PARROT (45004 "Have You Ever Been Lonely") 5-10 64
PARROT (45015 "Tore Up Over You") 5-10 65
CHESS 4-6 73
ERIC 4-6 73
MAISON DE SOUL 4-6 77
LPs: 10/12-inch
ARGO (4009 "You Always Hurt the One You Love") 75-125 61
CFH (101 "Bourbon St. New Orleans").....15-20
CADET (4009 "You Always Hurt the One You Love") 20-30 65
(Cadet 4009 LPs can be found in Argo 4009 covers.)
ROULETTE (42039 "Clarence 'Frogman' Henry Is Alive and Well") 15-25 69
Also see GAYTEN, Paul

HENRY, Earl
Singles: 7-inch
DOT (15756 "What'cha Gonna Do") 30-40 58

HENRY, Edd
(With the Nickels & Three Pennies)
Singles: 7-inch
BIG MACK (1286 "Crooked Woman") ..100-200
HEAVY HANK (123 "You Made Your Bed Baby") 10-15 69
NU-SOUND (180 "I Love Only You") 50-75

HENRY, Haywood
Singles: 7-inch
MERCURY (71674 "Midnight Alley") 10-20 60

HENRY, Henry
(Henry Lavoy)
Singles: 7-inch
STAFF (1002 "Baggie Maggie") 250-350

HENRY, Ja Neen
Singles: 7-inch
BLUE ROCK (4010 "Baby Boy") 15-25 65

HENRY, John, & Steel Drivers
Singles: 7-inch
ARLINGTON (100 "I'm Gonna Tell on You") 100-150
ARLINGTON (108 "Sweet and Neat") 30-40 59

HENRY, Little Man
Singles: 7-inch
CENTRAL (4701 "Wailin' Wildcat") 200-300

HENRY, Patrik, & Visions
Singles: 7-inch
LARK (5262 "Go Wherever Rainbows Go") ....500-750 '60s
Note: Label indicates "From the Album My Daughter the Model"; however, we have no other information about this LP. Any details, including value estimates, would be appreciated.

HENRY, Robert
Singles: 78 rpm
KING (4624 "Miss Anna B") 150-200 53
KING (4646 "Old Battle Ax") 150-200 53
Singles: 7-inch
KING (4624 "Miss Anna B") 550-650 53
KING (4646 "Old Battle Ax") 550-650 53

HENRY, Stacy, & Flip Jacks Orchestra
Singles: 7-inch
FLIPPIN' (108 "Sweetest Darling") 10-20 61
FLIPPIN' (203 "Magic Was the Night") 10-20 60
(With the Dream-Timers.)
Also see DREAM-TIMERS

HENRY, Thomas
Singles: 7-inch
HIT (73 "So Much in Love") 10-15 63

HENSKE, Judy
Singles: 7-inch
ELEKTRA 5-10 63
MERCURY 5-10 65
REPRISE 5-10 66
STRAIGHT 5-10 68
LPs: 10/12-inch
ELEKTRA 10-20 63
MERCURY 10-20 65
REPRISE 10-20 66
Also see COFFEE HOUSE
Also see GUARD, Dave, & Whiskeyhill Singers

HENSKE, Judy, & Jerry Yester
LPs: 10/12-inch
REPRISE 10-20 68
STRAIGHT 10-20 68
Also see HENSKE, Judy
Also see YESTER, Jerry

HENSLEE, Gene
Singles: 78 rpm
IMPERIAL (8227 "Dig'n & Datin' ") 15-25 54
Singles: 7-inch
BROWNSFIELD (1 "Shambles") 40-60
IMPERIAL (8227 "Dig'n & Datin' ") 40-60 54
JOSIE (982 "Soul of a Man") 5-10 67
LE CAM (334 "If You Really Want Me to I'll Go") 4-6 73
MEL-O-DY (110 "Beautiful Woman") 10-15 64
U.A. (946 "Shambles") 5-10 65

HENSLEY, Bill
Singles: 7-inch
KOOL (1007 "Come Closer to Me") 10-15 60

HENSON, Herb
(Cousin Herb Henson)
Singles: 78 rpm
ABBOTT 10-20 55
Singles: 7-inch
ABBOTT (179 "Out of Line") 25-50 55
(With Joyce Yours)
ABBOTT (182 "Old Jalopy") 25-50 55
TALLY (108 "Up Yonder") 25-50 57
TALLY (120 "Lose My Mind") 75-125 58

HEP CATS
Singles: 7-inch
DEL-FI (4159 "What in the World Can I Do") 250-350 61

HEP STARS
Singles: 7-inch
CAMEO (376 "Cadillac") 10-15 65

HEP STARS
Singles: 7-inch
CHARTMAKER (414 "It's Now Winter's Day") 8-10 69
DUNHILL (4040 "No Response") 12-15 66
Member: Benny Andersson.
Also see ABBA

HEPSTERS
Singles: 78 rpm
RONEL 50-100 55-56
Singles: 7-inch
RONEL (107 "I Had to Let You Go") 400-500 55
(Black vinyl.)
RONEL (107 "I Had to Let You Go") 4000-5000 55
(Red vinyl.)
RONEL (110 "I Gotta Sing the Blues") .500-600 56

HEPTONES
Singles: 78 rpm
ABBCO (401 "I'm So in Love Tonight") 150-250 56
Singles: 7-inch
ABBCO (401 "I'm So in Love Tonight") 500-750 56
(Serial numbers "105"/"106," are more prominent on label than selection no. "401.")

HERALD GOSPEL
Singles: 78 rpm
HERALD (412 "The Old Account") 15-20 53
Singles: 7-inch
HERALD (412 "The Old Account") 20-30 53

HERALDS
Singles: 78 rpm
HERALD (435 "Eternal Love") 50-75 54
Singles: 7-inch
HERALD (435 "Eternal Love") 100-200 54
HERALD (435 "Eternal Love") 10-20
(Has larger print.)
Member: Billy Dawn Smith.
Also see DAWN, Billy, Quartet
Also see FOUR DUKES

HERB & CRONIES
Singles: 7-inch
PERSONALITY (700 "Phantom") 15-25 60
TOP NOTCH (700 "Phantom") 5-10 66

HERB'S HALLUCINATIONS
Singles: 7-inch
MGM (13735 "Birds, Fish & Chips") 10-15 67

HERBIE & CLASS CUTTERS
Singles: 7-inch
RCA (7649 "Just a Summer Kick") 10-15 59

HERBS, The
Singles: 7-inch
SMOKE (602 "Never Never") 15-25 60
SMOKE (612 "There Must Be an Answer") 15-25 60

HERBST, Jack
Singles: 7-inch
DEL-FI (4228 "Jimmy's Party") 10-15 63

HERBY JOE
Singles: 78 rpm
ABCO (101 "Smokestack Lightning") 15-25 56
Singles: 7-inch
ABCO (101 "Smokestack Lightning") 30-50 56

HERD
Singles: 7-inch
FONTANA 5-10 67-69
Picture Sleeves
FONTANA (1602 "Sweet William") 10-15 67
LPs: 10/12-inch
FONTANA 15-25 68

HERD
Singles: 7-inch
OCTOPUS (257 "Things Won't Change") 20-30 67

HERDA, Al
Singles: 7-inch
EVE (9003 "Fuzzy Wuzzy") 50-100

HERDER, Pervis
(With the Combo Kings; with Leon "Fingers" Huff)
Singles: 7-inch
IMPERIAL (5989 "All That's Good")..........5-10 63
JAMIE (1254 "Soul City")......................... 15-25 63

HERMAN, Cleve / Don Rays
Singles: 7-inch
CAPCO (103 "In This Corner")................ 10-20 63

HERMAN, Hermy
Singles: 7-inch
BEE (1108 "Hey Hot Rod")..................... 75-125

HERMAN, Sticks
Singles: 7-inch
GOLDBAND (1047 "Long Gone Baby")... 40-60 57
GOLDBAND (1050 "Beautiful Doll")......... 40-60 57
GOLDBAND (1056 "Wipe the Tears from Your Eyes").. 40-60 58
HOLLYWOOD (1080 "Long Gone Baby").. 30-50 58
HOLLYWOOD (1082 "Beautiful Doll")..... 30-50 58
HOLLYWOOD (1085 "Wipe the Tears from Your Eyes").. 30-50 58
TIC TOC (103 "Give Me Your Love")....... 15-25 61

HERMAN, Woody, Orchestra *P&R '37*
Singles: 78 rpm
CAPITOL..3-6 54-56
COLUMBIA...3-6 45-48
DECCA..4-8 37-45
MGM...3-6 52
MARS...3-6 52-53
Singles: 7-inch
CADET (5634 "Light My Fire").....................4-6 69
CADET (5643 "Pontico")..............................4-6 69
CADET (5659 "I Can't Get Next to You")....4-6 69
CADET (5669 "My Cherie Amour")..............4-6 70
CAPITOL.. 10-15 54-56
CENTURY..3-5 79
CHURCHILL.......................................3-5 79
COLUMBIA...3-8 65-76
FANTASY...4-6 73-74
KENT (335 "Montmartre Bus Ride")............8-12 60
MCA..4-6 73
MGM... 10-15 52
MARS.. 10-15 52-53
PHILIPS..5-8 62
ROULETTE (4130 "Lullaby of Birdland")....5-10 59
EPs: 7-inch
CAPITOL..5-15 55-56
COLUMBIA...5-15 52-54
DECCA..5-15 56
MGM...5-15 52-55
LPs: 10/12-inch
ACCORD..5-10 82
ATLANTIC (1328 "At the Monterey Jazz Festival").. 20-30 60
ATLANTIC (90000 series)...........................5-10 82
BRIGHT ORANGE...................................5-10 73
CADET...8-12 69-71
CAPITOL..5-10 72-75
(With "M" or "SM" prefix.)
CAPITOL.. 15-30 55-62
(With "T" or "ST" prefix.)
CENTURY..5-10 78
CHESS..5-10 76
COLUMBIA (592 "The Three Herds")...... 15-25 55
COLUMBIA (651 "Music for Tired Lovers").. 15-25 55
COLUMBIA (683 "Twelve Shades of Blue").. 15-25 55
COLUMBIA (2300 & 2400 series)..............5-15 65-66
COLUMBIA (2500 series)....................... 20-30 52-54
(10-inch LPs.)
COLUMBIA (6000 series)....................... 20-30 49-55
COLUMBIA (9000 series)...........................5-15 65-67
COLUMBIA (32000 series)..........................5-10 74
CONCORD JAZZ......................................5-10 81-83
CROWN... 10-15 59
DECCA (4000 series).............................. 10-15 64
DECCA (8000 series).............................. 15-25 56
EVEREST (Except 200 & 300 series)...... 10-20 59-63
EVEREST (200 & 300 series)....................5-10 74-78
FPM...5-10 75
FANTASY...5-10 71-81
HARMONY..5-10 72
JAZZLAND (17 "Woody Herman and the Fourth Herd").. 15-25 60
(Monaural.)
JAZZLAND (917 "Woody Herman and the Fourth Herd")..15-25 60
(Stereo.)
MGM..10-25 55
METRO...5-12 65
PHILIPS..10-20 62-65
ROULETTE (25067 "At the Round-Table")..10-20 59
SURREY...8-12 66
TREND...5-10 81
TRIP..5-10 75
VSP...8-15 66-67
VERVE..10-20 63-68
WHO'S WHO IN JAZZ...............................5-10 78
WING...5-10
Also see BYRD, Charlie, & Woody Herman
Also see CLOONEY, Rosemary
Also see CROSBY, Bing
Also see ECKSTINE, Billy, & Woody Herman
Also see WISEMAN, Mac

HERMAN'S HERMITS *P&R '64*
Singles: 7-inch
ABKCO..4-6
BUDDAH...4-6 74-76
MGM..4-6 64-69
PRIVATE STOCK....................................4-6 75
ROULETTE (7213 "Heart Get Ready for Love")..4-6 77
Picture Sleeves
MGM..5-12 65-67
LPs: 10/12-inch
ABKCO..5-10 73-76
CAPITOL (90646 "Hold On!")....................10-20 66
(Soundtrack. Record club issue.)
MGM (E-4000 series, except 4478)..........10-20 65-67
(Monaural.)
MGM (SE-4000 series, except 4478).........8-15 65-68
(Stereo.)
MGM (E-4478 "Blaze").............................35-45 67
(Monaural.)
MGM (SE-4478 "Blaze")...........................10-15 67
(Stereo.)
Members: Peter Noone; Derek Leckenby; Karl Green; Keith Hopwood; Barry Whitwham.
Also see ALSTON, Shirley
Also see PAGE, Jimmy

HERMON & ROCKIN' TONICS
Singles: 7-inch
ROYAL (2871 "Been So Long")..............75-125

HERRERA, Little Julian
(With the Tigers; with Jim Balcom Orchestra; Ron Gregory)
Singles: 78 rpm
DIG..25-50 56-57
Singles: 7-inch
DIG (118 "Lonely Lonely Nights")............40-60 56
DIG (137 "Here in My Arms")...................50-75 57
ELDO (130 "Lonely Lonely Nights")...........8-12 62
EMMO (3302 "You Will Cry")....................15-25 '60s
ESSAR (1012 "Lonely Lonely Nights").....20-30 63
IRIS (137 "Here in My Arms").....................5-10
(Reissue of Dig 137.)
STARLA (6 "I Remember Linda")..............40-50 58
Also see BALCOM, Bill

HERRING, Red *C&W '60*
Singles: 7-inch
COUNTRY JUBILEE................................15-25 60

HERRINGS, Harry, & Radials
Singles: 7-inch
HIGHLAND ("A Crystal Ship")...................20-30
(Selection number not known.)

HERROLD, Dennis
Singles: 7-inch
IMPERIAL (5482 "Hip Hip Baby")............40-60 57

HESITATIONS *R&B '67*
Singles: 7-inch
GWP (504 "Yes I'm Ready").....................15-25 69
KAPP..8-15 66-68
LPs: 10/12-inch
KAPP..10-20 67-68
Members: George Scott; Fred Deal; Leonard Veal.
Also see METROTONES
Also see TURNER, Sonny, & Sound Ltd.

HESS, Bennie
(Big Ben Hess)
Singles: 7-inch
JET (1926 "Country Style Boogie").........50-100
MAJOR (1001 "Wild Hog Hop")...........150-250 58
MAJOR (1006 "Walking That Last Mile") .25-50 58
MUSICODE (5693 "Wild Hog Hop")........50-75 58
SHOWLAND...4-6 78
SPADE (1975 "Wild Hog Hop")..................5-10 75
SPADE (2202 "Elvis Presley Boogie")....75-125 58
TAP (1016 "Tennessee Mama Blues")...75-125 60

HESS, Chuck
(Ty Heston)
Singles: 7-inch
AMIGO (103 "Tijuana Guitar")..................10-20 66
Also see JODIMARS

HESSLER, Fred, & the U.C.L.A. Basketball Team
LPs: 10/12-inch
DOT (9501 "Perfect Season")..................10-20 64

HESTER, Carolyn
Singles: 7-inch
DOT (16660 "That's My Song")..................5-10 64
LPs: 10/12-inch
COLUMBIA (1796 "Carolyn Hester")........25-50 62
(Monaural.)
COLUMBIA (2032 "This Life I'm Living")..10-20 63
COLUMBIA (8596 "Carolyn Hester")........30-60 62
(Stereo. Has six "eye" logo boxes—three on each side.)
COLUMBIA (8596 "Carolyn Hester")........15-25 65
(Stereo. No "eye" logo boxes.)
DOT...10-15 64-65
Session: Bob Dylan (harmonica on 1962 Columbia LP.)
Also see DYLAN, Bob

HESTOR, Tony
(Tony Hester)
Singles: 7-inch
GIANT (707 "Watch Yourself").............100-150 66
KARATE (523 "Watch Yourself")..............50-75 66
LUCK...5-10 66

HEWITT, Ben
(Ben Davidson-Hewitt)
Singles: 7-inch
BROADLAND (2147 "Border City Call Girl")..4-8 75
(Canadian.)
MERCURY (Except 71612)......................10-20 58-59
MERCURY (71612 "Whirlwind Blues").....25-35 60
PLANTATION (133 "Border City Call Girl")..10-20 76

HEWITT, Dolph *C&W '49*
Singles: 78 rpm
RCA...5-10 49
Singles: 7-inch
JANIE (1 "You're the Keeper of My Heart")..8-12 59
JANIE (455 "Last Night Was the End of My World")..8-12 59
JANIE (459 "The Door to Your Love")........8-12 59
RCA (0107 "I Wish I Knew")....................15-25 49
RCA (0369 "I Hurt Inside").......................20-30 50
(Green vinyl.)

HEYBURNERS
Singles: 7-inch
TITANIC (5009 "Speedway")....................10-20 63
Session: Davie Allan; Mike Curb.

HEYMAN, Bill, & His Band
Singles: 78 rpm
ALADDIN (3323 "I Want My Baby")...........5-10 56
HERALD (427 "I'm Doin' Good Now")......15-20 54
Singles: 7-inch
ALADDIN (3323 "I Want My Baby").........10-15 56
HERALD (427 "I'm Doin' Good Now")......20-30 54

HI Cs
("HI C's")
Singles: 7-inch
3-4-5 (111 "Just How It Is")..................150-250

HI FIVES
Singles: 78 rpm
FLAIR-X (3000 "Throwing Pebbles in the Pond")..8-12 56
Singles: 7-inch
FLAIR-X (3000 "Throwing Pebbles in the Pond")..20-30 56

HI LIGHTERS
Singles: 78 rpm
WENDEE (1927 "Baby Don't Treat Me That Way")..10-15 55
Singles: 7-inch
WENDEE (1927 "Baby Don't Treat Me That Way")..40-60 55

HI-BALLERS
(Hi Ballers)
Singles: 7-inch
SUN STATE (103 "Day Train")..................10-20 62

HIBBLER, Al *R&B '48*
Singles: 78 rpm
ALADDIN..5-10 47-56
ATLANTIC...10-15 49-55
CHESS...8-12 51
CLEF...5-10 54
COLUMBIA..5-10 50
DECCA...5-10 55-57
MERCURY..5-10 52-56
MIRACLE..10-15 48
NORGRAN..5-10 54-55
ORIGINAL...5-10 55
Singles: 7-inch
ALADDIN (3328 "I Got It So Bad and That Ain't Good")..10-20 56
ATLANTIC (925 "The Blues Came Tumbling Down")..30-50 51
ATLANTIC (932 "Travelin' Light")............30-50 51
ATLANTIC (945 "This Is Always")............30-50 51
ATLANTIC (1071 "Danny Boy")................20-30 55
CHESS (1569 "Fat & Forty")................200-300 51
CLEF...10-20 54
COLUMBIA..5-10 50
DECCA...10-20 55-59
MCA..4-6 74
MERCURY...10-20 52-56
NORGRAN...10-20 54-55
ORIGINAL (1006 "After the Lights Go Down Low")..15-25 55
REPRISE (20035 "Look Away")..................5-10 61
REPRISE (20077 "Walk Away")..................5-10 62
SATIN (401 "Good for a Lifetime")..............4-8 66
TOP RANK (2089 "Stranger")....................8-12 60
VEGAS (711 "Early One Morning")..............4-8 67
EPs: 7-inch
CLEF...15-25 51
DECCA...15-25 55-57
NORGRAN...15-25 53
RCA..15-25 55
LPs: 10/12-inch
ATLANTIC (1251 "After the Lights Go Down Low – The Voice of Al Hibbler")..........................50-100 56
BRUNSWICK (54036 "Al Hibbler with the Ellingtonians")..30-40 57
DECCA (8328 "Starring Al Hibbler").........30-40 56
DECCA (8420 "Here's Hibbler")................30-40 56
DECCA (8697 "Torchy & Blue")................30-40 58
DECCA (8757 "Hits By Hibbler")..............30-40 58
DECCA (8862 "Al Hibbler Remembers [Big Songs of the Big Bands])..30-40 59
(Monaural.)
DECCA (7-8862 "Al Hibbler Remembers [Big Songs of the Big Bands])..40-50 59
(Stereo.)
DECCA (75000 series)...............................5-10 69
LMI (10001 "Early One Morning")...............8-12 65
MCA..5-10 76
NORGRAN (4 "Favorites").......................35-50 53
REPRISE (2005 "Monday Every Day")....10-15 61
SCORE (4013 "I Surrender Dear")..........30-40 56
TRIP..5-10 77
VERVE (4000 "Love Songs")...................20-30 55
Also see HOLIDAY, Billie, & Al Hibbler
Also see McSHANN, Jay
Also see RUSHING, Jimmy, & Al Hibbler

HIBBLER, Al, & Duke Ellington
Singles: 7-inch
COLUMBIA (33000 series)..........................4-6 76
LPs: 10/12-inch
COLUMBIA (2593 "Al Hibbler Sings with the Duke")..30-40 56
(10-inch LP.)
Also see ELLINGTON, Duke
Also see HIBBLER, Al

HI-BOYS
Singles: 7-inch
MALA (400 "Billy Boy").............................8-10 59

WOODRICH (1250 "So Good")................ 10-20 '60s

HICKEY, Ersel — P&R '58

Singles: 7-inch

APOLLO (761 "The Millionaire").............. 15-25 62
BLACK CIRCLE (845 "Slidin' Home")..........4-8 72
EPIC (9263 thru 9320)............................ 15-25 58-59
EPIC (9357 "What Do You Want")........... 20-30 60
EPIC (9395 "Stardust Brought Me You") . 15-25 60
JANUS (151 "Bluebirds Over the Mountain")..4-8 70
KAPP (372 "Teardrops at Dawn")........... 10-20 61
LAURIE (3165 "Some Enchanted Evening")...8-12 63
MAGNUM ("Country Tough") 4-6 89
(No selection number used.)
PARKWAY INT'L ("Let Me Be Your Radio").4-6 82
(No selection number used.)
RAMESES II (2003 "Waitin' for Baby") 4-6 75
TOOT (602 "Blue Skies")............................5-10 67
TOOT (607 "Strings of Gitarro") 5-10 68
UNIFAX (100 "How Unlucky Can You Get") 4-6 75

EPs: 7-inch

EPIC (7206 "Ersel Hickey in Lover's Land")... 100-200 58

LPs: 10/12-inch

BACK-TRAC (18750 "The Rockin' Bluebird") 65-75 85
Session: Mike Korda; Jimmy Mitchell.

HICKMAN, Beecher

Singles: 7-inch

COOL (165 "Hey Blues")..................... 100-200

HICKMAN, Dwayne

Singles: 7-inch

ABC-PAR (9908 "School Dance")..............5-10 58
CAPITOL 5-10 60

Picture Sleeves

ABC-PAR (9908 "School Dance")........... 10-20 58

LPs: 10/12-inch

CAPITOL (T-1441 "Dobie!") 15-25 60
(Monaural.)
CAPITOL (ST-1441 "Dobie!").................. 25-40 60
(Stereo.)

HICKORIES

Singles: 7-inch

BELL (125 "Teen Beat") 15-25 59

HICKORY WIND

LPs: 10/12-inch

GIGANTIC ("Hickory Wind")................ 550-650 69
(Reportedly 100 made. Number not known.)
Members: Mike McGuyer; Alan Jones; Bob Strehl.

HICKS, Al

EPs: 7-inch

BROADWAY (104 "Al Hicks") 50-75

HICKS, Bob
(With the Fenders; Bobby Hicks & Youngsters)

Singles: 7-inch

MIRASONIC (1001 "Rock, Baby, Rock") 450-500 59
SKYWAY (116 "Long Long Time")........... 30-40 58
Members (Youngsters): Leo Hicks; Linda Hicks; Freddy Countryman.

HICKS, Country Bill

Singles: 78 rpm

FORTUNE (188 "Blue Flame")................ 15-25 56

Singles: 7-inch

FORTUNE (188 "Blue Flame").............. 75-125 56

HICKS, Johnny

Singles: 78 rpm

COLUMBIA (21064 "Pick Up Blues")....... 10-20 53
COLUMBIA (21135 "I Swear") 8-12 53
COLUMBIA (21240 "Hey Now Honey")......8-12 54

Singles: 7-inch

COLUMBIA (21064 "Pick Up Blues")....... 25-50 53
COLUMBIA (21135 "I Swear") 10-20 53
COLUMBIA (21240 "Hey Now Honey") ... 10-20 54

HICKS, Major

Singles: 7-inch

SUN VALLEY ("Faded Levis")................ 50-75
(Selection number not known.)

HIDE-A-WAYS

Singles: 78 rpm

MGM (55004 "Cherie") 100-200 55
RONNI (1000 "Can't Help Loving That Girl of Mine")...300-400 54

Singles: 7-inch

LOST NITE...5-10
MGM (55004 "Cherie") 400-500 55
RONNI (1000 "Can't Help Loving That Girl of Mine")... 3000-4000 55

HIDEAWAYS

Singles: 7-inch

DUEL (521 "Loving Time") 10-15 63
MIRWOOD (5516 "Hideout").......................5-10 66

HI-FIDELITIES

Singles: 7-inch

HI-Q (5000 "Street of Loneliness")........500-750 57
Also see CONTOURS
Also see PARKS, Gino

HI-FI FOUR — P&R '56

Singles: 78 rpm

KING (4856 "Band of Gold")....................10-15 56

Singles: 7-inch

KING (4856 "Band of Gold")....................30-40 56
Members: Doug Harman; Jack McNicol; John Van Evera; Don Wainman.

HI-FIs

Singles: 78 rpm

LIBERTY...5-10 56

Singles: 7-inch

LIBERTY (55011 "Bridey Murphy")..........10-15 56
LIBERTY (55017 "Within My Heart")..........10-15 56
LIBERTY (55023 "Somebody's Gotta Lose")...10-15 56
LIBERTY (55037 "Dodie")........................10-15 56

HI-FIs
("Hi-Fi's")

Singles: 7-inch

MONTEL (1005 "My Dear")..................100-200 59
Also see SINGLETON, Jimmy, & Royal Satins

HI-FIs
(Hi-Fi's)

Singles: 7-inch

GAZA (122 "O-Oh Poopa Du Cha Cha")..50-100 60

HI-FIs

Singles: 7-inch

CAMEO (349 "I Keep Forgettin' ")..............5-10 65
INTERPHON (7701 "She's the One").......10-15 64
Members: Marilyn McCoo; La Monte McLemore; Floyd Butler; Harry Elston.
Also see FIFTH DIMENSION

HI-FIs

Singles: 7-inch

U.A. (50160 "I'm a Box").........................10-15 67

HI-Fis

Singles: 7-inch

CAM (100 "I Know This Love Is Real")...75-125

HI-FIVES

Singles: 7-inch

HITT (003 "Fujikami the Warrior").........400-600 61
LONDON (17200 "Mean Old Woman")..300-500 61
(Canadian.)
STAR-X (507 "The Hen Cackle")..............15-25 57
Members: Harry Walker; Tab Short; Bill Papuc; Larry Krashan; Freddy Carotenuto.

HI-FIVES

Singles: 7-inch

BINGO (1006 "Felicia")...........................20-30 60
DECCA (30576 "My Friend")....................20-30 58
DECCA (30657 "Dorothy") 50-75 58
(Pink label. Promotional issue only.)
DECCA (30657 "Dorothy") 40-50 58
(Black label. Has "Unbreakable 45 rpm Record" on right side. No star under middle "C" in Decca.)
DECCA (30657 "Dorothy").........................20-30 58
(Black label. No "Unbreakable 45 rpm Record" on label. Has a star under middle "C" in Decca.)
DECCA (30744 "Lonely") 20-30 58
Members: Dave Brigatti; Ron Menhardt; Peter Grieco; Howard Lanza; Rudy Jezerak; Joey Dee.
Also see DEE, Joey

HI-FIVES

Singles: 7-inch

HIT (0003 "Mo-Shun") 10-20 60
JERDEN (730 "Going Away") 10-15 64

HI-FIVES

Singles: 7-inch

BELL (634 "Julie").....................................20-30 65

HIGGINS, Ben

Singles: 7-inch

JAMIE (1217 "Really Paradise") 15-25 62
Also see FIVE SATINS

HIGGINS, Chuck
(With His Mellotones)

Singles: 78 rpm

ALADDIN..10-20 53
COMBO (Except 12 & 25) 8-12 51-55
COMBO (12 "Pachuko Hop")....................20-30 53
COMBO (25 "Real Gone Hound Dog").....20-30 52
DOOTONE...10-20 55-57
KICKS (6 "Shotgun Wedding")..................15-25 55
LOMA (706 "Double Dip") 10-20 56
LUCKY 10-20 53
MONEY..10-20 56
R&B 10-20 55
SPECIALTY 10-20 52-53

Singles: 7-inch

ALADDIN (3224 "Wiggie")........................20-30 53
ALADDIN (3283 "Pancho") 20-30 53
CADDY (108 "Flip Top Box") 15-25 57
COMBO (12 "Pachuko Hop")....................40-60 51
COMBO (13 "Love Me Baby")..................20-30 51
COMBO (14 "Cotton Picker")....................20-30 51
COMBO (17 "Stormy")...............................20-30 51
COMBO (25 "Real Gone Hound Dog").....50-75 52
COMBO (30 thru 176) 15-20 52-60
DOOTONE (361 thru 396) 15-25 55
KICKS (6F "Shotgun Wedding") 40-50 55
LOMA (706 "Double Dip") 15-25 56
LUCKY (003 "Greasy Pig") 15-25 53
MONEY (214 "Rock and Roll") 30-40 56
R&B (1314 "Chop-Chop")..........................15-25 55
ROLLIN' ROCK (011 "Big Bop Boom").........4-6 73
ROXBURY 4-6 75
SPECIALTY (532 "I'll Be There") 30-40 52
SPECIALTY (539 "One More Time")........15-25 53

EPs: 7-inch

COMBO (2 "Chuck Higgins") 35-50 55

LPs: 10/12-inch

COMBO (300 "Pachuko Hop").............400-600 55
(Cover pictures a woman wearing only a scarf.)
COMBO (300 "Pachuko Hop")...............75-100 55
(Cover pictures Higgins and a saxophone.)
ROLLIN' ROCK...8-10
Also see FLAMINGO, Johnny / Chuck Higgins
Also see FORREST, Gene, & Four Feathers

HIGGINS, Chuck / Roy Milton

EPs: 7-inch

DOOTO (208 "Rock 'N' Roll vs. Rhythm & Blues")..10-20 57
DOOTONE (208 "Rock 'N' Roll vs. Rhythm & Blues") 25-40 57

LPs: 10/12-inch

AUTHENTIC/DOOTO (223 "Rock 'N' Roll vs. Rhythm & Blues") 10-15
DOOTONE (223 "Rock 'N' Roll vs. Rhythm & Blues")...75-125 57
Members (Mellotones): John Watson; Eli Toney; Joe Ursery.
Also see HIGGINS, Chuck
Also see MILTON, Roy

HIGGINS, Chuck, & Mellomoods

Singles: 78 rpm

MONEY (214 "Beautiful Love")................15-25 56

Singles: 7-inch

MONEY (214 "Beautiful Love")................30-50 56
Also see MELLOMOODS

HIGGINS, Sally Ann

Singles: 7-inch

ERMINE (58 "Blue Angel").......................10-20 64

HIGH KEYES — P&R '63

Singles: 7-inch

ATCO 10-20 63-64
Members: Troy Keyes; Jim Williams; Bob Haggard; Cliff Rice.

HIGH KEYS

Singles: 7-inch

VERVE (10423 "Living a Lie")..................50-75 66

HIGH SCHOOLERS

Singles: 7-inch

QUILL (108 "Graduation Song") 10-20 66

HIGH SEAS

Singles: 7-inch

D-M-G (4000 "We Go Together") 75-100 60
Member: Adrian Torres.
Also see SATELLITES

HIGH SPIRITS

Singles: 7-inch

APEX (76972 "Love Light").......................20-30 65
(First issue.)
SOMA (1436 "Love Light") 10-20 65
SOMA (1446 "I Believe")..........................40-60 66

HIGH TENSIONS & TOMMY DAE

Singles: 7-inch

HITT (6601 "You Got It Made")................30-40 66
HITT (6603 "Poor Man")...........................15-25 66
Also see DAE, Tommy

HIGH TREASON

LPs: 10/12-inch

ABBOTT (1209 "High Treason")..............50-75 68
Members: Joe Cleary; Marcie Rauer; Sam Goodman.

HIGHBAUGH, Rev. John

Singles: 78 rpm

KING (4652 "Do What the Lord Says Do")..10-20 53

Singles: 7-inch

KING (4652 "Do What the Lord Says Do")..20-40 53

HIGHLANDERS

Singles: 7-inch

RAYS (36 "Sunday Kind of Love")........300-400 57

HIGHLIFES

Singles: 7-inch

PIT (403 "No One to Tell Her") 15-25 65

HIGHLIGHTERS
(With Fred Harris' Red Tops Organ Trio)

Singles: 7-inch

NEW SONG (115 "Flang Dang Do") 15-25 58
NEW SONG (133 "Well") 10-15 62

HIGHLIGHTS — P&R '56
(Featuring Frank Pizani; with Lew Douglas & Orchestra)

Singles: 78 rpm

BALLY 10-20 56-57

Singles: 7-inch

BALLY (1016 "City of Angels") 15-25 56
BALLY (1027 "To Be with You") 15-25 57
BALLY (1044 "Indiana Style").................. 10-15 57
Also see DOUGLAS, Lew
Also see PIZANI, Frank

HIGHLIGHTS

Singles: 7-inch

LODESTAR (7-29 "Whispering")............. 20-25 59
LODESTAR (15-60 "Hot Toddy")............. 20-25 59
PLAY (1004 "Ah, So") 20-25 59
Also see EDDY, Jim & Highlights

HIGHLIGHTS
(Bill Haley & Comets)

Singles: 7-inch

ARCADE (190 "Hot to Trot"/"All the Way with LBJ") 10-15 66
(Only *Hot to Trot* is by Bill Haley & the Comets, though the B-side is also credited to the Highlights.)
Also see HALEY, Bill

HIGHMINDED

Singles: 7-inch

RAIO & RAIO (1006 "The New E")........... 15-25

HIGHTOWER, Dean, & Twangin' Fools

Singles: 7-inch

ABC-PAR (10065 "Twangin' Fool") 10-20 59

LPs: 10/12-inch

ABC-PAR (312 "Guitar-Twangy with a Beat")... 25-35 59
(Monaural.)
ABC-PAR (S-312 "Guitar-Twangy with a Beat")... 35-45 59
(Stereo.)

HIGHTOWER, Donna
(Little Donna Hightower; with Sid Feller Orchestra; with Maxwell Davis Orchestra)
Singles: 78 rpm
DECCA....8-12 51
RPM....8-12 55-56
Singles: 7-inch
CAPITOL (4151 "Forgive Them")....8-12 59
DECCA (48254 "I Ain't in the Mood")....10-20 51
RPM....15-25 55-56
EPs: 7-inch
CAPITOL (1316 "Selections from *Gee, Baby ... Ain't I Good to You*")....20-30 59
(Promotional issue only.)
LPs: 10/12-inch
CAPITOL (1133 "Take One")....25-50 59
CAPITOL (1273 "Gee, Baby ... Ain't I Good to You")....25-50 59
Also see DAVIS, Maxwell

HIGHTOWER, Willie *R&B '69*
Singles: 7-inch
ADVENTURE ONE (8502 "Tell Me What You Want")....5-8
CAPITOL (2226 "It's a Miracle")....5-10 68
CAPITOL (2651 "It's Too Late")....4-6 69
ENJOY (2019 "Too Late")....8-12 65
FAME (1465 thru 1477)....4-8 70-71
FURY (5002 "If I Had a Hammer")....10-20 63
FURY (5004 "I Love You")....10-20 63
SOUND STAGE 7 (2503 "Chicago, Send Her Home")....4-6 76
(This same number is used on a 1963 release by Don Owens.)
Also see OWENS, Don

HIGHWAY
LPs:10/12-inch
HIGHWAY (584N11 "Highway")....30-50 74
Also see EPICUREANS

HIGHWAYMEN *P&R/LP '61*
Singles: 7-inch
ABC-PAR....5-10 65-66
LIBERTY....3-5 81
ORION (7403 "Michael")....4-6 74
(Canadian.)
U.A. 8-15 60-64
LPs: 10/12-inch
ABC-PAR....10-15 65-66
LIBERTY....5-8 82
U.A. 15-30 61-64
Members: Steve Butts; Chan Daniels; Dave Fisher; Steve Trott; Bob Burnett; Gil Robbins.

HIGNEY, Kenneth
LPs: 10/12-inch
KERBRUTNEY ("Attic Demonstration")....50-75 76

HI-HATS
(Hi Hats)
Singles: 7-inch
EVERLAST (5012 "Hoppin'")....15-25 57
HI HAT (123 "Big Wake")....8-12

HI-HATS
Singles: 7-inch
HI-HAT (123 "The Big Wake")....30-40

HI-JACKS
Singles: 78 rpm
ABC-PAR (9742 "The Letter I Wrote Today")....5-10 56
Singles: 7-inch
ABC-PAR (9742 "The Letter I Wrote Today")....10-15 56

HI-LARKS
(Hi Larks)
Singles: 7-inch
BEAT (50 "Mine")....200-300 59

HI-LIGHTERS
Singles: 7-inch
CANNON (371/372 "Mi Amor"/"Sweet Little Baby of Mine")....15-25 59
Also see HALL, Jimmy, & Hi-Lighters

HI-LIGHTS
Singles: 7-inch
JR (5004 "Oh Lover of Mine")....10-20 64

HI-LITERS
Singles: 78 rpm
BLEND (1004 "Baby I Miss You")....10-20 55
Singles: 7-inch
BLEND (1004 "Baby I Miss You")....50-100 55

HI-LITERS
Singles: 78 rpm
WEN DEE (1927 "Baby, Don't Treat Me That Way")....20-30 55
Singles: 7-inch
WEN DEE (1927 "Baby, Don't Treat Me That Way")....40-60 55

HI-LITERS
Singles: 78 rpm
CELESTE (3005 "Ain't Giving Up Nothing")....50-100 56
Singles: 7-inch
CELESTE (3005 "Ain't Giving Up Nothing")....200-300 56

HI-LITERS
Singles: 78 rpm
VEE-JAY (184 "Hello Dear")....300-400 56
Singles: 7-inch
VEE-JAY (184 "Hello Dear")....1000-1500 56

HI-LITERS
Singles: 7-inch
HANOVER (4506 "Dance Everybody Dance")....10-20 58
MERCURY (71342 "Dance Me to Death")....50-75 58
Members: Joe Franklin; Daryl Petty.

HI-LITERS
(With the Hamiltones; with King Bassie & Three Aces)
Singles: 7-inch
HICO (2432 "Let Me Be True to You")..100-200 58
(Black vinyl.)
HICO (2432 "Let Me Be True to You")..400-500 58
(Orange vinyl.)
HICO (2433 "Over the Rainbow")....250-350 58
HICO (2434 "Sandra")....500-600 58
Member: Ben Vereen.

HI-LITES
(With Leroy Kirkland & Orchestra)
Singles: 78 rpm
OKEH (7046 "I Found a Love")....75-125 54
Singles: 7-inch
OKEH (7046 "I Found a Love")....400-500 54

HI-LITES
(Hi Lites)
Singles: 78 rpm
MERCURY (70987 "Next Four Years")....5-10 56
Singles: 7-inch
BRUNSWICK (55102 "Friday Night, Go, Go")....10-15 58
JET (501 "The Pony")....8-12 61
JET (502 "4,000 Miles Away")....10-15 61
MERCURY (70987 "Next Four Years")....10-15 56
RENO (1030 "Please Believe I Love You")....50-100 '50s
SCOTTY (301 "The Party's Over")....10-15
TWISTIME (12 "Twistin' Time")....10-15 62
WASSEL (701 "Groovy")....5-10 65

HI LITES
Singles: 7-inch
KEY (M82 "Love You So Much")....10-20 59

HI-LITES
Singles: 7-inch
AUDIODISC ("Extinction")....10-20 61
(Selection number not known. Promotional issue only.)

HI-LITES
Singles: 7-inch
KING (5730 "Our Winter Love")....10-15 62

HI-LITES
Singles: 7-inch
JULIA (1105 "Gloria")....100-150 62
MONOGRAM (119 "Everybody's Somebody's Fool")....5-8 76
MONOGRAM (120 "To the Aisle")....5-8 76
MONOGRAM (121 "Maybe You'll Be There")....8-12 76
(Red vinyl.)
RECORD FAIR (500 "I'm Falling in Love")....20-30 61
RECORD FAIR (501 "For Your Precious Love")....10-20 62
LPs: 10/12-inch
DANDEE (206 "For Your Precious Love")....750-1000 62
Members: William Tucker; Shelton Highsmith; James Hodge; Eugene Hodge; Allen Gant.

HI-LITES
(Chi-Lites)
Singles: 7-inch
DARAN (011 "You Did That to Me")....50-100 64
DARAN (222 "I'm So Jealous")....50-100 64
OMEN (4 "You Did That to Me")....75-125 64
(First issue. Polystyrene pressing.)
Also see CHI-LITES

HILL, Billy
Singles: 7-inch
VITA (154 "Sunny Side Up")....15-20 57

HILL, Bobby *R&B '69*
Singles: 7-inch
LOLO (2305 "The Children")....5-8 69
LOLO (2307 "To the Bitter End")....25-50 70

HILL, Bunker *P&R/R&B '62*
Singles: 7-inch
MALA (451 "Hide and Go Seek")....8-12 62
MALA (457 "Nobody Knows")....40-60 62
MALA (464 "The Girl Can't Dance")....40-60 63
Also see MIGHTY CLOUDS OF JOY

HILL, Dave
Singles: 7-inch
APOGEE (106 "Only Boy on the Beach") 20-30 64

HILL, David *P&R '59*
Singles: 78 rpm
ALADDIN (3354 "Jelly Bean")....5-10 57
RCA....5-10 57
Singles: 7-inch
ALADDIN (3354 "Jelly Bean")....10-20 57
KAPP (266 "Two Brothers")....10-20 59
KAPP (280 "Sad, Sad World")....10-20 59
KAPP (293 "Living Doll")....10-20 59
KAPP (307 "Summertime")....10-20 59
RCA (7005 "Everywhere I Go")....10-20 57
RCA (7112 "Keep Me in Mind")....10-20 57
RCA (7181 "Big Guitar")....10-15 58
RCA (7430 "Christmas Bride")....10-15 59

HILL, Delores
Singles: 7-inch
COMPANION (104 "Roller Coaster")....10-20 61
COMPANION (105 "What He Used to Tell Me")....10-20 61

HILL, Eddie
Singles: 78 rpm
COLUMBIA (21556 "I'm Worried")....5-10 56
MERCURY....5-10 52-53
RCA (5809 "Same Old Dream")....5-10 54
Singles: 7-inch
COLUMBIA (21556 "I'm Worried")....10-20 56
GE GE (502 "I Can't Help It")....15-25 '60s
M&S (207 "Nothin' Sweeter Than You Girl")....35-55 68
MERCURY (6392 "Baby My Heart")....15-25 52
MERCURY (70142 "Live While You're Young Dream When You're Old")....10-20 53
RCA (5809 "Same Old Dream")....10-20 54
THELMA (105 "You Got the Best of Me")....50-100 64

HILL, Farris, & Madison Brothers
Singles: 7-inch
V-TONE (231 "Did We Go Steady Too Soon")....50-75 62
Also see MADISON BROTHERS

HILL, Freddie, Orchestra
Singles: 78 rpm
CHANCE (1159 "Knock Me Out")....50-75 54
Singles: 7-inch
CHANCE (1159 "Knock Me Out")....75-100 54

HILL, Grant
Singles: 7-inch
TOPAZ (1300 "She's Going Away")....10-20 59

HILL, Harvey
(Harvey Hill String Band)
Singles: 7-inch
SRC (104 "Boogie Woogie Woman")....150-250 51

HILL, Henry
Singles: 78 rpm
FEDERAL....15-25 51-52
Singles: 7-inch
FEDERAL (12030 "Wandering Blues")..75-100 51
FEDERAL (12037 "Hold Me, Baby")....75-100 51
FEDERAL (12044 "If You Love Me")....75-100 51
FEDERAL (12053 "My Baby's Back Home")....75-100 52

HILL, J.C.
Singles: 7-inch
ARGO (5311 "Only True Love")....5-10 58
MGM (12765 "Little Boy Blue")....10-15 59

HILL, Jaycee
Singles: 78 rpm
EPIC (Except 9185)....10-25 56-57
EPIC (9185 "Romp Stompin' Boogie")....10-20 56
Singles: 7-inch
EPIC (Except 9185)....20-40 56-57
EPIC (9185 "Romp Stompin' Boogie")....35-50 56

HILL, Jessie *P&R/R&B '60*
(With the Rhymaires)
Singles: 7-inch
BANDY (1500 "Ooh Poo Pah Doo")....4-6 '70s
BLUE THUMB (204 "Livin' a Lie")....5-10 72
CHESS (1999 "My Children, My Children")....8-12 67
DOWNEY....8-12 64
KERWOOD....10-15
MIDA (110 "Won't Have to Ask")....15-25 58
MINIT (607 thru 646)....10-20 60-62
WAND (1140 "Something Ought to Be Done")....5-10 66
YOGI-MAN (607 "Hey Now Mama")....10-15 65
LPs: 10/12-inch
BANDY (70006 "Jessie Hill")....10-15 '70s
BLUE THUMB....10-20 72

HILL, Jessie / Aaron Neville / Lee Diamond / Ernie K-Doe
LPs: 10/12-inch
MINIT (0001 "New Orleans, Home of the Blues, Vol. 1")....30-40 62
Also see DIAMOND, Lee
Also see HILL, Jessie
Also see NEVILLE, Aaron
Also see THOMAS, Irma / Ernie K-Doe / Showmen / Benny Spellman

HILL, Joel
(With the Strangers; with Invaders; Joel Scott Hill)
Singles: 7-inch
MONOGRAM (510 "I Ran")....10-20 63
MONOGRAM (515 "Monkey Business")..10-20 63
MONOGRAM (521 "Sticks & Stones")....10-20 64
TRANS-AMERICAN (519 "Little Lover")..35-55 60
Also see CANNED HEAT
Also see MONTEZ, Chris
Also see STRANGERS

HILL, John
Singles: 7-inch
AMY (972 "Get It")....10-20 67

HILL, Lance
Singles: 7-inch
ATOMIC (100 "Wailing Wind")....5-10 66
BANG BANG (4811 "Make My Love a Hurting Thing")....10-20

HILL, Lucky
(Lucky Hill / Betty Olive)
Singles: 78 rpm
TNT (109 thru 115)....10-15 54
Singles: 7-inch
TNT (109 "I'm Wondering")....15-25 54
TNT (111 "I'm the One")....15-25 54
TNT (115 "Wait for Me")....15-25 54

HILL, Maddy
Singles: 7-inch
COLUMBIA (43088 "When You Come Back to School")....10-15 64

HILL, Marty
Singles: 7-inch
ATCO (6145 "Don't Pretend")....10-20 59
CAPRICE (103 "Wanting You")....10-15 61
COLUMBIA (41936 "Mr. Oracle of Love")....20-40 61

HILL, Michael
Singles: 7-inch
CAPITOL (4504 "Beatnik Boogie")..........10-20 61

HILL, Murray
Singles: 7-inch
STAY (914 "Ooh Ginny Lou")..................30-40

HILL, Raymond
Singles: 78 rpm
SUN (204 "The Snuggle")....................100-200 54
Singles: 7-inch
SUN (204 "The Snuggle")....................250-350 54

HILL, Sam
(Gene Autry)
Singles: 78 rpm
GREYBULL (4281 "My Oklahoma Home")..25-50
GREYBULL (4310 "No One to Call Me Darling")..25-50
GREYBULL (4314 "Stay Away from My Chicken House")..25-50
VAN DYKE (5001 "Why Don't You Come Back Home")..25-50
VAN DYKE (7481 "My Oklahoma Home")..25-50
VAN DYKE (84310 "No One to Call Me Darling")..25-50
Also see AUTRY, Gene

HILL, Tiny, & His Orchestra *C&W '46*
Singles: 78 rpm
MERCURY..5-10 46-54
Singles: 7-inch
MERCURY..5-15 51-54
EPs: 7-inch
MERCURY..10-15 51-54
LPs: 10/12-inch
MERCURY (25126 "Tiny Hill")................20-35 52
(10-inch LP.)

HILL, Tom
Singles: 7-inch
DREEM (4465 "Stroll Through the Night with Me")..25-35

HILL, Windy
Singles: 7-inch
RCA (6985 "How Come").......................10-15 57

HILL SISTERS
Singles: 7-inch
ANNA (103 "Hit & Run Away Love")....250-350 59
ANNA (1103 "Hit & Run Away Love")......25-35 59
SPACE (309 "My Lover")......................10-20 '60s

HILLARD STREET
Singles: 7-inch
CAPITOL (4080 "River Love")................20-40 58
REPRISE (20052 "Indian Giver")............10-15 62

HILLIARD, Jimmy
Singles: 78 rpm
BALLY (1007 "My One & Only Love").........5-10 56
Singles: 7-inch
BALLY (1007 "My One & Only Love")......10-15 56

HILLIS, Clayton, & Rocket City Rockettes
Singles: 7-inch
LINCO (1319 "Don't You Know I Love You")..100-200 60

HILLOW HAMMET
LPs: 10/12-inch
HOUSE of FOX (2 "Hammer")...............75-150 68
L&BJ..5-10 78

HILLS, Clayton
Singles: 7-inch
LINCO (1319 "Rock, City, Rock")............35-50 61

HILLSIDERS
Singles: 7-inch
MEL-O-DY (120 "You Only Pass This Way One Time")..10-20 64

HILLTOPPERS *P&R '52*
(Featuring Jimmy Sacca; Hill Toppers)
Singles: 78 rpm
DOT..5-10 52-57
Singles: 7-inch
ABC..4-6 74
DOT (100 series)..............................5-10 63
DOT (15018 thru 15437)....................10-20 52-55
DOT (15451 thru 16054).....................8-12 56-60
DOT (16556 "Only You")........................5-10 63
3-J..4-6 66
EPs: 7-inch
DOT..10-15 54-56
LPs: 10/12-inch
DOT (105 "The Hilltoppers")....................30-40 54
(10-inch LP.)
DOT (106 "The Hilltoppers")....................30-40 54
(10-inch LP.)
DOT (3003 "Tops in Pops")......................20-30 55
DOT (3029 "Towering Hilltoppers")..........20-30 56
DOT (3073 "The Hilltoppers")..................20-30 57
SOUVENIR..8-15 73
Members: Jimmy Sacca; Billy Vaughn; Don McGuire; Seymour Spiegelman.
Also see SACCA, Jimmy
Also see VAUGHN, Billy

HI-LOs *P&R '54*
Singles: 78 rpm
COLUMBIA..5-10 57
STARLITE..3-8 55-56
TREND..3-8 54
Singles: 7-inch
COLUMBIA..5-10 57-60
REPRISE..4-8 62
STARLITE..5-12 55-56
TREND..8-15 54
EPs: 7-inch
COLUMBIA..5-15 57-58
KAPP..5-15 56
STARLITE..10-20 56
TREND (514 "The Hi-Los")......................10-20 54
LPs: 10/12-inch
COLUMBIA..15-25 57-60
KAPP..15-25 56-60
STARLITE (6004 "The Hi-Los")................20-30 55
STARLITE (6005 "The Hi-Los I Presume")..20-30 56
STARLITE (7005 "Under Glass")................20-30 56
Members: Clark Burroughs; Don Shelton; Bob Morse; Gene Puerling.
Also see CLOONEY, Rosemary, & Hi-Los

HILTON, Jerry, & Diadems
Singles: 7-inch
GOODIE (207 "My Little Darling").........200-300 63
Also see DIADEMS

HILTON, Valli
Singles: 7-inch
DOMME (022 "For a Lifetime")................40-50 57
RAMA (197 "For a Lifetime")....................20-30 56

HILTON & BELLHOPS
Singles: 7-inch
LOADSTONE (1849 "I'm Telling You True")..30-40

HINES, Donald
(Don Hines & Ben Branch Band)
Singles: 7-inch
HI (2043 "I'm So Glad")..........................5-10 62
HI (2056 "Stormy Monday Blues")...........10-20 62
HI (2068 "You Had to Pay")......................5-10 63
STARMAKER (1001 "Going Crazy").........50-60

HINES, Rev. J. Earl
Singles: 78 rpm
MONEY (213 "I Found Something")...........5-10 56
Singles: 7-inch
MONEY (213 "I Found Something").........10-20 56

HINES, Ronnie
Singles: 7-inch
ROCKET (7143 "I've Got a Woman")...150-200

HINES, Sonny
Singles: 7-inch
AIRTOWN (2005 "Nothing Like Your Love")..10-20
DECCA (31045 "It's Not a Game")...........10-20 60
TERRY (111 "Nothing Like Your Love")...10-20 63
TERRY (113 "All My Love Belongs to You")..10-20 64

HINGE
Singles: 7-inch
TEE PEE (75/76 "Come On Up"/"The Idols of Your Mind")..175-125 68

HINKLE, Kenny
Singles: 7-inch
WESTCO (5 "The Bee")........................100-200 63
(Yellow vinyl. First issued as by the Sentinals.)
Also see KARTER, Kenny
Also see SENTINALS

HINSON, Don
(With the Rigamorticians)
Singles: 7-inch
CAPITOL (5314 "Monster Jerk")................5-10 64
STARBURST..10-20 66
TREVA (222 "Protest Singer")..................10-15 66
LPs: 10/12-inch
CAPITOL (2219 "Monster Dance Party").15-20 64

HINTON, Joe *P&R/R&B '63*
(Little Joe Hinton)
Singles: 78 rpm
BACK BEAT (519 "I Know")....................40-60 58
Singles: 7-inch
ARVEE (5028 "My Love Is Real")............10-20 61
ARVEE (5029 "Let's Start a Romance")...10-20 61
BACK BEAT (519 "I Know")....................15-25 58
BACK BEAT (526 "Pretty Little Mama")...15-20 59
BACK BEAT (532 "If You Love Me")........10-20 60
BACK BEAT (535 "Come On Baby")..........10-20 61
BACK BEAT (537 thru 541)....................10-15 63-64
BACK BEAT (545 thru 594).....................5-10 65-68
KENT (368 "Tired of Walkin' ")..................8-12 62
HOTLANTA..8-10 74
SOUL (35080 "You Are Blue")....................5-10 71
(Black vinyl.)
SOUL (35080 "You Are Blue")..................15-20 71
(Colored vinyl. Promotional issue only.)
Picture Sleeves
BACK BEAT (526 "Pretty Little Mama")...15-25 59
LPs: 10/12-inch
BACKBEAT (60 "Funny")..........................20-25 65
DUKE..8-10 73

HINTON, Otis
Singles: 78 rpm
TIMELY (1003 "Walkin' Downhill")..........50-100 53
Singles: 7-inch
TIMELY (1003 "Walkin' Downhill")........200-250 53

HINTON, Sam
LPs: 10/12-inch
DECCA (8108 "Singing Across the Land")..20-30 55

HIORNS, Dick
Singles: 7-inch
CUCA (1047 "I'm Movin' On")..................50-75 61
CUCA (6815 "Cattle Call")........................5-10 68
CUCA (6816 "Two of a Kind")....................5-10 68

HIPP, Glynn
Singles: 7-inch
CLAUDRA (111 "Spit-Fire")......................10-15 59

HIPPIES / Reggie Harrison *P&R '63*
Singles: 7-inch
PARKWAY (863 "Memory Lane")..............15-20 63
Also see STEREOS
Also see TAMS

HI-SPEEDS
Singles: 7-inch
SAN WAYNE (1142 "Drag Race")............10-20 63
Member: Bob Tucker.

HIT PACK
Singles: 7-inch
COLPIX (745 "Summer Fever")................10-20 64
SOUL (35010 "Let's Dance")....................15-25 65

HITCH-HIKERS
Singles: 7-inch
HH (1 "Beavershot")................................20-30
HH (008 "S-O-M-F")................................20-30

HI-TENSIONS
(With the Downbeats; Hi Tensions)
Singles: 7-inch
AUDIO (201 "The Clock")......................100-150 60
(Purple label.)
AUDIO (201 "The Clock")........................15-25 60
(Red label.)
K&G (101 "The Clock")............................50-75 61
K&G (9000 "The Clock")..........................10-20 61

HI-TENSIONS
(Hi Tensions)
Singles: 7-inch
MILESTONE (2018 "Ebbing of the Tide")..50-100 63
WHIRLYBIRD (2005 "She'll Break Your Heart")..100-150 64
Also see PEELS, Leon

HI-TIMERS
(Hi Timers)
Singles: 7-inch
SONIC (1502 "You're Everything").......400-500 59

HITMAKERS
Singles: 7-inch
ANGLE TONE (1104 "I Can't Take It Anymore")..50-75 59
ORIGINAL SOUND (1 "Chapel of Love").60-80 58
(Flat black label.)
ORIGINAL SOUND (1 "Chapel of Love").15-25 58
(Glossy black label with outer color band.)
Also see NUGGETS

HI-TOMBS
Singles: 7-inch
CANNON (832 "Sweet Rockin' Mama")..750-1000 58
Member: Cody Reynolds.

HI-TONES
Singles: 7-inch
SKYLINE (701 "You Didn't Have to Laugh")..20-30 58

HI-TONES
(Hi Tones; Shy-Tones; with Madaro White & Orchestra)
Singles: 7-inch
CANDIX (307 "The Special Day")............10-20 60
EON (101 "What Was the Cause of It All")..150-200 61
FONSCA (201 "Lovers Quarrel")..............50-75 61
(Blue label. First issued as by the Shy-Tones.)
FONSCA (201 "Lovers Quarrel")..............15-25 61
(White label. Promotional issue only.)
FONSCA (202 "No More Pain")...........100-150 61
KING (5414 "Fool Fool Fool")..................10-15 60
SEG-WAY (105 "Sure As the Flowers")..250-350 61
Members: Graham True; Al Seavozzo; Fred Alvarez; Sal Covais; Bill Scarpa.
Also see EMOTIONS
Also see SHY-TONES
Also see TRENTONS

HI-TONES
LPs: 10/12-inch
HI (12011 "Raunchy Tones")..................15-20 63
(Monaural.)
HI (32011 "Raunchy Tones")....................20-25 63
(Stereo.)

HI-TONES
Singles: 7-inch
L&M (223 "I'm So Sorry")....................100-200

HITSON, Heron
Singles: 7-inch
MINIT (32072 "Yes You Did")..................10-15 69
MINIT (32096 "She's a Bad Girl")............10-15 70

HIX, Chuck, & Count Downs
Singles: 7-inch
FLAIR (101 "Loretta")..............................10-15 61
VERVE (708 "Sandy")..............................20-25 59
(Stereo.)
VERVE (10169 "Sandy")...........................10-15 59
(Monaural.)
VERVE (10190 "Is You Is").......................10-15 59

HOBART
Singles: 7-inch
VAULT (944 "Say Listen").........................10-20 68

HOBBITS
Singles: 7-inch
DECCA..5-10 68
LPs: 10/12-inch
DECCA (4920 "Down to Middle Earth")...20-25 68
DECCA (74920 "Down to Middle Earth").20-30 67
DECCA (75009 "Men and Doors")...........15-25 67
Also see CURTISS, Jimmy

HOBBS, Randy
Singles: 7-inch
APT (25059 "Signs of Love")....................8-12 61
GATOR (1000 "You Better Run")..........75-100 60
EMBER (1109 "Slowly but Surely")............5-10 64

HOBBS, Willie
Singles: 7-inch
BANDIT....................4-8 '70s
CHARAY (38 "Gloria")....................10-15 '60s
LE CAM (333 "Cry Cry Cry")....................15-25 79
SEVENTY-SEVEN (108 "Do Your Own Thing")....................4-8 72
SILVER FOX (5 "Game of Love")..............5-10 69
SILVER FOX (15 "Love 'Em and Leave 'Em")....................5-10 69
SOFT (1018 "Under the Pines")..............10-20 69
SOUND STAGE 7 (1510 thru 1513)...........4-8 73-74
Also see DIRTE FOUR

HOBECK, Curtis
Singles: 7-inch
CEE AND CEE (501 "Hey Everybody"). 75-125
LU (506 "Whole Town's Talking")........ 100-200 59
LU (508 "China Rock")....................200-300 59
TENNESSEE (301 "Tom Dooley Rock and Roll")....................40-60 59

HOBSON, Emmett, & Rag-Muffins
Singles: 78 rpm
CENTRAL (1001 "Looka Here, Mattie Bee")....................50-75 53
GROOVE (0124 "Mattie Bee")................35-45 55
Singles: 7-inch
CENTRAL (1001 "Looka Here, Mattie Bee")....................100-150 53
GROOVE (0124 "Mattie Bee")................45-55 55

HOBSON, George
Singles: 7-inch
SOUND CITY ("Let It Be Real")..............15-25

HOCKADAYS
Singles: 7-inch
SYMBOL (918 "Fairytales")....................20-30 62

HODGE, Bobby
Singles: 7-inch
CUCA (1066 "Sitting on Top of the World")....................30-50 62
CUCA (1140 "It's Almost Tomorrow").........8-12 63
CUCA (68101 "Blue Christmas")................8-12 68
GOLDEN WING (3040 "Alligator Man")......5-10 63
NASHVILLE (5014 "Carolina Bound").....50-75 61
REBEL (819 "Gonna Take My Guitar")....................100-200
STATURE (1101 "When")....................8-12 '60s
STOP (161 thru 1550)....................5-10 68-69
VOLUNTEER (4000 "Close Up the Honky Tonks")....................5-10

HODGE, Gary
Singles: 7-inch
DOLTON (7 "Too Old to Cry")................10-15 59

HODGES, Charles — R&B '70
(Charlie Hodges & Fi-Tones)
Singles: 7-inch
ALTO (2016 "There Is Love")...............15-20 65
ALTO (2017-2 "My Half a Heart")............15-20 65
ALTO (2022 "Who's Crying Now")...........20-25 65
ALTO (2024 "Charles' Shing-a-Ling")......15-20 65
CALLA....................4-8 69-72
Also see HUNT, Geraldine, & Charlie Hodges

HODGES, Eddie — P&R '61
(With Sue Wright)
Singles: 7-inch
AURORA....................5-10 65-66
BARNABY (536 "Made to Love")..................4-6 76
CADENCE....................10-15 60-62
COLUMBIA....................5-10 62-63
DECCA....................5-10 59
MGM....................5-8 64
Picture Sleeves
CADENCE....................10-15 61
COLUMBIA....................5-10 63
EPs: 7-inch
CADENCE (33-6 "Eddie Hodges")..........15-25 61
("Cadence Little LP." With cardboard insert in clear cover.)
Also see DE SHANNON, Jackie / Bobby Vee / Eddie Hodges
Also see MILLS, Hayley, & Eddie Hodges
Also see MILLS, Hayley, & Burl Ives

HODGES, Jesse
Singles: 7-inch
ASSOCIATED ARTISTS (116 "Till Then My Love")....................10-15 '60s
FABLE (609 "Until")....................20-30 58
Also see DRAKE, Larry, & His Vagabonds

HODGES, Johnny — P&R '37
(J. Hodges)
Singles: 78 rpm
BLUEBIRD....................5-8 40-44
CLEF....................4-6 53-56
COLUMBIA....................4-6 51
MERCURY....................4-6 51-53
NORGRAN....................4-6 54-56
VARIETY....................5-10 33
VOCALION....................5-10 37
Singles: 7-inch
CLEF....................8-15 53-56
COLUMBIA....................8-15 51
MERCURY....................10-20 51-53
NORGRAN....................8-15 54-56
VMC....................4-6 68
VERVE....................5-10 57-67
EPs: 7-inch
ATLANTIC....................20-30 54
EPIC....................15-25 55
NORGRAN....................25-50 54
RCA (3000 "Alto Sax")....................50-75 52
LPs: 10/12-inch
AMERICAN RECORDING (421 "Johnny Hodges & Ellington All Stars")....................40-60 57
CLEF (111 "Johnny Hodges Collates").100-200 52
(10-inch LP.)
CLEF (128 "Johnny Hodges Collates, Vol. 2")....................100-200 52
(10-inch LP.)
ENCORE....................10-15 68
EPIC (3105 "Hodge Podge")....................50-75 55
EPIC (22000 series)....................8-12 74
IMPULSE....................10-20 65
INSTANT....................15-20 64
MCA....................5-10 82
NORGRAN (1 "Swing with Johnny Hodges")....................150-250 53
(10-inch LP.)
NORGRAN (1004 "Memories of Ellington")....................100-200 54
NORGRAN (1009 "More Johnny Hodges")....................100-200 54
NORGRAN (1024 "Dance Bash").........100-200 55
NORGRAN (1045 "Creamy")...............100-200 56
NORGRAN (1048 "Castle Rock")..........100-200 56
NORGRAN (1055 "Ellingtonia")............75-150 56
NORGRAN (1059 "In a Tender Mood")..75-150 56
NORGRAN (1060 "Used to Be Duke")...75-150 56
NORGRAN (1061 "The Blues")..............75-150 56
PABLO....................5-10 78
RCA (500 series)....................10-20 66
RCA (3000 "Alto Sax")....................200-300 52
(10-inch LP.)
RCA (3800 series)....................10-20 67
VSP....................10-20 66-67
VERVE (8179 "Perdido")....................50-100 57
VERVE (8180 "In a Mellow Tone").........50-100 57
VERVE (8203 "Duke's in Bed")..............50-100 57
VERVE (8271 "Big Sound")....................50-100 58
(Reads "Verve Records, Inc." at bottom of label.)
VERVE (8271 "Big Sound")....................15-25
(Reads "MGM Records - A Division Of Metro-Goldwyn-Mayer, Inc." at bottom of label.)
VERVE (8314 thru 8358)....................25-45 59-60
(Reads "Verve Records, Inc." at bottom of label.)
VERVE (8314 thru 8358)....................15-25 61-69
(Reads "MGM Records - A Division Of Metro-Goldwyn-Mayer, Inc." at bottom of label.)
VERVE....................8-15 74-79
(Reads "Manufactured By MGM Record Corp.," or mentions either Polydor or Polygram at bottom of label.)
Also see ELLINGTON, Duke, & Johnny Hodges
Also see MULLIGAN, Gerry, & Johnny Hodges

HODGES, Johnny, & Lawrence Welk
LPs: 10/12-inch
DOT....................10-20 66
Also see WELK, Lawrence

HODGES, Johnny, & "Wild" Bill Davis — LP '65
LPs: 10/12-inch
RCA....................10-20 65-67
VERVE....................15-30 61-66
Also see DAVIS, "Wild" Bill
Also see HODGES, Johnny

HODGES, Ralph
Singles: 7-inch
WHISPERING PINES (101 "Honey Talk")....................300-400 58

HODGES, Russ
Singles: 78 rpm
("The Giants Win the Pennant")...............10-15 52
(No label name or selection number used.)
Singles: 7-inch
("The Giants Win the Pennant")...............15-25 52
(No label name or selection number used.)

HODGES, Sonny
Singles: 7-inch
GLOBAL (404 "Jamie")....................50-75 61
LARRY (802 "Shake a Leg")..................75-125 59
MYRL (404 "Jamie")....................50-75 61
(We're not sure yet whether Global or Myrl came first.)

HODGES BROTHERS
Singles: 78 rpm
TRUMPET (160 "It Won't Be Long").........15-20 52
TRUMPET (161 "Tennessee Baby")........15-20 52

HODGES BROTHERS
Singles: 7-inch
MISSISSIPPI (574 "I'm Gonna Rock Some Too")....................750-1000

HOFFMAN, Ron
Singles: 7-inch
SWAN (4012 "100,000 Times")...............15-25 58

HOFFMAN, Samuel J.
(With Leslie Baxter Orchestra & Chorus)
Singles: 7-inch
RCA (3215 "Jet")....................8-12
LPs: 10/12-inch
CAPITOL (2000 "Music Out of This World")....................50-75 52
(10-inch LP.)
Also see BAXTER, Les

HOFNER, Adolph
(With the San Antonians)
Singles: 7-inch
SARG (Except 207)....................10-15 57-62
SARG (207 "Milk Cow Blues")..................15-25 62
EPs: 7-inch
DECCA (2227 "Dance-O-Rama")............40-50
LPs: 10/12-inch
COLUMBIA (9017 "Dude Ranch Dances")....................40-50 51
(10-inch LP.)
DECCA (5564 "Dance-O-Rama")............40-50 55
(10-inch LP.)
Also see HOFNER, Bash

HOFNER, Bash
Singles: 78 rpm
SARG (131 "Tickle Toe Song")..................5-10 56
SARG (138 "Rockin' & a-Boppin'")..........20-30 56
Singles: 7-inch
SARG (131 "Tickle Toe Song")................10-20 56
SARG (138 "Rockin' & A-Boppin'")..........40-60 56
Also see HOFNER, Adolph

HOGAN, Billy
Singles: 7-inch
VENA (101 "Shake It Over Sputnik")......75-125 58

HOGAN, Carl, & Miracles
Singles: 78 rpm
FURY (1001 "I Love You So")..............100-200 57
Singles: 7-inch
FURY (1001 "I Love You So")..............300-400 57
Also see MIRACLES

HOGG, Andrew
Singles: 78 rpm
EXCLUSIVE (89 "He Knows How Much We Can Bear")....................30-40 47
Also see HOGG, Smokey

HOGG, John
Singles: 78 rpm
MERCURY (8230 "Got a Mean Woman")....................20-40 51
OCTIVE (705 "Black Snake Blues").........20-40 51
OCTIVE (706 "West Texas Blues")..........20-40 51

HOGG, Smokey — R&B '48
(Andrew Hogg)
Singles: 78 rpm
BULLET (285 "Hard Times")....................20-40 48
COLONY (103 "Need My Help")..............25-50 51
COMBO....................25-50 52
CROWN....................10-20 54
DECCA....................30-50 37
EXCLUSIVE....................25-50 47
FEDERAL....................20-30 52-53
FIDELITY....................15-25 52
IMPERIAL....................20-30 50-53
INDEPENDENT....................15-25 49
JADE....................25-35 51
MACY'S....................20-30 49
MERCURY....................40-60 51
METEOR....................30-50 55
MODERN....................20-30 48-52
RAY'S RECORD....................30-50 52
RECORDED IN HOLLYWOOD (130 "You'll Need My Help Someday")....................15-25 50
RECORDED IN HOLLYWOOD (131 "Ain't You Sorry Baby")....................15-25 50
RECORDED IN HOLLYWOOD (170 "Penitentiary Blues")....................15-25 51
SHOW TIME....................20-30 54
SITTIN' IN WITH....................10-20 51-52
SPECIALTY (300 series)....................30-40 49-50
TOP HAT....................15-25 52
Singles: 7-inch
COMBO (4 "Ooh Baby")....................75-125 52
COMBO (9 "Hello Little Girl")..................75-125 52
COMBO (11 "Believe I'll Change Towns")....................75-125 52
CROWN (122 "I Declare")....................50-100 54
EBB (127 "Sure 'Nuff")....................10-20 57
FEDERAL (12109 "Keep A-Walking")......50-75 52
FEDERAL (12117 "Your Little Wagon")...50-75 53
FEDERAL (12127 "Gone, Gone, Gone").50-75 53
IMPERIAL (5269 "When I've Been Drinkin'")....................50-75 53
IMPERIAL (5290 "My Baby's Gone").......50-75 53
MERCURY (8235 "Miss Georgia")...........50-75 51
MERCURY (8228 "She's Always on My Mind")....................50-75 51
METEOR (5021 "I Declare")....................50-75 55
MODERN (884 "Baby Don't You Tear My Clothes")....................50-75 51
MODERN (896 "Too Late, Old Man").......50-75 51
MODERN (924 "Can't Do Nothin'")..........50-75 52
RAY'S RECORD (33 "Penitentiary Blues")....................75-100 52
RAY'S RECORD (35 "I've Been Happy")....................75-100 52
SHOW TIME (1101 "Ain't Gonna Play Second No Mo'")....................50-75 54
LPs: 10/12-inch
CROWN (5526 "Smokey Hogg Sings the Blues")....................20-30 62
KENT....................10-15
TIME (6 "Smokey Hogg")....................40-50 62
UNITED....................5-10
Also see HOGG, Andrew

HOGS
Singles: 7-inch
HBR (511 "Blues Theme")....................25-50 67
Also see CHOCOLATE WATCH BAND
Also see ZAPPA, Frank

HOGSED, Roy — C&W '48
Singles: 78 rpm
CAPITOL (Except 40120)....................10-20 48-55
CAPITOL (40120 "Cocaine Blues").........30-40 51
COAST....................30-40 47
Singles: 7-inch
CAPITOL (1529 "Shuffleboard Boogie")..15-25 49
CAPITOL (1635 "Cocaine Blues")..........50-100 51
CAPITOL (1721 thru 3007)..................10-20 51-55

HOLDEN, Chuck
Singles: 78 rpm
UNIQUE (358 "My Last Melody")...............5-10 56
Singles: 7-inch
UNIQUE (358 "My Last Melody").............10-15 56

HOLDEN, Lorenzo
(With His Tenor Sax)
Singles: 78 rpm
CROWN................................ 10-15 54
FLASH (108 "Walking Down Swing Street")................................ 10-15 56
MAMBO................................ 10-15 55
Singles: 7-inch
CEE JAM (001 "Wig")................................8-12 65
CROWN (103 "Cry of the Wounded Juke Box")................................ 20-30 54
CROWN (105 "East Chester Flats")......... 20-30 54
FLASH (108 "Walking Down Swing Street")................................ 15-25 56
MAMBO (100 "Top Hat")................................ 20-30 55
MAMBO (103 "Stella by Starlight").......... 20-30 55

HOLDEN, Randy
LPs: 10/12-inch
HOBBIT (5002 "Population II")................ 75-125 68
Session: Chris Lockhead.
Also see BLUE CHEER
Also see FENDER IV
Also see KAK
Also see OTHER HALF

HOLDEN, Ron P&R/R&B '60
(With the Thunderbirds; with Twiliters)
Singles: 7-inch
ABC................................4-6 73
APEX (76645 "Love You So")................ 15-25 59
(Canadian.)
BARONET (3 "Things Don't Happen That Way")................................ 75-150 62
CHALLENGE (59360 "I Tried")............... 20-30 67
COLLECTABLES................................3-5
DONNA (1315 "Love You So")................ 15-20 59
(Blue or Green label.)
DONNA (1315 "Love You So")................ 10-15 60
(Black label.)
DONNA (1324 thru 1335)........................ 10-15 60-61
ELDO (117 "I'll Be Happy")...................... 10-20 61
LANA................................4-6 '60s
LOST NITE................................4-8
NITE OWL (10 "Love You So")........... 300-500 60
NOW................................4-6 74
RAMPART................................5-10 65
LPs: 10/12-inch
DONNA (DLP-2111 "Love You So")...... 75-125 60
(Monaural.)
DONNA (DLPS-2111 "Love You So").. 150-200 60
(Stereo.)
Session: Bruce Johnston.
Also see JOHNSTON, Bruce

HOLDER, Jimmy
Singles: 7-inch
LAKELAND (1001 "Foggy River")......... 75-125

HOLIDAY, Billie P&R '35
(With Teddy Wilson & His Orchestra; with Ray Ellis & Orchestra; "Lady Day"; with Tiny Grimes Sextet)
Singles: 78 rpm
ALADDIN (3094 "Be Fair to Me")............ 25-35 51
ALADDIN (3102 "Blue Turning Gray Over You")................................ 25-35 51
BRUNSWICK................................ 10-20 35-38
CAPITOL................................5-10 42
CLEF................................5-10 53-55
COLUMBIA................................5-10 51-52
COMMODORE................................ 10-15 39
DECCA................................ 10-20 45-52
MERCURY................................5-10 52-53
OKEH................................ 10-20 41
VOCALION................................ 10-15 36-38
Singles: 7-inch
CLEF................................ 10-20 53-55
COLUMBIA (30000 series)...................... 10-20 51-52
DECCA (250 "Lover Man")...................... 40-50 52
(Boxed set of four singles.)
DECCA (27000 series)........................... 10-20 50-52
DECCA (48000 series)........................... 10-20 51-52
KENT (3003 "God Bless the Child")............4-6 73
MCA................................4-6 73
MGM (12813 "Don't Worry 'Bout Me")..... 10-15 59
MERCURY (89000 series)...................... 10-20 52-53
RIC (129 "Strange Fruit")........................5-10 64
U.A.................................4-6 72
VERVE................................8-12 59-62
Picture Sleeves
MGM (12813 "Don't Worry 'Bout Me")..... 20-30 59
EPs: 7-inch
CLEF................................20-30 53-54
COLUMBIA................................15-25 54-58
DECCA................................5-15 56
LPs: 10/12-inch
AJ................................10-20 72
ALADDIN................................50-75 56
(Title and selection number not known.)
AMERICAN RECORDING SOCIETY (409 "Billie Holiday Sings")................................50-100 56
AMERICAN RECORDING SOCIETY (431 "Lady Sings the Blues")................................50-100 56
ATLANTIC................................5-10 72
AUDIO FIDELITY (312 "Billie Holiday")....10-20 84
(Picture disc.)
CLEF (118 "Favorites")........................150-250 53
(10-inch LP.)
CLEF (144 "Evening with Billie")..........150-250 54
(10-inch LP.)
CLEF (161 "Billie Holiday")...................150-250 54
(10-inch LP.)
CLEF (169 "Jazz at the Philharmonic")................................100-250 55
CLEF (669 "Music for Torching")............30-50 55
CLEF (686 "A Recital")........................100-150 56
CLEF (690 "Solitude")..........................100-150 56
CLEF (713 "Velvet Moods")..................100-150 56
CLEF (718 "Jazz Recital")....................100-150 56
CLEF (721 "Lady Sings the Blues")......100-150 56
COLUMBIA (21 "The Golden Years").......50-75 62
(Boxed, three-disc set.)
COLUMBIA (40 "The Golden Years, Vol. 2")................................25-35 66
(Boxed, three-disc set.)
COLUMBIA (637 "Lady Day")..............100-150 54
(Red label with gold printing. Includes tracks from CL-6040.)
COLUMBIA (637 "Lady Day")...................50-75 56
(Red label with black and white printing.)
COLUMBIA (2600 series)..........................8-15 67
COLUMBIA (6040 "Teddy Wilson Featuring Billie Holiday")................................150-200 49
(10-inch LP. Reissued as part of CL-637.)
COLUMBIA (6129 "Billie Holiday Sings")................................150-200 50
(10-inch LP.)
COLUMBIA (6163 "Billie Holiday Favorites")................................150-200 51
(10-inch LP.)
COLUMBIA (1157 "Lady in Satin")...........30-50 58
COLUMBIA (30000 series, except 32134).8-15 72-73
COLUMBIA (32134 "Billie Holiday Story, Vol. 2")................................15-25 73
(Two discs.)
DECCA (100 series, excep 161)..............10-20 65-72
DECCA (161 "Billie Holiday Story")..........30-40 65
(Two discs.)
DECCA (5345 "Lover Man")..................150-250 52
(10-inch LP.)
DECCA (8215 "The Lady Sings")...........50-100 56
DECCA (8701 "Blues Are Brewin'")........50-100 58
DECCA (75000 series)..............................8-15 68
ESP................................8-12 71-73
EVEREST................................5-10 73-75
HARMONY................................5-10 73
JAZZTONE (1209 "Billie Holiday Sings") .30-40 56
JOLLY ROGER (5020 "Billie Holiday")...75-100 54
KENT (600 "Billie Holiday Sings")..............5-10 73
MCA................................5-10 73
MFSL (201 "In Rehearsal")......................30-40 87
MFSL (247 "Body & Soul")......................25-35 95
MGM (100 series)................................6-10 70
MGM (3700 series)................................25-50 59
MGM (4900 series)................................5-10 74
MAINSTREAM................................10-20 65
METRO................................10-20 65
MONMOUTH-EVERGREEN (7046 "Gallant Lady")................................5-10 72
PARAMOUNT................................5-10 73
PICKWICK................................5-10
RIC................................10-20 64
SCORE................................25-50 57
SOLID STATE................................8-12 69
TRIP................................5-10 73
U.A. (5600 series)................................5-10 72
U.A. (14000 & 15000 series)....................20-30 62
VSP................................8-15 66
VERVE................................25-50 57-60
("Verve Records, Inc." at bottom of label.)
VERVE................................10-25 61-72
("MGM Records - a Division of Metro-Goldwyn-Mayer, Inc." at bottom of label.)
VERVE................................5-10 73-84
("Manufactured By MGM Record Corp.," or mentions either Polydor or Polygram at bottom of label.)
Also see FITZGERALD, Ella / Billie Holiday / Lena Horne

HOLIDAY, Billie, & Stan Getz
LPs: 10/12-inch
DALE (25 "Billie & Stan")......................150-250 51
(10-inch LP.)
Also see GETZ, Stan
Also see GOODMAN, Benny, Orchestra
Also see LYNNE, Gloria / Nina Simone / Billie Holiday

HOLIDAY, Billie, & Eddie Heywood
LPs: 10/12-inch
COMMODORE (20005 "Billie Holiday, Vol. 1")................................100-200 50
(10-inch LP.)
COMMODORE (20006 "Billie Holiday, Vol. 2")................................100-200 50
(10-inch LP.)
COMMODORE (30008 "Billie Holiday, Vol. 1")................................50-75 59
COMMODORE (30011 "Billie Holiday, Vol. 2")................................50-75 59

HOLIDAY, Billie, & Al Hibbler
LPs: 10/12-inch
IMPERIAL (9185 "Billie Holiday, Al Hibbler and the Blues")................................20-30 62
SUNSET (1147 "Shades of Blue")............8-10 67
(Monaural.)
SUNSET (5147 "Shades of Blue")...........10-15 67
(Stereo.)
Also see HIBBLER, Al
Also see HOLIDAY, Billie

HOLIDAY, Chico P&R '59
(With the Billy Mure Orchestra; Chico)
Singles: 7-inch
CORAL (62291 thru 62363).......................8-12 61-63
KARATE (512 thru 518)............................5-10 65
NEW PHOENIX (6190 "God, Country and My Baby")................................10-15 61
(First issue.)
RCA (7499 thru 7621)................................5-10 59
SHAMLEY (44108 "Now I Taste the Tears")................................5-10 69
EPs: 7-inch
RAYNARD (10065 "What Did I Do")........15-25 58
LP: 10/12-inch
ASEPH................................5-8 89
EAGLE WING................................5-8 89
MELODYLAND................................10-20 75-78
SONGSPIRATION................................5-10 73
Also see MURE, Billy
Also see VERLIN, Chico

HOLIDAY, Curly
Singles: 78 rpm
KING (1423 "Born to Be Lonely")............10-20 55
Singles: 7-inch
KING (1423 "Born to Be Lonely")............15-25 55

HOLIDAY, Gene
Singles: 7-inch
JOHNSON (125 "Scratch My Name Off the Mailbox")................................15-25 63

HOLIDAY, Gilbert, & Combo
Singles: 78 rpm
STATES (104 "Late One Night")................5-10 52
Singles: 7-inch
STATES (104 "Late One Night")..............10-20 52

HOLIDAY, Jim, & Futuretones
Singles: 7-inch
4 STAR (1720 "All I Want Is You")..........75-100 58

HOLIDAY, Jimmy P&R/R&B '63
(Jimmy Holliday)
Singles: 7-inch
DIAL (1004 "Sing a Song of Love")............4-8 71
DIPLOMACY (340 "New Breed")................8-12 65
EVEREST (2022 "How Can I Forget")......10-15 63
EVEREST (2027 thru 2056)......................8-12 63-65
KT................................5-10
KENT (482 "New Breed")..........................5-10 67
MINIT................................6-12 66-70
OLDIES 45................................4-6 '60s
TIP (1019 "A Friend of Mine")....................8-12
LPs: 10/12-inch
MINIT (24005 "Turning Point")..................20-30 66

HOLIDAY, Johnny
Singles: 78 rpm
UNITED (148 "Why Should I Cry")..........10-15 53
Singles: 7-inch
UNITED (148 "Why Should I Cry")..........20-30 53

HOLIDAY, Jon E.
Singles: 7-inch
ATLANTIC (2091 "Yes, I Will Love You Tomorrow")................................10-15 61

HOLIDAY, Kenny
Singles: 7-inch
FOUR WHEELS (0001 "Little Heart").......50-75

HOLIDAY, Marva
Singles: 7-inch
GNP (411 "It's Written All Over Your Face")................................10-20 68

HOLIDAYS
Singles: 78 rpm
SPECIALTY (522 "Irene")........................15-25 54
Singles: 7-inch
SPECIALTY (522 "Irene")........................40-50 54

HOLIDAYS
Singles: 78 rpm
KING (1520 "Listen")................................5-10 55
Singles: 7-inch
KING (1520 "Listen")................................10-20 55

HOLIDAYS
Singles: 7-inch
MUSIC CITY (818 "Never Go to Mexico")................................75-100 58

HOLIDAYS
Singles: 7-inch
BRUNSWICK (55084 "Sands of Gold")....10-15 58
MARK IV (725 "Down By the Shore").......50-75 '60s
MELBA (112 "The Robin")....................100-150 57
NIX (537 "One Little Kiss")......................20-30 61
(No "Pgh, Pa." on label.)
NIX (537 "One Little Kiss")......................15-25 61
(Has "Pgh, Pa." under label name.)
PAM (111 "Refreshing")........................150-200 61
ROBBEE (103 "Miss You").......................30-50 60
ROBBEE (107 "Lonely Summer")...........50-75 60
WONDER (115 "My Heart Never Knows")................................50-75 59

HOLIDAYS
Singles: 7-inch
COLT 45 (106 "Big Brown Eyes")............10-15 60

HOLIDAYS
Singles: 7-inch
ANDIE (5019 "The Stars Will Remember")................................50-75 60
BRENT (7018 "Come Back to Me")..........15-20 61
GALAXY (714 "Send Back My Love")......20-30 62
(Black vinyl.)
GALAXY (714 "Send Back My Love")......40-50 62
(Green vinyl. Promotional issue only.)

HOLIDAYS
Singles: 7-inch
MONUMENT (431 "Merry Christmas Song")................................8-12 60
TRACK ("Patty Ann")................................10-15 62
(No selection number used.)

HOLIDAYS
Singles: 7-inch
DIXIE (1156 "Little Miss Hurt")................15-25 60
SANTO (500 "Desparate")........................8-12 63

HOLIDAYS P&R/R&B '66
Singles: 7-inch
GOLDEN WORLD (36 "I Love You Forever")................................10-20 66
GOLDEN WORLD (47 "No Greater Love")................................10-20 66
GROOVE CITY (206 "Easy Living").........50-75 '60s
REVILOT (205 "Never Alone")..................15-25 66
REVILOT (210 "I Know She Cares").........15-25 67
REVILOT (226 "All That Is Required of You")................................15-25 69
Members: Edwin Starr; Steve Mancha; J.J. Barnes.
Also see BARNES, J.J., & Steve Mancha

Also see STARR, Edwin

HOLIDAYS
Singles: 7-inch
WILJER (6002 "Love That's True")......... 40-60

HOLLAND, Brian *R&B '72*
(Brian Holland with the Band; Holland-Dozier featuring Brian Holland)
Singles: 78 rpm
KUDO (667 "In Nature Boy")............... 100-200 58
Singles: 7-inch
INVICTUS...4-8 72-74
KUDO (667 "In Nature Boy")............... 500-600 58
Also see HOLLAND, Eddie
Also see HOLLAND - DOZIER
Also see SATINTONES

HOLLAND, Eddie *P&R/R&B '62*
(With the Rayber Voices)
Singles: 7-inch
MERCURY (71290 "You")..................... 75-100 58
MOTOWN (1021 thru 1063, except 1049).. 15-25 61-64
MOTOWN (1049 "I'm on the Outside Looking In").. 50-100 63
TAMLA (102 "Merry-Go-Round")......... 100-200 59
U.A. (172 thru 280)................................ 15-25 59-61
Picture Sleeves
MOTOWN (1030 "If Cleopatra Took a Chance").. 30-50 62
LPs: 10/12-inch
MOTOWN (604 "Eddie Holland")......... 150-200 63
Members (Rayber Voices): Brian Holland; Raynoma Gordy; Robert Bateman; Sonny Sanders; Gwen Murray.
Also see GRIFFIN, Herman
Also see HOLLAND, Brian
Also see JOHNSON, Marv
Also see REMUS, Eugene
Also see SATINTONES
Also see STRONG, Barrett

HOLLAND, Harry
Singles: 7-inch
RHYTHM (112 "Face of a Clown")....... 200-300 58

HOLLAND, Jimmy
Singles: 7-inch
BLUE ROCK (4036 "Baby Don't Leave Me")..5-10 65
SYCO (2001 "Sugar Baby").................... 10-20 65

HOLLAND, Lee
Singles: 7-inch
KING (5781 "Let's Stay Together")......... 10-20 63
(Black vinyl.)
KING (5781 "Let's Stay Together")......... 30-40 63
(Red vinyl.)

HOLLAND, Ray
Singles: 7-inch
AERTAUN (1106 "Gotta Go to Viet Nam").5-10 66
MARGO (101 "Surfboard Stag").............. 20-30 63
SAM.. 15-25

HOLLAND, Tex
Singles: 7-inch
IVORY (103 "Honey, Honey, Honey").... 50-100

HOLLAND – DOZIER *P&R '72*
(With the Andantes & Four Tops; featuring Lamont Dozier)
Singles: 7-inch
INVICTUS..4-6 72-73
MOTOWN (1045 "Come On Home")....... 15-20 63
Members: Brian Holland; Lamont Dozier
Also see FOUR TOPS
Also see HOLLAND, Brian
Also see KENT, Billy, & Andantes

HOLLER, Dick
(With His Rockets; with Holidays)
Singles: 7-inch
ACE (540 "Uh Uh Baby")......................... 20-30 58
COMET (913 "Hey Little Fool")............... 15-25 '60s
COMET (2146 "Hey Little Fool").............. 15-25 61
COMET (2152 "Double Shot").................. 15-25 62
HERALD (566 "Girl Next Door")............... 30-40 61
LAURIE (3487 "Amos-Ben-Haren-Hab-Seti-14").. 10-15 69
VITAL (108 "Rumble")............................ 10-20 65
LPs: 10/12-inch
ATLANTIC...8-15 70

HOLLERS, Wayne
Singles: 7-inch
DEL-FI (4121 "Why")...............................10-15 59

HOLLEY, Jackie
Singles: 7-inch
OWE MAN (107 "Heartbroken Lover").....50-75

HOLLEY, Peanut
Singles: 7-inch
K&C (106 "My One True Love")...............10-15 59

HOLLIDAY, Jay
Singles: 7-inch
EAST WEST (102 "Tell My Why")............5-10 57
GIANT (1100 "Wang Dang Doo")............10-20 57

HOLLIDAY, Jimmy
Singles: 7-inch
DRUM (2115 "Little Boy Little Boy")......100-200 '60s

HOLLIDAYS
(With the Gerald Wilson Orchestra)
Singles: 7-inch
PREP (136 "I'm Not Ashamed")...............30-40 58

HOLLIDAYS
(With the Blazers Band)
Singles: 7-inch
LYONS (107 "Got My Letter")..............200-300 61
(Black vinyl.)
LYONS (107 "Got My Letter")..............500-750 61
(Multi-color vinyl.)
Also see FOSTER, Eddie

HOLLIES *P&R '64*
Singles: 12-inch
ATLANTIC (502 "Stop in the Name of Love")...6-12 83
(Promotional issue only.)
EPIC (08157 "Draggin' My Heels")............8-10 77
Singles: 7-inch
ATLANTIC (89819 "Stop in the Name of Love")...3-5 83
EPIC (2000 series)..................................4-6 71
(Reissue series.)
EPIC (10180 thru 10613).............................4-8 67-70
EPIC (10677 "Dandelion Wine")...............5-10 70
EPIC (10716 "Survival of the Fittest").........8-12 71
EPIC (10754 "Row the Boat Together").....5-10 71
EPIC (10842 "The Baby")...........................5-10 72
EPIC (10871 thru 11100).............................4-8 72-74
EPIC (50000 series)...................................4-6 75-78
IMPERIAL (66026 thru 66070).................10-20 64-65
IMPERIAL (66099 "Yes I Will")................20-40 65
IMPERIAL (66119 thru 66258)....................5-10 66-68
IMPERIAL (66271 "If I Needed Someone")..20-40 65
LIBERTY (55674 "Stay")...........................30-40 64
Picture Sleeves
ATLANTIC (89819 "Stop in the Name of Love")...3-5 83
EPIC (10180 "Carrie-Anne")......................10-15 67
EPIC (10234 "King Midas in Reverse")......8-12 67
EPIC (10251 "Dear Eloise")........................8-12 67
EPIC (10842 "The Baby")............................8-12 72
IMPERIAL (66231 "On a Carousel")...........8-12 67
LPs: 10/12-inch
ATLANTIC (835216 "What Goes Around").5-10 83
CAPITOL (16056 "Greatest")......................6-10 80
EMI (92882 "Best of the Hollies")...............5-10 '80s
EPIC (24315 "Evolution")..........................25-35 67
(Monaural.)
EPIC (24344 "Dear Eloise"/"King Midas in Reverse")...25-35 67
(Monaural.)
EPIC (26315 "Evolution")..........................15-25 67
(Stereo.)
EPIC (26344 "Dear Eloise"/"King Midas in Reverse")...15-25 67
(Stereo.)
EPIC (26447 "Words and Music by Bob Dylan")..20-30 69
EPIC (26538 "He Ain't Heavy He's My Brother")..10-20 70
EPIC (30255 "Moving Finger")..................10-20 71
EPIC (KE-30958 "Distant Light")..............10-20 72
EPIC (AL-30958 "Distant Light")...............5-10 77
EPIC (31000 thru 35000 series)................6-12 73-78
IMPERIAL (9265 "Here I Go Again")....125-175 64
(Monaural. Black label with five stars under "Imperial" and straight lines from "10" to "2" [if label were a clock face].)
IMPERIAL (9265 "Here I Go Again")........50-75 64
(Monaural. Multi-color label.)
IMPERIAL (9299 "Hear! Here!")...............40-60 65
(Monaural.)
IMPERIAL (9312 "The Hollies [Beat Group]")..35-50 66
(Monaural.)
IMPERIAL (9330 "Bus Stop")...................35-50 66
(Monaural.)
IMPERIAL (9339 "Stop! Stop! Stop!").......35-50 67
(Monaural.)
IMPERIAL (9350 "Greatest Hits")............40-60 67
(Monaural.)
IMPERIAL (12265 "Here I Go Again")....75-125 64
(Stereo. Black "Imperial Stereo" label.)
IMPERIAL (12299 "Hear! Here!")............30-50 65
(Stereo.)
IMPERIAL (12312 "The Hollies [Beat Group]")..25-50 66
(Stereo.)
IMPERIAL (12330 "Bus Stop").................25-50 66
(Stereo.)
IMPERIAL (12339 "Stop! Stop! Stop!").....25-50 67
(Stereo.)
IMPERIAL (12350 "Greatest Hits")..........25-50 67
(Stereo.)
LIBERTY...5-10 84
U.A. (329 "Very Best")................................8-12 75
Members: Allan Clarke; Graham Nash; Bobby Elliott; Tony Hicks; Eric Haydock; Bernie Calvert; Terry Sylvester.
Also see BAMBOO
Also see EVERLY BROTHERS
Also see NASH, Graham
Also see PARSONS, Alan, Project
Also see SPRINGSTEEN, Bruce / Johnny Winter / Hollies
Also see SWINGING BLUE JEANS
Also see TREMELOES / Hollies

HOLLIES / Peter Sellers
Singles: 7-inch
U.A. (50079 "After the Fox")....................10-20 66
LPs: 10/12-inch
U.A. (286 "After the Fox")..........................8-10 74
(Soundtrack.)
U.A. (4148 "After the Fox").......................15-25 66
(Soundtrack. Monaural.)
U.A. (5148 "After the Fox").......................25-35 66
(Soundtrack. Stereo.)
Also see HOLLIES

HOLLIMAN, Earl
Singles: 7-inch
CAPITOL (3983 "A Teenager Sings the Blues")..10-20 58
CAPITOL (4042 "La La La Lovable")........10-20 58
PREP (127 "Nobody Knows How I Feel")..10-20 58

HOLLIMAN, Farris
Singles: 7-inch
ALEXANDER (101 "Pretty Woman")....100-200

HOLLINS, Tony
Singles: 78 rpm
DECCA...15-25 52
Singles: 7-inch
DECCA (48288 "Wine-O-Woman")............50-75 52
DECCA (48300 "Fishin' Blues")...............50-75 52

HOLLISTER, Bobby, & Rialtos
Singles: 7-inch
PIKE (5910 "Love's Gamble")..................15-20 61
Picture Sleeves
PIKE (5910 "Love's Gamble")..................20-30 61
Also see RIALTOS

HOLLOWAY, Alden
Singles: 7-inch
DIXIE (2020 "Blast Off").......................500-700 59
STARDAY (714 "Loving Is My Business")..75-100

HOLLOWAY, Brenda *P&R/R&B '64*
(With the Carrolls)
Singles: 7-inch
CATCH (109 You're My Only Love")........10-20 64
DONNA (1358 thru 1370).........................15-25 62
EUNICE (1009 "Crazy Little Heart").........15-25
MUSIC MERCHANT (1001 "Let Love Grow")...4-6 71
TAMLA (206312 "Play It Cool, Stay in School")...300-500 66
(Promotional issue only.)
TAMLA (54094 "Every Little Bit Hurts")......5-10 64
TAMLA (54099 "I'll Always Love You")......10-15 64
TAMLA (54099 "I'll Always Love You")...50-100 64
(Single-sided. Promotional issue only.)
TAMLA (54111 "When I'm Gone").............5-10 65
TAMLA (54115 thru 54137).....................10-20 65-66
TAMLA (54144 "Til Johnny Comes")....100-200 67
TAMLA (54148 "Just Look What You've Done")...10-20 67
TAMLA (54155 "You've Made Me So Very Happy")...10-20 67
Picture Sleeves
TAMLA (54111 "When I'm Gone")...........20-40 65
LPs: 10/12-inch
MOTOWN (5242 "Every Little Bit Hurts")...5-10 '80s
(Stereo.)
TAMLA (257 "Every Little Bit Hurts")....100-200 65
Also see DAVIS, Hal

HOLLOWAY, Brenda, & Jess Harris
Singles: 7-inch
BREVIT (641 "I Never Knew You Looked So Good until I Quit You")...25-35 63
Also see HOLLOWAY, Brenda

HOLLOWAY, Patrice
Singles: 7-inch
CAPITOL (5680 "Stolen Hours")..............50-75 66
CAPITOL (5778 "Love & Desire")............30-60 66
CAPITOL (5985 "Stay with Your Own Kind")...25-50 67
TASTE (125 "Do the Del Viking")............20-30 63
Also see JOSIE & PUSSYCATS

HOLLOWS
Singles: 7-inch
RENDEVOUS (141 "Revival Stomp").......10-20 61

HOLLY, Buddy *P&R/R&B '57*
(With the Crickets; with Three Tunes; with Picks)
Singles: 12-inch
SOLID SMOKE...10-20 79
(Picture disc.)
Singles: 78 rpm
BRUNSWICK (55009 "That'll Be the Day")...200-300 57
BRUNSWICK (55035 "Oh Boy")..........200-300 58
BRUNSWICK (55053 "Maybe Baby")..200-300 58
BRUNSWICK (55072 "Think It Over")..200-300 58
BRUNSWICK (55094 "It's So Easy")....200-300 58
CORAL (61852 "Words of Love").........400-500 57
CORAL (61885 "Peggy Sue")..............600-800 57
CORAL (61947 "Listen to Me")............150-250 58
CORAL (61985 "Rave On")..................150-250 58
CORAL (62006 "Early in the Morning")...600-800 58
CORAL (62051 "Heartbeat")................600-800 58
CORAL (62134 "Peggy Sue Got Married")..150-200 59
(Canadian.)
DECCA (29854 "Blue Days – Black Nights")...600-800 56
DECCA (30166 "Modern Don Juan")...600-800 56
DECCA (30434 "That'll Be the Day")....600-800 57
DECCA (30543 "Love Me").................400-500 58
DECCA (30650 "Ting-A-Ling")..............600-800 58
Singles: 7-inch
BRUNSWICK (55009 "That'll Be the Day")..40-60 57
BRUNSWICK (55035 "Oh Boy")..............40-60 58
BRUNSWICK (55053 "Maybe Baby").......30-50 58
BRUNSWICK (55072 "Think It Over").......30-50 58
BRUNSWICK (55094 "It's So Easy").........30-50 58
CORAL (61852 "Words of Love").........200-300 57
CORAL (61885 "Peggy Sue")...................25-40 57
CORAL (61947 "Listen to Me")................25-40 58
CORAL (61985 "Rave On").......................25-40 58
CORAL (62006 "Early in the Morning").....25-40 58
CORAL (62051 "Heartbeat").....................25-40 58
CORAL (62074 "It Doesn't Matter Anymore")...25-40 59
CORAL (62134 "Peggy Sue Got Married")...30-50 59
(Orange label.)
CORAL (62134 "Peggy Sue Got Married")...20-30 62
(Yellow label.)
CORAL (62210 "True Love Ways")..........30-50 60
CORAL (62329 "Reminiscing")................25-40 62

CORAL (62352 "Bo Diddley")...... 25-40 63
CORAL (62369 "Brown Eyed Handsome Man")...... 25-40 63
CORAL (62390 "Rock Around with Ollie Vee")...... 30-50 64
CORAL (62407 "Maybe Baby")...... 30-50 64
CORAL (62448 "Slippin' & Slidin' ")...... 50-75 65
CORAL (62554 "Rave On")...... 25-40 68
CORAL (62558 "Love Is Strange")...... 15-25 69
CORAL (65618 "That'll Be the Day")...... 15-25 69
DECCA (29854 "Blue Days – Black Nights")...... 300-400 56
(With silver lines on both sides of the name Decca.)
DECCA (29854 "Blue Days – Black Nights")...... 75-125 56
(With silver star and lines under the name Decca.)
DECCA (30166 "Modern Don Juan")... 300-400 56
(With silver lines on both sides of the name Decca.)
DECCA (30166 "Modern Don Juan")..... 75-125 56
(With silver star and lines under the name Decca.)
DECCA (30434 "That'll Be the Day")... 200-300 57
(With silver lines on both sides of the name Decca.)
DECCA (30434 "That'll Be the Day")..... 75-125 57
(With silver star and lines under the name Decca.)
DECCA (30543 "Love Me")...... 200-300 58
(With silver lines on both sides of the name Decca.)
DECCA (30543 "Love Me")...... 75-125 58
(With silver star and lines under the name Decca.)
DECCA (30650 "Ting-A-Ling")...... 200-300 58
(With silver lines on both sides of the name Decca.)
DECCA (30650 "Ting-A-Ling")...... 75-125 58
(With silver star and lines under the name Decca.)
MCA......4-6 73-78
MEMORY LANE......3-5

Promotional Singles

BRUNSWICK (55009 "That'll Be the Day")...... 50-100 57
BRUNSWICK (55035 "Oh Boy")...... 50-100 58
BRUNSWICK (55053 "Maybe Baby")...... 50-100 58
BRUNSWICK (55072 "Think It Over")... 50-100 58
BRUNSWICK (55094 "It's So Easy")..... 50-100 58
CORAL (61852 "Words of Love")...... 150-200 57
CORAL (61885 "Peggy Sue")...... 100-150 57
CORAL (61947 "Listen to Me")...... 50-100 58
CORAL (61985 "Rave On")...... 50-100 58
CORAL (62006 "Early in the Morning").... 50-75 58
CORAL (62051 "Heartbeat")...... 50-75 58
CORAL (62074 "It Doesn't Matter Anymore")...... 50-75 59
CORAL (62134 "Peggy Sue Got Married")...... 50-75 59
CORAL (62210 "True Love Ways")...... 50-75 60
CORAL (62329 "Reminiscing")...... 50-75 62
CORAL (62352 "Bo Diddley")...... 50-75 63
CORAL (62369 "Brown Eyed Handsome Man")...... 50-75 63
CORAL (62390 "Rock Around with Ollie Vee")...... 50-75 64
CORAL (62407 "Maybe Baby")...... 50-75 64
CORAL (62448 "Slippin' & Slidin' ")...... 50-75 65
CORAL (62554 "Rave On")...... 40-60 68
CORAL (62558 "Love Is Strange")...... 40-60 69
(Price doubles if accompanied by dee jay insert sheet.)
CORAL (65618 "That'll Be the Day")...... 40-60 69
DECCA (29854 "Blue Days - Black Nights")...... 150-250 56
DECCA (30166 "Modern Don Juan")... 150-250 56
DECCA (30434 "That'll Be the Day")... 150-250 57
DECCA (30543 "Love Me")...... 150-250 58
DECCA (30650 "Ting-A-Ling")...... 150-250 58

Picture Sleeves

BRUNSWICK (55009 "That'll Be the Day")
(Listed only because a recently made and widely circulated bootleg sleeve has confused some collectors. There is no authentic sleeve for this release.)
CORAL (61885 "Peggy Sue")......5-10 '90s
CORAL (62051 "Heartbeat")......5-10 '90s
CORAL (62074 "It Doesn't Matter Anymore")......5-10 '90s
CORAL (62210 "True Love Ways")...... 75-100 60
(Wrap-around type sleeve.)
CORAL (62558 "Love Is Strange")...... 30-40 69
MCA......4-6 78

EPs: 7-inch

BRUNSWICK (71036 "The Chirping Crickets")...... 300-400 57
(With printed back cover.)
BRUNSWICK (71036 "The Chirping Crickets")......350-450 57
(With blank back cover.)
BRUNSWICK (71038 "The Sound of the Crickets")......150-250 58
CORAL (81169 "Listen to Me")......250-350 58
CORAL (81182 "The Buddy Holly Story")......200-300 59
CORAL (81191 "Buddy Holly")......200-300 62
CORAL (81193 "Brown Eyed Handsome Man")......100-200 63
DECCA (2575 "That'll Be the Day")......500-750 58
(With liner notes on the back cover.)
DECCA (2575 "That'll Be the Day")......400-600 58
(With EP ads on the back cover.)

LPs: 10/12-inch

BRUNSWICK (54038 "The Chirping Crickets")......500-800 57
CORAL (8 "Best of Buddy Holly")......75-125 66
CORAL (57210 "Buddy Holly")......150-250 58
(Maroon label.)
CORAL (57210 "Buddy Holly")......25-50 63
(Black label.)
CORAL (57279 "The Buddy Holly Story")......125-175 59
(Maroon label. With red and black print on the back cover.)
CORAL (57279 "The Buddy Holly Story")......75-125 59
(Maroon label. With black print on the back cover.)
CORAL (57279 "The Buddy Holly Story") 30-40 63
(Black label. With pictures of other LPs, or black print, on the back cover.)
CORAL (57326 "The Buddy Holly Story, Vol. II")......100-200 60
(Maroon label.)
CORAL (57326 "The Buddy Holly Story, Vol. II")......25-50 63
(Black label.)
CORAL (57405 "Buddy Holly and the Crickets")......50-100 62
(Maroon label.)
CORAL (57405 "Buddy Holly and the Crickets")......25-45 63
(Black label.)
CORAL (57426 "Reminiscing")......50-75 63
(Maroon label.)
CORAL (57426 "Reminiscing")......20-40 63
(Black label.)
CORAL (57450 "Showcase")......40-50 64
CORAL (57463 "Holly in the Hills")......75-100 65
CORAL (57492 "Buddy Holly's Greatest Hits")......75-100 67
(Monaural.)
CORAL (757492 "Buddy Holly's Greatest Hits")......25-50 67
(Stereo.)
CORAL (757279 "The Buddy Holly Story")......25-50 63
(Stereo.)
CORAL (757405 "Buddy Holly and the Crickets")......50-75 62
(Maroon label. Stereo.)
CORAL (757405 "Buddy Holly and the Crickets")......25-50 63
(Black label. Stereo.)
CORAL (757463 "Holly in the Hills")......40-60 65
(Stereo.)
CORAL (757504 "Giant")......40-80 69
(Stereo.)
CREATIVE RADIO ("The Day the Music Died")......25-30
(Two discs. Includes poster.)
DECCA (207 "A Rock & Roll Collection").15-20 72
DECCA (8707 "That'll Be the Day")......500-750 58
(Black label.)
DECCA (8707 "That'll Be the Day")......150-250 61
(Multi-color label.)
LIFE (8707 "That'll Be the Day")......150-250 61
(Multi-color Decca label, but with "Life" on label instead of Decca. Cover shows Decca, not Life.)
MCA (Except 6-80000)......8-15 75-85
MCA (6-80000 "The Complete Buddy Holly")......30-40 81
(Boxed six-disc set.)
VOCALION (3811 "The Great Buddy Holly")......90-110 67
(Monaural.)
VOCALION (73811 "The Great Buddy Holly")......20-30 67
(Reprocessed stereo.)
VOCALION (73923 "Good Rockin' Buddy Holly")......100-125 71
(Reprocessed stereo.)

Promotional LPs

BRUNSWICK (54038 "The Chirping Crickets")......500-750 57
CORAL (Except 757504)......50-75 58-65
CORAL (757504 "Giant")......35-45 69
DECCA (8707 "That'll Be the Day")......400-600 58
(Pink label.)
PICK (1111 "Buddy Holly and the Picks") 10-12 86
Session: Bob Montgomery; Jerry Allison; Joe B. Mauldin; Sonny Curtis; Boots Randolph; Don Guess; Grady Martin; Niki Sullivan; Waylon Jennings; Larry Welborn; Ray "Slim" Corbin; George Atwood; Picks; Roses.
Also see BEATLES / Beach Boys / Buddy Holly
Also see CRAWFORD, Fred
Also see CRICKETS
Also see CURTIS, Sonny
Also see DAVIS, Sherry
Also see DON & HIS ROSES
Also see ENGLER, Jerry, & Four Ekkos
Also see FREED, Alan
Also see GIORDANO, Lou
Also see HUDDLE, Jack
Also see JENNINGS, Waylon
Also see KING, Ben E.
Also see MARTIN, Grady
Also see MONTGOMERY, Bob
Also see NIGHTHAWKS
Also see PETTY, Norman, Trio
Also see PHILLIPS, Charlie
Also see PICKS
Also see PRESLEY, Elvis / Buddy Holly
Also see RANDOLPH, Boots
Also see ROBINSON, Jim
Also see SULLIVAN, Niki
Also see TUCKER, Rick

HOLLY, Wes

Singles: 7-inch

IOWANA (809 "Shufflin' Shoes")......20-30 58
WES HOLLY ("Hop Rock")......15-25 '50s
(Selection number not known.)

HOLLY TWINS

Singles: 78 rpm

LIBERTY......15-25 56

Singles: 7-inch

LIBERTY (55015 "It's Easy")......15-25 56
LIBERTY (55048 "I Want Elvis for Christmas")......15-25 56
(With Eddie Cochran.)
RENDEZVOUS (180 "Potato Chips")......5-10 62
Also see COCHRAN, Eddie

HOLLYHAWKS

Singles: 7-inch

JUBILEE (5441 "I Cry All the Time")......20-30 63
Members: Niki Sullivan; Gene Evans.
Also see SULLIVAN, Niki

HOLLYHOCKS

Singles: 78 rpm

NASCO (6001 "Don't Say Tomorrow")......15-25 57

Singles: 7-inch

NASCO (6001 "Don't Say Tomorrow")......15-25 57

HOLLYRIDGE STRINGS *P&R/LP '64*

(Stu Phillips & Hollyridge Strings)

Singles: 7-inch

CAPITOL......5-10 61-68

EPs: 7-inch

CAPITOL (2626 "Selections from *Beatles Songbook*")......8-12 64
(Promotional issue only.)

LPs: 10/12-inch

CAPITOL (2116 thru 2998)......10-20 64-68
CAPITOL (839 thru 11830)......8-12 71-78
Also see BEACH BOYS / Hollyridge Strings
Also see GOLDEN GATE STRINGS
Also see PHILLIPS, Stu, & His Orchestra

HOLLYWOOD ALLSTARS

Singles: 7-inch

ADMIRAL (501 "Justine")......15-25 61
R-DELL (115 "My Dog Buddy")......10-15 59

HOLLYWOOD ARGYLES *P&R/R&B '60*

Singles: 7-inch

ABC......4-6 74
CHATTAHOOCHEE (691 "Longhair, Unsquare Dude Called Jack")......5-10 65
ERA......4-6 72
FELSTED (8674 "Bossynover")......5-10 63
FINER ARTS (1002 "Morning After")......5-10 61
LUTE (5905 thru 6002)......10-20 60
PAXLEY (751 "You Been Torturing Me")...8-12 61
TRILL (6311 "The Watermelon Song")......5-10 '60s
WHAM (7037 "Alley Oop")......8-12 '60s

Picture Sleeves

WHAM (7037 "Alley Oop")......15-25 '60s

LPs: 10/12-inch

LUTE (9001 "Alley Oop")......250-350 60
Members: Gary Paxton; Dallas Frazier; Buddy Mize; Scotty Turner. Session: Gary Webb; Bobby Rey; Gaynel Hodge; Ronnie Caleco; Harper Cosby; Sandy Nelson; Marshall Leib; Deary Weaver.
Also see FRAZIER, Dallas
Also see NEW HOLLYWOOD ARGYLES
Also see NELSON, Sandy
Also see PAXTON, Gary

HOLLYWOOD ARIST-O-KATS

(With the Red Callender Sextette)

Singles: 78 rpm

RECORDED IN HOLLYWOOD......150-250 53

Singles: 7-inch

RECORDED IN HOLLYWOOD (406 "I'll Be Home Again")......750-1000 53
Also see CALLENDER, Red

HOLLYWOOD BLUEJAYS

(Flairs)

Singles: 78 rpm

RECORDED IN HOLLYWOOD (185 "Cloudy and Raining")......50-100 52
RECORDED IN HOLLYWOOD (396 "I Had a Love")......50-100 53

Singles: 7-inch

RECORDED IN HOLLYWOOD (396 "I Had a Love")......300-500 53
Also see FIVE HOLLYWOOD BLUEJAYS
Also see FLAIRS

HOLLYWOOD CHAMBER JAZZ GROUP

EPs: 7-inch

RCA (4199 "Stakeout")......25-35 58
(Soundtrack.)

HOLLYWOOD FLAMES *P&R/R&B '57*

(Dave Ford & Hollywood Flames; "with Orchestra Acc.")

Singles: 78 rpm

DECCA......15-25 54-55
EBB......50-100 57-58
LUCKY (001 "One Night with a Fool")..150-250 54
LUCKY (006 "Peggy")......150-250 54
LUCKY (009 "I Know")......200-300 54
MONEY (202 "I'm Leaving")......75-100 54
RECORDED IN HOLLYWOOD (104 "Peggy")......250-450 50
SWING TIME (345 "Let's Talk It Over")......100-200 53

Singles: 7-inch

ATCO (6155 thru 6180)......10-15 59-60
CHESS (1787 "Gee")......8-12 61
CORONET (7025 "Believe in Me")......10-15 61
DECCA (29285 "Peggy")......50-100 54
DECCA (48331 "I Know")......100-150 55
EBB (119 "Buzz, Buzz, Buzz")......25-35 57
EBB (131 "Give Me Back My Heart")......15-25 58
EBB (144 "Strollin' on the Beach")......15-25 58
EBB (146 "Chains of Love")......20-30 58
EBB (149 "A Star Fell")......15-25 58
EBB (153 "Just for You")......20-30 59
EBB (158 "So Good")......10-20 59
EBB (162 "Now That You've Gone")......10-20 59
EBB (163 "In the Dark")......15-25 59
GOLDIE (1101 "Believe in Me")......10-15 62
LUCKY (001 "One Night with a Fool")..400-500 54
LUCKY (006 "Peggy")......400-500 54
LUCKY (009 "I Know")......800-1000 54
MONA-LEE (135 "Buzz, Buzz, Buzz")......10-15 59
MONEY (202 "I'm Leaving")......200-300 54
SWING TIME (345 "I Know")......300-500 53
SYMBOL (211 "Dance Senorita")......20-30 65
SYMBOL (215 "I'm Coming Home")......15-25 66
VEE-JAY (515 "Letter to My Love")......15-25 63

LPs: 10/12-inch

SPECIALTY (2166 "Buzz Buzz Buzz")......8-12 88

Members: David Ford; Bobby Byrd; Gaynel Hodge; Clyde Tillis; Earl Nelson; Donald Height; Curtis Williams; Ray Brewster; John Berry; George Home.
Also see BOB & EARL
Also see BYRD, Bobby
Also see FLAMES
Also see FOUR FLAMES
Also see HEIGHT, Donald
Also see HOLLYWOOD FOUR FLAMES
Also see JETS
Also see NELSON, Earl
Also see QUESTION MARKS
Also see SATELLITES
Also see TANGIERS
Also see TURKS

HOLLYWOOD FLAMES / Question Marks
Singles: 78 rpm
SWING TIME (346 "Go and Get Some More") 100-200 54

HOLLYWOOD FOUR FLAMES
(Hollywood Flames)
Singles: 78 rpm
RECORDED IN HOLLYWOOD (164 "I'll Always Be a Fool") 200-400 52
RECORDED IN HOLLYWOOD (165 "Young Girl") 200-400 52
UNIQUE (003 "Dividend Blues") 250-500 51
UNIQUE (005 "Tabarin") 250-500 51
(Reissued as by the Four Flames.)
UNIQUE (015 "Please Say I Am Wrong") 200-400 51
Also see FOUR FLAMES
Also see HOLLYWOOD FLAMES

HOLLYWOOD GAMBLERS
Singles: 7-inch
DON (201 "Moon Katt") 10-20 61
Also see GAMBLERS

HOLLYWOOD HURRICANES
Singles: 7-inch
PRIMA (1009 "Beavershot") 10-20 64

HOLLYWOOD PERSUADERS
Singles: 7-inch
ORIGINAL SOUND (39 "Grunion Run") .. 20-30 63
(First pressings credited to the Persuaders.)
ORIGINAL SOUND (44 "Juarez") 8-12 64
ORIGINAL SOUND (50 "Drums A-Go-Go") 8-12 64
ORIGINAL SOUND (58 "Hollywood A-Go-Go") 10-20 65
LPs: 10/12-inch
ORIGINAL SOUND (8874 "Drums A-Go-Go") 20-25 65
Also see PERSUADERS
Also see ZAPPA, Frank

HOLLYWOOD PLAYBOYS
Singles: 7-inch
RITA (118 "I'm Lonely") 40-50 61
SURE (105 "Ding Dong School Is Out") .. 25-35 60
Member: Nick Massi.

HOLLYWOOD PRODUCERS
Singles: 7-inch
PARKWAY (993 "You're Not Welcome") . 40-50 66
(Previously issued as by Jan Davis.)
Also see DAVIS, Jan

HOLLYWOOD REBELS
Singles: 7-inch
IMPACT (18 "Rebel Stomp") 15-20 63

HOLLYWOOD SAXONS
Singles: 7-inch
ELF (101 "Everyday's a Holiday") 15-25 62
ELF (103 "It's You") 20-30 62
HARECO (102 "Everyday Holiday" .. 3000-4000 61
(Note slight title variation on reissues.)
SWINGIN' (631 "Everyday's a Holiday") .. 10-20 61
SWINGIN' (651 "It's You") 10-20 63
SWINGIN' (654 "Laughing Girl") 35-45 63
TEEN (6 "Yes It's True") 5-10
20TH FOX (312 "Everyday's a Holiday") . 30-40 62
EPs: 7-inch
ACTION PAC (2023 "Hollywood Saxons") ...4-8
Also see BEVERLY, Stan, & Hollywood Saxons
Also see PORTRAITS
Also see SAXONS
Also see TUXEDOS

HOLLYWOOD SOUL COMFORTERS
Singles: 78 rpm
HOLLYWOOD (1042 "Silent Night") 20-30 55
Singles: 7-inch
HOLLYWOOD (1042 "Silent Night") 50-75 55

HOLLYWOOD SQUARES
Singles: 7-inch
SQUARE (001 "Hillside Strangler") 15-25 79
(Yellow vinyl.)
Picture Sleeves
SQUARE (001 "Hillside Strangler") 50-75 79

HOLLYWOOD SUNSETS BAND
(With the Sunset Choraliers)
EPs: 7-inch
RAINBOW (1001 "Teenage World of Music") 25-35 64
Also see ADRIAN & SUNSETS

HOLLYWOOD SURFERS / Dick Dale
LPs: 10/12-inch
DUBTONE (1246 "Surf Family") 20-30 63
Also see DALE, Dick

HOLLYWOOD TORNADOES
Singles: 7-inch
AERTAUN 15-25 62-63
Also see TORNADOES

HOLLYWOOD'S FOUR BLAZES
Singles: 78 rpm
EXCELSIOR 15-25 45-46
LAMPLIGHTER 15-25 46
Also see FOUR BLAZES

HOLMAN, Eddie *R&B '65*
Singles: 7-inch
ABC 5-10 69-71
AGAPE 3-5 82
ASCOT (2142 "Laughing at Me") 50-100 63
BELL (712 "I'll Cry 1,000 Tears") 10-20 68
DON-EL (124 "She's Beautiful") 15-25 63
GSF (6873 "My Mind Keeps Telling Me") 4-6 72
LEOPARD (5001 "I'm Counting Every Tear") 20-30 62
PARKWAY (106 thru 133) 5-10 66-67
PARKWAY (157 "Never Let Me Go") 30-40 67
PARKWAY (960 thru 994) 5-10 65
SALSOUL 4-6 77
SILVER BLUE 4-6 74
LPs: 10/12-inch
ABC-PAR (701 "I Love You") 10-15 70
SALSOUL (5511 "Night to Remember") 5-10 77

HOLMAN, Eddie / Lamplighters
Singles: 7-inch
SCRIPT (12212 "Never Let Go") 10-20
(Colored vinyl. Promotional issue only.)
Also see HOLMAN, Eddie
Also see LAMPLIGHTERS

HOLMAN, Jay
Singles: 7-inch
EMBER (1073 "My Love") 20-30 61
FALEW! (106 "Love Is a Sweet Thing") 10-20 64

HOLMAN, Rocky, & Romancers
Singles: 7-inch
FLIP (355 "My Precious Love") 35-45 61

HOLMES, Carl
(With the Commanders)
Singles: 7-inch
ATLANTIC (2140 "Mashed Potatoes") 5-10 62
PARKWAY (900 "I Want My Ya Ya") 5-10 64
VERVE (10510 "Telegram") 4-8 67
LPs: 10/12-inch
ATLANTIC 25-35 62
Carl Holmes; Marco King; Sports Lewis; Tommy Howard; Calvin Irons; John Holmes.

HOLMES, Eddie
Singles: 7-inch
EAGLE (1000 "Together Again") 10-20 58

HOLMES, Eldridge
Singles: 7-inch
ALON 8-12 62-65
ATCO (6701 "Cheatin' Woman") 5-10 69
DECCA 8-12
DEE-SU (300 thru 320) 15-25 66-67
JET SET (765 thru 1006) 15-25
SANSU (469 "Without a Word") 5-10

HOLMES, Fat Daddy
Singles: 7-inch
JET (505 "Chicken Rock") 25-35 60

HOLMES, Leon, & His Georgia Ramblers
Singles: 7-inch
PEACH (597 "She's My Baby") 1500-2500 59
PEACH (730 "Tears on My Pillow") 25-50 60
STARDAY (660 "Half a Chance") .... 150-200 '60s

HOLMES, Marvin
(With the Uptights; with Justice)
Singles: 7-inch
BROWN DOOR (6574 "Tell the Truth") 10-20
REVUE (11026 "Ride Your Mule") 5-10 68
UNI (55111 "Ooh Ooh the Dragon") 5-10 69
UNI (55177 "You're My Girl") 10-20 69
UNI (55233 "Sweet Talk") 10-20 69
LPs: 10/12-inch
UNI (73046 "Ooh Ooh the Dragon") 15-25 69

HOLMES, Richard "Groove" *P&R/R&B/LP '66*
Singles: 7-inch
BLUE NOTE 4-6 71
FLYING DUTCHMAN 4-6 76
GROOVE MERCHANT (1007 "American Pie") 4-6 75
GROOVE MERCHANT (1012 "Night Glider") 4-6 75
PACIFIC JAZZ 5-10 61-69
PRESTIGE 4-8 66-69
LPs: 10/12-inch
BLUE NOTE 5-10 71
FLYING DUTCHMAN 5-10 75-76
GROOVE MERCHANT 5-10 72-75
LOMA 10-15 66
MUSE 5-10 78-80
PACIFIC JAZZ (Except 20000 series) 15-25 61-62
PACIFIC JAZZ (20000 series) 8-15 68-69
PRESTIGE 8-15 66-70
VERSATILE 5-10 78
W.B. 10-20 64
WORLD PACIFIC JAZZ 8-12 70
Also see AMMONS, Gene, & Richard "Groove" Holmes
Also see McGRIFF, Jimmy
Also see WITHERSPOON, Jimmy

HOLMES, Richard "Groove," & Les McCann
LPs: 10/12-inch
PACIFIC JAZZ 15-25 62
Also see HOLMES, Richard "Groove"
Also see McCANN, Les

HOLMES, Sherlock
Singles: 7-inch
BRUNSWICK (55275 "Thought") 5-10 64
PART III (101 "Standing at a Standstill") .. 10-20 '60s
START (639 "Miss Fontaine") 5-10 64

HOLMES, Sonny Boy
Singles: 78 rpm
RECORDED IN HOLLYWOOD (223 "Walking and Crying Blues") 25-50 52
RECORDED IN HOLLYWOOD (225 "I Got Them Blues") 25-50 52

HOLMES, Tommy
Singles: 7-inch
CHERRY (112 "Wa-Chic-Ka-Naka") 200-300 58
CHERRY (113 "Witch Doctor's Wedding") 150-250 58

HOLMES, Wade
Singles: 78 rpm
4 STAR (1656 "You're Too Tired") 8-12 54
Singles: 7-inch
4 STAR (1656 "You're Too Tired") 15-25 54
LPs: 10/12-inch
CROWN ("The Memory of Hawkshaw Hawkins") 5-10 65
(Selection number not known.)

HOLMES, Wright
Singles: 78 rpm
GOTHAM (508 "Good Road Blues") 15-25 47
GOTHAM (511 "Alley Special") 25-50 47
MILTONE (5221 "Alley Special") 20-40 47

HOLOCAUST
Singles: 7-inch
RED ROBB (2025 "Savage Affection") 30-40

HOLT, Davey, & Hubcaps
Singles: 7-inch
U.A. (110 "Pittery Pat") 10-20 58
Also see SNOW MEN

HOLT, Jack
Singles: 7-inch
CHUCK GARNER (116 "Moonshine Still") 75-125

HOLT, Jim
Singles: 7-inch
GULFSTREAM (1061 "Paralyzed") ...... 100-150 '50s
GULFSTREAM (1062 "Money") .... 75-125 '50s
GULFSTREAM (1064 "Oh! My Linda") .. 75-125 '50s

HOLT, Will
Singles: 78 rpm
CORAL (Except 61789) 5-10 54
CORAL (61789 "M.T.A.") 10-20 57
Singles: 7-inch
CORAL (Except 61789) 8-12 54
CORAL (61789 "M.T.A.") 15-25 57

HOLTON, Bennie, Trio
Singles: 7-inch
STAFF (800 "Bennie's Boogie") .... 15-25 '50s

HOLY GHOST RECEPTION COMMITTEE #9
LPs: 10/12-inch
PAULIST PRESS ("Songs for Liturgical Worship") 50-75 68
(Selection number not known.)
PAULIST PRESS (4436 "Torchbearers"). 50-75 69

HOLY MODAL ROUNDERS
Singles: 7-inch
METROMEDIA 4-8 71
LPs: 10/12-inch
ESP (1068 "Indian War Whoop") 25-35 68
ELEKTRA (74026 "Moray Eels Eat the Holy Modal Rounders") 20-30 68
FANTASY (24711 "Stampfel & Weber") ... 15-20 72
METROMEDIA (1039 "Good Taste") 15-25 71
PRESTIGE (7410 "Holy Modal Rounders 2") 20-30 65
PRESTIGE (7451 "Holy Modal Rounders") 20-30 66
PRESTIGE (7720 "Holy Modal Rounders") 20-25 69
PRESTIGE (14031 "The Holy Modal Rounders") 25-35 64
ROUNDER 5-10
Members: Steve Weber; Pete Stampfel; Richard Tyler; Michael Hurley; Ken Crabtree.
Also see FUGS

HOMBRES *P&R/LP '67*
Singles: 7-inch
SUN 4-8 69
VERVE FORECAST (5058 "Let It All Hang Out") 5-10 67
VERVE FORECAST (5058 "Let It Out") 4-8 67
(Note shortened title.)
VERVE FORECAST (5076 thru 5093) 5-10 67-68
LPs: 10/12-inch
VERVE FORECAST (3036 "Let It Out") ... 20-30 67
VERVE FORECAST (S-3036 "Let It Out") 20-30 67

HOMBS, Jimmie / Twinkletones
(With the Invictas & Hollywood Rebels)
Singles: 7-inch
JACK BEE (1004 "Voo Doo Dolly") 30-40 59
Also see INVICTAS
Also see TWINKLETONES

HOME TOWNERS
Singles: 7-inch
FRATERNITY (842 "Ding Dong") 10-15 59
SAGE (240 "Prom Time") 10-15 58
SAGE (257 "Burning Bridges") 10-15 58
LPs: 10/12-inch
PALACE 10-20

HOMER
Singles: 7-inch
UNITED (123-6 "I Never Cared for You"). 10-20 69
UNITED (123-8 "Texas Lights") 10-20 70
UNITED (123-10 "Dandelion Wine") 10-20 70
LPs: 10/12-inch
UNITED (101 "Grown in USA") 100-150 70
Members: Phil Bepko; Frank Coy; Howard Gloor; Gene Coleman; Galen Niles.

HOMER, Chris

Singles: 7-inch

KICK (285 "Little Bull and Buttercup")...... 50-75

HOMER, Dennis

Singles: 7-inch

TRI-STATE ("Mean Woman Blues")........ 40-60
(Selection number not known.)

HOMER & JETHRO — C&W/P&R '49

Singles: 78 rpm

KING..5-15 46-53
FEDERAL..8-15 51
RCA...5-15 50-58

Singles: 7-inch

BLUEBIRD...4-8 59
KING..4-6 63
RCA (48-0113 thru 48-0349).................. 30-50 49-50
(Green vinyl.)
RCA (0100 thru 0468)........................... 20-30 50-51
(Black vinyl.)
RCA (0500 series) 4-6 71
RCA (4290 thru 7704)............................ 10-20 51-59
RCA (47-7744 "Sink the Bismarck")...........8-12 60
(Monaural.)
RCA (61-7744 "Sink the Bismarck")......... 15-25 60
(Stereo.)
RCA (7790 thru 9922)..............................4-8 60-70

Picture Sleeves

RCA (5456 "My Upper Plate")................. 20-30 53
RCA (8345 "I Want to Hold Your Hand"). 10-15 64

EPs: 7-inch

AUDIO LAB 10-20 59
KING.. 15-25 53-54
RCA... 15-25 53-57

LPs: 10/12-inch

AUDIO LAB (1513 "Musical Madness")... 25-50 58
CAMDEN 10-20 62-71
DIPLOMAT..8-12
GUEST STAR 10-15 63
KING (639 "Their Version of the
Standards")... 20-30 59
KING (800 series) 10-20 63
KING (1000 series)................................8-12 67
NASHVILLE..8-12 69
RCA (1412 "Barefoot Ballads")............... 20-40 57
RCA (1516 "Worst of Homer & Jethro")... 20-40 57
RCA (LPM-1880 "Life Can Be
Miserable")... 20-30 58
(Monaural.)
RCA (LSP-1880 "Life Can Be
Miserable")... 25-35 58
(Stereo.)
RCA (2100 thru 2900 series).................. 15-25 60-64
(Monaural. With "LPM" prefix.)
RCA (2100 thru 2900 series).................. 20-30 60-64
(Stereo. With "LSP" prefix.)
RCA (3112 "Homer & Jethro Fracture Frank
Loesser").. 30-60 53
(10-inch LP.)
RCA (3300 thru 4600 series).................. 15-30 65-72
Members: Henry "Homer" Haynes; Kenneth "Jethro" Burns.
Also see ANN-MARGRET
Also see FOUR LOVERS / Homer & Jethro
Also see HAYNES, Henry "Homer"
Also see JONES, Spike

HOMER & JETHRO WITH JUNE CARTER — C&W '49

Singles: 78 rpm

RCA (48-0075 "Country Girl") 5-10 49

Singles: 7-inch

RCA (48-0075 "Country Girl") 30-50 49
(Green vinyl.)
Also see HOMER & JETHRO

HOMER THE GREAT

(Pee Wee Crayton)

Singles: 78 rpm

HOLLYWOOD (1055 "Steppin' Out")....... 15-25 56

Singles: 7-inch

HOLLYWOOD (1055 "Steppin' Out")...... 35-50 56
Also see CRAYTON, Pee Wee

HOMESICK JAMES

(James Williamson)

Singles: 7-inch

BLUESVILLE (826 "The Woman I'm
Lovin' ")...8-12 64
COLT (632 "Can't Afford to Do It") 15-25 62
USA (746 "Crossroads")......................... 15-25 62

LPs: 10/12-inch

BLUES ON BLUE 8-10
BLUESWAY (6071 "Ain't Sick No More") ...8-10 73
PRESTIGE (7388 "Homesick James") 25-35 66
Also see WILLIAMSON, James

HOMESTEADERS

Singles: 7-inch

END (1017 "Riff Rock") 10-20 58

HONDAS

Singles: 7-inch

EDEN (4 "Twelve Feet High") 40-50 62

HONDELLS — P&R/LP '64

Singles: 7-inch

AMOS (131 "Legend of Frankie and
Johnny")..4-8 69
AMOS (150 "Shine on Ruby Mt.") 4-6 70
COLUMBIA (44361 "Just One More
Chance")..5-10 67
COLUMBIA (44557 "Another Woman")......5-10 68
MERCURY (72324 "Little Honda")...........10-15 64
MERCURY (72366 "My Buddy Seat") 10-15 64
MERCURY (72405 "Little Sidewalk Surfer
Girl")..8-12 65
MERCURY (72443 "Sea of Love")..............8-12 65
MERCURY (72479 "Sea Cruise") 5-10 65
MERCURY (72523 "Follow Your Heart")....5-10 66
MERCURY (72563 "Younger Girl")............5-10 67
MERCURY (72605 "Kissin' My Life
Away")..5-10 67

Promotional Singles

MERCURY (72324 "Hot Rod High")............20-25 64
(Shows *Hot Rod High* as the "A" side.)
MERCURY (72324 "Little Honda")............15-20 64
(Shows *Little Honda* as the "A" side.)
MERCURY (72366 "My Buddy Seat") 15-20 64
MERCURY (72405 thru 72605) 8-12 65-67

Picture Sleeves

MERCURY (72366 "My Buddy Seat") 15-25 64
MERCURY (72479 "Sea Cruise") 10-20 65

LPs: 10/12-inch

MERCURY (20940 "Go, Little Honda").....20-30 64
(Monaural.)
MERCURY (60940 "Go, Little Honda").....30-40 64
(Stereo.)
MERCURY (20982 "Hondells") 20-30 64
(Monaural.)
MERCURY (20982 "Hondells") 30-40 65
(Stereo.)
Members: Chuck Girard; Richard Burns; Brian Wilson; Wayne Edwards; Glen Campbell; Joe Kelly; Bruce Johnston; Terry Melcher; Jerry Naylor; Gary Usher.
Session: Davie Allan.
Also see ALLEN, Davie
Also see BRUCE & TERRY
Also see CAMPBELL, Glen
Also see FOUR SPEEDS
Also see NAYLOR, Jerry
Also see PENDLETONS
Also see SUNSETS
Also see USHER, Gary
Also see WILSON, Brian

HONDELLS / Del Shannon / Martha & Vandellas

EPs: 7-inch

PEPSI-COLA (8256 "Pepsi-Cola Ad Radio Youth
Market, 1966") 15-20 66
(Promotional issue only.)
Also see MARTHA & VANDELLAS
Also see SHANNON, Del

HONDELLS / Dusty Springfield

Singles: 7-inch

COLLECTABLES...3-5 86
Also see HONDELLS
Also see SPRINGFIELD, Dusty

HONEST MEN

Singles: 7-inch

V.I.P. (25047 "Cherie") 15-25 68

HONEY & BEES

Singles: 7-inch

PENTAGON (500 "Please Go Away")..... 20-30 59

HONEY & DEW-DROPS

Singles: 7-inch

MMC (005 "Come My Little Baby")..........20-30 59

Members: Scottie Stuart Cameron; Sandy Stuart Cameron; Jack Bieulisbach; Walter Roberts; Frank Zitske.
Also see STUART, Scottie

HONEY & TEARDROPS

Singles: 7-inch

VAL (202 "You Are the One")...................40-60 62
(Black vinyl.)
VAL (202 "You Are the One")...............100-150 62
(Colored vinyl.)

HONEY BEARS

Singles: 78 rpm

CASH (1004 "Cucamonga")......................25-35 55
SPARK 40-50 54-55

Singles: 7-inch

CASH (1004 "Cucamonga")......................50-75 55
SPARK (104 "It's a Miracle")..................75-125 54
SPARK (111 "I Shall Not Fail")............100-150 55

HONEY BEES

Singles: 78 rpm

IMPERIAL 10-15 56

Singles: 7-inch

IMPERIAL (5400 "Endless")......................20-30 56
IMPERIAL (5416 "Whats [sic] to Become of
Me") 20-30 56

HONEY BEES

Singles: 7-inch

FONTANA (1939 "One Wonderful
Night")..10-15 64
FONTANA (1505 "Some of Your
Lovin' ") 10-15 65
GARRISON (3005 "Never in a Million
Years")..100-150 66
(First issue.)
VEE-JAY (611 "No Guy") 10-20 64
WAND (1141 "Never in a Million Years") .20-40 66
Also see KING, Carole

HONEY BOY

(Frank Patt)

Singles: 78 rpm

SPECIALTY (476 "Bloodstains on the
Wall") 20-30 54

Singles: 7-inch

SPECIALTY (476 "Bloodstains on the
Wall")..50-75 54

HONEY BOYS

Singles: 78 rpm

MODERN (980 "Never Lose Faith in
Me") 10-15 56

Singles: 7-inch

BOOGIE MUSIC (1 "Unchained Melody")....4-6 74
MODERN (980 "Never Lose Faith in
Me") 20-30 56
Members: Calvin Kollette; John Billy; Diason Stokes; Roland Jackson; Eddie Rich.

HONEY DREAMERS

Singles: 7-inch

DOT (15925 "Time Was")...........................8-12 59

LPs: 10/12-inch

DOT (3175 "It's Dark on Observatory
Hill")..10-15 59
(Monaural.)
DOT (25175 "It's Dark on Observatory
Hill")..15-20 59
(Stereo.)

HONEY DRIPPERS

Singles: 7-inch

ALAGA (1017 "Impeach the
President")..100-150 73

HONEYBEES

(Featuring "La La")

Singles: 7-inch

BEE (1101 "Kiss Me My Love") 500-750 58

HONEYCOMBS — P&R '64

Singles: 7-inch

INTERPHON..5-10 64-65
W.B. 5-10 65-66

Picture Sleeves

INTERPHON (7713 "I Can't Stop")..........10-20 64

LPs: 10/12-inch

INTERPHON (88001 "Here Are the
Honeycombs")...20-30 64
VEE-JAY (88001 "Here Are the
Honeycombs")..35-45 64

Members: Honey Lantree; John Lantree; Martin Murray; Denis D'Ell; Alan Ward.

HONEYCONES — P&R '58

Singles: 7-inch

EMBER (Except 1036) 10-15 58-59
EMBER (1036 "Op")..................................15-25 58

HONEYCUTT, Glenn

Singles: 78 rpm

SUN (264 "I'll Be Around") 15-25 57

Singles: 7-inch

BLACK GOLD (100 "Right Gal, Right
Time") 50-75 57
FERNWOOD (142 "Campus Love")......75-100 64
SUN (264 "I'll Be Around") 30-40 57

HONEY-Dos

("Honey-Do's")

Singles: 7-inch

SUE (746 "Someone")..............................30-40 61

HONEYDREAMERS

(With Henri René & His Orchestra; with Elliot Lawrence Orchestra; Honey Dreamers)

Singles: 78 rpm

CAMDEN 5-10 56
COLUMBIA..5-10 55-56
DOUBLE AA 5-10 55
FANTASY...5-10 55
JUNIOR..5-10 51
MGM..5-10 56
MOOD..5-10 54
RCA..5-10 50

Singles: 7-inch

CAMDEN 10-20 56
COLUMBIA..10-20 55-56
CORONADO...10-15 59
DOUBLE AA 10-20 55
FANTASY..10-20 55
JUNIOR...10-20 51
MGM...10-20 56
MOOD...10-20 54
RCA...10-20 50

LPs: 10/12-inch

RKO UNIQUE 15-25
Also see RENÉ, Henri, & His Orchestra

HONEYS

Singles: 7-inch

CAPITOL (2454 "Tonight You Belong to
Me") 30-50 69
CAPITOL (4952 "Surfin' Down the Swanee
River")..75-125 63
CAPITOL (5034 "Pray for Surf") 100-125 63
CAPITOL (5093 "The One You Can't
Have")..100-125 63
RHINO..4-6 83
W.B. (5430 "He's a Doll")......................200-300 64

LPs: 10/12-inch

RHINO (851 "Ecstasy") 8-10 83

Picture Sleeves

CAPITOL (4952 "Surfin' Down the Swanee
River")..200-300 63
Members: Ginger Blake; Diane Rovell; Marilyn Rovell.
Also see ANNETTE
Also see BEACH BOYS
Also see CASEY, Al
Also see DAVE & MARKSMEN
Also see GINGER
Also see PETERSEN, Paul
Also see SPRING
Also see SURFARIS
Also see USHER, Gary

HONEYSTROLLERS

Singles: 7-inch

GLORY (272 "Honeystrollin").....................15-25 58

HONEYTONES

Singles: 78 rpm

MERCURY (70557 "Too Bad")....................5-10 55
WING (90013 "False Alarm")....................10-15 55

Singles: 7-inch

MERCURY (70557 "Too Bad") 25-30 55
WING (90013 "False Alarm") 20-25 55

HONEYTONES

Singles: 7-inch

BIG TOP (3002 "I Know I Know") 10-15 58

HONG KONG WHITE SOX / Brumley Prunk

Singles: 7-inch

TRANS-WORLD (6906 "Cholley-Oop"/"He'd Better Go") ... 10-15 60

HONG KONGS

Singles: 7-inch

COUNSEL (50 "Surfin' in the China Sea") ... 15-25 63
MELODY MILL (303 "Surfin' in the China Sea") ... 15-25 63

HONORABLES

Singles: 7-inch

HONOR (100 "Castles in the Sky") ... 50-75 61
HONOR (102 "Sunday Stroll") ... 15-25 62

HOOD, Darla
(With Bill Baker's Orchestra)

Singles: 7-inch

ACAMA (Except 122) ... 5-10 60-62
ACAMA (122 "No Secret Now") ... 10-20 60
ENCINO (1007 "No Secret Now") ... 40-50 57
Also see BAKER, Bill

HOOD, Robbin

Singles: 78 rpm

MGM (12138 "A Teen Age Prayer") ... 10-20 56

Singles: 7-inch

MGM (12138 "A Teen Age Prayer") ... 10-20 56

HOOK

Singles: 7-inch

UNI ... 5-10 68-69

LPs: 10/12-inch

UNI (73023 "The Hook Will Grab You") ... 20-25 68
UNI (73038 "Hooked") ... 20-25 68
Members: Bob Arlin; Craig Boyd; Dale Loyola; Buddy Skylar; Denny Provisor.
Also see PROVISOR, Denny

HOOKER, Earl
(With His Roadmasters; with Earlettes; with Soul Twisters; with Soul Thrillers)

Singles: 78 rpm

KING (4600 "Race Track") ... 50-75 53
ROCKIN' (513 "On the Hook") ... 50-75 53
ROCKIN' (519 "Sweet Angel") ... 50-75 53

Singles: 7-inch

AGE (29106 "Blue Guitar") ... 10-20 62
AGE (29111 "How Long Can This Go On") ... 10-20 62
AGE (29114 "That Man") ... 10-20 63
ARGO (5265 "Frog Hop") ... 20-30 57
ARHOOLIE (521 "Wah Wah Blues") ... 10-20 70
BEA & BABY (106 "Dynamite") ... 15-20 59
BLUE THUMB (103 "Boogie, Don't Blot") ... 5-10 69
CHECKER (1025 "Tanya") ... 5-10 62
CHIEF (7031 "Rockin' with the Kid") ... 15-25 61
C.J. (613 "Do the Chicken") ... 15-25 61
C.J. (643 "Chicken") ... 25-35 65
CUCA (1194 "Bertha") ... 30-40 64
CUCA (1445 "Dust My Broom") ... 10-15 69
CUCA (6793 "Dynamite") ... 10-15 67
JIM KO ... 10-15 65
KING (4600 "Race Track") ... 300-400 53
MEL (1005 "Messing with the Kid") ... 10-20 64
MEL-LON (1000 "Want You to Rock") ... 10-20 64
MEL-LON (1001 "The Leading Brand") ... 10-20 64
ROCKIN' (513 "Sweet Angel") ... 300-400 53
SUE (392 "Calling All Blues") ... 10-15 65

LPs: 10/12-inch

ARHOOLIE ... 8-10 70-73
BLUES ON BLUE ... 8-10
BLUESWAY (6032 "Don't Have to Worry") ... 8-10 69
BLUESWAY (6047 "Memorial Album") ... 8-10 70
BLUESWAY (6072 "Do You Remember the Great E.H.") ... 8-10 73
BLUE THUMB ... 12-18 68
CUCA (4100 "Genius of Earl Hooker") ... 10-15 65
Session: Earl Tidwell; Freddie Roulette.
Also see EVERETT, Betty
Also see MEMPHIS SLIM
Also see ROULETTE, Freddie
Also see TAYLOR, Hound Dog / Robert Nighthawk / John Littlejohn / Earl Hooker
Also see WATERS, Muddy

HOOKER, Earl, & A.C. Reed

Singles: 7-inch

AGE (29101 "This Little Voice") ... 20-30 61
Also see REED, A.C.

HOOKER, Earl, & Bobby Saxton

Singles: 7-inch

CHECKER (947 "Trying to Make a Living") ... 30-40 60

HOOKER, Earl / Junior Wells

Singles: 7-inch

CHIEF (7016 "Blues in D Natural") ... 35-45 60
CHIEF (7021 "Universal Rock") ... 15-25 60
CHIEF (7039 "Galloping Horses") ... 20-30 61
Also see HOOKER, Earl
Also see WELLS, Junior

HOOKER, John Lee R&B '49

Singles: 78 rpm

CHART ... 10-20 53
CHESS (1505 "High Priced Woman") ... 50-75 52
CHESS (1513 "Sugar Mama") ... 25-50 52
CHESS (1562 "It's My Own Fault") ... 20-30 54
JVB ... 20-30 53
MODERN ... 30-60 48-56
REGAL ... 40-60 50-51
SENSATION ... 25-40 49-50
SPECIALTY (528 "Everybody's Blues") ... 30-40 54
VEE-JAY ... 10-20 55-60

Singles: 7-inch

ABC ... 4-6 71-73
BATTLE (45901 "No More Doggin' ") ... 15-25 62
BLUESWAY (61010 "Motor City Is Burning") ... 5-10 67
BLUESWAY (61014 "Mr. Lucky") ... 5-10 68
BLUESWAY (61017 "Think Twice Before You Go") ... 5-10 68
BLUESWAY (61023 "Simply the Truth") ... 5-10 69
CHESS (1505 "High Priced Woman") ... 200-300 52
CHESS (1513 "Sugar Mama") ... 50-100 52
CHESS (1562 "It's My Own Fault") ... 100-150 54
CHESS (1965 "In the Mood") ... 5-10 66
ELMOR (303 "Blues for Christmas") ... 10-20 61
FEDERAL (12377 "Late Last Night") ... 10-20 60
FORTUNE (853 "Cry Baby") ... 10-20 60
GALAXY (716 "I Lost My Job") ... 10-15 63
HI-Q (5018 "Big Fine Woman") ... 15-25 61
IMPULSE (242 "Honey") ... 5-8 66
JVB (30 "Boogie Rambler") ... 150-250 53
JEWEL (824 "I Feel Good") ... 4-6 71
JEWEL (852 "Stand By") ... 4-6 77
KENT (332 "Boogie Chillen") ... 10-15 60
KING (6298 "Moanin' and Stompin' Blues") ... 4-6 70
LAUREN (361 "Mojo Hand") ... 10-15 61
MODERN (835 "How Can You Do It") ... 200-300 51
(Red label.)
MODERN (862 "Cold Chills All Over Me") ... 50-100 52
MODERN (886 "Bluebird Blues") ... 50-100 52
MODERN (893 "New Boogie Chillen") ... 50-100 52
MODERN (897 "Rock House Boogie") ... 50-100 53
MODERN (901 "It's a Stormin' and Rainin' ") ... 40-80 53
MODERN (908 "Love Money Can't Buy") ... 40-80 53
MODERN (916 "Too Much Boogie") ... 40-80 53
MODERN (923 "Down Child") ... 125-150 54
MODERN (931 "I Wonder Little Darling") ... 40-80 54
MODERN (935 "I Tried Hard") ... 35-50 54
MODERN (942 "Cool Little Car") ... 35-50 54
MODERN (948 "Half a Stranger") ... 35-50 55
MODERN (958 "You Receive Me") ... 35-50 55
MODERN (966 "Hug & Squeeze") ... 35-50 55
MODERN (978 "Lookin' for a Woman") ... 50-75 56
PLANET (114 "Don't Be Messing with My Bread") ... 5-10 66
SPECIALTY (528 "Everybody's Blues") ... 35-50 54
STAX (0053 "Slow and Easy") ... 5-10 69
VEE-JAY (164 "Mambo Chillun") ... 35-50 55
VEE-JAY (188 "Every Night") ... 35-50 56
VEE-JAY (205 "Baby Lee") ... 35-50 56
VEE-JAY (233 "I'm So Worried, Baby") ... 40-60 57
VEE-JAY (245 "I'm So Excited") ... 25-40 57
VEE-JAY (255 "Little Wheel") ... 25-40 57
VEE-JAY (265 "You Can Lead Me, Baby") ... 25-40 58
VEE-JAY (293 "I Love You Honey") ... 25-40 58
VEE-JAY (308 "Maudie") ... 25-40 59
VEE-JAY (319 "Tennessee Blues") ... 25-40 59
VEE-JAY (331 "Crawlin' Kingsnake") ... 25-40 59
VEE-JAY (349 "Solid Sender") ... 25-40 60
VEE-JAY (366 "Dusty Road") ... 25-40 60
VEE-JAY (397 "Want Ad Blues") ... 25-40 60
VEE-JAY (438 "Boom Boom") ... 20-30 62
VEE-JAY (453 "She's Mine") ... 20-30 62
VEE-JAY (493 "Frisco Blues") ... 20-30 63
VEE-JAY (538 "I'm Leaving") ... 20-30 63
VEE-JAY (575 "Send Me Your Pillow") ... 20-30 64
VEE-JAY (670 "Big Legs, Tight Skirt") ... 20-30 65
VEE-JAY (708 "It Serves Me Right") ... 20-30 65

EPs: 7-inch

IMPULSE ... 10-15 66
(Juke box issue only. Includes title strips.)

LPs: 10/12-inch

ABC (720 "Endless Boogie") ... 15-25 70
(Two discs.)
ABC (736 "Never Get Out of These Blues Alive") ... 10-20 72
ABC (761 "Soledad On My Mind") ... 10-20 72
ABC (768 "Born in Mississippi, Raised Up in Tennessee") ... 10-20 73
ABC (838 "Free Beer & Chicken") ... 10-20 74
ARCHIVE OF FOLK MUSIC (222 "John Lee Hooker") ... 10-12 68
ATCO (151 "Don't Turn Me from Your Door") ... 20-25 63
(Monaural.)
ATCO (SD-151 "Don't Turn Me from Your Door") ... 25-30 63
(Stereo.)
ATLANTIC (7228 "Blues Originals, Vol. 5 – Detroit Special") ... 8-10 72
BATTLE (6113 "John Lee Hooker") ... 30-50 60
BLUESWAY (6002 "Live At Café Au-Go-Go") ... 25-35 66
BLUESWAY (6012 "Urban Blues") ... 15-25 68
BLUESWAY (6023 "Simply the Truth") ... 15-25 69
BLUESWAY (6038 "If You Miss 'Im") ... 15-25 70
BLUESWAY (6052 "Live At Kabuki Wuki") ... 15-25 73
BRYLEN ... 5-10 84
BUDDAH (4002 "The Very Best of John Lee Hooker") ... 15-20 69
BUDDAH (7506 "Big Band Blues") ... 15-20 69
CHAMELEON ... 5-8 89
CHESS (1438 "House of the Blues") ... 200-300 61
CHESS (1454 "John Lee Hooker Plays and Sings the Blues") ... 200-300 61
CHESS (1508 "Real Folk Blues of John Lee Hooker") ... 15-20 66
CHESS (9000 series) ... 8-10
CHESS (60011 "Mad Man Blues") ... 10-15
(Two discs.)
CROWN (5157 "The Blues") ... 25-35 60
CROWN (5232 "John Lee Hooker Sings the Blues") ... 20-30 62
CROWN (5295 "Folk Blues") ... 15-25 63
CROWN (5353 "The Great John Lee Hooker") ... 15-25 63
CUSTOM (2048 "Driftin' Through the Blues") ... 10-15
EVEREST (347 "Hooked On the Blues") ... 5-10 79
EVEREST (369 "John Lee Hooker Sings John Lee Hooker") ... 5-8 83
EXODUS (325 "Is He the World's Greatest Blues Singer") ... 8-10
FANTASY (24706 "Boogie Chillun") ... 10-15 72
(Two discs.)
FANTASY (24722 "Black Snake") ... 5-10 77
(Two discs.)
GNP (10007 "Best Of") ... 10-15 74
(Two discs.)
GALAXY (201 "John Lee Hooker") ... 20-30 63
GALAXY (8205 "Live At Sugarhill") ... 100-150 '60s
(Stereo. White label promotional issue.)
GREEN BOTTLE (3130 "Johnny Lee") ... 10-15 72
(Two discs.)
IMPULSE (9103 "It Serves Me Right to Suffer") ... 12-15 66
JEWEL (5005 "I Feel Good") ... 10-12 71
KENT (559 "Greatest Hits") ... 10-12 71
KING (727 "John Lee Hooker Sings Blues") ... 50-75 61
KING (1085 "Moanin' and Stompin' Blues") ... 10-12 70
MCA (1365 "Jazz Heritage – Lonesome Mood") ... 5-10 83
MUSE (5205 "Sittin' Here Thinkin' ") ... 5-10 80
RIVERSIDE (321 "That's My Story") ... 100-150 60
RIVERSIDE (838 "Folk-Blues") ... 100-150 60
SPECIALTY (2125 "Alone") ... 10-15 70
(Black and gold label.)
SPECIALTY ... 5-10 88
(Black and white label.)
STAX (2013 "That's Where It's At") ... 10-12 69
STAX (4134 "That's Where It's At") ... 8-10 79
TOMATO (7009 "The Cream") ... 8-12 78
(Two discs.)
TRADITION (2089 "Real Blues") ... 10-12 69
TRIP (16-46 "16 Greatest Hits") ... 8-12 78
TRIP (9504 "Whiskey & Wimmen") ... 10-15 73
(Two discs.)
UNITED (7725 "The Blues") ... 10-12
UNITED (7729 "Folk Blues") ... 10-12
UNITED (7731 "The Great Blues Sound of John Lee Hooker") ... 10-12
UNITED (7746 "Greatest Hits") ... 10-12
UNITED (7769 "Original Folk Blues") ... 10-12
U.A. (5512 "Coast to Coast Blues Band") 12-15 71
U.A. (LA127-J "John Lee Hooker's Detroit") ... 15-20 73
(Three discs.)
VEE-JAY (1007 "I'm John Lee Hooker") ... 40-60 59
(Maroon label.)
VEE-JAY (1007 "I'm John Lee Hooker") ... 20-30 61
(Black label.)
VEE-JAY (1023 "Travelin' ") ... 30-40 60
VEE-JAY (1033 "Folk Lore Of") ... 30-40 61
VEE-JAY (1043 "Burnin' ") ... 30-40 62
VEE-JAY (1049 "Best Of") ... 15-25 62
VEE-JAY (1058 "Big Soul Of") ... 15-25 63
VEE-JAY (1066 "On Campus") ... 15-25 63
VEE-JAY (1078 "At Newport") ... 15-25 64
VERVE FOLKWAYS (3003 "And Seven Nights") ... 10-15 66
WAND (689 "On the Waterfront") ... 10-12 70
Also see BIG MACEO & JOHN LEE HOOKER
Also see BIRMINGHAM SAM & HIS MAGIC GUITAR
Also see BOOGIE MAN
Also see BOOKER, John Lee
Also see COOKER, John Lee
Also see COTTON, Sylvester
Also see DELTA JOHN
Also see GROUNDHOGS
Also see JOHN LEE
Also see JOHNNY LEE
Also see LITTLE PORK CHOPS
Also see MARTHA & VANDELLAS
Also see McGHEE, Sticks / John Lee Hooker
Also see MEMPHIS SLIM
Also see TEXAS SLIM
Also see WILLIAMS, Johnny

HOOKER, John Lee, & Canned Heat LP '71

Singles: 7-inch

U.A. (50779 "Let's Make It") ... 4-6 71

LPs: 10/12-inch

LIBERTY (35002 "Hooker 'N Heat") ... 10-15 71
(Two discs.)
RHINO ... 5-10 82
TRIP ... 5-10 74
Also see CANNED HEAT

HOOKER, John Lee / Lightnin' Hopkins / J. Carroll

LPs: 10/12-inch

GUEST STAR ... 15-20 64
Also see HOPKINS, Lightnin'

HOOKER, John Lee, & Little Eddie Kirkland

Singles: 78 rpm

MODERN (876 "It's Hurts Me So") ... 15-25 52

Singles: 7-inch

MODERN (876 "It's Hurts Me So") ... 40-60 52

HOOKER, John Lee / Eddie Kirkland / Eddie Burns / Sylvester Cotton

LPs: 10/12-inch

UNITED (7783 "Detroit Blues") ... 10-20
Also see BURNS, Eddie
Also see COTTON, Sylvester
Also see HOOKER, John Lee
Also see KIRKLAND, Eddie

HOOKS BROTHERS

Singles: 7-inch

HOOKS (526 "Natural Blues") ... 10-20 66
(Colored vinyl.)

HOOPER, Jess, & Daydreamers

Singles: 78 rpm

METEOR (5025 "All Messed Up") ... 100-200 56

Singles: 7-inch

METEOR (5025 "All Messed Up") ... 1000-1500 56
Session: Billy Lee Riley.
Also see RILEY, Billy Lee

HOOPER, Larry
(Lawrence Welk Presents Larry Hooper)

Singles: 78 rpm

BRUNSWICK ... 5-10 57
CORAL (61763 "Roger Boom") ... 10-15 56

Singles: 7-inch

BRUNSWICK ... 5-10 57
CORAL (61763 "Roger Boom") ... 15-25 56
(Orange label.)
CORAL (61763 "Roger Boom") ... 25-45 56
(Blue label. Promotional issue only.)
Also see WELK, Lawrence, & His Orchestra

HOOTCH

LPs: 10/12-inch

PROGRESS (4844 "Hootch") ... 200-300 74

HOPE, Bob — LP '76

Singles: 78 rpm

CAPITOL ... 3-5 52
RCA ... 3-5 56
("The Paleface") ... 75-100 44
(Label name and selection number not known. Santa Claus-shaped cardboard. Promotional issue only for the film *The Paleface*.)

Singles: 7-inch

CAPITOL ... 5-10 52
RCA ... 5-10 56

LPs: 10/12-inch

CAPITOL ... 5-10 76
DECCA ... 10-20 63
RCA ... 15-25 60
Also see BACKUS, Jim
Also see CROSBY, Bing, & Bob Hope
Also see MARTIN, Dean

HOPE, Dee D.

Singles: 7-inch

JOLUM (100 "California Surfer") ... 30-40 63

HOPE, Eddie, & Mannish Boys

Singles: 78 rpm

MARLIN (804 "A Fool No More") ... 50-75 56

Singles: 7-inch

MARLIN (804 "A Fool No More") ... 100-200 56

HOPE, Lynn — R&B '50
(Lynn Hope Quintet)

Singles: 78 rpm

ALADDIN ... 15-25 54-56
CHESS (1499 "Stardust") ... 5-10 52
PREMIUM (851 "Tenderly") ... 10-20 50
PREMIUM (861 "Poinciana") ... 5-10 50
PREMIUM (862 "Mona Lisa") ... 5-10 50

Singles: 7-inch

ALADDIN (Except 3155) ... 15-35 51-56
ALADDIN (3155 "Don't Worry 'Bout Me") ... 75-125 52
CHESS (1499 "Stardust") ... 15-25 52
KING ... 10-15 60

EPs: 7-inch

ALADDIN (505 "Lynn Hope") ... 20-40 55
ALADDIN (512 "Lynn Hope") ... 20-40 55

LPs: 10/12-inch

ALADDIN (707 "Lynn Hope & His Tenor Sax") ... 150-250 55
(10-inch LP.)
ALADDIN (850 "Lynn Hope") ... 100-150 56
IMPERIAL (9177 "Tenderly") ... 15-25 62
(Monaural.)
IMPERIAL (12177 "Tenderly") ... 20-30 62
(Stereo.)
KING (717 "Maharaja of the Saxophone") ... 20-40 61
SCORE (4015 "Tenderly") ... 50-100 57

HOPELESS HOMER

Singles: 78 rpm

GOLDBAND (1040 "New Way of Rockin'") ... 30-50 57

Singles: 7-inch

GOLDBAND (1040 "New Way of Rockin'") ... 100-150 57

HOPKIN, Mary — P&R '68
(Mary Hopkins)

Singles: 7-inch

APPLE/AMERICOM (238 "Those Were the Days") ... 250-350 69
(Four-inch flexi, "pocket disc.")
APPLE ... 5-10 68-72
ESKEE ... 5-10 66
RCA ... 4-6 76

Promotional Singles

ESKEE ... 5-10 66
RCA ... 4-6 76

Picture Sleeves

APPLE ... 5-10 68-70

LPs: 10/12-inch

AIR ... 8-10 72
APPLE ... 15-25 69-72
APPLE/CAPITOL RECORD CLUB (5-3351 "Postcard") ... 30-40 69

HOPKINS, Claude, Quartet

Singles: 78 rpm

RAINBOW ... 10-15 45
Also see COLE, Cozy

HOPKINS, Don

Singles: 7-inch

VANDAN (8030 "Evening in Paris") ... 10-20 '60s
VANDAN (8351 "That's No Way to Treat a Girl") ... 10-20 '60s

HOPKINS, Ford

Singles: 7-inch

APEX (7757 "She Was Not My Kind") ... 10-20

HOPKINS, Jerry

Singles: 7-inch

STARDAY (182 "Mamma Baby") ... 50-75 55

HOPKINS, Lightnin' — R&B '49
(With "His Guitar"; "Singing and Accompanying Himself on Guitar"; Sam "Lightnin'" Hopkins; Lightning Hopkins.)

Singles: 78 rpm

ACE ... 10-20 56
ALADDIN ... 25-50 47-54
CHART (636 "Walkin' the Streets") ... 10-15 55
DECCA ... 10-15 53
GOLD STAR (Except 671) ... 20-40 47-50
GOLD STAR (671 "Henny Penny Blues") ... 400-500 49
HARLEM ... 20-30 54-55
HERALD ... 25-35 54-55
LIGHTNING ... 100-150 55
MERCURY ... 15-25 52
MODERN ... 20-40 47-49
RPM ... 20-40 51-54
SITTIN' IN WITH ... 50-75 51-53
TNT ... 50-75 53-54

Singles: 7-inch

ACE (516 "Bad Boogie") ... 50-75 56
ALADDIN (3063 "Shotgun Blues") ... 100-200 50
ALADDIN (3077 "Moonrise Blues") ... 100-200 50
ALADDIN (3096 "Abilene") ... 100-200 51
ALADDIN (3117 "You Are Not Going to Worry My Life Anymore") ... 100-200 52
ALADDIN (3262 "My California") ... 50-100 54
ARHOOLIE (508 "Mama's Fight") ... 5-10 65
BLUESVILLE (813 thru 817) ... 10-20 61-62
BLUESVILLE (820 thru 823) ... 8-12 62-63
CANDID (603 "Mister Charlie") ... 8-12 62
CHART (636 "Walkin' the Streets") ... 15-25 55
DART (123 "Unsuccessful Blues") ... 10-20 60
DART (152 "Mary Lou") ... 10-20 61
DECCA (28841 "War Is Over") ... 15-25 53
DECCA (48306 "Merry Christmas") ... 15-25 53
DECCA (48312 "Highway Blues") ... 15-25 53
DECCA (48321 "I'm Wild About You, Baby") ... 15-25 53
FIRE (1034 "Mojo Hand") ... 10-20 61
FLASHBACK (18 "Mojo Hand") ... 5-10 65
HARLEM (2321 "Contrary Mary") ... 100-150 54
HARLEM (2324 "Lightnin's Boogie") ... 100-150 54
HARLEM (2331 "Fast Life") ... 100-150 55
HARLEM (2336 "Old Woman Blues") ... 100-150 55
HERALD (425 "Lightnin's Boogie") ... 25-50 54
HERALD (428 "Lightnin's Special") ... 25-50 54
HERALD (436 "Sick Feeling Blues") ... 25-50 54
HERALD (443 "Nothin' But the Blues") ... 25-50 54
HERALD (449 "They Wonder Who I Am") ... 25-50 55
HERALD (456 "My Baby's Gone") ... 25-50 55
HERALD (465 "I Had a Gal Called Sal") ... 25-50 55
HERALD (471 "Hopkins' Sky Hop") ... 25-50 55
HERALD (476 "Grandma's Boogie") ... 25-50 56
HERALD (483 "Finally Met My Baby") ... 25-50 56
HERALD (490 "Sitting & Thinking") ... 25-50 56
HERALD (497 "Remember Me") ... 25-50 57
HERALD (504 "Blues Is a Mighty Bad Feeling") ... 25-50 57
HERALD (520 "My Little Kewpie Doll") ... 25-50 58
HERALD (531 "Lightnin's Stomp") ... 25-50 58
HERALD (542 "Let's Move") ... 20-30 59
HERALD (547 "Gonna Change My Ways") ... 20-30 60
IMPERIAL (5834 "Feel So Bad") ... 10-15 62
IMPERIAL (5852 "Picture on the Wall") ... 10-15 62
INT'L ARTISTS (127 "Baby Child") ... 4-6 68
IVORY ... 8-12 61
JAX (315 "No Good Woman") ... 150-250 53
(Red vinyl.)
JAX (318 "Automobile") ... 150-250 53
(Red vinyl.)
JAX (321 "Contrary Mary") ... 150-250 54
(Red vinyl.)
JAX (661 "Down to the River") ... 150-250 53
(Red vinyl. Jax label has a Sittin' In With number.)
JEWEL ... 5-10 67-71
KIMBERLEY (2017 "If You Steal My Chickens, You Can't Make 'Em Lay") ... 10-20 60
LIGHTNING (104 "Unsuccessful Blues") ... 250-350 55
MERCURY (70081 "Ain't It a Shame") ... 50-75 52
MERCURY (70191 "My Mama Told Me") ... 50-75 52
MERCURY (8274 "Sad News from Korea") ... 50-75 52
MERCURY (8293 "Gone with the Wind") ... 50-75 52
PRESTIGE (326 thru 452) ... 5-10 64-67
RPM (337 "Beggin' You to Stay") ... 50-75 51
RPM (346 "Jake Head Boogie") ... 50-75 52
RPM (351 "Don't Keep My Baby Long") ... 50-75 52
RPM (359 "Needed Time") ... 50-75 52
RPM (378 "Another Fool in Town") ... 50-75 53
RPM (388 "Black Cat") ... 50-75 53
RPM (398 "Sante Fe") ... 50-75 54
SHAD (5011 "Hello Central") ... 10-20 59
SITTIN' IN WITH (621 "New York Boogie") ... 150-250 51
(Red vinyl.)
SITTIN' IN WITH (635 "Coffee Blues") ... 150-250 52
(Red vinyl.)
SITTIN' IN WITH (642 "You Caused My Heart to Weep") ... 50-75 52
(Black vinyl.)
SITTIN' IN WITH (644 "Jailhouse Blues") ... 150-250 52
(Red vinyl.)
SITTIN' IN WITH (647 "Dirty House") ... 150-250 52
(Red vinyl.)
SITTIN' IN WITH (652 "Papa Bones Boogie") ... 150-250 52
(Red vinyl.)
SITTIN' IN WITH (658 "Broken Hearted Blues") ... 150-250 53
(Red vinyl.)
SITTIN' IN WITH (660 "I've Been a Bad Man") ... 150-250 53
(Red vinyl.)
TNT (8002 "Late in the Evening") ... 200-300 54
TNT (8003 "Leavin' Blues") ... 200-300 54
TNT (8010 "Moanin' Blues") ... 200-300 55
VAULT (965 "No Education") ... 4-8 70

Note: There is some confusion regarding Jax and Sittin' In With singles. Some shown here as red vinyl may also exist as black. We have confirmed 642 as black. Additional information will appear as it becomes available.

LPs: 10/12-inch

ARHOOLIE (1034 "The Texas Bluesman") ... 10-15 68
ARHOOLIE (2007 "Early Recordings") ... 8-12
BARNABY (30247 "In New York") ... 8-10 71
BULLDOG (1010 "Live at the Bird Lounge") ... 12-18 65
CANDID (8010 "In New York") ... 20-30 61
(Monaural.)
CANDID (9010 "In New York") ... 25-40 61
(Stereo.)
COLLECTABLES ... 6-8 88
CROWN (5224 "Sings the Blues") ... 20-30 61
DART ... 10-15
EVEREST (241 "Lightnin' Hopkins") ... 10-15 69
EVEREST (342 "Autobiography in Blues") ... 5-10 79
FANTASY (24702 "Double Blues") ... 10-15 72
(Two discs. Gatefold.)
FANTASY (24725 "How Many More Years I Got") ... 8-12 81
(Two discs.)
FIRE (104 "Mojo Hand") ... 750-1000 62
FOLKWAYS (3822 "Lightnin' Hopkins") ... 50-75 59
GUEST STAR (1459 "Live at the Bird Lounge") ... 15-20 64
HARLEM HIT PARADE (5013 "Best Of") ... 5-10
HERALD (1012 "Lightnin' and the Blues") ... 500-1000 60
IMPERIAL (9180 "On Stage") ... 25-50 62
IMPERIAL (9186 "Lightnin' Hopkins Sings the Blues") ... 25-50 62
IMPERIAL (9211 "And the Blues") ... 25-50 62
(Monaural.)
IMPERIAL (12211 "And the Blues") ... 25-50 63
(Stereo.)
INT'L ARTISTS (6 "Free Form Patterns") ... 50-100 68
JAZZ MAN (5502 "Lightnin' Hopkins") ... 5-10 82
JEWEL (5000 "Blue Lightnin'") ... 10-12 67
JEWEL (5001 "Talkin' Some Sense") ... 10-12 68
JEWEL (5002 "Great Electric Show and Dance") ... 10-12 70
MAINSTREAM (311 "The Blues") ... 8-10 71
MAINSTREAM (326 "Dirty Blues") ... 8-10 71
MAINSTREAM (405 "Low Down Dirty Blues") ... 8-10 74
MOUNT VERNON (104 "Nothin' But the Blues") ... 15-20
OLYMPIC (7110 "Blues Giant") ... 8-10 73
PICKWICK ... 8-10
POPPY (60002 "Lightnin'") ... 15-20 69
(Two discs.)
PRESTIGE (7370 "Lightnin' Hopkins") ... 20-25 65
(Two discs.)
PRESTIGE (7377 "Soul Blues") ... 10-20 66
PRESTIGE (7592 "Greatest Hits") ... 10-20 69
PRESTIGE (7714 "Best Of") ... 10-20 69
PRESTIGE (7806 "Hootin the Blues") ... 10-20 70
PRESTIGE (7811 "Lightnin' – The Blues of Lightnin' Hopkins") ... 10-20 70
PRESTIGE (14021 "Hootin' the Blues") ... 10-20 64
PRESTIGE BLUESVILLE (1019 "Lightnin'") ... 30-50 61
PRESTIGE BLUESVILLE (1045 "Blues in My Bottle") ... 20-30 62
(Cover also indicates "OBC-506.")
PRESTIGE BLUESVILLE (1057 "Walkin' This Road By Myself") ... 20-30 62
PRESTIGE BLUESVILLE (1070 "Smokes Like Lightning") ... 15-25 63
PRESTIGE BLUESVILLE (1073 "Goin' Away") ... 15-25 64
PRESTIGE BLUESVILLE (1084 "His Greatest Hits") ... 15-25 64
PRESTIGE BLUESVILLE (1086 "Down Home Blues") ... 15-25 64
RHINO (103 "Los Angeles Blues") ... 5-10 82
SCORE (4022 "Strums the Blues") ... 300-500 59
SOUL PARADE ... 8-10
TIME (1 "Blues-Folk") ... 20-30 61
TIME (3 "More Blues-Folk") ... 20-30 61
TIME (70004 "Last of the Great Blues Singers") ... 25-35 60
TOMATO (7004 "Lightnin'") ... 5-10 77
(Two discs.)
TRADITION (1035 "Country Blues") ... 20-40 59
TRADITION (1040 "Autobiography in Blues") ... 20-40 60
TRADITION (1056 "Best Of") ... 10-15 67
(Monaural.)
TRADITION (2056 "Best Of") ... 10-20 67
(Stereo.)
TRADITION (2103 "Lightnin' Strikes") ... 8-12 72
TRIP (16-48 "16 Greatest Hits") ... 5-10 78
TRIP (8015 "Lightnin' Hopkins") ... 5-10 71
UNITED (7713 "Sings the Blues") ... 10-15
UNITED (7744 "Original Folk Blues") ... 10-15
UNITED (7785 "A Legend in His Time") ... 10-15
UPFRONT ... 8-12
VAULT (129 "California Mudslide") ... 10-15 69
VEE-JAY (1044 "Lightnin' Hopkins") ... 20-30 62
VERVE (8453 "Fast Life Woman") ... 20-30 62
VERVE FOLKWAYS (3013 "Something Blue") ... 10-15 67
VERVE FOLKWAYS (9000 "Roots") ... 12-18 65
VERVE FOLKWAYS (9022 "Lightnin' Strikes") ... 12-18 65
Also see HOOKER, John Lee / Lightnin' Hopkins / Johnny Carroll
Also see THOMAS, Andrew

HOPKINS, Lightnin,' & Sonny Terry

Singles: 7-inch

PRESTIGE BLUESVILLE ... 5-10 61

LPs: 10/12-inch
PRESTIGE BLUESVILLE (101 "Last Night Blues")........................ 30-40 63
PRESTIGE BLUESVILLE (1029 "Last Night Blues")........................ 40-50 61
Also see TERRY, Sonny

HOPKINS, Lightnin' / Brownie McGhee & Sonny Terry
LPs: 10/12-inch
HORIZON (WP-1617 "Blues Hoot")......... 20-25 63
(Monaural.)
HORIZON (ST-1617 "Blues Hoot")......... 25-30 63
(Stereo.)
Also see McGHEE, Brownie, & Sonny Terry

HOPKINS, Lightnin,' & Thunder Smith
Singles: 78 rpm
ALADDIN (165 "West Coast Blues")...... 75-100 47
ALADDIN (167 "Katie Mae Blues")....... 75-100 47
ALADDIN (168 "Feel So Bad")............. 75-100 47
Also see HOPKINS, Lightnin'
Also see SMITH, Thunder

HOPKINS, Linda
Singles: 12-inch
COLUMBIA....................................4-8 77
Singles: 7-inch
AMPEX (11008 "Walk Him Up the Stairs")...4-6 70
ATCO (6096 "Shiver and Shake")........... 15-25 57
ATCO (6154 "Sentimental Fool")............ 10-15 59
BRUNSWICK....................................6-12 61-65
COLUMBIA.......................................4-6 75
FEDERAL (12365 "Danny Boy")............. 10-15 59
RCA (0746 "Shake a Hand")....................4-6 72
LPs: 10/12-inch
COLUMBIA.......................................5-10 76
PALO ALTO.......................................5-10 83
RCA (4756 "Linda Hopkins")....................8-10 72
Also see WILSON, Jackie, & Linda Hopkins

HOPPI & BEAU HEEMS
Singles: 7-inch
LAURIE (3411 "So Hard")....................... 15-20 67
LAURIE (3439 "When I Get Home")........ 10-20 68

HORIZONS
Singles: 7-inch
REGINA (1321 "Hey Now Baby")............ 10-15 64

HORLICK, Maynard, & Hep Teens
Singles: 7-inch
V-I-R (7163 "Rollin' on Down the Street").. 300-400 57
Also see MAYNIE & HOWIE

HORN, Paul R&B '78
Singles: 7-inch
EPIC (11144 "Blue")...............................4-6 74
MUSHROOM......................................4-6 78
PARAMOUNT......................................4-6 72
LPs: 10/12-inch
COLUMBIA (36803 "Jingle Bell Jazz").........5-8 85
COLUMBIA (1677 thru 2050)................. 20-30 61-63
(Monaural.)
COLUMBIA (8477 thru 8850)................. 25-35 61-63
(Stereo.)
DOT (3091 "House of Horn")................... 40-60 57
DOT (9002 "Plenty of Horn")................... 40-60 58
EPIC..6-12 69-76
EVEREST...5-10 75
GPB...5-8 87
HI-FI JAZZ (615 "Something Blue")......... 30-50 60
IMPULSE...5-10 78
KUCKUCK..5-10 80-88
MUSHROOM......................................5-10 77-78
OVATION...8-12 70
RCA (3414 thru 3613).......................... 15-25 65-66
(With "LPM" prefix. Monaural.)
RCA (3414 thru 3613).......................... 15-30 65-66
(With "LSP" prefix. Stereo.)
SHELTER..8-12 71
WHO'S WHO IN JAZZ............................5-8 86-88
WORLD PACIFIC (Except 1266)............. 10-20 67-68
WORLD PACIFIC (1266 "Impressions").. 30-50 59
Also see TJADER, Cal

HORNE, Jimmy "Bo" R&B '75
Singles: 12-inch
SUNSHINE SOUND..............................4-8 79
Singles: 7-inch
ALSTON...4-6 72-77
DADE (235 "I Can't Speak")....................35-55 '60s
(At least one source shows this number as 2031. We don't know yet who's right.)
SUNSHINE SOUND..............................3-6 77-80
LPs: 10/12-inch
SUNSHINE SOUND..............................5-10 78-80

HORNE, Lena P&R '43
Singles: 78 rpm
RCA...3-5 52-57
Singles: 7-inch
BUDDAH..4-6 71
CHARTER (3 "Why Was I Born")...............4-8 63
DRG...3-5 86
GRYPHON...4-6 76
MCA...4-6 78
RCA (4000 thru 7000 series)..................5-10 52-61
20TH FOX...4-8 63-64
U.A..4-6 65-66
Picture Sleeves
RCA...8-12 62
EPs: 7-inch
MGM...5-10 54-55
RCA...5-10 56-59
LPs: 10/12-inch
BUDDAH..5-10 71
CAMDEN..10-20 56
CHARTER...10-15 63
CORONET...5-10
DRG...5-10 86
GOLDEN TONE....................................5-10
GRYPHON...5-10 75-76
LIBERTY..5-8 81
MFSL (094 "Lady & Her Music")..............30-40 82
MGM...15-30 54-55
POLYDOR...4-8
QWEST..5-10 81
RCA (Except 4300 series).....................10-30 52-63
RCA (4300 series)...............................4-8 81
RADIO CRAFTSMEN..............................10-20
SPRINGBOARD....................................4-8 77
TOPS..10-20 57
20TH FOX...8-15 64
U.A..8-15 65-66
Also see BELAFONTE, Harry, & Lena Horne
Also see FITZGERALD, Ella / Billie Holiday / Lena Horne
Also see FITZGERALD, Ella / Teddy Wilson / Lena Horne

HORNE, Lena, & Michel Legrand
LPs: 10/12-inch
GRYPHON...5-10 75
Also see LEGRAND, Michel

HORNE, Lena, & Gabor Szabo LP '70
(Lena & Gabor)
Singles: 7-inch
SKYE (4523 "Rocky Raccoon")..................4-6 70
LPs: 10/12-inch
SKYE (15 "Lena & Gabor")......................8-15 70
Also see HORNE, Lena
Also see SZABO, Gabor

HORNER, Jack
Singles: 7-inch
TREL (101 "If I Can")............................100-200

HORNETS
(Hornets & Orchestra)
Singles: 78 rpm
STATES (127 "I Can't Believe")....... 1000-2000 53
Singles: 7-inch
STATES (127 "I Can't Believe")....... 4000-6000 53
(Black vinyl.)
STATES (127 "I Can't Believe")..... 7500-10000 53
(Red vinyl.)
The wide price range here reflects both one known sale of, and one offer which was declined for the red vinyl pressing – though our valuation isn't quite as high as the 1988 sale price.
Members: James "Sonny" Long; Johnny Moore; Ben Iverson; Gus Miller.
Also see DRIFTERS
Also see IVERSON, Ben, & Hornets

HORNETS
Singles: 78 rpm
FLASH (125 "Crying Over You")..............50-75 57
Singles: 7-inch
FLASH (125 "Crying Over You")..........100-200 57

HORNETS
Singles: 7-inch
REV (3515 "Slow Dance").......................30-40 58

HORNETS
Singles: 7-inch
LIBERTY (55688 "Motorcycle U.S.A.").....10-15 64
LPs: 10/12-inch
LIBERTY..25-35 63-64

HORNETS
Singles: 7-inch
COLUMBIA (42999 "Fruit Cake")............15-25 64
V.I.P. (25004 "She's My Baby")...............25-35 64

HORNETS
Singles: 7-inch
EMERALD (501 "Runt").........................20-30

HORSEHAIRS
LPs: 10/12-inch
SHOWTOWN (5149 "Bach '69")..............10-15 69

HORSES
Singles: 7-inch
WHITE WHALE (301 "Class of '69")..........5-10 69
WHITE WHALE (320 "Freight Train").........5-10 69
LPs: 10/12-inch
WHITE WHALE (7121 "Horses").............25-35 70

HORTON, Big Walter
(With His Combo)
Singles: 78 rpm
COBRA (5002 "Have a Good Time").......20-30 54
Singles: 7-inch
COBRA (5002 "Have a Good Time").....75-100 54
LPs: 10/12-inch
ALLIGATOR.......................................10-20 72
ARGO..15-20 68
Also see BELL, Carey
Also see BIG WALTER
Also see HORTON, Shakey
Also see JIMMY & WALTER
Also see MUMBLES
Also see ROGERS, Jimmy
Also see SHINES, Johnny, & Big Walter Horton
Also see SUNNYLAND SLIM
Also see TAYLOR, Koko
Also see WATERS, Muddy

HORTON, Bill
(With the Silhouettes: with Dawns; Billy Horton)
Singles: 7-inch
ACE (563 "Never Will Part")...................75-125 59
KAYDEN (403 "I Wanna Know")..............10-20
LAWN (241 "Like to See You in That Mood")...30-50 64
Members: Bill Horton; Joe Moody; Robert Byrd.
Also see SILHOUETTES

HORTON, J.D.
Singles: 78 rpm
BULLET (350 "Cadillac Blues")..............50-100 52

HORTON, Jamie P&R '60
Singles: 7-inch
ERIC (118 "My Little Marine").....................4-8 68
JOY (234 "My Little Marine")..................10-15 59
JOY (237 "Heartbreakin' Doll")...............10-15 60
JOY (241 "Robot Man")..........................10-20 60
JOY (245 "Hands Off, He's Mine")...........10-20 60
JOY (252 thru 269)...............................10-15 61-62
Session: Boots Randolph.
Also see RANDOLPH, Boots

HORTON, Jay
Singles: 7-inch
MUSTANG (3010 "I Trip on You Girl").....20-25 65
MUSTANG (3021 "It's Love")..................10-15 66
Also see FULLER, Bobby

HORTON, Johnny C&W '56
Singles: 78 rpm
ABBOTT...15-25 51-52
COLUMBIA..10-25 56-57
CORMAC..25-50 51
MERCURY...10-20 54-55
Singles: 7-inch
ABBOTT (100 thru 109)..........................20-30 51-52
ABBOTT (135 "Plaid & Calico")...............15-20 53
CORMAC (1193 "Plaid & Calico")..........75-100 51
CORMAC (1197 "Birds and Butterflies") 75-100 51
COLUMBIA (21504 "Honky Tonk Man")...15-25 56
COLUMBIA (21538 "I'm a One-Woman Man")...15-25 56
COLUMBIA (40813 "I'm Coming Home").15-25 57
COLUMBIA (40919 "She Knows Why")...10-15 57
COLUMBIA (40986 "I'll Do It Every Time")..10-15 57
COLUMBIA (41043 "Lover's Rock").........15-25 57
COLUMBIA (41110 "Honky Tonk Hardwood Floor")...30-50 58
COLUMBIA (41210 "All Grown Up").........10-20 58
COLUMBIA (41308 thru 42302)................8-12 59-62
COLUMBIA (42653 thru 44156)................5-10 63-67
DOT (15996 "Plaid & Calico")....................8-12 59
MERCURY (6412 thru 70707).................15-25 52-55
Picture Sleeves
COLUMBIA (41308 "When It's Springtime in Alaska")...15-25 59
(Blue and white sleeve. Promotional only.)
COLUMBIA (41339 "The Battle of New Orleans")...15-25 59
(Standard sleeve.)
COLUMBIA (41339 "The Battle of New Orleans")...40-60 59
(Fold-out lyrics sleeve. Promotional issue only.)
COLUMBIA (41568 "Sink the Bismarck"). 10-15 60
COLUMBIA (41685 "Johnny Freedom")...10-15 60
COLUMBIA (41782 "North to Alaska").....10-15 60
COLUMBIA (41963 "Sleepy-Eyed John") 10-15 61
COLUMBIA (42302 "Honky Tonk Man")..10-15 62
COLUMBIA (42653 "All Grown Up").........10-15 63
COLUMBIA (42993 "Hooray for That Little Difference")..10-15 64
DOT (15996 "Plaid & Calico")..................10-15 59
EPs: 7-inch
COLUMBIA (2130 "Honky Tonk Man")....25-50 57
COLUMBIA (13621/22/23 "The Spectacular Johnny Horton ")..20-40 60
(Price is for either volume.)
COLUMBIA (14781/82/83 "Johnny Horton Makes History")...20-40 60
(Price is for either volume.)
MERCURY (3091 "Requestfully Yours")..25-50 55
SESAC (1201 "Free and Easy Songs")....30-50 59
LPs: 10/12-inch
BRIAR INT'L (104 "Done Rovin'")........100-150 '60s
COLUMBIA (CL-1362 "The Spectacular Johnny Horton")..20-30 60
(Monaural.)
COLUMBIA (CL-1478 "Johnny Horton Makes History")...20-30 60
(Monaural.)
COLUMBIA (CL-1596 "Johnny Horton's Greatest Hits")..20-30 61
(Monaural. Add $15 to $25 if accompanied by bonus photo.)
COLUMBIA (CL-1721 "Honky Tonk Man")..20-30 62
(Monaural.)
COLUMBIA (CL-2566 "Johnny Horton on the Louisiana Hayride")..20-25 66
(Monaural.)
COLUMBIA (CL-2566 "Johnny Horton on Stage")..10-20 66
(Monaural. Repackage of *Johnny Horton on the Louisiana Hayride.*)
COLUMBIA (CS-8167 "The Spectacular Johnny Horton ")..25-35 60
(Stereo.)
COLUMBIA (CS-8269 "Johnny Horton Makes History")...25-35 60
(Stereo.)
COLUMBIA (CS-8396 "Johnny Horton's Greatest Hits")..25-35 61
(Stereo. Add $15 to $25 if accompanied by bonus photo.)
COLUMBIA (PC-8396 "Johnny Horton's Greatest Hits")..5-10
COLUMBIA (CS-8779 "Honky Tonk Man")..25-35 62
(Stereo.)
COLUMBIA (CS-9099 "I Can't Forget You")...15-20 65
(Stereo.)
COLUMBIA (CS-9366 "Johnny Horton on the Louisiana Hayride")...............................20-25 66
(Stereo.)
COLUMBIA (CS-9366 "Johnny Horton on Stage")..10-15 66
(Stereo. Repackage of *Johnny Horton on the Louisiana Hayride.*)
COLUMBIA (CS-9940 "Johnny Horton on the Road")..10-15 69

COLUMBIA (KG-30884 "The World of Johnny Horton") 15-20 71
COLUMBIA (CG-30884 "The World of Johnny Horton") 10-15
COLUMBIA HOUSE (6418/19 "Johnny Horton, the Legend") 10-15 75
CROWN 10-20 63
CUSTOM .... 10-15 '60s
DOT (3221 "Johnny Horton") 30-50 59
(Monaural.)
DOT (25221 "Johnny Horton") 20-30 66
(Stereo.)
HARMONY (11291 "The Unforgettable Johnny Horton") 10-15 70
HARMONY (11384 "The Legendary Johnny Horton") 10-15 70
HARMONY (30394 "The Battle of New Orleans") 10-15 71
JUKE BOX 5-10
MERCURY (20478 "The Fantastic Johnny Horton") 35-50 59
PICKWICK/HILLTOP (6060 "All for the Love of a Girl") 10-15 65
PICKWICK/HILLTOP (6012 "The Voice of Johnny Horton") 10-15 68
SEARS (110 "Legend of Johnny Horton") .... 10-15 '60s
SESAC (1201 "Free and Easy Songs") . 75-125 59
Also see CLINE, Patsy / Cowboy Copas / Johnny Horton
Also see DEAN, Jimmy / Johnny Horton
Also see PRICE, Ray / Johnny Horton / Carl Smith / George Morgan

HORTON, Johnny / Sonny James

LPs: 10/12-inch

CUSTOM 6-12
Also see JAMES, Sonny

HORTON, Johnny / Texas Slim

LPs: 10/12-inch

CROWN .... 6-12 '60s
Also see HORTON, Johnny

HORTON, Shakey
(Walter Horton)

Singles: 78 rpm

COBRA 20-30 54

Singles: 7-inch

ARGO (5476 "Good Moanin' Blues") 5-10 64
COBRA (5002 "Have a Good Time") 75-100 56

LPs: 10/12-inch

ARGO (4037 "The Soul of Blues Harmonica") 25-35 64
Also see HORTON, Big Walter

HORTON, Willie
(With the Supremes)

Singles: 7-inch

CITY OF DETROIT (1900 "Detroit Is Happening") 100-200 67
(Promotional issue only.)
Also see SUPREMES

HOSEA, Don

Singles: 7-inch

CRYSTAL (501 "Everlasting Love") 100-150 58
RITA (1010 "John Henry") 10-20 60
SUN (368 "Since I Met You") 10-20 61

HOSS, Charlie, & Ponies

Singles: 7-inch

COLUMBIA (41855 "Madison Twist") 10-15 60
COLUMBIA (3-41855 "Madison Twist") ... 20-30 60
(Compact 33.)
Also see SINGLETON, Charlie

HOT DOG STAND

Singles: 7-inch

MALA (12014 "C'mon Summer's Happening") 10-20 68

HOT DOGGERS

LPs: 10/12-inch

EPIC (24054 "Surfin' U.S.A.") 50-75 63
(Monaural.)
EPIC (26054 "Surfin' U.S.A.") 75-100 63
(Stereo.)
Member: Bruce Johnston.
Also see JOHNSTON, Bruce

HOT HALF DOZEN

Singles: 7-inch

DUNWICH (134 "Angels Listened In") 40-60 65

SOMA 12-18 65
Also see DONN E. & KOSTIRS

HOT PEPPERS

Singles: 7-inch

BISCAYNE (001 "The Turnpike") 10-20 63
SEA-HORN (501 "New Orleans Surf") 15-25 63

HOT POOP

LPs: 10/12-inch

HOT POOP (3072 "Hot Poop Does Their Own Stuff!") 300-400 71
(500 made.)
Member: Thomas "Johnny Rockaway" Burke; Larry "Honyock" Praissman; Bruce "Flash Hammer" Lyons; Jim "Gabor Kovats" Anderson; Lisa "Gwendolyn Glopenstein" Hebard.
Session: J.A. Hurley.

HOT PROPERTY
(Magnificents)

Singles: 7-inch

CREW ("Too Hard to Handle") 15-20 68
(Promotional issue only.)
Also see MAGNIFICENTS

HOT ROD HAPPY
(James Bledsoe)

Singles: 78 rpm

PACEMAKER (1014 "Hot Rod Boogie") . 75-125 50
Also see COUNTRY JIM

HOT RODDERS

LPs: 10/12-inch

CROWN 15-25 63

HOT SOUP

Singles: 7-inch

RAMA RAMA (7775 "You Took Me By Surprise") 10-15 69

LPs: 10/12-inch

RAMA RAMA ("Hot Soup") 25-35 69
(Selection number not known.)

HOT TAMALES

Singles: 7-inch

ALPINE (68 "Mexican Twist") 5-10 60
DETROIT 4-8 64
DIAMOND (101 "Mr. Starlight") 15-25 66
DIAMOND (410 "Mr. Starlight") .... 5-10 '60s
PAC (3500 "No Help Wanted") 10-15 65
PAC (3501 "Hot Tamale") 10-20 65

HOT TODDYS — P&R '59
(Featuring Bill Pernell; Hot-Toddys)

Singles: 7-inch

BARREL (602 "Rockin' Crickets") 20-30 59
(Canadian.)
CORSICAN (0056 "Rockin' Crickets") 15-25 59
SHAN-TODD (0056 "Rockin' Crickets") 15-25 59
STRAND (25011 "Hoe-Down") 10-15 60
(Issued with two different flip sides.)
SWAN (4140 "Rockin' Crickets") 10-20 63
(Later issued as by the Rockin' Rebels.)
Also see ROCKIN' REBELS
Also see VINCENT, Rudy, Jr.

HOULE BROTHERS

Singles: 7-inch

CIRCLE DOT (1013 "Dream Night") 200-250

HOUND DOG CLOWNS

Singles: 7-inch

UNI (55047 "Superfox") 10-15 68

HOUND DOGS

Singles: 7-inch

DEE DEE (733 "I'm Beginning to Understand Them") 40-50 64

HOUND DOGS

Singles: 7-inch

HOUND DOG (1001 "Hound Dog Boogie") 100-150

HOUNDS

Singles: 7-inch

LARK (9003 "I'm Comin' Home") 10-15 60

HOUR GLASS
(Greg Allman & Hour Glass)

Singles: 7-inch

LIBERTY (56002 thru 56091) 10-15 67-69

Picture Sleeves

LIBERTY (56002 "Nothing But Tears") 40-60 67

LPs: 10/12-inch

LIBERTY 15-20 67-68
U.A. 10-15 73
Members: Duane Allman; Gregg Allman.
Also see ALLMAN BROTHERS BAND

HOUSE OF LORDS

Singles: 7-inch

BVA (101 "Last Stand") 15-25 67

HOUSE ROCKERS

Singles: 7-inch

FUN (102 "Say You'll Be Mine") 1000-2000

HOUSEHOLD SPONGE

Singles: 7-inch

MURBO (1017 "Scars") 15-25 67

HOUSTON, Cissy — R&B '70
(Sissie Houston; Cissie Houston)

Singles: 7-inch

COLUMBIA 3-6 79-80
COMMONWEALTH UNITED (3010 "I'll Be There") 4-8 70
CONGRESS (268 "Bring Him Back") 30-50 66
JANUS 4-6 70-75
KAPP (814 "Don't Come Running to Me") 15-25 67
PRIVATE STOCK 4-6 77-79

LPs: 10/12-inch

COLUMBIA 5-10 79-80
JANUS 8-10 70
PRIVATE STOCK 5-10 77-78
Also see BOWIE, David
Also see MANN, Herbie, & Cissy Houston
Also see SWEET INSPIRATIONS

HOUSTON, David — C&W '63
(With Calvin Crawford; with Sherri Jerrico)

Singles: 78 rpm

IMPERIAL 8-12 55
RCA (6611 "Sugar Sweet") 8-12 56
RCA (6696 "Blue Prelude") 8-12 56
RCA (6927 "One and Only") 15-25 57
RCA (7001 "Teenage Frankie and Johnny") 15-25 57

Singles: 7-inch

BLACK ROSE 3-5 82
COLONIAL 4-6 78
COUNTRY INT'L 3-5 80
DERRICK 4-6 79
ELEKTRA 4-6 78-79
EXCELSIOR 3-5 81
EPIC 4-8 63-76
IMPERIAL 10-20 55
NRC (005 "Waited So Long") 15-25 58
NRC (012 "The Key") 15-25 58
NRC (047 "It's Been So Long") 15-25 59
PHILLIPS INT'L (3583 "Sherry's Lips") 5-10 63
RCA (6611 "Sugar Sweet") 10-20 56
RCA (6696 "Blue Prelude") 10-20 56
RCA (6927 "One and Only") 30-40 57
RCA (7001 "Teenage Frankie and Johnny") 15-25 57
SOUNDWAVES 3-5 83
STARDAY 4-6 77
SUN (403 "Sherry's Lips") 5-10 66
SUN (1100 series) 4-6 72

Picture Sleeves

EPIC 5-10 66-69

LPs: 10/12-inch

CAMDEN 8-12 66
COLUMBIA 6-10 73
DELTA 5-10 82
EPIC 5-15 64-76
EXACT 5-10 80
EXCELSIOR 5-10 81
51 WEST 5-10 84
GUEST STAR 6-12 64
GUSTO 5-10 78
HARMONY 8-12 70-72
STARDAY 6-10 77
Session: Jordanaires.
Also see DEAN, Jimmy / David Houston / Warner Mack / Autry Inman
Also see JAMES, Sonny / David Houston
Also see JERRICO, Sherri
Also see JONES, George / David Houston / Sonny James
Also see JONES, George / Buck Owens / David Houston / Tommy Hill.
Also see JORDANAIRES
Also see WAGONER, Porter / David Houston

HOUSTON, David, & Barbara Mandrell — C&W '70

Singles: 7-inch

EPIC 4-6 70-74

LPs: 10/12-inch

EPIC 8-15 72-75
Also see MANDRELL, Barbara

HOUSTON, David, & Tammy Wynette — C&W '68

Singles: 7-inch

EPIC 4-6 67

LPs: 10/12-inch

EPIC 8-12 67
51 WEST 5-10 82
Also see HOUSTON, David
Also see WYNETTE, Tammy

HOUSTON, Eddie

Singles: 7-inch

CAPITOL (2170 "That's How Much") 15-25 68
CAPITOL (2397 "I Won't Be the Last to Cry") 15-25 69
OVATION (1051 "Knock and the Door Shall Be Opened") 8-10 78

HOUSTON, Freddie

Singles: 7-inch

CAPTAIN (692 "Willing to Try") 10-20 62
CARLTON (542 "Do You Feel It") 10-20 61
CARLTON (550 "Only Me") 10-20 61
OLD TOWN (1153 "Chills and Fever") 10-20 63
OLD TOWN (1156 "Only the Lonely One") 25-50 64
TOTO (101 "Soft Walkin'") 15-25 62
WHIZ-ON (7 "True") .... 15-25 '60s

HOUSTON, Joe — R&B '52
(With His Rockets; Mighty Joe Houston; Fabulous Joe Houston; Joe Houston Orchestra)

Singles: 78 rpm

BAYOU 10-15 53
CASH 10-15 55-56
COMBO 10-20 51-57
CROWN 10-20 56
FREEDOM (1526 "It's Really Wee Wee Hours") 30-40 49
FREEDOM (1535 "Jumping the Blues") ... 30-40 50
IMPERIAL 10-20 52-55
LUCKY 10-20 54
MACY'S (5017 "Cornbread and Cabbage Greens") 20-30 51
MERCURY (8248 "Worry, Worry, Worry") 10-20 51
MODERN 10-15 51-52
MONEY 10-15 55
RPM 10-15 55
RECORDED IN HOLLYWOOD 10-20 52-53
SPHINX (122 "Worry, Worry, Worry") 25-35 51

Singles: 7-inch

BAYOU (004 "Moody") 15-25 53
BAYOU (012 "Chittlin'") 15-25 53
BAYOU (015 "Blues Jump the Rabbit") 15-25 53
BAYOU (017 "Scramble") 15-25 53
BIG TOWN 4-6 79
CASH (1013 "Flying Home") 15-25 55
CASH (1018 "Rockin' 'N' Boppin'") 15-25 56
COMBO (6 thru 54) 15-25 51-55
COMBO (116 thru 185) 10-15 56-61
CROWN (102 "Hum Bug") 15-25 56
CROWN (109 "Dear Mom") 15-25 56
DOOTO (439 "Shindig") 15-25 58
IMPERIAL (5183 "Jumping the Blues") 20-30 52
IMPERIAL (5196 "Bobby Sox Ramble") ... 20-30 52
IMPERIAL (5201 "Earthquake") 20-30 52
IMPERIAL (5213 "Atom Bomb") 20-30 53
IMPERIAL (5334 "Tough Enough") 20-30 55
KEM (2761 "Ko Ko Mo") 8-12 61
KEM (2762 "Hush Your Mouth") 8-12 61
KENT (366 "Doing the Twist") 8-12 62
LUCKY (004 "Go, Joe, Go") 20-30 54
MAGNUM 10-20 64-65
MERCURY (8248 "Worry, Worry, Worry") 25-35 51
MODERN (830 "Blow Joe, Blow") 30-50 51
MODERN (850 "Have a Ball") 20-30 52
MODERN (863 "Doin' the Lindy Hop") 20-30 52
MODERN (879 "Boogie Woogie Woman") 20-30 52
MODERN (917 "Blowin' Crazy") 20-30 52

MONEY (203 "All Nite Long") 15-25 54
MONEY (207 "Celebrity Club Stomp") 15-25 55
RPM (422 "Celebrity Club Stomp") 10-20 55
RPM (426 "Joe's Gone") 15-25 55
RPM (427 "Riverside Rock") 15-25 55
RECORDED IN HOLLYWOOD (203 "All Night Long") 25-35 52
RECORDED IN HOLLYWOOD (423 "Jay's Boogie") 20-30 53
RONNEX (1103 "All Night Long") 15-25 55

EPs: 7-inch

COMBO (3 "Joe Houston") 50-75 54
COMBO (10 "Joe Houston") 50-75 55
MODERN/RPM (200 "The Fabulous Joe Houston") 50-75 55
(Cover shows Modern, but label shows RPM.)
TOPS (607 "Rock & Roll Party") 50-75 56

LPs: 10/12-inch

BIG TOWN (1004 "Kicking Back") 8-12 78
COMBO (100 "Joe Houston") 300-400 55
(Cover has titles and color photo of Houston)
COMBO (100 "Joe Houston") 100-200 56
(No photo or titles on cover. Has a saxophone as the "J" in Joe. No artist or title shown on label.)
COMBO (400 "Rockin' at the Drive-In") 200-300 55
CROWN (313 "Surf Rockin'") 15-30 63
CROWN (5006 "Joe Houston Rocks All Nite Long") 50-100 56
CROWN (5203 "Wild Man of the Tenor Sax") 25-35 62
CROWN (5319 "Limbo") 20-30 63
GOLD AWARD (8033 "Rock & Roll") 30-40
(Colored vinyl.)
MODERN (1206 "Joe Houston Blows All Night Long") 100-150 56
TOPS (1518 "Rock & Roll with Joe Houston") 50-100 56
Also see REYNOLDS, Teddy, & Twisters / Joe Houston

HOUSTON, Joe / Phantoms

Singles: 7-inch

PICO (2803 "All Night Long"/"Birdland") .. 10-20
Also see HOUSTON, Joe
Also see PHANTOMS

HOUSTON, Johnny
(With the Playboys; with the Capitals)

Singles: 7-inch

EAST WEST (100 "But It's Too Late") 15-25 57
EVENT (4277 "Playboy") 15-25 58
SURF (1001 "Rockin' on the Range") 15-25 59

HOUSTON, Lawyer

Singles: 78 rpm

ATLANTIC (916 "Dallas Be-Bop Blues") . 30-50 50
Also see HOUSTON, Soldier Boy

HOUSTON, Sammy & Alamos

Singles: 7-inch

CLEVELAND (104 "Summer Souvenir") .. 30-40 60

HOUSTON, Soldier Boy
(Lawyer Houston)

Singles: 78 rpm

ATLANTIC (971 "Western Rider Blues") 50-75 52

Singles: 7-inch

ATLANTIC (971 "Western Rider Blues") 100-200 52

HOUSTON, Thelma P&R '70
(With Pressure Cooker)

Singles: 12-inch

MCA 4-6 83
MOTOWN 4-8 76-78

Singles: 7-inch

CAPITOL (5767 "Baby Mine") 25-50 66
DUNHILL (Except 11) 4-8 70
DUNHILL (11 "Everybody Gets to Go to the Moon") 10-15 69
(Special Apollo 11 Mission promotional issue.)
MCA 3-5 83-84
MOTOWN 4-6 74-78
MOWEST 4-6 72-73
RCA 3-5 80-81
TAMLA 4-6 76-79

Picture Sleeves

DUNHILL (11 "Everybody Gets to Go to the Moon") 10-15 69
(Special Apollo 11 Mission promotional issue.)

LPs: 10/12-inch

DUNHILL 10-15 69
MCA 5-10 83
MOTOWN 5-10 81-82
MOWEST 8-12 72
RCA 5-10 80-81
SHEFFIELD (2 "I've Got the Music in Me") 25-30 74
SHEFFIELD (200 "I've Got the Music in Me") 5-10 82
TAMLA 5-10 76-79
MYRRH 8-10 74
Also see BUTLER, Jerry, & Thelma Houston

HOUSTON OUTLAWS

Singles: 7-inch

WESTBOUND (179 "Ain't No Telling") 10-20 69

HOWARD, Alvin

Singles: 7-inch

JET STREAM (707 "Work Baby") 10-15 62

HOWARD, Betty

Singles: 7-inch

ALTA (109 "Trifling Man") 50-75

HOWARD, Buddy

Singles: 7-inch

MIDA (115 "Be Sure You Know") 100-200 59

HOWARD, Camille R&B '48
(With Her Boy Friends; Camille Howard Trio)

Singles: 78 rpm

FEDERAL 10-15 53
IMPERIAL 10-15 53
SPECIALTY 10-15 48-53
VEE-JAY 8-12 56

Singles: 7-inch

FEDERAL (12125 "Excite Me, Daddy") 20-30 53
FEDERAL (12134 "Hurry Back, Baby") 20-30 53
FEDERAL (12147 "You're Lower Than a Mole") 200-300 53
GOTHAM (7261 "Sometimes I'm Happy") ..... 40-60 '50s
(Red vinyl.)
IMPERIAL 15-25 53
SPECIALTY (352 "O Sole Mio Boogie") ... 35-45 50
SPECIALTY (359 "Ferocious Boogie") 35-45 50
SPECIALTY (370 "Fire Ball Boogie") 35-45 51
SPECIALTY (378 "I Ain't Got the Spirit") 35-45 51
SPECIALTY (401 "Money Blues") 35-45 51
SPECIALTY (404 "Bangin' the Boogie") ... 35-45 51
SPECIALTY (417 "Million Dollar Boogie") 35-45 51
SPECIALTY (433 "Old Baldy Boogie") 35-45 52
SPECIALTY (449 "Bacarolle Boogie") 35-45 53
VEE-JAY (198 "Business Woman") 10-20 56
Members: Camille Howard; Roy Milton; Dallas Bartley.
Also see BROWN, Clarence "Gatemouth" / Camille Howard / Bill Johnson Quartet / Van "Piano Man" Walls
Also see MILTON, Roy

HOWARD, Chuck

Singles: 7-inch

BOONE (1049 "Easy to Say, Hard to Do") ... 5-8 66
BOONE (1057 "Anywhere the Wind Blows") 5-8 67
COLUMBIA (43108 "Thing Called Sadness") 5-10 64
ESA (1017 "Joe Gray") 50-75 57
FLAME (1020 "Gossip") 100-200 59
FRATERNITY (923 "Thing Called Sadness") 5-10 64
JOY (238 "Congratulations to You") 5-10 60
KIM (1045 "Congratulations to You") 10-15 60
(First issue.)
PORT (70002 "Crazy Crazy Baby") 40-60 58
SAND (266 "Crazy Crazy Baby") 75-100 58
SPOT (337 "The Promised Land") 5-10 69

HOWARD, Chuck

Singles: 7-inch

APEX (76915 "Johnny Be Good") 25-35 63
(First issue.)
GARRETT (4001 "Johnny Be Good") 10-20 63

HOWARD, Dave

Singles: 7-inch

CHOREO (105 "Dinah") 4-8 62
CHOREO (106 "A Hundred") 4-8 62
M.M.I. (1240 "While We Danced the Tango") 50-100 59
RCA (7004 "They Remind Me of You") 8-12 57

LPs: 10/12-inch

CHOREO (5 "I Love Everybody") 10-20 62

HOWARD, Don P&R '52

Singles: 78 rpm

ESSEX 4-8 53
MERCURY 3-5 56
TRIPLE A 10-15 52

Singles: 7-inch

ESSEX (311 "Oh Happy Day") 8-15 53
(Black vinyl.)
ESSEX (311 "Oh Happy Day") 15-25 53
(Colored vinyl.)
ESSEX (316 "Rain Rain") 8-15 53
MERCURY 5-10 56
MIDCO (1001 "My Wish") 15-25
TRIPLE A (2503 "Oh Happy Day") 20-30 52
TRIPLE A (2504 "Rain Rain") 15-25 52

HOWARD, Frank, & Commanders

Singles: 7-inch

BARRY (1008 "I'm So Glad") 15-25 67
EXCELLO (2291 "Judy") 10-20 68

HOWARD, Gregory

Singles: 7-inch

KAPP (536 "When in Love") 100-200 63
(Black label.)
KAPP (536 "When in Love") 50-75 63
(White label. Promotional issue only.)
Copies of *When in Love* on Gee, credited to the Gee-Tones, are boots from the mid-'70s.
Session: Cadillacs.
Also see CADILLACS

HOWARD, Harlan C&W '71

Singles: 7-inch

CAPITOL 5-10 61
MONUMENT (except 833) 4-8 64-65
MONUMENT (833 "I Can't Stand It") 20-25 64
NUGGET 4-6 71
RCA 4-6 67

LPs: 10/12-inch

CAPITOL (1631 "Harlan Howard Sings Harlan Howard") 20-40 61
MONUMENT 15-25 65
NUGGET 10-20 71
RCA (3729 "Mr. Songwriter") 40-50 67
RCA (3886 "Down to Earth") 40-50 68

HOWARD, Jan C&W '60

Singles: 7-inch

CHALLENGE 5-10 59-67
CAPITOL 4-8 63
CON BRIO 4-6 77-78
DECCA 4-6 65-72
GRT 4-6 74
FIRST GENERATION 3-5 81
JACKPOT (48018 "Weeping Willow") 5-10 59

LPs: 10/12-inch

A.V.I. 5-8 83-84
CAPITOL 15-25 62
CORAL 5-10 73
DECCA 10-20 66-72
FIRST GENERATION 5-10 81
FORUM 10-15
GRT 6-12 75-76
PHONORAMA 5-8 83
PICKWICK/HILLTOP ..... 6-12 '60s
TOWER 15-20 67-68
WRANGLER 10-20 62
Session: Jordanaires.
Also see ANDERSON, Bill, & Jan Howard
Also see JORDANAIRES
Also see MILLER, Ned, & Jan Howard
Also see STEWART, Wynn, & Jan Howard

HOWARD, Jeff

Singles: 7-inch

TITAN (1713 "I Can't Understand") 10-15 61
TITAN (1715 "Cookie Crumbles") 8-12 61

HOWARD, Jerry

Singles: 7-inch

DITTO (124 "My Every Heartbeat") 15-25 60
DITTO (128 "Wind of Love") 15-25 60
IMPERIAL (5632 "My Every Heartbeat") ... 5-10 59

LPs: 10/12-inch

IMPERIAL ..... 15-25 '60s

HOWARD, Jim C&W '64

Singles: 7-inch

DEL-MAR (1013 "Meet Me Tonight Outside of Town") 10-15 64

HOWARD, Johnny

Singles: 7-inch

DE LUXE (6044 "Vacation Blues") 50-75 53

HOWARD, Joltin' Joe

Singles: 7-inch

KUDO (666 "Searching for You Baby") .. 50-100 58

HOWARD, Lenny

Singles: 7-inch

REAL GEORGE (501 "Keep the Faith Baby") 10-20

HOWARD, Meredith

Singles: 7-inch

RCA (0028 "Easy Come, Easy Go Blues") 25-50 49
(Colored vinyl.)
RCA (0044 "Cold Potato") 25-50 49
(Colored vinyl.)

HOWARD, Paul Mason

Singles

("This Is How the Shrimp Boats Was Born") ..... 15-20 '50s
(Square cardboard picture disc. No label name or selection number used.)

HOWARD, Ronnie

Singles: 7-inch

BIG TOP (3093 "Give My Toy to the Boy Next Door") 10-15 62

HOWARD, Rosetta R&B '48
(With the Big Three Trio)

Singles: 78 rpm

COLUMBIA 8-15 48-55

Singles: 7-inch

COLUMBIA (Except 40494) 15-25 51-55
COLUMBIA (40494 "Ebony Rhapsody") .. 30-40 55
Also see BIG THREE TRIO

HOWARD, Van

Singles: 78 rpm

IMPERIAL 10-20 53-55

Singles: 7-inch

IMPERIAL (8202 thru 8293, except 8213) 20-30 53-55
IMPERIAL (8213 "Maybe Baby") 50-75 53

HOWARD, Willie, & Chordells

Singles: 7-inch

MASCOT (127 "Louise") 500-750 58

HOWARD & DARTS

Singles: 7-inch

DIXIE (1000 "Oh My Love") 50-75

HOWELL, Bill

Singles: 7-inch

PALLADIUM (513 "Rocket Rollin' Blues") 100-200
Also see WAYORES / Bill Howell

HOWELL, Leigh
(With the Uniques)

Singles: 7-inch

MEL-O-TONE (1000 "The Wind and the Sea") 200-300
STRETCH (5000 "Moving Too Slow") .. 200-300

HOWELL, Loyd

Singles: 7-inch

HI-Q (3756 "Truck Driving Jack") 20-30
NASHVILLE (5028 "Little Froggy") 150-200 61

HOWES, O'Neil

Singles: 7-inch

DART (116 "Miss Annette") 25-35 59

HOWIE & CRYSTALS

Singles: 7-inch

FLEETWOOD (4521 "Rockin' Hall") 10-20 62

HOWIE & SAPPHIRES

Singles: 7-inch

OKEH (7112 "More Than the Day Before") 10-20 59
Member: Howard Guyton.
Also see GUY, Bobby

HOWINGTON, Dub
Singles: 7-inch
QUINCY (934 "Don't Play with Love").. 200-300

HOWLIN' WOLF R&B '51
("The Howlin' Wolf"; Chester Burnett)
Singles: 78 rpm
CHESS (1479 "Moanin' at Midnight")..... 75-100 51
CHESS (1497 "Howlin' Wolf Boogie").... 75-100 52
CHESS (1510 "Mr. Highway Man")........ 75-100 52
CHESS (1515 "Saddle My Pony")........... 50-75 52
CHESS (1528 thru 1695)........................ 25-50 53-58
CHESS (1712 "I'm Leaving You")........... 50-75 58
CHESS (1726 "Howlin' Blues")............. 50-100 59
CHESS (1735 "I've Been Abused")........ 75-125 59
CHESS (1744 "The Natchez Burning") 150-200 59
CHESS (1750 "Who's Been Talking").. 200-250 60
RPM (333 "Riding in the Moonlight") ... 100-200 51
RPM (340 "Crying at Daybreak") 100-150 51
RPM (347 "My Baby Stole Off") 100-150 52
Singles: 7-inch
CADET CONCEPT (7013 "Evil")..................5-10 69
CHESS (1528 "My Last Affair")............. 75-125 53
CHESS (1557 "All Night Boogie")......... 75-125 53
CHESS (1566 "Rockin' Daddy")........... 100-150 54
CHESS (1575 "Baby How Long") 50-100 54
CHESS (1584 "I'll Be Around").............. 50-100 55
CHESS (1593 "Who Will Be Next")......... 50-75 55
CHESS (1607 "Come to Me Baby")......... 50-75 55
CHESS (1618 "Smokestack Lightning") .. 50-75 56
CHESS (1632 "I Asked for Water")......... 50-75 56
CHESS (1648 "Going Back Home")......... 40-60 57
CHESS (1668 "Somebody in My Home") 25-40 57
CHESS (1679 "Poor Boy")..................... 25-40 57
CHESS (1695 "I Didn't Know")............... 20-30 58
CHESS (1712 "I'm Leaving You")........... 20-30 58
CHESS (1726 "Howlin' Blues").............. 20-30 59
CHESS (1735 "I've Been Abused").......... 20-30 59
CHESS (1744 "The Natchez Burning")..... 20-30 59
CHESS (1750 "Who's Been Talking")...... 25-35 60
CHESS (1753 thru 1968)...................... 15-25 60-66
CHESS (2009 "I Had a Dream").............. 10-20 67
CHESS (2081 thru 2145)...........................5-10 70-73
LPs: 10/12-inch
CADET (319 "New Album")..................... 10-15 69
CHESS (201 "Howlin' Wolf") 15-25 76
(Two discs.)
CHESS (418 "Change My Way") 8-12 77
CHESS (1434 "Moaning in the Moonlight").. 100-200 58
(Black label.)
CHESS (1469 "Howlin' Wolf") 50-100 62
(Black label.)
CHESS (1469 "Howlin' Wolf") 200-300 62
(White label. Promotional issue only.)
CHESS (1502 "Real Folk Blues")............ 15-25 66
CHESS (1512 "More Real Folk Blues")... 15-25 67
CHESS (1540 "Evil")............................... 15-20 69
CHESS (50002 "Message to the Young") 10-12 71
CHESS (50015 "Live & Cookin'") 10-12 72
CHESS (50045 "Back Door Wolf").......... 10-12 74
CHESS (60008 "The London Howlin' Wolf Sessions")... 10-12 71
CHESS (60016 "Howlin' Wolf AKA Chester Burnett") 10-12 72
CHESS/MCA (Except 9332).....................5-8 89
CHESS/MCA (9332 "Howlin' Wolf")....... 35-45 91
(Boxed, five-disc set. Includes 32-page booklet.)
CROWN (5240 "Howlin' Wolf Sings the Blues").. 15-20 62
CUSTOM (2055 "Big City Blues") .... 10-12 '60s
KENT (526 "Original Folk Blues") 10-15 67
UNITED (7717 "Big City Blues")..................8-10
UNITED (7747 "Original Folk Blues") 8-10
Session: James Cotton; Ike Turner; Willie Steel; Pat Hare; Willie Johnson; Fred Below; Hubert Sumlin; Lee Cooper; Willie Dixon; Hosea Lee Kennard; Jody Williams; Earl Phillips.
Also see BERRY, Chuck, & Howlin' Wolf
Also see COTTON, James
Also see DIDDLEY, Bo, Howlin' Wolf & Muddy Waters
Also see DIXON, Willie
Also see ROBINSON, Freddy
Also see TURNER, Ike
Also see WATERS, Muddy, & Howlin' Wolf

HOYLE, Johnnie
Singles: 7-inch
RAY-BO (105 "What About Me")............. 15-25

HOYT, Dick
Singles: 78 rpm
ABBOTT (3020 "Never Doubt My Love") .10-15 56
Singles: 7-inch
ABBOTT (3020 "Never Doubt My Love") .15-25 56
CALDWELL (400 "Grass Is Green") 8-12 60

HUB KAPP & WHEELS
Singles: 7-inch
CAPITOL (5215 "Sigh, Cry, Almost Die") ...8-12 64
TAKE FIVE (631 "Let's Really Hear It") 10-20 63
FRAMAGRATZ ("Little Volks") 10-20 63
(Selection number not known.)
Picture Sleeves
CAPITOL (5215 "Sigh, Cry, Almost Die") .15-25 64
TAKE FIVE (631 "Let's Really Hear It") 20-30 63
Members: Pat McMahon; Michael Condello.
Also see CONDELLO

HUBBARD, Freddie LP '73
Singles: 12-inch
FANTASY..4-8 81
Singles: 7-inch
ATLANTIC...4-8 69
BLUE NOTE...5-10 61-64
COLUMBIA..5-7 74-76
LPs: 10/12-inch
ATLANTIC...8-15 67-76
BLUE NOTE...15-25 60-65
(Label reads "Blue Note Records Inc. - New York, U.S.A.")
BLUE NOTE..8-15 66-76
(Label shows Blue Note Records as a division of either Liberty or United Artists.)
CTI..6-12 70-75
COLUMBIA..5-10 74-83
ELEKTRA...5-8 82
ENJA...5-8 81
FANTASY...5-8 81-83
IMPULSE..10-20 63-73
LIBERTY..5-8 81
PABLO...5-8 82-83
PAUSA...5-8 82

HUBBARD, Freddie, & Oscar Peterson
LPs: 10/12-inch
PABLO..5-10 80
Also see PETERSON, Oscar

HUBBARD, Freddie, & Stanley Turrentine
LPs: 10/12-inch
CTI..6-12 74
Also see HUBBARD, Freddie
Also see TURRENTINE, Stanley

HUBBARD, Orangie
(Orangie Ray Hubbard)
Singles: 7-inch
DIXIE (662 "Sweet Love") 3000-4000
KING (6097 "Peepin' Tom") 5-8 67
KING (6140 "Big Cat")..............................5-8 67
LEE (4009 "In Search of You")...................4-8 79
LUCKY (0007 "Look What I Found") 350-450 60

HUBBARD, Tippy
Singles: 7-inch
FRANDY (607 "Our Winter Romance")..100-200 61

HUBBELL, Frank
(With the Hubbcaps; with the Stompers)
Singles: 7-inch
ATCO (6435 "Mame")..............................5-10 66
PHILIPS (40584 "How I Loved Her") 5-8 69
TOPIX (6005 "Broken Date")...................10-20 62
LPs: 10/12-inch
ATCO (196 "Penny Candy and Other Treats") 15-20 66
PHILIPS (600293 "The Night They Raided Minsky's & Other Show Stoppers") 10-15 69

HUBBINS, Aldo
Singles: 7-inch
RPR (110 "Sugar Man") ....55-65 '60s

HUBCAPS
Singles: 7-inch
LAURIE (3219 "Hot Rod City")................10-20 64
Members: Ernie Maresca; Tom Bogdany.
Also see MARESCA, Ernie

HUCKABYE, Gary
Singles: 7-inch
G&G ("Eager Lips") 450-550
(Selection number not known.)

HUDDERSFIELD TRANSIT HUDDLE, Jack
Singles: 7-inch
KAPP (207 "Starlight")............................75-125 58
PETSEY (1002 "Starlight")....................250-350 58
Session: Buddy Holly (lead guitar); Bowman Brothers.
Also see BOWMAN BROTHERS & NORMAN PETTY TRIO
Also see HOLLY, Buddy
Also see JACK & JIM

HUDGINS, Joe
Singles: 7-inch
ANTENNA (6437 "Where'd You Stay Last Night")..20-30 59
DECCA (30854 "Where'd You Stay Last Night")...10-20 59
NEW STAR (121 "You Tricked Me")........50-75
ROBBINS (1005 "Where'd You Stay Last Night")..40-60 58

HUDSON, Eddie
Singles: 7-inch
EXCELLO (2135 "She's Sugar Sweet") ...10-20 58

HUDSON, Frank
Singles: 7-inch
RED FEATHER (18402 "Fade Away") .200-300
(Blue vinyl.)

HUDSON, Glinda
Singles: 7-inch
SMALLTOWN (300 "I'll Wait")..................20-30

HUDSON, Joe, & His Rockin' Dukes
Singles: 78 rpm
EXCELLO (2112 "Baby Give Me a Chance")...10-20 57
Singles: 7-inch
EXCELLO (2112 "Baby Give Me a Chance")...20-30 57

HUDSON, Johnny, & Rip Tides
Singles: 7-inch
CHALLENGE (59062 "Hanky Panky")......10-15 59

HUDSON, Pookie P&R '63
(With the Spaniels)
Singles: 7-inch
CHESS..5-10 66
DOUBLE L (711 "I Know, I Know")..........15-20 63
DOUBLE L (720 "For Sentimental Reasons")...10-15 63
JAMIE (1319 "This Gets to Me") 25-50 66
NEPTUNE (124 "For Sentimental Reasons")...15-20 61
PARKWAY (839 "Turn Out the Lights")....10-15 62
Also see SPANIELS

HUDSON, Ray, & Western Rhythmaires
Singles: 7-inch
DIXIE (1043 "Jackhammer") 50-75 58
DIXIE ("The Blues Walked Away") 100-150
(No selection number used.)

HUDSON, Rock
Singles: 7-inch
DECCA (30966 "Pillow Talk") 8-10 59
Picture Sleeves
DECCA (30966 "Pillow Talk")..................15-25 59
LPs: 10/12-inch
STANYAN..10-15 71
Also see MARTIN, Dean / Rock Hudson

HUDSON, Tommy
(With the Savoys)
Singles: 78 rpm
CREST (1012 "Walkin' the Stroll") 5-10 55
Singles: 7-inch
CREST (1012 "Walkin' the Stroll") 10-15 55
D (1073 "Swanee River Gal")...................50-75 59
WHITE ROCK (1110 "Rock-It")..................50-75 58

HUERTA, Baldemar
(El Bebop Kid)
Singles: 7-inch
FALCON (838 "Encaje De Chantilly [Chantilly Lace]") 15-25 58
Also see FENDER, Freddy

HUESTON, Mel
Singles: 7-inch
CHANSON (1179 "Double Confusion")....10-20
Also see UNLIMITED FOUR

HUEY & JERRY
Singles: 7-inch
VIN (1000 "Little Chickie Wah Wah") 10-15 58
Members: Huey Smith; Jerry Vincent.
Also see SMITH, Huey

HUFF, Chauncey
Singles: 7-inch
FANTASY (587 "Swimmin' U.S.A.") 15-25 64

HUFF, Luther
Singles: 78 rpm
TRUMPET (132 "Dirty Disposition").........15-25 51
TRUMPET (141 "Rosalie Blues") 15-25 51

HUFF, Willie B.
Singles: 78 rpm
BIG TOWN (105 "I Love You Baby").........15-25 53
RHYTHM 15-25 53
Singles: 7-inch
BIG TOWN (105 "I Love You Baby").......50-75 53
RHYTHM (1770 "Beggar Man Blues") 50-75 53

HUFFMAN, Donnie
Singles: 7-inch
TAURUS (354 "Pink Cadillac")..................25-35 62
Also see DONNIE & DELCHORDS

HUFFMAN, Paul
Singles: 7-inch
WINSTON (1015 "She's Mine")..............50-100 57

HUFTON, Jimmy
Singles: 7-inch
FERNWOOD (201 "Shiver & Shake") ..150-250

HUG, Armand, & Ray Bauduc
Singles: 78 rpm
OKEH (6802 "Little Rock Getaway") 5-10 51
Singles: 7-inch
OKEH (6802 "Little Rock Getaway") 10-15 51
EPs: 7-inch
EPIC (7020 "Armand Hug and Ray Bauduc")...5-10 54

HUGGY'S ORR
Singles: 7-inch
MINIT (32045 "Help Wanted") 20-30 68

HUGH T. & JOHNNY
Singles: 7-inch
ASTRA (103 "Shirley Shirley")..................10-15 60

HUGHES, Ben
(With the Twigs; with René Hall's Orchestra)
Singles: 78 rpm
HOLLYWOOD 15-25 54
SPECIALTY...20-30 58
Singles: 7-inch
HOLLYWOOD (1014 "Someday, Somewhere, Somewhere")..150-200 54
SPECIALTY (616 "I Need Someone to Love Me")..15-25 58
SPECIALTY (630 "Sack")........................15-25 58
TRUE (101 "Crazy Man").........................10-20 59
Also see HALL, René
Also see HAYES, Linda
Also see WOODS, Sonny

HUGHES, Carol
Singles: 7-inch
CARLTON (571 "If She's Right For You")..5-10 62
DOT (15923 "Bobby")...............................10-15 59
RCA (7605 "Staying Young")......................8-12 59
RCA (7617 "It's Me It's Me It's Me")............8-12 59
ROULETTE (4032 "Pick Another Baby")..10-15 57
ROULETTE (4041 "Lend Me Your Comb")...10-15 58

HUGHES, Glenn, & D'Lighters
Singles: 7-inch
DYNASTY (623 "I Belong to You") 10-15 59

HUGHES, Jimmy P&R/R&B '64
Singles: 7-inch
ATLANTIC (2454 "Uncle Sam")..................5-10 67
COLLECTABLES 3-5 81
FAME 8-15 64-67
GUYDEN (2075 "I'm Qualified")..................8-12 62
JAMIE (1280 "My Loving Time")..............10-15 64
VOLT...5-10 68-71

LPs: 10/12-inch
ATCO (209 "Why Not Tonight")............... 15-20 67
STAX...5-10 85
VEE-JAY (1102 "Steal Away")................ 20-30 64
VOLT (6003 "Something Special")........... 10-20 69

HUGHES, Joe, & His Orchestra
Singles: 7-inch
KANGAROO (106 "Make Me Dance Little Ant").. 100-150 59
SOUND STAGE 7 (2571 "Can't Figure Out Women")..5-8 66

HUGHES, Johnny
Singles: 78 rpm
VALENTINE SOUND ("After Tonight").... 50-75 58
(No selection number used.)
VALENTINE SOUND ("First Dance")....... 50-75 58
(No selection number used.)
Singles: 7-inch
UBC (1017 "Pretty Little Girl")................. 15-25 61
UBC (1024 "Junior High Doll")................ 50-75 61
UBC (1034 "Doll Baby")......................... 25-35 62
VALENTINE SOUND ("After Tonight").... 30-40 58
(No selection number used.)
VALENTINE SOUND ("First Dance")....... 30-40 58
(No selection number used.)
Picture Sleeves
UBC (1024 "Junior High Doll")............ 75-100 61
UBC (1034 "Doll Baby")......................... 50-75 62

HUGHES, Judy
Singles: 7-inch
CRUSADER (128 "Ocean of Emotion")... 40-60 66
VAULT (917 "Crazy for You")................. 20-30 65

HUGHES, Pee Wee, & Delta Duo
Singles: 78 rpm
DELUXE (3228 "Country Boy")............... 20-40 49

HUGHLEY, George
(With the Cama Rockers)
Singles: 7-inch
BUDDAH (203 "That's Why I Cry")...............4-8 70
FAIRLANE (21012 "What Did I Do")........ 10-20 61
GAYE (004 "Do the Beatle")......................5-10 64

HUGO & LUIGI P&R '55
(Hugo & Luigi Chorus)
Singles: 78 rpm
MERCURY..4-8 55-56
Singles: 7-inch
MERCURY.. 10-15 55-56
RCA...8-12 59-60
ROULETTE..5-10 57-58
Picture Sleeves
ROULETTE (4074 "Cha-Hua-Hua")......... 10-15 58
LPs: 10/12-inch
FORUM.. 10-15 60
MERCURY.. 15-25 56
RCA... 10-20 60-63
ROULETTE (25283 "Cascading Voices") 10-20 59
WING... 10-15 60
Members: Hugo Peretti; Luigi Creatore.

HUHN, Billy, & Catalinas
Singles: 7-inch
LESLEY (1923 "Freshman Queen")........ 10-15 63

HULIN, T.K. P&R '63
Singles: 7-inch
L.K. (1001 "Little Bitty Boy")................. 75-125 60
L.K. (1112 thru 1120, except 1119)........ 15-25 62-63
L.K. (1119 "Baby, Be My Steady")....... 100-150 63
SMASH (1830 "I'm Not a Fool Anymore")..8-12 63
SMASH (1864 "Rain")..............................8-12 63
LPs: 10/12-inch
STARFLITE... 20-30

HULL, Terry, & Starfires
Singles: 7-inch
STAFF (103 "Those Pretty Brown Eyes").. 200-300 '60s

HULLABALOOS P&R '64
Singles: 7-inch
ROULETTE..5-10 64-65
Picture Sleeves
ROULETTE.. 10-20 64-65
LPs: 10/12-inch
ROULETTE (25297 "England's Newest Singing Sensations")................................ 25-30 65
ROULETTE (25310 "The Hullabaloos on Hullabaloo")..................................... 25-30 65

HUMAN BEINGS
Singles: 7-inch
IMPACT (1001 "An Inside Look")............20-30 65
IMPACT (1006 "Ling Ting Tong")............20-30 66
IMPACT (1022 "Can't Tell")....................10-15 67
W.B. (5622 "Because I Love Her")............5-10 65

HUMAN BEINZ P&R '67
(Human Beingz; with the Mammals)
Singles: 7-inch
CAPITOL..5-8 67-69
ELYSIAN (3376 "Hey Joe")......................15-25 67
ELYSIAN (8687 "My Generation")...........15-25 66
GATEWAY (828 "Gloria")..........................5-10 68
GATEWAY (838 "My Generation")..............5-10 68
Picture Sleeves
CAPITOL (2119 "Turn on Your Lovelight")..10-15 68
LPs: 10/12-inch
CAPITOL (2906 "Nobody But Me")..........15-25 68
CAPITOL (2926 "Evolutions")..................25-35 68
GATEWAY (3012 "Nobody But Me")........25-35 68
Members: Richard Belley; Mel Pachuta; Mike Tatman; Ting Markulin.

HUMAN EXPRESSION
Singles: 7-inch
ACCENT (1214 "Every Night")..................25-50 67
ACCENT (1226 "Optical Sound")..............25-50 67

HUMAN INSTINCT
Singles: 7-inch
TIME (503 "Renaissance Fair")..................5-10 69
LPs: 10/12-inch
AIR (107 "Stoned Guitar")....................500-600 70

HUMANE SOCIETY
Singles: 7-inch
LIBERTY (55968 "Knock Knock")............10-20 67

HUMANS
Singles: 7-inch
AUDITION (6109 "Warning")....................20-30 66

HUMBLE MIND
Singles: 7-inch
MUDWERK (10001 "African Judy")..........25-35 '60s
Also see LITTER
Also see STRANGELOVES

HUMDINGERS
Singles: 78 rpm
DALE (106 "Clock in Lovers Lane").........10-15 58
Singles: 7-inch
DALE (106 "Clock in Lovers Lane").........10-15 58

HUMDINGERS
Singles: 7-inch
DONNA (1386 "Corn Ball")..........................5-10 63
JAYE JOSEPH...10-20 63
Members: Larry Bright; Mike Rubini.
Also see BRIGHT, Larry

HUME, Don
Singles: 7-inch
FELSTED (8679 "Go Right Ahead").........10-15 63

HUMES, Anita
(With the Essex)
Singles: 7-inch
ROULETTE..5-15 64-67
LPs: 10/12-inch
ROULETTE..15-20 64
Also see ESSEX

HUMES, Bill
Singles: 7-inch
BEE HIVE (11504 "Bahama Isle")...........10-15

HUMES, Helen R&B '45
(With the Bill Doggett Octet)
Singles: 78 rpm
ALADDIN...10-20 45
DECCA...10-15 52
MODERN (779 "I'm Gonna Let Him Ride")..20-40 50
Singles: 7-inch
DECCA (28113 "They Raided the Joint").20-30 52
MODERN (779 "I'm Gonna Let Him Ride")..50-100 50
LPs: 10/12-inch
COLUMBIA..8-10
Members (Octet): Bill Doggett; Johnny Brown; Bill Moore; Ernest Thompson; Ross Butler; Alfred Moore; Charles Harris; Elmer Warner.

Also see DOGGETT, Bill
Also see MILTON, Roy

HUMMEL, Ray
(Ray Hummel III)
Singles: 7-inch
FENTON (2188 "Fine Day").....................15-25 67
RENEGADE...3-6 78-83
Picture Sleeves
FENTON (2188 "Fine Day").....................20-30 67
Also see JUJUs

HUMMINGBIRDS
(Humming Birds)
Singles: 7-inch
CANNON (4600 "You and Me")...............15-25 62
PANETTE (665 "Space Dance")................5-10 61

HUMOROUS DIANE
Singles: 7-inch
VELTONE (712 "Interview with Mr. K.")...10-20 62

HUMPERDINCK, Engelbert P&R/LP '67
(Gerry Dorsey)
Singles: 12-inch
EPIC/CBS (35020 "Last of the Romantics")...50-70 76
(Picture disc. Promotional issue only.)
Singles: 7-inch
EH (1 "For My Friends")..........................10-15
(Promotional issue only.)
EPIC...3-6 76-83
PARROT..4-8 67-73
Picture Sleeves
PARROT..4-8 67-71
EPs: 7-inch
PARROT..5-10 67-69
(Juke box issues.)
LPs: 10/12-inch
EPIC...5-10 76-83
LONDON..5-10 77
PARROT..5-15 67-77
TEE VEE..5-10
(TV mail order offer.)

HUMPHREY, Paul, & His Cool Aid Chemists P&R/R&B/LP '71
Singles: 7-inch
LIZARD...4-8 70-71
LPs: 10/12-inch
LIZARD...10-15 71
Members [Cool Aid Chemists]: Clarence MacDonald; David T. Walker; Bill Upchurch.
Also see WALKER, David T.

HUMPHREY, Phil
(With the Fendermen)
Singles: 7-inch
SASSY (0284 "Popeye")..........................20-25 62
Also see FENDERMEN

HUMPHRIES, Earl
LPs: 10/12-inch
VERVE (V-6136 "Earl Humphries").........40-60 60
(Monaural.)
VERVE (VS-6136 "Earl Humphries")........50-75 60
(Stereo.)

HUMPHRIES, Frank "Fat Man," & 4 Notes
Singles: 78 rpm
JUBILEE (5085 "Lulubell Blues")...........50-100 52
Singles: 7-inch
JUBILEE (5085 "Lulubell Blues")..........175-225 52
Note: The 4 Notes were actually the Crows.
Also see CROWS

HUMPHRIES, Teddy R&B '59
Singles: 7-inch
KING (5000 series)...............................10-15 59-61
(Monaural.)
KING (S-5205 "What a Night")..................20-30 59
(Stereo.)
Session: Mickey Baker.
Also see BAKER, Mickey

HUMPTY & IVANHOES
Singles: 7-inch
GRAMOPHONE (165 "Shy Guy")............40-50 65

HUNGER
Singles: 7-inch
PUBLIC (101 thru 1001)........................15-25 68-69
LPs: 10/12-inch
PUBLIC (1006 "Strictly from Hunger")..400-600 69

Members: Mike Parkison; Mike Lane; Steve Hansen; Bill Daffern; Tom Tanory; John Morton.

HUNGRI I's
Singles: 7-inch
PARIS TOWER (127 "Half Your Life")...... 15-25 67

HUNS
Singles: 7-inch
PYRAMID (6646 "Shakedown")............... 15-25 66

HUNS
Singles: 7-inch
ROCK 'N' JAZZ (8668 "Destination Lonely")..30-50 66
(Blue label.)
ROCK 'N' JAZZ (8668 "Destination Lonely")..10-20 66
(Red label.)

HUNS OF TIME
Singles: 7-inch
MAGIC TOUCH (2070 "Walking in the Vineyards")... 10-15 69
Also see ATTILA & HUNS

HUNT, Charlie
Singles: 7-inch
HUNT (1006 "I'm in the Dog House").......30-40

HUNT, D.A.
Singles: 78 rpm
SUN (183 "Lonesome Ol' Jail")............250-500 53

HUNT, Dennis
Singles: 7-inch
SAY (12 "A Story Untold")....................100-125

HUNT, Floyd, Quartette R&B '47
Singles: 78 rpm
MIRACLE (104 "Fool That I Am")............ 15-25 47
Members: Floyd Hunt; Tommy House; Clarence Hall; Al McDonald. Vocal: Gladys Palmer.
Also see PALMER, Gladys

HUNT, Geraldine R&B '70
Singles: 7-inch
ABC (10859 "Winner Take All")............... 15-25 67
BOMBAY (4501 "He's For Real")..............50-75 64
CHECKER (1028 "I Let Myself Go")......... 10-20 62
KATRON (829 "I Let Myself Go").............30-40 62
(First issue.)
PRISM..3-5 80
ROULETTE..4-6 70-73
USA (732 "Sneak Around")...................... 15-25 62
USA (737 "Sneak Around")...................... 10-20 63

HUNT, Geraldine, & Charlie Hodges
Singles: 7-inch
CALLA (173 "Together")...............................4-6 70
Also see HODGES, Charles
Also see HUNT, Geraldine

HUNT, Jackie
Singles: 7-inch
JET STREAM (702 "Since You've Been Gone")..10-15 '60s

HUNT, Kenneth
Singles: 7-inch
HEAP BIG (1000 "I'm the Wrong One")...100-200

HUNT, Lanny, & Themes
Singles: 7-inch
PANORAMA (42 "Stay")..............................8-12 66
SURE STAR (5001 "I Can't Say I Love You")..20-30 64

HUNT, Pee Wee P&R '48
Singles: 78 rpm
CAPITOL..3-5 48-57
Singles: 7-inch
CAPITOL..5-10 50-62
SAVOY..5-10 51
EPs: 7-inch
CAPITOL..5-10 50-56
SAVOY..5-10 51
LPs: 10/12-inch
CAPITOL..4-8 78
(With "SM" prefix.)
CAPITOL..15-30 50-63
(With "T" or "ST" prefix.)
GLENDALE..4-8 78
SAVOY (15042 "Dixieland")......................25-35 54
(10-inch LP.)

TOPS (1603 "Pee Wee Hunt") 15-25 57
Also see BLANC, Mel
Also see FOUR KNIGHTS

HUNT, Ricky, & Hunters
Singles: 7-inch
KATHY (101 "His Shoulder") 15-25

HUNT, Skipper, Combo
Singles: 7-inch
GLENN (1900 "Scalded") 50-75

HUNT, Slim
Singles: 78 rpm
EXCELLO (2005 "Welcome Home, Baby") 50-75 55
Singles: 7-inch
EXCELLO (2005 "Welcome Home, Baby") 125-175 55

HUNT, Tommy P&R/R&B '61
Singles: 7-inch
ATLANTIC 5-10 65
CAPITOL 5-10 66
DYNAMO 8-12 67
PRIVATE STOCK 4-6 76
SCEPTER 10-15 61-64
LPs: 10/12-inch
DYNAMO (8001 "Greatest Hits") 15-25 67
SCEPTER (506 "I Just Don't Know What to Do with Myself") 25-35 62
Also see FIVE ECHOES
Also see FLAMINGOS
Also see PLATTERS / Inez & Charlie Foxx / Jive Five / Tommy Hunt

HUNT, William
Singles: 7-inch
STREAMSIDE (100 "Would You Believe") 15-25 68

HUNT SISTERS
(Hunt Sisters & Mark)
Singles: 7-inch
FORTUNE (210 "Elvis Is Rocking Again") 75-100 60
FORTUNE (213 "I'm Not Going to Take it Anymore") 10-15 60
SAMPSON (415 "Christmas Piggy") 10-15 61
Also see HALL, Roy

HUNTER, Christine
Singles: 7-inch
ROULETTE (4589 "Santa, Bring Me Ringo") 10-15 64

HUNTER, Dean
Singles: 7-inch
CRYSTALETTE (732 "Double Date") 10-15 59

HUNTER, Fluffy
Singles: 78 rpm
FEDERAL 10-15 53-54
Singles: 7-inch
FEDERAL (12161 "Climb the Wall") 20-30 54
FEDERAL (12172 "Leave It to Me") 20-30 54
Also see POWELL, Jesse

HUNTER, Frank
(With the Huntsmen)
Singles: 7-inch
EPIC (9694 "Carnival") 5-8 64
LPs: 10/12-inch
EPIC (24052 "Watermelon Man") 15-25 63
(Monaural.)
EPIC (26052 "Watermelon Man") 25-30 63
(Stereo.)
Also see PRISCO, Tommy

HUNTER, Herbert
Singles: 7-inch
HIT .... 5-15 '60s
(Hit discs here may have other artists, such as Bill Austin or Joe Cash, on the flips.)
PONCELLO (711 "I'm So Satisfied") 10-20 61
PONCELLO (714 "Isn't It Wonderful to Dream") 10-20 61
SPAR (718 "Twistin' Party") 10-15 62
SPAR (723 "I Can't Help It") 10-20 62
SPAR (741 "Happy Go Lucky") 20-30 63
SPAR (9009 "I Was Born to Love You") .. 20-30

HUNTER, Ivory Joe R&B '45
(With the Ivorytones)
Singles: 78 rpm
ATLANTIC 20-30 55-58
EXCLUSIVE 15-25 45
4 STAR 25-50 48-51
KING 10-20 47-51
MGM 10-20 49-54
PACIFIC 20-30 45-47
Singles: 7-inch
ATLANTIC (1049 "It May Sound Silly") 20-30 55
ATLANTIC (1066 "Heaven Came Down to Earth") 25-35 55
ATLANTIC (1086 "A Tear Fell") 25-35 56
ATLANTIC (1095 "You Mean Everything to Me") 25-35 56
ATLANTIC (1111 thru 1191) 20-30 56-58
ATLANTIC (2020 "Now I Don't Worry No More") 15-25 59
CAPITOL (4587 thru 4688) 8-12 61-62
DOT (15880 thru 15986) 15-25 58-59
GOLDISC (3003 "It Must Be Love") 10-15 60
GOLDISC (3010 "You Satisfy Me Baby") . 10-15 60
GOLDWAX (307 "Every Little Bit Helps") . 15-25
JOIE 8-12
KING (4424 "False Friend Blues") 25-50 51
KING (4443 "She's Gone Blues") 25-50 51
KING (4455 "Old Gal and New Gal Blues") 25-50 51
KING (5280 "Guess Who") 10-15 59
MGM (500 series) 4-6 78
MGM (8011 "I Almost Lost My Mind") 25-50 49
MGM (10000 & 11000 series) 20-30 49-54
MGM (10578 "I Almost Lost My Mind") 25-50 49
PARAMOUNT 4-6 73
SMASH (1825 "Congratulations") 5-10 63
SMASH (1860 "My Lover's Prayer") 5-10 63
SOUND STAGE 7 .... 4-8 68-69
STAX (155 "This Kind of Woman") 5-10 64
VEE-JAY (452 "Somebody's Stealing My Love") 8-12 62
VEEP (1258 "Don't You Believe Me") 5-10 67
VEEP (1270 "Did She Ask About Me") 5-10 67
EPs: 7-inch
ATLANTIC (589 "Ivory Joe Hunter") 50-75 58
ATLANTIC (608 "Rock with Ivory Joe Hunter") 50-75 58
KING (265 "Ivory Joe Hunter") 50-75 54
MGM (1376/7/8 "I Get That Lonesome Feeling") 20-40 57
(Price is for any of three volumes.)
LPs: 10/12-inch
ATLANTIC (8008 "Ivory Joe Hunter") ... 100-200 58
(Black Label.)
ATLANTIC (8008 "Ivory Joe Hunter") 50-100 59
(Red Label.)
ATLANTIC (8015 "Ivory Joe Hunter Sings the Old and the New") 100-150 58
(Black Label.)
ATLANTIC (8015 "Ivory Joe Hunter Sings the Old and the New") 50-100 59
(Red Label.)
DOT (3569 "This Is Ivory Joe Hunter") 25-35 64
(Monaural.)
DOT (25569 "This Is Ivory Joe Hunter") ... 30-40 64
(Stereo.)
EPIC 8-10 71
EVEREST 8-10 74
GOLDISC (403 "Fabulous Ivory Joe Hunter") 40-60 61
GRAND PRIX 10-15
HOME COOKING 5-10 89
KING (605 "16 Greatest Hits") 75-125 58
LION 15-25
MGM (3488 "I Get That Lonesome Feeling") 50-100 57
PARAMOUNT 8-10 74
SAGE (603 "Ivory Joe Hunter") 35-50 59
SMASH (27037 "Golden Hits") 15-25 63
(Monaural.)
SMASH (67037 "Golden Hits") 20-30 63
(Stereo.)
SOUND (603 "Ivory Joe Hunter") 150-250 57
Also see CHARLES, Ray / Ivory Joe Hunter / Jimmy Rushing
Also see TURNER, Sammy / Ivory Joe Hunter

HUNTER, Ivory Joe / Memphis Slim
LPs: 10/12-inch
STRAND (1123 "The Artistry of Ivory Joe Hunter") 15-25

Also see HUNTER, Ivory Joe
Also see MEMPHIS SLIM

HUNTER, Jim
Singles: 7-inch
ADORE (904 "Bad Boy") 50-75

HUNTER, John
(Lost John Hunter & Blind Bats; Long John Hunter)
Singles: 78 rpm
4 STAR (1492 "Cool Down Mama") 20-40 50
4 STAR (1511 "Y-M and V Blues") 20-40 50
Singles: 7-inch
YUCCA (132 "Midnight Stroll") 10-15 61
YUCCA (138 "Grandma") 10-15 61
YUCCA (159 "Slash") 5-10 63
YUCCA (176 "It's Your Thing") 20-30
Also see LONG JOHN

HUNTER, Lee
Singles: 78 rpm
GOLD STAR (651 "Let's Boogie") 20-30 48

HUNTER, Robert
Singles: 7-inch
RELIX 3-5 86
ROUND 5-10 74
LPs: 10/12-inch
RELIX (Except 2002) 5-10 80-86
RELIX (2002 "Promontory Rider") 15-20 82
(Picture disc. 1000 made.)
ROUND 20-30 74-75
Members: Jerry Garcia; Mickey Hart.
Also see GARCIA, Jerry / Robert Hunter
Also see HART, Mickey
Also see OLD AND IN THE WAY / Keith & Donna / Robert Hunter / Phil Lesh & Ned Lagin

HUNTER, Shane, & Four Bars
Singles: 7-inch
CANDELO (379 "I've Lost Her") 10-20 59
IPS (101 "Follow Me") 30-40 59
Also see FOUR BARS

HUNTER, Shirlee
Singles: 7-inch
MERCURY (72599 "The Last Place You Go") 5-10 66
SALEM (516 "I Can't Do a Thing") 8-12 63
SALEM (535 "Why Do You Hesitate") 8-12 65
TIP TOP (720 "Hot Blood") 10-15 59
TOWER (130 "Why Do You Hesitate") 5-10 65

HUNTER, Tab P&R/R&B '57
Singles: 78 rpm
DOT 5-15 56-57
HEAR ("Tab Hunter") 20-30 56
(7-inch, cardboard disc, originally attached to front cover of *Hear* magazine. Double this price for magazine with record intact. Back cover has a similar disc by Jayne Mansfield.)
Singles: 7-inch
DOT 10-20 56-62
W.B. (Monaural) 10-20 58-59
W.B. (S-5032 "I'll Be with You in Apple Blossom Time") 25-35 59
(Stereo.)
W.B. (S-5051 "There's No Fool Like a Young Fool") 25-35 59
(Stereo.)
Picture Sleeves
W.B. (5008 "Jealous Heart") 10-20 58
W.B. (5093 "Waitin' for Fall") 10-20 60
W.B. (5160 "Again") 10-20 61
EPs: 7-inch
W.B. (EA-1221 "Tab Hunter") 15-25 58
(Monaural. Has one track not found on stereo version.)
W.B. (ESB-1221 "Tab Hunter") 20-35 58
(Stereo. Has one track not found on mono version.)
LPs: 10/12-inch
DOT (3370 "Young Love") 25-45 61
(Monaural.)
DOT (25370 "Young Love") 30-40 61
(Stereo. Includes some tracks originally recorded in mono – and found on 3370 – that were rerecorded in stereo especially for this LP.)
W.B. (1221 "Tab Hunter") 30-40 58
(Monaural.)
W.B. (1221 "Tab Hunter") 30-50 58
(Stereo.)
W.B. (1292 "When I Fall in Love") 30-40 58
(Monaural.)
W.B. (1292 "When I Fall in Love") 30-50 58
(Stereo.)
W.B. (1367 "R.F.D.") 30-40 60
(Monaural.)
W.B. (1367 "R.F.D.") 30-50 60
(Stereo.)
Also see MANSFIELD, Jayne

HUNTER, Ty R&B '60
(With the Voice Masters)
Singles: 7-inch
ANNA (1114 "Everything About You") 15-25 60
ANNA (1123 "Everytime") 10-15 60
CHECK MATE (1002 "Memories") 10-20 61
CHECK MATE (1015 "Lonely Baby") 15-25 62
CHESS (1857 "In Time") 10-20 63
CHESS (1881 "Am I Losing You") 10-20 63
CHESS (1893 "Bad Loser") 10-20 63
INVICTUS (9120 "Hey There Lonely Girl") 10-15 72
Also see ORIGINALS
Also see ROMEOS
Also see VOICE MASTERS

HUNTER MUSKETT
LPs: 10/12-inch
BRADLEY (1003 "Hunter Muskett") 35-45 73
Members: Danny Thompson; Jim McCarty; Chris George; Doug Morter; Roger Trevit; Terry Hiscock; Mike Giles; Ken Freeman.

HUNTERS
(Flairs)
Singles: 78 rpm
FLAIR (1017 "Down at Hayden's") 25-35 53
Singles: 7-inch
FLAIR (1017 "Down at Hayden's") 50-75 53
Also see FLAIRS

HUNTSMEN
Singles: 7-inch
SHUR-SHOT (6704 "So Long") .... 20-30 '60s

HURLEY, John
Singles: 7-inch
AKA (103 "Lonely Boy") 400-500 58

HURLEY, Mark
Singles: 78 rpm
RECORDED IN HOLLYWOOD 10-20 53
Singles: 7-inch
RECORDED IN HOLLYWOOD (418 "Are You From Dixie") 20-30 53

HURRICANE, Al, & Night Rockers
Singles: 7-inch
APT (25049 "South Bend") 10-15 60
CHALLENGE (9127 "Lobo") 10-15 61

HURRICANES
(Featuring Bob Gaye)
Singles: 78 rpm
AUDIVOX 8-12 54
Singles: 7-inch
AUDIVOX (109 "I Keep Crying") 10-20 54
AUDIVOX (112 "I'll Follow You") 10-20 54

HURRICANES
Singles: 78 rpm
KING 25-75 55-57
Singles: 7-inch
KING (4817 "Poor Little Dancing Girl") ... 75-125 55
KING (4867 "Maybe It's All for the Best") 75-125 56
KING (4898 "Raining in My Heart") 100-150 56
KING (4926 "Little Girl of Mine") 75-125 56
KING (4932 "Sentimental Heaven") 75-125 56
KING (4947 "Dear Mother") 100-150 56
(Does not have "High Fidelity" on label.)
KING (4947 "Dear Mother") 10-20 56
(Has "High Fidelity" on label.)
KING (5018 "Fallen Angel") 50-100 57
KING (5042 "Priceless") 100-150 57
Members: Henry Auston; James Brown; Frederick Williams; Vernon Britton.
Also see DORN, Jerry
Also see MEMOS
Also see TOPPERS

HURST, Larry, & Keys
Singles: 7-inch
ROMCO (102 "Linda Lou") 15-25

HURT, Harvey
Singles: 7-inch
MASTER (1226 "Big Dog, Little Dog"). 100-150

HURT, Jimmy, & Del Rios
Singles: 7-inch
DO-RA-ME (1401 "Oh What a Feeling").. 20-30 59

HURVITZ, Sandy
LPs: 10/12-inch
VERVE (5064 "Sandy's Album Is Here at Last") ... 15-20 68
Session: Frank Zappa.

HUSKY, Ferlin — C&W '55
(With the Hush Puppies; with Hushpuppies; with Coon Creek Girls; with Bettie Husky; Ferlin Huskey)
Singles: 78 rpm
CAPITOL ... 5-15 52-57
Singles: 7-inch
ABC ... 4-6 73-75
ABC/DOT ... 4-6 75
CAPITOL (2000 thru 3400) ... 4-8 67-72
(Orange labels.)
CAPITOL (2300 thru 4300) ... 10-20 52-60
(Purple labels.)
CAPITOL (4400 thru 5900) ... 5-10 60-67
CACHET ... 3-5 80
FIRST GENERATION ... 4-6 78
KING (5434 "Cotton Pickin' Heart") ... 10-15 60
KING (5476 "Guilty Feeling") ... 10-15 61
Picture Sleeves
CAPITOL ... 5-10 62-68
EPs: 7-inch
CAPITOL (609 "Ferlin Husky") ... 25-35 55
CAPITOL (1-2-3 718 "Songs of the Home and Heart") ... 20-40 56
(Price is for any of three volumes.)
CAPITOL (837 "Husky Hits") ... 15-25 57
CAPITOL (1-2-3 880 "Boulevard of Broken Dreams") ... 15-25 57
(Price is for any of three volumes.)
CAPITOL (921 "Songs from Country Music Holiday") ... 15-25 57
CAPITOL (1-2-3 1280 "Ferlin Favorites") 10-20 60
(Price is for any of three volumes.)
CAPITOL (1516 "Wings of a Dove") ... 15-25 60
LPs: 10/12-inch
ABC ... 5-10 73-75
AUDIOGRAPH ALIVE (6019 "Ferlin Husky") ... 5-10 82
CAPITOL (115 "White Fences and Evergreen Trees") ... 20-30 68
CAPITOL (718 "Songs of the Home and Heart") ... 30-50 56
CAPITOL (880 "Boulevard of Broken Dreams") ... 30-40 57
CAPITOL (1200 thru 2800 series) ... 15-25 60-68
(With "T" or "ST" prefix.)
CAPITOL (1200 thru 2800 series) ... 5-10 68-75
(With "DT" or "SM" prefix.)
FIRST GENERATION ... 5-10 81
KING (647 "Country Tunes Sung from the Heart") ... 25-35 59
KING (728 "Easy Livin' ") ... 25-35 60
PHONORAMA ... 5-8 83
PICKWICK (3651 "Hits of Ferlin Husky") ... 8-12 '70s
PICKWICK/HILLTOP (6005 "Ole Opry Favorites") ... 10-20 65
PICKWICK/HILLTOP (6099 "Wings of a Dove") ... 10-20 65
STARDAY (3018 "Favorites") ... 5-10 77
Also see CRUM, Simon
Also see FIVE KEYS / Ferlin Husky
Also see OWENS, Buck / Faron Young / Ferlin Husky
Also see PRESTON, Terry
Also see SHEPARD, Jean, & Ferlin Husky
Also see TUBB, Ernest
Also see VINCENT, Gene / Tommy Sands / Sonny James / Ferlin Husky

HUSKY, Ferlin / Pat Boone
Singles: 7-inch
U.S.A.F. ... 5-10 60
(Promotional issue only.)
Also see BOONE, Pat
Also see HUSKY, Ferlin

HUSTLERS
Singles: 7-inch
DOWNEY (118 "Inertia") ... 15-25 64
DOWNEY (125 "Kopout") ... 15-25 64
FASCINATION (6570 "Goodbye") ... 10-15 65
FINER ARTS ... 10-15 65-67
HOUSE OF NOTE (69 "Barefoot Venture") ... 25-35
ORLYN (1949 "She Waits for Me") ... 10-20
RICH (113 "Linda") ... 20-30 65
LPs: 10/12-inch
FINER ARTS (103 "Ski Country") ... 20-30 67
Also see ORIGINAL HUSTLERS

HUSTLERS 4
Singles: 7-inch
BARCLAY (19677 "Kind of Hurt") ... 25-35

HUTCH, Willie — P&R/R&B/LP '73
Singles: 7-inch
DUNHILL (4012 "The Duck") ... 25-50 65
MAVERICK (1003 "Use What You Got") ... 5-10 68
MODERN (1021 "I Can't Get Enough") ... 20-30 57
MOTOWN ... 4-6 73-82
RCA ... 4-8 69
SOUL CITY ... 5-10
WHITFIELD ... 4-6 78-79
Picture Sleeves
MOTOWN ... 4-6 75
LPs: 10/12-inch
MOTOWN ... 5-10 73-82
RCA ... 10-12 69
WHITFIELD ... 5-10 78-79
Also see PHONETICS

HUTTO, J.B.
(With the Hawks; J.B. & His Hawks; with Houserockers)
Singles: 78 rpm
CHANCE (1155 "Now She's Gone") ... 200-250 54
CHANCE (1160 "Pet Cream Man") ... 500-750 54
CHANCE (1165 "Things Are So Slow") ... 200-250 55
Singles: 7-inch
CHANCE (1155 "Now She's Gone") ... 500-750 54
CHANCE (1160 "Pet Cream Man") .. 1000-2000 54
CHANCE (1165 "Things Are So Slow") ... 500-750 55
LPs: 10/12-inch
DELMARK ... 10-15 72-73
BARON (Black vinyl.) ... 10-15 79
BARON (Colored vinyl.) ... 15-20 79

HUTTO, J.B., & Sunnyland Slim
LPs: 10/12-inch
DELMARK (617 "Hawk Squat") ... 30-40
Also see HUTTO, J.B.
Also see SUNNYLAND SLIM

HUTTON, Betty — P&R '44
Singles: 78 rpm
CAPITOL ... 4-8 44-56
RCA ... 4-6 50
VICTOR ... 4-8 46
Singles: 7-inch
CAPITOL ... 5-10 50-56
EPs: 7-inch
CAPITOL ... 10-20 50-54
LPs: 10/12-inch
CAPITOL (256 "Square in a Social Circle") ... 30-50 50
(10-inch LP.)
CAPITOL (547 "Satins & Spurs") ... 20-40 54
W.B. ... 15-25 59
Also see COMO, Perry, & Betty Hutton
Also see SHORE, Dinah, Tony Martin, Betty Hutton & Phil Harris

HUTTON, Betty, & Tennessee Ernie Ford
Singles: 78 rpm
CAPITOL ... 4-8 54
Singles: 7-inch
CAPITOL ... 5-10 54
Also see FORD, Tennessee Ernie
Also see HUTTON, Betty

HUTTON, Bobby
Singles: 7-inch
ABC (11441 "Loving You, Needing You") ... 4-6 74
BLUE ROCK (4055 "That's How Heartaches Are Made") ... 10-20 68
PHILIPS (40601 "Come See What's Left of Me") ... 15-20 69
PHILIPS (40657 "I've Got a Memory") ... 15-20 70
PHILIPS (40709 "Lonely in Love") ... 15-20 71

HUTTON, Danny — P&R '65
Singles: 7-inch
ALMO (213 "Home in Pasadena") ... 10-20 65
HBR (447 "Roses & Rainbows") ... 10-15 65
HBR (453 "Big Bright Eyes") ... 10-15 65
MGM (13502 "Funny How Love Can Be") .. 8-12 66
MGM (13613 "Hang on to a Dream") ... 8-12 66
Picture Sleeves
HBR (447 "Roses & Rainbows") ... 10-20 65
MGM (13502 "Funny How Love Can Be") ... 10-20 66
LPs: 10/12-inch
MGM (4664 "Pre-Dog Night") ... 10-15 70
Also see LYNNE, Jeff / Danny Hutton
Also see SWIFT, Basil, & Seegrams
Also see THREE DOG NIGHT

HUTTON, Neil
Singles: 7-inch
AVA (129 "It's Cold in This Dungeon") ... 10-20 63
Picture Sleeves
AVA (129 "It's Cold in This Dungeon") ... 15-25 63

HYLAND, Brian — P&R/R&B '60
("The Bikini Boy.")
Singles: 7-inch
ABC ... 4-6 73
ABC-PAR (10236 thru 10374) ... 8-12 61-62
ABC-PAR (10400 "If Mary's There") ... 8-12 63
(Black vinyl.)
ABC-PAR (10400 "If Mary's There") ... 15-25 63
(Colored vinyl. Promotional issue only.)
ABC-PAR (10427 "I Wish Today Was Yesterday") ... 8-12 63
ABC-PAR (10452 "Save Your Heart for Me") ... 10-20 63
ABC-PAR (10494 "Nothing Matters But You") ... 8-12 63
ABC-PAR (10549 "Act Naturally") ... 8-12 64
DOT ... 4-8 67-69
KAPP (342 thru 429) ... 10-20 60-61
LEADER (801 "Rosemary") ... 20-30 60
LEADER (805 "Itsy Bitsy Teenie Weenie Yellow Polkadot Bikini") ... 20-30 60
(First issue.)
MCA ... 4-6 73
PHILIPS ... 8-12 64-67
ROWE/AMI ... 5-10 66
("Play Me" Sales Stimulator promotional issue.)
ROULETTE ... 4-6
UNI ... 4-6 70-72
Picture Sleeves
ABC-PAR (10262 "I'll Never Stop Wanting You") ... 10-20 61
ABC-PAR (10294 "Ginny Come Lately") .. 10-20 62
ABC-PAR (10336 "Sealed with a Kiss") ... 10-20 62
ABC-PAR (10359 "Warmed Over Kisses") ... 10-20 62
ABC-PAR (10374 "I May Not Live to See Tomorrow") ... 10-20 62
ABC-PAR (10400 "If Mary's There") ... 10-20 63
KAPP (342 "Itsy Bitsy Teenie Weenie Yellow Polkadot Bikini") ... 15-25 60
KAPP (352 "Four Little Heels") ... 40-50 60
(Black and white sleeve. Refers to Hyland as "The Bikini Boy." Promotional issue only.)
KAPP (352 "Four Little Heels") ... 15-25 60
(Color sleeve. No mention of "Bikini Boy.")
KAPP (363 "I Gotta Go") ... 15-25 60
PHILIPS (40179 "Here's to Our Love") ... 10-15 64
PHILIPS (40203 "Devoted to You") ... 10-15 64
PHILIPS (40263 "He Don't Understand You") ... 10-15 65
PHILIPS (40424 "Hung Up in Your Eyes"). 8-12 67
LPs: 10/12-inch
ABC-PAR (400 "Let Me Belong to You") .. 30-40 61
ABC-PAR (431 "Sealed with a Kiss") ... 30-40 62
ABC-PAR (463 "Country Meets Folk") ... 30-40 62
DOT (25926 "Tragedy") ... 10-12 69
DOT (25954 "Stay and Love Me All Summer") ... 10-12 69
KAPP (1202 "The Bashful Blonde") ... 25-30 60
(Monaural.)
KAPP (3202 "The Bashful Blonde") ... 30-40 60
PHILIPS (200136 "Here's to Our Love") ... 15-20 64
(Monaural.)
PHILIPS (200158 "Rockin' Folk") ... 15-20 65
(Monaural.)
PHILIPS (200217 "The Joker Went Wild") ... 15-20 66
(Monaural.)
PHILIPS (600136 "Here's to Our Love") .. 20-25 64
(Stereo.)
PHILIPS (600158 "Rockin' Folk") ... 20-25 65
(Stereo.)
PHILIPS (600217 "The Joker Went Wild") ... 20-25 66
(Stereo.)
PICKWICK ... 5-10
PRIVATE STOCK (7003 "In a State of Bayou") ... 5-10 77
RHINO ... 5-8
UNI (73097 "Brian Hyland") ... 8-10 70
WING (16341 "Here's to Our Love") ... 10-12 67
Session: Trudy Packer.
Also see SMITH, Roy

HYLOR, Mary
(With Bill Rolle & Lighters)
Singles: 7-inch
EL-LOR (1058 "We Walked Down the Aisle") ... 400-500 63
MPRC (251 "We Walked Down the Aisle") ... 75-125 65

HYMAN, Dick — P&R '54
(Dick Hyman Trio; with His Electric Eclectics)
Singles: 78 rpm
MGM ... 3-5 54-57
Singles: 7-inch
COLUMBIA ... 4-6 74-75
COMMAND ... 5-8 61-70
EVEREST (19356 "Glow Worm") ... 4-8 60
MGM ... 5-10 54-62
RCA ... 4-8 62
Picture Sleeves
MGM (12149 "Mack the Knife") ... 10-15 55
LPs: 10/12-inch
ATLANTIC ... 5-10 75
COLUMBIA ... 5-10 74
COMMAND ... 10-20 60-73
EVEREST ... 5-10 60
FAMOUS DOOR ... 5-10 73
MCA ... 5-10 77
MGM ... 10-20 54-63
PROJECT 3 ... 5-10 71
RCA ... 4-8 80-83
SUNSET ... 5-10 66
Also see CLYDE
Also see HAYES, Bill
Also see ROUGH RIDERS
Also see TAYLOR, Sam "The Man," & Dick Hyman

HYPERIONS
Singles: 7-inch
CHATTAHOOCHEE (669 "Why Do You Wanna Treat Me Like You Do") ... 75-125 65

HYPERIONS
Singles: 7-inch
PARIS TOWER (102 "Theme") ... 15-25 67

HYPNOTICS
Singles: 7-inch
WAR KEE (905 "Eloise") ... 3000-4000 59

HYSTERICAL SOCIETY
Singles: 7-inch
TIPTON (100 "I Put a Spell on You") ... 15-25 66
U.A. (50147 "Come with Me") ... 10-20 67

HYSTERICS
Singles: 7-inch
BING (303 "Everything's There") ... 15-25 65
SWAN (4270 "Hey, Little Fink") ... 5-10 67
TOTTENHAM (500 "Won't Get Far") ... 20-30 66
Also see LOVE-INS

HYTONES
Singles: 7-inch
A-BET (9415 "Bigger & Better") ... 50-100 66

HY-TONES
(With Steve Samuel's Orchestra)
Singles: 7-inch
HY-TONE (120 "I'm a Fool") ... 50-75 59
Session: Frank Anderson.
Also see HARRIS, Georgia, & Hy-Tones

HY-TONES
Singles: 7-inch
BELL (627 "You Don't Even Know My Name") ... 15-25 65
SOUTHERN ARTISTS (2023 "You Don't Even Know My Name") ... 25-35 '60s

I

I.M. BROKE & TAXPAYERS
Singles: 7-inch
POVERTY (1 "Wiped Out") .... 25-50 '60s

I.N.I.T.I.A.L.S
Singles: 7-inch
BURDLAND (695 "You Taught Me to Cry") 15-25 62

I-V-LEAGUERS
(I.V. Leaguers)
Singles: 78 rpm
DOT (15677 "Ring Chimes") 10-15 57
PORTER (1004 "Ring Chimes") 30-40 57
Singles: 7-inch
DOT (15677 "Ring Chimes") 10-15 57
NAU-VOO (803 "Jim-Jamin' ") 100-200 59
NAU-VOO (803 "Jim-Jam") 50-150 59
(Note slight title change.)
PORTER (1004 "Ring Chimes") 30-40 57
Also see IVY LEAGUERS

IAN, Janis P&R/LP '67
Singles: 7-inch
CAPITOL (3107 "He's a Rainbow") 4-6 71
CASABLANCA 3-5 80
COLUMBIA 3-6 74-81
POLYDOR 4-6 78
VERVE (5027 "Society's Child") 5-10 67
VERVE FOLKWAYS (5027 "Society's Child") 5-10 67
VERVE FOLKWAYS (5041 "Younger Generation Blues") 5-10 67
VERVE FORECAST (5072 thru 5099) 5-10 67-68
Picture Sleeves
COLUMBIA (10154 "At Seventeen") 4-6 75
LPs: 10/12-inch
CAPITOL (683 "Present Company") 8-12 71
COLUMBIA 8-10 74-81
MGM 8-10 70
POLYDOR 8-10 75
VERVE FORECAST (3017 "Janis Ian") ... 10-20 67
VERVE FORECAST (3024 "For All the Seasons of Your Mind") 10-15 67
VERVE FORECAST (3048 "Secret Life of J. Eddy Fink") 10-15 68
VERVE FORECAST (3063 "Who Really Cares") 10-15 69

IAN & ZODIACS
Singles: 7-inch
PHILIPS 5-10 64-66
Picture Sleeves
PHILIPS (40291 "So Much in Love with You") 10-15 65
EPs: 7-inch
PHILIPS (807 "Ian & Zodiacs") 10-20 65
LPs: 10/12-inch
COLUMBIA (2172 "Exciting New Liverpool Sound") 20-30 64
PHILIPS (200176 "Ian and the Zodiacs") 15-25 65
(Monaural.)
PHILIPS (600176 "Ian and the Zodiacs") 15-25 65
(Stereo.)

ICE
Singles: 7-inch
BONNY (1212 "Chicago Blues") .... 10-20 '60s

ICEMEN
Singles: 7-inch
ABC 5-10 68
OLE 9 (1008 "It's Gonna Take Time") ...... 10-20 '60s

ID
Singles: 7-inch
JOLLY ROGER (101 "Rotten Apple") ....8-12 '60s
RCA 5-10 67
Picture Sleeves
JOLLY ROGER (101 "Rotten Apple") ...... 10-15 '60s
LPs: 10/12-inch
RCA (LPM-3805 "Inner Sounds") 30-40 67
(Monaural.)
RCA (LSP-3805 "Inner Sounds") 35-45 67
(Stereo.)
Members: Paul Arnold; Jerry Cole.
Also see COLE, Jerry

ID
LPs: 10/12-inch
AURA (1000 "Where Are We Going") 50-75 75
Members: Gary Oickle; Dave Oickle; Ralph Jenkins; Kevin Orson; James Albert.

IDAHO, Ken
Singles: 7-inch
FAME (506 "School of Love") 10-15 59

IDEALS
Singles: 7-inch
COOL (108 "Do I Have the Right") 250-350 58
Also see OVATIONS

IDEALS
Singles: 7-inch
DECCA (30720 "My Girl") 15-25 58
DECCA (30800 "Ivy League Lover") 15-25 58
STARS OF HOLLYWOOD (1001 "Always Yours") 15-25 59

IDEALS R&B '66
Singles: 7-inch
CHECKER (920 "Knee Socks") 15-25 59
CHECKER (979 "Knee Socks") 10-15 61
DUSTY DISC ("Magic") 5-10 64
(Selection number not known.)
PASO (6401 "Together") 20-30 61
PASO (6402 "Magic") 30-40 61
RED ROCKET (472 "Magic") 5-10 63
SATELLITE (2007 "You Hurt Me") 15-25 65
SATELLITE (2009 "Kissin' ") 15-25 65
SATELLITE (2011 "Kissing Won't Go Out of Style") 10-20 66
Members: Major Lance; Sam Stewart; Reggie Jackson; Leonard Mitchell.
Also see LANCE, Major

IDEALS
Singles: 7-inch
BOOGALOO (108 "Mighty Lover") ....15-25 '60s
DAISY (04 "Thunder Drums") 10-20 64
FARGO (1024 "Trans Zister") 5-10 62
ST. LAWRENCE (1001 "Cathy's Clown") .10-15 64
ST. LAWRENCE (1020 "I Got Lucky") 10-15 66

IDEALS
Singles: 7-inch
CORTLAND (110 "The Gorilla") 8-12 63
CORTLAND (113 "Mo Joe Hanna") 8-12 64
CORTLAND (115 "Mo Gorilla") 8-12 64
CORTLAND (117 "Local Boy") 8-12 64

IDENTICALS
Singles: 7-inch
FIREBIRD (101 "Jamie") 15-25 62

IDES
Singles: 7-inch
KEN-DEL (5309 "Psychedelic Ride") .....50-100 '60s

IDIOTS
(Sascha Burland & Mason Adams)
Singles: 7-inch
RIVERSIDE (4505 "School for Airplane Pirates") 5-10 61
LPs: 10/12-inch
RIVERSIDE (843 "In Our Own Image") 15-25 61

IDLE RACE
Singles: 7-inch
LIBERTY (55997 "Here We Go 'Round the Lemon Tree") 10-15 67
LIBERTY (56064 "The End of the Road") 10-15 68
LPs: 10/12-inch
LIBERTY (7603 "Birthday Party") 25-30 69
SUNSET 8-12 72
Members: Jeff Lynne; Greg Masters; Roger Spencer; Dave Pritchard.
Also see LYNNE, Jeff
Also see SHERIDAN, Mike, & Nightriders

IDOLS
Singles: 7-inch
RCA (7339 "30 Days") 10-15 58
REDD-E (1017 "You're Good for Me") 15-25 58

IDOLS
(With the Luca Trio)
Singles: 7-inch
E.Z (1 "Jeannine") 30-40 61

IDOLS
Singles: 7-inch
GALAXIE (77 "The Stars Will Remember") 100-150 61

IDOLS
Singles: 7-inch
L-U-V (201,306 "True Love Gone") 20-40 66

IDOLS / Swans
Singles: 7-inch
DOT (16210 "Just a Little Bit More"/"Why Must I Cry") 8-12 61
REVEILLE (1002 "Just a Little Bit More"/"Why Must I Cry") 15-25 61
(First issue.)

IDYLLS
Singles: 7-inch
SPINNING (6012 "Annette") 25-35 60

IFIELD, Frank P&R '62
Singles: 7-inch
CAPITOL 5-10 63-65
HICKORY 4-8 66-71
MAM (3612 "Lonesome Jubilee") 4-6 71
VEE-JAY 5-10 62-63
W.B. 4-6 79
LPs: 10/12-inch
CAPITOL 10-20 63
COLUMBIA 10-20
HICKORY 10-20 66-68
VEE-JAY 10-20 62
Also see BEATLES / Frank Ifield

IGUANAS
Singles: 7-inch
FORTE (201 "Mona") 25-35 66
Member: Don Swickerath.
Also see POP, Iggy

IGUANAS
Singles: 7-inch
IGUANA (101 "I Can Only Give You Everything") 20-30 67

IKETTES P&R/R&B '62
(With the Ike & Tina Revue)
Singles: 7-inch
ATCO (6212 "I'm Blue") 10-15 61
ATCO (6223 "Troubles on My Mind") 8-12 62
ATCO (6232 "Heavenly Love") 8-12 62
ATCO (6243 "I Do Love You") 8-12 62
INNIS (3000 "Here's Your Heart") 5-10 64
INNIS (6667 "So Blue Over You") 15-25
(Earlier version of *I'm Blue*.)
MODERN (1003 thru 1015) 5-10 64-66
PHI-DAN (5009 "What'cha Gonna Do") 8-12 66
POMPEII (66683 "Make 'Em Wait") 5-8 68
TEENA (1702 "Prisoner in Love") 8-12 63
U.A. (50866 "If You Take a Close Look") 4-6 71
U.A. (51103 "I'm Just Not Ready for Love") .4-6 72
LPs: 10/12-inch
MODERN (102 "Soul Hits") 15-25 65
U.A. 8-10 73-75
Members: Delores Johnson; Eloise Hester; Joshie Jo Armstead; Vanetta Fields; Jessie Smith; Robbie Montgomery.
Session: Tina Turner.
Also see MIRETTES
Also see TURNER, Ike & Tina

IL GRUPPO
LPs: 10/12-inch
RCA (3846 "Private Sea of Dreams") 10-15 67
Member: Ennio Morricone.

ILL WIND
Singles: 7-inch
ABC (11107 "In My Dark World") 10-20 68
LPs: 10/12-inch
ABC (641 "Flashes") 50-100 68
Members: Conny Devanney; Richard Griggs; Carey Mann; Ken Frankel; Dave Kinsman.

ILLUSIONS
Singles: 7-inch
AXTEL (101 "Better Late Than Never") 30-40 60
COLUMBIA (43700 "I Know") 5-10 66
CORAL (62173 "The Letter") 30-40 60
DIAL (4004 "I Don't Believe It") 5-10 65
DOT (16752 "Don't Put Me Down") 10-15 65
EMBER (1071 "Can't We Fall in Love") 25-35 61
(White label.)
EMBER (1071 "Can't We Fall in Love") ... 15-25 61
(Black label.)
KAPE (100 "The Closer You Are") 4-8 74
LAURIE (3245 "Maybe") 15-25 64
MALI (104 "Hey Boy") 75-150 62
(Label is black with silver top.)
MALI (104 "Hey Boy") 50-75 62
(Label is all black.)
NORTH-EAST (801 "Hey Boy") 10-20 62
RELIC (512 "Hey Boy") 5-10 64
SHERATON (104 "Hey Boy") 20-30 62
Also see 3 FRIENDS

ILLUSIONS
Singles: 7-inch
LITTLE DEBBIE (105 "Story of My Life") 400-500 64
PAMA (126 "Big Beat '65") 10-20 65
ROUND (1018 "Jezebel") 15-25 63

ILLUSIONS
Singles: 7-inch
AUDIO UNLIMITED (1000 "The Outcast") 25-50 66

ILLUSIONS
Singles: 7-inch
MICHELLE (1 "City of People") 15-25 66

ILMO SMOKEHOUSE
LPs: 10/12-inch
BEAUTIFUL SOUND (3002 "Ilmo Smokehouse") 25-35 71
ROULETTE (3002 "Ilmo Smokehouse") .. 15-20 71
Members: Freddie Tieken; Dennis Tieken; Slink Rand; Gerry Gabel; Craig Moore.
Also see GONN
Also see TIEKEN, Freddie, & Rockers

IMAGE
Singles: 7-inch
TWIN TOWN (738 "My Girl") ....10-20 '60s

IMAGINATIONS
Singles: 7-inch
BACON FAT (101 "I Want a Girl") 10-15 61

IMAGINATIONS
Singles: 7-inch
BALLAD (500 "Wait a Little Longer Son") ..5-10 62
BO MARC (301"Guardian Angel") 5-10 61
DUEL (507 "Guardian Angel") 10-15 62
HARVEY (101 "I'll Never Let You Go") 4-8 76
MUSIC MAKERS (103 "Goodnight Baby") 10-15 61
MUSIC MAKERS (108 "Guardian Angel") 10-15 61
LPs: 10/12-inch
RELIC 5-10
Members: Frank Mancuso; Bobby Bloom; Phillip Agtuca; Pete Agtuca; Richie Le Causi.
Also see DAY, Darlene
Also see EXPRESSIONS

IMAGINATIONS
Singles: 7-inch
FRATERNITY (1001 " I Just Can't Get Over Losing You") 20-30 67
FRATERNITY (1005 "No One Ever Lost More") 75-125 68
FRATERNITY (1006 "Be Near") 50-100 68

IMMORTALS
Singles: 7-inch
LAURIE (3099 "Moonshine") 10-20 61

IMON, Ben
Singles: 78 rpm
VEE-JAY (177 "Down in the Country") 10-15 56
Singles: 7-inch
VEE-JAY (177 "Down in the Country") 20-30 56

IMPACS
(Pat Scot & Impacs)
Singles: 7-inch
IMPAC (59 "Lost Love") 10-15 61
Members: Pat Scot; Vic Waters.

IMPACS
Singles: 7-inch
ARLEN (741 "Hold-Out") 5-10 63
KING (5851 thru 5965) 5-10 64
PARKWAY (865 "I'm Gonna Make You Cry") 10-20 63

LPs: 10/12-inch
KING (886 "Impact!") 20-35 64
KING (916 "Weekend with the Impacs") .. 20-35 64

IMPACT IV
Singles: 7-inch
AGAR (7171 "Island of Love") 20-25 63

IMPACTS
Singles: 7-inch
CARLTON (548 "Darling, No You're Mine") 50-60 61
("Now" is misspelled.)
CARLTON (548 "Darling, Now You're Mine") 40-50 61
("Now" is spelled correctly.)
RCA (7583 "Bobby Sox Squaw") 10-15 59
RCA (7609 "Canadian Sunset") 15-20 59
WATTS (5599 "Now Is the Time") 150-200 58

IMPACTS
LPs: 10/12-inch
DEL-FI (1234 "Wipe Out!") 20-30 63
DEL-FI (DLF-1234 "Wipe Out!") 10-12 98
(Thick, hard wax reissue.)
OCEAN (8701 "Wipe Out") 5-10 88
Members: Merrell Wayne Fankhauser; Joel Rose; Steve Lee Evans; Wayne Marty Brown; Steve Eric Metz.
Also see FANKHAUSER, Merrell

IMPACTS
(Impact Express)
Singles: 7-inch
DCP (1150 "Just Because") 8-12 65
LAVENDER (2005 "Don't You Dare") 10-15 66
LAVENDER (2007 "Don't You Dare") 10-15 67
NWI (2660 "Leavin' Here") 10-20 65
Members: Henry Brusco; Bruce Farquhar; Dan White; Ron Baldwin; Bill Uhlig; Steve Green; La Donna Lockner.

IMPACTS
Singles: 7-inch
ANDERSON (104 "Linda") 20-30
ANDERSON (201 "Speed Zone") 10-20

IMPAKS
Singles: 7-inch
EXPRESS (716 "Make Up Your Mind") ... 15-20 63

IMPALA SYNDROME
LPs: 10/12-inch
PARALLAX (4002 "Impala Syndrome") . 75-100 69

IMPALAS
("Featuring Bobby Byrd with Buddy T. & His T-Men")
Singles: 7-inch
CORVET (1017 "Why!") 200-300 58
Also see BYRD, Bobby

IMPALAS P&R/R&B '59
("Featuring Joe 'Speedo' Frazier")
Singles: 7-inch
CUB (9022 "I Ran All the Way Home") 50-75 58
CUB (9022 "Sorry I Ran All the Way Home") 15-25 59
(Note slightly different title.)
CUB (9033 "Oh What a Fool") 15-25 59
CUB (9053 "Peggy Darling") 15-25 60
HAMILTON (50026 "I Was a Fool") 15-25 59
MGM 4-6 64-78
U.G.H.A. (17 "My Hero") 3-5 82
Picture Sleeves
CUB (9022 "Sorry I Ran All the Way Home") .... 5-10 '90s
U.G.H.A. (17 "My Hero") 3-5 82
EPs: 7-inch
CUB (5000 "Sorry, I Ran All the Way Home") 150-250 59
LPs: 10/12-inch
CUB (CUB-8003 "Sorry, I Ran All the Way Home") 250-350 59
(Monaural.)
CUB (CUBS-8003 "Sorry, I Ran All the Way Home") 450-550 59
(Stereo.)
Members: Joe "Speedo" Frazier; Richard Wagner; Lenny Renda; Tony Carlucci.
Also see SPEEDO & IMPALAS

IMPALAS
("Vocal by Celeste Warren")
Singles: 7-inch
ECHO (6018 "Betty Jean") .... 50-100 '50s

IMPALAS
Singles: 7-inch
BO (001 "Raincheck") 10-20 62

IMPALAS
Singles: 7-inch
ELAART (3001 "Great Pretender") 4-6 75
FEATURE (107 "Spoonful") 10-20 66
PAGE (8083-26 "Teenager in Love") 4-6 77
Members: Jeff Moretti; Jerry Morcia; Ron Moen; Gene Schiller; Mike Price; Chuck Loth; Jerry Kueper; Jack Gebhardt; Steve Keppen; Phil Shields; Donnie Roberts; Emmit Smith.

IMPALOS
Singles: 7-inch
U.A. (327 "You're to Blame") 15-25 61
VAL (1002 "I Cried") 40-50 58

IMPERIAL C'S
Singles: 7-inch
PHIL-L.A. OF SOUL (308 "Someone Tell Her") 800-1200 68

IMPERIAL GENTS
Singles: 7-inch
LAURIE (3540 "Little Darlin' ") 15-25 70

IMPERIAL 7
Singles: 7-inch
ATHENS (207 "Midnight Tom") 10-20 62

IMPERIALITES
Singles: 7-inch
IMPERIAL (66015 "Have Love Will Travel") 10-15 64

IMPERIALS
Singles: 78 rpm
DERBY 50-100 54
GREAT LAKES (1201 "Life of Ease") ... 200-300 54
GREAT LAKES (1212 "You'll Never Walk Alone") 200-300 54
(Though Great Lakes 1201 exists on 45 rpm, this release is not yet verified as being on 45.)
Singles: 7-inch
BUZZY (1 "My Darling") 30-40 61
(Black vinyl.)
BUZZY (1 "My Darling") 15-25 61
(Purple vinyl.)
DERBY (858 "Why Did You Leave Me") 200-300 54
GREAT LAKES (1201 "Life of Ease") 750-1000 54
(This exact same track was also issued by the Four Arcs.)
SAVOY (1104 "My Darling") 150-200 54
Members: M. Harris; L. Goodwin; R. Adams; B. Knight.
Also see FOUR ARCS

IMPERIALS R&B/P&R '58
Singles: 78 rpm
END (1027 "Tears on My Pillow") 75-125 58
Singles: 7-inch
CAPITOL (4924 "I'm Still Dancing") 8-12 63
CARLTON (566 "Faithfully Yours") 15-25 61
END (1027 "Tears on My Pillow") 30-40 58
(First pressing. Quickly repressed, crediting "Little Anthony & Imperials.")
LIBERTY (55119 "Glory of Love") 15-20 58
Also see LITTLE ANTHONY & IMPERIALS

IMPERIALS
(With Richard Barrett)
Singles: 7-inch
NEWTIME (503 "A Short Prayer") 10-15 62
NEWTIME (505 "The Letter") 10-15 62
Also see BARRETT, Richard

IMPERIALS
Singles: 7-inch
JERDEN (745 "Backyard Compost") 15-20 64
Members: Alan Park; Jeff Beals; Dan Denton; Rocky Rhoades; Jeff La Brache; Jim Wolfe; George Mitroff.
Also see CITY LIMITS
Also see ROCKY & RIDDLERS

IMPERIALS
Singles: 7-inch
UNITED SOUND (2658 "Avalanche") .... 50-75 '60s

IMPERIALS MINUS 2
Singles: 7-inch
IMPERIAL (5787 "A Swingin' Dream") 10-20 61

IMPLACABLES
Singles: 7-inch
KAIN (1004 "Don't Call for Me") 500-750 61
(Reissued as by Johnny Williams.)
Also see WILLIAMS, Johnny

IMPOSSIBLES
Singles: 7-inch
BLANCHE (029 "Chapel Bells") 500-750 63
PELLEGRINO (1030 "Mr. Maestro") 10-15 59
RMP 15-20 59-61

IMPOSSIBLES
Singles: 7-inch
REPRISE (305 "Paint Me a Pretty Picture") 15-25 64
Also see NAPOLEON XIV

IMPOSSIBLES
Singles: 7-inch
ROULETTE (4745 "I Wanna Know") 10-20 67

IMPOSTERS
Singles: 7-inch
FROG DEATH (1 "Wipe In") 25-50 63

IMPRESSIONS R&B '58
("Featuring Jerry Butler"; with Riley Hampton's Orchestra)
Singles: 12-inch
20TH FOX 4-8 79
Singles: 78 rpm
ABNER (1017 "Come Back My Love") 50-75 58
Singles: 7-inch
ABC (10831 thru 11188) 5-10 66-68
ABC-PAR (10241 "Gypsy Woman") 15-20 61
ABC-PAR (10289 "Can't You See") 15-20 62
ABC-PAR (10328 "Never Let Me Go") 15-20 62
ABC-PAR (10357 thru 10647) 10-15 62-65
ABC-PAR (10670 thru 10789) 8-12 65-66
ABNER (1017 "Come Back My Love") 10-15 58
ABNER (1023 "The Gift of Love") 10-15 59
ABNER (1025 "Lonely One") 10-15 59
ABNER (1034 "Say That You Love Me") . 15-20 60
ADORE (901 "Popcorn Willie") 200-300 61
BANDERA (2504 "Listen") 25-35 59
CHI-SOUND (2418 "Sorry") 4-6 79
CHI-SOUND (2438 "Maybe I'm Mistaken") .. 3-5 80
COTILLION 4-6 76-77
CURTOM 4-8 68-76
ICHIBAN 3-5 94
MCA 3-5 87
PORT (70031 "Listen") 8-12 62
SWIRL (107 "I Need Your Love") 15-25 62
20TH FOX (172 "All Through the Night") . 10-20 62
20TH FOX (2491 "For Your Precious Love") 3-5 81
20TH FOX (2499 "Fan the Fire") 3-5 81
VEE-JAY (280 "For Your Precious Love"): see BUTLER, Jerry
VEE-JAY (424 "Say That You Love Me") . 10-15 62
VEE-JAY (621 "Say That You Love Me") ... 5-10 64
Picture Sleeves
CURTOM (1932 "Fool for You") 5-10 68
EPs: 7-inch
ABC-PAR (505 "People Get Ready") 10-20 64
(Juke box issue only. Includes title strips.)
CURTOM (5 "Mighty, Mighty Spade and Whitey") 5-10 69
(Promotional issue only.)
CURTOM (20 "Do You Want to Win") 5-10 71
(Promotional issue only.)
LPs: 10/12-inch
ABC (606 thru 30009) 10-20 66-76
ABC-PAR (450 "The Impressions") 20-30 63
ABC-PAR (468 "Never Ending") 20-30 64
ABC-PAR (493 "Keep On Pushing") 20-30 64
ABC-PAR (505 "People Get Ready") 20-30 65
ABC-PAR (515 "Greatest Hits") 20-30 65
ABC-PAR (523 "One By One") 20-30 65
ABC-PAR (545 "Ridin' High") 20-30 66
COTILLION (9911 "Funky Christmas") 8-12 76
CURTOM 8-10 68-76
EMUS 5-8
MCA 5-10 82
PICKWICK 8-10 75
SCEPTER/CITATION 8-10
SIRE (3717 "Vintage Years") 10-15 76
20TH FOX 5-10 79-81
UPFRONT 8-10
Members: Curtis Mayfield; Sam Gooden; Richard Brooks; Fred Cash; Leroy Hutson; Reggie Torian; Ralph Johnson; Nate Evans.
Also see BRADLEY, Jan
Also see EVERETT, Betty / Impressions
Also see MAYFIELD, Curtis
Also see O'KAYSIONS / Impressions
Also see RAMSEY, Gloria

IMPRESSORS
Singles: 7-inch
CUB (9010 "Do You Love Her") 30-40 58
ONYX (514 "Is It Too Late") 50-60 57

IMPS
Singles: 7-inch
DO-RA-ME (1414 "That'll Get It") 15-20 61
SCEPTER (1240 "That'll Get It") 8-15 62

IN
Singles: 7-inch
HICKORY (1413 "Just Give Me Time") 10-15 66

IN CROWD P&R '66
Singles: 7-inch
BRENT (7046 "Cat Dance") 5-10 65
HICKORY 10-15 65
MUSICOR (1111 "Do the Surfer Jerk") 10-20 65
RONN (1 "In the Midnight Hour") 10-20 67
SWAN (4204 "Let's Shindig") 5-10 65
TOWER 5-10 65-66
VIVA 5-8 66-67

INCIDENTALS
Singles: 7-inch
FORD (134 "All Night") 15-25 64
FORD (138 "Lucille") 15-25 65
GAR-LO (1000 "Barbara") 15-25 61

INCIDENTALS
Singles: 7-inch
PARIS TOWER (126 "It's in Your Mind") . 20-30 67

INCINERATORS
Singles: 7-inch
SOUND-DEX (100 "I Want to Know") ..... 75-100 '60s

INCOGNITOS
Singles: 7-inch
ZEE (001 "Dee Jay's Dilemma") 50-75 61

INCONQUERABLES
Singles: 7-inch
FLODAVIEUR (803 "Wait for Me") ... 1500-2000 64
(Yellow vinyl.)

INCREDABLES
Singles: 7-inch
KELRICH (851 "If You Gave a Party") 15-25

INCREDIBLE BONGO BAND P&R/R&B '73
Singles: 7-inch
MGM 4-6 73
PRIDE 4-6 72-74
LPs: 10/12-inch
PRIDE (0028 "Bongo Rock") 50-100 73
PRIDE (6010 "Return") 10-20 74

INCREDIBLE BROADSIDE BRASS BED BAND
Singles: 7-inch
POISON RING (717 "Little Dead Surfer Girl") 15-25 71
LPs: 10/12-inch
POISON RING (2240 "Great Gizzly Bear Hunt") 20-30 71

INCREDIBLE INVADERS
Singles: 7-inch
PROPHONICS (2028 "Boy Is Gone") 10-20 67
Also see LYN & INVADERS

INCREDIBLE UPSETTERS
EPs: 7-inch
AUDIO LAB (2 "Incredible Upsetters") 750-1000 57

INCREDIBLE VIKINGS
Singles: 7-inch
WINNDSOCK ("Love Will Be Mine") 2000-3000 55
(No selection number used.)

INDEX
(The Index)
LPs: 10/12-inch
DC ("The Index") 2500-3000 68
(No selection number used. Reportedly 100 made. Identification number in the trail-off is "DC-71.")

DC ("Index") 1500-2500 68
(No selection number used. Not issued with cover. Reportedly 100 made. Identification number in the trail-off is "DC-4736.")
Members: Jim Valice; John Ford; Gary Ballew.

INDIGOS
(With the Cornel Tanassy Orchestra)
Singles: 7-inch
ADMIRAL (906 "Get Up and Go") 8-12 61
ARCADE (1006 "Servant of Love") 4-8 77
CORNEL (515 "High School Social")....... 10-15 58
CORNEL (3001 "Servant of Love")...... 100-200 58
IMAGE (5001 "Girl By the Wayside")....... 10-20 61
Also see EPICS

INDIGOS
Singles: 7-inch
CADETTE (8003 "My Dream Girl") 10-15 63

INDIVIDUAL ACTIVITY
Singles: 7-inch
TEE PEE (73/74 "Ten O'Clock"/"Don't Let the Sun Catch You Cryin' ") 10-20 68
Members: Al Blau; Brian Olson; Bill Shaw; Dennis Moore.

INDIVIDUALISTS
Singles: 7-inch
ONDA (110 "A Blue Note") 15-25 57

INDIVIDUALS
(With the Curly Palmer Orchestra)
Singles: 7-inch
CHASE (1300 "Wedding Bells").......... 500-600 63

INDIVIDUALS
Singles: 7-inch
RED FOX (105 "Dear One") 5-10 65
SHOW TIME (595 "Met Her at a Dance") 25-35 59
SHOW TIME (598 "Dear One") 20-30 59
SPARROW (100 "Without Success")... 200-300 59
(Same number used on Beverly Noble release.)

INDIVIDUALS
Singles: 7-inch
RAVEN (2018 "I Want Love") 15-25
TEQUILA (101 "Heartbreak Hotel")......... 30-50 61
Also see RIO, Chuck

INDIVIDUALS
Singles: 7-inch
RENDEZVOUS (176 "Crazy Horse") 10-20 62
Members: Pat Vegas; Lolly Vegas.
Also see VEGAS, Pat & Lolly

INELIGIBLES
Singles: 7-inch
ANDERSON.. 10-20 65
CAPELLA (501 "Just the Things That You Do") 25-35 60

INEXPENSIVE HANDMADE LOOK
Singles: 7-inch
BRUNSWICK (55334 "Ice Cream Man") . 10-20 67

INFASCINATIONS
Singles: 7-inch
CLAUWELL (004 "I'm So in Love") 400-600 61
(Polystyrene pressing.)
CLAUWELL (004 "I'm So in Love") 20-30 61
(Vinyl pressing.)

INFATUATORS
Singles: 7-inch
DESTINY (504 "I Found My Love")...... 450-550 61
FELLATIO (201 "I Found My Love") 5-10
VEE-JAY (395 "I Found My Love") 50-75 61
Session: Leesures.
Also see LEE, Larry, & Leesures

INFERNO
Singles: 7-inch
DATE (1524 "Your Heart Is Too Big for Your Head") 10-20 66

INFERNOS
Singles: 7-inch
HAWK (13500 "Goin' Cruisin' ") 20-30 63
RUDY (001 "Little Willy's Monkey")............5-10 64

INFINITE STAIRCASE
Singles: 7-inch
BLACK SHEEP (1337 "Long Hair")......... 20-30

INFLAMMABLE, Dan, & Igniters
Singles: 7-inch
WINE (09 "High Flying") 40-60

INFLUENCE
LPs: 10/12-inch
ABC (630 "Influence")...............................25-35 68
Members: Andrew Keiler; Walter Rossi; Dave Wynne; Jack Geisinger; Louis McKelvey; Bobo Island.
Also see HAUNTED
Also see LUKE & APOSTLES

INFORMERS
Singles: 7-inch
DORE (562 "Don't Cry") 20-30 60

INFORMERS
(With Morris Bailey & Orchestra)
Singles: 7-inch
BLACKJACK (1402 "Baby, Set Me Free") 300-500 65
J-RUDE (1400 "If You Love Me")..........200-300 65
(Identification number shown since no selection number is used.)
Also see BAILEY, Morris, & Thomas Boys

INGLE, Red, & Natural Seven *C&W '47*
(With Jo Stafford as "Cinderella G. Stump")
Singles: 78 rpm
CAPITOL (1639 "Temptation")..................10-15 47-49
Singles: 7-inch
CAPITOL (1639 "Temptation")..................15-20 51
Also see JONES, Spike
Also see MARTIN, Dean / Red Ingle & Natural Seven
Also see STAFFORD, Jo

INGMANN, Jørgen *P&R/R&B '61*
(Grethe & Jørgen Ingmann)
Singles: 78 rpm
MERCURY 4-8 56
Singles: 7-inch
ATCO..5-15 60-66
MERCURY..8-12 56
PARROT 4-8 64
U.A. INT'L...4-6 68
LPs: 10/12-inch
ATCO...25-35 62
MERCURY...25-35 56
U.A. INT'L...8-12 68

INGRAM, Benny
Singles: 7-inch
BANDERA (1302 "Jello Sal") 350-400 58
TODD (1048 "Jello Sal")...........................25-50 59

INGRAM, Luther *R&B '69*
(With the G-Men)
Singles: 7-inch
DECCA (31794 "Ain't That Nice") 5-10 65
ERIC...4-6 '70s
HIB (698 "If It's All the Same to You Babe")...50-75 67
KO KO 5-10 67-78
PROFILE 3-5 86-87
SMASH (2019 "Foxy Devil")....................10-15 66
LPs: 10/12-inch
KO KO 8-10 71-76
(May also be shown as Koko—one word.)

INGREDIENTS
Singles: 7-inch
TODDLIN' TOWN (101 "Hey Who")..........15-25 67

IN-GROUP
LPs: 10/12-inch
IN (1002 "Swinging 12 String")..................15-25 64
Members: Glen Campbell; Leon Russell; Earl Palmer.
Also see CAMPBELL, Glen
Also see RUSSELL, Leon

INITIALS
("As Originated on the Terry Lee Show")
Singles: 7-inch
DEE (1001 "Bells of Joy").......................150-200 59
KEEL (100 "Giggling Girl") 150-200
SHERRY (2 "Bells of Joy") 20-30 59
(What appears to be the selection number actually reads "Teen Sound #2.")
VINTAGE (1006 "You Didn't Answer My Letter") 10-15 73
(Red vinyl.)

INK SPOTS *P&R '39*
(Charlie Fuqua's Ink Spots; Charlie Owens & Sensational Ink Spots)
Singles: 78 rpm
BLUEBIRD (6530 "Swingin' on the Strings") 15-25 36
DECCA (800 series) 10-15 36
DECCA (1000 thru 4000 series) 5-15 36-42
DECCA (18000 thru 30000 series) 5-10 42-57
GRAND AWARD 5-10 56
Singles: 7-inch
DECCA (25533 "All My Life") 5-10 61
DECCA (27000 thru 30000 series)..........10-20 50-56
FEATHER (099 "Into Each Life Some Rain Must Fall")..10-15
FLAGG (20117 "Someone Loves Someone")..15-25
FORD (115 "Hawaiian Wedding Song")...15-25 62
GRAND AWARD (1001 "Do I Worry")......15-25 56
KAY BEE (108 "Do I Worry") 15-25 63
SWIFT (1001 "If I Didn't Care"/"Into Each Life Some Rain Must Fall")....................................10-20
TOP RANK (2096 "Oh Yes") 10-15 61
VERVE (10071 "Darling Don't Cry") 10-15 57
VERVE (10094 "If I'd Only Known You Then") 10-15 58
VERVE (10198 "Secret Love")....................5-10 60
X-TRA (101 "Gimme the Key") 5-10 60
Picture Sleeves
GRAND AWARD (1001 "Do I Worry") 10-15 56
(Has die-cut center hole.)
EPs: 7-inch
DECCA...10-15 54-56
GRAND AWARD 10-20 56
TOPS (606 "Ink Spots") 10-15 59
(Two discs.)
WALDORF MUSIC HALL...........................10-15 55
LPs: 10/12-inch
AUDITION 15-25 56
COLORTONE 15-25 58
CORAL 4-8 73
CORONET ....10-15 '60s
CROWN (144 "Greatest Hits") 10-20 59
(Black vinyl.)
CROWN (144 "Greatest Hits") 40-60 59
(Colored vinyl.)
CROWN (175 "The Ink Spots")..................10-15 61
(Monaural.)
CROWN (217 "Sensational Ink Spots")....10-15 61
CROWN (448 "If I Didn't Care") 10-15 63
CROWN (5112 "Greatest Hits") 10-15 59
(Monaural.)
CROWN (5142 "The Ink Spots")................10-15 61
(Stereo.)
CROWN (5197 "Sensational Ink Spots")..10-15 62
DECCA (182 "Best of the Ink Spots") 15-25 65
(Monaural. Two discs.)
DECCA (7-182 "Best of the Ink Spots")....15-25 65
(Stereo. Two discs.)
DECCA (4297 "Our Golden Favorites")....15-25 63
(Monaural.)
DECCA (7-4297 "Our Golden Favorites") 15-25 63
(Stereo.)
DECCA (5000 series) 20-40 51-53
(10-inch LPs.)
DECCA (7000 & 8000 series) 15-30 54-59
DESIGN...5-10 '60s
DIPLOMAT...5-10 64
EVEREST...5-10 82
EVON ....10-20 '50s
EXACT 5-10 80
GOLDEN TONE..5-10
GRAND AWARD 10-25 56-59
HURRAH ....10-15 '60s
MCA..5-10 73
MAYFAIR 8-15
MODERN (7023 "Fabulous Ink Spots")..75-125
MONTGOMERY WARD'S........................10-20
(Colored vinyl.)
PRI (3 "In the Spotlight") 10-15
PAULA..5-10 72
PIROUETTE..10-20
SPIN-O-RAMA...5-10 '60s
TOPS (1561 "The Ink Spots") 20-30 57
TOPS (1668 "The Ink Spots, Vol. 2")........15-20 59
VENISE (10025 "4 of a Kind")...................15-25
(Gold vinyl.)
VERVE 15-25 56-60
VOCALION...8-15 59-65
WALDORF MUSIC HALL (144 "The Ink Spots Quartet") 30-50 55
(10-inch LP.)
WALDORF MUSIC HALL (152 "The Ink Spots Quartet, Vol. 2")...30-50 55
(10-inch LP.)
WESCO ("Hawaiian Wedding Song") 25-35 62
(Selection number not known.)
Members: Bill Kenny; Orville Jones; Charlie Fuqua; Herb Kenny; Ivory "Deek" Watson; Bernie Mackey; Cliff Givens; Billy Bowen; Charlie Owens.
Also see BROWN DOTS
Also see FITZGERALD, Ella, & Ink Spots
Also see FOUR DOTS
Also see KENNY, Bill
Also see OWENS, Charlie

INK SPOTS
Singles: 78 rpm
KING (1297 thru 1512)............................10-15 53-55
KING (4670 "Here in My Lonely Room")..20-30 53
(Blue label.)
KING (4670 "Here in My Lonely Room")..40-60 53
(White label with "Introducing the Ink Spots" bio. Promotional issue only.)
KING (4857 "Command Me")....................15-25 55
Singles: 7-inch
KING (1297 "Ebb Tide") 20-30 53
KING (1304 "Stranger in Paradise").........20-30 54
KING (1336 "Melody of Love")..................20-30 54
KING (1378 "Yesterday") 15-25 54
KING (1425 "When You Come to the End of the Day")..15-25 55
KING (1429 "Melody of Love")..................15-25 55
KING (1512 "Don't Laugh at Me")............15-25 55
KING (4670 "Here in My Lonely Room")..30-40 53
(Blue label.)
KING (4670 "Here in My Lonely Room")..50-75 53
(White label with "Introducing the Ink Spots" bio. Promotional issue only.)
KING (4857 "Command Me")....................15-25 55
EPs: 7-inch
KING (376 "Great Songs of Our Times Sung by Ink Spots") 50-100 56
LPs: 10/12-inch
KING (535 "Something Old, Something New") 100-200 57
KING (642 "Something Old, Something New") 75-125 59
Members: James Holmes; Charlie Fuqua; Harry Jackson; Isaac Royal; Leon Antoine.

INK SPOTS
Singles: 7-inch
FABULOUS (1003 "A Man") 40-50 63
PERIWINKLE (7307 "Reborn")....................5-10 73
(Canadian.)
PERIWINKLE (7330 "The Fabulous Ink Spots") 5-10 73
(Canadian.)
Members: Joe Van Loan; Ray Richardson; Napoleon Allen; Bob Moreland; Al Mayers; George Kelly; Al Williams; Bill Duncan
Also see MODERN INK SPOTS
Also see VAN LOAN, Joe

INMAN, Autry *C&W '53*
Singles: 78 rpm
BULLET (682 "It May Be") 5-10 49
DECCA (Except 28629 & 29936) 5-10 53-56
DECCA (28629 "That's All Right")............10-15 56
DECCA (29936 "Be Bop Baby") 15-20 56
Singles: 7-inch
DECCA (Except 28629 & 29936) 10-15 53-56
DECCA (28629 "That's All Right")............20-25 56
DECCA (29936 "Be Bop Baby") 40-60 56
EPIC...5-8 67-69
GLAD 10-15 60
JUBILEE...5-8 65-69
MERCURY...5-10 62
MILLION...4-6 72
RCA...10-15 58
RISQUE (103 "Niteclubbin' ") 5-10 67
RISQUE (105 "The Golf Game") 5-10 67
SIMS..5-10 63-64
U.A. 10-15 60
LPs: 10/12-inch
ALSHIRE..8-12 69
EPIC...10-15 68
GUEST STAR 8-12
JUBILEE..10-20 64-69

MOUNTAIN DEW....................................15-25 63
SIMS...15-20 64
Also see DEAN, Jimmy / David Houston / Warner Mack / Autry Inman

INMAN, Jimmy
(With the Impollos)
Singles: 7-inch
ALADDIN (3426 "I'm So Sorry")............75-125 58
NRC (5004 "Saving My Love")................15-25 59

IN-MEN LTD.
(Featuring Skip Hinshaw)
Singles: 7-inch
JOKERS THREE ("Voice Your Choice") . 20-30 '60s
(Selection number not known.)
PYRAMID (7200 "Take a Look at Me Baby")..................................15-25 66
PYRAMID (7454 "Little Girl")..................15-25 '60s

INMATES
Singles: 7-inch
COLUMBIA (44032 "You Tell Lies").........10-20 67
KOPIT (127 "This Is the Day")................10-20 66

INMATES
Singles: 7-inch
JCP (1029 "Baby, Come On").................10-20 64

IN-MEN
Singles: 7-inch
PYRAMID (7454 "Little Girl")..................15-25

INNER CIRCLE
Singles: 7-inch
DUNHILL (4128 "Goes to Show You").....10-20 68
IMPACT (1019 "Sally Go Round the Roses")...................................15-25 67
Members: Phil Sloan; Steve Barri.
Also see FANTASTIC BAGGYS

INNER THOUGHTS
Singles: 7-inch
PARIS TOWER (105 "Smokestack Lightning")...................................20-30 67

INNKEEPERS
Singles: 7-inch
GALIKO (895 "Wanted").........................20-30
SIX CENTS ("A Man Can Tell")...............30-40

INNOCENCE P&R '66
Singles: 7-inch
KAMA SUTRA..5-10 66-67
LPs: 10/12-inch
KAMA SUTRA..15-20 67
Members: Pete Anders; Vinnie Poncia.
Also see ANDERS & PONCIA

INNOCENTS P&R '60
Singles: 7-inch
DECCA (31519 "Don't Cry")....................10-15 63
ERA..4-6 72
INDIGO (105 thru 132)...........................15-25 60-61
PORT (3026 "Gee Whiz")........................5-10 68
REPRISE (20112 "Oh How I Miss My Baby"/"Be Mine")..10-15 62
REPRISE (20125 "Oh How I Miss My Baby"/ "You're Never Satisfied")...............................5-10 62
TRANS-WORLD (7001 "Tick Tock")........15-25 60
VIRGO (6019 "Gee Whiz")........................4-6 72
W.B. (5450 "My Heart Stood Still")..........20-30 64
EPs: 7-inch
INDIGO (1000 "The Innocents")..........150-250 61
(Issued with paper cover.)
LPs: 10/12-inch
INDIGO (503 "Innocently Yours")..........50-100 61
Members: Darron Stankey; Al Candaleria; Jim West.
Session: Gary Paxton.
Also see ECHOES
Also see PAXTON, Gary
Also see SUGAR BEATS
Also see WASHER WINDSHIELD
Also see YOUNG, Kathy

INNSMEN
Singles: 7-inch
WHEELS (3611 "I Don't Know")..............20-30 67

INSANE
Singles: 7-inch
ALLEN ASSOCIATES (201,347 "I Can't Prove It")..20-30 67

IN-SECT
LPs: 10/12-inch
CAMDEN (909 "Introducing the In-Sect Direct from England")..20-30 65

INSECT TRUST
Singles: 7-inch
ATCO (6764 "Reciprocity")........................5-10 70
DYNAMIC SOUND....................................5-10 67
LPs: 10/12-inch
ATCO (313 "Hoboken Saturday Night")....20-30 70
CAPITOL (0109 "Insect Trust")................15-25 68
Members: Nancy Jeffries; Luke Faust.

INSIDE OUT
LPs: 10/12-inch
FREDLO (6834 "Bringing It All Back")..100-200 68

INSIDERS
Singles: 7-inch
RCA (9225 "I'm Just a Man")...................10-15 67
RCA (9325 "If You Had a Heart").............10-15 67
RED BIRD (055 "Chapel Bells Are Calling")..10-15 66

INSIGHT
Singles: 7-inch
CASCADE ("Please Come Home for Christmas")...15-25 64

INSIGHTS
Singles: 7-inch
PALMETTO ARTISTS (9021 "I Need Your Loneliness")..15-25 68
RCA (9555 "Someday Girl").......................5-10 68

INSITES
Singles: 7-inch
VAGUE (901 "Nothing Is Wrong with Love")..10-20 66

INSPIRATIONS
(With Fats Gaines & Band)
Singles: 78 rpm
APOLLO (494 "Raindrops")......................50-75 56
Singles: 7-inch
APOLLO (494 "Raindrops")..................200-300 56
LAMP (2019 "Don't Cry")........................50-75 58

INSPIRATIONS
Singles: 78 rpm
JAMIE (1034 "Dry Your Eyes")................20-30 56
Singles: 7-inch
AL-BRITE (1651 "Angel in Disguise").......30-40 59
BELTONE (2037 "The Girl by My Side")..30-40 63
GONE (5097 "Angel in Disguise")............10-20 61
JAMIE (1034 "Dry Your Eyes")................50-60 56
JAMIE (1212 "Dry Your Eyes")................10-15 62
SPARKLE (102 "Angel in Disguise")....100-200 59
SULTAN (1 "The Genie")..........................20-30 59
Picture Sleeves
SULTAN (1 "The Genie")..........................30-40 59
Members: Carlton Brown; Cedric Wilson; Don Stevens; Jerry Johnson; Willie Wiggins.

INSPIRATIONS
Singles: 7-inch
RONDACK (9787 "Ring Those Bells")..400-500 61

INSPIRATIONS
Singles: 7-inch
FEATURE (110 "Baby Please Come Home")..25-35 66

INSPIRATIONS
Singles: 7-inch
BLACK PEARL (100 "Funny Situation").....5-10 67
BREAKTHROUGH ("No One Can Take Your Place")..20-30
(Selection number not known.)

INSPIRATIONS
Singles: 7-inch
MIDAS (9003 "Your Wish Is My Command")...400-500 67

INSPIRATIONS
Singles: 7-inch
PKC (1012 "Watermelon Man")...............10-20 68
Members: John Draws; Tom Bloom; Steve Fuchs; Ron Skaluta; Dean Hottinger; Dave Zylka; Bill Tate Tazinsky; Dale Streeter.

INSPIRATORS
Singles: 78 rpm
TREAT (502 "If Loving You Is Wrong").100-200 55

Singles: 7-inch
DUTCH (103 "If Loving You Is Wrong"/"Starlight Tonight")..50-75 99
LOST NITE..4-8
OLD TOWN (1053 "Starlight Tonight").150-200 58
TREAT (502 "If Loving You Is Wrong") 300-400 55

INSTANTS
Singles: 7-inch
RENDEZVOUS (193 "Always Be True")..10-15 62
RENDEZVOUS (201 "Gravy Train").........10-15 63

INSTRUMENTALS
Singles: 7-inch
FORWARD (500 "Jam Session Rock").....8-12 59
HANOVER (4502 "Chop Suey Rock")......10-15 58
RED FOX (100 "Chop Suey Rock")...........5-10 64

INTELLECTUALS
Singles: 7-inch
STARK (010 "One True Love")................10-20 66

INTENSIONS
Singles: 7-inch
BLUELIGHT (1212 "She's My Baby").......25-35
BLUELIGHT (1214 "I Don't Care Anymore")..25-35
BLUELIGHT (1234 "I Don't Get Down Like That")..25-35

INTENTIONS
Singles: 7-inch
JAMIE (1253 "Summertime Angel")....800-1000 63
JASON SCOTT (02 "Summertime Angel")...3-5 80
(500 made.)
Member: Rich Mignona.

INTENTIONS
Singles: 7-inch
UPTOWN (710 "Time")...........................10-15 65

INTENTIONS
Singles: 7-inch
KENT (455 "My Love, She's Gone").........10-20 66

INTENTIONS
Singles: 7-inch
PHILIPS (40428 "Don't Forget That I Love You")..10-20 67
Members: Brian Humble; Jack Vallati; Dennis Brennan; Ron Brennan; Greg Coates; Henry Urick; Rick Smith; Bob Siverling.
Also see EXCITING INVICTAS

INTENTIONS
Singles: 7-inch
MELRON (5014 "I'm in Love with a Go Go Girl")..150-200 68
Members: Chip Kopaczewski; Tony Avicoll; Charlie Votta; Ed Sachetti.

INTERIORS
Singles: 7-inch
WORTHY (1008 "Darling Little Angel")..75-125 61
WORTHY (1009 "Echoes").......................40-50 61

INTERLUDES
Singles: 7-inch
RCA (7281 "I Shed a Million Tears").......20-30 58
Members: Frankie Anderson; Kenny Loftman; Otha Sonnie; Eddie Adams; Fred Jackson.

INTERLUDES
Singles: 7-inch
STAR-HI (103 "Split a Kiss")....................10-15 59
VALLEY..10-15 59-60

INTERLUDES
Singles: 7-inch
ABC-PAR (10213 "No. 1 in the Nation")...10-20 61
KING (5633 "Darling I'll Be True")............30-40 62

INTERNATIONAL BOOGIE BAND
Singles: 7-inch
GAME (296 "Drinkin' Wine Spo-Dee-O-Dee")..15-25

INTERNATIONAL GTO's
Singles: 7-inch
ROJAC (1007 "I Love My Baby").............40-50 '60s

INTERNATIONAL SUBMARINE BAND
Singles: 7-inch
ASCOT (2218 "The Russians Are Coming, the Russians Are Coming ")..........................10-15 66
COLUMBIA...8-12 66
LHI (1205 "Blue Eyes")..............................5-10 68
LHI (1217 "I Must Be Somebody Else").....5-10 68
Picture Sleeves
ASCOT (2218 "The Russians Are Coming, the Russians Are Coming ")..........................30-50 66
(Counterfeits exist but those we've seen do not have the Ascot logo and number. Originals have these at lower right corner.)
LPs: 10/12-inch
LHI (12001 "Safe at Home")....................40-60 68
Members: Gram Parsons; Earl Ball; Bob Buchanan; Jon Corneal; John Nuese; J.D. Maness.
Also see PARSONS, Gram

INTERNATIONALS
Singles: 7-inch
ABC-PAR (9964 "Goin' to a Party").........10-20 58

INTERNS
Singles: 7-inch
CAPITOL (5747 "Just Like Me")..............10-20 66
PARADISE (1019 "Have Mercy").............50-75 66
PARADISE (1023 "Life with You")...........10-20 66
UPTOWN (730 "And I'm Glad")................10-20 66

INTERPRETERS
Singles: 7-inch
GEMINI/BOFUZ (100 "Stop That Man")...10-20 65
Picture Sleeves
GEMINI/BOFUZ (100 "Stop That Man")...10-20 65
Members: Sylvia; Beate.

INTERPRETERS
Singles: 7-inch
A-BET (9425 "Pretty Little Thing")...........10-15 67
CADET (5537 "The Knack")......................5-10 66
LPs: 10/12-inch
CADET (762 "The Knack").......................10-15 66

INTERVALS
(With Chick Morris & His Band)
Singles: 7-inch
AD (104 "I Still Love That Man")..............10-20 58
APT (25019 "I Still Love That Man")........10-15 58
CLASS (304 "Here's That Rainy Day")...750-1000 62
IRMA (820 "Love Me Sweet")..............250-350 58
Also see FIFTH DIMENSION

INTERVALS
Singles: 7-inch
WEST COAST (2 "I Envy These Things")..50-100 61

INTICERS
Singles: 7-inch
BABY LOV (003 "I've Got to Find My Baby")..15-25

INTIMATES
Singles: 7-inch
AMCAN (402 "Got You Where I Want You"/"Only Girl for Me")..40-50 64
AMCAN (402 "Got You Where I Want You")..10-20 64
(Single-sided. Promotional issue only.)
EPIC (9743 "I've Got a Tiger in My Tank")..20-30 64

INTREPIDES
Singles: 7-inch
MASCIO (120 "Golash")...........................20-30 65

INTRIGUES
Singles: 7-inch
BRUNSWICK (55247 "Checkmate")..........5-10 63
JOEY (6152 "Road Race").......................10-15 62

INTRIGUES
Singles: 7-inch
PORT (3018 "Girl Let's Stay Together")...10-20 66

INTROS
Singles: 7-inch
JAMIE (1350 "Stop, Look and Listen").....10-20 68

INTRUDERS P&R '59
(Intruders Trio)
Singles: 7-inch
BELTONE (1009 "Camptown Rock").........5-10 61
FAME (101 "Jeffries Rock").....................10-20 59
FAME (313 "Creepin").............................10-20 59
FAME (616 "Rock-A-Ma-Roll")................10-20 59
VALTONE (409 "Rockamaroll")................15-25 59

INTRUDERS
Singles: 7-inch
ANDERSON (103 "Intruder") ... 20-30 63
MUSIC VOICE (504 "But You Belong to Me") ... 15-25 64
SAHARA (101 "Wild Goose") ... 10-20 63

INTRUDERS
Singles: 7-inch
GALLANTRY ... 10-15 63
MOXIE ... 10-20 64
Also see BELOVED ONES
Also see DEARLY BELOVEDS

INTRUDERS
Singles: 7-inch
IT (2312 "She's Mine") ... 10-20 66
Picture Sleeves
IT (2312 "She's Mine") ... 20-30 66

INTRUDERS
Singles: 7-inch
CINEMA (6901 "Total Raunch") ... 25-50 66
MARLO (1545 "That's the Way") ... 30-40 66
Picture Sleeves
CINEMA (6901 "Total Raunch") ... 50-100 66

INTRUDERS
Singles: 7-inch
CLAREMONT (662 "Bringing Me Down") ... 10-20 66

INTRUDERS FIVE
Singles: 7-inch
GROG (2201 "Ain't Comin' Back") ... 20-30 66

INVADERS
("Featuring Johnny Burton")
Singles: 7-inch
BAMBOO (501 "Trouble on Main Street") ... 10-20 61
EL TORO (503 "Paradise") ... 100-200 59
INSTRO (1000 "Pam"/"Invasion") ... 75-100 62
(*Invasion* was also issued as *Surfer's Charge* by the Roulettes.)
MOHAWK (139 "One Step in the Darkness") ... 10-15 65
MUSICTONE ... 5-8 65
OO ... 4-6
PHILIPS ... 5-10 64
VAUGHN LTD. ... 10-20
WHINGDING ... 10-15
LPs: 10/12-inch
JUSTICE (125 "On the Right Track") ... 150-200 '60s
Member: Johnny Burton.
Also see ROULETTES

INVADERS
Singles: 7-inch
DELTA (2134 "You Can't Sit Down") ... 8-12
JCP (1027 "You Really Tear Me Up") ... 10-20 64
PHALANX (1028 "Set Me Free") ... 50-100 '60s

INVADERS
Singles: 7-inch
20TH FOX (469 "Mr. Guitar") ... 10-20 64
(Previously issued as *Crazy* by Buchanan & Goodman.)
Also see BUCHANAN & GOODMAN

INVADERS
Singles: 7-inch
TMS (7985 "Cryin' All Night Long") ... 15-20 67

INVADERS
Singles: 7-inch
CALENDAR (223 "I Won't Be Lanly [sic]") ... 15-25 68
CAPITOL (2292 "California Sun") ... 5-10 68
USA (902 "Flower Song") ... 5-10 68
Members: Dave Dobry; Mark Paulick; Pete Polzak; Jim Sawyer; John Sawyer.

INVALIDS
Singles: 7-inch
CRUTCH (14032 "I Love This Girl") ... 15-25

INVENTIONS
Singles: 7-inch
UP (111 "Hey, Peanuts") ... 15-25 60

INVERTS
Singles: 7-inch
TOWER (324 "Look Out Love") ... 15-25 67

INVICTAS
(With the Hollywood Rebels; "Featuring Sonny Patterson")
Singles: 7-inch
JACK BEE (1003 "Gone So Long") ... 30-40 59
VAULT (903 "Gone So Long") ... 15-25 63
(Also issued on Vault 101, credited to Sonny Patterson & the Invictas.)
Also see HOMBS, Jimmie / Twinkletones
Also see PASTEL SIX
Also see PATTERSON, Sonny, & Invictas

INVICTAS
Singles: 7-inch
MAVIS (221 "I Met Him at the Dance") ... 10-20 63
Also see RUTHANNE & INVICTAS

INVICTAS
Singles: 7-inch
20TH FOX (493 "Breakout") ... 10-15 64
LPs: 10/12-inch
20TH FOX (3132 "The Invictas") ... 30-40 64

INVICTAS
Singles: 7-inch
BENGEL ... 5-10 65
SAHARA (107 thru 117) ... 5-10 65
LPs: 10/12-inch
EVA (12016 "A-Go-Go") ... 10-15 83
SAHARA (101 "A-Go-Go") ... 50-100 65
Member: Herb McGovern.

INVICTAS
Singles: 7-inch
PIX (1101 "Lest You Forget") ... 500-750 60
RAMA RAMA (7779 "New Babe") ... 15-25 69

INVICTAS
LPs: 10/12-inch
INVICTAS (5816 "The Invictas") ... 150-200 '60s

INVICTORS
("Music by the Royal Dukes")
Singles: 7-inch
BEE (1117 "I'll Always Care for You") ... 400-500 59
Members: Barry Boswell; Ray Edwards; Bill Yuhas; Gene Yuhas; Robert Rohrbach.
Also see SILHOUETTES
Also see TERMITES

INVICTORS
Singles: 7-inch
TPE (8217 "This Thing Called Love") ... 100-150 62
TPE (8219 "Don't Take My Love") ... 200-300 62
TPE (8221 "Where All Lovers Meet") ... 2000-2500 62
(Reissued in '63 with a Victorio label added on top of this one, crediting the Vendors.)
TPE (8223 "I Took a Chance") ... 400-500 63
Also see VENDORS

INVINCIBLES
Singles: 7-inch
CHESS (1727 "Mr. Moonglow") ... 20-30 59
(Blue label.)
CHESS (1727 "Mr. Moonglow") ... 5-10 61
(Orange and yellow label.)
Members: David Richardson; Clifton Knight; Lester Johnson.

INVINCIBLES *R&B '65*
Singles: 7-inch
DOUBLE SHOT (131 "Keep on Trying") ... 5-10 68
LOMA (2032 thru 2057) ... 5-10 66
RAMPART (665 "Crystal Blue Persuasion") ... 15-25 69
STARDOM (3500 "Heart Full of Love 1970") ... 5-10 70
W.B. (5495 thru 7061) ... 5-10 64-67
Members: Lester Johnson; David Richardson; Clifton Knight.

INVITATIONS
Singles: 7-inch
DIAMOND ... 5-10 68
DYNO VOICE (206 thru 210) ... 15-25 65
DYNO VOICE (215 " Skiing in the Snow") ... 25-50 66
MGM (13574 "The Skate") ... 5-10 66
OUT OF THE PAST (9 "Skiing in the Snow") ... 5-10

IRBY, Jerry *C&W '48*
(With the Texas Ranchers)
Singles: 78 rpm
DAFFAN (106 "Time You Started Looking") ... 10-20 56
DAFFAN (108 "Clickety Clack") ... 50-100 56
MGM (10151 "Cryin' in My Beer") ... 8-12 48
MGM (10188 "Great Long Pistol") ... 8-12 48
Singles: 7-inch
DAFFAN (106 "Time You Started Looking") ... 30-40 56
DAFFAN (108 "Clickety Clack") ... 250-350 56
POLLY (201 "Forty Nine Women") ... 100-200

IRBY, Jerry & Jeanne
Singles: 7-inch
JER-RAY (222 "Chantilly Lace") ... 15-25
Also see IRBY, Jerry

IRENE & SCOTTS
Singles: 7-inch
SMASH (2138 "I'm Stuck on My Baby") ... 10-20 67

IRIDESCENTS
Singles: 7-inch
HUDSON (8102 "Three Coins in the Fountain") ... 20-30 63
(Black vinyl.)
HUDSON (8102 "Three Coins in the Fountain") ... 75-100 63
(Blue vinyl.)
HUDSON (8107 "I Found You") ... 30-40 63
ULTRASONIC (109 "The Angels Sang") ... 750-1000 60

IRMA & LARKS
Singles: 7-inch
FAIRMOUNT (1003 "Don't Cry") ... 10-15 66
PRIORITY (322 "Don't Cry") ... 30-40 63

IRON BUTTERFLY *P&R/LP '68*
Singles: 7-inch
ATCO ... 5-8 68-71
MCA ... 4-6 75
EPs: 7-inch
ATCO (4524 "Iron Butterfly") ... 20-30 68
(Promotional issue only. Issued with paper sleeve.)
LPs: 10/12-inch
ATCO (Except 227) ... 10-15 68-71
ATCO (227 "Heavy") ... 15-20 68
MCA ... 8-10 75
Members: Doug Ingle; Mike Pinera; Larry Reinhardt; Ron Bushy; Lee Dorman; Erik Brann.
Also see CAPTAIN BEYOND

IRON CITY HOUSEROCKERS
Singles: 7-inch
MCA ... 4-6 79-80
MCA ("Love's So Tough") ... 20-25 79
(Picture disc. Promotional issue only. Selection number not known.)
MCA (8418 "Hideaway") ... 8-15 79
(Picture disc. Promotional issue only.)
LPs: 10/12-inch
MCA (Except 1813) ... 5-10 79-81
MCA (8313 "Love's So Tough") ... 30-35 79
(Promotional only picture disc.)

IRON GATE
Singles: 7-inch
MARBELL (1001 "Feelin' Bad") ... 15-25 66

IRON GATE
Singles: 7-inch
MOBIE (3529 "Get Ready") ... 15-25 68

IRON MAIDEN *LP '81*
Singles: 7-inch
CAPITOL (Except V-15375) ... 3-5 88
CAPITOL (V-15375 "Can I Play with Madness") ... 10-20 88
(Shaped picture disc.)
LPs: 10/12-inch
CAPITOL (Except "SEAX" & "SJ" series) ... 4-8 82-88
CAPITOL (SEAX-12215 "Number of the Beast") ... 35-45 82
(Picture disc.)
CAPITOL (SEAX-12306 "Piece of Mind") 40-60 83
(Picture disc.)
CAPITOL (SJ-12321 "Powerslave") ... 8-12
("Special Limited Edition, Virgin Maiden Vinyl Pressing.")
EPIC ... 15-20 90
HARVEST (Except 15000) ... 8-12 80-82
HARVEST (15000 "Maiden Japan") ... 10-20 81
Members: Bruce Dickinson; Dave Murray; Adrian Smith; Niko Mc Brian; Steve Harris.

IRRIDESCENTS
Singles: 7-inch
HAWK (4001 "Bali Ha'i") ... 25-35 63
INFINITY (037 "Bali Ha'i") ... 15-25 63
OLDIES 45 (183 "Bali Ha'i") ... 8-10 63
Also see STRAWBERRY ALARM CLOCK

IRVIN, Curtis, & Sparks
Singles: 78 rpm
RPM (417 "Make a Little Love") ... 75-100 54
Singles: 7-inch
RPM (417 "Make a Little Love") ... 300-350 54

IRVINE, Robert
Singles: 7-inch
PRESTO (525 "Fastest Shot in Town") ... 50-75

IRVING, Gloria
Singles: 78 rpm
COBRA (5008 "I Need a Man") ... 5-10 56
Singles: 7-inch
COBRA (5008 "I Need a Man") ... 10-15 56
Also see KARI, Sax

IRVING, Lonnie *C&W '60*
Singles: 7-inch
LONNIE IRVING ... 10-20 '50s
STARDAY (505 "Gooseball Brown") ... 50-75 60

IRWIN, Big Dee *P&R '63*
(Difosco Erwin; Dee Irwin; with Little Eva)
Singles: 7-inch
BLISS (1003 "Anytime") ... 10-15 61
DIMENSION (1001 "Everybody's Gotta Dance But Me") ... 8-12 62
DIMENSION (1010 "Swinging on a Star") ... 10-20 63
DIMENSION (1015 thru 1028) ... 8-12 63-64
FAIRMOUNT (1005 "Sweet Young Thing Like You") ... 8-12 66
IMPERIAL ... 5-10 68-69
PHIL-L.A. OF SOUL (303 "Linda") ... 5-10 67
ROTATE (851 "You Satisfy My Needs") .. 10-20 65
ROTATE (853 "Follow My Heart") ... 10-20 65
20TH FOX (418 "Donkey Walk") ... 5-10 63
Also see ERVIN, Dee
Also see ERWIN, Dee
Also see IRWIN, Dee, & Mamie Galore
Also see LITTLE EVA
Also see PASTELLS

ISAAC, Esau
Singles: 7-inch
MELRON (Except 5002) ... 5-10 63-64
MELRON (5002 "All Because of You") ... 40-50 63
SWAN (4110 "Poison Pen") ... 5-10 62

ISABELL, Rusty
Singles: 7-inch
BRENT (7001 "Firewater") ... 15-20 59
BRENT (7006 "Manhunt") ... 15-20 59
Also see RIO ROCKERS

ISLANDERS *P&R '59*
(Featuring Randy Starr)
Singles: 7-inch
MAYFLOWER ... 5-10 59-60
LPs: 10/12-inch
MAYFLOWER ... 20-30 60
Members: Randy Starr; Frank Metis.
Also see BELAFONTE, Harry / Islanders
Also see STARR, Randy
Also see WARRIORS

ISLE, Jimmy
Singles: 78 rpm
BALLY ... 10-15 57
Singles: 7-inch
BALLY(1034 "Baby-O") ... 10-15 57
EVEREST (19320 thru 19383) ... 5-10 59-60
MALA (459 "Our Town") ... 10-15 63
ROULETTE (4065 "Goin' Wild") ... 20-30 58
SUN (306 thru 332) ... 8-12 58-59

ISLE, Ronnie
(With the Yo Yos)
Singles: 7-inch
IMAGE (1004 "Day We Marry") ... 10-20 60
MGM (12682 "Wicked") ... 15-25 58
METRO (20014 "Heaven Knows") ... 5-10 59
OKEH (7148 "Flame's Gone Out") ... 5-10 62

WARWICK (645 "Everybody Got a Little Shot") 5-10 61
Also see WOW WOWS

ISLEY BROTHERS P&R '59
("Featuring Ronald Isley")

Singles: 78 rpm

TEENAGE (1004 "Angels Cried") 200-400 57

Singles: 12-inch

T-NECK 4-8 79-83
W.B. 4-6 87

Singles: 7-inch

ATLANTIC (2092 thru 2122) 8-12 61
ATLANTIC (2263 thru 2277) 5-10 64-65
CINDY (3009 "Don't Be Jealous"/"This Is the End") 150-200 58
(Cindy logo is in block print with a shadow behind the letters.)
CINDY (3009 "Don't Be Jealous"/"This Is the End") 40-60 58
(Cindy logo is in a rectangular box at the top of the label.)
EARLY BIRD (007 "Don't Be Jealous") 3-5 96
(Lavender vinyl.)
GONE (5022 "Everybody's Gonna Rock & Roll") 40-50 58
GONE (5048 "My Love"/"The Drag") 30-40 58
MARK-X (7003 "Rockin' MacDonald") ...75-100 57
MARK-X (8000 "This Is the End"/"The Drag") 15-25 59
RCA (7537 "I'm Gonna Knock on Your Door") 10-15 59
RCA (47-7588 "Shout!") 15-25 59
(Monaural.)
RCA (61-7588 "Shout") 25-50 59
(Stereo.)
RCA (7657 thru 7787) 10-15 59-60
RCA GOLD STANDARD 5-8 61
(Black label, RCA dog on top.)
RCA GOLD STANDARD 4-6 65
(Black label, RCA dog on left side.)
T-NECK (Except 501) 3-6 69-84
T-NECK (501 "Testify") 5-10 64
TAMLA 5-15 66-69
TEENAGE (1004 "Angels Cried") 300-400 57
U.A. (605 thru 714) 10-20 63-64
V.I.P. (25020 "I Hear a Symphony") 300-500 65
VEEP (1230 "Love Is a Wonderful Thing").8-12 66
WAND (118 thru 131) 8-12 62-63
W.B. 3-5 85-89

Picture Sleeves

W.B. 3-5 87-89

LPs: 10/12-inch

BUDDAH 10-12 76
CAMDEN 8-10 73-75
COLLECTABLES 6-8 88
MOTOWN 5-10 80-82
PHILA. INT'L 5-10 78
PICKWICK 5-10 77
RCA (LPM-2156 "Shout!") 40-60 59
(Monaural.)
RCA (LSP-2156 "Shout!") 50-75 59
(Stereo.)
SCEPTER 10-20 66
SUNSET 8-10 69
T-NECK (Except 137) 8-10 69-84
T-NECK (137 "Everything You Always Wanted to Hear") 10-15 76
(Promotional issue only.)
TAMLA (269 "This Old Heart of Mine") 25-50 66
TAMLA (275 "Soul on the Rocks") 15-25 67
TAMLA (287 "Doin' Their Thing") 15-20 69
TRIP 8-10 76
U.A. (500 series) 8-10 75
U.A. (6000 series) 20-25 63
WAND (WD-653 "Twist & Shout") 20-30 62
(Monaural.)
WAND (WDS-653 "Twist & Shout") 30-40 62
(Stereo.)
W.B. 5-10 85-87
Members: Ron Isley; Rudy Isley; O'Kelly Isley; Ernie Isley; Marvin Isley. Session: Jimi Hendrix.
Also see CHRISTIE, Lou, & Classics / Isley Brothers / Chiffons
Also see HENDRIX, Jimi, & Isley Brothers
Also see RASCALS / Isley Brothers

ISLEY BROTHERS / Chiffons

LPs: 10/12-inch

SPIN-O-RAMA (127 "Isley Brothers and Chiffons") 15-25 64

ISLEY BROTHERS & DAVE "BABY" CORTEZ

LPs: 10/12-inch

T-NECK 8-10 69
Also see CORTEZ, Dave "Baby"

ISLEY BROTHERS / Brooklyn Bridge

LPs: 10/12-inch

T-NECK (3004 "Live at Yankee Stadium") 20-30 69
(With guests, Edwin Hawkins Singers; Five Stairsteps, Sweet Cherries, and Judy White.)
Also see BROOKLYN BRIDGE
Also see WHITE, Judy

ISLEY BROTHERS / Go-Go's

EPs: 7-inch

RCA/WURLITZER 10-15 64
(Promotional issue only.)
Also see GO-GOs

ISOM RAY
(Ray Agee)

Singles: 7-inch

RGA (114 "Rock Hard") 40-60 62
Also see AGEE, Ray

ISONICS

Singles: 7-inch

KAMMY (369 "He Needs Her") 20-30

IT'S A BEAUTIFUL DAY LP '69
(Featuring David LaFlamme)

Singles: 7-inch

COLUMBIA 4-8 69-73
SAN FRANCISCO SOUND 8-12 70

LPs: 10/12-inch

COLUMBIA (1058 "Marrying Maiden") 15-20 70
COLUMBIA (9768 "It's A Beautiful Day")..20-30 69
COLUMBIA (30734 "Choice Quality Stuff"/"Anytime") 10-15 71
COLUMBIA (31338 "Live at Carnegie Hall") 10-15 72
COLUMBIA (32181 "It's A Beautiful Day Today") 10-15 73
COLUMBIA (32660 "1001 Nights") 30-40 73
(Promotional issue only.)
SAN FRANCISCO SOUNDS (04800 "Marrying Maiden") ....30-40 '80s
(Half-speed mastered.)
SAN FRANCISCO SOUNDS (11790 "It's A Beautiful Day") ....30-40 '80s
(Half-speed mastered.)
Also see GARCIA, Jerry
Also see PABLO CRUISE

IT'S US

Singles: 7-inch

ARAB ("Don't Want Your Lovin'") 25-35
(Selection number not known.)

ITELS

Singles: 7-inch

MAGNIFICO (101 "Star of Paradise") 15-25 61

ITEMS

Singles: 7-inch

TELEDISC (63 "Foxy Lady") ....10-20 '60s

ITHICAS

Singles: 7-inch

FEE BEE (220 "If You Want My Love") 20-30 58

ITHICAS

Singles: 7-inch

VAL (6 "Michael's Madness") 10-20 66

ITO, Richie

Singles: 7-inch

STELLAR (711 "Don't Cry Linda") 40-50 61

IVAN P&R '58
(Jerry Ivan Allison)

Singles: 7-inch

CORAL (62017 "Real Wild Child") 50-100 58
CORAL (62017 "Real Wild Child") 150-250 58
(Light blue label. Promotional issue only.)
CORAL (62081 "Frankie Frankenstein") 50-100 59
CORAL (62081 "Frankie Frankenstein") 250-350 59
(Light blue label. Promotional issue only.)
CORAL (65607 "Real Wild Child") 20-30 67
Session: Buddy Holly (lead guitar); Jerry Allison; Joe B. Mauldin; Bo Clarke; Roses.
Also see CRICKETS

IVERSON, Ben, & Hornets

Singles: 7-inch

WAY OUT (4960 "Love Me") 250-350 62
(Identification number shown since no selection number is used.)
Also see HORNETS
Also see JOHNSON, Lester, & Hornets

IVES, Burl P&R '48
(With the Trinidaddies; "The Wayfaring Stranger")

Singles: 78 rpm

COLUMBIA 10-15 50-51
DECCA 10-15 47-57
STINSON (522 "Blue Tail Fly") 15-20 47

Singles: 7-inch

BELL 4-6 70
BIG TREE 4-6 71
BUENA VISTA 5-10 63
COLUMBIA (39000 series) 10-20 50-51
COLUMBIA (44000 series) 4-8 68-69
COLUMBIA (70000 series) 4-6 69
CYCLONE 4-6 70
DECCA (25000 series) 4-8 66-69
DECCA (27000 thru 30000 series) 10-20 50-59
DECCA (31000 thru 33000 series) 5-10 60-73
DISNEYLAND 4-8 64
MCA 4-6 73-74
MONKEY JOE 4-6 78
U.A. (429 "All Alone") 5-10 62

Picture Sleeves

BUENA VISTA (419 "On the Front Porch") 8-12 63
DECCA (31695 "A Holly Jolly Christmas").8-12 64

EPs: 7-inch

COLUMBIA 10-20 51-55
DECCA 10-20 49-65

LPs: 10/12-inch

BELL 5-10 71
CAEDMON 4-8 72
COLUMBIA (628 "Wayfaring Stranger") 15-25 55
COLUMBIA (1459 "Return of the Wayfaring Stranger") 10-20 60
COLUMBIA (2570 "Children's Favorites") 25-50 55
(10-inch LP.)
COLUMBIA (6058 "Wayfaring Stranger").25-50 50
(10-inch LP.)
COLUMBIA (6109 "Wayfaring Stranger, Vol. 2") 25-50 51
(10-inch LP.)
COLUMBIA (6144 "Wayfaring Stranger, Vol. 3") 25-50 51
(10-inch LP.)
COLUMBIA (9000 series) 8-12 68-69
CORAL 5-8 73
DECCA (100 series) 15-25 61
DECCA (4000 series) 10-20 62-68
(Decca LP numbers in this series preceded by a "7" or a "DL-7" are stereo issues.)
DECCA (5013 "Ballads and Folk Songs") 25-50 49
(10-inch LP.)
DECCA (5080 "Ballads and Folk Songs, Vol. 2") 25-50 49
(10-inch LP.)
DECCA (5093 "Ballads, Folk and Country Songs, Vol. 3") 25-50 49
(10-inch LP.)
DECCA (5490 "Women – Songs of the Fair Sex") 25-50 53
(10-inch LP.)
DECCA (8000 series) 10-20 55-59
DISNEYLAND 8-12 63-64
EVEREST 5-10 78
HARMONY 8-15 59-70
MCA 5-10 73-75
PICKWICK 5-10
SUNSET 5-10 70
UNART 6-12 67
U.A. 10-20 59-62
WORD 5-10 63-66
Session: Anita Kerr Singers.
Also see KERR, Anita
Also see MILLS, Hayley, & Burl Ives

IVES, Burl, with Grady Martin & His Slew Foot Five C&W '52

Singles: 78 rpm

DECCA (28055 "Wild Side of Life") 5-8 52

Singles: 7-inch

DECCA (28055 "Wild Side of Life") 10-20 52
Also see MARTIN, Grady

IVES, Burl, with Captain Stubby & Buccaneers C&W '49

Singles: 78 rpm

DECCA (24547 "Lavender Blue") 10-20 49
Also see IVES, Burl

IVES, Burl / Chad Willis & Beachstones

LPs: 10/12-inch

CORONET (271 "Burl Ives Sings") ....10-15 '60s

IVES, Jimmy

Singles: 7-inch

COMET (21 "My Fumbling Heart") 40-50 61

IVEY, Chet "Poison"
(With His Fabulous Avengers; Ivy Group; Chet Ivey)

Singles: 7-inch

ABC-PAR 5-10 60-61
ATCO (6148 "The Slop") 5-10 59
BEE CEE (304 "Is It Too Late") 15-25 63
BEE CEE (307 "Would It Be Wrong") 10-15 63
BEE CEE (315 "Soul Is My Game") 10-15 64
GATOR 4-8
SYLVIA 4-6
TANGERINE 4-6 68

IVEYS P&R '69
(Badfinger)

Singles: 7-inch

APPLE (1803 "Maybe Tomorrow") 10-15 69
APPLE/AMERICOM (301 "Maybe Tomorrow") 150-250 69
(Plastic, 4-inch flexi "Pocket Disc" soundsheet.)
Also see BADFINGER

IVIES

Singles: 7-inch

BRUNSWICK (55112 "Sunshine") 30-40 58
CORAL (62068 "Sunshine") 30-40 58
IVY (110 "Sunshine") 75-125 58
ROULETTE (4183 "Voodoo") 10-15 59

IVOLEERS
(With the Bobby Smith Orchestra & Chorus)

Singles: 7-inch

BUZZ (101 "Lovers' Quarrel") 400-500 59

IVORIES
(With the Sampson Horton Orchestra)

Singles: 7-inch

JAGUAR (3019 "Alone") 200-300 57
JAGUAR (3023 "Alone") 150-250 58

IVORIES

Singles: 7-inch

MERCURY (71239 "Me & You") 15-25 57

IVORY TONES

Singles: 7-inch

NORWOOD (101 "Little Fool") 400-500 60

IVORYS
(Ivory's)

Singles: 7-inch

DARLA (1000 "Wishing Well") 1000-2000 62
(First issue.)
SPARTA (001-BB "Why Don't You Write Me") 50-75 62
("BB" used because Sparta 001, without "BB," is *Wishing Well*, credited to the Blue Chips.)
Also see BLUE CHIPS

IVORYTONES

Singles: 7-inch

BAYOU (711 "Teen Love") 100-150 60

IVORYTONES

Singles: 7-inch

UNIDAP (448 "Wo Wo Wo Wo") 25-35 60

IVY, Sheron

Singles: 7-inch

COED (572 "Believe Me") 5-10 62
HERITAGE (106 "Believe Me") 10-20 62
(First issue.)

IVY, Sir Henry

Singles: 7-inch

FUTURE DIMENSION ("He Left You Standing There") 25-35
(Selection number not known.)

IVY, Sonny Joe

Singles: 7-inch

JEWEL (738 "Ruby and the Gambler") 15-20 64
JEWEL (746 "Take Me Back") 5-10 65

IVY JIVES
Singles: 7-inch
JARO (77036 "Knockout") 10-20 60

IVY LEAGUE *P&R '65*
Singles: 7-inch
CAMEO (343 thru 449) 10-15 65-66
Picture Sleeves
CAMEO (388 "Our Love Is Slipping Away") 20-30 65
LPs: 10/12-inch
CAMEO (2000 "Tossing & Turning") 25-35 65
(Monaural.)
CAMEO (S-2000 "Tossing & Turning") 30-40 65
(Stereo.)
Members: John Carter; Ken Lewis; Perry Ford.
Also see FLOWERPOT MEN
Also see PHILWIT & PEGASUS

IVY LEAGUE TRIO
Singles: 7-inch
CORAL (62301 "Take Me for a Ride in the Car Car") 5-10 62
CORAL (62327 "Deep Blue Sea") 5-10 62
LPs: 10/12-inch
CORAL (57399 "On and Off Campus") 10-20 62
CORAL (57404 "Folk Songs Rare and Well Done") 10-20 62

IVY LEAGUERS
Singles: 7-inch
FLIP (325 "Beware of Love") 30-40 57
Also see I.V. LEAGUERS

IVY THREE *P&R/R&B '60*
Singles: 7-inch
SHELL (302 "I Cried Enough for Two") 30-40 61
SHELL (306 "Bagoo") 10-15 61
SHELL (720 "Yogi") 15-20 60
(Blue label.)
SHELL (720 "Yogi") 10-15 60
(Multi-color label.)
SHELL (723 "Alone in the Chapel") 15-25 60

IVY TONES
Singles: 7-inch
RED TOP (105 "Oo-Wee Baby") 100-150 58
(Blue label. Label name in script.)
RED TOP (105 "Oo-Wee Baby") 50-75 58
(Blue label. No distributor.)
RED TOP (105 "Oo-Wee Baby") 30-40 58
(Blue label. Shows Liberty as distributor.)
RED TOP (105 "Oo-Wee Baby") 40-50 58
(White label.)
RED TOP (105 "Oo-Wee Baby") 8-12 58
(Red label.)
Members: John Ivy; William Brown; James Green; James Thomas; Little Joe Cook.
Also see COOK, Little Joe
Also see NAKED TRUTH

IVYLIERS
Singles: 7-inch
DONNA (3 "Echo from the Blue") 75-100 57

IVYMEN
Singles: 7-inch
TWIN TOWN (720 "La-Do-Da Da") 80-120 67

IVYS
Singles: 7-inch
COED (518 "All I Want") 10-15 59

J

J & SABERS
(With the Gents)
Singles: 7-inch
VAVRAY (1003 "Little One") 15-25 62

J. BROTHERS
(The "J" Brothers; with the Belltones)
Singles: 7-inch
MERMAID (3360 "The Girl I Used to Know") 75-150 58
("The Girl I Use [sic] to Know") 200-300 58
(First issue. No label name or selection number used. Issued for fan club use only.)
Members: John Tirino; Jim Tirino.
Also see 4 SEASONS / Neil Sedaka / J Brothers / Johnny Rivers

J.B. & HIS BAYOU BOYS
(J.B. Lenoir)
Singles: 7-inch
J.O.B. (1008 "The Mountain") 75-100 52
J.O.B. (1016 "I'll Die Trying") 50-75 52
Also see LENOIR, J.B.

J.B. & PLAYBOYS
Singles: 7-inch
RCA (3342 thru 3404) 8-12 65-66
Picture Sleeves
RCA (3342 "Chances") 10-15 65
RCA (3355 "Love, Happiness and Sweet You") 10-15 65
LPs: 10/12-inch
RCA (PC-1086 "J.B. & Playboys") 30-40 65
(Monaural.)
RCA (PCS-1086 "J.B. & Playboys") 20-30 65
(Stereo.)
Note: All above are Canadian releases.
Members: Al Nicholls; Doug West; Andy Kaye; Bill Hill; Lou Atkins.
Also see FREEDOM NORTH
Also see JAYBEES
Also see NICHOLLS, Al "J.B.", & Playboys

J.B.s *P&R '72*
(J.B.'s Internationals)
Singles: 7-inch
PEOPLE 5-10 72-76
POLYDOR 4-6 77-78
LPs: 10/12-inch
PEOPLE (5601 "Food for Thought") 50-75 72
PEOPLE (5603 "Doing It to Death") 50-75 73
Also see BROWN, James

J.B.G. & JULES
(Jules Blattner Group & Jules)
Singles: 7-inch
NORMAN (557 "Goodbye Baby") 10-15 65
Also see BLATTNER, Jules

J.C. THREE
Singles: 7-inch
SHASTA (172 "Lover's Farewell") 10-20 62

J.D. & IMPRESSIONS
Singles: 7-inch
STAR SATELLITE (1021 "Blues Kick") 10-20 62

J.K. & CO.
LPs: 10/12-inch
WHITE WHALE (7117 "Suddenly One Summer") 10-20 69

J.R. & ATTRACTIONS
Singles: 7-inch
HUNCH (928 "I'm Yours") 20-30 65
Also see RAND, Johnny

J.R. & GOLDEN NUGGETS
Singles: 7-inch
GOLDEN (101 "Lazy River Blues") 200-300

J's WITH JAMIE
Singles: 7-inch
COLUMBIA 5-10 62-64
Picture Sleeves
COLUMBIA (42855 "For the Last Time") 8-12 63
LPs: 10/12-inch
COLUMBIA 15-25 63-64
Members: Tom Jameson; Serena Jameson.
Also see JAMIES

JABLONSKI, Sir, & Unknowns
Singles: 7-inch
DUCAN (1500 "Merry Christmas Day") 400-500
M AND L ("Merry Christmas Day") 400-500
(No selection number used.)

JAC & JAY
(With the Tom Toms)
Singles: 7-inch
SHANE (47-2 "Peanut Butter") 25-50 64
Members: Jack (Jac) Castleberry; James (Jay) McClung; Gene Summers; Charlie Mendias; C.B. Williams; Ernest Walker.
Also see SUMMERS, Gene

JACEMEN
Singles: 7-inch
LARSON (5305 "You Can't Do That") 10-20 64

JACK, Bobby
Singles: 7-inch
TOP RANK (2009 "Early Mornin' ") 10-15 59

JACK, Buddy
(With Kathy Williams)
Singles: 7-inch
ARLEN (1001 "Lily White Hands") 100-200 61
ARLEN (1007 thru 1010) 10-20 61

JACK, Johnny
Singles: 7-inch
ASTRA (5003 "Beggar That Became a King") .... 3-5 '80s
DORE (617 "Love of My Own") 5-10 61
GONE (5132 "Beggar That Became a King") 15-20 62
GREAT (101 "Smack Madam") 50-75 59
LAWN (226 "True Love at First Sight") 30-40 64
LAWN (230 "Love Must Be") 20-30 64
RICKY (212 "Need You") 15-25 62
(Blue label.)
RICKY (212 "Need You") 8-10 62
(Silver label.)
Also see CHRISTIE, Lou
Also see YORK, Johnny

JACK & BEANSTALKS
Singles: 7-inch
LE RON (3601 "Don't Bug Me") 75-125 66
REVOLUTION (2914 "A Long Time Coming") 75-125 68
Members: Jack Tadych; John Conrath; Robert Kennedy; John Lyons; Pat Glass; Jim Dietrich; Doug Werginz.

JACK & BETTY
Singles: 78 rpm
TEEN (107 "This Is My Story") 8-12 55
Singles: 7-inch
TEEN (107 "This Is My Story") 15-20 55

JACK & JIM
Singles: 7-inch
BRUNSWICK (55141 "Midnight Monsters Hop") 40-60 59
Members: Jack Huddle; Jim Robinson.
Also see HUDDLE, Jack
Also see ROBINSON, Jim

JACK & KNIGHTS
Singles: 7-inch
MITCH (1612 "Rock the Blues Away") . 150-200

JACK LADS
Singles: 7-inch
KISKI (2050 "Hot Toddy") 10-15 63

JACKASSES
Singles: 7-inch
BRAY (2626 "Sugaree") 10-20 64

JACKIE & JILL
Singles: 7-inch
CUCA (64112 "I Want the Beatles for Christmas") 15-25 64
USA (791 "I Want the Beatles for Christmas") 10-20 65

JACKIE & RAINDROPS
Singles: 7-inch
COLPIX (738 "Down Our Street") 10-15 64
Members: Jackie Beadle; Len Beadle; Brian Adams.

JACKIE & STARLITES *R&B '62*
Singles: 78 rpm
FIRE & FURY (1000 "They Laughed at Me") 500-750 59
Singles: 7-inch
FIRE & FURY (1000 "They Laughed at Me") 1000-1500 59
FURY (1057 "I Found Out Too Late") 20-30 62
HULL (760 "I Still Remember") 15-25 64
LANA (120 "Valarie") 4-8 64
(First issued as by the Starlites.)
MASCOT (128 "For All We Know") 15-25 62
(No horseshoe on label.)
MASCOT (128 "For All We Know") 10-20 62
(Has horseshoe around hole.)
MASCOT (130 "You Keep Telling Me") 30-40 63
MASCOT (131 "Walking from School") 50-75 63
LPs: 10/12-inch
LOST NITE ("Jackie and the Starlites") 10-20 81
(10-inch LP. Red vinyl. 1000 made.)
RELIC (5090 "Jackie & Starlites") 10-15 91
Members: Jackie Rue; Alton Jones; George Lassu; John Felix; Billy Montgomery; Charles Hudson.
Also see 5 WINGS
Also see STARLITES

JACKIE & TONETTES
Singles: 7-inch
D-TOWN (1050 "Steady Boy") 15-25 65

JACK-O-LANTERNS
Singles: 7-inch
GOLDCREST (163 "Lori Anne") 1000-2000

JACKS *P&R/R&B '55*
Singles: 78 rpm
RPM (Except 428) 15-25 55-56
RPM (428 "Why Don't You Write Me"/"Smack Dab in the Middle") 50-75 55
RPM (428 "Why Don't You Write Me"/"My Darling") 25-35 55
(Note different flip side.)
Singles: 7-inch
KENT (344 "Why Don't You Write Me") 8-12 60
RPM (428 "Why Don't You Write Me"/"Smack Dab in the Middle") 75-125 55
RPM (428 "Why Don't You Write Me"/"My Darling") 50-75 55
(Note different flip side.)
RPM (433 "I'm Confessin' ") 50-75 55
RPM (444 "This Empty Heart") 40-50 55
RPM (454 "How Soon") 40-50 56
RPM (458 "Why Did I Fall in Love") 40-50 56
RPM (467 "Let's Make Up") 50-75 56
LPs: 10/12-inch
BEST 15-25
CROWN (372 "The Jacks") 50-75 62
(Stereo.)
CROWN (5021 "Jumpin' with the Jacks") 100-200 56
CROWN (5372 "The Jacks") 50-75 62
(Monaural.)
RPM (3006 "Jumpin' with the Jacks") ... 250-500 56
RELIC 10-15
UNITED .... 8-10 '70s
Members: Willie Davis; Ted Taylor; Aaron Collins; Will Jones; Lloyd McCraw; Prentice Moreland.
Also see BARRY, Dave, & Sara Berner
Also see CADETS
Also see JESSIE, Young
Also see MORELAND, Prentice
Also see ROCKETS

JACKS, A., & Cleansers
Singles: 7-inch
CLEAN (110 "Stronger Than Dirt") 10-20 65

JACKS & JILLS
(With the Ernie Freeman Orchestra)
Singles: 78 rpm
EMPIRE (101 "I Hear a Melody") 8-12 56
Singles: 7-inch
EMPIRE (101 "I Hear a Melody") 10-20 56
MGM (12671 "I Can't Forget") 5-10 58
Also see FREEMAN, Ernie

JACKSON, Al
Singles: 78 rpm
CORAL (65052 "Lonesome Lover Blues") 30-40 51
Singles: 7-inch
CORAL (65052 "Lonesome Lover Blues") 35-45 51

JACKSON, Bart
(George Jackson)
Singles: 7-inch
DECCA (32317 "Dancing Man") 10-20 68
Also see JACKSON, George

JACKSON, Bill
(Bill Jackson Quintet)
Singles: 78 rpm
BATON (239 "Traveling Stranger") 25-50 57
Singles: 7-inch
BATON (239 "Traveling Stranger") 25-50 57
LPs: 10/12-inch
TESTAMENT (201 "Long Steel Rail") 10-20 63

JACKSON, Bobby
Singles: 7-inch
BRUNSWICK (55026 "Wow Man") 20-30 57
BRUNSWICK (55060 "Dinah's Party") 20-30 58

JACKSON, Bull Moose *R&B '46*
(With His Buffalo Bearcats; with Flashcats; Moose Jackson)

Singles: 78 rpm

ENCINO 15-25 57
KING 20-40 45-55
MGM 10-20 47
QUEEN 10-20 45-46

Singles: 7-inch

BOGUS 4-6 85
ENCINO (1004 "Understanding") 15-25 57
ENCINO (1005 "Just As I Am") 15-25 57
GUSTO 3-5
KING (4181 "I Love You Yes I Do") 25-50 51
KING (4189 "I Want a Bowlegged Woman") 50-100 51
KING (4451 "Trust in Me") 25-50 51
KING (4462 "Unless") 25-50 51
KING (4472 "Cherokee Boogie") 25-50 51
KING (4493 "I'll Be Home for Xmas") 25-50 51
KING (4524 "Nosey Joe") 50-75 52
KING (4535 "Let Me Love You All Night") 25-50 52
KING (4551 "Bearcat Blues") 25-50 52
KING (4580 "Big Ten-Inch Record") 100-200 52
KING (4600 thru 4800 series) 15-25 53-55
7 ARTS (705 "Aw Shucks, Baby") 10-20 61
WARWICK (575 "I Found My Love") 5-10 60

Picture Sleeves

BOGUS 3-5 85

EPs: 7-inch

KING (211 "Bull Moose Jackson Sings His All-Time Hits") 50-100 52
KING (261 "Bull Moose Jackson Sings His All-Time Hits, Vol. 2") 50-100 54

LPs: 10/12-inch

AUDIO LAB (1524 "Bullmoose Jackson") 100-200 59
BOGUS 5-8 85

JACKSON, Chubby
(Chubby Jackson's Orchestra; Chubby Jackson Sextet; "Featuring Zoot Sims – Tenor Sax;")

Singles: 78 rpm

KING 5-10 45
NEW JAZZ (830 "Leavin' Town") 5-10 50

LPs: 10/12-inch

ARGO 15-25 60-62
EVEREST 15-25 62
LAURIE (2011 "Twist Calling") 15-25 62
Also see MARSHALL, Maria
Also see MERCURY ALL-STARS

JACKSON, Chuck *P&R/R&B '61*
(With the Vikings; with Kripp Johnson's Versatiles; Charles Jackson)

Singles: 7-inch

ABC 4-6 73-74
ALCAR (209 "Little Man") 10-12 63
ALCAR (210 "Never Let Me Go") 10-12 63
ALL PLATINUM 4-6 75-77
AMY (849 "Come On & Love Me") 10-15 62
AMY (868 "I'm Yours") 10-15 62
ATCO (6197 "Never Let Me Go") 8-12 61
BELTONE (1005 "Mister Pride") 10-20 61
CHANNEL (103 "Good Love") 5-10
CLOCK (1015 "Come On & Love Me") 15-25 59
CLOCK (1022 "I'm Yours") 15-25 60
CLOCK (1027 "This Is It") 15-25 60
DAKAR (4512 "I Forgot to Tell You") 4-8 72
EMI AMERICA (8042 "I Want to Give You Some Love") 3-5 80
EMI AMERICA (8056 "Let's Get Together") 3-5 81
FEE BEE (231 "Girl, Girl, Girl") 10-20 59
LOGO (1015 "Come On & Love Me") 5-10
MOTOWN (1118 thru 1152) 10-15 68-69
MOTOWN (1160 "The Day the World Stood Still") 150-250 70
PETITE (502 "Willette") 40-50 59
PETITE (503 "Cold Feet") 15-25 59
SCEPTER (21000 series) 4-6 73
(Reissues of Wand tracks.)
SUGAR HILL (764 "Sometimes When We Touch") 3-5 81
VIBRATION 4-6 77
V.I.P. (25052 thru 25059) 10-15 69-71
V.I.P. (25067 "Who You Gonna Run To") 100-200 71
WAND (106 "I Don't Want to Cry") 10-15 61
(Blue label.)
WAND (106 "I Don't Want to Cry") 4-6
(Multi-color label.)
WAND (108 thru 188) 8-15 61-65
WAND (1100 series) 5-10 65-68

Picture Sleeves

WAND (132 "Tell Him I'm Not Home") 10-20 63

LPs: 10/12-inch

ABC (798 "Through All Times") 8-12 73
ALL PLATINUM (3014 "Wanting You, Needing You") 8-10 76
EMI-AMERICA (17031 "I Wanna Give You Some Love") 5-10 80
MOTOWN (667 "Chuck Jackson Arrives") 25-40 67
MOTOWN (687 "Goin' Back to Chuck Jackson") 20-30 69
SCEPTER 8-10 72
SPINORAMA 10-15 '60s
U.A. 8-10 75
V.I.P. (403 "Teardrops Keep Fallin'") 20-40 70
WAND (650 "I Don't Want to Cry") 40-60 62
WAND (654 "Any Day Now") 40-60 62
WAND (655 "Encore") 25-35 64
WAND (658 "On Tour") 25-35 64
WAND (667 "Mr. Everything") 25-35 65
WAND (673 "Tribute to Rhythm & Blues, Vol. 1") 20-30 66
WAND (676 "Tribute to Rhythm & Blues, Vol. 2") 20-30 66
WAND (680 "Dedicated to the King") 25-50 67
WAND (683 "Greatest Hits") 15-25 67
Also see BENTON, Brook / Chuck Jackson / Jimmy Soul
Also see BONDS, Gary "U.S."
Also see FLAMINGO, Chuck
Also see FREEMAN, Bobby, & Chuck Jackson
Also see JOHNSON, Kripp, & Chuck Jackson

JACKSON, Chuck, & Maxine Brown *P&R/R&B '65*

Singles: 7-inch

WAND 10-15 65-67

LPs: 10/12-inch

COLLECTABLES 5-10 88
WAND (669 "Saying Something") 20-30 65
WAND (678 "Hold On, We're Coming") 20-30 67
Also see BROWN, Maxine

JACKSON, Chuck, & Chapelaires

Singles: 7-inch

GATEWAY (738 "Forever Is a Long, Long Time") 30-40 64
Also see CHAPELAIRES

JACKSON, Chuck, & Tammi Terrell

LPs: 10/12-inch

WAND (682 "The Early Show") 20-30 67
Also see TERRELL, Tammi

JACKSON, Chuck / Young Jesse

LPs: 10/12-inch

CROWN (5354 "Chuck Jackson & Young Jesse") 15-25 62
GUEST STAR 10-15 64
Also see JACKSON, Chuck
Also see JESSE, Young

JACKSON, Cleve

Singles: 78 rpm

HERALD (6000 "I Want Your Love") 40-60 53

Singles: 7-inch

HERALD (6000 "I Want Your Love") 200-300 53

JACKSON, Cliff, & Naturals

Singles: 7-inch

MIDNIGHT SUN (1 "Blues Walk") 20-30 69
MIDNIGHT SUN (2 "Nine Below Zero") 20-30 69

JACKSON, Cookie
(With the Flares)

Singles: 7-inch

CYCLONE (121 "Hot Dog") 10-20 61
OKEH (7279 "Your Good Girl's Gonna Go Bad") 5-10 67
OKEH (7292 "Fresh Out of Tears") 5-10 67
PRESS (2814 "Write a Song About Me") 5-10 64
PROGRESS (912 "Blind Love") 15-25 63
UPTOWN (700 "Uptown Jerk") 5-10 65
UPTOWN (714 "Find Me a Lover") 5-10 65
Also see FLARES

JACKSON, Cordell

Singles: 7-inch

MOON (80 "Rock and Roll Christmas") 40-60 58

JACKSON, Deacon
(Blind Lemon Jefferson)

Singles: 78 rpm

HERWIN (93031 "I Want to Be Like Jesus in My Heart") 150-200 26
(Previously issued as by Deacon L.J. Bates.)
Also see BATES, Deacon L.J.
Also see JEFFERSON, Blind Lemon

JACKSON, Dimples

Singles: 7-inch

GARDENA (114 "Where Are You") 15-25 60
OCTIVE (101 "Hold Me") 5-10

JACKSON, Earl
(With Kent Harian Orchestra)

Singles: 78 rpm

CARAVAN (15602 "Coyote") 10-15 56

Singles: 7-inch

CARAVAN (15602 "Coyote") 25-35 56

JACKSON, Earl

Singles: 7-inch

ABC (11142 "Self Soul Satisfaction") 15-25 68

JACKSON, Eddie

Singles: 78 rpm

FORTUNE (186 "Rock n' Roll Baby") 20-30 56

Singles: 7-inch

FORTUNE (186 "Rock n' Roll Baby") 40-60 56

JACKSON, Eddy

Singles: 7-inch

KING (5574 "Don't Call Me") 20-30 61

JACKSON, George

Singles: 78 rpm

ATLANTIC (1024 "Uh-Huh") 15-25 53
RPM (441 "Hold Me Up") 8-12 55

Singles: 7-inch

ATLANTIC (1024 "Uh-Huh") 25-35 53
RPM (441 "Hold Me Up") 10-20 55

JACKSON, George *R&B '70*
(With the Unisons)

Singles: 7-inch

CHESS 4-6 75
CAMEO (460 "That Lonely Night") 5-10 67
DOT 5-10 65
DOUBLE R 5-10
ER MUSIC 4-6 76
FAME (1468 "That's How Much You Mean to Me") 5-10 70
HAPPY HOOKERS 3-5 85
HI (2130 "I'm Gonna Wait") 5-10 67
HI (2200 series) 4-6 72-73
LESCAY (3006 "Watching the Rainbow") 75-125 62
MGM 4-6 73-74
MERCURY 10-20 67-68
MUSCLE SHOALS SOUNDS 4-6 79
PRANN 10-20 63
PUBLIC (1002 "Cold Cold Love") 10-15 68
VERVE (10658 "Love Highjacker") 15-25 70
WASHATAU 3-5 84
Also see JACKSON, Bart
Also see OVATIONS

JACKSON, George, & Dan Greer

Singles: 7-inch

GOLDWAX (313 "You Didn't Know It But You Had Me") 15-25 '60s
(Also issued as by George & Greer.)
Also see GEORGE & GREER
Also see JACKSON, George

JACKSON, Handy

Singles: 78 rpm

SUN (177 "Got My Application, Baby") 200-300 53

JACKSON, Harold

Singles: 7-inch

ALADDIN (3410 "Move It on Down the Line") 15-25 57

JACKSON, J.J. *P&R/R&B '66*
(With the Jackels; with Jackals; with Jackaels)

Singles: 7-inch

ABC 4-6 73
CALLA 5-10 66-67
CANDIX 12-18
CONGRESS (6008 "Fat, Black and Together") 5-10 69
EVEREST (2012 "False Face") 5-10 62
LOMA (2082 thru 2104) 5-10 67-68
MAGNA GLIDE 4-6 75
PRELUDE (502 "Oo-Ma-Liddi") 10-15 59
STORM (501 "That Look in Your Eye") 10-20 59
STORM (502 "Oo-Ma-Liddi") 15-20 59
W.B. 4-8 69

LPs: 10/12-inch

CALLA 15-25 67
CONGRESS 15-20 68
PERCEPTION 10-15 69-70
W.B. 10-20 69

JACKSON, Jerry

Singles: 7-inch

CAPITOL (2112 "Miss You") 5-10 68
COLUMBIA 5-10 64-65
KAPP 10-20 61-63
PARKWAY (100 "I'm Gonna Paint a Picture") 10-20 66
TOP RANK (2042 thru 2072) 10-15 60

JACKSON, Jerry "Count"

Singles: 7-inch

FROLIC (505 "Come Back Baby") 15-20 63
(First issue.)
VEE-JAY (563 "Come Back Baby") 8-10 63

JACKSON, Jill

Singles: 7-inch

REPRISE (297 thru 411) 10-15 64-65
Also see PAUL & PAULA

JACKSON, Jim

Singles: 7-inch

EVEREST (20001 "Foldin' Money") 10-15 62
FABLE (639 "I Want Your Love") 75-125 58
SANDBAG (102 "Some Love with Soul") 20-30

JACKSON, Jimmy
(With All Stars)

Singles: 78 rpm

DERBY (781 "Piano Boogie") 10-15 51
RPM 10-15 52

Singles: 7-inch

DERBY (781 "Piano Boogie") 15-25 51
RPM (349 "Stompin'") 15-25 52
RPM (352 "Deep Purple") 15-25 52

JACKSON, Jo-Ann, & Dreams

Singles: 7-inch

HARTHON (427 "Georgie Porgie") 20-30

JACKSON, Joe *P&R/LP '79*

Singles: 12-inch

A&M 4-6 82-86

Singles: 7-inch

A&M (Except 18000) 3-6 79-86
A&M (18000 "I'm the Man") 10-15 79
(Boxed set of five 45s with sleeves and poster. Labeled "The 7-inch Album.")

Picture Sleeves

A&M 3-6 79-86

LPs: 10/12-inch

A&M (3666 "Look Sharp") 10-20 79
(Double 10-inch LP set. Add $4 to $6 if "Look Sharp" button is included.)
A&M (3900 series) 5-8 87
A&M (4000 & 5000 series) 5-15 79-89
A&M (6000 series) 8-12 86-88
MFSL (080 "Night and Day") 30-40 82
VIRGIN 5-8 91

JACKSON, Johnnie, & Blazers

Singles: 7-inch

J-MER (101 "Wisdom of a Fool") 10-20 67

JACKSON, June

Singles: 7-inch

BELL (45173 "Little Dog Heaven") 10-20 72
BELL (45236 "Let's Try Dancin'") 10-20 72
IMPERIAL (66185 "It's What's Up Front That Counts") 15-25 66

JACKSON, Lee

Singles: 78 rpm

COBRA (5007 "Fishin' in My Pond") 50-75 57

Singles: 7-inch

ATLANTIC (2284 "Ad for Love") 5-10 65
BEA & BABY (132 "Apollo 15") 8-12 61
CJ (652 "Juanita") 15-25 65
COBRA (5007 "Fishin' in My Pond") 100-150 56
ROBIN RED 4-8

LPs: 10/12-inch

BLUESWAY (6083 "Lonely Girl") 8-10 74

Also see LASLEY, Clyde, & Cadillac Baby Specials / Lee Jackson & Cadillac Baby Specials

JACKSON, Lightning

Singles: 78 rpm

GOTHAM (311 "Fine Brown Groove") 10-15 56

Singles: 7-inch

GOTHAM (311 "Fine Brown Groove") 20-30 56

JACKSON, Lil' Son R&B '48

(With His Rockin' Rollers; Little Son Jackson)

Singles: 78 rpm

GOLD STAR 10-20 48-50
IMPERIAL 30-60 51-57
MODERN 10-20 49
POST (2014 "No Money") 10-20 55

Singles: 7-inch

IMPERIAL (5204 "Journey Back Home") 50-100 52
IMPERIAL (5218 "Black and Brown") 50-100 52
IMPERIAL (5229 "Lonely Blues") 50-100 53
IMPERIAL (5237 "Spending Money Blues") 50-100 53
IMPERIAL (5248 "Movin' to the Country") 50-100 53
IMPERIAL (5259 "Dirty Work") 50-100 53
IMPERIAL (5267 "Thrill Me, Baby") 50-75 53
IMPERIAL (5276 "Big Rat") 50-75 53
IMPERIAL (5286 "Trouble Don't Last Always") 50-75 53
IMPERIAL (5300 "Get High Everybody") . 50-75 53
IMPERIAL (5312 "How Long") 50-75 53
IMPERIAL (5319 "My Younger Days") 50-75 54
IMPERIAL (5339 "Sugar Mama") 50-75 54
IMPERIAL (5400 thru 5900 series) 15-25 56-63
POST (2014 "No Money") 25-35 55

EPs: 7-inch

BLACK DIAMOND (450 "Everybody Blues") 20-30

LPs: 10/12-inch

ARHOOLIE (1004 "Lil' Son Jackson") 15-30 60
IMPERIAL (9142 "Rockin' & Rollin'") ... 300-400 61

Also see CHARLES, Ray / Arbee Stidham / Li'l Son Jackson / James Wayne.

JACKSON, Louis

Singles: 78 rpm

C NOTE (110 "Tweedle Woofin' Boogie") ... 5-10 56

Singles: 7-inch

C NOTE (110 "Tweedle Woofin' Boogie") 10-20 56

Also see HAMPTON, Junior / Brother Jackson
Also see LOUIS & FROSTY

JACKSON, Mahalia P&R '48

(With the Melody Echoes)

Singles: 78 rpm

APOLLO 4-8 50-57
COLUMBIA 4-8 55-57
LLOYDS (103 "I Believe") 40-50 53

Singles: 7-inch

APOLLO (200 thru 500 series) 10-25 50-59
(Black vinyl.)
APOLLO (262 "In the Upper Room") 75-125 52
(Red vinyl.)
APOLLO (269 "Said He Would") 75-125 53
(Red vinyl.)
APOLLO (600 thru 700 series) 5-10 59-62
COLUMBIA 5-15 55-70
GRAND AWARD 5-10 58-59
KENWOOD 4-8 64-69
LLOYDS (103 "I Believe") 50-100 53
USA (109 "The Holy Bible") ..... 4-8 '60s

Picture Sleeves

APOLLO (42633 "Go Tell It on the Mountain") 4-8 62

EPs: 7-inch

APOLLO 5-10 54-59
COLUMBIA 5-10 55-60

LPs: 10/12-inch

APOLLO (201/2 "Spirituals") 15-20 54
APOLLO (482 "No Matter How You Pray") 10-15 59
APOLLO (499 "Mahalia Jackson") 10-15 62
APOLLO (1001 "Command Performance") 10-15 61
AUDIOFIDELITY 4-8
(Reissue of Apollo 499.)
CAEDMON 4-8 73
COLORTONE 5-8
(Reissue of Grand Award 265.)
COLUMBIA (CL-600 thru CL-2100 series) 10-20 55-64
COLUMBIA (CL-2400 thru CL-2600 series) 5-15 66-67
COLUMBIA (CS-8000 thru CS-8900 series) 10-20 59-64
(Stereo.)
COLUMBIA (CS-9200 thru CS-9900 series) 5-15 66-69
(Stereo. Reissues, with a "CSP," "JCS" or "PC" prefix, are in the $5 to $10 range.)
COLUMBIA (10000 series) 4-8 73
COLUMBIA (30000 series) 5-10 71-72
GRAND AWARD (265 "Spirtuals") 5-10 66
(Reissue of Grand Award 326.)
GRAND AWARD (326 "Spirtuals") 15-25 55
HARMONY 5-10 68-72
KENWOOD 5-10 64-73
PRIORITY 4-6 82

JACKSON, Mahalia, & Duke Ellington

LPs: 10/12-inch

COLUMBIA (CL-1162 "Black, Brown and Beige") 25-35 58
(Monaural.)
COLUMBIA (CS-8015 "Black, Brown and Beige") 35-40 58
(Stereo.)
COLUMBIA (JCS-1162 "Black, Brown and Beige") 5-10

Also see ELLINGTON, Duke
Also see JACKSON, Mahalia

JACKSON, Marvin, & Ozark Toppers

Singles: 7-inch

CRESTWOOD (200 "Gee Whiz, Miss Liz") 250-350
MARLO (1507 "Jay Bird") 15-25
MARLO (1512 "Sneaky") 15-25

JACKSON, Mel

Singles: 7-inch

JOSIE (815 "Move It Over Baby") 50-75 57

JACKSON, Michael P&R/R&B '71

Singles: 12-inch

EPIC 4-8 79-87

Singles: 7-inch

EPIC (03509 thru 04364) 3-6 83-84
EPIC (07253 "I Just Can't Stop Loving You") 3-5 87
(Black vinyl.)
EPIC (07253 "I Just Can't Stop Loving You") 5-8 87
(Colored vinyl. Promotional issue only.)
EPIC (07645 thru 08044) 3-6 87-88
EPIC (50654 thru 50871) 4-8 79-80
EPIC (74100 thru 78000) 3-5 91-95
MCA (1786 "Someone in the Dark") 25-50 83
(Promotional issue only.)
MOTOWN (1191 thru 1349) 4-8 71-75
MOTOWN (1512 "One Day in Your Life") 4-6 81
MOTOWN (1739 "Farewell My Summer Love") 3-6 84
MOTOWN (1914 "Twenty Five Miles") 4-8 87
(Colored vinyl. Promotional issue only.)

Picture Sleeves

EPIC 4-6 83-88
MCA (1786 "Someone in the Dark") 25-50 83
(Promotional issue only.)
MOTOWN (1202 "I Wanna Be Where You Are") 4-6 72
MOTOWN (1739 "Farewell My Summer Love") 4-6 84
MOTOWN (1914 "Twenty Five Miles") 4-8 87
(Promotional issue only.)

LPs: 10/12-inch

EPIC (35000 thru 40000, except 38867 & 44043) 5-10 79-87
EPIC (38867 "Thriller") 15-20 83
(Picture disc.)
EPIC (44043 "Bad") 10-20 87
(Picture disc. Includes poster.)
EPIC (45000 series) ..... 10-20 '80s
(Half-speed mastered.)
EPIC (68000 "Blood on the Dance Floor: History in the Mix") 10-15 97
MCA (70000 "E.T.") 50-100 82
(Boxed set with booklet & poster.)
MCA (6145 "E.T.") 50-100 85
(Boxed set with booklet & poster.)
MOTOWN (Except 6099) 5-15 72-85
MOTOWN (6099 "14 Greatest Hits") 10-15 84
(Picture disc. Has poster and glove.)

Also see JACKSONS
Also see JONES, Quincy
Also see McCARTNEY, Paul, & Michael Jackson
Also see ROSS, Diana, & Michael Jackson
Also see WONDER, Stevie, & Michael Jackson

JACKSON, Michael, & Mick Jagger / Jacksons P&R '84

Singles: 12-inch

EPIC (5022 "State of Shock") 8-12 84
(With special cover.)
EPIC (05022 "State of Shock") 15-20 84
(Promotional issue with cover.)

Singles: 7-inch

EPIC (4503 "State of Shock") 3-5 84

Picture Sleeves

EPIC (4503 "State of Shock") 3-5 84

Also see JACKSON, Michael
Also see JACKSONS
Also see JAGGER, Mick

JACKSON, Monroe "Moe"

Singles: 78 rpm

MERCURY (8127 "Move It on Over") 50-100 49

JACKSON, Ollie

Singles: 7-inch

MAGNUM (737 "The Day My Heart Stood Still") 35-45 65

JACKSON, Prentis

Singles: 7-inch

VEE-JAY (417 "Be Mine") 15-20 62

JACKSON, Preston, & Rhythm Aces

Singles: 7-inch

HERMITAGE (820 "Three Quarter Stomp") 10-20 63

JACKSON, Reuben (Tutti)

Singles: 7-inch

WHEEL CITY (05 "Come Home") ..... 10-20 '60s

JACKSON, Robert

Singles: 7-inch

JAN (101 "Oh Baby") 20-30 58
JAN (102 "You've Got Me Rocking and Rolling") 20-30 58

JACKSON, Roddy

(Sonny Bono)

Singles: 78 rpm

SPECIALTY (623 "I've Got My Sights Set on Someone New") 20-30 58

Singles: 7-inch

SPECIALTY (623 thru 666) 10-20 58-59

Also see SONNY

JACKSON, Rudy

(With the Mel-O-Aires)

Singles: 78 rpm

R&B (1310 "I'm Crying") 30-50 55

Singles: 7-inch

IMPERIAL (5425 "Teasin' Me") 15-25 63
R&B (1310 "I'm Crying") 100-150 55

Session: Vera Potts; Hattie Potts; Gladys Jackson; Mel-O-Aires.
Also see JEWELS

JACKSON, Sammy

Singles: 7-inch

ARVEE 8-15 60-63
ORBIT (536 thru 583) 10-15 59

Picture Sleeves

ORBIT (536 "Are You My Baby") 15-25 59
ORBIT (583 "Teen Age Miss") 15-25 59

JACKSON, Skip

(Skippy & Shantons; with Shantons)

Singles: 7-inch

CAPITOL (3397 "Peace of Mind") 4-6 72
DOT-MAR (324 "I'm on to You Girl") 10-15 69
DOT-MAR (575 "Christmas Song") 10-15 69

Also see BROWN, Skip, & Shantons

JACKSON, Stonewall C&W '58

Singles: 7-inch

COLUMBIA (41000 series) 8-15 58-61
COLUMBIA (42000 & 43000 series) 4-8 61-67
COLUMBIA (44000 & 45000 series) 4-6 67-73
FIRST GENERATION 3-5 81
GRT 4-6 74
LITTLE DARLIN' 4-6 78-79
MGM 4-6 73
PHONORAMA 3-5 83
UNIVERSAL 3-5 85

Picture Sleeves

COLUMBIA (41393 "Waterloo") 15-20 59

EPs: 7-inch

COLUMBIA (13911 "The Dynamic Stonewall Jackson, Vol. 1") 5-10 59
COLUMBIA (13912 "The Dynamic Stonewall Jackson, Vol. 2") 5-10 59
COLUMBIA (13913 "The Dynamic Stonewall Jackson, Vol. 3") 5-10 59

LPs: 10/12-inch

AUDIOGRAPH ALIVE 5-8 82
COLUMBIA (1391 "The Dynamic Stonewall Jackson") 20-30 59
(Monaural.)
COLUMBIA (1700 thru 2700 series) 8-15 62-67
(Monaural.)
COLUMBIA (8186 "The Dynamic Stonewall Jackson") 25-40 59
(Stereo.)
COLUMBIA (8500 thru 9900 series) 8-15 62-70
(Stereo.)
COLUMBIA (10000 series) 5-8 73
COLUMBIA (30000 series) 5-10 70-72
FIRST GENERATION 5-10 81
GRT 5-10 75-76
HARMONY 8-12 66-74
LITTLE DARLIN' 5-8 79
MYRRH 5-8 76
PHONORAMA 5-8 83
SUNBIRD 5-8 80

Session: Jordanaires.
Also see JORDANAIRES

JACKSON, Stoney

(With the V-Eights)

Singles: 7-inch

MUSICNOTE (124 "Where Is My Baby") ... 5-10 64
VIBRO (4007) 20-30 61
(Title unknown.)

Also see V-EIGHTS

JACKSON, Tommy

Singles: 7-inch

SUN-RAY (131 "Flat-Top Box") 25-50

JACKSON, Walter P&R/R&B '64

Singles: 7-inch

BRUNSWICK 4-6 73
CHI-SOUND 4-6 76-78
COLUMBIA (02000 series) 3-5 81
COLUMBIA (42000 series) 10-20 62-63
COTILLION 5-10 69
EPIC 5-10 66-68
KELLI-ARTS 3-5 82
OKEH (Except 7204) 5-10 64-67
OKEH (7204 "It's All Over") 5-10 64
(Black vinyl.)
OKEH (7204 "It's All Over") 15-25 64
(Colored vinyl.)
20TH FOX 4-6 79
U.A. 4-6 78
USA (104 "A Fool for You") ..... 8-12 '60s
WAND 4-6 72

Picture Sleeves

OKEH 8-12 66-67

LPs: 10/12-inch

CHI-SOUND 8-10 76-78
COLUMBIA 5-8 81
EPIC 8-10 77
OKEH 10-20 65-69
20TH FOX 5-8 79

JACKSON, Wanda C&W '56

(With the Party Timers)

Singles: 78 rpm

CAPITOL 15-40 56-57
DECCA 10-20 54-55

Singles: 7-inch

ABC 4-6 75
CAPITOL (2000 thru 3000 series) 4-8 67-72
(Orange or orange/yellow labels.)
CAPITOL (3400 thru 4600 series) 15-35 56-61
(Purple labels.)
CAPITOL (4700 thru 5900 series) 5-10 61-67
DECCA (29253 "Right to Love") 20-40 54
DECCA (29267 "You'd Be the First One to Know") 20-40 54
(Flip is a duet with Billy Gray.)

DECCA (29514 "Tears at the Grand Ole Op'ry") 20-40 55
DECCA (29677 "It's the Same World") 10-20 55
DECCA (29803 "Wasted") 20-40 55
DECCA (30153 "You Won't Forget") 10-20 56
JIN 4-6
MYRRH 4-6 73-75

Picture Sleeves

CAPITOL (4723 "If I Cried Everytime You Hurt Me") 10-15 62

EPs: 7-inch

CAPITOL (1041 "Wanda Jackson") 25-50 58

LPs: 10/12-inch

CAPITOL (100 thru 600 series) 15-20 69-71
CAPITOL (1041 "Wanda Jackson") 350-450 58
CAPITOL (1384 "Rockin' with Wanda"). 50-100 60
CAPITOL (1511 "There's a Party Goin' On") 40-80 61
(With "T" prefix. Monaural.)
CAPITOL (1511 "There's a Party Goin' On") 50-100 61
(With "ST" prefix. Stereo.)
CAPITOL (1596 "Right Or Wrong") 25-50 61
(With "T" prefix. Monaural.)
CAPITOL (1596 "Right Or Wrong") 30-55 61
(With "ST" prefix. Stereo.)
CAPITOL (1776 "Wonderful Wanda") 20-30 62
(With "T" prefix. Monaural.)
CAPITOL (1776 "Wonderful Wanda") 25-35 62
(With "ST" prefix. Stereo.)
CAPITOL (1911 "Love Me Forever") 20-30 63
(With "T" prefix. Monaural.)
CAPITOL (1911 "Love Me Forever") 25-35 63
(With "ST" prefix. Stereo.)
CAPITOL (2030 "Two Sides of Wanda Jackson") 25-35 64
(With "T" prefix. Monaural.)
CAPITOL (2030 "Two Sides of Wanda Jackson") 30-40 64
(With "ST" prefix. Stereo.)
CAPITOL (2300 thru 2900 series) 10-20 65-68
CAPITOL (11000 series) 5-8 72-73
DECCA (4224 "Lovin' Country Style") 40-50 62
GUSTO 5-8 80
MYRRH 5-8 73-76
PICKWICK/HILLTOP 8-12 65-68
VARRICK/ROUNDER 5-8 87
VOCALION 8-12 69
WORD 4-8 77

JACKSON, Wanda, & Billy Gray *C&W '54*

Singles: 7-inch

DECCA (29140 "You Can't Have My Love") 20-40 54
Also see GRAY, Billy
Also see JACKSON, Wanda

JACKSON, Willie

Singles: 78 rpm

BROADWAY (5050 "Telephone to Glory") 100-150
COLUMBIA 25-75
CROWN (3326 "Telephone to Glory") 40-60
HERWIN (92035 "Telephone to Glory") 100-200
HERWIN (93005 "Rock of Ages") 50-100

JACKSON, Willis *LP '66*

(Willis "Gator Tail" Jackson & His Orch.; vocal By the 4'Gaters; with Jack McDuff)

Singles: 78 rpm

APOLLO 10-20 50
ATLANTIC 20-50 51-53
DELUXE 4-8 53
MODERN 10-15 52

Singles: 7-inch

ATCO (6089 "Later 'Gator") 15-25 57
ATLANTIC (946 "Harlem Nocturne") 75-125 51
ATLANTIC (957 "Wine-O-Wine") 75-125 52
ATLANTIC (967 "Rock, Rock, Rock") 50-75 52
ATLANTIC (975 "Gator's Groove") 40-60 52
ATLANTIC (998 "Shake Dance") 40-60 53
CADET (5529 "Who Can I Turn To") 5-10 66
COTILLION 4-6 76
DELUXE 10-15 53
FIRE (1003 "Making It") 5-10 59
MODERN (906 "Let's Jump") 15-25 52
PAUL WINLEY (1101 "Bow Legged Daddy") 10-20 64
PRESTIGE 5-10 59-69
TRU SOUND (410 "Backtrack") 10-15 62
TRU SOUND (410 "That Twistin' Train") 8-12 62
(Retitled reissue.)
VERVE (10332 "I Almost Lost My Mind") ... 5-10 64

LPs: 10/12-inch

ATLANTIC 5-8 75
BIG CHANCE 5-10 75
CADET 10-20 66
COTILLION 5-8 76
MGM 10-20 64
MOODSVILLE 15-20 62
MUSE 5-8 76-81
PRESTIGE (2500 series) 5-8 82
PRESTIGE (7100 & 7200 series) 15-25 59-64
(Yellow label.)
PRESTIGE (7100 & 7200 series) 10-20 65
(Blue label.)
PRESTIGE (7300 thru 7800 series) 8-15 65-71
TRIP 5-10 73
VERVE 10-20 64-69
Also see BROWN, Ruth
Also see CLOVERS
Also see JENKINS, Bill, & Willis Jackson
Also see McDUFF, Brother Jack, & Willis Jackson

JACKSON, Willis, & Joe Holiday

Singles: 7-inch

AUDIO-LAB (1539 "Whole Lot of Blowin' ") 15-25 59

JACKSON BROTHERS

Singles: 78 rpm

DECCA (28055 "Wild Side of Life") 8-12 52

Singles: 7-inch

ATCO (6139 "Tell Him No") 8-12 59
DECCA (28055 "Wild Side of Life") 10-15 52

JACKSON BROTHERS

Singles: 7-inch

CANDY (002 "Baby, Baby") 10-20 59
CANDY (006 "I Only Know") 10-20 59
PROVIDENCE (409 "I've Gotta Hear It from You") 15-25 65

JACKSON BROTHERS ORCHESTRA

Singles: 7-inch

ARROW (1003 "The Wrong Door") 30-40 57

JACKSON INVESTMENT CO.

Singles: 7-inch

PARIS TOWER (125 "What Can I Do") 15-25 67
(Label error. Actual title: *What Can I Say.*)

JACKSON TRIO

Singles: 78 rpm

HOLLYWOOD 8-12 55-56

Singles: 7-inch

HOLLYWOOD (1046 "Jingle Bell Hop") ... 15-20 55
HOLLYWOOD (1062 "Jivarama Hop") 15-20 56

JACKSONS *P&R/R&B '69*

(Jackson 5; Michael Jackson & Jackson 5)

Singles: 12-inch

EPIC 5-10 79-84
MOTOWN 5-10 83

Singles: 7-inch

DYNAMO (146 "You Don't Have to Be Over 21") 15-25 71
EPIC 3-8 76-89
J5 (5 "Rappin' with the Jackson Five") 5-10
MCA 3-5 87
MOTOWN ("ABC") 20-30 71
(Cardboard cutout, 6-inch picture disc. No selection number used.)
MOTOWN ("Sugar Daddy") 10-20 71
(Cardboard cutout, 6-inch picture disc. No selection number used. Artists neither pictured nor credited.)
MOTOWN (1157 "I Want You Back") 5-10 69
MOTOWN (1157 "I Want You Back") 15-20 69
(Red vinyl. Promotional issue only.)
MOTOWN (1163 "ABC") 4-8 70
MOTOWN (1166 "The Love You Save") 4-6 70
(Black vinyl.)
MOTOWN (1166 "I Found That Girl") 15-20 70
(Red vinyl. Same song on both sides. Promotional issue only.)
MOTOWN (1166 "Love You Save") 15-20 70
(Red vinyl. Same song on both sides. Promotional issue only.)
MOTOWN (1171 thru 1310) 4-6 70-75
MOTOWN (1177 "Mama's Pearl") 12-18 71
(Colored vinyl. Promotional issue only.)
MOTOWN (1277 "Get It Together") 10-15 73
(Colored vinyl. Promotional issue only.)
MOTOWN (1356 "Forever Came Today") 4-6 75
(Black vinyl.)
MOTOWN (1356 "Forever Came Today") 10-15 75
(Colored vinyl. Promotional issue only.)
STEEL-TOWN (681 "Big Boy") 30-40 68
(Red or Orange label with no mention of Atco distribution.)
STEEL-TOWN (681 "Big Boy") 20-30 68
(Distribution by Atco noted on label.)
STEEL-TOWN (682 "We Don't Have to Be Over 21") 30-40 71
(First issue.)

Picture Sleeves

EPIC 3-8 76-84
MCA 3-5 87
MOTOWN 5-10 71-75

EPs: 7-inch

MOTOWN ("Jackson Five") 25-50 70
(Five track flexi-disc.)
MOTOWN ("Sugar Daddy") .... 20-40 '70s
(Three track, cardboard flexi-disc.)
MOTOWN (60718 "Jackson Five, Third Album") 15-25 70

LPs: 10/12-inch

EPIC (30000 series, except picture discs) . 5-10 76-84
EPIC (SAI-2561 "Kellogg's & the Jacksons, for the Taste of Victory") 100-200 85
("Victory Tour" picture disc in gatefold cover. Promotional issue, made for Kellogg's.)
EPIC (PAL 34835 "Goin' Places") 20-25 78
(Picture disc. Promotional issue only. Has same picture on both sides.)
EPIC (PAL 34835 "Goin' Places") 200-250 78
(Picture disc. Promotional issue only. Has "Radio Ten Q" logo on one side.)
EPIC (8E8-39576 "Victory") 15-25 84
(Picture disc.)
EPIC (40911 "2300 Jackson Street") 5-8 89
EPIC (46424 "Triumph") 10-15 81
(Half-speed mastered.)
MCA 5-8 87
MOTOWN (112 "Superstar Series") 5-10 80
MOTOWN (152 "ABC") 5-10 82
MOTOWN (157 "Third Album") 5-10 82
MOTOWN (700 "Diana Ross Presents the Jackson 5") 15-20 69
MOTOWN (709 "ABC") 10-20 70
MOTOWN (713 "The Jackson 5 Christmas Album") 15-25 70
MOTOWN (718 thru 829) 10-15 70-75
MOTOWN (868 "Anthology") 15-25 76
(Three discs.)
MOTOWN (5000 series) 5-8
MOTOWN (6099 "Michael Jackson and the Jackson 5 – 14 Greatest Hits") 5-10 84
NATURAL RESOURCES 8-12 79
(Promotional issues only.)
PHILLY INT'L (34229 "The Jacksons") 125-150 78
(Picture disc. Promotional issue only.)
PICKWICK .... 5-10 '70s
Members: Michael; Jermaine; Jackie; Marlon; Tito; Randy; Rebbie.
Also see JACKSON, Michael
Also see RIPPLES & WAVES PLUS MICHAEL
Also see ROSS, Diana, & Bill Cosby / Diana Ross & Jackson Five
Also see WONDER, Stevie

JACKY & LEE

Singles: 7-inch

TEEN-AGER (102 "Misery") 50-75

JACOBI, Lou *LP '66*

LPs: 10/12-inch

CAPITOL (2596 "Al Tijuana and His Jewish Brass") 10-20 66
VERVE (15058 "The Yiddish Are Coming! The Yiddish Are Coming!") 10-15 67
(With Frank Gallop, Phil Leeds, and Bob McFadden.)
Also see GALLOP, Frank
Also see McFADDEN, Bob

JACOBS, Bobby

("Toledo's Bobby Jacobs Accompanied By Rhythm Rascals")

Singles: 7-inch

(1 "How Deep Is the Ocean") .... 200-300 '60s
(No label name used.)

JACOBS, Dick, & His Orchestra *P&R '56*

Singles: 78 rpm

CORAL (Except 61705) 4-8 54-62
CORAL (61705 "Ballad of James Dean"). 15-20 56

Singles: 7-inch

CORAL (Except 61705) 8-12 54-62
CORAL (61705 "Ballad of James Dean"). 20-30 56

EPs: 7-inch

CORAL 8-15 56

LPs: 10/12-inch

CORAL 10-25 56-60
VOCALION 10-15 60
Also see BURNETT, Frances
Also see DIAMONDS
Also see KING, Teddi
Also see McGUIRE SISTERS
Also see McNAIR, Barbara
Also see MILES, Jackie
Also see ODOM, King

JACOBS, Donnie

Singles: 7-inch

JIN (212 "If You Want Good Lovin' ") 15-25 66

JACOBS, Eddy

(Eddy Jacobs Exchange)

Singles: 7-inch

CHESS (2014 "Tired of Being Lonely") 10-20 67
COLUMBIA (44821 "Pull My Coat") 5-10 69
COLUMBIA (45174 "Love") 8-12 70
KING (5574 "Don't Call Me") 10-15 61
KISS-KISS (222 "Was I So Young") 8-12 64

JACOBS, Hank *P&R/R&B '64*

Singles: 7-inch

CALL ME 4-6
IMPERIAL (5894 "Sting Ray") 10-15 62
SUE 5-10 63-64

LPs: 10/12-inch

SUE (1023 "So Far Away") 20-30 64

JACOBSON, Al

Singles: 7-inch

CAVE (555 "I Gotta Do It") 20-30
CAVE (18000 "Rockabilly Blues") 40-60

JACOBY BROTHERS

Singles: 78 rpm

TNT (1000 thru 1009) 8-12 53-54

Singles: 7-inch

TNT (186 "Alone Tonight") 8-12 61
TNT (1000 thru 1009) 15-25 53-54

JAC-O-LACS

Singles: 78 rpm

TAMPA (103 "Cindy Lou") 20-40 55

Singles: 7-inch

TAMPA (103 "Cindy Lou") 50-75 55
Members: Cornell Gunter; Charles Jackson; Thomas Fox; Obediah Donell; Randolph Jones.
Also see GUNTER, Cornell

JACONO, Jim, & J's

Singles: 7-inch

KAY-Y (66783 "Take My Money") 200-300 58
(Must have "Nicholas Music" on label.)
KAY-Y (66783 "Take My Money") 50-100 58
(Rigid pressing. No "Nicholas Music" on label.)
KAY-Y (66783 "Take My Money") 15-25 58
(Flexible vinyl pressing. No "Nicholas Music" on label.)

JACQUELINE & JILLS

Singles: 7-inch

GOLDISC (3023 "Gee But It's Great to Be in Love") 10-20 61

JACQUET, Illinois *R&B '52*

(With His All-Stars; Jacque Rabbit; with Russell Jacquet)

Singles: 78 rpm

ARA 5-10 46
ALADDIN 5-15 45-54
APOLLO 5-10 46-47
MERCURY 5-10 52
PHILO 5-10 45
RCA 5-15 48-51
SAVOY 5-10 46

Singles: 7-inch

ALADDIN 10-20 53-54
ARGO 5-10 63-65
CADET (5520 "Blues for Bunny") 5-10 66
MGM (89001 "One-Nighter Boogie") 15-25
MERCURY 10-15 52
PRESTIGE 5-10 68-69

RCA (0011 "Black Velvet") 10-20 49
(Black vinyl.)
RCA (50-0011 "Black Velvet") 20-30 49
(Cherry red vinyl.)
RCA (50-0021 "Big Foot") 20-30 49
(Cherry red vinyl.)
RCA (50-0047 "Blue Satin") 20-30 49
(Cherry red vinyl.)
RCA (50-0087 "My Old Gal") 20-30 49
(Cherry red vinyl.)
RCA (50-0097 "Slow Down Baby") 15-20 49
(Cherry red vinyl.)
VERVE (108 "Port of Rico") 5-10 62

EPs: 7-inch

ALADDIN (501 "Illinois Jacquet and His Tenor Sax") 50-75 53
ALADDIN (504 "Illinois Jacquet and His Tenor Sax") 50-75 54
ALADDIN (511 "Illinois Jacquet and His Tenor Sax") 50-75 54
APOLLO (602 "Jam Session") 50-75 50
CLEF (126 "Illinois Jacquet Collates") 25-40 51
CLEF (143 "Illinois Jacquet Collates") 25-40 51
CLEF (166 "Illinois Jacquet Collates, No. 2") 20-40 52
CLEF (167 "Illinois Jacquet Collates, No. 2") 20-40 52
CLEF (207 "Jazz Moods") 20-40 54
CLEF (374 "Illinois Jacquet and His Orchestra") 20-40 55
RCA (3236 "Black Velvet") 40-60 53
SAVOY 20-30 50-53

LPs: 10/12-inch

ACCORD 5-8 82
ALADDIN (708 "Illinois Jacquet and His Tenor Sax") 100-200 54
(10-inch LP.)
APOLLO (104 "Jam Session") 150-250 50
ARGO (722 "Message") 15-25 63
ARGO (735 "Desert Winds") 15-25 64
ARGO (746 "Illnois Jacquet Plays Cole Porter") 15-25 65
ARGO (754 "Spectrum") 15-25 65
CLEF (112 "Illinois Jacquet Collates") . 100-125 51
(10-inch LP. Has Mercury label with Clef logo and number.)
CLEF (129 "Illinois Jacquet Collates, No. 2") 100-125 52
(10-inch LP. Has Mercury label with Clef logo and number.)
CLEF (622 "Jazz Moods") 50-100 54
CLEF (676 "Illinois Jacquet and His Orchestra") 50-75 55
CLEF (680 "The Kid and Brute") 50-75 55
CLEF (700 "Jazz Moods") 40-60 56
CLEF (702 "Groovin'") 40-60 56
CLEF (750 "Swing's the Thing") 40-60 56
EPIC (16033 "Illinois Jacquet") 15-25 63
(Monaural.)
EPIC (17033 "Illinois Jacquet") 15-25 63
(Stereo.)
GRAND AWARD (315 "Uptown Jazz") 20-35 56
IMPERIAL (9184 "Flying Home") 15-25 62
JRC 5-10 79
MOSAIC (165 "Complete Illinois Jacquet Sessions 1945-50") .... 70-90 '90s
(Boxed, six-disc audiophile set. 5000 made.)
PRESTIGE 8-12 69-75
RCA (3236 "Black Velvet") 50-100 53
(10-inch LP.)
ROULETTE 20-30 60
SAVOY (15024 "Tenor Sax") 50-100 53
(10-inch LP.)
TRIP 5-8 79
VERVE (2500 series) 5-10 82-87
VERVE (8000 series) 25-50 57-58
(Reads "Verve Records, Inc." at bottom of label.)
VERVE (8000 series) 10-20 61-65
(Reads "MGM Records - a Division of Metro-Goldwyn-Mayer, Inc." at bottom of label.)
Session: Johnny Otis; Russell Jacquet; Arthur Dennis; Henry Coker; Sir Charles; Ulysses Livingston; William Hadnott; Miles Davis.
Also see COLE, Cozy, & Illinois Jacquet
Also see DAVIS, Miles
Also see DOGGETT, Bill
Also see HAMPTON, Lionel
Also see HEART BEATS QUINTET
Also see OTIS, Johnny
Also see X-RAYS

JACQUET, Illinois, & Count Basie

LPs: 10/12-inch

CLEF (701 "Port of Rico") 40-60 56
Also see BASIE, Count

JACQUET, Illinois / Lester Young

EPs: 7-inch

ALADDIN (501 "Battle of the Saxes") 50-100 54

LPs: 10/12-inch

ALADDIN (701 "Battle of the Saxes") ... 150-250 54
(10-inch LP. Black vinyl.)
ALADDIN (701 "Battle of the Saxes") 500-1000 54
(10-inch LP. Colored vinyl.)
ALADDIN (803 "Illinois Jacquet and His Tenor Sax") 75-100 56
(Eight tracks from *Battle of the Saxes*, plus four others.)
Also see JACQUET, Illinois
Also see YOUNG, Lester

JACQUET, Russell

(With His All Stars; with His Yellow Jackets; with His Bopper Band)

Singles: 78 rpm

GLOBE 5-10 45
JEWEL 5-10 47
KING 5-10 49-50
MODERN MUSIC 5-10 46
SENSATION 5-10 48

EPs: 7-inch

KING (308 "Russell Jacquet and His All Stars") 50-75 53
KING (309 "Russell Jacquet and His All Stars") 50-75 53

LPs: 10/12-inch

KING (8 "Russell Jacquet and His All Stars") 75-125 53
(10-inch LP.)
Also see HEART BEATS QUINTET
Also see JACQUET, Illinois

JACQUET, Russell, Orchestra, & Vernon Garrett

(Russell Jacquet Orchestra with Vernon & Jewell)

Singles: 7-inch

IMPERIAL (5722 "Sail On") 15-25 61
Also see GARRETT, Vernon
Also see JACQUET, Russell
Also see VERNON & JEWELL

JADE

LPs: 10/12-inch

GENERAL AMERICAN (11311 "Faces of Jade") 50-75 68

JADE

Singles: 7-inch

JADE (769 "I'm Leaving Here") .... 15-25 '60s

JADES

Singles: 7-inch

TIME (1002 "So Blue") 50-100 58
Member: Lou Reed.

JADES

(With the Pacers Band; with Pacer's Music; with Rocket Flames Band)

Singles: 7-inch

CHRISTY (110 "Oh Why!") 300-400 59
CHRISTY (111 "Tell Me Pretty Baby") .. 100-200 59
CHRISTY (113 "Don't Be a Fool") 150-250 59
CHRISTY (114 "Look for a Lie") 500-750 59
(Reportedly 100 made.)
CHRISTY (117 "Pretend") 100-150 59

EPs: 7-inch

CHRISTY (100 "The Jades") 5-8
(Colored vinyl. Issued with paper sleeve.)
Members: Louis Allen; Art Robinson; Ocie Watkins; Leroy Davis; David McShade.
Also see BERLIN, Joey, & Jades
Also see KLINT, Bobby
Also see McMILLIN BROTHERS & JADES

JADES

(With the Bluetone Orchestra)

Singles: 7-inch

NAU-VOO (807 "Walking All Alone") 150-250 59

JADES

Singles: 7-inch

DOT (15822 "I'm Pretending") 50-75 58
REO (825 "I'm Pretending") 50-75 58
(Canadian.)
REO (831 "I Sit Alone") 150-200 58
(Canadian only. Not issued in U.S.)

JADES

Singles: 7-inch

ADONA 15-25 62
DORE (687 "When They Ask About You") 20-25 63
PONCELLO (7703 "My Loss, Your Gain") .... 10-15 '60s

JADES

Singles: 7-inch

GAITY (2-23-64 "Surfin' Crow") 125-175 64
OXBORO (2002 "Surfin' Crow") 100-150 64
OXBORO (2005 "Little Marlene") 100-150 64

JADES

Singles: 7-inch

HOLIDAY (101 "I Cried") 20-30 65
MGM (13399 "You're So Right for Me") 5-10 65

JADES

LPs: 10/12-inch

JARRETT (21517 "Live at the Disco A-Go-Go") 35-50 65

JADES

Singles: 7-inch

ECTOR (101 "I'm All Right") 20-30 65
EMCEE (012 "Little Girl") 10-20 66
STRAWBERRY (10 "I'm Coming Home") 10-20 66

LPs: 10/12-inch

CICADELIC 5-10 82
Members: Gary Carpenter; Ron Brown; Jack Henry; Larry Earp; Alvin McCool.

JADES

Singles: 7-inch

NITE LIFE ("I'm Where It's At") 50-100 66
(Selection number not known.)
VERVE (10385 "For Just Another Day") 5-10 66

JADES

Singles: 7-inch

FENTON (2134 "Please Come Back") 15-25 67
FENTON (2208 "Surface World") 10-20 67
Also see RANK, Ken / Jades

JADES

Singles: 7-inch

MODE ("Lucky Fellow") 15-25
(Selection number not known.)

JADES LTD

Singles: 7-inch

TOWER (366 "Last Chance") 10-20 67

JADS

Singles: 7-inch

ASHLEY (770 "Miss Pretty") 15-25 66

JAGGED EDGE

Singles: 7-inch

GALLANT (3017 "You Can't Keep a Good Man Down") 15-25
RCA (8880 "Deep Inside") 5-10 66
TWIRL (2024 "Midnight-to-Six Man") 15-25 66

JAGGER, Mick *P&R/R&B/D&D/LP '85*

Singles: 12-inch

ATLANTIC ("Sweet Thing") 20-30 93
(Colored vinyl. Promotional issue only. Includes six versions.)
COLUMBIA (2060 "Lucky in Love") 4-8 85
(With special cover.)
COLUMBIA (2060 "Lucky in Love") 15-20 85
(Promotional issue with special cover.)
COLUMBIA (5181 "Just Another Night") 4-8 85
(With special cover.)
COLUMBIA (5181 "Just Another Night") .. 15-20 85
(Promotional issue with special cover.)
COLUMBIA (6926 "Let's Work") 5-10 87
COLUMBIA (7492 "Throwaway") 5-10 87
EPIC (5931 "Ruthless People") 10-15 86
(With special cover.)

Singles: 7-inch

COLUMBIA (04743 thru 07653) 3-5 85-87
EPIC (06211 "Ruthless People") 3-5 86

Picture Sleeves

COLUMBIA (04743 "Just Another Night") 3-5 85
COLUMBIA (04893 "Lucky in Love") 3-5 85
COLUMBIA (07306 "Let's Work") 3-5 87
COLUMBIA (07653 "Throwaway") 3-5 87
EPIC (06211 "Ruthless People") 3-5 86

Promotional Singles

COLUMBIA (04743 "Just Another Night") .. 8-10 85
COLUMBIA (04893 "Lucky in Love") 8-10 85
COLUMBIA (07306 "Let's Work") 8-10 87
COLUMBIA (07653 "Throwaway") 8-10 87
EPIC (06211 "Ruthless People") 5-10 86

LPs: 10/12-inch

COLUMBIA (39940 "She's the Boss") 8-10 85
COLUMBIA (40919 "Primitive Cool") 8-10 87
EPIC 8-12 86
LONDON WAVELENGTH (006 "The Mick Jagger Special") 75-100 81
(Promotional issue only.)
ROLLING STONES (164 "Interview with Mick Jagger") 75-100 71
(Promotional issue only.)
U.A. (300 "Ned Kelly") 10-15 74
(Soundtrack.)
U.A. (5213 "Ned Kelly") 15-20 70
(Soundtrack.)
Also see BOWIE, David, & Mick Jagger
Also see FRAMPTON, Peter
Also see JACKSON, Michael, & Mick Jagger
Also see OR, John
Also see ROLLING STONES
Also see SIMON, Carly
Also see TOSH, Peter, & Mick Jagger
Also see WEST, Leslie

JAGGERS

Singles: 7-inch

EXECUTIVE ("Feel So Good") 25-40 66
(No selection number used.)

JAGS

Singles: 7-inch

SOMA (1104 "Lost Woman") .... 40-60 '60s

JAGUARS

Singles: 78 rpm

AARDELL 20-40 55-56
R-DELL 50-100 56-57

Singles: 7-inch

AARDELL (0003 "Rock It, Davy, Rock It") 50-75 55
AARDELL (0006 "You Don't Believe Me") 75-100 56
BARONET (1 "The Way You Look Tonight") 50-75 62
CLASSIC ARTISTS (106 "Mellow Sunday") 5-8 88
(Black vinyl. 1000 made.)
CLASSIC ARTISTS (106 "Mellow Sunday") 5-10 88
(Brown vinyl.)
CLASSIC ARTISTS (113 "Play a Love Song") 5-8 89
(Black vinyl. 1000 made.)
CLASSIC ARTISTS (113 "Play a Love Song") 8-10 89
(Red vinyl. 1000 made.)
EBB (129 "Hold Me Tonight") 150-200 58
EBB (129 "Hold Me Tight") 50-75 58
ORIGINAL SOUND (6 "Thinking of You") 30-40 59
ORIGINAL SOUND (20 "Thinking of You") 10-15 62
ORIGINAL SOUND (59 "The Way You Look Tonight") 5-10 65
R-DELL (11 "The Way You Look Tonight"/ "Moonlight and You") 200-300 56
(Black vinyl.)
R-DELL (11 "The Way You Look Tonight"/ "Moonlight and You") 700-800 56
(Red vinyl.)
R-DELL (11 "The Way You Look Tonight"/ "Baby, Baby, Baby") 25-35 56
R-DELL (16 "I Love You Baby") 75-125 57
R-DELL (45 "Rock It Davy, Rock It") 50-75 58
R-DELL (107 "Rock It, Davy, Rock It") 25-50 58
R-DELL (117 "Don't Go Home") 50-75 60
Members: Val Poliuto; Herman Chaney; Manuel Chavez; Charles Middleton. Session: Tony Allen.
Also see ALLEN, Tony
Also see NUGGETS
Also see ROSS, Patty, & Jaguars
Also see STATON, Johnny, & Feathers / Jaguars

JAGUARS

Singles: 7-inch

EPIC (9308 "Jaguar") 10-15 59

EPIC (9325 "Drive-In") 10-15 59

JAGUARS

Singles: 7-inch

FARO (618 "Where Lovers Go") 5-10 65
RENDEZVOUS (159 "It Finally Happened") 15-25 61
RENDEZVOUS (216 "It Finally Happened") 8-12 63

JAGUARS

Singles: 7-inch

PIC (604 "Jaguar") 30-50 64

JAGUARS

Singles: 7-inch

CUCA (6542 "Boney Maronie") 15-25 65
SARA (6583 "Things We Said Today") 20-30 65
Members: Tom Sumner; Dave Peterson; Jim Flynn; Howie Market; Curt Johnson; Paul Nebel.
Also see UPSTAIRS

JAGUARS

Singles: 7-inch

SKOOP (1067 "It's Gonna Be Alright") 10-15 66

JAGUARS

Singles: 7-inch

WHIZZ (001 "Middle of a Heartache") ..... 10-20 '60s

JAGUARS

Singles: 7-inch

ALCO (1006 "The Metropolitan") 50-100
AZTEC 5-10
JAGUAR 5-10

JAGUARS

Singles: 7-inch

JANET (201 "I Could If I Would") 75-125

JAI, Lori

Singles: 78 rpm

RIM (2016 "Thrills & Heartaches") 10-15 56

Singles: 7-inch

RIM (2016 "Thrills & Heartaches") 40-50 56

JAIM

Singles: 7-inch

ETHEREAL 5-10

LPs: 10/12-inch

ETHEREAL (1001 "Prophesy Fulfilled") .. 30-40 69

JAMAICAN ALL STARS

LPs: 10/12-inch

ATLANTIC (8098 "Jamaica Ska") 10-20 64

JAMAL, Ahmad R&B/LP '58
(Ahmad Jamal Trio; Quintet; with Three Strings)

Singles: 78 rpm

PARROT (810 "But Not for Me") 8-12 55

Singles: 7-inch

ARGO (5294 thru 5379) 10-15 58-61
ARGO (5397 thru 5513) 5-10 61-65
CADET (5527 thru 5605) 5-10 66-68
CHESS 4-6 73
PARROT (810 "But Not for Me") 20-30 55
20TH CENTURY 3-6 73-80

EPs: 7-inch

ARGO 10-20 59-61

LPs: 10/12-inch

ABC 8-12 68
ARGO (610 thru 662) 40-75 56-60
ARGO (667 thru 758) 20-30 61-65
CADET 10-25 65-73
CATALYST 5-10 76
EPIC (600 series) 20-30 63-65
EPIC (3212 "Ahmad Jamal Trio") 50-75 56
EPIC (3631 "Piano Scene of Ahmad Jamal") 30-40 59
IMPULSE 10-20 69-73
MOTOWN 5-10 80
PARROT (245 "Ahmad Jamal Plays") 500-1000 55
PERSONAL CHOICE 5-8 82
SHUBRA 5-8 83
20TH FOX 5-10 73-80
WHO'S WHO IN JAZZ 5-10 81

JAMECOS

Singles: 7-inch

JAMECO (2004 "Second Hand Love") 10-15 65

JAMELLS

Singles: 7-inch

CROSLEY (350 "Beatle March") 15-25 64

JAMES, Artamer

Singles: 7-inch

CODE (711 "Congratulations") 50-75 58

JAMES, Betty

Singles: 7-inch

CEE=JAY (583 "I'm a Little Mixed Up") 20-30 61
(First issue.)
CHESS (1801 "I'm a Little Mixed Up") 10-20 61
CHESS (1837 "I'm Not Mixed Up Anymore") 10-20 62
CHESS (1970 "Salt in Your Coffee") 8-12 66

JAMES, Bill, & Hex-O-Tones

Singles: 7-inch

MUN RAB (104 "School's Out") 50-75 59

JAMES, Billy, & Crystaltones

Singles: 7-inch

MZ (111 "Meant for Me") 200-300 62
Also see CRYSTAL TONES

JAMES, Billy, & Stenotones

Singles: 7-inch

RUST (5038 "Phyllis") 50-75 61

JAMES, Bob P&R '74
(Bob James Trio)

Singles: 7-inch

CTI 4-6 74-77
COLUMBIA 3-6 79-83
TAPPAN ZEE/COLUMBIA 3-6 77-85

Picture Sleeves

COLUMBIA 3-6 79-80

LPs: 10/12-inch

CTI 5-10 74-77
COLUMBIA 5-8 83
ESP (1009 "Explosions") 10-15 65
MERCURY (20768 "Bold Conceptions") .. 15-25 63
TAPPAN ZEE/COLUMBIA 5-10 77-85

JAMES, Bobbie, & Four Buddies

Singles: 78 rpm

CLUB 51 (104 "I Need You So") 200-300 56

Singles: 7-inch

CLUB 51 (104 "I Need You So") 600-800 56
Also see FOUR BUDDIES

JAMES, Bobby

Singles: 7-inch

INDIGO (145 "5000 Tears Ago") 10-20 62
JOLUM (102 "Take This Lollipop") 10-20 63
KAROL 8-12
LANOR (530 thru 533) 5-10 67
LANT (66009 "True Blue") .... 20-30 '60s

JAMES, Calvin

Singles: 7-inch

STATURE (1104 "Find This Woman") .. 100-200

JAMES, Charles

Singles: 7-inch

ABC (10254 "Rockin' Chair") 5-10 61
LAB (102 "Rockin' Chair") 10-20 61
LAB (103 "One Mint Julep") 5-10 62

JAMES, Chick

Singles: 7-inch

PRIDE (1001 "She Doesn't Know") 10-15 59

JAMES, Chuck

Singles: 7-inch

STADIUM (2266 "Chuckles") 10-20 66

JAMES, Daniel

Singles: 78 rpm

ALLSTAR (7163 "Rock, Moon, Rock") .200-300 57

Singles: 7-inch

ALLSTAR (7163 "Rock, Moon, Rock") .200-300 57
ALLSTAR (7170 thru 7229) 25-50 58-61

JAMES, Denita

Singles: 7-inch

FLIP (364 "Wild Side") 10-20 63

JAMES, Deviny
(Jim Pewter)

Singles: 7-inch

BETA (1006 "Little Girl") 20-30 59
STUDIO CITY (1002 "That's All Right Mama") 10-20 61
Also see PEWTER, Jim

JAMES, Dian
(With the Satisfactions; with Greenbriar Boys)

Singles: 7-inch

GROOVE (53 "Welcome Stranger") 5-10 64
GROOVE (64 "Some Kind a' Wonderful") .. 5-10 65
RADIANT (1515 "Satisfaction") 10-20 62

LPs: 10/12-inch

ELEKTRA (233 "Dian and the Greenbriar Boys") 10-15 63

JAMES, Eddie

Singles: 7-inch

OAKRIDGE ("Think It Over") 50-75
(Selection number not known.)

JAMES, Elmore R&B '52
(With His Broomdusters; Elmo James)

Singles: 78 rpm

ACE (508 "My Time Ain't Long") 50-75 53
CHECKER (777 "Country Boogie") 200-300 53
CHIEF 25-50 57
FIRE (1011 "Make My Dreams Come True") 100-150 60
FLAIR 50-75 54-56
METEOR (5000 "I Believe") 200-300 52
METEOR (5003 "Sinful Woman") 50-100 53
MODERN (983 "Wild About You") 25-50 56
TRUMPET (146 "Dust My Broom") 300-400 52
VEE-JAY (249 "12-Year-Old Boy") 20-30 57
VEE-JAY (259 "It Hurts Me Too") 30-50 57

Singles: 7-inch

ACE (508 "My Time Ain't Long") 100-200 53
BELL (719 "Anna Lee") 20-25 68
CHECKER (777 "Country Boogie") 200-400 53
CHESS (1756 "The Sun Is Shining") 35-45 60
CHIEF (7001 "The Twelve Year Old Boy") 35-50 57
CHIEF (7004 "It Hurts Me Too") 35-50 57
CHIEF (7006 "Cry for Me Baby") 35-50 57
CHIEF (7020 "Knocking at Your Door") 50-75 60
ENJOY (2015 "Bleeding Heart"/"It Hurts Me Too") 20-30 65
ENJOY (2015 "It Hurts Me Too"/"Pickin' the Blues") 20-30 65
ENJOY (2020 "Bleeding Heart") 20-30 65
ENJOY (2022 "Shake Your Moneymaker") 15-25 65
ENJOY (2027 "Dust My Broom") 15-25 65
FIRE (504 "Shake Your Moneymaker") 20-30 62
FIRE (1011 "Make My Dreams Come True") 20-40 60
FIRE (1016 "The Sky Is Crying") 20-40 60
FIRE (1024 "I'm Worried") 20-40 60
FIRE (1031 "Fine Little Mama") 20-40 61
FIRE (1503 "Anna Lee") 30-50 62
FIRE (2020 "It Hurts Me Too") 8-12 68
FLAIR (1011 "Early in the Morning") 150-200 53
FLAIR (1014 "Can't Stop Lovin' ") 150-200 53
FLAIR (1022 "Strange Kinda Feeling"). 100-150 53
FLAIR (1031 "Make My Dreams Come True") 100-200 54
FLAIR (1039 "Sho'nuff, I Do") 100-200 54
FLAIR (1048 "Dark and Dreary") 100-200 54
FLAIR (1057 "Standing at the Crossroads") 100-200 55
FLAIR (1062 "Late Hours at Midnight") .. 75-125 55
FLAIR (1069 "Happy Home") 75-125 55
FLAIR (1074 "Dust My Blues") 250-350 55
FLAIR (1079 "Blues Before Sunrise") 50-75 55
FLASHBACK (15 "The Sky Is Crying") 5-10 65
JEWEL (764 "Dust My Broom") 5-10 66
JEWEL (783 "Catfish Blues") 5-10 67
(Though credited to Elmo James, the flip sides of Jewel 764 and 783 are actually by Big Boy Crudup.)
KENT (331 "Dust My Blues") 15-25 60
KENT (394 "Dust My Blues") 10-15 64
KENT (433 "Standing at the Crossroads") . 8-12 65
KENT (465 "Goodbye Baby") 8-12 67
KENT (508 "I Believe") 5-10 69
MEL (7011 "Cry for Me Baby") 10-20
METEOR (5000 "I Believe") 550-650 52
METEOR (5003 "Sinful Woman") 650-750 53
MODERN (983 "Wild About You") 150-250 56
M-PAC (7231 "Cry for Me Baby") 5-10 66
S&M 4-8
SPHERE SOUND (708 "Shake Your Moneymaker") 8-12 65
USA (815 "Cry for Me Baby") 8-12 65
VEE-JAY (249 "12-Year-Old Boy") 20-30 57
VEE-JAY (259 "It Hurts Me Too") 75-100 57
VEE-JAY (269 "Cry for Me Baby") 20-30 58

LPs: 10/12-inch

BELL (6037 "Elmore James") 10-15 69
BLUE HORIZON (46021 "Blues Masters, Vol. 1") 10-15
COLLECTABLES 5-10 88
CROWN (5168 "Blues After Hours") 50-100 61
CUSTOM 8-12
INTERMEDIA 5-10 84
KENT (5022 "Original Folk Blues") 20-30 64
KENT (9001 "Anthology") .... 15-20 '60s
KENT (9010 "The Resurrection of Elmore James") .... 15-20 '60s
KENT TREASURE SERIES 5-10 86
RELIC 5-10 88
SPHERE SOUND (7002 "The Sky Is Crying") .... 25-35 '60s
SPHERE SOUND (7008 "I Need You") .... 25-35 '60s
TRIP (1650 "16 Greatest Hits") 5-10 78
TRIP (8007-2 "History of Elmore James") 10-15 71
(Two discs.)
TRIP (9511 "History of Elmore James, Vol. 2") 10-15 73
(Two discs.)
UNITED (7716 "Blues in My Heart, Rhythm in My Soul") .... 10-15 '60s
UNITED (7743 "Original Folk Blues") .... 10-15 '60s
UNITED (7787 "The Resurrection of Elmore James") .... 10-15 '60s
UPFRONT (122 "The Great Elmore James") .... 8-10 '70s
Also see BROWN, J.T.
Also see CRUDUP, Big Boy
Also see JONES, Little Johnny

JAMES, Elmore, & John Brim

LPs: 10/12-inch

CHESS (1537 "Whose Muddy Shoes") 10-15 69
Also see BRIM, John
Also see JAMES, Elmore

JAMES, Etta R&B '55
(With the Peaches; Etta "Miss Peaches" James)

Singles: 78 rpm

MODERN 10-20 55-56

Singles: 7-inch

ABC 4-6 74
ARGO 10-15 60-64
CADET 4-8 66-70
CAPITOL (44333 "Avenue D") 3-5 89
CHESS 4-6 71-76
EPIC (68593 "Baby What You Want Me to Do") 3-5 89
KENT (304 thru 370) 10-15 58-62
MODERN (947 thru 998) 20-30 55
MODERN (1007 thru 1022) 10-20 57
REGENCY 10-20
T-ELECTRIC 3-5 80
W.B. 4-6 78

Picture Sleeves

CAPITOL (44333 "Avenue D") 4-6 89

LPs: 10/12-inch

ARGO 20-35 61-65
ARRIVAL 5-10 83
CADET 10-20 67-71
CHESS 10-12 71-76
CROWN (5209 "Miss Etta James") 20-30 61
CROWN (5234 "Best of Etta James") 20-30 62
CROWN (5250 "Twist with Etta James") .. 15-25 62
CROWN (5360 "Miss Etta James") 15-25 63
INTERMEDIA 5-10 84
KENT (3002 "Miss Etta James") 20-35 61
(Black vinyl.)
KENT (3002 "Miss Etta James") 50-100 61
(Colored vinyl.)
T-ELECTRIC 5-8 80
UNITED 10-12
W.B. 5-8 78
WESTBOUND 8-10
Session: Richard Berry; Riley Hampton's Orchestra.
Also see BERRY, Richard
Also see ETTA & HARVEY
Also see FLAIRS

JAMES, Gino

Singles: 7-inch

EPIC (9420 "New Girl") 10-15 60

JAMES, Harry, & His Orchestra P&R '38

Singles: 78 rpm

BRUNSWICK 3-6 38
COLUMBIA 3-6 40-57

VARIETY 4-8 40

Singles: 7-inch

CAPITOL (3849 "Andrea") 5-10 57
COLUMBIA (33000 series) 4-6 76
COLUMBIA (38000 thru 40000 series) 10-20 50-56
DOT 4-8 65-66
GOLD-MOR 4-6 73
MGM 5-10 59-63

EPs: 7-inch

COLUMBIA 5-15 50-56

LPs: 10/12-inch

BAINBRIDGE 5-8 83
BRIGHT ORANGE 5-8 73
CAPITOL (600 thru 1500 series) 20-40 55-61
(With "T", "ST," or "W" prefix.)
CAPITOL (1500 series) 10-20 62
(With "DT" prefix.)
CAPITOL (1500 series) 5-8 77
(With "M" prefix.)
COLUMBIA 10-30 50-67
COLUMBIA SPECIAL PRODUCTS 5-8 79
DOT 10-15 66-67
HARMONY 10-20 59-72
LONDON 8-12 68
MGM 10-20 59-65
METRO 8-15 65-67
PICKWICK .... 5-10 '70s
SHEFFIELD LAB 5-10 77-79
Also see CLOONEY, Rosemary, & Harry James
Also see KALLEN, Kitty
Also see SINATRA, Frank

JAMES, Jesse

Singles: 78 rpm

SITTIN' IN WITH (569 "Forgive Me Blues") 50-100 51
Also see JAMES, Sunny

JAMES, Jesse

Singles: 7-inch

DIXIE (1112 "Moonshine") .... 50-100 '60s
KENT (314 "Red Hot Rockin' Blues") ... 100-200 58

JAMES, Jesse — P&R/R&B '67

(With the Royal Aces; with the James Boys; Jessie James)

Singles: 7-inch

BUDDAH (315 "The Sweetest Little Thing") 5-10 72
HIT (6119 "I Call on You") .... 20-30 '60s
HIT (6120 "Believe in Me Baby") .... 15-25 '60s
MUSICOR (1008 "Dreams Never Hurt Nobody") 10-15 61
SHIRLEY (103 "I Will Go") 75-125 61
SHIRLEY (112 "I Wanna Full Time Love") 25-50 63
SHIRLEY (122 "I Want a Girl") 25-50 63
T.T.E.D. 3-5 87
20TH FOX 4-8 67-75
UNI 5-8 69
ZEA (ZAY) 4-8 70-71

LPs: 10/12-inch

20TH FOX 8-10 67

JAMES, Jimmy, & Candy Canes

Singles: 7-inch

COLUMBIA (41192 "Teen-Age Beauty") . 10-20 58

JAMES, Jimmy, & Vagabonds — P&R/R&B '68

Singles: 7-inch

ATCO (6551 "Come Softly to Me") 5-8 68
HBR (496 "Hi Diddley Dee Dum Dum") ... 10-20 66
PYE 4-6 75-76

LPs: 10/12-inch

ATCO (222 "New Religion") 10-15 67
PYE 5-8 75

JAMES, Joe

(With Bob Rush & Orchestra)

Singles: 7-inch

WAG (213 "A Fool for You") 50-100 59

JAMES, Johnny, & Tiaras

Singles: 7-inch

TOP TEN (45 "Tears") 30-40

JAMES, Joni — P&R '52

(With Lew Douglas & Orchestra; with Jack Halloran Singers; with Acquiviva & Orchestra; with Ray Charles Singers; with David Terry & Orchestra)

Singles: 78 rpm

MGM (222 "Let There Be Love") 100-200 53
(Four-disc boxed set.)
MGM (234 "Award Winning Album") 100-200 54
(Four-disc boxed set.)
MGM (272 "Little Girl Blue") 100-200 54
(Four-disc boxed set.)
MGM (11000 & 12000 series) 10-20 52-58
MGM (30000 series) 5-10 54
SHARP (46 "Let There Be Love") 25-50 52
SHARP (50 "You Belong to Me") 25-50 52

Singles: 7-inch

MGM (16 thru 19) 20-40 59-60
(Stereo compact 33 singles.)
MGM (11223 thru 12660) 15-25 52-58
MGM (12706 "There Goes My Heart") 10-15 58
(Monaural.)
MGM (12706 "There Goes My Heart") 20-30 58
(Stereo. Unusual numbering – most MGM stereo 45s are in the 50000 series. Billed as the industry's "First Single Stereo Disc.")
MGM (12746 thru 13304) 10-20 59-64
MGM (13288 "Sentimental Me") 50-75 64
(Promotional issue only.)
MGM (30000 series) 10-20 54
MGM (50111 "There Must Be a Way") 15-25 59
(Stereo.)
MGM/GOLDEN CIRCLE (101 thru 104) 5-10 61
SHARP (46 "Let There Be Love") 150-250 52
SHARP (50 "You Belong to Me") 100-200 52

Picture Sleeves

MGM (12565 "Never Till Now") 20-25 57
(Pictures Joni James as well as cast and scenes from the film *Raintree County*.)
MGM (12706 "There Goes My Heart") 30-50 58
(Reads: "MGM Records Is First with a Single Stereo Disc.")
MGM (12779 "I Still Get a Thrill") 10-20 59
MGM (12895 "We Know") 10-20 60
MGM (12933 "My Last Date") 10-20 60
MGM (12948 "Be My Love") 10-20 61
MGM (13037 "You Were Wrong") 10-20 62

EPs: 7-inch

MGM (222 "Let There Be Love") 50-75 53
MGM (234 "Award Winning Album") 50-75 54
MGM (272 "Little Girl Blue") 50-75 54
MGM (326 "When I Fall in Love") 20-40 55
(EPs 222 through 326 are two-disc sets.)
MGM (1160 "When I Fall in Love") 10-20 55
MGM (1172 "Have Yourself a Merry Little Christmas") 25-50 55
MGM (1211 thru 1617) 10-20 56-58
MGM (1652/3/4 "Songs of Hank Williams") 10-15 59
(Monaural. Price is for any of three volumes.)
MGM (1652/3/4 "Songs of Hank Williams") 30-40 59
(Stereo. Price is for any of three volumes.)
MGM (1656/7/8 "100 Strings and Joni") ... 10-15 59
(Monaural. Price is for any of three volumes.)
MGM (1656/7/8 "100 Strings and Joni") ... 30-40 59
(Stereo. Price is for any of three volumes.)
MGM (1672/3/4 "Joni Swings Sweet") 10-15 59
(Monaural. Price is for any of three volumes.)
MGM (1672/3/4 "Joni Swings Sweet") 30-40 59
(Stereo. Price is for any of three volumes.)
MGM (3328 "In the Still of the Night") 20-35 56
MGM (3533 "Songs by Jerome Kern and Harry Warren") 20-35 57

LPs: 10/12-inch

MGM (222 "Let There Be Love") 75-125 53
(10-inch LP.)
MGM (234 "Award Winning Album") 75-125 54
(10-inch LP.)
MGM (272 "Little Girl Blue") 75-125 54
(10-inch LP.)
MGM (3240 "When I Fall in Love") 30-50 55
MGM (3328 "In the Still of the Night") 30-50 56
MGM (3346 "Award Winning Album, Vol. 1") 30-50 56
MGM (3347 "Little Girl Blue") 30-50 56
MGM (3348 "Let There Be Love") 30-50 56
MGM (3449 "Songs by Victor Young & Frank Loesser") 30-50 56
MGM (3468 "Merry Christmas") 30-50 56
MGM (3528 "Give Us This Day") 25-45 57
MGM (3533 "Songs by Jerome Kern & Harry Warren") 25-45 57
MGM (3602 "Among My Souvenirs") 25-45 58
MGM (3623 "Ti Voglio Bene") 25-45 58
MGM (3706 "Award Winning Album, Vol. 2") 25-45 58
MGM (E-3718 "Je T'Aime") 25-45 58
(Monaural.)
MGM (SE-3718 "Je T'Aime") 35-55 58
(Stereo.)
MGM (E-3729 "Songs by Hank Williams") 25-45 59
(Monaural.)
MGM (SE-3729 "Songs by Hank Williams") 35-55 59
(Stereo.)
MGM (E-3749 thru E-4286) 20-40 59-65
(Monaural.)
MGM (SE-3749 thru SE-4286) 30-50 59-65
(Stereo.)
Also see CHARLES, Ray, Singers
Also see DOUGLAS, Lew
Also see HALLORAN, Jack, Singers

JAMES, Leon

Singles: 7-inch

BUMBLE BEE (501 "Baby, Let's Rock") 200-300

JAMES, Leonard

LPs: 10/12-inch

DECCA (8772 "Boppin' and A-Strollin' ") .. 40-50 58

JAMES, Leroy

Singles: 7-inch

GOLDBAND (1055 "Whoa Mule") 100-200 58

JAMES, Mark

(Mark James Trio)

Singles: 7-inch

BELL 4-6 73
CRS (1-8-35 "Blue Suede Heaven") 5-10 85
(Black vinyl.)
CRS (1-8-35 "Blue Suede Heaven") 10-20 85
(Colored vinyl.)
JAMIE (1261 "Running Back") 5-10 63
LIBERTY (55953 "Bimbo Knows") 5-10 67
MERCURY 4-6 75
NEW DESIGN 4-6 71
PRIVATE STOCK 4-6 78
SCEPTER (12221 "Suspicious Minds") 15-25 68
SCEPTER (12257 "Sunday Rain") 5-10 69
SPOTLIGHT (450 "Writing This Letter") ... 50-75 '60s

Picture Sleeves

CRS (1-8-35 "Blue Suede Heaven") 8-12 85

LPs: 10/12-inch

BELL 8-12 73

JAMES, Melvin

Singles: 7-inch

STAR (1623 "Do I Have a Chance") 50-75

JAMES, Ron

Singles: 7-inch

MAR-VEL (2500 "Please Be Mine") 15-25

JAMES, Sarah, & Soul Babies

Singles: 7-inch

FARO (628 "Takin' Care of Business") 10-20 67

JAMES, Skip

Singles: 78 rpm

PARAMOUNT (13065 "Cherry Ball Blues") 2000-2500
PARAMOUNT (13066 "22-20 Blues") 2000-2500
PARAMOUNT (13072 "How Long Buck") 2000-2500
PARAMOUNT (13083 "Devil Got My Woman") 2000-2500
PARAMOUNT (13085 "How Long Buck") 2000-2500
PARAMOUNT (13098 "Special Rider Blues") 2000-2500
PARAMOUNT (13106 "Hard Luck Child") 2000-2500
PARAMOUNT (13108 "Be Ready When He Comes") 2000-2500
PARAMOUNT (13111 "Drunken Spree") 2000-2500

LPs: 10/12-inch

BIOGRAPH 10-15 68-69
HISTORICAL 10-15
MELODEAN 10-15
VANGUARD 10-15 66-68

JAMES, Sonny — C&W '53

(With the Southern Gentlemen; with Silver; with Tennessee State Prison Band; the Southern Gentleman)

Singles: 78 rpm

CAPITOL 5-15 52-57

Singles: 7-inch

CAPITOL (2000 thru 3900) 4-6 67-74
(Orange labels.)
CAPITOL (2200 thru 3800) 10-20 52-57
(Purple labels.)
CAPITOL (3900 thru 5900, except 4178) ... 5-10 58-67
(Purple or orange/yellow swirl labels.)
CAPITOL (4178 "Talk of the School") 15-25 59
CAPITOL (6000 series) .... 4-6 '60s
CAPITOL CUSTOM ("Salute to KRAK") .. 15-25 67
(Promotional issue for a Sacramento radio station.)
COLUMBIA 4-6 72-78
DIMENSION 3-5 81-83
DOT (16381 thru 16419) 5-10 62
GROOVE (1 "Broken Wings") 5-10 61
MONUMENT 4-6 79
NRC (050 thru 061) 5-10 60
RCA (7858 thru 7998) 5-10 61-62

Picture Sleeves

CAPITOL (2155 thru 3232) 4-8 68-72
CAPITOL (4268 "Who's Next in Line) 10-20 59
CAPITOL (5129 "The Minute You're Gone") 8-12 63
CAPITOL (5375 thru 5987) 5-10 65-67
COLUMBIA 4-6 72-75
DIMENSION .... 3-5 '80s
NRC (050 "Jenny Lou") 10-20 60

EPs: 7-inch

CAPITOL 10-20 57-58
CAPITOL CREATIVE PRODUCTS 5-10 68

LPs: 10/12-inch

ABC 5-8 77
BROOKVILLE 8-12 75
CAMDEN .... 8-12 '60s
CAPITOL (100 thru 800 series) 8-12 68-71
CAPITOL (779 "Southern Gentleman") 25-35 57
CAPITOL (867 "Sonny") 20-30 57
CAPITOL (988 "Honey") 20-30 58
CAPITOL (1100 series) 15-25 59
CAPITOL (2000 thru 2800 series) 8-15 64-68
CAPITOL (11000 series) 5-8 72-75
COLUMBIA 5-10 72-78
CROWN .... 8-12 '60s
DIMENSION 5-8 82
DOT (3462 "Young Love") 15-25 62
(Monaural.)
DOT (25462 "Young Love") 15-25 62
(Stereo.)
GUEST STAR 10-15 64
HAMILTON 8-12 65
MONUMENT 5-8 79
PICKWICK 5-8 76-78
PICKWICK/HILLTOP 8-12 69
SUNRISE MEDIA 5-10
TEE VEE 8-12 79
TVP 8-12 75
WYNCOTE .... 8-12 '60s
Session: Darla Daret.
Also see DARET, Darla
Also see HAGGARD, Merle / Sonny James
Also see HORTON, Johnny / Sonny James
Also see JONES, George / David Houston / Sonny James
Also see VINCENT, Gene / Tommy Sands / Sonny James / Ferlin Husky
Also see VINCENT, Gene / Frank Sinatra / Sonny James / Ron Goodwin

JAMES, Sonny / Dave Dudley / Sunny Williams

LPs: 10/12-inch

DIPLOMAT .... 5-10 '60s
Also see DUDLEY, Dave

JAMES, Sonny / David Houston

LPs: 10/12-inch

PICKWICK/HILLTOP 8-12 67
Also see HOUSTON, David

JAMES, Sonny / Seekers

Singles: 7-inch

CAPITOL (5375 "I'll Keep Holding On"/"I'll Never Find Another You") 5-10 65
(These two tracks were unintentionally pressed back-to-back.)
Also see JAMES, Sonny
Also see SEEKERS

JAMES, Sunny
(Jesse James)
Singles: 78 rpm
DOWN TOWN (2010 "Please Mam, Forgive Me")....................50-100 48
Also see JAMES, Jesse

JAMES, Tammy
Singles: 7-inch
JANLENE (776 "Congratulations")..........15-25 63

JAMES, Tom
Singles: 78 rpm
RCA....................10-20 54
Singles: 7-inch
KLIX (001 "Track Down Baby")..........350-400 58
RCA (5695 "Your Kind of Lovin'")..........50-75 54
RCA (5790 "I'm a Pig About Your Lovin'")....................50-75 54

JAMES, Tommy P&R/R&B/LP '66
(With the Shondells)
Singles: 7-inch
ABC....................4-6 73
FANTASY....................3-6 75-80
MCA....................4-6 74
MILLENNIUM....................3-6 79-81
PHILCO (1 "Mirage"/"I Think We're Alone Now")....................10-20 67
PHILCO (2 "Hanky Panky"/"Gettin' Together")....................10-20 67
(Above two are "Hip Pocket" flexi-discs.)
ROULETTE....................10-15 66-73
TWENTY-ONE....................3-5 83
Picture Sleeves
FANTASY....................4-6 76
MILLENNIUM....................4-6 71
ROULETTE....................5-10 66-67
TWENTY-ONE....................3-5 83
LPs: 10/12-inch
FANTASY....................8-10 76-80
MILLENNIUM....................5-8 80
RHINO....................8-12 89
ROULETTE....................10-20 66-72
SCEPTER....................8-10 73
SCEPTER/CITATION....................5-8 82
TWENTY-ONE....................5-8 83
Members: Tommy James; Mike Vale; Ed Gray; Ron Rosman; Pete Lucia.
Also see SHONDELLS
Also see TOM & TORNADOS

JAMES, Tommy & Shondells / Lee Dorsey
Singles: 7-inch
ROULETTE (4710 "It's Only Love"/"Ya Ya")....................5-10 66
(Credits Tommy James & Shondells, but plays Lee Dorsey.)
Also see DORSEY, Lee
Also see JAMES, Tommy

JAMES, Ulysses / Lowell Fulson
Singles: 78 rpm
CAVATONE (250 "Poor Boy")..........40-60 48
Also see FULSON, Lowell

JAMES BOYS
Singles: 7-inch
GALLIANT (1002 "Back Rub")..........75-125 59
Members: Ralph Nielsen; Jame Druiett.
Also see NEILSEN, Ralph, & Chancellors

JAMES BOYS
Singles: 7-inch
COLPIX (702 "Another Lori")....................8-12 63
COLUMBIA (43488 "Sometimes")..........5-10 66
COLUMBIA (43717 "Keep the Fire Burning")....................5-10 66
EDSEL....................15-25 60
KAPP (502 "Stampede")....................8-12 63
PARK AVENUE (105 "Tears on My Pillow")....................10-15 63
PARK AVENUE (106 "Hey Sweet Girl")..10-15 63

JAMES QUINTET
Singles: 78 rpm
CORAL (60018 "Pleasing You")..........50-100 48
CORAL (60022 "Tell Me Why")..........50-100 49
CORAL (65002 "Pleasing You")..........50-100 48
CORAL (65016 "Tell Me Why")..........50-100 49
(We do not yet know whether the 60000 series precedes the 65000 series, or not.)
DECCA....................20-30 51
DERBY (726 "I'm Just a Fool")..........20-40 49
DERBY (732 "Don't Worry")..........20-40 50
Singles: 7-inch
DECCA (48218 "A Neighborhood Affair")....................200-300 51
DECCA (48237 "I Could Make You Care")....................200-300 51
Also see BROWN, Ruth
Also see POWELL, Austin

JAMESON, Bobby
(Robert Parker Jameson)
Singles: 7-inch
BRIT (7001 "I Wanna Know")..........5-10 65
CURRENT (103 "All Alone")..........5-10 64
LONDON (9730 "Each and Everyday")....20-30 65
PENTHOUSE (503 "Gotta Find My Roogalator")....................20-30 66
TALAMO (1934 "I Wanna Love You")......50-75 64
VERVE (10509 "New Age")..........5-10 67
VERVE (10542 "Right By My Side")..........5-10 67
LPs: 10/12-inch
GRT....................8-10
Also see ROLLING STONES

JAMIE & JANE
Singles: 7-inch
DECCA (30862 "Strolling")..........15-25 59
DECCA (30934 "Faithful Our Love")..........15-25 59
Members: Gene Pitney; Ginny Arnell.
Also see ARNELL, Ginny
Also see PITNEY, Gene

JAMIES P&R '58
Singles: 7-inch
EPIC....................10-15 58-63
EPIC (11000 series)....................4-6 74
U.A. (193 "Evening Star")..........5-10 59
Picture Sleeves
EPIC (9281 "Summertime Summertime")....................20-30 62
Members: Tom Jameson; Serena Jameson; Jeannie Roy; Arthur Blair.
Also see J's WITH JAMIE

JAMMERS
Singles: 7-inch
DEARBORN (519 "You're Gonna Love Me Too")....................25-35 65

JAMMIN' JIM
(Ed Harris)
Singles: 78 rpm
SAVOY (1106 "Shake Boogie")..........15-25 52
Singles: 7-inch
SAVOY (1106 "Shake Boogie")..........25-50 52
Also see CAROLINA SLIM
Also see COUNTRY PAUL
Also see LAZY SLIM JIM

JAN & ARNIE P&R '58
(With Don Ralke's Orchestra; with Adam Ross Orchestra)
Singles: 78 rpm
ARWIN (108 "Jennie Lee")..........250-300 58
QUALITY (1731 "Jennie Lee")..........100-200 58
(Canadian.)
QUALITY (1761 "Gas Money")..........100-200 58
(Canadian.)
Singles: 7-inch
ARWIN (108 "Jennie Lee")..........25-35 58
ARWIN (111 "Gas Money")..........30-40 58
ARWIN (113 "I Love Linda")..........50-75 58
DORE (522 "Baby Talk")..........350-450 59
(By Jan & Dean though shown on first pressings as by Jan & Arnie.)
DOT (16116 "Gas Money")..........40-50 58
QUALITY (1731 "Jennie Lee")..........35-50 58
(Canadian.)
QUALITY (1761 "Gas Money")..........35-50 58
(Canadian.)
EPs: 7-inch
DOT (1097 "Jan & Arnie")..........350-450 60
Members: Jan Berry; Arnie Ginsburg.
Also see BERRY, Jan
Also see GINSBURG, Arnie
Also see JAN & DEAN
Also see RALKE, Don
Also see RITUALS

JAN & DEAN P&R/R&B '59
Singles: 7-inch
AURAVISION (6723 "Linda")..........40-60 64
(Cardboard flexi-disc, one of six by six different artists. Columbia Record Club "Enrollment Premium." Set came in a special paper sleeve.)
CAPITOL (89 "Jennie Lee")..........5-10 89
(By Jan & Dean instead of Jan & Arnie.)
CHALLENGE (9120 "Wanted: One Girl")..10-20 61
CHALLENGE (9111 "Heart and Soul"/"Those Words")....................40-50 61
CHALLENGE (9111 "Heart and Soul"/ "Midsummer Night's Dream")....................15-25 61
(Note different flip side.)
CHALLENGE (59111 "Heart and Soul")...10-20 61
COLLECTABLES....................5-10 92
COLUMBIA (44036 "Yellow Balloon")......15-25 67
DORE (522 "Baby Talk")..........20-30 59
DORE (531 "There's a Girl")..........20-30 59
DORE (539 "Clementine")..........20-30 60
DORE (548 "White Tennis Sneakers")......20-30 60
DORE (555 "We Go Together")..........20-30 60
DORE (576 "Gee")..........25-35 60
DORE (583 "Baggy Pants")..........20-30 61
DORE (610 "Julie")..........20-30 61
J&D (1 "Oh What a Beautiful Morning")....................150-200 87
(Private, limited, promotional, red vinyl pressing by Dean Torrence which he used as Christmas gifts. With Chris Farmer and Phil Bardwell.)
J&D (001 "California Lullabye")..........20-30 66
J&D (402 "Like a Summer Rain")..........40-50 66
JAN & DEAN (10 "Hawaii")..........50-75 66
JAN & DEAN (11 "Fan Tan")..........50-75 66
LIBERTY (55397 "A Sunday Kind of Love")....................15-25 61
LIBERTY (55454 "Tennessee")..........15-25 62
LIBERTY (55496 "Who Put the Bomp")...30-40 62
LIBERTY (55522 "She's Still Talkin' Baby Talk")....................50-75 62
LIBERTY (55531 "Linda")..........15-25 63
LIBERTY (55580 "Surf City")..........15-20 63
LIBERTY (55613 "Honolulu Lulu")..........10-15 63
LIBERTY (55641 "Drag City")..........10-15 63
(Credits "Audio Engineers, Lanky & Bones.")
LIBERTY (55641 "Drag City")..........8-12 63
(No mention of "Lanky & Bones.")
LIBERTY (55672 "Dead Man's Curve")....10-15 64
LIBERTY (55704 "The Little Old Lady")...10-15 64
LIBERTY (55724 "Ride the Wild Surf")....10-15 64
LIBERTY (55727 "Sidewalk Surfin'")......10-15 64
LIBERTY (55766 "From All Over the World")....................10-15 65
LIBERTY (55792 "You Really Know How to Hurt a Guy")....................10-15 65
LIBERTY (55833 "I Found a Girl")..........10-15 65
LIBERTY (55849 "Folk City")..........10-15 65
LIBERTY (55856 "Norwegian Wood"/"I Can't Wait to Love You")....................10-15 66
LIBERTY (55860 "Batman")..........15-25 66
LIBERTY (55886 "Popsicle"/"Norwegian Wood")....................8-12 66
LIBERTY (55905 "Fiddle Around")..........8-12 66
LIBERTY (55923 "New Girl in School")......8-12 66
MAGIC LAMP (401 "California Lullabye") 35-45 66
ODE (66111 "Fun City")..........15-25 75
U.A....................10-20 72-76
W.B. (7151 "Only a Boy")..........35-50 67
W.B. (7219 "I Know My Mind")..........30-40 68
Picture Sleeves
DORE (555 "We Go Together")..........50-75 60
DORE (576 "Gee")..........75-125 60
LIBERTY (55580 "Surf City")..........15-25 63
LIBERTY (55613 "Honolulu Lulu")..........15-25 63
LIBERTY (55641 "Drag City")..........15-25 63
LIBERTY (55672 "Dead Man's Curve")....15-25 64
LIBERTY (55704 "The Little Old Lady")...15-25 64
LIBERTY (55727 "Sidewalk Surfin'")......15-25 64
LIBERTY (55766 "From All Over the World")....................80-125 65
LIBERTY (55792 "You Really Know How to Hurt a Guy")....................25-35 65
LIBERTY (55849 "Folk City")..........25-35 65
U.A. (50859 "Jenny Lee")..........15-25 71
EPs: 7-inch
ARTISTIC (227 "Original Golden Hits")....40-50 65
(Also contains tracks by Jerry Wallace; Champs; Ray Sharpe; Fireflies; Rosie & Originals; and Gene & Eunice.)
LAST RIDE (7801 "Jan & Dean Meet Batman")....................15-25 81
(Fan club issue only.)
LPs: 10/12-inch
ARTISTIC (227 "Original Golden Hits")..50-100 65
(Also contains tracks by Jerry Wallace; Champs; Ray Sharpe; Fireflies; Rosie & Originals; and Gene & Eunice.)
AUDIO ENCORE....................5-8 89
AXIS (45 "Very Best")....................5-10
COLUMBIA (9461 "Save for a Rainy Day")....................1500-2000 67
(At least one sale of this LP has been confirmed. It DOES exist but is probably not a U.S. issue. Tracks are remixed from what is heard on the J&D LP of the same title. Does have one track, *Lullaby in the Rain*, which is not on the J&D LP.)
DEADMAN'S CURVE ("Live at Keystone Berkeley")....................15-25 78
(With Papa Doo Ron Ron.)
DESIGN/STEREO SPECTRUM (181 "The Heart & Soul of Jan & Dean & Friends")..........20-25 63
DORE (101 "Jan & Dean")..........300-400 60
(With 12" x 12" bonus Jan & Dean color photo.)
DORE (101 "Jan & Dean")..........200-300 60
(Without bonus photo.)
EMI....................10-15 86
EMI/LIBERTY....................10-20 90
EXACT....................5-8 80
EXCELSIOR....................10-15 80
IMPERIAL HOUSE....................5-8 80
INTERNATIONAL AWARD....................8-10
J&D (101 "Save for a Rainy Day")........200-300 67
K-TEL....................5-10 70-89
LIBERTY (3248 thru 3403)..........20-25 62-65
(Monaural.)
LIBERTY (3414 "Pop Symphony Number 1")....................40-45 65
(Monaural. With Bel-Aire Pops Orchestra)
LIBERTY (3417 thru 3460)..........20-25 65-66
(Monaural.)
LIBERTY (7248 thru 7403)..........20-30 62-65
(Stereo.)
LIBERTY (7414 "Pop Symphony Number 1")....................40-50 65
(Stereo. With Bel-Aire Pops Orchestra)
LIBERTY (7417 thru 7460)..........20-30 65-66
(Stereo.)
LIBERTY (10000 series)..........8-12 81-82
MAGIC CARPET (1003 "Oddities")..........15-25 91
(Black vinyl. Without flexi-disc.)
MAGIC CARPET (1003 "Oddities")..........25-35 91
(Black vinyl. With flexi-disc "Surf Bunkey.")
MAGIC CARPET (1003 "Oddities")..........30-40 91
(Red vinyl. 10 made.)
MAGIC CARPET (1003 "Oddities")..........40-50 91
(Picture disc. No cover. 25 made.)
NEON (333006 "Greatest Hits")..........8-10 83
PAIR (1071 "California Gold")..........10-15
RHINO (1498 "One Summer Night Live") 25-45 82
SILVER EAGLE (1039 "Silver Summer").25-35 86
(Mail-order offer.)
SUNDAZED (5022 "Save for a Rainy Day")....................15-18 96
(Colored vinyl. Two-discs.)
SUNDAZED (5040 "Jan & Dean")..........8-10 96
(Colored vinyl. Includes poster.)
SUNSET....................10-15 67
U.A....................10-12 71-79
Members: Jan Berry; Dean Torrence. Session: Glen Campbell; Leon Russell; Hal Blaine; Sally Stevens; Carol Kaye; Phil Bardowell; Chris Farmer; Ray Pholman; Don Randi.
Also see BEACH BOYS
Also see BEACH BOYS / Jan & Dean
Also see BERRY, Jan
Also see BLAINE, Hal
Also see CAMPBELL, Glen
Also see JAN & ARNIE
Also see LAUGHING GRAVY
Also see LEGENDARY MASKED SURFERS
Also see MATADORS
Also see MIKE & DEAN
Also see OUR GANG
Also see RALLY PACKS
Also see RUSSELL, Leon

JAN & DEAN / Roy Orbison / 4 Seasons / Shirelles
EPs: 7-inch
COKE ("Let's Swing the Jingle for Coca-Cola")....................40-60 65

(Coca-Cola radio spots. Issued to radio stations only.)
Also see 4 SEASONS
Also see ORBISON, Roy
Also see SHIRELLES

JAN & DEAN & RANDELL KIRSCH
Singles: 7-inch
JAN & DEAN (1 "Wa Ichi Nichi Shiow")......5-10 87
Members: Jan Berry; Dean Torrence; Randell Kirsch; Gary Griffin; Chris Farmer; Mark Ward; John Cowsill; Phil Bardowell; Kevin Leonard; Bill Hollingshead; Dave Hoffman; Sue Nelson; members of Shanghai audience.

JAN & DEAN / Soul Surfers
LPs: 10/12-inch
L-J (101 "Jan & Dean with the Soul Surfers")........................ 35-45 61
Also see SOUL SURFERS / Delicates

JAN & DEAN / Ventures
Singles: 7-inch
DOLTON (57724381977071 "Frosty the Snowman")........................5-10 97
(Promotional issue only.)
Also see VENTURES

JAN & DEAN / Bobby Vinton / Andy Williams
Singles
AURAVISION (2 "Special Teen Preview Record #2")........................ 12-20 64
(Square cardboard picture disc. Columbia Record Club bonus. Has song excerpts by each artist, plus *Pipeline* by an unknown band.)
Also see JAN & DEAN
Also see VINTON, Bobby
Also see WILLIAMS, Andy

JAN & JERRY
Singles: 7-inch
METRO (20024 "Bandstand Baby")......... 10-15 59

JAN & KJELD P&R '60
Singles: 7-inch
ALONCA (6001 "Taste of Honey")...............4-8 66
IMPERIAL (5568 "Tiger Rag")....................5-10 59
JARO INT'L (77032 "Ting-a-Ling My Banjo Sings")........................5-10 60
KAPP (335 "Banjo Boy")........................5-10 60
KAPP (346 "Yes, Sir That's My Baby").......5-10 60
KAPP (373 "Oh, Mein Papa")....................5-10 61
Picture Sleeves
JARO INT'L (77032 "Ting-a-Ling My Banjo Sings")........................5-10 60
KAPP (335 "Banjo Boy")........................5-10 60
LPs: 10/12-inch
KAPP (1190 "Banjo Boy")........................ 20-30 60

JAN & LORRAINE
LPs: 10/12-inch
ABC-PAR (691 "Gypsy People")............. 15-25 69
Members: Jan Hendin; Lorraine Lefevre.

JANES, Bill
Singles: 7-inch
MUNRAB (104 "School's Out")............... 25-40

JANES, Roland
(Roland James)
Singles: 7-inch
JUDD (1012 "Guitarville")...................... 10-20 59
RITA (1007 "Down Yonder")..................... 10-15 60
Also see ALTON & JIMMY
Also see ANDERSON, Brother James
Also see BARTON, Ernie
Also see RILEY, Billy Lee
Also see WARREN, Randy

JANET & JAY
Singles: 7-inch
LEADER (810 "Pretend a Wedding")..........8-12 60
Picture Sleeves
LEADER (810 "Pretend a Wedding")....... 15-20 60
Also see LEONARD, Jay / Janet & Jay

JANIS, Johnny P&R '57
Singles: 78 rpm
ABC-PAR........................5-10 57
CORAL (61552 "Move It Or Lose It")..........5-10 55
Singles: 7-inch
ABC-PAR (9800 "Pledge of Love").......... 10-20 57
ABC-PAR (9840 "Later Baby")................. 10-20 57
BOMARC (304 "Willing to Learn")..............8-12 59
BOMARC (307 "I Said You")......................8-12 60
CARLTON (463 "The Better to Love You")........................10-20 58
COLUMBIA (41797 "Gina")........................8-12 60
COLUMBIA (41933 "Catch a Falling Star")........................8-12 61
COLUMBIA (42040 "I Get Ideas")...............8-12 61
CORAL (61552 "Move It Or Lose It")........10-20 55
MONUMENT........................5-10 66-68
LPs: 10/12-inch
ABC-PAR (140 "For the First Time").........50-75 57
COLUMBIA (1674 "Start of Something New")........................20-30 61
(Monaural.)
COLUMBIA (8474 "Start of Something New")........................30-40 61
(Stereo.)
MONUMENT (8036 "Once in a Blue Moon")........................10-15 65
(Monaural.)
MONUMENT (18036 "Once in a Blue Moon")........................15-20 65
(Stereo.)

JANIS & HER BOYFRIENDS
Singles: 7-inch
RCA (7318 "Please Be My Love") 10-20 58

JANO, Johnny
Singles: 78 rpm
EXCELLO (2099 "Having a Whole Lot of Fun")........................20-30 56
Singles: 7-inch
EXCELLO (2099 "Having a Whole Lot of Fun")........................50-100 56
(Orange label, blue print. Counterfeits can be identified by their orange label with black print.)
GOLDBAND (1062 "Mabel's Gone").........30-40 58
GOLDBAND (1087 "Mabel's Gone")..........20-25 59
(Same number used on a Sidney Ester release.)
HOLLYWOOD (1087 "Mabel's Gone") 50-75 58
(First issue.)
JADOR (101 "Shed So Many Tears").......10-20
JADOR (111 "Cajun Power")..................75-125
PAULA (1235 "Pool of Heartaches") 4-8 70

JANSSEN, Danny
Singles: 7-inch
STEPHENY (1841 "Mirror Mirror on the Wall")........................40-50 60

JANSSEN, David
(With the Tradewinds Orchestra)
Singles: 7-inch
STEPHENY (1841 "Blue Moon")................5-10 60
STEPHENY (1843 "Christmas All Alone")..5-10 60
LPs: 10/12-inch
EPIC (24150 "Hidden Island")..................10-20 65
(Monaural.)
EPIC (26150 "Hidden Island")..................15-25 65
(Stereo.)

JANUS
LPs: 10/12-inch
HARVEST (29433 "Gravedigger") 40-60 72

JAPANESE BEATLES
Singles: 7-inch
GOLDEN CREST (584 "Beatle Song").....15-20 64

JARETT, Peter, & Fifth Circle
Singles: 7-inch
MGM (13768 "Let's Dance Close") 30-40 67

JARLAYNS
Singles: 7-inch
GIANTSTAR (402 "Why Don't You Call Me")........................20-30

JARMELS P&R/R&B '61
Singles: 7-inch
LAURIE (3085 "Little Lonely One")...........15-20 61
LAURIE (3098 "A Little Bit of Soap") 15-20 61
LAURIE (3116 thru 3174)........................8-12 62-63
LPs: 10/12-inch
COLLECTABLES........................5-10 87
Members: Nate Ruff; Ray Smith; Tom Eldridge; Paul Burnett; Earl Christian; Major Harris.

JARRARD, Rick
Singles: 7-inch
CHATTAHOOCHEE (657 "Why")..............10-15 64
CHATTAHOOCHEE (700 "Traffic Jam") ..10-15 66
PLEBE (101 "Tell Me Not") 40-50 62
Also see JEFFERSON AIRPLANE

JARRE, Jean-Michael LP '77
Singles: 12-inch
POLYDOR........................4-6 86
Singles: 7-inch
POLYDOR........................3-6 78-87
LPs: 10/12-inch
DREYFUS........................5-8 85-86
MFSL (212 "Oxygene") 25-35 94
MFSL (227 "Equinoxe")...........................25-35 95
POLYDOR........................5-10 77-87
Also see ANDERSON, Laurie

JARREAU, Al R&B/LP '76
(Jarreau)
Singles: 7-inch
MCA........................3-5 87
RAYNARD (10022 "I'm Not Afraid")........50-100 65
RAYNARD (10024 "Shake Up")..............50-100 65
REPRISE........................3-6 76-88
W.B. 3-6 77-86
Picture Sleeves
MCA........................3-5 87
W.B. 3-5 83-84
LPs: 10/12-inch
MFSL (019 "All Fly Home") 50-75 78
REPRISE........................5-10 75-88
W.B. 5-10 77-86

JARREAU, Al, & Randy Crawford R&B '82
Singles: 7-inch
W.B. 3-5 82
Also see JARREAU, Al

JARRETT, Pete, & Fifth Circle
Singles: 7-inch
MGM (13768 "Let's Dance Closer")..........25-35 67

JARVIS, Carol P&R '57
Singles: 78 rpm
DITTO (101 "Loverboy")........................5-10 56
Singles: 7-inch
BALLY (1029 "Loverboy") 10-15 57
DITTO (101 "Loverboy")..........................10-15 56
(Black vinyl.)
DITTO (101 "Loverboy")..........................20-30 56
(Red vinyl.)
DOT........................10-15 57-59
ERA........................8-12 60-61

JARVIS, Felton
(With the Fel-Tones)
Singles: 7-inch
ABC-PAR 5-10 64-65
MGM (12982 "Goin' Downtown")...............5-10 61
THUNDER INT'L (1023 "Swingin' Cat")....50-75 60
THUNDER INT'L (1030 "Little Wheel")....25-50 61
VIVA (1001 "Don't Knock Elvis")..............15-25 59
Also see PRESLEY, Elvis

JARVIS, Kitty
LPs: 10/12-inch
SKYLINE (7701 "Kitty Jarvis Sings Supper Club Favorites") 15-25 59

JASPER WRATH
Singles: 7-inch
FUTURE MUSIC........................4-6 76
SUNFLOWER (107 "It's Up to You") 5-10 71
LPs: 10/12-inch
SUNFLOWER (5003 "Jasper Wrath") 40-60 71

JAVALANS
Singles: 7-inch
EVENT (4271 "Cynthia") 50-75 58

JAVALONS
(With the Respectable Three)
Singles: 7-inch
DIP (6901 "Took a Chance")....................30-40 61
TRU EKO (6901 "Took a Chance") 40-50 61
(Gold label.)
TRU EKO (6901 "Took a Chance") 20-30 61
(Light yellow label.)

JAVELINS
Singles: 7-inch
CAPITOL (5050 "Joe the Guitar Man").....10-20 63

JAVELS
Singles: 7-inch
JAIRO (500 "Distant Guitar")....................10-20 64

JAXON, Bob
(With Marty Gold & His Orchestra; Bob Jaxon & Hi Tones)
Singles: 78 rpm
CADENCE (1264 "Why Does a Woman Cry")........................5-10 55
RCA........................10-15 57
Singles: 7-inch
CADENCE (1264 "Why Does a Woman Cry")........................10-20 55
RCA (6945 "I'm Hangin' Around")............20-30 57
RCA (7006 "Come on Down") 20-30 57
RCA (7106 "I'm Hurtin' Inside")...............20-30 57
RCA (7168 "Me! Please! Me!") 10-20 58
20TH FOX (441 "Weep, Mary, Weep") 5-10 63

JAXON SISTERS
Singles: 78 rpm
BIG........................10-15 57
Singles: 7-inch
BIG (605 "For a Lifetime")......................10-15 57
BIG (606 "Thanks Mr. Moonbeam") 10-15 57

JAY, Bobby
(With the Runarounds)
Singles: 7-inch
ALTA........................4-6
EXCELLO (2225 "Tell Me Now")................8-12 62
IMPERIAL (5590 "Sweet Little Stranger") 10-20 59
RUSTONE (1407 "Because of You")..........8-12 61
TOWER (777 "Block Party") ....5-10 '60s
LP: 10/12-inch
W.B. 10-15

JAY, Bobby, & Hawks
EPs: 7-inch
W.B. (1438 "Bobby Jay and the Hawks")... 8-10 64
LPs: 10/12-inch
W.B. (1562 "Everybody's Doing the Watusi")........................10-15 64
W.B. (1563 "Everybody's Doing the Ska")........................10-15 64
W.B. (1564 "Everybody's Doing the Monkey")........................10-15 64

JAY, Brian
Singles: 7-inch
LAURIE (3228 "Tuff Enuff")......................10-20 64

JAY, Dale, & Storms
Singles: 7-inch
RAVEN (001 "Shakin' All Over")...............40-60 59

JAY, George, & Rockin' Ravens
Singles: 7-inch
DYNAMIC ("Say That You Love Me") 20-30
RAVE (103 "El Gringo") 10-20

JAY, Jerry
(Jerry Osborne)
Singles: 7-inch
QUALITY (201 "The King's Country")...200-300 66
(Six copies made as gifts.)
Also see OSBORNE, Jerry

JAY, Jimmie, & Moon-Reyes
(Jimie Jay & Moon-Reyes)
Singles: 7-inch
ALPAC (1912 "Highleggin Party") 15-25
DIXIETONE (1912 "Highleggin Party").200-300 65
Session: Romans.

JAY, Jimmy, & Blue Falcons
Singles: 7-inch
BELMONT (4006 "Turbine Drive")...........15-25 62

JAY, Johnny
(Johnny Huhta)
Singles: 78 rpm
MERCURY........................10-20 57-58
Singles: 7-inch
MERCURY........................15-25 57-58
NORCO (101 "Love of My Life")...............10-20 63
PLAY (1006 "That's What I Like")............10-20 58
STOP........................10-20 67-68
Also see HUHTA, Johnny

JAY, Karl
Singles: 7-inch
MARJON (503 "Unemployment Line") 30-40 62

JAY, Lonnie, & Jaynes
Singles: 7-inch
ARLEN (724 "Somewhere")......................10-15 63

JAY, Marty
Singles: 7-inch
MARTAY (2002 "That Little Old Wine Maker Me")....10-15 '60s

JAY, Morty, & Surfin' Cats / Jerry Norell & Beach Girls P&R '63
Singles: 7-inch
LEGEND (124 "Saltwater Taffy"/"What Is Surfin' All About")....15-25 63
Picture Sleeves
LEGEND (124 "Saltwater Taffy"/"What Is Surfin' All About")....15-25 63
Also see JAY, Morty
Also see NORELL, Jerry

JAY, Myrna
Singles: 7-inch
SAGE (310 "Savin' My Love")....10-15 59

JAY, P., & Haystackers
Singles: 7-inch
OAK (102 "High School Rock n' Roll")...50-100
OAK (103 "Little Heart Attacks")....75-125

JAY, Sammy
(With the Tiffineers)
Singles: 7-inch
PRINCESS (4021 "Candy Kisses")....5-10 63
PRINCESS (4032 "Blue Tears")....5-10 65
TRIBE (8311 "Never Let Me Go")....15-25 65

JAY, Tommy
Singles: 7-inch
DOVER (5001 "Going Steady Ring")....10-15 63
GOLBE (1258 "Sandie Jane")....10-15 59
HI (2088 "Tender Love")....8-12 65
M.O.C. (663 "Springtime's Coming")....8-12 64

JAY & AMERICANS P&R '62
Singles: 7-inch
COLLECTABLES....3-5 92-93
EEOC (1140 "Things Are Changing")....50-100 65
(Equal Employment Opportunity Center promotional issue.)
FUTURA....4-6 72
U.A. (353 thru 992)....6-12 61-66
U.A. (50000 series)....4-8 66-71
U.A. (1600 series)....3-6
U.A. SILVER SPOTLIGHT....3-5
Picture Sleeves
EEOC (1140 "Things Are Changing")....50-100 65
(Equal Employment Opportunity Center promotional issue.)
U.A. (919 "Some Enchanted Evening")....8-12 65
U.A. (919 "Sunday and Me")....10-20 65
U.A. (50016 "Crying")....8-12 66
U.A. (50046 "Livin' Above Your Head")....8-12 66
EPs: 7-inch
AMERICA'S (101 "America's Most Exciting Pop Concert Attraction")....20-30 '60s
(Promotional issue only.)
LPs: 10/12-inch
PAIR....8-10 88
RHINO....5-8 86
SUNSET....10-12 69-70
UNART....8-12 67
U.A. (300 series)....5-8 75
U.A. (1000 series)....5-8 80
U.A. (3222 "She Cried")....20-25 62
(Monaural.)
U.A. (3300 "At the Cafe Wha")....20-25 63
(Monaural.)
U.A. (3407 "Come a Little Bit Closer")....15-25 64
(Monaural.)
U.A. (3417 thru 3562)....15-20 64-67
(Monaural.)
U.A. (6222 "She Cried")....25-35 62
(Stereo.)
U.A. (6300 "At the Cafe Wha")....20-30 63
(Stereo.)
U.A. (6407 "Come a Little Bit Closer")....20-25 64
(Stereo.)
U.A. (6417 thru 6762, except 6671)....10-20 64-70
U.A. (6671 "Sands of Time")....20-30 69
U.A. (90814 "Greatest Hits")....15-20 '60s
(Record club issue.)
VACEL (007 "Jay Black's Favorites")....20-30 91
Members: Jay Traynor; Kenny Vance; Howard Kane; Jay Black; Marty Sanders; Sandy Yaguda.
Session: Donald Fagen; Walter Becker.
Also see BLACK, Jay
Also see HARBOR LIGHTS
Also see RAIN DROPS / Jay & Americans / Empires / Clusters
Also see STEELY DAN
Also see TRAYNOR, Jay
Also see VANCE, Kenny

JAY & DELTAS
Singles: 7-inch
W.B. (5404 "Bells Are Ringing")....40-50 64
Members: Jim Waller; Ed Atkinson; Jeff Christensen; Terry Christofferson; Roy Carlson.
Also see WALLER, Jim, & Deltas

JAY & DRIVING WHEELS
Singles: 7-inch
LANOR (528 "House of the Rising Sun").15-25

JAY & REBELS
Singles: 7-inch
SONORUS (7661 "Guitar Woman")....50-75

JAY & SHUFFLERS
Singles: 7-inch
CRACKERJACK (4010 "Always Be Mine")....20-30 63

JAY & TECHNIQUES P&R/R&B/LP '67
Singles: 7-inch
EVENT (222 "I Feel Love Coming On")....4-6 75
EVENT (228 "Number Onederful")....4-6 76
GORDY (7123 "I'll Be Here")....4-6 73
PHILCO (22 "Apples, Peaches, Pumpkin Pie"/"Loving for Money")....10-20 67
("Hip Pocket" flexi-disc.)
SILVER BLUE....4-8 74
SMASH (2086 thru 2237)....5-10 67-69
Picture Sleeves
SMASH (2124 "Keep the Ball Rollin' ")....8-12 67
SMASH (2142 "Strawberry Shortcake")....8-12 67
SMASH (2154 "Baby Make Your Own Sweet Music")....8-12 68
SMASH (2171 "Singles Game")....8-12 68
LPs: 10/12-inch
EVENT....8-12 75
SMASH....15-20 67-68
Members: Jay Proctor; John Walsh; Chuck Crowl; Ron Goosly; Dante Dancho; Karl Landis. Session: Harry "Hoag" Strother.
Also see COURIERS
Also see SINCERES

JAY BEE & KATS
Singles: 7-inch
BANGAR (606 "Tension")....25-35 64
Members: Robert Shaw; Lloyd Nerland; Steven Pugsley; Joe Unzicker.

JAY CEEs
Singles: 7-inch
ENJOY (1004 "The Waddle")....10-15 62

JAY JAY & SELECTONES
Singles: 7-inch
GUEST (6201 "Humpty Dumpty")....15-25 62

JAYBEES
Singles: 7-inch
COLUMBIA (2750 "Who Do You Think You Are")....15-20 67
(Canadian.)
RCA (3398 "I'm a Loner")....20-30 66
(Canadian.)
RCA (8904 "I'm a Loner")....15-20 66
RCA (9001 "I Think of Her")....15-20 66
(Canadian.)
Members: Al Nicholls; Doug West; Andy Kaye; Bill Hill; Lou Atkins.
Also see J.B. & PLAYBOYS

JAYE, Jerry
Singles: 7-inch
STEPHENY (1820 "How Could You Lose Your Trust in Me")....100-125 58
STEPHENY (1828 "How Could You Lose Your Trust in Me")....75-100 58

JAYE, Jerry
Singles: 7-inch
LABEL (2020 "Going to the River")....10-15 59

JAYE, Jerry P&R/LP '67
Singles: 7-inch
COLUMBIA....4-6 75
CONNIE (101 "Hello Josephine")....10-15 67
HI (2100 series)....5-10 67-69
HI (2300 series)....4-6 76-77
MEGA....4-6 71-74
RAINTREE....4-6 72
LPs: 10/12-inch
HI (32000 series)....15-20 67
HI (32100 series)....5-8 76

JAYE SISTERS
Singles: 7-inch
ATLANTIC (1171 "Going to the River")....10-15 58
ATLANTIC (1190 "Real Love")....10-15 58
ATLANTIC (2000 "Little Daddy")....10-15 58
DECCA (30236 "Have You Ever Been Lonely")....10-15 57
U.A. (187 "G-3")....10-15 59

JAYES
Singles: 7-inch
ARC (4443 "Panic Stricken")....75-100 58

JAYHAWKERS
Singles: 7-inch
DELTRON (1227 "Dawn of Instruction")....10-15 '60s
DELTRON (1228 "To Have a Love")....10-15 '60s
LUCKY ELEVEN (232 "Come On")....8-12 '60s
LYKE TIL (7147 "Love Have Mercy")....10-15 '60s

JAYHAWKS P&R/R&B '56
Singles: 78 rpm
ALADDIN (3393 "Everyone Should Know")....50-75 57
FLASH (Except 105)....10-15 56
FLASH (105 "Counting My Teardrops")...50-75 55
Singles: 7-inch
ALADDIN (3393 "Everyone Should Know")....75-125 57
EASTMAN (792 "I Wish the World Owed Me a Living")....50-150 59
EASTMAN (798 "New Love")....100-200 59
FIREFLY (327 "New Love")....3-5 74
FLASH (105 "Counting My Teardrops")....200-300 55
FLASH (109 "Stranded in the Jungle")....15-25 56
FLASH (111 "Love Train")....15-25 56
OLDIES 45....4-8 '60s
Members: James Johnson; Carl Fisher; Dave Govan; Carver Bunkern; Richard Owens.
Also see CURRY, James "King"
Also see MARATHONS
Also see PALMER, Earl
Also see VIBRATIONS

JAYHAWKS
Singles: 7-inch
ARGYLE (1005 "Lonely Highway")....10-20 61
ASSOCIATED ARTISTS (1064 "Creepin")....10-20 62

JAYNE, Betty
(With the Teenettes; with Dudley)
Singles: 7-inch
CARELLEN (2 thru 8)....5-10 62
CARELLEN (101 "The Sun Will Rise")....15-20 60
CARELLEN (107 thru 113)....10-15 61
CRUSADER (2440 "Dial L for Love")....10-20 '60s
MONA-LEE (139 "Lonely Teenager")....15-25 59
Picture Sleeves
CARELLEN (101 "The Sun Will Rise")....8-12 60

JAYNELLS
Singles: 7-inch
ANGELA (101 "Out of a Million Girls")....3-5 84
(Previously unreleased.)
ANGELA (102 "Portrait of Love")....3-5 84
(Previously unreleased.)
CAMEO (286 "I'll Stay Home")....15-25 63
DIAMOND (153 "I'll Stay Home")....50-75 63
(Brown vinyl. Reportedly 500 made.)

JAYNETTS P&R/R&B '63
(Jaynetts / Art Butler)
Singles: 7-inch
GOLDIE....3-5
J&S (1473 "Peepin' in and Out the Window")....5-10 65
J&S (1477 "That's My Boy")....5-10 65
TUFF (369 thru 377)....8-12 63-64
LPs: 10/12-inch
TUFF (13 "Sally, Go 'Round the Roses")....150-250 63
(Includes *Dear Abby* by the Hearts.)
Members: Ethel Davis; Johnnie Louise; Mary Sue Wells; Ada Ray; Yvonne Bushnell.
Also see HEARTS
Also see JOHNNIE & JOE

JAYSON, Buddy
Singles: 78 rpm
GROOVE (0017 "Hot Dog, She's Mine")....5-10 54
Singles: 7-inch
GROOVE (0017 "Hot Dog, She's Mine")..10-15 54

JAYTONES
Singles: 7-inch
BRUNSWICK (55087 "The Clock")....50-75 58
CUB (9057 "My Only Love")....40-50 60
TIMELY (1003 "The Bells")....750-1000 58
Also see CENTURIES / Jaytones

JAY-TONES
Singles: 7-inch
PARIS SKY (5000 "Cleopatra Cha-Cha") 20-30

JAYWALKER & PEDESTRIANS
Singles: 7-inch
AMY (848 "Never Happen")....10-15 62
Member: Peter Antell.
Also see ANTELL, Peter

JAYWALKERS
Singles: 7-inch
PAM (210 "Oh Babe")....10-15 62

JAZZ CRUSADERS P&R '66
Singles: 7-inch
CHISA (8010 "Jackson")....4-6 71
PACIFIC JAZZ....5-8 62-68
WORLD PACIFIC....5-8 64-65
LPs: 10/12-inch
BLUE NOTE....5-10 75-80
CHISA (804 "Old Socks New Shoes")....8-12 70
LIBERTY (11005 "Give Peace a Chance") 8-12 70
PACIFIC JAZZ (27 thru 87)....20-40 61-64
PACIFIC JAZZ (10000 & 20000 series)...10-20 65-69
PAUSA....5-8 82
WORLD PACIFIC....8-15 63-65
Members: Wilton Felder; Stix Hooper; Wayne Henderson; Joe Sample.
Also see CRUSADERS

JAZZ TRIBE
Singles: 7-inch
LITTLE STAR (127 "The Ritual")....10-15 63

JAZZBOMBERS
("Featuring Bobby Boyd")
Singles: 7-inch
TATTLER (1001 "Bad Boy")....50-75

JAZZNIX
Singles: 7-inch
RAKRIK (100 "Ballad of Al Capone")....10-15 59

JEAN, Miss Joy
("13 Yr. Old Miss Joy Jean")
Singles: 7-inch
JW (101 "Wherever You May Be")....10-20

JEANETTE
Singles: 7-inch
LAURIE (3094 "There's a Gleam")....10-15 61

JEANETTE, JOAN & KAY
Singles: 7-inch
TEEN-ED (5 "Christmas Time")....10-15 61

JEANIE & HER BOY FRIENDS
Singles: 7-inch
WARWICK (508 "Baby")....100-150 59
(White label. Promotional issue only.)
WARWICK (508 "Baby")....75-125 59
(Red label. Small print.)
WARWICK (508 "Baby")....30-40 59
(Red label. Ribbon design.)

JEANNIE & MILLER SISTERS
Singles: 7-inch
HULL (750 "Don't You Forget"/"Roll Back the Rug")....10-20 62
Also see MILLER SISTERS

JEANS
Singles: 7-inch
ZEFCO (4127 "My Own Time")....15-25 68

JEENS, Jimmy
Singles: 78 rpm
VULCAN (1001 "Ring Bells, Ring")....8-12 54
Singles: 7-inch
VULCAN (1001 "Ring Bells, Ring")....40-50 54

JEFF & ATLANTICS
Singles: 7-inch
SOUND PATTERNS (2501 "Twistin' Postman") .... 20-30 '60s

JEFF & CHARLES
Singles: 7-inch
JUNE ("Janet Ann") 20-40
(No selection number used.)
JUNE (100 "Sadie Hawkins Day in Tennessee") 20-40

JEFF & GINOS
Singles: 7-inch
MERCURY (72138 "One Summer in a Million") 10-15 63

JEFF & P.J.
Singles: 7-inch
ROYCE (0002 "Mr. Blues") 100-200 59

JEFFERS, Jimmy
Singles: 7-inch
DA-MOR (9220 "Raining Teardrops") 50-75
FRATERNITY (857 "Teardrops from My Eyes") 10-20 59
TARGET (850 "Purple Crackle") 10-20

JEFFERS, Sleepy
(With the Davis Twins)
Singles: 7-inch
STARDAY (319 "Pretending Is a Game") 100-200 57

JEFFERSON P&R '69
(Geoff Turton)
Singles: 7-inch
DECCA (32501 "The Colour of My Love") .. 5-10 69
JANUS (106 "Baby Take Me in Your Arms") 5-10 69
LPs: 10/12-inch
JANUS 10-20 69

JEFFERSON, Blind Lemon
Singles: 78 rpm
OKEH (8455 "Black Snake Moan") 300-400
PARAMOUNT 400-1000 26-30
LPs: 10/12-inch
BIOGRAPH 10-15 68
MILESTONE 8-10 74
OLYMPIC 8-10 75
RIVERSIDE (1014 "Folk Blues of Blind Lemon Jefferson") 100-200 53
(10-inch LP.)
RIVERSIDE (1053 "Blind Lemon's Penitentiary Blues") 100-200 55
(10-inch LP.)
RIVERSIDE (125 "Blind Lemon Jefferson") 75-125 60
RIVERSIDE (136 "Blind Lemon Jefferson, Vol. 2") 50-100 60
Also see BATES, Deacon L.J.
Also see JACKSON, Deacon

JEFFERSON, Eddie
(With James Moody & His Orchestra; with Walter Harper Orchestra)
Singles: 78 rpm
CHECKER (855 "Billie's Bounce") 8-12 57
HI-LO (1416 "Honeysuckle Rose") 8-12 53
Singles: 7-inch
CHECKER (855 "Billie's Bounce") 10-20 57
HI-LO (1416 "Honeysuckle Rose") 20-30 53
(Colored vinyl.)
STAX (147 "Uh Oh") 5-10 64
TRIUMPH (606 "Body and Soul") 8-12 59

JEFFERSON, Hilton
Singles: 78 rpm
RCA 10-15 57
Singles: 7-inch
RCA (7044 "Danny Boy") 15-25 57
RCA (7126 "Cole Slaw") 15-25 57

JEFFERSON AIRPLANE LP '66
Singles: 7-inch
ELEKTRA 3-5 88
GRUNT (0500 thru 0511) 4-6 71-72
GRUNT (10988 "White Rabbit") 10-20 77
(Colored vinyl. Promotional issue only.)
RCA (0150 thru 0343) 4-8 69-70
RCA (5156 "White Rabbit") 4-8 87
(Colored vinyl. Promotional issue only.)
RCA (8769 thru 9644) 5-10 66-68
(Dog on side of label.)
RCA (9000 series) 3-5 89
(Dog near top of label.)
Picture Sleeves
GRUNT (0500 "Pretty As You Feel") 5-10 71
GRUNT (0506 "Long John Silver") 10-15 72
RCA (Except 5156) 8-12 68-70
RCA (5156 "White Rabbit") 4-8 87
(Promotional issue only.)
EPs: 7-inch
RCA (SP33-564 "Jefferson Airplane") 30-50 69
(Promotional issue only.)
LPs: 10/12-inch
EPIC 5-8 89
GRUNT (0147 "Thirty Seconds Over Winterland") 10-15 73
GRUNT (1001 "Bark") 30-60 71
GRUNT (1007 "Long John Silver") 30-60 72
GRUNT (0437 "Early Flight") 10-15 74
GRUNT (4386 "Bark") 10-15 82
PAIR 8-10 84
RCA (0320 ("Volunteers") 15-20 73
(Quadraphonic.)
RCA (1511 "After Bathing at Baxter's") 20-30 67
(Black label. With "LSC" or "LSO" prefix.)
RCA (1511 "After Bathing at Baxter's") .... 10-12 '70s
(Orange or tan label.)
RCA (3584 "Jefferson Airplane Takes Off") 75-125 66
(Has 12 tracks. With "LPM" or "LSP" prefix.)
RCA (3584 "Jefferson Airplane Takes Off") 15-25 66
(Has 11 tracks. With "LPM" or "LSP" prefix.)
RCA (3584 "Jefferson Airplane Takes Off") 10-15 69
(Orange label.)
RCA (3661 "Worst of Jefferson Airplane") .. 5-10 80
RCA (3739 "Jefferson Airplane Takes Off") 5-10 80
RCA (3766 "Surrealistic Pillow") 20-30 67
(Black label. With "LPM" or "LSP" prefix.)
RCA (3766 "Surrealistic Pillow") 10-12 69
(Orange label.)
RCA (3766 "Surrealistic Pillow") .... 5-8 '80s
(With "AYL" prefix.)
RCA (3797 "Crown of Creation") 5-10 80
RCA (3798 "Bless Its Pointed Little Head") 5-10 80
RCA (3867 "Volunteers") 5-10 81
RCA (4058 "Crown of Creation") 10-15 68
RCA (4133 "Bless Its Pointed Little Head") 10-20 69
(Includes artwork insert.)
RCA (4238 "Volunteers") 10-15 69
RCA (4448 "Blows Against the Empire") .. 10-15 70
(Black vinyl. Add $4 to $6 if accompanied by booklet.)
RCA (4448 "Blows Against the Empire") 75-100 70
(Clear vinyl. Promotional issue only.)
RCA (LSP-4459 "Worst of Jefferson Airplane") 10-15 70
RCA (AFL1-4459 "Worst of Jefferson Airplane") .... 5-10 '80s
RCA (5724 "2400 Fulton Street") 8-12 87
Members: Signe Anderson; Marty Balin; Paul Kantner; Jack Casady; Jorma Kaukonen; Skip Spence; Grace Slick; Joey Covington; Spencer Dryden; Papa John Creach; Dave Freiberg; Craig Chaquico.
Also see BALIN, Marty
Also see GARCIA, Jerry
Also see GREAT!! SOCIETY!!
Also see JARRARD, Rick
Also see JEFFERSON STARSHIP
Also see QUICKSILVER
Also see SLICK, Grace
Also see STILLS, Stephen
Also see VIBRA-SONICS

JEFFERSON COUNTY
Singles: 7-inch
DEE GEE (3016 "Organized Confusion") . 15-20 66

JEFFERSON HANDKERCHIEF
Singles: 7-inch
CHALLENGE (59371 "I'm Allergic to Flowers") 10-20 67

JEFFERSON STARSHIP LP '74
Singles: 7-inch
GRUNT 3-6 74-84
Picture Sleeves
GRUNT 3-8 78-87
RCA 3-5 87-89
LPs: 10/12-inch
GRUNT (0717 thru 1557) 10-15 74-76
GRUNT (1255 "Flight Log, 1966-1976") ... 15-20 77
(With simulated leather cover. Also has Hot Tuna, Jefferson Airplane, Grace Slick and Paul Kantner tracks.)
GRUNT (1255 "Flight Log, 1966-1976") ... 10-20 81
(With standard cover.)
GRUNT (2515 thru 3247) 10-15 78-79
GRUNT (3363 "Gold") 15-20 79
(Picture disc.)
GRUNT (3452 thru 6413) 5-10 79-87
RCA 5-10 81-89
Members: Grace Slick; Marty Balin; Aynsley Dunbar; Paul Kantner; Pete Sears; Mickey Thomas; John Barbata.
Note: Cross references that already appear under Jefferson Airplane are not duplicated below.
Also see HART, Mickey
Also see JEFFERSON AIRPLANE
Also see STARSHIP
Also see STONEGROUND

JEFFERSON STARSHIP / Daryl Hall & John Oates / Evelyn "Champagne" King / Minglewood Band
EPs: 7-inch
COCA-COLA (1001 "Portraits in Gold") 5-10 80
(Canadian.)
Also see HALL, Daryl, & John Oates
Also see JEFFERSON STARSHIP

JEFFREY, Wally
Singles: 7-inch
DO-RA-ME (1402 "Oh Yeah") 200-300 57

JEFFRIES, Bob
(With "Marcels 123")
Singles: 7-inch
JODY (1048 "Take Me Back") 400-600 58
(We're not quite certain if the "123" has to do with the Marcels, or if it means something else. It does appear, however, that 1048 is the selection number.)
RHYTHM (110 "Never Let Me Go") 150-250 57

JEFFRIES, Fran
Singles: 7-inch
MONUMENT (1015 "Life Goes On") 5-10 67
WARWICK (567 "I'm Gonna Laugh You Right Out of My Life") 5-10 60
LPs: 10/12-inch
WARWICK (2020 "Fran Can Really Hang You Up the Most") 15-20 60

JEFFRIES, Herb
(With Eddie Beal's Orchestra)
Singles: 7-inch
MGM (12767 "Picture No Artist Can Paint") 5-10 59
RCA (6950 "Mailman, Bring Me No More Blues") 8-12 57
LPs: 10/12-inch
BCP (72 "Herb Jeffries") 50-75 57
CORAL (56044 "Time on My Hands") 25-40 51
(10-inch LP.)

JEFFRIES, Linc
Singles: 7-inch
KEY (1061 "Pitch Black") 400-600
KEY (1064 "On the Rampage") 300-500

JEKYLL & HYDE
Singles: 7-inch
DCP (1111 "My Baby Loves Monster Movies") 10-15 64
DCP (1126 "Frankenstein Meets the Beetles") 15-20 65
Member: Dickie Goodman.
Also see GOODMAN, Dickie

JEKYLL & HYDES
Singles: 7-inch
G.A.R. (107 "High Heeled Sneakers") 10-20 67
Members: John "Jekyll" Lohman; Gary Grimes; Chris Riley.
Also see NORSEMEN

JELLY & SLIM SEWARD
Singles: 78 rpm
APOLLO (412 "Sorry Women Blues") 20-40 47
Members: Louis Hayes; Alec Seward.
Also see SEWARD, Alec, & Fat Boy Hayes

JELLY BEAN BANDITS
Singles: 7-inch
MAINSTREAM (674 "Country Woman") .. 10-15 67
LPs: 10/12-inch
MAINSTREAM (6103 "Jelly Bean Bandits") 50-75 67
Members: Bill Donald; John Dougherty; Fred Buck; Mike Raab; Joe Scalfari.

JELLY BEANS P&R/R&B '64
Singles: 7-inch
ESKEE (001 "I'm Hip to You") 15-25 65
RED BIRD (003 "I Wanna Love Him So Bad") 8-12 64
RED BIRD (011 "Baby, Be Mine") 8-12 64
Members: Diane Taylor; Maxine Herbert; Elyse Herbert; Alma Brewer.

JENKINS, Bill, Quartet
(Bill Jenkins & Al)
Singles: 78 rpm
KING 10-15 54
Singles: 7-inch
KING (4760 "Danny Boy") 15-25 54
KING (4877 "Day Train") 15-25 55
PRESTIGE (175 "Billin' & Bluin'") 10-20 60
Also see JENKINS, Bill, & Willis Jackson

JENKINS, Bill, & Willis Jackson
Singles: 7-inch
KING (5087 "Wishbone") 15-25 57
Also see JENKINS, Bill, Quartet
Also see JACKSON, Willis

JENKINS, Blackie, & Satellites
Singles: 7-inch
RLS (71067 "Spaceship Life") .... 250-350 '60s

JENKINS, Bobby
(With the Jades)
Singles: 7-inch
ASTRO 5-10
BECKINGHAM (1080 "Hey Man") 8-12 65
HAMILTON (50001 "White Shorts and a Red Tee Shirt") 10-20 58
NASCO (6006 "My Baby's Gone") 10-20 57

JENKINS, Bobo
(Bobo Jenkins & Band)
Singles: 78 rpm
CHESS (1565 "Democrat Blues") 25-50 54
FORTUNE (838 "Baby, Don't You Want to Go") 30-60 56
Singles: 7-inch
BIG=STAR (001 "Tell Me Where You Stayed Last Night") 10-15 64
BOXER (202 "Nothing But Love") 20-30 59
CHESS (1565 "Democrat Blues") 125-150 54
FORTUNE (838 "Baby, Don't You Want to Go") 100-125 56
(Orange label.)
FORTUNE (838 "Baby, Don't You Want to Go") 15-25
(Red label)

JENKINS, Duke
(With the Roulettes)
Singles: 7-inch
BEE (1175 "Oh Boy") .... 5-10 '60s
COBRA (5009 "The Duke Walks") 15-25 57
COBRA (5020 "Shake It") 15-25 57
PENNANT (331 "Mambo Blues") .... 10-15 '50s
Also see GIBSON, Steve

JENKINS, Ella
LPs: 10/12-inch
FOLKWAYS (8273 "Adventures in Rhythm") 10-15 59

JENKINS, Gene
Singles: 78 rpm
TRINITY (102 "Short Stuff") 40-60 55
Singles: 7-inch
TRINITY (102 "Short Stuff") 150-250 55

JENKINS, George, & Tune Twisters
Singles: 78 rpm
SKYLARK (565 "Shufflin' Boogie") 5-10 54
TAMPA (113 "Drum Boogie") 5-10 56
Singles: 7-inch
SKYLARK (565 "Shufflin' Boogie") 10-20 54
TAMPA (113 "Drum Boogie") 10-20 56
Also see JOHNSON, Plas

JENKINS, Gordon, & Orchestra P&R '42
Singles: 78 rpm
CAPITOL 4-8 42-49
DECCA 3-6 50-56
Singles: 7-inch
COLUMBIA 4-6 64
DECCA 5-10 50-56
KAPP 4-8 60-64
TIME 4-6 62
"X" 4-8 55
EPs: 7-inch
DECCA 5-15 51-56
LPs: 10/12-inch
CAPITOL (700 series) 15-25 56
(With "T" prefix.)
CAPITOL (700 series) 10-15 61
(With "DT" prefix.)
CAPITOL (700 series) 4-8 75
(With "SM" prefix.)
COLUMBIA 10-20 62-63
CORAL 5-8 73
CUSTOM 5-10
DECCA 15-30 51-63
(Decca LP numbers in this series preceded by a "7" or a "DL-7" are stereo issues.)
DOT 5-10 66
GWP 5-10 71
MCA 5-8 73-75
SUNSET 5-10 67
TIME 10-15 62-64
Also see ARMSTRONG, Louis
Also see BOONE, Pat
Also see CARROLL, Bob
Also see LEE, Peggy
Also see WEAVERS

JENKINS, Gus P&R/R&B '56
(Gus Jinkins)
Singles: 78 rpm
COMBO 10-20 54
FLASH 10-20 56-57
Singles: 7-inch
CATALINA (711 "New Tricky") 10-15 63
COMBO (87 "I Been Working") 40-60 54
FLASH (115 thru 131) 20-30 56-58
GENERAL ARTIST 8-15 64-69
PIONEER INT'L (101 thru 1007) 15-25 59-61
PIONEER INT'L (1009 "Off the Road") 40-60 61
PIONEER INT'L (10011 "Too Tough") 10-20 62
PIONEER INT'L (10013 "Celebrate") 10-20 62
SAR (149 "Right Shakey") 10-15 64
TOWER (107 thru 122) 10-15 64
Also see HART, Haze, & Gus Jenkins
Also see LITTLE TEMPLE & HIS 88
Also see YOUNG WOLF

JENKINS, Haywood
Singles: 7-inch
MERCURY (71855 "You Can't Hear Me") 15-20 61

JENKINS, Johnny
(With the Pinetoppers)
Singles: 7-inch
ATLANTIC (2144 "Love Twist") 8-12 62
CAPRICORN 4-8 70
GERALD (1001 "Love Twist") 20-30 62
(First issue.)
TIFKO (825 "Love Twist") 10-20 62
VOLT (122 "Bashful Guitar") 5-10 64
LPs: 10/12-inch
CAPRICORN 10-15 70
Members: Johnny Jenkins; Otis Redding.
Also see REDDING, Otis

JENKINS, Marvin
Singles: 7-inch
PALOMAR (2202 "Big City") 10-15 64
PALOMAR (2208 "I've Got the Blues") 10-15 65
TANGERINE (929 thru 946) 5-10 63-64
LPs: 10/12-inch
PALOMAR (24001 "Big City") 10-15 65
(Monaural.)
PALOMAR (34001 "Big City") 15-20 65
(Stereo.)

JENKINS, Robert
Singles: 78 rpm
PARKWAY (103 "Steelin' Boogie") 100-200 50

JENKINS, Walter
Singles: 7-inch
FADER KAT (302 "Back in My Life") 15-25 75

JENNIE & JAY
Singles: 7-inch
JAY WING (5803 "Ruthie") 50-75 58
RESCUE (102 "Jo Baby") 15-25 62
(Reissue of David Gates & Accents' 1958 Perspective release.)
Member: David Gates.
Also see GATES, David

JENNINGS, Bill
(Bill Jennings Quartet)
Singles: 78 rpm
KING (4760 "Big Boy") 5-8 54
Singles: 7-inch
KING (4760 "Big Boy") 8-12 54
PRESTIGE (152 "Enough Said") 5-10 59
LPs: 10/12-inch
AUDIO LAB (1514 "Guitar-Vibes") 15-25 59
PRESTIGE (7164 "Enough Said") 15-25 59

JENNINGS, Lee
Singles: 7-inch
DOTTY'S (347 "Going & Get It") .... 25-35 '60s

JENNINGS, Lenny
Singles: 7-inch
ROULETTE (4704 "Last Laugh") 10-20 66

JENNINGS, Vee
Singles: 7-inch
ROYAL ROOST (630 "Whoopsie Daisy") 10-15 57

JENNINGS, Waylon C&W '65
(With the Waylors; with Crickets; Waylon)
Singles: 7-inch
A&M (739 "Four Strong Winds") 10-15 64
A&M (722 "Rave On") 10-20 63
A&M (753 "The Race Is On") 10-20 64
A&M (762 "The Real House of the Rising Sun") 10-20 65
BAT (121636 "White Lightning") 100-150 61
BAT (121639 "Dream Baby") 25-35 62
BRUNSWICK (55130 "Jole Blon") 100-150 59
(Maroon label. With Buddy Holly & King Curtis.)
BRUNSWICK (55130 "Jole Blon") 75-100 59
(Yellow label. Promotional issue only.)
COLUMBIA 3-5 83
EPIC 3-5 91
RCA (086 "You Ask Me To") 4-6 73
RCA (0105 "The Days of Sand & Shovels") 4-8 69
RCA (0157 "Delia's Gone") 4-8 69
RCA (0251 "This Time") 4-6 74
RCA (0281 "Brown Eyed Handsome Man") 4-8 69
RCA (0615 thru 0961) 4-6 72-73
RCA (1003 "Cedartown, Georgia") 4-6 71
RCA (8572 thru 9642) 5-10 65-68
RCA (9819 thru 9967) 4-8 70-71
RCA (10020 thru 14215) 3-6 74-85
RAMCO (1989 "Never Again") 8-12 67
RAMCO (1997 "My World") 8-12 68
TREND '61 (102 "Another Blue Day") 20-30 61
TREND '63 (106 "The Stage") 50-75 63
Picture Sleeves
RCA (11596 "Amanda") 3-6 79
RCA (12067 "Theme from the Dukes of Hazzard") 3-6 80
LPs: 10/12-inch
A&M (4238 "Don't Think Twice") 25-30 69
BAT (1001 "Waylon Jennings at JD's") 200-300 64
(500 copies were made on Bat, then another 500 were done on Sounds Ltd.)
CAMDEN 8-15 67-76
EPIC 5-8 90
MCA 5-8
PICKWICK 5-10 75
RCA (AFL-1 series) 5-10 78
RCA (0240 thru 3378) 5-10 73-79
RCA (3406 "Greatest Hits") 30-40 79
(Picture disc.)
RCA (3493 "What Goes Around Comes Around") 5-10 79
RCA (3523 "Folk Country") 15-25 66
RCA (3602 "Music Man") 5-10 80
RCA (3620 "Leavin' Town") 20-30 66
RCA (3660 "Waylon Sings Ol' Harlan") 15-20 67
RCA (3663 "Are You Ready for the Country") 5-8 80
RCA (3736 "Nashville Rebel") 15-25 66
(Soundtrack.)
RCA (3737 "Good Hearted Woman") 5-8 80
RCA (3825 "Love of the Common People") 15-25 67
RCA (3897 "Honky Tonk Heroes") 5-8 81
RCA (3918 "Hangin' On") 15-20 68
RCA (3942 "This Time") 5-8 81
RCA (4023 "Only the Greatest") 15-20 68
RCA (4072 "Dreaming My Dreams") 5-8 81
RCA (4073 "The Ramblin' Man") 5-8 81
RCA (4085 "Jewels") 15-20 68
RCA (4137 "Just to Satisfy You") 15-20 69
RCA (4163 "Waylon Live") 5-8 81
RCA (4164 "I've Always Been Crazy") 5-8 81
RCA (4180 "Country Folk") 15-25 69
RCA (4247 "Black on Black") 5-8 82
RCA (4250 "Music Man") 5-8 82
RCA (4260 "Waylon") 10-15 70
RCA (4341 "Best of Waylon Jennings") 8-10 77
RCA (4418 "Singer of Sad Songs") 10-15 70
RCA (4487 "The Taker/Tulsa") 10-15 71
RCA (4567 "Cedartown Georgia") 10-15 71
RCA (4647 "Good Hearted Woman") 10-15 72
RCA (4673 "It's Only Rock & Roll") 5-8 83
RCA (4751 "Ladies Love Outlaws") 10-15 72
RCA (4826 "Waylon & Co.") 5-8 83
RCA (4828 "Best of Waylon Jennings") 5-8 83
RCA (4854 "Lonesome, On'ry & Mean") 10-15 73
RCA (5473 "Collector's Series") 5-10 85
SEAGULL 5-8 83
SOUNDS (1001 "Waylon Jennings at JD's") 200-250 64
(First issued on Bat.)
TIME-LIFE 5-8 81
VOCALION 15-20 69
Session: Buddy Holly; King Curtis; James Burton.
Also see BARE, Bobby
Also see BURTON, James
Also see CASH, Johnny, & Waylon Jennings
Also see COE, David Allan
Also see CRICKETS
Also see DAVIS, Skeeter
Also see EDDY, Duane
Also see HARRIS, Emmylou
Also see HOLLY, Buddy
Also see KING CURTIS
Also see MANDRELL, Barbara
Also see MONROE, Bill
Also see NELSON, Willie
Also see RABBIT, Jimmy
Also see TUBB, Ernest
Also see WHITE, Tony Joe
Also see YOUNG, Neil

JENNINGS, Waylon, & Anita Carter C&W '68
Singles: 7-inch
RCA (9480 "I Got You") 5-10 68
Also see CARTER, Anita

JENNINGS, Waylon, & Jessi Colter LP '81
(Waylon & Jessi)
Singles: 7-inch
RCA (9920 "Suspicious Minds") 4-8 70
RCA (9992 "Under Your Spell Again") 4-8 71
LPs: 10/12-inch
RCA (3931 "Leather and Lace") 5-10 81
Also see COLTER, Jessi

JENNINGS, Waylon, & Willie Nelson P&R '77
(Waylon & Willie)
Singles: 7-inch
COLUMBIA 3-5 83
MCA 3-5 86
RCA 3-8 76-86
LPs: 10/12-inch
AURA 5-8 83
COLUMBIA 5-8 83
OUT OF TOWN DIST. .... 5-8 '80s
RCA (2686 "Waylon & Willie") 8-10 78
(Black vinyl.)
RCA (2686 "Waylon & Willie") 20-25 78
(Colored vinyl. Promotional issue only.)
RCA (4455 "Waylon & Willie II") 5-8 82
Also see NELSON, Willie

JENNINGS, Waylon, Willie Nelson, Jessi Colter, & Tompall Glaser LP '76
LPs: 10/12-inch
RCA (1321 "The Outlaws") 8-12 76
Also see COLTER, Jessi
Also see NELSON, Willie

JENNINGS, Waylon, Willie Nelson, Johnny Cash, & Kris Kristofferson LP '85
Singles: 7-inch
COLUMBIA 3-5 85-90
Picture Sleeves
COLUMBIA (04881 "Highwayman") 3-6 85
LPs: 10/12-inch
COLUMBIA 5-8 85-90
Also see CASH, Johnny
Also see KRISTOFFERSON, Kris
Also see NELSON, Willie

JENNINGS, Waylon / Johnny Paycheck
LPs: 10/12-inch
OUT OF TOWN DIST. 5-8 82
Also see PAYCHECK, Johnny

JENNINGS, Waylon, & Jerry Reed
Singles: 7-inch
RCA 3-5 83
Also see REED, Jerry

JENNINGS, Waylon, & Hank Williams Jr.
Singles: 7-inch
RCA 3-5 83
Also see JENNINGS, Waylon
Also see WILLIAMS, Hank, Jr.

JENNINGS BROTHERS
Singles: 7-inch
ATLANTIC (2245 "Believe in Me") 10-20 64

JENNY & JAY
Singles: 7-inch
TOWN (1980 "Jo Baby") 30-40 61

JENSEN, Curt
Singles: 7-inch
BIG B (1619 "How Could You Be") 5-10 62
DE WITT (5906 "Bobbie") 10-15 60
PET (806 "Just for You") 40-50 58
20TH FOX (183 "It Takes a Little Time") 10-20 60

JENSEN, Dick
(With the Imports; with Swamp Men)
Singles: 7-inch
AMBER (7001 "Waikiki Rumble") 15-25 63
LOMA (2021 thru 2055) 5-10 65-66
MAHALO (1012 "Surfin' in Hawaii") 15-25 63
MERCURY (72888 "Groove with What You've Got") 5-10 69
PHILA. INT'L (3504 thru 3542) 4-6 71-74
PROBE (468 thru 479) 5-10 69-70
Picture Sleeves
PROBE 5-10 69-70
LPs: 10/12-inch
PROBE (4512 "White Hot Soul") 10-12 69

JENSEN, Kris P&R '62
Singles: 7-inch
A&M (1204 "Dead End Street") 4-8 70
COLPIX (118 "Bonnie Baby") 10-15 59
HICKORY (1173 "Torture") 8-12 62
HICKORY (1195 thru 1311) 5-10 62-65
KAPP (393 thru 493) 5-10 61-62
LEADER (808 "Perfect Lover") 10-15 60
LEADER (813 "Please Let Me Love You") 10-15 61
WHITE WHALE (229 thru 240) 5-10 66
Picture Sleeves
HICKORY (1203 "Poor Unlucky Me") 10-20 63
HICKORY (1224 "Donna Donna") 10-20 63
LPs: 10/12-inch
HICKORY (110 "Torture") 40-50 62

JENSEN, Kurt, & His Orchestra
LPs: 10/12-inch
HOLLYWOOD (137 "An Evening with Jayne") .... 30-50 '50s
(Cover pictures Jayne Mansfield, although she is not heard on the disc.)
Also see MANSFIELD, Jayne

JENSON, Darryl
Singles: 7-inch
GONE (5088 "All Danced Out") 10-15 60

JENSON, Ken
Singles: 7-inch
AVA (158 "Box Cars") 15-25 57

JEREMIAH
Singles: 7-inch
PHILIPS (40321 "Goin' Lovin' with You") 10-20 65

JEREMY & SATYRS

Singles: 7-inch

REPRISE (664 "Movie Show")....................5-10 68

LPs: 10/12-inch

REPRISE (6282 "Jeremy & the Satyrs").. 10-20 68

JEREMY'S FRIENDS

LPs:10/12-inch

WARWICK (2019 "Jeremy's Friends")..... 25-35 60

Member: Alan Arkin.

JERICHO, Jerry

(Smilin' Jerry Jericho)

Singles: 78 rpm

4 STAR..5-10 50

STARDAY.. 10-15 53

Singles: 7-inch

ALLSTAR (7188 "When I'm Gone")........ 10-15 59

STARDAY (120 "Moanin' in the Morning")..................................... 20-30 53

STARDAY (133 "Lovin' Up a Storm")....... 20-30 53

JERMS

Singles: 7-inch

CASINO (1322 "Love Light").......................5-10

DEL MAR (521 "Since You Went Away").. 50-100 '60s

(At least one source gives 4 as the selection number.)

HONOR BRIGADE (1 "Green Door")..........5-10 69

HONOR BRIGADE (4 "Nobody")................5-10 69

JERMS INC. (2079 "Bald Headed Woman").. 25-50 '60s

SHANA (7195 "Not At All")...................... 10-20 68

Picture Sleeves

DEL MAR (521 "Since You Went Away").. 50-100 '60s

JERMS INC. (2079 "Bald Headed Woman").. 50-100 '60s

JERNIGAN, Wade

Singles: 7-inch

SANDY (1010 "Road of Love")................ 10-15 58

JEROME, Patti

(With the Sid Bass Orchestra)

Singles: 78 rpm

JOSIE (774 "Johnny Has Gone")..............5-10 55

WING (90038 "All Is Well").......................5-10 55

Singles: 7-inch

AMERICAN ARTS (10 "No More Tears")...5-10 64

BIG TOP (3080 "Mojo")........................... 10-20 61

JOSIE (774 "Johnny Has Gone")............ 15-25 55

JOSIE (908 "Only You")..............................5-10 63

WING (90038 "All Is Well")...................... 10-20 55

Also see P.J.

Also see PATTI & MICKEY

JEROME, Ralph

Singles: 7-inch

K.P. (1006 "Don't Destroy Me")............... 40-60 59

K.P. (1007 "Rockhouse")....................... 75-100 59

JEROMES, The

(With the John Abbot; The Jerome's)

Singles: 7-inch

DAR (300 "Rocking Chair").................... 75-125 61

JERRY & CAPRIS

Singles: 7-inch

GLENDALE (1007 "Dancing Dan")...... 100-200

JERRY & CASUALS / Rockin' Tones

Singles: 7-inch

BIG M (1001 "Battle of Three Blind Mice"/"What's the Score").. 25-50 61

STARS OF TOMORROW (2235 "Battle of Three Blind Mice"/"What's the Score")...................... 25-50 61

Also see PAGE, Jerry

Also see STOREY, Denny

JERRY & CATALINAS

Singles: 7-inch

VEROONA (101 "Away from It All")......... 10-20 63

JERRY & CONTINENTALS

Singles: 7-inch

NIGHT OWL (6791 "I've Had It")............. 15-20 67

Members: Jerry Karow; Larry Barden; Jerry Nennig; Tom Roland; Dean Packard; Rich Hartley; Mike Jordan; Tom Nennig.

JERRY & DEBORAH

Singles: 7-inch

EPIC (10087 "Come On In").................... 10-15 66

JERRY & DEL-FIs

Singles: 7-inch

HOUND (102 "Little Suzanne")............150-200

JERRY & DIAMONDS

(Jerry Swallow)

Singles: 7-inch

ARC (7456 "Sea-N-Shore").......................15-25 64

JERRY & PLAYMATES

Singles: 7-inch

ALVERA (677-4239 "Want-a Love You") .20-25 66

JERRY & RIALTOS

Singles: 7-inch

ALL BOY (8512 "It's All in Fun")................10-20 64

JERRY & SILVERTONES

Singles: 7-inch

COULEE (104 "Ce'ny")............................35-40 63

Picture Sleeves

COULEE (104 "Ce'ny")...............................15-25 63

Members: Jerry Grosskopf; Rollie Grosskopf; Calvin Grosskopf; Richard Krause; Tom Perry; Jerry Oliver.

Also see TOWNSMEN

JERRY & WAYNE

Singles: 78 rpm

ABC-PAR 10-15 57

Singles: 7-inch

ABC-PAR (9806 "Baby Baby Baby, Be Mine")...15-20 57

ABC-PAR (9806 "Baby Baby Baby") 25-35 57

(With shortened title.)

Members: Wayne Newton; Jerry Newton.

Also see NEWTON, Wayne

Also see NEWTON BROTHERS

Also see NEWTON RASCALS

JERRY DEE & INTRUDERS

Singles: 7-inch

SARA (6352 "Bo Diddley").......................15-25 63

Members: Wes Lamuska; Olie Wahl; Wayne Toske; Mick Zirngible; Mike Schelberger.

JESSE & MARVIN *R&B '53*

Singles: 78 rpm

SPECIALTY (447 "Dream Girl")................20-30 52

Singles: 7-inch

SPECIALTY (447 "Dream Girl")...............50-75 52

(Black vinyl.)

SPECIALTY (447 "Dream Girl")...........100-200 52

(Colored vinyl.)

Members: Jesse Belvin; Marvin Phillips.

Also see BELVIN, Jesse

Also see MARVIN & JOHNNY

Also see PHILLIPS, Marvin

JESSE & ROADRUNNERS

Singles: 7-inch

JARO (77034 "Sentimental")....................10-20 60

JESSE J. & BANDITS

Singles: 7-inch

RE CAR (9003 "Stomp Your Feet")..........60-80 '60s

LPs:10/12-inch

RE CAR (2001 "Top Teen Hits")..............30-50 65

Also see KING KRUSHER & TURKEYNECKS

JESSIE, Young

(Obediah Jessie)

Singles: 78 rpm

MODERN 8-12 54-56

Singles: 7-inch

ATCO (6101 "Make Believe")...................25-35 57

ATLANTIC (2003 "That's Enough for Me")..15-25 58

CAPITOL (4318 "Lula Belle")..................10-15 59

DCP (1117 "If You Love Me")....................8-12 65

MERCURY (71895 thru 72146)...............10-15 61-63

MODERN (921 thru 1010).......................15-25 54-57

VANESSA (101 "Brown Eyes")................10-20

Session: Cadets; Flairs.

Also see CADETS

Also see FLAIRS

Also see JACKS

Also see JACKSON, Chuck / Young Jessie

JESSIE & SEQUINS

(With Lefty Bates' Band)

Singles: 7-inch

BOXER (201 "Hold My Hand")................40-50 59

PROFILE (4008 "Hold My Hand")............15-25 59

Also see SEQUINS / Lefty Bates

JESSIE LEE & RHYTHMAIRES

Singles: 7-inch

MIDA (110 "Lonely Broken Heart")..........40-50 58

JESTER, Charlie

(With the Kilts)

Singles: 7-inch

LANAR (102 "Crazy Baby")....................75-100 61

LE CAM (722 "Sylvia") 10-15 61

LE CAM (726 "Once There Was a Time")....4-6 '70s

Session: Ron-Dels.

Also see RON-DELS

JESTERS *P&R '57*

(With David Clowney's Band)

Singles: 78 rpm

WINLEY...25-35 57

Singles: 7-inch

ABC 4-6 73

AMY (859 "Buffalo")..................................5-10 62

COLLECTABLES..3-5 '80s

CYCLONE (5011 "I Laughed").................50-75 58

(Title and artist in normal bold print. Songwriting credit is *directly* under title.)

CYCLONE (5011 "I Laughed")................10-20 61

(Title and artist in narrow, extra bold print. Songwriting credit is approximately centered between title and artist.)

LOST NITE...4-8 63

SPRY (118 "To Be or Not to Be") 5-10 59

WINLEY (218 "So Strange") 50-75 57

(Has "Winley" in 3/8-inch letters.)

WINLEY (218 "So Strange")....................20-30 61

(Has "Winley" in 1/4-inch letters.)

WINLEY (221 "I'm Fallin in Love") 50-75 57

WINLEY (221 "I'm Falling in Love")..........20-30 61

(Note slight title change.)

WINLEY (225 "The Plea").........................40-60 58

(Has "Winley" in 3/8-inch letters.)

WINLEY (225 "The Plea")..........................20-30 61

(Has "Winley" in 1/4-inch letters.)

WINLEY (242 "The Wind").........................40-60 60

WINLEY (248 "That's How It Goes") 100-200 61

(Colored vinyl.)

WINLEY (248 "That's How It Goes") 20-30 61

(Black vinyl.)

WINLEY (252 "Come Let Me Show You")..20-30 61

LPs: 10/12-inch

COLLECTABLES..6-8 86

LOST NITE (3 "The Jesters")...................10-20 81

(10-inch LP. Red vinyl. 1000 made.)

Members: Len McKay; Adam Jackson; Jimmy Smith; Noel Grant; Leo Vincent; Melvin Lewis; Don Lewis.

Also see HARPTONES / Paragons / Jesters / Clovers

Also see PARAGONS / Jesters

JESTERS

Singles: 7-inch

RIO (10 "Diesel") 10-20 61

VIV (1001 "Side Track") 10-20 62

JESTERS

Singles: 7-inch

FEATURE (101 "Panther Pounce") 20-30 64

ULTIMA (705 "Drag Bike Boogie")........... 15-25 64

Members: Jim Messina; Dave Archuleta; Bill Beckman; Larry Cundieff.

Also see MESSINA, Jim

JESTERS

Singles: 7-inch

SUN (400 "Cadillac Man")........................10-20 66

Members: Jim Dickinson; Teddy Paige; Jerry Phillips; Billy Wulfurs; Eddie Robertson.

JESTERS IV

Singles: 7-inch

FULLER (2684 "She Lied")...................15-25 66

JESTERS OF NEWPORT

Singles: 7-inch

SOLO (700 "Stormy")............................15-25 65

JET ACES

Singles: 7-inch

MONEY (230 "Forbidden Love")..........100-200 57

Also see TURBANS / Jet Aces

JET MEN

Singles: 7-inch

LINCOLN (300 "Mountain Dew") 10-20 60

JET STREAMS

Singles: 7-inch

DECCA (30743 "Who Me").......................15-25 58

JET TONES

Singles: 7-inch

PIX (1102 "Twangy")..............................50-100 59

PLAID (102 "Twangy").............................50-100 59

Also see OLSON, Rocky / Jet Tones

JETHRO TULL *LP '69*

Singles: 12-inch

CHRYSALIS..4-8 88-89

(Promotional only.)

Singles: 7-inch

CHRYSALIS..3-6 72-88

REPRISE/CHRYSALIS 5-10 69-72

Picture Sleeves

CHRYSALIS...4-6 74

EPs: 7-inch

CHRYSALIS...8-12 71

LPs: 10/12-inch

CHRYSALIS (Except CH4 & V5X series) ..5-15 73-89

CHRYSALIS (CH4-1044 "Aqualung") 35-45 73

(Quadraphonic.)

CHRYSALIS (CH4-1067 "War Child")......35-45 74

(Quadraphonic.)

CHRYSALIS (V5X-41653 "Twenty Years of Jethro Tull")...50-75 88

(Boxed, five-disc set.)

MFSL (061 "Aqualung") 40-60 82

MFSL (092 "Broadsword and the Beast") 30-50 82

MFSL (187 "Thick As a Brick") ....20-30 '80s

REPRISE (1024 "Hymn 43")......................10-20 71

REPRISE (2035 "Aqualung")....................10-20 71

REPRISE (2072 "Thick As a Brick")......... 10-20 72

(With color booklet.)

REPRISE (6336 "This Was Jethro Tull").. 10-20 69

REPRISE (6360 "Stand Up") 15-25 69

(With pop-up, or "Stand Up" cover.)

REPRISE (6400 "Benefit")........................10-15 70

REPRISE/CHRYSALIS (2106 "Living in the Past")...15-20 72

(With color booklet.)

Members: Ian Anderson; Clive Bunker; Glen Cormick; John Evan; Barry Barlow; David Palmer; John Glascock; Jeff Hammond; Mick Abrahams.

Also see WILD TURKEY

JETS

Singles: 78 rpm

RAINBOW (201 "The Lovers")..........2000-3000 53

Members: Buck Mason; Jim Walton; Walt Taylor; John Bowie; Charlie Booker; Herb Fisher.

Also see BACHELORS

JETS

Singles: 78 rpm

ALADDIN (3247 "I'll Hide My Tears") ...400-600 54

7-11 (2102 "Volcano")..........................200-300 53

Singles: 7-inch

ALADDIN (3247 "I'll Hide My Tears")..1000-2000 54

7-11 (2102 "Volcano").............................500-600 53

Members: David Ford; Gaynel Hodge; Bobby Byrd; Clyde Tillis.

Also see HOLLYWOOD FLAMES

JETS

Singles: 78 rpm

GEE (1020 "Heaven Above Me")..........400-500 56

Singles: 7-inch

GEE (1020 "Heaven Above Me")......4000-5000 56

JETS

Singles: 7-inch

JET (100 "Gonna Walk").........................75-125 57

JETS

Singles: 7-inch

PORT (3016 "Everything I Do") 10-20 66

JETT, Joan *LP '81*

(With the Blackhearts)

Singles: 12-inch

BLACKHEART/CBS 4-8 88

(Promotional only.)

MCA...4-8 83

Singles: 7-inch

BLACKHEART/CBS 3-5 83-90

BOARDWALK...3-5 81-82

MCA...3-5 83

Picture Sleeves
BLACKHEART/CBS....3-5 83-88
BOARDWALK....3-5 81-82
MCA....3-5 83
LPs: 10/12-Inch
BLACKHEART....50-75 80
(Red label with black heart. No mention of CBS. Number not known.)
BLACKHEART/CBS....5-8 83-90
BOARDWALK....5-8 81-82
MCA....5-8 83-84
RHINO (250 "Little Lost Girls")....15-20 82
(Picture disc.)
W.B. ....8-10 '90s
Also see BEACH BOYS
Also see RUNAWAYS

JETT, Tommy
Singles: 7-Inch
JOX (60 "Groovy Little Trip")....15-25 67

JEUJENE & JAYBOPS
Singles: 7-Inch
ZERO-O (3279 "Thunderin' Guitar")....200-300 '60s
(Colored vinyl. 50 made.)

JEWEL & EDDIE
Singles: 7-Inch
SILVER (1004 "Opportunity")....15-25 60
SILVER (1008 "Sixteen Tons")....15-25 60
Members: Jewel Akens; Eddie Daniels.
Also see AKENS, Jewel
Also see DANIELS, Eddie

JEWELL, Leonard
(Len Jewell)
Singles: 7-Inch
DRANDELL (001 "Doin' the Monster Mash")....8-12 63
FONTANA (1599 "Paint Me")....20-30 67
PZAZZ (050 "Elevator Song")....4-8 70

JEWELL & RUBIES
Singles: 7-Inch
ABC-PAR (10485 "Kidnapper")....5-10 63
LA LOUISIANNE (8041 "Kidnapper")....15-25 63
Member: Jewell Douglas.

JEWELS
(Crows)
Singles: 78 rpm
RAMA (10 "Heartbreaker")....200-250 53
Singles: 7-Inch
RAMA (10 "Heartbreaker")....500-750 53
(Black vinyl. May show *Heartbreaker* by the Crows and *Call a Doctor* by the Jewels on some labels.)
RAMA (10 "Heartbreaker")....1000-2000 53
(Red vinyl.)
Also see CROWS

JEWELS
Singles: 78 rpm
IMPERIAL....20-40 55-56
R&B....25-50 54
RPM....15-25 56
Singles: 7-Inch
ANTLER (1102 "The Wind")....10-15 59
BUCK RAM (1102 "The Wind")....20-30 59
IMPERIAL (5351 "Hearts Can Be Broken")....50-75 55
IMPERIAL (5362 "Natural, Natural Ditty") 30-40 55
IMPERIAL (5377 "How")....30-40 56
IMPERIAL (5387 "My Baby")....30-40 56
ORIGINAL SOUND (38 "Hearts of Stone")....5-10 63
R&B (1301 "Hearts of Stone")....50-75 54
R&B (1303 "A Fool in Paradise")....100-150 54
RPM (474 "She's a Flirt")....30-40 56
Members: Johnny Torrence; Dee Hawkins; James Brown; Rudy Jackson; Vernon Knight.
Also see JACKSON, Rudy
Also see TORRENCE, Johnny

JEWELS
Singles: 7-Inch
SHASTA (115 "Are You Comin' to the Party")....10-20 59

JEWELS
Singles: 7-Inch
FERN (806 "Space Guitar")....10-20 61

JEWELS
(With Johnny & the Sparks)
Singles: 7-Inch
OLIMPIC (244 "Jimmy Lee")....15-25 64
Also see STUDENTS

JEWELS P&R/R&B '64
Singles: 7-Inch
DIMENSION (1034 "Opportunity")....10-15 64
DIMENSION (1048 "But I Do")....10-15 65
Members: Sandra Bears; Margie Clark; Martha Harvin; Grace Ruffin.
Also see FOUR JEWELS

JEWELS
Singles: 7-Inch
DYNAMITE (2000 "Papa Left Mama Holding the Bag")....8-12 65
FEDERAL (12541 "My Song")....10-15 66
KING (6068 "Smokie Joe's")....5-10 66

JEWELS
Singles: 7-Inch
MGM (13577 "We Got Togetherness")....10-20 66

JIANTS
Singles: 7-Inch
CLAUDRA (112 "Tornado")....200-300 59
Members: Jerry Hedges; Andy Anderson; Bill Lee Balsbaugh; Ron Wolfe.
Also see SHONDELL, Troy

JILL & RAY
Singles: 7-Inch
LE CAM (979 "Hey Paula")....50-100 62
Members: Jill Jackson; Ray Hildebrand.
Also see HILDEBRAND, Ray
Also see JACKSON, Jill
Also see PAUL & PAULA

JILLETTES
Singles: 7-Inch
AMAZON (711 "Daddy Do")....10-15 62
CARBS (521 "Daddy Do")....15-25
PHILIPS (40140 "Why Did I Cry")....10-15 63

JIM & JOE
Singles: 7-Inch
FABOR (124 "Fireball Mail"/"Bimbo")....25-35 63
FABOR (124 "Fireball Mail"/"Daisy Mae")....20-30 63
Members: James Burton; Joe Osborn.
Also see GRASS ROOTS
Also see NELSON, Rick

JIM & LEE
Singles: 7-Inch
SMASH (2112 "Let's Go, Baby")....15-25 67

JIM & ROD
Singles: 7-Inch
CHALLENGE (59034 "Didn't It Rock")....75-125 58

JIM, JEFF & JAN
Singles: 7-Inch
CAPITOL (5059 "Star Bright")....30-40 63

JIM DANDIES
(Lawrence Piano Roll Cook, His Player Piano & Orch.)
Singles: 78 rpm
ABBEY (15003 "Why Do They Always Say No")....5-10 50
Singles: 7-Inch
ABBEY (15003 "Why Do They Always Say No")....10-20 50

JIMAE, Gene
Singles: 78 rpm
DOT (15478 "Riders in the Sky")....8-12 56
GENIE (1301 "Riders in the Sky")....10-15 55
Singles: 7-Inch
DOT (15478 "Riders in the Sky")....10-20 56
GENIE (1301 "Riders in the Sky")....15-25 55

JIMMIE & NIGHT HOPPERS
Singles: 7-Inch
KNIGHT (2006 "Cruising")....15-25 59
Member: Jimmie Haskell.

JIMMY & CRESTONES
(With the Al Browne Orchestra)
Singles: 7-Inch
AVENUE D (11 "Angel Maureen")....5-10 85
(Black vinyl. 1000 made.)
MARIA (101 "Angel Maureen")....75-100 64
Also see BROWNE, Al

JIMMY & DUANE
Singles: 7-Inch
EB X. PRESTON (212 "Soda Fountain Girl")....200-300 55
Members: Jimmy Delbridge; Duane Eddy.
Also see DELL, Jimmy
Also see EDDY, Duane

JIMMY & FABULOUS EARTHQUAKES
("Vocal By Jimmy Hopkins and the Starfires")
Singles: 7-Inch
MERIDIAN (1518 "In the Chapel in the Moonlight")....200-300 60
Member: Jimmy Hopkins.

JIMMY & GEMS
Singles: 7-Inch
TONE (7479 "Twisting Sadie")....50-75

JIMMY & ILLUSIONS
Singles: 7-Inch
JOLYNN (36 "Karen")....15-25 63

JIMMY & JACK
Singles: 78 rpm
ACE (507 "Love, Love, Love")....15-25 55
Singles: 7-Inch
ACE (507 "Love, Love, Love")....20-40 55

JIMMY & JAMES & TEMPOS
Singles: 7-Inch
DORA (123 "The Moon Will Shine")....100-200

JIMMY & JOHNNY C&W '54
Singles: 78 rpm
CHESS (4859 "If You Don't Somebody Else Will")....10-15 54
DECCA (29772 & 29954)....5-10 56
DECCA (30061 "Sweet Love on My Mind")....15-25 56
Singles: 7-Inch
CHESS (4859 "If You Don't Somebody Else Will")....20-30 54
D (1004 "I Can't Find the Door Knob")....40-60 58
D (1089 "My Little Baby")....10-20 59
DECCA (29772 "Sweet Singing Daddy")....10-20 56
DECCA (29954 "Till the End of the World")....10-20 56
DECCA (30061 "Sweet Love on My Mind")....75-125 56
TNT (184 "Two Empty Arms")....8-12 61
Members: Jimmy Lee Fautheree; "Country" Johnny Mathis.
Also see LEE, Jimmy, & Wayne Walker

JIMMY & OFFBEATS
Singles: 7-Inch
BOFUZ (1113 "Stronger Than Dirt")....15-25

JIMMY & ROMEOS
Singles: 7-Inch
SOUTHSIDE (1003 "Kathy")....10-15 62

JIMMY & SPARTANS
Singles: 7-Inch
SATELLITE (106 "You're My Girl")....200-300 60

JIMMY & SUNDIALS
Singles: 7-Inch
V-TONE (505 "All About You")....50-100 63
(Promotional issue only.)

JIMMY & TOWERS
Singles: 7-Inch
DEBANN (102 "One More Chance")....150-200

JIMMY & WALTER
Singles: 78 rpm
SUN (180 "Easy")....400-600 53
Singles: 7-Inch
SUN (180 "Easy")....1000-1500 53
Members: Jimmy DeBerry; Walter Horton.
Also see DE BERRY, Jimmy
Also see HORTON, Big Walter

JIMMY B. & ROCKATONES
Singles: 7-Inch
CUCA (6481 "Everything I Do")....10-15 64

JIMMY C. & CHELSEA 5
Singles: 7-Inch
ZERO (1003 "Play with Fire")....10-20 65

JIMMY "D" & "D"-LITES
Singles: 7-Inch
START (643 "Dream World")....30-40 63

JIMMY J & J's
Singles: 7-Inch
SALCO (647 "Please Be My Girlfriend")....30-50 61

JIMMY LEE
(Jimmy Lee Robinson)
Singles: 7-Inch
BANDERA (2506 "Chicago Jump")....25-50 60
Also see LONESOME LEE
Also see ROBINSON, Jimmy Lee

JINX
Singles: 7-Inch
RI-CATH (202 "Johnny's the Boy")....10-15 64

JIVE BOMBERS P&R/R&B '57
(Featuring Clarence "Bad Boy" Palmer; Clarence Palmer & Jive Bombers)
Single: 78 rpm
CITATION (1160 "It's Spring Again")....30-50 52
CITATION (1161 "Brown Boy")....30-50 52
SAVOY....25-35 56-57
Singles: 7-Inch
COLLECTABLES....3-5 85
MIDDLE-TONE (020 "Anytime")....40-50 64
SAVOY (1508 "Bad Boy")....15-25 56
SAVOY (1513 "If I Had a Talking Picture")....10-15 57
SAVOY (1515 "Cherry")....10-15 57
SAVOY (1535 "Is This the End")....15-20 58
SAVOY (1560 "Stardust")....15-20 59
Picture Sleeves
SAVOY (1508 "Bad Boy")....5-10 '90s
LPs: 10/12-Inch
SAVOY....8-10 86
Members: Clarence Palmer; Earl Johnson; Allen Tinney; William Tinney.

JIVE FIVE P&R/R&B '61
("Featuring Eugene Pitt"; Jive Fyve; with Horace & Orchestra)
Singles: 7-Inch
AMBIENT SOUND (02742 "Oh Baby"/"Magic Maker, Music Maker")....4-8 82
(Red vinyl.)
AMBIENT SOUND (03053 "Don't Believe in Him, Donna"/"Hey Sam")....4-8 82
BELTONE (1006 "My True Story")....20-30 61
BELTONE (1014 "Never Never")....15-25 61
BELTONE (2019 "No Not Again")....10-15 62
(Black vinyl.)
BELTONE (2019 "No Not Again")....15-25 62
(Brown vinyl.)
BELTONE (2024 "What Time Is It")....30-40 62
(White label. Vinyl is more brown than black.)
BELTONE (2024 "What Time Is It")....15-25 62
(Orange label.)
BELTONE (2029 "These Golden Rings")....30-40 62
(White label.)
BELTONE (2029 "These Golden Rings")....15-25 62
(Orange label.)
BELTONE (2030 "Lily Marlene")....10-20 63
(White and black label.)
BELTONE (2030 "Lily Marlene")....8-12 63
(Orange and black label.)
BELTONE (2034 "Rain")....10-15 63
(Black vinyl.)
BELTONE (2034 "Rain")....20-30 63
(Vinyl color is more brown than black.)
BELTONE (3000 series)....4-6 74
DECCA (32671 "You Showed Me the Light of Love")....5-10 70
DECCA (32736 "I Want You to Be My Baby")....5-10 70
LANA....4-6
LOST NITE....4-6 '70s
MUSICOR (1250 "Crying Like a Baby")....5-10 67
MUSICOR (1270 "No More Tears")....5-10 67
MUSICOR (1305 "Sugar")....5-10 68
OLDIES 45....4-8 '60s
RELIC....3-5 75-78
SIR RENDER (007 "Falling Tears")....5-8
(Colored vinyl.)
SKETCH (219 "United")....15-25 64
STOOP SOUNDS (101 "Where Do We Go from Here")....100-150 96
(Limited edition. Estimates range from less than 10 to a few dozen made.)
U.A. (807 thru 50107)....5-10 64-66
LPs: 10/12-Inch
AMBIENT SOUND....8-12 82
AMBIENT SOUND/ROUNDER....5-10 84

COLLECTABLES 6-8 85
RELIC 8-10
U.A. (3455 "The Jive Five") 50-75 65
(Monaural.)
U.A. (6455 "The Jive Five") 75-100 65
(Stereo.)
Members: Eugene Pitt; Norm Johnson; Richard Harris; Jerry Hannah; Billy Prophet; Johnny Watson; Casey Spencer; Webster Harris.
Also see CORVAIRS
Also see GENIES
Also see PITT, Eugene
Also see PLATTERS / Inez & Charlie Foxx / Jive Five / Tommy Hunt

JIVE KINGS
Singles: 7-inch
LU (918591 "Preacher Man") .... 200-250 '50s
WHITE STAR (105 "Preacher Man") ... 100-150 59

JIVE TONES
Singles: 7-inch
APT (25020 "Geraldine") 20-30 58
RHYTHM RECORDS (5000 "Geraldine") 50-75 58
Member: James Whittier.
Also see DESIRES

JIVE-A-TONES
(Jiv-A-Tones; with Bobby Wilson)
Singles: 7-inch
FELSTED (8506 "Flirty Girtie") 50-75 58
FOX (1 "Flirty Girtie") 100-150 57
FRATERNITY (823 "Wild Bird") 15-25 58

JIVERS
Singles: 78 rpm
ALADDIN (3329 "Cherie") 50-75 56
ALADDIN (3347 "Ray Pearl") 50-75 56
Singles: 7-inch
ALADDIN (3329 "Cherie") 100-150 56
ALADDIN (3347 "Ray Pearl") 150-200 56

JIVES
Singles: 7-inch
HOUR (102 "Ubangi Stomp") 25-40 62
Also see CHARLIE & JIVES

JIVIN' FIVE
Singles: 7-inch
NITA (129 "Basin Street Blues") 10-20 62

JIVIN' GENE *P&R '59*
(With the Jokers)
Singles: 7-inch
ABC 4-6 73
CHESS (1873 "Cryin' Towel") 5-10 64
HALLWAY (1202 "Lovelight Man") 5-10 64
JIN (109 "Going Out with the Tide") 20-30 59
JIN (116 "Breakin' Up Is Hard to Do") 20-40 59
JIN (7331 "Going Out with the Tide") 15-25 59
MERCURY (71485 thru 72403) 10-20 59-62
TCF/HALL (103 thru 121) 5-10 65
Member: Gene Bourgeois.
Also see MIZZELL, Bobby

JIVING JUNIORS
(With Duke Reid & His Group)
Singles: 7-inch
ASNES (103 "Sweet As an Angel") 15-25 61
BLUE BEAT (4 "Dearest Darling") 300-400 61
BLUE BEAT (5 "My Heart's Desire") 300-400 61
BLUE BEAT (24 "I Wanna Love") 200-300 62

JO-ANN
Singles: 7-inch
RAVEN (8006 "Baby Doll") 50-100 64
(Previously issued as by Del & the Escorts.)
Also see DEL & ESCORTS

JO ANN & TROY *P&R '64*
Singles: 7-inch
ATLANTIC (2256 "Who Do You Love") ... 10-15 64
ATLANTIC (2293 "Same Old Feeling") 10-15 65
Members: Jo Ann Campbell; Troy Seals.
Also see CAMPBELL, Jo Ann

JO BABY & DONNELLS
Singles: 7-inch
TY-TEX (114 "Little Sally Walker") 10-20 65

JO JO
Singles: 7-inch
ACE (113 "To-To-Mo-To") 25-50 57
RENDEZVOUS (206 "Slauson Shuffle") 5-10 63

JO JO & OUTCASTS
Singles: 7-inch
SOUND-O-RIFFIC (926 "Why Baby") 15-25

JOAN & HEARTS
Singles: 7-inch
HUNTER (3505 "Hully Gully, Twist Twist Twist") 75-125 61

JOANNE & TRIANGLES
Singles: 7-inch
V.I.P. (25003 "After the Showers Come Flowers") 25-50 64

JOBE, Don
Singles: 7-inch
TAR (1283 "Going to Have a Party") 15-25

JOBETTES
Singles: 7-inch
KENIN (2268 "What You Gonna Do") 10-15 66

JOBIM, Antonio Carlos *LP '65*
Singles: 7-inch
A&M 4-6 67
CTI 4-6 70
MCA 4-6 74
VERVE 4-6 63-65
LPs: 10/12-inch
A&M 8-12 67-70
CTI 8-12 70-71
CAPITOL 10-20 64
DISCOVERY 5-8 82
MCA 5-8 73
VERSATILE 5-8 78
VERVE (Except 3000 series) 10-20 63
VERVE (3000 series) 5-8 82
W.B. 8-15 65-80
Also see FITZGERALD, Ella, & Antonio Carlos Jobim
Also see SINATRA, Frank, & Antonio Carlos Jobim

JOCELYN
Singles: 7-inch
KNITE-LIFE (001 "Soldier in Saigon") 15-25

JODARETTES
Singles: 7-inch
JOCIDA (302 "What's in Da Box") ....10-20 '60s

JODIMARS
Singles: 78 rpm
CAPITOL 10-15 55-57
Singles: 7-inch
CAPITOL (3285 thru 3633, except 3512) .15-25 55-57
CAPITOL (3512 "Rattle Shakin' Daddy") ..20-30 56
PRESIDENT (1017 "Shoo-Sue") 8-12 58
Picture Sleeves
CAPITOL (3436 "Lot'sa Love") 25-35 56
(Promotional issue only.)
Members: Chuck Hess; Dick Richards; Marshall Lytle; Joey Ambrose; Max Daffner. Session: Billy Gussak.
Also see HALEY, Bill
Also see HESS, Chuck
Also see LYTELL, Marshall

JODY & BOOGIEMEN
Singles: 7-inch
TROLLEY (7301 "And I Love Him") 5-10 70
LPs:10/12-inch
TROLLEY (74-2 "Am I Blue") 15-25 70
Member: Gregory Dee.
Also see AVANTIES

JODY & ODIE
(Cousin Jody & Odie)
Singles: 78 rpm
CHIC 5-10 56
Singles: 7-inch
CHIC (1004 "Television Set") 10-15 56
CHIC (1006 "Money") 10-15 57

JOE, Gradie
(With the Western Gents)
Singles: 7-inch
BLUE MOON (407 "Rockabilly Music") 200-250 58

JOE, Willie
Singles: 78 rpm
SPECIALTY (618 "Flippin'") 10-15 56
Singles: 7-inch
SPECIALTY (618 "Flippin'") 15-25 56

JOE & ANN *R&B '60*
(Joe & Ann Trio)
Singles: 7-inch
ACE (577 thru 651) 10-20 60-62
HERMITAGE (770 "Eternity") 10-20 62
HERMITAGE (774 "Doubtful") 8-12 62
Members: Joe Joseph; Ann Tyler.

JOE & EDDIE *LP '64*
(With the Les Baxter Orchestra & Chorus)
Singles: 7-inch
CAPITOL (4149 thru 4288) 8-12 59
GNP 5-10 62-65
LPs: 10/12-inch
GNP 10-20 63-66
Members: Joe Gilbert; Eddie Brown.
Also see BAXTER, Les

JOE & FURIES
Singles: 7-inch
PARLIAMENT (9770 "Weasel") 15-25

JOE & SATELLITES
Singles: 7-inch
SAFARI (1003 "Say a Prayer") 150-200 57

JOE & URSULA
Singles: 78 rpm
IMPERIAL (5371 "The Good Book") 5-10 55
Singles: 7-inch
IMPERIAL (5371 "The Good Book") 10-15 55
Members: Joe Morris; Ursula Reed.
Also see MORRIS, Joe, & His Orch.
Also see REED, Ursula

JOE THE SHAKER
Singles: 7-inch
GLASS CITY (971 "Yea, Pretty Baby") 50-75

JOEL, Billy *P&R/LP '74*
Singles: 12-inch
COLUMBIA 5-8 83
Singles: 7-inch
COLUMBIA (2628 "She's Got a Way") 5-8 81
(Promotional issue only.)
COLUMBIA (02518 thru 06526) 3-5 81-86
COLUMBIA (10000 & 11000 series) 3-8 74-80
COLUMBIA (40000 series) 4-8 73-74
COLUMBIA (70000 series) 3-5 89-94
EPIC 3-5 86
FAMILY PRODUCTIONS (0900 "She's Got a Way") 10-20 72
FAMILY PRODUCTIONS (0906 "Tomorrow Is Today") 10-20 72
Picture Sleeves
COLUMBIA (Except 02628) 3-8 79-87
COLUMBIA (02628 "She's Got a Way") 8-10 81
(Promotional issue only.)
LPs: 10/12-inch
CBS 5-8
COLUMBIA (30000 & 40000 series) 5-12 73-89
(With "FC," "JC," "KC," "OC," "PC," "QC," or "TC" prefix.)
COLUMBIA (30000 series) 10-15 74-76
(With "CQ" or "PCQ" prefix. Quadraphonic.)
COLUMBIA (40121 "Greatest Hits") 8-12 85
(Two discs.)
COLUMBIA (40996 "Kohu,ept") 8-12 87
(Two discs.)
COLUMBIA (HC-40000 series) 10-15 80-87
(Half-speed mastered.)
FAMILY PRODUCTIONS (2700 "Cold Spring Harbor") 35-45 71
Promotional LPs
COLUMBIA (326 "Souvenir") 25-35 77
COLUMBIA (402 "Interchords") 25-35 77
COLUMBIA (452 "Now Playing") 20-30 78
COLUMBIA (1343 "Interview Album") 15-25 81
SKYCLAD (102 "A Tribute to Billy Joel") 6-8 91
(Clear vinyl. Intentionally has no music—by Billy Joel or anyone. Limited edition of 666 copies.)
Also see ATTILA
Also see HASSLES

JOEL, Billy, & Ray Charles *P&R '87*
Singles: 7-inch
COLUMBIA (06994 "Baby Grand") 3-5 87
Picture Sleeves
COLUMBIA (06994 "Baby Grand") 3-5 87
Also see CHARLES, Ray

JOELL & TOWN CRIERS
Singles: 7-inch
JAN ELL (465 "Secret Heart") 10-20 63

JOEY
(Joey Hall)
Singles: 7-inch
CAMEO (327 "Fool Fool Fool") 5-10 64
JOY (243 "Our Own Little World") 10-15 60
ROULETTE (7070 "Somewhere in the Rain") 4-8 70
TAURUS (353 "A Place in Your Heart") ...25-35 62
Also see LITTLE JOEY & FLIPS

JOEY, Guy
Singles: 7-inch
COED (563 "Anna") 10-20 62

JOEY & AMBERS
Singles: 7-inch
BIG TOP (3052 "Treasure in My Heart") ..10-15 60

JOEY & CONTINENTALS
Singles: 7-inch
CLARIDGE (304 "She Rides with Me") 5-10 65
KOMET (1001 "Will Love Ever Come My Way") 5-10 65
LAURIE (3294 "Sad Girl") 15-20 65
Member: Joey Porello.
Also see G.T.O.s

JOEY & DANNY
(With the Ali Baba & 4 Theives [sic])
Singles: 7-inch
SWAN (4147 "Rats in My Room") 10-20 63
SWAN (4157 "I Got Rid of the Rats") 10-20 63
Members: Joey Reynolds; Danny Neaverth.
Also see REYNOLDS, Joey / Joey & Danny

JOEY & IMPRESSIONS
Singles: 7-inch
CAGG (101 "Lonesome Teenager") 50-150

JOEY & LEXINGTONS
Singles: 7-inch
COMET (2154 "Heaven") 200-300 63
DUNES (2029 "Bobbie") 40-50 63

JOEY & OVATIONS
Singles: 7-inch
HAWK (153 "I Still Love You") 750-1000 64

JOEY & RODGE
(With the Crysteles; "With Guitar & Chorus")
Singles: 7-inch
TABBY (100 "I Should Live So Long") .100-200

JOEY & TEENAGERS
(With Herman, Jimmy & Sherman)
Singles: 7-inch
COLUMBIA (3-42054 "What's on Your Mind") 100-125 61
(Compact 33 Single.)
COLUMBIA (4-42054 "What's on Your Mind") 50-75 61
Members: Joey Pruitt; Jimmy Castor.
Also see CASTOR, Jimmy
Also see CASTOR, Jimmy / Joey & Teenagers / Sherman Garnes
Also see TEENAGERS

JOEY & TWISTERS
Singles: 7-inch
DUEL (505 "Mumblin'") 10-20 62
DUEL (509 "Last Dance") 10-20 62
Also see TWISTERS

JOGETTES
Singles: 7-inch
MAR (102 "Your Love") 15-25 62

JOHANNES & HIS ORCHESTRA
Singles: 7-inch
ATCO (6249 "Margarita") 10-20 63

JOHN, Billy, & Continentals
Singles: 7-inch
JIN (203 "The Alligator") 5-10 66
N-JOY (1012 "Ooh Poo Pah Doo") 15-20 65
N-JOY (1014 "Lover Blue Boy") 15-20 66

JOHN, Elton *P&R/LP '70*
Singles: 12-inch
GEFFEN 4-8 83-85
(Promotional only.)
MCA 4-8 78-88
(Promotional only.)

Singles: 7-inch

COLLECTABLES (4900 series)....................3-5 92
(Colored vinyl.)
CONGRESS (6017 "Lady Samantha") 20-30 70
CONGRESS (6022 "Border Song") 20-30 70
DJM (70008 "Lady Samatha")............. 250-300 69
(Commercial issue.)
DJM (70008 "Lady Samatha").............. 75-100 69
(Promotional issue only.)
EPIC...3-5 87
GEFFEN 3-5 81-86
MCA (40000 thru 40505)..............................4-8 72-76
MCA (40892 thru 40993)..............................4-6 78
MCA (41042 thru 41293)..............................4-6 79-80
MCA (53196 thru 53953)..............................3-5 87-90
MCA/ROCKET 4-8 76-77
ROCKET...4-8 76-77
UNI (55246 "Border Song") 8-12 70
UNI (55265 thru 55343)..............................5-10 70-72
UNI (55351 "Crocodile Rock")................... 25-50 72
(Canadian. In error, first issues were on UNI, instead of MCA.)
VIKING (1010 "From Denver to L.A.")...... 30-60 69
(Flip is by the Barbara Moore Singers.)

Picture Sleeves

GEFFEN 3-5 81-86
MCA (40344 thru 40505) 4-6 74-75
MCA (40892 thru 40973)...............................4-6 78
MCA (40993 "Song for Guy") 4-8 78
MCA (41042 thru 41293) 3-6 79-80
MCA (53196 thru 53000 series) 3-6 87-88
MCA/ROCKET 4-6 76-77
ROCKET...4-6 76-77

EPs: 7-inch

MCA (Except 40105) 8-10 73
(Juke box issues.)
MCA (40105 "Saturday Night's Alright for Fighting")..4-6 73
(Single with two tracks on side two. Not issued with EP cover.)
UNI.. 10-12 70
(Juke box issue only.)

LPs: 10/12-inch

COLUMBIA SPECIAL PRODUCTS 5-8 81
DCC (2004 "Madman Across the Water") 10-15 95
(Analog audiophile pressing.)
D.D.L. (16614 "Goodbye Yellow Brick Road") 50-75 73
(Half-speed mastered.)
DJLP (403 "Empty Sky")......................... 20-25 69
(U.K. issue, distributed in the U.S.A.)
GEFFEN (Except 2176).............................5-8 81-87
GEFFEN (2176 "Sasson")..........................5-10 84
(Single-sided. Promotional issue only.)
MCA (2015 thru 2130)...............................6-10 73-75
(Includes MCA reissues of UNI albums.)
MCA (2142 "Captain Fantastic and the Brown Dirt Cowboy").. 10-15 75
(Includes poster, lyrics booklet, bio scrapbook and comic insert. Deduct $3 to $5 if these items are missing.)
MCA (2142 "Captain Fantastic")............ 50-100 75
(Colored vinyl. Promotional issue only.)
MCA (2163 thru 5121) 5-10 75-80
MCA (6000 series).....................................5-8 88-89
MCA (8000 series)................................... 10-12 87
MCA (10003 "Goodbye Yellow Brick Road") 10-15 73
MCA (13921 "Thom Bell Sessions") 5-10 79
MCA (14591 "A Single Man") 15-20 79
(Picture disc. Both sides have front view of Elton.)
MCA (14591 "A Single Man")................... 50-60 79
(Promotional picture disc. B-side has back view of Elton.)
MCA (37000 series).....................................4-8 79
MCA/ROCKET (Except 1953 & 11004)... 10-12 76-77
MCA/ROCKET (1953 "Get Up and Dance").. 20-25 77
(Promotional issue only.)
MCA/ROCKET (11004 "Blue Moves") ....8-12 '70s
MFSL (160 "Goodbye Yellow Brick Road") 40-50 73
(Half-speed mastered.)
NAUTILUS (10003 "Goodbye Yellow Brick Road") 30-40 82
(Half-speed mastered.)
PARAMOUNT (6004 "Friends") 10-15 71
(Soundtrack.)
PICKWICK (966 "London and New York") .8-10 '70s
PICKWICK (3598 "Friends").......................8-10 '70s
(Soundtrack.)
SASSON/GEFFEN (2176 "Sasson Presents Elton John")..20-30 81
(Single-sided, four-track LP. Promotional issue only.)
UNI (73090 "Elton John") 15-20 70
(Includes booklet.)
UNI (73096 "Tumbleweed Connection")...15-20 71
(Includes booklet.)
UNI (93105 "11-17-70") 15-20 71
UNI (93120 "Madman Across the Water")..15-20 71
(Includes booklet.)
UNI (93135 "Honky Chateau") 15-20 72
VIKING (105 "The Games") 150-175 70
(Soundtrack. With Francis Lai & Barbara Moore Singers.)
Also see FRANKLIN, Aretha, & Elton John
Also see SEDAKA, Neil
Also see STARR, Ringo
Also see WONDER, Stevie

JOHN, Elton, & Kiki Dee — P&R '76

Singles: 7-inch

ROCKET (40585 "Don't Go Breaking My Heart")..4-6 76

Picture Sleeves

ROCKET (40585 "Don't Go Breaking My Heart")..4-8 76

JOHN, Elton / John Lennon — P&R '75

Singles: 7-inch

MCA (40364 "Philadelphia Freedom").........4-6 75

Picture Sleeves

MCA (40364 "Philadelphia Freedom").........4-6 75
MCA (40364 WFIL radio "Philadelphia Freedom")..30-40 75
(Promotional issue only.)
Also see LENNON, John

JOHN, Elton / Tina Turner

Singles: 7-inch

POLYDOR (002 "Pinball Wizard") 25-35 75
(Promotional issue only.)
Also see JOHN, Elton
Also see TURNER, Tina

JOHN, GEOFFREY, AND BROTHER TOM

Singles: 7-inch

MGM (13660 "You've Had Such a Good Life")...10-15 67

JOHN, Jimmie

Singles: 7-inch

TODD (1026 "Just Got Kids")....................10-20 59
Z Z (2392 "Solid Rock")........................100-200

JOHN, Little Willie — R&B '55

(Willie John with Three Lads & A Lass)

Singles: 78 rpm

KING (4818 thru 5091)..........................10-20 55-57
KING (5108 "Talk to Me, Talk to Me").......20-40 58
KING (5142 "You're a Sweetheart")..........50-75 58
KING (5147 "Tell It Like It Is")...............75-125 58
KING (5170 "I'll Carry Your Love Wherever I Go")..100-150 58
PRIZE (6900 "Mommy, What Happened to Our Christmas Tree") 100-200 54

Singles: 7-inch

GUSTO ("Fever")..3-5 87
(Selection number not known.)
GUSTO (2026 "Let Them Talk") 3-5 87
KING (500 series)..4-6
KING (4818 "All Around the World") 20-30 55
KING (4841 "Need Your Love So Bad") ...20-30 56
KING (4893 "I'm Stickin' with You Baby").20-30 56
KING (4935 "Fever")................................20-30 56
KING (4960 "Do Something for Me") 15-25 56
KING (4989 "I've Been Around")...............15-25 56
KING (5003 "A Little Bit of Loving")..........15-25 56
KING (5023 "Love, Life & Money") 15-25 57
KING (5045 "Look What You've Done to Me")..15-25 57
KING (5066 "Young Girl")..........................15-25 57
KING (5083 "Uh Uh Baby").......................15-25 57
KING (5091 "Person to Person") 15-25 57
KING (5108 "Talk to Me, Talk to Me")........15-25 58
KING (5142 "You're a Sweetheart")..........15-25 58
KING (5147 "Tell It Like It Is") 15-25 58
KING (5154 "Why Don't You Haul Off and Love Me")..15-25 58
KING (5170 "I'll Carry Your Love Wherever I Go")..15-25 58
KING (5179 "No More in Life")..................15-25 59
KING (5219 "Leave My Kitten Alone")......15-25 59
KING (5274 "Let Them Talk") 15-25 59
KING (5318 "Loving Care")........................10-20 60
KING (5342 "A Cottage for Sale")............10-20 60
KING (5356 "Heartbreak")..........................10-20 60
KING (5394 "Sleep")..................................10-20 60
KING (5428 "Walk Slow")..........................10-20 60
KING (5452 thru 5949)..............................8-15 61-64
KING (6000 series)....................................5-10 65-70

Picture Sleeves

GUSTO ("Fever")..3-5 87
KING (4935 "Fever")...................................5-10 '90s

EPs: 7-inch

KING (423 "Talk to Me")............................25-50 58
KING (767 "The Sweet, the Hot, the Teen-Age Beat")..15-25 61
(Stereo. Juke box issue only.)
KING (802 "At a Recording Session") 15-25 62
(Stereo. Juke box issue only.)

LPs: 10/12-inch

BLUESWAY...10-15 73
KING (564 "Fever")..................................100-200 56
(With brown cover.)
KING (564 "Fever")....................................40-60 59
(With blue cover.)
KING (596 "Talk to Me")..........................75-125 58
KING (603 "Mr. Little Willie John")..........50-100 58
KING (691 "In Action")............................100-125 60
KING (739 "Sure Things") 20-40 61
KING (767 "The Sweet, the Hot, the Teen-Age Beat")..20-40 61
KING (802 "At a Recording Session") 20-30 62
KING (895 "These Are My Favorite Songs")..20-30 64
KING (949 "All Originals") 20-30 66
KING (1081 "Free at Last") 20-30 70
Also see WILLIAMS, Paul

JOHN, Little Willie / Hank Ballard & Midnighters

Singles: 7-inch

KING (5428/5430 "Walk Slow"/"The Hoochi Coochi Coo")...20-30 60
Also see BALLARD, Hank, & Midnighters

JOHN, Little Willie / 5 Royales / Earl King / Midnighters

EPs: 7-inch

KING (387 "Rock & Roll Hit Parade").....75-100 56
Also see 5 ROYALES
Also see JOHN, Little Willie
Also see KING, Earl (Connelly)
Also see MIDNIGHTERS

JOHN, Mable — P&R/R&B '66

Singles: 7-inch

MOTOWN (54081 "Who Wouldn't Love a Man Like That") 300-400 63
(May have been promotional only. Should have been on Tamla, as selection number indicates.)
STAX 5-15 66-68
TAMLA (54031 "Who Wouldn't Love a Man Like That")..75-100 60
TAMLA (54040 "No Love")........................50-100 61
TAMLA (54050 "Take Me") 30-60 62
TAMLA (54081 "Who Wouldn't Love a Man Like That")..50-100 63
Also see RAELETTES

JOHN & JACKIE

Singles: 78 rpm

ALADDIN (3425 "Raging Sea")..................40-60 57

Singles: 7-inch

ALADDIN (3425 "Raging Sea")..................40-60 57

JOHN & PAUL

Singles: 7-inch

TIP (1021 "People Say") 10-15 64

JOHN LEE

(John Lee Hooker; John Lee's Groundhogs)

Singles: 78 rpm

GOTHAM (515 "Mean Old Train") 15-25 53

Singles: 7-inch

PLANET (104 "Over You Baby")................5-10 67
Also see GROUNDHOGS
Also see HOOKER, John Lee

JOHN LEE

(John Lee Henley)

Singles: 7-inch

J.O.B. (114 "Rhythm Rockin' Boogie") .150-250 58
Also see SPIRES, Big Boy

JOHN R.

Singles: 7-inch

SMASH (1982 "Mojo Blues") 5-10 65
SMASH (2013 "Stag 'O Lee") 5-10 65
USD (1041 "Keep Your Baby Home")...... 15-25 '60s

JOHN'S CHILDREN

Singles: 7-inch

WHITE WHALE (239 "Strange Affair")..... 10-15 66

LPs: 10/12-inch

WHITE WHALE (7128 "John's Children") 60-80 70

JOHNNIE & JACK — C&W '51

(With the Tennessee Mountain Boys; with Kitty Wells; Johnny & Jack)

Singles: 78 rpm

RCA...5-10 51-57

Singles: 7-inch

DECCA..4-8 62
RCA..8-15 51-59

EPs: 7-inch

DECCA..8-12 62
RCA..10-20 55-57

LP: 10/12-inch

ANTHOLOGY OF COUNTRY MUSIC 8-12
CAMDEN 10-20 63-64
COUNTRY CLASSICS.................................5-10
DECCA (4308 "Smiles and Tears") 15-25 62
GOLDEN COUNTRY 5-10
MCA ....5-8 '80s
RCA (1587 "Tennessee Mountain Boys") 25-35 57
RCA (LPM-2017 "Hits")............................20-30 59
(Monaural.)
RCA (LSP-2017 "Hits") 30-50 59
(Stereo.)
RCA (6022 "All the Best") 10-20 70
VOCALION 10-15 68
Members: John Wright; Jack Anglin.
Also see WELLS, Kitty
Also see WRIGHT, Johnny

JOHNNIE & JOE — P&R/R&B '57

(Johnny & Joe; Johnni & Joe; with Rex Garvin & His Orchestra; with Shytone 5 Orchestra)

Singles: 78 rpm

CHESS...40-60 57
J&S...40-60 57

Singles: 7-inch

ABC-PAR (10079 "I Adore You").............10-20 60
ABC-PAR (10117 "Your Love") 10-20 60
AMBIENT SOUND (03410 "Kingdom of Love") 5-10 82
BLUE ROCK (4084 "My Baby Is So Sweet")...5-8 69
CHESS (1641 "Feel Alright") 15-25 56
CHESS (1654 "Over the Mountain").........20-30 57
(Silver and blue label.)
CHESS (1654 "Over the Mountain")..........10-20 60
(Blue or multi-color label.)
CHESS (1677 "I Was So Lonely") 15-25 57
CHESS (1693 "Why Did She Go") 15-25 58
CHESS (1706 "Darling")...........................15-25 58
CHESS (1769 "Across the Sea")..............15-25 60
GONE (5024 "Who Do You Love")...........15-25 58
J&S (1008 "Over the Mountain, Cross the Sea")..4-6
J&S (1603 "I Was So Lonely")..................20-30 57
(First issue.)
J&S (1605 "Trust in Me")..........................20-30 57
J&S (1606 "Who Do You Love")...............20-30 57
J&S (1630 "Warm Soft & Lovely") 20-30 57
J&S (1631 "False Love Has Got to Go") ..20-30 57
J&S (1659 "It Was There").......................20-30 57
J&S (1664 "Over the Mountain, Cross the Sea")..35-45 57
(First issue. Though intended as 1654, selection number on label is 1664. Chess reissue has correct number. Has double horizontal lines across label.)
J&S (1664 "Over the Mountain, Across the Sea")...10-15 62
(Without horizontal lines across label.)
J&S (1684 "You're Just Right for the Part")..15-25 60
J&S (1701 "Red Sails in the Sunset") 15-25 59
J&S (1762 "Feel Alright") 20-40 56
J&S (1763 "I'll Be Spinning")....................20-40 56
(First issue.)
J&S (4420/4421 "The Devil Said No").........5-10 57
J&S (8718 "False Love Has Got to Go") 4-8 70
J&S (8719 "Tell Me")....................................4-8 70

J&S (42830 "Love Me Now")....................5-10 68
J&S (42832 "You're the Loveliest Song I've Ever Heard")....................5-10 68
LANA (121 "Over the Mountain, Across the Sea")....................5-8 65
OMEGA (237 "Speak Softly")....................8-12 63
OMEGA (967 "My Ideal")....................8-12 63
TUFF (379 "Here We Go Baby")....................8-12 64

LPs: 10/12-inch

AMBIENT SOUND....................8-12 82
Members: Johnnie Louise Richardson; Joe Rivers.
Also see CLIMBERS
Also see JAYNETTS

JOHNNIE & JOE / Jimmy Charles

Singles: 7-inch

TRIP (16 "Over the Mountain, Across the Sea"/"A Million to One")....................4-8 '70s
Also see CHARLES, Jimmy

JOHNNY & B.

Singles: 7-inch

RED WING (705 Meaner Than an Alligator")....................50-100

JOHNNY & BARB

Singles: 7-inch

DECCA (30663 "At the Prom")....................10-15 58

JOHNNY & BLUE BEATS

Singles: 7-inch

WINSOR (100 "Right On")....................15-20

LPs: 10/12-inch

WINSOR (1001 "Smile")....................30-40
Members: John Elizondo; Mike Elizondo, Jr.

JOHNNY & BLUE JAYS

Singles: 7-inch

DJ (1001 "Japanese Rock")....................10-20 60

JOHNNY & CANADIANS

Singles: 7-inch

COLUMBIA (43353 "Say Yeah")....................10-15 65

JOHNNY & DEBONAIRES

Singles: 7-inch

FENWAY (1711 "Bonecracker")....................10-15 62

JOHNNY & DELL

Singles: 7-inch

LUCK (101 "The Bounce")....................100-200 60

JOHNNY & DIALTONES

Singles: 7-inch

JIN (134 "I Ran Around")....................15-25 61

JOHNNY & DREAMS

Singles: 7-inch

RICHIE (457 "You're Too Young for Me")....................200-300 61
(Black vinyl. Orange label.)
RICHIE (457 "You're Too Young for Me")....................150-250 61
(Black vinyl. Green label.)
RICHIE (457 "You're Too Young for Me")....................350-500 61
(Red vinyl.)

JOHNNY & DUANE / Duane Carter

Singles: 7-inch

HEP (2002 "Can You")....................25-35 '60s
Also see CARTER, Duane

JOHNNY & HURRICANES *P&R/R&B '59*

Singles: 7-inch

ABC....................4-6 73
ATILA....................5-10 66-67
BIG TOP (3036 thru 3159)....................10-15 60-63
JA-DA....................8-12
JEFF....................5-10 64
MALA (470 "Shadows")....................5-10 63
MALA (483 "That's All")....................5-10 64
TWIRL (1001 "Crossfire")....................40-50 58
WARWICK (502 "Crossfire")....................20-30 59
("Warwick" in sans-serif, or block style print.)
WARWICK (502 "Crossfire")....................15-20 59
("Warwick" in serif style print, but does not extend across entire label. "Crossfire" in quotes.)
WARWICK (502 "Crossfire")....................10-15 59
("Warwick" in serif style print, extending across entire label. No quotes on Crossfire.)
WARWICK (509 "Red River Rock")....................10-15 59
(Monaural.)
WARWICK (509-ST "Red River Rock")....................20-30 59
(Stereo.)
WARWICK (513 "Reveille Rock")....................10-15 59
(Monaural.)
WARWICK (513-ST "Reveille Rock")....................20-30 59
(Stereo.)
WARWICK (520 "Beatnik Fly")....................15-25 60
("Warwick" in serif style print.)
WARWICK (520 "Beatnik Fly")....................10-15 60
(With Warwick horse and scroll logo.)

Picture Sleeves

BIG TOP (3036 "Down Yonder")....................10-20 60
BIG TOP (3051 "Rocking Goose")....................10-20 60
BIG TOP (3056 "You Are My Sunshine")....................10-20 60
BIG TOP (3063 "Ja-Da")....................10-20 61
BIG TOP (3076 "Old Smokie")....................10-20 61
WARWICK (520 "Beatnik Fly")....................15-25 60

EPs: 7-inch

WARWICK (700 "Johnny and the Hurricanes")....................100-200 59

LPs: 10/12-inch

ATILA (1030 "Live at the Star Club")....................75-125 64
(Price includes fan club insert.)
BIG TOP (1302 "The Big Sound of Johnny and the Hurricanes")....................45-55 60
(Monaural.)
BIG TOP (ST-1302 "The Big Sound of Johnny and the Hurricanes")....................75-100 60
(Stereo.)
TWIRL (5002 "Beatnik Fly")....................70-90 59
WARWICK (W-2007 "Johnny and the Hurricanes")....................50-75 59
(Monaural.)
WARWICK (WST-2007 "Johnny and the Hurricanes")....................75-100 59
(Stereo.)
WARWICK (W-2010 "Stormsville")....................45-60 60
(Monaural.)
WARWICK (WST-2010 "Stormsville")....................55-80 60
(Stereo.)
Members: Johnny Paris; Paul Tesluk; Dave Yorko; Lionel "Butch" Mattice; Bill Savitch; Eddie Fields.
Also see CRAFTSMEN
Also see FASCINATORS
Also see FREDDIE & PARLIAMENTS
Also see GIBSON, Johnny

JOHNNY & IMPALAS

Singles: 7-inch

KARRLETON (1069 "Blues Stay Away from Me")....................15-25 '60s

JOHNNY & JACKEY
(Johnny & Jackie)

Singles: 7-inch

ANNA (1108 "Lonely and Blue")....................10-20 60
ANNA (1120 "No One Else But You")....................10-20 60
TRI-PHI (1002 thru 1019)....................10-20 61-63
Members: Johnny Bristol [aka Johnny Bristoe]; Jackey Beavers.

JOHNNY & JACKS

Singles: 7-inch

TIKI (3501 "Baby I Love You So")....................75-100 63

JOHNNY & JAKE

Singles: 7-inch

BLUE ROCK (4058 "Driftin' Heart")....................5-10 68
MOD (1010 "I Need Your Help Baby")....................15-25 67
PHILIPS (40589 "I Need Your Help Baby")....................5-10 68

JOHNNY & JAMMERS

Singles: 7-inch

DART (131 "School Day Blues")....................200-250 60
Member: Johnny Winter.
Also see WINTER, Johnny

JOHNNY & JAYS

Singles: 7-inch

FAIRBANKS (2001 "Lugene")....................10-15 61

JOHNNY & JERRY

Singles: 7-inch

SILVER SLIPPER (1004 Cry Baby")....................10-20 60

Picture Sleeves

SILVER SLIPPER (1004 "Cry Baby")....................40-60 60

JOHNNY & JOKERS

Singles: 7-inch

BELTONE (2028 "I Know")....................10-20 62
(Brown vinyl.)
HARVARD (804 "Why Must It Be")....................30-40 59

JOHNNY & JONIE

Singles: 7-inch

CHALLENGE (59001 "Kee-Ro-Ryin' ")....................20-30 58
CHALLENGE (59024 "Still Going Steady")....................10-20 58
CHALLENGE (59041 "Tijuana Jail")....................8-12 59
Members: Johnny Mosby; Jonie Mosby.

JOHNNY & THE MARK V / Ron-Dels

Singles: 7-inch

CHARAY (95 "Sands of Malibu")....................15-25 68
REVUE (11055 "Sands of Malibu")....................10-15 69
Member: Sonny Threatt.
Also see RON-DELS
Also see SONNY & PHYLLIS

JOHNNY & NITE RYDERS

Singles: 7-inch

PERFECTION (558 "I Had a Girl")....................20-30 '60s

JOHNNY & SHY GUYS

Singles: 7-inch

CASCADE (1001 "Pretty Baby")....................15-25 64
CUCA (1145 "Moon Dawg")....................15-25 63
MA (101 "Shorty's Shack")....................15-25 64
REGAL (200 "What I'd Say")....................15-25 64
Members: Rudy Von Ruden; John Bernadot; Larry Ball Gaulke; Les King; Hal Atkinson; Tari Tovsen; Jan Hassman; Danny Baker.
Also see ATKINSON, Hal
Also see SHY GUYS
Also see VON RUDEN

JOHNNY & THUNDERBIRDS
(With the Trends)

Singles: 7-inch

CLOVER (1001 "They Say")....................100-150 59
RIC (160 "Fugitive")....................10-20 65

JOHNNY & TOKENS

Singles: 7-inch

WARWICK (658 "Taste of a Tear")....................10-15 61
Also see KINGS OF HOT RODS / Tokens / Hal Jones & Wheelers

JOHNNY & VIBRATIONS

Singles: 7-inch

W.B. (5372 "Bird Stompin' ")....................10-20 63

JOHNNY H. & SINCERES
(With Little Joe & the Latinaires)

Singles: 7-inch

EL ZARAPE (122 "Why Don't You Write Me")....................200-300 63
(Label is magenta at top, white on bottom. Has no address under label name.)
EL ZARAPE (122 "Why Don't You Write Me")....................200-300 63
(Label is purple with silver print. Has address under label name.)

JOHNNY LEE
(John Lee Hooker)

Singles: 78 rpm

DELUXE (6009 "I Came to See You Baby")....................30-60 52

Singles: 7-inch

DELUXE (6009 "I Came to See You Baby")....................75-100 52
Also see HOOKER, John Lee

JOHNNY Z.

Singles: 7-inch

DORE (667 "Midnight Beach Party")....................10-15 63

JOHNS, Johnny, & Three Jays

Singles: 7-inch

HI MAR (103/104 "I Found You"/"What Is Love")....................10-20 62
Also see ADMIRAL TONES

JOHNS, Liz
([Liz]Johns)

Singles: 7-inch

POWER (201 "To Prove My Love")....................10-15 64

JOHNS, Phill

Singles: 7-inch

RIVER (2012 "Ballad of a Juvenile Delinquent")....................50-75

JOHNS, Sammy, & DeVilles

Singles: 7-inch

CONSTELLATION (129 "Making Tracks")....................8-12 64
DIXIE (1107 "Making Tracks")....................20-30 60
KEDLEN (129 "Making Tracks")....................50-75 60
(First issue.)
Also see DEVILLES

JOHNSON, Al

Singles: 7-inch

BLUE ROCK (4079 "It's Soul Time")....................5-10 69
MARINA (500 "It's Not Too Late")....................5-10 66
RIC (956 "You Done Me Wrong")....................10-20 58
RIC (967 "Good Lookin' ")....................10-20 60
SOUTH CAMP (7002 "Love Waits for No Man")....................20-30

JOHNSON, Amos, & Rhythm Playboys

Singles: 7-inch

(01 "Rhythm Playboy's Stomp")....................10-20
(No label name is shown.)

JOHNSON, Arthur

Singles: 7-inch

WANGER (190 "Honey Please Believe Me")....................15-25 59

JOHNSON, Betty *P&R '54*
(With Charles Randolph Grean & Orchestra; with Jimmy Leyden & Orchestra)

Singles: 78 rpm

BALLY....................5-10 56-57
BELL....................10-15 54
COLUMBIA....................5-10 51-52
NEW DISC....................8-12 54-55
RCA....................5-10 55

Singles: 7-inch

ATLANTIC (1169 "The Little Blue Man")....................10-20 58
(With the song's writer, Fred Ebb, as the "Little Blue Man.")
ATLANTIC (1186 thru 2056)....................10-20 58-60
BALLY (1000 thru 1041)....................10-20 56-57
BELL (1054 "This Is the Thanks I Get")....................15-20 54
BELL (1074 "All of You")....................15-20 55
COED (532 "Take a Little Look")....................10-15 60
COLUMBIA....................10-15 51-52
DOT (16127 "Slipping Around")....................8-12 60
NEW DISC (10013 "I Want Eddie Fisher for Christmas")....................15-25 54
NEW DISC (10018 "Did They Tell You")....................15-25 55
RCA (6034 "Be a Lover")....................10-15 55
RCA (8143 "Betty's Bossa Nova")....................5-10 63
REPUBLIC (2011 thru 2025)....................10-15 61
SPARTAN....................10-20 56-57
(Canadian.)
WORLD ARTISTS (1014 "What's the Matter")....................5-10 63

EPs: 7-inch

ATLANTIC (611 "The Little Blue Man")....................25-50 58
RCA (4059 "Betty Johnson")....................25-50 57

LPs: 10/12-inch

ATLANTIC (8017 "Betty Johnson")....................25-50 58
ATLANTIC (8027 "Songs You Heard When You Fell in Love")....................25-35 59
BALLY (12011 "The Touch")....................30-50 57
HI-LIFE (57 "Make Yourself Comfortable")....................15-25 '50s

JOHNSON, Betty, with Three Beaus & A Peep / Anne Lloyd & Carillons

Singles: 78 rpm

BELL (1031 "Cross Over the Bridge")....................8-12 54
(7-inch 78 rpm.)
Also see LLOYD, Anne, & Michael Stewart

JOHNSON, Big Bill

Singles: 7-inch

BLUE ANGEL (2004 "Hot Rod Car")....................75-100

JOHNSON, Bill
(Bill Johnson Quartet; Bill Johnson Quintet)

Singles: 78 rpm

JUBILEE (5211 "We're Gonna Move")....................5-10 55
RONNEX (1001 "I Almost Lost My Mind")....................25-50 55

Singles: 7-inch

BATON (239 "Traveling Stranger")....................20-30 57
JUBILEE (5211 "We're Gonna Move")....................10-20 55
RONNEX (1001 "I Almost Lost My Mind")....................100-150 55

JOHNSON, Bill
(With Four Steps of Rhythm; with Gene Lowery Singers)

Singles: 7-inch

JOCIDA (301 "You Got Soul")....................8-12 65
SUN (340 "Bad Times Ahead")....................30-40 60
TALOS (402 "You Better Dig It")....................300-350 59
Also see BEETHOVEN 4

JOHNSON, Bill
Singles: 7-inch
STARDAY ("Um Boy, You're My Baby") 150-250
(Selection number not known.)

JOHNSON, Bill, & Musical Notes
(Bill Johnson Orchestra) R&B '47
Singles: 78 rpm
ALERT 15-20 46
HARLEM 10-15 46
KING 10-15 46-50
QUEEN 10-15 47
VICTOR 10-15 47-48
Singles: 7-inch
TRU-BLUE (414 "When Your Hair Has Turned to Silver") 75-100 54
(Colored vinyl.)

JOHNSON, Blind Boy, & His Rhythms
(Champion Jack Dupree)
Singles: 78 rpm
LENOX 15-25 46
Also see DUPREE, Champion Jack

JOHNSON, Blind Willie
LPs: 10/12-inch
FOLKWAYS (3585 "The Blues") 20-25 57
RBF/FOLKWAYS 15-20 65

JOHNSON, Bobby
Singles: 7-inch
MERCURY (71168 "Flat Tire") 10-15 57

JOHNSON, Brownie
Singles: 7-inch
LARK 10-15
LYNN (101 "The Sun Will Never Shine") 75-125 61

JOHNSON, Bubber P&R/R&B '55
(With the Dreamers)
Singles: 78 rpm
KING 10-15 55-57
MERCURY 10-15 52
Singles: 7-inch
KING (4000 series) 15-25 55-56
KING (5000 series) 10-20 57-60
MERCURY (8285 "Forget if You Can") 40-50 52
LPs: 10/12-inch
KING (569 "Come Home") 40-60 57
KING (624 "Sweet Love Songs") 30-40 59

JOHNSON, Budd
(Budd Johnson & Orchestra; with the Voices Five; with Boy & Girl)
Singles: 7-inch
ARGO (5458 "Theme from *The Cardinal*") .5-10 63
CRAFT (111 "You're Driving Me Crazy") 75-125 59
CRAFT (113 "Castle Rock") 15-25 59
(Monaural.)
CRAFT (116 "For Sentimental Reasons") 100-150 59
ROYAL AUDIO (20502 "For Sentimental Reasons") 5-10
STERE-O-CRAFT (111 "You're Driving Me Crazy") 40-50 59
STERE-O-CRAFT (113 "Castle Rock") ... 30-40 59
(Stereo.)
LPs: 10/12-inch
STERE-O-CRAFT (509 "Big Beat Dance Party") 400-600 58

JOHNSON, Buddy R&B '43
(Buddy Johnson & His Orchestra; with Bee Jays)
Singles: 78 rpm
ATLANTIC 4-8 53
COLUMBIA 4-8 48
DECCA 4-8 42-54
MERCURY 5-10 53-56
RCA 5-10 56
WING 5-10 56
Singles: 7-inch
ATLANTIC 10-20 53
DECCA (24996 "You Got to Walk That Chalk Line") 15-25 50
DECCA (27947 "Til' My Baby Comes Back") 30-40 52
DECCA (28293 "Baby You're On My Mind") 20-30 52
DECCA (28907 "Talkin' About Another Man's Wife") 10-20 53
DECCA (29058 "Handful of Stars") 10-20 54
MERCURY 10-20 53-56
RCA 10-20 56
WING 10-20 56
LPs: 10/12-inch
FORUM 10-15
MERCURY (20209 "Rock 'N' Roll") 30-40 58
MERCURY (20322 "Walkin'") 20-30 59
MERCURY (20330 "Buddy Johnson Wails") 25-35 59
(Monaural.)
MERCURY (60072 "Buddy Johnson Wails") 35-55 59
(Stereo.)
WING (12005 "Rock 'N' Roll") 35-50 56
WING (12234 "Buddy Johnson Wails") 15-25 63
(Monaural.)
WING (16234 "Buddy Johnson Wails") 15-25 63
(Stereo.)
Also see BROWN, Ruth
Also see PRYSOCK, Arthur

JOHNSON, Buddy & Ella P&R '60
Singles: 78 rpm
MERCURY 4-8 56-57
Singles: 7-inch
MERCURY 5-12 56-61
OLD TOWN (1173 "Like You Do") 5-10 64
ROULETTE (4134 "Don't Fail Me Baby") ... 5-10 59
ROULETTE (4188 "Keep My Love for You") 5-10 59
LPs: 10/12-inch
MERCURY (20347 "Swing Me") 25-35 58
ROULETTE (R-25085 "Go Ahead and Rock and Roll") 20-30 59
(Monaural.)
ROULETTE (SR-25085 "Go Ahead and Rock and Roll") 30-40 59
Also see JOHNSON, Buddy

JOHNSON, Buffalo
Singles: 7-inch
KENTUCKY (4520 "Tappin' Boogie") 75-125

JOHNSON, Byron
Singles: 7-inch
D (1031 "True Affection") 75-125
D (1058 "It's Wrong for Me to Love You"). 15-25 59

JOHNSON, Candy
(Candy Johnson Show; with Her Exciters)
Singles: 7-inch
CANJO (101 "Ooh Poo Paa Doo") 10-15 64
LPs: 10/12-inch
CANJO (1001 "Candy Johnson Show") 25-35 64
CANJO (1002 "Bikini Beach") 25-35 64
Also see MacRAE, Meredith, with Candy Johnson's Exciters

JOHNSON, Candy, Orchestra
(C. Johnson & Band)
Singles: 78 rpm
D.R.C. DANCELAND (399 "Stompin'") 20-30 49
D.R.C. DANCELAND (401 "Sunset Jump") 20-30 49

JOHNSON, Charles
Singles: 7-inch
TOWN (1501 "Dim the Lights Baby") 15-25

JOHNSON, Cliff
Singles: 78 rpm
COLUMBIA (40865 "Go 'Way Hound Dog") 20-40 57
Singles: 7-inch
COLUMBIA (40865 "Go 'Way Hound Dog") 30-60 57

JOHNSON, Conrad
Singles: 78 rpm
GOLD STAR 15-25 47
Also see CONNIE'S COMBO

JOHNSON, Curtis
Singles: 7-inch
EVENT (4268 "Baby Baby") 50-75 57

JOHNSON, Dave
Singles: 7-inch
APT (25054 "Angel of Mine") 20-30 60

JOHNSON, Dave
Singles: 7-inch
TRADE WIND (4313 "International Runway") 100-150 66

JOHNSON, Dave, & Shadows
Singles: 7-inch
SOMA (1154 "Maybe Baby") 15-25 60
Also see STRANGERS

JOHNSON, Dee
Singles: 7-inch
DIXIE (2012 "Just Look, Don't Touch") .. 50-100 58
DIXIE (2022 "Back to School") 50-75 59

JOHNSON, Deena, & Ricky Davis
Singles: 7-inch
SIMPSON (101 "Who Me, Yeah You") 15-20 65

JOHNSON, Delores
Singles: 7-inch
BOBBIN (132 "Give Me Your Love") 20-30 61

JOHNSON, Don
Singles: 7-inch
DOT (15812 "I'm Hypnotized") 20-30 58

JOHNSON, Dottie
Singles: 78 rpm
GEE (5 "Thank You Daddy") 10-15 54
Singles: 7-inch
GEE (5 "Thank You Daddy") 15-20 54

JOHNSON, Eddie
Singles: 78 rpm
CHESS (1488 thru 1512) 8-12 51-52
CHESS (1544 "Tiptoe") 10-20 53
COLONY (101 "Troubled Woman") 20-30 51
Singles: 7-inch
CHESS (1488 thru 1512) 15-20 51-52
CHESS (1544 "Tiptoe") 40-60 53
(Black vinyl.)
CHESS (1544 "Tiptoe") 100-200 53
(Red vinyl.)

JOHNSON, Edwin, & Mellow Fellows
Singles: 7-inch
CANDI (1023 "You Gave Me Love") 15-25 61

JOHNSON, F.D., & Missouri Valley Boys
Singles: 7-inch
JAN (58 "Be My Baby") 2000-3000

JOHNSON, Gene
(Gene Autry)
Singles: 78 rpm
TIMELY TUNES (1550 "High Steppin' Mama Blues") 25-75
TIMELY TUNES (1551 "Jimmie the Kid"). 25-75
TIMELY TUNES (1552 "Do Right Daddy Blues") 25-75
Also see AUTRY, Gene

JOHNSON, Glenn
Singles: 7-inch
OAK (360 "Little Heart Attacks") 50-75
OAK (7673 "Run Here Honey") 20-30

JOHNSON, Harry "Slick"
Singles: 78 rpm
PEACOCK (1560 "My Baby's Coming Home") 10-15 51

JOHNSON, Haven
Singles: 78 rpm
CABARET (101 "What Time Does This Party Get Started") 15-25

JOHNSON, Herb
(With the Cruisers; with Impacts)
Singles: 7-inch
ARCTIC (109 "Gloomy Day") 8-12 65
BRUNSWICK (55393 "I'm So Glad") 15-25 68
COLLECTABLES 3-5 82
LEN (1007 "Guilty") 10-20 60
PALM (301 "Help") 400-500 59
SWAN (4186 "Tell Me So") 10-15 64
TOXSAN (101 "Where Are You") 20-30
V-TONE (216 "Remember Me") 5-10 60
V-TONE (228 "That's the Way Life Goes") 5-10 61

JOHNSON, Hoyt
Singles: 7-inch
ERWIN (555 "Eenie Meany Minie Mo") 100-200 57
ERWIN (1000 "Where Are You") 50-75
RCA (7522 thru 7731) 10-20 59-60
SATELLITE (110 "I Just Can't Learn") 50-100 61
STATUE (609 "Cindy") .... 20-25 '70s

JOHNSON, Ike & Dee Dee
Singles: 7-inch
INNIS (3002 "You Can't Have Your Cake") 10-20 64
(Reportedly Ike Turner.)
Also see TURNER, Ike

JOHNSON, Jackie
Singles: 7-inch
TULANE (106 "Too Late") 15-25
WILLAMETTE (102 "Star Light, Star Bright") 50-100 59

JOHNSON, Jeanie
Singles: 7-inch
RCA (7782 "Wishing Well") 5-10 60
Picture Sleeves
RCA (7782 "Wishing Well") 15-20 60

JOHNSON, Jeff
Singles: 7-inch
RENEEK (116 "Doin' My Time") 50-100

JOHNSON, Jess
(Jesse Johnson)
Singles: 7-inch
CROSSROADS 5-10
SYMBOL (901 "So in Love Am I") 25-35 58

JOHNSON, Jesse
Singles: 7-inch
OLD TOWN (1195 "Left Out") 50-100 66

JOHNSON, Jimmy
(Jim Johnson)
Singles: 78 rpm
VIV (3000 "Cat Daddy") 50-75 56
Singles: 7-inch
CLASS (237 "Cool, Cool School") 10-20 58
MID WEST (1002 "Mean Woman Blues") 175-225
RENDEZVOUS (145 "Cool, Cool School") 15-25 61
STARDAY (561 "All Dressed Up") 1000-1500
VIV (3000 "Cat Daddy") 150-200 56
LPs: 10/12-inch
ALLIGATOR 8-10
DELMARK 10-20
Also see FLEETWOOD, Jimmy

JOHNSON, Jimmy R&B '65
(With His Band featuring Hank Alexander)
Singles: 7-inch
MAGNUM (719 "Don't Answer the Door") 10-15 64

JOHNSON, Joe
Singles: 7-inch
A-BET (9417 "Dirty Woman Blues") 5-10 66
CASCADE (5909 "Cool Love") 15-25 59
CRY (1102 "Got My Oil Well Pumpin'") 50-75 69
GALAXY (741 "Gold Digging Man") 5-10 65

JOHNSON, Joe D.
Singles: 7-inch
ACAME (45 "First After You") 75-100 62
(Black and silver label.)
ACAME (45 "First After You") 25-35 63
(Black and orange label.)
ACAME (46 "Last Letter") 50-75 63
(Black and silver label.)
ACAME (46 "Last Letter") 20-30 63
(Black and orange label.)
ACME (47 "Rattlesnake Daddy") 150-200 59
(Red label. Label reads "Acme," not "Acame" as on others.)
ACAME (47 "Rattlesnake Daddy") 50-75 63
(Black and silver label.)
ACAME (47 "Rattlesnake Daddy") 20-30 63
(Black and orange label.)
ACAME (48 "Beneath the Arizona Moon") 30-60 64
(Black and silver label.)
ACAME (48 "Beneath the Arizona Moon") 20-30 64
(Black and orange label.)
Picture Sleeves
ACAME (48 "Beneath the Arizona Moon") 40-60 64
Members: Joe D. Johnson; Leland Matthew; Dean Narramore; Bob Mack; Rudy Alcorts; David Bittick; Pete Pittman; Beau Pittman; George Edmunds; John Allan; Charlie Murphy; Brent Pace; Herschel Menchue; Joe Flood.

Also see PACE, Brent

JOHNSON, Joshua

Singles: 78 rpm

CAPITOL (1180 "Pile Driver Boogie")........8-12 50

Singles: 7-inch

CAPITOL (1180 "Pile Driver Boogie")...... 20-30 50

JOHNSON, Kripp

(With the Dell Vikings; Krip Johnson; "Lead Singer of Whispering Bells"; "The Del Viking Kripp Johnson"; "The Dell Viking Kripp Johnson.")

Singles: 7-inch

FEE BEE (218-A "I'm Spinning")......... 100-150 57
(Reissued as by the "Dell-Vikings.")
MERCURY (71436 "Everlasting")........... 10-15 59
MERCURY (71486 "Still I Forgive")......... 10-15 59
Also see RICHIE & RUNAROUNDS

JOHNSON, Kripp, & Chuck Jackson

("The Dell Viking Kripp Johnson and Charles Jackson")

Singles: 7-inch

DOT (15673 "Willette")........................ 15-20 57
FEE BEE (221 "Willette")..................... 50-75 57
(Reissued as by the "Dell-Vikings.")
Also see DEL-VIKINGS
Also see JACKSON, Chuck
Also see JOHNSON, Kripp

JOHNSON, Lee

Singles: 7-inch

ARNOLD (1005 "You Love Billy")........... 20-30 61
LASH (1126 "My Love")......................... 30-40 59

JOHNSON, Len

(With the Hi-Lighters)

Singles: 7-inch

RAY-CO (503 "Sweet Thing")................. 20-30 63
VENDED (107 "Nobody But You").......... 15-25 61

JOHNSON, Leroy

Singles: 78 rpm

FREEDOM.. 15-25 49
OKEH (6813 "Unlucky Blues")................ 10-15 51

Singles: 7-inch

OKEH (6813 "Unlucky Blues")................ 20-30 51

JOHNSON, Lester

(With the Hornets)

Singles: 7-inch

QUEEN (24009 "Heaven Only Knows").. 15-25 61
WAY OUT ("Wedding Day")................ 150-250 62
(No selection number used.)
Also see IVERSON, Ben, & Hornets

JOHNSON, Lonnie *P&R/R&B '48*

(With Victoria Spivey)

Singles: 78 rpm

ALADDIN.. 15-25 47
ARCO.. 15-25
BLUEBIRD... 15-25 38-44
DECCA.. 15-25 '30s
DISC.. 15-25 46-47
GROOVE... 15-25 55
HOLIDAY... 15-25 48
KING... 15-25 47-57
OKEH.. 25-75
PARADISE... 15-25 52
RCA.. 15-25 46-50
RAMA.. 10-20 56
SCORE.. 15-25 49

Singles: 7-inch

FEDERAL (12376 "What a Real Woman").. 10-15 60
GROOVE (5003 "He's a Jelly-Roll Baker")... 35-50 55
KING (4201 "Tomorrow Night")............ 50-75 51
KING (4400 thru 4600 series)............. 40-60 50-53
KING (4700 thru 4900 series)............. 30-40 54-56
KING (5000 series).............................. 10-25 57-65
KING (6000 series)................................... 4-8 70
PRESTIGE...5-10 60-64
RAMA (9 "My Woman Is Gone")............ 50-75 53
(Black vinyl.)
RAMA (9 "My Woman Is Gone")......... 100-200 53
(Red vinyl.)
RAMA (14 "Stick with Me Baby")............ 50-75 53
RAMA (19 "It's Been So Long")............. 50-75 53
RAMA (20 "This Love of Mine")............. 50-75 53
(Black vinyl.)
RAMA (20 "This Love of Mine")........... 100-200 53
(Red vinyl. Blue label.)

EPs: 7-inch

KING (267 "Lonnie Johnson")............... 50-100 54

LPs: 10/12-inch

BLUES BOY...8-12
COLLECTOR'S CLASSICS (30 "Masters of the Blues")..10-15
KING (520 "Lonesome Road")......... 1000-1500 56
KING (958 "12 Bar Blues").......................15-20 66
KING (1083 "Tomorrow Night")................10-15 70
PRESTIGE (7724 "Losing Game")..........10-15 69
PRESTIGE BLUESVILLE (1007 "Blues By Lonnie")...50-75 60
PRESTIGE BLUESVILLE (1024 "Losing Game")..50-75 61
PRESTIGE BLUESVILLE (1044 "Idle Hours")..50-75 61
PRESTIGE BLUESVILLE (1054 "Woman Blues")..50-75 63
PRESTIGE BLUESVILLE (1062 "Another Night to Cry")..50-75 63
ROOTS N' BLUES.......................................5-8 90
Also see SPIVEY, Victoria
Also see THREE KINGS & A QUEEN

JOHNSON, Lonnie, & Elmer Snowden

LPs: 10/12-inch

PRESTIGE BLUESVILLE (1011 "Blues and Ballads")..50-75 61

JOHNSON, Lonnie / George Dawson's Chocolateers

Singles: 78 rpm

PARADE..10-15 52
Also see JOHNSON, Lonnie

JOHNSON, Lorraine

Singles: 7-inch

ATLANTIC (2967 "Can I Hold You to It")..15-25 73

JOHNSON, Lou *P&R/R&B '63*

Singles: 7-inch

BIG HILL (552 thru 554)......................10-15 64-65
BIG TOP (3115 thru 3153)....................10-15 62-63
BIG TOP (101 thru 104)........................10-15 65-66
COTILLION..5-10 68-69
HILLTOP...8-12 64
VOLT (4055 "Who Am I").........................4-6 71

LPs: 10/12-inch

COTILLION..10-15 69
VOLT...8-12 71

JOHNSON, Luther / Mojo Buford

(With the Muddy Waters Blues Band)

LPs: 10/12-inch

DOUGLAS (781 "Muddy Waters Blues Band")..10-15 68
Also see BUFORD, Mojo
Also see WATERS, Muddy

JOHNSON, Marv *P&R/R&B '59*

(With the Band of Harold "Beans" Bowles; with Rayber Voices)

Singles: 78 rpm

U.A. (160 "Come to Me")........................50-75 59
(Canadian.)

Singles: 7-inch

GORDY...8-12 65-68
KUDO (663 "My Baby-O")...................200-300 58
TAMLA (101 "Come to Me").................200-300 59
(No company address shown.)
TAMLA (101-G1 "Come to Me")...........175-225 59
(Has Gladstone St. Address under "Tamla.")
U.A. 10-25 59-64

EPs: 7-inch

U.A. (10,007 "Marv Johnson")..............100-150 60
U.A. (10,009 "Marv Johnson")..............100-150 60

LPs: 10/12-inch

U.A. (3081 "Marvelous Marv Johnson")....50-75 60
(Monaural.)
U.A. (3081 "More Marv Johnson")...........50-75 60
(Monaural.)
U.A. (3187 "I Believe")............................25-50 62
(Monaural.)
U.A. (6081 "Marvelous Marv Johnson")..75-125 60
(Stereo.)
U.A. (6081 "More Marv Johnson").........60-100 60
(Stereo.)
U.A. (6187 "I Believe")............................40-60 62
(Stereo.)
Also see HOLLAND, Eddie
Also see PETERS, Nancy

JOHNSON, Marvin, & His Orchestra

(Vocal by Calvin Boze.)

Singles: 78 rpm

G&G (1029 "Safronia Bee").....................50-75 47
Also see BOZE, Calvin

JOHNSON, Meat Head

(Champion Jack Dupree)

Singles: 78 rpm

APEX...15-25 50
GOTHAM..10-12 50
Also see DUPREE, Champion Jack

JOHNSON, Mirriam

Singles: 7-inch

JAMIE (1181 "Lonesome Road").............10-20 61
JAMIE (1193 "Making Believe")...............10-20 61

Picture Sleeves

JAMIE (1181 "Lonesome Road").............25-35 61
Also see COLTER, Jessie
Also see EDDY, Duane & Mirriam

JOHNSON, Paul

(Guitar Red)

Singles: 7-inch

KELLMAC (1009 "Red Rock")..................10-20 63
Also see GUITAR RED

JOHNSON, Pete *R&B '45*

(Pete Johnson All-Star Orchestra)

Singles: 78 rpm

APOLLO...4-8 46-49
BRUNSWICK..4-8 44
DOWN BEAT..4-6 49
MODERN..4-6 47
NATIONAL..4-6 45-46

Singles: 7-inch

APOLLO...10-20 '50s

EPs: 7-inch

APOLLO (608 "Pete Johnson")................15-25 '50s
BRUNSWICK..10-20 55

LPs: 10/12-inch

SAVOY (14018 "Pete's Blues")................30-50 58
Also see AMMONS, Albert, & Pete Johnson
Also see BROOKS, Hadda / Pete Johnson
Also see TURNER, Joe

JOHNSON, Phil, & Duvals

Singles: 7-inch

KELIT (7033 "I Lied to My Heart")........400-500 58

JOHNSON, Phil, & Duvals / Royal Notes

(With Floyd Williams & Orchestra)

Singles: 7-inch

KELIT (7032 "Kisses Left Unkissed"/"Three Speed Girl")...100-150 58
Also see JOHNSON, Phil, & Duvals
Also see ROYAL NOTES / Phil Johnson & Duvals

JOHNSON, Plas

(With George Jenkins & Orchestra)

Singles: 78 rpm

BEDFORD (505 "Last Call").....................10-15 56
TAMPA...5-15 56-57

Singles: 7-inch

A.F.O. (501 "Lift Off")................................8-12 63
BEDFORD (505 "Last Call").....................15-25 56
CAPITOL...10-20 58-61
JET...5-10
TAMPA (116 thru 146)...............................15-25 56-58
YANKEE DOODLE (111 "Music from the House Next Door")..5-10 62

LPs: 10/12-inch

CAPITOL (1281 "This Must Be the Plas")..25-50 59
CAPITOL (1503 "Mood for the Blues").....25-50 61
TAMPA (24 "On Tenor Sax")....................50-75 57
Also see BEECHER, Johnny, & His Buckingham Road Quintet
Also see EDDY, Duane
Also see JENKINS, George
Also see JOHNSON, Ray
Also see NELSON, Rick
Also see PETERSEN, Paul
Also see SCOOBY DOO ALL STARS
Also see SUMMERS, Gene
Also see WILLIAMS, Larry

JOHNSON, Ralph

(With the Good Luck Charms)

Singles: 78 rpm

RALPH JOHNSON.......................................50-75 55

Singles: 7-inch

RALPH JOHNSON (639 "Henpecked Daddy")..200-400 55
WEDGE (1007 "Hemphill Mine Blues")..50-100 '50s

JOHNSON, Ray

(With the Hi-Liters; with Bystanders; Red Johnson; Ray Johnson Combo)

Singles: 78 rpm

ALADDIN...8-12 57
BLEND..15-25 55
DOT...8-12 56
MERCURY...10-15 52-53

Singles: 7-inch

ACCLAIM (1001 "After Hours")..................15-25 '50s
ALADDIN (3367 "Calypso Joe")................10-20 57
ALADDIN (3392 "Calypso Blues")............10-20 57
BLEND (104 "Baby I Miss You")...............50-75 55
BLEND (1002 "Gonna Roll Lucky Seven Tonight")..50-75 55
DEBB (202 "A Yellow Mellow Hardtop")..100-150 57
DEMON (1502 "A Yellow Mellow Hardtop")..15-25 57
DOT (15512 "Love A La Mode")..............10-15 56
FLIP (308 "Hop Scotch")...........................10-20 55
FLIP (310 "Longing")..................................10-20 55
FLIP (342 "Hop Scotch")...........................10-20 58
GOAD (1001 "Find Your Mind")................10-20 62
GOAD (1002 "Cee-Cee Rider")..................10-20 62
HEP (2936 "Hidden Feelings")..................10-15
IMPERIAL (5709 "Miss Mary")...................10-15 60
INFINITY (024 "Soul City")..........................8-10 63
LIBERTY (55135 "Can't Stop Loving You")..10-15 58
LOMA (2030 "Girl Talk")................................5-8 66
MERCURY (70203 "House of the Blues")..20-30 52
MERCURY (70231 "Boogin' the Blues")..20-30 53
RCA (7452 "After Hours")............................8-12 58
RCA (7498 "Baby, Won't You Please Come Home")..8-12 59
RCA (7573 "Prayer of a Fool")....................8-12 59
RCA (7737 "Sheik of Araby").......................8-12 60

LPs: 10/12-inch

GOAD (1001 "Birth of a Scene")................20-30 62
Session: Plas Johnson.
Also see DOSWELL, Kittie "Miss Soul"
Also see JOHNSON, Plas

JOHNSON, Rex

Singles: 7-inch

KEM (2754 "Discombobulated")................50-75 58

JOHNSON, Rick

Singles: 7-inch

COMET (102 "Eenie Meenie")..............100-200 57
COMET (103 "One Mistake")....................25-35 59
COMET (104 "Me and My Baby")..............10-20 59
RICE (5055 "Please Don't Love Me")..........4-6 73
RICE (5061 "One More Plane")....................4-6 73
TNT (174 "At Last")....................................10-20 59

JOHNSON, Robert *LP '90*

Singles: 78 rpm

ORIOLE (7-04-60 "32-20 Blues")......3500-4500 37
VOCALION (03416 "Terraplane Blues")..3000-4000 37
VOCALION (03475 "I Believe I'll Dust My Broom")..3000-4000 37
VOCALION (03445 "32/20 Blues")...3000-4000 37
VOCALION (03519 "Crossroads Blues")..4000-5000 37
VOCALION (03563 "Come On in My Kitchen")..3000-4000 37
VOCALION (03601 "Sweet Home Chicago")..4000-5000 37
VOCALION (03623 "Hell Hound on My Trail")...5000-6000 37
VOCALION (03665 "Milkcow's Calf Blues")..3000-4000 37
VOCALION (03723 "Stones in My Passway")..3000-4000 37
VOCALION (04002 "Stop Breakin' Down Blues")..3000-4000 38
VOCALION (04108 "Me and the Devil Blues")..3500-4500 38
VOCALION (04630 "Love in Vain Blues")..3500-4500 38

LPs: 10/12-inch

COLUMBIA (1654 "King of the Delta Blues Singers")..400-600 61

COLUMBIA (1654 "King of the Delta Blues Singers")....8-12 81
COLUMBIA (30034 "Robert Johnson, Vol. 2")....15-25 70
COLUMBIA (46222 "The Complete Recordings")....10-15 90
ROOTS 'N' BLUES....5-8 90

JOHNSON, Rockheart

Singles: 78 rpm

RCA....10-20 52

Singles: 7-inch

RCA (4967 "Evilest Woman in Town")...75-100 52
RCA (5136 "Black Spider")....150-250 52

JOHNSON, Roland C&W '59

Singles: 7-inch

BRUNSWICK (55110 "I Traded Her Love")....10-20 59
TODD (1056 "I've Got Seven Notches on My Gun")....4-8 60

JOHNSON, Ronnie

Singles: 7-inch

RIVERSIDE (4550 "Little Mary")....10-15 63

JOHNSON, Roy Lee

(With Doctor Feelgood & Interns; with Villagers)

Singles: 7-inch

COLUMBIA (43286 "My Best Just Ain't Good Enough")....15-25 65
COLUMBIA (43529 "Two Doors Down"). 25-35 66
EPIC (2250 "Too Many Tears")....8-12 66
OKEH (7160 "Too Many Tears")....15-25 62
OKEH (7182 "Busybody")....15-25 63
JOSIE (965 "Boogaloo No. 3")....10-15 66
PHILIPS (40558 "She Put the Wammy on Me")....10-20 68
STAX (0144 "The Dryer")....5-8 72
Also see DOCTOR FEELGOOD

JOHNSON, Rozetta P&R/R&B '70

(Rosetta Johnson)

Singles: 7-inch

ATLANTIC (2297 "It's Nice to Know")....40-80 65
CLINTONE....5-8 70-71

JOHNSON, Ruby R&B '66

Singles: 7-inch

NEBS (505 "Here I Go Again")....20-30 65
VOLT (133 "I'll Run Your Hurt Away")....10-15 66
VOLT (140 "When My Love Comes Down")....10-15 66
VOLT (147 "If I Ever Needed Love")....10-15 67
V-TONE (222 "Pleadin' Heart")....15-20 60

JOHNSON, Sam "Suitcase"

Singles: 78 rpm

SITTIN' IN WITH (608 "Sam's Coming Home")....20-40 51

JOHNSON, Sherman

(With His Clouds of Joy)

Singles: 78 rpm

NASHBORO (507 "Back Alley Boogie")..20-30 51
TRUMPET (189 "Sugar Blues")....15-25 53
TRUMPET (190 "Hot Fish")....15-25 53

JOHNSON, Sonny, & Sunglows

Singles: 7-inch

BABY J (13943 "All Over Town")....20-30
CARIB (1025 "If You Don't Want My Love")....400-500

JOHNSON, Sonny Boy, & His Blue Blazers

Singles: 78 rpm

MURRAY (505 "Come and Go with Me")....50-100 48
MURRAY (507 "I'm Drinking My Last Drink")....50-100 48

JOHNSON, Stacy

(Stacie Johnson)

Singles: 7-inch

M-PAC (7230 "Stand Alone")....8-12 66
MODERN (1001 "Consider Yourself")....15-25 64
MOWEST (5047 "Woman in My Eyes")....4-8 73
SONY (113 "Remove My Doubts")....25-50 63
Also see SHARPEES
Also see TURNER, Ike & Tina

JOHNSON, Stan

(With the Blue Chips)

Singles: 7-inch

RUBY (280 "Six White Horses")....750-1000 57
RUBY (530 "Shimmy & Shake")....100-150 58
RUBY (550 "Baby, Baby Doll")....50-75 58
RUBY (67100 "Big Black Train")....50-60 55

JOHNSON, Stella

Singles: 7-inch

ABC (10063 "John Henry")....8-12 59
CONCERTONE (250 "The Trial of Stagger Lee")....10-15 59
KRC (304 "Yeah, Baby")....10-15 58
KRC (5003 "Restless Year")....10-15 59
VIN (1022 "The Ways of Love")....8-12 60

JOHNSON, Sweetpea

(Billy Strange)

Singles: 7-inch

LIBERTY (55315 "The Crawdad Scene").15-25 61
Also see STRANGE, Billy

JOHNSON, Syl P&R/R&B '67

Singles: 12-inch

BOARDWALK (99904 "Ms. Fine Brown Frame")....4-6 82

Singles: 7-inch

CHA CHA....10-20
EPIC....8-10
FEDERAL....15-25 59-62
HI....4-6 71-79
SHAMA (1235 "Goodie-Goodie-Good Times")....4-6 77
SPECIAL AGENT (20079 "Do You Know What Love Is")....15-25
TAG LTD. (1 "Surround")....15-25
TMP-TING (115 "I've Got to Get Over")....8-12 65
TWILIGHT....5-10 67-68
TWINIGHT....5-10 68-71

LPs: 10/12-inch

HI....8-10 73-75
TWINIGHT....10-15 68
Also see DEACONS

JOHNSON, Terry

Singles: 7-inch

GORDY (7091 "My Springtime")....50-100 69
GORDY (7095 "What 'Cha Gonna Do")...10-20 70

JOHNSON, Tim

Singles: 7-inch

LEO (784 "Yes Indeed")....20-30

JOHNSON, Vicki

(With the Vals)

Singles: 7-inch

UNIQUE LABORATORIES ("Bells Are Ringing")....400-500 62
(No selection number used.)
Also see VALS

JOHNSON, Wallace

Singles: 7-inch

A.F.O. (308 "Clap Your Hands")....10-20 62
SANSU (476 "Baby Go Ahead")....5-10 68

JOHNSON, Willie

(Bill Johnson)

Singles: 78 rpm

IMPERIAL (5163 "Tears Come Falling Down")....20-30 51
JADE (201 "Boogie in Blues")....20-30 51
JADE (209 "That Boy's Boogie")....20-30 52
REGAL (3318 "Mad Money Blues")....20-30 47
SAVOY....15-25 52
SITTIN' IN WITH (570 "Sampson Street Boogie")....20-30 50
SPECIALTY (493 "That Night")....10-20 54

Singles: 7-inch

SAVOY (881 "Here Comes My Baby")....35-50 52
SAVOY (894 "Sometimes I Wonder Why")....35-50 52
SPECIALTY (493 "That Night")....25-35 54

JOHNSON BOYS

Singles: 7-inch

BETHLEHEM (3076 "Come Along Julie")..5-10 63
BETHLEHEM (3082 "Little Girl")....5-10 64

LPs: 10/12-inch

BETHLEHEM (4013 "Singin' & Pickin' ")..10-15 63

JOHNSON BROTHERS

Singles: 7-inch

IMPERIAL (5550 "Find Another Heart")....10-20 58

JOHNSON BROTHERS

Singles: 7-inch

VALOR (2006 "Zombie Lou")....30-50 59

JOHNSON BROTHERS

Singles: 7-inch

CUCA (1024 "Like Rachel")....10-20 61
Members: Cliff Johnson; Chuck Johnson; John Cooke.

JOHNSON BROTHERS

Singles: 7-inch

(106242 "Roll Over Beethoven")....20-25
(No label name used.)
(108412 "My Woman, My Wife")....20-25
(No label name used.)

JOHNSTON, Bruce

Singles: 12-inch 33/45

COLUMBIA (10567 "Pipeline")....8-10 77

Singles: 7-inch

COLUMBIA (10568 "Pipeline")....4-6 77
DEL-FI (4202 "The Original Surfer Stomp")....10-15 63
(First pressings credit the Surf Stompers.)
DONNA (1354 "Do the Surfer Stomp")....15-20 62
(First pressings credit the Surf Stompers.)
DONNA (1364 "Soupy Shuffle Stomp")....15-20 62
DONNA (1374 "Original Surfer Stomp")...15-20 62
RONDA (1003 "Do the Surfer Stomp")....50-75 62

Picture Sleeves

DONNA (1354 "Do the Surfer Stomp")....40-50 62

LPs: 10/12-inch

COLUMBIA (2057 "Surfin' 'Round the World")....50-100 63
(Monaural.)
COLUMBIA (8857 "Surfin' 'Round the World")....75-150 63
(Stereo.)
COLUMBIA (34459 "Going Public")....10-15 77
DEL-FI (DFLP-1228 "Surfer's Pajama Party")....40-60 63
(Monaural.)
DEL-FI (DFST-1228 "Surfer's Pajama Party")....50-75 63
(Del-Fi 1228 also may be found as by the Centurians — or may credit both Bruce Johnston and the Centurians on the same cover. Copies also exist with one artist's name on the cover and the other on the disc.)
DEL-FI (DLF-1228 "Surfer's Pajama Party")....10-12 98
("Thick, hard wax" reissue.)
Members (Centurians): Dennis Rose; Ernie Furrow; Jeff Lear; Joe Dominic; Ken Robinson; Pat Gaguebin.
Also see CATALINAS
Also see BEACH BOYS
Also see BRUCE & TERRY
Also see GAMBLERS
Also see HOLDEN, Ron
Also see HOT DOGGERS
Also see KUSTOM KINGS
Also see SIDEWALK SURFERS
Also see SLED, Bob & Toboggans
Also see SURF STOMPERS
Also see VETTES

JOHNSTON, Chuck

Singles: 7-inch

BRUNSWICK (55154 "Stop Baby")....10-15 59
HOT (1001 "Weepin' & Wailin' ")....75-125 59

JOHNSTON, Colonel Jubilation B., & His Mystic Knights Band & Street Singers

LPs: 10/12-inch

COLUMBIA (2532 "Attack the Hits")....15-20 66
(Monaural.)
COLUMBIA (9332 "Attack the Hits")....15-25 66
(Stereo.)
Members: Col. B. Johnston; O.X. Bellyman; Sir Wallace Bile; "Swine" Halbstarker; Tonto Levine.
Session: Charlie McCoy; Henry Strzelecki; Kenneth Buttrey; Mac Gayden; Wayne Butler; "Taps" Tidwell; Jerry Smith; Brenton Banks; Hargus "Pig" Robbins; Durl Glin; Lamar Fike; Tummy Hill; Mortuary Thomasson; Norma Jean Owen; Swamp Women.
Also see McCOY, Charlie
Also see SMITH, Jerry

JOHNSTON, Don

Singles: 78 rpm

CHIC (1014 "Whistle Bait")....10-20 57
MERCURY (70991 "Born to Love One Woman")....15-25 56

Singles: 7-inch

CHIC (1014 "Whistle Bait")....10-20 57
MERCURY (70991 "Born to Love One Woman")....35-50 56

JOHNSTON, Inez, & Florios

Singles: 7-inch

BRUNSWICK (55169 "A Feeling")....15-20 60
BRUNSWICK (55218 "Change of Heart")....15-20 61
Also see FOXX, Inez

JOHNSTON, Jay

Singles: 7-inch

FREEDOM (44018 "Livin' Doll")....10-15 59
LIBERTY (55176 "Early Autumn")....10-15 59

JOHNSTON, Jim

Singles: 7-inch

MIDWEST (1002 "Mean Woman Blues")....75-125

JOHNSTON BROTHERS

(With Malcolm Lockyer & Orchestra; with Johnny Douglas & Orchestra)

Singles: 78 rpm

LONDON (1423 "The Creep")....5-10 54
LONDON (1470 "The Bandit")....5-10 54
LONDON (1769 "Seven Bar Blues")....15-20 57

Singles: 7-inch

LONDON (1423 "The Creep")....10-15 54
LONDON (1470 "The Bandit")....10-15 54
LONDON (1769 "Seven Bar Blues")....20-30 57

JOINER, ARKANSAS JUNIOR HIGH SCHOOL BAND P&R '60

(Ernie Freeman)

Singles: 7-inch

LIBERTY (55244 "National City")....10-15 59
LIBERTY (55276 "Arkansas Traveler")....10-15 60
LIBERTY (55341 "Highland Rock")....10-15 61
Also see FREEMAN, Ernie

JOINT EFFORT

Singles: 7-inch

JOINT EFFORT (1 "Children")....20-30 67
RUBY DOO (10 "Loving You Could Be Magic")....10-20 '60s
SPIRIT (127 "The Square")....10-20 '60s

JOINT EFFORT

LPs: 10/12-inch

AMPHION SEAHORSE (8100 "Cannabis")....50-80 72
Members: Keith Tweedly; Gary Wilkinson; Bob Randell; Tony Rodriguez; Brian Kelly; Lonny Gasperini.

JOKERS

Singles: 7-inch

LIN (5027 "Dogfight")....15-25 60
Members: Dave Spencer; Bob Welz; Don Hosek; Joe Cook; Ray Cochran.

JOKERS

(With the Aztec Combo)

Singles: 7-inch

DANCO (117 "I Do")....500-1000 60
Also see DARLENE & JOKERS

JOKERS

Singles: 7-inch

DRUMFIRE (3 "One Million B.C.")....10-20 60

JOKERS

Singles: 7-inch

GRACE (510 "Little Mama")....35-50 61
GRECO (609 "Little Mama")....5-10 80
(Red vinyl.)
GRECO (610 "I Ain't Gonna Be Your Fool")....5-10 80
(Red vinyl.)
WAND (111 "Whisper")....400-600 61
(Black vinyl.)
WAND (111 "Whisper")....500-1000 61
(Red vinyl.)

JOKERS

Singles: 7-inch

BRO-KET (101 "Arkansas Twist")....10-20 '60s

JOKERS WILD

Singles: 7-inch

METROBEAT (4451 "All I See Is You")...25-35 67
PEAK (4456 "Sunshine")....25-35 68
PEAK (4459 "Peace Man")....25-35 68
Also see RAVE-ONS

JOLLY, Clarence
Singles: 78 rpm
COBRA (5016 "Don't Leave Me") 75-100 57
Singles: 7-inch
COBRA (5016 "Don't Leave Me") 75-100 57

JOLLY, Jack
(Jack "Big Daddy" Jolly)
Singles: 7-inch
MUSIC TOWN (212 "Johnnie Skid Row").. 40-60
TOF (1909 "Club Delight")........................ 20-30

JOLLY, Pete *LP '63*
(Pete Jolly Trio & Friends)
Singles: 7-inch
A&M 4-6 68-69
ÄVA...5-10 63-64
COLUMBIA...4-8 66
MAINSTREAM 4-6 69
EPs: 7-inch
RCA (636 "Pete Jolly Trio")........................8-12 55
LPs: 10/12-inch
A&M 8-12 68-71
ÄVA.. 10-20 63-64
CHARLIE PARKER.................................. 15-20 62
COLUMBIA... 10-20 65
MGM 8-15 63
METROJAZZ... 15-25 60
RCA (1100 thru 1300 series).................. 20-30 55-57
TRIP 5-8 75
Also see MONTEZ, Chris
Also see NELSON, Rick

JOLLY GREEN GIANTS
Singles: 7-inch
REDCOAT (101 "Caught You Red Handed").. 15-25 66

JOLLY JAX
Singles: 7-inch
AIRMASTER 5-10
DASHER (501 "This Day") 5-10 61
MONTICELLO..5-10 62
V-TONE (233 "There's Something on Your Mind")... 15-25 62

JOLLY OLLIE
Singles: 7-inch
JOHNSON (128 "That's What True Love Can Do") 15-25 63

JON, Vickie
Singles: 7-inch
ACCENT (1212 "Tears of Love") 10-20 67

JON & ROBIN *P&R '67*
(With the In Crowd)
Singles: 7-inch
ABNAK (Black vinyl) 5-10 65-69
ABNAK (119 "Do It Again a Little Bit Slower")... 15-25 68
(Gold vinyl. Promotional issue only.)
ABNAK (127 "Dr. Jon the Medicine Man").. 15-25 68
(Gold vinyl. Promotional issue only.)
LPs: 10/12-inch
ABNAK (2068 "Soul of a Boy and Girl") 15-25 67
ABNAK (2070 "Elastic Event") 15-25 68
Members: Jon Abnor; Robin Abnor.
Also see ABNOR, Jon

JONES, A.C.
(With the Atomic Aces)
Singles: 7-inch
IMPERIAL (66150 "Hole in Your Soul")......5-10 66
LULA (5587 "Ooh Baby")........................ 15-25 '60s
LUAU (5588 "Hole in Your Soul")............ 10-20 63

JONES, Arnold
Singles: 78 rpm
CHANCE (1100 "Sometime")................... 25-50 51
Singles: 7-inch
CHANCE (1100 "Sometime")................. 75-100 51

JONES, Billy, & Squires
(Billy Fortune)
Singles: 7-inch
DECK (478 "Listen to Your Heart") 50-75
(Purple label. Previously issued as by Billy Fortune.)
Also see FORTUNE, Billy

JONES, Billy, & Teenettes
Singles: 7-inch
CARELLEN (102 "Night Angel")................20-25 61
NET (101 "I Would Never Dare") 15-20 61
Also see BETTY JAYNE & TEENETTES

JONES, Bob
Singles: 7-inch
DIXIE (1070 "I Want 'Cha Baby")..........100-125 60

JONES, Bob, & Bobcats
Singles: 7-inch
BO-JO (100 "Tennessee Twister")...........10-20 62

JONES, Brian
LPs: 10/12-inch
ROLLING STONES (49100 "Pipes of Pan") 10-15 71
Promotional LPs
ROLLING STONES (49100 "Pipes of Pan") 30-35 71
(Includes poster and cue sheets.)
Also see ROLLING STONES

JONES, Buster
Singles: 7-inch
PHIL-L.A. OF SOUL (331 "Down Silent Streets") 5-10 69
SURE SHOT (5022 "Baby Boy")..............10-20 66
SURE SHOT (5033 "I'm Satisfied")..........10-20 67

JONES, Calvert
Singles: 78 rpm
CORAL (65056 "Tra La La").....................10-20 51
Singles: 7-inch
CORAL (65056 "Tra La La").....................35-50 51

JONES, Charles
Singles: 78 rpm
WING (90068 "My Silent Heart")................5-10 56
Singles: 7-inch
SULLY (108 "Whoo-ee and O So Fine")...50-75
WING (90068 "My Silent Heart")..............10-20 56

JONES, Chuck
Singles: 7-inch
BELLE MEADE (119 thru 442).................20-30 60-61
BELLE MEADE (1118 "I Flip for You Baby")..100-200 '60s
MEADE (6959 "Rockin' Around").........100-200

JONES, Commonwealth
(Ronnie Dawson)
Singles: 7-inch
BANNER 15-25 63
COLUMBIA (42217 "Do Do Do")..............10-15 62
Also see DAWSON, Ronnie

JONES, Corky
(Buck Owens)
Singles: 78 rpm
DIXIE (505 "Rhythm & Booze")................50-75 56
PEP (107 "Hot Dog") 50-100 56
Singles: 7-inch
DIXIE (505 "Rhythm & Booze")............200-300 56
PEP (107 "Hot Dog")............................200-300 56
(Rerecorded in 1958, credited to Buck Owens.)
Also see OWENS, Buck

JONES, Curtis
Singles: 78 rpm
CONQUEROR (9030 "You Got Good Business")..25-50 37
OKEH 15-30 36-41
PARROT (782 "Cool Playing Blues")......50-100 53
VOCALION..10-20 '30s
Singles: 7-inch
PARROT (782 "Cool Playing Blues")....300-400 53
LPs: 10/12-inch
BLUE HORIZON (7703 "Now Resident in Europe")...10-12 69
DELMARK (605 "Lonesome Bedroom Blues") 20-25 63
PRESTIGE BLUESVILLE (1022 "Trouble Blues") 25-35 61
Also see MEMPHIS SLIM & CURTIS JONES

JONES, David
(With the Dolphins; Davy Jones Quartet; Davey Jones)
Singles: 7-inch
APT (25013 "Love Your Way")..................10-15 58
APT (25064 "Let's Do It") 8-12 62
ARGO (5271 "The Love I Missed")...........10-15 57
AUDICON (116 "The Bull Fight")..............10-15 61
AUDICON (117 "Love Is Strange") 10-15 61
CHART (641 "A Night to Remember")......10-20 57
CHART (647 "The Love I Missed") 10-20 57
DADE (1801 "Love Me Some More") 10-20 59
DADE (1835 "Baby Please Love Me").......5-10 63
GLADES (601 "No More Tears") 15-25 59
GLADES (605 "I Was Blind") 15-25 59
MARLIN (6062 "Our Love")......................40-50 59
OLD TOWN (1095 "Come On and Get It")..8-12 61
SHEPHERD (2205 "My Son, the Surfer") 15-25 63
SINCLAIR (1005 "Annabelle Lee") 15-25 61
TOWER 5-10 68
20TH FOX (243 "Can't Get a Date")..........8-12 61

JONES, Davy *P&R '65*
(David Jones)
Singles: 7-inch
BELL (45111 "Rainy Jane") 15-25 71
BELL (45136 "I Really Love You")............15-25 71
BELL (45159 "Girl")................................50-75 72
BELL (45178 "I'll Believe in You")............15-25 72
COLPIX (764 "Dream Girl").....................10-20 65
COLPIX (784 "What Are We Going to Do")...10-20 65
COLPIX (789 "Girl from Chelsea")............10-20 65
MGM 10-15 72-73
MY FAVORITE MONKEE–DAVY JONES SINGS ("A Little Bit Me, a Little Bit You") 50-100 67
(Promotional issue only. No selection number used.)
Picture Sleeves
COLPIX (764 "Dream Girl")......................20-30 65
COLPIX (784 "What Are We Going to Do")..20-30 65
COLPIX (789 "Girl from Chelsea")............20-30 65
LPs: 10/12-inch
BELL (6067 "Davy Jones").......................15-25 71
COLPIX (CP-493 "David Jones")..............25-35 65
(Monaural.)
COLPIX (SCP-493 "David Jones") 30-40 65
(Stereo.)
Also see NILSSON, Harry

JONES, Davy, & Mickey Dolenz
Singles: 7-inch
BELL (986 "Lady Jane")..........................10-15 71
MCA...4-6 78
Picture Sleeves
MCA...4-6 78

JONES, Davy, Mickey Dolenz, & Peter Tork
LPs: 10/12-inch
RHINO/FOSHOFF (71110 "20th Anniversary Tour")...20-30 87
Also see JONES, Davy
Also see DOLENZ, Micky
Also see MONKEES

JONES, Dennis
Singles: 7-inch
PLUG (3225 "Raindrops") 10-20 65
PLUG (3226 "I Can't Understand")..........10-20 65

JONES, Dizzy
Singles: 7-inch
CHART (701 "You Left Me Here to Cry") .10-15 57

JONES, Dollar Bill
(With the Tempters)
Singles: 7-inch
VICTORIA (231 "You Are That Someone")...15-25 '50s

JONES, Dottie
("The Pride of Texas"; with Winston O'Neal)
Singles: 78 rpm
TNT (134 "I'll Be Yours") 10-15 56
TNT (139 "Honey Honey") 20-30 56
Singles: 7-inch
TNT (134 "I'll Be Yours") 15-25 56
TNT (139 "Honey Honey") 50-75 56

JONES, Dow
Singles: 7-inch
CHATTAHOOCHEE (709 "Bring It On Home")..10-20 66
EXCHANGE (101 "True Fine Mama") 50-100

JONES, Eddie
(Eddie "Guitar Slim" Jones; with His Playboys)
Singles: 78 rpm
IMPERIAL (5134 "Bad Luck Is Upon Me")..30-50 51
J-B (603 "Feelin' Sad") 75-125 52
Singles: 7-inch
ABC-PAR (10513 "That Will Never Do") ..30-40 63
J-B (603 "Certainly All")........................125-175 52
J-B (Black vinyl) 4-6 79
J-B (Colored vinyl) 4-8 79
TITAN (1722 "My Friend").......................10-20 61
Also see GUITAR SLIM

JONES, Elaine, & Tri-Dells
Singles: 7-inch
ANGEL-TOWN ("They're Doin' It") 25-35
(Selection number not known.)

JONES, Etta *P&R/R&B '60*
Singles: 7-inch
KING...5-10 61-62
PRESTIGE..5-10 60-65
ROULETTE (4699 "Lonely Crowd") 5-10 66
20TH FOX/WESTBOUND............................4-6 75
LPs: 10/12-inch
GRAND PRIX ....10-15 '60s
KING (544 "Etta Jones Sings") 40-60 58
KING (707 "Etta Jones Sings") 35-50 61
MUSE 5-8 77-81
PRESTIGE (7100 & 7200 series) 25-50 60-63
(Yellow labels.)
PRESTIGE (7100 & 7200 series) 15-25 65
(Blue labels.)
PRESTIGE (7400 thru 7700 series) 10-20 67-70
ROULETTE..10-20 66
20TH FOX/WESTBOUND............................5-10 75
Also see JONES, Jonah, / Etta Jones / Earl "Fatha" Hines / Rodney Jones

JONES, Floyd
(With His Trio)
Singles: 78 rpm
CHESS (1498 "Dark Road") 50-100 52
CHESS (1527 "You Can't Live Long")....50-100 53
JOB (1001 "Big World")..........................50-100 52
Singles: 7-inch
JOB (1013 "Skinny Mama") 100-200 53
VEE-JAY (111 "Schooldays on My Mind") 100-200 55
(Black vinyl.)
VEE-JAY (111 "Schooldays on My Mind") 200-400 55
(Colored vinyl.)
VEE-JAY (126 "Floyd's Blues")............200-400 55
(Black vinyl.)
VEE-JAY (126 "Floyd's Blues")............500-750 55
(Colored vinyl.)

JONES, George *C&W '55*
(With the Jones Boys; with Sonny Burns; Tina & Daddy)
Singles: 78 rpm
DIXIE (534) 25-50 56
(With Sleepy La Beef. Title not known. 78 rpm EP. Not issued with cover.)
DIXIE (535) 25-50 56
(78 rpm EP. Not issued with cover.)
MERCURY...10-25 57
STARDAY 10-25 54-57
Singles: 7-inch
D 5-8 65-66
EPIC...5-10 72-88
GUSTO 3-5 83
MCA 3-5 91
MERCURY (71000 series).....................15-25 57-62
MERCURY (72000 series).......................6-12 62-64
MUSICOR...6-12 65-71
PROMOTIONAL COPIES ("The Race Is On") 20-25 64
(No label name other than "Promotional Copies," is shown on disc.)
RCA...4-8 72-74
STARDAY (Except 100 & 200 series) 4-8 64-71
STARDAY (100 & 200 series) 20-30 54-57
(Black vinyl.)
STARDAY (264 "Just One More") 40-60 56
(Red vinyl.)
U.A. 8-12 62-67
Picture Sleeves
EPIC (68743 "Ya Ba Da Ba Do") 20-30 88
(Black and white sleeve shows George Jones, Fred Flintstone and Elvis Presley.)
MERCURY..8-12 62-64
MUSICOR..8-12 65
U.A. 8-12 62-63
EPs: 7-inch
DIXIE (501 "Why Baby Why")..................25-50 56
(Not issued with cover.)

DIXIE (505 "Heartbreak Hotel")...25-50 56
(Not issued with cover.)
DIXIE (516 "Poor Old Me")...25-50 56
(Not issued with cover.)
DIXIE (525 "Don't Do This to Me")...15-25 59
(Has one George Jones track. Not issued with cover.)
MERCURY...10-20 61
RECORD OF THE MONTH (280 "Heartbreak Hotel")...30-40 56
(Colored vinyl.)
STARDAY...8-15 65
(Juke box issues. May include title strips.)

LPs: 10/12-inch

ACCORD...4-6 82
ALBUM GLOBE...5-8 81
ALLEGIANCE...4-8 84
AMBASSADOR...5-8
AURA...5-8 82
BUCKBOARD...5-8 76
BULLDOG...8-10
CAMDEN...5-8 72-74
COLUMBIA...5-8 80-83
EPIC...10-20 72-82
EVEREST...5-8 79
51 WEST...5-8 79-82
GRASS COUNTRY...8-10 '80s
GUEST STAR...8-12 63
GUSTO...5-8 78-81
I&M...5-8 82
KOALA...5-8
K-TEL...5-8
LIBERTY...5-8 82
MCA...3-5 91-92
MERCURY (8000 series)...5-10 72
MERCURY (20306 "14 Country Favorites")...40-60 58
MERCURY (20462 "Country Church Time")...40-60 59
MERCURY (20477 "White Lightning")...40-60 59
MERCURY (20621 thru 20836)...20-30 60-63
(Monaural.)
MERCURY (20906 thru 21048)...20-30 64-65
(Monaural.)
MERCURY (60257 thru 60836)...35-45 60-63
(Stereo.)
MERCURY (60906 thru 61048)...15-25 64-65
(Stereo.)
MOUNTAIN DEW...5-8
MUSICO...10-15 69-70
MUSICOR...10-20 65-77
MUSICOR/RCA...10-20 74-75
NASHVILLE...10-20 70-71
PAIR...6-10 '70s
PHOENIX 10...5-8 81
PHOENIX 20...5-8 81
PICCADILLY...5-8 81
PICKWICK...4-8 80
PICKWICK/HILLTOP...8-12 69
POWER PAK...5-8 75
RCA...10-20 72-75
ROUNDER...5-8 82-84
RUBY...5-8
SEARS...8-12
STARDAY (101 "The Grand Ole Opry's New Star")...100-150 58
STARDAY (102 "George Jones")...50-75 59
STARDAY (125 "George Jones: Crown Prince of Country Music")...50-75 60
STARDAY (150 "George Jones Sings His Greatest Hits")...40-60 62
STARDAY (151 "Fabulous Country Music Sound of George Jones")...40-60 62
STARDAY (335 "George Jones")...25-35 65
STARDAY (344 "Long Live King George")...25-35 65
STARDAY (366 "The George Jones Story")...25-35 66
(With bonus 8" x 10" color photo.)
STARDAY (366 "The George Jones Story")...15-25 66
(Without bonus photo.)
STARDAY (400 series, except 401)...15-20 69
STARDAY (401 "George Jones Song Book and Picture Album")...35-45 67
(With 32-page song booklet.)
STARDAY (401 "George Jones Song Book and Picture Album")...15-25 68
(Without song booklet.)
STARDAY (3000 series)...5-8 77
STARDAY (90000 series)...8-12
SUNRISE...5-8 81
TIME-LIFE...5-15 81-82
TRIP...5-8 76
TROLLY CAR...5-8
UNART...8-12 67-68
U.A. (85 "Superpak")...10-15 71
U.A. (100 series)...5-8 73
U.A. (3000 series)...12-25 62-67
(Monaural.)
U.A. (6000 series)...15-30 62-69
(Stereo.)
WHITE LIGHTNING...12-18
WING...8-12 64-68
WING/PICKWICK...5-8
Session: Jordanaires; Oak Ridge Boys.
Also see CHARLES, Ray, George Jones & Chet Atkins
Also see HAGGARD, Merle, & George Jones
Also see JONES, Thumper
Also see JORDANAIRES
Also see OAK RIDGE BOYS
Also see PARTON, Dolly / George Jones
Also see SMITH, Hank
Also see TUBB, Ernest, & Loretta Lynn / Tubb, Ernest, & George Jones
Also see WILLIAMS, Hank, Jr.

JONES, George / Benny Barnes

EPs: 7-inch

DIXIE (518 "Stolen Moments")...25-50 56
(Not issued with cover.)
Also see BARNES, Benny

JONES, George / David Houston / Sonny James

LPs: 10/12-inch

PICKWICK/HILLTOP (6015 "Country Jamboree")...10-15 '60s
Also see HOUSTON, David
Also see JAMES, Sonny

JONES, George, & Brenda Lee C&W '84

Singles: 7-inch

EPIC (04723 "Hallelujah, I Love You So")...3-5 84
Also see LEE, Brenda

JONES, George, & Brenda Carter C&W '68

Singles: 7-inch

MUSICOR (1325 "Milwaukee, Here I Come")...8-12 68

JONES, George, & David Allan Coe

Singles: 7-inch

COLUMBIA...3-6 81
Also see COE, David Allan

JONES, George, & Lacy J. Dalton C&W '85

Singles: 7-inch

EPIC (04876 "Size Seven Round")...3-5 85

JONES, George, & Jeanette Hicks C&W '57

Singles: 7-inch

STARDAY (279 "Yearning")...20-30 57

JONES, George, & Alan Jackson

Singles: 7-inch

MCA...3-5 '90s

JONES, George, & Shelby Lynne C&W '88

Singles: 7-inch

EPIC (08011 "If I Could Bottle This Up")...3-5 88

JONES, George, & Melba Montgomery C&W '63

Singles: 7-inch

CURIO...5-10 '60s
MUSICO...10-15 69-70
MUSICOR...8-12 66-67
U.A....10-15 63-66

Picture Sleeves

CURIO (7020 "You're in My Heart")...8-12 '60s

LPs: 10/12-inch

BUCKBOARD (1035 "Down Home")...5-8 76
GUEST STAR (1465 "George Jones & Melba Montgomery")...8-10 '60s
LIBERTY (10169 "What's in Our Hearts")...5-8 82
MUSICO (1004 "Great Country Duets")...8-12 69
MUSICOR (3109 "Close Together")...10-20 66
MUSICOR (3127 "Let's Get Together")...10-20 67
MUSICOR (3259 "George Jones & Melba Montgomery")...8-12 74
MUSICOR/RCA (3127 "Party Pickin' ")...8-12 74
(Repackage of *Let's Get Together*.)
U.A. (201 "Rollin' in My Sweet Baby's Arms")...5-8 73
U.A. (3301 "What's in Our Hearts")...15-25 63
(Monaural.)
U.A. (3352 "Bluegrass Hootenanny")...15-25 64
(Monaural.)
U.A. (3472 "Blue Moon of Kentucky")...15-25 66
(Monaural.)
U.A. (6301 "What's in Our Hearts")...20-30 63
(Stereo.)
U.A. (6352 "Bluegrass Hootenanny")...20-30 64
(Stereo.)
U.A. (6472 "Blue Moon of Kentucky")...20-30 66
(Stereo.)

JONES, George / Buck Owens / David Houston / Tommy Hill

LPs: 10/12-inch

NASHVILLE...10-15 '60s
Also see HOUSTON, David
Also see OWENS, Buck

JONES, George, & Johnny Paycheck C&W '80
(With Janie Fricke)

Singles: 7-inch

EPIC...3-6 78-80

LPs: 10/12-inch

EPIC (35783 "Double Trouble")...5-10 80
Also see FRICKE, Janie
Also see PAYCHECK, Johnny

JONES, George, & Gene Pitney C&W/LP '65
(With Jordanaires; George & Gene)

Singles: 7-inch

MUSICOR (1066 "I've Got Five Dollars and It's Saturday Night")...10-15 65
MUSICOR (1097 "Louisiana Man")...10-15 65
MUSICOR (1115 "Big Job")...10-15 65
MUSICOR (1165 "That's All It Took")...10-15 66

Picture Sleeves

MUSICOR (1115 "Big Job")...5-10 65

LPs: 10/12-inch

DESIGN (199 "George Jones & Gene Pitney")...8-12 '60s
(Red label.)
DESIGN (629 "George Jones & Gene Pitney")...5-8 '60s
(Gold label.)
INTERNATIONAL AWARD (263 "George Jones & Gene Pitney")...8-10
MUSICO (1006 "America's Greatest Country Songs")...10-15 69
MUSICOR (2044 "George Jones & Gene Pitney")...15-25 65
(Monaural. Front cover shows title as "For the First Time! Two Great Stars, George Jones & Gene Pitney.")
MUSICOR (2044 "George Jones & Gene Pitney")...15-20 65
(Monaural. Front cover shows title as "Recorded in Nashville, Tennessee, George Jones & Gene Pitney.")
MUSICOR (2065 "It's Country Time Again")...10-20 65
(Monaural.)
MUSICOR (3044 "George Jones & Gene Pitney")...20-30 65
(Stereo. Front cover shows title as "For the First Time! Two Great Stars, George Jones & Gene Pitney.")
MUSICOR (3044 "George Jones & Gene Pitney")...15-25 65
(Stereo. Front cover shows title as "Recorded in Nashville, Tennessee, George Jones & Gene Pitney.")
MUSICOR (3065 "It's Country Time Again")...15-25 65
(Stereo.)
TS (439 "Country Cousins")...5-10
Session: Jordanaires.
Also see JORDANAIRES
Also see PITNEY, Gene

JONES, George, Gene Pitney, & Melba Montgomery

LPs: 10/12-inch

MUSICOR (3079 "Famous Country Duets")...10-20 66
(Contains duets by these artists, but there are no tracks where all three perform together.)

JONES, George, & Margie Singleton C&W '61

Singles: 7-inch

MERCURY...4-8 61-62

LPs: 10/12-inch

MERCURY (20747 "Duets")...15-25 62
(Monaural.)
MERCURY (60747 "Duets")...25-35 62
(Stereo.)
WING (16331 "Duets")...10-15 66

JONES, George, & Tammy Wynette C&W/LP '71
(George, Tammy & Tina)

Singles: 7-inch

EPIC (10815 thru 11151)...4-8 71-74
EPIC (50099 thru 50949)...3-6 75-80

LPs: 10/12-inch

COLUMBIA SPECIAL PRODUCTS (14105 "George & Tammy")...5-10 77
COLUMBIA SPECIAL PRODUCTS (15769 "The President and the First Lady")...5-10 81
EPIC (30802 thru 33351)...8-12 71-75
EPIC (33752 "We Go Together/Me and the First Lady")...8-12 75
EPIC (34291 thru 37348)...5-10 76-81
TEE VEE/CBS (1005 "Greatest Hits")...5-8 79
Also see JONES, George
Also see WYNETTE, Tammy

JONES, Geraldine

Singles: 7-inch

SONAR (101 "I'm Cracking Up")...15-25

JONES, Grandpa C&W '59

Singles: 78 rpm

KING...5-10 44-54
RCA...4-8 52-54

Singles: 7-inch

DECCA (30823 "Pickin' Time")...5-10 59
DECCA (30904 "Don't Bring Your Banjo Home")...5-10 59
KING...4-8 60-63
MONUMENT...4-6 62-67

EPs: 7-inch

DECCA (2648 "Grandpa Jones")...5-10 59
KING...5-15 '50s

LP: 10/12-inch

CMH...5-10 76-81
CORAL...5-10 73
DECCA (4364 "Evening with Grandpa Jones")...15-25 63
HARMONY...6-12 72
KING (554 "Greatest Hits")...25-35 58
KING (625 "Strictly Country Tunes")...20-30 59
KING (809 "Rollin' Along")...15-25 63
KING (822 thru 1042)...10-20 63-69
MONUMENT...10-20 62-74
POWER PAK...5-10 '80s
VOCALION...8-12 70

JONES, Grandpa / Minnie Pearl

LP: 10/12-inch

CAMDEN...5-10 74
Also see JONES, Grandpa
Also see MINNIE PEARL

JONES, Grant R&B '51
(Grant "Mr. Blues" Jones & Brown's Blues Blowers)

Singles: 78 rpm

DECCA...15-25 50
STATES...15-25 53
UNITED...15-25 52

Singles: 7-inch

DECCA (48129 "For You, My Love")...50-75 50
DECCA (48133 "Crying Good Morning Blues")...50-75 50
DECCA (48163 "Hospitality Blues")...50-75 50
DECCA (48169 "It's Been a Long Time, Baby")...50-75 50
DECCA (48179 "Night Time Is the Right Time")...50-75 50
STATES (114 "Stormy Monday")...30-50 53
UNITED (112 "Strange Man")...30-40 52
UNITED (133 "Hello Stranger")...30-50 52

JONES, Herman, & Kilts
("Featuring Tony La Mar")

Singles: 7-inch

GAYNOTE (105 "I'll Be True")...100-150 61
(Pink label.)
GAYNOTE (105 "I'll Be True")...30-40 61
(Orange and yellow label.)
GAYNOTE (105 "I'll Be True")...15-25
(Green label.)

JONES, Hilliard

Singles: 7-inch

CORTLAND (101 "Prison of Love")...10-15 62
ERMINE (52 "Wish I Were the Wind")...10-15 64

JONES, Horace DeBussey

Singles: 7-inch

SATCHITANANDA (1 "The O.J. Simpson Show") ... 10-15 96
(With bonus lyrics sheet. 250 made.)
SATCHITANANDA (1 "The O.J. Simpson Show") ... 8-10 96
(Without bonus lyrics sheet. 250 made.)

JONES, Inez

Singles: 78 rpm

RCA (5135 "Take a Back Seat Mister Jackson") ... 8-12 53

Singles: 7-inch

OMEGA DISK (145 thru 153) ... 5-10 59
RCA (5135 "Take a Back Seat Mister Jackson") ... 20-30 53

JONES, J., & Northernaires

Singles: 7-inch

JAS (321 "I Don't Know Why") ... 30-40

JONES, Jack *P&R '62*

Singles: 7-inch

APPLAUSE (101 "Love Boat") ... 3-5 82
CAPITOL ... 5-10 59-60
KAPP ... 4-8 60-67
MGM/POLYDOR ... 4-6 '70s
POLYDOR ... 3-5 83
RCA ... 4-6 67-77

Picture Sleeves

CAPITOL (4164 "Make Room for the Joy") ... 10-15 59
KAPP ... 5-8 63-69

LPs: 10/12-inch

CAMDEN ... 5-8 73
CAPITOL (1274 "This Love of Mine") ... 20-30 59
CAPITOL (2100 "In Love") ... 10-20 64
KAPP ... 10-25 61-69
MCA ... 5-10 77
MGM ... 5-10 79
RCA ... 5-15 67-77
SEARS ... 5-10
Also see ANDREWS, Julie & Andre Previn / Vic Damone / Jack Jones / Marian Anderson
Also see ANN-MARGRET

JONES, Janie

Singles: 7-inch

AWARD (156/7 "You Said Goodbye") ... 10-15 59
JAMA (501 "Dear Diary") ... 30-40 61
SMASH (2026 "Witch's Brew") ... 5-10 66

JONES, Jim, & Chaunteys

Singles: 7-inch

MANCO (1068 "Kiwi Boogie") ... 10-20 65
PACEMAKER (242 "Playboy") ... 5-10 65

LPs: 10/12-inch

SUNGLOW ... 10-15

JONES, Jimmy *P&R '59*
(With the Jones Boys; with Savoys; Jimmie Jones; Jimmy "Handyman" Jones; with Sensationals)

Singles: 7-inch

ARROW (717 "Heaven in Your Eyes") 250-350 57
BELL (682 "39-21-40") ... 5-10 67
BELL (689 "True Love Ways") ... 5-10 67
CUB (9049 thru 9102) ... 10-20 59-61
DEKE (5413 "I Don't Mind Confessing") ... 5-10
EPIC (9339 "Whenever You Need Me") 75-125 59
MGM (154 "Handy Man"/"Good Timin' ") ... 4-8 63
(Golden Circle reissue series.)
PARKWAY (988 "Don't You Just Know It") ... 5-10 66
ROULETTE (4232 "Lover") ... 20-30 60
ROULETTE (4608 "Walkin' ") ... 5-10 64
SAVOY (1553 "Somebody Bigger Than You and I") ... 10-15 58
SAVOY (1586 "Say You're Mine") ... 10-15 60
SAVOY (1586 " Please Say You're Mine") ... 10-15 61
(Rerecorded. Has slightly different title.)
SAVOY (4116 thru 4126) ... 5-10 59
VEE-JAY (505 "Mr. Fix-It") ... 8-10 63

Picture Sleeves

CUB (9072 "That's When I Cried") ... 15-20 60

LPs: 10/12-inch

JEN JILLUS ... 5-10 77
MGM (E-3847 "Good Timin' ") ... 40-50 60
(Monaural.)
MGM (SE-3847 "Good Timin' ") ... 50-75 60
(Stereo.)
Also see SAVOYS
Also see SPARKS OF RHYTHM

JONES, Jimmy, & Pretenders
(Jimmie Jones & Pretenders)

Singles: 78 rpm

RAMA (207 "Lover") ... 40-50 56
RAMA (210 "Lover") ... 20-30 56

Singles: 7-inch

RAMA (207 "Lover") ... 100-200 56
RAMA (210 "Lover") ... 50-100 56
ROULETTE (4232 "Lover") ... 20-30 60
(Different version than on Rama.)
Also see JONES, Jimmy
Also see PRETENDERS

JONES, Jo
(With Lucky Thompson; with Jimmy Forrest; with Ray Bryant; Jo Jones Trio; Jo Jones Plus Two)

Singles: 7-inch

EVEREST (19361 "Little Susie") ... 5-10 60

EPs: 7-inch

EVEREST (5023 "Jo Jones Trio") ... 15-25 59

LPs: 10/12-inch

EVEREST (1023 "Jo Jones Trio") ... 20-30 59
(Stereo.)
EVEREST (1099 "Vamp Till Ready") ... 20-30 59
(Stereo.)
EVEREST (1110 "Percussion & Bass") ... 20-30 59
(Stereo.)
EVEREST (5023 "Jo Jones Trio") ... 30-40 59
(Monaural.)
EVEREST (5099 "Vamp Till Ready") ... 30-40 59
(Monaural.)
EVEREST (5110 "Percussion & Bass") ... 30-40 59
(Monaural.)
VANGUARD (8503 "Special") ... 50-100 56
VANGUARD (2031 "Jo Jones Plus Two") ... 30-40 59
(Monaural.)
VANGUARD (8525 "Jo Jones Plus Two") ... 40-50 59
(Stereo.)
Also see BRYANT, Ray
Also see FOREST, Jimmy

JONES, Joe *P&R/R&B '60*

Singles: 78 rpm

CAPITOL ... 8-15 54
HERALD ... 10-15 56

Singles: 7-inch

ABC ... 4-6 73
CAPITOL ... 10-20 54
HERALD (488 "You Done Me Wrong") ... 15-25 56
RIC (972 "You Talk Too Much") ... 15-20 60
ROULETTE ... 10-15 58-61

LPs: 10/12-inch

PRESTIGE ... 10-15 69
ROULETTE (R-25143 "You Talk Too Much") ... 25-30 61
(Monaural.)
ROULETTE (SR-25143 "You Talk Too Much") ... 30-40 61
(Stereo.)

JONES, John Paul
(John Paul Jones Orchestra)

Singles: 7-inch

PARKWAY (915 "Baja") ... 20-30 64

LPs: 10/12-inch

COLUMBIA (32047 "John Paul Jones") ... 20-30 73
Also see LED ZEPPELIN

JONES, Johnn "Boris"
(John "Boris" Jones / John Burrton)

Singles: 7-inch

DORE (682 "Surfer Smash") ... 15-25 63

JONES, Jonah *LP '58*
(Jonah Jones Quartet; with Constellations)

Singles: 78 rpm

GROOVE ... 8-12 56

Singles: 7-inch

BETHLEHEM ... 4-8 58-62
CAPITOL ... 4-8 58-63
DECCA ... 4-6 65
GROOVE (0140 "Come Sit by Me") ... 30-40 56
MOTOWN (1144 "For Better Or Worse") ... 50-100 69

EPs: 7-inch

BETHLEHEM ... 5-15 55
CAMDEN ... 5-8 69
CAPITOL ... 5-10 58-59
RCA ... 5-10 59

LPs: 10/12-inch

ANGEL ... 20-30 56
BETHLEHEM ... 20-40 55-60
CAPITOL (1000 thru 2800 series) ... 10-25 58-67
(With "T" or "ST" prefix.)
CAPITOL (1600 series) ... 5-8 77
(With "SM" prefix.)
CAPITOL (11000 series) ... 5-8 75
DECCA ... 10-20 65-67
GROOVE ... 30-40 56
INNER CITY ... 5-8 81
MOTOWN (683 "Along Came Jonah") ... 30-50 69
MOTOWN (690 "Dis & Dat") ... 30-50 69
RCA ... 15-25 59-63
Also see CHRISTY, June
Also see SINATRA, Frank / Jonah Jones

JONES, Jonah, / Etta Jones / Earl "Fatha" Hines / Rodney Jones

LPs: 10/12-inch

CROWN (422 "Swings and Sings") ... 5-10 65
Also see JONES, Etta

JONES, Joyce

Singles: 7-inch

ATCO (6681 "Help Me Make Up My Mind") ... 10-15 69
V-8 (10001 "Help Me Make Up My Mind") ... 15-25

JONES, L. Sammy, & Eldorados

Singles: 7-inch

LIFETIME (1011 "Baby") ... 100-200 60

JONES, Lee

Singles: 7-inch

FLAME (633 "Cool, Cool Daddy") ... 50-75

JONES, Lefty

Singles: 7-inch

CADENCE (1395 "Tennessee Molly") ... 10-20 60

JONES, Leroy

Singles: 7-inch

GIANT (1001 "Peppermint Twist") ... 10-15 62
GIANT (1002 "Check Mr. Popeye") ... 8-12 62
GIANT (1004 "Slow Twistin' ") ... 10-15 62
HIT ... 5-10 64

JONES, Letha, & Rivals

Singles: 7-inch

ANNA (1113 "I Need You") ... 50-75 60
(Released with two different b-sides.)

JONES, Libby

LPs: 10/12-inch

STRAND (1072 "Strip Along with Us") ... 25-40 63

JONES, Linda *P&R/R&B '67*
(With the Whatnauts)

Singles: 7-inch

ATCO (6344 "I'm Taking Back My Love") 15-25 65
BLUE CAT (128 "Hit Me Like TNT") ... 15-25 66
LOMA (2070 thru 2105) ... 5-10 67-68
NEPTUNE ... 4-8 69
STANG (5039 "World Solution") ... 4-8 72
TURBO ... 4-6 71-72
W.B. (7278 "My Heart") ... 15-25 69

LPs: 10/12-inch

LOMA (5907 "Hyptomized") ... 20-30 67
TURBO ... 10-15 72
Also see LANE, Linda

JONES, Linda / Bessie Banks

Singles: 7-inch

COTIQUE (177 "Fugitive from Luv"/"Go Now") ... 10-15 69
Also see BANKS, Bessie
Also see JONES, Linda

JONES, Little Johnny
(Little Johnny & the Chicago Hound Dogs; Little Johnny)

Singles: 78 rpm

ARISTOCRAT (405 "Big Town Playboy") ... 50-100 50
ATLANTIC (1045 "Hoy, Hoy") ... 20-40 54
FLAIR (1010 "Sweet Little Woman") ... 50-75 53

Singles: 7-inch

ATLANTIC (1045 "Hoy, Hoy") ... 50-75 54
FLAIR (1010 "Sweet Little Woman) ... 150-250 53
(Credited to Jones but by Elmore James. Jones was Elmore's pianist.)
Session: Muddy Waters; Leroy Foster; J.T. Brown; Odie Payne.
Also see JAMES, Elmore
Also see WATERS, Muddy

JONES, Little Montie

Singles: 7-inch

JENN (100 "You're Just That Kind") ... 450-550 59
JENN (101 "Moonshine") ... 75-125 59

JONES, Little Sonny

Singles: 7-inch

IMPERIAL (5275 "I Got Booted") ... 50-75 53
IMPERIAL (5287 "Winehead Baby") ... 50-75 53
SPECIALTY (443 "Everything All Right") . 40-60 51

JONES, Little Willie

Singles: 7-inch

VRC (115 "When Will I Stop Loving You") ... 15-25

JONES, Mad Man

Singles: 7-inch

CAMEO (146 "Oh Henry") ... 10-15 58
M&M ... 10-15
MAD (1207 "Oh Henry") ... 15-25 58

JONES, Mari
(With Johnny Moore)

Singles: 78 rpm

RECORDED IN HOLLYWOOD ... 10-20 53

Singles: 7-inch

JET (102 "Riba Diba Doo"/"Teenage Quarrel") ... 250-350 56
RECORDED IN HOLLYWOOD (409 "There Is No Greater Love") ... 20-30 53
RECORDED IN HOLLYWOOD (424 "Keep Cool") ... 20-30 53
TAMPA (117 "Riba Diba Doo"/"Don't Cry") ... 100-200 57
TAMPA (122 "Riba Diba Doo"/"Teenage Quarrel") ... 200-300 57
Also see MOORE, Johnny

JONES, Mike, Group

Singles: 7-inch

JET (4001 "Funny Feelings") ... 20-30 67

JONES, Minnie, & Minuettes

Singles: 7-inch

SUGAR (100 "Shadow of a Memory") .. 100-125

JONES, Nyles

Singles: 7-inch

GEMINI (101 "Welfare Blues") ... 15-25

JONES, Oliver

Singles: 78 rpm

GEE (4 "What I Say") ... 10-15 54

Singles: 7-inch

GEE (4 "What I Say") ... 15-20 54

JONES, Palmer

Singles: 7-inch

EPIC (10321 "Dancing Master") ... 10-15 68

JONES, Quincy *LP '62*
(With Toots Thielemans)

Singles: 7-inch

A&M (1115 thru 1878) ... 4-8 69-76
A&M (1909 thru 2309) ... 3-8 77-81
A&M (9288 "Quincy Jones") ... 50-75 78
(Octagon picture disc. Promotional issue only.)
ABC ... 5-10 68
BELL ... 5-10 69
COLGEMS (1016 "Hangin' Paper") ... 5-10 68
IMPULSE (206 "Quintessence") ... 5-10 62
MERCURY (71425 thru 72105) ... 8-12 59-63
MERCURY (72160 thru 72533) ... 5-10 63-66
RCA ... 5-10 69
REPRISE ... 4-6 72
UNI ... 5-10 69
U.A. ... 4-8 70

Picture Sleeves

A&M (1743 "Is It Love That We're Missin' ") 4-6 75
A&M (1909 "Roots Medley") ... 4-6 77
COLGEMS (1016 "Hangin' Paper") ... 10-15 68
(Sleeve pictures characters from the film *In Cold Blood*.)

LPs: 10/12-inch

A&M ... 5-15 69-82
ABC (782 "Mode") ... 10-15 73
(Two discs.)
ABC-PAR (149 "How I Feel About Jazz") ... 75-100 56
ABC-PAR (186 "Go West, Man") ... 75-100 57
ALLEGIANCE ... 5-8 84

BELL (1200 "Bob & Carol & Ted & Alice") 12-18 70
BELL (1201 "Cactus Flower") 12-18 70
COLGEMS (107 "In Cold Blood") 20-30 68
EMARCY (36083 "Jazz Abroad") 75-100 56
IMPULSE (11 "Quintessence") 15-25 62
IMPULSE (9300 series) 8-12 78
LIBERTY (16004 "Enter Laughing") 15-25 67
(Monaural.)
LIBERTY (17004 "Enter Laughing") 20-30 67
(Stereo.)
MFSL (078 "You've Got It Bad") 30-40 82
MERCURY (623 "Ndeda") 15-20 72
MERCURY (2014 "Around the World") 20-30 61
(Monaural.)
MERCURY (20444 "Birth of a Band") 40-50 59
(Monaural.)
MERCURY (20561 "Great, Wide World") 40-50 60
(Monaural.)
MERCURY (20612 "I Dig Dancers") 40-50 60
(Monaural.)
MERCURY (20653 "Quincy Jones at Newport '61") 20-30 61
(Monaural.)
MERCURY (20751 "Big Band Bossa Nova") 20-30 62
(Monaural.)
MERCURY (20799 "Hip Hits") 20-30 63
(Monaural.)
MERCURY (20863 thru 21070) 10-20 64-66
(Monaural.)
MERCURY (6014 "Around the World") 25-35 61
(Stereo.)
MERCURY (60444 "Birth of a Band") 45-60 59
(Stereo.)
MERCURY (60561 "Great, Wide World") 45-55 60
(Stereo.)
MERCURY (60612 "I Dig Dancers") 45-55 60
(Stereo.)
MERCURY (60653 "Quincy Jones at Newport '61") 25-35 61
(Stereo.)
MERCURY (60751 "Big Band Bossa Nova") 25-35 62
(Stereo.)
MERCURY (60799 "Hip Hits") 25-35 63
(Stereo.)
MERCURY (60863 thru 61070) 15-25 64-66
NAUTILUS (52 "The Dude") 15-25 82
PRESTIGE (172 "Sweden-American All Stars") 200-250 53
(10-inch LP.)
QWEST 5-8 89
TRIP 5-8 74-76
U.A. (5214 "They Call Me Mr. Tibbs") 10-15 70
VERVE (8679 "Deadly Affair") 20-30 67
WING (16398 "Around the World") 6-12 69
Session: Brothers Johnson; Joe Newman.
Also see ASHFORD & SIMPSON
Also see AUSTIN, Patti
Also see ECKSTINE, Billy, & Quincy Jones
Also see FELICIANO, Jose, & Quincy Jones
Also see JACKSON, Michael
Also see MAYS, Willie, & Treniers
Also see SINATRA, Frank, with Quincy Jones & His Orchestra
Also see THIELEMANS, Toots
Also see VAUGHAN, Sarah, & Quincy Jones
Also see WASHINGTON, Dinah

JONES, Quincy, & Tevin Campbell *P&R '90*
Singles: 7-inch
QWEST (19881 "Tomorrow") 3-5 90

JONES, Quincy, Ray Charles & Chaka Khan *P&R '89*
Singles: 7-inch
QWEST (22697 "I'll Be Good to You") 3-5 89
Picture Sleeves
QWEST (22679 "I'll Be Good to You") 3-5 89
Also see CHARLES, Ray

JONES, Quincy, & James Ingram *P&R/R&B '81*
Singles: 7-inch
A&M (2357 "Just Once") 3-5 81
A&M (2387 "One Hundred Ways") 3-5 81

JONES, Quincy, James Ingram, Al B. Sure, El DeBarge & Barry White *P&R '90*
Singles: 7-inch
QWEST 3-5 90
Picture Sleeves
QWEST 3-5 90
Also see JONES, Quincy, & James Ingram
Also see WHITE, Barry

JONES, Quincy, & Letta Mbulu
Singles: 7-inch
A&M (1909 "Roots Mural Theme") 4-6 77
Also see JONES, Quincy
Also see MBULU, Letta

JONES, Rev. Jim
LPs: 10/12-inch
CHRISTIAN CRUSADERS (2017 "Message for the Total Man") 25-50
("Last Supper") 40-60
(Picture disc. Label name and selection number not known.)

JONES, Ricky
Singles: 7-inch
HERALD (498 "Hate to Say Goodbye") 40-60 57

JONES, Rocky
Singles: 7-inch
WASP (108 "Mule Skinner Blues") 40-60

JONES, Romeo
Singles: 7-inch
LITTLE STAR (119 "How 'Bout That") 15-25 62
Session: H.B. Barnum.
Also see BARNUM, H.B.

JONES, Ron
(With the 'C' Notes)
Singles: 7-inch
AURORA (1008 "When We Were Young and in Love") 10-15 62
MOBIE (3419 "Goodbye Linda") 20-30 66

JONES, Ronnie
Singles: 7-inch
PAN-OR (1126 "Falling Tears") 25-35
SMASH (2047 "Satisfy My Soul") 8-12 66

JONES, Ronnie, & Classmates
Singles: 7-inch
END (1002 "Little Girl Next Door") 75-125 57
END (1014 "Lonely Boy") 50-100 58
END (1125 "Teenage Rock") 10-15 63

JONES, Rosey, & Superiors
Singles: 7-inch
WICKETT (61472 "All I Need Is Half a Chance") 30-40

JONES, Roy
Singles: 7-inch
GLO-LIGHT (99 "Your Pilot Light Went Out") 50-75

JONES, Roy, & Shells
Singles: 7-inch
SWIRL (101 "Satisfied") 25-35 60

JONES, Rufus
LPs: 10/12-inch
CAMEO (1076 "Five On Eight") 12-15 64

JONES, Sam, Satch Sanders, & K.C. Jones
Singles: 7-inch
CEL (501 "Basketball Twist") .... 25-35 '60s

JONES, September
Singles: 7-inch
KAPP (802 "I'm Coming Home") 20-30 66

JONES, Sonny
Singles: 7-inch
CHART (601 "My Baby's Crying") 15-25 54
MALA (534 "Just Me") 5-10 66

JONES, Spike *P&R '42*
(With His City Slickers)
Singles: 78 rpm
BLUEBIRD 10-20 42-43
RCA 5-15 46-55
VICTOR 8-12 44-45
Singles: 7-inch
LIBERTY 5-10 59-65
MUSICAL POSTCARD .... 15-25 '50s
(Cardboard picture disc series.)
RCA (0030 "Cocktails for Two") .... 10-20 '50s
(Silver label, "Collector's Issue.")
RCA (0500 series) 4-6 71
RCA (3287-89 "Spike Jones Favorites") 40-60 49
(Boxed, three-disc set.)
RCA (2900 thru 6000 series) 10-20 49-55
(Black vinyl.)
RCA (Colored vinyl) .... 20-40 '50s
(We're not sure which specific numbers are colored vinyl.)
RCA (WY 417 "Christmas Fun with Spike Jones") 10-20 50
(Yellow vinyl. Little Nipper Junior Series.)
W.B. (5116 "Monster Movie Ball") 5-10 59
Picture Sleeves
RCA (5067 "I Saw Mommy Kissing Santa Claus") 20-30 53
RCA (5742 "I'm in the Mood for Love") 20-30 54
EPs: 7-inch
RCA 20-30 51-59
VERVE 15-25 56-57
LPs: 10/12-inch
GLENDALE 5-8 78
LIBERTY 15-25 60-65
MGM 8-12 70
PICKWICK 8-12
RCA (18 "Spike Jones Plays the Charleston") 50-100 51
RCA (1000 series) 5-10 75
RCA (2200 series) 20-25 60
RCA (2300 series) 5-10 77
RCA (3054 "Bottoms Up") 40-60 52
RCA (3128 "Spike Jones Kids the Classics") 40-60 53
RCA (3200 series) 8-12 71
RCA (3700 series) 4-8 80
RCA (3800 series) 10-15 67
(With "LPM" or "LSP" prefix.)
RCA (3800 series) 5-8 81
(With "AYL1" prefix.)
TIARA 8-12
U.A. 5-10 75
VERVE (Except 8500 series) 20-40 56-59
VERVE (8500 series) 12-20 63
W.B. 15-25 59-60
Session: Homer & Jethro.
Also see HOMER & JETHRO
Also see INGLE, Red, & Natural Seven
Also see KATZ, Mickey, & His Orchestra

JONES, Stan
Singles: 7-inch
DISNEYLAND (64 "Theme from *Sheriff of Cochise*"/"Theme from *Cheyenne*") 8-12 57
Picture Sleeves
DISNEYLAND (64 "Theme from *Sheriff of Cochise*"/"Theme from *Cheyenne*") 15-25 57
(Pictures TV series stars John Bromfield and Clint Walker.)

JONES, Sunny
Singles: 78 rpm
ORCHID (1211 "Don't Want Pretty Women") 50-100 50

JONES, Sweetie
Singles: 7-inch
FOX (3 "Oh Yeah") 50-75 58
NRC (017 "Cheryl Ann") 15-25 58
SCOTTIE (1312 "Baby Please Don't Leave") 75-125 60

JONES, Thumper
(George Jones)
Singles: 78 rpm
STARDAY (240 "Rock-It") 50-75 56
Singles: 7-inch
STARDAY (240 "Rock-It") 350-450 56
(Black vinyl.)
STARDAY (240 "Rock-It") 500-750 56
(Red vinyl.)
EPs: 7-inch
DIXIE (502 "Thumper Jones") 20-30 58
(Contains three Jones tracks. Not issued with cover.)
LPs: 10/12-inch
TEENAGE HEAVEN 8-12
Also see JONES, George

JONES, Tom *P&R/R&B/LP '65*
Singles: 7-inch
EPIC/MAM 4-8 76-80
LONDON 4-6 77
MCA 3-6 79
MERCURY 3-6 81-85
PARROT (9737 thru 9809) 8-12 65-66
PARROT (40000 series) 5-10 66-73
SYMBOL (205 "Nothing But Fine") 10-15 65
TOWER (126 thru 190) 10-15 65
Picture Sleeves
PARROT (9765 "What's New Pussycat") 10-20 65
PARROT (9787 "With These Hands") 10-20 65
PARROT (9801 "Thunderball") 10-20 65
PARROT (40000 series) 5-10 69-71
EPs: 7-inch
PARROT 5-10
(Juke box issues only. Includes title strips.)
LPs: 10/12-inch
EPIC 8-12 70-77
LONDON 5-10 77
MERCURY 5-10 81-85
PARROT 10-25 65-74

JONES, Tom / Freddie & Dreamers / Johnny Rivers
LPs: 10/12-inch
TOWER (5007 "Three at the Top") 15-25 65
Also see FREDDIE & DREAMERS
Also see JONES, Tom
Also see RIVERS, Johnny

JONES, Toni
Singles: 7-inch
SMASH (1814 "Love Is Strange") 25-35 63

JONES, Van
Singles: 7-inch
CONWAY (50138 "I Want to Groove You") 20-30

JONES, Wade
Singles: 7-inch
RAYBER (1001 "I Can't Concentrate") 200-300 59

JONES, Wailin' J.
Singles: 7-inch
FABLE ("Rock n' Roll Dice") 50-75
(Selection number not known.)

JONES, Will, & Cadets
Singles: 78 rpm
MODERN (1024 "Hands Across the Table") 15-25 57
Singles: 7-inch
MODERN (1024 "Hands Across the Table") 15-25 57
Also see CADETS

JONES, Willie
(Doc Jones; with Liza Smith)
Singles: 78 rpm
PEACOCK 10-15 50
Singles: 7-inch
BIG TOP (3050 "Mary") 8-12 60
METRO (20030 "Fast Choo Choo") 5-10 59
MR. PEACOCK (104 "Don't Leave Me") 10-15 62
SAVOY (1173 "My Promise") 10-15 55
UPSET (003 "Memories") 10-20
Also see SMITH, Liza

JONES BOYS
(With Ray Heath & His Orchestra)
Singles: 78 rpm
LIBERTY (55046 "Anastasia") 5-10 56
S&G 10-15 54-55
Singles: 7-inch
LIBERTY (55046 "Anastasia") 10-15 56
LIBERTY (55062 "Cherry Red") 10-15 57
LIBERTY (55093 "Good Night") 10-15 57
R-DELL (112 "The Song Is Ended") 5-10 59
S&G (5006 "Sweet and Low") 20-30 54
S&G (5007 "The Song Is Ended") 30-40 54
S&G (5008 "Marry a Rich Woman") 10-20 54
S&G (5009 "I Don't Stand a Chance with You") 30-40 55

JONES BROTHERS
Singles: 78 rpm
SUN (213 "Every Night") 200-300 54

JONES BROTHERS
Singles: 78 rpm
SILVER (100 "So Much Love") 5-10 50
Singles: 7-inch
SILVER (100 "So Much Love") 15-25 50

JONES BROTHERS
Singles: 7-inch
BELL (831 "That's All Over Baby")...8-12 69
SEEL (10 "That's All Over Baby")...25-30

JONSEY'S COMBO
Singles: 78 rpm
COMBO (79 "Ting Ting Boom Scat")...10-15 55
Singles: 7-inch
COMBO (79 "Ting Ting Boom Scat")...15-25 55

JOPLIN, Janis *P&R/LP '69*
(With Big Brother & Full Tilt)
Singles: 7-inch
COLUMBIA...4-8 69-72
SIMON & SHUSTER ("Janis")...3-5
(Soundsheet. Included with the book *Janis*.)
LPs: 10/12-inch
COLUMBIA (KCS-9913 "I Got Dem 'Ol Kozmic Blues Again, Mama")...20-25 69
COLUMBIA (PC-9913 "I Got Dem 'Ol Kozmic Blues Again, Mama")...5-8
COLUMBIA (30000 series)...10-15 71-75
(With "C2," "KC" or "PG" prefix.)
COLUMBIA (30000 series)...12-20 74
(With "CQ" prefix. Quad.)
COLUMBIA (30000 series)...5-8 82-84
(With "PC" prefix.)
MEMORY...5-10
Also see BIG BROTHER & HOLDING CO.

JOPLIN, Janis / Hot Tuna
LPs: 10/12-inch
GRUNT ("The Last Interview")...25-35 72
(Promotional issue only. Includes bonus Joplin home recording.)
Also see JOPLIN, Janis

JORDAN, Danny
Singles: 7-inch
CLIMAX (106 "Princess")...20-30 59
LEADER (811 "He Couldn't Resist Her with Her Pocket Transistor")...10-15 60
SMASH (1711 "Jeannie")...5-10 61

JORDAN, Don
Singles: 7-inch
SHAD (5014 "Hypnotized")...10-15 59

JORDAN, Jeri, & Jack Lewis
Singles: 7-inch
VITA (156 "Is That Bad")...15-25 57

JORDAN, Jimmy
Singles: 7-inch
NEW PHOENIX (6201 "Teenage Tears")...10-20 62
ROULETTE (4500 "My Girl")...10-20 63
ROULETTE (4501 "Tick Tock")...10-20 63
20TH FOX (436 "Some Kind of Girl")...10-20 63

JORDAN, Jimmy & Connie
Singles: 7-inch
AGAPE (9002 "Guess I Never Had It So Good")...20-25

JORDAN, Johnny
(John Faircloth)
Singles: 7-inch
JOLT (332 "Sweet, Sweet, Sweet")...50-75 59
Also see BROOKS, Donnie

JORDAN, Joy, & Jets
Singles: 7-inch
ORPHEUS (1103 "Keep Cool")...50-100 56
(At least one source shows this number as 1102; however, we have 1102 as being one side of a Bombers release. Confirmation either way would be welcome.)

JORDAN, Juanita
Singles: 7-inch
LAURIE (3235 "Some Sweet Day")...15-25 64
NOR VA JAK (1324 "Some Sweet Day")...25-35 59

JORDAN, King
LPs: 10/12-inch
CORAL (57372 "Phantom Guitar")...10-15 62

JORDAN, Lou
(With the Billy Mure Orchestra)
Singles: 7-inch
JOSIE (888 "Paradise for Two")...150-200 61
(Tan label.)
JOSIE (888 "Paradise for Two")...100-150 61
(White label. Promotional issue only.)
JOSIE (903 "Just to Look at You")...8-12 63
MUSICNOTE (122 "Just to Look at You")...8-12 64
20TH FOX (406 "Just to Look at You")...5-10 64
Also see CHAPERONES
Also see MURE, Billy

JORDAN, Louis *R&B '42*
(Louis Jordan's Elk Rendezvous Band; with His Tympani 5)
Singles: 78 rpm
ALADDIN...5-10 54
DECCA (7500 thru 8600 series)...5-15 38-43
DECCA (18000 thru 30000 series, except 28211)...5-10 44-54
DECCA (28211 "Junco Partner")...10-20 52
VIK...5-10 56
Singles: 7-inch
ALADDIN (3223 thru 3279, except 3243)...20-30 54
ALADDIN (3243 "A Dollar Down")...25-35 54
DECCA (20000 thru 30000 series, except 28211)...15-25 50-54
DECCA (28211 "Junco Partner")...30-50 52
LOU-WA...10-15 60
MERCURY...10-20 56-58
PZAZZ...4-8 68-69
TANGERINE...5-10 62-66
VIK...10-20 56
WARWICK...8-12 60-61
"X"...10-20 55
EPs: 7-inch
DECCA...15-25 56
MERCURY...15-25 57
LPs: 10/12-inch
CLASSICAL JAZZ...5-8 82
DECCA (5035 "Greatest Hits")...10-20 68
DECCA (8551 "Let the Good Times Roll")...30-40 56
MCA...5-8 75-80
MERCURY (20242 "Somebody Up There Digs Me")...25-30 57
MERCURY (20331 "Man, We're Wailin'")...25-30 58
SCORE (4007 "Go Blow Your Horn")...75-125 57
TANGERINE...10-20 64
TRIP...8-10 75
WING...15-20 63
Also see ARMSTRONG, Louis, & Louis Jordan
Also see CROSBY, Bing, & Louis Jordan
Also see DAVIS, Martha
Also see FITZGERALD, Ella, & Louis Jordan
Also see STURGIS, Rodney

JORDAN, Will
(With the Sicknicks)
Singles: 7-inch
HANOVER (4529 "Bye Bye Love")...10-15 59
JUBILEE (900 "Roast of the Town")...10-15 '50s
Picture Sleeves
JUBILEE (900 "Roast of the Town")...15-25 '50s
LPs: 10/12-inch
AMY (2 "Sick, No. 2")...20-30 61
JUBILEE (2032 "Ill Will")...20-30 61

JORDAN, Willie, & His Swinging Five
(Champion Jack Dupree)
Singles: 78 rpm
ALERT (207 "Cecelia Cecelia")...50-75 46
Also see DUPREE, Champion Jack

JORDAN & FASCINATIONS
(With the Sal Ditroia Orchestra)
Singles: 7-inch
CAROL (4116 "Once Upon a Time")...15-25 61
DAPT (203 "I'll Be Forever Loving You")...30-40 61
(With straight horizontal lines.)
DAPT (203 "I'll Be Forever Loving You")...15-25 61
(With jagged horizontal lines.)
DAPT (207 "Love Will make Your Mind Go Wild")...30-40 61
(With straight horizontal lines.)
DAPT (210 "She's Gone")...4-6 95
(Blue vinyl. 500 made.)
JOSIE (895 "If You Love Me, Really Love Me")...30-40 62

JORDAN BROTHERS
(Jordan)
Singles: 7-inch
CAMEO (370 "Good Love Goes Bad")...5-10 65
CHELTENHAM...5-10 65
GOLDEN CHARIOT (7000 series)...5-10 68
GOLDEN CHARIOT (73000 series)...5-8 68
HURRAH...4-6 84
JBP...3-5 80
JAMIE (1112 "Send Me Your Picture")...15-25 58
JAMIE (1125 thru 1205)...10-20 59-61
JAMIE (1390 "It's You Girl")...5-10 70
JORDAN (100 "Send Me Your Picture")...15-25 57
JORDAN (102 "Sloe Gin")...10-20 63
JOR-DAN (7 "Slow Thing")...5-10 66
MER-BRI (101 "Beach Party")...50-75 65
PARKWAY (945 "Jordan Theme")...5-10 65
PHILIPS (40415 "Gimme Some Lovin' ")...5-10 66
RUBY (475 "Revenge")...20-25 64
TURBO...5-8 68
VIM...5-10 64
SSS INT'L (723 "Good Time")...5-8 67
LPs: 10/12-inch
JBP...8-10 80
Members: Joe; Frank; Bob; Lew.

JORDAN HARMONIZERS
Singles: 7-inch
TRI-PHI (1009 "Do You Know Him")...20-30 62

JORDANAIRES
Singles: 78 rpm
CAPITOL...3-5 54-58
DECCA...3-5 52-54
RCA...3-5 51-53
"X"...3-5 54
Singles: 7-inch
CAPITOL...5-15 54-60
COLUMBIA (Except 43283)...5-8 64-66
(Columbia 43283, *Malibu Run*, is by another group of Jordanaires – listed in a separate section that follows.)
DECCA...5-15 52-54
SESAC...5-10 59
STOP...4-6 69
RCA...5-15 51-53
"X"...5-15 54
EPs: 7-inch
CAPITOL...5-15 55-59
RCA (3081 "Beautiful City")...15-25 53
LPs: 10/12-inch
CAPITOL...15-25 58-62
CLASSIC...10-15 78
COLUMBIA...5-15 64-66
DECCA...15-25 57
100% MUSIC...8-10 86
RCA (3081 "Beautiful City")...25-40 53
(10-inch LP.)
STEP ONE (0029 "Elvis' Favorite Spirituals")...8-10 90
SESAC...20-30 59
STEP ONE...5-8 87
STOP...5-10
VOCALION...5-10 69
Members: Gordon Stoker; Neal Matthews; Hoyt Hawkins; Hugh Jarrett; Ray Walker; Louis Nunley; Duane West.
Also see ACUFF, Roy
Also see ANDERSON, Bill
Also see ANDERSON, Lynn
Also see BANDY, Moe
Also see BEARD, Dean
Also see BRYANT, Soda, & Jordanaires
Also see CLINE, Patsy
Also see DAMON, Mark, & Jordanaires
Also see DONNER, Ral
Also see DRAGON, Paul
Also see FOLEY, Webb
Also see FORD, Tennessee Ernie
Also see FRANCIS, Connie
Also see FREDDIE & FISHSTICKS
Also see GIBSON, Don
Also see HAGGARD, Merle
Also see HOUSTON, David
Also see HOWARD, Jan
Also see JACKSON, Stonewall
Also see JONES, George
Also see JONES, George, & Gene Pitney
Also see LEE, Brenda
Also see LEE, Robin
Also see LOCKLIN, Hank
Also see LYNN, Loretta
Also see MACK, Warner
Also see McDOWELL, Ronnie
Also see MIZE, Billy
Also see NELSON, Rick
Also see PARTON, Dolly
Also see PAYCHECK, Johnny
Also see PRESLEY, Elvis
Also see PROFITT, Randy, & Beachcombers
Also see REEVES, Jim
Also see RICH, Charlie
Also see ROBBINS, Marty
Also see SAUCEDO, Rick
Also see SNOW, Hank
Also see STARR, Frank, & His Rock-Away Boys
Also see TIGRE, Terry
Also see TUBB, Ernest
Also see WEST, Dottie
Also see YOUNG, Faron

JORDANAIRES
Singles: 7-inch
COLUMBIA (43283 "Malibu Run")...10-15 65

JORGENSON, Christine
Singles: 7-inch
JOLT (101 "Nervous Jervis")...8-10 59
LPs: 10/12-inch
J ("Christine Jorgensen Reveals")...50-75 57
(No selection number used. Has date, "11-26-57" etched in trail-off.)

JOSEFUS
Singles: 7-inch
HOOKAH...5-10 79
MAINSTREAM (725 "Jimmy Jimmy")...10-15 70
LPs: 10/12-inch
EVA (12010 "Dead Man")...8-12 83
HOOKAH (330 "Dead Man")...200-300 69
MAINSTREAM (6127 "Josefus")...100-125 70
Members: Pete Bailey; Dave Mitchell; Ray Turner; Doug Tull.

JOSEPH, Mike
(With the Skylites; with Heartbeats)
Singles: 7-inch
GONE (5052 "Time Passes")...30-40 59
LUCKY FOUR (1017 "King of Wealth")...30-40 62
TA-RAH (102 "King of Wealth")...40-50 61
Also see SKYLITES

JOSEPHINE XIII
Singles: 7-inch
CAMEO (427 "Break the Drums")...10-15 66

JOSHUA FOX
Singles: 7-inch
TETRAGRAMMATON...5-10 69
LPs: 10/12-inch
TETRAGRAMMATON (125 "Joshua Fox")...20-30 69
Members: Mike Botts; Larry Hansen; Jo LaManno; Tom Menefee.
Also see BREAD

JOSIE, Lou
Singles: 7-inch
ARGO (5293 "Why Did You Leave Me")...75-125 58
ARGO (5312 "Time's a Wastin' ")...75-125 58
BATON (269 "Lonely Years")...20-30 59
RENDEZVOUS (143 "Talk to the Angels")...50-75 61

JOSIE & PUSSYCATS
Singles: 7-inch
CAPITOL (2900 & 3000 series)...10-20 70-71
CAPITOL CREATIVE PRODUCTS (50 thru 61)...10-20 70
(Kellogg's cereal promotional issues.)
Picture Sleeves
CAPITOL CREATIVE PRODUCTS (50 thru 61)...10-20 70
(Mailing envelope/sleeve from Kellogg's.)
LPs: 10/12-inch
CAPITOL (665 "Josie and the Pussycats")...100-150 70
(TV Soundtrack.)
Members: Patrice Holloway; Cherie Moor (a.k.a. Cheryl Ladd); Cathy Dougher.
Also see HOLLOWAY, Patrice

JOURNEY *LP '75*
Singles: 12-inch
COLUMBIA (A11-1728 "Don't Stop Believin' ")...5-10 82
(Picture disc. Promotional issue.)
Singles: 7-inch
COLUMBIA...3-6 74-87
GEFFEN...3-5 85
Picture Sleeves
COLUMBIA...3-5 81-87
GEFFEN...3-5 85

EPs: 7-inch
CSP....4-6 81
(Nestle's candy promotional issue.)
LPs: 10/12-inch
COLUMBIA ("Captured")....100-120 81
(10-inch picture disc. No selection number used. Promotional issue only.)
COLUMBIA (662 "Live Sampler")....12-15 75
(Promotional issue only.)
COLUMBIA (914 "Journey")....12-15 75
(Promotional issue only.)
COLUMBIA (30000 series)....5-10 75-82
COLUMBIA (KC2-37016 "Captured")....80-100 81
(Picture disc made for promotional use, but, due to a production error, the actual recordings are by unidentified artists.)
COLUMBIA (46000 & 47000 series)....20-40 81-82
(Half-speed mastered.)
MFSL (144 "Escape")....250-350 85
Members: Steve Perry; Neal Schon; Aynsley Dunbar; Gregg Rolie; Ross Valory; Jonathan Cain; Robert Fleishman.
Also see CAIN, Jonathan
Also see FRUMIOUS BANDERSNATCH

JOURNEYMEN
Singles: 7-inch
AMY (821 "Dust Storm")....5-10 61
CAPITOL....5-10 61-64
LPs: 10/12-inch
CAPITOL....15-20 61-63
Members: John Phillips; Scott McKenzie; Dick Weissman.
Also see McKENZIE, Scott
Also see PHILLIPS, John
Also see SMOOTHIES

JOURNEYMEN
(Baylanders)
Singles: 7-inch
IONA (1111 "Work Out")....10-20 63
IONA (1115 "Surfers Rule")....10-20 63
(Also issued as by the Baylanders.)
Member: Art Fisher.
Also see CHALLENGERS

JOURNEYMEN
Singles: 7-inch
TEE PEE (57/58 "You're a Better ManThan I"/ "Realities in Life")....50-100 68
Members: Dennis Pharis; Tom Halfpap; Mike Giese; Tobin Kraft; Donald Eastman.

JO-VALS
(Jovals)
Singles: 7-inch
ALWIL (101 "Ballerina")....10-15 64
GROVE (105 "Well It's Alright")....20-25 64
LAURIE (3229 "Sometimes I'm Happy")..15-20 64

JOVATIONS
Singles: 7-inch
TAURUS (362 "My Dreams")....20-30 63

JOWERS, Jerry
Singles: 7-inch
JOWERS (300 "Live and Learn")....150-250

JOY
Singles: 7-inch
EPIC (10528 "Bah Bah Bah")....10-15 69

JOY, Arlene
Singles: 7-inch
RENDEZVOUS (185 "Too Young")....10-15 62

JOY, Barbara
Singles: 7-inch
DYNAMIC (112 "Easy Come Easy Go Lover")....10-20 65
TAR-GET (1001 "Do This Do That")....10-20 62
U.C.S. (101 "Story of My Life")....100-150 62

JOY, Benny
(With Big John Taylor)
Singles: 7-inch
ANTLER (4011 "Crash the Party")....100-150 58
DECCA (31199 "New York, Hey Hey")....8-12 61
DECCA (31280 "You Go Your Way")....8-12 61
DIXIE (2001 "Steady with Betty")....600-800 58
DOT (16445 "Somebody Else's Heartache")....8-12 63
RAM (1107 "Ittie Bittie Everything")....150-200 59
TRI-DEC (8667 "Spin the Bottle")....400-600 58
Also see TAYLOR, Big John

JOY, Bobby
Singles: 7-inch
SENTRY (103 "You Sweet Devil You")....15-25
TANGERINE....5-10 68

JOY, Cee Cee
Singles: 7-inch
REGINA (293 "His Buddy's Girl")....10-15 63
W.B. (5343 "Harry's Harem")....5-10 63

JOY, Roddie *P&R/R&B '65*
Singles: 7-inch
PARKWAY....5-10 66-67
RED BIRD (021 "Come Back Baby")....8-12 65
RED BIRD (031 "He's So Easy to Love").10-20 65
RED BIRD (037 "If There's Anything Else You Want")....20-30 66

JOY ROCKERS
Singles: 7-inch
PENNY (9021 "The Gauster Bop")....10-20 62

JOY VENDORS
Singles: 7-inch
PAWN (1201 "Popeye Line")....10-20 62

JOYCE, Chuck
Singles: 7-inch
TREPUR (1006 "Mailman Blues")....250-350
TREPUR (1009 "Let's Rock")....350-450

JOYCE, Jo Ann
Singles: 7-inch
CARLTON (600 "Lonely Birthday")....10-20 64

JOYCE, Judy
Singles: 7-inch
CUPID (1001 "My Foolish Heart")....20-30 58

JOYCE & PRIVITEERS
(Joyce Heath)
Singles: 7-inch
AGON (1003 "Honor Roll of Love")....50-75 62
(Also issued as by Joyce Heath & Priviteers.)
Also see HEATH, Joyce
Also see TREMONTS

JOYETTES
Singles: 78 rpm
ONYX (502 "Story of Love")....20-40 56
Singles: 7-inch
ONYX (502 "Story of Love")....50-100 56

JOYFUL NOISE
Singles: 7-inch
RCA (9516 "Animals, Flowers and Children")....5-10 68
LPs: 10/12-inch
RCA (3963 "Joyful Noise")....10-12 68

JOYLARKS
Singles: 7-inch
CANDLELITE (426 "Betty My Love")....5-10 64
SNAG (107 "Betty My Love")....500-600 59

JOYRIDE
(The Joyride)
Singles: 7-inch
WORLD PACIFIC....10-15 67-68

JOYRIDE
LPs: 10/12-inch
RCA (4114 "Friend Song")....20-30 69
Also see REVERE, Paul, & Raiders

JOYS OF LIFE
Singles: 7-inch
COLUMBIA (44188 "Descent")....10-20 67

JOYTONES
Singles: 78 rpm
RAMA....50-75 56
Singles: 7-inch
RAMA (191 "All My Love Belongs to You")....30-40 56
RAMA (202 "Gee What a Boy")....50-75 56
RAMA (215 "My Foolish Heart")....200-300 56
STOOP SOUNDS (504 "My Foolish Heart")....100-150 96
(Limited edition. Estimates range from less than 10 to a few dozen made.)
Members: Lynn Middleton; Vicki Burgess; Margaret Moore; Toni Brown.
Also see CHARMERS
Also see HARPTONES

JOY-TONES
Singles: 7-inch
COED (600 "This Love")....10-15 65

JUBALAIRES
Singles: 78 rpm
CAPITOL....5-10 49-51
DECCA....5-10 44-46
LANG-WORTH....10-20 '40s
(16-inch transcriptions.)
Singles: 7-inch
CAPITOL (845 "That Old Piano Roll Blues")....30-40 50
CAPITOL (1054 "Little Mr. Big")....25-35 50
CAPITOL (1779 "Living Is a Lie")....40-50 51
CAPITOL (1888 "David and Goliath")....75-125 51
Members: Julius Ginyard; Ted Brooks; Bill Johnson; John Jennings; George McFadden.
Also see ROYAL HARMONY QUARTET
Also see SMITH, Johnny

JUBALAIRES *R&B '46*
(With Andy Kirk's Orchestra)
Singles: 78 rpm
CORAL....5-10 49
DECCA....5-10 46
KING....10-15 49-50
QUEEN (4163 thru 4172)....15-25 47
Also see KIRK, Andy, & His Clouds of Joy
Also see ORIGINAL JUBALAIRES

JUDAS PRIEST *LP '78*
Singles: 7-inch
ATLANTIC....3-5 88
COLUMBIA....3-6 79-84
Picture Sleeves
COLUMBIA....3-5 81
LPs: 10/12-inch
COLUMBIA (Except picture discs)....5-8 77-90
COLUMBIA (99-1543 "Screaming for Vengeance")....15-20 84
(World Tour picture disc.)
COLUMBIA (99-1543 "Screaming for Vengeance")....20-30 84
(Picture disc that, due to a production error, plays Neil Diamond's *Primitive* album.)
COLUMBIA (99-1851 "Love Bites")....60-70 84
(Picture disc with bite mark on outer edge.)
COLUMBIA (99-1851 "Love Bites")....15-25 84
(Picture disc.)
COLUMBIA (39926 "Great Vinyl and Concert Hits")....25-30 84
(Picture disc.)
JANUS (7019 "Sad Wings of Destiny")....8-12 76
OVATION (1751 "Sad Wings of Destiny")..5-10 80
RCA....5-8 83-84
VISA (7001 "Rocka Rolla")....15-25 74
(With bottle cap front cover.)
VISA (7001 "Rocka Rolla")....8-10 74
(No bottle cap on cover.)
Members: Rob Halford; K.K. Downing; Glenn Tipton; Ian Hill; Dave Holland; Scott Travis.
Also see DIAMOND, Neil

JUDDS *C&W '83*
Singles: 7-inch
CURB/RCA (2524 thru 2782)....3-5 90-91
CURB/RCA (8820 thru 9077)....3-5 89
RCA/CURB (5000 thru 8715)....3-5 86-88
RCA (13673 "Had a Dream")....4-6 83
(Black vinyl.)
RCA (13673 "Had a Dream")....15-20 83
(Brown vinyl.)
RCA/CURB (13772 "Mama He's Crazy")....3-5 84
RCA (13923 "Why Not Me")....4-6 84
(Black vinyl.)
RCA (13923 "Why Not Me")....10-20 84
(Brown vinyl.)
RCA/CURB (13991 thru 14362)....3-6 84-86
Picture Sleeves
RCA/CURB (5094 "Don't Be Cruel")....3-5 87
RCA/CURB (13772 "Mama He's Crazy")....3-5 84
LPs: 10/12-inch
RCA....5-8 83-88
RCA/CURB....5-8 89-89
Members: Naomi Judd; Wynonna Judd.

JUDGE 'N JURY
Singles: 7-inch
VERVE (10486 "Try Me")....10-15 67

JUDGE'S NEPHEWS
Singles: 7-inch
AUDIO (585 "Without Your Tender Love")....20-30

JUDY & AFFECTIONS
Singles: 7-inch
DODE (103 "Dum Dum De Dip")....30-40

JUDY & JADES
Singles: 7-inch
STARBURST (124 "Rooster")....15-20 67

JUDY, JOHNNY, & BILLY
Singles: 7-inch
SILVER (1003 "Beautiful Brown Eyes")...10-15 59

JUDY LEE & PLAYBOYS
Singles: 7-inch
DARLY (6382 "I Wonder Could It Be")....20-25
Members: Judy Lee Reeths; Pat Reeths; Dan Helland; Jim Jandrain; Tim Polzak; Dave Parpovich; Mike Larsheid.

JUDY LYNN *C&W '62*
(Judy Lynn Voiten)
Singles: 78 rpm
ABC-PAR....5-10 56
Singles: 7-inch
ABC-PAR (9767 "Tip Toe")....10-20 56
AMARET....4-6 71-73
COLUMBIA....4-8 68
JOSIE (849 "See If I Care")....10-15 58
MUSICOR....4-8 66-67
U.A.....5-10 62-66
W.B./CURB....4-6 75
LP: 10/12-inch
AMARET....5-10 71-73
COLUMBIA....8-12 69
MUSICOR....10-15 66-67
U.A.....10-20 62-66
UNART....10-15 67
Also see GRAMMER, Billy / Judy Lynn / Link Wray

JUICY GROOVE
LPs: 10/12-inch
PAYOLA ("First Taste")....10-15 78
(Picture disc. Up to 50 different graphics/color variations made. Selection number not known.)

JUJUS
Singles: 7-inch
FENTON (1004 "You Treat Me Bad")....35-45 65
UNITED (121570 "Do You Understand Me")....15-25 66
Picture Sleeves
UNITED (121570 "Do You Understand Me")....20-30 66
Members: Ray Hummell, Rod Shepard; Bill Gorski; Max Colley; Rick Stevens.
Also see HUMMEL, Ray

JULIAN
Singles: 7-inch
ONYX (519 "Whip")....15-25 58

JULIAN, Don & Meadowlarks
(Meadow Larks)
Singles: 78 rpm
DOOTO....30-40 57
DOOTONE....30-40 55-56
RPM (399 "Love Only You")....100-200 54
RPM (406 "LSMFT Blues")....100-200 54
Singles: 7-inch
CLASSIC ARTISTS (101 "Our Love")....5-8 88
(Black vinyl. 1000 made.)
CLASSIC ARTISTS (105 "White Christmas")....5-8 88
(Black vinyl. 1000 made.)
DOOTO (359 "Heaven & Paradise")....15-25 57
DOOTO (424 "Blue Moon")....40-50 57
DOOTONE (359 "Heaven & Paradise")....50-60 55
DOOTONE (367 "Always & Always")....65-75 55
(Red label.)
DOOTONE (367 "Always & Always")....30-40 55
(Maroon label.)
DOOTONE (372 "This Must Be Paradise")....65-75 55
DOOTONE (394 "Please Love a Fool")....65-75 56
DOOTONE (405 "I Am a Believer")....65-75 56
DYNAMITE (1112 "Heaven Only Knows")....50-75 62
JERK (100 "How Can You Be So Foul")..15-25 '60s
MAGNUM (716 "Lie")....15-25 64

ORIGINAL SOUND (3 "Please Say You Want Me")........ 30-40 58
ORIGINAL SOUND (12 "There's a Girl") . 30-40 60
RPM (399 "Love Only You")........ 400-500 54
RPM (406 "LSMFT Blues")........ 1500-2000 54

EPs: 7-inch

DOOTO (203 "Don Julian and the Meadowlarks")........ 25-50 58
DOOTONE (203 "Don Julian and the Meadowlarks")........ 100-150 56
DOOTONE (203 "Don Julian and the Meadowlarks")........ 10-20 '70s
(Reissues from the '70s, and later, can easily be identified by the "South Hope Street" Dootone address.)
Members: Don Julian; Ronald Barrett; Earl Jones; Randy Jones; Glen Reagan; Freeman Bralton; Benny Patricks.
Also see DEL-VIKINGS / Sonnets
Also see DOOTONES
Also see LARKS

JULIANA

Singles: 7-inch

RCA (7906 "You Can Have Any Boy")..... 50-60 61

JULITO & LATIN LADS
(Julio y Latin Lads)

Singles: 7-inch

RICO-VOX (27 "Nunca")........ 50-75 63

JULY FOUR

Singles: 7-inch

CAMEO (480 "Mr. Miff")........ 10-15 67

JUMPER, Ardon

Singles: 7-inch

FOREST (101 "Crawdad Song")........ 50-75

JUMPER, Johnny, & Rhythm Drifters

Singles: 7-inch

VANCE (480 "Walking-Talking")........ 150-200

JUMPIN' JACKS

Singles: 78 rpm

LLOYDS (101 "Do Let That Dream Come True")........ 300-400 53
Also see ROMEOS

JUMPIN' JACKS

Singles: 78 rpm

BRUCE (115 "Embraceable You")....... 150-250 54
1-0-1 (100 "Mop Job")........ 10-15 56

Singles: 7-inch

BRUCE (115 "Embraceable You")... 1000-2000 54
1-0-1 (100 "Mop Job")........ 20-30 56

JUMPIN' JAGUARS

Singles: 78 rpm

DECCA (29938 "Shut the Door")........ 5-10 56

Singles: 7-inch

DECCA (29938 "Shut the Door")........ 10-15 56

JUMPIN' JAY

Singles: 7-inch

TURBAN (101 "Come On Home")........ 40-50 61

JUMPIN' JUDGE & HIS COURT / Lafayette Thomas

Singles: 78 rpm

JUMPING (5000 "The Trial")........ 10-20 55

Singles: 7-inch

JUMPING (5000 "The Trial")........ 25-35 55
Also see THOMAS, Lafayette

JUMPIN' TONES

Singles: 7-inch

RAVEN (8004 "I Had a Dream")........ 40-50 64
RAVEN (8005 "Grandma's Hearing Aid") 40-50 64
Also see RAINDROPS

JUMPING JACKS

Singles: 78 rpm

CAPITOL (3496 "Toki Roll")........ 5-10 56

Singles: 7-inch

CAPITOL (3496 "Toki Roll")........ 10-15 56

JUMPING JACKS

Singles: 78 rpm

DECCA (29973 "You'll Wonder Where the Yellow Went")........ 10-15 56

Singles: 7-inch

DECCA (29973 "You'll Wonder Where the Yellow Went")........ 20-30 56

JUMPING JACKS

Singles: 7-inch

BERTRAM INT'L (221 "Roasted Peanuts")........ 20-25 61

JUNE, Rosemary

Singles: 7-inch

PARIS (507 thru 532)........ 10-15 57-59
PILGRIM (722 "Break Away")........ 15-20 56
TALENT (1001 "All of Me")........ 5-10 62
U.A. (197 thru 219)........ 5-10 59-60
Also see FOUR ESQUIRES

JUNIOR & HIS FRIENDS

Singles: 7-inch

ABC-PAR (10089 "Who's Our Pet, Annette")........ 20-30 60
(Written and produced by Paul Anka. Recorded by his younger brother.)

JUNIOR & STAR LITES

Singles: 7-inch

MEX MELODY (121 "Queen of My Heart")........ 50-75

JR. MISSES

Singles: 7-inch

RENDEZVOUS (101 "You Dream Too Much")........ 10-15 58

JUNIORS

Singles: 7-inch

LAURIE (3213 "On My Birthday")........ 5-10 64
MGM (13271 "Pocket Size")........ 5-10 64
TEXOMA (1900 "Dream Girl")........ 10-20 60

JUPP, Eric

Singles: 78 rpm

ESSEX (347 "Oop Dee Ooh")........ 8-12 54

Singles: 7-inch

ESSEX (347 "Oop Dee Ooh")........ 15-25 54

JURY, The

Singles: 7-inch

PLAY ME (1119 "Boogie Woogie Rock") .15-20 59
Session: Bill Justis.
Also see JUSTIS, Bill

JURY, The

Singles: 7-inch

PORT (3019 "Who Dat")........ 15-25 66

JUST BROTHERS

Singles: 7-inch

GARRISON (3003 "Carlena")........ 50-100 66
MUSIC MERCHANT (1002 "Tears Ago")........ 50-100 71
MUSIC MERCHANT (1008 "Things Will Be Better Tomorrow")........ 5-10 72
MUSIC MERCHANT (1010 "You've Got the Love to Make Me Over")........ 5-10 72
WAND (1144 "Carlena")........ 50-100 66

JUST LUV

Singles: 7-inch

M-S (216 "Valley of Hate")........ 30-50 66

JUST US *P&R '66*

Singles: 7-inch

ATLANTIC........ 4-6 71
COLPIX (803 "I Can't Grow Peaches on a Cherry Tree")........ 5-10 66
KAPP (768 thru 853)........ 5-10 66-67
MINUTEMAN (203 " I Can't Grow Peaches on a Cherry Tree")........ 10-20 66
(First issue.)
TCB (1001 "Only if You've Been Hurt")........ 5-10 '60s
VINCENT (132 "How I Love You")........ 5-10 '60s

Picture Sleeves

KAPP (853 "What Are We Gonna Do")........ 8-12 67

LPs: 10/12-inch

KAPP (1502 "I Can't Grow Peaches on a Cherry Tree")........ 10-20 66
(Monaural.)
KAPP (3502 "I Can't Grow Peaches on a Cherry Tree")........ 15-25 66
(Stereo.)
Members: Chip Taylor; Al Gorgoni.
Also see TAYLOR, Chip

JUSTICE, Jimmy

Singles: 7-inch

BLUE CAT (101 "Guitar Player")........ 5-10 64
KAPP (469 thru 514)........ 5-10 62-63

LPs: 10/12-inch

KAPP (1308 "Justice for All")........ 15-20 63
(Monaural.)
KAPP (3308 "Justice for All")........ 20-25 63
(Stereo.)

JUSTIFIERS

Singles: 7-inch

KIM (101 "Lonely Boy")........ 400-500 58

JUSTIS, Bill *P&R/R&B/C&W '57*
(With the Jury; Bill Justis Orchestra; with Roger Fakes & Spinners)

Singles: 78 rpm

PHILLIPS INT'L........ 15-30 57

Singles: 7-inch

BELL (921 "Electric Dreams")........ 4-6 70
MONUMENT........ 4-6 76
PHILLIPS INT'L (3519 thru 3544)........ 15-25 57-59
PLAY ME (3519 "Teensville")........ 10-15 59
MCA........ 4-6 77
MONUMENT (956 "Yellow Summer")........ 5-10 66
NRC (1119 "Boogie Woogie Rock")........ 8-12 60
SMASH........ 5-10 63-65

Picture Sleeves

SMASH (1812 "Tamoure")........ 8-12 63

LPs: 10/12-inch

HARMONY........ 8-10 72
PHILLIPS INT'L (1950 "Cloud 9")........ 50-100 57
SMASH........ 15-25 62-66
SUN........ 8-10 69
WING........ 10-20 65
Also see JURY, The
Also see POWERS, Johnny

JUSTIS, Bill / Jerry Reed

EPs: 7-inch

MCA (1961 "Music from *Smokey and the Bandit*")........ 10-15 77
(Promotional issue only.)
Also see JUSTIS, Bill
Also see REED, Jerry

JUSTIS BROTHERS

Singles: 7-inch

PARIS TOWER (121 "Count On Me")........ 15-25 67

JUVENILES
(With Al Caiola & Combo)

Singles: 7-inch

MODE (1 "Beat in My Heart")........ 100-150 57
(Black label with white print. Has "45 RPM" on two lines.)
MODE (1 "Beat in My Heart")........ 30-40 58
(Black label with silver print. Has 45 R.P.M." on one line.)
Also see CAIOLA, Al

K

K., Fred, & Chessmen

Singles: 7-inch

LOKI (6331 "Laurie")........ 100-200

K & D BOOTERY COMPANY

Singles: 7-inch

TEE PEE (1002 "Birthday")........ 10-20 69

KABIBBLE, Ish, & Shy Guys

Singles: 7-inch

REV (3501 "Calypso Rock")........ 25-35 57
(Red vinyl.)

KACHER, Del
(Del Katcher)

Singles: 7-inch

DENNY (347 "Night Bird")........ 10-20 62
MERRI (201 "Night Mist Over Highway No. 2")........ 10-20 60
Also see EXTERMINATORS

KAC-TIES

Singles: 7-inch

ATCO (6299 "Oh What a Night")........ 8-12 64
KAPE (502 "Smile")........ 20-30 63
KAPE (503 "Let Your Love Light Shine") . 10-15 63
KAPE (702 "Over the Rainbow")........ 4-8 72
KAPE (515632 "Girl in My Heart")........ 15-20 63
(Identification number shown since no selection number is used.)
SHELLEY (163 "Let Your Love Light Shine")........ 15-25 63
SHELLEY (165 "Oh What a Night")........ 15-25 63

KACT-TIES

Singles: 7-inch

TRANS ATLAS (695 "Walking in the Rain")........ 200-300 62
(With thunderstorm sound effects at beginning.)
TRANS ATLAS (695 "Walking in the Rain")........ 50-100 62
(Without thunderstorm effect.)

KADDO STRINGS

Singles: 7-inch

IMPACT (1005 "Cryin' Over You")........ 25-35 66
Also see BROWNER, Duke, & Kaddo Strings
Also see TARTANS

KAI, Lani

Singles: 7-inch

KEEN (2023 "Beach Party")........ 10-15 59
KEEN (2103 "Batnik")........ 10-15 59
KEEN (2109 "Isle of No Aloha")........ 10-15 59

KAIN, Buddy

Singles: 7-inch

BAND BOX (285 "The Dream Is Ended") .. 5-10 61
MYERS (106 "Jump Rope Hop")........ 20-30 60
20TH FOX (118 "Spider")........ 10-20 58

KAIN, Tasso
(With the Matadors; Tasso "The Great" Kain)

Singles: 7-inch

CAIN (9219 "Castro's Beat")........ 20-30 59
CY (0001 "Viet Nam Beat")........ 8-12 66
(Same track as *Castro's Beat.*)
Also see TASSO THE GREAT

KAK

Singles: 7-inch

EPIC (10383 "Everything's Changing")........ 10-15 68
EPIC (10446 "Disbelievin'")........ 10-15 69

LPs: 10/12-inch

EPIC (26429 "Kak")........ 75-125 69
Members: Chris Lockheed; Delmer Patten; Joe Damrell; Gary Yoder.
Also see BLUE CHEER
Also see HOLDEN, Randy

KALB, Buddy

Singles: 7-inch

SCOTTIE (1302 "Pony Tail")........ 10-20 59

KALEIDOSCOPE *LP '69*

Singles: 7-inch

A&M........ 4-6 73
EPIC (10117 thru 10500)........ 15-25 67-69
TSOP........ 4-8 75

LPs: 10/12-inch

BACK-TRAC........ 5-8 85
EPIC (24304 "Side Trips")........ 50-100 67
(Monaural.)
EPIC (24333 "Beacon from Mars")........ 50-100 67
(Monaural.)
EPIC (26304 "Side Trips")........ 50-75 67
(Stereo.)
EPIC (26333 "Beacon from Mars")........ 50-100 67
(Stereo.)
EPIC (26467 "Incredible Kaleidoscope")..20-40 69
EPIC (26508 "Bernice")........ 15-20 70
PACIFIC ARTS........ 5-10 78
Members: David Lindley; Solomon Feldthouse; John Vidican; John Welsh; Rick O'Neil; Brian Monsour; Chris Darrow.
Also see RODENTS
Also see WILLIAMS, Larry, & Johnny Guitar Watson

KALENDARS

Singles: 7-inch

TEE VEE (2510 "I'll Love Only You")........ 40-60

KALI, Satya Sai Maitreya

LPs: 10/12-inch

AKASHIC (2777 "Apache")........ 1000-1500 71
(Cover indicates "Sound Track from Yosemite, Dedicated to Jimi Hendrix.")
AKASHIC (2777 "Apache")........ 100-200 91
(Indicates "Limited second issue of 300 copies by the Rock & Roll Archives Club of Peru.")
Session: Mike Love.
Also see LOVE, Mike

KALIN TWINS *P&R/C&W/R&B '58*
Singles: 78 rpm
DECCA (30642 "When")....................50-75 58
Singles: 7-inch
AMY (969 "Thinkin' About You Baby")........5-10 66
DECCA (Except 30642)..............................8-15 58-62
DECCA (30642 "When")..........................15-25 58
(With silver lines on both sides of the name "Decca.")
DECCA (30642 "When")..............................8-15 58
(With a star and silver lines under the name "Decca.")
MCA...4-6 73
Picture Sleeves
DECCA (30977 "Why Don't You Believe Me")..10-20 59
EPs: 7-inch
DECCA (2623 "Kalin Twins")...................25-50 58
DECCA (2641 "Forget Me Not")................25-50 59
LPs: 10/12-inch
DECCA (8812 "Kalin Twins")...................50-75 58
VOCALION (73771 "Kalin Twins")...........30-40 66
Members: Hal Kalin; Herb Kalin.
Also see LEE, Brenda / Bill Haley & Comets / Kalin Twins / Four Aces

KALLABASH CORP
LPs: 10/12-inch
UNCLE BILL (311 "Kallabash Corp").......30-50 70
Members: Ted Keaton; Rick Oates.

KALLAN, Jackie
Singles: 7-inch
MOTION (1001 "Summer Romance")......40-50 63

KALLEN, Kitty *P&R '49*
(With Jack Pleis & Orchestra)
Singles: 78 rpm
DECCA...5-10 54-57
COLUMBIA..5-10 54
MERCURY...5-10 51-54
Singles: 7-inch
BELL (673 "Summer Summer Wind")...........4-6 67
DECCA...10-15 54-59
COLUMBIA (40000 series).......................10-15 54
COLUMBIA (41000 & 42000 series)..........8-12 59-61
MGM (13369 "So Many Others")..................4-8 65
MERCURY...10-15 51-54
PHILIPS (40375 "One Grain of Sand").........4-6 66
RCA..5-10 62-63
20TH-CENTURY-FOX..................................5-8 64
U.A. 4-8 65
Promotional Singles
DECCA (78094 "Personal Introduction by Kitty Kallen to '54 Christmas Seal Song")....................8-12 54
(Single-sided promotional pressing.)
Picture Sleeves
DECCA (290 "It's Not the Whistle")..........10-15 55
EPs: 7-inch
DECCA...10-15 54-56
COLUMBIA..10-15 54
MERCURY...10-15 55
LPs: 10/12-inch
COLUMBIA..10-20 60-61
DECCA (8397 "It's a Lonesome Old Town")...20-30 56
MCA (1544 "Little Things Mean a Lot")........5-8 83
MERCURY (25206 "Pretty Kitty Kallen Sings")..30-50 55
(10-inch LP.)
MOVIETONE (71026 "Delightfully")...........8-12 67
(Monaural.)
MOVIETONE (72026 "Delightfully")...........8-12 67
(Stereo.)
RCA (264 "My Coloring Book")................10-20 63
20TH-CENTURY-FOX (3151 "Quiet Nights")..10-15 64
(Monaural.)
20TH-CENTURY-FOX (4151 "Quiet Nights")..15-20 64
(Stereo.)
VOCALION (3679 "Little Things Mean a Lot")..10-20 59
WING (12241 "Sings")...............................10-20 63
(Monaural.)
WING (16241 "Sings")...............................15-25 63
(Stereo.)
Also see ANN-MARGRET / Kitty Kallen / Della Reese
Also see HAYES, Richard, & Kitty Kallen
Also see JAMES, Harry, & His Orchestra

KALLEN, Kitty, & Georgie Shaw
Singles: 78 rpm
DECCA (29776 "Go On with the Wedding")..5-10 55
Singles: 7-inch
DECCA (29776 "Go On with the Wedding")..10-15 55
Also see KALLEN, Kitty

KALLMAN, Dick
Singles: 7-inch
LIBERTY (55063 "I Cry to the Moon")..200-300 57
LIBERTY (55091 "7 Wonders of the World")...10-20 58

KAMA-DEL-SUTRA
Singles: 7-inch
ZIG ZAG (273 "Come On Up")................75-125 67

KAMPELLS
Singles: 7-inch
SELECT (736 "New Lock on My Door")...50-75 63

KAMPUS KIDS
Singles: 7-inch
ENSIGN (5000 "Leave Me Alone")...........10-15 '60s

KAN DELLS
Singles: 7-inch
BEAR (1971 "Do You Know")..............100-125 66
BOSS (6501 "Cry Girl")...........................25-35 65

KANDY KOLORED KONSPIRACY
Singles: 7-inch
MEDIA (007 "Konspiracy '68")..................10-20 68

KANE, Bernie, & Rockin' Rhythms
Singles: 7-inch
TABB (9133 "High Tide")..........................10-15 66

KANE, Eden
Singles: 7-inch
FONTANA..5-10 64-65
LONDON (1993 "Well I Ask You")............10-20 61
LONDON (9508 "Get Lost").....................10-20 61
LONDON (9516 "Forget Me Not")............10-15 62
LONDON (9532 "I Don't Know Why").......10-15 62
T.A. (193 "Reason to Believe")....................4-8 70

KANE, Gladys
Singles: 7-inch
PIXIE (800 "Mr. Policeman")....................10-20 62
Also see CAINE, Gladys

KANE, Jerry
Singles: 7-inch
AUDIO ARTISTS ("There's Not Enough Love")...10-20
(No selection number used.)

KANE, Paul
(Paul Simon)
Singles: 7-inch
TRIBUTE (128 "Carlos Dominguez")........50-75 63
(Copies crediting "Paul Simon" as the singer are bootlegs.)
Also see SIMON, Paul

KANE, Tommy, & Emeralds
Singles: 7-inch
DEAN (503 "Oh-Oh-Oh Rock")................10-15 60

KANE & ABEL
Singles: 7-inch
DESTINATION (607 "Break Down and Cry")..10-15 65
RED BIRD (059 "He Will Break Your Heart")...10-15 66
Members: Art Herrera; Al Herrera. Session: James Holvay; Gary Beiser.
Also see LITTLE ARTIE & PHAROAHS
Also see MOB

KANE'S COUSINS
Singles: 7-inch
SHOVE LOVE (069 "Take Your Love and Shove It")..10-15 69
(Colored vinyl.)
SHOVE LOVE (500 "Take Your Love and Shove It")..5-10 69
(Black vinyl.)
LPs: 10/12-inch
SHOVE LOVE (9827 "Undergum Bubbleground").....................................25-35 69

KANGAROO
Singles: 7-inch
MGM (13960 "I Never Tell Me Twice").......5-10 68
LPs: 10/12-inch
MGM (4586 "Kangaroo")..........................10-15 68
Members: Barbara Keith; N.D. Smart; John Hall.

KANISS, Chuck
Singles: 7-inch
IMPAC (6160 "Tru-Fine Twister")............50-75 61

KANNON, Ray, & Corals
Singles: 7-inch
CUCA (1078 thru 1164)...........................10-20 62-64
Member: James Curley Cooke; Dick Bartig; Ray Kannonberg; Buddy Bradford; Jim Marcotte; Tom Litzer.
Also see CORALS

KANSAS *LP '74*
Singles: 12-inch
CBS ASSOCIATED......................................5-10 83
(Promotional only.)
MCA...5-8 88
(Promotional only.)
Singles: 7-inch
CBS ASSOCIATED.......................................3-5 83
KIRSHNER...4-6 74-82
MCA (17290 "Power")..................................3-6 87
(CD mix on vinyl. Promotional issue only.)
MCA (50000 series)......................................3-5 86-87
Picture Sleeves
CBS ASSOCIATED.......................................3-5 83
KIRSHNER...3-5 82
MCA..3-5 86-87
LPs: 10/12-inch
CBS ASSOCIATED.......................................5-8 83-84
KIRSHNER (30000 series)............................8-12 74-82
KIRSHNER (40000 series)..........................15-25 81-82
(Half-speed mastered.)
MCA..5-8 86-88
Promotional LPs
BURNS MEDIA ("Two for the Show").......15-25 78
(Selection number not known.)
KIRSHNER (34929 "Point of Know Return")..50-100 79
(Picture disc.)
KIRSHNER (35660 "Two for the Show")..10-15 78
Members: Dave Hope; Rich Williams; Kerry Livgren; Phil Ehart; Robbie Steinhardt; Steve Walsh; Terry Brock.

KANSAS CITY PLAYBOYS
Singles: 7-inch
ROJAC (1004 "Loverman").......................40-50 '60s
RSVP (117 "Dancing Party")......................5-10 63

KANSAS CITY TURNPIKES
Singles: 7-inch
ANGLE TONE (537 "Douglas Blues").......10-20 59

KAPPALIERS / Noel Sookey
Singles: 7-inch
SHADOW (1229 "Down in Mexicali"/"Goodbye Baby")..300-400 '50s

KAPPAS
Singles: 7-inch
WONDER (112 "Sweet Juanita")............75-100 59

KARE TAKERS
Singles: 7-inch
WAM (5970 "Have You Seen My Baby").15-25 67

KAREN, Kenny *P&R '73*
(Ken Karen)
Singles: 7-inch
BIG TREE (16007 "That's Why You Remember")...4-6 73
COLUMBIA (3-42264 "Oh Susie, Forgive Me")..25-35 62
(Compact 33 Single.)
COLUMBIA (3-42452 "To Sandy, with Love")...25-35 62
(Compact 33 Single.)
COLUMBIA (3-42638 "16 Years Ago Tonight")...25-35 62
(Compact 33 Single.)
COLUMBIA (4-42264 "Oh Susie, Forgive Me")..10-20 62
COLUMBIA (4-42452 "To Sandy, with Love")...10-20 62
COLUMBIA (4-42638 "16 Years Ago Tonight")...10-20 62
STRAND..10-15 59-60
Picture Sleeves
COLUMBIA (42264 "Oh Susie, Forgive Me")...15-25 62
COLUMBIA (42452 "To Sandy, with Love")...15-25 62

KAREN & CUBBY
(Karen Pendleton & Cubby O'Brien)
Singles: 78 rpm
MICKEY MOUSE CLUB (75 "Karen & Cubby")..20-30 58
Singles: 7-inch
DISNEYLAND (112 "Ballad of Davy Crockett")...15-25 58
EPs: 7-inch
MICKEY MOUSE CLUB (75 "Karen & Cubby")..10-20 58
(Same number used on 78s and EPs.)
Also see MOUSEKETEERS

KARI, Harry, & His Six Saki Sippers *P&R '53*
(Harry Stewart)
Singles: 78 rpm
CAPITOL...5-10 53-55
Singles: 7-inch
CAPITOL (2392 "Yokohama Mama").......10-20 53
CAPITOL (2516 "Nishimoto at the Bat")...10-20 53
CAPITOL (3257 "Ragtime Cowboy Joe").10-20 55
Also see YORGESSON, Yogi

KARI, Sax
(With His Jivin' Jukes and Boogie Bob; Sax Kari Show Starring the Newports; with Codes; with Gloria Irving)
Singles: 78 rpm
APOLLO (389 "Play It Cool Blues")..........10-15 47
APOLLO (397 "I'll Never Leave You")......10-15 47
GREAT LAKES..5-10 54
STATES...5-10 53
Singles: 7-inch
AISLE (004 "T.V. Mama")............................3-5 94
AISLE (004 "T.V. Mama")............................5-10 94
(Red vinyl. 100 made.)
CONTOUR (301 "Chicky-Chop-Chop").....10-15 59
FLORIDA ROCK...4-6 80
GREAT LAKES (1205 "Train Ride").........25-50 54
INSTANT (3270 "Something You Got").....5-10 65
JOB (1118 "Chocolate Fizz")....................25-50 57
STATES (115 "Daughter").........................10-20 53
STATES (117 "Henry")..............................10-20 53
TUNE-KEL (600 "Siesta")............................5-10 67
TUNE-KEL (601 "Here & There")...............5-10 67
Picture Sleeves
AISLE (004 "T.V. Mama")............................3-5 94
Also see ALLEY KATS
Also see FALCONS
Also see IRVING, Gloria
Also see VON CARL, Jimmy
Also see WARD, Little Sammy
Also see WATKINS, Katie / Texas Red & Jimmy

KARI, Sax / Lena Gordon
Singles: 78 rpm
CHECKER (803 "Disc Jockey Jamboree")...10-15 54
Singles: 7-inch
CHECKER (803 "Disc Jockey Jamboree")...25-35 54
Also see KARI, Sax

KARI, Sax, & Quailtones
Singles: 78 rpm
JOSIE (779 "Tears of Love")......................40-50 55
Singles: 7-inch
JOSIE (779 "Tears of Love")..................100-200 55

KARL, Frankie *P&R/R&B '68*
(With the Dreams)
Singles: 7-inch
D.C. (180 "Don't Be Afraid")....................10-15 68
LIBERTY (56164 "Don't Sleep Too Long")..10-20 70
PHILTOWN (105 "You Should O' Held On")..5-10

KARLOFF, Boris
Singles: 7-inch
MOL (52 "He Is There")..............................5-10 67
EPs: 7-inch
COLUMBIA (1526 "Peter Pan")................25-50 50
LPs: 10/12-inch
CAEDMON (1088 "Just So Stories").........20-30 58
CAEDMON (1129 "Fairy Tales")................15-25 62

CAEDMON (1182 "Let' Listen")............... 15-25 63
(With Julie Harris.)
CAEDMON (1221 "Aesop's Fables") 10-15 68
COLUMBIA (4312 "Peter Pan").................. 50-75 50
DECCA (4833 "An Evening with Karloff and His Friends").. 10-20 67
MGM (901 "How the Grinch Stole Christmas").. 10-20 66
MERCURY (20815 "Tales of the Frightened, Vol. 1").. 25-50 63
(Monaural.)
MERCURY (20816 "Tales of the Frightened, Vol. 2").. 25-50 63
(Monaural.)
MERCURY (60815 "Tales of the Frightened, Vol. 1").. 25-50 63
(Stereo.)
MERCURY (60816 "Tales of the Frightened, Vol. 2").. 25-50 63
(Stereo.)
PLAYHOUR (22 "Tales of Mystery and Imagination")................................... 20-40 61

KARMEN, Steve

Singles: 7-inch

AUDIO FIDELITY (171 "You've Said It All")..8-12 68
ELDORADO (510 "Freight Train")........... 15-25 57
MERCURY (71164 "We Belong Together").. 10-20 57
MERCURY (71208 "How Soon")............ 10-20 57
MERCURY (71301 "River in My Blood") . 35-45 58
MERCURY (71386 "Oh! Oh!")................ 10-20 58

KARRIANNS
("Karriann's - Don & Neil with the Playboys")

Singles: 7-inch

PELPAL (118 "Don't Want Your Picture") .... 500-750 '50s

KARTER, Kenny
(Kenny Hinkle)

Singles: 7-inch

WESTCO (8 "Surfing with Bony Maronie")... 10-20 63
(Black vinyl. First issued as by the Sentinals.)
WESTCO (8 "Surfing with Bony Maronie")... 20-30 63
(Colored vinyl.)
Also see HINKLE, Kenny
Also see SENTINALS

KARTUNE KAPERS

Singles: 7-inch

SPACE (11 "Knock on Wood")................ 15-25 67

KARTUNES

Singles: 78 rpm

MGM (12598 "Raindrops") 20-30 57

Singles: 7-inch

MGM (12598 "Raindrops") 20-30 57
MGM (12680 "Dedicated to Love") 10-15 58

KASANDRA P&R/R&B/LP '68
(With the Midnight Riders; John W. Anderson; John Kasandra)

Singles: 7-inch

CAPITOL (2342 "Don't Pat Me On the Back and Call Me Brother")..5-10 68
IMPERIAL (5638 "I Couldn't Let You Down") 15-25 60
RESPECT (2503 "Ain't I Good")..................4-6 72
RESPECT (2504 "Mose Part III")................4-6 72

LPs: 10/12-inch

CAPITOL (2957 "John W. Anderson Presents Kasandra")... 10-15 68
RESPECT..8-12 71-72

KASEM, Casey

Singles: 7-inch

MGM (14214 "No Blade of Grass")..............4-6 71
W.B. (5474 "Letter from Elaina") 10-15 64

LPs: 10/12-inch

SIDEWALK (5905 "Astrology for Young Lovers").. 10-20 67

KASHMIRS

Singles: 7-inch

WONDER (104 "Heaven Only Knows")... 400-500 58

KASS, Steve, & Lovelarks

Singles: 7-inch

CLASS (10X "Darling My Love")......... 150-250 57

KASTY, Paul

Singles: 7-inch

FLEET ("Don't Rock Let's Roll")...............50-75
(Selection number not known.)

KATON, Larry

Singles: 78 rpm

HERALD (484 "Call Me Darling").............10-15 56

Singles: 7-inch

HERALD (484 "Call Me Darling")..............15-25 56

KATS

Singles: 7-inch

E&C (1002 "Wear Me Out")......................10-20 63

KATHY & CAROL

LPs: 10/12-inch

ELEKTRA (289 "Kathy & Carol")..............10-15 65

KATMANDU

LPs: 10/12-inch

MAINSTREAM (6131 "Katmandu")..........30-40 71
Members: Norman Harris; Ken Zale; Bob Jabo; Bob Caldwell.

KATZ, Mickey, & His Orchestra P&R '50

Singles: 78 rpm

CAPITOL..4-8 51-57

Singles: 7-inch

CAPITOL...5-12 51-62

EPs: 7-inch

CAPITOL..10-20 53-56

LPs: 10/12-inch

CAPITOL (Except SM-298)......................15-35 53-65
CAPITOL (SM-298 "Mickey Katz")..............5-8 78
Also see JONES, Spike

KAUFMAN, Murray
(Murray the "K"; Ludwig Von Kaufman)

Singles: 78 rpm

FRATERNITY (714 "Out of the Bushes") .10-15 55

Singles: 7-inch

FRATERNITY (714 "Out of the Bushes") .15-25 55
HAN-O-DISC ("A Salute to Murray the K")...25-35 79
(Picture disc. Promotional issue only.)
RED BIRD (045 "It's What's Happening, Baby")...5-10 66

KAUFMANN, Bob

LPs: 10/12-inch

LHI (12002 "Trip Thru a Blown Mind")......30-40 67

KAVETTES

Singles: 7-inch

OKEH (7194 "I'm Not Sorry for You") 20-40 64

KAY, Carol
(With Red Callender)

Singles: 78 rpm

RECORDED IN HOLLYWOOD................10-15 53

Singles: 7-inch

RECORDED IN HOLLYWOOD (424 "You Can't Do Boogie in School")..............................15-25 53
WRIGHT-SOUND (4479 "This Time You're Wrong")..15-25
Also see CALLENDER, Red

KAY, Eddie

Singles: 7-inch

BETHELEM (3063 "Cindy").......................10-20 63

KAY, Gary
(Billy Carlucci; Gary Kay & Passions-Echoes)

Singles: 7-inch

JASON SCOTT (20 "Cinderella")..................3-5 82
(500 made.)
RAN-DEE (116 "Cinderella").....................50-75 63
RAN-DEE (120 "Billy Bee").......................50-75 63
Session: Andre Williams.
Also see BILLY & ESSENTIALS
Also see WILLIAMS, Andre

KAY, Gene

Singles: 78 rpm

TNT...10-15 55

Singles: 7-inch

TNT (119 "Where Did You Get That Kiss")..15-25 55
TNT (124 "Name Your Price")..................15-25 55

KAY, Harriet

Singles: 78 rpm

DAWN (215 "Dear One")..........................10-15 56

Singles: 7-inch

DAWN (215 "Dear One")..........................15-20 56

KAY, Joey

Singles: 7-inch

JAMIE (1368 "It's a Miracle")....................5-10 69

LPs: 10/12-inch

LA BREA (1816 "Joey Kay")....................15-25 61

KAY, Johnny

Singles: 7-inch

A (103 "Oh Patti") 75-125 59
TIGER (105 "Starvation") 100-150 61

LPs: 10/12-inch

DIPLOMAT (1014 "The Night Before Christmas")..10-15 62
SPIN-O-RAMA.......................................10-15 '60s

KAY, Johnny
(With the Morty Jay Orchestra)

Singles: 7-inch

LEGEND (127 "A Christmas Love").........10-20 63

KAY, Tommy

Singles: 7-inch

EMBERS (1521 "Man Without a Name") .15-25 '60s
SARA (6754 "Oh, My Love").....................15-25 67

KAYE, Danny P&R '47
(Danny Kaye & Co.; with Earl Brown Singers; with Clinger Sisters; with Paul Weston Orchestra)

Singles: 78 rpm

COLUMBIA..4-8 49-54
DECCA..4-8 50-56
RCA..4-8 47-48

Singles: 7-inch

COLUMBIA...5-15 49-70
DECCA..10-20 50-56
REPRISE (20105 "D-o-d-g-e-r-s Song")...10-15 62

Picture Sleeves

DECCA (151 "Little White Duck")............10-15 '50s
REPRISE (20105 "D-o-d-g-e-r-s Song")...15-20 62

EPs: 7-inch

CAPITOL..5-10 58
COLUMBIA...10-20 49-54
DECCA..8-15 54-57

LPs: 10/12-inch

CAMDEN...15-25 57
CAPITOL...15-25 58
COLUMBIA (6000 series) 25-50 49-54
(10-inch LPs.)
DECCA (100 series)................................10-20 63
DECCA (5000 series)..............................20-40 54
(10-inch LPs.)
DECCA (8000 series)..............................20-40 54-59
DECCA (78000 series)............................10-15 67
DENA ("Danny Kaye")..............................15-25 63
(No selection number used and no label name other than Dena shown. Promotional issue only from Rambler dealers.)
GOLDEN..5-10 62
HARMONY (7000 series).........................15-25 57
HARMONY (7300 series)...........................8-15 64
Also see ARMSTRONG, Louis, & Red Nichols, & Danny Kaye
Also see BROWN, Earl
Also see WESTON, Paul, Orchestra

KAYE, Danny, & Louis Armstrong

Singles: 7-inch

DOT...5-10 59-64

Picture Sleeves

DOT (15941 "Five Pennies Saints") 8-12 59
Also see ARMSTRONG, Louis

KAYE, Danny, Jimmy Durante, Jane Wyman & Groucho Marx P&R '51
(With the Sonny Burke Orchestra; with 4 Hits And A Miss)

Singles: 78 rpm

DECCA...5-10 51

Singles: 7-inch

DECCA (27748 "Black Strap Molasses") .10-15 51
Also see DURANTE, Jimmy
Also see KAYE, Danny
Also see MARX, Groucho

KAYE, Jimmy

Singles: 7-inch

TNT (149 "I Wonder")..............................10-20 57

KAYE, Jimmy, & Coachmen

Singles: 7-inch

SOMA (1441 "Gloria")..............................25-35 '60s

KAYE, Jonie, & Chapelaires

Singles: 7-inch

ALPHA (1042 "Lonely Star")....................15-25 64
GATEWAY (744 "Lonely Star")................25-35 64
Also see CHAPELAIRES

KAYE, Kitty, & Cats

Singles: 7-inch

HAWK (72054 "Can't You Hear the Music")..40-60

KAYE, Mary P&R '52
(Mary Kaye Trio)

Singles: 78 rpm

CAPITOL...3-6 52
DECCA...3-6 55-56
RCA...3-6 54

Singles: 7-inch

BLUE-J (3 "I Want a Bracelet or a Diamond")..4-8
CAMELOT (132 "Can't Get You Off My Mind")...4-8 67
CAPITOL...10-15 52
DECCA..10-15 55-56
LECTRON (1963 "Actions Speak Louder Than Words")..4-8 65
RCA..10-15 54
VERVE (10228 "Kiss Me Again")...............5-10 60
W.B. 5-10 59

EPs: 7-inch

DECCA..5-10 56

LPs: 10/12-inch

COLUMBIA 10-15 62
DECCA..15-25 56
MOVIETONE 8-12 67
20TH FOX...10-15 64
VERVE..10-20 60-62
W.B. 10-20 59
Also see BYRNES, Edd "Kookie," with Joanie Sommers & Mary Kaye Trio

KAYE, Ronny

Singles: 7-inch

BAND BOX (336 "Flight for Drums") 15-25 63
BAND BOX (339 "Let There Be Drums") .15-25 63

KAYE, Sammy, & His Orchestra P&R '37

Singles: 78 rpm

COLUMBIA 3-6 50-57
RCA...3-6 52-53

Singles: 7-inch

COLUMBIA..5-10 50-60
DECCA...4-6 60-70
PROJECT 3 ....4-6 72
RCA...5-10 52-53

EPs: 7-inch

COLUMBIA..5-15 50-60
DECCA..4-6 64
RCA...5-15 52-53

LPs: 10/12-inch

CAMDEN 10-25 53-56
COLUMBIA..10-25 50-62
DECCA...8-15 60-70
HARMONY...5-10 59-68
MCA..5-10 74
PROJECT 3 ....5-8 72
RCA..5-10 68-72
VOCALION 5-10 71
Also see CORNELL, Don

KAYLI, Bob P&R '58
(With the Berry Gordy Orchestra; Robert Gordy)

Singles: 7-inch

ANNA (1104 "Never More") 25-35 59
CARLTON (482 "Everyone Was There") .20-30 58
GORDY (7008 "Toodle Loo"/"Hold On Pearl")...20-30 62
TAMLA (54051 "Small Sad Sam")...........20-30 62

KAYO & TRINITIES

Singles: 7-inch

SOUVENIR (1004 "Walking to School with My Love") 10-20 60

KAYS BAND
(With Rhythm Rogues; Kays; Kays Combo)

Singles: 7-inch

CAS LTD..3-5
CHOICE (3757 "To Be with You") 10-20
CREATIVE ARTS 3-5 80
HIT...4-8
JCP (1007 "Shout")..................................10-20 64
MGM (12630 "Baby") 10-20 58

K-DOE, Ernie *P&R/R&B '61*
(Ernest Kador; Ernie Kado; K-Doe)
Singles: 78 rpm
SPECIALTY (563 "Eternity")....................10-20 55
Singles: 7-inch
DUKE....................5-10 64-69
EMBER (1050 "My Love for You")..........15-20 59
EMBER (1075 "My Love for You")..........10-15 61
IMPERIAL (039 "Mother-in-Law")..............5-10 65
INSTANT (3260 "Sufferin' So")..............8-12 63
INSTANT (3264 "Reaping What I Sow").....8-12 64
MINIT (604 "There's a Will There's a Way")....................15-25 59
MINIT (614 "Hello My Lover")..................15-25 60
MINIT (623 "Mother-in-Law")..................15-25 61
MINIT (627 thru 665)....................10-15 61-63
MINIT (32042 "Te-Ta-Te-Ta-Ta")..............5-8 68
SANSU (1016 "She Gave It All to Me")....10-20
SPECIALTY (563 "Eternity")....................20-30 55
SYLA....................4-8
U.A. (110 "Mother-in-Law")....................4-6
LPs: 10/12-inch
BANDY (70004 "Ernie K-Doe, Vol. 1").....10-15 '70s
BANDY (70005 "Ernie K-Doe, Vol. 2").....10-15 '70s
JANUS....................8-10 71
MINIT (0002 "Mother-in-Law")..............75-100 61
Session: Benny Spellman.
Also see BLUE DIAMONDS
Also see SPELLMAN, Benny
Also see THOMAS, Irma / Ernie K-Doe / Showmen / Benny Spellman.

KEALOHA, Kalani
Singles: 7-inch
U.A. (212 "It Wasn't a Dream")................15-25 60

KEAN, Ronnie
Singles: 7-inch
FEDERAL (12424 "Chariot")....................10-20 61

KEARNS, Nick, & His Satellites
Singles: 7-inch
TOBE (1177 "T'was Down in Mexico")....40-60 58
(Identification number shown since no selection number is used.)

KEEBLER, Danny
Singles: 7-inch
SOUTH (101 "Match Box")....................50-75

KEEFE, Bob
Singles: 7-inch
SCOPE (1964 "Satellite Sadie")............75-125

KEEFER, Brenda
Singles: 7-inch
MARLO (1525 "Down the Line")..............10-15 62
Also see KEEFER SISTERS

KEEFER, Lyle
Singles: 7-inch
LINCOLN (758 "Come Back to Me")......75-125

KEEFER, Rusty, & His Greenlights
Singles: 78 rpm
CORAL....................5-10 55
Singles: 7-inch
CORAL (61421 "Sweet Corrina Blues")...10-20 55
CORAL (61499 "Rock-A-Way")..............10-20 55
Session: The Greenlights are Bill Haley's Comets. Rusty is the father of the Keefer Sisters.
Also see HALEY, Bill

KEEFER SISTERS
Singles: 7-inch
LAWN (101 "Wedding Bouquet")............10-20 60
SWAN (4015 "Summer Souvenir")..........10-20 58
VIRTUE....................4-8
Session: Bill Haley's Comets.
Also see KEEFER, Brenda
Also see KEEFER, Rusty, & His Greenlights

KEEGAN, Kathy
Singles: 7-inch
ABC (10806 thru 10877)....................5-10 66
AL BRITE (1305 "Nobody's Gonna Hurt You")....................10-15 60
COMPASS (7013 thru 7020)....................5-10 67-68
DCP (1006 thru 1127)....................5-10 64-65
MALIBU (1219 "Good Life")....................5-10 63
LPs: 10/12-inch
ABC (602 "Suddenly")....................10-20 66
DCP (3800 "When You're Young and in Love")....................15-25 64
(Monaural.)
DCP (6800 "When You're Young and in Love")....................20-30 64
(Stereo.)
MALIBU (100 "Good Life")....................20-30 63

KEEN, Billy
(Billy Keene; with Tradewinds)
Singles: 7-inch
ACCLAIM (1006 "Come a Little Closer")..15-25 61
DOTTIE (1134 "Somebody Please")........10-20
GALAXY (726 "Finally I Got Wise")...........8-12 64
KEEN (1922 "Don't Call Me")...................30-50 58
KEEN (82123 "Angel")....................5-10 61
LESLEY (1922 "Don't Call Me")...............10-15 61
PAULA (335 "Cross My Heart")...............8-12 70
VAULT (943 "Cross My Heart")................10-15 68

KEENAN, Ronny
Singles: 7-inch
SANDY (1005 "Juke Box Queen").........75-100 57

KEENE, Bobby
Singles: 7-inch
CORAL (62260 "Listen Little Girl")...........10-15 61
CORAL (62290 "Angel or Devil")..............10-15 61

KEENE, Nelson
Singles: 7-inch
CAPITOL (4540 "Teenage Troubles")......10-15 61

KEENEY, Chuck
Singles: 7-inch
FELSTED (8584 "Rockin' March")............15-25 59

KEENOS
Singles: 7-inch
LARK (4513 "Catwalk")....................10-20 59
(Colored vinyl.)

KEETIE & KATS
("The Rockinest of the Rockin;" "Vocal Jimmy Clendening)
Singles: 7-inch
HURON (22007 "Way Out")....................10-20 61
K-RECORDS (301 "Move")....................15-25 60
K-W (503 "That's the Way")....................50-100 59

KEGGS
Singles: 7-inch
ORBIT (20959 "To Find Out")..............200-300 67
(Identification number shown since no selection number is used. Reportedly 75 copies made.)
Note: Originals have "Produced by Yolanda Owens" at right. Counterfeits credit "Yalanda Owens" – Yolanda being misspelled.
Members: Art Lenox; Steve Cool; Bob Rich; Pat Amboyan.

KEITH *P&R '66*
(James Keefer)
Singles: 7-inch
DISCREET....................4-6 71-74
MERCURY....................5-10 66-68
PHILCO (20 "98.6"/"Ain't Gonna Lie")......10-20 67
("Hip Pocket" flexi-disc.)
RCA....................5-10 69
Picture Sleeves
MERCURY....................5-10 66-68
LPs: 10/12-inch
MERCURY....................15-20 67
RCA....................15-25 69
Also see TOKENS

KEITH, Anne
Singles: 7-inch
MEMO (897 "Lonely Girl")....................350-400 59
Session: El Venos.
Also see EL VENOS

KEITH, Bryan
Singles: 7-inch
DOT (16532 "Hound Dog")....................10-15 63
JOSIE (897 "Always Heartaches")............10-15 62

KEITH, Dusty
Singles: 7-inch
ARK (294 "Fool Over You")....................100-150

KEITH, Freeman, & Ramrods
Singles: 7-inch
KEY (15673 "I'll Find a New Love")..........10-15

KEITH, Larry
Singles: 7-inch
BLUE RIBBON (301 "Rattlesnake Boogie")....................50-75
NUMBER ONE....................4-6 79
RCA....................3-5 80-81

KELL & CHERRY
Singles: 7-inch
GLOWHILL (701 "That's What's Happenin' ")....................15-25
Member: Kell Osborne.
Also see OSBORNE, Kell

KELLER, Jerry *P&R '59*
Singles: 7-inch
CAPITOL....................5-10 61
CORAL....................5-10 63-64
KAPP (K-277 "Here Comes Summer").......8-12 59
(Monaural.)
KAPP (KS-277 "Here Comes Summer")..20-30 59
(Stereo.)
KAPP (310 thru 353)....................5-10 59-60
RCA....................5-10 67
REPRISE....................5-10 65
WEB....................5-10 58
Picture Sleeves
KAPP (277 "Here Comes Summer")........10-15 59
KAPP (295 "If I Had a Girl")....................10-15 59
LPs: 10/12-inch
KAPP (1178 "Here Comes Jerry Keller").20-30 59
(Monaural.)
KAPP (3178 "Here Comes Jerry Keller").25-35 59
(Stereo.)

KELLER, Jimmy
Singles: 7-inch
TRAIL (288 "Brush Pile Burns")...........300-400

KELLEY, Dean
Singles: 7-inch
CORAL (61969 "If The Shoe Fits")..........10-15 58

KELLOGS
Singles: 7-inch
LAURIE (3476 "Snap, Crackle, Pop").......10-15 69
Member: Vito Balsamo.
Also see VITO & SALUTATIONS

KELLUM, Murry / Glenn Sutton *P&R '63*
Singles: 7-inch
ABC....................4-6 73
M.O.C. (653 "Long Tall Texan"/"I Gotta Leave This Town")....................15-20 63
(No mention of London distribution.)
M.O.C. (653 "Long Tall Texan"/"I Gotta Leave This Town")....................10-15 63
(Label indicates "Distributed by London Records.")
Also see SUTTON, Glenn

KELLY, Calvin
Singles: 7-inch
CAMARO (3455 "I'm Begging You").........10-20

KELLY, Charles, & 3 Of Us Trio
Singles: 7-inch
YORK (3332 "Telegram")....................75-125 58

KELLY, Clyde
Singles: 7-inch
CUCA (6471 "I'll Cry Tomorrow")............15-25 64

KELLY, Dean
Singles: 7-inch
FASHION (1002 "Hey Baby")....................50-75

KELLY, Emmett
LPs: 10/12-inch
ROULETTE (R-25130 "Sing Along with Emmett Kelly")....................15-25 61
(Monaural.)
ROULETTE (SR-25130 "Sing Along with Emmett Kelly")....................20-30 61
(Stereo.)

KELLY, Jimmy
(With the Op Birds; with Rockabeats)
Singles: 78 rpm
IMPERIAL (8275 "Dunce Cap")...............10-20 54
Singles: 7-inch
ASTRA (101 "Little Chickie")....................15-25 58
CEVETONE (514 "Op Song")....................10-15 63
COBRA (5028 "Little Chickie")..................40-50 58
EPIC (9582 "Op Song")....................8-12 63
IMPERIAL (8275 "Dunce Cap")...............20-40 54
JIFFY (202 "Dunce Cap")....................50-75 53
MERCURY (72551 "Tubby Or Not Tubby")....................5-10 66

KELLY, Karol
Singles: 7-inch
JOY (272 "Slow Dance")....................20-30 62

KELLY, Leon, & Rhythm Rockers
Singles: 7-inch
SPACE (795 "You Put My Heart in Orbit")....................10-15 59

KELLY, Mike, & Legend
Singles: 7-inch
MEGAPHONE (705 "I Love the Little Girls")....................10-15 '60s
Also see LEGEND

KELLY, Monty, & His Orchestra *P&R '53*
Singles: 78 rpm
ESSEX....................3-5 53-55
Singles: 7-inch
CARLTON....................4-8 58-60
ESSEX....................5-10 53-55
LPs: 10/12-inch
ALSHIRE....................4-8 72
CARLTON....................10-20 59
ESSEX (106 "I Love")....................15-25 54
(10-inch LP.)
ESSEX (108 "Far Away Places")..............15-25 54
(10-inch LP.)
Also see MANNING, Bob

KELLY, Pat
Singles: 7-inch
CHIC....................10-15 57
JUBILEE (5315 "Hey Doll Baby")............40-60 58
JUBILEE (5333 "Patsy")....................8-12 58

KELLY, Paul *P&R/R&B '70*
Singles: 7-inch
DIAL....................5-10 65-68
EPIC (50555 "Everybody's Got a Jones")....4-6 78
HAPPY TIGER (568 "Hot Runnin' Soul").....4-6 71
PHILIPS....................10-20 66-68
TK....................10-20 60
W.B....................4-6 73-77
Picture Sleeves
PHILIPS....................10-20 66
LPs: 10/12-inch
HAPPY TIGER....................8-10 70
W.B....................8-10 72-76
Also see TEX, Joe
Also see VALADIERS

KELLY, Roy
Singles: 7-inch
MAIL CALL (1003 "Rock & Roll Rock")....................200-300 61
STANCHEL (028 "Draggin' It")..................50-75

KELLY, Sterling
Singles: 7-inch
KEL (1863 "Lonely Hearts")..................150-250

KELLY, Walt
LPs: 10/12-inch
SIMON & SCHUSTER ("Songs of the Pogo")....................50-75 56
(No selection number used.)

KELLY & SOUL EXPLOSIONS
Singles: 7-inch
DYNA MITE (110 "Talkin' 'Bout My Baby's Love")....................20-30 '60s

KELLY BROTHERS *R&B '66*
Singles: 7-inch
EXCELLO (2286 thru 2308)........................8-12 67-69
FEDERAL (12373 "I've Been Striving for So Long")....................25-50 60
FEDERAL (12404 "He's All Right")...........25-50 60
FEDERAL (12472 "I Couldn't Hear Nobody Pray")....................15-25 62
SIMS (210 thru 317)....................10-20 64-67
LPs: 10/12-inch
EXCELLO (8007 "Sweet Soul")...............25-35 68
Members: Andrew Kelly; Robert Kelly; Curtis Kelly.
Session: Charles Lee; Offe Reese.
Also see KING PINS

KELLY FOUR
Singles: 7-inch
CANDIX (325 "Annie Has a Party")..........10-15 63

SILVER (1001 "Strollin' Guitar") ... 15-25 59
SILVER (1006 "Annie Has a Party") ... 25-50 60
(Eddie Cochran plays guitar on *Annie Has a Party*, later issued as *Annie Had a Party*, by the Gee Cees. The Candix release is a different take of basically the same song.)
Also see COCHRAN, Eddie
Also see GEE CEES

KELLY SISTERS
Singles: 7-inch
COED (602 "Joey") ... 15-25 65

KELPER, Paul
Singles: 7-inch
DRUM (24 "Betty Lou") ... 100-200

KELSO, Dave
Singles: 7-inch
ROSE (112 "My Heart Goes Thump") ... 25-50 58

KELSO, Jackie
(With the Colts; Jackie Kelso & Orchestra)
Singles: 78 rpm
MAMBO ... 10-15 55
VITA ... 10-15 55-56
Singles: 7-inch
CENCO (121 "Baby Elephant Walk") ... 15-25 62
(First issue.)
MAMBO (104 "Piccadilly") ... 15-25 55
MAMBO (108 "Blue Moon") ... 15-25 55
RIVIERA (121 "Baby Elephant Walk") ... 10-15 62
SPRY (104 "Jumpin' Gee") ... 15-25 57
VITA ... 15-25 55-56
Also see SQUIRES

KELTON, Robert, & His Trio
Singles: 78 rpm
ALADDIN (3000 series) ... 10-20 50
Singles: 7-inch
ALADDIN (3187 "No, No, Baby") ... 20-30 50

KEMP, Eben
Singles: 7-inch
ARAGON (304 "Rootie Tootie") ... 50-75

KEMPER, Jim, & Four Tiers
("Music By the Renegades")
Singles: 7-inch
LE-MANS (002 "Lonely for Kathy") ... 125-150 64

KEMPY & GUARDIANS
Singles: 7-inch
LUCKY SOUND (1006 "Never") ... 20-30 '60s
ROMUNDA (1 "Never") ... 20-30 '60s

KEN & CORKY
Singles: 7-inch
BIG TOP (3031 "Nuttin' for Christmas") ... 10-20 59

KEN & FOURTH DIMENSION
Singles: 7-inch
STARBURST (128 "See If I Care") ... 15-25 66

KENDALL SISTERS *P&R/R&B '58*
Singles: 7-inch
ARGO (5278 "Don't Bother Me") ... 10-15 57
ARGO (5291 "Yea, Yea") ... 15-25 58
ARGO (5310 "Let's Wait") ... 8-12 58
CHECKER (884 "Make It Soon") ... 8-12 58
CHECKER (889 "Yea, Yea") ... 8-12 58

KENDRICK, Nat, & Swans *P&R/R&B '60*
Singles: 7-inch
DADE (1804 thru 1812) ... 10-15 59-60
DADE ... 8-10 63
Members: James Brown; King Coleman; J.C. Davis; Bobby Roach; Bernard Odum.
Also see BROWN, James

KENDRICK, Willie
Singles: 7-inch
GOLDEN WORLD (1 "Fine As Wine") ... 15-25 63
RCA (8947 "You Can't Bypass Love") ... 20-30 66
RCA (9212 "Change Your Ways") ... 25-50 67

KENDRIX, Bert
Singles: 7-inch
MARTAY (2003 "Zodico") ... 10-20 64

KENNARD
Singles: 7-inch
DORE (848 "What Did You Gain by That") ... 20-30 69

KENNEDY, Ace
(With the Candies)
Singles: 7-inch
PHILIPS (40091 "Down Where the Gang Hangs Out") ... 10-15 63
PHILIPS (40111 "As Time Goes By") ... 15-20 63
SWAN (4080 "I Made a Mistake") ... 10-15 61
XYZ (609 "You Promise") ... 10-15 60

KENNEDY, Billy
(Billie Kennedy)
Singles: 7-inch
SILVER (250 "If I Was a Kid") ... 10-20 '60s
THELMA (109 "Groovy Generation") ... 50-100 64

KENNEDY, Dave
(With the Blazers)
Singles: 7-inch
APEX (76071 "Joanie") ... 10-20 60
BOLO (721 "Where Did My Darling Go") ... 8-12 61
CUCA (1004 "Joanie") ... 15-20 60
(First issue. Later Cuca releases are by another Dave Kennedy, listed next.)
DINAMO (1002 "Pizza Pie") ... 10-20 59
JOB (502 "Night Train") ... 8-12 '60s
RAYNARD (1001 "Some Sweet Tomorrow") ... 15-25 66
RAYNARD (1002 "That Ring on Your Finger") ... 15-25 66
SOMA (1138 "Joanie") ... 8-12 60
LPs: 10/12-inch
PAGE ... 10-12

KENNEDY, Dave
(With Ambassadors; with Blazers; with Super-Phonics; with U.S.A. Band)
Singles: 7-inch
AUDEM ... 3-5 89
CUCA (1036 thru 1133, except 1107) ... 10-20 61-63
CUCA (1107 "Peepin' & Hidin'") ... 20-30 62
Note: Cuca 1004 is also by a Dave Kennedy, a completely different artist who is listed above.
Picture Sleeves
CUCA (1036 "Wooden Heart") ... 15-25 61
CUCA (1133 "Zombie Jamboree") ... 15-25 63
LPs:10/12-inch
COULEE (1001 "Breaking Up Is Hard to Do") ... 20-40 64
ELI ... 5-8 '80s
Members: Tari Tovsen; Ronnie Rink; Tom Neary; Tom Eisenman; Al Banasik; Chuck Sargeant; Jerry Oliver; George Eberdt.
Also see O'NEAL, Lance
Also see SARGENT, Chuck, & Ambassadors
Also see WALKER, Lonnie

KENNEDY, Dave, & Super-Phonics / Super-Phonics
Singles: 7-inch
LINDY (101 "B-L-U-E"/"Me Neither") ... 10-20 60
Also see KENNEDY, Dave
Also see SUPER-PHONICS

KENNEDY, Gene
(With the Dons)
Singles: 7-inch
HICKORY ... 5-10 64-66
INTREPID (75005 "Dreamin' Again") ... 5-10 69
OLD TOWN ... 10-15 60-63
PARADISE (112 "I'll Still Be Loving You") ... 15-25 59
VICTORIA (101 "Three's a Crowd") ... 5-10 63

KENNEDY, Jacqueline
LPs: 10/12-inch
AUDIO FIDELITY (703 "Jacqueline Kennedy") ... 15-25 66

KENNEDY, Jerry
Singles: 7-inch
DECCA ... 10-15 58
SMASH ... 5-10 63-64
LPs: 10/12-inch
MERCURY (692 "Jerry Kennedy and Friends") ... 5-10 74
MERCURY (61339 "Jerry Kennedy Plays") ... 8-12 71
SMASH (27004 "Jerry Kennedy's Dancing Guitars Rock Elvis' Hits") ... 15-20 62
(Monaural.)
SMASH (27024 "Golden Standards") ... 10-20 63
(Monaural.)
SMASH (27066 "From Nashville to Soulville") ... 10-20 65
(Monaural.)
SMASH (67004 "Jerry Kennedy's Dancing Guitars Rock Elvis' Hits") ... 20-25 62
(Stereo.)
SMASH (67024 "Golden Standards") ... 15-20 63
(Stereo.)
SMASH (67066 "From Nashville to Soulville") ... 15-20 65
(Stereo.)
Also see PAGE, Patti
Also see PRESLEY, Elvis
Also see TIDES
Also see TOM & JERRY

KENNEDY, John Fitzgerald *LP '63*
EPs: 7-inch
GOLDEN (766 "Voice of President John F. Kennedy") ... 5-10 '60s
LPs: 10/12-inch
CAEDMON ... 5-10 64
CHALLENGE ... 8-15 64
COLPIX ... 10-20 64
COLUMBIA ... 10-20 65
DECCA ... 10-20 63
DIPLOMAT ... 5-15 63
DOCUMENTARIES UNLIMITED ... 10-20 63
GATEWAY ... 8-15 64
GOLDEN ... 8-15 63
HARMONIA ... 8-15 64
LEGACY ... 10-20 65
MARK 56 ... 10-20 64
PALACE ... 8-15 64
PHILIPS ... 8-15 64
PICKWICK ... 8-12 63
PREMIER ... 10-20 63
RCA ... 8-15 64
REGINA ... 5-15 64
SOMERSET ... 5-15 63
20TH FOX ... 10-20 63
(Most of the albums listed above are a tribute of some type to President Kennedy after his assassination on November 22, 1963. Most contain excerpts of his speeches.)

KENNEDY, John Fitzgerald / Richard M. Nixon
LPs: 10/12-inch
COLUMBIA ... 10-15 68
Also see KENNEDY, John Fitzgerald
Also see NIXON, Richard

KENNEDY, Joyce *R&B/LP '84*
Singles: 7-inch
A&M ... 3-5 84-85
BLUE ROCK (4016 "I'm a Good Girl") ... 20-25 65
BLUE ROCK (4023 "Hi-Fi, Albums and I") ... 15-20 65
FONTANA (1924 "Could This Be Love") ... 15-25 64
RAN-DEE (110 "I Still Love You") ... 10-20 63
RAN-DEE (118 "How Old Is Old") ... 10-15 63
Picture Sleeves
A&M (2685 "Stronger Than Before") ... 3-5 84
A&M (2790 "Hold On") ... 3-5 85
LPs: 10/12-inch
A&M ... 5-8 84
Also see MOTHER'S FINEST

KENNEDY, Robert Francis *LP '69*
LPs: 10/12-inch
COLUMBIA (792 "A Memorial") ... 10-20 68
(Two discs.)

KENNEDY, Tiny
(Jesse Tiny Kennedy)
Singles: 7-inch
CAPITOL (840 "The Lady with the Black Dress On") ... 25-40 49
GROOVE (0106 "Country Boy") ... 30-50 55
GROOVE (0133 "Strange Kind of Feeling") ... 30-50 55
TRUMPET (187 "Strange Kind of Feeling") ... 15-25 53
TRUMPET (188 "Blues Disease") ... 15-25 53

KENNER, Chris *R&B '57*
Singles: 78 rpm
BATON (220 "Don't Let Her Pin That Charge") ... 10-20 56
IMPERIAL ... 10-20 57
Singles: 7-inch
BATON (220 "Don't Let Her Pin That Charge") ... 30-40 56
HEP ME (115 "We Belong Together") ... 4-8
IMPERIAL (5448 "Sick and Tired") ... 25-35 57
IMPERIAL (5488 "Will You Be Mine") ... 20-30 58
IMPERIAL (5767 "Sick and Tired") ... 10-15 61
INSTANT (3229 "I Like It Like That") ... 10-20 61
INSTANT (3234 thru 3257) ... 10-15 61-63
INSTANT (3263 thru 3290) ... 8-12 64-68
OLDIES 45 ... 4-8 '60s
PRIGAN (2002 "Right Kind of Girl") ... 10-20 61
RON (335 "Rocket to the Moon") ... 10-15 61
TRIP ... 4-6 '70s
UPTOWN (708 "Life of My Baby") ... 8-10 65
UPTOWN (716 "I'm the Greatest") ... 8-10 65
VALIANT (3229 "I Like It Like That") ... 40-60 61
LPs: 10/12-inch
ATLANTIC (8117 "Land of 1,000 Dances") ... 20-30 66
BANDY (70015 "The Name of the Place") ... 10-15 '70s

KENNINGTON, Ken
Singles: 7-inch
CONFEDERATE (130 "It Goes Without Saying") ... 150-250

KENNY, Bill
(With the Song Spinners)
Singles: 78 rpm
DECCA ... 4-6 50-53
VIK ... 4-6 56
"X" ... 4-6 55
Singles: 7-inch
DECCA ... 5-10 50-53
MERCURY (30106 "If I Didn't Care") ... 5-10 62
TEL (1004 "Oh What It Seemed to Be") ... 5-10 59
VIK (0195 "Two Little Candles") ... 5-10 56
VIK (0225 "Now You Say You Care") ... 5-10 56
WARWICK (541 "Into Each Life Some Rain Must Fall") ... 5-10 60
"X" (0124 "We Three") ... 5-10 55
"X" (0155 "The Gypsy") ... 5-10 55
LPs: 10/12-inch
DECCA (5333 "Precious Memories") ... 25-50 51
(10-inch LP.)
MERCURY (20691 "Golden Hits of the Ink Spots") ... 20-30 62
(Monaural.)
MERCURY (60691 "Golden Hits of the Ink Spots") ... 25-35 62
(Stereo.)
WING (12286 "Golden Hits of the Ink Spots") ... 10-20 64
(Monaural.)
WING (16286 "Golden Hits of the Ink Spots") ... 15-25 64
(Stereo.)
Also see INK SPOTS

KENNY, FRANK & RAY
Singles: 7-inch
CAMEO (144 "Everybody Loves Saturday Night") ... 15-25 58
PL (13 "If You Love Me") ... 50-75 58
Member: Kenny Bolognese; Frank Cacapardo; Ray Carlisle.
Also see CHANDLER, Kenny

KENNY, Herb
(With the Comets; with Rockets)
Singles: 78 rpm
FEDERAL (12083 "Only You") ... 40-60 52
MGM (11332 "My Song") ... 15-25 52
Singles: 7-inch
FEDERAL (12083 "Only You") ... 100-150 52
MGM (11332 thru 11648) ... 30-40 52-53

KENNY, Sue
Singles: 7-inch
TRIBUTE (118 "Look") ... 250-350 63
Session: Concords.
Also see CONCORDS

KENNY & BEBOPS
Singles: 7-inch
CHATEAU (116 "Lindy Lou") ... 200-300

KENNY & CADETS
Singles: 7-inch
RANDY (422 "Barbie") ... 350-450 62
(Black vinyl.)

RANDY (422 "Barbie")........................750-1000 62
(Red and yellow vinyl.)
Members: Kenny Doll; Brian Wilson; Carl Wilson; Al Jardine; Audree Wilson.
Also see BEACH BOYS

KENNY & CORKY
Singles: 7-inch
BIG TOP (3031 "Nuttin' for Christmas")......8-10 59
Picture Sleeves
BIG TOP (3031 "Nuttin' for Christmas")... 10-20 59

KENNY & DOOLITTLE
Singles: 7-inch
SIMS (123 "Kitty Kat")........................ 100-125 62

KENNY & FIENDS
(Kenny & the Beach Fiends)
Singles: 7-inch
DOT (16568 "House on Haunted Hill") 8-12 63
DOT (16596 "Moon Shot")..........................8-12 64
POSEA (80 "The Raven").......................... 15-25 63
POSEA (87 "House on Haunted Hill")...... 15-25 63
PRINCESS (51 "House on Haunted Hill")... 15-25 63
(First issue.)
PRINCESS (84 "Last Night")................... 15-25 63

KENNY & HO-DADDIES
Singles: 7-inch
INDIGO (134 "Surf Dance")..................... 10-15 61

KENNY & IMPACTS
Singles: 7-inch
DCP (1147 "Wishing Well") 25-35 65

KENNY & KASUALS
Singles: 7-inch
MARK (911 "Nothing Better to Do") 20-25 65
MARK (1002 "Don't Let Your Baby Go").. 20-30 66
MARK (1003 "It's All Right") 20-25 66
MARK (1004 "Strings of Time") 20-30 66
MARK (1006 "Journey to Tyme") 25-35 66
MARK (1008 "See-Saw Ride") 20-30 67
U.A. (50085 "Journey to Tyme").............. 10-15 66
EPs: 7-inch
MARK (400 "Kenny and the Kasuals Are Back").. 10-15 79
(Black vinyl.)
MARK (400 "Kenny and the Kasuals Are Back").. 10-15 79
(Clear vinyl.)
LPs: 10/12-inch
MARK (5000 "Impact Sound")............. 250-350 66
MARK (5000 "Impact Sound")....................8-12 77
(Cover reads "Reissue, 1977.")
MARK (6000 "Teen Dreams") 100-150 78
(Colored vinyl, signed, numbered limited edition.)
MARK (7000 "Garage Kings")............... 10-15 79
Members: Kenny Daniel; Tom Nichols; Jerry Smith; Richard Borgens; Paul Roach; David Blackley; Dan Green; Karl Tomorrow; Ron Mason; Greg Daniels.
Also see TRUTH

KENNY & KNIGHTS
Singles: 7-inch
EDMAC (106 "She's My Little Girl") .... 10-15 '60s

KENNY & MOE
(Blues Boys; Kenny & Mose)
Singles: 78 rpm
DELUXE 10-15 56
Singles: 7-inch
DELUXE (6101 thru 6154)........................ 15-25 56-57
JOSIE (854 "Tell Me That Your Love Is Real").. 10-15 59
Members: Kenny Ballard; Moses Pelham.

KENNY & NIGHT RIDERS
Singles: 7-inch
BRISTOL (102 "Andromeda") 10-20 63
Members: Kenny LeBlanc; Paul Anderson; Rene Goguen; Ron Roy; Richie Sbrega; Frank Dionne.

KENNY & SOCIALITES
(With the Joe René Orchestra)
Singles: 7-inch
CROSSTOWN (001 "I'll Have to Decide") 250-350 58
(White label. Promotional issue only.)
CROSSTOWN (001 "I'll Have to Decide") 200-300 58
(Pink label.)

KENNY & WHALERS
(With Vince Catalano & Orchestra)
Singles: 7-inch
WHALE (504 "Life Is But a Dream") 100-150 61
Also see CATALANO, Vinny
Also see DONNIE & DREAMERS

KENNY & YVONNE
Singles: 7-inch
COLUMBIA (43594 "Don't Go to Strangers")..10-15 66
Member: Kenny Rankin.
Also see RANKIN, Kenny

KENON, Abner
Singles: 78 rpm
JAY-DEE (804 "Baby Come Back to Me")..5-10 55
Singles: 7-inch
JAY-DEE (804 "Baby Come Back to Me")..10-15 55

KENSINGTON MARKET
Singles: 7-inch
W.B. (7221 "I Would Be the One") 5-10 68
LPs: 10/12-inch
W.B. 15-20 68-69

KENT, Adrienne
Singles: 78 rpm
BRUCE (2005 "I'll Remember April") 10-15 55
Singles: 7-inch
BRUCE (2005 "I'll Remember April") 15-20 55

KENT, Al *P&R/R&B '67*
Singles: 78 rpm
CHECKER (881 "Dat's Why") 15-25 57
Singles: 7-inch
BARITONE (942 "Hold Me")....................50-100 60
CHECKER (881 "Dat's Why") 15-25 57
RIC-TIC (123 "The Way You Been Acting Lately")..10-20 67
RIC-TIC (127 "You've Got to Pay the Price")..10-20 67
RIC-TIC (133 "Ooh! Pretty Lady") 10-20 67
WINGATE (004 "You Know I Love You") .15-25 65
WIZARD (100 "Hold Me") 75-100 59
Session: Dennis Coffey.
Also see FLAMING EMBERS / Al Kent
Also see NITECAPS
Also see WEAVER, Joe

KENT, Billy, & Andantes
Singles: 7-inch
BACK BEAT (512 "Ridin' on a Rainbow") 40-60 58
MAH'S (0002 "Your Love") 50-75 60
(No mention of Roulette Records.")
MAH'S (0002 "Your Love") 30-50 60
(With "Dist. By Roulette Records.")
Also see HOLLAND – DOZIER

KENT, Bob
Singles: 78 rpm
PAR (1303) 20-30 52
(Title not known.)

KENT, Bobby
Singles: 7-inch
BAY STATE (82159 "Don't Go Away") .100-200
MERCURY (71684 "Alabam") 10-20 60

KENT, Wayne
Singles: 7-inch
INSTRO (1000 "Pam")..............................50-75

KENT & CANDIDATES
("Vocal Backing: Ideals")
Singles: 7-inch
DOUBLE SHOT 5-10 67-68
LEISA (1001 "Never Let Me Go") ....75-125 '60s

KENTON, Stan, & His Orchestra *P&R '44*
Singles: 78 rpm
CAPITOL 3-6 45-57
Singles: 7-inch
CAPITOL (Purple labels) 5-15 50-61
CAPITOL (Orange & Yellow labels) 4-8 61-68
CAPITOL STARLINE ....4-6 '60s
Picture Sleeves
CAPITOL (386 "Stan Kenton Prologue: This Is an Orchestra") ....10-20 '50s
EPs: 7-inch
CAPITOL 5-15 50-59
LPs: 10/12-inch
BRIGHT ORANGE..5-8 73
CAPITOL (H-155 "Encores") 50-75 49
(10-inch LP.)
CAPITOL (T-155 "Encores") 25-50 55
CAPITOL (H-167 "Artistry in Rhythm") 50-75 49
(10-inch LP.)
CAPITOL (T-167 "Artistry in Rhythm") 25-50 55
CAPITOL (DT-167 "Artistry in Rhythm") 5-10 69
(Stereo.)
CAPITOL (SM-167 "Artistry in Rhythm") 5-8 75
CAPITOL (H-172 "Progressive Jazz") 50-75 50
(10-inch LP.)
CAPITOL (T-172 "Progressive Jazz") 25-50 55
CAPITOL (H-190 "Milestones") 50-75 50
(10-inch LP.)
CAPITOL (T-190 "Milestones") 25-50 55
CAPITOL (H-248 "Stan Kenton Presents") 50-75 50
(10-inch LP.)
CAPITOL (T-248 "Stan Kenton Presents") 25-50 55
CAPITOL (H-353 "City of Glass") 50-75 52
(10-inch LP.)
CAPITOL (T-353 "City of Glass") 25-50 55
CAPITOL (H-358 "Classics") 50-75 52
(10-inch LP.)
CAPITOL (T-358 "Classics") 25-50 55
CAPITOL (T-383 "New Concepts of Artistry in Rhythm") 25-50 54
CAPITOL (H-386 "This Is an Orchestra") .50-75 53
(10-inch LP.)
CAPITOL (T-421 "Popular Favorites By Stan Kenton") 25-50 54
CAPITOL (H-462 "Standards") 50-75 53
(10-inch LP.)
CAPITOL (T-462 "Standards") 25-50 55
CAPITOL (H-524 "Showcase") 50-75 54
(10-inch LP.)
CAPITOL (W-524 "Showcase") 25-75 55
CAPITOL (H-526 "Showcase") 50-75 54
(10-inch LP.)
CAPITOL (W-526 "Showcase") 25-50 55
CAPITOL (305 "Hair") 5-10 69
CAPITOL (600 thru 1200 series) 15-25 56-59
CAPITOL (1300 thru 2900 series) 10-20 60-68
CAPITOL (11000 & 12000 series) 5-8 72-80
CAPITOL (16000 series) 4-6 81
CREATIVE WORLD 5-8 71-80
HINDSIGHT 4-8 84
LONDON 5-8 72-77
MARK 56 ....5-8 77
MFSL (091 "Stan Kenton Plays Wagner") 20-30 82
Also see CHRISTY, June, & Stan Kenton
Also see COLE, Nat "King"
Also see FERGUSON, Maynard

KENTON, Stan, & Tex Ritter
LPs: 10/12-inch
CAPITOL (T-1757 "Stan Kenton & Tex Ritter") 40-60 62
(Monaural.)
CAPITOL (ST-1757 "Stan Kenton & Tex Ritter") 50-75 62
(Stereo.)
Also see KENTON, Stan
Also see RITTER, Tex

KENTONES
(With the Court Jesters)
Singles: 7-inch
SIROC (202 "Marie") 100-200 58

KENTS
Singles: 7-inch
ARGO (5299 "I Found My Girl") 15-25 58
DOME (501 "I Love You So") 400-500 58

KENTT, Klark
Singles: 7-inch
4 STAR (1729 "Superman") 10-15 59

KERN, Marcella
Singles: 7-inch
KAREN (1006 "If I Tell Them") 30-40 59

KERNELS
("With Orchestra")
Singles: 78 rpm
SELECT (333 "It's Written All over Your Face") 10-15 53
Singles: 7-inch
SELECT (333 "It's Written All over Your Face") 100-200 53

KEROUAC, Jack
LPs: 10/12-inch
HANOVER (5006 "Blues and Haikus")...50-100 60
VERVE (15005 "Readings by Jack Kerouac on the Beat Generation") 75-125 59

KEROUAC, Jack, & Steve Allen
LPs: 10/12-inch
DOT (3154 "Poetry for the Beat Generation") 100-150 59
HANOVER (5000 "Poetry for the Beat Generation") 75-125 59
Also see ALLEN, Steve
Also see KEROUAC, Jack

KERR, Anita *LP '69*
(Anita Kerr Singers; Quartette; with Royal Philharmonic Orchestra)
Singles: 78 rpm
DECCA 5-10 51-57
Singles: 7-inch
AMPEX 4-6 71
DECCA (27000 thru 30000 series) 10-20 51-60
DECCA (31000 thru 33000 series) 4-8 60-72
DOT 4-8 69-70
RCA 4-8 63-75
W.B. 4-8 66-68
Picture Sleeves
DECCA 10-20
EPs: 7-inch
SESAC 10-20 59
(Also has tracks by Buddy Hackett, Elliot Lawrence, and Bill Snyder.)
LPs: 10/12-inch
AMPEX (10136 "Grow to Know Me") 5-8 71
AMPEX (10142 "A Christmas Story") 5-8 71
BAINBRIDGE 5-8 81
CAMDEN 5-10 68
CENTURY 5-8 79
DECCA 10-20 60-69
DOT 8-12 69-70
RCA 5-15 62-77
VOCALION 5-10 70
W.B. 10-15 66
WORD 5-8 75-77
Also see ALLEN, Rex
Also see ANDERSON, Bill
Also see ANITA & SO-AND-SO'S
Also see ANN-MARGRET
Also see ATKINS, Chet
Also see ATKINS, Chet, Faron Young, & Anita Kerr Singers
Also see BARE, Bobby
Also see BOWERS, Chuck
Also see CHARLES, Tommy
Also see CLINE, Patsy
Also see COMO, Perry
Also see DAVIS, Jimmie
Also see ECHOES
Also see FOLEY, Red
Also see HELMS, Bobby
Also see IVES, Burl
Also see LEE, Brenda
Also see LEE, Robin
Also see LITTLE DIPPERS
Also see MACK, Warner
Also see MULLICAN, Moon
Also see NELSON, Willie
Also see PRESLEY, Elvis
Also see REEVES, Jim
Also see RICH, Charlie
Also see SHANNON, Pat
Also see SNOW, Hank
Also see STEWART, Wynn
Also see WILBURN BROTHERS
Also see WILLIAMS, Lawton
Also see YOUNG, Faron

KERR, Dick, & Sing-Along Teen-Agers
LPs: 10/12-inch
W.B. (1407 "Crazy, Top 40 and Cool") 25-35 60

KERRY, Marvin
Singles: 7-inch
HY SIGN (1111 "Sha-Marie") 50-75

KERRY'S AKOUSTIKS
Singles: 7-inch
MARKUS (6059 "I Can Tell") 20-30 65

KERSEY, Kenny, Trio
Singles: 78 rpm
MERCURY (8948 "Jatp Boogie") 10-15 52
Singles: 7-inch
MERCURY (8948 "Jatp Boogie") 15-25 52
Members: Kenny Kersey; Buddy Rich; Benny Fonville.

KERSHAW, Pee Wee
Singles: 7-inch
GOLDBAND (1118 "You're So Fine") 40-50 61

KESEY, Ken
LPs: 10/12-inch
SOUND CITY PROD. (27690 "The Acid Test") 100-150 67
Also see GRATEFUL DEAD

KESSEL, Barney / Grant Green / Oscar Moore / Mundell Lowe
LPs: 10/12-inch
PARKER (826 "Best Plucking in Town").. 25-40 '60s
Also see GRAPPELLI, Stephane, & Barney Kessel
Also see GREEN, Grant
Also see NELSON, Rick
Also see THOMPSON, Claudia
Also see WILDER BROTHERS

KESSLER, Keith
Singles: 7-inch
MTW (102 "Don't Crowd Me") 15-25 68

KESTRELS
Singles: 7-inch
LAURIE (3053 "There Comes a Time") ... 20-30 60

KETCHUM, Ben
Singles: 7-inch
UBC (1025 "I Don't Wanna") 40-60

KETCHUM, Robert
Singles: 78 rpm
PEACOCK (1623 "Stockade") 10-15 53
Singles: 7-inch
PEACOCK (1623 "Stockade") 15-25 53

KEVIN, Chris
(With the Comics)
Singles: 7-inch
COLT 45 (Except 103) 5-10 59-60
COLT 45 (103 "Haunted House") 25-50 59

KEVIN & GREGG
Singles: 7-inch
ASSOCIATED ARTISTS (116 "Boy You Oughta See Her Now") 8-10 63
ASSOCIATED ARTISTS (464 "I Know Just How You Feel") 8-10 64

KEY, Gary
Singles: 7-inch
RAN-DEE (116 "Cinderella") 50-75 63

KEY, Troyce
Singles: 7-inch
W.B. (5007 "Drown in Tears") 50-60 58
W.B. (5035 "Ain't I Cried Enough") 60-75 59
W.B. (5070 "Most of All") 50-60 59
Session: Sharps.
Also see COCHRAN, Eddie
Also see MELLOMOODS
Also see SHARPS
Also see VELOURS

KEY MEN
Singles: 7-inch
EM 10-20 64
GOLDUST (5019 "What Am I to Do") 20-30

KEY NOTES
Singles: 7-inch
LIN (1001 "Pyramid") 40-60 58

KEYES
Singles: 7-inch
TOP DOG (2314 "She's the One") .... 10-20 '60s

KEYES, Bert
(With His Trio; with Eddie Combs Quintet; with Teddy McRae & His Orchestra; Burt Keyes)
Singles: 78 rpm
RAMA 5-10 53-54
SAVOY 4-8 51
Singles: 7-inch
AMP 3 (133 "Stop Jivin', Start Drivin'") 10-15 57
CLOCK (1048 "Lady in My Heart") 5-10 61
CORAL 10-15 58
RAMA (4 "Wandering Blues") 15-25 53
RAMA (6 "After All I've Been to You") 15-25 53
(Black vinyl.)
RAMA (6 "After All I've Been to You") 40-60 53
(Red vinyl.)
RAMA (12 "Lonely") 15-25 53
RAMA (31 "Write Me Baby") 10-20 54
RAMA (32 "You Blame My Heart") 10-20 54
SIGN (1,000,000 "Peace of Mind") 8-12

KEYES, Larry
Singles: 7-inch
MASCARA (120 "Beatnik Boogie") 10-20 60

KEYES, Troy, & Norma Jenkins
Singles: 7-inch
ABC (11116 "A Good Love Gone Bad") ...10-20 68

KEYMEN
Singles: 7-inch
ABC-PAR (9977 "Miss You") 10-20 58
ABC-PAR (9977S "Miss You") 20-30 58
(Stereo.)
ABC-PAR (9991 "Gazachstahagen") 10-20 58
ABC-PAR (9991S "Gazachstahagen") 20-30 58
(Stereo.)
ABC-PAR (10016 "Dream") 10-20 59
ABC-PAR (10039 "Camilia") 10-20 59
ROULETTE (4433 "Five Weeks in a Balloon") 8-12 62
EPs: 7-inch
ABC-PAR (258 "Dance with Dick Clark") .20-30 58
LPs: 10/12-inch
ABC-PAR (ABC-258 "Dance with Dick Clark") 30-40 58
(Monaural.)
ABC-PAR (ABCS-258 "Dance with Dick Clark") 50-75 58
(Stereo.)

KEY-NOTERS
Singles: 7-inch
SWAN (4048 "Starlight & You") 50-75 60

KEYNOTERS
Singles: 7-inch
KEYNOTE (504 "Come Back Home") 10-15 63
KEYNOTE (629 "The Way You Look Tonight") 5-10 63

KEYNOTES
Singles: 78 rpm
DOT (15225 "Who") 5-10 54
Singles: 7-inch
DOT (15225 "Who") 10-15 54

KEYNOTES
Singles: 78 rpm
APOLLO 25-50 55
Singles: 7-inch
APOLLO (478 "Suddenly") 100-150 55
APOLLO (484 "I Don't Know") 50-100 55
APOLLO (493 "Really Wish You Were Here") 150-200 56
APOLLO (498 "Now I Know") 50-100 56
APOLLO (503 "In the Evening") 100-150 56
APOLLO (513 "One Little Kiss") 100-150 57
Members: Floyd Adams; Sam Kearney; Bernard Matthews.

KEYNOTES
(With Rubin & His Boys)
Singles: 7-inch
POP (111 "Congratulations Baby") 75-125 57

KEYNOTES
Singles: 7-inch
INDEX (101 "Dum-De-Dum-Dum") 10-15 58

KEYNOTES
Singles: 7-inch
TOP RANK (2005 "With These Rings") 15-25 59
LPs: 10/12-inch
SUPERIOR 10-15

KEYS
Singles: 78 rpm
MGM (11168 "Am I in Love") 5-10 52
Singles: 7-inch
MGM (11168 "Am I in Love") 15-25 52

KEYS
Singles: 7-inch
JAM (501 "Barbara") 30-40 64

KEYS
Singles: 7-inch
LEE (0759 "Lovely Roses") 10-20

KEYSTONERS
(Keystoner's)
Singles: 78 rpm
EPIC (9187 "The Magic Kiss") 5-10 56
G&M (102 "Magic Kiss") 10-20 56
Singles: 7-inch
EPIC (9187 "Magic Kiss") 40-50 56
G&M (102 "Magic Kiss") 200-300 56
OKEH (7210 "Magic Kiss") 10-15 64
RIFF (202 "Sleep & Dream") 400-500 61
Members: Norman Smith; Mitch Jackson; Al Singleton; Goliath James.

KEYTONES
Singles: 78 rpm
OLD TOWN (1041 "Wonder of the World") 100-150 57
OLD TOWN (1041 "Seven Wonders of the World") 50-75 57
Singles: 7-inch
OLD TOWN (1041 "Wonder of the World") 150-250 57
OLD TOWN (1041 "Seven Wonders of the World") 50-75 57
(Note slight title change.)

KEYTONES
(With Billy Costa & Orchestra; Key Tones)
Singles: 7-inch
CHELSEA (101 "I Don't Care"/"La Do Da") 10-15 62
CHELSEA (1002 "Don't Tell William") 10-15 61
CHELSEA (1004 "I Don't Care"/"I Was a Teen-Age Monster") 15-25 62
CHELSEA (1013 "Sweet Chariot") 10-15 63
CHELSEA (3066 "I Don't Care"/"La Do Da") 4-6 77
CHESS (1821 "Lover of Mine") 200-300 62
Picture Sleeves
CHELSEA (1004 "I Don't Care"/"I Was a Teen-Age Monster") 25-35 62
(Promotional issue only.)

KEYTONES
Singles: 7-inch
CHESS (1821 "Lover of Mine") 150-250 62

KHAZAD DOOM
LPs: 10/12-inch
LPL (892 "Level 6½") 800-1200 70
Members: Jack Eadon; Tom Sievers; Al Yates; Steve Hilkin.

KICK & TEEN BEATS
Singles: 7-inch
BIG TOP (3144 "Strawberries") 10-20 63

KICKSTANDS
Singles: 7-inch
CHINA 10-20 63
LPs: 10/12-inch
CAPITOL (T-2078 "Black Boots and Bikes") 35-50 64
(Monaural.)
CAPITOL (ST-2078 "Black Boots and Bikes") 40-60 64
(Stereo.)
Session: Gary Usher; Dick Burns; Jerry Cole; Dennis McCarthy; Steve Douglas; Glen Cass; Earl Palmer; William Oden; Stephen LaFever; Frank Capp; Ray Johnson; Benjamin Barrett.
Also see COLE, Jerry
Also see KNIGHTS
Also see USHER, Gary

KID, The
("The Kid"; Bobby Howard)
Singles: 7-inch
RUMBLE (1347 "Sleep Tight") 100-200 61

KID, The / Ponies
Singles: 7-inch
OKEH (7139 "The Pony") 10-15 60
Also see KID, The

KID ROCK
Singles: 7-inch
ARNO (100 "Look What You've Done") 100-150 58

KID THOMAS
Singles: 78 rpm
FEDERAL (12298 "The Spell") 75-100 57
Singles: 7-inch
FEDERAL (12298 "The Spell") 200-300 57
TRANSCONTINENTAL (1012 "Rockin' This Joint Tonight") 100-150 57
EPs: 7-inch
DNL (004 "Rockin' This Joint") 15-25

KIDD, Billy
(With the Madisons)
Singles: 7-inch
JANE (107 "Crazy Guitar") 15-25 59
MADISON (153 "First Time") 40-50 61

KIDD, Eddie
LPs: 10/12-inch
AZRA (001 "Eddie Kidd") 10-15 85
(Picture disc. 500 made.)

KIDD, Johnny, & Pirates
Singles: 7-inch
APT (25040 "Shakin' All Over") 20-30 60
CAPITOL (5065 "I'll Never Get Over You") 10-15 63

KIDDIE KA-DEES
Singles: 7-inch
KING (5181 "Ol Grey Goose") 15-25 58

KIDDS
Singles: 78 rpm
IMPERIAL (5335 "Are You Forgetting Me") 150-200 55
POST 75-125 55
Singles: 7-inch
IMPERIAL (5335 "Are You Forgetting Me") 800-1000 55
POST (2003 "You Broke My Heart") 400-500 55
POST (2010 "Miss Lucy") 4-8
(Red vinyl.)
Also see PELICANS

KIDS
EPs: 7-inch
RCA (4061 "Teenager's Dance the Hop-A-Do") 30-50 57
RCA (4188 "The Kids") 30-50 58

KIDS
Singles: 7-inch
CHROMA (1004 "Flipped Hair & Lace") 8-12 65
Picture Sleeves
CHROMA (1004 "Flipped Hair & Lace") ... 10-20 65

KIDS FROM CLEVELAND
Singles: 78 rpm
WHIPPET (204 "Someone in Love") 5-10 56
Singles: 7-inch
GNP (164 "Someone in Love") 10-20 61
WHIPPET (204 "Someone in Love") 15-25 56

KIDS FROM TEXAS
Singles: 7-inch
HANOVER (4500 "Long Legged Linda") 75-100 58

KILGORE, Merle C&W '60
(With "Friends")
Singles: 78 rpm
IMPERIAL 5-10 54-57
Singles: 7-inch
ASHLEY (6000 "Packing and Unpacking") .. 4-8
COLUMBIA (44279 "Fast Talkin' Louisiana Man") 4-8 67
COLUMBIA (44463 "Patches") 4-8 67
D (1042 "It'll Be My First Time") 8-12 59
ELEKTRA 3-5 81-82
EPIC 4-6 65-67
IMPERIAL (5379 "Teenager's Holiday") ... 15-25 56
IMPERIAL (5409 "Ernie") 45-55 56
IMPERIAL (5555 "Tom Dooley Jr.") 10-20 58
IMPERIAL (5584 "Static") 10-20 59
IMPERIAL (8256 "More & More") 10-20 54
IMPERIAL (8266 "Seeing Double Feeling Single") 10-20 54
IMPERIAL (8300 "Everybody Needs a Little Lovin'") 30-40 56
MGM 4-8 63-64
MERCURY (71839 "Wicked City") 5-8 61
MERCURY (71918 "42 in Chicago") 5-8 62
PARKWAY (864 "I Am") 4-8 63
STARDAY (400 thru 600 series) 6-12 59-61

STARDAY (950 "Good Rockin' Tonight") 4-6 72
W.B. 3-6 74-85

Picture Sleeves

EPIC (10049 "Nevada Smith") 15-20 65
(Sleeve pictures Steve McQueen, Karl Malden, Brian Keith, and others from the film.)

LPs: 10/12-inch

PICKWICK.. 10-20 '70s
STARDAY (251 "There's Gold in Them Thar Hills") 20-30 63
STARDAY (479 "Big Merle Kilgore")..........8-10 73
WING (12316 "The Tall Texan").............. 10-20 66
(Monaural.)
WING (16316 "The Tall Texan")............... 10-20 66
(Stereo.)
Session: Johnny Cash; Hank Williams Jr.

KILGORE, Theola *P&R/R&B '63*

Singles: 7-inch

CANDIX (311 "Later I'll Cry").................. 15-25 60
KT (501 "I'll Keep Trying") 8-12 64
MERCURY (72564 "I Can't Stand It") 5-10 66
SCEPTER (12170 "The Love of My Man").5-10 66
SEROCK (2004 "The Love of My Man").. 10-15 63
SEROCK (2006 "This Is My Prayer")....... 10-15 63

KILI JACKS

Singles: 7-inch

LONDON (10004 "China Rock")............. 10-20 62

KILLEN, Billy
(Billy J. Killen)

Singles: 7-inch

KAM (101 "Walkin' Talkin'") 15-25 60
MERIDIAN (1509 "It Makes No Difference").. 100-150 59
MERIDIAN (1511 "Georgia Boy")............. 30-40 59

KILLEN, Buddy

Singles: 7-inch

DIAL...5-10 68
SCARLET..5-10 '60s
UNIVERSITY (209 "Whatcha Gonna Do Tomorrow") 50-75 60

KILLEN, Ked

Singles: 7-inch

WESTERN RANCH (119 "Hey Pretty Mama")... 100-200

KILLER JOE ORCHESTRA

Singles: 7-inch

ATLANTIC (2279 "Killer Joe") 5-10 65
ATLANTIC (22282 "My Girl Sloopy") 5-10 65

LPs: 10/12-inch

ATLANTIC (8108 "Killer Joe's International Discotheque") 15-25 65

KILLOW, Gene

Singles: 7-inch

PLA ME (7383 "I'm off the Hook")........... 50-75

KILPATRICK, Milt
(With the Scott Johnson Orchestra)

Singles: 7-inch

CORVETTE (1007 "Come On In").......... 20-25 58
MAGNET (2006 "Fame and Fortune")...... 15-25 58
(Some copies of this disc have labels that were intended for a Johnny Ross release.)
Also see ROSS, Johnny

KILTS

Singles: 7-inch

GAYNOTE (105 "I'll Be True")................. 30-40 58
(Pink label.)
GAYNOTE (105 "I'll Be True")................. 15-25 58
(Green label.)

KIMBERLY, Adrian *P&R '61*
(Don Everly)

Singles: 7-inch

CALLIOPE (6501 "Pomp and Circumstance").. 25-35 61
CALLIOPE (6503 "Greensleeves") 25-35 61
CALLIOPE (6504 "Draggin' Dragon") 25-35 61

KIMBLE, Bobby

Singles: 7-inch

FAT FISH (8004 "A Good Fool Is Hard to Find")..5-10 66
JAB (1001 "Stop Right Here I Got Love") 25-50 58
(Blue vinyl.)

KIMBLE, Quinn, Orchestra

Singles: 78 rpm

RPM (400 "Blue Memories") 5-10 54

Singles: 7-inch

RPM (400 "Blue Memories") 10-20 54

KINETICS

Singles: 7-inch

STUDIO CITY (1033 "I'm Blue").............75-125 65

KINETICS

Singles: 7-inch

NASHVILLE (5334 "Put Your Loving on Me")..15-25 67

LPs: 10/12-inch

ETIQUETTE..5-8 86
Members: Roger Rogers; Daniel Davison; Roger Baldwin; Denney Goodhew.

KINFOLKS

Singles: 7-inch

DUO DISC (106 "Mustang") 10-20 64
REVIS (1012 "Do You Wanna Dance") 10-20 64

KING, Al *R&B '66*

Singles: 7-inch

DAVIS (448 "Melancholy Horn") 10-20 57
KENT (498 "The Thrill Is Gone")................5-10 68
KENT (509 "The World Needs Love") 5-10 69
MODERN (1046 "My Name Is Misery")......5-10 68
RONN (38 "I Can't Understand")................5-10 69
RONN (42 "High Cost of Living") 5-10 69
SAHARA (111 "Think Twice Before You Speak")..5-10 66
SAHARA (113 "My Money Ain't Long Enough") 5-10 66
SHIRLEY (117 "Reconsider Baby")...........8-12 64
TRIAD (501 "Reconsider Baby")..............10-15 '60s
Also see SMITH, Alvin

KING, Albert *R&B '61*
(Albert "Blues Boy" King)

Singles: 78 rpm

PARROT (798 "Bad Luck Blues") 200-300 54

Singles: 7-inch

ATLANTIC (2604 "The Hunter")..................5-10 69
BOBBIN...10-15 59-63
COUN-TREE..8-12 65
KING..6-12 61-69
PARROT (798 "Bad Luck Blues") 600-800 54
STAX 4-8 66-74
TOMATO...4-6 78-79
UTOPIA 4-6 76-77

Picture Sleeves

BOBBIN (143 "How About That Old Blue Ribbon") 100-200 63

LPs: 10/12-inch

ATLANTIC 8-12 69-82
FANTASY..5-8
KING (852 "Big Blues")............................50-75 63
KING (1000 series) 10-12 69
PARRALL (202 "At the Blues Festival Live")..8-12 '80s
STAX (Except 723 & 2000 series) 8-12 72-81
STAX (723 "Born Under a Bad Sign") 15-25 67
STAX (2000 series) 10-15 68-71
STAX (8000 series) 5-10 90
TOMATO...8-12 77-79
UTOPIA...10-15 76-77

KING, Albert, & Otis Rush

LPs: 10/12-inch

CHESS 10-15 69
Also see KING, Albert
Also see RUSH, Otis

KING, Alex, & Turnpikes

Singles: 7-inch

CENTRAL (314004 "Weightless")............10-20 63

KING, Anna *P&R/R&B '64*

Singles: 7-inch

END (1126 "Mama's Got a Bag of Her Own")..15-25 63
LUDIX (103 "Big Change") 20-30 63
MALIBU (1020 "In Between Tears") 10-20 61
RUST (5090 "Tears on My Pillow")............8-12 64
SMASH...5-10 63-65

LPs: 10/12-inch

SMASH (27059 "Back to Soul") 15-20 64
(Monaural.)
SMASH (67059 "Back to Soul") 20-25 64
(Stereo.)

KING, B.B. *R&B '51*
(With the King's Men; with Vocal Chords; "B.B. 'Blues Boy' King")

Singles: 78 rpm

BULLET (309 "Miss Martha King") 500-600 49
BULLET (315 "Got the Blues")..............300-400 49
KENT (301 "You Know I Go for You") 15-25 58
KENT (307 "Don't Look Now but You Got the Blues") 20-30 58
KENT (315 "Please Accept My Love") 30-40 58
RPM..15-25 49-57

Singles: 7-inch

ABC 4-8 66-78
ABC-PAR 8-12 62-66
BLUESWAY 5-10 67-70
KENT (300 series, except 315)................10-20 58-64
KENT (315 "Please Accept My Love") 20-30 58
KENT (400 & 500 series) 5-10 64-69
KENT (4000 series) 4-8 69-72
MCA...3-6 79-89
PAULA..3-6 81
RPM (339 "3 O'Clock Blues")................300-400 51
RPM (348 "Fine Looking Woman").......200-300 52
RPM (355 "Shake It Up and Go") 75-125 52
RPM (360 "Someday, Somewhere") 35-50 52
RPM (363 "You Didn't Want Me") 40-60 52
RPM (374 "Story from My Heart and Soul") 35-50 52
RPM (380 "Woke Up This Morning") 35-50 53
RPM (386 "Please Love Me")...................50-75 53
RPM (391 "Neighborhood Affair") 40-60 53
RPM (395 "Why Did You Love Me") 35-45 53
RPM (403 thru 479) 40-60 54-56
RPM (486 thru 501) 30-50 57

Picture Sleeves

BLUESWAY (61032 "The Thrill Is Gone")..5-10 69
MCA...3-5 85

EPs: 7-inch

ABC-PAR (456 "Mr. Blues") 10-20 63
(Juke box issue only.)
RPM (459 "Disc Jockey Special EP - Dark Is the Night")...75-125 56
(Not issued with cover. Promotional issue only.)

LPs: 10/12-inch

ABC (713 thru 1061)....................................8-12 70-78
ABC/COMMAND (40022 Friends")...........15-25 74
(Quadraphonic.)
ABC-PAR (456 "Mr. Blues") 30-40 63
ABC-PAR (509 "Live at the Regal")...........15-25 65
ABC-PAR (528 "Confessin' the Blues") 15-25 65
ACCORD 5-8 82
("B.B. King Live") 250-500
(Picture disc. No label name or selection number used. Promotional issue only.)
BLUESWAY (6001 thru 6050) 10-20 67-73
CROWN (147 "B.B. King Wails") 20-30 60
(Stereo. Black vinyl.)
CROWN (147 "B.B. King Wails") 100-200 60
(Stereo. Colored vinyl.)
CROWN (152 "Spirtuals") 15-25 60
(Stereo. Black vinyl.)
CROWN (152 "Spirtuals") 100-150 60
(Stereo. Colored vinyl.)
CROWN (195 "King of the Blues")............20-30 61
(Stereo. Black vinyl.)
CROWN (195 "King of the Blues")........100-150 61
(Stereo. Colored vinyl.)
CROWN (309 "Blues in My Heart") 15-25 62
(Stereo.)
CROWN (359 "B.B. King") 15-25 63
(Stereo.)
CROWN (5020 "B.B. King") 40-60 57
CROWN (5063 "The Blues") 30-50 58
CROWN (5115 "B.B. King Wails") 20-30 60
(Monaural.)
CROWN (5119 "Spirtuals") 15-25 60
(Monaural.)
CROWN (5120 "Singing the Blues").........20-30 60
CROWN (5143 "The Great B.B. King") 20-30 61
CROWN (5167 "King of the Blues")..........20-30 61
(Monaural.)
CROWN (5188 "My Kind of Blues")...........20-30 61
CROWN (5230 "B.B. King") 20-30 62
CROWN (5248 "Twist") 15-25 62
CROWN (5286 "Easy Listening Blues")...10-20 62
CROWN (5309 "Blues in My Heart") 15-25 62
(Monaural.)
CROWN (5359 "B.B. King") 15-25 63
(Monaural.)

Note: Though we lack specific titles, these Crown numbers may be other LPs featuring B.B. King: 5012, 5021, 5027, 5238, 5249, 5309, 5359 and 5405.

CRUSADERS 5-8 82
CUSTOM 8-10
FANTASY 5-10 81
GALAXY (202 "Best of B.B. King") 15-25 63
KENT 10-20 64-73
MCA 5-10 79-85
MFSL (235 "Lucille")..................................25-35 94
PICKWICK...5-10
UNITED ....10-20 '60s
Session: Ike Turner; Willie Mitchell; Calvin Newborn; Hank Crawford; Earl Forest; Floyd Jones; Connie McBooker; George Coleman; Charles Crosby; Ted Curry; Kenny Sands.
Also see BASIE, Count
Also see BLAND, Bobby, & B.B. King
Also see CRAWFORD, Hank
Also see FORREST, Earl
Also see KING, Carole
Also see McBOOKER, Connie
Also see MITCHELL, Willie
Also see TURNER, Ike
Also see U2 & B.B. KING

KING, Ben E. *P&R '60*

Singles: 7-inch

ATLANTIC...3-6 75-81
ATCO (6166 "Brace Yourself") 15-25 60
ATCO (6185 "Spanish Harlem") 15-20 60
ATCO (6194 "Stand By Me") 15-20 61
ATCO (6203 thru 6256)............................10-15 61-63
ATCO (6267 thru 6288)..............................8-12 63-64
ATCO (6303 thru 6666)..............................5-12 64-69
ELEKTRA..4-6 76
MANDALA..4-6 72-73
MAXWELL 5-10 69

LPs: 10/12-inch

ATCO (133 "Spanish Harlem") 30-40 61
(Monaural.)
ATCO (SD-133 "Spanish Harlem")...........35-45 61
(Stereo.)
ATCO (137 "For Soulful Lovers")..............25-35 62
(Monaural.)
ATCO (SD-137 "For Soulful Lovers") 30-40 62
(Stereo.)
ATCO (142 "Don't Play That Song") 20-30 62
(Monaural.)
ATCO (SD-142 "Don't Play That Song") ..25-35 62
(Stereo.)
ATCO (165 "Greatest Hits") 20-30 64
(Monaural.)
ATCO (SD-165 "Greatest Hits")................25-35 64
(Stereo.)
ATCO (174 "Seven Letters") 20-30 65
(Monaural.)
ATCO (SD-174 "Seven Letters") 25-35 65
(Stereo.)
ATLANTIC..8-12 75-81
CLARION (606 "Young Boy Blues") ....10-15 '60s
KING (3008 "Audio Biography")................10-15
MANDALA..8-12 72
MAXWELL 10-15 70
Also see BAKER, Lavern, & Ben E. King
Also see BOBBETTES
Also see BONDS, Gary "U.S."
Also see CHORDETTES
Also see DEL-VIKINGS
Also see DRIFTERS
Also see EARL-JEAN
Also see HALOS
Also see HOLLY, Buddy
Also see LEWIS, Jerry Lee
Also see LITTLE EVA
Also see SHIRLEY & LEE
Also see SILHOUETTES
Also see SOUL CLAN

KING, Ben E., & Dee Dee Sharp

Singles: 7-inch

ATCO (6557 "We Got a Thing Going On"). 5-10 68
Also see KING, Ben E.
Also see SHARP, Dee Dee

KING, Billy
("The Singingest Man You've Ever Seen")

Singles: 78 rpm

ABBOTT (1001 "Can't Get You Outta' My Mind") 10-15 54

Singles: 7-inch
ABBOTT (1001 "Can't Get You Outta' My Mind") 25-35 54

KING, Buzzy
Singles: 7-inch
TOP RANK (2027 "Your Picture") 15-25 59

KING, Carole P&R '62
Singles: 7-inch
ABC 4-6 74
ABC-PAR (9921 "Goin' Wild") 30-40 58
ABC-PAR (9986 "Baby Sittin'") 30-40 59
ALPINE (57 "Oh, Neil") 350-500 60
ATLANTIC 3-5 82-83
AVATAR 4-6 77-78
CAPITOL 3-6 77-80
COMPANION (2000 "It Might As Well Rain Until September") 100-150 62
DIMENSION (1004 "School Bells Are Ringing") 15-25 63
DIMENSION (1009 "He's a Bad Boy") 15-25 63
DIMENSION (2000 "It Might As Well Rain Until September") 10-20 62
(Purple label. Has black ring around center hole.)
DIMENSION (2000 "It Might As Well Rain Until September") 8-12 62
(Blue label. No black ring around center hole.)
ODE (Except 66112) 4-6 71-76
ODE (66112 "Pierre") 5-10 75
(Compact 33.)
RCA (7560 "Short Mort") 40-60 59
TOMORROW (7502 "A Road to Nowhere") 25-35 66
Picture Sleeves
ATLANTIC 3-5 82
AVATAR 4-6 77
CAPITOL 3-6 77-80
ODE 4-6 71-75
LPs: 10/12-inch
ATLANTIC 5-8 82-83
AVATAR 8-12 78
CAPITOL (Except 11000 series) 5-8 80
CAPITOL (11000 series) 8-10 77-79
EPIC/ODE (30000 series) 5-8 78-80
EPIC/ODE (40000 series) 12-15 80
(Half-speed mastered.)
ODE 10-12 70-78
Also see CITY
Also see COOKIES / Little Eva / Carole King
Also see DACHE, Bertell
Also see GERMZ
Also see HONEY BEES
Also see KING, B.B.
Also see PALISADES
Also see SHIRELLES

KING, Claude C&W/P&R '61
Singles: 7-inch
CINNAMON 4-6 74
COLUMBIA 4-8 61-71
DEE JAY (1248 "Run Baby Run") 150-250 57
TRUE 3-6 77-80
Picture Sleeves
COLUMBIA 5-10 61-69
LPs: 10/12-inch
COLUMBIA 10-20 62-70
GUSTO 5-8 80
HARMONY 8-12 68
TRUE 8-10 77
Also see YOUNG, Faron / Carl Perkins / Claude King

KING, Clyde
Singles: 7-inch
ASSAULT (1833 "Even a Man Can Cry") 10-15 62
ASSAULT (1846 "Wang Dang Do") 10-15 63

KING, Clydie R&B '71
(With the Sweet Things)
Singles: 78 rpm
SPECIALTY 10-20 57
Singles: 7-inch
IMPERIAL 10-20 65-66
LIZARD 4-6 71
MINIT 5-10 67-69
PHILIPS 8-12 62-63
SPECIALTY (605 "Our Romance") 30-40 57
SPECIALTY (642 "Young Fool in Love") . 20-30 58
LPs: 10/12-inch
LIZARD 8-12 71
Also see CARTER, Mel, & Clydie
Also see RAELETTS

KING, Curtis
Singles: 7-inch
COLUMBIA (44096 "Bad Habits") 10-20 67

KING, Dave, & Royal Knights
Singles: 7-inch
TEIA (1000 "Walkin' with David") 8-12 64
TEIA (1004 "The Beatle Walk") 10-20 64

KING, Earl R&B '55
Singles: 78 rpm
ACE 10-25 55-57
SPECIALTY 10-20 54-55
Singles: 7-inch
ACE (509 "Those Lonely, Lonely Nights") 40-60 55
ACE (514 "My Love Is Strong") 35-55 56
ACE (517 "It Must Have Been Love") 35-55 56
ACE (520 "Is Everything Alright") 35-55 56
ACE (529 "Those Lonely, Lonely Feelings") 25-50 57
ACE (543 "I'll Never Get Tired") 25-50 58
ACE (564 "Weary Silent Night") 20-30 59
ACE (598 "Buddy It's Time to Go") 15-25 60
AMY (942 "You'll Remember Me") 8-12 65
IMPERIAL (5713 "Come On") 15-25 60
IMPERIAL (5730 "Love Me Now") 15-25 61
IMPERIAL (5750 "Come Along with Me") 15-25 61
IMPERIAL (5774 "You Better Know") 10-15 61
IMPERIAL (5811 "Always a First Time") ... 10-15 62
IMPERIAL (5858 "We Are Just Friends") . 10-15 62
IMPERIAL (5891 "Come Along with Me") 10-15 62
REX (1015 "I Can't Help Myself") 15-25 61
SPECIALTY (495 "I'm Your Best Bet, Baby") 50-75 54
SPECIALTY (531 "Eating and Sleeping") . 50-75 54
SPECIALTY (558 "Funny Face") 50-75 55
Also see SMITH, Huey
Also see UNIQUES

KING, Earl
(Earl Connelly King)
Singles: 78 rpm
KING 10-15 55-57
Singles: 7-inch
KING (Except 5670) 15-25 55-57
KING (5670 "Big Blue Diamonds") 10-15 62
Also see JOHN, Little Willie / 5 Royales / Earl (Connelly) King / Midnighters

KING, Eddie
(With the Three Queens)
Singles: 7-inch
BIG WHEEL (170 "I Talk Too Much") 15-25 66
GALLIANT (1007 "Hear No Evil, See No Evil") 10-20 60
J.O.B. (1122 "Love You Baby") 150-250 58
PARKWAY (952 "If You Wish") 8-12 65

KING, Freddie P&R/R&B '61
(Freddy King)
Singles: 78 rpm
EL-BEE (157 "Country Boy") 20-30 56
Singles: 7-inch
COTILLION 4-8 68-70
EL-BEE (157 "Country Boy") 60-80 56
FEDERAL 15-25 60-65
GUSTO 4-6 78
KING 5-10 69
ROULETTE (7003 "Fortune Teller") 10-15 57
RSO 4-6 75
SHELTER 4-6 73
EPs: 7-inch
KING (773 "Let's Hide Away and Dance Away") 40-60 61
(Juke box issue only. Includes title strips.)
LPs: 10/12-inch
COTILLION 10-15 69-70
GUSTO (5033 "Hide Away") 10-12 78
KING (762 "Freddy King Sings the Blues") 30-40 61
KING (773 "Let's Hide Away and Dance Away") 35-50 61
KING (821 "Bossa Nova & Blues") 20-30 62
KING (856 "Freddy King Goes Surfin'") ... 20-30 63
KING (900 series) 15-20 65-66
KING (1000 series) 10-15 69
MCA .... 5-8 '80s
RSO 8-10 74-77
SHELTER 8-10 71-75
Also see ROGERS, Jimmy, & Freddie King
Also see RUSSELL, Leon

KING, Freddie, & Lula Reed
Singles: 7-inch
FEDERAL (12457 "Do the President Twist") 10-20 62
FEDERAL (12471 "Watch Over Me") 10-20 62
FEDERAL (12477 "Say Hey Pretty Baby") 10-20 62

KING, Freddie / Lula Reed / Sonny Thompson
LPs: 10/12-inch
KING (777 "Boy—Girl—Boy") 40-60 62
(Cover credits "Lula" Reed, label shows her as "Lulu" Reed.)
Also see KING, Freddie
Also see REED, Lulu
Also see THOMPSON, Sonny

KING, Gene
Singles: 7-inch
MICHELLE (941 "TV Show") 50-75

KING, Harold
Singles: 7-inch
MERRI (6004 "Buzz Me Baby") 40-60 63

KING, Hial
(Hyle King Movement)
Singles: 7-inch
LIBERTY (55984 "Flower Smile") 5-10 67
MBK (103 "Death Valley") 20-30 63
MBK (104 "Mailbu Sunset") 20-30 63

KING, J.D., & Dick Taylor Orchestra
Singles: 78 rpm
AARDELL (9 "Private Property") 10-15 56
Singles: 7-inch
AARDELL (9 "Private Property") 20-30 56

KING, Jack
Singles: 7-inch
COOL (144 "Dance Everybody") 150-250
4 STAR (1725 "I Just Learned to Rock") 100-150 58

KING, Jay W.
Singles: 7-inch
SKYSCRAPER (6001 "I Don't Have to Worry") 30-40

KING, Jeanie
Singles: 7-inch
GENERAL AMERICAN (717 "Everybody Knows") 10-15 64

KING, Jessie Lee, & His Crowns
Singles: 7-inch
PINE (652 "Rock & Roll Rover") 200-300

KING, Jewel R&B '50
(With Dave Bartholomew's Orchestra)
Singles: 78 rpm
IMPERIAL (5055 "3 X 7 = 21") 15-25 49
Also see BARTHOLOMEW, Dave

KING, Jimmy
Singles: 7-inch
HERALD (535 "Knocking on Your Door") . 35-50 59

KING, Joanne
Singles: 7-inch
CORAL (62463 "My Baby Left Me") 25-35 65
PHIL-L.A. OF SOUL 5-10 70
RCA 10-20 58

KING, Julius
Singles: 78 rpm
TENNESSEE (123 "I Want a Slice of Your Pudding") 100-150 52

KING, Kenny, & Be Bops
Singles: 7-inch
CUCA (1101 "You're Alright") 20-30 62
Members: Kenny King Jaeger; Ken Kleist; Dan Derfus; Tom Leininger; Rick Leigh.

KING, Keith
Singles: 78 rpm
LIBERTY BELL (9001 "I Can't Feel at Home") 5-10 54
Singles: 7-inch
LIBERTY BELL (9001 "I Can't Feel at Home") 10-15 54

KING, Kid R&B '53
(Kid King's Combo)
Singles: 78 rpm
EXCELLO 10-15 53-57
Singles: 7-inch
EXCELLO (2009 thru 2109) 20-30 53-57
EXCELLO (2185 "Shaggy Dog") 10-20 60
Members: Al Brooks; Tommy McGhee.
Also see BEASLEY, Good Rockin' Sam / Kid King's Combo
Also see McGHEE, Tommy

KING, Lefty
Singles: 7-inch
COOL (120 "Geraldine") 100-200 59

KING, Leon
Singles: 7-inch
EAST COAST (102 "You Little Old Turtle Dove") 100-200

KING, Leonard, & Soul Messengers
Singles: 7-inch
INFERNO 10-20 67

KING, Mabel
Singles: 78 rpm
RAMA 15-20 56
Singles: 7-inch
AMY (851 "Lefty") 35-45 62
AMY (874 "Love") 50-75 62
AMY (886 "I Could Cry") 35-45 63
RAMA (200 "Alabama Rock and Roll") ... 40-50 56
RAMA (204 "Symbol of Love") 30-40 56

KING, Mack
Singles: 7-inch
NUGGET (1004 "You Look Better Going") 150-200 59

KING, Maurice
(With the Wolverines)
Singles: 78 rpm
COLUMBIA 5-10 51
OKEH (6800 "I Want a Lavender Cadillac") 10-15 51
Singles: 7-inch
COLUMBIA 15-20 51
OKEH (6800 "I Want a Lavender Cadillac") 20-30 51
Also see RAY, Johnnie

KING, Morgana LP '64
Singles: 78 rpm
MERCURY 5-10 56
WING 5-10 56
Singles: 7-inch
MAINSTREAM 4-8 64
MERCURY 5-10 56
PARAMOUNT 4-6 73-74
REPRISE 4-6 66-67
20TH FOX 5-8 59
VERVE 4-6 68
WING (90073 "Delovely") 5-10 56
Picture Sleeves
PARAMOUNT 4-6 73
LPs: 10/12-inch
ASCOT 15-25 65-66
CAMDEN 15-25 60
EMARCY (36079 "For You, for Me, Forever More") 30-50 56
MAINSTREAM (300 series) 5-10 72
MAINSTREAM (6000 series) 15-25 64-65
MERCURY (20231 "Morgana King Sings the Blues") 30-40 57
MUSE 5-8 79-82
PARAMOUNT 5-10 73
REPRISE 15-25 65-67
TRIP 5-8 74
U.A. (3028 "Folk Songs ala King") 30-40 59
(Monaural.)
U.A. (3028 "Folk Songs ala King") 40-50 59
(Stereo.)
U.A. (30020 "Let Me Love You") 30-40 60
VERVE 10-15 68
WING 10-20 65

KING, Pee Wee C&W/P&R '48
(With Redd Stewart; with His Golden West Cowboys)
Singles: 78 rpm
BLUEBIRD 5-10 49
RCA 4-8 50-55
Singles: 7-inch
BRIAR (120 "Tennessee Waltz") 4-8 61

JARO (77025 "Vagabond Waltz") ... 5-10 60
CUCA ... 5-10 64-68
LANDA (668 "Slow Poke") ... 4-8 61
LANDA (673 "Bumming Around") ... 4-8 61
RCA ... 10-20 50-55
(Black vinyl.)
RCA (48-0037 thru 48-0379) ... 10-20 49-50
(Green vinyl.)
STARDAY ... 4-6 64-71
TODD (1009 "I Got a Wife") ... 8-12 59
TODD (1020 "Too Tall") ... 8-12 59
TOP RANK (2087 "Do You Remember") ... 4-8 60

EPs: 7-inch

RCA (797 "Swing West") ... 15-30 56
RCA (3028 "Country Classics") ... 15-30 53
RCA (3071 "Western Hits") ... 15-30 53
RCA (3109 "Country Classics, Vol. 2") ... 15-30 53
RCA (3280 "Swing West") ... 15-30 56

LPs: 10/12-inch

BRIAR (102 "Golden Olde-Tyme Dances") ... 50-70 62
CAMDEN ... 8-15 65-71
CUCA ... 20-40 64
DETOUR ... 5-10
LONGHORN ... 5-10
RCA (1237 "Swing West") ... 40-60 56
RCA (2464 "Swing West") ... 5-8 77
RCA (3071 "Western Hits") ... 25-50 53
(10-inch LP.)
RCA (3109 "Country Classics") ... 50-75 53
(10-inch LP.)
STARDAY (284 "Back Again") ... 15-20 64
STARDAY (900 series) ... 8-10 75-76
Also see WAYNE, Hal, & Pee Wee King

KING, Peggy — *P&R '55*
(With the Percy Faith Orchestra; with Jimmy Carroll Orchestra)

Singles: 78 rpm

COLUMBIA ... 4-6 54-56
MGM ... 4-6 52

Singles: 7-inch

BUENA VISTA (397 "Bon Voyage") ... 5-10 62
BULLET ... 4-6 71
CAMEO (152 "Beautiful Love") ... 5-10 58
COLUMBIA ... 8-12 54-56
MGM ... 8-12 52
ROULETTE (4327 "I'll Be Around") ... 5-10 61

Picture Sleeves

BUENA VISTA (397 "Bon Voyage") ... 5-10 62

EPs: 7-inch

COLUMBIA ... 8-12 55

LPs: 10/12-inch

COLUMBIA ... 15-25 55
IMPERIAL ... 10-20 59
Also see CARROLL, Jimmy
Also see FAITH, Percy, Orchestra
Also see VALE, Jerry, Peggy King & Felicia Sanders

KING, Ramona

Singles: 7-inch

AMY (989 "Stay Away from the Fire") ... 5-10 67
EDEN (3 "Oriental Garden") ... 50-60 62
EDEN (5 "What About You") ... 10-20 63
EDEN (6 "I Wanna Dance") ... 10-20 63
W.B. (5416 "It's in His Kiss") ... 5-10 64
W.B. (5432 "Blue Roses") ... 5-10 64
W.B. (5452 "Run Johnny Run") ... 5-10 64

KING, Randy

Singles: 78 rpm

TNT (108 "Crazy As a Loon") ... 10-20 54
TNT (9009 "Be-Boppin' Baby") ... 50-75 57

Singles: 7-inch

TNT (108 "Crazy As a Loon") ... 25-50 54
TNT (9009 "Be-Boppin' Baby") ... 200-300 57
WHIZ (1501 "Since You Came Back to Me") ... 50-100 57

KING, Ray

Singles: 7-inch

ACTION (100 "You've Gotta Stand Up") .. 15-25
KARL (222 "A Date at Eight") ... 150-250

KING, Rev. Martin Luther, Jr. — *LP '63*
(Rev. Martin Luther King)

Singles: 7-inch

DOOTO ... 4-6 68
MERCURY ... 4-6 68

EPs: 7-inch

GORDY (906 "Speech Excerpts") ... 15-25 63

LPs: 10/12-inch

AUDIO FIDELITY (343 "Martin Luther King") ... 15-20 84
(Picture disc.)
BLACK FORUM ... 5-10 70
BUDDAH ... 8-15 69
CREED ... 8-12 68-71
DOTTO ... 8-15 62-68
EXCELLO ... 8-15 68
GORDY (906 "The Great March") ... 25-50 63
GORDY (929 "Free at Last") ... 15-25 68
MERCURY ... 8-15 68
MR. MAESTRO ... 10-15 63
NASHBORO ... 5-8 72
20TH FOX ... 8-15 63-68
UNART ... 8-12 68
These recordings contain speeches or excerpts of speeches by King.
Also see LANDS, Liz / Martin Luther King

KING, Richard, & Orchestra

Singles: 78 rpm

KHOURY'S ... 10-20 51

KING, Rod, & Souls

Singles: 7-inch

SPACE ("Penniless Lover") ... 10-20 67
(Selection number not known.)
SPACE (15 "These Arms of Mine") ... 10-20 67
SPACE (21 "Don't Be Afraid") ... 40-60 68

Picture Sleeves

SPACE ("Penniless Lover") ... 30-40 67
(Selection number not known.)
Members: Rod King; Rick; Pat; Eddie; Johnny.

KING, Ronnie, & Passions

Singles: 7-inch

GATEWAY (786 "Girl, Break Away") ... 15-25 67

KING, Sandra

Singles: 7-inch

BELL (613 "Leave It Up to the Boys") ... 10-20 65

KING, Saunders, Orchestra — *R&B '49*

Singles: 78 rpm

ALADDIN ... 10-20 49
FLAIR ... 15-20 54
MODERN ... 10-20 48
RHYTHM ... 10-20 42-47

Singles: 7-inch

FLAIR (1035 "My Close Friend") ... 30-40 54
FLAIR (1045 "Quit Hangin' 'Round Me") ... 30-40 54
GALAXY (712 "S.K. Blues") ... 10-20 62
RPM (341 "Lazy Woman") ... 25-35 52
RPM (375 "New S.K. Blues") ... 25-35 53
RPM (497 "S.K. Blues") ... 15-25 57

KING, Sid
(With the Five Strings; Five Strings)

Singles: 78 rpm

COLUMBIA ... 15-25 55-57

Singles: 7-inch

COLUMBIA (21361 "I Like It") ... 30-40 55
COLUMBIA (21403 "Drinkin' Wine Spoli Oli") ... 40-50 55
COLUMBIA (21449 "Sag, Drag and Fall") ... 30-40 55
COLUMBIA (21489 "Mama, I Want You") ... 30-40 56
COLUMBIA (21503 "Blue Suede Shoes") ... 40-50 56
COLUMBIA (21564 "Good Rockin' Baby") ... 40-50 55
COLUMBIA (40680 "Oobie Doobie") ... 30-40 57
COLUMBIA (40833 "It's True, I'm Blue") ... 25-35 57
COLUMBIA (41019 "I've Got the Blues") .. 25-35 57
DOT (16293 "Once Upon a Time") ... 10-15 61
SOUNDWAVES ... 3-5 80
Members: Sid King; Billy King; Dave White; Melvin Robinson; Kenny Massey.
Also see SUMMERS, Gene

KING, Sleepy — *P&R '61*

Singles: 7-inch

AWAKE (852 "Rock Rock") ... 40-60
FELSTED (8541 "Come Home Maude") .. 10-15 59
JOY (257 "King Steps Out") ... 10-15 61
JOY (261 "Happy Music") ... 10-15 61
JOY (262 "Lovin' Time") ... 10-15 61
SUE (704 "One Legged Woman") ... 10-15 58
SYMBOL (904 "Begging") ... 40-50 59
VEEP (1236 "Hello Martha") ... 5-10 66

KING, Solomon

Singles: 7-inch

CAPITOL (2114 "She Wears My Ring") ... 4-8 69
RCA (8474 "I Believe") ... 5-10 64

LPs: 10/12-inch

CAPITOL (2923 "She Wears My Ring") ... 10-20 69
RCA (2837 "The Golden Voice of Gospel") ... 10-15 64
RCA (2985 "You'll Never Walk Alone") ... 10-15 65
RCA (3430 "Where He Leads Me") ... 10-15 65

KING, Susan

Singles: 7-inch

MIDTOWN (3501 "What a Love This Is") ... 10-20 66
TOY (104 "Building a Wall Around My Heart") ... 20-30 62
(Yellow label. Short version.)
TOY (104 "Building a Wall Around My Heart") ... 15-25 62
(Pink label. Short version.)
TOY (104 "Building a Wall Around My Heart") ... 10-20 63
(Red label. Long version.)
TOY (111 "Time Is Awastin' ") ... 8-12 64
TURNTABLE (711 "You Got Me in a Fix") ... 10-20 65

KING, Teddi — *P&R '56*
(With Dick Jacobs & Orchestra)

Singles: 78 rpm

CORAL ... 4-8 55
RCA ... 4-6 56-57

Singles: 7-inch

CHAMPION ... 5-15
CORAL (61350 "The Dragon") ... 8-12 55
RCA ... 5-15 56-57

EPs: 7-inch

RCA (1 "Teddi King Sings") ... 10-20 56
(Promotional issue, made for General Electric Flash Bulb buyers.)

LPs: 10/12-inch

CORAL (57278 "All the King's Songs") 40-60 59
(Monaural.)
CORAL (757278 "All the King's Songs") .. 50-75 59
(Stereo.)
RCA (1147 "Bidin' My Time") ... 50-75 56
RCA (1313 "From Teddi King") ... 50-75 57
RCA (1454 "A Girl & Her Songs") ... 50-75 57
STORYVILLE (302 "'Round Midnight") ... 100-200 54
(10-inch LP.)
STORYVILLE (314 "Storyville Presents Teddi King") ... 100-200 54
(10-inch LP.)
STORYVILLE (903 "Now in Vogue") ... 75-125 56
Also see FOUR LOVERS / Teddi King
Also see JACOBS, Dick, & His Orchestra

KING, Toby

Singles: 7-inch

FEDERAL (12573 "Mr. Tuff Stuff") ... 10-20 65

KING, Tom, & Starfires
(With the Ardells)

Singles: 7-inch

E.M.K. ... 5-10
PAMA (115 "Ring of Love") ... 10-20 61
PAMA (116 "I Know") ... 20-30 61
POP-SIDE (2 "Night Walk") ... 10-15 61
RESCUE (103 "Please Don't Leave Me") ... 20-30 63

KING, Tommy, & Starlites

Singles: 7-inch

CLAREMONT (661 "Bop Diddle in the Jungle") ... 50-75 66

KING, Vanda

Singles: 7-inch

GLORY (275 "Randy") ... 10-20 58
GLORY (280 "Kiss After Kiss") ... 10-20 58

KING, Willie
(With the Ike Turner Band.)

Singles: 78 rpm

VITA (123 "Peg Leg Woman") ... 35-40 56

Singles: 7-inch

VITA (123 "Peg Leg Woman") ... 50-100 56
Also see TURNER, Ike

KING & SHARPETTES

Singles: 7-inch

ALDO (503 "Did He Know") ... 10-20 62
Member: Windsor King.
Also see CASHMERES
Also see ROYAL SONS

KING BEES

Singles: 78 rpm

KRC (302 "Can't You Understand") ... 20-30 57

Singles: 7-inch

KRC (302 "Can't You Understand") ... 40-50 57

KING BEES
(With Lloyd Price's Orchestra)

Singles: 78 rpm

FLIP (323 "Puppy Love") ... 50-75 57

Singles: 7-inch

CHECKER (909 "Buzzin' ") ... 40-60 58
FLIP (323 "Puppy Love") ... 200-300 57
NOBLE (715 "Tender Love") ... 150-200 59
Also see MOORE, Jimmy, & Peacocks
Also see PRICE, Lloyd

KING BEES

Singles: 7-inch

PYRAMID (6217 "I Want My Baby") ... 15-25 66

KING BEEZ
(King Beezz)

Singles: 7-inch

JET ... 10-15 67
QUALITY (1792 "Gloria") ... 15-25 66
(Canadian.)
QUALITY (1817 "I Can't Explain") ... 15-25 66
(Canadian.)
QUALITY (1860 "Found & Lost") ... 15-25 66
(Canadian.)

KING BISCUIT ENTERTAINERS

Singles: 7-inch

BURDETTE (7 "Stormy") ... 10-15 68
BURDETTE (9 "Take My Thought Away") ... 10-15 68
KBE (1 "Courtship of Priscilla Brown") ... 10-15 68
REVUE (11066 "Rollin' Free") ... 10-15 69
Member: Ray Kennedy.
Also see AMERICAN CHEESE

KING BROTHERS

Singles: 7-inch

DECCA (30750 "I'll Die from Heartbreak") ... 10-20 58
Members: Jerry King; Bob King.

KING BUMBLE BEE SLIM & HIS PACIFIC COAST SENDERS
(Amos Easton)

Singles: 78 rpm

MARIGOLD ("Twin Beds") ... 25-50 51
(No selection number used.)
Also see EASTON, Amos, & His Orchestra

KING CHARLES
(With Left Hand Charlie.)

Singles: 7-inch

FOLK STAR (1131 "Bop Cat Stomp") ... 40-60 54

KING CHARLES & COUNTS

Singles: 7-inch

CRUSADER (117 "Salt and Pepper") ... 10-20 65

KING COBRAS

Singles: 7-inch

IRVANNE (117 "To Hold Your Hand") ... 750-1000 59

KING CRIMSON — *LP '69*

Singles: 12-inch

W.B. ... 4-6 84

Singles: 7-inch

ATLANTIC ... 4-6 70-74
W.B. ... 3-5 81-84

LPs: 10/12-inch

ATLANTIC (Except 18000 & 19000 series) ... 10-20 69-74
ATLANTIC (18000 & 19000 series) ... 8-10 74-75
EDITIONS ... 5-10
MFSL (075 "In the Court of the Crimson King") ... 40-60 82
W.B. ... 5-8 81-84
WIZARDO ... 10-12
WORLD RECORD CLUB ... 12-15
Members: Greg Lake; Robert Fripp; Michael Giles; Adrian Belew; Boz Burrell; Bill Bruford; Ian MacDonald; Peter Sinfield.
Also see YES

KING CROONERS
(Little Rico & King Krooners; King Crooner's)
Singles: 7-inch
EXCELLO (2168 "Now That She's Gone")....50-75 59
(Counterfeits can be identified by their lack of a number in the vinyl trail-off.)
EXCELLO (2187 "School Daze")....75-100 60
(Orange label, blue print. Counterfeits can be identified by their orange label with black print.)
HART (1002 "Lonely Nights")....400-500 59

KING CRUSHER & TURKEYNECKS
Singles: 7-inch
RASSLER (9008 "Fuzzy")....60-80 65
Also see JESSE J. & BANDITS

KING CURTIS P&R/R&B '62
(With the Kingpins; with Nobel Knights; King Curtis Combo; with His Tenor Sax)
Singles: 78 rpm
APOLLO (507 "King's Rock")....10-20 57
GEM (208 "Tenor in the Sky")....10-20 53
GROOVE (0160 "Movin' On'")....10-15 56
MONARCH (702 "Wine Head")....20-30 53
RPM (383 "Boogie in the Moonlight")....15-25 53
Singles: 7-inch
ABC-PAR (10133 "King Neptune's Guitar")....8-12 60
ALCOR (016 "Jay Walk")....5-10 62
APOLLO (507 "King's Rock")....15-25 57
ATCO (6100 series)....10-20 58-59
ATCO (6300 thru 6900 series)....4-8 65-72
CAPITOL....5-10 62-65
DELUXE (6142 "Steel Guitar Rag")....10-20 57
DELUXE (6157 "Wicky Wacky")....10-20 57
ENJOY (1000 "Soul Twist")....8-12 62
ENJOY (1001 "Wobble Twist")....8-12 62
EVEREST (19406 "Jay Walk")....8-12 61
EVERLAST (5030 "Soul Twist")....8-12 65
GEM (208 "Tenor in the Sky")....40-60 53
GROOVE (0160 "Movin' On'")....10-20 56
KING (5647 "Steel Guitar Rag")....8-12 62
MONARCH (702 "Wine Head")....50-75 53
NEW JAZZ (510 "Soul Meeting")....5-10 61
RPM (383 "Boogie in the Moonlight")....40-60 53
SEG-WAY....10-15 61
TRU SOUND....8-12 61-63
Picture Sleeves
CAPITOL (5377 "Bill Bailey")....5-10 65
EPs: 7-inch
ATCO (33-266 "Best of King Curtis")....5-10 68
(Stereo. Juke box issue only.)
CAPITOL....8-15 63
LPs: 10/12-inch
ATCO (113 "Have Tenor Sax Will Blow")....75-100 59
(Monaural.)
ATCO (SD-113 "Have Tenor Sax Will Blow")....100-125 59
(Stereo.)
ATCO (189 thru 385)....10-20 66-72
CAMDEN....10-15 68
CAPITOL (1756 "Country Soul")....10-20 62
CAPITOL (2000 series)....10-20 64-68
CAPITOL (11000 series)....5-8 78-79
CLARION....8-10 '60s
COLLECTABLES....6-8 88
ENJOY (2001 "Soul Twist")....30-50 62
EVEREST (1121 "Azure")....20-30 61
HARLEM HIT PARADE....8-10 '70s
MOUNT VERNON....10-12
NEW JAZZ (8237 "New Scene")....20-30 60
PRESTIGE (7200 series)....15-20 62
PRESTIGE (7700 series)....8-12 69-70
RCA....15-25 '60s
SCEPTER (18027 "The Best of")....10-15 73
TRU-SOUND....15-20 62
Also see BAKER, Lavern
Also see BARRY, Jeff
Also see BENTON, Brook
Also see BOBBETTES
Also see CLOVERS
Also see COASTERS
Also see COMSTOCK, Bobby
Also see COOPER, Horace
Also see DARIN, Bobby
Also see EMERSONS
Also see EVERETT, Bracy
Also see FACENDA, Tommy
Also see FREED, Alan
Also see JENNINGS, Waylon
Also see KING PINS
Also see LED ZEPPELIN / King Curtis
Also see MANN, Herbie
Also see McPHATTER, Clyde
Also see MICKEY & SYLVIA
Also see MR. BEAR
Also see MITCHELL, Freddie
Also see NOBLE KNIGHTS
Also see PAT & SATELLITES
Also see PRETTY BOY
Also see PRICE, Sam
Also see RAMRODS
Also see REDDING, Otis / King Curtis
Also see RESTIVO, Johnny
Also see RINKY DINKS
Also see SCOTT, Shirley
Also see SEDAKA, Neil
Also see SHARPE, Ray
Also see SHIRELLES & KING CURTIS
Also see SUNNYLAND SLIM
Also see TURNER, Joe
Also see TURNER, Sammy
Also see WASHBOARD BILL

KING DAVIS HOUSE ROCKERS
(Featuring Richard Thomas)
Singles: 7-inch
VERVE (10492 "Baby, You Satisfy Me")....15-25 67
Also see DAVIS, King

KING DIAMOND LP '87
LPs: 10/12-inch
ROADRACER (Except picture discs)....5-8 87-90
ROADRACER (9439 "Conspiracy")....15-20 89
(Picture disc.)
ROADRACER (9517 "Them")....20-25 89
(Picture disc. Promotional issue only.)
ROADRACER (65484 "Halloween")....15-20 '80s
(Picture disc.)

KING EDWARD & B.D.'s
(With the Bee Dees)
Singles: 7-inch
GROOVE (501 "Girls Are")....15-25
GROOVE (503 "I Do")....15-25
ROGA (69-14 "Working for My Baby")....15-25

KING V
Singles: 7-inch
FTP (410 "Purple Wall")....10-20 61
(We think this band is King "V," the Roman Numeral, and not "V" as in King Victor.)

KING FLOYD P&R/R&B '70
(With the Three Queens)
Singles: 7-inch
CHIMNEYVILLE....4-6 70-76
ORIGINAL SOUND....4-8 64-71
PULSAR (2404 "Heartaches")....5-10 69
PULSAR (2406 "You Got the Love I Need")....5-10 69
UPTOWN....5-10 65-66
V.I.P. (25061 "Heartaches")....10-15 71
Picture Sleeves
CHIMNEYVILLE (437 "Baby Let Me Kiss You")....4-6 71
LPs: 10/12-inch
ATCO....8-10 73
CHIMNEYVILLE....8-10 72
COTILLION....8-12 71
PULSAR....10-15 69
V.I.P. (407 "Heart of the Matter")....20-25 70

KING FLOYD & DOROTHY MOORE R&B '75
Singles: 7-inch
CHIMNEYVILLE (10207 "We Can Love")....4-6 75

KING GEORGE
(With the Fabulous Souls; with Jim Laurro & His Orchestra; King George / Jim Laurro)
Singles: 7-inch
AUDIO ARTS (60015 "Baby, I've Got It")....10-20 '60s
END (1023 "Jive Train")....15-25 58
RCA (8743 "I'm Gonna Be Somebody, Someday")....10-20 66
RCA (8846 "Ah Huh")....8-12 66

KING LEO & LIONS
Singles: 7-inch
DORAINE (1001 "Daddy's Gone Again")....10-15

KING LOUIE'S COURT
Singles: 7-inch
STICKY (1 "King Louie's Glue")....10-15 66
Members: Michael "Mad Man" Motz; Tony "The Greek" Drakey; Tom Holden; Pat Glossop.

KING LOUIS
Singles: 7-inch
UNIVERSAL ARTISTS (41562 "It Was Fun")....40-50

KING PHAROAH & EGYPTIANS
Singles: 7-inch
FEDERAL (12413 "By the Candlelight")....20-30 61
Members: Harold "King Pharoah" Smith; Morris Wade; Bernard Wilson; Pee Wee Lowrey.
Also see EGYPTIAN KINGS
Also see FOUR PHARAOHS

KING PINS
Singles: 7-inch
U.A. (111 "Ungaua")....15-25 58
RADIANT (1507 "Forever Lonely")....10-20 62

KING PINS P&R/R&B '63
(King-Pins; Kingpins)
Singles: 7-inch
ATCO (6516 "In the Pocket")....5-10 67
FEDERAL (12480 thru 12525)....15-25 62-64
VEE-JAY (494 "A Lucky Guy")....15-25 62
LPs: 10/12-inch
KING (865 "It Won't Be This Way Always")....35-50 63
Members: Andrew Kelly; Robert Kelly; Curtis Kelly.
Session: Charles Lee; Offe Reese.
Also see KELLY BROTHERS
Also see KING CURTIS
Also see LEE, T.C., & King Pins

KING PINS
Singles: 7-inch
LARSE (101 "Rod Hot Rod")....25-50 66
MGM (13535 "Rod Hot Rod")....10-20 66

KING PLEASURE R&B '52
(Clarence Beeks)
Singles: 78 rpm
ALADDIN (3352 "I'm in the Mood for Love")....10-15 57
JUBILEE (5226 "Evening Blues")....8-15 55
PRESTIGE....8-15 52-55
Singles: 7-inch
ALADDIN (3352 "I'm in the Mood for Love")....10-15 57
HI-FI (5004 "Golden Days")....5-10 60
JUBILEE (5226 "Evening Blues")....10-15 55
PRESTIGE (182 "Parker's Mood")....5-10 60
PRESTIGE (744 "I'm in the Mood for Love")....5-8 68
PRESTIGE (821 thru 924)....10-20 53-55
U.A. (527 "Mean to Me")....5-10 62
LPs: 10/12-inch
HI-FI (425 "Golden Days")....35-55 60
PRESTIGE (208 "King Pleasure Sings")....75-125 55
(10-inch LP.)
PRESTIGE (7128 "King Pleasure Sings")....50-75 57
(Includes four tracks by Annie Ross.)
PRESTIGE (7586 "Original Moody's Mood")....10-20 68
SOLID STATE (18021 "Mr. Jazz")....10-20 68
U.A. (14031 "Mr. Jazz")....30-40 62
(Monaural.)
U.A. (15031 "Mr. Jazz")....35-50 62
(Stereo.)

KING RICHARD & POOR BOYS
Singles: 78 rpm
APOLLO (1201 "I'm Not Ashamed")....5-10 55
Singles: 7-inch
APOLLO (1201 "I'm Not Ashamed")....10-15 55
Also see POOR BOYS

KING ROCK & KNIGHTS
Singles: 7-inch
ZOOM (003 "Scandal")....10-15 59

KING SOUND INTERPRETERS & TIPS
Singles: 7-inch
TALENT OF MUSIC (8253 "Hi Note")....100-150 66

KING TOPPERS
Singles: 78 rpm
JOSIE (811 "You Were Waiting for Me")....40-60 57
Singles: 7-inch
JOSIE (811 "You Were Waiting for Me")....50-75 57

KING TUT
Singles: 78 rpm
SITTIN' IN WITH (542 "Lonely Blues")....50-75 50
SITTIN' IN WITH (550 "Why Did You Leave Me Baby")....15-25 50
Singles: 7-inch
STARLINE....5-10 62
Members: Ed Wiley; Henry Hayes; Willie Johnson; Donald Cooks; Ben Turner.
Also see HAYES, Henry
Also see WILEY, Ed

KING VICTOR
Singles: 7-inch
MADISON (110 "Boppin' Bobbie Jean")....25-35 59

KINGBEATS
Singles: 7-inch
FLASH (1553 "I'll Tell My Mama on You")....100-200 59

KINGDOM
Singles: 7-inch
SPECIALTY (722 "Seven Fathoms Deep")....5-10 70
LPs: 10/12-inch
SPECIALTY (2135 "Kingdom")....35-50 70
(Black and gold label.)
Members: John Toyne; Ed Nelson; Tim Potkey; Gary Varga.

KINGDOM BOUND SINGERS
Singles: 7-inch
FEDERAL (12481 "It's Praying Time")....5-10 62
VEE-JAY (874 "I'll Be Standing")....10-15 59

KINGERY, Pat
Singles: 7-inch
VANCE (411 "Jam on the Lower Shelf")....50-75

KINGLETS
Singles: 78 rpm
CALVERT (101 "Six Days a Week")....40-60 56
Singles: 7-inch
BOBBIN (104 "Pretty Please")....75-125 59
CALVERT (101 "Six Days a Week")....75-125 56

KINGS
Singles: 78 rpm
SPECIALTY (497 "What Can I Do")....30-50 54
Singles: 7-inch
SPECIALTY (497 "What Can I Do")....100-200 54

KINGS
("Kings Featuring Bobby Hall"; King's; with Jack Gale Orchestra)
Singles: 78 rpm
GONE (5013 "Don't Go")....75-100 57
GOTHAM (316 "God Made You Mine")....30-40 56
Singles: 7-inch
BLUE SKY (105 "Sunday Kind of Love")....5-10 73
BLUE SKY (106 "Why? Oh Why")....5-10 73
EPIC (9370 "I Want to Know")....10-15 60
GONE (5013 "Don't Go")....200-300 57
GOTHAM (316 "God Made You Mine")....50-75 56
JALO (203 "Angel")....50-75 58
(Black vinyl.)
JALO (203 "Angel")....10-20 '60s
(Red vinyl.)
JAX (314 "Why? Oh Why?")....300-400 53
(Maroon label. Red vinyl.)
JAX (314 "Why? Oh Why?")....100-200 53
(Green label. Red vinyl.)
JAX (316 "Baby, Be There")....250-350 53
(Red vinyl.)
JAX (320 "Sunday Kind of Love")....200-300 53
(Red vinyl.)
JAY WING (5805 "Surrender")....75-125 59
LOOKIE (18 "I Want to Know")....40-50 60
(First issue.)
RCA (7419 "Till You")....15-25 58
RCA (7544 "Your Sweet Love")....30-40 59
Members: Robert Hall; Gil Wilkes; Adolphus Holcomb; Richard Holcomb.
Also see FOUR KINGS
Also see HALL, Bobby, & Kings

KINGS

Singles: 7-inch

JOX (045 "It's the LCB") 10-20 65
JOX (049 "Baby, You're the One") 15-25 65
JOX (052 "I've Got a License") 10-20 65

KINGS

Singles: 78 rpm

BATON (245 "Long Lonely Nights") 10-20 57

Singles: 7-inch

BATON (245 "Long Lonely Nights") 15-25 57
Members: Joe Van Loan; James Van Loan; Paul Van Loan; Dave Bowers.
Also see RAVENS
Also see VAN LOAN, Joe

KINGS & QUEENS

Singles: 7-inch

EVERLAST (5003 "Voices of Love") 15-25 57

KINGS IV

Singles: 78 rpm

MGM (12247 "You're On Trial") 5-10 56

Singles: 7-inch

MGM (12247 "You're On Trial") 10-15 56

KING'S HENCHMEN
(King's Henchmen)

Singles: 7-inch

CORAL (61979 "Deep Down and Low") .. 15-25 58
CORAL (61980 "Shufflin'") 15-25 58

KINGS MEN
(With Lefty Bates' Band)

Singles: 7-inch

CLUB 51 (108 "Don't Say You're Sorry") 1000-2000 57
Also see BATES, Lefty Guitar

KINGS OF HOT RODS / Tokens / Hal Jones & Wheelers

LPs: 10/12-inch

DIPLOMAT (2308 "King's of the Hot Rods") 15-25 64
(The two "Tokens" tracks on this LP are by Johnny & the Tokens.)
Also see JOHNNY & TOKENS

KINGS RANSOM

Singles: 7-inch

INTEGRA (101 "Shame") 10-20 68
INTEGRA (102 "Shadows of Dawn") 10-20 68

KINGSFIVE
(With the New Redtops Orchestra)

Singles: 7-inch

TROPHY (2 "I Hear the Rain") 800-1200 59

KINGSLEY, Pee Wee
(Featuring Sugar Pie De Santo)

Singles: 7-inch

MUSIC CITY (824 "Nickel and a Dime") .. 60-75 58
Also see DE SANTO, Sugar Pie

KINGSMEN

Singles: 78 rpm

ALL STAR (500 "Guardian Angel") 75-125 57
NEIL (102 "Stranded Love") 15-20 56

Singles: 7-inch

ALL STAR (500 "Guardian Angel") 75-125 57
NEIL (102 "Stranded Love") 30-40 56

KINGSMEN
(Kingsmen Quintet)

Singles: 7-inch

HILLSIDE 10-20 58
Members: Bob Shaw; Dick Greenberg; Jerry Swirsky; Hank Sargent; Howard Kurhan.
Also see ACADEMICS

KINGSMEN P&R '58

Singles: 7-inch

EAST WEST (115 "Week End") 15-20 58
EAST WEST (120 "Cat Walk") 15-20 58
Also see HALEY, Bill

KINGSMEN

Singles: 7-inch

F.D. ARNOLD (2106 "Good Night Sweetheart") 100-150 63

KINGSMEN P&R '63

Singles: 7-inch

CAPITOL (3576 "You Better Do Right") 4-8 72
EARTH 5-10 69
ERIC .... 4-6 '70s
JERDEN (712 "Louie Louie") 150-200 63
REO (028 "Louie Louie") 5-10 66
(Canadian.)
REO (8745 "Louie Louie") 35-50 63
(Canadian.)
WAND (143 "Louie Louie") 10-20 63
WAND (143 "Louie Louie '64-'65-'66") 8-10 66
WAND (150 "Money") 10-15 64
WAND (157 "Little Latin Lupe Lu") 8-12 64
WAND (164 "Death of an Angel") 8-12 65
WAND (172 "Jolly Green Giant") 8-12 65
WAND (183 "The Climb") 8-12 66
WAND (189 "Annie Fannie") 8-12 65
WAND (1107 "It's Only the Dog") 10-15 65
WAND (1115 "Killer Joe") 10-15 65
WAND (1118 "The Krunch") 8-12 66
WAND (1127 "Little Sally Tease") 8-12 66
WAND (1137 thru 1180) 6-12 66-68

Picture Sleeves

WAND (1118 "The Krunch") 15-20 66

LPs: 10/12-inch

ARISTA 8-10 81
HEAVY WEIGHT 20-25 67
PICADILLY 5-8 80
RHINO .... 5-8 '80s
SCEPTER/CITATION 8-12 72
WAND (657 "The Kingsmen in Person") .. 30-40 64
WAND (659 "The Kingsmen, Vol. 2") 50-100 64
(Without *Death of an Angel*.)
WAND (659 "The Kingsmen, Vol. 2") 25-35 64
(With *Death of an Angel*.)
WAND (662 "The Kingsmen, Vol. 3") 25-30 65
WAND (670 thru 681) 20-25 65-67
Members: Jack Ely; Lynn Easton; Mike Mitchell; Bob Nordby; Don Gallucci; Barry Curtis; Norm Sundholm; Gary Abbot; Dick Peterson; Kerry Magness; J.C. Reick; Pete Borg; Jeff Beals; Steve Friedson.
Also see DON & GOODTIMES
Also see ELY, Jack, & Courtmen

KINGSMILL, Steve

Singles: 7-inch

ALVIN (31 "Well, Come On") 200-300

KINGSTON, Jack

Singles: 78 rpm

QUALITY (1491 "I Got the Blues") 20-30 56
(Canadian.)

Singles: 7-inch

QUALITY (1491 "I Got the Blues") 50-100 56
(Canadian.)

KINGSTON TRIO P&R/R&B/LP '58

Singles: 7-inch

CAPITOL (856 "Merry Minuet") 20-30 59
(Promotional issue only.)
CAPITOL (1400 & 1800 series) 10-20 60-63
(Compact 33 Singles.)
CAPITOL (2006 "Farewell Adelita") 15-25 60
(Special products giveaway for Welgrume Sportswear.)
CAPITOL (2782 "Molly Dee") 15-25 59
(Promotional issue only.)
CAPITOL (3970 thru 4114) 10-15 58-59
CAPITOL (4167 "Tijuana Jail") 10-15 59
CAPITOL (S-4167 "Tijuana Jail") 20-30 59
(Stereo.)
CAPITOL (4221 "M.T.A.") 10-15 59
CAPITOL (4221 "M.T.A.") 25-35 59
(Promotional "Special Preview Record." Label pictures the Trio.)
CAPITOL (4271 "A Worried Man") 10-15 59
CAPITOL (4303 "Coo Coo-U") 8-12 59
CAPITOL (S-4303 "Coo Coo-U") 15-25 59
(Stereo.)
CAPITOL (4338 thru 5166) 5-10 59-64
CAPITOL (6000 series) 4-6 62-65
CAPITOL/LION OF TROY (2006 "Farewell Adelita") 10-20 60
(Capitol Special Products issue for Lion of Troy shirt buyers.)
DECCA 5-10 64-66
TETRAGRAMMATON (1526 "Scotch and Soda") 4-8 69
NAUTILUS 4-6 79
XERES 3-5 82

Picture Sleeves

CAPITOL (2006 "Farewell Adelita") 20-30 60
(Special products issue for Welgrume Sportswear.)
CAPITOL (2782 "Molly Dee") 20-30 59
(Promotional issue only.)
CAPITOL (4338 "El Matador") 15-25 60
CAPITOL (4740 "Scotch & Soda") 10-20 62
CAPITOL (4842 "One More Town") 10-20 62
CAPITOL/LION OF TROY (2006 "Farewell Adelita") 15-25 60
(Capitol Special Products issue for Lion of Troy shirts.)
DECCA (31702 "Hope You Understand") 15-25 65
DECCA (31790 "Yes, I Can Feel It") 15-25 65
DECCA (31860 "Runaway Song") 15-25 65
XERES 3-5 82

EPs: 7-inch

CAPITOL 15-30 58-61
CAPITOL CUSTOM (2670 "Cool Cargo") 30-40 60
(Special products issue for 7 Up.)

LPs: 10/12-inch

CANDLELITE (6971 "Historic Recordings") .... 15-25 '70s
CAPITOL (500 series) 8-15 70
CAPITOL (T-996 "The Kingston Trio") 50-75 58
(Green label. Monaural.)
CAPITOL (T-996 "The Kingston Trio") .100-125 58
(Yellow label. Monaural. Promotional issue only.)
CAPITOL (T-996 "The Kingston Trio") 20-30 58
(Black label. Monaural.)
CAPITOL (DT-996 "The Kingston Trio") 8-12 69
(Reprocessed stereo.)
CAPITOL (T-1107 "From the Hungry i") ... 20-30 59
(Monaural.)
CAPITOL (ST-1183 "Stereo Concert") 25-35 59
(Stereo.)
CAPITOL (T-1199 "Kingston Trio at Large") 20-30 59
(Monaural.)
CAPITOL (ST-1199 "Kingston Trio at Large") 25-35 59
(Stereo.)
CAPITOL (T-1258 "Here We Go Again") .20-30 59
(Monaural.)
CAPITOL (ST-1258 "Here We Go Again") 25-35 59
(Stereo.)
CAPITOL (T-1352 "Sold Out") 15-25 60
(Monaural.)
CAPITOL (ST-1352 "Sold Out") 20-30 60
(Stereo.)
CAPITOL (T-1407 "String Along") 15-25 60
(Monaural.)
CAPITOL (ST-1407 "String Along") 20-30 60
(Stereo.)
CAPITOL (T-1446 thru T-2081) 15-25 60-64
(Monaural.)
CAPITOL (ST-1446 thru ST-2081) 20-30 60-64
(Stereo.)
CAPITOL (T-2180 "Folk Era") 30-35 64
(Monaural. Three-disc set with bound-in booklet.)
CAPITOL (ST-2180 "Folk Era") 35-40 64
(Stereo. Three-disc set with bound-in booklet.)
CAPITOL (T-2280 thru T-2614) 10-20 65-66
(Monaural.)
CAPITOL (ST-2280 thru ST-2614) 15-25 65-66
(Stereo.)
CAPITOL (11000 series) 5-8 79
CAPITOL (16000 series) 4-6 81
DECCA (4613 "Kingston Trio") 10-20 64
(Monaural.)
DECCA (7-4613 "Kingston Trio") 15-25 64
(Stereo.)
DECCA (4656 "Stay Awhile") 10-20 65
(Monaural.)
DECCA (7-4656 "Stay Awhile") 15-25 65
(Stereo.)
DECCA (4696 "Somethin' Else") 10-20 65
(Monaural.)
DECCA (7-4696 "Somethin' Else") 15-25 65
(Stereo.)
DECCA (4758 "Children in the Morning"). 10-20 66
(Monaural.)
DECCA (7-4758 "Children in the Morning") 15-25 66
(Stereo.)
INTERMEDIA 5-10 85
NAUTILUS 20-25 79
PICKWICK .... 5-10 '70s
TETRAGRAMMATON (5101 "Once Upon a Time") 10-15 69
XERES 5-10 82
Members: John Stewart; Dave Guard; Nick Reynolds; Bob Shane.
Also see BEATLES / Beach Boys / Kingston Trio
Also see GUARD, Dave, & Whiskeyhill Singers
Also see STEWART, John
Also see STEWART, John, & Nick Reynolds

KINGSTON TRIO / Four Preps

Singles: 7-inch

U.S.A.F. (103 "El Matador") 20-25 60
(Promotional, radio station issue only.)
Also see FOUR PREPS

KINGSTON TRIO / Dinah Shore

Singles: 7-inch

U.S.A.F. (129 "Everglades") 20-25 60
(Promotional, radio station issue only.)
Also see SHORE, Dinah

KINGSTON TRIO / Frank Sinatra

EPs: 7-inch

CAPITOL (2229 "Excerpts from Great New Releases") 40-60 62
(Promotional issue only.)
Also see KINGSTON TRIO
Also see SINATRA, Frank

KINGTONES
("Vocal by Pete Mervenne"; King Tones)

Singles: 7-inch

COTILLION (44069 "It Doesn't Matter Anymore") 40-50 69
DERRY (101 "Twins") 30-50 64
DRUMMOND (105 "A Love I Had") 10-20 65
EUCALYPTUS (002 "It Doesn't Matter Anymore") 50-75 69
(First issue.)
KITOCO ("A Love I Had") 40-60 62
(No selection number used.)
KITOCO (355 "Twins") 40-60 63
MUSITONE (102 "Wish for an Angel") . 100-200 61
Members: Pete Mervenne; Dave Roberts; Phil Roberts, Jr; Bruce Snoap.

KINKS P&R/LP '64

Singles: 12-inch

ARISTA 5-10 79-83

Singles: 7-inch

ARISTA (0240 thru 0372) 4-8 77-78
ARISTA (0409 thru 9309) 4-6 79-84
CAMEO (308 "Long Tall Sally") 75-100 64
CAMEO (308 "Long Tall Sally") 50-75 64
(Promotional issue only.)
CAMEO (345 "Long Tall Sally") 40-60 65
CAMEO (345 "Long Tall Sally") 35-45 65
(Promotional issue only.)
CAMEO (348 "You Still Want Me") 150-200 65
CAMEO (348 "You Still Want Me") 100-150 65
(Promotional issue only.)
ERIC 3-5
MCA 3-5 86
RCA (0275 thru 10551) 5-10 72-76
REPRISE (0306 "You Really Got Me") 10-15 64
REPRISE (0334 "All Day and All of the Night") 10-15 64
REPRISE (0347 "Tired of Waiting for You") 10-15 65
REPRISE (0366 "Who'll Be the Next in Line") 10-15 65
REPRISE (0379 "Set Me Free") 10-15 65
REPRISE (0409 "Never Met a Girl Like You Before") 10-15 65
REPRISE (0420 "A Well Respected Man") 10-15 65
REPRISE (0454 "Till the End of the Day") 10-15 66
REPRISE (0471 "Dedicated Follower of Fashion") 10-15 66
REPRISE (0497 "Sunny Afternoon") 10-15 66
REPRISE (0540 "Deadend Street") 10-20 66
REPRISE (0587 "Mr. Pleasant") 10-20 67
REPRISE (0612 "Waterloo Sunset") 10-20 67
REPRISE (0647 "Autumn Almanac") 10-20 67
REPRISE (0691 "Polly") 10-20 68
REPRISE (0762 "She's Got Everything") . 10-20 68
REPRISE (0806 "Starstruck") 10-20 69
REPRISE (0847 "Village Green Preservation Society") 10-20 69
REPRISE (0863 thru 1017) 10-15 70-71

Picture Sleeves

ARISTA (0541 "Lola") 4-6 80
ARISTA (1054 "Come Dancing") 4-6 83
ARISTA (9309 "Do It Again") 4-6 84

EPs: 7-inch

ARISTA (22 "The Kinks Misfit Record")... 20-25 78
(Promotional issue only.)
REPRISE (352 "Arthur") 10-20 69
(Promotional issue only.)

LPs: 10/12-inch

ARISTA (69 "Low Budget Radio Interview") 40-50 79
ARISTA (4106 "Sleepwalker")....................6-12 77
ARISTA (4167 "Misfits")..............................6-12 78
ARISTA (4240 "Low Budget")......................6-12 79
ARISTA (8401 "One for the Road")............6-12 80
(Two discs.)
ARISTA (9567 "Give the People What They Want") 6-12 81
COMPLEAT...5-8
MCA...5-8 86-89
MFSL (070 "Misfits") 25-35 82
PICKWICK..5-10 72-79
RCA (APL1-1743 "Celluloid Heroes")...... 10-20 76
RCA (AYL1-1743 "Celluloid Heroes")..........5-8 81
RCA (3520 "Second Time Around")..............5-8 80
RCA (AYL1-3749 "Schoolboys in Disgrace") 5-8 80
RCA (AYL1-3750 "Soap Opera") 5-8 80
RCA (LSP-4644 "Muswell Hillbillies") 10-20 71
RCA (AYL1-4644 "Muswell Hillbillies") 5-8 82
RCA (LPL2-5002 "Preservation, Act 1") .. 10-20 73
(Two discs.)
RCA (CPL2-5040 "Preservation, Act 1").. 10-20 74
(Two discs.)
RCA (LPL1-5081 "Soap Opera").............. 10-20 75
RCA (LPL1-5102 "Schoolboys in Disgrace") 10-20 75
RCA (6065 "Everybody's in Show-Biz")... 10-20 72
REPRISE (2127 "The Great Lost Kinks Album") 20-30 73
REPRISE (2127 "The Great Lost Kinks Album") 50-75 73
(Promotional issue only.)
REPRISE (R-6143 "You Really Got Me")... 50-100 64
(Monaural.)
REPRISE (R-6143 "You Really Got Me")... 50-100 64
(White label, monaural. Promotional issue only.)
REPRISE (RS-6143 "You Really Got Me").. 20-30 64
(Stereo.)
REPRISE (RS-6143 "You Really Got Me").. 40-60 64
(White label, stereo. Promotional issue only.)
REPRISE (R-6158 "Kinks Size")............. 50-75 65
(Monaural.)
REPRISE (R-6158 "Kinks Size").......... 100-200 65
(White label, monaural. Promotional issue only.)
REPRISE (RS-6158 "Kinks Size") 20-30 65
(Stereo.)
REPRISE (RS-6158 "Kinks Size") 40-60 65
(White label, stereo. Promotional issue only.)
REPRISE (R-6173 "Kinda Kinks")........... 50-75 65
(Monaural.)
REPRISE (R-6173 "Kinda Kinks")........ 100-200 65
(White label, monaural. Promotional issue only.)
REPRISE (RS-6173 "Kinda Kinks") 20-30 65
(Stereo.)
REPRISE (RS-6173 "Kinda Kinks") 40-60 65
(White label, stereo. Promotional issue only.)
REPRISE (R-6184 "Kinks Kinkdom")....... 50-75 65
(Monaural.)
REPRISE (R-6184 "Kinks Kingdom") .. 100-200 65
(White label, monaural. Promotional issue only.)
REPRISE (RS-6184 "Kinks Kinkdom") 20-30 65
(Stereo.)
REPRISE (RS-6184 "Kinks Kinkdom") 40-60 65
(White label, stereo. Promotional issue only.)
REPRISE (R-6197 "Kink Kontroversy") ... 50-75 66
(Monaural.)
REPRISE (R-6197 "Kink Kontroversy") 100-200 66
(White label, monaural. Promotional issue only.)
REPRISE (RS-6197 "Kink Kontroversy"). 20-30 66
(Stereo.)
REPRISE (RS-6197 "Kink Kontroversy"). 40-60 66
(White label, stereo. Promotional issue only.)
REPRISE (R-6217 "The Kinks' Greatest Hits")... 50-75 66
(Monaural.)
REPRISE (R-6217 "The Kinks' Greatest Hits") 100-200 66
(White label, monaural. Promotional issue only.)
REPRISE (RS-6217 "The Kinks' Greatest Hits") 20-30 66
(Stereo.)
REPRISE (RS-6217 "The Kinks' Greatest Hits") 40-60 66
(White label, stereo. Promotional issue only.)
REPRISE (R-6228 "Face to Face") 50-75 66
(Monaural.)
REPRISE (R-6228 "Face to Face") 75-150 66
(White label, monaural. Promotional issue only.)
REPRISE (RS-6228 "Face to Face")........20-30 66
(Stereo.)
REPRISE (RS-6228 "Face to Face")........40-60 66
(White label, stereo. Promotional issue only.)
REPRISE (R-6260 "Live Kinks")..............50-75 67
(Monaural.)
REPRISE (R-6260 "Live Kinks")............75-150 67
(White label, monaural. Promotional issue only.)
REPRISE (RS-6260 "Live Kinks")............20-30 67
(Stereo.)
REPRISE (RS-6260 "Live Kinks")............40-60 67
(White label, stereo. Promotional issue only.)
REPRISE (R-6279 "Something Else")......50-75 67
(Monaural.)
REPRISE (R-6279 "Something Else")....75-150 67
(White label, monaural. Promotional issue only.)
REPRISE (RS-6279 "Something Else")....20-30 67
(Stereo.)
REPRISE (RS-6279 "Something Else")....40-60 67
(White label, stereo. Promotional issue only.)
REPRISE (6327 "Village Green Preservation Society")..25-35 69
REPRISE (6327 "Village Green Preservation Society")..30-50 69
(White label. Promotional issue only.)
REPRISE (6366 "Arthur")........................15-20 69
(Price includes lyrics insert.)
REPRISE (6366 "Arthur")........................30-50 69
(Price includes lyrics insert. White label. Promotional issue only.)
REPRISE (6423 "Lola vs. the Powerman")..10-20 69
(Blue and white cover.)
REPRISE (6423 "Lola vs. the Powerman")..30-50 69
(White label. Promotional issue only.)
REPRISE (6423 "Lola vs. the Powerman")..8-12 69
(Black, blue and white cover.)
REPRISE (6454 "The Kink Kronikles").....10-20 69
REPRISE (6454 "The Kink Kronikles").....30-50 69
(White label. Promotional issue only.)
Note: Original Reprise Kinks LPs from the '60s have a multi-colored label. All 11 of these LPs have been reissued with the brown Reprise label and are valued at $10 to $15.
W.B. (328 Complete "Kinks Kit"/"Then Now and In-Between") 325-375 69
(Boxed set, includes Then Now and In-Between LP, button, pin, postcard, letter, decal, and other materials. Promotional issue only.)
W.B. (328 "Then Now and In-Between") 75-100 69
(Price for LP only. Promotional issue.)
Members: Ray Davies; Dave Davies; Peter Quaife; Mick Avory; John Dalton; John Gosling; Ian Gibbons; Jim Rodford; Robert Henrit; John Beecham; Mike Cotton.
Also see ARGENT
Also see PAGE, Larry

KINKS / Hollywood Stars

Singles: 7-inch

ARISTA (5 "Sleepwalker"/"All the Kids on the Street")..8-12 77
(Colored vinyl. Promotional issue only.)

Picture Sleeves

ARISTA (5 "Sleepwalker"/"All the Kids on the Street")..10-15 77
(Promotional issue only.)
Also see KINKS

KINNEY, June

Singles: 7-inch

MILKY WAY (001 "The Hands You're Holding Now") 15-25 64
(With Arlie Neaville and Dave Marten.)
MILKY WAY (008 "Look Out Heart") 5-10 66
Also see NEAVILLE, Arlie

KINNEY, Mary

Singles: 7-inch

ANDEX (4031 "I'm Anxious") 25-35 59
DOT (15977 "I Wonder") 5-10 59
SPOT (106 "I Wonder")...............................5-10 59

KIPP, Dave

Singles: 7-inch

CORAL (61920 "No Sweat Baby")...........15-25 58

KIPPINGTON LODGE

Singles: 7-inch

CAPITOL (2236 "Rumors") 10-20 68
Member: Nick Lowe.

KIRBY, Durward

(With the Patriots)

Singles: 7-inch

DAVIS (999 "Crime Doesn't Pay!") ....10-20 '50s
(Red vinyl.)

Picture Sleeves

DAVIS (999 "Crime Doesn't Pay!!!") .... 10-20 '50s
(Sleeve has two more exclamation marks than shown on label.)

KIRBY, George

Singles: 7-inch

ARGO (5498 "No More")...............................5-10 65
CADET (5523 "What Can I Do") 40-50 66
CAMEO (317 "No Communication") 5-10 64

EPs: 7-inch

DOOTO (257 "Night in Hollywood, Part 1")..8-12 58
DOOTO (258 "Night in Hollywood, Part 2")..8-12 58

KIRBY, Glenn

Singles: 78 rpm

TNT (121 "I Love Blue Eyes")..................10-15 55

Singles: 7-inch

TNT (121 "I Love Blue Eyes")..................15-25 55

KIRBY, Larry

(With the Encores)

Singles: 7-inch

APOLLO (526 "Sweet Shop") 15-25 58
TODD (1080 "Make Believe You Do")......10-20 62
VEE-EIGHT (1050 "My Baby Don't Love Me")..75-125 59

KIRBY, Pat

(With Jack Pleis Orchestra)

Singles: 78 rpm

DECCA (29884 "What a Heavenly Night for Love")..5-10 56

Singles: 7-inch

DECCA (29884 "What a Heavenly Night for Love")..10-20 56

KIRIAE CRUCIBLE

Singles: 7-inch

NIGHT OWL (6836 "The Salem Witch Trial") 10-20 68
Also see CRUCIBLES

KIRK, Andy, & His Clouds of Joy — R&B '42

(With the Jubalaires; Andy Kirk & His Orchestra; with 12 Clouds; with June Richmond)

Singles: 78 rpm

CORAL...10-20 49
DECCA...10-20 42-46
Also see JUBALAIRES

KIRK, Curtis

Singles: 78 rpm

ABBOTT 5-10 53

Singles: 7-inch

ABBOTT (126 "The Little Things You Do")...10-15 53
ABBOTT (138 "Oh, So Lonesome Blues") 10-15 53

KIRK, Dave

Singles: 7-inch

HI-Q (5024 "Oh! Baby")...........................30-50 62

KIRK, Dee

Singles: 7-inch

VACA (104 "My Used to Be")...................50-75

KIRK, Eddie

(Eddie Kirkland)

Singles: 7-inch

HI-Q (5041 "The Grunt")...........................5-10 64
KING (5895 "Monkey Tonight")...................5-10 64
KING (5959 "Hog-Killin' Time")..................5-10 64
VOLT (106 "Hawg")....................................10-20 63
VOLT (111 "Them Bones") 10-20 63
Also see KIRKLAND, Eddie

KIRK, Ellis

Singles: 7-inch

FORTUNE (208 "Sweetie Pie") 100-150 59
HI-Q (5046 "Sweetie Pie")........................15-25 65

KIRK, James

Singles: 7-inch

GUYDEN (2126 "You Better Come Home") 20-30 65

KIRK, Larry

Singles: 7-inch

LARSON ("Been Cheated") 50-75
(Selection number not known.)

KIRK, Paul

(With the Pageants & Sandy Block Orchestra)

Singles: 7-inch

URANIA (5006 "Long Ago").......................30-40 59

KIRK, Red — C&W '49

Singles: 78 rpm

MERCURY...10-20 49-50
Session: Jerry Byrd.
Also see BYRD, Jerry

KIRK, Robie

Singles: 78 rpm

QUEEN 15-25 45

KIRKLAND, Danny, & His Band

Singles: 7-inch

J-V-B (60 "They Were Rockin'")...........500-700 57

KIRKLAND, Eddie

(With the Falcons; with His House Rockers; Little Eddie Kirkland)

Singles: 78 rpm

KING...40-60 53
RPM (367 "It's Time")..............................60-80 52
(7-inch 78 rpm.)

Singles: 7-inch

FORTUNE (848 "I Need You, Baby").......20-30 59
KING (4659 "No Shoes")......................100-150 53
KING (4680 "Please Don't Think I'm Nosey") 100-200 53
LU PINE (801 "I Tried") 5-10
PRESTIGE (316 "Chill Me Baby").............5-10 64
TRU SOUND (409 "Train Done Gone") 5-10 62

LPs: 10/12-inch

LU PINE (8003 "3 Shades of the Blues"). 10-20
TRIX...5-10 79
Also see FALCONS
Also see HOOKER, John Lee, & Little Eddie Kirkland
Also see KIRK, Eddie

KIRKLAND, Jimmy

(With the band of Stan Getz & Tom Cats)

Singles: 7-inch

FOX (919 "Come On Baby") 150-200 57
TEEN LIFE (919 "Come On Baby")......200-250 58
Also see GETZ, Stan

KIRKLAND, Leroy

Singles: 7-inch

APT (25056 "The Diddy Bop")................10-20 61

KIRKLAND, Mike James

Singles: 7-inch

BRYAN (9003 "Give It to Me")..................30-40 '60s

KIRSHNER, Don, Concept

Singles: 7-inch

RCA (0155 "Let the Sunshine In") 5-10 69

LPs: 10/12-inch

RCA (4174 "Don Kirshner Cuts 'Hair' ") ... 10-15 69

KISS — P&R/LP '74

Singles: 12-inch

CASABLANCA...10-20 78-82
MERCURY..10-20 83-88

Singles: 7-inch

CASABLANCA...4-8 74-82
MERCURY (Except 0002)............................3-6 85-88
MERCURY (0002 "World Without Heroes")...15-25 81
(Picture disc.)

Picture Sleeves

CASABLANCA (858 "Flaming Youth").......8-10 75
CASABLANCA (2365 "I Love It Loud") 8-10 81
MERCURY...4-8 85-87

LPs: 10/12-inch

CASABLANCA (7001 "Kiss") .... 10-20 '70s
(Reissue of 9001.)
CASABLANCA (7006 "Hotter Than Hell") 10-15 74
CASABLANCA (7016 "Dressed to Kill")... 10-15 75
CASABLANCA (7020 "Alive") 15-20 75
(With 8-page color booklet.)
CASABLANCA (7020 "Alive") 10-15 75
(Without booklet.)
CASABLANCA (7025 "Destroyer") 10-15 75
CASABLANCA (7032 "The Originals") 50-75 76
(With inserts: Army sticker; 16-page booklet; six trading cards.)
CASABLANCA (7032 "The Originals") 10-15 76
(Without inserts.)
CASABLANCA (7037 "Rock & Roll Over") 20-25 76
(With sticker-sheet order form.)
CASABLANCA (7037 "Rock & Roll Over") 10-15 76
(Without sticker-sheet.)
CASABLANCA (7057 "Love Gun") 50-75 77
(With cardboard gun. Apart from the LP unused cardboard gun is valued at $35 to $50. Labels on some pressings have tracks listed in the wrong sequence.)
CASABLANCA (7057 "Love Gun") 10-15 77
(Without cardboard gun.)
CASABLANCA (7076 "Alive II") 250-300 77
(Has three tracks not found on later issues: *Take Me, Hooligan*, and *Do You Love Me*. Reportedly 50 copies made.)
CASABLANCA (7076 "Alive II") 40-50 77
(With 8-page tatoo booklet. Add $20-30 if cover lists the three tracks, *Take Me, Hooligan*, and *Do You Love Me*, that are not on LP.)
CASABLANCA (7076 "Alive II") 10-15 77
(Without tatoo booklet. Add $20-30 if cover lists the three tracks, *Take Me, Hooligan*, and *Do You Love Me*, that are not on LP.)
CASABLANCA (7100 "Double Platinum") 30-40 78
(With platinum award order form.)
CASABLANCA (7100 "Double Platinum") 15-20 78
(Without platinum award order form.)
CASABLANCA (7152 "Dynasty") 8-12 79
CASABLANCA (7225 "Kiss Unmasked")....8-10 80
CASABLANCA (7261 "Music from the Elder") 25-35 81
(With lyric sheet.)
CASABLANCA (7261 "Music from the Elder") 8-12 81
(Without lyric sheet.)
CASABLANCA (7270 "Creatures of the Night") 30-45 82
(With make up.)
CASABLANCA (7270 "Creatures of the Night") 8-10 82
(Without make up.)
DYNASTY (7152 "Dynasty") 15-20 79
(With poster order form.)
DYNASTY (7152 "Dynasty") 8-12 79
(Without poster order form.)
CASABLANCA (9001 "Kiss") 30-50 74
(Does not contain *Kissin' Time*.)
CASABLANCA (9001 "Kiss") 10-20 74
(Contains *Kissin' Time*.)
MERCURY (814297 "Lick It Up") 5-8 83
MERCURY (822495 "Animalize") 5-8 84
MERCURY (826099 "Asylum") 5-8 85
MERCURY (832626 "Crazy Nights") 5-8 86
MERCURY (836887 "Smashes, Thrashes and Hits") 20-30 88
(Picture disc. Gatefold cover.)
MERCURY (836913 "Hot in the Shade")......5-8 89
MERCURY (522123 "Kiss My Ass") 25-30 94
(Colored vinyl, limited edition.)
POLYGRAM ("Kiss Alive III") 20-25 94
(Colored vinyl. Limited edition.)
POLYGRAM (832-903 "Crazy Nights").... 20-25 87
(Picture disc.)
UNMASKED (7225 "Kiss Unmasked")..... 15-20 80
(With poster order form.)
UNMASKED (7225 "Kiss Unmasked")........8-10 80
(Without poster order form.)

Promotional LPs

BURNS MEDIA ("Rock & Roll Over with Kiss") 50-75 76
CASABLANCA ("A Taste of Platinum") 30-50 78
CASABLANCA ("Rock & Roll Over") 30-50 76
CASABLANCA (76 "Kiss Tour Album") 30-50 76
CASABLANCA (7001 "Kiss") 40-60 74
(Without *Kissin' Time*.)
CASABLANCA (7001 "Kiss") 20-30 74
(With *Kissin' Time*.)
CASABLANCA (7032 "The Originals") .100-125 76
(With inserts.)
CASABLANCA (9001 "Kiss") 75-125 74
(Does not contain *Kissin' Time*.)
CASABLANCA (9001 "Kiss") 25-35 74
(Contains *Kissin' Time*.)
CASABLANCA (20137 "Criss, Frehley, Simmons, Stanley") 20-30 78
MERCURY (792-1 "First Kiss, Last Licks") 75-100 90
Members: Gene Simmons; Ace Frehley; Paul Stanley; Peter Criss; Bruce Kulick; Eric Carr; Vinnie Vincent.
Session: Mark St. John.
Also see CRISS, Peter
Also see FREHLEY, Ace
Also see GROUNDHOGS
Also see SIMMONS, Gene
Also see STANLEY, Paul

KISS / Mighty Bosstones

Singles: 7-inch

MERCURY (858894 "Detroit Rock City") 3-6 94
(Colored vinyl.)
Also see KISS

KIT & OUTLAWS

Singles: 7-inch

EMPIRE (1 "Mama's Gone") 15-25 66
PHILIPS (40420 "Midnight Hour") 8-12 66
Also see OUTLAWS

KIT KATS

Singles: 7-inch

JAMIE 5-10 66-68
LAURIE (3186 "Good Luck Charlie") 10-15 63
LAWN (249 "You're No Angel") 5-10 64
PARAMOUNT 4-6 71

LPs: 10/12-inch

JAMIE (3029 "It's Just a Matter of Time").20-30 67
JAMIE (3032 "The Kit Kats Do Their Thing, Live") 25-35 68
VIRTUE (102067 "Very Best") 30-35 67
Members: Kit Stewart; Carl Von Hausman; John Bradley; Ron Shane.
Also see NEW HOPE
Also see ROSCOE & LITTLE GREEN MEN
Also see TAK TIKS

KITCHEN, Jack, & Rock-A-Billies

Singles: 7-inch

("Hot Rod Boogie") 2000-3000
(No label name or selection number used.)

KITCHEN CINQ

Singles: 7-inch

DECCA (32262 thru 32374) 5-10 68
LHI (17005 thru 17015) 5-10 67

LPs: 10/12-inch

LHI (1200 "Everything But") 20-30 67
Also see Y'ALLS

KITT, Eartha *P&R '53*

Singles: 12-inch

STREETWISE 4-6 83

Singles: 78 rpm

RCA 4-8 53-57

Singles: 7-inch

DECCA 4-8 65
KAPP 5-10 59-66
RCA 10-20 53-57
STREETWISE 3-5 83

Picture Sleeves

RCA 15-25 54-55

EPs: 7-inch

RCA 20-30 53-57

LPs: 10/12-inch

CAEDMON 5-10 69
DECCA 10-15 65
GNP 10-15 65
KAPP 10-20 59-60
MGM 10-20 62
PHILIPS 8-15 68
RCA 25-50 53-57
STANYAN 5-10 72
SUNNYVIEW 5-8 84

KITT, Eartha, & Perez Prado

Singles: 78 rpm

RCA ....4-8 '50s

Singles: 7-inch

RCA ....10-15 '50s
Also see PRADO, Perez
Also see KITT, Eartha

KITTENS

Singles: 7-inch

ABC-PAR 5-10 65-66
ALPINE (64 "Dark Sunglasses") 10-15 60
ALPINE (67 "Broken Dreams") 10-15 60
CHESS 5-10 67-68
CHESTNUT (203 "I'm Worried") 40-50 63
DON EL (122 "Walter") 10-15 63
DON EL (205 "I Need Your Love Tonight") 10-15 63
MURBO (1015 "Lonely Summer") 5-10 67
SELECT (732 "Be Nice Tonight") 10-15 64
UNART (2010 "Letter to Donna") 20-30 59

KITTENS FIVE

Singles: 7-inch

HERALD (588 "Don't Let It Happen Again") 10-15 64

KITTENS THREE

Singles: 7-inch

NEWARK (215 "I'm Coming Apart at the Seams") ....20-30 '60s

KITTRELL, Christine
("With Band")

Singles: 78 rpm

REPUBLIC 15-25 53-55
TENNESSEE 20-40 52

Singles: 7-inch

FEDERAL (12540 "Call His Name") 5-10 65
KING (6045 "Call His Name") 5-10 66
REPUBLIC (7026 "Gotta Stop Loving You") 25-50 53
REPUBLIC (7044 "L&N Special") 25-50 53
REPUBLIC (7055 "Evil-Eyed Woman")....25-50 53
REPUBLIC (7096 "Sittin' Here Drinkin' Again") 25-50 54
REPUBLIC (7109 "Leave My Man Alone") 25-50 55
TENNESSEE (128 "Sittin' Here Drinking") 50-100 52
VEE-JAY (399 "Sittin' & Drinkin' ") 10-15 61
VEE-JAY (444 "I'm a Woman") 10-15 62

KITTY & KATS

Singles: 7-inch

COULEE (132 "Windy") 10-20 69

KLASSMEN

Singles: 7-inch

MUSICLAND USA (20016 "Can't You Hear the Music") 15-20 67

KLASSY, Kaye, & Kustoms

Singles: 7-inch

SURE PLAY (1002 "Karate Twist") 10-20 62

KLEIN, Mo
(With the Sergeants)

Singles: 7-inch

CRYSTALETTE (722 "Alright Private") 15-20 58
CRYSTALETTE (727 "Hot Saki") 5-10 59

KLINE, Bobby

Singles: 7-inch

MB (105 "Taking Care of Business") 100-200 67

KLINE, Burt

Singles: 7-inch

ORBIT (111 "Shove Off, Short Stuff") 50-75 57

KLINT, Bobby
(With the Jades)

Singles: 7-inch

CHRISTY (109 "Mona") 20-30 59
Also see JADES

KLINT, Pete, Quintet *P&R '67*

Singles: 7-inch

ATLANTIC (2533 "Hey Diddle Diddle") 8-12 68
IGL (127 "Very Last Day") 15-25 64
MERCURY (72709 "Walkin' Proud") 8-12 67
P.K.Q. (80-41 "Friday Night Band") ....8-12 '60s
TWIN SPIN (3001 "Walkin' Proud") ....12-18 '60s

KLIXS

Singles: 7-inch

MUSIC CITY (817 "It's All Over") 150-350 57
(Black vinyl.)
MUSIC CITY (817 "It's All Over") 1000-2000 57
(Colored vinyl.)
MUSIC CITY (823 "Elaine") 400-600 58

KLUGH, Earl *R&B/LP '77*

Singles: 7-inch

BLUE NOTE 4-6 76-77
LIBERTY 3-5 81
U.A. 4-6 78-79
W.B. 3-5 85

LPs: 10/12-inch

BLUE NOTE 5-8 76-77
CAPITOL 5-8 83-84
LIBERTY 5-8 80-81
MFSL (025 "Finger Paintings") 35-45 79
MFSL (UHQR 025 "Finger Paintings") 60-80 79
(Boxed set.)
MFSL (076 "Late Night") 30-40 82
U.A. 5-10 78-80
W.B. 5-8 84-91
Also see BENSON, George, & Earl Klugh

KNACKIN, Tommy, & Four Jets

Singles: 7-inch

CASCADE (5912 "Worry, Worry, Worry") 150-250 59

KNAVES

Singles: 7-inch

DUNWICH (147 "Leave Me Alone") 8-12 67
DUNWICH (164 "Inside Outside") 8-12 68
GLEN (8303 "Leave Me Alone") 15-25 67

KNICKERBOCKERS
(With the Buddy Lucas Band)

Singles: 78 rpm

IT'S a NATURAL (3000 "You Must Know") 75-125 53

Singles: 7-inch

IT'S a NATURAL (3000 "You Must Know") 200-300 53
Also see LUCAS, Buddy

KNICKERBOCKERS *P&R '65*

Singles: 7-inch

CHALLENGE (59268 "All I Need Is You") 10-20 65
CHALLENGE (59293 thru 59384) 5-10 65-67
ERIC ....4-6 '70s
LANA ....4-8 '60s

LPs: 10/12-inch

CHALLENGE (621 "Jerk and Twine Time") 45-55 66
CHALLENGE (622 "Lies") 50-75 66
CHALLENGE (12664 "Lloyd Thaxton Presents the Knickerbockers") 50-75 65
SUNDAZED 5-10 89
Members: Buddy Randell; Beau Charles; Jimmy Walker; John Charles.
Also see RANDELL, Buddy
Also see THAXTON, Lloyd
Also see WALKER, Jimmy

KNICK-KNACKS

Singles: 7-inch

COLUMBIA (43609 "Without You") 5-10 66
CUB (9030 "Baby Sittin' with You") 10-15 59

KNIGHT, Alan
(Winston Wheaton)

Singles: 7-inch

BAMBOO (519 "Baby Done What She Said") 5-10 62
TIDE 10-20 60-61
Also see WHEATON, Winston

KNIGHT, Baker
(With His Knightmares)

Singles: 78 rpm

DECCA (30135 "Bring My Cadillac Back") 25-35 56
DECCA (30213 thru 30426) 15-20 57

Singles: 7-inch

ANOTHER 4-6 75
CHALLENGE 8-10 63-65
CHECKER (1023 "Hungry for Love") 8-12 63
CHESS (1795 "Peek-a-Boo") 10-15 61
CORAL 10-15 59
DECCA (30135 "Bring My Cadillac Back") 25-35 56

DECCA (30213 "Reelin' and Rockin' ").... 15-20 57
DECCA (30306 "Just a Little Bit More")... 15-20 57
DECCA (30426 "Love-a-Love")............... 15-20 57
EVEREST (2033 "Big City Girls")...............5-10 63
JUBILEE.. 10-20 57-58
KIT (886 "Boppin' the Blues")................... 40-60 56
KIT (900 "Bring My Cadillac Back")......... 40-60 56
RCA (7814 "I Can Tell")........................... 10-15 60
RCA (37-7892 "Dum Dum Diddley Dum").. 15-25 61
(Compact 33 Single.)
RCA (47-7892 "Dum Dum Diddley Dum").. 10-15 61
REPRISE..5-10 65-68
Also see LIMELITERS
Also see SUGAR BEARS
Also see TRONICS

KNIGHT, Bob, Four

Singles: 7-inch

COMET (915 "Mr. Conscience") 4-6 95
(Black vinyl. 500 made.)
GOAL (4 "Willingly")................................. 30-40 64
JOSIE (899 "Memories")............................. 30-40 62
JUBILEE (5451 "Crazy Love")..................... 15-25 63
LAUREL (1020 "So So Long Good Goodbye").. 15-25 61
LAUREL (1023 "For Sale")......................... 15-25 61
LAUREL (1025 "Well I'm Glad")........... 100-150 61
(Single-sided.)
LAUREL (1030 "Mr. Conscience")...............3-5 93
TAURUS (100 "So So Long Good Goodbye").. 10-15 62
TAURUS (356 "I'm Selling My Heart") 15-20 62

EPs: 7-inch

NEMO (1009 "Acappella")...........................5-8 83
(Colored vinyl.)

LPs: 10/12-inch

KAPE (1001 "Greatest Hits")......................8-10 73
Members: Bob Bovino; John Ropers; Ralph Garone; Paul Ferrigno; Sandy Lynn; Charles Licarta; Frank Ivino.
Also see DELMAR, Eddie

KNIGHT, Chris, & Maureen McCormick

LPs: 10/12-inch

PARAMOUNT (6062 "Chris Knight & Maureen McCormick") 100-150 73
Also see BRADY BUNCH

KNIGHT, Curtis
(With the Squires)

Singles: 7-inch

BELL (45457 "Devil Made Me Do It")...........4-6 74
GULF (31 "That's Why") 15-25 61
HORTON (0001 "Baby That's Where It's At").. 10-20 60
RSVP (1111 "Ain't Gonna Be No Next Time")...8-12 66
RSVP (1120 "Welcome Home")...................8-12 66
RSVP (1124 "Knock Yourself Out") 10-20 66
SHELL (310 "You're Gonna Be Sorry") 8-12 62
SHELL (312 "When You've Got Love").......8-12 63

LPs: 10/12-inch

PARAMOUNT 10-15 70
Session: Jimi Hendrix.
Also see HENDRIX, Jimi, & Curtis Knight

KNIGHT, Earl, & George Kelly

Singles: 7-inch

WINLEY (238 "Let the Good Times Roll")... 15-25 59

KNIGHT, Evelyn
(With the Ray Charles Singers)

Singles: 78 rpm

DECCA (27182 "He Can Come Back Any Time He Wants To")...5-10 50

Singles: 7-inch

CANADIAN AMERICAN (110 "Speak for Yourself, Bill")..8-12 60
DECCA (27182 "He Can Come Back Any Time He Wants To") 10-20 50
Also see CHARLES, Ray, Singers

KNIGHT, Evelyn, & Red Foley C&W '51

Singles: 78 rpm

DECCA (27378 "My Heart Cries for You")..5-10 51

Singles: 7-inch

DECCA (27378 "My Heart Cries for You") 15-25 51
Also see FOLEY, Red

Also see KNIGHT, Evelyn

KNIGHT, Gladys P&R/R&B '61
(Pips; with the Pips)

Singles: 12-inch

COLUMBIA...4-8 79-85
MCA...4-6 86

Singles: 7-inch

ABC 4-6 73
BRUNSWICK (55048 "Whistle My Love")..50-75 58
BUDDAH 4-6 73-79
CASABLANCA...4-6 77-78
COLUMBIA..3-6 79-85
ENJOY(2012 "What Shall I Do") 10-20 64
ERIC...4-6 78
EVERLAST (5025 "Happiness") 15-25 63
FLASHBACK..4-6 67
FURY (1050 thru 1067) 10-15 61-62
FURY (1073 "Come See About Me")........20-30 63
HUNTOM (2510 "Every Beat of My Heart")...150-250 61
MCA...3-5 86-88
MAXX...10-20 64-65
SOUL...6-12 66-74
VEE-JAY (386 "Every Beat of My Heart")...10-15 61
VEE-JAY (545 "Queen of Tears") 10-20 63

Picture Sleeves

BUDDAH 4-6 73-75
COLUMBIA...3-5 81-85
MCA..3-5 86-87

LPs: 10/12-inch

ACCORD..5-8 81-82
ALLEGIANCE..5-8 84
BELL...10-15 68-75
BUDDAH 8-12 73-78
CASABLANCA...5-10 77-78
COLUMBIA..5-8 79-85
51 WEST...5-8 '80s
FURY (1003 "Letter Full of Tears") 200-300 62
LOST NITE (17 "Gladys Knight and the Pips")...10-20 81
(10-inch LP. Red vinyl. 1000 made.)
MCA...5-8 87
MCP...8-10 76
MAXX (3000 "Gladys Knight and the Pips")...20-30 64
MOTOWN (Except 792) 5-8 80-82
MOTOWN (792 "Anthology")......................8-12 74
NATURAL RESOURCES..............................5-8 78
PICKWICK..8-10 73
RELIC..5-10 90
SOUL (706 "Everybody Needs Love").....20-30 67
SOUL (707 "Feelin' Bluesy") 15-25 67
SOUL (711 "Silk 'N' Soul")......................15-25 69
SOUL (713 "Nitty Gritty")........................15-25 69
SOUL (723 thru 744)................................8-15 70-75
SPHERE SOUND (7006 "Gladys Knight and the Pips")..20-30 65
SPRINGBOARD...8-10 75
TRIP...8-10 73
U.A. 10-15 75
UPFRONT..10-12
VEE-JAY...10-15 75
Members: Gladys Knight; Merald Knight; William Guest; Edward Guest.
Also see GAYE, Marvin / Gladys Knight & Pips

KNIGHT, Gladys, & Johnny Mathis

Singles: 7-inch

COLUMBIA (11409 "When a Child Is Born")..3-6 80
Also see MATHIS, Johnny

KNIGHT, Gladys, & Bill Medley

Singles: 7-inch

SCOTTI BROS. 3-5 86
Also see KNIGHT, Gladys
Also see MEDLEY, Bill

KNIGHT, Gloria

Singles: 7-inch

EMERSON (2101 "Lonely Girl")...............50-75 64

KNIGHT, Jesse

Singles: 78 rpm

CHECKER (797 "Nothing But Money")....30-40 54

Singles: 7-inch

CHECKER (797 "Nothing But Money").....60-80 54

KNIGHT, Jim

Singles: 7-inch

BIG "M" (5002 "It's a Man Down There")..20-30 '60s
BIG "M" (5005 "You Cheated") ....20-30 '60s
DOME (1235 "The Lady in the Fine Feather Bed")...10-15 '60s
FAME (601 "Twist") ....25-50 '60s
STATUE (72676 "Magnolia Street") ....8-10 '70s
TEAR DROP (3253 "The Wrong Side of Town")..75-100 '60s

KNIGHT, Jimmy

Singles: 7-inch

GOOD (001 "Playmates")...........................10-20
KANGAROO (27 "Crankshaft")...................8-12 64
TOP ROCK (9140 "Flyin' High") 10-15 60

KNIGHT, Johnny
(With the Kingsmen; John Knight)

Singles: 7-inch

CHANCE (568 "Secret Heart")...............75-100 62
CONGRESS (205 "Sentimental Sweet and Gentle")...5-10 64
MOROCCO (1005 "Rock and Roll Guitar") 75-125 58
SSS INT'L (714 "Forbidden Affair")............5-10 67
20TH FOX (518 "Sweet Like a Rose") 5-10 64

KNIGHT, K.J.

Singles: 7-inch

SOUND PATTERNS ("Mo-Jo")................15-25 '60s
(Selection number not known.)
Also see AMBOY DUKES

KNIGHT, Knighty

Singles: 7-inch

IRVANNE (116 "Blue Diamond Cha Cha Cha")...10-15 59

KNIGHT, Larry, & Upsetters

Singles: 7-inch

GOLDEN WORLD (37 "Hurt Me") 10-20 66

KNIGHT, Little Sonny, & Cymbols

Singles: 7-inch

NEW TEENAGE (5001 "My Darling") .750-1000

KNIGHT, Marie R&B '49

Singles: 78 rpm

DECCA (Except 48315).............................5-15 49-54
DECCA (48315 "You Got a Way of Making Love")...10-20 54
MERCURY...5-10 56
WING (90069 "Tell Me Why")....................5-10 56

Singles: 7-inch

ADDIT (1016 "I Hope You Won't Hold It Against Me")...8-12 60
BATON (253 "September Song") 10-15 58
DECCA (Except 48315) 10-20 51-54
DECCA (48315 "You Got a Way of Making Love")...25-35 54
DIAMOND (171 "Make Yourself at Home")...8-12 64
MERCURY..10-15 56-57
MUSICOR (1076 "Cry Me a River")...10-20 65
MUSICOR (1106 "Say It Again")..............25-50 65
MUSICOR (1128 "You Lie So Well") 10-20 65
OKEH..5-10 61-65
WING (90069 "Tell Me Why") 15-20 56

Picture Sleeves

OKEH (7141 "Come Tomorrow")..............10-15 61

LPs: 10/12-inch

BLUE LABOR 15-25
CARLTON (119 "Lift Every Voice and Sing")..25-50 60
Session: Louisiana Red; Griffins; Millernaires.
Also see GRIFFINS
Also see MARIE & REX
Also see THARPE, Sister Rosetta, & Marie Knight

KNIGHT, Paul

Singles: 7-inch

BETHLEHEM (3022 "Fortune Teller") 5-10 62
DOT (16256 "Because")............................10-15 61
PLANET (1070 "Fortune Teller")................8-12 61

Picture Sleeves

PLANET (1070 "Fortune Teller")..............10-15 61

KNIGHT, Sherrie, & Knights

Singles: 7-inch

PLAYA DEL REY (101 "Too Young to Know") 75-100

KNIGHT, Sonny P&R '56
(With the Cleeshays; Sonny Knight Quartette)

Singles: 78 rpm

ALADDIN 15-25 53
DOT...10-20 56
SPECIALTY..15-25 57
VITA...15-25 56

Singles: 7-inch

A&M...5-10 63-64
ALADDIN (3195 "Dear Wonderful")..........25-50 53
ALADDIN (3207 "But Officer") 25-50 53
AURA (403 thru 4514)................................5-10 64-65
DOT (15507 "Confidential") 35-55 56
(Maroon label.)
DOT (15507 "Confidential") 15-25 57
(Black label.)
DOT (15542 "End of a Dream")...............10-15 57
DOT (15635 "Dedicated to You")...............8-12 57
EASTMAN (782 thru 791).........................10-20 59
FIFO (102 "Saving My Love") 20-30 61
FIFO (105 "Small Girl, Big World") 20-30 61
GO GO (711 "Teenage Party")..............50-100
JAN LAR (921 "Dear Debbie")..................40-50 59
KENT (312 "Lonely Room") 10-20 58
MERCURY (72033 "Just One More Chance")...10-15 62
ORIGINAL SOUND (2 "Once in Awhile") 25-35 58
ORIGINAL SOUND (18 "Those Oldies But Goodies Are Dedicated to You")............................15-20 62
SPECIALTY (547 "Keep a Walkin' ") 20-30 55
STARLA (1 "Dedicated to You") 15-25 57
STARLA (10 "Once in a While") 15-25 58
SWINGIN' (633 "Who in the World") 10-15 61
SWINGIN' (648 "Barbara")........................10-15 63
VITA (137 "Confidential") 75-125 56
WORLD PACIFIC (403 "If You Want This Love") 15-25 64
(Reissued a few months later on Aura 403.)
WORLD PACIFIC (77811 "If I May") 8-12 66
WORLD PACIFIC (77832 "If I Ruled the World")..50-100 66

Picture Sleeves

AURA (4505 "Love Me") 10-20 64

LPs: 10/12-inch

AURA (A-3001 "If You Want This Love") .30-40 64
(Monaural.)
AURA (AS-3001 "If You Want This Love") 40-50 64
(Stereo.)
Also see TYRELL, Danny, & Cleeshays

KNIGHT, Terry P&R/LP '66
(With the Pack; with Fabulous Pack)

Singles: 7-inch

A&M (769 "You Lie") 5-10 65
ABKCO...4-6 75
CAMEO (482 thru 495) 5-10 67
CAPITOL (2409 thru 2506).........................8-12 69
LUCKY ELEVEN (225 "How Much More")...15-25 66
LUCKY ELEVEN (226 "Better Man Than I")..15-25 66
LUCKY ELEVEN (228 "Lady Jane").........15-25 66
LUCKY ELEVEN (229 thru 236)..............10-15 66-67
Note: Label may be shown as either "Lucky 11" or "Lucky Eleven.

LPs: 10/12-inch

ABKCO...10-15 72
CAMEO (2007 "Reflections")....................20-30 67
LUCKY ELEVEN (8000 "Terry Knight and the Pack")..25-35 66
LUCKY ELEVEN (8001 "Reflections") 25-35 67
Members: Terry Knapp (a.k.a. Knight); Mark Farner; Don Brewer; Bob Caldwell; Curt Johnson.
Also see GRAND FUNK RAILROAD
Also see PACK

KNIGHT, Whitey

Singles: 78 rpm

DOT (15577 "Lately") 10-15 57
SAGE & SAND (205 "I Can't Stop Loving You")...5-10 55

Singles: 7-inch

DART (115 "Crazy Love Affair") 15-25 59
(First issue.)
DART (1210 "Crazy Love Affair") 10-20 59
DOT (15577 "Lately") 10-20 57
SAGE & SAND (205 "I Can't Stop Loving You")..10-20 55

KNIGHT BROTHERS P&R/R&B '65
Singles: 7-inch
CHECKER (Except 1107)....5-10 63-66
CHECKER (1107 "Temptation 'Bout to Get Me")....10-20 65
MERCURY....8-15 67-68
Members: Richard Dunbar; Jerry Diggs.

KNIGHT RIDERS
(Featuring Billy Vera)
Singles: 7-inch
1220 CLUB ("My Heart Crys")....30-40
(No selection number used. Labeled "Souvenir Copy.")
U.A. (366 "Annie's Place")....10-20 61
Also see VERA, Billy

KNIGHT RIDERS
Singles: 7-inch
TRAVEL (5303 "Roc-A-Nof")....10-20 66

KNIGHT RYDERS
Singles: 7-inch
CUCA (1197 "They'll Never Guess I'm Lonely")....10-20 '60s
CUCA (1264 "Talking in Your Sleep")....10-20 '60s
Members: Bill West; Mel West.

KNIGHT TRAINS
Singles: 7-inch
HART-VAN (126 "Beach Head")....20-30 63

KNIGHTBEATS
Singles: 7-inch
PLANET (55 "Hey Girl")....10-15 64

KNIGHTMARE II
Singles
AZRA (1 "Razor Love")....20-30 87
(Square picture disc. 25 made.)
MASQUE (1020 "Guillotine")....10-15 88
(Ram-shaped picture disc. 500 made.)
MASQUE (8806 "Down Town Brown")....5-10 89
(Hockey mask shaped picture disc. 500 made.)
LPs: 10/12-inch
MASQUE (8807 "Edge of Knight")....15-20 89
(Picture disc. Promotional issue only. 100 made.)

KNIGHTS
Singles: 7-inch
RED FEATHER (18401 "Cut Out")....10-20 61
RED FEATHER ("Lonely by the Sea")....10-20 61
(Selection number not known.)

KNIGHTS
Singles: 7-inch
CAPITOL (5302 "Hot Rod High")....10-20 64
LPs: 10/12-inch
CAPITOL (T-2189 "Hot Rod High")....40-50 64
(Monaural.)
CAPITOL (ST-2189 "Hot Rod High")....50-70 64
(Stereo.)
Session: Gary Usher; Chuck Girard; Joe Kelly; Dick Burns; Jerry Cole; Glen Campbell; Leon Russell; Hal Blaine; Steve Douglas; Tommy Tedesco; Bill Pitman; Charles Berghofer; Jay Migliori; Frank Capp.
Also see BLAINE, Hal
Also see CAMPBELL, Glen
Also see COLE,Jerry
Also see DOUGLAS, Steve
Also see KICKSTANDS
Also see RUSSELL, Leon
Also see TEDESCO, Tommy
Also see USHER, Gary

KNIGHTS
Singles: 7-inch
USA (800 "Forgive Me")....30-40 65

KNIGHTS
LPs: 10/12-inch
ACE (4763 "Cold Days, Hot Knights")....200-400 '60s
ACE (200854 "Across the Board")....200-400 66
ACE (201302 "Knights 1967")....200-400 67
CO (1269 "Off Campus")....300-500 65

KNIGHTS
Singles: 7-inch
TRAGAR (6806 "The Hump")....10-20 65

KNIGHTS BRIDGE QUINTET
Singles: 7-inch
K (101 "Sorrow in C Minor")....10-20 67
MARK VII (1019 "Sorrow in C Minor")....10-20 67
SALMAR....10-20
TRC (2072 "Sorrow in C Minor")....10-20 67

KNIGHTS OF DAY
Singles: 7-inch
TEE PEE (55/56 "Mr. Pitiful"/"Then There's You")....10-15 68
TOWER (245 "Everybody Needs Somebody to Love")....5-10 66

KNIGHTS OF THE ROAD
Singles: 7-inch
LEVE-WAY (4150 "Color of Dream")....10-15 '60s

KNIGHTSMEN
Singles: 7-inch
SOUND (142 "If I Really Loved You")....15-25 58

KNIGHTSMEN
("Featuring Johnny Trujillo")
Singles: 7-inch
BOCALDUN (1005/1006 "Darling Why?")....200-300 59
(Red vinyl.)
Member: Johnny Trujillo.

KNIPP, Lowell
Singles: 7-inch
DEWL (4260 "Pretty Brown Eyes")....15-25 65
DEWL (4266 "Goofy Little Bug")....75-125 65
MUSICOR....5-10 65-69
Picture Sleeves
DEWL (4260 "Pretty Brown Eyes")....20-30 65

KNOCKOUTS P&R '59
Singles: 7-inch
SCEPTER (1269 "Got My Mojo Working")....10-20 64
SHAD (5013 "Darling Lorraine")....50-75 59
(Has a long ending.)
SHAD (5013 "Darling Lorraine")....15-25 59
SHAD (5018 "Rich Boy, Poor Boy")....10-15 60
TRIBUTE (199 "Got My Mojo Working")....5-10 64
TRIBUTE (201 "What's on Your Mind")....10-15 64
TRIBUTE (216 "Falling from Paradise")....15-25 64
TRIBUTE (1039 "Don't Say Goodbye")....10-15 65
LPs: 10/12-inch
TRIBUTE (1202 "Go Ape")....75-100 64
Members: Robert D'Andrea; Eddie Parenti; Bob Collada; Harry Venuta.

KNOCKOUTS
(With Harry Hershey Orchestra)
Singles: 7-inch
COS-DE (1003 "Sweet Talk")....50-100 60

KNOTTS, Bobby
(With "Choral & Orch. Arr & Conducted by Squeak's")
Singles: 7-inch
GEE CLEF (077 "Too Young")....50-100 61

KNOWBODY ELSE
Singles: 7-inch
FLIP (8020 "Someone Something")....8-12 69
HIP (8020 "Someone Something")....10-20 69
LPs: 10/12-inch
HIP (7003 "Knowbody Else")....20-30 69
Member: James Mangrum.

KNOX, Buddy P&R/R&B '57
("Lieutenant Buddy Knox"; with the Rhythm Orchids)
Singles: 78 rpm
ROULETTE....15-40 57
Singles: 7-inch
ABC (2516 "Party Doll")....4-6 73
LIBERTY (55305 thru 55694)....10-15 61-64
REPRISE (395 thru 501)....5-10 65-66
ROULETTE (4002 "Party Doll")....30-40 57
(With roulette wheel circling label. Label may be either red/orange or maroon.)
ROULETTE (4002 "Party Doll")....15-25 57
(With roulette wheel on top half of label.)
ROULETTE (4002 "Party Doll")....10-20 58
(No roulette wheel on label.)
ROULETTE (4009 "Rock Your Little Baby to Sleep")....25-35 57
(With roulette wheel on label.)
ROULETTE (4009 "Rock Your Little Baby to Sleep")....10-20 58
(No roulette wheel on label.)
ROULETTE (4018 "Hula Love")....15-25 57
ROULETTE (4042 "Swingin' Daddy")....15-25 58
ROULETTE (4082 "C'mon Baby")....15-25 58
ROULETTE (4120 "Teasable, Pleasable You")....15-25 58
ROULETTE (4140 "To Be with You")....15-25 59
ROULETTE (4179 "Taste of the Blues")....15-25 59
ROULETTE (4262 "Long Lonely Nights")....15-25 60
RUFF (1001 "Jo-Ann")....5-10 65
SUNNYHILL ("I Named My Little Baby Holly")....5-10
(No selection number used.)
U.A. (50301 thru 50789)....5-10 68-71
Picture Sleeves
LIBERTY (55305 "Ling Ting Tong")....15-25 61
EPs: 7-inch
ROULETTE (301 "Buddy Knox")....50-75 57
LPs: 10/12-inch
ACCORD....5-8 82-83
LIBERTY (3251 "Golden Hits")....20-30 62
(Monaural.)
LIBERTY (7251 "Golden Hits")....25-35 62
(Stereo.)
ROULETTE (25003 "Buddy Knox")....75-100 57
U.A....10-15 69
Members (Rhythm Orchids): Buddy Knox; Jimmy Bowen; Dave Alldred; Don Lanier.
Also see LANIER, Don

KNOX, Buddy / Jimmy Bowen
(With the Rhythm Orchids) P&R/R&B '57
Singles: 78 rpm
ROULETTE (4001 "My Baby's Gone"/"I'm Stickin' with You")....30-50 57
TRIPLE-D (797 "Party Doll"/"I'm Stickin' with You")....50-100 57
Singles: 7-inch
BLUE MOON (402 "Party Doll"/"I'm Stickin' with You")....200-300 57
ROULETTE (4001 "My Baby's Gone"/"I'm Stickin' with You")....30-50 57
TRIPLE-D (797 "Party Doll"/"I'm Stickin' with You")....300-400 57
LPs: 10/12-inch
MURRAY HILL....5-8 '80s
ROULETTE (25048 "Buddy Knox & Jimmy Bowen")....75-125 58
Members (Rhythm Orchids): Buddy Knox; Jimmy Bowen; Dave Alldred; Don Lanier.
Also see BOWEN, Jimmy
Also see KNOX, Buddy

KNOX, Eugene
Singles: 7-inch
GALAXY (711 "Miss You")....400-500 63
(Green vinyl.)

KNOX, George, & Ultra Tones
Singles: 7-inch
EVEREST (19313 "Blessings")....20-30 59

KNULL, Ron, & His Rock-A-Kings
Singles: 7-inch
CARROLL (45-5 "G.I. Blues")....100-150 60

KO KOs
Singles: 78 rpm
COMBO (141 "First Day of School")....50-75 57
Singles: 7-inch
COMBO (141 "First Day of School")....100-150 58

KOALA
Singles: 7-inch
CAPITOL (2365 "Don't You Know What I Mean")....8-12 68
LPs: 10/12-inch
CAPITOL (176 "Koala")....15-25 69

KOATS OF MALE
Singles: 7-inch
IGL (134 "Life's Matter")....30-50 '60s

KODOKS
(Featuring Pearl McKinnon; with the Joy Vendors; Kadak's; Kodaks)
Singles: 78 rpm
FURY....25-75 57
Singles: 7-inch
FLASHBACK....4-6 65
FURY (1007 "Teenager's Dream")....50-75 57
(Maroon label.)
FURY (1007 "Teenager's Dream")....10-15 62
(Yellow label.)
FURY (1015 "Oh Gee Oh Gosh")....30-40 58
(Maroon label. Label name in small print.)
FURY (1015 "Oh Gee Oh Gosh")....15-25 58
(Maroon label. Label name in larger print.)
FURY (1015 "Oh Gee Oh Gosh")....10-15 62
(Yellow label. Black vinyl.)
FURY (1015 "Oh Gee Oh Gosh")....40-50 62
(Yellow label. Red vinyl.)
FURY (1019 "My Baby and Me")....50-75 58
FURY (1020 "Guardian Angel")....50-75 58
J&S (1684 "Look Up in the Sky")....75-125 60
(With straight horizontal lines.)
J&S (1684 "Look Up in the Sky")....50-75 60
(With wavy horizontal lines.)
WINK (1004 "Let's Rock")....15-20 61
WINK (1006 "Love Wouldn't Mean a Thing")....20-25 61
LPs: 10/12-inch
LOST NITE (14 "The Kodoks")....10-20 81
(10-inch LP. Red vinyl. 1000 made.)
RELIC....5-10 90
Members: Pearl McKinnon; Jean Miller; Larry Davis; Jim Patrick; Bill Franklin; Harold Jenkins; Bill Miller; Richard Dixon; Renaldo Gamble.
Also see SCHOOLBOYS
Also see PEARL & DELTARS

KODOKS / Starlites
LPs: 10/12-inch
SPHERE SOUND (7005 "The Kodoks Versus the Starlites")....100-150 65
Also see STARLITES

KOEN, Marvin
Singles: 7-inch
ATLAS (1204 "You Know")....50-100 59

KOENIG, Freddy, & Jades
Singles: 7-inch
GOLDEN EAGLE (115 "Lover's Prayer")....10-20 64
GOLDEN EAGLE (116 "Sweet Maureen")....10-20 64
LORI (9548 "Hey Clarice")....75-125 63
(First issue.)
VALERIE (225 "Hey Clarice")....50-100 63

KOERNER, Spider John
LPs: 10/12-inch
ELEKTRA (290 "Spider Blues")....10-20 65
SWEET JANE (5872 "Music Is Just a Bunch of Notes")....25-35
Also see KOERNER, RAY & GLOVER

KOERNER, Spider John, & Willie Murphy
LPs: 10/12-inch
ELEKTRA (2041 "Running, Jumping, Standing Still")....10-15 69

KOERNER, RAY & GLOVER
LPs: 10/12-inch
ELEKTRA (240 "Blues, Rags and Hollers")....10-20 63
ELEKTRA (267 "Lots More Blues, Rags and Hollers")....10-20 64
ELEKTRA (305 "The Return of Ray Koerner and Glover")....10-20 65
MIL CITY (172 "Good Old Koerner, Ray & Glover")....10-20
Members: John Koerner; Dave Ray; Tony Glover.
Also see KOERNER, Spider John

KOFFMAN, Moe P&R '58
(Moe Koffman Quartette; Quintet; Septette)
Singles: 7-inch
ABC....4-6 73
ASCOT....5-10 62-63
ATCO (6382 "Big Band Irving")....5-10 65
GOLD EAGLE....5-10 61
JUBILEE (5311 thru 5367)....8-12 58-59
JUBILEE (5471 thru 5632)....5-10 64-68
PALETTE....5-10 60-63
VIRGO....4-6 72
LPs: 10/12-inch
ASCOT (13001 "Plays for Teens")....10-20 62
(Monaural.)
ASCOT (16001 "Plays for Teens")....15-25 62
(Stereo.)
JANUS....5-10 78
JUBILEE (1037 "Cool & Hot Sax")....30-50 57
JUBILEE (1074 "The Shepherd Swings Again")....30-50 58
JUBILEE (8009 "Goes Electric")....8-12 68
JUBILEE (8016 "Turned On")....8-12 68
U.A. (13001 "Plays for Teens")....15-25 62
(Monaural. First issue.)
U.A. (14029 "Tales of Koffman")....15-25 63
(Monaural.)
U.A. (15029 "Tales of Koffman")....25-30 63
(Stereo.)
U.A. (16001 "Plays for Teens")....25-30 62
(Stereo. First issue.)

KOKOMOS
Singles: 7-inch
GONE (5134 "Mama's Boy")....................10-15 62
JOSIE (906 "Open House Party")..............5-10 63
Also see 4 SEASONS

KOLE, Kenny, & Huskies
Singles: 7-inch
KLIK (8205 "Sorry")....................50-60 58
Members: Jerry Cole; Ken Kolok; Jack Covert; Ed Hayden; Dave Jones; Dick Crane.

KOLETTES
Singles: 7-inch
BARBARA (1094 "Who's That Guy").......10-15 64
(First issue.)
CHECKER (1094 "Who's That Guy")..........5-10 64

KOLOC, Bonnie
Singles: 7-inch
OVATION 4-6 75
LPs: 10/12-inch
EPIC (35254 "Wild and Recluse")..............5-10 '80s
OVATION (1438 "You're Gonna Love Yourself in the Morning")....................................15-25 74
(Quadraphonic.)

KOLOR KORPORATION
Singles: 7-inch
HYPE (1015 "Sunshine on Our Love")....20-40 67
(Not commercially distributed. About 500 were made for sales at the group's concerts.)
Members: Mike Stegall; Wayne Proctor; Bob Pennington; Wayne Corbin; Steve Michaels; Jimmy Chambers.

KOMMOTIONS
Singles: 7-inch
BELL (630 "Little Black Egg").......10-15 65
(Also released as by Wayne Lacadisi.)

KOMONS
Singles: 7-inch
FEATURE (104 "Caught in the Trap")..... 15-25 66

KONDOS, John, & Galaxies
Singles: 7-inch
GALAXIE (5009 "Hip Snap")................... 20-30 66
Members: Mike Miller; Nick Kondos; Patrick McCarthy.

KONTRAST
Singles: 7-inch
KONTRAST (101 "Walkin' the Dog")....... 20-30

KOO KREW
Singles: 7-inch
ASCOT (2225 "Wet and Wild").................. 15-25 66

KOOBAS
Singles: 7-inch
CAPITOL (2416 "First Cut Is the Deepest")..5-10 69
KAPP (737 "Take Me for a Little While")....8-12 66
Picture Sleeves
KAPP (737 "Take Me for a Little While").. 15-25 66

KOOKIE
(Kookie & Satalites)
Singles: 7-inch
GMA (8 "Rebel Walk")............................ 10-20 64
MILKY WAY (2586 Ooby Dooby")............. 25-35 65
(Actually this was Milky Way 005, but that number was omitted from label.)
Also see CARTER, Dean

KOOKIE JOE
Singles: 7-inch
NERMEL (846 "Kookie Limbo")............... 10-20 61

KOOL & GANG *P&R/R&B '69*
Singles: 12-inch
DE-LITE..4-8 79-85
MERCURY 4-6 86-87
Singles: 7-inch
DE-LITE..3-8 69-85
MERCURY 3-5 86-88
Picture Sleeves
DE-LITE (880623 "Fresh")........................3-5 85
DE-LITE (880869 "Cherish")......................3-5 85
MERCURY 3-5 86-88
LPs: 10/12-inch
DE-LITE (2003 "Kool and the Gang")...... 60-80 69
DE-LITE (2008 "Live at the Sex Machine").. 20-40 71
DE-LITE (2009 "Best Of")........................ 20-30 71
DE-LITE (2010 "Live at P.J.'s")................20-30 72
DE-LITE (2012 "Good Times")..................20-30 73
DE-LITE (2013 thru 2023)........................10-20 73-76
DE-LITE (4001 "Kool Jazz")......................10-20 73
DE-LITE (8502 "Something Special")..........8-10 81
DE-LITE (8502 "History of Kool and the Gang")...15-20 81
(Promotional issue only. With interviews.)
DE-LITE (8505 "As One")..........................5-10 82
DE-LITE (8508 "In the Heart")....................5-10 83
DE-LITE (9501 thru 9518)...........................8-12 78-80
DE-LITE (822943 "Emergency")..................5-10 84
MERCURY (830398 thru 834780)...............5-8 86-88
POLYGRAM (001 "The 'Bull' Brings You Selections from Kool & the Gang's Past Hits")..........15-20 81
(Promotional issue only from Schlitz Malt Liquor.)
Members: Robert "Kool" Bell; George Brown; Ronald Bell; Curtis Williams; Charles Smith; James Taylor.

KOOL BLUES
Singles: 7-inch
CAPSOUL (35 "Keep on Loving You")......15-25

KOOL GENTS
Singles: 78 rpm
VEE-JAY...40-60 56
Singles: 7-inch
VEE-JAY (173 "This Is the Night").........200-300 56
VEE-JAY (207 "You Know")....................200-300 56
Members: Dee Clark; Johnny Carter; Ted Long; John McCall; Doug Brown.
Also see CLARK, Dee
Also see DELEGATES
Also see EL DORADOS

KOOL GENTS
Singles: 7-inch
BETHLEHEM (3061 "Picture on the Wall")...50-75 63

KOOL TOPPERS
Singles: 78 rpm
BEVERLY (702 "Cause I Love You So")...100-200 55
Singles: 7-inch
BEVERLY (702 "Cause I Love You So").. 750-1000 55

KOON, Larry
("Parkersburg's Larry Koon")
Singles: 7-inch
COUNTRY MUSIC CITY (50070 "The Heartaches")..3-5 82
HITVILLE (50067 "Easy to Say, Hard to Do")...15-25 66
HITVILLE (50069 "Oh How I Could Love You")...10-20 69

KOPE, Billy
(With the Quardells)
Singles: 7-inch
HARVARD (808 "Just You Wait and See")..20-30 59
KUDO (662 "It's All My Fault")................75-125 58

KORDS
(Buzz Sears & Kords; "Featuring Sharon LaMaster")
Singles: 7-inch
LAURIE (3403 "Boris the Spider")..............5-10 67
NWI (2765 "Mr. Someone")......................10-15 '60s
NWI (2793 "Worked Hard All My Life").....10-15 '60s

KORMAN, Jerry
Singles: 7-inch
ABC-PAR (10024 "Hurry Back")...............10-20 59
MEADOW (1001 "Hurry Back")..............50-100 59

KORNEGAY, Big Bob
Singles: 7-inch
HERALD (496 "The Man in the Phone Booth")...10-20 57
HERALD (499 "Come By Here")................20-30 57
HERALD (506 ("Stay with Me")..................10-20 57
JARO (77003 "Your Line Was Busy")........25-35 59
STACY (952 "Wowsville")..........................10-20 62

KORNERS OF TIME
Singles: 7-inch
REACTION (1009 "Cara Lin")..................40-60 '60s

K-OTICS
(K-Ottics)
Singles: 7-inch
BANG (521 "Double Shot").......................10-15 66
FORTUNE (1000 "Double Shot")..............20-30 66
RICK (10276 "Ooh-Wee")..........................5-10

KOTTKE, Leo *LP '71*
Singles: 7-inch
CAPITOL...4-6 75
LPs: 10/12-inch
CAPITOL (Except 16000 series)................8-12 71-76
CAPITOL (16000 series)..............................5-8 81
CHRYSALIS...5-10 76-81
OBLIVION (1 "12 String Blues")...............50-75 69
(Cover reads "12 String Blues" but label shows title as "Live At the Scholar Coffeehouse, Minneapolis, Minnesota.")
SYMPOSIUM (2001 "Circle 'Round the Sun")..15-25 70
TAKOMA..8-12 71-74

KOTTKE, Leo, John Fahey & Peter Lang
LPs: 10/12-inch
TAKOMA...8-10 74
Also see FAHEY, John
Also see KOTTKE, Leo

KOUNTS
Singles: 7-inch
VALMALCO (504 "Please Please Come Back")...75-100

KRACKER-BARREL-COMPLEX
Singles: 7-inch
PAGE (1087 "My World")............................15-25 68

KRAFTONES
Singles: 7-inch
MEDIEVAL (206 "Memories")..................30-40 64
(Black vinyl.)
MEDIEVAL (206 "Memories")..................50-75 64
(Yellow vinyl.)
Also see BEACHCOMBERS

KRAMER, Billy J., & Dakotas *P&R/LP '64*
Singles: 7-inch
EPIC..5-10 68
ERIC...3-5
IMPERIAL 5-10 64-66
LIBERTY (55586 "Do You Want to Know a Secret"/"I'll Be on My Way")...8-12 63
LIBERTY (55626 "Bad to Me")...................8-10 63
LIBERTY (55643 "I'll Keep You Satisfied").8-10 63
LIBERTY (55667 "Do You Want to Know a Secret"/ "Bad to Me")...5-10 64
Picture Sleeves
IMPERIAL (66051 "From a Window")......10-15 64
LPs: 10/12-inch
CAPITOL...8-10 78-79
IMPERIAL (9267 "Little Children")...........25-35 64
(Monaural.)
IMPERIAL (9273 "I'll Keep You Satisfied")..25-35 64
(Monaural.)
IMPERIAL (9291 "Trains and Boats and Planes")...25-35 65
(Monaural.)
IMPERIAL (12267 "Little Children")..........25-40 64
(Stereo.)
IMPERIAL (12273 "I'll Keep You Satisfied")..25-40 64
(Stereo.)
IMPERIAL (12291 "Trains and Boats and Planes")...25-40 65
(Stereo.)

KRANTZTONES
Singles: 7-inch
CRYSTAL BALL (140 "Zoop")......................4-8 81
(Black vinyl. 500 made.)
CRYSTAL BALL (140 "Zoop")......................8-12 81
(Red vinyl. 25 made.)
CRYSTAL BALL (140 "Zoop")..................30-40 81
(Multi-colored vinyl. Five made.)
Picture Sleeves
CRYSTAL BALL (140 "Zoop")..................20-25 81
(200 made.)

KRAZY KATS
Singles: 7-inch
DAMON (12350 "Beat Out My Love")......20-30 61
(Re-recording of tracks made first in 1959, which existed only on acetate. Has added sax and guitar.)
ECCO-FONIC (1006 "Beat Out My Love")...4-6 94
(First record release of 1959 version. Made from original acetate.)
Picture Sleeves
ECCO-FONIC (1006 "Beat Out My Love")...5-8 94
LPs: 10/12-inch
DAMON (12478 "Movin' Out")..................75-125 64
Members: Lee Dresser; Willie Carig; Fred Fletcher.
Also see DRESSER, Lee

KRAZY KRIS
Singles: 7-inch
KING (4991 "Floyd's Guitar Blues")..........15-25 57

KREED
LPs: 10/12-inch
VISION OF SOUND (71-56 "Kreed")...1000-1500 71
Members: David Cannon; Reed Boyd; Dean Sack; Doug Parent; Nigel Coff.

KREEG
Singles: 7-inch
LANCE (2229 "How Can I").......................15-25 67

KREIGER, Butch
Singles: 7-inch
GARDENA ("Betty Jean")........................75-125 '60s
(Selection number not known.)

KRISTOFFERSON, Kris *P&R/LP '71*
Singles: 7-inch
COLUMBIA...3-6 77-81
EPIC (10225 "Killing Time").......................8-12 67
MONUMENT...3-6 70-81
Picture Sleeves
COLUMBIA (10525 "Watch Closely Now")..4-6 77
EPs: 7-inch
MONUMENT (532 "Kristofferson")............5-10 71
(Promotional issue only.)
MONUMENT (31909 "Jesus Was a Capricorn")..5-10 72
(Juke box issue only. Includes title strips.)
LPs: 10/12-inch
COLUMBIA...5-10 77-81
MONUMENT (Except 18139)....................8-15 70-76
MONUMENT (18139 "Kristofferson").......25-35 70
(Green and yellow label.)
MONUMENT (18139 "Kristofferson").......15-25 70
(Brown label.)
Session: Larry Gatlin; Rita Coolidge.
Also see COE, David Allan
Also see JENNINGS, Waylon, Willie Nelson, Johnny Cash, & Kris Kristofferson
Also see NELSON, Willie, & Kris Kristofferson
Also see SCAGGS, Boz / Kris Kristofferson

KRISTOFFERSON, Kris, & Rita Coolidge *C&W '73*
Singles: 7-inch
A&M (1475 "A Song I'd Like to Sing").........4-6 73
A&M (1498 "Loving Arms")........................4-6 74
MONUMENT...4-6 74-75
Picture Sleeves
A&M (1475 "A Song I'd Like to Sing").........4-6 73
LPs: 10/12-inch
A&M (Except PR-4690).............................8-12 73-79
A&M (PR-4690 "Natural Act")..................10-15 79
(Picture disc, numbered edition. Promotional issue only.)
MONUMENT...8-12 74

KRISTOFFERSON, Kris, Willie Nelson, Dolly Parton, & Brenda Lee
LPs: 10/12-inch
MONUMENT...8-12 82
Also see KRISTOFFERSON, Kris
Also see NELSON, Willie
Also see PARTON, Dolly

KRISTYL
LPs: 10/12-inch
("Kristyl")..300-400 75
(No label name or selection number used.)

KROSS, Jack
Singles: 7-inch
HAP (102 "Mr. Blues")..............................50-75

KRUEGER, Bruce & Keith
Singles: 7-inch
CPO (112 "Tell Me a Story")....................15-20 '60s

KRUISERS
Singles: 7-inch
KISKI (2068 "Karen")...............................20-30 65

KRYSTYL
LPs: 10/12-inch
("Krystyl")....75-125 75
(No label name or number used.)
Members: Sonny DeVore; Bruce Whiteside; Bob Terrell; David Atherton.

KUBAN, Bob *P&R/LP '66*
(With the In-Men; Bob Kuban Band)
Singles: 7-inch
ERIC (153 "The Cheater")....4-6 73
MUSICLAND USA. (20001 "The Cheater")....10-20 66
("Vocal by Walter Scott" shown on both sides.)
MUSICLAND USA (20001 The Cheater")..5-10 66
("Vocal by Walter Scott" shown only on B-side, *Try Me Baby*.)
MUSICLAND USA (20001 "The Cheater").5-10 66
("Vocal by Walter Scott" not on either side.)
NORMAN (558 "Jerkin' Time")....5-15 65
(Walter Scott may be shown as "Little Walter.")
MUSICLAND USA (20003 thru 20017)....5-10 66-67
REPRISE....4-8 70
Picture Sleeves
MUSICLAND USA (20003 "The Pretzel") 10-15 66
LPs: 10/12-inch
MUSICLAND USA (3500 "Look Out for the Cheater")....25-35 66
MUSICLAND USA (3501 "Explosion")....20-30 66
Members: Walter Scott; Bob Kuban; John Krenski; Greg Hoeltzel.
Also see SCOTT, Walter

KUBIAK, Dan, & Sound Waves
Singles: 7-inch
DORRINGTON (100 "Finding You")....300-500 59

KUF-LINX *P&R '58*
("Featuring John Jennings"; Kuff-Linx)
Singles: 78 rpm
CHALLENGE....15-25 57-58
Singles: 7-inch
CHALLENGE (1013 "So Tough")....15-25 57
(Blue or white label.)
CHALLENGE (1013 "So Tough")....10-15 58
(Maroon label.)
CHALLENGE (59004 "Service with a Smile")....10-15 58
CHALLENGE (59015 "Climb Love's Mountain")....50-75 58
Member: John Jennings.

KUHN, Bob
Singles: 7-inch
IMPACT (8 "Rendezvous")....10-15 62
(Colored vinyl.)

KURRYETTES
Singles: 7-inch
KHOURY'S (722 "The Spook")....10-15 60

KURT & KAPERS
Singles: 7-inch
V-LEE (211 "Mongoose")....20-30 '60s

KUSTOM KINGS
Singles: 7-inch
SMASH (1883 "In My '40 Ford")....15-25 64
LPs: 10/12-inch
SMASH (27051 "Kustom City USA")....60-80 64
(Monaural.)
SMASH (67051 "Kustom City USA")....65-85 64
(Stereo.)
Members: Bruce Johnston; Steve Douglas.
Also see DOUGLAS, Steve
Also see JOHNSTON, Bruce

KYKS
Singles: 7-inch
RAF (1001 "Where Are You")....10-20 65
Picture Sleeves
RAF (1001 "Where Are You")....20-30 65

KYND
Singles: 7-inch
KYND (103169 "Clouds")....15-20 69

L

L.H. & MEMPHIS SOUNDS
Singles: 7-inch
HOLLYWOOD (1112 "Double Up")....40-50 67
HOLLYWOOD (1122 "I'm a Fool")....40-50 67

LRY
LPs: 10/12-inch
CONGRESS OF THE CROW (8031002 "The LRY Record")....150-250 68

LSD
Singles: 7-inch
MUSICOR (429 "Mystery of the Mystical Invasion")....15-25 67

LA BEEF, Sleepy *C&W '68*
(Tommy LaBeef)
Singles: 78 rpm
MERCURY (71112 "I'm Through")....50-100 57
MERCURY (71179 "All the Time")....50-100 57
STARDAY (292 "I'm Through")....50-100 57
Singles: 7-inch
COLUMBIA....5-10 65-68
CRESCENT (102 "Turn Me Loose")....100-200 57
GULF (62760 "Can't Get You Off My Mind")....50-75
MERCURY (71112 "I'm Through")....50-100 57
MERCURY (71179 "All the Time")....50-100 57
PLANTATION (Except 55)....5-10 70-71
PLANTATION (55 "Too Much Monkey Business")....15-25 70
STARDAY (292 "I'm Through")....50-100 57
(Issued the same month on both Mercury and Starday.)
SSS/SUN....4-8 68-79
(Black vinyl.)
SSS/SUN (1145 "Boogie Woogie Country Girl")....15-25 79
(Yellow vinyl. Promotional issue only.)
LPs: 10/12-inch
BARON....10-12 79
ROUNDER....5-8 81
SUN....8-10 74-78

LA BEEF, Tommy
Singles: 78 rpm
PICTURE (1937 "Ride On Josephine")....100-150 57
WAYSIDE (1651 "Ride On Josephine")....150-200 57
WAYSIDE (1654 "Tore Up")....200-300 57
Singles: 7-inch
PICTURE (1937 "Ride On Josephine")....100-150 57
WAYSIDE (1651 "Ride On Josephine")....150-200 57
WAYSIDE (1654 "Tore Up")....200-300 57
Also see LA BEEF, Sleepy

LABELLE, Patti *P&R '62*
(With the Blue-Belles; with Blue Belles; with Blue Bells; Pattie La Belle; Labelle; Patty La Belle)
Singles: 12-inch
EPIC....5-10 78-79
MCA....4-6 85
PHILA. INT'L....4-6 83-85
Singles: 7-inch
ATLANTIC....5-10 65-70
EPIC....3-6 74-80
KING (5777 "Down the Aisle")....8-12 63
MISTLETOE....4-6 73
PHILA. INT'L....3-5 81-85
PHILA. INT'L (02655 "Family")....10-20 82
(Red vinyl. Promotional issue.)
MCA....3-5 85-87
NEWTIME (510 "Love Me Just a Little")...10-15 62
NEWTOWN (5000 "I Sold My Heart to the Junkman")....10-15 62
NEWTOWN (5006 "I Found a New Love")....10-15 62
NEWTOWN (5007 "Tear After Tear")....10-15 62
NEWTOWN (5009 "When Johnny Comes Marching Home")....10-15 62
NEWTOWN (5019 "Decatur Street")....10-15 63
NEWTOWN (5777 "Down the Aisle")....10-15 63
(Reads "Pressed by King Records.")
NEWTOWN (5777 "Down the Aisle")....5-10 63
(No mention of King Records.)
NICETOWN (5020 "You'll Never Walk Alone"/"Where Are You")....15-20 63
NICETOWN (5020 "You'll Never Walk Alone"/"Decatur Street")....10-15 63
PARKWAY (896 thru 935)....8-10 64
RCA....4-6 73
TRIP....4-6 71
W.B....4-6 71-72
Picture Sleeves
MCA....3-5 85-87
LPs: 10/12-inch
ATLANTIC....15-25 65-67
EPIC....8-10 74-82
MCA....5-8 85-89
MISTLETOE....10-20
NEWTOWN (631 "Sweethearts of the Apollo")....50-100 63
NEWTOWN (632 "Sleigh Bells, Jingle Bells and Blue Bells")....50-100 63
PARKWAY (7043 "On Stage")....30-50 64
PHILA. INT'L....5-8 81-85
RCA (0200 series)....8-10 73
RCA (4100 series)....5-8 82
TRIP....8-10 71-75
U.A....8-10 74-75
UPFRONT....10-15
W.B....8-10 71-72
Also see BLUE BELLES
Also see NYRO, Laura
Also see WOMACK, Bobby, & Patti Labelle

LABELLE, Patti, & Michael McDonald *P&R/R&B '86*
Singles: 7-inch
MCA....3-5 86
Picture Sleeves
MCA....3-5 86
Also see McDONALD, Michael

LABELLE, Patti, & Grover Washington Jr. *R&B '82*
Singles: 7-inch
ELEKTRA....3-5 82
Also see LABELLE, Patti
Also see WASHINGTON, Grover, Jr.

LA BLANC, Red
Singles: 7-inch
CARMA (506 "I Love Her Right or Wrong")....50-75

LABOMBAS
Singles: 7-inch
NEW TEENAGE (5000 "Taboo")....25-35 '60s

LABRADORS
Singles: 7-inch
CHIEF (7009 "When Someone Loves You")....250-350 58

LACADISI, Wayne
(Wayne Logiudice)
Singles: 7-inch
BELL (630 "Little Black Egg")....10-15 65
(Also released as by the Kommotions.)

LA CHORDS
Singles: 7-inch
GAY (629 "To Be")....75-125 62
TAKE FIVE (631 "Hammer of My Heart")....75-125

LACKEY, Joe, & Ramrod Combo
Singles: 7-inch
BRIGHT (511 "Sittin' Alone")....100-200

LACOUR, Lenny
Singles: 78 rpm
ACADEMY....75-100 57
Singles: 7-inch
ACADEMY (3571 "Rockin' Rosalie")....75-100 57
ACADEMY (5732 "Jungle Rock")....75-100 57
LUCKY FOUR (1001 "Twinkle Toes")....15-25 61
MAGIC TOUCH (9001 "Mona Lisa")....4-6 76
Also see BIG ROCKER

LADD, Gaylan
Singles: 7-inch
MGM (13435 "Think About Me")....10-20 65
PACEMAKER (257 "Repulsive Situation")....25-35 66
VENTURAL (723 "Smokey Places")....15-30 65
VENTURAL (731 "Painted Lady")....15-30 65

LADDERS
Singles: 7-inch
HOLIDAY (2611 "Counting the Stars").100-200 57
(Glossy red label. Has double horizontal lines.)
HOLIDAY (2611 "Counting the Stars")....20-30 '60s
(Flat red label. Has single horizontal line.)
VEST (826 "My Love Is Gone")....75-125 58
(No stars are around the Vest logo.)
VEST (826 "My Love Is Gone")....20-30 58
(Has 11 stars around the Vest logo.)
Also see CHARTS / Bop-Chords / Ladders / Harmonaires

LADDINS
Singles: 7-inch
ANGIE (85713 "I'll Kiss Your Teardrops Away")....20-30 62
(Blue label. Identification number shown since no selection number is used. First issue.)
ANGIE (1790 "I'll Kiss Your Teardrops Away")....10-20 62
(Red label. Selection number is shown.)
BARDELL (776 "Push, Shake, Kick and Shout")....5-10 63
BUTANE (779 "Dream Baby")....5-10 64
CENTRAL (2602 "Now You're Gone").550-650 57
(Black label.)
CENTRAL (2602 "Now You're Gone").150-200 57
(Yellow label.)
CENTRAL (2602 "Now You're Gone")....40-50 57
(Pink label.)
GREY CLIFF (721 "Light a Candle")....10-15 59
GROOVE (4-5 "Try Try Again")....10-15 62
ISLE (801 "Come On")....40-60 60
MELLO (556 "Now You're Gone")....5-10 65
THEATRE (111 "There Once Was a Time")....30-40 61
TIMES SQUARE (3 "Now You're Gone").10-15 62
(Black vinyl.)
TIMES SQUARE (3 "Now You're Gone").25-35 62
(Blue or green vinyl.)
LPs: 10/12-inch
RELIC....10-15
Members: David Coleman; Ernest Gordy; Bob Jeffers; Earl Marcus; John Marcus.
Also see COLEMAN, David

LADDS
Singles: 7-inch
TEEN TOWN (4789/4790 "Bring Back the Days"/"Goodness Gracious Baby")....10-20 69
TRANSACTION (703 "Keep on Running")....15-25 67
UA (706 "I Found a Girl")....25-35 68
Picture Sleeves
TRANSACTION (703 "Keep on Running")....25-35 67
UA (706 "I Found a Girl")....40-60 68
Member: Alex Campbell. Session: Fax.
Also see FAX
Also see TODAY'S TOMORROW

LADELLES
Singles: 7-inch
DEBONAIR (309 "Hit'n Run Lover")....40-50 64
DEBONAIR (1218 "Borrowed Time")....15-25 '60s

LADMO
(With the La Chords)
Singles: 7-inch
LADMO (631 "Little Drummer Boy")....75-125

LADNER, Jerry, & Travelers
Singles: 7-inch
FLAME (127 "Give Me Your Love")....15-25

LA DONNA, Marie
Singles: 7-inch
GATEWAY (713 "Bobby Baby")....5-10 63
GATEWAY (730 "Georgie Porgie")....50-60 64
TRY ME (28009 "Bobby Baby")....8-12 63
(First issue.)
Also see DONNA MARIE

LADREW, John
Singles: 7-inch
ROULETTE (4688 "What's the Matter with Me")....10-20 66

LADY BUGS
(Ladybugs)
Singles: 7-inch
CHATTAHOOCHEE (637 "How Do You Do It") ... 5-10 64
DEL-FI (4233 "Sooner or Later") ... 10-15 64
LEGRAND (1033 "Who Sends This Love Note") ... 10-15 64

LADY FOX & FOXETTES
Singles: 7-inch
DON-EL (114 "Our Love") ... 10-15 62
DON-EL (118 "It Must Be Love") ... 10-15 62

LADY JANE & VERITY
Singles: 7-inch
PALETTE (5031 "Junior at the Senior Prom") ... 10-15 59
PALETTE (5040 "Cry Baby") ... 10-15 59

LADY NELL
(With Sunny's Nu Kat Orchestra)
Singles: 7-inch
NU-KAT (128 "Loving Daddy") ... 50-100 60

LADY REED
("Presented by Rudy Ray Moore")
LPs: 10/12-inch
KENT (004 "Lady Reed") ... 20-30
Also see MOORE, Rudy Ray

LA FAYETTE & LaSABRES
Singles: 7-inch
PORT (70036 "Cure for Love") ... 10-15 63
YOUR-PICK (1005 "Cure for Love") ... 20-30 63

LAFAYETTES P&R '62
Singles: 7-inch
BONA (1741 "I Lost My Way") ... 25-50
RCA (8044 "Life's Too Short") ... 15-25 62
RCA (8082 "Caravan of Lonely Men") ... 15-25 62
Member: Frank Bonarrigo.

LA FETS & KITTY
Singles: 78 rpm
APOLLO ... 100-150 57
Singles: 7-inch
APOLLO (520 "Christmas Letter") ... 250-350 57
APOLLO (520 "Christmas Letter") ... 400-500 57
(White label. Promotional issue only.)

LAINE, Bette
Singles: 7-inch
CHESS (1666 "Rock a Bye Rock") ... 20-25 57

LAINE, Brandi
Singles: 7-inch
BLOSSOM ("Haight St. Dream") ... 10-15 67
(No selection number used.)
Picture Sleeves
BLOSSOM ("Haight St. Dream") ... 15-25 67

LAINE, Cleo LP '74
Singles: 7-inch
LAURIE (3137 "I Only Have Eyes for You") ... 5-10 62
RCA ... 4-6 74-80
LPs: 10/12-inch
BUDDAH ... 8-12 74
FONTANA (27552 "Woman to Woman"). 10-20 66
(Monaural.)
FONTANA (67552 "Woman to Woman"). 15-25 66
(Stereo.)
GNP ... 5-10 74
QUINTESSENCE ... 5-10 80
RCA ... 5-10 73-80
Also see CHARLES, Ray, & Cleo Laine

LAINE, Frankie P&R/R&B '47
(With Paul Weston & the Mellomen)
Singles: 78 rpm
ATLAS ... 10-20 47
MERCURY ... 8-15 47-51
MERCURY/SAV-WAY (1027 "On the Sunny Side of the Street") ... 150-200 47
(Picture disc. Promotional issue only.)
MERCURY/SAV-WAY (1028 "West End Blues") ... 150-200 47
(Picture disc. Promotional issue only.)
MERCURY/SAV-WAY (5059 "Kiss Me Again") ... 100-200 47
(Picture disc. Promotional issue only.)
COLUMBIA ... 5-15 51-57
Singles: 7-inch
ABC ... 4-8 67-69
AMOS (138 "I Believe") ... 4-6 70
AMOS (153 "Put Your Hand in the Hand") ... 4-6 71
AMOS (161 "My God and I") ... 4-6 71
CAPITOL ... 5-8 64-66
COLUMBIA (39367 thru 41486) ... 10-20 51-59
COLUMBIA (41613 thru 42966) ... 5-10 60-64
MAINSTREAM ... 4-6 75
MERCURY (5000 series) ... 10-20 50-51
MERCURY CELEBRITY SERIES ... 4-6
SUNFLOWER ... 4-6 72
W.B. ... 4-6 74
Picture Sleeves
COLUMBIA ... 15-25 56-57
EPs: 7-inch
COLUMBIA ... 10-20 52-59
MERCURY ... 10-20 51-54
LPs: 10/12-inch
ABC (600 series) ... 8-15 67-69
ABC (30000 series) ... 5-8 76
AMOS ... 8-12 70-71
CAPITOL ... 10-15 65
COLUMBIA (600 thru 1200 series) ... 15-30 54-58
COLUMBIA (1300 thru 1900 series) ... 10-20 59-63
(Monaural.)
COLUMBIA (2500 series) ... 20-30 56
(10-inch LPs.)
COLUMBIA (6000 series) ... 20-40 53-54
(10-inch LPs.)
COLUMBIA (8100 thru 8700 series) ... 10-20 59-63
(Stereo.)
HARMONY ... 8-15 65-71
HINDSIGHT ... 4-8 84
MERCURY (20000 series) ... 20-40 54-61
MERCURY (25000 series) ... 50-75 51-52
(10-inch LPs.)
MERCURY (60000 series) ... 15-25 61
PICKWICK ... 5-10 78
TOWER ... 8-15 67
TRIP ... 5-8 75
WING ... 8-15 60-67
Also see DAY, Doris, & Frankie Laine
Also see MILLER, Mitch

LAINE, Frankie, & Jimmy Boyd P&R '53
Singles: 78 rpm
COLUMBIA (39945 "Tell Me a Story") ... 5-10 53
Singles: 7-inch
COLUMBIA (39945 "Tell Me a Story") ... 10-20 53
Also see BOYD, Jimmy

LAINE, Frankie, & Easy Riders P&R '57
Singles: 78 rpm
COLUMBIA (40856 "Love Is a Golden Ring") ... 4-8 57
Singles: 7-inch
COLUMBIA (40856 "Love Is a Golden Ring") ... 10-20 57
Also see GILKYSON, Terry

LAINE, Frankie, & Four Lads P&R '54
Singles: 78 rpm
COLUMBIA (40295 "Rain, Rain, Rain") ... 4-8 54
Singles: 7-inch
COLUMBIA (40295 "Rain, Rain, Rain") ... 10-20 54
EPs: 7-inch
COLUMBIA ... 10-20 56
LPs: 10/12-inch
COLUMBIA ... 20-30 56
Also see FOUR LADS

LAINE, Frankie, & Patti Page
(With Harry Geller & His Orchestra; Carl Fischer – piano)
Singles: 78 rpm
MERCURY (5442 "I Love You for That") ... 8-15 50
Singles: 7-inch
MERCURY (5442 "I Love You for That") .. 10-20 50

LAINE, Frankie, & Jo Stafford P&R '51
Singles: 78 rpm
COLUMBIA ... 4-8 51-53
Singles: 7-inch
COLUMBIA ... 10-20 51-53
EPs: 7-inch
COLUMBIA ... 10-20 54
LPs: 10/12-inch
COLUMBIA ... 20-40 54
Also see LAINE, Frankie
Also see STAFFORD, Jo

LAINE, Jeff
Singles: 7-inch
BATTLE (45906 "Baby, Come Back Home") ... 10-20 62
BATTLE (45918 "Carmelita") ... 10-20 63

LAINE, Linda, & Sinners
Singles: 7-inch
TOWER (108 "Low Grades and High Fever") ... 15-25 64

LAKE, Arthur
(With the Wheels)
Singles: 78 rpm
PREMIUM (406 "May I Count on You") ... 10-20 56
Singles: 7-inch
PREMIUM (406 "May I Count on You") ... 30-40 56
Also see WHEELS

LAKE, Bobby
Singles: 7-inch
LAP (1003 "Savannah") ... 20-30 62
(Colored vinyl. Also issued as by Bobby Angel.)
Also see ANGEL, Bobby

LAKE, Don, & Don Juans
Singles: 78 rpm
FORTUNE (520 "Ooh, Ooh, Those Eyes") ... 15-25 56
Singles: 7-inch
FORTUNE (520 "Ooh, Ooh, Those Eyes") ... 30-40 56
Also see LITTLE EDDIE & DON JUANS
Also see WEAVER, Joe, & Don Juans
Also see WILLIAMS, Andre, & Don Juans

LAKE, Hurdis
Singles: 7-inch
SCOTT ("Look Here Sweet Mama") ... 100-150
(Selection number not known.)

LAKE, Karen
Singles: 7-inch
ABC-PAR (10087 "When I'm Not Teenage Anymore") ... 10-15 60
BIG TOP (3077 "Air Mail Special Delivery") ... 10-15 61

LA LA & LALARETTS
Singles: 7-inch
ELPECO (2922 "This Day Is Ours") ... 20-30 63

LA LANNE, Jack
LPs: 10/12-inch
LA LANNE ("Glamour Stretcher Time") ... 15-25 59
(Blue vinyl. Selection number not known.)

LAM, Tommy
("With Glenn Douglass & His Orchestra & the Monograms")
Singles: 7-inch
NABOR (103 "Speed Limit") ... 150-250 58
R (303 "Blue Willow") ... 15-25 61
RANDALL (303 "Blue Willow") ... 50-75 59
SILVERBALL (102 "Speed Limit ") ... 4-6 93

LAMAR, Chris
Singles: 7-inch
DON-EL (121 "Love So True") ... 10-15 63

LAMAR, Lee
Singles: 7-inch
ERA (1041 "Teenage Pedal Pushers") ... 20-25 57

LA MAR, Tony
(With the Superiors; with Bachelors)
Singles: 7-inch
DUCO (5001 "Promises") ... 100-150 60
FIVE-FOUR (5440 "Don't Leave Me") ... 15-25 63
FIVE-FOUR (5450 "Ready for Your Love") ... 8-12 64
GO GO (1000 "Do the Whip") ... 15-25 65

LA MARR, Gene, & His Blue Flames
Singles: 7-inch
FLAME (102 "Just a Stranger") ... 75-100 58
SPRY (113 "Crazy Little House on the Hill") ... 175-225 59
SPRY (114 "Count On Me") ... 200-250 59
SPRY (115 "Close to Me") ... 25-35 59

LAMARR, Toni
Singles: 7-inch
BUDDAH (29 "I'd Do Anything") ... 10-20 68

LAMARS
Singles: 7-inch
GOLDWAX (120 "Patsy") ... 15-25 65

LAMBERT, Gloria
Singles: 7-inch
COLUMBIA (41216 "You Only Love Me") ... 15-25 58
COLUMBIA (41975 "Each Time I Hear, Don't Worry") ... 10-20 61

LAMBERT, Jerry, & Arcs
Singles: 7-inch
K&C (100 "Rockin' Strings") ... 50-60 58

LAMBERT, Lloyd
Singles: 78 rpm
SPECIALTY (553 "King Cotton") ... 10-20 55
Singles: 7-inch
SPECIALTY (553 "King Cotton") ... 20-40 55

LAMBERT, Rudy
(With the Mondellos)
Singles: 7-inch
RHYTHM (128 "That Old Feeling") ... 200-400 57
Also see MONDELLOS

LAMBERT, Tony
Singles: 7-inch
DAWN (232 "Hot Rod Scooter") ... 30-50 57

LAMBERTH, Jimmy, with the Saxons
Singles: 78 rpm
METEOR (5044 "Latch on to Your Baby") ... 50-100 57
Singles: 7-inch
METEOR (5044 "Latch on to Your Baby") ... 150-200 57
REKA (294 "Reelin' & Rockin") ... 50-75 61
REKA (400 "Step-Out") ... 10-20 65

LAMEGO, Danny, & Jumpin' Jacks
Singles: 78 rpm
ANDREA (101 "Hickory Dickory Rock") ... 50-75 56
Singles: 7-inch
ANDREA (101 "Hickory Dickory Rock") .75-100 56
JOSIE (816 "The Other Man") ... 25-35 57
LPs: 10/12-inch
FORGET-ME-NOT (105 "Big Weekend") 35-45 64
Also see PEPPERMINT, Danny, & His Jumping Jacks

LAMIE, Tony & Jackie
Singles: 7-inch
SUNSET (706 "Wore to a Frazzel [sic]") ... 150-250 '50s

LA MONT, Billy
Singles: 7-inch
BANG (502 "Shake and Jerk") ... 30-40 65
BRAN-T ... 10-15 '60s
CANDELO (376 "Tom Cat") ... 50-75 58
KING (5403 "Hear Me Now") ... 10-15 60
OKEH (7125 "Country Boy") ... 15-20 59
OKEH (7131 "I'm Gonna Try") ... 15-20 60
SAVOY (1522 "I Got a Rock 'N' Roll Gal") ... 10-15 57
THREE D (850 "Country Boy") ... 40-60 59
(First issue.)

LAMONT, Charles
(With the Extremes; Charles La Mont)
Singles: 7-inch
CHALLENGE (59290 "I've Got to Keep Moving") ... 20-30 65
REVUE (11047 "Before It's Over") ... 5-10 69
REVUE (11061 "Lefty") ... 5-10 69
LPs: 10/12-inch
VNI (73076 "Legend in His Own Mind") ... 10-15

LAMP, Buddy
Singles: 7-inch
ABC-PAR (10398 "Promised Land") ... 8-12 63
D TOWN (1064 "Next Best Thing") ... 15-25 66
DOUBLE L (716 "My Tears") ... 8-12 63
DUKE (438 thru 468) ... 5-10 68-69
GONE (5104 "Good News") ... 8-12 61
PEANUT (1001 "Have Mercy Baby") ... 10-20 61
PEANUT (1003 "Insanity") ... 10-20 61
WHEELSVILLE (113 "I Wanna Go Home") ... 25-50 66
WHEELSVILLE (120 "Confusion") ... 15-20 66
WHEELSVILLE (122 "Save You Love") ... 25-50 66

LAMPERT, Rudy
Singles: 7-inch
RHYTHM (128 "Sunday Kind of Love") ... 100-150 59

LAMPKIN, Tommy
Singles: 78 rpm
EBB (110 "Three Minus One") 10-15 57
IMPERIAL (5361 "Lover's Plea") 8-12 55
Singles: 7-inch
EBB (110 "Three Minus One") 20-30 57
IMPERIAL (5361 "Lover's Plea") 20-30 55

LAMPLIGHTERS
Singles: 78 rpm
DECCA (29669 "After All") 5-10 55
Singles: 7-inch
DECCA (29669 "After All") 10-15 55

LAMPLIGHTERS
Singles: 78 rpm
FEDERAL (Except 12149) 20-40 53-56
FEDERAL (12149 "Part of Me") 50-75 53
Singles: 7-inch
FEDERAL (12149 "Part of Me") 200-400 53
FEDERAL (12152 "Give Me") 100-200 53
FEDERAL (12166 "Smootchie") 100-200 54
FEDERAL (12176 "Tell Me You Care") 100-200 54
FEDERAL (12182 "Salty Dog") 100-200 54
FEDERAL (12192 "Five Minutes Longer") 100-200 54
FEDERAL (12197 "Yum! Yum!") 100-200 54
FEDERAL (12206 "I Wanna Know") 100-200 55
FEDERAL (12212 "Roll On") 100-200 55
FEDERAL (12242 "Don't Make It So Good") 100-200 55
FEDERAL (12255 "You Were Sent Down from Heaven") 75-125 56
FEDERAL (12261 "It Ain't Right") 75-125 56
GUSTO 3-5
Members: Al Frazier; Thurston Harris; Carl White; Willie Rockwell; Matthew Nelson.
Also see ELL, Carl, & Buddies
Also see HARRIS, Thurston
Also see HOLMAN, Eddie / Lamplighters
Also see RIVINGTONS
Also see TENDERFOOTS
Also see WITHERSPOON, Jimmy, & Lamplighters

LANCASTER, J.J.
Singles: 7-inch
DATE (1564 "So Unkind") 10-20 67

LANCASTRIANS
Singles: 7-inch
CAPITOL (5501 "There'll Be No More Goodbyes") 15-20 65
JERDEN (798 "World Keeps Going 'Round") 5-10 66

LANCE, Herb *R&B '49*
(With the Classics; with Roger Sherman & Orchestra)
Singles: 78 rpm
BRUCE 10-15 54
DELUXE 10-15 57
SITTIN' IN WITH (514 "Close Your Eyes") 20-40 49
SITTIN' IN WITH (519 "Because") 20-40 49
Singles: 7-inch
BRUCE (114 "No More Trouble") 15-20 54
DELUXE (6150 "You Can't Be Sure") 20-30 57
MALA (404 "Like a Baby") 10-20 59
MALA (405 "Some Love") 10-20 59
MALA (426 "Deep in My Heart") 10-20 61
PROMO (1010 "Blue Moon") 10-20 61
LPs: 10/12-inch
CHESS (1506 "Comeback") 20-30 66
Also see BEAVERS

LANCE, Major *P&R/R&B/LP '63*
Singles: 12-inch
KAT FAMILY 4-6 82
Singles: 7-inch
COLUMBIA 4-6 77
CURTOM 4-8 70
DAKAR (1450 "I Have No One") 5-10 69
EPIC (2242 "Hey Little Girl") 5-10 66
KAT FAMILY (04185 "Are You Leaving Me") 3-5 82
MERCURY (71582 "I've Got a Girl") 40-50 60
OKEH (7168 thru 7197) 5-10 63-64
OKEH (7200 "Think Nothing About It") 25-50 64
OKEH (7203 thru 7266) 5-10 64-66
OKEH (7284 "You Don't Want Me No More") 25-50 67
OKEH (7298 "Forever") 5-10 67
OSIRIS 4-6 75
PLAYBOY 4-6 75
SOUL (35123 "Chicago Disco") 4-6 77
VOLT (4069 thru 4085) 4-6 71-72
Picture Sleeves
OKEH 5-10 63-65
EPs: 7-inch
OKEH 10-15 64
(Juke box issue only.)
LPs: 10/12-inch
BACK-TRAC 5-8 85
CONTEMPO 10-12
KAT FAMILY 5-8 83
OKEH 15-20 63-64
SOUL 5-8 78

LANCE, Phil, & Versa-Tells
Singles: 7-inch
LANJO (6845 "Do the Stroll with Me") 15-25 59

LANCE, Ric
(With the Spirals)
Singles: 7-inch
MERCURY (72164 "Remember the Lonely") 40-50 63
PLAZA (501 "When You're in My Arms")..10-15 62
PLAZA (502 "The One Little Girl for Me")...8-12 62

LANCELOT, Rick
(With the 7 Knights)
Singles: 7-inch
RCA (8564 "Hoo Doo Man") 20-30 65
RCA (8680 "Homeless Heart") 5-10 65
TURBAN (1 "Hip Talk") 8-12 62
20TH FOX (549 "That's My Bag") 5-10 64

LANCELOT LINK & EVOLUTION REVOLUTION
Singles: 7-inch
ABC (11278 "Sha La Love You") 8-12 70
LPs: 10/12-inch
ABC (715 "Lancelot Link and the Evolution Revolution") 15-25 70

LANCERS *P&R '53*
Singles: 78 rpm
CORAL 5-10 54-56
STATE-CALLA 4-8 54
TREND 5-10 53-54
Singles: 7-inch
CORAL (61000 series) 10-20 54-57
IMPERIAL (5564 "Golden Years") 10-20 59
IMPERIAL (5578 "Don't Just Stand There") 10-20 59
IMPERIAL (5604 "Cindy Dee") 10-20 59
LANCELOT (122 "Can't Help Falling in Love with You") 5-10 62
LANCELOT/SWF ("See You in Seattle") 5-10 62
(Selection number not known.)
MONTCLARE (6003 "Lonesome Town") ...5-10 61
MONTCLARE (6013 "Rollin' River") 5-10 61
STATE-CALLA (1062 "He Answereth Prayer") 8-12 54
(With Jeanne Determan.)
STATE-CALLA (1063 "The Lord Is My Shepherd") 8-12 54
(With Jeanne Determan.)
TREND (63 "Sweet Mama Tree Top Tall") 10-15 53
TREND (70 "Stop Chasin' Me Baby") 5-10 54
TREND (73 "It's You, It's You I Love") 5-10 54
TREND (82 "So High, So Low, So Wide")..5-10 54
Picture Sleeves
LANCELOT/SWF ("See You in Seattle") 5-10 62
EPs: 7-inch
CORAL (81117 "Rhythm & Blues") 15-25 55
LPs: 10/12-inch
IMPERIAL (9075 "Concert in Contrasts") .15-25 59
(Monaural.)
IMPERIAL (12075 "Concert in Contrasts") 25-35 59
(Stereo.)
Members: Jerry Meacham; Dick Burr; Bob Porter; Corky Lindgren.
Also see McGUIRE SISTERS / Lancers / Dorothy Collins / Teresa Brewer

LANCERS
Singles: 7-inch
CENTRAL (6001 "The Moocher") ....15-25 '50s

LANCERS
Singles: 7-inch
LAWN (205 "Oh Little Girl") 15-25 63
(Also issued as by the Royal Lancers.)
Also see ROYAL LANCERS

LANCERS
Singles: 7-inch
CLOUD (500 "Baja") 20-30 65
OLD TIMER (604 "Baja") 10-20 65
(Black vinyl.)
OLD TIMER (604 "Baja") 20-30 65
(Colored vinyl.)
Also see DESTINAIRES / Lancers

LANCERS
Singles: 7-inch
VEE-JAY (654 "Hush-A-Bye") 10-15 65

LANCERS
Singles: 7-inch
PANTHER (1051 "Alone") 150-250

LAND, Billy
Singles: 7-inch
ESCO (100 "Shimmy Shake") 50-75 59
(First issue.)
SCOTTIE (1323 "Love at First Sight") 10-20 60
W.B. (5083 "Shimmy Shake") 10-20 59

LAND, Eddie
Singles: 7-inch
RON (320 "Easy Rockin'") 10-15 59

LANDERS, Bob, & Willie Joe
Singles: 78 rpm
SPECIALTY (576 "Cherokee Dance") 8-12 56
Singles: 7-inch
SPECIALTY (576 "Cherokee Dance") 15-25 56

LANDERS, Froggy, & Cough Drops
Singles: 7-inch
ENSIGN (4014 "River Rock") 10-15 58

LANDI, Tony
Singles: 7-inch
SAFARI (1001 "Angels Cried") 30-40 57

LANDIS, Jerry *P&R '63*
(Paul Simon)
Singles: 7-inch
AMY (875 "Lone Teen Ranger") 40-50 62
CANADIAN AMERICAN (130 "I'm Lonely") 75-125 61
CANADIAN AMERICAN (130 "I'm Lonely") 50-100 61
(White label. Promotional issue only.)
CHANCE (102 "Ask Me Why") 4-6 92
(Blue vinyl. 500 made.)
JASON SCOTT (22 "Lone Teen Ranger") ... 3-5 82
(1000 made.)
MGM (12822 "Anna Belle") 40-60 59
WARWICK (522 "Swanee") 25-50 60
WARWICK (552 "Just a Boy") 25-50 60
WARWICK (588 "Just a Boy") 25-50 60
WARWICK (619 "Play Me a Sad Song")..40-60 61
Also see SIMON, Paul

LANDIS, Junior
Singles: 7-inch
R&J (101 "Can't Wait") 75-125

LANDIS, Tommy
(With the Spinners)
Singles: 7-inch
WYN (1603 "Someone to Love") 50-75 59

LANDO, Jerry
Singles: 7-inch
PAM (1208 "Put My Mind at Ease") 50-75

LANDON, Buddy
(Bud Landon & the Rhythm Masters)
Singles: 7-inch
BELLE (109 "Get Away") 50-75 59
BELLE (111 "Running Man") 50-75 59
BELLE (113 "Walking") 20-40 59
CLARIDGE (425 "I Found It") 4-6 77
DONNA (1314 "Till the End of Time") 10-20 59
HOLLYWOOD (1052 "Foxy") 15-25 56
JAGUAR (3026 "Raunchy Little Baby") 100-150 59
JAGUAR (3028 "Oh Yes") 100-150 59
PAULA (1222 "Broken Heart USA") 5-8 70

LANDON, Michael
("Little Joe Cartwright of the NBC *Bonanza* Color TV Series")
Singles: 7-inch
FONO GRAF (1240 "Gimme a Little Kiss") 25-35 60
RCA (8330 "Linda Is Lonesome") 5-10 63
Picture Sleeves
FONO GRAF (1240 "Gimme a Little Kiss") 50-100 60

LANDS, Hoagy
Singles: 7-inch
ABC-PAR (10171 "Cry Some Tears") 10-20 60
(First issue.)
ABC-PAR (10392 "Tender Years") 8-12 63
ATLANTIC (2217 "Baby Let Me Hold Your Hand") 5-10 64
JUDI (054 "Cry Some Tears") 50-70 60
LAURIE (3349 "Friends and Lovers Don't Go Together") 10-15 66
LAURIE (3361 "Theme from the Other Side") 10-15 66
LAURIE (3372 "Yesterday") 10-15 67
LAURIE (3381 "The Next in Line") 10-20 67
LAURIE (3463 "Two Years and a Thousand Tears") 10-20 68
MGM (13041 "My Tears Are Dry") 10-15 61
MGM (13062 "Goodnight Irene") 10-15 62

LANDS, Liz
Singles: 7-inch
GORDY (7026 "What He Lived For") 40-50 63
ONE-DERFUL (4847 "One Man's Poison") 5-10 67
T&L 5-10

LANDS, Liz / Martin Luther King
Singles: 7-inch
GORDY (7023 "We Shall Overcome") 15-25 63
Also see KING, Rev. Martin Luther, Jr.

LANDS, Liz, & Temptations
Singles: 7-inch
GORDY (7030 "Keep Me") 35-50 64
Also see LANDS, Liz
Also see TEMPTATIONS

LANDSLIDE
LPs: 10/12-inch
CAPITOL (11006 "Two Sided Fantasy") ..25-35 72

LANE, Barry
Singles: 7-inch
ELKO (11 "Doggone Lonesome Town")...20-30 62
RA-Q (602 "Oh Geronimo") 10-15 60

LANE, Billy
(Billy Lane Quintet)
Singles: 7-inch
ROLLIN' (1003 "The New Night Train")....20-30 '50s
TABA (201 "Beginner in Love") 400-500 62

LANE, Bobby
Singles: 7-inch
AMCO (2 "You Shake Me") 50-100 62

LANE, Clarence
Singles: 7-inch
JOHNSON (113 "Take Me") 10-15 62

LANE, Damon
Singles: 7-inch
MERRI (6013 "Cry") 10-15 64

LANE, Ernest
Singles: 78 rpm
BLUES & RHYTHM (7000 "What's Wrong, Baby") 25-50 51
Singles: 7-inch
M.J.C. (1 "Slices Apples") 10-20 61
Also see TURNER, Ike

LANE, Gary & Mad Lads
Singles: 7-inch
SARA (6494 "Henrietta") 15-25 64
Also see MAD LADS

LANE, Jack
Singles: 7-inch
ELKO (102 "Mr. Blues") 10-20
ELKO (107 "Restless") 10-20
LAURIE (3129 "Restless") 5-10 62
YOLO (12 "King Fool") 50-100 60

LANE, Jeff
(With the Romans)
Singles: 7-inch
BATTLE (45906 "Baby Come Back Home")... 10-15 62
UNITED INT'L (1002 "The Day That You Left Me")... 15-25 63

LANE, Jimmy, & Sugartones
Singles: 7-inch
TIME (6602 "Constantly")... 50-75 59
(Also issued as by Jimmy Bailey. We're not yet sure which came first.)
Also see BAILEY, Jimmy

LANE, Johnny
Singles: 7-inch
G AND G (102 "Rockin' at the Dragstrip")... 200-300

LANE, Kenny
Singles: 7-inch
STRATE 8 (1504 "Froggy Went A-Courtin'")... 400-600 59

LANE, Laura
Singles: 7-inch
ARLEN (732 "I'll Pity You")... 5-10 63
CORVETTE (1001 "Soon I'll Wed My Love")... 10-15 60

LANE, Linda
(Linda Jones)
Singles: 7-inch
CUB (9124 "Lonely Teardrops")... 35-50 63
Also see JONES, Linda

LANE, Lois
Singles: 7-inch
SCEPTER (1270 "Till I Met My Man")... 5-10 64
WAND (166 "My Only Prayer")... 10-20 64

LANE, Mickey
Singles: 7-inch
BRUNSWICK (55098 "Daddy's Little Baby")... 10-20 58
(With Shonnie Lane.)
LAURIE (3071 "Dum Dee Dee Dum")... 10-20 60

LANE, Mickey Lee *P&R '64*
Singles: 7-inch
MALA (12032 "With Your Love")... 5-10 68
SWAN (4183 "Shaggy Dog")... 10-15 64
SWAN (4199 thru 4252)... 5-10 65-66

LANE, Morris, Band
Singles: 78 rpm
ROBIN (101 "Bobby's Boogie")... 10-15 51
Singles: 7-inch
RED ROBIN (101 "Bobby's Boogie")... 25-35 51

LANE, Ralph
Singles: 7-inch
COWTOWN (811 "You Gotta Show Me")... 50-100 59

LANE, Rusty
Singles: 7-inch
LAURIE (3031 "Karen")... 150-200 59

LANE, Theo
Singles: 7-inch
TENDER (517 "There's No Escape")... 30-40 58

LANE, Tommy
(With Tommy Sheridan & Orchestra; with El Ray & Night Beats)
Singles: 7-inch
ERRO (201 "Teen Ager's Lament")... 30-40 60
SURE (502 "Mine Alone")... 30-40 '50s
TIME (3 "Promises")... 15-25 61
Also see EL RAY & NIGHT BEATS

LANE, Willie
(Little Brother)
Singles: 78 rpm
STAR TALENT (805 "Prowlin' Ground Hog")... 40-60 49
STAR TALENT (806 "Howling Wolfe Blues")... 40-60 49

LANE BROTHERS *P&R '57*
Singles: 78 rpm
RCA... 8-15 57
Singles: 7-inch
FXL... 3-5 81
LEADER (804 "Mimi")... 8-12 60
RCA (6810 "Marianne")... 10-20 57
RCA (6900 "Uh-uh Honey")... 20-30 57
RCA (7220 "Boppin' in the Sack")... 20-30 58
RCA (7304 "Little Brother")... 20-30 58
EPs: 7-inch
RCA (4175 "Rockin' the Pops")... 75-100 57
Members: Pete Lane; Arthur Lane; Frank Lane.

LANE BROTHERS / Julius La Rosa
EPs: 7-inch
RCA... 10-20 57
(Promotional issue only.)
Also see LANE BROTHERS
Also see LA ROSA, Julius

LANE SISTERS
Singles: 7-inch
LANDA (672 "Birmingham Rag")... 10-20 61

LANEAR, Donnie
Singles: 7-inch
APT (25073 "Gangster of Love")... 10-20 62

LANEGAN, Mark
LPs: 10/12-inch
SUB POP (61 "Winding Street")... 15-25 90
(Colored vinyl.)
Session: Kurt Cobain; Krist Novoselic.
Also see NIRVANA

LANES
Singles: 78 rpm
GEE (1023 "You Alone")... 15-25 56
Singles: 7-inch
GEE (1023 "You Alone")... 40-50 56

LANG, Eddie
Singles: 78 rpm
RPM... 8-12 56
Singles: 7-inch
JEWEL (841 "Food Stamp Blues")... 5-10 73
RPM (466 "Come On Home")... 10-15 56
RPM (476 "I'm Tough to Resist")... 10-15 56
RON (324 "Troubles Troubles")... 15-25 59

LANG, Julie
(With the 4 Riffs)
Singles: 78 rpm
CAMPUS (104 "Exactly Like You")... 10-15 55
DELUXE (6111 "Elvis")... 10-20 57
Singles: 7-inch
CAMPUS (104 "Exactly Like You")... 30-40 55
(Red vinyl.)
DELUXE (6111 "Elvis")... 10-20 57

LANG, Leroy
Singles: 78 rpm
ROCKIN' (502 "Combos Boogie")... 10-20 52

LANGDON, Jim, Trio
Singles: 7-inch
CUCA (1129 "Billy Sol")... 10-20 63
EPs: 7-inch
CUCA (1149 "Maryann")... 15-25 63
LP: 10/12-inch
CUCA (1100 "Jim Langdon Trio")... 15-25 63
Members: Bill Lengacher; Don Tollefson; Steve MacEnroth; John Segerstrom; Steve Sperry; Dean Kaul.
Also see SPERRY, Steve

LANGFORD, Billie
(Emperor of the Blues; Billy Langford Combo)
Singles: 78 rpm
HARLEM... 10-20 46
LENOX... 10-20 45

LANGFORD, Frances
Singles: 78 rpm
UNIQUE (348 "When You Speak with Your Eyes")... 5-10 56
Singles: 7-inch
UNIQUE (348 "When You Speak with Your Eyes")... 10-15 56

LANGFORD, Jerry, & Ben Denton Singers
(Jerry Langford)
Singles: 7-inch
DEL-FI (4113 "Still of the Night")... 25-35 59

LANGLEY, Curley, & His Western All Stars
Singles: 78 rpm
ARCADIA... 30-50 56
Singles: 7-inch
ARCADIA (110 "Rockin' and Rollin'")... 100-200 56
ARCADIA (111 "She Wasn't Always Your Girl")... 75-125 56

LANHAM, Bob
Singles: 7-inch
ARK (202 "T for Texas")... 50-75

LANHAM, Richard
(With the Tempotones; "12 Year Old Richard Lanham"; "13 Year Old Richard Lanham")
Singles: 7-inch
ACME (712 "On Your Raido")... 150-250 57
("Radio" is misspelled.)
ACME (712 "On Your Radio")... 50-100 57
("Radio" is spelled right.)
ACME (712 "On Your Radio")... 15-25
(Has saw tooth lines on label.)
ACME (722 "Wishing All the Time")... 500-750 57
JOSIE (985 "Have a Little Faith")... 5-10 68
Also see TEMPO-TONES

LANHAM, Roy
(With the Whippoorwills)
Singles: 7-inch
RADIO (104 "Attitude")... 15-25 58
RADIO (109 "Boys Out of School")... 15-25 58
LPs: 10/12-inch
NRC (06 "Roy Lanham and Whippoorwills")... 50-75 58

LANIER, Don
(With the Rhythm Orchids)
Singles: 7-inch
GEE (1060 "Sweetness")... 10-15 60
ROULETTE (4021 "Pony Tail Girl")... 10-20 57
Also see DON & HIS ROSES
Also see KNOX, Buddy

LANO, Mickey
Singles: 7-inch
SINGULAR (718 "I Promise")... 50-75 59

LANTZ, Barbara
Singles: 7-inch
BIG TOP (3044 "One More Time")... 10-15 60
PHIL TONE (1103 "Tall Boy")... 5-10 60

LANZA, Mario *P&R '50*
Singles: 78 rpm
RCA... 3-5 50-57
Singles: 7-inch
RCA (0400 series)... 4-6 71
RCA (3200 thru 8500 series)... 5-10 51-59
RCA (1300 series)... 4-6 50
Picture Sleeves
RCA (3300 "The Loveliest Night of the Year")... 15-25 51
RCA (4209 "Song of India")... 15-25 51
RCA... 5-8 '50s
(For generic, die-cut paper sleeves with artist photo. Not for any specific release.)
EPs: 7-inch
RCA (Except 1837)... 8-15 53-61
RCA (1837 "Student Prince")... 15-25 54
(Soundtrack.)
LPs: 10/12-inch
CAMDEN (Except 400 series)... 5-15 63
CAMDEN (400 series)... 10-20 57
(With "CAL" prefix. Monaural.)
CAMDEN (400 series)... 8-15 63
(With "CAS" prefix. Stereo.)
RCA (75 "Toast of New Orleans")... 45-60 51
(Soundtrack. (10-inch LP.)
RCA (86 thru 1181)... 20-30 51-53
RCA (1750 "Legendary Performer")... 5-8 76
RCA (1837 "Student Prince")... 35-45 54
(Soundtrack.)
RCA (1860 thru 2090)... 15-25 54-57
(Black label.)
RCA (1860 thru 2090)... 6-12 68
(Orange label.)
RCA (2211 "Seven Hills of Rome")... 20-30 58
(Soundtrack tunes on side one, other Mario Lanza songs on side two.)
RCA (2331 thru 2333)... 15-25 59-61
(Black label.)
RCA (2331 thru 2333)... 6-12 68
(Orange label.)
RCA (2338 "For the First Time")... 20-30 59
(Soundtrack.)
RCA (2339 thru 2790)... 10-20 60-64
(Black or Red Seal label.)
RCA (2339 thru 2790)... 6-12 68
(Orange or Red Seal label.)
RCA (2800 series)... 4-8 78
RCA (2900 thru 3200)... 8-15 68-71
RCA (4158 "The Mario Lanza Collection")... 35-45 81
(Boxed, five-disc set.)
RCA/TELEHOUSE... 5-10 74
(Mail order offer.)
Also see LIMELITERS / Della Reese /Mario Lanza / Norman Luboff Choir

LANZO, Mike, & Blue Counts
(With "Landon" & Orchestra)
Singles: 7-inch
DEBRA (2006 "At the Fair")... 100-200 64
(Reportedly 1000 made.)
Members: Mike Lanzo; Lee Jacobs; Eddie Petro; Billy Sincavage; Spencer Smith; Joe Richards; Don Manzo.
Also see GENOVA, Tommy
Also see MAGICS

LAPELS
Singles: 7-inch
DOT (16129 "Sneakin' Around")... 5-10 60
FORTUNE (862 "Bad Luck")... 15-25 64
MELKER (103 "Sneakin' Around")... 15-25 60
MELKER (104 "I Want a True Friend"). 100-200 60

LA POINTE, Perry *C&W '86*
(With the Orange Playboys)
Singles: 7-inch
CRAZY CAJUN (501 "B.O. Rock")... 200-300 60
DOOR KNOB... 3-5 86-89
Also see BONSALL, Joe

LARA, Sammy
Singles: 7-inch
GAYLO (101 "Silly Sally")... 50-75 58

LARADOS
(With the Band of Lucky Lee)
Singles: 7-inch
DUSTY DISC (474 "Now the Parting Begins")... 8-12 64
FOX (962/963 "Now the Parting Begins")... 100-200 57
MADOG... 4-6 80
EPs: 7-inch
MADOG... 5-10 81
Members: Ronnie Morris; Don Davenport; Tom Hust; Bernie Turnbull; Bob Broderick; Tony Micale; Gary Banovitz; Rick Benko; John Dean.
Also see ROMEOS
Also see ZELLA, Danny

LARAINE, Little Rita
Singles: 7-inch
BLUE BONNETT (5284 "Stop")... 15-25

LARAMORE, Sylvia
Singles: 7-inch
MILLER (1142 "My Conscience")... 10-15 60

LARAND, Johnny
Singles: 7-inch
OCTAVIA (0005 "Heaven to Me")... 15-25 65

LA RELLS
Singles: 7-inch
LIBERTY (55430 "I Guess I'll Never Stop Loving You")... 15-25 62
ROBBEE (109 "Everybody Knew")... 20-30 61
ROBBEE (114 "I Just Can't Understand")... 25-35 61
ROBBEE (120 "Tomorrow Will Only Bring Sorrow")... 4-6 91

LARGOS
Singles: 7-inch
DOT (16292 "I Wonder Why")... 10-15 61
STARMAKER (1002 "I Wonder Why")... 40-50 61
(First issue.)
STARMAKER (1002 "Just a Picture")... 40-50 61
(Same number used twice.)

LARK, Frances
Singles: 7-inch
DORE (730 "Get Up and Dance")... 25-35 64

LARK, Toby
(Tobi Lark)
Singles: 7-inch
COTILLION... 5-10 69
PALMER (5000 "I'll Steal Your Heart")... 5-10 65
TOPPER (1011 "Talking About Love")... 15-20 '60s
TOPPER (1015 "Challenge My Love")... 15-20 '60s

LARKIN, Billy *LP '66*
(With the Delegates)
Singles: 78 rpm
MELODY HOUSE ... 20-30 56
Singles: 7-inch
BRYAN ... 4-6 75
CASINO ... 4-6 76
MELODY HOUSE (103 "Rock-it, Davy Crockett") ... 50-75 56
MERCURY ... 4-6 78-79
SUNBIRD ... 3-5 80-81
WORLD PACIFIC ... 4-8 66
LPs: 10/12-inch
AURA ... 15-25 65-66
BRYAN ... 5-10 75
WORLD PACIFIC ... 10-20 65-69

LARKS *R&B '51*
(With Bobby Smith & Orch.)
Singles: 78 rpm
APOLLO (427 "Eyesight to the Blind") . 200-300 51
APOLLO (429 "Little Side Car") ... 200-300 51
APOLLO (430 "Ooh . . . It Feels So Good") ... 100-200 51
APOLLO (435 "My Lost Love") ... 100-200 51
APOLLO (437 "Darlin' ") ... 100-200 52
APOLLO (475 "Honey from the Bee") ... 20-30 55
APOLLO (1177 "My Heart Cries for You") ... 150-250 51
APOLLO (1180 "Hopefully Yours") ... 100-200 51
APOLLO (1184 "My Reverie") ... 150-300 51
APOLLO (1189 "Shadrack") ... 100-200 52
APOLLO (1190 "Stolen Love") ... 100-200 52
APOLLO (1194 "Hold Me") ... 100-200 52
LLOYDS (108 "Margie") ... 100-200 54
LLOYDS (110 "If It's a Crime") ... 100-200 54
LLOYDS (112 "No Other Girl") ... 100-200 54
LLOYDS (114 "Forget It") ... 100-200 54
Singles: 7-inch
APOLLO (430 "I Don't Believe in Tomorrow") ... 2000-3000 51
APOLLO (435 "My Lost Love") ... 3000-4000 51
APOLLO (475 "No Mama No") ... 100-150 55
APOLLO (1180 "Hopefully Yours") ... 500-750 51
(Black vinyl.)
APOLLO (1180 "Hopefully Yours") .. 1000-2000 51
(Orange vinyl.)
APOLLO (1184 "My Reverie") ... 1000-2000 51
(Black vinyl.)
APOLLO (1184 "My Reverie") ... 3000-4000 51
(Orange vinyl.)
APOLLO (1184 "My Reverie") ... 30-40 '60s
(Red vinyl. Yellow label.)
APOLLO (1190 "Stolen Love") ... 1500-2000 52
(Black vinyl)
APOLLO (1190 "Stolen Love") ... 2500-3000 52
(Orange vinyl)
APOLLO (1194 "Hold Me") ... 2500-3000 52
LLOYDS (108 "Margie") ... 250-350 54
LLOYDS (110 "If It's a Crime") ... 400-500 54
LLOYDS (112 "No Other Girl") ... 1000-1200 54
LLOYDS (114 "Forget It") ... 400-500 54
Members: Gene Mumford; Allen Bunn; Ray Barnes; Thurmon Ruth; Dave McNeil; Hadie Rowe; Orville Brooks; David Bowers; Isaiah Bing; Glen Burgess.
Also see BUNN, Allen
Also see FIVE LARKS
Also see FOUR BARONS
Also see GALE, Barbara, & Larks
Also see KING ODOM
Also see MUMFORD, Gene
Also see SELAH JUBILEE QUARTET
Also see SOUTHERN HARMONAIRES

LARKS *P&R/R&B '61*
Singles: 7-inch
CROSS FIRE (74-50 "Fabulous Cars and Diamond Rings") ... 30-40 62
GUYDEN (2098 "I Want Her to Love Me") ... 8-12 63
GUYDEN (2103 "Fabulous Cars and Diamond Rings") ... 8-12 64
JETT (3001 "Love Me True") ... 30-40 65
SHERYL (334 "It's Unbelievable") ... 10-20 61
SHERYL (338 "There Is a Girl") ... 30-40 61
STACY (969 "Pogo Sticks") ... 5-10 63
VIOLET (1051 "I Want Her to Love Me") . 15-25 63
LPs: 10/12-inch
SHERYL ("It's Unbelievable") ... 100-200 62
(Selection number not known.)
Members: Weldon McDougal III; Earl Oxidine Jackie Marshall; Calvin Nichols.

LARKS
Singles: 7-inch
R&R (301 "Hippo") ... 10-20 63

LARKS *P&R '64*
(Meadowlarks)
Singles: 7-inch
ELEKTRA (101 "Mashin' Time") ... 5-10 '60s
JERK (103 "Baby My Love") ... 5-10 65
MONEY (106 "The Jerk") ... 15-20 64
MONEY (109 thru 127) ... 8-12 65-67
MONEY (601 "I Want You Back") ... 5-10 73
NASCO (028 "I Want You Back") ... 4-6 72
LPs: 10/12-inch
AMAZON (1009 "Greatest Hits") ... 45-55 63
MONEY ... 15-20 65-67
Also see JULIAN, Don, & Meadowlarks
Also see MASON, Barbara, & Larks
Also see SHIRELLES / Don Julian & Larks
Also see SMALL, Karen

LARKTONES
(With Teacho Wiltshire & Orchestra)
Singles: 7-inch
ABC-PAR (9909 "The Letter") ... 15-25 58
POPULAR REQUEST (109 "The Letter") ... 3-5 94
RIKI (140 "Why Are You Tearing Us Apart") ... 50-100 58
Also see WILTSHIRE, Teacho

LA ROC, Dallan
(Dal La Roc)
Singles: 7-inch
ARTEEN (102 "Margo") ... 10-15 61
ARTEEN (711 "Beginning of Love") ... 10-15 61
ARTEEN (1010 "Stop What You're Doing") ... 40-50 62

LA ROCCA, Pat
(With the Bellatones; with Savoys)
Singles: 7-inch
BELLA (15 "Rowena") ... 30-40 59
JAN ELL (1 "Cathy") ... 10-15 60
JAN ELL (6 "Cathy") ... 10-15 60

LA ROSA, Julius *P&R '53*
Singles: 78 rpm
CADENCE ... 3-6 53-55
Singles: 7-inch
ABC (10959 "Summer Love") ... 4-6 67
BARNABY (538 "Eh Cumpari") ... 4-6 76
CADENCE (1200 series) ... 5-10 53-55
CADENCE (1400 series) ... 4-8 63-64
KAPP ... 4-8 60-62
MGM ... 4-6 66-67
MGM CELEBRITY SCENE (CS5-5 "Julius La Rosa") ... 10-20 66
(Boxed set of five singles with bio insert and title strips.)
METROMEDIA ... 4-6 70
RCA (0900 series) ... 4-6 73
RCA (6000 & 7000 series) ... 5-10 56-58
ROULETTE (4110 "Until He Gets a Girl") .. 5-10 58
ROULETTE (4135 "Where's the Girl") ... 5-10 59
ROULETTE (4162 "Honey Bunch") ... 5-10 59
EPs: 7-inch
CADENCE ... 5-15 54-58
RCA (EPA-841 "Julius LaRosa") ... 5-10 56
RCA (EPB-1299 "Julius LaRosa") ... 15-25 56
LPs: 10/12-inch
CADENCE (1007 "Julie's Best") ... 20-30 55
FORUM (16012 "Just Say I Love Her") ... 10-15 60
KAPP ... 10-15 61
MGM ... 10-15 66-67
METROMEDIA ... 5-10 71
RCA (1299 "Julius LaRosa") ... 20-30 56
ROULETTE (25054 "Love Songs A La Rosa") ... 10-20 59
ROULETTE (25083 "On the Sunny Side") ... 10-20 59
Also see LANE BROTHERS / Julius La Rosa

LA ROSA, Julius, & Bob Crewe Generation
Singles: 7-inch
CREWE (335 "Where Do I Go") ... 4-8 69
Also see CREWE, Bob
Also see LA ROSA, Julius

LARRISON, Buddy
Singles: 7-inch
JABAR (103 "You Drive Me Out of My Mind") ... 50-75

LARRY, Dave
Singles: 7-inch
B'n KC (102 "Only a Dream") ... 15-25 63

LARRY & BLUE NOTES
Singles: 7-inch
CHARAY (20 "Talk About Love") ... 10-20 65
CHARAY (44 "In and Out") ... 10-20 65
TIRIS (101 "Night of the Phantom") ... 20-30 65
20TH FOX (573 "Night of the Phantom") .. 15-25 65
Also see MARK FIVE

LARRY & HANK
LPs: 10/12-inch
PRESTIGE (7472 "Blues, a New Generation") ... 10-20 66

LARRY & HEADLINERS
Singles: 7-inch
JAR ("Plastic Saddles") ... 100-150
(Selection number not known.)

LARRY & JOHNNY
Singles: 7-inch
JOLA (1000 "Beatle Time") ... 20-30 64
Members: Larry Williams; Johnny "Guitar" Watson.
Also see WILLIAMS, Larry, & Johnny Watson

LARRY & LEGENDS
(With the 4 Seasons)
Singles: 7-inch
ATLANTIC (2220 "Don't Pick On Me") ... 15-25 64
Also see 4 SEASONS

LARRY & LENORE
Singles: 7-inch
ABC-PAR (9994 "Part Time Love") ... 10-20 59
REQUEST (3005 "Sweet Kissin' Baby") ... 25-35 59
LPs: 10/12-inch
REQUEST (10037 "Traveling Guitars") ... 50-75 59

LARRY & MIKE
Singles: 7-inch
ERA (3135 "So Long Little Buddy") ... 10-15 64
PICADILLY (500 "Queen of the Starlight Dance") ... 50-75 63

LARRY & STANDARDS
Singles: 7-inch
LAURIE (3119 "Where Is She") ... 30-40 62

LARSEN, Key
(With Frank Slay's Orchestra & Chorus)
Singles: 7-inch
LAWN (106 "A Little Lovin' ") ... 10-20 60
Also see SLAY, Frank, & His Orchestra

LARSON, Jack
Singles: 7-inch
FRATERNITY (853 "Little Miss Starry Eyes") ... 10-15 59
FRATERNITY (865 "Autumn Heart") ... 10-15 60
FRATERNITY (875 "I Love the Way She Laughs") ... 10-15 61
FRATERNITY (884 "Back to School Blues") ... 10-15 61
Picture Sleeves
FRATERNITY (884 "Back to School Blues") ... 20-25 61

LARSON, Julia
Singles: 78 rpm
UNIQUE (311 "My Ideal") ... 5-10 55
Singles: 7-inch
UNIQUE (311 "My Ideal") ... 10-15 55

LARSON, Mike
Singles: 7-inch
CAMELLIA ... 10-15
TOM TOM (104 "Ghost Guitar") ... 10-20 60

LARSON, Tony Rodelle
Singles: 7-inch
BAND BOX (237 "Cool Yule") ... 5-10 60
Picture Sleeves
BAND BOX (237 "Cool Yule") ... 10-20 60

LA RUE, J.R.
(With the Goldtones)
Singles: 7-inch
PIKE (5914 "Jane") ... 5-10 63
PIKE (5915 "I Know Better") ... 10-20 63

LA RUE, Roc, & 3 Pals
Singles: 78 rpm
RAMA (226 "Teenage Blues") ... 75-125 57
Singles: 7-inch
RAMA (226 "Teenage Blues") ... 75-125 57
Also see CARDELL, Johnny, & 3 Pals

LA RUE, Roger
Singles: 7-inch
HOLLAND (7421 "If I Were in Your Shoes") ... 50-75 58

LA SABERS
Singles: 7-inch
RAYNARD (10011 "Lonely Days") ... 15-25 65

LA-SABERS / Echoes / Stoney Kilroy
EPs: 7-inch
CO-OP (1001 "Goodbye Johnny") ... 15-25 64
Members: Bill Meusy; Terry Lee Oman; Dennis Rinzel; Ken Erdeman; David Wenca; Richard Bucholz.

LA SALLE, John, Quartet
EPs: 7-inch
CAPITOL ... 5-10 59
LPs: 10/12-inch
CAPITOL ... 15-25 58-59

LA SALLE, Lynn
Singles: 7-inch
A&M (889 "Takin' Life Easy") ... 10-15 67
HY NIBBLE (0241 "Takin' Life Easy") ... 10-15 '60s
Also see DAYBREAK

LA SALLES
Singles: 7-inch
BACK BEAT (515 "Chopsticks") ... 200-300 58
MZ ... 5-10
V.I.P. (25036 "This Is True") ... 5-10 66

LASKY, Emanuel
(Emanuel Laskey)
Singles: 7-inch
NPC (303 "I Need Somebody") ... 30-40 63
THELMA (100 "Welfare Cheese") ... 15-25 63
THELMA (101 "Welfare Cheese") ... 15-25 63
THELMA (103 "Lucky to Be Loved") ... 100-200 64
THELMA (106 "Don't Lead Me On") ... 15-25 64
THELMA (108 "I'm a Peace Lovin' Man") 15-25 65
THELMA (110 "Run for My Life") ... 15-25 65
THELMA (2282 "I Need Somebody") ... 25-35 63
WESTBOUND (143 "More Love") ... 10-20 66
WILD DEUCE (1003 "Lucky to Be Loved") ... 20-30 '60s

LASLEY, Clyde, & Cadillac Baby Specials / Lee Jackson & Cadillac Baby Specials
Singles: 7-inch
BEA & BABY (121 "Santa Came Home Drunk") ... 15-25 61
Also see JACKSON, Lee

LASSIES *P&R '56*
(With the Ray Charles Singers; with Jack Pleis)
Singles: 78 rpm
DECCA (29868 "I Look at You") ... 5-10 56
Singles: 7-inch
DECCA (29868 "I Look at You") ... 10-20 56
Also see CHARLES, Ray, Singers

LASSITER, Art
Singles: 7-inch
BALLAD (1020 "Just Another Day in the Life of a Fool") ... 30-40 58
BALLAD (1024 "Just One Cure for the Blues") ... 30-40 59
BALLAD (1026 "It's Alright") ... 30-40 59
MARBO (0677 "Sum'n Nother") ... 100-150 62
SYMBOL (912 "It's Alright") ... 15-25 61
Also see TROJANS

LAST CALL OF SHILOH
LPs: 10/12-inch
LAST CALL (5136 "Last Call") ... 100-150

LAST DRAFT
Singles: 7-inch
TRANSACTION (711 "It's Been a Long, Long Time") ... 10-15 69
Picture Sleeves
TRANSACTION (711 "It's Been a Long, Long Time") ... 15-25 69

LAST FIVE
Singles: 7-inch
WAND (1122 "Kicking You") ... 10-20 66

LAST KNIGHT
Singles: 7-inch
ORLYN (3520 "Shadow of Fear") ... 20-30 67

LAST KNIGHTS
Singles: 7-inch
PARIS TOWER (116 "The Way You Do the Things You Do") ... 20-30 67
PARIS TOWER (131 "Twenty Four Hours a Day") ... 20-30 67

LAST NIKLE
Singles: 7-inch
MAINSTREAM ... 5-10 69
LPs: 10/12-inch
MAINSTREAM ... 10-15 69
Also see McDANIEL, Lenny, & Last Nikle

LAST RITUAL
Singles: 7-inch
CAPITOL (2495 "Delighted") ... 10-15 69
LPs: 10/12-inch
CAPITOL (206 "Last Ritual") ... 30-40 69

LATEEF, Yusef *LP '69*
(Yusef Lateef Quintet)
Singles: 7-inch
ARGO (5292 "Cookin' ") ... 8-12 58
ATLANTIC ... 4-6 68-70
IMPULSE ... 4-8 64
NEW JAZZ (506 "Sea Breeze") ... 5-8 60
PRESTIGE ... 4-8 63-69
LPs: 10/12-inch
ATLANTIC ... 8-15 68-76
CTI ... 5-8 77-79
CADET ... 10-15 69
CHARLIE PARKER ... 20-30 62
EVEREST ... 5-10 74
IMPULSE (56 thru 9125) ... 10-20 64-66
IMPULSE (9200 & 9300 series) ... 5-10 73-78
MILESTONE ... 8-12 73
MOODSVILLE ... 25-35 61
NEW JAZZ ... 25-40 59-61
PRESTIGE (7122 "The Sounds of Yusef Lateef") ... 50-100 57
(Yellow label.)
PRESTIGE (7400 thru 7800 series) ... 10-20 66-71
PRESTIGE (24000 series) ... 8-15 72-74
RIVERSIDE (300 series) ... 20-30 60
(Monaural.)
RIVERSIDE (3000 series) ... 10-20 68
RIVERSIDE (9300 series) ... 25-35 60
(Stereo.)
SAVOY (2200 series) ... 8-12 76-79
SAVOY (12000 series) ... 25-50 56-58
SAVOY (13000 series) ... 25-50 58
TRIP ... 5-10 73
VERVE (8217 "Before Dawn") ... 50-100 57
(Reads "Verve Records, Inc." at bottom of label.)
VERVE (8217 "Before Dawn") ... 25-35 '60s
(Reads "MGM Records - a Division of Metro-Goldwyn-Mayer, Inc." at bottom of label.)

LATHAM, Tommie
(Tommy Latham)
Singles: 7-inch
BANNON ("Put a Cricket in Your Ear") ... 50-75 '60s
(Selection number not known.)
DOT ... 5-10 69

LATHREM, Buddy
Singles: 7-inch
REM (308 "King of Rock and Roll") ... 200-300
SUN-RAY (102 "Bird Walk") ... 75-100

LATIN SOULS
Singles: 7-inch
KAPP (Except 844) ... 5-10 67-68
KAPP (844 "La Banda") ... 20-30 67
LPs: 10/12-inch
KAPP ... 10-15 67-68

LATONS
Singles: 7-inch
PORT (70030 "So in Love") ... 10-15 62

LATORRE, Johnny
Singles: 7-inch
BLACK GOLD (4613 "Atomic Bounce") ... 50-75

LAUGHING GRAVY
Singles: 7-inch
WHITE WHALE (261 "Vegetables") ... 30-40 68
Members: Dean Torrance; Rick Clingman; Durby Wheeler.
Also see ESQUIRES
Also see JAN & DEAN

LAUGHING KIND
Singles: 7-inch
HEAT WAVE (102 "Empty Heart") ... 15-25 67
JOX (066 "Show Me") ... 10-15 67
JOX (072 "Shotgun") ... 10-15 68

LAUGHING MATTERS
Singles: 7-inch
FUNTONE USA (23 "Tickets to Heaven") ... 15-25

LAUGHING WIND
Singles: 7-inch
TOWER (266 "Good to Be Around") ... 10-15 66

LAUNCHERS
Singles: 7-inch
CITE (5010 "Space Cowboy") ... 10-20 64
CITE (5011 "I See Her Face") ... 10-20 65
Also see LEE, Robin

LAUPER, Cyndi *P&R/LP '83*
Singles: 12-inch
PORTRAIT ... 4-6 83-87
Singles: 7-inch
EPIC ... 3-5 88-89
PORTRAIT ... 3-5 83-88
Picture Sleeves
EPIC ... 3-5 88
PORTRAIT ... 3-5 83-87
LPs: 10/12-inch
PORTRAIT (Except 39610) ... 5-8 83-86
PORTRAIT (39610 "She's So Unusual") ... 20-25 83
(Picture disc.)
Also see BLUE ANGEL

LAUREL & MILES
Singles: 78 rpm
ABBOTT (173 "A Rollin' Stone") ... 10-15 54
Singles: 7-inch
ABBOTT (173 "A Rollin' Stone") ... 15-25 54

LAURELS
Singles: 78 rpm
"X" (143 "Truly Truly") ... 50-75 55
Singles: 7-inch
"X" (143 "Truly Truly") ... 100-200 55
Member: Bobby Relf.
Also see BELVIN, Jesse
Also see BYRD, Bobby
Also see PEPPERMINT HARRIS
Also see PORTER, Jake, & Laurels
Also see RELF, Bobby

LAURELS
Singles: 7-inch
ABC-PAR (10048 "Picture of Love") ... 40-50 59
SPRING (1112 "Baby Talk") ... 100-150 59

LAUREN, Rod *P&R '59*
(With Shorty Rogers Orchestra & Chorus)
Singles: 7-inch
CHANCELLOR (1126 "I Ain't Got You") ... 5-10 62
RCA ... 8-12 59-62
Picture Sleeves
RCA (7645 "If I Had a Girl") ... 10-15 59
RCA (7720 "Listen My Love") ... 10-15 60
LPs: 10/12-inch
RCA (LPM-2176 "I'm Rod Lauren") ... 20-40 61
(Monaural.)
RCA (LSP-2176 "I'm Rod Lauren") ... 30-50 61
(Stereo.)
Also see COOKE, Sam / Rod Lauren / Neil Sedaka / Browns

LAURENCE, T., & Sherwood Greens
Singles: 7-inch
BANGAR (625 "For a Penny") ... 10-20 65
Also see ROSCOE & HIS LITTLE GREENMEN

LAURENZ, John / Starlighters
Singles: 78 rpm
MERCURY/SAV-WAY (3060 "Here We Are") ... 100-150 47
(Picture disc. Promotional issue only.)

LAURIE, Annie *R&B '49*
(With the Paul Gayten Trio)
Singles: 78 rpm
DELUXE ... 5-15 47-57
REGAL ... 5-10 49
OKEH ... 5-10 55
SAVOY ... 5-10 56
Singles: 7-inch
DELUXE ... 15-25 57-60
DOVE ... 4-6 68
GUSTO ... 4-6 78
OKEH ... 10-15 55
RITZ ... 4-8 62
SAVOY ... 15-20 56
LPs: 10/12-inch
AUDIO LAB (1510 "It Hurts to Be in Love") ... 100-150 58
Also see GAYTEN, Paul

LAURIE, Bob
Singles: 7-inch
STEPHENY (1824 "Ching a Ling") ... 10-15 58

LAURIE, Linda *P&R '59*
(With the Glen Stuart Orchestra)
Singles: 7-inch
ANDIE (5015 "Stay with Me") ... 10-15 60
GLORY (290 "Ambrose [Part 5]") ... 20-30 58
GLORY (294 "Forever Ambrose") ... 15-25 59
KEETCH (6001 "Chico") ... 5-10 64
RECONA (3502 "Lucky") ... 5-10 63
RUST (5022 "Prince Charming") ... 30-40 60
RUST (5042 "Stay-At-Home") ... 15-25 61
RUST (5061 "Return of Ambrose") ... 8-12 63
Also see DEL SATINS

LAURIE, Lou, & Harlequins
Singles: 7-inch
ESSAR (1011 "Deep Blue Sea") ... 40-50 61
(First issue.)
U.A. (336 "Deep Blue Sea") ... 10-15 61

LAURIE SISTERS *P&R '55*
Singles: 78 rpm
MERCURY ... 4-6 54-55
VIK ... 4-6 56
Singles: 7-inch
MGM ... 8-12 59-60
MERCURY ... 10-20 54-55
PORT (70033 "Something Old, Something New") ... 5-10 63
VIK (0220 "How Many Teardrops") ... 10-20 56
VIK (0247 "Give Me One Kiss") ... 10-20 56
LPs: 10/12-inch
CAMDEN (CAL-545 "Hits of the Great Girl Groups") ... 15-25 60
(Monaural.)
CAMDEN (CAS-545 "Hits of the Great Girl Groups") ... 25-35 60
(Stereo.)

LAURY, Johnny
Singles: 7-inch
RIDGE (1026 "Lotta Lovin' ") ... 150-250

LA VAH, Camille
Singles: 7-inch
WAX (18 "Let's Steal Away") ... 75-100
(Gold label, colored vinyl.)
WAX (18 "Let's Steal Away") ... 15-25
(Gold label, black vinyl.)
WAX (18 "Let's Steal Away") ... 3-6
(Green label.)

LAVELLE, Ronnie
Singles: 7-inch
PARKWAY (831 "Crazy Ways of Love") ... 5-10 61
PARKWAY (837 "Let Her Go") ... 5-10 62

LAVENDER HILL EXPRESS
Singles: 7-inch
SONOBEAT (102 thru 110) ... 10-20 67-68
Picture Sleeves
SONOBEAT (102 "Visions") ... 15-20 67
SONOBEAT (105 "Watch Out") ... 15-25 68
SONOBEAT (110 "Outside My Window") ... 15-25 68
Also see REASONS WHY

LAVENDER HOUR
Singles: 7-inch
STEFFEK (619 "Hang Loose") ... 10-15 67
STEFFEK (1929 "So Sophisticated") ... 10-15 67
TRIBE (8323 "Hang Loose") ... 5-10 67

Also see CLIQUE

LAVENDERS
Singles: 7-inch
CR (1003 "Angel") ... 50-75 61
CR (1005 "That Lucky Old Sun") ... 30-40 61
DOT (16584 "This I Feel") ... 5-10 64
LAKE (706 "The Bells") ... 15-25 61
MERCURY (72126 "One More Time") ... 10-15 63

LAVENDERS
Singles: 7-inch
CUCA (1130 "Aw Shucks") ... 15-25 63
CUCA (1152 "Maria") ... 15-25 63
Also see LEE, Robin
Also see ROD & TERRY

LAVERNE, Charles
(Charley LaVerne & Spitfires)
Singles: 78 rpm
MARK ... 8-12 57
Singles: 7-inch
ABEL (224 "Spitfire") ... 10-15 59
LITE (9008 "The Shoot 'Em Up Twist") ... 10-15 62
MARK ... 10-20 57

LAVETTE, Betty *R&B '62*
(Betty Lavett; Bettye LaVette)
Singles: 12-inch
WESTEND ... 5-10 78
Singles: 7-inch
ATCO ... 8-12 72-73
ATLANTIC ... 5-10 62-63
BIG WHEEL ... 5-8 66
CALLA ... 8-12 65
EPIC ... 4-6 75
KAREN ... 5-10 68-69
LU PINE (123 "Witch Craft in the Air") ... 20-30 64
LU PINE (1021 "Witch Craft in the Air") ... 10-20 64
MOTOWN ... 3-5 81-82
SSS INT'L ... 4-6 71
SILVER FOX ... 4-8 69-70
TCA ... 4-6 71
WEST END ... 4-8 78
LPs: 10/12-inch
MOTOWN ... 5-10 81

LA VON, Del
Singles: 7-inch
CAVALIER (870 "Rocking Chair Idol") ... 20-30 57

LAW, Art
Singles: 7-inch
GULFSTREAM (1050 "Big Train") ... 50-75 '50s
GULFSTREAM (1051 "Kitty Kat Rock") ... 100-200 '50s

LAW, Johnny, Four
Singles: 7-inch
PROVIDENCE (419 "Call on Me") ... 10-20 66
PROVIDENCE (421 "Underdog") ... 10-20 66
Also see CORRENTE, Sal

LAW, Tommy
Singles: 7-inch
CREST (1055 "Cool Juice") ... 75-85 58

LAWING, Mike, & Dissonaires
Singles: 7-inch
ALTAIR (101 "One Love") ... 50-100 59

LAWRENCE, Bernie
Singles: 7-inch
U.A. (388 "Collecting Girls") ... 15-25 61
W.B. (5216 "Stay Out of My Dreams") ... 8-12 61

LAWRENCE, Bill
(With the Lawrence Brothers; with Leon Marian & His Mood Recording Orchestra)
Singles: 78 rpm
MOOD (1013 "Little Girl") ... 5-10 53
Singles: 7-inch
BERTRAM INT'L (207 "Hey Baby") ... 100-125 58
BERTRAM INT'L (227 "Please Don't Leave Me") ... 40-60 64
FREEDOM (44004 "Hey Baby") ... 100-150 58
MOOD (1013 "Little Girl") ... 10-20 53
LP: 10/12-inch
TOPS (1576 "Bill Lawrence Sings I'm in the Mood for Love") ... 10-20 57
Also see LAWRENCE BROTHERS COMBO

LAWRENCE, Bill, & Five Finks
Singles: 7-inch
BERTRAM INT'L (227 "Please Don't Leave Me") ... 30-50 64

Also see LAWRENCE, Bill
Also see FIVE FINKS

LAWRENCE, Bob
Singles: 7-inch
MARK-X (7005 "Honey Dew")..................15-25 57

LAWRENCE, Carl, & Damons
Singles: 7-inch
JEAN (0001 "High School Dreams")........20-30 58

LAWRENCE, Eddie *P&R '56*
(Eddy Lawrence)
Singles: 78 rpm
CORAL..3-5 56-57
Singles: 7-inch
CORAL..10-20 56-63
EPIC (9804 "World's Fair Philosopher").....5-10 65
SHASTA (139 "Harlem Nocturne")..............5-10 60
SHASTA (144 "Cattle Call")........................5-10 60
SIGNATURE (12010 "Doctor's Philosopher")..5-10 59
SIGNATURE (12031 "Anyone for President")..5-10 60
Picture Sleeves
CORAL (61821 "Abner the Baseball")......10-20 56
EPIC (9804 "World's Fair Philosopher").....8-12 65
LPs: 10/12-inch
CORAL..15-30 55-62
EPIC..8-15 65
SIGNATURE..10-25 59

LAWRENCE, Linda
Singles: 7-inch
EPIC (9607 "A Tear for Tommy").........100-150 63

LAWRENCE, Robby
Singles: 7-inch
DONNA (1385 "Slow Bird")......................10-15 63
MGM (13081 "Why Did We Part")..............5-10 62

LAWRENCE, Steve *P&R '52*
(With Joe Guercio & Orchestra; with Sid Feller & Orchestra)
Singles: 78 rpm
CORAL..5-15 55-57
KING..5-10 52-54
Singles: 7-inch
ABC..4-6 73
ABC-PAR..8-12 58-60
CALENDAR..4-8 68
COLUMBIA..5-10 62-68
(Black vinyl.)
COLUMBIA (42865 "Walking Proud")......15-25 63
(Colored vinyl. Promotional issue only.)
COLUMBIA STEREO 33 SEVEN (31547 "It's a Sin to Tell a Lie")..5-10 62
CORAL..10-20 55-59
KING (1200 & 1300 series)......................10-20 53-54
KING (5000 series)..4-8 60-64
KING (15000 series)..10-20 52-53
MGM..4-6 71-73
RCA..4-8 69-70
ROULETTE..4-6 73
STAGE 2..3-5 84
20TH FOX..4-6 75-77
U.A. (200 & 300 series)..........................5-10 60-61
U.A. (900 thru 1100 series)......................4-6 76-78
W.B..4-6 78
Picture Sleeves
COLUMBIA..5-10 62-63
STAGE 2..3-5 84
U.A..10-15 60-61
EPs: 7-inch
COLUMBIA..5-10 64-69
(Juke box issues only.)
COLUMBIA STEREO 33 SEVEN (9565 "Steve Lawrence's Greatest Hit [sic]")......................4-8 68
CORAL..5-10 60
(Juke box issues only.)
KING..10-20 53
RCA..4-8 70
LPs: 10/12-inch
ABC-PAR..20-30 57-60
APPLAUSE..5-10 81
COLUMBIA..10-25 63-68
COLUMBIA RECORD CLUB......................8-15 75
CORAL (57050 "About That Girl")............20-40 56
CORAL (57182 "Songs By Steve Lawrence")..20-30 57
CORAL (57204 "Here's Steve Lawrence")..20-30 57
CORAL (57268 "All About Love")............20-30 58
(Monaural.)
CORAL (57434 "Songs Everybody Knows")..12-20 62
(Monaural.)
CORAL (757268 "All About Love")...........20-40 58
(Stereo.)
CORAL (757434 "Songs Everybody Knows")..15-25 62
(Stereo.)
GALA..5-10 77
GUEST STAR..5-10 64
HARMONY..6-12 68-71
KING (593 "Steve Lawrence")..................25-35 58
MGM..5-10 71
RCA..6-12 69-70
SESAC..10-20 59
SPINORAMA..8-15 63
U.A..10-20 61-64
VERSATILE..5-8 77
VOCALION..5-12 66-69

LAWRENCE, Steve / Tennessee Ernie Ford
LPs: 10/12-inch
CAMAY..5-15 60
Also see FORD, Tennessee Ernie

LAWRENCE, Steve, & Eydie Gorme *P&R '63*
(Steve & Eydie)
Singles: 78 rpm
CORAL..5-15 55
Singles: 7-inch
CALENDAR (1003 "Two of Us")..................4-6 68
COLUMBIA..4-8 62-67
CORAL..10-20 55
MGM..4-6 72-73
RCA..4-8 68-69
EPs: 7-inch
ABC..10-15 60
(Juke box issues only.)
ADVERTISING COUNCIL (5071 "Celebrity Spots")..15-30
(Promotional issue, with other artists.)
COLUMBIA..5-10 64-69
(Juke box issues only.)
CORAL..10-20 58
LPs: 10/12-inch
ABC..5-10 73-76
ABC/LONGINES ("Romantic Treasury")..30-45 67
(Boxed, six-disc set.)
ABC-PAR..15-25 59-64
CBS..10-15 63
CALENDAR..8-15 68
COLUMBIA..10-20 63-67
CORAL (57336 "Steve & Eydie")..............15-25 60
ENCORE..5-8 84
HARMONY..5-10 64-71
MCA..5-10
MGM..5-10 72-73
MATI-MOR (8003 "It's Us Again")............10-15
(Promotional issue made for Silvikrin Shampoo.)
PICKWICK..5-10 '70s
RCA..6-12 69-72
STAGE 2..5-10 78-84
U.A..10-20 61-62
VOCALION..5-12 67
Also see GORME, Eydie
Also see OSMONDS, Steve Lawrence & Eydie Gorme

LAWRENCE, Steve / Trini Lopez
LPs: 10/12-inch
DIPLOMAT..10-15 65
Also see LAWRENCE, Steve
Also see LOPEZ, Trini

LAWRENCE, Syd, & Friends / Billy Mure
(With Bill Buchanan)
Singles: 78 rpm
COSMIC (1001 "Answer to Flying Saucer")..10-20 58
Singles: 7-inch
COSMIC (1001 "Answer to Flying Saucer")..15-25 58
Also see MURE, Billy

LAWRENCE, Walt
Singles: 7-inch
HOLLYWOOD INT'L (2 "Cascade")..........20-30

LAWRENCE & ARABIANS
Singles: 7-inch
SHOUT (215 "Oooh Baby")......................15-25 67

LAWRENCE BROTHERS COMBO
Singles: 7-inch
BERTRAM INT'L (213 "Pyramid")............10-20 59
Member: Bill Lawrence
Also see LAWRENCE, Bill

LAWS, Lucy
Singles: 7-inch
LU-CEE (4001 "I'll Wait for You")..............15-25

LAWSON, Bobby
Singles: 7-inch
M.R.C. (600 "Baby Don't Be That Way")..250-350 58

LAWSON, George
Singles: 78 rpm
ROCKIN' (510 "Blue Memphis")..............10-20 53

LAWSON, Jimmie
Singles: 78 rpm
COLUMBIA..8-12 47
Singles: 7-inch
FABLE (583 "Fickle Fool")........................50-60 57
FABLE (584 "Ol' Jack Hammer Blues")....60-75 57

LAWSON, Robby
Singles: 7-inch
KYSER (2122 "Burning Sensation").1000-2000

LAWSON, Shirley
Singles: 7-inch
BACK BEAT (567 "The Star")..................10-20 66
ENTERPRISE..10-20

LAWSON, Teddy, & Lawson Boys
(Ted Lawson)
Singles: 7-inch
MANSFIELD (611 "There's No Return from Love")..300-400 57
ROULETTE (4033 "One Way Love")........15-25 57

LAWSON & 4 MORE
Singles: 7-inch
ARDENT (107 "Half Way Down the Stairs")..25-30

LAWTON, Luke, & Chickadees
Singles: 7-inch
STARR ("Look What Tears Have Done").25-35 60
(No selection number used.)

LAY, Dale
Singles: 7-inch
FLASH (105 "Country Style Twist")..........50-75 '60s

LAYNE, Herbie / Dick Warren
Singles: 7-inch
GATEWAY (1253 "Rebel Rouser"/"Little Star")..15-25 58

LAYNE, Judy
Singles: 7-inch
WREN (112 "Hard Headed Woman")...100-200

LAYNE, Ronnie
EPs: 7-inch
AIR (1649 "Ronnie Layne")....................75-100

LAYTONAIRS
Singles: 7-inch
TELA-STAR (102 "Another Night Alone") 10-15 63

LAZAR, Billy, & Woody Wagoners
LPs: 10/12-inch
SCARLETT (100 "Surfin' Around")..........40-60 '60s

LAZAR, Sam
(Sam Lazar Trio)
Singles: 7-inch
ARGO (5365 "Space Flight")......................8-12 60
ARGO (5427 "Camp Meetin' ")..................5-10 62
ARGO (5453 "See See Rider")..................5-10 63
CAWTHORN (507 "Space Flight")...........10-20 65
CHECKER (1030 "I Ain't Mad at You").....10-20 62

LAZY BILL & HIS BLUE RHYTHMS
Singles: 78 rpm
CHANCE (1148 "She Got Me Walkin' ")..100-200 53
Singles: 7-inch
CHANCE (1148 "She Got Me Walkin' ")..300-500 53
Member: Bill Lucas.

LAZY LESTER
(Leslie Johnson)
Singles: 78 rpm
EXCELLO..10-30 56-57
Singles: 7-inch
EXCELLO (2095 "I'm Gonna Leave You Baby")..30-40 56
(Orange & blue label. Company address at top.)
EXCELLO (2107 "They Call Me Lazy")....25-35 57
(Orange & blue label. Company address at top.)
EXCELLO (2107 "They Call Me Lazy")....15-25 58
(Orange & blue label. Company address at bottom.)
EXCELLO (2107 "They Call Me Lazy")......8-12 '60s
(Red, white & blue label. No address shown.)
EXCELLO (2129 "I Told My Little Woman")..20-30 58
(Orange & blue label.)
EXCELLO (2143 "I'm a Lover, Not a Fighter")..20-30 58
(Orange & blue label.)
EXCELLO (2155 "Through the Goodness of My Heart")..50-75 58
(Orange & blue label.)
EXCELLO (2166 "I Love You, I Need You")..15-25 59
(Orange & blue label.)
EXCELLO (2182 "Bye Bye Baby")..........25-35 60
(Orange & blue label.)
EXCELLO (2197 "You Got Me Where You Want Me")..30-40 61
(Orange & blue label.)
EXCELLO (2206 "I'm So Glad")...............15-20 61
(Orange & blue label.)
EXCELLO (2219 "If You Think I've Lost You")..15-20 62
EXCELLO (2230 "Lonesome Highway Blues")..10-15 63
EXCELLO (2235 "You're Gonna Ruin Me Baby")..10-15 63
EXCELLO (2243 "A Word About Women")..8-12 64
EXCELLO (2274 "Take Me in Your Arms")..8-12 65
EXCELLO (2277 "Because She's Gone")..8-12 66
LPs: 10/12-inch
EXCELLO..10-20 67
Session: Lionel Torrence; Guitar Gable; Bruce Broussard; Katie Webster.
Also see LIGHTNIN' SLIM
Also see WEBSTER, Katie

LAZY SLIM JIM
(Edward Harris)
Singles: 78 rpm
SAVOY..15-25 52
Singles: 7-inch
SAVOY (854 "Georgia Woman")..............25-50 52
SAVOY (868 "Slo Freight Blues")............25-50 52
SAVOY (887 "Wine Head Baby")..............25-50 52
Also see CAROLINA SLIM
Also see COUNTRY PAUL
Also see JAMMIN' JIM

LAZY SMOKE
LPs: 10/12-inch
ONYX (6903 "Corridor of Faces").....1000-1200 67
PONDICHERRY (6069 "Pictures in the Smoke")..50-100 96
Member: James L. Deveau.

L'CAP-TANS
(With the "Go" Boys; L'Captans; with Frank Motley's Orchestra)
Singles: 7-inch
DC (0416 "Say Yes")..............................20-30 59
HOLLYWOOD (1092 "The Bells Ring Out")..250-350 58
SAVOY (1567 "Say Yes")........................10-15 59
Also see CAP-TANS

LEA, Rebecca
Singles: 78 rpm
GROOVE (0157 "The Devil Hates You")....5-10 56
Singles: 7-inch
GROOVE (0157 "The Devil Hates You")..15-25 56

LEACH, Billy *P&R '57*
Singles: 78 rpm
BALLY (1039 "Lil's Grill")........................15-20 57
BREMNER..10-15 56
Singles: 7-inch
BALLY (1039 "Lil's Grill")........................15-20 57
BREMNER..15-20 56

LEACH, Lillian
(With the Jimmy Brokenshire Orchestra)
Singles: 7-inch
CELESTE (3002 "My "Darling") 400-600 56
Also see MELLOWS

LEADBELLY
(Lead Belly)
Singles: 78 rpm
ASCH.. 10-20
ATLANTIC (917 "Good Morning Blues").. 30-50 50
BLUEBIRD.. 10-20
CAPITOL .... 10-15 '50s
MUSICRAFT 5-10
PLAYBOY..4-6 73
Singles: 7-inch
ABC..4-6 76
EPs: 7-inch
CAPITOL (369 "Classics in Jazz") 15-25 53
LPs: 10/12-inch
ALLEGRO (4027 "Sinful Songs") 30-50
ARCHIVE OF FOLK MUSIC.................. 15-25 65
CAPITOL (H-369 "Classics in Jazz") 40-50 53
(10-inch LP.)
CAPITOL (1821 "Leadbelly")................... 20-30 62
COLUMBIA..8-10 70
ELEKTRA (301/302 "Leadbelly") 15-25 66
(Boxed, three-disc set.)
FANTASY..8-10 73
FOLKWAYS (4 "Memorial Album, Vol. 1: Take This Hammer").. 20-35 51
(10-inch LP.)
FOLKWAYS (14 "Memorial Album, Vol. 2: Rock Island Line").. 20-40 51
(10-inch LP.)
FOLKWAYS (24 "Memorial Album, Vol. 3").. 20-40 51
FOLKWAYS (34 "Memorial Album, Vol. 4").. 20-40 51
FOLKWAYS (42 "Last Sessions, Vols. 1 and 2").. 20-40 53
FOLKWAYS (2004 "Memorial Album, Vol. 1: Take This Hammer").. 15-25 '60s
(10-inch LP. With bio insert.)
FOLKWAYS (2014 "Memorial Album, Vol. 2: Rock Island Line").. 15-25 '60s
(10-inch LP. With bio insert.)
FOLKWAYS (2024 "Memorial Album, Vol. 3").. 15-25 '60s
(With bio insert.)
FOLKWAYS (2034 "Memorial Album, Vol. 4").. 15-25 '60s
(With bio insert.)
Note: The four LPs in the 2000 series are difficult to date. Folkways 2014 has, for example, "copyright 1951" on the bio insert; "copyright 1953" on the label; and another insert with a zip code in the address. Zip codes were not in use before 1963.
FOLKWAYS (2900 series)...................... 10-20 63-65
FOLKWAYS (3000 series)...................... 10-15 67-68
OLYMPIC 8-12 73
PLAYBOY.. 10-20 73-75
RCA (505 "Midnight Special") 15-25 64
STINSON.. 30-50 53-57
(10-inch LP.)
SUTTON..8-10
VERVE FOLKWAYS.............................. 10-20 63-67
Also see WHITE, Josh / Leadbelly / Bill Broonzy

LEADBELLY / Josh White / Sonny Terry
LPs: 10/12-inch
TRADITION 10-12 69
Also see LEADBELLY
Also see TERRY, Sonny
Also see WHITE, Josh

LEADER, Dottie
Singles: 78 rpm
ARCADIA (1951 "I Want a Pardon for Daddy").. 15-25 49

LEADERS
(With Abbie Baker Orchestra)
Singles: 78 rpm
GLORY 20-40 55-56
Singles: 7-inch
GLORY (235 "Stormy Weather")............ 20-30 55
GLORY (239 "Nobody Loves Me")........... 50-75 56
GLORY (243 "Can't Help Lovin' That Girl of Mine").. 30-40 56
Members: Harry Burton; Edward Alston; Nelson Shields; Joe Sheppard; Ronald Judge; Prince McKnight; Charles Simpson.
Also see CORVAIRS
Also see WESTSIDERS

LEADERS
Singles: 7-inch
PIV (1014 "Singapore Passage")..............10-15 57

LEAHY, Joe
(With the Teen Starlets; Joe Leahy Orch.)
Singles: 78 rpm
DAWN (219 "My Son John")....................10-15 56
UNIQUE 5-10 55-57
Singles: 7-inch
DAWN (219 "My Son John")....................15-20 56
FELSTED 5-10 58-59
MGM (13033 "Honeymoon Machine")..........4-8 61
RPC (503 "La Dolce Vita")..........................4-8 61
RPC (508 "Neapolitan Nights")....................4-8 62
RING-A-DING (704 "Happy Surfer")...........5-10 63
TOWER..4-8 65-66
UNIQUE 10-15 55-57
LPs: 10/12-inch
TOWER..15-25 66-67
Also see LINDEN, Kathy
Also see STEVENS, Tari
Also see TEEN STARLETS

LEAKE, Lafayette
Singles: 7-inch
VAL (02 "Disgusted")................................15-25 57

LEAP FROGS
(With Jimmy Johnson - Harmonica; Louis Campbell)
Singles: 78 rpm
EXCELLO (2014 "Dirty Britches")............20-30 54
Singles: 7-inch
EXCELLO (2014 "Dirty Britches")..........75-125 54
Also see CAMPBELL, Louis

LEAPER, Bob
(With the Prophets)
Singles: 7-inch
REPRISE (0274 "Come and Join Us") 5-10 64
LPs: 10/12-inch
LONDON (3391 "Big Band Beatle Songs") 15-20 64
(Monaural.)
LONDON (44056 "Big Band Beatle Songs") 20-25 64
(Stereo.)

LEAPING FERNS
(Chantays)
Singles: 7-inch
X-P-A-N-D-E-D SOUND (103 "Maybe Baby") 20-30 65
Also see CHANTAYS

LEAPING FLAMES
Singles: 7-inch
MRC (1201 "It's Been So Long")..........250-350 63
MAH'S (0008 "Dance Social")..................40-50 61

LEAPY LEE *C&W/P&R '68*
Singles: 7-inch
CADET (5635 "Light My Fire") 4-6 69
DECCA (32380 "Little Arrows")....................4-8 68
DECCA (32625 "Good Morning")...................4-8 70
MAM (3618 "Just Another Night")................4-6 72
MCA (40470 "Every Road Leads Back to You")..4-6 75
Picture Sleeves
MCA (40470 "Every Road Leads Back to You")..4-8 75
LPs: 10/12-inch
DECCA (75076 "Little Arrows")................10-20 68

LEARY, Dr. Timothy, PH.D.
LPs: 10/12-inch
DOUGLAS (1 "You Can Be Anyone This Time Around")..25-35 '60s
E.S.P. (1027 "Turn On, Tune In, Drop Out")..35-50 66
MERCURY (21131 "Turn On, Tune In, Drop Out")..20-25 67
(Monaural. Soundtrack.)
MERCURY (61131 "Turn On, Tune In, Drop Out")..25-30 67
(Stereo. Soundtrack.)
PIXIE (1069 "L.S.D.")..............................50-75 66

LEASEBREAKERS
Singles: 7-inch
U.A. (937 "Gabrielle") 5-10 65
U.A. (50050 "I Don't Wanna Go Home") 5-10 66
LPs: 10/12-inch
U.A. (3423 "Leasebreakers") 15-20 65
(Monaural.)
U.A. (6423 "Leasebreakers") 20-25 65
(Stereo.)

LEATHER BOY
(Leather Boy Milan)
Singles: 7-inch
FLOWER (100 "My Prayer") 30-40 66
MGM (13724 "I'm a Leather Boy")...........20-30 67
MGM (13790 "On the Go").......................20-30 67
PARKWAY (125 "Jersey Thursday")........20-30 66
Also see MILAN

LEATHER PAGES
Singles: 7-inch
BUSY-B ("Accept Me for What I Am") 10-20 68
(Selection number not known.)

LEATHERCOATED MINDS
LPs: 10/12-inch
VIVA (36003 "Trip Down Sunset Strip") ...50-75 67
Members: J.J. Cale; Roger Tillison; Terry Tillison.
Also see GYPSY TRIPS

LEATHERWOOD
Singles: 7-inch
LEMCO (103078 "Midnight Breakdown") .10-20 65

LEATHERWOOD, Bill *C&W '60*
Singles: 7-inch
COUNTRY JUBILEE (539 "The Long Walk") 10-15 60
JCD (103 "Prettiest Baby in Town")......200-300
PEACH (756 "Hillbilly Blues")......................8-12 62

LEAVES *P&R/LP '66*
Singles: 7-inch
CAPITOL (5799 "Lemon Princess")...........8-12 66
MIRA (202 "Too Many People")...............10-20 65
MIRA (207 "Hey Joe, Where You Gonna Go")..10-20 65
MIRA (213 thru 231)..................................5-10 66
PANDA (1003 "Hey Joe")..........................8-12 82
(Colored vinyl on one side, picture on flip. Leaf-shaped disc.)
LPs: 10/12-inch
CAPITOL (T-2638 "All the Good That's Happening")..25-50 67
(Monaural.)
CAPITOL (ST-2638 "All the Good That's Happening")..30-60 67
(Stereo.)
MIRA (LP-3005 "Hey Joe") 25-35 66
(Monaural.)
MIRA (LPS-3005 "Hey Joe")....................30-40 66
(Stereo.)
Members: John Beck; Bob Arlin; Jim Pons; Tom Ray; Bill Rheinhart; Robert Reiner; Jim Kern.
Also see MERRY-GO-ROUND
Also see MOTHERS OF INVENTION
Also see TURTLES

LEAVES OF GRASS
Singles: 7-inch
PLATINUM (2001 "All This Is Right")........10-20 '60s

LEAVES OF GRASS
Singles: 7-inch
MAAD (2668 "Crabs")..............................60-80 68

LEAVILL, Otis *R&B '65*
(Otis Leaville)
Singles: 7-inch
BLUE ROCK (4002 thru 4063).................10-20 64-68
BRUNSWICK (55337 "Baby")......................8-12 67
COLUMBIA (43661 "Keep On Loving")......8-12 66
DAKAR..5-10 69-70
LIMELIGHT (3020 "I'm Amazed")............10-20 64
LIMELIGHT (3037 "Jane Girl")..................10-20 64
LUCKY (1004 "Got a Right to Cry")..........20-30 64
SMASH (2141 "Nobody But You")..............8-12 67

LeBEAU, Bruce, & Wonderlands
Singles: 7-inch
B&S B-DISC-S (1793 "Make Up and Break Up")..15-25 '50s

LE BLANC
(Mel Blanc as "Pepé Le Pew")
Singles: 78 rpm
CAPITOL (2635 "I'm in the Mood for Love") 10-15 53
Singles: 7-inch
CAPITOL (2635 "I'm in the Mood for Love") 20-30 53
Also see BLANC, Mel

LED ZEPPELIN *P&R/LP '69*
Singles: 7-inch
ATLANTIC (2613 "Good Times Bad Times") 10-15 69
ATLANTIC (2690 "Whole Lotta Love")....... 8-10 69
(Long version [5:33].)
ATLANTIC (2690 "Whole Lotta Love")......... 5-8 69
(Edited version [3:12].)
ATLANTIC (2690 "Living Loving Maid") ... 10-15 69
(Single-sided. Promotional issue only.)
ATLANTIC (2777 "The Immigrant Song"/"Hey Hey, What Can I Do")..15-25 70
(Has "Do What Thou Wilt Shall Be the Whole of the Law" etched in the vinyl trail-off.)
ATLANTIC (2777 "The Immigrant Song"/"Hey Hey, What Can I Do")..10-15 70
(Does not have "Do What Thou Wilt Shall Be the Whole of the Law" etched in the vinyl trail-off.)
ATLANTIC (2849 thru 2986).......................5-10 71-73
ATLANTIC (13116 "Whole Lotta Love")....... 4-6 '70s
ATLANTIC (13131 "The Immigrant Song") .. 4-6 '70s
ATLANTIC (13129 "Black Dog") .... 4-6 '70s
ATLANTIC (13130 "Rock & Roll") .... 4-6 '70s
Note: Atlantic 13000 numbers are "Oldies Series" reissues.
SWAN SONG (70102 thru 71003)............... 4-6 75-79
Picture Sleeves
ATLANTIC (175 "Stairway to Heaven").... 50-75 72
(Promotional issue only.)
Promotional Singles
ATLANTIC (157 "Gallows Pole") 50-75 71
ATLANTIC (175 "Stairway to Heaven").... 50-75 72
ATLANTIC (269 "Stairway to Heaven").... 20-30 77
ATLANTIC (1019 "Dazed and Confused")..75-100 69
(With picture sleeve.)
ATLANTIC (2613 "Good Times Bad Times") 25-35 69
(Black and white label.)
ATLANTIC (2613 "Good Times Bad Times") 20-30 69
(Red and white label.)
ATLANTIC (2690 "Whole Lotta Love"/"Living Loving Maid") 15-25 69
ATLANTIC (2690 "Whole Lotta Love" [5:33] /"Whole Lotta Love" [3:12])..................................25-35 69
ATLANTIC (2777 "The Immigrant Song"/"The Immigrant Song")..................................15-25 70
ATLANTIC (2777 "The Immigrant Song"/ Blank) 15-25 70
(Single-sided.)
ATLANTIC (2849 "Black Dog") 15-20 71
ATLANTIC (2865 "Rock & Roll").............. 15-20 72
ATLANTIC (2970 "Over the Hills and Far Away") 10-20 73
ATLANTIC (2986 "D'yer Mak'er") 10-20 73
SWAN SONG (70102 "Trampled Under Foot") 10-15 75
SWAN SONG (70110 "Candy Store Rock") 10-15 76
SWAN SONG (71003 "Fool in the Rain"). 10-15 79
(Blue label. Side one runs 6:08; side two is edited [3:20].)
SWAN SONG (71003 "Fool in the Rain")... 8-12 79
(White label. Both sides run 6:08.)
EPs: 7-inch
ATLANTIC (7-7208 "Led Zeppelin") 50-75 71
(Juke box issue only.)
ATLANTIC (7-7255 "Houses of the Holy")..50-75 73
(Juke box issue only.)
LPs: 10/12-inch
ATLANTIC (7201 "Led Zeppelin III") 10-15 70
ATLANTIC (7208 "Led Zeppelin IV") 10-15 71
(Their fourth LP though no title is actually shown on cover.)
ATLANTIC (7255 "Houses of the Holy")... 15-20 73
(With "Led Zeppelin paper band around cover.)
ATLANTIC (7255 "Houses of the Holy")... 10-15 73
(Without "Led Zeppelin paper band around cover.)

ATLANTIC (8216 "Led Zeppelin")..........50-100 69
(Pink and brown label.)
ATLANTIC (8216 "Led Zeppelin")............10-20 69
(Red and green label.)
ATLANTIC (8236 "Led Zeppelin II")........10-15 69
ATLANTIC (19126 "Led Zeppelin")............5-10 '80s
ATLANTIC (19127 "Led Zeppelin II")..........5-10 '80s
ATLANTIC (19128 "Led Zeppelin III")........5-10 '80s
ATLANTIC (19129 "Led Zeppelin IV")........5-10 '80s
ATLANTIC (19130 "Houses of the Holy")...5-10 '80s
ATLANTIC (82144 "Led Zeppelin")..........50-75
(Boxed, six-disc set. Includes 36-page booklet.)
ATLANTIC MUSIC SERVICE..................10-15 69
(Record club issue.)
MFSL (065 "Led Zeppelin II")..................30-50 82
SWAN SONG (2-200 "Physical Graffiti") . 10-15 75
SWAN SONG (2-201 "The Song Remains the Same")....................................10-15 76
(Embossed print on cover. With bound-in eight-page booklet. Soundtrack.)
SWAN SONG (2-201 "The Song Remains the Same")..8-12 76
(Standard, not-embossed, cover.)
SWAN SONG (8416 "Presence")................8-12 76
SWAN SONG (16002 "In Through the Out Door")..8-12 79
(Issued with four different cover scene variations. Wiping cover with a damp cloth changes the cover colors. Packaged in a brown paper bag.)
SWAN SONG (90051 "Coda")...................8-10 82

Promotional LPs

ATLANTIC (7201 "Led Zeppelin III").... 100-150 70
(White label. Monaural.)
ATLANTIC (7201 "Led Zeppelin III").... 100-150 70
(White label. Stereo.)
ATLANTIC (7208 "Led Zeppelin IV").... 100-150 71
(White label. No title actually shown on cover; however, it was their fourth LP.)
ATLANTIC (7225 "Houses of the Holy")................................... 100-150 73
(White label. Monaural.)
ATLANTIC (7225 "Houses of the Holy")................................... 100-150 73
(White label. Stereo.)
ATLANTIC (8216 "Led Zeppelin")........ 100-150 69
(White label.)
ATLANTIC (8236 "Led Zeppelin II")..... 100-150 69
(White label.)
SWAN SONG (200 "Physical Graffiti")..... 15-20 75
(With "FT" suffix.)
SWAN SONG (2-201 "The Song Remains the Same")..15-20 76
(With "MO" suffix.)
SWAN SONG (8416 "Presence")............10-20 76
(With "MO" suffix.)
SWAN SONG (16002 "In Through the Out Door")..10-15 79
(With "MO" suffix.)
SWAN SONG (90051 "Coda")..................10-12 82
(With designate promo stamping on back cover.)
Members: Robert Plant; Jimmy Page; John Paul Jones; John Bonham.
Also see HARPER, Roy
Also see JONES, John Paul
Also see PAGE, Jimmy
Also see PLANT, Robert

LED ZEPPELIN / King Curtis

Singles: 7-inch

ATLANTIC/ATCO (2690/6779 "Whole Lotta Love")..40-50 71
(Promotional issue only. Atlantic label on Zep side; Atco label on flip, King Curtis' version of same song.)
Also see KING CURTIS
Also see LED ZEPPELIN

LEDO, Les
(With His Consorts; with Jerry Bruno Orchestra)

Singles: 7-inch

LAURIE (3510 "James Collins Shanty").....5-10 69
NINA (1601 "Nina")..............................35-40 59
SHELL (721 "Scarlet Angel")...................25-30 60
Members: Les Ledo; Nick Marco; Joe Walsh; Dennis Conboy; Bob Fava.
Also see MARCO, Nick, & Venetians

LEE, Abby

Singles: 7-inch

REED (1025 "Waitin' ")........................100-150

LEE, Ada

Singles: 7-inch

ATCO (6189 "Moanin' ")..............................5-10 61

LPs: 10/12-inch

ATCO (132 "Ada Lee Comes On")..........15-25 61

LEE, Addie

Singles: 7-inch

END (1018 "Please Buy My Record").......10-20 58
GLORY (267 "Buzzin' Around")...............10-15 57
KAPP (269 "Love Guaranteed")..................8-12 59
ROULETTE (4004 "One Little Kiss")........10-20 57

LEE, Alan

Singles: 7-inch

JEAN (1001 "Broken Hearted Baby").......25-50 58

LEE, Arty

Singles: 7-inch

FARGO (1060 "Shadago")........................20-30 64

LEE, Bella

Singles: 7-inch

LIGHTFOOT ("Two Timin' Man")..............50-75
(Selection number not known.)

LEE, Billy, & Ramblers

Singles: 7-inch

NORTHWAY (1003 "Tijuana Stomp").......15-20 59

LEE, Billy, & Rivieras

Singles: 7-inch

CARRIE (1515 "Fool for You")..................10-15 '60s
HYLAND (3016 "Won't You Dance with Me")...15-25 64
Members: Mitch Ryder; Joe Kubert; Jim McCarty; Earl Elliott.
Also see RYDER, Mitch

LEE, Bob
(Bobby Lee Trammell)

Singles: 7-inch

SKYLA (1117 "You Mostest Girl")............10-20 61
Also see TRAMMELL, Bobby Lee

LEE, Bob E.

Singles: 7-inch

WELLS (1 "Darling I Love You")..............10-15 '60s

LEE, Bobby

Singles: 7-inch

ACME (723 "This Is Goodbye")................50-75 57

LEE, Bobby

Singles: 7-inch

BRUNSWICK (55228 "Ain't That Right")..50-75 62
CONFEDERATE (125 "Run Fool Run").....5-10
CUCA (1065 "Connie")............................10-15 62
CUCA (1076 "Twist It")..........................10-15 62
MUSICOR..5-10 68-69
MUSTANG...8-12 62
RAMCO (1978 "Stand in My Shoes").........5-10 66
RAMCO (1996 "Big Big Day")....................5-10 67

LPs: 10/12-inch

LITTLE RICHIE..8-12 76
Session: Lloyd Green; Charlie McCoy; Pig Robbins; Bob Moore; Buddy Spicher; Buddy Harmon; Kelso Hersten; Billy Stanford; Nashville Edition.
Also see GREEN, Lloyd
Also see McCOY, Charlie
Also see MOORE, Bob

LEE, Bobby

Singles: 7-inch

A-B-S (106 "Miss Mary")......................150-200 61
DECCA (31181 "Little Flame")...................8-12 60
DECCA (31228 "Everyday").......................8-12 61
FALEW (102 "Tell It Like It Is")...................5-10 64
GOLD COAST INT'L.....................................5-10 '60s
PORT (3022 "Cut You Loose")...................5-10 67
VISTONE..5-10 '60s

LEE, Booker, Jr.

Singles: 7-inch

FEDERAL (12321 "Rockin' Blues").........75-100 58

LEE, Brenda
(Brenda Lee Jones)

Singles: 78 rpm

APOLLO (490 "I Ain't Gonna Give Nobody None")...10-20 56

Singles: 7-inch

APOLLO (490 "I Ain't Gonna Give Nobody None")...20-30 56

LEE, Brenda *P&R/C&W '57*
(With the Jordanaires; with Hollidays)

Singles: 78 rpm

DECCA...20-50 56-58

Singles: 7-inch

DECCA (30050 "Jambalaya")..................35-45 56
DECCA (30107 "Christy Christmas")........30-40 56
DECCA (30198 "One Step at a Time")......25-35 57
DECCA (30333 "Dynamite")....................25-35 57
DECCA (30411 "One Teenager to Another")..20-30 57
DECCA (30535 "Rock-A-Bye Baby Blues")...20-30 57
DECCA (30673 "Ring-A My Phone")........25-35 58
DECCA (30776 "Rockin' Around the Christmas Tree")..20-30 58
DECCA (30806 "Bill Bailey")....................10-20 59
DECCA (30885 "Let's Jump the Broomstick")..15-25 59
DECCA (30967 "Sweet Nothin's")...........10-20 59
(Price range of 30050 through 30967 is for black, pink or green label originals. Pink and green are promotional only. Decca multi-color labels in that series are $5 to $10 reissues.)
DECCA (31093 thru 31628)......................10-15 60-64
DECCA (31654 thru 32330)........................5-10 65-68
DECCA (32428 thru 32975)..........................4-8 69-72
DECCA (34063 "Fools Rush In)..............10-20 62
(Compact 33 stereo. As many as five other stereo singles, with tracks from the *Sincerely* LP, may exist – though we do not yet have those numbers and titles.)
DECCA (34330 "Interview").....................10-20 72
(Promotional issue only.)
DECCA (88215 "I'm Gonna Lasso Santa Claus")...20-30 56
(Decca "Children's Series.")
ELEKTRA..4-6 78
MCA..3-6 73-86
W.B. 3-5 91

Picture Sleeves

DECCA (30776 "Rockin' Around the Christmas Tree")..30-40 59
DECCA (30967 "Sweet Nothin's")...........25-35 59
DECCA (31093 "I'm Sorry")......................10-20 60
DECCA (31149 "I Want to Be Wanted")...40-60 60
DECCA (31195 "Emotions").....................10-20 60
DECCA (31231 "You Can Depend On Me")..10-20 61
DECCA (31309 "Fool #1")........................10-20 61
DECCA (31348 thru 32428)........................8-12 62-69
DECCA (88215 "I'm Gonna Lasso Santa Claus")...30-40 56
(For either 45 or 78 rpm single sleeve.)

EPs: 7-inch

DECCA...10-20 60-65

LPs: 10/12-inch

CORAL...5-10 73
DECCA (4039 thru 4104)........................20-35 60-61
(Monaural.)
DECCA (4176 thru 4755)........................15-30 61-66
(Monaural.)
DECCA (4757 "10 Golden Years")..........15-25 66
(Gatefold cover. Monaural.)
DECCA (4757 "10 Golden Years")..........10-15 '60s
(Standard cover. Monaural.)
DECCA (4825 thru 4955)........................10-20 66-68
(Monaural.)
DECCA (8873 "Grandma, What Great Songs You Sang")...30-40 59
(Monaural.)
DECCA (8873 "Songs Everybody Knows")...20-30 64
(Monaural. Repackage of *Grandma, What Great Songs You Sang.*)
DECCA (74039 thru 74104).....................25-40 60-61
(Stereo.)
DECCA (74176 thru 74755).....................20-35 61-66
(Stereo.)
DECCA (74757 "10 Golden Years")........20-30 66
(Gatefold cover. Stereo.)
DECCA (74757 "10 Golden Years")........10-15 '60s
(Standard cover. Stereo.)
DECCA (74825 thru 75232).....................10-20 66-70
(Stereo.)
DECCA (78873 "Grandma, What Great Songs You Sang")...35-45 59
(Stereo.)
DECCA (78873 "Songs Everybody Knows")...25-35 64
(Monaural. Repackage of *Grandma, What Great Songs You Sang.*)
MCA (Except 700 series)............................8-12 73-86
MCA (700 series)..5-8
PICKWICK..5-10 '70s
TEE-VEE...5-10 78
VOCALION...10-15 67-70
WARWICK (5083 "Little Miss Dynamite")..5-10 80
(TV mail order offer.)
Session: Anita Kerr; Bob Moore; Boots Randolph; Jordanaires; James "Buzz" Cason.
Also see JORDANAIRES
Also see KERR, Anita
Also see KRISTOFFERSON, Kris, Willie Nelson, Dolly Parton, & Brenda Lee
Also see MOORE, Bob
Also see NELSON, Willie, & Brenda Lee
Also see RANDOLPH, Boots

LEE, Brenda / Carl Dobkins, Jr.

EPs: 7-inch

DECCA (38169 "Datesetters, U.S.A.")..... 15-25 60
(Celanese Special Products issue.)
Also see DOBKINS, Carl, Jr.

LEE, Brenda / Bill Haley & Comets / Kalin Twins / Four Aces

EPs: 7-inch

DECCA (7-2661 "Top Teen Hits")...........20-30 59
(Stereo.)
Also see FOUR ACES
Also see HALEY, Bill
Also see KALIN TWINS

LEE, Brenda / Tennessee Ernie Ford

LPs: 10/12-inch

DECCA (9226 "Brenda Lee/Tennessee Ernie Ford Show for Christmas Seals").....................20-30
(Promotional issue only.)
Also see FORD, Tennessee Ernie

LEE, Brenda, & Pete Fountain *LP '68*

Singles: 7-inch

DECCA (32299 "Cabaret")..........................4-6 68

EPs: 7-inch

DECCA (734528 "Brenda & Pete")............5-10 68
(Juke box issue.)

LPs: 10/12-inch

DECCA (74955 "For the First Time")........10-20 68
PICKWICK..5-10 '70s
Also see FOUNTAIN, Pete

LEE, Brenda, & Oak Ridge Boys

Singles: 7-inch

MCA..3-5 82
Also see OAK RIDGE BOYS

LEE, Bryan, & Embers

Singles: 7-inch

TEST (101 "Watusi Lucy")........................10-20 '60s

LEE, Buddy
(With the Satellites)

Singles: 7-inch

BRUNSWICK (55228 "Teen Town").........15-25 62
COLUMBIA (43125 "Countdown")..............8-12 64
SCO-INA (89462 "All My Life")................10-15 63

LEE, Byron
(With the Dragonaires; with Dragonairs; with Ska Kings)

Singles: 7-inch

ATLANTIC (2236 "Watermelon Man Ska")..10-20 64
BATA ("Bata Cha-Cha-Cha")...................30-60
(Selection number not known.)
BRA (503 "You're So Good")...................40-50
DRAGON...4-6 72
DYNAMIC..4-8
JAD (210 "Every Day Will Be a Holiday")...5-10 68

LPs: 10/12-inch

ATCO (182 "Jump Up")............................10-20 66
BMN..10-20
BRA (3101 "Rock Steady").......................10-20 67
DYNAMIC..10-15
JAD...10-20 68
KENTONE..10-20
TOWERS HALL..10-20

LEE, Carol

Singles: 7-inch

TRIUMPH (104 "Just One Kiss")..............10-15 62
TRU SOUND (423 "Poor Little Rich Girl")..10-15 63

LEE, Chuck
Singles: 78 rpm
TNT.......10-15 54-56
Singles: 7-inch
TNT (117 "Maria").......15-25 54
TNT (125 "I Love You").......15-25 55
TNT (130 "Pretending").......15-25 56
TNT (143 "Open Your Heart").......15-25 57

LEE, Curley, Orchestra
Singles: 78 rpm
TRUMPET (133 "Jam Session Boogie").. 15-25 51

LEE, Curtis P&R '61
(With the Halos)
Singles: 7-inch
ABC.......4-6 74
DUNES (801 "California GL-903").......10-20 60
DUNES (1001 "Pretty Little Angel Eyes") 25-35 60
DUNES (2001 "Special Love").......10-20 60
DUNES (2003 "Pledge of Love").......10-20 61
DUNES (2007 "Pretty Little Angel Eyes") 15-25 61
DUNES (2008 "Under the Moon of Love").......15-25 61
DUNES (2012 "Just Another Fool").......10-15 62
DUNES (2015 "The Wobble").......10-15 62
DUNES (2020 "Lonely Weekends").......8-12 63
DUNES (2021 "Pickin' Up the Pieces of My Heart").......8-12 63
HOT (7 "Gotta Have You").......150-250 60
MCA.......3-5
MIRA (240 "Sweet Baby").......10-20 67
SABRA (517 "Let's Take a Ride").......15-25 61
WARRIOR (1555 "With All My Heart").......20-30 59
Picture Sleeves
DUNES (2003 "Pledge of Love").......20-30 61
Also see HALOS

LEE, Daaron
Singles: 7-inch
HIP (8008 "Long Black Train").......5-10 69
MYRL (410 "I've Been Searching").......10-15 61
Also see RILEY, Billy Lee

LEE, Damon, & Diablos
Singles: 7-inch
SOMA (1181 "Say Mama").......60-80 61

LEE, Darrel
Singles: 7-inch
EUNICE (1007 "Do You Really Care").......50-75

LEE, Davey
Singles: 7-inch
EMGE (1050 "Need You").......20-30 60
Also see FIVE DISCS

LEE, Diane
Singles: 7-inch
LIBERTY (55156 "You Upset Me").......10-20 58

LEE, Dick P&R '61
(With the Big Action Sound)
Singles: 78 rpm
ESSEX.......5-10 52-53
VIK.......4-8 56
"X".......4-8 55
Singles: 7-inch
ABC (11143 "One Rose").......5-8 68
ACTION.......4-6
BLUE BELL (503 "Oh Mein Papa").......10-15 61
CAPITOL (2107 "Only the Broken Hearted").......5-8 68
CENTAUR (852 "My First Kiss").......8-12 59
DOT (16896 "Chanson D'Amour").......4-8 66
DOT (16951 "Lost Chord").......4-8 66
ESSEX.......10-15 52-53
FELSTED (8603 "I Never Knew").......5-10 60
KAPP.......4-6 69
MGM (12774 "A Penny a Kiss").......8-12 59
METRO (20001 "My Love for You").......5-10 58
ROULETTE (4447 "How's the World Treating You").......5-10 62
ROULETTE (4473 "Susan").......5-10 63
20TH FOX (586 "Tears").......4-8 65
20TH FOX (6617 "You, You, You").......4-8 65
VIK (0200 "Serenade").......5-10 56
VIK (0238 "Love Is a King").......5-10 56
"X" (0145 "Daniel Boone").......5-10 55
"X" (0163 "I'll Miss You").......5-10 55
Picture Sleeves
FELSTED (8603 "I Never Knew").......8-12 60

LEE, Dickey P&R/R&B/LP '62
(With the Collegiates; Dickie Lee)
Singles: 78 rpm
SUN (280 "Good Lovin'").......15-25 57
SUN (297 "Dreamy Nights").......20-30 57
TAMPA (131 "Dream Boy").......15-25 57
Singles: 7-inch
ABC.......4-6 73
ATCO (6546 "Run Right Back").......5-10 67
ATCO (6580 "All My Life").......5-10 68
ATCO (6609 "Waitin' for Love to Come My Way").......5-10 68
DIAMOND.......5-10 69
("Dickie Lee Story").......15-20 77
(No label name or number used. Promotional issue only.)
DOT (16087 "Why Don't You Write Me")..15-25 60
ERIC (120 "Laurie").......3-6 73
HALL (1924 "Big Brother").......8-12 64
MERCURY.......3-6 79-82
OLDIES 45.......4-8 65
RCA.......4-8 70-78
RENDEZVOUS (188 "Stay True Baby")...15-25 62
SMASH (1758 thru 1913).......8-12 62-64
SUN (280 "Good Lovin'").......15-25 57
SUN (297 "Dreamy Nights").......75-100 57
TCF (102 "Laurie").......10-20 65
TCF (111 thru 128).......8-12 65
TAMPA (131 "Dream Boy").......15-25 57
TRACIE (2002 "Walk").......4-8 67
LPs: 10/12-inch
RCA.......6-12 71-76
MERCURY.......5-8 79-80
SMASH (27020 "Tale of Patches").......20-35 62
(Monaural.)
SMASH (67020 "Tale of Patches").......25-40 62
(Stereo.)
TCF (8001 "Dickey Lee Sings Laurie and Girl from Peyton Place").......15-20 65
Also see MIZZELL, Bobby

LEE, Emma Dell
Singles: 78 rpm
KHOURY'S (900 "How Much I Love You").......20-30 51

LEE, Ernie
Singles: 78 rpm
MGM (11517 "Hangin' My Heart Out to Dry").......5-10 53
Singles: 7-inch
MGM (11517 "Hangin' My Heart Out to Dry").......10-20 53
RCA (48-0158 "My Home Is the Dust of the Road").......20-30 50
(Green vinyl.)
RCA (48-0182 "Headin' Home").......20-30 50
(Green vinyl.)

LEE, Floyd
Singles: 7-inch
ENTERPRISE (1234 "Go Boy").......300-350 59

LEE, Gary
Singles: 7-inch
TIME (1009 "Why").......10-20 59

LEE, Gene, & Blues Rockers
Singles: 78 rpm
MUSIC CITY (803 "You're the One").......25-50 57
Singles: 7-inch
MUSIC CITY (803 "You're the One").......40-60 57

LEE, George
Singles: 78 rpm
BULLET (698 "Goodbye & Good Luck")...10-20 49
Singles: 7-inch
RUBY (170 "Heartbreak Trail").......8-12 57

LEE, Gloria
Singles: 7-inch
BLUEJAY (5000 "Just for Tonight").......40-50 65

LEE, Harold C&W '68
Singles: 7-inch
CARTWHEEL (198 "Mountain Woman").......4-6 71
COLUMBIA (44458 "Two Sides of Me").......4-8 68
COLUMBIA (44649 "Boys Kept Hangin' Around").......4-8 68
ESTA (293 "Blond Headed Woman")...300-400 58
MEGA (0009 "Ten O'Clock Train").......4-6 70

LEE, Harry
Singles: 7-inch
ACE (582 "Lynda Lynda").......10-15 60
ACE (615 "Are You Real").......10-15 61
IGLOO (101 "Rockin' on a Reindeer")..150-200 58
VIN (199 "Everytime I See You").......10-15 59
VIN (1007 "You Don't Know").......75-100 58
VIN (1014 "Undertow").......10-15 59
Picture Sleeves
IGLOO (101 "Rockin' on a Reindeer")....75-100 58

LEE, Herbie
Singles: 7-inch
EVENT (4286 "Champagne Charlene")...50-75 58

LEE, Honey
Singles: 78 rpm
CASH (1007 "Angel Cake").......10-15 55
Singles: 7-inch
CASH (1007 "Angel Cake").......20-30 55

LEE, Jackie P&R '59
(With the Pepe Lattanzi Orchestra; Jackie Lee Orchestra)
Singles: 78 rpm
CORAL.......4-8 54-56
ESSEX.......4-8 53
Singles: 7-inch
ARCADE (149 "Jumpin' Jackie").......10-20 58
CORAL.......8-12 54-57
ESSEX.......8-12 53
FAYETTE (1619 "Little Mary").......5-10 64
OASIS.......5-10
SURE (1738 thru 1767).......5-10 62
SWAN (4034 thru 4039).......8-12 59
SWAN (4260 "So Close to Heaven").......5-10 66

LEE, Jackie
Singles: 7-inch
TEENAGER (101 "Young & Dangerous") 25-35 59
Picture Sleeves
TEENAGER (101 "Young & Dangerous") 25-35 59

LEE, Jackie P&R/R&B '65
(Earl Nelson)
Singles: 7-inch
ABC.......10-20 68
KEYMAN.......5-10 67-68
MIRWOOD.......10-15 65-66
UNI.......4-8 70
LPs: 10/12-inch
MIRWOOD.......15-25 66
Also see BOB & EARL
Also see NELSON, Earl

LEE, Jackie, & Raindrops
Singles: 7-inch
JAYLEE (10684 "There Goes the Lucky One").......25-35 64
LONDON (10602 "Last One to Know").....30-40 62
LONDON (10604 "There Goes the Lucky One").......10-15 62

LEE, James Washington
Singles: 7-inch
L&M (1003 "I Need Somebody").......30-40 62

LEE, Jamie
Singles: 7-inch
J-LEE (1355 "Rock Bottom Boogie").......50-75

LEE, Jeanie
Singles: 7-inch
G&G ("Like in a Story").......50-75
(Selection number not known.)

LEE, Jerry, Trio
Singles: 7-inch
NORTHWAY (1001 "Warpath").......15-25 59
RENDEZVOUS (147 "Count 10").......8-12 61

LEE, Jimmy
(Jimmie Lee; with Playboys; with Jay Franks Orchestra)
Singles: 78 rpm
CAPITOL (Except 1709).......10-15 52-55
CAPITOL (1709 "Go Ahead and Go").......15-25 51
FORTUNE (191 "You Ain't No Good for Me").......30-50 56
Singles: 7-inch
APOLLO (525 "Intermission").......10-20 58
CAPITOL (1709 "Go Ahead and Go").......50-75 51
CAPITOL (1924 thru 2491).......20-30 52-53
CAPITOL (3012 "Open for Trade").......15-25 55
CLIX (100 "She's Gone").......100-150
DIXIE (2005 "Three Little Wishes").......150-250 58
FORTUNE (191 "You Ain't No Good for Me").......75-100 56
VIN (1010 "Look What Love Will Do").......15-25 59
Also see FRANKS, Jay, Orchestra
Also see LEE, Jimmy, & Artis

LEE, Jimmy, & Artis R&B '52
(Jimmie Lee & Artis)
Singles: 78 rpm
MODERN (870 "My Heart's Desire").......50-75 52
MODERN (885 "Let's Talk It Over Baby").......75-100 52
(Seven-inch disc.)
MODERN (899 "Why Do You Make Me Feel Blue").......50-75 53
MODERN (907 "That's Fat Jack").......50-75 53
Singles: 7-inch
MODERN (870 "My Heart's Desire").......50-75 52
MODERN (885 "Let's Talk It Over").......50-75 52
MODERN (899 "Why Do You Make Me Feel Blue").......50-75 53
MODERN (907 "That's Fat Jack").......50-75 53
Also see LEE, Jimmy

LEE, Jimmy
Singles: 7-inch
CANADIAN AMERICAN (122 "My Dear Little Doll").......15-25 61

LEE, Jimmy, & Wayne Walker
Singles: 78 rpm
CHESS (4863 "Love Me").......50-100 55
Singles: 7-inch
CHESS (4863 "Love Me").......150-250 55
Also see JIMMY & JOHNNY
Also see WALKER, Wayne

LEE, Joe
(Joe Lee Combo)
Singles: 7-inch
ALLEY.......5-10 64-65
FERNWOOD (108 "Ethel Mae").......50-100 58
FERNWOOD (112 "Hang-Out").......25-50 59
Member: Larry Donn.
Also see DONN, Larry

LEE, John
(John Arthur Lee)
Singles: 78 rpm
FEDERAL (10254 "Down at the Depot").......50-100 52
FEDERAL (10289 "Baby Blues").......50-100 52

LEE, Julia R&B '46
(With Her Boy Friends; with Her Scat Cats)
Singles: 78 rpm
CAPITOL.......10-20 46-52
DAMON (12151 "Scat You Cats").......10-20 53
Singles: 7-inch
CAPITOL (Except 2203).......20-30 49-52
CAPITOL (2203 "Last Call for Alcohol")...35-50 52
DAMON (12151 "Scat You Cats").......15-25 53
FOREMOST (104 "King Size Papa").......15-20 57
EPs: 7-inch
CAPITOL (EBF-228 "Party Time").......50-75 50
LPs: 10/12-inch
CAPITOL (H-228 "Party Time").......75-100 50
(10-inch LP.)
CAPITOL (T-228 "Party Time").......50-75 55
Session: Baby Lovett; Tommy Douglas; Clint Weaver; Jim Daddy Walker; Vic Dickenson; Bobby Sherwood; Red Norvo; Red Callender; Dave Cavanaugh; Benny Carter; Jack Marshall.
Also see CALLENDER, Red

LEE, Larry
(With the Four Bel-Aires; with Frankie Valli)
Singles: 7-inch
COLUMBIA.......3-5 82
GENIUS (2100 "Stoop Up").......20-30
M.Z. (006 "Stolen Love").......300-400 59
(First issued as *Can I Be in Love* and credited to the Four Bel'Aires.)
Also see FOUR BEL'AIRES
Also see VALLI, Frankie

LEE, Larry, & Leesures
("Vocal Background By the Infatuators")
Singles: 7-inch
CAMELOT (111 "Boot and Soul").......5-10 68
(Canadian.)
CANATAL (604 "Just a Little Too Much")..8-12 65
(Canadian.)

1.

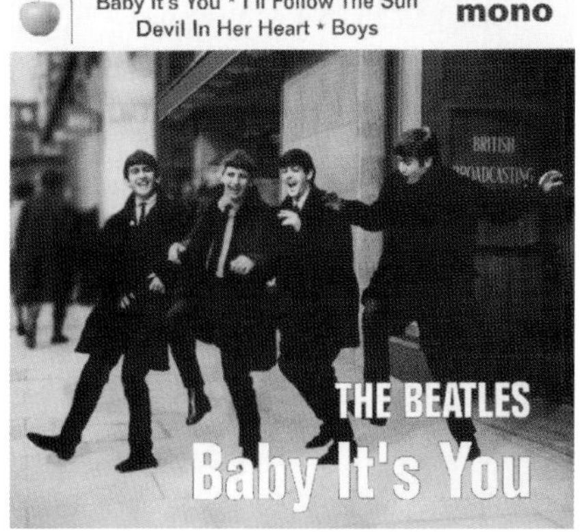

2.

3.

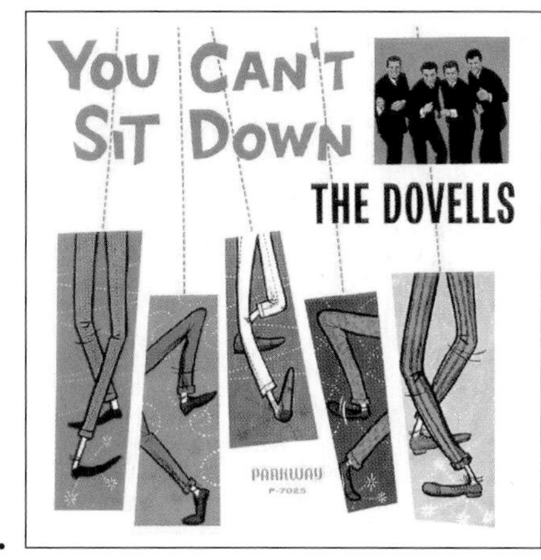

4.

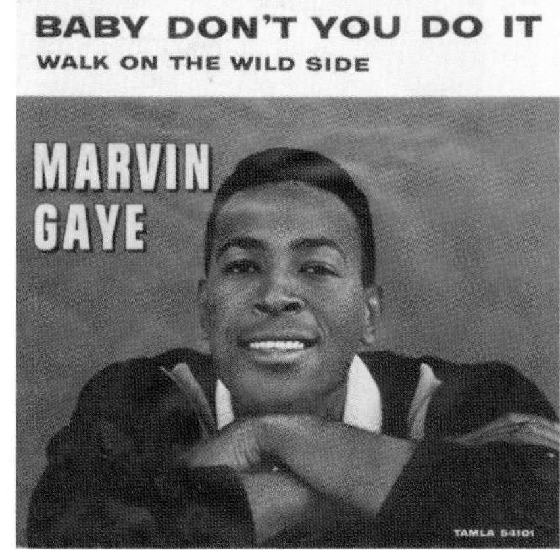

5.

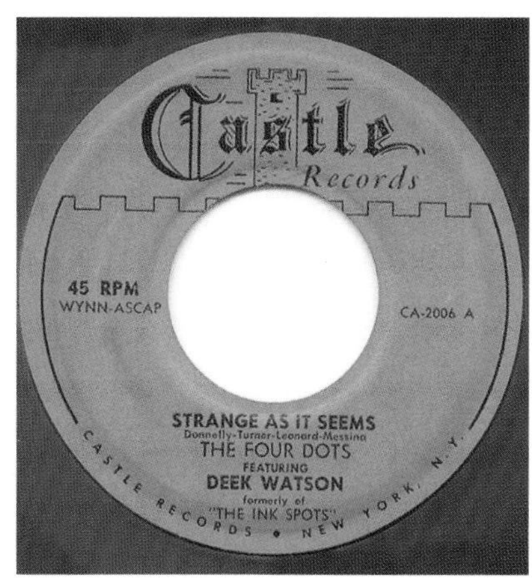

6.

1. Annette *Here's The Truth About Youth* ($35-$55). **2.** Beatles *Baby It's You* ($5-$10). **3.** Barrel House Blott & Lee with the St. Louisians *Brand New Man* ($300-$400). **4.** Dovells *You Can't Sit Down* ($30-$40). **5.** Marvin Gaye *Baby Don't You Do It* ($35-$55). **6.** Four Dots Featuring Deek Watson, formerly of the Ink Spots *Strange As It Seems* ($300-$400).

Price range reflects near-mint condition record with sleeve or insert pictured.

1.

2.

3.

4.

5.

6.

1. Brenda Lee *Sweet Nothin's* ($35-$55). **2.** Ray Price *Danny Boy* ($20-$40). **3.** Charlie Hoss & Ponies *The Madison Twist* ($20-$30). **4.** Five Stars *Baby, Baby* ($40-$60). **5.** Harry Belafonté with the Belafonté Singers *Annabelle Lee* ($10-$20). **6.** Snooky Pryor & His Trio *Cryin' Shame* ($450-$550).

Price range reflects near-mint condition record with sleeve or insert pictured.

1.

2.

3.

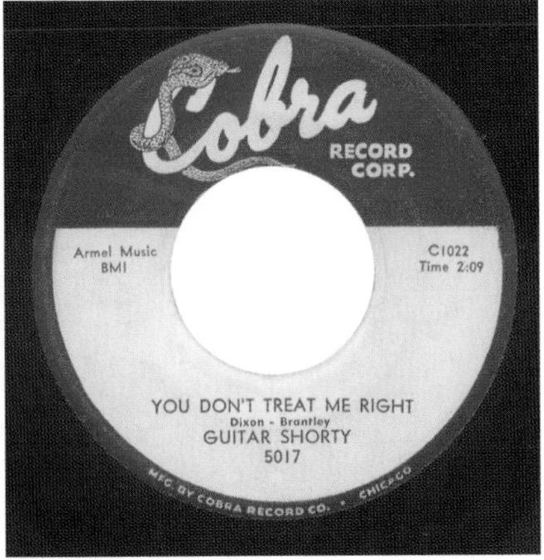

4.

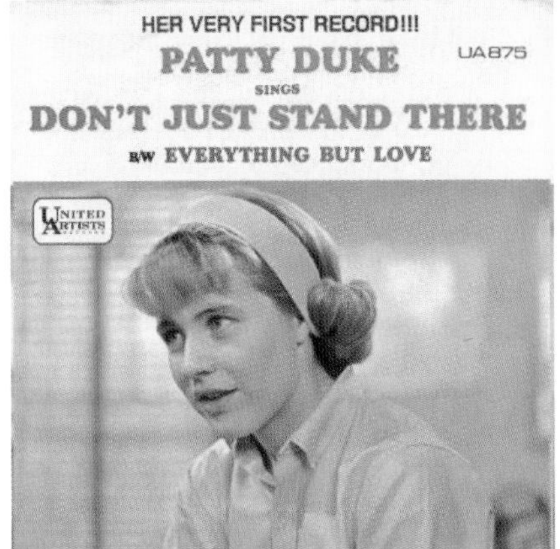

5.

6.

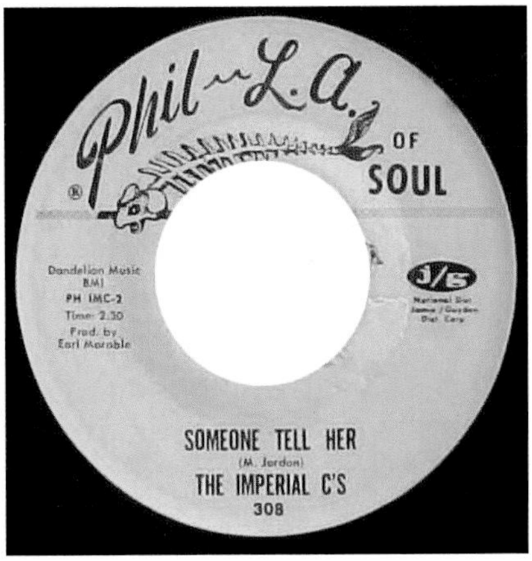

1. Eddie Sulik *Do I Love You* ($15-$18). **2.** B.B. King & the Vocal Chords *Please Accept My Love* ($30-$40). **3.** Guitar Shorty *You Don't Treat Me Right* ($50-$100). **4.** Patty Duke *Don't Just Stand There* ($15-$30). **5.** Five Keys *On Stage!* ($500-$750). **6.** Imperial C's *Someone Tell Her* ($800-$1,200).

Price range reflects near-mint condition record with sleeve or insert pictured.

1. 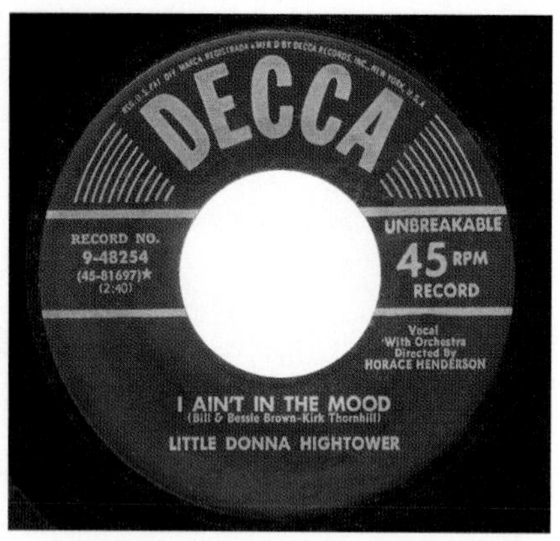

2. 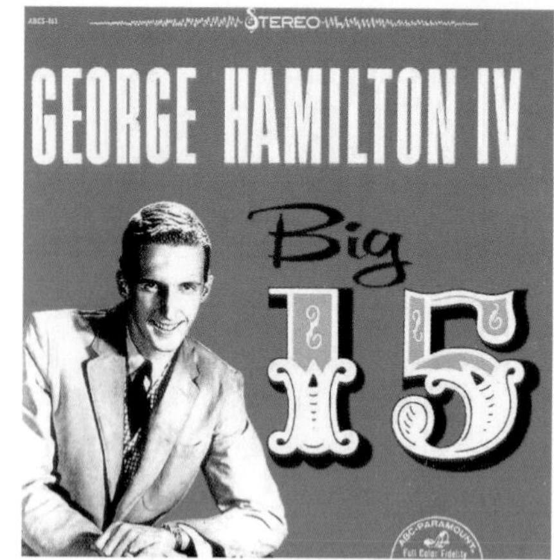

3. 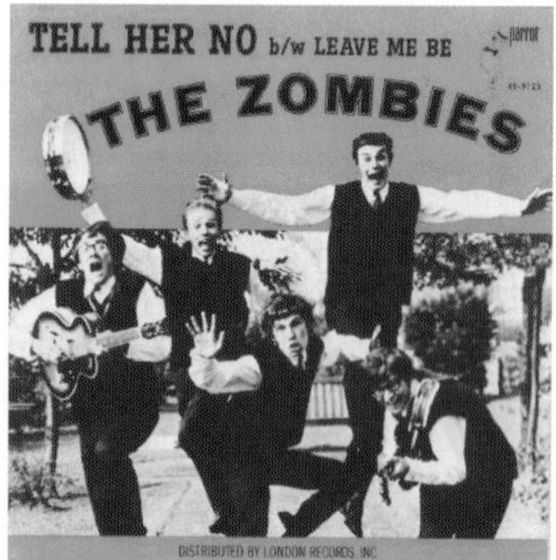

4. 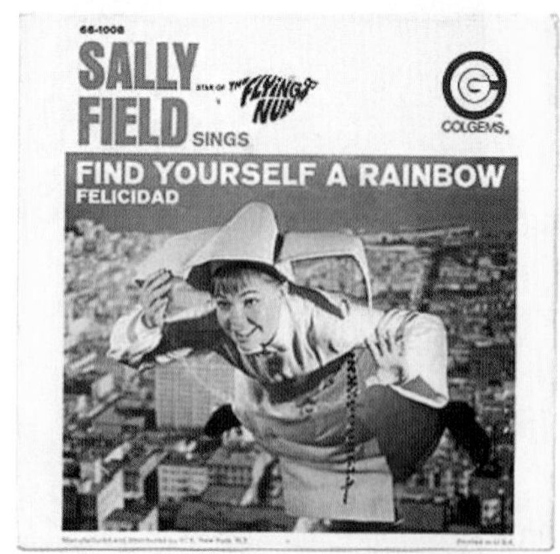

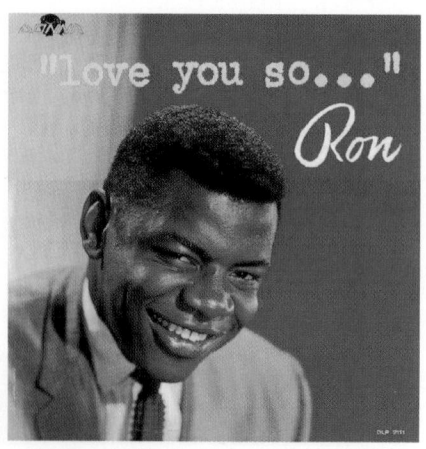

5.

6. 

1. Little Donna Hightower *I Ain't in the Mood* ($20-$30). **2.** George Hamilton IV *Big 15* ($25-$35). **3.** Zombies *Tell Her No* ($35-$45). **4.** Sally Field *Felicidad* ($25-$35). **5.** Ron Holden *Love You So …* ($75-$125). **6.** Confiners of Mississippi State Penitentiary *Harmonica Boogie* ($150-$200).

Price range reflects near-mint condition record with sleeve or insert pictured.

1. 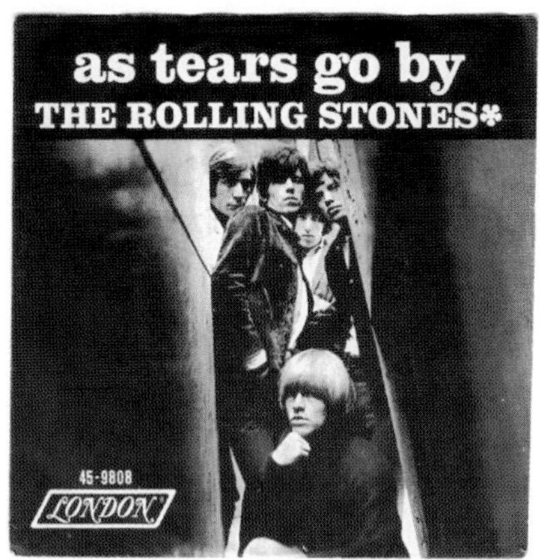

2. 

3. 

4. 

5. 

6. 

1. Rolling Stones *As Tears Go By* ($35-$50). **2.** 4 Dukes *Crying in the Chapel* ($1,000-$1,500). **3.** Blue Banana *Spicks and Specks* ($60-$80). **4.** Mom's Apple Pie *Mom's Apple Pie* ($10-$20). **5.** Dion and the Belmonts *A Teenager in Love* ($40-$60). **6.** Rivingtons *The Bird's the Word* ($30-$40).

Price range reflects near-mint condition record with sleeve or insert pictured.

1. 

2.

3. 

4. 

5.

6. 

1. Herd *From the Underworld* ($10-$20). **2.** Big Five *Wob-Ding-A-Ling* ($50-$75). **3.** Pilgrim Travelers *Look Up!* ($30-$50). **4.** Ral Donner *The Day the Beat Stopped* ($5-$10). **5.** John Lennon *Watching the Wheels* ($30-$40). **6.** Marvelettes *Playboy* ($50-$100).

Price range reflects near-mint condition record with sleeve or insert pictured.

1. 

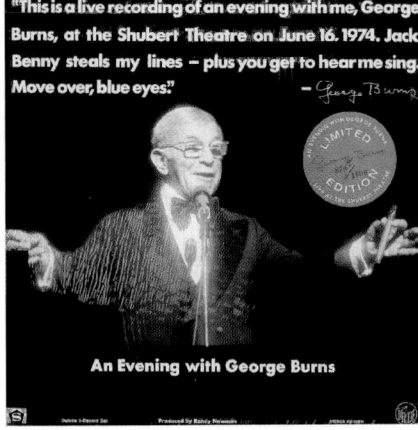

2.

3.

4.

5.

6. 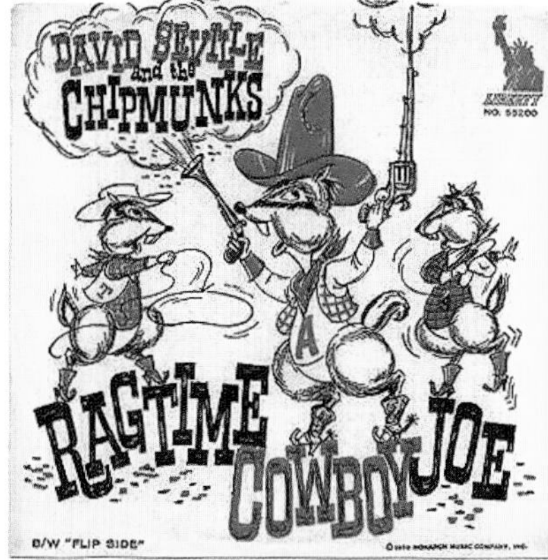

1. Delmar *Lizzie Mae* ($20-$30). **2.** Emotions *(By the Light of the) Silvery Moon* ($100-$150). **3.** George Burns *An Evening with George Burns* ($20-$30). **4.** Graham Bond *Solid Bond* ($15-$20). **5.** Rajahs *I Fell in Love* ($300-$400). **6.** David Seville and the Chipmunks *Ragtime Cowboy Joe* ($20-$30).

Price range reflects near-mint condition record with sleeve or insert pictured.

1.

2.

3.

4.

5.

6.

1. Larry Darnell *For You My Love* ($50-$100). **2.** Elvis Presley/Jaye P. Morgan *Elvis/Jaye P. Morgan* ($12,000-$15,000). **3.** Sam Cooke *Everybody Likes to Cha Cha Cha* ($35-$50). **4.** Falcons *You're So Fine* ($50-$100). **5.** Ozzy Osbourne *No Rest for the Wicked* ($5-$10). **6.** Wanda Jackson *If I Cried Every Time You Hurt Me* ($15-$25).

Price range reflects near-mint condition record with sleeve or insert pictured.

COLUMBIA (2690 thru 2740).....................5-10 66-67
(Canadian.)
DESTINY (503 "Desire")........................ 75-125 61
DESTINY (504 "I Get So Lonely")......... 75-125 61
GENIUS (2100 "Little Lana")................... 20-30 65
(Canadian.)
RED LEAF (601 "Little Lana")................. 20-30 65
(Canadian.)
TAMARAC (601 "Little Lana")................. 20-30 65
(Canadian.)

LPs: 10/12-inch

CANATAL (4016 "Number One")............ 25-35 65
(Canadian.)
COLUMBIA (314 "Club Date")................. 15-25 67
(Canadian.)

LEE, Larry & Nora

Singles: 78 rpm

TIN PAN ALLEY (155 "Those Cheating Eyes").. 10-15 56

Singles: 7-inch

TIN PAN ALLEY (155 "Those Cheating Eyes").. 15-25 56

LEE, Leonard

Singles: 78 rpm

LAMP (8001 "Tryin' to Fool Me")............. 15-20 54

Singles: 7-inch

LAMP (8001 "Tryin' to Fool Me")............. 20-30 54
7 ARTS (712 "Hard to Believe").............. 15-25 61

LEE, Little Frankie, & Saxons

Singles: 7-inch

GREAT SCOTT (0009 "Don't Make Me Over")..8-12 63
PEACOCK (1929 "Don't Make Me Cry").. 10-15 63
PEACOCK (1935 "I Gotta Come Back").....5-10 65
PEACOCK (1965 "I'm Making Love").........5-10 68

LEE, Lois

Singles: 7-inch

COOL (9035 "Am I Blue")...........................5-10
OKEH (7119 "I've Got It Bad for You Baby")... 10-15 59
Also see DEE, Joey, & Lois Lee
Also see ROCKETS

LEE, Lonnie

Singles: 7-inch

APT (25071 "Marilyn")............................. 15-25 62

LEE, Mabel

Singles: 78 rpm

HULL (712 "He's My Guy")...................... 10-15 55

Singles: 7-inch

HULL (712 "He's My Guy")...................... 20-30 55

LEE, Marva

Singles: 7-inch

ATCO (6320 "Can't We Talk It Over")...... 15-20 64
ATCO (6367 "If You Can't Be True")........ 15-20 65

LEE, Michele *P&R '68*
(With Sid Feller & Orchestra)

Singles: 7-inch

ABC (10365 "I'm Sorry Missus Murray").....8-12 62
ABC (10411 "He's Not Good Enough for You")...8-12 62
COLUMBIA..5-8 65-69

Picture Sleeves

ABC (10365 "I'm Sorry Missus Murray").. 15-25 62

LPs: 10/12-inch

COLUMBIA.. 10-20 66-68

LEE, Milliard

Singles: 7-inch

BLUES BOYS KINGDOM (105 "Waughely's Boogie")... 30-40 57
BLUES BOYS KINGDOM (106 "So Lonely, Baby").. 75-125 57
(Reissued as the Five Stars.)
Also see FIVE STARS

LEE, Myron
(With the Caddies; Mr. Lee & Caddies)

Singles: 7-inch

ABC-PAR (10610 "Everybody's Going to the Party")... 15-25 65
DEL-FI (4180 "Town Girl")....................... 25-35 62
FELSTED (8570 "Rona Baby")............... 25-35 59
GARRETT (4009 "Summertime Blues") .. 25-35 63
HEP (2076 "Rona Baby")........................ 50-75 59
(First issue.)
HEP (2102 "Magic in a Summer Night").. 40-60 60
HEP (2146 "Homicide")........................100-150 60
JARO (77037 "From Now On")................40-60 60
KEEN (2104 "Come Back Baby")............20-25 59
M&L (1004 "A Fella Needs a Girl")..........20-25 62
NOR VA JAK (1326 "Blue Lawdy Blue")...100-150 60
QUALITY (1308 "Blue Lawdy Blue").........50-75 60
(Canadian.)
SOMA (114 "Mary's Swingin' Lamb").......50-75 59
(Has photo of Myron Lee on label.)

LPs:10/12-inch

ML (1173 "Then and Now").......................10-20 80
ML (1174 "Still Packin' 'Em In")..................8-12 83
UNLIMITED (1004 "Rock and Roll Midwest Style")..5-10 84
Also see WINTER, Cyril

LEE, Nancy
(With the Tempo-Tones)

Singles: 7-inch

ACME (711 "So They Say").......................50-75 57
ACME (716 "You Asked Me Do I Love You")..100-150 57
ARC (6532 "First Date")...........................10-15 63
OJ (1004 "You're My Inspiration")............20-30 57
Also see LOVE LETTERS
Also see TEMPO-TONES

LEE, Nickie *R&B '68*

Singles: 7-inch

DADE (2011 "Late Shadows")...................5-10 67
MALA (12025 "And Black Is Beautiful")....10-15 68
MALA (12039 "Do Something About My Dream")...10-15 69

LEE, Norma

Singles: 7-inch

CAMEO (291 "God Bless Me")..................5-10 64
FILM (709 "Paper Boy")...........................50-75

LEE, Peggy *P&R '45*
(With Benny Goodman's Orchestra; with Billy May & Orchestra; with Jack Marshall & Orchestra)

Singles: 78 rpm

CAPITOL..5-15 41-58
OKEH...5-15 41-42

Singles: 7-inch

A&M...4-6 75
ATLANTIC...4-6 74
CAPITOL (801 thru 2000 series)...............8-12 49-51
CAPITOL (2100 thru 3400 series)...............4-6 68-72
CAPITOL (3800 thru 5900 series)...............4-8 58-67
CAPITOL (90000 series)............................4-8
COLUMBIA..4-6 76
DECCA (25000 series)...............................4-6 64
DECCA (28000 & 29000 series, except 29427 & 29460)...4-8 52-58
DECCA (29427 "Siamese Cat Song")......15-20 '50s
DECCA (29460 "Bella Notte")..................10-15 '50s
DECCA (30000 series)...............................4-8 58-59
DECCA (9-88186 "Siamese Cat Song")...10-20 '50s
(Children's Series.)

EPs: 7-inch

CAPITOL (Except 100 series)..................10-20 57-59
CAPITOL (100 series)..............................20-40 52
COLUMBIA..20-40 50-51
DECCA...15-30 52-55

LPs: 10/12-inch

A&M...5-8 75
ATLANTIC...5-8 74
CAMAY (3003 "Peggy Lee's Greatest")...10-15 '50s
CAPITOL (183 "A Natural Woman")..........8-12 69
CAPITOL (H-155 "Rendezvous with Peggy")..50-75 52
(10-inch LP.)
CAPITOL (T-155 "Rendezvous with Peggy")..25-50 55
CAPITOL (H-204 "My Best to You").........50-75 52
(10-inch LP.)
CAPITOL (377 thru 810)............................5-10 69-71
CAPITOL (864 "The Man I Love")............20-40 56
CAPITOL (979 "Jump for Joy")................20-40 57
CAPITOL (T-1049 thru T-1969)...............15-25 58-63
(Monaural.)
CAPITOL (ST-1049 thru ST-1969)..........20-30 58-63
(Stereo.)
CAPITOL (T-2096 thru T-2887)...............10-20 64-68
(Monaural.)
CAPITOL (ST-2096 thru ST-2887)..........10-20 64-68
CAPITOL (6600 series)..............................5-10 70
CAPITOL (11000 series)............................5-10 72-79
CAPITOL (16000 series)............................4-8 80
COLUMBIA (6033 "Benny Goodman & Peggy Lee")..40-60 50
(10-inch LP.)
DRG...5-8 79
DECCA (DXB-164 "Best of Peggy Lee")..15-25 60
(Monaural.)
DECCA (DXSB7-164 "Best of Peggy Lee")..10-20 66
(Stereo.)
DECCA (DL-4000 series).........................10-15 64
(Monaural.)
DECCA (DL7-4000 series).......................15-20 64
(Stereo.)
DECCA (5482 "Black Coffee").................50-75 53
(10-inch LP.)
DECCA (5539 "Songs in an Intimate Style")..50-75 53
(10-inch LPs.)
DECCA (8411 "Dream Street")................30-50 56
DECCA (8358 "Black Coffee")................30-50 57
DECCA (8591 "Sea Shells")....................30-50 58
DECCA (8816 "Miss Wonderful")............20-40 59
EVEREST..5-8 74
GLENDALE...4-8 82
HARMONY (7000 series)........................15-25 58
HARMONY (30000 series)........................5-10 70
HORIZON (1004 "Best of Peggy Lee").....25-35 62
MERCURY..5-8 77
VOCALION..6-12 66-70
Also see CROSBY, Bing, & Peggy Lee
Also see FITZGERALD, Ella, & Peggy Lee
Also see GOODMAN, Benny, Orchestra
Also see JENKINS, Gordon, & His Orchestra
Also see MARSHALL, Jack

LEE, Peggy, & Dean Martin

Singles: 78 rpm

CAPITOL (15349 "You Was")..................20-30 49
Also see MARTIN, Dean

LEE, Peggy, & Mills Brothers
(With Sy Oliver & Orchestra)

Singles: 78 rpm

DECCA (29359 "It Must Be So")..................4-8 55

Singles: 7-inch

DECCA (29359 "It Must Be So")................8-12 55
Also see MILLS BROTHERS
Also see OLIVER, Sy, & Orchestra

LEE, Peggy, & George Shearing

Singles: 7-inch

CAPITOL (4243 "You Came a Long Way from St. Louis")..5-10 59

LPs: 10/12-inch

CAPITOL (1219 "Beauty and the Beat")...20-30 59
(Capitol logo on left side of label.)
CAPITOL (1219 "Beauty and the Beat")...10-20 62
(Capitol logo at the top of label.)

LEE, Peggy, & Mel Torme

Singles: 78 rpm

CAPITOL (791 "Old Master Painter").........5-10 49

Singles: 7-inch

CAPITOL (791 "Old Master Painter").......10-20 49
Also see LEE, Peggy
Also see TORME, Mel

LEE, Perk

Singles: 7-inch

BOSS (2125 "The Docks")......................50-100 64

LEE, Pinky

Singles: 78 rpm

DECCA..5-10 55

Singles: 7-inch

DECCA..10-15 55

Picture Sleeves

DECCA (301 "Yoo-Hoo It's Me")..............15-20 55
DECCA (303 "Little Doggie with the Big Woof-Woof")..15-20 55

LEE, Randy

Singles: 7-inch

CUB (9056 "Just Give Me Time")..............5-10 60
EVEREST (19332 thru 19404)....................5-10 60-61
PHILIPS (40006 thru 40127)......................5-10 62-63
SPANN (402 "I Never Knew")..................40-50 59

LEE, Robert, & Exquisites

Singles: 7-inch

STEELTOWN (687 "Tears Are Falling")...15-25 69

LEE, Robin
(With Robins; with Royal Host; with Revels; with Wausau's Night Beats; with Jordanaires; with Anita Kerr Singers)

Singles: 7-inch

BIG SOUND...8-12 65-66
CIRCLE DOT (103 "Pretty Patty")...........15-25 60
CITE (5011 "I See Her Face")...................5-10 65
ESU..5-10 72
KARRYE (842 "Summertime's Finally Here")..30-40 61
PRO-GRESS (8357 "Sure I Will")..............8-12 69
REPRISE...5-10 62-63
TEE PEE (67/68 "To Hell with Love"/"The Urge for Going")..8-12 68
USA (2052 "Pretty Patty").........................8-12 67

LPs: 10/12-inch

EVERGREEN (1001 "Robin Lee")...........15-25
PRO-GRESS..15-25 69
STRAND...15-25 64
Members: Terry Christian; Rodney Means; Bob Oestreich; Jerry Suchomski; Curly Cooke.
Also see JORDANAIRES
Also see KERR, Anita
Also see LAUNCHERS
Also see LAVENDERS
Also see NIGHT BEATS
Also see ROYAL HOST
Also see SCHENZEL, Roger, & Flav-o-rites
Also see WINSTON, Roger, & Plaids

LEE, Robin

Singles: 7-inch

DOT (16773 "Great Wheel").......................5-10 65

LPs: 10/12-inch

DOT (3661 "Robin Lee").........................15-20 65
(Monaural.)
DOT (25661 "Robin Lee")........................20-25 65
(Stereo.)

LEE, Ronni

Singles: 7-inch

EVEREST (19427 "Teach Me Tiger")......10-15 61

LEE, Roosevelt

Singles: 78 rpm

EXCELLO (2022 "Lazy Pete")..................15-25 54

Singles: 7-inch

EXCELLO (2022 "Lazy Pete")..................30-50 54

LEE, Ruby

Singles: 7-inch

POPTONE (1901 "I Believe in You")........15-25 63

LEE, Sandy

Singles: 7-inch

SANTE FE ("Ballin' Keen")......................75-125
(Selection number not known.)

LEE, Sunnie
(Sunny Lee)

Singles: 7-inch

BOONE (1041 "Soft Rain").........................5-10 66
KARL (3008 "Puppy Love").......................50-75

LEE, Suzie

Singles: 7-inch

SEECO (6011 "In His Convertible")..........10-15 59

LEE, T.C., & Bricklayers

Singles: 7-inch

KING (6135 "Get Away from Here").....200-300 67

LEE, T.C., & King Pins

Singles: 7-inch

FEDERAL (12525 "I'm a Lonesome Rooster")..10-20 64
Also see KELLY BROTHERS
Also see KING PINS

LEE, Terry, & Poor Boys

Singles: 7-inch

SOMA (1002 Congo Bongo")................150-250 59
SOMA (1116 "My Little Sue")................150-200 59

LEE, Terry, & Revelers / Revelers

Singles: 7-inch

RED FOX (101 "Part III")........................15-20 64

LEE, Tipsie
("13 Yrs. Old")

Singles: 7-inch

ASWA (11 "How Could You")...................10-20 57

LEE, Tommy

Singles: 78 rpm

DELTA (403 "Packing Up My Blues")...250-350 53

LEE, Tony

Singles: 7-inch

DARRYL (723 "Walking Slow") ... 10-20
FORTUNE (530 "Suicide") ... 10-20 58
KING (5230 "I Don't Care What You Do") ... 10-15 59
MERCURY (71511 "Summer Love") ... 8-12 59

LEE, Vicki

Singles: 78 rpm

SPECIALTY (546 "Tears Keep a Falling") ... 10-20 55

Singles: 7-inch

COURT (6009 "Eddie My Love") ... 5-10 61
DRUM (017 "Cryin' My Heart Out") ... 50-75 59
SPECIALTY (546 "Tears Keep a Falling") ... 20-40 55

LEE, Vinnie, & Spunkys

Singles: 7-inch

ABC-PAR (10189 "Mule Train") ... 10-20 61
LEE ("Bustin' Through") ... 15-25 58
(Selection number not known.)
OLD TOWN (1061 "Mule Train Rock") ... 15-25 58
OLD TOWN (1083 "Whipper Snapper") ... 10-20 60
Also see LEEMEN

LEE, Wally, & Storms

Singles: 7-inch

NOW (1010 "Oh No Daddy") ... 100-200
SUNDOWN (123 "I Never Felt This Way") ... 300-400 59

LEE, Warren

(Warren Lee Taylor)

Singles: 7-inch

DEE-SU (302 "A Lady") ... 10-20 65
DEE-SU (305 "Waiting for a Bus") ... 10-20 65
DEE-SU (315 "Climb the Ladder") ... 10-20 66
NOLA (711 "Key to My Heart") ... 15-25 65
SOUNDEX (603 "Anna") ... 10-15 63
WAND (1194 "Funky Belly") ... 5-10 69

LEE, Wibby

Singles: 7-inch

JALYN (214 "I'm Lost Without Your Love") ... 100-150

LEE & BART

Singles: 7-inch

U.A. (140 "Knock at My Door") ... 10-20 58

LEE & CLARENDONS

Singles: 7-inch

H.S. ("Night Owl") ... 40-50
(Selection number not known.)

LEE & LEOPARDS

Singles: 7-inch

FORTUNE (867 "What About Me") ... 15-25 65
GORDY (7002 "Come Into My Palace") ... 20-30 62
LAURIE (3197 "Come Into My Palace") ... 5-10 63
Member: Lee Moore.

LEE & SOUNDS

Singles: 7-inch

LIDO (600 "Beautiful Romance") ... 20-30 59

LEE & VIBRATONES

Singles: 7-inch

DAROW (16013 "Too Cool") ... 10-20 60

LEE BROTHERS

(With Don Costa & Orchestra)

Singles: 78 rpm

COLUMBIA ... 8-15 51
PIC ... 8-15 54

Singles: 7-inch

COLUMBIA (39136 "If It Hadn't Been for You") ... 15-25 51
COLUMBIA (39144 "I Don't Want to Love You") ... 15-25 51
COLUMBIA (39303 "The Strange Little Girl") ... 15-25 51
COLUMBIA (39447 "Even As You & I") ... 15-25 51
COLUMBIA (39584 "If You've Forgotten Me") ... 15-25 51
PIC (0009 "Goodnight Sweetheart") ... 15-25 54
PIC (0022 "Sh' Says I Don't Know") ... 15-25 54
Also see COSTA, Don, Orchestra

LEE-ANNE

(Leeanne Leyden)

Singles: 7-inch

ANN (1000 "Never") ... 25-50 63

LEED TWINS

Singles: 7-inch

FLAME (109 "Rock and Roll Pizza Pie") ... 10-15 59

LEEDS

Singles: 7-inch

WAND (102 "Heaven Only Knows") ... 40-60 59

LEEDS, Brad

Singles: 7-inch

SIGNATURE (12021 "Teenage Love Is Born") ... 10-15 60

LEEDS, Mike

Singles: 7-inch

ABC-PAR (10101 "Working After School") ... 10-15 60

LEEDS, Randy

Singles: 7-inch

ROULETTE (4153 "Me, Oh My") ... 10-15 59
SUPERIOR (3303 "Love Talk") ... 15-20 57

LEEMEN

Singles: 7-inch

ABC-PAR (10210 "Hucklebuck") ... 10-15 61
Member: Vinnie Lee.
Also see LEE, Vinnie, & Vibratones

LEEN TEENS

Singles: 7-inch

IMPERIAL (5593 "So Shy") ... 50-75 59

LE FAWN, Paul

(With the Whippoorwills)

Singles: 78 rpm

ABBOTT ... 10-15 55-56

Singles: 7-inch

ABBOTT (3009 "Learning to Love") ... 15-25 55
ABBOTT (3013 "Sundown") ... 15-25 55
ABBOTT (3023 "Can't Get You Out of My Mind") ... 15-25 56
VANDAN (2323 "You Can Hold My Hand") ... 8-12 64

LEFT BANKE

P&R '66

Singles: 7-inch

CAMERICA (0005 "Queen of the Paradise") ... 3-5 80
SMASH (Except 2243) ... 5-10 66-69
SMASH (2243 "Myrah") ... 30-40 69

Picture Sleeves

SMASH (Except 2243) ... 10-20 67
SMASH (2243 "Myrah") ... 30-40 69

LPs: 10/12-inch

RHINO (123 "History of the Left Banke") ... 5-10 85
SMASH (27088 "Walk Away Renee") ... 75-125 67
(Monaural.)
SMASH (67088 "Walk Away Renee") ... 75-125 67
(Stereo.)
SMASH (67113 "Left Banke Too") ... 50-75 69
MERCURY ... 5-10 81
Members: Michael Brown; George Cameron; Tom Finn; Steve Martin; Rick Brand; Jeff Winfield; Tom Feher.
Also see MAGIC PLANTS
Also see MONTAGE
Also see STORIES

LEFTOVERS

Singles: 7-inch

CENCO (109 "Searchin' ") ... 30-40 60

LEFTY & LEADSMEN

Singles: 7-inch

CO & CE (103 "Wildwood Fun") ... 40-60 62

LEGAL EAGLES

Singles: 7-inch

ARCH (1607 "The Trial") ... 20-30 58
(Also issued as by Herb. B. Lou & Legal Eagles.)
Also see LOU, Herb B., & Legal Eagles

LE GARDES

C&W '78

(Le Garde Twins)

Singles: 7-inch

BEAR (194 "Crocodile Man") ... 4-6 88
BEL CANTO (725 "Hi-Di") ... 15-25 58
DOT (15608 "Freight Train Yodel") ... 10-15 57
4 STAR (1037 "I Can Almost Touch the Feelin' ") ... 3-5 79
INVITATION (101 "Daddy's Makin' Records in Nashville") ... 4-6 80
LIBERTY (55266 "Babysitter") ... 10-20 60
RAINDROP (012 "True Love") ... 4-8 78

LPs: 10/12-inch

CAPITOL ... 10-20
KOALA ... 8-10
PLATINUM PLATT ... 8-10

LE GAULT, Hank

Singles: 78 rpm

STARDALE (200 "I Knew") ... 50-100 56

Singles: 7-inch

STARDALE (200 "I Knew") ... 400-500 56

LEGEND

Singles: 7-inch

MEGAPHONE (701 "The Kids Are Alright") ... 10-15 68
MEGAPHONE (703 "Enjoy Yourself") ... 10-15 68

LPs: 10/12-inch

MEGAPHONE (101 "Legend") ... 50-75 70
Also see DRAGONFLY
Also see KELLY, Mike, & Legend

LEGEND, Tobi

Singles: 7-inch

MALA (591 "Heartbreaker") ... 25-45 68
MALA (12003 "No Good Cry") ... 10-20 68

LEGENDARY MASKED SURFERS

Singles: 7-inch

U.A. (270 "Summer Means Fun") ... 10-15 73
(Tan label. This track, previously included on the Jan & Dean LPs *The Little Old Lady from Pasadena* and *Popsicle* was mistakenly used for this single.)
U.A. (270 "Summer Means Fun") ... 10-15 73
(White label, promotional issue. Same incorrect track as noted above.)
U.A. (270 "Summer Means Fun") ... 100-125 73
(Tan label, promotional issue. Has the intended, new version with added vocal backing, not available elsewhere. Can be identified by playing, or visually by the following letters etched in the vinyl trail-off: Side 1 "BJ/TM/DT." Side 2 "GG/ILY/DOT.")
U.A. (270 "Summer Means Fun") ... 100-125 73
(White label, promotional issue. Has correct version as described above.)
U.A. (670 "Gonna Hustle You") ... 20-30 75
U.A. (50958 "Gonna Hustle You") ... 30-40 72

Picture Sleeves

U.A. (270 "Summer Means Fun") ... 20-30 73
(Add $5.00 if accompanied by explanatory note from Dean Torrence.)
Members: Jan Berry; Dean Torrence; Brian Wilson; Bruce Johnston; Terry Melcher; Leon Russell; Glen Campbell; Larry Knechtel.
Also see CAMPBELL, Glen
Also see JAN & DEAN
Also see RUSSELL, Leon
Also see WILSON, Brian

LEGENDARY STARDUST COWBOY

(Norman Odam)

Singles: 7-inch

MERCURY (72862 "Paralyzed") ... 10-20 69
MERCURY (72891 "Down in the Wrecking Yard") ... 10-20 69
MERCURY (72912 "Everything's Gettin' Bigger But Our Love") ... 10-20 69
NORTON (12 "I Hate CDs") ... 3-5 92
PSYCHO-SAUVE (1033 "Paralyzed") ... 25-35 68

LEGENDS

Singles: 78 rpm

MELBA (109 "I'll Never Fall in Love Again") ... 10-15 56

Singles: 7-inch

HULL (727 "The Legend of Love") ... 75-125 58
(Red label.)
HULL (727 "The Legend of Love") ... 10-15 62
(Multi-color label.)
MELBA (109 "I'll Never Fall in Love Again") ... 100-150 56
(Promotional issue only.)
MELBA (109 "I'll Never Fall in Love Again") ... 75-125 56
(Titles and artists shown in print approximately 1/8-inch letters. Label also has double horizontal lines.)
MELBA (109 "I'll Never Fall in Love Again") ... 10-20 '60s
(Titles and artists shown in print approximately 1/4-inch letters.)

LEGENDS

Singles: 7-inch

COLUMBIA (41949 "Later") ... 5-10 61

LPs: 10/12-inch

COLUMBIA (1707 "Hit Sounds of Today's Smash Hit Combos") ... 20-30 61
(Monaural.)
COLUMBIA (8507 "Hit Sounds of Today's Smash Hit Combos") ... 20-30 61
(Stereo.)
Member: Bill Ramal.
Also see RAMAL, Bill

LEGENDS

Singles: 7-inch

MAGENTA (02 "You Little Nothing") ... 10-15 61

LEGENDS

Singles: 7-inch

HART-VAN (18003 "Traction") ... 20-25 62

LEGENDS

Singles: 7-inch

CALDWELL (410 "Go Away with Me") ... 10-15 62
JAMIE (1228 "Tell the Truth") ... 10-15 62

LEGENDS

Singles: 7-inch

CAPITOL (5014 "Summertime Blues") ... 10-20 63
DATE (1521 "Raining in My Heart") ... 10-15 66
ERMINE (39 thru 45) ... 10-20 62-63
KEY (1002 "Lariat") ... 15-25 61
PARROT (45010 "Just in Case") ... 5-10 65
PARROT (45011 "Alright") ... 5-10 65
THAMES (104 "Raining in My Heart") ... 10-15 66
W.B. (5457 "Don't Be Ashamed") ... 5-10 64

Picture Sleeves

ERMINE (43 "Bop-A-Lena") ... 15-25 62

LPs: 10/12-inch

CAPITOL (T-1925 "Legends Let Loose") ... 50-100 63
(Monaural.)
CAPITOL (DT-1925 "Legends Let Loose") ... 50-100 63
(Reprocessed stereo.)
CAPITOL (2047 "Run to the Movies") ... 100-200 63
(Capitol Custom pressing.)
ERMINE (101 "Legends Let Loose") ... 100-200 63
Members: Larry Foster; Sam McCue; Jerry Schils; Jim Sessody. Session: John Rondell; Billy Joe Burnette.
Also see BIRDWATCHERS
Also see McCUE, Sam

LEGENDS

Singles: 7-inch

FALCO (305 "Well, Darling") ... 1000-2000 63

LEGENDS

Singles: 7-inch

DOC HOLIDAY (107 "Surfs Up") ... 15-25 63

Picture Sleeves

DOC HOLIDAY (107 "Surfs Up") ... 25-35 63

LEGENDS

Singles: 7-inch

FENTON (2512 "I'll Come Again") ... 15-25 67

LEGENDS

Singles: 7-inch

UP (2207 "Baby, Get Your Head Screwed On") ... 20-30 68
RAILROAD HOUSE (12003 "High Towers") ... 10-15 69

Picture Sleeves

RAILROAD HOUSE (12003 "High Towers") ... 20-30 69

LEGENDS

Singles: 7-inch

CHEECO (655 "Baby I Need Your Loving") ... 15-25
CHEECO (656 "If Ever") ... 15-25
MAGENTA (2 "You Little Nothing") ... 15-25
PUMPKIN (103 "Deep Inside") ... 15-20

LEGGS, Price

Singles: 7-inch

GLEN (101 "Teenage Fun") ... 20-40 58

LEHMAN, Billy

(With the Penn-Men; with Rock-Itts; Bill Lehman)

Singles: 7-inch

ARP (014 "Audrey") ... 5-10 59
PRIME 1 (316 "Take It Easy Greasy") ... 600-800 57

LEHMANN, Frankie

Singles: 7-inch

VJM RUSS (4424 "A Long Day's Flight"). 10-15 64

LEHRER, Tom LP '65

Singles: 7-inch

REPRISE....4-6 69

EPs: 7-inch

LEHRER (1 "Songs By Tom Lehrer") 50-100 52
(Two-discs. Gatefold.)
REPRISE (224 "An Evening Wasted with Tom Lehrer") 5-10 65
(Promotional issue only.)

LPs: 10/12-inch

LEHRER (101 "Songs By Tom Lehrer") .. 50-75 52
LEHRER (102 "More Songs By Tom Lehrer") 30-50 59
LEHRER (202 "An Evening Wasted with Tom Lehrer") 30-50 59
REPRISE (6179 "That Was the Year That Was") 10-20 65
REPRISE (6199 "An Evening Wasted with Tom Lehrer") 10-20 65
REPRISE (6216 "Songs By Tom Lehrer") 10-20 66

LEIBER, Jerry

LPs: 10/12-inch

KAPP (1127 "Scooby Doo") 30-40 59
Also see SCOOBY DOO ALL STARS

LEIBER & STOLLER BIG BAND

(Leiber-Stoller Orchestra)

Singles: 7-inch

U.A. (441 "Café Espresso") 5-10 62

LPs: 10/12-inch

ATLANTIC (847 "Yakety Yak") 20-30 61
(Monaural.)
ATLANTIC (SD-847 "Yakety Yak") 25-35 61
(Stereo.)
Members: Jerry Leiber; Mike Stoller.
Also see LEIBER, Jerry

LEIGH, Diane

Singles: 7-inch

FABOR (129 "Little Boy Lost") 10-15 64
TOWER (151 "It Won't Be a Lonely Summer") 10-15 65

LEIGH, Linda

(With Rosco Holland)

Singles: 7-inch

AMERICAN INT'L (540 "My Guy") 10-20 59
AMERICAN INT'L (543 "Beri Beri") 20-40 59
AMERICAN INT'L (546 "Foolish Dreams") 10-15 60
KASH (1028 "Heart") 5-10 65
MARK 56 (866 "That Old Black Magic") 5-10 64
RENDEZVOUS (103 "Move Out") 10-15 58
RENDEZVOUS (106 "Teardrops") 10-15 59
REPRISE (20060 "Please") 5-10 62
REPRISE (20078 "Lovers' Beach") 5-10 62

LEISURE LADS

(With Michael Francis & Orchestra)

Singles: 7-inch

DELCO (801 "A Teenage Memory") 40-50 59
(Reportedly 500 made.)

LEJEUNE, Iry

Singles: 78 rpm

TNT (105 "Bayou Pon Pon Special") 10-15 53

Singles: 7-inch

TNT (105 "Bayou Pon Pon Special") 15-25 53

LEMAY, Bob

Singles: 7-inch

FRANDY (601 "Chicken Shack") 15-25 61

LE MEL, Gary

Singles: 7-inch

MIRA (247 "Beautiful People") 5-10 68
REV (3509 "Man Overboard") 15-25 57
REV (3520 "Rockin' in the Halls") 40-60 58
VEE-JAY (648 "On Broadway") 8-12 65

LPs: 10/12-inch

VEE-JAY (1129 "Gary Le Mel Album") 10-20 65

LEMMON, Jack

LPs: 10/12-inch

CAPITOL (T-1943 "Jack Lemmon Plays Piano Selections from *Irma La Douce*") 30-50 63
(Monaural.)
CAPITOL (ST-1943 "Jack Lemmon Plays Piano Selections from *Irma La Douce*") 40-60 63
(Stereo.)
EPIC (LN-523 "Twist of Lemmon") 20-30 59
(Monaural.)
EPIC (BN-523 "Twist of Lemmon") 25-35 59
(Stereo.)
Also see NELSON, Rick, & Jack Lemmon

LEMON DROP BAND

Singles: 7-inch

TEEN TOWN (122 "Twist O Lemon") ....10-20 '60s
TEEN TOWN (123 "Chubby Mind") ....10-20 '60s

LEMON DROPS

Singles: 7-inch

REMBRANDT (5009 "I Love in the Springtime") 15-25 67

LPs: 10/12-inch

CICADELIC 8-10 85-87
Members: Dick Sidman; Danny Smola; Jeff Brand; George Sorenson; Rick Erickson.
Also see NUCHEZS

LEMON FOG

Singles: 7-inch

ORBIT (1117 "Lemon Fog") 20-30 67
ORBIT (1123 "Summer") 20-30 68
ORBIT (1127 "Day by Day") 20-30 68

LEMONS, Bill

Singles: 7-inch

CORT (1313 "Lorene") 100-125

LEMONS, George

Singles: 7-inch

GOLD SOUL (102 "Fascinating Girl") 1000-2000
(Promotional issue only.)

LEN & JUDY

Singles: 7-inch

DEER (3001 "I'm Leavin' Town, Baby") ..50-100 61

LEN-DELLS

Singles: 7-inch

REACH (02 "Mary Ann") 40-50 66
Also see LY-DELLS

LENNON, Freddie

Singles: 7-inch

JERDEN (792 "That's My Life") 20-30 66

LENNON, John P&R/LP '69

(John & Yoko; Plastic Ono Band; with Plastic Ono Nuclear Band; with Flux Fiddlers)

Singles: 12-inch

CAPITOL (9585/6 "Imagine"/"Come Together") 25-35 86
(Promotional issue only. With custom cover.)
CAPITOL (9894 "Happy Xmas") 150-200 86
(White vinyl. Promotional issue only. Black label. Has numbered cover for Food Bank Benefit.)
CAPITOL (9894 "Happy Xmas") 40-50 86
(White vinyl. Promotional issue only. Black label. Has unprinted clear plastic cover.)
CAPITOL (9917 "Rock & Roll People") 50-60 86
(Promotional issue only.)
CAPITOL (9929 "Happy Xmas") 35-45 86
(White vinyl. Promotional issue only. Silver label. Has custom clear plastic cover with title sticker on front.)
CAPITOL (79453 "Stand by Me") 30-40 88
(Promotional issue only. Has custom cover with title sticker)
GEFFEN (919 "Starting Over") 60-75 80
(Promotional issue only. With picture cover.)
GEFFEN (1079 "Happy Xmas") 25-30 82
(Promotional issue only. With custom cover)
POLYDOR (250 "Nobody Told Me") 25-30 83
(Promotional issue only. With custom cover)

Singles: 7-inch

AMERICOM (435 "Give Peace a Chance") 500-750 69
(Plastic "Pocket Disc" four-inch soundsheet.)
APPLE (1809 "Give Peace a Chance") 4-6 69
APPLE (1813 "Cold Turkey") 4-6 69
APPLE (1818 "Instant Karma") 15-30 70
(With Capitol logo.)
APPLE (1818 "Instant Karma") 5-10 70
(No Capitol logo.)
APPLE (1827 "Mother") 8-12 70
(No "Mono" print on label.)
APPLE (1827 "Mother") 30-40 70
(With "Mono" on label.)
APPLE (1830 "Power to the People") 8-12 71
APPLE (1840 "Imagine") 8-12 71
APPLE (1842 "Happy Xmas") 10-15 71
(Green vinyl. Label pictures John & Yoko.)
APPLE (1842 "Happy Xmas") 5-10 71
(Green vinyl. Standard Apple label.)
APPLE (1848 "Woman Is the Nigger of the World") 5-8 72
(With Elephant's Memory.)
APPLE (1868 "Mind Games") 4-6 73
APPLE (1874 "Whatever Gets You Through the Night") 4-6 74
APPLE (1878 "#9 Dream") 5-8 74
APPLE (1881 "Stand by Me") 5-8 75
CAPITOL (1830 "Power to the People") 5-10 78
(Purple label.)
CAPITOL (1830 "Power to the People") 5-10 83
(Black label.)
CAPITOL (1840 "Imagine") 10-15 76
(Orange label.)
CAPITOL (1840 "Imagine") 5-10 78
(Purple label.)
CAPITOL (1840 "Imagine") 5-10 83
(Black label.)
CAPITOL (1842 "Happy Xmas") 40-50 76
(Orange label.)
CAPITOL (1842 "Happy Xmas") 5-10 78
(Purple label.)
CAPITOL (1842 "Happy Xmas") 5-10 83
(Black label.)
CAPITOL (1868 "Mind Games") 10-15 76
(Orange label.)
CAPITOL (1868 "Mind Games") 5-10 78
(Purple label.)
CAPITOL (1868 "Mind Games") 5-10 83
(Black label.)
CAPITOL (1874 "Whatever Gets You Thru the Night") 5-10 78
(Purple label.)
CAPITOL (1874 "Whatever Gets You Thru the Night") 5-10 83
(Black label.)
CAPITOL (1878 "#9 Dream") 30-40 76
(Orange label.)
CAPITOL (1878 "#9 Dream") 5-10 76
(Purple label.)
CAPITOL (6244 "Stand by Me") 5-8 77
(Tan Starline label, circular Capitol logo.)
CAPITOL (6244 "Stand by Me") 4-6 78
(Tan Starline label, oval Capitol logo.)
CAPITOL (6244 "Stand by Me") 40-50 86
(Blue Starline series label.)
CAPITOL (6244 "Stand by Me") 40-50 86
(Black Starline series label.)
CAPITOL (17644 "Happy Xmas") 3-5 94
(Colored vinyl, 30th Anniversary juke box issue. Mistakenly has a slash following title: "Happy Xmas (War Is Over)/".)
CAPITOL (17644 "Happy Xmas") 3-5 95
(Colored vinyl, 30th Anniversary juke box issue. Erroneous slash removed from title.)
CAPITOL (17783 "Give Peace a Chance") 75-100 94
CAPITOL (44230 "Jealous Guy") 5-10 88
CAPITOL (57849 "Imagine") 30-50 92
COLLECTABLES (4307 "Nobody Told Me") 15-20 92
GEFFEN (0408 "Starting Over") 3-5 81
(Cream color label. Logo has narrow print.)
GEFFEN (0408 "Starting Over") 20-30 81
(Cream color label. Logo has bold print.)
GEFFEN (0408 "Starting Over") 15-30 80
(Black label.)
GEFFEN (0415 "Watching the Wheels") 3-5 81
(Cream color label. Logo has narrow print.)
GEFFEN (0415 "Watching the Wheels") ..30-40 82
(Cream color label. Logo has bold print.)
GEFFEN (0415 "Watching the Wheels") ..20-30 86
(Black label without bar code symbol.)
GEFFEN (0415 "Watching the Wheels") 5-10 88
(Black label with bar code symbol.)
GEFFEN (29855 "Happy Xmas") 3-5 82
GEFFEN (49604 "Starting Over") 3-5 80
GEFFEN (49644 "Woman") 3-5 80
GEFFEN (49695 "Watching the Wheels") 3-5 81
ORANGE (70078 "Interview") 15-20 81
(Picture disc. John is interviewed by David Peel.)
POLYDOR (817254 "Nobody Told Me") 4-8 84
POLYDOR (821107 "I'm Stepping Out") 4-8 84
POLYDOR (821204 "Borrowed Time") 4-8 84
POLYDOR (883927 "Nobody Told Me"/"I'm Stepping Out") 10-15 90
(Back-to-Back Hits series.)

Promotional Singles

APPLE (1818 "Instant Karma") 150-200 70
(Single-sided.)
APPLE (1868 "Mind Games") 40-50 73
APPLE (1874 "Whatever Gets You Through the Night") 35-45 74
APPLE (1878 "#9 Dream") 40-50 74
APPLE (1878 "What You Got") 75-100 74
(Two separate promo singles have the same selection number [1878]. On commercial issues these tracks were back to back.)
APPLE (1881 "Stand by Me") 40-50 75
APPLE (1883 "Ain't That a Shame") 150-200 75
APPLE (1883 "Slippin' and Slidin' ") 150-200 75
(Two separate promo singles are numbered 1883.)
APPLE (47663/4 "Happy Xmas") 600-750 71
(White label with black print.)
CAPITOL (44230 "Jealous Guy") 10-15 88
CAPITOL (57849 "Imagine") 30-50 92
COTILLION (104/5 "John Lennon On Ronnie Hawkins") 30-35 70
(John Lennon promotes a 1970 Ronnie Hawkins Atlantic/Cotillion release.)
EVA-TONE ("John Lennon Radio Play") 400-600 69
(Soundsheet only. Originally included with a boxed set issue of *Aspen* Magazine. Price for complete set would be double that of just the Lennon disc.)
EVA-TONE (101075 "The Rock Generation") 30-40 76
(Issued with the book *The Rock Generation* Has a brief Lennon interview. Price for book with disc would be double that of just the disc.)
GEFFEN (29855 "Happy Xmas") 10-15 82
GEFFEN (49604 "Starting Over") 15-20 80
GEFFEN (49644 "Woman") 15-20 80
GEFFEN (49695 "Watching the Wheels") 15-20 81
KYA ("KYA 1969 Peace Talk") 150-200 69
(Black vinyl. Radio KYA's Tom Campbell and Bill Holley's telephone interview with John Lennon. All colored vinyl copies are fakes.)
POLYDOR (817254 "Nobody Told Me") ..10-15 84
POLYDOR (821107 "I'm Stepping Out") ..10-15 84
POLYDOR (821204 "Borrowed Time") 10-15 84
QUAKER ("A Tribute to John Lennon") 10-15 86
(Picture disc, five-inch soundsheet, issued with Quaker Granola Dipps. See "Great Moments in Rock N Roll" in Picture Disc Chapter for other titles. No selection number used.)

Picture Sleeves

APPLE (1809 "Give Peace a Chance") 10-15 69
APPLE (1813 "Cold Turkey") 50-75 69
APPLE (1818 "Instant Karma") 10-15 70
APPLE (1827 "Mother") 100-125 70
APPLE (1830 "Power to the People") 20-30 71
APPLE (1842 "Happy Xmas") 10-20 71
APPLE (1848 "Woman Is the Nigger of the World") 15-25 72
APPLE (1868 "Mind Games") 10-15 73
CAPITOL (44230 "Jealous Guy") 3-5 88
GEFFEN (29855 "Happy Xmas") 3-5 82
GEFFEN (49604 "Starting Over") 3-5 80
GEFFEN (49644 "Woman") 3-5 80
GEFFEN (49695 "Watching the Wheels") 3-5 81
POLYDOR (817254 "Nobody Told Me") 4-8 84
POLYDOR (821107 "I'm Stepping Out") 4-8 84
POLYDOR (821204 "Borrowed Time") 4-8 84

LPs: 10/12-inch

ADAM VIII LTD. (8018 "Great Rock & Roll Hits – Roots") 750-1000 75
APPLE (3361 "Wedding Album") 150-175 69
(Price range is for complete boxed set with all inserts.)
APPLE (3361 "Wedding Album") 30-40 69
(Price for cover and disc only.)
APPLE (3362 "Live Peace in Toronto") ... 15-20 69
(No Capitol logo. Has 16-page photo calendar, valued separately at $20 to $40.)
APPLE (3362 "Live Peace in Toronto") 35-45 70
(With Capitol logo. Has 16-page photo calendar, valued separately at $20 to $40.)
APPLE (3372 "John Lennon, Plastic Ono Band") 15-20 70
APPLE (3379 "Imagine") 15-25 71
(Includes bonus poster and photo card.)

APPLE (3392 "Sometime in New York City")....................................... 30-40 72
(Includes an 8 ½" x 11" petition insert)
APPLE (3414 "Mind Games") 10-20 73
APPLE (3416 "Walls & Bridges") 10-20 74
(Includes booklet.)
APPLE (3419 "Rock 'N' Roll") 10-20 75
APPLE (3421 "Shaved Fish")................... 10-20 75
APPLE/TETRAGRAMMATON (5001 "Two Virgins").. 125-150 68
(With brown paper outer sleeve.)
APPLE/TETRAGRAMMATON (5001 "Two Virgins")......................................75-100 68
(Without paper outer sleeve.)
APPLE/TETRAGRAMMATON (5001 "Two Virgins").. 10-15 85
(Reissue, with brown paper outer sleeve that does NOT cover entire jacket.)
CAPITOL (3362 "Live Peace in Toronto") 10-15 82
(Purple label.)
CAPITOL (3362 "Live Peace in Toronto").. 50-60 83
(Black label.)
CAPITOL (3372 "John Lennon, Plastic Ono Band") 10-15 78
(Purple label with "Mfd. By Capitol, etc.")
CAPITOL (3372 "John Lennon, Plastic Ono Band") 15-20 83
(Black label.)
CAPITOL (3372 "John Lennon, Plastic Ono Band") 20-30 88
(Purple label with "Manufactured By Capitol, etc.")
CAPITOL (3379 "Imagine") 8-12 78
(Purple label with "Mfd. By Capitol, etc.")
CAPITOL (3379 "Imagine") 20-30 86
(Black or purple label with "Manufactured by Capitol, etc.")
CAPITOL (3392 "Sometime in New York City")... 25-35 72
(Gatefold cover. Purple label with "Mfd. By Capitol, etc.")
CAPITOL (3392 "Sometime in New York City")... 150-200 72
(Single-pocket cover. Purple label with "Mfd. By Capitol, etc.")
CAPITOL (3414 "Mind Games")............... 35-45 78
CAPITOL (3416 "Walls & Bridges") 10-15 78
(Purple label with "Mfd. by Capitol, etc.")
CAPITOL (3416 "Walls & Bridges") 30-40 78
(Black label.)
CAPITOL (3416 "Walls & Bridges") 10-15 78
(Purple label with "Manufactured by Capitol, etc.")
CAPITOL (3419 "Rock 'N' Roll") 25-35 75
CAPITOL (3421 "Shaved Fish")............... 10-15 78
(Purple label with "Mfd. by Capitol, etc." print. Without Capitol logo on back cover.)
CAPITOL (3421 "Shaved Fish")............... 25-35 78
(Purple label with "Mfd. by Capitol, etc." print. Has Capitol logo on back cover.)
CAPITOL (3421 "Shaved Fish")................ 10-20 83
(Black label. Without Capitol logo on back cover.)
CAPITOL (3421 "Shaved Fish")............... 30-40 83
(Black label. With Capitol logo on back cover.)
CAPITOL (3421 "Shaved Fish")................ 20-30 89
(Purple label with "Manufactured By Capitol, etc.")
CAPITOL (12239 "Live Peace in Toronto") 10-15 82
(Purple label with "Mfd. By Capitol, etc.")
CAPITOL (12239 "Live Peace in Toronto") 40-60 83
(Black label.)
CAPITOL (12451 "Live in New York City").. 10-20 86
CAPITOL (12533 "Menlove Ave.") 10-15 86
CAPITOL (16068 "Mind Games") 10-15 80
CAPITOL (16069 "Rock 'N' Roll") 10-15 80
CAPITOL (21954 "Lennon Legend")........ 30-40 98
(Two discs.)
CAPITOL (91425 "Double Fantasy") 15-25 89
GEFFEN (2001 "Double Fantasy") 10-15 80
(Cream color label. Logo has narrow print.)
GEFFEN (2001 "Double Fantasy") 50-60 80
(Cream color label with bold logo print.)
GEFFEN (2001 "Double Fantasy") 50-60 86
(Black label or purple label.)
GEFFEN (2023 "John Lennon Collection")...................................... 15-25 82
MFSL (153 "Imagine") 40-50 85
(Half-speed mastered.)
NAUTILUS (47 "Double Fantasy")............50-60 82
(Half-speed mastered.)
POLYDOR (817-160 "Milk & Honey").......10-20 84
(Black vinyl.)
POLYDOR (817-160 "Milk & Honey")...100-150 84
(Yellow vinyl.)
POLYDOR (817-160 "Milk & Honey")...150-175 84
(Green vinyl.)
POLYDOR (817-238 "Heart Play [Unfinished Dialogue]")..10-20 83
POLYDOR (Except 817160) 10-20 84
SILHOUETTE (10014 "Reflections and Poetry")..25-35 84
(Numbered edition.)
SILHOUETTE (10014 "Reflections and Poetry")..20-30 84
(Un-numbered edition.)
ZAPPLE (3357 "Life with the Lions") 25-30 69

Promotional LPs

APPLE (3392 "Sometime In New York City") 800-900 72
(White label.)
GEFFEN (2023 "John Lennon Collection") 35-45 82
(Quiex II "Limited Edition Pressing.")
NAUTILUS (47 "Double Fantasy")........300-400 82
(Issued in promotional white cover with blue print. Commercial disc.)
POLYDOR (817 238-1 "Heart Play") 20-30 83
(Has gold promo stamp on cover. Includes program notes and copy of a letter from Yoko on her stationary.)
SILHOUETTE (10014 "Reflections and Poetry")..60-75 84
U.A. (671010 "How I Won the War").....200-250 66
(Promotional issue only with radio spots.)
Also see BEATLES
Also see ELEPHANT'S MEMORY
Also see ELLIOT, Bill, & Elastic Oz Band
Also see HAWKINS, Ronnie
Also see JOHN, Elton / John Lennon
Also see ONO, Yoko
Also see PEEL, David, & Lower East Side / John Lennon & Yoko Ono

LENNON, John / Sean Lennon

Singles: 7-inch

POLYDOR (881378 "Every Man Has a Woman Who Loves Him"/"It's Alright") 4-8 84
POLYDOR (881378 "Every Man Has a Woman Who Loves Him"/"It's Alright") 12-15 84
(Promotional issue only.)

Picture Sleeves

POLYDOR (881378 "Every Man Has a Woman Who Loves Him"/"It's Alright") 5-10 84

LENNON SISTERS P&R '56

(With Lawrence Welk)

Singles: 78 rpm

BRUNSWICK...4-6 57
CORAL...4-6 56

Singles: 7-inch

BRUNSWICK...10-15 57-59
CORAL...10-15 56
DOT...5-10 58-67
MERCURY..4-8 68

EPs: 7-inch

BRUNSWICK..10-15 57

LPs: 10/12-inch

BRUNSWICK..20-30 57
DOT...10-20 59-67
HAMILTON..5-12 64
MERCURY...8-12 68-69
RANWOOD..4-8 68-81
VOCALION...5-10 69-70
WING...5-10 69
Members: Kathy; Peggy; Janet; Dianne.
Also see WELK, Lawrence

LENNY & CHIMES

(Lenny Cocco & the Chimes)

Singles: 7-inch

FREEDOM...5-10
TAG (450 "My Love").................................25-35 62
VEE-JAY (605 "Two Times Two")...............8-12 64

Picture Sleeves

VEE-JAY (605 "Two Times Two")............20-30 64
Also see CHIMES

LENNY & CONTINENTALS

("Featuring Dino & the Aladdins")

Singles: 7-inch

DOMAR (103 "Get Off the Road") 10-20 61
TRIBUTE (119 "Little Joe & LindaLee")....30-40 63
TRIBUTE (125 "Dance the Last Dance")...200-300 63

LENNY & STAR CHIEFS

Singles: 7-inch

MARK (149 "My Queen and Me") 300-400 60
PERFORMANCE (502 "My Queen and Me") 400-500 60

LENNY & THUNDERTONES

Singles: 7-inch

ASTRA (2002 "Homicidal") 25-40 60
COMMA (444 "Thunder Express")............25-35 61
COMMA (445 "On the Loose")..................25-35 61
DOT (16137 "Hot Ice") 10-20 60
DOT (16177 "Street Beat").......................10-20 61
Member: Lenny Drake.
Also see BROWN, Doug
Also see CARPENTER, Chris
Also see PRESTON
Also see THUNDERTONES

LENOIR, J.B. R&B '55

(J.B. Lenore; J.B. Lenor; with His African Hunch Rhythm)

Singles: 78 rpm

CHECKER...15-25 56-57
CHESS (1449 "My Baby Told Me") 25-50 51
CHESS (1463 "Deep in Debt Blues") 25-50 51
J.O.B...25-50 52
PARROT..25-50 54-55

Singles: 7-inch

CHECKER (844 "Let Me Die with the One I Love")...40-60 56
CHECKER (856 "Don't Touch My Head")...40-60 56
CHECKER (874 "Five Years")..................40-60 57
CHECKER (901 "Don't Talk to Your Son") 20-40 58
J.O.B. (1012 "The Mojo") 200-300 52
(Black vinyl.)
J.O.B. (1012 "The Mojo") 400-600 52
(Red vinyl.)
J.O.B. (1016 "I Want My Baby")............200-300 52
J.O.B. (1102 "Play a Little While") 200-300 52
PARROT (802 "Eisenhower Blues")........200-300 54
PARROT (802 "Tax Paying Blues")......200-300 54
(Black vinyl.)
PARROT (802 "Tax Paying Blues")....800-1200 54
(Red vinyl. *Eisenhower Blues* was retitled *Tax Paying Blues* and was issued using the same selection number. They are slightly different recordings.)
PARROT (809 "Mama, Talk to Your Daughter") 150-200 54
(Black vinyl. Maroon label.)
PARROT (809 "Mama, Talk to Your Daughter") 400-600 54
(Red vinyl. Maroon label.)
PARROT (809 "Mama, Talk to Your Daughter") 100-150 55
(Black vinyl. Red label.)
PARROT (814 "Mama, Your Daughter Is Going to Miss Me") 100-150 55
PARROT (821 "Fine Girls")...................150-175 55
SHAD (5012 "Back Door") 15-25 59
USA (744 "I Feel So Good").....................10-15 63
VEE-JAY (352 "Oh Baby") 30-40 60

LPs: 10/12-inch

CHESS (208 "J.B. Lenoir")......................15-25 76
(Two discs.)
CHESS (1410 "Natural Man") 50-75 63
POLYDOR (4011 "J.B. Lenoir")...............10-15 70
Session: Lorenzo Smith; Joe Montgomery; Al Garvin; Sunnyland Slim; Al Wallace; Junior Wells; Jesse Fowler; Ernest Cotton.
Also see SUNNYLAND SLIM
Also see J.B. & HIS BAYOU BOYS
Also see WELLS, Junior

LEO & PROPHETS

Singles: 7-inch

TOTEM (105 "Tilt-A-Whirl")......................20-30 66

LEON, Antoine (Lucky), & Key-Notes

Singles: 7-inch

BELL-O-TONIC (001 "A Sunday School Romance")..15-25 59

LEON, Eddie

Singles: 7-inch

FLIP (348 "Debbie Jill") 10-15 59

LEON, Randey

Singles: 7-inch

CONTE (824 "4th Dimension") 10-20 62

LEON & BURNERS

Singles: 7-inch

JOSIE (945 "Crack Up")...........................10-20 65

LEON & CARLOS

Singles: 7-inch

LIBERTY TONE (108 "Rock Everybody")..250-350 58
ROCKIN' STARS (101 "Rock Everybody") ......?
(Since we do not know the year of this disc, and are not positive it is a legit issue, we cannot yet price it. Suggestions welcome.)
Member: Carlos Jones.

LEON & DREAMERS

Singles: 7-inch

PARKWAY (843 "Haircut")........................10-15 62

LEON & HI-TONES

Singles: 7-inch

ARION (19169 "Rock & Roll in the Groove") 200-300

LEON & JAMES

Singles: 7-inch

THUNDER (1029 "Ella Rea").................75-100

LEONARD, Ben, & Furys

Singles: 7-inch

REO (1002 "Little Girl") 20-40

LEONARD, Bobby, & Explorers

Singles: 7-inch

UNITY (2114 "Project Venus")................ 10-15 62

LEONARD, Chuck

(Chuck Leonard Quartet)

Singles: 7-inch

CAPITOL (4016 "My Love") 10-20 58
CRACKERJACK (4017 "Nobody But You Girl")..5-10 64

LEONARD, Gloria

Singles: 7-inch

HIGH SOCIETY ("Head of the Class").....10-20
(Cardboard disc from *High Society* magazine. No selection number used.)

LEONARD, Harlan, & His Rockets

LPs: 10/12-inch

RCA (531 "Harlan & His Rockets")...........10-20 66

LEONARD, Jay / Janet & Jay

Singles: 7-inch

HANOVER (4549 "I Was Wrong"/"Have Some Popcorn").. 10-15 60

LEONE, Bobby, & Twilights

Singles: 7-inch

BOBBY (200 "My Girl Is an Angel")......... 15-25

LEONETTI, Tommy P&R '55

Singles: 78 rpm

CAPITOL...5-10 54-56

Singles: 7-inch

ATLANTIC...10-15 60
CAPITOL...10-20 54-56
COLUMBIA...4-8 67-73
DECCA...4-8 68-69
EPIC...4-6 74
RCA (Except 7455 thru 8799)....................4-8 75-77
RCA (7455 thru 8799)................................6-12 59-66
20TH FOX..4-6 77
VIK...10-20 57

Picture Sleeves

COLUMBIA (44568 "Let's Take a Walk")..... 4-8 68

LPs: 10/12-inch

CAMDEN (524 "Dream Street")............... 10-20 59
RCA..10-20 64-67

LEOPARDS

(With the Joe René Orchestra)

Singles: 7-inch

LEOPARD (5006 "Valerie")...................100-150 63
(Black vinyl.)
LEOPARD (5006 "Valerie")...................250-300 63
(Brown vinyl.)

LEOPOLD, Glenn
Singles: 7-inch
G.A.R. (108 "Someone New") ... 10-20 67

LEROY & DRIVERS
Singles: 7-inch
CORAL (62515 "L-o-v-e") ... 40-50 67
CORAL (62544 "Don't Ever Leave Me") ... 8-12 67

LES CHANSONETTES
Singles: 7-inch
SHRINE (114 "Deeper") ... 200-300 66

LES COMPAGNONS DE LA CHANSON *P&R '52*
Singles: 78 rpm
COLUMBIA ... 4-8 52
Singles: 7-inch
CAPITOL ... 8-12 59-60
COLUMBIA ... 10-15 52
LPs: 10/12-inch
ANGEL (64000 "Les Compagnons de la Chanson") ... 10-20 54
COLUMBIA (596 "The Three Bells") ... 10-20 55

LES FEMMES
Singles: 7-inch
POWER PAK (100 "Closer") ... 20-30

LES SABRES COMBO
Singles: 7-inch
RCT (1302 "Heaven in My Arms") ... 10-20 '60s

LES SOULES
Singles: 7-inch
KIM (102 "Nobody But You") ... 75-100 63
(500 made.)

LES SULTANS
Singles: 7-inch
TELEDISC ... 5-10 '60s
(Canadian.)
LPs: 10/12-inch
EXPRESS (16003 "Les Sultans") ... 40-60 '60s
TELEDISC ... 50-75 '60s
(Canadian.)
Members: Claude Reid; Denis Forcier; Roger Baudet; Ghislain Dufault; Pierre Belanger; Michael Dufault; Denis Pantis; Bruce Huard.

LESH, Phil, & Ned Lagin
LPs: 10/12-inch
ROUND ... 30-40 75
Also see OLD AND IN THE WAY / Keith & Donna / Robert Hunter / Phil Lesh & Ned Lagin
Also see RHYTHM DEVILS

LESLEY, Alis
Singles: 78 rpm
ERA (1034 "He Will Come Back to Me") . 15-25 57
Singles: 7-inch
ERA (1034 "He Will Come Back to Me") . 15-25 57

LESLIE, C. Vaughn
Singles: 7-inch
MASTERTONE (4014 "Hold It") ... 10-20 67

LESLIE, John
Singles: 7-inch
ABC-PAR (10293 "Fortune Teller") ... 10-15 62
EPIC (9217 "Mountain of Love") ... 15-25 57
LIBERTY (55152 thru 55205) ... 15-25 58-59

LESLIE, Laura
Singles: 7-inch
HANOVER ... 10-15 58-59
PRODUCTION (6364 "Bye, Bye Teach") ... 8-12 63
LPs: 10/12-inch
HANOVER ... 15-25 58

LESLIE, Pat
Singles: 7-inch
CHA CHA (707 "You Played with Love") . 10-20 '60s
GUARANTEED (215 "Fooling Me") ... 5-10 61

LESLIE BROTHERS
(Leslee Brothers)
Singles: 78 rpm
BAN ... 10-20 56
COLUMBIA (40651 "Ready, Rudy Rock & Roll") ... 10-20 56
KING (15222 "Say It Isn't True") ... 10-20 53
Singles: 7-inch
BAN ... 20-40 56
COLUMBIA (40651 "Ready, Rudy Rock & Roll") ... 20-40 56
KING (15222 "Say It Isn't True") ... 20-40 53

LESTER, Bobby
Singles: 7-inch
CHECKER (921 "Am I the Man") ... 15-25 59
COLUMBIA ... 4-8 70
LPs: 10/12-inch
COLUMBIA ... 10-15 70

LESTER, Bobby, & Moonglows
Singles: 7-inch
CHESS (1811 "Blue Velvet") ... 8-12 62
LPs: 10/12-inch
CHESS (1471 "Best of Bobby Lester and the Moonglows") ... 40-60 62
CHESS (1471 "Best of Bobby Lester and the Moonglows") ... 10-20 68
(Cover sticker indicates "Electronically Altered for Stereo.")
Also see MOONGLOWS

LESTER, Bobby, & Moonlighters
Singles: 78 rpm
CHECKER (806 "So All Alone") ... 20-30 54
CHECKER (813 "Hug and a Kiss") ... 8-12 55
Singles: 7-inch
CHECKER (806 "So All Alone") ... 75-125 54
(Checkerboard top label.)
CHECKER (806 "So All Alone") ... 10-20 58
(Vertical logo.)
CHECKER (813 "Hug and a Kiss") ... 20-30 55
Also see LESTER, Bobby

LESTER, Butch
Singles: 7-inch
BES (89 "The Car and the Keys") ... 50-75

LESTER, Carl
(With the Show Stoppers)
Singles: 7-inch
BRENT (7021 "When You See Me Hurt") ... 10-20 61

LESTER, Danny
(With the Margilators)
Singles: 7-inch
BLUE MOON (409 "Wait for Me") ... 40-50 58
CHRISTY (115 "Tomorrow Night") ... 5-10 59

LESTER, George
Singles: 7-inch
PACE (1014 "Cold Dark Night") ... 75-125

LESTER, Jimmie
Singles: 7-inch
CANON (224 "Granny Went Rockin'") . 100-150 59

LESTER, John, & Mello-Queens
Singles: 7-inch
C&M (500 "Getting Nearer") ... 8-12 59
C&M (505 "I Want to Know") ... 10-15 59

LESTER, Ketty *P&R/R&B/LP '62*
Singles: 7-inch
COLLECTABLES ... 3-5 '80s
ERA ... 5-10 62-63
EVEREST (20007 "I Said Goodbye to My Love") ... 4-8 62
PETE ... 4-6 68-69
RCA ... 4-6 64
TOWER ... 4-6 65-66
LPs: 10/12-inch
AVI ... 5-8 80
ERA (EL-108 "Love Letters") ... 25-35 62
(Monaural.)
ERA (ES-108 "Love Letters") ... 30-40 62
(Stereo.)
MEGA ... 5-8 85
PETE ... 10-15 69
RCA ... 10-20 64-65
SHEFFIELD ... 8-10 77
TOWER ... 10-15 66
Also see EVERETT, Betty, & Ketty Lester

LESTER, Larry
Singles: 7-inch
LOMA (2043 "Help Yourself") ... 50-75 66

LESTER, Lonnie, & Chuck Danzy
Singles: 7-inch
NUTONE (1209 "Ain't That a Shame") ... 15-25

LESTER, Robie
(With Sy Miller & His Orchestra)
Singles: 78 rpm
LIBERTY ... 5-10 56
Singles: 7-inch
CHATTAHOOCHEE (680 "Another Show, Another Town") ... 4-8 65
FINER ARTS (1004 "Miracle of Life") ... 5-10 61
LANDA (681 "Miracle of Life") ... 5-10 61
LIBERTY (55033 "With You Where You Are") ... 10-15 56
LIBERTY (55083 "My Love & I") ... 10-15 57
LUTE (5904 "Miracle of Life") ... 10-15 60

LESTER, Sonny
Singles: 7-inch
JARO (77019 "Anchors Aweigh") ... 5-10 60
ROULETTE (4437 thru 4470) ... 10-15 62-63
20TH FOX (304 "Creampuff") ... 10-20 62

LETT, Roy
Singles: 7-inch
SMITTY (4115 "Rosalie") ... 50-75

LETTERMEN
Singles: 7-inch
LIBERTY (55141 "Hey, Big Brain") ... 10-20 58

LETTERMEN *P&R '61*
Singles: 7-inch
ALPHA-OMEGA ... 3-6 78-88
APPLAUSE ... 3-5 83
CAPITOL (2054 thru 4226) ... 5-8 67-76
CAPITOL (4586 thru 5813) ... 5-10 61-67
W.B. (5152 "When") ... 10-20 60
W.B. (5178 "Two Hearts") ... 10-20 60
Picture Sleeves
CAPITOL (3192 "Love") ... 5-10 71
CAPITOL (4586 thru 5649) ... 10-15 61-66
LPs: 10/12-inch
ALPHA-OMEGA ... 5-15 77-88
APPLAUSE ... 5-8 82
CANDELITE ... 5-10 '70s
CAPITOL (138 thru 836 except 577) ... 5-15 68-71
CAPITOL (577 "The Lettermen") ... 15-20 68
(Boxed, three-disc set.)
CAPITOL (1669 thru 2934) ... 10-25 62-68
(With "T" or "ST" prefix.)
CAPITOL (2500 & 2700 series) ... 5-8 '80s
(With "SM" prefix.)
CAPITOL (11000 series) ... 5-10 71-75
CAPITOL (16000 series) ... 4-8 80-83
CAPITOL (90000 series) ... 10-20
LONGINES (220 "Time for Us") ... 20-30
(Boxed, five-disc set.)
LONGINES (220 "From the Lettermen, with Love") ... 5-8 72
(Bonus LP, issued with the above box set.)
PICKWICK (577 "The Lettermen") ... 10-15 70
(Three-disc set.)
PICKWICK (3000 series) ... 5-10 70-77
Members: Tony Butala; James Pike; Gary Pike; Bob Engemann; Donny Pike; Chad Nichols; Don Campo.
Also see BUTALA, Tony
Also see CAMPBELL, Glen / Lettermen / Ella Fitzgerald / Sandler & Young
Also see PETER & GORDON / Lettermen
Also see PIKE, Jim
Also see SONNY & CHER / Bill Medley / Lettermen / Blendells
Also see TONY, BOB & JIMMY

LEVEE SONGSTERS
(Levees)
Singles: 7-inch
KAREN (1004 "Our Love Is a Vow") ... 100-150 59
RELIC (515 "Our Love Is a Vow") ... 5-10 64
Also see MELLOHARPS
Also see TEENTONES

LEVERETT, Chico
(With the Satintones; with Rayber Voices of Detroit)
Singles: 7-inch
BETHLEHEM (3062 "Baby Don't Leave") ... 30-50 63
TAMLA (54024 "I'll Never Love Again") ... 300-500 60
(Same number used on a Swinging Tigers release.)
Also see SATINTONES

LEVETTES
Singles: 7-inch
UNITY (1002 "I'll Try Again") ... 30-50 63

LEVIATHAN
LPs: 10/12-inch
MACH (12501 "Leviathan") ... 20-25 74

LEVINS, Roosevelt
Singles: 7-inch
GG (520 "I'll Tell the World") ... 35-55

LEVINS, Susan
Singles: 7-inch
DEERO ("Saturday Night") ... 100-200 58
(Selection number not known. Reportedly 500 made.)

LEVON & HAWKS
(Featuring Levon Helm)
Singles: 7-inch
ATCO (6383 "Stones I Throw") ... 20-25 65
ATCO (6625 "Go Go Lisa Jane") ... 10-20 68
Also see BAND
Also see HAWKINS, Ronnie

LEWIE & 7 DAYS
Singles: 7-inch
SKIPPER (0774 "Night Train") ... 15-20 69
Member: Larry Lee.

LEWIS, Al, & Modernistics / Lord Luther
Singles: 7-inch
MUSIC CITY (829 "What Will the Outcome Be") ... 300-350 59
Also see LORD LUTHER

LEWIS, Artie
Singles: 7-inch
ATCO (6169 "Hey, Little School Girl") ... 10-15 60
FLING (714 "Alone, All Alone") ... 20-30 59
KENCO (5009 "Alone, All Alone") ... 20-30 60
LOMA (2073 "Ain't No Good") ... 8-12 67

LEWIS, Barbara *P&R/R&B '63*
Singles: 7-inch
ATLANTIC ... 5-10 62-67
COLLECTABLES ... 3-5 88
ENTERPRISE ... 4-8 70-71
KAREN (313 "My Heart Went Do Dat Da") ... 15-25 61
REPRISE ... 4-6 73
LPs: 10/12-inch
ATLANTIC (8086 thru 8173) ... 20-35 63-68
ATLANTIC (8286 "Best of Barbara Lewis") ... 10-15 71
COLLECTABLES ... 6-8 88
ENTERPRISE ... 10-12 70
SOLID SMOKE ... 8-10 '70s
Also see DELLS

LEWIS, Billy
("Billy" Lewis; Billy Lewis Group)
Singles: 7-inch
FIRE (1025 "Heart Trouble") ... 15-20 60
FLO=LOU (101 "I Won't Tell a Soul") ... 50-75 56

LEWIS, Bobby *P&R/R&B '61*
(With Dave Hamilton's Peppers)
Singles: 78 rpm
SPOTLIGHT ... 10-15 56
Singles: 7-inch
ABC-PAR (10565 thru 10592) ... 5-10 64
BELTONE (1002 thru 2035) ... 15-20 61-63
ERIC (141 "Tossin' and Turnin'") ... 4-6 73
LANA ... 4-6 '60s
MERCURY (71245 "Mumbles Blues") ... 10-20 57
PHILIPS (40519 "Soul Seekin'") ... 10-20 68
ROULETTE (4182 "You Better Stop") ... 8-12 59
ROULETTE (4382 "Solid As a Rock") ... 8-12 61
SPOTLIGHT (394 "Mumbles Blues") ... 20-40 56
SPOTLIGHT (397 "Solid As a Rock") ... 30-50 57
LPs: 10/12-inch
BELTONE (4000 "Tossin' and Turnin'") . 50-100 61

LEWIS, Buddy
(Ernest Lewis)
Singles: 78 rpm
SWING TIME (312 "Lonesome Bedroom") ... 30-50 52
Also see LEWIS, Ernest

LEWIS, Clarence, Jr.
Singles: 78 rpm
RED ROBIN ... 15-25 55
Singles: 7-inch
FURY (1032 "Half a Heart") ... 10-20 60
RED ROBIN (136 "Lost Everything") ... 50-75 55

LEWIS, Dana Lee
Singles: 7-inch
COZY (532 "A Lot of Lovin'") ... 50-75

LEWIS, Dave
Singles: 7-inch
A&M ... 8-12 64-69
JERDEN (711 "David's Mood") ... 5-8 66
NORTHGATE (1001 "Barney's Tune") ... 5-8 '60s
PANORAMA (51 "Searchin' ") ... 5-8 67
PANORAMA (1003 "Hi Heel Sneakers") ... 5-8 68
PICCADILLY (230 "Searchin' ") ... 5-10 66
PICCADILLY (235 "Mmm-Mmm-Mmm") ... 5-8 67
(Same number used for a Magic Fern release.)
SEAFAIR (105 "Candido") ... 10-15 62
LPs: 10/12-inch
A&M ... 15-25 64
FIRST AMERICAN ... 15-25 67
JERDEN ... 15-25 66
PANORAMA ... 15-25 65

LEWIS, Diane
Singles: 7-inch
LOVE (101 "Please Let Me Help You") ... 10-20 '60s

LEWIS, Donna
Singles: 7-inch
DECCA (Except 31554) ... 5-10 63
DECCA (31554 "Surfer Boy Blue") ... 10-15 63

LEWIS, Dorse
Singles: 7-inch
COZY ("Hot Rod Boogie") ... 300-400
(Selection number not known.)
COZY (433 "Mexican Twist") ... 200-300

LEWIS, Doug
Singles: 78 rpm
INTRO (6053 "Ice Worm Boogie") ... 15-25 52
Singles: 7-inch
INTRO (6053 "Ice Worm Boogie") ... 30-50 52

LEWIS, Ernest
Singles: 78 rpm
PARROT (791 "No More Lovin' ") ... 50-75 54
Singles: 7-inch
PARROT (791 "No More Lovin' ") ... 100-125 54
Also see COUNTRY SLIM
Also see LEWIS, Buddy
Also see WEST TEXAS SLIM

LEWIS, Furry
LPs: 10/12-inch
ADELPHI ... 10-12 70
AMPEX (10140 "Live at the Gaslight") ... 10-12 71
BIOGRAPH ... 10-12 70
BLUE HORIZON ... 10-12
FANTASY ... 10-12 72
PRESTIGE ... 8-10 70
PRESTIGE BLUESVILLE (1036 "Back on My Feet Again") ... 25-35 61
SOUTHLAND ... 8-10 76
Also see ALABAMA STATE TROUPERS

LEWIS, Gary, & Playboys — P&R '65
Singles: 7-inch
LIBERTY (Except 56144) ... 5-10 64-70
LIBERTY (56144 "I Saw Elvis Presley Last Night") ... 10-15 69
Picture Sleeves
LIBERTY ... 5-10 65-67
EPs: 7-inch
LIBERTY (227 "Doin' the Flake") ... 10-20 65
(Liberty/Kellogg's Premium Record. Issued with paper sleeve.)
LPs: 10/12-inch
GUSTO ... 5-8 72
LIBERTY (Except 10000 series) ... 15-30 65-69
LIBERTY (10000 series) ... 5-8 81
SUNSET ... 10-15 69
U.A. (Except 1000 series) ... 8-10 75
U.A. (1000 series) ... 5-8 81
Members: Gary Lewis; Dave Walker; Dave Costell; Al Ramsey; John West; Tommy Triplehorn.
Session: Leon Russell; Tommy Tedesco.
Also see RUSSELL, Leon
Also see TEDESCO, Tommy

LEWIS, Gene
Singles: 78 rpm
JOSIE (819 "Too Young to Settle Down") ... 25-35 57
Singles: 7-inch
JOSIE (819 "Too Young to Settle Down") ... 25-35 57
R-DELL (103 "Crazy Legs") ... 75-100 58

LEWIS, Grady
(With the Starlighters)
Singles: 7-inch
COLONIAL (7010 "Runaway Lover") ... 50-75 60
NATIONAL (14446 "I've Got a Feeling") ... 75-125
PINNACLE (84 "Oo-Poo-Pee-Doo") ... 50-75
STAR (13334 "Rompin' Stompin' ") ... 800-1200

LEWIS, Happy
(With Mae Questel)
Singles: 78 rpm
JUBILEE (5030 "Happy Boogie") ... 5-10 50
Singles: 7-inch
JUBILEE (5030 "Happy Boogie") ... 10-15 50

LEWIS, Huey, & News — P&R/LP '82
Singles: 12-inch
CHRYSALIS (Except 8V8-42795) ... 4-8 84-89
CHRYSALIS (8V8-42795 "The Heart of Rock and Roll") ... 8-12 84
(Picture disc.)
Singles: 7-inch
CHRYSALIS ... 3-5 80-89
Promotional Singles
CHRYSALIS (2589 "Do You Believe in Love") ... 8-12 80
(Colored vinyl. With Valentine card. Promotional issue only.)
CHRYSALIS (43065 "Hip to Be Square") ... 10-15 85
(Four-disc set, each of a different color vinyl.)
Picture Sleeves
CHRYSALIS ... 3-5 82-89
LPs: 10/12-inch
CHRYSALIS ... 5-8 80-89
MFSL ... 20-30 85
Members: Huey Lewis; Mario Cipollina; Sean Hopper; Chris Hayes; Bill Gibson; Johnny Colla.
Also see EDMUNDS, Dave

LEWIS, Hugh
Singles: 7-inch
FERN (802 "Two of a Kind") ... 10-20 61
FERN (803 "Rockin' Moon Men") ... 50-75 61
FERN (805 "Bingo") ... 10-20 61

LEWIS, James
Singles: 7-inch
ARROW (730 "I Cried Last Night") ... 15-25 58

LEWIS, Jerry — P&R/LP '56
Singles: 78 rpm
CAPITOL ... 4-8 50-53
DECCA ... 4-8 56-57
Singles: 7-inch
CAPITOL ... 10-20 50-53
DECCA ... 8-15 56-62
DOT ... 8-10 60
LIBERTY (55633 "Kids") ... 5-8 63
EPs: 7-inch
CAPITOL ... 10-15 56
DECCA ... 10-15 56
LPs: 10/12-inch
CAPITOL ... 10-15 64
DECCA ... 20-30 56
DOT ... 10-20 60
VOCALION ... 8-12 66
Also see MARTIN, Dean, & Jerry Lewis

LEWIS, Jerry Lee — P&R/C&W/R&B '57
(With "His Pumping Piano")
Singles: 78 rpm
SUN ... 50-100 56-58
Singles: 7-inch
AMERICA SMASH ... 3-5 86
BUDDAH ... 4-6 71
ELEKTRA ... 3-6 79-82
MCA ... 3-5 82-83
MERCURY ... 4-8 70-82
ORIGINAL SOUND (4538 "Great Balls of Fire"/"Breathless") ... 3-5 '80s
POLYDOR ... 3-5 89
SCR (386 "Get Out Your Big Roll, Daddy") ... 3-5 85
(Colored vinyl.)
SSS/SUN (1100 series) ... 4-8 69-78
SMASH (1857 "Pen & Paper") ... 10-15 63
SMASH (1886 "I'm On Fire") ... 25-35 64
SMASH (1906 "She Was My Baby") ... 8-12 64
SMASH (1930 "You Went Back on Your Word") ... 8-12 64
SMASH (1969 "I Believe in You") ... 10-20 65
SMASH (1992 thru 2053) ... 8-12 65-66
SMASH (2103 thru 2257) ... 4-8 67-70
SUN (169/213 "Whole Lotta Shakin' Going On"/"Great Balls of Fire") ... 5-10 94
(Gold vinyl. Promotional issue only.)
SUN (259 "Crazy Arms") ... 30-40 56
SUN (267 "Whole Lot of Shakin' Going On") ... 20-30 57
SUN (281 "Great Balls of Fire") ... 20-30 57
SUN (288 "Breathless") ... 20-30 58
SUN (296 "High School Confidential") ... 20-30 58
SUN (303 "Break-Up") ... 20-30 58
SUN (312 "I'll Sail My Ship Alone") ... 20-30 59
SUN (317 "Lovin' Up a Storm") ... 20-30 59
SUN (324 "Let's Talk About Us") ... 20-30 59
SUN (330 "Little Queenie") ... 20-30 59
SUN (337 thru 367) ... 15-25 60-61
SUN (371 thru 396) ... 10-20 62-65
Picture Sleeves
POLYDOR ... 3-6 89
SUN (267 "Whole Lot of Shakin' Going On") ... 5-10 '90s
SUN (281 "Great Balls of Fire") ... 35-50 57
SUN (296 "High School Confidential") ... 35-50 57
EPs: 7-inch
MERCURY (6 "Special Radio Cuts from *Would You Take Another Chance on Me*") ... 15-25 71
(Promotional issues only.)
MERCURY (14 "Special Radio Cuts from *The Killer Rocks On*") ... 15-25 72
(Promotional issues only.)
SCR ... 10-15 86
SSS/SUN (108 "Golden Cream of the Country") ... 15-25 69
(Juke box issue only.)
SSS/SUN (114 "A Taste of Country") ... 15-25 69
(Juke box issue only.)
SMASH (2 "Jerry Lee Lewis") ... 20-25 64
SMASH (28 "Open-End Interview") ... 30-40 64
(Promotional issue only.)
SUN (107 "Whole Lotta Shakin' Going On ") ... 75-125 57
(Issued with a paper sleeve.)
SUN (108 "Jerry Lee Lewis") ... 75-125 57
(Blue cover. First track listed is *Don't Be Cruel.*)
SUN (109 "Jerry Lee Lewis") ... 50-100 58
(Yellow cover. First track listed is *Ubangi Stomp.*)
SUN (110 "Jerry Lee Lewis") ... 50-100 58
(Red cover. First track listed is *High School Confidential.*)
LPs: 10/12-inch
ACCORD (7903 "Doin' Just Fine") ... 5-8 82
AURA (1021 "Louisiana Fireball") ... 5-8 82
BUCKBOARD (1025 "The 'Killer' Rocks On") ... 8-10 75
ELEKTRA (184 "Jerry Lee Lewis") ... 10-15 79
ELEKTRA (254 "When Two Worlds Collide") ... 10-15 80
ELEKTRA (291 "Killer Country") ... 10-15 81
ELEKTRA (60191 "Best of Featuring *39 and Holding*") ... 8-12 82
EVEREST (298 "Jerry Lee Lewis") ... 8-12 75
HILLTOP (6110 "Roll Over Beethoven") ... 10-12 72
HILLTOP (6120 "Rural Route #1") ... 10-12 72
KOALA (14109 "Great Balls of Fire") ... 5-10 81
KOALA (14120 "A Whole Lot of Shakin' ") ... 5-10 81
MCA (5387 "My Fingers Do the Talkin' ") ... 5-10 82
MCA (5478 "I Am What I Am") ... 5-10 84
MERCURY (3 "Southern Roots") ... 20-35 73
MERCURY (637 "The 'Killer' Rocks On") ... 10-15 72
MERCURY (677 "Sometimes a Memory Ain't Enough") ... 10-15 73
MERCURY (690 "Jerry Lee Lewis Radio Special") ... 40-50 73
(Promotional issue only.)
MERCURY (710 "I-40 Country") ... 10-15 74
MERCURY (803 "Session") ... 15-20 73
(Two discs.)
MERCURY (1030 "Boogie Woogie Country Man") ... 10-15 75
MERCURY (1064 "Odd Man In") ... 10-15 76
MERCURY (1109 "Country Class") ... 10-15 76
MERCURY (5004 "Country Memories") ... 10-15 77
MERCURY (5006 "Best of Jerry Lee Lewis, Vol. 2") ... 10-15 78
MERCURY (5010 "Jerry Lee Lewis Keeps Rockin' ") ... 10-15 78
MERCURY (61318 "In Loving Memories") ... 30-40 71
MERCURY (61323 "There Must Be More to Love Than This") ... 8-12 71
MERCURY (61343 "Touching Home") ... 15-20 71
(Cover is mostly an artist's drawing with a small photo of Lewis on the right side.)
MERCURY (61343 "Touching Home") ... 12-15 71
(Cover pictures Lewis standing in front of a brick wall.)
MERCURY (61346 "Would You Take Another Chance on Me") ... 8-12 71
MERCURY (61366 "Who's Gonna Play This Old Piano") ... 8-12 72
OUT OF TOWN DIST (8018 "Country Gold") ... 5-10 82
PICKWICK (1002 "Breathless") ... 10-12 74
(Two discs.)
PICKWICK (2055 "Breathless") ... 10-12 '70s
(Two discs. Completely different tracks than 1002.)
PICKWICK (3224 "High Heel Sneakers") .. 8-10 70
PICKWICK (3344 "Drinkin' Wine Spo-Dee-O-Dee") ... 8-10 73
POLYDOR (839516 "Great Ball of Fire") ... 5-8 89
(Includes tracks by other artists.)
POLYSTAR (102 "Best from Jerry Lee Lewis") ... 8-12
(Two discs.)
POWER PAK (247 "From the Vaults of Sun") ... 8-10 74
RHINO (255 "Original Sun Greatest Hits") ... 10-15 83
(Picture disc.)
SCR ... 5-10 85
SSS/SUN ... 5-15 69-84
SEARS (610 "Hound Dog") ... 10-15
SMASH (7001 "Golden Rock Hits") ... 5-8 82
SMASH (27040 "Golden Hits of Jerry Lee Lewis") ... 20-30 64
(Monaural.)
SMASH (27056 "Greatest Live Show on Earth") ... 15-20 64
(Monaural.)
SMASH (27063 "Return of Rock") ... 20-25 65
(Monaural.)
SMASH (27071 "Country Songs for City Folks") ... 15-20 65
(Monaural.)
SMASH (27079 "Memphis Beat") ... 20-25 65
(Monaural.)
SMASH (27086 "By Request") ... 15-20 66
(Monaural.)
SMASH (27097 "Soul My Way") ... 20-25 67
(Monaural.)
SMASH (67040 "Golden Hits of Jerry Lee Lewis") ... 25-35 64
(Stereo.)
SMASH (67040 "Golden Rock Hits of Jerry Lee Lewis") ... 20-30 '60s
(Reissue.)
SMASH (67056 "Greatest Live Show on Earth") ... 20-25 64
(Stereo.)
SMASH (67063 "Return of Rock") ... 25-30 65
(Stereo.)
SMASH (67071 "Country Songs for City Folks") ... 20-25 65
(Stereo.)
SMASH (67071 "All Country") ... 10-15 69
(Stereo. Reissue.)
SMASH (67079 "Memphis Beat") ... 25-30 65
(Stereo.)
SMASH (67086 "By Request") ... 20-25 66
(Stereo.)
SMASH (67097 "Soul My Way") ... 25-30 67
(Stereo.)
SMASH (67104 thru 67131) ... 8-15 68-70
SUN (1230 "Jerry Lee Lewis") ... 75-125 58
SUN (1265 "Jerry Lee's Greatest") ... 75-125 62
SUNNYVALE (9330-905 "Sun Story, Vol. 5") ... 8-10 77
TRIP (8501 "Best Of") ... 8-12 74
(Two discs.)
WING (125 "The Legend of Jerry Lee Lewis") ... 20-30 69
WING (12340 "In Demand") ... 15-20 66
(Monaural.)
WING (12406 "Unlimited") ... 15-20 67
(Monaural.)
WING (16340 "In Demand") ... 15-20 66
(Stereo.)
WING (16406 "Unlimited") ... 15-20 67
(Stereo.)
Also see CLANTON, Jimmy / Frankie Ford / Jerry Lee Lewis / Patsy Cline

Also see GEORGE & LOUIS
Also see HAWK
Also see KING, Ben E.
Also see McDOWELL, Ronnie, & Jerry Lee Lewis
Also see MEYERS, Augie
Also see NELSON, Willie / Jerry Lee Lewis / Carl Perkins / David Allan Coe
Also see TENNESSEE TWO & FRIEND

LEWIS, Jerry Lee / Curly Bridges / Frank Motley

LPs: 10/12-inch

DESIGN (165 "Rockin' ") 10-15 63

LEWIS, Jerry Lee / Johnny Cash

LPs: 10/12-inch

SSS/SUN (119 "Sunday Down South") 8-10 70
SSS/SUN (125 "Sing Hank Williams") 8-10 71
Also see CASH, Johnny
Also see CASH, Johnny / Jerry Lee Lewis / Jeanie C. Riley
Also see PERKINS, Carl, Jerry Lee Lewis, Roy Orbison & Johnny Cash

LEWIS, Jerry Lee, & Friends *C&W '79*

Singles: 7-inch

SSS/SUN (1139 "Save the Last Dance for Me") 4-6 78
(Gold vinyl. Credits only Jerry Lee Lewis.)
SSS/SUN (1141 "Cold, Cold Heart") 4-6 79

LPs: 10/12-inch

SSS/SUN (1011 "Duets") 8-12 78
(Colored vinyl.)
SSS/SUN (1011 "Duets") 8-12 78
(Black vinyl, even though cover indicates "Special Gold Vinyl." RCA Record Club issue.)
Members: Jerry Lee Lewis; Jimmy Ellis; Charlie Rich.
Also see ORION
Also see RICH, Charlie

LEWIS, Jerry Lee & Linda Gail *C&W '69*

Singles: 7-inch

SMASH (2220 "Don't Let Me Cross Over") ..4-8 69
SMASH (2254 "Roll Over Beethoven") 4-8 69
SUN (384 "Seasons of My Heart"/"Teenage Letter") 10-20 63
(Linda Gail is on A-side only.)

Picture Sleeves

SMASH (2220 "Don't Let Me Cross Over") 10-15 69

LPs: 10/12-inch

SMASH (67126 "Together") 15-25 69

LEWIS, Jerry Lee / Roger Miller / Roy Orbison

LPs: 10/12-inch

PICKWICK (3027 "Jerry Lee Lewis, Roger Miller & Roy Orbison") ....8-12 '60s
Also see MILLER, Roger
Also see ORBISON, Roy

LEWIS, Jerry Lee, Carl Perkins & Charlie Rich

LPs: 10/12-inch

SSS/SUN (1018 "Trio +") 8-10 78
(With Jimmy Ellis.)
Also see ELLIS, Jimmy
Also see LEWIS, Jerry Lee, & Friends
Also see PERKINS, Carl

LEWIS, Jerry Lee / Charlie Rich / Johnny Cash

LPs: 10/12-inch

POWER PAK (248 "Greatest Hits, Vol. 1 ...8-10 '80s
POWER PAK (249 "Greatest Hits, Vol. 2 ...8-10 '80s
Also see CASH, Johnny, Carl Perkins & Jerry Lee Lewis
Also see LEWIS, Jerry Lee

LEWIS, Jimmie

Singles: 7-inch

CYCLONE (123 "Teenage Sister") 5-10 62
LUCK (104 "Wishing Star") 10-15 60

LEWIS, Jimmy
(With the Jimmy Lewis Band)

Singles: 78 rpm

ATLANTIC 20-30 51
CAT (103 "Last Night") 10-20 54
RCA (4899 "Cherry Wine") 10-20 52

Singles: 7-inch

ACCENT (1059 "Go Go Go") 50-75 58
ATLANTIC (943 "Let's Get Together and Make Some Love") 50-100 51
CAT (103 "Last Night") 25-35 54
ERA 5-10 65-66
4J (503 "Wait Until Spring") 10-15 63
4J (508 "Feelin' in Mah Bones") 10-15 63
4J (512 "Don't Let 'Em") 10-15 64
MENT (02 "I Love You") ....100-150 '60s
MENT (1010 "I've Tried to Please You") ....50-100 '60s
MINIT 5-10 67-68
RCA (4899 "Cherry Wine") 35-50 52
TANGERINE (Except 1000) 4-8 68-69
TANGERINE (1000 "I Quit You Win") 20-30 69
Also see CHARLES, Ray, & Jimmy Lewis

LEWIS, Jimmy, & Volumes

Singles: 7-inch

IVY (104 "I Saw a Cottage in My Dreams") 30-40 57

LEWIS, Joe "Cannonball"

Singles: 78 rpm

KENTUCKY (574 "You Been Honky Tonkin' ") 20-30 53
MGM (11838 "Railroad Engineer") 5-10 54

Singles: 7-inch

KENTUCKY (574 "You Been Honky Tonkin' ") 40-60 53
MGM (11838 "Railroad Engineer") 10-20 54

LEWIS, Joe "Cannonball" / Eddie Moore

EPs: 7-inch

QUEEN CITY (43 "Big 4 Hits") ....20-30 '50s
Also see LEWIS, Joe "Cannonball"

LEWIS, Johnny
(Joe Hill Louis)

Singles: 78 rpm

ROCKIN' (517 "She's Taking All My Money") 100-150 53
Also see LOUIS, Joe Hill

LEWIS, Keni

Singles: 7-inch

BUDDAH (191 "Drug Traffic") 50-100 69
DE-VEL (6753 "Ain't Gonna Make It Easy") 10-20 73

LEWIS, Lavenia
(Levenia Lewis; Luvenia Lewis)

Singles: 7-inch

COTILLION (44048 "Find a Man That Satisfies") 5-10 69
GOLDEN EAGLE (108 "So Many Times") .5-10 64
VELERIE (227 "So Many Times") 10-20 64
WETSOUL 4-6

LEWIS, Lennie, & Orchestra *R&B '46*

Singles: 78 rpm

QUEEN (4133 "Blue Flame") 10-15 46

LEWIS, Little Junior

Singles: 7-inch

FURY (1039 "Come on Back Where You Belong") 10-15 60
FURY (1040 "Your Heart Must Be Made of Stone") 10-15 60

LEWIS, Louise

Singles: 7-inch

SKYWAY (137 "I Made a Mistake") 10-20 59
Also see HALL, René

LEWIS, Lovey

Singles: 78 rpm

DUKE (126 "Alright, Baby") 10-15 53

Singles: 7-inch

DUKE (126 "Alright, Baby") 15-25 53

LEWIS, Monica *P&R '47*
(With the Ray Bloch Orchestra)

Singles: 78 rpm

SIGNATURE (15078 "Midnight Masquerade") 10-20 47
Also see BLOCH, Ray, & Orchestra

LEWIS, Monica, & Ames Bros. *P&R '48*
(With the Mary Osborne Trio)

Singles: 78 rpm

DECCA (24411 "A Tree in the Meadow") ...5-10 48
Also see AMES BROTHERS
Also see LEWIS, Monica

LEWIS, Neil, Quintet

Singles: 78 rpm

GEE 10-15 54

Singles: 7-inch

GEE (2 "Long Gone") 15-20 54
GEE (3 "Harlem Nocturne") 15-20 54

LEWIS, Pat

Singles: 7-inch

GOLDEN WORLD (42 "Can't Shake It Loose") 10-20 66
SOLID HIT (101 "Look What I Almost Missed") 15-25 66
SOLID HIT (105 "Warning") 15-25 66
SOLID HIT (109 "No One to Love") 200-300 67

LEWIS, Paul, & Swans
(Paul Lewis "The Mighty Swamba" & Swans)

Singles: 78 rpm

FORTUNE 100-200 55

Singles: 7-inch

FORTUNE (813 "Wedding Bells, Oh Wedding Bells") 750-1200 55
(Purple label.)
Also see SWANS

LEWIS, Pete "Guitar"
(Carl Lewis)

Singles: 78 rpm

FEDERAL 25-50 52
PEACOCK 25-50 53

Singles: 7-inch

FEDERAL (12066 "Louisiana Hop") 50-100 52
FEDERAL (12076 "Harmonica Boogie") 50-100 52
FEDERAL (12103 "Ooh, Midnight") 50-100 52
FEDERAL (12112 "The Blast") 50-100 52
PEACOCK (1624 "Goin' Crazy") 50-100 53

LEWIS, Ramsey *LP '62*
(Ramsey Lewis Trio; Ramsey Lewis & Co.)

Singles: 12-inch

COLUMBIA 4-6 79-85

Singles: 7-inch

ABC 4-6 74
ARGO 5-15 58-65
ARGO (108-S "Scarlet Ribbons") ....15-25 '60s
(Stereo 33 Single.)
ARGO (110-S "These Foolish Things") ....15-25 '60s
(Stereo 33 Single.)
CADET 4-8 66-73
CHESS 4-6 73
COLUMBIA 3-8 72-87
EMARCY (5336 "I Love Paris") 10-15 59

EPs: 7-inch

ARGO (687 "Sound of Christmas") 15-25 61

LPs: 10/12-inch

ARGO (611 "Gentleman of Swing") 40-60 58
ARGO (627 "Gentleman of Jazz") 40-60 58
ARGO (642 "Ramsey Lewis Trio with Len Winchester") 40-60 59
ARGO (645 "An Hour with the Ramsey Lewis Trio") 30-50 59
ARGO (665 "Stretching Out") 30-50 60
ARGO (671 "In Chicago") 30-50 60
ARGO (680 "From the Soil") 30-50 61
ARGO (687 "Sound of Christmas") 30-50 61
ARGO (693 "Sound of Spring") 25-35 62
ARGO (700 series) 20-40 62-65
CADET 10-20 65-72
COLUMBIA 6-12 72-85
EMARCY (36150 "Down to Earth") 25-45 59
(Monaural.)
EMARCY (80029 "Down to Earth") 35-60 59
(Stereo.)
TRIP 5-8 75
Members: Ramsey Lewis; Eldee Young; Red Holt; Cleveland Eaton; Maurice White.
Also see DUSHON, Jean, & Ramsey Lewis Trio
Also see EARTH, WIND & FIRE & RAMSEY LEWIS
Also see YOUNG HOLT UNLIMITED

LEWIS, Ramsey, & Nancy Wilson *LP '84*

LPs: 10/12-inch

COLUMBIA (39326 "The Two of Us") 5-10 84
Also see LEWIS, Ramsey
Also see WILSON, Nancy

LEWIS, Richard

Singles: 78 rpm

ALADDIN 10-15 54

Singles: 7-inch

ALADDIN (3238 "Hey Little Girl") 20-30 54
ALADDIN (3261 "Sweet Dream") 20-30 54

LEWIS, Richard, & Dolores Gibson

Singles: 78 rpm

ALADDIN 10-15 54

Singles: 7-inch

ALADDIN (3239 "Let's Love Tonight") 20-30 54
ALADDIN (3255 "Hey Little Girl") 20-30 54
Also see LEWIS, Richard

LEWIS, Ricky

Singles: 7-inch

CINDY (100 "Stop, Think and Listen") 15-25
FURY (5051 "Cupid") 10-20 63
MERCURY (72640 "Dance All Night") 15-25 66

LEWIS, Robert Q.

Singles: 78 rpm

CORAL (61292 "Hard Hearted Hannah")...5-10 54

Singles: 7-inch

CORAL (61292 "Hard Hearted Hannah"). 10-15 54

LEWIS, Roy

LPs: 10/12-inch

MONTGOMERY WARD (005 "A Tribute to Hank Williams") ....10-20 '60s

LEWIS, Rudy, & Sputniks

Singles: 7-inch

ART (157 "Beer, Beer and More Beer") ... 15-25 60
(First issue.)
RCA (7792 "Beer, Beer and More Beer")...8-12 60

LEWIS, Sabby
(With the Vibra-Tones; with Uniques)

Singles: 78 rpm

ABC-PAR 10-20 56

Singles: 7-inch

ABC-PAR (9685 "Ding-A-Ling") 15-25 56
ABC-PAR (9697 "Forgive Me My Love")..40-50 56
GONE (5074 "Sabby") 15-25 59
Also see UNIQUES

LEWIS, Sammy
(With the Willie Johnson Combo)

Singles: 78 rpm

SUN (218 "I Feel So Worried") 50-75 55
UNITED (202 "I'm Heaven Bound") 5-10 56

Singles: 7-inch

8TH STREET 5-8
ST. LAWRENCE (704 "Hold On") 15-25
SUN (218 "I Feel So Worried") 100-150 55
UNITED (202 "I'm Heaven Bound") 10-20 56
(With the Lucy Smith Singers.)

LEWIS, Sidney Jo

Singles: 7-inch

ISLAND (6 "Boppin' to Grandfather's Clock") 100-200 58

LEWIS, Smiley *R&B '52*

Singles: 78 rpm

COLONY (106 "Sad Life") 50-75 52
COLONY (110 "Where Were You") 50-75 52
DELUXE (3099 "Turn Your Volume On, Baby") 50-75 47
IMPERIAL (5067 "Tee-Nah-Nah") 30-50 50
IMPERIAL (5072 "Slide Me Down") 60-80 50
IMPERIAL (5102 thru 5478) 20-40 50-57
QUALITY 25-50 56
(Canadian.)

Singles: 7-inch

DOT (16674 "I Wonder") 8-12 64
IMPERIAL (5124 "My Baby Was Right") 75-125 52
IMPERIAL (5194 "The Bells Are Ringing") 50-100 52
IMPERIAL (5208 "Gumbo Blues") 50-100 52
IMPERIAL (5224 "Gypsy Blues") 50-100 54
IMPERIAL (5234 "Play Girl") 50-100 53
(Black vinyl.)
IMPERIAL (5234 "Play Girl") 150-200 53
(Colored vinyl.)
IMPERIAL (5241 "Caldonia's Party") 200-300 53
IMPERIAL (5252 "Little Fernandez") 50-100 53
IMPERIAL (5268 "Down the Road") 50-100 54
IMPERIAL (5279 "I Love You for Sentimental Reasons") 100-150 54
IMPERIAL (5296 "Can't Stop Loving You") 50-100 54
IMPERIAL (5316 "Too Many Drivers") ...50-100 54
IMPERIAL (5325 "Jailbird") 50-100 54
IMPERIAL (5349 "Real Gone Lover") 50-100 55
IMPERIAL (5356 "I Hear You Knocking") 60-80 55
IMPERIAL (5372 "Queen of Hearts") 50-75 55

IMPERIAL (5380 "One Night") 50-75 56
IMPERIAL (5389 "She's Got Me Hook, Line and Sinker") 50-75 56
IMPERIAL (5404 "Down Yonder We Go Ballin'") 50-75 56
IMPERIAL (5418 "Shame, Shame, Shame") 50-75 56
IMPERIAL (5431 "You Are My Sunshine") 30-50 57
IMPERIAL (5450 "Go On Fool") 30-50 57
IMPERIAL (5478 "Bad Luck Blues") 30-50 57
IMPERIAL (5531 "My Love Is Gone") 30-50 58
IMPERIAL (5662 "Oh Red") 15-25 60
IMPERIAL (5676 "Last Night") 15-25 60
IMPERIAL (5719 "Stormy Monday") 15-25 61
IMPERIAL (5820 "Tee-Nah-Nah") 15-25 62
KNIGHT (2007 "Baby, Please") 15-25 59
KNIGHT (2011 "Lost Weekend") 15-25 59
LOMA (2024 "Bells Are Ringing") 8-10 65
OKEH (7146 "Tore Up") 10-15 62
QUALITY (1497 "She's Got Me Hook, Line and Sinker") 75-100 56
(Canadian.)

LPs: 10/12-inch

IMPERIAL (9141 "I Hear You Knocking") 250-300 61
Also see BARTHOLOMEW, Dave
Also see THOMAS, B.J., / Smiley Lewis

LEWIS, Tamala

Singles: 7-inch

MARTON (1002 "You Won't Say Nothing") 300-400

LEWIS, Ted

LPs: 10/12-inch

RKO (143 "Me and My Shadow") 10-20 59
RKO (144 "A Million Memories") 10-20 59

LEWIS, Texas Jim, & His Lone Star Cowboys C&W '44

Singles: 78 rpm

DECCA (6099 "Too Late to Worry, Too Blue to Cry") 10-20 44
VOCALION 5-10 37

LEWIS, Thelma

Singles: 7-inch

MAGIC CITY (005 "Why Weren't You There") 15-25

LEWIS, Tiny

Singles: 7-inch

LINDA (100 "Too Much Rockin' ") 75-125 59
TAP (502 "Too Much Rockin' ") 50-75 61

LEWIS, Wally

Singles: 78 rpm

DOT (15705 "Kathleen") 25-50 58

Singles: 7-inch

DOT (15705 "Kathleen") 15-25 58
DOT (15763 "White Bobby Sox") 15-25 58
LIBERTY (55178 thru 55370) 10-15 59-61
SIMS (139 "Kathleen") 5-10 63
TALLY (117 "Kathleen") 25-50 58
(First issue.)

LEWIS, Wink

Singles: 78 rpm

ABBOTT (119 "That's Me When I'm with You") 5-10 53
TONE (1121 "ZZZTT ZZZTT") 20-30 56

Singles: 7-inch

ABBOTT (119 "That's Me When I'm with You") 10-20 53
TONE (1121 "ZZZTT ZZZTT") 100-200 56

LEWIS & CLARKE P&R '67
(Lewis & Clarke Expedition)

Singles: 7-inch

CHARTMAKER (402 "For Your Freedom Tonight") 5-10 66
COLGEMS (1006 "I Feel Good") 5-10 67
COLGEMS (1011 "Destination Unknown") .8-12 67
COLGEMS (1022 "Why Need They Pretend") 8-12 68
COLGEMS (1028 "Daddy's Plastic Child") .8-12 68

Picture Sleeves

COLGEMS (1006 "I Feel Good") 8-12 67

LPs: 10/12-inch

COLGEMS (105 "Lewis & Clarke Expedition") 20-35 67
Members: Travis Lewis; Boomer Clarke (Castleman); John London. Session: Jim Pewter; Michael Murphey.
Also see MIKE, JOHN & BILL
Also see PEWTER, Jim

LEWIS CONNECTION

LP: 10/12-inch

("The Lewis Connection") 300-400 79
(No label name nor selection number used. Prince plays guitar and sings backup on *Got to Be Something Here.*)
Member: Sonny Thompson. Session: Prince.
Also see PRINCE

LEWIS FAMILY

Singles: 7-inch

HOLLYWOOD (1074 "Carry On") 10-15 57
HOLLYWOOD (1083 "You've Got a Chance") 10-15 58

LEWIS SISTERS
("The Singing School Teachers")

Singles: 7-inch

V.I.P. (25018 "He's an Oddball") 15-25 65
V.I.P. (25024 "You Need Me") 15-25 65
Members: Kay Lewis; Helen Lewis.
Also see CLARK, Chris

LEXINGTON PROJECT

Singles: 7-inch

SONIC (4626 "She Looks Much Older") ... 10-20 67

LEXINGTONS

Singles: 7-inch

EVEREST (19369 "I Found My Baby") 10-15 60

LEXINGTONS

Singles: 7-inch

INTERNATIONAL (500 "My Honey Loves Another Girl") 20-30 63

LEXONS

Singles: 7-inch

LEXINGTON (100 "Angels Like You") 50-75 58

LIBERACE P&R '52

Singles: 78 rpm

ADVANCE 5-8 55
COLUMBIA 3-6 52-57
DECCA 3-6 52
LIBERACE (25 "Lullaby") 10-15
(7-inch disc. Made for Ortmeyer Furniture Co.)

Singles: 7-inch

A.V.I. 4-6 76-77
COLUMBIA (39000 thru 41000 series) 5-15 52-58
COLUMBIA (48000 series) 3-6
CORAL 4-6 59-61
DECCA (28000 series) 10-15 52
DOT 4-8 64-67
MGM 4-6 73
W.B. 4-6 71

Picture Sleeves

COLUMBIA 10-20 54

EPs: 7-inch

COLUMBIA 5-15 52-56
DECCA 10-20 52

LPs: 10/12-inch

ABC 5-8 74
ADVANCE (7 "The Priceless Piano of Liberace") 75-100 51
(10-inch LP.)
A.V.I. (Except 6065) 5-8 73-79
A.V.I. (6065 "Liberace") 10-20 79
(Picture disc.)
BROOKVILLE 8-15
COLUMBIA (589 "Christmas") 35-45 54
COLUMBIA (600 "At the Hollywood Bowl") 35-45 55
COLUMBIA (645 "Hollywood Bowl Encore") 35-45 55
COLUMBIA (661 "By Candlelight") 35-45 55
COLUMBIA (800 "Sincerely Yours") 35-45 56
COLUMBIA (896 "At Home") 30-40 56
COLUMBIA (1000 thru 1200 series) 20-30 57-58
COLUMBIA (4000 series) 35-45 53
COLUMBIA (2516 "Piano Reverie") 50-75 56
(10-inch LP.)
COLUMBIA (2592 "Kiddin' on the Keys") .50-75 56
(10-inch LP.)
COLUMBIA (6217 "At the Piano") 50-100 52
(10-inch LP.)
COLUMBIA (6239 "Evening with Liberace") 50-100 53
(10-inch LP.)
COLUMBIA (6269 "Concertos for You") 50-100 53
(10-inch LP.)
COLUMBIA (6283 "Dream of Olwen") 50-100 54
(10-inch LP.)
COLUMBIA (6327 "Liberace Plays Chopin' ") 50-100 54
(10-inch LP.)
COLUMBIA (9800 series) 5-10 69
CORAL 8-15 59-64
DECCA 5-10 72
DOT 8-15 63-68
FAMOUS TWINSET (1032 "Liberace in Concert") 5-10
FORWARD 5-10 69
HARMONY 8-15 59-70
HAMILTON 5-10 65
MISTLETOE 5-8 74
PARAMOUNT 5-10 73-74
TRIP 4-8 76
VOCALION 5-10 68
W.B. 5-10 71
Also see PRESLEY, Elvis

LIBERACE, George
(George Liberace Orchestra)

LPs: 10/12-inch

COLUMBIA 15-30 54-55
IMPERIAL (9039 "George Liberace Goes Teenage") 30-45 57

LIBERMAN, Jeff

LPs: 10/12-inch

LIBRAH (1545 "Jeff Liberman") 15-25 75
LIBRAH (6969 "Solitude Within") 15-25 75
LIBRAH (12157 "Synergy") 10-20 78

LIBERTO, Ray

Singles: 7-inch

DOT (15848 "Wicked, Wicked Woman") .. 20-30 58
TNT (156 "Wicked, Wicked Woman") 50-75 58
(First issue.)
TNT (172 "I Want You to Love Me Tonight") 50-75 59

LIBERTY BELL

Singles: 7-inch

BACK BEAT (595 "Thoughts & Visions") ... 5-10 68
BACK BEAT (600 "Naw Naw Naw") 5-10 69
CEE BEE (1001 thru 1003) 20-30 67

LIBERTY LADS

Singles: 7-inch

DIXON (111 "Too Much Loving") .... 15-25 '60s

LIBRARY

Singles: 7-inch

EXCLUSIVE (1 "Temptation") 10-15 68

LICHTER, John

Singles: 7-inch

MIDWAY ("Mean-Eyed Cat") 30-50
(Selection number not known.)

LICK, SLICK & SLIDE

Singles: 78 rpm

SAVOY (1150 "I Got Drunk") 40-60 54

Singles: 7-inch

SAVOY (1150 "I Got Drunk") 75-100 54

LIDOS

Singles: 7-inch

BANDBOX (359 "Since I Last Saw You"). 10-15 64
MERCURY (72080 "Bashanova") 8-12 62
PRINCE (6407 "Drivin' Little Dragster") 15-20 64

LIFE

Singles: 7-inch

POLYDOR (540-005 thru 540-017) 10-20 69-70

Picture Sleeves

POLYDOR (540-009 "Hands of the Clock") 20-30 69
Note: All above are Canadian releases.
Members: J.P. Lauzon; Neil Sheppard; Michael Ship; Marty Simon; Danny Zimmerman.

LIFEGUARDS

Singles: 7-inch

ABC-PAR (10021 "Everybody Out'a the Pool") 10-20 59
CASA BLANCA (5535 "Everybody Out'a the Pool") 20-30 59
DR (69 "Everybody Out'a the Pool") 8-15 65

LPs: 10/12-inch

WYNCOTE 15-25 64
Also see HALEY, Bill

LIFEGUARDS

Singles: 7-inch

CATCH (104 "State Beach") 20-30 64
REPRISE (277 "Swim Time") 10-20 64
Members: Phil Sloan; Steve Barri.
Also see BARRI, Steve
Also see SLOAN, P.F.

LIGGETT, Larry

Singles: 78 rpm

CHESS 10-15 54-56
NOTE (1000 "The Flop") 10-15 56

Singles: 7-inch

CHESS 15-25 54-56
NOTE (1000 "The Flop") 15-25 56

LIGGINS, Jimmy R&B '48
(With His 3-D Music; with Joe Liggins; with His Guitar & Drops Of Joy Orchestra)

Singles: 78 rpm

ALADDIN 15-25 54
SPECIALTY 15-25 47-54

Singles: 7-inch

ALADDIN (3250 "I Ain't Drunk") 25-50 54
ALADDIN (3251 "No More Alcohol") 25-50 54
ASTRA (1034 "I Ain't Drunk") 5-10 73
(Yellow vinyl.)
DUPLEX (1004 "House Party") 4-6
SPECIALTY (434 "Brown Skin Baby") 40-60 49
SPECIALTY (470 "Drunk") 30-50 53
(Black vinyl.)
SPECIALTY (470 "Drunk") 50-100 53
(Red vinyl.)
SPECIALTY (484 "Going Away") 25-50 54

LIGGINS, Joe P&R/R&B '45
(With His Honeydrippers)

Singles: 78 rpm

DOT 8-15 51-56
EXCLUSIVE 15-25 45-48
SMASH 10-20 54
SPECIALTY 10-20 49-54

Singles: 7-inch

ALADDIN (3368 "Justina") 15-25 56
DOT (1031 "The Honey Dripper") 15-25 51
DOT (1032 "I've Got a Right to Cry") 15-25 51
DOT (1033 "Tanya") 15-25 51
DOT (15522 "The Honey Dripper") 10-15 56
MERCURY (70440 "Yeah, Yeah, Yeah") . 20-30 54
SPECIALTY (338 "The Honey Dripper") .. 20-40 49
SPECIALTY (379 "Little Joe's Boogie") 20-40 51
SPECIALTY (392 "Frankie Lee") 20-40 51
SPECIALTY (402 "Whiskey, Gin and Wine") 20-40 52
SPECIALTY (409 "Louisiana Woman") 20-40 52
SPECIALTY (413 "So Alone") 20-40 52
SPECIALTY (426 "Boogie Woogie Lou") . 20-40 52
SPECIALTY (430 "Tanya") 20-40 52
SPECIALTY (441 "Goin' Back to New Orleans") 20-40 52
SPECIALTY (453 "Freight Train Blues") .. 20-40 53
SPECIALTY (465 "Farewell Blues") 20-40 53
SPECIALTY (474 "Everyone's Down on Me") 20-40 53
SPECIALTY (529 "Whiskey, Women and Loaded Dice") 25-50 54

LPs: 10/12-inch

BLUES SPECTOR 15-25
Also see MILTON, Roy / Joe Liggins

LIGHT, Enoch, & His Orchestra
(Terry Snyder & All-Stars; Command All-Stars; Terry Snyder with His Orchestra, Chorus & Bagpipes; with Light Brigade; with Brass Menagerie) P&R '37

Singles: 78 rpm

VOCALION 4-6 37

Singles: 7-inch

COMMAND 4-6 59-65
GRAND AWARD 4-6 59
(Monaural.)
GRAND AWARD 8-10 59
(Stereo.)
PROJECT 3 .... 4-6 67-72
U.A. (298 "Tunes of Glory") 5-10 61

EPs: 7-inch

WALDORF .... 8-10 '50s

LPs: 10/12-inch

ABC (746 "Roaring Twenties") 5-10 71

COMMAND 10-20 59-67
GRAND AWARD 10-15 59-62
PROJECT 3 .... 5-10 67-72
REALISTIC 5-10
WALDORF (185 "Melody of Love") 50-100 54
(10-inch LP. Cover pictures Tina Louise, although she is not heard on the disc. Also issued credited to Vincent Lopez & His Orchestra.)
WALDORF (193 "Moments to Remember") 50-100 54
(10-inch LP. Cover pictures Tina Louise, although she is not heard on the disc. Also issued credited to Vincent Lopez & His Orchestra.)
WALDORF (1214 "Moments to Remember") 50-75 57
(Cover pictures Jayne Mansfield, although she is not heard on the disc. Also issued credited to Vincent Lopez & His Orchestra.)
WALDORF (1232 "Melody of Love") 30-50 57
(10-inch LP. Cover pictures Tina Louise, although she is not heard on the disc. Also issued credited to Vincent Lopez & His Orchestra.)
WALDORF (1329 "Moments to Remember") 30-50 58
(Cover pictures Tina Louise, although she is not heard on the disc. Also issued credited to Vincent Lopez & His Orchestra.)
Members: Enoch Light; Terry Snyder; Charles Magnante; Dick Hyman; Jack Lesberg; Teddy Sommer; Bob Haggart; Tony Mattola; Willie Rodriguez; Moe Wechsler; Urbie Green; Pee Wee Erwin; Bobby Byrne; Artie Marotti; Dominic Cortese; Ezelie Watson; Russ Banzer; Stanley Webb; Milt Yaner; Leonard Calderon; George Dessinger; Bernie Kaufman.
Also see LOPEZ, Vincent, & His Orchestra
Also see MANSFIELD, Jayne
Also see TINA LOUISE

LIGHT DRIVERS
Singles: 7-inch
GEMINI (1021 "Operator") 15-25

LIGHT NITES
Singles: 7-inch
DUNWICH (149 "Same Old Thing") 10-15 67

LIGHTFOOT, Charlie
Singles: 7-inch
SPOTLIGHT (5010 "Yes, Baby") 100-150 60

LIGHTFOOT, Gordon — *LP '69*
(Gord Lightfoot)
Singles: 7-inch
ABC-PAR (10352 "I'm the One") 10-20 62
ABC-PAR (10373 "Negotiations") 10-20 62
CHATEAU (142 "I'm the One") 30-40 62
(First issue.)
CHATEAU (148 "Negotiations") 30-40 62
(First issue.)
CHATEAU (152 "I'll Meet You in Michoocan") 30-40 62
REPRISE 4-8 70-77
U.A. 5-10 65-69
W.B. (Except 5621) 3-5 78-86
W.B. (5621 "For Lovin' Me") 10-15 65
Picture Sleeves
U.A. (50152 "The Way I Feel") 8-10 67
W.B. (28655 "Anything for Love") 3-5 86
LPs: 10/12-inch
AME (7000 "Early Lightfoot Collector's Album") 75-100 71
K-TEL 5-8
LIBERTY 5-8 80
MFSL (018 "Sundown") 30-50 78
PICKWICK 5-8 79
REPRISE (Except 93228) 8-12 70-76
REPRISE (93228 "Sit Down Young Stranger") 10-20 70
U.A. (243 "Very Best Of") 8-12 74
U.A. (3487 "Lightfoot") 10-15 66
(Monaural.)
U.A. (3587 "Way I Feel") 10-15 67
(Monaural.)
U.A. (6487 "Lightfoot") 10-15 66
(Stereo.)
U.A. (6587 "Way I Feel") 10-15 67
(Stereo.)
U.A. (6649 "Lightfoot") 10-15 68
U.A. (6672 "Back Here on Earth") 10-15 68
U.A. (6714 "Sunday Concert") 10-15 69
W.B. 5-10 78-86

LIGHTFOOT, Papa
(Papa George Lightfoot; with His Harmonica; Alexander Lightfoot)
Singles: 78 rpm
ALADDIN (3171 "After-While") 50-75 52
ALADDIN (3304 "Blue Lights") 40-60 52
IMPERIAL 40-60 54
SAVOY (1161 "Mean Old Train") 10-15 55
SULTAN 40-60 50
Singles: 7-inch
ALADDIN (3171 "After-While") 100-150 52
ALADDIN (3304 "Blue Lights") 75-125 52
IMPERIAL (5289 "Wine, Women, Whiskey") 75-125 54
SAVOY (1161 "Mean Old Train") 15-25 55
LPs: 10/12-inch
VAULT 10-15 69

LIGHTNER, Ken
Singles: 7-inch
DIXIE (913 "Corner of Love") 100-200
EMPEROR (220 "Mary Ann") 75-125

LIGHTNIN' JR.
(L.C. Williams)
Singles: 78 rpm
GOLD STAR (614 "Trying Trying") 25-50 47
Also see WILLIAMS, L.C.

LIGHTNIN' JR. & EMPIRES
(Champion Jack Dupree)
Singles: 78 rpm
HARLEM (2334 "Ragged & Hungry") 50-75 55
Singles: 7-inch
HARLEM (2334 "Ragged & Hungry") ... 150-200 55
Also see DUPREE, Champion Jack
Also see EMPIRES

LIGHTNIN' LEON
(Billy Lee Riley)
Singles: 7-inch
RITA (1005 "Repossession Blues") 10-20 60
Also see RILEY, Billy Lee

LIGHTNIN' ROD
LPs: 10/12-inch
U.A. (156 "Hustler's Convention") 50-80 73

LIGHTNIN' SLIM — *R&B '59*
(Otis Hicks; Lightning Slim)
Singles: 78 rpm
ACE (505 "Bad Feeling Blues") 50-75 55
EXCELLO (2066 thru 2096) 20-30 55-56
EXCELLO (2106 "Mean Ole Lonesome Train") 75-100 57
EXCELLO (2116 "I'm a Rollin' Stone") ... 75-100 57
EXCELLO (2131 "Hoo Doo Blues") 100-150 58
EXCELLO (2142 "My Starter Won't Work") 100-150 58
EXCELLO (2150 "I'm Leavin' You Baby") 150-250 59
FEATURE (3006 "Rock Me, Mama") 200-300 54
FEATURE (3008 "I Can't Live Happy") 10-25 54
FEATURE (3012 "Bugger Bugger Boy") .. 10-25 54
Singles: 7-inch
ACE (505 "Bad Feeling Blues") 75-125 55
EXCELLO (2066 "I Can't Be Successful") 50-75 55
EXCELLO (2075 "Sugar Plum") 50-75 56
EXCELLO (2080 "Goin' Home") 50-75 56
EXCELLO (2096 "Bad Luck & Trouble") .. 50-75 56
EXCELLO (2106 "Mean Ole Lonesome Train") 50-75 57
EXCELLO (2116 "I'm a Rollin' Stone") 50-75 57
EXCELLO (2131 "Hoo Doo Blues") 50-75 58
EXCELLO (2142 "My Starter Won't Work") 30-40 58
EXCELLO (2150 "I'm Leavin' You Baby") 20-30 59
EXCELLO (2160 "Sweet Little Woman") .. 20-30 59
EXCELLO (2169 "Rooster Blues") 20-30 59
EXCELLO (2173 "Tom Cat Blues") 20-30 60
EXCELLO (2173 "Tom Cat Blues") 75-100 60
(Shows address at top.)
EXCELLO (2179 "Too Close Blues") 20-30 60
EXCELLO (2186 "Cool Down Baby") 20-30 60
EXCELLO (2195 "Somebody Knockin' ") . 20-30 61
EXCELLO (2203 "I'm Tired Waiting Baby") 20-30 61
EXCELLO (2215 "Mind Your Own Business") 15-25 62
EXCELLO (2224 "I'm Warning You Baby") 15-25 62
EXCELLO (2228 thru 2272) 10-20 63-65
EXCELLO (2276 "Goin' Away Blues") 8-12 66
EXCELLO (2320 "My Babe") 5-10 72
FEATURE (3006 "Rock Me, Mama") 600-800 54
FEATURE (3008 "I Can't Live Happy") 100-200 54
FEATURE (3012 "Bugger Bugger Boy") 100-200 54
LPs: 10/12-inch
EXCELLO (8000 "Rooster Blues") 500-1000 60
EXCELLO (8004 "Bell Ringer") 15-25 65
EXCELLO (8018 "High and Low Down") .. 10-15 71
EXCELLO (8023 "London Gumbo") 10-15 72
QUICKSILVER 10-15
Session: Lazy Lester; Bobby McBride; Warren Storm; Slim Harpo; Katie Webster; Al Foreman; Rufus Thibodeaux; Austin Broussard.
Also see HARPO, Slim
Also see LAZY LESTER
Also see STORM, Warren
Also see WEBSTER, Katie

LIGHTNING
Singles: 7-inch
P.I.P. (8923 "Freedom") 10-20 71
LPs: 10/12-inch
P.I.P. (6807 "Lightning") 20-30 71
Also see LITTER
Also see WHITE LIGHTNING

LIL' BOYS BLUE
Singles: 7-inch
BAT WING (2003 "I'm Not There") 20-30 66

LIL DYNAMITE & EXPLOSIONS
Singles: 7-inch
LIL DYNAMITE (578 "Dancing Little Thing") 10-20 62

LIL' GEORGE & RAG DOLLS
Singles: 7-inch
IMPEL (70-004 "Well, It's Time") 50-75

LIL' MILLET & CREOLES
Singles: 78 rpm
SPECIALTY (565 "Rich Woman") 20-30 55
Singles: 7-inch
SPECIALTY (565 "Rich Woman") 40-60 55

LIL' SOUL BROTHERS
Singles: 7-inch
D-TOWN (10691 "I've Got Heartaches") .. 10-20 66
WHEELSVILLE (111 "I've Got Heartaches") 15-25 66

LILA & RONNIE
Singles: 7-inch
SEECO (6073 "My Steady") 40-50 59

LILE, Bobby
("With Music by Bob & Laverne;" with El Montes)
Singles: 78 rpm
SAGE & SAND 5-10 56
Singles: 7-inch
ALMO (227 "Man of the World") 15-25 65
CORONA (303 "Breakup") 5-10 64
4 STAR (1713 "Then You'll Know") 8-12 58
4 STAR (1723 "A Labor of Love") 8-12 58
4 STAR (1734 "All the Time") 8-12 59
IMPERIAL (5690 "My Big Mistake") 8-12 60
IMPERIAL (5754 "This Love") 8-12 61
ROLLO (642 "Breakaway") 5-10 65
SAGE & SAND (222 "Knockin' My Head") 10-20 56
SAGE & SAND (354 "Positive Thinking") ... 5-10 62
SIDEWALK (912 "Hard Way to Go") 4-8 67
TRILL 5-10 63
WHITE WHALE (267 "Down Comes the World") 4-8 68

LILLIE, Lonnie
Singles: 7-inch
MARATHON (5003 "Truck Driver's Special") 150-200 56
Session: Spud Goodall.

LILLY, Cletis
Singles: 7-inch
PATTIE (2661 "Southland Boogie") 200-300

LILY MAE & HOUSE ROCKERS
Singles: 78 rpm
MIRACLE 15-25 48

LIME
Singles: 7-inch
CHESS (2045 "Hey Girl") 10-15 68
WESTWOOD ("Love A-Go-Go") .... 5-10 '60s
(Selection number not known.)

LIME 3
LPs: 10/12-inch
ULTRASOUND/MATRA (006 "Guilty") 40-50 83
(Picture disc. Promotional issue only. Canadian.)

LIMELIGHTERS
Singles: 78 rpm
PIC (0006 "I Love a Melody") 5-10 54
Singles: 7-inch
PIC (0006 "I Love a Melody") 10-20 54

LIMELIGHTERS
Singles: 78 rpm
JOSIE (795 "Cabin Hideaway") 20-30 56
Singles: 7-inch
JOSIE (795 "Cabin Hideaway") 40-50 56
(Black vinyl.)
JOSIE (795 "Cabin Hideaway") 75-100 56
(Brown vinyl.)

LIMELIGHTERS
(With the Guitar-Billy Davis Orchestra)
Singles: 7-inch
GILCO (213 "This Lonely Boy") 300-400 57

LIMELITERS — *P&R/LP '61*
Singles: 7-inch
ELEKTRA 8-15 60-61
RCA 5-10 61-64
W.B. 4-8 68
Picture Sleeves
RCA 10-15 61-63
EPs: 7-inch
RCA (2445 "The Limeliters") 8-12 62
LPs: 10/12-inch
CAMDEN 5-10 74
ELEKTRA 15-25 60-61
LEGACY 8-10 70
PICKWICK 5-8 72
RCA (Except 2336) 15-25 61-68
RCA (2336 "Pure Gold") 5-8 77
STAX 6-10 74
W.B. 8-15 68
Members: Glen Yarbrough; Lou Gottlieb; Alex Hassilev; Ernie Sheldon.
Also see ANN-MARGRET
Also see GATEWAY SINGERS
Also see HASSILEV, Alex
Also see PENNY & JEAN
Also see YARBROUGH, Glen

LIMELITERS / Della Reese / Mario Lanza / Norman Luboff Choir
EPs: 7-inch
RCA (33-150 "Headline Hits") 8-12 61
(Promotional issue, made for Nestle's.)
Also see LANZA, Mario
Also see LIMELITERS
Also see REESE, Della

LIMEY & YANKS
Singles: 7-inch
LOMA (2059 "Gather My Things and Go") 25-40 66
STARBURST (127 "Guaranteed Love") ... 35-55 65

LIMEYS
Singles: 7-inch
AMCAN (406 "Somebody Help Me") 10-20 64
DOT (16725 "Don't Cry") 8-12 65
SCEPTER (12156 "Come Back") 5-10 66
SHERWOOD (1715 "Come Back") .... 15-25 '60s
Members: Andrea Gennard; Stephan Gennard.

LINC & LINNETTES
Singles: 7-inch
PALETTE (5112 "Big Eyed Baby") 15-20 63

LINCOLN FIG & DATES
Singles: 7-inch
WORTHY (1006 "Way Up") 150-200 58
(Black vinyl.)
WORTHY (1006 "Way Up") .... 50-75 '60s
(Red vinyl.)
Members: Ivan Figueroa; Steve Aspromonti; Manny Banuchi; Johnny Gigliono; Eddie Cruz.

LINCOLN STREET EXIT

Singles: 7-inch

ECCO (1001 "Bummer") 10-20 67
LANCE (102 "Paper Place") 15-25 66
LANCE (109 "Who's Been Driving My Yellow Taxi Cab") 15-25 66
MAINSTREAM (722 "Soulful Drifter") 5-10 69
SOULED OUT (104 "St. Louis Mama") 5-10 69

EPs: 7-inch

PSYCH OUT (101 "Lincoln Street Exit") 10-15 83

LPs: 10/12-inch

MAINSTREAM (6126 "Drive It") 30-50 70
Member: Michael Martin.
Also see XIT

LINCOLNS

Singles: 7-inch

ALJON (113 "I Cried") 500-750 61
ATLAS (1100 "Don't Let Me Shed Any More Tears") 100-125 58
BIM BAM BOOM (105 "I Cried") 4-6 72
MERCURY (71553 "Baby, Please Let Me Love You") 10-20 59

LINCOLNS

Singles: 7-inch

BUD (113 "Sukiyaki Rocki") 15-25 61

LINCOLNS

Singles: 7-inch

ABCO (1001 "Night Drag") 10-20 64
(Also issued as by the Vagabonds.)
Also see VAGABONDS

LINCOLNS QUINTETT

Singles: 7-inch

ANGLE TONE (522 "Dream of Romance") 250-350 58

LIND, Bob *P&R/LP '66*

Singles: 7-inch

AURA 10-20 65
CAPITOL 4-6 71
VERVE FOLKWAYS 5-10 66
WORLD PACIFIC 5-10 65-68

LPs: 10/12-inch

CAPITOL 10-15 71
VERVE FOLKWAYS 10-20 66
WORLD PACIFIC 10-20 66

LIND, Cory
(With the Jack Marshall Orchestra)

Singles: 7-inch

VITA (164 "Billy Loves Me") 10-15 57
Also see MARSHALL, Jack

LINDA

Singles: 7-inch

ANTLER (4020 "He's Mine") 10-15 63

LINDA & EPICS

Singles: 7-inch

BLUE MOON (415 "Memories of Love") 75-125 59

LINDA & PRETENDERS

Singles: 7-inch

ASSAULT (1879 "Believe Me") 15-25 63

LINDA & ROBERTA

Singles: 7-inch

JUNIOR (5001 "Grownup") 10-20 58
SHAD (5001 "Grownup") 10-20 58

LINDA & TEARS

Singles: 7-inch

CHALLENGE (59317 "Good Goodbye") 15-25 65

LINDA & VISTAS

Singles: 7-inch

SHRINE (100 "She Went Away") 200-300 65

LINDA JEAN

Singles: 7-inch

FAYETTE (1628 "Dream Boy") 10-15 65

LINDA JO & NOMADS

Singles: 7-inch

JULIAN (103 "Just Like You") 15-25 '60s

LINDA LOU & HITMAKERS

Singles: 7-inch

LAMA (7786 "The Torch Is Out") 50-100 61

LINDARELLA

Singles: 7-inch

T.E.A.M. (320 "I Don't Want to Walk Without You") 40-50 61

LINDEN, Kathy *P&R '58*
(With Joe Leahy's Orchestra)

Singles: 7-inch

CAPITOL 5-10 62-63
FELSTED 10-15 58-59
MONUMENT 5-10 60-61
NATIONAL 5-10 '60s
RPC (504 "Billy Is My Boyfriend") 8-12 61

Picture Sleeves

MONUMENT (420 "That's What Love Is") 10-20 60

EPs: 7-inch

FELSTED (35001 "Hits") 35-45 58

LPs: 10/12-inch

FELSTED (7501 "That Certain Boy") 40-60 59
Also see LEAHY, Joe

LINDER, Sy, & Cams / Cams

Singles: 7-inch

INDIE (1303 "Drag Race") 10-20 '60s

LINDSAY, Larry

Singles: 7-inch

KINBO ("Please Please Baby") 50-75
(Selection number not known.)

LINDSAY, Mark *P&R '69*

Singles: 7-inch

COLUMBIA 4-8 69-75
BUSCH MUSIC '76 (942 "Sing Your Own Song") 30-40 76
(Single-sided 33 speed promotional issue.)
ELKA (310 "Sing Your Own Song") 4-6
GREEDY 4-6 76
W.B. 4-6 77

LPs: 10/12-inch

COLUMBIA 10-15 70-71
Also see REVERE, Paul, & Raiders
Also see UNKNOWNS

LINDSAY, Merl
(Merle Lindsay)

Singles: 7-inch

D (1106 "Stolen Kisses") 10-20 60
D (1161 "Picks and Bows") 10-20 60
D (1164 "Rockin' Water Baby") 50-75 60
D (1231 "Tied to the Bottle") 10-20 62
SHASTA (117 "Born to Lose") 10-20 59

LINDSEY, Lewis

Singles: 7-inch

ALL AMERICAN (104 "So Sweet") 50-75
MANCO (1018 "The Push") 10-20 61

LINDSEY, Theresa

Singles: 7-inch

CORRECTONE (1053 "Good Idea") 10-20 '60s
CORRECTONE (5840 "Gotta Find a Way") 10-20 '60s
GOLDEN WORLD (43 "I'll Bet You") 15-25 66

LINDY & LAVELLS
(With the Lindells)

Singles: 7-inch

LAVETTE (5001 "Meet Me Tonight in Your Dreams") 15-25 64
RED FEATHER ("There's My Baby") 15-25
(No selection number used.)
Member: Lindy Blaskey.

LINE'S END

Singles: 7-inch

LOMPRI (90599 "Hey Little Girl") 15-25 68
Members: Steve Harkus; Pat James; Rocky Rockwell; Mike Tebeau; Bob Lakas.

LINK, Gary

Singles: 7-inch

ALVIC (764 "Rhythm Rock") 100-200

LINK EDDY COMBO *R&B '61*

Singles: 7-inch

REPRISE (20002 "Big Mr. C") 10-15 61

Singles: 12-inch

Members: Al Garcia; Fred Mendoza; Vince Bumatay; Art Rodriguez.
Also see RHYTHM KINGS

LINKLETTER, Bob

Singles: 7-inch

CHATTAHOOCHEE (702 "The Out Crowd") 10-15 66

LINKS

Singles: 7-inch

TEENAGE (1009 "She's the One") 1500-2500 57
Members: Herb Fisher; James Walton; Wilbert Dobson; Joe Woodley; John Terry.
Also see BACHELORS

LINKS

Singles: 7-inch

BRUNSWICK (55081 "Scraunch") 15-25 58

LINN & GINN
(With the Rocks)

Singles: 7-inch

TNT (9019 "Promise Me") 300-500 59

LINNEAS

Singles: 7-inch

DIAMOND (241 "Forever Baby") 10-20 68
DIAMOND (248 "Born to Be Your Baby") 10-20 68

LION, Johnny

Singles: 7-inch

COED (514 "Haunted Heart") 10-15 59

LION & LEPRECHAUNS

Singles: 7-inch

LITTLE FORT (8846 "Mouse Trap") 20-30 '60s

LIONS
(With René Hall Orchestra)

Singles: 7-inch

RENDEZVOUS (116 "Two Timing Lover") 100-200 60
(Red label.)
RENDEZVOUS (116 "Two Timing Lover") 75-125 60
(White label. Promotional issue only.)
RENDEZVOUS (116 "Two Timing Lover") 50-100
(Black label.)
Also see HALL, René

LIONS

Singles: 7-inch

EVEREST (19388 "No One") 8-12 61
IMPERIAL (5678 "Hickory Dickory") 5-10 60
MACK IV (2 "No One") 15-25 60
MACK IV (104 "Till the 13th of the Month") 10-15 62

LIONS

LPs: 10/12-inch

METRO (300 "Twist with the Lions") 10-20 62
Also see LIVERT, Paul, & Lions

LIPSCOMB, Mance

LPs: 10/12-inch

ARHOOLIE (1001 "Texas Sharecropper and Songster") 20-30 63
ARHOOLIE (1023 "Mance Lipscomb, Vol. 2") 20-30 64
ARHOOLIE (1026 "Mance Lipscomb, Vol. 3") 20-30 65
ARHOOLIE (1069 "Mance Lipscomb, Vol. 6") 15-25 73
REPRISE (2012 "Trouble in Mind") 20-25 61
(Monaural.)
REPRISE (R9-2012 "Trouble in Mind") 25-30 61
(Stereo.)
REPRISE (6404 "Trouble in Mind") 10-15 70

LIPSCOMB, Max K.

Singles: 7-inch

DOT (16324 "Baby I Don't Care") 25-35 62
SQUIRE (102 "Baby, You're So Square") 100-200 62
(First issue.)
Also see McKAY, Scotty

LIPTON, Peggy

Singles: 7-inch

ODE 4-8 68-70

Picture Sleeves

ODE (114 "Stoney End") 8-12 69
ODE (66001 "Wear Your Love Like Heaven") 5-10 70

LPs: 10/12-inch

ODE (44006 "Peggy Lipton") 10-20 68

LIQUID SMOKE *P&R '70*

Singles: 7-inch

AVCO EMBASSY (4522 "I Who Have Nothing") 4-8 70
ROULETTE (7166 "Where Is Our Love") 4-6 75

LPs: 10/12-inch

AVCO EMBASSY (33005 "Liquid Smoke") 20-30 70
Member: Sandy Dantaleo.

LISA & LULLABIES
(Concords)

Singles: 7-inch

COED (589 "Why Do I Cry") 10-15 64
Also see CONCORDS

LISS, Tommy, & Matadors
(Tommy Lysaght)

Singles: 7-inch

SAXONY (1005 "Just in Make Believe") 10-20 63
SAXONY (2007 "Just in Make Believe") 4-6 97
Also see CABARETS
Also see MARTIN, Fred, & Matadors

LISTEN

Singles: 7-inch

COLUMBIA (43967 "You Better Run") 200-300 67
(Red label.)
COLUMBIA (43967 "You Better Run") 150-250 67
(White label. Promotional issue only.)
Member: Robert Plant.
Also see PLANT, Robert

LISTENING

Singles: 7-inch

VANGUARD (35077 "I Can Teach You") 10-15 68
VANGUARD (35094 "Life Stories") 10-15 69

LPs: 10/12-inch

VANGUARD (6504 "Listening") 40-60 68
Members: Ernie Kamanis; Peter Malick; Walter Powers; Michael Tschudin.

LISTER, Big Bill

Singles: 78 rpm

CAPITOL (1488 "Beer Drinking Blues") 10-15 51

Singles: 7-inch

CAPITOL (1488 "Beer Drinking Blues") 15-25 51

LITE, "Uncle" Buck

Singles: 7-inch

RONMAR (1000 "Mr. Ducktail") 550-650 '50s

LITE, Tippo, & His All Stars

Singles: 78 rpm

BACK ALLEY (202 "Dark Skin Woman Blues") 25-50 50

LITE NITES

Singles: 7-inch

DUNWICH (149 "One, Two Bugaloo") 10-20 67
Also see AMERICAN BREED
Also see GARY & NITE LITES

LITE STORM

LPs: 10/12-inch

BEVERLY HILLS (1135 "Lite Storm Warning") 40-60 73

LITTER *LP '69*

Singles: 7-inch

PROBE (461 "Silly People") 15-25 69
PROBE (467 "Blue Ice") 15-25 69
SCOTTY (6710 "Action Woman") 75-100 67
WARICK (6711 "Somebody Help Me") 150-200 67
WARICK (6712 "Action Woman") 100-150 67

LPs: 10/12-inch

EVA (12013 "Rare Tracks") 10-15 83
HEXAGON (681 "$100 Fine") 150-250 69
K-TEL (835-1 "Distortions") 5-10 90
(Includes three additional tracks not on the Warick release: *The Mummy, The Egyptian,* and *Blues One.*)
PROBE (4504 "Emerge the Litter") 30-50 69
WARICK (671 "Distortions") 200-400 68
Members: Dan Rinaldi; Tom Caplan; Denny Waite; Ray Melina; Jim Kane; Tom Murray; Mark Gallagher.
Also see HUMBLE MUD
Also see TROYS
Also see WHITE LIGHTNING

LITTERBUGS

Singles: 7-inch

OKEH (7164 "Valerie") 50-60 62

LITTLE, Ben, & Four Kings
Singles: 7-inch
REVIVAL (635 "Forever Mine")................ 30-40 61

LITTLE, Connie
Singles: 7-inch
ELMOR (307 "Billy")................................ 20-30 61

LITTLE, Jimmy
Singles: 7-inch
BIG TOP (517 "Hornets") 10-15 64

LITTLE, Lee Roy
Singles: 7-inch
CEE=JAY (578 "I'm a Good Man But a Poor Man")... 10-20 60
CEE=JAY (579 "Hurry Baby, Please Come Home")... 30-40 60

LITTLE, Olen
Singles: 7-inch
PEACH (712 "You'll Find Me")................ 20-30 59
PEACH (721 "The World Belongs to Me").. 50-100 59

LITTLE, Paul
Singles: 7-inch
PEAK (188 "I Want to Walk with You") 50-75

LITTLE, Rod
Singles: 7-inch
BOOK (112 "Sweet Lookin' Mama") 100-150

LITTLE, Victor
Singles: 7-inch
RICHLAND ("Papa Lou")........................ 10-20
(Selection number not known.)

LITTLE AL
(Al Gunter)
Singles: 78 rpm
EXCELLO (2098 "No Jive")..................... 40-60 57
EXCELLO (2128 "Easy Ridin' Buggy") 40-60 58
Singles: 7-inch
EXCELLO (2098 "No Jive")..................... 50-75 57
(Orange and blue label.)
EXCELLO (2098 "No Jive")..................... 15-20 62
(Red, white and blue label.)
EXCELLO (2128 "Easy Ridin' Buggy") 40-60 58

LITTLE ALFRED
(With the Berry Cup)
Singles: 7-inch
JEWEL (744 "Even Though")................... 15-25 65
KHOURY'S (726 "Miss Ann")................... 10-15 60
LYRIC (733 "Mashed Potatoes Back Again") 10-15 62
LYRIC (1007 "Broken Heart")................... 15-20 63
Also see COOKIE & HIS CUPCAKES / Little Alfred

LITTLE ALICE
Singles: 7-inch
4J (502 "So What If I Can't Cook").......... 30-40 62

LITTLE ALTON & VELVATONES
Singles: 7-inch
J-M-O (1004 "She Said Yeah") 20-30 66

LITTLE ANGEL
Singles: 7-inch
AWARD (126 "Help Me Baby") 10-20 59

LITTLE ANGELS
Singles: 7-inch
CAPITOL (4490 "Says You").................... 10-20 60
WARWICK (672 "Santa Parade") 8-12 61

LITTLE ANN
Singles: 7-inch
RIC-TIC (142 "Going Down a One-Way Street") 15-25 68
Also see TARHEEL SLIM & LITTLE ANN

LITTLE ANTHONY & IMPERIALS R&B/P&R '58
(Anthony & Imperials; Imperials)
Singles: 78 rpm
END (1027 "Tears on My Pillow") 75-125 58
Singles: 7-inch
APOLLO (755 "The Fires Burn No More") 10-15 61
AVCO...4-6 74-75
C&G ("Tears on my Pillow") ....4-8 '70s
(No selection number used.)
DCP..5-10 64-66
EMBER (1090 "Dear Jesu Bambino").........5-10 62
(With the M. Dodds Choir.)
END (1027 "Tears on My Pillow") 15-25 58
(First issued as by the Imperials.)
END (1036 "So Much")..............................15-25 58
END (1038 "The Diary")..............................15-25 59
END (1039 "Wishful Thinking") 15-25 59
END (1047 "A Prayer and a Juke Box") ...15-25 59
(Monaural.)
END (1047 "A Prayer and a Juke Box") ...40-50 59
(Stereo.)
END (1053 "I'm Alright") 15-25 59
END (1060 "Shimmy Shimmy Ko-Ko Bop")..15-25 59
END (1067 "My Empty Room") 15-25 60
END (1074 thru 1104) 10-20 60-61
JANUS..4-6 71-72
MCA...3-5 80
NEWTIME (503 "A Short Prayer") 5-10 62
NEWTIME (505 "The Letter") 5-10 62
OLD HIT 3-5
PCM..3-5 83
PURE GOLD (101 "Running with the Wrong Crowd")..30-50 76
ROULETTE (4379 "It Just Ain't Fair").........8-12 61
ROULETTE (4477 "I've Got a Lot to Offer Darling")..5-10 63
ROULETTE (GG-16 "Tears on My Pillow") ..4-6 71
STOOP SOUNDS (115 "What Did I Do")..100-150 97
U.A. 4-8 69-70
VEEP 5-10 66-69
Picture Sleeves
DCP (1128 "Hurt So Bad") 10-20 65
VEEP (1228 "Better Use Your Head") 10-20 66
EPs: 7-inch
END (203 "Little Anthony and the Imperials")..50-100 58
END (204 "We Are the Imperials Featuring Little Anthony") 50-100 59
LPs: 10/12-inch
ACCORD (7216 "Tears on My Pillow").......5-10 83
AVCO (11012 "On a New Street") 8-10 73
DCP (3801 "I'm On the Outside Looking In")...20-30 64
(Monaural.)
DCP (3808 "Goin' Out of My Head").........20-30 65
(Monaural.)
DCP (3809 "Best of Little Anthony & the Imperials")..15-25 66
(Monaural.)
DCP (6801 "I'm On the Outside Looking In")...25-40 64
(Stereo.)
DCP (6808 "Goin' Out of My Head").........25-40 65
(Stereo.)
DCP (6809 "Best of Little Anthony & the Imperials")..20-35 66
(Stereo.)
EMUS 5-10 79
END (303 "We Are the Imperials Featuring Little Anthony") 75-125 59
(Monaural.)
END (303 "We Are the Imperials Featuring Little Anthony") 50-100 59
(Reprocessed stereo.)
END (311 "Shades of the '40s")..............50-100 60
FORUM CIRCLE (9107 "Their Big Hits")..20-30 64
LIBERTY (10133 "Best of Little Anthony & the Imperials")..5-10 81
ROULETTE (25294 "Greatest Hits").........20-30 65
SUNSET (5287 "Little Anthony & the Imperials")..10-15 70
U.A. (026 "Legendary Masters") 12-18 73
(Two discs.)
U.A. (255 "Very Best") 10-12 74
U.A. (382 "Very Best") 8-10 74
U.A. (1017 "Out of Sight, Out of Mind") 5-10 80
U.A. (6720 "Out of Sight, Out of Mind") 10-15 69
VEEP (13510 "I'm On the Outside Looking In")...15-20 66
VEEP (13513 "Payin' Our Dues") 15-20 66
(Monaural.)
VEEP (13514 "Reflections").......................15-20 67
(Monaural.)
VEEP (13516 "Movie Grabbers").............15-20 67
(Monaural.)
VEEP (16510 "I'm On the Outside Looking In")...15-25 66
(Stereo.)
VEEP (16513 "Payin' Our Dues") 15-25 66
(Stereo.)
VEEP (16514 "Reflections").......................15-25 67
(Stereo.)
VEEP (16516 "Movie Grabbers").............15-25 67
(Stereo.)
VEEP (16519 "Best of Little Anthony & the Imperials, Vol. 2") 15-25 68
Members: Anthony Gourdine; Tracy Lord; Sam Strain; Clarence Collins; Gloucester Rogers; Ernie Wright.
Also see CHESTERS
Also see CHIPS
Also see DUPONTS
Also see IMPERIALS
Also see LITTLE ANTHONY
Also see O'JAYS

LITTLE ANTHONY & IMPERIALS / Platters
LPs: 10/12-inch
EXACT (231 "Little Anthony & the Imperials & the Platters")..5-10 80
Also see LITTLE ANTHONY & IMPERIALS
Also see PLATTERS

LITTLE ARTIE & PHAROAHS
Singles: 7-inch
CUCA (1142 "Fox & the Hound")..............10-20 63
CUCA (1157 "It Puzzles Me") 10-20 63
CUCA (1162 "Foxy Devil") 10-20 64
Members: Artie Herrera; Mike Morgan; Phil Zinos; Jim Lombard; Dick Baradic; Al Herrera; Pete Psiroupolis; Andy Bakiris; Chuck Matson; Tom Markin; Pat Short Cibarrich.
Also see KANE & ABEL
Also see MOB

LITTLE BEATS
Singles: 7-inch
MERCURY (71155 "Love Is True")..........50-75 57

LITTLE BEN & CHEERS
Singles: 7-inch
BELL (731 "I Don't Have to Cry")...............5-10 68
LAREDO (2518 "Beggar of Love")............15-20 58
RUSH (601 thru 604)..................................10-15 '60s

LITTLE BEN & FOUR KINGS
Singles: 7-inch
REVIVAL (635 "Forever Mine")..................50-75 61

LITTLE BENNY
(With the Stereos; with Dickie Thompson's Orchestra)
Singles: 7-inch
SPOT (106 "My Sweetheart") 50-75 61
TRI-ODE (100 "Astronaut Glenn") 8-12 62

LITTLE BERNIE & BLAZERS
Singles: 7-inch
JOSIE (884 "My Love I Have You") 100-150 61

LITTLE BERNIE & CAVALIERS
Singles: 7-inch
ASCOT (2183 "Do You") 5-10 65
JOVE (100 "Lonely Soldier") 15-25 62

LITTLE BESSIE
Singles: 7-inch
AMY (816 "Broken Hearted") 10-15 61

LITTLE BETTY
Singles: 7-inch
ALTO (2006 "Twistin' School")..................10-15 61
SAVOY (1603 "I May Be Wrong")..............8-12 61

LITTLE BILL & BLUENOTES P&R '59
(With the Adventurers & Shalimars; Little Bill)
Singles: 7-inch
BOLO (725 "Little Angel")..........................20-30 62
DOLTON (4 "I Love an Angel") 15-25 59
TOPAZ (1303 "Sweet Cucumber") 25-50 60
TOPAZ (1305 "Louie Louie")......................50-75 61
LPs: 10/12-inch
CAMELOT (102 "The Fiesta Club Presents Little Bill & the Blue Notes") 250-350 60
Members: Bill Engelhart; Frank Dutra; Tom Giving; Buck Ormsby; Lassie Aanes; Buck England; Tom Morgan.

LITTLE BILLY & TRADERS
Singles: 7-inch
BIG BEAT (101 "Champagne")..................15-25 62

LITTLE BIT OF SOUND
Singles: 7-inch
CAROLE (1002 "Incense and Peppermints")..10-15 67
ROULETTE (4744 "Girls Who Paints Designs") 10-15 67

LITTLE BITS
Singles: 7-inch
DYNO VOICE (919 "Feeling of Love") 5-10 68
TIGER EYE (101 "Girl, Give Me Love") ...20-25 '60s
Member: Karyl Mann.

LITTLE BOB & LOLLIPOPS
(Lil Bob & Lollipops; Little Bob)
Singles: 7-inch
B&L (1 "Rock the Uke")............................10-20 66
DECCA (31412 "Twisting Home") 10-15 62
HIGH-UP (101 "Are You Ever Coming Home") ....10-20 '60s
JIN (222 thru 227)......................................10-20 67-68
LA LOUISIANNE (8067 "I Got Loaded") 5-10 66
Also see CAMILLE, Bob, & Lollipops

LITTLE BOOKER
(James Booker)
Singles: 78 rpm
IMPERIAL (5293 "Thinkin' 'Bout My Baby")..25-45 54
Singles: 7-inch
ACE (547 "Teen-Age Rock")......................15-25 58
IMPERIAL (5293 "Thinkin' 'Bout My Baby")..50-75 54

LITTLE BOPPERS
Singles: 7-inch
GLENDALE (1001 "Chattanooga Drummer Man")..75-100

LITTLE BOY BLUES
Singles: 7-inch
FONTANA (1623 "It's Only You") 5-10 68
IRC (6929 "Look at the Sun")....................10-15 66
IRC (6936 "I'm Ready")..............................15-25 66
IRC (6939 "I Can Only Give You Everything")..15-25 66
RONKO (6996 "The Great Train Robbery") 15-25 67
Picture Sleeves
IRC (6939 "I Can Only Give You Everything")..25-35 66
LPs: 10/12-inch
FONTANA (67578 "In the Woodland of Weir")..15-25 68

LITTLE BUBBER
Singles: 78 rpm
IMPERIAL 25-45 53
Singles: 7-inch
IMPERIAL (5225 "High Class Woman")...50-75 53
IMPERIAL (5238 "Runnin' 'Round") 50-75 53

LITTLE BUSTER
Singles: 7-inch
JUBILEE (5491 "Lookin' for a Home")......10-20 64
JUBILEE (5502 "I'm So Lonely") 10-20 65
JUBILEE (5510 "T.C.B.") 10-20 65
JUBILEE (5527 "It's Loving Time") 10-20 66
JUBILEE (5537 "All Night Worker") 10-20 66

LITTLE BUTCH & VELLS
(Butchie Saunders)
Singles: 7-inch
ANGLE TONE (535 "Over the Rainbow") 20-30 58
(Black vinyl.)
ANGLE TONE (535 "Over the Rainbow") 50-75 58
(Red vinyl.)
Also see SAUNDERS, Little Butchie

LITTLE CAESAR R&B '52
(With Maxwell Davis & His Orchestra; with Rusty; Horace Caesar)
Singles: 78 rpm
BIG TOWN 15-25 53
RPM 15-25 53
RECORDED IN HOLLYWOOD 15-25 52
Singles: 7-inch
BIG TOWN (106 "Big Eyes")......................25-50 53
BIG TOWN (110 "What Kind of Fool Is He")...25-50 53
RPM (393 "Tried to Reason with You Baby")..25-50 53
RECORDED IN HOLLYWOOD (234 "The River")..125-175 52
RECORDED IN HOLLYWOOD (235 "Goodbye Baby")..50-75 52
RECORDED IN HOLLYWOOD (236 "Talking to Myself")..25-50 52
RECORDED IN HOLLYWOOD (238 "Do Right")..25-50 52

RECORDED IN HOLLYWOOD (239 "Atomic Love") ... 25-50 52
SKYLARK (611 "Adorable") ... 3-5
Also see CALLENDER, Red
Also see DAVIS, Maxwell
Also see WILSON, Jimmy / Thrillers / Little Caesar

LITTLE CAESAR

Singles: 7-inch

RCA (7270 "I'm Reachin' ") ... 10-20 58

LITTLE CAESAR

(With the Ark Angels)

Singles: 7-inch

JACK BEE (1005 "I Hope That It's Me") .. 10-20 60
JACK BEE (1008 "The Ghost of Mary Meade") ... 10-20 60

LITTLE CAESAR & CONSPIRATORS

Singles: 7-inch

STUDIO CITY (1023 "New Orleans") ... 40-60 '60s

LITTLE CAESAR & EMPIRE

Singles: 7-inch

PARKWAY (152 "Everybody Dance Now") ... 10-20 67

LITTLE CAESAR & ROMANS P&R/R&B '61

(Caesar & the Romans; Ceasar & Romans)

Singles: 7-inch

DEL-FI (4158 "Those Oldies But Goodies") ... 20-30 61
DEL-FI (4164 "Hully Gully Again") ... 20-30 61
DEL-FI (4166 "Memories of Those Oldies But Goodies") ... 15-25 61
DEL-FI (4170 "Ten Commandments of Love") ... 30-40 61
DEL-FI (4176 "Popeye One More Time") 10-15 62
ESSAR (7803 "We Belong Together") ... 4-6 78
GJM ... 10-20 68
HI-NOTE (194 "What's Wrong with You")...5-10
LOST NITE ... 4-8
SCEPTER (12237 "Baby Love") ... 5-10 68

LPs: 10/12-inch

DEL-FI (1218 "Memories of Those Oldies But Goodies") ... 50-75 61
Members: Carl Burnett; David Johnson; Early Harris; Leroy Sanders; Johnny Simmons.
Also see BLUE JAYS / Little Caesar & Romans
Also see BURNETT, Carl, & Hustlers

LITTLE CAL

Singles: 7-inch

GOLDEN CREST (553 "Young School Girl") ... 15-20 60

LITTLE CAL / Mad Lads

Singles: 7-inch

GOLDEN CREST (533 "Young School Girl") ... 15-25 59
(Reissued on Golden Crest 553 with Little Cal on both sides.)
Also see LITTLE CAL

LITTLE CAMERON

Singles: 7-inch

STYLO (2016 "She's Leaving") ... 40-60 59

LITTLE CHARLES

(With the Sidewinders)

Singles: 7-inch

BOTANIC (1001 "Shanty Town") ... 5-10 68
DECCA (31980 I'm Available") ... 20-30 66
DECCA (32095 Taste of the Good Life") . 10-20 67
DECCA (32233 The Loner") ... 10-15 67
DECCA (32321 Sweet Lorene") ... 10-15 68
JEWEL (752 "Give Me a Chance") ... 10-15 65
RED SANDS (701 "You're a Blessing") ... 8-12
STRIPE (333 "I Don't Like the Game") ... 10-15 62

LITTLE CHARLES & GENTS

Singles: 7-inch

VISCOJON (6425 "Oh What a Dream")... 50-75

LITTLE CHERYL

(Cheryl Williams)

Singles: 7-inch

CAMEO (270 "Heaven Only Knows") ... 20-30 63
CAMEO (276 thru 307) ... 8-12 63-64
REPRISE (20109 "Jim") ... 8-12 62
Also see WILLIAMS, Little Cheryl

LITTLE CHICO & CORONDOLAYS

Singles: 7-inch

STYLE (1927 "My Wishes") ... 20-30 65

LITTLE CHIPS & CHORDELLS

Singles: 7-inch

HULL (746 "Amazon Girl") ... 30-40 61

LITTLE CINDY

Singles: 7-inch

COLUMBIA (41346 "He's Around") ... 8-10 59

Picture Sleeves

COLUMBIA (41346 "He's Around") ... 10-20 59

LITTLE CINDY & WILLIS SISTERS

Singles: 7-inch

COLUMBIA (41320 "Blue Christmas") ... 8-10 59

Picture Sleeves

COLUMBIA (41320 "Blue Christmas") ... 10-20 59
Also see LITTLE CINDY
Also see WILLIS SISTERS

LITTLE CLEM & DEW DROPS

Singles: 7-inch

ZYNN (504 "Waiting in the Chapel") ... 100-150 58
(Reissued as by the Gay Notes.)
Also see GAYNOTES

LITTLE CLYDIE & TEENS

Singles: 78 rpm

RPM (462 "A Casual Look") ... 40-50 56

Singles: 7-inch

RPM (462 "A Casual Look") ... 75-125 56

LITTLE COOLBREEZES

Singles: 7-inch

EBONY (1004 "Downstairs") ... 150-200 59
EBONY (1005 "Won't You Come In") ... 200-250 59

LITTLE COOPER & DRIFTERS

Singles: 7-inch

STEVENS (105 "Evening Train") ... 75-125 59
Member: Sonny Cooper.

LITTLE "D" & BEL-AIRES

Singles: 7-inch

RAFT (604 "Are You My Girl") ... 100-200 62

LITTLE D & DELIGHTERS

Singles: 7-inch

LITTLE "D" (1010 "Oh My Darling") ... 200-300 58

LITTLE DANNY

Singles: 7-inch

SHARP (112 "Your Precious Love") ... 10-15 60

LITTLE DAVID

(David Wylie)

Singles: 78 rpm

REGAL (3271 "Shackels 'Round My Body") ... 25-50 50

LITTLE DAVID

Singles: 78 rpm

INTERNATIONAL ... 10-15 52
RPM (371 "Crying Blues") ... 25-50 52
(7-inch 78rpm.)
RPM (371 "Crying Blues") ... 10-15 52

LITTLE DAVID

(With the Harps)

Singles: 78 rpm

SAVOY (1178 "I Won't Cry") ... 10-15 56

Singles: 7-inch

521 (1001 "Love Me") ... 5-10
SAVOY (1178 "I Won't Cry") ... 15-25 56
SAVOY (1617 "So Long") ... 10-15 63
SAVOY (1622 "Work of Art") ... 10-15 63
Member: David Baughan.
Also see DRIFTERS

LITTLE DAVID

Singles: 7-inch

MERCURY (71323 "I'm Glad I Waited") ... 10-15 58

LITTLE DAVID

Singles: 7-inch

SYMPHONY (40 "Call On Me") ... 25-35
Also see CORRENTE, Sal

LITTLE DEAN'S COMBO

Singles: 7-inch

PEORIA (101 "Happy Bullfrog") ... 10-20 64

LITTLE DENNY

(With the Torkays)

Singles: 7-inch

PERRY (1 "Rock & Roll Blues") ... 40-60 58
PERRY (2 "I'd Love to Take You Walking") ... 50-75 58

LITTLE DIPPERS P&R '60

(Anita Kerr Singers)

Singles: 7-inch

DOT (16602 "For Just a Little While Tonight") ... 5-10 64
UNIVERSITY (210 "Forever") ... 10-20 59
UNIVERSITY (211 "Forever") ... 10-20 59
UNIVERSITY (603 "Be Sincere") ... 10-20 60
UNIVERSITY (608 "Lonely") ... 10-20 60
Also see KERR, Anita

LITTLE DIXIE

("11 Year-Old International Prince of Rhythm")

Singles: 7-inch

LAS VEGAS STRIP (101 "Be Fair") ... 100-200 59

LITTLE DOOLEY & FABULOUS TEARS

Singles: 7-inch

BAYLOR (101 "I Love You") ... 15-25 65
NORTH BAY ... 5-10
Member: Dooley Silverspoon.

LITTLE DOUG

(Doug Sahm)

Singles: 78 rpm

SARG (113 "A Real American Joe") ... 15-25 55

Singles: 7-inch

SARG (113 "A Real American Joe") ... 50-75 55
Also see SAHM, Doug

LITTLE DUCK & DRAKES

Singles: 7-inch

KINGSTON (419 "Ramblin' Guy") ... 50-75 60
PEE VEE (139 "Every Beat of My Heart") ... 75-100 66
X-BAT (2001 "Ramblin' Guy") ... 4-8 2000
(Red vinyl.)
Members: Ronnie Aungst; Donald "Duck" Hunter; Gordy Snyder; Charlie Brinkman; Reed Dombach; Mike Wickenheiser; Rick Huxta; Doug Dempsey; Jack Lovinger; Glenn Corvelle; Bo Eddy; Bobby Nolt; Bill Teats.

LITTLE "E" & MELLO-TONE 3

Singles: 7-inch

FALCO (302 "Candy Apple Red Impala") 15-25 61
FALCO (304 "I'm Knockin' Love") ... 15-25 61

LITTLE EDDIE

(With the Johnny Mann Singers)

Singles: 7-inch

BIG BEAT ... 5-10 '60s
LIBERTY (55433 "Look No More") ... 5-10 62
MONUMENT (827 "Cozy Inn") ... 5-10 63
REGINALD ... 10-20 65
Also see MANN, Johnny, Singers

LITTLE EDDIE & DON JUANS

Singles: 7-inch

FORTUNE (836 "This Is a Miracle") ... 40-50 57
Also see LAKE, Don, & Don Juans
Also see LITTLE EDDIE & FIVE DOLLARS

LITTLE EDDIE & FIVE DOLLARS

Singles: 7-inch

FORTUNE (845 "Yellow Moon") ... 30-40 58
Also see FIVE DOLLARS
Also see LITTLE EDDIE & DON JUANS

LITTLE EDITH

Singles: 7-inch

JESSICA (1602 "I Couldn't Take It") ... 10-20

LITTLE ELLIS & L7s

Singles: 7-inch

CLW (6578 "Barb Wire") ... 15-25 62

LITTLE ERNIE

(With the Park Williams Combo)

Singles: 7-inch

SUMIT (0008 "You Lied and I Cried") ... 60-80 63

LITTLE ESTHER R&B '50

(Esther Phillips; Little Esther Phillips; with Earle Warren Orchestra; with Johnny Otis Orchestra)

Singles: 78 rpm

DECCA ... 15-25 54
FEDERAL ... 25-50 51
SAVOY ... 8-12 56

Singles: 7-inch

ATLANTIC ... 8-15 64-67
DECCA (28804 "Talkin' All Out of My Head") ... 20-30 54
DECCA (48305 "Stop Cryin' ") ... 20-30 54
DECCA (48314 "He's a No Good Man") .. 50-75 54
FEDERAL (12023 "I'm a Bad Girl") ... 75-125 51
FEDERAL (12042 "Crying and Singing the Blues") ... 75-125 51
FEDERAL (12055 "Crying Blues") ... 75-125 52
FEDERAL (12063 "Summertime") ... 75-125 52
FEDERAL (12065 "Better Beware") ... 75-125 52
(Black vinyl.)
FEDERAL (12065 "Better Beware") ... 200-300 52
(Blue vinyl.)
FEDERAL (12078 "Aged and Mellow") .. 75-125 52
FEDERAL (12090 "Ramblin' Blues") ... 75-125 52
FEDERAL (12126 "Hound Dog") ... 75-125 53
FEDERAL (12142 "Cherry Wine") ... 75-125 53
GUSTO ... 3-5
KUDU ... 4-6 72-76
LENOX (5555 thru 5577) ... 10-15 62-63
MERCURY ... 4-6 77-79
ROULETTE (7031 thru 7059) ... 5-10 69
SAVOY (1193 thru 1563) ... 10-15 56-59
WARWICK (559 "The Chains") ... 10-20 60
WARWICK (610 "Gee Baby") ... 10-20 61
WINNING ... 3-5 83

LPs: 10/12-inch

ATLANTIC (1500 & 1600 series) ... 8-12 70-76
ATLANTIC (8100 series) ... 20-30 65-66
KING (622 "Memory Lane") ... 1500-2000 59
KUDU ... 8-12 72-76
LENOX (227 "Release Me") ... 30-50 62
MERCURY ... 5-10 78-81
YORKSHIRE ... 8-12
Also see ADAMS, Faye / Little Esther / Shirley & Lee
Also see OTIS, Johnny, Quintette, with Little Esther & Robins

LITTLE ESTHER & DOMINOES WITH EARLE WARREN ORCHESTRA / Little Esther with Earle Warren Orchestra

Singles: 78 rpm

FEDERAL ... 100-200 51

Singles: 7-inch

FEDERAL (12036 "Heart to Heart") ... 350-500 51
Also see DOMINOES

LITTLE ESTHER & BIG AL DOWNING

Singles: 7-inch

LENOX (5565 "You Never Miss the Water") ... 10-15 63
Also see DOWNING, Al

LITTLE ESTHER & JUNIOR WITH THE JOHNNY OTIS ORCHESTRA / Johnny Otis Orchestra with the Vocaleers

Singles: 78 rpm

SAVOY (824 "Get Together Blues") ... 25-50 51
Also see VOCALEERS

LITTLE ESTHER & LITTLE WILLIE LITTLEFIELD

Singles: 78 rpm

FEDERAL ... 40-60 52-53

Singles: 7-inch

FEDERAL (12108 "Last Laugh Blues") .. 75-125 52
FEDERAL (12115 "Turn the Lamps Down Low") ... 75-125 53
Also see LITTLEFIELD, Little Willie

LITTLE ESTHER & CLYDE McPHATTER

Singles: 7-inch

FEDERAL (12344 "Heart to Heart") ... 40-60 58
Also see McPHATTER, Clyde

LITTLE ESTHER & BOBBY NUNN

Singles: 78 rpm

FEDERAL ... 50-100 52-53

Singles: 7-inch

FEDERAL (12100 "Saturday Night Daddy") ... 250-450 52
FEDERAL (12122 "You Took My Love Too Fast") ... 250-450 53
Also see NUNN, Bobby

LITTLE ESTHER WITH JOHNNY OTIS & HIS ORCHESTRA / Johnny Otis & His Orchestra

Singles: 7-inch

MODERN (748 "Mean Ole Gal") ... 15-25 50

LITTLE ESTHER & MEL WALKER

(Esther & Mel; with Johnny Otis Orchestra)

Singles: 78 rpm

FEDERAL (12055 "Ring-A-Ding Doo") ... 20-40 52
SAVOY (735 "Mistrustin' Blues") ... 20-40 50
SAVOY (759 "Deceivin' Blues") ... 20-40 50

SAVOY (1146 "My Christmas Blues")...... 10-20 56
Singles: 7-inch
FEDERAL (12055 "Ring-A-Ding Doo") 100-150 52
SAVOY (735 "Mistrustin' Blues")......... 100-150 50
SAVOY (759 "Deceivin' Blues") 100-150 50
SAVOY (1146 "My Christmas Blues")...... 25-50 56
Also see OTIS, Johnny
Also see WALKER, Mel

LITTLE ESTHER & EARLE WARREN ORCHESTRA
("Vocal By Little Esther and the Dominoes"/"Vocal By Little Esther with Orchestra")
Singles: 78 rpm
FEDERAL.................................. 150-250 51
Singles: 7-inch
FEDERAL (12016 "The Deacon Moves In")................................ 400-600 51
Also see DOMINOES

LITTLE EVA P&R/R&B/LP '62
Singles: 7-inch
ABC..4-6 74
AMY (943 "Stand by Me")......................5-10 65
BELL (45264 "Loco-Motion")......................4-6 72
DIMENSION (1000 thru 1019)................ 15-25 62-63
DIMENSION (1035 "Makin' with the Magilla") 10-20 64
DIMENSION (1042 "Takin' Back What I Said")....................................... 10-20 64
MCA..3-5 80
SPRING......................................4-6 70
VERVE (10529 "Everything Is Beautiful About You") 5-10 67
Picture Sleeves
DIMENSION (1035 "Makin' with the Magilla") 25-35 64
LPs: 10/12-inch
DIMENSION (DLP-6000 "L-L-L-L-Locomotion")........................ 40-60 62
(Monaural.)
DIMENSION (DLPS-6000 "L-L-L-L-Locomotion")........................ 50-80 62
(Stereo.)
Also see BOYD, Idalia
Also see COOKIES / Little Eva / Carole King
Also see IRWIN, Big Dee
Also see KING, Ben E.

LITTLE FAY
Singles: 7-inch
TOP-POP (260 "I Don't Care What the People Say").. 75-125 66

LITTLE FEAT LP '74
Singles: 7-inch
W.B. 4-6 70-78
LPs: 10/12-inch
MFSL (2-013 "Waiting for Columbus"). 100-150 78
NAUTILUS (24 "Time Loves a Hero")...... 25-35 '70s
(Half-speed mastered.)
W.B. (984 "Hoy Hoy") 15-20 81
(Promotional issue only.)
W.B. (1890 thru 2884) 8-15 70-76
W.B. (3015 thru 3538) 6-12 77-81
W.B. (25000 & 26000 series)....................5-8 88-90
Members: Lowell George; Ken Gradney; Sam Clayton; Richard Hayward; Fred Tackett; Paul Barrere; Bill Payne; Roy Estrada.
Also see COODER, Ry
Also see HARRIS, Emmylou
Also see MOTHERS OF INVENTION
Also see TOWER OF POWER
Also see ZEVON

LITTLE FRANKIE
Singles: 7-inch
ABC-PAR (10510 "Going, Going, Gone") 10-15 63
CAPITOL (5416 "The Kind of Boy You Can't Forget")..................................... 10-15 65
INTERSTATE.....................................5-10 '60s
SMASH (2067 "I Want to Marry You")........5-10 66

LITTLE FREDDIE & GENTS
Singles: 7-inch
SHOWCASE (402 "Betty")..................... 10-15 65

LITTLE FREDDY & ROCKETS
Singles: 7-inch
CHIEF (33 "All My Love")...................... 400-600 58
Also see WOOD, Brenton

LITTLE G.
LPs: 10/12-inch
TOP RANK (316 "Bahama Bash")...........10-20 60
(Monaural.)
TOP RANK (616 "Bahama Bash")...........20-25 60
(Stereo.)

LITTLE GIGI
(With Vernon Harrell)
Singles: 7-inch
DECCA (31721 "Baby, Dont'cha Worry")...5-10 64
DECCA (31760 "I Volunteer")...................10-20 65
SELECT (731 "I'm Hurt and So Is My Heart")..8-12 64
Also see HARRELL, Vernon

LITTLE GINO & JINKS
Singles: 7-inch
.007 (101 "Beggar of Love")......................15-25 '60s

LITTLE GIRL BLUE
Singles: 7-inch
UNIVERSAL (5004 "But It's True")...........20-30 64

LITTLE GIRLS
LPs: 10/12-inch
FTM ("Little Girls")....................................75-100 85
(Clear vinyl. Promotional issue only. Issued with two 8" x 10" photos, and three bio-credits pages. Three tracks. 100 made. No selection number used. With Clem Burke and Nigel Harrison.)
PVC (5904 "Thank Heaven")....................15-20 83
(Six tracks.)
Members: Kip Brown; Caron Maso; Michele Maso; Jon Gerlach; Jeff Fair; Steve Sicular.
Also see BLONDIE
Also see SHOCK

LITTLE GREGORY & CONCEPTS
Singles: 7-inch
LOMPRI (270 "Go Away")..........................15-25 69

LITTLE GUY & GIANTS
Singles: 7-inch
LAWN (103 "So Young") 150-250 60
Members: Harold Johnson; Arthur Crier; Carl Spencer.
Also see HALOS

LITTLE HANK & RHYTHM KINGS
Singles: 7-inch
RHYTHM & RANGE (101 "Christene").....20-30

LITTLE HENRY & SHAMROCKS
Singles: 7-inch
KENT (398 "Come to Me")......................10-15 64

LITTLE HERBERT & ARABIANS
Singles: 7-inch
TEEK (1/2 "Bouncing Ball")..................150-250 64
Member: Herbert Reeves.
Also see SHARPEES

LITTLE HERBIE
(With the Sandabs; with Wise Guys)
Singles: 7-inch
BAMBOO (522 "Crab Louie")..................10-20 62
CATCH (107 "Crab Louie") 5-10 64
IN-SOUND (412 "Beach Ball")....................5-10 68

LITTLE HERMAN
Singles: 7-inch
ARLEN (749 "One Out of a Hundred").....15-25 64
ARLEN (751 "I'm Gonna Put the Hurt on You")..15-25 64
GINA (751 "I'm Gonna Put the Hurt on You")..15-25

LITTLE HITE & SOUL ROCKERS
Singles: 7-inch
JA-WES (0116 "Soul Blues")....................10-20 '60s
JA-WES (3007 "Fine")...............................10-20 '60s

LITTLE HOOKS & KINGS
(With the Sentries)
Singles: 7-inch
CENTURY (1300 "Count Your Blessings")...10-15 63
(Second issue.)
CHESS (1867 "Count Your Blessings")......5-10 63
(Third issue.)
CLARIDGE (303 "Jerk Train")....................8-12 65
LITTLE RICK (909 "Count Your Blessings")..15-25 63
(First issue.)
U.A. (50932 "Give the Drummer Some Time")...5-10 72

LITTLE HUDSON & HIS RED DEVIL TRIO
(Hudson Shower)
Singles: 78 rpm
J.O.B. (1015 "Rough Treatment")............50-75 53
Singles: 7-inch
J.O.B. (1015 "Rough Treatment").........125-175 53

LITTLE HYMIE
Singles: 7-inch
LIBERTY (55256 "Clock Rock")................10-15 60

LITTLE IKE
Singles: 7-inch
CHAMPION (1011 "She Can Rock")......75-100 59

LITTLE ISIDORE & INQUISITORS
(Little Isldore & Golden Inquisitors)
Singles: 7-inch
EARLY BIRD (5000 "Woo Woo Train")........3-5 95
(Blue vinyl.)
EARLY BIRD (5001 "Bongo Stomp") 3-5 95
(Gold vinyl.)
GOLDEN GUP (101/102 "Harlem Hit Parade")..5-10 99
(Yellow vinyl. 700 made.)
STOOP SOUNDS (116 "My Love for You")...100-125 98
STOOP SOUNDS (117 "Peppermint Stick")..100-125 98
Picture Sleeves
GOLDEN GUP (101/102 "Harlem Hit Parade")..8-12 99
(350 made.)

LITTLE IVA & HER BAND
Singles: 7-inch
MIRACLE (2 "When I Needed You") ..500-1000 60
Member: Raynona Gordy.

LITTLE J & MONOTONES
Singles: 7-inch
SESAME STREET ("Sad").........................50-75
(Selection number not known.)

LITTLE JAN & RADIANTS
(Jan & Radiants)
Singles: 7-inch
CLOCK (1028 "Is It True")..........................20-30 60
GOLDISC (G-15 "If You Love Me") 10-15 63
QUEEN (24007 "If You Love Me")...........15-20 61
VIM (507 "If You Love Me")......................30-40 60
(Yellow label.)
VIM (507 "If You Love Me")......................10-15 60
(Pink label.)

LITTLE JEANETTE
Singles: 7-inch
GREEN LIGHT (0040 "Crazy Crazy") 15-25

LITTLE JERRY
(Jerry Williams)
Singles: 7-inch
ALDO (502 "Chapel on the Hill")..............15-25 62
EMBER (1081 "Don't You Feel") 8-12 61
Also see WILLIAMS, Jerry
Also see WILLIAMS, Little Jerry

LITTLE JESSIE
Singles: 7-inch
EBB (136 "Huggin'")................................15-25 58

LITTLE JIMMY & SPARROWS
Singles: 7-inch
VAL-UE (101 "Two Hearts Together")..200-300 58
(300 made.)

LITTLE JIMMY & TOPS
(Little Jimmy Rivers)
Singles: 7-inch
LEN (1011 "Puppy Love") 15-20 61
(Black vinyl.)
LEN (1011 "Puppy Love") 50-75 61
(Red vinyl.)
V-TONE (102 "Puppy Love")...................75-125 59
(First pressings credit only the Tops.)
V-TONE (102 "Puppy Love")....................40-50 59
("Philadelphia" under label name.)
Member: Jimmy Rivers.
Also see RIVERS, Little Jimmy, & Tops
Also see TOPS

LITTLE JOE
(Joe Hill Louis)
Singles: 7-inch
HOUSE OF SOUND (500 "Glamour Girl")...75-125 57
Also see LOUIS, Joe Hill

LITTLE JOE
Singles: 7-inch
BRUNSWICK (55369 "Fool on the Hill") 5-10 68
LPs: 10/12-inch
BRUNSWICK (54135 "Little Joe Sure Can Sing")..10-15 68

LITTLE JOE & LATINAIRES
Singles: 7-inch
TOMI 10-15
WHITE WHALE (304 "Crazy Baby").......50-100 69
LPs: 10/12-inch
GOOD LUCK (0001 "Chicanos Can, Too!")...30-50 68

LITTLE JOE & MOROCCOS
Singles: 78 rpm
BUMBLE BEE (500 "Trouble in the Candy Shop")...10-15 58
Singles: 7-inch
BUMBLE BEE (500 "Trouble in the Candy Shop")...15-25 58
Member: Joe Cook.
Also see LITTLE JOE & THRILLERS
Also see PEPS
Also see UNDISPUTED TRUTH

LITTLE JOE & MUSTANGS
Singles: 7-inch
CHALLENGE (59258 "I Dig You Baby")... 10-15 64
CHALLENGE (59273 "South Swell")........ 10-15 64

LITTLE JOE & RAMRODS
Singles: 7-inch
SOMA (1403 "Yogi Twist")......................20-25 '60s
STUDIO CITY (1014 "Hurtin' Inside").......25-35 '60s
STUDIO CITY (1019 "Ooh Poo Pah Doo")..25-35 '60s
Members: Joe Hupp; Leland Grieves; Gene Hammerlun; Larry Young; Doug Spiedel.
Also see SMOKE RING

LITTLE JOE & THRILLERS P&R '57
(Little Joe; Little Joe the Thriller)
Singles: 78 rpm
OKEH 15-25 56-57
Singles: 7-inch
ENJOY (2011 "Peanuts & Popcorn")..........5-10 64
EPIC (2206 "Peanuts")...............................8-10 63
EPIC (7088 "Peanuts").............................15-25 57
(Canadian. Has same number as on Okeh)
EPIC (9292 "It's Too Bad We Had to Say Goodbye") 10-15 58
(Canadian.)
EPIC (9431 "Run Little Girl")....................10-15 61
MGM...4-6 70-73
OKEH (7075 "This I Know")......................20-30 56
OKEH (7088 "Peanuts")...........................20-30 57
(Purple label.)
OKEH (7088 "Peanuts")...........................10-15 57
(Yellow label.)
OKEH (7094 "Echoes Keep Calling Me") 10-15 57
(Yellow label.)
OKEH (7099 thru 7140)..........................10-15 57-61
PEANUT..5-10
REPRISE (20142 "Peanuts")......................5-10 63
ROSE (835 "I'll Do Anything")....................8-12 63
TWENTIETH CENTURY (1214 "For Sentimental Reasons")...25-35 61
EPs: 7-inch
EPIC (7198 "Little Joe and the Thrillers") 75-125 58
Members: Joe Cook; Richard Frazier; Farris Hill; Don Burnett; Harry Pascle.
Also see COOK, Little Joe
Also see LITTLE JOE & MOROCCOS

LITTLE JOE BLUE R&B '66
(Joe Valery Jr.)
Singles: 7-inch
CHECKER (1141 "Dirty Work Going On") 10-15 66
CHECKER (1150 "Once a Fool")...............5-10 66
CHECKER (1173 "Me and My Woman")....5-10 67
JEWEL 4-6 69-76
KRIS 4-6
MILES AHEAD..5-10
MOVIN' (132 "Dirty Work Going On").......35-40 66
MOVIN' (134 "Once a Fool")......................5-10 66
MOVIN' (135 "Little Baby").........................5-10 66

SOUL SET (103 "Why I Sing the Blues")......4-6 74
RONN..3-5 84
SOUND STAGE 7 (2662 "Lonely") 4-6 70

LITTLE JOEY & FLIPS P&R '62
(Joey Hall)
Singles: 7-inch
JOY (262 "Bongo Stomp")..................... 10-15 62
JOY (268 "Bongo Gully")...................... 10-15 62
Members: Joey Hall; James Meagher; John Smith; Jeff Leonard; Fred Gerace; Jimmy Dilks.
Also see JOEY

LITTLE JOHN
Singles: 7-inch
GO GATE (2 "Just Wait & See") 50-100
MARTAY (4508 "Heart Breakin' Time") ... 20-30 '60s

LITTLE JOHN & SHERWOOD MEN
Singles: 7-inch
BANGAR (608 "Movin' Out") 25-35 63
FLEETWOOD.. 10-20
Members: Rick Sundvick; Jerry Phillips; John Hamilton; Bill Berg.

LITTLE JOHN & TONY
Singles: 7-inch
VOLKANO (5001 "All I Ask")................... 50-75 65

LITTLE JOHN & UNFORGETTABLES
Singles: 7-inch
ALAN K (6901 "Funny What a Little Kiss Can Do") 100-200 62
(First issued as by the Untouchables.)
Also see UNTOUCHABLES

LITTLE JOHNNY & RUMBLERS
Singles: 7-inch
DOWNEY (119 "Hustler")........................ 10-15 64
Member: Johnny Kirkland.
Also see RUMBLERS

LITTLE JUAREZ
Singles: 7-inch
NORTH BEACH (1002 "El Jefe")............. 15-25 66

LITTLE JUNE & HIS JANUARYS
(Lil' June & January's)
Singles: 7-inch
PROFILE (4009 "Oh My Love")........... 100-150 59
SALEM (188 "Hello")........................ 1000-1500 63
(Commercial issue. Green-gold label.)
SALEM (188 "Hello")............................ 500-750 63
(Reads: "Free Sample." Promotional issue only.)
Members: Johnny "June" Coleman; Wilbert Johnson; Lewis Johnson; Claudie Johnson.

LITTLE JUNIOR'S BLUE FLAMES R&B '53
(Junior Parker)
Singles: 78 rpm
SUN 100-150 53
Singles: 7-inch
SUN (187 "Feelin' Good")..................... 150-250 53
SUN (192 "Love My Baby")................... 150-250 53
Also see PARKER, Little Junior

LITTLE KIDS
Singles: 7-inch
TOWER (298 "Santa Claus Is Stuck in the Chimney")... 10-15 66
Also see VENTRILLS

LITTLE L. & STREETLIGHTERS
Singles: 7-inch
BONDED (22 "Later for the Twist")........... 20-30 62

LITTLE LADY BEATLES / Insects
Singles: 7-inch
APPLAUSE (1002 "Dear Beatles"/"Let's Bug the Beatles").. 15-25 64

LITTLE LATOURS
Singles: 7-inch
FOLK STAR (1205 "Ho Ho Ho Babe")..... 10-20

LITTLE LISA
(Lisa Miller)
Singles: 7-inch
V.I.P. (25023 "Hang On Bill")................... 15-25 65
Also see MILLER, Lisa

LITTLE LOU & HIS BAND
LPs: 10/12-inch
BIG TOP 25-35 62
Member: James Gary "Little Lou" Fowler.

LITTLE LOUIE
Singles: 7-inch
SIMS ("Short Trip")...................................15-25 59
(Selection number not known.)

LITTLE LOUIE & LOVERS
Singles: 7-inch
VISCOUNT (102 "Someday You'll Pay")..10-20 62

LITTLE LUTHER
Singles: 7-inch
APT (25060 "Cryin' Blues") 10-20 61
CHECKER (1090 "Twirl") 10-15 64
CHECKER (1096 "Twirl")..............................8-10 64
CRISS CROSS 5-10
DOT (16325 "Du Dee Squat").......................8-12 62
TARX (1002 "Doggin' Me")..........................10-15 62

LITTLE MAC
(With the Bravadoes; "Mac" McCardle)
Singles: 7-inch
JAYBIRD 15-25
LITTLE MAC (101 "Dance Baby")...........75-125
LUCKY..10-20

LITTLE MACK
(Little Mac; Little Mack & His Boys; Mack Simmons & His Boys; Mack Simmons; Mack Sims)
Singles: 7-inch
BEA & BABY (109 "Time Is Getting Tougher")...20-30 60
BEA & BABY (113 "You Mistreated Me")...20-30 60
BEA & BABY (118 "Let's Hootenanny Blues")...20-30 61
C.J. (606 "Come Back")..............................20-30 59
C.J. (607 "Jumpin' at the Cadillac") 20-30 59
CHECKER (984 "I Need Love") 10-20 61
DUD SOUND (4220 "Hard Times")............10-20 65
EL SATURN (144 "I'm Making Believe") 8-10 67
HY-TONE (119 "Sad Lover")......................30-50 58
PACER (1201 "Drivin' Wheel")...................15-25 61
PALOS (1201 "Drivin' Wheel")...................50-75 61
(First issue.)

LITTLE MAN & VICTORS
Singles: 7-inch
ROULETTE (4576 "Smile") 15-25 64
TARHEEL (064 "I Need an Angel")...........25-35 63

LITTLE MAN HENRY
Singles: 7-inch
CENTRAL (4701 "Wailin' Wildcat").......500-750

LITTLE MANNY
Singles: 7-inch
VELTONE (110 "Chuke Baby")..................40-60

LITTLE MARCUS & DEVOTIONS
Singles: 7-inch
GORDIE (1001 "I'll Always Remember") 150-200 64

LITTLE MAXIE
Singles: 7-inch
DEE DEE (732 "Clap Along with Max") 10-20

LITTLE MELVIN
Singles: 7-inch
AMA (502 "Life Is Miserable") 20-30
VEE-EIGHT (1001 "Too Slick").............100-150 '60s
Also see SHAW, Timmy, & Little Melvin

LITTLE MELVIN & BOLEROS
Singles: 7-inch
VALERIE (4397 "Jealous Lover") 20-30

LITTLE MIGUEL'S GOLDEN FIVE
Singles: 7-inch
DRUMMOND (106 "Garlic Breath") 10-20 67

LITTLE MILTON
(Milton Anderson)
Singles: 78 rpm
DELTA (403 "Little Milton's Boogie") 50-75 53

LITTLE MILTON R&B '62
(Milton Campbell; with Playmates of Rhythm)
Singles: 78 rpm
BOBBIN (101 "That Will Never Do") 100-150 58
METEOR...50-100 57
SUN (194 "Beggin' My Baby")..................75-125 53
SUN (200 "If You Love Me")....................75-125 54
SUN (220 "Homesick for My Baby") 100-150 55
Singles: 7-inch
BOBBIN (101 "That Will Never Do") 40-50 58
BOBBIN (103 thru 125) 20-30 59-60
BOBBIN (128 "Cross My Heart") 50-60 61
CHECKER (0124 thru 0252).........................4-8 72-76
CHECKER (977 thru 1096)..........................8-12 61-65
CHECKER (1105 thru 1239).........................5-10 65-71
CHESS 4-8 73-76
GLADES...4-8 76-78
GOLDEN EAR 3-6 80
MCA..3-5 83
MALACO 3-5 84-86
METEOR (5040 "Love at First Sight") ..300-400 57
METEOR (5045 "Let My Baby Be")......150-250 57
MIER...4-6 78
STAX...3-8 71-83
SUN (194 "Beggin' My Baby")..............200-300 53
SUN (200 "If You Love Me") 250-350 54
SUN (220 "Homesick for My Baby").....300-500 55
LPs: 10/12-inch
CHECKER (2995 "We're Gonna Make It")..20-30 65
CHECKER (3002 "Big Blues") 20-30 66
CHECKER (3011 "Grits Ain't Groceries").15-20 69
CHECKER (3012 "If Walls Could Talk")...20-30 70
CHESS (204 "Little Milton").......................15-25 76
(Two discs.)
CHESS (50013 "Greatest Hits")................10-15 72
GLADES...8-10 76-77
GOLDEN EAR 5-10 80
MCA..5-8 83
MALACO 5-10 84-92
STAX...6-12 73-81
Also see MANN, Herbie

LITTLE MISS CORNSHUCKS
Singles: 78 rpm
ALADDIN (3126 "Waiting in Vain") 30-40 52
MILTONE (243 "In the Rain")....................50-75 48
Singles: 7-inch
ALADDIN (3126 "Waiting in Vain") 40-60 52
CHESS (1785 "No Teasin' Around").........10-20 61
LPs: 10/12-inch
CHESS (1453 "Loneliest Girl in Town")....50-75 61
Also see DAVIS, Maxwell

LITTLE MISS JESSIE / Benny Sharp & His Band
Singles: 7-inch
MEL-O (101 "My Baby's Gone") 25-50 61

LITTLE MISS WANDA
(With the Joe Wade Orchestra)
Singles: 7-inch
ARIES (1020 "My Johnny")...................400-500 61

LITTLE MOJO
(With the Jesters; with Caravans; George Buford)
Singles: 7-inch
INDIGO (139 "Something on Your Mind")..15-25 62
MOJO (0513 "Paula")............................75-100 60
(Identification number shown since no selection number is used.)
NORMAN (505 "Paula")..............................40-50 61
Also see BUFORD, Mojo
Also see MOJO

LITTLE MOOSE & HUNTERS
Singles: 7-inch
SMC (1373 "Granny Rock") 25-35 59

LITTLE MUMMY
Singles: 7-inch
FEDERAL (12371 "Where You At, Jack?")..10-20 60

LITTLE NAT
Singles: 7-inch
PIK (242 "Do This Do That") 10-15 61

LITTLE NAT & ETIQUETTES
Singles: 7-inch
CLOCK (2001 "You're So Close")............10-15 67
Member: Nathaniel Burknight.
Also see LITTLE NATE & CHRYSLERS

LITTLE NATALIE & HENRY
(With the Gifts)
Singles: 7-inch
ROULETTE (4540 "Teardrops Are Falling")..10-15 63
Member: Henry Ford.

LITTLE NATE & CHRYSLERS
Singles: 7-inch
JOHNSON (318 "Someone Up There") .50-100 59
Member: Nathaniel Burknight.
Also see LITTLE NAT & ETIQUETTES
Also see SHELLS

LITTLE OTIS
(Otis Hayes)
Singles: 7-inch
TAMLA (54058 "I Out-Duked the Duke") . 15-25 62

LITTLE PAPA JOE
(Joseph Leon Williams)
Singles: 78 rpm
BLUE LAKE (116 "Lookin' for My Baby")..40-60 55
Singles: 7-inch
BLUE LAKE (116 "Lookin' for My Baby")..75-100 55
Also see WILLIAMS, Jody
Also see WILLIAMS, Sugar Boy

LITTLE PATRICK & SIG-A-LERTS
Singles: 7-inch
EBB TIDE (416 "Freeway Strut")..............40-50 62

LITTLE PATTIE & STATESMEN
Singles: 7-inch
WORLD HITS (150 "He's My Blonde-Headed, Stompie Wompie [Real Gone Surfer Boy]" 15-20 64

LITTLE PETE & YOUNGSTERS
(With the Aristocrats)
Singles: 7-inch
LESLEY (1925 "You Told Another Lie").50-100 63
Also see YOUNGSTERS

LITTLE PIA
(Pia Zadora)
Singles: 7-inch
LAP INT'L (1002 "Bye Bye Boy")..............20-30
(May have been a promo issue only.)
Also see ZADORA, Pia

LITTLE PORK CHOPS
(John Lee Hooker)
Singles: 78 rpm
D.R.C. DANCELAND (403 "Wayne County Ramblin' Blues")..200-300 49
Also see HOOKER, John Lee

LITTLE PRINCE & FREELOADERS / Freddie & Freeloaders
Singles: 7-inch
M&M (1263 "Nursery Love")............2000-3000 62
Also see FREDDIE & FREELOADERS

LITTLE RALPHIE
Singles: 7-inch
20TH FOX (6654 "Half Way Lover")......... 10-20 66

LITTLE RAY
Singles: 7-inch
CLOVER (1003 "Give Me Your Love")..... 15-25 59

LITTLE RAY
(With the Midnighters; with Premiers; Lil' Ray)
Singles: 7-inch
ATCO (6355 "I Who Have Nothing") 5-10 65
DONNA (1404 "I Who Have Nothing") 10-20 65
(First issue.)
DORE (590 "My Rainbow")........................ 10-15 61
FARO (617 "Karen").................................. 10-20 64
IMPACT (26 "Soul & Stomp") 20-30 64
IMPACT (30 "Loretta")...............................20-30 64
W.B. (5351 "Come Baby Dance").............. 8-10 63
Member: Ray Jiminez.

LITTLE RICHARD P&R '56
Singles: 78 rpm
PEACOCK 50-100 53
RCA (4392 "Taxi Blues")......................100-200 51
RCA (4582 "Get Rich Quick")..............100-200 52
RCA (4772 "Ain't Nothing Happenin'").100-200 52
RCA (5025 "Please Have Mercy on Me")..100-200 52
SPECIALTY...25-75 55-58
Singles: 7-inch
ABC..4-6 73
ATLANTIC (2181 "Crying in the Chapel" ..5-10 63
ATLANTIC (2192 "It Is No Secret") 5-10 63
BELL (45385 "Good Golly Miss Molly")........ 4-6 73
BRUNSWICK...5-10 68
CORAL (62366 "Milky White Way")............5-10 63
END (1057 "Save Me Lord")......................10-20 59

END (1058 "Milky White Way") 10-20 59
GREEN MOUNTAIN 4-6 73
KENT (4568 "In the Name") 4-6 72
MCA 3-5 86
MAINSTREAM (5572 "Try to Help Your Brother") 4-6 75
MANTICORE (7007 "Call My Name") 4-6 75
MERCURY (71884 thru 71965) 5-10 61-62
MODERN (1018 thru 1043) 5-10 66-67
MYSTIC VALLEY (551 "Every Night About This Time") 10-15
OKEH 5-10 66-69
PEACOCK (1658 "Little Richard's Boogie") 125-175 53
PEACOCK (1673 "Maybe I'm Right") 75-125 54
RCA (4392 "Taxi Blues") 200-300 51
(Turquoise label.)
RCA (4582 "Get Rich Quick") 200-300 52
(Turquoise label.)
RCA (4772 "Ain't Nothing Happenin' ") 100-200 52
(Black label.)
RCA (5025 "Please Have Mercy on Me") 300-400 52
(Black label.)
REPRISE 4-6 70-72
SPECIALTY (561 "Tutti-Frutti") 50-75 55
SPECIALTY (572 "Long Tall Sally") 25-35 56
SPECIALTY (579 "Rip It Up") 25-35 56
SPECIALTY (584 "Heeby Jeebies") 25-35 56
SPECIALTY (591 "All Around the World") 25-35 56
SPECIALTY (598 "Lucille") 20-30 57
SPECIALTY (606 "Jenny Jenny") 20-30 57
SPECIALTY (611 "Keep a-Knockin' ") 20-30 57
SPECIALTY (624 "Good Golly Miss Molly") 25-35 58
SPECIALTY (624 "True Fine Mama"/"Ooh! My Soul") 25-45 58
(*True Fine Mama* mis-numbered. *Ooh! My Soul* correctly numbered 633.)
SPECIALTY (633 "Ooh! My Soul"/"True Fine Mama") 20-30 58
(Both sides numbered 633.)
SPECIALTY (645 "Baby Face") 20-30 58
SPECIALTY (652 "She Knows How to Rock") 20-30 58
SPECIALTY (660 "By the Light of the Silvery Moon") 20-30 59
SPECIALTY (664 "Lonesome and Blue") 20-30 59
SPECIALTY (670 "Shake a Hand") 15-25 59
SPECIALTY (680 "Whole Lotta Shakin' ") 10-20 60
SPECIALTY (681 "Baby") 10-20 60
SPECIALTY (686 "Directly from My Heart") 10-20 60
SPECIALTY (692 "Bama Lama Bama Loo") 15-25 64
SPECIALTY (697 "Bama Lama Bama Loo"/"Keep a-Knockin' ") .... 5-10 '60s
SPECIALTY (699 "Wonderin' ") .... 5-10 '60s
SPECIALTY (734 "Oh Why?") .... 4-6 '70s
SPECIALTY (SPBX series) 15-20 85
(Boxed sets of six colored vinyl 45s.)
TRIP 4-6 71
VEE-JAY (612 thru 665) 5-10 64-65
VEE-JAY (698 "I Don't Know What You've Got") 15-25 65
W.B. 3-5 87
WOODMAN (1001 "Hold in the Wall") .... 10-15 '60s

Picture Sleeves

MCA (52780 "Great Gosh A'Mighty") 3-5 86
MODERN (1018 "Holy Mackeral") 25-35 57
OKEH (7251 "Poor Dog") 10-15 66
SPECIALTY (606 "Jenny Jenny") 25-50 57
SPECIALTY (611 "Keep a Knockin' ") 50-75 57
SPECIALTY (624 "Good Golly Miss Molly") 25-50 58
SPECIALTY (633 "Ooh! My Soul") 25-50 58
SPECIALTY (736 "All Around the World") 4-6 85

EPs: 7-inch

CAMDEN (416 "Little Richard") 150-200 56
CAMDEN (446 "Little Richard Rocks") 100-150 56
KAMA SUTRA (17 "Little Richard") 10-20 70
SPECIALTY (400 "Here's Little Richard") 40-60 56
SPECIALTY (401 "Here's Little Richard") 40-60 56
SPECIALTY (402 "Here's Little Richard") 40-60 56
SPECIALTY (403 "Little Richard") 40-60 57
SPECIALTY (404 "Little Richard") 40-60 57
SPECIALTY (405 "Little Richard") 40-60 57

LPs: 10/12-inch

ACCORD 5-10 81
AUDIO ENCORES 20-25 80
BUDDAH 10-12 69
CAMDEN (420 "Little Richard") 150-250 56
CAMDEN (2430 "Every Hour") 20-30 70
CORAL 20-30 63
CROWN 15-25 63
CUSTOM .... 10-12 '60s
EPIC 10-12 71
EVEREST 5-8 82
EXACT 5-10 80-81
EXODUS 5-10
51 WEST .... 5-8 '80s
GNP .... 5-8 '90s
GRT 5-8 77
GOLD DISC 10-15
GUEST STAR 10-15 64
KAMA SUTRA 10-12 70
KOALA 8-15
MERCURY 20-30 61
MODERN 10-20 66
OKEH 10-20 67
PICKWICK 10-15 72
REPRISE 10-15 70-72
ROULETTE 10-15 68
SCEPTER 10-15
SPECIALTY (100 "Here's Little Richard") 300-500 57
(Reissued as Specialty 2100.)
SPECIALTY (2100 "Here's Little Richard") 50-100 57
(Label indicates "Natural Sound.")
SPECIALTY (2100 "Here's Little Richard") .... 25-50 '60s
(Label indicates "Stereo Natural Sound.")
SPECIALTY (2103 "Little Richard") 50-100 57
SPECIALTY (2104 "The Fabulous Little Richard") 50-100 58
SPECIALTY (2111 "Biggest Hits") 20-30 63
SPECIALTY (2113 "Grooviest 17 Original Hits") 10-15 68
SPECIALTY (2136 "Well Alright!") 8-10
SPECIALTY (2154 "The Essential Little Richard") 8-12 84
SPIN-O-RAMA .... 10-15 '60s
SPRINGBOARD (6002 "Little Richard") .... 5-10 '70s
SUMMIT 10-15
TRIP 10-15 71-78
20TH FOX (5010 "Gospel Songs") 15-25 63
UNITED .... 8-10 '70s
U.A. 8-10 75
UPFRONT (123 "Best of Little Richard") .. 10-15 77
VEE-JAY 15-25 64-65
VEE-JAY/DYNASTY 10-12
W.B. 5-8 87
WING 10-20 64

Session: Lee Allen; Robins; Jimi Hendrix; Billy Preston.
Note: Many Specialty reissues exist, some of which are very similar in appearance to '50s originals. Any with a zip code on covers are obviously post-1963 reissues. Discs from the '50s are heavier than reissues. Many reissues have a raised vinyl ridge around the record's outer edge—originals do not. Any on colored, or semi-transparent vinyl are reissues. Some reissues do have an identifying copyright date.
Also see ALLEN, Lee
Also see BEACH BOYS / Little Richard
Also see CANNED HEAT
Also see CHARLES, Ray / Little Richard / Sam Cooke
Also see COOKE, Sam / Lloyd Price / Larry Williams / Little Richard
Also see DUCES OF RHYTHM & TEMPO TOPPERS
Also see HENDRIX, Jimi, & Little Richard
Also see McPHATTER, Clyde / Little Richard / Jerry Butler
Also see ROBINS
Also see UPSETTERS
Also see UPSETTERS Featuring Little Richard

LITTLE RICHARD / John Cougar Mellancamp

Singles: 7-inch

ELEKTRA 3-5 88

Picture Sleeves

ELEKTRA 4-6 88
Also see MELLENCAMP, John Cougar

LITTLE RICHARD / Arthur Crudup / Red Callendar Sextet

LPs: 10/12-inch

CAMDEN (371 "Little Richard, Arthur Crudup & Red Callendar Sextet") 75-125 56
Also see CRUDUP, Big Boy

LITTLE RICHARD / Sister Rosetta

LPs: 10/12-inch

GUEST STAR 10-15
Also see LITTLE RICHARD
Also see THARPE, Sister Rosetta

LITTLE RICHIE

Singles: 7-inch

SOUND STAGE 7 (2554 "Just Another Heartache") 75-125 65
SOUND STAGE 7 (2567 "I Catch Myself Crying ") 15-25 66

LITTLE RITA

Singles: 7-inch

MAGNIFICENT (100 "Dear Love") 75-125 60

LITTLE RIVER BAND — P&R/LP '76

(LRB)

Singles: 12-inch

CAPITOL 4-6 83

Singles: 7-inch

CAPITOL 3-6 79-85
HARVEST 4-8 76-78
MCA 3-5 89-90

Picture Sleeves

CAPITOL 3-5 81-85
HARVEST 4-8 78
MCA 3-5 89

LPs: 10/12-inch

CAPITOL 5-10 79-85
HARVEST 5-10 75-80
MFSL (036 "First Under the Wire") 30-40 79
Members: Glenn Shorrock; Rick Formosa; Beeb Birtles; Graham Goble; Roger McLachlan; Derek Pellicci; George McArdle; David Briggs; Wayne Nelson; John Farnham; Steve Housden; Steven Prestwich; David Hirschfelder; Peter Becket.

LITTLE ROCK COACHMEN

Singles: 7-inch

MY (2924 "I've Had Enough") .... 10-20 '60s

LITTLE ROGER & GOOSEBUMPS

Singles: 7-inch

RICHMOND (5 "Kennedy's Girls") 4-8 79
SPLASH (315 "Stairway to Gilligan's Island") 5-10 94
SPLASH (901 "Stairway to Gilligan's Island") 25-50 78

LITTLE ROMEO & CASANOVAS

Singles: 7-inch

ASCOT (2192 "Remember Lori") 15-25 65
VEEP (1224 "Remember Lori") 8-10 66
Also see OVATIONS

LITTLE RONNIE & CHROMATICS

Singles: 7-inch

EARLY BIRD .... 10-20 '60s
H-L-S .... 5-10 '60s

LITTLE ROY & LONG JOHNS

Singles: 7-inch

EVEREST (19421 "It's Heaven") 15-25 61

LITTLE ROYAL

(With Swingmasters; "Horns by: Andrew Simms")

Singles: 7-inch

BLACK PRIDE (105 "Don't Want Nobody Standing Over Me") 4-6 73
CARNIVAL (531 "I Can Tell") 10-20 67
TRI-US 4-6 72-73

EPs: 7-inch

FLAME (1001 "Groovin") 25-35 67
Also see 4 SEASONS / Little Royal

LITTLE SAM

(Big Bill Broonzy)

Singles: 78 rpm

HUB (3003 "Please Believe Me") 30-40 45
HUB (3023 "Just a Dream") 30-40 45
Session: Don Byas; Kenny Watts; Slick Jones; John Levy.
Also see BROONZY, Big Bill
Also see BYAS, Don, Quartet

LITTLE SAMMY

Singles: 7-inch

RESTORED (1000 "Can You Love Me") 5-10
SHADE (1002 "Can You Love Me") 250-300 60
Also see YATES, Little Sammy

LITTLE SAMMY & TONES

Singles: 7-inch

JACLYN (1161 "Christine") 25-35 62
(First issued as by Little Sammy Rozzi and the Guys.)
Member: Sammy Rozzi.
Also see ROZZI, Little Sammy, & Guys

LITTLE SAMMY & WHEELETTS

Singles: 7-inch

RIP-COR (6001 "Good By [sic] My Love") .... 25-35 '60s

LITTLE SANDY

Singles: 7-inch

JC-ENT. (0001 "Devotion") .... 40-50 '60s

LITTLE SHERMAN & MOD SWINGERS

Singles: 7-inch

ABC-PAR (11233 "The Price of Love") 10-15 69
SAGPORT (105 "The Price of Love") 25-35 69
(First issue.)

LITTLE SHY GUY & HOT RODS

Singles: 7-inch

CALVERT (107 "My Little Baby") 75-125 57

LITTLE SISTERS

(Little Sisters with Chubby Checker)

Singles: 7-inch

LIBERTY (55220 "A Little Star Came Down") 10-15 59
PARKWAY (815 "The Twist") 10-20 60
WEE 5-10

LPs: 10/12-inch

MGM (4116 "Joys of Love") 15-25 63
Also see CHECKER, Chubby

LITTLE SONNY

(Aaron Willis)

Singles: 78 rpm

DUKE (186 "I Gotta Find My Baby") 25-50 58

Singles: 7-inch

DUKE (186 "I Gotta Find My Baby") 40-60 58
ENTERPRISE 4-8 70-72
EXCELLO (2209 "Love Shock") 10-20 62
JVB (5001 "Love Shock") 30-40 58
REVILOT (209 "Creeper") 5-10 66
SPEEDWAY 4-8 72
SWINGIN' (614 "There Is Something on Your Mind") 10-20 59
WHEELSVILLE (103 "Let's Have a Good Time") 10-20 65

LPs: 10/12-inch

ENTERPRISE (1018 "Black and Blue") 8-12 71

LITTLE STEVE

Singles: 7-inch

GUYDEN (2060 "I See a Star") 75-125 62

LITTLE SUSIE

Singles: 78 rpm

MGM (12396 "Christmas Season") 5-10 56

Singles: 7-inch

MGM (12396 "Christmas Season") 10-15 56

LITTLE SUZIE

Singles: 7-inch

BURBANK (6006 "Young Love") 10-15 61

LITTLE SYLVIA

(With the Heywood Henry Orchestra; Sylvia Vanderpool)

Singles: 78 rpm

CAT (102 "Fine Love") 10-20 53
JUBILEE 10-20 52
SAVOY (816 "Little Boy") 15-25 51

Singles: 7-inch

CAT (102 "Fine Love") 15-25 53
JUBILEE (5093 "Drive, Daddy, Drive") 25-35 52
Also see MICKEY & SYLVIA
Also see PAGE, Hot Lips

LITTLE T-BONE

Singles: 78 rpm

MILTONE (5223 "Love's a Gamble") 20-40 47

LITTLE TED & NOVAS

Singles: 7-inch

KAY-GEE (440 "All Your Lovin' ") .... 30-40 '60s

LITTLE TEMPLE & HIS 88
(Gus Jenkins)
Singles: 78 rpm
SPECIALTY (475 "I Ate the Wrong Part") 50-100 54
Singles: 7-inch
SPECIALTY (475 "I Ate the Wrong Part") 100-200 54
Also see JENKINS, Gus

LITTLE TERRY
Singles: 7-inch
SAVOY (1520 "Shake Me Up, Baby") 15-25 57

LITTLE THUMPERS
Singles: 7-inch
RCA (47-7440 "Buck Dance") 10-15 59
(Monaural.)
RCA (61-7440 "Buck Dance") 20-30 59
(Stereo.)

LITTLE TOIANS / Tornados
Singles: 7-inch
SMALLTOWN ("I Love You"/"Beans") . 500-750 56
(No selection number used.)

LITTLE TOM & HIS VALENTINES
Singles: 7-inch
MR. BIG (222 "School Girl") 20-30 61

LITTLE TOMMY
Singles: 7-inch
JIM-KO .... 15-25 '60s
LAURIE (3077 "All I Want for Christmas") ..5-10 60
SOUND OF SOUL (100 "I'm Hurt") 30-60 65
SOUND OF SOUL (104 "Baby Can't You See") 50-100 66
WAN-DELL (1715 "I Played a Trick on Santa Claus") 5-10 60

LITTLE TOMMY & ELGINS
Singles: 7-inch
ABC-PAR (10358 "Never Love Again") ... 10-20 62
ELMAR (1084 "Never Love Again") 75-100 62
Also see ELGINS

LITTLE VICTOR
Singles: 7-inch
LANOR (511 "Can't Stop My Loving You") 15-25 62

LITTLE VICTOR
Singles: 7-inch
RICHLAND (123 "Papa Lou and Gran") 50-100

LITTLE VICTOR & VISTAS
Singles: 7-inch
RENDEZVOUS (183 "No More") 25-30 62

LITTLE WALKIN' WILLIE
(Walkin' Willie)
Singles: 78 rpm
JAGUAR (3012 "Clayhouse Blues") 20-30 55
Singles: 7-inch
EVERLAST (5031 "Did You Hear What I Say 5-10 65
JAGUAR (3012 "Clayhouse Blues") 10-15 55
JAGUAR (3015 "Heart Attack") 10-15 56
JAGUAR (3017 "Easy Does It") 10-15 56
RSVP (113 "It Sounds So Funny") 5-10 61
WEBCOR (102 "If You Woulda Said Goodbye") 8-12 61

LITTLE WALTER R&B '52
(With His Jukes; with Night Caps; with Night Cats; Little Walter Trio; Little Walter J., Guitar & Harmonica; Little Walter Jacobs; Marion Walter Jacobs)
Singles: 78 rpm
CHANCE (1116 "That's Allright") 300-500 52
CHECKER (758 thru 867) 30-40 52-57
CHECKER (890 thru 938) 50-100 58-59
ORA NELLE (711 "Ora-Nelle Blues [That's Allright]") 250-350 47
REGAL (3296 "Muskadine Blues") 25-50 50
Singles: 7-inch
CHANCE (1116 "That's Allright") 1000-2000 52
CHECKER (758 "Juke") 100-200 52
CHECKER (764 "Mean Old World") 100-200 52
CHECKER (770 "Off the Wall") 100-200 53
(Black vinyl.)
CHECKER (770 "Off the Wall") 800-1000 53
(Red vinyl.)
CHECKER (780 "Blues with a Feeling") 75-125 53
CHECKER (786 "You're So Fine") 75-125 53
CHECKER (793 "Oh Baby") 75-125 54
CHECKER (799 "You Better Watch Yourself") 75-125 54
(Black vinyl.)
CHECKER (799 "You Better Watch Yourself") 800-1000 54
(Red vinyl.)
CHECKER (805 "Last Night") 50-100 54
CHECKER (811 "My Babe") 50-100 55
CHECKER (817 "Roller Coaster") 50-100 55
CHECKER (825 "Too Late") 50-100 55
CHECKER (833 "Who") 50-100 56
CHECKER (838 "One More Chance with You") 50-100 56
CHECKER (845 "Teenage Beat") 50-100 56
CHECKER (852 "It's Too Late Brother") 50-100 56
CHECKER (859 "Everybody Needs Somebody") 50-75 57
CHECKER (867 "Boom Boom, Out Goes the Lights") 50-75 57
CHECKER (890 "The Toddle") 50-75 58
CHECKER (904 "Key to the Highway") 40-60 58
CHECKER (919 "Crazy Mixed-Up World") 40-60 59
CHECKER (930 "Everything's Gonna Be Alright") 40-60 59
CHECKER (938 "Break It Up") 40-60 59
CHECKER (945 "Ah'w Baby") 20-30 60
CHECKER (955 "My Babe") 20-30 60
CHECKER (968 "I Don't Play") 20-30 61
CHECKER (986 "Crazy Legs") 20-30 61
CHECKER (1013 thru 1117) 15-25 62-65
LPs: 10/12-inch
CHESS (202 "Little Walter") 15-25 76
(Two discs.)
CHESS (416 "Confessin' the Blues") 10-15 74
CHESS (1428 "Best of Little Walter") ...200-300 57
CHESS (1535 "Hate to See You Go") 15-25 69
CHESS (9000 series) .... 8-10 '80s
CHESS (60014 "Boss Blues Harmonica") 15-25 72
(Two discs.)
DELMARK 10-20
LE ROI DU BLU 10-20
Session: Louis Myers; Dave Myers; Robert Lockwood Jr.; Fred Below; Leonard Caston; Willie Dixon; Othum Brown.
Also see BRIM, John
Also see DIXON, Willie
Also see ROBINSON, Freddy
Also see ROGERS, Jimmy
Also see SUNNYLAND SLIM

LITTLE WALTER
(Leroy Foster)
Singles: 78 rpm
PARKWAY (502 "I Just Keep Loving Her") 100-200 50
Singles: 7-inch
HERALD (403 "I Just Keep Loving Her") 200-300 53
HERALD (404 "Boll Weevil") 200-300 53
Also see BABY FACE

LITTLE WALTER JR.
(George Smith)
Singles: 78 rpm
LAPEL (100 "Miss O'Mally's Rally") 20-30 55
Singles: 7-inch
LAPEL (100 "Miss O'Mally's Rally") 40-60 55
Also see ALLEN, George
Also see HARMONICA KING

LITTLE WHEELS
Singles: 7-inch
TAB (1016 "Something Special") 10-20 60

LITTLE WHEELS
Singles: 7-inch
DOT (16676 "Four Wheeled, Ball Bearing Surfing Board") 10-20 64
Members: Ray Hildebrand; Jill Jackson.
Also see PAUL & PAULA

LITTLE WILLIE & ADOLESCENTS
Singles: 7-inch
TENER (1009 "Get Out of My Life") 15-25 66
TENER (1013 "Looking for Love") 15-25 66

LITTLE WORLEY & DROPS
Singles: 7-inch
RAMCO (3710 "Who Stole My Girl") 75-125 61

LITTLEFIELD, Little Willie R&B '48
Singles: 78 rpm
BULLSEYE (1005 "Ruby-Ruby") 15-25 58
EDDIE'S (1202 "Little Willie's Boogie") 50-75 48
EDDIE'S (1205 "Chicago Bound") 50-75 48
EDDIE'S (1212 "Swanee River") 50-75 49
FEDERAL 40-60 52-57
MODERN 40-60 49-50
Singles: 7-inch
ARGYLE (1013 "Ruby-Ruby") 8-12 59
BLUES CONNOISSEUR 5-8
BULLSEYE (1005 "Ruby-Ruby") 10-15 58
FEDERAL (12101 "Sticking on You, Baby") 75-125 52
FEDERAL (12110 "K.C. Loving") 75-125 52
FEDERAL (12137 "The Midnight Hour Was Shining") 75-125 53
FEDERAL (12148 "Miss K.C.'s Fine") 75-125 53
FEDERAL (12163 "Please Don't Go-o-o-o-oh") 75-125 54
FEDERAL (12174 "Goofy Dust Blues") .. 75-125 54
FEDERAL (12221 "Jim Wilson's Boogie") 50-100 55
FEDERAL (12351 "Kansas City") 15-25 59
RHYTHM (107 "Mistreated") 100-200 57
RHYTHM (108 "Ruby-Ruby") 100-200 57
RHYTHM (115 "I Need a Pay Day") 100-200 58
RHYTHM (124 "Theresa") 100-200 58
RHYTHM (130 "I Wanna Love You") 100-200 59
Also see LITTLE ESTHER & LITTLE WILLIE LITTLEFIELD

LITTLEFIELD, Little Willie / Goree Carter
Singles: 78 rpm
FREEDOM (1502 "Littlefield Boogie") 50-75 49
Also see CARTER, Goree
Also see LITTLEFIELD, Little Willie

LITTLES, Hattie
(With the Fayettes)
Singles: 7-inch
GORDY (7004 "Back in My Arms Again") 150-250 62
GORDY (7007 "Here You Come") 10-15 62

LITTLETON, Glen, & Fascinators
Singles: 7-inch
LAKE (1003 "Sherry My Love") 30-40

LITTLETON, John, & Capistranos
Singles: 7-inch
DUKE (179 "Po Mary") 40-50 58
Members: James Brown; Johnny Littleton.

LITTRELL, Bubba
Singles: 7-inch
MANCO (1037 "Ain't That Cool") 40-60 62
MANCO (1048 "Worlds Apart") 20-30 63
PAULA (410 "Cross I'll Have to Bear") 4-6 74
RENNER (241 "Only for You") 5-10 63

LIVE FIVE
Singles: 7-inch
PANORAMA (31 "Shake a Tail Feather") 10-20 66
PANORAMA (46 "Let's Go") 10-20 66
JERDEN (797 "Shake a Tail Feather") 5-10 66
PICCADILLY (233 thru 248) 8-12 67

LIVE WIRES
Singles: 7-inch
BOOM (60015 "The Mask") 5-10 66
R.E.F. (110 "Kick Off") 15-20 62
R.E.F. (300 "One Cycle Venture") 20-25 65
R.E.F. (301 "Love") 20-25 65

LIVELY ONES
Singles: 7-inch
DEL-FI (4184 "Guitarget") 15-25 62
DEL-FI (4189 "Miserlou"/"Blue Tears") 10-20 62
DEL-FI (4189 "Miserlou"/"Livin' ") 10-15 62
(Note different flip side.)
DEL-FI (4196 thru 4217) 10-15 63
MGM (13691 "Bugalu Movement") 5-10 67
SMASH (1880 "Night and Day") 5-10 64
LPs: 10/12-inch
DEL-FI (DFLP-1226 "Surf Rider") 35-45 63
(Monaural.)
DEL-FI (DFST-1226 "Surf Rider") 40-60 63
(Stereo.)
DEL-FI (DFLP-1231 "Surf Drums") 35-45 63
(Monaural.)
DEL-FI (DFST-1231 "Surf Drums") 40-60 63
(Stereo.)
DEL-FI (DLF-1231 "Surf Drums") 10-12 98
("Thick, hard wax" reissue.)
DEL-FI (DFLP-1237 "Surf City") 35-45 63
(Monaural.)
DEL-FI (DLF-1237 "Surf City") 10-12 98
("Thick, hard wax" reissue.)
DEL-FI (DFLP-1238 "Great Surf Hits") 35-45 63
(Monaural.)
DEL-FI (DFST-1238 "Great Surf Hits") 40-60 63
(Stereo.)
DEL-FI (DFLP-1240 "Surfin' South of the Border") 35-45 63
(Monaural.)
DEL-FI (DFST-1240 "Surlfin' South of the Border") 40-60 63
(Stereo.)
MGM (E-4449 "Bugalu Party") 20-25 67
(Monaural.)
MGM (SE-4449 "Bugalu Party") 25-30 67
(Stereo.)
Members: Jim Masener; Ron Griffith; Jim Fitzpatrick; Ed Chiaverini; Joe Willenbring.
Also see SURFMEN

LIVELY TIM & PROFITS
Singles: 7-inch
PROFIT (067 "Simon Sez") 15-25 67

LIVERPOOL BEATS
(Beats)
LPs: 10/12-inch
RONDO (2026 "New Merseyside Sound") 25-35 64
(Also issued as by the Beats.)
Also see BEATS

LIVERPOOL FIVE P&R '66
Singles: 7-inch
RCA 8-12 65-67
LPs: 10/12-inch
RCA (LPM-3583 "The Liverpool Five Arrive") 20-25 66
(Monaural.)
RCA (LSP-3583 "The Liverpool Five Arrive") 20-30 66
(Stereo.)
RCA (LPM-3682 "Out of Sight") 20-25 67
(Monaural.)
RCA (LSP-3682 "Out of Sight") 20-30 67
(Stereo.)
Also see ASTRONAUTS / Liverpool Five

LIVERPOOL KIDS
(Schoolboys)
LPs: 10/12-inch
PALACE (777 "Beatle Mash") 35-45 64
Also issued as by the Schoolboys.)
Also see SCHOOLBOYS

LIVERPOOL SCENE
Singles: 7-inch
RCA 5-10 69
LPs: 10/12-inch
EPIC (24336 "Incredible New Liverpool Scene") 20-25 67
(Monaural.)
EPIC (26336 "Incredible New Liverpool Scene") 20-30 67
(Stereo.)
RCA 15-20 69-70

LIVERPOOLS
LPs: 10/12-inch
WYNCOTE (9001 "Beatle Mania in the U.S.A.") 15-25 64

LIVERT, Paul
(With the Lions; with the Dawn All Stars)
Singles: 7-inch
DAWN (214 "Bye Bye Baby") 40-60 55
LPs: 10/12-inch
METRO (318 "Chicken Twist") 15-20 62
Also see LIONS

LIVIN' ENDS
Singles: 7-inch
ATLANTIC (2622 "I Love You More Than You Know") 10-20 69

LIVING CHILDREN
Singles: 7-inch
MTA (140 "Crystalize Your Mind") 10-20 68

LIVING END
Singles: 7-inch
MIRA (215 "Turkey Stomp") 15-25 66

LIVING ENDS
Singles: 7-inch
HUDSON (707 "I Don't Mind") 15-25 66
Member: Larry Gonsky.

LIVINGSTON, Buddy, & Versatones
Singles: 7-inch
SCOTTIE (1313 "Fumbling") 15-25 59

LIVINGSTON, Patty
Singles: 7-inch
DIMENSION (1044 "Playin' with Fire") 10-20 65

LIZARDS
Singles: 7-inch
20TH FOX (519 "Hot Rod") 10-15 64

LLOIDS OF LON-DEN
Singles: 7-inch
FENTON (1000 "Girls Can Really Dance") 20-30 65

LLOYD, Adrian
Singles: 7-inch
CHARGER (112 "Lorna") 8-12 65
SUNSET (603 "Justine") 50-75

LLOYD "Fatman"
Singles: 78 rpm
OKEH ("7073 "Where You Been") 10-20 56
Singles: 7-inch
OKEH ("7073 "Where You Been") 25-35 56

LLOYD, Jack
Singles: 78 rpm
EASTMAN (779 "Real Crazy") 8-12 56
Singles: 7-inch
EASTMAN (779 "Real Crazy") 10-20 56

LLOYD, Jackie
Singles: 7-inch
HERO (342 "Warm Love") 150-200 60

LLOYD, Jimmy
Singles: 78 rpm
ROULETTE 10-20 57
Singles: 7-inch
AIR (1003 "Baby Won't You Listen") 10-20 59
ROULETTE (4062 "Rocket in My Pocket") 40-60 58
ROULETTE (7001 "Where the Rio De Rosa Flows") 40-60 57

LLOYD, Johnny, & Essentials
Singles: 7-inch
LORRAINE (1000 "I Want Your Lovin' ") 8-12 65
READING (16000 "On Our Wedding Day") 20-30 65

LLOYD, Leroy, & Swinging Dukes
Singles: 7-inch
CAROL (105 "Party Time") 10-20 67
MINARET (146 "Taste of the Blues") 5-10 68

LLOYD & GLEN
Singles: 7-inch
WIRL (159 "What You've Got") 15-25

LLOYD & WILLIE
Singles: 78 rpm
MAMBO (101 "Don't Know Where She Went") 20-40 55
Singles: 7-inch
MAMBO (101 "Don't Know Where She Went") 50-75 55
Member: Willie Egans.
Also see EGANS, Willie

LOAD
Singles: 7-inch
OWL (740501 "Wow, We'll Say We Tried") .... 15-25 '60s

LOAD OF MISCHIEF
Singles: 7-inch
HOLIDAY INN (2205 "I'm a Lover") 10-15 68
SUN (407 "I'm a Lover") 75-100 68

LOADING ZONE
Singles: 7-inch
COLUMBIA (43938 "I Couldn't Care Less") 5-10 66
RCA (9538 "Don't Lose Control") 5-10 68
RCA (9620 "No More Tears") 5-10 69
UMBRELLA (1001 "One for All") 5-10 67
LPs: 10/12-inch
RCA (3959 "Loading Zone") 15-25 68
UMBRELLA (101 "One for All") 40-60 67
Members: Linda Tillery; Paul Faverso; Steve Busfield; Steve Downer; George Marsh.
Also see TILLERY, Linda, & Loading Zone

LOAFERS
Singles: 7-inch
PHONOGRAPH (1025 "The Best Thing"/"Crazy Talk") 75-125

LOBO
Singles: 7-inch
REX (1002 "Never Let Me Go") 10-15 59

LOCKE, Rusty
Singles: 78 rpm
TNT (1012 "Milk Cow Blues") 10-20 54
Singles: 7-inch
TNT (1012 "Milk Cow Blues") 20-30 54

LOCKETTES
Singles: 7-inch
FLIP (334 "Puddin' Pie") 15-25 58
Also see BERRY, Richard

LOCKLIN, Hank *C&W '49*
Singles: 78 rpm
DECCA 5-10 52
4 STAR 5-10 49-54
RCA 5-10 55-57
Singles: 7-inch
COUNTRY ARTISTS 3-5 83
DECCA (29000 series) 10-15 52
4 STAR (1500 & 1600 series) 10-15 52-54
KING (5000 series) 5-8 59
MGM 4-6 74
PLANTATION 4-6 76-77
RCA (0030 thru 0900 series) 4-6 72-74
RCA (6100 thru 7600 series) 8-15 55-59
RCA (7700 thru 9900 series) 4-8 60-71
EPs: 7-inch
RCA 8-15 58-61
LPs: 10/12-inch
ARCADE 5-8
CAMDEN 8-15 62-74
DESIGN 10-15 62
INTERNATIONAL AWARD .... 8-12 '60s
KING (600 & 700 series) 15-25 61
MGM 5-10 75
METRO 10-15 65
PICKWICK/HILLTOP 8-15 65-68
PLANTATION 5-8 77-81
RCA (Except 1673 series) 10-20 62-71
RCA (1673 "Foreign Love") 15-25 58
SEARS .... 8-12 '60s
STEREO SPECTRUM .... 5-10 '60s
WRANGLER 8-12 62
Session: Jordanaires.
Also see CLINE, Patsy / Hank Locklin / Miller Brothers / Eddie Marvin
Also see JORDANAIRES
Also see SNOW, Hank / Hank Locklin / Porter Wagoner

LOCKLIN, Hank, with Danny Davis & Nashville Brass *C&W '70*
Singles: 7-inch
RCA 4-6 69-70
LPs: 10/12-inch
RCA 8-10 70
Also see DAVIS, Danny
Also see LOCKLIN, Hank

LOCKWOOD, Robert, Jr.
(Robert Jr. Lockwood)
Singles: 78 rpm
J.O.B. (1107 "Aw Aw Baby") 50-75 54
MERCURY (8260 "I'm Gonna Dig Myself a Hole") 50-75 51
Singles: 7-inch
J.O.B. (1107 "Aw Aw Baby") 100-200 54
LPs: 10/12-inch
TRIX 10-15
Also see DIXON, Floyd
Also see SPANN, Otis, & Robert Lockwood Jr.
Also see SUNNYLAND SLIM

LOCKYER, Malcolm
Singles: 78 rpm
WING 5-10 55
Singles: 7-inch
WING (90002 "Careless Lips") 10-20 55
WING (90026 "Back Track") 10-20 55

LOCO, Joe
(With His Piano; with His Quintet)
Singles: 78 rpm
TICO 5-10 53-54
Singles: 7-inch
FANTASY (543 "St. Louis Blues Cha Cha") 5-10 59
IMPERIAL (5573 "Ka Da Cha Cha Cha") ... 5-10 59
TICO (173 "Bandstand Mambo") 8-12 53
TICO (222 "Cha-Cha-Cha No. 5") 8-12 54
TICO (1091 "Apple Blossom Time") 8-12 54
LPs: 10/12-inch
GNP (64 "Poco Loco") 15-25 62
FANTASY (3294 "Latin Jewels") 15-25 60
(Monaural.)
FANTASY (8041 "Latin Jewels") 20-30 60
(Stereo.)
IMPERIAL (9166 "Pachanga Twist") 15-25 62
(Monaural.)
IMPERIAL (12079 "Pachanga Twist") 20-30 62
(Stereo.)
MERCURY (60071 "Calypso Dance") 20-30 59
SUNSET (1133 "Dance") 10-15 66
(Monaural.)
SUNSET (5133 "Dance") 15-20 66
(Stereo.)
TICO (1006 "Mambo Moods") 20-40 55

LOCOMOTIONS
Singles: 7-inch
GONE (5142 "Adios My Love") 15-25 63
SWAN (4237 "Make it Sat. Night") 5-10 65

LOCOMOTIVE
Singles: 7-inch
BELL (754 "Never Set Me Free") 5-10 69
BELL (778 "There's Got to Be a Way") 5-10 69
MGM (14102 "Roberta") 5-10 69
LPs: 10/12-inch
MGM (4653 "Locomotive") 10-15 69

LOCOS
Singles: 7-inch
RCA (8931 "Guantanamera Rock") 5-10 66
20TH FOX (102 "Oh Yes, Indeed I Do") ... 30-40 58

LOE & JOE
Singles: 7-inch
HARVEY (112 "Little Ole Boy, Little Ole Girl") 10-20 61
Members: Lorri Rudolph; Joe Charles.
Also see RUDOLPH, Lorri
Also see SATINTONES
Also see SPINNERS

LOFGREN, Nils *LP '75*
Singles: 7-inch
A&M 4-6 75-77
LPs: 10/12-inch
A&M (Except 8362) 8-10 75-82
A&M (8362 "Authorized Bootleg") 25-30 76
(Promotional issue only.)
BACKSTREET 5-8 81
COLUMBIA 5-8 85
EPIC 8-10 76
RYKODISC 5-8 91

LOFTIN, Willie, & Discords
Singles: 7-inch
SMOKE (101 "Bad Habit") 25-50 59
(Also issued as by Eddie Corner & Discords.)

LOFTON, Cripple Clarence
Singles: 78 rpm
SESSION 10-20 43
Also see YANCEY, Jimmy / Cripple Clarence Lofton

LOFTON, Rohny
Singles: 7-inch
IMPACT (4292 "El Diablo") 10-20 61

LOGAN, Dorothy, & Gems
Singles: 78 rpm
DREXEL (902 "Since I Fell for You") 20-30 54
Singles: 7-inch
DREXEL (902 "Since I Fell for You") 75-125 54
Also see GEMS

LOGAN, Willie & Plaids
Singles: 7-inch
JERRY-O (103 "You Conquored [sic] Me") 30-40 64
(Reissued as by Charles McCline.)
Also see McCLINE, Charles

LOGAN VALLEY BOYS
Singles: 78 rpm
EXCELLENT (279 "Rock n' Roll Country Style") 50-75 56
Singles: 7-inch
EXCELLENT (279 "Rock n' Roll Country Style") 125-150 56

LOGGINS & MESSINA *P&R/LP '72*
Singles: 7-inch
COLUMBIA 4-6 72-76
LOS ANGELES KINGS COLUMBIA (10444 "Angry Eyes") 4-6 76
(Promotional issue for "Columbia/Kings Record Night" at the L.A. Forum.)
Picture Sleeves
LOS ANGELES KINGS COLUMBIA (10444 "Angry Eyes") 4-6 76
(Promotional issue for "Columbia/Kings Record Night" at the L.A. Forum.)
LPs: 10/12-inch
COLUMBIA (31044 "Sittin' In") 10-15 72
COLUMBIA (31748 "Loggins with Messina") 10-15 72
COLUMBIA (KC-31748 "Loggins and Messina") 8-12 72
(Repackage of *Loggins with Messina*.)
COLUMBIA (CQ-31748 "Loggins and Messina") 10-20 73
(Quadraphonic.)
COLUMBIA (KC-32540 "Full Sail") 15-25 73
COLUMBIA (CQ-32540 "Full Sail") 25-35 74
(Quadraphonic.)
COLUMBIA (33175 "Mother Lode") 8-12 74
COLUMBIA (32848 "On Stage") 10-15 74
(Two discs.)
COLUMBIA (PC-33578 "Native Sons") 8-12 76
COLUMBIA (PCQ-33578 "Native Sons") . 10-20 76
(Quadraphonic.)
COLUMBIA (33810 "So Fine") 10-20 75
COLUMBIA (34167 "Finale") 10-15 77
(Two discs.)
COLUMBIA (34388 "Best of Friends") 8-12 76
COLUMBIA (44388 "Best of Friends") 30-40 82
(Half-speed mastered.)
DIRECT-DISK (16606 "Full Sail") 30-40 82
(Half-speed mastered.)
Members: Kenny Loggins; Jim Messina. Session: Larry Sims; Vince Denham; Merle Bregante; Jon Clarke; Don Roberts; Steve Forman.
Also see MESSINA, Jim

LOGICS
Singles: 7-inch
EVERLAST (5015 "One Love") 30-40 62
GAIT (1004 "Ain't That a Mess") .... 30-40 '60s

LOGSDON, Jimmy
Singles: 78 rpm
DECCA 5-10 54
Singles: 7-inch
DECCA (29075 "Good Deal Lucille") 10-15 54
DECCA (29122 "My Sweet French Baby") 10-15 54
STARDAY (286 "No Longer") 50-100 57
LPs: 10/12-inch
KING (843 "Howdy Neighbors") 15-25 63

LOLITA *P&R '60*
Singles: 7-inch
4 CORNERS 4-8 63-65
KAPP 8-12 60-61
Picture Sleeves
KAPP (349 "Sailor") 20-25 60
KAPP (370 "Cowboy Jimmy Joe") 10-15 61
LPs: 10/12-inch
KAPP (1219 "Sailor") 15-25 61
(Monaural.)
KAPP (1229 "Songs You Will Never Forget") 15-25 61
(Monaural.)
KAPP (3219 "Sailor") 20-30 61
(Stereo.)

KAPP (3229 "Songs You Will Never Forget") 20-30 61
(Stereo.)

LOLLAR, Bobby
Singles: 7-inch
BENTON (101 "Bad Bad Boy") 1500-2500 58

LOLLIPOP SHOPPE
Singles: 7-inch
SHAMLEY (44005 "Someone I Knew") 5-10 68
UNI (55050 "You Must Be a Witch") 8-12 68
Picture Sleeves
UNI (55050 "You Must Be a Witch") 10-20 68
LPs: 10/12-inch
UNI (73019 "Just Colour") 40-60 68
Members: Ron Buzzel; Bob Atkins; Edward Bowen; Fred Cole; Carl Fortina; Tim Rockson.
Also see WEEDS

LOLLIPOPS
Singles: 7-inch
ATCO (6787 "I Believe in Love") 4-8 70
ATCO (6841 "Love a Little Longer") 4-8 71
GORDY (7089 "Cheating Is Telling on You") 200-300 69
IMPACT (1021 "Lovin' Good Feeling") 20-30 67
RCA (8390 "Love Is the Only Answer") ... 15-20 64
RCA (8344 "Peggy Got Engaged") 15-20 64
RCA (8430 "Big Brother") 10-15 64
SMASH (2057 "Gee Whiz") 5-10 66
VAULT (926 "Words Ain't Enough") 5-10 66
V.I.P. (25051 "Cheating Is Telling on You") 10-20 69

LOLLIPOPS
Singles: 7-inch
SSS INT'L (777 "You Don't Know") 10-15 69

LOLLYPOPPERS
Singles: 78 rpm
ALADDIN (3291 "A Bottle of Pop and a Lollipop") 10-20 55
HARLEM 10-15 55
Singles: 7-inch
ALADDIN (3291 "A Bottle of Pop and a Lollipop") 30-40 55
HARLEM 20-30 55

LOLLYPOPS
Singles: 7-inch
HOLLAND (7420 "My Love Is Real") 1000-1200 58
UNIVERSAL INT'L (7420 "My Love Is Real") 2000-3000 58

LOMAS, Bobby Joyce
(Joyce Lomas)
Singles: 7-inch
MICHELLE (602 "Cry Fool") 10-15 65
ULTRA D'OR (202 "Cry Fool") 100-150 56

LOMAX, Jackie *LP '69*
Singles: 7-inch
APPLE (1802 "Sour Milk Sea") 15-20 68
APPLE (1807 "New Day") 60-80 69
APPLE (1819 "How the Web Was Woven") 5-10 70
APPLE (1834 "Sour Milk Sea") 5-10 71
CAPITOL 4-6 77
EPIC (10270 "One Minute Woman") 5-10 67
W.B. 4-6 71-73
Promotional Singles
APPLE (6240 "Sour Milk Sea") 25-30 68
W.B. (514 "Let the Play Begin") 5-10 72
Picture Sleeves
APPLE (1819 "How the Web Was Woven") 5-10 70
W.B. (514 "Let the Play Begin") 5-10 72
(Promotional only issue.)
LPs: 10/12-inch
APPLE (3354 "Is This What You Want") . 12-20 69
CAPITOL 5-10 76-77
W.B. 8-12 71-72
Also see CLAPTON, Eric
Also see McCARTNEY, Paul
Also see STARR, Ringo

LOMBARD, Watsie, & Eastmen
Singles: 7-inch
GLOW (100 "Passion") 15-25

LOMBARD, Wilbert, & Kartels
Singles: 7-inch
DEB (1002 "That's How It Will Be") 200-300 57

LOMBARDIE, Joe
Singles: 7-inch
NEW ENGLAND (1015 "Let's All Rock & Roll") 40-60

LOMBARDO, Guy *P&R '27*
(With the His Royal Canadians)
Singles: 78 rpm
BRUNSWICK 4-8 32-34
COLUMBIA 4-8 27-31
DECCA 3-8 34-57
VICTOR 3-6 36-38
Singles: 7-inch
CAPITOL 5-10 57-67
DECCA 5-15 50-73
EPs: 7-inch
CAMDEN 5-10
CAPITOL 5-10 56-59
DECCA 5-10 50-59
RCA 5-10 60
LPs: 10/12-inch
CAMDEN 10-30 54-65
CAPITOL (Except 739 thru 1598) 5-15 61-81
CAPITOL (739 thru 1598) 10-30 56-61
DECCA 10-30 50-67
LONDON 5-8 73
MCA 5-8 75
PICKWICK 5-8
RCA 5-8 72-77
SUFFOLK 5-8
VOCALION 5-10 66-68
Also see ARMSTRONG, Louis, & Guy Lombardo

LOMONTE, Tommy
Singles: 7-inch
IMPERIAL (5524 "Yeah, Yeah, Yeah") 40-60 58

LONDON, Bob
(With the Mike Stoller & Orchestra)
Singles: 78 rpm
DOT (15442 "Reckless") 5-10 55
SPARK (109 "Lola") 5-10 55
VITA (118 "Love Words") 5-10 55
Singles: 7-inch
DOT (15442 "Reckless") 8-12 55
SPARK (109 "Lola") 8-12 55
(Red label.)
SPARK (109 "Lola") 10-15 55
(Blue label. This may be the only blue label Spark release.)
VITA (118 "I Sailed the 7 Seas") 15-25 55

LONDON, Clarence
Singles: 78 rpm
FIDELITY (3009 "Goin' Back to Mama") ...25-50 53

LONDON, Dutch
Singles: 7-inch
FAWN (6003 "Each Day") 100-200 59

LONDON, Johnny
("Alto Wizard")
Singles: 78 rpm
SUN (175 "Drivin' Slow") 1000-2000 52
(First commercial issue on the Sun label.)
Session: Johnny London; Charles Keel; Joe Louis Hall; Julius Drake.

LONDON, Julie *P&R '55*
(With Barney Kessel, Roy Leatherwood & Felix Slatkin's Orchestra; with Russ Garcia & His Orchestra; with Bobby Troup's Quintet; Spencer-Hagen Orchestra; with Pete King & Orchestra)
Singles: 78 rpm
LIBERTY 5-10 55-57
Singles: 7-inch
BETHLEHEM 5-10 59
LIBERTY (55006 thru 55512) 10-15 55-62
LIBERTY (55605 thru 56085) 5-10 63-69
Picture Sleeves
LIBERTY (55076 "Dark") 20-30 57
LIBERTY (55269 "Time for Lovers") 10-15 61
EPs: 7-inch
BETHLEHEM (133 "Julie London") 10-20 59
LIBERTY (1001 "Cry Me a River") 10-20 56
LIBERTY (1-2-3 3006 "Julie Is Her Name") 10-20 56
(Price is for any of three volumes.)
LIBERTY (1-2-3 3012 "Lonely Girl") 10-20 56
(Price is for any of three volumes.)
LIBERTY (1-2-3 3060 "Make Love to Me") 10-20 57
(Price is for any of three volumes.)
LIBERTY (1-2-3 9002 "Calendar Girl") 10-20 56
(Price is for any of three volumes.)
LPs: 10/12-inch
GUEST STAR 5-10 64
LIBERTY (1 "By Myself") 12-18 65
(Columbia Record Club exclusive.)
LIBERTY (3006 "Julie Is Her Name") 35-50 56
(Monaural.)
LIBERTY (3012 "Lonely Girl") 35-50 56
(Monaural.)
LIBERTY (3043 "About the Blues") 20-40 57
(Monaural.)
LIBERTY (3060 "Make Love to Me") 20-40 57
(Monaural.)
LIBERTY (3096 "Julie Swings") 20-40 58
(Monaural.)
LIBERTY (3100 "Julie Is Her Name, Vol. 2") 20-40 58
(Monaural.)
LIBERTY (3105 "London By Night") 15-30 59
(Monaural.)
LIBERTY (3119 "Swing Me an Old Song") 15-30 59
(Monaural.)
LIBERTY (3130 "Your Number Please") ..15-30 59
(Monaural.)
LIBERTY (3152 "Julie at Home") 15-30 60
(Monaural.)
LIBERTY (3164 "Around Midnight") 15-30 60
(Monaural.)
LIBERTY (3171 "Send for Me") 15-30 61
(Monaural.)
LIBERTY (3192 "Whatever Julie Wants") 15-30 61
(Monaural.)
LIBERTY (3203 "Sophisticated Lady") 15-25 62
(Monaural.)
LIBERTY (3231 "Love Letters") 15-25 62
(Monaural.)
LIBERTY (3249 "Love on the Rocks") 15-25 62
(Monaural.)
LIBERTY (3278 "Latin in a Satin Mood") ..15-25 63
(Monaural.)
LIBERTY (3291 "Golden Hits") 15-25 63
(Monaural.)
LIBERTY (3300 "End of the World") 15-25 63
(Monaural.)
LIBERTY (3324 "Wonderful World of Julie London") 15-25 63
(Monaural.)
LIBERTY (3342 "Julie London") 15-25 64
(Monaural.)
LIBERTY (3375 "Julie London in Person at the Americana") 15-25 64
(Monaural.)
LIBERTY (3392 "Our Fair Lady") 15-25 65
(Monaural.)
LIBERTY (3416 "Feeling Good") 15-25 65
(Monaural.)
LIBERTY (3478 "For the Night People") ...15-25 66
(Monaural.)
LIBERTY (3493 "Nice Girls Don't Stay for Breakfast) 15-25 67
(Monaural.)
LIBERTY (3514 "With Body and Soul") 15-25 67
(Monaural.)
LIBERTY (5501 "Best of Julie") 20-30 62
(Monaural.)
LIBERTY (6601 "Best of Julie") 25-35 62
(Stereo.)
LIBERTY (7004 "Julie") 50-75 57
(Stereo.)
LIBERTY (7012 "About the Blues") 50-75 57
(Stereo.)
LIBERTY (7027 "Julie Is Her Name") 75-100 60
(Stereo. Colored vinyl.)
LIBERTY (7029 "Lonely Girl") 20-35 60
(Stereo.)
LIBERTY (7060 "Make Love to Me") 20-35 60
(Stereo.)
LIBERTY (7100 "Julie Is Her Name, Vol. 2") 20-35 59
(Stereo.)
LIBERTY (7105 "London By Night") 20-35 59
(Stereo.)
LIBERTY (7119 "Swing Me an Old Song") 20-35 59
(Stereo.)
LIBERTY (7130 "Your Number Please") ..20-35 59
(Stereo.)
LIBERTY (7152 "Julie at Home") 20-35 60
(Stereo.)
LIBERTY (7164 "Around Midnight") 20-35 60
(Stereo.)
LIBERTY (7171 "Send for Me") 20-35 61
(Stereo.)
LIBERTY (7192 "Whatever Julie Wants") 20-35 61
(Stereo.)
LIBERTY (7203 "Sophisticated Lady") 20-30 62
(Stereo.)
LIBERTY (7231 "Love Letters") 20-30 62
(Stereo.)
LIBERTY (7249 "Love on the Rocks") 20-30 62
(Stereo.)
LIBERTY (7278 "Latin in a Satin Mood") ..20-30 63
(Stereo.)
LIBERTY (7291 "Golden Hits") 20-30 63
(Stereo.)
LIBERTY (7300 "End of the World") 20-30 63
(Stereo.)
LIBERTY (7324 "Wonderful World of Julie London") 20-30 63
(Stereo.)
LIBERTY (7342 "Julie London") 20-30 64
(Stereo.)
LIBERTY (7375 "Julie London in Person at the Americana") 20-30 64
(Stereo.)
LIBERTY (7392 "Our Fair Lady") 20-30 65
(Stereo.)
LIBERTY (7416 "Feeling Good") 20-30 65
(Stereo.)
LIBERTY (7478 "For the Night People") ..20-30 66
(Stereo.)
LIBERTY (7493 "Nice Girls Don't Stay for Breakfast) 15-25 67
(Stereo.)
LIBERTY (7514 "With Body and Soul") 15-25 67
(Stereo.)
LIBERTY (7546 "Easy Does It") 15-20 68
LIBERTY (7609 "Yummy, Yummy, Yummy") 15-20 69
LIBERTY (9002 "Calendar Girl") 40-60 56
SUNSET 8-15 66-68
U.A. (437 "Very Best of Julie London") 5-10 75
Session: Barney Kessel; Ray Leatherwood; Bobby Troup; Howard Roberts; Buddy Collette; Bob Enevoldsen; Don Heath.
Also see CONNOR, Chris / Julie London / Carmen McRae

LONDON, Julie, & Bud Shank Quintet
LPs: 10/12-inch
LIBERTY (3434 "All Through the Night") ..10-20 66
(Monaural.)
LIBERTY (7434 "All Through the Night") ..15-25 66
(Stereo.)
Also see LONDON, Julie
Also see SHANK, Bud

LONDON, Laurel
Singles: 7-inch
GULF REEF (1007 "Don't Knock the Rock") 25-50 62

LONDON, Laurie *P&R/R&B '58*
(With the 4 Jacks)
Singles: 7-inch
CAPITOL (3891 "He's Got the Whole World") 8-12 58
CAPITOL (3973 "Joshua") 8-12 58
CAPITOL (4133 "My Mother") 8-12 59
ROULETTE (4176 "Pretty Eyed Baby") 5-10 59
EPs: 7-inch
CAPITOL (10182 "Laurie London") 20-30 58
CAPITOL (10191 "Laurie London") 20-30 58
LPs: 10/12-inch
CAPITOL (10169 "Laurie London") 30-50 58

LONDON, Lloyd, & Yachtsmen
Singles: 7-inch
DESTINY (530 "Will There Ever Be a Girl for Me") 50-100 59
Also see YACHTSMEN

LONDON, Mark
Singles: 7-inch
CAMEO (362 "Moonin' ") 8-12 65

LONDON, Mel

Singles: 78 rpm

CHIEF (7000 "Doggin Me Around") 10-15 57

Singles: 7-inch

CHIEF (7000 "Doggin Me Around") 10-15 57

LONDON, Paul, & Capers

Singles: 7-inch

CHECK MATE (1006 "Sugar Baby") 40-50 62
LIMELIGHT (3015 "Keep Your Heartaches to Yourself") 10-20 64
LIMELIGHT (3028 "Drummer Boy") 5-10 64

LONDON, Ralph

Singles: 7-inch

COED (588 "Lovely, Lovely Girl") 75-150 64

LONDON, Robb, & Rogues

Singles: 7-inch

BECKINGHAM (1085 "It Should Have Been Me") 15-25 65
SUZUKI (1001 "Gloria") .... 15-25 '60s

LONDON FOG
(With the Continentals)

Singles: 7-inch

COULEE (118 "Mr. Baldi") 15-25 66
GOLD STARS (90852 "Trippin' ") 10-20 68
IMPERIAL (66440 "Trippin' ") 5-10 70

LPs: 10/12-inch

POMPEI 8-12

LONDON KNIGHTS

Singles: 7-inch

MIKE (4200 "Go to Him") 15-25 66

LONDONS

Singles: 7-inch

PYRAMID (7211 "Old Man") 10-15 66

LONELY BOYS

Singles: 7-inch

NU-WAY (555 "My Girl") 25-35 59

LONELY GUYS

Singles: 7-inch

CADDY (117 "The Way You Look Tonight") 150-200 58

LONELY ONE

Singles: 7-inch

CAROL (103 "A Letter to My Love") 5-10 66
CAROL (4110 "A Letter to My Love") 10-15 61

LONELY ONES

Singles: 7-inch

BATON (270 "My Wish") 15-20 59
SIR (270 "My Wish") 10-15 59

LONELY ONES

Singles: 7-inch

RENDEVOUS (125 "Swanee River Fling") 10-15 60

LONELY ONES

EPs: 7-inch

STUB'S PUB (2277 "Stub's Pub") 35-50

LONELY RIDERS

Singles: 7-inch

MTA (139 "Lonely Rider") 10-15 68

LONELY SOULS

Singles: 7-inch

PARIS TOWER (137 "I Can't Stop Now") 20-30 68

Picture Sleeves

PARIS TOWER (137 "I Can't Stop Now") 25-35 68

LONERO, Bobby

Singles: 7-inch

APT (25043 "No More Money") 8-12 60
LIBERTY (55180 "Little Bit") 15-25 59
SPINETT (1003 "Wham Bam") 8-12 60
SPINETT (1006 "No More Money") 8-12 60

LONESOME DRIFTER

Singles: 78 rpm

K (5812 "Eager Boy") 400-500 56

Singles: 7-inch

K (5812 "Eager Boy") 1500-2000 56
R.A.M. (1738 "What Do You Think of Me") 75-100

LONESOME LARRY

Singles: 7-inch

TILT (779 "Cool Today") 10-20 62

LONESOME LEE
(Jimmy Lee Robinson)

Singles: 7-inch

BANDERA (2501 "Cry Over Me") 25-35 59
Also see JIMMY LEE
Also see ROBINSON, Jimmy Lee

LONESOME RHODES

Singles: 7-inch

RCA (9305 "Delight of My Day") 10-15 67

LONESOME SUNDOWN

Singles: 78 rpm

EXCELLO 25-75 56-57

Singles: 7-inch

EXCELLO (2092 "Lost Without Love") 50-75 56
EXCELLO (2102 "My Home Is a Prison") 50-75 57
(Orange and blue label.)
EXCELLO (2102 "My Home Is a Prison") 4-6 70
(Blue label.)
EXCELLO (2117 "Don't Say a Word") 50-75 57
EXCELLO (2132 "Lonely Lonely Me") 50-75 58
EXCELLO (2145 "I Stood By") 50-75 58
EXCELLO (2154 "You Know I Love You") 50-75 59
EXCELLO (2163 "Gonna Stick It to You Baby") 50-75 59
EXCELLO (2174 "Love Me Now") 50-75 60
EXCELLO (2202 "Lonesome Lonely Blues") 20-30 61
EXCELLO (2213 "I Woke Up Crying") 10-20 62
EXCELLO (2236 thru 2264) 10-20 63-65
REO (8311 "I Stood By") 100-150 58
(Canadian.)

LPs: 10/12-inch

ALLIGATOR (4716 "Been Gone Too Long") 5-10 80
EXCELLO (8012 "Lonesome Sundown") . 10-20 69
JOLIET (6002 "Been Gone Too Long") 10-15 78
Also see CHENIER, Clifton

LONESOME SUNDOWN & PHILIP WALKER

LPs: 10/12-inch

ROUNDER 8-12
Also see LONESOME SUNDOWN
Also see WALKER, Philip

LONETTE

Singles: 7-inch

M-S (208 "Veil of Mystery") 15-25 68

LONG, Barbara

LPs: 10/12-inch

SAVOY (12161 "Soul") 15-25 61

LONG, Bill

Singles: 78 rpm

UNIQUE (332 "Blow the Whistle") 5-10 56

Singles: 7-inch

UNIQUE (332 "Blow the Whistle") 10-15 56

LONG, Bobby
(With the Cherrios; with Satelites; Joe Erskine)

Singles: 7-inch

ARROW (727 "Patty") 15-25 58
CUB (9120 "Flip Flop") 8-10 63
EVERLAST (5020 "Ooh Poo Pah Doo") 5-10 63
FOUNTAINHEAD (105 "I Need You") 10-15 60
GLOW-HILL (503 "Don't You Run") 10-15 58
GLOW-HILL (504 "Hold Me") 10-15 59
GLOW-HILL (505 "Calling") 10-15 59
(First issue.)
SKYMAC (1007 "Just for a Day") 10-15 64
SKYMAC (1011 "I Had to Come Back") 5-10 64
TEIA (1001 "Jenny Lee") 8-12 64
UNART (2023 "Calling") 8-12 59
VEGAS (500 "Mojo Workout") 5-10 64
VEGAS (700 "Stir It Up") 5-10 64
(Black vinyl.)
VEGAS (700 "Stir It Up") 15-25 64
(Red vinyl.)
Also see ERSKINE, Joe

LONG, Curtis
(With the Rhythm Rockers)

Singles: 7-inch

LINCO (1314 "Hootchey Cootchey") 300-400 59
STARDALE (600 "Goin' Out on the Town") 100-150 58

LONG, Dewey

Singles: 7-inch

BIG SOUND (22849 "Feelings on Paper") 30-50

LONG, Huey

Singles: 7-inch

FIDELITY (4054 "Waiting for a Letter") 8-12 62
FIDELITY (4055 "Elvis Stole My Gal") 40-50 62
ROCK IT (17077 "Elvis Stole My Baby") 5-10 78
(At least one source shows this number as 100. We don't know yet which is correct.)

LONG, Joey
(Joey Longoria)

Singles: 7-inch

ARGO (5363 "I Need Someone") 10-20 60
CRAZY CAJUN 4-6 77
PACEMAKER (228 "The Rains Came") 5-10 64
RUNNING BEAR (8300 "I'm Glad for Your Sake") 10-15 62
TRIBE (8302 "Hurtin' Inside") 10-15 62

LPs: 10/12-inch

CRAZY CAJUN 10-15 77
Also see MEYERS, Augie
Also see SIR DOUGLAS QUINTET

LONG, Johnny

Singles: 7-inch

SOMA (1149 "Rock and Roll Nursery Rhyme") 10-20 61
STARDUST .... 10-20 '60s
TWIN TOWN .... 8-12 '60s

LONG, Shorty C&W '48
(With the Happy Fellows; with Santa Fe Rangers; with Searchers)

Singles: 78 rpm

DECCA 4-8 48
DOLLO 10-20
RCA 10-20 49-57
VALLEY (108 "I Got Nine Little Kisses") ... 10-20 54
(Promotional issue only.)

Singles: 7-inch

K-SON ("Redstone John"") 50-75
(Selection number not known.)
MALVERN (2 "Empty Bottles") 4-6
RCA (59 "Jesse James"/"Wyatt Earp") 10-20 56
RCA (63 "Tales of the Texas Rangers") ... 10-20 55
RCA (48-0057 thru 48-0347) 25-50 49-50
(Green or blue vinyl.)
RCA (6572 "Vacation Rock") 40-60 56
RCA (6873 "You Don't Have to Be a Baby to Cry") 30-50 57
VALLEY (108 "I Got Nine Little Kisses") ... 50-75

Picture Sleeves

RCA (59 "Wyatt Earp") 25-35 56
RCA (63 "Tales of the Texas Rangers") ... 25-35 55
(Sleeve pictures TV series cast.)
Also see WELLINGTON, Rusty

LONG, Shorty P&R/R&B '66
(With the Santa Fe Rangers)

Singles: 7-inch

JAMIE (1315 "Greetings") 8-12 66
SOUL (35001 "Devil with a Blue Dress") .. 20-25 64
SOUL (35005 "It's a Crying Shame") 15-25 64
SOUL (35021 thru 35064) 6-12 66-69
SOUL (35054 "I Had a Dream") 10-20 69
(Red vinyl. Promotional issue.)
TRI-PHI (1006 "I'll Be There") 25-35 62
TRI-PHI (1015 "Too Smart") 25-35 62
TRI-PHI (1021 "Going My Way") 25-35 62
VALLEY (108 "I Got Nine Little Kisses") . 50-100 59

LPs: 10/12-inch

SOUL (709 "Here Comes the Judge") 10-20 68
SOUL (719 "The Prime") 10-15 69

LONG, Tom
(Gene Autry)

Singles: 78 rpm

Sunrise (33070 "I'll Be Thinking Of You Little Girl") 25-75
Also see AUTRY, Gene

LONG HAIRS

Singles: 7-inch

MEMPHIS (110 "Go Go Go") 50-75 62

LONG ISLAND SOUNDS
(Long Island Soundes)

Singles: 7-inch

BALBOA (021 "Pancho's Villa") 5-10

DYNO VOICE (903 "One, Two, Three and I Fell") 5-10 68
WONDER (165 "Tiger") 10-15 65
WONDER (166 "Don't Cry Linda") 10-15 65
Members: Tony Pragano; Andelo Frisketti; Tom Hanlon; Jack Russell; Bob Pasternak; Fred O'Brien.

LONG JOHN
(John Hunter)

Singles: 78 rpm

DUKE (122 "Crazy Girl") 10-20 53

Singles: 7-inch

DUKE (122 "Crazy Girl") 20-30 53
Also see HUNTER, John

LONG JOHN & SILVERMEN

Singles: 7-inch

WANTED (001 "Heart Filled with Love") .. 15-25 66
WANTED (4581 "I'll Come Back") 10-15 66

LONG TALL LESTER
(Lester Foster)

Singles: 7-inch

DUKE (197 "All Because of You") 10-20 58

LONG TALL MARVIN
(Marvin Phillips)

Singles: 78 rpm

MODERN (993 "Have Mercy Miss Percy") 30-40 56

Singles: 7-inch

MODERN (993 "Have Mercy Miss Percy") 50-75 56
Also see PHILLIPS, Marvin

LONGBRANCH PENNYWHISTLE

Singles: 7-inch

AMOS (121 thru 148) 5-10 69-70

LPs: 10/12-inch

AMOS (7007 "Longbranch Pennywhistle") 25-40 69
Members: John David Souther; Glenn Frey; Ry Cooder; James Burton.
Also see BURTON, James
Also see COODER, Ry

LONGO, Bobby

Singles: 7-inch

ZIP (102 "A Night to Remember") 200-300 57

LONNIE
(Irving Brofsky)

Singles: 7-inch

MOHAWK (122 "Beeline") 10-15 61
Also see LONNIE & CAROLLONS

LONNIE & CAROLLONS
(With the Irv Spice Orchestra)

Singles: 7-inch

MOHAWK (108 "Chapel of Tears") 75-125 58
(Green label.)
MOHAWK (108 "Chapel of Tears") 15-25 59
(Red label.)
MOHAWK (111 "Trudy") 30-40 58
MOHAWK (112 "You Say") 40-50 58
MOHAWK (113 "The Gang All Knows") 200-300 59
STREET CORNER (101 "Chapel of Tears") 8-12 73
Members: Irving Brofsky; Richie Jackson; Eric Nathanson; Jimmy Laffey.
Also see LONNIE

LONNIE & CAROLLONS / Barons

Singles: 7-inch

MOHAWK (902 "Chapel of Tears"/"Wild Weekend") 15-25 63
Also see BARONS

LONNIE & CAROLLONS / Deans

LPs: 10/12-inch

CRYSTAL BALL (126 "Lonnie & the Carollons Meet the Deans") 15-20 88
(Black vinyl. 1000 made.)
Also see DEANS
Also see LONNIE & CAROLLONS

LONNIE & CRISIS
(With Bob Alfieri & Orchestra)

Singles: 7-inch

RELIC (532 "Bells in the Chapel") 5-10 65
TIMES SQUARE (25 "Bells in the Chapel") 10-15 63
UNIVERSAL (103 "Bells in the Chapel") 150-200 61

LONNIE & LEGENDS

Singles: 7-inch

IMPRESSION (109 "I Cried") 20-30 66
REV (1005 "Penguin Walk") 15-25 63

LONNIE THE CAT

Singles: 78 rpm

RPM (410 "I Ain't Drunk") 15-25 54

Singles: 7-inch

RPM (410 "I Ain't Drunk") 30-50 54

LONNIE'S LEGENDS

Singles: 7-inch

PLAYBOY (108 "Trying So Hard to Forget") 10-20 65

LONZO & OSCAR C&W '48
(With the Winston County Pea Pickers)

Singles: 78 rpm

DECCA 4-8 53-54
DOT 4-8 54
RCA (2563 I'm My Own Grandpa") 15-25 48

Singles: 7-inch

DECCA 5-10 53-54
DOT 5-10 54
GRC (1006 "Traces of Life") 4-8 74
NUGGET 4-8 62-64
STARDAY (Except 543) 4-8 60-61
STARDAY (543 "Country Music Time") 10-20 61

LPs: 10/12-inch

BRYLEN 5-10 82
COLUMBIA 10-20 68
DECCA 15-25 63
GRC 6-12 75
NUGGET 6-12
PICKWICK/HILLTOP 10-20 65
STARDAY (119 "America's Greatest Country Comedians") 35-45 60
STARDAY (244 "Country Music Time") 25-35 63
Members: Rollin Sullivan; Ken Marvin; John Sullivan; David Hooten.

LOOKING GLASS

Singles: 7-inch

MEDIA (414 "Kathy's Dream"/"Migada Bus") 10-20 67
(Also issued, using the same number, but credited to the Looking Glasses.)
Also see LOOKING GLASSES

LOOKING GLASSES

Singles: 7-inch

MEDIA (414 "Visions"/"Migada Bus") 20-30 67
(Also issued, using the same number, but credited to the Looking Glass.)
Also see CLOUDS
Also see LOOKING GLASS

LOOK OUTS

Singles: 7-inch

SEEBURG (3012 "Roll Over Beethoven") 10-15 65

LOOMS

Singles: 7-inch

MONTGOMERY (0009 "It's True") .... 25-35 '60s

LOOSE ENDS

Singles: 7-inch

BELL (671 "Dead End Kid") 5-10 67
MALA (538 "He's a Nobody") 10-20 66
MEADOW BROOK (69 "Hey Sweet Baby") 10-15 69

LOOSE ENZ

Singles: 7-inch

DB (18963 "A World Outside") 30-50 67
VIRTUE (2502 "Easy Rider") 10-20 68
Members: Al Gutierrez; Eric Gutierrez; Bill Kauffman; Rich Viara.

LOOSE WIG

Singles: 7-inch

RESIST (506 "I'll Always Love You Darlin'") .... 10-20 '60s

LOPEZ, Trini P&R/R&B/LP '63

Singles: 12-inch

ROULETTE 5-8 77

Singles: 7-inch

CAPITOL 4-6 71-72
D.R.A. (7008 "Rosita") 10-15 61
GRIFFIN 4-6 73
KING (5173 "Yes You Do") 10-20 59
KING (5187 "Rock On") 15-25 59
KING (5198 "Here Comes Sally") 10-20 59
KING (5234 thru 5487) 10-15 59-61
KING (5800 series) 5-10 63-64
KING (6000 series) 4-8 65-66
MARIANNE 4-6 77
PRIVATE STOCK 4-6 75
REPRISE 5-10 63-71
ROULETTE (7214 "Helplessly") 4-6 77
UNITED MODERN (106 "If") 5-8 64
VOLK (101 "The Right to Rock") 15-25 58

Picture Sleeves

REPRISE 10-15 62-66

EPs: 7-inch

COLUMBIA/W.B. (124178 "Trini Lopez Sings His Greatest Hits") 10-15 67
(Special products issue for Coca-Cola/Fresca.)
KING (483 "Teenage Idol") 15-25 63
REPRISE 8-12 63-68

LPs: 10/12-inch

CAPITOL 5-10 72
CROWN 8-12 65
EXACT 5-8 81
GRIFFIN 8-10 72
HARMONY 8-10 70
KING (863 "Teenage Love Songs") 20-30 63
KING (877 "More of Trini Lopez") 20-30 63
REPRISE 10-20 63-69
ROULETTE 5-8 78
SILVER EAGLE 5-10 82
WEA LATINA 5-8 91
Also see BIG BEATS
Also see LAWRENCE, Steve / Trini Lopez
Also see RIVERS, Johnny / Trini Lopez

LOPEZ, Trini / Scott Gregory

LPs: 10/12-inch

GUEST STAR (1499 "Trini Lopez / Scott Gregory [Bill Haley]") 30-50 64
Also see HALEY, Bill

LOPEZ, Trini, with the Ventures & Nancy Ames

LPs: 10/12-inch

REPRISE (6361 "Trini Lopez Show") 10-15 70
Also see LOPEZ, Trini
Also see VENTURES

LOPEZ, Vincent, & His Orchestra

LPs: 10/12-inch

MERCURY .... 15-25 '50s
WALDORF (185 "Melody of Love") 35-55 54
(10-inch LP. Cover pictures Tina Louise, although she is not heard on the disc. Also issued credited to Enoch Light & His Orchestra.)
WALDORF (193 "Moments to Remember") 35-55 54
(10-inch LP. Cover pictures Tina Louise, although she is not heard on the disc. Also issued credited to Enoch Light & His Orchestra.)
WALDORF (1214 "Moments to Remember") 25-50 57
(Cover pictures Jayne Mansfield, although she is not heard on the disc. Also issued credited to Enoch Light & His Orchestra.)
WALDORF (1232 "Melody of Love") 20-40 57
(10-inch LP. Cover pictures Tina Louise, although she is not heard on the disc. Also issued credited to Enoch Light & His Orchestra.)
WALDORF (1329 "Moments to Remember") 20-40 58
(Cover pictures Tina Louise, although she is not heard on the disc. Also issued credited to Enoch Light & His Orchestra.)
Also see LIGHT, Enoch, & His Orchestra
Also see MANSFIELD, Jayne

LOR, Denise P&R '54

Singles: 78 rpm

LIBERTY 5-10 56
MAJAR 5-10 54
MERCURY 5-10 55

Singles: 7-inch

LIBERTY (55020 thru 55047) 8-12 56
MAJAR (27-X45 "If I Give My Heart to You") 10-15 54
MERCURY (70573 thru 70644) 10-15 55

EPs: 7-inch

MERCURY (4008 "Tops in Pops") 10-20 55

LORAN, Kenny
(With the Laurels)

Singles: 7-inch

CAPITOL (4230 "Stop Me") 10-20 59
CAPITOL (4276 "Magic Star") 25-35 59
CAPITOL (4305 "Look Who's Lonely") 10-20 59
CHALLENGE (59010 "Lonely Boy") 15-25 58

LORBER, Alan

Singles: 7-inch

VERVE (10537 "Hang On to a Dream") 5-10 67
VERVE (10538 "Look of Love") 5-10 67
MGM (13926 "Congress Alley") 5-10 68

LPs: 10/12-inch

MGM 10-15 69
VERVE (8711 "Lotus Palace") 10-15 67
Also see CLIFFORD, Mike

LORD, Bobby C&W '56

Singles: 78 rpm

COLUMBIA (21000 series, except 21339 & 21539) 5-10 55-56
COLUMBIA (21339 "No More, No More") 10-15 55
COLUMBIA (21539 "Everybody's Rockin' But Me") 10-20 56
COLUMBIA (40000 series) 10-15 56

Singles: 7-inch

COLUMBIA (21339 "No More, No More") 40-60 55
COLUMBIA (21339 "No More") 10-20 55
COLUMBIA (21367 "I'm the Devil Who Made Her That Way") 10-20 55
COLUMBIA (21397 "Something's Missing") 10-20 55
COLUMBIA (21437 "Hawk-Eye") 20-30 55
COLUMBIA (21498 "So Doggone Lonesome") 10-20 55
COLUMBIA (21459 "I Can't Do Without You Anymore") 10-20 55
COLUMBIA (21539 "Everybody's Rockin' But Me") 50-75 56
COLUMBIA (40666 "Fire of Love") 20-30 56
COLUMBIA (40819 "Your Sweet Love") 10-20 57
COLUMBIA (40927 "High Voltage") 25-35 57
COLUMBIA (41030 "Am I a Fool") 10-20 57
COLUMBIA (41155 "Sack") 15-25 58
COLUMBIA (41288 "Walking Alone") 10-20 58
COLUMBIA (41352 "Party Pooper") 15-25 59
COLUMBIA (41505 "Too Many Miles") 15-25 59
COLUMBIA (41596 "Give Me a Woman") 15-25 60
COLUMBIA (41824 "Before I Lose My Mind") 15-25 60
COLUMBIA (42012 "A Rose and a Thorn") 15-25 61
DECCA 4-8 68-71
HICKORY 5-10 61-64
RICE 4-6 73-74

LPs: 10/12-inch

DECCA 8-10 70
HARMONY (7322 "Bobby Lord's Best") 10-20 64
HICKORY (126 "The Bobby Lord Show") 10-12 65

LORD, Brian, & Midnighters

Singles: 7-inch

CAPITOL (4981 "Big Surfer") 20-40 63
VIGAH (0001 "Big Surfer") 75-125 63
Members: Brian Lord; Frank Zappa; Paul Buff; Ray Collins: David Aerni.
Also see MOTHERS OF INVENTION
Also see NED & NELDA
Also see ROTATIONS

LORD, Cindy

Singles: 78 rpm

CADENCE (1276 "Put Your Lips to Mine") 5-10 55

Singles: 7-inch

CADENCE (1276 "Put Your Lips to Mine") 10-15 55

LORD, Emmett

Singles: 7-inch

ANTEL (520 "Been So Long") .... 5-10 '60s
LIBERTY (55491 "Women") 15-20 62

LORD, Janet

Singles: 78 rpm

UNIQUE (305 "Reward, Reward") 5-10 55

Singles: 7-inch

UNIQUE (305 "Reward, Reward") 10-15 55

LORD, Peggy

LPs: 10/12-inch

STEREODDITIES (1903 "Lusty Trusty Buster") 15-20 63

LORD & FLIES

Singles: 7-inch

USA (828 "You Made a Fool Out of Me") 5-10 66
USA (857 "Echoes") 10-20 66

LORD & HIS BARONS

Singles: 7-inch

FLEETWOOD (4566 "Foolish Lies") 15-25 66

LORD DENT & INVADERS

Singles: 7-inch

SHELLEY (1001 "Wolf Call") .... 10-20 '60s
SHELLEY (1810 "Wolf Call") .... 10-15 '60s

Picture Sleeves

SHELLEY (1001 "Wolf Call") .... 10-20 '60s
Member: Clayton "Lord Dent" Watson.

LORD DOUGLAS & SERFS

Singles: 7-inch

HR (606 "Your Turn to Cry") 15-25

LORD LUTHER
(With the Counts; with Garnets; with Kingsmen; Luther McDaniel)

Singles: 7-inch

FRANTIC (102 "Turn the Key") 15-25 58
FRANTIC (112 "Truth") 25-50 59
(First issue.)
IMPERIAL (5596 "Truth") 15-25 59
LUSAN (101 "Two of a Kind") 15-25
MUSIC CITY (833 "Tell Ya What") 250-350 58
SCHIRECK (101 "My Mistake") 15-25
Also see GAYLARKS
Also see LEWIS, Al, & Modernistics / Lord Luther

LORD ROCKINGHAM'S XI P&R '58

Singles: 7-inch

LONDON (1810 "Fried Onions") 10-15 58

LORD SITAR

Singles: 7-inch

CAPITOL (5972 "Black Is Black") 5-10 67

LPs: 10/12-inch

CAPITOL (2916 "Lord Sitar") 10-20 68

LORD SUTCH LP '70
(With His Heavy Friends; Screaming Lord Sutch)

Singles: 7-inch

CAMEO (341 "Bye Bye Baby") 5-10 65

LPs: 10/12-inch

COTILLION (9015 "Lord Sutch and His Heavy Friends") 20-30 70
COTILLION (9049 "Hands of Jack the Ripper") 15-25 72
Member: Daniel Edwards.
Also see BECK, Jeff
Also see MOON, Keith
Also see PAGE, Jimmy

LORD WESTBROOK

Singles: 7-inch

BIG TOP (3138 "Quiet Please") 10-20 63

LORDAN, Jerry

Singles: 7-inch

CAPITOL (4389 "Do I Worry") 10-15 60

LORDS

Singles: 7-inch

VALIANT (725 "She Belongs to Me") 10-20 66

LORDS

Singles: 7-inch

ALDRICH (1001 "Light Rain") 15-25 66

LORDS OF LONDON

Singles: 7-inch

APEX (21809 "Candy Rainbow") 15-20
(Canadian.)
APEX (77054 "Cornflakes & Ice Cream") 15-20 67
(Canadian.)
APEX (77068 "Popcorn Man") 15-20 67
(Canadian.)
APEX (77074 "Candy Rainbow") 15-20 68
(Canadian.)
DECCA (32196 "Cornflakes and Ice Cream") 10-15 67
DOMAIN (1421 "Broken Heart") 15-20 65
MGM (13919 "Candy Rainbow") 10-15 68

LORELEIS P&R '55
(With the George Annis Orchestra)
Singles: 78 rpm
BALLY....5-15 57
DOT (15268 "Have Fun Baby")....5-10 54
SPOTLIGHT (390 "You're So Nice to Be Near")....5-10 55
Singles: 7-inch
BALLY (1024 "Your Love")....5-15 57
BALLY (1032 "But Why?")....5-15 57
BRUNSWICK (55271 "Why Do I Put Up with You")....10-15 64
DOT (15268 "Have Fun Baby")....10-15 54
SPOTLIGHT (390 "You're So Nice to Be Near")....20-30 55

LOREN, Donna
Singles: 7-inch
CAPITOL....8-12 64-65
CHALLENGE....8-12 62-64
CREST (1095 "I'm So Lonely")....5-10 62
CREST (1106 "Sailor, Sailor")....5-10 62
REPRISE (586 "Let's Pretend")....5-10 67
REPRISE (634 "As Long As I'm Holding You")....5-10 67
Picture Sleeves
CAPITOL (5250 "Blowing Out the Candles")....10-15 64
LPs: 10/12-inch
CAPITOL (T-2323 "Beach Blanket Bingo")....20-25 65
(Monaural.)
CAPITOL (ST-2323 "Beach Blanket Bingo")....20-30 65
(Stereo.)

LOREN, Frankie
Singles: 7-inch
MERCURY (71444 "Hey Little Girl")....10-20 59
PORTER....10-20 59

LOREN, John
Singles: 7-inch
GEE (1059 "Tell the World")....10-15 60

LOREN, Keith
Singles: 7-inch
MARK IV (8800 "Born to Ramble")....50-75

LOREN, Kenny
(With the Cordairs)
Singles: 7-inch
DAWN (1113 "My Girl Doesn't Care")....40-50 59

LOREN, Sophia
Singles: 78 rpm
RCA (6385 "Woman of the River")....5-10 56
Singles: 7-inch
COLUMBIA (41200 "Love Song from *Houseboat*")....10-20 58
RCA (6385 "Woman of the River")....10-20 56

LORENZ, Hans
Singles: 7-inch
CREST (1041 "Buttercup a Golden Hair")....10-15 57

LORENZ, John / Starlighters
Singles: 78 rpm
MERCURY (3060 "Here We Are")....100-200 47
(Picture disc. Promotional only issue.)

LORI, Fran
Singles: 7-inch
CHANCELLOR (1035 "True, True Love")...5-10 59
CHANCELLOR (1050 "Will I Always Be Your Sweetheart")....5-10 60
EMBER (1103 "I Never Knew")....10-15 64
LENOX (5573 "Better to Have Loved and Lost You")....5-10 63
SUNNYBROOK (3 "Teenage Prayer")....5-10 61

LORI & LANCE
Singles: 7-inch
FEDERAL (12548 "I Don't Have to Worry")....15-25 64

LORI ANN
Singles: 7-inch
MELRON (5004 "The Same Thing Could Happen to You")....10-20 62
MELRON (5007 "Darling")....10-20 63

LORIN, Tempi, & Candy Girls
Singles: 7-inch
ROTATE (5005 "Runaround")....10-15 64
Also see CANDY GIRLS

LORING, Randy
Singles: 7-inch
ROWENA (113 "Happy Birthday, Seventeen")....10-15 64

LORNETTES
Singles: 7-inch
GALLIO (105 "I Don't Deny It")....10-15 65
GALLIO (110 "His Way with the Girls")....10-15 66

LORRAINE & DELIGHTS
Singles: 7-inch
BARRY (1002 "Baby I Need You")....10-20 65

LORRAINE & SOCIALITES
Singles: 7-inch
MERCURY (72163 "Any Old Way")....10-15 63

LORRIE, Myrna
Singles: 78 rpm
ABBOTT....10-15 55-56
Singles: 7-inch
ABBOTT (185 "Listen to My Heart Strings")....15-25 55
ABBOTT (187 "Moonshy")....15-25 56
LPs: 10/12-inch
HARMONY....20-40

LORRIE, Myrna, & Buddy DeVal C&W '55
Singles: 78 rpm
ABBOTT....10-15 54-55
Singles: 7-inch
ABBOTT (172 "Are You Mine")....15-25 54
ABBOTT (177 "I'm Your Man")....15-25 55
Also see DEVAL, Buddy

LORRY LEE & DELLA
Singles: 7-inch
MECCA (2699 "Let Him Go, Go, Go")....10-20 '60s

LORY, Dick
Singles: 78 rpm
DOT (15496 "Cool It Baby")....15-25 56
Singles: 7-inch
COLUMBIA (41224 "Wild Blooded Women")....15-25 58
COLUMBIA (41276 "Crazy Little Daisy")..15-25 58
DOT (15496 "Cool It Baby")....25-50 56
LIBERTY (55293 thru 55415)....10-15 60-62
LIBERTY (55529 thru 55707)....8-12 63-64

LOS ADMIRADORES LP '60
LPs: 10/12-inch
COMMAND (809 "Bongos Bongos Bongos")....10-20 60
COMMAND (812 "Bongos/Flutes/ Guitars")....10-20 60

LOS ANGELES
Singles: 7-inch
CARAVAN-FORTY (6601 "I Can Read Between the Lines")....50-100 62

LOS BRAVOS P&R/LP '66
Singles: 7-inch
PARROT (3020 thru 3023)....8-12 68-69
PRESS (60002 "Black Is Black")....8-12 66
PRESS (60003 "Going Nowhere")....8-12 66
PRESS (60004 "You'll Never Get the Chance Again")....8-12 66
LPs: 10/12-inch
PARROT (71021 "Bring a Little Lovin'")...20-30 68
PRESS (83003 "Black Is Black")....30-40 66
Members: Mike Kogel; Manuel Fernandez; Miguel Danus; Pablo Sanllehi; Tony Martinez.
Also see DRIFTERS / Lesley Gore / Roy Orbison / Los Bravos
Also see NASHVILLE TEENS / Los Bravos

LOSERS
Singles: 7-inch
CONGRESSIONAL ("Saxy Guitar")....8-12
(Selection number not known.)
PARLEY (711 "Snake Eyes")....20-30 63
SPHINX (6109 "Pourquoi")....10-20 65

LOS INDIOS TABAJARAS P&R/LP '63
Singles: 7-inch
RCA....5-10 63-64
EPs: 7-inch
RCA (488 "Los Indios Tabajaras")....8-12
LPs: 10/12-inch
ARAVEL....20-30
CAMDEN....8-12
RCA (LPM-1788 "Sweet and Savage")....20-30 58
(Monaural.)
RCA (LSP-1788 "Sweet and Savage")....30-50 58
(Stereo.)
RCA (Except 2800 thru 4649)....5-10
RCA (2800 thru 4649)....10-20 63-66
VOX....10-20
Members: Natalicio; Antenor Moreyra Lima (a.k.a. Musaperi & Herundy).

LOS LOCOS DEL RITMO
LPs: 10/12-inch
DIMSA (8178 "Rock!")....75-100 '60s
(Mexican garage band.)

LOS MOSQUITOS
Singles: 7-inch
CANYON STATE (114 "Wipe Out")....25-35 '60s

LOS SILVER ROCKETS
Singles: 7-inch
IDEAL (2538 "Señorita Dizzy Livy [Dizzy Miss Lizzy]")....10-20 58

LOS STARDUSTERS
(Sunglows)
LPs: 10/12-inch
TEAR DROP (3113 "El Papalote")....10-15 64
Also see SUNGLOWS

LOST AGENCY
Singles: 7-inch
USA (881 "One Girl Man")....15-25 67

LOST & FOUND
Singles: 7-inch
INT'L ARTISTS (120 "Everybody's Here")....10-20 67
INT'L ARTISTS (125 "Professor Black")...10-20 67
PINS (1 "Don't Move Girl")....10-20 '60s
LPs: 10/12-inch
INT'L ARTISTS (3 "Everybody's Here")..75-100 68
TEMPO....10-15 73
Members: Peter Black; Jim Frost; Steve Webb; James Harrell.

LOST CHORDS
Singles: 7-inch
VAUGHN LTD. (725 "I Want to Be Her Man")....10-20 66

LOST GENERATION
Singles: 7-inch
PARIS TOWER (109 "I'd Gladly Pay")....10-15 67

LOST ONES
Singles: 7-inch
MERSEY (002 "I Can't Believe You")....15-25 66
VALIANT (721 "Trouble in the Streets")....8-12 65

LOST SOUL
Singles: 7-inch
RAVEN (2016 "A Secret of Mine")....15-25
RAVEN (2032 "I'm Gonna Hurt You")....20-30

LOST SOULS
Singles: 7-inch
DAWN (809 "Artificial Rose")....20-30 68
GLORIA (778 "It's Not Fair")....10-20 67
LIBERTY (56024 "Artificial Rose")....10-20 68

LOST SOULS
Singles: 7-inch
BANG (509 "Simple to Say")....15-25 65
BANG (513 "If She Remembers Me")....15-25 65
GLASCO (101 "Give Me Your Love")....10-15 67

LOST WEEKEND
Singles: 7-inch
USA (101 "Bridge of Love")....10-20 '60s
USA (102 "Little Black Child")....10-20 '60s

LOT
Singles: 7-inch
CADET (5613 "Ann")....5-10 68
STANAL (7887 "Call Me Your Baby")....15-20 67

LOTHAR & HAND PEOPLE
Singles: 7-inch
CAPITOL (2008 "Have Mercy")....15-25 67
CAPITOL (2376 "Milkweed Love")....15-25 68
CAPITOL (2556 "Midnight Ranger")....15-25 69
CAPITOL (5874 "L-o-v-e")....15-25 67
CAPITOL (5945 "Comic Strip")....15-25 68
LPs: 10/12-inch
CAPITOL (247 "Space Hymn")....30-50 69
CAPITOL (ST-2997 "Presenting Lothar and the Hand People")....30-50 68
CAPITOL (SM-2997 "Presenting Lothar and the Hand People")....5-10 77

LOTSA POPPA
(Lots-A-Poppa)
Singles: 7-inch
JET STREAM (710 "I Found a Love")....10-20 63
JET STREAM (714 "Tribute to Sam")....10-20 64
TRIBE (8305 "That's Where It's At")....8-12 64

LOU, Herb B., & Legal Eagles / Legal Eagles
(Herb Alpert)
Singles: 7-inch
ARCH (1607 "The Trial")....20-30 58
(Also issued as by the Legal Eagles.)
Also see ALPERT, Herb
Also see LEGAL EAGLES

LOU & GINNY
Singles: 7-inch
HEP (2141 "Do It Right")....15-25 58

LOUDERMILK, John D. P&R '61
Singles: 7-inch
COLUMBIA....5-10 58-60
MUSIC IS MEDICINE....4-6 78-79
RCA....5-10 61-69
W.B.....4-6 71
Picture Sleeves
COLUMBIA (41165 "Yearbook")....10-20 58
RCA (8101 "Road Hog")....5-10 62
LPs: 10/12-inch
MUSIC IS MEDICINE....10-20 78
RCA....15-30 61-69
W.B.....8-12 71
Also see DEE, Johnny
Also see SNEEZER, Ebe, & Epidemics

LOUIE & AMBASSADORS
Singles: 7-inch
HILLTOP (1879 "Talk That Talk")....10-15 63

LOUIS, Bobby
Singles: 7-inch
CAPITOL (4224 "Adult Western")....15-25 59
CAPITOL (4272 "Call of Love")....15-25 59

LOUIS, Dwain, & Classmates
Singles: 7-inch
CAROLE (111 "That's All Right")....400-600

LOUIS, Jimmy
Singles: 7-inch
HAWKEYE (104 "Willadean")....75-125
PHILLIPS INT'L (3565 "Your Fool")....15-25 60
TOPIC (8019 "Tonight's the Night My Angel's Halo Fell")....5-10 66

LOUIS, Joe Hill
Singles: 78 rpm
BIG TOWN (401 "Hydramatic Woman")....100-150 54
CHECKER (763 "Dorothy Mae")....200-300 52
COLUMBIA (30182 "Railroad Blues")....50-75 49
COLUMBIA (30221 "Don't Trust Your Best Friend")....50-75 49
IT'S THE PHILLIPS (9001 "Gotta Let You Go")....4000-6000 50
MODERN (795 "I Feel Like a Million")....50-75 51
MODERN (813 "Boogie in the Park")....50-75 51
MODERN (822 "Walkin' Talkin' Blues")....50-75 52
MODERN (828 "Eyesight to the Blind")....50-75 51
MODERN (839 "Gotta Go, Baby")....50-75 51
MODERN (856 "Peace of Mind")....50-75 52
SUN (178 "We All Gotta Go Sometime")....200-400 53
Singles: 7-inch
BIG TOWN (401 "Hydramatic Woman")....200-300 54
CHECKER (763 "Dorothy Mae")....1000-1500 52
Also see CHICAGO SUNNY BOY
Also see LEWIS, Johnny
Also see LITTLE JOE
Also see MEMPHIS MINNIE

LOUIS, Leslie
Singles: 78 rpm
ROCKIN' (509 "Ridin' Home") 15-25 53
Singles: 7-inch
ROCKIN' (509 "Ridin' Home") 100-200 53

LOUIS, Tommy, & Rhythm Rockers
Singles: 7-inch
MURIEL (1002 "Wail Baby Wail") 200-300

LOUIS & FROSTY
Singles: 78 rpm
C-NOTE (109 "Lonesome & Confused") . 10-20 55
Singles: 7-inch
C-NOTE (109 "Lonesome & Confused") . 20-30 55
Members: Louis Jackson; William Pyles.
Also see JACKSON, Louis

LOUIS & INNIS CLAN
Singles: 78 rpm
STERLING (207 "Oklahoma City") 15-25 47
STERLING (209 "Foggy River") 15-25 47

LOUISE, Anita
Singles: 7-inch
HICKORY (1334 "Jim Dandy") 10-20 65

LOUNGERS
Singles: 7-inch
HERALD (534 "Remember the Night") 100-150 58
(Original has a multi-color label.)
Members: Dave Concepcion; Pat Russo; Vinnie Santorelli; Steve Murphy; Frank DelCavo.
Also see FIVE SECRETS
Also see SECRETS

LOURDES
Singles: 7-inch
MERCURY (71655 "My Favorite Dream") 10-15 60

LOUVIN, Ira C&W '65
Singles: 7-inch
CAPITOL (5428 "Yodel, Sweet Molly") 5-10 65
LPs: 10/12-inch
CAPITOL (2413 "Unforgettable") 25-35 65
Also see LOUVIN BROTHERS

LOUVIN BROTHERS C&W '55
(Ira and Charlie Louvin)
Singles: 78 rpm
CAPITOL 5-10 52-57
MGM 8-12 52
Singles: 7-inch
CAPITOL (2296 thru 3871) 15-20 52-57
CAPITOL (3974 thru 5296) 10-15 58-64
MGM 10-20 52
EPs: 7-inch
CAPITOL 10-20 55-60
LPs: 10/12-inch
ACM 5-10
CMF 5-10
CAPITOL (T-769 "Tragic Songs of Life") 50-100 56
(Monaural.)
CAPITOL (DT-769 "Tragic Songs of Life") 25-50 68
(Reprocessed stereo.)
CAPITOL (825 "Nearer My God to Thee") 30-40 57
CAPITOL (910 "Ira & Charlie") 30-40 58
CAPITOL (T-1061 "Family Who Prays") .. 20-40 58
(Monaural.)
CAPITOL (DT-1061 "Family Who Prays") 10-15 68
(Reprocessed stereo.)
CAPITOL (SM-1061 "Family Who Prays") .. 5-10
(Reprocessed stereo.)
CAPITOL (1106 "Country Love Ballads") 30-40 59
CAPITOL (1385 "My Baby's Gone") 30-40 60
CAPITOL (1277 "Satan Is Real") 30-40 60
CAPITOL (1449 "Tribute to the Delmore Brothers") 50-75 60
CAPITOL (1547 "Encore") 30-40 61
CAPITOL (1616 "Country Christmas") 20-40 61
CAPITOL (1721 "Weapon of Prayer") 10-20 62
CAPITOL (1834 "Keep Your Eyes on Jesus") 15-25 63
CAPITOL (2091 "Current Hits") 20-40 64
CAPITOL (2331 "Thank God for My Christian Home") 20-40 65
CAPITOL (2827 "The Great Roy Acuff Songs") 20-30 67
CAPITOL (11193 "Great Gospel Singing") 10-15 73
COUNTRY CLASSICS 5-10
GOLDEN COUNTRY 5-10
GUSTO 5-10
MGM (3426 "Louvin Brothers") 75-150 57
METRO (598 "The Louvin Brothers") 20-40 67
PICKWICK/HILLTOP 10-15 66-67
ROUNDER 5-10 79-80
TOWER (5038 "Two Different Worlds") 20-40 66
TOWER (5122 "Country Heart and Soul") 20-40 68
Members: Charlie Louvin; Ira Louvin
Also see LOUVIN, Ira

LOVE P&R/LP '66
Singles: 7-inch
BLUE THUMB 4-8 69-70
ELEKTRA (45603 "My Little Red Book") 5-10 66
ELEKTRA (45605 "7 & 7 Is") 5-10 66
ELEKTRA (45608 "Stephanie Knows Who") 10-20 66
ELEKTRA (45608 "She Comes in Colors") 5-10 67
(Same number and flip used again.)
ELEKTRA (45613 "Que Vida") 15-25 67
ELEKTRA (45629 thru 45700) 5-10 68-70
RSO 4-6 74-75
LPs: 10/12-inch
BLUE THUMB (8822 "False Start") 20-30 70
BLUE THUMB (9000 "Out Here") 15-25 69
ELEKTRA (4001 "Love") 30-40 66
(Monaural.)
ELEKTRA (4005 "Da Capo") 30-40 66
(Monaural.)
ELEKTRA (4013 "Forever Changes") 30-40 67
(Monaural.)
ELEKTRA (74001 "Love") 25-35 66
(Stereo.)
ELEKTRA (74005 "Da Capo") 25-35 67
(Stereo.)
ELEKTRA (74013 "Forever Changes") 20-30 67
(Stereo.)
ELEKTRA (74049 "Four Sail") 20-30 69
(Stereo.)
ELEKTRA (74058 "Revisited") 20-30 70
(Gatefold cover.)
ELEKTRA (74058 "Revisited") 5-8 81
(Standard cover.)
MCA 5-8 82
RSO 8-10 74
RHINO (251 "Love Live") 8-10 82
RHINO (251 "Love Live") 10-15 82
(Picture disc.)
RHINO (800 "Best of Love") 5-8 80
Members: Arthur Lee; John Fleckenstein; Don Conka; John Echols; Ken Forssi; Al Pfisterer; Michael Stuart; Tjay Contrelli; Bryan Maclean; Gary Rowles.
Also see AMERICAN FOUR

LOVE, Billy
Singles: 78 rpm
HART'S BREAD (66 "Hart's Bread Boogie") 750-1000
(Used in radio commercial for bread. Recorded at Sun Studios.)

LOVE, Billy
Singles: 7-inch
GLEE (1005 "Sweet Talkin'") 20-30 61
GLEE (1010 "I'll Find My Way") 20-30 62
SMAK (5777 "Tough Lover") 5-10 67
SMOGVILLE (02 "Tough Lover") 5-10 67

LOVE, Billy, & Lovers
Singles: 7-inch
DRAGON (4403 "Legend of Love") 50-75 64
DRAGON (4403 "Legend of Love") 5-10 95
(Yellow vinyl. 500 made.)

LOVE, Billy "Red"
Singles: 78 rpm
CHESS (1508 "Drop Top") 50-75 52
CHESS (1516 "My Teddy Bear Baby") 50-75 52

LOVE, Buddy, & Blue Flames
Singles: 7-inch
PROUD (101 "Heartbreak Hotel") 50-75
THUNDER (1 "I Love You") 100-150 62

LOVE, Clayton
Singles: 78 rpm
ALADDIN (3148 "Chained to Your Love") 15-25 52
GROOVE (0162 "Mary Lou") 10-20 56
MODERN (929 "Wicked Little Baby") 10-20 54
TRUMPET (138 "Susie") 20-30 51
Singles: 7-inch
ALADDIN (3148 "Chained to Your Love") 35-55 52
BOBBIN (108 "Bye Bye Baby") 30-40 59
BOBBIN (122 "It's You") 30-40 60
(With the Ross Marker Orchestra.)
GROOVE (0162 "Mary Lou") 25-50 56
MODERN (929 "Wicked Little Baby") 25-50 54
Also see MARKS, Roosevelt, Orchestra

LOVE, Cyndy
Singles: 7-inch
SPACE (00013 "You Never Knew") 10-20 67

LOVE, Darlene P&R '63
Singles: 7-inch
COLUMBIA (07984 "He's Sure the Man I Love") 3-5 88
ELEKTRA (79647 "River Deep, Mountain High") 3-5 85
(Promotional issue only.)
PHILLES (111 "The Boy I'm Gonna Marry"/"My Heart Beat a Little Bit Faster") 25-50 63
PHILLES (111 "The Boy I'm Gonna Marry"/ "Playing for Keeps") 20-30 63
PHILLES (114 "Wait Till My Bobby Gets Home") 20-30 63
PHILLES (117 "A Fine, Fine Boy") 20-30 63
PHILLES (119 "Christmas [Baby Please Come Home]") 20-30 64
(Same selection number used for a Crystals release.)
PHILLES (123 "He's a Quiet Guy") 750-1000 64
(Yellow label. Same selection number later used for a Ronettes release.)
PHILLES (123 "He's a Quiet Guy") 100-200 64
(White label. Promotional issue only.)
PHILLES (125 "Christmas [Baby Please Come Home]") 15-25 65
REPRISE (0534 "If") 8-12 66
RHINO 5-8 86
W.B./SPECTOR (0401 "Christmas") 4-6 74
W.B./SPECTOR (0410 "Stumble & Fall") 4-6 77
Picture Sleeves
COLUMBIA (07984 "He's Sure the Man I Love") 3-5 88
ELEKTRA (79647 "River Deep, Mountain High") 3-5 85
(Promotional issue only.)
LPs: 10/12-inch
COLUMBIA (40605 "Paint Another Picture") 10-15 88
RHINO (855 "Live at Hop Singh's") 8-10 85
Also see BLOSSOMS
Also see BOB B. SOXX & BLUE JEANS
Also see CRYSTALS
Also see HALE & HUSHABYES
Also see MOOSE & PELICANS
Also see RONETTES / Crystals / Darlene Love / Bob B. Soxx & Blue Jeans
Also see 6680 LEXINGTON

LOVE, Darlene / Ronettes
Singles: 7-inch
CHRYSALIS (3202 "Phil Spector's Christmas Mix") 3-5 87
Picture Sleeves
CHRYSALIS (3202 "Phil Spector's Christmas Mix") 3-5 87
Also see LOVE, Darlene
Also see RONETTES

LOVE, Frankie
Singles: 7-inch
LA ROSA (101 "First Star") 20-30 62
LA ROSA (102 "Stranger at the Dance") 100-150 62
LOMA (2033 "First Star") 8-12 66

LOVE, Honey, & Love Notes
Singles: 7-inch
CAMEO (380 "Mary Ann") 8-12 65
CAMEO (409 "Beg Me") 10-15 66

LOVE, Hot Shot
Singles: 78 rpm
SUN (196 "Wolf Call Boogie") 400-500 54
Singles: 7-inch
SUN (196 "Wolf Call Boogie") 2000-2500 54

LOVE, Johnny
(With the Way Singers)
Singles: 7-inch
MERCURY (71492 "Lead Me") 10-20 59
MERCURY (71575 "Because You Love Me") 10-20 60
MERCURY (71667 "There Goes My Heart") 10-20 60
STARTIME (5001 "Chills & Fever") 35-50 60
(Reissued as by Ronnie Love.)
TEE PEE (395 "Consolation") 15-20
Also see LOVE, Ronnie

LOVE, Mary R&B '66
Singles: 7-inch
JOSIE (999 "Hurt Is Just Beginning") 5-10 68
MODERN 10-20 65-67

LOVE, Mike, & Dean Torrence / Paul Revere & Raiders
Singles: 7-inch
PREMORE (2 "Jingle Bell Rock") 20-30 83
Picture Sleeves
PREMORE (2 "Jingle Bell Rock") 20-30 83
Also see REVERE, Paul, & Raiders

LOVE, Nancy
Singles: 7-inch
DECCA (32338 "Hangin' On") 10-20 68
VEE-JAY (432 "Rescue Me") 8-12 62
VEE-JAY (458 "Proove It to Me") 8-12 62

LOVE, Preston
(With the Love Bugs; "Vocal Beverly Wright")
Singles: 78 rpm
FEDERAL 15-25 51-53
SPIN (103 "Feel So Good") 15-25
ULTRA 10-20 55
Singles: 7-inch
DIG (101 thru 116) 15-25 56
FEDERAL (12069 "Wango Blues") 50-100 52
FEDERAL (12085 "Like a Ship at Sea") . 50-100 52
FEDERAL (12132 "You Got Me Drinkin' ") 50-100 53
FEDERAL (12145 "My Love Is Draggin' ") 50-100 53
KING (5787 "Blues in the Night") 10-15 63
MEXIE (103 "Tough Walk") 15-25 62
("Mexie" is the mother of Preston Love.)
ULTRA (101 "If You Ever Get Lonesome") 75-100 55
ULTRA (103 "That's All Right Baby") 50-75 55
(Credited to Preston Love, but vocalist is really Johnny Otis.)
LPs: 10/12-inch
KENT 10-20 68
Also see HANK & SUGAR PIE
Also see LOVE BUGS
Also see SAILOR BOY / Preston Love

LOVE, Ronnie P&R/R&B '61
Singles: 7-inch
ALMERIA (4001 "Nothing to It") 15-25
D-TOWN (1021 "Judy") 150-200 64
D-TOWN (1047 "Judy") 30-40 65
DOT (16144 "Chills & Fever") 10-20 60
(First issued as by Johnny Love.)
DOT (16186 "Just to Be Loved") 10-20 61
STARTIME (5003 "Shakin' and a Breakin' ") 75-100 61
Also see LOVE, Johnny

LOVE, Sybil, & Love Notes
Singles: 7-inch
VALEX (505 "I Love You Darling") 250-350 59

LOVE, Tommy
("Dead Beats")
Singles: 7-inch
BAGDAD (1002 "Take My Hand") 10-15 63
DONDEE (1937 thru 1947) 10-15 61-62
FEDERAL (12331 "My Crazy Heart") 10-20 58
ORBIT (4889 "Wow! Wow!") 100-200 62
REV (1001 "Love Bug Is Buggin' Me") 10-15 63
EPs: 7-inch
DONDEE (10835 "Tommy Love Sings") .. 20-30 62
DONDEE (10836 "Tommy Love Sings") .. 20-30 62

LOVE, Vince
Singles: 7-inch
AMAZON (713 "Sunday Kind of Love")... 40-50 62

LOVE, Willie
(With His Three Aces; Willie Love's Three Aces)
Singles: 78 rpm
TRUMPET (137 "Little Car Blues") 25-35 51
TRUMPET (147 "My Own Boogie") 25-35 51
TRUMPET (Except 137 & 147) 20-30 52-53
Singles: 7-inch
TRUMPET (172 "Falling Rain") 40-60 52
TRUMPET (173 "Vanity Dresser Boogie") 40-60 52
TRUMPET (174 "Shady Lane Blues") 40-60 52
TRUMPET (175 "Nelson Street Blues")... 40-60 52
TRUMPET (209 "Shout, Brother, Shout") 40-60 53

LOVE BROTHERS
Singles: 7-inch
BY LOVE (843 "Baby, I'll Never Let You Go") 150-200

LOVE BUGS
Singles: 78 rpm
FEDERAL (12216 "Boom Diddy Wawa Baby") 20-30 55
Singles: 7-inch
FEDERAL (12216 "Boom Diddy Wawa Baby") 40-60 55
Members: Preston Love; Hank Huston; Peylia Balinton.
Also see HANK & SUGAR PIE
Also see LOVE, Preston

LOVE CHAIN
Singles: 7-inch
MINIT (32065 "I'm Loving You Baby") 15-25 69
U.A. (50582 "The Sun") 5-10 69

LOVE COLUMN
Singles: 7-inch
DUO (7460 "Can't Get Enough") 20-30

LOVE EXCHANGE
Singles: 7-inch
UPTOWN (755 "Swallow the Sun") 15-25 67
LPs: 10/12-inch
TOWER (5115 "Love Exchange") 15-25 68

LOVE INS
Singles: 7-inch
CURTIS BROS (101 "Everything's There") 15-25 67
LAURIE (3415 "You're Supposed to Be Mine") 10-20 67
LAURIE (3456 "Groove Me") 10-20 68
Also see HYSTERICS

LOVE LARKS
Singles: 7-inch
FELLATIO (301 "Diddle-Le-Bom") 5-10
MASON'S (3-070 "Diddle-Le-Bom"). 1000-1500 57

LOVE LETTERS
Singles: 7-inch
ACME (714 "Walking the Streets Alone") 500-800 57
(Small print on label.)
ACME (714 "Walking the Streets Alone") 75-125 57
(Large print on label.)
Also see LEE, Nancy

LOVE LORDS
(With the Fauntleroy Five; "Jimmie Holmes, Tenor")
Singles: 7-inch
AL KING (11021 "Burning Love") 200-300 62

LOVE NOTES
("On Tenor Sax Lucky Warren")
Singles: 78 rpm
IMPERIAL (5254 "Surrender Your Heart") 300-400 53
RAINBOW (266 "I'm Sorry") 75-150 54
RIVIERA (970 "I'm Sorry") 150-250 54
RIVIERA (975 "Since I Fell for You") ... 200-300 54
Singles: 7-inch
IMPERIAL (5254 "Surrender Your Heart") 3000-4000 53
LOST NITE 5-10
RAINBOW (266 "I'm Sorry") 250-300 54
RIVIERA (970 "I'm Sorry") 800-1000 54
RIVIERA (975 "Since I Fell for You") 2000-2500 54
(Original label color is a mixture of magenta [red] and cyan [blue] – giving a lavender-pink look. Counterfeits are just light pink.)
Member: Ronald Gill. Session: Lucky Warren.
Also see GILL, Ronnie, & Pastel Keys
Also see WARREN, Lucky

LOVE NOTES / Ronald Gill / Nats Walker Orchestra / Margie Anderson
EPs: 7-inch
FAMILY LIBRARY OF RECORDED MUSIC (1040 "Crawling") 200-300 53
Also see LOVE NOTES

LOVE NOTES — R&B '57
Singles: 78 rpm
HOLIDAY (2605 "United") 75-100 57
Singles: 7-inch
HOLIDAY (2605 "United") 30-50 57
(Glossy label stock.)
HOLIDAY (2605 "United") ....10-15 '60s
(Flat label stock.)
HOLIDAY (2607 "If I Could Make You Mine") 20-30 57

LOVE NOTES
(With Vinny Catalano & Orchestra)
Singles: 7-inch
WILSHIRE (200 "Nancy") 20-40 63
WILSHIRE (203 "Gloria") 50-75 63
Also see CATALANO, Vinny

LOVE POTION
Singles: 7-inch
KAPP (979 "This Love") 10-15 69
TCB (1601 "This Love") 20-30 69
(Selection number shown only in the vinyl trail-off area. First issue.)

LOVE SCULPTURE
Singles: 7-inch
PARROT 8-12 68-70
LPs: 10/12-inch
PARROT (71035 "Forms and Feelings")..20-25 70
RARE EARTH (505 "Blues Helping") 20-40 69
(Rounded-top cover.)
RARE EARTH (505 "Blues Helping") 15-20 69
(Standard cover.)
Members: Dave Edmunds; John Williams; Bob Jones.
Also see EDMUNDS, Dave

LOVE SOCIETY
Singles: 7-inch
MERCURY (73130 "America") 8-12 70
RCA 5-10 69-70
SCEPTER 5-10 68-69
TARGET (1006 "Let's Pretend") 10-20 69
TARGET (1009 "Hey Bulldog") 10-20 69
TEE PEE (49/50 "Do You Wanna Dance"/"Without You") 15-25 68
Members: Dave Steffen; Mike Holdridge; Keith Abler; Steve Giles; Mike Deliger.

LOVE SPECIAL DELIVERY
Singles: 7-inch
LANCE ("Babe") ....25-50 '60s
(Selection number not known.)

LOVED ONES
Singles: 7-inch
AMBASSADOR (212 "Surprise Surprise") 15-25 66
BROOKMONT (556 "Country Club Life") .20-30 '60s

LOVEHORN
Singles: 7-inch
ZODIAC (1031 "If") ....10-15 '60s

LOVEJOY, Tony
Singles: 7-inch
SCOTT (1001 "Traffic Jam") 10-20 61

LOVEJOY, Louie
Singles: 7-inch
CHICO (6305 "Midnight Blues") 10-20 63

LOVEJOYS
(Leola & the Lovejoys)
Singles: 7-inch
RED BIRD (003 "Payin' ") 5-10 64
TIGER (101 "He Ain't No Angel") 5-10 63
TIGER (105 "Payin' ") 10-15 64
(First issue.)

LOVELITES
Singles: 7-inch
PHI-DAN (5008 "I Get Scared") 10-15 66

LOVELITES — R&B '69
(Patti & the Lovelites; Patti Hamilton & Lovelites)
Singles: 7-inch
BANDERA (2515 "I Found Me a Lover")..10-15 67
COTILLION (44145 "I'm the One That You Need") 4-6 72
COTILLION (44161 "Is That Lovin' in Your Heart") 4-6 72
LOCK (723 "How Can I Tell My Mom and Dad") 8-10 69
LOVELITE (01 "My Conscience") 10-15 70
LOVELITE (02 "Bumpy Road Ahead") 4-8 71
LOVELITE (03 "The Way That You Treat Me Baby") 4-8 72
LOVELITE (1008 "Oh My Love") ....4-8 '70s
20TH FOX (2068 "Love Is So Strong") 4-8 73
UNI (55181 thru 55222) 4-8 69-70
LPs: 10/12-inch
UNI (73081 "The Lovelites") 10-20 70
Members: Patti Hamilton; Rozena Petty; Dell McDaniel; Barbara Peterman; Joni Berlman; Rhonda Grayson.

LOVENOTES
Singles: 7-inch
PREMIUM (611 "A Love Like Yours") 750-1000 57
(Reissued almost immediately with artist credit changed to the Trueloves.)
Member: David Haywood.
Also see TRUELOVES

LOVER, Joe
Singles: 7-inch
PARLIAMENT (1001 "I Hope So") 15-25 61

"LOVER BOY"
Singles: 78 rpm
RPM (409 "Love Is Scarce") 10-15 54
Singles: 7-inch
CRYSTALETTE (758 "Dance a Little Closer") 10-20 63
RPM (409 "Love Is Scarce") 20-30 54

LOVERS — P&R/R&B '57
Singles: 78 rpm
DECCA (29862 "Don't Touch Me") 20-25 56
LAMP (Except 2005) 20-40 57-58
LAMP (2005 "Darling It's Wonderful") 40-60 57
Singles: 7-inch
ALADDIN (3419 "Tell Me") 30-40 58
DECCA (29862 "Don't Touch Me") 40-50 56
IMPERIAL (5845 "Darling It's Wonderful") 15-25 62
IMPERIAL (5960 "Let's Elope") 10-15 63
IMPERIAL (66055 "Darling It's Wonderful") 10-15 64
KELLER (101 "Strange As It Seems") ..300-400 61
LAMP (2005 "Darling It's Wonderful") 30-40 57
LAMP (2013 "Let's Elope") 40-60 58
LAMP (2018 "Tell Me") 40-60 58
POST (10007 "Darling It's Wonderful") 10-20 63
Member: Tarheel Slim.
Also see TARHEEL SLIM & LITTLE ANN

LOVERS
Singles: 7-inch
CASINO (103 "Let's") 15-25 58

LOVERS
Singles: 7-inch
SUNNY (1 "Temptation") 15-25 63

LOVERS
Singles: 7-inch
AGON (1011 "Caravan of Lonely Men")...10-20 65
CHECKER (1100 "It's Too Late") 5-10 65
GATE (501 "Someone") 40-50 65
HERMITAGE (818 "It's Too Late") 5-10 64
PHILIPS (40353 "Someone") 8-12 66

LOVETONES
Singles: 7-inch
PLUS (108 "Talk to an Angel") 400-500 57

LOVETONES
Singles: 7-inch
LOVE-TONE (101 "When I Asked My Love") 15-25 61
MARLO (1515 "It's Mighty Nice") 15-25 61

LOVETT, Glenda
Singles: 7-inch
RAWSON (1001 "You Treat Me Like a Baby") 50-75

LOVETT, Lyle — C&W '86
(With His Large Band)
Singles: 7-inch
ATLANTIC (1058 Unchained Melody") 20-30
CURB/MCA 3-5 86-89
LPs: 10/12-inch
CURB/MCA 5-10 86-89
Also see CARNES, Kim

LOVETTES
Singles: 7-inch
CARNIVAL (518 "Lonely Girl") 5-10 66
CHECKER (1033 "One More Year") 5-10 63
CHECKER (1053 "Hands Off") 5-10 63
KNIGHT (2010 "Puzzling Love") 20-30 59
(Issued with two different flip sides.)

LOVIN' MACHINE
Singles: 7-inch
POWELL (2 "The Lovin' Machine") 100-200

LOVIN' SPOONFUL — P&R/LP '65
Singles: 7-inch
ERIC 4-6 78
KAMA SUTRA 4-8 65-76
Picture Sleeves
KAMA SUTRA 5-10 65-67
EPs: 7-inch
KAMA SUTRA (1 "Nashville Cats") 10-15 67
(Promotional issue only.)
LPs: 10/12-inch
AZZURRA (5801 "Anthology") 5-10 83
BACK-TRAC 5-8 85
BUDDAH 8-10 73
EMUS 5-8
51 WEST ....5-8 '80s
GRT 8-15 76
GUSTO ....5-8 '80s
KAMA SUTRA (750 "24 Karat Hits") 10-15 68
KAMA SUTRA (2000 series) 8-15 70-76
KAMA SUTRA (8050 thru 8054) 15-25 65-66
KAMA SUTRA (8056 "Best of the Lovin' Spoonful") 15-25 67
(Add $10 to $20 if accompanied by four color photos.)
KAMA SUTRA (8058 thru 8073) 15-25 67-69
KAMA SUTRA (91102 "Best of the Lovin' Spoonful") 8-10
Members: John Sebastian; Zalman Yanovsky; Joe Butler; Steve Boone; Jerry Yester.
Also see SEBASTIAN, John
Also see YANOVSKY, Zalman
Also see YESTER, Jerry

LOW EBB
Singles: 7-inch
PATTEN BENNETT (1001 "Can't Make Up My Mind") 15-20

LOW ROCKS
Singles: 7-inch
SABRE (101 "Blueberry Jams") 10-20 61
S.A.K. (1048 "Snooker") 10-20 63

LOWE, Bernie — P&R '58
(Bernie Lowe Orchestra)
Singles: 7-inch
CAMEO (153 thru 289) 5-10 58-63
LPs: 10/12-inch
CAMEO 15-25 62-63
Also see GRACIE, Charlie

LOWE, Buddy
Singles: 7-inch
CREST (1049 "Kiss Me Goodnight") 15-25 58
ENSIGN (4037 "Sherry Lee") 10-20 59
IMPERIAL (5680 "A Teenager Feels It Too") 5-10 60

LOWE, Jim — P&R '53
Singles: 78 rpm
DOT 5-15 55-57
MERCURY 5-10 53-54
Singles: 7-inch
BUDDAH (44 "Michael J. Pollard for President") 4-8 68
DECCA (31153 "Someone Else's Arms") ..8-12 60
DECCA (31198 "That Do Make It Nice") ...8-12 61
DOT (132 "The Green Door") 5-10 63
DOT (15381 thru 15611, except 15486) ..10-15 55-57

DOT (15486 "The Green Door")............ 15-20 56
DOT (15693 thru 16074) 8-12 58-60
DOT (16636 "Have You Ever Been Lonely")..5-10 64
MERCURY (70168 "Gamblers and the Guitar").. 10-20 53
MERCURY (70208 "Go and Leave Me"). 10-20 53
MERCURY (70265 "Santa Claus Rides a Strawberry Roan")................................. 10-20 53
MERCURY (70319 "Riverboat")............... 10-20 54
20TH FOX (426 "Hootenanny Granny") 5-10 63
U.A. 4-8 65-67

EPs: 7-inch

DOT (1061 "Rainbow")......................... 10-20 57
MERCURY (3222 "Jim Lowe")................ 10-20 57

LPs: 10/12-inch

DOT (3051 "The Green Door")............... 25-35 57
DOT (3114 "Wicked Women").................. 25-35 58
DOT (3681 "The Green Door")............... 10-20 66
(Monaural.)
DOT (25681 "The Green Door")............. 10-20 66
(Stereo.)
KATS KARAVAN (100 "Old Favorites"). 50-100 '50s
MERCURY (20246 "Door of Fame")........ 25-35 57

LOWE, Max

Singles: 7-inch

WATERFALL ("Ain't Got a Nickel")......... 50-75
(Selection number not known.)

LOWE, Mundell

Singles: 7-inch

CHARLIE PARKER (203 "Lost & Lonely")..5-10 62

LPs: 10/12-inch

CHARLIE PARKER (406 "Satan in High Heels") 15-20 62
(Monaural. Gatefold cover.)
CHARLIE PARKER (406S "Satan in High Heels")... 25-30 62
(Stereo. Gatefold cover.)
CHARLIE PARKER (406 "Satan in High Heels")... 10-15 62
(Monaural. Standard cover.)
CHARLIE PARKER (406S "Satan in High Heels").. 15-20 62
(Stereo. Standard cover.)

LOWE, Sammy
(Sammy Lowe & Orchestra)

Singles: 7-inch

CANDLELIGHT (1014 "Easy My Love").. 40-50 57
NEWPORT (7001 "Speak Up")................ 10-20 58
NEWPORT (7003 "Moon Glide")............ 10-20 58

LPs: 10/12-inch

RCA (2770 "Hitsville USA")................... 15-25 63
Also see FIDELITYS
Also see IMPRESSORS
Also see MARQUIS
Also see PEARLS
Also see SPARKS, Milton
Also see TOKENS
Also see VALETS
Also see VELOURS
Also see WANDERERS

LOWE, Virginia

Singles: 78 rpm

MELBA (107 "I'm in Love with Elvis Presley").. 25-35 56

Singles: 7-inch

JOSIE (818 "I Believe in You")................ 15-20 57
MELBA (107 "I'm in Love with Elvis Presley")... 50-75 56

LOWELL, Bobby, & Rock-A-Boogie Boys

Singles: 7-inch

ROTO (5972 "Um Baby, Baby")......... 100-200 58

LOWELL, Jackie

Singles: 7-inch

BAND BOX (226 "Rocket Trip") 40-60 61

LOWERY, Frankie
(With the Golden Rocks)

Singles: 7-inch

COLUMBIA (41168 "Little Girl") 8-12 58
DART (142 "She's Fine")....................... 10-15 61
KHOURY'S (716 "Kansas City Train")..... 20-30 60

LOWERY, Sonny

Singles: 78 rpm

SPECIALTY.. 10-20 57-58

Singles: 7-inch

SPECIALTY (621 "Thank You for Your Kisses")...10-20 57
SPECIALTY (648 "Goodbye, Baby, Goodbye")...10-20 58

LOYAL OPPOSITION

Singles: 7-inch

TARGET (1002 "Telling Lies") 25-35 69
Members: Carl Weinberger; Rick Gustafson; Greg Rakun; Mike Eubank; Steve Hofschield.

LOYD, James, & Whirlwinds

Singles: 7-inch

EMPALA (117 "I Can't Stand Another Broken Heart")..20-30 63

LOYD, Jay B.

Singles: 7-inch

ABC-PAR (9922 "You're Just My Kind").75-125 58
HI (2017 "I'm So Lonely") 50-75 59
U.A. (314 "No Other Baby")......................5-10 61
Also see BLACK, Bill

LOYE, Bobby, Jr.
(Robert Loye Jr.)

Singles: 7-inch

EMBER (1111 "I Just Stand There")...........8-12 64
LAURIE (3222 "I'm Startin' Tonight") 40-50 64
WILSHIRE (202 "Lovin' Tree")..................15-25 '60s

LUBRANO, Bill
(With Malcolm Dodds Orchestra)

Singles: 7-inch

ASCOT (2123 "I'm Way Ahead of You Baby") 8-12 63
DIAMOND (117 "She Didn't Invite Me")....10-20 62
Also see DODDS, Malcolm

LUCAS, Al

Singles: 78 rpm

JUBILEE..5-10 51-52
RCA..5-10 53

Singles: 7-inch

CHALLENGE (59042 "She's My Baby")...10-15 59
CHALLENGE (59050 "Sweet Tooth for Baby Ruth")..10-15 59
JUBILEE...10-20 51-52
RCA...10-15 53
Also see PRICE, Sam

LUCAS, Buddy *R&B '52*
(Big Buddy Lucas; Buddy Lucas Orchestra; with All Stars; with His Band of Tomorrow; with Wigglers; with Studio "B" Orchestra; Buddy Lucas Show)

Singles: 78 rpm

BELL..10-15 57
GROOVE..10-15 54
JUBILEE..10-15 51-53
RCA..10-15 53
SAVOY..5-10 56

Singles: 7-inch

BELL..8-12 57
CAPRICE (120 "I Can't Go") 5-10 63
CARLTON (506 "Crazy Baby") 10-15 59
GONE (5025 "Boppin' Hop") 10-15 58
GROOVE (0003 thru 0030)........................15-25 54
JUBILEE (5058 thru 5111) 15-25 51-53
LAWN (227 "Bump Te Bump")....................5-10 64
LUNIVERSE (104 "Bo-Lee").......................15-25 57
PIONEER (71850 "Get Away Fly") 50-75 61
PIONEER (1760 "Packin' My Grip")............5-10 62
RCA..15-25 53
SAVOY (1180 "Oh Mary Ann")...................10-20 56
TRU SOUND (416 "Hocus Pocus") 5-10 62
TRU SOUND (420 "April Showers") 5-10 63
VIM (502 "Deacon John")..........................10-15 59
VIM (505 "Night Train")..............................10-15 60

LPs: 10/12-inch

CAMDEN (2146 "Honkin' Sax") 10-15 67
U.A. (3482 "Fifty Fabulous Harmonica Favorites")..10-20 66
(Monaural.)
U.A. (6482 "Fifty Fabulous Harmonica Favorites") 10-20 66
(Stereo.)
Also see BUDDY & EDNA
Also see GAY KNIGHTS
Also see GONE ALL STARS
Also see GOOD BUDDY
Also see KNICKERBOCKERS
Also see MALVIN, Artie / Buddy Lucas
Also see McGRIFF, Edna

LUCAS, Ernie

Singles: 7-inch

OKEH (7315 "Love Thief") 10-20 68
OKEH (7321 "What We Pay for Love").... 10-20 68

LUCAS, Jim
(Jimmy Lucas)

Singles: 78 rpm

REPUBLIC (7123 "Tutti Frutti")..................5-10 56

Singles: 7-inch

BIG (1018 "Words Are Not Enough for Me")...5-10 59
NRC (458 "You Can't Have Seconds").....50-75
REPUBLIC (7123 "Tutti Frutti")...............10-15 56

LUCAS, Matt *P&R '63*

Singles: 7-inch

CJC (504 "Put Me Down")..........................5-10 77
DOT (16564 "Maybellene") 10-20 63
DOT (16614 "Turn On Your Love Light") .10-20 64
GOOD (003 "Tradin' Kisses")....................50-75 62
KANATA (1008 "The Old Man")...................5-10 72
KAREN (321 "The M.C. Twine")...............15-25 65
KAREN (2524 "Baby You Better Go-Go") 200-300 65
QUALITY (2129 "You Gotta Love") 5-10 75
(Canadian.)
QUALITY (2159 "I Need Your Lovin' ").......5-10 75
(Canadian.)
RENAY (304 "I'm Movin On")..................75-125 63
(First issue.)
SMASH (1813 "I'm Movin' On") 10-15 63
SMASH (1840 "Ooby Dooby") 10-15 63
UNDERGROUND (3001 "I'm Movin' On")....4-8 81
UNDERGROUND (3002 "Peepin' Tom Blues")...4-8 82

LPs: 10/12-inch

BLUEJAM (1001 "White Blues Wonder") .10-20 79
BLUEJAM (1002 "A Legend in His Time – Back with the Blues")..10-20 83

LUCE, Bob

Singles: 7-inch

LOVE LOCK (111 "Hot Shot Baby") 50-75 60

LUCE, Milson

Singles: 78 rpm

ARGO (5260 "I Got You")..........................5-10 56

Singles: 7-inch

ARGO (5260 "I Got You")..........................10-15 56

LUCIANO, Danny

Singles: 7-inch

LU-MAR (121467 "Get in to It")................10-20 67

LUCIE, Don

Singles: 7-inch

EMPALA (119 "Just a Walkin' ")...............10-20 '60s

LUCIFER
(Mort Garson)

LPs: 10/12-inch

GALLO ("Lucifer")...................................200-300 70
(Selection number not known.)

LUCIFER & PEPPERMINTS

Singles: 7-inch

RHM (1001 "The Green Itch Got the Bear")...15-25 60

LUCKY CHARMS

Singles: 7-inch

RUBBERTOWN (100 "I Want a Love of My Own")..40-60

LUDAWAY, Rudy
(Ludaway)

Singles: 7-inch

DUEL (530 "Hello Lady")..........................5-10 64
GALIKO (102 "What's Wrong Baby").........15-25 69
U.A. (50590 "What's Wrong Baby").........10-15 69

LUDWIG & CLASSICS

Singles: 7-inch

IMPERIAL (66163 "I Forgot")...................15-25 66

LUGEE & LIONS

Singles: 7-inch

ROBBEE (112 "The Jury") 50-75 61
Members: Lou Christie; Kay Chick; Amy Sacco; Bill Faveck.
Also see CHRISTIE, Lou
Also see CLASSICS

LUKAS LOLLIPOP

Singles: 7-inch

LOMA (2067 "Don't Hold on to Someone") 20-30 67

LUKE, Billy

Singles: 7-inch

RODEO (126 "Long Time No See") 25-35

LUKE, Jimmy

Singles: 7-inch

BIG C (1002 "Joanie")..............................20-30
RAZORBACK (104 "Ruby Baby")..............5-10 58
UNI (55036 "Billie Sue")............................5-10 67

LUKE, Jimmy, & Bruce Channel

Singles: 7-inch

LE CAM...4-6 78
Also see CHANNEL, Bruce
Also see LUKE, Jimmy

LUKE, Robin *P&R/R&B '58*

Singles: 7-inch

BERTRAM INT'L (206 "Susie Darlin'")...50-100 58
BERTRAM INT'L (208 "My Girl")..............20-30 58
BERTRAM INT'L (210 "Strollin' Blues")....20-30 58
BERTRAM INT'L (212 "Five Minutes More")...20-30 58
DOT (15899 thru 16229)..........................10-15 59-61

Picture Sleeves

BERTRAM INT'L (206 "Susie Darlin' ").150-200 58
DOT (16096 "Well Oh, Well Oh ")...........50-100 60

EPs: 7-inch

DOT (1092 "Susie Darlin' ")....................75-125 60

LPs: 10/12-inch

STARFIRE (1002 "Boppin' with Robin Luke") 10-15 81

LUKE, Robin, & Roberta Shore

Singles: 7-inch

DOT (16366 "Foggin Up the Windows")......5-10 62
Also see LUKE, Robin

LUKE & APOSTLES

Singles: 7-inch

BOUNTY (105 "Been Burnt")...................15-25 67
(First issue.)
ELEKTRA (45605 "Been Burnt") 8-12 67
TRUE NORTH (101 "You Make Me High")..15-25 '60s
Members: Walter Rossi; Jack Geisinger.
Also see INFLUENCE

LUKE & DISCIPLES

Singles: 7-inch

FANNIN (1003 "Three") 10-20 64

LULLABYES

Singles: 7-inch

DIMENSION (1039 "You Touch Me")...... 10-20 64

LULU *P&R '64*
(With the Luvers; with Dixie Flyers)

Singles: 7-inch

ALFA 3-6 79-82
ATCO 4-8 69-72
CHELSEA..4-6 73-76
EPIC...5-10 67-68
PARROT (Except 9678 & 40021)..............5-10 64-65
PARROT (9678 "Shout")...........................15-20 64
PARROT (40021 "Shout")..........................10-15 67
ROCKET..4-6 78

Picture Sleeves

ALFA (7006 "I Could Never Miss You More")..4-6 81
(Pictures Lulu without headband.)
ALFA (7006 "I Could Never Miss You More")...3-5 81
(Pictures Lulu wearing headband.)
ALFA (7011 "If I Were You").......................3-5 81
EPIC (10260 "Best of Both Worlds") 5-10 67
EPIC (10302 "Me, the Peaceful Heart") 5-10 68

EPs: 7-inch

EPIC (26339 "To Sir with Love")...............5-10 67
(Juke box issue only. Includes title strips.)

LPs: 10/12-inch

ALFA 5-10 81
ATCO 10-12 70-72
CAPRICORN 8-10 74
CHELSEA..10-12 73-77
EPIC..10-15 67-70
HARMONY...10-12 70

PARROT (61016 "From Lulu with Love") 50-100 67
(Monaural.)
PARROT (71016 "From Lulu with Love") 50-100 67
(Stereo.)
PICKWICK 8-10 73
ROCKET 5-8 78
Also see CLARK, Dave, Five / Lulu
Also see MOORE, Jackie

LUMAN, Bob C&W/P&R/R&B '60

Singles: 78 rpm

IMPERIAL 20-50 57

Singles: 7-inch

CAPITOL (4059 "Svengali") 15-25 58
EPIC 4-8 68-77
HICKORY (1200 series) 5-10 63-64
HICKORY (1300 thru 1500 series) 4-8 65-70
IMPERIAL (5705 "Red Cadillac and a Black Mustache") 10-20 60
(Black label. Reissue of 8311.)
IMPERIAL (8311 "Red Cadillac and a Black Mustache") 50-75 57
(Maroon label.)
IMPERIAL (8313 "Red Hot") 40-60 57
(Maroon label.)
IMPERIAL (8313 "Red Hot") 30-40 59
(Black label.)
IMPERIAL (8315 "Make Up Your Mind Baby") 20-30 57
(Maroon label.)
IMPERIAL (8315 "Make Up Your Mind Baby") 10-15 59
(Black label.)
POLYDOR 4-6 77-78
W.B. (5081 thru 5233) 15-25 59-61
W.B. (5255 thru 5299) 10-20 62

Picture Sleeves

W.B. (5105 "Dreamy Doll") 40-60 59
W.B. (5172 "Let's Think About Livin' ") 25-35 60
W.B. (5184 "Oh Lonesome Me") 25-35 60
W.B. (5204 "The Great Snow Man") 25-35 61
W.B. (5233 "Private Eye") 25-35 61

EPs: 7-inch

HICKORY (124-006 "Selections from Livin' Lovin' Sounds") 25-35 65
("Six-Pac." Promotional issue only.)
ROLLIN' ROCK (34 "Bob Luman") .... 5-8 '80s
W.B. (1396 "Let's Think About Livin' ") 50-75 60
W.B. (5506 "Bob Luman") 40-50 61
(Promotional issue only.)

LPs: 10/12-inch

EPIC 8-15 68-77
HARMONY 10-15 72
HICKORY (124 "Livin' Lovin' Sounds") 15-25 65
HICKORY (4000 series) 8-12 74
POLYDOR 8-12 78
W.B. (W-1396 "Let's Think About Livin' ") 30-40 60
(Monaural.)
W.B. (WS-1396 "Let's Think About Livin' ") 40-60 60
(Stereo.)
Also see THOMPSON, Sue, & Bob Luman

LUMLEY, Rufus

Singles: 7-inch

AFFORD (10441 "Minneapolis, Minn.") .... 5-10 '60s
HOLTON .... 8-12 '60s
RCA (9230 "Michelle") 5-10 67
RCA (9396 "Annabella") 10-20 67

Picture Sleeves

RCA 5-10 67

LPs: 10/12-inch

RCA (3898 "Rufus Lumley") 40-50 67

LUMPKIN, Billy

Singles: 78 rpm

HERALD (405 "Mary Lou") 15-20 53

Singles: 7-inch

HERALD (405 "Mary Lou") 20-30 53

LUMPKIN, Bobby

Singles: 7-inch

FELCO (102 "One Way Ticket") 400-600 57
Also see CROWN, Bobby, & Capers

LUMPKIN, Henry
(With the Love Tones)

Singles: 7-inch

BUDDAH (55 "Honey Hush") 5-10 68
MOTOWN (1005 "We Really Love Each Other") 40-50 61
MOTOWN (1013 "Don't Leave Me") 20-30 61
MOTOWN (1029 "Mo Jo Hanna") 20-30 62
PAGEANT (605 "Make a Change") 30-40 63

LUNA

LPs: 10/12-inch

ARHOOLIE (8001 "Space Swell") 10-15 67

LUND, Garrett

LPs: 10/12-inch

("Almost Grown") 150-250 75
(No label or number used.)

LUNDBERG, Victor P&R '67

Singles: 7-inch

LIBERTY (55996 "An Open Letter to My Teenage Son") 4-8 67

LPs: 10/12-inch

LIBERTY 10-15 68

LUNELL, Mary

Singles: 78 rpm

VITA (140 "I Can't Win for Losing") 8-12 56

Singles: 7-inch

VITA (140 "I Can't Win for Losing") 15-25 56

LUNSFORD, Mona

Singles: 7-inch

VAN-DECK (117 "You're No Warden") 75-100

LUREX, Larry

Singles: 7-inch

ANTHEM (104 "I Can Hear Music") 40-60 73
Also see MERCURY, Freddie

LUTCHER, Joe R&B '48
(With His Society Cats)

Singles: 78 rpm

CAPITOL 10-15 48
MODERN 10-15 49
SPECIALTY 10-15 48-51

Singles: 7-inch

SPECIALTY (303 "Rockin' Boogie") 50-75 51

LUTCHER, Nellie P&R/R&B '47
(With Her "Rhythm"; with Sy Oliver Orchestra)

Singles: 78 rpm

CAPITOL 5-10 47-50
DECCA 5-10 55
LIBERTY 5-10 56

Singles: 7-inch

CAPITOL 10-20 50-59
DECCA (29464 "Please Come Back") 10-20 55
LIBERTY (55018 "Blue Skies") 10-20 56
LIBERTY (55027 "All of a Sudden") 10-20 56

EPs: 7-inch

CAPITOL (232 "Real Gone") 20-40 50
LIBERTY (3014-1/2/3 "Our New Nellie") 10-20 56
(Price is for any of three volumes.)

LPs: 10/12-inch

CAPITOL (H-232 "Real Gone!") 35-55 50
(10-inch LP.)
CAPITOL (T-232 "Real Gone!") 20-30 55
EPIC (1108 "Whee! Nellie") 25-35 55
(10-inch LP.)
LIBERTY (3014 "Our New Nellie") 20-40 56
Also see OLIVER, Sy, & Orchestra

LUTCHER, Nellie, & Nat "King" Cole R&B '50

Singles: 78 rpm

CAPITOL (847 "For You My Love") 5-10 50

Singles: 7-inch

CAPITOL (847 "For You My Love") 10-20 50
Also see COLE, Nat "King"
Also see LUTCHER, Nellie

LUTHER & LITTLE EVA

Singles: 7-inch

KING (5010 "Love Is Strange") 15-25 57

LUV BANDITS

Singles: 7-inch

PARROT (316 "Blues No. 2") 10-15 67

LUV'D ONES

Singles: 7-inch

DUNWICH (121 "I'm Leaving You") 10-20 66
DUNWICH (130 "Come Back") 10-20 66
DUNWICH (136 "Dance Kid Dance") 10-20 66
WHITE OAK (759101 "Up and Down Sue") .... 20-30 '60s

LUVS

Singles: 7-inch

STALLION (1002 "We Kiss in the Shadow") 100-150 63

LUZER, Tony

Singles: 7-inch

LAURIE (3019 "Darling Goodbye") 40-50 58

LY-DELLS P&R '61
(Lydells; with Frank Slay Orchestra; with Paul Swain Orchestra)

Singles: 7-inch

CLIFTON (67 "Book of Songs") 3-5 81
KING TUT (177 "Sherry") 5-10 78
LOST NITE 10-15 64
MASTER (111 "Genie of the Lamp") 100-200 61
MASTER (251 "Wizard of Love") 50-150 61
(Label name in block print.)
MASTER (251 "Wizard of Love") 10-15 61
("Distr. by Roulette Records Inc." on label.)
PAM (103 "There Goes the Boy") 100-150 59
PARKWAY (897 "There Goes the Boy") 10-20 64
ROULETTE (4493 "Karen") 20-30 63
SCA (18001 "Book of Songs") 15-25 62
SOUTHERN SOUND (122 "Hide and Seek") 15-25 65

LPs: 10/12-inch

CLIFTON (2002 "Greatest Hits") 8-10 81
Also see LEN-DELLS
Also see SLAY, Frank, & His Orchestra

LYKES OF US

Singles: 7-inch

MOLT (6801 "7:30 Said") 15-25 68

LYLE, Rudy

Singles: 7-inch

ECHO (101 "Missing and Kissing") 50-75

LYMAN, Arthur LP '58
(Arthur Lyman Group; with Kapiolani)

Singles: 7-inch

GNP (315 "Pearly Shells") 5-10 64
GNP (497 "Puka Shells") 4-6 75
HI-FI (533 thru 5083) 5-10 59-63
HI-FI (5065 thru 5105) 4-8 64-69
ORBIT 8-12 58

LPs: 10/12-inch

GNP (605 "Exotic Sounds") 8-15 63
GNP (606 "Paradise") 8-15 64
GNP (2091 "Puka Shells") 5-10 75
HI-FI (806 "Taboo") 15-25 58
HI-FI (813 thru 1018) 10-20 59-63
HI-FI (1023 thru 1040) 8-15 64-69
OLYMPIC 5-8 79

LYMAN, Joni

Singles: 7-inch

REPRISE (378 "Happy Birthday Blue") 20-30 65

LYMAN, Tiny, & Jukes

Singles: 7-inch

RUNNIN' WILD (1940 "Left Overs") 250-350

LYMON, Frankie P&R/R&B '56
(With the Teenagers; with Jimmy Wright & His Orchestra; with Hugo Peretti & His Orchestra)

Singles: 78 rpm

GEE (1002 "Why Do Fools Fall in Love") 30-60 55
(Red label, gold print.)
GEE (1002 "Why Do Fools Fall in Love") 15-25 55
(Red label, black print.)
GEE (1012 thru 1039) 20-30 56-57
ROULETTE 15-25 57

Singles: 7-inch

ABC 4-6 73
BIG KAT (7008 "I Want You to Be My Girl") 5-10 68
COLUMBIA (43094 "Somewhere") 8-12 64
GEE (1002 "Why Do Fools Fall in Love") 400-500 55
(Colored vinyl.)
GEE (1002 "Why Do Fools Fall in Love") 50-100 55
(Red label, gold print.)
GEE (1002 "Why Do Fools Fall in Love") 20-30 55
(Red label, black print. Credits three writers.)
GEE (1002 "Why Do Fools Fall in Love") 10-15 55
(Red label, black print. Credits two writers.)
GEE (1002 "Why Do Fools Fall in Love") 10-20 58
(White label, black print. Not a promo.)
GEE (1012 "I Want You to Be My Girl") 40-50 56
GEE (1018 "I Promise to Remember") 30-40 56
GEE (1022 "The ABCs of Love") 30-40 56
GEE (1026 "I'm Not a Juvenile Delinquent") 30-40 57
GEE (1032 "Paper Castles") 25-35 57
GEE (1035 "Love Is a Clown") 25-35 57
GEE (1036 "Out in the Cold Again") 25-35 57
GEE (1039 "Goody Goody") 30-40 57
(Credits "Frankie Lymon & the Teenagers.")
GEE (1039 "Goody Goody") 20-25 59
(No mention of the Teenagers.)
GEE (1052 "Goody Good Girl") 25-30 59
MURRAY HILL .... 3-5 '80s
RAMA (34 "I Want You to Be My Girl") 5-10 64
(Golden Goodies Series.)
ROBIN HOOD (155 "Fortunate Fellow") 4-6 77
ROULETTE (4026 "So Goes My Love") 15-25 57
ROULETTE (4035 "Little Girl") 15-25 57
ROULETTE (4044 "Footsteps") 15-25 58
ROULETTE (4068 "Portable on My Shoulder") 15-25 58
ROULETTE (4093 "Melinda") 15-25 58
ROULETTE (4128 "No Matter What You've Done") 15-25 59
ROULETTE (4150 "Before I Fall Asleep") 15-25 59
ROULETTE (4257 "Little Bitty Pretty One") 10-20 60
ROULETTE (4283 "Buzz Buzz Buzz") 10-20 60
ROULETTE (4310 "Silhouettes") 10-20 60
ROULETTE (4348 "So Young") 10-20 61
ROULETTE (4391 "I Put the Bomp") 10-20 61
TCF (11 "To Each His Own") 8-12 64

Picture Sleeves

BIG KAT (7008 "I Want You to Be My Girl") 8-12 68

EPs: 7-inch

GEE (601 "The Teenagers Go Rockin' ") 100-150 56
GEE (602 "The Teenagers Go Romantic") 100-150 56
ROULETTE (304 "Frankie Lymon at the London Palladium") 50-100 58

LPs: 10/12-inch

ACCORD 5-10 82
GEE (701 "The Teenagers Featuring Frankie Lymon") 200-300 57
(Red or white label.)
GEE (701 "The Teenagers Featuring Frankie Lymon") 75-125 61
(Gray label.)
GUEST STAR 5-10
MURRAY HILL (148 "Frankie Lymon and the Teenagers") .... 50-75 '80s
(Boxed, five-disc set, with booklet and bonus single.)
ROULETTE (25013 "Frankie Lymon at the London Palladium") 100-150 58
ROULETTE (25036 "Rock & Roll") 50-100 58
ROULETTE (25250 "Frankie Lymon's Greatest") 25-50 64
Members: Frankie Lymon; Herman Santiago; Sherman Garnes; Jim Merchant; Joe Negroni.
Also see WRIGHT, Jimmy
Also see TEENAGERS

LYMON, Lewis, & Teenchords
(With the Teenchords)

Singles: 78 rpm

END 25-35 57
FURY 25-50 57

Singles: 7-inch

BIM BAM BOOM (114 "Them There Eyes") 4-6 73
END (1003 "Too Young") 50-75 57
END (1007 "I Found Out Why") 50-75 58
END (1113 "Too Young") 10-15 62
FURY (1000 "I'm So Happy") 75-125 57
(Maroon label.)
FURY (1000 "I'm So Happy") .... 20-30 '60s
(Yellow label.)
FURY (1003 "Please Tell the Angels") 100-150 57
(Maroon label. Thick and thin lines.)
FURY (1003 "Please Tell the Angels") .... 15-25 '60s
(Maroon label. Only thin lines.)
FURY (1003 "Please Tell the Angels") 10-15 62
(Yellow label.)
FURY (1006 "Falling in Love") 100-150 57
(Maroon label. Thick and thin lines.)
FURY (1006 "Falling in Love") 75-100 57
(Maroon label. Only thin lines.)
FURY (1006 "Falling in Love") 10-15 62
(Yellow label.)

JUANITA (101 "Them There Eyes")....... 75-100 58
(Black vinyl.)
JUANITA (101 "Them There Eyes")......... 40-50 '60s
(Red vinyl.)
PARK AVENUE (09 "I Found Out Why")......4-6 '90s
(Yellow vinyl. 1000 made.)

LPs: 10/12-inch

COLLECTABLES..5-10 88
LOST NITE (13 "Lewis Lymon and the Teenchords").. 10-20 81
(10-inch LP. Red vinyl. 1000 made.)
Members: Lewis Lymon; Ralph Vaughan; David Lyttle; Ross Rocco; Lyndon Harold; Jimmy Castor; John Pruitt; Ed Pellegrino.
Also see CASTOR, Jimmy
Also see TOWNSMEN / Louie Lymon

LYN, Ronnie
(Ronnie Lynn Quartet)

Singles: 7-inch

SPANGLE (2006 "Burning Eyes")........... 10-15 58
V.A.C...5-10

LYN & INVADERS

Singles: 7-inch

FENTON (2040 "Secretly")...................... 25-35 66
Also see INCREDIBLE INVADERS

LYND, Johnny, & Madisons

Singles: 7-inch

ARC (4455 "Little Angel Blue")................ 15-25 60

LYNDON, Frank

Singles: 7-inch

BANG (531 "Earth Angel")..........................5-10 66
JAB (1004 "Cry Cry Cry")......................... 30-40 '60s
LAURIE (3322 "Santa's Jet").......................8-12 65
SABINA (520 "Earth Angel")..................... 15-25 64
STRAWBERRY..3-5 '80s
UPTOWN (758 "Lisa")............................. 10-20 69
Session: Guy Valari.
Also see BELMONTS
Also see REGENTS

LYNN, Barbara *P&R/R&B '62*

Singles: 7-inch

ATLANTIC...4-8 67-72
COLLECTABLES...3-5 '80s
COPYRIGHT..4-8
ERIC (7004 "Dina & Patrina").................. 15-25 62
JAMIE...8-12 62-65
JET STREAM (804 "I'll Suffer")...................5-10 67
TRIBE (8316 "I'm a Good Woman")......... 15-25 66
TRIBE (8319 "Until I'm Free")....................8-10 66
TRIBE (8322 "Watch the One")...................8-10 67
TRIBE (8324 "I Don't Want a Playboy")......8-10 67
(Though a higher number, this disc came out about three months before 8322.)

LPs: 10/12-inch

ATLANTIC.. 10-20 68
FONTANA... 10-20
JAMIE.. 20-30 62-64

LYNN, Barbara, & Lee Maye

Singles: 7-inch

JAMIE (1295 "Just Lay It On the Line")......5-10 65
Also see LYNN, Barbara
Also see MAYE, Arthur Lee

LYNN, Billy

Singles: 7-inch

AMY (820 "Little Pony Tail").................... 40-50 61
CR (1001 "Barbara")................................ 50-75 61
Session: Rick & Masters.
Also see RICK & MASTERS

LYNN, Blow Top, & His House Rockers
(With Melvin Smith)

Singles: 78 rpm

RCA... 15-25 51

Singles: 7-inch

RCA (0110 "School Boy Blues")............... 20-30 51
RCA (0124 "Up on the Hill")..................... 20-30 51
RCA (0139 "Rampaging Mama")............... 20-30 51
RCA (4328 "Come Back My Darlin' ")...... 20-30 51

LYNN, Bobbi

Singles: 7-inch

CR (1002 "Charleston")........................... 20-30 61

LYNN, Bobbi

Singles: 7-inch

ELF (90009 "Earthquake")........................ 10-20 67

LYNN, Cherri

Singles: 78 rpm

APOLLO..10-15 54

Singles: 7-inch

APOLLO (456 "If It Hadn't Been for You")..15-25 54
APOLLO (463 "Baby I'm Gone")..............15-25 54

LYNN, Debra
(Debbie Lynn)

Singles: 7-inch

FLIGHT (10001 "Fujiyama Mama")...........20-30 62
SAM (116 "Half Finished Wedding Gown")..5-10 62

LYNN, Donna *P&R '64*
(With Jack Wolf, "Bugs" Bower & Orchestra)

Singles: 7-inch

CAPITOL (5087 thru 5456, except 5127)...5-10 63-65
CAPITOL (5127 "My Boyfriend Got a Beatle Haircut")...15-20 64
EPIC (9580 "Donna Loves Jerry")..............8-12 63
PALMER (5016 "Don't You Dare")............15-25 67

LPs: 10/12-inch

CAPITOL (2085 "Java Jones"/"My Boyfriend Got a Beatle Haircut")...20-30 64

LYNN, Jeannie, & Friends

Singles: 7-inch

REX (1001 "You Can Dance")..................15-25 59
REX (1009 "Dream Dream").....................10-15 60

LYNN, Jerry

Singles: 7-inch

D (1041 "Bugger Burns")..........................50-60 59
KRC (102 "Don't Want Your Money Honey")..50-60 59

LYNN, Kari

Singles: 7-inch

AUBURN (600 "I'm Sincere").......................8-12 61
AUBURN (601 "Summer Day")....................8-12 61
AUBURN (602 "Lonesome and Sorry").......8-12 61
AUBURN (3800 "Lonesome and Sorry")....8-12 62
AUBURN (3801 "Joey, I'll Be Around").......8-12 62
AUBURN (3802 "Tell Him I'm Blue")..........8-12 62

LYNN, Kathy
(With the Playboys)

Singles: 7-inch

SWAN (4175 "Rock City")..........................30-50 64
SWAN (4193 "I Got a Guy").......................30-50 64
SWAN (4209 "Little Baby").........................30-50 65
Also see ROCKIN' REBELS

LYNN, Laura

Singles: 7-inch

DE'BESTH (1112 "Let the Past")..............50-75 58
Also see FIVE CROWNS

LYNN, Lorelei, & Sparkles

Singles: 7-inch

AWARD (128 "Rock-a-Bop")......................10-20 59

LYNN, Loretta *C&W '60*
(With the Coal Miners)

Singles: 7-inch

DECCA (31384 thru 31966).......................5-15 62-66
DECCA (32045 thru 32851).........................4-8 66-71
DECCA (32900 "Here in Topeka")...........10-15 71
DECCA (32900 "One's on the Way")...........4-8 71
(Reissue, with different title.)
DECCA (32974 thru 33039)..........................4-8 72
MCA..3-6 73-86
ZERO (107 "I'm a Honky Tonk Girl")....400-500 60
ZERO (110 "New Rainbow")................300-400 60
ZERO (112 "The Darkest Day")...........300-400 61

Picture Sleeves

DECCA (32043 "It Won't Seem Like Christmas")...10-20 66
DECCA (32749 "Coal Miner's Daughter")..5-10 70
MCA (40954 "We've Come a Long Way Baby")..4-6 78
MCA (52621 "Heart Don't Do This to Me")...4-6 85
MCA (52706 "Wouldn't It Be Great")............4-6 85

EPs: 7-inch

DECCA..10-20 64-65

LPs: 10/12-inch

CORAL (20056 "Here's Loretta Lynn").........5-8 73
CORAL (20064 "Alone with You")................5-8 73
COUNTRY MUSIC MAGAZINE (1043 "Best of Loretta Lynn")..15-20 76
(Two discs. Mail-order LP sold by *Country Music* magazine.)

DECCA (DL-4457 "Loretta Lynn Sings")..40-60 63
(Monaural.)
DECCA (DL7-4457 "Loretta Lynn Sings")...45-65 63
(Stereo.)
DECCA (DL-4541 "Before I'm Over You")..30-40 65
(Monaural.)
DECCA (DL7-4541 "Before I'm Over You")..35-45 65
(Stereo.)
DECCA (DL-4620 "Songs from My Heart")...30-40 65
(Monaural.)
DECCA (DL7-4620 "Songs from My Heart")...35-45 65
(Stereo.)
DECCA (DL-4665 "Blue Kentucky Girl")...15-25 65
(Monaural.)
DECCA (DL7-4665 "Blue Kentucky Girl") 20-30 65
(Stereo.)
DECCA (DL-4655 "Hymns")......................15-25 65
(Monaural.)
DECCA (DL7-4655 "Hymns")....................20-30 65
(Stereo.)
DECCA (DL-4744 "I Like 'Em Country")...15-25 66
(Monaural.)
DECCA (DL-4744 "I Like 'Em Country")...15-25 66
(Monaural.)
DECCA (DL7-4744 "I Like 'Em Country").15-25 66
(Stereo.)
DECCA (DL7-4783 "You Ain't Woman Enough")..15-25 66
(Monaural.)
DECCA (DL7-4783 "You Ain't Woman Enough")..15-25 66
(Stereo.)
DECCA (DL7-4817 "A Country Christmas")..15-25 66
(Monaural.)
DECCA (DL7-4817 "A Country Christmas")..15-25 66
(Stereo.)
DECCA (DL-4842 "Don't Come Home a Drinkin' ")..15-25 67
(Monaural.)
DECCA (DL7-4842 "Don't Come Home a Drinkin' ")..15-25 67
(Stereo.)
DECCA (DL-4928 "Who Says God Is Dead")...15-25 67
(Monaural.)
DECCA (DL7-4928 "Who Says God Is Dead")...15-25 67
(Stereo.)
DECCA (DL-4930 "Singin' with Feeling").15-25 67
(Monaural.)
DECCA (DL7-4930 "Singin' with Feeling")..15-25 67
(Stereo.)
DECCA (DL-4997 "Fist City")...................15-25 68
(Monaural.)
DECCA (DL7-4997 "Fist City")................10-20 68
(Stereo.)
DECCA (75000 "Greatest Hits")..............12-25 68
DECCA (75113 "Woman of the World/To Make a Man")...25-35 69
DECCA (75198 "Loretta Lynn Writes 'Em and Sings 'Em")...12-25 70
DECCA (75163 "Wings Upon Your Horns")...12-25 70
DECCA (75253 "Coal Miner's Daughter")...10-20 71
DECCA (75282 "I Want to Be Free").......12-25 71
DECCA (75310 "You're Looking at Country")..12-25 71
DECCA (75334 "One's on the Way")........12-25 72
DECCA (75351 "God Bless America Again")...12-25 72
DECCA (75381 "Here I Am Again")..........12-25 72
DECCA (75084 "Your Squaw Is on the Warpath")..25-35 69
(Has *Barney*.)
DECCA (75084 "Your Squaw Is on the Warpath")..15-20 69
(Without *Barney*.)
L.L. (1001 "On the Road").......................20-30 76
MCA...5-10 73-86
TEE VEE (1024 "All My Best")...................8-12 78
(Two discs. Mail-order offer.)

TROLLEY CAR (5000 "Loretta")..................8-10 81
VOCALION (73853 "Here's Loretta Lynn")...10-15 68
VOCALION (73925 "Alone with You")........8-12 72

Promotional LPs

MCA (1934 "Loretta Lynn's Greatest Hits")..30-40 74
(Cover shows title as simply *Loretta Lynn*.)
MCA (35013 "Allis-Chalmers Presents Loretta Lynn")..30-40 78
MCA (35018 "Crisco Presents Loretta Lynn's Country Classics")..30-40 79
Session: Bob Hempker; Chuck Flynn; Ken Riley; Dave Thornhill; Gene Dunlap; Don Ballenger; Jordanaires.
Also see BEATLES / Loretta Lynn
Also see PIERCE, Webb / Loretta Lynn
Also see STARR, Kenny
Also see TUBB, Ernest, & Loretta Lynn
Also see TUBB, Ernest, & Loretta Lynn / Tubb, Ernest, & George Jones
Also see TWITTY, Conway, & Loretta Lynn
Also see WEBB, Jay Lee
Also see WILBURN BROTHERS

LYNN, Loretta, & Conway Twitty *C&W/P&R '71*

Singles: 7-inch

CRLX (7211281"Seasons Greetings")...50-100 '80s
(Picture disc. Promotional issue only.)
DECCA..4-6 71-72
MCA...3-6 73-81

LPs: 10/12-inch

DECCA (75251 "We Only Make Believe").8-15 71
DECCA (75326 "Lead Me On")..................8-15 72
MCA..5-10 73-84
TVP (1010 "Great Country Hits")...............8-12 76
(Two discs. Mail-order offer.)
Also see LYNN, Loretta
Also see TWITTY, Conway

LYNN, Loretta / Tammy Wynette

LPs: 10/12-inch

RADIANT (2003 "Loretta Lynn /Tammy Wynette")..5-10 81
Also see LYNN, Loretta
Also see WYNETTE, Tammy

LYNN, Ray

Singles: 7-inch

GLENN (2300 "Mean Mean Woman")....75-125 '60s
LIL' (1002 "Forbidden")............................10-20 '60s

LYNN, Robby, & Teens

Singles: 7-inch

CUCA (1086 "The Angel Sent Me").........10-15 62
SUNDERLAND (1086 "Angel, You Sent Me")..10-20 62

LYNN, Sandra
(Sandy Lynn)

Singles: 7-inch

CONSTELLATION (140 "Where Would I Be")..5-10 64
LAUREL (1024 "Hurry Home")...............150-200 61
LEMAY (1002 "I Can't Escape")..................5-10 64
Also see CORVETS

LYNN, Sandy / Timmy Reynolds

Singles: 7-inch

OPERATORS (2007 "Break It to Me Gently"/"Dear Lady Twist")...5-10 62
Also see LYNN, Sandra
Also see REYNOLDS, Timmy

LYNN, Smiling Smokey

Singles: 78 rpm

PEACOCK...10-20 51-52
SPECIALTY...10-20 49

LYNN, Tami

Singles: 7-inch

A.F.O. (310 "Where Can I Go")..................8-12 63
ATCO (6342 "I'm Gonna Run Away from You")..10-20 65
MOJO (001 "I'm Gonna Run Away from You")..5-8 71

LPs: 10/12-inch

COTILLION...10-15 72
Also see A.F.O. EXECUTIVES & TAMI LYNN

LYNN, Vera *P&R '48*
(With the Johnston Singers; with Roland Shaw & Orchestra)

Singles: 78 rpm

LONDON...3-5 51-57

Singles: 7-inch
ARCO 4-6 67
DJM (70009 "Fool on the Hill") 4-6 69
LONDON 5-10 51-64
U.A. 4-6 67
EPs: 7-inch
LONDON 10-20 52-56
LPs: 10/12-inch
LONDON 15-30 52-64
MGM 8-12 61
U.A. 5-10 67
Also see SHAW, Roland, Orchestra

LYNN, Vicki
Singles: 7-inch
APPLAUSE (1011 "Don't Break My Heart") 10-15 64
APPLAUSE (1015 "Darling I Love You") 10-15 65
APPLAUSE (1101 "Waiting") 10-15 65
INDIGO (118 "Cry Baby Heart") 8-12 61

LYNN, Windie
Singles: 7-inch
LACONIC (500 "My Boyfriend") 10-15 61

LYNN & FOUR RIVERS
Singles: 7-inch
MUSIC CITY (845 "Send My Records C.O.D.") 100-150 62

LYNNE, Gloria *P&R/R&B/LP '61*
(Gloria Alleyne; with Wheels)
Singles: 7-inch
CANYON 4-6 70
EMBER (1002 "Cool Daddy") 5-10 56
EVEREST 5-10 59-65
FONTANA 5-10 64-69
HI FI 4-8 66
IMPULSE 4-6 76
MERCURY 4-6 72
PREMIUM (412 "Run for Your Love") 30-40 57
SEECO 5-8 59-61
Picture Sleeves
FONTANA (1890 "Be Anything") 5-10 64
LPs: 10/12-inch
CANYON 5-10 70
DESIGN 10-15 62
EVEREST (300 series) 5-10 75
EVEREST (1000 series) 20-30 58-65
(Stereo.)
EVEREST (5000 series) 15-25 58-65
(Monaural.)
FONTANA 10-20 64-69
HI FI 10-15 66
IMPULSE 5-10 76
MERCURY 8-12 69-72
PAUL WINLEY 5-10 74
SUNSET 8-15 66-67
UPFRONT 5-10 72
Also see ALLEYNE, Gloria

LYNNE, Gloria / Nina Simone / Billie Holiday
LPs: 10/12-inch
ALMOR 10-15
Also see HOLIDAY, Billie

LYNNE, Jeff *P&R '84*
(Jeff Lynn)
Singles: 12-inch
JET 5-8 77
Singles: 7-inch
JET 4-6 77
REPRISE 5-8 90
TWIN-SPIN (102 "I Need Your Love") 30-40 65
VIRGIN 3-5 84
Also see ELECTRIC LIGHT ORCHESTRA
Also see IDLE RACE
Also see MOVE, The
Also see TRAVELING WILBURYS

LYNNE, Jeff / Danny Hutton
Singles: 7-inch
WHAT'S IT ALL ABOUT (1429 "Interviews") 15-25 '70s
(Issued only to radio stations.)
Also see HUTTON, Danny
Also see LYNNE, Jeff

LYNNE, Lina, & Storms
Singles: 7-inch
TOPPA (1008 "Five Golden Charms") 40-50 59

LYNNE, Susan
Singles: 7-inch
CAPITOL (5201 "In His Car") 5-10 64
DUEL (506 "Such a Short Time") 10-15 62
DUEL (514 "Even Though") 5-10 62
DUEL (523 "Just a Number") 5-10 63

LYNX
Singles: 7-inch
THUNDERBALL (135 "You Lie") 20-30 67
THUNDERBALL (137 "Show Me") 20-30 67

LYNYRD SKYNYRD *LP '73*
Singles: 7-inch
ATNIA (129 "Need All My Friends") 4-8 78
MCA (Except 1966) 4-6 74-78
MCA (1966 "Gimmie Back My Bullets") 8-12 77
(Promotional concert souvenir issue.)
EPs: 7-inch
MCA (1988 "Skynyrd's First ... and Last") 10-20 76
(Tracks from their first, and last albums. Promotional issue only.)
LPs: 10/12-inch
MCA (2000 & 3000 series, except 3029) 8-10 75-78
MCA (3029 "Street Survivors") 30-40 77
(Front cover pictures the group in flames.)
MCA (3029 "Street Survivors") 8-10 77
(Pictures the group without flames.)
MCA (5000 series) 5-8 79-82
MCA (6000 series) 10-15 76-81
MCA (8011 "Live at the Fox") 10-15 76
MCA (8027 "Southern by the Grace of God") 8-12 88
MCA (10000 series) 10-15 79-81
MCA (37000 series) 5-8 79-82
MCA (42000 series) 5-8 87
MCA/SOUNDS OF THE SOUTH (300 & 400 series) 8-15 73-74
Promotional LPs
MCA (1946 "Special Advance Preview *Live* Album") 25-35 76
(White label.)
MCA (1988 "Lynyrd Skynyrd") 25-35 76
(White label.)
MCA (2170 "Gimmie Back My Bullets") 25-35 76
(White label. Concert souvenir copy.)
Members: Ronnie Van Zant; Gary Rossington; Allen Collins; Steve Gaines; Cassie Gaines; Ed King; Rick Medlocke; Greg Walker; Artimus Pyle; Leon Wildeson; Billy Powell; Bob Burns; Johnny Van Zant.
Also see STRAWBERRY ALARM CLOCK

LYON, Barbara
Singles: 78 rpm
CAPITOL (3497 "Puppy Love") 5-10 56
Singles: 7-inch
CAPITOL (3497 "Puppy Love") 10-15 56

LYON, Bob, & Cubs
Singles: 7-inch
LYON (4721 "Ram Charger") 15-20 61

LYON, Don
(With Regus Patoff & Orchestra)
Singles: 78 rpm
COLUMBIA (28 "Little Black Sambo") 20-30
(Two discs.)

LYON, Ken
Singles: 7-inch
EPIC (9446 "Fallen Idol") 25-35 61

LYONS, Billy
Singles: 7-inch
AVA (144 "My Angel Debbie") 15-25 63
CANDIX (330 "Little Fool") 10-20 62

LYONS, Cleve
Singles: 7-inch
VIK (0276 "Out of the Closet") 15-25 57

LYONS, Dolly
Singles: 7-inch
APOLLO (518 "Call Me Darling") 20-30 57
BELTONE (2039 "Lots of Lovin' ") 5-10 63

LYONS, Joe, & Arrows
Singles: 7-inch
HIT MAKER (600 "Bob-O-Loop") 75-125 59
HOLLYWOOD (1071 "No End to True Love") 40-50 57
Also see ARROWS
Also see FLOWERS, Phil, / Joe Lyons & Arrows

LYONS, Lonnie
(Lonnie Lyons Combo)
Singles: 78 rpm
FREEDOM 15-25 49

LYONS, Marie
(Marie "Queenie" Lyons)
Singles: 7-inch
DELUXE 8-12 68-70
LPs: 10/12-inch
DELUXE (12001 "Soul Fever") 15-25 70

LYRES
(Nutmegs)
Singles: 78 rpm
J&G (101 "Ship of Love") 300-500 53
Members: Leroy Griffin; Sonny Griffin; Leroy McNeil; Bill Embery; Walter Singleterry.
Also see NUTMEGS

LYRICS
(With Ray's Combo)
Singles: 7-inch
HY-TONE (111 "I'm in Love") 1000-2000 57
Also see HARRIS, Georgia

LYRICS
Singles: 7-inch
MARVELS (1005 "Did She Leave You") 15-25 58
MID-SOUTH (1500 "Down in the Alley") 20-30 59
RHYTHM (126/127 "Come Back Baby"/"Every Night") 1200-1800 59
(Different selection number on each side of disc. Rhythm also used the number 126 for a Carol Gray release.)
RHYTHM (127 "Every Night"/"Come Back Baby") 1500-2000 59
(Same number on both sides. Has an alternative take of *Every Night* compared to track used on 126/127, listed above.)
VEE-JAY (285 "Come On Home") 40-60 58
Also see GRAY, Carol

LYRICS
Singles: 7-inch
CORAL (62322 "Oh, Please Love Me") 20-30 62
HARLEM (101 "Oh, Please Love Me") 500-600 59
(First issue.)
HARLEM (104 "The Beating of My Heart") 600-700 59
(Thick wax.)
HARLEM (104 "The Beating of My Heart") 10-15
(Thin wax.)
WILDCAT (0028 "Oh, Please Love Me") 50-100 59
LPs: 10/12-inch
HARLEM 8-10 79

LYRICS
Singles: 7-inch
FERNWOOD (129 "Let's Bee [sic] Sweethearts Again") 500-750 61
FLEETWOOD (233 "Let's Be Sweethearts Again") 250-350 61
STOOP SOUNDS (507 "Let's Be Sweethearts Again") 100-150 97
(Limited edition.)

LYRICS
(Ida Valentine & Lyrics; Leo Valentine & Lyrics)
Singles: 7-inch
SKYLIGHT (200 "Why Did You Lie to Me") 1500-2000 62
SKYLIGHT (201 "Please Don't Leave Me This Way") 1000-1500 62
Also see WIGFALL, William, & Lyrics

LYRICS
Singles: 7-inch
ABC-PAR (10560 "So Hard to Get Along") 5-10 64
DAN-TONE (1002 "I Can't Get Along Without You") 15-25 63
GOLDWAX (101 "Darling") 40-50 63
GOLDWAX (105 "So Hard to Get Along") 10-20 63

LYRICS
Singles: 7-inch
J.W.J. (19792 "They Call That Love") 10-20 67

LYRICS
Singles: 7-inch
ERA (3153 "So What") 50-75 65

FEATHER (1968 "Wake Up to My Voice") 15-25 68
GNP (381 "My Son") 8-12 66
GNP (393 "Mr. Man") 8-12 67
Members: Chris Gaylord; Steve Khailer; Bill Garcia; Michael Allen; Gary Neves.
Also see MAGIC MUSHROOM

LYTATIONS
Singles: 7-inch
TIMES SQUARE (107 "Over the Rainbow") 10-20 64

LYTE
Singles: 7-inch
BOLO (761 "It's Gonna Work Out Fine") 10-15 68

LYTELL, Marshall
(Marshall Lytle)
Singles: 7-inch
CAMEO (163 "Just Pretend") 10-20 59
Also see HALEY, Bill
Also see JODIMARS
Also see MARSHALL & WES

LYTHGOE, John, & Tri-Five
Singles: 7-inch
VARBEE (2002 "Oh Baby") 20-30 61

LYTLE, Johnny *P&R/LP '66*
(Johnny Lytle Quintet; J Trio)
Singles: 7-inch
CONSTELLATION (145 "Big Bill") 5-10 65
JAZZLAND (709 "Lela") 5-8 62
PACIFIC JAZZ (88143 "Gonna Get That Boat") 4-6 68
RIVERSIDE (4551 "Lela") 4-8 63
RIVERSIDE (4570 "Solitude") 4-8 63
SOLID STATE (2523 "Be Proud") 4-6 68
TUBA (2004 "The Loop") 8-12 65
TUBA (2117 "Screamin' Loud") 5-10 66
EPs: 7-inch
NEOPHON 10-15
LPs: 10/12-inch
JAZZLAND 15-25 60-62
MILESTONE 5-10 72
MUSE 5-8 78-81
PACIFIC JAZZ (20129 "Swingin' at the Gate") 8-15 67
RIVERSIDE 10-20 63-68
SOLID STATE (18026 "Sound of Velvet Soul") 8-15 68
SOLID STATE (18044 "Be Proud") 8-15 68
TUBA (5001 "The Loop") 10-15 66

LYTLE, Johnny, & Ray Barretto
LPs: 10/12-inch
JAZZLAND (81 "Moon Child") 15-25 62
Also see BARRETTO, Ray
Also see LYTLE, Johnny

I'M MOVIN ON
(Hank Snow)
RENAY
R-45-207
Hill and Range
BMI
Time: 2:20
MATT LUCAS
304
RENAY RECORDS, P.O. BOX 897, MEMPHIS, TENN.

The Kingsmen
Volume II
MORE GREAT SOUNDS FROM THE
GROUP THAT GAVE YOU "LOUIE, LOUIE"

JAN & DEAN
JAN & DEAN
FROM ALL OVER THE WORLD

COMPLIMENTARY
KING
DEE JAY
SPECIAL
(Cedarwood-BMI)
Time: 2:42
45—K4036
HIGH FIDELITY
NOT FOR SALE
Vocal by
Moon Mullican
For the first eight years of his life, it looked like young Moon Mullican was destined to help his father run their 87-acre farm down in Polk County, Texas. Moon had a love for music though—a love
that was stimulated by Joe Jones, a talented Negro guitar player who worked on the farm. Joe taught Moon how to sing the blues—the only music lessons he ever took.
ROCK AND ROLL MR. BULLFROG
(Moon Mullican)
MOON MULLICAN
With Boyd Bennett And His Rockers
4915

M

MC 5 *P&R/LP '69*
(Motor City 5)
Singles: 7-inch
A² (333 "Looking at You") 50-75 68
(Reportedly 500 made.)
A² (3012 "Looking at You") 5-8 98
AMG (1001 "I Can Only Give You Everything"/"One of the Guys") 35-55 67
AMG (1001 "I Can Only Give You Everything"/"I Just Don't Know") 15-25 69
ATLANTIC (2678 "Tonight") 4-8 69
ATLANTIC (2724 "Shakin' Street") 4-8 70
ELEKTRA (MC5-1 "Kick Out the Jams") . 50-75 68
(Promotional issue only. Given away at a 1968 New York concert.)
ELEKTRA (45648 "Kick Out the Jams") 5-10 69
(We would like to know more about a picture sleeve for *Kick Out the Jams*, which may be a foreign issue. From the small photo we have, a label name can't be read. Besides the title and group name, it appears to have "Super Stereo Sound" at upper right.)
Picture Sleeves
A² (333 "Looking at You") 100-125 68
(Reportedly 500 made.)
LPs: 10/12-inch
ALIVE/TOTAL ENERGY (0005 "Power Trip") 5-10 94
(10-inch LP.)
ALIVE/TOTAL ENERGY (0008 "Ice Pick Slim") 5-10 95
(10-inch LP.)
ALIVE/TOTAL ENERGY (0051 "Alive") 5-10 95
(10-inch LP.)
ALIVE/TOTAL ENERGY (2010 "American Ruse") 5-10 95
(10-inch LP.)
ALIVE/TOTAL ENERGY (3005 "Looking at You") 5-10 95
(10-inch LP.)
ALIVE/TOTAL ENERGY (3008 "Teenage Lust") 5-10 96
ALIVE/TOTAL ENERGY (3018 "Starship Live") 5-10 98
ATLANTIC (8247 "Back in the USA") 25-50 70
ATLANTIC (8285 "High Time") 25-50 71
ELEKTRA (74042 "Kick Out the Jams") .. 30-40 69
(Title track has X-rated intro. Gatefold cover. With John Sinclair's liner notes inside cover.)
ELEKTRA (74042 "Kick Out the Jams") .. 15-20 69
(Title track has censored intro. Cover does not have John Sinclair liner notes.)
ELEKTRA (74042 "Kick Out the Jams") 5-8 91
(Title track has censored intro. Cover does not have John Sinclair liner notes.)
Members: Rob Tyner; Robert Derminer; Fred "Sonic" Smith; Michael Davis; Wayne Kramer; Sigrid Dobat; Dennis Thompson.

MDC
(Multi-Death Corportation)
EPs: 7-inch
R RADICAL (2 "Multi-Death Corporation") 10-15 83
LPs: 10/12-inch
R RADICAL 5-10 81-86

MFQ
Singles: 7-inch
W.B. (5481 "If All You Think") 5-10 64
W.B. (5623 "That's Alright with Me") 5-10 65
Members: Chip Douglas; Cyrus Faryar.
Also see GUARD, Dave, & Whiskeyhill Singers

MG & ESCORTS
Singles: 7-inch
MALA (582 "Next to Nowhere") 5-10 68
REO (8936 "Please Don't Ever Change") 10-20 67
(Canadian.)
REO (8960 "I Can't Go On") 10-20 67
(Canadian.)
REO (8975 "A Someday Fool") 10-20 67
(Canadian.)
REO (8998 "Next to Nowhere") 10-20 67
(Canadian.)

M.H. ROYALS
Singles: 7-inch
ABC (10907 "Tomorrow's Dead") 10-20 68
ABC (10957 "Old Town") 10-20 68

M&Ms
(M-M's & the Peanuts)
Singles: 7-inch
MONEY (101 "Open Up Your Eyes") 10-15 64
MONEY (107 "I Found My Love") 10-15 65
MONEY (111 "Without a Word") 5-10 65

MJT PLUS 3
(Walter Perkins & MJT Plus 3)
Singles: 7-inch
VEE-JAY ("The Whiffenpoof Song") 8-12 60
(No selection number used. Promotional issue only.)
LPs: 10/12-inch
ARGO (621 "Daddy-O Presents") 50-75 57
VEE-JAY (1013 "Walter Perkins & MJT Plus 3") 40-60 59
(Maroon label.)
VEE-JAY (1013 "Walter Perkins & MJT Plus 3") 25-50 60
(Black label.)
VEE-JAY (3008 "Make Everybody Happy") 25-50 60
VEE-JAY (3014 "MJT Plus 3") 25-50 60
Members: Walter Perkins; Bob Cranshaw; Frank Strozier; Paul Serrano; Nicky Hill.

M-3s
Singles: 7-inch
ABC-PAR (10772 "So Give Me Love") 10-20 66
U.A. (889 "I See a Rainbow") 5-10 65

M.V.P.s
Singles: 7-inch
BUDDAH (262 "Turning My Heartbeat Up") 15-25 72

MABASA, Lemmy
Singles: 7-inch
PHILIPS (40335 "The Mad Kids") 10-20 65

MABE, Robby, & Outcasts
Singles: 7-inch
ROTAB (1013 "I'm Lonely") 8-12

MABLEY, Moms *LP '61*
Singles: 7-inch
MERCURY 4-8 69-71
EPs: 7-inch
CHESS (5136 "I Got Somethin' to Tell You") 5-10 63
LPs: 10/12-inch
CHESS 15-25 61-64
MERCURY 10-20 64-70

MABLEY, Moms / George Kirby / Heartbreakers / Keynotes
LPs: 10/12-inch
VANGUARD (9093 "Comedy Night at the Apollo") 50-100 61
(Demand is primarily for the R&B tracks by the Heartbreakers and the Keynotes.)

MABLEY, Moms, & Pigmeat Markham
LPs: 10/12-inch
CHESS 10-20 64-71
Also see MABLEY, Moms
Also see MARKHAM, Pigmeat

MABON, Willie *R&B '52*
(With His Combo)
Singles: 78 rpm
CHESS 10-20 52-56
FEDERAL 15-25 57
PARROT 50-100 53
Singles: 7-inch
CHESS (1531 "I Don't Know") 100-200 53
(Red vinyl.)
CHESS (1531 "I Don't Know") 40-60 53
(Black vinyl.)
CHESS (1538 "I'm Mad") 100-200 53
(Red vinyl.)
CHESS (1538 "I'm Mad") 40-60 53
(Black vinyl.)
CHESS (1548 "You're a Fool") 40-60 53
CHESS (1554 "I Got to Go") 40-60 53
CHESS (1564 "Would You, Baby") 40-60 54
CHESS (1580 "Poison Ivy") 40-60 54
CHESS (1592 "Come On Baby") 40-60 54
CHESS (1608 "The Seventh Son") 40-60 55
CHESS (1627 "Knock on Wood") 30-50 56
DELTA (3004 "Light Up Your Lamp") 5-10
FEDERAL (12306 "Light Up Your Lamp") 15-25 57
FORMAL 4-8 62
MAD (1298 "I Gotta Go Now") 10-20 60
MAD (1300 "I Don't Know") 10-20 60
PARROT (1050 "I Don't Know") 150-250 53
SOLAR (54001 "Fannie Mae") 10-20
(Number 1052 is also on the label.)
USA 5-10 63-65
LPs: 10/12-inch
CHESS (1439 "Willie Mabon") 75-125 59
Also see BIG WILLIE

MAC, Barbara Lee
Singles: 7-inch
CUCA (6635 "Big Fat Mama") 15-25 66

MAC, Billy
(Billy Mack)
Singles: 7-inch
MISS BETTY (34 "I Can't Sleep") 8-12
MUSIC MAKERS (107 "Tomorrow Night") 10-20 61
PHILIPS (40301 "Too Much") 5-10 65

MAC, Bobby
(Bobby Mac Trio)
Singles: 7-inch
AUDITION (6108 "Maria") 10-20 66
ORIGINAL SOUND (68 "Walkin' Together") 15-25 67
VENDED (104 "How Was Your Weekend") 300-400 62

MAC, George
Singles: 7-inch
MAC (512966 "I Want to Be with You Baby") 20-40

MAC, Johnny
Singles: 7-inch
J&M (2655 "There Goes Another Rocket") 50-75
SELECT (739 "Pink Champagne and a Room of Roses") 5-10 65
STUDIO 5-10
Also see McKEOWN, John

MAC, Lou
(Lou Mack; Lu Mac; with Palms)
Singles: 78 rpm
BLUE LAKE (108 "Come Back, Little Daddy") 25-75 54
BLUE LAKE (114 "Slow Down") 25-75 55
BLUE LAKE (117 "Albert Is His Name") ... 25-75 55
BLUE LAKE (119 "Move Me") 25-75 56
Singles: 7-inch
BLUE LAKE (108 "Come Back, Little Daddy") 50-75 54
(Black vinyl.)
BLUE LAKE (108 "Come Back, Little Daddy") 100-200 54
(Red vinyl.)
BLUE LAKE (114 "Slow Down") 200-300 55
(Black vinyl.)
BLUE LAKE (114 "Slow Down") 300-400 55
(Red vinyl.)
BLUE LAKE (117 "Albert Is His Name") ... 50-75 55
(Black vinyl.)
BLUE LAKE (117 "Albert Is His Name") 100-200 55
(Red vinyl.)
BLUE LAKE (119 "Move Me") 50-75 56
(Black vinyl.)
BLUE LAKE (119 "Move Me") 100-200 56
(Red vinyl.)

MAC, Marti
(With the Sandslingers; with Whiskey)
Singles: 7-inch
LAURIE (3269 "Ready, Aim, Kiss") 5-10 64
LAURIE (3384 "The Joint") 5-10 67

MAC & MIKE
Singles: 7-inch
GLORY (273 "Be My Next") 10-20 58

MAC TRUQUE
Singles: 7-inch
CAPITOL (5951 "Mickey's Monkey") 5-10 67
LPs: 10/12-inch
CAPITOL (275 "Truqued Up") 10-15 69

MACAMBO, J.J.
Singles: 7-inch
CONQUEST (1001 "Kitty") 10-20 63

MacARTHUR, James *P&R '63*
Singles: 7-inch
SCEPTER (1241 " Story of the In-Between Years") 8-12 62
SCEPTER (1250 "Ten Commandments of Love") 8-12 63
TRIODEX (112 "Story of the In-Between Years") 15-20 61

MacDONALD, Bruce
Singles: 7-inch
HURRICANE (101 "Drag Race Mama") 100-150

MacDONALD, Jeanette, & Nelson Eddy *LP '59*
Singles: 78 rpm
RCA 4-8 50
Singles: 7-inch
RCA (0200 "Indian Love Call") 8-10 50
(Red vinyl.)
EPs: 7-inch
RCA (Except 220) 5-10 59-61
RCA (220 "Rose Marie") 10-20 52
LPs: 10/12-inch
RCA (16 "Rose Marie") 40-50 52
RCA (526 "16 Nostalgic Original Recordings") 10-20 66
RCA (1000 series) 5-10 75
RCA (1700 series) 10-20 59
RCA (2400 series) 5-8 77
RCA (3900 series) 5-8 81

MACEO & ALL THE KING'S MEN *R&B '70*
Singles: 7-inch
EXCELLO (2325 "Dreams") 5-10 72
HOUSE OF FOX (1 "Got to Get'cha") 8-10 70
HOUSE OF FOX (8 "Thank You for Letting Me Be Myself Again") 8-10 71
HOUSE OF FOX (10 "Funky Women") 8-10 71
LPs: 10/12-inch
EXCELLO (8022 "Funky Music Machine") 15-25 72
Member: Maceo Parker.

MACEO & MACKS *R&B '73*
(Maceo)
Singles: 7-inch
PEOPLE 5-8 73-74
LPs: 10/12-inch
PEOPLE (6601 "Us") 50-75 74
Member: Maceo Parker.
Also see MACEO & ALL THE KING'S MEN
Also see PARLIAMENT
Also see SWEAT BAND

MACH, Leon
Singles: 7-inch
LAVENDER (1554 "You Hurt Me So") ... 75-100 60

MACHE, Billy
Singles: 7-inch
IMPALA (1156 "It Makes No Difference") 20-30 59

MACIAS, George, & Original Royal Bops
Singles: 7-inch
R-B (501 "So Alone") 300-500

MACK, Bill
Singles: 78 rpm
IMPERIAL 15-30 52-54
JUBILEE 8-12 54
STARDAY 35-50 56
Singles: 7-inch
IMPERIAL (8174 "Play My Boogie") 50-75 52
IMPERIAL (8212 "I'm Not Free") 15-25 53
IMPERIAL (8225 "That's How I Feel") 15-25 54
IMPERIAL (8242 "We Waltzed in My Dreams") 15-25 54
IMPERIAL (8278 "Sue Suzie Boogie") 50-75 54
JUBILEE (9002 "Paper Doll") 10-20 54
SHAH (303 "Honky Tonk Band") 8-12
STARDAY (231 "Kitty Kat") 75-125 56
STARDAY (252 "Cat Just in Town") 75-125 56
STARDAY (280 "It's Saturday Night") .. 125-150 56
STARDAY (300 & 400 series) 10-20 57-59

MACK, Billy
(With Bobby Anderson & Band)
Singles: 7-inch
R&H (001 "I Refuse to Cry") .... 20-30 '50s

MACK, Bobby
Singles: 7-inch
ACE OF HEARTS (0462 "Heartaches Caused by You") 4-6 73
ACE OF HEARTS (0467 "A Love Nobody Knows") 4-6 73
ACE OF HEARTS (0475 "Lovin' Feeling") 4-6 73
ACE OF HEARTS (0483 "The Same Old Way") 4-6 73
B-MAC (723 "Waitin' for You to Call") .. 100-125 59
DIXIE (2026 "Who Put the Blues in Your Heart") 25-35 59
MIDAS .... 8-12 '60s
TEMPUS (1508 "No One Like You") 50-75 59

MACK, Dell
Singles: 7-inch
GOLDBAND (1064 "The Way Love Goes") 10-15 58

MACK, Floyd
(Floyd McDaniel)
Singles: 7-inch
SANDSPUR (25406 "I Like to Go") 500-600
(Rerecorded and issued on Dixie as by Floyd McDaniel.)
Also see McDANIEL, Floyd

MACK, Gene
Singles: 7-inch
ZERO (103 "I'm Going Crazy") 5-10 60

MACK, George
Singles: 7-inch
MAC (27510 "I Want to Be with You Baby") 50-75

MACK, Jamie
Singles: 7-inch
SIDE WINDER (110 "Another Lonely Night") 10-20

MACK, Jeani
Singles: 7-inch
CLASS (230 "Dirty Dishes") 10-15 58
CLASS (242 "Tonight You'll Have Your Dream") 10-15 59

MACK, Jimmie, & Watts
Singles: 7-inch
ELGIN (1028 "True Lover Girl") 75-125 59
GEE (1056 "True Lover Girl") 10-15 60

MACK, Jimmy
Singles: 7-inch
PALMER (5019 "My World Is on Fire") 100-200 67

MACK, Jimmy, & Music Factory
Singles: 7-inch
ATLANTIC (2552 "Baby I Love You") 5-10 68

MACK, Lonnie *P&R/R&B/LP '63*
(With Pismo)
Singles: 7-inch
ABC 4-6 73
A.M.G. 4-6
BARRY 4-6
BUCCANEER (3001 "Memphis") 5-10 66
CAPITOL 4-6 77
COLLECTABLES .... 3-5 '80s
ELEKTRA 4-6 71
FRATERNITY 6-12 63-68
ROULETTE (7175 "Highway 56") 4-6 75
LPs: 10/12-inch
ALLIGATOR 5-8 85-86
CAPITOL 8-10 77
ELEKTRA 10-20 69-71
FRATERNITY (SF-1014 "Wham of That Memphis Man") 25-50 63
(Monaural.)
FRATERNITY (SSF-1014 "Wham of That Memphis Man") 50-100 63
(Stereo.)
TRIP 8-10 75
Members: Lonnie Mack; Jim Keltner; Tim Drummond.
Also see ALABAMA STATE TROUPERS

MACK, Lonnie, & Rusty York
LPs: 10/12-inch
QCA 10-15 73
Also see MACK, Lonnie
Also see YORK, Rusty

MACK, Oscar
Singles: 7-inch
AMY (11007 "I'm Glad It's Over") 5-10 68
STAX (152 "Dream Girl") 10-20 64
VOLT (107 "Don't Be Afraid of Love") 8-12 63

MACK, Patti
Singles: 7-inch
CINEMA (101 "Handy Andy") 50-100

MACK, Teddy, & Mackinteers
Singles: 7-inch
MONROE ("Is There Any Doubt") 40-50
(No selection number used.)

MACK, Warner *C&W/P&R '57*
Singles: 78 rpm
DECCA 15-20 57
Singles: 7-inch
DECCA (30301 "Is It Wrong) 20-30 57
DECCA (30471 "Roc-a-Chicka) 20-30 57
DECCA (30587 "Fallin' in Love") 15-25 58
DECCA (30645 "Your Fool") 10-20 58
DECCA (30714 "Going Away to School") .15-25 59
DECCA (30841 thru 31684) 8-15 59-64
DECCA (31774 thru 33045) 4-6 65-73
KAPP 5-10 61-62
LOST GOLD (1024 "Bring Your Own Blues") 3-5 93
MCA 4-6 73-76
PAGEBOY 3-6 77-81
SCARLET (4002 "My Love for You") 10-20 60
TOP RANK (2053 "I'll Run Back to You") ... 8-12 60
Picture Sleeves
DECCA (30471 "Roc-a-Chicka) 10-20 58
(Has die-cut center hole. Reads: "The Exciting Warner Mack.")
EPs: 7-inch
DECCA 5-10 65
LPs: 10/12-inch
CORAL 5-10 73
DECCA 10-25 65-70
KAPP 15-25 61-66
PAGEBOY 5-10
SAPPHIRE 5-10
Session: Anita Kerr Singers; Jordanaires.
Also see DEAN, Jimmy / David Houston / Warner Mack / Autry Inman
Also see JORDANAIRES
Also see KERR, Anita

MACK, Wally
Singles: 7-inch
GROOVE (7 "Crazy Love") 5-10 62

MACK & GWEN
Singles: 7-inch
PHIL (1200 "Baby I Want Another Date with You") 30-40

MACK TWINS
Singles: 7-inch
LAURIE (3051 "Goodbye") 5-10 60

MacKAY, Bruce
LPs: 10/12-inch
ORO 10-15

MacKAY, Rabbit
(With the Somis Rhythm Boyze)
Singles: 7-inch
UNI (55074 "Big Sur Country") 5-10 68
UNI (55112 "Somebody Beat Me") 5-10 69
LPs: 10/12-inch
UNI (73064 "Passing Through") 10-15 69

MACKEY, Linda, & Soul Strings
Singles: 7-inch
VEE-JAY (721 "Gotta Find My Man") 5-10 66

MacKENZIE, Fred
(With Carl Stevens & His Orchestra)
Singles: 78 rpm
MERCURY (70962 "Talk to Me") 10-15 56
Singles: 7-inch
MERCURY (70962 "Talk to Me") 15-25 56

MacKENZIE, Gisele *P&R '52*
Singles: 78 rpm
CAPITOL 3-5 51-54
VIK 3-5 56
"X" 3-5 55
Singles: 7-inch
CAPITOL 10-20 51-54
EVEREST (19352 "In Milano") 5-10 60
MERCURY (72113 "Loser's Lullaby") 5-10 63
VIK 5-10 56
"X" 5-10 55
Picture Sleeves
VIK (300 "Too Fat for the Chimney") 10-20 56
"X" (137 "Hard to Get") 10-20 55
EPs: 7-inch
CAPITOL 10-15 53-59
VIK 10-15 56
LPs: 10/12-inch
CAMDEN (532 "Gisele MacKenzie") 10-20 59
EVEREST (1069 "In Person at the Empire Room") 10-15 60
(Monaural.)
EVEREST (5069 "In Person at the Empire Room") 15-20 60
(Stereo.)
GLENDALE 5-8 78
MERCURY (20790 "Loser's Lullabies") 10-20 63
RCA (2006 "Christmas with Gisele") 10-20 59
SUNSET (1155 "In Person at the Empire Room") 8-12 67
(Monaural.)
SUNSET (5155 "In Person at the Empire Room") 10-15 67
(Stereo.)
VIK 15-25 56

MacMURRAY, Fred
Singles: 7-inch
BUENA VISTA (381 "Flubber") 5-10 61
Picture Sleeves
BUENA VISTA (381 "Flubber") 15-25 61
(Sleeve pictures Annette.)
Also see ANNETTE

MacRAE, Gordon *P&R '47*
Singles: 78 rpm
CAPITOL 3-5 47-57
Singles: 7-inch
CAPITOL 5-10 50-68
EPs: 7-inch
CAPITOL 5-10 54-57
ROYALE 5-10
LPs: 10/12-inch
CAPITOL 10-25 54-69
EVON .... 10-15 '50s
RONDO-LETTE 15-30
SUTTON (292 "Broadway Best") .... 10-20 '60s
Also see DESMOND, Johnny / John Gary / Gordon MacRae
Also see MARTIN, Dean / Bob Eberly / Gordon MacRae

MacRAE, Gordon, & Jo Stafford *P&R '48*
Singles: 78 rpm
CAPITOL 5-10 48-50
Singles: 7-inch
CAPITOL 5-10 62
LPs: 10/12-inch
CAPITOL (1600 & 1900 series) 10-20 62-63
CAPITOL (11000 series) 4-8 79
Also see BRYANT, Anita / Jo Stafford & Gordon MacRae
Also see MacRAE, Gordon
Also see STAFFORD, Jo

MacRAE, Johnny
Singles: 7-inch
CANDIX (302 "Lonely Years") 8-12 60
FELSTED (8654 "Honest John") 5-10 62
FELSTED (8657 "Tag Along") 5-10 62
FELSTED (8675 "Whoever You Are") 5-10 63
LANDA (682 "Such a Fool") 5-10 61
MUSICOR (1091 "Cryin' Machine") 5-10 65

MacRAE, Meredith, with Candy Johnson's Exciters
Singles: 7-inch
CANJO (103 "Image of a Boy") 10-15 64
Also see JOHNSON, Candy

MACREE, Vincent
(With the Rhythm Kings; with Chords)
Singles: 7-inch
GAMETIME (103 "Candy Doll") 10-20 57
GAMETIME (110 "My Love for You Will Never Change") 15-25 57

MAD ANDY'S TWIST COMBO
Singles: 7-inch
ORIGINAL SOUND (85 "Painted Smile") . 10-15 69

MAD ANGEL
Singles: 7-inch
BASF (15345 "Can't Run, Can't Hide") 10-15 74

MAD CAPS
Singles: 7-inch
COOL (100 "Chit Chat") 10-20 58
COOL (101 "Jam Sam") 10-20 58

MAD ENGLISHMEN & FURYS
Singles: 7-inch
VEE SIX (1023 "Beatle Mania") 10-20 64

MAD HATTERS
Singles: 7-inch
ASCOT (2197 "I Need Love") 10-20 65
ASCOT (2220 "Go Find a Love") 10-20 66
FONTANA (1582 "I'll Come Running") 10-15 67
LPs: 10/12-inch
20TH FOX (4141 "At Midnight") 20-30 64
Also see FALLEN ANGELS

MAD LADS *P&R/R&B '65*
Singles: 7-inch
CAPITOL (5284 "Don't Cry at the Party") ... 8-12 64
STAX (160 "Sidewalk Surf") 10-20 64
VOLT (100 series) 8-15 65-68
VOLT (4000 series) 4-8 68-73
LPs: 10/12-inch
COLLECTABLES 6-8 86
VOLT (400 series) 15-25 66
VOLT (6000 series) 10-15 69-73
Members: Julius Green; John Williams; Robert Phillips; Sam Nelson; Cliff Billops Jr.; William Brown.
Also see OLLIE & NIGHTINGALES

MAD LADS
Singles: 7-inch
MARK-FI (1934 "Why") 100-150 62
Session: H.B. Barnum.
Also see BARNUM, H.B.

MAD LADS
(Fabulous Mad Lads)
Singles: 7-inch
RAYNARD (10020 "Rock Around the Clock") 5-10 65
Members: Gary Lane; Norm Sherian; Larry Lynne; Paul Frederick; Wayne Walters; Jerry Mallon; Al Babicky.
Also see DARNELLS
Also see LANE, Gary, & Mad Lads

MAD LADDS
Singles: 7-inch
TREY (300 "Midnight Terror") 10-20 64

MAD MARTIANS
Singles: 7-inch
SATELLITE (33617 "Outer Space Looters") 20-30 57

MAD MEN
Singles: 7-inch
GAMBLE (212 "Do the African Twist") 5-10 68

MAD MIKE & MANIACS
Singles: 7-inch
HUNCH (345 "Quarter to Four") 10-15 61

MAD MILO
Singles: 7-inch
COMBO (131 "Elvis on Trial") 25-40 57

MAD MILO / Roy Tan & Combo
Singles: 7-inch
MILLION (20018 "Elvis for Christmas") 20-30 57
Also see MAD MILO

MAD MODS
Singles: 7-inch
COBRA (1131 "The Mad Mod") 10-20 65
JOX (069 "No One Like Me") 15-25 65

MAD PERFESSER
Singles: 7-inch
BIG TOP (3009 "Silent Movies") 5-10 59

MAD PLAIDS
Singles: 7-inch
GOLDEN CREST (533 "Blood Rare") 15-20 59

MAD RIVER LP '69
Singles: 7-inch
CAPITOL (2310 "High All the Time") 5-10 68
CAPITOL (2559 "Copper Plates") 5-10 69
EPs: 7-inch
WEE (10021 "Mad River") 25-50 68
LPs: 10/12-inch
CAPITOL (185 "Paradise Bar and Grill") . 25-35 69
CAPITOL (2985 "Mad River") 25-35 68
Members: David Robinson; Tom Manning; Lawrence Hammond; Rick Bochner; Greg Dewey; Ron Wilson.

MADADORS
Singles: 7-inch
FEATURE (105 "Girl, Don't Leave Me") .. 15-25 66
Members: Phil Holzbauer; Larry Black; Jerry Adams; Gene Bell; Nels Christiansen; Jerry Stefani; Ron Buchek.
Also see EASY STREET

MADAM
LPs: 10/12-inch
KENT (012 "Sensuous Black Woman") ... 10-12 72

MADARA, Johnny
(Johnny Madera)
Singles: 78 rpm
PREP (110 "Lovesick") 15-25 57
Singles: 7-inch
BAMBOO (503 "Good Golly Miss Molly") 10-15 61
BAMBOO (511 "Story Untold") 10-15 61
BAMBOO (515 "Dream") 10-15 61
LANDA (687 "Heavenly") 10-20 62
MATT (163 "You're So Dear to Me") 10-15 60
PREP (110 "Lovesick") 15-25 57
PREP (129 "My Big Thrill") 15-25 58
SWAN (4063 "Teenager's Dream") 10-20 60
Also see SPOKESMEN

MADDEN, Chuck
Singles: 7-inch
CEE BEE JAY (1661 "Girls That Shake") 50-75

MADDEN, Doyle
Singles: 7-inch
HU-SE-CO (757 "Gonna Learn to Rock") 300-400

MADDEN, Eddie "Trombone"
Singles: 7-inch
TAMPA (164 "Carmen's Rock") 10-15 59

MADDEN, John
Singles: 7-inch
TOMORROW (0621 "Heat and Hot Water Supplied") 50-100

MADDEN, Margie
Singles: 7-inch
SCOPE (103 "If I Could Make a String of Pearls") 10-15 59

MADDENING CROWD
Singles: 7-inch
PARROT (329 "Happy Days") 5-10 68

MADDIN, Jimmy
(With Sundowners; Jimmy Madden)
Singles: 78 rpm
TAMPA (102 "Let 'Em Rock") 25-50 55
Singles: 7-inch
AMERICAN INT'L (525 "Bird Dog") 50-100 59
AMERICAN INT'L (529 "Leadfoot") 20-30 59
AMERICAN INT'L (542 "Tongue Tied") . 50-100 59
CONCERT ROOM 8-12 63
DOT (15641 "Tongue Tied") 75-125 57
FABOR (207 "This Dance Is Mine") 8-12 61
FREEDOM (44007 "I'm Studyin' You") 10-20 59
IMPERIAL (5494 "Party Line") 10-20 58
IMPERIAL (5496 "Shirley Purley") 10-20 58
RADAR 5-10
TAMPA (102 "Let 'Em Rock") 50-100 55
Also see EXTERMINATORS

MADDOX, Johnny P&R '52
(With the Rhythmasters)
Singles: 78 rpm
DOT 4-8 50-57
Singles: 7-inch
ABC..4-6 74
DOT 5-15 50-63
EPs: 7-inch
DOT 5-10 52-56
LPs: 10/12-inch
DOT (Except 102) 10-25 55-67
DOT (102 "Authentic Ragtime") 20-30 52
(10-inch LP.)
HAMILTON (115 "Twelve Ragtime Greats") 8-10 64
(Monaural.)
HAMILTON (12115 "Twelve Ragtime Greats") 10-15 64
(Stereo.)
PARAMOUNT 5-10 74

MADDOX, Rose C&W '59
Singles: 7-inch
CAPITOL 8-15 58-63
CATHAY (1153 "House of the Rising Sun") 10-20 66
CATHAY (1156 "I Don't Really Want to Know") 5-10 66
PORTLAND (1004 "Tomorrow I'll Be Gone") 4-6 72
PORTLAND (1011 "Baby Hang On") 4-6 72
UNI (55040 "Bottom of the Glass") 5-10 67
EPs: 7-inch
CAPITOL 10-20 58-60
COLUMBIA 10-20 58
LPs: 10/12-inch
ARHOOLIE (5024 "This Is Rose Maddox") ....10-15 '60s
CAPITOL (T-1312 "The One Rose") 25-35 60
(Monaural.)
CAPITOL (ST-1312 "The One Rose") 30-40 60
(Stereo.)
CAPITOL (ST-1437 "Glory Bound Train") 30-40 60
(Monaural.)
CAPITOL (ST-1437 "Glory Bound Train") 35-55 60
(Stereo.)
CAPITOL (T-1548 "Big Bouquet of Roses") 30-40 60
(Monaural.)
CAPITOL (ST-1548 "Big Bouquet of Roses") 35-45 60
(Stereo.)
CAPITOL (T-1799 "Rose Maddox Sings Bluegrass") 30-40 62
(Monaural.)
CAPITOL (ST-1799 "Rose Maddox Sings Bluegrass") 35-45 62
(Stereo.)
CAPITOL (T-1993 "Alone with You") 15-25 63
(Monaural.)
CAPITOL (ST-1993 "Alone with You") 20-30 63
(Stereo.)
COLUMBIA (1159 "Precious Memories") .40-50 58
HARMONY (7312 "Rose Maddox's Best") 10-20 64
PICKWICK/HILLTOP ....10-15 '60s
STARDAY (463 "Rosie") 10-20 70
VARRICK 6-12 83
Session: Emmylou Harris; Bill Monroe; Vern Williams; Merle Haggard and the Strangers.
Also see HAGGARD, Merle
Also see HARRIS, Emmylou
Also see MONROE, Bill
Also see OWENS, Buck, & Rose Maddox

MADDY BROTHERS
Singles: 7-inch
CELESTIAL (109 "Rockin' Party") 100-150 58
RA-RA (900 "Mixed Up") 15-25

MADHATTANS
(With Ray Ellis Orchestra)
Singles: 7-inch
ATLANTIC (1142 "Wowie") 10-20 57
Also see ELLIS, Ray, Orchestra

MADHATTERS
Singles: 7-inch
CARDINAL (72 "Game Is Done") 25-35 67
CARDINAL (77 "You May See Me Cry") ..25-35 67
Member: Dale Menton.
Also see BEST THINGS
Also see GESTURES
Also see MASON, Tommy, & Madhatters
Also see MENTON, Dale

MADISON, Al
Singles: 7-inch
GOLDEN CREST ("The Society") 10-20 61
(Selection number not known.)

MADISON, Glen
Singles: 7-inch
EBONY (105 "When You Dance") 50-75 64
Also see DELCOS

MADISON, Jerry
Singles: 7-inch
RENDEZVOUS (217 "Love Her") 5-10 63

MADISON, Ronnie
(With the Valmars, Skip Esterly & Orchestra)
Singles: 78 rpm
CORAL 10-20 57
Singles: 7-inch
CORAL (61812 "True Love Gone") 20-30 57
STORM (987 "Linda") 20-30 59

MADISON, Rosalind
Singles: 7-inch
LIBERTY (55749 "Teasin' and Cheatin' Again") 5-10 64
LIBERTY (55795 "Neighborhood Girl") 5-10 65
LIBERTY (55824 "Inconceivable") 5-10 65
REVIS (1008 "My Eyes Are Crying") 40-50
SILVER FOX (20 "Fancy") 5-10 69

MADISON & WRUBEL
Singles: 7-inch
SOULVILLE (1011 "The Masquerade Is Over") ....5-10 '60s

MADISON BROTHERS
Singles: 7-inch
APT (25050 "Trusting in You") 40-50 60
CEDARGROVE (314 "Trusting in You") 150-250 60
SURE (1002 "Give Me Your Heart") 150-250 58
V-TONE (231 "Did We Go Steady Too Soon") 40-60
Members: Farris Hill; Don Burnett; Rich Frazier; Harry Pascall.
Also see BELLTONES
Also see HILL, Farris, & Madison Brothers

MADISON REVUE
Singles: 7-inch
MADISON (4130 "Another Man") 15-25 67

MADISONS
Singles: 7-inch
JOMADA (601 "Only a Fool") 10-15 65
LAWN (240 "The Wind and the Rain") 30-40 64
LIMELIGHT (3018 "Because I Got You") . 10-15 64
MGM (13312 "Cheryl Anne") 15-25 65
Also see MADISONS / Monterays
Also see SANTOS, Larry

MADISONS / Monterays
Singles: 7-inch
TWIN-HIT (2685 "Valerie"/"I'll Be Around") 25-35 65
Also see MADISONS
Also see MONTERAYS

MADNESS, Bernie
Singles: 7-inch
BANG (529 "Bikini Beach") 10-15 66

MADONNA P&R/R&B/D&D/LP '83
Singles: 12-inch
MAVERICK (6074 "Fever") 15-20 92
(Two colored vinyl discs. Promotional issue only.)
MAVERICK (40585 "Erotica") 4-8 92
SIRE (20212 "Borderline") 5-10 84
SIRE (20239 "Like a Virgin") 5-10 84
SIRE (20304 "Material Girl") 5-10 85
SIRE (20335 "Angel") 5-10 85
SIRE (20369 "Dress You Up") 5-10 85
SIRE (20461 "Live to Tell") 5-10 86
SIRE (20597 "Open Your Heart") 5-10 87
SIRE (20633 "La Isla Bonita") 5-10 87
SIRE (20762 "Causing a Commotion") 5-10 87
SIRE (21170 "Like a Prayer") 5-10 89
SIRE (21225 "Express Yourself") 5-10 89
SIRE (21427 "Keep It Together") 5-10 90
SIRE (21513 "Vogue") 5-10 90
SIRE (21820 "Justify My Love") 5-10 91
SIRE (21813 "Rescue Me") 5-10 91
SIRE (23867 "Holiday") 5-10 83
SIRE (26553 "True Blue") 5-10 86
SIRE (29715 "Physical Attraction") 5-10 83
SIRE (29899 "Everybody") 8-12 82
(Promotional issue only.)
Singles: 7-inch
GEFFEN 3-5 85
SIRE (Black vinyl) 3-6 83-92
SIRE (28591 "True Blue") 5-8 86
(Colored vinyl.)
Picture Sleeves
GEFFEN 3-5 85
SIRE (Except 29354) 3-8 83-90
SIRE (29354 "Borderline") 5-10 84
(Poster sleeve.)
LPs: 10/12-inch
Sire (7311 "Bedtime Stories") 45-55 94
(Two colored vinyl discs. Promotional issue only.)
SIRE (23867 "Madonna") 5-8 83
SIRE (25157 "Like a Virgin") 5-8 83
(Black vinyl.)
SIRE (1-25157 "Like a Virgin") 75-125 83
(Colored vinyl. Promotional issue only.)
SIRE (25442 "True Blue") 5-8 86
SIRE (25611 "Who's That Girl") 5-8 87
SIRE (25535 "You Can Dance") 5-8 87
SIRE (25844 "Like a Prayer") 5-8 89
SIRE (26209 "I'm Breathless") 5-8 90
Also see BERLIN / Madonna

MADRI HI FIVE
Singles: 7-inch
VEE-JAY (523 "Putti Putti") 10-20 63

MADURA LP '71
Singles: 7-inch
COLUMBIA (45483 "Johnny B. Goode") 4-6 71
LPs: 10/12-inch
COLUMBIA (30794 "Madura") 15-20 71
(Two discs.)
COLUMBIA (32545 "Madura II") 5-10 73

MADURI, Carl
Singles: 7-inch
CAMEO (202 "What a Night") 5-10 61
MERCURY (71084 "A Girl in Her Teens") . 5-10 57
ROULETTE (4667 "I Love You More Than Yesterday") 5-8 66
WARWICK (604 "The Joker") 5-10 60

MAEDER, Gene
Singles: 7-inch
VANDA (702 "Gremlin in the Kremlin") 8-12

MAESTRO, Johnny P&R '61
(With the Crests; with Coeds; with Del Satins; Johnny Mastro)
Singles: 7-inch
APT (25075 "She's All Mine Alone") 30-40 65
BUDDAH 5-10 71-72
CAMEO (256 "I'll Be True") 15-25 63
CAMEO (305 "Lean On Me") 15-25 64
COED (545 "Model Girl") 15-25 61
COED (549 "What a Surprise") 15-25 61
COED (552 "Mr Happiness") 15-25 61
COED (557 "I.O.U.") 30-40 61
COED (562 "Besame Baby") 300-400 62
COLLECTABLES ....3-5 '80s
PARKWAY (118 "Is It You") 5-10 67
PARKWAY (987 "Heartburn") 5-10 66
PARKWAY (987 "Heartburn") 10-15 66
(Single sided disc. Promotional issue only.)
PARKWAY (999 "Come See Me") 5-10 66
POPULAR REQUEST (103 "I'll Be True") 3-5 94
SCEPTER (12112 "I'm Stepping Out of the Picture") 20-30 65
U.A. (474 "Before I Loved Her") 20-30 62
LPs: 10/12-inch
BUDDAH (5091 "The Johnny Maestro Story") 25-35 71
(Price includes inserts.)
HARVEY (1000 "His Biggest Hits with the Crests and Brooklyn Bridge") 10-20 81
(Two-LP set. Black vinyl. Issued with three different covers: two gatefold and one standard.)
HARVEY (1000 "His Biggest Hits with the Crests and Brooklyn Bridge") 10-20 81
(Two-LP set. Colored vinyl.)
Also see BROOKLYN BRIDGE
Also see CRESTS
Also see DEL SATINS
Also see MASTERS, Johnny

MAESTRO, Johnny, / Tymes
Singles: 7-inch
POPULAR REQUEST 3-5 94
Also see MAESTRO, Johnny
Also see TYMES

MAFFITT & DAVIES
Singles: 7-inch
CAPITOL (2311 "Forest Lawn")..........5-10 68
LPs: 10/12-inch
CAPITOL (2999 "Rise and Fall of Honesty")..........10-15 68

MAGEE, Al
Singles: 7-inch
ARIES (7-10-2 "You Can Count On Me") 20-30 61
(Maroon label.)
ARIES (1262 "You Can Count On Me")... 10-20 61
(Light blue label.)

MAGEE, Sterling
Singles: 7-inch
TANGERINE (968 "Get in My Arms Little Girl")..........5-10 67
TANGERINE (975 "Tighten Up")..........5-10 67

MAGESTRO, Miss Toni
Singles: 7-inch
U.S.A. (1223 "Broken Hearted Over You")..........20-30 59

MAGI
Singles: 7-inch
WAND (197 "Rockin' Crickets")..........8-12 65

MAGI
LPs: 10/12-inch
UNCLE DIRTY'S (6102 "Win Or Lose")..........250-350 72
Members: Tom Stevens; Larry Stutzman.

MAGI
Singles: 7-inch
CLARIDGE (431 Overnight Sensation").. 15-25 77
FARR (71271 "Rock & Roll Lady")..........10-20 71
MONSTER (0001 "I Think I Love You")... 10-20 '60s

MAGIC
Singles: 7-inch
ARMADILLO (22 "One Minus Two")..........10-20 69
ARMADILLO (23 "California")..........10-20 70
MONSTER (0001 "I Think I Love You")... 15-25
LPs: 10/12-inch
ARMADILLO (8031 "Enclosed")..........200-400 70
RARE EARTH (527 "Magic")..........10-15 71
Members: Nick King; Duane King; Joey Myrcia; Gary Harger.

MAGIC, Awood
Singles: 7-inch
MINIT (621 "It's Better to Dream")..........5-10 61

MAGIC CHRISTIANS
Singles: 7-inch
COMMONWEALTH UNITED (3006 "Come and Get It")..........5-10 69
Member: Trevor Burton.
Also see MOVE, The

MAGIC CIRCLE
Singles: 7-inch
MIRA (216 "I Was Bewitched")..........5-10 66
PARIS TOWER (119 "I Put a Spell on You")..........10-15 67

MAGIC FERN
Singles: 7-inch
JERDEN (813 "Maggie")..........15-20 66
PICCADILLY (235 "Maggie")..........10-15 67
(Same number used for a Dave Lewis release.)
PICCADILLY (240 "Nellie")..........10-15 67
LPs: 10/12-inch
PANORAMA (108 "Magic Fern")..........100-150 80

MAGIC FLEET
Singles: 7-inch
HOT BISCUIT (1453 "So Is Our Song")......5-10 68

MAGIC GRASS
Singles: 7-inch
DECCA (32544 "Ain't It Nice")..........5-10 69

MAGIC KNIGHTS
Singles: 7-inch
CEE=JAY (577 "Searching for Tomorrow")..........20-30 60

MAGIC LANTERNS *P&R '68*
Singles: 7-inch
ATLANTIC..........5-10 68-70
BIG TREE (109 "One Night Stand")..........4-8 70
BIG TREE (113 "Let the Sunshine In")..........4-8 71
CHARISMA (100 "Country Woman")..........4-6 72
EPIC (10062 "Excuse Me Baby")..........5-10 66
EPIC (10111 "Simple Things")..........5-10 66
Picture Sleeves
EPIC (10062 "Excuse Me Baby")..........10-15 66
LPs: 10/12-inch
ATLANTIC (8217 "Shame Shame")..........12-15 69
Members: Jim Bilsbury; Bev Beveridge; Mike "Ozzy" Osborne; Peter Garner; Harry Paul Ward; Albert Hammond.

MAGIC MUSHROOM
Singles: 7-inch
W.B. (5846 "I'm Gone")..........15-25 66
Also see SONS

MAGIC MUSHROOMS *P&R '66*
Singles: 7-inch
A&M (815 "Never More")..........10-15 66
EAST COAST (1001 "Let the Rain Be Me")..........10-15 68
PHILIPS (40483 "Look in My Face")..........10-15 67
Members: Chris Gaylord; Michael Allen.
Also see LYRICS

MAGIC NOTES
Singles: 7-inch
ERA (1035 "Never Again")..........50-60 57

MAGIC NOTES
Singles: 7-inch
BLUE BEAT (51 "Rosabel")..........150-250 64

MAGIC PLANTS
Singles: 7-inch
VERVE (10377 "I'm a Nothing")..........20-30 66
Member: Tom Finn.
Also see LEFT BANKE

MAGIC REIGN
Singles: 7-inch
JAMIE (1364 "Mirrors")..........5-10 68
JAMIE (1374 "Jefferson Street")..........5-10 69

MAGIC RING
Singles: 7-inch
MUSIC FACTORY (404 "Do I Love You")..5-10 68
SMASH (2128 "Frodo Lives")..........5-10 67
TANTRA (3105 "Do I Love You")..........10-20 '60s

MAGIC SAM
(Sam Maghett)
Singles: 78 rpm
COBRA..........15-25 57
Singles: 7-inch
BRIGHT STAR (1037 "I'll Pay You Back") .5-10 69
CHIEF (7013 "Mr. Charlie")..........30-40 60
CHIEF (7017 "Square Dance Rock")..........30-40 60
CHIEF (7026 "Every Night About This Time")..........30-40 61
CHIEF (7033 "Blue Light Boogie")..........30-40 61
COBRA (5013 "All Your Love")..........40-60 57
COBRA (5021 "Everything Gonna Be Alright")..........20-30 58
COBRA (5025 "All Night Long")..........20-30 58
COBRA (5029 "Easy, Baby")..........40-60 58
CRASH (425 "Out of Bad Luck")..........8-12 66
MINIT (32070 "I'll Pay You Back")..........5-8 69

MAGIC SAM BLUES BAND
LPs: 10/12-inch
DELMARK (615 "West Side Soul")..........10-15 68
DELMARK (620 "Black Magic")..........10-15 68
INTERMEDIA..........5-10 84

MAGIC SAND
LPs: 10/12-inch
UNI (73094 "Magic Sand")..........10-12 71

MAGIC SHIP
Singles: 7-inch
B.T. PUPPY (548 "Green Plant")..........10-20 68
Members: Tom Nikosey; Cosmo Riozzi; Phil Polimeni; Mike Garrigan; Rob Buckman.
Also see MAJIC SHIP

MAGIC SLIM & TEARDROPS
Singles: 7-inch
JA-WES (0105 "Love My Baby")..........25-50 68
MEAN MISTREATER..........8-12
EPs: 7-inch
ROOSTER BLUES..........5-8 81
LPs: 10/12-inch
ALLIGATOR..........5-8 82

MAGIC STRAY
Singles: 7-inch
TRY (630 "Give Me Your Love")..........20-30

MAGIC SWIRLING SHIP
Singles: 7-inch
CADET (5642 "Love in Your Eyes")..........15-25 68

MAGIC TONES
(Magic-Tones)
Singles: 78 rpm
KING..........100-150 53
Singles: 7-inch
HOWFUM (3686 "Tears in My Eyes")..........2500-3500 57
(Identification number shown since no selection number is used.)
KING (4665 "When I Kneel Down to Pray")..........500-750 53
KING (4681 "How Can You Treat Me This Way")..........500-750 53
Members: Gene Hawkins; Arthur Williams; James Williams; Willie Stokes; Joseph Reed.

MAGIC TONES / Mustangs
Singles: 7-inch
STOOP SOUNDS (502 "Tears in My Eye"/"Over the Rainbow")..........100-150 96
(Limited edition. Estimates range from less than 10 to a few dozen made.)
Also see MAGIC TONES
Also see MUSTANGS

MAGIC TONES
(Magictones)
Singles: 7-inch
MAH'S (1037 "It's Better to Love")..........10-15 68
WESTBOUND (152 "How Can I Forget You")..........10-20 69
WESTBOUND (180 "I've Changed")..........10-20 71
WHEELSVILLE (106 "Got to Get a Little Closer")..........15-25 66
WHEELSVILLE (114 "How Can I Forget You")..........75-125 66
Also see UNDISPUTED TRUTH

MAGIC TYMES
Singles: 7-inch
MALA (541 "Happy Feet Night")..........5-10 66

MAGICHORDS
Singles: 78 rpm
DOMINO (311 "Be Sure")..........10-15 50
REGAL (3238 "Darling")..........10-15 49

MAGICIANS
Singles: 7-inch
COLUMBIA (43435 "An Invitation to Cry") .5-10 65
COLUMBIA (43608 "About My Love")..........5-10 66
COLUMBIA (43725 "And I'll Tell the World")..........5-10 65
COLUMBIA (44061 "Double Good Feeling")..........5-10 67
Picture Sleeves
COLUMBIA (43435 "An Invitation to Cry")..........10-20 65
Members: Mike Appell; Garry Bonner; Everett Jacobs; Alan Gordon; John Townley; Jake Jacobs.
Also see TEX & CHEX

MAGICIANS
Singles: 7-inch
VILLA (703 "Love, Let's Try Again")..........25-50 66
VILLA (704 "Why Do I Do These Foolish Things")..........75-100 66
VILLA (706 "Why Must You Cry")..........50-75 66
(Has "Villa Records" on two lines at top.)
VILLA (706-A "Why Must You Cry")..........15-25 66
(Has "Villa Records" on one line at top.)

MAGICIANS
Singles: 7-inch
LONDON (1006 "Tarzan")..........5-10 66

MAGICS
Singles: 7-inch
DEBRA (1003 "Chapel Bells")..........40-50 63
(First issued as by the Palisades. Some copies have "Magics" label applied on top of "Palisades" one.)
Also see GENOVA, Tommy
Also see LANZO, Mike, & Blue Counts
Also see PALISADES
Also see PRECISIONS

MAGICS
Singles: 7-inch
BELL (606 "Zombie Walk")..........5-10 64

MAGICS
Singles: 7-inch
RFA (100 "If I Didn't Have You")..........10-20 '60s

MAGISTRATES *P&R '68*
Singles: 7-inch
MGM..........8-12 68-69
Member: Jean Hillary; Arnie Silver; Jerry [Summers] Gross; Mike [Dennis] Freda.
Also see DOVELLS

MAGNA CARTA
Singles: 7-inch
DUNHILL (4257 "Airport Song")..........4-8 70
LPs: 10/12-inch
ARIOLA AMERICA (50014 "Puttin' It Back")..........8-12
DUNHILL (50091 "Seasons")..........10-15 70
VERTIGO (6360-040 "Songs from Wasties Orchard")..........10-15 71

MAGNATONES
Singles: 7-inch
CEDARGROVE (313 "I Need You")..........100-150 60
TIME (108 "I Need You")..........30-40

MAGNATONES
Singles: 7-inch
FORTUNE (555 "Adios, My Desert Love")..........25-35 63

MAGNETIC FORCE
Singles: 7-inch
MALBEE (7801 "Touch Me")..........50-75 '60s

MAGNETICS
Singles: 7-inch
ALLRITE (620 "Where Are You")..........30-40 62
BONNIE (107374 "Lady in Green")..........500-1000
(We're not sure if this is the selection number or identification number.)
J.V. (2501 "Oh Love")..........10-20

MAGNETICS
LPs: 10/12-inch
ROLLIN' ROCK..........5-10 82
Members: Tom Svornich; Freda Johnson; Jeff Poskin; Steve Grindle; Tom Berghan.

MAGNETS
Singles: 7-inch
GROOVE (0058 "You Just Say the Word")..........30-40 65
RCA (7391 "When the School Bells Ring")..........15-20 58

MAGNETS
Singles: 7-inch
KEYS (3 "Swingin' Organ")..........10-15 59

MAGNETS
Singles: 7-inch
LONDON (10036 "Drag Race")..........8-12 63

MAGNIFICENT FOUR
Singles: 7-inch
BLAST (210 "The Closer You Are")..........10-20 63
COLLECTABLES..........3-5 '80s
WHALE (506 "The Closer You Are")..........30-40 61

MAGNIFICENT MALOCHI
Singles: 7-inch
BRUNSWICK (55359 "As Time Goes By")..........5-10 68

MAGNIFICENT MEN *P&R/LP '67*
Singles: 7-inch
CAPITOL..........5-10 66-68
MERCURY (72988 "Holly Go Softly")..........4-8 70
LPs: 10/12-inch
CAPITOL..........10-20 67-68
MERCURY..........8-12 70
Members: Dave Bupp; Buddy King; Tom Pane; Bob Angelucci; Tommy Hoover; Jimmy Seville; Terry Crousore; Billy Richter.
Also see DEL-CHORDS

MAGNIFICENT MONTA-GUE
Singles: 7-inch
ERA (1069 "The Breather")..........8-12 58

MAGNIFICENT SEVEN
Singles: 7-inch
THELMA (12282 "The Groove")............ 50-75 63
(Previously issued as *Let's Do It*, by Don Davis & His Groovers.)
VEE-EIGHT (1003 "Baby Doll")........... 250-300 '60s
Also see DAVIS, Don, & His Groovers

MAGNIFICENT 7
(Magnificent VII)
Singles: 7-inch
DIAL (4074 "Ooh Baby Baby")................ 10-20 68
DIMENSION (1050 "Show Me").............. 10-15 65
EASTERN (611 "Since You've Been Gone").. 20-30 66
LEMCO (882 "Stubborn Kind of Fellow"). 10-20 65

MAGNIFICENT SIX
Singles: 7-inch
L BROWN (01659 "Forever More")......... 20-30 '60s
(Identification number shown since no selection number is used.)

MAGNIFICENTS *R&B '56*
Singles: 78 rpm
VEE-JAY.. 25-75 56-58
Singles: 7-inch
CHECKER (1016 "Do You Mind")..............5-10 62
COLLECTABLES..3-5 '80s
KANSOMA (03 "Do You Mind")............... 15-25 62
VEE-JAY (183 "Up on the Mountain")...... 50-75 56
(Black vinyl.)
VEE-JAY (183 "Up on the Mountain").. 400-500 56
(Red vinyl.)
VEE-JAY (208 "Caddy Bo")..................... 50-75 56
VEE-JAY (235 "Off the Mountain")........... 50-75 57
VEE-JAY (367 "Up on the Mountain")...... 15-25 60
Also see EL DORADOS

MAGNIFICENTS
Singles: 7-inch
VEE-JAY (281 "Don't Leave Me")......... 75-125 58
(Not the same group as listed above.)
Member: Al Smith.

MAGNIFICENTS
Singles: 7-inch
DEE GEE (3008 "My Heart Is Calling").... 10-20 65
SYMBOL (221 "Take Me On")................ 10-15 66

MAGNIFICENTS
Singles: 7-inch
BIRTH 5-10 69
Members: Richard Bogan; Helen Wrice; Tony Rogers; Howard West; Ron Morgan; Richard Osborne; Jake Kowal.
Also see HOT PROPERTY

MAHADY, Jack
Singles: 7-inch
DIXIE (882 "I Don't Want Two Timin' Love").. 50-75

MAHAFFAY, Chuck, & Individuals
LP: 10/12-inch
21 RECORDS 10-15 64

MAHAL, Taj *LP '69*
Singles: 7-inch
COLUMBIA (10000 series)........................4-6 75
COLUMBIA (44000 series)......................5-10 67-69
COLUMBIA (45000 series).........................4-6 69-74
Picture Sleeves
COLUMBIA (44051 "I Wish I Could Shimmy Like My Sister Kate")...5-10 67
LPs: 10/12-inch
COLUMBIA...6-12 68-81
W.B. 5-10 77
Also see RISING SONS
Also see SPRINGSTEEN, Bruce / Albert Hammond / Loudon Wainwright III / Taj Mahal

MAHALIC, Johnny
(Johnny Mihalic)
Singles: 7-inch
SELECT (725 "Cotton Fields")...................5-10 63
Also see GILREATH, James
Also see NITE-LITERS

MAHAN, Benny
Singles: 7-inch
MONUMENT (1220 "Sand Man")..................4-8 70
POMPEII (66690 "She Knows How")...........5-8 69
SCRATCH (5582 "She Knows How") 10-20

MAHAR, Jamie
Singles: 7-inch
W.B. (5479 "Slippin' and Slidin' ") 5-10 64

MAHARAJAHS
Singles: 7-inch
FLIP (332 "I Do Believe").........................10-20 58
FLIP (335 "Oh Shirley") 100-150 58

MAHARREY, Moe
Singles: 7-inch
HI (2019 "Just for a Moment")..................20-30 60
MARLO (1527 "Giddy-Upa-Ding Dong") 8-12 62

MAHOGANY
LPs: 10/12-inch
EPIC (26498 "Mahogany") 10-12 70

MAHOGANY RUSH *LP '74*
Singles: 7-inch
COLUMBIA...3-6 76-82
20TH FOX..4-6 74-75
LPs: 10/12-inch
COLUMBIA..8-12 76-82
20TH FOX..15-25 73-75
Member: Frank Marino.

MAHONEY, Bob
Singles: 7-inch
SAHARA (101 "Come Along with Me").....20-30 59

MAHONEY, John Culliton
Singles: 7-inch
AMHERST (701 "Ballad of Evil Knievel") 4-6 74
Picture Sleeves
AMHERST (701 "Ballad of Evil Knievel") .10-20 74

MAIDEN, Sidney
(With the Ramblers)
Singles: 78 rpm
FLASH...15-25 55
IMPERIAL...20-30 52
Singles: 7-inch
FLASH (101 "Hurray, Hurray Baby").........30-50 55
IMPERIAL (5189 "Honey Bee Blues").......50-75 52
LPs: 10/12-inch
PRESTIGE BLUESVILLE (1035 "Trouble an' Blues") 75-100 63

MAIDEN, Sidney / Al Simmons
Singles: 78 rpm
DIG (138 "Hand Me Down Baby")............15-25 56
Singles: 7-inch
DIG (138 "Hand Me Down Baby")............25-50 56
Also see MAIDEN, Sidney
Also see SIMMONS, Al, & Slim Green

MAIN CHANGE
Singles: 7-inch
NEBULA (Sunshine Is Her Way") 50-75 71
(Selection number not known.)

MAIN EVENTS
Singles: 7-inch
U.A. (50810 "Girl I Want You to Remember") 20-30 71

MAIN INGREDIENT *P&R/R&B/LP '70*
("Featuring Cuba Gooding")
Singles: 7-inch
POLYDOR...3-5 89-90
RCA (0046 thru 0939)..............................4-8 70-74
RCA (10095 thru 12060)...........................3-6 74-80
ZAKIA (015 "Do Me Right").........................3-6 86
Picture Sleeves
RCA (0517 "Black Seeds Keep On Growing")...5-8 71
LPs: 10/12-inch
COLLECTABLES...5-8 88
RCA (0335 thru 1558).................................8-12 74-77
RCA (3641 "Ready for Love") 8-10 80
RCA (3963 "I Only Have Eyes for You").....8-10 81
RCA (4253 thru 4834) 10-15 70-73
Members: Cuba Gooding; Don McPherson; Luther Simmons; Tony Sylvester.
Session: Stevie Wonder.
Also see WONDER, Stevie

MAINSTREETERS
Singles: 7-inch
HANOVER (4518 "Tony's Folly") 15-25 59

MAJESTEES
Singles: 7-inch
MUTT (18382 "Let Her Go").......................15-25 68

MAJESTIC
Singles: 7-inch
EQUATOR (1401 "Send My Baby Back to Me") 40-50

MAJESTICS
Singles: 78 rpm
MARLIN (802 "Nitey Nite")...................300-400 56
Singles: 7-inch
MARLIN (802 "Nitey Nite")................1200-1500 56
Members: John McArthur; Sam Moore.
Also see CULMER, Little Iris
Also see SAM & DAVE

MAJESTICS
(With the Nightwinds; Majestic's)
Singles: 7-inch
CONTOUR (501 "Hard Times") 10-20 60
EIGHT BALL (7591 "Big Time")...............10-20 59
FOXIE (7004 "Lone Stranger") 5-10 61
NRC (502 "Please Don't Say No")........100-200 58
SIOUX (91459 "Lone Stranger")..............30-40 59
20TH FOX (171 "Lone Stranger")............10-15 59

MAJESTICS
(With Al Rogers & His Combo)
Singles: 7-inch
KNIGHT (105 "Pennies for a Beggar") .300-400 60
(Reportedly 200 made.)

MAJESTICS
Singles: 7-inch
BOARDWALK (121 "Girl of My Dreams") 3-5 91
JORDAN (123 "Angel of Love") 40-50 61
(Black vinyl. First issue.)
JORDAN (123 "Angel of Love") 100-150 61
(Yellow vinyl.)
LINDA (111 "Strange World")....................20-30 63
LINDA (121 "Girl of My Dreams") 75-125 65
NU-TONE (123 "Angel of Love")...............20-30 61
PIXIE (6901 "Angel Of Love") 10-15 61

MAJESTICS
Singles: 7-inch
SALVATION (11 "Movin' On")....................8-12 62

MAJESTICS
Singles: 7-inch
CHANSON (1007 "Safari")..........................10-15 62
CHANSON (1008 "Blue Flame")..............10-15 62
CHESS (1802 "Oasis")...............................10-15 61

MAJESTICS
(Johnny Mitchell & Majestics)
Singles: 7-inch
CHEX (1000 "Give Me a Cigarette").........50-60 62
CHEX (1000 "So I Can Forget")...............30-40 62
(Same number used twice.)
CHEX (1004 "Unhappy & Blue")...............30-40 62
CHEX (1006 "Lonely Heart")....................30-40 62
CHEX (1009 "Baby") 15-25 63
V.I.P. (25028 "Say You") 400-600 65
(Promotional issue only.)
Also see MITCHELL, Johnny

MAJESTICS
Singles: 7-inch
BOSS (1001 "Let's Make It")....................10-20 '60s
DUNES (2014 "Boss Walk").......................10-20 62
SAM (112 "Jaguar")...................................20-30 62
SAM (117 "Riptide")...................................20-30 62
SAM (123 "XL-3") 20-30 62
Also see PHANTOMS

MAJESTICS
Singles: 7-inch
DAMEN ("Judy") 10-20 63
(No selection number used.)

MAJESTICS
Singles: 7-inch
JCP (1018 "Round & Round")...................10-20 64

MAJESTICS
Singles: 7-inch
MGM (13488 "Love Has Forgotten Me") 5-10 66

MAJESTICS
Singles: 7-inch
MALA (574 "Doin' the Best I Can") 5-10 67

MAJESTICS
Singles: 7-inch
VINTAGE (1002 "Symbol of Love") 10-15 73
(Blue vinyl.)

MAJIC SHIP
Singles: 7-inch
B.T. PUPPY (548 "Green Plant")..................5-10 68
CRAZY HORSE (1311 "Hummin'")..........10-20 69
CRAZY HORSE (1317 "On the Edge")....10-20 69
CRAZY HORSE (1322 "Night Time Music")...10-20 70
MAGIC-L (519 "Hummin' ") 20-30 66
P.I.P. (8936 "Wednesday Morning Dew") ..8-12 73
LPs: 10/12-inch
BEL AMI (711 "Majic Ship") 300-500 67
Members: Tom Nikosey; Cosmo Riozzi; Phil Polimeni; Mike Garrigan; Rob Buckman.
Also see MAGIC SHIP

MAJIC STRAY
Singles: 7-inch
TRY (630 "Give Me Your Love")..................5-10 69

MAJOR & LIEUTENANTS
Singles: 7-inch
NIGHT OWL (6812 "The Thing") 10-20 68

MAJOR ARCANA
LP: 10/12-inch
A MAJOR...10-15 76
Members: Jim Spencer; Jay Borkenhagen; Sigmund Snopek; Tom Ruppenthal.
Also see BAROQUES
Also see BLOOMSBURY PEOPLE

MAJOR IV
Singles: 7-inch
VENTURE (606 "Down in the Ghetto") 25-40 67
VENTURE (608 "I Don't Believe in Losing") 10-15 67
VENTURE (619 "Just Another Lonely Night")..10-15 68

MAJOR SIX / Glass Opening
Singles: 7-inch
DONDEE (1 "Virgin of Time"/"All Those Lies")..20-25 '70s
Also see GLASS OPENING

MAJORETTES
Singles: 7-inch
TROY (1000 "White Levis") 15-25 63
TROY (1004 "Let's Do the Kangaroo")..... 10-15 63
Picture Sleeves
TROY (1000 "White Levis") 25-35 63
Member: Becky Page; Sheila Page; Joanna Page; Suzy Page.

MAJORITY
Singles: 7-inch
LONDON (9779 "Pretty Little Girl")............5-10 65

MAJORS
Singles: 78 rpm
DERBY (763 "At Last")...........................300-400 51
DERBY (779 "Laughing on the Outside")...300-400 51
Members: Bernard Beckum; Scott Alvin; Clyde Lee; Billy Bee Bee.

MAJORS
Singles: 7-inch
FELSTED (8501 "Rockin' the Boogie") 15-25 58
FELSTED (8576 "Les Qua") 20-30 59
FELSTED (8707 "Les Qua") 5-10 65
FELSTED (8707 "I Found My Love")........10-15 65

MAJORS / Belltones
Singles: 7-inch
EXCALIBUR (500 "Les Qua"/"Swingin' Little Chickie")...3-5 88
Also see BELLTONES
Also see MAJORS

MAJORS *P&R/R&B '62*
Singles: 7-inch
IMPERIAL (5855 "A Wonderful Dream") .. 15-20 62
IMPERIAL (5879 "A Little Bit Now") 15-20 62
IMPERIAL (5914 "What in the World")..... 10-15 63
IMPERIAL (5936 "Tra La La")................... 10-15 63
IMPERIAL (5968 "Get Up Now") 10-15 63
IMPERIAL (5991 "Your Life Begins")....... 10-15 63
IMPERIAL (66009 "I'll Be There")............ 10-15 63
LPs: 10/12-inch
IMPERIAL (9222 "Meet the Majors")........50-75 63
(Monaural.)
IMPERIAL (12222 "Meet the Majors")....50-100 63
(Stereo.)

Members: Ricky Cordo; Eugene Glass; Idella Morris; Frank Troutt; Ronald Gathers.

MAJORS
(With the Osie Johnson Orchestra)
Singles: 78 rpm
ORIGINAL (1003 "Big Eyes") 75-100 54
Singles: 7-inch
ORIGINAL (1003 "Big Eyes") 150-250 54
(Colored vinyl.)

MAJORS
Singles: 7-inch
BIG THREE (403 "Lost in the City") .... 40-50 '60s
MAGNET 10-20

MAKEBA, Miriam LP '63
("Milton Okun, Conductor")
Singles: 7-inch
KAPP (452 "Can't Cross Over") 5-10 62
MERCURY (72642 "Mommy, Mommy What Is Heaven Like") 4-6 66
RCA (8326 "Forbidden Games") 5-8 64
REPRISE (0578 "Reza") 4-8 67
REPRISE (0606 "Pata Pata") 4-8 67
REPRISE (0654 "Malayisha") 4-8 68
REPRISE (0671 "What Is Love") 4-8 68
REPRISE (0732 "Pata Pata"/"Malayisha") ... 4-8 69
REPRISE (0804 "I Shall Be Released") 4-8 69
EPs: 7-inch
RCA (100 "Miriam Makeba") 5-10 60
LPs: 10/12-inch
KAPP (1274 "Many Voices Of") 10-15 62
(Monaural.)
KAPP (3274 "Many Voices Of") 15-20 62
(Stereo.)
MERCURY 10-15 66
PETERS INT'L 5-8 81
RCA 10-20 60-68
REPRISE 10-15 67
Also see BELAFONTE, Harry, & Miriam Makeba
Also see MANHATTAN BROTHERS & MIRIAM MAKEBA

MAKEM, Tommy
LPs: 10/12-inch
TRADITION 20-40 61
Also see CLANCY BROTHERS & TOMMY MAKEM

MALABOUS RON
Singles: 7-inch
TOMI (8-9019 "Start All Over") 8-12 68

MALACHI
LPs: 10/12-inch
VERVE (5024 "Holy Music") 20-30 67
(Monaural.)
VERVE (6-5024 "Holy Music") 30-40 67
(Stereo.)

MALCOLM & CHRIS
LPs: 10/12-inch
BLUES TIME (9008 "Just the Blues") 10-12 70

MALCONTENTS
Singles: 7-inch
GEMS (18348 "Motivated Action") 8-12

MALDONEERS
(With the Deltairs)
Singles: 7-inch
VINTAGE (1015 "Maria My Love") 10-15 73
(Yellow vinyl.)
Member: Johnny Maldon.
Also see DELTAIRS

MALEMEN
Singles: 7-inch
P.H. (3455 "My Little Girl") 15-25

MALIBUS
Singles: 7-inch
MALIBU (1 "Cry") 15-25 65
PLANET (58 "Cry") 10-15 65

MALIBUS
Singles: 7-inch
DUKE (457 "I Just Can't Stand It") 10-20
SURE SHOT (5008 "A Chance for You and Me") 10-15 65
SURE SHOT (5014 "I Had a Dream") 10-15 66
SURE SHOT (5028 "Gee Babe") 8-12 67
SURE SHOT (5037 "Summertime") 8-12 68

MALIBUS
Singles: 7-inch
ORLYN (66312 "Baby, Let Me Take You Home") 8-12
QUILL (104 "Runaway") 10-20 65

MALIBUS
(Malibu's)
Singles: 7-inch
WHITE WHALE (289 "Broken Man") 5-10 68

MALIBU-BUS
(Malibu-Bu's)
Singles: 7-inch
CRH (101 "Caravan") 10-20 62

MALLARD, Sax
Singles: 78 rpm
CHECKER (750 "Slow Caboose") 25-50 52
CHECKER (755 "I'm Yours") 25-50 52
MERCURY (70002 "Bunny Hop") 10-15 52
Singles: 7-inch
MERCURY (70002 "Bunny Hop") 15-25 52
Also see CHICAGO ALL STARS
Also see CORONETS

MALLETT, Saundra, & Vandellas
Singles: 7-inch
TAMLA (54067 "Camel Walk") 400-600 62
(Reissued as by LaBrenda Ben.)
Also see BEN, LaBrenda
Also see ELGINS
Also see MARTHA & VANDELLAS

MALONE, Mike
(With the Misters)
Singles: 7-inch
SIMS (266 "Don't Lecture Me") 5-10 66
TOKEN (1002 "It Must Be Raining") 20-30 63

MALONE, Penny
LPs: 10/12-inch
JUBILEE (16 "Penny Malone Sings an Album of Sophisticated Songs") 25-50 55
(10-inch LP.)

MALONE, Ronnie
Singles: 7-inch
FLAGSHIP (914 "My Snow Man") 10-20 57
JUDD (1004 "Lightning Bug") 10-20 58

MALONE, Tommie
(Blind Tom Malone)
Singles: 78 rpm
DECCA 10-20 55
Singles: 7-inch
DECCA (29442 "I'm Wading in Deep Water") 15-25 55
EBONY (1055 "Cow Cow Shake") 20-30 60

MALONE, Tommy
Singles: 7-inch
STERLING (901 "It's Been So Long Baby") 100-200 55
(Red vinyl.)

MALONEY, Annie
Singles: 7-inch
WHIPPET (205 "Now Hear This") 8-12 57

MALOY, Vince
Singles: 7-inch
ANGLE TONE (520 "Flying Love") 75-125 57
END (1019 "Hubba Hubba Ding Dong") 450-550 58
FELSTED (8569 "Draggin' All Night") 50-75 59
1223 (475 "I've Been 'Round Your Door Before") 75-100 57
WEB ("Falling in Love") 150-250
(Selection number not known.)

MALTAIS, Gene
(With the Gibson String Band)
Singles: 78 rpm
DECCA (30387 "Crazy Baby") 100-150 57
Singles: 7-inch
DECCA (30387 "Crazy Baby") 100-200 57
DEEP RIVER (1001 "Begone Come the Dawn") 10-15 77
(500 made.)
LILAC (3159 "The Raging Sea") 200-300 57
MASSABESIC (101 "Raging Sea") 10-15 75
REGAL (7502 "Lovemakin'") 100-150 58
Picture Sleeves
DEEP RIVER (1001 "Begone Come the Dawn") 10-15 77
(200 made.)

MALTEES FOUR
Singles: 7-inch
PACIFIC CHALLENGER (111 "You") 10-15 66

MAMA & SOUL BABIES
Singles: 7-inch
LAURIE (3485 "Soul Babies") 5-10 69

MAMA CATS
Singles: 7-inch
HIDEOUT (1225 "Miss You") 10-20 66

MAMA LION
Singles: 7-inch
FAMILY PRODUCTIONS 4-6 72-73
LPs: 10/12-inch
FAMILY PRODUCTIONS (2702 "Mama Lion") 15-20 72
FAMILY PRODUCTIONS (2713 "Give It Everything I've Got") 10-15 73

MAMAS & PAPAS P&R/LP '66
Singles: 7-inch
ABC 4-6 70
DUNHILL (4020 "California Dreamin' ") 5-10 65
DUNHILL (4026 "Monday Monday") 5-10 66
DUNHILL (4031 "I Saw Her Again") 5-10 66
DUNHILL (4050 "Look Through Any Window") 5-10 66
DUNHILL (4057 "Words of Love") 5-10 66
DUNHILL (4077 "Dedicated to the One I Love") 5-10 67
DUNHILL (4083 "Creeque Alley") 5-10 67
(Commercial issue.)
DUNHILL (4083 "Creeque Alley") 25-35 67
(Promotional issue, alternate mix.)
DUNHILL (4099 "Twelve Thirty") 5-10 67
DUNHILL (4107 "Glad to Be Unhappy") 5-10 67
DUNHILL (4113 "Dancing Bear") 5-10 67
DUNHILL (4125 "Safe in My Garden") 5-10 68
DUNHILL (4145 "Dream a Little Dream of Me") 5-10 68
DUNHILL/ABC (13 "Special Radio Interview with Mama Cass and Papa John") 25-50 70
DUNHILL/ABC (4150 "For the Love of Ivy") 5-10 68
DUNHILL/ABC (4171 "Do You Wanna Dance") 5-10 68
DUNHILL/ABC (4301 "Step Out") 5-8 72
MCA 3-5 80-82
Picture Sleeves
DUNHILL/ABC (13 "Special Radio Interview with Mama Cass and Papa John") 40-60 70
DUNHILL (4020 "California Dreamin' ") .. 50-100 65
(Promotional issue only.)
DUNHILL (4083 "Creeque Alley") 35-45 67
(Promotional issue only.)
DUNHILL (4113 "Dancing Bear") 8-10 67
EPs: 7-inch
ABC (50106 "People Like Us") 8-15 71
(Juke box issue.)
DUNHILL ("If You Can Believe Your Eyes and Ears") 10-20 66
(Juke box issue. Selection number not known.)
LPs: 10/12-inch
ABC (30005 "The Mamas and the Papas") 5-10 76
DUNHILL (50006 "If You Can Believe Your Eyes and Ears") 10-20 66
DUNHILL (50010 "The Mamas and the Papas") 10-20 66
DUNHILL (50014 "The Mamas and the Papas Deliver") 10-20 67
DUNHILL (50025 "Farewell to the First Golden Era") 10-20 67
DUNHILL (50031 "Presented By") 10-20 68
DUNHILL (50038 "Golden Era, Vol. 2") 10-20 68
DUNHILL (50064 "16 of Their Greatest Hits") 10-20 69
DUNHILL (50073 "Gathering of Flowers") 10-20 70
DUNHILL (50100 "Historic Performances") 10-20 70
DUNHILL (50106 "People Like Us") 10-20 71
DUNHILL (50145 "20 Golden Hits") 10-20 73
(Two discs.)
MCA (709 "Farewell to the First Golden Era") 5-10 80
MCA (710 "Presented By") 5-10 80
MCA (6019 "Best of the Mamas and the Papas") 8-10 82
(Two discs.)
MCA (37145 "16 of Their Greatest Hits") ... 5-10 80
MCA (50145 "20 Golden Hits") 5-10 73
PICKWICK (3352 "California Dreamin' ") ... 5-10 72
PICKWICK (3380 "Monday Monday") 5-10 72
TEE VEE (50145 "20 Greatest Hits") 5-10 73
Members: John Phillips; "Mama" Cass Elliot; Denny Doherty; Michelle Phillips.
Also see BIG THREE
Also see ELLIOT, Cass
Also see PHILLIPS, John

MAMAS & PAPAS / Association / Fifth Dimension
LPs: 10/12-inch
TEE VEE/W.B. SPECIAL PRODUCTIONS 10-20 79
Also see ASSOCIATION
Also see FIFTH DIMENSION

MAMAS & PAPAS / Barry McGuire
EPs: 7-inch
DUNHILL (50005 "This Precious Time") .. 10-15 66
Also see MAMAS & PAPAS
Also see McGUIRE, Barry

MAMMARELLA, Tony
Singles: 7-inch
SWAN (4226 "Eve of Tomorrow") 5-10 65

MAMMOUTH
Singles: 7-inch
TIRINO 50-100 73

MAM'SELLES
Singles: 7-inch
ABC (11040 "It Won't Take Much to Bring Me Back") 5-10 68
BISON 4-8
DIAMOND (172 "Love Him") 10-15 64

MAN
Singles: 7-inch
COLUMBIA (44806 "Sister Salvation") 5-8 69
LPs: 10/12-inch
COLUMBIA (9803 "Man") 10-12 69
Member: Richard Supa.

MANCHA, Steve R&B '66
(Clyde Wilson)
Singles: 7-inch
GROOVESVILLE (1001 "You're Still in My Heart") 10-20 65
GROOVESVILLE (1002 "I Don't Want to Lose You") 8-12 66
GROOVESVILLE (1004 "Friday Night") ... 50-75 66
GROOVESVILLE (1005 "Don't Make Me a Story Teller") 8-12 67
GROOVESVILLE (1007 "Sweet Baby") ... 10-20 67
WHEELSVILLE (102 "Did My Baby Call") 50-100 65
Also see BARNES, J.J., & Steve Mancha
Also see 100 PROOF Aged in Soul
Also see TWO FRIENDS

MANCHESTER, Melissa LP '73
Singles: 12-inch
ARISTA 4-6 82
CASABLANCA 4-6 84
MCA 4-6 85
Singles: 7-inch
ARISTA 3-6 75-84
BELL 4-6 73-74
CASABLANCA 3-5 84
MB (1005 "Beautiful People") 5-10 67
MCA 3-5 85
LPs: 10/12-inch
ARISTA 8-10 75-83
BELL 10-12 73-74
CASABLANCA 5-8 84
MCA 5-8 79-85
MFSL 30-50 79
Also see NATIONAL LAMPOON

MANCHESTER, Melissa, & Peabo Bryson P&R '81
Singles: 7-inch
ARISTA (0587 "Lovers After All") 3-5 81
Also see MANCHESTER, Melissa

MANCHESTERS
Singles: 7-inch
PEAK (7043 "I Wanna Hold Your Hand") ...8-12 64
Picture Sleeves
PEAK (7043 "I Wanna Hold Your Hand") 15-25 64
LPs: 10/12-inch
DIPLOMAT (2307 "Beatlerama") 10-20 64
(Shows title only. No artist credited.)
DIPLOMAT (2307 "Beatlerama") 10-20 64
(Shown as by the Manchesters.)
GUEST STAR (2307 "Beatlerama")........ 10-20 64
(Shows title only. No artists credited.)

MANCHESTERS
Singles: 7-inch
VEE-JAY (700 "I Don't Come from England") 10-20 65
Member: David Gates.
Also see GATES, David

MANCHILD
LPs: 10/12-inch
AZRA/DIPIAZZA (1001 "Manchild")........ 10-15 84
(Picture disc.)

MANCINI, Henry LP '59
(Henry Mancini's Orchestra & Chorus)
Singles: 78 rpm
LIBERTY..5-10 56
Singles: 7-inch
LIBERTY (1400 series)............................3-5 82
LIBERTY (55045 "Four Girls in Town").... 10-15 56
LIBERTY (55060 "Hot Rod") 8-12 57
LIBERTY (55184 "Pow")..............................5-10 59
RCA (Except 8184)....................................3-8 59-85
RCA (8184 "Banzai Pipeline") 8-10 63
U.A. 4-6 78
W.B. 3-6 79-83
Picture Sleeves
RCA (Except 8184)....................................5-15 59-77
RCA (8184 "Banzai Pipeline") 10-15 63
W.B. 4-6 79
EPs: 7-inch
RCA 5-15 60-62
LPs: 10/12-inch
AVCO EMBASSY....................................... 10-20 70
CAMDEN...5-15 66-74
LIBERTY (3000 series)........................... 15-25 57-59
LIBERTY (51000 series)..............................4-8 82
MCA...6-12 75-76
PARAMOUNT 10-15 70
RCA (0013 thru 0098)..................................5-10 72-73
RCA (0270 "Country Gentleman") 5-8 74
RCA (0672 thru 1928)..................................5-10 74-76
RCA (1956 "Music from Peter Gunn") 15-25 59
RCA (2040 "More Music from Peter Gunn") 15-25 59
RCA (2101 "The Mancini Touch") 15-25 60
RCA (2147 "The Blues and the Beat")..... 15-25 60
RCA (2198 "Music from Mr. Lucky") 15-25 60
RCA (2258 "Combo")................................ 15-25 62
RCA (2314 "High Time")........................... 15-25 60
RCA (2360 "Mr. Lucky Goes Latin")......... 15-25 61
RCA (2362 "Breakfast at Tiffany's") 15-25 61
RCA (2442 "Experiment in Terror")......... 25-30 62
RCA (2559 "Hatari!")................................. 25-30 62
RCA (2600 & 2700 series)....................... 10-20 63-64
RCA (2800 & 2900 series).........................8-15 64-65
RCA (3000 series) 4-8 78
RCA (3356 "The Latin Sound of Henry Mancini") 10-20 65
RCA (3347 "Best of Henry Mancini, Volume 3") 5-8 79
RCA (3500 series) 6-12 66
RCA (3612 "Merry Mancini Christmas")... 10-15 66
RCA (3667 "Pure Gold")..............................4-8 80
RCA (3668 "Mancini Country")....................4-8 80
RCA (3694 thru 3713)............................. 10-20 66-67
RCA (3756 "Warm Shade of Ivory")............4-8 80
RCA (3822 "Best of Henry Mancini") 4-8 80
RCA (3877 "Music of Hawaii")......................4-8 81
RCA (3887 "Encore")...................................8-15 67
RCA (3943 "The Mancini Sound")................4-8 68
RCA (3954 "Country Gentleman") 4-8 67
RCA (3997 thru 4689)................................5-15 68-72
RCA (5000 series) 4-8 85
RCA (6000 series) 8-15 66-72
SUNSET...5-10 66
U.A. 10-12 70
W.B. 10-20 59-73
Also see ANN-MARGRET
Also see MATHIS, Johnny, & Henry Mancini
Also see PRIDE, Charley

MANCINI, Henry / Al Hirt / Robert Russell Bennett / Melachrino Strings
EPs: 7-inch
RCA (33-151 "Headline Hits") 8-12 61
(Promotional issue, made for Nestle's.)

MANCINI, Henry, & Doc Severinsen LP '73
LPs: 10/12-inch
RCA 5-12 72-80
Also see MANCINI, Henry

MANCINI, Nan, & JBD
LPs: 10/12-inch
WINDSONG (3498 "It's a Man's World") 8-12

MANDALA
LPs: 10/12-inch
ATLANTIC (8184 "Soul Crusade")...........20-25 68

MANDEL, Harvey LP '69
Singles: 7-inch
PHILIPS (40566 "Cristo Redentor")............5-10 68
PHILIPS (40579 "Wade in the Water") 5-10 68
LPs: 10/12-inch
JANUS..8-12 70-74
OVATION 10-15 71
PHILIPS.. 10-15 68-69
Also see CANNED HEAT

MANDELLS
Singles: 7-inch
CHESS (1794 "Darling I'm Home")..........40-50 61
HOURGLASS (004 "Now I Know")............5-10
SMART (323 "Darling I'm Home")........250-350 61
(First issue.)
SMART (325 "Because I Love You") 50-100 61
TRANS WORLD SOUND (222 "I Miss You Baby") ....25-50 '60s
TRANS WORLD SOUND (701 "There Will Be Tears)...15-20 '60s
YORK (202 "It's No Good") 150-250 63
Also see WILLIAMS, Marie

MAN-DELLS
Singles: 7-inch
DANDY (5308 "Bonnie")..........................50-75

MANDELS
Singles: 7-inch
LILLY (502 "My Kissin' Cousin") 30-40 61

MANDERINS
Singles: 7-inch
BAND BOX (236 "Going Away")..............50-75 60

MANDO & CHILI PEPPERS
EPs: 7-inch
GOLDEN CREST (3023 "On the Road with Rock & Roll") 300-400 57
LPs: 10/12-inch
GOLDEN CREST (3023 "On the Road with Rock & Roll") 500-750 57
Members: Armando Mandarez; Jesse Perales; Rudy Martinez; Joe Elizando; Jesse Garcia.
Also see BOSSMEN

MANDOLPH, Bobby
Singles: 78 rpm
SPECIALTY (603 "Malinda")......................5-10 56
Singles: 7-inch
IMPERIAL (5949 "This Thing Called Love")..10-20 63
SPECIALTY (603 "Malinda") 10-20 56
VAULT (949 "Gotta Get You Back") 5-15 69

MANDOLPH, Margaret
Singles: 7-inch
PLANETARY (102 "Silly Little Girl")..........10-20 65
PLANETARY (106 "Something Beautiful") 50-75 65

MANDRAKE
Singles: 7-inch
COLUMBIA (41858 "Witch's Twist") 5-10 60
COLUMBIA (41928 "Lost Love")................5-10 61
COLUMBIA (42004 "Thank Goodness It's Friday") 5-10 61
Member: Vic Rogers.

MANDRAKE MEMORIAL
Singles: 7-inch
POPPY 5-10 69-70
LPs: 10/12-inch
POPPY (40002 "Mandrake Memorial") 15-25 68
POPPY (40003 "Medium").......................15-25 69
POPPY (40006 "Puzzle") 20-30 70
Members: Randy Monaco; Michael Kac.

MANDRAKES
Singles: 7-inch
NOLTA (349 "Summer's End")...................5-10 61

MANDRELL, Barbara C&W '69
Singles: 7-inch
ABC 4-6 78-79
ABC/DOT 4-6 75-78
COLUMBIA 4-8 69-75
EMI 3-5 87-88
KFC (003 "Sweet Weekend Encounter")....8-12 79
(Coincides with "National Winners Kentucky Fried Chicken Song Writing Contest." Promotional issue only.)
MCA (Black vinyl) 3-6 79-86
MCA (8950 "3 Out of 3 Ain't Bad")...........40-60 79
(Picture disc. Promotional issue only.)
MCA (52737 "Fast Lanes and Country Roads")..15-20 85
(Colored vinyl. Promotional issue only.)
MCA (52802 "When You Get to the Heart")..15-20 86
(Colored vinyl. Promotional issue only.)
MOSRITE (190 "Queen for a Day") 50-75 66
Picture Sleeves
MCA..3-6 79-85
LPs: 10/12-inch
ABC 8-10 78-79
ABC/DOT 8-12 76-77
COLUMBIA 6-15 71-81
COLUMBIA SPECIAL PRODUCTS.............5-8 82
EMI 5-8 88
MCA..5-10 79-86
SONGBIRD 5-8 82
TIME-LIFE...5-8 81
Session: Waylon Jennings; Randy Wright.
Also see FRICKE, Janie
Also see HOUSTON, David, & Barbara Mandrell
Also see JENNINGS, Waylon
Also see McCOY, Charlie
Also see WRIGHT, Randy

MANDRELL, Barbara, & Lee Greenwood C&W/LP '84
Singles: 7-inch
MCA..3-5 84
Picture Sleeves
MCA (52415 "To Me") 3-6 84
LPs: 10/12-inch
MCA...5-8 84

MANDRELL, Barbara, & Oak Ridge Boys C&W '86
Singles: 7-inch
MCA (52802 "When You Get to the Heart"). 3-5 86
Also see MANDRELL, Barbara
Also see OAK RIDGE BOYS

MANGIONE, Chuck P&R/LP '71
(Chuck Mangione Quintet)
Singles: 7-inch
A&M 3-6 75-80
COLUMBIA 3-5 82-84
MERCURY...4-6 71-77
Picture Sleeves
A&M 3-6 78-80
LPs: 10/12-inch
A&M 5-10 75-81
COLUMBIA 5-8 82-84
JAZZLAND (84 "Recuerdo") 40-50 62
(Monaural.)
JAZZLAND (984 "Recuerdo") 50-60 62
(Stereo.)
MFSL..30-50 82
MERCURY...6-12 71-78
MILESTONE 5-8 77

MANGIONE BROTHERS SEXTET
Singles: 7-inch
RIVERSIDE (446 "Struttin' with Sandra")...5-10 60
LPs: 10/12-inch
RIVERSIDE (335 "Jazz Brothers") 50-75 60
RIVERSIDE (371 "Jazz Brothers") 40-60 61
Members: Chuck Mangione; Gap Mangione.
Also see MANGIONE, Chuck

MANHATTAN BROTHERS & MIRIAM MAKEBA P&R '56
Singles: 78 rpm
LONDON (1610 "Lovely Lies") 4-8 56
Singles: 7-inch
LONDON (1610 "Lovely Lies") 8-12 56
Also see MAKEBA, Miriam

MANHATTAN STRINGS
(With Bob Summers)
LPs: 10/12-inch
TOWER (5067 "Manhattan Strings Play Instrumental Versions of Hits Made Famous by the Monkees") 8-12 67

MANHATTAN TRANSFER P&R/LP '75
Singles: 7-inch
ATLANTIC (3277 "Clap Your Hands")........5-10 75
ATLANTIC (3292 "Operator") 4-6 75
ATLANTIC (3349 "Helpless") 4-6 76
ATLANTIC (3374 "Chanson D'Amour")........4-6 76
ATLANTIC (3491 "It's Not the Spotlight")..... 4-6 78
ATLANTIC (3636 "Birdland") 4-6 79
ATLANTIC (3649 "Twilight Zone")...............3-5 80
ATLANTIC (3772 "Trickle Trickle")............8-12 80
ATLANTIC (3855 "Smile Again") 3-5 81
ATLANTIC (3816 "Boy from New York City")...3-5 81
ATLANTIC (4034 "Route 66")......................3-5 82
ATLANTIC (89094 "So You Say") 3-5 88
ATLANTIC (89156 "Soul Food to Go").........3-5 87
ATLANTIC (89533 "Ray's Rockhouse").......3-5 85
ATLANTIC (89594 "Baby Come Back to Me") 8-12 85
ATLANTIC (89695 "Mystery").......................3-5 84
ATLANTIC (89720 "American Pop")..............3-5 85
ATLANTIC (89786 "Spice of Life") 3-5 83
CAPITOL (2968 "Care for Me") 8-12 70
CAPITOL (3108 "Java Jive")......................8-12 71
STOOP SOUNDS (102 Gloria") 100-150 96
(Limited edition. Estimates range from less than 10 to a few dozen made.)
STOOP SOUNDS (106 "Unchained Melody") 100-150 97
(Limited edition. Estimates range from less than 10 to a few dozen made.)
Picture Sleeves
ATLANTIC (89156 "Soul Food to Go").........3-6 87
ATLANTIC (89786 "Spice of Life") 3-6 83
LPs: 10/12-inch
ATLANTIC (16036 "Mecca for Moderns")..8-12 81
ATLANTIC (18133 "The Manhattan Transfer")..8-12 75
ATLANTIC (18183 "Coming Out") 8-12 76
ATLANTIC (19163 "Pastiche")....................8-12 78
ATLANTIC (19319 "The Best of Manhattan Transfer")..8-12 81
ATLANTIC (19258 "Extensions")................8-12 79
ATLANTIC (80104 "Bodies and Souls").....8-12 83
ATLANTIC (81233 "Bop Doo-Wopp") 10-15 84
ATLANTIC (81266 "Vocalese")...................8-12 85
ATLANTIC (81723 "Live")...........................8-12 87
ATLANTIC (81803 "Brasil").........................8-12 87
COLLECTABLES 6-8 88
MFSL (022 "Live") 40-60 78
MFSL (199 "Extensions")........................25-35 90s
Members: Tim Hauser; Alan Paul; Gary Chester; Garnett Brown; Ken Buttrey; Cheryl Bentyne; Janis Siegel; Don Roberts.
Also see CRITERIONS
Also see MASON, Dave
Also see YOUNG GENERATION

MANHATTANS
("Vocal By Herman Carter")
Singles: 78 rpm
PINEY (107 "Go Baby Go") 10-15 55
Singles: 7-inch
PINEY (107 "Go Baby Go") 40-60 55

MANHATTANS
Singles: 7-inch
WARNER RECORDS (1015 "How Do You Say I'm Sorry")..150-250 58

MANHATTANS
Singles: 7-inch
DOOTO (445 "My Big Dream")................40-50 59
Member: Eli Price.
Also see PRICE, Eli, & Manhattans

MANHATTANS
Singles: 7-inch
BOSS (404 "Far East Rock")................... 15-25 59

MANHATTANS
Singles: 7-inch
COLPIX (115 "Big Wheel Express")......... 10-15 59
Member: Jim Ford.
Also see FORD, Jim

MANHATTANS
Singles: 7-inch
GOLDEN WORLD (14 "Just a Little Loving")..5-10 64

MANHATTANS *P&R/R&B '65*
Singles: 12-inch
COLUMBIA...4-6 84-85
Singles: 7-inch
AVANTI (1601 "What Should I Do")......... 10-15 63
CAPITOL (4591 "I Ain't Down Yet")......... 10-15 62
CAPITOL (4730 "Sing all the Day")......... 10-15 62
CARNIVAL (504 "For the Very First Time")... 10-15 64
CARNIVAL (506 "Call Somebody Please")... 40-50 64
(Identification number is CA-1010. Credits "A Joe Evans Production.")
CARNIVAL (506 "Call Somebody Please")... 20-30 64
(Identification number is CA-1010x. Credits "A Joe Evans-Bob McGhee Production.")
CARNIVAL (507 thru 542)...................... 10-25 65-69
COLUMBIA..3-6 73-87
DELUXE...4-8 69-73
Picture Sleeves
COLUMBIA..3-5 85
LPs: 10/12-inch
CARNIVAL (201 "Dedicated to You") .. 100-200 66
CARNIVAL (202 "For You and Yours") 100-150 66
COLUMBIA..8-12 73-85
DELUXE 10-15 70-72
SOLID SMOKE..5-8 81
UPFRONT (120 "Doing Their Thing")...... 10-15 '70s
Members: George Smith; Ken Kelly; Sonny Bivens; Winfred Scott; Richard Taylor; Gerald Alston; Regina Bell.

MANHATTENS
Singles: 7-inch
BIG MACK (823 "Why Should I Cry") .. 400-500 63

MANIFEST DESTINY
Singles: 7-inch
CHAMP (3404 "Silly Me")....................... 10-20 66
CHAMP (3405 "I Hear Bells").................. 10-20 66

MANILOW, Barry *P&R/LP '74*
Singles: 12-inch
ARISTA..5-10 78-87
Singles: 7-inch
ARISTA (1 "One Voice")......................... 25-35 83
(Profile-shaped picture disc, made for Fox Photo. Promotional issue only.)
ARISTA (11 "It's Just Another New Year's Eve")..5-10 77
ARISTA (0108 thru 1025)........................3-8 75-82
ARISTA (2094 "Because It's Christmas").....3-5 90
ARISTA (9003 thru 9185)........................3-6 83-84
ARISTA (9318 "Paradise Cafe")................3-5 84
(Black vinyl.)
ARISTA (9318 "Paradise Cafe")................5-8 84
(Clear vinyl.)
ARISTA (9838 thru 9948)........................3-5 89-90
BELL (45422 "Could It Be Magic")............5-10 73
BELL (45613 "Mandy")..............................4-6 74
FLASHBACK...4-6 76
RCA..3-5 85-86
Picture Sleeves
ARISTA (11 "It's Just Another New Year's Eve")..4-8 77
(Promotional issue only.)
ARISTA (0330 "Even Now")......................4-8 78
ARISTA (9318 "Paradise Cafe")................3-5 84
RCA (14397 "I'm Your Man")......................3-6 86
LPs: 10/12-inch
ARISTA (2500 "Oh, Julie")........................5-10 82
ARISTA (4007 thru 4164)..........................8-12 74-78
ARISTA (8102 thru 8274)..........................5-10 83-85
ARISTA (8500 "Live")............................... 10-12 77
(Two discs.)
ARISTA (8527 "Swing Street")...................5-10 87
ARISTA (8570 "Barry Manilow")................5-10 89
ARISTA (8601 "Greatest Hits")................10-12 78
(Two discs.)
ARISTA (A2L-8601 "Greatest Hits")........10-20 78
(Two picture discs.)
ARISTA (8638 thru 9573)..........................5-10 79-90
ARISTA (18687 "Showstoppers")................5-8 91
BELL (1129 "Barry Manilow")...................15-25 73
BELL (1314 "Barry Manilow II")................10-15 74
MFSL (097 "I")..30-40 82
RCA (7044 "Manilow")...............................5-10 85
Also see FEATHERBED

MANILOW, Barry / Atlanta Rhythm Section
Singles: 7-inch
WHAT'S IT ALL ABOUT..............................4-6 79
Also see ATLANTA RHYTHM SECTION

MANILOW, Barry / Firefall
Singles: 7-inch
WHAT'S IT ALL ABOUT..............................4-6 79

MANILOW, Barry / Kid Creole & Coconuts *P&R '88*
Singles: 7-inch
ARISTA (9666 "Hey Mambo")......................3-5 88
Picture Sleeves
ARISTA (9666 "Hey Mambo")......................3-6 88
Also see MANILOW, Barry

MANIN BROTHERS
Singles: 7-inch
APT (25033 "Hot Rod Susie")..................10-20 59

MANIS, Georgie
Singles: 7-inch
ECLAIRE ("Hep 2, 3, 4").......................150-200 58
GIZMO (66347 "High School Love")..........8-12 61

MANLEY, Lorenzo
Singles: 7-inch
ORIGINAL SOUND (60 "Swoop Down on You")..5-10 66

MANN, Allen, & Mustangs
Singles: 7-inch
MUSTANG (1 "First Love").......................10-15 65

MANN, Barbara
Singles: 7-inch
BUZZ (106 "All I Want for Christmas Is a Steady Eddie")..8-12 60
COUNT...8-12 59

MANN, Barry *P&R '61*
Singles: 7-inch
ABC...4-6 73
ABC-PAR (10143 "Counting Teardrops").10-20 60
ABC-PAR (10180 "Happy Birthday, Broken Heart")...10-20 61
ABC-PAR (10237 "Who Put the Bomp")...15-25 61
ABC-PAR (10263 "Little Miss U.S.A.")......10-20 61
ABC-PAR (10356 "Hey Baby I'm Dancing")..10-20 62
ABC-PAR (10380 "Bless You")................10-20 62
ARISTA...4-6 76
CAPITOL...5-10 66-68
CASABLANCA..4-6 80
COLPIX (691 "Johnny Surfboard")...........10-20 63
JDS (5002 "All the Things You Are")........15-25 59
MCA...3-5 '80s
NEW DESIGN..4-8 71-72
RCA...4-6 74-76
RED BIRD (015 "Amy")..............................8-12 64
ROULETTE..4-6 '70s
SCEPTER (12281 "Feelings")......................4-8 70
U.A. 4-6 77-78
W.B. 4-6 79
LPs: 10/12-inch
ABC-PAR (ABC-399 "Who Put the Bomp in the Bomp Bomp Bomp")..................................50-80 62
(Monaural.)
ABC-PAR (ABCS-399 "Who Put the Bomp in the Bomp Bomp Bomp")..................................75-100 62
(Stereo.)
CASABLANCA..5-8 80
NEW DESIGN..10-12 71
RCA (0860 "Survivor")..............................8-12 75
RCA (1162 "Interview")...........................12-15 75
(Promotional issue only.)
U.A. 8-10 77
Also see HALOS

MANN, Billy
Singles: 78 rpm
DIG..10-20 56
Singles: 7-inch
DIG (111 "Lost Angel")...........................15-25 56
DIG (120 "Just Like Before")...................25-35 56

MANN, Carl *P&R/R&B '59*
(With the Kool Kats)
Singles: 7-inch
ABC...4-6 74
ABC/DOT..4-6 76
JAXON (502 "Gonna Rock and Roll Tonight")..400-600 57
MONUMENT (974 "Serenade of the Bells")...5-10 66
PHILLIPS INT'L (3539 thru 3579).............15-25 59-62
SUN...4-6 '70s
LPs: 10/12-inch
GRT/SUNNYVALE......................................6-10 77
PHILLIPS INT'L (1960 "Like Mann")......400-500 60

MANN, Charles *R&B '73*
Singles: 7-inch
ABC (11347 "I Can Feel It")........................4-6 73
LANOR (524 "I'm Just Wondering")............8-15
LANOR (526 "A Good Thing")....................8-15
LANOR (529 "Hey, Little Girl")...................8-15
LANOR (535 "I'm Too Far Gone")..............8-15
LANOR (540 "I've Got Dreams to Remember")..8-15
LANOR (543 "Red Red Wine")....................5-15
LANOR (550 "Only Sometimes")..................5-15
LANOR (556 "Make Me Smile")...................5-15
LANOR (562 "People Say").........................5-15
LANOR (565 "Any Man Can Be a Fool")....5-15
LANOR (574 "Pretty Poison")......................5-15
LANOR (575 "My Little Home Town")........5-15
LANOR (591 "Tomorrow Never Comes")...5-15
LANOR (605 "From a Jack to a King").......5-15
LANOR (621 "Walk of Life").........................5-15
LPs: 10/12-inch
ABC (786 "Say You Love Me Too").........10-15 73

MANN, Chuck
Singles: 7-inch
LEONA (3699 "Little Miss Muffett").......100-200

MANN, Cindy
Singles: 7-inch
HERALD (530 "You Can't Fool Me Baby")..10-20 58

MANN, Frankie
Singles: 7-inch
APT (25024 "Toe to Toe").........................10-15 59

MANN, George
LPs: 10/12-inch
CROWN ("Born Free")...............................8-12 66
(Selection number not known.)
CROWN ("That's Life")..............................8-12 66
(Selection number not known.)

MANN, Glen
Singles: 7-inch
COOL (104 "It's Good to Know")............50-100

MANN, Gloria *P&R '55*
(With the Carter Rays; with Don Costa's Orchestra)
Singles: 78 rpm
ABC-PAR...10-15 57
DECCA...10-15 56
DERBY...10-15 56
JUBILEE...10-15 54
SLS..10-15 54
SOUND...10-15 54-55
Singles: 7-inch
ABC-PAR (9805 "My Heart Has a Mind of Its Own")..15-25 57
ABC-PAR (9866 "Foolish Pride")..............15-25 57
DECCA (29832 "Why Do Fools Fall in Love")..15-25 56
DECCA (29896 "One Heart")....................15-25 56
DECCA (29961 "My Secret Sin")..............15-25 56
DECCA (30069 "It Happened Again")......15-25 56
DERBY (841 "All Dressed Up")................10-20 56
JUBILEE (5142 "Goodnight Sweetheart Goodnight")..20-30 54
SLS (102 "Goodnight Sweetheart Goodnight")..75-125 54
(First issue.)
SOUND (102 "The Waltz You Save for Me")..40-50 54
SOUND (109 "I Love You, Yes I Do").......20-30 55
SOUND (114 "Pretty Eyes")......................20-30 55
SOUND (121 "I Can Tell")........................20-30 55
SOUND (122 "My Gift from Heaven").......20-30 55
SOUND (126 "A Teenage Prayer")............20-30 55
Also see CARTER RAYS
Also see COSTA, Don, Orchestra
Also see MELLO-TONES / Gloria Mann

MANN, Herbie *LP '62*
Singles: 12-inch
ATLANTIC...4-6 83
Singles: 7-inch
A&M..4-6 68
ATLANTIC...3-8 60-83
BETHLEHEM..5-10 59-62
COLUMBIA..4-6 70
EMBRYO...4-6 71
PRESTIGE...4-8 66
Picture Sleeves
ATLANTIC...4-6 79
LPs: 10/12-inch
A&M..8-12 68
ATLANTIC (300 series).............................8-12 72
ATLANTIC (1300 & 1400 series).............10-20 60-66
ATLANTIC (1500 thru 1600 series)...........8-12 69-76
ATLANTIC (8000 series)............................8-15 67
ATLANTIC (18000 and 19000 series).......5-10 77-83
BETHLEHEM (24 "Flamingo")................50-100 55
BETHLEHEM (40 "Herbie Mann")..........50-100 56
BETHLEHEM (63 "Love and the Weather")..50-100 56
BETHLEHEM (1018 "East Coast Jazz") 75-100 54
(10-inch LPs.)
BETHLEHEM (6001 "The Bethlehem Years")..5-8 76
BETHLEHEM (6067 "The Epitome of Jazz")...25-35 63
COLUMBIA..8-18 65-81
EMBRYO...8-12 70-71
EPIC (3395 "Salute to the Flute")............60-80 57
EPIC (3499 "Herbie Mann")......................50-70 58
FINNADAR..5-10 76
INTERLUDE...20-35 59
JAZZLAND (5 "Californians")...................35-55 60
MILESTONE...8-12 73
MODE (114 "Flute Fraternity")..................40-60 57
NEW JAZZ (8211 "Just Wailin'")...............50-60 58
PREMIER..20-30 63
PRESTIGE (7101 "Flute Souffle")..........75-100 57
PRESTIGE (7124 "Flute Flight")............75-100 57
PRESTIGE (7136 "Mann in the Morning")...75-100 58
PRESTIGE (7432 "Best of Herbie Mann")...20-30 65
RIVERSIDE (03 "Blues for Tomorrow")........5-8 82
RIVERSIDE (234 "Sultry Serenade").......50-75 57
RIVERSIDE (245 "Great Ideas")...............50-75 57
RIVERSIDE (3000 series)..........................8-12 69
ROULETTE..10-15 67
SAVOY (1100 series).................................5-8 76
SAVOY (12107 "Mann Alone")..................30-40 57
SAVOY (12108 "Yardbird Suite")..............35-50 57
SOLID STATE...8-12 68
SURREY...10-15 65
U.A. (4000 & 5000 series).......................20-40 59
U.A. (5300 series)....................................8-10 72
U.A. (14000 & 15000 series)...................20-40 62-63
VSP..8-15 66
VERVE...20-40 57-61
(Reads "Verve Records, Inc." at bottom of label.)
VERVE...15-25 63
(Reads "MGM Records - A Division of Metro-Goldwyn-Mayer, Inc." at bottom of label.)
VERVE..5-10 69-73
(Reads "Manufactured By MGM Record Corp.," or mentions either Polydor or Polygram at bottom of label.)
Session: King Curtis; Little Milton.
Also see AYERS, Roy
Also see KING CURTIS
Also see LITTLE MILTON

MANN, Herbie, & Cissy Houston *R&B '76*
Singles: 7-inch
ATLANTIC (3343 "Cajun Moon")..................4-6 76
Also see HOUSTON, Cissy

MANN, Herbie / Maynard Ferguson
LPs: 10/12-inch
ROULETTE 8-12 71
Also see FERGUSON, Maynard
Also see MANN, Herbie

MANN, Jerry
Singles: 7-inch
HANOVER (4542 "Baby, Come Back to Me") 8-12 60

MANN, Joey, & Statesmen
Singles: 7-inch
CLEVETOWN (220 "Cry a Million Tears") ..5-10 66

MANN, Johnny
(With the Tornados; with Bill Eisenhauer & Orchestra)
Singles: 7-inch
DONNIE (27746 "Breaker of Dreams").... 50-75 58
(Identification number shown since no selection number is used.)
SHREVE (1214 "Sorry") 15-25 60
SWAN (4018 "Breaker of Dreams") 10-15 58
TIARA (6118 "Too Young to Cry") 40-50 58

MANN, Johnny, Singers LP '63
(Johnny Mann Children's Chorus; with John Addison)
Singles: 7-inch
DECCA (31992 "Green Years") 4-8 66
EPIC....4-6 72
EUREKA (1202 "Lord Help Me") 5-10 60
LIBERTY....5-10 59-69
LPs: 10/12-inch
EPIC....5-10 72
LIBERTY.... 10-25 59-69
LIGHT....5-10 76
SUNSET....5-10 66-70
U.A. 6-12 71-72
Session: George Hale.
Also see DARET, Darla
Also see LITTLE EDDIE
Also see McDANIELS, Gene
Also see VEE, Bobby
Also see ZENTNER, Si

MANN, Johnny, Singers / Allyn Ferguson Orchestra
EPs: 7-inch
KPRC/HOUSTON COLTS ("Shoot 'Em Down .... 10-15 '60s
(No selection number used.)
Also see MANN, Johnny, Singers

MANN, Manfred P&R/LP '64
(Manfred Mann's Earth Band)
Singles: 7-inch
ARISTA....3-5 84-85
ASCOT (Except 2157 & 2165) 6-12 64-67
ASCOT (2157 "Do Wah Diddy Diddy") 5-10 64
ASCOT (2165 "Sha La La") 5-10 64
MERCURY 4-8 66-69
POLYDOR....4-6 71-74
PRESTIGE (312 "Without You") 8-10 64
U.A. (50040 "Pretty Flamingo") 5-10 66
U.A. (50066 "Do You Have to Do That") 5-10 66
W.B. 3-6 76-81
Picture Sleeves
ASCOT (2165 "Sha La La") 10-20 64
ASCOT (2170 "Come Tomorrow") 10-20 64
MERCURY (72882 "My Name Is Jack") 8-15 68
W.B. (8252 "Blinded By the Light") 4-6 76
EPs: 7-inch
U.A. (10030 "Manfred Mann") 10-20 64
(Promotional issue only. Not issued with cover.)
LPs: 10/12-inch
ARISTA....5-8 83
ASCOT (13015 "Manfred Mann") 25-35 64
(Monaural.)
ASCOT (13018 "Five Faces of Manfred Mann") 25-35 65
(Monaural.)
ASCOT (13021 "My Little Red Book of Winners") 25-35 66
(Monaural.)
ASCOT (13024 "Mann Made") 25-35 66
(Monaural.)
ASCOT (16015 "Manfred Mann") 35-45 64
(Stereo.)
ASCOT (16018 "Five Faces of Manfred Mann") 35-45 65
(Stereo.)
ASCOT (16021 "My Little Red Book of Winners") 35-55 66
(Stereo.)
ASCOT (16024 "Mann Made") 35-45 66
(Stereo.)
CAPITOL 5-8 80
EMI AMERICA 10-12 77
JANUS....12-15 74
MERCURY 15-20 68
POLYDOR....10-15 70-74
U.A. 20-35 66-68
W.B. 5-8 74-81
Members: Manfred Mann; Mike D'Abo; Paul Jones; Tom McGuinnes; Mick Rogers; Mick Vickers; Chris Slade; Colin Pattenden; Mike Hugg; Steve York; Mick Rogers.
Also see BELL, Madeline

MANN, Pete
Singles: 7-inch
CHRISTY (133 "Heavenly Father") 10-20 60
POPLAR (116 "Call On Me") 8-12 59

MANN, Plez Gary
Singles: 7-inch
PLAYBOY (698 "Cheer Me Up") 400-600

MANN, Reverend Columbus
(With His Pentecostal Choir)
Singles: 7-inch
CYE (1001 "Soon Very Soon") ....15-25 '60s
TAMLA (54047 "Jesus Loves") 25-35 61
LPs: 10/12-inch
TAMLA (227 "They Shall Be Mine") 300-400 61
WINGATE (701 "He Satisfies Me") ....200-300 '60s

MANN, Rosalie
Singles: 7-inch
JAMIE (1192 "Mr. So and So") 5-10 61

MANN, Sandy
Singles: 7-inch
ROULETTE (4651 "Bright Lights, Big City") 5-10 65

MANN, Scotty, & Masters
Singles: 78 rpm
PEACOCK....5-10 56
Singles: 7-inch
PEACOCK (1665 "Just a Little Bit of Loving") 40-60 56
Members: Scotty Mansfield; Frank Newman; Fred Council; Pavel Bess.
Also see CLEFS

MANN, Shadow
Singles: 7-inch
TOMORROW....5-10 74
LPs: 10/12-inch
TOMORROW (69001 "Come Live with Me") 40-60 74

MANN, Steve
LPs: 10/12-inch
CUSTOM FIDELITY....10-12

MANN, Tony
Singles: 7-inch
DECCA (32720 "Alabama Song") 10-15 70

MANNA, Charlie LP '61
Singles: 7-inch
DECCA (31320 "I Want My Crayons") 4-8 61
DECCA (38338 "The Astronaut") 8-12 61
(Promotional issue only.)
JUBILEE (5498 "Give Me a Chance to Explain") 4-6 65
Picture Sleeves
DECCA (38338 "The Astronaut") 10-20 61
(Promotional issue only.)
LPs: 10/12-inch
DECCA (4159 "Manna Overboard") 15-25 61
DECCA (4213 "Manna Live") 15-25 62
VERVE (15051 "Rise and Fall of the Great Society") 10-15 66

MANNA, Paddy
Singles: 7-inch
USA (1776 "Ain't That a Shame") 5-10 62

MANNING, Bob
(With Bobby Hackett; with Monty Kelly & Orchestra)
Singles: 78 rpm
CAPITOL....5-10 53-55
RCA....5-10 56
Singles: 7-inch
CAPITOL....10-15 53-55
RCA....10-15 56-57
Also see KELLY, Monty, & His Orchestra

MANNING, Chuck
Singles: 7-inch
CORBY (232 "Let's Go") 150-250

MANNING, Dick
Singles: 7-inch
FELSTED (8650 "Dancing Princess") 5-10 62

MANNING, Linda C&W '68
Singles: 7-inch
BULLETIN (1000 "Our World of Rock and Roll") 5-10 61
DOKE (106 "Boy I Can't Forget") 5-10 60
FRATERNITY (895 "Lovin' Kind") 5-10 62
GAYLORD (6425 "Johnny Kiss and Tell") ..5-10 62
MERCURY (72803 "Hurt Me Now") 4-8 68
RICE....4-8 64-67
ROULETTE (4638 "You're Loving Me to Death") 5-10 65

MANNO, Tommy
Singles: 7-inch
ATLANTIC (2149 "Too Good to Be True") .5-10 62
CLEOPATRA (4 "Gloria") 10-20 62
FLIPPIN' (311 "Too Good to Be True") 10-15 62

MANOR, A.J., & Jets
Singles: 7-inch
TWIRL (105 "I Know the Blues Are Blues") ....10-20 '60s

MANPOWER
LPs: 10/12-inch
PHILIPS (600313 "Revelation") 10-15 69
Also see MAN

MANSEL, Red
Singles: 7-inch
ALLSTAR (7160 "Johnny on the Spot") 40-60 57
ALLSTAR (7162 "Love Starved") 15-25 57
ALLSTAR (7165 "Angel of Love") 15-25 57

MANSFIELD, Jayne
Singles: 78 rpm
HEAR ("Tab Hunter") 20-30 56
(7-inch, cardboard disc, originally attached to back cover of *Hear* magazine. Double this price for magazine with record intact. Front cover has a similar disc by Tab Hunter.)
Singles: 7-inch
ORIGINAL SOUND (51 "Little Things Mean a Lot") 5-8 64
Picture Sleeves
ORIGINAL SOUND (51 "Little Things Mean a Lot") 10-20 64
EPs: 7-inch
RCA (1046 "Music for Bachelors") 20-30 55
LPs: 10/12-inch
MGM (4202 "Shakespeare, Tchaikovsky and Me") 25-50 64
RCA (1046 "Music for Bachelors") 50-100 55
20TH FOX (3049 "Jayne Mansfield Busts Up Las Vegas") 75-100
Also see HUNTER, Tab
Also see JENSEN, Kurt, & His Orchestra
Also see LIGHT, Enoch, & His Orchestra
Also see LOPEZ, Vincent, & His Orchestra
Also see REGENT CONCERT ORCHESTRA
Also see RENÉ, Henri, & His Orchestra
Also see WASHBURN, Frank, & His Orchestra

MANSFIELD, Keith
(Keith Mansfield Orchestra)
Singles: 7-inch
EPIC (10504 "Soul Confusion") 5-10 69

MANSHIP, Jimmy & Judy
Singles: 7-inch
BLUE HEN (233 "Teenage Sweetie") 35-50 59

MANSHIP, Jimmy, & Allison Sisters / Bill Price
Singles: 7-inch
BLUE HEN (236 "Broken Heart") 10-15 59
Also see MANSHIP, Jimmy & Judy

MANSO, Burrie, & Bonnivilles
Singles: 7-inch
TOWN-CRIER (200 "My Woman") 800-1200

MANSON, Charles
LPs: 10/12-inch
AWARENESS (1 "Charles Manson") 5-10 87
AWARENESS (2144 "The Love and Terror Cult") ....200-300 '60s
ESP DISK (2003 "The Love and Terror Cult") 100-200 70

MANTOVANI P&R '35
(Mantovani & His Orchestra)
Singles: 78 rpm
COLUMBIA....3-8 35-36
LONDON (Except 1761) 3-5 51-65
LONDON (1761 "Let Me Be Loved") 4-6 57
Singles: 7-inch
LONDON (Except 1761) 4-8 51-65
LONDON (1761 "Let Me Be Loved") 8-12 57
Picture Sleeves
LONDON (Except 1761) 4-8 57-65
LONDON (1761 "Let Me Be Loved") 30-45 57
(*Let Me Be Loved* is the main theme from the film, *The James Dean Story*. Sleeve pictures Dean.)
EPs: 7-inch
LONDON....5-10 51-59
LPs: 10/12-inch
BAINBRIDGE....5-10 82
LONDON....5-20 51-72
Also see DEAN, James
Also see PRESLEY, Elvis
Also see WHITFIELD, David

MANUEL, Larry
Singles: 7-inch
STOMPER TIME (1159 "You Say I Was a Fool") 50-75

MANUEL & RENEGADES
Singles: 7-inch
PIPER (7000 "Surf Walk") 25-35 63
PIPER (7001 "Rev-Up") 25-35 63

MANZAREK, Ray LP '75
Singles: 7-inch
MERCURY....4-6 73-74
LPs: 10/12-inch
A&M....5-10 84
MERCURY....8-12 74-75
Also see DOORS
Also see RICK & RAVENS

MAPLES
(With Von Freeman Combo)
Singles: 78 rpm
BLUE LAKE (111 "I Must Forget You") 300-400 55
Singles: 7-inch
BLUE LAKE (111 "I Must Forget You") 1500-2000 55
Members: Johnny Jones; Albert Hunter; Andrew Smith.
Also see CLOUDS
Also see FASCINATORS
Also see FIVE CHANCES

MAPP, Norman
Singles: 7-inch
JARO (77021 "Fools Rush In") 8-12 60

MacQUINN, Steve
Singles: 7-inch
WYNNE (113 "Wonder Why") 5-10 59

MARA, Tommy P&R '58
(With LeRoy Holmes Orchestra & Chorus)
Singles: 78 rpm
MGM (11931 "Honey Bunch") 5-10 55
UNIQUE (343 "First Traveling Saleslady") . 5-10 56
Singles: 7-inch
B&F (1334 "Secret Love") 8-10 60
FELSTED (8505 "Hello, Goodbye") 10-15 58
FELSTED (8532 "Where the Blue of the Night") 10-15 58
FELSTED (8547 "Marie") 10-15 58
FELSTED (8561 "With Someone You Love") 10-15 59
FELSTED (8579 "Until I Hear It from You") 10-15 59
MGM (11931 "Honey Bunch") 10-15 55
MGM (12002 "Captured") 10-15 55
UNIQUE (343 "First Traveling Saleslady") 10-15 56
UNIQUE (377 "Nobody Understands Me") 10-15 57

MARA, Tony
Singles: 7-inch
ATCO (6172 "Ramblin' ") 10-20 60

MARAINEY, Big Memphis
Singles: 78 rpm
SUN 200-300 53
Singles: 7-inch
SUN (184 "Call Me Anything, But Call Me") 800-1200 53

MARATHONS
Singles: 7-inch
J.C. (101 "Don't Know Why") 40-50 59
(Publishing credit mentions only Robin Hood Music.)
J.C. (101 "Don't Know Why") 20-30 59
(Publishing credit mentions both Lach Music and Robin Hood Music.)
SABRINA (108 "Don't Know Why") 150-200 59
(First issue.)
SABRINA (334 "Don't Know Why") 100-150 59

MARATHONS *P&R/R&B '61*
Singles: 7-inch
ARGO (5389 "Peanut Butter") 10-20 61
ARVEE (5027 "Peanut Butter") 15-25 61
(Other Arvee releases by the Marathons are by a different group. See the following section.)
CHESS (1790 "Peanut Butter") 5-10 61
EPs: 7-inch
MARK 56 ("Laura Scudder's Magic Record") 4-8 69
(Laura Scudder's potato chip mail-order, coupon giveaway item. Has three tracks, including *Peanut Butter*, imbedded in a single band on each side. When needle begins tracking, it's unknown which song will play. Price includes paper picture sleeve.)
LPs: 10/12-inch
ARVEE (428 "Peanut Butter") 50-75 61
Members: James Johnson; Carl Fisher; Dick Owens; Dave Govan; Don Bradley.
Also see JAYHAWKS
Also see VIBRATIONS

MARATHONS
Singles: 7-inch
ARVEE (5038 "Tight Sweater") 10-15 61
ARVEE (5048 "Chicken Spaceman") 10-15 62
(Arvee 5027 is by a different group and is listed in the preceding section.)
PLAZA (507 "Little Pancho") 5-10 62

MARAUDERS
Singles: 7-inch
HAWK (4002 "Sand Flea") 20-30 62
Member: Steve Wildermuth.

MARAUDERS
Singles: 7-inch
KISKI (2067 "Slidin' ") 10-20 63

MARAUDERS
Singles: 7-inch
COULEE (110 "I Can Tell") 25-35 64
(Blue vinyl.)
Members: Rick Przywojski; Rick Miller; Jim Young; Terry Gardner.
Also see SATISFACTIONS

MARAUDERS
Singles: 7-inch
ROCKLAND (2 "Bad Girl") 15-25 65

MARAUDERS
Singles: 7-inch
LEE (9449 "Nightmare") 15-25 65

MARAUDERS
Singles: 7-inch
ALMO (221 "Like You") 8-10 65
FR (6143 "Motorcycle Bug") 25-35

MARAUDERS
Singles: 7-inch
SKYVIEW (001 "Since I Met You") 10-15 66
Picture Sleeves
SKYVIEW (001 "Since I Met You") 10-20 66

MARAUDERS
Singles: 7-inch
LAURIE (3356 "Jugband Music") 10-15 66

MARAUDERS
Singles: 7-inch
JIVE TIME (28 "White Lines") 8-12 70

STUDIO CITY (1035 "She Threw My Love Away") 10-15 65

MARBLE COLLECTION
Singles: 7-inch
COTIQUE 5-10 68
MARBLE DISC 5-10 69
Members: Charles Byrd; Len Eldridge; Jim White; Bruce Webb; Dave Coviello.

MARBLE PHROGG
Singles: 7-inch
DERRICK (8568 "Fire") 40-60 68
LPs: 10/12-inch
DERRICK (8868 "Marble Phrogg") 800-1200 68

MARBLES
Singles: 78 rpm
LUCKY (002 "Golden Girl") 300-400 54
Singles: 7-inch
LUCKY (002 "Golden Girl") 3000-4000 54
Members: Johnny Torrence; Dee Hawkins; James Brown; Rudy Jackson.
Also see JEWELS

MARCEL, Eddie
Singles: 7-inch
GLAD-HAMP (2034 "I Go Crazy") .... 100-200 '60s

MARCEL, Pete
Singles: 7-inch
FUTURA (104 "Sloppy Twist a Fish") 5-10 61

MARCEL, Vic
Singles: 7-inch
DONBUT (17349 "Come Back to These Arms") 30-50 64
RCA (0317 "Funky Lover") 10-20 70

MARCELL, Beverly
Singles: 7-inch
GONE (5145 "Monkey Dance") 5-10 63

MARCELL, Professor, & Collegians
Singles: 7-inch
MAYHAMS (21422 "Be No Fool, Play It Cool, Stay in School") 5-10 67

MARCELLE, Lydia
Singles: 7-inch
ATCO (6366 "Everybody Dance") 10-20 65
MANHATTAN (805 "Come On and Get It") 10-20 67
MANHATTAN (809 "It's Not Like You") 10-20 67

MARCELLINO, Muzzy
Singles: 78 rpm
CRYSTALETTE 10-15 56
Singles: 7-inch
CRYSTALETTE (707 "That's a Plenty") ... 15-25 56
Also see GOON BONES / Muzzy Marcellino

MARCELS *P&R/R&B '61*
(With the Stu Phillips Orchestra; Marcelles)
Singles: 7-inch
ALL EARS (810085 "Blue Moon") 3-5 81
COLPIX (147 "Blue Moon") 8-12 62
(Torchlight Series.)
COLPIX (186 "Blue Moon") 20-30 61
COLPIX (186 "Blue Moon") 25-35 61
(Mistakenly credits "Marcelles." Canadian.)
COLPIX (196 "Summertime") 20-30 61
COLPIX (606 "You Are My Sunshine") 20-30 61
COLPIX (612 "Heartaches") 20-30 61
COLPIX (617 "Merry Twist-Mas") 20-30 61
COLPIX (621 "My Melancholy Baby") .. 100-200 62
(Promotional issue only. Has wrong number.)
COLPIX (624 "My Melancholy Baby") 10-20 62
COLPIX (629 "Footprints in the Sand") 10-20 62
COLPIX (640 "Hold On") 40-60 62
COLPIX (651 "Friendly Loan") 15-25 62
COLPIX (665 "Alright, Okay, You Win") ... 10-15 62
COLPIX (683 "That Old Black Magic") 10-15 63
COLPIX (687 "I Want to Be the Leader") .15-25 63
COLPIX (694 "One Last Kiss") 50-75 63
COLPIX (15015 "Summertime") 10-15 61
CYCLE (2001 "Crazy Bells in My Heart") .10-20
888 (101 "Lonely Boy") 10-15 63
ERIC (113 "Blue Moon") 4-6 73
KYRA ("Comes Love") 40-60 64
(Black vinyl. No selection number used.)
KYRA ("Comes Love") 75-125 64
(Red vinyl. No selection number used.)
MONOGRAM (113 "Over the Rainbow") .. 15-20 75
(Colored vinyl.)

MONOGRAM (115 "Two People in the World") 5-8 75
OWL (324 "Crazy Bells") 4-6 74
QUEEN BEE (47001 "In the Still of the Night") 10-15 73
SIR RENDER (005 "A Fallen Tear") 5-8
(Colored vinyl.)
ST. CLAIR 5-10 75
Picture Sleeves
COLPIX (186 "Blue Moon") 50-75 61
COLPIX (612 "Heartaches") 50-75 61
COLPIX (617 "Merry Twist-Mas") 150-200 61
LPs: 10/12-inch
COLPIX (416 "Blue Moon") 75-125 61
(Gold label.)
COLPIX (416 "Blue Moon") 30-50 63
(Blue label.)
CRYSTAL BALL (111 "Lucky Old Sun") ... 15-18 83
(Black vinyl. 2000 made.)
CRYSTAL BALL (120 "Marcels") 15-20 85
(Black vinyl. 1000 made.)
EMUS 8-10 79
MURRAY HILL 8-10
Members: Cornelius Harp; Fred Johnson; Ron Mundy; Gene Bricker; Richard Knauss; Walt Maddox; Al Johnson.
Also see MONDELLOS / Marcels
Also see REGAN, Tommy

MARCH, Little Peggy *P&R/R&B/LP '63*
(Peggy March)
Singles: 7-inch
OLDE WORLD 4-8 75
RCA (0136 "Boom Bang-a-Bang") 4-8 69
RCA (8107 thru 9718) 8-12 62-69
Picture Sleeves
RCA (8189 "I Wish I Were a Princess") 10-20 63
RCA (8221 "Hello Heartache, Goodbye Love") 10-20 63
EPs: 7-inch
RCA (4376 "I Wish I Were a Princess") 20-25 63
LPs: 10/12-inch
RCA (129 "Her German Hits") 15-25 65
RCA (LPM-2732 "I Will Follow Him") 50-60 63
(Monaural.)
RCA (LSP-2732 "I Will Follow Him") 75-100 63
(Stereo.)
RCA (3883 "No Foolin' ") 15-25 68
Also see MARCH, Peggy, & Gary Marshal

MARCH, Little Peggy, & Bennie Thomas
LPs: 10/12-inch
RCA (3408 "In Our Fashion") 15-25 65
Also see MARCH, Little Peggy
Also see THOMAS, Bennie

MARCH, Myrna
Singles: 7-inch
COLUMBIA (43050 "Parade of Broken Hearts") 5-10 64
ROULETTE (4463 "Warm Are Your Lips") . 5-10 62
ROULETTE (4486 "Baby") 5-10 63
ROULETTE (4522 "I Can't Say No") 5-10 63
WARWICK (525 "Cryin' Up a Storm") 5-10 60
WARWICK (576 "Don't Be Angry") 5-10 60
LPs: 10/12-inch
KAPP (3603 "Night They Raided Myrna's") 10-20 69
STRAND (1033 "Explosive Vocal Percussion") 15-25 61

MARCH, Peggy, & Gary Marshal
Singles: 7-inch
RCA (8877 "Play a Simple Melody") 5-10 66
Also see MARCH, Little Peggy
Also see MARSHAL, Gary

MARCH, Tony
(With the Rockets)
Singles: 7-inch
CHECKER (887 "Stompen Rock") 15-25 58
CROSSWAY (447 "Beatle Mania Blues") 10-20 64
TAMMY (1003 "Show Down") 15-25 60
Also see MONORAYS

MARCHAN, Bobby *P&R/R&B '60*
(With the Tick Tocks; with Clowns; Bobby Marchon)
Singles: 78 rpm
ACE 10-20 56
ALADDIN 10-20 53
DOT 10-20 54
FIRE (1022 "There's Something on Your Mind") 300-400 60

GALE 10-20 57
Singles: 7-inch
ABC 4-6 73
ACE (523 "Chickie Wah Wah") 20-30 56
ACE (532 "I'll Never Let You Go") 20-30 57
ACE (557 "Rockin' Behind the Iron Curtain") 10-15 59
ACE (595 "Quit My Job") 10-15 60
ACE (3004 "My Day Is Coming") 4-8 74
ACE (3016 "What Can I Do") 4-8 74
ALADDIN (3189 "Just a Little Walk") 30-40 53
BOBBY ROBINSON 4-6 73
CAMEO (405 "There's Something About My Baby") 5-10 66
CAMEO (429 "Just Be Yourself") 5-10 66
CAMEO (453 "Hooked") 5-10 67
CAMEO (469 "Help Yourself") 5-10 67
CAMEO (489 "Rockin' Pneumonia") 5-10 67
DIAL 4-10 64-74
DOT (1203 "Just a Little Ol' Wine") 20-30 54
FIRE 10-20 60-62
FLASHBACK 4-6 65
GALE 20-30 57
GAMBLE (216 "For Girls to Be Lonely") 5-10 68
MERCURY 4-6 77
RIVER CITY 10-20
SANSU .... 5-10 '60s
SPHERE SOUND (706 "All in My Mind") ... 5-10 65
VOLT 8-12 63-64
LPs: 10/12-inch
COLLECTABLES 5-8 88
SPHERE SOUND (7004 "There's Something on Your Mind") 100-200 64
Also see SMITH, Huey

MARCHAN, Bobby, & Willie Dixon
Singles: 7-inch
ACE (3008 "My Days Are Coming") 4-8 75
Also see DIXON, Wylie, & Wheels
Also see MARCHAN, Bobby

MARCHAND, Donny
(Donnie Marchand)
Singles: 7-inch
CRAFT (3000 "Round in Circles") 60-80 60
MOHAWK (125 "I Confess") 10-15 61
TRANS ATLAS (693 "Round in Circles") 400-500 62

MARCHAND, Glen
Singles: 7-inch
DORE (763 "Your Ship of Fools") 25-50 65

MARCHAND, Yvette
Singles: 7-inch
BETHLEHEM (3037 "Rock-A-Daddy-O") ... 5-10 62

MARCI & MATES
Singles: 7-inch
BIG TOP (3116 "Let Us Part for a Year") ... 8-12 62
BIG TOP (3136 "Suddenly We're Strangers") 8-12 63

MARCIA & LYNCHMEN
Singles: 7-inch
SCOTTY (94456740 "Ain't Gonna Eat Out My Heart") .... 25-35 '60s
Also see PLASTIC ICE CUBE

MARCO
Singles: 7-inch
MOHAWK (135 "I'm So Lonely") 5-10 63

MARCO, Nick, & Venetians
Singles: 7-inch
DWAIN (813 "Little Boy Lost") 20-30 60
Members: Nick Marco; Joe Walsh; Dennis Conboy; Bob Fava.
Also see LEDO, Les

MARCUS, Steve
LPs: 10/12-inch
VORTEX (2001 "Tomorrow Never Knows") 10-20 68
VORTEX (2009 "Count's Rock Band") 10-20 68

MARCUS BROTHERS
Singles: 7-inch
EBB (150 "Sugar Booger") 50-75 58

MARCY
LPs: 10/12-inch
ZONDERVAN (693 "Sing Along") 10-20 66

MARCY JO & EDDIE RAMBEAU

Singles: 7-inch

SWAN (4136 "Those Golden Oldies")..... 10-15 63
SWAN (4145 "The Car Hop & the Hard Top")..... 15-25 63
Also see MARCY JOE
Also see RAMBEAU, Eddie

MARCY JOE P&R '61
(Marcy Jo)

Singles: 7-inch

ROBBEE (110 "Ronnie")..... 10-15 61
ROBBEE (115 "Since Gary Went into the Navy")..... 10-15 61
ROBBEE (117 "Take a Word")..... 10-15 61
SWAN (4116 "First Kiss")..... 8-12 62
SWAN (4128 "Night")..... 8-12 62
SWAN (4148 "The Next Time")..... 8-12 63
Session: Lou Christie.
Also see CHRISTIE, Lou

MARENO, Lee
(Lee)

Singles: 7-inch

NEW ART (103 "Goddess of Love")..... 50-75 61
(First issue.)
SCEPTER (1222 "Goddess of Love")..... 20-30 61
SCEPTER (12222 "Goddess of Love")..... 5-10 68
Also see RUNAROUNDS

MARESCA, Ernie P&R/R&B '62
(With the Billy Mure Orchestra)

Singles: 7-inch

LAURIE (3345 "The Good Life")..... 5-10 66
LAURIE (3371 "My Son")..... 5-10 67
LAURIE (3447 "What Is a Marine")..... 5-10 68
LAURIE (3496 "Blind Date")..... 5-10 69
LAURIE (3519 "The Spirit of Woodstock")..5-10 69
LAURIE (3671 "Please Don't Play Me a Seven")..... 4-6 78
PROVIDENCE (417 "Rockin' Boulevard Street")..... 30-40 65
RUST (5076 "The Beetle Dance")..... 8-12 64
SEVILLE (107 "Lonesome Blues")..... 10-20 60
SEVILLE (117 "Shout! Shout!")..... 5-10 62
SEVILLE (119 "Down on the Beach")..... 5-10 62
SEVILLE (122 "Something to Shout About")..... 5-10 62
SEVILLE (125 "Love Express")..... 20-30 63
SEVILLE (129 "Rovin' Kind")..... 15-25 63
SEVILLE (138 "I Can't Dance")..... 8-12 65

Picture Sleeves

SEVILLE (119 "Down on the Beach")..... 15-25 62

LPs: 10/12-inch

LAURIE (4006 "Original Songs of Ernie Maresca")..... 10-15 78
SEVILLE (77001 "Shout! Shout! [Knock Yourself Out]")"..... 30-60 62
(Monaural.)
SEVILLE (87001 "Shout! Shout! [Knock Yourself Out]")"..... 40-80 62
(Stereo.)
Also see CHICAGO, Artie
Also see DEL SATINS
Also see DESIRES
Also see HUBCAPS

MARGARET & CAROL

Singles: 7-inch

CHECKER (1116 "That Guy Is Mine")..... 5-10 65

MARGARET & CHARMETTES

Singles: 7-inch

MARKAY (101 "Donnie")..... 10-20 62
Also see CHARMETTES

MARGIE & FORMATIONS

Singles: 7-inch

COED (601 "Sad Illusion")..... 20-30 65

MARGO & MARVETTES

Singles: 7-inch

AMERICAN ARTS (8 "Cherry Pie")..... 8-12 64

MARGULIS, Charles

Singles: 7-inch

CARLTON (456 "Gigi")..... 5-10 58
CARLTON (494 "Malagueña")..... 5-10 59

LPs: 10/12-inch

CARLTON (103 "Marvelous Margulis")..... 15-25 59

MARIA, Vonda

Singles: 7-inch

PHIL-L.A. OF SOUL (319 "Open Arms, Closed Heart")..... 5-10 68

MARIA ELENA & TWILIGHTS

Singles: 7-inch

COUNTESS (113 "I Was Too Careful")..... 50-75 62

MARIA MAE
(With the Chaperones; with Peptones; with Maybees)

Singles: 7-inch

JAMIE (1293 "Try My Love")..... 5-10 65
PHANTOM (986 "Teenage Love")..... 75-125 61
SAVOY (1613 "Hic-Cups")..... 5-10 62

MARIACHI BRASS
("Featuring Chet Baker") LP '66

Singles: 7-inch

WORLD PACIFIC..... 5-10 66-67

LPs: 10/12-inch

WORLD PACIFIC..... 10-15 66-67

MARIANI

LPs: 10/12-inch

SONOBEAT (1004 "Perpetuum Mobile")..... 2000-2500 '70s
(Promotional issue only.)
Member: Vince Mariani.

MARIANNE

Singles: 7-inch

A-BET (9432 "The Woman in Me")..... 5-10 68
BELL (729 "You Know My Name")..... 5-10 68
BELL (745 "Gloria's Sun")..... 5-10 68

MARIE & REX P&R '59

Singles: 7-inch

CARLTON (502 "I Can't Sit Down")..... 10-15 59
Members: Marie Knight; Rex Garvin.
Also see GARVIN, Rex, & Mighty Cravers
Also see KNIGHT, Marie

MARIE ANN

Singles: 7-inch

EPIC (9465 "Your Heart's Not Made of Wood")..... 8-10 61
WARWICK (605 "Dream Boy")..... 8-10 60

MARIE SISTERS

Singles: 7-inch

BRUNSWICK (55146 "Oh, Tony")..... 15-25 59

MARIGOLDS R&B '55

Singles: 78 rpm

EXCELLO..... 15-25 55

Singles: 7-inch

EXCELLO (2057 "Rollin' Stone")..... 50-100 55
EXCELLO (2061 "Two Strangers")..... 30-40 55
EXCELLO (2078 "Foolish Me")..... 30-40 56
EXCELLO (2091 "It's You, Darling, It's You")..... 30-40 56
Members: Johnny Bragg; Henry Jones; Hal Hebb; Al Brooks; Willie Wilson.
Also see BRAGG, Johnny

MARINI, Perla

Singles: 78 rpm

GROOVE..... 5-10 54

Singles: 7-inch

GROOVE (0007 "I'll Never Be Free")..... 10-15 54
GROOVE (0025 "Candy")..... 10-15 54

MARINO, Del

Singles: 7-inch

COLPIX (163 "One Girl")..... 15-25 60
SCEPTER (1221 "Cupid's Arrow")..... 5-10 61
Also see CASTRO, Bernadette

MARINO, Joe

Singles: 78 rpm

BELL (1090 "Wedding Bells")..... 5-10 55

Singles: 7-inch

BELL (1090 "Wedding Bells")..... 10-15 55
ELECTRO VOX (2173 "Trying So Hard to Forget")..... 5-10 62

MARINO, Lita

Singles: 7-inch

W.B. (5302 "Big Daddy")..... 5-10 62

MARINO, Ronnie

Singles: 7-inch

BRITE STAR (3645 "I Can Help It")..... 5-10 67

MARINO, Sandy

Singles: 7-inch

ARAGON (407 "Hopin' and a-Prayin' ")..75-125

MARIO & FLIPS

Singles: 7-inch

CROSS COUNTRY (100 "Once in Awhile")..... 10-15 59
DECCA (31252 "Twistin' Train")..... 8-12 61

MARION
(Marion Carpenter)

Singles: 7-inch

SANDY (1021 "Happy Lonesome")..... 10-15 59
SANDY (1026 "Cutie")..... 10-15 59
SANDY (1041 "Happy Lonesome")..... 8-10 61

MARION, Al

Singles: 7-inch

GAY (624 "Kay")..... 50-75

MARION & HERBIE

Singles: 7-inch

ULTRA-SONIC (1717 "Going Steady By the Numbers")..... 10-15 60

MARIONETTES

Singles: 7-inch

LONDON (9738 "Nobody But You")..... 5-10 65

MARIS, Tommy

Singles: 7-inch

CAMEO (406 "Wait for Me My Love")..... 5-10 66
SHOWCASE (2001 "I Want You Back Again")..... 5-10 65
SURE (503 "Teenage Lover")..... 25-35 '50s

MARK

Singles: 7-inch

SUPER K (103 "Good 'N Plenty")..... 5-10 69
TEAM..... 5-10 69
Also see 1910 FRUITGUM COMPANY

MARK, Jon

Singles: 7-inch

DECCA (31929 "Little Town Girl")..... 5-10 66

LPs: 10/12-inch

COLUMBIA..... 8-10 75
Also see MARK - ALMOND BAND
Also see SWEET THURSDAY

MARK, Ronald

Singles: 7-inch

GATEWAY (102 "Moonlight Sky")..... 200-250 64

MARK - ALMOND BAND LP '71

Singles: 7-inch

ABC..... 4-6 75
BLUE THUMB..... 4-6 72
COLUMBIA..... 4-6 72-73

LPs: 10/12-inch

A&M..... 8-10 78
ABC..... 8-10 76
BLUE THUMB..... 8-12 70-73
COLUMBIA..... 8-12 72-73
MCA..... 5-8
PACIFIC ARTS..... 8-10 81
Members: Jon Mark; Johnny Almond.
Also see MARK, Jon
Also see MAYALL, John

MARK & ESCORTS

Singles: 7-inch

GNP (350 "Tuff Stuff")..... 5-10 65
GNP (358 "Dance with Me")..... 5-10 65

MARK II P&R '60

Singles: 7-inch

ROULETTE (4784 "Night Theme")..... 5-10 67
WYE (1001 "Night Theme")..... 10-15 60
WYE (1004 "Blue Fantasy")..... 8-12 61
Members: Wayne Cogswell; Ray Peterson.
Also see POWERS, Wayne

MARK III

Singles: 7-inch

ABC-PAR (10280 "Valerie")..... 5-10 61
BRB (100 "Valerie")..... 15-25 61
(First issue.)
CENTURY..... 5-10 '60s
FULLER (2729 "Thunderball")..... 5-10 65

MARK III

Singles: 7-inch

NIGHT OWL (108 "Jaw Breaker")..... 10-20 68

MARK III TRIO

Singles: 7-inch

ATCO (6451 "All the Things You Are")..... 5-10 66
ATCO (6468 "The Sleeper")..... 5-10 67
IN (6308 "G'wan")..... 10-20 66
(First issue.)
IN (6309 "The Sleeper")..... 10-20 66
(First issue.)
WINGATE (015 "G'wan")..... 8-12 66

MARK IV P&R '58

Singles: 7-inch

COSMIC (704 "The Shake")..... 15-20 58
MERCURY (71000 series)..... 10-15 59

MARK FOUR

Singles: 7-inch

PACIFIC CHALLENGER (1002 "Swingin' Hangout")..... 30-40 65

MARK IV

Singles: 7-inch

GIANT STAR (404 "Hey Girl, Won't You Listen")..... 10-15 66
GIANT STAR (405 "Won't You Believe Me")..... 10-15 66

MARK IV

Singles: 7-inch

COLUMBIA (43911 "Better Than That")..... 5-10 66

MARK IV

Singles: 7-inch

TEE PEE (59/60 "Rollin' Stone"/"The Wayward Wind")..... 10-20 68

MARK IV R&B '72

Singles: 7-inch

MERCURY (73000 series)..... 4-6 72-73

LPs: 10/12-inch

MERCURY..... 10-12 73
Members: James Ponder; Larry Jones.

MARK IVs

Singles: 7-inch

BARRY (105 "Tide Has Turned")..... 10-20 62

MARK FOURS

Singles: 7-inch

ONE-DERFUL (4809 "Washington and Lee Swing")..... 5-10 62

MARK 4'S

Singles: 7-inch

BONUS (7041 "Bonneville")..... 15-25

MARK V
(Mark Five)

Singles: 7-inch

ABC-PAR (10433 "Night Rumble")..... 5-10 63
CARMEN (1 "Baby Patsy")..... 5-10 63
CHARAY (20 "The Phantom")..... 10-20 65
CHARAY (20 "Talk About Love")..... 10-20 65
(Same selection number used twice.)
COUNTERPART (813 "Hey Conductor")..... 5-10 '60s
HEARTBEAT (58 "Jacqueline")..... 5-10 63
MILO (110 "Cry Baby")..... 5-10 60
SUNNY (1 "Jacqueline")..... 5-10 63
Also see LARRY & BLUE NOTES

MARK V

Singles: 7-inch

BLAST (215 "I Want to Say")..... 10-20 64

MARK V

Singles: 7-inch

BOLO (746 "Ooh Poo Pah Doo")..... 5-10 64
JANI (1258 "It's Your Heart")..... 5-10 65
JANI (1265 "Maggie's Farm")..... 5-10 65
NWI (2700 "Search Your Mind")..... 5-10 66

MARK V

Singles: 7-inch

IMPRESSION (102 "I'll Keep On Trying")..5-10 65

MARK V

Singles: 7-inch

COUNTERPART (2591 "Hey Conductor")..... 20-25
JCP (102 "Pay")..... 10-20 '60s

MARK V COMBO

Singles: 7-inch

VARIETY..... 5-10 62-65

MARK VI
Singles: 7-inch
ZEST (100 "Cleo") 20-40

MARKAY, Grace
Singles: 7-inch
CAPITOL 5-10 67-68
PARAMOUNT (0137 "Time Have Changed") 4-8 71
U.A. (50478 "Come to the Sun") 5-10 68
LPs: 10/12-inch
CAPITOL 10-15 67
U.A. 10-15 69

MARKEES
Singles: 7-inch
GONE (5028 "Along Came Love") 30-40 58

MARKEES
(Marquees)
Singles: 7-inch
GRAND (141 "The Bells") 40-50 61
(Yellow label. No company address shown.)
Also see MARQUEES

MARKEETS
(With the Leon Ross Band)
Singles: 7-inch
MELATONE (1005 "Tear Drops") 250-350 57
Member: Fred Hughes.

MAR-KELLS
Singles: 7-inch
JCP (1036 "Call") 10-20 64
JCP (1041 "Don't You Realize") 10-20 65

MARKELS
(With Bob Bravin's Orchestra)
Singles: 7-inch
R&M (407-617 "The Letter of Love") 300-400 58

MARKER, Morty
Singles: 7-inch
BACK BEAT (521 "Tear Down the House") 40-60 59

MARKETTS P&R '62
(Mar-Kets)
Singles: 7-inch
ARVEE (5063 "Beach Bum") 15-20 62
LIBERTY (55401 "Surfer's Stomp") 15-20 62
LIBERTY (55443 "Balboa Blue") 15-20 62
LIBERTY (55506 " Canadian Sunset ") ... 15-20 62
MERCURY (73433 "Sister Candy") 4-6 73
SEMINOLE (501 "M*A*S*H Theme") 4-6 76
UNI (55173 "Undefeated") 5-10 69
UNION (501 "Surfer's Stomp") 30-40 61
UNION (504 "Balboa Blue") 30-40 62
UNION (507 "Canadian Sunset") 30-40 62
W.B. (5365 "Woody Wagon") 8-12 63
W.B. (5391 "Outer Limits") 15-25 63
W.B. (5391 "Out of Limits") 10-15 63
(Note title change.)
W.B. (5423 "Vanishing Point") 10-15 64
W.B. (5468 "Come See, Come Ska") 10-15 64
W.B. (5641 "Miami's Blue") 10-15 65
W.B. (5670 "Ready Steady Go") 10-15 65
W.B. (5696 "Batman Theme") 8-12 66
W.B. (5814 "Theme from *The Avengers*") .. 8-12 66
WORLD PACIFIC (77874 "Sun Power") 8-12 67
LPs: 10/12-inch
DORE (501 "Summer Means Love") 5-10 82
LIBERTY (3226 "Surfer's Stomp") 30-40 62
(Monaural.)
LIBERTY (3226 "Surfing Scene") 20-25 62
(Monaural. Reissue.)
LIBERTY (7226 "Surfer's Stomp") 35-45 62
(Stereo.)
LIBERTY (7226 "Surfing Scene") 25-30 62
(Stereo. Reissue.)
MERCURY (679 "AM, FM, Etc.") 10-15 73
PHONORAMA 5-10 84
W.B. (W-1509 "Take to Wheels") 20-30 63
(Monaural.)
W.B. (WS-1509 "Take to Wheels") 30-40 63
(Stereo.)
W.B. (W-1537 "Out of Limits") 25-35 64
(Monaural.)
W.B. (WS-1537 "Out of Limits") 35-45 64
(Stereo.)
W.B. (W-1642 "Batman Theme") 20-30 66
(Monaural.)
W.B. (WS-1642 "Batman Theme") 30-40 66
(Stereo.)
WORLD PACIFIC (1870 "Sun Power") 15-25 67
Members: Ben Benay; Mike Henderson; Ray Pohlman; Tommy Tedesco; Bill Pittman; Gene Pello; Tom Hensley; Richard Hobaica.
Also see BEACH BOYS / Marketts / Frogmen
Also see TEDESCO, Tommy

MARKEYS
Singles: 7-inch
RCA (7256 "Hot Rod") 10-15 58
RCA (7412 "A Time to Love") 10-15 58

MAR-KEYS P&R/R&B '61
Singles: 7-inch
SATELITE (107 "Last Night") 10-15 61
STAX 5-10 61-66
LPs: 10/12-inch
ATLANTIC 20-25 61-62
STAX 10-20 66-71
Members: Donald Dunn; Steve Cropper; Terry Johnson; Smoochie Smith; Wayne Jackson; Joe Arnold; Charles Axton; Don Nix; Andrew Love.
Also see PACKERS
Also see TRIUMPHS

MAR-KEYS / Booker T. & MGs LP '67
LPs: 10/12-inch
STAX (720 "Back to Back") 12-18 67
Also see BOOKER T. & MGs
Also see MAR-KEYS

MARKEYS
Singles: 7-inch
TWENTIETH CENTURY (1210 "Eternal Love") 40-50 61

MARKHAM, Don, & Marksmen
Singles: 7-inch
DONNA (1323 "The Shuck") 10-15 60
DONNA (1325 "The Goose") 10-15 60

MARKHAM, Junior, & Tulsa Review
Singles: 7-inch
UPTOWN (759 "Let 'Em Roll") 5-10 69
UPTOWN (762 "Black Cherry") 5-10 69

MARKHAM, Mark
(With the Jesters)
Singles: 7-inch
POWER (4225 "Marlboro Country") 20-30 66
(First issue.)
RCA (8992 "Marlboro Country") 10-15 66
LPs: 10/12-inch
ATHENS FIRE 15-25
Session: Mark Markham; Scott Austin.

MARKHAM, Pigmeat P&R/R&B/LP '68
Singles: 7-inch
ABC 4-6 74
CHESS 4-8 64-70
WIG 6-12
EPs: 7-inch
CHESS (5128 "Pigmeat Markham – *The Trial Excerpts*") 10-15 61
LPs: 10/12-inch
CHESS 10-20 61-69
JEWEL 5-10 72-73
Also see MABLEY, Moms, & Pigmeat Markham

MARKLEY, Bob
(Markley)
Singles: 7-inch
W.B. (5140 "Tia Juana Ball") 15-25 60
W.B. (5167 "It Should've Been Me") 15-25 60
LPs: 10/12-inch
FORWARD (1007 "A Group") 15-25 69
Also see WEST COAST POP ART EXPERIMENTAL BAND

MARKS, Guy P&R '68
(With the Peter DeAngelis Orchestra)
Singles: 7-inch
ABC 4-8 68
ARIOLA AMERICA 4-6 76
RADNOR 4-6 70
LPs: 10/12-inch
ABC 10-20 66-68

MARKS, J.
(J. Marks & Shipen Lebzelter)
LPs: 10/12-inch
COLUMBIA (7193 "Rock and Other Four-Letter Words") 15-25 68
COLUMBIA (30006 "First National Nothing") 10-15 70

MARKS, Lou
Singles: 7-inch
ABC (10857 "Just Dance") 5-10 66

MARKS, Richard
Singles: 7-inch
ROULETTE (7034 "Funky Four Corners") . 5-10 69
TUSKA (101 "Funky Four Corners") .... 30-50 '60s

MARKS, Roosevelt, Orchestra
(With Clayton Love)
Singles: 7-inch
BOBBIN (102 "Unlimited Love") 8-12 59
BOBBIN (108 "Bye Bye Baby") 8-12 59
Also see LOVE, Clayton

MARKS, Steve / Jack Richards / Vic Corwin Orchestra
EPs: 7-inch
GILMAR (214 "Six Hits") 20-30 57
Also see CORWIN, Vic, Orchestra

MARKS, Zachary
Singles: 7-inch
REEL (102 "Daddy-O") 5-10 60

MARKSMEN
Singles: 78 rpm
CORAL (61453 "Hot Rod") 8-12 55
Singles: 7-inch
CORAL (61453 "Hot Rod") 15-25 55

MARKSMEN
Singles: 7-inch
STARDAY (320 "Don't Gamble with My Heart") 250-350 57

MARKSMEN
Singles: 7-inch
BLUE HORIZON (6052 "Night Run") 30-50 61
Members: Nokie Edwards, Howie Johnson.
Also see VENTURES

MARKSMEN
Singles: 7-inch
WESTCO (10 "Down the Tubes") 10-20
(Black vinyl.)
WESTCO (10 "Down the Tubes") 20-40
(Colored vinyl.)

MARKSMEN
Singles: 7-inch
SARA (65128 "Black Pepper") 15-25 65
Members: Dick Neu; Ken Locke; Bob Allen Humpa; Ed Porcaro; Dan Vance; Jerry Bellamy.

MARKSMEN
Singles: 7-inch
DEARBORN (536 "Castle Rock") 5-10 66

MARKTONES
Singles: 78 rpm
EMBER 30-50 57-58
Singles: 7-inch
EMBER (1022 "Hold Me Close") 40-50 57
EMBER (1030 "Yes, Siree") 30-40 58

MARLAND, Cletus
Singles: 7-inch
GENEVA (109 "Every Now and Then") 10-20
ROULETTE (4388 "I'll Take Care Of You") 5-10 61

MARLEE, Dan
Singles: 7-inch
CONSTELLATION (125 "You Left Me") 5-10 64

MARLENA
Singles: 7-inch
JAMIE (1313 "I Don't Want to Go On Without You") 5-10 66

MARLENE, Donna
Singles: 7-inch
SPANGLE (501 "Only Forever") .... 5-10 '60s

MARLENE, Gary
Singles: 7-inch
MAVERICK (591 "Look for a Star") 8-12 60

MARLENE & DEBANETTES
Singles: 7-inch
SUNBURST (1111 "Play Something Slow") 10-20
SUNBURST (9780 "Bad Love") 15-25 65

MARLETTES
(With the Imperial Orchestra)
Singles: 7-inch
HOWFUM ("Just the Way You Are") .. 750-1000 58
(No selection number used.)

MARLEY, Bob, & Wailers LP '75
(Wailers)
Singles: 7-inch
COTILLION 3-5 81
ISLAND 3-6 76-84
SHELTER 4-6 71
TUFF GONG 4-6 74
Picture Sleeves
ISLAND 3-5 83
LPs: 10/12-inch
AUDIO FIDELITY (350 "Bob Marley") 10-15 83
(Picture disc.)
CALLA (1200 series) 10-15 76
CALLA (34000 series) 8-10 77
COTILLION 5-10 81
ISLAND (11 "Babylon By Bus") 10-12 78
ISLAND (9000 series, except 9329) 8-12 75-80
ISLAND (9329 "Catch a Fire") 15-25 75
(Shaped cover.)
ISLAND (9329 "Catch a Fire") 8-10 75
(Standard cover.)
ISLAND (90000 series) 5-10 83-86
LYNN ("Soul Revolution II") 10-20
(No selection number used.)
MFSL (221 "Exodus") 25-35 94
MFSL (236 "Catch a Fire") 25-35 95
Also see TOSH, Peter

MARLEY, Lloyd
Singles: 7-inch
UNITED SOUTHERN ARTISTS (109 "Ooh Poo Pah Doo") 8-12 61

MARLEY, Rita
Singles: 7-inch
STUDIO ONE (5 "You Lied") 25-50

MARLIN, Milton
Singles: 7-inch
CAROL (104 "Working On a New Love") ... 5-10 66

MARLIN & MERMAIDS
Singles: 7-inch
ABC-PAR (10493 "At Weeki Wachee") 5-10 63
Picture Sleeves
ABC-PAR (10493 "At Weeki Wachee") 15-20 63

MARLIN SISTERS
Singles: 7-inch
METRO (20009 "Sunshine & Laughter") 8-12 58

MARLINS
Singles: 7-inch
SANDY (1002 "Now I'm So Lonesome I Could Die") 75-125 57

MARLINS
Singles: 7-inch
CAMEO (333 "Swim") 8-12 64

MARLINS
Singles: 7-inch
SCOTTY (818 "Let Down") .... 5-10 '60s

MARLO, Bob
Singles: 7-inch
RONCO (104 "Straighten Up and Fly Right") 15-25

MARLO, Micki P&R '57
Singles: 78 rpm
ABC-PAR (Except 9841) 5-10 57
ABC-PAR (9841 "What You've Done to Me") 10-20 57
(With "Vocal assist by Paul Anka.")
ABC-PAR (9841 "What You've Done to Me") 5-10 57
(Has the singer humming the lines done by Paul Anka on first pressing.)
CAPITOL 5-10 54-56
Singles: 7-inch
ABC-PAR (Except 9841) 5-10 57
ABC-PAR (9841 "What You've Done to Me") 10-20 57
(With "Vocal assist by Paul Anka.")
ABC-PAR (9841 "What You've Done to Me") 5-10 57
(Has the singer humming the lines done by Paul Anka on first pressing.)

CAPITOL ... 10-15 54-56
LPs: 10/12-inch
ABC-PAR (295 "Married I Can Always Get") ... 15-25 60
Also see ANKA, Paul

MARLO, Russ
Singles: 7-inch
JAX (106 "Down by the Riverside") ... 15-25 61
U.A. (112 "Tom Cattin'") ... 30-40 58

MARLOW, Jerry, & Full House
Singles: 7-inch
TRUMP (004 "What Are Little Girls Made Of") ... 10-15 61

MARLOW, Ricky
(Ric Marlow)
Singles: 7-inch
LIBERTY (55098 "Pretty Baby") ... 10-15 57
PAT (760 "She's Gone") ... 15-25

MARLOW, Ric
Singles: 7-inch
ZEPHYR (7 "That's What I'm Gonna Be") ... 75-125

MARMALADE P&R/LP '70
Singles: 7-inch
ARIOLA AMERICA ... 4-6 76
EMI ... 4-6 74
EPIC ... 4-8 67-69
LONDON ... 4-6 70-72
LPs: 10/12-inch
EPIC ... 10-15 70
G&P ... 8-10 81
LONDON ... 10-15 70
Members: Dean Ford; Junior Campbell.

MARONI, Chuck, & Preludes
Singles: 7-inch
ESSAR (1006 "Don't Tell Me") ... 5-10 62
IMPERIAL (5498 "Flap Flap") ... 8-12 58

MAROONS
Singles: 7-inch
QUEEN (24012 "Someday I'll Be the One") ... 20-30 62

MARQUE V
Singles: 7-inch
W.B. (7009 "Can't Buy My Soul") ... 5-10 67

MARQUEE MONSTERS
Singles: 7-inch
OUR BAG (102 "Laws & Restrictions") ... 20-30

MARQUEES
Singles: 78 rpm
GRAND (141 "The Bells") ... 50-100 56
Singles: 7-inch
COLLECTABLES ... 3-5 '80s
GRAND (141 "The Bells") ... 400-500 56
(Yellow label. Rigid disc. No company address shown. Reissued as by the Markees.)
Also see MARKEES

MARQUEES
Singles: 78 rpm
OKEH (7096 "Hey Little School Girl") ... 75-100 57
Singles: 7-inch
OKEH (7096 "Hey Little School Girl") ... 75-100 57
Members: Marvin Gaye; Reese Palmer; Bob Hawkins; Chester Simmons; Nolan Ellison.
Also see GAYE, Marvin
Also see MOONGLOWS
Also see SPINNERS
Also see STEWART, Billy

MARQUEES
(With the Gene Joseph Trio)
Singles: 7-inch
DAYSEL (1001 "Close to Me") ... 200-300 58

MARQUEES
Singles: 7-inch
LEN (100 "Say Hey") ... 100-125 58

MARQUEES
Singles: 7-inch
DO-RA-ME (1407 "In the Halo of Your Love") ... 10-20 59

MARQUEES
(With the "Big Sound of Don Ralke")
Singles: 7-inch
W.B. (5072 "Who Will Be the First One") ... 20-30 59
W.B. (5127 "Christmas in the Congo") ... 20-30 59
W.B. (5139 "Until the Day I Die") ... 40-60 60
Also see RALKE, Don

MARQUEES
(With the Rosco Weathers Orchestra)
Singles: 7-inch
JO ANN (128 "Stay with Me") ... 100-200 60
JO ANN (130 "I Need a Helping Hand") ... 75-125 61

MARQUIS
Singles: 78 rpm
RAINBOW ... 40-50 55
Singles: 7-inch
RAINBOW (358 "I Don't Want Your Love") ... 150-200 55

MARQUIS
(With the Sammy Lowe Orchestra)
Singles: 78 rpm
ONYX (505 "Bohemian Daddy") ... 200-300 56
Singles: 7-inch
ONYX (505 "Bohemian Daddy") ... 1000-2000 56
RELIC (505 "Bohemian Daddy") ... 5-10 64
(Yellow vinyl.)
Also see BATEMAN, June
Also see LOWE, Sammy, Orchestra

MARQUIS
Singles: 7-inch
NOBLE (719 "Never Forget") ... 750-1000 59
(Repressed crediting the Tabs.)
Also see TABS

MARQUIS
Singles: 7-inch
CLASS (251 "Strange Is Love") ... 10-15 59
EARL ... 5-10

MARQUIS
Singles: 7-inch
TEEN GRAVE (201,159 "Broken Mirror") ... 20-30 66

MARQUIS
Singles: 7-inch
JCP (1024 "Walking a Stranger") ... 10-20 64

MARR, Hank
(Hank Marr Trio; Quartet)
Singles: 7-inch
FEDERAL ... 5-10 61-64
KING ... 4-8 68-69
WINGATE (012 "The Out Crowd") ... 8-12 66
LPs: 10/12-inch
KING ... 10-20 63-69

MARR, Hank / Sonny Stitt
Singles: 7-inch
WINGATE (011 "Marr's Groove"/"Stitt's Groove") ... 5-10 66
Also see MARR, Hank
Also see STITT, Sonny

MARRELL'S MARAUDERS
Singles: 7-inch
FAN JR (1003 "I Wanta Do It") ... 25-50 66
(Reissued twice as by Robin and the Three Hoods.)
Also see ROBIN & THREE HOODS

MARREN, Howard
Singles: 7-inch
FARGO (1006 "I'm Getting to Be a Big Boy Now") ... 15-25 59

MARRIOTS
Singles: 7-inch
ABC (11218 "Ooh Baby Baby") ... 5-10 69

MARRO, Brad
Singles: 78 rpm
ABBOTT ... 10-15 55
Singles: 7-inch
ABBOTT (3010 "Heart of Gold") ... 15-25 55

MARRS, Troy
Singles: 7-inch
SURE SHOT (5019 "Rhythm Message") ... 5-10 66

MARS, Marlina
Singles: 7-inch
CAPITOL ... 5-10 63
MGM ... 10-20 65-66
OKEH (7213 "It's Love That Really Counts") ... 15-25 65

MARS, Mitzi R&B '53
Singles: 78 rpm
CHECKER (773 "I'm Glad") ... 15-25 53
Singles: 7-inch
CHECKER (773 "I'm Glad") ... 20-40 53

MARS, Sylvia
LPs: 10/12-inch
LYRIC (124 "Blues Walk Right In") ... 40-60

MARSDEN, Beryl
Singles: 7-inch
CAPITOL (5552 "Gonna Make Him My Baby") ... 5-10 65

MARSDEN, Gerry
Singles: 7-inch
COLUMBIA (44309 "Please Let Them Be") ... 5-10 67
Also see GERRY & PACEMAKERS

MARSH, Billy
Singles: 7-inch
ARROW (716 "Don't Tell Me") ... 20-30 57
ARROW (722 "Tell Me") ... 10-15 58

MARSH, Nettie
Singles: 7-inch
INSTANT (3274 "String of Lies") ... 5-10 65

MARSH, Richie
(Dick Marsh; with Hoodwinks)
Singles: 7-inch
ACAMA (125 "Half Angel") ... 10-20 61
ÄVA (122 "Goodbye") ... 10-15 63
ROSCO (412 "There's Only One Girl") ... 10-20 60
SHEPHERD ... 10-20 '60s
Also see SAXON, Sky

MARSHAL, Gary
Singles: 7-inch
RCA (8849 "After the Laughter") ... 5-10 66
RCA (9083 "This Year") ... 5-10 67
LPs: 10/12-inch
RCA (3487 "You're Gonna Hear from Me") ... 10-15 66
RCA (3602 "Show Stopper") ... 10-15 66
Also see MARCH, Peggy, & Gary Marshal

MARSHAL, A.J.
LPs: 10/12-inch
MGM (4648 "There's a Lot of Lovin' in This Old Boy Yet") ... 5-10 69

MARSHALL, Bill
Singles: 7-inch
R-DELL (108 "It Was Just One of Those Things") ... 8-12 58

MARSHALL, Bob
Singles: 78 rpm
DAWN ... 5-10 54
Singles: 7-inch
DAWN (206 "Bewitched Am I") ... 10-15 54
DAWN (207 "Sweet Perfumed Letter") ... 10-15 54

MARSHALL, Dick, & Nighthawks
Singles: 7-inch
CUCA (6311 "Jitterbug Joe") ... 20-40 62

MARSHALL, Dodi
Singles: 7-inch
PULSE (1006 "Good Good Gravy") ... 5-10 65

MARSHALL, Eddie
Singles: 7-inch
RCA (48-0357 "Tom Cat Blues") ... 10-20 50
(Green vinyl.)

MARSHALL, Eric, & Chymes
Singles: 7-inch
SIRE (4101 "I Can't Love You Anymore") ... 10-15 68
Also see T.C. ATLANTIC

MARSHALL, Frank
Singles: 7-inch
ARCADE (160 "Louisiana Shuffle") ... 5-10 61

MARSHALL, Frankie
Singles: 78 rpm
ATCO ... 5-10 55-56
SPARK (117 "Just Say the Word") ... 5-10 55
Singles: 7-inch
ATCO ... 10-15 55-56
JACKPOT (48009 "Don't Go") ... 10-15 58
SPARK (117 "Just Say the Word") ... 10-15 55
SPRY (102 "Walk with Me") ... 10-15 57

MARSHALL, George
Singles: 7-inch
GAIETY (87718 "Do We Know") ... 50-75

MARSHALL, Jack
Singles: 78 rpm
EKKO ... 5-10 54
Singles: 7-inch
EKKO (101 "Bye Bye My Baby") ... 10-20 54
EKKO (104 "Choo Choo Guitar") ... 10-20 54

MARSHALL, Jack
("Tuff Jack")
Singles: 7-inch
CAPITOL ... 5-10 60-64
LPs: 10/12-inch
CAPITOL (T-1727 "Twangy, Shoutin', Fantastic Big-Band Sounds of Tuff Jack") ... 20-30 62
(Monaural.)
CAPITOL (ST-1727 "Twangy, Shoutin', Fantastic Big-Band Sounds of Tuff Jack") ... 25-35 62
(Stereo.)
CAPITOL (T-1939 "My Son the Surf Nut") ... 20-30 63
(Monaural.)
CAPITOL (ST-1939 "My Son the Surf Nut") ... 25-35 63
Stereo.)
Also see LEE, Peggy
Also see LIND, Cory

MARSHALL, Lynn
Singles: 7-inch
CREST (1034 "Borrowed Love") ... 8-12 57
(Black vinyl.)
CREST (1034 "Borrowed Love") ... 15-20 57
(Colored vinyl.)
CREST (1035 "The Hat") ... 8-12 57
CREST (1036 "My Only One") ... 8-12 57
CREST (1046 "As Years Go By") ... 8-12 58

MARSHALL, Maria
Singles: 7-inch
KENT (347 "You Fall in Love with Everybody") ... 5-10 60
LPs: 10/12-inch
CROWN (208 "Chubby Jackson Discovers Maria Marshall") ... 10-20 61
(Black vinyl.)
CROWN (208 "Chubby Jackson Discovers Maria Marshall") ... 20-35 61
(Colored vinyl.)
Also see JACKSON, Chubby

MARSHALL, Percy
Singles: 7-inch
MARSHALL (101 "Leaving Town") ... 15-25

MARSHALL, Peter, & Deputies
Singles: 78 rpm
MELBA (103 "Nice and Cozy") ... 10-15 56
Singles: 7-inch
MELBA (103 "Nice and Cozy") ... 20-30 56

MARSHALL, Ron
Singles: 7-inch
INTREPID (75004 "Let Me Be Free") ... 4-8 69
LAURIE (3697 "Dear Mr. President") ... 3-5 '80s
LAURIE (3700 "Castles in the Sand") ... 3-5 '80s
MOHAWK (134 "Hold Me Close") ... 5-10 63
SWAN (4056 "I Know This Place") ... 5-10 60
TOP RANK (2056 "Please Don't Say Goodbye") ... 5-10 60

MARSHALL, Sammy
(With the Sun Rays; with Rays; with Kris Arden & the Rays; Singing Sammy Marshall; with Party Crashers; with Nute James)
Singles: 78 rpm
SILVER ... 5-10 '50s
Singles: 7-inch
BLUE HILL (2896 "Blue Hill Twist") ... 5-10 62
BROSH BROS. (900 "Yellow Gold") ... 5-10 63
CHEYENNE (601 "Game of Love") ... 5-10 63
DOTTIE (1008 "Give Me Music") ... 5-10 61
JABAR ... 10-15
KEEPSAKE (1006 "Salton Sea") ... 5-10 63
MAYHAMS (213 "My College Girl") ... 5-10 63
PLEDGE (104 "Tears and Champagne") ... 5-10 62
RANCHWOOD (2230 "Game of Love") ... 5-10 62
ROXIE (301 "Be Optimistic") ... 5-10 61

ROXIE (302 "Please Believe") 5-10 61
ROXIE (324 "It's Christmas Time Again")...5-10 62
ROXIE (325 "Out of the Blue") 5-10 62
ROXIE (326 "Be Optimistic") 5-10 62
SHOW (2244 "Little Girl") 5-10 62
SILVER.. 10-15 '50s
TJB (101 "Jingle Mint Twist").......................5-10 62
VALE (1001 "Bender Song") 5-10 61
WORLD'S FAIR (1001 "World Fair Wiggle Walk")..5-10 64
WORLD'S FAIR (1004 "World Fair Honeymoon")...5-10 64

MARSHALL, Sammy / Key Tones

Singles: 7-inch

BROSH BROS. (400 "Love Song for You"/"Until Eternity") 15-25 62

MARSHALL, Sammy / Cara Stewart

EPs: 7-inch

AIR (5027 "I'll Always Love You") 4-6
Also see MARSHALL, Sammy

MARSHALL, Wayne
(With the Members)

Singles: 7-inch

JOSIE (937 "Her Final Letter") 5-10 65

MARSHALL & CHI-LITES

Singles: 7-inch

DAKAR (600 "The Price of Love")..............5-10 68
Member: Marshall Thompson.
Also see CHI-LITES

MARSHALL & WES

Singles: 7-inch

MILESTONE (2004 "Time")...................... 10-20 60
Member: Marshall Lytle.
Also see LYTELL, Marshall

MARSHALL BROTHERS

Singles: 78 rpm

SAVOY (825 "Who'll Be the Fool from Now On") 25-50 51
(Reissued as by the Marshalls.)
SAVOY (833 "Why Make a Fool Out of Me")... 25-50 52
Member: Maithe Marshall; Rich Cannon; Ray Johnson; Willis Saunders.
Also see COOK, Bill, & Marshalls
Also see MARSHALLS
Also see RAVENS

MARSHALL TUCKER BAND *LP '73*

Singles: 7-inch

CAPRICORN...4-6 73-78
ERIC ....3-5 '70s
MERCURY 3-5 87-88
W.B. 3-6 79-83

Picture Sleeves

W.B. 4-6 79

LPs: 10/12-inch

CAPRICORN...8-12 73-78
MERCURY 5-10 87
W.B. 5-10 79-83
Members: Doug Gray; Tom Caldwell; Troy Caldwell; Franklin Wilkie; Jack Eubanks; Paul Riddle.

MARSHALLS

Singles: 7-inch

SAVOY (825 "Who'll Be the Fool from Now On") 15-25 62
(First issue by the Marshall Brothers.)
Also see MARSHALL BROTHERS

MARSHANS

Singles: 7-inch

ETIQUETTE (8 "I Remember") 10-15 64
JOHNSON (736 "Main Man") 15-25 66

MARSHMALLOW HIGHWAY

Singles: 7-inch

KAPP (904 "Loving You Makes Everything Alright") 5-10 68

MARSHMALLOW WAY

Singles: 7-inch

U.A. (50611 "Good Day") 5-10 69

LPs: 10/12-inch

U.A. (6708 "Marshmallow Way")............. 10-20 69
Member: Billy Carl.
Also see BILLY & ESSENTIALS

MARSHMELLOW STEAMSHOVEL

Singles: 7-inch

HEAD (1908 "Steamshovel")...................10-20 64

MARSHMELLOW TUGBOAT

Singles: 7-inch

BLUE CORAL (5474 "Michelle, Be My Girl")..10-15 67

MARSHMELLOWS

Singles: 7-inch

COLUMBIA (44159 "Just You & I")............5-10 67
VEEP (1212 "When I Look at My Love") 5-10 65

MARTEL, Bill

Singles: 7-inch

IMPALA (207 "Now or Never") 40-50 59

MARTEL, Johnny

Singles: 7-inch

GONE (5071 "Exactly Like You")..............10-15 59

MARTEL, Rick

Singles: 7-inch

ARWIN (119 "Love, Return to Me") 5-10 59

MARTELL, Freddie

Singles: 7-inch

TOP RANK (2033 "Perfect Fool") 5-10 60

MARTELL, Joy

Singles: 7-inch

JARO (77002 "The One I Love")................8-12 59

MARTELLS
(Martels; Eulis Mason & Martells with Bellatones Orchestra)

Singles: 7-inch

ATCO (6336 "What Can I Do")...................5-10 65
BELLA (20 "Carol Lee")...........................75-125 61
BELLA (21 "Va Va Voom") 100-150 61
CESSNA (477 "Va Va Voom") 200-250 61
NASCO (6026 "Where Did My Woman Go")..10-15 59
RELIC (517 "Va Va Voom")........................5-10 64

MARTELLS

Singles: 7-inch

A-LA-CARTE (283 "In the Morning").........10-20

MARTHA & BOB

Singles: 7-inch

GOLDEN CREST (542 "Tweenager") 8-12 60

MARTHA & VANDELLAS *P&R/R&B/LP '63*
(Martha Reeves & Vandellas)

Singles: 7-inch

GORDY (7011 "I'll Have to Let Him Go")..30-40 62
GORDY (7014 "Come and Get These Memories") 10-20 63
GORDY (7022 thru 7062)...........................8-15 63-67
(Black vinyl.)
GORDY (7062 "Love Bug Leave My Heart Alone") 8-15 67
(Colored vinyl. Promotional issue only.)
GORDY (7067 thru 7127).........................4-8 67-73
(Black vinyl.)
GORDY (7113 "In and Out of My Life") 8-15 71
(Colored vinyl. Promotional issue only.)
MOTOWN...3-5
MOTOWN/TOPPS (7 "Dancing in the Street")...50-75 67
(Topps Chewing Gum promotional item. Single-sided, cardboard flexi, picture disc. Issued with generic paper sleeve.)
MOTOWN/TOPPS (14 "Heat Wave").......50-75 67
(Topps Chewing Gum promotional item. Single-sided, cardboard flexi, picture disc. Issued with generic paper sleeve.)
TAMLA/MOTOWN 4-8

Picture Sleeves

GORDY (7033 "Dancing in the Street")..150-200 64

EPs: 7-inch

GORDY (60920 "Watchout")....................15-25 67
MOTOWN (2009 "Martha & the Vandellas") 15-25
MOTOWN (2017 "Hittin' ")........................15-25

LPs: 10/12-inch

ERA 5-10 79
GORDY (902 "Come and Get These Memories") 100-200 63
(Monaural.)
GORDY (S-902 "Come and Get These Memories") 200-300 63
(Stereo.)
GORDY (907 "Heat Wave") 60-80 63
(Monaural.)
GORDY (S-907 "Heat Wave") 75-100 63
(Stereo.)
GORDY (915 "Dance Party") 50-75 65
(Monaural.)
GORDY (S-915 "Dance Party") 60-80 65
(Stereo.)
GORDY (917 "Greatest Hits") 20-30 66
GORDY (920 "Watchout")........................20-30 67
GORDY (925 "Live")................................15-25 66
GORDY (926 thru 958).............................15-20 68-72
MOTOWN (Except 100 & 200 series) 12-15 74
MOTOWN (100 & 200 series)......................5-8 81-82
PICKWICK 5-8
Members: Martha Reeves; Rosalind Ashford; Annette Beard; Betty Kelly; Lois Reeves; Sandra Tilley.
Also see ALAN, Lee, & Vandellas
Also see BEN, LaBrenda
Also see BROWN, James / Martha & Vandellas
Also see DEL-PHIS
Also see GAYE, Marvin
Also see HONDELLS / Del Shannon / Martha & Vandellas
Also see HOOKER, John Lee
Also see MALLETT, Sandra, & Vandellas
Also see VELLS
Also see VELVELETTES

MARTIANS

Singles: 7-inch

ADMIRAL (110 "Martian's Rock") 5-10 64

MARTIN, Aston, & Moon Discs

Singles: 7-inch

DEL RIO (2301 "Fallout") 20-30 61

MARTIN, Barry

Singles: 7-inch

FREEDOM (44019 "Minnie the Moocher").5-10 59
LIBERTY (55137 "Hello Love") 8-12 57
RCA (7834 "Got a Whole Lot of Loving to Do")..10-15 61
RCA (7864 "Little Lonely One") 10-15 61

MARTIN, Benny *C&W '63*
(Bennie Martin)

Singles: 78 rpm

MERCURY...5-10 54-56

Singles: 7-inch

ASTRO (109 "Darling Goodbye") 100-150 60
DECCA (30935 "Untrue Your")..................8-12 59
GULF REEF (1005 "Man Next Door") 10-15 62
HI (2062 "Love You Too Much") 5-8 63
JAB (9002 "Salvation Army") 4-6 67
MERCURY...10-15 54-56
RCA (7100 "Do Me a Favor")....................10-15 58
STARDAY 5-10 60-65

LPs: 10/12-inch

CMH 5-10
FLYING FISH..8-10
GUEST STAR ....10-15 '60s
MARATHON 8-10
(Canadian.)
WING..8-10 '60s

MARTIN, Benny, & Bobby Sykes

LPs: 10/12-inch

PICKWICK/HILLTOP 10-15 65
Also see MARTIN, Benny
Also see SYKES, Bobby

MARTIN, Bet E.

Singles: 7-inch

BRUNSWICK (55107 "Pretty Lies")............8-12 58
EPIC (9333 "Maybe You'll Be There") 20-30 59
EPIC (9362 "I Know a Girl")......................10-15 60
EPIC (9414 "I Can't Find My Keys") 10-15 60
ERA (3163 "You've Got to See Mama Every Night")..5-10 66
FORD (107 "Mrs. Santa Claus") 5-10 61

MARTIN, Bill / James Lane

Singles: 7-inch

CHART (1004 "Meet Me Halfway").......250-350

MARTIN, Billy
(With the Corvairs; Bill Martin)

Singles: 7-inch

LUCKY (0009 "If It's Lovin' That You Want")...25-50 60
MONITOR (1402 "I Found My Baby") ......15-25 '60s
TRIBUTE (115 "Come On") 10-15 62

MARTIN, Bobby
(Bob Martin)

Singles: 7-inch

BEL-KAY (600 "Jo Jo Rock & Roll") 50-100 58
BEL-KAY (605 "Back to School Rock")..50-100 58
MAR-TONE (0001 "The World I Left Behind")..5-10 62
RUBY (390 "Sleepy Time Blues")......... 100-200 57
RUBY (400 "There Ain't No Nothing Tonight")...50-100 57
TIDE (0015 "My Heart Is Thumpy")..........10-20 61
TODD (1013 "Hunk of Dynamite")............10-20 59
TREND (3973 "Slowly") 5-10 66

MARTIN, Chuck

Singles: 78 rpm

NASCO (6004 "Emma Lee")......................20-30 57

Singles: 7-inch

JIN (128 "As Long As I Have You") 15-25 60
NASCO (6004 "Emma Lee")......................20-30 57

MARTIN, Cliff, & Cliff Dwellers

Singles: 7-inch

CREST (16 "The Prairie") 8-10 58
CREST (500 "Full Time Job") 8-10 59
CREST (502 "Older and Bolder") 8-10 59
CREST (504 "Back Street Affair")...............8-10 59

MARTIN, Danny

Singles: 7-inch

RIOT (431 "Rockin' Memphis Mama")......25-30 57

MARTIN, Dave

Singles: 7-inch

VIRTUE (1 "Old Man River")......................20-30 60

MARTIN, Dean *P&R '49*
(With Orchestras of: Dick Stabile; Gus Levene; Nelson Riddle; Neal Hefti; Marty Paich; Chuck Sagle; Don Costa; Ernie Freeman)

Singles: 78 rpm

APOLLO (1088 "Oh Marie")..................100-150 47
APOLLO (1116 "Santa Lucia") 100-150 48
CAPITOL (545 thru 2001) 15-25 49-52
CAPITOL (2037 "Hey, Brother, Pour the Wine")...20-30 54
(Seven-inch 78 rpm. Promotional issue only.)
CAPITOL (2071 thru 3841) 10-20 52-57
CAPITOL (15000 series)...........................20-40 48-49
DIAMOND (2035 "Which Way Did My Heart Go")..100-150 46
DIAMOND (2036 "I Got the Sun in the Morning")...100-150 46
EMBASSY (124 "One Foot in Heaven")...500-1000 49

Singles: 7-inch

CAPITOL (401 "Dean Martin Sings")......75-100 53
(Boxed, four-disc set.)
CAPITOL (247 "Silver Bells")....................10-15 66
(Promotional issue only.)
CAPITOL (691 thru 981) 25-35 49-50
CAPITOL (987 "Sleep Warm")................50-100 59
(Promotional issue only.)
CAPITOL (1002 thru 1458).......................20-30 50-51
CAPITOL (1609 "I Met a Girl")...............50-100 60
(Promotional issue only.)
CAPITOL (1703 thru 3238).......................15-25 51-55
CAPITOL (3295 thru 4570).......................10-20 55-61
CAPITOL (6000 series)................................4-6 64
CAPITOL (44153 "That's Amore")...............3-5 88
MCA (52662 "L.A. Is My Home")..............50-75 85
REPRISE (190 thru 193).............................6-12 64
(Compact 33 singles. Promotional issues only.)
REPRISE (200 "Sophia") 150-200 65
(Promotional issue only.)
REPRISE (0252 thru 1178).........................5-10 64-73
REPRISE (20,000 series) 8-12 62-63
REPRISE (40,015 "Gigi")...........................15-25 62
(Stereo 33 single.)
REPRISE (40,016 "C'est Si Bon") 15-25 62
(Stereo 33 single.)
REPRISE (40,017 "Mimi")..........................15-25 62
(Stereo 33 single.)
REPRISE (40,018 "The River Seine")......15-25 62
(Stereo 33 single.)
REPRISE (40,019 "Mam'Selle") 15-25 62
(Stereo 33 single.)
TEXAS DESERT CIRCUS WEEK (2160 "It's 1200 Miles from Texas to Palm Springs").......75-125 58
(Single-sided promotional disc. Made especially for play in Palm Springs, promoting a circus. Incorrect title is shown on label—should read *It's 1200 Miles from Palm Springs to Texas.*)

W.B. (29584 "My First Country Song") 3-5 83
(With Conway Twitty.)
W.B. (29480 "Drinking Champagne") 3-5 83

Picture Sleeves

CAPITOL (987 "Sleep Warm") 100-200 59
CAPITOL (1609 "I Met a Girl") 50-100 60
(Promotional issue only. Sleeve reads: "From the Soundtrack of the Motion Picture *Bells are Ringing.*")
CAPITOL (4028 "Volare") 15-25 58
CAPITOL (4222 "On an Evening in Roma") 15-25 59
REPRISE (20,116 "Who's Got the Action") 15-20 62

EPs: 7-inch

CAPITOL (EAP-401 "Dean Martin Sings") 25-50 53
(Price is for either of two volumes.)
CAPITOL (EBF-401 "Dean Martin Sings") 75-125 53
(Boxed, two-disc set.)
CAPITOL (481 "Sunny Italy") 25-50 53
CAPITOL (576 "Swingin' Down Yonder") 20-40 59
(Price is for any of three volumes.)
CAPITOL (701 "Memories Are Made of This") 25-50 55
CAPITOL (702 "Artists & Models") 25-50 55
CAPITOL (806 "Hollywood Or Bust") 25-50 57
CAPITOL (840 "Ten Thousand Bedrooms") 25-50 57
CAPITOL (849 "Pretty Baby") 20-40 58
(Price is for any of three volumes.)
CAPITOL (939 "Return to Me") 20-40 58
CAPITOL (1027 "Volare") 20-40 58
CAPITOL (1285 "Winter Romance") 20-40 59
(Price is for any of three volumes.)
CAPITOL (1580 "Dean Martin") 20-30 61
(Compact Double 33.)
CAPITOL (EAP-1659 "Dino – Italian Love Songs") 15-25 61
CAPITOL (SU-1659 "Dino – Italian Love Songs") 15-25 61
(Juke box issue only. Includes title strips.)
CAPITOL (DU-2601 "The Best of Dean Martin") 15-25 61
(Juke box issue only. Includes title strips.)
CAPITOL (9123 "Dean Martin") 25-50 54
18 TOP HITS (27 "Dean Martin") 20-40 55
(Price for either 45 and 78 rpm EPs.)
LLOYDS (705 "Dean Martin") 25-50 54
(Mail-order offer.)
REPRISE.. 10-20 62-73
(Juke box 33 compact issues. Include title strips.)

LPs: 10/12-inch

CAPITOL (140 "The Best of Dean Martin, Vol. 2") 8-15 69
CAPITOL (378 "Dean Martin's Greatest")...8-15 69
CAPITOL (H-401 "Dean Martin Sings") . 50-100 53
(10-inch LP.)
CAPITOL (T-401 "Dean Martin Sings").... 25-50 55
(Red cover.)
CAPITOL (TT-401 "Dean Martin Sings") . 10-20 59
(Pink cover.)
CAPITOL (523 "Return to Me"/"You're Nobody Till Somebody Loves You") 8-12 70
(Two discs.)
CAPITOL (524 "You're Nobody Till Somebody Loves You") 8-12 70
CAPITOL (576 "Swingin' Down Yonder") 30-40 55
CAPITOL (849 "Pretty Baby") 25-35 57
CAPITOL (T-1047 "This Is Dean Martin") 25-35 58
(Monaural.)
CAPITOL (DT-1047 "This Is Dean Martin") 8-12 63
(Stereo. Reprocessed.)
CAPITOL (1150 "Sleep Warm") 25-35 59
CAPITOL (1285 "A Winter Romance") 25-35 59
CAPITOL (1435 "Bells Are Ringing") 15-25 60
(Soundtrack.)
CAPITOL (1442 "This Time I'm Swingin' ") 15-25 60
CAPITOL (1659 "Italian Love Songs") 15-25 62
CAPITOL (1702 "Cha Cha De Amor") 15-25 62
CAPITOL (2212 "Hey Brother, Pour the Wine") 15-25 64
CAPITOL (2297 "Dean Martin Sings – Sinatra Conducts") 10-15 65
(Repackage of *Swingin' Down Yonder.*)
CAPITOL (2333 "Dean Martin Southern Style") 10-15 65
(Repackage of *Sleep Warm.*)
CAPITOL (2343 "Holiday Cheer") 10-15 65
(Repackage of *A Winter Romance.*)
CAPITOL (2601 "Best of Dean Martin")....10-15 66
CAPITOL (2815 "Dean Martin Deluxe Set") 20-25 67
(Boxed, three-disc set.)
CAPITOL (2941 "Dean Martin Favorites")..8-12 68
CAPITOL (4563 "Italian Love Songs")..........5-8 '80s
CAPITOL (91285 "Winter Romance").......10-20 65
(Capitol Record Club series.)
COSMIC (450 "Dean Martin") 15-20
LONGINES (5234 "Memories Are Made of This") 25-50 73
(Boxed, five-disc set. Includes booklet.)
LONGINES (5235 "That's Amore") 8-15 73
PAIR (1029 "Dreams & Memories") 8-10 83
(Two discs.)
PICKWICK..6-12 '70s
REPRISE (2053 thru 2267) 8-15 72-78
REPRISE (5228 "Songbook") 10-15 70
(Two discs.)
REPRISE (6021 thru 6123) 15-25 62-64
REPRISE (6130 thru 6428) 10-20 64-70
REPRISE (93929 "On the Sunny Side")...10-20 68
(Capitol Record Club series.)
S.M.I. 10-20
SEARS ....15-25 '60s
TALKING BOOK (58007 "Look: December 26, 1967") 15-25 67
(Reading of a Dean interview/story in *Look.* Produced by the American Foundation for the Blind. Plays at 16 2/3 rpm.)
TEE VEE 10-20 78
TOWER (5006 "The Lush Years") 20-30 65
TOWER (5018 "Relaxin' ") 20-30 66
TOWER (5036 "Happy in Love") 20-30 66
TOWER (5059 "Like Never Before") 20-30 67
WALDORF (27 "Dean Martin Sings") 50-75 53
(10-inch LP.)
W.B. (23870 "Nashville Sessions") 15-25 83

Promotional LPs

("Dean Martin Testimonial Dinner") 200-300 59
(Presented by the Friars Club, and sold as a "Collectors Item" for $25 at the dinner. Three LPs in triple pocket jacket. No label name nor selection number used. Appearances by Jimmy Durante, Joey Bishop, Tony Martin, George Burns, Dinah Shore, Mort Sahl, Judy Garland; Sammy Cahn, Danny Thomas, Sammy Davis Jr., Bob Hope, Frank Sinatra and others.)
REPRISE ("Dean Martin as Matt Helm in the Silencers – Special Open-End Interview Record") ..50-75 66
(Includes one-page script.)
REPRISE (246 "Dean Martin Radio Sampler") 35-50 66
Session: Ken Lane; Herman McCoy Singers.
Also see COSTA, Don, Orchestra
Also see DURANTE, Jimmy
Also see FREEMAN, Ernie
Also see GARLAND, Judy
Also see GILKYSON, Terry
Also see HEFTI, Neal
Also see HOPE, Bob
Also see LEE, Peggy, & Dean Martin
Also see MARTIN, Tony
Also see PAICH, Marty
Also see SHORE, Dinah
Also see SINATRA, Frank, Sammy Davis Jr. & Dean Martin
Also see SINATRA, Nancy
Also see THOMAS, Danny
Also see TWITTY, Conway

MARTIN, Dean / Glen Campbell

LPs: 10/12-inch

ZENITH/CAPITOL.......................................10-20 72
(Issued with paper cover. Special products.)
Also see CAMPBELL, Glen

MARTIN, Dean / Jeff Clark / Arlene James

EPs: 45/78 rpm

POPULAR (1035 "Oh Marie") 10-15 54
(78 rpm. Not issued with special cover.)
VICTORY (1031 "Walking My Baby Back Home") 10-15 54
(78 rpm. Not issued with special cover.)
POPULAR (1035 "Oh Marie") 10-20 54
(45 rpm. Not issued with special cover.)
VICTORY (1031 "Walking My Baby Back Home") 20-40 54
(45 rpm. Colored vinyl. Not issued with special cover.)

MARTIN, Dean, & Nat "King" Cole

(With Billy May & Orchestra)

Singles: 78 rpm

CAPITOL..5-10 54

Singles: 7-inch

CAPITOL (2985 "Long Long Ago")...........10-15 54
Also see COLE, Nat "King"

MARTIN, Dean / Bob Eberly / Gordon MacRae

LPs: 10/12-inch

BRIGADE (1310 "Dino, Gordon & Bob Sing") ....20-40 '50s
Also see DORSEY, Jimmy, Orchestra & Chorus
Also see MacRAE, Gordon

MARTIN, Dean / Jane Froman

Singles: 78 rpm

CAPITOL..5-10 53

Singles: 7-inch

CAPITOL (20030 "Who's Your Little Who Zis") 10-20 53
(Promotional issue only.)

MARTIN, Dean / Jackie Gleason

LPs: 10/12-inch

CAPITOL SPECIAL MARKETS..................8-10
Also see GLEASON, Jackie

MARTIN, Dean / Rock Hudson

Singles: 7-inch

NATIONAL FEATURES (2785 "Showdown") 20-30 73
(Interviews with *Showdown* film stars. Promotional issue only. Includes script.)
Also see HUDSON, Rock

MARTIN, Dean / Red Ingle & Natural Seven

Singles: 78 rpm

CAPITOL (726 "Vieni Su") 10-15 49
(Promotional issue only.)
Also see INGLE, Red, & Natural Seven

MARTIN, Dean, & Jerry Lewis — P&R '48

Singles: 78 rpm

CAPITOL (15000 series)..............................5-10 48
NATIONAL MASK & PUPPET CORP. ("Puppet Show") ....10-20 '50s
(Promotional issue only.)

EPs: 7-inch

CAPITOL (533 "Living It Up")................100-150 54
CAPITOL (752 "Pardners") 100-150 56

LPs: 10/12-inch

MEMORABILIA (714 "Dean Martin & Jerry Lewis - First Show") 10-15 74
RADIOLA (1102 "Dean Martin & Jerry Lewis on the Radio") 10-15
Also see LEWIS, Jerry

MARTIN, Dean / Nicolini Lucchesi

LPs: 10/12-inch

AUDITION (5936 "Dean Martin Sings, Nicolini Lucchesi Plays") 25-50 56

MARTIN, Dean / Johnny Mathis / St. James Pop Orchestra

EPs: 7-inch

JIMMY McHUGH (400 "Music by Jimmy McHugh") 10-15 81
(Promotional issue only.)
Also see MATHIS, Johnny

MARTIN, Dean, & Ricky Nelson

Singles: 7-inch

W.B. (2262 "My Rifle, My Pony and Me") 400-500 59
(Promotional issue only.)
Also see NELSON, Rick

MARTIN, Dean, & Nuggets

(With Dick Stabile & Orchestra)

Singles: 78 rpm

CAPITOL..8-12 55

Singles: 7-inch

CAPITOL (3468 "I'm Gonna Steal You Away") 20-30 55
Also see NUGGETS

MARTIN, Dean, & Helen O'Connell

Singles: 78 rpm

CAPITOL..5-10 51

Singles: 7-inch

CAPITOL (1575 "We Never Talk Much") .15-25 51
Also see O'CONNELL, Helen

MARTIN, Dean / Patti Page

LPs: 10/12-inch

DECCA (79224 "Christmas Seals for 1962") 30-40 62
(Public service program for TB. Dean's show on one side, Patti's on flip.)
DECCA (79235 "Christmas Seals for 1962") 20-30 62
(Public service program for TB. Dean's and Patti's shows on one side, flip has Si Zentner and Vaughn Monroe.)
Also see MONROE, Vaughn
Also see PAGE, Patti
Also see ZENTNER, Si

MARTIN, Dean, & Line Renaud

(With Dick Stabile & Orchestra)

Singles: 78 rpm

CAPITOL..5-10 55

Singles: 7-inch

CAPITOL (3196 "Two Sleepy People") 10-20 55

MARTIN, Dean / Nelson Riddle

EPs: 7-inch

CAPITOL (1063 "Rio Bravo")................250-350 59
(Promotional only. Has special paper sleeve.)

MARTIN, Dean, & Margaret Whiting

Singles: 78 rpm

CAPITOL..5-10 50

Singles: 7-inch

CAPITOL (1160 "Don't Rock the Boat") ... 15-25 50
Also see MARTIN, Dean
Also see WHITING, Margaret

MARTIN, Deana

Singles: 7-inch

REPRISE (506 "Baby I See You") 5-10 66

MARTIN, Derek — P&R/R&B '65

Singles: 7-inch

BUTTERCUP (009 "You Blew It Baby").....5-10 70
BUTTERCUP (011 "Your Love Made a Man Out of Me") 5-10 70
CRACKERJACK (4013 "Daddy Rollin' Stone") 10-20 63
ROULETTE (4631 "You Better Go").........10-15 65
ROULETTE (4647 "I Won't Cry Anymore") 8-12 65
ROULETTE (4670 "Don't Resist") 8-12 66
ROULETTE (4743 "Breakaway") 8-12 67
ROULETTE (7017 "You Know") 8-12 68
SUE (118 "Cha Cha Skate") 8-10 65
SUE (143 "Count to Ten") 10-20 66
TUBA (2010 "Soul Power") 8-12 67
VIBRATION (522 "Falling Out of Love")...... 4-6 73
VOLT (160 "Soul Power") 5-10 68
Also see FIVE PEARLS

MARTIN, Dewey, & Medicine Ball

Singles: 7-inch

RCA 5-8 71
UNI 5-8 70

LPs: 10/12-inch

UNI 10-15 70
Also see BUFFALO SPRINGFIELD
Also see SIR WALTER RALEIGH

MARTIN, Dick, & Swinging Strings

Singles: 7-inch

FILM CITY (2065 "Come Home")........150-200 59

MARTIN, Dude

Singles: 78 rpm

MERCURY 8-10 50

Singles: 7-inch

MERCURY 10-20 50
RCA (48-0102 "Tennessee Baby")...........10-20 50
(Green vinyl.)
Also see THOMPSON, Sue

MARTIN, Fred, & Matadors

Singles: 7-inch

SAXONY (1003 "Sharin' Sharon")............20-30 62
Also see LISS, Tommy, & Matadors
Also see WILLIS, Rollie, & Contenders

MARTIN, George, & Orchestra — P&R/LP '64

Singles: 7-inch

U.A. (745 "Ringo's Theme") 25-35 64
U.A. (745 "Ringo's Theme") 40-60 64
(Both sides credit "The Beatles." Canadian.)
U.A. (745 "Ringo's Theme") 15-20 64
(Credits George Martin. Canadian.)

U.A. (750 "A Hard Day's Night") ... 75-125 64
U.A. (800 series) ... 4-8 65
U.A. (50148 "Love in the Open Air") ... 20-25 67

Picture Sleeves

U.A. (745 "Ringo's Theme") ... 75-100 64
U.A. (750 "A Hard Day's Night") ... 1000-1200 64

Promotional Singles

U.A. (745 "Ringo's Theme") ... 20-30 64
(White label.)

LPs: 10/12-inch

U.A. (3377 "Off the Beatle Track") ... 30-40 64
(Monaural.)
U.A. (3383 "A Hard Day's Night") ... 20-30 64
(Monaural.)
U.A. (3420 "George Martin") ... 15-25 65
(Monaural.)
U.A. (3448 "Help") ... 20-30 65
(Monaural.)
U.A. (3539 "The Beatle Girls") ... 25-35 66
(Monaural.)

Note: Promotional copies of 3383, 3448 & 3539 can be worth twice the above price ranges. We have yet to verify promo copies of the stereo versions, though, if any exist, at least the same increase would apply.

U.A. (6377 "Off the Beatle Track") ... 30-40 64
(Stereo.)
U.A. (6383 "A Hard Day's Night") ... 20-30 64
(Stereo.)
U.A. (6420 "George Martin") ... 15-25 65
(Stereo.)
U.A. (6448 "Help") ... 20-30 65
(Stereo.)
U.A. (6539 "The Beatle Girls") ... 25-35 66
(Stereo.)
U.A. (6647 "London by George") ... 10-15 68
(Stereo.)
Also see BEATLES
Also see GERRY & PACEMAKERS

MARTIN, Grady
(With His Slew Foot Five; with Winging Strings)

Singles: 78 rpm

DECCA ... 4-8 53-55

Singles: 7-inch

DECCA ... 5-15 53-66

EPs: 7-inch

DECCA ... 8-18 55-64
MCA ... 4-6 73-78

LPs: 10/12-inch

DECCA ... 15-35 55-67
Also see CROSBY, Bing
Also see ECHOES
Also see FOLEY, Red
Also see HOLLY, Buddy
Also see IVES, Burl, with Grady Martin & His Slew Foot Five
Also see TUBB, Ernest

MARTIN, Jack

Singles: 7-inch

CHART (3101 "Rocket Baby") ... 40-60

MARTIN, Janis — P&R '56
(Janis & Her Boyfriends)

Singles: 78 rpm

RCA (Except 6652) ... 10-20 56-57
RCA (6652 "My Boy Elvis") ... 15-25 56

Singles: 7-inch

BIG DUTCH ... 4-6 77
PALETTE (5058 "Hard Times Ahead") ... 25-35 60
PALETTE (5071 "Teen Street") ... 5-10 61
RCA (6400 & 6500 series) ... 25-35 56
RCA (6652 "My Boy Elvis") ... 30-40 56
RCA (6700 thru 7300 series) ... 15-25 56-58

Promotional Singles

BIG DUTCH ... 4-6 77
PALETTE (5071 "Teen Street") ... 10-20 61
RCA (6400 & 6500 series) ... 20-40 56
RCA (6652 "My Boy Elvis") ... 35-45 56
RCA (6700 thru 7300 series) ... 20-40 56-58

EPs: 7-inch

RCA (4093 "Just Squeeze Me") ... 75-100 58

MARTIN, Janis / Otto Bash

EPs: 7-inch

RCA (38 "Dealer's Prevue") ... 50-75 56
(Promotional issue only.)
Also see BASH, Otto

MARTIN, Janis / Hank Snow

EPs: 7-inch

RCA (76 "Love Me to Pieces") ... 25-50 56
(Promotional issue only.)
Also see MARTIN, Janis
Also see SNOW, Hank

MARTIN, Jay

Singles: 7-inch

TOWER (403 "By Yourself") ... 20-30 67

MARTIN, Jean

Singles: 78 rpm

DOT ... 5-10 55
UNIQUE ... 5-10 56

Singles: 7-inch

ADONIS (100 "I'll Wait for You") ... 5-10 59
CHART (1008 "Rock-A-Knock") ... 20-30 '50s
CORAL (61838 "Another Door Opens") ... 10-15 57
DOT (15322 "Sneakin' Around") ... 10-15 55
OKLAHOMA (106 "Another Door Opens") ... 20-25 57
(First issue.)
UNIQUE (352 "Please Be Gentle with Me") ... 10-15 56

MARTIN, Jerry
(With the Sounds; with Danny Mendelssohn & Orchestra & Chorus)

Singles: 7-inch

FREDLO (5901 "Janet") ... 150-250 57
R (504 "Hold My Hand") ... 20-30 59
R (507 "Lover's Promise") ... 15-25 59
R (510 "Deep in My Heart") ... 15-25 59
Session: Scotty Moore; D.J. Fontana.
Also see MENDELSOHN, Danny
Also see MOORE, Scotty
Also see ZBORNIK, Layton Redell, Jr.

MARTIN, Jerry

Singles: 7-inch

PRESIDENT (827 "Shake-a Take-a") ... 5-10 63

MARTIN, Jesse

Singles: 7-inch

IMPALA (101 "Love Can't Be Bad") ... 5-10 63

MARTIN, Jimmie

Singles: 7-inch

D (1219 "Signifyin' Monkey") ... 20-30 61

MARTIN, Jimmy — C&W '58
(With the Sunny Mountain Boys; with J.D. Crowe)

Singles: 7-inch

DECCA (Except 30703) ... 5-10 59-72
DECCA (30703 "Rock Hearts") ... 10-15 58
GONE (5044 "Jack Cobb") ... 5-10 58

EPs: 7-inch

DECCA ... 5-15 59-64

LPs: 10/12-inch

ANTHOLOGY OF COUNTRY MUSIC ... 10-20
DECCA ... 10-30 60-72
GUSTO ... 5-10
MCA ... 5-10 72-81
Also see MONROE, Bill
Also see NITTY GRITTY DIRT BAND & JIMMY MARTIN
Also see OSBORNE BROTHERS

MARTIN, Jimmy, Combo
(Vocal by Sandie Karman)

Singles: 7-inch

JAXON (501 "Rock the Bop") ... 600-800 57

MARTIN, Kenny — R&B '58
(With the Bluenotes)

Singles: 78 rpm

FEDERAL (12330 "I'm Sorry") ... 15-35 58

Singles: 7-inch

BIG TOP (3053 "Lovin' Man") ... 10-20 60
BIG TOP (3072 "Fever") ... 10-20 61
FEDERAL (12310 "I'm the Jivin' Mr. Lee") ... 20-30 57
FEDERAL (12330 "I'm Sorry") ... 10-20 58
FEDERAL (12341 "My Sugar Queen") ... 10-20
FEDERAL (12350 "Now I Know") ... 10-20 59
FEDERAL (12354 "My Wish") ... 10-20 59
FEDERAL (12362 "Ask Me") ... 50-100 59
FEDERAL (12379 "Last Words of the Jivin' Mr. Lee") ... 10-15 60
PJ (1732 "Star Eyes") ... 5-10 66

MARTIN, Kenny Lee

Singles: 7-inch

DECCA (30754 "The Rock Keeps Rollin' On") ... 15-25 58
MGM (12846 "One Night Stand") ... 10-20 59

MARTIN, Lee
(With the Vikings; with Velvet-Tones)

Singles: 7-inch

JIN (149 "I Lost Again") ... 15-25 61
JIN (159 "Lover's Plea") ... 40-50 62

MARTIN, Lela
(With the Soul Providers)

Singles: 7-inch

MELA-TONE (401 "You Can't Have Your Cake") ... 25-35 63
STIGERS ... 5-10 '60s

MARTIN, Lucia

Singles: 7-inch

KING (5608 "Star from Heaven") ... 10-15 62

MARTIN, Mandi

Singles: 7-inch

COLUMBIA (43254 "Don't Let Him Get Away from You") ... 10-15 65

MARTIN, Mary

Singles: 7-inch

BUENA VISTA (332 "Makin' Believe It's Christmas Eve") ... 10-15 58

LPs: 10/12-inch

DISNEYLAND (1038 "Hi-Ho, Mary Sings & Swings") ... 15-25 58

MARTIN, Marv

Singles: 7-inch

LIMELIGHT (3021 "Way Down") ... 5-10 64

MARTIN, Red

Singles: 7-inch

SAGE (371 "Keep a Movin' ") ... 15-25 64

MARTIN, Ricky

Singles: 7-inch

BLAINE (4001 "When I Lost You") ... 5-10 65

MARTIN, Roberta, Singers

Singles: 78 rpm

APOLLO ... 5-10 53

Singles: 7-inch

APOLLO (270 "Oh Lord") ... 8-10 53
(Black vinyl.)
APOLLO (270 "Oh Lord") ... 20-30 53
(Red vinyl.)

MARTIN, Robin

Singles: 7-inch

EBB (137 "I'm a Flop") ... 8-12 58

MARTIN, Rodge

Singles: 7-inch

BRAGG (227 "When She Touches Me") ... 5-10 '60s
DOT (16394 "I'm Standing By") ... 8-12 62
DOT (16776 "I'm Standing By") ... 5-8 65
NEWARK ... 8-12 '60s

MARTIN, Roger

Singles: 7-inch

DRIFT (1442 "Wella, Wella Baby") ... 50-75

MARTIN, Ronnie
(With the Timbers)

Singles: 78 rpm

PILGRIM (721 "Hey, Doc") ... 5-10 56

Singles: 7-inch

BILLIE FRAN (4 "Storm of Love") ... 8-12 '60s
CALDWELL (409 "Soiree") ... 5-10 62
PILGRIM (721 "Hey, Doc") ... 10-15 56

MARTIN, Seth

Singles: 7-inch

PAGE ONE (21004 "Day in the Life") ... 5-10 68

MARTIN, Sonny

Singles: 7-inch

EXCELLO (2207 "Life Will Be So Hard to Bear") ... 10-15 61
FELSTED (8507 "Rockabye Baby") ... 15-20 58
ROCKO (518 "When True Love Is Gone") ... 10-20 61

MARTIN, Steve
(With the Five Discs)

Singles: 7-inch

EMGE (1010 "Adorable One") ... 40-50 59

MAGNASOUND (700 "Lonely Little Girl") ... 5-10 63
Also see FIVE DISCS

MARTIN, Tommy

Singles: 7-inch

TUNEGLOW (3 "Hootchie Cootchie") ... 50-75

MARTIN, Tony — P&R '38

Singles: 78 rpm

BRUNSWICK ... 5-10 38
DECCA ... 3-8 39-42
MERCURY ... 3-8 46-56
RCA ... 3-8 47-57

Singles: 7-inch

CHART (5059 "Hills of Yesterday") ... 4-6 70
CHART (5078 "Coast of California") ... 4-6 70
DOT ... 5-10 61-66
DUNHILL ... 4-8 67
MERCURY ... 10-15 '50s
MOTOWN ... 5-10 64-66
NAN ... 5-10 64
PARK AVENUE ... 5-10 63
RCA ... 10-20 50-60

EPs: 7-inch

DECCA ... 5-10 51-56
MERCURY ... 5-10 54-56
RCA ... 5-10 51-57

LPs: 10/12-inch

CAMDEN ... 10-20 59-60
CHART ... 5-10 70
CHARTER ... 10-20 63
CORAL ... 5-8 73
DECCA ... 15-30 51-56
DOT ... 10-20 61-62
MERCURY ... 10-25 54-61
RCA ... 15-30 51-60
20TH FOX ... 10-15 64
WING ... 10-20 59-60
Also see BABBITT, Harry / Tony Martin
Also see MARTIN, Dean
Also see SHORE, Dinah, Tony Martin, Betty Hutton & Phil Harris

MARTIN, Trade — P&R '62

Singles: 7-inch

COED (570 "That Stranger Used to Be My Girl") ... 10-15 62
COED (573 "Hula Hula Dancin' Doll") ... 20-30 62
COED (575 "Strategy") ... 10-15 63
COED (579 "Hot Diggity") ... 10-15 63
COED (590 "Send for Me") ... 10-15 64
COED (594 "Joanne") ... 25-35 64
GEE (1053 "La Mer") ... 10-15 59
RCA ... 5-10 66-67
ROULETTE (4258 "Pomp and Circumstance") ... 8-10 60
STALLION ... 4-6
TOOT (610 "You're the Cause") ... 5-10 68

LPs: 10/12-inch

BUDDAH ... 10-15 72
Session: Tantones.
Also see PIXIES THREE

MARTIN, Vicky

Singles: 7-inch

BAND BOX (272 "Roller Coaster") ... 10-20

MARTIN, Vince — P&R '56
(With the Tarriers; with Fred Neil)

Singles: 78 rpm

GLORY ... 5-10 56

Singles: 7-inch

ABC-PAR ... 5-10 59
GLORY ... 10-15 56-58
ELEKTRA ... 5-10 64

LPs: 10/12-inch

CAPITOL ... 5-10 73
ELEKTRA ... 10-20 64
Also see NEIL, Fred
Also see TARRIERS

MARTIN, Vinnie Jay

Singles: 7-inch

REPRISE (225 "She's Everything You're Looking For") ... 5-10 68
V.J.M. RUSS (4435 "Let the Love Light In") ... 5-10 65

MARTIN BROTHERS

Singles: 7-inch

LIBERTY TONE (107 "Where Have You Been All Night") ... 50-75

MARTIN SISTERS

Singles: 7-inch

BARRY (1006 "Only Seventeen")..............8-12 66
DUB..10-20 57

MARTIN'S MUSTANGS

Singles: 7-inch

VRC (1001 "Funky Boardwalk")..................8-12 '60s
Also see REVLONS

MARTINDALE, Donny

Singles: 7-inch

QUINTET (101 "Go Jenny")................ 300-400

MARTINDALE, Wink *P&R/C&W '59*

Singles: 7-inch

ABC/DOT..3-6 76
DOT (150 "Deck of Cards")..........................5-8 64
DOT (15728 "All Love Broke Loose")...... 15-25 58
DOT (15968 "Deck of Cards")................. 10-20 59
DOT (16020 "I Never See Maggie Alone") .8-12 59
DOT (16051 "Blue Bobby Socks")..............8-12 60
DOT (16083 "Love's Old Sweet Song")......8-12 60
DOT (16138 "Glory of Love")................... 10-15 60
DOT (16243 "Black Land Farmer")..............8-12 61
DOT (16282 "Man Needs a Woman")..........8-12 61
DOT (16313 "The Thing")...........................8-12 62
DOT (16347 "Sweet Little Loveable You")..8-12 62
DOT (16435 "I Saw Me")............................8-12 63
DOT (16491 "Deck of Cards").......................5-10 63
DOT (16500 "The Next Time").....................8-12 63
DOT (16531 "Nevertheless")........................8-12 63
DOT (16597 "Why Don't They Understand")..................................5-10 64
DOT (16698 "My True Love")......................5-10 65
DOT (16821 "Giddy Up Go")........................5-10 66
DOT (16863 "To a Sleeping Beauty")..........5-10 66
OJ (1009 "Thought It Was Moonlove") .. 50-100 58
RANWOOD...4-6 73

Picture Sleeves

DOT (15968 "Deck of Cards")................ 10-20 59
DOT (16051 "Blue Bobby Socks")........... 10-20 60
DOT (16083 "Love's Old Sweet Song")... 10-20 60

LPs: 10/12-inch

DOT (3245 "Deck of Cards").................... 15-25 59
(Monaural.)
DOT (3293 "The Bible Story")................ 15-25 60
(Monaural.)
DOT (3403 "Big Bad John")...................... 15-25 61
(Monaural.)
DOT (3692 "Giddy Up Go")....................... 15-25 66
(Monaural.)
DOT (25245 "Deck of Cards").................. 25-35 59
(Stereo.)
DOT (25293 "The Bible Story")............... 20-30 60
(Stereo.)
DOT (25403 "Big Bad John")................... 20-30 61
(Stereo.)
DOT (25692 "Giddy Up Go").................... 20-30 66
(Stereo.)
HAMILTON (128 "Deck of Cards")........... 10-20 64
(Monaural.)
HAMILTON (12128 "Deck of Cards")........ 15-25 64
(Stereo.)

MARTINDALE, Wink, & Robin Ward

Singles: 7-inch

DOT (16555 "Our Love Affair")....................8-12 63
DOT (16628 "Hey Girl, Hey Boy")...............8-12 64

LPs: 10/12-inch

DOT (3571 "My True Love")..................... 15-25 64
(Monaural.)
DOT (25571 "My True Love").................. 20-30 64
(Stereo.)
Also see MARTINDALE, Wink
Also see WARD, Robin

MARTINE, Layng *P&R '71*
(Layng Martine Jr.)

Singles: 7-inch

BARNABY...4-6 71-74
DATE (1511 "Crazy Daisy")........................5-10 66
GENERAL INT'L (351 "Pick All the Flowers That You Can")...5-10 66
PLAYBOY (6069 "Don Juan")......................4-6 76
PLAYBOY (6081 "Summertime Lovin' ") 4-6 76
Also see PROFESSOR MORRISON'S LOLLIPOP

MARTINELS

Singles: 7-inch

SUCCESS (110 "Baby Think It Over")..... 10-15 63

MARTINEQUES

Singles: 7-inch

DANCELAND (777 "Tonight Is Just Another Night")..50-75 61
DANCELAND (779 "Broken Hearted Me")...75-100 62
DANCELAND (1002 "I Need Love").........40-50 62
ME-O (1002 "If You Want to Call Me")......15-25 65

MARTINEZ, Frank, & Pharomen

Singles: 7-inch

SOMA (1419 "Jeanette")............................40-60 '60s

MARTINEZ, Oberia

Singles: 7-inch

KEITH (6503 "Gotta Think It Over")..........10-15 62

MARTINEZ, Tony "Pepino"

LPs: 10/12-inch

DEL-FI (1205 "Many Sides of Pepino")....15-25 59

MARTINI, Bernardo

Singles: 7-inch

PHILIPS (40090 "Silver Dust")..................10-20 63

MARTINIQUES

Singles: 7-inch

DANCELAND (777 "Tonight Is Just Another Night")..50-75 62
DANCELAND (779 "Broken Hearted Me")...75-100 62
DANCELAND (1002 "I Need Love").........40-50 62
ROULETTE (4423 "Tonight Is Just Another Night")..10-15 62

MARTINIS

Singles: 7-inch

BAR (101 "Hung Over").............................15-25 67
USA (893 "Holiday Cheer").........................5-10 67

MARTINO, Al *P&R '52*

Singles: 78 rpm

BBS...5-10 52
CAPITOL...3-5 52-57

Singles: 7-inch

BBS (101 "Here in My Heart")...................10-20 52
(Black vinyl.)
BBS (101 "Here in My Heart")...................25-35 52
(Colored vinyl.)
CAPITOL (Except F-2122 thru F-5060)........3-8 64-81
CAPITOL (F-2122 thru F-5060) 10-20 52-63
JUBILEE (Black vinyl)...............................5-10 53
JUBILEE (Colored vinyl)............................15-20 53
MAZE (7025 "There's No Tomorrow")........5-10 62
20TH FOX..5-10 59-64
VERVE (10104 "A Little Love a Little Kiss")..10-20 57

Picture Sleeves

CAPITOL..5-10 63-66
MAZE (7025 "There's No Tomorrow")......10-15 62

EPs: 7-inch

CAPITOL..10-15 63-64
(Juke box issues & Compact 33s.)

LPs: 10/12-inch

CAPITOL..5-20 62-80
GUEST STAR......................................5-10 64
MONTGOMERY WARD...........................10-15 '60s
MOVIETONE..5-10 67
PICKWICK (3115 "We Could")....................5-10 69
SPRINGBOARD.....................................5-8 78
20TH FOX..10-20 59-65

MARTINO, Johnny

Singles: 7-inch

CHAM...10-20 58

MARTINO, Lou

Singles: 7-inch

COLUMBIA (43126 "Please")......................50-75 64

MARTINSON, Vick, & 3 Bears

Singles: 7-inch

CUCA (1083 "Boo on You").......................20-30 62

MARTONI, Bobby

Singles: 7-inch

DORE (796 "Dear Angie").........................30-40 67

MARTY

Singles: 78 rpm

NOVELTY...10-15 56

Singles: 7-inch

NOVELTY (101 "Marty on Planet Mars")..20-30 56

MARTY

Singles: 7-inch

DI VENUS (103 "Mom and Dad")............10-15 67
Also see REGENTS

MARTY & MUFF-TONES

Singles: 7-inch

MUFF-TONE.......................................10-15 86
(Pink vinyl.)

MARTY'S MISFITS

Singles: 7-inch

TAPA (1651 "Hey Little Girl").....................8-10 65

MARV & HARV

Singles: 7-inch

FILM (1020 "Sing Little Bird, Sing")............5-10 61

MARVA & SAVOYS

Singles: 7-inch

COED (582 "Don't Let Him Go")...............10-15 63

MARVEL, Tina

Singles: 7-inch

LU PINE (121 "Promises You Made to Me")..20-30 64

MARVELEERS

Singles: 78 rpm

DERBY..10-15 53
DOT..5-10 55

Singles: 7-inch

DERBY (829 "For the Longest Time")......15-25 53
DERBY (842 "All My Heart")....................15-25 53
DERBY (844 "Love Me, Want Me")..........20-30 53
DOT (15320 "These Are the Things We'll Share")..10-15 55

MARVELETTES *P&R/R&B '61*

Singles: 7-inch

COLLECTABLES.....................................3-5
MOTOWN...3-5
MOTOWN/TOPPS (12 "Please Mr. Postman")...50-75 67
(Topps Chewing Gum promotional item. Single-sided, cardboard flexi, picture disc. Issued with generic paper sleeve.)
TAMLA (54046 thru 54088).....................10-12 61-62
TAMLA (54091 "He's a Good Guy [Yes He Is]")...8-12 64
(With subtitle.)
TAMLA (54091 "Yes He Is")......................40-60 64
(No subtitle. Single-sided. Promotional issue only.)
TAMLA (54097 thru 54198)........................5-10 64-72
(Black vinyl.)
TAMLA...8-12 69
(Colored vinyl. Promotional issues only.)

Picture Sleeves

TAMLA (54046 "Please Mr. Postman").....40-60 61
TAMLA (54054 "Twistin' Postman")..........70-90 62
TAMLA (54097 "You're My Remedy").......15-25 64

EPs: 7-inch

MOTOWN (2003 "Marvelettes")................15-25 '60s
TAMLA (60253 "Greatest Hits")................15-25 66
TAMLA (60274 "Marvelettes")..................15-25 67

LPs: 10/12-inch

MOTOWN (Except 100 series)................10-15 75
MOTOWN (100 series)...............................5-8 82
TAMLA (228 "Please Mr. Postman") 150-250 61
TAMLA (229 "Marvelettes Sing Smash Hits of '62")..750-1000 62
TAMLA (229 The Marvelettes Sing")......75-125 62
(Reissue with shorter title. May show the Marvelettes as "Marvelets.")
TAMLA (231 "Playboy")..........................50-100 62
TAMLA (237 "Marvelous Marvelettes") ..50-100 63
TAMLA (243 "On Stage")..........................50-75 63
TAMLA (253 "Greatest Hits")...................15-20 66
TAMLA (274 "The Marvelettes")...............15-20 67
TAMLA (286 thru 305)..............................10-20 68-70
Members: Gladys Horton; Kathy Anderson; Georgeanna Tillman; Wanda Young; Juanita Cowart; Ann Bogan.
Also see DARNELLS
Also see THEM / Marvelettes
Also see WESTON, Kim / Marvelettes

MARVELETTES / Mary Wells / Miracles / Marvin Gaye

Singles: 7-inch

TAMLA/MOTOWN ("Album Excerpts").....30-40 63
(Though from Tamla/Motown, no label name is shown, nor is there a title. Promotional issue only.)
Also see GAYE, Marvin
Also see MARVELETTES
Also see MIRACLES
Also see WELLS, Mary

MARVELIERS

Singles: 7-inch

COUGAR (1868 "Down").......................100-200 60
Also see WEST, Johnny

MARVELIERS

Singles: 7-inch

JOANY (4439 "The Spider").....................10-20

MARVELLE & BLUE MATCH

Singles: 7-inch

DYNAMIC SOUND (2000 "The Dance Called the Motion")...8-12 66
MAGIC TOUCH (2076 "Don't End Up Like Me")..5-10 69
Member: Marvelle Love.

MARVELLO, Bruce, & Red Coats

Singles: 7-inch

NIKKO (610 "Teen-Age Broken Hearts")..300-400 58

MARVELLOS
(Mar-Vellos; with "Jimmy Johnson Rhythm Acc.")

Singles: 78 rpm

THERON...100-200 55

Singles: 7-inch

CHA CHA (756 "Come Back My Love").....5-10 67
MARVELLO (5005 "Red Hot Mama")...100-200 '50s
MARVELLO (5005 "Cloud Nine").........100-200 '50s
STEPHENY (1818 "Come Back My Love")...75-125 58
THERON (117 "You're the Dream").....400-500 55

MARVELLOS

Singles: 7-inch

EXODUS (6214 "She Told Me Lies").....75-125 62
EXODUS (6216 "I Ask of You").............50-100 62
REPRISE (20088 "She Told Me Lies")......10-15 62

MARVELLOS

Singles: 7-inch

LOMA (2045 "We Go Together")...............5-10 66
LOMA (2061 "Why Do You Want to Hurt the One You Love")..5-10 66
MODERN (1054 "In the Sunshine")...........5-10 68
W.B. (7011 "Let Me Keep You Satisfied")..5-10 67
W.B. (7054 "Yes I Do")..............................5-10 67

MARVELLS
(With the Scott Johnson Orchestra)

Singles: 7-inch

MAGNET (1005 "Did She Leave You")...200-300 59

MAR-VELLS

Singles: 7-inch

CARLSON INT'L (5105 "If I'm a Fool")......15-25 62

MARVELLS

Singles: 7-inch

FINER ARTS (2019 "The Miracle of Life")..10-20 67
FINER ARTS (2024 "How Could You Hurt Me So")..10-20 68
FINER ARTS (2026 "I'm a Fool for Losing You")..10-20 68

MARVELOUS RAY

Singles: 7-inch

FALCON (1003 "I Believe in Miracles")...... 8-12 57

MARVELOWS *P&R/R&B '65*
(Mighty Marvelows)

Singles: 7-inch

ABC..5-10 66-69
ABC-PAR..10-15 64-66

LPs: 10/12-inch

ABC..15-25 68
Members: Melvin Mason; Frank Paden; Johnny Paden; Jesse Smith; Andrew Thomas; Sonny Stevenson.
Also see NATURALS

MARVELS

Singles: 78 rpm

ABC-PAR...100-150 56

Singles: 7-inch

ABC-PAR (9771 "I Won't Have You Breaking My Heart")..500-700 56
Members: Richard Blandon; Jake Miller; Cleveland Still; Cordell Brown; Tom Gardner.

Also see DUBS

MARVELS
(Marvells)
Singles: 7-inch
LAURIE (3016 "So Young So Sweet")..... 30-40 58
WINN (1916 "For Sentimental Reasons") 150-200 62
(Artist credit not printed on label.)
WINN (1916 "For Sentimental Reasons") 100-150 62
(Artist credit printed on label.)
Also see SENATORS

MARVELS
Singles: 7-inch
MUNRAB (1008 "Just Another Fool").......... 1000-2000 59

MAR-VELS
(Mar-vells; with Larry & the Lads; with D. Jones & Continentals)
Singles: 7-inch
ANGIE (1005 "Go On and Have Yourself a Ball").......... 8-12 63
(First issue.)
BUTANE (778 "Go On and Have Yourself a Ball").......... 5-10 63
FOUR SONS (4105 "Lookin' at the Ceiling").......... 8-12 63
LOVE (5011 "Cherry Lips").......... 40-50 58
(White label. Promotional issue only.)
LOVE (5011 "Cherry Lips").......... 25-35 58
(Red label.)
TAMMY (1016 "Somewhere in Life") ... 300-400 61
TAMMY (1019 "My Guardian Angel") .. 200-300 62
VEL (100 "Somewhere Love Is Waiting").......... 50-100

MARVELS / Buzz Clifford
Singles: 7-inch
JASON SCOTT (21 "Guiding Angel"/"I'll Never Forget") 4-8 82
(500 made.)
Also see CATTIVA, Savina / Marvels
Also see CLIFFORD, Buzz

MARVELS
Singles: 7-inch
SENSATION (007 "Forget About That Mess") .... 10-15 '60s

MARVELS
Singles: 7-inch
BLUE BIRD ("Sonya").......... 75-125
(Selection number not known.)

MAR-VELS
Singles: 7-inch
IN (102 "Endless Nights").......... 30-40 64

MAR-VELS
Singles: 7-inch
MELBOURNE (1538 "Someone Else").... 15-25 66

MARVELS FIVE
Singles: 7-inch
UPTOWN (722 "Forgive Me") 5-10 66

MARVELTONES
Singles: 78 rpm
REGENT.......... 10-20 52
Singles: 7-inch
REGENT (194 "So").......... 30-40 52
REGENT (196 "Care").......... 30-40 52

MARVELUSS MICKEY
Singles: 7-inch
MARLO (1535 "I Feel So Good") 300-400 63
Picture Sleeves
MARLO (1535 "I Feel So Good") 450-650 63

MAR-VILLES
Singles: 7-inch
INFINITY (027 "The Drag").......... 15-25 63
(First issued by Eddie Ford. Reissued as by Rick & Rick-A-Shays.)
Also see FORD, Eddie
Also see RICK & RICK-A-SHAYS

MARVIN, Eddie
Singles: 7-inch
OAKRIDGE ("I'm Packin' My Duds").... 150-250
(Selection number not known.)

MARVIN, Lee / Lee Marvin & Clint Eastwood
Singles: 7-inch
PARAMOUNT (0010 "Wand'rin' Star"/"Best Things").......... 5-10 69
Also see EASTWOOD, Clint

MARVIN, Paul
Singles: 7-inch
RON (322 "Cinderella") 8-12 59

MARVIN & BUDDY
Singles: 7-inch
TWIN (923 "A Wonderful One") 5-10 59

MARVIN & CHIRPS
("Vocal by Marvin Williams")
Singles: 78 rpm
TIP TOP.......... 75-125 58
Singles: 7-inch
TIP TOP (202 "I'll Miss You This Xmas") 100-200 58
Member: Marvin Williams.

MARVIN & FARRAR
LPs: 10/12-inch
EMI AMERICA.......... 8-10
Members: Hank Marvin; John Farrar.
Also see SHADOWS

MARVIN & JOE
Singles: 7-inch
DORE (615 "The Picture Was Crying") 8-10 61

MARVIN & JOHNNY *R&B '53*
Singles: 78 rpm
ALADDIN.......... 10-20 56
MODERN 15-30 54-56
RAYS.......... 10-20 54
SPECIALTY.......... 15-25 53-55
Singles: 7-inch
ALADDIN (3335 "My Dear, My Darling") .. 20-30 56
ALADDIN (3371 "Yak-Yak") 30-40 57
ALADDIN (3408 "Smack Smack") 40-50 58
ALADDIN (3439 "It's Christmas Time") 40-50 58
ERIC.......... 4-6 '70s
FELSTED (554 "I'm Tired of Being Alone") 15-20 63
(White label. Promotional issue.)
FELSTED (8681 "I'm Tired of Being Alone") 10-15 63
FIREFLY (333 "Second Helping of Cherry Pie") 10-20 60
JAMIE (1188 "Tick Tock") 10-15 61
KENT (2 "Cherry Pie") 5-8
KENT (303 "Cherry Pie") 10-20 58
KENT (436 "Baby You're the One") 5-10 65
LANA (127 "Cherry Pie") 5-8 65
LIBERTY.......... 3-5 80
MODERN (933 "Tick Tock").......... 50-75 54
MODERN (941 "Kiss Me").......... 40-60 55
MODERN (946 "Little Honey") 30-50 55
MODERN (949 "Ko Ko Mo").......... 30-50 55
MODERN (952 "I Love You, Yes I Do").... 30-50 55
MODERN (959 "Sugar Mama").......... 30-50 55
MODERN (968 "Sweet Dreams") 30-50 55
MODERN (974 "Let Me Know") 30-50 55
OLDIES 45 (80 "Cherry Pie") 5-10 63
RAYS (34 "Baby, Baby, Baby").......... 20-30 54
RENCO (102 "Be Mine Tonight") 4-8
SPECIALTY (479 "Baby Doll") 50-75 53
(Black vinyl.)
SPECIALTY (479 "Baby Doll") 100-150 53
(Colored vinyl.)
SPECIALTY (488 "Jo Jo") 25-35 54
SPECIALTY (498 "School of Love") 25-35 54
SPECIALTY (530 "Day In, Day Out") 25-35 54
SPECIALTY (554 "Mamo Mamo") 25-35 55
SWINGIN' (641 "I'm Tired of Being Alone") 10-15 62
SWINGIN' (645 "Second Helping of Cherry Pie") 10-15 63
LPs: 10/12-inch
CROWN (5381 "Marvin and Johnny") 35-55 63
UNITED (7796 "R&B Hits of the '50s") 10-15
Members: Marvin Phillips; Johnny Dean.
Also see JESSE & MARVIN
Also see PHILLIPS, Marvin

MARVIN & JOHNNY / Frankie Ford
Singles: 7-inch
TRIP (131 "Cherry Pie"/"Sea Cruise") .... 3-5 '90s
Also see FORD, Frankie
Also see MARVIN & JOHNNY

MARX
(The Marx with Norman Baker Orchestra)
Singles: 7-inch
CHANTÉ (1002 "One Minute More") 50-100 59
(Same number used on a Misters release.)
DAHLIA (1002 "One Minute More") 100-200 59

MARX, Dick
Singles: 7-inch
OMEGA DISK (135 "Joey, Joey") 5-10 59
OMEGA DISK (137 "Cool") 5-10 59

MARX, Groucho *LP '72*
Singles: 78 rpm
DECCA.......... 4-8 51
YOUNG PEOPLE'S RECORDS 3-6 54
Singles: 7-inch
A&M.......... 4-6 73
DECCA.......... 10-20 51
YOUNG PEOPLE'S RECORDS 5-10 54
LPs: 10/12-inch
A&M (3515 "An Evening with Groucho") 5-10 72
A&M (PR-3515 "An Evening with Groucho") 15-20 78
(Picture disc. Includes booklet. Limited numbered edition.)
DECCA (5405 "Hooray for Captain Spaulding") 100-150 52
(10-inch LP.)
Also see KAYE, Danny, Jimmy Durante, Jane Wyman & Groucho Marx
Also see MARX BROTHERS

MARX, Harpo
EPs: 7-inch
RCA (329 "Harp by Harpo") 15-25 50
LPs: 10/12-inch
MERCURY (20232 "Harpo in Hi-Fi") 25-45 57
(Monaural.)
MERCURY (20363 "Harpo at Work") 25-35 58
(Monaural.)
MERCURY (60232 "Harpo in Hi-Fi") 40-60 57
(Stereo.)
MERCURY (60363 "Harpo at Work") 30-50 58
(Stereo.)
RCA (27 "Harp by Harpo") 50-75 50
(10-inch LP.)
RCA (2720 "Harp by Harpo") 15-25 63
WING (12164 "Harpo") 30-40 59
Also see MARX BROTHERS

MARX BROTHERS *LP '69*
LPs: 10/12-inch
DECCA (9169 "Marx Brothers") 8-12 69
(With Gary Owens.)
Also see MARX, Groucho
Also see MARX, Harpo

MARY & DESIRABLES
Singles: 7-inch
CHECKER (1126 "Hurtin' Hurts") 5-10 65

MARY B.
Singles: 7-inch
ENJOY (1014 "Cut It Out") 5-10 64
FLING (725 ("Since I Fell for You") 8-12 62

MARY BUTTERWORTH
Singles: 7-inch
CUSTOM FIDELITY ("Phase II") 10-20 69
(Selection number not known.)
LPs: 10/12-inch
CUSTOM FIDELITY (2092 "Mary Butterworth") 175-275 69
Members: Mike Hunt; Mike Ayling; Mike Eachus; Jim Giordano.

MARY Ds
Singles: 7-inch
ECHO (1003 "Just One Kiss") 5-10 61
PRESIDENT (430 "Brr-Um") 5-10 60

MARY ELLEN
(With Maxwell Davis Orchestra)
Singles: 7-inch
GRAMO (5502 "Moon Rocket") 20-30 63
GRAMO (5504 "This Love of Mine") 20-30 63
Also see DAVIS, Maxwell

MARY LOU & NEW WORLD
Singles: 7-inch
VAULT (951 "Small Town Girl") 5-10 69

MARY LOU & TEMPTEES
Singles: 7-inch
EVERLAST (5024 "Hippy Dippy") 5-10 63

MARYLANDERS
Singles: 78 rpm
JUBILEE.......... 100-150 52-53
Singles: 7-inch
JUBILEE (5079 "I'm a Sentimental Fool") 400-500 52
JUBILEE (5091 "Make Me Thrill Again") 400-500 52
JUBILEE (5114 "Fried Chicken") 100-150 53
(Black vinyl.)
JUBILEE (5114 "Fried Chicken") 250-350 53
(Red vinyl.)

MASCOTS
Singles: 7-inch
KING (5377 "Story of My Heart") 40-50 60
KING (5435 "Lonely Rain") 30-40 60
Members: Eddie Levert; William Powell; Walter Williams; Bob Massey; Bill Isles.
Also see FERGUSON, H-Bomb / Escos / Mascots

MASCOTS
(With Vinny Catalano & Orchestra)
Singles: 7-inch
BLAST (206 "Once Upon a Love") 15-25 62
(Red or white label.)
MERMAID (107 "Bluebirds Over the Mountain") 40-50 62
Also see CATALANO, Vinny

MASEKELA, Hugh *P&R/LP '67*
(With the Union of South Africa)
Singles: 12-inch
JIVE AFRIKA.......... 4-6 84
Singles: 7-inch
BLUE THUMB.......... 4-6 74
CASABLANCA.......... 4-6 75-77
CHISA.......... 4-6 67-71
JIVE AFRIKA.......... 3-5 84
MGM.......... 4-6 66-68
MERCURY.......... 4-8 63-68
UNI.......... 4-6 67-69
LPs: 10/12-inch
BLUE THUMB.......... 5-10 72-74
CASABLANCA.......... 5-10 75-77
CHISA.......... 8-15 67-71
IMPULSE.......... 5-10 78
MGM.......... 8-15 66-68
MERCURY.......... 8-18 63-67
UNI.......... 8-12 67-69
UPFRONT.......... 5-8 77
VERVE.......... 8-15 68
WING.......... 6-12 68
Also see ALPERT, Herb, & Hugh Masekela

MASHBURN, Billy
("A Spectorious Production")
Singles: 7-inch
ATLANTIC (2208 "Don't It Sound Good") .. 8-12 63

MASHERS
Singles: 7-inch
HAMILTON (50038 "The Mash") 10-15 63

MASK, James
Singles: 7-inch
ARBEL (500 "I Miss My Teen Angel") 10-20
BANDERA (1306 "Save Your Love") 40-60 60

MASKED DEMONS
Singles: 7-inch
R.R.E. (1016 "Hi Surfin'") 20-30 63

MASKED MARAUDERS *LP '70*
Singles: 7-inch
DEITY.......... 5-10 69
LPs: 10/12-inch
DEITY (6378 "Masked Marauders") 15-20 69
Also see CLEANLINESS & GODLINESS SKIFFLE BAND

MASKED MARVEL
(Charlie Patton)
Singles: 78 rpm
PARAMOUNT (12805 "Screamin' and Hollerin' the Blues") 5000-7500
Also see PATTON, Charlie

MASKED MARVELS
LPs: 10/12-inch
BETHLEHEM (4007 "Dance to the Music") ... 20-30 62

MASKMAN & AGENTS R&B '68
Singles: 7-inch
DYNAMO ... 5-10 68-69
GAMMA ... 4-8 68
HITBOUND (2921 "In My Diary") ... 30-50
LOOP (701 "Crowded Station") ... 15-25 65
MUSICOR ... 4-6 70
VIGOR (707 "Stand Up") ... 5-10
LPs: 10/12-inch
DYNAMO ... 10-15 69
MUSICOR ... 10-15 70
Members: Harmon Bethea; Paul Williams; John Hood; Ty Gray.

MASON
LPs: 10/12-inch
ELEVENTH HOUR (1001 "Harbour") ... 50-75 71
Members: Jim Gaylon; Steve Arcese; Marg Hampton.

MASON, Barbara P&R/R&B/LP '65
(With the Futures)
Singles: 12-inch
WEST END ... 4-8 83-84
Singles: 7-inch
ARCTIC ... 15-25 64-69
BUDDAH ... 4-6 71-75
CHARGER (111 "Trouble Child") ... 4-8 65
CRUSADER (111 "Trouble Child") ... 5-10 64
NATIONAL GENERAL ... 4-6 70
PHONORAMA ... 3-5 84
PRELUDE ... 4-6 78
WMOT ... 3-5 80-81
WEST END ... 3-5 83-84
Picture Sleeves
BUDDAH (481 "We Got Each Other") ... 4-6 75
LPs: 10/12-inch
ARCTIC ... 15-25 65-68
BUDDAH ... 8-12 72-75
GNC ... 10-15 70
NATIONAL GENERAL ... 10-15 70
PHONORAMA ... 5-8 84
PRELUDE ... 8-10 78
WMOT ... 8-10 81
W.B. ... 8-12 77
WIND ... 8-10 81

MASON, Barbara, & Larks
Singles: 7-inch
CRUSADER (111 "Dedicated to You") ... 8-12 65
Also see LARKS

MASON, Barbara, & Bunny Sigler
Singles: 7-inch
W.B. ... 4-6 77
Also see MASON, Barbara
Also see SIGLER, Bunny

MASON, Bonnie Jo
(Cher)
Singles: 7-inch
ANNETTE (1000 "Ringo, I Love You"). 400-600 64
Also see CHER

MASON, Clint
Singles: 7-inch
S.P.Q.R. (3307 "Please Don't Release Me") ... 8-12 63

MASON, Dave P&R/LP '70
Singles: 12-inch
COLUMBIA ... 4-6 77
Singles: 7-inch
ABC ... 4-6 74
BLUE THUMB ... 4-8 70-78
COLUMBIA ... 3-6 73-81
MARBLE (75205-993 "Break Away") ... 3-5 83
LPs: 10/12-inch
ABC ... 8-10 75
BLUE THUMB (19 "Alone Together") ... 10-12 70
(Black vinyl.)
BLUE THUMB (19 "Alone Together") ... 20-30 70
(Multi-colored vinyl.)
BLUE THUMB (34 "Headkeeper") ... 10-15 72
BLUE THUMB (54 "Dave Mason Is Alive") ... 10-15 73
BLUE THUMB (880 "Dave Mason at His Best") ... 8-10 75
BLUE THUMB (6013 "Best of Dave Mason") ... 8-10 74
COLUMBIA (PC-31721 "It's Like You Never Left") ... 8-12 73
COLUMBIA (PCQ-31721 "It's Like You Never Left") ... 10-20 74
(Quadraphonic.)
COLUMBIA (PC-33096 "Dave Mason") ... 8-12 74
COLUMBIA (PCQ-33096 "Dave Mason"). 10-20 74
(Quadraphonic.)
COLUMBIA (PC-33698 "Split Coconut") ... 8-12 75
COLUMBIA (PCQ-33698 "Split Coconut") ... 10-20 75
(Quadraphonic.)
COLUMBIA (34174 "Certified Live") ... 10-12 76
(Two discs.)
COLUMBIA (34680 "Let It Flow") ... 8-10 77
COLUMBIA (35285 "Mariposo de Oro") ... 8-10 78
COLUMBIA (36144 "Old Crest on a New Wave") ... 8-10 80
Session: Graham Nash; Stevie Wonder; David Crosby; Manhattan Transfer; Leon Russell; Jim Capaldi; Rita Coolidge; Delaney & Bonnie.
Also see MERRYWEATHER, Neil
Also see TRAFFIC

MASON, Dave / Les Dudek / Southside Johnny & Asbury Jukes / Walter Egan
EPs: 7-inch
COLUMBIA (AE7-1119 "June Is CBS Records Month at Tower Records") ... 8-12 77
(Columbia/Epic promotional issue only.)

MASON, Dave, & Cass Elliot LP '71
(Mason & Cass)
Singles: 7-inch
DUNHILL (4266 "Next to You") ... 4-6 70
DUNHILL (4271 "Too Much Truth, Too Little Love") ... 4-6 71
LPs: 10/12-inch
BLUE THUMB (8825 "Dave Mason and Cass Elliot") ... 12-15 71
Also see ELLIOT, Cass
Also see MASON, Dave

MASON, Jerry
Singles: 7-inch
CHESS (1766 "You Are Lonely") ... 8-12 60
KAPP (276 "Strange Feeling") ... 8-12 59
SWAN (4129 "Jones Street") ... 5-10 62
VANCO ... 5-10 68

MASON, Kenny
Singles: 7-inch
CANARY (2004 "Person to Person") ... 8-12 65

MASON, Little Billy
Singles: 78 rpm
APEX (Canadian.) ... 5-10 56-57
RAMA ... 5-10 56-57
Singles: 7-inch
APEX (Canadian.) ... 10-15 56-57
GEE (1042 "School Kid") ... 15-25 57
RAMA (212 "Make Me Your Own") ... 15-25 56
RAMA (223 "Thinking of You") ... 15-25 57
Also see DAVIS, Bob

MASON, Peter
Singles: 7-inch
LAWN (105 "Lonely Drummer Boy") ... 15-25 60

MASON, Ronnie
Singles: 7-inch
CRYSTALETTE (719 "Kinda Like Love") . 10-15 58

MASON, Sharon
Singles: 7-inch
DORE (525 "Eddie, Can I Park in Your Lot") ... 10-15 59

MASON, Ted
Singles: 7-inch
LAURIE (3073 "Deep Inside") ... 5-10 60

MASON, Tommy, & Madhatters
Singles: 7-inch
CARDINAL (72 "The Game Is Done") ... 15-25 67
Also see MADHATTERS

MASON PROFFIT LP '71
Singles: 7-inch
AMPEX (11048 "Hope") ... 4-8 71
HAPPY TIGER (545 "Voice of Change") ... 4-8 70
HAPPY TIGER (570 "Hard Luck Woman") ... 4-8 70
LPs: 10/12-inch
AMPEX (10138 "Last Night I Had the Strangest Dream") ... 8-12 71
HAPPY TIGER ... 8-12 70-71
W.B. ... 8-10 72-73
Members: John Talbot; Terry Talbot.
Also see SOUNDS UNLIMITED

MASONICS
Singles: 7-inch
INTERPHON (7714 "Call It a Day") ... 5-10 64

MASQUE
Singles: 7-inch
BELL (647 "Sweet Soul") ... 5-10 66

MASQUERADERS P&R/R&B '68
Singles: 7-inch
ABC/HBS ... 4-8 75-76
A.G.P. (108 "I'm Just an Average Guy") ... 5-10 68
A.G.P. (114 "Say It") ... 5-10 69
A.G.P. (122 "Tell Me You Love Me") ... 5-10 69
BANG (4806 "Desire") ... 4-6 80
BELL (733 "I Ain't Got to Love Nobody Else") ... 8-12 68
BELL (874 "Please Take Me Back") ... 5-10 70
BELL (932 "Brotherhood") ... 5-10 70
L.A. BEAT (6605 "A Family") ... 25-50 '60s
WAND (1168 "Let's Face Facts") ... 15-25 67
WAND (1172 "Sweet Lovin' Woman") ... 25-35 67
LPs: 10/12-inch
ABC ... 10-15 75
Members: Lee Hatim; Robert Wrightsil; David Sanders; Harold Thomas; Sam Hutchins.

MASQUERADERS
Singles: 7-inch
HI ... 4-6 73-74
HOT BUTTERED SOUL ... 4-6 75-76
MK (101 "Man's Temptation") ... 10-15 '60s
STAIRWAY ... 10-20 '60s
TOWER (281 "Family") ... 5-10 66

MASQUERADERS
Singles: 7-inch
LABEAT ... 8-12
SOULTOWN ... 8-12

MASQUERADES
Singles: 7-inch
FORMAL (1011 "These Red Roses") ... 200-300 60
(Blue label.)
FORMAL (1012 "These Red Roses") ... 40-60 60
(Green label. Note number change.)

MASQUERADES
Singles: 7-inch
BOYD (1027 "The Whip") ... 600-800 64

MASSENGALE, Joey
Singles: 7-inch
JAA DEE (500 "Ma'm Selle") ... 100-150 62

MASSEY, Barbara
Singles: 7-inch
BRUT (801 "I'm So Glad") ... 4-6 73
IMPERIAL (5786 "You Call Me Angel") ... 15-25 61

MASSEY, Bill
Singles: 7-inch
GUYDEN (2063 "Still Walkin' ") ... 5-10 62
LANIER (002 "Ghost Town") ... 15-25 57

MASSEY, Edith
Singles: 7-inch
EGG (001P "Punks Get Off the Grass") ... 15-20 84
(Picture disc.)

MASSEY, Jimmy
(Jimmy Massi)
Singles: 7-inch
ROBBEE (104 "If I Had You") ... 10-20 60
ROBBEE (113 "Moon Rock") ... 10-20 61

MASSEY, Sally
Singles: 7-inch
SIMS (166 "I Miss Those Little Things") ... 5-10 64

MASSEY, Vince
Singles: 78 rpm
HERALD (414 "Smile") ... 15-20 53
Singles: 7-inch
HERALD (414 "Smile") ... 40-50 53

MASSIEL
Singles: 7-inch
BELL (725 "He Gives Me Love") ... 5-10 68

MASTER, Ronnie, & Rainbows
Singles: 7-inch
LANDA (667 "Loose Ends") ... 15-25 61
LANDA (669 "I Don't Know") ... 15-25 61

MASTER FLEET
Singles: 7-inch
SUSSEX (516 "Well Phase I") ... 8-15 74

MASTER FOUR
Singles: 7-inch
TAY-STER (6012 "It's Not the End") ... 50-75 67

MASTER FREDDY & PLEDGES
Singles: 7-inch
KAREN (1007 "Great Campus Raid") ... 10-20 60

MASTER KEYS
Singles: 78 rpm
JUBILEE (5004 "I Got the Blues in the Morning") ... 15-25 49
20TH CENTURY ... 15-25 49

MASTERETTES
Singles: 7-inch
LE SAGE (715/716 "Follow the Leader") . 50-75 61
Members: Brenda Reid; Sylvia Wilbur; Carol Johnson; Lillian Walker.
Also see EXCITERS

MASTERKEYS
Singles: 78 rpm
ABBEY (2017 "Mr. Blues") ... 30-40
SPORT (109 "If You Haven't Got Love") .. 15-25 67

MASTERS
Singles: 7-inch
LEN (103 "Til I Return") ... 50-75 59

MASTERS
Singles: 7-inch
END (1100 "A Man's Not Supposed to Cry") ... 150-200 61
LE SAGE (713/714 "I'm Searching") ... 200-300 61
Member: Herb Rooney.

MASTERS
(Featuring Willie Morris)
Singles: 7-inch
BINGO (1008 "A Lovely Way to Spend an Evening") ... 30-40 60

MASTERS
Singles: 7-inch
EMMY (10082 "Breaktime") ... 35-50 62

MASTERS, Johnny
(Johnny Maestro)
Singles: 7-inch
COED (527 "Say It Isn't So") ... 15-20 60
Also see MAESTRO, Johnny

MASTERS, Ken
Singles: 7-inch
DECCA (31084 "Too Late") ... 10-15 60

MASTERS, Mike
Singles: 7-inch
DRA (316 "Whole Wide World") ... 50-75 62

MASTERS, Sammy P&R '60
Singles: 78 rpm
DECCA ... 8-12 57
4 STAR ... 25-50 57
Singles: 7-inch
DECCA (30402 "The Drifter") ... 10-20 57
DOT (16123 "Charolette") ... 8-12 60
DOT (16865 "Dream Chaser") ... 5-10 66
4 STAR (1695 "Pink Cadillac") ... 50-75 57
4 STAR (1697 "Whop-T-Bop") ... 50-75 57
GALAHAD (506 "Stars Without a Heaven") ... 5-10 62
GALAHAD (526 "On Tour in Heaven") ... 5-10 63
GALAHAD (538 "Little Ben") ... 5-10 65
GALAHAD (600 "Carnival Is Over") ... 4-8 72
KAPP (613 "I Fought the Law") ... 5-10 64
KAPP (638 "Louisiana Jane") ... 5-10 65
LODE (108 "Rockin' Red Wing") ... 15-25 60
LODE (109 "Charolette") ... 10-20 60
LODE (114 "Never") ... 10-20 61
TJB BRANDES ... 5-10
W.B. (5102 "Rockin' Red Wing") ... 20-30 59

EPs: 7-inch

4 STAR (26 "Sammy Masters")............... 50-75 57
(Promotional issue only. Not issued with cover.)

MASTERS OF DECEIT

LPs: 10/12-inch

VANGUARD (6522 "Electric Jazz Band") 20-30 69
Member: Tom Hensley.

MASTERS OF SOUL

Singles: 7-inch

CAPITOL...5-10 68-69
DUKE...4-8 70-71
OVIDE (241 "Do You Really Love Me")... 10-20 67
OVIDE (247 "I Need You")..................... 10-20 68
OVIDE (251 "The Vow")........................ 10-20 68
OVIDE (253 "Sad Face")........................ 10-20 68

MASTERS OF STONEHOUSE

Singles: 7-inch

DISCOTEQUE (2 "If You Treat Me Bad Again")...................................8-12

MASTERSOUNDS

Singles: 7-inch

FANTASY (550 "Golden Earrings")............5-10 61
WORLD PACIFIC (103 "Fate")..................5-10 '60s

LPs: 10/12-inch

FANTASY.. 10-15 61
WORLD PACIFIC.................................... 10-15 59-64

MASTER-TONES

Singles: 78 rpm

BRUCE (111 "What'll You Do")........... 100-200 54

Singles: 7-inch

BRUCE (111 "What'll You Do")........ 1500-2000 54
(Black vinyl. With "45 R.P.M." above the top horizontal line. Reads: "N.Y. 19, N.Y.")
BRUCE (111 "What'll You Do")............... 50-75 62
(Blue vinyl. With "45 R.P.M." between the parallel horizontal lines. Reads: "N.Y. 19, N.Y.")
BRUCE (111 "What'll You Do")............... 10-20 62
(Black vinyl. With "45 R.P.M." between the parallel horizontal lines. Reads: "New York.")

MASTRIO, Johnny
(Johnny Mastrio Quartet; Quintet)

Singles: 7-inch

FRANKIE (1 "I Wish")............................. 15-20 57
Also see CLASSMATES

MASTRO, Andy
("Mister Charm"; with Lew Douglas Orchestra & Art Long Singers)

Singles: 7-inch

PANLIN (8302 "Cry, Cry, Baby")................5-10 '60s

Picture Sleeves

PANLIN (8302 "Cry, Cry, Baby")............. 15-20 '60s
Also see DOUGLAS, Lew

MATADORS

Singles: 7-inch

SUE (700 "Vengeance")..................... 100-200 57
SUE (700 "Vengeance")................... 2000-3000 57
(Red vinyl.)
SUE (701 "Be Good to Me")................ 100-200 57

MATADORS

Singles: 7-inch

CHAVIS (1034 "Carmen, I Wish You Were Here").. 10-20 62
DUCHESS (1005 "If I Had Another Chance")... 10-20 61
JAMIE (1226 "Listen").................................8-12 62
KEITH (6502 "If You Left Me Today")...... 15-25 62
KEITH (6504 "My Foolish Heart")........... 30-40 63

MATADORS

Singles: 7-inch

COLPIX (698 "Perfidia").............................8-12 63
COLPIX (718 "I've Gotta Drive")............. 40-50 63
(*I Gotta Drive* is actually by Jan Berry, Dean Torrance & Jill Gibson.)
COLPIX (741 "C'mon, Let Yourself Go")....8-12 64
Members: Tony Minichiello; Vic Diaz; Manuel Sanchez.
Also see GIBSON, Jill
Also see JAN & DEAN

MATADORS

Singles: 7-inch

EKO (1960 "Moments Like This")......... 75-125 64

MATADORS
(Featuring John Lopacinski)

Singles: 7-inch

LEE (5466 "Should I Ever Love Again").. 40-50 65

MATADORS

Singles: 7-inch

FEATURE (109 "You're a Better Man Than I")...15-25 66
Members: Ronnie Thone; Roman Brotz; Greg Busch; Lee McGlade; Tommy Raml.

MATADORS

Singles: 7-inch

CHART MAKER (404 "Let Me Dream")..75-100 66
FORBES (230 "Let Me Dream")..................8-12 67

MATCH, Billy

Singles: 7-inch

STARFIRE (664 "I Want My Baby")......200-300

MATCHES

Singles: 7-inch

JAGUAR (712 "Gonna Build Myself a Castle")...15-25 66

MATEO, Gia

Singles: 7-inch

RCA (8845 "With His Plinkity Plink Plink Banjo and Her Dum Diddy Dum Dum Drum")..................15-25 66
RCA (9138 "If You Can't Say Anything Nice")...15-25 67

MATERLYN & CUPONS

Singles: 7-inch

IMPACT (28 "I'll Be Your Love Tonight")..10-20 64

MATHERS, Jerry "Beaver"

Singles: 7-inch

ATLANTIC (2156 "Don't Cha Cry")............5-10 62

MATHEWS, Bill, & Balladeers
(Billy Mathews & Balladiers)

Singles: 78 rpm

ARLINGTON (201 "Please Give My Heart a Break")...15-25 49
JUBILEE (5021 "Red Sails in the Sunset")..200-300 50
JUBILEE (5024 "I Never Knew I Loved You")...200-300 50
MERCURY (8073 "I Love You, Yes I Do")...20-30 48
WRIMUS..10-15 56

Singles: 7-inch

CLIFTON (96 "Red Sails in the Sunset")......3-5 92
WRIMUS (701 "Dance the Rhythm and Blues")..75-125 56
Members: Bill Mathews; Joe Cleary; Dave Moore; Harold Leiter; John Paloney; Pat Yocalano.

MATHEWS, Hank
(With the Twilight Ramblers)

Singles: 7-inch

HOLLY (210 "Alabama Boogie")..........200-300 '50s
WINDS (101 "Alabama Boogie")..........300-400 '50s

MATHEWS, Morley

Singles: 7-inch

HAMILTON (50034 "Give My Love a Chance")...5-10 63

MATHEWS, Ronnie

Singles: 7-inch

DAYHILL (2004 "Lonesome Teenager")..20-30 62

MATHEWS, Tobin P&R '60
(Tobin Mathews & Co.; Tobin Matthews)

Singles: 7-inch

CHIEF (7022 "Ruby Duby Du")..................8-12 60
CHIEF (7024 "Steel Guitar Rag")...............8-12 61
COLUMBIA (42489 "Susan").....................5-10 62
COLUMBIA (42771 "Break It Easy")...........5-10 63
USA (718 "Think It Over").......................10-20 61
W.B. (5398 "When You Came Along").......5-10 63

MATHIS, Bobby, & Sevilles

Singles: 7-inch

SIOUX (51860 "Girl in the Drug Store")..75-125 60

MATHIS, Johnny P&R/R&B/LP '57
(With Ray Conniff)

Singles: 78 rpm

COLUMBIA...20-40 57-58

Singles: 7-inch

AURAVISION (6726 "Starbright")..............8-12 64
(Cardboard flexi-disc, one of six by six different artists. Columbia Record Club "Enrollment Premium." Set came in a special paper sleeve.)
COLUMBIA (04468 thru 07797).....................3-5 84-88
COLUMBIA (10112 thru 11313)....................3-6 75-80
COLUMBIA (33000 series)..........................4-8 '60s
(Hall of Fame series. With "13" prefix.)
COLUMBIA (40784 thru 41491)..................10-20 57-59
COLUMBIA (41583 thru 42916)..................8-15 60-63
COLUMBIA (44266 thru 46048)....................4-8 67-74
MERCURY (71202 "Moonlight Magic")....15-25 57
MERCURY (71273 "Harbor of Love")........15-25 58
MERCURY (72000 series)...........................5-10 63-66

Picture Sleeves

COLUMBIA (40993 "Chances Are")..........20-30 57
COLUMBIA (41060 thru 42799)...............10-20 58-63
MERCURY...8-12 63-66

EPs: 7-inch

COLUMBIA (Except 8800 series)............10-20 57-59
COLUMBIA (8871 thru 8873)....................15-25 56

LPs: 10/12-inch

COLUMBIA (Except 887)............................5-15 57-87
COLUMBIA (887 "Johnny Mathis")...........35-50 56
COLUMBIA HOUSE (6030 "Johnny Mathis")..15-25 73
(Boxed 6-disc set. Record club offer.)
COLUMBIA SPECIAL PRODUCTS.............5-8
CONCERT...8-12
(TV mail-order offer.)
HARMONY..5-10
MFSL (171 "Heavenly")...........................25-35 85
MERCURY..8-15 64-67
Also see CONNIFF, Ray
Also see FAITH, Percy, Orchestra / Johnny Mathis
Also see KNIGHT, Gladys, & Johnny Mathis
Also see NELSON, Willie / Nat "King" Cole / Johnny Mathis / Shirley Bassey

MATHIS, Johnny / Tony Bennett / North Carolina Ramblers / Ray Conniff & Jerry Vale

Singles

AURAVISION ("Most Beautiful Girl")..........8-12 63
(Square cardboard picture disc. Sampler with highlights from each artist's new album.)
Also see BENNETT, Tony
Also see CONNIFF, Ray
Also see VALE, Jerry

MATHIS, Johnny, & Henry Mancini LP '87

LPs: 10/12-inch

COLUMBIA (40372 "Hollywood Musicals")..5-8 87
Also see MANCINI, Henry

MATHIS, Johnny, & Jane Olivor P&R '79

Singles: 7-inch

COLUMBIA (10902 "The Last Time I Felt Like This")...3-6 79

MATHIS, Johnny, & Dionne Warwick P&R '82

Singles: 7-inch

ARISTA (0673 "Friends in Love")................3-5 82
Also see WARWICK, Dionne

MATHIS, Johnny, & Deniece Williams P&R/R&B/LP '78

Singles: 7-inch

COLUMBIA (04379 "Love Won't Let Me Wait")...3-5 84
COLUMBIA (10693 "Too Much, Too Little, Too Late")...3-6 78
COLUMBIA (10772 "You're All I Need to Get By")...3-6 78

LPs: 10/12-inch

COLUMBIA (35435 "That's What Friends Are For")...5-10 78
(Standard vinyl disc.)
COLUMBIA (35435 "That's What Friends Are For")...30-50 78
(Picture disc. Promotional issue only.)
Also see MATHIS, Johnny
Also see WILLIAMS, Deniece

MATHIS, Lucille
(Lucille Matthis)

Singles: 7-inch

A-BET (9427 "I'm Not Your Regular Woman")...10-15 68
A-BET (9431 "Somewhere Out There")....10-15 68

MATHIS, Mike

Singles: 7-inch

BLUE RIVER (203 "Am I to Blame").........10-20 63

MATHIS BROTHERS

Singles: 7-inch

HICKORY (1414 "When I Stop Dreaming")..10-20 66

MATSON, Judy

Singles: 7-inch

SURF (5015 " '86' Out")..............................8-12 57

MATT, Dee, & Fabulous Cenders

Singles: 7-inch

PRIMOS (1006 "Searching for You")........10-20

MATTE, Bill

Singles: 7-inch

LANOR (503 "Cher P'tit Coeur")................5-10 61
LANOR (519 "Restless Night")...................5-10 64

MATTHEW, Otis

Singles: 7-inch

EXOTIC (8004 "Style of My Own")..........15-25

MATTHEWS, Dino

Singles: 7-inch

DOT (16365 "The Girl That I Love").........30-40 62

MATTHEWS, Fat Man
(Fats Matthews)

Singles: 78 rpm

BAYOU..50-75 52
IMPERIAL..40-60 52

Singles: 7-inch

BAYOU (016 "I'm Thankful")..................100-150 52
IMPERIAL (5235 "Down the Line").........75-125 52

MATTHEWS, Fat Man, & Four Kittens

Singles: 78 rpm

IMPERIAL..500-750 52

Singles: 7-inch

IMPERIAL (5211 "When Boy Meets Girl")..3000-5000 52
Also see MATHEWS, Fat Man

MATTHEWS, Ian LP '72

Singles: 7-inch

DECCA..4-6 70-71
COLUMBIA..4-6 76-77
ELEKTRA...4-6 73
MUSHROOM..4-6 78-79
VERTIGO...4-6 71-72

LPs: 10/12-inch

CAPITOL...8-10 71
COLUMBIA..8-10 77
DECCA..8-12 71
ELEKTRA...8-10 73-74
MUSHROOM (Except 5012)......................8-10 78
MUSHROOM (5012 "Stealin' Home")......10-20 78
(Picture disc. Promotional issue only.)
MUSHROOM (5012 "Stealin' Home")........8-10 78
(Standard vinyl disc.)
VERTIGO...10-12 71-72
Also see MATTHEWS' SOUTHERN COMFORT

MATTHEWS, Jerry

Singles: 7-inch

KOOL (1001 "Long Long Gone").............50-75 59
KOOL (1012 "Lonely Dreamer")..............15-25 62

MATTHEWS, Joannie Mae
(Johnnie Mae Mathews)

Singles: 7-inch

ART..8-12
ATCO (6528 "Cut Me Loose")....................5-10 67
BLUE ROCK (4001 "Baby What's Wrong")...10-20 64
BLUE ROCK (4011 "My Man")..................10-20 65
NORTHERN (3736 "Ooh Wee")................30-40 60
NORTHERN (3742 "So Lonely")...............15-25 60
NORTHERN (10039 "It's Good")..............15-25 '60s
REEL (112 "My Little Angel").....................20-30 61
SPOKANE (4008 "Itty Bitty Heart")..........10-15 64
SUE (755 "My Little Angel")......................10-15 62

Picture Sleeves

BLUE ROCK (4001 "Baby What's Wrong")...10-20 64

MATTHEWS, Joannie Mae, & Dapps

Singles: 7-inch

NORTHERN (3729 "Someday")................30-40 59
Also see DAPPS
Also see MATTHEWS, Joannie Mae

MATTHEWS, Joe

Singles: 7-inch

KOOL KAT (1001 "Ain't Nothing You Can Do")...100-200 59
THELMA (104 "She's My Beauty Queen")..100-200 64
THELMA (107 "Sorry Ain't Good Enough")..25-50 64

MATTHEWS, Little Arthur
Singles: 78 rpm
DIG ... 15-25 56
FEDERAL ... 15-25 55
Singles: 7-inch
DIG (117 "Bad Bad Bulldog") ... 20-40 56
FEDERAL (12232 "I'm Gonna Whale on You") ... 20-40 55

MATTHEWS, Renee
Singles: 7-inch
SQUARE (201 "What'll I Do") ... 5-10 61

MATTHEWS, Shirley
(With the Big Town Girls)
Singles: 7-inch
AMY (910 "Feel So Pretty") ... 5-10 64
AMY (921 "Stop the Clock!") ... 5-10 65
ATLANTIC (2210 "Big Town Boy") ... 10-20 63
ATLANTIC (2224 "Wise Guys") ... 10-20 64
TAMARAC (602 "Big Town Boy") ... 15-25 63
Also see 4 SEASONS

MATTHEWS BROTHERS
Singles: 7-inch
ABC-PAR (10473 "Stupid") ... 20-30 63

MATTHEWS FAMILY
Singles: 7-inch
CAMTONE (102 "Crocodile Chile") ... 5-10 59
OKEH (7128 "Crocodile Chile") ... 5-10 60

MATTHEWS' SOUTHERN COMFORT *P&R/LP '71*
(Featuring Ian Matthews)
Singles: 7-inch
DECCA ... 4-8 71
LPs: 10/12-inch
DECCA ... 10-15 70-71
MCA ... 5-10 78
Also see MATTHEWS, Ian
Also see SOUTHERN COMFORT

MATTHEWSON, Guy
Singles: 7-inch
MCM (6969 "Blues Has Got Me") ... 50-75

MATTICE, Bob, & Phaetons
Singles: 7-inch
CUCA (1016 "What's All This") ... 35-55 61
CUCA (1034 "Safari") ... 15-25 61
Members: Tom Loos; Jim Kelly; Tom Reischl; Ralph Barfell; Jerry Kowall.

MATTINA, Tony
Singles: 7-inch
ACE (614 "Forever and Forever") ... 10-15 61
LANOR (512 "Don't Ever Break My Heart") ... 5-10 62

MATTINGLY, Jesse
Singles: 7-inch
THRONE (509 "'Til My Money Runs Out") ... 50-75

MATTISON, Ti
Singles: 7-inch
ENJOY (1012 "Don't Make Me Cry") ... 5-10 63

MATTS, Merle, III
Singles: 7-inch
COOL (111 "Shake with Me Baby") ... 300-400
COOL (142 "Pink Shoes") ... 200-300

MATTSON, Bart
Singles: 7-inch
TAMPA (137 "Love Slave") ... 10-20 58
Picture Sleeves
TAMPA (137 "Love Slave") ... 30-50 58

MATTSON, Marilyn
Singles: 7-inch
ALLIED (102 "He Means So Much to Me") ... 15-20

MATTY, Jay
Singles: 7-inch
ERA (3008 "Janie, My Lover") ... 10-15 59
LUTE (6021 "Merry Twist-Mas") ... 8-10 61

MATYS BROS. *P&R '63*
Singles: 78 rpm
CORAL (61941 "Crazy Street") ... 20-40 57
DECCA ... 5-10 56
ESSEX ... 5-10 54
SOUND ... 5-10 54-55
20TH CENTURY ... 5-10 55
Singles: 7-inch
ASTRO (13 "Boom Biddy Biddy Boom") ... 5-10
BEE-BEE ... 5-10
CORAL (61941 "Crazy Street") ... 25-50 57
DECCA ... 10-20 56
ESSEX (369 "Muskrat Ramble") ... 10-20 54
FAYETTE ... 5-10 64
SELECT ... 5-10 62-64
SOUND ... 10-20 54-55
20TH CENTURY (75024 "You're the Moment of a Lifetime") ... 10-20 55
Session: Bill Haley's Comets.
Also see HALEY, Bill

MAUCK, Carl, & Oilers
Singles: 7-inch
BELLAIRE (PD4 "Oiler Cannonball") ... 10-15 80
(Picture disc.)

MAUDS *P&R '68*
Singles: 7-inch
DUNWICH (160 "Hold On") ... 5-10 67
MERCURY ... 4-8 67-69
RCA ... 4-8 70
LPs: 10/12-inch
MERCURY ... 15-25 67

MAULDIN, Dickie
Singles: 7-inch
TAGG (502 "Falling in Love Again") ... 5-10 59

MAUNDY QUINTET
Singles: 7-inch
PARIS TOWER (103 "2's Better Than 3") ... 20-30 67
Member: Bernie Leadon.

MAUPIN, Ramon
Singles: 78 rpm
FERNWOOD (101 "No Chance") ... 50-75 58
FERNWOOD (105 "Rockin' Rufus") ... 50-75 58
Singles: 7-inch
FERNWOOD (101 "No Chance") ... 75-100 58
FERNWOOD (105 "Rockin' Rufus") ... 150-250 58
MEMPHIS (101 "Hey Rena") ... 100-150 61

MAURICE & MAC
Singles: 7-inch
BROWN SUGAR (0103 "Use That Good Thing") ... 4-8 72
CHECKER ... 10-15 67-70
Members: Maurice McAlister; Green McLauren.
Also see RADIANTS

MAURO, Vince
Singles: 7-inch
POP-SIDE (4 "Don't You Cry") ... 5-10 61

MAUVE
Singles: 7-inch
CORI (31006 "You've Got Me Cryin'") ... 15-25 66

MAVERICKS
Singles: 7-inch
HARMON (1008 "Chicken Back") ... 10-15 62
YUCCA (146 "Don't Run Away") ... 100-150 62
YUCCA (155 "Spanish Fandango") ... 15-25 63

MAVERICKS
Singles: 7-inch
SOMA (1406 "Tell Me How") ... 25-35 64
(Blue vinyl.)
SOMA (1408 "Cold Cold Darling") ... 10-20 64
Also see TIBOR BROTHERS

MAVERICKS
Singles: 7-inch
20TH FOX (595 "When I'm Gone") ... 5-10 65

MAVERICKS
Singles: 7-inch
CUCA (69103 "Patty Joanne, Christine") ... 10-15 69

MAVRICKS
(Gary Paxton)
Singles: 7-inch
CAPITOL (4507 "Angel with a Heartache") ... 10-20 61
CAPITOL (4560 "Going to the River") ... 10-20 61
Note: If the Mavricks' 1958 recording of *You're Ruining My Gladness* is on record, we would like to know its label name and number.)
Also see PAXTON, Gary

MAXIM TRIO *R&B '49*
(Maxin Trio)
Singles: 78 rpm
DOWNBEAT (171 "Confession Blues") ... 40-60 49
Members: Ray Charles; Gosady McKee; Milton Garred.
Also see CHARLES, Ray

MAXIMAS
Singles: 7-inch
CREST (666 "Gladly") ... 10-15 '70s

MAXIMILLIAN
(Max Crook)
Singles: 7-inch
BIG TOP (3068 "The Wanderer") ... 10-15 61
BIG TOP (3095 "Peter Gunn Theme") ... 10-15 62
CUB (9046 "Gee Baby, You're the Utmost") ... 5-10 59
TWIRL (2003 "Autumn Mood") ... 5-10 60
Also see SHANNON, Del

MAXIMILLIAN
LPs: 10/12-inch
ABC (696 "Maximillian") ... 20-40 69

MAXINE, Ernest
Singles: 7-inch
TOP RANK (2030 "On the Beach") ... 5-10 60

MAXTED, Billy
(With His Manhattan Jazz Band)
Singles: 7-inch
CADENCE ... 8-12 57-59
K&H (505 "Watermelon Man") ... 5-10 64
LIBERTY ... 5-10 65-67
SEECO (6017 "Wedding Bells") ... 5-10 59

MAXWELL, Bobby, & Exploits
Singles: 7-inch
FARGO (1009 "Stay with Me") ... 50-75 59
FARGO (1010 "You're Laughing") ... 40-60 59

MAXWELL, Claude
Singles: 7-inch
W.B. (5509 "Limbo Number Two") ... 5-10 61

MAXWELL, Delores
Singles: 7-inch
BUMBLE BEE (506 "My Man") ... 30-40 60

MAXWELL, Diane *P&R '59*
Singles: 7-inch
CAPITOL ... 8-12 61
CHALLENGE ... 10-20 58-59
LPs: 10/12-inch
CHALLENGE (607 "Almost Seventeen") ... 30-40 59
(Monaural.)
CHALLENGE (2501 "Almost Seventeen") ... 40-60 59
(Stereo.)
Also see FULLER, Jerry, & Diane Maxwell

MAXWELL, Holly
Singles: 7-inch
CONSTELLATION (152 "One Thin Dime") ... 10-20 65
CONSTELLATION (162 "Only When You're Lonely") ... 10-20 65
CURTOM ... 5-10 69
STAR (100 "Philly Barracuda") ... 8-12 66

MAXWELL, Len
Singles: 7-inch
20TH FOX (551 "Merry Monster Christmas") ... 5-10 64

MAY, Gloria
Singles: 7-inch
CHESS (1719 "Boy in My Dreams") ... 15-25 59

MAY, Patricia
Singles: 7-inch
PARKWAY (858 "Angel of Love") ... 5-10 62

MAYALL, John *LP '68*
(With the Blues Breakers Featuring Eric Clapton)
Singles: 7-inch
ABC ... 4-6 76
IMMEDIATE ... 4-8 67
LONDON ... 5-10 66-68
POLYDOR ... 4-8 69-74
LPs: 10/12-inch
ABC ... 8-12 76-78
BLUE THUMB ... 8-12 74
DJM ... 8-12 79
ISLAND ... 5-8 90
LONDON ... 10-15 67-78
MCA ... 5-8
MFSL (183 "Bluesbreakers Featuring Eric Clapton") ... 30-40 85
MFSL (246 "Blues Alone") ... 25-35 95
POLYDOR ... 10-12 69-74
Session: Jon Mark; Johnny Almond.
Also see CLAPTON, Eric
Also see FLEETWOOD MAC
Also see GROUNDHOGS
Also see MARK - ALMOND BAND

MAYBEE, Charley
Singles: 7-inch
RIMROCK (202 "Little Judy") ... 75-125

MAYBERRY, Howard
Singles: 7-inch
DIXIE (908 "Proof of Love") ... 300-400

MAYE, Arthur Lee
(With the Crowns; Lee Maye; "Lee Maye of the Milwaukee Braves")
Singles: 78 rpm
DIG ... 25-75 56-57
FLIP ... 50-100 58
MODERN ... 75-125 54
RPM ... 50-75 55
SPECIALTY ... 20-30 56
Singles: 7-inch
ABC ... 5-8 68
ANTRELL (102 "Moonlight") ... 8-12 85
(Yellow label, green or blue vinyl.)
ANTRELL (102 "Moonlight") ... 3-5 85
(Gold label, blue vinyl.)
BUDDAH (141 "He'll Have to Go") ... 5-10 69
CASH (1063 "Will You Be Mine") ... 600-800 58
CASH (1065 "All I Want Is Someone to Love") ... 100-200 58
DIG (124 "This Is the Night for Love") ... 100-200 56
DIG (133 "A Fool's Prayer") ... 50-100 57
(Original 45s of Dig 146, 149 and 151 were not issued, though unauthorized discs do exist.)
FLIP (330 "Cause You're Mine Alone") ... 100-150 58
IMPERIAL (5790 "Will You be Mine") ... 40-50 61
JAMIE (1272 "Loving Fool") ... 10-15 64
JAMIE (1276 "How's the World Treating You") ... 10-15 64
JAMIE (1284 "Only a Game") ... 10-15 64
JAMIE (1287 "Even a Nobody") ... 10-15 64
JET STREAM (735 "Loving Fool") ... 5-10 68
KENT (406 "Love Me Always") ... 30-40 64
LENOX (5566 "Half Way") ... 10-15 63
MODERN (944 "Set My Heart Free") ... 1000-1500 54
PACEMAKER (252 "Fools Rush In") ... 5-10 65
RPM (424 "Truly") ... 100-200 55
RPM (429 "Love Me Always") ... 150-250 55
RPM (438 "Please Don't Leave Me") ... 200-300 55
SPECIALTY (573 "Gloria") ... 50-75 56
(With saw-tooth horizontal lines.)
SPECIALTY (573 "Gloria") ... 25-35 '50s
(Without saw-tooth horizontal lines.)
TOWER (243 "At the Party") ... 8-12 66
Members: Arthur Lee Maye; Richard Berry; Charles Colbert; Joe Moore; Johnny Coleman.
Also see BERRY, Richard
Also see LYNN, Barbara, & Lee Maye
Also see RAMS

MAYER, Nathaniel *P&R/R&B '62*
(With the Fabulous Twilights; with Fortune Braves; Nathaniel "Nay Dog" Mayer & Filthy McNasty Group Plus Free Style)
Singles: 7-inch
FORTUNE (449 "Village of Love") ... 15-25 62
FORTUNE (487 "Hurting Love") ... 30-40 62
FORTUNE (500 series) ... 10-20 62-69
LOVE DOG (101 "Raise the Curtain High") ... 4-6 80
LPs: 10/12-inch
FORTUNE (8014 "Goin' Back to the Village of Love") ... 100-200 64

MAYES, Jimmy, & Soul Breed
Singles: 7-inch
PORT (3014 "Drums for Sale") ... 5-10 66

MAYES, Zilla
Singles: 7-inch
CHECKER (973 "A Prayer for Jackie") ... 15-25 61

MAYFAIR VOICES
Singles: 7-inch
VIVA (629 "Day I Say I Love You") ... 5-10 68

MAYFIELD, Charles, & Casuals
Singles: 7-inch
GAME (392 "Throw It Out of Your Mind") 25-35

MAYFIELD, Chuck
Singles: 7-inch
ABBOTT (191 "Four Faces High") ... 10-15 57

MAYFIELD, Curtis *P&R/R&B/LP '70*
Singles: 7-inch
ARISTA ... 3-5 89
BOARDWALK ... 3-5 81-82
CRC (001 "Baby It's You") ... 3-5 85
CURTOM ... 3-6 70-80
Picture Sleeves
ARISTA ... 3-5 89
CURTOM (0135 "You Are, You Are") ... 4-6 78
CURTOM (1968 "We Got to Have Peace") ... 4-6 72
CURTOM (1978 "Superfly") ... 5-8 72
CURTOM (1999 "Kung Fu") ... 4-6 74
EPs: 7-inch
CURTOM (8018 "Curtis in Chicago") ... 10-15 73
("Collector's Edition.")
LPs: 10/12-inch
ABC (780 "His Early Years") ... 10-20 73
(Two discs.)
BOARDWALK ... 5-10 81-82
CURTOM ... 8-15 70-78
RSO ... 5-10 79-80
Also see IMPRESSIONS
Also see REED, Jimmy

MAYFIELD, Curtis, & Linda Clifford *R&B '79*
Singles: 7-inch
RSO/CURTOM (941 "Between You Baby and Me") ... 4-6 79
RSO/CURTOM (1029 "Love's Sweet Sensation") ... 4-6 80
LPs: 10/12-inch
RSO (3084 "Right Combination") ... 8-12 80
Also see MAYFIELD, Curtis

MAYFIELD, Curtis, & Ice-T
Singles: 7-inch
CAPITOL (PRO-79205 "Superfly 1990") ... 3-5 90

MAYFIELD, Joe
Singles: 7-inch
EXCELLO (2256 "I'm On the Move") ... 8-12 64
ROCKET ... 5-10

MAYFIELD, Percy *P&R/R&B '50*
Singles: 78 rpm
CASH (1041 "Bluest Blues") ... 10-15 56
CHESS (1599 "Double Dealing") ... 25-50 55
KING (4480 "Two Years of Torture") ... 25-35 51
RECORDED IN HOLLYWOOD (228 "Two Years of Torture") ... 15-25 52
SPECIALTY ... 10-30 50-57
Singles: 7-inch
ATLANTIC ... 4-6 74
BRUNSWICK ... 5-10 68
CASH (1041 "Bluest Blues") ... 20-30 56
CHESS (1599 "Double Dealing") ... 50-100 55
IMPERIAL (5577 "One Love") ... 10-15 59
IMPERIAL (5620 "My Memories") ... 10-15 59
KING (4480 "Two Years of Torture") ... 50-100 51
RCA ... 4-6 70
7 ARTS (715 "Say You Love Me") ... 5-10 61
SPECIALTY (375 "Please Send Me Someone to Love") ... 40-60 50
SPECIALTY (390 "Lost Love") ... 40-60 51
SPECIALTY (400 "Nightless Lover") ... 40-60 51
SPECIALTY (408 "My Blues") ... 40-60 51
SPECIALTY (416 "Cry Baby") ... 40-60 52
SPECIALTY (425 "Big Question") ... 40-60 52
SPECIALTY (432 "Louisiana") ... 40-60 52
SPECIALTY (439 "My Heart") ... 40-60 53
SPECIALTY (451 "I Dare You, Baby") ... 40-60 54
SPECIALTY (460 "Lonely One") ... 40-60 54
(Black vinyl.)
SPECIALTY (460 "Lonely One") ... 100-200 54
(Red vinyl.)
SPECIALTY (473 "How Deep Is the Well") ... 40-60 54
(Black vinyl.)
SPECIALTY (473 "How Deep Is the Well") ... 100-200 54
(Red vinyl.)
SPECIALTY (485 "I Need You So Bad") ... 40-60 54
SPECIALTY (499 "You Don't Exist No More") ... 40-60 55
SPECIALTY (537 "You Were Lyin' to Me") ... 25-50 55
SPECIALTY (544 "Voice Within") ... 25-35 55
SPECIALTY (607 "Please Believe Me") ... 20-30 57
SPECIALTY (690 "What Must I Do") ... 15-25 60
SPECIALTY (723 "Lost Mind") ... 4-6 '70s
TANGERINE ... 5-15 62-67
LPs: 10/12-inch
BRUNSWICK ... 10-20 69
RCA ... 10-15 70-71
SPECIALTY ... 8-12 70
TANGERINE ... 15-25 66-67

MAYMIE & ROBERT
(With Able Baker Orchestra)
Singles: 7-inch
GLORY (260 "Parting Tears") ... 10-20 57
MGM (12702 "Sweet Lips") ... 8-12 58
ROULETTE (4347 "That's When") ... 5-10 61
Members: Maymie Roberts; Robert Mosley.
Also see MOSLEY, Robert

MAYNARD, Lloyd
(With the Paramounts)
Singles: 7-inch
FERN (810 "I Want a True Love") ... 50-75 61

MAYNIE & HOWIE
Singles: 7-inch
SHO-MI (13083 "Library Rock") ... 900-1000 58
Members: Maynard Horlick; Howard Sandler.
Also see HORLICK, Maynard, & Hep Teens

MAYO, Andy
Singles: 7-inch
TITAN (1726 "I'm Coming Back to You") ... 5-10 62

MAYO, Bobby
Singles: 7-inch
ROULETTE (4315 "Arrivederci") ... 5-10 60

MAYO, Danny
Singles: 7-inch
MONITOR (103 "Pretty Baby Rock") ... 250-350

MAYO, Mary
Singles: 7-inch
COLUMBIA (41190 "It Seemed So Right Last Night") ... 8-12 58
Also see VALE, Jerry

MAYORGA, Lincoln
(With Distinguished Colleagues)
Singles: 7-inch
CAPITOL (5400 "Lord Jim") ... 5-10 65
WHITE WHALE (339 "Suite: Judy Blue Eyes") ... 4-8 70
LPs: 10/12-inch
SHEFFIELD LABS (10 "The Missing Linc") ... 20-30
(Half-speed mastered.)
Also see FOUR PREPS

MAYPOLE
Singles: 7-inch
COLOSSUS (131 "Show Me the Way") ... 4-8 70
LPs: 10/12-inch
COLOSSUS (1007 "Maypole") ... 30-50 71

MAYRO, Jackie
(Jacqueline Mayro)
Singles: 7-inch
MALA (529 "Giant Step") ... 5-10 66
ROULETTE (4548 "Who Am I") ... 5-10 65

MAYS, Bredice
Singles: 7-inch
TWIN (33 "Miami Boogie") ... 50-75

MAYS, Carl
Singles: 7-inch
AZTEC (101 "Report Card Time") ... 20-30 64

MAYS, Jean
Singles: 7-inch
DIAMOND (170 "He Makes Me Feel So Crazy") ... 10-20 64
(Brown vinyl.)

MAYS, Willie
Singles: 7-inch
DUKE (350 "My Sad Heart") ... 5-10 62
MATTEL ("Willie Mays") ... 5-15 71
(Selection number not known. Picture disc. This is only known picture disc in the "Instant Replay Series." Only playable on special Mattel phonograph because of its small size without a play hole.)
Also see BASEBALL ("HOW TO" SERIES)

MAYS, Willie, & Treniers
("Willie Mays of the New York Giants"; with Quincy Jones & Orchestra)
Singles: 78 rpm
EPIC (9066 "Say Hey") ... 10-15 54
Singles: 7-inch
EPIC (9066 "Say Hey") ... 25-50 54
Also see JONES, Quincy
Also see MAYS, Willie
Also see TRENIERS

MAYTALS
Singles: 7-inch
SHELTER (7311 "54-46 Was My Number") . 4-6 71
LPs: 10/12-inch
BMN (003 "Sensational Maytals") ... 75-125 65

MAYS, Zilla
(With the Four Students)
Singles: 78 rpm
GROOVE ... 8-15 55
MERCURY ... 8-15 54
Singles: 7-inch
GROOVE (0127 "Right Now") ... 20-30 55
MERCURY ... 10-20 54
Also see FOUR STUDENTS

MAZE
Singles: 7-inch
CALLA (135 "I Got Love") ... 5-10 67

MAZE
LPs: 10/12-inch
MTA (5012 "Armageddon") ... 40-60 69

MAZZA, Mary
(With Chuck Sagle & Orchestra)
Singles: 7-inch
ALPINE (55 "Cha Cha Italiano") ... 15-25 59
ALPINE (63 "Schoolgirl's Prayer") ... 15-25 60

MBULU, Letta *R&B/LP '77*
Singles: 7-inch
A&M ... 4-6 77-78
CAPITOL (2070 "Aredze") ... 10-12 68
LPs: 10/12-inch
A&M (4609 "There's Music in the Air") ... 5-10 77
CAPITOL (2874 "Letta Mbulu") ... 10-15 68
CAPITOL (2929 "Free Soul") ... 10-15 68
FANTASY (9428 "Naturally") ... 8-10 73
Also see JONES, Quincy, & Letta Mbulu

McADAMS, Johnny
Singles: 7-inch
SPADE (1929 "Nine O'Clock") ... 200-300

McAFEE, Bill
Singles: 7-inch
GALAXY (710 "I Don't Know Why") ... 10-20 62

McALISTER, Maurice
Singles: 7-inch
CHESS (1988 "Baby Hang On") ... 5-10 67
Also see RADIANTS

McALISTER, Mike
Singles: 7-inch
HOB NOB (441 "I Don't Dig It") ... 150-250

McALLISTER, Billie
LPs: 10/12-inch
KENT (011 "What a Big Piece of Meat") .. 10-15 73

McALLISTER, Red
Singles: 78 rpm
KING (4598 "Eggs & Grits") ... 25-50 52
Singles: 7-inch
KING (4598 "Eggs & Grits") ... 50-100 52

McALLISTERS
Singles: 7-inch
VIV (7 "But I Was Cool") ... 10-15 63

McAULIFFE, Leon *C&W '49*
(With His Western Swing Band; with His Cimmaron Boys; Leon McAuliffe)
Singles: 78 rpm
COLUMBIA ... 5-10 49-54
Singles: 7-inch
CAPITOL ... 4-8 64-65
CIMARRON ... 5-10 59-62
COLUMBIA ... 10-15 52-54
EPs: 7-inch
CAPITOL ... 8-12 '60s
DOT ... 8-12 58
LPs: 10/12-inch
ABC-PAR (ABC-394 "Cozy Inn") ... 25-35 61
(Monaural.)
ABC-PAR (ABCS-394 "Cozy Inn") ... 35-45 61
(Stereo.)
CAPITOL (2016 "Dancin'est Band Around") ... 20-30 64
CAPITOL (2148 "Everybody Dance, Everybody Swing") ... 20-30 64
CIMARRON (2002 "Swingin' Western Strings") ... 35-55 60
COLUMBIA ... 5-8 84
DELTA ... 5-10 82
DOT (3139 "Take Off") ... 25-50 58
DOT (3689 "Golden Country Hits") ... 15-20 66
PINE MOUNTAIN ... 6-12
SESAC (225 "Just a Minute") ... 50-75 59
SESAC (1601 "Points West") ... 50-75 59
STARDAY (171 "Mister Western Swing") 20-40 62
STARDAY (280 "Swinging West") ... 20-40 64
STARDAY (309 "Swingin' Western Strings") ... 20-40 65
STONEWAY ... 10-20
Member: Sam D. Bass.
Also see WILLS, Bob

McBEE, Ronnie
Singles: 7-inch
SPANGLE (2007 "Midnight Sun") ... 8-12 58

McBOOKER, Connie
(Connie Mac Booker; Connie Mack Booker with His Orchestra)
Singles: 78 rpm
EDDIE'S ... 15-25 49
FREEDOM ... 15-25 49
RPM ... 20-30 53
Singles: 7-inch
RPM (401 "Love Me Pretty Baby") ... 100-200 54
Also see KING, B.B.
Also see WILLIAMS, L.C.

McBRIDE, Jimmy
Singles: 7-inch
MADISON (101 "Rockin' Guitar") ... 10-15 58

McBRIDE, Lee
Singles: 7-inch
MARLO (1502 "Confusin'") ... 750-1000 '50s

McBURNEY & ORIGINAL FOUR JACKS
Singles: 78 rpm
ALADDIN (3274 "Tired of Your Sexy Ways") ... 50-75 55
HOLLYWOOD (1058 "Let Me Get Next to You") ... 50-100 56
Singles: 7-inch
ALADDIN (3274 "Tired of Your Sexy Ways") ... 200-300 55
HOLLYWOOD (1058 "Let Me Get Next to You") ... 150-250 56
Also see FOUR JACKS

McCAIN, Benny, & Ohio Untouchables
Singles: 7-inch
LU PINE (126 "You Were on My Mind") ... 8-12 64
Also see OHIO UNTOUCHABLES

McCAIN, Jerry
(With His Upstarts; Jerry "Boogie" McCain)
Singles: 78 rpm
EXCELLO ... 50-100 56-57
TRUMPET ... 40-60 54
Singles: 7-inch
CONTINENTAL (777 "Love Me Right") ... 5-10 65
EXCELLO (2068 "Courtin' in a Cadillac") ... 100-150 56
EXCELLO (2079 "You Don't Love Me No More") ... 100-150 57
EXCELLO (2081 "Run, Uncle John, Run") ... 100-150 57
EXCELLO (2103 "Trying to Please") ... 100-150 58
EXCELLO (2111 "Bad Credit") ... 100-150 58
EXCELLO (2127 "Groom Without a Bride") ... 75-125 59
JEWEL (753 "728 Texas") ... 5-10 65
JEWEL (761 "Sugar Baby") ... 5-10 66

JEWEL (773 "Love Ain't Nothin' to Play With") … 5-10 66
JEWEL (790 "Juicy Lucy") … 5-10 67
JEWEL (828 "Soul Spasm") … 5-10 72
OKEH (7150 "Twist '62") … 10-15 62
OKEH (7157 "Run Back Home") … 10-15 62
OKEH (7158 "Popcorn") … 10-15 62
REX (1014 "She's Tough") … 15-25 60
RIC (153 "Here's Where You Get It") … 5-10 65
TRUMPET (217 "Wine-O-Wine") … 100-200 54
TRUMPET (231 "Stay Out of Automobiles") … 100-200 54

LPs: 10/12-inch

ICHIBAN … 5-10
Also see DIDDLEY, Bo

McCAIN, Ronnie

Singles: 7-inch

TRIODEX (116 "Too Much of a Good Thing") … 5-10 62

McCALL, C.W. — C&W/P&R '74

Singles: 7-inch

AFR (18391 "Pine Tar Wars") … 5-10
AMERICAN GRAMOPHONE (351 "Old Home Fill-Er Up an' Keep on Truckin' Café") … 10-15 74
MGM … 4-6 74-75
POLYDOR … 4-6 76-79

LPs: 10/12-inch

MGM … 5-10 75
POLYDOR … 5-8 76-79
Session: Fort Calhoun Nuclear Power Plant Band, later known as Mannheim Steamroller.

McCALL, Cash — R&B '66

Singles: 7-inch

CHECKER (1184 "I'm in Danger") … 5-10 67
COLUMBIA … 4-6 76-77
EXECUTIVE … 5-10 '60s
PAULA (404 "I Need Your Love") … 4-6 74
RONN (76 "Stoop Down") … 4-6 75
THOMAS … 5-10 66
TOPIC … 5-10 65-66

McCALL, Little Johnny

Singles: 7-inch

DONNA (1334 "My Love I Can't Hide") … 40-50 60
WOW (1060 "My Love I Can't Hide") … 150-250 60
(First issue.)

McCALL, Toussaint — P&R/R&B '67

Singles: 7-inch

COLLECTABLES … 3-5 '80s
RONN (3 "Nothing Takes the Place of You") … 8-12 67
RONN (9 "I'll Do It for You") … 8-12 67
RONN (13 "Step By Step") … 8-12 67
RONN (20 "Never Like Before") … 8-12 68
RONN (23 "King for a Day") … 8-12 68
RONN (26 "My Love Is a Guarantee") … 8-12 68
RONN (31 "Baby You Got It") … 8-12 69

LPs: 10/12-inch

RONN (7527 "Nothing Takes the Place of You") … 10-12 67

McCALLISTER, Lon

Singles: 7-inch

APT (25061 "Empty Heart") … 20-30 62

McCANN, Les — LP '69

Singles: 7-inch

ATLANTIC … 4-6 69-75
LIMELIGHT … 4-6 65-67
PACIFIC JAZZ … 5-10 60-65
WORLD PACIFIC … 4-8 '60s

LPs: 10/12-inch

ATLANTIC … 5-10 69-75
LIMELIGHT … 15-25 65
PACIFIC JAZZ (2 thru 91) … 15-30 60-65
PACIFIC JAZZ (893 "Les McCann") … 5-10 78
Also see HOLMES, Richard "Groove," & Les McCann
Also see JAZZ CRUSADERS
Also see RAWLS, Lou, & Les McCann Ltd.

McCANN, Les, & Eddie Harris — LP '69

Singles: 7-inch

ATLANTIC … 4-6 69-70

LPs: 10/12-inch

ATLANTIC … 5-10 69-71
Also see HARRIS, Eddie
Also see McCANN, Les

McCANNON, George

(George McCannon III)

Singles: 7-inch

AMOS (135 "I Fall to Pieces") … 4-8 70
AMOS (151 "No Love at All") … 4-8 70
BELL (702 "I Miss Her") … 5-8 68
DYNO VOICE (228 "I'll Love Love My Friend") … 5-10 66
FUN 45 (008 "Seven Million People") … 5-10 65
MERCURY (72021 "Shy Boy") … 5-10 62
MERCURY (72072 "Candle in the Wind") … 5-10 63
PARKWAY (883 "Lana") … 15-20 63
PHI-DAN (5007 "Seven Million People") … 15-20 65
TOWER (198 "Look for the Rainbow") … 5-10 66

McCARTER, Al

Singles: 7-inch

TWO GUITARS (900 "His True Love for You") … 200-300

McCARTNEY, Paul — LP '70

(Wings; with Wings; with Linda McCartney)

Singles: 12-inch

CAPITOL (15212 "Spies Like Us") … 10-20 85
(With custom cover.)
CAPITOL (15235 "Press") … 10-15 86
(With custom cover.)
CAPITOL (15499 "Ou Est Le Soleil") … 10-15 89
COLUMBIA (03019 "Take It Away") … 8-12 82
(With custom cover.)
COLUMBIA (05077 "No More Lonely Nights") … 8-12 84
("Playout version." With custom cover.)
COLUMBIA (05077 "No More Lonely Nights") … 20-30 84
("Special Dance Mix." With custom cover.)
COLUMBIA (10940 "Goodnight Tonight") … 70-90 79
(Plain white cover with large title sticker.)
COLUMBIA (10940 "Goodnight Tonight") … 8-10 79
(Plain white cover without title sticker.)
COLUMBIA (10940 "Goodnight Tonight") … 15-20 79
(With custom picture cover.)
COLUMBIA (39927 "No More Lonely Nights") … 15-20 84
(Picture disc.)

Promotional 12-inch Singles

CAPITOL (8574 "Maybe I'm Amazed") … 60-80 77
(With custom cover.)
CAPITOL (9556 "Spies Like Us") … 20-30 85
CAPITOL (9763 "Press") … 15-20 86
CAPITOL (9797 "Angry") … 20-25 86
CAPITOL (9861 "Stranglehold") … 20-25 86
CAPITOL (9928 "Pretty Little Head") … 40-50 86
COLUMBIA (775 "Coming Up") … 50-60 80
(Red label.)
COLUMBIA (775 "Coming Up") … 40-50 80
(White label.)
COLUMBIA (1940 "No More Lonely Nights") … 15-20 84
COLUMBIA (10940 "Goodnight Tonight") … 15-25 79

Singles: 7-inch

APPLE (1829 "Another Day") … 8-12 71
APPLE (1837 "Uncle Albert Admiral Halsey") … 10-20 71
(With sliced apple on flip side.)
APPLE (1837 "Uncle Albert Admiral Halsey") … 40-50 71
(With unsliced apple on flip side.)
APPLE (1847 "Give Ireland Back to the Irish") … 10-20 72
APPLE (1851 "Mary Had a Little Lamb") … 8-10 72
APPLE (1857 "Hi Hi Hi") … 8-10 73
APPLE (1861 "My Love") … 5-8 73
APPLE (1863 "Live and Let Die") … 5-8 73
APPLE (1869 "Helen Wheels") … 5-8 73
APPLE (1871 "Jet"/"Mamunia") … 100-125 74
(Label has "2:49" on A-side.)
APPLE (1871 "Jet"/"Mamunia") … 8-10 74
(Label has "4:08" on A-side.)
APPLE (1871 "Jet"/"Let Me Roll It") … 5-8 74
APPLE (1873 "Band on the Run") … 5-8 74
APPLE (1875 "Junior's Farm") … 5-8 74
CAPITOL (1829 "Another Day") … 10-15 76
CAPITOL (1837 "Uncle Albert Admiral Halsey") … 10-15 76
CAPITOL (1847 "Give Ireland Back to the Irish") … 15-20 76
CAPITOL (1851 "Mary Had a Little Lamb") … 10-15 76
CAPITOL (1857 "Hi Hi Hi") … 10-15 76
CAPITOL (1861 "My Love") … 15-20 76
CAPITOL (1863 "Live and Let Die") … 10-15 76
CAPITOL (1869 "Helen Wheels") … 10-15 76
CAPITOL (1871 "Jet") … 10-15 76
CAPITOL (1873 "Band on the Run") … 10-15 76
CAPITOL (1875 "Junior's Farm") … 10-15 76
CAPITOL (4091 "Listen to What the Man Said") … 4-6 75
CAPITOL (4145 "Letting Go") … 4-6 75
CAPITOL (4175 "Venus & Mars Rock Show") … 4-6 75
CAPITOL (4256 "Silly Love Songs") … 4-6 76
(Capitol custom label.)
CAPITOL (4256 "Silly Love Songs") … 5-8 76
(Black label.)
CAPITOL (4293 "Let 'Em In") … 4-6 76
(Capitol custom label.)
CAPITOL (4293 "Let 'Em In") … 5-8 76
(Black label.)
CAPITOL (4385 "Maybe I'm Amazed") … 4-6 77
(Capitol custom label.)
CAPITOL (4385 "Maybe I'm Amazed") … 15-20 77
(Black label.)
CAPITOL (4504 "Mull of Kintyre") … 100-125 77
(Purple label.)
CAPITOL (4504 "Mull of Kintyre") … 4-6 77
(Black label.)
CAPITOL (4559 "With a Little Luck") … 4-6 78
CAPITOL (4594 "I've Had Enough") … 4-6 78
CAPITOL (4625 "London Town") … 4-6 78
CAPITOL (5537 "Spies Like Us") … 5-8 85
CAPITOL (5597 "Press") … 4-6 86
CAPITOL (5636 "Stranglehold") … 4-6 86
CAPITOL (5672 "Only Love Remains") … 4-6 87
CAPITOL (17318 "Off the Ground") … 4-6 94
CAPITOL (17318 "Off the Ground") … 4-6 93
(Black vinyl or colored vinyl.)
CAPITOL (17319 "Biker Like an Icon") … 4-6 93
(Black vinyl.)
CAPITOL (17319 "Biker Like an Icon") … 4-6 93
(Colored vinyl.)
CAPITOL (17489 "C'mon People") … 4-6 94
(Colored vinyl.)
CAPITOL (17643 "Wonderful Christmastime") … 4-6 94
(Colored vinyl.)
CAPITOL (44367 "My Brave Face") … 5-10 89
CAPITOL (56785 "Biker Like an Icon") … 4-6 93
CAPITOL (58823 "Try Not to Cry") … 6-8 99
COLUMBIA (02171 "Silly Love Songs") … 15-25 81
COLUMBIA (03018 "Take It Away") … 4-6 82
COLUMBIA (03235 "Tug of War") … 8-10 82
COLUMBIA (04127 "Wonderful Christmastime") … 20-30 83
COLUMBIA (04296 "So Bad") … 4-6 83
COLUMBIA (04581 "No More Lonely Nights") … 4-6 84
COLUMBIA (10939 "Goodnight Tonight") … 4-6 79
COLUMBIA (11020 "Getting Closer") … 4-6 79
COLUMBIA (11070 "Arrow Through Me") … 4-6 79
COLUMBIA (11162 "Wonderful Christmastime") … 5-10 79
COLUMBIA (11263 "Coming Up") … 4-6 80
(Listed with the singles even though there are two tracks on the B-side.)
COLUMBIA (11335 "Waterfalls") … 4-6 80
COLUMBIA HALL OF FAME (33409 "Band on the Run") … 10-15 80
(Red label.)
COLUMBIA HALL OF FAME (33409 "Band on the Run") … 25-35 85
(Gray label.)

Picture Sleeves

APPLE (1847 "Give Ireland Back to the Irish") … 20-30 72
APPLE (1851 "Mary Had a Little Lamb") … 25-35 72
(Has "Little Woman Love" printed under photo, on reverse side of sleeve.)
APPLE (1851 "Mary Had a Little Lamb") … 15-25 72
("Little Woman Love" is not printed under photo, on reverse side of sleeve.)
CAPITOL (4091 "Listen to What the Man Said") … 8-12 75
CAPITOL (4504 "Mull of Kintyre") … 8-12 77
CAPITOL (5537 "Spies Like Us") … 4-6 85
CAPITOL (5597 "Press") … 4-6 86
CAPITOL (5636 "Stranglehold") … 4-6 86
CAPITOL (5672 "Only Love Remains") … 4-6 87
CAPITOL (44637 "My Brave Face") … 4-6 89
COLUMBIA (03018 "Take It Away") … 5-8 82
(Reads "Not for Sale" on back side. Promotional issue only.)
COLUMBIA (03018 "Take It Away") … 4-6 82
COLUMBIA (04296 "So Bad") … 4-6 83
COLUMBIA (04296 "So Bad") … 5-10 83
(Reads "Not for Sale" on back side. Promotional issue only.)
COLUMBIA (04581 "No More Lonely Nights") … 4-6 84
(Title has white print.)
COLUMBIA (04581 "No More Lonely Nights") … 20-30 84
(Title has gray print.)
COLUMBIA (11020 "Getting Closer") … 20-30 79
COLUMBIA (11162 "Wonderful Christmastime") … 10-15 79
COLUMBIA (11263 "Coming Up") … 4-6 80
COLUMBIA (11335 "Waterfalls") … 15-20 80

Promotional Singles

APPLE (1829 "Another Day") … 60-75 71
APPLE (1837 "Uncle Albert Admiral Halsey") … 60-75 71
APPLE (1851 "Mary Had a Little Lamb") … 300-350 72
APPLE (1861 "My Love") … 150-200 73
APPLE (1871 "Jet") … 40-50 74
APPLE (1873 "Band on the Run") … 30-35 74
(Long [5:09] and short [3:50] versions.)
APPLE (1873 "Band on the Run") … 100-150 74
(Both sides have short [3:50] version.)
APPLE (1875 "Junior's Farm") … 40-50 74
APPLE (1875 "Sally G") … 60-80 74
APPLE (6786 "Helen Wheels") … 40-50 73
APPLE (6787 "Country Dreamer") … 300-350 73
CAPITOL (4145 "Letting Go") … 25-30 75
CAPITOL (4175 "Venus & Mars Rock Show") … 25-30 75
CAPITOL (4256 "Silly Love Songs.") … 20-25 76
CAPITOL (4293 "Let 'Em In") … 20-25 76
CAPITOL (4594 "I've Had Enough") … 40-50 78
(With special promotional flyer.)
CAPITOL (4594 "I've Had Enough") … 20-25 78
(Without special promotional flyer.)
CAPITOL (4625 "London Town") … 20-30 78
CAPITOL (5597 "Press") … 10-15 86
CAPITOL (5636 "Stranglehold") … 10-15 86
CAPITOL (5672 "Only Love Remains") … 10-15 87
CAPITOL (8138 "Listen to What the Man Said") … 20-30 75
CAPITOL (8570/1 "Maybe I'm Amazed") … 20-30 77
CAPITOL (8746/7 "Mull of Kintyre") … 20-30 77
CAPITOL (8812 "With a Little Luck") … 20-25 78
CAPITOL (9765 "Press") … 200-250 86
CAPITOL (9952 "Spies Like Us") … 15-20 85
CAPITOL (44367 "My Brave Face") … 10-15 89
CAPITOL (79700 "This One") … 300-350 89
COLUMBIA (1204 "Coming Up") … 5-8 80
(Single-sided.)
COLUMBIA (03018 "Take It Away") … 8-10 82
COLUMBIA (03235 "Tug of War") … 15-20 82
COLUMBIA (04296 "So Bad") … 10-15 83
COLUMBIA (04581 "No More Lonely Nights") … 8-10 84
COLUMBIA (10939 "Goodnight Tonight") … 10-15 79
COLUMBIA (11020 "Getting Closer") … 10-15 79
COLUMBIA (11070 "Arrow Through Me") … 10-15 79
COLUMBIA (11162 "Wonderful Christmastime") … 10-15 79
COLUMBIA (11263 "Coming Up") … 10-15 80
COLUMBIA (11335 "Waterfalls") … 10-15 80
MIRAMAX (4202 "Rock Show") … 500-600 75
(Contains three radio spots. Issued to radio stations only.)

LPs: 10/12-inch

APPLE (3363 "McCartney") … 25-35 70
(Label shows Paul's full name beneath LP title. No Capitol logo.)
APPLE (3363 "McCartney") … 75-85 70
(Label with Capitol logo shows Paul's full name beneath LP title.)
APPLE (3363 "McCartney") … 20-25 70
(Label doesn't show Paul's name beneath LP title.)
APPLE (3375 "Ram") … 20-30 71
(No Capitol logo. No "All Rights Reserved, etc." perimeter print.)

APPLE (3375 "Ram")................................ 40-50 71
(With Capitol logo.)
APPLE (3375 "Ram")............................ 75-100 75
(With "All Rights Reserved, etc." perimeter print.)
APPLE (3386 "Wild Life") 15-20 71
APPLE (3409 "Red Rose Speedway")..... 15-20 73
APPLE (3415 "Band on the Run")........... 15-25 73
(Price includes bonus poster.)
CAPITOL (3363 "McCartney")................. 15-25 '70s
CAPITOL (3375 "Ram")........................... 20-30 '70s
CAPITOL (3386 "Wildlife")....................... 20-30 '70s
CAPITOL (3409 "Red Rose Speedway"). 20-30 '70s
CAPITOL (3415 "Band on the Run")........ 30-50 76
(Price includes bonus poster.)
CAPITOL (11419 "Venus & Mars") 15-20 75
(Gatefold. Includes bonus posters and stickers.)
CAPITOL (11525 "Wings at the Speed of Sound") 8-10 76
CAPITOL (11593 "Wings Over America").. 30-35 76
(Three discs. Gatefold. Has two bonus posters.)
CAPITOL (11777 "London Town")........... 10-20 78
(Includes bonus poster.)
CAPITOL (11901 "Band on the Run")...... 25-35 78
(Picture disc.)
CAPITOL (11905 "Wings Greatest")........ 10-20 78
(Price includes bonus poster.)
CAPITOL (12475 "Press to Play")..............8-12 87
CAPITOL (48287 "All the Best!")............. 20-30 87
(Two discs.)
CAPITOL (91653 "Flowers in the Dirt")..... 15-25 89
CAPITOL (94778 "Tripping the Live Fantastic").. 50-60 90
(Three discs. Includes booklet. 3000 made.)
CAPITOL (595379 "Tripping the Live Fantastic: Highlights").. 15-20 90
(Single disc. Capitol Record Club issue.)
COLUMBIA (36057 "Back to the Egg").......8-12 79
(Photo label.)
COLUMBIA (36057 "Back to the Egg").... 50-75 84
(Red label.)
COLUMBIA (36478 "McCartney")........... 15-20 80
COLUMBIA (36479 "Ram")...................... 15-20 80
COLUMBIA (36480 "Wild Life")............... 15-20 80
COLUMBIA (36481 "Red Rose Speedway")... 15-20 80
COLUMBIA (JC-36482 "Band on the Run").. 10-15 80
(Photo label.)
COLUMBIA (36482 "Band on the Run") .. 50-75 80
(Red label. With "JC" or "PC" prefix.)
COLUMBIA (HC-36482 "Band on the Run").. 60-75 80
(Red label. Half-speed mastered.)
COLUMBIA (FC-36511 "McCartney II")... 10-15 80
(Issued with bonus single [1204] *Coming Up*, which represents $5 to $8 of the price range. Photo label. Gatefold.)
COLUMBIA (FC-36511 "McCartney II")... 15-25 80
(Red label.)
COLUMBIA (PC-36511 "McCartney II")................................... 100-125 80
(Red label.)
COLUMBIA (36801 "Venus & Mars")....... 15-20 80
(Includes bonus posters.)
COLUMBIA (36987 "The McCartney Interview")..8-12 80
COLUMBIA (37409 "Wings at the Speed of Sound")15-20 81
COLUMBIA (TC-37462 "Tug of War") 8-10 82
(Custom label. Has "TC" prefix on both label and cover.)
COLUMBIA (PC-37462 "Tug of War") 30-40 84
(Custom label. Has "TC" prefix on label and "PC" prefix on cover.)
COLUMBIA (PC-37462 "Tug of War") . 100-150 85
(Red label. Has "PC" prefix on both label and cover.)
COLUMBIA (37990 "Wings Over America").. 40-50 82
COLUMBIA (39149 "Pipes of Peace")........8-12 83
COLUMBIA (39613 "Give My Regards to Broad Street") 10-15 84
COLUMBIA (46482 "Band on the Run") .. 10-15 80
(Half-speed mastered.)
LIBERTY (50100 "Live and Let Die")...........5-8 84
(With McCartney on title track only.)
LONDON (76007 "Family Way")............ 80-90 67
(Soundtrack. Monaural.)
LONDON (82007 "Family Way")........... 90-120 67
(Soundtrack. Stereo.)

U.A. (100 "Live and Let Die") 15-20 73
(Copies with cut corners are valued at about one-half of the above price range. McCartney is heard on title track only.)

Promotional LPs

APPLE (3375 "Ram")...................... 3000-3500 71
(Monaural.)
APPLE (6210 "Brung to Ewe By")........400-500 71
CAPITOL (2955 "Band on the Run Radio Interview").. 1000-1500 73
CAPITOL (11525 "Wings at the Speed of Sound")..200-250 76
(White label.)
COLUMBIA (821 "The McCartney Interview")..30-40 80
(Two discs. White label.)
COLUMBIA (36057 "Back to the Egg").....25-35 79
COLUMBIA (36511 "McCartney II")..........20-30 80
(White label.)
W.B. ("The Family Way").....................350-450 67
(10-inch LP. Ad spots for radio stations.)
Also see BAND AID
Also see BEATLES
Also see COUNTRY HAMS
Also see HARPER, Roy
Also see LOMAX, Jackie
Also see COSTELLO, Elvis
Also see NEWMAN, Thunderclap
Also see PERKINS, Carl
Also see SUN FERRY AID
Also see SUZY & RED STRIPES
Also see THORNTON, FRADKIN & UNGER
Also see TUDOR MINSTRELS

McCARTNEY, Paul, & Michael Jackson

P&R/R&B '82

Singles: 12-inch

COLUMBIA (1758 "Say Say Say")...........10-15 83
(With plain, black unprinted cover. Has designate promo stamping.)
COLUMBIA (04169 "Say Say Say").........10-15 83
(With custom picture cover.)

Promotional 12-inch Singles

COLUMBIA (04169 "Say Say Say").........15-20 83
(With custom picture cover.)
COLUMBIA (04169 "Say Say Say")............8-10 83
(With plain, unprinted cover.)

Singles: 7-inch

COLUMBIA (04168 "Say Say Say")............4-6 83
EPIC (03288 "The Girl Is Mine") 4-6 82
EPIC (03372 "The Girl Is Mine") 8-12 82
(Single-sided, with small, LP size, hole.)

Picture Sleeves

COLUMBIA (04168 "Say Say Say")............4-6 83

Promotional Picture Sleeves

COLUMBIA (04168 "Say Say Say")...........5-10 83
EPIC (03288 "The Girl Is Mine") 5-10 82

Promotional Singles

COLUMBIA (04168 "Say Say Say")...........8-12 83
EPIC (03288 "The Girl Is Mine") 8-12 82
(Identification number shown as 169138.)
EPIC (03288 "The Girl Is Mine") 20-30 82
(Identification number shown as 169202. Reads "New Edited Version.")
Also see JACKSON, Michael

McCARTNEY, Paul / Rochestra / Who / Rockpile

Singles: 12-inch

ATLANTIC (388 "Every Night") 150-250 81
(Promotional issue only.)
Also see WHO

McCARTNEY, Paul, & Stevie Wonder

P&R/R&B '82

Singles: 12-inch

COLUMBIA (02878 "Ebony & Ivory").........8-12 82

Promotional 12-inch Singles

COLUMBIA (1444 "Ebony & Ivory").........20-30 82

Singles: 7-inch

COLUMBIA (02860 "Ebony & Ivory")........20-30 82
COLUMBIA (02860 "Ebony and Ivory") 4-6 82
(Ampersand [&] in title is replaced by "and.")

Promotional Singles

COLUMBIA (02860 "Ebony & Ivory")........25-30 82
COLUMBIA (02860 "Ebony and Ivory")....10-15 82
(Ampersand [&] in title is replaced by "and.")

Picture Sleeves

COLUMBIA (02860 "Ebony and Ivory")......8-10 82
(Lists both A-side and B-side titles.)

COLUMBIA (02860 "Ebony and Ivory")....12-15 82
(Lists only "Ebony and Ivory." Promotional issue only.)
Also see McCARTNEY, Paul
Also see WONDER, Stevie

McCAULEY, Chi Chi

Singles: 7-inch

RED BIRD (004 "I Know He Loves Me") .. 15-25 64

McCLAM, Pro, & Orchestra

Singles: 78 rpm

VEE-JAY 10-20 53-54

Singles: 7-inch

VEE-JAY (102 "Boot-Um").......................20-30 53
(Black vinyl.)
VEE-JAY (102 "Boot-Um").......................40-60 53
(Colored vinyl.)
VEE-JAY (112 "Cinemascope Baby") 20-30 54
(Black vinyl.)
VEE-JAY (112 "Cinemascope Baby") 40-60 54
(Colored vinyl.)

McCLANAHAN, Mac

Singles: 7-inch

TIGER (104 "That Nonsense Stuff").......75-100 61

McCLAREN, Ted

Singles: 7-inch

UFO ("Gemini Jump")...........................10-20 64
(Selection number not known.)

McCLARY, Butch

(Don Curtis)

Singles: 7-inch

KLIFF (103 "Rockin' Rockin Hall") 50-100 58
Also see CURTIS, Don

McCLAY, Ernest

(With His Trio)

Singles: 78 rpm

MURRAY (506 "Big Timing Woman").....50-100 48

McCLAY, Yul, & Mondellos

Singles: 7-inch

RHYTHM (105 "Over the Rainbow").....150-250 57
Also see MONDELLOS

McCLEESE, James

Singles: 7-inch

MARCO (106 "A Million Tears")................20-30
Also see SOUL, Jimmy

McCLELLAND, Clark

Singles: 7-inch

VERSATILE (110 "A Little Dog Cried").......5-10 62

McCLENDON, Charlie, & Magnificents

(With the Magnificents)

Singles: 7-inch

COLOSSUS (101 "We're Gonna Hate Ourselves" 10-15 69
L-REV (62068 "Need Love") ....20-30 '60s

McCLENDON, Clark

Singles: 7-inch

AUDICON (114 "Eileen")............................5-10 61

McCLENNEY, Lloyd

Singles: 7-inch

SEVILLE (127 "Cruel World").....................5-10 63

McCLINE, Charles

Singles: 7-inch

LARRY-O (103 "You Conquored [sic] Me")..15-25 64
(First issued as by Willie Logan & the Plaids.)
Also see LOGAN, Willie, & Plaids

McCLINTON, Delbert

LP '79

(With the Ron-Dels; Del McClinton)

Singles: 7-inch

ABC 4-6 75-77
BOBILL (101 "I Know She Knows")...........8-10 67
BROWNFIELD 8-12 65
CAPITOL..3-5 80-81
CAPRICORN (0302 "Take It Easy") 4-6 78
JUBILEE (9012 "I Know She Knows")........8-12 65
LE CAM (717 "Hey Baby") 4-6 79
LE CAM (1220 "Mr. Pitiful") 4-6 79
LONDON (9544 "Angel Eyes") 15-25 62
PARAMOUNT (0016 "Fannie Mae")...........5-10 70
SOFT (1041 "100 Pounds of Honey") 4-6 70

LPs: 10/12-inch

ABC 10-20 75-77
ACCORD...8-12 81
CAPITOL..8-12 80-81

CAPRICORN 10-15 78-79
INTERMEDIA...5-10 84
MCA..5-10 81
POLYDOR 10-20 79
Also see CHANNEL, Bruce
Also see CLINTON, Mac, & Straitjackets
Also see RONDELLS

McCLURE, Bobby

P&R/R&B '66

Singles: 7-inch

CHECKER (1130 "I'll Be True to You") 8-12 65
CHECKER (1152 "Peak of Love")..............8-12 66
CHECKER (1169 "Don't Get Your Signals Crossed")..8-12 67
EDGE (005 "You Never Miss Your Water")...5-10
FEBRUARY 11 (280 "Sitting in the Park")...10-15
HI...4-6 76-78
Also see BASS, Fontella, & Bobby McClure

McCOLLOUGH, Charles

(With the Silks; Charles McCullough)

Singles: 7-inch

DOOTO (462 "My Girl")............................15-20 61
DOOTO (465 "You're Not Too Young")....15-20 61
DOOTO (467 "I Cried All Night")..............10-15 62

McCOLLOUGH, Lloyd

Singles: 78 rpm

EKKO 8-12 56
REPUBLIC (7129 "Gonna Love My Baby")..100-200 56

Singles: 7-inch

EKKO (1023 "What Goes On in Your Heart") 15-25 56
REPUBLIC (7129 "Gonna Love My Baby")..600-800 56
STARDAY (686 "Half My Fault")..........200-300
VANITY ("Half My Fault") 300-400
(First issue. Selection number not known.)
VON (1002 "Oh Darling") 100-200

McCOLLOUGH, Rod

Singles: 7-inch

DOMINO (902 "My Lonely Night") 5-10 60

McCOLLUM, Tyrone, & Inclines

Singles: 7-inch

ATCO (6674 "Pressure Cooker")...............5-10 69
ATCO (6699 "Who's Lovin' You")..............5-10 69

McCONNVILLE, Jimmy, & Shamrocks

Singles: 7-inch

FARRALL (691 "Scorpion").......................10-20 60

McCOOK, Johnny

Singles: 7-inch

GONE (5143 "By and By") 5-10 63

McCOOK, Tommy, & Super-Sonics

Singles: 7-inch

YEW (1005 "Liquidator") 8-12 70

McCORMACK, Franklyn

LPs: 10/12-inch

LIBERTY (3086 "The Torch Is Burning")..20-40 57

McCORMICK, Gayle

P&R/LP '71

Singles: 7-inch

DECCA..4-6 72
DUNHILL...4-8 71-72
MCA..4-6 73

LPs: 10/12-inch

DECCA..10-12 72
DUNHILL..10-12 71
FANTASY...8-10 74
Also see SMITH

McCORMICK, George / Rusty Adams

LPs: 10/12-inch

SOMERSET..5-10 '60s
Also see ADAMS, Rusty
Also see McCORMICK, George

McCORMICK, Johnnie

Singles: 7-inch

TIARA (6125 "Pink Lady")..........................8-12 59

McCORMICK, Patty

Singles: 7-inch

RIC (152 "Take All the Kisses") 5-10 65

McCORMICK BROTHERS

Singles: 78 rpm

HICKORY..5-10 54-57

Singles: 7-inch
HICKORY (1000 series)..........10-20 54-58
HICKORY (1103 thru 1203)..........8-12 59-63
HICKORY (1245 "Are You Feeling Blue")..5-10 64

McCOY, Carl
(Carl McVoy)
Singles: 7-inch
HI (2054 "It's a Crime")..........8-12 62
Also see McVOY, Carl

McCOY, Charlie *P&R '61/C&W '72*
Singles: 7-inch
CADENCE..........5-10 60-62
MONUMENT..........3-8 68-83
EPs: 7-inch
MONUMENT (0001 "Charlie McCoy")..........5-10 72
(Promotional issue only.)
LPs: 10/12-inch
EPIC..........5-8 82
MONUMENT..........5-15 69-78
Session: Barefoot Jerry.
Also see DYLAN, Bob
Also see FOWLER, Wally
Also see GAS LANTERN
Also see JOHNSTON, Colonel Jubilation B., & His Mystic Knights Band & Street Singers
Also see LEE, Bobby
Also see MANDRELL, Barbara
Also see McDOWELL, Ronnie
Also see TUBB, Ernest

McCOY, Joe
Singles: 7-inch
TIARA (6115 "Hey Hey Loretta")..........75-100 58

McCOY, Johnny
Singles: 7-inch
FELSTED (8540 "Give Me a Chance")..........10-15 58

McCOY, Patty, & Renegades
Singles: 7-inch
COUNSEL (116 "Goodbye")..........20-30 62
COUNSEL (119 "I Love Him So")..........10-20 62

McCOY, Ray
Singles: 7-inch
FABLE (615 "Rockin' Baby")..........75-100 58

McCOY, Robert
(With His Five Sins)
Singles: 7-inch
SOUL-O (112 "Bye Bye Baby")..........5-10 64
SOUL-O (114 "Goodbye")..........5-10 64
VULKAN..........5-10 58-63

McCOY, Rose Marie
Singles: 78 rpm
CAT..........10-20 55
Singles: 7-inch
BRUNSWICK (55541 "I Do the Best I Can with What I Got")..........4-6 78
CAT (111 "Dippin in My Business")..........20-30 55

McCOY, Rube
Singles: 7-inch
TESTAMENT..........5-10 65
Also see WILLIAMS, Joe Big

McCOY, Van *R&B '74*
(With the Soul City Symphony; Van McCoy Strings)
Singles: 12-inch
H&L..........4-8 76
MCA..........4-8 79
Singles: 7-inch
AMHERST..........4-6 '70s
AVCO..........4-6 74-75
CGC..........4-6 70
COLUMBIA..........5-8 65-66
EPIC..........4-6 69
H&L..........4-6 76
LIBERTY (55457 "Follow Your Heart")..........5-10 62
MCA..........4-6 78-79
ROCK'N (100 "That's How Much You Mean to Me")..........75-100 61
ROCK'N (101 "Mr. D.J.")..........10-20 61
ROCK'N (1012 "Girls Are Sentimental")..10-15 61
SHARE..........4-8 69
SILVER BLUE..........4-6 73
LPs: 10/12-inch
AVCO..........8-10 74-75
BUDDAH..........8-10 72-75
COLUMBIA..........12-18 66
H&L..........8-10 76
MCA..........8-10 77-79
Also see SHELDON, Sandi
Also see TWYLIGHTS

McCOY BOYS
Singles: 7-inch
VERVE (10208 "Our Man in Havana")..........10-15 60
Members: Gil Garfield; Perry Botkin Jr; Ray Campi.
Also see CAMPI, Ray
Also see GOOD GUYS
Also see WOODS, Billy

McCOYS
Singles: 7-inch
RCA (7354 "Throwing Kisses")..........10-15 58

McCOYS *P&R/LP '65*
Singles: 7-inch
BANG (Except 543)..........5-10 65-67
BANG (543 "Beat the Clock")..........25-35 67
COLLECTABLES..........3-5 '80s
MERCURY (72843 "Jesse Brady")..........8-15 68
PHILCO (6 "Fever"/"Hang on Sloopy")..........10-20 67
("Hip Pocket" flexi-disc.)
SOLID GOLD..........4-6 73
LPs: 10/12-inch
BANG (212 "Hang on Sloopy")..........25-35 65
(Monaural.)
BANG (S-212 "Hang on Sloopy")..........35-45 65
(Stereo.)
BANG (213 "You Make Me Feel So Good")..........25-35 66
(Monaural.)
BANG (S-213 "You Make Me Feel So Good")..........35-45 66
(Stereo.)
MERCURY (61163 "Infinite McCoys")..........20-25 68
MERCURY (61207 "Human Ball")..........20-25 69
Members: Rick Derringer; Randy Zehringer; Randy Hobbs; Ron Brandon.
Also see STRANGELOVES

McCRACKEN, Hugh
(With the Funatics)
Singles: 7-inch
CONGRESS (257 "Buzz in My Head")..........10-20 65
CONGRESS (261 "What I Gotta Do to Satisfy You")..........10-20 66
Also see POWERS OF BLUE

McCRACKLIN, Jimmy *P&R/R&B '58*
(With His Blues Blasters; Jimmie McCracklin)
Singles: 78 rpm
ALADDIN..........20-30 51
CAVATONE..........25-50 47
COURTNEY..........25-50 45
DOWN TOWN..........20-30 48
EXCELSIOR..........25-50 45
GLOBE..........25-50 45
HOLLYWOOD..........15-25 54-55
IRMA..........15-30 56-57
MODERN..........20-30 49
PEACOCK..........15-25 52-54
RPM..........20-30 51
SWING TIME..........15-25 51-52
TRILON..........25-50 49
Singles: 7-inch
ART-TONE (825 "Just Got to Know")..........10-20 61
ART-TONE (826 "Christmas Time")..........10-20 61
ART-TONE (827 "I'm the One")..........10-20 62
ART-TONE (831 "Susie & Pat")..........10-20 62
CHECKER (885 "The Walk")..........15-25 58
CHECKER (893 "Everybody Rock")..........15-25 58
CHESS (1809 "I Know")..........10-15 61
CHESS (1826 "One Track Love")..........10-15 62
GEDINSON'S (6121 "Club Savoy")..........10-15 61
HI (2023 "Things I Meant to Say")..........10-20 60
HOLLYWOOD (1025 "I Found That Woman")..........25-35 54
HOLLYWOOD (1054 "It's All Right")..........25-35 56
IMPERIAL..........8-12 62-67
IRMA (102 "You're the One")..........20-40 56
IRMA (103 "Take a Chance")..........20-40 56
IRMA (107 "I'm the One")..........20-40 57
IRMA (109 "Love for You")..........20-40 57
KENT (369 "I Got Eyes for You")..........8-12 62
LIBERTY (56198 "Believe Me")..........4-6 70
MERCURY (71412 "The Wobble")..........10-15 59
MERCURY (71516 "Let's Do It")..........10-15 59
MERCURY (71613 "By Myself")..........10-15 60
MERCURY (71666 "No One to Love Me")..........10-15 60
MERCURY (71747 "The Bridge")..........10-15 61
MERCURY (71766 "No One to Love Me")..........10-15 61
MINIT..........5-10 67-70
MODERN (926 "Blues Blasters Boogie")..20-40 54
MODERN (934 "Darlin' Share Your Love")..........20-40 54
MODERN (951 "Forgive Me Baby")..........20-40 54
MODERN (967 "Gonna Tell Your Mother")..........20-40 55
OAK CITY..........4-6
PEACOCK (1605 "She's Gone")..........30-40 52
PEACOCK (1615 "Share and Share Alike")..........30-50 53
PEACOCK (1634 "The End")..........30-50 53
PEACOCK (1639 "The Cheater")..........30-50 53
PEACOCK (1683 "The Swinging Thing")..15-25 58
PREMIUM (101 "You're the One")..........15-25
PREMIUM (102 "I Don't Care")..........15-25
SWING TIME (291 "House Rockin' Blues")..........30-50 51
LPs: 10/12-inch
CHESS (1464 "Jimmy McCracklin Sings")..........40-60 62
CROWN..........15-20 61
IMPERIAL..........20-35 63-66
MINIT..........12-18 67-69
STAX..........8-12 72-81
Also see BROWN, Charles, & Jimmy McCracklin

McCRACKLIN, Jimmy / T-Bone Walker / Charles Brown
LPs: 10/12-inch
IMPERIAL (9257 "Best of the Blues, Vol. 1")..........15-25 64
Also see BROWN, Charles
Also see WALKER, T-Bone

McCRAY, Mack
Singles: 7-inch
FORD (1074 "Shorts Crazy")..........50-75

McCREA, Darlene
Singles: 7-inch
JUBILEE (5524 "Soulful Feeling")..........5-10 66
ROULETTE (4173 "You")..........8-12 59
TOWER (104 "Don't Worry Baby")..........5-10 64

McCREA, Jody
Singles: 7-inch
CANJO (106 "Chicken Surfer")..........10-15 64

McCRILL, Chandos
Singles: 7-inch
STARDUST (655 "Money Lovin' Woman")..........75-125

McCRORY, Jim
Singles: 7-inch
KEY (5803 "Parking Lot")..........100-125 58
KEY (5805 "Rock Ya Baby")..........125-150 58

McCUE, Sam
Singles: 7-inch
FLIGHT (616 "Valley of Tears")..........5-10 64
Also see LEGENDS

McCULLERS, Mickey
(With the Miracles)
Singles: 7-inch
TAMLA (54064 "Same Old Story")..........25-35 62
V.I.P. (25009 "Same Old Story")..........25-35 64
Also see MIRACLES

McCULLOUGH, Cecil
Singles: 7-inch
MANCO (1011 "Pick 'Em Up and Shake 'Em Up")..........50-100 61

McCULLOUGH, Jonnie
Singles: 7-inch
LOG CABIN (2971 "Who Shot Sam")..........30-40

McCURDY, Ed
LPs: 10/12-inch
DAWN (1127 "Folk Singer")..........20-30 58
ELEKTRA (108 "Blood, Booze 'N' Bones")..........25-35 56
ELEKTRA (110 "When Dalliance Was in Flower, Vol. 1")..........20-30 56
ELEKTRA (112 "Songs of the Old West")..........15-25 56
ELEKTRA (124 "Sin Songs, Pro and Con")..........15-25 57
ELEKTRA (140 "When Dalliance Was in Flower, Vol. 2")..........15-25 58
ELEKTRA (989 "When Dalliance Was in Flower, Vol. 3")..........15-25 '60s
RIVERSIDE (601 "Ballad Record")..........20-30 56
RIVERSIDE (807 "Bar Room Songs")..........20-30 56
RIVERSIDE (810 "Legend of Robin Hood")..........15-25 57
TRADITION (1003 "Ballad Singer's Choice")..........20-30 56
TRADITION (1027 "Children's Songs")..........15-25 58

McCURN, George *P&R '63*
Singles: 7-inch
A&M..........5-10 63-64
LIBERTY (55418 "Your Daughter's Hand")..........5-10 62
REPRISE (479 "Too Many Tears")..........5-8 66
REPRISE (533 "America")..........5-8 66
LPs: 10/12-inch
A&M (102 "Country Boy Goes to Town")..15-25 63

McDANIEL, Floyd
Singles: 7-inch
DIXIE (2159 "I Like to Go")..........400-500
Also see MACK, Floyd

McDANIEL, Willard
Singles: 78 rpm
CROWN (107 "My Sin")..........10-20 54
SPECIALTY..........10-20 51
Singles: 7-inch
CROWN (107 "My Sin")..........20-30 54
SPECIALTY (415 "Blues On the Delta")..40-50 51
SPECIALTY (424 "Ciri-Biri-Bin Boogie")..40-50 51
LPs: 10/12-inch
CROWN (5024 "88 A La Carte")..........75-125 58

McDANIELS, Gene *P&R/R&B '61*
(Eugene McDaniels)
Singles: 7-inch
COLUMBIA..........5-8 66-67
LIBERTY..........8-15 59-65
MGM..........4-6 73
ODE (66107 "Lady Fair")..........4-6 75
EPs: 7-inch
LIBERTY..........10-20 '60s
LPs: 10/12-inch
ATLANTIC (8259 "Outlaw")..........20-30 70
ATLANTIC (8281 "Headless Heroes of the Apolcalypse")..........100-150 71
LIBERTY..........15-25 60-67
ODE..........8-12 75
SUNSET..........10-15 66
U.A...........8-12 75
Also see MANN, Johnny, Singers
Also see SULTANS
Also see UNIVERSAL JONES

McDANIELS, Jimmie
Singles: 7-inch
DOT (16248 "Cat Walk")..........5-10 61

McDANIELS, Lenny, & Last Nikle
(Lenny McDaniel)
Singles: 7-inch
MAINSTREAM..........5-10 69
SEVEN B..........10-15
Also see LAST NIKLE

McDANIELS, Luke
(Jeff Daniels)
Singles: 78 rpm
KING..........10-20 53-55
TRUMPET..........15-25 52
Singles: 7-inch
KING..........15-25 53-55
TRUMPET (184 "Tribute to Hank Williams")..........25-50 52
TRUMPET (185 "Whoa, Boy")..........25-50 52
Also see DANIELS, Jeff

McDEVITT, Charles, Skiffle Group *P&R '57*
(With Nancy Wiskey; with Shirley Douglas)
Singles: 7-inch
BELL (644 "Don't Blame Me")..........5-10 66
CHIC (1008 "Freight Train")..........10-20 57
KAPP (238 "Stack-O-Lee")..........8-12 58
ORIOLE..........8-12 57

McDONALD, Cleve
Singles: 7-inch
JULENE (403 "Tell Me That You Love Me")..........200-300

McDONALD, Country Joe *P&R '75*
Singles: 7-inch
FANTASY ... 4-6 75-79
VANGUARD ... 4-6 71-74
LPs: 10/12-inch
FANTASY ... 5-10 75-79
MFSL ... 30-50 81
PICCADILLY ... 10-15 78
VANGUARD ... 8-12 69-76
Also see COUNTRY JOE & FISH

McDONALD, Jerry
Singles: 7-inch
FERNWOOD (123 "Am I a Fool") ... 5-10 60

McDONALD, Jim
Singles: 7-inch
KCM (3700 "Let's Have a Ball") ... 50-100
Also see TENNESSEE JIM

McDONALD, Ken
Singles: 78 rpm
DELUXE ... 8-12 57
Singles: 7-inch
ABC-PAR (10049 "Teenage Years") ... 10-15 59
DELUXE (6109 "Only Me") ... 15-20 57
DELUXE (6121 "Candy from a Baby") ... 10-15 57
PREP (128 "One Love Alone") ... 10-15 58

McDONALD, Marie
Singles: 7-inch
RCA (7068 "He Took Me by Storm") ... 8-12 57
LPs: 10/12-inch
RCA (1585 "The Body Sings") ... 50-75 57

McDONALD, Michael *P&R/R&B/LP '82*
Singles: 7-inch
MCA ... 3-5 86
W.B. ... 3-5 82-85
Picture Sleeves
MCA ... 3-5 86
W.B. ... 3-5 82-85
LPs: 10/12-inch
MCA ... 5-8 86
MFSL (149 "If That's What It Takes") ... 25-35 85
REPRISE ... 5-8 90
W.B. ... 5-8 82-85
Also see DOOBIE BROTHERS
Also see LABELLE, Patti, & Michael McDonald
Also see STEELY DAN

McDONALD, Michael, & James Ingram *P&R/R&B '83*
Singles: 7-inch
QWEST ... 3-5 83
Also see McDONALD, Michael

McDONALD, Rusty
Singles: 78 rpm
INTRO (6035 "Baby Sittin' Boogie") ... 25-50 52
Singles: 7-inch
INTRO (6035 "Baby Sittin' Boogie") ... 50-75 52

McDONALD, Scott
Singles: 7-inch
TREND (30007 "Don't Make It Hurt") ... 10-20 58

McDONALD, Skeets *C&W '52*
Singles: 78 rpm
CAPITOL (Except 3461) ... 10-20 51-57
CAPITOL (3461 "You Oughta See Grandma Rock") ... 20-40 56
FORTUNE ... 10-20 50
Singles: 7-inch
CAPITOL (Except 3461) ... 10-20 51-59
CAPITOL (3461 "You Oughta See Grandma Rock") ... 60-80 56
COLUMBIA ... 5-10 60-67
EPs: 7-inch
CAPITOL ... 15-25 54-58
LPs: 10/12-inch
CAPITOL (1040 "Goin' Steady with the Blues") ... 50-100 58
COLUMBIA ... 15-25 64
FORTUNE (3001 "Tattooed Lady Plus Other Songs") ... 30-50 69
HILLYBILLY HEAVEN ... 5-10
SEARS (116 "Skeets") ... 15-20 '60s
Also see STEWART, Wynn

McDONALD & GILES
LPs: 10/12-inch
COTILLION ... 10-15 71
Members: Ian McDonald; Peter Giles; Mike Giles; Steve Winwood.
Also see GILES, GILES & FRIPP
Also see WINWOOD, Steve

McDONALD SISTERS
Singles: 78 rpm
MODERN (5000 "If It's Love") ... 8-10 54
Singles: 7-inch
MODERN (5000 "If It's Love") ... 15-20 54

McDOWELL, Bobby
Singles: 7-inch
ABC-PAR (10447 "Running Away") ... 10-15 63
AMY (964 "Cry Softly Little One") ... 5-10 66
AMY (979 "You Bet Your Life") ... 5-10 67
AMY (995 "I'm Coming Home") ... 5-10 67
GOLD WAX (103 "Our Last Quarrel") ... 8-12 64
SUPREME (101 "Lonely") ... 50-75

McDOWELL, Chester
(Chet McDowell)
Singles: 7-inch
DART (150 "You're Gone for Good") ... 10-15 61
DUKE (302 "I Wonder Why") ... 10-20 59
DUKE (316 "Tell Me Now") ... 8-12 60

McDOWELL, Paul
Singles: 7-inch
LIFETIME (1028 "Standing Room Only") ... 50-75

McDOWELL, Ronnie *P&R/C&W '77*
Singles: 7-inch
EPIC ... 3-6 79-85
GRT ... 4-6 77
MCA/CURB ... 3-5 86
SCORPION (Except 0533) ... 4-6 77-79
SCORPION (0533 "Only the Lonely") ... 4-8 77
LPs: 10/12-inch
DICK CLARK (79 "Elvis") ... 8-12 79
(TV soundtrack.)
EPIC ... 5-10 79-85
MCA/CURB ... 5-8 86
SCORPION (0010 "Live at the Fox") ... 10-15 78
SCORPION (8021 "The King Is Gone") ... 10-20 77
(Includes copy of front page of newspaper with news that 'The King' is gone.)
SCORPION (8028 "I Love You, I Love You, I Love You") ... 10-15 78
STRAWBERRY ... 8-10 '70s
Session: Jordanaires; Conway Twitty; Kathy Westmoreland; Charlie McCoy; David Briggs; Chip Young; Dale Sellers; Bobby Ogden; Mike Leech.
Also see JORDANAIRES
Also see TWITTY, Conway

McDOWELL, Ronnie, & Jerry Lee Lewis *C&W '89*
Singles: 7-inch
CURB (10521 "Never Too Old to Rock 'N' Roll") ... 3-5 88
Also see LEWIS, Jerry Lee
Also see McDOWELL, Ronnie

McDUFF, Brother Jack *LP '63*
(With George Benson)
Singles: 7-inch
ATLANTIC ... 4-8 66-67
CADET (5614 "Let My People Go") ... 4-6 68
CADET (5632 "Black Is?") ... 4-6 69
CADET (5693 "Ain't No Sunshine") ... 4-6 72
BLUE NOTE (1953 "Down Home Style") ... 4-6 69
PRESTIGE ... 5-10 62-65
LPs: 10/12-inch
ATLANTIC (1472 "Tobacco Road") ... 10-20 67
BLUE NOTE (84322 "Down Home Style") ... 8-12 69
PRESTIGE (7000 series) ... 25-50 60-64
(Yellow label.)
PRESTIGE (7000 series) ... 15-25 64-68
(Blue label.)
Also see BENSON, George
Also see BURRELL, Kenny, & Brother Jack McDuff

McDUFF, Brother Jack, & Gene Ammons
LPs: 10/12-inch
PRESTIGE (7228 "Brother Jack McDuff Meets the Boss") ... 50-75 61
(Yellow label.)
Also see AMMONS, Gene

McDUFF, Brother Jack, & Willis Jackson *LP '66*
LPs: 10/12-inch
PRESTIGE (7364 "Together Again") ... 15-25 66
Also see JACKSON, Willis

McDUFF, Brother Jack, Quintet, & David Newman
Singles: 7-inch
ATLANTIC (2488 "But It's Alright") ... 4-8 68
LPs: 10/12-inch
ATLANTIC (1498 "Double Barrelled Soul") ... 10-12 68
Also see McDUFF, Brother Jack
Also see NEWMAN, David "Fathead"

McDUFF, Eddie
Singles: 7-inch
ARGO (5335 "Car Trouble") ... 5-10 59
ARLISS (1002 "Goodbye Betty Lou") ... 5-10 61
GIANT (1101 "Whup It On Out") ... 8-12 57
GIANT (1102 "Colored Glass") ... 8-12 57
GIANT (1105 "Merry Christmas Mr. Heartache") ... 8-12 57
TOLLIE (9031 "Hello Lonesome") ... 5-10 64

McDUFF, Freddy
Singles: 7-inch
SHORE BIRD (7002 "Jack Daddy") ... 40-60

McEACHERN, Murray
Singles: 7-inch
SIGNATURE (12036 "Have You Met Miss Jones") ... 5-10 60

McELROY, Sollie
Singles: 7-inch
JA-WES (101 "Angel Girl") ... 25-50 '60s
Also see CHANTEURS
Also see FLAMINGOS
Also see MOROCCOS
Also see NOBLES

McENTIRE, Reba *C&W '76*
Singles: 7-inch
MCA ... 3-5 84-92
MERCURY (55036 thru 57062) ... 5-10 76-81
MERCURY (73788 "I Don't Want to Be a One Night Stand") ... 10-15 76
MERCURY (73879 "Between a Woman and a Man") ... 10-15 77
Picture Sleeves
MCA (52349 "Just a Little Love") ... 3-6 84
MCA (52527 "Somebody Should Leave") ... 3-6 85
MCA (52604 "Have I Got a Deal for You") ... 3-6 85
MERCURY (57062 "Only You") ... 5-10 81
LPs: 10/12-inch
MCA ... 5-10 84-90
MERCURY (1177 "Reba McEntire") ... 50-100 77
MERCURY (4047 "Unlimited") ... 15-25 82
MERCURY (5002 "Reba McEntire") ... 25-50 77
MERCURY (5017 "Out of a Dream") ... 25-50 79
MERCURY (5029 "Feel the Fire") ... 20-30 80
MERCURY (6003 "Heart to Heart") ... 20-30 81
MERCURY (57062 thru 76157) ... 10-15 81-82
MERCURY (812781 "Behind the Scene") ... 10-15 83
Session: Chris Austin; Pake McEntire.
Also see AUSTIN, Chris

McFADDEN, Bob *P&R '59*
("Bob McFadden & Dor"; with Jack Hansen & Transylvanians)
Singles: 7-inch
BRUNSWICK (55140 "The Mummy") ... 15-20 59
BRUNSWICK (55156 "Shake, Rattle and Roll") ... 15-20 59
CORAL (62209 "Dracula Cha-Cha") ... 10-15 60
U.S. RUBBER CO. ("Noah's Ark and What's a Nauga?") ... 5-10
(Promotional only issue. Square cardboard picture disc. Made for U.S. Naugahyde & Naugaweave Co.)
Picture Sleeves
BRUNSWICK (55140 "The Mummy") ... 30-40 59
CORAL (62209 "Dracula Cha-Cha") ... 25-35 60
LPs: 10/12-inch
BRUNSWICK (54056 "Songs Our Mummy Taught Us") ... 75-125 59
(Monaural.)
BRUNSWICK (7-54056 "Songs Our Mummy Taught Us") ... 100-150 59
(Stereo.)
Members: Bob McFadden; Rod McKuen.
Also see DOR & CONFEDERATES
Also see JACOBI, Lou
Also see McKUEN, Rod

McFADDEN, Ruth
(With the Supremes; with Royaltones)
Singles: 78 rpm
OLD TOWN ... 20-40 56
Singles: 7-inch
APT (25057 "Lovin' Time") ... 20-30 61
CAPITOL (4802 "Pencil & Paper") ... 5-10 62
GAMBLE (2503 "Ghetto Woman") ... 4-6 71
OLD TOWN (1017 "Darling, Listen to the Words of This Song") ... 50-100 56
(The "Supremes" credited here are reportedly the Solitaires. Old Town also had another Supremes group on their label in 1956.)
OLD TOWN (1020 "Two in Love") ... 50-75 56
OLD TOWN (1030 "School Boy") ... 150-250 56
RECONA (3502 "He Hurt Me Again") ... 5-10 64
SURE SHOT (5011 "I'll Cry") ... 5-10 65
TIARA ... 10-20 58
Also see ROYALTONES
Also see SOLITAIRES

McFARLAND, Gary *LP '69*
(With Bill Evans; Gary McFarland Sextet)
Singles: 7-inch
IMPULSE (250 "Winter Samba") ... 5-10 66
PRESTIGE (331 "Dreamer") ... 5-10 64
SKYE (453 "Flea Market") ... 4-8 68
SKYE (4516 "Slaves") ... 4-8 69
VERVE ... 5-10 62-66
LPs: 10/12-inch
IMPULSE (46 "Point of Departure") ... 10-15 64
IMPULSE (9112 "Profiles") ... 10-15 66
SKYE (2 "Does the Sun Really Shine on the Moon") ... 10-15 68
SKYE (8 "America the Beautiful") ... 10-15 69
VERVE ... 10-20 61-69

McFARLAND, Gary, & Gabor Szabo
LPs: 10/12-inch
IMPULSE (9122 "Simpatico") ... 10-15 66
Also see SZABO, Gabor

McFARLAND, Gary, & Clark Terry
LPs: 10/12-inch
IMPULSE (9104 "Tijuana Jazz") ... 10-15 66
Also see McFARLAND, Gary
Also see TERRY, Clark

McFARLIN, Ronnie
(Ron McFarlin)
Singles: 7-inch
CORBY (227 "Forty Days") ... 8-12 68
SLIM-SLO-SLIDER (1 "Mr. Toad's Ride") ... 10-15
SLIM-SLO-SLIDER (230 "Let It Rock") ... 75-125
LPs: 10/12-inch
SLIM-SLO-SLIDER ("Spirit of '76") ... 20-30
(Selection number not known. Date used in title may or may not indicate time of release. We do not yet know.)

McFERRON, Robert
Singles: 7-inch
SUNBEAM (101 "Water Boy") ... 10-15 58

McGEE, Al
Singles: 7-inch
DONNA (1348 "Tender Beloved") ... 10-20 61

McGEE, Butch
Singles: 7-inch
REV (3519 "Stacked") ... 10-15 58

McGEE, Jerry
(Gerry Mc Gee)
Singles: 7-inch
A&M (771 "Moonlight Surfin' ") ... 8-12 65
PACEMAKER (236 "Twilight Zone") ... 5-10 65
REPRISE ... 5-10 62-63
Also see VENTURES

McGEE, Sam
LPs: 10/12-inch
ARHOOLIE (5012 "Grand Dad of the Country Guitar Pickers") ... 8-12

McGHEE, Brownie *R&B '48*
(With His Jook Block Busters; with His Sugar Men)
Singles: 78 rpm
ALERT ... 10-20 46-47
DERBY ... 10-20 52
DISC ... 10-20 47
DOT ... 50-75 53
ENCORE ... 10-20 53
HARLEM ... 20-30 54
LONDON ... 10-20 51

PAR ... 10-20 52
RED ROBIN ... 50-75 52-53
SAVOY ... 20-40 44-57
SITTIN' IN WITH ... 15-25 48

Singles: 7-inch

DOT (1184 "Cheatin' & Lying") ... 150-200 53
HARLEM (2323 "Christina") ... 30-50 54
HARLEM (2329 "Bluebird") ... 30-50 54
JACKSON (2304 "Mean Old Frisco") ... 100-150 52
(Red vinyl.)
JAX (304 "I Feel So Good") ... 75-100 52
(Red vinyl.)
JAX (307 "Meet You in the Morning") ... 75-100 52
(Red vinyl.)
JAX (310 "Stranger's Blues") ... 75-100 52
(Red vinyl.)
JAX (312 "I'm 10,000 Years Old") ... 75-100 52
(Red vinyl.)
JAX (322 "New Bad Blood") ... 75-100 52
(Red vinyl.)
RED ROBIN (111 "Don't Dog Your Woman") ... 100-200 52
SAVOY (778 "True Blues") ... 35-55 51
SAVOY (835 "Diamond Ring") ... 20-40 52
SAVOY (844 "Bottom Blues") ... 20-40 52
SAVOY (872 "Bad Nerves") ... 20-40 52
SAVOY (899 "Sweet Baby Blues") ... 20-40 53
SAVOY (1177 "I'd Love to Love You") ... 15-25 55
SAVOY (1185 "Love's a Disease") ... 15-25 56
SAVOY (1564 "Living with the Blues") ... 15-25 59

LPs: 10/12-inch

BLUESVILLE (1042 "Brownie's Blues") ... 30-50 '60s
FOLKWAYS (Except 20, 30 & 2000 series) ... 8-10
FOLKWAYS (20, 30 & 2000 series) ... 20-40 54-55
STORYVILLE ... 5-8
VANGUARD ... 8-12 '60s

Session: Sonny Terry; Mickey Baker.
Also see BAKER, Mickey
Also see COLLINS, Big Tom
Also see DUPREE, Champion Jack
Also see SPIDER SAM
Also see WILLIAMS, Blind Boy

McGHEE, Brownie, & Sonny Terry LP '73
(Sonny Terry & Brownie McGhee)

Singles: 78 rpm

SAVOY ... 10-20 44-48

Singles: 7-inch

BRUT (804 "Blueboy's Holler") ... 4-6 73
FANTASY (546 "Just a Closer Walk with Thee") ... 5-10 60
OLD TOWN (1075 "She Loves So Easy") ... 15-25 60
PRESTIGE BLUESVILLE ... 5-10 60-62

LPs: 10/12-inch

A&M ... 8-10 73
BLUESWAY (6028 "A Long Way from Home") ... 10-12 69
ELEKTRA (14 "Folk Blues") ... 50-100 53
ELEKTRA (15 "City Blues") ... 50-100 53
EVEREST ... 10-12 69
FANTASY (3000 series) ... 15-25 61-62
(Black vinyl.)
FANTASY (3000 series) ... 25-50 61-62
(Red vinyl.)
FANTASY (8000 series) ... 15-20 62
(Black vinyl.)
FANTASY (8000 series) ... 25-40 62
(Red vinyl.)
FANTASY (24000 series) ... 8-10 72-81
FOLKWAYS (2000 & 3000 series) ... 15-30 55-61
FOLKWAYS (31000 series) ... 8-10
FONTANA (67599 "Where the Blues Begin") ... 10-15 69
MFSL (233 "Sonny & Browny") ... 25-35 94
MAINSTREAM (6049 "Hometown Blues") ... 15-20 65
MAINSTREAM (308 "Hometown Blues") ... 8-10 71
MUSE (5177 "Hootin' ") ... 5-8 81
OLYMPIC (7108 "Hootin' and Hollerin' ") ... 8-10 73
PRESTIGE (1000 series) ... 25-30 60
PRESTIGE (7000 series) ... 8-10 69-70
PRESTIGE BLUESVILLE ... 20-40 60-62
PRESTIGE FOLKLORE ... 12-15
ROULETTE (25074 "Folk Songs") ... 25-35 59
SAVOY (1100 series) ... 5-8 84
SAVOY (12000 series) ... 8-10 73
SAVOY (14000 series) ... 25-30 58
SHARP (2003 "Down Home Blues") ... 25-50 59
SMASH (67067 "At the Bunkhouse") ... 15-20 65
VERVE (3008 "Blues Is My Companion") ... 20-25 61
VERVE FOLKWAYS (9019 "Guitar Highway") ... 15-20 65
WORLD PACIFIC (1294 "Blues Is a Story") ... 25-30 60

Also see BROONZY, Big Bill
Also see GADDY, Bob
Also see HOPKINS, Lightnin' / Brownie McGhee & Sonny Terry
Also see McGHEE, Brownie
Also see TERRY, Sonny
Also see WILLIS, Ralph

McGHEE, Brownie, Sonny Terry & Earl Hooker

LPs: 10/12-inch

BLUESWAY (6059 "I Couldn't Believe My Eyes") ... 10-15 73

McGHEE, Howard
(With the Blazers; Howard McGhee Quintet)

Singles: 7-inch

ARGO (5422 "House Warmin' ") ... 8-12 62
BETHLEHEM (11034 "Lover Man") ... 5-10 59
BETHLEHEM (11035 "Don't Blame Me") ... 5-10 59
BETHLEHEM (11061 "You're Teasing Me") ... 5-10 60
(With Philly Joe Jones.)
BETHLEHEM (11095 "With Malice Towards None") ... 5-10 61
WINLEY (245 "Into Somethin' ") ... 10-20 60
WINLEY (264 "House Warmin' ") ... 10-20 62
(First issue.)

LPs: 10/12-inch

ARGO (4020 "House Warmin' ") ... 10-15 63
BETHLEHEM (6055 "Dusty Blue") ... 10-15 61
FELSTED (7512 "Music from *The Connection*") ... 10-15 60
(Monaural.)
FELSTED (17512 "Music from *The Connection*") ... 15-20 60
(Stereo.)

McGHEE, Paul, & Rock-E-Teers

Singles: 7-inch

FLAME (305 "You Are My Sunshine") ... 100-125 59

McGHEE, Stick P&R/R&B '49
(With His Buddies; with Ramblers; Sticks McGhee)

Singles: 78 rpm

ATLANTIC ... 25-75 49-52
DECCA (48104 "Drinkin' Wine Spo-Dee-O-Dee") ... 15-25 47
ESSEX ... 10-15 52
HARLEM (1018 "Blues Mixture") ... 15-25 47
KING ... 20-30 53-55
LONDON ... 25-75 51
SAVOY ... 10-15 55

Singles: 7-inch

ATLANTIC (955 "Wee Wee Hours") ... 50-75 52
ATLANTIC (991 "New Found Love") ... 40-60 52
ATLANTIC CLASSICS (873 "Drinkin' Wine Spo-Dee-O-Dee") ... 10-20 71
("Classics Revisited" reissue series. Original Atlantic 45s of this number—from 1949—do not exist.)
GUSTO ... 3-5
HERALD (553 "Money Fever") ... 5-10 60
KING (4610 "Little Things We Used to Do") ... 50-75 53
KING (4628 "Blues in My Heart") ... 50-75 53
KING (4672 "Dealin' from the Bottom") ... 50-75 53
KING (4700 "I'm Doin' All the Time") ... 50-75 53
KING (4783 "Double Crossin' Liquor") ... 50-100 55
KING (4800 "Get Your Mind Out of the Gutter") ... 50-75 55
LONDON (978 "You Gotta Have Something on the Ball") ... 100-200 51
SAVOY ... 15-25 55

McGHEE, Sticks / John Lee Hooker

LPs: 10/12-inch

AUDIO LAB (1520 "Highway of Blues") ... 100-125 59

Also see DUPREE, Champion Jack
Also see HOOKER, John Lee
Also see McGHEE, Stick

McGHEE, Tommy

Singles: 78 rpm

EXCELLO (2027 "Late Every Evening") ... 15-25 54

Singles: 7-inch

EXCELLO (2027 "Late Every Evening") ... 30-40 54

Also see KING, Kid

McGILL, Connie, & Visions
(With Roland Parker & Strollers)

Singles: 7-inch

EDGE (502 "My Love Will Never Change") ... 15-25 64
SUGAR (502 "A Million Years") ... 20-30 62
TOY (107 "A Million Years") ... 10-20 63
UNITED INT'L (1009 "No I Won't Believe It") ... 15-25 64
WATCH (1786 "No I Won't Believe It") ... 10-15 65

McGILL, Clarence, & Blue Devils

Singles: 7-inch

TENER (1027 "Pauline") ... 8-12 '60s

McGILL, Jerry, & Top Coats

Singles: 7-inch

SUN (326 "Lovestruck") ... 15-25 59

McGILL, Rollee R&B '55
(With the Rhythm Rockers; with Whippoorwills; Rollie McGill)

Singles: 78 rpm

CAMEO (119 "People Are Talking") ... 10-20 57
MERCURY ... 10-15 55-56
PINEY ... 15-25 55

Singles: 7-inch

CAMEO (119 "People Are Talking") ... 10-20 57
CHELSEA (531 "That's My Girl") ... 50-75 59
JUNIOR (396 "Go On Little Girl") ... 40-60 58
(Same number used on a Silhouettes release.)
KAISER (1039 "People Are Talking") ... 4-8 77
LANDA (702 "Come Home") ... 8-10 64
MERCURY (70582 "There Goes That Train") ... 20-30 55
MERCURY (70652 "Rhythm Rockin' Blues") ... 20-30 55
MERCURY (70725 "There's Madness in My Heart") ... 20-30 55
MERCURY (70807 "Oncoming Train") ... 20-30 56
MERCURY (70914 "Come On In") ... 20-30 56
PINEY (104 "There Goes That Train") ... 50-100 55
(First issue.)

McGINNIS, Wayne, & Swing Teens

Singles: 78 rpm

METEOR ... 50-75 56

Singles: 7-inch

METEOR (5035 "Rock, Roll and Rhythm") ... 150-200 56

McGONNIGLE, Mel

Singles: 7-inch

ROCKET (101 "Rattle Shakin' Mama") ... 550-650 58

McGREGOR, Billy

Singles: 7-inch

MELLOTONE (1000 "It's My Turn Now") . 10-20

McGRIFF, Edna
(With Buddy Lucas & His Band of Tomorrow; with Four Spooners)

Singles: 78 rpm

BELL (4 "Born to Be with You") ... 10-20 57
(7-inch 78 rpm.)
JOSIE (764 "Ooh Little Daddy") ... 10-20 54
JUBILEE ... 10-15 51-53

Singles: 7-inch

BELL (4 "Born to Be with You") ... 10-20 57
BELL (7 "Just Walking in the Rain") ... 20-30 57
CAPITOL ... 4-8 64-65
FELSTED (8519 "Oh Joe") ... 5-10 58
JOSIE (764 "Ooh Little Daddy") ... 20-30 54
JUBILEE (5062 "Note Droppin' Papa") ... 20-30 51
JUBILEE (5073 "Heavenly Father") ... 20-30 52
JUBILEE (5087 "It's Raining") ... 20-30 52
JUBILEE (5089 "In a Chapel by the Side of the Road") ... 20-30 52
JUBILEE (5099 "Good") ... 20-30 52
JUBILEE (5109 "Edna's Blues") ... 20-30 53
(Black vinyl.)
JUBILEE (5109 "Edna's Blues") ... 50-75 53
(Red vinyl.)
WILLOW (23001 "Heavenly Father") ... 5-10 61

Picture Sleeves

BELL (4 "Born to Be with You") ... 25-35 57
(Sleeve for either 45 or 78 rpm.)

Also see BUDDY & EDNA
Also see LUCAS, Buddy

McGRIFF, Edna, & Sonny Til

Singles: 78 rpm

JUBILEE ... 10-20 52

Singles: 7-inch

JUBILEE (5090 "Once in a While") ... 20-30 52
JUBILEE (5099 "Good") ... 20-30 52

Also see McGRIFF, Edna
Also see TIL, Sonny

McGRIFF, Jimmy P&R/R&B/LP '62
(Jimmy McGriff Trio)

Singles: 7-inch

BLUE NOTE ... 4-6 71
CAPITOL ... 4-6 70-71
COLLECTABLES ... 3-5 '80s
GROOVE MERCHANT ... 4-6 75
JELL (190 "I've Got a Woman") ... 8-12 62
JELL (502 "Jungle Cat") ... 5-10 65
LRC ... 4-6 78
MILESTONE ... 3-5 83
SOLID STATE ... 4-6 66-70
SUE ... 5-10 62-65
U.A. ... 4-6 71-78

EPs: 7-inch

SOLID STATE ... 8-12 66

LPs: 10/12-inch

BLUE NOTE ... 8-12 70-71
COLLECTABLES ... 6-8 88
51 WEST ... 5-8 '80s
GROOVE MERCHANT ... 8-12 71-76
LRC ... 8-10 77-78
MILESTONE ... 5-8 81-83
SOLID STATE ... 10-15 66-70
SOUL SUGAR ... 10-12 70
SUE ... 20-30 62-65
U.A. ... 8-12 71
VEEP ... 10-15 68

Also see ADAMS, Faye / Jimmy McGriff
Also see HOLMES, Richard "Groove"
Also see PARKER, Little Junior, & Jimmy McGriff

McGUINN, Roger LP '73

Singles: 7-inch

COLUMBIA ... 4-6 73-77

LPs: 10/12-inch

ARISTA ... 5-10 90
COLUMBIA (Except "Airplay Anthology") ... 8-12 73-77
COLUMBIA ("Airplay Anthology") ... 20-30 77
(Promotional issue only.)

Also see BYRDS
Also see MITCHELL, Chad, Trio

McGUIRE, Barry P&R/LP '65
(With the Horizon Singers)

Singles: 7-inch

ABC ... 4-6 70
DUNHILL ... 4-8 65-66
HORIZON ... 4-8 63
ODE (66010 "Old Farm") ... 4-6 70
MCA ... 4-6
MIRA (205 "Greenback Dollar") ... 4-6 65
MOSAIC ... 4-8 61-62
MYRRH ... 4-6 73
ROULETTE ... 3-5

Picture Sleeves

DUNHILL (4014 "Child of Our Times") ... 5-10 65

EPs: 7-inch

DUNHILL (50005 "This Precious Time") ... 8-12 65
(Juke box issue.)

LPs: 10/12-inch

BIRDWING ... 5-8 80
DUNHILL ... 20-30 65
HORIZON ... 15-25 63
MYRRH ... 5-8 73-75
ODE ... 8-10 70
SPARROW ... 5-8 78
SURREY ... 12-15 65

Also see MAMAS & PAPAS / Barry McGuire
Also see NEW CHRISTY MINSTRELS

McGUIRE, Barry, & Barry Kane

Singles: 7-inch

HORIZON (354 "Another Man") ... 4-8 62

LPs: 10/12-inch

HORIZON (1608 "Here & Now") ... 15-25 62
SURREY (1022 "Star Folk Volume") ... 12-18 66

McGUIRE, Lowell

Singles: 7-inch

NASCO (6007 "Spellbound") ... 10-15 57

McGUIRE, Marian
Singles: 7-inch
DOT (15999 "Hold My Hand")....................5-10 59

McGUIRE, Phyllis P&R '64
Singles: 7-inch
ABC-PAR (10826 "My Happiness")...........5-10 66
REPRISE (310 "That's Life")......................5-10 64
REPRISE (354 "Run to My Arms")..............5-10 65
ORPHEUM (4502 "Just a Little Lovin' ").....5-10 68
LPs: 10/12-inch
ABC-PAR (552 "Phyllis McGuire Sings"). 10-20 66
Also see McGUIRE SISTERS

McGUIRE SISTERS P&R '54
(With Lawrence Welk; with Dick Jacobs Orchestra)
Singles: 78 rpm
CORAL...4-8 54-58
Singles: 7-inch
ABC-PAR...4-6 66
CORAL (Except 61000 & 98000 series).......4-8 58-65
CORAL (61000 series)...........................5-10 54-58
CORAL (98000 series)........................... 10-15 60
(Stereo.)
MCA...4-6 '70s
REPRISE...4-6 63-65
Picture Sleeves
CORAL..5-15 56-61
EPs: 7-inch
CORAL.. 10-15 55-60
LPs: 10/12-inch
ABC-PAR.. 10-20 66
CORAL (6 "Best of the McGuire Sisters")... 15-25 65
CORAL (56123 "By Request")................ 25-50 55
CORAL (57000 series).......................... 15-25 56-65
MCA...5-8 78
VOCALION... 10-20 60-67
Members: Phyllis; Dorothy; Christine.
Also see DESMOND, Johnny, Eileen Barton & McGuire Sisters
Also see JACOBS, Dick, & His Orchestra
Also see McGUIRE, Phyllis
Also see WELK, Lawrence, & His Orchestra

McGUIRE SISTERS / Lancers / Dorothy Collins / Teresa Brewer
EPs: 7-inch
CORAL (98015 "Christmas Alphabet").... 15-25 '50s
(Promotional issue only.)
Also see BREWER, Teresa
Also see COLLINS, Dorothy
Also see LANCERS
Also see McGUIRE SISTERS

McGUIRE SISTERS & DE JOHN SISTERS
LPs: 10/12-inch
CORONET (24 "Starring the McGuire Sisters with the De John Sisters")................................... 15-25 56

McHOUSTON, Big Red
("Vocal by Larry Dale"; Mickey Baker)
Singles: 78 rpm
GROOVE (0020 "I'm Tired").................... 15-25 54
Singles: 7-inch
GROOVE (0020 "I'm Tired").................... 30-40 54
Also see BAKER, Mickey
Also see DALE, Larry

McHUGH, Jimmy
Singles: 7-inch
DEE CAL (501 "Rock-A-Billie")..................5-10 61
HUNCH (346 "I Don't Want Everything")....5-10 65
SUCCESS (106 "I Don't Want Everything").. 10-15 63

McHUGH, Richie
Singles: 7-inch
RAEWOOD (587 "Joann")....................... 15-25 63

McILWAIN, Ed, & Travelers
Singles: 7-inch
ALLISON (922 "We Made a Promise")..75-125 62

McINTYRE, Chester
(Chet McIntyre)
Singles: 7-inch
RENNER (219 "Chet's Twist")................. 10-15 62
SARG (180 "I'm Gonna Rock with My Baby")..75-100 61

McKAY, Rufus
(With the Red Tops)
Singles: 7-inch
ACE (602 "Boll Weevil Junction")..............8-12 60
SKY (703 "Swanee River Rock")..............15-25 60
Also see RED TOPS

McKAY, Scotty
(Scott McKay)
Singles: 7-inch
ACE (603 "Little Liza Jane")....................10-15 60
ACE (608 "Brown-eyed Handsome Man")..10-15 60
ACE (623 "Pull Down the Sky")................10-15 61
ACE (636 "Shattered Dreams")................10-15 61
ACE (652 "Olive Learned to Popeye")......10-15 62
ACE (8003 "Little Miss Blue")..................10-15 62
CAPRI..8-12 63
CHARAY (1004 "High on Life")................10-20 70
CLARIDGE (309 "Batman")......................10-20 66
DESK...8-12 63
EVENT (4295 "Rollin' Dynamite").........100-200 59
FALCON (101 "Train Kept a-Rollin' ").......50-75 68
HBR (495 "I'm Gonna Love Ya")..............10-15 66
LAWN (102 "I've Been Thinkin' ")............10-15 60
MASTERS MAGIC..................................4-8 72
PARKWAY (806 "Rollin' Dynamite")......75-125 59
PHILIPS (40109 "Mess Around")...............8-12 63
POMPEII...10-15 69
STARLING..8-12 63
SWAN (4049 "Little Lump of Sugar")........10-15 60
UNI...5-10 70
LPs: 10/12-inch
ACE (1017 "Tonight in Person")...............40-50 61
MASTERS MAGIC...................................10-20 72
Also see LIPSCOMB, Max K.

McKAY, Tony
Singles: 7-inch
CLARIDGE (307 "Nobody's Perfect").........5-10 66
CLARIDGE (318 "Ten Past Twelve Cinderella Blues")..5-10 66
JOSIE (979 "Ticking of the Clock")............5-10 67

McKEE, Rick
Singles: 7-inch
LE CAM (713 "What Went Wrong").........10-20 61

McKEE, Ron, & Rivieres
Singles: 7-inch
LINCOLN (710 "Summertime Fun")...........8-12 64

McKENNA, Val
Singles: 7-inch
ASCOT (2245 "House for Sale")................5-10 68

McKENNON, Kenny
Singles: 7-inch
FABLE (564 "Call Your Daddy, Baby").100-200 57

McKENZIE, Don
Singles: 7-inch
MIRACLE (10 "Whose Heart").................50-75 61
RIDGE (6602 "Beauty")...........................50-75
Also see SUPREMES

McKENZIE, Lil, & Four Students
Singles: 78 rpm
GROOVE (0113 "Run Along")....................8-12 55
Singles: 7-inch
GROOVE (0113 "Run Along")..................20-30 55
Also see FOUR STUDENTS

McKENZIE, Mike, & Embers
Singles: 7-inch
CRASH (101 "My Summer Star")............15-25

McKENZIE, Scott P&R/LP '67
(McKenzie's Musicians)
Singles: 7-inch
CAPITOL..4-8 65-67
EPIC...4-6 67-72
ODE (103 "San Francisco [Wear Some Flowers in Your Hair]")..8-10 67
ODE (103 "San Francisco [Be Sure to Wear Flowers in Your Hair]")..4-8 67
(Note slight change in title.)
ODE (105 "Like an Old Time Movie")..........4-8 67
ODE (107 "Holy Man")..............................4-8 68
ODE (66012 "Going Home Again")..............4-6 71
LPs: 10/12-inch
ODE (44000 series)................................15-25 67
ODE (34000 series)................................8-10 77
ODE (77000 series)................................10-15 70

Also see JOURNEYMEN

McKEOWN, John
Singles: 7-inch
HI LITE (510 "The Tug Boat Song").........50-75
Also see MAC, Johnny

McKINLEY, David Pete
(Pete McKinley)
Singles: 78 rpm
FIDELITY (3008 "Black Snake Blues").....25-35 52
GOTHAM (505 "Shreveport Blues").........25-35 52

McKINLEY, L.C.
Singles: 78 rpm
STATES (135 "Companion Blues")..........10-20 55
VEE-JAY..10-15 55
Singles: 7-inch
BEA & BABY (102 "Nit Wit")...................40-60 59
STATES (135 "Companion Blues")..........40-60 55
VEE-JAY (133 "Strange Girl")..................30-40 55
VEE-JAY (159 "I'm So Satisfied")............30-40 55

McKINLEY, Wilson
Singles: 7-inch
ELIJAH ("On Stage")............................75-125
(Selection number not known.)
ELIJAH ("Heaven's Gonna Be a Blast").75-125
(Selection number not known.)
ELIJAH ("The Spirit")...........................75-125
(Selection number not known.)

McKINLEYS
Singles: 7-inch
SWAN (4185 "Million Miles Away")............8-12 64
SWAN (4194 "Then I'll Know It's Love").....8-12 64

McKINNEY, John, & Premiers
Singles: 7-inch
MAD (1009 "Angels in the Sky")..........125-150 58

McKINNEY, Johnny
Singles: 7-inch
CLOCK (1043 "If You Leave Me")..............5-10 61

McKINNEY, Mike
Singles: 7-inch
SPOT (102 "Teen Town Hop")..................40-60 59

McKINNEY, Nathan
(With Valleyites)
Singles: 7-inch
DESERT BONE (40 "Very Special Lady")..5-10
RAYCO (526 "Weep No More")...............10-15 64
RAYCO (532 "I'm Gonna Cry")................10-15 65

McKINNON, Don
Singles: 7-inch
ANTENNA (6442 "Fat Fat Fat")..............50-100 59
BELTONE (1013 "Should I Kiss You").....10-15 61
SOUND STAGE 7 (2529 "Sing Me a Sad Song Willie")..5-10 64

McKINNON, Harold, & Rimm Shots
Singles: 7-inch
CARTER (4215 "Little Jump Joint")....800-1200

McKINNON, Preston
Singles: 7-inch
SHARP (104 "Till I Met You Sweet")........15-25 60

McKINZIE, Larry
Singles: 7-inch
VIM (1091 "Chubie Dubie")....................50-100

McKNIGHT
Singles: 7-inch
CUSTOM (127 "You're Doin' Me Wrong")..25-35

McKNIGHT, Billy Wade
Singles: 7-inch
CONGRESS (6020 "Stacey").....................4-8 70
INT'L ARTISTS (116 "I Need Your Lovin' ")..5-10 67

McKNIGHT, June
Singles: 7-inch
JEANNIE (1225 "Twist Me Henry")...........10-15 62

McKNIGHT, Tammy
Singles: 7-inch
TUNE-KEL (603 "Don't Rub It In")..............5-10 67

McKOWN, Gene
Singles: 7-inch
AGGIE (1001 "Rockabilly Rhythm")......100-200 58
AGGIE (1003 "Little Mary")..................100-200 58

BRASS (238 "Ghost Memories")...........75-125 60
RICH (106 "I'm Out on the Town")...........10-15 '60s
SIMS (228 "Keeper of Heartaches")..........5-10 65

McKUEN, Rod P&R '62
(With the Keytones; with Horizon Singers)
Singles: 7-inch
A&M..5-10 63
BUDDAH...4-6 73-74
BUENA VISTA.......................................4-8 71
DECCA..10-15 59
HORIZON..5-10 63
JUBILEE..5-10 62
KAPP..5-10 61
LIBERTY...10-20 56
RCA..4-8 66-67
SPIRAL...5-10 61-62
STANYAN...4-6 74
W.B..4-8 68-72
Picture Sleeves
BUENA VISTA (482 "Scandalous John")..... 4-8 71
W.B..4-8 71
LPs: 10/12-inch
BUENA VISTA.......................................20-30 71
DECCA (4900 series).............................10-15 68
DECCA (8800 series).............................20-30 59
DECCA (75000 series)...........................10-12 69
CAPITOL...15-20 64
HARMONY..8-10 71
HI FI...20-30 58-59
EPIC (600 & 3800 series)......................15-20 62
EPIC (26000 series)..............................10-12 68
EVEREST..10-12 68
HORIZON..15-25 63
IN...15-20 64
JUBILEE..20-25 62
KAPP (1200 & 3200 series)....................15-25 61
KAPP (1500 & 3500 series)....................10-20 67
LIBERTY (Except 3011)..........................10-15 67
LIBERTY (3011 "Songs for a Lazy Afternoon")...25-40 56
PICKWICK..5-10 '70s
RCA...10-20 65-69
STANYAN..10-15 66-72
SUNSET...8-10 70
TRADITION..10-12 68
W.B...8-15 67-76
Also see DALEY, Jimmy, & Ding-A-Lings
Also see DOR & CONFEDERATES
Also see McFADDEN, Bob

McKUSICK, Hal, Quartet
Singles: 7-inch
GLORY (292 "Just Keep Walking, Ambrose")..5-10 59

McLAIN, Tommy P&R '66
Singles: 7-inch
COLLECTABLES.....................................3-5 '80s
JIN (Except 197).....................................5-8 66-69
JIN (197 "Sweet Dreams")......................10-20 66
MSL (197 "Sweet Dreams").....................5-10 66
STARFLITE..4-6 79
LPs: 10/12-inch
STARFLITE..10-15 79
Also see FENDER, Freddy, & Tommy McLain

McLANE, Jimmy
Singles: 7-inch
SWAY (900 "Born to Be with You")...........5-10 61

McLAURIN, Bette P&R '52
(With the Four Fellows; with Striders; Betty McLaurin)
Singles: 78 rpm
CENTRAL...10-15 54
CORAL..10-15 53
DERBY (700 series)................................10-15 50-52
DERBY (804 "My Heart Belongs to Only You")..20-40 52
GLORY...10-15 55
JUBILEE..10-15 55
Singles: 7-inch
ALMONT (309 "You're the Greatest")....50-100 58
ATCO (6099 "What a Night for Love")......40-50 57
CAPITOL (4320 "Remember")..................15-25 59
CENTRAL (1004 "It's Easy to Remember")..20-30 54
CORAL (60906 "My Dreams of You").......15-25 53
CORAL (61129 "If You Believed in Me")..15-25 53
DERBY (790 "I May Hate Myself in the Morning")..15-25 52

DERBY (804 "My Heart Belongs to Only You") 75-100 52
GLORY (233 "Grow Old Along with Me") 20-30 55
GLORY (237 "Just Come a Little Bit Closer") 30-40 55
GLORY (241 "I'm Past Sixteen") 30-40 55
JUBILEE (5139 "Please Don't Leave Me") 15-25 55
JUBILEE (5155 "Ever So Lonely") 15-25 55
JUBILEE (5179 "How Can I") 40-50 55
O GEE (100 "The Masquerade Is Over") 15-25 59
PULSE (1004 "Never") 5-10 65
Also see FOUR FELLOWS
Also see STRIDERS

McLAURIN, Sonny
Singles: 7-inch
FAYETTE (1623 "Things to Do") 5-10 64

McLAWLER, Sarah
Singles: 78 rpm
BRUNSWICK 5-10 53
KING 25-40 52
VEE-JAY 10-15 56
Singles: 7-inch
BRUNSWICK (84018 "Your Fool Again") 10-15 53
KING (4561 "Romance in the Dark") 50-100 52
VEE-JAY (199 "Flamingo") 15-25 56

McLEAN, Don *P&R/LP '71*
Singles: 7-inch
ARISTA 4-6 78
CAPITOL 3-5 87-88
EMI AMERICA (Except 9100) 3-5 87
EMI AMERICA (9100 "American Pie") 4-8 92
(Full length [8:30] version.)
LIBERTY 3-5
MEDIARTS 4-6 70
MILLENNIUM 3-5 81-83
RCA 3-5 83
U.A. 4-8 71-75
Picture Sleeves
U.A. 4-8 71-73
LPs: 10/12-inch
ARISTA (4149 "Prime Time") 5-10 77
(Black vinyl.)
ARISTA (4149 "Prime Time") 10-15 77
(Colored vinyl. Promotional issue only.)
CASABLANCA 8-10 79
GOLD CASTLE ("For the Memories") 20-30 89
(Selection number not known.)
LIBERTY 5-8 82-83
MEDIARTS (41-4 "Tapestry") 15-20 70
MILLENNIUM 5-8 81
RCA (3933 "Special Radio Series") 10-15 81
(Promotional issue only.)
U.A. 10-15 71-74

McLEAN, Phil *P&R '61*
Singles: 7-inch
VERSATILE (107 "Small Sad Sam") 5-10 61
VERSATILE (108 "Big Mouth Bill") 5-10 61

McLIN, Claude
(Claude McLin Combo)
Singles: 7-inch
ALLEGRO (1462 "Kansas City") 5-10 62
DOOTO (476 "Jambo") 5-10 63

McLOLLIE, Oscar
(With the Honey Jumpers; with Bobby Smith Combo; Oscar Lollie)
Singles: 78 rpm
CLASS 10-15 53-57
MERCURY 10-15 51-56
MODERN 10-20 52-55
WING 10-15 56
Singles: 7-inch
CLASS (206 "Say") 15-20 57
CLASS (216 "King of the Fools") 15-20 57
CLASS (238 "Rock-a-Cha") 15-20 58
CLASS (243 "Convicted") 15-20 58
CLASS (265 "Honey Jump") 10-20 60
CLASS (501 "Honey Jump") 15-25 53
CLASS (503 "Rain") 15-25 53
JET (517 "You Belong to Me") 10-20 61
MERCURY (70964 "The Penalty") 20-30 56
MODERN (902 "Honey Jump") 30-40 52
MODERN (915 "Be Cool, My Heart") 20-30 52
MODERN (920 "Lollypop") 30-40 54
MODERN (928 "Mama Don't Like") 20-30 54
MODERN (938 "Hot Banana") 10-20 54
MODERN (940 "Love Me Tonight") 15-25 54
MODERN (943 "Dig That Crazy Santa Claus") 10-20 54
MODERN (950 "Hey Lolly Lolly") 10-20 55
MODERN (955 "Eternal Love") 15-25 55
MODERN (970 "Convicted") 10-20 55
SHOW TIME (600 "Ignore Me") 10-20 59
WING (90083 "God's Green Earth") 15-25 56
LPs: 10/12-inch
CROWN (5016 "Oscar McLollie and His Honey Jumpers") 150-250 56

McLOLLIE, Oscar, & Jeanette Baker / Oscar McLollie *P&R '58*
Singles: 7-inch
CLASS (228 "Hey Girl – Hey Boy"/"Let Me Know, Let Me Know") 15-20 58
HI OLDIES 3-6
Also see BAKER, Jeanette

McLOLLIE, Oscar, & Nancy Lamarr
Singles: 7-inch
SAHARA (100 "Love's a Funny Little Game") 10-15 63
Also see McLOLLIE, Oscar

McLUHAN, Marshall
LPs: 10/12-inch
COLUMBIA (2701 "The Medium Is the Message") 15-20 67
(Monaural.)
COLUMBIA (9501 "The Medium Is the Message") 20-25 67
(Stereo.)
Also see McLUHAN

McMAHON, Ed
Singles: 7-inch
CAMEO (474 "Beautiful Girl") 5-10 67
LPs: 10/12-inch
CAMEO (2009 "I'm Ed McMahon") 10-20 67

McMAKEN, Bill
Singles: 7-inch
REDWING (14204 "Call My Name") 15-25

McMANUS, Ross
Singles: 7-inch
IMPERIAL (66042 "I'm the Greatest") 5-10 64

McMILLAN, Cab, & His Fadaways
Singles: 78 rpm
MACY'S (5011 "3 Women Blues") 15-25 50

McMILLIN BROTHERS & JADES
Singles: 7-inch
CHRISTY (120 "Let It Be Me") 20-30 60
Also see JADES

McMULLAN, Jim
Singles: 7-inch
SHAD (5004 "I Get So Jealous") 10-15 59

McMURRY, Beverly
Singles: 7-inch
ASSOCIATED ARTISTS (1264 "Taking My Baby's Love") 5-10 64

McNABB, Cecil
Singles: 7-inch
KING (5516 "Clock Tickin' Rhythm") 100-200 58

McNAIR, Barbara
(With Milton De Lugg & Orchestra; with Dick Jacobs & Orchestra)
Singles: 7-inch
AUDIO FIDELITY 4-8 69
CORAL (61923 "Bobby") 15-30 58
CORAL (61972 "He's Got the Whole World in His Hands") 15-25 58
CORAL (62071 "Going Steady with the Moon") 10-20 59
CORAL (62116 "Lover's Prayer") 10-20 59
KC (109 "Cross Over the Bridge") 20-40 62
KC (112 "Nobody Rings My Bell") 20-40 63
MOTOWN (Except 1112) 10-20 65-69
MOTOWN (1112 "Steal Away Tonight") 100-200 67
ROULETTE (4346 "That's All I Want from You") 8-12 61
ROULETTE (4372 "Honeymoonin '") 8-12 61
SIGNATURE 5-15 60
W.B. (5633 "Wanted") 15-25 65
LPs: 10/12-inch
AUDIO FIDELITY (6222 "More Today Than Yesterday") 10-15 69
CORAL 15-25 59
MOTOWN (644 "Where I Am") 25-50 66
MOTOWN (680 "The Real Barbara McNair") 20-30 69
SIGNATURE (1042 "Love Talk") 20-30 60
W.B. (1541 "I Enjoy Being a Girl") 15-25 64
W.B. (1570 "Living End") 15-25 64
Also see DE LUGG, Milton
Also see JACOBS, Dick, & His Orchestra

McNAMARA, Robin *P&R '70*
Singles: 7-inch
RCR 3-6 76-77
STEED 4-8 69-71
LPs: 10/12-inch
STEED 10-15 70

McNEELY, Big Jay *R&B '49*
(With His Blue Jays; with Little Sonny Warner)
Singles: 78 rpm
ALADDIN 20-30 49-54
BAYOU 20-30 53
FEDERAL 15-25 52-54
EXCLUSIVE 15-25 46
IMPERIAL 15-25 51-53
SAVOY 15-25 48-54
VEE-JAY 15-25 55-56
Singles: 7-inch
ALADDIN (3242 "Real Crazy Cool") 15-25 54
BAYOU (014 "Teenage Hop") 40-60 53
BAYOU (018 "Catastrophe") 40-60 53
FEDERAL (12102 "The Goof") 25-50 52
FEDERAL (12111 "Penthouse Serenade") 25-50 52
FEDERAL (12141 "Nervous, Man Nervous") 25-50 53
FEDERAL (12151 "3-D") 25-50 53
FEDERAL (12168 "Mule Walk") 25-50 54
FEDERAL (12179 "Hot Cinders") 25-50 54
FEDERAL (12186 "Let's Work") 25-50 54
FEDERAL (12191 "Beachcomber") 25-50 54
IMPERIAL (5219 "Deacon's Express") 25-35 53
SAVOY (798 "The Deacon's Hop") 25-50 51
SWINGIN' (614 "There's Something On Your Mind") 15-25 59
SWINGIN' (618 "I Got the Message") 10-20 59
SWINGIN' (622 "My Darling Dear") 10-20 60
SWINGIN' (627 "Oh What a Fool") 20-30 60
SWINGIN' (629 "After Midnight") 10-20 61
SWINGIN' (637 "Without a Love") 10-20 62
VEE-JAY (142 "Big Jay's Hop") 25-35 55
VEE-JAY (212 "Jay's Rock") 25-35 56
W.B. (5401 "Big Jay's Count") 8-12 63
EPs: 7-inch
FEDERAL (246 "Go! Go! Go! with Big Jay McNeely") 100-200 53
FEDERAL (301 Big Jay McNeely, Vol. 2") 100-150 54
FEDERAL (332 Wild Man of the Saxophone") 100-150 54
FEDERAL (373 Just Crazy") 75-100 55
LPs: 10/12-inch
BIG J (101 "Loose on Sunset") 8-10 84
COLLECTABLES 5-8 88
FEDERAL (96 "Big Jay McNeely") 600-800 54
(10-inch LP.)
FEDERAL (530 "Big Jay in 3-D") 300-500 57
KING (650 "Big Jay in 3-D") 50-100 59
SAVOY (15045 "Rhythm and Blues Concert") 250-350 55
(10-inch LP.)
W.B. (W-1523 "Big Jay McNeely") 25-35 63
(Monaural.)
W.B. (WS-1523 "Big Jay McNeely") 30-40 63
(Stereo.)
Also see DELEGATES / Big Jay McNeely
Also see OTIS, Johnny
Also see THREE DOTS & A DASH & BIG JAY McNEELY & HIS ORCHESTRA
Also see WARNER, Sonny

McNEELY, Big Jay, with Jesse Belvin & Three Dots and A Dash
Singles: 78 rpm
IMPERIAL (5115 "All That Wine Is Gone") 75-125 51
Singles: 7-inch
IMPERIAL (5115 "All That Wine Is Gone") 500-750 51
Also see BELVIN, Jesse

McNEELY, Big Jay / Paul Williams
Singles: 78 rpm
SAVOY 10-15 54
Singles: 7-inch
SAVOY (1143 "The Deacon's Hop"/"The Hucklebuck") 20-40 54
Also see McNEELY, Big Jay
Also see WILLIAMS, Paul

McNEIL, Aaron
(With the Tornados)
Singles: 7-inch
C.J. (615 "Carolyn") 15-25 60
CAPITOL (5105 "Crying on My Shoulder") 15-25 64
CAPITOL (5268 "Draculena") 15-25 65
TOWER 5-10 66-67
UPTOWN (737 "Then You'll Know") 5-10 66

McNEIL, Angela
Singles: 7-inch
FELSTED (8503 "Please Daddy") 10-20 58
PREP (126 "The Phone Call") 8-12 58

McNEIL, Landy
(With the Corsairs; Landy McNeal)
Singles: 7-inch
KAPP (600 "Move It") 5-10 64
TUFF (402 "The Change in You") 8-12 65
Also see CORSAIRS

McNEIL, Lloyd
Singles: 7-inch
STACY (963 "Run Johnny Run") 5-10 63

McNEIR, Ronnie *R&B '75*
Singles: 7-inch
CAPITOL 3-5 84
DETO (2878 "Sitting in My Class") 75-125
PRODIGAL 4-6 75
RCA (0958 "In Summertime") 4-6 73
Picture Sleeves
PRODIGAL (619 "For Your Love") 4-6 75
LPs: 10/12-inch
CAPITOL 5-8 84

M'COOL, Shamus *P&R '81*
Singles: 7-inch
PERSPECTIVE (107 "American Memories") 25-50 81
PERSPECTIVE (777 "Santa's Little Helper, Dingo") 5-10 76
PERSPECTIVE (6002 "Santa's Little Helper, Dingo") 25-50 73
(Some have shown this as by Richard Doyle. We're not yet certain which is correct, or if it came out both ways. For now, we will list both.)
Also see DOYLE, Richard

McPEAK, Henry
Singles: 7-inch
H.G. (771 "I Feel Like Yelling") 200-300
H.G. (851 "When You Kissed Me") 200-300

McPHATTER, Clyde *P&R/R&B '56*
(With Cookie & the Cues)
Singles: 78 rpm
ATLANTIC (1081 thru 1185) 20-30 56-57
ATLANTIC (1199 "A Lover's Question") 40-60 58
Singles: 7-inch
AMY 5-15 65-67
ATLANTIC (1070 "Everyone's Laughing") 30-40 56
ATLANTIC (1081 "Seven Days") 25-35 56
ATLANTIC (1092 "Treasure of Love") 20-30 56
ATLANTIC (1106 "Thirty Days") 20-30 56
ATLANTIC (1117 "Without Love") 20-30 57
ATLANTIC (1133 "Just to Hold My Hand") 15-25 57
ATLANTIC (1149 "Long Lonely Nights") 15-25 57
ATLANTIC (1158 "Rock and Cry") 15-25 57
ATLANTIC (1170 "That's Enough for Me") 15-25 58
ATLANTIC (1185 "Come What May") 15-25 58
ATLANTIC (1199 "A Lover's Question") 15-25 58
ATLANTIC (2018 "Lovey Dovey") 10-20 59
ATLANTIC (2028 "Since You've Been Gone") 10-20 59
ATLANTIC (2038 "You Went Back On Your Word") 10-20 59
ATLANTIC (2049 "Just Give Me a Ring") 10-20 60
ATLANTIC (2060 "Deep Sea Ball") 10-20 60
ATLANTIC (2082 "If I Didn't Love You Like I Do") 10-20 60

DECCA 4-8 70
DERAM 4-8 68-69
MGM (12780 "I Told Myself a Lie") 10-20 59
MGM (12816 "Twice As Nice") 10-20 59
MGM (12843 "Let's Try Again") 10-20 60
(Monaural.)
MGM (12877 "Think Me a Kiss") 10-20 60
MGM (12949 "This Is Not Goodbye") 10-20 60
MGM (50134 "Let's Try Again") 20-40 60
(Stereo.)
MERCURY 10-20 60-65

Picture Sleeves

MGM (12949 "This Is Not Goodbye") 15-25 60
MERCURY 10-20 60-65

EPs: 7-inch

ATLANTIC (584 "Clyde McPhatter") 100-200 58
ATLANTIC (605 "Rock with Clyde McPhatter") 100-200 58
ATLANTIC (618 "Clyde McPhatter") 50-100 59
MERCURY ("Golden Blues Hits") 10-15 62
(Has paper sleeve. Number not known. Promotional issue only.)

LPs: 10/12-inch

ALLEGIANCE 5-8 '80s
ATLANTIC (8024 "Love Ballads") 100-200 59
(Black label.)
ATLANTIC (8024 "Love Ballads") 25-50 59
(Red label.)
ATLANTIC (8031 "Clyde") 75-125 59
ATLANTIC (8077 "Best of Clyde McPhatter") 25-40 63
DECCA 15-25 70
MGM (E-3775 "Let's Start Over Again") 30-40 59
(Monaural.)
MGM (SE-3775 "Let's Start Over Again") 40-50 59
(Stereo.)
MGM (E-3866 "Greatest Hits") 30-40 60
(Monaural.)
MGM (SE-3866 "Greatest Hits") 40-50 60
(Stereo.)
MERCURY 20-35 60-64
WING 20-30 62
Session: King Curtis.
Also see BROWN, Ruth, & Clyde McPhatter
Also see DOMINOES
Also see DRIFTERS
Also see KING CURTIS
Also see LITTLE ESTHER & CLYDE McPHATTER
Also see WARD, Billy, & Dominoes

McPHATTER, Clyde / Little Richard / Jerry Butler

LPs: 10/12-inch

PICKWICK (3233 "Rhythm & Blues and Greens") 15-20 '70s
Also see BUTLER, Jerry
Also see LITTLE RICHARD
Also see McPHATTER, Clyde

McPHERSON, Ted

Singles: 7-inch

PEACH (724 "You Were Laughing") 5-10 59

McPHERSON, Wyatt "Earp"

P&R/R&B '61

Singles: 7-inch

SAVOY (1599 "Here's My Confession") 10-20 61

McPHERSON, Wyatt "Earp," & Paul Williams

Singles: 7-inch

BATTLE (45907 "You Broke My Heart") 5-10 63
Also see McPHERSON, Wyatt "Earp"
Also see WILLIAMS, Paul

McQUAID, Betty

Singles: 7-inch

GO (5013 "Tongue Tied") 40-60

McQUITTY, Dave

Singles: 7-inch

VEE CEE (503 "Bony Moronie") 75-125
Also see VISCOUNTS

McRAE, Arvis

Singles: 7-inch

RANGER (823 "Me and My Love") 50-75

McRAE, Carmen

P&R '56

Singles: 78 rpm

DECCA 3-6 55-57
VENUS 4-8 54

Singles: 7-inch

BETHLEHEM (11009 "Tip Toe Gently") 5-10 58
COLUMBIA 4-6 62
DECCA 5-10 55-57
FOCUS (3331 "Cutie Pants") 4-8 64
MAINSTREAM (605 "Too Good") 4-8 65
MERCURY (71764 "Belonging to You") 5-10 61
VENUS 5-10 54

Picture Sleeves

COLUMBIA (42292 "Take Five") 4-8 62

EPs: 7-inch

DECCA 5-10 55

LPs: 10/12-inch

BETHLEHEM (1023 "Carmen McRae") 75-125 54
(10-inch LP.)
COLUMBIA 15-25 61-65
DECCA (8100 thru 8800 series) 40-60 55-58
(Black and silver label.)
DECCA (8100 thru 8800 series) 15-25 64
(Black label with horizonal rainbow stripe.)
FOCUS 15-25 65
KAPP 20-40 58-59
MAINSTREAM 10-20 65-67
TIME 15-25 63
Also see CONNOR, Chris / Julie London / Carmen McRae
Also see DAVIS, Sammy, Jr., & Carmen McRae

McRAE, Teddy

Singles: 7-inch

AMP 3 (129 "Hi' Fi' Baby") 75-100 '50s
Also see BUTANES

McREYNOLDS, Galen, Quintet

Singles: 7-inch

NOLTA 5-10 61
Members: Hal Champ; Galen McReynolds; Jimmy Buettner; Keith Purvis; Al Turay.

McRILL, Chandos

Singles: 78 rpm

STARDUST 20-30 56

Singles: 7-inch

STARDUST (655 "Money Lovin' Woman") 75-100 56
STARDUST (805 "Poor Me") 100-125 57

McSHANN, Jay

P&R '41

(With His Orchestra; Combo; Trio; Quartet; Sextet; Kansas City Stompers; Jazz Men)

Singles: 78 rpm

ALADDIN 10-15 50
CAPITOL 10-20 44-45
DECCA 10-15 41-43
DOWN BEAT 10-15 48-49
MERCURY 10-15 45-46
MODERN 10-15 50
PHILO/ALADDIN 10-20 45
PREMIER 10-15 45
SWING TIME 10-15 48-52
VEE-JAY 5-10 55-56

Singles: 7-inch

SWING TIME (314 "Jeronimo") 20-25 52
VEE-JAY 10-20 55-56

EPs: 7-inch

DECCA (742 "Kansas City Memories") 50-100 54

LPs: 10/12-inch

CAPITOL (2645 "McShann's Piano") 15-20 67
DECCA (5503 "Kansas City Memories") 200-300 54
(10-inch LP. With Charlie Parker, Al Hibbler, Walter Brown, & Paul Paul Quinichette.)
DECCA (9000 series) 10-15 68
Also see ADAMS, Faye / Jay McShann
Also see BROWN, Walter
Also see HIBBLER, Al
Also see WATERFORD, Crown Prince
Also see WITHERSPOON, Jimmy

McSHANN, Jay, With Johnny Moore's Three Blazers

Singles: 78 rpm

MODERN 10-15 50
Also see MOORE, Johnny

McSHANN, Jay, & Priscilla Bowman

Singles: 78 rpm

VEE-JAY 5-10 55

Singles: 7-inch

VEE-JAY 10-15 55
Also see BOWMAN, Priscilla
Also see McSHANN, Jay

McTELL, Blind Willie

(Blind Willie)

Singles: 78 rpm

DECCA (7078 "Ticket Agent Blues") 200-300
DECCA (7093 "Dying Gambler") 200-300
DECCA (7117 "Hillbilly Willie's Blues") 200-300
DECCA (7140 "We Got to Meet Death One Day") 200-300
DECCA (7180 "Cold Winter Day") 200-300
REGAL (3260 "River Jordan") 100-200 50
REGAL (3272 "It's My Desire") 100-200 50
REGAL (3277 "Love Changing Blues") 100-200 50
VICTOR (21124 "Mr. McTell Got the Blues") 250-500
VICTOR (21474 "Writin' Paper Blues") 250-500
VICTOR (38001 "Three Women Blues") 250-500
VICTOR (38032 "Dark Night Blues") 250-500
VICTOR (38580 "Drive Away Blues") 250-500

LPs: 10/12-inch

ATLANTIC 8-12 72
BIOGRAPH 10-15 69-73
MELODEON (7323 "1940") 15-25 66
PRESTIGE 8-12 70
PRESTIGE BLUESVILLE (1040 "Last Session") 25-35 62
Also see BARRELHOUSE SAMMY
Also see PIG 'N WHISTLE BAND

McTELL, Blind Willie, & Memphis Minnie

LPs: 10/12-inch

BIOGRAPH 10-15 70
Also see McTELL, Blind Willie
Also see MEMPHIS MINNIE

McVEA, Jack

P&R/R&B '47

(With His All-Stars)

Singles: 78 rpm

APOLLO 15-20 45
BLACK & WHITE 15-25 45-47
EXCLUSIVE 10-15 47
COMBO 8-12 56
COMET (100 "B.B. Boogie") 10-15 48
MELODISC 15-25 45

Singles: 7-inch

COMBO (Except 55) 10-20 56
COMBO (55 "Let's Ride, Ride, Ride") 15-25 55
TAG 10-15 56
Also see BROWN, Clarence "Gatemouth"
Also see PHILLIPS, Gene
Also see SAVOYS / Jack McVea
Also see SHARPS / Jack McVea

McVOY, Carl

Singles: 7-inch

HI (2001 "Tootsie") 15-25 57
HI (2002 "Daydreamin' ") 10-20 58
PHILLIPS INT'L (3526 "Tootsie") 10-20 58
TRI (212 "Rainin' in My Heart") 10-15 61
Also see BLACK, Bill
Also see McCOY, Carl

ME & DEM GUYS

(Me & Them Guys)

Singles: 7-inch

CORAL GABLES (2082 "Black Cloud") 25-35 66
(First issue.)
DEARBORN (550 "Black Cloud") 10-15 66
PALMER (5007 "Black Cloud") 5-10 66
PYRENEES (2 "Mercy Mercy") 10-15 '60s
PYRENEES (6 "Simple Thoughts of Love") 10-15 '60s
PYRENEES (41 "She Cried") 10-15 '60s

ME & GUYS

Singles: 7-inch

PLA ME (101 "I Can't Take It") 15-25 66

ME & HIM DUO

Singles: 7-inch

PAZA (867 "On the Money") 10-20 66

ME & THE REST

Singles: 7-inch

BRASS CITY (2027 "Mark Time") 15-25 67

ME & YOU

Singles: 7-inch

PARKWAY (121 "Let the World In") 8-15 66

MEAD, Glenn

Singles: 7-inch

PONZI (100 "Blue Suede Shoes") 100-200

MEAD, Montie

(Monty Mead)

Singles: 7-inch

FORTUNE (1001 "Cape Canaveral") 75-125 '60s
KING (5848 "She's Gone Away") 5-10 64

MEADE, Freddie, & Calenders

Singles: 7-inch

20TH FOX (287 "Just Give Her My Love") 20-30 61
Session: Bill Haley's Comets.
Also see HALEY, Bill

MEADER, Vaughn

LP '62

Singles: 7-inch

MGM (13169 "No Hiding Place") 5-10 63
VERVE (10309 "St. Nick Visits the White House") 5-10 63

EPs: 7-inch

VERVE (5082 "Have Some Nuts") 5-10 63

LPs: 10/12-inch

CADENCE (3060 "First Family") 20-30 62
(Monaural.)
CADENCE (3065 "First Family, Vol. 2") 20-30 63
(Monaural.)
CADENCE (25060 "First Family") 30-40 62
(Stereo.)
CADENCE (25065 "First Family, Vol. 2") 30-40 63
(Stereo.)
CONGRESSIONAL RECORDS ("First Family, Vols. 1 & 2") 30-40
(No selection number used. "Congressional Records Presents a Priceless Collectors Album in Its Original Package – Specially Certified Limited Edition Pressing.")
KAMA SUTRA 8-12 '70s
LAURIE (2035 "Take That, You No Good") 10-15 66
VERVE (15042 "Have Some Nuts") 10-15 63
VERVE (15050 "If the Shoe Fits") 10-15 65
VERVE (15054 "The New First Family") 10-15 66

MEADOWBROOKS

Singles: 7-inch

CATAMOUNT (106 "Time After Time") 8-12 65
CATAMOUNT (108 "Lover's Quarrel") 5-10 65
(Black vinyl.)
CATAMOUNT (108 "Lover's Quarrel") 8-12 65
(Yellow or purple vinyl.)

MEADOWLARKS

Singles: 78 rpm

IMPERIAL (5146 "Brother Bill") 15-25 51

MEADOWS, Dave, & Neanderthals

Singles: 7-inch

MAGNUM (41160 "Angel") 10-20 '60s

MEADOWS, Larry

Singles: 7-inch

REGENCY (25 "Don't Hide Your Love") 20-30 62
REGENCY (27 "Pretending") 10-20 63
STRAT O LITE (969 "Phyllis") 30-40 59

MEANS, Keith, & Knighters

Singles: 7-inch

RENA (3001 "Sham-Bam") 8-12 61

MEANTIME

Singles: 7-inch

ATCO (6524 "Friday Kind of Monday") 8-12 67
Member: Ellie Greenwich.
Also see GREENWICH, Ellie

MEAT LOAF

LP '77

(With Ellen Foley; Marvin Lee Aday)

Singles: 12-inch

EPIC (477 "Meat Loaf") 5-8 77
(Promotional issue only.)

Singles: 7-inch

EPIC 3-6 77-83
RCA 3-5 85
RSO 4-6 74

Picture Sleeves

RCA 3-5 85

LPs: 10/12-inch

CLEVELAND INT'L (38444 "Midnight at the Lost and Found") 5-10 83
EPIC (34974 "Bat Out of Hell") 5-10 77
EPIC (E99-34974 "Bat Out of Hell") 20-25 77
(Picture disc. With bats on front cover.)
EPIC (E99-34974 "Bat Out of Hell") 25-35 77
(Picture disc. Without bats on front cover. Promotional issue only.)

EPIC (34974 "Bat Out of Hell")................ 25-35 77
(Picture disc. Canadian.)
EPIC (36007 "Dead Ringer")................... 25-35 81
(Picture disc. Promotional issue only.)
EPIC (44974 "Bat Out of Hell")............... 15-20 80
(Half-speed mastered.)
RCA (5451 "Bad Attitude")........................5-10 85
Also see POPCORN BLIZZARD
Also see STONEY & MEAT LOAF

MEAT PUPPETS

EPs

LONDON (1111 "Raw Meat")................. 20-30 94
(10-inch EP.)
SST...4-6 85
WORLD IMITATION ("In a Car")........... 50-100 81
(No selection number used.)

LPs: 10/12-inch

LONDON (Except 484)...............................5-8 91-95
LONDON (484 "Too High to Die")........... 25-35 94
(With 10-inch *Raw Meat* EP.)
LONDON (484 "Too High to Die")................5-8 94
(Without 10-inch *Raw Meat* EP.)
SST...5-8 81-87
Members: Curt Kirkwood; Cris Kirkwood; Derrick Bostrom.

MEAUX, Huey

Singles: 7-inch

JIN (104 "73 Special")........................... 15-25 59

MECHANICAL SWITCH

Singles: 7-inch

ONE WAY (906 "Everything Is Red")....... 20-40 '60s

Picture Sleeves

ONE WAY (906 "Everything Is Red")....... 30-60 '60s

MECHANICS

Singles: 7-inch

JAMIE (1305 "Co-Co Mo-Mo")....................5-10 65
NORMAN (501 "Fastest Thing on Wheels")...................................... 15-25 61

MECKI MARK MEN

Singles: 7-inch

LIMELIGHT (3083 "Love Feeling").............5-10 68

LPs: 10/12-inch

LIMELIGHT (86054 "Mecki Mark Men")... 10-20 68

MEDALLIONAIRES

Singles: 7-inch

MERCURY (71309 "Magic Moonlight").. 75-100 58

MEDALLIONS

Singles: 78 rpm

ESSEX (901 "I Know")........................... 50-100 55

Singles: 7-inch

ESSEX (901 "I Know")......................... 300-400 55

MEDALLIONS

Singles: 7-inch

CARD (1 "Since You've Gone Away")..... 30-40 60
SINGULAR (1002 "Broken Heart").......... 40-50 57
SULTAN (1004 "Love That Girl")............ 20-30 59

MEDALLIONS

Singles: 7-inch

SARG (191 "I Love You True")................ 20-30 61
SARG (194 "Lovin' Time")...................... 20-30 61

MEDALLIONS

Singles: 7-inch

LENOX (5556 "Why Do You Look at Me").. 15-25 63
NOLA (701 "Why Do You Look at Me").. 100-150 63

MEDALLIONS

Singles: 7-inch

WARPED (1001 "Leave Me Alone")........ 20-30 '60s

MEDALLIONS

Singles: 7-inch

MEDALLION (010 "Hot Ice")......................8-12

MEDELL, Jack, Orchestra

Singles: 7-inch

UNITED (213 "Enchantment")....................8-12 57

MEDICINE MEN

Singles: 7-inch

DUEL (510 "Fever")............................... 10-20 62
LAUREL (1016 "Teen Fever")....................5-10 61

MEDINA, Renee

Singles: 7-inch

CHALLENGE (59226 "Boy I Love")...........5-10 64

MEDITATIONS

Singles: 7-inch

WORLD PACIFIC (77876 "Transcendental Meditation")...5-10 67

MEDLEY, Bill *P&R/R&B/LP '68*

("Bill Medley of the Righteous Brothers")

Singles: 7-inch

A&M...4-8 71-73
CURB/MCA (10542 "Most of All You").........3-5 89
LIBERTY...3-5 81
MCA/CURB (53443 "You've Lost That Lovin' Feelin'")...3-5 88
MGM (13931 "I Can't Make It Alone").........5-10 68
MGM (13959 "Brown Eyed Woman").........5-10 68
MGM (14000 "Peace Brother Peace")........5-10 68
MGM (14025 thru 14202).......................5-10 68-70
MGM BAND OF GOLD (531 "Brown Eyed Woman")..3-6 75
MGM GOLDEN CIRCLE (207 "Brown Eyed Woman")..4-8 70
MOONGLOW (221 "Gotta Tell You How I Feel")..5-10 63
PARAMOUNT (0089 "Swing Low Sweet Chariot")...4-8 71
PLANET...3-5 82-83
RCA...3-5 83-85
REPRISE (413 "Leavin' Town")..................5-10 65
SCOTTI BROTHERS (07938 "He Ain't Heavy, He's My Brother")..3-5 88
U.A...4-6 78-80
VERVE (10569 "That Lucky Old Sun").......5-10 67

LPs: 10/12-inch

A&M (3505 "A Song for You")..................10-15 71
A&M (3517 "Smile")...................................8-12 73
LIBERTY (1097 "Sweet Thunder")..............5-10 81
MCA/CURB (42257 "Best of Bill Medley")..5-10 88
MGM (4583 "Bill Medley 100%")..............10-20 68
MGM (4603 "Soft and Soulful")................10-20 69
MGM (4640 "Someone Is Standing Outside")..10-20 69
MGM (4702 "Nobody Knows")..................25-35 70
MGM (4741 "Gone")..................................10-15 70
(Repackage of MGM 4702, *Nobody Knows*.)
MGM (91609 "Bill Medley 100%")............10-20 68
(Capitol Record Club issue.)
PLANET (4434 "Right Here and Now")......5-10 82
RCA (5352 "Still Hung Up on You")............5-8 85
RCA (8519 "I Still Do")...............................5-8 84
U.A. (929 "Lay a Little Lovin' on Me")........8-10 78
U.A. (1024 "Sweet Thunder")...............150-250 80
(Canadian.)
Also see CLOUDS
Also see KNIGHT, Gladys, & Bill Medley
Also see RIGHTEOUS BROTHERS
Also see ROGERS, Kenny
Also see 6680 LEXINGTON
Also see SONNY & CHER / Bill Medley / Lettermen / Blendells

MEDLEY, Bill, & Jennifer Warnes / Mickey & Sylvia *P&R '87*

Singles: 7-inch

RCA (5224 "The Time of My Life"/"Love Is Strange")..3-5 87

Picture Sleeves

RCA (5224 "The Time of My Life"/"Love Is Strange")..3-5 87
Also see MEDLEY, Bill
Also see MICKEY & SYLVIA
Also see WARNES, Jennifer

MEDWICK, Joe

Singles: 7-inch

ALL BOY (8504 "You Ain't Treatin' Her Right")..5-10 62
DUKE (189 "You Still Send Me")..............10-20 58
DUKE (311 "Searchin' in Vain")..................8-12 60
PACEMAKER (232 "Wedding Bells")...........5-8 65
MONUMENT (875 "Have Fun Baby")...........5-8 65

MEECHAN, Don

Singles: 7-inch

BIG TOP (3096 "Twistin' at the Waldorf").10-15 62

MEEFORD, Ray

Singles: 7-inch

ACCENT (1197 "Honky Tonk Sweetheart")..5-10 66

MEEP MEEP & ROADRUNNERS

Singles: 7-inch

BOOMERANG (651 "Justine")....................5-10 65

MEGATONES

Singles: 7-inch

AZRA (119 "Don't Drop the Bomb on My Boyfriend")..5-10 83
(Rectangular picture disc.)
AZRA (119 "Don't Drop the Bomb on My Boyfriend")..5-10 83
(Octogon or hexagon picture disc.)
AZRA (DTR 119 "Don't Drop the Bomb on My Boyfriend")..5-10 83
(8-inch picture disc.)

MEGATONS *P&R '62*

Singles: 7-inch

CHECKER (1005 "Shimmy, Shimmy Walk")..10-15 62
DODGE (808 "Shimmy, Shimmy Walk")..15-20 61
FOREST (046 "Little Atom").......................5-10 63
JELL (189 "Isis")...5-10 62
Members: Billy Lee Riley; Jimmy Wilson; Martin Willis.
Also see RILEY, Billy Lee

MEGATRONS *P&R '59*

Singles: 7-inch

ACOUSTICON (101 "Velvet Waters")......30-40 59
(First issue.)
AUDICON (101 "Velvet Waters").............10-20 59
AUDICON (104 "Whispering Winds").......10-20 60
AUDICON (107 "Ranchero")....................10-20 60
AUDICON (110 "By the Waters of Minnetonka")..10-20 61
LAURIE (3291 "Velvet Waters")..................8-12 65
LAURIE (3310 "Detroit Sound")..................8-12 65
Members: John Summers; Heywood Henry.

MEI, Hao, & Rickshaw 5

Singles: 7-inch

ENCORE (73 "Skip School Flu")..................8-12 64

MEL & BLUE ACES

Singles: 7-inch

HOLL-STAR (8-8640 "Cold Sweat")...........5-10 68

MEL & JERRY

Singles: 7-inch

W.B. (5195 "Double Whammy")..................5-10 61

MEL & MARY

Singles: 7-inch

GRAMO (5501 "The Plea").........................8-12 63

MEL & TIM *P&R/R&B '69*

Singles: 7-inch

BAMBOO...4-6 69-71
COLLECTABLES...3-5 '80s
ERIC...4-6 '70s
STAX...4-6 72-74

LPs: 10/12-inch

BAMBOO...10-15 70
STAX...8-12 72-74
Members: Mel Harden; Tim McPherson.

MELA, Denny

Singles: 7-inch

PARKWAY (802 "Blondie").........................8-12 59

MELANIE *LP '69*

(With the Edwin Hawkins Singers)

Singles: 7-inch

ABC/MCA...4-6 75
AMHERST...3-5 85
ATLANTIC...4-6 77
BLANCHE...3-5 82
BUDDAH...4-8 69-73
CASABLANCA...4-6 74
COLUMBIA (44349 "God's Only Daughter")..10-15 67
COLUMBIA (44524 "Garden in the City")...8-12 68
ERIC...3-6 78
FLASHBACK...3-6 '70s
GOLDIES 45...3-6 73
GORDIAN...5-10 85
MIDSONG INT'L...4-6 78-79
NEIGHBORHOOD...4-6 71-75
PORTRAIT (51001 "One More Try")............3-5 81
RADIO ACTIVE GOLD...................................3-5 '80s
STORK...5-10 70
(Promotional issue only.)
TOMATO...4-6 78-79
WHAT'S IT ALL ABOUT..................................4-6 '70s
(Promotional issue only.)
WORLD UNITED...4-6 78

Picture Sleeves

BUDDAH...4-8 70-72
NEIGHBORHOOD...4-8 72-73

EPs: 7-inch

BUDDAH...5-8 70
(Juke box issue.)

LPs: 10/12-inch

ABC..8-10 75
ACCORD...5-8 81-82
AMHERST...8-10 85
ARISTA..5-10 75-77
ATLANTIC...8-10 76
BELL..8-10 71
BLANCHE..5-8 82
BUDDAH..10-15 69-77
51 WEST...5-8 79
KOALA..5-10 79
MCA/MIDSONG..5-10 77-78
NEIGHBORHOOD..8-10 71-75
PAIR...5-10 88
PICKWICK..8-10 71
TELLENHOUSE..15-25 78
TOMATO..5-10 79
Also see MOMMY

MELCHER, Terry

Singles: 7-inch

RCA/EQUINOX (10587 "Fire in a Rainstorm")..4-8 76

LPs: 10/12-inch

RCA/EQUINOX (0948 "Royal Flush")......10-15 76
REPRISE(2185 "Terry Melcher")............10-15 74
Also see DAY, Terry

MELCHER, Terry, & Bruce Johnston

Singles: 7-inch

RCA/EQUINOX (10238 "Take It to Mexico")...4-8 75
Also see BRUCE & TERRY
Also see JOHNSTON, Bruce
Also see MELCHER, Terry

MELCHIOR, Dean

Singles: 7-inch

MEL (1000 "Baby Sister")............................8-12 '50s

MELI, Debbie

Singles: 7-inch

RCA (9043 "Forever Yours").....................10-15 66

MELINDA & MISFITS

Singles: 7-inch

U-NEK (711 "Don't Take Your Love Away")..15-25 '60s

MELIS, Jose

Singles: 78 rpm

MERCURY/SAV-WAY (5038 "Stardust")..100-150 47
(Picture disc. Promotional issue only.)

Singles: 7-inch

SEECO...5-10 58-59

MELL, Bobby

Singles: 7-inch

DORE (612 "Dedication Time")..................5-10 61
DORE (625 "Lost the One I Love")..............5-10 62
DORE (644 "Truly, Truly True")..................5-10 62

MELLENCAMP, John Cougar *P&R/LP '79*

(John Cougar; Johnny Cougar; John Mellencamp)

Singles: 12-inch

MAIN MAN (4001 "Kid Inside")............100-125 83
(Picture disc. Has four tracks. Promotional issue only.)
MAIN MAN (4001 "Kid Inside")..............75-100 83
(Picture disc. Has two tracks. Promotional issue only. Autographed.)
MAIN MAN (4001 "Kid Inside")................60-80 83
(Picture disc. Has two tracks. Promotional issue only. Not Autographed.)

Singles: 7-inch

MERCURY...3-5 87-90
RIVA (Except 211 & 215)................................3-6 79-85
RIVA (211 "Hand to Hold on To")..................3-5 82
RIVA (211 "Hand to Hold on To")..............20-25 82
(Promotional only picture disc.)

RIVA (215 "Pink Houses") 5-10 83
(Colored vinyl.)

Picture Sleeves

MERCURY 3-6 87-90
RIVA 4-8 79-86

EPs: 7-inch

GULCH (005 "U.S. Male") 150-200 78

LPs: 10/12-inch

MCA (2225 "Chestnut Street Incident") ... 15-20 77
MAIN MAN ("Chestnut Street Incident") .. 30-40 76
(Selection number not known.)
MAIN MAN (601 "Kid Inside") 5-10 83
MERCURY (Except 349) 5-8 87-90
MERCURY (349 "Let It All Hang") 25-35 87
(Interview LP. Promotional issue only.)
MFSL (222 "Lonesome Jubilee") 25-35 94
RIVA 5-10 79-85
Members: John Cougar Mellencamp; Wayne Hall; Larry Crane; David Parman; Terrence Sala; Tom Wince; Michael Wanchic; George Perry; Doc Rosser; Ken Aronoff; Toby Myers; John Cascalle.
Also see LITTLE RICHARD / John Cougar Mellencamp

MELLO, Dennie

Singles: 7-inch

BLUE BELL (500 "Wailin' Guitar") 10-15 60

MELLO DROPS

Singles: 78 rpm

IMPERIAL 100-200 54

Singles: 7-inch

IMPERIAL (5324 "When I Grow to Old to Dream") 400-500 54

MELLO KINGS

Singles: 78 rpm

IMPERIAL (5105 "Shirley") 40-60 50

MELLO-CHORDS

Singles: 7-inch

LYCO (1001 "Golden Vanity") 15-25 61

MELLO-FELLOWS

Singles: 78 rpm

LAMP (8006 "Iddy Biddy Baby") 10-15 54

Singles: 7-inch

LAMP (8006 "Iddy Biddy Baby") 25-30 54

MELLOHARPS
(Mello-Harps)

Singles: 78 rpm

DO-RE-MI (203 "Love Is a Vow") 200-400 56
TIN PAN ALLEY 100-200 55-56

Singles: 7-inch

CASINO (104 "No Good") 40-50 58
DO-RE-MI (203 "Love Is a Vow") 2000-3000 56
TIN PAN ALLEY (145/146 "I Love Only You") 200-300 55
TIN PAN ALLEY (157/158 "What Good Are My Dreams") 500-700 56
TIN PAN ALLEY (159/160 "I Couldn't Believe") 400-600 56
Also see LEVEE SONGSTERS
Also see TEENTONES
Also see WILTSHIRE, Teacho, & Melloharps

MELLO-KINGS P&R '57
(Mellokings; Mello Kings; Mellotones)

Singles: 78 rpm

HERALD (502 "Tonite Tonite") 150-250 57
(Credits "The Mellotones.")
HERALD (502 "Tonite Tonite") 75-125 57
(Credits "The Mello-Kings.")

Singles: 7-inch

COLLECTABLES ....3-5 '80s
FLASHBACK (2 "Tonite Tonite"/"Thrill Me") 8-12 65
(*Thrill Me* is a previously unissued Herald track.)
HERALD (502 "Tonite Tonite") 300-500 57
(Credits "The Mellotones.")
HERALD (502 "Tonite Tonite") 50-60 57
(Credits "The Mello-Kings." Has logo in script print inside the flag.)
HERALD (502 "Tonite Tonite") 30-40
(Credits "The Mello-Kings." Has logo in block print inside the flag.)
HERALD (507 "Chapel on the Hill") 20-30 57
HERALD (511 "The Only Girl") 20-30 58
HERALD (518 "Valerie") 20-30 58
HERALD (536 "Running to You") 15-25 59
HERALD (548 "Our Love Is Beautiful") 15-25 60
HERALD (554 "Kid Stuff") 15-25 60
(Yellow label, small print.)
HERALD (554 "Kid Stuff") 10-20 60
(Multi-color label.)
HERALD (554 "Kid Stuff") 10-15 60
(Yellow label, large print.)
HERALD (561 "Penny") 15-25 61
HERALD (567 "Love At First Sight") 20-30 61
LANA (124 "Tonite Tonite") 4-6 64
LESCAY (3009 "Walk Softly") 20-30 62

EPs: 7-inch

HERALD (451 "The Fabulous Mello-Kings") 200-250 60

LPs: 10/12-inch

COLLECTABLES 5-10 84
HERALD (1013 "Tonight Tonight") 350-500 60
RELIC ....5-10 '80s
Members: Larry Esposita; Bob Scholl; Jerry Scholl; Eddie Quinn; Neil Areana.

MELLO-LARKS

Singles: 78 rpm

EPIC 5-10 54-56

Singles: 7-inch

EPIC 10-15 54-56

LPs: 10/12-inch

CAMDEN (530 Just for a Lark") 20-40 59
EPIC (1106 "The Mello-Larks & Jamie") .. 20-40 55
(10-inch LP.)
Members: Tom Hamm; Adele Castle; Bob Wolter; Joseph Eich.

MELLO-LARKS & DELORES HAWKINS

LPs: 10/12-inch

EPIC (1122 "Broadway Success Story") .. 20-40 55
Also see HAWKINS, Dolores
Also see MELLO-LARKS

MELLO-MAIDS

Singles: 78 rpm

BATON 8-12 56-57

Singles: 7-inch

BATON (231 "Will You Ever Say You're Mine") 10-15 56
BATON (238 "I Remember, Dear") 10-15 57

MELLOMEN

Singles: 7-inch

FULTON (113 "Daddy's Lullaby") 10-15
(Colored vinyl.)

MELLO-MOODS R&B '52
(Mellow Moods; Mello Moods; Mellomoods; with Teacho Wiltshire & Band; with Schubert Swanston Trio)

Singles: 78 rpm

PRESTIGE (799 "Call on Me") 100-200 53
PRESTIGE (856 "I'm Lost") 100-200 53
RED ROBIN (104 "I Couldn't Sleep a Wink Last Night") 200-400 52
RED ROBIN (105 "Where Are You") 400-500 52
ROBIN (105 "Where Are You") 200-300 52

Singles: 7-inch

GAMBLE (2512 "Stop Taking My Love for Granted") 5-10 72
PRESTIGE (799 "Call on Me") 750-1000 53
PRESTIGE (856 "I'm Lost") 750-1000 53
ROBIN (105 "Where Are You") 2000-3000 51
(We have yet to verify any **Red** Robin issues of this on 45 rpm.)
Members: Ray "Buddy" Wooten; Bobby Williams; Monte Owens; Bobby Baylor; Jimmy Bethea.
Also see PERSONALITIES
Also see SOLITAIRES
Also see WILTSHIRE, Teacho

MELLO-MOODS / Rainbows

Singles: 7-inch

HAMILTON (143 "I'm Lost"/"They Say") ... 10-15
Also see MELLO-MOODS
Also see RAINBOWS

MELLOMOODS

Singles: 78 rpm

RECORDED IN HOLLYWOOD (399 "Song of Love") 50-100 53
Member: Al Frazier.
Also see HIGGINS, Chuck, & Mellomoods
Also see KEY, Troyce
Also see RIVINGTONS
Also see SHARPS

MELLON, LeGrand

Singles: 7-inch

COLUMBIA (43528 "Everybody But Me") ..5-10 66
COLUMBIA (43655 "Summertime") 5-10 66
COLUMBIA (43848 "Move It On Over") 5-10 66

MELLO-TONES

Singles: 78 rpm

COLUMBIA 25-40 50-51
OKEH 20-30 51

Singles: 7-inch

COLUMBIA (39051 "What Are They Doing in Heaven") 200-300 50
COLUMBIA (39215 "Flying Saucers") .. 100-200 51
OKEH (6828 "Rough & Rocky Road") .. 100-200 51

MELLO-TONES
(With Reginald Ashby Orchestra)

Singles: 78 rpm

DECCA 50-100 54

Singles: 7-inch

DECCA (48319 "I'm Just Another One in Love with You") 400-500 54
DECCA (48319 "I'm Just Another One in Love with You") 10-20
(Multi-colored label.)
Also see BENITEZ, Marga, & Mello-Tones
Also see MELLO-TONES / Gloria Mann

MELLO-TONES / Gloria Mann

EPs: 7-inch

DECCA (2399 "Rhythm and Blues Bit") ... 50-75 56
Also see MANN, Gloria
Also see MELLO-TONES

MELLO-TONES P&R '57
(With Hank Ivory's Orchestra)

Singles: 78 rpm

FASCINATION 50-75 57
GEE 15-25 57

Singles: 7-inch

FASCINATION (1001 "Rosie Lee") 200-300 57
GEE (1037 "Rosie Lee") 50-60 57
GEE (1040 "Ca-Sandra") 15-25 57

MELLOTONES

Singles: 7-inch

MINARET (105 "He's a Friend") 10-20 62
TURRET (102 "Everything's Gonna Be Alright") ....25-50 '60s

MELLOW BRICK RODE

Singles: 7-inch

U.A. (50333 "Don't Put All Your Eggs in One Basket") 5-10 68
Members: Jerry Hudson; Phil Hudson; Joseph Hesse; Jim Hesse; Ralph Parker; Nick Distefano.

MELLOW DROPS

Singles: 78 rpm

IMPERIAL 50-75 54

Singles: 7-inch

IMPERIAL (5324 "When I Grow Too Old to Dream") 100-125 54

MELLOW FELLOWS

Singles: 7-inch

DOT (17135 "My Baby Needs Me") 8-12 68
DOT (17240 "Me Tarzan, You Jane") 8-12 69

MELLOW KEYS

Singles: 78 rpm

GEE (1014 "Listen, Baby") 8-12 56

Singles: 7-inch

GEE (1014 "Listen, Baby") 15-25 56

MELLOW JACKS

Singles: 7-inch

ASCOT (2115 "Gina Baby") 10-15 62
MARQUEE (83695 "Gina Baby") 20-30 62
(Identification number shown since no selection number is used.)

MELLOW LARKS
(With Clue J. & His Blues Blasters)

Singles: 7-inch

WORLDISC (104 "I'll Be True") 750-1000 58

MELLOW MOODS

Singles: 7-inch

NORTH BAY (300 "If You See Him") 5-10 73
WE MAKE ROCK & ROLL RECORDS (1602 "When You Go, Take Your Memories Too") 5-10 68

MELLOW TONES

Singles: 7-inch

("Bally's Blues") .... 15-25 '50s
(Neither label name nor number shown.)

MELLOWLARKS

Singles: 78 rpm

ARGO (5285 "Farewell to You") 10-15 58

Singles: 7-inch

ARGO (5285 "Farewell to You") 10-15 58

MELLOWS
(Featuring Lillian Leach; Featuring Lillian Lee; with Sammy Lowe & His Orchestra; Featuring Harold Johnson; with Jimmy Brokenshire Orchestra)

Singles: 78 rpm

CELESTE (3002 "My Darling") 200-300 56
JAY-DEE (793 "Nothin' to Do") 50-75 55

Singles: 7-inch

APOLLO (542 "Be Mine") 3-5 87
(Previously unissued.)
CANDLELIGHT (1011 "Moon of Silver") 75-125 57
CELESTE (3004 "I'm Yours") 600-800 56
CELESTE (3008 thru 3014) 4-6 74
DAVIS 5-10
JAY-DEE (793 "How Sentimental Can I Be") 100-200 54
(Yellow label. Has lines on label.)
JAY-DEE (793 "How Sentimental Can I Be") 15-25
(Yellow label. No lines on label.)
JAY-DEE (797 "Smoke from Your Cigarette") 50-100 55
(Yellow label.)
JAY-DEE (797 "Smoke from Your Cigarette") .... 25-50 '50s
(Orange label.)
JAY-DEE (801 "I Was a Fool to Let You Go") 50-100 55
JAY-DEE (807 "Yesterday's Memories") 75-125 55
(Yellow label. Has lines on label.)
JAY-DEE (807 "Yesterday's Memories") .. 15-25
(Yellow label. No lines on label.)

LPs: 10/12-inch

RELIC 8-10
Members: Lillian Leach; Harry Johnson; John Wilson; Carl Spencer; Arthur Crier.
Also see CRICKETS / Mellows / Deep River Boys
Also see LEACH, Lillian
Also see PRE-HISTORICS

MELO GENTS

Singles: 7-inch

W.B. (5056 "Baby Be Mine") 40-60 59

MELOAIRES

Singles: 7-inch

NASCO (6019 "You Know Baby") 15-20 58

MELODEARS

Singles: 7-inch

GONE (5033 "Summer Romance") 10-20 58
GONE (5040 "It's Love Because") 20-30 58

MELODEERS P&R '60
(Mellodeers)

Singles: 7-inch

SHELLEY (127 "The Letter") 10-20 61
SHELLEY (161 "Born to Be Mine") 10-20 62
STUDIO (9908 "Rudolph the Red-Nosed Reindeer") 15-25 60
STUDIO (9909 "Happy Teenage Times") 15-25 60

Picture Sleeves

STUDIO (9908 "Rudolph the Red-Nosed Reindeer") 20-40 60
(Sleeve credits "Mellodeers.")
STUDIO (9909 "Happy Teenage Times") 15-25 60

MELODEES

Singles: 7-inch

NU KAT (124 "Daddy Daddy") 15-25 60

MELODICS

Singles: 7-inch

M.O.C. (674 "I'd Never Thought I'd Lose You") ....5-10 '60s

MEL-O-DOTS
(Featuring Ricky Wells)

Singles: 78 rpm

APOLLO 200-300 52

Singles: 7-inch

APOLLO (1192 "One More Time") 800-1200 52
(Black vinyl.)
APOLLO (1192 "One More Time") ... 2000-2500 52
(Dark brown vinyl.)
Member: Ricky Wells.

MELO-D-RAYS + TWO
Singles: 7-inch
CUCA (6828 "Ma Cher Amie") ... 5-10 68

MELO-DS
(Melo-D's with Chuck Hamilton)
Singles: 7-inch
MEL-O-D (201 "A Thousand Stars") ... 20-30

MELODY MAKERS
(With Larry Clinton & Orchestra)
Singles: 78 rpm
HOLLIS ... 30-40 57
Singles: 7-inch
HOLLIS (1001 "Carolina Moon") ... 40-50 57
HOLLIS (1002 "Gotta Go") ... 40-50 57

MELODY MAIDS
Singles: 7-inch
LANIER (001 "Harry, Will You Marry Me") ... 10-20 58

MELOTONES
Singles: 78 rpm
LEE TONE (700 "Prayer of Love") ... 200-250 52
Singles: 7-inch
LEE TONE (700 "Prayer of Love") ... 2000-2500 52

MELO-TONES
Singles: 7-inch
IMAGE (1009 "Special Delivery") ... 30-40 60

MEL-O-TONES
Singles: 7-inch
KEY (5804 "A Little Bit More") ... 15-25 '60s

MELSON, Joe
Singles: 7-inch
EMP (002 "Heartbreak") ... 35-45
HICKORY (1121 "Oh Yeah") ... 20-30 60
HICKORY (1128 "Shook Up") ... 20-30 60
HICKORY (1143 "Hey Mr. Cupid") ... 15-25 61
HICKORY (1155 "Wake Up Little Susie") 15-25 61
HICKORY (1175 "Love Is a Dangerous Thing") ... 10-20 62
HICKORY (1200 "Any Little Thing") ... 10-15 63
HICKORY (1229 "His Girl") ... 10-15 63

MELSON, Lee "Red," & Missouri Nighthawks
EPs: 7-inch
RIDGECREST (1007 "Carmen Sue Rock"/"I'm Being Haunted"/"Rockin' Through the Tunnel of Love") ... 300-400 59

MELTON, Barry
LPs: 10/12-inch
MUSIC IS MEDICINE (9007 "We Are Like the Ocean") ... 8-12 77
MUSIC IS MEDICINE (9014 "Level with Me") ... 8-12 78
VANGUARD (6551 "Bright Sun Is Shining") ... 10-20 70
Also see COUNTRY JOE & FISH

MELTON, Ray
Singles: 7-inch
HOPE (1001 "Only Once") ... 15-25 60
IMAGE (1005 "Boppin' Guitar") ... 100-150 60

MEL-TONES
Singles: 7-inch
NEW (7780 "I'll Go") ... 8-12 60

MELTZER, David & Tina
LPs: 10/12-inch
VANGUARD (6519 "Poet Song") ... 20-30 69
Also see SERPENT POWER

MELVETTES
(With Curtis Freeman & Orchestra)
Singles: 7-inch
TELA-STAR (110 "Take One Step") ... 200-250 '50s

MELVIN, Harold *R&B '75*
(With the Blue Notes)
Singles: 12-inch
PHILA. INT'L ... 4-8 80
SOURCE ... 4-8 79-80
Singles: 7-inch
ABC ... 4-6 76-78
ARCTIC (135 "Go Away") ... 5-10 67
LANDA (703 "Get Out") ... 15-25 64
MCA ... 3-5 81
PHILA. INT'L ... 4-6 72-76
PHIL-L.A. OF SOUL (372 "Get Out") ... 4-6 75
PHILLY WORLD ... 3-5 84-85
SOURCE ... 4-6 79-80
Picture Sleeves
PHILA. INT'L ... 4-6 72-75
EPs: 7-inch
PHILA. INT'L (31648 "I Miss You") ... 5-10 72
LPs: 10/12-inch
ABC ... 8-10 77
MCA ... 5-8 81
PHILA. INT'L ... 8-12 72-76
PHILLY WORLD ... 5-8 84-85
SOURCE ... 5-10 80
Member: Lloyd Parkes.
Also see BLUE NOTES
Also see EPSILONS
Also see PENDERGRASS, Teddy

MELVIN, Joe
Singles: 7-inch
JET STREAM (727 "You Made Me Love You") ... 5-10 66
PACEMAKER (237 "You Made Me Love You") ... 5-10 65

MELVIN & LEE
Singles: 7-inch
PANCHO (11 "I Need Your Love") ... 8-12 63

MEMORIES
Singles: 7-inch
WAY=LIN (101 "Love Bells") ... 300-400 59

MEMORIES
Singles: 7-inch
OLD SOUND (809 "Little Bitty Girl") ... 5-10 62

MEMORIES
Singles: 7-inch
TIMES SQUARE (11 "Darling, You're My Angel") ... 20-30 64
(Red vinyl.)

MEMORIES
Singles: 7-inch
FLASHBACK (2001 "Dedication Time") ... 20-30 63

MEMORIES
Singles: 7-inch
K.O. (107852 "Mercy Mercy") ... 10-20 66
Members: Tom Noffke; Chuck Posniak; Bob Fusfeld; Dennis Becker; Charles Reitzner; George Baer; Kip Kruse; Frank Criclear.

MEMORY
Singles: 7-inch
AVENUE D (5 "Street Corner Serenade") .. 8-15 81
(Black vinyl. 500 made.)
AVENUE D (5 "Street Corner Serenade") ... 20-30 81
(Red vinyl. 50 made.)
AVENUE D (5 "Street Corner Serenade") ... 75-100 81
(Multi-colored vinyl. Two made.)
AVENUE D (6 "Under the Boardwalk") ... 8-15 81
(Black vinyl. 450 made.)
AVENUE D (6 "Under the Boardwalk") ... 20-30 81
(Red vinyl. 50 made.)
Members: Jaime DeJesus; Louis Benito; Bobby Hepburn; Herb Olson; Otis Harper; Leslie Uhl.

MEMORY LANE
Singles: 7-inch
CRYSTAL BALL (149 "Little Star") ... 4-8 85
(500 made.)
Picture Sleeves
CRYSTAL BALL (149 "Little Star") ... 10-15 85
(200 made.)

MEMOS
Singles: 7-inch
MEMO (5001 "I'm Going Home") ... 15-20 59
MEMO (34891 "My Type of Girl") ... 10-15 59
Members: Henry Austin; James Brown; Eugene Williams; Vernon Britton.
Also see HURRICANES

MEMPHIS BELLS Featuring Shirley
Singles: 7-inch
PHILLIPS INT'L (3547 "The Midnite Whistle") ... 10-20 59

MEMPHIS JIMMY
(James Clarke)
Singles: 78 rpm
BLUEBIRD ... 10-20 46
RCA ... 10-20 46-47
Also see CLARKE, James "Beale Street"

MEMPHIS JUG BAND
Singles: 78 rpm
VICTOR (38620 "Cocaine Habit Blues") ... 100-200 30
Members: Hattie Hart; Ben Ramey; Val Stevens.

MEMPHIS MEN
Singles: 7-inch
MIRAMAR (109 "Oh What a Night") ... 5-10 65

MEMPHIS MINNIE
(With Her Combo; Memphis with Little Joe & His Band; with Kansas Joe; Lizzie Douglas)
Singles: 78 rpm
CHECKER (771 "Broken Heart") ... 75-125 52
COLUMBIA ... 15-25 44-49
J.O.B. (1101 "Kissing in the Dark") ... 75-125 54
OKEH ... 15-25 44-45
REGAL (3259 "Why Did I Make You Cry") ... 15-25 50
Singles: 7-inch
CHECKER (771 "Broken Heart") ... 300-400 52
J.O.B. (1101 "Kissing in the Dark") ... 300-400 54
LPs: 10/12-inch
BLUES CLASSICS ... 8-10
Also see LOUIS, Joe Hill
Also see McTELL, Blind Willie, & Memphis Minnie

MEMPHIS NOMADS
Singles: 7-inch
STAX (243 "Don't Pass Your Judgment") 15-25 68
(March of Dimes charity record.)

MEMPHIS SLIM *R&B '48*
(With His House Rockers; Peter Chatman)
Singles: 78 rpm
BLUEBIRD (8584 "Beer Drinking Woman") ... 50-100 40
BLUEBIRD (8615 "Empty Room Blues") ... 50-100 41
BLUEBIRD (8645 "Shelby County Blues") ... 50-100 41
BLUEBIRD (8749 "Two of a Kind") ... 50-100 41
BLUEBIRD (8784 "Me, Myself and I") ... 50-100 41
BLUEBIRD (8834 "Whiskey Store Blues") ... 50-100 41
BLUEBIRD (8903 "Old Taylor") ... 50-100 42
BLUEBIRD (8945 "Whiskey and Gin Blues") ... 50-100 42
BLUEBIRD (8974 "Caught the Old Coon") ... 50-100 42
BLUEBIRD (9028 "Lend Me Your Love") ... 50-100 42
CHESS (1491 "Rockin' the Pad") ... 25-50 52
FEDERAL (12007 "Life Is Like That") ... 25-50 51
FEDERAL (12015 "Pacemaker Boogie") .25-50 51
FEDERAL (12021 "Midnight Jump") ... 25-50 51
FEDERAL (12033 "Darling, I Miss You So") ... 25-50 51
HY-TONE (10 "Mistake in Life") ... 25-50 46
HY-TONE (17 "Slim's Boogie") ... 25-50 46
HY-TONE (19 "Cheatin' Around") ... 25-50 46
KING (4284 "Cheatin' Around") ... 25-50 49
KING (4312 "A Letter Home") ... 25-50 49
KING (4324 "Little Mary") ... 25-50 49
KING (4327 "Grinder Man Blues") ... 25-50 49
MASTER (1010 "Believe I'll Settle Down") ... 25-50 48
MASTER (1020 "Restless Nights") ... 25-50 49
MASTER (1030 "Love at Sight") ... 25-50 49
MELODY LANE (10 "Mistake in Life") ... 25-50 46
MERCURY ... 10-20 51-52
MIRACLE (102 "Kilroy's Been Here") ... 25-50 47
MIRACLE (103 "Rockin' the House") ... 25-50 47
MIRACLE (110 "Pacemaker Boogie") ... 25-50 47
MIRACLE (111 "Harlem Bound") ... 25-50 47
MIRACLE (125 "Midnight Jump") ... 25-50 48
MIRACLE (132 "Frisco Baby") ... 25-50 49
MIRACLE (136 "Help Me Some") ... 25-50 49
MIRACLE (145 "Nobody Loves Me") ... 25-50 49
MIRACLE (153 "Throw This Dog a Bone") ... 25-50 49
MONEY (212 "My Country Gal") ... 15-25 54
OLD SWINGMASTER (1010 "Believe I'll Settle Down") ... 50-100 48
PEACOCK ... 20-40 49-52
PREMIUM (850 "Flock Rocker") ... 20-40 50
PREMIUM (860 "Slim's Blues") ... 20-40 50
PREMIUM (867 "Really Got the Blues") ... 20-40 50
PREMIUM (873 "Trouble Trouble") ... 20-40 51
PREMIUM (878 "My Baby Left Me") ... 20-40 51
PREMIUM (903 "I'm Crying") ... 20-40 52
UNITED ... 15-25 52-54
Singles: 7-inch
JEWEL (831 "I Wanna Dance") ... 4-8 73
JOSIE (973 "Little Lonely Girl") ... 5-10 67
KING (6301 "Messin' Around with the Blues") ... 4-8 70
MERCURY (8251 "Train Time") ... 50-75 51
MERCURY (8266 "No Mail Blues") ... 50-75 51
MERCURY (8281 "The Question") ... 50-75 51
MERCURY (70063 "The Train Is Comin'") ... 50-75 51
MONEY (212 "My Country Gal") ... 50-75 54
PEACOCK (1602 "Sittin' and Thinkin'") ... 50-75 52
STRAND (25041 "Lonesome") ... 15-25 61
UNITED (138 "Back Alley") ... 50-75 52
UNITED (156 "The Comeback") ... 50-75 53
(Black vinyl.)
UNITED (156 "The Comeback") ... 100-200 53
(Red vinyl.)
UNITED (166 "Call Before You Go Home") ... 50-75 53
(Black vinyl.)
UNITED (166 "Call Before You Go Home") ... 100-200 53
(Red vinyl.)
UNITED (176 "Sassy Mae") ... 50-75 54
(Black vinyl.)
UNITED (176 "Sassy Mae") ... 100-200 54
(Red vinyl.)
UNITED (182 "I Love My Baby") ... 50-75 54
UNITED (186 "Memphis Slim U.S.A.") ... 50-75 54
UNITED (189 "She's Alright") ... 50-75 55
UNITED (201 "Got to Find My Baby") ... 50-75 56
VEE-JAY (271 "Stroll On Little Girl") ... 10-15 58
VEE-JAY (294 "What's the Matter") ... 10-15 58
VEE-JAY (330 "Steppin' Out") ... 10-15 59
VEE-JAY (343 "The Comeback") ... 10-15 60
W.B. (7500 "Chicago Seven") ... 4-6 71
LPs: 10/12-inch
BATTLE (6118 "Alone with My Friends") . 20-30 63
BARNABY (31291 "Bad Luck and Troubles") ... 8-12 72
BLACK LION (155 "Rock Me Baby") ... 8-12 74
BUDDAH (7505 "Mother Earth") ... 10-20 69
CANDID (8024 "Memphis Slim U.S.A.") ... 40-50 62
(Monaural.)
CANDID (9024 "Memphis Slim U.S.A.") ... 50-75 62
(Stereo.)
CHESS (1455 "Memphis Slim") ... 50-75 61
CHESS (1510 "Real Folk Blues") ... 20-35 66
EVEREST (215 "Memphis Slim") ... 15-20 68
EVEREST (286 "Memphis Slim, Vol. 2") ... 8-12 74
FANTASY (24705 "Raining the Blues") ... 10-15 72
(Two discs.)
FOLKWAYS (2387 "Favorite Blues Singers") ... 8-12 74
GNP (10002 "The Blues Is Everywhere") .. 8-12 74
JAZZMAN (5500 "Memphis Slim") ... 5-8 82
JEWEL (5004 "Born with the Blues") ... 10-15 71
JUBILEE (8003 "Legend of the Blues") ... 15-20 67
KING (885 "Memphis Slim") ... 40-60 64
KING (1082 "Messin' Around with the Blues") ... 10-15 70
MUSE (5219 "I'll Just Keep On Singing the Blues") ... 5-10 81
PEARL (10 "Memphis Slim, U.S.A.") ... 5-10 78
PRESTIGE BLUESVILLE (1018 "Just Blues") ... 20-40 61
PRESTIGE BLUESVILLE (1031 "No Strain") ... 20-40 61
PRESTIGE BLUESVILLE (1053 "All Kinds of Blues") ... 20-40 63
PRESTIGE BLUESVILLE (1075 "Steady Rollin' Blues") ... 20-40 64
SCEPTER (535 "Self-Portrait") ... 15-25 66
SPIN-O-RAMA (149 "Lonesome Blues") .. 10-20 '60s
STORYVILLE (4044 "Blues Roots") ... 5-8 82
STRAND (1046 "World's Foremost Blues Singer") ... 25-40 61
TRIP (8025 "Right Now") ... 8-12 '70s
U.A. (3137 "Broken Soul Blues") ... 40-50 61
(Monaural.)
U.A. (6137 "Broken Soul Blues") ... 50-60 61
(Stereo.)
VEE-JAY (1012 "Memphis Slim at the Gate of Horn") ... 100-200 59
W.B. (1899 "Blue Memphis") ... 10-15 71
W.B. (2646 "South Side Reunion") ... 10-15 72

Session: Alex Atkins; Ernest Cotton; Willie Dixon; Ernest Crawford; Tim Overton; Betty Overton; Leon Hooper; Vagabonds; Floyd Hunt; Neil Green; Henry Taylor; Otho Allen.
Also see DIXON, Willie, & Memphis Slim
Also see HOOKER, Earl
Also see HOOKER, John Lee
Also see HUNTER, Ivory Joe / Memphis Slim
Also see JONES, Curtis
Also see WILLIAMSON, Sonny Boy, & Memphis Slim

MEMPHIS SLIM & LOWELL FULSOM
LPs: 10/12-inch
INNER CITY....5-10
Also see FULSON, Lowell

MEMPHIS SLIM & CURTIS JONES
LPs: 10/12-inch
CANDID (8023 "Tribute to Big Bill Broonzy")....40-50 61
(Monaural.)
CANDID (9023 "Tribute to Big Bill Broonzy")....50-75 62
(Stereo.)
Also see JONES, Curtis

MEMPHIS SLIM & ROOSEVELT SYKES
LPs: 10/12-inch
OLYMPIC (7136 "Memphis Blues")....8-12 75
Also see SYKES, Roosevelt

MEMPHIS SLIM / Muddy Waters / Jimmy Driftwood & Stoney Mountain Boys
LPs: 10/12-inch
U.A. (3050 "Folk Song Festival at Carnegie Hall")....50-60 59
(Monaural.)
U.A. (6050 "Folk Song Festival at Carnegie Hall")....60-80 59
(Stereo.)
Also see DRIFTWOOD, Jimmy
Also see MEMPHIS SLIM

MEN AT WORK P&R/LP '82
Singles: 12-inch
COLUMBIA....4-6 82-83
Singles: 7-inch
COLUMBIA....3-5 82-85
Picture Sleeves
COLUMBIA (Except 1633)....3-5 83-85
COLUMBIA (1633 "Overkill")....5-10 83
(Promotional issue only.)
LPs: 10/12-inch
COLUMBIA (1650 "Cargo World Premier Weekend")....10-15 83
(Promotional issue only.)
COLUMBIA (37978 "Business As Usual")..5-10 82
(With "ARC" or "FC" prefix.)
COLUMBIA (PAL-37978 "Business As Usual")....35-45 83
(Picture disc. Promotional issue only.)
COLUMBIA (38167 "Business As Usual")....5-8 82
COLUMBIA (38660 "Cargo")....5-8 83
COLUMBIA (40078 "Two Hearts")....5-8 85
COLUMBIA (47978 "Business As Usual")....30-50 85
(Half-speed mastered.)
COLUMBIA (48660 "Cargo")....10-15 85
Members: Colin Hay; Ron Strykert; John Rees; Jerry Speiser; Greg Ham.

MEN IN SPACE
Singles: 7-inch
ERA (3203 "Apollo 8")....10-15 69

MEN OF CHANCE
Singles: 7-inch
GATEWAY CUSTOM (105 "Count Down")....10-20 64

MENDELBAUM
Singles: 7-inch
SMACK (6963 "Try So Hard")....10-20 69

MENDELL, Johnny
(With the Premiers)
Singles: 7-inch
COLUMBIA (42154 "The Strut")....40-50 61
JAMIE (1208 "Jingle Bell Twist U.S.A.")..10-15 61
JAMIE (1214 "Please Be My Love")....40-50 62

MENDELSOHN, Danny
Singles: 7-inch
X (0050 "Good Boogie Woogie")....10-20 55

Also see MARTIN, Jerry

MENDES, Sergio P&R/LP '66
(With Brasil '66; Brasil '77; Brasil '86; Trio)
Singles: 12-inch
A&M....4-8 82
Singles: 7-inch
A&M (807 thru 1257)....4-8 66-71
A&M (1279 thru 2917)....3-6 71-87
ATLANTIC....4-6 67-68
BELL....4-6 73
ELEKTRA....4-6 75-80
Picture Sleeves
A&M....4-6 68-69
LPs: 10/12-inch
A&M (Except 4100 series)....5-12 69-84
A&M (4100 series)....10-15 66-69
ATLANTIC (1434 "Swinger from Rio")....20-30 65
ATLANTIC (8177 "Favorite Things")....15-20 68
BELL....8-10 73-74
CAPITOL (T-2294 "In a Brazilian Bag")....40-50 65
(Monaural.)
CAPITOL (ST-2294 "In a Brazilian Bag") .50-60 65
(Stereo.)
ELEKTRA....8-10 75-79
EVEREST....8-10 74
MFSL....20-30 84
PHILIPS....10-15 68
TOWER (T-5052 "In a Brazilian Bag")....30-40 65
(Monaural.)
TOWER (ST-5052 "In a Brazilian Bag")...40-50 65
(Stereo.)
Session: Joe Pizzulo.
Also see ADDERLEY, Julian "Cannonball," & Sergio Mendes

MENDOLA, Dom, & Lovers
(With the Mickey Moroni Orchestra)
Singles: 7-inch
MC (003 "You Are Welcome to My Heart")....40-50

MENERALS
Singles: 7-inch
HEAT WAVE (001 "Hot Night Down in Texas")....15-25 '60s

MENG, Jimmy
Singles: 7-inch
JAY EM (1000 "True & Faithful")....20-30 61
(First issue.)
LIBERTY (55346 "True & Faithful")....10-15 61

MENN
Singles: 7-inch
TWO & TWO (1 "One-Way Deal")....15-25 '60s

MENTON, Dale
(With Batch; Dale Menten)
Singles: 7-inch
GROOVE SHOP....5-10 '60s
MCA (40478 "Too Much a Lady")....4-6 '70s
MISCIDE (7216 "Downtown Bloomington")....25-35 '60s
(100 made.)
LPs: 10/12-inch
MCA/TALLY (2151 "I Really Wanted to Make a Movie")....8-10 75
Also see BEST THINGS
Also see GESTURES
Also see MADHATTERS

MERCADO, Mike
Singles: 7-inch
DYNO VOICE (235 "Popcorn")....5-10 67

MERCED BLUE NOTES
Singles: 7-inch
ACCENT (1069 "Rufus")....15-25 61
GALAXY (738 "Rufus Jr.")....10-20 65
GALAXY (744 "Mama Rufus")....10-20 65
MAMMOTH (5331 "Rufus Jr.")....15-25 '60s
SOUL (35007 "Do the Pig")....200-300 65
TRI-PHI (1011 "Midnite Sessions")....15-25 62
TRI-PHI (1023 "Whole Lotta Nothing")....15-25 63

MERCER, Barbara
Singles: 7-inch
GOLDEN WORLD....10-20 65

MERCER, Johnny P&R '38
Singles: 78 rpm
CAPITOL....4-8 42-52
DECCA....4-8 38

Singles: 7-inch
CAPITOL....5-10 50-52
EPs: 7-inch
CAPITOL (210 "Music of Kern")....10-20 50
LPs: 10/12-inch
CAPITOL (210 "Music of Kern")....40-50 50
(10-inch LP.)
CAPITOL (214 "Mercer Sings")....40-50 50
(10-inch LP.)
CAPITOL (907 "Ac-Cent-Tchu-Ate the Positive")....25-40 57
JUPITER (1001 "Just for Fun")....25-45 56
Also see CROSBY, Bing, & Johnny Mercer
Also see DARIN, Bobby, & Johnny Mercer

MERCER, Johnny, Jo Stafford & Pied Pipers
Singles: 78 rpm
CAPITOL....4-8 45
Also see PIED PIPERS
Also see STAFFORD, Jo

MERCER, Mabel
Singles: 7-inch
ATLAS (1207 "Sweet Little Angel")....10-20 60
(For records that actually play Mabel Mercer.)
ATLAS (1207 "Sweet Little Angel")....200-300 60
(For records that play a different song, by an unidentified R&B group.)
EPs: 7-inch
ATLANTIC (501 "Mabel Mercer Sings, Vol. 1")....10-20 55
ATLANTIC (522 "Mabel Mercer Sings, Vol. 2")....10-20 55
ATLANTIC (541/542/543 "Mabel Mercer Sings Cole Porter")....10-20 55
(Price is for any of three volumes.)
LPs: 10/12-inch
ATLANTIC (402 "Songs by Mabel Mercer, Vol. 1")....30-40 52
ATLANTIC (403 "Songs by Mabel Mercer, Vol. 2")....30-40 53
ATLANTIC (602 "The Art of Mabel Mercer")....30-40 57
ATLANTIC (1213 "Mabel Mercer Sings Cole Porter")....20-35 54
ATLANTIC (1244 "Midnight")....20-35 56
ATLANTIC (1300 series)....15-30 59-60

MERCER, Tommy
Singles: 7-inch
VOLCANO (1 "Volcano Rock")....200-300 59

MERCER, Wally
Singles: 78 rpm
DOT....15-25 52
MERTON....15-25 47
TRUMPET....15-25 54
Singles: 7-inch
DOT (1099 "Rock Around the Clock")....25-50 52
DOT (1120 "Looped")....25-50 52
RING (1502 "Hey, Miss Lula")....25-50 57
TRUMPET (226 "Sad and Blue")....25-50 54
TRUMPET (227 "Too Old to Get Married")....25-50 54

MERCER, Will
Singles: 7-inch
CONSTELLATION (109 "Penny Candy")...5-10 63
HI (2011 "Teenage Love")....5-10 58
SUN (329 "You're Just My Kind")....25-35 59

MERCHANTS OF DREAM
Singles: 7-inch
A&M....5-10 68
LPs: 10/12-inch
A&M (4199 "Strange Night Voyage")....15-25 68
CAPITOL (102 "Soul Knight")....15-25 68
Also see DREAM MERCHANTS

MERCURY, Eric
LPs: 10/12-inch
AVCO EMBASSY....10-15 69
CAPITOL....5-10 81
ENTERPRISE....8-12 72-73
SACK (1 "Lonely Girl")....300-500

MERCURY, Freddie P&R/D&D '84
Singles: 12-inch
COLUMBIA....4-6 84
Singles: 7-inch
CAPITOL (5696 "The Great Pretender")....3-5 87
COLUMBIA....3-5 84-85

EMI (6151 "Great Pretender")....30-40 87
(Antique radio-shaped picture disc.)
Picture Sleeves
CAPITOL....3-6 87
COLUMBIA....4-8 84-85
LPs: 10/12-inch
COLUMBIA....5-8 85
Also see LUREX, Larry
Also see QUEEN

MERCURY, Freddie / Giorgio Moroder
Singles: 12-inch
COLUMBIA....4-6 84
Also see MERCURY, Freddie

MERCURY ALL-STARS
Singles: 78 rpm
MERCURY (70385 "I Got Rhythm")....5-10 54
Singles: 7-inch
MERCURY (70385 "I Got Rhythm")....10-15 54
Members: Chubby Jackson; Mike Simpson; Dick Marks; Red Saunders.
Also see JACKSON, Chubby
Also see SAUNDERS, Red

MERCURYS
Singles: 7-inch
MADISON (119 "Someone Touched Me")....40-50 59
MADISON (161 "Someone Touched Me")....25-35 61

MERCY P&R/LP '69
Singles: 7-inch
SUNDI....4-8 69
W.B.....4-8 69
LPs: 10/12-inch
SUNDI....15-20 68
W.B.....10-15 69
Members: James Marvell; Ronnie Coudill; Roger Fuentes; Buddy Good; Debbie Lewis; Brenda McNish.

MERCY & JUSTICE
Singles: 7-inch
XYZ (101 "Rockabilly Walk")....20-30 57
Members: Hank Mercy; Frank Justice.

MERCY BABY
(J. Mercy Baby)
Singles: 78 rpm
ACE....10-20 57
RIC....10-20 58
Singles: 7-inch
ACE (528 "Rock & Roll Baby")....10-20 57
ACE (535 "Mercy's Blues")....10-20 57
MERCY BABY....10-20 58
RIC (955 "Don't Lie to Me")....10-20 58

MERCY BOYS
Singles: 7-inch
MERRILIN (5300 "Spoonful")....15-25 65
PANORAMA (24 "Mercy Mercy")....8-12 66
PANORAMA (45 "Long Tall Shorty")....8-12 66

MERCY DEE R&B '49
(Mercy Dee Walton)
Singles: 78 rpm
BAYOU (003 "Anything in This World")....25-50 53
BAYOU (013 " Happy Bachelor")....40-60 53
COLONY (102 "Happy Bachelor")....25-50 51
COLONY (107 "Old Fashioned Ways")....20-40 52
COLONY (111 "Honey Baby")....20-40 52
FLAIR....15-25 55
IMPERIAL (5104 "Honey Baby")....20-40 50
IMPERIAL (5110 "Big Foot Country")....20-40 50
IMPERIAL (5118 "Bought Love")....20-40 50
IMPERIAL (5127 "Danger Zone")....20-40 50
RHYTHM....50-75 54
SPECIALTY....15-25 53
SPIRE (001 "Lonesome Cabin Blues")....25-50 49
SPIRE (002 "Evil & Hanky")....25-50 49
Singles: 7-inch
BAYOU (003 "Anything in This World")....600-750 53
BAYOU (013 "Happy Bachelor")....500-700 53
FLAIR (1073 "Romp & Stomp Blues")....40-60 55
FLAIR (1077 "True Love")....40-60 55
FLAIR (1078 "Have You Ever")....40-60 55
RHYTHM (1774 "Trailing My Baby")....150-200 54
SPECIALTY (Except 458, 466 and 481)..20-40 53-54
SPECIALTY (458 "One Room Country Shack")....25-50 53
SPECIALTY (466 "Rent Man Blues")....25-50 53
(Black vinyl.)

SPECIALTY (466 "Rent Man Blues")... 100-200 53
(Red vinyl.)
SPECIALTY (481 "Get to Gettin' ") 25-50 53

LPs: 10/12-inch

ARHOOLIE (1007 "Mercy Dee") 40-60 61
PRESTIGE BLUESVILLE (1039 "Pity and a Shame") 50-75 62
Also see THOMAS, Marcellus, & His Rhythm Rockets

MERCYFUL FATE

Singles: 12-inch

MEGAFORCE (369 "Melissa") 15-20 87
(Picture disc.)

Singles: 7-inch

WESSELS ("Black Masses") ....5-10 '80s
(Picture disc. No selection number used.)

MEREDITH, Buddy *C&W '62*

Singles: 7-inch

GUYDEN (2128 "For the Love of Mike") 5-10 66
NASHVILLE (5042 "I May Fall Again") 10-20 62
RICE 5-10 64-67

LPs: 10/12-inch

DAVIS UNLIMITED 8-12
STARDAY 15-25 63

MEREDITH, J.W.

Singles: 78 rpm

ACE (513 "I Love You So Much") 10-15 56

Singles: 7-inch

ACE (513 "I Love You So Much") 15-25 56

MERIAN, Leon

Singles: 7-inch

SEECO (6041 "Let Me Know") 5-10 59
SEECO (6043 "Marie's Law") 5-10 60
20TH FOX (129 "Rockin' Bee") 5-10 59

MERIDIANS
(With R. Lopez & Orchestra)

Singles: 7-inch

PARNASO (107 "Have You Forgotten") 1000-2000 63
PARNASO (120 "Blame My Heart") .... 75-125 '60s

MERIWETHER, Roy, Trio

LPs: 10/12-inch

CAPITOL (102 "Soul Knight") 10-20 68
Also see CLARK, Dave, Five / Roy Meriwether Trio / Bobby Vinton / Bob Dylan

MERKIN

LPs: 10/12-inch

WINDI (1005 "Music from Merkin") 250-350 72
Members: Ralph Hemingway; Robert Bouney; Rocky Baum; Kent Balog; Gary Balog; Richard Leavitt.

MERLIN, Jack
(With the Valiants)

Singles: 7-inch

CAMEO (311 "Drip Drop Shala La Blues") 10-15 64
DOT (16332 "Girl of My Dreams") 15-25 62
HICKORY (1296 "One Song") 5-10 65
HICKORY (1322 "Are You") 5-10 65
NEW PHOENIX ....8-12 '60s

MER-LYN

Singles: 7-inch

ABC-PAR (10660 "Promise") 5-10 65

MERRELL & EXILES
(Merrell & Xiles)

Singles: 7-inch

GLENN (426 "Tomorrow's Girl") 30-40 67
GOLDEN CROWN (102 "That's All I Want from You") 20-30 65
INTERLUDE (317 "Sorry for Yourself") 15-25 65

LPs: 10/12-inch

AMERICAN SOUND (1000 "The Early Years: 1964-1967") 20-40 94
Members; Merrell Fankhauser; Dan Parrish; Bill Dodd; Dick Lee.
Also see FANKHAUSER, Merrell

MERRIAM, Chuck

Singles: 7-inch

CAMEO (301 "Broken Glass") 5-10 64

MERRIL, Lee

Singles: 7-inch

BOOM (60003 "Boys from Madrid") 5-10 66
BOOM (60013 "Green Hornet") 5-10 66

Picture Sleeves

BOOM 10-15 66

MERRILL, Adgis

Singles: 7-inch

RON TODD (102 "Close to My Heart") 15-25 59

MERRILL, Bob

Singles: 7-inch

ROULETTE (4043 "Nairobi") 5-10 58
ROULETTE (4085 "Swimmin' Suit") 5-10 58

MERRILL, Bobby "Mr. Blues"

Singles: 7-inch

BARGAIN (5002 "I Ain't Mad at You") 10-20 61

MERRILL, Helen

Singles: 78 rpm

MERCURY 5-10 56

Singles: 7-inch

ATCO (6159 "You Don't Know") 5-10 60
MERCURY (70798 "Love Comes") 8-12 56
MERCURY (70844 "Anything Goes") 8-12 56

LPs: 10/12-inch

ATCO (112 "American Country Songs") ...10-15 59
EMARCY (36006 "Helen Merrill") 15-25 54
METRO JAZZ (1010 "You've Got a Date with the Blues") 10-15 59

MERRILL, Jimmy

Singles: 7-inch

QUALITY (1239 "A Woman's Mind") 50-75

MERRILL, Ray
(With the Musical Merrills)

Singles: 78 rpm

VITA (147 "Ooh What Santa Said") 8-12 56

Singles: 7-inch

VITA (147 "Ooh What Santa Said") 15-25 56
VITA (159 "Big Deal") 15-25 57

MERRILL, Roy

Singles: 7-inch

TOP RANK (3006 "Teenage Love") 8-12 61

MERRILL, Toni

Singles: 7-inch

SAFARI (1005/1006 "You Can Make Things Right"/"Ba Dum, Ba Dum") 20-30 58

MERRILL BROTHERS

Singles: 7-inch

GM (102 "Mercy Blues") 20-40

MERRI-MEN

Singles: 7-inch

APT (25051 "Big Daddy") 10-20 60
Also see HALEY, Bill

MERRITT, Gaye, & Elligibles

Singles: 7-inch

PILLAR (1 "This Is the Kiss") 50-75 59

MERRITT, Jerry
(With the Crowns; with Royal Crowns; with John Ballard)

Singles: 7-inch

AMERICAN 5-10 65
LAVENDER 10-15 61-62
SCORPIO 4-6 68
SMART 4-8 67
TELL INT'L (300 series) 5-10 67-68
TELL INT'L (400 series) 3-5 85

Picture Sleeves

LAVENDER (1676 "Bass Fever") 15-25 62
Also see CARTER, Dean
Also see VINCENT, Gene

MERRITT, Little Jimmie
(With Cuba Sanchez Orchestra)

Singles: 78 rpm

CASH (1025 "Sharecropper") 10-15 56

Singles: 7-inch

CASH (1025 "Sharecropper") 20-30 56
KRC (5004 "Fancy Free") 30-50 59

MERRITT, Neal

Singles: 78 rpm

SARG 5-10 54-55

Singles: 7-inch

BOONE (1053 "Ain't Love a Hurtin' Thing") 5-10 67
MANCO (1014 "Stop Talking") 5-10 61
MANCO (1027 "Is This Love") 5-10 62
MANCO (1040 "No Longer in My Heart") ...5-10 62
SARG 10-15 54-55

MERRITT, Terry, & Normanaires

Singles: 78 rpm

SEGER (7005 "Alone Again") 50-75 52

Singles: 7-inch

SEGER (7005 "Alone Again") 200-300 52
Also see NORMANAIRES

MERRY ELVES

Singles: 7-inch

ARGUS (250 "Rock and Roll Around the Christmas Tree") 8-12 64
Members (Elves): Milton; Sleepy; Ringo.

MERRY-GO-ROUND *P&R/LP '67*

Singles: 7-inch

A&M 5-10 67-69

LPs: 10/12-inch

A&M (4132 "Merry-Go-Round") 20-30 67
RHINO 5-8 85
Members: Emitt Rhodes; Joel Larson; Gary Kato; Bill Reinhart.
Also see GRASS ROOTS
Also see LEAVES

MERRYLANDERS

Singles: 7-inch

MERGER (100 "Rattlesnake") 10-20 60

MERRYWEATHER, Neil *LP '69*
(With Friends; Merryweather)

Singles: 7-inch

CAPITOL 4-6 69
KENT (4520 "Are You Ready") 4-6 70

LPs: 10/12-inch

CAPITOL 10-20 69
MERCURY 10-15 74-75
Also see GOLDBERG, Barry / Harvey Mandell / Charlie Musselwhite / Neil Merryweather
Also see MASON, Dave
Also see MILLER, Steve

MERSEY BEATS OF LIVERPOOL
(Merseybeats)

LPs: 10/12-inch

ARC INT'L (834 "England's Best Sellers") 25-35 64
Also see MERSEYBEATS

MERSEY LADS

Singles: 7-inch

MGM (13481 "Johnny No Love") 8-12 66

MERSEY MEN

Singles: 7-inch

WILD WOODS (2001 "I Can Tell") ....20-30 '60s

MERSEY SOUNDS

Singles: 7-inch

MONTEL (966 "Get on Your Honda and Ride") 5-10 66

MERSEYBEATS

Singles: 7-inch

FONTANA 5-10 64-65

LPs: 10/12-inch

ARC INT'L (834 "England's Best Sellers") 25-35 64
Members: Bill Kinsley; John Banks; Aaron Williams; Tony Crane; Peter Clarke; John Gustafson.
Also see MERSEY BEATS OF LIVERPOOL

MERSEYBOYS

LPs: 10/12-inch

VEE-JAY (1101 "15 Greatest Songs of the Beatles") 35-45 64
(Monaural.)
VEE-JAY (1101 "15 Greatest Songs of the Beatles") 40-60 64
(Stereo.)
VEE-JAY (1101 "15 Greatest Songs of the Beatles") 50-75 64
(White label. Promotional issue only.)

MESMERIZING EYE

LPs: 10/12-inch

SMASH (27090 "Psychedelia – A Musical Light Show") 20-30 67
(Monaural.)
SMASH (67090 "Psychedelia – A Musical Light Show") 25-35 67
(Stereo.)

MESSENGERS

Singles: 7-inch

BEAM (700 "Don't Cha Quit School") 10-15 64
ERA (3143 "Let Me Be Your Man") 5-10 65
MGM (13293 "I'm Stealin' Back") 5-10 64
MGM (13346 "When Did You Leave Heaven") 5-10 65
NEWGET (700 "Don't Cha Quit School"). 15-25 61

MESSENGERS

Singles: 7-inch

SOMA (1427 "My Baby") 30-50 65
Members: Greg Jeresek; Greg Bambenek; Roy Burger; Chip Andrus; Mike Murphy.

MESSENGERS *P&R '71*

Singles: 7-inch

HOME MADE (01 "Right On") 15-25 69
RARE EARTH (5032 "That's the Way a Woman Is") 4-6 71
USA (866 "Midnight Hour"/"Hard Hard Year") 10-15 67
(Reissued, with a different flip, by Michael & the Messengers.)

LPs: 10/12-inch

RARE EARTH (509 "Messengers") 10-12 69
(Standard cover.)
RARE EARTH (509 "Messengers") 20-30 69
(Rounded-top cover. Promotional issue.)
Members: Greg Jennings [Jeresek]; Jesse Roe; Peter Barans; Jeff Taylor; Rob Leslie; Augie Jurishica; John Hoier; Michael Morgan; Mike Demling; Bob Cavallo.
Also see MICHAEL & MESSENGERS

MESSER, Richard, & Question Marks

Singles: 7-inch

CINCY (104 "Sad Sack") 15-20

MESSINA, Jim *LP '79*
(With the Jesters; Jimmy Messina)

Singles: 7-inch

AUDIO FIDELITY (098 "Strange Man") 15-25 64
COLUMBIA 4-6 79-80
VIV 10-15
W.B. 3-5 81-83

LPs: 10/12-inch

AUDIO FIDELITY (7037 "Dragsters") 60-80 64
COLUMBIA 5-8 79
THIMBLE 10-12 73
W.B. 5-8 81-83
Also see BUFFALO SPRINGFIELD
Also see JESTERS
Also see LOGGINS & MESSINA
Also see POCO
Also see ULTIMATES
Also see YOUNG, Neil, & Jim Messina

MESSNER, Bud, & His Sky Line Boys *C&W '50*

Singles: 78 rpm

ABBEY 10-15 50

Singles: 7-inch

ABBEY (15004 "Slippin' Around with Jole Blon") 20-30 50

METALLICA *LP '84*

Singles: 7-inch

ELEKTRA (Except 69357) 3-5 88-89
ELEKTRA (69357 "Eye of the Beholder") ..5-10 88

Picture Sleeves

ELEKTRA (Except 69357) 3-5 88-89
ELEKTRA (69357 "Eye of the Beholder") 10-15 88

LPs: 10/12-inch

ELEKTRA (Except 60757) 5-10 84-89
ELEKTRA (60757 "Garage Days Revisited") 25-50 87
MEGAFORCE 12-25 84-86
Members: James Hetfield; Kirk Hammett; Lars Ulrich; Cliff Burton; Jason Newsted.

METALLICS

Singles: 7-inch

BARONET (2 "Need Your Love") 40-60 62
(No ribbon shown on label.)
BARONET (2 "Need Your Love") 10-15 62
(Ribbon shown on label.)
BARONET (14 "Drop By") 30-50 62
(No ribbon shown on label.)
BARONET (14 "Drop By") 10-15 62
(Ribbon shown on label.)
BARONET (16 "Let Me Love You") 30-40 62
BARONET (18 "It Hurts Me") 30-40 62

METAPHORS

Singles: 7-inch

RAD ("Come On Baby") ....30-40 '60s
(Selection number not known.)

METCALFE, Ronn
Singles: 7-inch
DUNES (2011 "Big Band Twist")................5-10 62

METEORS
Singles: 7-inch
AXE (1302 "El Paso Guitar") 15-25 58
AXE (1313 "The Death of Geronimo") 15-25 58

METEORS
Singles: 7-inch
PIXIE (7411 "Don't Hurt Me No More").... 20-30 61

METEORS
Singles: 7-inch
BELTONE (2041 "Let's Start Anew") ... 300-400 63
(Black vinyl.)
BELTONE (2041 "Let's Start Anew") ... 500-750 63
(Brown vinyl.)

METERS *P&R/R&B/LP '69*
Singles: 7-inch
JOSIE 5-10 68-71
REPRISE...5-10 74-76
SANSU 4-6
W.B. 4-6 77
LPs: 10/12-inch
ISLAND (9250 "Cissy Strut") 10-15 75
JOSIE (4010 "The Meters") 50-75 69
JOSIE (4011 "Look-Ka Py Py") 50-75 70
JOSIE (4012 "Struttin' ") 50-75 70
REPRISE (2076 "Cabbage Alley") 75-100 72
REPRISE (2200 "Rejuvenation") 50-75 74
VIRGO (6005 "Sophisticated Cissy") 10-20 73
VIRGO (12002 "Best of the Meters") 10-20 75
W.B. (3042 "New Directions") 10-15 77
Members: Arthur Neville; Leo Nocentelli; George Porter; Joe Modeliste.
Also see NEVILLE BROTHERS

METER-TONES
Singles: 7-inch
JAX (1002 "Talk to Me") 50-60 59

METHENY BROTHERS
Singles: 7-inch
RENNER (270 "It's Only Love") 5-10 65

METHUSELAH
LPs: 10/12-inch
ELEKTRA 10-15 69

METIS, Frank
Singles: 7-inch
MAYFLOWER (13 "Black Smoke").............5-10 60
MAYFLOWER (14 "Open House")..............5-10 60
Also see STARR, Randy, & Frank Metis

METOYER, Herb
LPs: 10/12-inch
VERVE FOLKWAYS (9012 "Something New").. 12-15 65

METRICS
Singles: 7-inch
CHADWICK (101 "I Found You") 50-100 64

METRO-CHORDS
Singles: 7-inch
ADMIRAL (300 "It's a Shame")............ 100-200 61

METRONOMES
(With the Dave McRae Orchestra.)
Singles: 78 rpm
CADENCE (1310 "I Love My Girl") 25-35 57
CADENCE (1339 "How Much I Love You") 40-60 57
Singles: 7-inch
CADENCE (1310 "I Love My Girl") 25-35 57
CADENCE (1339 "How Much I Love You") 40-60 57
Member: Harold Wright.
Also see DIAMONDS
Also see REGALS

METRONOMES
Singles: 7-inch
BROADCAST (1131 "Blue")..................... 15-25 75
RIVERSIDE (4523 "Back Door Blues").. 80-100 62
EPs: 7-inch
WYNNE (101 "The Metronomes")........... 40-60 60
LPs: 10/12-inch
JAZZLAND (3978 "The Metronomes")..... 40-60 56
WYNNE (WLP-106 "And Now...the Metronomes")......................................50-100 60
(Monaural.)
WYNNE (WLPS-106 "And Now...the Metronomes")....................................200-300 60
(Stereo.)
Also see BUCCANEERS

METRONOMES
Singles: 7-inch
CHALLENGE (9157 "Tears Tears Tears")..10-20 62
MAUREEN (1000 "My Dearest Darling")..20-30 62
Also see ELLIS, Shirley

METROPOLITANS
Singles: 7-inch
JUNIOR (395 "So Much in Love")............15-25 58

METROS
Singles: 7-inch
JUST (1502 "All of My Life")................150-250 59
(Blue label.)
JUST (1502 "All of My Life")................100-200 59
(White label.)

METROS *P&R/R&B '67*
Singles: 7-inch
1-2-3 (1720 "If You Can Tell") 5-10 69
RCA (8994 "Sweetest One")....................10-15 66
RCA (9159 "Since I Found My Baby")......70-90 67
RCA (9333 "Let's Groove")......................20-30 67
LPs: 10/12-inch
RCA (3776 "Sweetest One")....................15-25 67

METROTONES
Singles: 78 rpm
COLUMBIA...5-10 55
Singles: 7-inch
COLUMBIA...10-15 55
EPs: 7-inch
COLUMBIA (2026/2027 "Tops in Rock and Roll")..15-25 55
(Price is for either of two volumes.)
LPs: 10/12-inch
COLUMBIA (6341 "Tops in Rock and Roll")..30-40 55
(10-inch LP.)

METROTONES
(With the Little Walkin' Willie Quartet)
Singles: 7-inch
RESERVE (114 "More & More")..........150-250 57
(Same number also used for a Tracey Twins release.)
RESERVE (116 "Please Come Back").150-250 57
Members: Sonny Turner; Melvin Smith; James Frierson; Leonard Veal; Leuvenia Eaton.
Also see HESITATIONS
Also see PLATTERS
Also see TRACEY TWINS

MEYER, Chuck
Singles: 7-inch
VALENTINE (1002 "An Hour Away")........30-50

MEYERS, Augie *C&W '88*
(Augie)
Singles: 7-inch
ATLANTIC AMERICA.................................3-5 88
AXBAR 3-5 83
PARAMOUNT..4-6 73
TEXAS RE-CORD CO.................................4-6 75-79
SUPER BEET (Except 102) 3-5 87
SUPER BEET (102 "Velma from Selma") ..5-10 87
SUPER BEET (102 "Mathilda")..................3-5 87
(Same number used twice.)
VOL..4-8 68
LPs: 10/12-inch
ATLANTIC AMERICA.................................5-8 88
PARAMOUNT..15-20 73
POLYDOR...10-20 71
SUPER BEET..5-8 87
TEXAS RE-CORD CO..............................10-15 75-77
Also see COPELAND, Johnny
Also see EZBA, Danny
Also see LEWIS, Jerry Lee
Also see LONG, Joey
Also see MEYERS, Bernie
Also see NELSON, Willie
Also see SIR DOUGLAS QUINTET
Also see VINCENT, Gene

MEYERS, Bernie
(Augie Meyers)
Singles: 7-inch
JET STREAM (1 "As the World Turns Around")..10-20 62
Also see MEYERS, Augie

MEYERS, Brad, & Citations
Singles: 7-inch
SARA (101 "Just for You") 15-25 64
Also see CITATIONS

MEYERS, Jerry
Singles: 7-inch
GES (0880 "Teen Age Heart")..................40-50 59
VASSAR (309 "Honey Bun")....................50-75 60

MEYERS, Jimmy
Singles: 78 rpm
FORTUNE...10-20 52
Singles: 7-inch
FORTUNE (162 "Drunk Man's Wiggle")...40-60 52
FORTUNE (211 "Pretty Baby Rock") ...100-200 60
FORTUNE (212 "Oh Baby Babe")...........50-75 60
FORTUNE (214 "Bouncy")......................10-15 61

MEYERS, Johnny
Singles: 7-inch
INSTANT (3243 "Lonely Fool")...................5-10 62
INSTANT (3249 "Waiter")...........................5-10 62
PEACOCK (1954 "T.C.B.")...........................4-8 67
SPINETT (1004 "Laughing")........................5-10 60

MEYERS, Louie, & Aces
Singles: 78 rpm
ABCO (104 "Just Wailin' ") 20-40 56
Singles: 7-inch
ABCO (104 "Just Wailin' ") 50-75 56

MIAMI SOUND MACHINE *P&R/R&B/D&D/LP '85*
(Gloria Estefan & Miami Sound Machine)
Singles: 12-inch
EPIC 4-6 84-88
Singles: 7-inch
EPIC 3-5 84-88
Picture Sleeves
EPIC 3-5 85-88
LPs: 10/12-inch
AUDIOFON (5426 "Live Again, Renacher") 25-50 77
EPIC 5-8 84-88
Members: Gloria Estefan (née Fajardo); Merci Navarro; Marcos Avila; Emilio Estefan Jr.; Kiki Garcia.

MIAMIANS
Singles: 7-inch
AMP 3 (1005 "Call Me a Coward") 10-20 58

MICHAEL
Singles: 7-inch
ROULETTE (4735 "Gotta Make My Heart Turn Away")...5-10 67

MICHAEL, Al, & Medallions
Singles: 7-inch
BRAGG (222 "I Wanna Talk to You") 15-25

MICHAEL, Spike
Singles: 7-inch
CUCA (1151 "Billy Boy") 10-15 63

MICHAEL, Teddy Lee
Singles: 7-inch
FLEETWOOD (7001 "My Love Is Yours")...150-250 63

MICHAEL & CONTINENTALS
Singles: 7-inch
AUDIO FIDELITY (139 "Little School Girl")...10-20 68

MICHAEL & MAJESTICS
Singles: 7-inch
RAY (1 "I've Got an Angel") 30-40

MICHAEL & MESSENGERS
Singles: 7-inch
SOUL (35037 "California Soul")..................8-10 67
USA (866 "Midnight Hour"/"Up Till News").8-12 67
(First issued, with a different flip, by the Messengers.)
USA (874 "Lies")...8-10 67
USA (889 "Run and Hide")..........................8-10 67
USA (897 "I Need Her Here")......................8-10 68
Members: Jack DeCarolis; Ron Gagnon; Paul Cosenza; Ken Menehan; Jerry Goodman; Tom Fini.
Also see MESSENGERS

MICHAEL & RAYMOND
Singles: 7-inch
RCA (9244 "Walking the Dog")................15-25 67

MICHAELS, Dick
(With the Serenaders)
Singles: 7-inch
BANYAN (198 "Goodbye to Yesterday")....5-10 66
CROSS COUNTRY (1820 "How Do You Mend a Broken Heart") 15-25 59
EXPLOSIVE (101 "Teenage Blues")..........8-12 61
KENT (425 "Timin' Man")...........................5-10 65

MICHAELS, Jerri
Singles: 7-inch
CAMEO (414 "Give It All to Me") 5-10 66

MICHAELS, Joey
Singles: 7-inch
ARCADE (150 "16 Cats")........................50-100 58

MICHAELS, Johnny "Mad Man"
Singles: 7-inch
MICHAELS (1194 "Czarnina Kid")...........15-25 54
RAYNARD (8838 "Qwiazdop") 15-25 55

MICHAELS, Lee *LP '69*
Singles: 7-inch
A&M...4-6 67-71
COLUMBIA..4-6 73
Picture Sleeves
A&M...4-6 70-71
LPs: 10/12-inch
A&M (Except 3158 & 4140) 10-15 67-73
A&M (3158 "Lee Michaels").......................5-8 82
A&M (4140 "Carnival of Life")..................15-25 67
COLUMBIA...10-12 73-75
Promotional LPs
COLUMBIA ("In Hawaii")..........................35-45 75

MICHAELS, Lindy
LPs: 10/12-inch
VAULT (123 "Ragamuffin Child").............10-15 69

MICHAELS, Marilyn
Singles: 7-inch
RCA (7771 "Tell Tommy I Miss Him") 10-15 60

MICHAELS, Mickey
Singles: 7-inch
FELSTED (8509 "Always") 8-12 58

MICHAELS, Tony
(Tony Micale)
Singles: 7-inch
DEBBIE..4-8
GOLDEN WORLD (41 "I Love the Life I Live")..10-20 66
Also see REFLECTIONS

MICHEL, George
Singles: 7-inch
JANSON (6001 "Another Start")..............20-30
NEW VOICE (802 "Gotta Be Right Some Time")..5-10 65

MICK, Fred
Singles: 7-inch
HILLTOP (1876 "Daddy-O Goose")..........40-60 62

MICK & SHAMBLES
Singles: 7-inch
VERVE FOLKWAYS (5010 "Lonely Nights Again")..8-12 66

MICKEY & BONNIE
Singles: 7-inch
JERDEN (723 "Ma, He's Making Eyes At Me") 5-10 63

MICKEY & KITTY
Singles: 7-inch
ATLANTIC (2024 "Ooh-Sha-La-La") 10-15 59
ATLANTIC (2036 "First Love")..................10-15 59
ATLANTIC (2046 "Buttercup")..................10-15 59
Members: Mickey Baker; Kitty Noble.
Also see BAKER, Mickey

MICKEY & MIKES
Singles: 7-inch
BELL (750 "Little Green Apples") 5-10 68

MICKEY & SOUL GENERATION
Singles: 7-inch
MAXWELL (806 "Joint Session")..............10-15 70

MICKEY & SYLVIA R&B '56
("Little" Sylvia Vanderpool & Mickey Baker)
Singles: 78 rpm
CAT (102 "Fine Love")... 10-20 54
GROOVE (0164 "No Good Lover")... 25-35 56
GROOVE (0175 "Love Is Strange")... 35-55 56
RAINBOW... 10-20 55
VIK (Except 0267)... 10-20 57
VIK (0267 "There Ought to Be a Law")... 35-45 57
Singles: 7-inch
ALL PLATINUM (2307 "Because You")... 5-8 68
ALL PLATINUM (2310 "Anytime")... 5-8 69
CAT (102 "Fine Love")... 25-35 54
GROOVE (0164 "No Good Lover")... 25-35 56
GROOVE (0175 "Love Is Strange")... 25-35 56
KING (6006 "Love Is Strange")... 5-10 65
RCA (0080 "Love Is Strange")... 4-6 73
RCA (7403 "To the Valley")... 10-15 58
RCA (47-7774 "Sweeter As the Day Goes By")... 10-15 60
RCA (61-7774 "Sweeter As the Day Goes By")... 20-30 60
(Stereo.)
RCA (47-7811 "What Would I Do")... 10-15 60
RCA (61-7811 "What Would I Do")... 20-40 60
(Stereo.)
RCA (37-7877 "Love Lesson")... 20-40 61
(Compact 33 Single.)
RCA (47-7877 "Love Lesson")... 8-12 61
RCA (8517 "Let's Shake Some More")... 8-10 65
RCA (8582 "From the Beginning of Time")... 8-10 65
RAINBOW (316 "I'm So Glad")... 20-30 55
RAINBOW (318 "Rise Sally Rise")... 15-25 55
RAINBOW (330 "Where Is My Honey")... 15-25 55
STANG (5004 "Rocky Raccoon")... 4-8 69
STANG (5047 "Baby, You're So Fine")... 4-8 73
VIK (0252 "Love Is Strange")... 15-25 57
VIK (0267 "There Ought to Be a Law")... 15-25 57
VIK (0280 "Love Will Make You Fail in School")... 15-25 57
VIK (0290 "Love Is a Treasure")... 15-25 57
VIK (0297 "There'll Be No Backing Out"). 15-25 57
VIK (0324 "Bewildered")... 15-25 58
VIK (0334 "True, True Love")... 15-25 58
WILLOW (23000 "Baby, You're So Fine". 10-15 61
WILLOW (23002 "Darling")... 10-15 61
WILLOW (23004 "Since I Fell for You")... 10-15 62
WILLOW (23006 "Love Is Strange")... 10-15 62
(Overdubbed reissue of the Groove release.)
EPs: 7-inch
GROOVE (18 "Love Is Strange")... 50-100 57
VIK (262 "Mickey and Sylvia")... 40-60 57
LPs: 10/12-inch
CAMDEN (863 "Love Is Strange")... 35-50 65
RCA (0327 "Do It Again")... 15-20 73
VIK (1102 "New Sounds")... 200-300 57
Members: Mickey Baker; Sylvia Vanderpool.
Session: King Curtis.
Also see BAKER, Mickey
Also see KING CURTIS
Also see LITTLE SYLVIA
Also see MEDLEY, Bill, & Jennifer Warnes / Mickey & Sylvia
Also see MICKEY & KITTY

MICKLE, Elmon
(With His Rhythm Aces)
Singles: 7-inch
E.M. (132 "Short 'N' Fat")... 50-75 59
E.M. (132 "Jackson Blues")... 40-60 59
ELKO (003 "Flatfoot Sam")... 40-60 59
J. GEMS (1908 "Independent Walk")... 25-35 59
Also see DRIFTIN' SLIM
Also see MODEL T. SLIM

MID AMERICANS
Singles: 7-inch
PABLO (7014 "Lonely Surfer")... 25-35 62
(First issue.)
TEARDROP (3103 "Lonely Surfer")... 15-25 62

MID AMERICANS / Bonnie & Treasures
Singles: 7-inch
PABLO (7014 "Lonely Surfer")... 20-25 '60s
Also see BONNIE & TREASURES
Also see MID AMERICANS

MIDDLETON, Gary
Singles: 7-inch
HARLEM (102 "Don'T Be Shy")... 100-200 59

MIDDLETON, Rex
(Red Middleton's Hi-Fi's; with the Art Foxall Combo)
Singles: 7-inch
CAM (100-14 "Wow")... 40-60 54
(Identification number shown since no selection number is used.)
LPs: 10/12-inch
VERVE/CLEF (2035 "Rex Middleton's Hi-Fi's")... 150-250 57

MIDDLETON, Tony
(With the Willows; with Dave Rhodes Orchestra & Chorus; with Hal Mooney & Orchestra)
Singles: 7-inch
A&M (1084 "Angelea")... 10-20 69
A&M (1123 "Harlem Lady")... 10-20 69
ABC-PAR (10695 "You Spoiled My Reputation")... 20-30 65
ALFA (113 "My Home Town")... 15-25 62
ALTO (2001 "I Need You")... 10-20 60
BIG TOP (3037 "Unchained Melody")... 15-25 60
ELDORADO (508 "First Taste of Love")... 15-25 57
GONE (5015 "Let's Fall in Love")... 75-100 57
MAGGIE (715 "I'm Jack and I'm Back")... 10-15 '60s
MALA (544 "Out of This World")... 10-20 66
MGM (13493 "To the Ends of the Earth"). 25-35 66
MR. G (811 "Let Me Down Easy")... 5-10 68
MR. G (815 "Good Morning World")... 5-10 68
PHILIPS (40151 "Send Me Away")... 8-12 63
PHILIPS (40184 "Too Hot to Handle")... 8-12 64
ROULETTE (4345 "I'm Gonna Try Love")... 15-25 61
SAXONY (104 "I'm On My Way")... 40-60 58
SCEPTER (12290 "Border Song")... 4-6 70
TRIUMPH (600 "Count Your Blessings"). 20-30 59
TRIUMPH (605 "The Universe")... 20-30 59
U.A. (410 "Drifting")... 125-175 62
Also see FIVE WILLOWS
Also see WILLOWS

MIDKNIGHTS
Singles: 7-inch
STYLE (2001 "Pain")... 15-25 66

MID-KNIGHTERS
Singles: 7-inch
KEY (1003 "Baby My Heart")... 15-25 61
PARAGON (814 "Charlena")... 20-30 62
Members: Jimmy Rosetti; Keith Dreher; Charlie Lewondowski; Bill Hakow; Mel Lundie; Johnny Verbraken.

MIDNIGHT ANGELS
Singles: 7-inch
APEX (77073 "I'm Sufferin'")... 15-25 67
Picture Sleeves
APEX (77073 "I'm Sufferin'")... 25-35 67

MIDNIGHT MAIL
Singles: 7-inch
AUDIO ARTS (60003 "I Can't Get It")... 10-20 '60s
Member: Jim Webb.
Also see WEBB, Jimmy

MIDNIGHT SHIFT
Singles: 7-inch
MSI (1001 "Every Day Without You")... 25-50

MIDNIGHT SONS
Singles: 7-inch
JERDEN ("Draft Time Blues")... 5-10 66
(Selection number not known.)
KG (100 "Draft Time Blues")... 10-15

MIDNIGHT SUN
Singles: 7-inch
SONIC (5476 "I'll Find a Way")... 10-20 68

MIDNIGHTERS R&B '54
("The Midnighters, Formerly the Royals.")
Singles: 78 rpm
FEDERAL... 25-50 54-57
Singles: 7-inch
FEDERAL (12169 "Work with Me Annie")... 100-150 54
(Silver top label.)
FEDERAL (12169 "Work with Me Annie")... 50-75 55
(Green label.)
FEDERAL (12177 "Give It Up")... 50-100 54
FEDERAL (12185 "Sexy Ways")... 50-100 54
FEDERAL (12195 "Annie Had a Baby"). 50-100 54
FEDERAL (12200 "Annie's Aunt Fannie")... 50-100 54
FEDERAL (12202 "Tell Them")... 50-100 54
FEDERAL (12205 "Moonrise")... 50-100 54
FEDERAL (12210 "Ashamed of Myself")... 50-100 55
FEDERAL (12220 "Switchie, Witchie, Titchie")... 50-100 55
FEDERAL (12224 "Henry's Got Flat Feet")... 50-100 55
FEDERAL (12227 "It's Love Baby")... 50-100 55
FEDERAL (12230 "Give It Up")... 30-50 55
FEDERAL (12240 "That House on the Hill")... 50-100 55
FEDERAL (12243 "Don't Change Your Pretty Ways")... 50-100 55
FEDERAL (12251 "Partners for Life")... 50-100 56
FEDERAL (12260 "Rock Granny Roll").. 50-100 56
FEDERAL (12270 "Tore Up Over You")... 50-75 56
FEDERAL (12285 "Come on and Get It"). 50-75 56
FEDERAL (12288 "Let Me Hold Your Hand")... 50-75 56
FEDERAL (12293 "In the Doorway Crying")... 50-75 57
FEDERAL (12299 "Oh So Happy")... 40-60 57
FEDERAL (12305 "Let 'Em Roll")... 40-60 57
FEDERAL (12317 "Stay By My Side")... 40-60 58
FEDERAL (12339 "Baby Please")... 40-60 58
Members: Henry Booth; Hank Ballard; Sonny Woods; Charles Sutton; Lawson Smith; Alonzo Tucker.
Also see BALLARD, Hank, & Midnighters
Also see BOOTH, Henry
Also see JOHN, Little Willie / 5 Royales / Earl (Connelly) King / Midnighters
Also see ROYALS

MIDNIGHTERS
Singles: 7-inch
LUCKY STAR (100 "Rock These Blues Away")... 15-25 59

MIDNIGHTERS
Singles: 7-inch
20TH FOX (182 "Road Home")... 10-15 60

MIDNIGHTERS
Singles: 7-inch
SARG (187 "Rockin' Romance")... 50-75 61

MIDNIGHTERS
Singles: 7-inch
CAPITOL (4981 "The Big Surfer")... 10-15 63
Member: Dave Aerni.

MIDNIGHTERS
Singles: 7-inch
BARRY (3028 "Slow Walk")... 15-25 '60s
(Canadian.)
RCA (3308 "Goofy Foot")... 10-20 63
(Canadian.)
Also see RONNIE & COMETS

MIDNIGHTS
Singles: 78 rpm
MUSIC CITY... 30-60 54
Singles: 7-inch
MUSIC CITY (746 "Annie Pulled a Hum-Bug")... 50-75 54
MUSIC CITY (762 "She Left Me")... 40-50 54
(Black vinyl.)
MUSIC CITY (762 "She Left Me")... 75-125 54
(Red or blue vinyl.)

MID SOUTH SINGERS
Singles: 7-inch
DUKE (202 "See About Me")... 35-45 58

MIDWEST
Singles: 7-inch
METROBEAT (4460 "Alibis")... 8-12 68
Member: Danny Holien.
Also see SHADES

MIFFLIN TRIPLETS
Singles: 7-inch
EMBER (1045 "I Do")... 50-75 58
IMPACT (1003 "Rock a Baby Rock")... 5-10 65

MIGHTY ACCENTS
Singles: 7-inch
RODALA (69 "Sabre Stomp")... 15-25 63
Member: Ray Salaz.

MIGHTY BABY
LPs: 10/12-inch
HEAD (025 "Mighty Baby")... 35-50 69
Members: Reg King; Alan "Bam" King; Mike Evans; Martin Stone; Pete Watson; Roger Powell; Ian Whiteman.

MIGHTY DUKES
Singles: 78 rpm
DUKE (104 "No Other Love")... 50-100 52
Members: Billy Dawn Smith; Donny Miles; Tommy Smith; Sonny Benton.
Also see DAWN, Billy, Quartet
Also see DUKES

MIGHTY FIVE
Singles: 7-inch
FLEETWOOD (1000 "Daddy Guitar")... 10-15 58

MIGHTY HANNIBAL R&B '66
(James T. Shaw)
Singles: 7-inch
DECCA (31876 "I Found a Way")... 8-12 65
DECCA (31955 "Get Back")... 8-12 66
JOSIE (964 "Hymn No. 5")... 10-15 66
(First issue.)
JOSIE (977 "Shame, Shame")... 8-12 67
KENT (397 "Come Back")... 8-12 64
LOMA (2093 "Get in the Groove")... 8-12 68
LOMA (2103 "Good Time")... 8-12 68
SHURFINE (021 "Hymn No. 5")... 8-12 66
Also see HANNIBAL

MIGHTY JUPITERS
Singles: 7-inch
WARNER RECORDS (1020 "Your Love")... 100-150 59

MIGHTY MANFRED & WONDERDOGS
Singles: 7-inch
ATCO (6823 "You Can, I Can")... 4-8 71
PARIS TOWER (140 "Bo Diddley")... 15-25 68

MIGHTY SPARROW
LPs: 10/12-inch
RCA (3006 "Sparrow Come Back")... 15-25 62
W.B. (2771 "Hot & Sweet")... 8-12 74

MIGHTY VIKINGS
Singles: 7-inch
WINCOX (7 "Your Love Is Mine")... 40-60

MIKE & DEAN
Singles: 7-inch
BUDWEISER (8246 "Budweiser Fight Song"/"Be True to Your Bud")... 35-45 83
(Add $8 to $12 if accompanied by two Mike & Dean posters and a story insert. Promotional issue only.)
HITBOUND... 10-20 82
PREMORE (23/24 "Da Doo Ron Ron"/"Baby Talk")... 20-30 83
Picture Sleeves
PREMORE (23/24 "Da Doo Ron Ron"/"Baby Talk")... 20-30 83
LPs: 10/12-inch
PREMORE (983 "Rock'n Roll Again")... 30-50 83
(Also has tracks by the Association, Rip Chords, and Paul Revere & Raiders.)
PREMORE (3009 "Rock'n Roll City")... 30-50 83
(Also has tracks by other artists.)
Members: Mike Love; Dean Torrence.
Also see ASSOCIATION
Also see JAN & DEAN
Also see LOVE, Mike, & Dean Torrence / Paul Revere & Raiders
Also see RIPCHORDS

MIKE & JAYS
Singles: 7-inch
DOYL (1001 "Dingle Dangle Doll")... 75-100 60
(Reissued as by Ron Bennet.)
Also see BENNET, Ron

MIKE & JOKERS
Singles: 7-inch
CHASE (6000 "There's Got to Be a Girl")... 20-30
CHASE (6001 "Bound for Love")... 15-25

MIKE & MODIFIERS
Singles: 7-inch
GORDY (7006 "I Found Myself a Brand New Baby")... 20-30 62
Member: Mike Valvano.

MIKE & RAVENS
Singles: 7-inch
EMPIRE (1 "Mr. Heartbreak")... 10-15 62

MIKE & UTOPIANS
(Mike Lasman)
Singles: 7-inch
CEE=JAY (574 "Erlene"/"I Wish") 250-350 60
CEE=JAY (574 "Erlene"/"I Found a Penny") 100-200 60

MIKE, JOHN & BILL
Singles: 7-inch
OMNIBUS (239 "How Can You Kiss Me") 100-200 65
Members: Mike Nesmith; John London; Bill Sleeper.
Also see LEWIS & CLARKE
Also see NESMITH, Mike

MIKE'S MESSENGERS
Singles: 7-inch
EL-EZ-DE 10-20

MIKEL, J., & Hepcats
Singles: 7-inch
SONIC (1 "Bettyjean Rock") 600-800

MIKIE & ARDONS
Singles: 7-inch
GALLANT (3016 "Three's a Crowd") 40-50 64
MAM'SELLE 10-15 62
Session: Joe Bill Loudermilk.

MIKKELSEN, Don
(With the Birds; with Edell & the T-Birds)
Singles: 7-inch
DECK (600 "Chapel of Love") 40-50 59
IMPACT (15 "Now You're Gone") 15-25 63

MILAN
(Leather Boy Milan; World of Milan)
Singles: 7-inch
ABC-PAR (10718 "Cry, Lonely Boy") 10-15 65
BRUNSWICK (55292 "Follow the Sun") .. 10-15 66
BRUNSWICK (55298 "One Track Mind") 15-25 66
END (1123 "Innocence") 5-10 63
20TH FOX (487 "I Am What I Am") 10-15 64
20TH FOX (552 "Angel's Lullaby") 10-15 65
Also see LEATHER BOY

MILAN, Mickey
(With the Montclairs)
Singles: 7-inch
KARATE (538 "This Heart") 5-10 66
PHILLIPS INT'L (3533 "Somehow without You") 10-15 58

MILANO, Bobby
Singles: 78 rpm
CAPITOL 5-10 55
Singles: 7-inch
CAPITOL 10-15 55
CHALLENGE (59005 "Life Begins At Four O'Clock") 40-60 58
ROULETTE (4361 "Everybody Loves My Baby") 5-10 61
TIME (1019 "Ruby") 10-15 60
W.B. (5027 "Water Under the Bridge") 5-10 59

MILBURN, Amos *R&B '48*
(With the Aladdin Chickenshackers)
Singles: 78 rpm
ALADDIN 10-40 45-56
Singles: 7-inch
ALADDIN (3014 "Chicken-Shack Boogie") 400-500 48
ALADDIN (3018 "Bewildered") 300-400 48
ALADDIN (3023 "Hold Me Baby") 300-400 49
ALADDIN (3026 "In the Middle of the Night") 300-400 49
ALADDIN (3032 "Roomin' House Blues") 300-400 49
ALADDIN (3038 "Real Pretty Mama Blues") 300-400 49
ALADDIN (3043 "I'm Just a Fool in Love") 300-400 50
ALADDIN (3049 "Walkin' Blues") 300-400 50
ALADDIN (3056 "Anybody's Blues") 300-400 50
ALADDIN (3059 "Hard Luck Blues") 300-400 50
ALADDIN (3064 "Remember") 300-400 50
ALADDIN (3068 "Bad Bad Whiskey") .. 200-300 50
ALADDIN (3080 "Let's Rock Awhile") 50-75 51
ALADDIN (3090 "Everybody Clap Hands") 50-75 51
ALADDIN (3093 "Ain't Nothing Shaking") 50-75 51
ALADDIN (3105 "Boogie Woogie") 50-75 51
ALADDIN (3124 "Drinkin' and Thinkin'") .. 40-60 52
ALADDIN (3125 "Flying Home") 40-60 52
ALADDIN (3133 "Roll Mr. Jelly") 40-60 52
ALADDIN (3146 "Button Your Lip") 40-60 52
ALADDIN (3150 "Greyhound") 100-125 52
ALADDIN (3159 "Rock Rock Rock") 100-125 52
ALADDIN (3164 "Let Me Go Home, Whiskey") 50-75 53
ALADDIN (3168 "Please, Mr. Johnson") .. 50-75 53
ALADDIN (3197 "One Scotch, One Bourbon, One Beer") 50-75 53
ALADDIN (3218 "Good Good Whiskey") .. 50-75 53
ALADDIN (3226 "Rocky Mountain") 40-60 54
ALADDIN (3240 "Milk & Water") 40-60 54
ALADDIN (3248 "Glory of Love") 40-60 54
ALADDIN (3253 "Vicious Vicious Vodka") 40-60 54
ALADDIN (3269 "That's It") 40-60 54
ALADDIN (3281 "I Love You Anyway") 25-45 55
ALADDIN (3293 "My Happiness Depends on You") 25-45 55
ALADDIN (3306 "House Party") 25-45 55
ALADDIN (3320 "I Need Someone ") 25-35 56
ALADDIN (3332 "Chicken Shack Boogie") 35-45 56
ALADDIN (3340 "Girl of My Dreams") 20-40 56
ALADDIN (3363 "Run and Coca-Cola") 25-35 57
ALADDIN (3370 "Dear Angel") 20-40 57
ALADDIN (3383 "Thinking of You Baby") . 20-40 57
IMPERIAL 5-10 62
KING (5000 series) 5-10 60-61
KING (6000 series) 4-8 67
MOTOWN (1038 "My Baby Gave Me Another Chance") 15-25 63
MOTOWN (1046 "My Daily Prayer") 15-25 63
LPs: 10/12-inch
ALADDIN (704 "Rockin' the Boogie") 500-1000 55
(Black vinyl. 10-inch LP.)
ALADDIN (704 "Rockin' the Boogie") 2500-3500 55
(Red vinyl. 10-inch LP.)
ALADDIN (810 "Rockin' the Boogie") ... 300-500 56
IMPERIAL (9176 "Million Sellers") 100-200 62
MOSAIC (155 "Complete Aladdin Recordings of Amos Milburn") 140-150 90s
(Boxed 10-disc audiophile set. 3500 made.)
MOTOWN (608 "The Blues Boss") 500-750 63
SCORE (4012 "Let's Have a Party") 100-200 57
Also see BROWN, Charles, & Amos Milburn

MILBURN, Amos / Wynonie Harris / Velma Nelson / Crown Prince Waterford
LPs: 10/12-inch
ALADDIN (703 "Party After Hours"). 1000-1500 56
(Black vinyl. 10-inch LP.)
ALADDIN (703 "Party After Hours"). 3000-4000 56
(Red vinyl. 10-inch LP.)
Also see HARRIS, Wynonie
Also see MILBURN, Amos
Also see WATERFORD, Crown Prince

MILBURN, Amos, Jr.
Singles: 7-inch
BROWNFIELD 5-10 65
HOLLYWOOD (1124 "Gloria") 4-8 68
LE CAM (947 "Dance Her By Me") 5-10 62
SHALIMAR (105 "Gloria") 8-12 63
Session: Ron-Dels.
Also see RON-DELS

MILE, Chuck, & Styles
Singles: 7-inch
DORE (630 "Be Mine Or Be a Fool") 75-125 62

MILE ENDS
Singles: 7-inch
5TH ESTATE (8447 "Bottle Up and Go") . 15-25 '60s

MILEM, Percy
Singles: 7-inch
GOLDWAX (315 "Cry Cry Baby") 5-10 67
GOLDWAX (326 "She's About a Mover") ... 5-10 67

MILES, Buddy *P&R/LP '69*
(Buddy Miles Express; with Freedom Express)
Singles: 7-inch
CASABLANCA 4-6 75-76
COLUMBIA 4-6 73-74
MERCURY 4-8 68-72
Picture Sleeves
MERCURY 4-8
LPs: 10/12-inch
CASABLANCA 8-10 75
COLUMBIA 8-12 73-74
MERCURY 10-15 68-72
Also see FIDELITYS
Also see HENDRIX, Jimi

MILES, Garry *P&R '60*
(With the Statues; with Buzzettes; Gary Miles; Buzz Cason)
Singles: 7-inch
LIBERTY (54564 "Look for a Star") 5-10 68
LIBERTY (55261 "Look for a Star") 10-15 60
LIBERTY (55279 "Dream Girl") 10-15 60
LIBERTY (55596 "Candy") 10-15 63
LIBERTY (55685 "What's New") 10-15 64
LIBERTY (55714 "Ecstacy") 10-15 64
LIBERTY (55738 "How Are Things in Paradise") 10-20 64
Picture Sleeves
LIBERTY (55261 "Look for a Star") 10-20 60
EPs: 7-inch
LIBERTY (1005 "Look for a Star") 50-75 60
Also see STATUES

MILES, Jackie
(With Dick Jacobs Orchestra)
Singles: 78 rpm
CORAL (61249 "I'm a Rollin' ") 5-10 54
Singles: 7-inch
CORAL (61249 "I'm a Rollin' ") 10-20 54
LPs: 10/12-inch
IMPERIAL (9154 "120 Pounds Dripping Wet") 15-25 61
Also see JACOBS, Dick, & His Orchestra

MILES, Lenny *P&R '60*
Singles: 7-inch
GROOVE (0001 "Stay with Me") 8-12 62
GROOVE (0010 "I Wouldn't Be Here") 8-12 62
RCA (8011 "Donna's Gone") 8-12 62
SCEPTER (1212 "Don't Believe Him, Donna") 10-20 60
SCEPTER (1218 "In Between Tears") 10-20 61

MILES, Lizzy
LPs: 10/12-inch
COOK (1183 "Hot Songs") 30-60

MILES, Luke "Long Gone"
(Long Gone Miles & Boys from 25th St.)
Singles: 7-inch
KENT (500 "Hello Josephine") 5-10 68
SMASH (1755 "Long Gone") 10-15 62
TWO KINGS 8-12 65
WORLD PACIFIC (408 "Long Gone") 8-12 64
LPs: 10/12-inch
WORLD PACIFIC 15-25 64

MILES, Mary Ann
(With the Zeke Strong Band)
Singles: 7-inch
CELESTE (201 "I'll Be Gone") 8-12 65
CELESTE (801 "Without Someone to Love") 8-12 64
Also see AGEE, Ray, & Mary Ann Miles

MILES, Shan
Singles: 7-inch
SHOUT (222 "Soul People") 8-12 67

MILES & ANDREW
(With the Gay Clifs)
Singles: 7-inch
PLAY (1002 "Till the End of Time") 20-30 59
(Same number used on a Toneblenders release.)

MILES & ANDREW / Little Leroy
Singles: 7-inch
DEVILLE (002 "It's Heaven"/"She's a Wonder") 8-12 61

MILEY, Lonnie
Singles: 7-inch
KIX (102 "Rockum Beat") 50-100

MILK
Singles: 7-inch
BUDDAH (80 "Angela Jones") 5-10 69
Member: Johnny Cymbal.
Also see CYMBAL, Johnny

MILKWOOD
LPs: 10/12-inch
A&M (4226 "Under Milkwood") 15-20 69

MILKWOOD
LPs: 10/12-inch
PARAMOUNT (6046 "How's the Weather") 30-40 73
Also see CARS

MILKWOOD TAPESTRY
LPs: 10/12-inch
METROMEDIA (1007 "Milkwood Tapestry") 20-25 69

MILKY WAYS
Singles: 7-inch
LIBERTY (55255 "Teenage Island") 15-25 60

MILLARD & DYCE
LPs: 10/12-inch
KAYMAR (265 "Millard & Dyce") 25-50 73

MILLBURNAIRES '63
LPs: 10/12-inch
BATTLE (6126 "Teenage Hootenanny") .. 15-25 63

MILLENNIUM
Singles: 7-inch
COLUMBIA 5-8 68-69
Picture Sleeves
COLUMBIA 10-15 68
LPs: 10/12-inch
COLUMBIA 15-20 68
Members: Curt Boetcher; Michael Fennelly; Sandy Salisbury.
Also see SALISBURY, Sandy

MILLER, Arlie, & Bullets
Singles: 7-inch
LUCKY (6197 "Lou Ann") 300-400 60
Also see CARTER, Dean
Also see NEAVILLE, Arlie

MILLER, Big
(With the Five Pennies; Clarence Miller)
Singles: 78 rpm
SAVOY 10-15 56
Singles: 7-inch
COLUMBIA (42411 "Sam's Song") 5-10 62
SAVOY (1181 "Try to Understand") 15-25 56
LPs: 10/12-inch
COLUMBIA 20-25 61-62
U.A. (3047 "Did You Ever Hear the Blues") 30-35 58
(Monaural.)
U.A. (6047 "Did You Ever Hear the Blues") 40-60 58
(Stereo.)
Also see FIVE PENNIES

MILLER, Bingo, & Velvetones
Singles: 7-inch
YOUNG ARTISTS (103 "Martha Sue") .. 50-100 58

MILLER, Bob
Singles: 7-inch
JUBILEE (5329 "Crazy Dreamer") 10-15 58
JUBILEE (5336 "Lonesome Lover") 10-15 58

MILLER, Bobby
Singles: 7-inch
CONSTELLATION (103 "The Big Question") 10-20 63
CONSTELLATION (111 "The Big Question ") 10-20 63
CONSTELLATION (116 "Whoa") 10-20 64
CONSTELLATION (127 "This Is My Dance") 10-20 64
CONSTELLATION (134 "I'm for the Girls") 15-25 64

MILLER, Brad
LP: 10/12-inch
MFLS (004 "Power & Majesty") 25-50 78

MILLER, Buddy
Singles: 7-inch
BAND BOX (311 "Teen Twist") 10-20 62
BAND BOX (322 "Little Bo Peep") 40-60 62
BAND BOX (335 "Walking Slowly from You") 10-20 62
EKO (401 "Honey Baby") 75-100 58
FELSTED (8557 "Buddy Boy") 25-35 59
GEM (102 "Little Bo Peep") 40-60 59
SECURITY (108 "Rock & Roll Irene") 1200-1800 58
SECURITY (110 "Little Bo Peep") 100-200 58
VEM (2226 "Teen Twist") 15-25 60
VEM (2228 "Little Bo Peep") 50-100 60
Picture Sleeves
BAND BOX (335 "Walking Slowly from You") 25-35 62
Also see TWITTY, Conway

MILLER, Carl
Singles: 7-inch
LU (503 "Rhythm Guitar") 300-400 58

MILLER, Chuck P&R '55
Singles: 78 rpm
CAPITOL 5-10 54-55
MERCURY 5-15 55-58
Singles: 7-inch
CAPITOL (2700 "After All") 10-15 54
CAPITOL (2841 "Hopahula Boogie") 10-15 54
CAPITOL (3187 "No Baby Like You") 10-15 55
MERCURY (70627 "The House of Blue Lights") 10-20 55
MERCURY (70697 "Hawk-Eye") 10-20 55
MERCURY (70767 "Boogie Blues") 10-20 55
MERCURY (70842 "Bright Red Convertible") 10-20 56
MERCURY (70942 "Cool It Baby") 10-20 56
MERCURY (71001 "Auctioneer") 10-20 56
MERCURY (71308 "Down the Road Apiece") 10-20 58
LPs: 10/12-inch
MERCURY (20195 "After Hours") 50-75 56
(10-inch LP.)

MILLER, Clint P&R '58
Singles: 7-inch
ABC-PAR (9878 "Bertha Lou") 20-30 58
ABC-PAR (9938 "Polka-Dotted Poliwampus") 10-20 58
BIG TOP (3013 "Lonely Traveler") 10-15 59
HEADLINE (1010 "Do You Remember") . 10-15 60
HEADLINE (1011 "Till the End of the World Rolls 'Round") 8-12 61
HEADLINE (1013 "Girl with the Ribbon in Her Hair") 8-12 61
LENOX (5557 "Forget-Me-Nots") 8-12 62
LENOX (5574 "Bridge Across the River") ... 8-12 63

MILLER, Dave
Singles: 7-inch
INDIO (3 "Froggy Went a-Courtin' ") 50-100 61

MILLER, Dick
Singles: 7-inch
AGGIE (1002 "Now I'm Gone") 15-25 58
AGGIE (1007 "Cold Hearted Stranger") .. 15-25 60
MERCURY (71658 "Make Room for the Blues") 8-10 60
TOPPA (1016 "Make Room for the Blues") 10-15 60
(First issue.)

MILLER, Dick
(With the Rhythmasters)
Singles: 7-inch
PAGEANT (717 "A Tear, a Heartbreak, a Love") .... 15-25 '60s
SUNDOWN (121 "Wishful Thinking") 10-15 59

MILLER, Dick, & Saddle-Ites
Singles: 7-inch
GOLD STAR (105 "It") .... 15-25 '60s
Also see WRANGLERS

MILLER, Frankie C&W '59
(Frank Miller)
Singles: 78 rpm
COLUMBIA 5-10 54-56
Singles: 7-inch
COLUMBIA 10-20 54-56
MANCO (1013 "Cheatin' & Hidin' ") 5-10 61
STARDAY (Except 469 & 577) 5-15 59-67
STARDAY (469 "Rain, Rain") 100-125 59
STARDAY (577 "Gotta Win My Baby Back Again") 50-75 62
U.A. (514 "Losing By a Hair") 5-10 62
EPs: 7-inch
STARDAY (122 "Frankie Miller") 10-15 60
LPs: 10/12-inch
AUDIO LAB (1562 "Fine Country Singing") 40-50 63
STARDAY (134 "Country Music's New Star") 40-50 61
STARDAY (199 "Country Style") 40-50 62
STARDAY (338 "Blackland Farmer") 40-50 65

MILLER, Glenn, & His Orchestra P&R '35
(New Glenn Miller Orchestra with Ray McKinley; with Buddy DeFranco)
Singles: 78 rpm
BLUEBIRD 5-10 38-44
BRUNSWICK 5-10 37-38
COLUMBIA 5-10 35
DECCA 15-25 37
RCA 4-8 47-58
VICTOR 5-10 42-46
Singles: 7-inch
DECCA (25000 series) .... 5-15 '50s
EPIC 4-6 65-69
RCA 5-15 50-67
EPs: 7-inch
EPIC 5-15 54-56
RCA (Except 6700 boxed series) 5-15 50-61
RCA (6700 "Anthology Limited Edition, Vol. 1") 35-50 56
(Boxed, 10-disc set.)
RCA (6701 "Anthology Limited Edition, Vol. 2") 45-60 56
(Boxed, 15-disc set.)
RCA (6702 "Army Air Force Band") 45-60 56
(Boxed, 15-disc set.)
LPs: 10/12-inch
BRIGHT ORANGE 5-8 73
CAMDEN 5-10 63-74
COLUMBIA 5-8 82
EPIC (1000 & 3000 series) 20-40 54-56
EPIC (16000 series) 12-25 60
EPIC (24000 & 26000 series) 10-20 65-66
EVEREST (Except 4004) 5-8 82
EVEREST (4004 "Glenn Miller") 20-30 82
(Boxed, five-disc set.)
GREAT AMERICAN 5-10 77
HARMONY 5-10 70
KORY 5-8 77
MOVIETONE 8-15 67
RCA (16 thru 30) 25-50
(10-inch LPs.)
RCA (0600 thru 3800 series) 5-10 74-81
(With "ANL," "AYL" or "CPL" prefix.)
RCA (LPT-3000 series) 25-50 52-54
(10-inch LP.)
RCA (1000 thru 1500 series) 20-40 54-57
(Black label.)
RCA (1100 thru 1500 series) 5-10 68-69
(Orange label.)
RCA (1600 thru 3900 series) 10-25 58-68
(Black label. With "LPM" or "LSP" prefix.)
RCA (1900 thru 4100 series) 5-10 68-69
(Orange or gold label.)
RCA (5000 series) 5-10 75-80
RCA (6000 series) 5-15 69-73
RCA (6100 series) 15-30 59-63
RCA (LPT-6700 "Anthology-Limited Edition, Vol. 1") 100-200 56
(Five-disc set with booklet and special gold or silver case.)
RCA (LPT-6700 "Anthology-Limited Edition, Vol. 1") 50-75 62
(Reissue, has '60s RCA labels.)
RCA (LPT-6701 "Anthology-Limited Edition, Vol. 2") 100-200 56
(Five-disc set with booklet and special gold or silver case.)
RCA (LPT-6701 "Anthology-Limited Edition, Vol. 2") 50-75 62
(Reissue, has '60s RCA labels.)
RCA (LPT-6702 "Army Air Force Band") 100-200 56
READER'S DIGEST (64 "The Unforgettable Glenn Miller") 20-30 66
(Six discs. Includes booklet.)
SPRINGBOARD 4-8 77
20TH FOX (100 series) 20-30 59
20TH FOX (900 series) 5-10 73
20TH FOX (3000 series) 15-25 59
20TH FOX (3100 series) 10-15 65
20TH FOX (4100 series) 10-15 65
20TH FOX (72000 series) 6-12 73
Also see HELLER, Jackie / Glenn Miller
Also see SINATRA, Frank / Fontaine (sic) Sisters / Glenn Miller & His Orchestra

MILLER, Hal
(With the Rays)
Singles: 7-inch
AMY (900 "Love Another Girl") 20-30 64
AMY (909 "On My Own Two Feet") 75-100 64
AMY (920 "Blessing in Disguise") 50-75 65
TOPIX (6003 "An Angel Cried") 20-30 61
(With the 4 Seasons.)
Also see 4 SEASONS
Also see RAYS

MILLER, Jerry
Singles: 7-inch
SARA (6742 "Honky Tonk Song") 50-75

MILLER, Jody P&R '64/C&W '65
Singles: 7-inch
CAPITOL 5-10 63-70
EPIC 4-6 70-79
Picture Sleeves
CAPITOL 5-10 65
LPs: 10/12-inch
CAPITOL (1913 "Wednesday's Child Is Full of Woe") 15-25 63
CAPITOL (2349 thru 2996) 10-20 65-69
CAPITOL (11000 series) 5-10 73
EPIC 5-10 70-77
PICKWICK/HILLTOP 10-15 66
SEARS 8-12

MILLER, Jody, & Johnny Paycheck C&W '72
Singles: 7-inch
EPIC 4-6 72
Also see MILLER, Jody
Also see PAYCHECK, Johnny

MILLER, Joe
Singles: 78 rpm
HERALD (464 "Dumplin' Darlin' ") 10-15 55
Singles: 7-inch
HERALD (464 "Dumplin' Darlin' ") 15-25 55

MILLER, Johnny
Singles: 78 rpm
SABRE (109 "Always") 5-10 54
Singles: 7-inch
SABRE (109 "Always") 10-20 54

MILLER, June
Singles: 7-inch
CARVEL (858 "How Bad Can Bad Luck Be") 50-100

MILLER, Kenny
(Ken Miller)
Singles: 7-inch
FARO (581 "Zonbeeshe Blues") 10-15 58
IMPERIAL (5740 "Spring Vacation") 8-12 61
20TH FOX (315 "Rollin' Stone") 8-12 62
VIKING (1001 "The Letter") 8-12 61

MILLER, Lisa
Singles: 7-inch
CANTERBURY (519 "Loneliest Christmas Tree") 10-20 67
TRIDENT (223 "Does She Know") .... 20-30 '60s
Also see LITTLE LISA

MILLER, Mac
Singles: 7-inch
TEMPWOOD (1036 "It's My Way") 5-10 62
VIN (1008 "To My Lover Sorrow") 8-12 58
VIN (1011 "Love Is the Reason") 8-12 59

MILLER, Mandy
(With Maury Laws' Orchestra & Chorus)
Singles: 78 rpm
FLAIR-X (5005 "Oh Promise") 10-15 56
Singles: 7-inch
FLAIR-X (5005 "Oh Promise") 15-25 56

MILLER, Maurice
Singles: 7-inch
JERRY-O (801 "Fly Me to the Moon") 20-30

MILLER, Mickey
LPs: 10/12-inch
FOLKWAYS 15-25 59

MILLER, Mike, & Reflections
Singles: 7-inch
M-PAC (7227 "Shake a Tail Feather") 5-10 65

MILLER, Mike, & Jack Casey
Singles: 78 rpm
CAMEO (137 "Don't Mess Up My Hair") .. 25-50 58
Singles: 7-inch
CAMEO (137 "Don't Mess Up My Hair") .. 15-25 58
STARR ("Don't Mess Up My Hair") 50-100
(Selection number not known.)

MILLER, Mrs. Elva P&R/LP '66
(Mrs. Miller)
Singles: 7-inch
AMARET 4-8 69-70
CAPITOL (5640 "Downtown"/"Lover's Concerto") 5-10 66
LPs: 10/12-inch
AMARET 10-20 69
CAPITOL 20-35 66-67

MILLER, Mr.
Singles: 7-inch
SWAN (4256 "I'm Henry VIII, I Am") 5-10 66

MILLER, Mitch P&R '50
(Mitch Miller's Orchestra & Chorus; Mitch Miller & Sing-Along Gang)
Singles: 78 rpm
COLUMBIA 3-6 50-57
Singles: 7-inch
("Christmas Carol Medley") .... 5-8 '50s
(Rectangular picture disc. Three other Christmas titles were made. Same value for each. No label name or selection numbers used.)
COLUMBIA 4-10 50-65
DECCA 4-8 65-66
DIAMOND 4-8 68
DJM (1006 "It's Only Love") 4-6 76
GOLD-MOR 4-6 73
U.A. 4-8 68
Picture Sleeves
COLUMBIA 5-8 59-63
EPs: 7-inch
COLUMBIA 5-10 55-61
LPs: 10/12-inch
ATLANTIC 5-8 70
COLUMBIA (Except 2780/6380) 5-20 56-82
COLUMBIA (2780 "Major Dundee") 35-45 65
(Soundtrack. Monaural.)
COLUMBIA (6380 "Major Dundee") 45-55 65
(Soundtrack. Stereo.)
DECCA 5-12 66
HARMONY 5-12 65-71
Also see LAINE, Frankie
Also see SANDPIPERS with Mitch Miller & Orchestra / Mitch Miller & Orchestra

MILLER, Ned C&W/P&R '62
Singles: 78 rpm
DOT (Except 15601) 10-20 57
DOT (15601 "From a Jack to a King") 15-25 57
Singles: 7-inch
CAPITOL (2000 series) 4-6 68
CAPITOL (4600 series) 5-10 61
CAPITOL (5400 thru 5800 series) 4-8 65-67
DOT (Except 15601) 10-20 57
DOT (15601 "From a Jack to a King") 15-25 57
FABOR (114 thru 139) 5-10 62-65
FABOR (143 "Old Mother Nature") 10-20 57
RADIO (105 "With Enough Love") 10-20 58
REPUBLIC 4-6 69-70
LPs: 10/12-inch
CAPITOL 10-15 65-67
FABOR (1001 "From a Jack to a King") ... 15-25 63
(Black vinyl.)
FABOR (1001 "From a Jack to a King") . 50-100 63
(Colored vinyl.)
PLANTATION 5-8 81
REPUBLIC 8-10 70

MILLER, Ned, & Jan Howard
Singles: 7-inch
JACKPOT (48020 "Ring the Bell for Johnny") 8-12 59
Also see HOWARD, Jan
Also see MILLER, Ned

MILLER, Red, Trio R&B '48
Singles: 78 rpm
BULLET 15-25 48
SWING BEAT 10-20 49
Singles: 7-inch
PRIZE (801 "Mary Jo") .... 20-30 '50s
Also see GLENN, Lloyd

MILLER, Rex
Singles: 7-inch
ABNAK (107 "Ringo's Doctor") 10-20 65
NORMAN (537 "Weather Lady") 5-10 63

MILLER, Roger C&W '60
Singles: 7-inch
BUENA VISTA (493 "Whistle Stop") 4-6 73
COLUMBIA 4-6 73-74
DECCA 5-10 59
ELEKTRA 3-5 81
MCA 3-5 85-86
MERCURY 4-6 70-72
MUSICOR (1102 "You're Forgettin' Me") 4-8 65

RCA (7000 series)....8-15 60-63
RCA (8000 series)....4-6 62-65
SMASH....4-8 64-76
STARDAY (356 "You're Forgettin' Me")... 10-15 58
STARDAY (718 "Playboy")....4-8 65
STARDAY (7029 "Under Your Spell Again")....4-8 65
20TH CENTURY....4-6 79
WINDSONG....4-6 77

Picture Sleeves

BUENA VISTA (493 "Whistle Stop")....5-8 73
SMASH....5-10 64-68

LPs: 10/12-inch

CAMDEN....8-10 64-65
COLUMBIA....5-10 73
EVEREST....5-8 75
HILLTOP....8-12 '60s
MCA....5-8 86
MERCURY....5-10 72
NASHVILLE....8-12
PICKWICK....5-10 '70s
SMASH (Except 7000 series).... 10-20 64-70
SMASH (7000 series)....5-8 82
STARDAY.... 10-20 65
20TH FOX....5-8 79
WINDSONG....5-8 77
WING....6-12 69

Also see LEWIS, Jerry Lee / Roger Miller / Roy Orbison
Also see NELSON, Willie, & Roger Miller
Also see TUBB, Justin / Roger Miller
Also see YOUNG, Donny, & Roger Miller

MILLER, Roger, & Willie Nelson C&W '82
(With Ray Price)

Singles: 7-inch

COLUMBIA....3-5 82

LPs: 10/12-inch

COLUMBIA....5-8 82

Also see MILLER, Roger
Also see NELSON, Willie
Also see PRICE, Ray

MILLER, Ronnie

Singles: 7-inch

DIXIE (1126 "Dang You Pride").... 150-250 '60s

MILLER, Russ

Singles: 7-inch

VIP (1006 "I Sit in My Window").... 15-25 59

MILLER, Scott

Singles: 7-inch

GREY CLIFF (722 "I Got School").... 30-50 59
MOHAWK (109 "It's Love").... 20-30 58

MILLER, Steve P&R/LP '68
(Steve Miller Band)

Singles: 12-inch

CAPITOL (Except 9992)....4-8 81-85
CAPITOL (9992 "I Wanna Be Loved")....5-10 86
(Colored vinyl. Promotional issue only.)

Singles: 7-inch

CAPITOL (2156 "Sittin' in Circles")....5-10 68
CAPITOL (2287 "Living in the USA")....5-10 68
CAPITOL (2447 thru 3344)....4-8 69-72
CAPITOL (3732 thru 4496)....4-6 73-77
CAPITOL (5000 series)....3-5 81-87
CAPITOL (44000 series)....3-5 88

Picture Sleeves

CAPITOL (2156 "Sittin' In Circles")....8-12 67
CAPITOL....3-5 80-88

LPs: 10/12-inch

CAPITOL (184 thru 748).... 10-15 69-71
CAPITOL (2900 series).... 15-20 68
CAPITOL (11000 thru 16000)....5-10 72-86
CAPITOL (11872 "Greatest Hits").... 20-30 78
(Colored vinyl. Promotional issue only.)
CAPITOL (11903 "Book of Dreams").... 15-20 78
(Picture disc.)
CAPITOL (48000 series)....5-8 88
MFSL (021 "Fly Like an Eagle").... 60-80 78
MERCURY....5-10 81

Also see BERRY, Chuck
Also see DAVIS, Tim
Also see FRUMIOUS BANDERSNATCH
Also see GOLDBERG - MILLER BLUES BAND
Also see MERRYWEATHER, Neil
Also see SCAGGS, Boz

MILLER, Steve, Band / Band / Quicksilver Messenger Service

LPs: 10/12-inch

CAPITOL (288 "Steve Miller Band / The Band / Quicksilver Messenger Service")....35-45 69
(Three-disc set, with one by each group.)

Also see BAND
Also see MILLER, Steve
Also see QUICKSILVER

MILLER, Tal

Singles: 7-inch

GOLDBAND (1059 "Mean Old Kokamoo")....10-20 58
HOLLYWOOD (1086 "You Move Me")....10-20 58
HOLLYWOOD (1094 "B-A-B-Y")....10-20 58
HOLLYWOOD (1097 "Scorched")....10-20 59

MILLER, Terry

Singles: 7-inch

CAVALIER (877 "Teenage Lingo Jive")....15-25 59
E.D.S. (32062 "My Doll")....40-60 59
LIBERTY (55146 "Single 'n' Searchin' ")..10-20 58
LUTE (5903 "I'm Available")....5-10 60
REVEILLE (1001 "Sweet Lovin' ")....5-10 61

MILLER, Walter
(With the Barons; with Yellow Jackets; Walter Wise Miller)

Singles: 78 rpm

GOLDBAND....20-30 57
METEOR....20-30 56

Singles: 7-inch

GOLDBAND (1033 "I Was Wrong")....50-75 57
GOLDBAND (1039 "Wanna Rock and Roll")....50-75 57
METEOR (5037 "My Last Mile")....50-75 56

MILLER, Warren

Singles: 7-inch

U.A. (104 "Everybody's Got a Baby But Me")....50-100 58

Picture Sleeves

U.A. (104 "Everybody's Got a Baby But Me")....100-200 58

MILLER BROTHERS

Singles: 78 rpm

4 STAR....5-10 54-57

Singles: 7-inch

COED (577 "Let Me Now")....5-10 63
4 STAR....10-20 54-61
LAYNE (203 "Don't Break My Heart")....75-125
MERCURY (71293 "Try")....15-20 58
MERCURY (71391 "Let Me See You Smile")....10-15 59
STRAND (25004 "Molly Pitcher")....10-15 59

EPs: 7-inch

4 STAR (32 "The Miller Brothers")....10-15 '50s

Members: Jimmy Miller; Paul Miller.

MILLER SISTERS

Singles: 78 rpm

FLIP (504 "Someday You Will Pay")....50-100 55
SUN (230 "There's No Right Way to Do Me Wrong")....25-50 55
SUN (255 "Ten Cats Down")....25-50 55
SUN (504 "Someday You Will Pay")....50-75 55

Singles: 7-inch

FLIP (504 "Someday You Will Pay")....200-300 55
(First issue.)
SUN (230 "There's No Right Way to Do Me Wrong")....50-100 55
SUN (255 "Ten Cats Down")....75-125 55
SUN (504 "Someday You Will Pay")....100-150 55

Members: Elsie Jo Miller; Mildred Wages.

MILLER SISTERS

Singles: 78 rpm

EMBER (1004 "Guess Who")....10-15 56
HERALD (455 "Until You're Mine")....10-15 55
HULL (718 "Do You Wanna Go")....10-15 56
ONYX (507 "Sugar Daddy")....25-50 57

Singles: 7-inch

ACME (717 "You Made Me a Promise")...30-40 57
ACME (721 "Let's Start Anew")....30-40 57
EMBER (1004 "Guess Who")....20-30 56
GMC (10006 "I'm Telling It Like It Is")....5-8 67
GLODIS (1003 "You Got to Reap What You Sow")....10-20 61
HERALD (455 "Until You're Mine")....20-30 55
HERALD (527 "Until You're Mine")....8-12 58
HULL (718 "Do You Wanna Go")....30-40 56
HULL (752 "I Cried All Night")....10-20 62
MILLER (1140 "Oh Lover")....15-20 60
MILLER (1141 "Pony Dance")....15-20 60
ONYX (507 "Sugar Daddy")....75-100 57
RAYNA (5001 "I Miss You So")....10-15 62
RAYNA (5004 "Oh Why")....10-15 62
RIVERSIDE (4535 "Tell Him")....10-20 62
ROULETTE (4491 "Baby Your Baby")....5-10 63
STARDUST (3001 "Feel Good")....5-10 64
YORKTOWN....5-10 65

Also see JEANNIE & MILLER SISTERS

MILLER SISTERS / Leo Price

Singles: 7-inch

HULL (736 "Just Wait and See"/"Black Pepper")....10-20 60

Also see MILLER SISTERS

MILLET, Lil, & Creoles

Singles: 78 rpm

SPECIALTY (565 "Hopeless Love")....10-15 55

Singles: 7-inch

SPECIALTY (565 "Hopeless Love")....35-45 55

MILLET, Lou

Singles: 78 rpm

ACE....50-75 55
DOT (203 "Heart of Stone")....8-12 52
EKKO (1024 "Shape of My Heart")....40-60 56
REPUBLIC (7130 "Slip, Slip, Slippin' In")....100-150 56

Singles: 7-inch

ACE (506 "Just You and Me")....200-250 55
ACE (510 "Hummingbird")....175-200 55
DOT (203 "Heart of Stone")....25-35 52
EKKO (1024 "Shape of My Heart")....100-200 56
REPUBLIC (7130 "Slip, Slip, Slippin' In")....300-500 56
TRACE (107 "Johnny Reb")....25-50 59

MILLIKIN, Curley, & Sundowners

Singles: 7-inch

TALOS (401 "Rock and Roll Country Boy")....100-150 59

MILLINDER, Lucky, & His Orchestra P&R/R&B '42

Singles: 78 rpm

DECCA....5-15 41-48
KING....10-30 51-57
RCA....10-20 49-51

Singles: 7-inch

KING (4449 "Chew Tobacco Rag")....25-45 51
KING (4453 "I'm Waiting Just for You")....25-45 51
KING (4476 "The Grape Vine")....25-45 51
KING (4496 "The Right Kind of Lovin' ")....25-45 51
(Black vinyl.)
KING (4496 "The Right Kind of Lovin' ").50-100 51
(Blue vinyl.)
KING (4545 "When I Have You")....50-75 52
KING (4557 "Lords Knows I Tried") 50-75.... 52
KING (4571 "Please Be Careful")....50-75 52
KING (4803 "Goody Good Love")....15-25 55
KING (5240 "Honey Dripper")....5-10 59
RCA (0054 "D Natural Blues")....30-50 49
(Red vinyl.)
WARWICK (582 "Big Fat Mama")....5-10 60

EPs: 7-inch

KING (268 "Lucky Millinder")....25-50 54
KING (336 "Lucky Millinder, Vol. 2")....25-50 54

Also see ALLEN, Annisteen, & Melvin Moore
Also see HARRIS, Wynonie
Also see STIDHAM, Arbee

MILLINDER, Lucky, & Admirals

Singles: 78 rpm

KING (4792 "It's a Sad Sad Feeling")....25-35 55

Singles: 7-inch

KING (4792 "It's a Sad Sad Feeling")....40-60 55

Also see ADMIRALS
Also see MILLINDER, Lucky

MILLIONAIRES

Singles: 78 rpm

DAVIS (441 "Somebody's Lyin' ")....10-15 55

Singles: 7-inch

DAVIS (441 "Somebody's Lyin' ")....20-30 55

Members: Ollie Jones; Napoleon Allen; Abe DeCosta; James DeLoache.

Also see BLENDERS

MILLIONAIRES

Singles: 7-inch

SHAR (355 "Haunted Train")....10-20 59

MILLIONAIRES

Singles: 7-inch

CUCA (6463 "I Got a Woman")....10-20 64
SOUNDS OF WISCONSIN (6814 "Packer Backer")....8-12 68

MILLS, Chuck
(With the Monarchs)

Singles: 7-inch

BAND BOX (221 "She's Mine")....50-75 60
BAND BOX (227 "Ding Dong")....20-30 60
TOPPA (1116 "You Name It")....5-10 67

Also see DAVIS, Gene / Chuck & Gene

MILLS, Denise, & Satinettes

Singles: 7-inch

CALJO (501 "Meet Me in the Moonlight") 20-30 62

MILLS, Everett

Singles: 7-inch

PROTONE (113 "Close Your Eyes")....15-25 59
PROTONE (114 "My Vision")....20-30 60

MILLS, Garry P&R '60

Singles: 7-inch

IMPERIAL (5674 "Look for a Star")....10-15 60
LONDON (9504 "I'll Step Down")....5-10 62
TOP RANK (2071 "Top Teen Baby")....15-25 60

MILLS, Gene

Singles: 7-inch

JIN (284 "Rocking Rolling Ocean")....15-25

MILLS, Hank

Singles: 7-inch

BLAZE (103 "Mean Mean Mama")....75-100 59

MILLS, Hayley P&R '61

Singles: 7-inch

BUENA VISTA....10-15 61-62
MAINSTREAM (656 "Gypsy Girl")....5-10 66

Picture Sleeves

BUENA VISTA (385 "Let's Get Together")....10-20 61
BUENA VISTA (395 "Johnny Jingo")....10-20 62
BUENA VISTA (401 "Side by Side")....10-20 62
BUENA VISTA (408 "Castaway")....10-20 62

LPs: 10/12-inch

BUENA VISTA (3311 "Let's Get Together")....20-25 62
(Monaural.)
BUENA VISTA (STER-3311 "Let's Get Together")....25-35 62
(Stereo.)
MAINSTREAM (6090 "Gypsy Girl")....15-25 66
(Soundtrack.)

Also see ANNETTE / Hayley Mills
Also see WAYFARERS

MILLS, Hayley, & Kevin Corcoran

EPs: 7-inch

DISNEYLAND (93 "Pollyanna Songs")....15-25 60

MILLS, Hayley, & Maurice Chevalier

Singles: 7-inch

BUENA VISTA (409 "Enjoy It")....8-12 62

MILLS, Hayley, & Eddie Hodges

Singles: 7-inch

BUENA VISTA (420 "Flittering")....8-12 63

Picture Sleeves

BUENA VISTA (420 "Flittering")....10-20 64

Also see HODGES, Eddie

MILLS, Hayley, & Burl Ives
(With Eddie Hodges & Deborah Walley)

Singles: 7-inch

BUENA VISTA (4023 "Summer Magic")....5-10 63
(Alcoa Wrap promotional issue.)

Picture Sleeves

BUENA VISTA (4023 "Summer Magic")..10-15 63
(Alcoa Wrap promotional issue.)

EPs: 7-inch

ALCOA WRAP (701 "Music from *Summer Magic*")....15-25 63
(Promotional issue only.)

Also see HODGES, Eddie
Also see IVES, Burl
Also see MILLS, Hayley

MILLS, James, with Bailey's Nervous Kats

Singles: 7-inch

CAMELIA (100 "Cobra")....20-40 63
(First issue.)
MAGNET (106 "Cobra")....10-20 63

MAGNET (235 "Drummer Boy Blues ") ... 10-20 '60s

MILLS, Margie
(With the Executives)

Singles: 7-inch

GROOVE (59 "What About Mine")..............5-10 65
RCA (8673 "Goodbye, Boys, Goodbye")....8-12 66
RCA (8802 "You'll Know I'm Around ") 5-10 66
VEE-JAY (549 "Knock on Any Door")........8-12 63

MILLS, Steve

Singles: 7-inch

LEAF (852 "Nothing to Do with Love")..... 50-75 64

MILLS BROTHERS — P&R '31

Singles: 78 rpm

BANNER..5-10 34
BRUNSWICK 5-10 31-47
CONQUEROR 5-10
DECCA (100 thru 4300 series)....................5-10 34-42
DECCA (11000 thru 24000 series) 5-10 42-57

Singles: 7-inch

ABC...4-6 74
DECCA (25516 "Across the Alley from the Alamo") 5-10 61
DECCA (27000 & 28000 series) 15-25 50-53
DECCA (29000 thru 31000 series) 8-12 54-58
DOT (250 "My Shy Violet")..........................5-10 68
(Colored vinyl.)
DOT (15000 series) 10-15 58-59
DOT (16000 series) 5-10 60-67
DOT (17000 series) 4-8 68-69
GOLDIES 45 ....3-6 73
MCA..4-6 73-74
PARAMOUNT 4-6 70-72
RANWOOD 4-6 73-76

EPs: 7-inch

DECCA...5-15 50-63
DOT (1073 "Mmmmmm")..............................5-10 58
DOT (1087 "Great Hits")...............................5-10 59

LPs: 10/12-inch

ABC...5-8 74
DECCA (193 "Best Of") 10-20 66
(Two discs. Monaural.)
DECCA (7193 "Best Of") 10-20 66
(Two discs. Stereo.)
DECCA (4000 series) 10-20 61-67
DECCA (5000 series) 20-50 49-55
(10-inch LPs.)
DECCA (7019 "Curtain Call") 25-35 55
DECCA (8000 series)................................ 20-35 55-59
DECCA (75000 series) 5-10 70
DOT (3103 "Mmmmmm")........................... 20-30 58
(Monaural.)
DOT (25103 "Mmmmmm")........................ 30-50 58
(Stereo.)
DOT (3157 thru 3809)............................. 10-20 59-67
DOT (25157 thru 25809) 10-25 59-67
DOT (25872 thru 25960) 8-12 68-70
EVEREST...5-10 75-77
GNP 5-8 73
MCA...5-10 73
MFP/MCA...5-8 82
PARAMOUNT 5-10 72-74
PICKWICK...5-10 '70s
RANWOOD 5-10 74-81
SONGBIRD 6-12 74
VOCALION 8-15 66-69
Members: Harry; Herb; Donald; John.
Also see CROSBY, Bing, & Mills Brothers
Also see FITZGERALD, Ella, & Mills Brothers
Also see LEE, Peggy, & Mills Brothers

MILLS BROTHERS & LOUIS ARMSTRONG — P&R '38

Singles: 78 rpm

DECCA (1876 "Flat Foot Floogee") 5-10 38

Singles: 7-inch

DECCA (25536 "Cherry") 5-10 61
Also see ARMSTRONG, Louis

MILLS BROTHERS & COUNT BASIE

LPs: 10/12-inch

ABC..5-10 74
DOT (25838 "Board of Directors")............ 10-15 68
Also see BASIE, Count
Also see MILLS BROTHERS

MILNER, Jimmy

Singles: 7-inch

EMBER (1052 "A Place in Your Heart")... 10-20 59
YORK (101 "A Place in Your Heart") 40-50 59

MILO, Skip
(With the Bel-Aires—Dynamics)

Singles: 7-inch

A (107 "Smallest Heart")............................10-15 60
ARC (4453 "What's Wrong with Me") 15-25 59
Also see BEL-AIRES
Also see DYNAMICS

MILS, Telli .W.
(T.W. Mills; Slim Willet)

Singles: 7-inch

CARLTON (470 "Sneaky Pete")................15-25 58
WINSTON (1017 "Ain't Goin' Home") 50-75 57
WINSTON (1021 "Sneaky Pete").............25-45 58
Note: "Telli W. Mils" is essentially "Slim Willet" spelled backwards.
Also see WILLETT, Slim

MILSAP, Ronnie — R&B '65/C&W '73

Singles: 7-inch

BOBLO 4-6 77
CAPITOL...3-5 90s
CHIPS...5-10 70
FESTIVAL 4-6 77
PACEMAKER (246 "Wishing You Were Here")..5-10 65
RCA (Black vinyl) 3-8 74-92
RCA (Colored vinyl) 5-10 74-89
(Promotional only.)
SCEPTER 10-20 65-70
W.B. (5405 "It Went to Your Head")...........5-10 63
W.B. (8000 series).......................................4-6 75-76

Picture Sleeves

RCA (10112 "A Legend in My Time") 4-8 74
RCA (14135 "Lost in the Fifties Tonight").....3-6 85

LPs: 10/12-inch

BUCKBOARD 8-10 76
CRAZY CAJUN...8-10 75
51 WEST...5-8 '80s
HSRD 8-10 82
RCA..5-10 74-92
TIME-LIFE...5-10 81
TRIP..8-10 76
W.B...8-10 71-75
Also see PRESLEY, Elvis

MILTON, Bobby, & Debutones

Singles: 7-inch

ARROW (1009 "A Place in My Heart") 50-75 57

MILTON, Buddy, & Twilighters

Singles: 78 rpm

RPM (418 "Please Understand")..............50-75 54
RPM (419 "Oo Wah").................................30-40 54

Singles: 7-inch

RPM (418 "Please Understand")...........300-350 54
RPM (419 "Oo Wah")..............................200-250 54

MILTON, Fred

Singles: 7-inch

SKYWAY (129 "Barbie Barbie") 25-45 61

MILTON, Roy — P&R/R&B '46
(With His Solid Senders; Roy Milton Sextet)

Singles: 78 rpm

DOOTONE..20-30 55-56
DELUXE...15-25 '50s
HAMP-TONE..20-40 45
JUKE BOX...20-40 46
KING..10-15 56-57
MILTONE (202 "When I Grow Too Old to Dream")..50-75 47
(Cartoon label.)
MILTONE (219 "Pack Your Sack, Jack")..50-75 47
(Cartoon label.)
ROY MILTON (111 "Groovin' with Joe")...20-40 46
(Cartoon label.)
ROY MILTON (207 "Them There Eyes")..20-40 46
(Cartoon label.)
SPECIALTY..15-25 47-55

Singles: 7-inch

CENCO (112 "I Wonder")...........................10-20 61
DOOTONE (363 "Fools Are Getting Scarcer")...30-40 55
DOOTONE (369 "You Got Me Reeling and Rocking") 30-40 55
DOOTONE (377 "I Want to Go Home")....30-40 55
DOOTONE (378 "Bam-a-Lam") 40-50 55
(Vocal by Mickey Champion.)
DOOTONE (398 "Baby I'm Gone") 30-40 56
KING (4993 "You're Gonna Suffer") 15-25 56
KING (5035 "Succotash")...........................15-25 57
KING (5069 "Skid Row")............................15-25 57
KING (5074 "R.M. Blues").........................15-25 57
KING (5663 "R.M. Blues").........................10-15 62
SPACE (310 "Always Want You Around") . 8-12 '60s
SPECIALTY (414 "Short, Sweet and Snappy"/"Best Wishes") 20-40 50
SPECIALTY (429 "So Tired")....................40-60 51
SPECIALTY (436 "Flying Saucer")...........30-50 52
SPECIALTY (438 "Night & Day")..............30-50 52
SPECIALTY (446 "Believe Me Baby")......50-75 52
SPECIALTY (458 "Some Day") 30-50 53
(Black vinyl.)
SPECIALTY (458 "Some Day") 75-125 53
(Red vinyl.)
SPECIALTY (464 "Let Me Give You All My Love")..30-50 53
(Black vinyl.)
SPECIALTY (464 "Let Me Give You All My Love")..75-125 53
(Red vinyl.)
SPECIALTY (480 "I Stood By")..................20-30 53
SPECIALTY (489 "Make Me Know It") 20-30 54
SPECIALTY (526 "It's Too Late") 20-30 54
SPECIALTY (538 "Tell It Like It Is")..........40-50 54
SPECIALTY (545 "What Can I Do") 20-30 55
SPECIALTY (721 "R.M. Blues")..................5-10 69
THUNDERBIRD (104 "Driveway Blues")..10-15 62
WARWICK (549 "Early in the Morning")...10-20 60
WARWICK (591 "R.M. Blues")..................10-20 60
WARWICK (662 "So Tired").......................10-20 61

LPs: 10/12-inch

KENT (554 "Great Roy Milton") 40-60 63
Also see CHAMPION, Mickey
Also see HIGGINS, Chuck, & Roy Milton
Also see HOWARD, Camille, Trio
Also see HUMES, Helen

MILTON, Roy / Joe Liggins

Singles: 78 rpm

SPECIALTY 10-20 53

Singles: 7-inch

SPECIALTY (414 "Short, Sweet and Snappy"/"So Alone") 20-40 53
Also see LIGGINS, Joe
Also see MILTON, Roy

MIMMS, Garnet — P&R/R&B/LP '63
(With the Enchanters; with Trucking Co.)

Singles: 7-inch

ARISTA 4-6 77
GSF 4-6 72
LIBERTY 3-5 81
U.A. 10-15 63-66
VEEP..5-8 66-67
VERVE..5-10 68-70

Picture Sleeves

U.A. (658 "For Your Precious Love")..10-20 63

LPs: 10/12-inch

ARISTA (4153 "Garnett Mimms Has It All")..8-12 78
GUEST STAR (1907 "Garnet Mimms") 20-25 64
U.A. (3305 "Cry Baby")..............................25-40 63
(Monaural.)
U.A. (3396 "As Long As I Have You") 25-40 64
(Monaural.)
U.A. (3498 "I'll Take Good Care of You") .35-50 66
(Monaural.)
U.A. (6305 "Cry Baby")..............................35-50 63
(Stereo.)
U.A. (6396 "As Long As I Have You") 35-50 64
(Stereo.)
U.A. (6498 "I'll Take Good Care of You") .35-50 66
(Stereo.)
Members: Garnet Mimms; Samuel Bell; Charles Boyer; Zola Pearnell.
Also see GAINORS

MIMMS, Garnet / Maurice Monk

LPs: 10/12-inch

GRAND PRIX (424 "Garnett Mimms & Maurice Monk")..15-20 63
Also see MIMMS, Garnet

MIMS, Paul

Singles: 7-inch

SHELL (121 "I Blowed My Top")..............50-75

MIMS, T.S., & Mystics
("Vocal by Sabu")

Singles: 7-inch

COIN (1500 "Love You Betty")..................20-30 59

MINCY TWINS

Singles: 7-inch

GROOVE (0048 "School Girl") 5-10 64
PHILIPS (40136 "Dream")...........................5-10 63

MIND EXPANDERS

LPs: 10/12-inch

DOT (3773 "What's Happening")............50-100 67
(Monaural.)
DOT (25773 "What's Happening")............30-40 67
(Stereo.)

MIND RATION

Singles: 7-inch

TENER (1020 "Always and a Day")........... 8-12 67

MIND'S EYE

Singles: 7-inch

JOX (58 "Help, I'm Lost") 15-25 67
Also see CHILDREN

MIND'S EYE

Singles: 7-inch

AMY (11050 "Mystic Woman") 10-20 69

MINDBENDERS — P&R/LP '66

Singles: 7-inch

FONTANA..5-10 66-68

LPs: 10/12-inch

FONTANA (27554 "A Groovy Kind of Love") 30-40 66
(Monaural. With *Ashes to Ashes*)
FONTANA (27554 "A Groovy Kind of Love") 20-30 66
(Monaural. Without *Ashes to Ashes*)
FONTANA (67554 "A Groovy Kind of Love") 30-40 66
(Stereo. With *Ashes to Ashes*)
FONTANA (67554 "A Groovy Kind of Love") 20-30 66
(Stereo. Without *Ashes to Ashes*)
Members: Eric Stewart; Ric Rothwell; Bob Lang.
Also see FONTANA, Wayne, & Mindbenders

MINEO, Sal — P&R '57

Singles: 78 rpm

EPIC..15-25 57

Singles: 7-inch

DECCA (31692 "Girl Across the Way") 5-10 64
EPIC (9216 "Start Movin' ")......................15-25 57
EPIC (9227 "Lasting Love").......................15-25 57
EPIC (9246 "Party Time") 15-25 57
EPIC (9260 "Little Pigeon").......................10-20 58
EPIC (9327 "Make Believe Baby") 10-20 59
EPIC (9345 "I'll Never Be Myself Again") . 10-20 59
FONTANA (1504 "Take Me Back") 5-10 65

Picture Sleeves

EPIC (9216 "Start Movin' ")......................20-30 57
EPIC (9227 "Lasting Love").......................20-30 57
EPIC (9246 "Party Time") 20-30 57

EPs: 7-inch

EPIC (27284 "Sal Sings").........................40-60 57
(Promotional issue, made for Scotch Brand Tape. Identification number shown since no selection number is used.)
EPIC (7187 "Sal Mineo")...........................30-50 57
EPIC (7194/7195 "Sal")............................30-50 58
(Price is for either volume.)
EPIC (7194 "Sal") 20-30 58
EPIC (7204 "Souvenirs of Summertime"). 20-30 58

LPs: 10/12-inch

EPIC (3405 "Sal") 75-100 58

MINETS

Singles: 7-inch

ROCK-IT (200054 "Secret of Love").........20-30

MINIMI, Ross

Singles: 7-inch

GULFSTREAM (7269 "Oh Janet") 200-300

MINKS
(With the Darrell Balasty Orchestra)

Singles: 7-inch

ERMINE (788 "Lotsa' Luck")......................20-30 60
(Reissued crediting "Susan Dwight & the Minks." Label refers to both "Ermine" and "Erman" Records.)
Also see DWIGHT, Susan, & Minks

MINNELLI, Liza — LP '64

Singles: 7-inch

A&M...4-8 68-71
ABC...4-6 73

CADENCE (1436 "What Do You Think I Am") 10-20 63
CAPITOL (4900 thru 5700 series).......... 8-12 63-65
COLUMBIA.......... 4-6 72-75
U.A. 4-6 77

LPs: 10/12-inch

A&M 10-15 68-73
ABC (752 "Cabaret").......... 10-15 72
(Soundtrack. With Joel Grey.)
ARISTA (4069 "Lucky Lady") 8-10 76
(Soundtrack.)
CADENCE (4012 "Best Foot Forward")... 30-40 63
(Monaural. Original cast.)
CADENCE (24012 "Best Foot Forward"). 40-60 63
(Stereo. Original cast.)
CAPITOL (T-2100 and T-2400 series)..... 10-20 64-66
(Monaural.)
CAPITOL (ST-2100 and ST-2400 series) 15-25 64-66
(Stereo.)
CAPITOL (2200 series) 5-8 78
CAPITOL (11000 series) 5-10 72-78
COLUMBIA.......... 8-15 72-77
DRG (6101 "The Act") 8-10 78
EPIC.......... 5-8 89
MCA (752 "Cabaret").......... 5-8
(Soundtrack. With Joel Grey.)
STET.......... 8-10
TELARC 10-12 87
Also see GARLAND, Judy, & Liza Minnelli

MINNER, Prentice

Singles: 7-inch

DOT (16173 "Sincerely") 10-20 61

MINNESODA

LPs: 10/12-inch

CAPITOL (11102 "Minnesoda") 8-10 72

MINNESOTA MARV & VANGUARDS

Singles: 7-inch

CUCA (1023 "Nobody's Darling But Mine").......... 100-200 61
Also see BLIHOVDE, Marv
Also see DENNIS, Marv

MINNESOTA MARV & ED CREE

Singles: 7-inch

CUCA (1025 "White Lightning") 50-75 61
Also see DENNIS, Marv, & Ed Cree
Also see MINNESOTA MARV & VANGUARDS

MINNIE PEARL *C&W '66*

Singles: 78 rpm

BULLET (613 "Jealous Hearted Me") 10-20 46
RCA.......... 5-10 54-56

Singles: 7-inch

RCA.......... 8-15 54-56
STARDAY.......... 4-6 66

LPs: 10/12-inch

NASHVILLE.......... 10-15 '60s
PICKWICK/HILLTOP.......... 10-15 '60s
STARDAY (224 thru 397) 15-25 63-66
SUNSET.......... 10-15 67
Also see JONES, Grandpa / Minnie Pearl
Also see STEVENS, Ray

MINOR, Dorothy

Singles: 7-inch

TEX (104 "Bye Bye Baby") 25-35 58

MINOR CHORDS

Singles: 7-inch

FLICK (005 "Fire").......... 10-20 59
FLICK (006 "Don't Let Me Down").......... 30-40 59
LU PINE (112 "Many a Day") 30-40 63
Also see ELMO, Sunnie, & Minor Chords

MINOR TONES

Singles: 78 rpm

CHOLLY (7094 "Burning Desire") 50-75 56

Singles: 7-inch

MUSIC CITY (816 "I Need You Baby") 200-300 57

MINORBOPS

Singles: 7-inch

LAMP (2012 "Need You Tonight") 100-150 57

MINORS
(Featuring Yvonne Lee; with Richard Meister & His Orchestra)

Singles: 78 rpm

CELESTE (3007 "Jerry") 300-400 57

Singles: 7-inch

CELESTE (3007 "Jerry") 1000-2000 57
CHAMP (2004 "Lonely Boy").......... 10-15
MELLO (554 "Jerry").......... 10-15 65

MINT, Little Eddie

Singles: 7-inch

MEMO (17911 "Two More Days").......... 15-25 59

MINT JULEP

Singles: 7-inch

BARNABY (5025 "Angel in Your Eyes") 4-6 73
TY (7772 "Riptide").......... 10-15

MINT JULEPS

Singles: 78 rpm

HERALD (481 "Bells of Love").......... 40-60 56

Singles: 7-inch

HERALD (481 "Bells of Love").......... 50-75 56
(Yellow label with script logo in flag. Has "45 rpm" on both sides of hole.)
HERALD (481 "Bells of Love").......... 75-125 56
(White label. Promotional issue only. Has "45 rpm" on both sides of hole.)
HERALD (481 "Bells of Love").......... 10-15 '60s
(Has "45 rpm" on left side only.)
Members: William Terrel; Charles Thomas; Al Clarke; George Poitier; Emra Clemmons.

MINT TATOO

Singles: 7-inch

DOT (17242 "I'm Talking About You") 5-10 69

LPs: 10/12-inch

DOT (25918 "Mint Tatoo").......... 15-25 69
Members: Bruce Stephens; Burns Kellogg.
Also see BLUE CHEER

MINTS

Singles: 7-inch

AIRPORT (103 "The Magic of Love") 10-20 58
Also see COPELAND, Ken / Mints

MINTZ, Junier
(Frank Zappa)

Singles: 7-inch

REPRISE/STRAIGHT (1027 "Tears Began to Fall").......... 20-30 71
Also see ZAPPA, Frank

MIRACLES

Singles: 78 rpm

BATON (210 "A Lovers' Chant") 20-30 55

Singles: 7-inch

BATON (210 "A Lovers' Chant") 50-75 55
Also see HOGAN, Carl, & Miracles

MIRACLES

Singles: 78 rpm

CASH (1008 "You're an Angel").......... 50-75 55

Singles: 7-inch

CASH (1008 "You're an Angel").......... 100-150 55
Members: Val Poliuto; Herman Chaney; Manuel Chavez; Charles Middleton.

MIRACLES *P&R '59*
(Smokey Robinson & Miracles; featuring Bill Smokey Robinson; featuring Billy Griffin)

Singles: 78 rpm

END (1016 "Got a Job") 150-250 58

Singles: 12-inch

COLUMBIA.......... 4-6 77

Singles: 7-inch

CHESS (119 "Bad Girl").......... 3-5 84
CHESS (1734 "Bad Girl") 50-75 59
(Black label.)
CHESS (1734 "Bad Girl") 20-30 59
(Blue label.)
CHESS (1768 "All I Want").......... 15-25 60
COLUMBIA.......... 4-6 77-78
END (1016 "Got a Job") 30-40 58
END (1029 "Money") 30-40 58
(No mention of Roulette Records.)
END (1029 "Money") 10-20 58
(Has "A Division of Roulette Records Inc".)
END (1084 "Money") 5-10 61
MOTOWN (G1 "Bad Girl").......... 1000-1500 59
(May or may not have TLX-2207 on label.)
MOTOWN (400 & 500 series).......... 3-5 '80s
MOTOWN (2207 "Bad Girl").......... 400-450 59
MOTOWN/TOPPS (11 "Shop Around").... 50-75 67
(Topps Chewing Gum promotional item. Single-sided, cardboard flexi, picture disc. Issued with generic paper sleeve.)
ROULETTE GOLDEN GOODIES.......... 4-6 '70s
STANDARD GROOVE (13090 "I Care About Detroit").......... 150-200 68
(Tamla logo at top, Artist credit at bottom. Promotional issue only.)
STANDARD GROOVE (13090 "I Care About Detroit").......... 100-150 68
(Artist credit at top. Promotional issue only.)
TAMLA (009 "The Christmas Song").... 200-250 63
(Promotional issue only.)
TAMLA (54028 "The Feeling Is So Fine"/"You Can Depend on Me") 300-400 60
(With common version of *You Can Depend on Me*.)
TAMLA (54028 "The Feeling Is So Fine"/"You Can Depend on Me") 400-500 60
(With alternate take of *You Can Depend on Me*. Can be identified by the letter "A" following the identification number in the trail-off.)
TAMLA (54028 "Way Over There"/"Depend on Me") 100-200 60
(With alternate take of *Way Over There*, sans strings. Not available elsewhere.)
TAMLA (54028 "Way Over There"/"Depend on Me") 40-50 60
(With the hit version of *Way Over There*, the same as is heard on their Tamla LPs.)
TAMLA (54034 "Shop Around").......... 100-150 61
(Horizontal lines across top half of label. Has an alternate take of *Shop Around*. Has either "H55518 A-2" or "45-L1 37003" etched in the trail-off.)
TAMLA (54034 "Shop Around") 75-125 61
(No horizontal lines and Tamla globe logo at top. Has an alternate, slower take of *Shop Around*. Etched in trail-off is "H55518 A-2.")
TAMLA (54034 "Shop Around") 10-20 61
(Has the hit version of *Shop Around*. Etched in trail-off is "L1" or "ARP L-1.")
TAMLA (54036 "Ain't It Baby").......... 50-75 61
TAMLA (54044 "Broken Hearted").......... 25-50 61
TAMLA (54048 "You Gotta Pay Some Dues").......... 50-100 61
(Note title variation.)
TAMLA (54048 "Everybody's Gotta Pay Some Dues").......... 25-50 61
TAMLA (54053 "What's So Good About Goodbye") 15-25 62
(Black vinyl.)
TAMLA (54053 "What's So Good About Goodbye") 20-30 62
(Colored vinyl. Promotional issue only.)
TAMLA (54059 "I'll Try Something New"). 10-20 62
TAMLA (54069 "Way Over There") 10-20 62
TAMLA (54073 thru 54184).......... 5-10 62-69
TAMLA (54189 "Point It Out") 4-8 69
(Black vinyl.)
TAMLA (54189 "Point It Out") 15-20 69
(Colored vinyl. Promotional issue only.)
TAMLA (54194 thru 54268).......... 4-6 70-76

Picture Sleeves

MOTOWN (411 "Tracks of My Tears") 4-8 87
TAMLA (54034 "Shop Around").......... 5-10 '90s
TAMLA (54044 "Broken Hearted").......... 75-125 61
TAMLA (54048 "Everybody's Gotta Pay Some Dues").......... 50-75 61
TAMLA (54059 "I'll Try Something New"). 40-60 62
TAMLA (54098 "I Like It Like That") 15-25 64
TAMLA (54127 thru 54194).......... 10-20 65-70

EPs: 7-inch

TAMLA (60254 "Greatest Hits from the Beginning") 30-50 66
(Juke box issue only. Includes title strips.)
TAMLA (60267 "Going to a Go Go").......... 30-50 66
(Juke box issue only. Includes title strips.)

LPs: 10/12-inch

COLUMBIA 8-10 77-78
IMPERIAL HOUSE 8-12 79
MOTOWN (Except 793 & 8238) 5-10 82-84
MOTOWN (793 "Anthology") 12-18 74
MOTOWN (8238 "Greatest Hits from the Beginning").......... 8-12
NATURAL RESOURCES.......... 5-10 78
TAMLA (220 "Hi! We're the Miracles").. 250-500 61
(White label.)
TAMLA (220 "Hi! We're the Miracles").. 250-350 61
(Yellow label with globes.)
TAMLA (223 "Cookin' with the Miracles").......... 250-500 61
(White label.)
TAMLA (223 "Cookin' with the Miracles").......... 200-300 62
(Yellow label with globes.)
TAMLA (230 "I'll Try Something New"). 250-500 62
(White label.)
TAMLA (230 "I'll Try Something New"). 100-150 62
(Yellow label with globes.)
TAMLA (236 "Christmas with the Miracles").......... 150-200 62
TAMLA (238 "Fabulous Miracles") 150-200 63
TAMLA (238 "You Really Got a Hold on Me").......... 75-125 63
(Reissue with new title.)
TAMLA (241 "On Stage").......... 50-100 63
TAMLA (245 "Mickey's Monkey") 50-75 63
(Monaural.)
TAMLA (245 "Mickey's Monkey") 75-125 63
(Stereo.)
TAMLA (254 "Greatest Hits from the Beginning").......... 25-35 63
(Monaural.)
TAMLA (254 "Greatest Hits from the Beginning").......... 35-45 63
(Stereo.)
TAMLA (267 "Going to a Go Go").......... 40-50 65
(Tamla globe label.)
TAMLA (271 thru 297).......... 15-30 66-70
TAMLA (301 thru 344).......... 10-20 71-76
Members: William "Smokey" Robinson; Pete Moore; Bobby Rogers; Ron White; Claudette Rogers; Billy Griffin; Marv Tarplin.
Also see MARVELETTES / Mary Wells / Miracles / Marvin Gaye
Also see McCULLERS, Mickey
Also see ROBINSON, Smokey
Also see RON & BILL

MIRACLE-TONES

Singles: 7-inch

J&M (5803 "Tell Me My Darling").......... 400-600 58

MIRANDA, Billy

Singles: 7-inch

CHECKER (957 "Go Ahead") 10-15 60
QUEENS (721 "You Could've Had a Good Time") 50-75

MIRANDA, Bob
(With the Happenings)

Singles: 7-inch

ALLEGIANCE (75708 "Oh Diane").......... 5-10 89
(Promotional issue only.)
B.T. PUPPY (544 "Girl on a Swing") 5-10 68
L.A. ROCK.......... 4-8 87
MIDLAND INT'L.......... 4-6 77
Also see HAPPENINGS

MIRANDA, Ralph
(Ralph Miranda & Del Toro's)

Singles: 7-inch

ROGO (1025 "The Flame").......... 100-200 59
ROGO ("A Little Bit of Love").......... 25-50 61
(Selection number not known.)
ROGO ("Angel of My Dreams") 25-50 62
(Selection number not known.)

MIRETTES *P&R/R&B '68*

Singles: 7-inch

MIRWOOD (5514 "Your Kind Ain't No Good") 5-10 66
MIRWOOD (5531 "Now That I Found You Baby").......... 5-10 67
REVUE (11004 "In the Midnight Hour")...... 5-10 67
REVUE (11017 "Real Thing") 5-10 68
REVUE (11029 "First Love").......... 5-10 68
UNI 4-8 69

LPs: 10/12-inch

REVUE.......... 12-18 68
UNI 10-15 69
Members: Vanetta Fields; Jessie Smith; Robbie Montgomery.
Also see IKETTES

MISFITS
("Misfits & Band")

Singles: 7-inch

ARIES (7-10-4 "Midnight Star") 50-150 61
HUSH (105 "Give Me Your Heart").......... 40-60 61

MISFITS

Singles: 7-inch

JOEY (117 "Chicago Confidential") 10-15 61

MISFITS

Singles: 7-inch

AGAR (7130 "Mess Around").......... 25-35 62

MISFITS
Singles: 7-inch
IMPERIAL (66054 "Lost Love")....................5-10 64
SOUND STAGE 7 (2538 "It's Up to You")..5-10 65

MISFITS
Singles: 7-inch
TRUMP (356 "Two, Three or Twelve").... 30-40 66
(500 made.)

MISFITS
LPs: 10/12-inch
RUBY (804 "Walk Among Us")........... 100-200 78
(Red cover. No bar code on cover.)
RUBY (804 "Walk Among Us").............. 10-20 78
(Green cover. Has bar code on cover.)
Members: Glenn Danzig; Franche Coma; Jerry Only; Mr. Jim.

MISFITS
Singles: 7-inch
TIRIS (707 "Please Believe Me")............ 20-30

MISHAPS
Singles: 7-inch
HEMPHILL ("Come On Up")................... 35-55 '60s
(Selection number not known.)

MISHOE, Watson
Singles: 7-inch
DIXIE (1011 "She Told a Lie")............... 50-100 60

MISQUEZ, Isidro
Singles: 7-inch
CREST (1048 "House of Lords")................8-12 58

MISS DEE
LPs: 10/12-inch
DAVIS (120 "Sexarama Joe")................ 50-100 '50s

MISS GEORGIA
Singles: 7-inch
CIRCLE DOT (1003 "Rockin' After School")... 150-250 60

MISS L.L. & 3 MICE
Singles: 7-inch
SKYWAY (138 "No Cheese").....................8-12 63

MISS LA VELL
Singles: 7-inch
DUKE (307 "Yes, I've Been Crying")........ 10-15 59
DUKE (322 "Stolen Love")....................... 10-15 60
DUKE (334 "Tide of Love")...................... 10-15 61
DUKE (372 "Run to You")...........................5-10 64
DUKE (382 "Best Part of Me")...................5-10 64

MISS PEACHES
(Elsie Griner)
Singles: 78 rpm
GROOVE.. 15-20 54
RCA 10-15 56
Singles: 7-inch
GROOVE (0009 "Calling Moody Field") .. 30-40 54
NRC (064 "Calling Moody Field")............ 10-20 61
RCA (6543 "Mama Done Said")............... 10-20 56

MISS RHAPSODY
(Viola Underhill)
Singles: 78 rpm
SAVOY (534 "Sweet Man")...................... 10-20 45
SAVOY (536 "Blues in My Heart")........... 10-20 45
SAVOY (565 "We're Sisters Under the Skin").. 10-20 45
SAVOY (5510 "Bye Bye Baby")............... 10-20 44
SAVOY (5511 "Hey Lawdy Mama")......... 10-20 44
SAVOY (5532 "He May Be Your Man")... 10-20 46

MISS SHARECROPPER
(Dolores Williams)
Singles: 78 rpm
NATIONAL (9151 "I've Tried").................. 15-25 47
NATIONAL (9153 "Take Out Some Time").. 15-25 47

MISSILES
Singles: 7-inch
LAWN (213 "Singing Flute")........................5-10 63

MISSING LINKS
Singles: 7-inch
ROSCOE (418 "I Cried Goodbye") 15-25 65

MISSING LINKS
Singles: 7-inch
DISCOVERY (102265 "You've Got Your Posies On")... 15-25 65
SOCK-IT (203 "Don't Hang Me Up").........15-25 65

MISSING LINKS
Singles: 7-inch
AMY (960 "I Told You I Loved You")...........5-10 66
JOWAR (105 "I Told You I Loved You")...25-35 66
Members: George Mesecke; Al Vertucci; Joe Parisi; Larry Rubenstein; Dennis Raffelock.

MISSING LINKS
Singles: 7-inch
PYRO (53 "Midnight Hour").......................10-15 66

MISSING LINKS
Singles: 7-inch
PARIS TOWER (115 "Where Were You Last Night")..15-25 67
SIGNET (931 "You Hypnotize Me")..........10-15 67

MISSING LYNX
Singles: 7-inch
UNITED SOUNDS (100 "Hang Around")..10-20 67

MISSLES
(Cadillacs)
Singles: 7-inch
NOVEL (200 "Space Ship").......................15-25 60
Also see CADILLACS

MISTAKES
Singles: 7-inch
LO-FI (2312 "Chapel Bells")......................40-50 59
(Black vinyl.)
LO-FI (2312 "Chapel Bells").......................10-15
(Red vinyl.)

MR. BEAR
(With His Bearcats; Teddy McRae)
Singles: 78 rpm
GROOVE...10-15 55
Singles: 7-inch
GROOVE (0125 "I'm Gonna Keep My Good Eye On You")..40-60 55
GROOVE (0138 "Peek-a-Boo")..................25-35 56
GROOVE (0150 "Mr. Bear Comes to Town")..25-35 56
Session: King Curtis; Mickey Baker; Sam Taylor; Sticks Evans; Teacho Wiltshire; Milt Hinton; Al Lucas.
Also see BAKER, Mickey
Also see DUPREE, Jack, & Mr. Bear
Also see KING CURTIS
Also see TAYLOR, Sam "The Man"
Also see WILTSHIRE, Teacho

MR. CLEAN
Singles: 7-inch
ORIGINAL SOUND (40 "Mr. Clean")....150-200 63
Also see ZAPPA, Frank

MR. FORD & MR. GOON-BONES
(Ralph Ford & Ted Goon) *P&R '49*
Singles: 78 rpm
CRYSTALETTE (601 "Ain't She Sweet")..10-15 49
Singles: 7-inch
CRYSTALETTE (601 "Ain't She Sweet")..15-25 49
DOT (15920 "Ain't She Sweet")..................5-10 59
Also see MR. GOON BONES

MR. GASSER & WEIRDOS
Singles: 7-inch
CAPITOL ("Doin' the Surfing"/"Finksville") .5-10 64
(Bonus promotional single, packaged with an LP by the Super Stocks.)
LPs: 10/12-inch
CAPITOL (T-2010 "Hot Rod Hootenanny")...30-50 63
(Monaural.)
CAPITOL (ST-2010 "Hot Rod Hootenanny")...40-60 63
(Stereo.)
CAPITOL (T-2057 "Rods 'N' Ratfinks")...75-100 63
(Monaural.)
CAPITOL (ST-2057 "Rods 'N' Ratfinks") 100-150 63
(Stereo.)
CAPITOL (T-2114 "Surfink") 40-60 63
(Monaural. With *Midnight Run*, a bonus single by the Super Stocks.)
CAPITOL (T-2114 "Surfink") 35-55 63
(Monaural. Without bonus single.)
CAPITOL (ST-2114 "Surfink")...................50-70 63
(Stereo. With *Midnight Run*, a bonus single by the Super Stocks.)
CAPITOL (ST-2114 "Surfink")...................45-55 63
(Stereo. Without bonus single.)
Also see DALE, Dick / Jerry Cole / Super Stocks / Mr. Gasser & Weirdos
Also see SUPER STOCKS8-12........................ 58

MR. GOON BONES
Singles: 78 rpm
REPUBLIC (7116 "Goon Bones Ditty")......5-10 55
Singles: 7-inch
REPUBLIC (7116 "Goon Bones Ditty")....10-15 55
Also see GOON BONES / Muzzy Marcellino
Also see MR. FORD & MR. GOON-BONES

MISTER HIPP
Singles: 7-inch
USA (867 "Sloopy and the Red Moron")..15-20 67
(Single-sided. Promotional issue only.)

MR. LEE
(Little Mr. Lee & Cherokees)
Singles: 7-inch
ADDIT (1229 "Dear One")........................10-20 60
GNP CRESCENDO (331 "Lucille, Lucille")...5-10 64
IMPERIAL (5931 "Thank You")................10-15 63
SURE SHOT (5002 "Party Time")...........25-35 64
SURE SHOT (5006 "Come Closer")...........5-10 65
SURE SHOT (5015 "Young Love")............5-10 66
WINTER (501 "The Decision")..................25-35 60

MR. LEE & EL CAMINOS
Singles: 7-inch
NOLTA (355 "My Darling I Love You").....40-50 64

MR. LEE & FRANK ANDRADE 5
Singles: 7-inch
SKYLARK (503 "Hey Mrs. Jones")..........15-25 64

MR. LOVE
Singles: 7-inch
IGL (119 "Hot Pepper")............................15-25 '60s

MR. LUCKY & GAMBLERS
Singles: 7-inch
DOT (16930 "Take a Look at Me")..........10-20 66
JERDEN (799 "Take a Look at Me").........15-25 66
(Some question the existence of this number. We cannot yet confirm its release.)
KASINO (1001 "New Orleans")................15-25 65
PANORAMA (37 "Take a Look at Me")....10-20 66
PANORAMA (52 "Alice Designs")...........10-15 66
UNITED INT'L (1001 "Searching")............10-20 65
UNITED INT'L (4404 "Koko Joe")............10-20 66
Members: Willy Reiner; Alan Gunter; Jim Dunlap.

MR. M.B.
(Mack Banks)
Singles: 7-inch
ELMORE (101 "Yo Yo")..........................50-100
Also see BANKS, Mack

MISTER MYSTIC
("?Mister Mystic?"; Ronnie Armstrong)
Singles: 7-inch
PICTURE (10001 "Mister Mystic")...........15-25 61

MR. P.T. & PARTY-TIMERS
Singles: 7-inch
FEDERAL (12418 "Aunt Susie")..............40-60 61

MR. PERCY
Singles: 78 rpm
DOT (1205 "Full of Misery").....................15-25 54
Singles: 7-inch
DOT (1205 "Full of Misery").....................25-50 54

MR. PITIFUL
Singles: 7-inch
JOSIE (987 "One Dollar Man")..................5-10 68

MR. SAD HEAD
Singles: 78 rpm
RCA...25-50 52-53
Singles: 7-inch
RCA (4938 "Butcher Boy").....................50-100 52
RCA (5089 "Hot Weather Blues")............40-60 52
RCA (5230 "I'm High")............................40-60 53
RCA (5388 "Make Haste").......................40-60 53

MR. SAKS & BLUE STRINGS
(Tom Brown & Tom Toms)
Singles: 7-inch
LE CAMP (1900 "Are You Lonesome Tonight")...15-25 60
Members: Joe "Mr. Saks" Donnell; Bill Smith Combo.
Also see BROWN, Tom, & Tom Toms
Also see SMITH, Bill

MR. SHORT STUFF & BIG JOE WILLIAMS
LPs: 10/12-inch
SPIVEY 15-25
Also see MR. SHORT STUFF
Also see WILLIAMS, Big Joe, & Short Stuff Macon

MR. STRINGBEAN
(With Joe Morris & His Orchestra)
Singles: 78 rpm
HERALD 15-25 53
Singles: 7-inch
HERALD (418 "Pass the Juice, Miss Lucy")..20-30 53
(Black vinyl.)
HERALD (418 "Pass the Juice, Miss Lucy")..50-100 53
(Red vinyl.)
Also see MORRIS, Joe, & His Orchestra

MR. SUNSHINE & HIS GUITAR PICKERS
Singles: 78 rpm
R.F.D. (5082 "Marijuana – The Devil's Flower")..30-40 51

MR. SWING
(With Bobby Plater's Orchestra)
Singles: 78 rpm
BULLET (327 "Beer Bottle Boogie").........50-75 50

MR. TEARS
Singles: 7-inch
4J (509 "Don't Lead Me On")...................20-30 63

MR. TWELVE STRING
(Glen Campbell)
Singles: 7-inch
WORLD PACIFIC (77803 "All I Really Want to Do")..5-10 65
LPs: 10/12-inch
WORLD PACIFIC (1835 "Mr. 12-String Guitar")..10-15 65
Also see CAMPBELL, Glen

MR. X
Singles: 7-inch
VITA (152 "Rock Doc")............................25-50 57

MR. "X" & EX-TONES
Singles: 7-inch
H.O.B. (1000 "I'm in Love").....................50-100 59

MR. ZULU & WARRIORS
Singles: 7-inch
SCORE (7-11 "Anna")...........................250-500
(Colored vinyl.)

MISTERS
Singles: 7-inch
CHANTE (1002 "Too Many Girls")...........20-30 59
(First issue. Same number used on a Marx release.)
DECCA (31026 "Too Many Girls")............10-15 59

MISTERS VIRTUE
Singles: 7-inch
VECTOR (4979 "Captured")......................20-30

MISTICS
Singles: 7-inch
CAPRI (631 "Memories")..........................10-15 63

MISTICS
Singles: 7-inch
KIRK (636 "You'll Be There")....................10-15 64

MISTREATER
Singles: 7-inch
700 WEST (16507 "Hell's Fire")..................5-10 80
LPs: 10/12-inch
CPI (1280 "Hell's Fire").........................200-300 '80s
(10-inch LP.)
ERIKA ("Mistreater")..............................15-25 85
(Black vinyl. Selection number not known.)
ERIKA ("Mistreater")..............................25-35 85
(Red vinyl. Selection number not known.)
Members: Dane Alex; Johnny Rainbow; Steven E.; Gregory Jay.

MISTY & DO-DROPS
Singles: 7-inch
IMPERIAL (5975 "Answer Me, My Love")..8-12 63

MISTY BLUES
Singles: 7-inch
STATURE (5-7 "I Feel No Pain")..............15-25 66

MISTY FOUR
Singles: 7-inch
DEL MORAL (6001 "The Legend of Sleepy Hollow") .... 15-25 '60s

MISUNDERSTOOD
Singles: 7-inch
BLUES SOUND (13 "You Don't Have to Go") .... 20-25 '60s
Member: Glenn Campbell.
Also see GOLDTONES

MITCH & GAIL
Singles: 7-inch
REPRISE (520 "Blame It On the Times") ...5-10 66
Member: Mitchell Torok.
Also see TOROK, Mitchell

MITCHELL, Billy *R&B '69*
(Billy Mitchell Group)
Singles: 78 rpm
ATLANTIC 50-75 51-52
Singles: 7-inch
ATLANTIC (933 "My Love, My Desire") 150-250 51
CALLA (165 "Oh Happy Day") 5-10 69
CALLA (167 "Too Busy Thinking 'Bout My Baby") 5-10 69
JUBILEE (5400 "Short Skirts") 10-15 61
POPLAR (105 "Bottomless Pit") 15-25 57
SMASH (1802 "Just Waiting") 5-10 62
U.A. (235 "Call to Me") 8-12 60
WARWICK (501 "It Doesn't Matter to Me") 10-15 59
Also see CLOVERS
Also see MORRIS, Joe, & His Orchestra
Also see WILSON, Sonny

MITCHELL, Billy
Singles: 7-inch
IMPERIAL (5520 "Satellite Beep Bop") 10-20 58

MITCHELL, Billy
EPs: 7-inch
DOOTONE (210 "Party Songs") 10-15 56
LPs: 10/12-inch
DOOTONE (212 "Songs for Fun") 30-40 56

MITCHELL, Blue
Singles: 7-inch
BLUE NOTE (1921 "Fungii Mama") 5-10 65
MAINSTREAM (5506 "Soul Village") 4-6 71
MAINSTREAM (5538 "Last Tango in Paris") 4-6 72
MAINSTREAM (5552 "Graffiti Blues") 4-6 72
RCA (10462 "Satin Soul") 4-6 76
RIVERSIDE 5-10 61-63
LPs: 10/12-inch
BLUE NOTE (4257 "Boss Horn") 8-12 67
BLUE NOTE (84272 "Heads Up") 8-12 68
MAINSTREAM (400 "Graffiti Blues") 5-10 73
RIVERSIDE 10-15 59-63
Members: Blue Mitchell; Junior Cook; Chick Corea; Gene Taylor; Aloysius Foster.

MITCHELL, Bobby
Singles: 78 rpm
DERBY 10-15 49
MERCURY 10-15 49

MITCHELL, Bobby *R&B '56*
(With the Toppers; with Basie-Ites)
Singles: 78 rpm
IMPERIAL 25-50 53-57
Singles: 7-inch
IMPERIAL (5236 "I'm Cryin'") 150-250 53
IMPERIAL (5250 "One Friday Morning") 150-250 53
IMPERIAL (5270 "Baby's Gone") 100-200 54
IMPERIAL (5282 "Angel Child") 75-125 54
IMPERIAL (5295 "The Wedding Bells Are Ringing") 100-200 54
IMPERIAL (5309 "I'm a Young Man") .. 100-200 54
IMPERIAL (5326 "I Wish I Knew") 50-75 55
IMPERIAL (5346 "I Cried") 75-125 55
IMPERIAL (5378 "Try Rock and Roll") 15-25 56
IMPERIAL (5412 "You're My Angel") 15-25 56
IMPERIAL (5378 "No No No") 15-25 57
IMPERIAL (5392 "I Try So Hard") 50-100 57
IMPERIAL (5412 "I've Got My Fingers Crossed") 15-25 57
IMPERIAL (5440 "You Always Hurt the One You Love") 15-25 57
IMPERIAL (5475 "I'm Gonna Be a Wheel Someday") 15-25 57
IMPERIAL (5511 "I Love to Hold You") 15-25 58
IMPERIAL (5558 "Hearts of Fire") 15-25 58
IMPERIAL (5882 "When First We Met") ... 10-20 62
IMPERIAL (5923 "I Don't Want to Be a Wheel No More") 10-20 63
RIP (576 "Walking in Circles") 10-15 63
RON (337 "Send Me Your Picture") 10-20 61
RON (342 "There's Only One of You") 10-20 61
SHOW-BIZ (717 "Well, I Done Got Over It") 15-25 59
Also see MITCHUM, Billy

MITCHELL, Chad, Trio *P&R/LP '62*
Singles: 7-inch
COLPIX 5-10 59-61
KAPP 5-10 61-63
MAY (116 "Sally Ann") 4-8 62
MERCURY 4-8 63-64
Picture Sleeves
KAPP 10-15 61-62
MERCURY 8-12 63-65
LPs: 10/12-inch
COLPIX 20-30 60
KAPP 15-25 61-64
MERCURY 15-20 63-64
Members: Chad Mitchell; Joe Frazier; Mike Kobluk; Jim [Roger] McGuinn.
Also see McGUINN, Roger
Also see MITCHELL, Chad
Also see MITCHELL TRIO

MITCHELL, Chad, Trio, & Gatemen
LPs: 10/12-inch
COLPIX (7296 "In Concert, Everybody's Listening") 20-25 64
Also see GATEMEN
Also see MITCHELL, Chad, Trio

MITCHELL, Dave
(David Mitchell)
Singles: 7-inch
CRYSTAL (7733 "Temptation") 10-20 63
CRYSTAL ("Under the Rug") 10-20 63
(Selection number not known.)
FELSTED (8636 "Target") 15-25 61
MET (2768 "The Trip") 10-20 65

MITCHELL, Duke
Singles: 78 rpm
LIBERTY 5-10 56
Singles: 7-inch
ALADDIN (3427 "I Love You Much Too Much") 15-25 58
CRYSTALETTE (743 "The Lion") 10-20 61
(Reissued as *Surf Stomp*, by the Crestriders.)
LIBERTY (55031 "Be Mine Tonight") 10-15 56
LIBERTY (55086 "Crazy Heart") 8-12 57
LIBERTY (55158 "Be Mine Tonight") 8-12 58
VERVE (10206 "Tik-a-Tee, Tik-a-Tay") 5-10 60
VERVE (10215 "Pagan Love Song") 5-10 60
Also see CRESTRIDERS
Also see SPINNERS

MITCHELL, Freddie, Orchestra *R&B '49*
(With Rip Harrigan; Freddie Mitchell)
Singles: 78 rpm
ABC-PAR 5-10 57
BRUNSWICK 5-10 53
CORAL 5-10 53
DERBY (Except 713) 5-10 49-52
DERBY (713 "Doby's Boogie") 20-30 49
MERCURY 5-10 52
Singles: 7-inch
ABC-PAR 10-15 57-61
BRUNSWICK (84023 "Mr. Freddie's Boogie") 15-25 53
CORAL (61740 "Snow Blues") 10-20 53
DERBY (Except 733 & 777) 20-30 49-52
DERBY (733 "Easter Parade") 30-40 50
DERBY (777 "Hot Ice") 20-30 51
(Black vinyl.)
DERBY (777 "Hot Ice") 40-60 51
(Red vinyl.)
MERCURY (8286 "Perfidia") 10-20 52
MERCURY (70018 "Later Gator") 10-20 52
ROCK 'N ROLL (609 "Preachin'") 50-100 56
EPs: 7-inch
DERBY (102 "Boogie Woogie") .... 15-25 '50s
LPs: 10/12-inch
ALLEGRO/ROYAL (1600 "That Boogie Beat") .... 30-50 '50s
TRIP .... 10-15 '60s
"X" (1030 "Boogie Bash") 50-75 56
Session: King Curtis; Joe Black.
Also see BLACK, Joe
Also see KING CURTIS

MITCHELL, Guy *P&R '50*
(Al Cernick; with Sauerbraten Five)
Singles: 78 rpm
COLUMBIA 5-15 50-57
KING (15125 "Cabaret") 10-15 51
Singles: 7-inch
CHALICE (711 "My Angel"/"Bit of Love") .15-25 63
CHALICE (711 "My Angel"/"Mr. Hobo") 15-25 63
(Note different flip.)
CHALICE (712 "Take Your Time") 15-25 63
CHALICE (713 "Your Imagination") 15-25 63
COLLECTABLES .... 3-5 '80s
COLUMBIA 10-20 50-61
ERIC 3-5 83
GMI 4-6 74
JOY 4-8 62-63
KING (15125 "Cabaret") 20-30 51
(Previously issued as by Al Grant, Al Cernick's pseudonym before using Guy Mitchell.)
REPRISE 4-6 66
STARDAY 4-6 67-69
Picture Sleeves
COLUMBIA (40769 "Singing the Blues") .. 15-20 56
COLUMBIA (40820 "Knee Deep in the Blues") 15-20 57
COLUMBIA (40877 "Rock-a-Billy") 10-20 57
COLUMBIA (41476 "Heartaches by the Number") 10-15 60
COLUMBIA (41853 "Sunshine Guitar") 10-15 60
COLUMBIA (42231 "Soft Rain") 10-15 61
EPs: 7-inch
COLUMBIA 10-15 54-57
LPs: 10/12-inch
COLUMBIA (1211 "Guy in Love") 15-25 58
(Monaural.)
COLUMBIA (1226 "Greatest Hits") 15-25 59
COLUMBIA (1552 "Sunshine Guitar") 15-25 60
(Monaural.)
COLUMBIA (6231 "Open Spaces") 25-50 53
(10-inch LP.)
COLUMBIA (8011 "Guy in Love") 20-30 58
(Stereo.)
COLUMBIA (8352 "Sunshine Guitar") 20-30 60
(Stereo.)
KING (644 "Sincerely Yours") 150-250 59
(Mitchell pictured but not identified on cover. Includes tracks recorded as Al Grant.)
NASHVILLE 5-10 70
STARDAY 10-15 68-69
Also see CAVALLARO, Carmen, Featuring Al Cernick
Also see CLOONEY, Rosemary, & Guy Mitchell
Also see GRANT, Al

MITCHELL, Jeff, & His Dad Duke
("10 Year Old Wonder;" with Duke Mitchell & Orchestra)
Singles: 7-inch
CLICK (728 "Fountain of the Bells") 8-12

MITCHELL, Jimmy
Singles: 7-inch
MERCURY (71522 "At This Moment") 20-30 59
RCA (7528 "I Only Live for Your Love") ... 20-30 59

MITCHELL, Jock
(With the Fabulous Angels)
Singles: 7-inch
GOLDEN HIT (103 "Free at Last") .... 75-125 '60s
IMPACT (1004 "Work with Me Annie") 10-20 66
IMPACT (1023 "Not a Chance in a Million") 50-100 67

MITCHELL, Johnny
Singles: 7-inch
TEAR DROP (3085 "A Letter to the President") 25-75 62
Also see MAJESTICS

MITCHELL, Joni *LP '68*
Singles: 7-inch
ASYLUM 3-6 72-80
ELEKTRA 4-6 75
GEFFEN 3-5 82-91
REPRISE 4-8 68-72
Picture Sleeves
GEFFEN 3-6 82-85
LPs: 10/12-inch
ASYLUM 6-12 72-80
GEFFEN 5-10 82-91
REPRISE 10-20 68-71

MITCHELL, Joni, & L.A. Express
LPs: 10/12-inch
ASYLUM (202 "Miles of Aisles") 20-30 74
Also see MITCHELL, Joni

MITCHELL, Lee
(With the Curley Money Combo)
Singles: 7-inch
MUSICOR (1479 "You and You Alone") .. 10-15 73
PHILLIPS INT'L (3530 "The Frog") 10-20 58
ROLL 5-10 75
SHARP (8062 "Rootie Tootie Baby") .. 750-1000 59
SURE SHOT (5030 "Where Does Love Go") 5-10 67
TRACKDOWN 8-12
Also see MONEY, Curley

MITCHELL, Marlon "Madman," & Rocketeers
Singles: 7-inch
VENA (100 "Ice Cold Baby") 450-550 57

MITCHELL, McKinley *R&B '62*
(With the Honey Duo Twins; McKinley "Soul" Mitchell)
Singles: 7-inch
BIG BOY (85 "I Need to See You") 4-6 85
BIG 3 (6141 "Trouble Blues") 5-10 75
BLACK BEAUTY (301 "Party Across the Hall") 4-8 72
BOXER (204 "Rock Everybody Rock") 100-200 59
CHESS (2046 "Playboy") 5-10 67
CHIMNEYVILLE (10213 "Trouble Blues") .. 5-10 77
CHIMNEYVILLE (10219 "The End of the Rainbow") 4-8 77
CHIMNEYVILLE (10225 "The Town I Live In") 4-6 78
MALACO (2067 "Trouble Blues"/"Run to Love") 8-10 78
MALACO (2067 "Trouble Blues"/"Poverty") . 4-6 80
(Note different flip side.)
MALACO (2071 "A Slave for Your Love") 3-6 80
MIDAS (2029 "The Town I Live In") 20-30 61
(Identification number shown since no selection number is used.)
ONE-DERFUL (4804 "The Town I Live In") 10-15 62
ONE-DERFUL (4808 "All of a Sudden") ... 10-15 62
ONE-DERFUL (4810 "I'm So Glad") 10-15 62
ONE-DERFUL (4812 "Darling That's What You Said") 10-15 63
ONE-DERFUL (4817 "A Bit of Soul") 10-15 63
ONE-DERFUL (4822 "Tell It Like It Is") 10-15 63
ONE-DERFUL (4826 "You Know I've Tried") 10-15 64
ONE-DERFUL (4832 "Watch Over Me") .. 10-15 65
RETTAS (005 "Road of Love") 4-6 82
RETTAS (007 "Watch Over Me") 4-6 83
RETTAS (009 "I Don't Know Which Way to Turn") 4-6 83
SOUTHERN BISCUIT (104 "Fallin' for Your Love") 4-6 80
SANDMAN (702 "This Place Ain't Getting No Better") 5-10 71
SPOONFUL (777-26 "Good Time Baby") 4-8 74
SPOONFULL (777-20 "That Last Home Run") 5-10 74
(Label name misspelled. Identification number shown since no selection number is used.)
TODDLIN' TOWN (117 "The Town I Live In") 5-8 69

MITCHELL, Ronnie
Singles: 7-inch
ATLANTIC (2061 "Still Waters") 5-10 60
BLUE CAT (111 "Having a Party") 5-8 65
BRUNSWICK (55308 "Come On Home to Me Baby") 5-8 66
COLUMBIA (42336 "It's the Talk of the Town") 5-10 62
LAURIE (3395 "I Don't Want to Go On Without You") 4-8 67
LAURIE (3420 "I'm Having a Party") 4-8 68
LAURIE (3436 "My Kind of People") 4-8 68
SEVILLE (108 "How Many Times") 5-10 60
SEVILLE (115 "But Are You Sure") 5-10 61

SEVILLE (116 "More Than My Share")........5-10 61

MITCHELL, Rose

Singles: 78 rpm

IMPERIAL...15-25 54

Singles: 7-inch

IMPERIAL (5243 "Slippin' In")..............30-50 54
IMPERIAL (5260 "Live My Life")..............30-50 54

MITCHELL, Stan

Singles: 7-inch

GONE (5106 "Devil in Disguise")..............15-25 61

MITCHELL, Stanley
(With the Tornados)

Singles: 78 rpm

CHESS 30-40 57

Singles: 7-inch

CHESS (1649 "Would You, Could You"). 50-75 57
DYNAMO (111 "Get It Baby")..................30-40 67

MITCHELL, Steve

Singles: 7-inch

MAST (100 "Linda, Linda").........................5-10 62

MITCHELL, Thomas

Singles: 7-inch

FLASH (108 "I'm a Wise Old Cat")..........50-75

MITCHELL, Tommy

Singles: 78 rpm

MERCURY 15-25 56

Singles: 7-inch

MERCURY (70930 "Juke Box, Help Me Find My Baby")..................................25-35 56

MITCHELL, Tony

Singles: 7-inch

LIBERTY (55110 "Tell Me Tell Me")...........8-12 57

MITCHELL, Tony

Singles: 7-inch

CANADIAN-AMERICAN (143 "Write Me a Letter")..15-25 62
CANADIAN-AMERICAN (157 "A Million Drums")..10-15 63
CANADIAN-AMERICAN (162 "Ponchinello")..5-10 63

MITCHELL, Walter

Singles: 78 rpm

J.V.B. (75827 "Stop Messing Around") 100-150 48

MITCHELL, Willie P&R/R&B '64
(With the Four Kings, "Vocal D. Bryant"; Willie Mitchell Orchestra; "Vocal by Billy Taylor")

Singles: 7-inch

HI 4-8 62-73
HOME OF THE BLUES..............................5-10 60-61
MOTOWN...3-5
SKIPPER (1001 "Wasting My Time").......15-25
STOMPER TIME (1160 "Walking at Your Will")...500-1000 58
STOMPER TIME (1163 "Walkin' Alone")..1000-1500 59

Picture Sleeves

HI (2151 "Up-Hard")....................................5-10 68

EPs: 7-inch

HI (72 "Willie Mitchell")..........................10-15 '60s
HI (32021 "Hold It!!!")..............................10-15 64
(Stereo. Juke box issue only.)
HI (32026 "It's Dance Time")..................10-15 65
(Stereo. Juke box issue only.)

LPs: 10/12-inch

BEARSVILLE 5-8 81
HI (12010 thru 12042)..........................10-20 63-68
(Monaural.)
HI (32010 thru 32058)..........................10-25 63-71
(Stereo.)
HI (8000 series)...5-8 77
MOTOWN..8-10 82
Also see KING, B.B.
Also see TAYLOR, Billy
Also see YURO, Timi

MITCHELL TRIO LP '64

Singles: 7-inch

MERCURY...4-8 65-66
REPRISE..4-8 67

Picture Sleeves

MERCURY...5-10 63-66

LPs: 10/12-inch

MERCURY (20944 "Slightly Irreverent Mitchell Trio")...15-20 64
(Monaural.)
MERCURY (20992 "Typical American Boys")...15-20 65
(Monaural.)
MERCURY (21049 "That's the Way It's Gonna Be")..15-20 65
(Monaural.)
MERCURY (21067 "Violets of Dawn")......15-20 65
(Monaural.)
MERCURY (60944 "Slightly Irreverent Mitchell Trio")..20-25 64
(Stereo.)
MERCURY (60992 "Typical American Boys")...20-25 65
MERCURY (61049 "That's the Way It's Gonna Be")..20-25 65
(Stereo.)
MERCURY (21067 "Violets of Dawn")......20-25 65
(Stereo.)
REPRISE (6354 "Alive")..........................15-20 67
Members: Chad Mitchell; Joe Frazier; Mike Kobluk; John Denver; David Boise; Michael Johnson.
Also see DENVER, John
Also see MITCHELL, Chad, Trio

MITCHUM, Billy
(Billy Mitchell)

Singles: 7-inch

IMPERIAL (5616 "Twelve and Three Quarters")...10-20 59
Also see MITCHELL, Bobby

MITCHUM, Jim

Singles: 7-inch

CANDIX (324 "Lonely Birthday")..............30-40 61
20TH FOX (277 "Lonely Birthday")..........10-20 60

Picture Sleeves

20TH FOX (277 "Lonely Birthday")..........20-40 60

MITCHUM, Robert P&R '58
(With the Calypso Band)

Singles: 78 rpm

CAPITOL 5-15 57-58

Singles: 7-inch

CAPITOL (Except 3986)............................5-10 57
CAPITOL (3986 " Thunder Road")..............8-12 58
(Purple label.)
CAPITOL (3986 "The Ballad of Thunder Road")..4-8 62
(Orange/yellow label. Note title change.)
CAPITOL STARLINE...................................4-8 '60s
MONUMENT...4-6 67

EPs: 7-inch

CAPITOL (853 "Calypso Is Like So")........15-25 57
(Price is for any of three volumes.)

LPs: 10/12-inch

CAPITOL (853 "Calypso Is Like So")........25-50 57
MONUMENT (8086 "That Man")..............15-20 67
(Monaural.)
MONUMENT (18086 "That Man")............20-25 67
(Stereo.)

MITLO SISTERS

Singles: 7-inch

KLIK (8405 "Let Me Tell You")..................30-40 58
Also see DREAMTONES

MIXED EMOTIONS

Singles: 7-inch

KUSTOM KUT (1 "I'll Fade Away")...........25-35 '60s

MIXED EMOTIONS

Singles: 7-inch

ROCK HOUSE (5709 "Gold of My Life")..100-150 84

MIXED UP ZOMBIES

Singles: 7-inch

REL (105 "It's Incredible")..........................5-10 63

MIXERS

Singles: 7-inch

BOLD (101 "You Said You're Leaving")..300-500 58
BOLD (102 "Love and Kisses")...............300-500 59

MIXTURES

Singles: 7-inch

LINDA..10-15 62-64

LPs: 10/12-inch

LINDA (3301 "Stompin' at the Rainbow")..50-100 62

MIZE, Billy C&W '66

Singles: 78 rpm

DECCA...5-10 56

Singles: 7-inch

COLUMBIA 4-8 66-68
DECCA (29812 "Who Will Buy the Wine")..10-15 56
IMPERIAL 4-8 69-70
MEGA...4-6 74-75
U.A...4-6 70-74
ZODIAC..4-6 76-77

Picture Sleeves

COLUMBIA (43546 "Don't Let the Blues Make You Bad")..8-12 66

LPs: 10/12-inch

IMPERIAL 10-15 69
U.A. 8-12 71
ZODIAC..5-10 76
Session: Jordanaires.
Also see BILLY & CLIFF
Also see JORDANAIRES

MIZELL, Hank

Singles: 7-inch

AMAZON (711 "Jungle Rock")..................35-45 63
EKO (506 "Jungle Rock")....................700-900 58
(Some copies credit Jim Bobo.)
KING (101 "Jungle Rock")........................15-25 76
KING (5236 "Jungle Rock")..................100-200 59

MIZELL, Hank, & Jim Bobo

Singles: 7-inch

KING (5445 "What Is Life Without You")..15-25 61
Also see BOBO, Jim
Also see MIZELL, Hank

MIZZELL, Bobby

Singles: 7-inch

CENTURY LIMITED (604 "San Antonio Rose")..4-8 69
HEART ("Same Thing")............................50-75
(Selection number not known.)
KIM (307 "Knockout")............................75-125 57
KIM (308 "Rocket in My Pocket")..................4-8 86
(Colored vinyl.)
PHILIPS (40018 "High Noon")..................10-15 62
REED (1028 "Same Thing")..................100-150 59
20TH FOX (160 "Same Thing")..................50-75 59
Also see ACORN, Bobby, & Leaves
Also see BERNARD, Rod
Also see JIVIN' GENE
Also see LEE, Dickie
Also see NEAL & NEWCOMERS
Also see PRESTON, Johnny
Also see WINTER, Johnny
Also see WOODARD, Jerry

MIZZELL, Bobby, & Glenn Layne

Singles: 7-inch

CENTURY LTD (604 "Sunset Blues")......15-25 60
Also see MIZZELL, Bobby

MO & JO

Singles: 7-inch

LITA (1002 "The Yo Yo Song")...................5-10 62
Members: Gaynel Hodge; Bobby Gross.

MOANIN' GLORIES

Singles: 7-inch

YORKSHIRE (1001 "She Took the Rain Out of My Mind")...30-50 67

MOB P&R '71

Singles: 7-inch

CAMEO (421 "Mystery Man")....................5-10 66
COLOSSUS..4-6 70-71
DAYLIGHT (1000 "Open the Door to Your Heart")..8-12 '60s
MGM...4-6 72-73
MERCURY..4-8 68
PRIVATE STOCK..4-6 75-77
TWINIGHT (111 "Unbelievable")...............8-12 68

Picture Sleeves

COLOSSUS (134 "Give It to Me")................4-8 71

LPs: 10/12-inch

COLOSSUS 10-15 71
MGM (4839 "The Mob").............................10-15 72
PRIVATE STOCK...8-12 75
Members: Art Herrera; Al Herrera; Jimmy Ford; James Holvay; Gary Beiser; Mike Sistak; Tony Nedza; Bobby Raffino.
Also see ARTIE & PHARAOHS
Also see KANE & ABEL

MOBILE STRUGGLERS

Singles: 78 rpm

AMERICAN MUSIC (104 "Memphis Blues")..25-35 49

MOBLEY, John

Singles: 7-inch

TOWN & COUNTRY (6601 "Tunnel of Love")..40-60

MOBLEY, Sylvia

Singles: 7-inch

SANTO (502 "All by Myself")....................15-25 62

MOBY DICK & WHALERS

Singles: 7-inch

FOREST (2009 "You've Got a Bull")........35-45 '60s

MOBY GRAPE P&R/LP '67

Singles: 12-inch

SAN FRANCISCO SOUND 100-125 84
(Set of six picture discs.)

Singles: 7-inch

COLUMBIA..6-12 67-69

Picture Sleeves

COLUMBIA (44173 "Omaha")....................20-25 67

LPs: 10/12-inch

COLUMBIA (2698 "Moby Grape")............40-50 67
(Monaural. Cover pictures Don Stevenson's middle finger over washboard. Price includes bonus poster, which represents about $5 to $10 of the value.)
COLUMBIA (2698 "Moby Grape")............10-20 67
(Monaural. Cover pictures Don Stevenson's hand closed. Price includes bonus poster.)
COLUMBIA (9498 "Moby Grape")............40-50 67
(Stereo. Cover pictures Don Stevenson's middle finger over washboard. Price includes bonus poster, which represents about $5 to $10 of the value.)
COLUMBIA (9498 "Moby Grape")............10-20 67
(Stereo. Cover pictures Don Stevenson's hand closed. Price includes bonus poster.)
COLUMBIA (9613 "Wow")..........................10-15 68
COLUMBIA (9696 "Moby Grape '69")......10-15 69
COLUMBIA (9912 "Truly Fine Citizen")....10-15 69
COLUMBIA (31098 "Great Grape")..........10-15 72
ESCAPE (A1A "Live Grape").......................8-10 78
HARMONY (30393 "Omaha")....................10-12 71
REPRISE (6460 "20 Granite Creek").......10-12 71
SAN FRANCISCO SOUND 10-15 83
(Black vinyl.)
SAN FRANCISCO SOUND (04830 "Moby Grape '84")..20-25 83
(Picture disc.)

Promotional LPs

COLUMBIA (MGS-1 "Grape Jam")...........15-25 68
(With Mike Bloomfield and Al Kooper.)
ESCAPE (95018 "Live Grape")..................15-25 78
(Colored vinyl.)
Members: Don Stevenson; Jerry Miller; Peter Lewis; Skip Spence; Jeff Blackburn; Bob Mosley.
Also see BLOOMFIELD, Mike, & Al Kooper
Also see FRANKLIN, Aretha / Union Gap /Blood, Sweat & Tears / Moby Grape
Also see FRANTICS

MOCKERS

Singles: 7-inch

MONTE VISTA (65-1 "Children of the Sun")..20-30 65

MOCKINGBIRDS

Singles: 7-inch

ABC-PAR (10653 "That's How")...............10-15 65
Members: Graham Gouldman; Kevin Godley.
Also see 10CC

MOD & ROCKERS

LPs: 10/12-inch

JUSTICE (153 "Now")..........................200-300 69

MOD IV

Singles: 7-inch

EMERALD (121 "What Can I Do")...........10-20 '60s

MOD ROCKERS

Singles: 7-inch

DOT (16907 "Lover's Lane").......................5-10 66

MOD SINGERS

Singles: 7-inch

USA (108 "Mr. Thunder")............................5-10 '60s

MOD VI
Singles: 7-inch
EMERALD (127 "What Can I Do") 15-25 67

MOD SQUAD
Singles: 7-inch
TANGERINE (1004 "Charge") 5-10 69

MODDS
Singles: 7-inch
AMERICAN NATIONAL (3041 "Leave My House") 25-35 66

MODEL T. SLIM
(Elmon Mickle)
Singles: 7-inch
AUDIO BLUES .... 5-10 '60s
KENT (504 "Christine") 5-10 69
KIM (1001 "15 Years My Love Was in Vain") 8-12
MAGNUM (739 "Good Morning Little Schoolgirl") 10-15 66
WONDER (15001 "Shake Your Boogie") 20-30 66
Also see MICKLE, Elmon

MODELS
Singles: 7-inch
MGM (13775 "Bend Me, Shape Me") 10-15 67

MODERN FOLK QUARTET
Singles: 7-inch
ALOHA 3-5
LPs: 10/12-inch
HOMECOMING 5-10 87
W.B. 15-25 63-64
Members: Chip Douglas; Stan White; Henry Diltz.
Also see MONKEES
Also see TURTLES
Also see WILCOX THREE

MODERN INK SPOTS
Singles: 7-inch
RUST (5052 "Together") 500-1000 62
(Promotional issue only.)
Members: Al Turner; Reginald Grant; Oscar Drummand; Lynn Thomas; R. Foreman; Gary Evans.
Also see EQUADORS

MODERN LOVERS
LPs: 10/12-inch
BESERKLEY 10-20 76-77
BOMP 8-12 82
HOME OF THE HITS (1910 "Modern Lovers") 20-40 75
MOHAWK 10-15 81
ROUNDER 5-8 88
Members: Jonathan Richman; Jerry Harrison; David Robinson; Ernie Brooks.
Also see CARS
Also see TALKING HEADS

MODERN RED CAPS
Singles: 7-inch
LAWN (254 "Empty World") 10-15 65
PENNTOWNE (101 "Never Kiss a Good Man Good-By") 15-20 65
SWAN (4243 "Golden Teardrops") 30-40 66
Also see GIBSON, Steve
Also see TINDLEY, George, & Modern Red Caps

MODERN TIMES
Singles: 7-inch
GOLDEN WORLD (115 "Stompin' Crazy Legg") 10-20 73
Member: Ed Wingate.

MODERNISTICS
Singles: 7-inch
PIONEER (7315 "Who Can I Turn To") ... 10-15 65

MODS
Singles: 7-inch
KNIGHT (105 "Empty Heart") 20-30 66

MODS
Singles: 7-inch
CEE THREE (10001 "It's for You") 20-30 66

MODS
Singles: 7-inch
PECK (331 "I Give You an Inch") 20-30 66

MODS
Singles: 7-inch
DEE-DEE (812 "Get It Now") .... 8-12 '60s
PLAINS (811 "My Girl") .... 8-12 '60s

MODULATION CORPORATION
Singles: 7-inch
ATOM (1001 "Worms") 25-35 67

MOE, ADRIAN, & SCULPTORS
Singles: 7-inch
COLUMBIA (43445 "Love Train") 5-10 65
Picture Sleeves
COLUMBIA (43445 "Love Train") 8-12 65

MOFFATT, Tom
(With the Flames)
Singles: 7-inch
BERTRAM INT'L (204 "Beyond the Reef") 20-30 57
MAHALO 5-10 63

MOGAMBOS
(Mogambo's)
Singles: 7-inch
SUNBEAM (107 "Wa'tch You Mean") 15-25 58
Note: We're not yet sure what the Bobby Darin connection is here, but we are told there is one.
Also see DARIN, Bobby

MOGEN DAVID & GRAPES OF WRATH
Singles: 7-inch
CHA CHA (757 "Little Girl Gone") 1500-2000 67

MOHAWKS
Singles: 7-inch
COLPIX (117 "Night Run") 15-25 59
Member: Jim Ford.
Also see FORD, Jim

MOHAWKS
Singles: 7-inch
MUTUAL (504 "Shopliftin' Molly") 25-50 64
VAL-UE (211 "I Got a Gal") 50-75 60
(Reco Art in dead wax.)
VAL-UE (211 "I Got a Gal") 10-15 60

MOHAWKS
Singles: 7-inch
MARK (147 "Shaggin'") 10-20 60

MOJO
(George Buford)
Singles: 7-inch
ADELL 15-25 64
FOLK ART (101 "Knockin' on My Door") .. 10-15 '60s
LPs: 10/12-inch
FOLK ART (101 "Shades of Folk Blues") .20-30 '60s
Also see BUFORD, Mojo
Also see LITTLE MOJO

MOJO MEN
Singles: 7-inch
TIDE (2000 "Surfin' Fat Man") 20-30 64
Members: Denny King; Vic Blunt; Paul Case; Bruce Pollard.
Also see CANADIAN BEADLES
Also see DARNELLS

MOJO MEN — P&R '65
(Mojo)
Singles: 7-inch
AUTUMN 10-15 65
GRT 5-8 69
REPRISE 5-10 66-68
LPs: 10/12-inch
GRT (10003 "Mojo Magic") 15-20 69
Members: Dennis DeCarr; Paul Curcio; Jim Alaimo; Don Metchick.

MOJOS
Singles: 7-inch
PARROT (45001 "Everythin's Al'Right") 5-10 64
PARROT (45002 "Why Not Tonight") 5-10 64

MOJOS
Singles: 7-inch
MOJO ("Love Does Its Harm") 15-25 65
(No selection number used.)
MOJO (88 "What She's Done to Me") .... 10-20 '60s
Picture Sleeves
MOJO ("Love Does Its Harm") 25-35 65
Members: Matt Lewis; Jon Earl; Skip Brown; John Percival.

MOLES
Singles: 7-inch
PAGE ONE (21023 "The Moles") 5-10 69
LPs: 10/12-inch
NO LABEL CO. (1566 "Moles") 15-25

MOLES, Gene
(With the Softwinds; Gene "The Draggin' King" Moles)
Singles: 7-inch
CHALLENGE (59249 "Burning Rubber") . 10-20 64
(Also issued as *Batmobile*, by the Bats.)
GARPAX (44176 "Kaha Huna [Goddess of Surfing]") 15-25 63
MOSRITE (210 "Durango") 8-12 66
STARVIEW (1001 "Fingerlickin'") 5-10 68
THREE STAR (4304 "Raunchy") 10-15 63
Also see BATS

MOLINA, Little Ralphie
Singles: 7-inch
CLEF-TONE (154 "Rock & Roll Vowels") .20-40 58

MOLITTERI, Pat
Singles: 7-inch
TEEN (414 "The USA") 20-30 61

MOLLEEN, Ronnie
Singles: 7-inch
KING (5365 "Rockin' Up") 75-100 60

MOLLY HATCHET — LP '78
Singles: 7-inch
EPIC 3-6 79-86
Picture Sleeves
EPIC 4-6 79
EPs: 7-inch
CSP ("Molly Hatchet") 4-8 81
(Promotional issue only. Made for Nestle's candy.)
LPs: 10/12-inch
EPIC (Except picture discs and 40137) 5-10 78-87
EPIC (694 "Flirtin' with Disaster") 40-50 79
(Picture disc. Has die-cut cover. Promotional issue only.)
EPIC (844 "Beatin the Odds") 30-40 80
(Picture disc. Promotional issue only. 1350 made.)
EPIC (1320 "Take No Prisoners") 20-25 81
(Picture disc. Promotional issue only.)
EPIC (35347 "Molly Hatchet") 40-50 78
(Picture disc. Promotional issue only.)
EPIC (36110 "Flirtin' with Disaster") 50-60 79
(Picture disc. Promotional issue only. 450 made.)
EPIC (40137 "Double Trouble Live") 10-15 79
EPIC (40137 "Double Trouble Live") 15-25 79
(White label. Promotional issue only.)
Members: Danny Joe Brown; Jimmy Farrar.

MOLLY MAGUIRES
Singles: 7-inch
TRANSACTION (709 "First Spring Rain") 10-20 69
TRANSACTION (713 "Our Favorite Melodies") 10-20 70
Picture Sleeves
TRANSACTION (709 "First Spring Rain") 10-20 69
Members: Art Mcclure; Jim Davidson; Dirk Weber; Eric Hartwig; Tom Franzini; Steve Kunes; Neil Wang.

MOLOCH
Singles: 7-inch
BOOGER (1 "Cocaine Katy") 50-80
LPs: 10/12-inch
ENTERPRISE 10-15 69

MOM'S APPLE PIE
Singles: 7-inch
BROWN BAG (90000 "Dawn of a New Day") 4-6 72
LPs: 10/12-inch
BROWN BAG (14200 "Mom's Apple Pie") 10-20 72
(Cover pictures a vulva in pie.)
BROWN BAG (14200 "Mom's Apple Pie") 10-15 72
(Reworked cover has wire covering the vulva. Demand is more for the first issue, yet this is actually the rarer cover.)
BROWN BAG (073 "Mom's Apple Pie #2") 8-12 73

MOMENTOS
Singles: 7-inch
REPRISE (20091 "Do the Mashed Potatoes") 5-10 62

MOMENTS — P&R '63
Singles: 7-inch
ERA 5-10 62-64
HIT (101 "Don't Take Your Love from Me") 15-25 63
WORLD ARTISTS (1032 "You Really Got Me") 5-10 64
Also see SHACKLEFORDS

MOMMY
Singles: 7-inch
U.A. (50219 "Love in My Mind") 5-10 67
Also see MELANIE

MONACLES
Singles: 7-inch
VARIETY (301 "I Can't Win") 15-25 66
(Black vinyl.)
VARIETY (301 "I Can't Win") 15-25 66
(Colored vinyl.)
VARIETY (401 "Debbie") 10-15 66
VARIETY (501 "I Found a Way") 10-15 66
VARIETY (601 "Everybody Thinks I'm Lonely") 10-15 66

MONAGRAMS
Singles: 7-inch
CHARRINGTON (1000 "Go-Go Marlin") .. 20-30

MONARCHS
Singles: 78 rpm
WING (90040 "Angels in the Sky") 25-50 55
Singles: 7-inch
WING (90040 "Angels in the Sky") 50-75 55

MONARCHS
Singles: 78 rpm
MELBA 5-10 56
NEIL 10-15 56
Singles: 7-inch
MELBA (101 "Pretty Little Girl") 15-25 56
NEIL (101 "Pretty Little Girl") 50-75 56
(Brown vinyl.)
NEIL (101 "Pretty Little Girl") 40-50 56
(Label name is in slightly smaller print.)
NEIL (101 "Pretty Little Girl") 15-25 56
(Label name in larger print.)
NEIL (103 "Always Be Faithful") 30-40 56

MONARCHS
Singles: 7-inch
JUKE BOX (110 "Yes! Uh! Huh Or Even Maybe") 50-75 57

MONARCHS
(Monarch's)
Singles: 7-inch
LIBAN (1002 "Love You That's Why") 800-1000 59

MONARCHS
Singles: 7-inch
REEGAL (512 "Over the Mountain") 50-75 62

MONARCHS
Singles: 7-inch
ZONE (1067 "Friday Night") 10-15 63

MONARCHS
(Monarchs IV)
Singles: 7-inch
ERWIN (1069 "Surge") 15-25 64

MONARCHS
Singles: 7-inch
YUCCA (172 "Forever Lost") 20-30 64

MONARCHS — P&R '64
Singles: 7-inch
JAM (104 "This Old Heart") 20-30 63
SOUND STAGE 7 (2502 "This Old Heart") 5-10 63
SOUND STAGE 7 (2516 "Look Homeward Angel") 10-15 64
SOUND STAGE 7 (2530 "Climb Every Mountain") 5-10 64
Member: Bob Lange.
Also see ORIGINAL GROUP

MONARCHS
Singles: 7-inch
KENTONE ("Last Night I Dreamed") 50-75

MONARCHS
Singles: 7-inch
ROMAN (4040 "Needles & Pins") 20-30

MONARCHS OF WINSTON-SALEM
Singles: 7-inch
TRIBUNE (1002 "Army of Love") 50-60 65

MON—CLAIRES
Singles: 7-inch
JOEY (6101 "Please Come Back") 150-250 62

MONDAY, Danny
(Dan Monday)
Singles: 7-inch
MODERN (1025 "Baby Without You") . 100-150 64
PREVIEW 4-8

MONDAY, Florian, & Mondos
Singles: 7-inch
REALM (006 "Mondo") 40-60 64
REALM (007 "Rip It, Rip It Up") 100-125 64

MONDAY, Paul
Singles: 7-inch
DOOTO (444 "Are You Ready to Go Steady") 15-25 58

MONDELL, Len
Singles: 7-inch
SMASH (1836 "That's What Girls Are Made Of") 8-12 63

MONDELLOS
Singles: 7-inch
RHYTHM (106 "That's What I Call Love") 250-350 57
RHYTHM (109 "Hard to Please") 300-400 57
RHYTHM (114 "My Heart") 3000-4000 58
Also see ALICE JEAN & MONDELLOS
Also see McCLAY, Yul, & Mondellos

MONDELLOS / Marcels
Singles: 7-inch
RHYTHM (118 "You'll Never Know"/"Hard to Please") 4-6 84
Also see MARCELS
Also see MONDELLOS

MONDO
Singles: 7-inch
ARCY (886 "Red Lips") 40-50 60

MONDO, Joe, & His Combo
Singles: 7-inch
EPI (1003 "Last Summer Love") 40-50 63

MONEY, Curley
(Lee Mitchell)
Singles: 7-inch
MONEY (101 "Honky Tonk Man") 50-75 57
MONEY (105 "Little Queenie") 25-50 57
MONEY (8812 "Gonna Rock") 25-50 58
RAMBLER (552 "Gonna Rock") 50-75 58
RAMBLER (554 "That's My Darlin' ") 8-12 59
RAMBLER (2331 "Rambler") 25-50 59
RAMBLER (2471 "Hurricane Baby") 50-75 59
RAMBLER (2509 "Lover's Blues") 25-50 59
RAMBLER (3407 "Bo Jangles Rock") 25-50 60
RAMBLER (5466 "Shortnin' Bread") 25-50 60
Also see MITCHELL, Lee

MONEY, Eddie P&R/LP '78
Singles: 12-inch
COLUMBIA 5-10 84
Singles: 7-inch
CBS (165196 "Maybe I'm a Fool") 20-30 79
(Picture disc. Promotional issue only.)
COLUMBIA 3-6 78-89
POLYDOR 3-5 85
Picture Sleeves
COLUMBIA 3-5 82-88
LPs: 10/12-inch
COLUMBIA 6-12 77-89
POLYDOR 5-10 85

MONEY, Eddie, / Zane Buzby
Singles: 7-inch
COLUMBIA (11064 "Get a Move On"/"Don't You Ever Say No") 4-6 79

MONEY, Eddie, & Valerie Carter P&R '80
Singles: 7-inch
COLUMBIA (11377 "Let's Be Lovers Again") 3-6 80

MONEY, Eddie, & Ronnie Spector
Singles: 7-inch
COLUMBIA (06231 "Take Me Home Tonight") 3-6 86
Also see MONEY, Eddie
Also see SPECTOR, Ronnie

MONEY, Zoot
Singles: 7-inch
EPIC (10077 "Big Time Operator") 5-10 66
LPs: 10/12-inch
CAPITOL 15-20 69
EPIC (24241 "All Happening") 15-20 67
(Monaural.)
EPIC (26241 "All Happening") 15-20 67
(Stereo.)
Also see SCAFFOLD

MONFORTE, Pat "The Cat"
Singles: 7-inch
BRUNSWICK (55076 "Blow Pat Blow") 15-25 58

MONGRELS
Singles: 7-inch
FRANKLIN (307 "Death of a Salesman") .10-20
FRANKLIN (619 "My Woman") 10-20
FRANKLIN (624 "Funny Day") 10-20
FRANKLIN (632 "Do You Know Your Mother") 10-20 69
M&L (101 "My Woman") 20-30 68
NICO (107 "Funny Day") ....10-20 '60s
RCA (1036 "Ivy in Her Eyes") ....8-12 '60s
Picture Sleeves
FRANKLIN (632 "Do You Know Your Mother") 25-35 69

MONIQUES
Singles: 7-inch
BENN-X (15 "Love So Wonderful") 15-25 62
BENN-X (55 "Hey Girl") 10-20 62

MONIQUES
Singles: 7-inch
CENTAUR (104 "Halo") 8-12 63
CENTAUR (105 "Rock Pretty Baby") 8-12 63

MONITORS
Singles: 78 rpm
ALADDIN (3309 "Tonight's the Night") 40-50 55
Singles: 7-inch
ALADDIN (3309 "Tonight's the Night") ...75-125 55

MONITORS
Singles: 78 rpm
SPECIALTY 25-50 57-58
Singles: 7-inch
SPECIALTY (595 "Our School Days") 50-75 57
SPECIALTY (622 "Closer to Heaven") .100-125 58
SPECIALTY (636 "Hop Scotch") 25-35 58

MONITORS
Singles: 7-inch
CIRCUS (219 "Boy Friend's Prayer") 100-125 58

MONITORS P&R/R&B '66
Singles: 7-inch
BUDDAH 4-6 72
MOTOWN 3-5
SOUL (35049 "Step by Step") 8-15 68
V.I.P. (25028 thru 25046) 10-20 65-68
V.I.P. (25049 "Step by Step") 20-40 68
LPs: 10/12-inch
SOUL (714 "Greetings") 50-75 69
Members: John Fagin; Richard Street; Warren Harris; Sandra Fagin.

MONK, Thelonious LP '63
Singles: 7-inch
COLUMBIA 4-8 63-69
PRESTIGE 5-10 60-69
RIVERSIDE (434 "Blue Monk") 5-10 59
EPs: 7-inch
PRESTIGE 20-40 52
LPs: 10/12-inch
BLACK LION 5-10 74
BLUE NOTE (100 thru 500 series) 6-12 73-76
BLUE NOTE (1510 "Genius of Modern Music, Vol. 1") 50-75 56
(Label has Lexington Ave. street address for Blue Note Records.)
BLUE NOTE (1510 "Genius of Modern Music, Vol. 1") 40-50 58
(Label reads, "Blue Note Records Inc. New York, U.S.A.")
BLUE NOTE (1510 "Genius of Modern Music, Vol. 1") ....15-25 '60s
(Label reads "Blue Note Records - a Division of Liberty Records Inc.")
BLUE NOTE (1511 "Genius of Modern Music, Vol. 2") 50-75 56
(Label has Lexington Ave. street address for Blue Note Records.)
BLUE NOTE (1511 "Genius of Modern Music, Vol. 2") 40-50 58
(Label reads, "Blue Note Records Inc. New York, U.S.A.")
BLUE NOTE (1511 "Genius of Modern Music, Vol. 2") ....15-25 '60s
(Label reads "Blue Note Records - a Division of Liberty Records Inc.")
BLUE NOTE (5002 "Theolonious Monk") 200-400 52
(10-inch LP.)
BLUE NOTE (5009 "Theolonious Monk") 200-400 52
(10-inch LP.)
COLUMBIA (1900 thru 2600 series) 12-25 63-67
(Monaural.)
COLUMBIA (8700 thru 9800 series) 15-30 63-69
(Stereo.)
COLUMBIA (32000 thru 38000 series) 5-15 74-83
EVEREST 5-10 78
MILESTONE 5-15 75-84
PAUSA 5-10 83
PRESTIGE (142 "Thelonious Monk Trio") 100-200 52
(10-inch LP.)
PRESTIGE (180 "Thelonious Monk with Frank Foster") 100-200 54
(10-inch LP.)
PRESTIGE (189 "Thelonious Monk with Art Blakey") 100-200 54
(10-inch LP.)
PRESTIGE (7053 thru 7245) 30-60 56-62
(Yellow labels.)
PRESTIGE (7000 thru 7600 series) 15-25 65-69
(Blue labels.)
PRESTIGE (24000 series) 8-12 72
RIVERSIDE (12-201 thru 12-323) 30-60 55-60
RIVERSIDE (400 series) 15-30 62-67
RIVERSIDE (1100 series) 25-50 58-60
RIVERSIDE (3000 series) 10-20 68-69
RIVERSIDE (9400 series) 15-30 62-63
TOMATO 5-10 78
TRIP 5-10 73
Also see COLTRANE, John, & Thelonious Monk
Also see DAVIS, Miles, & Thelonious Monk
Also see MULLIGAN, Gerry, & Thelonious Monk

MONK, Thelonious, & Sonny Rollins
EPs: 7-inch
PRESTIGE 20-40 52
LPs: 10/12-inch
PRESTIGE (166 "Thelonious Monk & Sonny Rollins") 150-250 52
(10-inch LP.)
PRESTIGE (200 series) 50-75 57-58
PRESTIGE (7000 series) 50-75 57-59
PRESTIGE (1100 series) 40-60 58

MONKEES P&R/LP '66
Singles: 12-inch
ARISTA 8-12 86
(Promotional issue only.)
Singles: 7-inch
ARISTA (0201 "Daydream Believer") 5-10 76
ARISTA (9000 series) 4-8 76-86
COLGEMS 20-30 67
(Cardboard 5½-inch picture disc cutouts from cereal boxes. Four different graphic designs were used. Each lists four tracks, but only plays one. Song on any given disc is indicated by a number stamped into label area. A total of four different songs with four different pictures totals 16 variations.)
COLGEMS (1001 "Last Train to Clarksville") 8-12 66
COLGEMS (1002 " I'm a Believer ") 8-12 66
COLGEMS (1004 "A Little Bit Me, a Little Bit You") 8-12 67
COLGEMS (1007 "Pleasant Valley Sunday") 8-12 67
COLGEMS (1012 "Daydream Believer") 8-12 67
COLGEMS (1019 "Valleri") 8-12 68
COLGEMS (1023 "D.W. Washburn") 8-12 68
COLGEMS (1031 "Porpoise Song") 15-25 68
COLGEMS (5000 "Tear Drop City") 20-30 69
COLGEMS (5004 "Listen to the Band") 15-25 69
COLGEMS (5005 "Mommy and Daddy") .30-50 69
COLGEMS (5011 "Oh My My") 30-50 70
COLLECTABLES (0904300717 "18 Great Singles, Vol. 1") 30-40 94
(Colored vinyl.)
FLASHBACK 4-6 73
RHINO (Except 74411) 3-5 87
RHINO (74411 "Every Step of the Way"). 15-20 87
(Picture disc.)
Picture Sleeves
ARISTA 3-5 86
COLGEMS (1001 "Last Train to Clarksville") 25-35 66
COLGEMS (1002 "I'm a Believer") 10-15 66
COLGEMS (1004 "A Little Bit Me, a Little Bit You") 10-15 67
COLGEMS (1007 "Pleasant Valley Sunday") 10-15 67
COLGEMS (1012 "Daydream Believer") ..10-15 67
COLGEMS (1019 "Valleri") 10-15 68
COLGEMS (1023 "D.W. Washburn") 10-15 68
COLGEMS (1031 "Porpoise Song") 25-35 68
COLGEMS (5000 "Tear Drop City") 30-40 69
COLGEMS (5004 "Listen to the Band") ...25-35 69
COLGEMS (5005 "Mommy and Daddy") .40-60 69
COLGEMS (5011 "Oh My My") 40-60 70
RHINO 3-5 87
EPs: 7-inch
COLGEMS (Cardboard discs) 5-10 67
(Single-sided, four track discs, originally attached to cereal boxes. Not issued with covers, although discs were illustrated.)
COLGEMS (101 "The Monkees") 50-75 66
(Stereo 33 compact. Juke box issue.)
COLGEMS (102 "More of the Monkees") 50-75 67
(Stereo 33 compact. Juke box issue.)
LPs: 10/12-inch
ARISTA (4089 "Greatest Hits") 8-12 76
(Repackage of Bell 6081.)
ARISTA (8313 "Greatest Hits") 5-10 86
ARISTA (8432 "Then and Now") 8-12 86
BELL (6081 "Refocus") 40-50 73
(Cover pictures group in a camera lens.)
BELL (6081 "Refocus") 35-45 73
(Pictures group on stage, from TV show.)
COLGEMS (101 "The Monkees") 40-50 66
(Monaural or stereo. With *Papa Gene's Blues.*)
COLGEMS (101 "The Monkees") 20-30 66
(Monaural or stereo. Without *Papa Gene's Blues.*)
COLGEMS (102 "More of the Monkees") 20-30 67
(Monaural or stereo.)
COLGEMS (103 "Headquarters") 20-30 67
(Monaural or stereo.)
COLGEMS (104 "Pisces, Aquarius, Capricorn and Jones") 20-30 67
(Monaural or stereo.)
COLGEMS (109 "The Birds, The Bees, and the Monkees") 50-75 68
(Monaural.)
COLGEMS (109 "The Birds, The Bees, and the Monkees") 20-30 68
(Stereo.)
COLGEMS (113 "Instant Replay") 25-35 69
COLGEMS (115 "Monkees Greatest Hits") 30-50 69
COLGEMS (117 "Monkees Present") 50-75 69
COLGEMS (119 "Changes") 75-100 70
COLGEMS (329 "Golden Hits") 100-125 71
(RCA Special Products issue.)
COLGEMS (1001 "Barrel Full of Monkees") 50-75 71
COLGEMS (5008 "Head") 35-45 68
LAURIE HOUSE (8009 "The Monkees") ..20-30 73
(Mail-order offer.)
PAIR (0188 "The Monkees") 15-25 82
RCA (329 "Golden Hits") 50-75 72
RCA (7868 "More of the Monkees") 8-10
RCA (7912 "Pisces, Aquarius, Capricorn and Jones") 8-10
RHINO (Except 701) 5-10 82-87
RHINO (701 "Monkee Business") 15-20 82
(Picture disc.)
SILHOUETTE (10012 "Tails of the Monkees") 10-15 83
(Picture disc.)
Members: Michael Nesmith; Davy Jones; Micky Dolenz; Peter Tork.
Also see DOLENZ, Micky
Also see DOLENZ, JONES & TORK
Also see JONES, Davy
Also see MODERN FOLK QUARTET
Also see NESMITH, Michael

MONN-KEYS

Singles: 7-inch

OMEGA (176 "Catch a Falling Star") .... 10-20 '60s

MONOCLES

Singles: 7-inch

CHICORY (407 "Spider & the Fly") 20-30 67
DENCO .... 8-12 '60s

MONOGRAMS

(With Count Fisher Trio)

Singles: 7-inch

MONOGRAM (105 "Baby") 4-6 75
MONOGRAM (106 "Tears in My Eyes") 4-6 75
RUST (5036 "Baby Blue Eyes") 10-15 61
SAFIRE (102 "Tears & Dreams") 15-25 60
SAGA (1000 "My Baby Dearest Darling") 75-100 57

MONORAILS

Singles: 7-inch

LUTE (6017"Come to Me Darlin' ") 250-300 61

MONORAYS

Singles: 7-inch

NASCO (6020 "It's Love Baby") 15-20 58

MONORAYS

(With Tony March & Orchestra)

Singles: 7-inch

RED ROCKET (476 " Five Minutes to Love You") 10-15 63
TAMMY (1005 "Five Minutes to Love You") 100-200 59
(Reads: "Tammy Records" at top.)
TAMMY (1005 " Five Minutes to Love You") 50-75 59
(Reads only "Tammy" at top. No mention of distribution by Jubilee.)
TAMMY (1005 " Five Minutes to Love You") 20-30 59
("Tammy" at top. Also indicates: "Nationally Distributed by Jubilee Records.")
Member: Tony March.
Also see MARCH, Tony

MONORAYS

Singles: 7-inch

20TH FOX (594 "You're No Good") 30-40 65

MONOTONES — P&R/R&B '58

Singles: 78 rpm

ARGO (5290 "Book of Love") 50-100 58

Singles: 7-inch

ARGO (5290 "Book of Love") 30-40 58
ARGO (5301 "Tom Foolery") 20-30 58
ARGO (5321 "The Legend of Sleepy Hollow") 15-25 58
ARGO (5339 "Tell It to the Judge") 40-50 59
CHESS 4-6 73
COLLECTABLES .... 3-5 '80s
ERIC (241 "Book of Love") 4-6 77
HICKORY 5-10 64-65
HULL (735 "Reading the Book of Love") . 40-50 60
HULL (743 "Daddy's Home But Momma's Gone") 20-30 61
MASCOT (124 "Book of Love") 600-700 57
(Yellow label. Counterfeits with a white label exist.)
OWL (323 "Book of Dance") 5-10 74
ROULETTE GOLDEN GOODIES 4-6 73

LPs: 10/12-inch

MURRAY HILL 5-8
Members: Warren Davis; Frank Smith; John Raynes; George Malone; Charles Patrick; James Patrick.

MONRO, Matt — P&R/LP '61

(Matt Manro)

Singles: 7-inch

CAPITOL 4-6 66-72
LIBERTY 4-8 62-66
U.A. 4-6 74
WARWICK 5-10 61

LPs: 10/12-inch

CAP LATINO (19006 "Todo Pasara") 8-15
CAPITOL 8-15 67-70
LIBERTY 10-20 62-66
LONDON (1611 "Blue and Sentimental") 20-30 57
WARWICK (2045 "My Kind of Girl") 15-25 61

MONROE, Bill — C&W '46

(With His Blue Grass Boys)

Singles: 78 rpm

BLUEBIRD .... 15-30 '30s
COLUMBIA 10-20 45-49
DECCA 10-15 50-57

Singles: 7-inch

DECCA (20000 series) 12-25 52-56
DECCA (30000 series) 5-15 56-64
DECCA (40000 series) 20-30 52
GLOBE (45 "Pelota") 10-15 81
(Picture disc. Has photo of Fernando Valenzuela of L.A. Dodgers.)
MCA 4-6 73

EPs: 7-inch

COLUMBIA 10-15 52-57
DECCA 5-15 56-65

LPs: 10/12-inch

ALBUM GLOBE .... 5-10 '80s
CAMDEN 5-12 62-64
CORAL .... 5-8 '80s
COUNTY 5-10
DECCA (Except 8731) 10-25 60-71
DECCA (8731 "Knee Deep in Bluegrass") 15-25 58
HARMONY 10-20 61-69
MCA 5-12 73-84
VOCALION 8-15 64-70
Members: Bill Monroe; Birch Monroe; Charles Monroe; Lester Flatt; Earl Scruggs; Chubby Wise; Cedric Rainwater; L.E. White; Waylon Jennings.
Also see JENNINGS, Waylon
Also see MARTIN, Jimmy
Also see MADDOX, Rose, & Bill Monroe
Also see WHITE, L.E., & Lola Jean Dillon

MONROE, Homer

Singles: 7-inch

SILVIA (1161 "It's Many a Mile from Me to You") 300-500

MONROE, Jill

Singles: 7-inch

PRINCE (0001 "Somebody – Anybody") .... 200-300 '60s

MONROE, Marilyn — P&R '54

Singles: 78 rpm

RCA (5745 "River of No Return") 8-12 54
RCA (5745 "River of No Return") 150-200 54
(Has picture of Marilyn on label. Promotional issue only.)
RCA (6033 "Heat Wave") 10-20 55
RCA/SIMON HOUSE (5745 "River of No Return") 100-200 54
(Has "Who Is She?" label. Promotional issue only.)
U.A. (161 "I Wanna Be Loved By You") 25-50 59

Singles: 7-inch

CAPITOL (204 "Invitation to National Conference Los Angeles 1955") 250-350 55
(Dialogue only, no music. Made for Southern California Chapter P.R.S.A. Promotional issue only.)
DELL PUBLISHING (MM-SS 1 "Sidney Skolsky Interviews Marilyn Monroe") 2500-5000 54
(Single-sided disc. Promotional issue only. Includes *Diamonds Are a Girl's Best Friend* and a portion of *File My Claim.*)
RCA (5745 "River of No Return") 15-25 54
RCA (5745 "River of No Return") 150-200 54
(Has picture of Marilyn on label. Promotional issue only.)
RCA (6033 "Heat Wave") 15-25 55
20TH FOX (311 "River of No Return") 10-15 62
U.A. (161 "I Wanna Be Loved By You") 10-15 59

Picture Sleeves

RCA (5745 "River of No Return") 50-100 54
RCA (6033 "Heat Wave") 50-100 55
20TH FOX (311 "River of No Return") 50-75 62

EPs: 7-inch

MGM (208 "Gentlemen Prefer Blondes") .25-50 53
(Soundtrack. With Jane Russell.)
RCA (593 "There's No Business Like Show Business") 30-40 55
U.A. (1005 "Some Like It Hot") 25-35 59
(With "This Is Hot!" publicity insert for the film.)
U.A. (1005 "Some Like It Hot") 15-25 59
(Without film publicity insert.)

LPs: 10/12-inch

ASCOT (13500 "Some Like It Hot") 20-30 64
(Monaural. Soundtrack.)
ASCOT (16500 "Some Like It Hot") 30-40 64
(Stereo. Soundtrack. Also has selections from other films.)
AUDIO FIDELITY (50005 "The Ten") 25-35 84
(Picture disc.)
COLUMBIA (1527 "Let's Make Love") 30-50 60
(Monaural. Soundtrack.)
COLUMBIA (8327 "Let's Make Love") 40-60 60
(Stereo. Soundtrack.)
COLUMBIA/CSP (8327 "Let's Make Love") 8-12
(Soundtrack. With Yves Montand and Frankie Vaughan.)
MGM (208 "Gentlemen Prefer Blondes") 75-100 53
(10-inch LP.)
MGM (3231 "Gentlemen Prefer Blondes") 40-60 55
(Soundtrack. With Jane Russell. One side has music from *Till the Clouds Roll By.)*
MOVIETONE (72016 "Unforgettable") 15-25 67
SANDY HOOK (Except 2013) 5-10 79
SANDY HOOK (2013 "Rare Recordings 1948-'62") 30-40 84
STET (15005 "Never Before and Never Again") 8-12
(Soundtrack. With Jane Russell.)
20TH FOX (5000 "Marilyn") 75-125 62
(With bonus photo of Marilyn nude.)
20TH FOX (5000 "Marilyn") 50-75 62
(Without bonus photo.)
U.A. (272 "Some Like It Hot") 8-12 74
(Soundtrack.)
U.A. (4030 "Some Like It Hot") 35-55 59
(Monaural. Soundtrack.)
U.A. (5030 "Some Like It Hot") 50-75 59
(Stereo. Soundtrack.)

MONROE, Smiley

(With Ruby)

Singles: 78 rpm

VITA (131 "Wigwam Wipwop") 20-30 56
VITA (149 "The Snake Song") 20-30 57
VITA (163 "Teenage Doll") 20-30 57

Singles: 7-inch

PORTLAND (1010 "Sorry, Mary Ann") .... 4-6 '70s
SAGE (403 "Pickin' Pete") 10-15 64
VITA (131 "Wigwam Wipwop") 20-30 56
VITA (149 "The Snake Song") 20-30 57
VITA (163 "Teenage Doll") 20-30 57
VITA (177 "No Love at All") 15-20 58
VITA (183 "Heaven's Earth Angel") 10-15 59
VITA (189 "Happy Happy Birthday") 10-15 59

MONROE, Vaughn — P&R '40

Singles: 78 rpm

BLUEBIRD 5-10 40-42
RCA 4-8 47-58
VICTOR 4-8 42-47

Singles: 7-inch

AMY (11016 "God Is Alive") 4-8 68
DOT 5-10 62-63
JUBILEE (5412 "Bye Bye Blackbird") 8-12 61
MGM (12968 "Song of the Skier") 8-12 60
RCA 10-20 50-59
ROD (105 "God Is Alive") 4-8 68
U.A. (214 "Ballerina") 5-10 60

Picture Sleeves

RCA (6895 "The Ride Back") 15-25 57

EPs: 7-inch

CAMDEN 10-15 56
RCA 10-20 50-56

LPs: 10/12-inch

CAMDEN 15-25 56
DOT 10-20 62-64
HAMILTON 10-20 65
KAPP 10-20 65
RCA (11 thru 3066) 25-50 50-53
(10-inch LPs.)
RCA (1400 thru 1700 series) 20-40 56-58
(12-inch LPs.)
RCA (1100 series) 5-10 75
RCA (3800 series) 10-20 67
RCA (6000 series) 8-12 72
Also see MARTIN, Dean / Patti Page
Also see PRESLEY, Elvis / Vaughn Monroe / Gogi Grant / Robert Shaw

MONROE, Vince

Singles: 78 rpm

EXCELLO (2089 "Give It Up") 10-15 56

Singles: 7-inch

EXCELLO (2089 "Give It Up") 15-25 56

MONROE BROTHERS

Singles: 78 rpm

BLUEBIRD .... 20-30 '30s
Members: Bill; Birch; Charles.
Also see MONROE, Bill

MONSTERS

LPs: 10/12-inch

ROYAL (3507 "Beat'n Hits") .... 35-50 '60s
(Title on label is "Tribute to the Beatles".)

MONSTERS FOUR

Singles: 7-inch

VEE-JAY (600 "Russian Roulette") 5-10 64

MONSTROSITIES

Singles: 7-inch

MONSTER (001 "Dance Along with Dracula") 10-15 65
(With foldout lyrics/dance instruction insert.)
MONSTER (001 "Dance Along with Dracula") 8-10 65
(Without insert.)

Picture Sleeves

MONSTER (001 "Dance Along with Dracula") 15-25 65
Members: Wellington; Ashley; Gainsborough; Montague.

MONTAGE

Singles: 7-inch

LAURIE (3438 "I Shall Call Her Mary") 5-10 68
LAURIE (3453 "Wake Up, Jimmy") 5-10 68

LPs: 10/12-inch

LAURIE (2049 "Montage") 15-20 69
Members: Michael Brown; Vance Chapman; Mike Smyth; Lance Cornelius; Bob Steurer.
Also see LEFT BANKE

MONTALVO, Lenny, & Crystal Chords

(With Leroy Kirkland & Orchestra)

Singles: 7-inch

3D (373 "Be Mine Again") 150-250 58
Also see SOTOLONGO, Edward

MONTANAS — P&R '68

Singles: 7-inch

INDEPENDENCE 5-10 67-69
W.B. 4-8 66-68

MONTCLAIRS

("Featuring Eugene Arnold with Ted Walker & Orchestra"; with Douglas DuBois, Chico Chism & His Jettinaires)

Singles: 7-inch

HI-Q (5001 "Golden Angel") 75-125 57
(Has double horizontal lines. Indicates "Unbreakable 45 R.P.M.")
HI-Q (5001 "Golden Angel") 15-25 57
(Has single horizontal line. No mention of "Unbreakable 45 R.P.M.")
PREMIUM (404 "Give Me a Chance") .. 300-400 56
SONIC (104 "All I Want Is Love") 3000-4000 56
Also see SMITH, Floyd, & Montclairs

MONTCLAIRS

Singles: 7-inch

TNT (154 "The Bells") 1500-2000 58

MONTCLAIRS

Singles: 7-inch

AUDICON (111 "Goodnight") 30-40 61

MONTCLAIRS

Singles: 7-inch

ABC-PAR (10463 "I Believe") 10-15 63

MONTCLAIRS

Singles: 7-inch

UNITED INT'L (1007 "Lisa") 25-35 64
UNITED INT'L (1013 "Young Wings Can Fly") 10-20 64

MONTE, Del

Singles: 7-inch

1ST (102 "No Fooling Around") 8-12 61

MONTE, Lou — P&R '54

Singles: 78 rpm

RCA (Except 6704) 3-5 53-56
RCA (6704 "Elvis Presley for President"). 10-20 56

Singles: 7-inch

GWP 4-6 71-72
JAMIE (1407 "Old Fashioned Girl") 4-6 72
LAURIE (3643 "Paul Revere's Horse") 4-6 76
LAURIE (3652 "Crabs Walk Sideways") 4-6 77
RCA (5382 thru 6600 series) 10-20 53-56
RCA (6700 thru 7600 series, except 6704) 5-15 56-60
RCA (6704 "Elvis Presley for President"). 20-30 56

RCA (8700 thru 9000 series).......5-10 65-67
RAGALIA.......4-6 69
REPRISE.......5-10 62-65
ROULETTE.......5-10 60-68

Picture Sleeves

REPRISE.......8-12 62-63

EPs: 7-inch

RCA (Except 18)....... 10-20 57-59
RCA (18 "Elvis Presley for President") 25-35 56
(Promotional issue only. Not issued with cover.)

LPs: 10/12-inch

CAMDEN....... 15-20 58
DESIGN....... 10-15
HARMONY....... 10-15 68
RCA (1600 thru 1900 series)....... 20-35 57-59
RCA (3000 series) 10-20 66-67
ROULETTE....... 15-25 60
REPRISE....... 15-25 61-65
Also see PRESLEY, Elvis / Martha Carson / Lou Monte / Herb Jeffries

MONTE, Michael

Singles: 7-inch

CHRISTY (103 "Rock My Rockin' Chair")....... 25-50 58

MONTE, Vinnie

(With the Jay Birds; with Charles Calello & Orchestra)

Singles: 78 rpm

JOSIE 5-10 56

Singles: 7-inch

DECANTER (101 "A Love of My Own")... 10-20 58
DECANTER (103 "Excite Me")....... 10-20 59
DECANTER (104 "I'll Walk You Home").. 10-20 59
DECANTER (350 "After You've Gone")... 10-20 59
DECANTER (351 "You'll Never Know")... 10-20 60
FARGO (1000 "I Wrote a Poem") 100-200 58
HARMON (1009 "Take Good Care of Her")....... 10-20 62
HARMON (1013 "It's the End")....... 10-20 63
JOSIE (793 "Your Cute Little Ways")....... 10-20 56
JOSIE (810 "Telegram")....... 10-20 57
JUBILEE (5391 "Red Ink")....... 10-20 60
JUBILEE (5398 "One Alone")....... 10-20 61
JUBILEE (5403 "Follow That Girl") 10-20 61
JUBILEE (5408 "Rocco's Theme")....... 10-20 61
JUBILEE (5410 "Ask Your Heart") 10-20 61
JUBILEE (5417 "One of the Guys") 10-20 62
JUBILEE (5428 "Mashed Potato Girl")....... 15-25 62
RCA (8611 "I Walk Alone").......5-10 65
TCF (7 "Hey, Look at the Winter Snow") . 60-80 64

MONTEGOS

Singles: 7-inch

ABC (11101 "Most of All").......5-10 68
BLACK FALCON (19101 "Most of All").......8-12 68

MONTELLS

Singles: 7-inch

GOLDEN CREST (582 "A Ring a Ling").. 10-15 63
GOLDEN CREST (585 "Gee Baby")....... 10-15 63
Member: Charles Dell.
Also see H.M. SUBJECTS

MONTELS

Singles: 7-inch

KINK (9365 "Rondevous [sic]") 75-100 61
UNIVERSAL (101 "Union Hall") 200-300 61
Also see FRANKIE & C-NOTES / Montels

MONTENEGRO, Hugo *LP '66*

(With Orchestra & Chorus; with Don Sebesky)

Singles: 7-inch

RCA.......4-6 64-75
TIME.......4-6 61-64
20TH FOX.......5-8 59

LPs: 10/12-inch

CAMDEN....... 10-20 62
GWP 5-10 70
MAINSTREAM 10-15 67-68
MOVIETONE.......8-12 67
PICKWICK.......5-10 '70s
RCA (0025 thru 2300 series).......5-10 72-77
RCA (LOC-1113 "Hurry Sundown") 35-40 67
(Monaural. Soundtrack.)
RCA (LSO-1113 "Hurry Sundown") 40-50 67
(Stereo. Soundtrack.)
RCA (2900 series) 10-15 64
RCA (LPM-3475 "Man from U.N.C.L.E.") 25-35 65
(Monaural. Soundtrack.)
RCA (LSP-3475 "Man from U.N.C.L.E."). 30-40 65
(Stereo. Soundtrack.)
RCA (LPM-3574 "Man from U.N.C.L.E., Volume 2")....... 30-40 66
(Monaural. Soundtrack.)
RCA (LSP-3574 "Man from U.N.C.L.E., Volume 2")....... 35-45 66
(Stereo. Soundtrack.)
RCA (3500 thru 4600 series) 5-15 66-71
RCA (6000 series) 5-10 71
TIME.......10-20 60-64
20TH FOX.......10-25 59-68
Also see SEBESKY, Don, & Jazz-Rock Syndrome

MONTERAYS

Singles: 7-inch

BUFF.......10-20 '60s
SAHARA (118 "You Belong to My Heart")....... 10-15 '60s
SURE STAR (5000 "Deep Within My Heart")....... 25-35 64
(First issue.)
ULTIMA (704 "Deep Within My Heart") 15-25 64
Also see MADISONS / Monterays

MONTERAYS

Singles: 7-inch

PLANET (57 "You Never Cared")....... 10-15 64

MONTERAYS

Singles: 7-inch

RONDACK (8657 "Why Do You Cry")...... 15-25

MONTEREYS

Singles: 78 rpm

NESTOR (15 "Someone Like You")......400-600 54
TEENAGE (1001 "Someone Like You")....... 150-250 56

Singles: 7-inch

TEENAGE (1001 "Someone Like You")....... 450-550 56
Members: Dean Barlow; Bill Lindsay; Ed Jordan.
Also see BARLOW, Dean, & Montereys

MONTEREYS

Singles: 7-inch

ARWIN (130 "Goodbye My Love")....... 15-25 59
ASTRA (1018 "Step Right Up")....... 15-25 65
BLAST (219 "Step Right Up")....... 250-350 65
DOMINION (1019 "First Kiss")....... 50-75 64
EAST WEST (121 "I'll Love You Again") .. 15-25 58
GNP (314 "For Sentimental Reasons") 10-20 63
HILLSIDE (826 "Oh Cheryl") 20-30
IMPALA (213 "Without a Girl") 100-150 63
MAJOR (1009 "A Crowded Room")....... 50-60 59
PRINCE (5060 "Rita")....... 10-20 60
ROSE (109 "You're the Girl for Me")....... 40-50 58
SATURN (1002 "My Girl") 25-35 60
TRANS AMERICAN (1000 "Darlin'")....... 1500-2000 60
Also see PATRICK, Sandra, & Montereys

MONTEREYS

Singles: 7-inch

CUCA (1002 "Rockin' Fool") 20-30 62
GOLD STAR (1001 "Whiplash")....... 20-30 62
Members: Kenny Loehrke; Wes Phillips; Orville Luebke; Rudd Hoger; Don Pinnow; Jimmy Thiele.

MONTEREYS

Singles: 7-inch

DEE-JAY (1013 "Party")....... 15-25 '60s
T-HEE (700/1 "Bo-Did-It") 10-20 66

MONTEREYS QUARTET

Singles: 7-inch

J.C. (9317 "The Ballad of Take Me Back to Baltimore")....... 40-50 60

MONTERO, Andre

LPs: 10/12-inch

OMEGA (4 "Music for Heavenly Bodies") 50-100 58

MONTERO, Juan

Singles: 7-inch

EMBER (1088 "Freckles")....... 10-20 62

MONTEZ, Chris *P&R/R&B '62*

Singles: 7-inch

A&M.......4-6 65-68
COLLECTABLES.......3-5 '80s
ERA.......4-6 72
ERIC (129 "Let's Dance").......4-6 73
GUARANTEED (217 "They Say")....... 5-10 61
JAMIE (1410 "Let's Dance")....... 4-6 73
MONOGRAM.......5-10 62-64
PARAMOUNT.......4-6 71-72

LPs: 10/12-inch

A&M.......10-20 66-67
MONOGRAM (100 "Let's Dance")....... 50-100 63
Members: Joel Hill; Carol Kaye; Tom Tedesco; Julius Wechter; Pete Jolly; Hal Blaine.
Also see BLAINE, Hal
Also see CHRIS & KATHY
Also see HILL, Joel
Also see JOLLY, Pete
Also see TEDESCO, Tommy

MONTGOMERY, Bob

Singles: 7-inch

BRUNSWICK (55157 "Because I Love You")....... 20-30 59
Also see HOLLY, Buddy

MONTGOMERY, Carol

Singles: 7-inch

SOUND STAGE 7....... 5-10 63-64
Also see BOB & CAROL

MONTGOMERY, Christopher

Singles: 7-inch

DOLTON (84 "My Paradise")....... 10-20 63

MONTGOMERY, Gray

Singles: 7-inch

BEAGLE (101 "Right Now")....... 200-250

MONTGOMERY, Harold

Singles: 7-inch

WOLF TEX (103 "How Much Do You Miss Me") 350-450 61

MONTGOMERY, Jack

Singles: 7-inch

BARRACUDA (2-8030 "Don't Turn Your Back on Me") .... 30-50 '60s
REVUE (11009 "Baby, Baby Take a Chance on Me") 10-20 68
SCEPTER (12152 "Do You Believe It")....30-40 66

MONTGOMERY, Joe

Singles: 78 rpm

ABBOTT (189 "Cool Cat")....... 25-50 56

Singles: 7-inch

ABBOTT (189 "Cool Cat")....... 50-100 56
LIBERTY BELL (9020 "Planetary Run").75-125 57

MONTGOMERY, Joe

Singles: 7-inch

BARONET (13 "Snake Pit") 10-15 62

MONTGOMERY, Little Brother

(With His Vicksburgers; with His Bogalusa Boys; Quintet)

Singles: 78 rpm

CENTURY.......10-20 47
EBONY.......10-15 56
WINDIN' BALL 10-15 54

Singles: 7-inch

BLACKBIRD (705 "Pine Top Boogie Woogie")....... 10-20 61
EBONY.......10-20 56-60
F.M. (1002 "Mini-Skirt Blues")....... 10-15 66
WINDIN' BALL 15-25 54

LPs: 10/12-inch

ADELPHI.......10-12
PRESTIGE.......5-8
PRESTIGE BLUESVILLE (1012 "Tasty Blues") 50-75 61
RCA.......10-15 77
RIVERSIDE (9410 "Chicago, Living Legend")....... 20-30
Session: Lafayette Thomas.
Also see SUNNYLAND SLIM
Also see SYKES, Roosevelt, & Little Brother Montgomery

MONTGOMERY, Little Brother, & Mama Yancey

LPs: 10/12-inch

RIVERSIDE (403 "Southside Blues") 30-40 60
Also see MONTGOMERY, Little Brother
Also see YANCEY, Mama

MONTGOMERY, Rick

Singles: 7-inch

MELMAR (120 "Waitin' ") 150-200 64

MONTGOMERY, Sam (King of Spades)

Singles: 78 rpm

MELOTONE (6-11-55 "Baby Please Don't Go")....... 150-250 36

MONTGOMERY, Tammy *P&R '63*

(Tana Montgomery; Tammi Terrell)

Singles: 7-inch

CHECKER (1072 "If I Would Marry You")....... 25-35 64
(Maroon label.)
CHECKER (1072 "If I Would Marry You")....... 15-25 64
(Multi-color label.)
SCEPTER (1224 "If You See Bill") 30-50 61
TRY ME (28001 "I Cried")....... 20-30 63
WAND (123 "Voice of Experience")....... 20-30 62
Also see TERRELL, Tammi

MONTGOMERY, Wes *LP '65*

(Wes Montgomery Quartet)

Singles: 7-inch

A&M.......4-6 67-70
PACIFIC JAZZ 4-8 60
RIVERSIDE.......4-8 60-64
VERVE.......4-6 65-68
WORLD PACIFIC.......5-10 58

EPs: 7-inch

A&M (126 "Greatest Hits") 5-10 70
(Juke box issue only. Includes title strips.)
A&M (3001 "A Day in the Life")....... 5-10 67
(Juke box issue only. Includes title strips.)

LPs: 10/12-inch

A&M.......10-15 67-70
ACCORD 5-8 82
BLUE NOTE.......6-12 75
MFSL (508 "Bumpin' ")....... 20-30
MGM.......10-15 70
MILESTONE.......8-15 73-83
PACIFIC JAZZ (5 "Montgomeryland")......35-45 60
PACIFIC JAZZ (10000 & 20000 series) ... 10-20 66-68
RIVERSIDE (034 thru 089) 5-8 82-83
RIVERSIDE (300 & 400 series) 15-30 59-67
RIVERSIDE (3000 series)....... 10-15 68-69
VERVE.......10-20 65-72
(Reads "MGM Records - A Division of Metro-Goldwyn-Mayer, Inc." at bottom of label.)
VERVE.......5-10 73-84
(Reads "Manufactured By MGM Record Corp.," or mentions either Polydor or Polygram at bottom of label.)
Also see MONTGOMERY BROTHERS
Also see SMITH, Jimmy, & Wes Montgomery

MONTGOMERY BROTHERS

Singles: 7-inch

RIVERSIDE (466 "Groove Yard")....... 5-10 61

EPs: 7-inch

RIVERSIDE (9362 "Groove Yard")....... 10-20 61
(Stereo. Juke box issue only.)

LPs: 10/12-inch

FANTASY (3308 "Montgomery Brothers") 30-40 60
(Monaural.)
FANTASY (3323 "In Canada")....... 30-40 61
(Monaural.)
FANTASY (8052 "Montgomery Brothers") 35-45 60
(Stereo.)
FANTASY (8066 "In Canada")....... 35-45 61
(Stereo.)
PACIFIC JAZZ (17 "Montgomery Brothers") 25-35 60
(Reissue of World Pacific 1240.)
RIVERSIDE (362 "Groove Yard")....... 25-35 61
(Monaural.)
RIVERSIDE (9362 "Groove Yard")....... 30-40 61
(Stereo.)
WORLD PACIFIC (1240 "Montgomery Brothers")....... 50-75 58
Members: Wes; Buddy; Monk.
Also see MONTGOMERY, Wes
Also see SHEARING, George, & Montgomery Brothers

MONTGOMERYS, The

(Montgomery's; with Tommy Falcone & Orchestra)

Singles: 7-inch

AIRWAY (174 "Storybook Lines")....... 50-75
AMY (883 "Promise of Love")....... 400-500 63
Also see FALCONE, Tommy, & Centuries

MONTICELLOS

Singles: 7-inch

RED CAP (102 "Don't Hold Back")....... 15-25 67

MONTRELL, Roy

Singles: 78 rpm

SPECIALTY (583 "Ooh, Wow!")............ 10-20 56

Singles: 7-inch

MINIT (619 "The Montrell")....................5-10 61
SPECIALTY (583 "Ooh, Wow!")............ 15-25 56

MONTY PYTHON *LP '75*

Singles: 7-inch

ARISTA...4-6 80

LPs: 10/12-inch

ARISTA (4039 "Matching Tie and Handkerchief")........................ 10-20 75
ARISTA (4050 "Album of the Soundtrack of the Trailer of the Film of *Monty Python and the Holy Grail*")........................ 10-20 75
ARISTA (4073 "Monty Python Live! at the City Center")........................ 10-20 76
ARISTA (9536 "Monty Python's Contractual Obligation Album")........................ 10-20 80
CHARISMA/BUDDAH (1049 "Another Monty Python Record")........................ 15-25 72
CHARISMA/BUDDAH (1063 "Monty Python's Previous Record")........................ 15-25 72
MCA (6121 "Meaning of Life")..............8-12 83
W.B. (3396 "Life of Brian")............... 10-15 79
PYE (12116 "Monty Python's Flying Circus")........................ 15-20 75
Members: John Cleese; Graham Chapman; Eric Idle; Michael Palin; Terry Jones; Terry Gilliam.
Also see RUTLES

MON-VALES

Singles: 7-inch

PEN JOY (501 "Carol-Ann").................. 75-125 58

MONUMENTS

Singles: 7-inch

ALVERA (2 "I Need You")..................... 20-30 66

MONZAS

Singles: 7-inch

A-LA-CARTE.......................................8-12
MOON (5321 "Stubborn Kind of Fella")... 20-25 '60s
MOON (7330 "You Know You Turn Me On")........................ 10-20 '60s
PACIFIC (1002 "Instant Love")............. 30-50 60
PACIFIC (1120 "Hey I KnowYou")........... 15-20
PACIFIC (1999 "Baby You Know")........... 15-20
PACIFIC (7731 "In My Lonely Room")..... 20-25
WAND (1120 "Forever")........................5-10 66
Members: Al Wilks; Bobby Cooper; Jimmy Lane; Jack Ferrell; Jerry McIntosh; Phil Mullins.

MONZELS

Singles: 7-inch

PRISM (1898 "Sharkskin")..................... 15-25 64

MOOD

Singles: 7-inch

B&G (101 "In the Amber Fields")........... 20-30 '60s

MOOD, Barbara

Singles: 7-inch

GLORY (295 "The Fool")....................... 75-125 59

MOOD MAKERS
(With Rocky G. Bralter Orchestra)

Singles: 7-inch

BAMBI (8000 "Dolores")........................ 75-100 61

MOODS

Singles: 7-inch

RENCO (3003 "Here I Stand")............... 10-15 62
SARG (162 "Little Alice")..................... 15-25 59
SARG (176 "Easy Going")..................... 15-25 59
SARG (179 "Let Me Have Your Love").... 15-25 59
SARG (184 "Rockin' Santa Claus")......... 10-20 59
SARG (185 "Teenager's Past")............. 10-20 59
TNT (189 "It's Goodbye and Not Goodnight")........................ 40-50 62

MOODS

Singles: 7-inch

KOOL (1024 "High School Days")..............5-10 64
KOOL (1028 "Stay with Me")...................5-10 65
KOOL (1029 "Stay with Me")...................5-10 65
KOOL (1032 "Only the Young")................5-10 66
Also see EXCEPTIONS

MOODY, Doc

Singles: 7-inch

DEMON (1505 "Crazy Wonderful")......... 10-15 58

MOODY, James

Singles: 7-inch

ARGO (5347 "Little Girl Blue")....................8-12 59
SCEPTER (1290 "Giant Steps")................5-10 65

MOODY, Joan

Singles: 7-inch

TCF (122 "Big Time Operator")..................5-10 65
TCF (125 "Lend a Helpin' Hand")..............5-10 65
20TH FOX (6649 "Lend a Helpin' Hand").....5-8 66

MOODY, Ron, & Centaurs

Singles: 7-inch

ABC (11411 "Lonely Weekends")..............8-12 73
COLUMBIA (44908 "If I Didn't Have a Dime")........................5-10 69
COLPAR (39 "If I Didn't Have a Dime")....10-20

MOODY & DELTAS

Singles: 7-inch

DAISY (504 "Monkey Climb")..................15-25 64

MOODY BLUES *P&R '65*

Singles: 12-inch

THRESHOLD.......................................8-10 '80s

Singles: 7-inch

DERAM...4-8 68-72
LONDON (200 series)...............................4-6 78
LONDON (1005 "This Is My House")..........8-12 67
LONDON (9726 "Go Now"/"It's Easy Child")........................10-20 65
(Purple and white label.)
LONDON (9726 "Go Now"/"It's Easy Child")........................25-35 65
(Orange label. Promotional issue only.)
LONDON (9726 "Go Now"/"Lose Your Money")........................8-12 65
(Purple and white label.)
LONDON (9726 "Go Now"/"Lose Your Money")........................5-8 65
(Blue and white label.)
LONDON (9764 "From the Bottom of My Heart")........................10-15 65
LONDON (9799 "Ev'ry Day")...................10-15 65
LONDON (9810 "Stop").........................10-15 66
LONDON (20000 series).........................8-12 66
POLYDOR (Black vinyl)..........................3-5 86-88
POLYDOR (7078 "The Other Side of Life")..4-6 86
(Colored vinyl.)
THRESHOLD (600 series)........................3-5 81-85
THRESHOLD (67000 series).....................4-6 71-73

Picture Sleeves

POLYDOR (7078 "The Other Side of Life")..4-6 86
POLYDOR (870990 "No More Lies")...........3-5 88
POLYDOR (883906 "Your Wildest Dreams")........................3-5 86
POLYDOR (885201 "The Other Side of Life")........................3-5 86
POLYDOR (887600 "I Know You're Out There Somewhere")........................3-5 88
THRESHOLD (602 "The Voice")..................3-5 81
THRESHOLD (604 "Sitting at the Wheel")...3-5 81
THRESHOLD (67006 "The Story in Your Eyes")........................4-6 71

LPs: 10/12-inch

DERAM (16012 "Days of Future Passed")........................30-40 68
(Monaural.)
DERAM (18012 "Days of Future Passed")........................10-20 68
(Stereo.)
DERAM (18017 "In Search of the Lost Chord")........................10-20 68
(Gatefold cover.)
DERAM (18017 "In Search of the Lost Chord")........................5-10
(Standard cover.)
DERAM (18025 "On the Threshold of a Dream")........................10-20 69
(Gatefold cover.)
DERAM (18025 "On the Threshold of a Dream")........................5-10 69
(Standard cover.)
DERAM (18051 "In the Beginning").........10-20 69
DERAM (820006 "Days of Future Passed")........................5-10
LONDON (428 "Go Now")........................20-25 65
(Stereo.)
LONDON (690/1 "Caught Live")...............10-20 77
LONDON (708 "Octave")..........................8-10 78
(Black vinyl.)
LONDON (708 "Octave").........................20-25 78
(Colored vinyl. Promotional issue only.)
LONDON (3428 "Go Now")......................25-45 65
(Monaural.)
MFSL (042 "Days of Future Past")...........60-80 80
MFSL (151 "Seventh Sojourn")................60-80 85
MFSL (215 "On the Threshold of a Dream")........................25-35 94
MFSL (232 "Every Good Boy Deserves Favour")........................25-35 95
POLYDOR (835765 "Sur la Mer")..............5-10 88
POLYDOR (849433 "Keys of the Kingdom")........................5-10 91
THRESHOLD (1 "To Our Children's Children's Children")........................8-12 69
(Gatefold cover.)
THRESHOLD (1 "To Our Children's Children's Children")........................5-10
(Standard cover.)
THRESHOLD (3 "A Question of Balance") 8-12 70
(Gatefold cover.)
THRESHOLD (3 "A Question of Balance") 5-10
(Standard cover.)
THRESHOLD (5 "Every Good Boy Deserves Favor")........................8-10 71
(Gatefold cover.)
THRESHOLD (7 "Seventh Sojourn")..........8-10 72
(Gatefold cover.)
THRESHOLD (12/13 "This Is the Moody Blues")........................10-12 74
(Two LPs.)
THRESHOLD (2901 "Long Distance Voyager")........................5-10 81
(Gatefold cover.)
THRESHOLD (2902 "The Present")...........5-10 83
THRESHOLD (820155 "Voices in the Sky")........................5-10 85
THRESHOLD (820517 "Prelude")..............5-10 86
THRESHOLD (829179 "Other Side of Life")........................5-10 86
THRESHOLD (840659 "Greatest Hits").....5-10 89
Members: Michael Pinder; Ray Thomas; Graeme Edge; Brian Hines (a.k.a. Denny Laine); Clint Warwick; John Lodge; Justin Hayward; Patrick Moraz; Rod Clarke.
Also see HAYWARD, Justin, & John Lodge
Also see THOMAS, Ray

MOODY WALKERS

Singles: 7-inch

RAYNARD (10043 "We Never Loved Before")........................15-25 65

MOOG MACHINE *LP '69*

LPs: 10/12-inch

COLUMBIA (9921 "Switched-On Rock")..10-15 69

MOOHAH

Singles: 78 rpm

STARMAKER (501 "All Shook Out").........50-75 54

Singles: 7-inch

STARMAKER (501 "All Shook Out")....150-250 54

MOON

Singles: 7-inch

IMPERIAL (66285 "Mothers & Fathers")..15-25 68
IMPERIAL (66330 "Faces")......................10-20 68
IMPERIAL (66415 "Pirate").....................10-20 69

LPs: 10/12-inch

IMPERIAL (12381 "Without Earth")..........20-30 68
IMPERIAL (12444 "The Moon")...............20-30 69
Members: Matthew Moore; David Marks; Larry Brown; Dave Jackson.
Also see DAVE & MARKSMEN
Also see MOORE, Matthew

MOON, Derryl

Singles: 7-inch

FARGO (1001 "I Was Wrong")................25-35 '60s

MOON, Joe

Singles: 7-inch

HILLCREST (120 "Live It Up")..............200-300

MOON, Keith *LP '75*

Singles: 7-inch

MCA (40316 "Don't Worry Baby").............20-30
(Promotional issue.)
TRACK...4-6 75

LPs: 10/12-inch

MCA...8-10 75
Also see LORD SUTCH
Also see NELSON, Rick
Also see WHO

MOON, Mickey

Singles: 7-inch

CORAL (62088 "That's My Daisy")..........10-20 59

MOON, Smiley, & Moontunes

Singles: 7-inch

STAR (601 "You Don't Understand")........40-50 '60s

MOON, Sonny

Singles: 7-inch

W.B. (5018 "Countdown")......................10-20 59

MOON, Tony, & Aktones

Singles: 7-inch

PAN WORLD (513 "L-O-V-E")..................50-75 60

MOON & MARS

Singles: 7-inch

DOOTO (477 "Copper Penny")..................5-10 63

MOON MEN

Singles: 7-inch

SOUTHERN SOUND (114 "Other Side of the Moon")........................15-25 64
Also see WRAY, Link

MOON PEOPLE

Singles: 7-inch

ROULETTE (7065 "Kippy, Skippy Moon Strut")........................5-10 69
SPEED (003 "Land of Love")......................5-10 68

MOON STARS BAND

Singles: 7-inch

GOOD SOUND (108 "Hot Footsie")...........5-10 62

MOON STONES

Singles: 7-inch

DOLTON (70 "My True Love")...............10-15 63
Session: Nokie Edwards.
Also see VENTURES

MOON SURFERS / Michael Dominico

Singles: 7-inch

GENIUS (2101 "Surfin' on the Moon")......20-30 '60s

MOON'S TRAIN

Singles: 7-inch

MGM (13654 "It's in My Mind")..................5-10 67

MOONBEAMS

Singles: 7-inch

GREAT (100 "A Lover's Plea")..............75-125 59

MOONBEEMS

Singles: 7-inch

CHECKER (912 "Cryin' the Blues")............8-12 59
SAPPHIRE (1003 "Cryin' the Blues")......75-100 58
SAPPHIRE (1053 "Teen Age Baby")........50-75 58
Members: Simon Washington; John Meyers; Fontelle Land; Bill Turicot; Elaine Edwards.
Also see OTIS, Johnny

MOONBEEMS / Hawkettes

Singles: 7-inch

SAPPHIRE (2250 "Cryin' the Blues"/"Mardi Gras Mambo")........................10-20 58
Also see HAWKETTES
Also see MOONBEEMS

MOONBILLIES

Singles: 7-inch

REPUBLIC (2003 "Fall of the Planet Earth")........................20-30 60
Member: Pat Buttram.
Also see BUTTRAM, Pat

MOON-DAWGS

Singles: 7-inch

BOFUZ (1115 "You're No Good")............25-35 '60s
ROUND (69 "Keep on Pushing")..............20-30 '60s

MOONDOG
(With His Friends; with Louis T. Hardin)

EPs: 7-inch

BRUNSWICK (86000 "Improvisations at a Jazz Concert")........................25-50 53
(Issued with a paper sleeve.)
EPIC (7015 "Moondog & His Friends")....15-25 54
MARS (A2 "Moondog on the Streets of New York")........................20-30 55
MOONDOG (2 "Moondog and His Honking Geese")........................25-50 '50s
SMC (11 "Moondog in the Wide Open Spaces")........................25-50 53

LPs: 10/12-inch

COLUMBIA.......... 10-15 70-71
EPIC (1002 "Moondog & His Friends").. 75-125 54
(10-inch LP.)
MUSICAL HERITAGE SOCIETY (3803 "Moondog").......... 15-25 78
PRESTIGE (7042 "Caribea").......... 30-60 56
PRESTIGE (7069 "More Moondog")........ 30-60 56
PRESTIGE (7099 "Story of Moondog") ... 30-60 57

MOONEY, Art, & His Orchestra P&R '48
(With Cloverleafs)

Singles: 78 rpm

MGM.......... 3-5 48-57
VOGUE (Except R711 & R713).......... 25-40 46-48
(Picture discs.)
VOGUE (R711 "Seems Like Old Times"/ "Warsaw Concerto").......... 300-400 46
(Picture disc.)
VOGUE (R711/R713 "Seems Like Old Times"/ "I've Been Working on the Railroad").......... 60-80 46
(Picture disc.)
VOGUE (R713 "I've Been Working on the Railroad"/You're Nobody 'Til Somebody Loves You").......... 350-450 46
(Picture disc.)
VOGUE (R713/R732 "I've Been Working on the Railroad"/"I Don't Know Why").......... 60-80 46
(Picture disc.)
VOGUE (R-713-2/R-732-13 "I've Been Working on the Railroad"/"I Don't Know Why").......... 60-80 46
(Picture disc.)
VOGUE (R730 "Piper's Junction").......... 70-80 46
(Picture disc.)
VOGUE (R732 "In the Moonmist").......... 60-80 46
(Picture disc.)
VOGUE (R732-13/R732 "In the Moonmist").......... 70-90 46
(Picture disc.)

Singles: 7-inch

DECCA.......... 5-10 61-62
KAPP.......... 4-8 64-65
MGM (Except 12312).......... 5-15 50-64
MGM (12312 "Rebel Without a Cause"/"East of Eden").......... 10-15 56
RIVERSIDE.......... 5-10 62

Picture Sleeves

MGM (12312 "Rebel Without a Cause"/"East of Eden").......... 30-40 56
(Billed as a "Tribute to James Dean.")

EPs: 7-inch

MGM (Except 1342).......... 5-10 55-56
MGM (1342 "Music from Movies Starring James Dean").......... 30-40 55-56

LPs: 10/12-inch

DECCA.......... 10-20 62
DIPLOMAT.......... 6-12 '60s
KAPP.......... 10-15 64
MGM.......... 15-30 55-61
RCA.......... 10-15 67
SPINORAMA.......... 10-15 62
Also see AMES BROTHERS
Also see DEAN, James
Also see GORDON, Barry

MOONEY, Glenn

Singles: 7-inch

FRATERNITY (898 "Go Steady with Me").......... 10-15 62

MOONEY, Joe

LPs: 10/12-inch

ATLANTIC (1255 "Lush Life").......... 30-50 57

MOONEY, Ralph

Singles: 7-inch

CHALLENGE (59105 "Moonshine").......... 10-15 61
Also see BURTON, James, & Ralph Mooney
Also see STEWART, Wynn

MOONGLOWS R&B '54
(With Red Holloway Orchestra)

Singles: 78 rpm

CHAMPAGNE (7500 "I Just Can't Tell No Lie").......... 200-300 52
(Reportedly 2,500 made.)
CHANCE (1147 "Baby Please").......... 50-100 53
CHANCE (1150 "Just a Lonely Christmas").......... 50-100 54
CHANCE (1152 "Secret Love").......... 50-100 54
CHANCE (1156 "I Was Wrong").......... 50-100 54
CHANCE (1161 "219 Train").......... 50-100 54
CHESS (1500 & 1600 series).......... 30-50 54-57
QUALITY.......... 25-50 56
(Canadian.)

Singles: 7-inch

BIG P.......... 4-6 71
CHAMPAGNE (7500 "I Just Can't Tell No Lie").......... 1000-2000 53
(Reportedly 1500 made.)
CHANCE (1147 "Baby Please").......... 1000-2000 53
(Red vinyl.)
CHANCE (1150 "Just a Lonely Christmas").......... 1000-2000 54
(Red vinyl.)
CHANCE (1152 "Secret Love").......... 750-1200 54
(Blue and silver label.)
CHANCE (1152 "Secret Love").......... 500-700 54
(Yellow and black label.)
CHANCE (1156 "I Was Wrong").......... 500-1000 54
(Yellow and black label.)
CHANCE (1156 "I Was Wrong").......... 300-400 54
(White and black label.)
CHANCE (1161 "219 Train").......... 2500-3500 54
(White and black label.)
CHESS (1581 "Sincerely").......... 40-60 54
(Silver top label with chess pieces.)
CHESS (1581 "Sincerely").......... 10-15 '60s
(Blue label.)
CHESS (1589 "Most of All").......... 40-60 54
(Silver top label with chess pieces.)
CHESS (1589 "Most of All").......... 10-15 '60s
(Blue label.)
CHESS (1598 "Foolish Me").......... 40-60 55
(Silver top label with chess pieces.)
CHESS (1598 "Foolish Me").......... 10-15 '60s
(Blue label.)
CHESS (1605 "Starlite").......... 40-60 55
(Silver top label with chess pieces.)
CHESS (1605 "Starlite").......... 10-15 '60s
(Blue label.)
CHESS (1611 In My Diary").......... 40-60 55
(Silver top label with chess pieces.)
CHESS (1611 In My Diary").......... 10-15 '60s
(Blue label.)
CHESS (1619 "We Go Together").......... 30-50 56
(Silver top label with chess pieces.)
CHESS (1619 "We Go Together").......... 10-15 '60s
(Blue label.)
CHESS (1629 "See Saw").......... 30-50 56
(Silver top label with chess pieces.)
CHESS (1629 "See Saw").......... 10-15 '60s
(Blue label.)
CHESS (1646 "Over and Over Again")..... 30-50 56
(Silver top label with chess pieces.)
CHESS (1646 "Over and Over Again")..... 10-15 '60s
(Blue label.)
CHESS (1651 "I'm Afraid the Masquerade Is Over").......... 30-50 56
(Silver top label with chess pieces.)
CHESS (1651 "I'm Afraid the Masquerade Is Over").......... 10-15 '60s
(Blue label.)
CHESS (1661 "Please Send Me Someone to Love").......... 30-50 57
(Silver top label with chess pieces.)
CHESS (1661 "Please Send Me Someone to Love").......... 10-15 '60s
(Blue label.)
CHESS (1669 "Beating of My Heart")....... 25-35 57
CHESS (1681 "Too Late").......... 15-25 58
CHESS (1689 "In the Middle of the Night").......... 15-25 58
CHESS (1701 "This Love").......... 15-25 58
CHESS (1717 "I'll Never Stop Wanting You").......... 15-25 59
CHESS (1770 "Junior").......... 10-15 60
CHESS (1781 "Mama").......... 10-15 61
CRIMSON (1003 "My Imagination").......... 15-20 64
LANA (130 thru 135).......... 4-6 64
MELLO (69 "Just a Lonely Christmas")........ 3-5
QUALITY (1524 "See Saw").......... 40-60 56
(Canadian.)
RCA (0759 "Sincerely '72").......... 4-6 72
RCA (0839 "When I'm with You").......... 4-6 72
RELIC (1024 "I Pray for Love").......... 3-5 73
SKYLARK (552 "Thrill Me").......... 4-6 79
(Black or red vinyl.)
TIMES SQUARE (30 "I've Got the Right").......... 10-15 64
VEE-JAY (423 "Secret Love").......... 10-15 61

EPs: 7-inch

CHESS (5122 "Look! It's the Moonglows").......... 150-250 59
CHESS (5123 "Look! It's the Moonglows, Vol. 2").......... 100-200 59

LPs: 10/12-inch

CHESS (701 "The Moonglows").......... 10-15 76
CHESS (1430 "Look, It's the Moonglows").......... 200-300 59
CHESS (8403 "Their Current Sides")......... 5-10 83
CONSTELLATION (2 "Collectors Showcase").......... 20-30 64
LOST NITE (23 "Moonglows").......... 10-20 81
(10-inch LP. Red vinyl. 1000 made.)
RCA.......... 10-15 72
SUGARHILL/MCA.......... 5-10 84
Members: Harvey Fuqua; Bobby Lester; Alexander "Pete" Graves; Prentiss Barnes; Marvin Gaye; Buddy Johnson; Reese Palmer; James Knowland; Chester Simmons; Berle Ashton; Dock Green; George Thorpe; Danny Coggins.
Also see CROWNS
Also see DIDDLEY, Bo
Also see DRIFTERS
Also see FLAMINGOS / Moonglows
Also see GAYE, Marvin
Also see HARVEY & MOONGLOWS
Also see LESTER, Bobby, & Moonglows
Also see MARQUEES

MOONGOONERS

Singles: 7-inch

CANDIX (335 "Moongoon Stomp").......... 20-30 62
DONNA (1373 "Moongoon Twist").......... 10-20 62
ESSAR (1007 "Moongoon Twist").......... 25-50 62
Members: Scott Engel; John Stewart.
Also see ENGEL, Scott, & John Stewart

MOONLIGHTERS

Singles: 7-inch

JOSIE (843 "Broken Heart").......... 15-25 58
TARA (100 "Broken Heart").......... 75-100 58
TARA (102 "Rock-A-Bayou Baby").......... 60-75 58

MOONRAKERS

Singles: 7-inch

SHAMLEY (44012 "Love Train").......... 8-12 68
SHAMLEY (44015 "No Number to Call").... 8-12 68
SHAMLEY (44021 "No Hidin'").......... 8-12 68
TOWER (157 "I Was Wrong").......... 15-25 65
TOWER (180 "I'm Alright").......... 15-25 66
TOWER (222 "Trip and Fall").......... 15-25 66
TOWER (230 "Baby Please Don't Go").... 15-25 66

LPs: 10/12-inch

SHAMLEY (704 "Together").......... 25-35 68
Members: Van Dorn; Randy Walrath; Dennis Flanagan; Joel Brandes.

MOONSHINERS

Singles: 7-inch

SABINA (515 "Little Boat").......... 5-10 63
VILLAGE GATE (104 "Draft Dodger Rag") 5-10 65

LPs: 10/12-inch

VILLAGE GATE (2002 "Break Out")......... 10-20 65

MOORE, Abe

Singles: 78 rpm

DIG (125 "Moore Boogie").......... 10-15 56

Singles: 7-inch

DIG (125 "Moore Boogie").......... 15-25 56

MOORE, Ada

LPs: 10/12-inch

DEBUT (15 "Jazz Workshop").......... 25-50 55
Also see RUSHING, Jimmy, Ada Moore & Buck Clayton

MOORE, Alexander

Singles: 78 rpm

RPM (326 "If I Lose You Woman").......... 25-50 51

LPs: 10/12-inch

ARHOOLIE.......... 10-20

MOORE, Bernie
(With the Rockets)

Singles: 7-inch

BURDETT (1911 "45 RPMs").......... 5-10 66
PLANET X (9622 "Rock Guitar Rock").100-150 57

MOORE, Betty
(With Ambassadors; with Esquires)

Singles: 7-inch

CUCA (1134 "Long Hot Summer").......... 15-25 63
CUCA (1467 "Long Hot Summer").......... 10-15 69
Also see ESQUIRES
Also see MOORER, Betty

MOORE, Bill R&B '48

Singles: 78 rpm

SAVOY (666 "We're Gonna Rock").......... 20-30 48
Also see WILLIAMS, Paul

MOORE, Bob P&R/R&B/LP '61

Singles: 7-inch

HICKORY.......... 4-8 65-68
MONUMENT (Except 446).......... 5-10 59-64
MONUMENT (446 "Mexico").......... 10-15 61

Picture Sleeves

MONUMENT.......... 5-10 62-63

LPs: 10/12-inch

HICKORY.......... 10-15 66
MONUMENT.......... 10-20 61-67
Also see ATKINS, Chet
Also see BOX, David
Also see DRAGON, Paul
Also see LEE, Bobby
Also see LEE, Brenda
Also see NASHVILLE ALL-STARS
Also see NELSON, Willie
Also see PRESLEY, Elvis
Also see STARR, Frank, & His Rock-Away Boys
Also see STEWART, Wynn
Also see TIGRE, Terry

MOORE, Bob, & Temps

Singles: 7-inch

DAISY (502 "Trophy Run").......... 25-35 63
(Also released as by the Temptations.)
Member: Roy Buchanan.
Also see BUCHANAN, Roy
Also see TEMPTATIONS

MOORE, Bobby, & Foremost

Singles: 7-inch

D.W. (105 "Girl, You Do Something to Me").......... 8-12 66
FANTASY (585 "You Got to Live for Yourself").......... 30-40 64
RED BIRD (071 "Girl, You Do Something to Me").......... 5-10 66

MOORE, Bobby P&R/R&B '66
(With the Rhythm Aces; Bob Moore)

Singles: 7-inch

CHECKER (1129 "Searching for My Love").......... 10-15 65
(Maroon label.)
CHECKER (1129 "Searching for My Love").......... 5-10 65
(Blue label.)
CHECKER (1156 "Try My Love Again")..... 5-10 66
CHECKER (1180 "Chained to Your Heart").......... 5-10 67

LPs: 10/12-inch

CHECKER (3000 "Searching for My Love").......... 20-25 66

MOORE, Buel, & Garnets

Singles: 7-inch

VITA (174 "Really Really Baby").......... 20-30 58

MOORE, Candy

Singles: 7-inch

SABLE (101 "It's Your Turn Now").......... 5-10 62

MOORE, Cathy

Singles: 7-inch

MAJESTY (302 "I'll Wait").......... 10-20 62

MOORE, Cecil
(With the Diamond Backs; with Notes)

Singles: 7-inch

ATCO (6309 "Rise and Shine").......... 5-10 64
LU TEX.......... 4-6 78
SARG (150 "Walkin' Fever").......... 25-50 57
SARG (165 "Moonshine").......... 25-50 59
SARG (192 "My Money's Gone").......... 20-30 60
SARG (200 series, except 206 & 211)....... 5-10 '60s
SARG (206 "Rise and Shine").......... 15-25 61
SARG (211 "Stormy").......... 15-25 62
TOTEM (103 "Stuff").......... 10-20 66

MOORE, Craig

EPs: 7-inch

RUMBLE.......... 4-8 81

LPs: 10/12-inch

MCCM (8901 "Agonnagain".......... 25-30 89
(Two splash, multi-color vinyl discs.)

Also see GONN

MOORE, Curly
(Curley Moore)
Singles: 7-inch
INSTANT (3295 "Sophisticated Sissy") 5-8 68
NOLA (707 "Soul Train")............................5-10 64
SANSU (468 "Goodbye")............................5-10 67
SANSU (473 "Don't Pity Me")......................5-10 67

MOORE, Danny
Singles: 7-inch
ALLRITE (625 "Somebody New")........ 300-400 63
LPs: 10/12-inch
EVEREST (1211 "Folk Songs from Here and There") 10-20 63
(Monaural.)
EVEREST (5211 "Folk Songs from Here and There") 15-25 63
(Stereo.)

MOORE, David
Singles: 7-inch
LYNN (501 "Crazy Dream")........................5-10 60

MOORE, Debby
Singles: 7-inch
TOP RANK (2039 "I Got a Feeling") 5-10 60
LPs: 10/12-inch
TOP RANK (301 "Debby Moore") 15-25 59
(Monaural.)
TOP RANK (601 "Debby Moore") 20-30 59
(Stereo.)

MOORE, Det
Singles: 7-inch
GALLANT (3004 "Blue Sax")......................5-10 62
LPs: 10/12-inch
GALLANT (4001 "Great Jazz from Great TV") 20-30 62

MOORE, Donny Lee
Singles: 7-inch
GOLDEN CREST (512 "Fire")................. 25-50 59
GOLDEN CREST (527 "I'm Buggin' Out Little Baby") 100-200 59
SHELLEY (1000 "I'm Buggin' Out Little Baby") 75-125 59

MOORE, Eddie
Singles: 7-inch
20TH FOX (101 "Phone Chick")............. 10-20 58
Also see LEWIS, Joe "Cannonball" / Eddie Moore

MOORE, Frank, Four
Singles: 7-inch
ALMO (202 "Look Here Baby") 5-10 64

MOORE, Gary *LP '83*
(Gary Moore Band)
Singles: 7-inch
JET...4-6 79
MIRAGE...3-5 83-86
VIRGIN 3-5 87-89
LPs: 10/12-inch
CHARISMA..5-8 90
JET...5-10 78
MIRAGE...5-8 83-86
PETERS INT'L (9004 "Grinding Stone").. 12-15 73
(Red label.)
PETERS INT'L (9004 "Grinding Stone").. 10-12 73
(Orange label.)
VIRGIN 5-8 87-89
Also see SKID ROW
Also see THIN LIZZY

MOORE, Gatemouth
Singles: 78 rpm
CHEZ PAREE 10-20 45
KING 10-20 47-48
NATIONAL.. 10-20 45-46
LPs: 10/12-inch
BLUESWAY (6074 "After Twenty-One Years") 10-15 73
KING (684 "Gatemouth Moore Sings Blues")... 4000-6000 60

MOORE, Gene, & Metronomes
Singles: 78 rpm
SPECIALTY (472 "She's Gone")........... 75-125 53
Singles: 7-inch
SPECIALTY (472 "She's Gone")...... 3000-4000 53
(Has wavy line through center of black line.)
SPECIALTY (472 "She's Gone").................4-8
(Reissue has solid black line.)

MOORE, Gene, & Chimes / Jake Porter with Gene Moore & Chimes
Singles: 78 rpm
COMBO (63 "Only a Dream"/"Reap What You Sow")..75-125 55
Singles: 7-inch
COMBO (63 "Only a Dream"/"Reap What You Sow")..250-350 55
Also see MOORE, Gene
Also see PORTER, Jake

MOORE, Hank
Singles: 7-inch
5-4 (5425 "Reconsider, Baby")................15-25
5-4 (5426 "Sour Mash")..........................15-25

MOORE, Harv
Singles: 7-inch
AMERICAN ARTS (20 "Interview of the Fab Four")..30-40 65

MOORE, Henry
Singles: 7-inch
AFADA...10-15
JET STREAM (711 "Am I Wrong")............5-10 63
JET STREAM (720 "I Can't Forget You") ...5-10 64
JET STREAM (731 "I'm Losing You").........5-10 68
KING (5449 "Rock Junction")....................5-10 61
HERMITAGE (805 "She's a Lover")...........5-10 63
Also see BALLARD, Hank, & Midnighters

MOORE, Jack
Singles: 7-inch
CAPRI (62-2 "Half Angel").......................10-20
TROJAN (5001 "Bad Bad Blues")............15-25

MOORE, Jackie *P&R/R&B '70*
(With the Memphis Horns; with Dixie Flyers)
Singles: 12-inch
COLUMBIA...4-8 79-84
Singles: 7-inch
ATLANTIC...4-8 70-73
CATAWBA...3-5 83
COLUMBIA...3-6 79-84
KAYVETTE...3-6 75-81
SHOUT (232 "Here I Am")........................5-10 68
LPs: 10/12-inch
ATLANTIC...8-12 73
COLUMBIA...5-10 79
Also see LULU

MOORE, James
Singles: 7-inch
SOFT (1014 "Cool")..................................8-12 69

MOORE, James, & Pretenders
Singles: 7-inch
TISHMAN (905 "To Be Loved")................50-75 64

MOORE, Jan
Singles: 7-inch
BOYD (3271 "Deep Water").......................5-10 61
WINSTON (1035 "Play It Cool")...............50-75 59

MOORE, Jerry
Singles: 7-inch
COLUMBIA (44072 "High Hemlines").........5-10 67
LPs: 10/12-inch
ESP (1061 "Life Is a Constant Journey Home")..10-15 67

MOORE, Jimmy
Singles: 7-inch
LEGRAND (1037 "Crawlin' ") 15-25 65
S.P.Q.R. (1106 "Church Street Sally")........8-12 67

MOORE, Jimmy, & Peacocks
Singles: 7-inch
NOBLE (711 "Tender Love")........... 1000-1500 58
Also see KING BEES

MOORE, Joe
Singles: 7-inch
TIME (1053 "I Believe") 5-10 62

MOORE, Johnny *R&B '46*
(With the Blazers; with Three Blazers; with New Blazers; with Twigs; with Rudy Toombs; with Eddie Williams; with Floyd Dixon; with Mari Jones; Johnny Moore's Orchestra with Mal Hogan & Twigs)
Singles: 78 rpm
ALADDIN...20-50 45-48
BLAZE...10-20 54
COMBO...10-20 55
EXCLUSIVE...20-40 46-48
HOLLYWOOD...10-20 53-56
MODERN...10-20 48-50
MODERN MUSIC..10-20 45-46
MONEY...10-15 55
PHILO...10-20 46
RCA..15-25 50
SWING TIME 10-20 51
Singles: 7-inch
ALADDIN (112 "Drifting Blues")...........150-200 51
AMPEN (222 "Every Street's a Boulevard")...50-75 63
BLAZE (101 "Miss Mosey")......................30-40 54
BLAZE (108 "Pretty Please") 50-75 54
BRUNSWICK...4-6 71
COMBO (69 "Take Off My Wig")..............25-50 55
(Vocal by Floyd Dixon.)
HOLLYWOOD (1001 "Strange Love")......40-50 53
HOLLYWOOD (1012 "Diesel Drive").......40-50 54
HOLLYWOOD (1045 "Christmas Eve Baby")...40-50 55
HOLLYWOOD (1056 "I Send My Love")..50-60 56
MODERN (800 & 900 series)...................20-30 53
MONEY (205 "Lonesome Gal") 20-30 55
RCA (50-0009 "This Is One Time Baby")...75-125 50
(Cherry red vinyl.)
RCA (50-0018 "Bop-a-Bye Baby").........75-125 50
(Cherry red vinyl.)
RCA (50-0026 "Walkin' Blues")..............75-125 50
(Cherry red vinyl.)
RCA (50-0031 "Shuffle Shuck")..............75-125 50
(Cherry red vinyl.)
RCA (50-0043 "So Long") 75-125 50
(Cherry red vinyl.)
RCA (50-0073 "Misery Blues")................75-125 50
(Cherry red vinyl.)
RCA (50-0086 "Rain-Check")..................75-125 50
(Cherry red vinyl.)
RCA (50-0095 "Jumping Jack") 75-125 50
(Cherry red vinyl.)
RENDEZVOUS (115 "Bullfrog")................10-15 60
SUE (726 "You're My Queen")..................15-25 60
Members: Johnny Moore; Charles Brown; Eddie Williams.
Also see BELL, Hugh, & Twiggs
Also see BROWN, Charles
Also see COMPOSERS
Also see DIXON, Floyd, & Johnny Moore's Three Blazers
Also see FEATHERS
Also see JONES, Mari
Also see McSHANN, Jay, & Johnny Moore's Three Blazers
Also see WILLIAMS, Eddie
Also see WOODS, Sonny

MOORE, Johnny, & Linda Hayes
Singles: 78 rpm
HOLLYWOOD 10-20 55
Singles: 7-inch
HOLLYWOOD (1031 "Why, Johnny [Ace], Why")...30-50 55
Also see HAYES, Linda
Also see MOORE, Johnny

MOORE, Johnny
Singles: 7-inch
VADEN (111 "Country Girl")..................100-200 60

MOORE, Johnny
Singles: 7-inch
BLUE ROCK (4053 "Such a Wonderful Feeling") 5-10 68
BLUE ROCK (4070 "That's What You Said") 5-10 68
DATE (1562 "Walk Like a Man")..............15-25 67
WAND (1165 "Haven't I Been Good to You") 8-12 67

MOORE, Johnny
Singles: 7-inch
BRIGHT STAR (145 "Sold on You")...........8-12 66
BRIGHT STAR (148 "Your Love's Got Power") 8-12 66
CHI-CITY...8-12
MERCURY (72939 "Your Love Is Fading") 8-12 69

MOORE, Joseph
Singles: 7-inch
MAR-V-LUS (6008 "I Still Can't Get You") .8-12 65

MOORE, Kenzie
Singles: 78 rpm
SPECIALTY...10-15 53-56
Singles: 7-inch
SPECIALTY (Black vinyl.)......................15-20 53-56
SPECIALTY (Red vinyl.) 20-30 53

MOORE, Larry
Singles: 7-inch
ORIGINAL SOUND (30 "Hooray for Music") 5-10 63
ORIGINAL SOUND (31 "Two Young Lovers") 5-10 63

MOORE, Lattie *C&W '61*
(With His Allen County Boys)
Singles: 78 rpm
ARROW ("Hideaway Heart").....................20-30 51
KING (4955 "Lonesome Man Blues").......10-20 56
SPEED (101 "Juke Joint Johnny").........50-100 52
Singles: 7-inch
ARC (8005 "Juke Joint Johnny") 100-200 57
KING (4955 "Lonesome Man Blues").......25-35 56
KING (5370 "Cajun Doll").........................20-30 60
KING (5413 "Drunk Again") 5-10 61
KING (5723 "Just About Then") 5-10 63
OLIMPIC ("Skinny Minnie Shimmy") ......75-125 '60s
(Selection number not known.)
SPEED (101 "Juke Joint Johnny")........300-400 52
SPEED (105 "Baby I'll Soon Be Gone")...150-250
STARDAY (403 "Why Did You Lie to Me")...50-100 58
STARDAY (441 "Too Hot to Handle") 50-100 59
EPs: 7-inch
SAGA (500 "Lattie Moore") ....50-75 '50s
LPs: 10/12-inch
AUDIO LAB (1555 "Best of Lattie Moore")...30-40 60
AUDIO LAB (1573 "Country Side")..........25-35 62
DERBYTOWN (102 "Lattie Moore") ....10-20 '60s

MOORE, Lee
(With the Hank Trotter's Happy Rangers)
Singles: 78 rpm
CROSS COUNTRY.......................................25-50 55
Singles: 7-inch
CROSS COUNTRY (506 "The Cat Came Back") 50-100 55

MOORE, Little Bobby
Singles: 7-inch
KING (5668 "Ginger Snap") 10-20 62

MOORE, Lucky
Singles: 7-inch
WAY-VEE (900 "Walking & Talking")...200-300 58

MOORE, Martha
Singles: 78 rpm
DELUXE...8-12 54
Singles: 7-inch
DELUXE (6038 "Yo Yo Yo") 15-25 54
DELUXE (6049 "Baby I'm Through")........15-25 54

MOORE, Matthew
(Matthew Moore Plus Four)
Singles: 7-inch
CAPITOL..8-12 66-67
CARIBOU..4-6 78-79
GNP (343 "I Know You Girl").....................5-10 65
WHITE WHALE (223 "Codyne") 20-30 65
LPs: 10/12-inch
CARIBOU..5-10 78
Members: Matthew Moore; David Marks.
Also see MOON

MOORE, Melba *LP '71*
Singles: 12-inch
CAPITOL..4-6 83-86
EPIC..4-8 79-80
Singles: 7-inch
BUDDAH..4-6 75-78
CAPITOL..3-5 82-87
EMI...3-5 90
EMI AMERICA...3-5 81-82
EPIC...3-6 78-80
MERCURY...4-6 69-72
MUSICOR...4-8 66
Picture Sleeves
BUDDAH..4-6 76-77
CAPITOL..4-6 84-87
LPs: 10/12-inch
ACCORD..5-10 81

BUDDAH 8-10 75-79
CAPITOL 5-8 83-86
EMI AMERICA..5-10 81
EPIC..5-10 78-80
MERCURY 10-15 70-72

MOORE, Melba, & Freddie Jackson *R&B '88*

Singles: 7-inch

CAPITOL 3-5 86-88

MOORE, Melba, & Kashif *R&B '86*

(Melba & Kashif)

Singles: 7-inch

CAPITOL 3-5 86-88

Picture Sleeves

CAPITOL (5577 "Love the One I'm With")....4-6 86
CAPITOL (44195 "I'm in Love")....................4-6 88
Also see MOORE, Melba

MOORE, Melvin

(With the Bill Hendricks Orchestra)

Singles: 78 rpm

JUBILEE.. 10-15 56
KING 25-50 52

Singles: 7-inch

JUBILEE (5250 "That's All There Is to That").. 15-25 56
KING (4539 "Possessed")...................... 50-100 52

MOORE, Merrill

Singles: 78 rpm

CAPITOL 10-15 52-57

Singles: 7-inch

CAPITOL.. 15-20 52-57

EPs: 7-inch

CAPITOL (608 "Merrill Moore")............... 50-75 56

MOORE, Mike

Singles: 7-inch

CYCLONE (503 "The Chick")................ 75-100 '60s

MOORE, Nunnie, & Peacocks

Singles: 7-inch

L&M (1002 "Bouquet of Roses") 400-600 57

MOORE, Phil

(With the Phil Moore Four)

Singles: 78 rpm

BLACK & WHITE 10-15 47
RCA 10-15 53

Singles: 7-inch

RCA 15-25 53
Members: Marty Wilson; Jimmy Lyons; Milt Hinton; Johnny Letman.

MOORE, Phil, & Chords

Singles: 7-inch

TIME (101 "Little Angel") 100-200 57

MOORE, Phil, III, & Afro-Latin Soultet

LPs: 10/12-inch

TOWER (5085 "Afro-Brazil Ora") 10-20 67

MOORE, Red

Singles: 7-inch

RED (840 "Crawdad Song") .... 500-600 '50s

MOORE, Robert

Singles: 7-inch

DELUXE...5-10 69
HOLLYWOOD (1127 "Am I Wasting My Time")..5-10 68
HOLLYWOOD (1134 "Searching for Your Love")..5-10 68

MOORE, Ronnie

Singles: 7-inch

JARO (77009 "When You Lose Your Love").. 10-20 59
STOMPER TIME (1157 "You Have This and More") 50-75 58
TEEN'S CHOICE (7 "Sweet Shop Doll")... 100-150

MOORE, Rudy

Singles: 78 rpm

FEDERAL.. 10-15 56

Singles: 7-inch

FEDERAL (12253 "My Little Angel")........ 20-30 56
FEDERAL (12259 "Buggy Ride")............. 20-30 56
FEDERAL (12276 "Step It Up and Go")... 20-30 56
FEDERAL (12280 "I'll Be Home to See You Tomorrow Night") 20-30 56

MOORE, Rudy Ray

(With the Raytones; with Seniors)

Singles: 7-inch

BALL (500 "Dear Ruth") 10-20
BALL (503 "My Baby")...............................10-20
BALL (504 "Your Tender Touch") 10-20
CASH (1059 "Until You're in My Arms") .75-100 58
CASH (1060 "I'm Ready") 75-100 58
COMEDIANS INC. (103 "You Could Be Ugly Too")..4-8
IMPERIAL (66022 "Baby That's Why I'm Your Fool")..5-10 64
KENT (363 "Driveway Blues")....................5-10 61
KENT (4570 "Great Pretender")..................4-6 72
KENT (4579 "Miss Wonderful")...................4-6 72
LEE (501 "Honey Hush")..........................50-75 58
VERMONT (205 "Your Tender Touch")....20-30
WORLD PACIFIC (821 "Easy Easy Baby")..10-20 60
Also see LADY REED
Also see WHEATSTRAW, Peetie, & Rudy Ray Moore

MOORE, Rudy Ray / Carl Otis & Castlerockers

Singles: 7-inch

CASH (1058 "It Hurts to My Heart"/ "Josephine") 25-35 58
Also see MOORE, Rudy Ray

MOORE, Sandee

Singles: 7-inch

BRUNSWICK (55065 "Autograph") 10-15 58

MOORE, Scotty

(Scotty Moore Trio)

Singles: 7-inch

FERNWOOD (107 "Have Guitar Will Travel") 20-25 58

LPs: 10/12-inch

EPIC (24103 "The Guitar That Changed the World")..50-75 64
(Monaural.)
EPIC (24103 "The Guitar That Changed the World")..60-80 64
(White label. Promotional issue only.)
EPIC (26103 "The Guitar That Changed the World")..60-80 64
(Stereo.)
GUINNESS..20-30 77
Also see DONNER, Ral
Also see DRAGON, Paul
Also see MARTIN, Jerry
Also see POINDEXTER, Doug, & Starlite Wranglers
Also see PRESLEY, Elvis
Also see TIGRE, Terry

MOORE, Shelly, & Eddie Harris

LPs: 10/12-inch

ARGO (4016 "For the First Time") 30-40 62
Also see HARRIS, Eddie

MOORE, Sonny

Singles: 7-inch

ASCOT (2103 "Have Fun") 5-10 62
OLD TOWN (1063 "My True Love and I")...10-20 58
ROULETTE (4441 "Bloodshed in Tombstone") 5-10 62
U.A. (382 "Bloodshed in Tombstone")......15-25 61

MOORE, Sparkle

(With the Dan Belloc Orchestra)

Singles: 7-inch

FRATERNITY (751 "Skull and Cross Bones") 50-60 57
FRATERNITY (766 "Killer")......................40-50 57

MOORE, Turner

Singles: 7-inch

MEL-O-TONE (1500 "I'll Be Leavin' You") 1000-1500 57

MOORE, Wendell

Singles: 7-inch

RIM (4103 "Send Me a Little Girl").............5-10 62

MOORE, Wild Bill

(Wild Bill Moore Quintet; with Twistets)

Singles: 78 rpm

KING...10-15 50
OLD TOWN (1035 "Wild One") 10-15 56
SENSATION 17 "Blue Journey")..............25-35 49

Singles: 7-inch

JAZZLAND (706 "Bubbles") 5-10 61
OLD TOWN (1035 "Wild One").................15-25 56

LPs: 10/12-inch

JAZZLAND (38 "Wild Beat's Beat") 10-15 61
POPSIDE 15-20 62

MOORE, Woo Woo

Singles: 78 rpm

MERCURY..10-15 53

Singles: 7-inch

MERCURY (70204 "Something's Wrong")..35-50 53

MOORE & MOORE

Singles: 7-inch

VALIANT (749 "Leave Him and Come to My Arms") 5-10 66
Session: Davie Allan.

MOORER, Betty

Singles: 7-inch

WAND (11202 "It's My Thing")..................10-15 69
Also see ESQUIRES
Also see MOORE, Betty

MOORHOUSE, Walter, & Mighty Magnificent 7

Singles: 7-inch

KIMM (9322 "Come into My Heart") 5-10 68
STUDIO CITY (726 "Our Love") ....5-10 '60s

MOORPARK INTERSECTION

Singles: 7-inch

CAPITOL (2115 "Yesterday Holds On").....5-10 68

MOOSE & PELICANS

Singles: 7-inch

VANGUARD (35110 "We're Rockin' ").......5-10 71
VANGUARD (35129 "He's a Rebel")........12-15 71
Member: Darlene Love.
Also see LOVE, Darlene

MOOSE JOHN

(John Walker)

Singles: 78 rpm

ULTRA (102 "Wrong Doin' Woman")........10-20 55

Singles: 7-inch

ULTRA (102 "Wrong Doin' Woman")........20-30 55

MOOVE SOCIETY

EPs: 7-inch

JOYZEE (101 "Moove Society") 10-15 90

MOP TOPS

Singles: 7-inch

TEEN (518 "Flipper")..................................10-20 63

MORALES, Ernie, & Lavenders

Singles: 7-inch

CRYSTAL BALL (100 "Little Bit of Everything")..5-10 77
(Black vinyl. 500 made.)
CRYSTAL BALL (100 "Little Bit of Everything") 8-12 77
(Red vinyl. 25 made.)

MORDOR

Singles

WORLD METAL (003 "Rock Warrior").......8-12 89
(Octagon picture disc. 500 made.)
WORLD METAL (003 "Rock Warrior").....15-20 89
(Square picture disc. 100 made.)

MORELAND, Prentice

Singles: 78 rpm

RPM..8-12 56-57

Singles: 7-inch

CHALLENGE (9134 "Holy Mack'rel") 8-12 62
CHALLENGE (9154 "Chubby Ain't Chubby No More") 8-12 62
CHALLENGE (9176 "More Your Love").....8-12 62
CHALLENGE (9181 "Limbo Party")............8-12 63
DONNA (1320 "Looking for Your Heart") .10-15 60
EDSEL (778 "Oh Pretty Baby")................15-25 59
RPM (475 "I've Never BeenThere").........15-25 56
RPM (487 "Marie My Love").....................15-25 57
Also see CHANTECLAIRS
Also see JACKS

MORELAND, Richie

(Little Richard Moreland & Pyramids; Richard Moreland)

Singles: 7-inch

CAPITOL (5849 "Gotta Travel On")............5-10 67
DART (108 "Things I'll Never Know") 10-20 59
DART (153 "Let Me In")............................10-20 61
IMPERIAL (66105 "Bells in My Heart").......8-12 65
IMPERIAL (66126 "I Forgot to Remember to Forget")..8-12 65
PICTURE (7722 "Bells in My Heart")........50-75 65
(First issue.)

MORELAND, Tommy

Singles: 7-inch

COLUMBUS (1501 "Tennessee Blues")..75-85
SKOOP (1054 "Bang Bang") 75-85 60

MORENO, Buddy

Singles: 78 rpm

CHESS (1535 "One Dozen Roses").........10-20 53

Singles: 7-inch

CHESS (1535 "One Dozen Roses").........40-60 53
(Black vinyl.)
CHESS (1535 "One Dozen Roses").....100-200 53
(Red vinyl.)
NORMAN (522 "Money Talks") 5-10 62

MORE-TISHANS

Singles: 7-inch

PEAK (4453 "I've Got Nowhere to Run") .25-35 67

MORGAN

Singles: 7-inch

LAUREL (1013 "High School Steady").......8-12 60

MORGAN

Singles: 7-inch

BELL (798 "Who Am I") 5-10 69

MORGAN, Al *C&W '49*

Singles: 78 rpm

CHANCE 8-12 53
LONDON...4-8 49
UNIVERSAL..6-12 49

Singles: 7-inch

CHANCE (3002 "Disappointed in You")...20-30 53
RENDEZVOUS (113 "Me and the Moon") .5-10 60

MORGAN, Bill

Singles: 7-inch

DART (137 "Red Hot Rhythm") 25-50 61
DELTA (501 "I Need Your Love")............25-50

MORGAN, Billie *C&W '59*

Singles: 7-inch

STARDAY (420 "Life to Live")....................8-12 59

MORGAN, Charlie

(Charlie Feathers)

Singles: 7-inch

WALMAY (100 "Dinky John")...............150-250 60
Also see FEATHERS, Charlie

MORGAN, Chris

(With the Togas)

Singles: 7-inch

BELL (798 "Now I Taste the Tears") 5-10 69
BELL (851 "Trouble Maker").........................4-8 70
CHALLENGE (59330 "There She Goes")...15-25 66
Also see 6680 LEXINGTON
Also see TOGAS

MORGAN, Dean

Singles: 7-inch

RARE (101 "Good Rockin' Tonight")......75-125
TOP RANK (2065 "Come What May")...... 15-25 60

MORGAN, Gene

Singles: 7-inch

GEMINI ("Ten Wheeler Blues") 75-125
(Selection number not known.)

MORGAN, George *C&W '49*

(With Little Roy Wiggins)

Singles: 78 rpm

COLUMBIA...5-10 52-57

Singles: 7-inch

COLUMBIA...15-25 52-65
DECCA..4-6 71-73
4 STAR...4-6 75-79
MCA...4-6 73-74
STARDAY 5-10 67-68
STOP...4-8 69-70

EPs: 7-inch

COLUMBIA...15-25 52-58

LPs: 10/12-inch

COLUMBIA (Except 1044)........................15-30 61-75
COLUMBIA (1044 "Morgan, By George")..30-40 57
4 STAR...6-12 75-77
HARMONY 8-15 67-69
MCA 5-10 74

NASHVILLE ... 6-12 69-71
POWER PAK ... 5-10 74
STARDAY (400 series) ... 10-20 67-69
STARDAY (900 series) ... 5-10 74
STOP ... 8-12 69

MORGAN, George, & Marion Worth

LPs: 10/12-inch

COLUMBIA (2197 "Slippin' Around") ... 15-25 64
(Monaural.)
COLUMBIA (8997 "Slippin' Around") ... 20-30 64
(Stereo.)
Also see MORGAN, George
Also see WORTH, Marion

MORGAN, Jane — P&R/LP '57

(With the Troubadors)

Singles: 78 rpm

KAPP ... 3-8 54-57

Singles: 7-inch

ABC ... 4-6 67-68
ELEKTRA ... 3-5 82
EPIC ... 4-6 65-68
COLPIX ... 4-8 63-65
KAPP ... 5-10 54-62
RCA ... 4-6 69-70

EPs: 7-inch

KAPP ... 5-10 55-59

Picture Sleeves

COLPIX ... 5-10 63
ELEKTRA ... 3-5 82
EPIC ... 4-8 65
KAPP ... 5-12 57-59

LPs: 10/12-inch

ABC ... 5-10 68
COLPIX ... 10-20 63-66
EPIC ... 10-15 65-67
KAPP ... 10-20 56-63
MCA ... 5-10 73
RCA (Except 1160) ... 8-12 69-70
RCA (1160 "Marry Me, Marry Me") ... 10-15 69
(Soundtrack.)
HARMONY ... 5-8 70
Also see WILLIAMS, Roger, & Jane Morgan

MORGAN, Janice

Singles: 7-inch

MARLEE (101 "Money Honey") ... 50-75 60
MARLEE (103 "Sittin' in a Corner") ... 50-75 60

MORGAN, Jaye P. — P&R '53

Singles: 78 rpm

DECCA ... 5-10 54-55
DERBY ... 5-10 53
RCA ... 5-10 54-56

Singles: 7-inch

ABC-PAR ... 5-10 65
BEVERLY HILLS ... 4-6 69-72
DECCA (29501 "Have You Ever Been Lonely") ... 10-20 55
DECCA (29611 "Life Is Just a Bowl of Cherries") ... 5-10 55
DECCA (29722 "Nobody Met the Train") ... 5-10 55
DERBY (828 "Just a Gigolo") ... 5-10 53
DERBY (837 "Life Is Just a Bowl of Cherries") ... 5-10 53
DERBY (843 "Ring Telephone Ring") ... 5-10 54
DERBY (852 "Nobody Met the Train") ... 5-10 54
DERBY (855 "I Ain't Got the Man") ... 5-10 54
GIGOLO ... 3-5
MGM ... 5-15 59-63
RCA (5896 "That's All I Want from You") ... 10-20 54
RCA (6016 "Danger! Heartbreak Ahead") ... 10-20 55
RCA (6182 "The Longest Walk") ... 10-20 55
RCA (6282 "If You Don't Want My Love") ... 10-20 55
RCA (6329 "Not One Goodbye") ... 10-20 55
RCA (6441 "Sweet Lips") ... 10-20 56
RCA (6505 "Lost in the Shuffle") ... 10-20 56
RCA (6565 "Johnny Casanova") ... 10-20 56
RCA (6653 "Just Love Me") ... 10-20 56
RCA (6798 "I Thought It Was Over") ... 10-20 56
RCA (7064 "Take a Chance") ... 10-20 57
RCA (7178 "Tell Me More") ... 10-20 58

EPs: 7-inch

DECCA ... 10-20 55
DERBY ... 10-20 53

LPs: 10/12-inch

BAINBRIDGE (6236 "What Are You Doing the Rest of Your Life") ... 5-10 82
BEVERLY HILLS (24 "What Are You Doing the Rest of Your Life") ... 8-12 70
MGM (3774 "Slow and Easy") ... 15-25 59
MGM (3830 "Up North") ... 15-25 60
MGM (3867 "Down South") ... 15-25 60
MGM (3940 "That Country Sound") ... 15-25 61
RCA (1155 "Jaye P. Morgan") ... 25-35 55
RCA (1682 "Just You, Just Me") ... 25-35 55
RONDO-LETTE (13 "Jaye P. Morgan Sings") ... 15-20 58
ROYALE (18122 "Jaye P.Morgan") ... 20-30 55
(10-inch LP. Side 2 has uncredited instrumentals.)
Also see ARNOLD, Eddy, & Jaye P. Morgan
Also see COMO, Perry, & Jaye P. Morgan
Also see PRESLEY, Elvis / Jaye P. Morgan

MORGAN, Jaye P., & Frank De Vol Orchestra

LPs: 10/12-inch

ALLEGRO (1604 "Jaye P. Morgan Sings with the Frank De Vol Orchestra") ... 10-20 '50s
Also see DE VOL, Frank, Orchestra
Also see MORGAN, Jaye P.

MORGAN, King

Singles: 7-inch

JOHANSON (321 "We're Goin' Out to Rock Tonight") ... 50-75

MORGAN, Lee — P&R/R&B/LP '64

Singles: 7-inch

BLUE NOTE ... 4-6 64-69
BUZZ ... 3-6 79-80
VEE-JAY ... 4-8 60

LPs: 10/12-inch

BLUE NOTE (200 series) ... 8-12 74
BLUE NOTE (900 & 1000 series) ... 5-10 79-81
BLUE NOTE (1500 series) ... 50-75 56-58
(Label gives New York street address for Blue Note Records.)
BLUE NOTE (1500 series) ... 25-50 58
(Label reads: "Blue Note Records Inc. - New York, USA.")
BLUE NOTE (1500 series) ... 15-25 66
(Label shows Blue Note Records as a division of either Liberty or United Artists.)
BLUE NOTE (4000 series) ... 30-40 61
(Label gives New York street address for Blue Note Records.)
BLUE NOTE (4000 series) ... 15-25 62
(Label reads: "Blue Note Records Inc. - New York, USA.")
BLUE NOTE (4000 series) ... 10-20 66
(Label shows Blue Note Records as a division of either Liberty or United Artists.)
BLUE NOTE (4100 thru 4200 series) ... 15-25 63
(Label reads: "Blue Note Records Inc. - New York, USA.")
BLUE NOTE (4100 thru 4200 series) ... 10-20 66-67
(Label shows Blue Note Records as a division of either Liberty or United Artists.)
BLUE NOTE (84000 series) ... 30-40 61
(Label gives New York street address for Blue Note Records.)
BLUE NOTE (84000 series) ... 20-30 62
(Label reads: "Blue Note Records Inc. - New York, USA.")
BLUE NOTE (84000 series) ... 10-20 66
(Label shows Blue Note Records as a division of either Liberty or United Artists.)
BLUE NOTE (84100 thru 84200 series) ... 15-30 63-69
(Label reads: "Blue Note Records Inc. - New York, USA.")
BLUE NOTE (84100 thru 84300 series) ... 10-20 66-70
(Label shows Blue Note Records as a division of either Liberty or United Artists.)
BLUE NOTE (89000 series) ... 10-15 71
GNP ... 6-12 73
JAZZLAND (80 "Take Twelve") ... 15-25 62
MCA ... 5-8 74
PACIFIC JAZZ ... 5-8 81
PRESTIGE ... 5-8 81
SAVOY (12091 "Introducing...") ... 50-75 56
SUNSET ... 5-10 69
TRADITION (2079 "Genius Of") ... 8-15 68
TRIP ... 6-10 73
VEE-JAY ... 25-50 60-65

MORGAN, Loumell

Singles: 78 rpm

ATLANTIC (953 "Charmaine") ... 50-75 51

Singles: 7-inch

ATLANTIC (953 "Charmaine") ... 100-200 51

MORGAN, Maggie

Singles: 7-inch

FABLE ("Stop Your Running Around") ... 50-75
(Selection number not known.)

MORGAN, Oliver

Singles: 7-inch

GNP (318 "Hold Your Dog") ... 5-10 64

MORGAN, Paula

Singles: 7-inch

DEMON (1506 "Only a Fool") ... 10-15 58

MORGAN, Rocket

Singles: 7-inch

ZYNN (502 "You're Humbuggin' Me") ... 100-200 58
ZYNN (507 "Tag Along") ... 200-300 59

MORGAN, Rocky

Singles: 7-inch

PIC (907 "Wolf Whistle Baby") ... 150-250

MORGAN, Vicki

Singles: 78 rpm

CHICAGO (111 "New Meat") ... 15-25 46

MORGAN TWINS

Singles: 7-inch

PEAK (1008 "Sittin' in the Drive-In") ... 10-20 59
RCA (7300 "TV Hop") ... 15-25 58
RCA (7373 "Let's Get Goin' ") ... 15-25 58

MORGEN

(Steve Morgen)

Singles: 7-inch

PROBE (474 "Of Dreams") ... 8-12 69

LPs: 10/12-inch

PROBE (4507 "Morgen") ... 75-100 69

MORGUS & 3 GHOULS / Frankie & Mac

Singles: 7-inch

VIN (1013 "Morgus the Magnificent"/"Lonely Boy") ... 15-20 59

MORIER, Debra, & Lennettes

Singles: 7-inch

ZEPP (1472 "Mathematics of Love") ... 100-200 62

MORISETTE, Johnnie — P&R/R&B '62

(Johnny Morisette)

Singles: 7-inch

BAY-TONE (116 "Run") ... 15-25 65
CHECKER ... 5-10
ICEPAC (302 "My Change Done Come") ... 5-10 '60s
SAR (104 "Never") ... 10-20 60
SAR (107 "Always on My Mind") ... 10-20 60
SAR (113 "Don't Cry Baby") ... 10-15 61
SAR (121 "Your Heart Will Sing") ... 10-15 61
SAR (126 "Anytime, Anyplace, Anywhere") ... 10-15 62
SAR (133 "Wildest Girl in Town") ... 10-15 62
SAR (139 "Blue Monday") ... 10-15 63
SAR (147 "Black Night") ... 10-15 63
SAR (151 "Never") ... 8-12 64
Also see COOKE, Sam / Johnny Morisette

MORLEY, Cozy — P&R '57

Singles: 78 rpm

ABC-PAR (9811 "I Love My Girl") ... 10-20 57
CAMEO (147 "I Chicken Out") ... 10-20 58

Singles: 7-inch

ABC-PAR (9811 "I Love My Girl") ... 10-20 57
CAMEO (147 "I Chicken Out") ... 10-20 58
COZY (101 "Bill Bailey Won't You Please Come Home") ... 8-12

MORLOCKS

(Mor-Loks)

Singles: 7-inch

DECCA (31950 "What My Baby Wants") ... 10-15 66
LIVING LEGEND (100 "Elaine") ... 30-40 65

MORLY GREY

LPs: 10/12-inch

STARSHINE (6900 "The Only Truth") ... 15-25 69

MORNING AFTER

Singles: 7-inch

TAM (201, 369 "Things You Do") ... 15-25 '60s

MORNING DEW

Singles: 7-inch

FAIRYLAND (1001 "No More") ... 25-50 67
FAIRYLAND (1003 "Be a Friend") ... 25-50 67

MORNING DEW

LPs: 10/12-inch

ROULETTE (R-41045 "Morning Dew") ... 75-125 70
(Monaural.)
ROULETTE (RS-41045 "Morning Dew") ... 100-150 70
(Stereo.)
Members: Malcolm Robinson; Tommy Smith; Ken Tebow; Blair Honeyman.

MORNING GLORIES

Singles: 7-inch

W.B. (7045 "Love-In") ... 5-10 67

MORNING GLORY

Singles: 7-inch

FONTANA (1613 "I See a Light") ... 8-12 68

LPs: 10/12-inch

FONTANA (67573 "Two Suns Worth") ... 15-20 68

MORNING STARR

Singles: 7-inch

LION (1003 "Virgin Lover") ... 5-10 69
MOUTH (514 "Artful Joker") ... 5-10

Picture Sleeves

LION (1003 "Virgin Lover") ... 20-30 69

MORNING SUN

Singles: 7-inch

CORBY (218 "Someday") ... 5-10 67
VMC (739 "Together") ... 5-10 69

MORNING TYMES

Singles: 7-inch

MAAD (52268 "Every Day") ... 40-60 68

MORNINGLORY

Singles: 7-inch

TOYA (100 "Happiness to the Homeland") ... 5-10 72

LPs: 10/12-inch

TOYA (2001 "Growing") ... 15-25 72

MORNINGSTAR, Jackie

Singles: 7-inch

ORANGE (1018 "Rockin' in the Graveyard") ... 450-500 59
SANDY (1018 "Rockin' in the Graveyard") ... 150-250 59

MOROCCOS

(With Al Smith & His Band; with the Lefty Bates Band)

Singles: 78 rpm

UNITED ... 50-100 55-56

Singles: 7-inch

B&F (193 "Somewhere Over the Rainbow") ... 15-25 60
(Mistakenly credits "*Sally* McElroy, Vocalist."
B&F (1347 "What Is a Teen-Ager's Prayer") ... 15-25 61
UNITED (188 "Pardon My Tears") ... 100-200 55
UNITED (193 "Somewhere Over the Rainbow") ... 75-150 55
UNITED (204 "What Is a Teen-Ager's Prayer") ... 100-200 56
UNITED (207 "Sad, Sad Hours") ... 200-300 57
(Black vinyl.)
UNITED (207 "Sad, Sad Hours") ... 800-1000 57
(Red vinyl.)
Member: Sollie McElroy.
Also see BATES, Lefty "Guitar"
Also see BROOKS, Lillian
Also see CHANTEURS
Also see McELROY, Sollie
Also see MORROCANS
Also see SMITH, Al

MORRA, Tony

(With the Do-Wells; with Beltones; "Featuring Frankie Gray & His Orchestra")

Singles: 7-inch

ARCADE (152 "Claire") ... 15-25 59
DU-WELL (1005 "Looking for My Baby") ... 75-100 60

MORRIE, Tiny

Singles: 7-inch

CHALLENGE (9136 "My Lonely Heart") ... 5-10 62
CHALLENGE (9210 "Choo Choo") ... 5-10 63
DOT (16847 "Bernadine") ... 5-10 66
DOT (16937 "I Get Jealous") ... 5-10 66
HURRICANE (except 2) ... 10-15 59-64
HURRICANE (2 "Everybody Rocks") ... 50-75 59

MORRILL, Kent
Singles: 7-inch
BRC ... 4-8 71
CONGRESS (6016 "I Cannot Live without Her") ... 5-10 70
ETIQUETTE (5 "I Had a Dream") ... 10-15 63
LPs: 10/12-inch
CREAM ... 10-12
SUSPICIOUS ... 5-8 88
Also see WAILERS

MORRIS, Andy
Singles: 78 rpm
FIRE (108 "I Need Her Love") ... 20-30 56
Singles: 7-inch
FIRE (108 "I Need Her Love") ... 75-100 56

MORRIS, Artie, & Combinations
Singles: 7-inch
COCO ... 20-30 59

MORRIS, Cam
Singles: 7-inch
DORE (552 "Look Around") ... 15-25 60

MORRIS, Charlene, & Dreamers
Singles: 7-inch
CAMPUS (113 "Forever and a Day") ... 30-40 59

MORRIS, Chick
(Chick Morris Five)
Singles: 78 rpm
DELCRO ... 10-15
Singles: 7-inch
LEE (503 "Rattlesnake Daddy") ... 50-100 57
Also see SEVILLES

MORRIS, Eddie
Singles: 7-inch
DISC MASTERS (2101 "Chimes of My Heart") ... 100-150 '60s

MORRIS, Elmore
(With the Spinners)
Singles: 78 rpm
PEACOCK ... 5-10 56
Singles: 7-inch
CRACKERJACK (4006 "It Seemed Like Heaven to Me") ... 10-20 62
LANDA (670 "Paradise Hill") ... 15-25 61
PEACOCK ... 8-15 56-60

MORRIS, Ernie
Singles: 7-inch
ERMO (54 "Please Don't Hurt Me") ... 50-75

MORRIS, Floyd
Singles: 7-inch
BBS (0578 "Bee Hive") ... 10-15 68
(First issue.)
BUNKY (7757 "Bee Hive") ... 5-10 68
DILLIE (102 "Dillie's Blues") ... 15-25 58
SELECT (737 "Pompton Turnpike") ... 10-20 64

MORRIS, Gene
(With the Pages)
Singles: 7-inch
EDMORAL (1012 "Lovin' Honey") ... 150-250 57
VIK (0287 "Lovin' Honey") ... 50-75 57
WINSTON (1020 "I Need It") ... 20-30 58
WINSTON (1032 "I Crawfished") ... 20-30 59
WINSTON (1046 "If You Need My Love") ... 50-75 60

MORRIS, Glenn
Singles: 7-inch
LIBERTY BELL (9017 "I Got the Blues") . 30-40 57

MORRIS, Jack
Singles: 7-inch
PEP (116 "She's Gone, She's Gone") ... 50-75

MORRIS, Joe, & His Orch. *R&B '50*
(With Laurie Tate; Mr. Stringbean; Al Savage; Joe Morris Blues Cavalcade Featuring Billy Mitchell)
Singles: 78 rpm
ATLANTIC (855 thru 892) ... 10-20 47-50
ATLANTIC (914 "Anytime, Any Place, Anywhere") ... 40-60 50
ATLANTIC (923 "Don't Take Your Love Away from Me") ... 40-60 50
ATLANTIC (933 "Pack Up All Your Bags") ... 10-20 51
ATLANTIC (940 "Midnight Grinder") ... 10-20 51
ATLANTIC (942 "You're Mine Darling") ... 10-20 51
ATLANTIC (950 "Verna Lee") ... 20-30 51
ATLANTIC (954 "Someday You'll Be Sorry") ... 20-30 52
ATLANTIC (974 "Bald Headed Woman") . 20-30 52
ATLANTIC (985 "I'm Going to Leave You") ... 15-25 53
DECCA ... 10-15 49-50
HERALD ... 10-20 53-54
MANOR ... 10-15 46-47
Singles: 7-inch
ATLANTIC (933 "Pack Up All Your Bags") ... 100-150 51
(Vocal by Billy Mitchell.)
ATLANTIC (940 "Midnight Grinder") ... 25-50 51
ATLANTIC (942 "You're Mine Darling") ... 25-50 51
ATLANTIC (950 "Verna Lee") ... 100-150 51
ATLANTIC (954 "Someday You'll Be Sorry") ... 50-100 52
ATLANTIC (974 "Bald Headed Woman") ... 50-100 52
ATLANTIC (985 "I'm Going to Leave You") ... 30-50 53
ATLANTIC (1007 Watch Out, I Told You) ... 20-40 53
ATLANTIC (1160 "Sinner Woman) ... 10-20 57
HERALD (420 "Travelin' Man") ... 20-30 54
(Black vinyl.)
HERALD (420 "Travelin' Man") ... 50-75 54
(Red vinyl.)
HERALD (446 "Be Careful") ... 15-25 55
Also see ADAMS, Faye
Also see JOE & URSULA
Also see MR. STRINGBEAN
Also see MITCHELL, Billy
Also see REED, Ursula
Also see SAVAGE, Al
Also see TATE, Laurie

MORRIS, Joe "Guitar"
Singles: 7-inch
RON (343 "Git Back") ... 5-10 61

MORRIS, Melvin
Singles: 7-inch
SNOW CAP (602 "Heartaches of a Love Untrue") ... 300-400

MORRIS, Pete
Singles: 7-inch
END (1006 "Walkin' Together") ... 20-30 57

MORRIS, Robert
Singles: 7-inch
IN CIRCLE (1 "Ain't That Easy") ... 25-35

MORRIS, Rod
Singles: 78 rpm
CAPITOL ... 5-10 53
Singles: 7-inch
CAPITOL (2651 "I'm Not a Kid Anymore") ... 10-20 53
CAPITOL (2669 "Bimbo") ... 10-20 53
LUDWIG (1002 "Ghost of Casey Jones") ... 100-200 58
LUDWIG (1011 "Bimbo") ... 10-15 59
LUDWIG (1015 "Half Shot in Sioux Falls") ... 10-15 59
LUDWIG (1364 "Alabama Jail House") ... 100-200

MORRIS, Rose, & Delighters
Singles: 7-inch
PUFF (1002 "I Love the Life I Live") ... 75-100 62

MORRIS & BETTY
Singles: 7-inch
FIRMA (625 "This House") ... 10-20 62
Members: Morris Jones; Betty Everett.
Also see EVERETT, Betty

MORRIS BROTHERS BAND
Singles: 7-inch
MOBRO (101 "Rockin' Country Fever") ... 300-400

MORRISON, Bill
(With His Band)
Singles: 7-inch
TNT (9029 "Set Me Free") ... 350-400 60
TNT (9030 "Baby Be Good") ... 300-350 60

MORRISON, Dorothy *P&R '69*
Singles: 7-inch
BUDDAH (196 "Spirit in the Sky") ... 4-6 70
ELEKTRA (45671 "All God's Children Got Soul") ... 4-8 69
MGM (14381 "Higher and Higher") ... 4-6 72
Picture Sleeves
ELEKTRA (45671 "All God's Children Got Soul") ... 5-10 69
LPs: 10/12-inch
BUDDAH ... 10-15 70

MORRISON, Freddy
Singles: 7-inch
VACA (108 "Twistin' Little Baby") ... 50-100

MORRISON, Jim
(Curley Jim Morrison)
Singles: 7-inch
CURLEY-Q (5707 "My Old Standby") ... 50-100

MORRISON, Jim / Gerry Fiander
Singles: 7-inch
ARCTIC (2100 "Ready to Rock") ... 400-500 59

MORRISON, Van *P&R/LP '67*
Singles: 7-inch
BANG ... 5-10 67-71
MERCURY ... 3-5 85-90
PHILCO (16 "Brown Eyed Girl"/"Midnight Special") ... 10-20 67
("Hip Pocket" flexi-disc.)
SOLID GOLD ... 3-6 73
W.B. ... 4-8 70-83
LPs: 10/12-inch
BANG (BLP-218 "Blowin' Your Mind") ... 20-25 67
(Monaural.)
BANG (BLPS-218 "Blowin' Your Mind") ... 25-30 67
(Stereo. White label. Has 45 rpm version of *Brown-Eyed Girl*, with "makin' love in the green grass behind the stadium" lyrics.)
BANG (BLPS-218 "Blowin' Your Mind") ... 25-30 67
(Stereo. White label. Has edited *Brown-Eyed Girl*, with "laughin' and a runnin' behind the stadium" lyrics.)
BANG (BLPS-218 "Blowin' Your Mind") ... 10-15 70
(Yellow label.)
BANG (222 "Best Of...") ... 15-20 70
BANG (400 "T.B. Sheets") ... 10-15 73
LONDON ... 10-15 74
MERCURY ... 5-10 85-90
W.B. ... 8-15 68-83
Also see THEM

MORRISON, Van, & Chieftains *LP '88*
LPs: 10/12-inch
MERCURY ... 5-8 88
Also see MORRISON, Van

MORRISSEY, Pat
(Pat Morrisey)
Singles: 78 rpm
DECCA ... 10-15 54-55
Singles: 7-inch
DECCA (28879 "Baby, It Must Be Love") . 15-25 54
DECCA "29594 "House of Blue Night") ... 15-25 55
LPs: 10/12-inch
MERCURY (20197 "I Sing") ... 50-100 56

MORRO, Phil
Singles: 7-inch
MOHAWK (115 "Where Are You") ... 5-10 60

MORROCANS
(With Teddy Phillips Orchestra)
Singles: 7-inch
SALEM (1014 "Believe in Tomorrow") .. 100-200 57
Member: Sollie McElroy.
Also see MOROCCOS

MORROCCO MUZIK MAKERS
Singles: 7-inch
MOTOWN (1047 "Back to School Again") ... 40-60 63

MORROW, Bruce
(With D. Clock)
Singles: 7-inch
CLOCK (1029 "Tea with the Shakes") ... 8-12 60
GLAD-HAMP (1015 "More Shimmy") ... 8-12 61
Also see RILEY, Bob

MORROW, Buddy, & Orchestra *P&R '51*
(With Shaye Cogan; with Frankie Lester)
Singles: 78 rpm
MERCURY ... 3-5 54-57
RCA ... 3-5 50-57
Singles: 7-inch
EPIC ... 4-6 64
MERCURY ... 4-8 54-62
RCA ... 5-10 50-59
U.A. ... 4-8 68
WING ... 4-8 55-56
EPs: 7-inch
MERCURY ... 5-15 54-61
RCA ... 5-15 52-61
LPs: 10/12-inch
EPIC (Except 24095 & 26095) ... 5-15 64-65
EPIC (24095 "Big Band Beatlemania") ... 15-25 64
(Monaural.)
EPIC (26095 "Big Band Beatlemania") ... 20-30 64
(Stereo.)
MERCURY ... 20-30 54-62
RCA (1400 thru 2100) ... 15-30 59-60
RCA (2200 & series) ... 10-20 60
RCA (3100 & 3200 series) ... 25-50 52-54
(10-inch LPs.)
U.A. ... 5-10 68
WING ... 10-20 56
Also see COGAN, Shaye

MORROW, Liza
(With Sid Feller & Orchestra)
Singles: 78 rpm
KING (15186 "Washing Machine Blues") ... 5-10 52
Singles: 7-inch
KING (15186 "Washing Machine Blues"). 10-15 52

MORSE, Ella Mae *P&R/R&B '43*
(With Freddie Slack; with Big Dave & His Orchestra)
Singles: 78 rpm
CAPITOL ... 5-15 42-57
Singles: 7-inch
CAPITOL (1500 thru 3400 series) ... 5-15 50-57
EPs: 7-inch
CAPITOL ... 10-20 54-57
LPs: 10/12-inch
CAPITOL (H-513 "Barrelhouse Boogie, and the Blues") ... 100-150 54
(10-inch LP.)
CAPITOL (T-513 "Barrelhouse Boogie, and the Blues") ... 50-75 55
CAPITOL (898 "Morse Code") ... 50-75 57
CAPITOL (1802 "Hits") ... 30-45 62
Also see FORD, Tennessee Ernie, & Ella Mae Morse

MORTICIANS
Singles: 7-inch
MORTICIAN (101 "Little Latin Lupe Lu") .. 15-25 '60s
PALMER (5027 "It's Gonna Take Awhile") ... 15-25 68
ROULETTE (4702 "Now That You've Left Me") ... 5-10 66

MORTIMER
Singles: 7-inch
PHILIPS (20 "Dedicated Music Man") ... 10-15 68
(Stereo. Promotional issue only.)
PHILIPS (40524 "Dedicated Music Man") .. 5-10 68
(Monaural.)
Picture Sleeves
PHILIPS (40524 "Dedicated Music Man") ... 15-25 68
LPs: 10/12-inch
PHILIPS (200267 "Mortimer") ... 15-25 68
(Monaural.)
PHILIPS (600267 "Mortimer") ... 15-25 68
(Stereo.)
Also see TEDDY BOYS

MORTIMER, Azie
(A.Z. Mortimer)
Singles: 7-inch
BIG TOP (3041 "Lips") ... 200-300 60
(White label. Promotional issue only.)
BIG TOP (3041 "Lips") ... 8-12 60
EPIC (9584 "Little Boy") ... 5-10 63
OKEH (7336 "One Way Love") ... 5-8 69
OKEH (7337 "I Don't Care") ... 5-8 69
PALETTE (5097 "When You're Talking Love") ... 5-10 62
RCA (8985 "Best Years") ... 5-10 66
REGATTA (2002 "Brother Love") ... 5-10 61
SWAN (4158 "Bring Back Your Love") ... 5-10 63
TROY (104 "Forever Kind of Love") ... 40-50 62
U.A. (847 "The Other Half of Me") ... 15-25 65

MORTON, Richard
Singles: 7-inch
MORTON (1 "Sad Sad Song") ... 50-75

MORY STORM BAND
LPs: 10/12-inch
SOUND MACHINE (49007 "Cry for the Dreamer") 35-55

MOSAIC TWEED
Singles: 7-inch
CAPITOL (2566 "You and Me") 5-10 69

MOSELY, Little Joe, & Sequins
Singles: 7-inch
DEL-FI (4107 "Lookin' for a Job") 15-20 58

MOSES, Johnny
Singles: 78 rpm
IMPERIAL (5329 "You're Torturing Me") . 10-20 55
Singles: 7-inch
IMPERIAL (5329 "You're Torturing Me") . 20-30 55

MOSES & JOSHUA
(Moses & Joshua Dillard)
Singles: 7-inch
MALA (575 "My Elusive Dreams") 5-10 67
MALA (598 "Get Out of My Heart") 5-10 68
Also see DILLARD, Moses, & Dynamic Showmen

MOSES & TEN COMMANDMENTS
Singles: 7-inch
RAYNARD (1061 "Monkey Time") 15-25 67

MO-SHUNS
Singles: 7-inch
20TH FOX (6645 "What Can I Say") 25-50 65

MOSLEY, Ernest
Singles: 7-inch
LA-CINDY (225 "Keep on Loving Me") 100-200

MOSLEY, Johnny
Singles: 7-inch
JEWEL (763 "Mistreated by You") 5-10 66

MOSLEY, Robert
Singles: 7-inch
CAPITOL (4961 "Crazy 'Bout My Baby") . 10-20 63
COED (524 "Just a Little More") 8-12 60
COED (528 "Crazy Moonlight") 8-12 60
Also see MAYMIE & ROBERT

MOSLEY, Tommy
Singles: 7-inch
ARVEE (5021 "My Melancholy Baby") 10-20 61
ERA (317 "Wishing Well") 20-30 67
MOONGLOW (226 "Just Hold My Hand") 10-20 63
UPTOWN (706 "For Her Love") 10-20 65

MOSQUITOS
Singles: 7-inch
HERALD (587 "Blind Date") 10-15 64

MOSS, Gene
Singles: 7-inch
RCA (8438 "Ghoul Days") 8-12 64
LPs: 10/12-inch
RCA (LPM-2977 "Dracula's Greatest Hits") 20-35 64
(Monaural.)
RCA (LSP-2977 "Dracula's Greatest Hits") 30-45 64
(Stereo.)

MOSS, Keith
Singles: 7-inch
HARVEY (122 "Satisfaction Guaranteed") 100-200 63

MOSS, Lord Beverly, & Mossmen
Singles: 7-inch
TARGET (107/108 "Please, Please What's the Matter"/"The Kids Are Alright") 25-50 67
Members: Bob Timmers; Gary Laabs; Vic Wendt; Tom Gebheim.

MOSS, Roy
Singles: 78 rpm
MERCURY 20-30 56
Singles: 7-inch
FASCINATION (1002 "Wiggle Walkin' Baby") 50-75 58
MERCURY (70770 "You're My Big Baby Now") 50-75 56
MERCURY (70858 "Corinne Corinna") 50-75 56

MOSS & ROCKS
Singles: 7-inch
CHATTAHOOCHEE (703 "There She Goes") 5-10 66

MOST
Singles: 7-inch
COLUMBIA (43712 "Sea of Misery") 5-10 66

MOST, Mickie
Singles: 7-inch
LAWN (236 "Sea Cruise") 10-20 64

MOTE, Danny
Singles: 7-inch
OPAL (001 "Done You Wrong") 100-200 61
(First issue.)
VEE-JAY (381 "Done You Wrong") 50-75 61

MOTEN, Bus, & His Men
Singles: 78 rpm
CAPITOL (831 "That Did It") 10-15 50
Singles: 7-inch
CAPITOL (831 "That Did It") 25-35 50

MOTHER EARTH LP '69
Singles: 7-inch
MERCURY 5-10 68-69
REPRISE 4-8 71
U.A. (50303 "Revolution") 5-10 68
LPs: 10/12-inch
MERCURY 10-20 69-70
REPRISE 10-15 71
Members: Tracy Nelson; John Andrews; Bob Arthur; George Rains. Session: Boz Scaggs.
Also see SCAGGS, Boz

MOTHER HEADS FAMILY REUNION
Singles: 7-inch
MARION (669 "Reunion Blues") 5-10 67

MOTHER HEN
LPs: 10/12-inch
RCA (4641 "Mother Hen") 5-10 71

MOTHER HUBBARD
Singles: 7-inch
COLUMBIA (44445 "Children") 5-10 68
Picture Sleeves
COLUMBIA (44445 "Children") 8-12 68

MOTHER LOVE
Singles: 7-inch
EPIC (10379 "Goodbye Mary") 5-10 68
20TH FOX (6687 "Flim-Flam Man") 10-20 67
LPs: 10/12-inch
EPIC (26520 "Carousel of Daydreams") .. 10-15 70

MOTHER TUCKER'S YELLOW DUCK
Singles: 7-inch
CAPITOL (2707 "Times Are Changing") .. 15-25 69
CAPITOL (72583 "One Ring Jane"/"Funny Feeling") 10-15 69
(Canadian.)
CAPITOL (72614 "Starting a New Day") .. 10-15 70
(Canadian.)
DUCK (001 "I") 25-50 68
(Canadian.)
DUCK (002 "One Ring Jane"/"Kill the Pig") 25-50 68
(Canadian.)
TCP (106 "I") 15-25 69
(Canadian.)
LPs: 10/12-inch
CAPITOL (6304 "Homegrown Stuff") 75-100 69
(Canadian.)
CAPITOL (6352 "Starting a New Day") .. 75-100 70
(Canadian.)
DUCK (1 "Homegrown Stuff") 200-250 68
(Canadian. Issued in plain white cover with seven-page bio and 8"x10" b/w photo.)

MOTHER'S COOKIES
Singles: 7-inch
VALHALLA (691 "Great Crusade") 5-10 69

MOTHER'S FINEST P&R/LP '76
Singles: 12-inch
EPIC 4-8 77-79
Singles: 7-inch
EPIC 4-6 76-79
LPs: 10/12-inch
ATLANTIC 5-10 81
EPIC 5-10 76-79
RCA 8-12 72
Members: Glenn Murdock; Gary Moore; Joyce Kennedy; Jerry Seay; Barry Borden; Michael Keek.
Also see KENNEDY, Joyce

MOTHER'S HEROS
Singles: 7-inch
THE LABEL (1113 "Brother John") 5-10 67

MOTHER'S LITTLE HELPERS
Singles: 7-inch
POPPY (505 "Walk with Me") 5-10 68

MOTHER'S WORRY
Singles: 7-inch
LOOK (5012 "Funky Good") 5-10 68
LOOK (5013 "It's a Long Way Back") 5-10 68
Members: Rick Purcell; John Zaffiro; Ernest Mathies; Keith Cravillion; Peter Alioto.

MOTHERLODE P&R/LP '69
Singles: 7-inch
BUDDAH 4-6 69
EPs: 7-inch
BUDDAH (11 "When I Die") 8-12 69
LPs: 10/12-inch
BUDDAH 10-15 69-72

MOTHERS OF INVENTION LP '67
(Mothers)
Singles: 7-inch
BIZARRE/REPRISE (840 "My Guitar") 30-40 69
BIZARRE/REPRISE (889 "Peaches En Regalia") 30-40 70
BIZARRE/REPRISE (892 "WPLJ") 30-40 70
BIZARRE/REPRISE (967 "Tell Me You Love Me") 30-40 70
BIZARRE/REPRISE (1052 "Tears Began to Fall") 30-40 71
BIZARRE/REPRISE (1127 "Cletus Awreetus Awrightus") 30-40 71
DISCREET (1180 "I'm the Slime") 20-30 73
DISCREET (1312 "Don't Eat the Yellow Snow") 20-30 74
VERVE (10418 "How Could I Be Such a Fool") 100-150 66
VERVE (10458 "Trouble Comin' Everyday") 100-150 66
VERVE (10513 "Big Leg Emma") 100-150 67
VERVE (10570 "Lonely Little Girl") 100-150 67
Promotional Singles
BIZARRE/REPRISE (840 "My Guitar") 20-30 69
BIZARRE/REPRISE (889 "Peaches En Regalia") 20-30 70
BIZARRE/REPRISE (892 "WPLJ") 20-30 70
BIZARRE/REPRISE (967 "Tell Me You Love Me") 20-30 70
BIZARRE/REPRISE (1052 "Tears Began to Fall") 20-30 71
BIZARRE/REPRISE (1127 "Cletus Awreetus Awrightus") 20-30 71
DISCREET (1180 "I'm the Slime") 20-25 73
DISCREET (1312 "Don't Eat the Yellow Snow") 20-25 74
VERVE (10418 "How Could I Be Such a Fool") 40-60 66
VERVE (10458 "Trouble Comin' Everyday") 30-50 66
VERVE (10513 "Big Leg Emma") 30-50 67
VERVE (10570 "Lonely Little Girl") 30-50 67
EPs: 7-inch
REPRISE (332 "Uncle Meat") 35-45 69
(Promotional issue only.)
LPs: 10/12-inch
BIZARRE (2024 "Uncle Meat") 35-45 69
(Blue label. With 12-page booklet.)
BIZARRE (2024 "Uncle Meat") 20-30 69
(Blue label. Without booklet.)
BIZARRE (2024 "Uncle Meat") .... 10-15 '70s
(Brown label.)
BIZARRE (2028 "Weasles Ripped My Flesh") 20-30 70
(Blue label.)
BIZARRE (2028 "Weasles Ripped My Flesh") .... 5-10 '70s
(Brown label.)
BIZARRE (2042 "The Mothers Live"/"Fillmore East") 20-30 71
(Blue label.)
BIZARRE (2042 "The Mothers Live"/"Fillmore East") .... 5-10 '70s
(Brown label.)
BIZARRE (2075 "Just Another Band from L.A.") 20-30 72
(Blue label.)
BIZARRE (2093 "Grand Wazoo") 20-30 72
(Blue label.)
BIZARRE (2093 "Grand Wazoo") .... 5-10 '70s
(Brown label.)
BIZARRE (6370 "Burnt Weeny Sandwich") 30-40 69
(Blue label. With folder of bonus photos.)
BIZARRE (6370 "Burnt Weeny Sandwich") 15-25 69
(Blue label. Without folder of photos.)
BIZARRE (6370 "Burnt Weeny Sandwich") .... 5-10 '70s
(Brown label.)
DISCREET (2149 "Over-Nite Sensation") 15-25 73
DISCREET (MS4-2149 "Over-Nite Sensation") 30-40 73
(Quadraphonic.)
MGM (112 "Mothers of Invention") 30-40 70
MGM (4754 "Worst of the Mothers") 25-35 71
REPRISE 8-12 73-74
(Reissues of Bizarre catalog.)
VERVE (5005 "Freak Out!") 75-125 66
(Monaural. With mail-order "Freak Out - Hot Spots" map/poster offer printed on inside of cover.)
VERVE (5005 "Freak Out!") 50-100 67
(Monaural. Without mail-order map/poster offer printed on inside of cover.)
VERVE (V6-5005 "Freak Out!") 50-100 66
(Stereo. With mail-order "Freak Out - Hot Spots" map/poster offer printed on inside of cover.)
VERVE (V6-5005 "Freak Out!") 40-80 67
(Stereo. Without mail-order map/poster offer printed on inside of cover.)
VERVE (5013 "Absolutely Free") 60-80 67
(Monaural. Includes Libretto or Freak Map.)
VERVE (5013 "Absolutely Free") 50-75 67
(Monaural. Without Libretto or Freak Map.)
VERVE (V6-5013 "Absolutely Free") 50-75 67
(Stereo. Includes Libretto or Freak Map.)
VERVE (V6-5013 "Absolutely Free") 40-50 67
(Stereo. Without Libretto or Freak Map.)
VERVE (5045 "We're Only in It for the Money") 50-75 67
(Monaural. With "Only Money" insert.)
VERVE (5045 "We're Only in It for the Money") 30-50 67
(Monaural. Without "Only Money" insert.)
VERVE (V6-5045 "We're Only in It for the Money") 50-75 67
(Stereo. With "Only Money" insert.)
VERVE (V6-5045 "We're Only in It for the Money") 30-50 67
(Stereo. Without "Only Money" insert.)
VERVE (5068 "Mothermania") 20-40 69
VERVE (5074 "XXXX of the Mothers") 20-25 69
Notes: Price range of Verve LPs is for commercial copies on the blue & black labels as well as white MGM/Verve labels. Several reissues came out in the early '80s that are nearly identical to originals, except their cover stock is glossier than are '60s issues. Among the reissues we have verified are: *Freak Out, We're Only in It for the Money,* and *Absolutely Free.*)
W.B. 8-10 77
Promotional LPs
BIZARRE (2024 "Uncle Meat") 40-60 69
BIZARRE (2028 "Weasles Ripped My Flesh") 35-45 70
BIZARRE (2042 "The Mothers Live/Fillmore East") 35-45 71
BIZARRE (2075 "Just Another Band from L.A.") 30-40 72
BIZARRE (2093 "Grand Wazoo") 30-40 72
BIZARRE (6370 "Burnt Weeny Sandwich") 30-30 69
VERVE (5005 "Freak Out!") 100-200 66
VERVE (5013 "Absolutely Free") 75-125 67
VERVE (5045 "We're Only in It for the Money") 75-125 67
VERVE (5068 "Mothermania") 50-100 69
VERVE (5074 "XXXX of the Mothers") ... 50-100 69
Members: Frank Zappa; Jimmy Carl Black; Roy Estrada; Ray Collins; Elliot Ingber; Jim Pons; Lowell George.
Also see CAPTAIN BEEFHEART
Also see FISCHER, Wild Man
Also see GAMBLERS

Also see GRANDMOTHERS
Also see LEAVES
Also see LORD, Brian, & Midnighters
Also see NED & NELDA
Also see PRESTON, Billy
Also see RUBEN & JETS
Also see ZAPPA, Frank

MOTIFS

Singles: 7-inch

LEJAC (3004 "Someday") .... 25-35 '60s

MOTIONS

Singles: 7-inch

LAURIE (3112 "Mr. Night") 75-125 61
Also see EMOTIONS

MOTIONS

Singles: 7-inch

ABC-PAR (10529 "Big Chief") 5-10 64
CONGRESS (237 "It's Gone") 5-10 65
MERCURY (Except 72297) 5-10 64-65
MERCURY (72297 "Beatle Drums") 10-20 64

MOTIONS

Singles: 7-inch

PHILIPS (40624 "Freedom") 5-10 69

LPs: 10/12-inch

PHILIPS (600317 "Electric Baby") 10-15 69

MOTIVATIONS

Singles: 7-inch

PRIDE (301 "Motivate") 10-20 63
Members: Greg Sevigny; Pete Johnson; Mike Wells.

MOTLEY, Frank

(Jimmy Crawford Vocal; Frank Motley "Dual Trumpeter" & His Crew; Frank "Dual Trumpet" Motley & His Motley Crew-vocal, Curley Bridges)

Singles: 78 rpm

BIG TOWN (116 "Snatch It") 15-25 54
BIG TOWN (119 "Frantic Love") 15-25 55
DC (6004 "That Ain't Right") 25-50 54
HAWKEYE 10-15 56
HOLLYWOOD (1067 "Last Time") 15-25 56
JOSIE (761 "Crying, Crying") 10-15 54

Singles: 7-inch

BIG TOWN (116 "Snatch It") 25-50 54
BIG TOWN (119 "Frantic Love") 25-50 55
COOKIN' (604 "Crying All Alone") 8-12 63
DC (0404 "Don't Go") 30-40 57
DC (0415 thru 0437) 10-20 59-62
DC (6004 "That Ain't Right") 50-100 54
(Also issued as by Jimmy Crawford with Frank Motley & His Crew.)
HAWKEYE (4015 "Rock 'n' Roll's Gotta Beat") 20-30 56
HOLLYWOOD (1067 "Last Time") 15-25 56
JOSIE (761 "Crying, Crying") 15-25 54
Also see BRIDGES, Curly, & Frank Motley
Also see CRAWFORD, Jimmy, Frank Motley & His Crew
Also see FREEMAN, Ernie, & Frank Motley
Also see PARAKEETS / Frank Motley
Also see ONTARIOS
Also see TRIBBLE, TNT, with Frank Motley & His Crew
Also see TWILIGHTERS

MOTLEY, Frank, / Angel Face

Singles: 78 rpm

BIG TOWN (114 "Don't Ever Leave Me") 15-20 54
GEM (219 "Don't Ever Leave Me") 20-35 53

Singles: 7-inch

BIG TOWN (114 "Don't Ever Leave Me") 50-75 54
GEM (219 "Don't Ever Leave Me") 60-80 53
Also see ANGEL FACE

MOTLEY BLUES BAND

Singles: 7-inch

SCEPTER (12177 "Ain't That a Funny Thing") 5-10 66

MOTLEY CRUE — LP '83

Singles: 12-inch

WEA/ELEKTRA (60395 "Helter Skelter") 50-60 84
(Picture disc. Includes poster.)

Singles: 7-inch

ELEKTRA 3-5 83-88

Picture Sleeves

ELEKTRA 3-5 84-89

LPs: 10/12-inch

ELEKTRA 5-10 82-89
LEATHÜR ("Too Fast for Love") 50-75 81
(Black lettering on cover.)
LEATHÜR ("Too Fast for Love") 25-50 81
(White lettering on cover.)
Member: Vince Neil; Nikki Sixx; Tommy Lee; Mick Mars; John Corabi.

MOTORMEN

Singles: 7-inch

MOMENTUM (661 "Rat Fink") 15-25

MOTS MEN

Singles: 7-inch

LOREN (1005 "Comin' Or Goin'") 15-25 66

MOTT THE HOOPLE — LP '70

Singles: 7-inch

ATLANTIC 4-8 70
COLUMBIA 4-6 72-74

LPs: 10/12-inch

ATLANTIC 12-18 70-74
COLUMBIA 10-15 72-75
Member: Ian Hunter.

MOTTOLA, Tony — LP '62

Singles: 7-inch

PROJECT 3 (1323 "Spanish Harlem") 5-10 67

LPs: 10/12-inch

COMMAND 10-20 62-65
PROJECT 3 .... 8-12 67-70
Also see ALLISON, Fran

MOULTRIE, Mary

(With Hutch's Trio)

Singles: 7-inch

AMERICANA (1002 "You Gotta Hum") ..... 10-15 '60s
KING (6038 "Last Year, Senior Prom") 10-15 66

MOULTRIE, Sam

Singles: 7-inch

ROULETTE (7038 "Funky Jerk") 5-10 69
WARREN (108 "I'll Always Love You") 15-20

MOUNT RUSHMORE

Singles: 7-inch

DOT (17158 "Stone Free") 5-10 68

LPs: 10/12-inch

DOT (25898 "High on MountRushmore") . 10-20 68
DOT (25934 "Mount Rushmore '69") 10-20 69
Members: Mike Bolan; Glen Smith; Travis Fullerton; Terry Kimball.

MOUNTAIN — P&R/LP '70

Singles: 7-inch

WINDFALL 4-8 69-71

LPs: 10/12-inch

COLUMBIA 10-15 73-74
SCOTTI BROTHERS 5-8 85
WINDFALL 10-15 69-72
Members: Leslie West; Corky Laing; Steve Knight; Felix Pappalardi; David Perry.
Also see WEST, Leslie

MOUNTAIN BUS

LPs: 10/12-inch

GOOD (101 "Sundance") 50-75 71
Members: Tom Jurkens; Bill Kees; Lee Sims; Ed Mooney.

MOUNTAIN SMOKE

LPs: 10/12-inch

SMOKE ("On Blue Ridge") 50-75 75
(No selection number used. Reportedly 500 made.)
Members: Vince Gill; Jim Wagoner; Dave Coe; Russ Christopher; Bob Cuadrado, Hal Clifford.

MOURNING REIGN

Singles: 7-inch

CONTOUR (601 "Evil-Hearted You") 15-25 67
LINK (1 "Satisfaction Guaranteed") 20-30 66
LINK (2 "Evil-Hearted You") .... 20-30 '60s

Picture Sleeves

LINK (1 "Satisfaction Guaranteed") 40-60 67

MOUSE

(With the Traps; Chris St. John)

Singles: 7-inch

BELL (850 "And I Believe Her") 10-15 70
BELL (870 "Knock on My Door") 10-15 70
BELL (918 "Woman or a Girl") 10-15 70
FRATERNITY 10-20 65-68
SMUDGE (0703 "Bottom Line") 10-15 81

Picture Sleeves

FRATERNITY (1005 "Sometimes You Just Can't Win") 30-50 68
Members: Ronnie Weiss; Dave Stanley; Bugs Henderson; Ken Murray; Bobby Dale; Doug Rhone.
Also see POSITIVELY 13 O'CLOCK
Also see UNIQUES

MOUSEKETEERS

Singles: 78 rpm

MICKEY MOUSE CLUB (50 "Mickey Mouse Club March") 20-30 55
(Black vinyl. Cardboard cover.)
MICKEY MOUSE CLUB (50 "Mickey Mouse Club March") 40-50 55
(Orange vinyl. Cardboard cover.)
MICKEY MOUSE CLUB (51 thru 55) 15-25 55
(Black vinyl. Cardboard cover.)
MICKEY MOUSE CLUB (51 thru 55) 25-30 55
(Orange vinyl. Cardboard cover.)
MICKEY MOUSE CLUB (62 thru 87) 25-35 56-58

Singles: 7-inch

BUENA VISTA (346 "Hey Batter Batter") . 10-15 59
BUENA VISTA (569 "Disco Mouse") 4-6 77
DISNEYLAND 15-25 61-75
MICKEY MOUSE CLUB 10-15 78

Picture Sleeves

BUENA VISTA (569 "Disco Mouse") 4-6 77

EPs: 7-inch

DISNEYLAND (71 "We're the Mouseketeers") 75-100 58

LPs: 10/12-inch

DISNEYLAND (3918 "How to Be a Mouseketeer") 20-30 62
Also see ANNETTE
Also see CRAWFORD, Johnny
Also see DODD, Jimmy
Also see GILLESPIE, Darlene
Also see KAREN & CUBBY

MOUSERS

Singles: 7-inch

APPLAUSE (1004 "Little Princess") 5-10 64

MOUTH & MacNEAL — P&R/LP '72

Singles: 7-inch

PHILIPS 4-6 72

Picture Sleeves

PHILIPS 4-6 72

LPs: 10/12-inch

PHILIPS 10-12 72-73
Members: Will Duyn; Maggie MacNeal.

MOUZAKIS

(Fabulous Pharaohs)

Singles: 7-inch

BRITISH MAIN (7771 "Lady") 15-20 71
BRITISH MAIN (31671 "Looking Back") ... 15-20 71
BRITISH MAIN (51970 "Don't Want You No More") 15-20 70
BRITISH MAIN (101472 "Hey, Hey, Hey") 10-15 72
THREE STAR (32374 "Gonna Give You Rock & Roll") 10-15 74

LPs: 10/12-inch

BRITISH MAIN (90069 "Magic Tube") .. 225-275 72
Member: Eddie Stevenson.
Also see FABULOUS PHARAOHS

MOVE, The — P&R '72

Singles: 7-inch

A&M (884 "Flowers in the Rain") 5-10 67
A&M (966 "Something"/"Yellow Rainbow") 5-10 68
A&M (1020 "Blackberry Way"/ "Something") 5-10 69
A&M (1119 "Curly") 5-10 69
CAPITOL (3126 "Tonight") 10-20 71
DERAM (7504 "The Disturbance") 5-10 67
DERAM (7506 "I Can Hear the Grass Grow") 5-10 67
MGM (14332 "Chinatown") 8-12 71
U.A. (202 "Tonight") 5-10 73
U.A. (50876 "Chinatown") 5-10 72
U.A. (50928 "Do Ya") 5-10 73

EPs: 7-inch

A&M ("Something Else") 75-125 68
(May have been released only in the U.K. If issued in the U.S., may have been a promo only. Verification needed. Selection number also needs to be verified from actual EP.)

LPs: 10/12-inch

A&M (3181 "Shazam") 5-8 82
A&M (3625 "Best of the Move") 15-25 74
A&M (4259 "Shazam") 20-25 70
CAPITOL (658 "Looking On") 15-25 71
CAPITOL (811 "Message from the Country") 15-25 71
PICKWICK .... 10-15 '70s
U.A. (5666 "Split Ends") 10-15 73
Members: Jeff Lynne; Roy Wood; Bev Bevan; Denny Cordell; Richard Tandy; Carl Wayne; Rick Price; Trevor Burton; Ace Kefford.
Also see LYNNE, Jeff
Also see MAGIC CHRISTIANS

MOVEMENT

Singles: 7-inch

TINKER (3921 "Green Knight") 15-25 67

MOVERS

Singles: 7-inch

1-2-3 (1700 "Leave Me Loose") 15-25 68
1-2-3 (1705 "Hello L.A., Goodbye Birmingham") 15-25 68

MOVIN' MORFOMEN

Singles: 7-inch

DELTA (2242 "Run Girl Run") 15-25 67
NEL-RIC (301 "We Tried, Try It") 15-25 67

MOVING PARTS

Singles: 7-inch

BOBBY (14001 " Sock-A-Lu") 5-10 68

MOVING SIDEWALKS

Singles: 7-inch

TANTARA (3101 "99th Floor") 25-35 67
TANTARA (3103 "I Want to Hold Your Hand") 25-35 68
TANTARA (3113 "Flashback") 20-30 69
WAND (1156 "99th Floor") 15-20 67
WAND (1167 "Need Me") 10-20 67

EPs: 7-inch

MUTT (1030 "The Moving Sidewalks") .. 75-125 '60s

LPs: 10/12-inch

EVA (12002 "99th Floore") 8-12 82
TANTARA (6919 "Flash") 200-300 68
Members: Billy Gibbons; Tom Moore; Don Summers; Lanier Greig; Dan Mitchell.
Also see ZZ TOP

MOVING VIOLATIONS

Singles: 7-inch

ATLANTIC (3030 "Spinning Top") 4-6 74
GEM (101 "This Time") .... 35-55 '60s
SSS INT'L (733 "You'd Better Move On") 10-20 68

MOWREY, Al

Singles: 7-inch

FINE (257 "Girl of My Dreams") 10-15 59

MOXIES

Singles: 7-inch

MONZA (1124 "I Must Apologize") 5-10 65

MOY, June

(With the Feathers)

Singles: 78 rpm

SHOW TIME 50-75 54

Singles: 7-inch

SHOW TIME (1103 "Desert Winds") 75-125 54
Also see FEATHERS

MOYA, Monte, & Surfers

LPs: 10/12-inch

EVEREST (1212 "Percussionata") 15-20 63
(Monaural.)
EVEREST (5212 "Percussionata") 20-25 63
(Stereo.)

MU

Singles: 7-inch

MANTRA (101 "Ballad of Brother Lew") ... 15-25 71
MU (101 "One More Day") 10-15 72
MU (103 "Too Naked for Demetrius") 10-15 73

LPs: 10/12-inch

APPALOOSA (071 "Last Album") 8-12 81
BLUE FORM (1 "Children of the Rainbow") 8-12 85
CASS (100 "Mu") 75-100 72
RTV (300 "Mu") 150-250 71
RECKLESS (7 "End of an Era") 10-15 88
U.A. (27909 "Mu") 30-40 74
Members: Merrell Fankhauser; Jeff Cotton; Jeff Parker; Randy Wimer; Mary Lee; Larry Willey.
Also see CAPTAIN BEEFHEART
Also see FANKHAUSER, Merrell

MUDCRUTCH
Singles: 7-inch
SHELTER (40357 "Depot Street") 10-20 75
Member: Tom Petty.
Also see PETTY, Tom, & Heartbreakers

MUDD FAMILY
Singles: 7-inch
SCEPTER (12151 "Stand Back and Look At Yourself") 5-10 66

MUDLARKS
Singles: 7-inch
ROULETTE (4143 "Love Game") 5-10 59

MUDSLINGER, Roger
Singles: 7-inch
RED BIRD (013 "Election Year 1964") 5-10 64

MUFFETS
Singles: 7-inch
CHELSEA LTD. (2002 "Make It Alright") . 10-20
COUNTERPART (813 "Heather Girl") 10-20

MUFFINS
Singles: 7-inch
RCA (9211 "Subway Traveler") 5-10 67

MUGWUMPS
(Mugwump Establishment)
Singles: 7-inch
SIDEWALK (900 "Bald Headed Woman") 10-20 66
SIDEWALK (909 "My Gal") 10-20 67
SIDEWALK (931 "Bo Weevil") 10-20 67
W.B. 5-10 64-67
LPs: 10/12-inch
W.B. (W-1697 "Mugwumps") 15-25 67
(Monaural.)
W.B. (WS-1697 "Mugwumps") 20-30 67
(Stereo.)
Members: Cass Elliot; Denny Doherty; James Hendricks; John Sebastian; Zal Yanovsky.
Also see ELLIOT, Cass
Also see SEBASTIAN, John
Also see YANOVSKY, Zal

MUHOBERAC, Larry
Singles: 7-inch
COVER (8201 "Tailspin") 10-15 63
Also see PRESLEY, Elvis

MULDAUR, Maria — LP '73
Singles: 7-inch
REPRISE 4-6 73-76
W.B. 4-6 78-79
LPs: 10/12-inch
MYRRH 5-8 82
REPRISE 8-12 73-76
TAKOMA 5-8 80
W.B. 5-10 78-79

MULESKINNERS
Singles: 7-inch
CUCA (1139 "Galloping Paul Revere") 5-10 63
SARA (63101 "Brody's 97") 8-12 63
SOMA (1414 "Wolfman") 8-12 64
TWIN TOWN (708 "Muleskinner Blues '65") 8-12 65
WATER STREET (8596 "Muleskinner Blues") 5-10 70
Member: Jim Sundquist.
Also see FENDERMEN
Also see VASSER, Dave

MULL, Regis
Singles: 7-inch
VERVE FOLKWAYS (5049 "I Saw Your Face") 5-10 67

MULLANEY, Dave, & Sounds Extraordinaire
Singles: 7-inch
LAURIE (3473 "An Extra Gas") 10-20 68

MULLER, Rich
Singles: 7-inch
AMBER ("What Cha Gonna Say") 50-75
(Selection number not known.)

MÜLLER BROTHERS
Singles: 7-inch
BULLSEYE (1007 "Ho-La-Hee") 10-20 58

MULLICAN, Moon — C&W/P&R '47
(With the Showboys)
Singles: 78 rpm
KING 15-25 46-56
Singles: 7-inch
CORAL 62042 "Moon's Rock") 20-30 58
DECCA (30962 "Cush Cush Ky-Yay") 10-20 59
HALL/HALLWAY 10-20 62-65
KING (830 "I'll Sail My Ship Alone") 35-50 50
KING (839 thru 996) 30-40 50-51
KING (1006 "Memphis Blues") 20-40 51
KING (1007 "Country Boogie") 20-40 51
KING (1043 "Shoot the Moon") 40-60 51
(Red vinyl.)
KING (1060 thru 1481) 20-30 52-55
KING (4894 "Honolulu Rock-A Roll-A") 20-30 55
KING (4915 "Rock and Roll Mr. Bullfrog") 20-30 55
KING (4915 "Rock and Roll Mr. Bullfrog") 40-60 55
(Promotional issue only, with bio on label.)
KING (4937 "Hey Shah") 20-30 56
KING (4979 "If You Don't Want No More of My Loving") 20-30 56
KING (5172 "I'll Sail My Ship Alone") 10-20 59
KING (5223 "Goodnight Irene") 10-20 59
KING (5328 "Jambalaya") 10-20 60
KING (5354 "Sweeter Than the Flowers") 10-20 60
KING (5379 "Rocket to the Moon") 10-20 60
KING (5473 "I Don't Know What to Do") ...10-20 61
STARDAY (527 "New Jole Blon") 8-12 60
STARDAY (545 "Ragged But Right") 8-12 61
STARDAY (556 "Just Plain Lonesome") 8-12 61
STARDAY (562 "I'll Sail My Ship Alone") ...8-12 61
TCF (106 "Just to Be with You") 5-10 65
EPs: 7-inch
KING (214 "King of the Hillbilly Piano Players") ....20-30 '50s
KING (227 "Piano Solos") ....15-25 '50s
KING (314 "Moon Mullican") ....15-25 '50s
STARDAY (154 "Moon Mullican") 20-30 60
LPs: 10/12-inch
AUDIO LAB 50-75
CORAL (57235 "Moon Over Mullican") 150-250 58
KAPP 20-30 69
KING (555 "All-Time Greatest Hits") 50-100 57
KING (628 "16 Favorite Tunes") 50-75 59
KING (681 "Many Moods") 50-75 60
KING (937 "24 Favorite Tunes") 40-60 65
NASHVILLE 10-20 70
PHONORAMA 5-8 83
PICKWICK/HILLTOP 10-15 66
SPUR (3005 "Moon Mullican Sings and Plays") 100-150
STARDAY (398 "Unforgettable") 20-40 67
STERLING (601 "I'll Sail My Ship Alone") ....50-75 '50s
WESTERN 5-8
Also see KERR, Anita

MULLICAN, Moon / Cowboy Copas
Singles: 7-inch
DIXIE (594 "Good Times Gonna Roll Again") ....40-50 '50s

MULLICAN, Moon / Cowboy Copas / Red Sovine
LPs: 10/12-inch
DIPLOMAT ....5-10 '60s
Also see COPAS, Cowboy
Also see SOVINE, Red

MULLICAN, Moon / Cotton Thompson
Singles: 78 rpm
KING 10-20 48
Also see MULLICAN, Moon
Also see THOMPSON, Cotton

MULLIGAN, Gerry — LP '59
(Gerry Mulligan Quartet; Jazz Combo)
Singles: 7-inch
A&M (1377 "Country Beaver") 3-5 72
LIMELIGHT (3061 "Downtown") 4-6 65
PACIFIC JAZZ 4-6 61
PHILIPS 4-6 64
VERVE 4-8 60
EPs: 7-inch
CAPITOL 30-45 53
COLUMBIA 10-20 59
EMARCY 10-20 56
FANTASY (4008 "Gerry Mulligan Quartet") 25-50 53
(Purple vinyl.)
FANTASY (4028 "Gerry Mulligan Quartet") 25-50 53
(Probably purple vinyl.)
PACIFIC JAZZ 25-50 53-57
PRESTIGE (1317 "Gerry Mulligan Blows") 50-100 52
PRESTIGE (1318 "Gerry Mulligan Blows") 50-100 52
U.A. 10-20 58
LPs: 10/12-inch
A&M (3036 "The Age of Steam") 8-12 72
ABC-PAR (225 "Jazz Concerto") 75-125 58
BLUE NOTE 5-8 81
CTI 8-12 75
CAPITOL (H-439 "Gerry Mulligan") 150-250 53
(10-inch LP.)
CAPITOL (691 "Modern Sounds") 100-150 56
(One side is by Shorty Rogers.)
CAPITOL (2000 series) 20-40 63
CAPITOL (11000 series) 8-12 72
CHIAROSCURO 5-10 77
COLUMBIA (1307 thru 1932) 20-45 59-63
(Monaural.)
COLUMBIA (8116 thru 8732) 25-50 59-63
(Stereo.)
COLUMBIA (34000 series) 5-10 77
CROWN 10-20 63-64
DRG 5-8 80
EMARCY (1000 series) 5-8 81
EMARCY (36056 "Gerry Mulligan Sextet") 100-150 56
EMARCY (36101 "Mainstream") 100-150 57
FANTASY (3-6 "Gerry Mulligan Quartet") 100-150 53
(10-inch LP.)
FANTASY (3-220 "Gerry Mulligan Quartet") 150-250
(Red vinyl.)
GRP 5-8 83
GENE NORMAN (3 "Gerry Mulligan Quartet") 150-250 52
(10-inch LP.)
GENE NORMAN (26 "Gerry Mulligan/Chet Baker/ Buddy DeFranco") 50-100 57
GENE NORMAN (56 "Gerry Mulligan/Chet Baker/ Buddy DeFranco") 20-40 61
INNER CITY 5-8 80
KIMBERLY 20-30 63
LIMELIGHT (82000 series) 12-25 65-66
(Monaural.)
LIMELIGHT (86000 series) 15-30 65-66
(Stereo.)
MERCURY (20453 "Profile") 40-60 59
ODYSSEY 10-20 68
PACIFIC JAZZ (1 "Gerry Mulligan Quartet") 200-300 53
(10-inch LP.)
PACIFIC JAZZ (2 "Gerry Mulligan Quartet") 200-300 53
(10-inch LP.)
PACIFIC JAZZ (5 "Gerry Mulligan") 200-300 53
(10-inch LP.)
PACIFIC JAZZ (10 "Gerry Mulligan") ...150-250 54
(10-inch LP.)
PACIFIC JAZZ (1201 "California Concert") 100-150 55
PACIFIC JAZZ (1207 "Original Quartet") 100-150 55
PACIFIC JAZZ (1210 "Paris Concert") .100-150 56
PACIFIC JAZZ (1228 "Mulligan at Storyville") 100-150 57
PACIFIC JAZZ (1237 "Songbook") 100-150 57
PACIFIC JAZZ (1241 "Reunion") 100-150 57
PACIFIC JAZZ (10000 & 20000 series) ...10-20 66
PAUSA 5-10 76
PHILIPS 10-20 63-64
PRESTIGE (003 "Mulligan Plays Mulligan") 5-8 82
PRESTIGE (120 "Gerry Mulligan Blows") 200-300 52
(10-inch LP.)
PRESTIGE (141 "Mulligan Too Blows") 200-300 53
(10-inch LP.)
PRESTIGE (7006 "Gerry Plays Mulligan") 75-100 56
(Yellow label.)
PRESTIGE (7251 "Historically Speaking") 30-40 63
(Yellow label.)
SUNSET (5117 "Concert Days") 10-15 66
TRIP 6-12 75-76
U.A. (4006 "I Want to Live") 30-40 58
(Monaural.)
U.A. (4006 "I Want to Live") 40-50 58
(Stereo.)
V.S.P. (6 "Gerry's Time") 10-20 66
VERVE 25-50 58-60
(Reads "Verve Records, Inc." at bottom of label.)
VERVE 10-25 61-72
(Reads "MGM Records - A Division Of Metro-Goldwyn-Mayer, Inc." at bottom of label.)
VERVE 5-12 73-84
(Reads "Manufactured By MGM Record Corp.," or mentions either Polydor or Polygram at bottom of label.)
WHO'S WHO IN JAZZ 5-8 78
WING (16335 "Night Lights") 10-20 67
WORLD PACIFIC (1241 "Reunion") 50-100 58
WORLD PACIFIC (1253 "Annie Ross Sings with Mulligan") 50-100 59
Members: Chet Baker; Chico Hamilton; Carson Smith.
Also see BRUBECK, Dave, & Gerry Mulligan
Also see GETZ, Stan, & Gerry Mulligan
Also see HAMILTON, Chico

MULLIGAN, Gerry, & Paul Desmond
(Gerry Mulligan / Paul Desmond)
LPs: 10/12-inch
FANTASY (220 "Gerry Mulligan/Paul Desmond") 100-150 56
(Colored vinyl.)
RCA (2642 "Two of a Mind") 40-60 62
VERVE (8246 "Gerry Mulligan/Paul Desmond") 50-100 58
(Reads "Verve Records, Inc." at bottom of label.)
VERVE (8246 "Gerry Mulligan/Paul Desmond") 25-50 62
(Reads "MGM Records - A Division Of Metro-Goldwyn-Mayer, Inc." at bottom of label.)
Also see DESMOND, Paul

MULLIGAN, Gerry, & Johnny Hodges
LPs: 10/12-inch
VERVE 30-40 60
(Reads "Verve Records, Inc." at bottom of label.)
VERVE 15-25 62
(Reads "MGM Records - A Division of Metro-Goldwyn-Mayer, Inc. at bottom of label.)
Also see HODGES, Johnny

MULLIGAN, Gerry, & Thelonious Monk
LPs: 10/12-inch
MILESTONE 8-12 82
RIVERSIDE (247 "Mulligan Meets Monk") 50-100 57
RIVERSIDE (1106 "Mulligan Meets Monk") 40-60 58
Also see MONK, Thelonious

MULLIGAN, Gerry, & Oscar Peterson
LPs: 10/12-inch
VERVE (8235 "Gerry and Oscar at Newport") 50-100 57
VERVE (8559 "Gerry and Oscar at Newport") 30-40 63
(Monaural.)
VERVE (68559 "Gerry and Oscar at Newport") 30-40 63
(Stereo.)
Also see PETERSON, Oscar

MULLIGAN, Gerry, & Ben Webster
LP: 10/12-inch
MFSL (234 "Gerry Mulligan Meets Ben Webster") 25-35 94
(Half-speed mastered.)
Also see MULLIGAN, Gerry

MULLINS, Hank "Soul Man"
Singles: 7-inch
AUDEL (362 "He Upset Your Dreams") ... 10-20

MULLINS, Lonnie
Singles: 7-inch
LOGAN (3111 "It Was You") 10-15 59

MULLINS, Moon
(With the Night Raiders)
Singles: 7-inch
LANCE (005 "Gonna Dance Tonight")..... 15-25 61
MART (113 "Bip Bop Boom") 700-900 58
PIEDMONT (2044 "Baby, I Got You")...... 50-75
Also see HAWKS, Mickey

MULLINS, Tony
Singles: 7-inch
TRI-STATE (1824 "Coal Mine Mama") .. 50-100

MULVANEY, Gary "Happo"
(With Baron Mack Ferguson & Orchestra)
Singles: 7-inch
TEEN-TIME (1001 "Every Little Thing I Do") 50-100 61

MUMBLES
(Walter Horton)
Singles: 78 rpm
MODERN (809 "Little Boy Blue") 50-100 51
RPM (338 "Black Gal") 100-125 51
Also see HORTON, Big Walter

MUMFORD, Gene
(With the Serenaders)
Singles: 7-inch
COLUMBIA (41233 "Please Give Me One More Chance") 40-60 59
(Rerecorded—not reissue of Whiz track.)
LIBERTY (55241 "I'm Getting Sentimental Over You") 10-15 59
LIBERTY (55274 "I Gotta Have My Baby Back") 10-15 60
WHIZ (1500 "Please Give Me One More Chance") 300-400 57
Also see LARKS
Also see WARD, Billy, & Dominoes

MUNGO JERRY P&R/LP '70
Singles: 7-inch
BELL 4-6 71-74
FLASHBACK 4-6 73
JANUS 4-8 70-71
PYE 4-6 72-75
LPs: 10/12-inch
JANUS (7000 "Mungo Jerry") 10-15 70
PYE (504 "Mungo Jerry") .... 8-12 '70s
Members: Paul King; Colin Earl; Mike Cole; Ray Dorset.

MUNI, Scott
Singles: 7-inch
RCA (9291 "Letter to an Unborn Child") 8-12 67
Picture Sleeves
RCA (9291 "Letter to an Unborn Child") .. 10-20 67
(Promotional issue only.)

MUNRO, Chad
Singles: 7-inch
DECCA (32256 "After All Is Said and Done") 5-10 68

MUNRO, Janet, & Sean Connery
Singles: 7-inch
DISNEYLAND (124 "Pretty Irish Girl") 10-20 59
Picture Sleeves
DISNEYLAND (124 "Pretty Irish Girl") 40-50 59

MUNRO, Sonny
Singles: 7-inch
EPIC (50174 "Open the Door to Your Heart") 10-20 75

MUNSTERS
Singles: 7-inch
DECCA (31670 "Munster Creep") 5-10 64
LPs: 10/12-inch
DECCA (4588 "The Munsters") 25-30 64
(Monaural.)
DECCA (7-4588 "The Munsters") 25-35 64
(Stereo.)
GOLDEN (139 "At Home") 10-20 64

MUNX
Singles: 7-inch
JUBILEE (5612 "Girls, Girls, Girls") 5-10 68
JUBILEE (5634 "So Much in Love") 5-10 68

MUPHETS
Singles: 7-inch
SOUND SPECTACTULAR (36001 "Why Can't You Go") 10-15

MURALS
Singles: 7-inch
CLIMAX (110 "See You in September") ... 25-50 59
Member: Billy Mure.
Also see MURE, Billy

MURE, Billy P&R '59
(With the Wild-Cats; with Trumpeteers; with 7 Karats)
Singles: 78 rpm
RCA 5-10 57-58
Singles: 7-inch
DANCO (506 "Rose of Cherry Bay") 5-8 65
EVEREST (19335 "Jambalaya") 5-10 60
JUBILEE (5388 "Stranger in Paradise") 5-10 60
MGM 4-8 60-66
PARIS (545 "Ambush") 5-10 60
RCA 10-15 57-58
RIVERSIDE (4547 "Diamonds") 5-10 63
SRG (102 "Theme for the Lonely") 5-10 61
SPLASH 8-12 58
STRAND (25037 "Pink Hawaii") 5-10 61
EPs: 7-inch
RCA 10-15 58
LPs: 10/12-inch
EVEREST 15-20 60-61
KAPP 15-20 61
MGM 15-20 59-66
RCA 25-30 57-58
STRAND 15-20 61
SUNSET 10-12 67
U.A. (3031 "Bandstand Record Hop") 30-40 59
(Monaural.)
U.A. (6031 "Bandstand Record Hop") 40-50 59
(Stereo.)
Also see CASTLE SISTERS
Also see DE MARCO, Ralph
Also see DESIRES
Also see DOVERS
Also see EMOTIONS
Also see FOUR BARS
Also see GALLAHADS
Also see HOLIDAY, Chico
Also see JORDAN, Lou
Also see LAWRENCE, Syd / Billy Mure
Also see MARESCA, Ernie
Also see MURALS
Also see PYRAMIDS
Also see SHANTONS
Also see SHAW, Ricky
Also see SUPERTONES
Also see TEMPOS
Also see TRUMPETEERS
Also see WILD-CATS

MURE, Billy & Benny
Singles: 7-inch
MGM (13252 "Sticky Fingers") 5-10 64
Also see MURE, Billy

MURE, Gary
Singles: 7-inch
VERVE (10356 "Crack Up") 10-15 65

MURE, Sal
Singles: 7-inch
U.A. (153 "Desire") 20-30 59

MURFREESBORO
(With Jimmy Beck & Orchestra)
Singles: 7-inch
CHAMPION (1007 "Oh My Love") 50-150 59

MURMAIDS P&R '63
(Mermaids)
Singles: 7-inch
CHATTAHOOCHEE (628 "Popsicles and Icicles"/"Blue Dress") 15-25 63
CHATTAHOOCHEE (628 "Popsicles and Icicles"/"Huntington Flats") 5-10 63
CHATTAHOOCHEE (628 "Popsicles and Icicles"/"Tragedy") 5-10 63
CHATTAHOOCHEE (636 "Heartbreak Ahead") 5-10 64
CHATTAHOOCHEE (641 "Wild and Wonderful") 5-10 64
CHATTAHOOCHEE (650 "Wild and Wonderful") 5-10 64
CHATTAHOOCHEE (668 "Little White Lies") 5-10 65
CHATTAHOOCHEE (711 "Go Away") 5-10 66
LIBERTY (56078 "Paper Sun") 4-8 68
LPs: 10/12-inch
CHATTAHOOCHEE 8-10 81
Members: Cathy Fischer; Terry Fischer; Sally Gordon.

MURPHEY, Chuck
Singles: 78 rpm
COLUMBIA (21305 "Rhythm Hall") 10-15 54
Singles: 7-inch
COLUMBIA (21305 "Rhythm Hall") 15-25 54

MURPHEY, Jim
Singles: 7-inch
RAMCO (3703 "Nobody's Darlin' But Mine") 5-10 60

MURPHY, Beth, & Downbeats
Singles: 7-inch
GOLDBAND (1083 "Where Were You") ... 10-15 58

MURPHY, Don
Singles: 7-inch
COSMOPOLITAN (2264 "Mean Mama Blues") 100-150

MURPHY, Donnie, & Ambassadors
Singles: 7-inch
REDBUG (0005 "My Love for You") 25-35 61

MURPHY, Jim, & Accents
Singles: 78 rpm
REV (3508 "I'm Gone Mama") 20-30 57
Singles: 7-inch
REV (3508 "I'm Gone Mama") 30-40 57

MURPHY, Jimmy C&W '86
Singles: 78 rpm
COLUMBIA 25-50 56
RCA 10-20 51-52
Singles: 7-inch
ARK (260 "My Feet's on Solid Ground") 8-12 63
COLUMBIA (21486 "Here Kitty Kitty") .. 100-150 56
COLUMBIA (21534 "16 Tons Rock and Roll") 100-150 56
COLUMBIA (21569 "Baboon Boogie") . 100-150 56
ENCORE 3-5 86-87
RCA 20-40 51-52
REM (340 "Half a Loaf") 10-20 62
SUGAR HILL 4-6 78
LPs: 10/12-inch
SUGAR HILL 5-10 78

MURPHY, Joe
Singles: 7-inch
VIVID (106 "It's a Weakness") 5-10 64

MURPHY, Keith, & Daze
Singles: 7-inch
KING (6171 "Dirty Ol' Sam") 500-1000 68
(Less than 100 made.)
Also see O'CONNER, Keith

MURPHY, Mark
Singles: 7-inch
FONTANA (1510 "The Best Is Yet to Come") 5-10 65
RIVERSIDE (4526 "Why Don't You Do Right") 5-10 62

MURPHY, Marvin
Singles: 7-inch
M.M. (103 "Crying for My Baby") 20-30 63

MURPHY, Ron
Singles: 7-inch
ABC-PAR (10667 "Let's Pretend") 5-10 65
BEVMAR (962 "Long, Long Way") 8-12 61
MGM (12848 "Holding Hands and Making Love") 8-12 59
MGM (12898 "Forever Young") 8-12 60
20TH FOX (437 "Hollow Man") 5-10 63
20TH FOX (470 "To Wait for Love") 5-10 64

MURPHY, Rose R&B '48
(With the Selah Jubilee Quartette; Rose Murphy Trio)
Singles: 78 rpm
DECCA 5-10 55
MAJESTIC 5-10 48
Singles: 7-inch
DECCA (29000 series) 8-12 55
DECCA (32030 "Three Little Words") 4-8 66
REGINA (292 "Love My Baby") 4-8 63
LPs: 10/12-inch
MUSE 5-8
ROYALE (1835 "Rose Murphy") 30-40 52
(10-inch LP.)
VERVE 20-30 57
Also see BAILEY, Pearl / Rose Murphy / Ivie Anderson
Also see SELAH JUBILEE QUARTETTE

MURPHY, Rose, & Slam Stewart
Singles: 7-inch
DECCA (31257 "Dinah") 5-10 61
LPs: 10/12-inch
U.A. (14025 "Jazz, Joy and Happiness") . 15-25 63
Also see MURPHY, Rose

MURPHY & MOB
Singles: 7-inch
TALISMAN (1823 "Born Loser") 15-25 66

MURPHY'S R&B '82
Singles: 7-inch
GRT (130 "Dancin'") 4-6 77
THUNDERBIRD (514 "Great Pretender") 10-20 '60s
VENTURE 3-5 82

MURRAY, Al. B
Singles: 7-inch
MOHAWK (110 "Whistle Bait") 8-12 58

MURRAY, Anne C&W/P&R/LP '70
(With Doug Mallory)
Singles: 7-inch
ARC 5-10 69
(Canadian.)
CAPITOL 3-6 70-86
Picture Sleeves
CAPITOL 3-8 79-86
LPs: 10/12-inch
ARC (782 "What About Me") 10-20 69
(Canadian.)
AURA 5-8 83
CAPITOL (Except "Let's Keep It That Way" picture disc) 5-15 70-87
CAPITOL ("Let's Keep It That Way") 50-100 78
(Picture disc. Promotional issue only. One of a four-artist, four-disc set. 250 made.)
SESAME ST. 5-10 79
Also see CAMPBELL, Glen, & Anne Murray
Also see CAMPBELL, Glen / Anne Murray / Kenny Rogers / Crystal Gayle
Also see WINCHESTER, Jesse

MURRAY, Bill "Winehead Willie," & George "Sweet Lucy" Copeland
Singles: 7-inch
ANNA (1121 "Bigtime Spender") 10-20 60

MURRAY, Billy, & Four Cousins
Singles: 78 rpm
20TH CENTURY 15-25 54
Singles: 7-inch
20TH CENTURY (75020 "Time and Time Again") 30-40 54

MURRAY, Clarence
Singles: 7-inch
FEDERAL (12562 "Book of Love") 4-8 71
SSS INT'L (730 "One More Chance") 5-10 68
Also see MURRAY, Mickey & Clarence

MURRAY, Eddie
(With Mark Donald & Orchestra)
Singles: 7-inch
E-M (4058 "Stepping High Dance") .... 8-12 '60s

MURRAY, Jack
Singles: 7-inch
GOLD ARROW (214 "Every Little Twister") 5-10 63
LAURIE (3199 "Surfin' with Me") 5-10 63

MURRAY, Joan
Singles: 7-inch
APPLAUSE (1243 "Oh Johnny") 5-10 61

MURRAY, Mickey P&R/R&B '67
Singles: 7-inch
FEDERAL (12558 "Going Back to Alabama") 4-8 71
FEDERAL (12560 "Fat Gal") 4-8 71
SSS INT'L (715 "Shout Bamalama") 5-10 67
SSS INT'L (727 "Hit Record") 5-10 67
SSS INT'L (755 "Flat Foot Sam") 5-10 68
LPs: 10/12-inch
FEDERAL (13000 "People Are Together") 8-12 71

MURRAY, Mickey & Clarence
Singles: 7-inch
SSS INT'L (743 "Pig and the Pussycat") 5-10 68
Also see MURRAY, Clarence

Also see MURRAY, Mickey

MURRAY, Mitch
Singles: 7-inch
MGM (13512 "Whatever Happened to Music")....5-10 66
Also see MURRAY'S MONKEY

MURRAY, Ray
(With the Dynamics)
Singles: 7-inch
ARBO (222 "With All My Love")....100-150 60
FLEETWOOD (7005 "Warm")....30-40 63

MURRAY'S MONKEY
(Mitch Murray)
Singles: 7-inch
HBR (469 "I'll Be There")....5-10 66
Also see MURRAY, Mitch

MUSCLEMEN
Singles: 7-inch
MUSICOR (1001 "Plunkin'")....10-20 61
Member: Al Kooper.

MUSCRAT RAMBLERS
LPs: 10/12-inch
CROWN ("Dixieland One-Step")....5-10 66
(Selection number not known.)

MUSE, Cynthia
Singles: 7-inch
DOT (16335 "High School Play")....8-12 62

MUSHROOMS
Singles: 7-inch
HIDEOUT (1121 "Burned")....15-25 '60s

MUSIAL, Stan
EPs: 7-inch
RCA (141 "Stan the Man's Hit Record")..10-15 61
(Promotional issue, made for Phillips 66.)

MUSIC CITY SOUL BROTHERS
(Soul Brothers)
Singles: 7-inch
MUSIC CITY (855 "Looking for My Baby")....10-15 64
MUSIC CITY (856 "Every Night I See Your Face")....10-15 64

MUSIC EMPORIUM
Singles: 7-inch
SENTINEL (501 "Nam Myo Ho Renge Kyo")....30-40 68
LPs: 10/12-inch
PSYCHO (11 "Music Emporium")....8-10 83
SENTINEL (100 "Music Emporium") 1000-1500 68
SENTINEL (69001 "Music Emporium")....10-15 84
Members: Casey Cosby; Dave Padwin; Dora Wahl; Carolyn Lee.

MUSIC EXPLOSION P&R/LP '67
Singles: 7-inch
ATTACK (1404 "Little Black Egg")....10-20 66
LAURIE (3380 "Little Bit O' Soul")....8-12 67
LAURIE (3400 "Sunshine Games")....8-12 67
LAURIE (3414 "We Gotta Go Home")....8-12 67
LAURIE (3429 thru 3500)....5-10 68-69
LPs: 10/12-inch
LAURIE (2040 "Little Bit O' Soul")....20-30 67
Members: Jamie Lyons; Don Atkins; Bob Avery; Rick Nesta; Butch Stahl.

MUSIC MACHINE P&R '66
Singles: 7-inch
BELL (764 "Advise & Consent")....5-10 69
ORIGINAL SOUND....5-10 66-68
RED COACH (812 "By the Hair of My Chinny Chin Chin")....4-6 75
W.B. (7199 "To the Light")....5-10 68
W.B. (7234 "Time Out")....5-10 68
Picture Sleeves
ORIGINAL SOUND (82 "Hey Joe")....15-25 68
(Has die-cut center hole on both sides.)
LPs: 10/12-inch
ORIGINAL SOUND (5015 "Turn on the Music Machine")....20-30 66
(Monaural.)
ORIGINAL SOUND (8875 "Turn on the Music Machine")....75-100 66
(Stereo.)
Members: Sean Bonniwell; Mark Landon; Keith Olsen (shown on LP as "Kieth"); Ron Edgar; Doug Rhodes.
Also see BONNIWELL'S MUSIC MACHINE

MUSIC MACHINE / Bubble Puppy
Singles: 7-inch
ORIGINAL SOUND....3-5 85
Also see BUBBLE PUPPY
Also see MUSIC MACHINE

MUSIC MAKERS
Singles: 7-inch
N.A.M. (2001 "Hawaii Tattoo")....5-10 64

MUSIC MAKERS P&R '67
Singles: 7-inch
GAMBLE (210 "United")....5-10 67
GAMBLE (215 "Spring Fever")....5-10 68
MOWEST (5044 "Follow Me – Mother Nature")....4-6 73
LPs: 10/12-inch
GAMBLE (5003 "Music Makers Are United")....12-18 68

MUSIC MASTERS
Singles: 7-inch
BATON (267 "Tempest")....8-12 59
MARK 1 (1010 "Vapor Trails")....5-10 60

MUSIC MEN
Singles: 7-inch
BIG TOP (3006 "Blue Bird")....10-15 58
BIG TOP (3014 "An Open Fire")....10-15 59

MUSIC VANNS
Singles: 78 rpm
GLORY (245 "Book of Love")....10-15 56
Singles: 7-inch
GLORY (245 "Book of Love")....50-75 56

MUSICAL LYNN TWINS
Singles: 7-inch
BLUE FEATHER (294 "Double Trouble").20-30 59
BLUE FEATHER ("Rockin' Out the Blues")....100-150
(Selection number not known.)

MUSICAL WADES
Singles: 7-inch
JANIE (458 "Homicidal Maniac")....8-12 60

MUSICS
Singles: 7-inch
COLUMBIA (43634 "It's the Little Things").5-10 66

MUSIL, Jim, Combo
Singles: 7-inch
JAY EMM (423 "North Beach")....15-25 62

MUSIQUE & LYRICS
Singles: 7-inch
VALIANT (740 "Talkin' About Love")....5-10 66

MUSKATEERS
Singles: 7-inch
DOT (15926 "Poor Boy No. 2")....8-12 59

MUSKETEERS
Singles: 78 rpm
ROXY (801 "Goodbye My Love")....2000-2500 52
SWING TIME (331 "Deep in My Heart")....200-400 53
Members: Norman Thrasher; Noah Howell.
Also see ROYAL JOKERS

MUSSELWHITE, Charles
(Charley Musselwhite; Charles Musselwhite Blues Band)
Singles: 7-inch
VANGUARD....5-10 68-69
LPs: 10/12-inch
PARAMOUNT....10-15 69
VANGUARD....10-15 69
Also see GOLDBERG, Barry / Harvey Mandell / Charlie Musselwhite / Neil Merryweather

MUSSIES
Singles: 7-inch
FENTON (2216 "Louie Go Home")....100-200 67

MUSSO, Vido
(Vido Musso Sextette)
Singles: 78 rpm
CROWN....10-15 54
RPM....10-15 53-57
Singles: 7-inch
CROWN (100 "Roseland Boogie")....15-25 54
CROWN (110 "Musso's Boogie")....15-25 54
CROWN (130 "Powerhouse Boogie")....15-25 54
GALAXY (704 "Cutting the Nut")....5-10 61
RPM (387 "Vido's Boogie")....15-25 53
RPM (404 "Vido's Drive")....15-25 54
RPM (493 "Blues for Two")....15-25 57
LPs: 10/12-inch
CROWN (5029 "Teenage Dance Party") .30-50 57

MUSTACHE WAX
Singles: 7-inch
INNER (501 "I'm Gonna Get You")....5-10 65

MUSTANG
Singles: 7-inch
ASCOT (2231 "Here, There and Everywhere")....15-25 67

MUSTANG, Harry, Singers
Singles: 7-inch
EPIC (9688 "Rat Fink")....8-12 64

MUSTANGS
Singles: 7-inch
VEST (8005 "Over the Rainbow")....500-1000 65
Also see MAGIC TONES / Mustangs

MUSTANGS P&R '64
Singles: 7-inch
KEETCH (6002 "Baby Let Me Take You Home")....5-10 64
PROVIDENCE (401 "Dartell Stomp")....15-20 64
PROVIDENCE (407 Topsy '65")....8-12 64
SURE SHOT (5004 "First Love")....5-10 64
LPs: 10/12-inch
PROVIDENCE (1 "Dartel Stomp")....40-60 64

MUSTANGS
Singles: 7-inch
JETSTAR (120 "How Funky Can You Get")....5-10 69
(Black vinyl.)
JETSTAR (120 "How Funky Can You Get")....10-20 69
(Colored vinyl. Promotional issue only.)
Also see PATTERSON, Bobby

MUSTANGS
Singles: 7-inch
SMEK (3051 "Jack the Ripper")....40-60 '60s
Picture Sleeves
SMEK (3051 "Jack the Ripper")....50-75 '60s
(Two different sleeves exist for this issue.)

MUSTANGS
Singles: 7-inch
DALE (101 "Don't Take Your Love")....25-45

MUSTARD MEN
Singles: 7-inch
RAYNARD (10036 "I Lost My Baby")....20-30 65
Members: Keith Paplham; Warren Wiegratz; Stan Kellicut; Jerry Wimmer; George Welik.
Also see PEASANTS

MUS-TWANGS
Singles: 7-inch
NERO (1-61 "Marie")....20-30 61
(First issue.)
NERO (1002 "Nova Blues")....15-25 62
NERO (1700 "Marie")....10-20 61
SMASH (1700 "Marie")....10-20 61
SMASH (1709 "Frankie and Johnny")....10-15 61

MUTIMER, Steve, & Rhythm Kings
Singles: 7-inch
CUCA (1009 "Maj")....15-25 60
INT'L ARTISTS (2121 "Stuck on Me")....15-25 60

MUTZIE
LPs: 10/12-inch
SUSSEX (7001 "Light of Your Shadow") .20-25 70
Members: "Mutzie" Lavenburg; Andy Lavenburg.

MYDDLE CLASS
Singles: 7-inch
BUDDAH (150 "I Happen to Love You")....5-10 69
TOMORROW (912 "Don't Look Back")....10-20 66
TOMORROW (7501 "Gates of Eden")....10-20 66
TOMORROW (7503 "I Happen to Love You")....15-25 66
Member: Dave Palmer.

MYERS, Bernie
Singles: 7-inch
JET STREAM (736 "As the World Turns Around")....8-12 68

MYERS, Dave
(With the Surftones; with Disciples; Dave Meyers' Effect)
Singles: 7-inch
HARMONY PARK (251 "Come On Luv")....5-10 66
IMPACT (20 "Moment of Truth")....15-25 64
IMPACT (27 "Church Key")....15-25 64
WICKWIRE (13008 "Gear!")....20-30 64
LPs: 10/12-inch
CAROLE (8002 "Greatest Racing Themes")....20-30 67
DEL-FI (DFLP-1239 "Hangin' 20")....30-40 63
(Monaural.)
DEL-FI (DFST-1239 "Hangin' 20")....50-75 63
(Stereo.)
DEL-FI (DLF-1239 "Hangin' 20")....10-12 98
("Thick, hard wax" reissue.)
Members: Dave Myers; Johnny Curtis; Dennis Merritt; Ed Quarry; Seaton Blanco; Bob Colwell.

MYERS, Dave, & Surftones / Rhythm Kings
LPs: 10/12-inch
GNP (85 "Surf Battle")....25-50 63
Also see MYERS, Dave
Also see RHYTHM KINGS

MYERS, Gary
Singles: 7-inch
EDIT (2005 "Poor Little Baby")....15-25 63
Also see DARNELLS
Also see PAUL & PACK / Mad Doctors
Also see PORTRAITS

MYERS, Jim
(With His Gems)
Singles: 7-inch
ATHENA (103 "Gem Rock")....10-15 60
FLING (722 "Needless to Say")....10-20 61
FORTUNE (214 "Bouncy")....10-20 61

MYERS, Jim, & Tex Regan
Singles: 7-inch
FORTUNE (211 "Pretty Baby Rock")....15-25 60
Also see MYERS, Jim

MYERS, Orella
Singles: 7-inch
ZERO (101 "Give a Little, Take a Little")..50-75 60
ZERO (105 "Ask Lucille")....50-75 60

MYERS, Sam
(With the King Mose Royal Rockers. Sammy Myers)
Singles: 78 rpm
ACE....20-30 57
Singles: 7-inch
ACE (536 "My Love Is Here to Stay")....25-50 57
FURY (1035 "Sad, Sad, Lonesome Day")....20-40 60

MYLES, Big Boy
(With the Shaw-Wees)
Singles: 78 rpm
SPECIALTY....20-30 55-56
Singles: 7-inch
ACE (605 "New Orleans")....10-20 60
ACE (637 "Oh Mary")....10-20 61
PIC-1 (101 "Big Break")....5-10 64
SPECIALTY (564 "Who's "Been Fooling You")....50-75 55
SPECIALTY (590 "Just to Hold My Hand")....50-75 56
V-TONE (232 "She's So Fine")....10-15 62
Also see GAYTEN, Paul
Also see SHA-WEEZ

MYLES, Billy P&R '57
Singles: 78 rpm
EMBER....15-25 57-58
Singles: 7-inch
COLLECTABLES....3-5 '80s
DOT (15809 "King of Clowns")....10-20 58
EMBER (1026 "The Joker")....15-25 57
EMBER (1040 "Piece of Your Love")....10-20 58
EMBER (1046 "I'm Gonna Walk")....10-20 58
KING (5395 "Dance Little Girl")....8-12 60

MYLES, David
Singles: 7-inch
GALLO (105 "Only to Be Loved")....30-40 58

MYLES & DUPONT
Singles: 7-inch
ARGO (5326 "Loud Mouth Annie")....8-12 59

MYRON, Mitch
Singles: 7-inch
BAY-TONE (109 "True Love Is Hard to Find") 10-20 62

MYRON & VAN DELLS
Singles: 7-inch
FLO-RUE (15 "Crazy Little Mama") 10-20 63

MYSTERIANS
Singles: 7-inch
JOREL (101 "The Fuzzy One") 5-10 64

MYSTERIES
Singles: 7-inch
JDL (3554 "Pink Panther") 10-20 65

MYSTERIES
Singles: 7-inch
MANHATTAN (815 "Please Agree") 15-25 68
MANHATTAN (817 "I Can't Wait for Love") 15-25 68

MYSTERIONS
Singles: 7-inch
JOX (40 "Is It a Lie") 25-35 65
Also see ? (Question Mark) & Mysterians

MYSTERIONS
Singles: 7-inch
BRS (1011 "Jerico Rock") 10-15
FASCINATION (1004 "Transylvania") 15-25 59
FASCINATION (1009 "Down Hill") 10-20 60
WARWICK (521 "Transylvania") 10-15 60
ZORDAN (101 "A-Bomb") .... 10-20 '60s

MYSTERY MEN
(With Joseph Ricci & Orchestra)
Singles: 7-inch
POW (1001 "Feel Like a Million") 75-125 63
(Reissued as by Tyrone & the Nu Ports)
Also see TYRONE & NU PORTS

MYSTERY MEN
Singles: 7-inch
CEVA (1020 "Pier X") .... 10-20 '60s

MYSTERY TREND
Singles: 7-inch
VERVE (10499 "Johnny Was a Good Boy") 10-15 67
Members: Ron Nagel; Bob Cuff.
Also see SERPENT POWER

MYSTERY TRIO
Singles: 7-inch
CAMELLIA (100 "Willie Joe") 100-200

MYSTIC ASTROLOGIC CRYSTAL BAND
Singles: 7-inch
CAROLE (1004 "Flowers Never Cry") 10-20 67
LPs: 10/12-inch
CAROLE (8001 "Mystic Astrologic Crystal Band") 20-30 67
CAROLE (8003 "Clip On, Put On Book"). 20-30 68
Members: Steve Hoffman; Ron Roman; John Leighton; John Moreland; Bob Phillips.
Session: Phil Alagna; Gary Myers.

MYSTIC CRASH
Singles: 7-inch
ABC (11012 "Love-In Kind") 5-10 67
ABC (11069 "Land of Love") 5-10 68

MYSTIC FIVE
Singles: 7-inch
GO-GO (26000 "I'm Gonna Love You Too") 15-25 66

MYSTIC FIVE
Singles: 7-inch
MYSTIC (1 "It Doesn't Matter") 15-25 66

MYSTIC KNIGHTS OF OINGO BOINGO
Singles: 7-inch
PELICAN (1001 "You Got Your Baby Back") .... 10-15 '70s
(Add $5 to $10 if accompanied by an insert sheet of Patty Hearst cut-out paper dolls.)

MYSTIC NUMBER NATIONAL BANK
Singles: 7-inch
PROBE (457 "St. James Infirmary") 5-10 69
LPs: 10/12-inch
PROBE (4501 "Mystic Number National Bank") 10-15 69

MYSTIC SIVA
LPs: 10/12-inch
VO (19713 "Mystic Siva") 900-1000 71
(With gatefold cover.)
Members: Dave Mascarin; Al Tozzie; Mark Heckert; Art Trienel;

MYSTIC TIDE
Singles: 7-inch
ESQUIRE (719 "Mystic Eyes") 50-100 66
ESQUIRE (4677 "Stay Away") 50-100 65
SOLID SOUND (156 "Frustration") 50-100 66
SOLID SOUND (157 "Psychedelic Journey") 50-100 66
SOLID SOUND (158 "Running Through the Night") 50-100 67
SOLID SOUND (321 "Mystery Ship") 50-100 67
SOLID SOUND ("Mystic Eyes") 50-100 66
(Selection number not known.)
LPs: 10/12-inch
DISTORTIONS 8-10 91
Members: Joe Docko; James Thomas; Paul Picell; John Williams.

MYSTICS
Singles: 7-inch
CHATAM (350 "Teenage Sweetheart") 1500-2000 58
(Reissued as by the Champs.)
Also see CHAMPS

MYSTICS *P&R '59*
Singles: 7-inch
AMBIENT SOUND (02871 "Now That Summer Is Here") 4-6 82
COLLECTABLES .... 3-5 '80s
LAURIE (3028 "Hushabye") 20-30 59
LAURIE (3028S "Hushabye") 40-50 59
(Stereo.)
LAURIE (3038 "Don't Take the Stars") 15-25 59
LAURIE (3047 "All Through the Night") 15-25 60
LAURIE (3058 "White Cliffs of Dover") 15-25 60
LAURIE (3086 "Goodbye Mister Blues") .. 10-15 61
LAURIE (3104 "Sunday Kind of Love") 10-15 61
LPs: 10/12-inch
AMBIENT SOUND (37716 "Crazy for You") 8-12 82
COLLECTABLES 6-8 87
Members: Phil Cracolici; Albee Cracolici; Bob Ferrante; George Galfo.
Also see DEMOLYRS / Mystics / Five Discs / Fascinators
Also see GARRETT, Scott
Also see RESOLUTIONS

MYSTICS / Passions
LPs: 10/12-inch
LAURIE 5-10 79
Also see MYSTICS
Also see PASSIONS

MYSTICS
Singles: 7-inch
KING (5678 "Mashed Potatoes with Me") 10-20 62
KING (5735 "Just for Your Love") 10-20 63

MYSTICS
Singles: 7-inch
CONSTELLATION (138 "She's Got Everything") 5-10 64
DOT (16862 "Didn't We Have a Good Time") 5-10 66
NOLTA (353 "Fox") 15-25 63
SAFICE (331 "She's Got Everything") 15-25 64
(First issue.)

MYSTICS
Singles: 7-inch
TEAKO (370 "That's the Kind of Love") 25-50 64

MYSTICS
Singles: 7-inch
AFC (4778 "Cryin' Over You") 5-10 64
BEAR (1965 "You Ran Away") 15-25 66
CHARLIE .... 10-20 '60s
METROMEDIA 8-12 69
Picture Sleeves
CHARLIE .... 20-25 '60s

MYSTICS
Singles: 7-inch
BLACK CAT (501 "Snoopy") 20-30 66
Also see RATS

MYSTICS
Singles: 7-inch
MARQUETTE (1001 "Jealous of You") .... 50-75 '60s
STAFF (1001 "Peace of Mind") .... 15-25 '60s

MYSTICS
Singles: 7-inch
SPECTRA (707 "Didn't We Have a Good Time") .... 20-25 '60s

MYSTICS
Singles: 7-inch
JENNY LYNN (101 "Get a Job") 15-25

MYSTIFYING MONARCHS
Singles: 7-inch
CENTURY (27913 "Soldier of Fortune") ... 40-60 '60s

N

N. GROUP
Singles: 7-inch
WES MAR (1021 "Keep On Running") .... 15-25 '60s

NAIF GROUP
(North Atlantic Invasion Force)
Singles: 7-inch
CONGRESSIONAL (999 "Blue and Green Gown") 10-20 66
MAJESTIC (998 "Sweet Bird of Love") 10-20 67
MR. G. (808 "Black on White") 10-15 68
MR. G. (819 "Rainmaker") 5-10 68
STAFF (1006 "Love's No Game") 10-15 69
Members: George Morgio; Nick Tirozzi; Neil Mitchell; Jim Gaffney; Edward Dumbrowski.

NGC-4594
Singles: 7-inch
SMASH (2104 "Going Home") 10-20 67

N.J. ORANGE
Singles: 7-inch
VANGUARD (35074 "Pretty Sunshine Girl") 5-10 68

NRBQ *LP '69*
(New Rhythm & Blues Quintet)
Singles: 7-inch
BEARSVILLE 3-5 83
BUDDAH 4-6 74
COLUMBIA 5-10 69
KAMA SUTRA 4-6 72-74
MERCURY 4-6 78
RED ROOSTER 4-6 77
ROUNDER 3-5 80-83
VIRGIN 3-5 89-90
Picture Sleeves
RED ROOSTER 4-6 77
ROUNDER 3-5 80
EPs: 7-inch
ROUNDER 5-10 82
LPs: 10/12-inch
ANNUIT COEPTIS 10-15 76
BEARSVILLE 5-8 83
KAMA SUTRA 10-15 72-73
MERCURY 8-12 78
COLUMBIA 10-15 69
RED ROOSTER 8-10 77-83
ROUNDER 5-10 79-80
VIRGIN 5-8 89
Members: Frank Gadler; Terry Adams; G.T. Stanley; Jody St. Nicholas; Steve Ferguson; Don Adams; Al Anderson; Tom Staley; Joey Spampinato; Tommy Ardolino.
Also see DAVIS, Skeeter, & NRBQ
Also see PERKINS, Carl, & NRBQ
Also see SEVEN OF US

NABAY
Singles: 7-inch
IMPACT (1032 "Believe It Or Not") 100-200 67

NABBIE, Jimmie
Singles: 7-inch
CARLTON (561 "Sweet Thing") 8-12 61
Also see BROWN DOTS
Also see FOUR TUNES

NACE, Johnny
Singles: 7-inch
JAN (131158 "You Got the Blues") 100-150
(Identification number shown since no selection number is used.)
JAN (131159 "Bashful Sorta Guy") 300-500
(Identification number shown since no selection number is used.)

NAKED TRUTH
Singles: 7-inch
DERAM (85061 "Two Little Room") 8-12 70
JUBILEE (5642 "The Wall") 5-10 68
RCA (9327 "Shing-a-Ling Thing") 5-10 67
Session: Tony Burrows.

NALL, Clint
Singles: 7-inch
CASE (1003 "Your Eyes") 15-25 59

NANTON, Morris
(Morris Nanton Trio)
Singles: 7-inch
PRESTIGE (345 "Ja Da") 5-10 65
PRESTIGE (368 "Black Orpheus") 5-10 65
PRESTIGE (384 "Something We've Got") ... 5-8 66
PRESTIGE (434 "Shadow of Your Smile") .. 5-8 67
LPs: 10/12-inch
PRESTIGE (7345 "Preface") 10-20 65
PRESTIGE (7409 "Something We've Got") 10-20 65
PRESTIGE (7467 "Soul Fingers") 10-20 67
W.B. (1256 "Flower Drum Song") 10-20 59
W.B. (1279 "Roberta – Original Jazz Performance") 10-20 59

NANTOS, Nick, & Fireballers
(Nick Nastos; Nick Masters)
LPs: 10/12-inch
STRAND 15-25 62
SUMMIT .... 10-15 '60s
Session: Bill Haley's Comets.
Also see HALEY, Bill

NANTZ, Pete
Singles: 7-inch
CLIX (3873 "Flip, Flop and Fly") 300-350

NAOMI & HARRIS
Singles: 7-inch
ATCO (6465 "You're My Baby") 5-10 67
ATCO (6543 "We Belong Together") 5-10 67

NAPOLEON
Singles: 7-inch
A.P.I. (334 "Magic Glasses") 5-10 65

NAPOLEON XIV *P&R '66*
(Jerry Samuels)
Singles: 7-inch
ERIC 4-6 76
W.B. (5800 series) 5-10 66
W.B. (7700 series) 4-6 73
LPs: 10/12-inch
RHINO .... 5-8 '80s
W.B. (W-1661 "They're Coming to Take Me Away") 50-60 66
(Monaural.)
W.B. (W-1661 "They're Coming to Take Me Away") 75-100 66
(White label. Promotional issue only.)
W.B. (WS-1661 "They're Coming to Take Me Away") 75-100 66
(Stereo.)
Also see IMPOSSIBLES
Also see SAMUELS, Jerry

NARDONE, Joe, & All Stars
Singles: 7-inch
MADISON (124 "Caravan") 8-12 60
RED BIRD (070 "Shake a Hand") 5-10 66
TIMES SQUARE (123 "Wiggle") 8-12 60

NARVIE, Don, & Visions
Singles: 7-inch
ALLEY (1027 "Little Latin Lupe Lu") 5-10 67

NASH, Cliff, & Rockaways
(Cliffie Nash)
Singles: 7-inch
DO-RA-ME (5027 "No Time for Sisters") . 40-60 61
DO-RA-ME (5028 "Jennie Lou") 50-75 61
KIM (1048 "This Little Boy's Gone Looking") 25-30
NASH (600 "Rampage") 50-75

NASH (601 "Cincinnati Rock") 40-60
NASH (602 "Band Stand") 40-60
Also see ROCKAWAYS

NASH, Gene

Singles: 78 rpm
JOSIE (826 "Beeline") 20-30 57
JUBILEE (5285 "Dandy Lion") 10-20 57
Singles: 7-inch
CAPITOL (4215 "I'm an Eskimo Too") 5-10 59
JOSIE (826 "Beeline") 20-30 57
JUBILEE (5285 "Dandy Lion") 10-20 57

NASH, Graham — P&R/LP '71

Singles: 7-inch
ATLANTIC (2000 series) 4-6 71-73
ATLANTIC (89000 series) 3-5 86
CAPITOL 3-6 79-80
Picture Sleeves
ATLANTIC 3-5 86
CAPITOL 4-6 79
LPs: 10/12-inch
ATLANTIC (7000 series) 8-12 71-73
ATLANTIC (81000 series) 5-8 86
CAPITOL 8-10 80
Also see CROSBY, STILLS & NASH
Also see HOLLIES
Also see MASON, Dave
Also see YOUNG, Neil, & Graham Nash

NASH, Johnny — P&R '57

Singles: 12-inch
EPIC 5-8 79
Singles: 7-inch
ABC-PAR 8-15 57-61
ARGO (5471 "Talk to Me") 5-10 64
ARGO (5479 "Always") 5-10 64
ARGO (5492 "Spring Is Here") 5-10 65
ARGO (5501 "I Know What I Want") 5-10 65
ATLANTIC (2344 "Big City") 5-10 66
BABYLON 5-10 69
CADET (5528 "Teardrops in the Rain") ... 10-20 66
EPIC 3-6 72-80
GROOVE (0018 "Helpless") 5-10 63
GROOVE (0021 "Deep in the Heart of Harlem") 20-40 63
GROOVE (0026 "It's No Good for Me") 5-10 63
GROOVE (0030 "I'm Leaving") 5-10 64
JAD (207 "Hold Me Tight") 5-10 68
JAD (209 "You Got Soul") 5-10 68
JAD (220 "Cupid") 5-10 69
JAD (223 "Groovey Feeling") 4-8 70
JANUS (136 "Falling in and out of Love") 4-8 70
JODA (102 "Let's Move and Groove") 5-10 65
JODA (105 "One More Time") 5-10 66
JODA (106 "Somewhere") 5-10 66
MGM (13637 "Amen") 5-10 66
MGM (13683 "You Never Know") 5-10 67
MGM (13805 "Stormy") 5-10 67
W.B. (5270 "Moment of Weakness") 5-10 62
W.B. (5301 "Ol' Man River") 5-10 62
W.B. (5336 "I'm Movin' On") 5-10 63
Picture Sleeves
ABC-PAR (9996 "As Time Goes By") 15-25 59
GROOVE (0018 "Helpless") 10-15 63
EPs: 7-inch
ABC-PAR 10-20 58-61
LPs: 10/12-inch
ABC-PAR 20-30 58-61
ARGO (4038 "Composer's Choice") 15-20 64
CADET 10-15 73
EPIC 10-15 72-74
JAD (1001 "Prince of Peace") 10-20 69
JAD (1006 "Soul Folk") 10-20 69
JAD (1207 "Hold Me Tight") 10-20 68
Also see ANKA, Paul, George Hamilton IV & Johnny Nash

NASH, Johnny, & Kim Weston

Singles: 7-inch
BANYAN TREE (1001 "We Try Harder") 5-10 69
Also see NASH, Johnny
Also see WESTON, Kim

NASH, Lloyd, & Cavaliers

Singles: 7-inch
GUM (1004 "The Right Time") 10-15 62
Also see CAVALIERS

NASH, Marvin, & Chevelles

Singles: 7-inch
COURIER (111 "Dina") 30-40 64
PHARAOH (115 "Dina") 50-75 61

NASHVILLE ALL-STARS

LPs: 10/12-inch
RCA (0126 "That Happy Nashville Sound") 8-12 67
RCA (LPM-2302 "After the Riot at Newport") 20-30 60
(Monaural.)
RCA (LSP-2302 "After the Riot at Newport") 25-35 60
(Stereo.)
Members: Chet Atkins; Boots Randolph; Hank Garland; Bob Moore; Floyd Cramer; Buddy Harman; Gary Burton; Brenton Banks.
Also see ATKINS, Chet
Also see CRAMER, Floyd
Also see MOORE, Bob
Also see RANDOLPH, Boots

NASHVILLE GUITARS

LPs: 10/12-inch
MONUMENT (8058 "Nashville Guitars") ..10-15 66
(Monaural.)
MONUMENT (18058 "Nashville Guitars") 15-20 66
(Stereo.)

NASHVILLE TEENS — P&R '64

Singles: 7-inch
LONDON (9689 "Tobacco Road") 10-20 64
(Blue label with silver print. Canadian.)
LONDON (9689 "Tobacco Road") 8-10 64
LONDON (9736 "Find My Way Back Home") 8-10 65
MGM 5-10 65-67
U.A. 4-6 72
LPs: 10/12-inch
LONDON (407 "Tobacco Road") 40-50 64
(Stereo.)
LONDON (3407 "Tobacco Road") 50-60 64
(Monaural.)
Members: Arthur Sharp; John Allen; Roger Groom; Ray Phillips; Barry Jenkins.

NASHVILLE TEENS / Los Bravos

Singles: 7-inch
LONDON (1058 "Tobacco Road"/"Black Is Black") ....4-6 '70s
Also see LOS BRAVOS
Also see NASHVILLE TEENS

NASTY SAVAGE

LPs: 10/12-inch
RESTLESS (72213 "Indulgence") 15-20 87
(Picture disc.)

NAT "THE COOL CAT"

Singles: 7-inch
TALOS ("Come By Here") 40-60
(Selection number not known.)

NATHUNE, Joe

Singles: 7-inch
JAY TONE (808 "Crazy") 5-10 61

NATION, Kerry

Singles: 78 rpm
WING (90059 "Half Your Heart") 5-10 56
Singles: 7-inch
WING (90059 "Half Your Heart") 10-20 56

NATIONAL GALLERY

LPs: 10/12-inch
PHILIPS (600266 "National Gallery") 20-30 68

NATIONAL LAMPOON — P&R/LP '72

Singles: 7-inch
BLUE THUMB 4-6 72-73
EPIC (193 "Have a Kung-Fu Christmas") 4-6 75
(Promotional issue only.)
LABEL 21 ....3-6 78-80
Picture Sleeves
EPIC (193 "Have a Kung-Fu Christmas") 4-6 75
(Promotional issue only.)
LABEL 21 ....3-6 78-80
EPs: 7-inch
EPIC (1095 "A History of the Beatles") 10-15 75
(Promotional issue only.)
LPs: 10/12-inch
BANANA 10-15 72-74
BLUE THUMB 10-15 72-74
EPIC 8-12 75-76
IMPORT 8-10 77
LABEL 21 (Except PIC-2001) 5-8 78-80
LABEL 21 (PIC-2001 "That's Not Funny, That's Sick") 20-30 80
(Picture disc.)
NATIONAL LAMPOON 15-20 74
PASSPORT 5-8 82
VISA 5-8 78
Members: John Belushi; Chevy Chase; Melissa Manchester; Tony Hendra; Jim Payne; John Lopresti.
Also see MANCHESTER, Melissa

NATIONAL OPINION POLL

Singles: 7-inch
PLANET (111 "Make Your Mark Little Man") 5-10 66

NATIONAL SALON GROUP

LPs: 10/12-inch
HALO (5010 "Music to Love By") 15-25

NATIONAL SOULS

Singles: 7-inch
LANOR (546 "Since I Met You Baby") 5-10 68

NATIVE BOYS

Singles: 78 rpm
COMBO 20-40 55-56
MODERN (939 "Native Girl") 75-125 54
Singles: 7-inch
COMBO (113 "Cherrlyn") 30-40 55
(Purple label.)
COMBO (113 "Cherrlyn") 10-15 56
(Red label.)
COMBO (115 "Tears") 75-125 56
(Purple label. Black wax.)
COMBO (115 "Tears") 15-20
(Red label. Red wax.)
COMBO (119 "Laughing Love") 50-75 56
(Purple label.)
COMBO (119 "Laughing Love") 10-15
(Red label.)
COMBO (120 "Oh Let Me Dream") 75-125 56
(Purple label.)
COMBO (120 "Oh Let Me Dream") 15-20
(Red label.)
MODERN (939 "Native Girl") 500-750 54
Members: Fred Romain; Vince Weaver.

NATO, Ray, & Kings

Singles: 7-inch
ENJAY (10 "I Don't Want to Leave You") .15-25

NATURAL FOUR — R&B '69

Singles: 7-inch
ABC (11205 "Why Should We Stop Now") ...4-6 69
ABC (11236 "Same Thing in Mind") 8-12 69
ABC (11253 "Hurt") 20-40 70
BOOLA BOOLA (2382 "I Thought You Were Mine") 40-60 69
BOOLA-BOOLA (6384 "Why Should We Stop Now") 40-60 69
(First issue. Note hyphen added to label name.)
CHESS 5-10 72
CURTOM 4-8 73-76
PATH 8-12
LPs: 10/12-inch
CURTOM 8-12 74-75
Members: Chris James; Steve Striplin; Del Mos Whitley; Darryl Canady.

NATURALE, Ralph

Singles: 7-inch
JEREE (2 "Go Find a Love") 10-15 65
WHITE ROCK (1059 "My Baby's Gone and Left Me") 50-75

NATURALS

Singles: 7-inch
MGM (11970 "Marty") 8-12 55
MGM (12358 "The Buccaneers") 8-12 56
Picture Sleeves
MGM (11970 "Marty") 25-35 55
(Pictures film stars Ernest Borgnine, Betsy Blair and other cast members.)
MGM (12358 "The Buccaneers") 20-30 56
(Pictures TV series stars from *The Buccaneers* and *Sir Lancelot.*)

NATURALS

Singles: 7-inch
BEACON (462 "You Gave Me So Much") 25-35 58

NATURALS

Singles: 7-inch
ERA (1089 "The Mummy") 10-15 59

NATURALS

Singles: 7-inch
HUNT (325 "Blue Moon") 8-12 59
RED TOP (113 "Blue Moon") 15-25 58
Also see FOUR NATURALS

NATURALS

Singles: 7-inch
SMASH (1875 "Let Love Be True") 8-12 64
SMASH (1925 "Different Girls") 8-12 64
SMASH (1972 "I'm the One") 8-12 65
Members: Carlton Black; Arthur Cox; Charles Perry; Charles Woolridge; Andrew Thomas.
Also see DUVALS
Also see MARVELOWS

NATURALS

Singles: 7-inch
JOWAR (120 "Internationally Me") 10-20 67
JOWAR (123 "Maiden in the East") 10-20 67

NATURE BOY & FRIENDS

Singles: 7-inch
BERTRAM INT'L (255 "Surfer John") 25-35 64

NAUTICALS

Singles: 7-inch
POLO (210 "Rockin' Chopin' ") 10-15 61

NAVARRO, Danny, & Corvels

Singles: 7-inch
N.J.N. (175 "La Bomba") 50-75 64

NAVARRO, Tommy

LPs: 10/12-inch
URANIA (5900 "Twist Around") 25-50 61

NAYLOR, Jerry — P&R '70/C&W '75

Singles: 7-inch
COLUMBIA 4-8 68-71
HITSVILLE 4-6 76
MC/CURB 4-6 78
MGM 6-6 71-72
MELODYLAND 4-6 74-75
OAK 3-5 80
PACIFIC CHALLENGER 3-5 82
SKYLA 10-15 61-62
SMASH (1971 "I Found You") 5-10 65
TOWER 5-15 65-68
W.B./CURB 4-6 79
WEST 3-5 86
Session: Davie Allan.
Also see ALLAN, Davie
Also see CRICKETS
Also see HONDELLS

NAYLOR, Jerry, & Kelli Warren — C&W '79

Singles: 7-inch
JEREMIAH (1002 "Don't Touch Me") 4-6 79
Also see NAYLOR, Jerry

NAZY, Ron Cameron

(Ron Cameron Nasey)
Singles: 7-inch
RENDEZVOUS (137 "The Panic") 10-20 60
TREY (3013 "The Great Debate") 10-20 60

NAZZ

Singles: 7-inch
VERY RECORD (001 "Lay Down and Die, Goodbye") 750-1000 67
Members: Vince "Alice Cooper" Furnier; M. Bruce; G. Buxton; D. Dunaway; Tom Speer.
Also see COOPER, Alice

NAZZ — LP '68

Singles: 7-inch
SGC (001 "Hello It's Me") 10-20 68
(Light yellow label. No horizontal lines.)
SGC (001 "Hello It's Me") 8-12 69
(Dark yellow label. With horizontal lines.)
SGC (001 "Hello It's Me") 4-8 70
(Green label with yellow top.)
SGC (006 "Not Wrong Long") 8-10 69
SGC (009 "Some People") 8-10 69
Picture Sleeves
SGC (001 "Hello It's Me") 30-40 68
SGC (006 "Not Wrong Long") 30-40 69
Promotional Singles
SGC (001 "Hello It's Me") 10-20 68
SGC (006 "Not Wrong Long") 10-15 69

SGC (009 "Some People") 10-15 69
SGC (009 "Kicks") 15-25 70
LPs: 10/12-inch
SGC (5001 "Nazz") 30-50 68
SGC (5002 "Nazz Nazz") 40-60 69
(Black vinyl.)
SGC (5002 "Nazz Nazz") 50-100 69
(Colored vinyl. Pink and orange label. SGC logo is blue. Identification number is 691531.)
SGC (5002 "Nazz Nazz") 50-100 69
(Colored vinyl. White label. Promotional issue only.)
SGC (5002 "Nazz Nazz") 75-100 69
(Colored vinyl. Mail-order edition. Red and orange label. SGC logo is purple. Identification number is 691531-MO.)
SGC (5004 "Nazz III") 30-50 71
(Black vinyl.)
SGC (5004 "Nazz III") 40-50 81
(Picture disc.)
Members: Todd Rundgren; Robert "Stewkey" Antoni; Carson Van Osten; Thom Mooney.
Also see RUNDGREN, Todd

NEAL, Abbie, & Her Ranch Girls
Singles: 7-inch
ADMIRAL (15000 "Hillbilly Beat") 15-25

NEAL, Debi
EP: 10-inch
PLEADEIANS (9164 "Not This Girl") 30-35 81
(Picture disc. Promotional issue only. 250 numbered copies made.)

NEAL, Jerry
(Jerry Capehart)
Singles: 7-inch
DOT (15810 "I Hates Rabbits") 50-75 58
KW (501 "Oh Baby") 50-75 59
Session: Eddie Cochran.
Also see CAPEHART, Jerry
Also see COCHRAN, Eddie

NEAL, Meredith
Singles: 7-inch
BLAZE (101 "Gertrude") 50-75

NEAL, Pamela
LPs: 10/12-inch
FREE FLIGHT (11555 "Charlie Hustle").. 25-30 79
(Picture disc. Promotional issue only.)
FREE FLIGHT (11555 "Charlie Hustle").. 40-45 79
(Picture disc. Promotional issue only. Autographed by Pete Rose.)

NEAL, Screamin' Joe
Singles: 7-inch
SHIPPINGS (1329 "Rock and Roll Deacon") 500-1000

NEAL & NEWCOMERS
Singles: 7-inch
HALLWAY (1206 "Rockin' Pneumonia").. 15-20 65
KIM (Colored vinyl) 4-6 86
Member: Bobby Mizzell.
Also see MIZZELL, Bobby

NEALY, Pepper
(With the Ace Trio)
Singles: 78 rpm
BULLET (297 "Fanny Brown") 15-25 48
BULLET (1056 "Rendezvous with a Rose") 15-25 48
Members: Pepper Nealy; Phil Ryan Osborne; Al Crocker; John Davis.

NEAVILLE, Arlie
(The Rockin' "A"; with Lindsey Sisters; Arlie Nevil)
Singles: 7-inch
FRATERNITY (900 "Alone on a Star") 10-15 62
FRATERNITY (1202 "Don't Throw Any Stones") 20-30 73
FRATERNITY (21122 "Gospel Music Man") 30-40 72
PING (8001 "Angel Love") 75-100 61
SHOUT N SHINE (143 "Sweet Side of Life") 4-6 75
SHOUT N SHINE (294 "It's Only Make Believe") 30-40 76
TELL INT'L (375 "Sunday Mornin'") 10-20 69
TELL INT'L (378 "Drink My Wine") 30-40 70
LPs: 10/12-inch
FRATERNITY (1021 "The Birth of Christ") 50-75 73
FRATERNITY (1025 "The Gospel Music Man") 75-100 73
FRATERNITY (3121 "He Saved My Soul") 15-25 74
Also see BARNES, Dorothy
Also see CARTER, Dean
Also see KINNEY, June
Also see MILLER, Arlie, & Bullets

NED & CAROLYN
Singles: 78 rpm
TNT (9004 "Old Rendezvous") 10-15 56
Singles: 7-inch
TNT (9004 "Old Rendezvous") 15-25 56

NED & GARY
Singles: 7-inch
LIBERTY (55160 "Lovin'") 25-50 58

NED & NELDA
Singles: 7-inch
VIGAH (002 "Hey Nelda") 75-100 63
Members: Frank Zappa; Ray Collins.
Also see LORD, Brian, & Midnighters
Also see ZAPPA, Frank

NEDD, Ramona
Singles: 7-inch
LIN (5009 "Rendezvous") 8-12 57

NEDITCH, Stan, & Relations
Singles: 7-inch
REGENCY (8001 "Honestly") 300-500

NEEVETS
Singles: 7-inch
REON (1303 "You're Gonna Pay") 10-15 64

NEIGHBORHOOD *P&R '70*
Singles: 7-inch
BIG TREE (102 "Big Yellow Taxi") 4-8 70
BIG TREE (106 "Laugh") 4-8 70
BULLET (102269 "Why Can't You See").. 15-25 69
LPs: 10/12-inch
BIG TREE (2001 "Debut") 10-15 70

NEIGHB'RHOOD CHILDR'N
(Neighborhood)
Singles: 7-inch
ACTA (813 "Maintain") 10-20 67
ACTA (823 "Happy Child") 10-15 68
ACTA (828 "Behold the Lilies") 10-20 68
DOT (17238 "Women Think") 10-15 69
NAM (2014 "Dancing in the Street") 10-15 '60s
LPs: 10/12-inch
ACTA (38005 "Neighb'rhood Childr'n") 60-90 68
Members: Rick Bolz; Dyan Hoffmann.

NEIGHBORS, Tex
Singles: 7-inch
EMERALD (2019 "Rock & Roll Dot") 250-300 58
EMERALD (2021 "Rockin' Beat") 150-200 58

NEIGHBORS COMPLAINT
EPs: 7-inch
KORNER BOYS (601 "Neighbors Complaint") 4-6 '80s
LPs: 10/12-inch
COLLECTABLES (5012 "Remember Then") 5-10 84
(Black vinyl.)
COLLECTABLES (PDR 15 "Remember Then") 10-15 82
(Picture disc.)

NEIL, Fred
(Freddie Neil)
Singles: 7-inch
BRUNSWICK (55117 "Listen Kitten") 15-25 59
CAPITOL (2047 "Dolphins") 15-25 68
CAPITOL (2091 "Felicity") 15-25 68
CAPITOL (2256 "Everybody's Talkin'") 15-25 68
CAPITOL (2604 "Everybody's Talkin'") 10-20 69
EPIC (9334 "Love's Funny") 10-15 59
EPIC (9403 "You Don't Have to Be a Baby to Cry") 10-15 60
EPIC (9435 "Rainbow and the Rose") 10-15 59
LOOK (1002 "You Ain't Treatin' Me Right") 50-60 58
LPs: 10/12-inch
CAPITOL (294 "Everybody's Talkin'") 20-30 69
CAPITOL (2665 "Fred Neil") 30-40 67
CAPITOL (2862 "Sessions") 30-40 68
Also see MARTIN, Vince

NEIL & JACK
Singles: 7-inch
DUEL (508 "You Are My Love at Last") 300-400 62
DUEL (517 "I'm Afraid") 300-400 62
Members: Neil Diamond; Jack Parker.
Also see DIAMOND, Neil

NEISWANDER, Oscar
Singles: 7-inch
AZALEA (139 "King of Hearts") 50-75

NELLIS, Jimmy
Singles: 7-inch
TOJON (101 "Rockin' Rocket") 550-650

NELSON, Bobby, Quartet
Singles: 7-inch
LE RON (101 "There Ain't Nothin' True About You") 200-300

NELSON, Carrie
Singles: 7-inch
COED (534 "It's Me") 8-12 60

NELSON, Chip
(Earl Nelson)
Singles: 7-inch
ASTRA (1011 "Honey for Sale") 5-10 65
EDSEL (783 "Honey for Sale") 20-30 60
Also see NELSON, Earl

NELSON, Clare
Singles: 7-inch
EPIC (9250 "Shake Me I Rattle") 10-15 57
Picture Sleeves
EPIC (9250 "Shake Me I Rattle") 20-30 57

NELSON, Clarence
Singles: 7-inch
MGM (13752 "Good Times") 5-10 67
PEN (352 "I Hurt") 5-10 64

NELSON, Darwin, & Blaze Makers
Singles: 7-inch
FIRE (5001 "Good Gosh Gertie") 200-300 '50s
FIRE (5002 "Lazy Lu") 300-400 '50s
TEK (1014 "Lazy Lu") 100-150 59

NELSON, Earl
(With the Pelicans)
Singles: 78 rpm
CLASS (209 "I Bow to You") 100-200 57
Singles: 7-inch
CLASS (209 "I Bow to You") 200-300 57
EBB (164 "Come On") 20-30 59
Also see BOB & EARL
Also see CHURCH, Eugene
Also see HOLLYWOOD FLAMES
Also see LEE, Jackie
Also see NELSON, Chip
Also see SATELLITES
Also see VOICES

NELSON, Jay
(With His Jumpers)
Singles: 7-inch
DREW-BLAN 5-10 61-62
EXCELLO (2149 "Fool That Was Blind") 5-10 59
EXCELLO (2165 "To You My Darlin'") 5-10 59
EXCELLO (2178 "Don't You Wanna Man Like Me") 5-10 60
HOLLYWOOD (1088 "Raise Some Sand") 50-75 58

NELSON, Jimmie *R&B '51*
(With the Peter Rabbit Trio; Jimmy Nelson)
Singles: 78 rpm
CHESS 15-25 53
OLLIET (100 "Baby Chile") 100-200 48
RPM 10-20 51-54
Singles: 7-inch
ALL BOY (8502 "She Was So Good to Me") 5-10 62
CHESS (1587 "Free & Easy Mind") 25-50 53
CHESS (1877 "Tell Me Who") 8-12 63
KENT (354 "Unlock the Door") 5-10 61
RPM (325 "T-99 Blues") 100-200 51
RPM (329 "Baby Child") 500-750 51
(Only two known copies.)
RPM (353 "Big Eyed, Brown Eyed Girl of Mine") 100-200 52
RPM (368 "Little Rich Girl") 50-75 52
RPM (377 "Little Miss Teasin' Brown") 50-75 53
RPM (385 "Meet Me with Your Black Dress On") 25-50 53
RPM (389 "Second Hand Fool") 25-50 53
RPM (397 "Mean Poor Girl") 25-50 54
RPM (463 "T-99 Blues") 25-50 56
Also see TURNER, Joe / Jimmy Nelson

NELSON, Johnny
Singles: 7-inch
UP TOWN (757 "I'd Rather Lose You") 40-60 59

NELSON, Lady, & Lords
Singles: 7-inch
DUNHILL (4121 "Monday Monday") 5-10 68
LPs: 10/12-inch
DUNHILL (50028 "Piccadilly Pickle") 10-15 68
Member: Porta Nelson.

NELSON, Larry
LPs: 10/12-inch
WORLD PACIFIC (1836 "In Harmonica") 10-20 65

NELSON, Lloyd
Singles: 78 rpm
ABBOTT (3026 "Sentimental Dreamer") 5-10 57
Singles: 7-inch
ABBOTT (3026 "Sentimental Dreamer").. 10-15 57
SYMBOL (903 "Blues After Midnight") 20-30 59

NELSON, Martha
Singles: 7-inch
RIC (975 "Bless You Darling") 10-15 60
Also see CARTER, Martha

NELSON, Nate
Singles: 7-inch
PRIGAN (2001 "Once Again") 10-20 61
Also see FLAMINGOS
Also see PLATTERS

NELSON, Peppermint
(Harrison Nelson)
Singles: 78 rpm
GOLD STAR (626 "Peppermint Boogie") 30-50 47
Also see PEPPERMINT HARRIS

NELSON, Rick *P&R/R&B/LP '57*
(With the Stone Canyon Band; with Jordanaires; Ricky Nelson)
Singles: 12-inch
CAPITOL 5-10 82
Singles: 78 rpm
IMPERIAL (5463 "Be-Bop Baby") 50-75 57
IMPERIAL (5483 "Stood Up") 50-75 57
IMPERIAL (5503 "Believe What You Say") 75-100 58
IMPERIAL (5528 "Poor Little Fool") 100-150 58
VERVE (10047 "A Teenager's Romance") 50-100 57
VERVE (10070 "You're My One and Only Love") 100-150 57
(Flip side is a Barney Kessel instrumental.)
Singles: 7-inch
DECCA (31475 "I Got a Woman") 8-12 63
DECCA (31495 "String Along") 8-12 63
DECCA (31533 "Fools Rush In") 8-12 63
DECCA (31574 "For You") 8-12 63
DECCA (31612 "The Very Thought of You") 8-12 64
DECCA (31656 "There's Nothing I Can Say") 5-10 64
DECCA (31703 "A Happy Guy") 5-10 64
DECCA (31756 "Mean Old World") 5-10 65
DECCA (31800 "Yesterday's Love") 5-10 66
DECCA (31845 "Love & Kisses") 5-10 66
DECCA (31900 "Fire Breathin' Dragon") 5-10 66
DECCA (31956 "Louisiana Man") 5-10 66
DECCA (32026 "Alone") 5-10 67
DECCA (32055 "They Don't Give Medals") 5-10 66
DECCA (32120 "Take a City Bride") 5-10 67
DECCA (32176 "Suzanne on a Sunday Morning") 5-10 67
DECCA (32222 "Dream Weaver") 5-10 67
DECCA (32284 "Don't Blame It on Your Wife") 5-10 68
DECCA (32298 "Don't Make Promises") 5-10 68
DECCA (32550 "Promises") 5-10 69
DECCA (32635 "Easy to Be Free") 5-10 70
DECCA (32676 "I Shall Be Released") 5-10 70
DECCA (32711 "Look at Mary") 5-10 70
DECCA (32779 "California") 5-10 71
DECCA (32860 "Thank You Lord") 5-10 71
DECCA (32906 "Gypsy Pilot") 5-10 71

DECCA (32980 "Garden Party")..................5-10 72
DECCA (34193 "Gypsy Woman"/"For Your Sweet Love")... 15-25 63
(Compact 33 stereo. As many as five other stereo singles, with tracks from the *For Your Sweet Love* LP, may exist – though we do not yet have those numbers and titles.)
DECCA (732635 "Easy to Be Free")........ 10-20 70
(Stereo.)
CAPITOL...4-8 82
EPIC...3-6 77-86
IMPERIAL (008 thru 032)..............................5-8 '60s
(Back-to-Back Hits series.)
IMPERIAL (5463 "Be-Bop Baby")........... 40-50 57
(Red label.)
IMPERIAL (5463 "Be-Bop Baby")........... 30-40 57
(Maroon label.)
IMPERIAL (5463 "Be-Bop Baby")........... 10-20 58
(Black label.)
IMPERIAL (5483 "Stood Up").................. 25-35 57
(Maroon label.)
IMPERIAL (5483 "Stood Up").................. 10-20 58
(Black label.)
IMPERIAL (5503 "Believe What You Say").. 15-25 58
IMPERIAL (5528 "Poor Little Fool")......... 15-25 58
IMPERIAL (5545 "Lonesome Town")....... 15-25 58
(Black vinyl.)
IMPERIAL (5545 "Lonesome Town")... 150-200 58
(Colored vinyl.)
IMPERIAL (5565 "It's Late")..................... 15-25 59
IMPERIAL (5595 "Just a Little Too Much")... 10-20 59
IMPERIAL (5614 "Mighty Good")............ 10-20 59
IMPERIAL (5663 "Young Emotions")....... 10-20 60
IMPERIAL (5685 "I'm Not Afraid")........... 10-20 60
IMPERIAL (5707 "You Are the Only One").. 10-20 60
IMPERIAL (5741 "Travelin' Man")........... 10-15 61
(Black vinyl.)
IMPERIAL (X5741 "Travelin' Man") 400-600 61
(Red vinyl.)
IMPERIAL (5770 "A Wonder Like You").. 10-15 61
IMPERIAL (5805 "Young World")............ 10-15 62
IMPERIAL (5864 "Teen Age Idol").......... 10-15 62
IMPERIAL (5901 "It's Up to You")........... 10-15 62
IMPERIAL (5910 "That's All").................. 10-15 63
IMPERIAL (5935 "Old Enough to Love") . 10-15 63
IMPERIAL (5958 "Long Vacation") 8-12 63
(Black vinyl.)
IMPERIAL (5958 "Long Vacation") 50-100 63
(Colored vinyl.)
IMPERIAL (5985 "Time After Time")........ 10-12 63
IMPERIAL (54031 "It's Late").......................5-8 '60s
(Back-to-Back Hits series.)
IMPERIAL (66004 "Today's Teardrops") . 10-15 63
IMPERIAL (66017 "Congratulations").................................... 10-15 64
IMPERIAL (66039 "Lucky Star").............. 10-15 64
LIBERTY...3-5 '80s
MCA...3-8 73-86
VERVE (10047 "A Teenager's Romance")... 35-45 57
VERVE (10070 "You're My One and Only Love").. 35-45 57
(Flip side is a Barney Kessel instrumental.)

Picture Sleeves

DECCA (31475 "I Got a Woman") 10-20 63
DECCA (31495 "String Along") 10-20 63
DECCA (31533 "Fools Rush In") 10-20 63
DECCA (31574 "For You") 10-20 63
DECCA (31612 "The Very Thought of You").. 10-20 64
DECCA (31656 "There's Nothing I Can Say").. 30-40 64
DECCA (31703 "A Happy Guy") 30-40 64
DECCA (31756 "Mean Old World")......... 10-20 65
DECCA (31800 "Yesterday's Love")........ 10-20 66
DECCA (31845 "Love & Kisses")............ 10-20 66
DECCA (31900 "Fire Breathin' Dragon").. 500-750 66
DECCA (31956 "Louisiana Man") 10-20 66
DECCA (32026 "Alone")........................... 10-20 67
DECCA (32120 "Take a City Bride")........ 10-20 67
DECCA (32635 "Easy to Be Free")........... 10-20 70
EPIC...3-5 86
IMPERIAL (5463 "Be-Bop Baby") 40-50 57
IMPERIAL (5483 "Stood Up").................. 30-40 57
IMPERIAL (5503 "Believe What You Say").. 20-30 58
IMPERIAL (5528 "Poor Little Fool")............5-10 '90s
IMPERIAL (5545 "Lonesome Town") 20-30 58
IMPERIAL (5565 "It's Late").......................15-25 59
IMPERIAL (5595 "Just a Little Too Much")..15-25 59
IMPERIAL (5614 "Mighty Good")..............15-25 59
IMPERIAL (5663 "Young Emotions")..........15-20 60
IMPERIAL (5685 "I'm Not Afraid")............15-20 60
IMPERIAL (5707 "You Are the Only One")..15-20 60
IMPERIAL (5741 "Travelin' Man")..............15-20 61
IMPERIAL (5770 "A Wonder Like You")...15-20 61
IMPERIAL (5805 "Young World") 10-20 62
IMPERIAL (5864 "Teen Age Idol")............10-20 62
IMPERIAL (5901 "It's Up to You")..............10-20 62
IMPERIAL (5935 "Old Enough to Love") ..10-20 63
IMPERIAL (66004 "Today's Teardrops") ..10-20 63
MCA...3-6 86

EPs: 7-inch

DECCA (2760 "One Boy Too Late") 25-50 63
DECCA (4419 "For Your Sweet Love") 25-50 63
(Juke box issue only. Includes title strips.)
DECCA (4460 "Best Always")...................25-50 65
(Juke box issue only. Includes title strips.)
IMPERIAL (153/154/155 "Ricky") 50-75 58
(Price is for any of three volumes.)
IMPERIAL (156/157/158 "Ricky Nelson") .50-75 58
(Price is for any of three volumes.)
IMPERIAL (159/160/161 "Ricky Sings Again")..50-75 58
(Price is for any of three volumes.)
IMPERIAL (162/163/164 "Songs By Ricky")..50-75 59
(Price is for any of three volumes.)
IMPERIAL (165 "Ricky Sings Spirituals") .50-75 60
VERVE (5048 "Ricky")............................75-100 57
(Includes one track by Barney Kessell.)

LPs: 10/12-inch

CAPITOL...5-8 81
DECCA (DL-4419 "For Your Sweet Love")..25-50 63
(Monaural.)
DECCA (DL7-4419 "For Your Sweet Love")..25-50 63
(Stereo.)
DECCA (DL-4479 "For You") 25-50 63
(Monaural.)
DECCA (DL7-4479 "For You") 25-50 63
(Stereo.)
DECCA (DL-4559 "The Very Thought of You")..25-50 64
(Monaural.)
DECCA (DL7-4559 "The Very Thought of You")..25-50 64
(Stereo.)
DECCA (DL-4608 "Spotlight on Rick") 25-50 64
(Monaural.)
DECCA (DL7-4608 "Spotlight on Rick") ...25-50 64
(Stereo.)
DECCA (DL-4660 "Best Always") 25-50 65
(Monaural.)
DECCA (DL7-4660 "Best Always") 25-50 65
(Stereo.)
DECCA (DL-4678 "Love and Kisses")......25-50 65
(Monaural.)
DECCA (DL7-4678 "Love and Kisses") 25-50 65
(Stereo.)
DECCA (DL-4779 "Bright Lights and Country Music")..25-50 66
(Monaural.)
DECCA (DL7-4779 "Bright Lights and Country Music")..25-50 66
(Stereo.)
DECCA (DL-4827 "Country Fever")..........25-50 67
(Monaural.)
DECCA (DL7-4827 "Country Fever")........25-50 67
(Stereo.)
DECCA (DL-4944 "Another Side of Rick")..25-50 67
(Monaural.)
DECCA (DL7-4944 "Another Side of Rick")..25-50 67
(Stereo.)
DECCA (75014 "Perspective")..................15-25 68
DECCA (75162 "In Concert")...................15-25 70
DECCA (75236 "Rick Sings Nelson") 15-25 70
DECCA (75297 "Rudy the Fifth") 15-25 71
DECCA (75391 "Garden Party")................15-25 72
EPIC...8-15 77-86
EPIC/NU-DISK...10-15 81
IMPERIAL (9048 "Ricky")..........................50-80 57
("Imperial" across top of label.)
IMPERIAL (9048 "Ricky")..........................15-25 64
("IR-Imperial" logo on left.)
IMPERIAL (9050 "Ricky Nelson") 45-65 58
("Imperial" across top of label.)
IMPERIAL (9050 "Ricky Nelson") 15-25 64
("IR-Imperial" logo on left.)
IMPERIAL (9061 "Ricky Sings Again").....25-50 59
(Monaural.)
IMPERIAL (9082 "Songs By Ricky").........25-50 59
(Monaural.)
IMPERIAL (9122 "More Songs By Ricky")..25-50 60
(Monaural.)
IMPERIAL (9152 "Rick Is 21") 20-40 61
(Monaural.)
IMPERIAL (9167 "Album Seven")............20-40 62
(Monaural.)
IMPERIAL (9218 "Best Sellers")...............20-40 63
(Monaural.)
IMPERIAL (9223 "It's Up to You")............20-40 63
(Monaural.)
IMPERIAL (9232 "Million Sellers By Rick Nelson")..20-40 63
(Monaural.)
IMPERIAL (9244 "Long Vacation") 20-40 63
(Monaural.)
IMPERIAL (9251 "Rick Nelson Sings for You")..20-40 63
(Monaural.)
IMPERIAL (12030 "Songs By Ricky").....50-100 59
(Stereo.)
IMPERIAL (12059 "More Songs By Ricky")..40-60 60
(Stereo. Black vinyl.)
IMPERIAL (12059 "More Songs By Ricky")..300-400 60
(Stereo. Blue vinyl.)
IMPERIAL (12071 "Rick Is 21") 20-40 61
(Stereo.)
IMPERIAL (12082 "Album Seven")...........20-40 62
(Stereo.)
IMPERIAL (12090 "Ricky Sings Again")...20-30 64
(Stereo.)
IMPERIAL (12218 "Best Sellers") 20-40 63
(Stereo.)
IMPERIAL (12223 "It's Up to You")...........20-40 63
(Stereo.)
IMPERIAL (12232 "Million Sellers By Rick Nelson")..20-40 64
(Stereo.)
IMPERIAL (12244 "Long Vacation").........20-40 63
(Stereo.)
IMPERIAL (12251 "Rick Nelson Sings for You")..20-40 64
(Stereo.)
LIBERTY...5-10 81-83
MCA (Except 1517) 10-15 73-74
MCA (1517 "The Decca Years") 5-10 82
MCA/SILVER EAGLE...................................5-10 86
RHINO (Except 259)....................................5-10 85
RHINO (259 "Greatest Hits").......................8-12 85
(Picture disc.)
SESSIONS (1003 "Ricky Nelson Story")..15-30 79
(Three-disc, mail-order offer.)
SUNSET (1118 "Rick Nelson") 10-20 66
SUNSET (5205 "I Need You") 10-20 68
TIME-LIFE...10-15 86
U.A. (330 "Very Best of Rick Nelson")......10-15 75
U.A. (1004 "Ricky")......................................5-10 80
U.A. (9960 "Legendary Masters") 15-25 71
VERVE (2083 "Teen Time")..................200-300 57
(Also contains tracks by Randy Sparks; Gary Williams; Jeff Allen; Rock Murphy; and Barney Kessel.)
Session: Four Preps; Barney Kessel; Tiny Timbrell; Jack Marshall; Plas Johnson; Gloria Woods; Joe Maphis; James Burton; Joe Osborn; Randy Meisner; Richie Frost; Jerry Fuller; Jordanaires; Al Kemp; Steve Duncan; Dave Burgess; Glen Campbell; Pete Jolly; Tommy Tedesco; Blossoms; Jack Halloran Singers.
Also see APPLETREE THEATRE CO.
Also see BLOSSOMS
Also see BURGESS, Dave
Also see BURTON, James
Also see DILLARDS
Also see FLEAS
Also see FOUR PREPS
Also see FULLER, Jerry
Also see GRAPPELLI, Stephane, & Barney Kessel
Also see HALLORAN, Jack, Singers
Also see JIM & JOE
Also see JOHNSON, Plas
Also see JOLLY, Pete
Also see JORDANAIRES
Also see KESSEL, Barney / Grant Green / Oscar Moore / Mundell Lowe
Also see MARTIN, Dean, & Ricky Nelson
Also see MOON, Keith
Also see RIVERS, Johnny / Ricky Nelson / Randy Sparks
Also see SZIGETI, Sandy
Also see TEDESCO, Tommy
Also see TROPHIES

NELSON, Rick, & Jack Lemmon

Singles: 7-inch

THEATRE PROMOTION RECORD (760 "Do You Know What It Means to Miss New Orleans") 150-200 60
(Promotional issue, made for theater play.)
Also see LEMMON, Jack

NELSON, Rick / Joannie Sommers / Dona Jean Young

LPs: 10/12-inch

DECCA (DL-4836 "On the Flip Side") 20-30 66
(Monaural.)
DECCA (DL7-4836 "On the Flip Side") 25-35 66
(Stereo.)
Also see NELSON, Rick
Also see SOMMERS, Joannie

NELSON, Sandy *P&R/R&B '59*

Singles: 7-inch

COLLECTABLES ....3-5 '80s
ERA..4-6 72
IMPERIAL 4-8 61-69
LIBERTY ....3-5 '80s
ORIGINAL SOUND (5 "Teen Beat")........10-15 59
U.A. 4-6 74
VEEBLETRONICS 3-5 81

EPs: 7-inch

IMPERIAL 10-20 65
(Stereo juke box "Little LPs.")

LPs: 10/12-inch

IMPERIAL (Except 9105/12044) 10-25 61-69
IMPERIAL (9105 "Teen Beat") 20-30 60
(Monaural.)
IMPERIAL (12044 "Teen Beat") 20-30 60
(Stereo.)
LIBERTY 5-10 82-83
SKYCLAD 5-8 89
SUNSET...10-20 66-70
U.A. 8-12 75
Also see A'KIES
Also see ALLEN, Richie
Also see GAMBLERS
Also see HOLLYWOOD ARGYLES
Also see TEDDY BEARS
Also see TYLER & FLIPS

NELSON, Tommy

Singles: 7-inch

DIXIE (814 "Hobo Hop")......................750-1000 '50s
DIXIE (919 "Like Let's Get Out")............50-100 '50s

NELSON, Vikki

(Vikki Nelson & Sounds)

Singles: 78 rpm

PREMIUM (402 "By My Side")..................10-15 55

Singles: 7-inch

MALA (434 "Playboy")................................8-12 61
PREMIUM (402 "By My Side")..................30-40 55
VIK (0273 "Like a Baby")........................10-20 57

NELSON, Willie *C&W '62*

(Willy Nelson)

Singles: 78 rpm

SARG (260 "A Storm Has Just Begun")..100-200 55

Singles: 7-inch

AMERICAN GOLD 4-6 76
ATLANTIC...4-6 73-75
BETTY (5702 "Misery Mansion")..............10-15 64
BETTY (5703 "A Man with the Blues")......10-15 64
BELLAIRE (107 "Night Life")....................15-25 63
(Black vinyl.)
BELLAIRE (107 "Night Life")....................40-50 63
(Colored vinyl.)
BELLAIRE (5000 series)...............................4-6 76
CAPITOL...4-6 78
COLUMBIA 3-6 75-91

COLUMBIA (1183 "Rudolph the Red-Nosed Reindeer")....5-10 79
(Red vinyl. Promotional issue only.)
D (1084 "Man With the Blues")....15-25 59
D (1131 "What a Way to Live")....15-25 60
DOUBLE BARREL....4-8
EVATONE/MUSIGRAM (92828 "Blue Christmas")....4-6 79
(Flexi-disc.)
LIBERTY (55155 "No Dough")....15-25 58
LIBERTY (55386 "Mr. Record Man")....10-20 61
LIBERTY (55439 thru 55697)....8-12 62-64
LIBERTY (56143 "I Hope So")....5-10 69
LONE STAR....4-6 78
MONUMENT (800 series)....5-10 64
RCA (0100 thru 0800 series)....4-8 69-72
RCA (8500 thru 9900 series)....5-10 65-71
RCA (10000 thru 12000 series)....3-6 75-81
SARG (260 "A Storm Has Just Begun")....200-300 55
SONGBIRD....3-5 80
U.A. (641 "Night Life")....5-10 63
U.A. (700 thru 1200 series)....4-6 76-78
WILLIE NELSON (628 "No Place for Me")....150-250 57
(Reportedly 3,000 made.)

Picture Sleeves

COLUMBIA....3-5 84
RCA (12254 "Good Times")....4-6 81

EPs: 7-inch

COLUMBIA (2687 "Red Headed Stranger")....8-12 75
(Promotional only issue.)

LPs: 10/12-inch

ACCORD....5-8 82-83
ALLEGIANCE....5-8 83
ATLANTIC....8-12 73-76
AUDIO FIDELITY (213 "Willie Nelson")...15-20
(Picture disc.)
AURA....5-8 82-83
BACK-TRAC....5-8
CAMDEN....8-12 70-74
CASINO....8-10 84
COLUMBIA (30000 series, except 38250 and picture discs)....5-15 75-91
COLUMBIA (38250 "Willie Nelson")....75-100 83
(Boxed, 10-disc set. Includes poster. Nine are black vinyl and one, *Always on My Mind*, is a picture disc.)
COLUMBIA (35305 "Stardust")....30-50 78
(Picture disc.)
COLUMBIA (39943 "Always on My Mind")....15-25 83
(Picture disc.)
COLUMBIA (40000 series, except "HC," half-speed mastered series)....5-10 85-90
COLUMBIA (HC-40000 series)....20-35 82-83
(Half-speed mastered.)
DELTA....5-8 82
DOUBLE BARRELL....15-25
EXACT....5-8 83
HBO (171010 "Willie Nelson & Family")..30-40 83
(Picture disc. Promotional issue only.)
H.S.R.D....8-10 84
HEARTLAND....10-15 87
HOT SCHATZ....5-10 84
LIBERTY (3239 "And Then I Wrote")....25-35 62
(Monaural.)
LIBERTY (7239 "And Then I Wrote")....30-40 62
(Stereo.)
LIBERTY (10000 series)....5-10 '80s
LONE STAR....8-12 78
MCA....5-10 80
MASTERS....5-10
OUT OF TOWN DIST....5-10
PICKWICK....5-10 74-76
PICKWICK/CAMDEN....5-10 '70s
PLANTATION....5-10 82
POTOMAC....10-15 82
PREMORE....5-10
RCA (1100 thru 3200 series)....5-15 75-79
RCA (LPM-3400 thru LPM-3900 series)..15-25 65-68
(Monaural.)
RCA (LSP-3400 thru LSP-4700 series)...10-25 65-72
(Stereo.)
RCA (3600 thru 4800 series)....5-8 80-83
(With "AYL1" prefix.)
RCA (7158 "Willie")....5-8 85
RCA/CANDELITE....8-10 80
SHOTGUN....20-30 77
SOLID GOLD....5-10
SONGBIRD....5-10 80
SUNSET....10-20 66
TAKOMA....5-8 83
TIME-LIFE (16000 series)....15-25 83
(Three discs.)
U.A. 8-12 73-78
Session: Paul Buskirk; Herb Remington; Bob White; Clyde Brewer; Dick Shannon; Pete Wade; Ray Edenton; Jimmy Day; Hargus "Pig" Robbins; Bob Moore; Willie Ackerman; Billy Strange; Glen Campbell; Leon Russell; Red Callender; Muddy Berry; Harold Bradley; David Briggs; Anita Kerr Singers; Ernie Freeman; Cal Smith; Jerry Reed; Buddy Emmons; Velma Smith; Johnny Bush; Chet Atkins; Bill Pursell; Roy Huskey; Buddy Harman; Buddy Spicher.
Also see ATKINS, Chet
Also see BRUCE, Ed
Also see BUSH, Johnny
Also see BUSKIRK, Paul, & His Little Men
Also see CAMPBELL, Glen
Also see CHARLES, Ray, & Willie Nelson
Also see COCHRAN, Hank, & Willie Nelson
Also see COE, David Allan, & Willie Nelson
Also see EDDY, Duane
Also see GATLIN, Larry
Also see FREEMAN, Ernie
Also see HAGGARD, Merle, & Willie Nelson
Also see HARRIS, Emmylou
Also see JENNINGS, Waylon, & Willie Nelson
Also see KERR, Anita
Also see KRISTOFFERSON, Kris, Willie Nelson, Dolly Parton, & Brenda Lee
Also see LEE, Brenda, & Willie Nelson
Also see MILLER, Roger, & Willie Nelson
Also see MOORE, Bob
Also see MYERS, Augie
Also see PARTON, Dolly, & Willie Nelson
Also see PRICE, Ray, & Willie Nelson
Also see REED, Jerry
Also see SAHM, Doug
Also see STEELE, Don / Willie Nelson
Also see STRANGE, Billy
Also see TUBB, Ernest

NELSON, Willie / Nat "King" Cole / Johnny Mathis / Shirley Bassey

EPs: 7-inch

JIMMY McHUGH (300 "Three Guys and a Gal")....8-12 81
(Promotional issue only. Includes Jimmy McHugh bio insert)
Also see BASSEY, Shirley
Also see COLE, Nat "King"
Also see MATHIS, Johnny

NELSON, Willie, & Shirley Collie — C&W '62

Singles: 7-inch

LIBERTY (55403 "Willingly")....15-20 62
LIBERTY (55468 "You Dream About Me")..8-12 62
Also see COLLIE, Shirley

NELSON, Willie, & Kris Kristofferson — C&W/LP '84

LPs: 10/12-inch

COLUMBIA....5-8 84
Also see KRISTOFFERSON, Kris

NELSON, Willie, & Brenda Lee — C&W '83

Singles: 7-inch

MONUMENT....3-5 83
Also see LEE, Brenda

NELSON, Willie / Johnny Lee / Mickey Gilley

LPs: 10/12-inch

PLANTATION....5-8 82
Also see GILLEY, Mickey

NELSON, Willie / Jerry Lee Lewis / Carl Perkins / David Allan Coe

LPs: 10/12-inch

PLANTATION....5-10 75
Also see COE, David Allan
Also see LEWIS, Jerry Lee
Also see PERKINS, Carl

NELSON, Willie, & Webb Pierce — C&W '82

Singles: 7-inch

COLUMBIA....3-5 82

LPs: 10/12-inch

COLUMBIA....5-8 82
Also see PIERCE, Webb

NELSON, Willie, & Ray Price — C&W/LP '80

Singles: 7-inch

COLUMBIA....3-5 80

LPs: 10/12-inch

COLUMBIA....5-8 80
Also see PRICE, Ray

NELSON, Willie, & Leon Russell — C&W '79

Singles: 7-inch

COLUMBIA....4-6 79

LPs: 10/12-inch

COLUMBIA....5-10 79
Also see RUSSELL, Leon

NELSON, Willie, & Hank Wilson — C&W '84

Singles: 7-inch

PARADISE....3-5 84

NELSON, Willie / Faron Young

LPs: 10/12-inch

COLUMBIA....5-10
ROMULUS (6056 "Willie Nelson and Faron Young")....5-10
Also see NELSON, Willie
Also see YOUNG, Faron

NEON PHILHARMONIC — P&R '69

Singles: 7-inch

MCA....4-6 76
TRX (5039 "Love Will Find a Way")....4-6 72
W.B. 4-8 69-71

LPs: 10/12-inch

W.B. 10-15 69

NEONS

Singles: 78 rpm

TETRA....25-35 56-57

Singles: 7-inch

CHALLENGE (9147 "Magic Moment")....50-75 62
(White label. Promotional issue only.)
CHALLENGE (9147 "Magic Moment")....40-60 62
(Green label.)
CHALLENGE (59147 "Magic Moment")...10-20 63
(Black label.)
GONE (5090 "Angel Face")....15-25 60
ROULETTE GOLDEN GOODIES....4-6 '70s
TETRA (4444 "Angel Face")....15-25 56
(Yellow label.)
TETRA (4444 "Angel Face")....40-50 56
(Light pink label.)
TETRA (4449 "Road to Romance")....30-40 57
VINTAGE (1016 "Golden Dreams")....10-15 73
(Purple vinyl.)
Members: Frank Vignari; Jeff Pearl; Norm Isacoff; Ron Derin.

NEONS

Singles: 7-inch

WALDON (1001 "My Lover")....400-600 61

NEOPHONIC STRING BAND

LPs: 10/12-inch

DIRECT to DISK (105 "Neophonic String Band")....10-20 79
Member: Jim Glaser.
Also see GLASER, Jim

NEPENTHE

Singles: 7-inch

DIRECTION (4003 "Good Morning Baby")....10-20 '60s

NEPTUNES

Singles: 78 rpm

GLORY (269 "As Long As")....15-25 57

Singles: 7-inch

GLORY (269 "As Long As")....30-40 57

NEP-TUNES

Singles: 7-inch

THREE RIVERS (111 "Don't Condemn Me")....50-75 '50s

NEP-TUNES

LPs: 10/12-inch

FAMILY (FLP-152 "Surfer's Holiday")....50-75 63
(Monaural.)
FAMILY (SFLP-152 "Surfer's Holiday")..75-100 63
(Stereo.)
Members: Al Torzelli; Steve Marcus; Ed Hawkins; Richard Schweitzer.

NEPTUNES

Singles: 7-inch

CHECKER (967 "So Little Time")....10-15 60
(Same number used on a Vibrations release.)
GEM (100 "Turn Around")....15-25 63
INSTANT (3255 "Make a Memory")....15-25 63
PAYSON (102 "If You Care")....15-25 58
RCA (7931 "This Is Love")....8-12 61
VICTORIA (102 "I Don't Cry Anymore")..50-100 64
Also see VIBRATIONS

NEPTUNES

Singles: 7-inch

MARLO (1534 "I Met You")....30-40 64

NEPTUNES

Singles: 7-inch

W.B. (5453 "Shame Girl")....5-10 64

NERO, Frances

Singles: 7-inch

SOUL (35020 "Keep on Lovin' Me")....10-20 66

NERO, Paul

(Paul Nero's Blues Sounds)

Singles: 7-inch

FONTANA (1951 "Nut Shaker")....5-10 64
LIBERTY (56082 "Light My Fire")....5-10 68

NERVOUS BREAKDOWNS

Singles: 7-inch

TAKE 6 (1001 "I Dig Your Mind")....15-25 67

NERVOUS KATS

LPs: 10/12-inch

EMMA ("Nervous Kats")....250-300 64
(Selection number not known.)

NERVOUS NORVUS — P&R '56

(With Red Blanchard; Jimmy Drake)

Singles: 12-inch

BIG BEAT (12 "Transfusion")....10-15 85
(Includes picture cover.)

Singles: 78 rpm

DOT....10-25 56-57
QUALITY....20-30 56

Singles: 7-inch

BIG BEN (101 "Pure Gold")....10-15
DOT (15470 "Transfusion")....20-30 56
(Maroon label.)
DOT (15470 "Transfusion")....10-15 56
(Black label.)
DOT (15485 "Ape Call")....20-30 56
(Maroon label.)
DOT (15485 "Ape Call")....10-15 56
(Black label.)
DOT (15500 "The Fang")....20-30 56
(Maroon label.)
DOT (15500 "The Fang")....10-15 56
(Black label.)
DOT (16765 "Transfusion")....5-10 65
EMBEE (117 "I Like Girls")....10-20 59
QUALITY ("Transfusion")....25-50 56
(Canadian. Selection number not known.)
QUALITY ("Ape Call")....25-50 56
(Canadian. Selection number not known.)
QUALITY (1548 "The Fang")....25-50 56
(Canadian.)
Also see BLANCHARD, Red

NESBITT, Ike

Singles: 7-inch

FURY (1046 "I Want You")....10-15 61

NESMITH, Michael — P&R/LP '70

(With the First National Band; with Second National Band)

Singles: 7-inch

EDAN (1001 "Just a Little Love")....50-100 65
ISLAND....5-8 77
OMNIBUS....15-25 63
PACIFIC ARTS....8-10 75-79
RCA....10-20 70-75

Picture Sleeves

RCA (0453 "Nevada Fighter")....15-25 71

LPs: 10/12-inch

PACIFIC ARTS ("Conversation with Michael Nesmith – Music Radio Special")....25-35 78
(Promotional issue only.)
PACIFIC ARTS (101 "The Prison")....25-50 78
(Boxed edition. With booklet.)
PACIFIC ARTS (101 "The Prison")....10-20 78
(Standard LP. With booklet.)
PACIFIC ARTS (106 thru 130)....10-20 78-79

PACIFIC ARTS (9486 "From a Radio Engine to the Photon Wing")........ 15-25 77
RCA........ 20-30 70-75
RHINO........ 8-10 89
Also see BLESSING, Michael
Also see EZBA, Denny
Also see MIKE, JOHN & BILL
Also see MONKEES
Also see RHODES, Red
Also see TRINITY RIVER BOYS
Also see WICHITA TRAIN WHISTLE

NESTRO, Frankie

Singles: 7-inch

COUNT (1009 "I Don't Wanna Wait")...... 20-30 '60s
FRAN-CO (1000 "You Cheated, You Lied")........ 30-40 62
FRAN-CO (1004 "My Love")........ 40-50 62

NETHERTON, Fred

EPs: 7-inch

RURAL RHYTHM (540 "Fred Netherton")........ 200-300
Also see WILDWOOD TRIO

NETHERWORLD

LPs: 10/12-inch

REM (441 "Netherworld")........ 20-30 '60s

NETTLES, Bill, & Dixie Blue Boys — C&W '49

Singles: 78 rpm

BRUNSWICK........ 10-15 37
BULLET........ 8-12
MERCURY........ 5-10 49
STARDAY........ 25-35 55
VOCALION........ 10-15

Singles: 7-inch

NETT (1005 "Old Age Pension Blues").... 50-75
STARDAY (174 "Wino Boogie")........ 75-125 55

NETTLES, Joe

Singles: 7-inch

CIRCLE (1174 "Oh Baby")........ 50-75

NETTLES, Norma

Singles: 7-inch

DELTA (1174 "I've Got the Right Key Baby")........ 50-75

NETTLES, Roosevelt

Singles: 7-inch

BAMBOO (510 "Yes, Your Honor")........ 10-20 61
CAPITOL (5033 "Sorry for Me")........ 8-12 63
CHESS (1846 "Drifting Heart")........ 8-12 63
FELSTED (8700 "Miracles")........ 5-10 64
MASCOT (105 "Got You on My Mind").... 15-25 57

NEUMAN, Alfred E., & Furshlugginer Five

Singles: 7-inch

ABC-PAR (10013 "What-Me Worry?").... 15-25 59
MAD ("It's a Gas")........ 10-15 '60s
(Square cardboard cutout picture disc with Mad Magazine. No selection number used.)

Picture Sleeves

ABC-PAR (10013 "What-Me Worry?").... 30-50 59

NEUROTIC SHEEP

Singles: 7-inch

BOFUZ (1117 "Season of the Witch")..... 25-35 '60s
CAPITOL........ 10-20 '60s

NEVEGANS

(Nevegan's)

Singles: 7-inch

X-P-A-N-D-E-D (101 "Russian Roulette") 15-25 63
(Also issued as *Surf Bound* by the Teenbeats.)
Also see CHANTAYS
Also see TEENBEATS

NEVILLE, Aaron — R&B '60

(Arron Neville)

Singles: 7-inch

AIRECORDS (333 I've Done It Again").... 25-30 63
BANDY (1501 "Let's Live")........ 5-10
BELL........ 8-10 68-69
HEAD........ 3-5
IMPERIAL (035 "Over You")........ 5-8 65
INSTANT (3282 "I've Done It Again")...... 10-15 67
MERCURY........ 4-6 72-73
MINIT (612 "Over You")........ 5-10 60
MINIT (618 "Show Me the Way")........ 5-10 60
MINIT (624 "Reality")........ 5-10 61
MINIT (631 "Let's Live")........ 5-10 61
MINIT (639 "I'm Waitin' at the Station")....... 5-10 62
MINIT (650 "Sweet Little Mama")........ 5-10 62
MINIT (657 "How Could I Help But Love You")........ 5-10 63
PAR-LO........ 5-10 66-67
POLYDOR........ 4-6 77
SAFARI (201 "Forever More")........ 5-10 67
WHO DAT?........ 4-6

LPs: 10/12-inch

COLLECTABLES........ 6-8 88
MINIT (40007 "Like It 'Tis")........ 15-25 67
(Monaural.)
MINIT (40007 "Like It 'Tis")........ 15-25 67
(Stereo.)
PAR-LO (1 "Tell It Like It Is")........ 20-30 67
(Monaural.)
PAR-LO (1 "Tell It Like It Is")........ 25-35 67
(Stereo.)
Also see HILL, Jessie / Aaron Neville / Lee Diamond / Ernie K-Doe
Also see NEVILLE BROTHERS
Also see RONSTADT, Linda, & Aaron Neville

NEVILLE, Art

Singles: 78 rpm

SPECIALTY........ 10-20 57

Singles: 7-inch

CINDERELLA (1400 "My Dear, Dearest Darling")........ 20-30 65
(Has two different flip sides.)
INSTANT........ 8-15 61-66
SANSU (481 "Bo Diddley")........ 5-10 68
SANSU (482 "Heartaches")........ 5-10 68
SPECIALTY (592 "Oooh-Wee Baby")...... 20-30 57
SPECIALTY (637 "Zing Zang")........ 10-20 58
SPECIALTY (656 "What's Going On")...... 15-25 59
Also see NEVILLE BROTHERS
Also see WILLIAMS, Larry

NEVILLE, Art / Aaron Neville

LPs: 10/12-inch

BANDY (70013 "Best of Art & Aaron")...... 10-15 '70s
Also see NEVILLE, Aaron
Also see NEVILLE, Art

NEVILLE BROTHERS — LP '81

Singles: 7-inch

A&M........ 3-5 81-90
CAPITOL........ 4-6 78

LPs: 10/12-inch

A&M........ 5-10 81-90
BLACK TOP........ 5-10 86
CAPITOL (11865 "Neville Brothers")........ 20-30 78
EMI AMERICA........ 5-8 87
RHINO........ 5-8 87
SPINDLE TOP........ 5-8 87
Members: Aaron; Art; Charles; Cyril.
Also see HAWKETTS
Also see METERS
Also see NEVILLE, Aaron
Also see NEVILLE, Art

NEW, Paul, & Steel City

EPs: 7-inch

(371 "Minnesota")........ 4-6 '70s
(No label name used. Bonus EP, packaged with *Catch This!* LP. Pittsburgh Steelers promotional issue.)

LPs: 10/12-inch

(371 "Catch This!")........ 15-25 '70s
(No label name used. Includes bonus EP. Pittsburgh Steelers promotional issue.)

NEW BAG

Singles: 7-inch

DATE (1512 "Norwegian Wood")........ 5-10 66

NEW BIRTH — P&R/R&B/LP '71

Singles: 7-inch

ARIOLA AMERICA........ 4-6 79
BUDDAH........ 4-6 75
RCA........ 4-6 71-75
W.B........ 4-6 76-78

LPs: 10/12-inch

ARIOLA AMERICA........ 5-10 79
BUDDAH........ 8-12 75
COLLECTABLES........ 5-10 88
RCA (Except APD1-0285 & LSP-4000 series)........ 5-10 73-82
RCA (APD1-0285 "It's Been a Long Time")........ 15-25 74
(Quadraphonic.)
RCA (LSP-4000 series)........ 10-15 70-72
W.B........ 8-12 76-77
Members: Harvey Fuqua; Tony Churchill; Alan Frye; Robert Jackson; Joe Porter; Mel Wilson; Leslie Wilson; Londee Loren; Bobby Downs; Ann Bogan; Austin Lander; James Baker; Ben Boytel; Leroy Taylor; Robin Russell; Roger Voice; James Hall.
Also see HARVEY
Also see NITE-LITERS

NEW BLOCKBUSTERS

Singles: 78 rpm

ANTLER (4001 "Rock & Roll Guitar")....... 20-25 55

Singles: 7-inch

ANTLER (4001 "Rock & Roll Guitar")....... 40-60 56
Also see BLOCKBUSTERS

NEW BLOODS

Singles: 7-inch

20TH FOX (554 "Self Service")........ 15-20 65

NEW BREED

Singles: 7-inch

IMPACT (29 "John Birch American")........ 5-10 64

NEW BREED

Singles: 7-inch

DIPLOMACY (22 "Green Eyed Woman"). 20-30 65
HBR (508 "Want Ad Reader")........ 5-10 66
MERCURY (72556 "I've Been Wrong Before")........ 5-10 66
WORLD UNITED (001 "Want Ad Reader")........ 5-10 67
WORLD UNITED (003 "Fine with Me")...... 5-10 67

LPs: 10/12-inch

CICADELIC (985 "Want Ad Reader")........ 8-10 85

NEW BREED

Singles: 7-inch

POLARIS (711 "Wasting My Time")........ 20-30 66

NEW BREED

Singles: 7-inch

BOYD (156 "You'll Be There")........ 5-10 66
FRATERNITY (1003 "High Society Girl"). 10-20 68
IN CROWD (001 "Sunny")........ 20-30 67
IN CROWD (1234 "Big Time")........ 15-25 67
IN CROWD (1235 "Little Bit of Soul")....... 15-25 67
JAMIE (1341 "Sunny")........ 5-10 67

NEW BREED

Singles: 7-inch

NEW BREED (13635 "Don't Jive")........ 15-25 '60s

NEW CHRISTY MINSTRELS — P&R/LP '62

Singles: 7-inch

COLUMBIA (42000 series)........ 4-8 62-63
COLUMBIA (43000 & 44000 series)........ 4-6 64-69
GREGAR........ 4-6 70-72
W.B........ 4-6 79

Promotional Singles

COLUMBIA (Colored vinyl)........ 5-10 63-65

Picture Sleeves

COLUMBIA........ 4-8 62

LPs: 10/12-inch

COLUMBIA (1800 thru 2500 series)........ 10-20 62-66
(Monaural.)
COLUMBIA (8600 thru 9300 series)........ 10-30 62-66
(Stereo.)
COLUMBIA (9600 & 9700 series)........ 10-15 68
GREGAR........ 8-12 70
HARMONY........ 8-12 68-72
Members: Randy Sparks; Barry McGuire; Larry Ramos; Kenny Rogers; Mike Settle; Thelma Lou Camacho; Terry Williams; Mickey Jones; Jackie Miller; Gayle Caldwell; Gene Clark; Rex Kramer.
Also see ASSOCIATION
Also see CLARK, Dave, Five / New Christy Minstrels / Bobby Vinton / Jerry Vale
Also see CLARK, Dave, Five / Simon & Garfunkel / Yardbirds / New Christy Minstrels
Also see CLARK, Gene
Also see FIRST EDITION
Also see McGUIRE, Barry
Also see SPARKS, Randy

NEW COLONY SIX — P&R '66

Singles: 7-inch

CENTAUR (1201 "I Confess")........ 10-20 66
CENTAUR (1202 "I Lie Awake")........ 10-20 66
CENTAUR (1203 "Cadillac")........ 10-20 66
MCA........ 4-6 74
MERCURY ("Attacking a Straw Man")..... 10-20 69
(Promotional issue only. Number not known.)
MERCURY (72737 thru 73004)........ 5-10 67-70
MERCURY (73063 "People & Me")........ 10-15 70
MERCURY (73093 "Close Your Eyes Little Girl")........ 10-15 70
SENTAR (1204 "Power of Love")........ 10-20 66
SENTAR (1205 "Love You So Much")..... 10-20 66
SENTAR (1206 "Woman")........ 10-20 67
SENTAR (1207 "Hello Lonely")........ 10-20 67
SUNLIGHT........ 4-6 71-72
TWILIGHT........ 4-6 73

Picture Sleeves

MERCURY........ 8-12 67-68

LPs: 10/12-inch

EVA (12008 "Breakthrough")........ 5-10 '80s
MERCURY (61165 "Revelations")........ 20-30 68
MERCURY (61228 "Attacking a Strawman")........ 20-30 69
SENTAR (101 "Breakthrough")........ 150-250 66
SENTAR (3001 "Colonization")........ 50-75 67
SENTAR (61165 "Revelations")........ 30-40 68
Members: Ronnie Rice; Ray Graffia; Craig Kemp; Jerry Kollenberg; Pat McBride; Chick James; Billy Herman; Chuck Lobes; Wally Kemp.
Also see RICE, Ronnie

NEW DAWN

Singles: 7-inch

MAINSTREAM (664 "Slave of Desire").... 10-20 66

NEW DAWN

Singles: 7-inch

IMPERIAL (66397 "Melody Fair")........ 5-10 69
RCA (9569 "Someday")........ 5-10 68

NEW DAWN

Singles: 7-inch

GARLAND (2020 "Tears")........ 10-20 70

LPs: 10/12-inch

HOOT (4569 "A New Dawn")........ 450-500 70

NEW DIMENSIONS

LPs: 10/12-inch

SUTTON........ 40-60 63-64

NEW DYNAMICS

Singles: 7-inch

CUCA (1081 "Come Go with Me")........ 15-25 62
CUCA (1095 "Oh, I Like It Like That")...... 15-25 64
Members: Bobby Price; Don Anderson; Dick Ford; John Thompson; Jack Rygg; Dennis Murphy; John Murray.
Also see DYNAMICS

NEW ERA

Singles: 7-inch

GREAT LAKES (2532 "We Ain't Got Time")........ 10-15 67

NEW ESTABLISHMENT — P&R '69

Singles: 7-inch

AVALANCHE (36007 "Ridin' High")........ 4-6 71
COLGEMS (5006 "Sunday's Gonna' Come On Tuesday")........ 5-8 69
COLGEMS (5009 "I'll Build a Bridge")........ 5-8 70
MERCURY (72705 "And We Were Strangers")........ 5-10 67

NEW FACES

Singles: 7-inch

DOT (16777 "You'll Be Too Late")........ 10-20 65
PARROT (40030 "If You Love Me")........ 5-8 68

NEW FORMULA

Singles: 7-inch

ROULETTE (7023 "Burning in the Background of My Mind")........ 10-15 68

NEW FOURTH REICH

Singles: 7-inch

PLANET (68 "That Girl")........ 15-25 67

NEW FUGITIVES

Singles: 7-inch

GLO (5241 "That's Queer")........ 20-25 66

NEW HARLEQUINS

Singles: 7-inch

PACIFIC CHALLENGER (124 "Zelda Klotz")........ 20-30 '60s

NEW HAWKS

Singles: 7-inch

BLACK ROSE (3002 "Walk Don't Run-Pipeline [Medley]")........ 10-20 '60s

NEW HOLIDAYS

Singles: 7-inch

WESTBOUND (157 "My Baby Ain't No Play Thing")........ 20-30 69

NEW HOLLYWOOD ARGYLES
Singles: 7-inch
KAMMY (105 "Alley Oop '66")....................5-10 65
Also see HOLLYWOOD ARGYLES

NEW HOPE *P&R '70*
Singles: 7-inch
JAMIE...4-8 69-74
LAURIE (3608 "Green Green Grass")..........4-6 73
LPs: 10/12-inch
JAMIE (3034 "The New Hope")............... 20-30 69
Members: Kit Stewart; Carl Von Hausman; John Bradley; Ron Shane.
Also see KIT KATS

NEW HUDSON EXIT
Singles: 7-inch
DATE (1576 "Come with Me")....................5-10 67

NEW INVICTORS
Singles: 7-inch
HALE (500 "Deeply in Love with You").. 750-1000 62

NEW LEGION ROCK SPECTACULAR
Singles: 7-inch
SPECTACULAR..4-8 75
LPs: 10/12-inch
SPECTACULAR (7777 "Wild")................. 30-40 75
Also see BOOZE BROTHERS REVUE

NEW LIME
Singles: 7-inch
COLUMBIA (44017 "That Girl")............... 10-20 67
COLUMBIA (44597 "Donna")......................8-12 68
COUNTERPART (2495 "Walkin' the Dog")... 10-20 '60s
FRATERNITY (947 "And She Cried").........5-10 65
MINARET (150 "Sunny")...........................5-10 69

NEW LONDON RHYTHM & BLUES BAND
LPs: 10/12-inch
VOCALION (73880 "Soul Cookin' ")........ 10-12 69

NEW LOST CITY RAMBLERS
LPs: 10/12-inch
VERVE FOLKWAYS (5263 "American Moonshine and Prohibition").. 40-50 65
(Includes lyrics sheet.)
VERVE FOLKWAYS (9003 "Rural Delivery No. 1")... 10-20 65
Members: Tracy Schwarz; Mike Seeger; John Cohen.

NEW LUVS
Singles: 7-inch
BARCLAY ("It's All Over")......................... 20-30 '60s
(Selection number not known.)

NEW MASON DIXONS
Singles: 7-inch
CENTENNIAL (1863 "Totaled")............... 75-85 '60s

NEW MIX
LPs: 10/12-inch
U.A. (6678 "The New Mix")...................... 10-20 68

NEW ORDER
(Featuring Roger Joyce)
Singles: 7-inch
W.B. (5816 "You've Got Me High")......... 15-25 66
W.B. (5870 "Sailing Ship")........................5-10 67

NEW ORLEANS PUBLIC LIBRARY
Singles: 7-inch
WHITE WHALE (230 "Trippin' Down the Street")...5-10 66

NEW PHOENIX
Singles: 7-inch
WORLD PACIFIC (77884 "Give to Me Your Love")...8-10 68
Also see HARD TIMES
Also see T.I.M.E.

NEW RAGING STORM
Singles: 7-inch
TEE PEE (15/16 "Cry Girl"/"Monkey Time")... 10-20 67
Members: Ron Besaw; Dick Schelk; Rollie Ritchie; Roger Loos; Bob Anderson; Denny Noie.
Also see BESAW, Ron, & Mojo Men

NEW RENAISSANCE SOCIETY
LPs: 10/12-inch
HBR (8504 "Baroque N' Stones")............ 10-15 66
(Monaural.)
HBR (9504 "Baroque N' Stones")............15-20 66
(Stereo.)

NEW RIDERS OF THE PURPLE SAGE *LP '71*
Singles: 7-inch
COLUMBIA..4-6 71-74
MCA...4-6 76-77
LPs: 10/12-inch
A&M...5-8 81
BUDDAH...8-12 75
COLUMBIA..10-15 71-75
MCA...8-10 76-77
RELIX (Except 2025)..................................5-8 86-87
RELIX (2025 "Vintage")..............................5-8 87
(Black vinyl.)
RELIX (2025 "Vintage")............................30-50 87
(Picture disc.)
Members: Skip Battin; David Turbert. Also, assorted Grateful Dead members guested on Columbia and Relix issues.
Also see BATTIN, Skip
Also see GRATEFUL DEAD

NEW ROADRUNNERS
Singles: 7-inch
A-OK (1036 "Tired of Living")...................10-15 67

NEW SEEKERS *P&R '70*
Singles: 7-inch
COCA-COLA (2601 "By the World a Coke")..5-10 71
(Promotional issue only.)
ELEKTRA..4-6 70-72
MGM/VERVE..4-6 72-73
Picture Sleeves
MGM/VERVE..4-6 72-73
EPs: 7-inch
COCA-COLA...5-10 71
(Promotional issue only.)
LPs: 10/12-inch
ELEKTRA..10-12 71-72
MGM/VERVE..8-10 73
Member: Keith Potger.
Also see SEEKERS

NEW SILHOUETTES
Singles: 7-inch
GOODWAY (101 "Not Me Baby")................4-8 68
JAMIE (1333 "We Belong Together").......15-25 67

NEW SMYRNA BEACH HIGH / Campus Choir
Singles: 7-inch
CAMPUS (106 "Comes a Cuda"/"My Senior Year")..8-12 '60s

NEW SOCIETY
Singles: 7-inch
GRAMOPHONE (3 "Lovin' Kind")..............5-10 65
RCA (8807 "Buttermilk").............................5-8 66
RCA (8958 "Dawn of Sorrow")....................5-8 66
RCA (9149 "Love Thee Till I Die")...............5-8 67
LPs: 10/12-inch
RCA (3676 "Barock Sound of the New Society")..10-15 66

NEW STRING-A-LONGS
Singles: 7-inch
OHN-J (1009 "How Lovely Will You Be")...5-10 66
Also see STRING-A-LONGS

NEW SURVIVORS
Singles: 7-inch
KANWIC (147 "Pickle Protest")..................5-10 68
SCEPTER (12227 "Pickle Protest")...........5-10 68
Member: Tony Teebo.

NEW THINGS
Singles: 7-inch
ACCENT (1228 "Dumbo")........................20-30 67

NEW TRADITION
Singles: 7-inch
CAPITOL (2589 "Leavin' on a Jet Plane")..5-10 69
U.A. (50608 "I'm Happy Again")..................5-10 69

NEW TRAVELERS
Singles: 7-inch
YELLOW SAND (451 "Groovy")..................5-10 64

NEW TWEEDY BROTHERS
Singles: 7-inch
DOT (16910 "Good Time Car")................15-25 66
LPs: 10/12-inch
RIDON (234 "The New Tweedy Brothers").....................................1800-2000 66
(With hex cover.)

NEW VAUDEVILLE BAND *P&R/LP '66*
Singles: 7-inch
FONTANA (1562 "Winchester Cathedral")...4-8 66
FONTANA (1573 "Peek-A-Boo")..................4-8 67
FONTANA (1589 "Finchley Central")...........4-8 67
FONTANA (1598 "Green Street Green")......4-8 67
FONTANA (1612 "Bonnie & Clyde")............4-8 68
LPs: 10/12-inch
FONTANA (27560 "Winchester Cathedral")...10-15 66
(Monaural.)
FONTANA (67560 "Winchester Cathedral")...15-20 66
(Stereo.)
FONTANA (27568 "New Vaudeville Band on Tour")..10-15 67
(Monaural.)
FONTANA (67568 "New Vaudeville Band on Tour")..15-20 67
(Stereo.)

NEW WANDERERS
Singles: 7-inch
READY (1001 "Let Me Render My Service")..40-50
READY (1006 "This Man in Love")...........40-50

NEW WAVE
Singles: 7-inch
CANTERBURY (503 "Not from You").........5-10 67
CANTERBURY (512 "Little Dreams").........5-10 67

NEW WORLD CONGREGATION
Singles: 7-inch
ATCO (6667 "My World Is Empty Without You")...5-10 69
COULEE (123 "My World Is Empty Without You")...10-15 68
Picture Sleeves
COULEE (123 "My World Is Empty Without You")...15-20 68

NEW YORK CITY *P&R/R&B/LP '73*
Singles: 7-inch
CHELSEA 4-6 73-75
LPs: 10/12-inch
CHELSEA 10-15 73-77
Also see CADILLACS
Also see FIVE SATINS

NEW YORK DOLLS *LP '73*
Singles: 7-inch
MERCURY...4-6 73-76
Picture Sleeves
MERCURY...4-8 73
LPs: 10/12-inch
MERCURY (675 "New York Dolls")..........30-40 73
MERCURY (1001 "Too Much, Too Soon")...30-40 74
REACH OUT INT'L.......................................5-10 81
Members: David Johansen; Jerry Nolan; Arthur Kane; Johnny Thudners; Sylvain Sylvain.

NEW YORK ROCK & ROLL ENSEMBLE
(New York Rock Ensemble)
Singles: 7-inch
ATCO 5-10 67-69
LPs: 10/12-inch
ATCO 10-15 68-70
COLUMBIA...8-12 70-72

NEW YORK ROCK EXCHANGE
Singles: 7-inch
U.A. (50326 "Hey Baby")..............................5-10 68

NEW YORK SOUNDS
Singles: 7-inch
RED BIRD (060 "Drag Street") 8-12 66

NEW YORK THREE
Singles: 7-inch
AESOP'S (6045 "Cool Breeze")..................5-10 66

NEW YORK THRUWAY
Singles: 7-inch
MGM (14071 "Jack B. Nimble")..................5-10 69

NEW YORKERS *P&R '61*
Singles: 7-inch
WALL (547 "Miss Fine")...........................15-25 61
WALL (548 "Tears in My Eyes")...............15-25 61
Members: Fred Parris; Louis Peebles; Richard Freeman; Wesley Forbes; Silvester Hopkins.
Also see FIVE SATINS

NEW YORKERS
Singles: 7-inch
PARK AVENUE (100 "I Know Why")........50-75 61

NEW YORKERS
Singles: 7-inch
TAC-FUL (101 "You Shold Have Told Me")..25-50 64
TAC-FUL (102 "There's Going to Be a Wedding")..12-25 65

NEW YORKERS
Singles: 7-inch
DECCA (32569 "Do Wah Diddy")...............5-10 69
JERDEN...8-12 68-69
SCEPTER (Except 12199).........................5-10 67-68
SCEPTER (12199 "Seeds of Spring")......15-25 67
Members: Bill Hudson; Brett Hudson; Mark Hudson.

NEW YORKERS
(With Horace Ott & Orchestra)
Singles: 7-inch
W.B. (7318 "Lonely")...................................5-10 69

NEW YORKERS 5
(With Jessie Powell & His Band; New Yorker's 5)
Singles: 78 rpm
DANICE...100-150 55
Singles: 7-inch
DANICE (801 "Gloria My Darling").......250-350 55
Members: J.R. Bailey; Shelly Dupont; Fred Barksdale; Rocky Smith.
Also see POWELL, Jesse

NEW ZEALAND TRADING CO.
Singles: 7-inch
CADET (5637 "Could Be")..........................5-10 69

NEWBAG, Johnny
Singles: 7-inch
ATLANTIC (2355 "Got to Get You Back")..5-10 66
PORT (3008 "Sweet Thing")....................10-20 65

NEWBEATS *P&R/LP '64*
Singles: 7-inch
ABC...4-6 74
HICKORY...4-8 64-72
PLAYBOY 4-6 74
EPs: 7-inch
HICKORY (120-005 "Bread & Butter").....20-30 65
(Compact 33. Promotional issue only.)
LPs: 10/12-inch
HICKORY (LP-120 "Bread & Butter").......25-45 65
(Monaural.)
HICKORY (LPS-120 "Bread & Butter")..75-125 65
(Stereo.)
HICKORY (LP-122 "Big Beat Sound").....25-45 65
(Monaural.)
HICKORY (LPS-122 "Big Beat Sound")...50-75 65
(Stereo.)
HICKORY (LP-128 "Run Baby Run").......25-45 65
(Monaural.)
HICKORY (LPS-128 "Run Baby Run").....50-75 65
(Stereo.)
Members: Larry Henley; Dean Mathis; Mark Mathis.
Also see DEAN & MARC

NEWBORN, Phineas, Jr.
Singles: 7-inch
CONTEMPORARY (382 "For Carl")...........5-10 62
Session: Sam Jones; Louis Hayes; Paul Chambers; Philly Joe Jones.

NEWBURY, Mickey *P&R/LP '71*
Singles: 7-inch
ABC/HICKORY..4-6 77-79
AIRBORNE...3-5 88
ELEKTRA...4-6 71-73
HICKORY (1312 thru 1463).......................5-10 65-67
HICKORY (1600 series)..............................3-5 80
MCA...4-6 79
MERCURY...4-6 69-70
RCA...4-6 68-70
Picture Sleeves
RCA...4-6 68
LPs: 10/12-inch
ABC/HICKORY..5-10 77-79
MCA...5-8 79
ELEKTRA...8-10 71-75

MERCURY (4024 "After All These Years")...5-8 81
MERCURY (61236 "Looks Like Rain") 10-12 69
RCA 8-12 68-72

NEWBY

Singles: 7-inch

BLUE CAT (124 "I Can't Grow Peaches on a Cherry Tree") 5-10 66

NEWELL, Skip, & Mustangs

Singles: 7-inch

TREND (4107 "Roadrunner") 15-25 63
Also see RIGHTEOUS BROTHERS

NEWHART, Bob *LP '60*

Singles: 7-inch

W.B. (142 "Introducing Tobacco to Civilization") 5-10 62
(Promotional issue only.)

LPs: 10/12-inch

HARMONY 10-15 69
W.B. (1300 thru 1500 series) 20-30 60-65
W.B. (1600 thru 1700 series) 15-25 66-67

NEWKIRK, Bob

Singles: 7-inch

CLINTON (1001 "Dance of Love") 5-10 61
CLINTON (1003 "Once Again") 5-10 62
PHILIPS 4-8 62-69
TRIP UNIVERSAL (83 "For the Good Times") ....4-6 '70s

NEWLAND, Dickie "Bird"

Singles: 7-inch

FAME (504 "Don't Be Funny Honey") 50-75 58
FAME (508 "Pearlie Mae") 50-75 60

NEWLEY, Anthony *P&R '60*

Singles: 7-inch

KAPP 4-8 69
LONDON 5-15 58-63
MGM 4-6 71-74
RCA 4-8 66-67
U.A. 4-6 76-77
W.B. 4-8 68

EPs: 7-inch

BELL 5-8 71

LPs: 10/12-inch

BELL 8-12 71
LONDON 10-20 62-66
MGM 8-12 71-73
RCA 10-20 64-69
U.A. 5-10 77

NEWLYWEDS

Singles: 7-inch

HOMOGENIZED SOUL (601 "Love Walked Out") 1500-2500 61

NEWMAN, Carl

Singles: 7-inch

JET (802 "Until I'm with You") 25-50
MAR-VEL (2350 "Rockin' and a-Boppin'") 150-200 62
TRIO (849 "Tom-Tom"/"Ethel") 15-25 60
(Side one also issued as *Tom-Tom, Pt. 2* by the Rocking Rebels.)
Also see ROCKING REBELS

NEWMAN, David "Fathead"

Singles: 7-inch

ATLANTIC (2554 "Yesterday") 4-6 68
ATLANTIC (2966 "Killing Me Softly with his Song") 4-6 73
ATLANTIC (5002 "Hard Times") 8-12 59

LPs: 10/12-inch

ATLANTIC (1304 "Ray Charles Presents David 'Fathead' Newman") 40-60 59
ATLANTIC (1366 "Straight Ahead") 30-50 60
ATLANTIC (1399 "Fathead Comes On") . 25-40 61
ATLANTIC (1505 "Bigger and Better")... 10-150 68
RIVERSIDE (327 "Sounds of the Wide Open Spaces") 25-50 60
(Monaural.)
RIVERSIDE (1178 "Sounds of the Wide Open Spaces") 35-55 60
(Stereo.)
Also see McDUFF, Brother Jack, Quintet, & David Newman
Also see SCOTT, Shirley

NEWMAN, Floyd

Singles: 7-inch

STAX (143 "Frog Stomp") 10-20 64

NEWMAN, Herb, & Co.

Singles: 7-inch

HAPPY TIGER (100 "Alice's Restaurant") .5-10 69

NEWMAN, Jeanne

Singles: 7-inch

PHILLIPS INT'L (3585 "The Boy I Met Today") 10-15 63

NEWMAN, Jimmy *C&W '54*
(Jimmy C. Newman; with Cajun Country)

Singles: 78 rpm

DOT 10-15 54-57
KHOURY'S (630 "Darling") 10-20 54

Singles: 7-inch

CAJUN COUNTRY (45101 "Hadacol Boogie") 4-6 75
DECCA 5-10 60-71
DOT (Except 15766) 10-20 54-57
DOT (15766 "Carry On") 50-75 58
KHOURY'S (630 "Darling") 20-25 54
LA LOUISIANNE 4-6 73-75
MGM 10-15 58-60
MONUMENT 4-6 72
PLANTATION 3-6 76-80
SHANNON 4-6 73

EPs: 7-inch

DECCA (2772 "Jimmy Newman") 10-15 64

LPs: 10/12-inch

CROWN (329 "Guest Star of the Grand Ole Opry") ....10-15 '60s
(Includes tracks by Billy Carson.)
DECCA 10-25 62-70
DELTA 5-8 82
DOT (3690 "A Fallen Star") 15-25 66
(Monaural.)
DOT (3736 "Country Crossroads") 15-25 66
(Monaural.)
DOT (25690 "A Fallen Star") 15-25 66
(Stereo.)
DOT (25736 "Country Crossroads") 15-25 66
(Stereo.)
LA LOUISIANNE 5-10 73-75
MGM (E-3777 "This Is Jimmy Newman") .25-30 59
(Monaural.)
MGM (SE-3777 "This Is Jimmy Newman") 35-45 59
(Stereo.)
MGM (E-4045 "Songs By Jimmy Newman") 25-30 62
(Monaural.)
MGM (SE-4045 "Songs By Jimmy Newman") 30-40 62
(Stereo.)
PICKWICK/HILLTOP 8-12
PLANTATION 5-10 77-81
RIDGEWOOD (34001 "Louisiana Love") ...5-10
SWALLOW 5-8

NEWMAN, Randy *LP '71*

Singles: 78 rpm

REPRISE (0284 "I Think It's Gonna Rain Today") 8-10 78
(Promotional issue only.)

Singles: 7-inch

DOT (16411 "Country Boy") 4-8 62
REPRISE (Except 0771) 3-8 68-88
REPRISE (0771 "Last Night I Had a Dream") 10-20 68
W.B. 3-6 77-85

Picture Sleeves

REPRISE 3-5 88
W.B. 4-6 78

LPs: 10/12-inch

EPIC (147 "Peyton Place") 20-30 65
(TV Soundtrack.)
REPRISE (Except 6286) 5-10 70-88
REPRISE (6286 "Randy Newman") 15-20 68
(Cover pictures Randy in sweater and coat.)
REPRISE (6286 "Randy Newman") 10-15 68
(Cover picture is a close-up of Randy.)
W.B. 5-10 77-85
Also see EAGLES
Also see RONSTADT, Linda
Also see SEGER, Bob

NEWMAN, Ted *P&R '57*

Singles: 78 rpm

REV (7251 "Hey Little Freshman") 20-30 57

Singles: 7-inch

RCA (7251 "Hey Little Freshman") 10-20 58
REV (3505 "Plaything") 10-20 57
REV (3511 "I Double Dare You") 10-20 57

NEWMAN, Thunderclap *P&R '69*

Singles: 7-inch

MCA ....3-5 '80s
TRACK (2000 series) 4-8 69-70
TRACK (60000 series) 4-6 75

LPs: 10/12-inch

ATLANTIC/TRACK 10-20 70
MCA/TRACK 5-10 73
Members: Andy Newman; Jimmy McCulloch; Speedy Keen.
Also see McCARTNEY, Paul

NEWMAN, Wayne

Singles: 7-inch

NEW RANK (1847 "Midnight Train") 75-85

NEWMARKS

Singles: 7-inch

CHATTAHOOCHEE (627 "Goody Goody Gumdrop") 50-100 63

NEWPORT NOMADS

Singles: 7-inch

PRINCE (6304 "Blue Mallard") 20-30 62

NEWPORTERS

Singles: 7-inch

SCOTCHTOWN (500 "Adventures in Paradise") 30-40 63
Members: Scott Engel; John Stewart.
Also see ENGEL, Scott, & John Stewart

NEWPORTS

Singles: 7-inch

MAP (2527 "Dream") 100-200 58
(Identification number shown since no selection number is used.)

NEWPORTS

Singles: 7-inch

AVENUE D (18 "I Dreamt I Dwelt in Heaven") 4-6 93
(Black vinyl. 500 made.)
AVENUE D (18 "I Dreamt I Dwelt in Heaven") 8-10 93
(Pink swirl vinyl. 100 made.)
AVENUE D (20 "My Movie Queen") 4-6 94
(Black vinyl. 900 made.)
AVENUE D (20 "My Movie Queen") 5-8 94
(Blue/gray swirl vinyl. 100 made.)
CRYSTAL BALL (108 "Go to Sleep My Little Girl") 4-8 78
(Black vinyl. 500 made.)
CRYSTAL BALL (108 "Go to Sleep My Little Girl") 8-12 78
(Red vinyl. 25 made.)
CRYSTAL BALL (113 "Looking for Love") ...4-8 78
(Black vinyl. 500 made.)
CRYSTAL BALL (113 "Looking for Love") .8-12 78
(Red vinyl. 25 made.)
CRYSTAL BALL (129 "My Juanita") 4-8 78
(Black vinyl. 500 made.)
CRYSTAL BALL (129 "My Juanita") 8-12 78
(Red vinyl. 25 made.)
CRYSTAL BALL (134 "Denise") 4-8 80
(Black vinyl. 500 made.)
CRYSTAL BALL (143 "Gloria") 4-8 81
(Black vinyl. 500 made.)
CRYSTAL BALL (143 "Gloria") 8-12 81
(Red vinyl. 25 made.)
CRYSTAL BALL (143 "Gloria") 30-40 81
(Multi-colored vinyl. Five made.)
GUYDEN (2067 "If I Could Tonight") 20-30 62
GUYDEN (2116 "Tears") 100-150 64
KANE (008 "If I Could Tonight") 40-50 62
(First issue. Black vinyl.)
KANE (008 "If I Could Tonight") 100-150 62
(First issue. Red vinyl.)

Picture Sleeves

CRYSTAL BALL (143 "Gloria") 20-25 81
(200 made.)

NEWPORTS

Singles: 7-inch

KENT (380 "The Wonder of You") 10-20 62

NEWPORTS

Singles: 7-inch

PARROT (45008 "Party Night") 10-20 65

NEWPORTS

Singles: 7-inch

LAURIE (3327 "The Trouble Is You") 5-10 66

NEWPORTS

Singles: 7-inch

ZEBB (155 "Feelin' Low") 8-12 67

NEWPORTS

Singles: 7-inch

IMAGE (501 "Wishing Star") 10-15 78
(Black vinyl. 300 made.)
Members: LiCalsi; Pace; Ed Engel.

NEWSOM, Chubby *R&B '49*
(With Her Hip Shakers; with Lee Allen)

Singles: 78 rpm

DELUXE (3199 "Hip Shakin' Mama") 15-25 49
DELUXE (3204 "Back-Bitin' Woman") 15-25 49
MILTONE 15-25 49

Singles: 7-inch

WINLEY (216 "Toodle Luddle Baby") 25-40 57
Also see ALLEN, Lee
Also see GAYTEN, Paul

NEWSOME, Cuddles C.

Singles: 7-inch

ADCO (791 "So Long Baby") 50-75

NEWSOME, Frankie *R&B '69*

Singles: 7-inch

GWP (515 "My Lucky Day") 4-6 69
PORT (202 "My Lucky Day") 10-20
SAVERN (103 "Don't Mess with My Lovemaker") 8-12
USA (911 "Taunting Love") 5-10 68
W.B. (8056 "We're on Our Way") 4-6 74
Also see PARKER, Willie

NEWSOME, Jimmy

Singles: 78 rpm

MGM (11849 "Do That Thing") 15-25 54
MGM (55005 "Long Gone Lonesome Blues") 10-15 55

Singles: 7-inch

MGM (11849 "Do That Thing") 25-35 54
MGM (55005 "Long Gone Lonesome Blues") 15-25 55

NEWTON, Chris, & Jades / Notables

Singles: 7-inch

MIKESELL (134 "Impala"/"Hello and Goodbye") 20-30 61

NEWTON, Ernie, & Spielers

Singles: 7-inch

CALDWELL (401 "Yeah, Yeah, Yeah") 15-25 60

NEWTON, Holder
(With the Apes; with Pygmies)

Singles: 7-inch

CAPITOL (4601 "On Safari") 5-10 61

NEWTON, Johnny, & Tags

Singles: 7-inch

BELL (114 "Sorry I Ran All the Way Home"/"Am I Better Off") 20-30 59
BELL (114 "Sorry I Ran All the Way Home"/"Teenager in Love") 15-25 59

NEWTON, Ronnie

Singles: 7-inch

ARMONEER (1003 "Workingman Blues") 200-300

NEWTON, Ted

Singles: 7-inch

BELLWOOD ("Save Me the Label") 75-125
(Selection number not known.)
SALEM (530 "Tennessee Rhythm") 75-125

NEWTON, Wayne *P&R/LP '63*

Singles: 7-inch

ARIES II 3-6 79-80
CAPITOL (Except 5124 & 5338) 4-8 63-71
CAPITOL (5124 "Dream Baby") 10-15 64
CAPITOL (5338 "Comin' on Too Strong") 10-20 64
(With Bruce Johnston & Terry Melcher.)
CHALLENGE 5-10 64
CHELSEA 4-6 72-78
GEORGE (7777 "Little White Cloud That Cried") 10-15 62
MGM 4-6 68
20TH FOX 4-6 78

W.B. 4-6 70-77
Picture Sleeves
CAPITOL 5-10 65-66
LPs: 10/12-inch
AIRES II 5-8 79-80
CAMDEN 5-10 74
CAPITOL (573 "Wayne Newton") 15-25 70
(Three-disc set.)
CAPITOL (600 series) 5-10 71
CAPITOL (T-1973 thru T-2847).... 10-20 63-68
(Monaural.)
CAPITOL (ST-1973 thru ST-2847).... 15-25 63-68
(Stereo.)
CAPITOL (SM-2300 series) 5-8 75
CAPITOL (SPC-3400 series) 5-8
CAPITOL (11000 series) 5-8 79
CAPITOL (16000 series) 5-8 80
CHELSEA.... 10-15 72-75
MGM 6-12 68-72
MUSICOR....5-8 79
SILVER EAGLE....8-10
20TH FOX 5-8 78
Also see BRUCE & TERRY
Also see NEWTON BROTHERS
Also see NEWTON RASCALS

NEWTON, Wayne, & Tammy Wynette
C&W '89
Singles: 7-inch
CURB....3-5 89
Also see JERRY & WAYNE
Also see NEWTON, Wayne
Also see WYNETTE, Tammy

NEWTON BROTHERS
(Featuring Wayne)
Singles: 7-inch
CAPITOL (4236 "The Real Thing") 50-75 59
GEORGE (7778 "Little Juke box") 15-20 61
GEORGE (7780 "You're Much Too Lovely to Cry") 25-35 61
LAMA (7794 "I Was Born When You Kissed Me") 25-50 63
Members: Wayne Newton; Jerry Newton.
Also see JERRY & WAYNE
Also see NEWTON, Wayne
Also see NEWTON RASCALS

NEWTON RASCALS
Singles: 7-inch
RANGER (401 "Rascals Boogie") 75-125 58
(Issued with a paper insert picturing 12-year-old Wayne and 14-year-old Jerry as "The Rascals in Rhythm." Value of insert is about the same as for disc.)
Members: Wayne Newton; Jerry Newton.
Also see JERRY & WAYNE
Also see NEWTON, Wayne
Also see NEWTON BROTHERS

NEWTON-JOHN, Olivia
P&R/LP '71
Singles: 12-inch
MCA (Except 1150)....4-6 81-84
MCA (1150 "Twist of Fate") 5-10 83
(Promotional issue only.)
Singles: 7-inch
GEFFEN 3-5 89
KIRSHNER (5005 "Goin' Back") 10-15 70
MCA (Except 40043) 3-8 73-88
MCA (40043 "Take Me Home Country Roads") 5-10 73
RSO (903 "Hopelessly Devoted to You")....4-6 78
UNI (55281 "If Not for You") 5-10 71
UNI (55304 "Banks of the Ohio") 5-10 71
UNI (55317 "What Is Life") 5-10 72
UNI (55348 "Just a Little Too Much") 10-15 72
Promotional Singles
MCA (1810 "Deeper Than the Night")...... 30-40 79
(Picture disc. Promotional issue only.)
WHAT'S IT ALL ABOUT 5-10 74
Picture Sleeves
MCA (Except 40418) 3-6 75-88
MCA (40418 "Please Mr. Please") 6-10 75
EPs: 7-inch
MCA.... 12-15 73
(Promotional issues only.)
LPs: 10/12-inch
GEFFEN 5-8 89
MCA (389 "Let Me Be There") 10-12 73
MCA (411 "If You Love Me, Let Me Know") 12-15 74
(With *I Love You, I Honestly Love You.* Note longer title.)
MCA (411 "If You Love Me, Let Me Know") 8-10 74
(With *I Honestly Love You.* Note shorter title.)
MCA (2000 & 3000 series) 8-10 75-78
MCA (5000 & 6000 series) 5-8 80-83
MCA (37000 series) 5-8 80-83
MFSL (040 "Totally Hot") 40-60 80
UNI (73117 "If Not for You") 50-75 71
(Cover depicts a field scene.)
UNI (73117 "If Not for You") 20-30 71
(Field scene removed from cover.)
Also see DENVER, John, & Olivia Newton-John
Also see TOOMORROW

NEWTON-JOHN, Olivia / Dion
Singles: 7-inch
WHAT'S IT ALL ABOUT (347/8 "Interviews") ....15-25 '70s
(Issued only to radio stations.)
Also see DION

NEWTON-JOHN, Olivia, & Electric Light Orchestra
P&R/LP '80
Singles: 7-inch
MCA (41285 "Xanadu") 3-5 80
Picture Sleeves
MCA (41285 "Xanadu") 3-5 80
LPs: 10/12-inch
MCA (6100 "Xanadu") 8-12 80
MCA (10384 "Xanadu") 750-1000 80
(Picture disc. Promotional issue only. Also has Cliff Richard, Gene Kelly, and the Tubes.)
Also see ELECTRIC LIGHT ORCHESTRA
Also see RICHARD, Cliff

NEWTON-JOHN, Olivia, & Andy Gibb
P&R '80
Singles: 12-inch
POLYDOR (104 "Rest Your Love on Me") 10-15 79
Singles: 7-inch
RSO (1026 "I Can't Help It") 3-5 80

NEWTON-JOHN, Olivia, & Cliff Richard
P&R '80
Singles: 7-inch
MCA (51007 "Suddenly") 4-6 80
(Custom MCA/Xanadu label. Has artist credit at top, title at bottom.)
MCA (51007 "Suddenly") 3-5 80
(Standard MCA label. Has artist credit at bottom, title at top.)
Picture Sleeves
MCA (51007 "Suddenly") 4-6 80
Also see RICHARD, Cliff

NEWTON-JOHN, Olivia, & John Travolta
P&R '78
Singles: 7-inch
RSO 4-6 78
Picture Sleeves
RSO 4-6 78
Also see NEWTON-JOHN, Olivia

NEWTONES
Singles: 7-inch
BATON (260 "Remember the Night"/"Going Steady") 1000-1500 58
(White label. Promotional issue only.)
BATON (260 "Remember the Night"/"Going Steady") 750-1000 58
(Yellow label.)
RELIC (1009 "Remember the Night") 5-10 65
RELIC (1010 "Going Steady") 5-10 65

NEXT EXIT
Singles: 7-inch
SPIRIT ....5-10 '60s

NEXT FIVE
Singles: 7-inch
DESTINATION (637 "He Stole My Love") 10-20 67
WAND (1170 "Talk to Me Girl") 10-20 68
Members: Steve Thomas; Eric Olson; Gordon Wayne; Mark Buscaglia; Tom Stewart; John Peter; Gary Cooper; John Crook.
Also see TOY FACTORY

NEXT MORNING
LPs: 10/12-inch
CALLAS (2002 "Next Morning") 50-100 71

NIC NACS
Singles: 78 rpm
RPM (313 "Found Me a Sugar Daddy") .75-125 51
RPM (316 "Found Me a Sugar Daddy") .50-100 51
RPM (342 "Found Me a Sugar Daddy") ...40-60 52
Members: Mickey Champion; Ty Terrell; Bobby Nunn; Bill Richards; Roy Richards.
Also see CHAMPION, Mickey
Also see ROBINS

NICHOLLS, Al "J.B.", & Playboys
Singles: 7-inch
DJ (1002 "All My Loving") 15-25 64
Also see J.B. & Playboys

NICHOLLS, Dave, & Coins
Singles: 7-inch
SPARTON (1062 "Bells Will Ring") 50-75 61
(Canadian.)

NICHOLS, Ann
(With the Bluebirds; with Sentimentals)
Singles: 78 rpm
SITTIN' IN WITH (552 "Let Me Know")....25-50 50
SITTIN' IN WITH (561 "Those Magic Words") 25-50 50
Singles: 7-inch
TUXEDO (926 "Lover, I'm Waiting for You") 50-75 58
Also see CARTER, James, & Sentimentals

NICHOLS, Joey, & Rock-A-Fellas
Singles: 7-inch
ABC-PAR (9951 "Steady Love") 10-20 58
Also see ROCK-A-FELLAS

NICHOLS, Little Al
Singles: 7-inch
STATUE (7004 "You Ought to Be Ashamed") ....20-30 '60s

NICHOLS, Mann
Singles: 78 rpm
FBC (125 "Walking Talking Blues") 100-200 49
IMPERIAL (5162 "Get Going") 50-100 49
IMPERIAL (5173 "Worried Life Blues") ..50-100 49

NICHOLS, Nichelle
Singles: 7-inch
R-WAY 5-8
EPs: 7-inch
AMERICANA (1 "Dark Side of the Moon") 25-35
(Double EP set.)
LPs: 10/12-inch
EPIC (26351 "Down to Earth") 40-50 68
R-WAY 10-15

NICHOLS, Rick
Singles: 7-inch
SOUND (231 "Infatuation") 5-10
Also see RICKY & LEXINGTONS

NICHOLS, Sonny
Singles: 7-inch
PATCO (1316 "Young in Years") 10-20 59

NICHOLSON, J.D.
(With His Jivin' 5)
Singles: 78 rpm
ELKO (204 "Black Night Is Gone") 25-35 51
Singles: 7-inch
IMCO (110 "Annie Jo") 15-25 63
Also see CALLENDER, Red

NICK & DINO
Singles: 7-inch
IMPACT (1016 "Wish I Was a Kid Again") 15-25 66

NICK & JAGUARS
Singles: 7-inch
TAMLA (5501 "Cool & Crazy") 200-250 60

NICK & NACKS
Singles: 7-inch
BARRY (108 "The Night") 250-350 64

NICK & STING-RAYS
Singles: 7-inch
MILL-MONT (1628 "You Are So Beautiful") ....100-150 '60s

NICKEL REVOLUTION
Singles: 7-inch
PHILIPS (40569 "Oscar Crunch") 25-35 69

NICKELL, Betty
Singles: 7-inch
ABBEY (102 "Hot Dog") 100-200 58
SNAP (058 "I'm Ready") 50-100

NICKERSON, Cleve
Singles: 7-inch
SAVOY (1626 "Big Bob") 10-20 62

NICKIE & NITELITES
Singles: 7-inch
BRUNSWICK (55155 "Tell Me You Care") 75-125 59
Member: Nick Massi.

NICKS, Lefty
Singles: 7-inch
NICKTONE (6020 "Model A Ford Blues") 1000-1500 58

NICKS, Stevie
LP '81
Singles: 12-inch
MODERN 4-8 81-86
Singles: 7-inch
MODERN 3-5 81-89
Picture Sleeves
MODERN 3-5 82-89
LPs: 10/12-inch
MFSL (121 "Bella Donna") 30-40 84
MODERN 5-10 81-89
Also see BUCKINGHAM NICKS
Also see FLEETWOOD MAC
Also see STEWART, John

NICKS, Stevie, & Don Henley
P&R '81
Singles: 7-inch
MODERN (7341 "Leather & Lace") 3-5 81
Picture Sleeves
MODERN (7341 "Leather & Lace") 4-6 81

NICKS, Stevie, & Tom Petty & Heartbreakers
P&R '81
Singles: 7-inch
MODERN 3-5 81-86
Picture Sleeves
MODERN 4-6 81-86
Also see PETTY, Tom, & Heartbreakers

NICKS, Stevie, & Sandy Stewart
Singles: 7-inch
MODERN (99799 "Nightbird") 3-5 83
Picture Sleeves
MODERN (99799 "Nightbird") 4-6 83
Also see NICKS, Stevie

NICKY & NOBLES
Singles: 7-inch
END (1021 "Schoolhouse Rock") 25-35 58
END (1098 "School Bells") 15-25 61
GONE (5039 "School Days") 75-100 58
(Mistake in title.)
GONE (5039 "School Bells") 40-50 58
(Black label.)
GONE (5039 "School Bells") 10-15 61
(Multi-color label.)
RELIC (544 "School Bells") 5-10 66
ROULETTE GOLDEN GOODIES ....4-6 '70s
TIMES SQUARE (37 "School Bells") 20-30 64
Also see NOBLES

NICKY C. & CHATEAUX
Singles: 7-inch
BAY SOUND (67012 "Try Some Soul") ...50-75 69

NICO
LPs: 10/12-inch
ELEKTRA (74029 "Marble Index") 15-20 68
ISLAND 8-10 75
REPRISE 10-15 70
VERVE (5032 "Chelsea Girl") 25-40 67
(Monaural.)
VERVE (V6-5032 "Chelsea Girl") 35-45 67
(Stereo.)
Also see VELVET UNDERGROUND & NICO

NICOL, Jimmy
(With the Shubdubs; Sound of Jimmy Nicol)
Singles: 7-inch
MAR MAR (313 "Night Train") 100-150 64
(Nicol played drums for the Beatles in 1964, sitting in

briefly for an ailing Ringo Starr. Label reads "Now with the Beatles.")
PARROT (9752 "Roaring Blue")............. 10-20 65
Also see BEATLES

NICOLLET, Miss
(With the Novelairs; Nicollet)
Singles: 7-inch
DECCA (31402 "I Can Tell")......................5-10 62
SHAR (3 "Crazy Over You")................... 15-25 60

NIELSEN, Merlin
Singles: 7-inch
CUCA (6834 "How Long Must I Wait")..... 10-15 68

NIELSEN, Ralph, & Chancellors
Singles: 7-inch
CRYPT...4-6
SURF (5302 "Scream")...................... 200-300 66
Picture Sleeves
CRYPT...4-8
Also see JAMES BOYS

NIGH TRANES
Singles: 7-inch
CUCA (1012 "Hangover")...................... 15-25 60
Members: Ken Adamany; Jerry Chase; Denny Gerg; Bob Shebesta; Frank Ellefson; Ron Boyer.

NIGHT, Johnny
Singles: 7-inch
APRIL (1101 "Secret Place")................... 15-25 59

NIGHT, Rocky
Singles: 7-inch
PEARL (708 "Teenage Bop")............. 100-200 57

NIGHT BEATS
Singles: 7-inch
SOUND (100 "Exotic")........................... 10-20 65
Also see EL RAY & NIGHT BEATS
Also see NOBLEMEN
Also see ROLLETTES ORCHESTRA

NIGHT BEATS
Singles: 7-inch
CUCA (1001 "Johnny B. Goode")........... 10-20 59
Picture Sleeves
CUCA (1001 "Johnny B. Goode")........... 15-25 59
Members: Dick Lodholz; Jim Drwek; Paul Pritzl; Dick Sternberg; Ken Heldt.
Also see LEE, Robin

NIGHT CAPS
Singles: 7-inch
ARC (1181 "Keep on Runnin'")............... 20-30 '60s

NIGHT CRAWLERS
Singles: 7-inch
MAAD (1566 "You Say")......................... 10-20 66

NIGHT CRAWLERS
Singles: 7-inch
SHADOW (101 "Let's Move")................. 20-30 66

NIGHT HAWKS
Singles: 7-inch
STARS (550 "You're My Baby")........... 125-150 57

NIGHT HAWKS
Singles: 7-inch
DEL-FI (4122 "Big Top")......................... 10-20 59

NIGHT HAWKS
Singles: 7-inch
ALON (9001 "Rockin' Hawk")................. 10-20 62

NIGHT HAWKS
Singles: 7-inch
PACIFIC (352 "Bunny Ride")................... 15-25

NIGHT OWLS
Singles: 7-inch
NRC (015 "Loop the Hoop")................... 10-15 58

NIGHT OWLS
Singles: 7-inch
CLIMAX (103 "Stompin'")....................... 10-15 59

NIGHT OWLS
Singles: 7-inch
VALMOR (14 "Be My Guest")....................5-10 62
VALMOR (14 "Be My Guest")................. 10-15 62
(Single-sided. Promotional issue only.)
LPs: 10/12-inch
VALMOR (79 "Twistin' the Oldies")......... 25-40 62

NIGHT OWLS
Singles: 7-inch
CUCA (1075 "Waitin' by the School").......15-25 62
Also see ALLEN, Dick, & Fairlanes

NIGHT OWLS
Singles: 7-inch
BETHLEHEM (3087 "Bells Ring")............10-15 64
(5206 "The Country Inn")..........................15-25 '60s
(No label name used.)

NIGHT OWLS
Singles: 7-inch
MICHELLE (916 "Muddy").........................10-20 64

NIGHT PASTOR & SEVEN FRIENDS
LP: 10/12-inch
CLAREMONT (672 "Music to Lure Pigeons By")..15-20 67
Member: Dick Ruedebush.

NIGHT PEOPLE
Singles: 7-inch
BERMA..5-10 61
OUTLAW..5-10 '60s
SEAFAIR (103 "Istanbul").......................15-25 61
Picture Sleeves
SEAFAIR (103 "Istanbul").......................20-30 61

NIGHT RIDERS
LPs: 10/12-inch
JUSTICE (157 "Introducing ... the Night Riders")..200-250 66

NIGHT SHADOWS
(Night Shadow; Little Phil & Nightshadows)
Singles: 7-inch
BAJA (4504 "Turned On").......................15-25 67
BANNED (6T9 "Hot Dog Man")................25-50 66
DOT (16912 "So Much")..........................15-25 66
GAYE (3031 "60 Second Swinger").........25-50 66
NA-R-CO (100 "Station Break")..................8-12 '60s
NATIONAL (187 "Garbage Man")............10-15 '60s
Picture Sleeves
GAYE (3031 "60 Second Swinger").........40-60 66
LPs: 10/12-inch
HOTTRAX (1414 "The Square Root of Two")..30-40 79
HOTTRAX (1430 "Live at the Spot").........15-20 81
HOTTRAX (1450 "Invasion of the Acid Eaters")..10-20 82
ROTT ("Rock Anomaly")............................8-12 88
(Selection number not known.)
SPECTRUM STEREO (2001 "The Square Root of Two").. 1200-1400 68
(Executive edition. Includes bonus psychedelic poster *and* bonus 45 rpm – *The Hot Dog Man/The Hot Rod Song* [Banned 6T9]. Six made.)
SPECTRUM STEREO (2001 "The Square Root of Two").. 1000-1200 68
(Promotional edition, made for radio stations. Includes bonus psychedelic poster. 294 made.)
SPECTRUM STEREO (2001 "The Square Root of Two").. 775-1050 68
(Commercial edition. Includes bonus 45 rpm – *The Hot Dog Man/The Hot Rod Song* [Banned 6T9]. 700 made.)
SPECTRUM STEREO (2001 "The Square Root of Two")...750-1000 68
(LP without either of the two bonus inserts.)
Members: Little Phil Ross; Ronnie Farmer; Charles Spinks; Bobbie Newell.
Session; Aleck Janoulis; Pat Andrews; Jimi Callaway; Electric Bob.

NIGHT WATCH
Singles: 7-inch
ABC (10862 "Cloud Time").......................10-20 66

NIGHTBEATS
Singles: 7-inch
ZOOM (002 "Lonesome Road Rock")..100-125 59
ZOOM (004 "Cryin' All Night")..............100-125 59
Members: Peter Ronstadt; Nate Foster; Bert Roberts; Lance Hoops; Don Grossberndt.

NIGHTCAPS
Singles: 7-inch
MUSICOR (1057 "Nightcap Rock")..........10-15 64
VANDAN (3223 "Thunderbird")................10-15 61
VANDAN (3587 "24 Hours")......................10-15 61
VANDAN (4280 "Next Time You See Me")..5-10 66
VANDAN (4733 "Wine Wine Wine #2")......5-10 66
VANDAN (7066 "Darlin'")..........................10-20 61
VANDAN (7491 "Wine Wine Wine")........10-15 60
(Reissued in 1963 and again in 1966, using the same selection number.)
LPs: 10/12-inch
BARON (Black vinyl)................................10-12 80
BARON (Colored vinyl).............................15-20 80
VANDAN (8124 "Wine Wine Wine").....100-125 61

NIGHTCRAWLERS
Singles: 7-inch
JAM (109 "A Fool in Love")......................15-25 64

NIGHTCRAWLERS *P&R '67*
Singles: 7-inch
KAPP (110 "Little Black Egg")...................8-12 67
KAPP (709 "Little Black Egg")....................5-10 65
KAPP (746 "Basket of Flowers")................5-10 66
KAPP (826 "My Butterfly")..........................8-12 67
LEE (101 "Cry")...20-30 64
LEE (1012 "Little Black Egg")..................10-20 65
MARLIN (1904 "Basket of Flowers").........10-15 66
SCOTT (28 "I Don't Remember")................8-12 66
LPs: 10/12-inch
KAPP (1520 "Little Black Egg")..............75-125 67
(Monaural.)
KAPP (3520 "Little Black Egg")................50-75 67
(Stereo.)
Members: Chuck Conlon; Rob Rouse; Sylvan Wells; Tom Ruger; Pete Thomason.
Also see CONLON & CRAWLERS

NIGHTHAWK, Robert *R&B '49*
(With His Nighthawks Band; Robert McCollum)
Singles: 78 rpm
ARISTOCRAT (413 "Six Three O")......100-200 48
CHESS (1484 "My Sweet Lovin' Woman")..50-100 48
STATES (131 "The Moon Is Rising")......50-100 54
UNITED (102 "Kansas City Blues").......50-100 51
UNITED (105 "Feel So Sad")..................50-100 51
Singles: 7-inch
STATES (131 "The Moon Is Rising")....300-400 53
LPs: 10/12-inch
ROUNDER..5-10
Also see NIGHTHAWKS
Also see TAYLOR, Hound Dog / Robert Nighthawk / John Littlejohn / Earl Hooker
Also see TAYLOR, Koko

NIGHTHAWKS
Singles: 78 rpm
ARISTOCRAT (2301 "Black Angel Blues")..100-200 48
Members: Robert McCollum; Willie Dixon.
Also see DIXON, Willie
Also see NIGHTHAWK, Robert

NIGHTHAWKS
Singles: 7-inch
STARS (550 "You're My Baby")................20-30 57

NIGHTHAWKS
Singles: 7-inch
HAMILTON (50006 "All'a Your Love"/"When Sin Stops")...50-100 58
(At least one report claims Buddy Holly plays lead guitar on these tracks.)
Also see HOLLY, Buddy

NIGHTHOPPERS
Singles: 7-inch
AMERICAN INT'L (526 "Girls, Girls, Girls")..10-15 59

NIGHTINGALES
Singles: 78 rpm
DECCA (48225 "Guide My Mind")...........10-15 51
Singles: 7-inch
DECCA (48225 "Guide My Mind")...........40-50 51

NIGHTINGALES
Singles: 7-inch
RAY STAR (784 "Love in Return")...........10-15 62
TAMPA (162 "I Love You Oh So Much")..10-15 59

NIGHTMARES
Singles: 7-inch
AMERICAN INT'L (531 "Horrors of the Black Museum")..10-15 59

NIGHTMARES
Singles: 7-inch
UNITED RECORD ("Love of My Lady")...50-75
(No selection number used.)

NIGHTRIDERS
Singles: 78 rpm
SOUND (128 "Never")..............................10-20 55
Singles: 7-inch
SOUND (128 "Never")..............................25-35 55

NIGHTRIDERS
Singles: 7-inch
HUNCH..10-20 63
SUE (713 "Pretty Plaid Skirt")................40-50 59
SUE (719 "Lookin' for My Baby")............25-35 59
SUE (731 "Talk to Me Baby")...................25-35 60
Also see SMITH, Melvin

NIGHTROCKERS
Singles: 7-inch
ARCO (105 "Junction #1").......................15-25 66
Picture Sleeves
ARCO (105 "Junction #1").......................25-35 66

NIGHTSHADES
Singles: 7-inch
GEAR (744 "Flying High")..........................5-10 '60s
GEAR (747 "Summertime")..........................5-10 '60s
GEAR (751 "Sweet Cecelia").......................5-10 '60s

"NIGHTS OF LOVE IN LESBOS"
LPs: 10/12-inch
FAX (1009 "Nights of Love in Lesbos – a Frank Description of a Young Girl")...................25-35
(A collection of poetry with music. Title used since no artist is credited.)

NIGHTWALKERS
Singles: 7-inch
JCP (1058 "It'll Only Hurt for a Little While")..20-30 65

NIGHTWALKERS
Singles: 7-inch
VISCOUNTS (4503 "In Our Time")..........10-20 '60s

NIKITA THE "K"
Singles: 7-inch
W.B. (7005 "Go Go Radio Moscow").......20-25 67

NILSSON, Harry *P&R/LP '69*
(With the New Salvation Singers; Nilsson)
Singles: 7-inch
POLYDOR 3-5 85
RCA...4-8 67-77
TOWER (100 series).................................8-12 64-65
TOWER (500 series)..................................5-10 69
Picture Sleeves
RCA...4-6 74-77
EPs: 7-inch
RCA (248 "Excerpts from *The Point*)..........8-10 71
(Promotional issue only.)
LPs: 10/12-inch
51 WEST..5-8 '80s
MUSICOR...8-10 77
PICKWICK..5-10 '70s
POLYDOR...5-8 85
RCA (0097 thru 0817, except "APD1" series)...8-15 73-75
RCA ("APD1" series)..............................10-20 74-75
(Quadraphonic.)
RCA (1003 "The Point")............................10-12 71
(With Davy Jones and Mickey Dolenz.)
RCA (1031 thru 3811)...............................5-10 76-80
RCA (3874 "Pandemonium Shadow Show")...15-20 67
RCA (3956 "Aerial Ballet").......................10-20 68
RCA (4197 thru 4717)................................8-15 69-72
RAPPLE..8-12 74
SPRINGBOARD..5-10 78
TOWER (5095 "Spotlight")........................10-15 69
Promotional LPs
RCA (567 "Scatalogue")............................30-40 '60s
RCA ("Pandemonium Shadow Show - Boxed Set")..50-100 67
(Includes two black and white 8" x 10" photos, two balloons, two lyrics sheets, three-page biography, 16" x 12" poster, and 2" x 4" fan club card. Monaural.)
Also see BO PETE
Also see CHER & NILSSON
Also see DOLENZ, Mickey
Also see FOTO-FI FOUR
Also see JONES, Davy
Also see RIC-A-SHAYS
Also see STARR, Ringo, & Harry Nilsson

NIMBLE, Jack B.
(With the Quicks)
Singles: 7-inch
DEL-RIO (2303 "Like Keyed")................. 10-20 61
DEL-RIO (2305 "Nut Rocker")................. 15-25 62
DOT (16319 "Nut Rocker")........................8-12 62

NIMOY, Leonard *LP '67*
Singles: 7-inch
DOT...8-12 67-69
Picture Sleeves
DOT (17038 "A Visit to a Sad Planet")..... 20-30 67
LPs: 10/12-inch
CAEDMON... 10-15 '70s
DOT.. 25-50 67-69
JRT ("The Mysterious Golem")................ 20-40 82
PARAMOUNT... 20-40 74
PICKWICK.. 15-25 '60s
SEARS.. 15-25 '60s

9W NORTH
Singles: 7-inch
KIM (104 "Eileen")................................. 75-100 65
(500 made.)

9TH STREET MARKET
Singles: 7-inch
FENTON (2136 "I'm a Baby")............. 100-150 67

98 PER CENT AMERICAN MOM & Apple Pie 1929 Crash Band
LPs: 10/12-inch
LHI.. 10-15 67

1910 FRUITGUM CO. *P&R/LP '68*
Singles: 7-inch
ATTACK..4-8 70
BUDDAH...4-8 67-69
SUPER K..4-8 70
LPs: 10/12-inch
BUDDAH.. 15-25 68-70

1910 FRUITGUM COMPANY / Lemon Pipers
LPs: 10/12-inch
BUDDAH.. 15-20 68-70
Also see 1910 FRUITGUM COMPANY

1929 DEPRESSION
Singles: 7-inch
PROVIDENCE (422 "You've Been Cheatin' on Me Baby").. 10-15 66
Also see CORRENTE, Sal

NINJA
Singles
IRON WORKS (1015 "Eye on You")..........8-12 86
(Square, logo-picture disc.)
IRON WORKS (1015 "Eye on You")........ 10-15 86
(Weapon-shaped picture disc.)
IRON WORKS (1015 "Eye on You")........ 15-25 86
(Two rectangular picture discs.)

NINO & EBB TIDES *P&R '61*
(Nino & Ebb-Tides)
Singles: 7-inch
MADISON (162 "Those Oldies But Goodies")... 40-50 61
MADISON (166 "Juke Box Saturday Night")... 30-40 61
MALA (480 "Linda Lou")......................... 10-15 64
MARCO (105 "Someday")........................ 40-50 61
MR. PEACOCK (102 "Wished I Was Home").. 15-25 61
MR. PEACOCK (117 "Lovin' Time")..........8-12 62
MR. PEEKE (123 "Tonight")..................... 20-30 63
RECORTE (405 "Puppy Love")................ 15-25 58
RECORTE (408 "The Real Meaning of Christmas").. 200-300 59
RECORTE (409 "I'm Confessin' ")............ 40-50 59
RECORTE (413 "I Love Girls")................ 40-50 59
Member: Nino Aiello.
Also see COLEMAN, Lenny
Also see EBB TIDES
Also see EBBS
Also see WINCHELL, Danny

NINO & EBB TIDES / Miss Frankie Nolan
Singles: 7-inch
MADISON (151 "A Week from Sunday"). 10-20 61
Also see NINO & EBB TIDES
Also see NOLAN, Frankie

NINO & PULASKI HIGHWAYMEN
Singles: 7-inch
MIRA (214 "Michelle")................................5-10 66

NINTH STREET BRIDGE
Singles: 7-inch
CECILE (1968 "Wild Illusions")................20-30 68

NINTH STREET BRIDGE
Singles: 7-inch
FENTON (2136 "I'm a Baby")...............125-150 '60s

NIP 'N' TUCK
Singles: 7-inch
DITTO (123 "I Know What Side My Bread Is Buttered")..5-10 59

NIPTONES
Singles: 7-inch
LORRAINE (1001 "Angie")........................10-15 65

NIRVANA
Singles: 7-inch
BELL (715 "Pentecost Hotel")....................5-10 68
LPs: 10/12-inch
BELL..15-25 68-69
METROMEDIA..10-20 70

NIRVANA *LP '91*
Singles: 12-inch
DGC (21673 "Smells Like Teen Spirit")......5-10 91
DGC (21707 "Come As You Are")...............5-10 92
DGC (21818 "Lithium")...............................5-10 92
Singles: 7-inch
DGC (19050 "Smells Like Teen Spirit")........4-8 91
DGC (19120 "Come As You Are")................4-8 92
SUB POP (23 "Love Buzz")....................50-100 88
(1,000 made.)
SUB POP (73 "Sliver")..............................15-25 90
(Colored vinyl.)
EPs: 7-inch
TUPELO (8 "Blew")....................................20-30 89
LPs: 10/12-inch
DGC (24425 "Nevermind").........................10-15 91
DGC (24540 "Incesticide")..........................8-12 92
DGC (24607 "In Utero")..............................8-12 93
DGC (24727 "Unplugged")...........................8-12 94
DGC (25105 "From the Muddy Banks of the Wishkah")..8-12 96
DGC/SUB POP (24607 "In Utero")...........20-30 93
(Clear vinyl, limited edition.)
MCA (24727 "Unplugged")..........................8-10 90s
MFSL (258 "Nevermind")...........................25-35 96
SUB POP (34 "Bleach")........................100-200 89
(Colored vinyl.)
SUB POP (34 "Bleach")...............................25-50 89
(Black vinyl. Includes poster.)
Members: Kurt Cobain; Krist "Chris" Novoselic; Jason Everman; Chad Channing; Dave Grohl; Dave Foster.
Also see LANEGAN, Mark

NIRVANA / The Fluid
Singles: 7-inch
SUB POP (97 "Molly's Lips")....................10-20 91
(Black vinyl. 3,500 made.)
SUB POP (97 "Molly's Lips")....................10-20 91
(Colored vinyl. 4,000 made.)
Picture Sleeves
SUB POP (97 "Molly's Lips")....................10-20 91

NIRVANA / Jesus Lizard
Singles: 7-inch
TOUCH & GO (83 "Puss")............................5-10 93

NIRVANA / The Melvins
Singles: 7-inch
COMMUNION (25 "Here She Comes Now")..10-15 91
(Black vinyl.)
COMMUNION (25 "Here She Comes Now")..10-15 91
(Colored vinyl.)
Also see NIRVANA

NIRVANA BANANA
Singles: 7-inch
ATLANTIC (2422 "Rainy Day Stage Door Mama")..5-10 67

NIRVANA SITAR & STRING GROUP
Singles: 7-inch
MR. G (806 "Never My Love").....................5-10 68

NISWONGER, Larry
Singles: 7-inch
DALLAS (100 "The Two Step")..............75-125

NITE & LITERS
Singles: 7-inch
VERVE (10256 "Jealous Hearts")............10-15 62

NITE, Ken
Singles: 7-inch
TNT (158 "All Those Lovely Stars").........10-20 58

NITE CAPS
Singles: 7-inch
CHESS (1694 "Haunted Sax")..................15-25 58

NITE CAPS
Singles: 7-inch
BRYTE (307 "Wildcat")...............................15-25 62
CMP (1 "Skip School Flu").........................50-75

NITE HAWKS
Singles: 7-inch
BROOKE (112 "Hawk's Hop")....................10-20 59

NITE LITES
Singles: 7-inch
SOUTHERN SOUND (106 "Bust Out")....10-20 61

NITE OWLS
Singles: 7-inch
REMBRANDT..8-12 '60s
TAKE 3 (777 "Hip Monkey").......................10-20 63
TOP DOG...8-12 66

NITE PEOPLE
Singles: 7-inch
AMSTERDAM (85008 "Hot Smoke and Sassafrass")...15-25 70

NITE RIDERS
Singles: 78 rpm
APOLLO...10-20 54
MGM..15-25 57
Singles: 7-inch
APOLLO (460 "Say Hey").........................40-50 54
CHERRY (7886 "Aleph Beth")...................15-25
MGM (12487 "Sittin' Sippin' Coffee").........15-25 57
RIFF (101 "In My Dream").......................50-100
TEEN (116 "Starlight and You")...............25-35 58
TEEN (118 "Don't Hang Up the Phone")..20-30 58
TEEN (120 "When a Man Cries")..............20-30 58
Member: James "Doc" Starks.
Also see STARKS, Doc, & Nite Riders

NITE RIDERS
Singles: 7-inch
("Tornado")..15-25 '60s
(No label name or number shown.)

NITE ROCKERS
Singles: 7-inch
RCA (7323 "Oh Baby")..............................10-20 58
SUPER (003 "Little Mama")....................50-100

NITE SOUNDS
Singles: 7-inch
FORTUNE (548 "I Love You with Tender Passion")..30-40 62
FORTUNE (552 "Harem Girl")..................10-15 63
Member: Butch Vaden.
Also see DAVIS, Melvin
Also see VADEN, Butch

NITE SOUNDS
Singles: 7-inch
SEAFAIR (112 "On Broadway")...............10-15 62
Members: Paul Goldsmith; Luther Rabb; Jim Walters.
Also see EMERGENCY EXIT

NITE WALKERS
Singles: 7-inch
RUSSELL (43107 "High Class")...............20-30 66

NITEBEATS
Singles: 7-inch
PEACH (718 "Teen-Age Lover")...........175-200 59

NITEBEATS
Singles: 7-inch
TIDE (1088 "I Think It's Love")..................10-15 63

NITE-CAPPERS
Singles: 7-inch
PAL (1150 "Out of Sight")........................15-25 '60s
PAL (9158 "Everything")...........................15-25 '60s

NITECAPS
Singles: 78 rpm
GROOVE..25-50 55
Singles: 7-inch
GROOVE (0134 "A Kiss and a Vow")..150-200 56
GROOVE (0147 "Tough Mama")..............40-50 56
GROOVE (0158 "Bamboo Rock & Roll").50-75 56
GROOVE (0176 "Let Me Know Tonight")..100-150 56
Members: Ronnie Savoy; Bob Hamilton; Al Kent; Freddy Price.
Also see DILLARD, Varetta
Also see SAVOY, Ronnie

NITE-LITERS
Singles: 7-inch
SUDDEN (101 "Fat Sally")........................15-25 60

NITE-LITERS
Singles: 7-inch
STATUE (601 "Jericho Road")...................8-12 '60s
STATUE (608 "What's Happening")...........8-12 '60s
VEE EIGHT (8 "Nervous")........................10-15 62
VERVE (10256 "Nervous")..........................5-10 62
LPs: 10/12-inch
STATUE (6254 "The Nite-Liters")............15-25 76
Members: Johnny Mihalic; Jerry Hood; Thomas Kelly; Jimmy Ellis; Roy Cayson; Charles Watts.
Also see MAHALIC, Johnny

NITE-LITERS *P&R/R&B/LP '71*
Singles: 7-inch
RCA...4-8 69-72
LPs: 10/12-inch
RCA...8-15 71-72
Members: Harvey Fuqua; Austin Lander; Tony Churchill; James Baker; Robert Jackson; Leroy Taylor; Robin Russell; Roger Voice; James Hall; Ben Boytel.
Also see NEW BIRTH

NITE-LITES
(With the Rock-A-Fellas)
Singles: 7-inch
SEQUOIA (502 "Lovers Twist")...............50-75

NITE-NIKS
Singles: 7-inch
LAWN (207 "Shawnee")...........................10-20 63

NITERIDERS
Singles: 7-inch
STAR-BRIGHT (3055 "Just "Call on Me")...15-20 65

NITEWALKERS
Singles: 7-inch
NITE (115 "Corner of the World")............20-30 '60s

NITTY GRITTY DIRT BAND *P&R/LP '67*
(Dirt Band)
Singles: 78 rpm
LIBERTY (2889 "Mr. Bojangles")..............20-30 70
(Promotional issue only.)
U.A. (69 "All the Good Times")..................20-30 71
(Promotional issue only. Includes script and booklet.)
Singles: 7-inch
LIBERTY (1000 series).................................3-6 81-84
LIBERTY (55948 "Buy for Me the Rain")....5-10 67
LIBERTY (55982 "Truly Right")...................5-10 67
LIBERTY (56054 "Collegiana")....................5-10 68
LIBERTY (56134 "Some of Shelley's Blues")..5-10 69
LIBERTY (56159 "Cure").............................5-10 70
LIBERTY (56197 "Mr. Bojangles")..............5-10 70
U.A. 4-8 71-80
W.B. 3-5 84-86
Picture Sleeves
LIBERTY (1000 series).................................3-5 81-84
LIBERTY (55982 "Truly Right")...................8-12 67
U.A. 3-6 71-80
EPs: 7-inch
LIBERTY (37 "Special Radio Interview with the N.G.D.B.")...10-15 70
(Promotional issue only. Issued with paper cover.)
U.A. (69 "All the Good Times")...................20-30 71
(Promotional issue only. Includes script and booklet.)
LPs: 10/12-inch
LIBERTY (1100 series).................................5-10 81
LIBERTY (3501 "Nitty Gritty Dirt Band")...15-25 67
(Monaural.)
LIBERTY (7501 "Nitty Gritty Dirt Band")...15-25 67
(Stereo.)
LIBERTY (7501 thru 7611).........................15-20 67-69
LIBERTY (7642 "Uncle Charlie").........100-125 70
(Gatefold promotional edition. Includes two bonus singles, photos and booklet.)
LIBERTY (LST-7642 "Uncle Charlie")......10-20 70

LIBERTY (LATO-7642 "Uncle Charlie") ... 5-8
LIBERTY (51146 "Let's Go") ... 5-8 83
U.A. (117 "Interview") ... 15-25 75
(Promotional issue only.)
U.A. (UA-LA184 "Stars and Stripes Forever") ... 10-20 74
U.A. (LWB-184 "Stars and Stripes Forever") ... 8-10
U.A. (469 "Dream") ... 8-12 75
U.A. (469 "Dream - Programmers Guide") ... 15-25 75
(Promotional issue only.)
U.A. (UA-LA670 "Dirt, Silver and Gold") .. 15-20 76
U.A. (LKCL-670 "Dirt, Silver and Gold") ... 8-12
U.A.(854 thru 1042) ... 5-10 78-80
U.A. (5500 series) ... 8-12 71
U.A. (9801 "Will the Circle Be Unbroken") ... 30-40 72
(Three-disc set.)
UNIVERSAL (12500 "Will the Circle Be Unbroken, Vol. 2") ... 10-15 89
W.B. ... 5-10 84-86
Members: Jeff Hanna; John McEuen; Bernie Leadon; Jimmy Ibbotson; Bob Carpenter; Jimmie Fadden.
Session: Nicolette Larson; Al Garth; Merle Bregante.
Also see DENVER, John, & Nitty Gritty Dirt Band
Also see SKAGGS, Ricky

NITTY GRITTY DIRT BAND & ROY ACUFF
C&W '71

Singles: 7-inch

U.A. ... 4-6 71
Also see ACUFF, Roy

NITTY GRITTY DIRT BAND & JIMMY MARTIN
C&W '73

Singles: 7-inch

U.A. ... 4-6 73
Also see MARTIN, Jimmy

NITTY GRITTY DIRT BAND & LINDA RONSTADT

Singles: 7-inch

U.A. ... 4-6 79
Also see NITTY GRITTY DIRT BAND
Also see RONSTADT, Linda

NITZINGER
LP '72
(John Nitzinger)

Singles: 7-inch

CAPITOL ... 4-6 72-73
20TH FOX ... 4-6 76

LPs: 10/12-inch

CAPITOL ... 10-15 72-73
20TH FOX ... 8-10 76
Members: John Nitzinger; Bugs Henderson.
Also see HENDERSON, Bugs

NITZSCHE, Jack
P&R '63

Singles: 7-inch

FANTASY ... 4-6 76
MCA ... 4-6 78
REPRISE ... 10-20 63-65

Picture Sleeves

REPRISE (20,202 "Lonely Surfer") ... 15-25 63

LPs: 10/12-inch

MCA ... 5-10 78
REPRISE (2000 series) ... 8-12 73
REPRISE (R-6101 "Lonely Surfer") ... 30-40 63
(Monaural.)
REPRISE (RS-6101 "Lonely Surfer") ... 40-60 63
(Stereo.)
REPRISE (R-6115 "Dance to the Hits of the Beatles") ... 15-25 64
(Monaural.)
REPRISE (RS-6115 "Dance to the Hits of the Beatles") ... 25-30 64
(Stereo.)
REPRISE (6200 "Chopin '66") ... 10-20 66
Also see ALLEY CATS
Also see HALE & HUSHABYES
Also see SINNERS
Also see VERONICA

NIX, Billy

Singles: 7-inch

BEN (132 "I'm Gonna Please My Baby") .. 50-75
GLENN (1800 "I'm a Lucky Guy") ... 10-20 59
GLENN (1802 "An Old Flame") ... 10-20 60
GLENN (1804 "Get with the Beat") ... 50-75 60
MAR-VEL (1803 "Your Flame of Love") .. 10-15 63

NIX, Donnie

Singles: 7-inch

WILROD (1001 "Ain't About to Go Home") ... 125-175

NIX, Ford, & Moonshiners

Singles: 7-inch

CLIX (621 "Nine Times Out of Ten") ... 250-350

NIX, Hoyle

Singles: 7-inch

BO-KAY (110 "I Don't Lov'a Nobody") ... 15-25 60
CAPROCK (103 "My Wasted Love") ... 10-20 58
CAPROCK (105 "My Mary") ... 10-20 58
CAPROCK (109 "Summit Ridge Drive") ... 10-20 58

NIX, Willie
(With His Combo; the Memphis Blues Boy)

Singles: 78 rpm

CHANCE (1163 "Nervous Wreck") ... 100-200 55
CHECKER (756 "Truckin' Little Woman") ... 100-200 52
RPM (327 "Lonesome Bedroom Blues") ... 100-200 51
SABRE (104 "Just Can't Stay") ... 75-125 53
SUN (179 "Baker Shop Boogie") ... 400-500 53

Singles: 7-inch

CHANCE (1163 "Nervous Wreck") ... 300-500 55
SABRE (104 "All By Yourself") ... 250-400 53

NIXON, Elmore
(With Henry Hayes; with His Hadacol Boys)

Singles: 78 rpm

IMPERIAL ... 15-25 55
LUCKY ... 15-25 49
MERCURY ... 15-25 51
PEACOCK (1537 "My Wish for You") ... 15-25 50
PEACOCK (1572 "You See Me Smiling") ... 15-25 51
POST ... 15-25 55
SAVOY ... 15-25 53
SITTIN' IN WITH (546 "Foolish Love") ... 15-25 50
SITTIN' IN WITH (580 "I'm Moving Out") .. 15-25 50
SITTIN' IN WITH (601 "Shout & Rock") ... 15-25 51

Singles: 7-inch

IMPERIAL (5388 "You Left Me") ... 20-40 55
MERCURY (70061 "Playboy Blues") ... 30-50 51
POST (2008 "Don't Do It") ... 20-40 55
SAVOY (878 "Over Here Pretty Lady") ... 20-40 53
SAVOY (889 "Elmore's Blues") ... 20-40 53
SAVOY (1105 "Last Nite") ... 20-40 53
Also see CHENIER, Clifton
Also see HAYES, Henry

NIXON, Richard

Singles: 7-inch

CBS/AURAVISION ("Nixon's the One") ... 10-20 68
(Picture disc postcard.)

LPs: 10/12-inch

CAPITOL (11350 "Resignation of a President") ... 10-15 74
Also see KENNEDY, John Fitzgerald / Richard M. Nixon

NIXON, Roy, & Down Beats

Singles: 7-inch

DEE-CEE ("Hard-Rockin' Daddy") ... 75-125
(Selection number not known.)
Members: Roy Nickson; Mel Thomas; Barry Steinberg; Brian Steinberg.

NO DEPOSIT, NO RETURN

Singles: 7-inch

PHILIPS (40451 "Your Love Is My Love") .. 5-10 67

NO NAME BAND

Singles: 7-inch

SCORPIO (472 "Israeli Stomp") ... 10-20 63

NO NAMES

Singles: 7-inch

GUYDEN (2114 "Love") ... 50-100 64
(Black vinyl.)
GUYDEN (2114 "Love") ... 400-500 64
(Red vinyl.)
Also see DANNY & DIAMONDS / No Names

NO NAMES

Singles: 7-inch

TEE PEE (51/52 "Take It from Me"/"I Never Realized") ... 10-20 68

NO STRINGS ATTACHED

Singles: 7-inch

ACCENT (1240 "You're More Than a Miracle") ... 5-10 68
ACCENT (1246 "Leave My Baby Alone") ... 5-10 68

NOACK, Eddie
C&W '58

Singles: 78 rpm

MERCURY ... 10-20 55
STARDAY ... 10-25 54-57
TNT ... 15-25 54

Singles: 7-inch

ALLSTAR ... 5-10 62-65
D (1019 "Have Blues, Will Travel") ... 15-25 58
D (1037 "Walk 'Em Off") ... 30-50 59
D (1060 "A Thinking Man's Woman") ... 15-25 59
D (1094 "Relief Is Just a Swallow Away"). 15-25 59
D (1100 series) ... 10-20 59-61
D (1200 series) ... 5-10 61-72
K-ARK ... 4-6 69
MERCURY ... 15-25 55
STARDAY (except 213) ... 15-25 54-57
STARDAY (213 "Don't Worry 'Bout Me") .. 50-75 55
TNT (110 "Too Hot to Handle") ... 50-75 54
TNT (1010 "Too Hot to Handle") ... 50-75 54
(Both 110 and 1010 exist; however, we're not sure which came first.)
WIDE WORLD ... 4-6 70-72

LPs: 10/12-inch

WIDE WORLD ... 10-20 70

NOAH'S ARK

Singles: 7-inch

DECCA (32153 "Love-On") ... 5-10 67
DECCA (32217 "Paper Man") ... 5-10 67
Members: Ron Elliott; Buddy Richardson.

NOAH'S ARK

Singles: 7-inch

ROULETTE (4703 "I Think I Wanna Love You Baby") ... 5-10 66
Member: Ron Dante.

NOAH'S DOVE

Singles: 7-inch

PICCADILLY (253 "Noah's Dove") ... 5-10 67
PICCADILLY ("Camels & Dragons") ... 5-10 67
(Selection number not known.)

NOBELLS

Singles: 7-inch

MAR (101 "Cryin' Over You") ... 50-75 62

NOBELMEN

Singles: 7-inch

BEE (1826 "Vibration") ... 15-25 67

NOBELS

Singles: 7-inch

CUCA (6375 "Tossing & Turning") ... 10-20 63

NOBLE, Beverly

Singles: 7-inch

RALLY (502 "Better Off Without You") ... 8-12 65
SPARROW (100 "You Cheated") ... 10-15 62
(Same number used on Individuals release.)

NOBLE, Eddy

Singles: 7-inch

TOP HAT (1002 "There Go Frankie") ... 15-25

NOBLE, Kitty

Singles: 78 rpm

HERALD ... 10-15 54

Singles: 7-inch

HERALD (422 "Can't See Nobody But You") ... 15-25 54
MAY (119 "I'll Be Yours") ... 5-10 62
MAY (124 "Toodle Ooh") ... 5-10 62

NOBLE, Nick
P&R '55

Singles: 78 rpm

MERCURY ... 5-15 56-57
WING ... 5-10 55

Singles: 7-inch

CAPITOL ... 4-6 73
CHESS ... 5-10 63-64
CHURCHILL ... 3-6 77-80
COLUMBIA ... 5-10 69
CORAL ... 8-12 59-66
DATE ... 5-10 67-68
EPIC ... 4-6 77
FRATERNITY ... 10-20 58
LIBERTY ... 5-10 62-63
MERCURY ... 10-20 56-57
PARAMOUNT ... 4-6 71
TMS ... 4-6 79
20TH FOX ... 5-10 65
WING ... 10-15 55

LPs: 10/12-inch

COLUMBIA ... 8-12 69
LIBERTY ... 10-15 63
WING ... 15-25 60
Also see PLATTERS / Nick Noble / Rusty Draper / Ralph Marterie

NOBLE KNIGHTS

Singles: 7-inch

COTILLION (44030 "Movin', Pt. 4") ... 5-10 69
Session: King Curtis.
Also see KING CURTIS

NOBLEMEN

Singles: 7-inch

PROFILE (4012 "Dirty Robber") ... 20-40 60
USA (1002 "Thunder Wagon") ... 30-50 59
(USA logo has no periods on this label.)
U.S.A. (1213 "Thunder Wagon") ... 20-30 59
U.S.A. (1222 "Dirty Robber") ... 15-25 60
Members: Brand Shank; Chuck Lalicata; Bob Stange; Jerry Sworske; Raymond Ojeda; Bruce Rudan.
Also see NIGHT BEATS

NOBLEMEN

Singles: 7-inch

PRISM (1930 "She Still Thinks I Love Her") ... 10-20 65

NOBLEMEN

Singles: 7-inch

IGL (130 "Things Aren't the Same") ... 20-40 67
CJL (101 "Stop Your Running Around") ... 10-15 67

NOBLEMEN

Singles: 7-inch

PARIS TOWER (110 "Two-Faced Woman") ... 20-30 67

NOBLEMEN

Singles: 7-inch

CLARITY (103 "Everytime") ... 30-40 '60s

NOBLEMEN / Toni Magestro

Singles: 7-inch

U.S.A. (1215 "Sleep Beauty Sleep") ... 20-30 63
(Not the same group of Noblemen as heard on other U.S.A. issues.)
Also see MAGESTRO, Miss Toni

NOBLEMEN 4

Singles: 7-inch

RECAP (291 "What's Your Name") ... 20-30 '60s
RECAP (292 "I Can Hear Raindrops") ... 20-30 '60s

NOBLES

Singles: 78 rpm

SAPPHIRE (151 "Do You Love Me") ... 25-35 56

Singles: 7-inch

SAPPHIRE (151 "Do You Love Me") ... 75-125 56

NOBLES

Singles: 7-inch

KLIK (305 "Poor Rock 'N Roll") ... 100-200 57
LOST NITE ... 4-6 '70s
TIMES SQUARE (1 "Poor Rock 'N Roll"). 25-30 62
(Blue vinyl.)
TIMES SQUARE (1 "Poor Rock 'N Roll"). 20-25 62
(Green vinyl.)
TIMES SQUARE (12 "Crime Don't Pay"). 20-25 63
(Blue vinyl.)
TIMES SQUARE (33 "Why Be a Fool") ... 20-25 64
Members: Dick Bernardo; Pat Cosenza; Sal Tramauche; Joey Kakulis.
Also see NICKY & NOBLES

NOBLES

Singles: 7-inch

ABC-PAR (9984 "Standing Alone") ... 10-15 58
ABC-PAR (10012 "Just for Me") ... 10-15 58

NOBLES

Singles: 7-inch

STACY (926 "You Ain't Right") ... 30-40 61
Member: Sollie McElroy.
Also see McELROY, Sollie

NOBLES

Singles: 7-inch

SELBON (1005 "Black Widow") ... 20-30 63

NOBLES
Singles: 7-inch
USA (788 "Marlene") ... 10-20 64
Also see CHICK & NOBLES

NOBLES
Singles: 7-inch
MARQUIS (4991 "Something Else") ... 20-30 66

NOBLES, Cliff P&R/R&B/LP '68
(Cliff Nobles & Co.)
Singles: 7-inch
ATLANTIC (2352 "My Love Is Getting Stonger") ... 45-65 66
ATLANTIC (2380 "Everybody Is Weak for Somebody") ... 10-15 67
J-V (1034 "My Love Is Getting Stronger") ... 5-10
JAMIE (1406 "The Horse") ... 4-6 72
MOONSHOT (6710 "Pony the Horse") ... 5-10 69
PHIL-L.A. OF SOUL (310 "This Love Will Last") ... 5-10 68
PHIL-L.A. OF SOUL (313 "The Horse") ... 5-10 68
PHIL-L.A. OF SOUL (318 "Horse Fever") ... 5-10 68
PHIL-L.A. OF SOUL (324 Switch It On") ... 5-10 69
PHIL-L.A. OF SOUL (329 "The Camel") ... 5-10 69
ROULETTE (7142 "This Feeling of Loneliness") ... 4-6 73
LPs: 10/12-inch
MOON SHOT (601 "Pony the Horse") ... 15-25 '60s
PHIL-L.A. OF SOUL (4001 "The Horse"). 15-25 68

NOBLETONES
Singles: 7-inch
BIM BAM BOOM (118 "Who Cares About Love") ... 4-6 73
(Black vinyl.)
BIM BAM BOOM (118 "Who Cares About Love") ... 5-8 73
(Blue vinyl.)
C&M (182 "I Love You") ... 50-75 58
C&M (182 "Who Cares About Love") ... 40-60 58
(Same number used twice.)
C&M (188 "I'm Crying") ... 20-30 58
RELIC (529 "I Love You") ... 5-10 65
TIMES SQUARE (17 "I Love You") ... 15-20 63
(Blue vinyl.)
TIMES SQUARE (18 "Who Cares About Love") ... 15-20 63
VINTAGE (1014 "I Still Love You") ... 10-15 73
(Blue vinyl.)
Member: Dottie Watkins.

NOBODYS
Singles: 7-inch
SAMAR (119 "Thinkin' About It") ... 5-10 67

NOBODY'S CHILDREN
Singles: 7-inch
BUDDAH (36 "I Can't Let Go") ... 5-10 68
BULLET (10000 "I Can't Let Go") ... 8-12 68
U.A. (50090 "Junco Partner") ... 15-25 67

NOBODY'S CHILDREN
Singles: 7-inch
GPC (1944 "Good Times") ... 10-20 67

NOBODY'S CHILDREN
Singles: 7-inch
DELTA (2207 "St. James Infirmary") ... 20-30 '60s

NOC-A-BOUTS
Singles: 7-inch
COSMIC (706 "Session") ... 10-20 58

NOCTURNAL DAYDREAM
Singles: 7-inch
COCONUT GROOVE (2039 "Had a Dream Last Night") ... 30-50 68

NOCTURNALS
Singles: 7-inch
BAT (101 "Twister's Stomp") ... 15-25 62
REVIVE (101 "Twister's Stomp") ... 10-15 63
REVIVE (104/5 "Stag Line") ... 10-20 64
Members: Mike Metko; Bill Caldwell; Tom Waldrup; Jack Griffin; Stan Seymore.
Also see VANCE, Chico

NOCTURNALS
Singles: 7-inch
EMBASSY (1967 "Detroit") ... 5-10 67

NOCTURNES
Singles: 7-inch
KAREN (1009 "Sh-Boom") ... 10-20 60

NOCTURNES
("Featuring Dana Powers")
Singles: 7-inch
CARLSON INT'L (4105 "My Christmas Star") ... 50-100 64

NOCTURNES
Singles: 7-inch
CUCA (6373 "Cyclone") ... 10-20 63
CUCA (64103 "Little One") ... 10-20 64
SOMA (1108 "Hot Night") ... 15-25 59
Picture Sleeves
CUCA (64103 "Little One") ... 15-25 64

NOCTURNS
Singles: 7-inch
FONTANA (1528 "Sha La La") ... 5-10 65
LTD (405 "Saturday") ... 5-10 66

NODAENS
Singles: 7-inch
GOLD (1001 "Beach Girl") ... 50-75 '60s
Member: Dave Nowlen.
Also see SURVIVORS

NOE, Dale
Singles: 78 rpm
SMART (1016 "Hound Dog Boogie") ... 10-20 52
Singles: 7-inch
SMART (1016 "Hound Dog Boogie") ... 20-40 52

NOEL, Dick
Singles: 78 rpm
FRATERNITY ... 5-10 55-56
Singles: 7-inch
AVA (136 "Brush Those tears from Your Eyes") ... 5-10 63
CUCA (1301 "Little Lost Angel") ... 10-15 65
EVEREST (2048 "Little Lost Angel") ... 15-20 64
FRATERNITY ... 10-20 55-58
LIBERTY (55254 "Sugar Beat") ... 10-20 60

NOEL, Didi
Singles: 7-inch
BLUE CAT (129 "No More Tears to Cry") .. 5-10 66

NOEL, Fats
Singles: 78 rpm
HERALD (401 "High Tide") ... 15-20 53
Singles: 7-inch
HERALD (401 "High Tide") ... 20-30 53
HERALD (402 "Duck Soup") ... 20-30 53

NOEL, Hattie
Singles: 7-inch
DOOTO (461 "My Passionate Man") ... 5-10 61

NOEL, Sid
Singles: 78 rpm
ALADDIN (3331 "Flying Saucer") ... 10-20 56
ATCO (6065 "Take Five") ... 5-10 56
Singles: 7-inch
ALADDIN (3331 "Flying Saucer") ... 20-30 56
ATCO (6065 "Take Five") ... 10-15 56

NOIE, Denny
(With the In-Crowd; with 4th of Never; with Catalinas)
Singles: 7-inch
KNIGHT (100 "Dee Dee") ... 50-100 65
TENER (150 "Dee Dee") ... 25-50 67
Also see CATALINAS

NOISEMAKERS
Singles: 7-inch
ASTRA (102 "Zoobie") ... 10-15 61
(Black vinyl.)
ASTRA (102 "Zoobie") ... 15-25 61
(Colored vinyl.)
SWIRL INT'L (2 "Zoobie") ... 15-20 61

NOISES & SOUNDS
Singles: 7-inch
PICCADILLY (222 "How Much Lovin' ") ... 5-10 66

NOLA, Larry, & Monroe Playboys
Singles: 78 rpm
FLAIR (1004 "What's the Reason") ... 8-12 53
Singles: 7-inch
FLAIR (1004 "What's the Reason") ... 10-20 53

NOLAN, Frankie
(Miss Frankie Nolan)
Singles: 7-inch
ABC-PAR (10231 "I Still Care") ... 40-50 61
(With Frankie Valli.)
MADISON (151 "A Week from Sunday") .. 30-40 61
Also see NINO & EBB TIDES / Miss Frankie Nolan
Also see VALLI, Frankie

NOLAN, Kenny P&R '76
Singles: 7-inch
CASABLANCA ... 3-6 79-80
DOT ... 5-10 68
FORWARD ... 5-10 69
HIGHLAND ... 5-10 68
LION ... 4-6 72
MGM ... 4-6 71
POLYDOR ... 4-6 78
20TH FOX ... 4-6 76-77
LPs: 10/12-inch
CASABLANCA ... 5-10 79
MCA ... 5-10 82
POLYDOR ... 5-10 78
20TH FOX ... 5-10 77

NOLAND, Terry
Singles: 7-inch
BRUNSWICK (55010 "Hypnotized") ... 20-30 57
Singles: 7-inch
APT (25065 "Long Gone Baby") ... 10-15 62
BRUNSWICK (55010 "Hypnotized") ... 25-50 57
BRUNSWICK (55036 "Patty Baby") ... 15-25 57
BRUNSWICK (55054 "Look at Me") ... 20-30 58
BRUNSWICK (55069 "Everyone But Me") ... 20-30 58
BRUNSWICK (55092 "There Was a Fungus Among Us") ... 20-30 58
BRUNSWICK (55122 "Guess I'm Gonna Fall") ... 10-20 59
CORAL (62274 "There Was a Fungus Among Us") ... 10-15 61
LPs: 10/12-inch
BRUNSWICK (54041 "Terry Noland") .. 200-250 58
Also see FREED, Alan

NOLEN, Bob
Singles: 7-inch
FARO (594 "Bucket Full of Tears") ... 5-10 59

NOLEN, Jimmy
Singles: 78 rpm
ELKO ... 20-40 55
FEDERAL ... 15-25 55-56
IMPERIAL ... 10-15 55
Singles: 7-inch
ELKO (254 "Slow Freight Back Home") ... 50-75 55
FEDERAL ... 15-25 55-56
IMPERIAL ... 15-25 55

NOLEN, Larry
Singles: 78 rpm
STARDAY (233 "Lady Luck") ... 10-15 56
Singles: 7-inch
RADIO (112 "Hey Mr. Heartache") ... 15-20 58
RENNER (211 "Remember Me") ... 10-15 61
RENNER (214 "Hey Mr. Heartache") ... 10-15 61
RENNER (223 My Real Love") ... 10-15 62
STARDAY ("King of the Ducktails") ... 300-400
(Selection number not known.)
STARDAY (233 "Lady Luck") ... 20-30 56

NOLEN, Lloyd
Singles: 7-inch
KING (5651 "Fun Fun") ... 5-10 62
KING (5680 "I Don't Know About You") ... 5-10 62

NOMADS
Singles: 7-inch
BALBOA (006 "The Perfect Crime") ... 20-30 59
(First issue.)
JOSIE (851 "The Perfect Crime") ... 15-25 59
JOSIE (905 "Rainbow's End") ... 15-25 63
NORTHERN (503 "Heart Attack") ... 100-150 59

NOMADS
Singles: 7-inch
ABC-PAR (10191 "I'm Popeye the Sailor Man") ... 5-10 61
GENIE (7817 "I'm Popeye the Sailor Man") ... 8-12 61
PHAROS (101 "Oh Jennie") ... 5-10 64
RUST (5028 "Bounty Hunter") ... 5-10 61

NOMADS
Singles: 7-inch
ARLEN (714 "Watch Dog") ... 5-10 62

NOMADS
Singles: 7-inch
KEL (1000 "You Come Around") ... 15-25 65
Members: Jack Litjens; Joe Litjens; Mike Yanke; Larry Wolfe.

NOMADS
Singles: 7-inch
SOFT (958 "I Saw You Go") ... 10-20 65
SPOTLIGHT (5019 "Be Nice") ... 20-25 66
Picture Sleeves
SPOTLIGHT (5019 "Be Nice") ... 25-35 66
Also see YELLOW PAYGES

NO-MADS
Singles: 7-inch
BATTLE OF THE BANDS (201,353 "Liverpool Lover") ... 15-25 66

NOMADS
Singles: 7-inch
STARK (009 "Not for Me") ... 20-30 66
TORNADO (159 "Thoughts of a Madman") ... 25-35 67

NOMADS
Singles: 7-inch
MO-GROOV ... 5-10 67
Members: Sonny Threatt; Phyllis Brown; Andy McKinney; Hugg Martin; Carroll Cox; Darrel McClinton.
Also see SONNY & PHYLLIS
Also see TANGENTS

NOMADS
Singles: 7-inch
DAMON (1 "Cry Baby") ... 15-25 67
(Canadian.)
DAMON (2 "Dizzy Miss Lizzy") ... 15-25 67
(Canadian.)
DAMON (3 "Come on Now") ... 15-25 67
(Canadian.)
DAMON (4 "Hey Joe") ... 15-25 67
(Canadian.)
DAMON (101 "I Walk Alone") ... 15-25 67
(Canadian.)
MAINSTREAM ... 10-20 '60s
(Canadian.)
ORBIT (1121 "Three O'Clock") ... 15-25 68
LP: 10/12-inch
POINT (333 "Hits of the Nomads") ... 30-50 '60s
Also see SMOKE

NOMADS
Singles: 7-inch
DISCOTEK ... 10-15 '60s
PRELUDE (1112 "Last Summer Day") ... 20-30 '60s
SAMTER ... 10-15 '60s

NON CONFORMISTS
Singles: 7-inch
SCEPTER (12184 "Two-Legged Big-Eyed Canary") ... 15-25 67

NO-NA-MEES
Singles: 7-inch
ERA (3165 "Gotta Hold On") ... 10-20 66

NONCHALANTS
Singles: 7-inch
CHROMA (1000 "Honky Tonk Joe") ... 50-75

NOON EXPRESS
Singles: 7-inch
EMBASSY (1970 "Flashback") ... 15-25 67

NORDINE, Ken
(With His Kinsmen; with Fred Katz Group)
Singles: 7-inch
DOT ... 8-12 57-59
LPs: 10/12-inch
BLUE THUMB ... 8-12 72
DECCA (8550 "Concert in the Sky") ... 40-50 57
DOT (3075 thru 3301) ... 30-50 57-60
(Monaural.)
DOT (25115 thru 25301) ... 30-50 58-60
(Stereo.)
DOT (25880 "Best of Word Jazz") ... 10-20 67
HAMILTON (102 "Voice of Love") ... 20-30 59
(Monaural.)
HAMILTON (12102 "Voice of Love") ... 30-40 59
(Stereo.)
SNAIL (1001 "Stare with Your Ears") ... 15-25 79
(Gatefold cover.)
PHILIPS (200224 "Colors") ... 15-25 67
(Monaural.)

PHILIPS (600224 "Colors") 15-25 67
(Stereo.)
Also see VAUGHN, Billy

NORELKOS

Singles: 7-inch

KINGSWOOD (102 "Tell Me Baby") 400-500 61

NORELL, Jerry

Singles: 7-inch

AMY (822 "Wanderin' ") 5-10 61
AMY (827 "Yo Yo") 5-10 61
BRUNSWICK (55148 "Freshman") 10-15 59
HAMILTON (50022 "Freshman") 10-20 59
KAMA (13 "It's Goodies Time") 5-10 62
Also see JAY, Morty, & Surfin' Cats / Jerry Norell & Beach Girls

NORFLEET BROTHERS

Singles: 7-inch

RUSH (2703 "The Story of Martin Luther King") 8-12 61

EPs: 7-inch

JERICO (701 "Norfleet Brothers") 15-25 61

NORFLEET COUSINS

Singles: 7-inch

GEMINI STAR (30007 "Brown Eyed Devil") 5-10 68
Also see NORFLEET BROTHERS

NORMA & LINDA

Singles: 7-inch

FABOR (4039 "Stop Right Here Where You Are") 10-20 58
RADIO (113 "Do Dee Doodle Dee Do I'm in Love") 10-20 58

NORMA JEAN *C&W '64*
(Norma Jean Beasler-Taylor)

Singles: 7-inch

COLUMBIA 5-10 58-62
RCA 4-8 63-72
RIVERSIDE 5-10 63

LPs: 10/12-inch

CAMDEN 8-15 68-71
HARMONY 10-15 66
RCA (2961 thru 3977) 20-30 64-67
RCA (4060 thru 4695) 12-25 68-72
Also see BARE, Bobby, Liz Anderson & Norma Jean
Also see WAGONER, Porter

NORMA JEAN *R&B/LP '78*
(Norma Jean Wright)

Singles: 12-inch

BEARSVILLE (Black vinyl.) 4-8 79-80
BEARSVILLE (Colored vinyl.) 10-15 79-80

Singles: 7-inch

BEARSVILLE 3-6 78-80

LPs: 10/12-inch

BEARSVILLE 5-10 78
Also see CHIC

NORMAN, Don

Singles: 7-inch

MGM (13562 "All of My Life") 5-10 66

NORMAN, Fred, & Abnormals

Singles: 7-inch

CARLTON (458 "Crazy Short'nin") 10-20 58

NORMAN, Fred, & Orchestra

Singles: 78 rpm

JAY-DEE (778 "Jump Town") 5-10 53
MGM (12231 "Cherry Coke") 5-10 56

Singles: 7-inch

JAY-DEE (778 "Jump Town") 10-20 53
MGM (12231 "Cherry Coke") 10-15 56

NORMAN, Gene, & Rockin' Rockets

Singles: 7-inch

SNAG (101 "Snaggle Tooth Ann") 550-650 59

NORMAN, Jimmy *P&R/R&B '62*
(With the Hollywood Teeners; with Viceroys; with H.B. Barnum; Jimmy Norman / Willie "The Moon Man" Echols)

Singles: 7-inch

DOT (16016 "Green Stamps") 15-20 59
FUN (101 "A Boy and a Girl") 10-20 61
FUN (102 "My Thanks") 10-20 61
GOOD SOUND (105 "Here Comes the Night") 15-20 61
GOOD SOUND (120 "True Love") 15-20 61
JOSAN (711 "Green Stamps") 30-40 59
(First issue.)
JOSIE (994 "Gangster of Love") 5-10 68
LITTLE STAR (113 "I Don't Love You No More") 8-12 62
LITTLE STAR (121 "You Crack Me Up") .. 10-15 62
MERCURY (72658 "It's Beautiful") 5-10 67
MERCURY (72727 "I'm Leaving") 20-30 67
MUN RAB (102 "Thank Him") 10-20 59
POLO (211 "You Crack Me Up") 40-50 64
RAY STAR (781 "I'll Never Be Free") 10-15 61
RAY STAR (783 "One of TheseDays") 10-15 62
SAMAR (116 "Can You Blame Me") 5-10 66

LPs: 10/12-inch

BADCAT 5-10
Also see BARNUM, H.B.
Also see BERRY, Dorothy, & Jimmy Norman
Also see CHARGERS
Also see COASTERS
Also see DYNA-SORES

NORMAN, Jimmy, & O'Jays

Singles: 7-inch

LITTLE STAR (126 "Love Is Wonderful") . 10-15 63
Also see NORMAN, Jimmy
Also see O'JAYS

NORMAN, Ray

Singles: 7-inch

NASCO (6030 "Mystery of a Kiss") 10-20 59

NORMAN, Val

Singles: 7-inch

VALOR (2005 "The Ballad of Barbara Graham") 10-20 59

NORMAN, Van

Singles: 7-inch

DART (141 "Shortnin' Bread") 5-10 61

NORMAN, Zack

Singles: 7-inch

POPLAR (111 "Hey Doll") 50-75 58
(This same number was also used for a Clovers release.)
Also see CLOVERS

NORMANAIRES

Singles: 78 rpm

MGM (11622 "My Greatest Sin") 10-15 53

Singles: 7-inch

MGM (11622 "My Greatest Sin") 20-30 53
Also see MERRITT, Terry, & Normanaires

NORRIS, Bob
(Bobby Norris)

Singles: 7-inch

ARLEN (501 "Lonely Woman") 15-25 58
CAPITOL (3945 "I Went Rockin' ") 20-30 58
CASCADE (5907 "Party Time") 100-150 59
NAME (1 "Yellow Pages") 10-15 60

NORRIS, Chuck

Singles: 78 rpm

ATLANTIC (994 "Messin' Up") 20-30 52

Singles: 7-inch

ATLANTIC (994 "Messin' Up") 30-50 52

NORRIS, Joe

Singles: 7-inch

SOM (1001 "Rock Out of This World") . 250-350 58

NORSEMEN

Singles: 7-inch

M&M .... 10-15 '60s
Members: Jim Walden; Bob Liles; Gary Grimes; Chris Riley.
Also see JEKYLL & HYDES
Also see VANDALS

NORTH, Freddie *P&R/R&B '71*

Singles: 7-inch

A-BET 5-8 67-70
CAPITOL (4832 "Just to Please You") 10-15 62
CAPITOL (4873 "Just to Please You") 8-12 62
MANKIND 4-6 71-76
PHILLIPS INT'L (3574 "Don't Make Me Cry") 10-20 61
RIC (119 "The Hurt") 20-30 64
UNIVERSITY (605 "How to Cry") 10-20 60

LPs: 10/12-inch

A-BET 10-15
MANKIND 8-12 71-75
PHONORAMA 5-8 84

NORTH, Jay

Singles: 7-inch

KEM (2757 "Little Boy Blues") 5-10 60

LPs: 10/12-inch

COLPIX (204 "Dennis the Menace") 25-35 60
KEM (27 "Look Who's Singing") 20-30 60

NORTH, Jimmy

Singles: 7-inch

INDIO (1 "Leavin' Town") 50-75

NORTH, Nicki, & Citations

Singles: 7-inch

CANADIAN AMERICAN (136 "Magic Eyes") 10-20 62
JASON SCOTT (23 "Magic Eyes") 3-5 82
(500 made.)

NORTH, Ricky

Singles: 7-inch

VERSATILE (102 "The Angels Bring Me Dreams") 15-25 60

NORTHWEST COMPANY

Singles: 7-inch

GRENADIER (1 "Hard to Cry") .... 20-30 '60s

NORTON, Hal

Singles: 7-inch

TREND (30003 "Hocus Pocus") 30-50 58

NORTONES

Singles: 7-inch

STACK (502 "I'm Gonna Find You") 5-10 60
W.B. (5065 "Susie Jones") 10-15 59
W.B. (5115 "Smile, Just Smile") 10-15 59

NOR-TRONS

Singles: 7-inch

CUCA (1104 "Hey There") 15-25 62

NORVELLS

Singles: 7-inch

CHECKER (1037 "As I Walk Alone") 50-100 63

NOTATIONS

Singles: 7-inch

CLARITY (106 "On the Other Side of the World") .... 30-40 '60s
JASON SCOTT (03 "Chapel Doors") 3-5 80
(500 made.)
WONDER (100 "Chapel Doors") 300-400 58

NOTATIONS

Singles: 7-inch

RELIC (1019 "Danny Boy") 5-10 65

NOTATIONS *R&B '70*

Singles: 7-inch

C.R.A. 4-6 73
GEMIGO 4-6 75-76
MERCURY 4-6 77
SUE 5-10 69
TAD 5-10 68
TWINIGHT 4-8 70

LPs: 10/12-inch

GEMIGO 8-12 76
Members: Clifford Curry; Bobby Thomas; Jimmy Stroud; Lasalle Matthews; Walter Jones.
Also see CURRY, Clifford

NOTATIONS

Singles: 7-inch

BEVERLY (1555 "Miserlou") .... 25-35 '60s
CAMELOT (101 "Ram Charger") .... 20-25 '60s

NOTEABLES

Singles: 7-inch

RIBBON (6908 "Tonto") 15-20 60

NOTEABLES

Singles: 7-inch

SOUND CITY (1001 "Get Ready") 5-10 69

NOTEMAKERS

Singles: 7-inch

SOTOPLAY (007 "Do I Have a Chance") 250-350 58
(Previously issued on Sotoplay's 006, credited to the Webs.)
Also see WEBS

NOTES

Singles: 78 rpm

CAPITOL 50-100 56
MGM 50-75 56

Singles: 7-inch

CAPITOL (3332 "Don't Leave Me Now") 150-250 56
MGM (12338 "Trust in Me") 100-150 56
Members: Ray McIlwain; Boyd Becks; Dave Wilson; Clarence Becks.

NOTES

Singles: 7-inch

SARG (177 "Little Girl") 30-40 61
Member: Charlie England.

NOTES FROM THE UNDERGROUND

Singles: 7-inch

VANGUARD (35073 "Down in the Basement") 5-10 68

LPs: 10/12-inch

VANGUARD (6502 "Notes from the Underground") 50-100 68
WING (16337 "Psychedelic Visions") 75-100 67

NOTE-TORIALS

Singles: 7-inch

IMPALA (201 "My Valerie") 400-600 59
(First issue.)
SUNBEAM (119 "My Valerie") 50-150 58

NOTORIOUS NOBLEMEN

Singles: 7-inch

BEDELL (80405 "If I Needed Someone") 40-60 67
IGL (130 "Night Rider") 40-60 67

NOUBARIAN, Johnny, Quartet

Singles: 7-inch

RKO UNIQUE (407 "Susie") 8-12 57

NOVA, Aldo *P&R/LP '82*

Singles: 12-inch

PORTRAIT 5-8 82
(Black vinyl.)
PORTRAIT (1427 "Fantasy") 15-20 82
(Picture disc. Promotional issue only.)

Singles: 7-inch

PORTRAIT 3-5 82

Picture Sleeves

PORTRAIT 3-5 82

LPs: 10/12-inch

PORTRAIT 5-10 82-83
Also see CHEAP TRICK / Aldo Nova / Saxon

NOVA LOCAL

Singles: 7-inch

DECCA (32138 "Games") 10-20 67
DECCA (32194 "Other Girls 10-20 67

LPs: 10/12-inch

DECCA (74977 "Nova 1") 30-50 68
Members: Joe Mendyk; Randy Winburn; Ken Schinhan; Jim Opton; Bill Levasseur.
Also see BETTER DAYS

NOVAK, Binky

Singles: 7-inch

TODD (1036 "If This Is Love") 5-10 59

NOVAS *P&R '65*

Singles: 7-inch

MEAN MT. (1427 "The Crusher") 4-8 82
(Canadian.)
PARROT (45005 "The Crusher") 30-50 64
TWIN TOWN (713 "Novas Coaster") 25-35 65

NOVAS

Singles: 7-inch

S.T.A.R. (001 "And It's Now") 25-35 66

NOVAS IX
(Nova's Nine)

Singles: 7-inch

ABC (11127 "Pain") 5-10 68
HERITAGE (8876 "Pain") 10-15 68
(First issue.)

NOVA-TONES

Singles: 7-inch

ROSCO (417 "Walk on the Surfside") 20-30 63

NOVATONES

Singles: 7-inch

RODEO (184 "Mary Lee") 50-75

NOV-ELITES

Singles: 78 rpm

SHARP (55 "Angels Never Leave Heaven") 200-300 53

NOVELLS

Singles: 7-inch

MOTHERS (1312 "Almost There") 8-12 68

LPs: 10/12-inch
MOTHERS (73 "A Happening")................30-40 68
(Title also shown as *That Did It.*)
Members: Bob Archer; Ed Benson; Chip Moore; Terry Tibbets.

NOVELLS
Singles: 7-inch
WESTCHESTER (271 "Billy Boy")..............5-10 67

NOVY, Len
Singles: 7-inch
ATCO (6672 "Rain and Snow")....................5-8 69
LPs: 10/12-inch
ATCO (274 "No Explanations")..................8-12 69

NOVY, Len & Judy
LPs: 10/12-inch
PRESTIGE (7355 "Folk Songs, Sweet and Bittersweet")...10-20 65
Also see NOVY, Len

NO-YZ
LPs: 10/12-inch
AZRA (112 "Sheer Electronic Den")........15-20 83
(Promotional only picture disc. 500 made.)

NOW
Singles: 7-inch
COTILLION (44005 "Déjà vu")...................5-10 68

NOW GENERATION
LPs: 10/12-inch
SOMERSET (30800 "Sock It to Me").......10-15 68

NOWLIN, Ernie
Singles: 7-inch
MISSOURI (640 "Tally Ho")................150-175

NU BEATS
Singles: 7-inch
SOMA (1159 "Carlotta")..........................25-35 61

NU-COACHMEN
Singles: 7-inch
READING (16001 "A Letter from Margie")..15-25 65

NU LUVS
(Nu Luv's; Nu-Luvs)
Singles: 7-inch
CLOCK (2003 "Baby You Belong to Me")..30-50 67
MERCURY (72569 "Take My Advice").......5-10 66

NU SOUNDS & GARY RAY
Singles: 7-inch
LINCOLN (8426 "To the Aisle")..................8-12 67

NU TORNADOS *P&R '58*
Singles: 7-inch
CARLTON (492 "Philadelphia U.S.A.")....10-20 58
CARLTON (497 "Let's Have a Party")..........8-12 58
FELSTED (8577 "Cry, Baby, Cry")..........8-12 59
Members: Ed Dono; Phil Dale; Tom Dell; Louie Mann; Mike Perna.

NUBIN, Katie Bell
LPs: 10/12-inch
VERVE (3004 "Soul, Soul Searching")....10-20 61

NUCHEZS
Singles: 7-inch
REMBRANDT (5001 "Open Up Your Mind")..25-35 66
Member: Rick Erickson.
Also see LEMON DROPS

NUCLEAR VISION
Singles: 7-inch
LAURIE (3518 "Night Time Child").............8-12 69
SKEE (7771 "Night Time Child").............15-25 69

NUCLEUS
LPs: 10/12-inch
MAINSTREAM (6120 "Nucleus")............40-60 68
Members: Hugh Leggat; Danny Taylor; Bob Horne; John Richardson.

NU-DEMENSIONS
Singles: 7-inch
BURDETTE (1 "Look Thru Any Window")..5-10 67

NUGENT, Ted *LP '75*
(With the Amboy Dukes; with Brian Howe)
Singles: 7-inch
ATLANTIC..3-5 84-88
DISCREET..4-6 74
EPIC..3-6 76-80
Picture Sleeves
ATLANTIC..3-5 84
LPs: 10/12-inch
ATLANTIC..5-10 82-88
DISCREET..8-10 74
EPIC (Except 607)......................................8-15 75-81
EPIC (607 "State of Shock")......................25-50 79
(Picture disc.)
MAINSTREAM (10-01 "Ted Nugent and the Amboy Dukes")..5-10 82
MAINSTREAM (421 "Ted Nugent and the Amboy Dukes")..8-12
POLYDOR (4035 "Survival of the Fittest")..10-20 71
Also see AMBOY DUKES

NUGGETS
Singles: 78 rpm
CAPITOL..5-10 54-56
Singles: 7-inch
CAPITOL..10-20 54-56
Member: Ollie Jones.
Also see CUES
Also see MARTIN, Dean, & Nuggets
Also see SINATRA, Frank

NUGGETS
Singles: 7-inch
JOY (256 "Popcorn Baby")........................8-12 61

NUGGETS
Singles: 7-inch
RCA (7930 "Before We Say Goodnight").30-40 61
RCA (8031 "Just a Friend")........................8-12 62
Member: Val Poliuto.
Also see CALVANES
Also see HITMAKERS
Also see JAGUARS

NUGGETS
Singles: 7-inch
VINTAGE (1003 "Whisper")......................10-15 73
(Yellow vinyl.)

NULL, Jimmy
(With the Inversions)
Singles: 7-inch
RENAY (302 "My Girl")..........................75-125 '60s
USA (870 "Good Good Lovin' ")..................8-12 67

NUMBERS
Singles: 7-inch
BONNEVILLE (101 "My Pillow")..........250-350 62
DORE (641 "My Pillow")..........................30-50 62

NUNN, Bobby
(With the Robbins; with Ginny Tyler)
Singles: 78 rpm
MODERN (807 "Rockin' ")......................75-125 51
Singles: 7-inch
TITAN (1703 "Like")..................................5-10 59
Also see BYRD, Bobby
Also see COASTERS
Also see FOUR BLUEBIRDS / Johnny Otis & His Orchestra
Also see LITTLE ESTHER & BOBBY NUNN
Also see ROBINS

NUNN, Earl, & His Alabama Ramblers
(With Billy Lee) *C&W '49*
Singles: 78 rpm
SPECIALTY (701 "Double Talkin' Woman")..20-30 49

NURSE, Allan
(Allan Nurse's Blues Band)
Singles: 78 rpm
EBONY..15-25 44
SOUTHERN..15-25 45

NUTMEGS *R&B '55*
Singles: 78 rpm
HERALD..25-50 55-57
Singles: 7-inch
BABY GRAND (800 "Story Untold '72")........4-8 72
CLIFTON (104 "Nutmeg's Medley")............3-5 92
COLLECTABLES..3-5 '80s
FLASHBACK ("Story Untold")....................5-10 65
(Selection number not known.)
HERALD (452 "Story Untold")..................40-50 55
(White label. Promotional issue only.)
HERALD (452 "Story Untold")..................15-25 55
(Yellow label.)
HERALD (452 "Story Untold")....................8-12 55
(Multi-color label.)
HERALD (459 "Ship of Love")..................15-25 55
(Yellow label.)
HERALD (459 "Ship of Love")....................8-12
(Multi-color label.)
HERALD (466 "Whispering Sorrows")......25-35 55
HERALD (475 "Key to the Kingdom").......40-50 56
HERALD (492 "A Love So True")............15-25 56
HERALD (538 "My Story")........................30-40 59
HERALD (574 "Rip Van Winkle")..............10-15 62
LANA (128 "Beautiful Dreamer")..................4-8 64
LANA (129 "Ting a Ling")..........................4-8 64
NIGHTRAIN (905 "Shifting Sands")..............4-6 73
RELIC (528 "Down in Mexico")..................5-10 65
RELIC (531 "Let Me Tell You")..................5-10 65
RELIC (533 "The Way Love Should Be")...5-10 65
RELIC (1006 "Shifting Sands")..................5-10 65
TEL (1014 "A Dream of Love")............150-200 60
TIMES SQUARE (6 "Let Me Tell You")....30-50 63
(Green or yellow vinyl.)
TIMES SQUARE (14 "The Way Love Should Be")..30-50 63
(Blue vinyl.)
TIMES SQUARE (27 "Down in Mexico")..15-25 64
TIMES SQUARE (103 "You're Crying")....20-30 64
EPs: 7-inch
HERALD (452 "The Nutmegs")............150-250 60
LPs: 10/12-inch
COLLECTABLES..5-10 84
LOST NITE ("Nutmegs")..........................10-20 81
(10-inch LP. Red vinyl. 1000 made.)
RELIC..8-12 '70s
Members: Leroy Griffin; Jimmy Tyson; Leroy McNeil; James "Sonny" Griffin; Bill Emery; Ed Martin; Sonny Washburn; Harold Jones.
Also see LYRES
Also see RAJAHS

NUTMEGS / Admirations
Singles: 7-inch
CANDLELITE (434 "Down to Earth"/"Coo Coo Cuddle Coo")..4-6
TIMES SQUARE (19 "Down to Earth"/"Coo Coo Cuddle Coo")..20-30 64
Also see ADMIRATIONS

NUTMEGS / Volumes
Singles: 7-inch
RELIC (535 "Why Must We Go to School")..5-10 65
TIMES SQUARE (22 "Why Must We Go to School"/"Ink Dries Quicker Than Tears").50-75 63
Also see NUTMEGS
Also see VOLUMES

NUTMEGS
LPs: 10/12-inch
QUICKSILVER (1001 "Shoo-Wop-A-Doo-Wop")..10-15
(Reissue of Strawberry LP.)
STRAWBERRY (6003 "Street Corner Soul")..40-60
YVONNE (609 "Live")..............................50-100 71
Member: Harry Jaynes.

NU TONES
Singles: 7-inch
CHA CHA (716 "Sharon Lee")..................10-20 61
DART (135 "Time and Again")..................5-10 61

NUTONES
(Nu-Tones)
Singles: 78 rpm
COMBO (127 "At Midnite")....................50-100 56
HOLLYWOOD STAR (797 "Goddess of Love")..500-750 54
(45 rpm not yet known to exist.)
HOLLYWOOD STAR (798 "Annie Kicked the Bucket"/"Believe")..................................500-750 54
HOLLYWOOD STAR (798 "You're No Barking Dog"/"Believe")......................................100-200 55
20TH CENTURY (75030 "I Never Dream")..10-15 55
Singles: 7-inch
COMBO (127 "At Midnite")....................400-600 56
(Does not show address on label.)
COMBO (127 "At Midnite")......................30-40
(Shows address on label.)
HOLLYWOOD STAR (798 "Annie Kicked the Bucket")......................................4000-5000 54
HOLLYWOOD STAR (798 "You're No Barking Dog")..3000-4000 54
(Same number used twice.)
SPIN-TIME (1001 "Teen-Age Heart").......50-75 59
20TH CENTURY (75030 "I Never Dream")..20-40 55
Members: Don Ballard; Joe Green.
Also see SHARPS

NU-TRENDS
Singles: 7-inch
LAWN (216 "Together")....................1000-1500 63

NU-TRONS
Singles: 7-inch
ELDEE (85 "Beat")..................................10-20 63
FEDERAL (12495 "Tension")....................5-10 63

NUTTY NOVELTIES
LPs: 10/12-inch
DYNA (105 "Nutty Novelties")..................20-30 61

NUTTY SQUIRRELS *P&R/R&B '59*
Singles: 7-inch
COLUMBIA (3-41818 "Please Don't Take Our Tree for Christmas")..10-20 60
(Compact 33.)
COLUMBIA (41818 "Please Don't Take Our Tree for Christmas")..5-10 60
(45 rpm.)
HANOVER (4540 "Uh Oh")........................8-12 59
HANOVER (4551 "Eager Beaver")............8-12 60
RCA (8287 "Hello Again")........................5-10 64
Picture Sleeves
COLUMBIA (41818 "Please Don't Take Our Tree for Christmas")..10-20 60
(Color sleeve.)
COLUMBIA (41818 "Please Don't Take Our Tree for Christmas")..20-30 60
(Black-and-white sleeve. Promotional issue only.)
HANOVER (4540 "Uh Oh")......................10-20 59
EPs: 7-inch
HANOVER (301 "Nutty Squirrels")..........15-25 60
LPs: 10/12-inch
COLUMBIA (1589 "Bird Watching").........20-25 61
(Monaural.)
COLUMBIA (8389 "Bird Watching").........20-30 61
(Stereo.)
HANOVER (8014 "Nutty Squirrels")........25-35 60
MGM..15-25 64
Members: Don Elliott; Sascha Burland.

NYE, Lonnie, & Silvertones
Singles: 7-inch
LO-LON (101 "I Gotta Know")..................20-30 60
LO-LON (103 "Lonely Train")..................20-30 60

NYE, Louis
(With the Status Seekers)
Singles: 7-inch
CORAL (61836 "Hi-Ho Steve-O")............10-15 57
U.A. (356 "Emotional Newspaper")...........5-10 61
WIG (103 "Teenage Beatnik")....................5-10 59
LPs: 10/12-inch
RIVERSIDE..15-25 60
U.A..15-25 61
Also see ALLEN, Steve

NYLONS
(Rumblers)
Singles: 7-inch
DOWNEY (109 "Maid-in-Japan")............10-20 63
Also see RUMBLERS

NYRO, Laura *LP '68*
Singles: 7-inch
COLUMBIA..4-8 68-71
VERVE FOLKWAYS..................................5-10 66-67
VERVE FORECAST....................................4-8 68-69
Picture Sleeves
COLUMBIA..5-10 68
LPs: 10/12-inch
COLUMBIA..5-15 68-84
VERVE FOLKWAYS..................................10-20 67
VERVE FORECAST....................................10-15 69
Also see LABELLE, Patti

O

O.C. & ALL STARS
Singles: 7-inch
SAVOY (1533 "Stone Down") 15-25 58

O.C. & HOLIDAYS
Singles: 7-inch
W.B. (1019 "The Tuttle") 10-20 58

O.K.s
Singles: 78 rpm
SUMMER (290 "Don't Leave Me Now")... 15-25 57
Singles: 7-inch
SUMMER (290 "Don't Leave Me Now")... 15-25 57

OAK RIDGE BOYS C&W '76
(Oak Ridge Quartet; Oaks)
Singles: 7-inch
ABC 3-6 78-79
ABC/DOT 4-6 77
CADENCE (1362 "Mocking Bird") 8-12 59
COLUMBIA 4-6 73-79
HEARTWARMING 4-6 71
IMPACT 4-6 71
MCA (Except 51247) 3-6 79-90
MCA (51247 "Sail Away") 25-50 79
(Picture disc. Promotional issue only. Made for Western Merchandiser's 11th Annual Convention.)
RCA 3-5 90-91
W.B. (5359 "This Ole House") 5-10 63
Picture Sleeves
MCA 3-5
LPs: 10/12-inch
ABC 5-10 78-79
ABC/DOT 8-10 77
ACCORD 5-10 81-82
CADENCE (3019 "The Oak Ridge Quartet") 35-55 58
CANAAN 8-15 66
COLUMBIA 5-10 74-83
EXACT 5-10 83
51 WEST 5-8
HEARTWARMING 5-8 71-74
INTERMEDIA 5-10 84
LIBERTY 5-8
MCA 5-10 80-86
NASHVILLE 8-10 70
OUT OF TOWN DIST 5-10 82
PHONORAMA 5-8 83
PICKWICK 5-8 '70s
POWER PAK 5-10 '70s
PRIORITY 5-10 82
SKYLITE 10-20 64-66
STARDAY 10-20 65
U.A. 10-20 66
VISTA 5-8
W.B. (1497 "Oak Ridge Boys") 10-20 63
W.B. (1521 "Folk Minded Spirituals") 10-20 63
Members: William Lee Golden; Duane Allen; Rich Sterban; Joe Bonsall; Steve Sanders; Willie Wynn.
Also see BONSALL, Joe
Also see CASH, Johnny, Carter Family & Oak Ridge Boys
Also see JONES, George
Also see LEE, Brenda, & Oak Ridge Boys
Also see MANDRELL, Barbara, & Oak Ridge Boys
Also see STEVENS, Even
Also see SUMNER, J.D., & Stamps

OAKES, Bob, & Sultans
Singles: 78 rpm
REGENT 10-20 56
Singles: 7-inch
REGENT (7502 "Church Bells May Ring") 20-30 56

O'BANION, Sammy, & Features
Singles: 7-inch
DELPHI (0012 "Mistaken Identity") 10-20

O'BRIEN, Betty
Singles: 7-inch
ABC-PAR (10410 "True True Love") 8-12 63
ABC-PAR (10461 "I Don't Feel a Thing") 8-12 63
LIBERTY (55365 "She'll Be Gone") 10-20 61
LIBERTY (55434 "Money Honey") 10-20 62

O'BRIEN, Hugh
EPs: 7-inch
ABC-PAR ("Wyatt Earp Sings") 10-20 57
LPs: 10/12-inch
ABC-PAR (203 "Wyatt Earp Sings") 40-60 57

O'BRIEN, Skip
Singles: 7-inch
LAURIE (3514 "Baby Shake Your Whoop Whoop") 10-15 69

O'BRIEN, Timmy
(With the Premiers)
Singles: 7-inch
LOOP (113 "Pitter Patter") 30-40 '60s
RASON (1001 "I've Been a Good Boy") 10-15 59

OBSESSIONS
Singles: 7-inch
ACCENT (1182 "Love Always") 50-75 65

OBVIOUS
Singles: 7-inch
CHALLENGE (59372 "Fate") 10-20 67

OCAPELLOS
("Ocapello's"; with Hayes Thompson Orchestra)
Singles: 7-inch
CHECKER (1144 "The Stars") 5-10 66
GENERAL (107 "The Stars") 100-150 66
(Has a drawing of a general, saluting.)
GENERAL (107 "The Stars") 75-125 66
(No drawing of a general.)

OCEAN P&R/LP '71
Singles: 7-inch
KAMA SUTRA 4-6 71-72
YORKVILLE (45033 "Put Your Hand in the Hand") 8-12 71
(Canadian.)
LPs: 10/12-inch
KAMA SUTRA 8-12 71-72
Members: Janice Morgan; Greg Brown; David Tamblyn; Charles Slater.

OCHS, Phil LP '66
(With the Pan African Ngembo Rumba Band)
Singles: 7-inch
A&M 5-10 67-73
SPARKLE (9966 "Bwatue") 3-5 91
(Canadian. 1,000 numbered copies made.)
Picture Sleeves
SPARKLE (9966 "Bwatue") 3-5 91
(Canadian. 1,000 numbered copies made.)
LPs: 10/12-inch
A&M 10-20 67-76
ELEKTRA 15-25 64-66

O'CONNELL, Helen P&R '51
Singles: 78 rpm
CAPITOL 3-5 51-54
KAPP 3-5 55
VIK 3-5 57
Singles: 7-inch
CAMEO (245 "Witchcraft") 4-8 63
CAPITOL 5-10 51-54
KAPP 5-8 55
VIK 5-8 57
EPs: 7-inch
CAPITOL 8-12 54
VIK 8-12 57
LPs: 10/12-inch
CAMDEN 10-20 59-62
CAMEO 10-15 63
LONGINES 5-10 '70s
MARK 56 5-10 77
RCA 5-10 72
VIK (1093 "Helen O'Connell") 25-35 57
W.B. 10-20 61
Also see MARTIN, Dean, & Helen O'Connell

O'CONNER, Keith
(Keith Murphy)
Singles: 7-inch
STACY (958 "Cindy Lou") 15-25 63
Also see MURPHY, Keith, & Daze
Also see TORKAYS

OCTAVES
Singles: 7-inch
VAL (1001 "You're Too Young") 100-150 58

OCTOBER, Johnny
(Johnny Ottobre)
Singles: 7-inch
CAPITOL (4267 "Growin' Prettier") 8-12 59
CAPITOL (4345 "So Mean") 8-12 60
CAPITOL (4417 "Uh-Huh") 8-12 60
FIRST (103 "Little Boy Blue") 8-12 59
FIRST (106 "First Time") 8-12 59
Picture Sleeves
CAPITOL (4267 "Growin' Prettier") 15-25 59
Also see FOUR DATES

OCTOBER COUNTRY
Singles: 7-inch
EPIC (10252 "October Country") 5-10 67
EPIC (10320 "My Girlfriend Is a Witch") 5-10 68
EPIC (10373 "Cowboys & Indians") 5-10 68
LPs: 10/12-inch
EPIC (26381 "October Country") 15-25 68

OCTOBERS
Singles: 7-inch
CHAIRMAN (4402 "I Should'a Listened to Mama") 8-12 63

ODA
LPs: 10/12-inch
LOUD (80011 "Oda") 50-100 73
Members: Randy Oda; Kevin Oda.

O'DAY, Anita P&R '47
Singles: 78 rpm
CLEF 5-10 53
CORAL 5-10 52
LONDON 5-10 51
SIGNATURE 5-10 47
MERCURY 5-10 52-53
VERVE 5-10 56-57
Singles: 7-inch
CLEF 5-15 53
CLOVER 4-6 66
COLUMBIA 4-6 76
CORAL 5-15 52
EMILY 4-6 79
LONDON 5-15 51
MERCURY 5-15 52-53
VERVE 5-15 56-62
EPs: 7-inch
CLEF 25-50 53
NORGRAN 20-40 54
LPs: 10/12-inch
ADVANCE (8 "Specials") 150-200 51
(10-inch LP.)
AMERICAN RECORDING SOCIETY (426 "For Oscar") 50-75 57
CLEF (130 "Anita O'Day") 100-150 53
COLUMBIA 8-10 74
CORAL (56073 "Singin' & Swingin' ") 100-150 53
DOBRE 5-10 78
EMILY 5-10 79-82
FLYING DUTCHMAN 5-10 74
GNP 5-10 79
MPS 5-10 73
NORGRAN (30 "Anita O'Day") 75-100 54
(10-inch LP.)
NORGRAN (1049 "Anita O'Day Sings Jazz") 50-75 55
NORGRAN (1057 "An Evening with Anita O'Day") 50-75 56
PAUSA 5-10 81
SIGNATURE 5-10 75
VERVE (2000 series) 30-60 56
(Has "Verve Records Inc." at bottom of label.)
VERVE (2100 series) 25-50 58-61
(Has "Verve Records Inc." at bottom of label.)
VERVE (6000 series) 25-50 59-60
(Has "Verve Records Inc." at bottom of label.)
VERVE (8200 thru 8500 series) 15-30 59-64
(Has "Verve Records Inc." at bottom of label.)
VERVE (2000 series) 30-60 56
(Has "Verve Records Inc." at bottom of label.)
VERVE 12-25 61-72
(Has "MGM Records - A Division Of Metro-Goldwyn-Mayer, Inc." at bottom of label.)
VERVE 5-10 79-82
(Has "Manufactured By MGM Record Corp." or mentions either Polydor or Polygram at bottom of label.)

O'DAY, Anita, & Cal Tjader
LPs: 10/12-inch
VERVE 15-25 62
(Has "MGM Records - A Division Of Metro-Goldwyn-Mayer, Inc." at bottom of label.)
Also see O'DAY, Anita
Also see TJADER, Cal

ODDBALLS
Singles: 7-inch
COLUMBIA (43024 "Suzy") 5-10 64
ROCKET (110 "Rockin' in the Jungle") 75-125 64

ODDIS, Ray
Singles: 7-inch
V.I.P. (25012 "Happy Ghoul Tide") 10-15 64

ODDS & ENDS
Singles: 7-inch
SOUTHBAY (102 "Cause You Don't Love Me") 15-25 66

ODDS & ENDS
Singles: 7-inch
RED BIRD (083 "Before You Go") 5-10 67

O'DELL, Brooks P&R/R&B '63
Singles: 7-inch
BELL (612 "Walkin' in the Shadow") 10-20 65
BELL (618 "Slow Motion") 10-20 65
GOLD (214 "Watch Your Step") 10-15 63
MANKIND (12010 "Got to Travel On") 4-6

O'DELL, Doye C&W '48
(With the Cass County Boys)
Singles: 78 rpm
EXCLUSIVE 5-10 48
Singles: 7-inch
INTRO (6047 "Diesel Smoke") 15-25 52
LIBERTY (55310 "Run Thief Run") 5-10 61
LIBERTY (55347 "Dreamboat, Still Afloat") 5-10 61
RADIO (115 "Bring a Hammer and a Needle") 10-20 58
SAGE (297 "Everybody Likes a Little Lovin") 30-40
LPs: 10/12-inch
CROWN 10-20 '60s
ERA (20004 "Doye O'Dell") 20-30 '60s
(Colored vinyl.)
LONGHORN 5-10 83
SAGE (297 "If the Devil Wants to Talk") 10-20 59
SAGE (314 "Count Down") 10-20 60
SUNSET 6-12

O'DELL, Kenny P&R '67
Singles: 7-inch
ABC 4-6 73
CAPRICORN 4-6 73-79
KAPP (2169 "Why Don't We Go Somewhere") 4-8 72
KAPP (2178 "Homecoming Queen") 8-12 72
MAR-KAY (3696 "Take Another Look") 8-12 65
VEGAS (718 "Beautiful People") 5-10 67
VEGAS (722 "Springfield Plane") 5-10 68
VEGAS (724 "Happy with You") 5-10 68
WHITE WHALE (319 "No Obligation") 5-10 69
WHITE WHALE (331 "Groovy Relationship") 5-10 69
LPs: 10/12-inch
CAPRICORN (0140 "Kenny O'Dell") 5-10 74
CAPRICORN (0211 "Let's Shake Hands and Come Out Lovin' ") 5-8 78
VEGAS (401 "Beautiful People") 15-25 68

ODETTA LP '63
(Odetta & Larry; Odetta Holmes)
Singles: 7-inch
DUNHILL 4-6 69
POLYDOR 4-6 70
RCA 4-8 63
RIVERSIDE 4-8 62
VANGUARD 5-10 59
VERVE FOLKWAYS 4-6 66
VERVE FORECAST 4-6 68
EPs: 7-inch
FANTASY (4017/4018 "Odetta & Larry") 15-20 54
(Price is for either of two volumes.)
LPs: 10/12-inch
EVEREST 5-10 73
FANTASY (15 "Odetta & Larry") 40-60 54
(10-inch LP.)

FANTASY (3252 "Odetta") 35-50 58
(Colored vinyl.)
POLYDOR 5-10 70
RCA 10-25 62-66
RIVERSIDE (400 series) 15-25 62
RIVERSIDE (3000 series) 10-20 68
RIVERSIDE (9400 series) 20-30 62
TRADITION (1010 "Odetta Sings Ballads and Blues") 25-35 57
TRADITION (1025 "At the Gate of Horn") 20-30 58
TRADITION (1052 "Best of Odetta") 10-15 67
(Monaural.)
TRADITION (2052 "Best of Odetta") 10-20 67
(Stereo.)
U.A. 5-10 76
VANGUARD 10-20 59-67
VERVE FOLKWAYS 10-15 67

ODOM, King
(King Odom Four; Quartette; with Dick Jacobs Orchestra)
Singles: 78 rpm
ABBEY (15064 "Don't Trade Your Love for Gold") 150-250 52
DERBY 10-20 50-51
MUSICRAFT 10-20 49-49
PERSPECTIVE 10-20 52
Singles: 7-inch
ABBEY (15064 "Don't Trade Your Love for Gold") 800-1200 52
Members: Dave Odom; David Bowers; Isaiah Bing; Cleveland Bing.
Also see CHURCHILL, Savannah
Also see LARKS
Also see RAVENS

ODYSSEY
Singles: 7-inch
HI (2259 "No One Else") 4-6 74
IMPERIAL (66323 "Everything Will Be Alright") 5-10 68
WHITE WHALE (263 "Little Girl Little Boy") 10-20 68

ODYSSEY P&R/R&B/LP '77
Singles: 12-inch
RCA 4-8 77-82
Singles: 7-inch
MOWEST (5022 "Broken Road") 4-8 72
RCA 3-6 77-82
LPs: 10/12-inch
MOWEST 10-12 72
RCA 8-10 77-82
Members: Lillian Lopez; Louise Lopez.

OEDIPUS & MOTHERS
Singles: 7-inch
BEACON (1001 "How It Used to Be") 20-30 67

OERTLING, Jim
(With the Bayou Boys)
Singles: 7-inch
HAMMOND (267 "Old Moss Back") 250-350 59

OFF KEYS
Singles: 7-inch
ROWE (003 "Our Wedding Day") 50-75 62
TECHNICHORD (1001 "Our Wedding Day") 20-30 62
Also see EVANS, Jerry, & Off Keys

OFF SET
Singles: 7-inch
BRENT (7051 "Just a Little Smile") 15-25 65
BRENT (7053 "You're a Drag") 15-25 66
JUBILEE (5542 "A Change Is Gonna Come") 5-10 66

OFFBEATS
Singles: 7-inch
TROPICAL (109 "Double Trouble") 15-25 64

OFF-BEATS
Singles: 7-inch
MERRITT (0001 "Mister Machine") 15-25 63
MERRITT (0002 "Grind") 15-25 63
Also see CAHILL, Graig, & Off-Beats

OFFENBACH
Singles: 7-inch
PAULA (293 "No Letter Today") 5-10 68

OFFITT, Lillian P&R/R&B '57
Singles: 78 rpm
EXCELLO (2104 "Miss You So") 20-30 57
Singles: 7-inch
CHIEF (7012 "The Man Won't Work") 15-25 59
CHIEF (7015 "Oh Mama") 15-25 60
CHIEF (7029 "Troubles") 15-25 61
EXCELLO (2104 "Miss You So") 20-30 57
EXCELLO (2124 "Darling I'll Forgive You") 15-25 57
EXCELLO (2139 "Can't Go On") 15-25 58

OGLETREE, Leo
Singles: 7-inch
STARDAY ("Crooked Dice") 100-200
(Selection number not known.)

OGNIR & NITE PEOPLE
Singles: 7-inch
SAMRON (102 "I Found a New Love") 15-25 65
W.B. (5682 "I Found a New Love") 10-20 65

OGSBURY, Jay
Singles: 7-inch
SONGS UNLIMITED (13 "Our Teenage Prayer") 25-35
SONGS UNLIMITED (17 "How Do We Know") 30-40

O'GWYNN, James C&W '58
Singles: 78 rpm
STARDAY (266 "Losing Games") 10-20 56
Singles: 7-inch
D (1006 "Talk to Me Lonesome Heart") 20-30 58
D (1022 "Blue Memories") 20-30 58
HICKORY 5-10 65-66
MERCURY 10-15 59-62
STARDAY (266 "Losing Games") 40-60 56
U.A. 8-12 63-64
LPs: 10/12-inch
MERCURY 20-30 62
PLANTATION 5-10 76-78
WING 10-20 64

O'HARA, Maureen
LPs: 10/12-inch
RCA (1953 "Love Letters") 25-40 59

O'HARA, Sandy
("The Improper Bostonian;" with the Nick Spencer Orchestra, David Haller conducting; "Introducing Ray Suarez, Vocalist: Johnny Campbell")
EPs: 7-inch
TEIA (0001 "Miss Sandy O'Hara 'Live' from Las Vegas") 10-20 70
(Compact 33 stereo. One track on each side, though 10 songs are heard. Issued with paper sleeve.)

O'HENRY, Lenny P&R/R&B '64
(With Short Stories; Lenny O. Henry)
Singles: 7-inch
ABC-PAR (10222 "Billy the Continental") 10-15 61
ABC-PAR (10272 "The Touch of Your Lips") 10-15 61
ATCO (6291 "Across the Street") 10-15 64
ATCO (6312 "Savin' All My Love") 5-10 64
ATCO (6525 "Across the Street") 5-10 67
SMASH (1800 "Burning Memories") 5-10 63

OHIO EXPRESS P&R '67
(Ohio Ltd.)
Singles: 7-inch
ATTACK 4-6 70
BUDDAH 4-8 68-73
CAMEO (483 "Beg, Borrow & Steal") 8-12 67
(Reissue of Attack 1401 by Rare Breed.)
CAMEO (2001 "Try It") 8-12 67
ERIC 4-6 78
SUPER K 4-8 69-70
LPs: 10/12-inch
BUDDAH 10-20 68-70
CAMEO (20,000 "Beg, Borrow & Steal") 20-30 68
Member: Joey Levine.
Also see RARE BREED
Also see REUNION
Also see 10CC

OHIO PLAYERS R&B '68
Singles: 7-inch
AIR CITY 3-5 84
ARISTA 4-6 79
BOARDWALK 3-5 81
CAPITOL 5-10 69
COMPASS (7015 "Trespassin' ") 5-10 67
COMPASS (7018 "It's a Crying Shame") 5-10 68
MERCURY 4-6 74-78
TRC 4-8 70
TRIP (3006 "Trespassin' ") 4-6 72
TANGERINE (978 "Neighbors") 5-10 67
TRACK 3-5 88
WESTBOUND 4-6 71-76
LPs: 10/12-inch
ACCORD 5-10 81
ARISTA 5-10 79
BOARDWALK 5-10 81
CAPITOL (192 "Observations in Time") 10-20 69
CAPITOL (11291 "Ohio Players") 8-12 74
MERCURY 8-12 74-78
SPRINGBOARD .... 8-10 '70s
TRIP 8-10 72
U.A. 8-10 75
WESTBOUND 8-12 72-75
Members: Joe Harris; Marshall Jones; Jimmy Williams; Clarence Satchell; Marvin Pierce; Billy Beck; Ralph Middlebrook; Leroy Bonner.
Also see OHIO UNTOUCHABLES
Also see UNDISPUTED TRUTH

OHIO UNTOUCHABLES
Singles: 7-inch
LU PINE (109 "She's My Heart's Desire") 10-20 62
LU PINE (110 "Forgive Me Darling") 10-20 63
LU PINE (116 "I'm Tired") 10-20 64
LU PINE (1009 "She's My Heart's Desire") 20-30 62
(First issue.)
LU PINE (1010 "Forgive Me Darling") 20-30 62
(First issue.)
LU PINE (1011 "I'm Tired") 20-30 64
(First issue.)
Also see FABULOUS PEPS
Also see FALCONS
Also see McCAIN, Benny, & Ohio Untouchables
Also see OHIO PLAYERS
Also see WARD, Robert, & Ohio Untouchables

OILAR, Bev
Singles: 7-inch
G&G (120 "Sixteen ") 40-60

O'JAHS
Singles: 7-inch
SOUND STAGE 7 (2599 "Let It All Out") 5-10 67

O'JAYS P&R/R&B '63
Singles: 12-inch
PHILA. INT'L 4-8 83
Singles: 7-inch
ALL PLATINUM 4-6 74
APOLLO (759 "Miracles") 10-15 61
ASTROSCOPE 4-6 74
BELL 4-8 67-73
CBS 4-6 72
DAYCO ("Miracles") 30-40 60
(Selection number not known.)
EMI (17491 "Somebody Else Will") 3-5 93
EMI (18914 "Have Yourself a Merry Little Christmas") 3-5 95
EMI (50180 "Have You Had Your Love Today") 3-5 89
EMI (50212 "Out of My Mind") 3-5 89
EMI (50230 "Serious Hold on Me") 3-5 90
EPIC 3-5 83
IMPERIAL (5942 "How Does It Feel") 10-15 63
IMPERIAL (5976 "Lonely Drifter") 10-15 63
IMPERIAL (66007 thru 66131) 10-15 64-65
IMPERIAL (66145 "I'll Never Let You Go") 30-50 65
IMPERIAL (66162 "I'll Never Forget You") 25-35 66
IMPERIAL (66177 "Blowing Wind") 5-10 66
IMPERIAL (66197 "Stand in for Love") 10-15 66
IMPERIAL (66200 "Lonely Drifter") 5-10 66
LIBERTY 3-5 81
LITTLE STAR (124 "How Does It Feel") 15-25 63
LITTLE STAR (125 "Dream Girl") 15-25 63
LITTLE STAR (1401 "Just to Be with You") 15-25 63
MANHATTAN 3-5 89-90
MINIT (32015 "Hold On") 5-10 67
NEPTUNE 5-10 69-70
PHILA. INT'L 3-8 72-87
SARU 4-6 71
TSOP 3-6 80-81
LPs: 10/12-inch
BELL (6014 "Back on Top") 10-20 68
BELL (6082 "The O'Jays") 8-12 73
EMI 5-8 89-90
EPIC 5-8 83
IMPERIAL (9290 "Coming Through") 30-35 65
(Monaural.)
IMPERIAL (12290 "Coming Through") 35-40 65
(Stereo.)
KORY 8-10 77
MINIT (24008 "Soul Sounds") 20-30 67
(Stereo.)
MINIT (40008 "Soul Sounds") 15-25 67
(Monaural.)
PHILA. INT'L 5-10 72-86
SUNSET 10-15 68
TSOP 5-10 80
TRIP 8-10 73
U.A. 8-12 72
Members: Bob Massey; Eddie LeVert; Walt Williams; Bill Powell; Bill Isles; Sam Strain.
Also see CHIPS
Also see LITTLE ANTHONY & IMPERIALS
Also see MASCOTS
Also see NORMAN, Jimmy, & O'Jays

O'KAYSIONS P&R/R&B/LP '68
Singles: 7-inch
ABC (11094 "Deal Me In") 5-10 68
ABC (11207 "Colors") 5-10 69
COTILLION (44089 "Watch Out Girl") 4-8 70
NORTH STATE (1001 "Girl Watcher") 20-30 68
ROULETTE GOLDEN GOODIES (130 "Girl Watcher") 4-6 73
SPARTON (1676 "Girl Watcher") 5-10 68
(Canadian.)
Picture Sleeves
NORTH STATE (1001 "Girl Watcher") 50-75 68
EPs: 7-inch
ABC (664 "Girl Watcher") 15-25 68
(Juke box issue.)
LPs: 10/12-inch
ABC (664 "Girl Watcher") 15-25 68
Members: Donnie Weaver; Jim Spidel; Jim Hennant; Ron Turner; Bruce Joyner.

O'KAYSIONS / Impressions
EPs: 7-inch
ABC (18201 "O'Kaysions & Impressions") 8-12 68
Also see IMPRESSIONS
Also see O'KAYSIONS

O'KEEFE, Danny P&R/C&W/LP '72
Singles: 7-inch
ATLANTIC 4-6 75
COTILLION 4-6 71
JERDEN (806 "That Old Sweet Song") 5-10 66
PICCADILLY (228 "That Old Sweet Song") 5-10 66
PICCADILLY (237 "Today, One Day Later") 5-10 66
SIGNPOST (70006 "Good Time Charlie's Got the Blues") 4-6 72
W.B. 4-6 77-78
Picture Sleeves
W.B. 4-6 77-78
LPs: 10/12-inch
ATLANTIC 8-12 73-75
COTILLION 10-15 70
FIRST AMERICAN .... 8-10 '70s
PANORAMA (105 "Introducing Danny O'Keefe") 20-30 66
SIGNPOST (8404 "O'Keefe") 10-12 72
W.B. 5-10 77-79

O'KEEFE, Johnny
Singles: 7-inch
BRUNSWICK (55067 "Real Wild Child") 50-75 58
LIBERTY (55223 "She's My Baby"/"Own True Self") 15-20 59
LIBERTY (55228 "She's My Baby"/"It's Too Late") 10-15 60
(Note different flip side.)
LIBERTY (55262 "Take My Hand") 10-20 60
MR. PEACOCK (111 "I'm Counting on You") 5-10 62
RA-O 4-8
SIMS (337 "So Why") 5-10 68
Picture Sleeves
LIBERTY (55228 "She's My Baby") 25-30 60

O'KEEFE, Larry
Singles: 7-inch
FREEDOM (44020 "Love's Dream") 5-10 59
PAT-O-RITE (15384 "Rolling Stone") 100-200

OL' THOROUGHBRED
Singles: 7-inch
THOROUGHBRED (1001 "Mean Mouthin' Mama")....................50-75

OLA & JANGLERS *P&R '69*
Singles: 7-inch
GNP....................4-8 68-69
LONDON....................5-10 67
LPs: 10/12-inch
GNP....................15-20 69
Member: Ola Hakansson.

O'LAY, Ruth
(Ruth Olay)
Singles: 7-inch
ABC (10870 "God Bless the Child")..........5-10 66
EVEREST (2037 "Scarlet Bird")..........5-10 64
ZEPHYR (002 "Good Love")..........10-20 57
LPs: 10/12-inch
ABC....................10-20 67
EMARCY....................20-40 58
EVEREST....................20-30 63
MERCURY....................20-40 59
U.A....................20-40 60

OLD AND IN THE WAY *LP '75*
LPs: 10/12-inch
ROUND (103 "Old and in the Way")..........20-25 75
SUGAR HILL....................5-8 85
Members: Peter Rowan; Jerry Garcia; Vassar Clements; David Grisman.
Also see GARCIA, Jerry
Also see ROWANS

OLD AND IN THE WAY / Keith & Donna / Robert Hunter / Phil Lesh & Ned Lagin
Singles: 7-inch
ROUND (02 & 03 "Sampler for Dead Heads")....................40-60 75
(Promotional, fan club two-disc set. Price also includes a letter from Anton Round, a letter about members of the Grateful Dead, several miniature LP covers, and a mailer advertising posters.)
ROUND (02 & 03 "Sampler for Dead Heads")....................20-30 75
(Price is for both discs, without inserts. Divide in half for either one of the two records.)
Also see GRATEFUL DEAD
Also see HUNTER, Robert
Also see LESH, Phil, & Ned Lagin
Also see OLD AND IN THE WAY

OLDFIELD, Mike *LP '73*
(With Sally Oldfield)
Singles: 7-inch
EPIC....................3-5 81-82
VIRGIN....................3-8 73-82
Picture Sleeves
VIRGIN....................4-6 74
EPs: 7-inch
VIRGIN (199 "Tubular Bells")..........5-10 74
(Promotional issue only.)
LPs: 10/12-inch
EPIC (37358 "QE2")..........5-10 81
EPIC (37983 "Five Miles Out")..........5-10 82
EPIC (44116 "Tubular Bells")..........20-40 73
(Half-speed mastered.)
VIRGIN (2001 "Tubular Bells")..........10-15 73
(Picture disc.)
VIRGIN (13105 "Tubular Bells")..........8-12 73
VIRGIN (13109 "Hergest Ridge")..........8-12 74
VIRGIN (13143 "Airborne")..........10-15 80
(Two discs.)
VIRGIN (PZ-33913 "Ommadawn")..........8-12 75
VIRGIN (PZQ-33913 "Ommadawn")..........10-20 75
(Quadraphonic.)
VIRGIN (90645 "Islands")..........5-8 88
Session: Maggie Reilly; Bonnie Tyler.

OLDHAM, Andrew, Orchestra
Singles: 7-inch
PARROT (9745 "I Get Around")..........10-15 65
LPs: 10/12-inch
LONDON (457 "Rolling Stones Songbook")....................30-45 65
(Stereo.)
LONDON (3457 "Rolling Stones Songbook")....................35-50 65
(Monaural.)
PARROT (61003 "East Meets West")..........25-35 65
(Monaural.)
PARROT (71003 "East Meets West")..........30-40 65
(Stereo.)

OLDSMOBUICKS
LPs: 10/12-inch
TONEMASTER (101 "Rockin' 'N' Boppin'")....................10-15 89
TONEMASTER (102 "Oldsmobuicks")..........8-10 90
Members: Brian Dardeen; Rob Santos; Stan Kozlowski; Haney Kozlowski.

OLE JOSE & GOLDEN LEAVES
Singles: 7-inch
CHALLENGE (59388 "Tequila '68")..........5-10 68

OLE MISS DOWN BEATS
Singles: 7-inch
ARDENT (103 "Mister Crump")..........40-60 61

OLE MOON DADDY
Singles: 7-inch
RALLY (595 "Moon Daddy")..........5-10 67

OLE SONNY BOY
Singles: 78 rpm
EXCELLO (2086 "Blues and Misery")..........25-35 56
Singles: 7-inch
EXCELLO (2086 "Blues and Misery")..........50-100 56

O'LEARY, Lilith
Singles: 7-inch
AMARET (105 "8 Miles to Tijuana")..........5-10 69

OLENN, Johnny
(With the Blockbusters; with Jokers)
Singles: 78 rpm
TNT....................15-25 55-56
Singles: 7-inch
ANTLER (1101 "My Sweetie Pie") 20-30.....59
ANTLER (1105 "Born Reckless")..........20-30 59
ANTLER (4009 "Smile")..........20-30 58
ANTLER (4012 "My Sweetie Pie")..........20-30 59
ANTLER (4018 "The Magic Touch")..........20-30 61
GLENCO (700 "Sally Let Your Bangs Hang")....................50-70
LIBERTY (55053 "Candy Kisses")..........15-25 57
LIBERTY (55467 "Candy Kisses")..........8-12 62
PERSONALITY (1002 "Teenie")..........15-25 59
TNT (1016 "Sally Let Your Bangs Hang") 50-60 55
TNT (1018 "I Ain't Gonna Cry No More")..50-60 56
LPs: 10/12-inch
LIBERTY (3029 "Just Rollin'")..........100-200 58
Also see BLOCKBUSTERS

OLIVER *P&R/LP '69*
(Bill Oliver Swofford)
Singles: 7-inch
CREWE....................4-8 69-70
JUBILEE....................5-10 69
LIBERTY....................3-5
PARAMOUNT....................4-6 73
PEOPLE SONG....................3-5 82
U.A....................4-6 70-71
Picture Sleeves
CREWE (334 "Jean")..........5-10 69
LPs: 10/12-inch
CREWE....................10-15 69-70
U.A....................8-12 71
Also see BILLY & SUE
Also see VIRGINIANS

OLIVER, Big Danny
Singles: 7-inch
KAPP (721 "Sapphire")..........20-30 65
TREND (30012 "Sapphire")..........40-50 58
TREND (30016 "Blues for the 49")..........20-40 59

OLIVER, Bobby
Singles: 7-inch
LUCKY FOUR (1004 "All Around the World")....................15-25 61
LUCKY FOUR (1006 "Lucille")..........15-25 61

OLIVER, Chet
Singles: 78 rpm
FORTUNE....................20-30 56
Singles: 7-inch
FORTUNE (829 "Cool As a Cucumber")....................100-200 56

OLIVER, Dale
Singles: 7-inch
SANGELO (105 "Long Gone Daddy")..100-125 58

OLIVER, Jimmy
(With the Rockers)
Singles: 7-inch
PORT (70016 "Slim Jim")..........10-15 60
SUE (707 "The Sneak")..........15-25 58
SYMBOL (207 "Bye Bye Baby")..........5-10 65
LPs: 10/12-inch
SUE (1041 "Hits Au Go Go")..........15-25 65

OLIVER, Johnny
(With Johnny Brantley Orchestra & Chorus; with Joe Lipman Orchestra & Chorus)
Singles: 78 rpm
MGM....................5-10 55-56
Singles: 7-inch
JOSIE (860 "Sweet Sugar")..........10-15 59
LIBERTY (55349 "Mail Man, Where's My Check")....................5-10 61
LIBERTY (55463 "As Long As Time Goes On")....................5-10 62
MGM (12164 "Chain Gang")..........10-20 56
MGM (12230 "Six Feet of Heaven")..........10-20 56
MGM (12319 "I Need You So")..........10-20 56
MGM (55001 "Lemonade Baby")..........15-25 55
MGM (55012 "Darling, Is It True")..........20-30 55
MERCURY (71570 "That's All I'm Living For")....................8-12 60
MERCURY (71662 "I Gave Him Back His Ring")....................8-12 60
MIRA (981 "Walk a Chalk Line")..........10-15
(Identification number shown since no selection number is used.)

OLIVER, O. Jay
(With the Crackerjacks; with Groove Riders)
Singles: 7-inch
COED (500 "Good Gravy")..........10-20 58

OLIVER, Sy, & Orchestra
("Vocal Jim Brown")
Singles: 78 rpm
BELL (1102 "Ain't That a Shame")..........10-20 55
Singles: 7-inch
BELL (1102 "Ain't That a Shame")..........10-20 55
Also see LEE, Peggy, & Mills Brothers
Also see LUTCHER, Nellie

OLIVER, Tommy
Singles: 7-inch
W.B. (5011 "Rendezvous Rock")..........15-25 58

OLIVER & TWISTERS
Singles: 7-inch
COLPIX (615 "Mother Goose Twist")..........5-10 61
Picture Sleeves
COLPIX (615 "Mother Goose Twist")..........10-15 61
LPs: 10/12-inch
COLPIX (423 "Look Who's Twistin'")..........25-35 61

OLIVERS
Singles: 7-inch
PHALANX (1022 "Bleeker Street")..........40-60 66
RCA (9113 "Bleeker Street")..........10-20 67

OLLER, Shadie
Singles: 7-inch
SUMMIT (114 "Come to Me Baby")..........200-250 59

OLLIE & NIGHTINGALES *P&R/R&B '68*
Singles: 7-inch
STAX....................5-10 68-69
LPs: 10/12-inch
STAX....................10-15 69
Members: Ollie Nightingale; Quincy Billops, Jr.; Nelson Lesure; Bill Davis; Rochester Neal; Sir Mack Rice.
Also see MAD LADS
Also see OVATIONS
Also see RICE, Mack

OLNESS, Gunner
Singles: 7-inch
GO (101 "Caravan")..........8-12 66
LPs:10/12-inch
GO (101 "Gunner Olness")..........15-25 67
Also see GAMINS

OLSON, Dick
Singles: 7-inch
MARK (104 "Hearts Are Never Meant to Be Broken")....................30-40 57

OLSON, Jimm
Singles: 7-inch
VELVET PEN (44635 "Red Teardrops")....................150-250 68
(Identification number shown since no selection number is used.)

OLSON, Reggie
Singles: 7-inch
SURF (5039 "You Upset Me")..........5-10 60

OLSON, Rocky / Jet Tones *P&R '59*
Singles: 7-inch
CHESS (1723 "Kansas City"/"Jet Tone Boogie")....................15-25 59
Also see JET TONES

OLVERA, Frankie
Singles: 7-inch
LOLA (104 "Huggie's Bunnies")..........8-12 64

OLYMPICS *P&R/R&B '58*
Singles: 78 rpm
DEMON (1508 "Western Movies")..........60-80 58
Singles: 7-inch
ABC....................4-6 73
ARVEE (562 "Hully Gully")..........15-25 59
ARVEE (595 "Big Boy Pete")..........15-25 60
ARVEE (5006 "Shimmy Like Kate")..........10-20 60
(Credits "Piron" as songwriter.)
ARVEE (5006 "Shimmy Like Kate")..........10-20 60
(Credits "Smith & Goldsmith" as songwriters.)
ARVEE (5020 "Dance By the Light of the Moon")....................10-20 61
ARVEE (5023 "Little Pedro")..........10-20 61
ARVEE (5031 "Dooley")..........30-40 61
(Orange and black label.)
ARVEE (5031 "Dooley")..........40-50 61
(Pink label. Promotional issue only.)
ARVEE (5044 "The Stomp")..........10-15 61
ARVEE (5051 "Twist")..........10-15 62
ARVEE (5056 "The Scotch")..........10-15 62
ARVEE (5073 "What'd I Say")..........10-15 63
ARVEE (6501 "Big Boy Pete '65")..........8-12 65
COLLECTABLES....................3-5 '80s
DEMON (1508 "Western Movies")..........20-30 58
DEMON (1512 "Dance with the Teacher")....................20-30 58
DEMON (1514 "Your Love")..........20-30 59
DUO DISC (104 "The Boogler")..........5-10 64
DUO DISC (105 "Return of Big Boy Pete")....................5-10 64
ERIC....................4-6 '70s
JUBILEE (5674 "Cartoon Song")..........5-10 69
LOMA (2010 "I'm Comin' Home")..........8-12 65
LOMA (2013 "Good Lovin'")..........8-12 65
LOMA (2017 "Baby I'm Yours")..........8-12 65
MGM (14505 "The Apartment")..........4-6 73
MIRWOOD (5504 "We Go Together")..........5-10 65
MIRWOOD (5513 "Mine Exclusively")..........5-10 66
MIRWOOD (5523 "Baby, Do the Philly Dog"/"Western Movies")....................5-10 66
MIRWOOD (5525 "The Duck")..........5-10 66
MIRWOOD (5529 "The Same Old Thing")..5-10 67
MIRWOOD (5533 "Big Boy Pete")..........5-10 67
PARKWAY (6003 "Good Things")..........5-8 68
TITAN (1718 "The Chicken")..........15-25 61
TRI DISC (105 "Return of Big Boy Pete") 10-15 62
TRI DISC (106 "The Bounce")..........10-15 62
TRI DISC (107 "Dancin' Holiday")..........10-15 62
TRI DISC (110 "Bounce Again")..........10-15 63
TRI DISC (112 "Broken Hip")..........10-15 63
W.B. (7639 "Please Please Please")..........4-8 70
EPs: 7-inch
ARVEE (423 "Doin' the Hully Gully")..........50-100 60
LPs: 10/12-inch
ARVEE (423 "Doin' the Hully Gully")..........100-200 60
ARVEE (424 "Dance by the Light of the Moon")....................100-125 61
ARVEE (429 "Party Time")..........100-125 61
EVEREST....................5-10 81
MIRWOOD (M-7003 "Something Old, Something New")....................20-30 66
(Monaural.)
MIRWOOD (MS-7003 "Something Old, Something New")....................25-35 66
(Stereo.)
POST....................8-10 '70s
RHINO....................5-8 '80s
TRI-DISC (1001 "Do the Bounce")..........40-60 63
Members: Walter Ward; Eddie Lewis; Melvin King; Charles Figer; Julius McMichaels.
Also see PARAGONS
Also see REYNOLDS, Jody / Olympics
Also see WARD, Walter, & Challengers

OMAR & VILLAGE IDIOTS
Singles: 7-inch
PACIFIC CHALLENGER ....5-10 '60s

O'MARY, Slim
Singles: 7-inch
H&K (20 "Sink Or Swim") 40-60

OMEGAS
Singles: 7-inch
U.A. (50247 "I Can't Believe") 15-25 68

OMENS
Singles: 7-inch
CODY (007 "Searching") 25-35 66

ONCOMERS
Singles: 7-inch
GATEWAY (103 "Every Day Now") ....20-30 '60s

ONDIOS
Singles: 7-inch
EVEREST (19414 "Black Widow") 5-10 61

ONE
(No. 1)
Singles: 7-inch
COLUMBIA (44256 "Hey Taxi") 10-20 67
KAPP (824 "The Collector") 8-12 67
LPs: 10/12-inch
GRUNT 10-15 72
STARBORNE 8-12 78
VILLAGE 20-30 77
Also see BLUE BEATS

ONE, Bobby
Singles: 7-inch
DECCA (30515 "Tell Me Again") 10-20 57
NRC (021 "Hummingbird") 15-25 59
NRC (5010 "Sure Do Know Her Now") 15-25 60

ONE EYED JACKS
(One-Eyed Jacks)
Singles: 7-inch
LAKESIDE 4-8
ROULETTE (7025 "Together We're in Love") 5-10 68
ROULETTE (7035 "Gettin' in the Groove") .5-10 69
TY TEX 5-10
WHITE CLIFFS (265 "Love") 20-30 67
Members: Bill Schneider; Barry Fasman; Buddy Carr; George Gedzun; Mike Murphy.
Also see FAT WATER

ONE OF HOURS
Singles: 7-inch
CHETWYD (45001 "It's Best") 50-100 66
CHETWYD (45005 "Psychedelic Illusion") 50-100 67

100 PROOF Aged in Soul *P&R/R&B '69*
Singles: 7-inch
HOT WAX 4-6 69-72
LPs: 10/12-inch
HOT WAX 10-15 70-73
Members: Steve Mancha; Joe Stubbs; Eddie Anderson.
Also see FALCONS
Also see MANCHA, Steve
Also see ORIGINALS
Also see STUBBS, Joe

100 PROOF Aged in Soul / New York Port Authority
Singles: 7-inch
HOT WAX (9256 "I'm Mad As Hell") 4-6 77

125TH ST. CANDY STORE
Singles: 7-inch
UP TITE (Except 0025) 5-10 68-69
UP TITE (0025 "If You Wanna Dream") .. 30-40 69

ONE STRING SAM
Singles: 78 rpm
J.V.B. (40 "My Baby Ooo") 100-200 56
Singles: 7-inch
J.V.B. (40 "My Baby Ooo") 400-500 56

ONE WAY STREET
Singles: 7-inch
SUNRISE (103 "We All Love Peanut Butter") 25-35 66

ONE WAY STREET
Singles: 7-inch
APOLLO (100 "Yard Dog") 10-15 67
SMASH (2155 "Girls Girls Girls") 10-20 68
SMASH (2187 "What's Your Name") 10-20 68

ONE WAY STREET
Singles: 7-inch
BOTIQUE (160 "I Wanted to Be with You Girl") 5-10 68
SMASH (2155 "Girls Girls Girls") 5-10 68
SMASH (2187 "What's Your Name") 5-10 68

ONE WAY STREET
Singles: 7-inch
DEEK (101 "I Know I Love") 15-25 67
DEEK (103 "Joy and Sorrow") 15-25 68

O'NEAL, Jackie, & Rebel Rockers
Singles: 7-inch
CAPA (111 "I Cry") 40-60 62

O'NEAL, Johnny
Singles: 78 rpm
KING (4599 "Johnny Feels the Blues") ...75-125 52
Singles: 7-inch
KING (4599 "Johnny Feels the Blues") .250-350 52

O'NEAL, Lance
(With the Dave Kennedy & Ambassadors)
Singles: 7-inch
NORKO (1113 "I'm Twistin' Alone") ....50-75 '60s
Also see KENNEDY, Dave

O'NEAL, Tom
Singles: 7-inch
PETAL (1001 "St. Louis Blues") 10-20 62

O'NEIL, Grady
(Grady O'Neal)
Singles: 7-inch
BELLA (2205 "Baby Oh Baby") 200-300 59
JAN ELL 5-10 60-62

O'NEIL, Jackie
Singles: 7-inch
CAPA (111 "You Broke My Heart") 10-20

O'NEILL, Steve
Singles: 7-inch
UPP (501 "I Want You to Be My Baby") ...15-25 60

ONES, The
LPs: 10/12-inch
ASHWOOD HOUSE (1105 "The Ones") 300-500 66
CONTRAPOINT (9010 "Maybe It's Both of Us") ....30-50 '60s

ONES, The
Singles: 7-inch
FENTON (2514 "You Haven't Seen My Love") 40-60 67
MOTOWN (1117 "You Haven't Seen My Love") 8-15 67
(Black vinyl.)
MOTOWN (1117 "You Haven't Seen My Love") 15-25 67
(Colored vinyl. Promotional issue only.)
MOTOWN (1130 "Don't Let Me Lose This Dream") 8-15 68
(Black vinyl.)
MOTOWN (1130 "Don't Let Me Lose This Dream") 15-25 68
(Colored vinyl. Promotional issue only.)
SPIRIT (0001 "You Haven't Seen My Love") 25-50 69

ONION RINGS
Singles: 7-inch
BLUE ONION (102 "She's Gonna Cry") ...20-30 67

ONLY ONES
Singles: 7-inch
SIGHT (5416 "With This Kiss") 20-25 65
Also see GLIEDEN, Mike

ONLY ONES
Singles: 7-inch
PANIK (5112 "Find a Way") 5-10 66

ONLY ONZ
Singles: 7-inch
TIME (1076 "When Teardrops Fall") 25-35 64

ONO, Yoko *LP '71*
(With the Plastic Ono Band)
Singles: 12-inch
POLYDOR 5-10 85-86
Singles: 7-inch
APPLE 4-8 71-73
GEFFEN 3-5 81
POLYDOR 3-5 82-86
Promotional Singles
APPLE (OYB-1 "Open Your Box") 600-800 70
APPLE (1853 "Now Or Never") 25-30 72
APPLE (1867 "Woman Power") 20-25 73
GEFFEN 5-8 81
POLYDOR 4-6 82-86
Picture Sleeves
APPLE (1853 "Now Or Never") 8-12 72
GEFFEN 3-5 81
LPs: 10/12-inch
APPLE 15-20 71-73
GEFFEN 5-10 81
POLYDOR 5-10 82-86
Promotional LPs
GEFFEN (934 "Walking on Thin Ice") 20-25 81
GEFFEN (975 "No No No") 25-30 81
Also see LENNON, John

ONTARIO, Art
(Art Buchanan)
Singles: 7-inch
CRUSADE (299 "Truck Driving Man") 4-8 84
(500 made.)
DIXIE (823 "Queen of Bowling Green") 150-250 59
DIXIE (1002 "Hi-Yo Silver") 25-50 62
DIXIE (2019 "It Must Have Been Me") ..200-250 59
FLAME (1 "Time Will Tell") 100-200 58
ILLINOIS (725 "Wiggle Walkin' Boogie") 500-750 58
Also see BUCHANAN, Art

ONTARIOS
(With Frank Motley & His Crew)
Singles: 78 rpm
BIG TOWN (121 Memories of You") 50-75 55
Singles: 7-inch
BIG TOWN (121 "Memories of You") ...300-400 55
FIREFLY (Black vinyl) 3-5 74
FIREFLY (Red vinyl) 4-8 74
Also see MOTLEY, Frank

ONTEARE, Troy
Singles: 7-inch
MAXWELL (56 "Marry the Money") 50-75

ONYX
Singles: 7-inch
BURDETTE (6 "You've Got to Be with Me") 5-10 68
GREAT NORTHWEST (708 "I Could Really Make You Happy") ....5-10 '60s

OOGUM B. & TRICKS
Singles: 7-inch
PENTAGRAM (101 "You Are My Woman") 25-30 69

OPALS
Singles: 78 rpm
APOLLO 25-35 54
Singles: 7-inch
APOLLO (462 "My Heart's Desire") 250-300 54
(Flat label color.)
APOLLO (462 "My Heart's Desire") 20-30 58
(Glossy label color.)
LUNA (5001 "Come to Me Darling") 50-60
("Opals Formerly Knowns as the Crystals.")
Members: Earl Wade; John Hopson; Marty Brown; Ted Williams.
Also see CADILLACS
Also see CRYSTALS
Also see ORIGINAL CADILLACS

OPALS
Singles: 7-inch
BELTONE (2025 "Love") 10-20 62
(Brown vinyl.)

OPALS
Singles: 7-inch
OKEH (7184 "Losers Weepers") 15-20 63
OKEH (7188 "Does It Matter") 15-20 64
OKEH (7202 "You Can't Hurt Me No More") 10-15 64
OKEH (7224 "I'm So Afraid") 10-15 65

OPALS
Singles: 7-inch
LAURIE (3288 "Just Like a Little Bitty Baby") 8-12 65

OPALS & BELAIRS 4
Singles: 7-inch
SALEM (006 "I Want You More") ....15-25 '60s

OPELS
EPs: 7-inch
TREX (060 [four Christmas songs]) 50-75

OPEN SLOWLY
Singles: 7-inch
ROULETTE (7026 "Where Are You Now My Love") 5-10 68

OPKIS, Cenith
Singles: 7-inch
HEARTBREAK (620 "Funny Honey") 50-75

OPPER, Wolf
Singles: 7-inch
ACADEMY (1437 "Stompin' to the Beat") 100-200 59

OPPOSITE SIX
Singles: 7-inch
DOT (16700 "All Night Long") 8-10 65
SOUTH SHORE (720 "Down the Tubes") ....15-25 '60s
SOUTH SHORE (721 "Church Key") ....15-25 '60s

OPUS 1
Singles: 7-inch
MUSTANG (3017 "Dodge in My Mind") ...15-20 66

OR, John
(With Mick Jagger)
LPs: 10/12-inch
ATCO 15-25 71
Also see JAGGER, Mick

ORACLE
Singles: 7-inch
VERVE FORECAST (5075 "The Night We Fell in Love") 5-10 67

ORANG UTAN
LPs: 10/12-inch
BELL (6054 "Orang Utan") 20-25 71

ORANGE, Allen
Singles: 7-inch
MINIT (615 "Just a Little Love") 5-10 60
MINIT (630 "When You're Lonely") 5-10 61
MINIT (640 "The Letter") 5-10 62
SOUND STAGE 7 (2573 "V.C. Blues") 5-10 66

ORANGE COLORED SKY
Singles: 7-inch
MGM (14578 "Morning Light") 4-6 73
PEOPLE (1007 "Help") 5-10 69
UNI 5-10 68-69
LPs: 10/12-inch
UNI (73031 "Orange Colored Sky") 10-20 68
Member: Ernie Hernandez.
Also see YOUNGER BROTHERS

ORANGE WEDGE
Singles: 7-inch
BLUE FLAT (95097 "From the Womb to the Tomb") 50-75 68

ORANGE WEDGE
LPs: 10/12-inch
("No One Left But Me") ....200-300 '70s
(Label and number not known.)
("Wedge") ....200-300 '70s
(Label and number not known.)

ORBISON, Roy *P&R '56*
(With the Teen Kings; with Candy Men; with Roses; with Friends)
Singles: 78 rpm
QUALITY 20-40 56
SUN (242 "Ooby Dooby") 100-200 56
SUN (251 "Rockhouse") 75-100 56
SUN (265 "Sweet & Easy to Love") 75-100 56
SUN (284 "Chicken Hearted") 75-100 58
Singles: 12-inch
VIRGIN (2667 "She's a Mystery to Me") ..10-15 89
(Includes cover.)
Singles: 7-inch
ASYLUM 4-6 78-79

COLLECTABLES 3-5 85
MGM (13386 "Ride Away")....................8-12 65
MGM (13410 "Crawling Back")....................8-12 65
MGM (13446 "Breakin' Up Is Breakin' My Heart")....................8-12 66
MGM (13498 "Twinkle Toes") 8-12 66
MGM (13549 "Too Soon to Know")............8-12 66
MGM (13634 "Communication Breakdown") 8-12 66
MGM (13685 "Memories")....................8-12 67
MGM (13756 thru 13760)....................5-8 67
(Five reissues which are also found in the "MGM Celebrity Scene" boxed set.)
MGM (13764 "Cry Softly Lonely One") 8-12 67
MGM (13817 "She")....................8-12 67
MGM (13889 "Shy Away")....................5-10 68
MGM (13950 "Flowers") 5-10 68
MGM (13991 "Heartache")....................5-10 68
MGM (14039 "Southbound Jericho Parkway")....................5-10 69
MGM (14079 "Penny Arcade")....................5-10 69
MGM (14105 "She Cheats on Me")..........5-10 70
MGM (14121 "So Young")....................5-10 70
MGM (14293 "Close Again") 5-10 71
MGM (14358 "Changes") 5-10 72
MGM (14413 "Remember the Good")..........5-10 72
MGM (14441 "I Can Read Between the Lines")....................5-10 72
MGM (14552 "Blue Rain") 5-10 73
MGM (14626 "You Lay So Easy on My Mind")....................5-10 73
MGM CELEBRITY SCENE (CSN9-5 "Roy Orbison").................... 50-75 66
(Boxed set of five singles [13756 thru 13760] with bio insert and juke box title strips.)
MERCURY 4-8 74
MONUMENT (409 "Paper Boy") 20-30 59
MONUMENT (412 "Uptown")................ 15-25 59
MONUMENT (421 "Only the Lonely")...... 15-25 60
MONUMENT (425 "Blue Angel")........... 15-25 60
MONUMENT (433 "I'm Hurtin' ")........... 15-25 60
MONUMENT (438 "Running Scared")..... 10-20 61
MONUMENT (447 "Crying").................. 10-20 61
MONUMENT (456 "Dream Baby").......... 10-20 62
MONUMENT (461 "The Crowd") 10-20 62
MONUMENT (467 "Léah") 10-20 62
MONUMENT (500 series) 5-8 63-65
(Oldies reissue series.)
MONUMENT (806 "In Dreams")............ 10-15 63
MONUMENT (815 "Falling").................. 10-15 63
MONUMENT (824 "Mean Woman Blues").................... 10-15 63
MONUMENT (830 "Pretty Paper")......... 10-15 63
MONUMENT (837 "It's Over")............... 10-15 64
MONUMENT (851 "Oh, Pretty Woman"). 10-15 64
MONUMENT (873 "Goodnight")............. 10-15 65
MONUMENT (891 "You're My Girl") 10-15 65
MONUMENT (906 "Let the Good Times Roll")....................8-12 65
MONUMENT (8600 series) 4-6 76
MONUMENT (8900 series) 4-6 72
(Oldies reissue series.)
MONUMENT (45000 series) 4-6 76-77
QUALITY (1499 "Ooby Dooby")........... 50-100 56
(Canadian.)
QUALITY (1559 "Rockhouse").............. 50-100 56
(Canadian.)
RCA (7381 "Sweet & Innocent").............. 20-30 58
RCA (7447 "Jolie").................... 20-30 59
SSS/SUN....................4-6 69
SUN (242 "Ooby Dooby").................... 40-60 56
SUN (251 "Rockhouse") 40-60 56
SUN (265 "Sweet and Easy to Love")...... 25-50 56
SUN (284 "Chicken Hearted")............... 25-50 58
SUN (353 "Sweet and Easy to Love")...... 15-25 61
(Yellow label.)
SUN (353 "Sweet and Easy to Love")...... 25-50 61
(White label. Promotional issue only.)
VIRGIN 3-5 87-89

Picture Sleeves

MGM (13386 "Ride Away").................... 30-40 65
MGM (13410 "Crawling Back")............... 30-40 65
MGM (13446 "Breakin' Up Is Breakin' My Heart").................... 30-40 66
MGM (13498 "Twinkle Toes") 30-40 66
MGM (13549 "Too Soon to Know")........ 30-40 66
MGM (13764 "Cry Softly Lonely One") 30-40 67
MONUMENT (433 "I'm Hurtin' ")............ 20-30 60
MONUMENT (438 "Running Scared")..... 15-25 61
MONUMENT (447 "Crying").................. 15-25 61
MONUMENT (456 "Dream Baby")..........15-25 62
MONUMENT (461 "The Crowd") 15-25 62
MONUMENT (467 "Léah") 15-25 62
MONUMENT (806 "In Dreams") 10-20 63
MONUMENT (815 "Falling")....................10-20 63
MONUMENT (837 "It's Over")..................10-20 64
VIRGIN (99202 "California Blues") 4-6 89
VIRGIN (99227 "She's a Mystery to Me").....4-6 89
VIRGIN (99245 "You Got It")....................4-6 89

EPs: 7-inch

MGM (4379 "Classic Roy Orbison").........30-50 66
(Juke box issue only.)
MONUMENT (2 "Crying")....................20-30 62
(Compact 33, "Special Promotional Six-Pac." Not issued with special cover.)
MONUMENT (3 "Roy Orbison")..............20-30 62
(Compact 33, "Special Promotional Six-Pac." Not issued with special cover.)
MONUMENT (526 "Roy Orbison")...........15-25 64
(Compact 33. Juke box issue only.)
STARS INC. (101 "Roy Orbison and the Teen Kings") 300-400 59
(Promotional issue, distributed to fan club members.)

LPs: 10/12-inch

ACCORD....................5-8 81
ASYLUM....................5-8 78-79
BUCKBOARD 8-10
CANDLELITE MUSIC....................10-15 '70s
DESIGN....................10-20 '60s
LIVING LEGEND (05013 "Living Legend")....................30-50 80
(Soundtrack.)
MGM (E-4308 "There Is Only One Roy Orbison")....................15-20 65
(Monaural.)
MGM (SE-4308 "There Is Only One Roy Orbison")....................15-25 65
(Stereo.)
MGM (E-4322 "The Orbison Way").........15-20 65
(Monaural.)
MGM (SE-4322 "The Orbison Way")........15-25 65
(Stereo.)
MGM (E-4379 "Classic Roy Orbison") 15-20 66
(Monaural.)
MGM (SE-4379 "Classic Roy Orbison") ...15-25 66
(Stereo.)
MGM (E-4424 "Roy Orbison Sings Don Gibson")....................15-20 66
(Monaural.)
MGM (SE-4424 "Roy Orbison Sings Don Gibson")....................15-25 66
MGM (E-4475 "The Fastest Guitar Alive")....................15-20 67
(Monaural.)
MGM (SE-4475 "The Fastest Guitar Alive")....................15-25 67
(Stereo.)
MGM (4636 "Roy Orbison's Many Moods")....................10-20 69
MGM (4659 "Great Songs of Roy Orbison")....................10-20 70
MGM (4835 "Roy Orbison Sings")...........10-15 72
MGM (4867 "Memphis")....................10-15 72
MGM (4934 "Milestones") 10-15 73
MGM/CAPITOL (90454 "There Is Only One Roy Orbison")....................20-30 65
(Label reads "Mfd. by Capitol Records." Record club issue.)
MGM/CAPITOL (90928 "Classic Roy Orbison")....................20-30 66
(Label reads "Mfd. by Capitol Records." Record club issue.)
MERCURY....................8-12 75
MONUMENT (4002 "Lonely & Blue")....100-200 61
(Monaural.)
MONUMENT (4007 "Crying"....................50-100 62
(Monaural.)
MONUMENT (4009 "Greatest Hits")........30-40 62
(Monaural.)
MONUMENT (6600 series) 8-10
MONUMENT (7600 "Regeneration") 8-10 76
MONUMENT (8000 "Greatest Hits").........25-30 63
(Monaural.)
MONUMENT (8003 "In Dreams") 30-40 63
(Monaural.)
MONUMENT (8023 "Early Orbison")........30-40 64
(Monaural.)
MONUMENT (8024 "More Greatest Hits")....................20-25 64
(Monaural.)
MONUMENT (8035 "Orbisongs") 25-30 65
(Monaural.)
MONUMENT (8045 "Very Best") 30-40 66
(Blue cover. Monaural.)
MONUMENT (8045 "Very Best") 20-30 66
(Purple cover. Monaural.)
MONUMENT (14002 "Lonely and Blue")....................200-300 61
(Stereo.)
MONUMENT (14007 "Crying") 150-250 62
(Stereo.)
MONUMENT (14009 "Greatest Hits") 40-50 62
(Stereo.)
MONUMENT (18000 "Greatest Hits") 35-40 63
(Stereo.)
MONUMENT (18003 "In Dreams") 40-50 63
(Stereo.)
MONUMENT (18024 "More Greatest Hits")....................25-30 64
(Stereo.)
MONUMENT (18035 "Orbisongs") 35-40 65
(Stereo.)
MONUMENT (18023 "Early Orbison")......30-40 64
(Stereo.)
MONUMENT (18045 "Very Best") 30-40 66
(Blue cover. Stereo.)
MONUMENT (18045 "Very Best") 20-30 66
(Purple cover. Stereo.)
MONUMENT (31484 "All-Time Greatest Hits")....................8-12 72
MONUMENT (38384 "All-Time Greatest Hits")....................6-10 82
RHINO....................5-8 88
SPECTRUM....................15-20 '60s
SSS/SUN (113 "Original Sound") 8-12 69
SUN (1260 "Rock House")...................300-400 62
SUNNYVALE 8-10 77
TIME-LIFE....................10-15 86
TRIP 8-10 74
VIRGIN 6-12 87-89
Session: Bobby Goldsboro; James Burton; Glen D. Hardin; Ronnie Tutt; Jerry Scheff; Elvis Costello; k.d. lang; Bonnie Raitt; Jennifer Warnes; Bruce Springsteen.
Also see BURTON, James
Also see CANDYMEN
Also see COOK, Ken
Also see COSTELLO, Elvis
Also see CRICKETS
Also see DRIFTERS / Lesley Gore / Roy Orbison / Los Bravos
Also see GOLDSBORO, Bobby
Also see JAN & DEAN / Roy Orbison / 4 Seasons / Shirelles
Also see LEWIS, Jerry Lee / Roger Miller / Roy Orbison
Also see PERKINS, Carl, Jerry Lee Lewis, Roy Orbison & Johnny Cash
Also see RAITT, Bonnie
Also see SPRINGSTEEN, Bruce
Also see TEEN KINGS
Also see TRAVELING WILBURYS
Also see TUCKER, Rick
Also see WARNES, Jennifer
Also see WILSON, Peanuts

ORBISON, Roy / Bobby Bare / Joey Powers

LPs: 10/12-inch

CAMDEN (820 "Special Delivery") 15-25 64
Also see BARE, Bobby
Also see POWERS, Joey

ORBISON, Roy, & Emmylou Harris / Craig Hundley C&W/P&R '80

Singles: 7-inch

W.B. (49262 "That Lovin' You Feelin' Again")....................3-5 80
Also see HARRIS, Emmylou

ORBISON, Roy, & k.d. Lang C&W '87

Singles: 7-inch

VIRGIN (99388 "Crying")....................3-5 87
Also see ORBISON, Roy

ORBIT ROCKERS

Singles: 7-inch

WILLAMETTE (106 "Windfall") 10-15 59
WILLAMETTE (107 "Rock It")...................10-15 59
Also see SMITH, Leon

ORBITEERS

Singles: 7-inch

FILM (716 "Landslide")....................10-20 61

ORBITS

Singles: 78 rpm

ARGO....................15-25 58
FLAIR-X 10-15 56

Singles: 7-inch

ARGO (5286 "Mr. Hard Luck")....................20-30 58
FLAIR-X (5000 "Message of Love") 20-30 56
FRIDDELL (102 "My Rosa-Lee")..........150-250
NU KAT (116/117 "Knock Her Down"/"My Love") 30-40 59

ORBITS

(Tommy Lee & Orbits)

Singles: 7-inch

GAITY (181 "Jingle Rock")....................25-35 61
SPACE (1116 "Queen Bee")................300-350 60

ORBITS

Singles: 7-inch

CUCA (1006 "Orbit Rock")....................10-20 66
(This is a different band than the Cuca one that follows.)
Member: Jerry Raimer; Bill Alexander; Bob Hoffer.

ORBITS

Singles: 7-inch

BIG SOUND (304 "Fuzzy") 10-20 66
CUCA (6744 "Don't")....................10-20 67
Member: Ron Hanson.

ORBITS

(With the Rockin' Royals)

Singles: 7-inch

DON-J (48798 "I'm Home")................750-1000

ORCHARDS

Singles: 7-inch

T&K (1001 "We're in Love") 10-15 65

ORCHIDS

Singles: 78 rpm

KING (4661 "Oh Why") 50-100 53
KING (4663 "I've Been a Fool from the Start")....................50-100 53
PARROT (815 "Newly Wed")...................50-100 55
PARROT (819 "You Said You Loved Me")....................50-100 55

Singles: 7-inch

KING (4661 "Oh Why") 250-300 53
KING (4663 "I've Been a Fool from the Start")....................250-300 53
LOST NITE 4-8
PARROT (815 "Newly Wed")................250-300 55
PARROT (819 "You Said You Loved Me") 250-300 55
SAVOY (964 "My Story")....................4-8
(Previously unreleased.)
Members: Gilbert Warren; Buford Wright; Robert Nesbary.

ORCHIDS

Singles: 7-inch

HARLOW (101 "I Don't Think You Missed Me")....................10-20 62
ROULETTE (4412 "Pony Walk") 5-10 62
ROULETTE (4633 "Good Good Time")......5-10 65
WALL (549 "Good Golly") 5-10 61

LPs: 10/12-inch

ROULETTE (25169 "Twistin' at the Roundtable") 20-30 62

ORCHIDS

Singles: 7-inch

COLUMBIA (42913 "That Boy Is Messin' Up My Mind") 5-10 63
COLUMBIA (43066 "From Bad to Worse") 5-10 64
COLUMBIA (43175 "It Doesn't Matter") 5-10 64

ORDELLS

Singles: 7-inch

DIONN (505 "Big Dom")....................10-15 67

ORE'S HALYCON DAYS

LPs: 10/12-inch

AKASHIC (10-2-49-79 "Ore's Halycon Days")....................8-12 79
(Picture disc.)

ORGAN GRINDERS

Singles: 7-inch

SMASH (2227 "Daylight") 5-10 69

SMASH (2242 "Babylon")............................5-10 69

LPs: 10/12-inch

MERCURY (61282 "Out of the Egg")....... 15-25 70

ORIENT EXPRESS

LPs: 10/12-inch

MAINSTREAM (6117 "Orient Express").. 50-75 69

Members: Liz Damon; Guy Duris.
Also see DAMON, Liz

ORIENTALS

Singles: 7-inch

KAYO (346 "Please Come Back Home"). 30-50 58

KAYO (927 "Get Yourself to School")...... 30-40 58

(White label. Promotional issue only.)

KAYO (927 "Get Yourself to School")...... 10-20 58

(Blue label.)

NEW DAWN (413 "Misty Summer Night").. 20-30 '60s

ORIENTS

Singles: 7-inch

LAURIE (3232 "Queen of Angels")......... 15-25 64

(Promotional issue only.)

LAURIE (3232 "Queen of Angels")............5-10 64

Members: Al Mickens; Bobby Lee Hollis; Robert Colman; James Davis; Johnny Cumbo; William Edwards.
Also see SUNBEAMS

ORIGINAL CADILLACS

Singles: 7-inch

JOSIE (821 "Hurry Home")...................... 15-25 57

JOSIE (915 "I'll Never Let You Go")......... 15-25 64

Members: Earl Carroll; Charles Brooks; Bobby Phillips; Earl Wade; Junior Glanton; Roland Martinez.
Also see CADILLACS
Also see CARROLL, Earl, & Original Cadillacs
Also see OPALS

ORIGINAL CASUALS *P&R/R&B '58*

(Casuals; "Featuring Gary Mears"; with Alex Sample & Orchestra)

Singles: 78 rpm

BACK BEAT 15-25 57

Singles: 7-inch

ABC ("So Tough")....................................4-6 73

(Selection number not known.)

BACK BEAT (503 "So Tough")................ 20-30 57

(Credits the "Casuals.")

BACK BEAT (503 "So Tough")................ 15-25 57

BACK BEAT (510 "Ju-Judy")................... 10-20 58

BACK BEAT (514 "Three Kisses Past Midnight")..................................... 10-20 58

JARRETT (101 "So Tough").......................5-10

Picture Sleeves

BACK BEAT (503 "So Tough")................ 20-30 57

EPs: 7-inch

BACK BEAT (40 "Three Kisses Past Midnight")..................................... 50-100 58

Members: Gary Mears; Paul Kearney; Jay Adams.
Also see CASUALS

ORIGINAL CHARMERS

Singles: 7-inch

ANGLE TONE (550 "For Sentimental Reasons") 100-200 60

ORIGINAL CHARMERS

Singles: 7-inch

BLUE SKY (102 "Fools Rush In") 4-6 72

(Black vinyl.)

BLUE SKY (102 "Fools Rush In") 20-25 72

(Blue vinyl. Reportedly 3 made.)

BLUE SKY (102 "Fools Rush In") 15-20 72

(Red vinyl. Reportedly 5 made.)

ORIGINAL CHECKERS

(Checkers)

Singles: 7-inch

KING (5592 "Over the Rainbow")............ 10-15 61

Also see CHECKERS

ORIGINAL DUKES

Singles: 7-inch

DOWN HOME (106 "Ain't About to Lose My Cool") .... 20-30 '60s

ORIGINAL FIVE BLIND BOYS

Singles: 78 rpm

VEE-JAY (225 "Oh Why")....................... 10-15 56

Singles: 7-inch

VEE-JAY (225 "Oh Why")....................... 50-75 56

ORIGINAL FOUR ACES

Singles: 78 rpm

BIG TOWN 10-20 54-55

Singles: 7-inch

BIG TOWN (112 "Release Me")...............30-40 54

BIG TOWN (118 "I Can See an Angel") ...40-50 55

Also see FOUR ACES

ORIGINAL GROUP

(Monarchs)

Singles: 7-inch

SMASH (2219 "Look Homeward Angel"/"Climb Every Mountain") 5-10 69

Picture Sleeves

SMASH (2219 "Look Homeward Angel"/"Climb Every Mountain") 10-12 69

Also see MONARCHS

ORIGINAL HAUNTED

(Featuring Bob Burgess)

Singles: 7-inch

JET (4002 "Mona") 20-30 67

(Canadian.)

Also see HAUNTED

ORIGINAL HUSTLERS

Singles: 7-inch

LA BELLE (64121 "Cueball")....................10-20 64

Also see HUSTLERS

ORIGINAL JUBALAIRES

Singles: 78 rpm

CROWN 20-30 54

Singles: 7-inch

CROWN (111 "Waiting All My Life for You") 50-75 54

CROWN (118 "You Won't Let Me Go").....50-75 54

Also see JUBALAIRES

ORIGINAL LIVERPOOL BEAT

LPs: 10/12-inch

20TH FOX (3144 "Original Liverpool Beat") 10-20 64

(Listed by title since there is no artist credited.)

ORIGINAL MUSTANGS

Singles: 7-inch

HI-Q (5040 "Jump Lula") 10-20 64

ORIGINAL PLAYBOYS

Singles: 7-inch

LEISURE TIME (0001 "I'll Always Be By Your Side") 50-100

Also see VACANT LOT

ORIGINAL PROPHETS

Singles: 7-inch

CIA (4509 "Ain't That Lovin' You Baby")...15-25 66

ORIGINAL PYRAMIDS

Singles: 7-inch

SHELL (304 "Ankle Bracelet")...................25-35 61

Also see PYRAMIDS

ORIGINAL ROCKETS

Singles: 7-inch

RENDEZVOUS (164 "Garbage Can") 10-20 62

ORIGINAL SINNERS

Singles: 7-inch

DISCOTECH (1001 "You'll Never Know") 15-25 66

ORIGINAL SMOKEHOUSE BAND

Singles: 7-inch

GLOW STAR (901 "Don't Let Your Mind Go Astray") ....20-30 '60s

ORIGINAL SOUNDTRACKS

Singles: 7-inch

LAWN (214 "Come On Let's Go")............10-15 63

ORIGINAL TURKS

Singles: 78 rpm

CASH (1042 "Wagon Wheels")................10-15 56

Singles: 7-inch

CASH (1042 "Wagon Wheels")................20-30 56

ORIGINALES

Singles: 7-inch

POOR BOY (110 Lend Me Your Ear")......50-75 60

Members: Tom Smalley; Ron Bonham; Sonny Johnson; Sam Dargo; Jan Conway.

ORIGINALS

Singles: 7-inch

JACKPOT (48007 "The Whip") 15-25 58

JACKPOT (48012 "Anna") 15-25 58

Also see RIO, Chuck

ORIGINALS

EPs: 7-inch

SOMERSET (6000 "The Originals") 10-15 58

ORIGINALS

Singles: 7-inch

BRUNSWICK (55171 "A Kiss from Your Lips")..75-100 60

(Same number used on a Valentinos release.)

ORIGINALS

Singles: 7-inch

ORIGINAL SOUND (10 "Wishing Star")...20-30 60

Also see ALLEN, Tony

ORIGINALS

Singles: 7-inch

DIAMOND (102 "At Times Like This")......20-30 61

(Black vinyl.)

DIAMOND (102 "At Times Like This")......30-40 61

(Brown vinyl.)

DIAMOND (116 "You and I")....................15-25 62

(Black vinyl.)

DIAMOND (116 "You and I")....................30-40 62

(Brown vinyl.)

ORIGINALS

Singles: 7-inch

VAN (02165 "Blast Off!") 10-20 65

VAN (03065 "Night Flight")........................10-20 65

ORIGINALS

Singles: 7-inch

RAYNARD (10039 "Now's the Time") 5-10 65

Members: Dan Helland; Jim Morrison; Pete Polzak; Jim Jandrain; Tim Polzak.

ORIGINALS *P&R/R&B '69*

Singles: 7-inch

FANTASY..4-6 78

MOTOWN (1 "Young Train")................100-200 73

(Promotional issue only.)

MOTOWN (1300 series).............................4-6 75

PHASE II 3-5 81

SOUL (35029 thru 35061)...........................6-12 67-69

SOUL (35066 thru 35121)...........................4-8 69-77

(Black vinyl.)

SOUL (Colored vinyl)..................................8-15

(Promotional issue only.)

LPs: 10/12-inch

FANTASY..5-10 78-79

MOTOWN 5-10 74-80

SOUL (716 "Baby I'm for Real")...............20-40 69

SOUL (724 "Portrait")..................................15-20 70

SOUL (729 "Naturally Together") 15-20 70

SOUL (734 thru 746)...................................8-15 73-76

Members: Ty Hunter; Henry Dixon; Joe Stubbs; Walt Gaines; C.P. Spencer; Freddie Gorman.
Also see CONTOURS
Also see FIVE STARS
Also see GORMAN, Freddie
Also see HUNTER, Ty
Also see STUBBS, Joe
Also see VOICE MASTERS

ORIOLES *P&R/R&B '48*

(With the Sid Bass Orchestra; Sonny Til & Orioles; Sonny Til's Orioles)

Singles: 78 rpm

IT'S A NATURAL (5000 "It's Too Soon to Know") 100-200 48

JUBILEE (5000 "It's Too Soon to Know").50-75 48

JUBILEE (5001 "Dare to Dream").........100-200 48

JUBILEE (5001 "A Lonely Christmas")......25-75 48

(Same selection number used twice.)

JUBILEE (5002 "Please Give My Heart a Break")..25-75 49

JUBILEE (5005 "Tell Me So") 25-75 49

JUBILEE (5008 "I Challenge Your Kiss") .25-75 49

JUBILEE (5009 "A Kiss and a Rose") 25-75 49

JUBILEE (5016 "So Much")......................25-75 49

JUBILEE (5017 "What Are You Doing New Year's Eve")..25-75 49

JUBILEE (5018 "Would You Still Be the One in My Heart")..25-75 50

JUBILEE (5025 "At Night").......................25-75 50

JUBILEE (5026 "Moonlight")....................25-75 50

JUBILEE (5028 "You're Gone")................25-75 50

JUBILEE (5031 "I'd Rather Have You Under the Moon") 20-60 50

JUBILEE (5037 "I Need You So")............20-60 50

JUBILEE (5040 "I Cross My Fingers")......20-60 50

JUBILEE (5045 "Oh Holy Night")..............20-60 50

JUBILEE (5051 "I Miss You So")..............20-60 51

JUBILEE (5055 "Pal of Mine") 20-60 51

JUBILEE (5057 "Would I Love You")........20-60 51

JUBILEE (5061 "I'm Just a Fool in Love")..20-60 51

At least 10 of the above 78 rpm singles were reissued around 1951 on 45s. It's likely that others in the 5001-5061 series appeared on early '50s Jubilee 45s, but those listed below are the only ones we have verified.

JUBILEE (5061 thru 5231).......................15-45 51-56

QUALITY..20-30 53

(Canadian.)

VEE-JAY 15-35 56-57

Singles: 7-inch

ABNER (1016 "Sugar Girl") 75-100 58

CHARLIE PARKER 8-15 62-63

CLIFTON (105 "Danny Boy")......................3-5 92

COLLECTABLES ....3-5 '80s

JUBILEE (5000 "It's Too Soon to Know")..1500-2500 51

JUBILEE (5005 "Tell Me So")...........1000-1500 51

JUBILEE (5016 "So Much") 750-1000 51

JUBILEE (5017 "What Are You Doing New Year's Eve") 500-1000 51

JUBILEE (5025 "At Night")...................500-750 51

JUBILEE (5040 "I Cross My Fingers")..1000-1500 51

JUBILEE (5045 "Oh Holy Night")..........300-400 51

JUBILEE (5051 "I Miss You So") 500-750 51

(Black vinyl.)

JUBILEE (5051 "I Miss You So")......1000-2000 51

(Red vinyl.)

JUBILEE (5061 "I'm Just a Fool in Love")..700-800 51

JUBILEE (5065 "Baby, Please Don't Go") 200-300 51

(Black vinyl.)

JUBILEE (5065 "Baby, Please Don't Go") 600-800 51

(Red vinyl.)

JUBILEE (5071 "When You're Not Around") 500-750 51

JUBILEE (5074 "Trust in Me") 300-400 52

(Black vinyl.)

JUBILEE (5074 "Trust in Me") 650-750 52

(Red vinyl.)

JUBILEE (5082 "Waiting").....................550-650 52

JUBILEE (5084 "Barfly") 300-500 52

JUBILEE (5092 "Don't Cry Baby")........300-400 52

(Black vinyl.)

JUBILEE (5092 "Don't Cry Baby") 800-1000 52

(Red vinyl.)

JUBILEE (5102 "You Belong to Me") ...500-750 52

JUBILEE (5107 "I Miss You So") 300-400 53

(Reissued in 1963, using the same catalog number, but credited to Sonny Til & Orioles. Black vinyl.)

JUBILEE (5107 "I Miss You So") 800-1000 53

(Red vinyl.)

JUBILEE (5108 "Teardrops on My Pillow")...300-400 53

(Black vinyl.)

JUBILEE (5108 "Teardrops on My Pillow")...600-800 53

(Red vinyl.)

JUBILEE (5115 "Bad Little Girl")...........200-300 53

JUBILEE (5120 "I Cover the Waterfront") 300-400 53

(Black vinyl.)

JUBILEE (5120 "I Cover the Waterfront")..800-1000 53

(Red vinyl.)

JUBILEE (5122 "Crying in the Chapel") ...50-75 53

(Black vinyl.)

JUBILEE (5122 "Crying in the Chapel")..2000-2500 53

(Red vinyl.)

JUBILEE (5127 "In the Mission of St. Augustine")..40-60 53

JUBILEE (5134 "There's No One But You")..40-60 54

JUBILEE (5137 "Secret Love") 40-60 54

JUBILEE (5143 "Maybe You'll Be There")..75-100 54

JUBILEE (5154 "In the Chapel in the Moonlight")..50-75 54

JUBILEE (5161 "If You Believe") 40-60 54

JUBILEE (5172 "Runaround")..................40-60 54

JUBILEE (5177 "I Love You Mostly") 40-60 55

JUBILEE (5189 "I Need You Baby") 40-60 55
JUBILEE (5221 "Please Sing My Blues Tonight") 50-75 55
JUBILEE (5231 "Angel") 40-60 56
JUBILEE (5363 "Tell Me So") 10-20 59
JUBILEE (5384 "Come On Home") 10-15 60
JUBILEE (5394 "Night and Day") 40-60 60
JUBILEE (6001 "Crying in the Chapel") ... 10-15 59
(Jubilee 5066 & 5076 are credited to Sonny Til. Same number used on an earlier release by the Johnny Dee Trio.)
MAXI (003 "For All We Know") 3-5 80
QUALITY (1139 "Crying in theChapel") ... 50-75 53
(Canadian.)
ROULETTE GOLDEN GOODIES .... 4-6 '70s
SHAG (104 "Bring the Money Home") 4-8
(Previously unissued.)
VEE-JAY (196 "Happy Till the Letter") 25-35 56
VEE-JAY (228 "For All We Know") 25-35 56
VEE-JAY (244 "Sugar Girl") 400-500 57
VIRGO .... 4-8 '70s

Picture Sleeves

JUBILEE (5017 "What Are You Doing New Year's Eve") 300-500 54
(Sleeve for 78 rpm.)
JUBILEE (5017 "What Are You Doing New Year's Eve") 550-650 54
(Sleeve for 45 rpm.)
JUBILEE (5045 "Oh Holy Night") 550-650 54
(Both Jubilee sleeves were issued in late 1954 and sold with 1954 pressings – actually second pressings of both. These were blue script Jubilee labels with the line under the logo.)
LANA (109 "What Are You Doing New Year's Eve") 4-6 63

EPs: 7-inch

JUBILEE (5000 "The Orioles Sing"). 1000-2000 53

LPs: 10/12-inch

BIG A RECORDS (2001 "Greatest All Time Hits") 20-30 69
CHARLIE PARKER (816 "Modern Sounds") 50-100 62
COLLECTABLES 5-10 84
MURRAY HILL .... 30-40 '80s
(Boxed, five-disc set. Number not known.)
MURRAY HILL (61277 "The Orioles Featuring Sonny Til") .... 30-40 '80s
(Boxed, five-disc set.)
ROULETTE 5-10
Members: Sonny Til; George Nelson; Johnny Reed; Tom Gaither; Alex Sharp; Greg Carroll; Charles Harris; Billy Adams; Jerry Holman; Al Russell; Jerry Rodriguez; Bill Taylor.
Also see CADILLACS / Orioles
Also see REED, Johnny
Also see REGALS
Also see TIL, Sonny

ORION *C&W '79*
(Jimmy Ellis)

Singles: 7-inch

KRISTAL 4-6 85
ORCHID 4-6 89
SUN 5-10 79-84
(Most, if not all, on colored vinyl – usually gold.)

Promotional Singles

SUN (1142 "Ebony Eyes"/"Honey") 10-20 79
(With unprinted white label. Includes flyer explaining blank label idea.)

EPs: 7-inch

ORION ("Merry Christmas") .... 10-15 '80s
(Fan club issue.)
SUN (1152 "A Stranger in My Place") 15-25 80
(Promotional issue only. Price includes explanatory flyer. Not issued with cover.)

LPs: 10/12-inch

ARON 10-15 89
(Canadian.)
SUFFOLK MARKETING 10-15 81
(TV mail-order LP.)
SUN (Except 1012) 10-20 79-81
(Most Sun LPs are colored vinyl)
SUN (1012 "Orion Reborn") 20-30 78
(White cover. Often referred to as with the "Coffin Cover.")
SUN (1012 "Orion Reborn") 10-15 78
(Blue cover.)
Also see ELLIS, Jimmy
Also see LEWIS, Jerry Lee, & Friends

ORION, P.J., & Magnates

LPs: 10/12-inch

MAGNATE (122459 "P.J. Orion and the Magnates") .... 75-125 '60s

ORION THE HUNTER *P&R/LP '84*

Singles: 7-inch

PORTRAIT 3-5 84-85

LPs: 10/12-inch

PORTRAIT (39239 "Orion the Hunter") 20-40 84
Member: Barry Goudreau.
Also see BOSTON

ORK, Jay Hodge

Singles: 7-inch

CORNUTO (1000 "Goatsville") 10-20
(Colored vinyl.)

ORLANDO, Tony

Singles: 7-inch

MILO (101 "Ding Dong") 75-100 59
Also see SIMON, Paul

ORLANDO, Tony *P&R '61*

Singles: 12-inch

CASABLANCA 5-10 79

Singles: 7-inch

ATCO (6376 "She Loves Me") 5-10 65
CAMEO (471 "Sweet Sweet") 5-10 67
CASABLANCA 3-6 79-80
EPIC (2202 "Halfway to Paradise") 5-10 63
EPIC (9441 "Halfway to Paradise") 10-15 61
EPIC (9452 "Bless You") 10-15 61
EPIC (9476 "Happy Times Are Here to Stay") 10-15 61
EPIC (9491 "My Baby's a Stranger") 10-15 61
EPIC (9502 "I'd Never Find Another You") 10-15 62
EPIC (9519 "Chills") 10-15 62
EPIC (9562 "Beautiful Dreamer") 10-15 62
EPIC (9570 "Shirley") 10-15 63
EPIC (9622 "I'll Be There") 10-15 63
EPIC (9668 "She Doesn't Know It") 10-15 64
EPIC (9715 "To Wait for Love") 10-15 64
EPIC (55299 "Happy Times Are Here to Stay") 20-30 61
(Promotional issue only.)

Picture Sleeves

EPIC (9441 "Halfway to Paradise") 15-25 61
EPIC (9452 "Bless You") 15-25 61
EPIC (9476 "Happy Times Are Here to Stay") 15-25 61
EPIC (9491 "My Baby's a Stranger") 15-25 61

LPs: 10/12-inch

EPIC (611 "Bless You") 40-60 61
(Stereo.)
EPIC (3808 "Bless You") 35-50 61
(Monaural.)
EPIC (33785 "Before Dawn") 10-12 75
CASABLANCA 5-10 79-80
Also see DACHE, Bertell
Also see SHIELDS, Billy
Also see WIND

ORLANDO, Tony, & Dawn *P&R/LP '70*

Singles: 7-inch

ARISTA 4-6 75
BELL 4-6 71-74
ELEKTRA 4-6 75-78
FLASHBACK .... 4-6 '70s

LPs: 10/12-inch

ARISTA 8-10 75-76
ASYLUM 8-10 75
BELL (6000 series) 10-12 70-71
BELL (1000 series) 8-10 73-75
ELEKTRA 8-10 75-78
KORY 8-10 74-77
Members: Telma Hopkins; Joyce Wilson.
Also see ORLANDO, Tony

ORLANDOS

Singles: 7-inch

CINDY (3006 "Old MacDonald") 100-200 57
(Cindy logo is in block print with a shadow behind the letters.)
CINDY(3006 "Old MacDonald") 30-40 57
(Cindy logo is in a rectangular box at the top of the label.)
Note: Any colored vinyl pressings are unauthorized issues.

ORLIE & SAINTS

Singles: 7-inch

BAND BOX (253 "King Kong") 10-20 61
BAND BOX (264 "Annette") 10-20 61

ORLONS *P&R/R&B/LP '62*

Singles: 7-inch

ABC (10894 "Everything") 5-10 67
ABC (10948 "Kissin' Time") 5-10 67
ABKCO 4-6
CALLA (113 "Spinnin' Top") 8-12 66
(First issue.)
CAMEO (198 "I'll Be True") 30-40 61
CAMEO (211 "Mr. Twenty-One") 40-50 62
CAMEO (218 thru 384, except 346) 10-20 62-65
CAMEO (346 "Envy") 40-50 64
JUKE BOX (509 "I'll Be True") 8-10
PLANET (117 "Spinnin' Top") 5-10 66
TEEN (3 "Over the Mountain") 3-5

Picture Sleeves

CAMEO 15-20 62-64

LPs: 10/12-inch

CAMEO (1020 "Wah Watusi") 50-100 62
CAMEO (1033 "All the Hits") 50-100 62
CAMEO (1041 "South Street") 50-100 63
CAMEO (1054 "Not Me") 50-100 63
CAMEO (1061 "Biggest Hits") 50-100 63
CAMEO (1073 "Memory Lane") 50-100 63
Members: Shirley Brickley; Rosetta Hightower; Steve Caldwell; Marlena Davis.
Also see SHARP, Dee Dee
Also see ZIP & ZIPPERS

ORLONS / Dovells

LPs: 10/12-inch

CAMEO (1067 "Golden Hits") 25-50 63
Also see DOVELLS
Also see ORLONS

ORLONS / Dale Hawkins

Singles: 7-inch

TEEN (3 "Over the Mountain"/"Little Pig") .. 5-10
Also see HAWKINS, Dale
Also see ORLONS

ORMANDY

Singles: 7-inch

DECCA (32741 "Good Day") 10-15 70
KASABA (100 "Good Day") 10-20 70
STARSHINE (7203 "The Banker") .... 8-12 '70s
Member: Alto Reed.
Also see SEGER, Bob

ORO, Emmy, & Her Rhythm Escorts

Singles: 7-inch

CHELSEA (1001 "Is It a Sin") 15-25 61

ORPHAN EGG

LPs: 10/12-inch

CAROLE (8004 "Orphan Egg") 15-25 68

ORPHANS

Singles: 7-inch

EPIC (10288 "One Spoken Word") 5-10 68
EPIC (10348 "This Is the Time") 5-10 68

ORPHEUS

Singles: 7-inch

RED BIRD (041 "My Life") 5-10 65

ORR, Chet, & Rumbles

Singles: 7-inch

STUDIO CITY (1012 "Be Satisfied") 40-60 64
Members: Chet Orr; Dennis Konkel; Don Fenn; Dave Lindemann; John Rookey; John Grindal.

ORR, J.D. & Lonesome Valley Boys

Singles: 7-inch

SUMMIT (105 "Hula-Hoop Boogie") 200-300 58

ORRELL, David

Singles: 7-inch

FELSTED (8515 "Be My Baby") 50-75 58

ORSI, Phil
(With the Little Kings)

Singles: 7-inch

LUCKY (1009 "Oh My Darling") 100-200 63
LUCKY (1015 "Don't You Just Know It") .. 15-25 64
SONIC 4-6 77
USA (837 "Stay") 15-25 66
USA (841 "Sorry") 15-25 66
WISE WORLD (62770 "Oh My Darling") .. 50-75 63

ORTEGA, Frankie

Singles: 7-inch

JUBILEE (5365 "77 Sunset Strip") 8-10 59

LPs: 10/12-inch

JUBILEE (JLP-1106 "77 Sunset Strip") 15-25 59
(Monaural.)
JUBILEE (SDJLP-1106 "77 Sunset Strip") 25-40 59
(Stereo.)

ORTEGA, Palito

LPs: 10/12-inch

RCA (196 "Boogaloo – Nashville Style") .. 10-15 67
RCA (3661 "Palito Ortega") 10-15 67

ORTEZ, Anita

Singles: 7-inch

COLUMBIA (43695 "He's All Mine") 5-10 66

ORTON, Irv

LPs: 10/12-inch

LIBERTY (3069 "Alone with You") 15-25 58
(Monaural.)
LIBERTY (7016 "Alone with You") 25-35 58
(Stereo.)

O'RYAN, Jack, & Al Tercek

Singles: 78 rpm

NOCTURNE (8 "Political Circus") 20-30 56

Singles: 7-inch

NOCTURNE (8 "Political Circus") 25-50 56

OSBORN, Dave

Singles: 7-inch

COOL (125 "Shake It") 200-300

OSBORN, Richetta

Singles: 7-inch

BLUE RIVER (226 "My Sweet Baby") 5-10 67

OSBORNE, Arthur

Singles: 7-inch

BRUNSWICK (55068 "Hey Ruby") 50-75 58

OSBORNE, B., & Tracers

Singles: 7-inch

RIC (165 "My Baby Gives Me Lovin'") 10-20

OSBORNE, Billy
(With the Tracers)

Singles: 7-inch

CYCLONE (1000 "My Baby Blues") 200-300
RIC (165 "Is This Really Me") 10-20 65

OSBORNE, Bobby

Singles: 7-inch

DATE (1527 "From L.A. to New Orleans"). 5-10 66

OSBORNE, Chuck
(With the Baby Dolls)

Singles: 7-inch

ABC-PAR (10474 "Come and Walk with Me") 5-10 63
ALANNA (565 "Give Me Your Hand") 15-25 61
(Same number used in an Elroy & Excitements release.)

OSBORNE, Jerry

Singles: 7-inch

JELLYROLL (10676 "The Country Side of '76") 4-6 76
(With Bruce Hamilton. 500 made.)
RECORD DIGEST (25794 "The Graceland Tour") 8-12 79
(Elvis break-in soundsheet, given as a bonus to *Presleyana III* book buyers. 500 made)
Also see JAY, Jerry
Also see PRESLEY, Elvis

OSBORNE, Jimmie *C&W '48*

Singles: 78 rpm

KING 5-10 48-55

Singles: 7-inch

KING 10-20 52-55

EPs: 7-inch

AUDIO LAB (3 "Jimmie Osborne") 10-15 59

LPs: 10/12-inch

AUDIO LAB (1527 "Songs He Wrote") 25-35 59
KING 15-25 61-65

OSBORNE, Johnny, & Mello Jacks

Singles: 78 rpm

TUNE (1002 "Sax Maniac") 5-10 54

Singles: 7-inch

TUNE (1002 "Sax Maniac") 15-25 54

OSBORNE, Kell
(With the Chicks; Kell Osborne's Band)
Singles: 7-inch
CLASS (302 "Do You Mind") 10-15 62
GLOWHILL (702 "That's What's Happening") .... 8-12 '60s
LOMA (2023 "You Can't Outsmart a Woman") 8-10 65
LOMA (2033 "You Can't Outsmart a Woman") 8-10 66
REVIS (1010 "Somethin' for the Books") .... 8-12 '60s
TITANIC (5008 "Quicksand") 50-100 63
TREY (3006 "Bells of St. Mary's") 25-35 60
Also see KELL & CHERRY

OSBORNE, Mary
Singles: 7-inch
WARWICK (531 "I Love Paris") 5-10 60
LPs: 10/12-inch
WARWICK (2004 "Girl and Her Guitar") .. 15-25 60

OSBORNE, Tony
Singles: 7-inch
DERAM (85030 "Sun Spot") 8-12 68
KING (5525 "Swinging Gypsies") 10-20 61
ROULETTE (4189 "Windows of Paris") ... 10-20 59

OSBORNE BROTHERS *C&W '58*
(With Red Allen)
Singles: 7-inch
CMH 3-5 80
DECCA 4-8 63-72
MCA 4-6 73-75
MGM (100 series) 4-8 64
(Golden Circle reissue series.)
MGM (12000 & 13000 series) 5-10 59-63
EPs: 7-inch
MGM 10-15 59
LPs: 10/12-inch
CMH 5-10 76-82
CORAL 5-10 73
DECCA 10-20 65-72
MCA 5-10 73-75
MGM (100 series) 5-10 70
MGM (3700 series) 25-35 59
MGM (4000 series) 15-25 62-63
PICKWICK .... 5-10 '70s
ROUNDER .... 5-8 '80s
SUGAR HILL 5-8 84
Members: Bobby Osborne; Sonny Osborne; Benny Birchfield. Session: Ronnie Reno; Jimmy Martin.
Also see MARTIN, Jimmy

OSBORNE BROTHERS & MAC WISEMAN
(With Red Allen) *C&W '79*
Singles: 7-inch
CMH 4-6 79
Also see OSBORNE BROTHERS
Also see WISEMAN, Mac

OSBOURNE, Ozzy *LP '81*
Singles: 12-inch
EPIC (37640 "Mr. Crowley Live") 30-40 82
(Picture disc.)
JETT (6400 "Mr. Crowley Live") 20-30 81
(Picture disc. Promotional issue only.)
JET (7670 "Diary of a Madman") 30-40 81
(Picture disc. Promotional issue only.)
JET (7670 "Diary of a Madman") 45-55 81
(Picture disc. Promotional issue only. Has KMET logo on one side.)
Singles: 7-inch
CBS ASSOCIATED 3-5 83-86
JET 3-5 82
Picture Sleeves
CBS ASSOCIATED 3-5 86
JET 3-5 82
LPs: 10/12-inch
CBS ASSOCIATED (Black vinyl) 5-8 83-90
CBS ASSOCIATED (40543 "Ultimate Live Ozzy") 25-35 86
(Picture disc. Promotional issue only.)
JET (Black vinyl) 5-10 81-82
JET (1327 "Diary of a Madman") 45-50 81
(Promotional only picture disc.)
Also see BLACK SABBATH

OSBOURNE, Ozzy, & Randy Rhoads *LP '87*
LPs: 10/12-inch
CBS ASSOC 5-8 87

OSBURN, Bob
(Bobby Osburn)
Singles: 7-inch
ARLEN (747 "My Heart's Been Broken") .. 40-50 64
KNICKERBOCKER 5-10
LE CAM (136 "Baby Lou") 5-10 64
Also see CLASSICS 4

OSBURNE, Elvis
Singles: 7-inch
MANCO (1075 "Shackled and Chained") ... 5-10 65

OSCAR & MAJESTICS
Singles: 7-inch
USA (851 "I Can't Explain") 15-25 66
Members: Oscar Hamod; Sam Hamod; Robert Wheeler; John Toda; Vince Jimkimzak.

OSCAR 5
Singles: 7-inch
D&C (171 "I Won't Be Your Fool") 15-25 67

O'SHEA, Paul, with Four Jacks & A Jill
LPs: 10/12-inch
RIVERSIDE 25-35 60

OSHINS, Milt
Singles: 78 rpm
PELVIS (169 "All About Elvis") 20-30 56
Singles: 7-inch
PELVIS (169 "All About Elvis") 40-60 56
(Some pressings have no artist credited.)

OSHUN
Singles: 7-inch
MERCURY (72685 "Battle of Life") 10-20 67

OSMONDS *P&R/R&B/LP '71*
(Osmond Brothers)
Singles: 7-inch
BARNABY 4-8 68-69
CURB/EMI 3-5 85-86
EMI AMERICA 3-5 85-86
ELEKTRA/CURB 3-5 82-83
MGM (13126 thru 14159) 5-10 63-70
MGM (14193 thru 14831) 4-6 70-75
MERCURY 4-6 79
POLYDOR 4-6 76-77
UNI (55015 "I Can't Stop") 5-8 67
UNI (55276 "I Can't Stop") 4-6 71
W.B./CURB 3-5 83-85
Picture Sleeves
MGM 4-8 73-74
LPs: 10/12-inch
EMI AMERICA 5-8 86
ELEKTRA 5-10 82
MGM (7 "Preview – the Osmond Brothers") .... 15-20 '70s
(Promotional issue only.)
MGM (9 "We Sing You a Merry Christmas") .... 15-20 '70s
(Monaural. Promotional issue only.)
MGM (4100 & 4200 series) 25-35 63-65
MGM (4724 thru 5012) 8-12 70-75
MERCURY 5-10 79
METRO 10-20 65
POLYDOR 5-10 76-77
W.B./CURB 5-8 83-85
Members: Donny; Alan; Merrill; Wayne; Jimmy; Marie.
Also see CURB, Mike

OSMONDS, Steve Lawrence & Eydie Gorme *P&R '72*
Singles: 7-inch
MGM 4-6 72
Also see LAWRENCE, Steve, & Eydie Gorme
Also see OSMONDS

OSMUS, Gib
Singles: 7-inch
CUCA (67115 "Bad Love") 10-15 67

OSPREYS
Singles: 7-inch
EAST WEST (110 "It's Good to Me") 15-25 58

OSSER, Glenn, & Orchestra with Chorus
Singles: 7-inch
METS (1 "Meet the Mets") 8-12 69

OSTER, Al
Singles: 7-inch
TUNDRA (101 "Midnight Sun Rock") 200-300
LPs: 10/12-inch
ALKON (1001 "Alaska Purchase Centennial: Ballads of the North") 150-200 67
ALKON (1002 "Northland Ballads") .... 150-200 '60s
ALKON (1003 "Alaska, Star 49") .... 150-200 '60s
DOMINION (1321 "Echo of the Yukon") 150-200
FRONTIER (1006 "Yukon Ballads") 100-150
KLONDIKE (1 "Yukon Gold") 150-200

O'SULLIVAN, Gilbert *P&R/LP '72*
Singles: 7-inch
EPIC 3-6 77-81
MAM 4-8 71-75
Picture Sleeves
MAM 4-6 72
LPs: 10/12-inch
EPIC 5-10 81
MAM 10-15 72-73

OSWALD, Lee Harvey, vs Carlos Bringuier
(With narrator, Dr. Billy James Hargis)
LPs: 10/12-inch
EYEWITNESS (1002 "Lee Harvey Oswald Speaks") 35-55 64
(From a 1963 radio interview in New Orleans.)
KEY (880 "The President's Assassin Speaks") 35-55 64
(Debate between Oswald and Bringuier, taped three months before the assassination.)

OTHER BROTHERS
Singles: 7-inch
AMY (11005 "Mini Dress") 5-10 68
AMY (11033 "Little Girl") 5-10 68
MODERN (1027 "Hole in the Wall") 8-12 67

OTHER HALF
Singles: 7-inch
7/2 (1 "Aspens of the Night") 100-200 66
(Reportedly 50 made.)
LPs: 10/12-inch
RESURRECTION (1266 "The Other Half") 8-10 84
7/2 (1 "The Other Half") 1000-1500 66
(Reportedly 150 to 200 made.)
Members: Andrea Inganni; Bob Collett; Don Karr.

OTHER HALF
Singles: 7-inch
ACTA (801 "Wonderful Day") 10-20 67
ACTA (806 "I Need You") 10-20 67
ACTA (819 "Bad Day") 10-20 68
ACTA (825 "Morning Fire") 10-20 68
GNP (378 "I've Come So Far") 10-15 66
LPs: 10/12-inch
ACTA (38004 "Other Half") 50-100 68
Members: Randy Holden; Jeff Nowlen; Craig Tawater; Mike Port.
Also see HOLDEN, Randy
Also see SONS OF ADAM

OTHER ONES
Singles: 7-inch
ABC-PAR (10793 "Dreaming Out Loud") ... 8-12 66
KNOLL .... 10-20 '60s

OTHER SIDE
Singles: 7-inch
BRENT (7061 "Street Car") 8-12 66
Also see WILDFLOWER / Harbinger Complex / Euphoria / Other Side

OTHER SIDE
Singles: 7-inch
MOTION (6946 "I Wanna Be There") 5-10 69

OTHER TIKIS
Singles: 7-inch
AUTUMN (18 "If I've Been Dreaming") 5-10 65
AUTUMN (28 "Bye Bye Bye") 5-10 65
Also see TIKIS

OTHER VOICES
Singles: 7-inch
ATLANTIC (2479 "Hung Up On Love"/"May My Heart Be Cast into Stone") 5-10 68
ATLANTIC (2523 "Hung Up On Love"/"No Olympian Heights") 5-10 68

OTHERS
Singles: 7-inch
FONTANA (1944 "Oh Yeah") 10-20 64

OTHERS
Singles: 7-inch
JUBILEE (5550 "My Friend the Wizard") 5-10 66
RCA (8669 "I Can't Stand This Love, Goodbye") 15-25 65
RCA (8776 "Lonely Street") 5-10 66

OTHERS
Singles: 7-inch
MERCURY (72602 "Revenge") 15-25 66

OTIS, Johnny *R&B '48*
(Johnny Otis Show; Quintette; with Peacocks; with Debbie Lindsay; with Barbara Morrison; with Joe Swift; with Mel Williams)
Singles: 78 rpm
CAPITOL 10-25 57
DIG 10-25 55-57
EXCELSIOR 15-25 45-47
EXCLUSIVE (51 "That's Your Last Boogie") 10-15 48
EXCLUSIVE (64 "I'll Just Laugh") 10-15 48
MERCURY 10-25 51-53
PEACOCK (Except 1625) 10-25 52
PEACOCK (1625 "Young Girl") 20-40 52
REGENT 10-25 50-51
SAVOY 10-20 50-54
UNITED ARTIST (142 "Harlem Nocturne") .... 15-25 '40s
Singles: 7-inch
CAPITOL (3799-3802 "The Johnny Otis Show") 400-600 57
(Four discs with special four-pocket cover.)
CAPITOL (3799 thru 3802) 20-40 57
(Price for four records without cover.)
CAPITOL (3852 "Good Golly") 10-20 57
CAPITOL (3889 "Well, Well, Well, Well!") 10-20 58
CAPITOL (3966 "Willie and the Hand Jive"/"Ring-A-Ling") 10-20 58
CAPITOL (3966 "Willie and the Hand Jive"/"Willie and the Hand Jive") 20-30 58
(Blue label. Promotional issue only.)
CAPITOL (4060 "Crazy Country Hop") 10-20 58
CAPITOL (4168 "Castin' My Spell") 10-20 59
(Monaural.)
CAPITOL (S-4168 "Castin' My Spell") 25-35 59
(Stereo.)
CAPITOL (4226 thru 4326) 10-20 59-60
CAPITOL (6040 "Willie and the Hand Jive") 5-8 63
(Starline Series.)
DIG (119 "Let the Sunshine in My Life") ... 25-50 56
DIG (122 "Midnight Creeper") 25-50 56
DIG (131 "Tough Enough") 25-50 57
DIG (132 "My Eyes Are Full of Tears") 25-50 57
DIG (134 "Wa-Wa") 25-50 57
DIG (139 "The Night Is Young") 25-50 57
ELDO (106 "New Bo Diddley") 10-20 60
ELDO (152 "Keep the Faith") 5-10 67
ELDO (153 "Long Distance") 5-10 67
EPIC 4-8 70
HAWK SOUND 4-6 75
IT WILL STAND 3-5 82
JAZZ WORLD 4-6 78
KENT (506 "Country Girl") 5-10 69
KING 8-12 61-63
MERCURY (8263 "Oopy Doo") 50-100 51
MERCURY (8273 "Goomp Blues") 50-100 51
MERCURY (8289 "Call Operator 210") .. 50-100 52
MERCURY (8295 "Gypsy Blues") 50-100 52
MERCURY (70038 "Why Don't You Believe Me") 50-100 52
MERCURY (70050 "The Love Bug Boogie") 50-75 52
OKEH (7332 "Watts Breakaway") 5-10 69
PEACOCK (1625 "Young Girl") 50-75 52
PEACOCK (1636 "Shake It") 40-60 52
PEACOCK (1648 "Sittin' Here Drinkin'") .. 40-60 52
PEACOCK (1675 "Butterball") 40-60 52
RED HOT 15-25
SAVOY 25-50 51-54
EPs: 7-inch
CAPITOL (940 "Johnny Otis Show") 75-100 58
CAPITOL (1134 "Johnny Otis") 50-75 59
RITZ-EE (5214 Blackouts of 1959) 40-60 59
(Has one Johnny Otis track, *Backstage at the Blackouts*. Promotional issue only. Not issued with cover.)
LPs: 10/12-inch
ALLIGATOR (4726 "The New Johnny Otis Show") 5-10 82

BLUES SPECTRUM 10-15
CAPITOL (940 "The Johnny Otis Show") 200-300 58
DIG (104 "Rock and Roll Hit Parade") . 500-750 57
(Mustard color cover, black and white print. Counterfeits exist, some of which have a yellow cover, others have a gold cover. Regardless, the discs of originals are rigid – noticeably thicker than the more flexible ones found on fakes.)
EPIC 10-15 70-71
JAZZ WORLD 5-10 78
KENT 10-20 70
RED HOT 5-10
SAVOY 5-10 78-80
Session: Jackie Kelso; Freddie Harmon; George Washington; Jimmy Nolan; Johnny Parker; Don Johnson; "Lady Dee" Williams; Shuggie Otis; "Kansas City" Bell; Jayos; Three Tons Of Joy Featuring Marie Adams; Arthur Lee Maye; Jeannie Sterling & Moonbeams; Mel Williams; Marci Lee; Delmar Evans; Lee Graves.
Referenced below are some of the artists who performed with the Johnny Otis Show, or with whom he or his orchestra appears.
Also see ACE, Johnny
Also see ADAMS, Marie
Also see ALLEN, Tony
Also see AUGUST, Joseph
Also see FOUR BLUEBIRDS / Johnny Otis Orchestra
Also see FREEMAN, Ernie
Also see GLADIATORS
Also see JACQUET, Illinois
Also see McNEELY, Big Jay
Also see MOONBEEMS
Also see ROBINS / Mel Walker & Bluenotes
Also see RUSHING, Jimmy
Also see RYDER, Junior, & Peacocks
Also see SCOTT, Marilyn
Also see SKILLET & LEROY
Also see SWIFT, Joe
Also see WALKER, Mel
Also see WATSON, Johnny
Also see WILSON, Faye
Also see WILLIAMS, Mel

OTIS, Johnny, Orchestra, with Little Esther & Mel Walker R&B '50
Singles: 78 rpm
REGENT 30-50 51
SAVOY 20-40 50-51
Singles: 7-inch
REGENT (1036 "I Dream") 100-125 51
SAVOY (750 "Cupid's Boogie") 50-75 50
SAVOY (775 "Love Will Break Your Heart") 50-75 51
Also see LITTLE ESTHER & MEL WALKER

OTIS, Johnny, Quintette, with Little Esther & Robins R&B '50
Singles: 78 rpm
SAVOY 50-75 50
Singles: 7-inch
SAVOY (731 "Double Crossing Blues") 100-150 50
Also see LITTLE ESTHER
Also see OTIS, Johnny
Also see ROBINS

OTIS, Laura, & Satinettes
Singles: 7-inch
MEXIE (102 "I'm Gonna Make You Love Me") 50-75 62
(Reportedly, approximately 100 made.)
Session: Johnny Otis (Laura's father).
Also see OTIS, Johnny

OTIS & CARLA P&R/R&B/LP '67
Singles: 7-inch
ATCO (6665 "When Something Is Wrong with My Baby") 5-10 69
STAX 5-10 67-68
LPs: 10/12-inch
STAX (716 "King & Queen") 10-20 67
Members: Otis Redding; Carla Thomas.
Also see REDDING, Otis
Also see THOMAS, Carla

OTT, Paul C&W '79
Singles: 7-inch
ELEKTRA 4-6 79
MONUMENT 4-6 75
SHOW BIZ 4-6 72

THUNDER INT'L (1022 "Kitty Kat") 50-75 60

OUR GANG
Singles: 7-inch
BR'ER BIRD (001 "Summertime Summertime") 100-150 66
Members: Jan Berry; Dean Torrance.
Also see JAN & DEAN

OUR GANG
Singles: 7-inch
WARRIOR (166 "Careless Love") 15-25 66

OUR GENERATION
Singles: 7-inch
FENTON (970 "Baby Boy") .... 100-150 '60s

OUR PATCH OF BLUE
Singles: 7-inch
W.B. (7257 "Zoom, Zoom, Zoom") 10-20 69

OUT CROWD
Singles: 7-inch
OMEN (11 "Get Yourself Together") 5-10 66

OUTCASTS
Singles: 7-inch
VETTE (425 "Under Tow") 20-30 63

OUTCASTS
Singles: 7-inch
ASKEL (102 "I'm in Pittsburgh") 40-60 65
ASKEL (104 "I'll Set You Free") 10-20 66
ASKEL (107 "Route 66") 15-25 66
GALLANT (101 "1523 "Blair") 20-30 67
OUTCAST (6865 "Nothing Ever Comes Easy") 8-12 65

OUTCASTS
Singles: 7-inch
KARATE (531 "I Found Out About You") .. 10-20 66

OUTCASTS
Singles: 7-inch
SHORE BIRD (1005 "I Wanted You") 10-15 66

OUTCASTS
Singles: 7-inch
SOLA (12 "People") 15-25 66

OUTCASTS
Singles: 7-inch
STUDIO CITY (1040 "You Do Me Wrong") 15-25 66

OUTCASTS
Singles: 7-inch
CAMEO (477 "Today's the Day") 10-20 67
DECCA (32036 "Set Me Free") 8-12 66
LPs: 10/12-inch
CICADELIC (987 "Meet the Outcasts") 8-10 85
CICADELIC (988 "The Outcasts Live! Standing Room Only") 8-10 85

OUTCASTS
Singles: 7-inch
PLATO (80285 "Loving You Sometimes") .. 8-12 68

OUTER LIMITS
Singles: 7-inch
DERAM (7508 "Help Me Please") 15-25 67

OUTER LIMITS
Singles: 7-inch
GOLDUST (5014 "Don't Need You No More") 15-25 67

OUTER MONGOLIAN HEARD
Singles: 7-inch
DAISY (4846 "Hey Joe") 20-30 67

OUTERKIRK, Ron
Singles: 7-inch
SITATION (1055 "My Kind of Woman") .. 50-100

OUTLAW BLUES BAND
LPs: 10/12-inch
BLUESWAY (6021 "Outlaw Blues Band") 10-20 68
BLUESWAY (6030 "Breakin' In") 10-20 69

OUTLAWS
Singles: 7-inch
DOT (16512 "Hold Up") 10-20 63

OUTLAWS
Singles: 7-inch
CRUSADE (92765 "Chains") 10-20 65

SMASH (2025 "Don't Cry") 5-10 66

OUTLAWS LP '76
Singles: 7-inch
ARISTA 3-6 75-83
PASHA 3-5 86
LPs: 10/12-inch
ARISTA 5-10 75-83
DIRECT DISC (16617 "Outlaws") .... 15-25 '80s
(Half-speed mastered.)
PASHA 5-8 86
PEAR 8-12 84
Members: Hughie Thomasson; Henry Paul; David Dix; Billy Jones; Fred Salem; Rick Cua; Harvey Dalton Arnold; Frank O'Keefe; Monte Yoho; Chuck Glass; Steve Grisham.

OUTLAWS
Singles: 7-inch
BLACKNIGHT (902 "Midnight Hour") 25-50
(Credits the Outlaws.)
BLACKNIGHT (902 "Midnight Hour") 15-25
(Credits Kit & Outlaws.)
Also see KIT & OUTLAWS

OUTLAWS
Singles: 7-inch
JRE (226 "Run Rudolph Run") 75-125

OUTLAWS
Singles: 7-inch
KAYGIN (101 "Ain't Got No Home") 50-75

OUTSIDE IN
Singles: 7-inch
RIGHT RPM (6612 "You Ain't Gonna Bring Me to My Knees") 20-30 66

OUTSIDERS
Singles: 7-inch
EASTMAN (9802 "Shortnin' Bread Twist") 15-25 62

OUTSIDERS P&R/LP '66
Singles: 7-inch
BELL (904 "Changes") 4-8 70
CAPITOL 5-10 66-68
KAPP (6165 "Time Won't Let Me") 4-8 70
Picture Sleeves
CAPITOL 8-12 66-67
LPs: 10/12-inch
CAPITOL 20-30 66-67
Members: Sonny Geraci; Bill Bruno; Tom King; Rickey Baker; Merdin Madsen.
Also see STARFIRES

OUTSIDERS
Singles: 7-inch
ELLEN 10-15
KARATE (505 "The Guy with the Long Liverpool Hair") 10-15 65

OUTSIDERS
Singles: 7-inch
CHA CHA ("Go Go Ferrari") .... 20-30 '60s
(Selection number not known.)
KNIGHT (103 "Just Let Me Be") 10-20 66
KNIGHT (104 "Summertime Blues") 10-20 66
Also see SOUL TRIPPERS

OVATIONS
Singles: 7-inch
ANDIE (5017 "My Lullaby") 30-40 60
BARRY (101 "The Day We Fell in Love") . 20-30 61
EPIC (9470 "Oh What a Day") 30-40 61
Also see IDEALS

OVATIONS
Singles: 7-inch
CAPITOL (5082 "I Don't Wanna Cry") 10-20 63

OVATIONS
Singles: 7-inch
JOSIE (916 "Who Needs Love") 20-30 64
LPs: 10/12-inch
CRYSTAL BALL (125 "High School Reunion") 10-15 85
(Black vinyl. 1000 made.)
Members: Sammy Cantos; Greg Malmeth; Gary Willet; Frank Cox; Nick Kassy; Tony Clementa; Ronnie Brecheter.
Also see LITTLE ROMEO & CASANOVAS

OVATIONS P&R/R&B '65
(Ovation)
Singles: 7-inch
CHESS (2166 "Pure Natural") 4-6 75
GOLDWAX (110 "Pretty Little Angel") 8-12 64
GOLDWAX (113 "It's Wonderful to Be in Love") 8-12 65
GOLDWAX (117 "I'm Living Good") 8-12 65
GOLDWAX (300 "Don't Cry") 8-12 66
GOLDWAX (306 "Qualifications") 8-12 66
GOLDWAX (314 "They Say") 8-12 66
GOLDWAX (332 "I've Gotta Go") 8-12 67
GOLDWAX (342 "I'm Living Good") 5-10 69
MGM 4-8 73
SOUNDS OF MEMPHIS 4-8 72-73
LPs: 10/12-inch
MGM 10-15 73
SOUNDS OF MEMPHIS 10-20 72
Members: George Jackson; Louis Williams; Bill Davis; Rochester Neal; Quincy Billops Jr.
Also see JACKSON, George
Also see OLLIE & NIGHTINGALES

OVATIONS
Singles: 7-inch
HAWK (153 "I Still Love You") 75-125 63

OVELLA & OVERTURES
Singles: 7-inch
COLUMBIA (43687 "Trust Me") 5-10 66

OVERBEA, Danny R&B '53
Singles: 78 rpm
ARGO 10-20 56
CHECKER 25-50 53-55
Singles: 7-inch
APEX (7751 "Don't Laugh at Me") 20-30 59
ARGO (5252 "Hear My Story") 25-50 56
CHECKER (774 "40 Cups of Coffee") 50-100 53
(Black vinyl.)
CHECKER (774 "40 Cups of Coffee") .. 150-200 53
(Red vinyl.)
CHECKER (768 "Train Train Train") 75-125 53
CHECKER (784 "Sorrento") 75-125 54
CHECKER (788 "Stomp and Whistle") ... 75-125 54
CHECKER (796 "Roamin' Man") 75-125 54
CHECKER (808 "A Toast to Lovers") 75-125 55
CHECKER (816 "Hey, Pancho") 50-100 55
FEDERAL (12434 "Book of Tears") 15-25 61
FEDERAL (12455 "Rosebud") 15-25 62
SHEP (101 "Like Crazy") 15-25 60

OVERBY, Lee, & Red Toppers
Singles: 7-inch
DAN (3214 "I Never Had a Girl Like You") 10-15 61

OVERLAND STAGE
(Overland Stage Company)
Singles: 7-inch
EPIC (10860 "I'm Beginning to Feel It") 5-10 72
EPIC (10924 "To the Park") 5-10 72
FRANKLIN (630 "Airplane") 25-35 68
LPs: 10/12-inch
EPIC (31319 "Overland Stage") 15-25 72

OVERLANDERS P&R '64
Singles: 7-inch
HICKORY 10-15 64-66
MERCURY (72165 "Call of the Wild") 5-10 63

OVERMAN, Rune
Singles: 7-inch
ARGO (5505 "Bobsled") 5-10 65
PARKWAY (859 "Big Bass Boogie") 5-10 62
STACY (970 "Beatnik Walk") 5-10 63

OVERTONES
Singles: 7-inch
SLATE (3068 "I Wonder, I Wonder") 10-20 61
SLATE (3072 "This Old Love of Mine") 10-20 61

OVERTONES / Bob Fitzgerald
Singles: 7-inch
SLATE (4013 "This Old Love of Mine") 10-20 62
Also see OVERTONES

OVERTONES
Singles: 7-inch
AJAX (173 "Please Let Me Know") 15-25 66
AJAX (174 "From My Heart") 15-25 66
AJAX (175 "Home Type Girl") 10-20 67
AJAX (176 "I've Been There Before") 10-20 67

OVERSTREET, Tommy *C&W '69*
(With the Nashville Express)
Singles: 7-inch
ABC ... 3-5 78-79
ABC/DOT ... 4-6 74-78
AMI ... 3-5 83
DOT ... 4-8 69-74
ELEKTRA ... 3-6 79-80
GERVASI ... 3-5 84
SILVER DOLLAR ... 3-5 86
TINA ... 4-6 79
LPs: 10/12-inch
ABC (1066 "A Better Me") ... 8-12 78
ABC/DOT (2016 "I'm a Believer") ... 8-12 75
ABC/DOT (2027 "Greatest Hits") ... 8-12 75
ABC/DOT (2038 "Live from the Silver Slipper") ... 8-12 75
ABC/DOT (2065 "Turn On to Tommy Overstreet") ... 8-12 76
ABC/DOT (2071 "Vintage '77") ... 8-12 77
ABC/DOT (2086 "Hangin' 'Round") ... 8-12 77
AUDIOGRAPH ALIVE (6020 "Tommy Overstreet") ... 5-8 82
CMH (6244 "I Can Hear Kentucky Calling Me") ... 5-10 80
DEJA VU ... 5-8 84
DOT (25992 "Gwen") ... 15-25 71
DOT (25994 "This Is Tommy Overstreet") ... 10-20 72
DOT (26003 "Heaven Is My Woman's Love") ... 10-20 72
DOT (26012 "My Friends Call Me T.O.") . 10-20 73
DOT (26021 "Woman, Your Name Is My Song") ... 10-20 74
ELEKTRA (178 "I'll Never Let You Down") . 5-10 79
ELEKTRA (226 "The Real Tommy Overstreet") ... 5-10 79
ELEKTRA (292 "Best of Tommy Overstreet") ... 5-10 80
MCA ... 5-8 '80s
PINNACLE (2006 "There'll Never Be Another First Time") ... 8-10 78

OWEN-B *P&R '70*
Singles: 7-inch
JANUS (107 "Mississippi Mama") ... 4-8 70
JANUS (123 "Never Goin' Home") ... 4-8 70
LPs: 10/12-inch
MUS-I-COL (101209 "Owen-B") ... 40-60 70
Members: Tom Zinser; Bob Tousignant; Jim Krause; Terry Van Auker.

OWEN, Jim
Singles: 7-inch
FINE (1004 "Simon Shuffle") ... 50-75

OWEN, Rudy, & Ravens
Singles: 7-inch
STARTIME (3287 "Pretty Linda") ... 100-125 58

OWENS, Bonnie *C&W '63*
(With the Strangers)
Singles: 7-inch
CAPITOL ... 4-8 65-69
DEL-FI ... 5-10 60
TALLY ... 5-10 63-64
LPs: 10/12-inch
CAPITOL (195 thru 557) ... 10-20 69-70
CAPITOL (2403 thru 2861 ... 15-30 65-68
Also see HAGGARD, Merle, & Bonnie Owens

OWENS, Buck *C&W '59*
(With the Buckaroos)
Singles: 78 rpm
CAPITOL ... 25-50 57
Singles: 7-inch
CAPITOL (2000 thru 4000 series) ... 5-10 67-75
(Orange label.)
CAPITOL (3824 "Come Back") ... 15-25 57
(Purple label.)
CAPITOL (3957 "Sweet Thing") ... 15-25 58
(Purple label.)
CAPITOL (4000 series) ... 10-20 59-63
(Purple or orange/yellow label.)
CAPITOL (5000 series) ... 8-12 63-67
CHESTERFIELD (44223 "Leavin' Dirty Tracks") ... 100-200 '60s
HILLTOP (6027 "Hot Dog") ... 25-50 '60s
NEW STAR (6418 "Hot Dog") ... 150-200 58
(Rerecorded version of "Corky Jones" track.)
PEP (105 "Down on the Corner of Love") 25-50 56
PEP (106 "Right After the Dance") ... 25-50 56
PEP (109 "There Goes My Love") ... 25-50 57
STARDAY (588 "Down on the Corner of Love") ... 10-20 61
STARDAY (5000 series) ... 4-8 64
W.B. (Except 8316) ... 3-6 76-80
W.B. (8316 "World Famous Holiday Inn") .. 5-10 77
W.B. (8316 "World Famous Paradise Inn") .. 4-6 77
(Note title change.)
Picture Sleeves
CAPITOL ... 10-25 66-69
EPs: 7-inch
CAPITOL ... 15-30 61-65
LPs: 10/12-inch
BUCKBOARD ... 5-10
CAPITOL (131 thru 550 series) ... 10-20 69-70
CAPITOL (574 "Buck Owens") ... 20-30 70
(Three-disc set.)
CAPITOL (628 thru 860) ... 10-15 70-72
CAPITOL (T-1482 thru T-1989) ... 30-40 61-63
(Monaural.)
CAPITOL (ST-1482 thru ST-1989) ... 35-50 61-63
(Stereo.)
CAPITOL (DT-1400 series) ... 10-20 69
CAPITOL (2100 thru 2700 series) ... 12-25 64-67
CAPITOL (2800 thru 2900 series) ... 10-20 68
CAPITOL (2980 "Buck Owens Minute Masters") ... 30-40 66
(Promotional issue only.)
CAPITOL (11000 series) ... 5-8 72-78
COUNTRY FIDELITY ... 5-8 83
GUEST STAR ... 8-12 '60s
HALL OF MUSIC ... 8-12
LA BREA (8017 "Buck Owens") ... 100-200 61
OUT OF TOWN DIST ... 5-8 82
PICKWICK/HILLTOP ... 5-10 78
SPRINGBOARD ... 5-10
STARDAY (172 "Fabulous Country Music Sound of Buck Owens") ... 15-25 62
STARDAY (300 series) ... 15-20 64-65
STARDAY (400 series) ... 10-15 75
STARPAK ... 5-8 79
SUNRISE MEDIA ... 5-8 81
TIME-LIFE ... 5-10 82
TRIP ... 5-8 76
W.B. ... 5-10 76-77
Also see COLLINS, Tommy
Also see JONES, Corky
Also see JONES, George / Buck Owens / David Houston / Tommy Hill
Also see STEWART, Wynn
Also see WEBBER, Rollie
Also see YOAKAM, Dwight, & Buck Owens

OWENS, Buck, & Buddy Alan *C&W '68*
(Buck & Buddy; with the Buckaroos)
Singles: 7-inch
CAPITOL (2237 "Let the World Keep On A Turnin' ") ... 5-10 68
LPs: 10/12-inch
CAPITOL (874 "Too Old to Cut the Mustard") ... 10-15 72
Also see ALAN, Buddy

OWENS, Buck / Tennessee Ernie Ford
LPs: 10/12-inch
CAPITOL (6720 "Music Hall") ... 10-15
Also see FORD, Tennessee Ernie

OWENS, Buck, & Emmylou Harris
Singles: 7-inch
W.B. (8830 "Play Together Again Again") 4-6 79
Also see HARRIS, Emmylou

OWENS, Buck, & Rose Maddox *C&W '63*
Singles: 7-inch
CAPITOL (4992 "We're the Talk of the Town") ... 10-15 63
Also see MADDOX, Rose

OWENS, Buck, & Susan Raye *C&W/LP '70*
Singles: 7-inch
CAPITOL ... 4-8 70-73
LPs: 10/12-inch
CAPITOL ... 5-10 70-73

OWENS, Buck, & Ringo Starr *C&W '89*
Singles: 7-inch
CAPITOL (79805 "Gonna Have Love") ... 5-8 89
(Commercial issue.)
CAPITOL (79805 "Gonna Have Love") ... 8-10 89
(Promotional issue.)
Also see STARR, Ringo

OWENS, Buck / Faron Young / Ferlin Husky
LPs: 10/12-inch
PICKWICK/HILLTOP (6027 "Buck Owens, Faron Young and Ferlin Husky") ... 10-15 65
Also see HUSKY, Ferlin
Also see OWENS, Buck
Also see YOUNG, Faron

OWENS, Charlie
(With the Sensational Ink Spots)
Singles: 7-inch
KENT (355 "Diane") ... 75-125 61
Also see INK SPOTS

OWENS, Clyde
(With His Moonlight Ramblers)
Singles: 7-inch
LINCO (1313 "Swing It, Little Katy") ... 200-300 59
PARADOX (1974 "If This Should Be Our Last Day Together") ... 5-10 '60s
SPARTAN (200 "Right and Ready") ... 100-200 58

OWENS, Danny
Singles: 7-inch
IMPERIAL (5700 "Drifting Blues") ... 5-10 60
MGM (12821 "Melinda") ... 5-10 59
MANHATTAN (804 "I Can't Be a Fool for You") ... 15-25 67

OWENS, Dawn
Singles: 7-inch
STAR ("Hang Up My Rock and Roll Shoes") ... 50-75
(Selection number not known.)

OWENS, Don
Singles: 7-inch
GREGMARK (4 "I Don't Want to Lose Her") ... 5-10 61
SOUND STAGE 7 (2503 "Your Fool") ... 5-10 63
(This same number is used on a 1976 release by Willie Hightower.)
STARDAY (607 "Last Chance") ... 50-75
Also see HIGHTOWER, Willie

OWENS, Donnie *P&R '58*
(Donny Owens)
Singles: 7-inch
ARA ... 4-8
GUYDEN (2001 "Need You") ... 15-25 58
GUYDEN (2006 "Tomorrow") ... 10-15 58
GUYDEN (2013 "Between Midnight and Dawn") ... 10-15 59
OLDIES 45 (144 "Need You") ... 4-8 '60s
RAMCO (1975 "Useless") ... 5-10 66
TREY (3015 "What a Dream") ... 10-15 61
Session: Duane Eddy.
Also see EDDY, Duane

OWENS, Dusty
Singles: 78 rpm
COLUMBIA ... 5-10 54-55
Singles: 7-inch
ADMIRAL (1004 "Hey Honey") ... 20-30 57
COLUMBIA (21202 "Hello Operator") ... 10-15 54
COLUMBIA (21260 "Just Call On Me") ... 10-15 54
COLUMBIA (21310 "They Didn't Know the Difference") ... 10-15 54
COLUMBIA (21362 "Give Me a Little Chance") ... 10-15 55
COLUMBIA (21440 "Who Do You Think They Would Blame") ... 10-15 55

OWENS, Freddy
Singles: 7-inch
BETHLEHEM (3036 "What Kind of Heart") ... 5-10 62
WALL (550 "Heavenly One") ... 40-50 61

OWENS, Garland
Singles: 7-inch
LEGRAND (1024 "Food of Love") ... 15-25 62
LE MONDE (1502 "I Want to Know If You Love Me") ... 15-25 62

OWENS, Hughie, & Blue Notes
(With Joe Tanner & Orchestra)
Singles: 7-inch
RENOWN (108 "Time Will Tell") ... 40-50 59

OWENS, Jack
(With Al Allen's Orchestra)
Singles: 7-inch
ORBIT (520 "You Flip Me") ... 10-20 58

OWENS, Jackye
Singles: 7-inch
GROOVY (3006 "You're Doing Something Awfully Good") ... 5-10 66
GROOVY (3008 "Love That Guy") ... 5-10 66

OWENS, Kelly
(Kelly Owens Combo)
Singles: 78 rpm
FLAIR-X ... 5-10 56
RAINBOW ... 10-15 54
Singles: 7-inch
ARROW (725 "Tweety") ... 15-25 58
FLAIR-X (5004 "The Sweeper") ... 10-20 56
RAINBOW (248 "Sweeper Shuffle") ... 15-25 54
U.A. (181 "Charlie's Dance") ... 15-25 59

OWENS, Kenny
(Kenny Owen)
Singles: 7-inch
POPLAR (106 "I Got the Bug") ... 75-125 57
REKA (401 "Wrong Line") ... 100-150
RUTH (442 "Frog Man Hop") ... 300-400 58

OWL
Singles: 7-inch
AXIS LTD. ("Spirits") ... 25-35
(Colored vinyl. Selection number not known.)

OWLS
Singles: 7-inch
ARDEN (1000 "So Lost") ... 200-300

OX TONES
Singles: 7-inch
PHONOGRAPH (1024 "Mickey") ... 30-50 58

OXFORD BLUE
Singles: 7-inch
HYPE (1043 "Will You Still Love Me Tomorrow") ... 8-12 '60s

OXFORD CIRCLE
Singles: 7-inch
WORLD UNITED (002 "Mind Destruction") ... 50-75 '60s
Members: Paul Whaley; Gary Yoder.
Also see BLUE CHEER

OXFORD CIRCUS
Singles: 7-inch
ZIG ZAG (101 "Tracy") ... 20-25 67

OXFORD 12
Singles: 7-inch
WORLD ARTISTS (1039 "Goldfinger") ... 5-10 65

OXFORDS
Singles: 7-inch
GOLDEN CREST (569 "Toy Balloons") ... 10-20 63
MALA (550 "Time and Place") ... 5-10 67
MALA (563 "Chicago Woman") ... 5-10 67
NATIONAL (15881 "It's You") ... 8-12
PAULA (331 "Come on Back to Beer") ... 5-10 70
UNION JACK ... 8-12
LPs: 10/12-inch
UNION JAC (6497 "Flying Up") ... 20-30 68
Members: Jill DeMarco; Jay Petrech.

OZ & ENDS
Singles: 7-inch
PACEMAKER (753 "Look Away") ... 15-25 66

OZ & SPERLINGS
Singles: 7-inch
VILLA (701 "Mo Jo Hanna") ... 10-20 '60s

OZ BAND
Singles: 7-inch
CUB (9158 "I Am Not the Same") ... 8-12 68

OZ KNOZZ
LPs: 10/12-inch
OZONE (1000 "Ruff Mix") ... 350-500 75
Members: Richard Heath; Duane Massey; Monty Haul; Newton Bildo.

OZARKS
Singles: 7-inch
CALIFORNIA (304 "The Saints") ... 15-25 63
Reissued as *The Saints Go Surfin' In*, and shown as by the Woodys.)
Also see WOODYS

OZARKS / Billy & Carol
Singles: 7-inch
CALIFORNIA (303 "Who Stole My Bird Dog") 5-10 63

OZELLS
Singles: 7-inch
CUB (9126 "Please Don't Go") 8-12 63

P

P&J REVIEW BAND
Singles: 7-inch
JET STREAM (805 "Right On Brother Right On") 20-30 67

P.F. FLYERS
Singles: 7-inch
REVEILLE (103 "Heartaches of Love") 40-60 62

PHDs
Singles: 7-inch
LAMP (87 "Way It Used to Be") .... 75-125 '60s

PH PHACTOR
Singles: 7-inch
PICCADILLY (241 "Minglewood Blues") .. 10-15 67
LPs: 10/12-inch
PICCADILLY ("Merryjuana") 50-100 82
(Selection number not known.)

P.J.
(Patti Jerome)
Singles: 7-inch
TAMLA (54215 "T.L.C.") 10-20 72
V.I.P. (25062 "The Best Years of My Life") 15-25 71
Also see JEROME, Patti

P.J. & GALAXIES
Singles: 7-inch
P.M. (47 "Tally Ho!") 10-20 63
Member: Paul Johnson.

P.J. & GENTS
Singles: 7-inch
BEAVER (12632 "She Said No") 75-125

P.J. MURPHY
LP: 10/12-inch
LEAF (6475 "P.J. Murphy") 15-25 64
Members: Kathy McBroon; Gary Sagamiller; Ron Hileman; Jim Kasdorf; Andy Duvall.

P.T.s
Singles: 7-inch
OUTSTANDING (1 "Dragon Walk") .... 10-15 '60s

PABLO CRUISE *LP '75*
Singles: 7-inch
A&M 3-6 75-84
Picture Sleeves
A&M 3-6 77-84
LPs: 10/12-inch
A&M 5-10 75-84
MFSL (029 "A Place in the Sun") 30-40 79
(Half-speed mastered.)
NAUTILUS 10-20 81
Members: Dave Jenkins; Steven Price; Cory Lerios; Bud Cockrell.
Also see IT'S A BEAUTIFUL DAY
Also see STONEGROUND

PAC MAN
LPs: 10/12-inch
KID STUFF (6012 "Sing Along with Mr. & Mrs. Pac Man") 10-15 80
(Picture disc.)

PACE, Brent
Singles: 7-inch
ACME (101 "Take Back a Fool") 25-50 65
(Has a large "A" in the middle of "Acme.")
Also see JOHNSON, Joe D.

PACE, Glen, & Gliders
Singles: 7-inch
ABC-PAR (10091 "Next Year") 10-15 60
SATELLITE ("My Night Off") 15-25
(Selection number not known.)

PACE, Nick & Pacers
Singles: 7-inch
BIL-JON (101 "I'm in Love with a Girl") 200-300 62

PACE, Roger
Singles: 7-inch
SELECT (744 "The Minute My Back Was Turned") 5-10 65
TWIRL (2023 "You Better Know What You're Doing") 5-10 66

PACE SETTERS
Singles: 7-inch
AURORA (1971 "Ooh-Poo-Pah-Doo") 15-25 65

PACEMAKERS
Singles: 7-inch
CLOCK (2000 "Take Off") 10-15 61

PACERS
Singles: 7-inch
CALICO (101 "I Found a Dream") 75-125 58

PACERS
(Pacers with Bobby Crawford)
Singles: 7-inch
RAZORBACK (103 "Front Street") 10-20 59
RAZORBACK (108 "Confound It") 10-20 60
RAZORBACK (112 "Don't Get Around Much") 10-20 62
RAZORBACK (115 "West Memphis") 10-20 64
RAZORBACK (118 thru 139) 5-15 64-68
LPs: 10/12-inch
RAZORBACK (121 "You Asked for It") 30-50 65
RAZORBACK (139 "Pacers Go Hog Wild") 20-30 67
Members: Joe Cyr; Jim Aldridge; Fred Douglas; Bob Dalton; Bobby Crafford; Jerry Little.
Also see BURGESS, Sonny
Also see CRAFFORD, Bobby

PACERS & RIVERMEN
LPs: 10/12-inch
RAZORBACK (124 "Big Red") 30-50 65
Also see PACERS

PACERS
Singles: 7-inch
UNITED SOUTHERN ARTISTS (112 "New Wildwood Flower") 10-15 61

PACERS
Singles: 7-inch
GUYDEN (2064 "How Sweet") 1000-1500 62
JASON SCOTT (01 "How Sweet") 3-5 80
(500 made.)

PACERS
Singles: 7-inch
ALLEY (1013 "Skeeter Dope") 10-20 64
GEMINI (6301 "Settin' the Pace") 10-20 63

PACESETTERS
Singles: 7-inch
CORREC-TONE (3476 "Around the World") 5-10 63
MINIT (32043 "I'm Gonna Make It") 8-12 68
WINK (1008 "That's All") 10-15 62

PACE-SETTERS
Singles: 7-inch
AVA (161 "Mustang") 20-30 64

PACETTES
Singles: 7-inch
REGINA (306 "Don't Read the Letter") 10-15 64

PACIFIC DRIFT
LPs: 10/12-inch
DERAM (18040 "Feelin' Free") 8-12 70

PACIFIC GAS & ELECTRIC *LP '69*
(PG&E; Pacific Gas & Electric Blues Band)
Singles: 7-inch
BRIGHT ORANGE (1701 "Get It On") 5-10 68
COLUMBIA 4-8 69-72
KENT (4538 "The Hunter") 4-6 71
POWER 5-10 69
LPs: 10/12-inch
ABC .... 8-10 '70s
BRIGHT ORANGE (701 "Get It On") 40-80 68
COLUMBIA 8-12 69-73
KENT (547 "Get It On") 10-20 68
POWER 10-15 69
Members: Charlie Allen; Frank Cook; Brent Block; Tom Marshall; Glenn Schwartz.
Also see SEEGER, Pete, & Pacific Gas & Electric

PACIFIC OCEAN
Singles: 7-inch
VMC (732 "I Can't Stand It") 5-10 68
VMC (738 "My Shrink") 5-10 69
LPs: 10/12-inch
VMC (135 "Pacific Ocean") 10-15 69

PACK
Singles: 7-inch
SOUND TEX (650529 "Time") 20-30 65

PACK
Singles: 7-inch
LUCKY ELEVEN (003 "Harlem Shuffle") 8-12 68
WINGATE (007 "The Color of Our Love") 10-15 65
Also see KNIGHT, Terry

PACK, Charlie
Singles: 7-inch
TRC (2819 "Fluffy Dog") 25-35

PACKARDS
(With Paul Boyers Band)
Singles: 78 rpm
PARADISE 25-50 56
PLA-BAC 200-300 56
Singles: 7-inch
PARADISE (105 "Dream of Love") 200-300 56
PLA-BAC (106 "Ladise") 1000-2000 56

PACKERS *P&R/R&B '65*
Singles: 7-inch
HBR (478 "Pink Chiffon") 5-10 66
IMPERIAL 5-8 69
PURE SOUL MUSIC (1107 "Hole in the Wall") 10-15 65
SOUL BABY .... 5-10 '60s
TAG LTD. 5-10 67
TANGERINE (982 "Soul Time") 5-10 68
LPs: 10/12-inch
IMPERIAL (12409 "Hitch It Up") 10-15 68
PURE SOUL MUSIC (1001 "Hole in the Wall") 15-20 66
Member: Charles Axton.
Also see MAR-KEYS

PAC-KEYS
Singles: 7-inch
HOLLYWOOD (1108 "Dig In") 5-10 66
HOLLYWOOD (1118 "Hip Pocket") 5-10 67

PACO & CITATIONS
Singles: 7-inch
SARA (5036 "Cheryl Moana Marie") .... 15-25 '60s
Members: Leroy "Paco" Beribeau; Jim Delongchamp; Dick Bjorkman.

PADDLES
(With Sam Pruitt & Orchestra)
Singles: 7-inch
CLOWN (3090 "You're My Love") 100-200 63

PADDY, KLAUS & GIBSON
Singles: 7-inch
CHESS (1956 "Rejected") 10-15 66

PADGETT, Linda
Singles: 7-inch
DOT (16191 "Along Came Love") 5-8 61
TOPPA (1033 "Along Came Love") 8-12 61
(First issue.)
TOPPA (1045 "When You Go") 8-12 61
TOPPA (1049 "Somewhere, Someday") ... 8-12 61

PADUA, Tony
Singles: 7-inch
CHRISTY (116 "Barbara Ann") 20-30 59

PAEGENS
Singles: 7-inch
RAMPRO (122 "Good Day Sunshine") 10-20 67
Picture Sleeves
RAMPRO (122 "Good Day Sunshine") 20-30 67
Member: Bun E. Carlos.
Also see CHEAP TRICK

PAGANS
Singles: 7-inch
MUSIC CITY (832 "Lover's Plea") 400-500 60

PAGANS
Singles: 7-inch
STUDIO CITY (1034 "Stop Shakin' Your Head") 50-75 65

PAGE, Allen
(With the Crowns; with Deltones; with Moonbeams)
Singles: 7-inch
MOON (301 "Honeysuckle") 75-100 59
MOON (302 "Dateless Night") 75-100 59
MOON (303 "She's the One That Got It") 75-100 59
MOON (307 "Oh Baby") 75-100 59

PAGE, Billy
Singles: 7-inch
PALOMAR (2214 "American Girl") 5-10 65

PAGE, Bobby
Singles: 78 rpm
VITO 10-15 54
Singles: 7-inch
RAM (1338 "Hippy Ti-Yo") .... 20-30 '50s
VITO ("Carioca") 10-20 54
(No selection number used.)

PAGE, Charles
Singles: 7-inch
GOLDBAND 10-15 61-64
TIC TOC (501 "Sweet Little Girl") 5-10 62

PAGE, Cleo
Singles: 7-inch
GOODIE TRAIN (007 "Goodie Train") ..... 20-30 '60s

PAGE, Hot Lips
(Oran Page)
Singles: 78 rpm
APOLLO 5-10 46
BLUEBIRD 10-20 38
COLUMBIA 4-8 47-50
COMMODORE 5-10 44-45
CONTINENTAL 5-10 44
HARMONY 4-8 47
HUB 5-10 45
SAVOY 5-10 44-45
V-DISC 8-12 44
Singles: 7-inch
KING (1404 "The Cadillac Song") 50-75 53
KING (4584 "Last Call for Alcohol") 100-200 52
KING (4594 "Ruby") 50-100 53
KING (4616 "What Shall I Do") 50-100 53
KING (15000 series) 15-25 52
RCA (50-0120 "Let Me In") 50-75 51
RCA (50-0129 "I Want to Ride Like the Cowboys Do") 50-75 51
EPs: 7-inch
BRUNSWICK (97102 "Jazztime U.S.A.") . 15-25 54
REMINGTON (82 "Rhythm Blues") .... 15-25 '50s
LPs: 10/12-inch
BRUNSWICK (54002 "Jazztime U.S.A.") . 35-50 54
Also see ABERNATHY, Marion
Also see BOSTIC, Earl
Also see DOGGETT, Bill
Also see LITTLE SYLVIA

PAGE, Hot Lips, & Cozy Cole
LPs: 10/12-inch
CONTINENTAL (16007 "Hot and Cozy") . 30-40 62
Also see COLE, Cozy
Also see PAGE, Hot Lips

PAGE, Howard, & Pearls
Singles: 7-inch
ASTOR (1005 "I Just Can't Stand It") 10-20

PAGE, Jerry
("Featuring the Kentuckians")
Singles: 7-inch
SONIC (209 "Be What You Want") .... 8-12 '60s
Also see JERRY & CASUALS

PAGE, Jimmy *LP '82*
Singles: 7-inch
GEFFEN 3-5 88
Picture Sleeves
GEFFEN 4-6 88
(Promotional issue only.)
LPs: 10/12-inch
GEFFEN 5-8 88
SPRINGBOARD (4038 "Early Works") ...... 8-12 '70s
SWAN SONG 5-10 82
Also see CLAPTON, Eric, Jeff Beck & Jimmy Page
Also see HERMAN'S HERMITS

Also see LED ZEPPELIN
Also see LORD SUTCH
Also see SPANN, Otis
Also see STEWART, Al
Also see YARDBIRDS

PAGE, Jimmy, & Robert Plant
LPs: 10/12-inch
W.B. (62706 "No Quarter") ... 10-15 94
Also see PLANT, Robert

PAGE, Jimmy, and Sonny Boy Williamson
LPs: 10/12-inch
SPRINGBOARD ... 10-20 72
Also see WILLIAMSON, Sonny Boy, & Yardbirds

PAGE, Joey
Singles: 7-inch
ROULETTE (4373 "Blue Velvet") ... 30-40 61

PAGE, Larry
(Larry Page Orchestra)
Singles: 7-inch
CALLA (126 "Waltzing to Jazz") ... 5-10 66
CALLA (144 "Last Waltz") ... 5-10 68
PAGE ONE (21010 "Hey Jude") ... 5-10 68
PAGE ONE (21018 "Promises Promises") .5-10 69
PAULA (291 "Somebody Knows") ... 5-10 68
LPs: 10/12-inch
RHINO (257 "Kinky Music") ... 10-15 84
(Picture disc with Kinks photo. Has instrumental versions of Kinks' songs.)
Also see KINKS

PAGE, Mike
Singles: 7-inch
ROYCE (0005 "Long Black Shiny Car") .. 75-85 59

PAGE, Patti
(With Al Clauser & the Oklahomans)
Singles: 78 rpm
OKLA (66 "My Sweet Papa") ... 5-10 '40s
(Listed primarily to distinguish this singer from the following Patti Page.)

PAGE, Patti P&R '48
(With the George Barnes Trio; with Jack Rael Quartet/Orchestra; with Merrie Melody Singers; with Jerry Kennedy & Orchestra)
Singles: 78 rpm
MERCURY (A-95 thru A-1025) ... 5-15 50-52
(Boxed set of singles.)
MERCURY (505 "Confess") ... 5-10 50
MERCURY (1219 "The Prisoners Song")...5-10 '50s
MERCURY (5061 thru 5899) ... 5-10 47-52
MERCURY (70025 thru 71101) ... 5-10 52-57
MERCURY (71177 thru 71331) ... 10-20 57-58
PLAYCRAFT ... 5-10 53-55
Singles: 7-inch
AVCO ... 4-6 74-75
COLUMBIA ... 4-8 62-70
EPIC ... 4-6 73-74
LANGWORTH ... 10-20 49
(8-inch, 33 rpm transcriptions.)
MERCURY (A-95 thru A-1025) ... 10-20 50-52
(Boxed set of singles.)
MERCURY (505 "Confess") ... 10-15 50
MERCURY (1219 "The Prisoners Song") 10-20 '50s
MERCURY (5344 thru 5899) ... 15-25 50-52
MERCURY (7000 series) ... 10-20 61
(Compact 33 stereo.)
MERCURY (10000 series) ... 5-10 58-60
(Stereo.)
MERCURY (30000 series) ... 5-10 58
MERCURY (70025 thru 72123) ... 12-25 52-62
MERCURY (73000 series) ... 4-6 70-72
PLANTATION (Black vinyl.) ... 3-5 81-83
PLANTATION (Green vinyl.) ... 4-8 81-83
PLAYCRAFT ... 15-25 53-55
Picture Sleeves
MERCURY (70302 "Cross Over the Bridge") ... 15-25 54
MERCURY (70458 "The Mama Doll Song") ... 15-25 55
MERCURY (71355 thru 72123) ... 15-25 58-63
EPs: 7-inch
MERCURY ... 10-20 52-61
PLAYCRAFT ... 8-12 59
LPs: 10/12-inch
ACCORD ... 5-10 82
AHED ... 5-8 76
BRYLEN ... 5-8 82
CANDLELITE ... 8-12 73
COLUMBIA (Except "CL" & "CS" series) ... 8-15 70-77
COLUMBIA (CL-2049 thru CL-2761) ... 10-20 63-68
(Monaural.)
COLUMBIA (CS-8849 thru CS-9999) ... 15-25 63-69
(Stereo.)
EMARCY (2-100 "The East Side The West Side") ... 50-80 58
(Two discs.)
EMARCY (36074 "In the Land of Hi Fi")...40-60 56
(No Mercury logo on cover or label.)
EMARCY (36074 "In the Land of Hi Fi")...30-40 58
(Mercury logo on cover and label.)
EMARCY (80000 "In the Land of Hi Fi")...35-45 58
(Stereo.)
EMARCY (36116 "West Side") ... 20-30 58
(Monaural.)
EMARCY (36136 "East Side") ... 20-30 58
(Monaural.)
EMARCY (60113 "East Side") ... 20-30 59
(Stereo.)
EMARCY (60114 "West Side") ... 20-30 59
(Stereo.)
EVEREST ... 5-8 83
EXACT ... 5-8 80
51 WEST ... 5-8 79
GOOD MUSIC ... 5-8 85
HARMONY ... 5-12 69-70
HARTLAND ... 5-8 86
HINDSIGHT ... 5-8 86
IMPACT ... 5-8 79
MERCURY (100 series) ... 8-12 69
MERCURY (20076 thru 20226) ... 20-40 55-56
MERCURY (20318 thru 20952) ... 15-30 57-64
(Monaural.)
MERCURY (25059 thru 25210) ... 20-40 50-54
(10-inch LPs.)
MERCURY (60049 thru 60011) ... 20-40 57-58
(Stereo.)
MERCURY (60025 thru 60952) ... 20-35 58-64
(Stereo.)
MERCURY (61344 "I'd Rather Be Sorry") ... 10-20 71
PAIR ... 5-8 87
PICKWICK ... 5-8 72
PILLSBURY (001 "Big Records") ... 15-25 57
(Special products issue made for Pillsbury.)
PLANTATION ... 5-10 81-82
PLAYCRAFT (1300 "Patti Page") ... 15-25 58
SUFFOLK ... 5-8 88
WING (2-100 series) ... 5-12 72
WING (12121 thru 12174) ... 15-25 58-59
(Monaural.)
WING (12250 thru 12295) ... 10-20 65
(Monaural.)
WING (16000 series) ... 10-25 61-68
(Stereo.)
Also see KENNEDY, Jerry
Also see MARTIN, Dean / Patti Page

PAGE, Priscilla
Singles: 7-inch
ALCOR (015 "Dreaming") ... 10-15 62
ROSE (500 "Dreaming") ... 15-25 61

PAGE, Rickie
Singles: 7-inch
EPIC (9841 "I'm His Girl") ... 5-10 65
LANDA (683 "Je Vous Aime") ... 5-10 61
ZEPHYR (020 "Gee How I Love You") ... 8-12 57
Also see PICKETT, Bobby

PAGE, Ricky
Singles: 7-inch
DOT (16261 "I Understand") ... 5-10 61
LIBERTY (55094 "I'm Old Enough Now")...8-12 57
RENDEZVOUS (139 "Yes, I'm Lonesome Tonight") ... 8-12 60
SPAR (301 "Harper Valley P.T.A.") ... 5-10 68

PAGE BOYS
Singles: 7-inch
ABC-PAR (10323 "Lonely Sea") ... 5-10 62
CAMELOT ... 5-10 65
DECCA (31505 "If Tears Could Speak") .. 10-15 63
HAMILTON (50025 "Peter Gunn") ... 5-10 59
PREP (117 "This I Give to You") ... 10-15 57
SEVILLE (135 "I Have Love") ... 15-20 65
TEL (1007 "Hey Now Baby") ... 15-20 59

PAGE BOYS
Singles: 7-inch
RUFF (1020 "All I Want") ... 15-20 67

PAGE SISTERS
Singles: 7-inch
LIBERTY (55133 "Dream Boy") ... 8-12 58
ZEPHYR (012 "Sweet Sweetheart") ... 10-15 57

PAGEANTS
Singles: 7-inch
GOLDISC (3013 "Happy Together") ... 400-500 61
Also see DEE, Tony

PAGEANTS
Singles: 7-inch
BAMBOO (525 "Sad and Lonely") ... 5-10 63
PAXLEY (753 "Theme from *Sleeping Moondog*") ... 40-50 61
Members: Roy Bronson; Barbara Reeves; Mel Riley.
Also see DEE, Tony
Also see REEVES, Barbara, & Pageants

PAGEANTS
Singles: 7-inch
GROOVE (0056 "Make It Last") ... 10-15 65
RCA (8601 "Are You Ever Coming Home") ... 5-10 65

PAGEBOYS
Singles: 7-inch
SEVILLE (135 "I Have Love") ... 15-20 65

PAGENTS
Singles: 7-inch
ERA (3119 "Enchanted Surf") ... 8-12 63
ERA (3124 "Glenda") ... 8-12 64
ERA (3134 "Sad and Lonely") ... 8-12 64
I.K.E. (631 "Enchanted Surf") ... 15-25 63

PAGES
Singles: 7-inch
DON TAN (0001 "Donna Marie") ... 15-25 59
(Reportedly, the first issue.)
EAGLE (1006 "Donna Marie") ... 10-20 59

PAGES
Singles: 7-inch
UA (667 "Sugar on the Road") ... 10-15 '60s
UA ("Train Pulling Mama") ... 10-15 '60s
(Selection number not known.)

PAICH, Marty
Singles: 7-inch
GROOVE (0002 "Love Is in the Air") ... 5-10 62
Also see MARTIN, Dean

PAIGE, Hal
(With the Whalers)
Singles: 78 rpm
ATLANTIC ... 50-75 52-53
FURY ... 50-75 57
J&S ... 30-40 57
Singles: 7-inch
ATLANTIC (996 "Drive It Home") ... 100-125 52
ATLANTIC (1032 "Big Foot May") ... 100-125 53
CHECKER (873 "Don't Have to Cry No More") ... 10-15 57
FURY (1002 "Don't Have to Cry No More") ... 40-50 57
FURY (1024 "After Hours Blues") ... 20-30 59
J&S (1601 "Thunder Bird") ... 15-25 57
Session: Mickey Baker.
Also see BAKER, Mickey
Also see WILLOWS / Hal Paige

PAIGE, Joey
Singles: 7-inch
MIRA (211 "Goes to Show") ... 5-10 66
PHILIPS (40449 "Just a Boy in Love") ... 5-10 67
TOLLIE (9025 "Gone Back to Tennessee") ... 5-10 64
TOLLIE (9045 "Yeah, Yeah, Yeah") ... 5-10 65
VEE-JAY (704 "Goodnight My Love") ... 10-20 65
W.B. (5377 "Surfer from Tennessee") ... 10-20 63
Also see DICKEY DOO & DONT'S

PAIGE, Joy
Singles: 7-inch
MONITOR (1408 "Boll Weevil Twist") ... 5-10 62

PAIGE, Kiki
Singles: 7-inch
GNP (181 "Crazy New Love") ... 5-10 62

PAIGE, Ray
Singles: 7-inch
RCA (9047 "Don't Stop Now") ... 10-20 66

PAINTED FACES
Singles: 7-inch
MANHATTAN (808 "Anxious Color") ... 15-25 67
MANHATTAN (811 "I Think I'm Going Mad") ... 15-25 67
MANHATTAN (814 "In the Heat of the Night") ... 15-25 68

PAINTED GARDEN
Singles: 7-inch
STEADY (123 "Red, Red Wine") ... 5-10 69

PAINTED SHIP
Singles: 7-inch
LONDON (17351 "Frustration") ... 10-20 67
(Canadian.)
LONDON (17354 "Audience Reflections") ... 10-20 67
(Canadian.)
MERCURY (72663 "Frustration") ... 10-20 67

PAIR EXTRAORDINAIRE
(The Pair)
Singles: 7-inch
LIBERTY (55748 "Patience Baby") ... 5-10 64
LIBERTY (55910 "Girl, I Think I Love You") ... 5-10 66
LPs: 10/12-inch
LIBERTY (3440 "Pair Extraordinaire") ... 10-20 66
(Monaural.)
LIBERTY (3461 "In-Citement") ... 10-20 66
(Stereo.)
LIBERTY (7440 "Pair Extraordinaire") ... 10-20 66
(Monaural.)
LIBERTY (7461 "In-Citement") ... 10-20 66
(Stereo.)

PAIR OF KINGS
Singles: 7-inch
RCA (7659 "Once") ... 10-15 59
WARWICK (608 "I Wonder Where My Baby Is Tonight") ... 10-15 61
WARWICK (647 "Ev'rytime") ... 10-15 61
Member: Jerry Vance.

PAISLEYS
Singles: 7-inch
PEACE (70 "Wind") ... 10-20
LPs: 10/12-inch
AUDIO CITY (70 "Cosmic Mind at Play") ... 150-200 70

PAL, Ricki
(With Adam Ross Orchestra)
Singles: 7-inch
ARWIN (115 "No Need for Crying") ... 8-12 58

PAL & PROPHETS
Singles: 7-inch
JAMIE (1382 "Peace Pipe") ... 5-10 69
PHIL-L.A. OF SOUL (328 "Lotta Good Lovin' ") ... 5-10 69
PHIL-L.A. OF SOUL (332 "Whip") ... 5-10 69
SCEPTER (1287 "Shame, Shame, Shame") ... 10-15 64
Member: Pal Rakes.

PALACE, Eddie
Singles: 7-inch
JUKE BOX (109 "Kangaroo") ... 40-60 57

PALACE GUARDS
Singles: 7-inch
WHITE CLIFFS (269 "Gas Station Boogaloo") ... 20-25 67

PALISADES
Singles: 7-inch
CALICO (113 "Close Your Eyes") ... 10-15 60
DORE (609 "Oh My Love") ... 10-15 61
LEADER (806 "Dear Joan") ... 15-25 60
MEDIEVAL (205 "This Is the Night") ... 5-10 64

PALISADES
Singles: 7-inch
DEBRA (1003 "Chapel Bells") ... 100-200 63
(Reissued as by the Magics. Reportedly 100 made.)
Also see MAGICS

PALISADES
Singles: 7-inch
CHAIRMAN (4401 "Make the Night a Little Longer") ... 15-25 63
Session: Carole King.
Also see KING, Carole

PALM, Horace M., with Lefty Bates Orchestra
Singles: 7-inch
APEX (952 "Why Can't You Love Me").... 10-15 59
Also see BATES, Lefty "Guitar"

PALM, Tommy
Singles: 7-inch
BOP (101 "Stroll with Me Baby")............ 35-50 57

PALMER, Don
Singles: 7-inch
ABNER (1021 "Goodbye Lolita")................8-12 59
ABNER (1027 "Explosion").........................8-12 59
FAY (201 "Hey Yea Baby")...................... 50-75

PALMER, Earl
(With His Ten Piece Rockin' Band; with Jayhawks)
Singles: 78 rpm
ALADDIN (3379 "Johnny's House Party") 10-15 57
Singles: 7-inch
ALADDIN (3379 "Johnny's House Party") 10-20 57
CAPITOL (3899 "Drum Village")............ 10-20 58
LIBERTY (55356 "New Orleans") 5-10 61
ROULETTE (4440 "Summer")...................5-10 62
LPs: 10/12-inch
LIBERTY (3201 "Drumsville")................. 20-30 61
(Monaural.)
LIBERTY (7201 "Drumsville").................. 25-35 61
(Stereo.)
LIBERTY (3227 "Percolator Twist") 20-30 62
(Monaural.)
LIBERTY (7227 "Percolator Twist") 25-35 62
(Stereo.)
Also see GAYTEN, Paul
Also see JAYHAWKS
Also see WILLIAMS, Larry
Also see WOODS, Donald

PALMER, Gladys
Singles: 78 rpm
FEDERAL (12006 "Ain't That Just Like a Man").. 10-15 51
FEDERAL (12018 "Fool That I Am")....... 10-15 51
Also see HUNT, Floyd, Quartette

PALMER, Jerry
Singles: 7-inch
CARLTON (581 "Hey Sweet Baby")....... 15-25 62
CHATTAHOOCHEE (671 "That'll Be the Day") 10-15 65
CHATTAHOOCHEE (676 "That'll Be the Day") 8-12 65
GAIETY (102 "Head Over Heels in Love")... 50-100
GAIETY (105 "Walkin' Home")............ 50-100
GAIETY (109 "Don't Ever Leave Me") 10-20 65
GAIETY (111 "Walking the Dog")........ 10-20 66
GAIETY (113 "Ice Cream Man").............. 10-20 66

PALMER, Rick
Singles: 7-inch
CARLTON (491 "You Threw a Dart")...... 20-30 58
Also see RICK & LEGENDS

PALMER, Robert LP '75
Singles: 12-inch
ISLAND...4-6 83-86
Singles: 7-inch
EMI/MANHATTAN 3-5 88
ISLAND..3-6 75-86
Picture Sleeves
EMI/MANHATTAN 3-5 88
ISLAND..3-5 83-88
LPs: 10/12-inch
EMI..5-10 88-90
ISLAND (Except 819) 5-10 75-86
ISLAND (819 "Secrets").................... 35-40 79
(Picture disc. Promotional issue only.)
Also see VINEGAR JOE

PALMER, Sal
(Butch Palmer)
Singles: 7-inch
VASSAR (325 "Baby Come Back to Me")... 20-30 62

PALMER, Sy
Singles: 7-inch
EAGLE (1005 "Can't Cha Tell")............ 75-100 58

PALMIERI, Charlie
Singles: 7-inch
ATLANTIC (2384 "Uptight")......................8-12 67

PALMORE, Lil, & Her Caldonia Boys
Singles: 78 rpm
EBONY (1004 "I Believe I'll Go Back Home")...25-35 48
SITTIN' IN WITH (540 "I Believe I'll Go Back Home")...15-20 49

PALMS
Singles: 78 rpm
UNITED (208 "Edna")..............................50-100 57
Singles: 7-inch
UNITED (208 "Edna")............................150-250 57
Also see WILKINS, Artie, & Palms

PALS
(With Andy Gibson & His Orchestra)
Singles: 7-inch
GUYDEN (2019 "Summer Is Here") 15-25 59
TURF (1000 "Summer Is Here") 40-50 58

PAM & JANE
Singles: 7-inch
PETAL (1230 "There Goes Linda")............5-10 64

PANASSI, Tony
Singles: 7-inch
JAMIE (1252 "Bye Bye Baby")...................5-10 63

PANDAS
Singles: 7-inch
SWINGTIME (1001 "Walk")......................15-25 67

PANICKS
Singles: 7-inch
KYRA (1001 "Bad Doreen") 20-30 64

PANICKS
Singles: 7-inch
DUPREE (102 "Work") 15-25 66
DUPREE (200 "You're My Baby")............10-15 67

PANICS
Singles: 7-inch
CHANCELLOR (1109 "Panicsville") 5-10 62
PHILIPS (40230 "It Ain't What You Got") ...5-10 64
SWAN (4247 "Show Her You Care")..........5-10 66
LPs: 10/12-inch
CHANCELLOR (5026 "Panicsville") 20-30 62
PHILIPS (200159 "Discotheque Dance Party")..15-25 64
(Monaural.)
PHILIPS (600159 "Discotheque Dance Party")..20-30 64
(Stereo.)
Member: Sonny Richards.

PANICS
Singles: 7-inch
BOBBY (2004 "Love Riot").......................10-20 66

PANTHERS
Singles: 7-inch
D&C (12 "Bridgestone")...........................10-20 65
(Canadian.)
Picture Sleeves
D&C (12 "Bridgestone")...........................20-30 65
(Canadian.)

PAPA DON ASSOCIATION
Singles: 7-inch
AMY (11011 "Souled Out")......................5-10 68

PAPER GARDEN
LPs: 10/12-inch
MUSICOR (3175 "Paper Garden Presents")..20-30 69

PARADE P&R '67
Singles: 7-inch
A&M...5-10 67-69
Members: Jerry Riopelle; Murray MacLeod; Smokey Roberds.

PARADISE, Earl
Singles: 7-inch
ATCO (6326 "You're All I Need")............10-20 64

PARADONS P&R/R&B '60
(With the Rockets Combo)
Singles: 7-inch
COLLECTABLES......................................3-5 '80s
ERA...4-6 72
MILESTONE (2003 "Diamonds & Pearls") 20-30 60
(Maroon label.)
MILESTONE (2003 "Diamonds & Pearls") 15-20 60
(Red label.)
MILESTONE (2003 "Diamonds & Pearls").8-12 60
(Green label.)
MILESTONE (2005 "Bells Ring")............15-25 60
MILESTONE (2015 "I Had a Dream") 40-50 62
TUFFEST (102 "This Is Love") 250-350 61
(Reissued as by the Trend-Tones.)
W.B. (5186 "Take All of Me") 10-15 61
Members: Bill Myers; Chuck Weldon; Wes Tyler; Bill Powers.
Also see TREND-TONES

PARAGONS P&R '61
("Featuring Mack Starr")
Singles: 78 rpm
WINLEY (215 "Florence").........................40-60 57
WINLEY (220 "Let's Start All Over Again")...50-75 57
Singles: 7-inch
ABC...4-6 73
BUDDAH...4-6 75
COLLECTABLES......................................3-5 '80s
LOST NITE..4-8
MUSIC CLEF (3001 "Time After Time") ...15-20 63
MUSICRAFT (1102 "Wedding Bells").......15-20 60
(Maroon label.)
MUSICRAFT (1102 "Wedding Bells").......10-15 60
(Red label.)
ROBIN HOOD (145 "Danny Boy"/"Florence, Don't Leave Me")..5-10 77
STARLIGHT (23 "Florence, Don't Leave Me"/"Blue Velvet")...5-10 84
STARLIGHT (46 "Hey Little School Girl"/"Danny Boy")..5-10 86
SUPREME (3 "Love at Last")...............100-125 '60s
TAP (500 "If")..25-35 61
TAP (503 "Begin the Beguine")................30-40 61
TAP (504 "These Are the Things I Love")..75-100 61
TIMES SQUARE (9 "So You Will Know").15-25 63
VIRGO...4-6 72-73
WINLEY (215 "Florence").......................50-100 57
(Has "Winley" in 3/8-inch letters.)
WINLEY (215 "Florence")..........................25-50 61
(Has "Winley" in 1/4-inch sans serif letters.)
WINLEY (215 "Florence").........................15-25 61
(Has "Winley" in 1/4-inch serif letters.)
WINLEY (215 "Florence")..........................10-20 61
(Has "Winley" in 5/8-inch letters.)
WINLEY (220 "Let's Start All Over Again")..50-100 57
(Has "Winley" in 3/8-inch letters.)
WINLEY (220 "Let's Start All Over Again")...20-30 61
(Has "Winley" in 1/4-inch letters.)
WINLEY (223 "Two Hearts Are Better Then [sic] One")..50-100 58
(Has "Winley" in 3/8-inch letters.)
WINLEY (223 "Two Hearts Are Better Then [sic] One")..20-30 61
(Has "Winley" in 1/4-inch letters.)
WINLEY (227 "Twilight"/"The Wows of Love")..1000-1500 58
(Note spelling error on "Vows.")
WINLEY (227 "Twilight"/"The Vows of Love")...20-30 61
(Title error corrected.)
WINLEY (228 "So You Will Know") 25-50 58
(Has "Winley" in 3/8-inch letters.)
WINLEY (228 "So You Will Know") 20-30 61
(Has "Winley" in 1/4-inch letters.)
WINLEY (240 "So You Will Know") 20-30 59
WINLEY (250 "Just a Memorie")..........100-200 61
(Note spelling error on "Memory.")
WINLEY (250 "Just a Memory")...............20-30 61
(Title error corrected.")
LPs: 10/12-inch
COLLECTABLES......................................6-8 86
LOST NITE (4 "Paragons") 10-20 81
(10-inch LP. Red vinyl. 1000 made.)
RARE BIRD (8002 "Simply the Paragons")..35-50
Members: Julius McMichaels; Mack Starr; Al Brown; Don Travis; Ben Frazier; Bill Witt; Rick Jackson.
Session: Dave "Baby" Cortez.
Also see COLLINS, Tommy, & Paragons
Also see CORTEZ, Dave "Baby"
Also see HARPTONES / Paragons
Also see OLYMPICS
Also see STARR, Mack

PARAGONS / Jesters
LPs: 10/12-inch
JOSIE ("Paragons Meet the Jesters") ......50-75 '60s
(Selection number not known.)
JUBILEE (1098 "Paragons Meet the Jesters") 250-350 59
PAUL WINLEY PROD. (102 "Paragons Meet the Jesters") 20-40 65
WINLEY (6003 "War! The Paragons vs. the Jesters") 150-250 60
Also see JESTERS
Also see PARAGONS

PARAGONS
Singles: 7-inch
LAFAYETTE ("Scramble") 10-20 61
(Selection number not known.)

PARAGONS
Singles: 7-inch
EXIT (12 "Pretty Words") 50-100 63

PARAGONS / Samohi Serenaders
Singles: 7-inch
CENTURY CUSTOM (19317 "Surf Drums") ....20-30 '60s
Members: Mike Faulkner; Forrest Peque.

PARAKEETS
Singles: 7-inch
BIG TOP (3130 "I Want You Right Now") .. 8-12 62
JUBILEE (5407 "Come Back")................. 15-25 61

PARAKEETS / Frank Motley
Singles: 78 rpm
GEM (218 "Give Me Time") 100-150 54
Singles: 7-inch
GEM (218 "Give Me Time") 250-350 54

PARAKEETS QUINTET
Singles: 78 rpm
ATLAS..50-75 56
Singles: 7-inch
ANGLE TONE (1068 thru 1075)................4-7
ATLAS (1068 "I Have a Love") 100-150 56
ATLAS (1069 "My Heart Tells Me") 100-150 56
Also see DONNA, Vic

PARALLELS
Singles: 7-inch
TWILIGHT (404 "Sax-A-Nova") 10-15 63
TWILIGHT (405 "Surf-A-Nova")............... 20-25 63
(Reissued on Twilight 406 as by the Tri-Tones.)
Also see TRI-TONES

PARAMONTS
Singles: 7-inch
CENTAUR (103 "When I Dream") 40-50 63
EMBER (1099 "In a Dream") 150-200 64

PARAMOUNTS
Singles: 7-inch
COMBO (156 "Take My Heart").............50-100 59

PARAMOUNTS
(With Stan Vincent Orchestra)
Singles: 7-inch
FLEETWOOD (1014 "I Know You'll Be My Love") 30-40 60
Also see VINCENT, Stan

PARAMOUNTS
Singles: 7-inch
PAM (110 "Judy") 30-40 61

PARAMOUNTS
Singles: 7-inch
AVENUE D (7 "Tell Me Why")..................... 8-10 82
(Black vinyl. 800 made.)
AVENUE D (7 "Tell Me Why").................. 15-25 82
(Blue vinyl. 100 made.)
CARLTON (524 "Trying") 10-20 60
LAURIE (3201 "Just to be with You") 15-25 63
EPs: 7-inch
AVENUE D (101 "We Belong Together"). 20-25 85
(Black vinyl. 987 made.)
Members: Willy Mendez; Kenny Demmo; Guy Tann; Joe Regusa; Larry Gilliam; Steve Alous; Kevin Prothro.
Also see DE MARCO, Ralph

PARAMOUNTS
Singles: 7-inch
DOT (16175 "Congratulations")............... 10-15 61
DOT (16201 "When You Dance") 15-25 61
Member: Robert Knight.

PARAMOUNTS
Singles: 7-inch
MAGNUM (722 "Under Your Spell") 15-25 64

PARAMOUNTS
Singles: 7-inch
LIVERPOOL SOUND (903 "Poison Ivy"). 20-30 64
Also see PROCOL HARUM

PARAMOUNTS
Singles: 7-inch
SARA (6567 "Shake a Tail Feather")....... 10-20 65
Member: Greg Berndt.

PARAMOURS
Singles: 7-inch
MOONGLOW (214 "There She Goes") ... 15-25 62
(Black vinyl.)
MOONGLOW (214 "There She Goes") . 75-125 62
(Red vinyl. Promotional issue only.)
SMASH (1701 "That's the Way We Love") 15-25 61
SMASH (1718 "Cutie Cutie") 15-25 61
Members: Bill Medley; Bobby Hatfield (only on Moonglow).
Also see RICHARDS, Penny
Also see RIGHTEOUS BROTHERS

PARCHMAN, Kenny
Singles: 7-inch
JAXON (503 "Treat Me Right")......... 1000-2000
LU (504 "Satellite Hop") 350-450 58
ROCK IT (102 "You Call Everybody Darlin' ") 4-8 78

PAREE, Paul
Singles: 7-inch
ZENITH (100 "Big Daddy") 10-15 59

PARETTI SISTERS
Singles: 7-inch
AL-BRITE (1500 "Undiscovered Love")... 10-20 60

PARHAM, Baby "Pee Wee"
Singles: 78 rpm
FLAIR............ 10-15 54
Singles: 7-inch
FLAIR (1036 "People Are Wondering").... 25-50 54

PARIGI, Gastone, Quintet
Singles: 7-inch
JARO INT'L (77033 "Be Mine Tonight")......8-12 60

PARIS
Singles: 7-inch
DOC (102 "Sleepless Nights")............ 100-125 '60s
UNI (55243 "Gone Again") 10-20 70

PARIS, Bobby
(With the Centuries; with Parisians)
Singles: 7-inch
CAMEO (396 "Night Owl")............ 50-75 66
CAPITOL (5929 "I Walked Away") 25-35 67
CHATTAHOOCHEE (631 "Little Miss Dreamer") 10-20 63
CHATTAHOOCHEE (672 "Love Passed Me By") 10-20 65
INT'L GUILD (13007 "How Did Your Vacation Go") 100-150 60
JAIRICK (204 "Are You the One")........... 40-60 63
MAGENTA (03 "Dark Continent") 10-20 61
TETRAGRAMMATON 5-10 68-69

PARIS, Freddie
Singles: 7-inch
RCA (9232 "Take Me As I Am") 5-10 67
RCA (9358 "Little Things Can Make a Woman Cry") 5-10 67
RCA (9571 "There She Goes") 10-15 68
LPs: 10/12-inch
RCA (4064 "Lovin' Mood") 10-15 68
(This artist is not Fred Parris, who performed with the Five Satins.)

PARIS, Laurie
Singles: 7-inch
ABC-PAR (10441 "Stay") 10-15 63

PARIS, Richie
Singles: 7-inch
TIP TOP (403 "I'm Gonna Get My Own Love") 15-25 61

PARIS BROTHERS
Singles: 7-inch
BRUNSWICK (55132 "This Is It")............20-30 59
CORAL (62220 "Funny Feeling")............10-20 60

PARIS SISTERS P&R '61
Singles: 78 rpm
CAVALIER............10-15 53
DECCA............10-15 54-56
IMPERIAL............10-15 57-58
Singles: 7-inch
ABC 4-6 73
CAPITOL (2081 "Golden Days")............5-8 68
CAVALIER (828 "Bully, Bully Man")..........15-25 53
CAVALIER (829 "Christmas in My Home Town")............15-25 53
COLLECTABLES............3-5 '80s
DECCA (29000 series)............15-25 54-56
DECCA (30554 "Don't Tell Anybody") 10-20 58
ERIC............3-6 '70s
GNP (410 "Greener Days") 5-8 68
GREGMARK (2 "Be My Boy")............15-25 61
GREGMARK (6 "I Love How You Love Me")............15-25 61
GREGMARK (10 "He Knows I Love Him Too Much")............15-25 62
GREGMARK (12 "Let Me Be the One")....15-25 62
GREGMARK (13 "Yes I Love You")..........15-25 62
IMPERIAL (5465 "Old Enough to Cry") 10-20 57
IMPERIAL (5487 "Someday") 10-20 58
MGM (13236 "Dream Lover")............5-10 64
MERCURY (72320 "When I Fall in Love")..5-10 64
MERCURY (72468 "Why Do I Take It from You")............5-10 65
REPRISE (440 "Sincerely")............5-10 65
REPRISE (472 "You")............5-10 66
REPRISE (511 "It's My Party")............5-10 66
REPRISE (548 "Long After Tonight Is Over")............5-10 67
Picture Sleeves
GREGMARK (6 "I Love How You Love Me")............5-10 '90s
MGM (13236 "Dream Lover")............10-20 64
MERCURY (72320 "When I Fall in Love")..8-10 64
LPs: 10/12-inch
REPRISE (R-6259 "Everything Under the Sun") 15-20 67
(Monaural.)
REPRISE (RS-6259 "Everything Under the Sun")............20-25 67
(Stereo.)
SIDEWALK............12-18
UNIFILMS............10-15
Members: Priscilla Paris; Sherrell Paris; Albeth Paris.
Session: Davie Allan.
Also see ALLAN, Davie
Also see PRISCILLA

PARISIAN SEXTET
Singles: 7-inch
CHALLENGE (9151 "Baby Elephant Walk")............8-12 62

PARISIANS
Singles: 7-inch
ARGYLE (1006 "Silhouettes")............5-10 61
BULLSEYE (1028 "Silhouettes")............8-12 59
FELSTED (8627 "Ambush")............5-10 61
Member: Jimmy Wisner.
Also see WISNER, Jimmy

PARISIANS
Singles: 7-inch
POVA (1004 "Why")............30-40 62

PARKAYS P&R '61
Singles: 7-inch
ABC-PAR (10242 "Last Date")............8-12 61
ABC-PAR (10285 "Green Monkeys") 8-12 61
FONTANA (1526 "You've Got a Good Thing Goin' ")............15-25 65
SAFIRE (101 "Last Date") 30-40 61
(First issue.)

PARKER, Arnold
Singles: 7-inch
STARDAY (570 "Find a New Baby")......200-300

PARKER, Bill / Blues Boy Palmer
Singles: 7-inch
HOLLYWOOD (1090 "Busted") 10-15 58
HOLLYWOOD (1095 "Sweet Potato Cha Cha")............10-15 59
Also see SHOWBOATS

PARKER, Bobby P&R '61
Singles: 7-inch
AMANDA (1001 "Foolish Love") 50-100 59
SABU (100/101 "It's Too Late Darling"/"Get Right")............75-125 63
VEE-JAY (279 "You Got What It Takes") .20-30 58
V-TONE (223 "Watch Your Step") 15-20 61
(Hit version. Has "45-V-Tone 223A" etched in the vinyl trail-off.)
V-TONE (223 "Watch Your Step") 8-12 61
(Alternative take. Has "223AAX" in trail-off.)

PARKER, Bobby / Larry Green
Singles: 7-inch
LU-GREEN (101 "Watch Your Step"/"Sittin' Here")............10-15 '60s
Also see GREEN, Larry
Also see PARKER, Bobby

PARKER, Deanie
Singles: 7-inch
VOLT (105 "My Imaginary Guy") 8-12 63
VOLT (115 "Each Step I Take")............8-12 64

PARKER, Eddie
Singles: 7-inch
ASHFORD (1 "I Love You Baby")............15-25
MIKO 10-20
PRODIGAL (0617 "Body Chains")............4-8 75
TRIPLE B 10-20

PARKER, Elbie
Singles: 7-inch
VEEP (1246 "Lucky Guy")............25-50 66

PARKER, Fess P&R '55
(With Buddy Ebsen)
Singles: 78 rpm
COLUMBIA............5-10 55
DISNEYLAND 5-10 57
Singles: 7-inch
BUENA VISTA (426 "Ballad of Davy Crockett")............5-10 63
CASCADE (5910 "Eyes of an Angel") 8-12 59
COLUMBIA (242 "Ballad of Davy Crockett")............10-15 55
(Columbia Children's Series.)
COLUMBIA (40449 "Ballad of Davy Crockett")............10-15 55
COLUMBIA (40450 "Farewell")............10-15 56
COLUMBIA (40510 "Be Sure You're Right")............10-15 56
COLUMBIA (40568 "King of the River") ...10-15 56
DISNEYLAND (43 "Wringle Wrangle") 8-12 57
GUSTO (426 "Ballad of Davy Crockett") 5-10 63
RCA............5-8 64-69
Picture Sleeves
BUENA VISTA (426 "Ballad of Davy Crockett")............8-12 63
COLUMBIA (242 "Ballad of Davy Crockett")............15-25 55
(Columbia Children's Series.)
DISNEYLAND 10-20 57
RCA (8429 "Davy Crockett") 5-10 64
EPs: 7-inch
COLUMBIA (2031 "Indian Fighter")............20-25 55
COLUMBIA (2032 "Davy Crockett Goes to Congress")............20-25 55
COLUMBIA (2033 "At the Alamo")............20-25 55
LPs: 10/12-inch
COLUMBIA (666 "Davy Crockett") 50-75 55
DISNEYLAND (1007 "Yarns & Songs")....15-25 59
DISNEYLAND (1200 series) 10-20 64-65
DISNEYLAND (1300 series) 5-10 70
DISNEYLAND (1926 Davy Crockett") 10-20 63
DISNEYLAND (3007 "Yarns & Songs")....25-35 57
DISNEYLAND (3900 series) 10-20 64
HARMONY............10-20 60
RCA (2973 "Fess Parker Sings")............10-20 64

PARKER, Fess, & Buddy Ebsen / Gene Autry
Singles: 7-inch
COLUMBIA/CHRYSLER (3 "Story of Davy Crockett")............5-10 55
(Promotional issue, made by Columbia for Chrysler. Plays at 16 2/3 rpm.)
Picture Sleeves
COLUMBIA/CHRYSLER (3 "Story of Davy Crockett")............10-15 55
(Promotional issue, made by Columbia for Chrysler.)
Also see AUTRY, Gene
Also see EBSEN, Buddy
Also see PARKER, Fess

PARKER, Frenda
Singles: 7-inch
NORMAN (518 "All You Have to Do") 5-10 62

PARKER, Gigi
(With the Lovelies)
Singles: 7-inch
CORAL (62314 "Little Girl Blue")............20-30 62
MGM (13225 "Beatles Please Come Back") 10-15 64

PARKER, Graham P&R/LP '77
(With Rumour; with Shot)
Singles: 7-inch
ARISTA............3-6 79-83
ELEKTRA............3-5 85
MERCURY............4-6 76-77
Picture Sleeves
ARISTA............3-5 80-83
ELEKTRA............3-5 85
MERCURY............4-6 77
EPs: 7-inch
MERCURY (74000 "Hold Back the Night") .. 5-8 77
(Colored vinyl.)
LPs: 10/12-inch
ARISTA............5-10 78-83
ELEKTRA............5-8 85
MERCURY............5-10 77-78
RCA............5-8 88-89
Promotional LPs
ARISTA (41 "Mercury Poisoning")............25-35 78
ARISTA (63 "Live Sparks") 25-35 79
Also see SPRINGSTEEN, Bruce

PARKER, Jack "The Bear"
(Featuring H-Bomb Ferguson; Featuring Emmet Davis)
Singles: 78 rpm
DERBY............20-30 50
PRESTIGE............10-15 '50s
7-11 (2100 "Cheap Old Wine Whiskey") ..50-75 53
7-11 (2101 "One More Kiss")............35-60 53
Singles: 7-inch
7-11 (2100 "Cheap Old Wine Whiskey")............100-150 53
7-11 (2101 "One More Kiss")............50-75 53
Also see DAVIS, Emmett
Also see FERGUSON, H-Bomb

PARKER, Jimmy
Singles: 7-inch
COMET (2156 "It's Wrong")............8-10 63
DIAMOND (104 "No Word from Betty")...... 8-12 61
HERALD (589 "They Say") 5-10 64
20TH FOX (6647 "Drown in My Own Tears")............5-10 66

PARKER, Johnny
(Johnny "Bird" Parker & the Fabulous Zircons)
Singles: 78 rpm
CORAL............10-15 54
RPM 10-15 54
Singles: 7-inch
BRUNSWICK (55043 "I Must Be in Love")............30-50 58
CT (302 "Oongawa")............40-50
(Selection number not known.)
CORAL (61290 "Hurts Me to My Heart").. 15-25 54
RPM (407 "Tired of Everybody")............ 15-25 54
WELLS (199 "Beach Time USA")............ 10-20 62

PARKER, Lee
Singles: 7-inch
BIRTHSTONE (21622 "Mary-Lou") 100-150
CASCADE (5265 "Boy Meets Girl")........... 10-15 59
GOLDEN CREST (561 "Girl of My Dreams") 10-20 60
T-KAY (111 "We're Gonna Dance All Night")............50-75

PARKER, Leo
Singles: 78 rpm
UNITED (141 "Leo's Boogie")............5-10 53
Singles: 7-inch
UNITED (141 "Leo's Boogie")............20-30 53

PARKER, Leroy

Singles: 7-inch

CHALLENGE (9123 "I Know")................. 10-20 61
CHALLENGE (9167 "Cross My Heart") . 50-100 62
(Vinyl pressing.)
CHALLENGE (9167 "Cross My Heart")... 40-60 62
(Polystyrene pressing.)

PARKER, Little Bobby

Singles: 7-inch

SHRINE ("I Won't Believe It Till I See").. 50-100 66
(Selection number not known.)

PARKER, Little Junior R&B '57
(With His Blue Flames; with Blue Blowers; with Bill Johnson's Blue Flames; Junior Parker)

Singles: 78 rpm

DUKE (120 thru 184)............................ 30-40 54-58
MODERN (864 "Bad Women, Bad Whiskey").. 25-50 52

Singles: 7-inch

ABC...4-6 73
BLUE ROCK..5-10 68-69
CAPITOL 4-8 70-71
DUKE (120 "Dirty Friend Blues")............. 25-50 54
DUKE (127 "Pretty Baby Blues")............. 25-50 54
DUKE (137 "Backtrackin'")...................... 25-50 55
DUKE (147 "Driving Me")......................... 20-40 55
DUKE (157 "Mother-in-Law Blues")......... 20-40 56
DUKE (164 "My Dolly Bee") 20-40 56
DUKE (168 "Pretty Baby") 20-30 57
DUKE (177 "Peaches")............................. 15-25 57
DUKE (184 "Wondering")......................... 15-25 58
DUKE (193 "Barefoot Rock").................... 15-25 58
DUKE (301 "Sweet Home Chicago") 15-25 59
DUKE (306 "Five Long Years") 15-25 59
DUKE (309 "Stranded")............................ 15-25 59
DUKE (315 "Dangerous Woman") 15-25 60
DUKE (317 "Next Time") 15-25 60
DUKE (326 "That's Just Alright").............. 15-25 60
DUKE (330 "Stand By Me") 15-25 60
DUKE (335 "Seven Days") 15-25 61
DUKE (341 "In the Dark")......................... 15-25 61
DUKE (345 "Mary Jo").............................. 15-25 61
DUKE (351 "I Feel Alright Again")............ 10-20 62
DUKE (357 "Foxy Devil")........................... 10-20 62
DUKE (362 "It's a Pity") 10-20 63
DUKE (364 "I Can't Forget About You") .. 10-20 63
DUKE (367 "Tables Have Turned").......... 10-20 63
DUKE (371 "I'm Gonna Stop")................. 10-20 64
DUKE (376 "Things I Used to Do") 10-20 64
DUKE (384 "I'm in Love") 10-20 64
DUKE (389 "Crying for My Baby")............ 10-20 65
DUKE (394 "These Kind of Blues")........... 10-20 65
DUKE (398 "Goodbye Little Girl") 10-20 66
DUKE (406 "Get Away Blues")....................5-10 66
GROOVE MERCHANT (1010 "A Losing Battle")..4-6 75
MCA...3-5
MERCURY...5-15 66-68
MINIT (32080 "Worried Life Blues")...............4-8 69
U.A. (50855 "Funny How Time Slips Away")..4-6 72

LPs: 10/12-inch

ABC..8-10 76
BLUE ROCK (64004 "Honey-Drippin' Blues")... 10-15 69
BLUESWAY (6066 "Sometime Tomorrow My Heart Will Die")..8-12 73
CAPITOL (64 "The Outside Man") 10-15 70
DUKE (76 "Driving Wheel") 60-100 62
(Cover pictures a Cadillac.)
DUKE (76 "Driving Wheel") 35-55 62
(Cover pictures a Wagon Wheel.)
DUKE (83 "Best of Junior Parker").............8-12 74
GROOVE MERCHANT........................... 10-15
MCA..5-8
MERCURY (61101 "Like It Is")................. 10-20 67
MINIT (24024 "Blues Man")...................... 10-15 69
U.A. (6823 "I Tell Stories, Sad & True")... 10-20 71
Also see BLAND, Bobby / Little Junior Parker
Also see LITTLE JUNIOR'S BLUE FLAMES

PARKER, Little Junior, & Jimmy McGriff

LPs: 10/12-inch

CAPITOL (569 "Dudes Doin' Business") . 10-15 71
U.A. (6814 "100 Proof Black Magic")....... 10-15 71
Also see McGRIFF, Jimmy
Also see PARKER, Little Junior

PARKER, Little Willie
(With the Lorenzo Smith Orchestra)

Singles: 7-inch

MAR-VEL (2700 "Lookin' in from the Outside")...10-20 64
Also see SMITH, Lorenzo

PARKER, Malcolm

Singles: 7-inch

CODE (301 "Come Along with Me") 50-75

PARKER, Monister

Singles: 78 rpm

NUCRAFT (100 "Black Snake Blues")....75-100 52

PARKER, Otis

Singles: 7-inch

NEW STAR (529 "You Don't Have to Operate") 25-50

PARKER, Pat, & Way-Mates

Singles: 7-inch

SKYLAND (1000 "Boy Watcher").............10-15 '60s

Picture Sleeves

SKYLAND (1000 "Boy Watcher")..............15-25 '60s

PARKER, Penny
(With the Lew Douglas Orchestra & Chorus)

Singles: 7-inch

GUARANTEED (212 "Heartache Weather")..10-20 60

PARKER, Richard

Singles: 7-inch

COMMONWEALTH UNITED (3013 "You're All I Need")...10-20 70
PHILIPS (40133 "Monkey All Over")...........8-12 63
RIGHT ON (106 "You're All I Need") 8-12 71

PARKER, Robert P&R/R&B '66

Singles: 7-inch

HEAD (1050 "Barefootin'") 4-6 72
IMPERIAL (5842 "Mash Potatoes All Night Long")...10-15 62
IMPERIAL (5889 "Little Things Mean a Lot")..10-15 62
ISLAND (015 "Get Ta Tappin'") 4-6 75
ISLAND (074 "Little Bit Something")............4-6 76
NOLA (721 "Barefootin'")...............................5-10 66
NOLA (726 "Happy Feet")..............................5-10 66
NOLA (729 "Tip Toe")....................................5-10 67
NOLA (730 "Letter to Santa").........................5-10 67
NOLA (733 "Yak Yak Yak")............................5-10 67
NOLA (735 "Foxy Mama")..............................5-10 67
NOLA (738 "Holdin' Out")...............................5-10 67
RON (327 "All Nite Long")..............................5-10 59
RON (331 "Walkin'") 5-10 59
SILVER FOX (12 "You See Me")....................5-10 69

LPs: 10/12-inch

NOLA (1001 "Barefootin'")..........................20-30 66
(Monaural.)
NOLA (S-1001 "Barefootin'") 30-40 66
(Stereo.)
Also see BO, Eddie

PARKER, Ronald

Singles: 7-inch

RICH-R-TONE (8010 "The Walking Blues") 50-75

PARKER, Sonny
(With His All Stars)

Singles: 78 rpm

ALADDIN (3033 "Pretty Baby") 10-15 50
ALADDIN (3062 "Sad Feeling") 10-15 50
BRUNSWICK..15-25 53
COLUMBIA (30151 "Lay Right Down and Die")..10-15 49
COLUMBIA (30154 "Tossin' & Turnin'") ..10-15 49
PEACOCK...15-25 51

Singles: 7-inch

BRUNSWICK (84025 "Jealous Blues") 30-50 53
PEACOCK (1595 "Money Ain't Everything")..40-60 51
PEACOCK (1620 "Disgusted Blues") 40-60 51

PARKER, Terrie, & Plushpups

Singles: 7-inch

QUEEN (24011 "A Dream in the Night")...10-15 61

PARKER, Tim

Singles: 7-inch

EMMONS (1005 "That's All Right Mama") 100-150

PARKER, Wayne / Dal-Tones

EPs: 7-inch

VELVET VOICE (58 "Ginger") 200-300
(We have yet to learn if the tracks on the other side are by the same artists, or others. May not have been issued with cover.)

PARKER, Willie
(With the Sensational Souls; Frankie Newsome)

Singles: 7-inch

B and B (7401 "Why Not Tonight") 10-15
M-PAC (7233 "I've Got to Fight It") 8-12 66
M-PAC (7235 "Salute to Lovers")..................8-12 67
M-PAC (7236 "You Got Your Finger in My Eye")..15-25 67
M-PAC (7237 "Town I Live In")......................8-12 67
Also see NEWSOME, Frankie

PARKER, Willis

Singles: 78 rpm

SITTIN' IN WITH (589 "733 Blues")..........15-25 51

PARKER, Winfield R&B '71
(With the Skydell Band)

Singles: 7-inch

ARCTIC (151 "Brand New Start")..................5-8 69
ATCO (6474 "Sweet Little Girl")....................5-10 67
GSP (6883 "Baby, Don't Get Hooked On Me")...4-6 72
RU-JAC (20 "Sweet Little Girl")..................10-15 67
RU-JAC (24 "Fallen Star")..........................10-15 68
SPRING (116 "S.O.S.") 4-6 71
SPRING (126 "Starvin'") 4-6 72

PARKER, Winnie

Singles: 7-inch

RUBY (350 "Down Boy Boogie") 50-75 57
(At least one source shows this artist as Wanda Parker. We don't know yet which is correct.)

PARKETTES

Singles: 7-inch

LUDIX (105 "El Matador") 10-15 63

PARKINS, Barbara

Singles: 7-inch

BARONET (15 "Tiny Little Teardrop") 5-10 62

PARKS, Andy

LPs: 10/12-inch

CAPITOL (2799 "Sex, School...and Like Other Pressures")...15-20 67

PARKS, Gino
(With the Hi Fidelities; with Love-Tones; Gino Purifoy)

Singles: 7-inch

CRAZY HORSE (1303 "Nerves of Steel")..15-25 68
FORTUNE (528 "Last Night I Cried") 30-40 57
GOLDEN WORLD (32 "My Sophisticated Lady")..10-15 66
MIRACLE (3 "Don't Say Bye Bye").......200-400 60
TAMLA (54042 "That's No Lie")................25-50 61
TAMLA (54066 "For This I Thank You")...25-50 62
Also see HI-FIDELITIES
Also see PURIFOY, Gino
Also see WILLIAMS, Andre, & Gino Parks

PARKS, Ray

Singles: 78 rpm

CAPITOL...40-60 57

Singles: 7-inch

CAPITOL (3580 "You're Gonna Have to Bawl")..50-75 57
DIADON (60 "Rock Around the Barn").....30-40 58

PARKS, Russ

Singles: 7-inch

LEE (003 "Jealous-Hearted Me")...........75-125

PARKS, Sonny

Singles: 7-inch

ANOTHER FEATURE PRESENTATION (103 "Raindrops on a River") ....10-20 '60s
W.B. (5358 "New Boy in Town") 5-10 63

PARKS, Van Dyke

Singles: 7-inch

MGM (13441 "Number One")...................10-20 65
MGM (13570 "Come to the Sunshine") 5-10 66
W.B. (1727 "Song Cycle")...........................5-8 68
W.B. (2589 "Discover America")..................4-6 72
W.B. (2878 "Clang of Yankee Reaper") 4-6 75

LPs: 10/12-inch

W.B. 10-20 67-75
Also see BEAU BRUMMELS
Also see BYRDS
Also see COLLINS, Judy
Also see COODER, Ry
Also see RAITT, Bonnie
Also see STARR, Ringo

PARKTOWNS

Singles: 7-inch

CRIMSON (1006 " You Hurt Me Inside")..50-75 64
IMPALA (214 "You Hurt Me Inside").....100-150 63
(First issue.)
THOR (3258 "You Hurt Me Inside").......75-125 63

PARLAMENTS

Singles: 7-inch

USA (719 "My Only Love")....................75-125 61

PARLAY BROTHERS
(With the Avantis)

Singles: 7-inch

VALJAY (2725 "My Girl") 20-30 65

PARLETTES

Singles: 7-inch

JUBILEE (5467 "Tonight I Met an Angel")..10-15 64

PARLEYS

Singles: 7-inch

COUNSEL (4901 "Big Ben")....................10-20 64

PARLIAMENT R&B '71
(Parliament Thang)

Singles: 12-inch

CASABLANCA...5-10 78

Singles: 7-inch

CASABLANCA..3-6 74-81
INVICTUS 5-10 70-72
SOULTOWN 4-6

Picture Sleeves

CASABLANCA (950 "Aqua Boogie")...........4-6 79

LPs: 10/12-inch

CASABLANCA (Except NBPIX-7125).......8-12 74-80
CASABLANCA (NBPIX-7125 "Motor Booty Affair")..10-15 79
(Picture disc.)
INVICTUS (7302 "Osmium")....................50-75 70
Members: George Clinton; Raymond Davis; Calvin Simon; Clarence Haskins; Pedro Bell; Grady Thomas; Glen Collins; Mahalia Franklin; Shirley Hayden; Debbie Wright; Lynn Marby; William "Bootsy" Collins; Dawn Silva; Ron Banks; Larry Demps; Junie Morrison; Donny Sterling; Fred Wesley; Gary Shider; Eddie Hazell; Michael Brecker; Randy Brecker; Peter Chase; Jerome Bailey; Tiki Fulwood; Grady Thomas; Michael Hampton; Willie Nelson; Maceo Parker; Gary Cooper; Cordell Mosson.
Also see MACEO & MACKS
Also see PARLIAMENTS
Also see PARLET

PARLIAMENTS

Singles: 7-inch

FLIPP (100 "Lonely Island").......................40-60 60
(Yellow label. First issue.)
FLIPP (100 "Lonely Island")....................75-100 60
(Red label. Slightly longer version.)
LEN (101 "Don't Need You Anymore")...75-125 58
SYMBOL (917 "I'll Get You Yet").............15-20 62

PARLIAMENTS P&R/R&B '67

Singles: 7-inch

APT (25036 "Party Boys")..........................15-25 59
ATCO (6675 "A New Day Begins")..............8-12 69
GOLDEN WORLD (46 "Heart Trouble")...25-50 66
REVILOT (207 "Testify") 10-20 66
REVILOT (211 "All Your Goodies Are Gone")...10-20 67
REVILOT (214 "The Goose")....................10-20 68
REVILOT (217 "Sentimental Lady") 10-20 68
(Same number may have been used twice. We have verified *What You Been Growing*, but have yet to verify *Sentimental Lady* as #217.)
REVILOT (217 "What You Been Growing")...10-20 68
REVILOT (223 "Good Old Music") 10-20 68
REVILOT (228 "A New Day Begins").......10-20 69
Members: George Clinton; Ray Davis; Calvin Simon; Clarence Haskins; Grady Thomas; Bernie Worrell; Bootsy Collins; Frank Waddy; Maceo Parker; Fred Wesley.
Also see FUNKADELIC
Also see PARLIAMENT

PARNELL, Guy, & Nite Beats
Singles: 7-inch
DOT (16323 "Dudy's Place") 8-10 62
VEE-JAY (480 "Easy") 8-10 62
Also see SUMMERS, Gene

PARR, Johnny
(With the Singing Strings)
Singles: 7-inch
I-NEZZ (002 "In a Dream") 30-40 61
LAWN (201 "I Know a Girl") 25-35 63
ROULETTE (4523 "Monkey See, Monkey Do") 5-10 63

PARRIS, Fred P&R '82
(With the Satins; with Five Satins; with "Scarlets Originally the Five Satins"; with Passionettes; with Black Satin; with Restless Hearts; Fred Paris)
Singles: 7-inch
ATCO (6439 "Land of Broken Hearts") 5-10 66
BIRTH 4-8
BUDDAH 4-6 75
CANDLELITE (411 "She's Gone") 5-10 63
(Black vinyl.)
CANDLELITE (411 "She's Gone") 8-12 63
(Red vinyl.)
CHECKER (1108 "No Use in Crying") 30-50 65
ELEKTRA (47411 "Memories of Days Gone By") 4-6 82
GREEN SEA 5-10 66
KLIK (7905 "She's Gone") 100-150 58
MAMA SADIE (1001 "In the Still of the Night") 5-10 67
RCA (9232 "It's Okay to Cry") 5-10 67
(A Freddie Paris also recorded for RCA at this time. Note slightly different spelling.)
LPs: 10/12-inch
BUDDAH 30-50 75
ELEKTRA 10-15 82
Also see FIVE SATINS
Also see PARIS, Freddie

PARRISH, Darrell, & Wildcats
Singles: 7-inch
WAYNE-WAY (119 "Rockin' Pneumonia") 10-20 63

PARRISH, Dean P&R '66
(Dean Parish; with Roy Glover Orch.)
Singles: 7-inch
BOOM (60012 "Tell Her") 10-20 66
LAURIE (3418 "I'm On My Way") 5-10 68
MUSICOR (1099 "I'm Over 18") 5-10 65

PARRISH, Gene, & Orchestra
Singles: 78 rpm
RCA (4240 "Dream Blues") 10-20 51
RPM (302 "Left Behind Blues") 30-50 50
RPM (307 "Street of Dreams") 30-50 50
Singles: 7-inch
RCA (4240 "Dream Blues") 25-35 51

PARRISH, Troy
Singles: 7-inch
BARONET (10 "Gloria") 30-40 62

PARRISH & WILDE
Singles: 7-inch
INVADER (407 "Don't Fight It") 15-25 65

PARRISH BROTHERS
LPs:10/12-inch
CUCA (5174 "The Variety Songs of the Parrish Brothers") 15-20 74

PARRISH TWINS
Singles: 7-inch
VISTONE (2016 "All Alone") 15-25 61
(Black vinyl.)
VISTONE (2016 "All Alone") 25-50 61
(Yellow vinyl.)

PARROTS
Singles: 78 rpm
CHECKER 100-200 53
Singles: 7-inch
CHECKER (772 "Please Don't Leave Me") 400-500 53

PARROTS
Singles: 7-inch
MALA (558 "They All Got Carried Away") 5-10 67

PARRY, Kent, & Rogues
Singles: 7-inch
ALTON (600 "Stop, Then Rock") 40-60 59

PARSON, Gene
(Gene Parson's Band)
Singles: 7-inch
SOUTHFIELD (4501 "Night Club Rock and Roll") 300-400 59
SOUTHFIELD (4502 "I Found Out What Love Can Do"/"Please Don't Wait Til Tomorrow") 10-20 59
SOUTHFIELD (4503 "Please Be Mine"/"Wreck of Ol' No. 9") 10-20 59
Members: Kimble Janes; Wanda Janes.

PARSONS, Al
Singles: 78 rpm
SARG (140 "Wait for Me Baby") 20-25 56
Singles: 7-inch
SARG (140 "Wait for Me Baby") 40-50 56

PARSONS, Alan, Project P&R/LP '76
(Alan Parsons)
Singles: 12-inch
ARISTA (Except 66 & 9348) .... 4-8 '80s
ARISTA (66 "Damned If I Do") 5-10 79
(Promotional issue only.)
ARISTA (9348 "Days Are Numbers") 4-8 85
(Promotional issue only.)
Singles: 7-inch
ARISTA 3-6 77-89
20TH FOX 4-6 76
Picture Sleeves
ARISTA 3-5 84-87
LPs: 10/12-inch
ARISTA (111 "No Gambler") 15-20 80
ARISTA (68 "Complete Audio Guide") 50-75 82
(Boxed, five-disc set.)
ARISTA (140 "Complete Audio Guide") 75-100 82
(Boxed, eight-disc set.)
ARISTA (4000 series) 5-10 78
(Black vinyl.)
ARISTA (4180 "Pyramid") 15-20 78
(Colored vinyl. Promotional issue only.)
ARISTA (7002 "I Robot") 5-10 77
ARISTA (8000 series, except 8263) 5-8 83-89
ARISTA (8263 "Vulture Culture") 5-8 85
ARISTA (PD-8263 "Vulture Culture") 30-40 85
(Picture disc. Promotional issue only.)
ARISTA (9000 series) 5-10 79-82
MERCURY (832 820 "Tales of Mystery and Imagination") 8-12 87
(Remastered limited edition with booklet.)
MFSL (084 "I Robot") 40-60 82
MFSL (UHQR 084 "I Robot") 100-125 82
(Boxed set.)
MFSL (175 "Best of the Alan Parsons Project") 30-40 85
MFSL (204 "Tales of Mystery and Imagination") 25-35 94
20TH FOX (508 "Tales of Mystery and Imagination") 15-25 76
(Includes 8-page booklet.)
20TH FOX (508 "Tales of Mystery and Imagination") 8-12 76
20TH FOX (539 "Tales of Mystery and Imagination") 5-10 77
Members: Alan Parsons; Eric Woolfson; David Paton; Stuart Tosh; Lenny Zakatek; B.J. Cole; Stuart Elliott; Ian Bairnson; Allan Clarke; Colin Blunstone; Andrew Powell; John Miles; Gary Brooker; Christopher Rainbow; Laurie Cottle; Duncan Mackay; Geoff Barradale; Richard Cottle; William Lyall.
Also see HOLLIES

PARSONS, Bill P&R '58
(Bobby Bare)
Singles: 7-inch
ABC 4-6 73
COLLECTABLES .... 3-5 '80s
FRATERNITY (835 "The All American Boy") 10-20 58
(Fraternity 838, by the real Bill Parsons – not Bobby Bare – is listed in the following section.)
Also see BARE, Bobby

PARSONS, Bill
Singles: 7-inch
FRATERNITY (838 "Educated Rock and Roll") 10-20 59
(Fraternity 835, credited to Bill Parsons [Bobby Bare], is listed in the preceding section.)
STARDAY (526 "Hot Rod Volkswagen") 25-35 60
STARDAY (544 "A-Waitin'") 40-60 61

PARSONS, Gram LP '74
(With the Fallen Angels)
Singles: 7-inch
REPRISE 4-6 73
SIERRA 3-5 79
EPs: 7-inch
SIERRA 8-10 82
(Promotional issue only.)
LPs: 10/12-inch
REPRISE 10-15 73
SHILOH 10-15 73
SIERRA 8-12 79-82
Also see BYRDS
Also see GUILBEAU & PARSONS
Also see HARRIS, Emmylou
Also see INTERNATIONAL SUBMARINE BAND

PARSONS, Jerry, & Blue Jeans
Singles: 7-inch
AMP (791 "Don't Need No Job") 200-300 59

PARTNERSHIP
Singles: 7-inch
CUB (9161 "Angels in the Dark") 5-10 68
MGM (13854 "Baby, If I Had You") 5-10 67
RCA (9226 "I Miss You Dixie") 10-20 67

PARTON, Dolly C&W '67
Singles: 12-inch
RCA (Black vinyl) 4-8 78-83
RCA (Colored vinyl) 10-20 78
Singles: 7-inch
COLUMBIA 3-5 90s
GOLDBAND (1086 "Puppy Love") 800-1000 59
MERCURY (71982 "It's Sure Gonna Hurt") 300-400 62
MONUMENT (869 thru 1047) 5-10 65-68
RCA (0132 thru 0950) 4-6 69-76
RCA (5000 series) 3-5 86
RCA (9500 thru 9900 series) 4-6 68-71
RCA (10031 thru 11240) 4-6 74-78
RCA (11296 "Heartbreaker") 5-10 78
(Label mistakenly reads: "From the *Sure Thing* album.")
RCA (11296 "Heartbreaker") 4-6 78
(Label reads: "From the *Heartbreaker* album.")
RCA (11420 thru 14297) 3-6 78-86
RCA GOLD STANDARD 3-5 80
Promotional Singles
RCA (Colored vinyl) 4-8 77-85
Picture Sleeves
RCA 3-8 69-85
LPs: 10/12-inch
ALSHIRE 8-12 69-71
CAMDEN 5-10 72-78
COLUMBIA 5-8 87
MONUMENT (7600 series) 5-10 78
MONUMENT (8085 "Hello, I'm Dolly") 15-20 67
MONUMENT (18000 series) 12-20 67
MONUMENT (18100 series) 8-15 70
MONUMENT (31000 series) 8-15 72
MONUMENT (33000 series) 8-10 75
RCA (812 "HBO Presents") 15-20 83
(Picture disc. Promotional issue only.)
RCA (0033 thru 5000 series) 5-12 73-87
(With "AFL1," "AHL1," "APD1," "APL1," or "AYL1" prefix.)
RCA (2314 "Personal Music Dialogue") 10-20 77
(Interview. Promotional issue only.)
RCA (CPL1-3413 "Great Balls of Fire") 15-20 79
(Picture disc. Promotional issue only.)
RCA (LPM-3949 "Just Because I'm a Woman") 15-25 68
(Monaural.)
RCA (LSP-3949 "Just Because I'm a Woman") 15-20 68
(Stereo.)
RCA (LSP-4188 "My Blue Ridge Mountain Boy") 15-20 69
RCA (LSP-4099 "In the Good Old Days") 15-20 69
RCA (LSP-4288 "Fairest of Them All") 10-20 70
RCA (LSP-4387 "A Real Live Dolly") 20-30 70
RCA (LSP-4398 "Golden Streets of Glory") 30-50 71
RCA (4422 "Greatest Hits") 25-50 82
(Without *Islands in the Stream*)
RCA (4422 "Greatest Hits") 5-8 82
(With *Islands in the Stream.*)
RCA (LSP-4449 "Best of Dolly Parton") 10-20 70
RCA (LSP-4507 "Joshua") 10-20 71
RCA (LSP-4603 "Coat of Many Colors") 10-20 71
RCA (LSP-4686 "Touch Your Woman") 10-20 72
RCA (LSP-4752 "Dolly Parton Sings [Porter Wagoner]") 10-20 72
RCA ("HBO Presents Dolly") 15-25 83
(Picture disc. Promotional issue only.)
SOMERSET 10-20 63-68
STEREO-FIDELITY 10-20 63-68
TIME-LIFE 5-8 81
Session: Jordanaires; Ricky Skaggs; Porter Wagoner.
Also see HARRIS, Emmylou
Also see JORDANAIRES
Also see KRISTOFFERSON, Kris, Willie Nelson, Dolly Parton, & Brenda Lee
Also see PHILLIPS, Bill
Also see ROGERS, Kenny, & Dolly Parton
Also see WAGONER, Porter, & Dolly Parton

PARTON, Dolly / George Jones
LPs: 10/12-inch
STARDAY (429 "Dolly Parton and George Jones") 30-40 68
Also see JONES, George

PARTON, Dolly, & Willie Nelson C&W '82
Singles: 7-inch
MONUMENT (3408 "Everything's Beautiful") 3-5 82
Also see NELSON, Willie

PARTON, Dolly, Linda Ronstadt, & Emmylou Harris LP '87
Singles: 7-inch
W.B. (27970 "Wildflowers") 3-5 88
W.B. (28248 "Those Memories of You") 3-5 87
W.B. (28302 "Someday My Ship Will Sail") 3-5 87
W.B. (28371 "Telling Me Lies") 3-5 87
W.B. (28492 "To Know Him Is to Love Him") 3-5 87
Picture Sleeves
W.B. (28248 "Those Memories of You") 3-5 87
W.B. (28492 "To Know Him Is to Love Him") 3-5 87
LPs: 10/12-inch
W.B. (25491 "Trio") 5-8 87
Also see HARRIS, Emmylou
Also see RONSTADT, Linda
Also see PARTON, Dolly

PARTRIDGE FAMILY P&R/LP '70
("Starring Shirley Jones," "Featuring David Cassidy")
Singles: 7-inch
ARISTA/COLLECTIBLES .... 3-5 '80s
BELL 4-8 70-73
FLASHBACK .... 4-6 '70s
Picture Sleeves
BELL (910 "I Think I Love You") 5-10 70
BELL (963 "Doesn't Somebody Want to Be Wanted") 5-10 70
LPs: 10/12-inch
BELL (1107 "Their Greatest Hits") 15-25 72
BELL (1111 "Notebook") 15-25 72
BELL (1122 "Crossword Puzzle") 15-25 73
BELL (1137 "Bulletin Board") 15-25 73
BELL (1319 "The World of the Partridge Family") 15-25 74
BELL (6050 "The Partridge Family Album") 20-30 70
(With bonus photo.)
BELL (6050 "The Partridge Family Album") 10-20 70
(Without bonus photo.)
BELL (6059 "Up to Date") 20-30 71
(With booklet cover.)
BELL (6059 "Up to Date") 10-20 71
(Standard cover.)
BELL (6064 "The Partridge Family Sound Magazine") 15-25 71
BELL (6066 "Christmas Card") 15-25 71
BELL (6072 "The Partridge Family Shopping Bag") 20-30 72
(With shopping bag.)
BELL (6072 "The Partridge Family Shopping Bag") 10-20 72
(Without shopping bag.)
Also see CASSIDY, David

PASH, Richard, & Back Door Society
Singles: 7-inch
SHOREMEN (1900 "I'm the Kind") 15-25 67

PASQUALE, Jessie
Singles: 7-inch
COMBO (148 "Pepperoni") 15-25 58

PASQUALE & LUNARTIKS
Singles: 7-inch
DINO (229 "La Pizza with Sazziza") 8-12
Member: Jessie Pasquale.
Also see PASQUALE, Jessie

PASSENGERS
Singles: 7-inch
MALA (454 "Round Table") 10-15 62
MUSE (001 "Sand in Your Eye") 15-25 60
Members: Johnny Seastrand; Johnny Fisco; Jerry Greenberg; Charles Williams; Howie Liebewicz; Larry Mendelson; Al Flamer.
Also see ACADEMICS

PASSERALLO, Dave, & 4 Escorts
Singles: 7-inch
BI-MI (102 "By the Fire") 100-200 61

PASSIONETTES
Singles: 7-inch
PATH (101 "My Plea") .... 15-25 '60s

PASSIONS *P&R '59*
Singles: 7-inch
ABC-PAR (10436 "The Empty Seat") 10-20 63
AUDICON (102 "Just to Be with You") 30-40 59
AUDICON (105 "I Only Want You") 15-25 60
AUDICON (106 "Gloria") 15-25 60
AUDICON (108 "Beautiful Dreamer") 30-40 60
AUDICON (112 "Made for Lovers") 40-50 61
COLLECTABLES .... 3-5 '80s
CRYSTAL BALL (157 "Brooklyn") 3-5 90
(500 made.)
DIAMOND (146 "16 Candles") 10-20 63
(Black vinyl.)
DIAMOND (146 "16 Candles") 30-40 63
(Brown vinyl.)
DORE (505 "Tango of Love") 10-20 58
JASON SCOTT (09 "Aphrodite") 3-5 81
(500 made.)
JUBILEE (5406 "Lonely Road") 20-30 61
(One-sided release.)
JUBILEE (5406 "Lonely Road") 10-20 61
OCTAVIA (8005 "Aphrodite") 400-600 62
LPs: 10/12-inch
CLIFTON 5-10
CRYSTAL BALL (138 "Legendary Hits") . 10-15 91
(Black vinyl. 1000 made.)
Members: Jim Gallagher; Tony Armato; Al Galione; Vince Acerno; Louis Rotondo.
Also see ALADDIN, Johnny
Also see HART, Rocky
Also see MYSTICS / Passions
Also see RESOLUTIONS
Also see SABER, Johnny, & Passions

PASSIONS
Singles: 7-inch
CAPITOL (3963 "Jackie Brown") 15-20 58
ERA (1063 "Jackie Brown") 15-20 57

PASSIONS
Singles: 7-inch
PIC 1 (117 "Lively One") 20-30 65

PASSIONS
Singles: 7-inch
FANTASTIC (79 "The Reason Why I Love You") 10-15 65
UNIQUE (79 "The Reason Why I Love You") 15-25 65
(First issue.)

PASSIONS
Singles: 7-inch
ELVITRUE (27916 "You Better Make a Move") 15-25

PASTEL SIX *P&R '62*
Singles: 7-inch
CHATTAHOOCHEE (696 "I Can't Dance") 8-12 66
DOWNEY (101 "Twitchin'"/"Wino Stomp") 10-20 62
DOWNEY (101 "Twitchin' "/"Open House at the Cinder") 10-20 62
DOWNEY (102 "Brahm's Nightmare") 10-20 62
ERA 4-6 72
ZEN (102 "Cinnamon Cinder") 5-10 62
ZEN (105 "A Sing-Along Song") 10-20 63
ZEN (108 "The Milkshake") 10-20 63
ZEN (111 "Miss Sue") 10-20 63
LPs: 10/12-inch
ZEN (1001 "Cinnamon Cinder") 50-100 62
Member: Sonny Patterson.
Also see INVICTAS
Also see PATTERSON, Sonny, & Invictas

PASTELS
("Fred Buckley, Vocalist")
Singles: 78 rpm
UNITED (196 "If You Put Your Arms Around Me") 75-100 55
UNITED (196 "Put Your Arms Around Me") 25-50 55
Singles: 7-inch
UNITED (196 "If You Put Your Arms Around Me") 150-250 55
UNITED (196 "Put Your Arms Around Me") 50-100 55
Member: Fred Buckley.

PASTELS *P&R/R&B '58*
Singles: 78 rpm
ARGO (5287 "Been So Long") 40-50 58
Singles: 7-inch
ARGO (5287 "Been So Long") 20-30 58
ARGO (5297 "You Don't Love Me Anymore") 10-15 58
ARGO (5314 "So Far Away") 10-15 58
CADET .... 4-6 '70s
CHESS 4-6 73
MASCOT (123 "Been So Long") 200-300 57
OWL (332 "Oh Me, Oh My") 4-6 74
Members: Big Dee Irwin; Richard Travis; Tony Thomas; J.B. Wellington.
Also see ERVIN, Dee
Also see IRWIN, Big Dee
Also see REED, Lula

PASTELS
Singles: 7-inch
LIMELIGHT (3007 "King of Fools") 10-15 63

PASTELS
Singles: 7-inch
ARK .... 8-12 '60s
PASTEL (506 "Sleep Tight") 10-15 64
PUSH (110 "Weird Sounds") .... 15-25 '60s

PASTELS
Singles: 7-inch
PHALANX (1006 "Cause I Love You") 10-20 66

PASTELS
Singles: 7-inch
CENTURY (22103 "Why Don't You Love Me") 10-20 65
CENTURY (23507 "Mirage") 15-25 66

PASTRAMI MALTED
Singles: 7-inch
METROMEDIA (101 "Wiwwian Wevy") 15-25 69

PAT & DEE
Singles: 7-inch
DIXIE (2006 "Gee Whiz") 50-100 58

PAT & ROYAL LANCERS
Singles: 7-inch
TUFF ("A Fool") 30-40
(No selection number used.)

PAT & SATELLITES *P&R '59*
Singles: 7-inch
ATCO (6131 "Jupiter-C") 10-20 59
Members: Pat Otts; King Curtis; Wayne Lips.
Also see KING CURTIS

PAT & WILDCATS
Singles: 7-inch
CRUSADER (100 "The Giggler") 8-12 64
Member: Pat Vegas
Also see VEGAS, Pat

PAT THE CAT & HIS KITTENS featuring VIC FONTAINE
Singles: 78 rpm
BSD (1009 "Little Rock Special") 50-100 52
BULLSEYE (106 "Jesse James") 30-50 56
Singles: 7-inch
BSD (1009 "Little Rock Special") 150-250 52
BULLSEYE (106 "Jesse James") 60-80 56
Also see FONTAINE, Vic

PATACHEK, John
Singles: 7-inch
PAGE (4101 "Bartender") .... 10-15 '70s

PATCH, Billy, & Pirates
Singles: 7-inch
JOY (244 "Splittin' ") 10-20 60

PATE, Gus, & Jokers
Singles: 7-inch
SUMMIT (111 "Man Alive") 150-250 59

PATE, Johnny *P&R/R&B '58*
(Johnny Pate Trio: Johnnie Pate)
Singles: 78 rpm
FEDERAL 5-10 57
GIG 5-10 56
Singles: 7-inch
ARGO (5468 "Bluesette") 5-10 64
DRAKE 8-12 61
FEDERAL 10-20 57-59
GIG 15-25 56
LPs: 10/12-inch
GIG 40-50 56
KING (561 "Jazz Goes Ivy League") 30-50 58
(Monaural.)
KING (KSD-561 "Jazz Goes Ivy League") 50-75 59
(Stereo.)
KING (584 "Swingin' Flute") 30-50 58
KING (611 "A Date with Johnny Pate") 30-50 58
SALEM 25-35 58
STEPHENY (4002 "Johnny Pate at the Blue Note") 45-55 57
Also see CANDLES
Also see DAYLIGHTERS
Also see UNIQUES

PATE, Ray
Singles: 7-inch
GULFSTREAM (6654 "My Shadow") ... 200-300

PATENTS
Singles: 7-inch
HART-VAN (0127 "Blue Surf") 15-25 63

PATERNO, Pat
Singles: 7-inch
YALE (233 "Girl in Her Teens") 10-15 60

PATEY BROTHERS
Singles: 7-inch
RON-MAR (1004 "Jeanie") 50-75 59

PATIENCE & PRUDENCE *P&R '56*
(Patience & Prudence / Prudence)
Singles: 78 rpm
LIBERTY 15-25 56-57
Singles: 7-inch
CHATTAHOOCHEE (659 "Apples on the Lilac Tree") 5-8 64
CHATTAHOOCHEE (665 "How Can I Tell Him") 5-8 65
LIBERTY (55022 "Tonight You Belong to Me") 15-25 56
LIBERTY (55040 "Gonna Get Along Without Ya Now") 15-25 56
LIBERTY (55058 "We Can't Sing Rhythm and Blues") 10-20 57
LIBERTY (55084 "You Tattletale") 10-20 57
LIBERTY (55107 "Over Here") 10-20 57
LIBERTY (55125 "Heavenly Angel") 10-20 58
LIBERTY (55154 "All I Do Is Dream of You") 10-20 58
LIBERTY (55169 "Golly Oh Gee") 10-20 58
U.A. .... 4-6 '70s
Picture Sleeves
LIBERTY (55084 "You Tattletale") 30-40 57
Members: Patience McIntyre; Prudence McIntyre.
Also see CLIFFORD, Mike, with Patience & Prudence

PATRICK
Singles: 7-inch
RSVP (1117 "Five Different Girls") 5-10 65
RSVP (1119 "Don't Let This Room Become Your World") 5-10 66
RSVP (1122 "We Gotta Stick It Out") 5-10 66
Picture Sleeves
RSVP (1119 "Don't Let This Room Become Your World") 8-12 66

PATRICK, Gladys
(With the Charioteers; Gladys "Glad Rag" Patrick)
Singles: 78 rpm
MGM (55015 "Somebody Please") 20-30 56
Singles: 7-inch
ATLANTIC 5-10 69
CENTRAL .... 5-10 '60s
MGM (55010 "The Blues") 30-40 55
MGM (55015 "Somebody Please") 40-50 56
O-GEE (100 "A Letter to You") 40-50 59
O-GEE (102 "Balmy Breezes") 10-15 59
O-GEE (430 "Willow Weep for Me") 10-15 59
Also see CHARIOTEERS

PATRICK, Jimmy
Singles: 7-inch
RENAUD (540315 "$20 Dollar Bill") 200-300

PATRICK, Ken
Singles: 7-inch
SUMMIT ("Night Train") 100-150
(Selection number not known.)

PATRICK, Kirk
Singles: 7-inch
FABOR (150 "Fall in Love") 5-10 66

PATRICK, Milt
Singles: 7-inch
CAPITOL (4634 "When I Met You") 5-10 61
DEMON (1518 "Fountain of Love") 10-15 59
EVEREST (2014 "I Don't Think I Wanna Do It") 5-10 63
TERRI ANN (101 "Merry Christmas") 5-10 62

PATRICK, Sandra, & Montereys
Singles: 7-inch
DOMINION (1008 "I Want Your Love") .. 50-100 58
Also see MONTEREYS

PATRICK, Sue
Singles: 7-inch
PROCESS (139 "You Found a New Love") 50-75

PATRIDGE, Prince
(With the Monroe Tucker Orchestra)
Singles: 78 rpm
BLAZE (104 "Cooperation") 25-35 54
CREST 20-30 55-56
Singles: 7-inch
CAT (105 "Cooperation") 25-35 54
CREST (1006 "How Come My Dog Don't Bark When You Come Round") 25-35 55
CREST (1009 "Hen Party") 15-20 55
CREST (1022 "Mabel Was") 15-20 56
CREST (1114 "How Come My Dog Don't Bark") 10-15 62

PATRIOTS
Singles: 7-inch
CHART (1315 "I'm No Communist") 4-8 66
LOOK (5005 "Close Your Eyes") 5-10 67
MAINSTREAM (631 "I'll Be There") 10-20 65
MURBO (1025 "What a Drag It Is") 10-15 68
WHITE CLIFFS (238 "Eagle Feathers") ... 10-15 67

PATT, Gerry, & His Pals
Singles: 7-inch
ASCOT (2189 "Dancing By Myself") 5-10 65
ASCOT (2212 "Someone") 5-10 66

PATTERNS
Singles: 7-inch
ABC-PAR (10284 "It's So Nice") 5-10 61
CHATTAHOOCHEE (662 "Late Show") 5-10 65
CREST (603 "Blue Lawdy Blue") 75-125

PATTERSON, Bobby *R&B '69*
(With the Mustangs)
Singles: 7-inch
ABNAK (112 "Till You Give In") 8-12 65
ABNAK (117 "You've Just Got to Understand") 8-12 66
ALL PLATINUM 4-6 77
GRANITE 4-6 76
JETSTAR (Black vinyl) 5-10 66-70
JETSTAR (109 "Let Them Talk") 10-20 67
(Colored vinyl. Promotional issue only.)
JETSTAR (111 "Funky No More") 10-20 68
(Colored vinyl. Promotional issue only.)
JETSTAR (113 "Sweet Taste of Love") 10-20 69
(Colored vinyl. Promotional issue only.)
PAULA 6-12 71-73
PROUD 5-10

Also see MUSTANGS

PATTERSON, Earl, & Darts

Singles: 7-inch

MOON (305 "Nightmare Hop") ... 50-75 59

PATTERSON, Mike

(Mike Patterson & Fugitives)

Singles: 7-inch

IMPERIAL (66083 "Jerry") ... 5-10 65
IMPERIAL (66118 "Don't You Just Know It") ... 5-10 65
Also see RHYTHM ROCKERS
Also see 6680 LEXINGTON

PATTERSON, Pat

Singles: 78 rpm

STARDAY (142 "Mr. Hillbilly") ... 10-15 54

Singles: 7-inch

STARDAY (142 "Mr. Hillbilly") ... 25-50 54

PATTERSON, Sonny, & Invictas

Singles: 7-inch

VAULT (101 "Gone So Long") ... 10-20 62
(Reissue of Jack Bee 1003, a '59 release credited to the Invictas. Also on Vault 903, a '63 issue.)
Also see INVICTAS
Also see PASTEL SIX

PATTERSON, Ted

Singles: 7-inch

KLUB (3112 "I Love My Baby") ... 50-75

PATTERSON SINGERS

Singles: 78 rpm

KING ... 10-20 54

Singles: 7-inch

KING (4693 "All Day and All Night") ... 20-40 54
KING (4705 "He Answered My Prayer") .. 20-40 54

PATTI & MARGIE

Singles: 7-inch

ROULETTE (4111 "Sentimental Journey") .8-12 58

PATTI & MICKEY

Singles: 7-inch

IMPACT (1027 "My Guy"/"My Girl") ... 10-20 67
Members: Patti Jerome; Mickey Denton.
Also see DENTON, Mickey
Also see JEROME, Patti

PATTI & XLs

Singles: 7-inch

DOT (16849 "Cross My Heart") ... 5-10 66
DOT (16942 "You've Got a Hold On Me") ..5-10 66

PATTI ANNE

Singles: 78 rpm

ALADDIN (3198 "Sorrowful Heart") ... 75-125 53
ALADDIN (3280 "Shtiggy Boom") ... 15-25 55

Singles: 7-inch

ALADDIN (3198 "Sorrowful Heart") ... 200-300 53
ALADDIN (3280 "Shtiggy Boom") ... 50-75 55

PATTI ANNE & FLAMES

Singles: 78 rpm

ALADDIN (3162 "Midnight") ... 40-60 53

Singles: 7-inch

ALADDIN (3162 "Midnight") ... 100-150 53
Member: Patti Anne Mesner.
Also see PATTI ANNE
Also see FLAMES

PATTON, Alexander

(Alexander Patten)

Singles: 7-inch

CAPITOL (5677 "No More Dreams") ... 15-25 66
DUO DISC (113 "Make the Best of What You've Got") ... 5-10 65

PATTON, Big John

Singles: 7-inch

BLUE NOTE (1888 "Silver Meter") ... 10-20 63
BLUE NOTE (1889 "I'll Never Be Free") .. 10-20 63

PATTON, Charlie

Singles: 78 rpm

PARAMOUNT (12792 "Banty Rooster Blues") ... 250-500 '20s
PARAMOUNT (12854 "It Won't Be Long") ... 250-500 '20s
PARAMOUNT (12869 "Spoonful Blues") ... 250-500 '20s
PARAMOUNT (12877 "Pea Vine Blues") ... 250-500 '20s
PARAMOUNT (12883 "Lord I'm Discouraged") ... 250-500 '20s
PARAMOUNT (12909 "High Water Everywhere") ... 250-500 '20s
PARAMOUNT (12924 "Rattlesnake Blues") ... 250-500 '20s
PARAMOUNT (12943 "Magnolia Blues") ... 250-500 '20s
PARAMOUNT (12953 "Mean Black Moan") ... 250-500 '20s
PARAMOUNT (12972 "Green River Blues") ... 250-500 '20s
PARAMOUNT (12986 "I Shall Not Be Moved") ... 250-500 '20s
PARAMOUNT (12998 "Hammer Blues") ... 250-500 '20s
PARAMOUNT (13014 "Moon Going Down") ... 250-500 '20s
PARAMOUNT (13031 "Some Happy Day") ... 250-500 '20s
PARAMOUNT (13040 "The Devil Sent the Rain") ... 250-500 '20s
PARAMOUNT (13070 "Dry Well Blues") ... 250-500 '20s
PARAMOUNT (13080 "Some Summer Day") ... 250-500 '20s
PARAMOUNT (13110 "Frankie and Albert") ... 250-500 '20s
PARAMOUNT (13133 "Joe Kirby") ... 250-500 '20s
VOCALION (02651 "Poor Me") ... 200-400 '30s
VOCALION (02680 "High Sheriff Blues") ... 200-400 '30s
VOCALION (02782 "Love My Stuff") ... 200-400 '30s
VOCALION (02931 "Revenue Man Blues") ... 200-400 '30s

LP: 10/12-inch

YAZOO ... 15-25
Also see MASKED MARVEL

PATTON, Freddie

Singles: 7-inch

CUCA (1147 "Have Mercy") ... 15-25 63

PATTON, Jimmy

Singles: 78 rpm

SIMS ... 10-20 55

Singles: 7-inch

HILLIGAN (001 "Okie's in the Pokie") ... 300-500 60
(First issue.)
SAGE (261 "Yea, I'm Movin'") ... 75-125 58
(At least one source shows this number as 241. We don't know yet which is correct.)
SAGE (282 "Ocean Full of Tears") ... 25-35 59
SIMS (103 "Guilty") ... 20-30 55
(With Ann Jones.)
SIMS (104 "Teenage Heart") ... 20-30 55
SIMS (105 "Ocean of Tears") ... 20-30 55
SIMS (117 "Okie's in the Pokie") ... 150-250 60
SIMS (227 "Blue Darling") ... 5-10 65
SIMS (256 "Can't Shake the Blues") ... 5-10 65

LPs: 10/12-inch

MOON (101 "Make Room for the Blues") .25-30
SIMS (127 "Blue Darlin'") ... 30-40 65
SOURDOUGH (127 "Blue Darlin'") ... 35-50 65

PATTY & EMBLEMS *P&R/R&B '64*

(Patti & Emblems)

Singles: 7-inch

COLLECTABLES ... 3-5 '80s
CONGRESS (263 "Easy Come, Easy Go") ... 5-10 66
HERALD (590 "Mixed-Up, Shook-Up Girl") ... 10-20 64
HERALD (593 "You Took Advantage of a Good Thing") ... 10-15 64
HERALD (595 "And We Danced") ... 10-15 64
KAPP ... 10-20 66-68
LOST NITE ... 3-5
SPHERE SOUND ... 10-20 64

PATTY & PETER

Singles: 7-inch

COLUMBIA (41924 "Goody Goody") ... 5-10 61
SANDS (2761 "Can't Get a Date") ... 5-10 62

PATTY ANNE

Singles: 78 rpm

ALADDIN ... 10-20 53

Singles: 7-inch

ALADDIN (3162 "My Heart Is Free Again") ... 25-35 53

PATTY CAKES

Singles: 7-inch

TUFF (378 "I Understand Them") ... 8-12 64

PATTY FLABBIE'S COUGHED ENGINE

Singles: 7-inch

DIAMOND (252 "Billy's Got a Goat") ... 10-20 68

PAUL

(Ray Hildebrand)

Singles: 7-inch

CHARAY (48 "Happy Music") ... 8-12 66
(First issue.)
DOT (16936 "Happy Music") ... 5-8 66
LE CAM ... 5-10 '60s
PHILIPS (40174 "It's All Over, Paula") ... 5-10 64
TOWER (304 "Paper Clown") ... 5-8 67
Also see PAUL & PAULA

PAUL / Paul & Paula

Singles: 7-inch

JOSIE (935 "Happiness Across the Street"/"Last One") ... 5-10 65
Also see PAUL
Also see PAUL & PAULA

PAUL / Ron-Dels

Singles: 7-inch

CHARAY (94 "Lollipops and Teardrops") ... 5-10 69
Also see PAUL
Also see RON-DELS

PAUL, Billy *LP '70*

Singles: 12-inch

PHILA. INT'L ... 4-8 79

Singles: 7-inch

FINCH (1005 "I'm Always a Brother") ... 8-12 60
GAMBLE (232 "Somewhere") ... 5-10 69
JUBILEE (5081 "That's Why I Dream") ... 10-20 52
JUBILEE (5086 "You Didn't Know") ... 10-20 52
NEPTUNE (30 "Let's Fall in Love All Over") 4-6 70
PHILA. INT'L ... 4-8 71-81
TOTAL EXPERIENCE (2419 "Lately") ... 3-5 85

LPs: 10/12-inch

GAMBLE (5002 "Feelin' Good at the Cadillac Club") ... 10-20 67
NEPTUNE ... 10-15 70
PHILA. INT'L ... 5-10 71-80

PAUL, Buddy *C&W '60*

Singles: 7-inch

MURCO (1018 "This Old Town") ... 15-25 60

PAUL, Bunny *P&R '53*

("With Billy May's Music;" "with Marty Manning's Music")

Singles: 78 rpm

CAPITOL ... 8-12 55
DOT ... 8-12 53
DYNAMIC ... 10-20 49
ESSEX ... 10-15 54-55
POINT ... 10-20 56

Singles: 7-inch

BRUNSWICK (55022 "Beedle-Lump-Bump") ... 10-15 57
CAPITOL (3074 "Please Have Mercy") ... 10-20 55
CAPITOL (3109 "Leave My Heart Alone") ... 10-20 55
CAPITOL (3178 "Song of the Dreamer") .. 10-20 55
CAPITOL (3224 "Take a Chance") ... 10-20 55
CAPITOL (3288 "Open the Door") ... 10-20 55
DOT (15107 "Magic Guitar") ... 10-20 53
ESSEX (344 "New Love") ... 25-50 54
ESSEX (371 "You Are Always in My Heart") ... 20-30 54
ESSEX (385 "Brown Jug") ... 15-25 55
GORDY (7017 "I'm Hooked") ... 15-25 63
POINT (5 "Sweet Talk") ... 25-50 56
ROULETTE (4101 "Love Birds") ... 8-12 58
ROULETTE (4186 "Such a Night") ... 8-12 59

PAUL, Bunny, & Harptones

(Bunny Paul)

Singles: 78 rpm

ESSEX (352 "Such a Night") ... 20-30 54
ESSEX (359 "Lovey Dovey") ... 20-30 54
ESSEX (364 "I'll Never Tell") ... 30-50 54

Singles: 7-inch

ESSEX (352 "Such a Night") ... 50-100 54
ESSEX (359 "Lovey Dovey") ... 50-100 54
ESSEX (364 "I'll Never Tell") ... 100-200 54
Also see HALEY, Bill
Also see HARPTONES
Also see PAUL, Bunny

PAUL, Clarence

(With the Members; Clarence Pauling)

Singles: 7-inch

FEDERAL (12402 "Baby Don't You Leave Poor Me") ... 20-40 61
HANOVER (4519 "I Need Your Lovin' ") .. 10-20 59
LONDON (218 "I'm in Love Again") ... 4-6 75
PRIDE (3 "Operation Breadbasket") ... 10-20 60
ROULETTE (4196 "Falling in Love Again") ... 20-30 59
Also see FIVE ROYALES
Also see WONDER, Stevie, & Clarence Paul

PAUL, Darlene

Singles: 7-inch

CAPITOL (5119 "Little Bit of Heaven") ... 5-10 64
CAPITOL (5200 "All Cried Out") ... 5-10 64
KAPP (422 "Say It Isn't So") ... 5-10 61
LUTE (5907 "You're Just You") ... 5-10 60

PAUL, Dennis

(With Wes Dakus' Rebels)

Singles: 7-inch

KAPP (815 "Peggy Sue") ... 5-10 67
Also see DAKUS, Wes

PAUL, Jerry

Singles: 7-inch

GREAT (103 "Sparkling Blue") ... 30-40 59
HOLIDAY (1001 "Step Out") ... 40-60 60

PAUL, John, & Liberators

Singles: 7-inch

CUCA (66104 "Midnite Hour") ... 10-20 66
NIGHT OWL (6732 "Around & Around") .. 10-20 67

PAUL, Johnnie, Combo

Singles: 7-inch

EBONY (1075 "My Rock and Roll Man") .. 10-20 63

PAUL, Joyce *C&W '68*

Singles: 7-inch

DOT (16246 "Cold Cold Heart") ... 5-10 61
G&G ("I Love My Baby") ... 100-200
(Red vinyl.)
IMPERIAL (66024 "Lasting Love") ... 5-10 64
IMPERIAL (66050 "Walk Away") ... 5-10 64
U.A. ... 5-10 65-68

LPs: 10/12-inch

U.A. (6684 "Heartaches, Laughter and Tears") ... 10-15 69

PAUL, Larry

Singles: 7-inch

MALA (411 "You're So Far Away") ... 10-20 59
MALA (450 "Makings of a Man") ... 10-20 62

PAUL, Les *P&R '45*

(Les Paul Trio)

Singles: 78 rpm

CAPITOL ... 5-10 50-53
DECCA ... 5-10 54

Singles: 7-inch

CAPITOL ... 5-15 50-53
DECCA ... 5-15 54
LONDON (120 "Los Angeles") ... 4-6 68

EPs: 7-inch

DECCA ... 10-20 50-53

LPs: 10/12-inch

CAPITOL (200 series) ... 5-10 77
CAPITOL (16000 series) ... 5-8
DECCA (5018 "Hawaiian Paradise") ... 50-100 49
(10-inch LP.)
DECCA (5376 "Galloping Guitars") ... 50-75 52
(10-inch LP.)
DECCA (8589 "More of Les") ... 30-50 57
GLENDALE ... 5-8 78
LONDON ... 6-12 71-79
TOPS (1602 "Les Paul Trio") ... 20-25 57
VOCALION (3849 "Guitar Artistry of Les Paul") ... 6-12 68
Also see ANDREWS SISTERS & LES PAUL
Also see ATKINS, Chet, & Les Paul
Also see CROSBY, Bing

PAUL, Les, & Mary Ford *P&R '50*

(Mary Ford with Les Paul; Mary Ford)

Singles: 78 rpm

CAPITOL ... 5-15 50-57

Singles: 7-inch

CALENDAR ... 4-6
CAPITOL ... 10-20 50-57
COLUMBIA ... 5-10 58-64

Picture Sleeves
COLUMBIA....................5-15 58-64
EPs: 7-inch
CAPITOL....................10-20 50-57
LPs: 10/12-inch
CAPITOL (SM-200 series)....................5-8 78
CAPITOL (H-226 thru H-577)....................25-50 50-55
(10-inch LPs.)
CAPITOL (T-226 thru T-802)....................20-40 55-57
CAPITOL (T-1400 & T-1500 series)....................15-25 60-61
(Monaural.)
CAPITOL (ST-1400 & ST-1500 series)...20-30 60-61
(Stereo.)
CAPITOL (11000 series)....................5-10 74
COLUMBIA....................10-20 61-63
HARMONY....................8-12 61-65
MURRAY HILL (979462 "All Time Greatest Hits")....................15-25 80
(Boxed, three-disc set.)
Also see PAUL, Les

PAUL, Marvin
Singles: 7-inch
VAN (02965 "None of Your Business")....40-50

PAUL & FOURMOST
Singles: 7-inch
SHELLEY (170 "Cut Out")....................10-20 63

PAUL & PACK / Mad Doctors
Singles: 7-inch
TOWER (304 "Paper Clown")....................8-12 67
(Promotional issue only.)
TOWER (4261 "Hiding from Myself"/"Dr. Goldfoot's Igloo")....................5-10 67
Members: Paul Stefan; Gary Myers; Phil Alagna; Pat Cibbarrich; John Rondell.
Also see MYERS, Gary
Also see STEFAN, Paul

PAUL & PAULA P&R/R&B '62
Singles: 7-inch
LE CAM (300 series)....................3-6 74-82
LE CAM (99 "Beginning of Love")....................8-12 63
PHILIPS (40000 series)....................5-10 62-66
PHILIPS (44000 series)....................4-6 '70s
SOFT (106 "Hey Paula '69")....................8-12 69
UNI (55052 "All These Things")....................5-8 68
U.A. (50712 "Moments Like These")....................4-8 70
Picture Sleeves
PHILIPS (40096 "Young Lovers")....................10-15 63
PHILIPS (40114 "First Quarrel")....................10-15 64
LPs: 10/12-inch
PHILIPS (200078 "For Young Lovers")....30-40 63
(Monaural.)
PHILIPS (200089 "We Go Together")....30-40 63
(Monaural.)
PHILIPS (200101 "Holiday for Teens")....30-40 63
(Monaural.)
PHILIPS (600078 "For Young Lovers")....40-50 63
(Stereo.)
PHILIPS (600089 "We Go Together")......40-50 63
(Stereo.)
PHILIPS (600101 "Holiday for Teens")....40-50 63
(Stereo.)
Members: Ray Hildebrand; Jill Jackson.
Also see CHANNEL, Bruce / Paul & Paula
Also see JACKSON, Jill
Also see JILL & RAY
Also see PAUL

PAUL & PAULA
Singles: 7-inch
KARAT....................5-10 67
Members: Sonny Threatt; Phyllis Brown-Threatt.
Also see SONNY & PHYLLIS

PAUL'S HIGH SCHOOL BAND
Singles: 7-inch
ROULETTE (4298 "Recess")....................10-15 60
Member: Paul Vance.
Also see VANCE, Paul

PAULA, Marlena
Singles: 78 rpm
REGENT (7506 "I Wanna Spend Christmas with Elvis")....................15-25 56
Singles: 7-inch
REGENT (7506 "I Wanna Spend Christmas with Elvis")....................25-35 56

PAULEY, Everett
Singles: 7-inch
EVERETT PAULEY (11429 "Little Girl")....................1000-2000

PAULINE & BOBBY
Singles: 7-inch
EXPO (102 "No Messin' Around")....................5-10 68
LP: 10/12-inch
EXPO....................15-25 68
Members: Pauline Shivers Banks; Bobby Jones.
Also see BIRDLEGS & PAULINE & THEIR VERSATILITY BIRDS

PAULING, Ed, & Exciters
Singles: 7-inch
SAVOY (1625 "Soul House")....................10-15 65

PAULSON, Butch
Singles: 7-inch
VIRGELLE (708 "Man from Mars")........75-100
VIRGELLE (718 "Candy Lou")....................35-50

PAUPERS
Singles: 78 rpm
MELFORD (258 "Blue Sunday Morning")....................100-125 49

PAUPERS LP '67
Singles: 7-inch
VERVE ("If I Called You By Some Name")....................20-30 66
(Canadian. Selection number not known.)
VERVE FOLKWAYS....................8-15 66-67
VERVE FORECAST....................5-10 67-68
Picture Sleeves
VERVE FOLKWAYS (5062 "Magic People")....................10-20 67
LPs: 10/12-inch
VERVE FORECAST....................15-25 67-68
Also see THOMAS, David Clayton / Paupers / Shays

PAWNBROKERS
Singles: 7-inch
BIG SOUND (103 "Smell of Incense")......40-60 '60s
IGL (143 "Someday")....................10-20 67

PAWNS
(Featuring Ron Nowlan)
Singles: 7-inch
BAY-STATE (1267 "Summer")....................15-25

PAXTON, Gary C&W '76
(With the Road Runners; with Nashville Mavericks; with the Bakersfield Sound; Gary S. Paxton; Gary Sanford Paxton)
Singles: 7-inch
BAKERSFIELD CENTENNIAL (1001 "Bakersfield")....................15-25 69
("Collector's Edition" promo. Indicates being given "Compliments of Bakersfield Business.")
CAPITOL....................4-8 65-67
FELSTED (8691 "Kansas City")....................5-10 63
GARPAX (44172 "It Had to Be You")..........5-10 63
GARPAX (44177 "How to Be a Fool")..........5-10 63
GARPAX (44180 "Your Past Is Back")........5-10 64
LIBERTY (55407 "Teen Age Crush")..........5-10 62
LIBERTY (55485 "Stop Twistin' Baby")......5-10 62
LIBERTY (55584 "Spookie Movies")..........5-10 63
LONDON (5208 "Super Torque")..........5-10 64
LUTE (5801 "The Way I See It")..........5-10 60
MGM....................4-6 71
PRIVATE STOCK....................4-6 75
RCA....................4-6 73-76
W.I.N. (28-45 "The Racedrivers Song")......3-5 80
Picture Sleeves
W.I.N. (28-45 "The Race Drivers Song")......3-5 80
(Promotional item made for NAPA Auto Parts. Note, sleeve shows title as "Race Driver," whereas disc label reads "Racedriver.")
LPs: 10/12-inch
GASLIGHT....................10-15
NEW PAX....................5-10 76-80
PARAGON....................5-10 79
PAX....................5-10 78-79
Also see BERRY, Richard
Also see CASSIDY, Ted
Also see GARY, Clyde, & His Orchestra
Also see GARY & CLYDE
Also see FIVE SUPERIORS
Also see HOLLYWOOD ARGYLES
Also see INNOCENTS
Also see MAVRICKS
Also see PICKETT, Bobby
Also see ROAD RUNNERS
Also see SKIP & FLIP
Also see YORK, Dave, & Beachcombers

PAXTON, Les
Singles: 7-inch
SPRING DALE (102 "Tall Texas Woman")....................50-100

PAYCHECK, Johnny C&W '65
(With Charnissa; with Micki Evans)
Singles: 7-inch
ABC....................3-6 74
AMI....................3-5 84-85
CERTRON....................4-8 70
CUTLASS....................4-6 72
DAMASCUS....................3-5 89
DESPERADO....................3-5 88
EPIC....................3-8 71-82
HILLTOP....................10-15 64-66
LITTLE DARLIN' (008 thru 0072)..........5-10 66-69
LITTLE DARLIN' (7804 thru 7918)..........4-6 78-79
MERCURY....................3-5 86-87
LPs: 10/12-inch
ACCORD....................5-10 82
ALLEGIANCE....................5-10 83
CERTRON....................8-15 70
EPIC....................5-15 71-83
EXCELSIOR....................5-8 80
GUSTO....................5-10 83
IMPERIAL....................5-10 80
LAKESHORE....................5-8
LITTLE DARLIN' (0571 thru 0792)..........5-10 79-80
LITTLE DARLIN' (4001 "Johnny Paycheck at Carnegie Hall")....................20-30 66
(Monaural.)
LITTLE DARLIN' (4001 "Johnny Paycheck in Concert")....................10-15 66
(Repackage of *At Carnegie Hall.* Monaural.)
LITTLE DARLIN' (8001 "Johnny Paycheck at Carnegie Hall")....................20-30 66
(Stereo.)
LITTLE DARLIN' (8001 "Johnny Paycheck in Concert")....................15-20 66
(Repackage of *At Carnegie Hall.* Stereo.)
LITTLE DARLIN' (4003 thru 4006)..........10-20 66-67
(Monaural.)
LITTLE DARLIN' (8003 thru 8023)..........10-20 66-69
(Stereo.)
LITTLE DARLIN' (10000 series)..........8-12 79
MERCURY....................5-8 86
PICKWICK/HILLTOP....................5-10 72
POWER PAK....................5-8
Session: Jordanaires.
Also see HAGGARD, Merle, & Johnny Paycheck
Also see JENNINGS, Waylon / Johnny Paycheck
Also see JONES, George, & Johnny Paycheck
Also see JORDANAIRES
Also see MILLER, Jody, & Johnny Paycheck
Also see STEWART, Wynn, & Johnny Paycheck
Also see TUBB, Ernest
Also see YOUNG, Donny

PAYCHECK & HAGGARD C&W '81
Singles: 7-inch
EPIC (51012 "I Can't Hold Myself in Line")..3-5 81
Members: Johnny Paycheck; Merle Haggard.
Also see HAGGARD, Merle
Also see PAYCHECK, Johnny

PAYMENTS
Singles: 7-inch
LANDA (686 "Brand New Automobile")......5-10 62
(Flip, *Cantina*, was first issued as flip of Landa 676, as by the Tronics.)
Also see TRONICS

PAYNE, Benny
LPs: 10/12-inch
KAPP (1004 "Sunny Side Up")....................20-30 55

PAYNE, Cecil, Orchestra R&B '50
(Cecil Payne Sextet)
Singles: 78 rpm
DECCA (48127 "Block Buster Boogie")....30-40 50
Singles: 7-inch
CHARLIE PARKER (206 "Yes She's Gone")....................5-10 62

PAYNE, Chuck
Singles: 78 rpm
ATLAS (1057 "Escape")....................10-15 56
Singles: 7-inch
ATLAS (1057 "Escape")....................20-30 56
ATLAS (1072 "Baby")....................50-100 57

PAYNE, Dennis, & Renegades
Singles: 7-inch
GARPAX (4545 "California Girl")..........5-10 81
RED MAN (1492 "Token")....................50-100 69
LPs: 10/12-inch
RED MAN (1492 "We're Indian")..........100-200 69
(LP and Red Man single, *Token*, have the same selection number.)

PAYNE, Diane
Singles: 7-inch
ROULETTE (4290 "One Kiss Affair")......10-15 60
ROULETTE (4363 "Lover")....................10-15 61

PAYNE, Don
Singles: 78 rpm
STARDAY (150 "Pogo the Hobo")..........10-15 54
Singles: 7-inch
STARDAY (150 "Pogo the Hobo")..........15-25 54

PAYNE, Dusty
(With the Rhythm Rockers)
Singles: 78 rpm
FIRE (111 "Walkin' Shoes")....................20-30 56
Singles: 7-inch
BAKERSFIELD (119 "Long Time Gone")....................100-200
FIRE (111 "Walkin' Shoes")....................100-200 56

PAYNE, Freda R&B '69
Singles: 12-inch
CAPITOL....................4-8 79
Singles: 7-inch
ABC....................4-6 75
ABC-PAR....................5-10 62-63
CAPITOL....................4-6 77-78
DUNHILL....................4-6 74
IMPULSE....................5-10 63
INVICTUS....................4-8 69-73
MGM....................10-20 66
RIPETE....................3-6
SUTRA....................3-5 82
Picture Sleeves
CAPITOL....................4-6 77-78
INVICTUS....................5-8 71-73
LPs: 10/12-inch
ABC....................8-10 75
CAPITOL....................5-10 78-79
DUNHILL....................8-10 74
IMPULSE....................15-25 64
INVICTUS....................10-15 70-72
MGM....................10-20 66-70
USA....................10-15 71

PAYNE, Gordon
LPs: 10/12-inch
A&M (4725 "Gordon Payne")....................10-15 78

PAYNE, Hal
Singles: 7-inch
STARDAY (727 "Honky Tonk Stomp").500-700

PAYNE, Leon C&W '49
Singles: 78 rpm
CAPITOL (40238 "I Love You Because").10-15 49
DECCA....................5-10 54
STARDAY....................5-10 55-56
Singles: 7-inch
DECCA (29046 "Face in the Crowd")......15-25 54
DECCA (29333 "Lifetime to Regret")......15-25 54
STARDAY (208 "We're on the Main Line")....................15-25 55
STARDAY (215 "Christmas Everyday")...15-25 55
STARDAY (220 "You Are the One")........15-25 56
STARDAY (232 "Two By Four")..........15-25 56
STARDAY (250 "All the Time")..........15-25 56
STARDAY (637 "Close to You")..........15-25 57
TNT (168 "My Ship of Dreams")..........10-20 59
TNT (192 "We'll Break the Tie")..........8-12 62
EPs: 7-inch
DIXIE (506 "Leon Payne")....................50-100 '50s
LPs: 10/12-inch
STARDAY (231 "Living Legend of Country Music")....................25-50 63
STARDAY (236 "Americana")....................20-40 63
Also see ROGERS, Rock

PAYNE, Louis, Orchestra
(Vocal By Bonnie Buckner & Danny [Run Joe] Taylor; Lou Payne)
Singles: 78 rpm
SAXONY....................8-12 55

Singles: 7-inch
FEDERAL (12387 "Hand Out") 10-15 60
SAXONY (102 "That's Alright with Me")... 20-30 55
Also see TAYLOR, Danny "Run Joe"

PAYNE, Tommy
Singles: 7-inch
FELSTED (8531 "I Go Ape") 15-25 59
XYZ (601 "Shy Boy").............................. 10-15 59
XYZ (603 "Cruisin' Around") 15-25 59

PEABODY
Singles: 7-inch
BUSY B (7 "Forever Eyes")...................... 10-15 68

PEACE, Elroy "Shadow"
Singles: 7-inch
KEEN (2106 "Oh Yeah").......................... 10-15 59
Also see SHADOWS

PEACE, Joe
LPs: 10/12-inch
RITE (29917 "Finding Peace") 100-200 72

PEACE, Mike
(With Filet of Soul)
Singles: 7-inch
MAGIC TOUCH (2078 "Proud Mary")...... 10-15 69
WAVEMAKERS (001 "The Tape Player Song") 3-5 84
Also see FILET OF SOUL

PEACE & LOVE
Singles: 7-inch
EX-PLO (011 "I Touched Her") 10-20 72

PEACE & QUIET
LPs: 10/12-inch
KINETIC (30315 "Peace & Quiet").......... 10-15 71

PEACHEROOS
Singles: 78 rpm
EXCELLO 250-350 54
Singles: 7-inch
EXCELLO (2044 "Be Bop Baby")..... 2500-3000 54
(Black vinyl. Bootlegs we've seen are red vinyl and spell the group name with one "o" – "Peacheros.")

PEACHES
Singles: 7-inch
BUMP'S (1503 "I'm Living in a Dream")... 15-20 63
CONSTELLATION (171 "Music to My Ears") 5-10 66

PEACHES & HERB ***P&R/R&B '66***
Singles: 7-inch
COLUMBIA...4-6 71-74
COLUMBIA (03972 "Come to Me")..............3-5 83
DATE 5-10 66-70
MCA (40701 "We're Still Together")............4-6 77
MCA (40782 "I'm Counting On You")...........4-6 77
MERCURY (73350 "I'm Hurting Inside").......4-6 73
MERCURY (73388 "Can't It Wait")...............4-6 73
Picture Sleeves
DATE 5-10 67-68
LPs: 10/12-inch
DATE 10-20 67-68
EPIC..8-10 79
MCA..8-10 77
Members: Francine Barker; Herb Fame.
Also see BARKER, Francine "Peaches"
Also see SWEET THINGS

PEACOCKS
Singles: 7-inch
4 STAR (1718 "My New Hi-Fi") 75-100 58

PEAK, Buford
Singles: 7-inch
FERNWOOD (102 "Knock Down Drag Out") 100-200 58

PEANUT BUTTER CONSPIRACY ***P&R/LP'67***
Singles: 7-inch
CHALLENGE (500 "Back in L.A.") 5-8 69
COLUMBIA (43985 "It's a Happening Thing")...8-10 67
COLUMBIA (44063 "Dark on You") 8-10 67
COLUMBIA (44356 "Turn On a Friend").....8-10 67
VAULT (933 "Floating Dream") 10-15 66
Picture Sleeves
COLUMBIA (43985 "It's a Happening Thing")... 15-25 67
LPs: 10/12-inch
CHALLENGE (200 "For Children of All Ages") 20-25 69
COLUMBIA (2654 "Peanut Butter Conspiracy Is Spreading")...20-25 67
(Monaural.)
COLUMBIA (2790 "The Great Conspiracy") 20-30 68
(Monaural.)
COLUMBIA (9454 "Peanut Butter Conspiracy Is Spreading")...25-30 68
(Stereo.)
COLUMBIA (9590 "The Great Conspiracy") 20-25 68
(Stereo.)
COLUMBIA (38000 series)........................8-10 82
Members: Sandi Robison; Alan Brackett; Lance Fent; Bill Wolf; Jim Voight; John Merrill.

PEANUT BUTTER CONSPIRACY / Ashes / Chambers Brothers
LPs: 10/12-inch
VAULT (113 "West Coast Love-In")..........30-50 67
Also see ASHES
Also see CHAMBERS BROTHERS

PEANUTS
Singles: 7-inch
PIC 1 (110 "Peanuts") 10-20 65
(First issue.)
PIC 1 (113 "Sylvia") 10-20 65
SMASH (1974 "Peanuts") 8-12 65
LPs: 10/12-inch
LONDON (91362 "Peanuts")....................15-25 65

PEARL & DELTARS
Singles: 7-inch
FURY (1048 "Teenager's Dream")...........20-30 61
Member: Pearl McKinnon.
Also see KODOKS

PEARL JAM ***LP '92***
Singles: 7-inch
EPIC (5610 "Angel") 5-10 94
(Promotional issue only.)
Picture Sleeves
EPIC (5610 "Angel") 10-15 94
(Promotional issue only.)
LPs: 10/12-inch
EPIC 5-10 91-95
Members: Eddie Vedder; Mike McCready; Jeff Ament; Stone Gossard; Dave Krusen.
Also see GREEN RIVER

PEARLESCENTS
Singles: 7-inch
JOC (101 "Ronnie's Night House")..........10-20 63

PEARLETTES ***P&R '62***
Singles: 7-inch
CRAIG (502 "He's Gone") 10-20 61
GO (712 "Can I Get Him") 25-35 61
(First issue.)
SEG-WAY (1003 "He's Gone") 5-10 62
VAULT (100 "Can This Be Love") 15-25 62
VEE-JAY (422 "Can I Get Him") 10-20 61
VEE-JAY (435 "Duchess of Earl") 10-20 62
Members: Lynda Galloway; Sheila Galloway; Mary Meade; Priscilla Kennedy.

PEARLS
Singles: 78 rpm
ATCO...15-25 55
ONYX (503 "Let's You and I Go Steady").15-25 56
ONYX (506 "Tree in the Meadow")...........50-75 56
ONYX (510 "Your Cheatin' Heart") 30-50 57
ONYX (511 "Ice Cream Baby") 40-60 57
ONYX (516 "The Wheel of Love")...........75-100 57
Singles: 7-inch
ATCO (6057 "Shadows of Love") 40-60 55
ATCO (6066 "Bells of Love")....................50-75 56
ON THE SQUARE (320 "Band of Angels") 15-25 59
ONYX (503 "Let's You and I Go Steady").50-60 56
ONYX (506 "Tree in the Meadow").......150-200 56
ONYX (510 "Your Cheatin' Heart") 40-50 57
ONYX (511 "Ice Cream Baby") 50-75 57
ONYX (516 "The Wheel of Love").........150-200 57
RELIC...5-10 64
Members: Howard Guyton; Dave "Baby" Cortez; Bob Spencer; Robert Gu; Earl Carroll.
Also see CADILLACS
Also see CORTEZ, Dave "Baby"
Also see FIVE PEARLS
Also see GUY, Bobby

PEARLS
Singles: 7-inch
AMBER (2003 "I Cried") 1000-1500 61
(Identification number, "M-114," is stamped in vinyl trail-off.)
AMBER (2003 "I Cried") ....30-40 '60s
(No identification number in vinyl trail-off.)

PEARLS
Singles: 7-inch
W.B. (5300 "Happy Over You")................10-15 62

PEARLS
Singles: 7-inch
LAMP (653 "Shooting Star")......................20-30

PEARLS BEFORE SWINE ***LP '69***
Singles: 7-inch
ESP (4554 "Morning Song")......................20-30 67
ESP (4576 "I Saw the World") 20-30 68
REPRISE (0873 "These Things Too")........5-10 69
W.B./REPRISE (0949 "Rocket Man")..........4-8 70
LPs: 10/12-inch
ADELPHI...8-12 80
ESP (1054 "One Nation Underground") ...30-50 67
ESP (1075 "Balaklava")............................20-40 68
W.B./REPRISE 10-20 69-71
Members: Tom Rapp; Richard Alderson; Bob Elizabeth; Warren Smith; Charlie McCoy; Lane Lender; Wayne Harley.

PEARLY, Don
Singles: 7-inch
CORVETTE (1004 "Drag Race") 15-25 57

PEARSON, Duke ***LP '69***
Singles: 7-inch
BLUE NOTE...4-8 60-67
LPs: 10/12-inch
ATLANTIC (3002 "Honey Buns") 10-20 66
ATLANTIC (3005 "Prairie Dog")...............10-20 66
BLUE NOTE..25-40 59-61
(Label gives New York street address for Blue Note Records.)
BLUE NOTE..20-30 63-64
(Label reads "Blue Note Records Inc. - New York, USA.")
BLUE NOTE..10-20 66-74
(Label shows Blue Note Records as a division of either Liberty or United Artists.)
PRESTIGE 10-15 70

PEARSON, Jimmy
Singles: 7-inch
DIXIE (824 "Nobody Cares")..................50-100

PEARSON, Melvin
Singles: 7-inch
REDWING (1046 "Wasting Time") 40-60

PEARSON, Ronnie
Singles: 7-inch
HERALD (500 "Hot Shot").........................50-75 57
HERALD (514 "She Bops a Lot").............50-75 58
HERALD (516 "Teenage Fancy") 50-75 58
MART 5-10

PEASANTS
Singles: 7-inch
RAYNARD (6289 "Big Boss Man")...........10-20 '70s
Also see MUSTARD MEN

PEBBLES
Singles: 78 rpm
MIDDLE-TONE...75-100 55
Singles: 7-inch
MIDDLE-TONE (002 "Let Me Hear It Again")..200-300 55

PEBBLES & BAMM BAMM
Singles: 7-inch
HBR (449 "Open Up Your Heart") 8-12 65
HBR (484 "Daddy")....................................8-12 66
Picture Sleeves
HBR (449 "Open Up Your Heart") 20-30 65
LPs: 10/12-inch
HBR (2040 "On the Good Ship Lollipop").25-35 65

PEDESTRIANS
Singles: 7-inch
ATCO (6567 "Think Twice") 5-10 67
BUYIT (2556 "Think Twice") 15-25 67
FENTON (2102 "Think Twice")................15-25 66
FENTON (2116 "It's Too Late") 15-25 66
FENTON (2226 "You Aren't Going to Say You Know") 10-20 67
Member: Tony Cooper.

PEDESTRIANS / Association / Five Americans / Soulblenders
EPs: 7-inch
WLAV (6873 "Think Twice")......................10-20 '60s
(Promotional issue only.)
Also see ASSOCIATION
Also see FIVE AMERICANS
Also see PEDESTRIANS
Also see SOULBLENDERS

PEDICIN, Mike ***P&R '56***
(Michael Pedicin, Jr; Mike Pedicin Quintet; Quartet)
Singles: 78 rpm
CAMEO (125 "Shake a Hand")................10-20 58
MALVERN (100 "Dickie-Doo")..................15-25 57
RCA..5-10 55-56
20TH CENTURY 5-10 54-55
Singles: 12-inch
PHILA. INT'L...4-8 79-82
Singles: 7-inch
ABC-PAR (10303 "Gotta Twist")................5-10 62
APOLLO (534 "Hey Pop, Give Me the Keys") 25-35 59
CAMEO (125 "Shake a Hand")................15-25 58
FEDERAL (12417 "Burnt Toast and Black Coffee") 8-12 61
MALVERN (100 "Dickie-Doo")..................15-20 57
PHILA. INT'L...3-6 79-82
RCA (6000 series)....................................15-25 55-57
20TH CENTURY (75019 "Is That What You Call Love") 10-20 54
20TH CENTURY (75029 "Sweet Georgia Brown")...10-20 55
Picture Sleeves
RCA (6546 "The Beat")...........................20-30 56
("This Is Their Life" sleeve makes no reference to this particular release. Promotional issue only.)
EPs: 7-inch
RCA (2 "Rock 'n Roll with Mike Pedicin").20-30 56
(Promotional issue, made for General Electric Flash Bulb buyers.)
LPs: 10/12-inch
APOLLO (484 "Musical Medicine").........75-125 59
PHILA. INT'L...5-10 79
Members: Al Mauro; Mike Pedicin; Sammy Cooke; Lou DeFrancis; Bobby Stevens.

PEDIGO, Tommy
Singles: 7-inch
OLO (103 "Red Headed Woman") 200-300 66

PEDIGO BROTHERS & TENNESSEE RHYTHM BOYS
Singles: 7-inch
ATWELL (100 "She's Gone")...............100-200 '50s
Member: Tommy Pedigo.
Also see PEDIGO, Tommy

PEDRICK, Bobby ***P&R '58***
(Bobby Pedrick Jr.)
Singles: 7-inch
BIG TOP (3004 "White Bucks and Saddle Shoes")..8-12 58
BIG TOP (3008 "Pajama Party")................8-12 59
BIG TOP (3024 "Summer Nights") 8-12 59
DUEL (504 "I'm Scared") 5-10 62
DUEL (516 "Two Ton Tessie")....................5-10 62
DUEL (525 "If Mary Only Knew")...............5-10 63
MGM (13384 "Don't Try to Change My Ways")..4-8 65
SHELL (722 "School Crush")...................15-20 60
VERVE (10402 "Maybe") 40-50 66
Also see BOBBY & CONSOLES

PEE, Eddie
(Memphis Eddie; Memphis Eddie P. & His Trio)
Singles: 78 rpm
FOTO 20-25 48
GLOBE..10-20 45
RPM 10-20 50-51

PEE WEE & PROPHETS
Singles: 7-inch
CENTENNIAL (1863 "Tell Me") 40-50

PEEBLES, Robert
Singles: 7-inch
JAX (1001 "This Little Light of Mine") .. 100-125 59

PEEK, Billy
(With the Love-Ins)
Singles: 7-inch
CARTER (5230 "Pretty Blue-Eyed Baby") 100-200
DARSA (133 "Colors of the Rainbow") 10-15 63
MARLO (1521 "Twistin' Johnny B. Goode") 50-75 62
PEEK (101 "Rock to the Top") 50-75
ROYAL CREST 10-15 62
WHITE WHALE (357 "Population Explosion") 5-10 70

PEEK, John, & His Orchestra
(Featuring Arlene Harris)
Singles: 78 rpm
CHESS (1471 "Long Tall Papa") 15-25 51

PEEK, Paul P&R '61
Singles: 78 rpm
NRC (001 "Sweet Skinny Jenny") 15-25 58
NRC (008 "I'm Not Your Fool Anymore"). 25-45 58
Singles: 7-inch
COLUMBIA (43527 "Rockin' Pneumonia and Boogie Woogie Flu") 5-10 66
COLUMBIA (43771 "I'm Movin' Uptown") ... 5-10 66
FAIRLANE (702 "Brother-in-Law") 10-15 61
FAIRLANE (21005 "Watermelon") 10-15 61
MERCURY (72064 "Young Hearts") 8-12 62
MERCURY (72118 "You're Just in Love") .. 8-12 63
MERCURY (72181 "Good of Love") 8-12 63
NRC (001 "Sweet Skinny Jenny") 15-25 58
NRC (008 "I'm Not Your Fool Anymore"). 15-25 58
NRC (025 "Shortnin' Bread") 10-20 59
NRC (033 "Waikiki Beach") 10-20 59
NRC (048 "Hurtin' Inside") 10-20 59
NRC (059 "I'm a Happy Man") 10-20 60
1-2-3 (1714 "Sweet Lorraine") 4-6 69

PEEKS
Singles: 7-inch
LE JAC (3005 "Once Upon a Time") .... 25-35 '60s

PEEL, David, & Lower East Side LP '69
Singles: 7-inch
APPLE (6498 "F Is Not a Dirty Word"). 100-125 72
(Promotional issue only.)
APPLE (6545 "Hippie from New York City") 100-125 72
(Promotional issue only.)
ORANGE 4-6 77
ORANGE PEEL (70078PD "Interview") ... 15-20 80
(Picture disc. With John Lennon.)
LPs: 10/12-inch
APPLE (3391 "Pope Smokes Dope") 50-75 72
ELEKTRA (74032 "Have a Marijuana") ... 15-25 68
ELEKTRA (74069 "American Revolution") 15-25 70
ORANGE 8-12 77

PEEL, David, & Lower East Side / John Lennon & Yoko Ono
Singles: 7-inch
ORANGE (8374 "Amerika") 3-5 90
(Promotional bonus with book purchase.)
ORANGE (789001 "Ballad of New York City") 3-5 87
Picture Sleeves
ORANGE (8374 "Amerika") 3-5 90
(Promotional bonus with book purchase.)
Also see LENNON, John
Also see PEEL, David, & Lower East Side

PEELE, Steve, Five
Singles: 7-inch
F.G.I. (1000 "Frankie's Got It") 15-25

PEELS P&R '66
Singles: 7-inch
KARATE (522 "Juanita Banana") 8-12 66
KARATE (527 "Scrooey Mooey") 5-10 66
KARATE (533 "Juanita Banana II") 5-10 66
LPs: 10/12-inch
KARATE (1402 "Juanita Banana") 55-65 66
(Monaural.)
KARATE (5402 "Juanita Banana") 65-75 66
(Stereo.)

PEELS, Leon
(With the Hi Tensions)
Singles: 7-inch
WHIRLY BIRD (2002 "A Casual Kiss") 20-30 64
WHIRLY BIRD (2008 "A Magic Island") 50-75 64
Also see BLUE JAYS
Also see HI TENSIONS

PEERS
Singles: 7-inch
LEJAC (3005 "Once Upon a Time") 20-25 68

PEGGY & BOB
Singles: 7-inch
HARVARD (802 "What You Do to Me") 25-35 59

PEIL, Danny
(With the Tigers; with Apollos; with Sound Majority)
Singles: 7-inch
CURTIS ("Four Days to St. Paul") .... 10-20 '60s
(No selection number used.)
RAYNARD (602 "Jingle Jump") 10-15 65
(With the Apollos.)
RAYNARD (602 "Jingle Jump") 15-20 65
(With the Tigers.)
Picture Sleeve
RAYNARD (602 "Jingle Jump") 15-20 65
(With the Tigers. Sleeve shows record as being by the Jingle Jumpers.)
Members: Denny McCarthy; Duane Lundy; Bobby Ray; Roland Stone Oeller; Pete Miller.
Also see CORPORATION
Also see STEFAN, Paul

PEJOE, Morris
Singles: 78 rpm
ABCO 15-25 56
CHECKER 100-150 54
VEE-JAY 15-25 55
Singles: 7-inch
ABCO (106 "Screaming and Crying") 25-50 56
ATOMIC-H ("She Walked Right In") 200-300 60
(No selection number used.)
CHECKER (766 "Tired of Crying Over You") 300-400 54
(Black vinyl.)
CHECKER (766 "Tired of Crying Over You") 1500-2000 54
(Red vinyl.)
CHECKER (781 "Can't Get Along") 250-350 54
(Black vinyl.)
CHECKER (781 "Can't Get Along") 500-750 54
(Red vinyl.)
VEE-JAY (148 "You Gonna Need Me") 25-50 55

PELICANS
Singles: 78 rpm
IMPERIAL (5307 "Chimes") 300-500 54
PARROT (793 "Aurelia") 300-500 54
Singles: 7-inch
IMPERIAL (5307 "Chimes") 2000-3000 54
LOST NITE 5-10
PARROT (793 "Aurelia") 750-1000 54
(Black vinyl.)
PARROT (793 "Aurelia") 2000-3000 54
(Red vinyl.)
Also see KIDDS

PELL BROTHERS
Singles: 7-inch
JAY (59 "I'm the One You Love") 20-30 59
EPs: 7-inch
JAY (45 "Pell Brothers") 50-100

PEMBERTON, Jimmy
Singles: 7-inch
END (1052 "Rags to Riches") 25-35 59
MARK-X (8002 "Rags to Riches") 15-25 60
ORCHID (5002 "Ko-Ko-Mo Girl") 10-20 58
Session: Chantels.
Also see CHANTELS

PEN ETTS
Singles: 7-inch
BECCO (1001 "If I Never See You Again") 40-60
Member: G. Penney.

PENDARVIS, Tracy
(With the Blue Notes; with Swampers; with Gene Lowery Singers)
Singles: 7-inch
DES CANT (1234 "First Love") 10-15 62
SCOTT (1202 "One of These Days") 25-35 58
SCOTT (1203 "Give Me Lovin' ") 600-800 58
SUN (335 "A Thousand Guitars") 25-35 60
SUN (345 "Southbound Line") 25-35 60
SUN (359 "Eternally") 25-35 61

PENDERGRASS, Teddy P&R/R&B/LP '77
Singles: 12-inch
PHILA. INT'L 4-8 78-82
Singles: 7-inch
ASYLUM 3-5 84-88
ELEKTRA 3-5 88-90
PHILA. INT'L 3-6 77-84
Picture Sleeves
ELEKTRA 3-5 89
LPs: 10/12-inch
ASYLUM 5-8 84-86
ELEKTRA 5-8 88-90
EPIC 5-10 83
PHILA. INT'L (30000 series, except JZ-30595) 5-10 77-84
PHILA. INT'L (JZ-35095 "Life Is a Song Worth Singing") 15-25 78
(Picture disc. Promotional issue only.)
PHILA. INT'L (40000 series) 10-20 82
(Half-speed mastered.)
Also see MELVIN, Harold

PENDERGRASS, Teddy, & Whitney Houston P&R '84
Singles: 7-inch
ASYLUM (69720 "Hold Me") 3-5 84
Picture Sleeves
ASYLUM (69720 "Hold Me") 3-5 84
Also see PENDERGRASS, Teddy

PENDLETONS
Singles: 7-inch
DOT (16511 "Blue Surf") 20-35 63
RENDEZVOUS (194 "Waddle") 15-25 62
Member: Richie Burns.
Also see HONDELLS

PENDULUMS
Singles: 7-inch
AURORA (160 "Love Is Summertime") 15-25 66

PENETRATIONS
Singles: 7-inch
ICON (1002 "Bring 'Em In") 20-25
(Black vinyl.)
ICON (1002 "Bring 'Em Back Alive") 20-25
(Black vinyl. Note title variation.)
ICON (1002 "Bring 'Em In") 35-50
(Colored vinyl.)

PENETRATIONS
Singles: 7-inch
CROYDEN (583 "Sweeter Than Wine") ... 20-30

PENETRATORS
Singles: 7-inch
SKYLARK (100 "Caravan") 10-20 60
SKYLARK (111 "One Love") 10-20 60
(First issued as by the Dissonaires.)
Also see DISSONAIRES

PENETRATORS
Singles: 7-inch
FENTON (992 "What Won't Go Wrong") .. 20-30 65

PENGUINS P&R/R&B '54
("Featuring Cleve Duncan"; Penquins)
Singles: 78 rpm
ATLANTIC 25-50 57
DOOTO 20-30 57
DOOTONE 25-75 54-55
MERCURY 25-50 55-57
WING 10-20 56
Singles: 7-inch
ATLANTIC (1132 "Pledge of Love") 20-30 57
DOOTO (348 "Earth Angel") 8-10 62
(Reissue of DooTONE 348.)
DOOTO (362 "Baby Let's Make Love") .... 5-7 '60s
(Reissue of DooTONE 362.)
DOOTO (428 "That's How Much I Need You") 30-50 57
DOOTO (432 "Let Me Make Up Your Mind") 15-25 58
DOOTO (435 "Do Not Pretend") 20-30 58
(Dootone 345 is found in the following section: PENGUINS / Dootsie Williams Orchestra.)
DOOTONE (348 "Earth Angel") 50-75 54
(Red label.)
DOOTONE (348 "Earth Angel") 40-50 54
(Maroon label.)
DOOTONE (348 "Earth Angel") 35-45 54
(Blue label. Black vinyl.)
DOOTONE (348 "Earth Angel") 400-500 54
(Blue label. Red vinyl.)
DOOTONE (348 "Earth Angel") 15-25 54
(Black label.)
DOOTONE (353 "Love Will Make Your Mind Go Wild") 50-60 54
(Red label.)
DOOTONE (353 "Love Will Make Your Mind Go Wild") 30-40 54
(Maroon label.)
DOOTONE (353 "Love Will Make Your Mind Go Wild") 15-25 54
(Blue label.)
DOOTONE (353 "Love Will Make Your Mind Go Wild") 10-15 54
(Black label.)
DOOTONE (362 "Baby Let's Make Love") 40-50 55
ELDO (119 "To Keep Our Love") 5-10 62
GLENVILLE 4-6
MERCURY (70610 "Be Mine Or Be a Fool") 30-40 55
MERCURY (70654 "It Only Happens with You") 25-35 55
MERCURY (70703 "Devil That I See") 20-30 55
MERCURY (70762 "Christmas Prayer") .. 40-50 55
MERCURY (70799 "My Troubles Are Not at an End") 25-35 56
(Maroon label.)
MERCURY (70799 "My Troubles Are Not at an End") 10-15 56
(Black label.)
MERCURY (70943 "Earth Angel") 15-25 56
MERCURY (71033 "Will You Be Mine") ... 15-25 57
ORIGINAL SOUND (27 "Memories of El Monte") 30-40 63
ORIGINAL SOUND (54 "Heavenly Angel") 25-35 65
POWER (7023 "Earth Angel") 4-8
SUN STATE (001 "Believe Me") 25-35 62
WING (90076 "Peace of Mind") 30-40 56
Picture Sleeves
POWER (7023 "Earth Angel") 5-10
EPs: 7-inch
DOOTO (241/243/244 "Cool, Cool Penguins") 40-60 59
(Price is for any of three volumes.)
DOOTONE (101 "The Penguins") 100-150 55
LPs: 10/12-inch
COLLECTABLES .... 5-8 '80s
DOOTO (242 "Cool, Cool Penguins") .. 150-250 59
(Yellow label with red lettering. Full-color cover.)
DOOTO (242 "Cool, Cool Penguins") ...... 10-15 '60s
(Multi-color label.)
Members: Cleve Duncan; Curtis Williams; Ted Harper; Dexter Tisby; Bruce Tate; Walter Saulsberry; Randy Jones.
Also see DUNCAN, Cleve
Also see GUNTER, Cornell
Also see JULIAN, Don, & Meadowlarks
Also see VICEROYS

PENGUINS / Meadowlarks / Medallions / Dootones
LPs: 10/12-inch
COLLECTABLES (5048 "Dootone Rhythm & Blues") .... 5-10 '80s
DOOTONE (204 "Best in Rhythm & Blues") 300-400 57
(Black vinyl.)
DOOTONE (204 "Best in Rhythm & Blues") 1000-1200 57
(Red vinyl.)
DOOTO (204 "Best in Rhythm & Blues") . 25-50 '60s
Also see DOOTONES
Also see PENGUINS

PENGUINS / Medallions
Singles: 7-inch
DOOTO (456 "Penguins/Medallions") 75-125 60
(Not issued with specially printed cover or sleeve.)
Also see GREEN, Vernon, & Medallions

PENGUINS / Dootsie Williams Orchestra
Singles: 78 rpm
DOOTONE 25-40 54

Singles: 7-inch
DOOTONE (345 "No There Ain't No News Today")................................ 200-300 54
Also see WILLIAMS, Dootsie, Orchestra

PENIGAR, Eddie
(Eddie "Sugarman" Penigar & His Band)
Singles: 78 rpm
RCA (20-2700 and 22-0000 series)......... 25-35 47-49
Singles: 7-inch
RCA (50-0020 "Easy Baby")................ 100-125 50
(Cherry red vinyl.)
Also see CHICAGO ALL STARS

PENIX, William
Singles: 7-inch
DAFFAN (116 "Dig That Crazy Driver")... 50-75 59

PENN, Little "Lambsie"
Singles: 78 rpm
ATCO (6082 "I Want to Spend Christmas with Elvis").. 10-20 56
Singles: 7-inch
ATCO (6082 "I Want to Spend Christmas with Elvis").. 20-25 56
ATCO (6082 "I Want to Spend Christmas with Elvis").. 30-50 56
(Promotional issue only. Reads "Test Pressing" at left.)

PENN, William
(With the Quakers; William Penn Fyve)
Singles: 7-inch
DUANE (104 "Coming Up My Way")....... 25-35 '60s
HUSH (230 "Little Girl")..................... 20-40 '60s
MELRON (5013 "California Sun")........... 15-25 67
MELRON (5024 "Philly")....................... 25-50 67
MELRON (5024 "Sweet Caroline")........... 25-50 67
(Selection number 5024 used twice.)
THUNDERBIRD (502 "Blow My Mind")... 50-75 66
TWILIGHT (410 "Ghost of the Monks...... 15-25 67
UPTOWN (745 "Chrome Dome Wheeler Dealer")....................................... 20-30 67

PENN BOYS
Singles: 7-inch
BOBBY (502 "Have a Party")................. 30-40 59

PENNA, Dennis
(With the Freebees; Denny Penna; D.R. Penna Mississippi Jook Band)
Singles: 7-inch
DE-MAT... 10-15 62
MUSITRON (103 "Mean to Me").............. 40-50 60
MUSITRON (105 "Battle of the Duals")... 40-50 60
P&M.. 10-15
Picture Sleeves
MUSITRON (105 "Battle of the Duals")... 40-60 60

PENNANTS
Singles: 7-inch
WORLD (102 "Don't Go")...................... 250-350 61
WORLD (102 "Don't Go")...................... 4-6 89
(Blue vinyl. 500 made.)

PENNDULUMS
("Members of U of Penn. Glee Club")
Singles: 7-inch
MAY (109 "Time Marches On")........... 100-150 61

PENNER, Dick
Singles: 78 rpm
SUN (282 "Your Honey Love")................ 25-50 57
Singles: 7-inch
SUN (282 "Your Honey Love")................ 30-60 57
Also see WADE & DICK

PENNINGTON, Ray C&W '66
Singles: 7-inch
CAPITOL.. 4-8 66-68
DIMENSION (1039 "For Christmas")........... 4-8
KING (5783 "Your Diary")........................ 5-10 63
LEE (502 "Boogie Woogie Country Girl")... 150-250 56
LEE (504 "My Steady Baby")................ 50-75 58
LEE (505 "Billy Jo")............................. 60-75 58
MONUMENT.. 4-6 69-71
RUBY (290 "Fancy Free")...................... 30-50 57
LPs: 10/12-inch
MONUMENT.. 10-15 69-71

PENNSYLVANIA PLAYERS
Singles: 7-inch
ORON (101 "Washington Uptight")............. 8-12
Also see GOODMAN, Dickie

PENNY, Dayward
Singles: 7-inch
BIG HOWDY (8102 "Come Back Baby")..50-75 58
RUBY (330 "Bee Bop Song")..................50-75 57

PENNY, Edward, & Larry Forbes
Singles: 78 rpm
ESSEX (376 "What Is Christmas")..............8-12 54
Singles: 7-inch
ESSEX (376 "What Is Christmas")...........15-25 54

PENNY, Hank C&W '46
Singles: 78 rpm
DECCA..5-10 55-56
KING...5-10 46-52
RCA..5-10 50-53
Singles: 7-inch
DECCA (29560 "I Can't Get You Out of My Mind")...10-15 55
DECCA (29597 "Bloodshot Eyes")..........10-15 56
KING (1020 "Alabama Jubilee")...............10-20 52
(Black vinyl.)
KING (1020 "Alabama Jubilee")...............20-30 52
(Red vinyl.)
RCA..10-20 50-53
WASP (117 "A Letter from Home")............5-10
LPs: 10/12-inch
AUDIO LAB (1508 "Hank Penny")...........20-40 58
RAMBLER..8-12
Session: Noel Boggs; Boudleaux Bryant; Eddie Duncan; Sheldon Bennett.
Also see THOMPSON, Sue

PENNY, Joe C&W '64
Singles: 7-inch
DEL MAR (1021 "What's the Score")..........5-10 65
FEDERAL (12322 "Bip a Little, Bop a Lot")...100-200 58
SIMS (173 "Frosty Window Pane")..........15-20 64

PENNY, Paul
Singles: 7-inch
JAM (108 "True Fine Mama")..................60-80 '60s
TILT (786 "Honey")................................5-10 61

PENNY & EKOS
Singles: 7-inch
ARGO (5295 "Gimme What You Got").....25-50 58
Member: Penny Smith.

PENNY & JEAN
Singles: 7-inch
RCA (7844 "I Forgot More Than You'll Ever Know")..5-10 61
LPs: 10/12-inch
RCA (2244 "Two for the Road")...............15-25 61
Also see LIMELITERS

PENNY & OVERTONES
Singles: 7-inch
RIM (2020 "What Made You Forget").....50-100 58

PENNY & PACEMAKERS
Singles: 7-inch
TEMPO (125936 "I Can't Stay")...............25-30

PENNY ARCADE
Singles: 7-inch
SMASH (2190 "Bubble Gum Tree")............5-10 68
U.A. (50221 "Me and My Piano")...............5-10 67
Also see ANDERS & PONCIA

PENSE, Janie
Singles: 7-inch
ABC-PAR (10490 "Big You, Little Me").....10-15 64

PENSE, Lydia, & New Invaders
Singles: 7-inch
INVADER ("Forgive You, Then Forget You")..10-20
(Selection number not known.)

PENTAGONS P&R '61
Singles: 7-inch
CALDWELL (411 "I'm in Love")...............20-30 62
(First issue.)
DONNA (1337 "To Be Loved")..................15-25 61
DONNA (1344 "For a Love That Is Mine")..20-30 61
ERIC..4-6 '70s
FLEET INT'L (100 "To Be Loved").......100-150 60
JAMIE (1201 "I Wonder").........................15-25 61
JAMIE (1210 "I'm in Love").......................8-12 62
ORIGINAL SOUND (4560 "To Be Loved")...3-5 '80s
SPECIALTY (644 "It's Spring Again").......20-30 58
SUTTER (100 "Forever Yours")..............50-100 61

PENTAGONS / Earl Phillips
Singles: 7-inch
OLDIES 45 (67 "To Be Loved"/"Oop-De-Oop")..5-10 64
Also see PENTAGONS
Also see PHILLIPS, Earl

PENTAGONS
Singles: 7-inch
AUDIO DYNAMICS (153 "About the Girl I Love")..15-20 67

PENTANGLE LP '68
Singles: 7-inch
REPRISE...5-10 68-69
TRANSATLANTIC.....................................4-6
LPs: 10/12-inch
REPRISE...10-20 68-72
Members: Jacqui McShee; Bert Jansch; Danny Thompson; John Renbourn; Terry Cox.
Also see RENBOURN, John

PENTHOUSE FIVE
Singles: 7-inch
SOLAR (4211 "Bad Girl").........................15-25 66

PEOPLE P&R/LP '68
Singles: 7-inch
CAPITOL (2078 "I Love You")...................8-12 68
CAPITOL (2251 "Apple Cider")..................8-12 68
CAPITOL (2499 "Turnin' Me In")...............8-12 69
CAPITOL (5920 "Organ Grinder")..............8-12 67
PARAMOUNT (0005 "Love Will Take Us Higher and Higher")..5-10 69
PARAMOUNT (0011 "Sunshine Lady")......5-10 69
PARAMOUNT (0019 "For What It's Worth")...5-10 70
PARAMOUNT (0028 "Keep It Alive")..........5-10 70
POLYDOR (14087 "Chant for Peace").........5-10 71
ZEBRA (102 "Come Back Beatles")...........5-10 78
(Includes a note suggesting the Beatles reunite.)
LPs: 10/12-inch
CAPITOL (151 "Both Sides")...................20-30 69
CAPITOL (2924 "I Love You")..................25-35 68
PARAMOUNT (5013 "There Are People and There Are People")..10-20 70
Members: Larry Norman; John Tristao; Robb Levin; Tom Tucker; Gene Mason; Geoff Levin.
Also see NORMAN, Larry

PEOPLE'S CHOICE P&R/R&B '71
Singles: 7-inch
CASABLANCA.......................................3-5 80
PALMER (5009 "Hot Wire")..................100-200 66
PALMER (5020 "Easy to Be True")......100-200 67
PALMER (5031 "Saving All My Love")...50-100 68
PHIL-L.A. OF SOUL.................................4-8 71-72
PHILA. INT'L..4-8 78
PHILIPS (40615 "Lost and Found")............5-10 69
PHILIPS (40653 "Just Look What You've Done")..5-10 69
TSOP..4-6 74-77
LPs: 10/12-inch
CASABLANCA.......................................5-10 80
PHILA. INT'L..5-10 78
TSOP..8-10 75-76
Members: Roger Andrews; Guy Fiske; David Thompson; Leon Lee; Frankie Brunson; Donell Jordan; Donald ford.
Also see BRUNSON, Frankie
Also see FASHIONS

PEPE, Diane
Singles: 7-inch
DWAIN (810 "I Watch the Rain")..............40-50 60

PEPE & ASTROS
Singles: 7-inch
SWAMI (554 "Judy My Love")..............100-125 61

PEPETTES ALL GIRL TRIO
Singles: 7-inch
FENTON (995 "Peppett Rock")................20-30 65

PEPPEL, Harry
(With His Shenandoah Valley Rangers; "Vocal by Dick Dorn")
Singles: 7-inch
ARC (4449 "Sugar Doll")..........................8-10 59
EPs: 7-inch
COWTOWN (700 "Harry Peppel and His Shenandoah Valley Rangers")................................200-300

PEPPER, Jim
LPs: 10/12-inch
EMBRYO (731 "Pepper's Powwow")........20-30 71

PEPPER & RED HOTS
(With Lew Douglas & Orchestra)
Singles: 7-inch
WHITE STAR (1104 "Rock and Roll On Forever")...100-200 59
Also see DOUGLAS, Lew

PEPPER & SHAKERS
Singles: 7-inch
CHETWYD (45002 "Need Your Love") 300-400 66
(Black vinyl.)
CHETWYD (45002 "Need Your Love")...750-1000 66
(Red vinyl.)
CORAL (62523 "I'll Always Love You")....30-40 67

PEPPERMINT, Danny, & Jumping Jacks P&R '61
Singles: 7-inch
CARLTON (565 "Peppermint Twist")........10-20 61
(Different from the Joey Dee song.)
LAURIE (3249 "Toot Toot Tootsie")...........5-10 64
LPs: 10/12-inch
CARLTON (LP-20001 "Danny Peppermint")...25-35 62
(Monaural.)
CARLTON (STLP-20001 "Danny Peppermint")...35-50 62
(Stereo.)
Member: Danny Lamego.
Also see LAMEGO, Danny, & Jumpin' Jacks

PEPPERMINT HARRIS R&B '50
(With the Cross Town Blues Band; Harrison Nelson)
Singles: 78 rpm
ALADDIN...20-40 51-52
CASH...50-75 55
COMBO..15-30 56
MODERN..20-40 51
MONEY..20-40 56
SITTIN' IN WITH....................................25-50 50-51
"X"..20-40 55
Singles: 7-inch
ALADDIN (3097 "I Got Loaded")............50-100 51
(Black vinyl.)
ALADDIN (3097 "I Got Loaded")..........400-500 51
(Colored vinyl.)
ALADDIN (3107 "Have Another Drink and Talk to Me")...75-125 51
ALADDIN (3108 "P. H. Blues")...............75-125 51
ALADDIN (3130 "Right Back On It")......75-125 52
(Black vinyl.)
ALADDIN (3130 "Right Back On It")...750-1000 52
(Green vinyl.)
ALADDIN (3141 "There's a Dead Cat on the Line")...75-125 52
ALADDIN (3154 "I Sure Do Miss My Baby")...75-125 51
ALADDIN (3177 "Wasted Love")............75-125 51
ALADDIN (3183 "Don't Leave Me All Alone")..75-125 53
ALADDIN (3206 "I Never Get Enough of You")..75-125 51
CASH (1003 "Cadillac Funeral")...........100-150 55
COMBO (114 "Love at First Sight")........50-100 56
DART (103 "Messin' Around with the Blues")..15-25 59
DUKE (319 "Ain't No Business")..............15-25 60
JEWEL..5-10 65-68
LUNAR..4-6
MAISON DE SOUL...................................5-10
MODERN (936 "Black Cat Bone").............50-100 51
MONEY (214 "Cadillac Funeral")............50-100 56
SITTIN' IN WITH (543 "Rainin' in My Heart")...100-125 51
"X" (0142 "I Need Your Lovin' ")...........100-150 55
LPs: 10/12-inch
TIME (5 "Peppermint Harris")................50-100 62
Session: Laurels.
Also see LAURELS
Also see NELSON, Peppermint
Also see REED, Jimmy / Peppermint Harris

PEPPERMINT TROLLEY CO. P&R '68
Singles: 7-inch
ACTA..8-12 67-69
VALIANT (752 "Lollipop Train")...............10-15 66

LPs: 10/12-inch
ACTA (38007 "Peppermint Trolley Co.") . 15-25 68
Members: Danny Faragher; Jimmy Faragher; Casey Cunningham; Greg Tornquist.

PEPPERMINTS
Singles: 78 rpm
MERCURY (70681 "Shuf-A-Lin") 10-15 55
Singles: 7-inch
MERCURY (70681 "Shuf-A-Lin") 15-25 55

PEPPERMINTS
(With the House of Beauty Orchestra)
Singles: 7-inch
HOUSE OF BEAUTY (1 "Believe Me") 50-60 59
PEPPERMINT (1001 "Cherryl Ann") 15-25 65
RSVP (1112 "Peppermint Jerk") 15-25 65
Also see BARONS
Also see BLUE, Katie, & Peppermints

PEPPERS
Singles: 78 rpm
CHESS (1577 "Rocking Chair Baby") 75-125 54
Singles: 7-inch
CHESS (1577 "Rocking Chair Baby") .. 400-500 54

PEPPERS
Singles: 7-inch
ENSIGN (1706 "One More Chance") 15-25 61
PRESS (2809 "It Wouldn't Be the Same") 10-15 63
Members: Willie Davis; Aaron Collins; George Hollis; Tom Miller; Robbie Robinson; Beverley Harris.
Also see CADETS
Also see FLARES

PEPPERS
Singles: 7-inch
HOLLY (105 "Soul and Inspiration") .... 15-25 '60s
(May predate Righteous Brothers version.)
Also see RIGHTEOUS BROTHERS

PEPS
Singles: 7-inch
D-TOWN (1049 "Detroit, Michigan") 20-40 65
D-TOWN (1060 "Thinkin' About You") 20-40 66
Members: Joe Harris; Richard Street;.
Also see FABULOUS PEPS
Also see LITTLE JOE & MOROCCOS
Also see STORM, Tom, & Peps
Also see TEMPTATIONS
Also see UNDISPUTED TRUTH

PEPSI-TONES
Singles: 7-inch
PEPSI (15890 "Keep on Walking") .... 15-25 '60s

PERCELLS *P&R '63*
Singles: 7-inch
ABC-PAR (10401 "What Are Boys Made Of") 10-20 63
ABC-PAR (10449 "Boy Friends") 8-12 63
ABC-PAR (10476 "My Guy") 8-12 63
ABC-PAR (10516 "I Stand Alone") 8-12 64

PERCY & ROCKIN' ACES
Singles: 7-inch
LIUVIA (5051 "Don't Cry in Vain") 50-75 61

PERDEW, Wayne
Singles: 78 rpm
ZIPP (103 "Up Beam Baby") 10-20 56
Singles: 7-inch
ZIPP (103 "Up Beam Baby") 100-150 56

PERE UBU
Singles: 7-inch
HEARTHAN (101 "30 Seconds over Tokyo") 15-25 75
Picture Sleeves
HEARTHAN (101 "30 Seconds over Tokyo") 50-75 75

PERENNIALS
Singles: 7-inch
BALL (1016 "My Big Mistake") 1000-1500 63

PEREZ, Manny
(With the Emeralds; with Stony Starr)
Singles: 7-inch
MAGNET (1002 "Theme for Moongazers") 10-20 61
VISTONE (2011 "Coffee Rock") 10-20 59

PERFECTIONS
Singles: 7-inch
LOST NITE (111 "My Baby") 40-50 62
(Yellow vinyl.)
SVR (1005 "I Love You My Love") 75-125 64
Also see DURETTES / Perfections

PERFECTIONS
Singles: 7-inch
PAM-O (101 "No More Love for You") 15-20

PERFIDIANS
Singles: 7-inch
HUSKY (1 "La Paz") 15-25 62
(Black vinyl.)
HUSKY (1 "La Paz") 40-60 62
(Colored vinyl.)

PERFORMERS
("With Orchestra")
Singles: 78 rpm
ALLSTAR 50-100 56
TIP TOP 75-100 57
Singles: 7-inch
ALLSTAR (714 "I'll Make You Understand") 150-250 56
TIP TOP (402 "I'll Make You Understand") 50-75 57
(Black vinyl.)
TIP TOP (402 "I'll Make You Understand") 15-25 61
(Red or yellow vinyl.)

PERIGENTS
Singles: 7-inch
MALTESE (101 "One Girl Too Many") 20-30 65
MALTESE (106 "Love On a Rampage") ...20-30 65

PERILS
Singles: 7-inch
VELVA (7484 "Hate") 15-25 66

PERISCOPES
Singles: 7-inch
DESERT WELLS (2274 "Beavershot") 15-25 65

PERKINS, Al *R&B '69*
(With Betty Bibbs)
Singles: 7-inch
ATCO 5-10 69-71
BUDDAH 4-6 77
C.J. (000 "Don't Deceive Me") 5-10
C.J. (612 "You Cost Too Much") 10-20 61
COLT (623 "Please Come Back") ....10-20 '60s
CONSTELLATION (168 "Thanks to You") .8-12 66
HI 4-6 72
JIVE (1003 "So Long") 30-40 66
SALEM 10-20 61
USA (Except 822) 8-12 64-65
USA (822 "So Long") 15-25 65
Also see DAYLIGHTERS
Also see EVERETT, Bettie, & Daylighters
Also see EVERETT, Betty

PERKINS, Archie & Al
Singles: 7-inch
USA (757 "You Can Belong to Someone") .8-12 64
Also see PERKINS, Al

PERKINS, Billy
Singles: 7-inch
ALCO (1003 "Campus Cutie") 200-300

PERKINS, Carl *C&W/P&R/R&B '56*
(The "Rockin' Guitar Man"; with the C.P. Express)
Singles: 78 rpm
FLIP (501 "Movie Magg") 200-300 55
QUALITY (Except 1571) 25-75 56-57
(Canadian.)
QUALITY (1571 "Gone Gone Gone") 50-100 56
(Canadian.)
SUN (224 "Gone Gone Gone") 50-100 56
SUN (234 thru 287) 35-75 56-57
Singles: 7-inch
AMERICA/SMASH 4-6 86-87
BANTAM 4-6
COLUMBIA (41131 "Pink Pedal Pushers") 25-35 58
COLUMBIA (41207 "Levi Jacket") 25-35 58
COLUMBIA (41296 "Y-O-U") 20-30 58
COLUMBIA (41379 "Pointed Toe Shoes") 20-30 59
COLUMBIA (41449 "One Ticket to Loneliness") 20-30 59
COLUMBIA (41651 "Loveville") 15-25 60
COLUMBIA (41825 "Just for You") 50-100 60
(With "3" prefix. Compact 33 Single.)
COLUMBIA (41825 "Just for You") 15-25 60
COLUMBIA (42061 "Any Way the Wind Blows") 50-100 61
(With "3" prefix. Compact 33 Singles.)
COLUMBIA (42061 "Any Way the Wind Blows") 15-25 61
COLUMBIA (42403 "Forget Me Next Time Around") 15-25 62
COLUMBIA (42405 "The Fool I Used to Be") 50-100 62
(With "3" prefix. Compact 33 Singles.)
COLUMBIA (42405 "The Fool I Used to Be") 15-25 62
COLUMBIA (42514 "Hambone") 50-100 62
(With "3" prefix. Compact 33 Singles.)
COLUMBIA (42514 "Hambone") 15-25 62
COLUMBIA (42753 "Forget Me") 15-25 63
COLUMBIA (44723 "Restless") 8-12 69
COLUMBIA (45347 "Me Without You") 5-10 71
COLUMBIA (45466 "Cotton Top") 5-10 71
COLUMBIA (45582 "High On Love") 5-10 72
COLUMBIA (45694 "Someday") 5-10 72
DECCA (31548 "For a Little While") 10-15 63
DECCA (31591 "After Sundown") 10-15 64
DECCA (31709 "Monkeyshine") 10-15 64
DECCA (31786 "One of These Days") 10-15 65
DOLLIE (505 "Country Boy's Dream") 10-20 67
DOLLIE (508 "Almost Love") 10-20 67
DOLLIE (512 "You Can Take the Boy Out of the Country") 15-25 67
DOLLIE (514 "Back to Tennessee") 10-20 67
DOLLIE (516 "It's You") 10-20 67
FLIP (501 "Movie Magg") 500-1000 55
JET (5054 "Blue Suede Shoes") 4-6 79
MERCURY (73393 "Help Me Dream") 4-8 73
MERCURY (73425 "Dixie Fried") 4-8 73
MERCURY (73489 "Ruby Don't Take Your Love to Town") 4-8 74
MERCURY (73653 "You'll Always Be a Lady to Me") 4-8 74
MERCURY (73690 "E.P. Express") 8-12 75
MUSIC MILL 4-8 76
QUALITY (1473 "Blue Suede Shoes") 40-60 56
(Canadian.)
QUALITY (1571 "Gone Gone Gone") ...100-200 56
(Canadian.)
QUALITY (1557 "Dixie Fried") 50-75 56
(Canadian.)
QUALITY (1570 "Boppin' the Blues") 50-75 56
(Canadian.)
QUALITY (1579 "Matchbox") 40-60 57
(Canadian.)
QUALITY (1654 "Forever Yours") 40-60 57
(Canadian.)
QUALITY (1701 "Glad All Over") 40-60 57
(Canadian.)
SSS/SUN ....4-8 '70s
SUEDE 3-6 81
SUN (224 "Gone Gone Gone") 100-150 56
SUN (234 "Blue Suede Shoes") 35-50 56
SUN (235 "Sure to Fall") 1000-2000 56
SUN (243 "Boppin' the Blues") 35-50 56
SUN (249 "Dixie Fried") 40-60 56
SUN (261 "Matchbox") 35-50 57
SUN (274 "Forever Yours") 35-50 57
SUN (287 "Glad All Over") 35-50 57
UNIVERSAL 3-6 89
Picture Sleeves
AMERICA/SMASH 4-6 86
COLUMBIA (41131 "Pink Pedal Pushers") 35-50 58
COLUMBIA (42405 "Hollywood City") 20-30 62
COLUMBIA (42514 "Hambone") 40-60 62
EPs: 7-inch
COLUMBIA (12341 "Whole Lotta Shakin'") 250-350 58
SUN (115 "Blue Suede Shoes") 250-350 58
LPs: 10/12-inch
ACCORD 8-12 82
ALBUM GLOBE 8-12
ALLEGIANCE 5-10 84
COLUMBIA (1234 "Whole Lotta Shakin'") 100-200 58
(Red label.)
COLUMBIA (1234 "Whole Lotta Shakin'") 150-250 58
(White label. Promotional issue only.)
COLUMBIA (9833 "Greatest Hits") 10-20 69
COLUMBIA (10117 "Greatest Hits") 8-10 74
DESIGN ....15-25 '60s
DOLLIE (4001 "Country Boy's Dream") ...15-25 67
GRT/SUNNYVALE 8-12 77
HARMONY 8-12 72
HILLTOP 8-12
JET 8-12 78
KOALA 8-12 80
MERCURY 10-15 73
PICKWICK/HILLTOP 8-12
ROUNDER 8-12 89
SSS/SUN 8-15 69-84
SUEDE 8-12 81
SUN (1225 "Dance Album") 750-1000 57
SUN (1225 "Teen Beat") 200-400 61
(Repackage of *Dance Album*.)
TRIP 8-12 74
UNIVERSAL 8-12 89
Also see McCARTNEY, Paul
Also see NELSON, Willie / Jerry Lee Lewis / Carl Perkins / David Allan Coe
Also see STATLER BROTHERS
Also see YOUNG, Faron / Carl Perkins / Claude King

PERKINS, Carl / Sonny Burgess
LPs: 10/12-inch
SSS/SUN 8-12
Also see BURGESS, Sonny

PERKINS, Carl, Jerry Lee Lewis, Roy Orbison & Johnny Cash *LP '86*
LPs: 10/12-inch
AMERICA ("Class of '55") 20-30 86
(Mail-order edition. Has souvenir booklet and audio cassette with interviews of the singers.)
AMERICA/SMASH (830002 "Class of '55") 8-12 86
AMERICA/SMASH (830002 "Class of '55") 30-40 86
(Picture disc. Promotional issue only.)
Also see CASH, Johnny, Carl Perkins & Jerry Lee Lewis
Also see LEWIS, Jerry Lee, Carl Perkins & Charlie Rich
Also see ORBISON, Roy

PERKINS, Carl, & NRBQ
Singles: 7-inch
COLUMBIA (45107 "All Mama's Children") 5-10 70
LPs: 10/12-inch
COLUMBIA (9981 "Boppin' the Blues") 10-15 70
Also see NRBQ
Also see PERKINS, Carl

PERKINS, Dal *C&W '68*
Singles: 7-inch
COLUMBIA (44343 "Helpless") 5-10 67
VIV (102 "Shy") 10-20 57

PERKINS, George *P&R/R&B '70*
(With the Silver Stars)
Singles: 7-inch
ACE (7102 "Baby I'm Fed Up") 5-10 71
SILVER FOX (18 Cryin' in the Streets") 8-12 69
SOUL POWER (113 "Baby You Saved Me") 4-6 73
LPs: 10/12-inch
SSS INT'L (25 "Cryin' in the Streets") .... 8-12 '70s

PERKINS, Harold, & Don Clairs
Singles: 7-inch
AMP 3 (1001 "I Lost My Job") 20-30 58

PERKINS, Howard
Singles: 7-inch
SHAWNEE (102 "Lovin' Baby") 600-800
Also see BOGGS, Lucky / Howard Perkins

PERKINS, Ike
Singles: 7-inch
APT (26012 "Annabelle") 4-8 72
C.J. (101 "These Kissable Lips") .... 8-12 '50s
Also see DU PUY, Helda & Ike Perkins Orchestra

PERKINS, Jerry, & His Blues Blasters
Singles: 78 rpm
W&W (204 "Katherine Blues") 40-60 50

PERKINS, Joe *P&R '63*
("Featuring the Memphis Sound")
Singles: 7-inch
BERRY ....5-10 '60s

BLUFF CITY ... 4-6 74
MUSICOR (1064 "Natalie Would") ... 5-10 65
PLUSH (100 "Wrapped Up in Your Love") . 5-10
SOUND STAGE 7 (2511 "Little Eeefin' Annie") ... 10-15 63

PERKINS, Joe, & Rookies
Singles: 78 rpm
KING ... 30-75 56-57
Singles: 7-inch
KING (5005 "Time Alone Will Tell") ... 30-40 56
KING (5030 "How Much Love Can One Heart Hold") ... 50-75 57
(Blue label.)
KING (5030 "How Much Love Can One Heart Hold") ... 75-125 57
(White bio label. Promotional issue only.)

PERKINS, Laura Lee
Singles: 7-inch
IMPERIAL (5493 "Kiss Me Baby") ... 20-35 58
IMPERIAL (5507 "Don't Wait Up") ... 20-35 58

PERKINS, Reggie
Singles: 7-inch
GEM (1201 "Saturday Night Party") ... 75-100 59
RAY NOTE (9 "High School Caesar") ... 20-30 59

PERKINS, Roy
(Roy "Boogie Boy" Perkins)
Singles: 78 rpm
MELADEE (112 "You're Gone") ... 50-75 56
Singles: 7-inch
DART (112 "Sweet Lilly") ... 50-75 59
MELADEE (111 "Bye Bye Baby") ... 75-100
MELADEE (112 "You're Gone") ... 300-400 56
MERCURY (71278 "Drop Top") ... 20-30 58
RAM (10821 "Drop Top") ... 200-300 57

PERKINS, Tony *P&R '57*
(Anthony Perkins)
Singles: 78 rpm
RCA ... 10-15 57-58
Singles: 7-inch
EPIC (9181 "Friendly Persuasion") ... 10-15 57
RCA (7020 "Moonlight Swim") ... 10-20 57
RCA (7078 "When School Starts Again") 10-20 57
RCA (7155 "Indian Giver") ... 10-20 58
RCA (7244 "Prettiest Girl in School") ... 10-20 58
Picture Sleeves
RCA (7155 "Indian Giver") ... 20-30 58
LPs: 10/12-inch
EPIC (3394 "Tony Perkins") ... 25-35 57
RCA (1679 "From My Heart") ... 30-40 58
RCA (LPM-1853 "On a Rainy Afternoon") ... 30-40 58
RCA (LSP-1853 "On a Rainy Afternoon") ... 40-60 58

PERKINS, Tony / James Dean
Singles: 78 rpm
RAINBO (5-21-57 "Hear Hollywood") ... 40-60 57
(Cardboard picture disc.)
Also see DEAN, James
Also see PERKINS, Tony

PERKINS, Walter
Singles: 7-inch
PLA-ME (666 "Solid Rock") ... 75-100

PERNELL, Larry, & Kings Of Rhythm
Singles: 78 rpm
SHOWCASE (100 "Hot Nuts") ... 20-30 '50s
Singles: 7-inch
SHOWCASE (100 "Hot Nuts") ... 200-300 '50s

PERPETUAL MOTION
Singles: 7-inch
DIAL (4078 "Neckin' Don't Make It") ... 5-10 68
ROCK 'N' JAZZ (9188 "Sally Brown") ... 10-20 67

PERRI'S
Singles: 7-inch
MADISON (105 "Jerilee") ... 15-20 58

PERRIN, Sue
Singles: 7-inch
GOLDEN WORLD (2 "Candy Store Man") ... 10-20 62
GOLDEN WORLD (101 "I Wonder") ... 10-20 62
J.W. (1001 "Can't Let Go") ... 50-75 '60s

PERRINE, Pep
LPs: 10/12-inch
HIDEOUT (1003 "Live and in Person") .. 75-100 '60s

PERRY, Berlin, & Gleams
Singles: 7-inch
RIBBON (6902 "Put That Tear Back") .. 100-200 59
Also see GLEAMS

PERRY, Bill
Singles: 7-inch
REED (1029 "You Hit the Nail on the Head") ... 50-100

PERRY, Bill, & Bel-Airs
Singles: 78 rpm
G.G. ... 20-30 56
Singles: 7-inch
G.G. (521 "You'll Never Be Mine Again") ... 100-150 56

PERRY, Chris
Singles: 7-inch
VIBRO (4003 "I Want to Know Where I Stand") ... 20-30 60

PERRY, Ike, & His Lyrics
Singles: 7-inch
ANN (101 "Lovin' Poppa") ... 30-40 63
AZALEA (101 "Don't Let It Get You Down") ... 5-10 64
BEE (1875 "Lovin' Poppa") ... 10-20 65
BRIDGE (110 "Star Steps to Heaven") . 100-200 58
COURIER (828 "Don't Let It Get You Down") ... 15-20 64
COWTOWN (801 "I Got You Covered") ... 25-35 60
KING TUT ... 4-8 79
MAMA (1 "In My Letter to You") ... 50-100 63
MAMA (3614 "Don't Let It Get You Down") ... 30-40 63
(Identification number shown since no selection number is used.)
NAURLENE (100 "Don't Let It Get You Down") ... 10-15 65
Also see FIVE LYRICS

PERRY, Jesse
Singles: 78 rpm
MODERN ... 15-25 45

PERRY, Jim, & Hesitations
Singles: 7-inch
BAND BOX (310 "Surfside Twist") ... 15-25 62

PERRY, Johnny, Orchestra
(Featuring Ida Haymes)
Singles: 78 rpm
ATLAS (1038 "I Left My Baby") ... 10-15 54
JUBILEE (5125 "Terrible Feeling") ... 10-15 53
Singles: 7-inch
ATLAS (1038 "I Left My Baby") ... 15-25 54
JUBILEE (5125 "Terrible Feeling") ... 15-25 53
MILO (101 "Milk Shake") ... 10-20 63

PERRY, King
(With the Pied Pipers; King Perry Quintet)
Singles: 78 rpm
DELUXE (3216 "Going to California Blues") ... 30-40 47
DOT (15010 "Going to California Blues") . 15-25 52
EXCELSIOR (522 "Rocks in My Bed") ... 20-30 45
EXCELSIOR (524 "The Ice Man") ... 20-30 45
EXCELSIOR (600 "Big Fat Mama") ... 15-25 51
HOLLYWOOD (1030 "Back to Kansas City") ... 10-20 55
LUCKY (003 "Things Ain't What They Used to Be") ... 10-20 54
MELODISC ... 20-30 45
RPM (381 "Everybody Jump") ... 10-20 53
SPECIALTY ... 25-35 50-51
UNITED ARTIST (504 "Stardust") ... 20-30 46
Singles: 7-inch
DOT (15010 "Going to California Blues") . 25-35 52
EXCELSIOR (4 "Big Fat Mama") ... 100-200 51
HOLLYWOOD (1030 "Back to Kansas City") ... 15-25 55
LUCKY (003 "Things Ain't What They Used to Be") ... 20-30 54
RPM (381 "Everybody Jump") ... 30-40 53
RPM (392 "Card Playin' Blues") ... 30-40 53
SPECIALTY (367 "Everything Gotta Be Alright") ... 40-60 50
SPECIALTY (398 "Blue and Lonesome") . 40-60 51
SPECIALTY (412 "I Ain't Got a Dime to My Name") ... 40-60 51
TRILYTE (4001 "Come Back Baby") ... 20-30 56

PERRY, Lou
Singles: 7-inch
BELLA (2207 "Cupid's Arrow") ... 50-75 59
CORDAK (1703 "Him") ... 5-10 66

PERRY, Paul
Singles: 7-inch
NU SOUND (1008 "Got a Girl Named Dee") ... 150-250 61

PERRY, Rosetta
Singles: 78 rpm
BLUES BOYS KINGDOM (107 "Farewell Blues") ... 25-30 57
Singles: 7-inch
BLUES BOYS KINGDOM (107 "Farewell Blues") ... 30-40 57

PERRY, Tony
Singles: 7-inch
EMBER (1015 "I'm Your Forever") ... 20-30 57

PERRY & PETE
Singles: 7-inch
BRENT (7036 "Rockin' Wobble") ... 10-20 62

PERRY & HARMONICS
Singles: 7-inch
MERCURY (72476 "Do the Monkey with James") ... 5-10 65
LPs: 10/12-inch
MERCURY (21037 "Intrigue with Soul") ... 10-20 65
(Monaural.)
MERCURY (61037 "Intrigue with Soul") ... 15-25 65
(Stereo.)

PERRYMAN, Paul
Singles: 78 rpm
DUKE ... 10-20 56-57
Singles: 7-inch
DUKE (158 "Just to Hold My Hand") ... 30-40 56
DUKE (169 "Long Enough") ... 30-40 56
DUKE (181 "Satellite Fever, Asiatic Flu") . 50-75 57
DUKE (195 "While You Wait") ... 15-25 57
DUKE (305 "Teenage Romeo") ... 15-25 59
FIRE (1018 "Look At My Baby") ... 10-20 60

PERRYMATES
(Perry Mates)
Singles: 7-inch
LANAR (103 "Little Darlin'") ... 20-25
MARKETTE (1050 "Hang Your Head") ... 10-15 '60s

PERRYWELL, Charles, & Fairlanes
Singles: 7-inch
TIC-TOC (104 "You're Lonesome Now") .. 50-75

PERSIA, Judee
Singles: 7-inch
COLUMBIA (42073 "Please Love Me") ... 10-20 61

PERSIAN MARKET
Singles: 7-inch
LIGHTNING (103 "Flash in the Pan") ... 15-25 67

PERSIANETTES
Singles: 7-inch
SWAN (4271 "What Good Is It") ... 5-10 67
Also see CARR, Timmy, & Persianettes
Also see TIMMY & PERSIANETTES

PERSIANS
Singles: 7-inch
GOLD EAGLE (1813 "Love Me Tonight") 10-15 62
GOLDISC (G-1 "Teardrops Are Falling") .. 30-40 63
GOLDISC (G-17 "When You Said Let's Get Married") ... 10-15 63
MUSIC WORLD (102 "Let's Get Married") ... 10-15 63
PAGEANT (601 "Steady Kind") ... 15-25 63
RSVP (114 "Tears of Love") ... 30-40 62
RTO (100/101 "Sunday Kind of Love"/"When We Get Married") ... 10-20 62
SIR RAH (501 "Don't Let Me Down") ... 25-35 63

PERSIANS / Clifton Chenier
Singles: 7-inch
MASTERPIECE (1111 "Tears of Love") ... 5-10
(Colored vinyl.)
Also see CHENIER, Clifton
Also see PERSIANS

PERSIANS *R&B '68*
Singles: 7-inch
ABC (11087 "Too Much Pride") ... 5-10 68
ABC (11145 "I Only Have Eyes for You") . 20-40 68
CAPITOL (3230 "Your Love") ... 5-10 71
CAPITOL (3333 "Baby Come Back Home") ... 5-10 72
GRAPEVINE (201 "Detour") ... 5-10 70
GWP (201 "Detour") ... 5-10 70
GWP (509 "I Don't Know How") ... 5-10 69
Members: James Gill; Freddie Lewis; James Harlee; Jim Brown.

PERSONALITIES
(Featuring Ralph Molina; with Teacho Wiltshire Orchestra)
Singles: 78 rpm
SAFARI ... 100-200 57
Singles: 7-inch
SAFARI (1002 "Woe Woe Baby") ... 100-200 57
(Giraffe is pictured on label.)
SAFARI (1002 "Woe Woe Baby") ... 30-40 57
(No giraffe on label.)
Also see MELLO-MOODS

PERSPECTIVES
Singles: 7-inch
TRANS-WORLD (1101 "Git-Git Guitar") .. 10-20

PERSUADERS
Singles: 7-inch
RELIC (1002 "Tears") ... 5-10 65
WINLEY (235 "Tears") ... 150-200 59

PERSUADERS
(Featuring Chuck "Tequila" Rio)
Singles: 7-inch
SATURN (404 "Surfing Strip") ... 15-25 63
SATURN (405 "Gremmie Bread") ... 15-25 63
LPs: 10/12-inch
SATURN (5000 "Surfer's Nightmare") .. 125-150 63
(Monaural.)
SATURN (S-5000 "Surfer's Nightmare") ... 150-175 63
(Stereo.)
Also see RIO, Chuck "Tequila"

PERSUADERS
Singles: 7-inch
ORIGINAL SOUND (39 "Grunion Run") ... 25-35 63
(Reissued as by the Hollywood Persuaders.)
Also see HOLLYWOOD PERSUADERS

PERSUASIONS
Singles: 7-inch
CROWN POINT (1 "The Magic of Love"). 15-25 64

PERSUASIONS *LP '71*
Singles: 7-inch
A&M ... 4-6 74-75
CAPITOL ... 4-8 71-72
CATAMOUNT (Black vinyl) ... 4-6 '70s
CATAMOUNT (Colored vinyl) ... 8-12 '70s
ELEKTRA (45396 "Papa-Oom-Mow-Mow"). 3-5 77
ERICA ... 10-20
KING TUT (171 "The Sun") ... 4-8 78
MCA (40080 "Good Old Acappella") ... 4-8 73
MCA (40118 "Love You") ... 4-8 73
MINIT (32067 "Party in the Woods") ... 8-12 69
PAY-4-PLAY (100 "Echo") ... 5-10 72
(Red vinyl. Shown as "Four Persuasions.")
REPRISE (0977 "Since I Fell for You") ... 4-8 70
TOWER ... 5-10 65-66
LPs: 10/12-inch
A&M ... 10-15 74
CAPITOL ... 15-25 71-72
CATAMOUNT ... 8-10 '70s
ELEKTRA ... 10-12 77
FLYING FISH ... 5-10 79
MCA ... 8-12 73
ROUNDER ... 5-8 '80s
STRAIGHT (6394 "Acapella") ... 25-35 70
Members: Jerry Lawson; Jimmy Hayes; Jayotis Washington; Joe Russell; Herb Rhoad.

PERY MATES
Singles: 7-inch
CA-JO (210 "It Was You") ... 40-50 59

PET SHOP BOYS *P&R/R&B/LP '86*
Singles: 12-inch
BOB CAT ... 5-10 84
EMI ... 4-8 86-87
Singles: 7-inch
EMI ... 3-6 86-90
Picture Sleeves
EMI ... 3-6 86-89
LPs: 10/12-inch
EMI (Except 90263) ... 5-10 86-90

EMI (90263 "Actually")........................ 10-15 88
(With bonus 12-inch single, *Always on My Mind.*)
Members: Neil Tennant; Chris Lowe.

PET SHOP BOYS & DUSTY SPRINGFIELD
Singles: 7-inch
EMI.. 3-5 87
Also see PET SHOP BOYS
Also see SPRINGFIELD, Dusty

PETE, Peter, & Lovers
("Music with the Travelers")
Singles: 7-inch
DERBY (1030 "A Lonely Island")......... 100-150 60

PETE & ERNIE
Singles: 7-inch
KING (5493 "Donkey Trot")..................... 10-15 61
KING (5640 "The Hunch")....................... 15-25 61

PETE & JIMMY
Singles: 7-inch
CASTLE (504 "So Wild")..................... 200-250 58

PETE & VINNIE
Singles: 7-inch
BIG TOP (3155 "Hand Clappin' Time").... 10-15 63
Members: Pete Anders; Vinnie Poncia.
Also see ANDERS & PONCIA

PETER & GORDON — P&R/LP '64
Singles: 7-inch
CAPITOL.. 8-12 64-69
SOUND CLASSICS.............................. 3-5
Picture Sleeves
CAPITOL.. 10-15 64-67
LPs: 10/12-inch
CAPITOL (T-2115 thru T-2882)............... 15-25 64-68
(Monaural.)
CAPITOL (ST-2115 thru ST-2882)........... 20-30 64-68
(Stereo.)
CAPITOL (SM-2549 "Best of Peter & Gordon").. 5-10 77
CAPITOL (SN-16084 "Best of Peter & Gordon").. 5-8 80
Members: Peter Asher; Gordon Waller.
Also see WALLER, Gordon

PETER & GORDON / Lettermen
Singles: 7-inch
CAPITOL CREATIVE PRODUCTS............ 5-10 66
(Fritos Company promotional issue.)
Also see LETTERMEN
Also see PETER & GORDON

PETER & PROPHETS
Singles: 7-inch
FENTON (2050 "Johnny of Dreams")...... 20-30 66

PETER & RABBITS
Singles: 7-inch
BELL (670 "Bless You Little Girl")............... 5-10 67

PETER, PAUL & MARY — P&R/LP '62
Singles: 7-inch
("Eugene McCarthy for President")......... 10-20 68
(Promotional issue only. No label name used.)
W.B. (5000 series).............................. 5-10 62-66
W.B. (7000 series).............................. 4-8 67-70
Picture Sleeves
W.B. (5325 "Big Boat")......................... 15-25 62
W.B. (5402 "A'Soalin' ")........................ 15-25 63
EPs: 7-inch
W.B. (1507 "In the Wind")...................... 5-10 62
(Promotional issue only.)
LPs: 10/12-inch
GOLD C.. 5-8 87
W.B. (1449 thru 1648)........................... 20-30 62-66
(Gold or gray labels.)
W.B. (1700 thru 2552)........................... 8-15 67-70
W.B. (3000 series)................................ 5-10 77-78
Members: Peter Yarrow; Paul Stookey; Mary Travers.
Also see STOOKEY, Paul
Also see TRAVERS, Mary

PETERS, Nancy
(With the Band of Harold "Beans" Bowles)
Singles: 7-inch
KUDO (664 "Cry Baby Heart").............. 75-100 58
Also see JOHNSON, Marv

PETERS, Pete
(With the Rhythmakers)
Singles: 7-inch
DIXIE (836 "Rockin' 'N My Sweet Baby's Arms").. 300-400 '50s
P&J (100 "Wig Walk")........................... 100-200
P&J (101 "Fanny Brown")...................... 100-200

PETERS, Preston
Singles: 7-inch
LU JAY (218 "Lingie Ching")..................... 25-35 '60s

PETERS, Sandra
Singles: 7-inch
PAC (102 "Rock Away My Blues")............ 50-75

PETERSEN, Paul — P&R '62
Singles: 7-inch
ABC.. 4-6 74
COLPIX (Except 720)........................... 10-20 62-65
COLPIX (720 "Poorest Boy in Town")...... 50-75 64
ERIC... 4-6 '70s
MCA.. 4-6
MOTOWN.. 10-20 67-68
Picture Sleeves
COLPIX (620 "She Can't Find Her Keys").. 15-25 62
COLPIX (632 "Keep Your Love Locked"). 15-25 62
COLPIX (663 "My Dad")......................... 15-25 62
LPs: 10/12-inch
COLPIX (CP-429 "Lollipops & Roses")..... 25-35 62
(Monaural.)
COLPIX (SCP-429 "Lollipops & Roses").. 35-45 62
(Stereo.)
COLPIX (CP-442 "My Dad")..................... 30-40 63
(Monaural.)
COLPIX (SCP-442 "My Dad").................. 35-45 63
(Stereo.)
Session: Beach Boys; Honeys; Billy Strange; Hal Blaine; Tommy Tedesco; Plas Johnson; Steve Douglas; David Gates; Richie Frost.
Also see BEACH BOYS
Also see DARREN, James / Shelly Fabares / Paul Petersen
Also see DOUGLAS, Steve
Also see GATES, David
Also see HONEYS
Also see JOHNSON, Plas
Also see STRANGE, Billy

PETERSEN, Paul, & Shelly Fabares
Singles: 7-inch
COLPIX (631 "What Did They Do Before Rock & Roll").. 5-10 62
Also see FABARES, Shelly
Also see PETERSEN, Paul

PETERSON, Bobby — P&R '59
(Bobby Peterson Quintet)
Singles: 7-inch
ATLANTIC (2152 "Every Now and Then").. 5-10 62
GRAND (164 "It's Been So Long Baby").... 8-12 63
JAMIE (1249 "Love or Misery")................ 5-10 63
V-TONE (205 "The Hunch")..................... 10-15 59
V-TONE (210 "Rockin' Charlie")............... 10-15 60
V-TONE (214 "Irresistible You")............... 10-15 60
V-TONE (217 "Three Street").................. 10-15 61
V-TONE (221 "One Day")........................ 10-15 61
V-TONE (226 "Smooth Sailing")............... 10-15 61
Members: Bobby Peterson; James Thomas; Joe Pyatt; Chico Green; David Butler.

PETERSON, Earl
(Michigan's Singing Cowboy)
Singles: 78 rpm
COLUMBIA... 10-20 55
SUN (197 "Boogie Blues")..................... 200-300 54
Singles: 7-inch
COLUMBIA (21364 "Boogie Blues")......... 30-40 55
COLUMBIA (21406 "You're Going to Break").. 15-25 56
COLUMBIA (21540 "You Gotta Be My Baby").. 20-30 56
SUN (197 "Boogie Blues")..................... 400-500 54

PETERSON, Jackie, & Paramounts
(With Dominic Apollito & Orchestra)
Singles: 7-inch
WARWICK (127 "Funny Man").................. 10-20 61

PETERSON, James
Singles: 7-inch
FANTASTIC (1007 "Cheating Woman")... 25-35

PETERSON, Jimmy
Singles: 7-inch
ATHENS (210 "Help Me")........................ 15-25

PETERSON, Leon
Singles: 7-inch
BOBBIN (137 "Searchin' ")..................... 10-20 62
HOB (117 "This Creation")..................... 20-40 61

PETERSON, Oscar — LP '63
(Oscar Peterson Trio; with Milt Jackson; with Clark Terry)
Singles: 78 rpm
CLEF... 4-6 53-56
MERCURY... 4-8 51-52
NORGRAN... 4-6 55
VERVE... 4-8 57
Singles: 7-inch
CLEF... 5-15 53-56
LIMELIGHT.. 4-8 65-66
MERCURY (8900 series)........................ 5-15 51-52
MERCURY (72000 series)...................... 4-8 64
MERCURY (89000 series)...................... 5-15 52-53
NORGRAN... 5-15 55
PRESTIGE... 4-6 69
VERVE... 5-10 57-64
EPs: 7-inch
CLEF... 25-50 52-55
RCA (3006 "This Is Oscar Peterson").... 75-125 51
LPs: 10/12-inch
BASF... 8-12 74-76
CLEF (106 "Piano Solos")...................... 100-200 52
(10-inch LP.)
CLEF (107 "At Carnegie Hall")............... 100-200 52
(10-inch LP.)
CLEF (110 "Collates")........................... 100-200 52
(10-inch LP.)
CLEF (116 "Oscar Peterson Quartet"). 100-200 52
(10-inch LP.)
CLEF (119 "Oscar Peterson Plays Pretty").. 100-200 52
(10-inch LP.)
CLEF (127 "Collates, No. 2")................. 100-150 53
(10-inch LP.)
CLEF (145 "Oscar Peterson Sings")..... 100-150 54
(10-inch LP.)
CLEF (155 "Oscar Peterson Plays Pretty, No. 2").. 100-150 54
(10-inch LP.)
CLEF (168 "Oscar Peterson Quartet, No. 2").. 100-150 55
(10-inch LP.)
CLEF (600 series)............................... 50-100 53-56
EMARCY... 8-12 76
LIMELIGHT (1000 series)...................... 5-8 82
LIMELIGHT (82000 & 86000 series)........ 10-20 65-67
MFSL (243 "Very Tall")......................... 25-35 95
(Half-speed mastered.)
MGM (100 series)................................ 8-12 70
MPS.. 8-12 72-76
MERCURY (20975 "Trio+One")................ 20-30 64
(Monaural.)
MERCURY (60975 "Trio+One")................ 25-35 64
(Stereo.)
METRO.. 10-15 65
PABLO... 6-12 75-83
PAUSA... 5-10 79-81
PRESTIGE... 8-15 69-74
RCA (3006 "This Is Oscar Peterson").. 200-250 51
(10-inch LP.)
TRIP.. 5-8 75-76
VSP... 10-20 66-67
VERVE... 35-75 56-60
(Reads "Verve Records, Inc." at bottom of label.)
VERVE... 10-25 61-72
(Reads "MGM Records - A Division of Metro-Goldwyn-Mayer, Inc." at bottom of label.)
VERVE... 5-15 73-83
(Reads "Manufactured By MGM Record Corp.," or mentions either Polydor or Polygram at bottom of label.)
WING.. 8-12 67
Members (Oscar Peterson Trio): Oscar Peterson; Ray Brown; Herb Ellis.
Also see ARMSTRONG, Louis, & Oscar Peterson
Also see BASIE, Count, & Oscar Peterson
Also see FITZGERALD, Ella, & Oscar Peterson
Also see GETZ, Stan, & Oscar Peterson
Also see HENDERSON, Bill, & Oscar Peterson Trio
Also see HUBBARD, Freddie, & Oscar Peterson
Also see MULLIGAN, Gerry, & Oscar Peterson
Also see TERRY, Clark
Also see YOUNG, Lester, & Oscar Peterson

PETERSON, Pigmeat
Singles: 78 rpm
FEDERAL.. 25-40 52
Singles: 7-inch
FEDERAL (12081 "Everybody Loves a Fat Man").. 50-75 52

PETERSON, Ray — P&R '59
(With Hugo Winterhalter Orchestra & Chorus; with Shorty Rogers & His Orchestra; with the Jack Halloran Singers)
Singles: 7-inch
CLOUD 9... 4-6 75
DECCA... 4-6 71
DUNES... 10-20 60-63
MGM... 5-10 64-66
MGM (100 series)............................... 4-8 64
(Golden Circle reissue series.)
POLYDOR... 4-6 '70s
QUALITY... 10-20 60-63
(Canadian.)
RCA (7087 "Fever").............................. 15-25 57
RCA (7165 "Shirley Purley")................... 40-60 58
RCA (7255 "Tail Light")......................... 15-20 58
RCA (7303 "My Blue Eyed Baby")............ 15-20 58
RCA (7336 "Dream Away")..................... 15-20 58
RCA (7404 "Richer Than I")................... 15-20 58
RCA (7513 "Wonder of You").................. 15-20 59
RCA (7578 "My Blue Angel").................. 15-20 59
(Monaural. With "47" prefix.)
RCA (7578 "My Blue Angel").................. 25-35 60
(Stereo. With "61" prefix.)
RCA (7635 "Goodnight My Love")........... 15-20 59
RCA (7703 "Answer Me My Love")........... 15-20 60
RCA (7745 "Tell Laura I Love Her")......... 15-20 60
(Monaural. With "47" prefix.)
RCA (7745 "Tell Laura I Love Her")......... 30-50 60
(Stereo. With "61" prefix.)
RCA (7779 "Teenage Heartache")........... 15-20 60
(Monaural. With "47" prefix.)
RCA (7779 "Teenage Heartache")........... 25-35 60
(Stereo. With "61" prefix.)
RCA (7845 "My Blue Angel").................. 15-20 61
RCA (8333 "Wonder of You").................. 10-15 64
REPRISE.. 5-10 69
UNI... 4-6 70-71
Picture Sleeves
DUNES (2002 "Corrina Corrina")............. 20-30 60
MGM (13269 "Oh No")........................... 8-10 64
MGM (13336 "House Without Windows").. 8-10 64
RCA (7635 "Goodnight My Love")............ 20-30 59
EPs: 7-inch
RCA (4367 "Tell Laura I Love Her")......... 50-75 60
LPs: 10/12-inch
CAMDEN (2119 "Goodnight My Love, Pleasant Dreams").. 10-20 66
DECCA... 8-12 71
MGM... 20-30 64-65
RCA (LPM-2297 "Tell Laura I Love Her").. 50-100 60
(Monaural.)
RCA (LSP-2297 "Tell Laura I Love Her").. 75-125 60
(Stereo.)
Also see HALLORAN, Jack, Singers
Also see ROGERS, Shorty
Also see WINTERHALTER, Hugo, & His Orchestra

PETITE TEENS
Singles: 7-inch
BRUNSWICK (55119 "We're in Our Teens").. 10-20 59

PETITES
Singles: 7-inch
ASCOT (2166 "I'm Gonna Love Him")....... 5-10 64
COLUMBIA (41662 "Get Your Daddy's Car Tonight").. 8-12 60
COLUMBIA (42053 "Little Love")............. 8-12 61
CUB (9153 "Don't Go Changing Your Mind").. 5-10 68
ELMOR (304 "The Beating of My Heart").. 100-150 62
SPINNING (6003 "Marguerite")............... 10-20 58
SPINNING (6005 "Sweetie Pie")............. 10-20 58

PETITES
Singles: 7-inch
TROY (1001 "Baby Blue Mustang")......... 15-25 63

PETRI, Barry
(Barry Petricoin)
Singles: 7-inch
AL-STAN (388 "All My Love") 30-40 59
MONT-AL (604 "Dance Baby Dance") 10-15
SWAN (4111 "Pretty Little Angel") 20-30 62
Also see PETRICOIN, Barry, & Belairs

PETRICOIN, Barry, & Belairs
Singles: 7-inch
AL-STAN (103 "Pretty Little Angel") 50-75 58
AL-STAN (103 "Pretty Little Angel") .... 4-6 '80s
(Black vinyl. 500 made.)
Also see PETRI, Barry

PETS P&R '58
Singles: 7-inch
ARWIN (109 "Cha-Hua-Hua") 10-20 58
ARWIN (112 "Wow-Ee") 10-15 58
ARWIN (116 "Guitaro") 10-15 58
Member: Seph Acre.
Also see WARREN, Jerry

PETS / Searchers
Singles: 7-inch
STOOP SOUNDS (506 "Never Let You Go"/ "Yvonne") 75-100 97
Also see SEARCHERS

PETTIBONE, Art
Singles: 7-inch
TEE PEE (102 "Newest Sound") 50-75

PETTICOATS
Singles: 7-inch
CHALLENGE (9211 "Surfin' Sally") 10-20 63

PETTIS, Ray
Singles: 78 rpm
DREXEL 5-10 56
Singles: 7-inch
BOSS ("Power of Love") 50-100
(No selection number used.)
DEE DEE (3903 "Hello There Pretty Baby") 10-20
DEE DEE (73173 "Together Forever") 10-20
DREXEL (908 "Please Tell Me When") ... 10-20 56
DREXEL (911 "Does It Have to Be Christmas") 10-20 56

PETTISON, Mike, Quartet
Singles: 78 rpm
20TH CENTURY 15-25 52
Singles: 7-inch
20TH CENTURY (75006 "I'll Always Love You So") 30-40 52

PETTIT, Mike
Singles: 7-inch
1001 (102 "I've Cried Before") 15-25 63

PETTY, Al
(With Patti Lewis)
Singles: 7-inch
4-STAR (1761 "My Lips Won't Talk") 10-20 60

PETTY, Daryl
Singles: 7-inch
HORNET (502 "Flaming Love") 75-100 59

PETTY, Eddie "Prince"
Singles: 7-inch
GUEST (1003 "That's You, That's Me") ... 15-25 57

PETTY, Norman, Trio P&R '54
(Vi Petty)
Singles: 78 rpm
ABC-PAR 5-10 57
COLUMBIA (Except 41039) 5-10 57
COLUMBIA (41039 "Moondreams") 50-75 57
NOR VA JAK 15-20 57
"X" 5-10 54-55
Singles: 7-inch
ABC-PAR (9787 "Almost Paradise") 10-20 57
COLUMBIA (40929 "First Kiss") 10-20 57
COLUMBIA (41039 "Moondreams") 50-100 57
(Has Buddy Holly on lead guitar.)
COLUMBIA (41176 "Hey Punkin") 10-20 57
FELSTED (8647 "Mood Indigo") 8-12 62
JARO (77027 "Bring Your Heart") 8-12 60
NOR VA JAK (1313 "Mood Indigo") 15-20 57
NOR VA JAK (1316 "Almost Paradise") .. 15-20 57
NOR VA JAK (1322 "Little Black Sambo") 15-20 58
NOR VA JAK (1325 "True Love Ways") .. 50-75 60
NORMAN (500 "Weird") 10-15 60
PRISM (101 "The Plane Crash") 5-10
"X" (0040 "Mood Indigo") 10-20 54
"X" (0071 "On the Alamo") 10-20 56
"X" (0104 "I Wonder Why") 10-20 55
"X" (0130 "Hey Good Lookin' ") 10-20 55
"X" (0167 "Darkness on the Delta") 10-20 55
EPs: 7-inch
COLUMBIA (2139 "Four Hits") 15-25 58
COLUMBIA (10921 "Moon Dreams") 50-100 58
"X" (82 "In Full Fidelity") 15-25 55
LPs: 10/12-inch
COLUMBIA (1092 "Moon Dreams") 50-100 58
TOP RANK (R-639 "Petty for Your Thoughts") 25-40 60
(Monaural.)
TOP RANK (RS-639 "Petty for Your Thoughts") 35-50 60
(Stereo.)
VIK (1073 "Corsage") 50-75 57
Members: Norman Petty; Vi Petty; Jack Petty; Bowman Brothers.
Also see BOWMAN BROTHERS & NORMAN PETTY TRIO
Also see HOLLY, Buddy
Also see PICKS

PETTY, Tom, & Heartbreakers P&R/LP '77
Singles: 7-inch
BACKSTREET 3-6 79-83
(Black vinyl.)
BACKSTREET (52181 "Change of Heart") .. 5-8 83
(Colored vinyl.)
MCA 3-5 85-93
SHELTER 4-6 77-78
Picture Sleeves
BACKSTREET 3-6 79-83
MCA 3-5 85-90
SHELTER 4-6 77-78
LPs: 10/12-inch
BACKSTREET 5-10 79-82
MCA 5-8 85-93
SHELTER 8-15 76-78
W.B. 5-12 94-96
Promotional LPs
SHELTER (12677 "Official Live Leg") 15-25 76
SHELTER (52029 "You're Gonna Get It") 15-25 78
(Colored vinyl.)
Members: Tom Petty; Mike Campbell; Stan Lynch; Benmont Tench; Ron Blair; Howie Epstein.
Also see DYLAN, Bob, & Heartbreakers / Michael Rubini
Also see MUDCRUTCH
Also see NICKS, Stevie, & Tom Petty & Heartbreakers

PEWTER, Jim
(With the Saturday Revue)
Singles: 7-inch
CIRCUS 15-20 61
MGM 4-8 72-73
RCA 5-8 69
Session: Davie Allan.
Also see ALLAN, Davie
Also see ALLISON, Jerry, & Crickets
Also see CURTIS, Sonny
Also see JAMES, Deviny
Also see LEWIS & CLARKE
Also see PEWTER PALS
Also see TEMPO, Nino, & April Stevens

PEWTER PALS
Singles: 7-inch
MANHATTAN (807 "Childhood") 5-10 67
Member: Jim Pewter.
Also see PEWTER, Jim

PHAETONS
Singles: 7-inch
HI-Q (5012 "Fling") 10-15 59
VIN (1015 "I Love My Baby") 75-100 59

PHAFNER
Singles: 7-inch
DRAGON (1001 "Overdrive") 50-100 71
LPs: 10/12-inch
DRAGON ("Overdrive") 1800-2200 71
Members: Greg Smith; Steve Smith; Dale Shultz; Tom Shultz; Steve Gustafson.

PHANTOM
Singles: 7-inch
DOT (16056 "Love Me") 75-100 60
Picture Sleeves
DOT (16056 "Love Me") 400-600 60
Members: Marty Lott; H.H. Brooks; Bill Yates; Frank Holmes; Pete McCord.

PHANTOM
Singles: 7-inch
CAPITOL (3857 "Calm Before the Storm") 5-10 74
HIDEOUT (1080 "Calm Before the Storm") 10-15 73
LPs: 10/12-inch
CAPITOL (11313 "Divine Comedy") 40-60 74
GHOST ("The Lost Album") 8-10 90
(Selection number not known.)

PHANTOM FIVE
Singles: 7-inch
SKULL (817002 "Graveyard") .... 40-60 '60s
(Identification number used since no selection number is shown.)

PHANTOMS
(Majestics)
Singles: 7-inch
SAM (123 "XL-3") 20-25 62
Also see MAJESTICS

PHANTOMS
Singles: 7-inch
GRAVES ("Hallucinogenic Odyssey") ...... 40-60 '60s
(Selection number not known.)
IRC (6937 "My Generation") 20-30 66

PHANTONES
(Phantones & Combo)
Singles: 7-inch
BALE (105 "Waiting for Your Love") 75-100 59
CODE (707 "This Is Love") 150-200 58

PHARAOHS
("Featuring Rickey")
Singles: 7-inch
CLASS (202 "Teenagers Love Song") .300-400 57

PHARAOHS
Singles: 7-inch
FASCINATION (001 "Walking Sad") 300-400 57

PHARAOHS
Singles: 7-inch
FLIP (352 "I'll Never Love Again") 25-35 60
Members: Byron Gipson Jr; Judge Dennis; Eugene Jackson; Clarence Alexander; Alexander Lee.
Also see BERRY, Richard
Also see GIPSON, Slick, & Sliders

PHARAOHS
Singles: 7-inch
PYRAMID (101 "Jack-Knife") 15-25 60

PHARAOHS
Singles: 7-inch
PHARAOH ("Come to Me") 15-25 61
(No selection number used.)

PHARAOHS
Singles: 7-inch
CHATTAHOOCHEE (660 "The Friendly Martian") 10-15 64
IONA (1002 "Green Werewolf") .... 10-15 '60s

PHARAOS
Singles: 7-inch
DONNA (1327 "The Tender Touch") 25-35 60

PHAROS
Singles: 7-inch
DEL-FI (4208 "Rhythm Surfer") 10-20 63

PHAROTONES
Singles: 7-inch
TIMELY (1002 "Give Me a Chance") 1000-1500 58
Also see CHANELLS / Butterballs
Also see FIVE SATINS / Pharotones

PHAROTONES / Citadels
Singles: 7-inch
STOOP SOUNDS (509 "Give Me a Chance"/"Let's Fall in Love") 100-150 97
Also see CITADELS
Also see PHAROTONES

PHEASANTS
(With Bobby Eli & Orchestra)
Singles: 7-inch
THRONE (802 "Out of the Mist") 30-40 63

PHELPS, James P&R/R&B '65
(With the Du-Ettes; Jimmy Phelps)
Singles: 7-inch
ARGO (5499 "Love Is a Five-Letter Word") 8-12 65
ARGO (5509 "Wasting Time") 8-12 65
CADET (5534 "Action") 5-10 66
FONTANA (1581 "Don't Be a Cry Baby") ... 5-10 67
FONTANA (1600 "Wrong Number") 5-10 67
MECCA (5 "Blue Point Drive") 20-30 60
PARAMOUNT (0136 "My Lovers Prayer") . 5-10 71
Also see SOUL STIRRERS

PHELPS, Johnny
Singles: 7-inch
SKI (5505 "Tom Kat") 75-125

PHIL & BEA BOPP
Singles: 7-inch
AMC .... 25-35 '60s
Members: Phillip Walker; Ivor Beatrice.
Also see WALKER, Phillip

PHIL & CATALINAS
(With the Neutrons)
Singles: 7-inch
OLIMPIC (4479 "June 30th") 20-30 60
(Identification number shown since no selection number is used.)
Member: Phil Gary.
Also see GARY, Phil

PHIL & FLAKES
Singles: 7-inch
IO (1010 "Chrome Reversed Rails") 25-30 63
(Because complete selection number is "Fink 1010," label name is sometimes shown as "Fink.")
Member: Phil Pearlman.

PHIL & FRANTICS
Singles: 7-inch
ARA (1968 "Til You Get What You Want") 15-25 65
LA MAR (100 "She's My Gal") 10-15 64
RABBITT (1219 "I Must Run") 20-30 66
RAMCO (1970 "I Must Run") 10-20 66
SOUNDS LTD. .... 25-30 '60s
LPs: 10/12-inch
VOXX 5-8
Member: Phil Kelsey.

PHILADELPHIANS
Singles: 78 rpm
CAMPUS 10-15 55
Singles: 7-inch
CAMPUS (101 "Dear") 20-30 55
CAMPUS (103 "Church Bells") 20-30 55

PHILADELPHIANS
Singles: 7-inch
CAMEO (216 "The Vow") 10-15 62
Also see BIG JOHN & PHILADELPHIANS / Vince Montana

PHILHARMONICS
Singles: 7-inch
FUTURE (2200 "Why Don't You Write Me") 10-20 58

PHILIP & STEPHAN
Singles: 7-inch
INTERPHON (7711 "Meet Me Tonight Little Girl") 15-20 64
Members: Philip Sloan; Stephan Barri.
Also see FANTASTIC BAGGYS

PHILIPS, Terry
Singles: 7-inch
CORAL (62247 "Find a Horseshoe") 5-10 61
U.A. (351 "My Foolish Ways") 40-60 61

PHILLEY STOMPERS
Singles: 7-inch
PAJ ("Two Step Stomp") .... 50-75 '60s
(Selection number not known.)

PHILLINGANES, Greg / Cool Change
Singles: 7-inch
STOOP SOUNDS (120 "Countdown to Love"/"Streets of the Bronx") 75-125 98

PHILLIPS, Anthony LP '77
Singles: 7-inch
PASSPORT 4-6 77-78

LPs: 10/12-inch
PASSPORT (Except 9828)........................5-10 77-78
PASSPORT (9828 "Wise After the Event") 15-20 78
(Picture disc.)
Also see GENESIS

PHILLIPS, Bill *C&W '64*
(With Dolly Parton)
Singles: 7-inch
COLUMBIA (41954 "Blues Are Settin' In").. 20-30 61
DECCA (Except 31901)................................4-8 64-71
DECCA (31901 "Put It Off Until Tomorrow") 8-10 66
SOUNDWAVES 4-6 78-79
U.A. 4-6 72-73
LPs: 10/12-inch
DECCA (Except 4792)........................... 15-25 67-70
DECCA (DL-4792 "Put It Off Until Tomorrow") 15-20 66
(Monaural.)
DECCA (DL7-4792 "Put It Off Until Tomorrow") 20-25 66
(Stereo.)
HARMONY 12-18 64
GUINNESS..5-10
SEA SHELL..8-10
Also see PARTON, Dolly
Also see TILLIS, Mel, & Bill Phillips
Also see WELLS, Kitty / Bill Phillips / Bobby Wright / Johnny Wright

PHILLIPS, Buddy
Singles: 7-inch
CKM (1000 "Coffee Baby")................. 100-200

PHILLIPS, Carl
Singles: 7-inch
BOBBIN (110 "Wigwam Willie") 300-400 59
K-ARK (607 "Salty Dog Blues")............... 15-25

PHILLIPS, Charlie *C&W '62*
Singles: 7-inch
COLUMBIA (42289 "I Guess I'll Never Know")...5-10 62
COLUMBIA (42526 "You're Moving Away")...5-10 62
COLUMBIA (42691 " 'Til Sunday")..............5-10 63
COLUMBIA (42851 "This Is the House")....5-10 63
CORAL (61970 "Be My Bride") 30-40 58
Also see HOLLY, Buddy

PHILLIPS, Earl, Orchestra
Singles: 78 rpm
VEE-JAY (158 "Oop De Oop") 10-20 55
Singles: 7-inch
VEE-JAY (158 "Oop De Oop") 20-30 55
Also see PENTAGONS / Earl Phillips

PHILLIPS, Gene
(With His Rhythm Aces; with Jack McVea & His Orchestra)
Singles: 78 rpm
EXCLUSIVE 15-25 50
IMPERIAL.. 10-20 51
MODERN.. 15-25 47-49
RPM 15-25 51
LPs: 10/12-inch
CROWN... 20-30 63
Also see McVEA, Jack

PHILLIPS, John *P&R/C&W/LP '70*
Singles: 7-inch
ATCO (6960 "Green-Eyed Lady")................4-6 74
COLUMBIA..4-6 73
DUNHILL 4-8 70
LPs: 10/12-inch
DUNHILL 10-15 70
Also see JOURNEYMEN
Also see MAMAS & PAPAS

PHILLIPS, Marvin
(With the Men from Mars)
Singles: 78 rpm
MODERN...8-12 56
PARROT.. 50-75 53-54
SPECIALTY... 25-50 52
SWING TIME... 20-30 54
Singles: 7-inch
MODERN (982 "Yes I Do")...................... 15-25 56
PARROT (786 "Salty Dog")................... 100-150 53
PARROT (795 "Anne Marie") 75-125 54
SPECIALTY (445 "Wine Boogie")........... 50-75 52
SPECIALTY (479 "Baby Doll")..................50-75 53
(Black vinyl.)
SPECIALTY (479 "Baby Doll") 75-100 53
(Red vinyl.)
SPECIALTY (488 "Jo Jo") 50-75 52
SPECIALTY (498 "School of Love") 50-75 52
SPECIALTY (530 "Day in Day Out")..........50-75 52
SPECIALTY (554 "Ding Dong Daddy")......50-75 52
SWING TIME (339 "Salty Dog")................40-60 54
SWINGIN' (621 "The Big Dance").............10-15 60
Also see JESSE & MARVIN
Also see LONG TALL MARVIN
Also see MARVIN & JOHNNY

PHILLIPS, Phil *P&R/R&B '59*
(With the Twilights)
Singles: 78 rpm
MERCURY (71465 "Sea of Love")............40-60 59
(Canadian.)
Singles: 7-inch
CLIQUE (100 "Please Forgive Me")..............5-8 66
KHOURY'S (711 "Sea of Love") 200-300 59
LANOR (551 "That's What My Heart Needs")..15-25 72
LANOR (559 "It's All Right")....................15-25 72
MERCURY (10021 "Verdi Mae")..............20-30 59
(Stereo.)
MERCURY (71465 "Sea of Love")..............15-25 59
MERCURY (71531 "Verdi Mae")................10-15 59
MERCURY (71550 "Don't Leave Me").......10-15 59
MERCURY (71611 "What Will I Tell My Heart")...10-15 60
MERCURY (71649 "Don't Cry Baby").......10-15 60
MERCURY (71657 "Come Back My Darling") 10-15 60
MERCURY (71746 "I Love to Love You")..10-15 61
MERCURY (71817 "Sweet Affection")......10-15 61
MERCURY CELEBRITY SERIES................4-6
Picture Sleeves
CLIQUE (100 "Please Forgive Me").........15-25 66

PHILLIPS, Sandra
Singles: 7-inch
BROADWAY (402 "When Midnight Comes") 15-30 65
BROADWAY (403 "World Without Sunshine")...15-30 66
BROWN DOG (9004 "I Need You Back Home")..4-6 75
OKEH (7310 "I Wish I Had Known") 5-10 68

PHILLIPS, Shawn *LP '72*
Singles: 7-inch
A&M..5-10 70-75
ASCOT (2152 "Cloudy Summer Afternoon")..15-25 64
LPs: 10/12-inch
A&M..10-20 70-77
RCA (3028 "Transcendence")....................8-12 78
RCA (3873 "Transcendence")....................8-12 78

PHILLIPS, Steve
LPs: 10/12-inch
CRAFTSMAN (8010 "Organ Favorites") ..20-40 '50s
(Cover pictures Mary Tyler Moore, although she is not heard on the disc.)

PHILLIPS, Stu *C&W '66*
Singles: 7-inch
PARAGON 4-6 76
RCA...4-8 66-69
W.B. 4-8 69
LPs: 10/12-inch
BANFF...15-30
PARAGON 5-10 76
RCA...15-30 66-68
RODEO 30-50

PHILLIPS, Stu, & His Orchestra
Singles: 7-inch
CAPITOL (5466 "Feels Like Lovin' ").........5-10 65
CAPITOL 4-6 72-73
COLPIX 10-20 60-63
COLUMBIA...5-10 62-64
MCA...4-6 78
SMASH 8-12 67
LPs: 10/12-inch
CAPITOL (2356 "Feels Like Lovin' ")........15-20 65
SMASH (27094 "Hell's Angels On Wheels") 20-25 67
(Monaural. Soundtrack.)
SMASH (67094 "Hell's Angels On Wheels") 25-30 67
(Stereo. Soundtrack.)
WALDORF MUSIC HALL (1409 "Strings in Stereo")...10-15 59
WALDORF MUSIC HALL (1414 "Organ and Strings in Stereo")...10-15 59
Also see HOLLYRIDGE STRINGS
Also see WILLIAMS, Beverly

PHILLIPS, T., & Sharps
Singles: 7-inch
FIREFLY (332 "Someone to Love")..........40-50 60

PHILLIPS, Teddy
(With His Orchestra; with the Montereys)
Singles: 78 rpm
BALLY 5-10 57
KING..8-12 54
Singles: 7-inch
ALADDIN (3467 "Don't Do Anything") 10-15 60
BALLY (1036 "Melody #9") 10-15 57
CRYSTALETTE (740 "Crazy Fever Blues")...15-25 60
(First issue.)
DOT (1690 "Crazy Fever Blues")................8-12 60
DRUM BOY (106 "Happy Go Lucky").........5-10 64
DRUM BOY (113 "Goodnight Sweetheart")..5-10 65
KING (1333 "Please Unlock the Door")....15-25 54
LIMELIGHT (3004 "Melancholy Mood") 4-8 63
SALEM (1014 "Believe in Tomorrow")..100-150 57
THANKS (251 "31 Steps") 60-75
EPs: 7-inch
DECCA (715 "Concert in the Sky")...........15-25 '50s

PHILLIPS, Walt, & Barry Young
Singles: 7-inch
DELTONE (5023 "Surfin' Annie")..............15-25 63
Also see YOUNG, Barry

PHILLIPSON, Larry Lee
(With the Larry Lee Trio)
Singles: 7-inch
CINCH (3858 "Bitter Feelings")..............75-100 64
CUCA (6541 "Bitter Feelings")..................50-75 65
CUCA (6565 "Milwaukee Road") 50-75 65
DEMO (1029 "Bitter Feelings") 50-75 64
PHILLIPSON (1002 "Absent Minded You")..10-20
PHILLIPSON (1004 "First Night Back in Milwaukee")...10-20
PHILLIPSON (1005 "Milwaukee Road")...10-20
PHILLIPSON (1006 "Double Time Heart")..10-20
PHILLIPSON (2001 "Charlene")...............10-20
PHILLIPSON (2004 "Baby Sitter's Christmas")...10-20
RAYNARD (770 "Milwaukee") 50-75 65
RAYNARD (1053 "Baby Sitter's Christmas")...10-20 66
TARGET (1010 "Barney") 5-10 69

PHILMON, Hiram
Singles: 7-inch
PHILMON (1000 "You Gotta Love Me, Baby")..150-250 60

PHILOSOPHERS
LPs: 10/12-inch
PHILO (1001 "After Sundown")............100-150 69
(Front cover is identical to *White Light*, by White Light.)
Also see WHITE LIGHT

PHILWIT & PEGASUS
LPs: 10/12-inch
CHAPTER 1 ....8-12 70
Members: Roger Greenaway; Guy Fletcher; Peter Lee Sterling; John Carter; Chas Mills.
Also see DAVID & JONATHAN
Also see IVY LEAGUE

PHLUPH
Singles: 7-inch
VERVE (10564 "Another Day")...................8-15 67
VERVE (10575 "Patterns")..........................8-15 68
LPs: 10/12-inch
VERVE (5054 "Phluph")............................15-25 68
Members: Benson Blake; Joel Maisano; John Pell; Lee Dudley.

PHONETICS
Singles: 7-inch
TRUDEL (1005 "Pretty Girl")....................25-35
TRUDEL (1008 "Just a Boy's Dream").100-200
TRUDEL (1012 "What Good Am I Without You")..50-75
Member: Willie Hutch.
Also see HUTCH, Willie

PIAF, Edith *P&R '50*
(With Theo Sarapo)
Singles: 78 rpm
CAPITOL..5-8 56-58
COLUMBIA 5-8 50-52
Singles: 7-inch
CAPITOL (Except 3368) 10-20 56-61
CAPITOL (3368 "Black Denim Trousers & Mororcycle Boots")..20-30 56
(With "Capitol Introduces Edith Piaf" insert. Promotional issue only.)
CAPITOL (3368 "Black Denim Trousers & Mororcycle Boots")..10-20 56
(Without insert.)
CAPITOL STARLINE ....4-6 '60s
COLUMBIA..5-15 50-52
EPs: 7-inch
ANGEL..5-15 55-56
COLUMBIA..5-15 50-52
DECCA...5-15 54
LPs: 10/12-inch
ANGEL..25-40 55-56
CAPITOL (10210 "Piaf")..........................15-25 59
CAPITOL (10283 "Piaf of Paris")..............10-20 61
CAPITOL (10295 "Potpourri Par Piaf").....10-20 62
CAPITOL (10348 "Piaf & Sarapo")...........10-20 63
CAPITOL STARLINE ....5-10 '60s
CAPITOL (16000 series)............................5-10 81-82
COLUMBIA (898 "La Vie En Rose").........20-40 56
COLUMBIA (6223 "Encore Parisiennes")..25-50 52
(10-inch LP.)
COLUMBIA (9500 series)........................25-50 51-52
(10-inch LPs.)
COLUMBIA (37000 series) 5-10 81
DECCA (6004 "Chansons des Cafes de Paris")..25-50 54
(10-inch LP.)
DISCOS 20-30 56
PHILIPS 10-20 64-67
RCA (123 "Edith Piaf") 10-15 64
VOX (3050 "Edith Piaf Sings")..................25-50 53
(10-inch LP.)
VOX (3060 "Edith Piaf Favorites")............25-50 53
(10-inch LP.)

PIANO RED *R&B '50*
(Willie Perryman)
Singles: 78 rpm
CHECKER (911 "Get Up Mare")..............20-40 58
GROOVE 10-15 54-57
RCA (4265 thru 5544).............................15-25 51-53
RCA (6856 "Wild Fire") 20-30 57
RCA (6859 "Rock Baby") 20-30 57
RCA (6953 "Please Don't Talk About Me") 20-30 57
RCA (7065 "South") 20-30 57
RCA (7217 "One Glimpse of Heaven") 40-60 58
Singles: 7-inch
CHECKER (911 "Get Up Mare")..............15-25 58
GROOVE (0023 "Decatur Street Blues") . 15-25 54
GROOVE (0101 "Pay It No Mind") 15-25 55
GROOVE (0118 "Six O'Clock Bounce")... 15-25 55
GROOVE (0126 "Red's Blues")................15-25 55
GROOVE (0136 "She Knocks Me Out")... 15-25 56
GROOVE (0145 "I'm Nobody's Fool") 15-25 56
GROOVE (0169 "You Were Mine for Awhile") 15-25 56
JAX (1000 "I Feel Good")...........................8-12 59
RCA (50-0099 "Red's Boogie")............100-150 50
(Cherry red vinyl.)
RCA (50-0099 "Red's Boogie")................50-75 51
(Black vinyl.)
RCA (50-0106 "Wrong Yo-Yo") 40-60 51
RCA (50-0118 "Jumpin' the Boogie") 40-60 51
RCA (50-0130 "Baby What's Wrong")......40-60 51
RCA (4265 "Let's Have a Good Time") 40-60 51
RCA (4380 "Hey Good Lookin' ") 40-60 51
RCA (4524 "Bouncin' with Red") 40-60 52
RCA (4766 "Sales Tax Boogie")...............40-60 52
RCA (4957 "Voo Doopee Doo")................40-60 52
RCA (5101 "I'm Gonna Rock Some More")..35-45 52
RCA (5224 "I'm Gonna Tell Everybody") .35-45 53

RCA (5337 "Your Mouth's Got a Hole in It")....35-45 53
RCA (5544 "Right and Ready")....35-45 53
RCA (6856 "Wild Fire")....20-30 57
RCA (6859 "Rock Baby")....20-30 57
RCA (6953 "Please Don't Talk About Me")....20-30 57
RCA (7065 "South")....20-30 57
RCA (7217 "One Glimpse of Heaven")....20-30 58
EPs: 7-inch
GROOVE (3 "Jump Man, Jump")....40-60 56
GROOVE (10026/27/28 "Piano Red in Concert")....35-50 56
(Price is for any of three volumes.)
RCA (587 "Rockin' with Red")....50-100 54
RCA (5091 "Rockin' with Red")....40-60 59
(Black label.)
RCA (5091 "Rockin' with Red")....50-100 59
(Maroon label.)
LPs: 10/12-inch
ARHOOLIE....8-10
BLACK LION....8-10 76
GROOVE (1001 "Jump Man, Jump")....500-750 56
GROOVE (1002 "Piano Red in Concert")....200-400 56
KING (1117 "Underground Atlanta")....10-20 70
RCA....8-10 74
Also see DOCTOR FEELGOOD
Also see SHIRLEY, Danny, & Piano Red

PIANO RED / June Valli
EPs: 7-inch
RCA (92 "Dealer's Prevue")....15-25 56
(Promotional issue only.)
Also see PIANO RED
Also see VALLI, June

PIANO SLIM
(Willard Burton)
Singles: 7-inch
C&P (103 "Lot of Shakin' Lot of Jivin'")....100-200 59
DART (148 "Squeezing")....10-20 61
JET STREAM (705 "Stagecoach to Boothill")....10-20 62
MYRIL (405 "Heartbeat of Love")....10-20 61
Also see BURTON, Willard

PICADILLY PIPERS
Singles: 78 rpm
CHART (615 "I Loved Only You")....10-20 56
Singles: 7-inch
CHART (615 "I Loved Only You")....50-60 56

PICADILLYS
Singles: 78 rpm
CHART (619 "Lonely Lover's Prayer")....15-25 56
Singles: 7-inch
CHART (619 "Lonely Lover's Prayer")....75-100 56
Also see PICADILLY PIPERS

PICK, Al
Singles: 7-inch
PINK (703 "Lover's Confession")....40-50 60

PICKARD, Jimmy
Singles: 7-inch
JIFFY (209 "I Got Another You")....100-200

PICKENS, Slim
(Eddie Burns)
Singles: 78 rpm
HOLIDAY (202 "Papa's Boogie")....50-100 48
Also see BURNS, Eddie
LPs: 10/12-inch
NIGHTHAWK....5-8 82
Also see MITCHELL, Walter

PICKETT, Bobby *P&R/R&B/LP '62*
(Bobby [Boris] Pickett & Crypt-Kickers; Featuring Bobby Paine)
Singles: 12-inch
EASY STREET....4-8 84
Singles: 7-inch
ANTHEM....4-6
ATMOSPHERE....5-10 65
CAPITOL....5-10 63-64
EASY STREET....3-5 84
GARPAX (1 "Monster Mash")....10-15 62
(With distribution picked up by London, this was quickly reissued as Garpax 44167.)
GARPAX (724 "I'm Down to My Last Heartbreak")....5-10
GARPAX (44000 series)....5-10 62-65
LONDON....4-6 '70s
METROMEDIA (0089 "Me & My Mummy")....4-8 68
METROMEDIA (9989 "Me & My Mummy")....4-6 73
PARROT....4-8 70-73
RCA (8312 "Smoke, Smoke, Smoke")....5-10 64
RCA (8459 "Werewolf Watusi")....5-10 64
WHITE WHALE (363 "Monster Man Jam")....4-8 70
WHITE WHALE (365 "Monster Concert")....4-8 70
Picture Sleeves
GARPAX (44167 "Monster Mash")....10-20 62
GARPAX (44171 "Monster's Holiday")....10-20 62
GARPAX (44175 "Graduation Day")....10-20 63
LPs: 10/12-inch
GARPAX (GPX-57001 "Monster Mash")....30-50 62
(Monaural.)
GARPAX (SGP-57001 "Monster Mash")....50-75 62
(Stereo.)
PARROT....10-20 73
Members [Crypt-Kickers]: Leon Russell; Johnny MacCrae; Rickie Page; Gary Paxton.
Session: David Gates; Larry Nectal; Jesse Salles; Chuck Hamilton.
Also see CORDIALS
Also see GATES, David
Also see PAGE, Rickie
Also see PAXTON, Gary
Also see RUSSELL, Leon
Also see STOMPERS

PICKETT, Dan
Singles: 78 rpm
GOTHAM (201 "Baby, Laughing Rag")....25-50 48
GOTHAM (242 "Baby, How Long")....25-50 48
GOTHAM (510 "Ride to a Funeral in a V-8")....25-50 48
GOTHAM (512 "Baby, Something's Gone Wrong")....25-50 48
GOTHAM (516 "Lemon Man")....25-50 48

PICKETT, Lee
Singles: 7-inch
JOLT (331 "Fatty Patty")....100-200 58

PICKETT, Wilson *P&R/R&B '63*
(With Elwood Blues Revue)
Singles: 7-inch
ATLANTIC (2200 thru 2400 series)....6-12 64-67
ATLANTIC (2500 thru 2900 series)....4-8 68-73
ATLANTIC (8000 series)....3-5 88
BIG TREE....4-6 78
CORREC-TONE (501 "Let Me Be Your Boy")....40-60 62
CUB (9113 "Let Me Be Your Boy")....10-20 62
DOUBLE L (713 "If You Need Me")....10-20 63
DOUBLE L (717 "It's Too Late")....10-20 63
DOUBLE L (724 "I'm Down to My Last Heartbreak")....10-20 63
EMI AMERICA....3-6 79-81
MOTOWN....3-5 87-88
PHILCO (11 "Land of 1000 Dances"/"Midnight Hour")....10-20 67
("Hip Pocket" flexi-disc.)
RCA....4-6 73-74
ROWE/AMI....5-10 66
("Play Me" Sales Stimulator promotional issue.)
VERVE (10378 "Let Me Be Your Boy")....10-20 66
WICKED....4-8 75-76
Picture Sleeves
ATLANTIC....3-5 88
EPs: 7-inch
ATLANTIC (SD-8250 "Right On")....10-15 70
(Stereo. Juke box issue only. With paper envelope-sleeve.)
LPs: 10/12-inch
ALA....8-10
ATLANTIC (Except 8100 series)....10-15 69-73
ATLANTIC (8100 series)....12-25 65-68
BIG TREE....5-10 78
BROOKVILLE....8-12 77
DOUBLE L (DL-8300 "It's Too Late")....25-35 63
(Monaural.)
DOUBLE L (SDL-8300 "It's Too Late")....30-40 63
(Stereo.)
EMI AMERICA....5-10 79-81
RCA....8-12 73-77
WAND....10-15 68
WICKED....8-12 76
Also see FALCONS

PICKETT, Wilson / Sam & Dave
LPs: 10/12-inch
ATLANTIC (ST-136 "Excerpts from *Hey Jude*")....15-25 69
(Promotional issue for in-store use.)
Also see PICKETT, Wilson
Also see SAM & DAVE

PICKS
Singles: 7-inch
COLUMBIA (41039 "Moondreams")....50-75 57
(White label, promotional issue. Copies credited to the **Picks** may exist only on promo copies.)
COLUMBIA (41096 "Moondreams")....25-50 58
(Previously issued as by the Norman Petty Trio.)
Members: John Pickering; Bill Pickering; Bob Lapham.
Also see HOLLY, Buddy
Also see PETTY, Norman, Trio
Also see TUCKER, Rick

PICO PETE
Singles: 7-inch
GROOMS (312 "Can't Go for That")....10-15 64
GROOMS (503 "Going to Work")....10-15 62
JET (100 "Hot Dog")....75-100 57

PICONE, Vito
(Vito)
Singles: 7-inch
ADMIRAL (103 "I Like to Run")....10-20 63
ADMIRAL (302 "Still Waters Run Deep")....15-25 63
I.P.G. (1016 "Path in the Wilderness")....10-20 63
Also see CORDEL, Pat
Also see ELEGANTS

PICTORIAN SKIFFULS
Singles: 7-inch
SKIFFUL (15587 "In Awhile")....15-25 65

PIECES OF EIGHT *P&R '67*
Singles: 7-inch
A&M (854 "Lonely Drifter")....5-10 67
A&M (879 "Come Back Girl")....5-10 67
A&M (907 "It Will Stand")....5-10 68
ACTION....5-10 '60s
MALA (12024 "I'd Pay the Price")....5-10 68
MALA (12037 "Double Shot")....5-10 69
Also see SWINGIN' MEDALLIONS

PIED PIPERS *P&R '44*
(With Paul Weston's Orchestra)
Singles: 78 rpm
CAPITOL....5-10 44-55
RCA....4-8 48
Singles: 7-inch
CAPITOL....8-12 49-55
RCA....5-10 48
EPs: 7-inch
CAPITOL....10-20 50-55
LPs: 10/12-inch
CAPITOL (H-212 "Harvest Moon")....30-50 50
(10-inch LP.)
GOLDEN TONE....5-10
TOPS (1570 "Pied Pipers in a Tribute to Tommy Dorsey")....15-25 57
Members: Jo Stafford; Chuck Lowry; Clark Yocum; Hal Hopper; June Hutton; Sue Allen.
Also see MERCER, Johnny, Jo Stafford & Pied Pipers
Also see PERRY, King
Also see SINATRA, Frank, & Pied Pipers
Also see STAFFORD, Jo

PIED PIPERS
Singles: 7-inch
HAMLIN TOWN (2510 "Stay in My Life")....15-25 '60s

PIERCE, Alan, & Tone Kings
Singles: 7-inch
CHALLENGE (59093 "Swamp Water")....8-12 60
TOM TOM (101 "Swamp Water")....15-25 60
(First issue.)

PIERCE, Bobby, Combo
Singles: 7-inch
STAR-LIGHT (1021 "I Cried Over You")....10-20 60

PIERCE, Eddie
Singles: 7-inch
FARRELL (689 "It's You, Only You")....75-100

PIERCE, Henry, & Five Notes
Singles: 78 rpm
SPECIALTY....50-75 52
Singles: 7-inch
SPECIALTY (461 "Thrill Me Baby")....200-300 52
(Black vinyl.)
SPECIALTY (461 "Thrill Me Baby")....500-750 52
(Red vinyl.)

PIERCE, Otis
Singles: 7-inch
KINGS RIVER (304 "Blue Eyed Darlin' ")....75-100

PIERCE, Webb *C&W '52*
Singles: 78 rpm
DECCA....5-15 51-52
4 STAR....10-20 51-52
Singles: 7-inch
DECCA (28091 thru 29804)....10-20 52-56
DECCA (30045 "Teenage Boogie")....25-35 56
DECCA (31000 thru 33000 series)....5-10 59-73
DECCA (46000 series)....10-20 51-52
KING (5366 "It's All Between the Lines")....5-10 60
KING (5429 "Jilted Love")....5-10 60
MCA....4-6 73-74
PLANTATION....4-6 75-77
SOUNDWAVES....3-5 83
EPs: 7-inch
DECCA....10-20 53-65
LPs: 10/12-inch
BULLDOG....5-10
CASTLE....5-10
CORAL....5-10 73
DECCA (181 "Webb Pierce Story")....15-25 64
(Includes booklet.)
DECCA (DL-4015 "Webb with a Beat")....20-30 60
(Monaural.)
DECCA (DL7-4015 "Webb with a Beat")....20-40 60
(Stereo.)
DECCA (DL-4079 thru 4964)....10-25 60-67
DECCA (DL7-4079 thru 4964)....15-30 60-67
DECCA (5536 "Wondering Boy")....40-60 53
(10-inch LP.)
DECCA (8129 "Webb Pierce")....20-40 55
DECCA (8295 "Wondering Boy")....20-40 56
DECCA (8728 "Just Imagination")....20-40 57
DECCA (DL-8889 "Bound for the Kingdom")....20-40 59
(Monaural.)
DECCA (DL7-8889 "Bound for the Kingdom")....25-50 59
(Stereo.)
DECCA (DL-8899 "Webb!")....20-30 59
(Monaural.)
DECCA (DL7-8899 "Webb!")....25-35 59
(Stereo.)
DECCA (74000 & 75000 series)....8-12 68-73
KING (648 "The One and Only Webb Pierce")....20-40 59
KOALA....5-8 80
MCA....5-12 73-78
MUSIC MASTERS....5-10
PICCADILLY....5-8 80
PICKWICK/HILLTOP....10-15 65
PLANTATION....5-8 76-77
SEARS....8-12 '60s
SESAC....30-50 59
SKYLITE....5-8 77
VOCALION....5-15 66-70
Also see NELSON, Willie, & Webb Pierce
Also see SOVINE, Red, & Webb Pierce
Also see WELLS, Kitty, & Webb Pierce

PIERCE, Webb / Patsy Cline / T. Texas Tyler
LPs: 10/12-inch
DESIGN (901 "Three of a Kind")....8-12 63
Also see CLINE, Patsy
Also see TYLER, T. Texas

PIERCE, Webb / Loretta Lynn
LPs: 10/12-inch
PHILCO/MCA....15-25 69
Also see LYNN, Loretta

PIERCE, Webb / Wynn Stewart
LPs: 10/12-inch
DESIGN....8-12 62
Also see STEWART, Wynn

PIERCE, Webb, & Mel Tillis *C&W '63*
Singles: 7-inch
DECCA (31445 "How Come Your Dog Don't Bite Nobody But Me")....5-10 62
Also see TILLIS, Mel

PIERCE, Webb, & Wilburn Brothers *C&W '54*
Singles: 78 rpm
DECCA (29107 "Even Tho")....................5-10 54
Singles: 7-inch
DECCA (29107 "Even Tho")....................20-25 54
Also see PIERCE, Webb
Also see WILBURN BROTHERS

PIERMEN
Singles: 7-inch
JESSE (1000 "Piermen Stomp")............15-25 62

PIERSON, Con
(With the Ekhoes)
Singles: 7-inch
FORD (144 "Somewhere Down the Line")....................10-15 67
LE-MANS (007 "I Heard Those Bells")....15-25 64

PIERSON LAKE
Singles: 7-inch
CENTURY (35501 "Just Give Me a Chance")....................8-12 69
SOUND (1373 "People Are Dying")............4-6 73
Also see EMBERMEN FIVE

PIG 'N WHISTLE BAND
Singles: 78 rpm
REGAL (3277 "Love Changing Blues").. 50-100 50
Member: Willie McTell.
Also see McTELL, Blind Willie

PIGEONS
LPs: 10/12-inch
WAND (687 "While the World Was Eating Vanilla Fudge")....................15-25 68
Members: Tim Bogert; Vince Martell; Mark Stein; Joe Brenan.
Also see VANILLA FUDGE

PIKE, Jim
(With the Damons)
Singles: 7-inch
CAPITOL (3006 "Morning Girl")..................4-8 70
W.B. (5048 "Lucy D")....................10-20 59
Also see LETTERMEN

PIKE, Jim, & Kephart Rockets
Singles: 7-inch
JEROME (7336 "Shaken' and a Shuddern' ")....................800-1200 '50s

PIKE, Travis
(Travis Pike's Tea Party)
Singles: 7-inch
ALMA (201,680 "If I Didn't Love You Girl")....................15-25 67

PILGRIM HARMONEERS
Singles: 78 rpm
J&S (1754 "Wooden Church")................10-20 56
Singles: 7-inch
J&S (1754 "Wooden Church")................25-35 56

PILGRIMS
Singles: 7-inch
BATON....................8-12 56-57
Singles: 7-inch
BATON (225 "Mister Fiddler")................10-20 56
BATON (235 "Careless Love")................10-20 57

PILOT
Singles: 7-inch
RCA....................4-6 72
LPs: 10/12-inch
RCA (4730 "Pilot")....................10-15 72
RCA (4825 "Point of View")....................15-20 73
Members: Bruce Stephens; Leigh Stephens; Martin Quittenton; Mickey Waller; Neville Whitehead.
Also see BLUE CHEER

PILTDOWN FIVE
Singles: 7-inch
PARLIAMENT (102 " '32 Ford")............75-100 63

PILTDOWN MEN *P&R '60*
Singles: 7-inch
CAPITOL....................10-20 60-62
Members: Lincoln Mayorga; Bob Bain; Earl Palmer; Jack Kel.
Also see BAIN, Bob

PINEAPPLE HEARD
Singles: 7-inch
DIAMOND (231 "Valerie")....................15-25 68

PINETOP SLIM
Singles: 78 rpm
COLONIAL (106 "Applejack Boogie").......50-75 49

PING PONGS
Singles: 7-inch
CUB (9062 "In the Chapel in the Moonlight")....................20-30 60
G-NOTE (100 "You and Only You")..........20-30 61
MARCO (107 "You Belong to Me")..........30-40 61
MUSICANZA....................5-10
U.A. (236 "Summer Reverie")....................8-12 60

PINK FLOYD *LP '67*
Singles: 12-inch
COLUMBIA (1334 "Money")....................25-35 81
(Pink vinyl. Promotional issue only.)
COLUMBIA (1635 "Selections/Final Cut")....................15-20 83
(Promotional issue only.)
COLUMBIA (2878 "On the Turning Away")....................8-12 87
(Promotional issue only.)
Singles: 7-inch
CAPITOL....................5-15 71-78
COLUMBIA (Black vinyl)....................3-8 75-94
COLUMBIA (Colored vinyl)....................5-10 87
(Promotional issue only.)
HARVEST....................5-15 73-74
TOWER (333 "Arnold Layne")....................35-55 67
TOWER (356 "See Emily Play")................35-55 67
TOWER (378 "The Gnome")....................35-55 67
TOWER (426 "It Would be So Nice")........35-55 68
TOWER (440 "Let There Be More Light")....................35-55 68
Picture Sleeves
TOWER (356 "See Emily Play")...........300-400 67
COLUMBIA....................3-8 80-87
EPs: 7-inch
HARVEST (6746/7 "Pink Floyd, from *Dark Side of the Moon*)....................75-125 73
(Promotional issue only. Issued with paper sleeve.)
LPs: 10/12-inch
CAPITOL (Except 11902)....................5-8 78-83
CAPITOL (11902 "Dark Side of the Moon")....................30-40 78
(Picture disc.)
COLUMBIA (Except Half-Speed Mastered, Quadraphonic, & Colored vinyl)..............6-10 75-88
COLUMBIA (HC-43453 "Wish You Were Here")....................25-50 80
(Half-speed mastered.)
COLUMBIA (PCQ-43453 "Wish You Were Here")....................40-60 75
(Quadraphonic.)
COLUMBIA (HC-47680 "Collection of Great Dance Songs")....................20-40 '80s
(Half-speed mastered.)
COLUMBIA (H2C-46183 "The Wall")...150-200 '80s
(Half-speed mastered.)
COLUMBIA (64200 "Division Bell")............8-12 94
(Blue vinyl.)
HARVEST (STBB-388 "Ummagumma")....................25-35 69
HARVEST (SMAS-382 "Atom Heart Mother")....................15-20 70
HARVEST (759 "Relics")....................10-15 71
HARVEST (832 "Meddle")....................10-15 71
HARVEST (11078 "Obscured By Clouds")....................10-15 72
HARVEST (11163 "Dark Side of the Moon")....................8-12 73
HARVEST (11198 "More")....................10-15 73
(Soundtrack.)
HARVEST (11000 series)....................10-15 72-73
HARVEST (11257 "A Nice Pair")............10-15 73
HARVEST (16234 "Relics")....................5-10 82
MFSL (017 "Dark Side of the Moon")......75-100 78
MFSL/UHQR (017 "Dark Side of the Moon")....................125-175 78
(Boxed set.)
MFSL (190 "Meddle")....................50-75 79
MFSL (202 "Atom Heart Mother")............25-35 94
(Half-speed mastered.)
TOWER (T-5093 "Piper at the Gates of Dawn")....................100-125 67
(Monaural.)
TOWER (ST-5093 "Piper at the Gates of Dawn")....................50-75 67
(Orange label. Stereo.)
TOWER (5093 "Piper at the Gates of Dawn")....................40-50 67
(Striped label.)
TOWER (5131 "A Saucerful of Secrets")....................50-100 68
(Orange label.)
TOWER (5131 "A Saucerful of Secrets")....................50-100 68
(Striped label.)
TOWER (5169 "More")....................25-40 69
(Soundtrack.)
Promotional LPs
CAPITOL (8116 "Tour '75")....................30-50 75
COLUMBIA (1 "Animals")....................75-100 77
(With inserts.)
COLUMBIA (1636 "Final Cut")................15-20 83
(Tracks not banded for airplay.)
COLUMBIA (1636 "Final Cut")................30-40 83
(Tracks are banded for easy airplay.)
COLUMBIA (33453 "Wish You Were Here")....................50-75 75
COLUMBIA (34474 "Animals")................40-60 77
(Quadraphonic.)
COLUMBIA (36183 "The Wall")................50-75 79
Members: David Gilmour; Roger Waters; Rick Wright; Nick Mason; Syd Barrett.
Also see WRIGHT, Richard

PINKERTON'S ASSORTED COLOURS
Singles: 7-inch
PARROT (40001 "Will Ya")....................10-20 66

PINKINY CANANDY
LPs: 10/12-inch
UNI (73049 "Pinkiny Canandy")................10-15 69

PINKNEY, Bill
(With the Original Drifters; with O.D.'s; with Turks; with Originals; with Perks; Bill Pinckney)
Singles: 7-inch
FONTANA (1956 "I Do the Jerk")..............5-10 64
GAME (393 "Ol' Man River")....................30-40 64
(Logo at left. With "O.D.'s.")
GAME (394 "Ol' Man River")....................50-75 64
(Logo on top. With "Original Drifters.")
PHILLIPS INT'L (3524 "After the Hop")....15-25 58
VEEP (1264 "Masquerade Is Over")..........5-10 67
Also see DRIFTERS
Also see FLYERS

PIPER, Jimmie
Singles: 7-inch
ROYCE (0001 "Bonfire")....................40-50 59
ROYCE (0008 "Wasted Life")..................30-40 60
SUMMIT (108 "Don't Play Around with My Ear")....................150-250

PIPES
Singles: 78 rpm
DOOTONE....................50-75 56
Singles: 7-inch
DOOTO (388 "Be Fair")....................15-25 '60s
DOOTO (401 "You Are an Angel")..........15-25 '60s
DOOTONE (388 "Be Fair")................100-200 56
DOOTONE (401 "You Are an Angel")..100-200 56

PIPES
Singles: 7-inch
JACY (001 "So Long")....................400-500 58

PIPKIN, Chester
Singles: 7-inch
AZUZA (1003 "Slow Jerk")....................10-20 '60s

PIPKIN, Jimmy
(With Gallahads; Jim Pipkin; Jim Pipkin & Boss)
Singles: 7-inch
CAMELOT (128 "I'm Just a Lonely Guy").10-20 '60s
(Since we've yet to learn exact year of release – especially with regard to Gallahads Del-Fi and Donna issues – price is subject to change.)
DONNA (1361 "This Letter to You")........50-75 62
NORMAN (579 "Mr. Clean '67")..................5-10 67
Also see GALLAHADS

PIRATES
(Temptations)
Singles: 7-inch
MEL-O-DY (105 "Mind Over Matter")......40-50 62
Also see TEMPTATIONS

PIRATES
Singles: 7-inch
BACK STAGE (5001 "Naughty Girl").......25-35 65
(May have been promo only.)

DEAUX (1150 "Big Boy Pete")................10-20 '60s

PIT MEN
Singles: 7-inch
PIT (402 "Surf Bored")....................40-60 65

PITCHE BLENDE
Singles: 7-inch
VALLEY (1102 "My World Has Stopped")....................40-60 '60s

PITLIK'S CONSTRUCTION CO.
Singles: 7-inch
MISTER ED (7502 "Your Nose Is Gonna Grow")....................10-20 65
Members: Bob Moes; Hohn Pitlik; Jim Roehling; Mike Vlahakis.

PITMEN
Singles: 7-inch
EARTH (401 "Susie Q")....................15-20

PITNEY, Gene *P&R '61*
Singles: 7-inch
COLLECTABLES....................3-5 '80s
EPIC....................4-6 77
ERIC....................4-6 '70s
FESTIVAL (25002 "Please Come Back Baby")....................10-15 61
MUSICOR (1002 "Love My Life Away")...15-20 60
(Gray label.)
MUSICOR (1002 "Love My Life Away")...15-20 60
(Beige label.)
MUSICOR (1006 "Louisiana Mama").......20-25 60
MUSICOR (1009 "Town Without Pity")....10-15 61
MUSICOR (1011 "Every Breath I Take")..30-40 61
(Gray label.)
MUSICOR (1011 "Every Breath I Take")..15-25 61
(Beige label.)
MUSICOR (1020 "The Man Who Shot Liberty Valance")....................10-15 62
MUSICOR (1022 "Only Love Can Break a Heart")....................10-15 62
MUSICOR (1026 "Half Heaven - Half Heartache")....................10-15 62
MUSICOR (1028 "Mecca")....................10-15 62
MUSICOR (1032 "True Love Never Runs Smooth")....................10-15 63
MUSICOR (1034 "Twenty-Four Hours from Tulsa")....................10-15 63
MUSICOR (1036 "That Girl Belongs to Yesterday")....................10-15 64
MUSICOR (1038 "Yesterday's Hero")......10-15 64
MUSICOR (1039 "I'm Gonna Find Myself a Girl")....................10-15 64
MUSICOR (1040 "It Hurts to Be in Love")....................10-15 64
MUSICOR (1045 "I'm Gonna Be Strong")....................10-15 64
MUSICOR (1065 "Amici Miei")................8-12 65
MUSICOR (1070 "I Must Be Seeing Things")....................8-12 65
MUSICOR (1093 "Last Chance to Turn Around")....................8-12 65
MUSICOR (1103 "Looking Through the Eyes of Love")....................8-12 65
MUSICOR (1130 "Princess in Rags")........8-12 65
MUSICOR (1150 "Hojas Muertas")............8-12 66
MUSICOR (1155 "Lei Mi Aspetta")............8-12 65
MUSICOR (1171 "Backstage")..................8-12 66
MUSICOR (1200 "Cold Light of Day")........8-12 66
MUSICOR (1219 "Just One Smile")...........8-12 66
MUSICOR (1233 "I'm Gonna Listen to Me")....................8-12 67
MUSICOR (1235 "Animal Crackers")..........8-12 67
MUSICOR (1245 "Where Did the Magic Go")....................8-12 67
MUSICOR (1252 "Building Up My Dream World")....................8-12 67
MUSICOR (1299 "The More I Saw of Her")....................8-12 68
MUSICOR (1306 "She's a Heartbreaker").8-12 68
MUSICOR (1308 "Lonely Drifter")............8-12 68
MUSICOR (1331 "Billy You're My Friend")....................10-20 68
MUSICOR (1348 "Baby, You're My Kind of Woman")....................10-20 69
MUSICOR (1361 "California")................10-20 69
MUSICOR (1384 "She Lets Her Hair Down")....................10-20 69
MUSICOR (1394 "I Remember")..............10-20 70
MUSICOR (1405 "Think of Us")...............10-20 70

MUSICOR (1419 "Shady Lady") 10-20 70
MUSICOR (1439 "Higher and Higher") 10-20 71
MUSICOR (1442 "A Thousand Arms") 10-20 71
MUSICOR (1453 "I Just Can't Help Myself") 10-20 72
MUSICOR (1474 "Shady Lady") 10-20 73

Picture Sleeves

MUSICOR (1002 "Love My Life Away")... 15-20 60
MUSICOR (1011 "Every Breath I Take"). 15-20 61
MUSICOR (1028 "Mecca") 10-20 63
MUSICOR (1034 "Twenty-Four Hours from Tulsa") 10-20 63
MUSICOR (1036 "That Girl Belongs to Yesterday") 10-20 64
MUSICOR (1040 "It Hurts to Be in Love") 10-20 64
MUSICOR (1045 "I'm Gonna Be Strong") 10-20 64
MUSICOR (1070 "I Must Be Seeing Things") 10-20 65
MUSICOR (1171 "Backstage") 10-20 66
MUSICOR (1331 "Billy You're My Friend") 10-20 68

EPs: 7-inch

MUSICOR (500 "Looking Through the Eyes of Love") 15-20 65
(Issued without cover. Promotional issue only.)

LPs: 10/12-inch

COLUMBIA HOUSE (6397 "The Fabulous Gene Pitney") 10-15 75
(Two discs. Columbia Record Club issue.)
EVEREST (4100 "Gene Pitney") 5-10 81
KOALA 5-10 79
MUSICO (1003 "Liberty Valance") 10-15 69
MUSICO (1005 "Town Without Pity") 10-15 69
MUSICO (1008 "Twenty-Four Hours From Tulsa") 10-15 69
MUSICO (1014 "Baby I Need Your Lovin' ") 10-15 69
MUSICOR (2001 "The Many Sides of Gene Pitney") 25-35 62
(Monaural.)
MUSICOR (2003 "Only Love Can Break a Heart") 25-35 62
(Monaural.)
MUSICOR (2004 "Just for You") 20-35 63
(Monaural.)
MUSICOR (2005 "World-Wide Winners") 20-35 63
(Monaural.)
MUSICOR (2006 "Blue Gene") 20-35 63
(Monaural.)
MUSICOR (2007 "Dedicated to My Teen Queens") 35-55 63
(First issue. Monaural.)
MUSICOR (2007 "The Fair Young Ladies of Folkland") 20-35 63
(Retitled. Monaural.)
MUSICOR (2008 "Big 16") 20-35 64
(Monaural.)
MUSICOR (2015 "Gene Italiano") 15-25 64
(Monaural.)
MUSICOR (2019 "It Hurts to Be in Love") 15-25 64
(Monaural.)
MUSICOR (2043 "Big 16, Vol. 2") 15-25 66
(Monaural.)
MUSICOR (2056 "I Must Be Seeing Things") 15-25 66
(Monaural.)
MUSICOR (2069 "Looking Through the Eyes of Love") 15-25 66
(Monaural.)
MUSICOR (2072 "Gene Pitney Español") 15-25 66
(Monaural.)
MUSICOR (2085 "Big 16, Vol. 3") 15-25 66
(Monaural.)
MUSICOR (2095 "Backstage") 15-25 66
(Monaural.)
MUSICOR (2100 "Nessuno Mi Puo Giudicare") 15-25 66
(Monaural.)
MUSICOR (2102 "Greatest Hits of All Time") 15-25 66
(Monaural.)
MUSICOR (2104 "The Country Side") 15-25 66
(Monaural.)
MUSICOR (2101 "Gene Pitney Show") ... 15-25 66
(Monaural.)
MUSICOR (2108 "Young, Warm and Wonderful") 15-25 66
(Monaural.)
MUSICOR (2117 "Just One Smile") 15-25 66
(Monaural.)
MUSICOR (2134 "Golden Greats") 15-25 66
(Monaural.)
MUSICOR (3001 "The Many Sides of Gene Pitney") 30-45 62
(Stereo.)
MUSICOR (3003 "Only Love Can Break a Heart") 25-40 62
(Stereo.)
MUSICOR (3004 "Just for You") 25-40 63
(Stereo.)
MUSICOR (3005 "World-Wide Winners").25-40 63
(Stereo.)
MUSICOR (3006 "Blue Gene") 25-40 63
(Stereo.)
MUSICOR (3007 "Dedicated to My Teen Queens") 45-60 63
(First issue. Stereo.)
MUSICOR (3007 "The Fair Young Ladies of Folkland") 25-40 63
(Retitled. Stereo.)
MUSICOR (3008 "Big 16") 20-35 64
(Stereo.)
MUSICOR (3015 "Gene Italiano") 15-25 64
(Stereo.)
MUSICOR (3019 "It Hurts to Be in Love") 15-25 64
(Stereo.)
MUSICOR (3043 "Big 16, Vol. 2") 15-25 66
(Stereo.)
MUSICOR (3056 "I Must Be Seeing Things") 15-25 66
(Stereo.)
MUSICOR (3069 "Looking Through the Eyes of Love") 15-25 66
(Stereo.)
MUSICOR (3072 "Gene Pitney Español") 15-25 66
(Stereo.)
MUSICOR (3085 "Big 16, Vol. 3") 15-25 66
(Stereo.)
MUSICOR (3095 "Backstage") 15-25 66
(Stereo.)
MUSICOR (3100 "Nessuno Mi Puo Giudicare") 15-25 66
(Stereo.)
MUSICOR (3102 "Greatest Hits of All Time") 15-25 66
(Stereo.)
MUSICOR (3104 "The Country Side") 15-25 66
(Stereo.)
MUSICOR (3101 "Gene Pitney Show") 15-25 66
(Stereo.)
MUSICOR (3108 "Young, Warm and Wonderful") 15-25 66
(Stereo.)
MUSICOR (3117 "Just One Smile") 15-25 66
(Stereo.)
MUSICOR (3134 "Golden Greats") 15-25 66
(Stereo.)
MUSICOR (3148 "The Gene Pitney Story") 15-25 68
(Two discs.)
MUSICOR (3154 "Pitney Español") 15-25 68
MUSICOR (3161 "Gene Pitney Sings Burt Bacharach") 15-25 68
MUSICOR (3164 "She's a Heartbreaker") 15-25 68
MUSICOR (3174 "Greatest Hits") 15-25 68
MUSICOR (3183 "This Is Gene Pitney") .. 15-25 70
MUSICOR (3206 "Ten Years After") 8-12 71
MUSICOR (3200 series) 8-12 71-73
MUSICOR (4600 "The Best of Gene Pitney") 10-15
MUSICOR (5025 "This Is Gene Pitney") .. 15-25 66
(Two discs. Columbia Record Club issue.)
MUSICOR (5600 "Double Gold") 10-15 78
(Two discs.)
PHOENIX 10 .... 5-10 81
RHINO 5-8 85
SPRINGBOARD 5-10 76
TRIP (16-16 "16 Greatest Hits") 5-10 76
51 WEST (16055 "The Pick of Gene Pitney") 5-10 79
Also see BRYAN, Billy
Also see JAMIE & JANE
Also see JONES, George, & Gene Pitney
Also see ROE, Tommy / Bobby Rydell / Gene Pitney

PITNEY, Gene, & Burt Bacharach

LPs: 10/12-inch

MUSICO 10-15 70

PITNEY, Gene, & Melba Montgomery C&W '66

Singles: 7-inch

MUSICOR (1135 "Baby, Ain't That Fine") .. 5-10 65
MUSICOR (1173 "Being Together") 5-10 65

LPs: 10/12-inch

BUCKBOARD 8-10 76
MUSICOR (3077 "Being Together") 15-20 66

PITNEY, Gene / Newcastle Trio

LPs: 10/12-inch

DESIGN (160 "Spotlight on Gene Pitney") .... 10-15 '60s
Also see PITNEY, Gene

PITRELLO, Carne

(Lynn Pratt.)

Singles: 7-inch

HORNET (1004 "The Saints") 30-40 63
Also see PRATT, Lynn

PITT, Eugene

(With the Jyve Fyve; with Teacho Wiltshire & Orchestra)

Singles: 7-inch

AVCO 4-6 71-72
BELTONE (2027 "She's My Girl") 10-15 62
VEEP (1229 "Another Rainy Day") 10-15 66
Also see JIVE FIVE
Also see WILTSHIRE, Teacho

PITTMAN, Al "Dr. Horse"

Singles: 7-inch

CLOWN (3008 "Crazy Beat") 40-60 59

PITTMAN, Barbara

(With the Gene Lowery Singers)

Singles: 78 rpm

SUN (253 "I Need a Man") 25-50 56

Singles: 7-inch

PHILLIPS INT'L (3518 "Two Young Fools in Love") 20-40 57
PHILLIPS INT'L (3527 "Cold Cold Heart") 20-40 58
PHILLIPS INT'L (3553 "Handsome Man") 10-15 60
SUN (253 "I Need a Man") 50-100 56

PITTMAN, Jackie, & Fugitives

Singles: 7-inch

PIXIE (6355 "Do the Jerk") 20-30 65

PITTS, Beverly, & Cheaters

Singles: 7-inch

RAYNARD (10055 "Satisfaction") 15-25 66
Also see CHEATERS

PITTS, Clyde

Singles: 7-inch

CHALLENGE (9165 "Better Side of Him") .5-10 62
COLUMBIA (43713 "Let Me Be Me") 4-8 66
COLUMBIA (43820 "Would You Believe It") 4-8 66
COLUMBIA (43945 "Lover Let Go") 4-8 66
EVEREST (20002 "Heartbroken") 5-10 62
FOUR STAR (1751 "Lonely Side of Town") 8-12 61
MONUMENT (1068 "If the Song Fits") 4-8 68
TOPPA (1018 "Shakin' Like a Leaf") 50-100 60

PITTS, Gloria Jean

Singles: 78 rpm

IMPERIAL 15-25 56

Singles: 7-inch

IMPERIAL (5406 "I Don't Stand No Quittin' ") 30-40 56

PITTS, Jerry

Singles: 7-inch

CROC-A-GATOR (101 "Elvis Medley") 15-25 69
JPRM (100 "Keep Ole Central Rolling") ... 50-75
TOMBIGBEE 5-10 69

PITTS, Nolan

Singles: 7-inch

MINIT (603 "What Is Life") 10-20 59

PIXIES

Singles: 7-inch

BALBOA (007 "Santa's Too Fat for the Hula Hoop") 10-15 58

PIXIES

Singles: 7-inch

AMC (102 "Cry Like a Baby") 15-20 62
DON-DEE (102 "Cry Like a Baby") 10-15 63

PIXIES THREE P&R '63

Singles: 7-inch

MERCURY 10-15 63-64

Picture Sleeves

MERCURY (72130 "Birthday Party") 10-20 63
MERCURY (72208 "Cold, Cold Winter") .. 15-20 63
MERCURY (72288 "It's Summertime") 10-20 64

LPs: 10/12-inch

MERCURY (20912 "Party") 50-75 64
(Monaural.)
MERCURY (60912 "Party") 75-100 64
(Stereo.)
Members: Debra Swisher; Midge Bollinger; Kaye McCool; Bonnie Long. Session: Leon Huff; Trade Martin; Vinnie Bell.
Also see MARTIN, Trade
Also see SWISHER, Debra

PIZANI, Frank P&R '57

(With Lew Douglas & Orchestra; with Del Rondos)

Singles: 78 rpm

BALLY (1040 "Angry") 5-10 57

Singles: 7-inch

AFTON (616 "Wanna Dance") 20-30 59
AFTON (617 "The Stars Will Remember") 40-50 59
BALLY (1040 "Angry") 10-15 57
WARWICK (518 "Play a Slow One") 5-10 59
Also see DOUGLAS, Lew
Also see HIGHLIGHTS

PLAGUE

Singles: 7-inch

BIRCHMONT ("Love and Obey") 20-30 67
(Canadian. Selection number not known.)
REO (8962 "The Face of Time") 20-30 67
(Canadian.)
REO (8981 "Love and Obey") 15-25 67
(Canadian.)

LP: 10/12-inch

BIRCHMONT 25-50 67
(Canadian.)

PLAGUE

Singles: 7-inch

WRIGHT (6863 "Mr. White Collar Man") .. 15-25 68

PLAGUE

Singles: 7-inch

EPIDEMIC (2164 "Go Away") 15-25 66

PLAGUES

Singles: 7-inch

FENTON (2070 "I've Been Through It Before") 40-60 66
QUARANTINED (2020 "Why Can't You Be True") 10-20 66
QUARANTINED (41369 "That'll Never Do") 10-20 66

PLAGUES

Singles: 7-inch

RON (1000 "To Wander") 10-15 66

PLAGUES

Singles: 7-inch

SMITTY'S (1293 "Somebody Help Me") 50-100 '60s

PLAIDS

Singles: 7-inch

MARK (119 "Out to Lunch") 20-30 58

PLAIDS

Singles: 7-inch

ERA (3002 "Around the Corner") 10-15 59
LIBERTY (55167 "Hungry for Your Love") 40-50 58
(White label. Promotional issue only.)
LIBERTY (55167 "Hungry for Your Love") 100-200 58
(Green label.)
NASCO (6011 "My Pretty Baby") 10-15 58

PLAIN BROWN WRAPPER
Singles: 7-inch
MONSTER (0002 "Junior Saw It Happen") ... 25-35 69
SPIRIT (0010 "Stretch Out Your Hand") .. 15-25 '70s
THIS IS MUSIC (2114 "And Now You Dream") ... 30-40 '60s
Member: Gary Story.
Also see ZOOKIE & POTENTATES

PLAIN JANE
Singles: 7-inch
HOBBIT (42000 "Who's Drivin' This Train") ... 5-10 69
LPs: 10/12-inch
HOBBIT (5000 "Plain Jane") ... 15-25 69
Members: Barry Ray; Jerry Schoenfeld; David Schoenfeld; Don Gleicher.

PLANETEERS
("Vocal: Dan Smith")
Singles: 7-inch
SPEAR (1 "Sail On") ... 300-400

PLANETS
("Featuring Bill Steward;" "Featuring Vince Howard")
Singles: 7-inch
ERA (1038 "Never Again") ... 20-30 57
ERA (1049 "Be Sure") ... 15-25 57
NU-CLEAR (7422 "Sharin' Lockers") ... 15-25 59
Members: Bill Steward; Vince Howard.

PLANETS
Singles: 7-inch
ALJON (1244 "Once in a Lifetime") ... 200-300 62

PLANK, Lucky
Singles: 7-inch
BLUE JAY (110 "Hey Hey Baby") ... 350-400

PLANNED OBSOLESCENCE
Singles: 7-inch
JETSET (2 "Exit Sticky Icky") ... 25-50
JETSET (4296 "Still in Love with You Baby") ... 25-50

PLANT, Robert — P&R/LP '82
Singles: 12-inch
ES PARANZA ... 5-8 85
Singles: 7-inch
ATLANTIC ... 3-5 83
ES PARANZA ... 3-5 83-89
SWAN SONG ... 3-5 82
Picture Sleeves
ATLANTIC ... 3-5 83
ES PARANZA ... 3-5 83-88
SWAN SONG ... 3-5 82
LPs: 10/12-inch
ES PARANZA (Except 2244) ... 5-8 83-90
ES PARANZA (2244 "Non-Stop, Go!") ... 30-50 88
(Interview on 2 LPs. Promotional issue only.)
SWAN SONG ... 5-10 82
Also see BAND OF JOY
Also see LED ZEPPELIN
Also see LISTEN
Also see PAGE, Jimmy, & Robert Plant

PLANT & SEE
Singles: 7-inch
WHITE WHALE (309 "Henrietta") ... 8-12 69
LPs: 10/12-inch
WHITE WHALE (7120 "Plant and See") .. 15-25 69

PLANTS
("With Orchestra")
Singles: 7-inch
J&S (1602 "Dear, I Swear") ... 400-500 57
(Label has company address under logo.)
J&S (1602 "Dear, I Swear") ... 40-50 61
(No company address on label.)
J&S (1617/1618 "From Me") ... 500-750 58
Note: Despite having the same name, this is a different group than on J&S 248.

PLANTS
Singles: 7-inch
J&S (248/249 "I Searched the Seven Seas") ... 400-600 59
Members: James Lawson; Steve McDowell; George Jackson; Thurmon Thrower.

PLASTIC ICE CUBE
Singles: 7-inch
WARICK (6750 "Won't Turn Back") ... 25-35 67
Also see FORREST, Andrea
Also see MARCIA & LYNCHMEN

PLASTIC LAUGHTER
Singles: 7-inch
HEAVY (705 "I Don't Live Today") ... 75-100 67

PLATO & PHILOSOPHERS
Singles: 7-inch
FAIRYLAND (1002 "Thirteen O'Clock Flight to Psychedelphia") ... 300-400 66
G.A.R. (104 "I Don't Mind") ... 20-30 67
I.T. (2313 "I Don't Mind") ... 20-30 67
Members: Ken "Plato" Tebow; Barry Orscheln; Mike Imbler; Ben White; Mark Valentine.

PLATTERS — P&R/R&B '55
(Featuring Tony Williams)
Singles: 78 rpm
FEDERAL (12153 "Give Thanks") ... 50-100 53
FEDERAL (12164 "I Need You All the Time") ... 75-125 54
FEDERAL (12181 "Roses of Picardy") ... 50-100 54
FEDERAL (12188 "Tell The World") ... 50-100 54
FEDERAL (12198 "Voo-Vee-Ah-Bee") ... 50-100 54
FEDERAL (12204 "Take Me Back") ... 50-100 54
FEDERAL (12244 "Only You") ... 100-200 55
FEDERAL (12250 "Tell the World") ... 30-50 55
FEDERAL (12271 "I Need You All the Time") ... 30-50 56
MERCURY (Except 71289) ... 30-40 55-58
MERCURY (71289 "Twilight Time") ... 75-125 58
Singles: 7-inch
ANTLER (3000 "I Do It All the Time") ... 3-5 82
COLLECTABLES ... 3-5
FEDERAL (12153 "Give Thanks") ... 150-250 53
FEDERAL (12164 "I Need You All the Time") ... 1000-1500 54
FEDERAL (12181 "Roses of Picardy") . 150-250 54
FEDERAL (12188 "Tell The World") ... 150-250 54
FEDERAL (12198 "Voo-Vee-Ah-Bee") . 150-250 54
FEDERAL (12204 "Take Me Back") ... 150-250 54
FEDERAL (12244 "Only You") ... 200-300 55
FEDERAL (12250 "Tell The World") ... 100-150 55
FEDERAL (12271 "I Need You All the Time") ... 50-100 56
GUSTO ... 3-5 '80s
KING (2241 "Smoke Gets in Your Eyes") ... 3-5 84
MERCURY (10001 "Smoke Gets in Your Eyes") ... 25-50 58
(Stereo.)
MERCURY (10018 "Where") ... 25-50 59
(Stereo.)
MERCURY (10038 "Red Sails in the Sunset") ... 25-50 60
(Stereo.)
MERCURY (70633 "Only You") ... 40-60 55
(Pink label.)
MERCURY (70633 "Only You") ... 20-30 55
(Black label.)
MERCURY (70753 "Great Pretender") ... 20-30 55
(Maroon label.)
MERCURY (70753 "Great Pretender") ... 10-20 56
(Black label.)
MERCURY (70819 "Magic Touch") ... 20-30 56
(Maroon label.)
MERCURY (70819 "Magic Touch") ... 10-20 56
(Black label.)
MERCURY (70893 "My Prayer") ... 20-30 56
(Maroon label.)
MERCURY (70893 "My Prayer") ... 10-20 56
(Black label.)
MERCURY (70948 "You'll Never Never Know") ... 15-25 56
MERCURY (71011 "One in a Million") ... 20-30 56
(Maroon label.)
MERCURY (71011 "One in a Million") ... 10-20 56
(Black label.)
MERCURY (71032 "I'm Sorry") ... 20-30 56
(Maroon label.)
MERCURY (71032 "I'm Sorry") ... 10-20 56
(Black label.)
MERCURY (71093 "My Dream") ... 20-30 56
(Maroon label.)
MERCURY (71093 "My Dream") ... 10-20 56
(Black label.)
MERCURY (71184 "Only Because") ... 10-20 57
MERCURY (71246 "Helpless") ... 10-20 57
MERCURY (71289 "Twilight Time") ... 10-20 58
MERCURY (71320 "You're Making a Mistake") ... 10-20 58
MERCURY (71353 "I Wish") ... 10-20 58
MERCURY (71383 "Smoke Gets in Your Eyes") ... 10-20 58
MERCURY (71427 "Enchanted") ... 10-20 59
MERCURY (71467 "Remember When") .. 10-20 59
MERCURY (71502 "Wish It Were Me") ... 10-20 59
MERCURY (71538 "My Secret") ... 10-20 59
MERCURY (71563 "Harbor Lights") ... 10-20 60
MERCURY (71624 "Ebb Tide") ... 10-15 60
MERCURY (71656 "Red Sails in the Sunset") ... 10-15 60
MERCURY (71697 "To Each His Own") .. 10-15 60
MERCURY (71749 "If I Didn't Care") ... 10-15 60
MERCURY (71791 "Trees") ... 8-12 61
MERCURY (71847 "I'll Never Smile Again") ... 8-12 61
MERCURY (71904 "You'll Never Know") ... 8-12 61
MERCURY (71921 thru 72359) ... 8-15 62-64
MERCURY (30,000 series) ... 5-8 '60s
(Celebrity Series reissues.)
MUSICOR ... 5-10 66-71
OWL (320 "Are You Sincere") ... 4-6 73
POWER (7012 "Only You") ... 5-10 '60s
Picture Sleeves
MERCURY ... 15-25 60-64
POWER (7012 "Only You") ... 8-12 '60s
EPs: 7-inch
FEDERAL (378 The Platters Sing for Only You") ... 300-400 56
KING (378 "The Platters") ... 100-200 56
KING (651 "The Platters") ... 100-200 56
(All copies of **Federal** 651 are bootlegs. Originals are only on King.)
MERCURY ... 25-75 56-61
LPs: 10/12-inch
CANDLELITE ("The Platters") ... 30-40 '70s
(Boxed, four-disc set.)
EVEREST ... 5-10 81
FEDERAL (549 "The Platters") ... 800-1200 57
51 WEST ... 5-10 '80s
GUEST STAR ... 10-15 '60s
KING (651 "The Platters") ... 200-400 59
KING (5002 "10 Hits") ... 8-12 59
MERCURY (4000 series) ... 5-8 82
MERCURY (8000 series) ... 5-8
MERCURY (20146 "The Platters") ... 75-100 56
MERCURY (20216 "The Platters, Vol. 2") ... 75-100 56
MERCURY (20298 "Flying Platters") ... 50-75 57
MERCURY (20410 thru 20983) ... 15-30 59-65
(Monaural.)
MERCURY (60043 thru 60983) ... 20-50 59-65
(Stereo.)
MUSICO ... 10-12 69-70
MUSICOR (2000 & 3000 series) ... 15-20 66-69
MUSICOR (4600 series) ... 10-15 77
PHOENIX 20 (615 "The Platters") ... 5-8 '80s
PICKWICK ... 8-10 '70s
RHINO ... 8-12 '80s
SPRINGBOARD ... 8-10 76
TRIP ... 8-10 76
WING ... 12-25 62-67
Members: Tony Williams; David Lynch; Sandra Dawn; Linda Hayes; Herb Reed; Nate Nelson; Sonny Turner; Zola Taylor; Paul Robi; Alex Hodge.
Also see GUNTER, Cornel
Also see HAYES, Linda, & Platters
Also see LITTLE ANTHONY & IMPERIALS / Platters
Also see METROTONES
Also see NELSON, Nate
Also see RAM, Buck
Also see TAYLOR, Zola
Also see TURNER, Sonny, & Sound Ltd.
Also see WILLIAMS, Tony

PLATTERS / Exotic Guitars
LPs: 10/12-inch
GUEST STAR ... 10-15 64

PLATTERS / Inez & Charlie Foxx / Jive Five / Tommy Hunt
LPs: 10/12-inch
MUSICOR (2142 "Quartet of Soul") ... 10-15 67
(Monaural.)
MUSICOR (3142 "Quartet of Soul") ... 15-20 67
(Stereo.)
Also see FOXX, Inez
Also see HUNT, Tommy
Also see JIVE FIVE

PLATTERS / Nick Noble / Rusty Draper / Ralph Marterie
EPs: 7-inch
MERCURY (4023 "Platters / Nick Noble / Rusty Draper / Ralph Marterie") ... 30-40 56
Also see DRAPER, Rusty
Also see NOBLE, Nick

PLATTERS / Red Prysock / Dinah Washington
EPs: 7-inch
MERCURY (4020 "Platters / Red Prysock / Dinah Washington") ... 30-40 56
Also see PLATTERS
Also see PRYSOCK, Red
Also see WASHINGTON, Dinah

PLAYBOYS
Singles: 78 rpm
CAT ... 10-15 54-55
Singles: 7-inch
CAT (108 "Tell Me") ... 20-30 54
CAT (115 "Good Golly, Miss Molly") ... 20-30 55
Member: Charlie White.
Also see RAVENS

PLAYBOYS
Singles: 78 rpm
TETRA (4447 "One Question") ... 50-100 57
Singles: 7-inch
TETRA (4447 "One Question") ... 75-100 57

PLAYBOYS
Singles: 78 rpm
MERCURY ... 10-15 57
Singles: 7-inch
MERCURY (71228 "Don't Do Me Wrong") ... 10-15 57

PLAYBOYS — P&R '58
(Playboys/Cousins)
Singles: 7-inch
CAMEO (142 "Over the Weekend") ... 15-25 58
CHANCELLOR (1074 "Boston Hop") ... 10-15 61
CHANCELLOR (1106 "Duck Walk") ... 10-15 62
COTTON (1008 "Girl of My Dreams") ... 15-25 62
MARTINIQUE (101 "Over the Weekend") ... 40-50 58
MARTINIQUE (400 "Please Forgive Me") ... 25-35 59

PLAYBOYS
Singles: 7-inch
SOUVENIR (1001 "Believe It Or Not") ... 25-35 59

PLAYBOYS
Singles: 7-inch
CUCA (6371 "Look at Me") ... 15-25 63
Members: Jim Peterman; Rick Kludt; Wayne Champion; Paul Zoerb; Rick Bruhn; Kevin Peterman; Bill Patterson; Nels Christiansen; Steve Sperry; Mike Warner.

PLAYBOYS
Singles: 7-inch
LEGATO (101 "Mope De Mope") ... 10-15 63

PLAYBOYS
Singles: 7-inch
CATALINA ... 10-20 64
JEWEL (737 "Boogie Children") ... 50-75 64
TITAN (1732 "Cat Walk") ... 5-10 65

PLAYBOYS
Singles: 7-inch
CORSAIR (403 "Cry Cry") ... 50-75 64

PLAYBOYS
Singles: 7-inch
TRI-DEC (8557 "I Can Tell") ... 75-125

PLAYBOYS OF EDINBURG
(P.O.E.)
Singles: 7-inch
CAPITOL (2890 "La Bamba") ... 8-12 70
COLUMBIA ... 10-15 66-67
1-2-3 ... 4-8 69-70
PHARAOH (141 "Wish You Had a Heart") ... 15-25 65
PHARAOH (142 "Look at Me Girl") ... 15-25 66
UNI (73099 "Up Through the Spiral") ... 5-10 71
Members: Michael Williams; Jim Williams; Val Curl; Jerry McCord.

PLAYERS

Singles: 7-inch

TARX (1007 "You Need a Love")......... 100-200 63

PLAYGIRLS

Singles: 7-inch

GALAXY (713 "Donnie")....................... 200-300 62

(Green vinyl.)

RCA (7546 "Hey Sport")..............................8-12 59

RCA (7719 "Gee But I'm Lonesome").........8-12 60

Also see BLOSSOMS

PLAYGROUND

Singles: 7-inch

PEE-GEE...5-10 85

LPs: 10/12-inch

PEE-GEE (1000 "Images")....................... 50-75 85

PLAYGUE

Singles: 7-inch

REBIC (19653 "I Gotta Be Goin' ")........... 40-50 65

PLAYMAKERS

Singles: 7-inch

TAP (501 "Bubble Gum")......................... 30-50 61

PLAYMATES *P&R '58*

(With Hugo Peretti & Orchestra; with Joe Reisman & Orchestra)

Singles: 78 rpm

RAINBOW 10-15 56

ROULETTE.. 15-25 57-58

Singles: 7-inch

ABC-PAR...5-10 63-64

BELL (45149 "Foundation of Love") 4-6 71

COLPIX...5-10 64-65

CONGRESS (245 "Ballad of Stanley the Lifeguard") 5-10 65

RAINBOW (360 "Nickelodeon Rag") 20-30 56

ROULETTE (4003 thru 4136).................. 10-20 57-59

ROULETTE (4160 "What Is Love")......... 10-20 59

(Monaural.)

ROULETTE (4160 "What Is Love")......... 30-40 59

(Stereo.)

ROULETTE (4200 thru 4464)......................8-12 59-62

LPs: 10/12-inch

FORUM (16001 "Playmates Visit the West Indies").. 15-25 60

ROULETTE... 20-40 57-61

Members: Donny Conn; Morey Carr; Chic Hetti.

PLEASE, Bobby

(Bob Please & Pleasers)

Singles: 7-inch

ERA (1044 "Heartache Street")............. 10-25 57

IMPERIAL (5508 "I'm Girl Crazy")............ 15-25 58

JAMIE (1118 "The Switch") 10-15 59

PLEASURE *R&B/LP '76*

Singles: 12-inch

FANTASY..4-8 76-80

Singles: 7-inch

FANTASY..3-6 75-80

RCA 3-5 82-83

LPs: 10/12-inch

FANTASY (9473 "Dust Yourself Off")...... 25-50 75

FANTASY (9506 "Accept No Substitutes")... 25-50 76

FANTASY (9526 "Joyous")...................... 25-50 77

FANTASY (9550 "Get to the Feeling")..... 25-50 78

FANTASY (9578 "Future Now") 25-50 79

FANTASY (9600 "Special Things")......... 25-50 80

RCA (4209 "Give It Up")......................... 10-20 82

Members: Sherman Davis; Nate McClain; Marlon McClain; Michael Hepburn; Donald Hepburn; Bruce Carter; Bruce Smith; Dennis Springer.

PLEASURE FAIR

Singles: 7-inch

UNI (55016 "Fade In Fade Out")................5-10 67

UNI (55078 "Let You Go") 5-10 68

LPs: 10/12-inch

UNI (3009 "Pleasure Fair")...................... 15-20 67

Members: Robb Royer; Michele Cochrane; Tim Hallinan; Steve Cohn.

Also see BREAD

PLEASURE SEEKERS

Singles: 7-inch

CAPITOL (2050 "If You Climb the Tiger's Back").. 10-15 67

HIDEOUT (1006 "Never Thought You'd Leave Me")... 50-75 66

MERCURY (72800 "Good Kind of Hurt"). 10-20 68

PLEASURES

Singles: 7-inch

CATCH (100 "Music City") 20-30 63

RSVP (1102 "Plaything")............................10-20 64

RSVP (1113 "Let's Have a Beach Party") 10-20 65

PLEBIAN REBELLION

Singles: 7-inch

COLUMBIA (44231 "Good Sweet Love") .15-25 67

PLEDGES

Singles: 78 rpm

REV (3517 "Betty Jean")......................100-200 58

Singles: 7-inch

REV (3517 "Betty Jean")......................100-200 58

Members: Gary Paxton; Clyde Batton.

Also see SKIP & FLIP

PLUM NELLY

LPs: 10/12-inch

CAPITOL (692 "Deceptive Lines")............15-25 71

PLUMMER, Dave, & Plungers

Singles: 7-inch

MAYBROOK (320 "Surfin' Monster")........25-35 '60s

PLURALS

(Plural's)

Singles: 7-inch

BERGEN (186 "Donna My Dear")............10-15 58

WANGER (186 "Donna My Dear")...........50-75 58

(Has "Wanger" in sans serif typeface, and songwriters names in parentheses.)

WANGER (186 "Donna My Dear")...........25-50 58

(Has "Wanger" in serif typeface. Songwriters names are not in parentheses.)

WANGER (188 "Goodnight")....................25-50 58

PLUSHTONES

Singles: 7-inch

PLUSH (601 "Penny Loafers")..................10-20 60

PLYMOUTH ROCK

Singles: 7-inch

PLYMOUTH ROCK (206321 "Comin' Down")...20-30

TIGER ("Comin' Down") 25-35

(Selection number not known.)

POCO *LP '69*

Singles: 7-inch

ABC 4-6 75-79

ATLANTIC..3-5 82-84

EPIC..4-6 69-75

MCA..3-6 79-82

RCA...3-5 89

Picture Sleeves

EPIC 4-6 70-72

MCA..3-5 80

RCA...3-5 89

LPs: 10/12-inch

ABC 8-12 75-78

ATLANTIC..5-8 82-84

EPIC (26460 "Pickin' Up the Pieces").......10-15 69

EPIC (26522 "Poco") 10-15 70

EPIC (30209 "Deliverin' ")..........................8-12 71

EPIC (EQ-30209 "Deliverin' ") 15-25 71

(Quadraphonic.)

EPIC (30753 "From the Inside")................5-10 71

EPIC (31601 "A Good Feelin' to Know").....5-10 72

EPIC (32354 "Crazy Eyes")........................5-10 73

EPIC (EQ-32354 "Crazy Eyes")...............10-15 73

(Quadraphonic.)

EPIC (32895 "Seven")................................5-10 74

EPIC (33192 "Cantamos")..........................5-10 74

(Quadraphonic.)

EPIC (PEQ-33192 "Cantamos")...............10-15 74

EPIC (33537 thru 36210) 5-10 75-81

MCA...5-10 80-82

MFSL (020 "Legend")..............................30-50 78

RCA..5-8 89

Members: Richie Furay; Jim Messina; Rusty Young; Timothy Schmit; Paul Cotton.

Also see BOENZEE CRYQUE

Also see BUFFALO SPRINGFIELD

Also see EAGLES

Also see GLAD

Also see MESSINA, Jim

PODOLOR, Dickie

(Richard Podolor)

Singles: 7-inch

RADIO (112 "Samoa")..............................15-25 58

RADIO (116 "She's My Baby").................15-25 58

Also see ALLEN, Richie

Also see REVELLS

Also see SURFARIS

POE, Bobby

Singles: 7-inch

WHITE ROCK (1112 "Rock and Roll Boogie") 150-250 58

POET

(The Poet)

Singles: 7-inch

PULL (305 "Vowels of Love")...............250-300 58

(First issued as by the Poets.)

Also see POETS

POETS

Singles: 7-inch

SHADE (1001 "Never Let You Go")......500-750 60

POETS / Searchers

Singles: 7-inch

STOOP SOUNDS (506 "Never Let You Go"/ "Yvonne")...75-125 97

POETS

Singles: 7-inch

FLASH (129 "Vowels of Love") 50-150 58

(Black label.)

FLASH (129 "Vowels of Love") 25-35 58

(Maroon label. Reissued as by the Poet.)

Also see POET

POETS

Singles: 7-inch

IMPERIAL (5664 "I'm in Love")................10-15 60

SPOT (107 "I'm in Love") 50-75 60

(First issue.)

POETS

(James Brown & His Band)

Singles: 7-inch

TRY ME (28006 "Devil's Den") 10-15 63

Also see BROWN, James

POETS *P&R/R&B '66*

Singles: 7-inch

CHAIRMAN (4408 "Number One")............8-12 63

J-2 (1302 "Wrapped Around Your Finger")...75-125

SYMBOL (214 "She Blew a Good Thing") 10-15 66

SYMBOL (216 "So Young") 10-15 66

SYMBOL (219 "I'm Particular")................10-15 66

VEEP (1286 "The Hustler")......................10-20 68

Members: Ronnie Lewis; Melvin Bradford; Paul Fulton; Johnny James.

POINDEXTER, Doug, & Starlite Wranglers

Singles: 78 rpm

SUN...200-300 54

Singles: 7-inch

SUN (202 "Now She Cares No More for Me") 800-1200 54

Members: Doug Poindexter; Bill Black; Scotty Moore.

Also see BLACK, Bill

Also see MOORE, Scotty

POINTER SISTERS *P&R/R&B/LP '73*

Singles: 12-inch

PLANET 4-8 78-85

RCA...4-6 85-86

Singles: 7-inch

ABC 4-6 75-78

ATLANTIC (2845 "Don't Try to Take the Fifth")..10-20 72

ATLANTIC (2893 "Destination, No More Heartaches")...10-20 72

BLUE THUMB..4-6 73-78

MCA...3-5 87

PLANET 3-6 78-85

RCA..3-5 85-88

Picture Sleeves

MCA...3-5 87

PLANET 3-6 78-85

RCA..3-5 85-86

LPs: 10/12-inch

BLUE THUMB..8-12 73-77

MCA..5-10 81

PLANET 5-10 78-84

RCA..5-8 85-88

Members: Bonnie; Anita; Ruth; June.

POLICE *P&R/LP '79*

Singles: 12-inch

A&M (4401 "Don't Stand So Close to Me")...200-250 81

(Picture disc. Promotional issue only. 25 made.)

A&M (17122 "Message in a Bottle") 5-8 79

(Promotional issue only.)

Singles: 7-inch

A&M (Except 25000, and picture discs) 3-6 79-84

A&M (25000 "De Do Do Do, De Da Da Da")..10-20 80

(Spanish/Japanese language version.)

A&M ("Roxanne") 250-500 79

(Rose-shaped picture disc. Production pressing.)

A&M (2096 "Roxanne")..............................35-40 79

(Badge-shaped picture disc. Promotional issue only. Includes custom folder.)

A&M (4401 "Don't Stand So Close to Me") 25-30 81

(Star-shaped picture disc.)

A&M (4401 "Don't Stand So Close to Me") 30-35 81

(Star-shaped picture disc. Promotional issue only. Identified by promo sticker on cover.)

SIRE 3-5 86

Picture Sleeves

A&M (Except 25000)....................................3-5 80-86

A&M (25000 "De Do Do Do, De Da Da Da")...4-6 80

LPs: 10/12-inch

A&M (Except 3713 & 3735) 5-15 79-86

A&M (3713 "Reggatta de Blanc") 10-20 79

(Two 10-inch LPs. Includes poster. Promotional issue only.)

A&M (3735 "Synchronicity")....................75-100 83

(Black and white cover.)

A&M (3735 "Synchronicity")......................40-50 83

(Gold, gray and brown cover.)

NAUTILUS (40 "Ghost in the Machine")...40-50 '80s

NAUTILUS (19 Zenyata Mondata")..........25-35 81

Members: Gordon "Sting" Sumner; Stewart Copeland; Andy Summers.

POLK BROTHERS

Singles: 7-inch

FLAG (117 "Going to the Hop") 250-350

POLKA DOTS

Singles: 7-inch

ROLLS (1002 "Go Chase a Moonbeam") ..5-10 60

POLLARD, Bill

Singles: 7-inch

OZARK (2001 "Night Spot Rock") 350-450

POLLARD, Donnie, & Marauders

Singles: 7-inch

MI-JA (1001 "Hang Loose") 15-25 58

POLLARD, Ray

Singles: 7-inch

DECCA (32111 "Lie, Lips, Lie") 40-60 67

DECCA (32189 "Wanderlust")..................10-20 67

SHRINE (103 "No More Like Me")........150-250 65

U.A. (856 "My Girl and I")..........................15-25 65

U.A. (916 "Let Him Go") 25-35 65

U.A. (50012 "It's a Sad Thing")................30-50 65

Also see WANDERERS

POMUS, Doc

Singles: 78 rpm

APOLLO (393 "Blues in the Red") 20-30 45

APOLLO (401 "Naggin' Wife Blues").........20-30 45

CHESS (1440 "No Home Blues") 15-25 50

SAVOY (5545 "Doc's Boogie")...................15-25 48

SELMER (7146 "Pomus Blues")................15-25 48

Also see SMITH, Tab

PONDER, Carl

Singles: 7-inch

DESTINY (1202 "Greatest Hurt")...........75-125

PONDIROSAS

Singles: 7-inch

CO & CE (236 "Everybody's Surfin' ") 40-60 66

PONI-TAILS *P&R/R&B '58*

(With Al Tercek & His Orchestra; Pony-tails)

Singles: 78 rpm

ABC-PAR 20-40 57

MARC...10-20 57

POINT 10-20 57

Singles: 7-inch

ABC 4-6 73

ABC-PAR (9846 "It's Just My Luck to Be 15")....10-20 57
ABC-PAR (9934 "Born Too Late")....30-40 58
(Credits "Pony-Tails.")
ABC-PAR (9934 "Born Too Late")....10-20 58
ABC-PAR (9969 "Seven Minutes in Heaven")....10-20 58
ABC-PAR (9995 "Early to Bed")....10-20 59
ABC-PAR (10027 "Moody")....10-20 59
ABC-PAR (10047 "I'll Be Seeing You")....10-20 59
ABC-PAR (10077 "Before We Say Goodnight")....10-20 60
ABC-PAR (10114 "Oh My You")....10-20 60
MCA....4-6
MARC (1001 "Still in Your Teens")....10-20 57
POINT (8 "Your Wild Heart")....10-20 57
Members: Toni Cistone; LaVerne Novak; Patti McCabe.

POOKAH
LPs: 10/12-inch
U.A. (6737 "Pookah")....8-12 70

POOLE, Brian P&R '64
(With the Tremeloes)
Singles: 7-inch
DATE (1539 "I Need Her Tonight")....5-10 66
LONDON....5-10 63
MONUMENT....5-10 64-65
LPs: 10/12-inch
AUDIO FIDELITY....15-25 66-67
Also see TREMELOES

POOLE, Johnny
Singles: 7-inch
WIDE (430 "Barefoot Baby")....75-100

POOR
Singles: 7-inch
DECCA (32318 "Come Back Baby")....5-10 68
LOMA (2062 "Once Again")....8-12 66
YORK (402 "Love Is Real")....15-25 67
YORK (404 "My Mind Goes High")....15-25 67

POOR BOY
(James Oden)
Singles: 78 rpm
BLACK & WHITE....20-40 47
Also see ST. LOUIS JIMMY

POOR BOY'S PRIDE
Singles: 7-inch
FENTON (3060 "I'm Here")....15-25 68
SWADE ("The Place")....10-15 67
(Selection number not known.)

POOR BOYS
Singles: 78 rpm
APOLLO (1203 "Washboard")....5-10 55
Singles: 7-inch
APOLLO (1203 "Washboard")....10-15 55
SOMA (1116 "Driftin'")....10-15 59
Also see KING RICHARD & POOR BOYS

POOR BOYS
LPs: 10/12-inch
RARE EARTH (519 "Ain't Nothin' in Our Pocket But Love")....8-12 70

POOR BOYS
Singles: 7-inch
GENERAL AMERICAN (005 "Over the Hill")....10-20 65

POOR SOULS
Singles: 7-inch
IT WILL STAND (4602 "Over the Rainbow")....10-15 81
SURFSIDE (820302 "I Want You")....3-5 80

POORE BOYES
Singles: 7-inch
PATTY (1375 "Give")....20-25 '60s
SUMMER (181 "It's Love")....20-25 67
UPTOWN (739 "It's Love")....20-25 67

POOTHER UNLIMITED
Singles: 7-inch
CADET (5653 "Tastee Freeze")....15-25 69

POOVEY, Joe
(Groovy Joe Poovey)
Singles: 7-inch
DIXIE (733 "Move Around")....400-600 58
DIXIE (2018 "Ten Long Fingers")....200-300 59
SIMS....5-10 62-66

POP, Iggy LP '73
(Iggy & Stooges)
Singles: 12-inch
A&M....4-8 86
Singles: 7-inch
A&M....3-5 86
BOMP....4-6 78
RCA....4-6 77
SIAMESE....4-6 77
Picture Sleeves
A&M....3-5 86
EPs: 7-inch
BOMP....5-10 78
LPs: 10/12-inch
A&M....5-8 86
ANIMAL....5-10 82
ARISTA....8-12 79-81
BOMP (1018 "Kill City")....10-15 78
(Black vinyl.)
BOMP (1018 "Kill City")....20-30 78
(Colored vinyl.)
COLUMBIA....10-20 73
ENIGMA....5-8 84
IMPORT....8-10 77
INVASION....8-10 83
RCA....5-10 77-78
VIRGIN....5-8 90
Also see BOWIE, David / Iggy Pop
Also see IGUANAS
Also see STOOGES

POPCORN BLIZZARD
Singles: 7-inch
DE-LITE (516 "Good Thing Going")....10-20 69
DE-LITE (522 "Good, Good Day")....10-20 69
(Having two groups with such a distinctive name, we have them listed together. However, while we have confirmed Meat Loaf's involvement with the Magenda issue, we are not yet certain about this release. Readers?)
MAGENDA (7411 "Once Upon a Time")..20-30 67
Member: Marvin Lee Aday.
Also see MEAT LOAF

POPE, Raymond, & Love Tones
(With the Andrew McPherson's Band)
Singles: 7-inch
SQUALOR (1313 "I Love Nadine")....75-125 58

POPPA HOP
(Poppy Hop)
Singles: 7-inch
IVORY (127 "I'm a Stranger")....30-40 60
IVORY (134 "Merry Christmas Darling")...30-40 60
Also see WILSON, Hop, & His Two Buddies

POPPIES P&R '66
Singles: 7-inch
EPIC (9893 "Lullaby of Love")....5-10 66
EPIC (10019 "He's Ready")....5-10 66
EPIC (10059 "Do It with Soul")....5-10 66
EPIC (10086 "There's a Pain in My Heart")....10-20 66
TUFF (372 "Johnny Don't Cry")....10-15 63
Picture Sleeves
EPIC (10019 "He's Ready")....10-15 66
LPs: 10/12-inch
EPIC (24200 "Lullaby of Love")....20-30 66
(Monaural.)
EPIC (26200 "Lullaby of Love")....25-35 66
(Stereo.)
Members: Dorothy Moore; Rosemary Taylor; Pet McCune.

POPSICLES
Singles: 7-inch
KNIGHT (2002 "Thumb Print")....30-40 58

POPULAIRS
Singles: 7-inch
MARVELLO (5001 "I Lost My Heart")...200-300 '50s

PORCELAIN BEARMEAT
LPs: 10/12-inch
DILL PICKLE (3468 "Free Love, Free Sex, Free Music")....15-20 71

PORGY & MONARCHS
Singles: 7-inch
MALA (462 "Stay")....10-15 63
(Black vinyl.)
MALA (462 "Stay")....40-50 63
(Colored vinyl.)
MUSICOR (1179 "That Girl")....15-25 66
MUSICOR (1221 "My Heart Cries for You")....20-30 66
SYLVES (123 "That's My Girl")....5-10 68
VERVE (10597 "Love Chain")....5-10 68
VERVE (10609 "That's My Girl")....5-10 68

PORTER, Bruce
(With the Bell Hops)
Singles: 7-inch
LEE (100 "Rattlesnake")....100-150 58
LEE (101 "I'm Not Ashamed")....50-100 58
LEE (103 "Double Trouble")....50-100 58
LEE (104 "Go Little Go Go Girl")....50-100 58
LEE (5687 "Please Please Darling")....15-25 59

PORTER, Jake
(With the Combo-Nettes; Jake Porter Combo)
Singles: 78 rpm
COMBO....10-15 50-54
Singles: 7-inch
COMBO....20-40 50-54
KEM (2760 "Saturday Blues")....5-10 61
Also see DUCHESS / Jake Porter
Also see MOORE, Gene, & Chimes / Jake Porter with Gene Moore & Chimes

PORTER, Jake, & Buzzards
Singles: 78 rpm
COMBO (91 "The Bop")....15-25 55
Singles: 7-inch
COMBO (91 "The Bop")....30-40 55

PORTER, Jake, & Ebbonairs
Singles: 78 rpm
COMBO (110 "Doodle Doo Doo")....15-25 55
COMBO (111 "You")....25-35 55
COMBO (126 "Rosetta")....15-25 56
Singles: 7-inch
COMBO (110 "Doodle Doo Doo")....40-60 55
COMBO (111 "You")....50-75 55
COMBO (126 "Rosetta")....40-60 56

PORTER, Jake, & Laurels / Jake Porter
Singles: 78 rpm
COMBO (66 "Fine Fine Baby"/"T.J.")...100-150 55
Singles: 7-inch
COMBO (66 "Fine Fine Baby"/"T.J.")...300-400 55
Also see LAURELS
Also see PORTER, Jake

PORTER, Johnny
(Johnny Schoolboy Porter & His Schoolboys; with Chanceteers)
Singles: 78 rpm
CHANCE....15-25 51-53
Singles: 7-inch
CHANCE (1101 "Schoolboy's Boogie")....30-40 51
CHANCE (1103 "Tennessee Waltz")....30-40 51
CHANCE (1104 "Walk Heavy")....30-40 51
CHANCE (1105 "Kayron")....30-40 51
CHANCE (1111 "Stairway to the Stars")..30-40 52
CHANCE (1114 "Soft Shoulder")....100-150 52
CHANCE (1117 "Fire Dome")....30-40 52
CHANCE (1119 "Break Through")....30-40 52
CHANCE (1132 "Small Squall")....30-40 53
Also see CHANCETEERS

PORTER, Lulu
Singles: 7-inch
MOONGLOW (5008 "I Gotta Be with You")....5-10 65
MUSIC MAN (102 "You've Turned On the Light")....5-10 66
MUSIC MAN (103 "Mr. Music Man")....5-10 66
PEP (101 "Love Came Walking In")....5-10 65

PORTER, Ralph
Singles: 7-inch
MERIDAN ("Hey Mr. Porter")....50-100
(Selection number not known.)

PORTER, Robert
Singles: 7-inch
DIAMOND (151 "Casanova")....20-30 63

PORTER, Rocky
Singles: 7-inch
STARS (549 "First Sight")....50-100

PORTER, Royce
Singles: 7-inch
D (1026 "Lookin'")....50-100 58
LOOK (1001 "Yes I Do")....150-200 57
MERCURY (71314 "Good Time")....50-75 58

SPADE (1931 "A Woman Can Make You Blue")....150-200 '50s

PORTO, Billy
Singles: 78 rpm
MERCURY (71205 "Ruby Ruby")....5-10 57
Singles: 7-inch
MERCURY (71205 "Ruby Ruby")....15-25 57

PORTRAITS
Singles: 7-inch
CAPITOL (4181 "Close to You")....10-20 59
Also see HOLLYWOOD SAXONS
Also see TUXEDOS

PORTRAITS
Singles: 7-inch
NIKE ("It Had to Be You")....30-50 67
(No selection number used. 100 made.)
Members: Emil Rakovich; Peter Lewna; Bill Watson; Greg Stupek; Michael Szymborski.

PORTRAITS
(Jerry & Portraits)
Singles: 7-inch
SIDEWALK (928 "Million to One")....10-20 67
SIDEWALK (935 "Runaround Girl")....10-20 68
Members: Jerry Tawney; Phil Anthony; Gary Myers; John Rondell.
Also see DARNELLS
Also see MYERS, Gary
Also see TAWNEY, Jerry

PORTUGUESE JOE & TENNESSEE ROCKABILLYS
Singles: 7-inch
SURF (5016 "Sugar Sugar Honey")....40-60 57
SURF (5018 "Teenage Riot")....75-100 57

POSEY, Clarence / Henry Smith
Singles: 78 rpm
FORTUNE (802 "Rockin' Chair Boogie") .50-75 52
Also see SMITH, Henry

POSEY, Ralph
Singles: 7-inch
BEAVER (9631 "Don't Leave Me Here")....100-200

POSIES
LPs: 10/12-inch
GEFFEN (24305 "Dear 23")....10-15 90
POPLLAMA (2323 "Failure")....25-35 88
(Blue vinyl.)
Members: Jonathan Auer; Kenneth Stringfellow.

POSITIVELY THIRTEEN O'CLOCK
Singles: 7-inch
HBR (500 "Psychotic Reaction")....25-35 66
Session: Jimmy Rabbitt.
Also see MOUSE
Also see RABBITT, Jimmy

POSSESSIONS
Singles: 7-inch
BRITTON (1003 "No More Love")....15-25 64
(Black vinyl.)
BRITTON (1003 "No More Love")....40-50 64
(Blue vinyl.)
PARKWAY (930 "No More Love")....8-12 64
Also see VITO & SALUTATIONS

POSSUMS
Singles: 7-inch
JM (3824 "She's Loving Me")....15-25 66

POT OF FLOWERS
LPs: 10/12-inch
MAINSTREAM (56100 "With Love")....25-35 67
(Monaural.)
MAINSTREAM (6100 "With Love")....30-40 67
(Stereo.)

POTITO, Joe, & Satellites
Singles: 7-inch
SAFARI (1003 "Say a Prayer")....50-60 57

POTTER, Bob
Singles: 7-inch
RURAL RHYTHM (45 "Leavin' a Laughin' ")....50-75

POTTER, Curtis
Singles: 7-inch
DOT....4-6 71
FOX (409 "Real Glad Daddy")....150-250 58

HILLSIDE....3-5 80
WINSTON (1042 "Can I Be Sure")....10-15 59
LPs: 10/12-inch
DOT....10-20 71
HILLSIDE....5-10 80
Also see SANDERS, Ray / Curtis Potter / Darrell McCall

POTTER - ST. CLOUD
LPs: 10/12-inch
MEDIARTS....10-15 71
Members: D.F. Potter; Endle St. Cloud; James Harrell; Danny Baker.

POULSEN, Skip, & Beach Continentals
Singles: 7-inch
DEAUVILLE (1006 "A Pretzel Ain't Nothin' But a Twist")....8-12 62

POULTON, Dick, Trio
Singles: 7-inch
VIN (1016 "Susie")....10-20 59

POUND
LPs: 10/12-inch
A.M.S. (74840 "Odd Man Out")....35-55 74
Members: Dave Bither; Dave Franson; Greg Shannon; Pam Petros.

POWDER PUFFS
(Angels)
Singles: 7-inch
IMPERIAL (66014 "My Boyfriend's Woody")....15-25 64
Also see ANGELS

POWDRILL, Pat
Singles: 7-inch
DOWNEY (139 "Do It")....15-25 66
DOWNEY (141 "Together Forever")....15-25 66
REPRISE....10-15 63-64

POWELL, Austin
(With the James Quintet; Austin Powell Quintet)
Singles: 78 rpm
ATLANTIC (968 "Wrong Again")....100-150 52
DECCA (48206 "All This Can't Be True") 20-30 51
DECCA (48206 "All This Can't Be True")....75-100 51
(White label promotional issue.)
Singles: 7-inch
ATLANTIC (968 "Wrong Again")....500-700 52
DECCA (48206 "All This Can't Be True")....150-250 51
Also see CATS & FIDDLE
Also see JAMES QUINTET

POWELL, Bobby *P&R/R&B '65*
Singles: 7-inch
EXCELLO....5-10 72-74
HEP' ME (151 "A Fool for You")....5-10
HEP' ME (155 "The Glory of Love")....5-10
HEP' ME (155 "Glory of Love [Short Version]"/ "Glory of Love [Long Version]")....10-15
(Labeled "For Juke Box Only.")
JEWEL (785 "Our Love")....5-10 67
WHIT....6-12 65-71
LPs: 10/12-inch
EXCELLO....10-15 73

POWELL, Chris, & Blue Flames
(With "Vocal Chorus by Johnny Echo, Sax Solo by Vance Wilson;" with Five Blue Flames)
Singles: 78 rpm
COLUMBIA (Except 39407)....25-50 49-51
COLUMBIA (39407 "My Love Has Gone")....400-500 51
GRAND....15-25 54-55
GROOVE....8-12 55-56
OKEH (Except 6818)....40-50 51-52
OKEH (6818 "The Masquerade Is Over")....75-125 51
Singles: 7-inch
COLUMBIA (39272 "Country Girl Blues")....50-100 51
COLUMBIA (39407 "My Love Has Gone")....300-500 51
GRAND (108 "Sweet Sue Mambo")....25-35 54
GRAND (112 "Secret Love Mambo")....25-35 54
GRAND (116 "Dinah [Mambo]")....25-35 54
GRAND (124 "Sweet Georgia Brown")....25-35 55
GRAND (127 "Mandoline Mambo")....25-35 55
GROOVE (0105 "Break It Up")....10-20 55
GROOVE (0111 "Unchained Melody")....10-20 55
GROOVE (0128 "Chinatown")....10-20 55
GROOVE (0144 "Moritat")....10-20 56
OKEH (6818 "The Masquerade Is Over")....75-125 51
OKEH (6850 "October Twilight")....50-75 51
OKEH (6875 "Ida Red")....50-75 52
OKEH (6900 "Blue Boy")....50-75 52
Member: Joe Van Loan.
Also see VAN LOAN, Joe

POWELL, Curt
Singles: 7-inch
SONIC (138 "Impossible to Find")....5-10 67

POWELL, Dick, Orchestra & Chorus
Singles: 7-inch
RPC (501 "Wonderful Teens")....8-12 61
LPs: 10/12-inch
RPC (105 "Wonderful Teens")....10-15 62

POWELL, Doug
Singles: 7-inch
JUDI (051 "Crazy Georgia Shake")....15-25 60
KETO (102 "Love We Feel")....10-20 61
MERCURY (71949 "Fort Lauderdale")....40-60 62
TIP TOP (713 "Loud Mufflers")....100-150 58

POWELL, Freddy, & Citrones
Singles: 7-inch
SHERATON (105 "Flip to the Twist")....30-40 62

POWELL, George, & Troopers
Singles: 7-inch
LUMMTONE (101 "My Choice for a Mate")....200-300 59

POWELL, James
Singles: 7-inch
CHRISTY (137 "Beverly Angel")....40-50 60
CHRISTY (61151 "Beverly Angel")....20-30 61
(Different version than above.)

POWELL, Jesse
(With the Caddys; with Majors; "Vocal By Dan Taylor;" Jessie Powell)
Singles: 78 rpm
FEDERAL (12056 "Walkin' Blues")....25-50 52
(With Fluffy Hunter.)
FEDERAL (12060 "My Natch'l Man")....25-50 52
(With Fluffy Hunter.)
FEDERAL (12159 "Rear Bumper")....15-25 53
FEDERAL (12171 "Hot Box")....15-25 53
JOSIE....5-10 55-58
Singles: 7-inch
FEDERAL (12056 "Walkin' Blues")....100-200 52
(With Fluffy Hunter.)
FEDERAL (12060 "My Natch'l Man")....100-200 52
(With Fluffy Hunter.)
FEDERAL (12159 "Rear Bumper")....50-100 53
FEDERAL (12171 "Hot Box")....50-100 53
FLING (715 "Kingfish Rock")....10-20 60
JOHNSON (122 "Searching")....5-10 63
JOSIE....15-25 55-58
KAPP (476 "Taste of Honey")....5-10 62
RONNEX....5-10 '60s
TRU SOUND (404 "Jumpin' Salty")....8-12 61
TRU SOUND (407 "Tonight")....8-12 61
TRU SOUND (414 "Hot Stuff")....8-12 62
LPs: 10/12-inch
JUBILEE (1113 "Blow Man Blow")....40-60 60
KAPP (1301 "Taste of Honey with a Dash of Jazz")....20-30 62
(Monaural.)
KAPP (3301 "Taste of Honey with a Dash of Jazz")....20-30 62
(Stereo.)
TRU-SOUND (15007 "It's Party Time with Jesse Powell")....20-30 62
Also see CADILLACS
Also see EXECUTIVE FOUR
Also see GUY, Bobby
Also see HUNTER, Fluffy
Also see NEW YORKERS 5

POWELL, Keith, & Valets
Singles: 7-inch
STELLAR (1503 "Tore Up")....20-30 '60s

POWELL, Sandy
(Sandra Powell)
Singles: 7-inch
HERALD (557 "Bon Bon")....150-200 61
IMPALA (211 "Bon Bon")....300-400 61
SINGULAR (714 "My Jimmie")....20-30 58
Also see STREET, Mel, & Sandy Powell

POWER, Mike
Singles: 7-inch
ZELMAN (5301 "I Left My Love in Paris")....300-500

POWERHOUSE
LPs: 10/12-inch
ALADDIN....20-30 75
POWERHOUSE....5-10 83-87
Member: Tom Principato.

POWERS, Donna
Singles: 7-inch
MIDCO (2200 "Loving You")....15-25 61

POWERS, Eddie
Singles: 7-inch
RONN (11 "Tears in My Eyes")....5-10 67
SIMS....5-10 64-65

POWERS, Freddy, & Powerhouse IV
LPs: 10/12-inch
W.B. (W-1488 "The Good Life")....15-25 63
(Monaural.)
W.B. (WS-1488 "The Good Life")....25-35 63
(Stereo.)
Members: Freddy Powers; Glenn Keener.
Also see SUMMERS, Gene

POWERS, Jackie
Singles: 7-inch
MOPIC (7707 "Heeby Jeeby Blues")....50-60 62
SAHARA (103 "Heebie Jeebie Blues")....10-15 62

POWERS, Jett
(James Smith)
Singles: 7-inch
BETA (1008 "Loud Perfume")....75-100 60
DESIGN (811 "Go Girl Go")....75-100 57
Session: Bumps Blackwell.
Also see PROBY, P.J.

POWERS, Joey *P&R '63*
(Joey Powers' Flower)
Singles: 7-inch
AMY....5-15 63-67
MGM (13421 "Leave Me Alone")....5-10 65
RCA (8039 "Jenny, Won't You Wake Up").8-10 62
RCA (8119 "Don't Envy Me")....8-10 62
RCA (9790 "Hard to Be Without You")....4-8 69
LPs: 10/12-inch
AMY (8001 "Midnight Mary")....20-25 64
Also see ORBISON, Roy / Bobby Bare / Joey Powers

POWERS, Johnny
(With His Rockets; with the band of Stan Getz & Tom Cats)
Singles: 78 rpm
FORTUNE (199 "Honey Let's Go [To a Rock and Roll Show]")....25-50 56
Singles: 7-inch
FORTUNE (199 "Honey Let's Go [To a Rock and Roll Show]")....100-200 56
FOX (917 "Rock Rock"/"Long Blonde Hair, Red Rose Lips")....750-1000 57
HI-Q (5044 "Rock the Universe")....75-100 64
OLYMPIC....4-6 76-78
SUN (327 "Be Mine All Mine")....50-75 59
SUN (600 series)....4-6 75
TEE PEE (398 "Seventeen")....20-30 61
TRIODEX (103 "A Teenager's Prayer")....10-15 60
Also see BROWN, Johnny "Scat"
Also see GETZ, Stan
Also see JUSTIS, Bill
Also see RICH, Charlie

POWERS, Roni
Singles: 7-inch
LT PRODUCTIONS (1022 "An Angel Up in Heaven")....50-100 61

POWERS, Tina
Singles: 7-inch
PARKWAY (847 "Making Up Is Fun to Do")....10-20 62

POWERS, Wayne
(Wayne Cogswell)
Singles: 7-inch
PHILLIPS INT'L (3523 "My Love Song")..10-20 58
Also see MARK II

POWERS, Wendy
Singles: 7-inch
KEEN (2004 "Auctioneer Lover")....10-20 58

POWERS OF BLUE
Singles: 7-inch
MTA....5-10 66-67
LPs: 10/12-inch
MTA (5002 "Flip Out")....20-30 67
Member: Hugh McCracken.
Also see McCRACKEN, Hugh

POYNTER, Joyce
Singles: 7-inch
GOLDEN ROD (301 "Chili Dippin' Baby")....50-75 57

POZO - SECO SINGERS *P&R/LP '66*
(Susan Taylor & the Pozo Seco Singers; Pozo Seco; Pozo-Seco Singers Featuring Don Williams)
Singles: 7-inch
CERTRON....4-8 70-71
COLUMBIA....5-8 65-70
COLUMBIA (43437 "Time")....10-20 65
(Red vinyl. Promotional issue.)
EDMARK (10017 "Down the Road I Go"/ "Time")....10-20 65
LPs: 10/12-inch
CERTRON....10-15 70
COLUMBIA....10-20 66-68
EXCELSIOR....5-10 80
Members: Don Williams; Susan Taylor; Lofton Kline.
Also see WILLIAMS, Don

PRADO, Perez, & His Orchestra *P&R '53*
Singles: 78 rpm
RCA....4-6 50-58
Singles: 7-inch
RCA....5-15 50-64
U.A.....5-8 64
Picture Sleeves
RCA (7540 "My Roberta")....10-15 59
EPs: 7-inch
BELL (2 "Perez Prado")....5-10
RCA....8-15 54-61
LPs: 10/12-inch
CAMDEN (547 "Latino")....10-15 60
RCA....5-10 76
(With "ANL1" prefix.)
RCA....10-30 54-72
(With "LPM," "LSP" or "VPS" prefix.)
SPIN-O-RAMA....8-12 62
SPRINGBOARD....5-10 77
U.A.....10-15 65-68
Also see CLOONEY, Rosemary, & Perez Prado
Also see KITT, Eartha, & Perez Prado

PRAEGER, Billy
Singles: 7-inch
CRYSTAL (106 "Everybody's Rockin'")....200-300 59

PRAIRIE CHIEFS
Singles: 78 rpm
RCA....5-10 57
Singles: 7-inch
RCA (69 "Broken Arrow")....5-10 57
RCA (79 "Tales of Wells Fargo")....5-10 57
Picture Sleeves
RCA (69 "Broken Arrow")....20-30 57
(Pictures TV series stars John Lupton and Michael Ansara.)
RCA (79 "Tales of Wells Fargo")....15-25 57
(Pictures TV series star Dale Robertson.)

PRATT, Lynn
Singles: 78 rpm
HORNET (1000 "Tom Cat Boogie")....75-100
Singles: 7-inch
HORNET (1000 "Tom Cat Boogie")....100-200
HORNET (1001 "Troubles")....100-125
HORNET (1002 "Come Here Mama")..250-350
HORNET (1003 "Red Headed Woman")....100-125
Also see PITRELLO, Carne

PRATT, Scrapper
Singles: 7-inch
FALCON ("Guitar Man's Struggle")....100-200
(Selection number not known.)

PRATT BROTHERS
Singles: 7-inch
BURDETTE (3000 "Go Find Your Love") ... 100-150

PREACHERS
Singles: 7-inch
RE (491 "Girls, Girls, Girls") ... 15-20 66
RIGHTEOUS ENT. (1001 "Inspiration"/"Who's That Hiding in the Closet") ... 20-25 65
RIGHTEOUS ENT. (1003 "Inspiration"/"Hallowed Ground") ... 15-20 66
Note: Righteous Enterprises, also known as RE, was formed by the Righteous Brothers.
Also see RIGHTEOUS BROTHERS

PREACHERS
Singles: 7-inch
CHALLENGE (501 "Till the Dawn") ... 5-10 69
MOONGLOW (240 "Who Do You Love") 50-75 65
MOONGLOW (5006 "Pain and Sorrow") . 10-20 65
PEP (102 "Zeke") ... 8-12 65

PRECIOUS FEW
Singles: 7-inch
NASCO (001 "The Carnival") ... 5-10 69
SALEM (501 "The Train Kept A-Rollin'") . 20-30 66

PRECIOUS FEW
Singles: 7-inch
BEAR (1978 "You Don't Need Me") ... 20-25 '60s

PRECISIONS
(With Herchel Dwellingham & Orchestra)
Singles: 7-inch
WILD (903 "The Love") ... 25-50

PRECISIONS
Singles: 7-inch
GOLDEN CREST (571 "Someone to Watch Over Me") ... 15-25 62
STRAND (25038 "Dream On") ... 40-50 61

PRECISIONS
Singles: 7-inch
HIGHLAND (300 "Eight Reasons Why I Love You") ... 200-300 62
(Counterfeits have 45 RPM between the lines.)

PRECISIONS
Singles: 7-inch
DEBRA (1001 "Sweet Dreams") ... 15-25 63
Also see MAGICS

PRECISIONS *P&R/R&B '67*
Singles: 7-inch
ATCO (6643 "Into My Life") ... 5-10 69
ATCO (6669 "New York City") ... 5-10 69
D-TOWN (1033 "My Lover Come Back"). 40-60 65
D-TOWN (1055 "Mexican Love Song") ... 10-20 65
DREW (1001 "Such Misery") ... 15-25 66
DREW (1002 "Why Girl") ... 15-25 67
DREW (1003 "If This Is Love") ... 15-25 67
DREW (1004 "Instant Heartbreak") ... 15-25 68
DREW (1005 "A Place") ... 15-25 68
HEN-MAR (4501 "Take a Good Look") ... 4-6 73

PRECISIONS
Singles: 7-inch
RAYNA (1001 "White Christmas") ... 50-75
Members: Pat Gerlardi; Ronnie Gerlardi; Gil Pabon; Billy Reid.
Also see CHYMES

PRE-HISTORICS
Singles: 7-inch
EDSEL (779 "Alley Oop Cha-Cha-Cha") . 15-25 60
Members: Arthur Crier; Carl Spencer.
Also see FIVE CHIMES
Also see HALOS
Also see MELLOWS

PREHLE, Michelle / Dee Lites
Singles: 7-inch
MAGIC CARPET (506 "Letter to Elvis") ... 8-12 79
(Black vinyl. 400 made.)
MAGIC CARPET (506 "Letter to Elvis") ... 15-20 79
(Colored vinyl. 100 made.)

PRELUDES
Singles: 78 rpm
EMPIRE ... 20-30 56
Singles: 7-inch
EMPIRE (103 "Don't Fall in Love Too Soon") ... 40-50 56
Members: Charles Everidge; Harold Murray; James Warren; Homer Green.
Also see YOUNGSTERS

PRELUDES
Singles: 7-inch
ACME (730 "Kingdom of Love") ... 150-200 58
(First issue.)
CUB (9005 "Kingdom of Love") ... 50-100 58

PRELUDES
Singles: 7-inch
ARLISS (1004 "Lorraine") ... 40-50 61
OCTAVIA (8008 "A Place for You") ... 25-35 62

PRELUDES FIVE *P&R '61*
(Preludes)
Singles: 7-inch
PIK (231 "Starlight") ... 25-30 61

PREMEERS
Singles: 7-inch
HERALD (577 "Diary of Our Love") ... 30-40 63

PREMIER, Ronnie
(Ronnie Premier & the Royal Lancers)
Singles: 7-inch
LAURIE (3091 "Angel in My Eyes") ... 10-20 61
SARA (1020 "Angel in My Eyes") ... 30-50 60
Also see ROYAL LANCERS

PREMIERS
Singles: 78 rpm
DIG (106 "New Moon") ... 20-30 56
DIG (113 "My Darling") ... 20-30 56
FORTUNE (527 "When You Are in Love") ... 10-20 56
RCA (6958 "Run Along Baby") ... 20-30 57
Singles: 7-inch
BEST (1004 "False Love") ... 100-150 59
CINDY (3008 "Life Is Grand") ... 50-100 58
DIG (106 "New Moon") ... 50-100 56
DIG (113 "My Darling") ... 75-125 56
DIG (141 "Red Sails in the Sunset") ... 3-5
(Previously unissued.)
ECHO (6013 "Until") ... 750-1000 '50s
FORTUNE (527 "When You Are in Love") ... 40-50 56
GONE (5009 "Is It a Dream") ... 500-600 57
GONE (5009 "Is It a Dream") ... 200-300 57
(Due to a production error, *Let Me Share Your Dream* [Delta 5010] appears on this side instead of *Is it a Dream*.)
IRIS (113 "My Darling") ... 5-10
(Reissue of Dig 113.)
RCA (6958 "Run Along Baby") ... 30-40 57
Also see DELTAS
Also see STEVENS, Julie

PREMIERS
Singles: 7-inch
BOND (5803 "Hop and Skip") ... 50-100 58

PREMIERS
(Premieres)
Singles: 7-inch
NU-PHI (367 "Cruisin'") ... 30-40 59
NU-PHI (701 "Firewater") ... 30-40 60
Also see WALTERS, Bucky & Jukes

PREMIERS
Singles: 7-inch
ALERT (703 "Linda") ... 3-5
(Previously unissued.)
ALERT (706 "Jolene") ... 40-50 58
FURY (1029 "I Pray") ... 15-25 60
RUST (5032 "Falling Star") ... 50-100 61
Members: Roger Koob; Billy Koob; Gus Delcos; Frank Polimus; Vinny Klump; Barbara Klump; Tim Vail; Joe Vece.
Also see ROGER & TRAVELERS

PREMIERS
(With John Medora & Orchestra)
Singles: 7-inch
MINK (21 "Tonight") ... 40-50 59
PARKWAY (807 "Tonight") ... 15-25 59

PREMIERS
Singles: 7-inch
DICE (115 "Crazy Bells") ... 15-25 61

PREMIERS
Singles: 7-inch
DORE (547 "True Deep Love") ... 15-25 60
DORE (603 "Evening Star") ... 15-25 61
DORE (614 "What Makes Little Girls Cry") ... 15-25 61

PREMIERS *P&R '64*
Singles: 7-inch
FARO ... 6-12 64-67
FINE ... 4-8 '60s
LEO (501 "Run Along Baby") ... 5-10 64
W.B. ... 4-8 64
LPs: 10/12-inch
RAMPART ("Farmer John") ... 25-35 64
(Selection number not known.)
W.B. (1565 "Farmer John") ... 15-25 64

PREMIERS
Singles: 7-inch
KING (6061 "I'm Better Off Now") ... 10-20 66
STAX (177 "Make It Me") ... 15-25 65

PREMIERS
Singles: 7-inch
ODEX (1711 "Speaking of You") ... 15-25 '60s

PREMIERS & INVICTAS
Singles: 7-inch
F-M (677 "Magic of Love") ... 50-75 59

PREMONITIONS
Singles: 7-inch
JADE (711 "Baby Baby") ... 75-125 67

PREPARATIONS *R&B '68*
Singles: 7-inch
HEART AND SOUL (201 "Get-E-Up [The Horse]") ... 8-12 68
MAINSTREAM (720 "That's When He Remembers") ... 8-12 69

PREPS
Singles: 7-inch
ANOTHER LOSER (176 "Pam Pam") ... 5-10 64
DOT (16663 "Night Theme") ... 5-10 64
SOUTHBAY ... 5-10 '60s
WARPED (5000 "Night Theme") ... 15-25 64
(First issue.)

PREPS
Singles: 7-inch
COAST ("Moon Racers") ... 30-40 '60s
(Selection number not known.)

PRESCOTT, Ralph
Singles: 7-inch
ABS (204 "Little Boy Bop") ... 250-350 '50s
LANOR (564 "Hot Hot Lips") ... 75-125 '50s

PRESENT, The
Singles: 7-inch
PHILIPS (40466 "I Know") ... 15-25 67

PRESIDENTS
Singles: 7-inch
MERCURY (72016 "Pots & Pans") ... 15-20 62
W.B. (5240 "I Do Love You") ... 5-10 61

PRESIDENTS *P&R/R&B '70*
Singles: 7-inch
DELUXE (113 "I Want My Baby") ... 5-8 69
HOLLYWOOD (1137 "Shoeshine") ... 5-8 68
SUSSEX ... 4-8 70-71
LPs: 10/12-inch
SUSSEX ... 15-25 70
Members: Tony Boyd; Archie Powell; Bill Shorter.

PRESIDENTS BANNED
Singles: 7-inch
YORK TOWN (1000 "Gotcha Babe") ... 20-30 '60s

PRESLEY, Elvis *C&W '55*
(With Scotty & Bill; with Jordanaires; with Imperials; with J.D. Sumner & Stamps; with Mello Men; with Amigos; with Jubilee Four & Carol Lombard Trio)
Singles: 12-inch
RCA (0517 "Little Sister") ... 125-150 83
(Promotional issue only.)
RCA (60575-1 "A Little Less Conversation") ... 8-12 2002
(Issued with custom sleeve.)
Singles: 78 rpm
(Commercial and Promotional)
RCA (6357 "Mystery Train") ... 100-150 55
RCA (6380 "That's All Right") ... 100-150 55
RCA (6381 "Good Rockin' Tonight") ... 100-150 55
RCA (6382 "Milkcow Blues Boogie") ... 100-150 55
RCA (6383 "Baby, Let's Play House") .. 100-150 55
RCA (6420 "Heartbreak Hotel") ... 75-100 56
(Black label.)
RCA (6420 "Heartbreak Hotel") ... 400-500
(White label. Promotional issue only.)
RCA (6492 "Blue Suede Shoes") ... 100-200 56
(Canadian. This number not used for any U.S. RCA release.)
RCA (6540 "I Want You, I Need You, I Love You") ... 75-100 56
(Black label.)
RCA (6540 "I Want You, I Need You, I Love You") ... 400-500
(White label. Promotional issue only.)
RCA (6604 "Don't Be Cruel") ... 75-100 56
(Black label.)
RCA (6604 "Don't Be Cruel") ... 400-500
(White label. Promotional issue only.)
RCA (6636 "Blue Suede Shoes") ... 75-100 56
RCA (6637 "I Got a Woman") ... 75-100 56
RCA (6638 "I'll Never Let You Go") ... 75-100 56
RCA (6639 "Tryin' to Get to You") ... 75-100 56
RCA (6640 "Blue Moon") ... 75-100 56
RCA (6641 "Money Honey") ... 75-100 56
RCA (6642 "Lawdy, Miss Clawdy") ... 75-100 56
RCA (6643 "Love Me Tender") ... 50-100 56
(Black label.)
RCA (6643 "Love Me Tender") ... 400-500
(White label. Promotional issue only.)
RCA (6800 "Too Much") ... 75-125 57
(Black label.)
RCA (6800 "Too Much") ... 400-500
(White label. Promotional issue only.)
RCA (6870 "All Shook Up") ... 75-125 57
(Black label.)
RCA (6870 "All Shook Up") ... 400-500
(White label. Promotional issue only.)
RCA (7000 "Teddy Bear") ... 75-125 57
(Black label.)
RCA (7000 "Teddy Bear") ... 400-500
(White label. Promotional issue only.)
RCA (7035 "Jailhouse Rock") ... 75-125 57
(Black label.)
RCA (7035 "Jailhouse Rock") ... 400-500
(White label. Promotional issue only.)
RCA (7066 "Mean Woman Blues") ... 100-200 57
(Canadian. Not issued as a U.S. single.)
RCA (7150 "Don't") ... 75-150 58
RCA (7240 "Wear My Ring Around Your Neck") ... 200-300 58
RCA (7280 "Hard Headed Woman") ... 200-300 58
RCA (7410 "One Night") ... 600-800 58
RCA (7506 "I Need Your Love Tonight") ... 400-600 59
(Canadian.)
RCA (7600 "Big Hunk O' Love") ... 400-600 59
(Canadian.)
ROYAL ("Elvis Presley Show") ... 200-300 56
(Single-sided disc, issued to radio stations to promote Elvis in concert. Includes an excerpt of *Heartbreak Hotel*.)
SUN (209 "That's All Right") ... 1500-2500 54
SUN (210 "Good Rockin' Tonight") ... 1500-2500 54
(Credits "Elvis Presley, Scotty and Bill")
SUN (210 "Good Rockin' Tonight") ... 1200-1500 54
(Credits "Elvis Presley")
SUN (215 "Milkcow Blues Boogie") .. 2000-3000 55
SUN (217 "Baby Let's Play House"). 1500-2500 55
SUN (223 "Mystery Train") ... 1000-1500 55
Notes: All Elvis RCA and Sun 78s were simultaneously issued on 45 rpm singles. For 78 rpm plastic soundsheets and flexi-discs, see a separate section that follows. RCA and Sun 78s can be found with many label variations. Sun promotional singles were marked with the word "sample" rubber stamped on the label. White label promotional 78s are still listed; however, their authenticity has been challenged by some experts.
Singles: 7-inch
(Commercial)
COLLECTABLES (Black vinyl) ... 3-5 86-87
COLLECTABLES (Gold vinyl) ... 3-5 92
MEMPHIS FLASH (92444 "Beginnings – Elvis Style") ... 10-20 78
RCA (0088 "Raised on Rock") ... 10-15 73
RCA (0130 "How Great Thou Art") ... 25-30 69
RCA (0196 "Take Good Care of Her") ... 8-10 74
RCA (0280 "If You Talk in Your Sleep") ... 15-20 74
(Has full title on one line.)
RCA (0280 "If You Talk in Your Sleep") ... 8-10 74
(Two lines are used for title.)

RCA (0572 "Merry Christmas Baby")....... 20-25 71
RCA (0619 "Until It's Time for You to Go").. 10-15 72
RCA (0651 "He Touched Me")............ 150-175 72
(Has the *He Touched Me* side pressed at about 35 rpm instead of 45. These copies – the result of a production error – are commercial issues. Flip, *Bosom of Abraham*, plays at 45 rpm.)
RCA (0651 "He Touched Me")................ 25-30 72
RCA (0672 "An American Trilogy")......... 20-25 72
RCA (0769 "Burning Love")................. 350-400 72
(Gray label.)
RCA (0769 "Burning Love")..........................5-8 72
(Orange label.)
RCA (0815 "Separate Ways")......................5-8 71
RCA (0910 "Fool")..5-8 73
RCA (1017 "It's Only Love")................... 10-15 71
RCA (2458 "My Boy"/"Loving Arms")... 700-750 74
(Add $150 to $200 if accompanied by insert, which reads: "Elvis Presley" and "My Boy." Produced in the U.S. for European distribution.)
RCA (6357 "Mystery Train")................... 50-75 55
RCA (6380 "That's All Right")................. 50-75 55
(Black label.)
RCA (6380 "That's All Right").............. 100-200 55
(Canadian. Pale blue.)
RCA (6381 "Good Rockin' Tonight")....... 50-75 55
RCA (6382 "Milkcow Blues Boogie")....... 50-75 55
RCA (6383 "Baby Let's Play House")...... 50-75 55
RCA (6420 "Heartbreak Hotel")........... 250-300 56
(Turquoise label.)
RCA (6420 "Heartbreak Hotel")............... 35-45 56
(Black label.)
RCA (6420 "Heartbreak Hotel")........... 100-200 56
(Canadian. Pale blue.)
RCA (6540 "I Want You, I Need You, I Love You")... 35-45 56
(Black label.)
RCA (6540 "I Want You, I Need You, I Love You")... 100-200 56
(Canadian. Pale blue.)
RCA (6604 "Don't Be Cruel")................... 35-45 56
(Black label.)
RCA (6604 "Don't Be Cruel").............. 100-200 56
(Canadian. Pale blue.)
RCA (6636 "Blue Suede Shoes")........... 80-100 56
RCA (6637 "I Got a Woman")................. 50-70 56
RCA (6638 "I'll Never Let You Go")......... 50-70 56
RCA (6639 "Tryin' to Get to You")........... 50-70 56
RCA (6640 "Blue Moon")......................... 50-70 56
RCA (6641 "Money Honey")..................... 50-70 56
RCA (6642 "Lawdy, Miss Clawdy")........... 50-70 56
(Dog is pictured on label.)
RCA (6642 "Lawdy, Miss Clawdy")...... 200-250 56
(Dog is not shown on label.)
RCA (6643 "Love Me Tender")................ 35-45 56
RCA (6800 "Too Much")........................... 35-45 57
(Dog is pictured on label.)
RCA (6800 "Too Much").................... 200-250 57
(Dog is not shown on label.)
RCA (6870 "All Shook Up")...................... 35-45 57
RCA (7000 "Teddy Bear")......................... 35-45 57
RCA (7035 "Jailhouse Rock")................... 35-45 57
(Black label, black vinyl.)
RCA (7035 "Jailhouse Rock")........... 3500-4000 57
(Gold label, gold vinyl.)
Note: All RCA singles from 6357 through 7035 can be found on various black labels, both with or without a horizontal silver line. Some folks may add a $5 to $10 premium for copies with a line; however, first issues came without the line.)
RCA (7150 "Don't")................................... 15-20 58
RCA (7240 "Wear My Ring Around Your Neck").. 15-20 58
RCA (7280 "Hard Headed Woman")........ 15-20 58
RCA (7410 "One Night").......................... 15-20 58
RCA (7506 "I Need Your Love Tonight"). 15-20 59
RCA (7600 "A Big Hunk O' Love")........... 15-20 59
RCA (47-7740 "Stuck on You")..................8-12 60
RCA (61-7740 "Stuck on You")........... 400-500 60
(Living Stereo.)
RCA (47-7777 "It's Now Or Never")... 750-1000 60
(Due to mixing error, piano track is omitted.)
RCA (47-7777 "It's Now Or Never")............8-10 60
RCA (61-7777 "It's Now Or Never")..... 500-700 60
(Living Stereo.)
RCA (47-7810 "Are You Lonesome To-night")...8-10 60
RCA (61-7810 "Are You Lonesome To-night")..700-750 60
(Living Stereo.)
RCA (37-7850 "Surrender")..................500-700 61
(Compact 33 Single.)
RCA (47-7850 "Surrender")........................8-10 61
RCA (61-7850 "Surrender")............. 1000-1200 61
(Living Stereo. Has "Living Stereo" twice on label, once on each side.)
RCA (61-7850 "Surrender")............. 1200-1500 61
(Living Stereo. Has "Living" on left and "Stereo" on right side.)
RCA (68-7850 "Surrender")............. 1000-1500 61
(Stereo Compact 33 Single.)
RCA (37-7880 "I Feel So Bad")........ 1000-1500 61
(Compact 33 Single.)
RCA (47-7880 "I Feel So Bad")...................8-10 61
RCA (37-7908 "His Latest Flame").. 5000-6000 61
(Compact 33 Single.)
RCA (47-7908 "His Latest Flame")............8-10 61
RCA (37-7968 "Can't Help Falling in Love")... 6000-8000 61
(Compact 33 Single.)
RCA (47-7968 "Can't Help Falling in Love")...8-10 61
RCA (37-7992 "Good Luck Charm").. 8000-12000 62
(Compact 33 Single.)
RCA (47-7992 "Good Luck Charm")...........8-10 62
RCA (8041 "She's Not You").......................8-10 62
RCA (8100 "Return to Sender")..................8-10 62
RCA (8134 "One Broken Heart for Sale")...8-10 63
RCA (8188 "Devil in Disguise")............600-800 63
(Flip side title is incorrectly shown as *Please Don't Drag That String ALONG.*)
RCA (8188 "Devil in Disguise")..................8-10 63
(Flip side title correctly shown as *Please Don't Drag That String AROUND.*)
RCA (8243 "Bossa Nova Baby")..................8-10 63
RCA (8307 "Kissin' Cousins")......................8-10 64
RCA (8360 "Viva Las Vegas")......................8-10 64
RCA (8400 "Such a Night").........................8-10 64
RCA (8440 "Ask Me")..................................8-10 64
RCA (8500 "Do the Clam")...........................8-10 65
RCA (8585 "Easy Question").......................8-10 65
RCA (8657 "I'm Yours")...............................8-10 65
RCA (8740 "Tell Me Why")...........................8-10 65
RCA (8780 "Frankie and Johnny")...............8-10 66
RCA (8870 "Love Letters")..........................8-10 66
RCA (8941 "Spinout")..................................8-10 66
RCA (8950 "If Everyday Was Like Christmas")..8-10 66
RCA (9056 "Indescribably Blue")................8-10 67
RCA (9115 "Long Legged Girl")..................8-10 67
RCA (9287 "Judy").......................................8-10 67
RCA (9341 "Big Boss Man")........................8-10 67
RCA (9425 "Guitar Man")............................8-10 68
RCA (9465 "U.S. Male")..............................8-10 68
RCA (9547 "Your Time Hasn't Come Yet Baby")..8-10 68
RCA (9600 "You'll Never Walk Alone").......8-10 68
RCA (9610 "A Little Less Conversation") .20-25 68
Note: Commercial issues of all RCA singles from 6357 through 9600 are on black labels.
RCA (9670 "If I Can Dream").......................5-8 68
RCA (9731 "Memories")...............................5-8 69
RCA (9741 "In the Ghetto")..........................5-8 69
RCA (9747 "Clean Up Your Own Back Yard")...5-8 69
RCA (9764 "Suspicious Minds")...................5-8 69
RCA (9768 "Don't Cry Daddy")....................5-8 69
RCA (9791 "Kentucky Rain").........................5-8 70
RCA (9835 "The Wonder of You")................5-8 70
RCA (9873 "I've Lost You")...........................5-8 70
RCA (9916 "You Don't Have to Say You Love Me")..5-8 70
RCA (9960 "I Really Don't Want to Know")..5-8 70
RCA (9980 "Rags to Riches").........................5-8 71
RCA (9985 "Life")..5-8 71
RCA (9998 "I'm Leavin'")..............................5-8 71
Note: RCA numbers in the 10000 to 14000 series with a "GB" prefix are Gold Standards and are listed in a separate Gold Standard Singles section.
RCA (10074 "Promised Land")................15-20 74
(Orange label.)
RCA (10074 "Promised Land")................10-15 74
(Gray label.)
RCA (10191 "My Boy")...........................15-20 75
(Orange label.)
RCA (10191 "My Boy")...........................20-25 75
(Tan or brown label.)
RCA (10278 "T-r-o-u-b-l-e")....................25-30 75
(Orange label.)
RCA (10278 "T-r-o-u-b-l-e")........................8-10 75
(Tan label.)
RCA (10278 "T-r-o-u-b-l-e")................300-400 75
(Gray label.)
RCA (10401 "Bringing It Back")...........250-300 75
(Orange label.)
RCA (10401 "Bringing It Back")................8-10 75
(Tan label.)
RCA (10601 "For the Heart").......................5-8 76
(Tan label.)
RCA (10601 "For the Heart")................90-100 76
(Black label.)
RCA (10857 "Moody Blue")..........................4-6 76
(Black vinyl. Colored vinyl 45s of *Moody Blue*, were experimental and are listed in the Promotional Singles section that follows.)
RCA (10998 "Way Down")...........................4-6 77
RCA (11099 thru 11113)...............................4-6 77
(Discs in this series were originally packaged in either 11301 and/or 11340, both of which are boxed sets of singles with sleeves.)
RCA (11165 "My Way").................................4-6 77
(Flip side shown as *America.*)
RCA (11165 "My Way")...............................20-25 77
(Fith flip side shown as *America the Beautiful.*)
RCA (11212 " Unchained Melody")..............4-6 78
RCA (11301 "15 Golden Records").........65-75 77
(Boxed set of 15 Elvis singles with picture sleeves.)
RCA (11320 "Teddy Bear")..........................4-6 78
RCA (11340 "20 Golden Hits")................65-75 77
(Boxed set of 10 Elvis singles with picture sleeves.)
RCA (11533 "Are You Sincere")...................4-6 79
RCA (11679 "I Got a Feelin' in My Body")...12-18 79
(With production and backing credits shown on label.)
RCA (11679 ("I Got a Feelin' in My Body")...4-6 79
(With backing credits removed, leaving only production credits.)
RCA (12158 "Guitar Man")...........................3-5 81
RCA (12205 "Lovin' Arms")..........................3-5 81
RCA (13058 "You'll Never Walk Alone")......3-5 82
RCA (13351 "The Elvis Medley")..................3-5 82
RCA (13500 "I Was the One").......................3-5 83
RCA (13547 "Little Sister")...........................3-5 83
RCA (13875 "Baby, Let's Play House")....15-20 84
(Gold vinyl.)
RCA (13885 thru 13890)...............................3-5 84
(Gold vinyl. Discs in this series were originally packaged in 13897, *Golden Singles, Vol. I.* May include juke box title strips.)
RCA (13891 thru 13896)...............................3-5 84
(Gold vinyl. Discs in this series were originally packaged in 13898, *Golden Singles, Vol. II.* May include juke box title strips.)
RCA (13897 "Golden Singles, Vol. I").......20-30 84
(Package of six gold vinyl singles with sleeves.)
RCA (13898 "Golden Singles, Vol. II")......20-30 84
(Package of six gold vinyl singles with sleeves.)
RCA (13929 "Blue Suede Shoes"/"Promised Land")..15-20 84
(Blue vinyl. Incorrectly shows *Blue Suede Shoes* as stereo and *Promised Land* as mono.)
RCA (13929 "Blue Suede Shoes"/"Promised Land")...8-12 84
(Blue vinyl. Correctly shows *Blue Suede Shoes* as mono and *Promised Land* as stereo.)
RCA (14090 "Always on My Mind")..........30-40 85
(Purple vinyl.)
RCA (14237 "Merry Christmas Baby").......8-12 85
(Black vinyl.)
RCA (14237 "Merry Christmas Baby").....15-20 85
(Green vinyl.)
RCA (60575-7 "A Little Less Conversation")..4-6 2002
(White label. Jukebox issue only.)
RCA (62402 "Don't Be Cruel")...................5-10 92
(Colored vinyl.)
RCA (62403 "Blue Christmas")..................5-10 92
(Colored vinyl.)
RCA (62449 "Heartbreak Hotel")..............5-10 92
(Colored vinyl.)
Note: RCA numbers in the 10000-14000 series with a "GB" prefix are Gold Standard Series and are listed in a separate Gold Standard Singles section. Regular series issues are in the preceding section.
SPOKEN WORD (100 "1955 Texarkana Interview")..8-12 78
SUN (209 "That's All Right")............1500-2000 54
SUN (210 "Good Rockin' Tonight")....1500-2000 54
SUN (215 "Milkcow Blue Boogie")....1800-2200 55
SUN (217 "Baby Let's Play House").1500-2000 55
SUN (223 "Mystery Train")................1000-1500 55
TRIBUTE (501 "A Tribute to Elvis Presley")..50-100 56
(Besides Elvis, has guest appearances by Edward R. Murrow, Steve Allen, Ed Sullivan, Danny Kaye, Jimmy Durante, Gabriel Heater, Sid Ceaser, Liberace, Mantovani, Jack Benny, Gene Vincent, Gloria DeHaven, Nat King Cole, Nelson Eddy, and Jane Russell.)
Note: Plastic soundsheets or flexi-discs are listed in a separate section that follows.

Picture Sleeves
(Commercial and Promotional)

LAUREL (41 623 "Treat Me Nice").5000-10000 57
(Pictures Elvis but credits Vince Everett. Black and white sleeve made as a prop for the *Jailhouse Rock* film. The printed sheets have no reverse side, but are applied to a randomly selected EP. No Laurel records of this title exist.)
LAUREL (41 624 "Jailhouse Rock").......75-100 57
LAUREL (41 625 "Young and Beautiful")..75-100 57
(Above two picture Elvis but credit Vince Everett. Black-and-white, cardboard, EP-like cover. May have been made as a film prop. While many researchers question the authenticity – and therefore the actual date of production – of these, these prices have been paid. No Laurel records of these titles exist.).
PECA ("Could I Fall in Love")..........4000-8000 66
(Pictures Elvis but credits Guy Lambert with George and His G-Men. A full color sleeve made as a prop for the *Double Trouble* film. No Peca records of this title exist.)
RCA (76 "Don't"/"Wear My Ring Around Your Neck")..1500-2000 60
(Promotional issue only.)
RCA (0088 "Raised on Rock")...................30-40 73
RCA (118 "King of the Whole Wide World")..200-250 62
(Promotional issue only.)
RCA (0130 "How Great Thou Art").......150-200 69
RCA (162 "How Great Thou Art").........150-200 67
(Promotional issue only.)
RCA (0196 " Take Good Care of Her")....20-25 74
RCA (0280 "If You Talk in Your Sleep")...30-40 74
RCA (0572 "Merry Christmas Baby").......50-75 71
RCA (0619 "Until It's Time for You to Go")...30-35 71
RCA (0651 "He Touched Me")..............150-200 71
RCA (0672 "An American Trilogy").........75-100 72
RCA (0769 "Burning Love").....................10-15 72
RCA (0815 "Separate Ways")..................10-15 71
RCA (0910 "Fool")...................................10-15 73
RCA (1017 "It's Only Love")....................30-35 71
RCA ("This Is His Life")......................1500-2000 55
(No specific titles are indicated on sleeve. For many years we reported this being issued with 6540 [*I Want You, I Need You, I Love You*]. A few years ago, certain facts persuaded us to change it to 6357 [*Mystery Train*]. Now, as more RCA sleeves in this "Life Story" series are found, the truth becomes even more elusive. Here are some facts from which you may draw your own conclusion:
1. RCA issued promo sleeves in the "Life" series from early 1955 through mid-'56. Those we've seen from '55 came with a white label "Record Prevue" disc. Many have the song titles printed on the sleeve (i.e. 6077, Dinah Shore *Whatever Lola Wants*), and many from '55 are duotone (black plus one color). Since the only U.S. "Record Prevue" by Elvis is *Mystery Train,* the sleeve may have come with that disc. Also, 6357 was RCA's first Presley single, making this sleeve quite appropriate.
2. All of the "Life" sleeves we've seen from early-to-mid-'56, when *I Want You, I Need You, I Love You* (6540) came out are black and white, as is the Elvis "This Is His Life" sleeve. Two in particular recently verified, one on each side of 6540, are for the Rhythmettes (6539) and the Mike Pedicin Quintet (6546). Both are identical in format to the Presley sleeve.
Although not often suggested, who's to say this sleeve wasn't used with any of several Elvis discs, including *Heartbreak Hotel?*

For now, and until we are further enlightened, we will list the sleeve without a specific record title attached to it.
RCA (6604 "Don't Be Cruel")................. 75-100 55
(Shows "*Don't Be Cruel c/w Hound Dog.*")
RCA (6604 "Hound Dog")....................... 65-75 56
(Shows "*Hound Dog c/w Don't Be Cruel.*")
RCA (6643 "Love Me Tender")............ 100-150 56
(Black and white sleeve.)
RCA (6643 "Love Me Tender").............. 75-100 56
(Black and green sleeve.)
RCA (6643 "Love Me Tender")................ 50-75 56
(Black and dark pink sleeve.)
RCA (6643 "Love Me Tender")................ 40-60 56
(Black and light pink sleeve.)
RCA (6800 "Too Much")........................ 50-100 57
RCA (6870 "All Shook Up").................... 50-100 57
RCA (7000 "Teddy Bear")...................... 50-100 57
RCA (7035 "Jailhouse Rock")............... 50-100 57
(Sleeve only.)
RCA/MGM "Jailhouse Rock").......... 1000-1500 57
(MGM *Jailhouse Rock* film preview invitation ticket. A promotional item for the media, the ticket came wrapped around a commercial single and sleeve. Deduct about 50% if ticket stub is detached. Counterfeits exist.)
RCA (7150 "Don't")................................ 50-75 58
RCA (7240 "Wear My Ring Around Your Neck").. 50-75 58
RCA (7280 "Hard Headed Woman")........ 50-75 58
RCA (7410 "One Night")........................ 50-75 58
RCA (7506 "I Need Your Love Tonight").. 400-500 59
(Has advertising for the *Elvis Sails* EP on reverse.)
RCA (7506 "I Need Your Love Tonight") . 40-50 59
(Lists Elvis EPs and 45s on reverse.)
RCA (7600 "A Big Hunk O' Love").......... 40-50 59
RCA (7740 "Stuck on You")................... 40-50 60
(Die-cut sleeve which displays record label.)
RCA (7777 "It's Now Or Never")............ 30-40 60
RCA (7810 "Are You Lonesome To-night")... 30-40 60
RCA (37-7850 "Surrender")................. 500-700 61
(Compact 33 Single sleeve. Copies without some ring wear are very scarce.)
RCA (47-7850 "Surrender").................... 30-40 61
RCA (37-7880 "I Feel So Bad")........ 1000-1500 61
(Compact 33 Single sleeve.)
RCA (47-7880 "I Feel So Bad")............... 30-40 61
RCA (37-7908 "His Latest Flame") .. 5000-6000 61
(Compact 33 Single sleeve.)
RCA (47-7908 "His Latest Flame") 30-40 61
RCA (37-7968 "Can't Help Falling in Love")....................................... 6000-8000 61
(Compact 33 Single sleeve.)
RCA (47-7968 "Can't Help Falling in Love").. 30-40 61
RCA (37-7992 "Good Luck Charm")....................................... 8000-12000 62
(Compact 33 Single sleeve.)
RCA (47-7992 "Good Luck Charm")........ 30-40 62
RCA (8041 "She's Not You").................. 30-40 62
RCA (8100 "Return to Sender").............. 30-40 62
RCA (8134 "One Broken Heart for Sale") 30-40 63
RCA (8188 "Devil in Disguise")............... 30-40 63
RCA (8243 "Bossa Nova Baby")............. 30-40 63
(Reads: "Coming Soon! *Fun in Acapulco* LP Album.")
RCA (8243 "Bossa Nova Baby")......... 200-300 63
(No mention of *Fun in Acapulco* Album.")
RCA (8307 "Kissin' Cousins")................. 30-40 64
RCA (8360 "Viva Las Vegas")................. 30-40 64
(Reads "Coming Soon" regarding the *Viva Las Vegas* EP.)
RCA (8360 "Viva Las Vegas")............. 100-150 64
(Reads "Ask For" regarding the *Viva Las Vegas* EP.)
RCA (8400 "Such a Night").................... 30-40 64
RCA (8440 "Ask Me")............................ 30-40 64
(Reads: "Coming Soon! *Roustabout* LP Album.")
RCA (8440 "Ask Me")............................ 40-50 64
(Reads: "Ask For *Roustabout* LP Album.")
RCA (8500 "Do the Clam")..................... 30-40 65
RCA (8585 "Easy Question")................. 30-40 65
(Reads "Coming Soon! Special *Tickle Me* EP."
RCA (8585 "Easy Question")................. 50-75 65
(Reads "Ask For Special *Tickle Me* EP."
RCA (8657 "I'm Yours")......................... 30-40 65
RCA (8740 "Tell Me Why")..................... 30-40 65
RCA (8780 "Frankie & Johnny")............. 30-40 66
RCA (8870 "Love Letters").................... 30-40 66
(Reads "Coming Soon – *Paradise Hawaiian Style.*"
RCA (8870 "Love Letters").......................60-80 66
(Reads "Ask For – *Paradise Hawaiian Style.*"
RCA (8941 "Spinout")..............................30-40 66
(Reads "Watch For Elvis' *Spinout* LP."
RCA (8941 "Spinout")..............................40-50 66
(Reads "Ask For Elvis' *Spinout* LP."
RCA (8950 "If Everyday Was Like Christmas")..40-50 66
RCA (9056 "Indescribably Blue")............30-40 67
RCA (9115 "Long Legged Girl")...............30-40 67
(Reads "Coming Soon – *Double Trouble* LP Album."
RCA (9115 "Long Legged Girl")...............50-75 67
(Reads "Ask For – *Double Trouble* LP Album."
RCA (9287 "Judy")...................................30-40 67
RCA (9341 "Big Boss Man").....................30-40 67
RCA (9425 "Guitar Man").........................30-40 68
(Reads "Coming Soon, *Elvis' Gold Records, Volume 4.*")
RCA (9425 "Guitar Man").........................40-50 68
(Reads "Ask For *Elvis' Gold Records, Volume 4.*")
RCA (9465 "U.S. Male")...........................20-30 68
RCA (9547 "Your Time Hasn't Come Yet Baby")..30-40 68
(Reads "Coming Soon – *Speedway* LP."
RCA (9547 "Your Time Hasn't Come Yet Baby")..50-75 68
(Reads "Ask For – *Speedway* LP."
RCA (9600 "You'll Never Walk Alone").100-150 68
RCA (9610 "A Little Less Conversation") .40-60 68
RCA (9670 "If I Can Dream")...................30-40 68
RCA (9731 "Memories")...........................30-40 69
RCA (9741 "In the Ghetto").....................20-30 69
(Reads "Coming Soon *From Elvis in Memphis* LP Album."
RCA (9741 "In the Ghetto").....................30-40 69
(Reads "Ask For *From Elvis in Memphis* LP Album."
RCA (9747 "Clean Up Your Own Back Yard")..25-35 69
RCA (9764 "Suspicious Minds")...............20-25 69
RCA (9768 "Don't Cry Daddy")................20-25 69
RCA (9791 "Kentucky Rain")....................20-25 70
RCA (9835 "The Wonder of You")............20-25 70
RCA (9873 "I've Lost You").......................10-15 70
RCA (9916 "You Don't Have to Say You Love Me")..20-25 70
RCA (9960 "I Really Don't Want to Know")..20-30 70
(Reads "Coming Soon – New Album.")
RCA (9960 "I Really Don't Want to Know")..30-40 70
(Reads "Now Available – New Album.")
RCA (9980 "Rags to Riches")..................30-40 71
RCA (9985 "Life").....................................30-40 71
RCA (9998 "I'm Leavin'")..........................30-40 71
RCA (10074 "Promised Land")................20-25 74
RCA (10191 "My Boy")..............................40-50 75
RCA (10278 "T-r-o-u-b-l-e")......................20-25 75
RCA (10401 "Bringing It Back")................20-25 75
RCA (10601 "For the Heart")....................20-30 76
RCA (10857 "Moody Blue").......................20-25 76
RCA (10998 "Way Down")........................15-20 77
RCA (11099 thru 11113)...............................4-6 77
(Sleeves in this series were originally packaged in either RCA 11301 and/or 11340, both boxed sets of singles with sleeves.)
RCA (11165 "My Way").............................10-15 77
(Flip side title shown as *America*.)
RCA (11165 "My Way").............................40-50 77
(Flip side title shown as *America the Beautiful*)
RCA (11212 "Unchained Melody")............10-15 78
RCA (11320 "Teddy Bear")..........................8-10 78
RCA (11533 "Are You Sincere")..................8-10 79
RCA (11679 "I Got a Feelin' in My Body")..8-10 79
RCA (12158 "Guitar Man")...........................8-10 81
RCA (13058 "There Goes My Everything")..20-25 82
RCA (13302 "The Impossible Dream")...75-100 82
(Promotional issue only.)
RCA (13351 "The Elvis Medley")..............10-15 82
RCA (13500 "I Was the One")....................5-10 83
RCA (13547 "Little Sister")........................5-10 83
RCA (13875 "Baby, Let's Play House")....10-20 84
RCA (13885 thru 13896)..............................3-5 84
(Sleeves in this series were originally packaged in RCA 13897 and 13898, *Golden Singles.*)
RCA (13929 "Blue Suede Shoes")............20-30 84
RCA (14090 "Always on My Mind")............8-10 85
RCA (14237 "Merry Christmas Baby")......10-15 85
Notes: There may be slight price differences for assorted variations in colors and paper stock used. Often, the difference is simply which one is needed to complete a run. Regardless, sleeve variations within the price range given do not require separate listings. If the value varies beyond the given range, a separate listing will be added. Sleeves for the RCA "447" Gold Standard Series are listed in a separate section following the Gold Standard Singles. A slight premium – perhaps $3 to $5 – may be placed on RCA's "Living Stereo" paper sleeves. These were used for many different RCA stereo singles and were not exclusively an Elvis item.

Gold Standard Singles with "447" prefix (Commercial)

RCA (0600 thru 0639)..............................15-25 59-64
(Black label, dog on top.)
RCA (0600 thru 0639)..............................30-50 65-66
(Black label, dog on side.)
RCA (0600 thru 0639)..........................100-150 68-69
(Orange label.)
RCA (0600 thru 0639)..............................10-15 70-74
(Red label.)
RCA (0600 thru 0639)..................................3-5 77
(Black label, dog near top.)
RCA (0640 thru 0642)..............................20-25 64
(Black label, dog on top.)
RCA (0640 thru 0642)..............................30-50 65-66
(Black label, dog on side.)
RCA (0640 thru 0642)............................75-125 68-69
(Orange label.)
RCA (0640 thru 0642)..............................10-15 70-74
(Red label.)
RCA (0640 thru 0642)..................................3-5 77
(Black label, dog near top.)
RCA (0643 "Crying in the Chapel")..........20-30 65
(Black label, dog on side.)
RCA (0643 "Crying in the Chapel")..........10-15 '70s
(Red label.)
RCA (0643 "Crying in the Chapel")..............3-5 77
(Black label, dog near top.)
RCA (0644 thru 0646)..............................20-25 65
(Black label, dog on top.)
RCA (0644 thru 0646)..............................30-50 65
(Black label, dog on side.)
RCA (0644 thru 0646)............................75-125 68-69
(Orange label.)
RCA (0644 thru 0646)..............................10-15 70-74
(Red label.)
RCA (0644 thru 0646)..................................3-5 77
(Black label, dog near top.)
RCA (0647 thru 0650)..............................40-50 65
(Black label, dog on side.)
RCA (0647 thru 0650)..............................10-15 70-74
(Red label.)
RCA (0647 thru 0650)..................................3-5 77
(Black label, dog near top.)
RCA (0651 & 0652)..................................40-50 66
(Black label, dog on side.)
RCA (0651 & 0652)..................................15-25 '70s
(Red label.)
RCA (0651 & 0652)......................................3-5 77
(Black label, dog near top.)
RCA (0653 thru 0658)..............................40-50 66-68
(Black label, dog on side.)
RCA (0653 thru 0658)............................75-125 68-69
(Orange label.)
RCA (0653 thru 0658)..............................10-15 70-74
(Red label.)
RCA (0653 thru 0658)..................................3-5 77
(Black label, dog near top.)
RCA (0659 "Indescribably Blue")..........100-150 68
(Orange label.)
RCA (0659 "Indescribably Blue")............10-15 70
(Red label.)
RCA (0660 "Long Legged Girl")...............40-50 70
(Red label.)
RCA (0661 "Judy")....................................20-25 70
(Red label.)
RCA (0662 "Big Boss Man")....................10-15 70
(Red label.)
RCA (0662 "Big Boss Man")........................3-5 77
(Black label, dog near top.)
RCA (0663 thru 0685)..............................10-15 70-73
(Red label.)
RCA (0663 thru 0685)..................................3-5 77
(Black label, dog near top.)
RCA (0720 "Blue Christmas")..................15-20 64
(Black label, dog on top.)

Gold Standard Singles with "GB" prefix (Commercial)

RCA (10156 thru 10489)...........................10-15 75-76
(Red label.)
RCA (10156 thru 10489)...............................3-5 77
(Black label, dog near top.)
RCA (11326 thru 13275)...............................3-5 77
(Black label, dog near top.)
Gold Standard *promotional* singles are in numerical sequence in the section for Promotional Singles.

Gold Standard Picture Sleeves

RCA (0601 "That's All Right")..............250-300 64
RCA (0602 "Good Rockin' Tonight")....250-300 64
RCA (0605 "Heartbreak Hotel")...........250-300 64
RCA (0608 "Don't Be Cruel")...............250-300 64
RCA (0618 "All Shook Up")..................250-300 64
RCA (0639 "Kiss Me Quick")...................50-75 64
RCA (0643 "Crying in the Chapel")..........20-30 65
RCA (0647 "Blue Christmas")..................40-50 65
(Pictures Elvis on a Christmas card among wrapped gifts.)
RCA (0647 "Blue Christmas")....................8-10 77
(Pictures Elvis in a circle among colored ornaments.)
RCA (0650 "Puppet on a String")............40-50 65
RCA (0651 "Joshua Fit the Battle")......250-300 66
RCA (0652 "Milky White Way")............250-300 66
RCA (0651 & 0652 "Special Easter Programming Kit")..1000-1500 66
(Picture sleeve-mailer. Contained both 1966 Easter singles, *Joshua Fit the Battle* and *Milky White Way* in their sleeves and an Easter greeting card from Elvis. Price is for the complete kit.)
RCA (0651 & 0652 "Special Easter Programming Kit")..800-1000 66
(Picture sleeve-mailer only.)
RCA (0720 "Blue Christmas")..................50-75 64

Promotional Singles

CREATIVE RADIO ("Elvis 10th Anniversary"/"The Elvis Hour")..15-20 87
(Demonstration disc, promoting the syndicated 10th anniversary radio special.)
CREATIVE RADIO ("Memories of Elvis"/"The Elvis Hour")..15-20 87
(Demonstration disc, promoting the syndicated 10th anniversary radio special.)
For *Elvis 50th Birthday Special*, see PRESLEY, Elvis / Buddy Holly.
For *The Elvis Hour*, see PRESLEY, Elvis / Gary Owens.
CREATIVE RADIO ("Nearer My God to Thee")..10-20 89
(Promotional souvenir only. Issued as a bonus single with the LP, *Between Takes with Elvis.*)
CREATIVE RADIO ("Mystery Train")........5-10 92
(Single-sided demonstration disc, taken from the syndicated 15th anniversary radio special.)
PARAMOUNT PICTURES ("Easy Come, Easy Go")..800-1000 67
(Issued only to select theatres, designed for lobby play.)
PARAMOUNT PICTURES (1800 "Blue Hawaii")..500-750 61
(Single-sided pressing. Issued only to select theatres, designed for lobby play. Has excerpts of songs from the film.)
PARAMOUNT PICTURES (2017 "Girls! Girls! Girls!")..800-1000 64
(Issued only to select theatres, designed for lobby play.)
PARAMOUNT PICTURES (2413 "Roustabout")....................................2000-3000 64
(Issued only to select theatres, designed for lobby play. Track is an alternate take.)
RCA (15 "Old Shep")...............................700-800 56
RCA (76 "Don't"/"Wear My Ring Around Your Neck")..800-1000 60
(Issued with special sleeve, listed in the Picture Sleeves section.)
RCA (0088 "Raised on Rock")..................25-30 73
(Yellow label.)
RCA (118 "King of the Whole Wide World")..200-250 62
(Issued with a special sleeve, which is listed in the Picture Sleeves section. Includes "Deejay Notes from RCA Victor" one-page insert.)
RCA (0130 "How Great Thou Art").......125-150 69
(Yellow label.)
RCA (139 "Roustabout")........................250-300 64

RCA (162 "How Great Thou Art")......... 150-200 67 (Issued with a special sleeve, listed in the Picture Sleeves section.)

RCA (0196 "Take Good Care of Her")..... 25-30 74 (Yellow label.)

RCA (0280 "If You Talk in Your Sleep")... 25-30 74 (Yellow label.)

RCA (0572 "Merry Christmas Baby")....... 30-40 71 (Yellow label.)

RCA (0601 "That's All Right").............. 100-150 64 (White label.)

RCA (0602 "Good Rockin' Tonight").... 100-150 64 (White label.)

RCA (0605 "Heartbreak Hotel")........... 100-150 64 (White label.)

RCA (0608 "Don't Be Cruel")................ 100-150 64 (White label.)

RCA (0618 "All Shook Up")................. 100-150 64 (White label.)

RCA (0619 "Until It's Time for You to Go")... 30-40 72 (Yellow label.)

RCA (0639 "Kiss Me Quick").................. 40-50 64 (White label.)

RCA (0643 "Crying in the Chapel")......... 40-50 65 (White label.)

RCA (0647 "Blue Christmas")................. 40-50 65 (White label.)

RCA (0650 "Puppet on a String")............ 40-50 65 (White label.)

RCA (0651 "Joshua Fit the Battle")...... 150-200 66 (White label.)

RCA (0652 "Milky White Way")........... 150-200 66 (White label. See Gold Standard Picture Sleeves section for special mailing sleeve used with 0651 & 0652.)

RCA (0651 "He Touched Me")............ 100-150 72 (Yellow label.)

RCA (0672 "An American Trilogy")......... 40-50 72 (Yellow label.)

RCA (0720 "Blue Christmas")................. 40-50 64 (White label.)

RCA (0769 "Burning Love")..................... 15-20 72 (Yellow label.)

RCA (0808 "Blue Christmas")..........2000-3000 57 (Identification number shown since no selection number is used.)

RCA (0815 "Separate Ways")................. 20-30 72 (Yellow label.)

RCA (0910 "Fool")................................... 20-25 73 (Yellow label.)

RCA (6357 "Mystery Train")................ 400-500 55 (White "Record Prevue" label. Add $50 to $100 if accompanied by *Dee Jay Digest* Vol 2, No. 50, dated Dec. 2, 1955 – a four-page RCA record newsletter)

RCA (8360 "Viva Las Vegas")................ 40-50 64 (White label.)

RCA (8400 "Such a Night")............. 7000-8000 64 (White label.)

RCA (8440 "Ask Me")............................. 40-50 64 (White label.)

RCA (8500 "Do the Clam")...................... 40-50 65 (White label.)

RCA (8585 "Easy Question").................. 40-50 65 (White label.)

RCA (8657 "I'm Yours")........................... 40-50 65 (White label.)

RCA (8740 "Tell Me Why")...................... 40-50 65 (White label.)

RCA (8780 "Frankie & Johnny")............. 40-50 66 (White label.)

RCA (8870 "Love Letters")...................... 40-50 66 (White label.)

RCA (8941 "Spinout")............................. 40-50 66 (White label.)

RCA (8950 "If Everyday Was Like Christmas").. 40-50 66 (White label.)

RCA (9056 "Indescribably Blue")............ 40-50 67 (White label.)

RCA (9115 "Long Legged Girl").............. 50-75 67 (White label.)

RCA (9287 "Judy")................................... 40-50 67 (White label.)

RCA (9341 "Big Boss Man")................... 40-50 67 (White label.)

RCA (9425 "Guitar Man")....................... 40-50 68 (Yellow label.)

RCA (9465 "U.S. Male")......................... 40-50 68 (Yellow label.)

RCA (9547 "Your Time Hasn't Come Yet Baby")..40-50 68 (Yellow label.)

RCA (9600 "You'll Never Walk Alone").....40-50 68 (Yellow label.)

RCA (9610 "A Little Less Conversation") .50-60 68 (Yellow label.)

RCA (9670 "If I Can Dream")...................40-50 68 (Yellow label.)

RCA (9731 "Memories")..........................40-50 69 (Yellow label.)

RCA (9741 "In the Ghetto")......................30-40 69 (Yellow label.)

RCA (9747 "Clean Up Your Own Back Yard")..30-40 69 (Yellow label.)

RCA (9764 "Suspicious Minds")...............30-40 69 (Yellow label.)

RCA (9768 "Don't Cry Daddy")................30-40 69 (Yellow label.)

RCA (9791 "Kentucky Rain")....................30-40 70 (Yellow label.)

RCA (9835 "The Wonder of You")...........30-40 70 (Yellow label.)

RCA (9873 "I've Lost You")......................30-40 70 (Yellow label.)

RCA (9916 "You Don't Have to Say You Love Me")...20-30 70 (Yellow label.)

RCA (9960 "I Really Don't Want to Know")..20-30 70 (Yellow label.)

RCA (9980 "Rags to Riches")..................20-30 71 (Yellow label.)

RCA (9985 "Life")....................................30-40 71 (Yellow label.)

RCA (9998 "I'm Leavin'")........................30-40 71 (Yellow label.)

RCA (10074 "Promised Land")................20-30 74 (Yellow label.)

RCA (10191 "My Boy")............................30-40 75 (Yellow label.)

RCA (10278 "T-r-o-u-b-l-e")....................30-40 75 (Yellow label.)

RCA (10401 "Bringing It Back")...............20-30 75 (Yellow label.)

RCA (10601 "For the Heart")....................20-25 76 (Yellow label.)

RCA (10700 "Don'cha Think It's Time").. 3000-4000 76 (Experimental only. Made when RCA was testing a process whereby the label information is actually stamped right into the vinyl itself, rather than printed on paper and affixed to the disc during the stamping procedure. Though the vinyl contains the 1958 Elvis tune on both sides, "labels" used in this experiment are for *One for the Money*, by the Whispers – a summer '76 hit.)

RCA (10857 "Moody Blue")......................20-25 76 (Yellow label. Black vinyl.)

RCA (10857 "Moody Blue")............. 1000-2000 77 (Experimental colored vinyl pressings. Not intended for distribution.)

RCA (10951 "Let Me Be There")..........200-250 77

RCA (10998 "Way Down")...................150-200 77 (White label.)

RCA (10998 "Way Down")......................15-20 77 (Yellow label.)

RCA (11165 "My Way")............................10-20 77 (Yellow label.)

RCA (11212 "Unchained Melody")...........10-15 78 (Yellow label.)

RCA (11320 "Teddy Bear")......................10-15 78 (Yellow label.)

RCA (11533 "Are You Sincere")..............10-15 79 (Yellow label.)

RCA (11679 "I Got a Feelin' in My Body")..10-15 79 (Yellow label.)

RCA (12158 "Guitar Man").......................10-15 81 (Yellow label. Black vinyl.)

RCA (12158 "Guitar Man")...................150-200 81 (Yellow label. Red vinyl.)

RCA (12205 "Lovin' Arms")......................10-15 81 (Yellow label. Black vinyl.)

RCA (12205 "Lovin' Arms")..................250-300 81 (Yellow label. Green vinyl.)

RCA (13058 "There Goes My Everything")..10-15 82 (Yellow label.)

RCA (13302 "The Impossible Dream")...75-100 82

RCA (13351 "Elvis Medley")....................10-15 82 (Yellow label. Black vinyl.)

RCA (13351 "Elvis Medley")..................75-125 82 (Gold label. Gold vinyl.)

RCA (13500 "I Was the One")................10-15 83 (Yellow label. Black vinyl.)

RCA (13500 "I Was the One")............150-200 83 (Yellow label. Colored vinyl.)

RCA (13547 "Little Sister")......................10-15 83 (Yellow label. Black vinyl.)

RCA (13547 "Little Sister")..................200-250 83 (Blue label. Blue vinyl.)

RCA (13875 "Baby, Let's Play House")...350-400 84 (Gold label on *Baby Let's Play House* and white label on *Hound Dog*. Gold vinyl.)

RCA (13875 "Baby, Let's Play House")..75-100 84 (Gold label on both sides. Neither side indicates mono or stereo. Gold vinyl.)

RCA (13875 "Baby, Let's Play House")....30-40 84 (Gold label on both sides. Both sides shown as "Stereo." Gold vinyl.)

RCA (13929 "Blue Suede Shoes)............20-30 84 (Gold label. Blue vinyl.)

RCA (14090 "Always on My Mind").........30-40 85 (Gold label. Purple vinyl.)

RCA (14237 "Merry Christmas Baby").......8-10 85

Note: Elvis 50th Anniversary singles – RCA 13875 through 14237 – used the same gold label for both commercial and promotional issues. Promo singles have "Not For Sale" printed on the label.

RCA (4-834-115 "I'll Be Back").........6000-8000 66 (White label. Single-sided disc. Reads "For Special Academy Consideration Only." Made for submission to the Academy of Motion Picture Arts and Sciences.)

ROYAL CARIBBEAN CRUISE LINES (12690 "Follow That Dream - Take 2")...........................10-15 90 (Souvenir disc for Elvis cruise passengers.)

UNITED STATES AIR FORCE (125 "It's Now Or Never"): see PRESLEY, Elvis / Jaye P. Morgan.

UNITED STATES AIR FORCE (159 "Surrender"): see PRESLEY, Elvis / Lawrence Welk.

WHAT'S IT ALL ABOUT (78 "Life"): see PRESLEY, Elvis / Helen Reddy

WHAT'S IT ALL ABOUT (1840 "Elvis Presley")..70-75 80

WHAT'S IT ALL ABOUT (3025 "Elvis Presley")..50-60 82

Note: Plastic soundsheets and flexi-discs are listed in a separate section that follows. Promotional 78s are included with Singles: 78 rpm, at the beginning of the Presley section.

Plastic Soundsheets/Flexi-discs

EVA-TONE (38713 "Elvis Speaks! The Truth About Me")..30-40 (Eva-Tone number is not on label but is etched in the trail-off.)

EVA-TONE (52578 "The King Is Dead Long Live the King")...50-100 78

EVA-TONE (831942 "50,000,000 Elvis Fans Weren't Wrong!")..5-10 83

EVA-TONE (726771 "The Elvis Presley Story")...8-15 77

EVA-TONE (1037710 "Elvis Live")...........25-30 78 (Price for magazine, titled *Collector's Issue*, with bound-in soundsheet.)

EVA-TONE (1037710 "Elvis Live")...........10-15 78 (Price for soundsheet only.)

EVA-TONE (1227785 "Thompson Vocal Eliminator")..15-20 78 (Has segments of songs by three artists including Elvis.)

EVA-TONE (10287733 "Elvis: Six Hour Special")..15-20 77

EVA-TONE/RCA ("Love Me Tender")......25-35 74 (Price for April 1974 issue of *Teen Magazine* with bound-in soundsheet.)

EVA-TONE/RCA ("Love Me Tender")......15-25 74 (Price for soundsheet only.)

LYNCHBURG AUDIO ("The Truth About Me")...125-150 56 (Lynchburg Audio number is not on label but is etched in the trail-off.)

RAINBO ("Elvis Speaks, in Person")....300-400 56 (Price for magazine, *Elvis Answers Back*, with 78 rpm flexi-disc still attached to front cover.)

RAINBO ("Elvis Speaks, in Person")....100-150 56 (Price for flexi-disc only.)

RAINBO ("The Truth About Me")..........300-400 56 (Price for magazine, *Elvis Answers Back*, with 78rpm paper flexi-disc still attached to front cover.)

RAINBO ("The Truth About Me")..........100-150 56 (Price for flexi-disc only.)

RAINBO ("Elvis Show")........................150-250 56 (Promotional issue for a June 3, 1956 concert.)

Note: All soundsheets and flexi-discs were used for some type of promotional purpose.

EPs: 7-inch (Commercial and Promotional)

MEMPHIS FLASH (92444 "Elvis – My Life")...50-75 78 (Two 7-inch picture discs in gatefold, die-cut cover. Spoken word content from interviews, etc. "Collector Series" number on front cover. Reportedly 3,000 made.

RCA (2 "Dealers' Prevue"): see PRESLEY, Elvis / Martha Carson / Lou Monte / Herb Jeffries.

RCA (15 "Title Not Known")...............800-1000 55 (Exact title, if one, not yet known to us. SPD-15 is a set of 10 EPs. May be found with either black or gray labels. Presumably packaged in a box with inserts; however, we have yet to verify these. A complete set would easily top $7,500. For just the Elvis disc from this set, see RCA 9089.)

RCA (19 "The Sound of Leadership").......................................1800-2200 56 (Boxed eight-EP set. Includes box, four-page booklet and nine separator inserts. Promotional issue only. For just the Elvis EP from this set, see RCA 9113.)

RCA (22 "Elvis Presley")..................2000-2500 56 (May have "Elvis" in either light or dark pink letters on front cover. Two-EP bonus promotional item. Discs are numbered 9121 & 9122.)

RCA (23 "Elvis Presley")..................4000-5000 56 (Three-EP bonus promotional item. Includes "How to Use and Enjoy Your RCA Victor Elvis Presley Autograph Automatic 45 Victrola Portable Phonograph," which represents $75 to $100 of the value. Discs are numbered 9123, 9124 & 9125.)

RCA (26 "Great Country/Western Hits")..800-1200 56 (Boxed 10-EP set. Includes box and separator inserts. Includes tracks by other artists. Promotional issue only. For just the Elvis EP from this set, see RCA 9141.)

RCA (27 "Save-On Records: Bulletin for June")...400-500 56 (Includes paper sleeve. Promotional mail order only offer. Has tracks by other artists.)

RCA (37 "Perfect for Parties Highlight Album")..125-150 56 (Includes paper sleeve. Promotional mail order only offer. Has tracks by other artists.)

RCA (39 "Dealers' Prevue")..............2500-3000 57 (Includes envelope/sleeve. Includes tracks by other artists. Promotional issue only.)

RCA (39 "Dealers' Prevue")...............800-1000 57 (Disc only, without envelope/sleeve.)

RCA (61 "Untitled EP Sampler").......1000-1500 57 (Promotional issue only. Includes tracks by other artists. Not issued with special cover.)

RCA (121 "RCA Family Record Center")..1500-2000 62 (Promotional issue only. Includes tracks by other artists. Not issued with special cover.)

RCA (128 "Elvis by Request")................75-100 61

RCA (747 "Elvis Presley")....................100-125 56 (Black label, dog on top. Has song title strip across the top of front cover.)

RCA (747 "Elvis Presley")....................250-300 56 (Black label, without dog.)

RCA (747 "Elvis Presley")......................75-125 65 (Black label, dog on side.)

RCA (747 "Elvis Presley")....................100-150 69 (Orange label.)

RCA (747 "Blue Suede Shoes").......1800-2000 56 (Temporary paper sleeve for 1956 issue of EPA-747. Price is for sleeve only.)

RCA (821 "Heartbreak Hotel")............100-125 56 (Black label, dog on top. Has song title strip across the top of front cover.)

RCA (821 "Heartbreak Hotel")............250-300 56 (Black label, without dog.)

RCA (821 "Heartbreak Hotel")..............75-125 65 (Black label, dog on side.)

RCA (821 "Heartbreak Hotel")............100-150 69 (Orange label.)

RCA (830 "Elvis Presley") 100-125 56
(Black label, dog on top. Has song title strip across the top of front cover.)

RCA (830 "Elvis Presley") 250-300 56
(Black label, without dog.)

RCA (830 "Elvis Presley") 75-125 65
(Black label, dog on side.)

RCA (830 "Elvis Presley") 100-150 69
(Orange label.)

RCA (940 "The Real Elvis") 100-125 56
(Black label, dog on top. Has song title strip across the top of front cover.)

RCA (940 "The Real Elvis") 250-300 56
(Black label, without dog. Reissued as Gold Standard 5120.)

RCA (965 "Any Way You Want Me") ... 100-125 56
(Black label, dog on top. Has song title strip across the top of front cover.)

RCA (965 "Any Way You Want Me") ... 250-300 56
(Black label, without dog.)

RCA (965 "Any Way You Want Me") 75-125 65
(Black label, dog on side.)

RCA (965 "Any Way You Want Me") ... 100-150 69
(Orange label.)

RCA (992 "Elvis, Vol. 1") 100-125 56
(Black label, dog on top. Has song title strip across the top of front cover.)

RCA (992 "Elvis, Vol. 1") 250-300 56
(Black label, without dog.)

RCA (992 "Elvis, Vol. 1") 75-125 65
(Black label, dog on side.)

RCA (992 "Elvis, Vol. 1") 100-150 69
(Orange label.)

RCA (993 "Elvis, Vol. 2") 100-125 56
(Black label, dog on top. Has song title strip across the top of front cover.)

RCA (993 "Elvis, Vol. 2") 250-300 56
(Black label, without dog.)

RCA (993 "Elvis, Vol. 2") 75-125 65
(Black label, dog on side.)

RCA (993 "Elvis, Vol. 2") 100-150 69
(Orange label.)

RCA (994 "Strictly Elvis") 100-125 56
(Black label, dog on top. Has song title strip across the top of front cover.)

RCA (994 "Strictly Elvis") 250-300 56
(Black label, without dog.)

RCA (994 "Strictly Elvis") 75-125 65
(Black label, dog on side.)

RCA (994 "Strictly Elvis") 100-150 69
(Orange label.)

RCA (1023 "Pop Transcribed Spot") 500-750 57
(Price for disc only. No sleeve or special cover exists for this disc. Has 30-second radio spots for various RCA releases, including two spots for *Elvis' Christmas Album.* Identification number, H08W-1023, shown since no selection number is used. Promotional issue only.)

RCA (1254 "Elvis Presley") 550-650 56
(Black label, without dog. Two EP set.)

RCA (1254 "Elvis Presley") 325-425 56
(Black label, dog on top. Two EP set.)

RCA (1254 "Most Talked-About New Personality") 4000-5000 56
(Two EPs, also numbered 0793 & 0794, in a single pocket paper sleeve. Promotional issue only. Includes a copy of *Dee-Jay Digest*, which represents $50 to $75 of the value.)

RCA (1254 "Most Talked-About New Personality") 1000-2000 56
(Price for the two EPs without the sleeve. Either disc would be worth about half the amount shown for both. Discs, numbered 0793 & 0794, are untitled. Promotional issue only.)

RCA (1-1515 "Loving You, Vol. 1") 100-125 57
(Black label, dog on top. Has song title strip across the top of front cover.)

RCA (1-1515 "Loving You, Vol. 1") 75-125 65
(Black label, dog on side.)

RCA (1-1515 "Loving You, Vol. 1") 100-150 69
(Orange label.)

RCA (2-1515 "Loving You, Vol. 2") 100-125 57
(Black label, dog on top. Has song title strip across the top of front cover.)

RCA (2-1515 "Loving You, Vol. 2") 75-125 65
(Black label, dog on side.)

RCA (2-1515 "Loving You, Vol. 2") 100-150 69
(Orange label.)

RCA (2006 "Aloha from Hawaii Via Satellite") 150-200 74
(Includes sheet of 10 title strips. Made for juke box operators only.)

RCA (4006 "Love Me Tender") 100-125 56
(Black label, dog on top. Has song title strip across the top of front cover.)

RCA (4006 "Love Me Tender") 250-300 56
(Black label, without dog. Has song title strip across the top of front cover.)

RCA (4006 "Love Me Tender") 75-125 65
(Black label, dog on side.)

RCA (4006 "Love Me Tender") 100-150 69
(Orange label.)

RCA (4041 "Just for You") 100-125 57
(Black label, dog on top. Has EP title strip across the top of front cover.)

RCA (4041 "Just for You") 250-300 57
(Black label, without dog. Has EP title strip across the top of front cover.)

RCA (4041 "Just for You") 75-125 65
(Black label, dog on side.)

RCA (4041 "Just for You") 100-150 69
(Orange label.)

RCA (4054 "Peace in the Valley") 100-125 57
(Black label, dog on top. Has EP title strip across the top of front cover. Reissued as Gold Standard 5121.)

RCA (4108 "Elvis Sings Christmas Songs") 100-125 57
(Black label, dog on top. Has EP title strip across the top of front cover.)

RCA (4108 "Elvis Sings Christmas Songs") 75-125 65
(Black label, dog on side.)

RCA (4108 "Elvis Sings Christmas Songs") 150-200 69
(Orange label.)

RCA (4114 "Jailhouse Rock") 100-125 57
(Black label, dog on top.)

RCA (4114 "Jailhouse Rock") 75-125 65
(Black label, dog on side.)

RCA (4114 "Jailhouse Rock") 100-150 69
(Orange label.)

RCA (4319 "King Creole") 100-125 58
(Reissued as Gold Standard 5122.)

RCA (4321 "King Creole, Vol. 2") 100-125 58
(Black label, dog on top.)

RCA (4321 "King Creole, Vol. 2") 75-125 65
(Black label, dog on side.)

RCA (4321 "King Creole, Vol. 2") 100-150 69
(Orange label.)

RCA (4325 "Elvis Sails") 100-150 58
(Reissued as Gold Standard 5157.)

RCA (4340 "Christmas with Elvis") 200-250 58
(Black label, dog on top.)

RCA (4340 "Christmas with Elvis") 150-200 65
(Black label, dog on side.)

RCA (4340 "Christmas with Elvis") 150-200 69
(Orange label.)

RCA (4368 "Follow That Dream") 75-125 62
(Black label, dog on top. Playing times are incorrectly listed for three of the four tracks: *Follow That Dream* shown as 1:35, should be 1:38; *Angel* shown as 2:35, should be 2:40; and *I'm Not the Marrying Kind* shown as 1:49, should be 2:00.)

RCA (4368 "Follow That Dream") 50-100 62
(Black label, dog on top. All playing times are correctly shown.)

RCA (4368 "Follow That Dream") 200-250 62
(Special paper sleeve, issued to radio stations and juke box operators. Promotional issue only. Price is for sleeve only.)

RCA (4368 "Follow That Dream") 75-125 65
(Black label, dog on side.)

RCA (4368 "Follow That Dream") 100-150 69
(Orange label.)

RCA (4371 "Kid Galahad") 100-125 62
(Black label, dog on top.)

RCA (4371 "Kid Galahad") 75-125 65
(Black label, dog on side.)

RCA (4371 "Kid Galahad") 100-150 69
(Orange label.)

RCA (4382 "Viva Las Vegas") 100-125 64
(Black label, dog on top.)

RCA (4382 "Viva Las Vegas") 75-125 65
(Black label, dog on side.)

RCA (4382 "Viva Las Vegas") 100-150 69
(Orange label.)

RCA (4383 "Tickle Me") 75-100 65
(Black label, dog on side. Mentions "Special Elvis Anniversary LP Album" at bottom on front cover.)

RCA (4383 "Tickle Me") 100-125 65
(Black label, dog on side. No mention of "Special Elvis Anniversary LP Album.)

RCA (4383 "Tickle Me") 400-500 69
(Orange label.)

RCA (4387 "Easy Come, Easy Go") 75-125 67
(Black label, dog on side.)

RCA (4387 "Easy Come, Easy Go") 150-200 67
(White label. Promotional Issue Only.)

RCA (5088 "A Touch of Gold, Vol. I") ... 500-750 59
(Maroon label.)

RCA (5088 "A Touch of Gold, Vol. I") ... 100-125 59
(Black label, dog on top. Add $25 to $50 if accompanied by "I am a loyal Elvis fan" insert card.)

RCA (5088 "A Touch of Gold, Vol. I") ... 100-150 65
(Black label, dog on side.)

RCA (5088 "A Touch of Gold, Vol. I") ... 250-300 69
(Orange label.)

RCA (5101 "A Touch of Gold, Vol. II") .. 500-750 59
(Maroon label.)

RCA (5101 "A Touch of Gold, Vol. II") .. 100-125 59
(Black label, dog on top. Add $25 to $50 if accompanied by "I am a loyal Elvis fan" insert card.)

RCA (5101 "A Touch of Gold, Vol. II") .. 100-150 65
(Black label, dog on side.)

RCA (5101 "A Touch of Gold, Vol. II") .. 100-200 69
(Orange label.)

RCA (5120 "The Real Elvis") 700-800 59
(Maroon label. Reissue of 940.)

RCA (5120 "The Real Elvis") 100-150 59
(Black label, dog on top.)

RCA (5120 "The Real Elvis") 75-125 65
(Black label, dog on side.)

RCA (5120 "The Real Elvis") 100-150 69
(Orange label.)

RCA (5121 "Peace in the Valley") 500-750 59
(Maroon label. Reissue of 4054.)

RCA (5121 "Peace in the Valley") 75-125 59
(Black label, dog on top.)

RCA (5121 "Peace in the Valley") 75-125 65
(Black label, dog on side.)

RCA (5121 "Peace in the Valley") 150-200 69
(Orange label.)

RCA (5122 "King Creole") 5000-7500 59
(Maroon label. Listed based on one — and only one — person's report of it. Many collectors have doubts about the existence of a maroon label of this EP. We can't confirm it; however, if one should turn up, price range is a reality..)

RCA (5122 "King Creole") 100-125 59
(Black label, dog on top.)

RCA (5122 "King Creole") 75-125 65
(Black label, dog on side.)

RCA (5122 "King Creole") 100-150 69
(Orange label.)

RCA (5141 "A Touch of Gold, Vol. 3") .. 500-750 60
(Maroon label.)

RCA (5141 "A Touch of Gold, Vol. 3") .. 100-125 60
(Black label, dog on top.)

RCA (5141 "A Touch of Gold, Vol. 3") 75-125 65
(Black label, dog on side.)

RCA (5141 "A Touch of Gold, Vol. 3") .. 100-200 69
(Orange label.)

RCA (5157 "Elvis Sails") 100-125 65
(Black label, dog on top. Reissue of 4325.)

RCA (5157 "Elvis Sails") 150-200 69
(Orange label.)

RCA (8705 "TV Guide Presents Elvis") 1000-1500 56
(Price for disc only. Insert sheets are priced separately below. No sleeve or special cover exists for this disc. Promotional issue only.)

RCA (8705 "TV Guide Presents Elvis") 200-300 56
(Price for "Elvis Exclusively" gray insert.)

RCA (8705 "TV Guide Presents Elvis") 200-300 56
(Price for *Elvis Exclusively* pink insert, with suggested continuity.)

RCA (9089 "SPD-15 Elvis EP") 400-500 56
(Black label. Just the Elvis disc from SPD-15.)

RCA (9089 "SPD-15 Elvis EP") 400-500 56
(Gray label. The Elvis disc from SPD-15. Gray label pressings were for juke box operators.)

RCA (9113 "SPD-19 Elvis EP") 300-400 56
(The Elvis disc from SPD-19, *The Sound of Leadership.*)

RCA (9141 "SPD-26 Elvis EP") 200-250 56
(Black label. The Elvis disc from SPD-15, *Great Country/Western Hits.*)

RCA (64476 "Heartbreak Hotel") 4-8 96
(Issued with paper sleeve.)

SHOW-LAND (1001 "The Beginning of Elvis") 60-80 79

TUPPERWARE (11973 "Tupperware's Hit Parade") 50-75 73
(Promotional issue only. Includes tracks by other artists. Not issued with special cover.)

Notes: Unless listed and priced separately, all EP values include both disc and cover with approximately half of the total attached to each. Some of the rarer pieces that are often traded individually (disc or sleeve), as well as those sleeves that have an exceptionally higher value than their disc, are listed separately in this section. All EPs in the 5000 series are Gold Standard Series issues although none are identified as such on the labels, only on the covers. Remember, if you don't find the EP in this section it may contain two, three or four artists, and will be listed following the Presley LP section.

LPs: 10/12-Inch
(Commercial and Promotional)

ABC RADIO (1003 "Elvis Memories") .. 425-525 78
(Boxed, three-disc set. Add $25 to $50 if accompanied by a 16-page programmer's booklet and four pages of added information. Issued only to radio stations. Add $40 to $50 if accompanied by a 7-inch reel tape, with spots and promo announcements. Program Highlights issue on Michelob 810.)

ASSOCIATED BROADCASTERS (1001 "Legend of a King") 125-150 80
(White label. Advance pressing.)

ASSOCIATED BROADCASTERS (1001 "Legend of a King") 50-75 80
(Picture disc. First pressings are numbered from 3000 through 6000. Number appears under "Side One" on the disc itself. Cover is standard, die-cut, picture disc cover. Has several spelling errors on back cover, including "idle" for idol and "Jordinaires" instead of Jordanaires.)

ASSOCIATED BROADCASTERS (1001 "Legend of a King") 30-50 80
(Picture disc. Second pressings are numbered from 6001 through 9000. Most of the spelling errors were corrected on this cover.)

ASSOCIATED BROADCASTERS (1001 "Legend of a King") 25-30 80
(Picture disc. Third pressings are numbered from 00001 through 02999 and 09001 through 15000. Cover errors have all been corrected.)

ASSOCIATED BROADCASTERS (1001 "Legend of a King") 15-20 84
(Picture disc. Fourth pressings are also numbered from 3000 through 6000, but were packaged in a clear plastic sleeve instead of a conventional cover.)

ASSOCIATED BROADCASTERS (1001 "Legend of a King") 8-15 85
(Picture disc. Discs are not numbered. Packaged in a plastic sleeve.)

ASSOCIATED BROADCASTERS ("Legend of a King") 200-250 85
(Three-hour, three-disc set. Not boxed. Price includes six pages of cue sheets. Available to radio stations only.)

ASSOCIATED BROADCASTERS ("Legend of a King") 300-350 85
(Same as above, but packaged in a specially printed box.)

ASSOCIATED BROADCASTERS ("Legend of a King") 300-350 86
(Boxed, three-disc set, same as above except time on segment 1-B is increased from 14:25 to 15:15 in order to include a Johnny Bernero interview.)

ASSOCIATED PRESS (1977 "The World in Sound") 80-100 78
(News highlights of 1977, including coverage of Elvis' death.)

BOXCAR ("Having Fun with Elvis on Stage") 150-200 74
(No selection number used. Sold in conjunction with Elvis' concert appearances. Reissued as RCA CPM1-0818.)

CAEDMON (1572 "On the Record") 60-80 78
(Various news items and artists featured.)

CAMDEN (2304 "Flaming Star") 30-40 69
(First issued as RCA PRS-279, reissued in 1975 as Pickwick 2304.)

CAMDEN (2408 "Let's Be Friends") 30-40 70
(Reissued in 1975 as Pickwick 2408.)

CAMDEN (2428 "Elvis' Christmas Album") ... 30-40 70
(Eight songs on this LP were first issued on RCA LOC-1035. Reissued in 1975 as Pickwick 2428.)
CAMDEN (2440 "Almost in Love") ... 30-40 70
(With *Stay Away Joe*.)
CAMDEN (2440 "Almost in Love") ... 20-30 73
(*Stay Away* replaces *Stay Away Joe*.)
Note: Reissued in 1975 as Pickwick 2440.
CAMDEN (2472 "You'll Never Walk Alone") ... 30-40 71
(Reissued in 1975 as Pickwick 2472.)
CAMDEN (2518 "C'mon Everybody") ... 25-30 71
(Reissued in 1975 as Pickwick 2518.)
CAMDEN (2533 "I Got Lucky") ... 25-30 71
(Reissued in 1975 as Pickwick 2533.)
CAMDEN (2567 "Elvis Sings Hits from His Movies") ... 20-30 72
(Reissued in 1975 as Pickwick 2567.)
CAMDEN (2595 "Burning Love") ... 35-45 72
(Cover has "Special Bonus Photo Inside" at lower left. Add $40 to $45 if accompanied by the bonus 8" x 10" Elvis photo.)
CAMDEN (2595 "Burning Love") ... 10-20 72
(No mention of "Special Bonus Photo Inside." Reissued in 1975 as Pickwick 2595.)
CAMDEN (2611 "Separate Ways") ... 20-30 73
(Add $20 if accompanied by 3" x 5" color greeting card. Reissued in 1975 as Pickwick 2611.)
CREATIVE RADIO (E1 "Elvis Exclusive Interview") ... 175-200 88
(Price for *complete* 1956 Little Rock concert copies. Only the first 100 copies were pressed with the full concert. The only way to visually identify these is to check the disc. On the full concert pressings, the grooves take up nearly the entire disc.)
CREATIVE RADIO (E1 "Elvis Exclusive Interview") ... 20-30 88
(Has edited concert songs. On this pressing the grooves occupy only about two-thirds of the disc.)
CREATIVE RADIO ("Between Takes with Elvis") ... 150-250 89
(Three-disc set. Promotional issue only. Though not packaged inside covers—shrink wrapped at the factory—each LP set came with the bonus single, *Nearer My God to Thee/You Gave Me a Molehill*.)
CURRENT AUDIO MAGAZINE (1 "Elvis: Press Conference") ... 50-75 72
(Includes 8-page, fold-out insert.)
EMR ENTERPRISES (8 "The Age of Rock") ... 100-125 69
(Promotional issue only.)
ELEKTRA (60107 "Diner") ... 10-20 82
(Soundtrack.)
FRANKLIN MINT (4 "The Official Grammy Award Winners") ... 150-200 85
(Boxed set of four colored vinyl discs. One in a series of 14 boxed sets, but only this one (titled *The Great Singers*) has Elvis. Includes booklet.)
GOLDEN EDITIONS LIMITED (1 "The First Year") ... 8-15 79
(Print in upper corners on front cover is in white. Label is black. Add $5 to $8 if accompanied by a 12-page booklet and one-page copy of the 1954 Elvis/Scotty Moore contract.)
GOLDEN EDITIONS LIMITED (101 "The First Year") ... 15-25 79
(Print in upper corners on front cover is in gold. Label is white. Add $5 to $8 if accompanied by a 12-page booklet and one-page copy of the 1954 Elvis/Scotty Moore contract. Most of the material on this LP was previously issued on HALW 00001.)
GREAT NORTHWEST (4005 "The Elvis Tapes") ... 10-15 77
(Repackaged on Starday 995.)
GREAT NORTHWEST (4006 "The King Speaks") ... 8-10 77
(First issued as Green Valley 2001.)
GREEN VALLEY (2001 "Elvis 1961 Press Conference") ... 30-50 77
(Cover is thin, soft stock and does not have black bar on spine. Label does not show selection number.)
GREEN VALLEY (2001 "Elvis 1961 Press Conference") ... 12-15 77
(Cover is standard stock and has black bar on spine. Label has the selection number. Repackaged as one half of Green Valley 2001/2003.)
Note: Repackaged as Great Northwest 4006.

GREEN VALLEY (2001/2003 "Elvis Speaks to You") ... 25-30 78
(GV-2001 was first issued as a single LP.)
HALW (00001 "The First Years") ... 25-30 78
(Repackaged in 1979 on Golden Editions 1.)
INTERNATIONAL HOTEL PRESENTS ELVIS 1969 ... 3500-4000 69
(Custom gift box prepared by Col. Parker and RCA for International Hotel guests. Originally contained: RCA LPM-4088 & LSP-4155, three 8" x 10" Elvis photos, RCA Elvis catalog, calendar and a nine-page letter. Price is for complete set but box itself represents 90-95% of value.)
INTERNATIONAL HOTEL PRESENTS ELVIS 1970 ... 3500-4000 70
(Custom gift box prepared by Col. Parker and RCA for International Hotel guests. Originally contained: RCA LSP-6020 & 45-9791, one 8" x 10" Elvis photo, photo album, RCA Elvis catalog, calendar, menu and letter. Price is for complete set but box itself represents 90-95% of value.)
INTERNATIONAL HOTEL PRESENTS ELVIS 1969 or 1970 ... 3500-4000 69
(Known as "V.I.P. Box." Same contents as described in two preceding listings; however, this box has no printing in top right corner of front cover. Thus it may have been used for either engagement. Price is for complete set but box itself represents 90-95% of value.)
K-TEL (9900 "Elvis Love Songs") ... 15-20 81
LOUISIANA HAYRIDE (3061 "The Beginning Years") ... 400-500 84
(White label advance pressing from RCA, Indianapolis, where this LP was manufactured.)
LOUISIANA HAYRIDE (3061 "The Beginning Years") ... 20-25 84
(Price includes 20-page *D.J. Fontana Remembers Elvis* booklet, a four sheet copy of Elvis' Hayride contract and a 10" x 10" *Presleyana, Second Edition* flyer, all of which represent about $5 to $10 of the value.)
Note: Selections from this LP are also on the Music Works 3601 & 3602.
LOUISIANA HAYRIDE (8454 "The Louisiana Hayride") ... 500-700 76
(Yellow label. A program of various artists including Elvis. Issued to radio stations only.)
LOUISIANA HAYRIDE (8454 "The Louisiana Hayride") ... 300-350 81
(Gold label. A program of various artists including Elvis.)
MFSL (059 "From Elvis in Memphis") ... 50-80 82
(First issued as RCA LSP-4155.)
MARVENCO (101 "1954-1955, The Beginning") ... 10-15 88
(Tracks first issued on Golden Editions 101.)
MICHELOB (810 "Highlights of Elvis Memories") ... 100-200 78
(A Michelob in-house promotional issue only.)
Elvis Memories was first issued on ABC Radio 1003.
MUSIC WORKS (3601 "The First Live Recordings") ... 15-20 84
(First issued on Louisiana Hayride 3061.)
MUSIC WORKS (3602 "Hillbilly Cat") ... 15-20 84
(First issued on Louisiana Hayride 3061.)
MUTUAL BROADCAST SYSTEM (4082 "The Frantic Fifties") ... 400-500 59
(Various news items and artists featured. Promotional issue only.)
OAK (1003 "Vintage 1955") ... 40-60 91
PAIR (1010 "Double Dynamite") ... 30-40 82
(First issued as Pickwick 5001.)
PAIR (1037 "Remembering Elvis") ... 30-40 83
PICKWICK (2304 "Flaming Star") ... 8-10 75
(First issued as RCA PRS-279.)
PICKWICK (2408 "Let's Be Friends") ... 8-10 75
(Black vinyl.)
Note: First issued as Camden 2408.
PICKWICK (2408 "Let's Be Friends") 750-1000 '70s
(Colored vinyl. Experimental pressing only. There is no colored vinyl commercial or promotional edition of this issue.)
PICKWICK (2428 "Elvis' Christmas Album") ... 8-10 75
(First issued as Camden 2428.)
PICKWICK (2428 "Elvis' Christmas Album") ... 20-40 86
(Has RCA Special Products on label and cover.)
PICKWICK (2440 "Almost in Love") ... 8-10 75
(First issued as Camden 2440.)

PICKWICK (2472 "You'll Never Walk Alone") ... 8-10 75
(First issued as Camden 2472.)
PICKWICK (2518 "C'mon Everybody") ... 8-10 75
(First issued as Camden 2518.)
PICKWICK (2533 "I Got Lucky") ... 8-10 75
(First issued as Camden 2533.)
PICKWICK (2567 "Elvis Sings Hits from His Movies") ... 8-10 75
(First issued as Camden 2567.)
PICKWICK (2595 "Burning Love") ... 8-12 75
(First issued as Camden 2595.)
PICKWICK (2611 "Separate Ways") ... 8-10 75
(First issued as Camden 2611.)
PICKWICK (5001 "Double Dynamite") ... 25-30 75
(Repackaged in 1982 as Pair 1010.)
PICKWICK (7007 "Frankie & Johnny") ... 10-15 75
(First issued as RCA 3553.)
PICKWICK (7064 "Mahalo from Elvis") ... 15-25 78
PREMORE (589 "Early Elvis") ... 20-40 89
(Mail-order album from the Solo Cup Company.)
RCA (EPC-1 "Special Christmas Program" Reel Tape) ... 350-400 67
(Price includes programming inserts, which represent $25-35 of the value.)
Note: Never issued commercially on disc, all 10–inch red vinyl LPs of this material are bootlegs.
RCA (TB-1 "Collectors Edition") ... 100-150 76
(Boxed, five-disc set.)
RCA (0001 "Robert W. Sarnoff") ... 2000-3000 73
(Promotional RCA in-house issue only. Includes tracks by other artists.)
RCA (4 "Untitled RCA Sampler") ... 1000-1500 56
(Promotional issue only. Includes tracks by other artists. Not issued with special cover.)
RCA (7 "February Sampler") ... 600-800 59
(Promotional issue only. Includes tracks by other artists. Full number: 59-7. Not issued with special cover.)
RCA (10 "Untitled RCA Sampler") ... 900-1200 58
(Promotional issue only. Includes tracks by other artists. Not issued with special cover.)
RCA (010 "Elvis! His Greatest Hits") ... 400-500 79
(White box edition. Boxed, eight-disc set, sold mail-order by *Reader's Digest*.)
RCA (010 "His Greatest Hits") ... 50-80 83
(Yellow box edition. Boxed, seven-disc set, sold mail-order by *Reader's Digest*. See RCA 181 for the bonus LP offered with this set.)
RCA (27 "August 1959 Sampler") ... 750-1000 59
(Promotional issue only. Includes tracks by other artists. Not issued with special cover.)
RCA RBA-040: see READER'S DIGEST 040
RCA (41 "October Christmas Sampler") ... 600-750 59
(Promotional issue only. Includes tracks by other artists. Full number: 59-40-41. Not issued with special cover.)
RCA (0056 "Elvis") ... 45-55 73
(Mustard color label. Cover shows "Brookville Records" in upper right. A mail-order LP offer.)
RCA (0056 "Elvis") ... 25-35 73
(Blue label. Cover doesn't show "Brookville Records." Mail-order LP offer. Repackaged in 1978 and titled *Elvis Commemorative Album*.)
RCA (0056 "Elvis Commemorative Album") ... 80-100 78
(Price includes a "Registered Certificate of Ownership." A mail-order LP offer. First titled *Elvis*, using the same selection number.)
RCA (66 "Christmas Programming from RCA") ... 1000-1200 59
(Price includes paper sleeve, which represents half the value. Promotional issue only. Includes tracks by other artists.)
RCA (072 "Great Hits of 1956-'57") ... 20-30 87
(Offered as a bonus LP from *Reader's Digest*, with the purchase of one of their non-Elvis boxed sets.)
RCA (96 "October 1960 Popular Stereo Sampler") ... 500-750 60
(Promotional issue only. Includes tracks by other artists. Not issued with special cover.)
RCA (0108 "E-Z Country No. 2") ... 300-350 55
(Promotional issue only. Includes tracks by other artists. Identification number shown since no selection number is used. Not issued with special cover.)
RCA (141 "October '61 Pop Sampler"). 500-750 61
(Promotional issue only. Includes tracks by other artists. Not issued with special cover.)

RCA (0168 "Elvis in Hollywood") ... 50-75 76
(Add $10 to $15 is accompanied by a 20-page photo booklet.)
RCA (181 "Elvis Sings Inspirational Favorites") ... 15-20 83
(Special Products, Reader's Digest mail-order bonus LP for buyers of the 1983 edition of RCA 010. Price includes 24-page Reader's Digest Music catalog.)
RCA (191 "Elvis, the Legend Lives On") .. 50-75 86
(Boxed, seven-disc set, sold mail-order by Reader's Digest. Includes booklet.)
RCA (0197 "E-Z Pop No. 6") ... 300-350 56
(Promotional issue only. Includes tracks by other artists. Identification number shown since no selection number is used. Not issued with special cover.)
RCA (0199 "E-Z Country No. 3") ... 300-350 56
(Promotional issue only. Includes tracks by other artists. Identification number shown since no selection number is used. Not issued with special cover.)
RCA (219 "September '63 Pop Sampler") ... 500-750 63
(Promotional issue only. Includes tracks by other artists.)
RCA (242 "Elvis Sings Country Favorites") ... 50-75 84
(Bonus LP from Reader's Digest, given with the purchase of their seven-disc boxed set, *The Great Country Entertainers*, which has no Elvis tracks.)
RCA (247 "December '63 Pop Sampler") ... 500-750 63
(Promotional issue only. Includes tracks by other artists. Not issued with special cover.)
RCA (0263 "Elvis Presley Story") ... 50-75 77
(Special Products five-disc boxed set. A Candelite Music mail-order offer.)
RCA (0264 "Songs of Inspiration") ... 15-20 77
(Special Products issue. A Candelite Music mail-order bonus LP for buyers of RCA 0263.)
RCA (272 "April '64 Pop Sampler") ... 500-750 64
(Promotional issue only. Includes tracks by other artists. Not issued with special cover.)
RCA (279 "Singer Presents Elvis") ... 100-125 68
(Reissued in 1969 as Camden 2304 and in 1975 as Pickwick 2304.)
RCA (0283 "Elvis, Including Fool") ... 40-50 73
RCA (331 "April '65 Pop Sampler") ... 500-750 65
(Promotional issue only. Includes tracks by other artists. Not issued with special cover.)
RCA (0341 "Legendary Performer, Vol. 1") ... 25-30 74
(With die-cut cover. Add $5 to $10 if accompanied by *The Early Years* booklet.)
RCA (0341 "Legendary Performer, Vol. 1") ... 15-25 83
(With standard cover—not die-cut.)
RCA (0341 "Legendary Performer, Vol. 1") ... 1000-2000 78
(Picture discs of the 0341 material but with pictures from any of about six different LP covers pressed on the disc. RCA in-house, experimental items.)
RCA (347 "August '65 Pop Sampler") .. 500-750 65
(Promotional issue only. Includes tracks by other artists. Not issued with special cover.)
RCA (0347 "Memories of Elvis") ... 60-70
(Special Products five-disc boxed set. A Candelite Music mail-order offer. Add $8 to $10 if accompanied by a 16-page booklet and an Elvis print. Not all sets came with the print and booklet.)
RCA (0348 "Greatest Show on Earth") ... 15-20 78
(Special Products issue. A Candelite Music mail-order bonus LP for buyers of RCA 0347.)
RCA (0388 "Raised on Rock") ... 30-40 73
(Orange label.)
RCA (0388 "Raised on Rock") ... 40-50 76
(Tan label.)
RCA (0388 "Raised on Rock") ... 10-20 77
(Black label.)
RCA (403 "April '66 Pop Sampler") ... 500-750 66
(Promotional issue only. Includes tracks by other artists. Not issued with special cover.)
RCA (0401 RCA Radio Victrola Division Spots") ... 1500-2000 56
(Single-sided disc with four 50-second radio commercials for RCA's Victrolas, as well as for the SPD-22 and SPD-23 EPs that were offered as a bonus. Elvis is the announcer on all of the spots, which include excerpts of some of his songs. Issued only to radio stations scheduling the spots.)
RCA (0412 "The Legendary Recordings") ... 100-125 79

(Special Products six-disc boxed set. A Candelite Music mail-order offer.)
RCA (0413 "Greatest Moments in Music") 15-20 80
(Special Products issue. A Candelite Music mail-order bonus LP for buyers of RCA 0412.)
RCA (0437 "Rock 'N Roll Forever") 15-20 81
(Candelite Music mail-order LP offer.)
RCA (461 "Special Palm Sunday Programming") 800-1000 67
(With programming packet. Promotional issue only.)
RCA (0461 "The Legendary Magic")........ 15-20 80
(Candelite Music mail-order LP offer.)
RCA (CPL1-0475 "Good Times")............ 45-65 74
VICTOR (AFL1-0475 "Good Times")....... 10-20 77
RCA (571 "Elvis As Recorded at Madison Square Garden").......... 300-400 72
(Two-disc, double pocket issue. Promotional issue only. Commercially issued as RCA LSP-4776.)
RCA (CPL1-0606 "On Stage in Memphis")........ 25-30 74
(Orange label.)
RCA (APD1-0606 "On Stage in Memphis")........ 200-300 74
(Quadradisc. Orange label.)
RCA (DJL1-0606 "On Stage in Memphis")........ 400-500 74
(Banded edition. Promotional issue only.)
RCA (CPL1-0606 "Recorded Live on Stage in Memphis")........ 50-75 76
(Tan label.)
RCA (AFL1-0606 "Recorded Live on Stage in Memphis")........ 10-20 77
RCA (0632 "The Elvis Presley Collection")........ 75-100 84
(Special Products three-disc boxed set, produced for Candlelite Music. Includes booklet. A mail-order LP offer.)
RCA (DPL1-0647 "Elvis Country") 25-35 84
(Special Products issue for ERA Records.)
RCA (DPK1-0679 "Savage Young Elvis")........ 20-30 84
(Cassette tape of a package that was never available on LP. Price is for tape still attached to 12" x 12" photo card.)
RCA (0704 "Elvis, HBO Special") 50-60 84
(Includes color poster. Special Products issue for HBO cable TV subscribers. This material was first issued as RCA LPM-4088.)
RCA (0710 "50 Years-50 Hits") 30-40 85
(Three-disc set. Offered by TV mail-order and through the RCA Record Club.)
RCA (0728 "Elvis, His Songs of Faith and Inspiration")........ 50-80 86
(Two-disc, mail-order offer.)
RCA (CPM1-0818 "Having Fun with Elvis on Stage")........ 30-40 74
(Orange label.)
RCA (CPM1-0818 "Having Fun with Elvis on Stage")........ 30-40 76
(Tan label.)
RCA (AFM1-0818 "Having Fun with Elvis on Stage")........ 40-60 77
(Black label.)
Note: First issued on Boxcar without a selection number.
RCA (0835 "Elvis Presley Interview Record – An Audio Self-Portrait")........ 80-100 84
(Promotional issue only.)
RCA (APL1-0873 "Promised Land") 50-60 75
(Orange label.)
RCA (APD1-0873 "Promised Land")........ 200-300 75
(Quadradisc. Orange label.)
RCA (APL1-0873 "Promised Land") 20-30 76
(Tan label.)
RCA (AFL1-0873 "Promised Land")......... 10-20 77
(Black label.)
RCA (APD1-0873 "Promised Land").... 100-200 77
(Quadradisc. Black label.)
RCA (ANL1-0971 "Pure Gold") 20-30 75
(Orange label.)
RCA (ANL1-0971 "Pure Gold") 10-20 76
(Yellow label.)
Note: Reissued in 1980 as AYL1-3732.
RCA (1001 "The Sun Collection") 15-25 75
(Label does not have "Starcall" on it. Back cover pictures other LPs.)
RCA (1001 "The Sun Collection") 10-20 75
(Label has "Starcall" on it. Back cover with liner notes.)

Note: This English import was distributed throughout the U.S. Repackaged in 1976 as RCA 1675.
RCA (LOC-1035 "Elvis' Christmas Album")........ 15000-18000 57
(Red vinyl. Experimental pressing only.)
RCA (LOC-1035 "Elvis' Christmas Album")........ 600-800 57
(Black vinyl. With gold foil, gift-giving sticker.)
RCA (LOC-1035 "Elvis' Christmas Album")........ 200-400 57
(Black vinyl. Without gold foil, gift-giving sticker.)
Note: Repackaged in 1958 as RCA 1951, in 1970 as Camden 2428 and in 1985 as RCA 5486. May be found with either gold or silver print on the spine.
RCA (APL1-1039 "Today")........ 60-75 75
(Orange label.)
RCA (APD1-1039 "Today")........ 300-350 75
(Quadradisc. Orange label.)
RCA (APL1-1039 "Today")........ 40-50 76
(Tan label.)
RCA (AFL1-1039 "Today")........ 10-20 77
(Black label.)
RCA (APD1-1039 "Today")........ 150-200 77
(Quadradisc. Black label.)
RCA (LPM-1254 "Elvis Presley") 350-450 56
(Monaural. Black label, "Long Play" at bottom. Cover has selection number in upper right corner.)
RCA (LPM-1254 "Elvis Presley") 350-450 56
(Canadian. Pale blue label.)
RCA (LPM-1254 "Elvis Presley")........ 200-250 63
(Black label, "Mono" at bottom. Cover has selection number on left.)
RCA (LPM-1254 "Elvis Presley")........ 75-100 64
(Black label, "Monaural" at bottom. Cover has selection number on left.)
RCA (LSP-1254e "Elvis Presley")........ 200-300 62
(Stereo. Black label, all print on label is silver.)
RCA (LSP-1254e "Elvis Presley")........ 50-100 64
(Black label, RCA logo is white, other label print is silver.)
RCA (LSP-1254e "Elvis Presley")........ 50-75 68
(Orange label. Rigid vinyl.)
RCA (LSP-1254e "Elvis Presley")........ 30-40 71
(Orange label. Flexible vinyl.)
RCA (LSP-1254e "Elvis Presley")........ 40-50 76
(Tan label.)
RCA (LSP-1254e "Elvis Presley")........ 10-20 77
(Black label, dog near top.)
RCA (AFL1-1254e "Elvis Presley")........ 10-20 77
Note: Digitally remastered in 1984 on RCA 5198.
RCA (ANL1-1319 "His Hand in Mine")...... 10-20 76
(First issued as LPM/LSP-2328.)
RCA (1349 "Legendary Performer, Vol. 2")........ 25-30 76
(With die-cut cover. Includes false starts and outtakes on *Such a Night* and *Cane and a High Starched Collar*. Add $5 to $10 if accompanied by *The Early Years Continued* booklet.)
RCA (1349 "Legendary Performer, Vol. 2")........ 50-75 76
(Does not have the false starts and outtakes on *Such a Night* and *Cane and a High Starched Collar*. Mistakenly has only the complete take of both songs. Add $5 to $10 if accompanied by *The Early Years Continued* booklet.)
RCA (1349 "Legendary Performer, Vol. 2")........ 30-40 86
(With standard cover—not die-cut.)
RCA (LPM-1382 "Elvis")........ 600-800 56
(Monaural. Black label, "Long Play" at bottom. Cover has selection number in upper right corner. Mistakenly pressed with an alternative take of *Old Shep*, not available on any other authorized U.S. vinyl release. Any copy with a "15S," "17S" or "19S" matrix on side 2 (following identification number stamped in the vinyl trail-off – matrix on side 1 is irrelevant) is likely to have the alternative; however, playing the track is the way to be certain. Alternative is different throughout, instrumentally and vocally – especially Elvis' phrasing – but here are two lyric variations. Words in all upper case are exclusive to the alternative take (which can be heard on the 1992 CD boxed set *Elvis – The King of Rock 'N' Roll, The Complete '50s Masters*): 1) "As the years fast did roll, Old Shep he grew old AND his eyes were fast growing dim." 2) "He came to my side and he looked up at me, and HE laid his old head on my knee.")
RCA (LPM-1382 "Elvis")........ 300-400 56
(Black label, selections numbered as "Band 1" through "Band 6.")

RCA (LPM-1382 "Elvis")........ 300-400 56
(Black label, "Long Play" at bottom. Cover has selection number in upper right corner.)
RCA (LPM-1382 "Elvis")........ 200-250 63
(Black label, "Mono" at bottom. Cover has selection number on left.)
RCA (LPM-1382 "Elvis")........ 75-100 64
(Black label, "Monaural" at bottom. Cover has selection number on left.)
RCA (LSP-1382e "Elvis")........ 200-300 62
(Stereo. Black label, all print on label is silver.)
RCA (LSP-1382e "Elvis")........ 50-100 64
(Black label, RCA logo is white, other print on label is silver.)
RCA (LSP-1382e "Elvis")........ 50-75 68
(Orange label. Rigid vinyl.)
RCA (LSP-1382e "Elvis")........ 30-40 71
(Orange label. Flexible vinyl.)
RCA (LSP-1382e "Elvis")........ 40-50 76
(Tan label.)
RCA (LSP-1382e "Elvis")........ 10-20 77
(Black label, dog near top.)
RCA (AFL1-1382e "Elvis")........ 10-20 77
Note: Digitally remastered in 1984 on RCA 5199.
RCA (APL1-1506 "From Elvis Presley Boulevard")........ 30-40 76
(Tan label.)
RCA (APL1-1506 "From Elvis Presley Boulevard")........ 10-20 77
(Black label.)
RCA (AFL1-1506 "From Elvis Presley Boulevard")........ 10-20 77
RCA (LPM-1515 "Loving You")........ 300-400 57
(Monaural. Black label, "Long Play" at bottom. Cover has selection number in upper right corner.)
RCA (LPM-1515 "Loving You")........ 200-250 63
(Black label, "Mono" at bottom. Cover has selection number on left.)
RCA (LPM-1515 "Loving You")........ 4000-6000 '60s
(Picture disc, but with the cover of a European *G.I. Blues* album being the picture imbeded in the vinyl. Possibly an experimental disc, with only one copy known. Has just five *Loving You* tracks, the others being randomly selected instrumentals which have nothing at all to do with Elvis.)
RCA (LPM-1515 "Loving You")........ 75-100 64
(Black label, "Monaural" at bottom. Cover has selection number on left.)
RCA (LSP-1515e "Loving You")........ 200-300 62
(Stereo. Black label, all print on label is silver.)
RCA (LSP-1515e "Loving You")........ 50-100 64
(Black label, RCA logo is white, other label print is silver.)
RCA (LSP-1515e "Loving You")........ 50-75 68
(Orange label. Rigid vinyl.)
RCA (LSP-1515e "Loving You")........ 30-40 71
(Orange label. Flexible vinyl.)
RCA (LSP-1515e "Loving You")........ 40-50 76
(Tan label.)
RCA (AFL1-1515e "Loving You")........ 10-20 77
RCA (APM1-1675 "The Sun Sessions")... 20-25 76
(Tan label.)
RCA (APM1-1675 "The Sun Sessions")... 15-20 76
(Black label.)
RCA (AFM1-1675 "The Sun Sessions")... 10-15 77
Note: First issued as RCA HY-1001 and reissued in 1981 as RCA AYM1-3893.
RCA (LPM-1707 "Elvis' Golden Records")........ 300-400 58
(Monaural. Black label, "Long Play" at bottom. Cover has selection number in upper right corner and LP title in light blue letters.)
RCA (LPM-1707 "Elvis' Golden Records")........ 200-250 63
(Black label, "Mono" at bottom. Cover has selection number on left and LP title in white letters.)
RCA (LPM-1707 "Elvis' Golden Records")........ 75-100 64
(Black label, "Monaural" at bottom. Cover has selection number on left.)
RCA (LSP-1707e "Elvis' Golden Records")........ 200-300 62
(Stereo. Black label, all print on label is silver.)
RCA (LSP-1707e "Elvis' Golden Records")........ 50-100 64
(Black label, RCA logo is white, other label print is silver.)
RCA (LSP-1707e "Elvis' Golden Records")........ 50-75 68
(Orange label. Rigid vinyl.)

RCA (LSP-1707e "Elvis' Golden Records")........ 30-40 71
(Orange label. Flexible vinyl.)
RCA (LSP-1707e "Elvis' Golden Records")........ 40-50 76
(Tan label.)
RCA (AFL1-1707e "Elvis' Golden Records")........ 15-20 77
RCA (AQL1-1707e "Elvis' Golden Records")........ 10-15 79
Note: Digitally remastered in 1984 on RCA 5196.
RCA (1785 "WRCA Plays the Hits")..... 300-350 76
(Promotional issue only. Includes tracks by other artists. Not issued with special cover.)
RCA (LPM-1884 "King Creole")........ 300-400 58
(Monaural. Black label, "Long Play" at bottom. Cover has selection number in upper right corner. Add $250 to $300 if accompanied by an 8" x 10" black and white photo of Elvis in uniform, which reportedly did not come packaged inside this LP, but was given to buyers by dealers at time of purchase.)
RCA (LPM-1884 "King Creole")........ 200-250 63
(Black label, "Mono" at bottom. Cover has selection number on left.)
RCA (LPM-1884 "King Creole")........ 75-100 64
(Black label, "Monaural" at bottom. Cover has selection number on left.)
RCA (LSP-1884e "King Creole") 200-300 62
(Stereo. Black label, all print on label is silver.)
RCA (LSP-1884e "King Creole") 50-100 62
(Black label, RCA logo is white, other label print is silver.)
RCA (LSP-1884e "King Creole") 50-75 68
(Orange label. Rigid vinyl.)
RCA (LSP-1884e "King Creole") 30-40 71
(Orange label. Flexible vinyl.)
RCA (LSP-1884e "King Creole") 40-50 76
(Tan label.)
RCA (AFL1-1884e "King Creole")........ 10-20 77
Note: Reissued in 1980 as RCA AYL1-3733.
RCA (ANL1-1936 "Wonderful World of Christmas")........ 100-125 76
(Tan label. First issued as RCA LSP-4579.)
RCA (ANL1-1936 "Wonderful World of Christmas")........ 40-50 76
(Black label.)
RCA (LPM-1951 "Elvis' Christmas Album")........ 250-300 58
(Monaural. Black label, "Long Play" at bottom. Cover has selection number in upper right corner.)
RCA (LPM-1951 "Elvis' Christmas Album")........ 150-200 63
(Black label, "Mono" at bottom. Cover has selection number on left.)
RCA (LPM-1951 "Elvis' Christmas Album")........ 40-50 64
(Black label, "Monaural" at bottom. Cover has selection number on left.)
RCA (LSP-1951e "Elvis' Christmas Album")........ 40-50 64
(Stereo. Black label, RCA logo is white, other label print is silver.)
RCA (LSP-1951e "Elvis' Christmas Album")........ 100-150 68
(Orange label. Rigid vinyl.)
Note: Repackage of RCA LOC-1035. Repackaged again in 1970 as Camden 2428 and then again in 1985 as RCA AFM1-5486.
RCA (1981 "Felton Jarvis Talks About Elvis")........ 250-350 81
(Price includes three script sheets. Add $25 to $50 if accompanied by silver and black *Guitar Man* engraved Elvis belt buckle.)
RCA (LPM-1990 "For LP Fans Only") .. 300-400 59
(Monaural. Black label, "Long Play" at bottom. Cover has selection number in upper right corner.)
RCA (LPM-1990 "For LP Fans Only") .. 200-250 63
(Black label, "Mono" at bottom. Cover has selection number on left.)
RCA (LPM-1990 "For LP Fans Only") 75-100 65
(Black label, "Monaural" at bottom. Cover has selection number on left.)
RCA (LPM-1990 "For LP Fans Only") .. 400-500 65
(Black label. Cover has same Elvis photo on front and back.)
RCA (LSP-1990 "For LP Fans Only")... 400-500 65
(Black label. Cover has same Elvis photo on front and back.)

RCA (LSP-1990e "For LP Fans Only") 200-250 65
(Stereo. Black label, RCA logo is white, other label print is silver.)
RCA (LSP-1990e "For LP Fans Only") 50-75 68
(Orange label. Rigid vinyl.)
RCA (LSP-1990e "For LP Fans Only") 40-50 76
(Tan label.)
RCA (LSP-1990e "For LP Fans Only") 10-20 76
(Black label, dog near top.)
RCA (AFL1-1990e "For LP Fans Only") .. 10-20 77
RCA (LPM-2011 "A Date with Elvis"). 900-1000 59
(Monaural. Black label, "Long Play" at bottom. Has gatefold cover and 1960 calendar. With "New Golden Age of Sound" wrap-around banner.)
RCA (LPM-2011 "A Date with Elvis") ... 400-500 59
(Black label, "Long Play" at bottom. Has gatefold cover and 1960 calendar, but *does not* have "New Golden Age of Sound" banner.)
RCA (LPM-2011 "A Date with Elvis") ... 200-250 65
(Black label, "Mono" at bottom. Cover has selection number on left.)
RCA (LPM-2011 "A Date with Elvis") 75-100 65
(Black label, "Monaural" at bottom. Cover has selection number on left.)
RCA (LSP-2011e "A Date with Elvis") ... 50-100 65
(Stereo. Black label, RCA logo is white, other label print is silver.)
RCA (LSP-2011e "A Date with Elvis") 50-75 68
(Orange label. Rigid vinyl.)
RCA (LSP-2011e "A Date with Elvis") 30-40 71
(Orange label. Flexible vinyl.)
RCA (LSP-2011e "A Date with Elvis") 40-50 76
(Tan label.)
RCA (LSP-2011e "A Date with Elvis") 10-20 77
(Black label, dog near top.)
RCA (AFL1-2011e "A Date with Elvis") 10-20 77
RCA (LPM-2075 "Elvis' Golden Records, Vol. 2") 300-400 59
(Monaural. Black label, "Long Play" at bottom. Cover has selection number in upper right corner.)
RCA (LPM-2075 "Elvis' Golden Records, Vol. 2") 200-250 63
(Black label, "Mono" at bottom. Cover has selection number on left.)
RCA (LPM-2075 "Elvis' Golden Records, Vol. 2") 75-100 64
(Black label, "Monaural" at bottom. Cover has selection number on left.)
RCA (LSP-2075e "Elvis' Golden Records, Vol. 2") 200-300 62
("Stereo Electronically Reprocessed." Black label, all print on label is silver.)
RCA (LSP-2075e "Elvis' Golden Records, Vol. 2") 650-750 63
(Stereo. Black label. Has "Stereo" at bottom. All print on label – including RCA logo – is silver.)
RCA (LSP-2075e "Elvis' Golden Records, Vol. 2") 50-100 64
(Black label, RCA logo is white, other label print is silver.)
RCA (LSP-2075e "Elvis' Golden Records, Vol. 2") 50-75 68
(Orange label. Rigid vinyl.)
RCA (LSP-2075e "Elvis' Golden Records, Vol. 2") 30-40 71
(Orange label. Flexible vinyl.)
RCA (LSP-2075e "Elvis' Golden Records, Vol. 2") 40-50 76
(Tan label.)
RCA (LSP-2075e "Elvis' Golden Records, Vol. 2") 10-20 76
(Black label, dog near top.)
RCA (AFL1-2075e "Elvis' Golden Records, Vol. 2") 10-20 77
Note: May also be shown as *50,000,000 Elvis Presley Fans Can't Be Wrong.* Digitally remastered in 1984 on RCA 5197.
RCA (2227 "Great Performances") 30-40 90
RCA (LPM-2231 "Elvis Is Back") 300-400 60
(Monaural. Black label, "Long Play" at bottom. No song titles printed on cover. Does not have yellow sticker on cover showing song titles, nor are contents printed on cover.)
RCA (LPM-2231 "Elvis Is Back") 250-300 60
(Monaural. Black label, "Long Play" at bottom. No song titles printed on cover. Has yellow sticker, listing titles, on cover.)
RCA (LPM-2231 "Elvis Is Back") 200-250 63
(Black label, "Mono" at bottom. Cover has selection number on left.)
RCA (LPM-2231 "Elvis Is Back") 75-100 64
(Black label, "Monaural" at bottom. Cover has selection number on left.)
RCA (LSP-2231 "Elvis Is Back") 500-600 60
(Stereo. Black label, "Living Stereo" at bottom. Front and back cover slicks are transposed. No song titles printed on cover. May or may not have yellow sticker on cover showing song titles.)
RCA (LSP-2231 "Elvis Is Back") 300-400 60
(Stereo. Black label, "Living Stereo" at bottom. Front and back cover slicks are correctly applied. No song titles printed on cover. May or may not have yellow sticker on cover showing song titles.)
RCA (LSP-2231 "Elvis Is Back") 50-100 64
(Black label, RCA logo is white, other label print is silver.)
RCA (LSP-2231 "Elvis Is Back") 50-75 68
(Orange label. Rigid vinyl.)
RCA (LSP-2231 "Elvis Is Back") 30-40 71
(Orange label. Flexible vinyl.)
RCA (LSP-2231 "Elvis Is Back") 40-50 76
(Tan label.)
RCA (LSP-2231 "Elvis Is Back") 10-20 76
(Black label, dog near top.)
RCA (AFL1-2231 "Elvis Is Back") 10-20 77
RCA (LPM-2256 "G.I. Blues") 80-100 60
(Monaural. Black label, "Long Play" at bottom. Add $15 to $25 if accompanied by "Elvis Is Back" inner sleeve. Add $400 to $500 if cover has a heart-shaped announcement for *Wooden Heart.)*
RCA (LPM-2256 "G.I. Blues") 200-250 63
(Black label, "Mono" at bottom.)
RCA (LPM-2256 "G.I. Blues") 75-100 64
(Black label, "Monaural" at bottom.)
RCA (LSP-2256 "G.I. Blues") 100-125 60
(Stereo. Black label, "Living Stereo" at bottom. Add $15 to $25 if accompanied by "Elvis Is Back" inner sleeve. Add $400 to $500 if cover has a heart-shaped announcement for *Wooden Heart.)*
RCA (LSP-2256 "G.I. Blues") 650-750 63
(Stereo. Black label. Has "Stereo" at bottom. All print on label – including RCA logo – is silver.)
RCA (LSP-2256 "G.I. Blues") 50-100 64
(Black label, RCA logo is white, other label print is silver.)
RCA (LSP-2256 "G.I. Blues") 50-75 68
(Orange label. Rigid vinyl.)
RCA (LSP-2256 "G.I. Blues") 30-40 71
(Orange label. Flexible vinyl.)
RCA (LSP-2256 "G.I. Blues") 40-50 76
(Tan label.)
RCA (LSP-2256 "G.I. Blues") 10-20 76
(Black label, dog near top.)
RCA (AFL1-2256 "G.I. Blues") 10-20 77
(Reissued in 1980 as RCA AYL1-3735.)
Note: For *G.I. Blues* picture disc, see *Loving You* (RCA LPM-1515).
RCA (APL1-2274 "Welcome to My World") 15-20 77
RCA (AFL1-2274 "Welcome to My World") 10-15 77
RCA (AQL1-2274 "Welcome to My World") 20-25 79
RCA (LPM-2328 "His Hand in Mine") ... 150-200 60
(Monaural. Black label, "Long Play" at bottom.)
RCA (LPM-2328 "His Hand in Mine") ... 150-200 63
(Black label, "Mono" at bottom.)
RCA (LPM-2328 "His Hand in Mine") 75-100 64
(Black label, "Monaural" at bottom.)
RCA (LSP-2328 "His Hand in Mine") 250-300 60
(Stereo. Black label, "Living Stereo" at bottom.)
RCA (LSP-2328 "His Hand in Mine") 650-750 63
(Stereo. Black label. Has "Stereo" at bottom. All print on label – including RCA logo – is silver.)
RCA (LSP-2328 "His Hand in Mine") 50-100 64
(Black label, RCA logo is white, other label print is silver.)
RCA (LSP-2328 "His Hand in Mine") 50-75 68
(Orange label. Rigid vinyl.)
RCA (LSP-2328 "His Hand in Mine") 10-20 76
(Orange label. Flexible vinyl.)
RCA (LSP-2328 "His Hand in Mine") 40-50 76
(Tan label.)
Note: Repackaged in 1976 as RCA ANL1-1319 and in 1981 as RCA AYM1-3935.
RCA (2347 "Elvis-Greatest Hits, Vol. One") 15-25 81
(Has embossed letters on front cover.)
RCA (2347 "Elvis-Greatest Hits, Vol. One") 10-15 83
(Standard flat cover print – not embossed.)
RCA (LPM-2370 "Something for Everybody") 150-200 61
(Monaural. Black label, "Long Play" at bottom. Back cover promotes Compact 33s.)
RCA (LPM-2370 "Something for Everybody") 200-250 63
(Black label, "Mono" at bottom.)
RCA (LPM-2370 "Something for Everybody") 75-100 64
(Black label, "Monaural" at bottom.)
RCA (LSP-2370 "Something for Everybody") 250-300 61
(Stereo. Black label, "Living Stereo" at bottom. Back cover promotes Compact 33s.)
RCA (LSP-2370 "Something for Everybody") 650-750 63
(Stereo. Black label. Has "Stereo" at bottom. All print on label – including RCA logo – is silver.)
RCA (LSP-2370 "Something for Everybody") 75-100 64
(Black label, RCA logo is white, other label print is silver.)
RCA (LSP-2370 "Something for Everybody") 50-75 68
(Orange label. Rigid vinyl.)
RCA (LSP-2370 "Something for Everybody") 30-40 71
(Orange label. Flexible vinyl.)
RCA (LSP-2370 "Something for Everybody") 40-50 76
(Tan label.)
RCA (LSP-2370 "Something for Everybody") 10-20 76
(Black label, dog near top.)
RCA (AFL1-2370 "Something for Everybody") 10-20 77
Note: Reissued in 1981 as RCA AYM1-4116.
RCA (LPM-2426 "Blue Hawaii") 125-175 61
(Monaural. Black label, "Long Play" at bottom. Has red sticker announcing the inclusion of *Rock-A-Hula Baby* and *Can't Help Falling in Love.* Sticker is permanently affixed to cover.)
RCA (LPM-2426 "Blue Hawaii") 75-100 63
(Monaural. Black label, "Long Play" at bottom. Does not have red sticker announcing the inclusion of *Rock-A-Hula Baby* and *Can't Help Falling in Love.)*
RCA (LPM-2426 "Blue Hawaii") 100-150 63
(Black label, "Mono" at bottom.)
RCA (LPM-2426 "Blue Hawaii") 70-80 64
(Black label, "Monaural" at bottom.)
RCA (LSP-2426 "Blue Hawaii") 150-200 61
(Stereo. Black label, "Living Stereo" at bottom. Has red sticker announcing the inclusion of *Rock-A-Hula Baby* and *Can't Help Falling in Love.* Sticker is permanently affixed to cover)
RCA (LSP-2426 "Blue Hawaii") 75-100 63
(Stereo. Black label, "Living Stereo" at bottom. Does not have red sticker announcing the inclusion of *Rock-A-Hula Baby* and *Can't Help Falling in Love.)*
RCA (LSP-2426 "Blue Hawaii") 650-750 63
(Stereo. Black label. Has "Stereo" at bottom. All print on label – including RCA logo – is silver.)
RCA (LSP-2426 "Blue Hawaii") 50-75 64
(Black label, RCA logo is white, other label print is silver.)
RCA (LSP-2426 "Blue Hawaii") 50-60 68
(Orange label. Rigid vinyl.)
RCA (LSP-2426 "Blue Hawaii") 25-30 71
(Orange label. Flexible vinyl.)
RCA (LSP-2426 "Blue Hawaii") 30-40 76
(Tan label.)
RCA (LSP-2426 "Blue Hawaii") 10-20 76
(Black label, dog near top.)
RCA (LSP-2426 "Blue Hawaii") 800-1000 77
(Blue vinyl. Experimental pressing only.)
RCA (AFL1-2426 "Blue Hawaii") 10-20 77
Note: Reissued in 1981 as RCA AYL1-3683.
RCA (AFL1-2428 "Moody Blue") 800-1200 77
(Colored vinyl – any color *other than blue or black.* Includes, but not limited to: white, red, green, yellow, gold, as well as combinations of colors. Experimental production discs for RCA in-house use only.)
RCA (AFL1-2428 "Moody Blue") 15-25 77
(Blue vinyl.)
RCA (AFL1-2428 "Moody Blue") 200-250 77
(Black vinyl. Reportedly 25,000 made.)
RCA (AQL1-2428 "Moody Blue") 15-25 79
RCA (LPM-2523 "Pot Luck") 100-150 62
(Monaural. Black label, "Long Play" at bottom.)
RCA (LPM-2523 "Pot Luck") 75-100 64
(Black label, "Monaural" at bottom.)
RCA (LSP-2523 "Pot Luck") 150-200 62
(Stereo. Black label, "Living Stereo" at bottom.)
RCA (LSP-2523 "Pot Luck") 650-750 63
(Stereo. Black label. Has "Stereo" at bottom. All print on label – including RCA logo – is silver.)
RCA (LSP-2523 "Pot Luck") 75-100 64
(Black label, RCA logo is white, other label print is silver.)
RCA (LSP-2523 "Pot Luck") 50-75 68
(Orange label. Rigid vinyl.)
RCA (LSP-2523 "Pot Luck") 30-40 71
(Orange label. Flexible vinyl.)
RCA (LSP-2523 "Pot Luck") 40-50 76
(Tan label.)
RCA (LSP-2523 "Pot Luck") 10-20 76
(Black label, dog near top.)
RCA (AFL1-2523 "Pot Luck") 10-20 77
RCA (APL1-2558 "Harum Scarum") 10-20 77
(First issued as RCA LPM/LSP-3468. Reissued in 1980 as RCA AYL1-3734.)
RCA (APL1-2559 "Frankie & Johnny") . 400-500 77
(Cover slicks only – discs never made. First issued as RCA LPM/LSP-3553.)
RCA (APL1-2560 "Spinout") 10-20 77
(First issued as RCA LPM/LSP-3702. Reissued in 1980 as RCA AYL1-3684.)
RCA (APL1-2564 "Double Trouble") 10-20 77
(First issued as RCA LPM/LSP-3787.)
RCA (APL1-2565 "Clambake") 10-20 77
(First issued as RCA LPM/LSP-3893.)
RCA (APL1-2568 "It Happened at the World's Fair") 10-20 77
(First issued as RCA LPM/LSP-2697.)
RCA (APL2-2587 "Elvis in Concert") 15-25 77
RCA (APL2-2587 "Elvis in Concert") 3500-4000 77
(Blue vinyl. Experimental pressing only.)
RCA (CPL2-2587 "Elvis in Concert") 50-100 82
RCA (LPM-2621 "Girls! Girls! Girls!") ... 100-150 62
(Monaural. Black label, "Long Play" at bottom. Add $150 to $200 if accompanied by 11" x 11" 1963 calendar.)
RCA (LPM-2621 "Girls! Girls! Girls!") ... 150-200 63
(Black label, "Mono" at bottom.)
RCA (LPM-2621 "Girls! Girls! Girls!") 75-100 64
(Black label, "Monaural" at bottom.)
RCA (LSP-2621 "Girls! Girls! Girls!") ... 100-150 62
(Stereo. Black label, "Living Stereo" at bottom. Add $150 to $200 if accompanied by 11" x 11" 1963 calendar.)
RCA (LSP-2621 "Girls! Girls! Girls!") 50-100 64
(Black label, RCA logo is white, other label print is silver.)
RCA (LSP-2621 "Girls! Girls! Girls!") 50-75 68
(Orange label. Rigid vinyl.)
RCA (LSP-2621 "Girls! Girls! Girls!") 30-40 71
(Orange label. Flexible vinyl.)
RCA (LSP-2621 "Girls! Girls! Girls!") 40-50 76
(Tan label.)
RCA (LSP-2621 "Girls! Girls! Girls!") 10-20 76
(Black label, dog near top. Add $400 to $450 if with green cover sticker reading "Contains the Hit! Return to Sender.")
RCA (AFL1-2621 "Girls! Girls! Girls!") 10-20 77
RCA (CPD2-2642 "Aloha from Hawaii") ... 30-40 75
(Orange label.)
RCA (CPD2-2642 "Aloha from Hawaii") ... 20-30 77
(Black label. Add $50 to $75 if with cover sticker reading "Memories of Elvis.")
Note: First issued as RCA VPSX-6089.
RCA (LPM-2697 "It Happened at the World's Fair") 100-150 63
(Monaural. Black label, "Long Play" at bottom. Add $200 to $250 if accompanied by 8" x 10" bonus color photo.)
RCA (LSP-2697 "It Happened at the World's Fair") 100-150 63
(Stereo. Black label, "Living Stereo" at bottom. Add $200 to $250 if accompanied by an 8" x 10" bonus color photo.)
RCA (LPM/LSP-2697 "It Happened at the World's Fair") 300-400 63
(Souvenir envelope only. Reads "It Happened at the World's Fair Souvenir Package Complements of Elvis and the Colonel.")
RCA (LSP-2697 "It Happened at the World's

Fair")... 50-100 64
(Black label, RCA logo is white, other label print is silver. Reissued in 1977 as RCA APL1-2568.)

RCA (LPM-2756 "Fun in Acapulco")... 100-150 63
(Monaural. Black label, "Mono" at bottom.)

RCA (LPM-2756 "Fun in Acapulco")... 70-80 64
(Black label, "Monaural" at bottom.)

RCA (LSP-2756 "Fun in Acapulco")... 100-150 63
(Stereo. Black label, all print on label is silver.)

RCA (LSP-2756 "Fun in Acapulco")... 70-80 64
(Black label, RCA logo is white, other label print is silver.)

RCA (LSP-2756 "Fun in Acapulco")... 50-75 68
(Orange label. Rigid vinyl.)

RCA (LSP-2756 "Fun in Acapulco")... 50-75 76
(Tan label.)

RCA (LSP-2756 "Fun in Acapulco")... 10-20 76
(Black label, dog near top.)

RCA (AFL1-2756 "Fun in Acapulco")... 10-20 77

RCA (LPM-2765 "Elvis' Golden Records, Vol. 3")... 100-150 63
(Monaural. Black label, "Mono" at bottom.)

RCA (LPM-2765 "Elvis' Golden Records, Vol. 3")... 75-100 64
(Black label, "Monaural" at bottom.)

RCA (LSP-2765 "Elvis' Golden Records, Vol. 3")... 100-150 63
(Stereo. Black label, all print on label is silver.)

RCA (LSP-2765 "Elvis' Golden Records, Vol. 3")... 50-75 64
(Black label, RCA logo is white, other label print is silver.)

RCA (LSP-2765 "Elvis' Golden Records, Vol. 3")... 50-75 68
(Orange label. Rigid vinyl.)

RCA (LSP-2765 "Elvis' Golden Records, Vol. 3")... 40-50 76
(Tan label.)

RCA (LSP-2765 "Elvis' Golden Records, Vol. 3")... 10-20 76
(Black label, dog near top.)

RCA (AFL1-2765 "Elvis' Golden Records, Vol. 3")... 10-20 77

RCA (AFL1-2772 "He Walks Beside Me")... 15-25 77

RCA (LPM-2894 "Kissin' Cousins")... 100-150 64
(Black label, "Mono" at bottom. Pictures film cast in lower right corner photo on cover.)

RCA (LPM-2894 "Kissin' Cousins")... 200-250 64
(Monaural. Black label, "Mono" at bottom. *Does not* picture film cast in lower right corner photo on cover.)

RCA (LPM-2894 "Kissin' Cousins").. 1600-1800 64
(Black label, "Mono Dynagroove" at bottom.)

RCA (LPM-2894 "Kissin' Cousins")... 75-100 64
(Black label, "Monaural" at bottom.)

RCA (LSP-2894 "Kissin' Cousins")... 100-150 64
(Black label, all print on label is silver. Pictures film cast in lower right corner photo on cover.)

RCA (LSP-2894 "Kissin' Cousins")... 200-250 64
(Stereo. Black label, all print on label is silver. *Does not* picture film cast in lower right corner photo on cover.)

RCA (LPM/LSP-2894 "Kissin' Cousins")... 300-400 64
(Souvenir envelope only. Reads "Souvenir Package Complements of Elvis and the Colonel.")

RCA (LSP-2894 "Kissin' Cousins")... 50-100 64
(Black label, RCA logo is white, other label print is silver.)

RCA (LSP-2894 "Kissin' Cousins")... 50-75 68
(Orange label. Rigid vinyl.)

RCA (LSP-2894 "Kissin' Cousins")... 30-40 71
(Orange label. Flexible vinyl.)

RCA (LSP-2894 "Kissin' Cousins")... 75-125 76
(Tan label.)

RCA (LSP-2894 "Kissin' Cousins")... 10-20 77
(Black label, dog near top.)

RCA (LSP-2894 "Kissin' Cousins").. 1000-1500 77
(Blue vinyl. Experimental pressing only.)

RCA (AFL1-2894 "Kissin' Cousins")... 10-20 77

Note: Reissued in 1981 as RCA AYM1-4115.

RCA (CPL1-2901 "Elvis Sings for Children")... 10-20 78
(Includes "Special Memories" greeting card.)

RCA (CPL1-2901 "Elvis Sings for Children")... 10-20 78
(Gatefold with "Special Memories" greeting card printed on cover.)

RCA (CPL1-2901 "Elvis Sings for Children")... 40-50 78
(Single pocket jacket with "Special Memories" greeting card printed on cover.)

RCA (LPM-2999 "Roustabout")... 300-350 64
(Monaural. Black label, "Mono" at bottom.)

RCA (LPM-2999 "Roustabout")... 75-100 65
(Black label, "Monaural" at bottom.)

RCA (LSP-2999 "Roustabout")... 650-750 64
(Stereo. Black label. All print on label – including RCA logo – is silver.)

RCA (LSP-2999 "Roustabout")... 50-100 64
(Black label, RCA logo is white, other label print is silver.)

RCA (LSP-2999 "Roustabout")... 50-75 68
(Orange label. Rigid vinyl.)

RCA (LSP-2999 "Roustabout")... 30-40 71
(Orange label. Flexible vinyl.)

RCA (LSP-2999 "Roustabout")... 75-125 76
(Tan label.)

RCA (LSP-2999 "Roustabout")... 10-20 77
(Black label. Dog near top.)

RCA (AFL1-2999 "Roustabout")... 10-20 77

RCA (3078 "Legendary Performer, Vol. 3")... 20-25 78
(Picture disc. Add $3 to $5 if accompanied by *Yesterdays* booklet. Has picture art pressed on blue vinyl.)

RCA (3078 "Legendary Performer, Vol. 3")... 30-40 78
(Picture disc. Add $3 to $5 if accompanied by *Yesterdays* booklet. Has picture art pressed on black vinyl. Also issued on standard black vinyl as CPL1-3082.)

RCA (3082 "Legendary Performer, Vol. 3")... 10-15 78
(Add $3 to $5 if accompanied by *Yesterdays* booklet. Also issued on a picture disc, as RCA 3078.)

RCA (3082 "Legendary Performer, Vol. 3")... 75-100 86
(Does not have die-cut cover.)

RCA (3279 "Our Memories of Elvis")... 20-25 79
(Add $60 to $80 if with "Featuring the Hit Single: Are You Sincere" shrink sticker. Add $90 to $100 if with "Contains the Hit Single: Are You Sincere" shrink sticker.)

RCA (LPM-3338 "Girl Happy")... 75-100 65
(Monaural.)

RCA (LSP-3338 "Girl Happy")... 75-100 65
(Stereo. Black label.)

Note: Though not packaged with the LP, a 16" x 20" June Kelly print was given by some record stores with the purchase of this LP. Add $75 to $100 for this print.

RCA (LSP-3338 "Girl Happy")... 50-75 68
(Orange label. Rigid vinyl.)

RCA (LSP-3338 "Girl Happy")... 30-40 71
(Orange label. Flexible vinyl.)

RCA (LSP-3338 "Girl Happy")... 50-75 76
(Tan label.)

RCA (LSP-3338 "Girl Happy")... 10-20 76
(Black label, dog near top.)

RCA (AFL1-3338 "Girl Happy")... 10-20 77

RCA (3448 "Our Memories of Elvis, Vol. 2")... 15-25 79
(Add $90 to $100 if with "There's a Honky Tonk Angel" shrink sticker. A sampling of these tracks is on RCA 3455, *Pure Elvis*.)

RCA (LPM-3450 "Elvis for Everyone")... 75-100 65
(Monaural.)

RCA (LSP-3450 "Elvis for Everyone")... 75-100 65
(Stereo. Black label.)

RCA (LSP-3450 "Elvis for Everyone")... 50-75 68
(Orange label. Rigid vinyl.)

RCA (LSP-3450 "Elvis for Everyone")... 30-40 71
(Orange label. Flexible vinyl.)

RCA (LSP-3450 "Elvis for Everyone")... 40-50 76
(Tan label.)

RCA (LSP-3450 "Elvis for Everyone")... 10-20 76
(Black label, dog near top.)

RCA (AFL1-3450 "Elvis for Everyone")... 10-20 77
(Reissued in 1982 as RCA AYL1-4232.)

RCA (3455 "Pure Elvis")... 600-800 79
(Cover reads "Pure Elvis," but label shows "Our Memories of Elvis - Vol. 2." Promotional issue only.)

RCA (LPM-3468 "Harum Scarum")... 50-75 65
(Monaural. Add $50 to $75 if accompanied by bonus 12" x 12" photo, and $20 to $25 if with sticker announcing the bonus photo.)

RCA (LSP-3468 "Harum Scarum")... 45-65 65
(Stereo. Add $50 to $75 if accompanied by bonus 12" x 12" photo, and $20 to $25 if with sticker announcing the bonus photo.)

Note: Reissued in 1977 as APL1-2558 and in 1980 as AYL1-3734.

RCA (LPM-3553 "Frankie & Johnny")... 50-75 66
(Monaural. Add $50 to $75 if accompanied by bonus 12" x 12" photo, and $20 to $25 if with sticker announcing the bonus photo.)

RCA (LSP-3553 "Frankie & Johnny")... 45-65 66
(Stereo. Add $50 to $75 if accompanied by bonus 12" x 12" photo, and $20 to $25 if with sticker announcing the bonus photo.)

Note: Reissued in 1977 as RCA APL1-2559. A repackage appeared in 1976 as Pickwick 7007.

RCA (LPM-3643 "Paradise Hawaiian Style")... 50-75 66
(Monaural.)

RCA (LSP-3643 "Paradise Hawaiian Style")... 50-75 66
(Stereo. Black label. Rigid vinyl.)

RCA (LSP-3643 "Paradise Hawaiian Style")... 75-85 66
(Stereo. Black label. Flexible vinyl, similar to '70s Dynaflex issues.)

RCA (LSP-3643 "Paradise Hawaiian Style")... 50-75 68
(Orange label. Rigid vinyl.)

RCA (LSP-3643 "Paradise Hawaiian Style")... 30-40 71
(Orange label. Flexible vinyl.)

RCA (LSP-3643 "Paradise Hawaiian Style")... 50-75 76
(Tan label.)

RCA (LSP-3643 "Paradise Hawaiian Style")... 10-20 76
(Black label, dog near top.)

RCA (AFL1-3643 "Paradise Hawaiian Style")... 10-20 77

RCA (AYL1-3683 "Blue Hawaii")... 10-15 80
(First issued as RCA LPM/LSP-2426.)

RCA (AYL1-3684 "Spinout")... 10-15 80
(First issued as RCA LPM/LSP-3702, reissued in 1977 as RCA APL1-2560.)

RCA (CPL8-3699 "Elvis Aron Presley").. 80-100 80
(Boxed, eight-disc set. Add $10 to $15 if accompanied by 20-page booklet, and $3 to $5 if with "25th Anniversary" shrink sticker.)

RCA (CPL8-3699 "Elvis Aron Presley")... 250-275 80
(REVIEWER SERIES edition. Silver sticker on back also identifies the Reviewer Series copy as "NS-3699." Add $10 to $15 if accompanied by 20-page booklet, and $3 to $5 if with "25th Anniversary" shrink sticker.)

RCA (CPK8-3699 "Elvis Aron Presley") . 80-100 80
(Boxed, four-cassette tape set. Add $10 to $15 if accompanied by 20-page booklet, and $3 to $5 if with "25th Anniversary" shrink sticker. Add $20 to $30 if accompanied by eight 12" x 12" Elvis photos.)

RCA (CPS8-3699 "Elvis Aron Presley") . 90-125 80
(Boxed, four 8-track tape set. Add $10 to $15 if accompanied by 20-page booklet, and $3 to $5 if with "25th Anniversary" shrink sticker. Add $20 to $30 if accompanied by eight 12" x 12" Elvis photos.)

Note: *Excerpts* of songs in this set appear on RCA 3729. *Selections* from this LP are on RCA 3781.

RCA (LPM-3702 "Spinout")... 50-75 66
(Monaural. Add $40 to $60 if accompanied by bonus 12" x 12" photo.)

RCA (LSP-3702 "Spinout")... 50-75 66
(Stereo. Add $40 to $60 if accompanied by bonus 12" x 12" photo.)

Note: Reissued in 1977 as APL1-2560.

RCA (3729 "Elvis Aron Presley Excerpts")... 100-125 80
(Has 37 excerpts from RCA 3699. Promotional issue only.)

RCA (AYL1-3732 "Pure Gold")... 10-20 80
(First issued as RCA ANL1-0971.)

RCA (AYL1-3733 "King Creole")... 10-20 80
(First issued as RCA LSP-1884.)

RCA (AYL1-3734 "Harum Scarum")... 10-20 80
(First issued as RCA LPM/LSP-3468.)

RCA (AYL1-3735 "G.I. Blues")... 10-20 80
(First issued as RCA LPM/LSP-2256.)

RCA (LPM-3758 "How Great Thou Art") .. 70-80 67
(Mono Dynagroove. Add $40 to $50 if with "Grammy Award Winner" cover sticker.)

RCA (LSP-3758 "How Great Thou Art")... 70-80 67
(Stereo Dynagroove. Black label. Add $40 to $50 if with "Grammy Award Winner" cover sticker.)

RCA (LSP-3758 "How Great Thou Art"). 50-100 68
(Orange label. Rigid vinyl.)

RCA (LSP-3758 "How Great Thou Art")... 30-40 71
(Orange label. Flexible vinyl.)

RCA (LSP-3758 "How Great Thou Art")... 40-50 76
(Tan label.)

RCA (LSP-3758 "How Great Thou Art")... 10-20 76
(Black label, dog near top.)

RCA (AFL1-3758 "How Great Thou Art"). 10-20 77

RCA (3781 "Elvis Aron Presley Selections")... 100-125 80
(Has 12 selections from RCA 3699. Promotional issue only.)

RCA (LPM-3787 "Double Trouble")... 40-60 67
(Monaural. Front cover reads "Special Bonus Full Color Photo." Add $40 to $50 if accompanied by bonus 7" x 9" photo.)

RCA (LPM-3787 "Double Trouble")... 50-75 68
("Special Bonus Full Color Photo" is replaced by "Trouble Double.")

RCA (LSP-3787 "Double Trouble")... 45-65 67
(Stereo. Front cover reads "Special Bonus Full Color Photo." Add $40 to $50 if accompanied by bonus 7" x 9" photo. Black label.)

RCA (LSP-3787 "Double Trouble")... 50-75 68
("Special Bonus Full Color Photo" is replaced by "Trouble Double.")

RCA (LSP-3787 "Double Trouble")... 35-40 68
(Orange label.)

RCA (LSP-3787 "Double Trouble")... 150-200 76
(Tan label.)

Note: Reissued in 1977 as RCA APL1-2564.

RCA (AYL1-3892 "Elvis in Person")... 8-10 81
(First issued as RCA LSP-4428.)

RCA (LPM-3893 "Clambake")... 200-250 67
(Monaural. Add $40 to $50 if accompanied by bonus 12" x 12" photo.)

RCA (LSP-3893 "Clambake")... 40-60 67
(Stereo. Add $40 to $50 if accompanied by bonus 12" x 12" photo.)

Note: Reissued in 1977 as RCA APL1-2565.

RCA (AYM1-3893 "Sun Sessions")... 5-10 81
(First issued as RCA APM1-1675.)

RCA (AYM1-3894 "Elvis TV Special")... 5-10 81
(First issued RCA LPM-4088.)

RCA (3917 "Guitar Man")... 25-35 81
(Includes a "This Is Elvis" flyer. Producer Felton Jarvis talks about Elvis as well as the making of this LP on RCA 1981.)

RCA (LPM-3921 "Elvis' Gold Records, Vol. 4")... 1500-2000 68
(Monaural.)

RCA (LSP-3921 "Elvis' Gold Records, Vol. 4")... 30-50 68
(Stereo. Black label.)

RCA (LSP-3921 "Elvis' Gold Records, Vol. 4")... 30-40 68
(Orange label. Rigid vinyl.)

RCA (LSP-3921 "Elvis' Gold Records, Vol. 4")... 20-30 71
(Orange label. Flexible vinyl.)

RCA (LSP-3921 "Elvis' Gold Records, Vol. 4")... 20-30 76
(Tan label.)

RCA (LSP-3921 "Elvis' Gold Records, Vol. 4")... 10-18 76
(Black label, dog near top.)

RCA (AFL1-3921 "Elvis' Gold Records, Vol. 4")... 8-15 77

RCA (AYM1-3935 "His Hand in Mine")... 5-10 81
(First issued as RCA LPM/LSP-2328.)

RCA (AYL1-3956 "That's The Way It Is")... 5-10 81
(First issued as RCA LSP-4460.)

RCA (LPM-3989 "Speedway")... 1500-2000 68
(Monaural. Add $25 to $50 if accompanied by bonus 8" x 10" photo, and $20 to $25 if with shrink sticker announcing bonus photo.)

RCA (LSP-3989 "Speedway")... 40-60 68
(Stereo. Black label. Add $25 to $50 if accompanied by bonus 8" x 10" photo, and $20 to $25 if with shrink sticker announcing bonus photo.)

RCA (LSP-3989 "Speedway")... 35-40 68
(Orange label. Rigid vinyl.)

RCA (LSP-3989 "Speedway")... 15-25 71
(Orange label. Rigid vinyl.)

RCA (LSP-3989 "Speedway")... 10-20 76
(Tan label.)

RCA (LSP-3989 "Speedway")... 10-28 76
(Black label, dog near top.)

RCA (AFL1-3989 "Speedway")... 8-15 77

RCA (4031 "This Is Elvis")........................ 15-25 80
(Add $10 to $15 if with "Contains Previously Unreleased Material" shrink sticker.)
RCA (LPM-4088 "Elvis TV Special")........ 40-50 68
(Orange label. Rigid disc.)
RCA (LPM-4088 "Elvis TV Special")........ 25-35 71
(Orange label. Flexible disc.)
RCA (LPM-4088 "Elvis TV Special")........ 15-25 76
(Tan label. Add $40 to $50 if with "Memories of Elvis" TV show shrink sticker.)
RCA (LPM-4088 "Elvis TV Special")........ 12-22 76
(Black label. Add $40 to $50 if with "Memories of Elvis" TV show shrink sticker.)
RCA (AFM1-4088 "Elvis TV Special").........8-15 77
Note: Reissued in 1981 as RCA AYM1-3894. Repackaged for HBO as RCA 0704.
RCA (AYL1-4114 "That's The Way It Is") ...5-10 81
(First issued as RCA LSP-4445.)
RCA (AYM1-4115 "Kissin' Cousins").........5-10 81
(First issued as RCA LPM/LSP-2894.)
RCA (AYM1-4116 "Something for Everybody")..5-10 81
(First issued as RCA LPM/LSP-2370.)
RCA (LSP-4155 "From Elvis in Memphis").. 40-50 69
(Orange label. Rigid disc. Add $30 to $40 if accompanied by 8" x 10" Elvis photo, and $5 to $10 if with shrink sticker announcing photo.)
RCA (LSP-4155 "From Elvis in Memphis").. 30-45 72
(Orange label. Flexible disc.)
RCA (LSP-4155 "From Elvis in Memphis").. 25-30 69
(Tan label.)
RCA (LSP-4155 "From Elvis in Memphis").. 10-18 69
(Black label.)
RCA (AFL1-4155 "From Elvis in Memphis")..8-15 77
Note: A half-speed mastered issue of this LP was released in 1982 as MFSL 059.
RCA (AYL1-4232 "Elvis for Everyone") 5-10 82
(First issued as RCA LPM/LSP-3450.)
RCA (LSP-4362 "On Stage").................... 35-45 70
(Orange label. Rigid disc.)
RCA (LSP-4362 "On Stage").................... 20-30 72
(Orange label. Flexible disc.)
RCA (LSP-4362 "On Stage").................... 25-35 76
(Tan label.)
RCA (LSP-4362 "On Stage").................... 25-35 76
(Black label.)
RCA (AFL1-4362 "On Stage")................. 10-12 77
RCA (AQL1-4362 "On Stage")....................5-10 83
RCA (4395 "Memories of Christmas") 10-15 82
(Add $5 to $8 if accompanied by 7" x 9" greeting card with Elvis' photo, and $3 to $5 if with shrink sticker announcing bonus card.
RCA (LSP-4428 "Elvis in Person").......... 45-55 70
(Orange label. Rigid vinyl.)
RCA (LSP-4428 "Elvis in Person").......... 40-50 71
(Orange label. Flexible vinyl.)
RCA (LSP-4428 "Elvis in Person").......... 20-25 76
(Tan label.)
RCA (LSP-4428 "Elvis in Person").......... 10-18 76
(Black label.)
RCA (AFL1-4428 "Elvis in Person")...........8-15 77
Note: First released as half of RCA LSP-6020, then reissued in 1981 as RCA AYL1-3892.
RCA (LSP-4429 "Elvis Back in Memphis").. 30-40 70
(Orange label. Rigid vinyl.)
RCA (LSP-4429 "Elvis Back in Memphis").. 25-35 71
(Orange label. Flexible vinyl.)
RCA (LSP-4429 "Elvis Back in Memphis").. 20-25 76
(Tan label.)
RCA (LSP-4429 "Elvis Back in Memphis").. 10-18 76
(Black label.)
RCA (AFL1-4429 "Elvis Back in Memphis")..8-12 77
Note: First issued as half of RCA LSP-6020.
RCA (LSP-4445 "That's the Way It Is").. 50-100 70
(Orange label. Rigid vinyl.)
RCA (LSP-4445 "That's the Way It Is").... 15-25 71
(Orange label. Flexible vinyl.)
RCA (LSP-4445 "That's the Way It Is").... 15-25 76
(Tan label.)
RCA (LSP-4445 "That's the Way It Is").....10-18 77
(Black label.)
RCA (AFL1-4445 "That's the Way It Is").....8-10 77
Note: Reissued in 1981 as RCA AYL1-4114.
RCA (LSP-4460 "Elvis Country") 30-40 71
(Orange label. Rigid vinyl. Add $10 to $15 if accompanied by 7" x 9" Elvis photo, and $15 to $20 if with shrink sticker announcing bonus photo.)
RCA (LSP-4460 "Elvis Country") 15-25 71
(Orange label. Flexible vinyl. Add $10 to $15 if accompanied by 7" x 9" Elvis photo, and $15 to $20 if with shrink sticker announcing bonus photo.)
RCA (LSP-4460 "Elvis Country") 20-30 76
(Tan label. Black vinyl.)
RCA (LSP-4460 "Elvis Country") 1000-2000 77
(Tan label. Green vinyl. Experimental pressing only.)
RCA (LSP-4460 "Elvis Country") 10-20 76
(Black label.)
RCA (AFL1-4460 "Elvis Country") 8-12 77
Note: Reissued in 1981 as RCA AYL1-3956.
RCA (LSP-4530 "Love Letters")................35-45 71
(Orange label. Full title, *Love Letters From Elvis*, on TWO lines on front cover.)
RCA (LSP-4530 "Love Letters")................20-35 71
(Orange label. Full title, *Love Letters From Elvis*, on THREE lines on front cover.)
RCA (LSP-4530 "Love Letters")................25-35 76
(Tan label.)
RCA (LSP-4530 "Love Letters")................20-30 76
(Black label.)
RCA (AFL1-4530 "Love Letters")..............15-25 77
Note: Reissued in 1981 as RCA AYL1-3956.
RCA (AHL1-4530 "Elvis Medley")............10-15 82
RCA (LSP-4579 "Wonderful World of Christmas")...20-30 71
(Orange label. Add $20 to $25 if accompanied by a 5" x 7" Elvis postcard, and $15 to $20 if with shrink sticker announcing bonus photo. Reissued in 1977 as RCA ANL1-1936.)
RCA (LSP-4671 "Elvis Now")..................80-100 72
(Has white titles/times sticker on front cover. Promotional issue only.)
RCA (LSP-4671 "Elvis Now")....................25-35 72
(Orange label.)
RCA (LSP-4671 "Elvis Now")....................20-30 76
(Tan label.)
RCA (LSP-4671 "Elvis Now")....................10-18 76
(Black label.)
RCA (AFL1-4671 "Elvis Now")....................8-15 77
RCA (LSP-4690 "He Touched Me")........80-100 72
(Has white titles/times sticker on front cover. Promotional issue only.)
RCA (LSP-4690 "He Touched Me")..........30-40 72
(Orange label.)
RCA (LSP-4690 "He Touched Me")..........10-20 76
(Tan label.)
RCA (LSP-4690 "He Touched Me")..........10-18 76
(Black label.)
RCA (AFL1-4690 "He Touched Me")..........8-15 77
RCA (4678 "I Was the One")......................8-10 83
RCA (LSP-4776 " Elvis As Recorded at Madison Square Garden")................................80-100 72
(Orange label. Has white programming stickers applied to front cover. Promotional issue only. Counterfeit stickers exist but can be identified by the misspelling of the title *Love Me*, which reads: "Live Me."For double disc promotional issue, see RCA 571.)
RCA (LSP-4776 " Elvis As Recorded at Madison Square Garden") 20-30 72
(Orange label.)
RCA (LSP-4776 " Elvis As Recorded at Madison Square Garden") 10-20 76
(Tan label.)
RCA (LSP-4776 " Elvis As Recorded at Madison Square Garden") 10-18 76
(Black label.)
RCA (AQL1-4776 " Elvis As Recorded at Madison Square Garden") 8-10 77
RCA (4848 "Legendary Performer, Vol. 4") 25-35 83
(Embossed cover. Price includes a 12-page *Memories of the King* booklet.)
RCA (4848 "Legendary Performer, Vol. 4") 15-25 86
(Standard flat print – not embossed – on cover.)
RCA (4941 "Elvis' Gold Records, Vol. 5")...5-10 84
RCA (5172 "Golden Celebration") 75-100 84
(Boxed, six-disc set. Price includes custom inner sleeves and an envelope containing an 8" x 10" Elvis photo and a 50th Anniversary flyer.)
RCA (5172 "Golden Celebration") 25-35 84
(Special "Advance Cassette" boxed set sampler.)
RCA (5182 "Rocker")...................................20-25 84
RCA (5196 "Elvis' Golden Records")........15-20 84
(Digitally remastered, quality mono pressing. Price includes gold "The Definitive Rock Classic" banner. First issued as RCA LPM-1707.)
RCA (5197 "Elvis' Gold Records, Vol. 2") 15-20 84
(Digitally remastered, quality mono pressing. Price includes gold "The Definitive Rock Classic" banner. First issued as RCA LPM-2075.)
RCA (5198 "Elvis Presley").......................15-20 84
(Digitally remastered, quality mono pressing. Price includes gold "The Definitive Rock Classic" banner. First issued as RCA LPM-1254.)
RCA (5199 "Elvis") 15-20 84
(Digitally remastered, quality mono pressing. Price includes gold "The Definitive Rock Classic" banner. First issued as RCA LPM-1382.)
RCA (5353 "Valentine Gift for You").........18-22 85
(Red vinyl. Add $4 to $5 if with shrink sticker announcing red vinyl.)
RCA (5353 "Valentine Gift for You")...........5-10 85
(Black vinyl.)
RCA (5418 "Reconsider Baby")................18-22 85
(Blue vinyl. Add $4 to $5 if with shrink sticker announcing blue vinyl and "New Versions.")
RCA (5430 "Always on My Mind")............18-22 85
(Purple vinyl. Add $4 to $5 if with shrink sticker announcing purple vinyl and contents.)
RCA (5486 "Elvis' Christmas Album") 18-22 85
(Green vinyl. Add $4 to $5 if with shrink sticker announcing green vinyl.)
RCA (5486 "Elvis' Christmas Album") 12-20 85
(Black vinyl. Thus far, all black vinyl copies discovered are packaged with stickers reading "pressed on green vinyl.")
RCA (5600 "Return of the Rocker")..........10-20 86
RCA (5697 "Special Christmas Programming") 2000-3000 67
(Identification number shown since no selection number is used. Promotional issue only.)
RCA (LSP-6020 "From Memphis to Vegas") 100-150 69
(Orange label. Rigid vinyl. Incorrectly shows writers of *Words* as Tommy Boyce & Bobby Hart. Also shows writer of *Suspicious Minds* as Frances Zambon. Add $40 to $50 if accompanied by two 8" x 10" black and white Elvis photos.)
RCA (LSP-6020 "From Memphis to Vegas") 80-120 69
(Orange label. Rigid vinyl. Correctly shows writers of *Words* as Barry, Robin & Maurice Gibb, and writer of *Suspicious Minds* as Mark James. Add $40 to $50 if accompanied by two 8" x 10" Elvis photos.)
RCA (LSP-6020 "From Memphis to Vegas") 25-50 69
(Orange label. Flexible vinyl.)
RCA (LSP-6020 "From Memphis to Vegas") 30-40 76
(Tan label.)
RCA (LSP-6020 "From Memphis to Vegas") 15-25 77
(Black label.)
Note: Each of the two LPs in this set was reissued individually, *Elvis in Person at the International Hotel* as LSP-4428 and *Elvis Back in Memphis* as LSP-4429, both in 1970.
RCA (VPSX-6089 "Aloha from Hawaii") 3000-5000 73
(Has "Chicken of the Sea" sticker on cover. Quadradisc and contents stickers also are on cover. Includes programming insert card, which is valued at $100 to $200. Promotional in-house issue by the Van Camps Company.)
RCA (VPSX-6089 "Aloha from Hawaii") 1000-2000 73
(Has white titles/times sticker on front cover. Promotional issue only.)
RCA (VPSX-6089 "Aloha from Hawaii").75-100 73
(Has Quadradisc and contents stickers on cover. Red/orange label.)
RCA (VPSX-6089 "Aloha from Hawaii")...30-40 74
(Has Quadradisc/RCA logo in lower right corner of front cover. Titles are printed on back cover. Orange label.)
RCA (VPSX-6089 "Aloha from Hawaii")...25-30 76
(Tan label.)
Note: Issued through the RCA Record Club as RCA 213736 and later (1977) as RCA CPD2-2642.
RCA (6221 "Memphis Record")................25-35 87
(Includes a bonus color 15" x 22" poster and *Elvis Talks* LP flyer.)
RCA (6313 "Elvis Talks!") 20-30 87
(Mail-order offer.)
RCA (6382 "Number One Hits") 20-30 87
(Includes a bonus color 15" x 22" poster and *Elvis Talks* LP flyer.)
RCA (6383 "Top Ten Hits")........................25-35 87
(Includes a bonus color 15" x 22" poster and *Elvis Talks* LP flyer.)
RCA (LPM-6401 "Worldwide 50 Gold Hits, Vol. 1") 70-90 70
(Orange label. Rigid vinyl. Boxed, four-disc set. Add $30 to $40 if accompanied by a 16-page Elvis photo booklet.)
RCA (LPM-6401 "Worldwide 50 Gold Hits, Vol. 1") 70-90 70
(Orange label. Flexible vinyl. Boxed, four-disc set. Add $30 to $40 if accompanied by a 16-page Elvis photo booklet.)
RCA (LPM-6401 "Worldwide 50 Gold Hits, Vol. 1") 30-40 76
(Tan label.)
RCA (LPM-6401 "Worldwide 50 Gold Hits, Vol. 1") 20-35 77
(Black label.)
Note: Two discs in this set were repackaged for the RCA Record Club in 1974 as RCA 213690. The remaining two came out in 1978 as RCA 214657.
RCA (LPM-6402 "Worldwide 50 Gold Hits, Vol. 2") 60-75 71
(Orange label. Boxed, four-disc set. Add $25 to $50 if accompanied by an Elvis print, and an envelope with piece of material.)
RCA (LPM-6402 "Worldwide 50 Gold Hits, Vol. 2") 30-40 76
(Tan label. With bonus items shown as included.)
RCA (LPM-6402 "Worldwide 50 Gold Hits, Vol. 2") 25-35 76
(Tan label. No bonus items shown as being included.)
RCA (LPM-6402 "Worldwide 50 Gold Hits, Vol. 2") 20-25 77
(Black label.)
Note: Two discs in this set were repackaged for the RCA Record Club in 1978 as RCA 214567.
RCA (6414 "The Complete Sun Sessions") 20-30 87
(Includes a bonus color 15" x 22" poster and *Elvis Talks* LP flyer.)
RCA (6738 "Essential Elvis")....................15-25 88
RCA (6985 "The Alternate Aloha") 15-20 88
RCA (7031 "Elvis Forever") 30-45 74
(TV mail-order offer.)
RCA (9681 "E-Z Pop No. 5").................300-350 55
(Promotional issue only. Includes tracks by other artists. Identification number shown since no selection number is used. Not issued with special cover.)
RCA (7065 "Canadian Tribute")................15-20 78
(Price includes photo inner-sleeve. Canadian issues of this have the same number, but are clearly marked on back cover as Canadian.)
RCA (8468 "Elvis in Nashville") 20-40 88
RCA (9408 "Stay Away Joe")........20000-25000 67
(Identification number shown since no selection number is used. White label, black print. Single-sided. Reads: "Special Location Radio Program. MGM's *Stay Away Joe* on Location Sedona, Arizona Compliments of Elvis and the Colonel." Plain white inner sleeve has track titles typewritten, along with: "For KVIO broadcast, Sunday, November 5, 1967. Property of All Star Shows. Return to Col. Parker's office after airing." Promotional issue only, made for one-time broadcast by one radio station – KVIO, Cottonwood, Ariz. Self-contained program includes eight of Elvis' gospel tunes along with an announcer thanking the communities of Sedona and Cottonwood for the hospitality shown the cast and crew there during production of *Stay Away Joe*. Also includes publicity for Elvis' two gospel albums as well as the upcoming [December 3] Special Christmas Radio Program.)
RCA (9586 "Elvis Gospel") 20-40 89
RCA (9589 "Stereo '57, Essential Elvis, Vol. 2") 15-25 89
RCA (213690 "Worldwide Gold Award Hits, Parts 1&2") 100-150 74
(Orange label. RCA Record Club issue only.)
RCA (213690 "Worldwide Gold Award Hits, Parts 1&2") 30-40 76
(Tan label. RCA Record Club issue only.)

RCA (213690 "Worldwide Gold Award Hits, Parts 1&2")....................15-25 77
(Black label. RCA Record Club issue only. The two discs in this set were first issued as half of RCA LPM-6401.)
RCA (213736 "Aloha from Hawaii") 50-75 73
(Orange label.)
RCA (213736 "Aloha from Hawaii") 40-60 76
(Tan label.)
RCA (214657 "Worldwide Gold Award Hits, Parts 3&4")....................15-20 78
(RCA Record Club issue only. The two discs in this set were first issued as half of RCA LPM-6401.)
RCA (233299 "Country Classics")........... 30-40 80
(RCA Record Club issue only.)
RCA (234340 "From Elvis with Love") 30-40 78
(RCA Record Club issue only.)
RCA (244047 "Legendary Concert Performances")....................30-40 78
(RCA Record Club issue only.)
RCA (244069 "Country Memories") 30-40 78
(RCA Record Club issue only.)
SILHOUETTE (10001/10002 "Personally Elvis")....................30-40 79
STARDAY (995 "Interviews with Elvis")... 40-60 78
(Previously issued on Great Northwest 4005.)
SUN (1001 "The Sun Years")................. 15-25 77
(Light yellow label, "Memphis" at bottom. Light yellow cover with light brown printing.)
SUN (1001 "The Sun Years")................. 10-15 77
(Darker yellow label, four target circles. Dark yellow cover with dark brown printing.)
SUN (1001 "The Sun Years")................. 10-15 77
(White cover with brown printing.)
TM ("The Presley Years")................... 100-200 81
(Boxed, 12-disc syndicated radio show. Includes script and cue sheets.)
TIME-LIFE (106 "Elvis Presley: 1954-1961")....................25-30 86
(Boxed, three-disc set. Part of the *Rock 'N' Roll Era* series of sets available from Time-Life by mail-order. Includes brochure.)
UNITED STATIONS ("Elvis Presley Birthday Tribute")....................125-150 89
(Four hour radio show. Includes four pages of cue sheets. Promotional issue only.)
WATERMARK ("The Elvis Presley Story, 1975")....................800-900 75
(13-disc set. White label, pink letters. Includes a 48-page operations manual. Promotional issue only. Not issued with a special cover or package.)
WATERMARK ("The Elvis Presley Story, 1977")....................700-800 77
(13-disc set. White label, pink letters. Includes a 48-page operations manual, which represents about $100 of the value. Promotional issue only. Not issued with a special cover or package.)
WESTWOOD ONE ("A Golden Celebration")....................200-250 84
(Boxed, three-disc set. Price includes instructions and cue sheets, which represent $5-10 of the value. Issued to radio stations only.)
WORLD OF ELVIS PRESLEY 50-100 83
(One hour weekly radio show, numbered as program 1 through program 30. The show ceased operation after 30 programs. Each disc is accompanied by a single cue sheet. Price is for any one of the discs, although Program #3 is by far the rarest of them all.)
Session: Chet Atkins; Johnny Bernero; Bill Black; Hal Blaine; Blossoms; David Briggs; James Burton; Floyd Cramer; D.J. Fontana; Glen Hardin; Jordanaires; Jerry Kennedy; Anita Kerr; Ronnie Milsap; Bob Moore; Scotty Moore; Larry Muhoberac; Shaun Neilsen; Boots Randolph; Jerry Reed; Ray Stevens; J.D. Sumner & Stamps; Sweet Inspirations; Kathy Westmoreland; John Wilkinson; Bobby Wood.
Also see ALLEN, Steve
Also see ATKINS, Chet
Also see AUDREY
Also see BLACK, Bill
Also see BLAINE, Hal
Also see BLOSSOMS
Also see BURTON, James
Also see COLE, Nat "King"
Also see CRAMER, Floyd
Also see CRICKETS
Also see DONNER, Ral
Also see DURANTE, Jimmy
Also see FOWLER, Wally
Also see HARRIS, Emmylou
Also see JARVIS, Felton
Also see JORDANAIRES
Also see KENNEDY, Jerry
Also see KERR, Anita
Also see LIBERACE
Also see MANTOVANI
Also see MILSAP, Ronnie
Also see MOORE, Bob
Also see MOORE, Scotty
Also see MUHOBERAC, Larry
Also see OSBORNE, Jerry
Also see RANDOLPH, Boots
Also see REED, Jerry
Also see ROMANS, Charlie
Also see SINATRA, Nancy
Also see STEVENS, Ray
Also see SUMNER, J.D., & Stamps
Also see SWEET INSPIRATIONS
Also see VINCENT, Gene
Also see WHISPERS
Also see WOOD, Bobby

• Prefix letters or numbers are used on some LP listings in order to more quickly identify the variations available.

• A few items that have no label name are listed by title, such as the International Hotel boxed sets.

• LPs with a sticker applied over the selection number, showing a new number, are valued approximately the same as those without the sticker.

• If you don't find a record in the preceding sections, it may contain two, three or four artists, and is listed in a section that follows.

• As imposing as our Presley section here may seem, it is but a drop in the bucket. For a far more in-depth study of Elvis Presley collectibles, including records, compact discs and memorabilia, get Jerry Osborne's *Presleyana: The Elvis Presley Records, CD, and Memorabilia Price Guide.*

PRESLEY, Elvis / Beatles

Singles: 7-inch

OSBORNE ENTERPRISES ("The 1967 Elvis Medley")....................10-15 88
(Flip side is titled *The #1 Hits Medley, 1956-69.* Includes insert. 400 made.)
OSBORNE ENTERPRISES ("The 1967 Elvis Medley")....................15-25 89
(Flip side is titled *The #1 Hits Medley, 1956-70.* 100 made.)

LPs: 10/12-inch

UNITED DISTRIBUTORS (2382 "Lightning Strikes Twice")....................25-50 81
(Promotional issue only. Has five songs by each artist.)
Also see BEATLES

PRESLEY, Elvis / Martha Carson / Lou Monte / Herb Jeffries

EPs: 7-inch

RCA (2 "Dealer's Prevue") 2300-3000 57
(With paper envelope/sleeve. Promotional issue only.)
RCA (2 "Dealer's Prevue") 800-1000 57
(Disc only, without paper envelope/sleeve. Promotional issue only.)
Also see CARSON, Martha
Also see MONTE, Lou

PRESLEY, Elvis / Jean Chapel

EPs: 7-inch

RCA (7 "Love Me Tender")....................150-200 56
(Not issued with a special sleeve or cover. Promotional issue only.)
Also see CHAPEL, Jean

PRESLEY, Elvis / Buddy Holly

Singles: 7-inch

CREATIVE RADIO ("Elvis 50th Birthday Special")....................10-20 85
(Demonstration disc. A promotional issue.)
Also see HOLLY, Buddy

PRESLEY, Elvis / Fear

LPs: 10/12-inch

DISCONET (309 "The Original Elvis Presley Medley"/"Fear Medley")....................25-50 80
(Promotional issue only.)

PRESLEY, Elvis / David Keith

Singles: 7-inch

RCA (8760 "Heartbreak Hotel") 50-100 88
(White label. Promotional issue only.)
RCA (8760 "Heartbreak Hotel") 4-6 88
(Red label. Printing on both sides of label.)
RCA (8760 "Heartbreak Hotel") 4-8 88
(Red label. Printing on Elvis side only.)
RCA (8760 "Heartbreak Hotel") 4-8 88
(Red label. Printing on David Keith side only.)

Picture Sleeves

POPULAR LIBRARY/FAWCETT ("Heartbreak Hotel")....................300-400 88
(Produced by the publisher of the book that inspired the screenplay. Promotional issue only.)
RCA (8760 "Heartbreak Hotel") 20-40
(Pictures, but doesn't identify, RCA's Butch Waugh. Promotional issue only.)
RCA (8760 "Heartbreak Hotel") 4-8 88
(Pictures Elvis and others in a Cadillac.)

LPs: 10/12-inch

RCA (8533 "Heartbreak Hotel") 20-25 88
(Includes tracks by other artists.)

PRESLEY, Elvis / Vaughn Monroe / Gogi Grant / Robert Shaw

EPs: 7-inch

RCA (3736 "Pop Transcribed 30 Sec. Spot")....................500-700 58
(Not issued with a special sleeve or cover. Promotional issue only.)
Also see GRANT, Gogi
Also see MONROE, Vaughn

PRESLEY, Elvis / Jaye P. Morgan

Singles: 7-inch

UNITED STATES AIR FORCE (125 "It's Now Or Never")....................300-400 61
(Add $100 to $125 if accompanied by printed, cardboard mailing box. Issued only to radio stations.)

EPs: 7-inch

RCA (992 & 689 "Elvis/Jaye P. Morgan")....................8000-12000 56
(Two-disc set, coupling EPA-992 by Presley and EPA-689 by Jaye P. Morgan in a promotional package. Gatefold cover. Since the discs are standard pressings, nearly all of the value is represented by the custom cover.)
Also see MORGAN, Jaye P.

PRESLEY, Elvis / Gary Owens

Singles: 7-inch

CREATIVE RADIO ("Elvis Hour") 20-30 86
(Demonstration disc. A promotional issue.)

PRESLEY, Elvis / Helen Reddy

Singles: 7-inch

WHAT'S IT ALL ABOUT (78 "Life") 45-55 77
(Issued only to radio stations.)

PRESLEY, Elvis / Dinah Shore

EPs: 7-inch

RCA (56 "Too Much")....................150-200 57
(Not issued with a special sleeve or cover. Promotional issue only.)
Also see SHORE, Dinah

PRESLEY, Elvis / Frank Sinatra / Nat King Cole

EPs: 7-inch

CREATIVE RADIO ("Elvis Remembered")....................40-45 79
(Promotional demonstration disc.)
Also see COLE, Nat "King"
Also see SINATRA, Frank

PRESLEY, Elvis / Hank Snow / Eddy Arnold / Jim Reeves

EPs: 7-inch

RCA (12 "Old Shep")....................2000-3000 56
(Issued with a paper, "WOHO Featuring RCA Victor" sleeve. Deduct $1,500 to $2,000 if sleeve is missing. Promotional only.)
Also see ARNOLD, Eddy
Also see REEVES, Jim
Also see SNOW, Hank

PRESLEY, Elvis / Lawrence Welk

Singles: 7-inch

UNITED STATES AIR FORCE (159 "Surrender")....................300-400 61
(Add $100 to $125 if accompanied by printed, cardboard mailing box. Issued only to radio stations.)
Also see WELK, Lawrence

PRESLEY, Elvis / Hank Williams

LPs: 10/12-inch

SUNRISE MEDIA (3011 "History of Country Music")....................15-25 81
(Has four songs by each artist.)
Also see PRESLEY, Elvis
Also see WILLIAMS, Hank

PRESLEY, Elvis
(Michael Conley)

Singles: 7-inch

ELVIS CLASSIC (5478 "Tell Me Pretty Baby")....................4-8 78
(Despite being labeled as a 1954 recording by Elvis Presley, this track is simply a 1978 recording by Michael Conley, performing in an Elvis style. It is listed separately to eliminate confusion.)

Picture Sleeves

ELVIS CLASSIC (5478 "Tell Me Pretty Baby")....................8-10 78
(Sleeve pictures an artist's sketch of Elvis Presley.)

PRESLEY, Gaylon

Singles: 7-inch

UNITED SOUTHERN ARTISTS (107 "College Love Affair")....................5-10 61

PRESLEY, Jesse Dee
(Grandpa Jesse Presley)

Singles: 7-inch

LEGACY ("The Billy Goat Song") 20-30 59
(Selection number not known.)

EPs: 7-inch

LEGACY PARK (2000 "Roots of Elvis").....5-10 78

PRESS, Don

Singles: 7-inch

LAURIE (3036 "More Than Ever")........100-200 59

PRESTON
(Preston Carnes)

Singles: 7-inch

SOUND PATTERN (110 "This World Is Closing in on Me")....................10-20 68
(Colored vinyl.)
Also see CARPENTER, Chris
Also see LENNY & THUNDERTONES

PRESTON, Billy — *LP '65*

Singles: 12-inch

MEGATONE 4-6 84
MONTAGE....................4-6 84

Singles: 7-inch

A&M....................4-8 72-78
APPLE/AMERICOM (1808/433 "That's the Way God Planned It")....................300-400 69
(4-inch flexi, "pocket disc.")
APPLE....................6-12 69-71
APPLE (1808/6555 "That's the Way God Planned It")....................50-60 69
CAPITOL....................4-8 66-69
CONTRACT (5101 "My Kind of Music").....8-12 61
DERBY (1002 "Greazee")....................8-12 63
MOTOWN....................3-6 79-86
VEE-JAY....................5-10 65

Picture Sleeves

A&M....................5-10 72-75
APPLE (1808 "That's the Way God Planned It")....................8-12 69
APPLE (1817 "All That I've Got").............10-15 70

LPs: 10/12-inch

A&M....................8-12 71-82
APPLE (3359 "That's the Way God Planned It")....................40-50 69
(With portrait cover photo.)
APPLE (3359 "That's the Way God Planned It")....................15-25 69
(Full figure cover photo.)
APPLE (3370 "Encouraging Words") 10-20 70
BUDDAH....................10-15 69
CAPITOL (T-2532 "Wildest Organ").........10-15 66
CAPITOL (ST-2532 "Wildest Organ")......10-20 66
CAPITOL (SM-2532 "Wildest Organ")..........5-8 75
DERBY (701 "16-Year-Old Soul") 50-75 63
EXODUS....................15-20 65
GNP....................10-15 73
MOTOWN 5-10 79-82
MYRRH....................5-10 78
PEACOCK 8-12 73
PICKWICK ....5-8 '70s
SPRINGBOARD....................5-10 78
TRIP....................8-12 73

VEE-JAY (1123 "Most Exciting Organ Ever") 15-25 65
Also see BEATLES
Also see MOTHERS OF INVENTION

PRESTON, Jimmy, & His Prestonians
(With Burnetta Evans) R&B '49
Singles: 78 rpm
DERBY (748 "Oh Babe!") 25-35 50
DERBY (751 "Rock with It Baby") 25-35 50
GOTHAM 15-25 49-50
Singles: 7-inch
GOTHAM (175 "Hucklebuck Daddy") 25-35 49
GOTHAM (188 "Rock the Joint") 25-35 49
Also see WILLIAMS, Cootie / Jimmy Preston

PRESTON, Johnny P&R '59
Singles: 7-inch
ABC 4-6 68-73
HALL/HALLWAY 5-10 64-65
IMPERIAL (5924 "The Day the World Stood Still") 10-15 63
IMPERIAL (5947 "I Couldn't Take It Again") 5-10 63
MERCURY (10027 "Cradle of Love") 15-25 60
(Stereo [reprocessed].)
MERCURY (10036 "Feel So Fine") 20-30 60
(Stereo.)
MERCURY (71474 thru 72049) 10-20 59-62
(Monaural.)
TCF (101 "Sound Like Trouble") 5-10 65
TCF (120 "Good Good Lovin' ") 5-10 65
Picture Sleeves
MERCURY 10-20 60-62
EPs: 7-inch
MERCURY (3397 "Johnny Preston") 75-125 60
LPs: 10/12-inch
MERCURY (20592 "Running Bear") 50-70 60
(Monaural.)
MERCURY (20609 "Come Rock with Me") 50-70 60
(Monaural.)
MERCURY (60250 "Running Bear") 60-90 60
(Stereo. Black label)
MERCURY (60250 "Running Bear") 8-12 81
(Chicago "Skyline" label)
MERCURY (60609 "Come Rock with Me") 60-90 60
(Stereo.)
WING (12246 "Running Bear") 20-30 63
(Monaural.)
WING (16246 "Running Bear") 25-35 63
(Stereo.)
Also see MIZZELL, Bobby

PRESTON, Kenny
Singles: 7-inch
ABBCO (46300 "Can't You Change Your Mind") 200-300

PRESTON, Mike P&R '58
Singles: 7-inch
LONDON (1834 "A House, a Car and a Wedding Ring") 15-20 58
LONDON (1865 thru 9601) 8-12 59-63

PRESTON, Robert
Singles: 7-inch
CAPITOL CUSTOM (1000 "Chicken Fat") 8-12 62
JAYCEES (1000 "Chicken Fat") 10-15 62

PRESTON, Rudy
EPs: 7-inch
KATONA (1375 "Rudy Preston") 200-300

PRESTON, Terry
(Ferlin Husky)
Singles: 78 rpm
CAPITOL 8-15 52-53
FOUR STAR 10-15 49-51
Singles: 7-inch
CAPITOL 10-20 52-53
FOUR STAR 15-25 49-51
Also see HUSKY, Ferlin

PRESTON, Vic
Singles: 7-inch
ELITE (1 "Hot Rod") 15-25

PRESTON & PACEMAKERS
Singles: 7-inch
NEW SONG (128 "Stop & Go") 10-20 60

PRESTOS
Singles: 78 rpm
MERCURY 25-35 55
Singles: 7-inch
MERCURY (70747 "Till We Meet Again") 50-75 55
Also see EMPIRES
Also see WHIRLERS

PRE-TEENS
(With the Shytan Five)
Singles: 78 rpm
J&S 300-400 56
Singles: 7-inch
J&S (1756 "What Makes Me Love You Like I Do") 1000-1500 56

PRETENDERS
("Featuring Jimmy Jones with Rhythm Accompaniment")
Singles: 78 rpm
RAMA 25-35 56
WHIRLIN' DISC 50-75 57
Singles: 7-inch
ABC-PAR (10094 "Blue & Lonely") 75-100 60
APT (25026 "Blue & Lonely") 200-300 59
CENTRAL (2605 "Blue & Lonely") 4000-5000 58
HOLIDAY (2610 "Tonight") 400-500 57
PORT (70040 "Close Your Eyes") 5-10 64
RAMA (198 "Possessive Love") 50-75 56
WHIRLIN' DISC (106 "Close Your Eyes") 50-100 57
Members: Jimmy Jones; Bobby Moore; Kerry Saxton; Bill Walker; Mel Walton; Irving Lee Gail.
Also see JONES, Jimmy, & Pretenders
Also see SAVOYS
Also see VOCALTONES

PRETENDERS
Singles: 7-inch
POWER-MARTIN (1001 "I'm So Happy") 50-75 61
POWER-MARTIN (1006 "A Very Precious Love") 4-6 76
RELIC (1004 "I'm So Happy") 5-10 65

PRETENDERS
Singles: 7-inch
AGAR (7169 "Surfer's Dream") 25-35 63

PRETENDERS
Singles: 7-inch
ROSE INT'L (100 "Answer to My Prayers") 650-750 63

PRETENDERS P&R/LP '80
Singles: 12-inch
SIRE 4-6 84
Singles: 7-inch
SIRE 3-6 79-90
Picture Sleeves
SIRE 3-5 80-87
LPs: 10/12-inch
NAUTILUS (38 "Pretenders") .... 25-35 '80s
SIRE 5-10 80-90
Members: Chrissie Hynde; Robbie MacIntosh; Pete Farndon; Martin Chambers; Malcomb Foster; James Honeyman Scott.

PRETENDERS
Singles: 7-inch
AL-STAN (1005 "Ding Dong Bells") 3-5 95
(Colored vinyl.)
BETHLEHEM (3050 "Ding Dong Bells") 30-40 62
Picture Sleeves
AL-STAN (1005 "Ding Dong Bells") 3-5 95
Members: Skip Pietrobone; Kenny Shott; Dan Wisniewski; Sam Talarico; Mick Diana.
Also see PETRICOIN, Barry, & Pretenders

PRETTY BOY
(Don Covay; with Johnny Fuller's Band)
Singles: 78 rpm
ATLANTIC (1147 "Bip Bop Bip") 50-75 57
BIG (617 "Rockin' the Mule") 50-75 58
RHYTHM (1768 "I'm Bad") 30-50 54
Singles: 7-inch
ATLANTIC (1147 "Bip Bop Bip") 50-75 57
BIG (617 "Rockin' the Mule") 75-100 58
Session: King Curtis.
Also see COVAY, Don
Also see FULLER, Johnny
Also see KING CURTIS

PRETTY THINGS LP '75
Singles: 7-inch
FONTANA 5-10 64-66
LAURIE (3458 "Talkin' About the Good Times") 5-8 68
RARE EARTH (5005 "Private Sorrow") 4-8 69
SWAN SONG 4-6 75-76
LPs: 10/12-inch
FONTANA (27544 "Pretty Things") 35-55 66
(Monaural.)
FONTANA (67544 "Pretty Things") 35-55 66
(Stereo.)
MOTOWN 10-15 76
RARE EARTH (506 "S.F. Sorrow") 15-25 69
(With standard square cover.)
RARE EARTH (506 "S.F. Sorrow") 20-40 69
(With rounded-top cover. Promotional issue.)
RARE EARTH (515 "Parachute") 15-20 70
RARE EARTH (549 "Rare Earth") 8-12 76
(Reissue of material from 506 & 515.)
SIRE 8-10 76
SWAN SONG 8-10 75-76
W.B. 8-10 73-80

PREVETTE, Colin
Singles: 7-inch
LEO (1824 "The Hillbilly Bop") 50-75

PREVIN, André P&R/LP '59
(With the David Rose Orchestra; with Leontyne Price; with the Mitchells; André Previn Jazz Trio)
Singles: 78 rpm
MODERN 3-6 51
RCA 5-10 49-51
Singles: 7-inch
COLUMBIA 4-8 60-64
DECCA 4-8 61
MGM 5-10 59
MODERN 10-20 51
RCA (214 "André Previn") 10-20 49
(Boxed, three-disc set.)
RCA (4354 "I'll String Along with You") 10-20 51
RCA (9122 "Theme from *Hotel*") 4-6 67
EPs: 7-inch
MGM (1669 "Secret Songs for Young Lovers") 5-10 59
LPs: 10/12-inch
ALLEGIANCE 5-8 84
ANGEL 5-8 80-81
CAMDEN 5-10 64
COLUMBIA 10-20 60-65
CONTEMPORARY 15-30 57-60
CORONET .... 5-10 '60s
DECCA (4000 series) 8-15 61-63
(Decca LP numbers in this series preceded by a "7" or a "DL-7" are stereo issues.)
DECCA (8000 series) 20-40 55-56
EVEREST 5-10 70
GUEST STAR .... 5-15 '60s
HARMONY 5-10 67
MFSL 30-50 82
MGM 10-15 59-64
METRO JAZZ (1012 "Get Those elephants Out'a Here") 10-20 59
MONARCH (203 "All Star Jazz") 60-80 54
(10-inch LP.)
MONARCH (204 "André Previn Plays Duke") 60-80 54
(10-inch LP.)
ODYSSEY 8-12 68
RCA (1000 series) 5-10 75
(With an "ARL1" prefix.)
RCA (1000 series) 20-45 54
(With an "LPM" prefix.)
RCA (1356 "Three Little Words") 40-60 56
RCA (2983 "Right As Rain") 6-12 67
RCA (3002 ("André Previn Plays Harry Warren") 75-100 51
(10-inch LP.)
RCA (3400 thru 3800 series) 10-20 65-67
TOPS 10-20 57
U.A. (5200 series) 5-10 71
VERVE (8565 "Essential André Previn") 15-25 63
Also see ANDREWS, Julie, & André Previn / Vic Damone / Jack Jones / Marian Anderson
Also see ASTAIRE, Fred, & Red Skelton / Helen Kane
Also see CARROLL, Diahann, & André Previn
Also see DAY, Doris, & André Previn
Also see ROSE, David
Also see SHORE, Dinah, & André Previn

PRICE, Alan P&R '66
(Alan Price Set)
Singles: 7-inch
COTILLION 4-8 69
EPIC 3-5 84
JET 4-6 79
PARROT 5-10 66-68
W.B. 4-6 72
LPs: 10/12-inch
ACCORD 5-10 82
JET 8-12 77-80
PARROT 15-25 68
TOWNHOUSE 5-10 81
W.B. 8-12 73
Also see ANIMALS

PRICE, Bobby, & Dynamics
Singles: 7-inch
CUCA (1095 "Oh, I Like It Like That") 15-25 62
Also see DYNAMICS

PRICE, Eli, & Manhattans
Singles: 7-inch
DOOTO (445 "My Big Dream") 50-75 59
(Yellow label. Reissued on a multi-color label as by the Manhattans.)
Also see MANHATTANS

PRICE, Gene
Singles: 7-inch
ROBIN (101 "Duck Call Boogie") 200-300

PRICE, Herb, & Darts
(With Jay Peabody & Orchestra)
Singles: 7-inch
TEMPUS (1506 "Gone Too Long") 125-175 58
TEMPUS (1506 "Gone Too Long") 150-200 58
(White label. Promotional issue only.)

PRICE, Joe
Singles: 7-inch
STARDAY (177 "Typhoon") 50-75

PRICE, Leo
Singles: 7-inch
GMC (10008 "Hard Times") 5-10 67
HULL (739 "Hey Now Baby") 8-12 61
UP & DOWN (712 "Quick Down") 20-30 65
Also see MILLER SISTERS / Leo Price

PRICE, Lloyd R&B '52
(Lloyd Price Orchestra; with the Dukes; with Erma Franklin)
Singles: 78 rpm
ABC-PAR (9792 "Just Because") 15-20 57
ABC-PAR (9972 "Stagger Lee") 15-20 58
KRC (301 "Lonely Chair") 25-40 57
KRC (587 "Just Because") 50-75 57
SPECIALTY 15-25 55-56
Singles: 7-inch
ABC 4-8 67-73
ABC-PAR (9792 "Just Because") 15-25 57
ABC-PAR (9972 "Stagger Lee") 15-25 58
(Monaural.)
ABC-PAR (S-9972 "Stagger Lee") 50-75 58
(Stereo.)
ABC-PAR (9997 "Where Were You") 15-25 59
(Monaural.)
ABC-PAR (S-9997 "Where Were You") 50-75 59
(Stereo.)
ABC-PAR (10018 "Personality") 15-25 59
(Monaural.)
ABC-PAR (10018 "Personality") 50-75 59
(Stereo.)
ABC-PAR (10032 "I'm Gonna Get Married") 15-25 59
ABC-PAR (10062 "Come into My Heart") 10-20 59
ABC-PAR (10075 "Lady Luck") 10-20 60
ABC-PAR (10102 "For Love") 10-20 60
ABC-PAR (10123 "Question") 10-20 60
ABC-PAR (10139 "Just Call Me") 10-20 60
ABC-PAR (10162 "Know What You're Doin' ") 10-20 60
ABC-PAR (10177 "I Made You Cry") 10-20 61
ABC-PAR (10197 "Say I'm the One") 10-20 61
ABC-PAR (10206 "Chantilly Lace") 10-20 61
ABC-PAR (10221 "I Ain't Givin' You Nothin' ") 10-20 61
ABC-PAR (10229 "Talk to Me") 10-20 61
ABC-PAR (10288 "Be a Leader") 10-20 62
ABC-PAR (10299 "Twistin' the Blues") 10-20 62
ABC-PAR (10342 "Your Picture") 10-20 62

ABC-PAR (10372 "Under Your Spell Again") 10-20 62
ABC-PAR (10412 "Who's Sorry Now") 10-20 63
COLLECTABLES .... 3-5 '80s
DOUBLE L 8-15 63-66
GSF 4-6 72-73
JAD (208 "Take All") 5-10 68
KRC (301 "Lonely Chair") 30-50 57
KRC (303 "Hello Little Girl") 30-50 57
KRC (305 "How Many Times") 30-50 58
KRC (587 "Just Because") 50-75 57
KRC (5000 "No Limit to Love") 15-25 58
KRC (5002 "Down by the River") 15-25 59
LPG (111 "Love Music") 4-6 76
LUDIX 8-12 63
MCA .... 4-6 '70s
MONUMENT 5-10 64-65
PARAMOUNT 4-6 72
RCA (5937 "Gold Cadillac Song") 50-75 54
(Single-sided. Promotional issue only.)
REPRISE (499 "Man Who") 5-10 66
ROULETTE 4-6 70s
SCEPTER 4-6 71
SPECIALTY (SPBX series) 15-25 86
(Boxed set of six colored vinyl 45s.)
SPECIALTY (428 "Lawdy, Miss Clawdy") 100-150 52
(Black vinyl.)
SPECIALTY (428 "Lawdy, Miss Clawdy") 400-600 52
(Red vinyl.)
SPECIALTY (440 "Oooh Oooh Oooh") .. 50-100 52
(Black vinyl.)
SPECIALTY (440 "Oooh Oooh Oooh") 150-250 52
(Red vinyl.)
SPECIALTY (452 "Ain't It a Shame") 50-100 53
(Black vinyl.)
SPECIALTY (452 "Ain't It a Shame") ... 150-250 53
(Red vinyl.)
SPECIALTY (457 "What's the Matter Now") 50-100 53
(Black vinyl.)
SPECIALTY (457 "What's the Matter Now") 150-250 53
(Red vinyl.)
SPECIALTY (463 "Where You At") 50-100 53
(Black vinyl.)
SPECIALTY (463 "Where You At") 150-250 53
(Red vinyl.)
SPECIALTY (471 "I Wish Your Picture Was You") 50-75 54
SPECIALTY (483 "Let Me Come Home, Baby") 50-75 54
(Black vinyl.)
SPECIALTY (483 "Let Me Come Home, Baby") 150-250 54
(Red vinyl.)
SPECIALTY (494 "Walkin' the Track") 50-75 54
SPECIALTY (535 "Oo Ee Baby") 25-35 55
SPECIALTY (540 "Trying to Find Someone to Love") 25-40 55
SPECIALTY (571 "Woe Ho Ho") 25-40 56
SPECIALTY (578 "Country Boy Rock") ... 25-40 56
SPECIALTY (582 "Forgive Me Clawdy") . 25-40 56
SPECIALTY (602 "Baby Please Come Home") 25-40 57
SPECIALTY (661 "Lawdy, Miss Clawdy") 15-25 59
TURNTABLE (506 "Bad Conditions") 5-10 69
TURNTABLE (509 "Lawdy Miss Clawdy") .. 5-10 69

Picture Sleeves

ABC-PAR (10018 "Personality") .... 5-10 '90s
DOUBLE L (729 "Billie Baby") 10-20 64

EPs: 7-inch

ABC-PAR (14 "Rockin' on 5th Ave.") 25-50 59
(Promotional issue, made for Luden's Inc., maker of 5th Ave. candy bars.)
ABC-PAR (277 "The Exciting Lloyd Price") 25-50 59
ABC-PAR (315 "Mr. Personality Sings the Blues") 25-50 60
ABC-PAR (324 "Four Songs from Mr. Personality's Big 15 Hits") 25-50 60

LPs: 10/12-inch

ABC 8-10 72-76
ABC-PAR (ABC-277 "The Exciting Lloyd Price") 25-45 59
(Monaural.)
ABC-PAR (ABCS-277 "The Exciting Lloyd Price") 30-50 59
(Stereo.)
ABC-PAR (ABC-297 "Mr. Personality") 25-45 59
(Monaural.)
ABC-PAR (ABCS-297 "Mr. Personality") .. 30-50 59
(Stereo.)
ABC-PAR (ABC-315 "Mr. Personality Sings the Blues") 25-45 60
(Monaural.)
ABC-PAR (ABCS-315 "Mr. Personality Sings the Blues") 30-50 60
(Stereo.)
ABC-PAR (ABC-324 "Mr. Personality's Big 15") 25-45 60
(Monaural.)
ABC-PAR (ABCS-324 "Mr. Personality's Big 15") 30-50 60
ABC-PAR (ABC-346 "The Fantastic Lloyd Price") 25-45 60
(Monaural.)
ABC-PAR (ABCS-346 "The Fantastic Lloyd Price") 30-50 60
(Stereo.)
ABC-PAR (ABC-366 "Lloyd Price Sings the Million Sellers") 25-45 61
(Monaural.)
ABC-PAR (ABCS-366 "Lloyd Price Sings the Million Sellers") 25-45 61
(Stereo.)
ABC-PAR (ABC-382 "Cookin'") 25-45 61
(Monaural.)
ABC-PAR (ABCS-382 "Cookin'") 30-50 61
(Stereo.)
ABC-PAR (ABCX-763 "16 Greatest Hits") 10-15 72
DOUBLE L (2303 "Misty") 20-25 63
(Monaural.)
DOUBLE L (8303 "Misty") 25-30 63
(Stereo.)
GRAND PRIX .... 10-15 '60s
GUEST STAR 10-15 64
JAD 10-15 69
MCA 5-10 82
MONUMENT (8032 "Lloyd Swings for Sammy") 10-15 65
(Monaural.)
MONUMENT (18032 "Lloyd Swings for Sammy") 15-20 65
(Stereo.)
OLDE WORLD 8-10 78
PICKWICK 10-15 67
SPECIALTY (2105 "Lloyd Price") 40-50 59
TSG (802 "Golden Dozen") 8-12 76
TRIP 8-10 76
TURNTABLE 10-15 69
UPFRONT .... 8-12 '70s
Also see ANKA, Paul / Lloyd Price
Also see COOKE, Sam / Lloyd Price / Larry Williams / Little Richard
Also see DOMINO, Fats
Also see DUKES
Also see FRANKLIN, Erma
Also see KING BEES

PRICE, Mel

(With His Santa Fe Rangers)

Singles: 7-inch

DIXIE (887 "Jailed") 25-50
DIXIE (2016 "Little Dog Blues") 75-125 59
STARDAY (226 "Gonna See My Baby") .. 50-75

PRICE, Ray — C&W '52

(With the Cherokee Cowboys)

Singles: 78 rpm

BULLET (701 "Jealous Lies") 75-125 52
COLUMBIA 5-15 52-57

Singles: 7-inch

ABC 4-6 75
ABC/DOT 4-6 75-77
COLUMBIA (10000 series) 4-6 74-77
COLUMBIA (20000 & 21000 series) 10-20 52-56
COLUMBIA (40000 thru 43000 series) 5-15 57-66
COLUMBIA (44042 "Danny Boy") 4-8 67
(Black vinyl.)
COLUMBIA (44042 "Danny Boy") 8-10 67
(Green vinyl. Promotional issue only.)
COLUMBIA (44100 thru 45000 series) 4-6 67-73
COLUMBIA HALL OF FAME 3-5
GOLDIES 45 .... 3-6 73
DIMENSION 3-5 81-82
MONUMENT 4-6 78-79
MYRRH 4-6 74-75
STEP ONE 3-5 85-86
W.B. 3-5 82-83
WORD 4-6 78

Picture Sleeves

COLUMBIA (44042 "Danny Boy") 8-12 67
(Promotional issue only.)

EPs: 7-inch

COLUMBIA (1700 thru 2800 series) 15-25 53-57
COLUMBIA (8556 "Ray Price") .... 10-20 '50s
COLUMBIA (10000 thru 14000 series) 10-20 57-60
(White label. Promotional issue only.)

LPs: 10/12-inch

ABC/DOT 6-12 75-77
ARTCO 20-40
(Titel and selection number not known.)
CBS 5-10
COLUMBIA (28 "The World of Ray Price") 8-12 70
COLUMBIA (157 "The Same Old Me") 10-15 66
(Record club exclusive.)
COLUMBIA (1015 "Heart Songs") 30-40 57
COLUMBIA (1148 "Talk to Your Heart") ... 25-35 58
COLUMBIA (1400 thru 2600 series) 10-25 60-67
(Monaural)
COLUMBIA (8200 thru 9400 series, except 9422) 15-30 60-67
(Stereo)
COLUMBIA (9422 "Heart Songs") 25-35 67
(Stereo.)
COLUMBIA (9700 thru 9900 series) 8-12 68-70
COLUMBIA (10000 series) 5-10 73-79
COLUMBIA (30000 thru 37000 series) 5-10 70-81
COLUMBIA SPECIAL PRODUCTS 5-10
COLUMBIA STAR SERIES 5-15
DIMENSION 5-8 81
51 WEST 5-8 84
HARMONY 8-15 66-71
MONUMENT 5-10 79
MYRRH 5-8 74
PAIR 8-10 82
RADIANT 5-8 81
SEASHELL 5-10
STEP ONE 5-10 86
SUNRISE MEDIA 5-8 81
VIVA 5-10
W.B. 5-8 83
WORD 5-8 77
Session: Johnny Bush; Willie Nelson; Johnny Gimble.
Also see ANDERSON, Lynn / Ray Price
Also see BUSH, Johnny
Also see MILLER, Roger, & Willie Nelson
Also see NELSON, Willie, & Ray Price
Also see ROBBINS, Marty / Johnny Cash / Ray Price

PRICE, Ray / Lefty Frizzell / Carl Smith

LPs: 10/12-inch

COLUMBIA (1257 "Greatest Western Hits") 20-30 59
(Monaural.)
COLUMBIA (8776 "Greatest Western Hits") 15-25 63
(Stereo.)
Also see FRIZZELL, Lefty
Also see SMITH, Carl

PRICE, Ray / Johnny Horton / Carl Smith / George Morgan

EPs: 7-inch

COLUMBIA (2157 "4 Big Hits") 20-25 60
Also see HORTON, Johnny
Also see SMITH, Carl

PRICE, Ronnie, & Velvets

Singles: 7-inch

CAROUSEL (1001 "White Bucks") 20-30

PRICE, Ruth

(With the Johnny Smith Quartet; with Shelly Manne & His Men)

Singles: 7-inch

CONTEMPORARY 5-10 61

LPs: 10/12-inch

AVA (54 "Live and Beautiful") 30-40 63
(Monaural.)
AVA (S-54 "Live and Beautiful") 35-45 63
(Stereo.)
CONTEMPORARY (3590 "At the Manne Hole") 35-45 61
(Monaural.)
CONTEMPORARY (7590 "At the Manne Hole") 40-50 61
(Stereo.)
KAPP (1006 "My Name Is Ruth Price") 50-60 58
ROOST (2217 "Sing!") 50-75 58

PRICE, Sam

(With His Texas Bluesicians; Sam Price All Stars)

Singles: 78 rpm

SAVOY 8-10 56

Singles: 7-inch

SAVOY 10-20 56-59
Session: King Curtis; Mickey Baker; Leonard Gaskin; Bobby Donaldson; Al Casey; Al Lucas; Panama Francis.
Also see BAKER, Mickey
Also see CASEY, Al
Also see KING CURTIS
Also see LUCAS, Al

PRICE, Vincent

LPs: 10/12-inch

CAPITOL (342 "Witchcraft Magic") 20-30 69

PRIDE

LPs: 10/12-inch

WARNER (1848 "Pride") 15-25 70

PRIDE, Adrian

(Bernie Schwartz)

Singles: 7-inch

CALLIOPE 15-25
W.B. (5867 "Her Name Is Melody") 8-12 66
Also see ATELLO, Don

PRIDE, Charley — C&W '66

(With the Pridesmen; with Henry Mancini; Country Charley Pride)

Singles: 7-inch

RCA (0073 thru 0942 series) 4-8 69-73
RCA (8700 & 8800 series) 5-10 66
RCA (9000 thru 9996) 4-8 66-71
RCA (10030 thru 11655) 4-6 74-79
RCA 11736 "Dallas Cowboys") 4-6 79
(Black label.)
RCA 11736 "Dallas Cowboys") 8-12 79
(Gray and blue label. Special Dallas Cowboys Edition.)
RCA (11751 thru 14296) 3-6 79-86
RCA GOLD STANDARD 4-6
16TH AVE. 3-5 87-89

Picture Sleeves

RCA 4-6 71-74

EPs: 7-inch

RCA .... 5-10 '60s
(Juke box issues.)

LPs: 10/12-inch

CAMDEN 5-10 72
RCA (Except LPM/LSP 3700 thru 4800 series) 5-10 74-86
RCA (3700 thru 4800 series) 10-20 66-73
(With "LPM" or "LSP" prefix.)
RCA SPECIAL PRODUCTS (0208 "Charley's Favorites") 8-12
READER'S DIGEST/RCA ("Charley Pride") 30-40
(Six-disc, boxed set with booklet. Mail order offer.)
TELEHOUSE 5-10
Also see MANCINI, Henry

PRIESMAN, Magel

Singles: 7-inch

SUN (294 "I Feel So Blue") 15-20 58

PRIMA, Louis — P&R '35

(With Gia Malone)

Singles: 78 rpm

BRUNSWICK 5-10 35
COLUMBIA 4-6 52-53
DECCA 4-8 54
HIT 5-10 44-45
MAJESTIC 4-8 45
MERCURY 4-8 50
RCA 4-8 47
ROBIN HOOD 4-8 50
SAVOY 4-8 53
VOCALION 5-10 37

Singles: 7-inch

ABC 4-6 68-74
BUENA VISTA 4-6 66-74
CAPITOL 4-8 62
COLUMBIA 5-10 52-53
DECCA 5-10 54
DOT 4-8 59-62

HBR (452 "See That You're Born an Italian")....4-6 65
HBR (454 "Santa, How Come Your Eyes Are Green")....4-6 66
HBR (467 "Civilization")....4-6 66
KAMA SUTRA....4-6 66
MERCURY....8-12 50
PRIMA....4-8 63-64
ROBIN HOOD....8-12 50
SAVOY....8-12 53
U.A.....4-6 67

EPs: 7-inch

CAPITOL....5-15 56
JUBILEE....5-15 55
VARSITY....5-15 54

LPs: 10/12-inch

BUENA VISTA....8-18 65-74
CAPITOL....10-20 56-62
DE-LITE....5-10 68
DOT....10-20 60
HBR (8502 "Golden Hits")....5-10 66
(Monaural.)
HBR (9502 "Golden Hits")....10-15 66
(Stereo.)
HAMILTON....5-10 65
MERCURY (25142 "For the People")....30-40 53
(10-inch LP.)
PRIMA....5-8 72-76
RONDO/RONDOLETTE....10-20 59
TOPS....10-20 56
U.A.....5-10 67

PRIMA, Louis, & Keely Smith *P&R/R&B/LP '58*
(With Sam Butera & the Witnesses)

Singles: 78 rpm

ROBIN HOOD....5-10 50

Singles: 7-inch

CAPITOL....10-15 58-59
DOT....8-12 59-61
TOD (123 "Oh Babe")....30-50

Picture Sleeves

CAPITOL (4063 "That Old Black Magic")...8-12 58
(Sleeve has a die-cut center hole)
DOT (15978 "I'm Confessin' ")....10-15 59

EPs: 7-inch

CAPITOL....8-12 58
DOT (103 "The Frantic '40s")....10-20 60
(Promotional issue, made for the Desert Inn as a giveaway.)
DOT (1093 "Louis & Keely")....5-10 60

LPs: 10/12-inch

CAPITOL (With "SM" prefix.)....5-8 75
CAPITOL (With "T" or "ST" prefix.)....20-35 58-61
COLUMBIA (1206 "Breaking It Up")....20-30 58
CORONET....10-15 '60s
DESIGN....10-15 '60s
DOT....15-25 59-60
Also see SMITH, Keely

PRIMA, Louis, & Keely Smith / Louis Prima & Sam Butera

Singles: 7-inch

CAPITOL (719 "Album Highlights")....10-15 57
(Promotional issue only.)
Also see BUTERA, Sam
Also see PRIMA, Louis
Also see PRIMA, Louis, & Keely Smith

PRIMATES

Singles: 7-inch

MARKO (923 "Knock on My Door")....15-25 65
MARKO (924 "Don't Press Your Luck")....20-30 66

PRIMATES

Singles: 7-inch

LEAF (667 "Girl Don't Tell Me")....15-25 66
Members: Mike Eubank; Tom Schilder; Clark Wessel; Gary Hildebrand; John Doll.

PRIMETTES
(Supremes)

Singles: 7-inch

LU PINE (120 "Tears of Sorrow")....75-125 64
(Lu-Pine [hyphenated] 120 is also a Joe Stubbs single.)
Also see STUBBS, Joe
Also see SUPREMES

PRIMITIVES

Singles: 7-inch

PICKWICK CITY (1001 "The Ostrich")....100-125 64
Members: Lou Reed; John Cale; Tony Conrad; Walter DeMaria.
Also see REED, Lou

PRINCE *P&R/R&B/LP '78*
(With the Revolution; "Artist Formerly Known As Prince")

Singles: 12-inch

BELLMARK (71003 "Beautiful Experience")....15-20
(Includes 10" x 10" booklet.)
HOT PINK (3223 "Just Another Sucker")..20-25 86
(Promotional issue only.)
PAISLEY PARK (1082 "Let's Pretend We're Married")....30-50 84
(Promotional issue only. With title sleeve.)
PAISLEY PARK (2300 "America")....15-20 85
(Promotional issue only. With title sleeve.)
PAISLEY PARK (2313 "Raspberry Beret")....15-20 85
(Promotional issue only. With title sleeve.)
PAISLEY PARK (2331 "Pop Life")....15-20 85
(Promotional issue only. With title sleeve.)
PAISLEY PARK (2448 "Kiss" [Edit])....8-12 86
(Promotional issue only.)
PAISLEY PARK (2458 "Kiss" [Extended])..8-12 86
(Promotional issue only.)
PAISLEY PARK (2476 "Mountains")....8-10 86
(Promotional issue only.)
PAISLEY PARK (2687 "Sign O' the Times")....8-10 87
(Promotional issue only.)
PAISLEY PARK (2758 "If I Was Your Girlfriend")....8-10 87
(Promotional issue only.)
PAISLEY PARK (2770 "I Could Never Take the Place of Your Man")....8-10 87
(Promotional issue only.)
PAISLEY PARK (2771 "U Got the Look")...8-10 87
(Promotional issue only.)
PAISLEY PARK (3704 "Scandalous Sex Suite")....8-10 89
(Promotional issue only.)
PAISLEY PARK (4345 "Thieves in the Temple")....10-15 90
(Promotional issue only. With picture cover.)
PAISLEY PARK (4515 "New Power Generation")....8-10 90
(Promotional issue only.)
PAISLEY PARK (4578 "New Power Generation" [Remix])....8-10 90
(Promotional issue only.)
PAISLEY PARK (4977 "Gett Off")....10-15 91
(Promotional issue only.)
PAISLEY PARK (4977 "Gett Off")....250-300 91
(Special birthday issue, with artwork by Prince. Promotional issue only.)
PAISLEY PARK (5141 "Insatiable")....15-25 91
(Promotional issue only. With picture cover.)
PAISLEY PARK (5148 "Diamonds & Pearls")....8-12 91
(Promotional issue only.)
PAISLEY PARK (5298 "Money Don't Matter")....15-25 91
(Promotional issue only. With picture cover.)
PAISLEY PARK (5570 "Sexy M-F")....10-15 91
(Promotional issue only.)
PAISLEY PARK (5770 "My Name Is Prince")....15-25 92
(Promotional issue only. With picture cover.)
PAISLEY PARK (20170 "Let's Pretend We're Married")....5-10 84
(With picture cover.)
PAISLEY PARK (20355 "Raspberry Beret") 5-8 85
(With picture cover.)
PAISLEY PARK (20357 "Pop Life")....5-8 85
(With picture cover.)
PAISLEY PARK (20389 "America")....5-8 85
(With picture cover.)
PAISLEY PARK (20516 "Anotherloverholenyohead")....5-8 85
(With picture cover.)
PAISLEY PARK (20728 "I Could Never Take the Place of Your Man")....8-10 87
(With picture cover.)
PAISLEY PARK (20930 "Alphabet St.")....5-8 88
(With picture cover.)
PAISLEY PARK (21074 "I Wish U Heaven")....5-8 88
(With picture cover.)
PAISLEY PARK (21422 "Scandalous Sex Suite")....5-8 89
(With picture cover.)
PAISLEY PARK (21598 "Thieves in the Temple")....5-8 90
(With picture cover.)
PAISLEY PARK (21783 "New Power Generation")....4-6 90
(With picture cover.)
PAISLEY PARK (40138 "Gett Off")....4-6 91
(With picture cover.)
PAISLEY PARK (40197 "Cream")....4-6 88
(With picture cover.)
PAISLEY PARK (41833 "Space")....4-6 94
(With picture cover.)
W.B. (741 "Just As Long As We're Together")....75-100 78
(Promotional issue only.)
W.B. (832 "I Wanna Be Your Lover")....50-75 79
(Promotional issue only.)
W.B. (848 "Why You Wanna Treat Me So Bad")....75-100 80
(Promotional issue only.)
W.B. (870 "Still Waiting")....75-100 79
(Promotional issue only.)
W.B. (904 "Uptown")....40-60 80
(Promotional issue only.)
W.B. (915 "Head")....50-75 80
(Promotional issue only. Single-sided.)
W.B. (916 "When You Were Mine")....50-75 80
(Promotional issue only.)
W.B. (937 "Head")....50-75 80
(Promotional issue only. Double-sided.)
W.B. (980 "Controversy")....30-50 81
(Promotional issue only. With title sleeve.)
W.B. (1004 "Let's Work")....50-75 81
(Promotional issue only.)
W.B. (1035 "Do Me Baby")....50-75 81
(Promotional issue only.)
W.B. (1070 "1999")....30-50 82
(Promotional issue only. With title sleeve.)
W.B. (1082 "Let's Pretend We're Married")....30-50 84
(Promotional issue only. With title sleeve.)
W.B. (2001 "Little Red Corvette")....30-50 83
(Promotional issue only. With title sleeve.)
W.B. (2080 "Delirious")....30-50 83
(Promotional issue only. With title sleeve.)
W.B. (2042 "1999")....30-50 82
(Promotional issue only. With title sleeve.)
W.B. (2139 "When Doves Cry")....15-25 84
(Black vinyl. Promotional issue only. With title sleeve.)
W.B. (2139 "When Doves Cry")....20-30 84
(Colored vinyl. Promotional issue only. With title sleeve.)
W.B. (2173 "Let's Go Crazy" [Edit])....15-25 84
(Promotional issue only. With title sleeve.)
W.B. (2182 "Let's Go Crazy" [Dance Mix])....15-25 84
(Promotional issue only. With title sleeve.)
W.B. (2192 "Purple Rain")....20-30 84
(Purple vinyl. Promotional issue only. With title sleeve.)
W.B. (2233 "I Would Die 4 U")....15-25 84
(Promotional issue only.)
W.B. (2263 "Take Me with U")....15-20 85
(Promotional issue only. With title sleeve.)
W.B. (3579 "Batdance")....5-8 89
(Promotional issue only.)
W.B. (3702 "Batdance")....8-12 89
(Promotional issue only.)
W.B. (3705 "Partyman")....8-12 89
(Promotional issue only.)
W.B. (20228 "When Doves Cry")....8-10 84
(With picture cover.)
W.B. (20246 "Let's Go Crazy")....5-8 84
(With picture cover.)
W.B. (20267 "Purple Rain")....5-8 85
(With picture cover.)
W.B. (20291 "I Would Die 4 U")....25-35 84
W.B. (21257 "Batdance")....4-6 89

Note: Designate promotional copies – as indicated by a gold sticker – of any 12-inch singles *not* listed separately, are roughly in the same price as commercial issues. Also, some may have picture covers or title sleeves, even though not shown here as with them.

Singles: 7-inch

PAISLEY PARK....4-8 85-93
W.B. (8619 "Soft and Wet")....15-25 78
W.B. (8713 "Just As Long As We're Together")....10-20 78
W.B. (20129 "Little Red Corvette")....20-25 83
(Picture disc.)
W.B. (22757 "Arms of Orion")....4-6 89
W.B. (22814 "Partyman")....3-6 89
W.B. (22824 "Scandalous")....3-6 89
W.B. (22924 "Batdance")....3-6 89
W.B. (28751 "Kiss")....4-6 86
W.B. (29079 "Take Me with U")....4-6 85
W.B. (29121 "I Would Die 4 U")....4-6 84
W.B. (29174 "Purple Rain")....4-6 84
(Black vinyl.)
W.B. (29174 "Purple Rain")....8-10 84
(Purple vinyl.)
W.B. (29216 "Let's Go Crazy")....4-6 84
W.B. (29286 "When Doves Cry")....4-6 84
(Black vinyl.)
W.B. (29286 "When Doves Cry")....5-10 84
(Colored vinyl.)
W.B. (29503 "Delirious")....4-6 83
W.B. (29548 "Let's Pretend We're Married")....4-6 84
W.B. (29746 "Little Red Corvette")....5-10 83
(Black vinyl.)
W.B. (29746 "Little Red Corvette")....10-15 83
(Picture disc.)
W.B. (29896 "1999")....10-15 82
W.B. (49050 "I Wanna Be Your Lover")...10-20 79
W.B. (49178 "Why You Wanna Treat Me So Bad")....10-15 80
W.B. (49226 "Still Waiting")....20-30 80
W.B. (49559 "Uptown")....10-15 80
W.B. (49638 "Dirty Mind")....10-15 81
W.B. (49808 "Controversy")....10-15 81
W.B. (50002 "Let's Work")....10-15 81
W.B. BACK TO BACK HITS....3-5

Promotional Singles

PAISLEY PARK (Except 2939 & 29052)....4-8 85-93
PAISLEY PARK (2939 "Hot Thing")....15-25 87
PAISLEY PARK (29052 "Paisley Park")...15-25 85
W.B. (8619 "Soft and Wet")....15-25 78
W.B. (8713 "Just As Long As We're Together")....10-20 78
W.B. (22757 "Arms of Orion")....4-6 89
W.B. (22814 "Partyman")....3-6 89
W.B. (22824 "Scandalous")....3-6 89
W.B. (22924 "Batdance")....3-6 89
W.B. (29079 "Take Me with U")....4-6 85
W.B. (29121 "I Would Die 4 U")....4-6 84
W.B. (29174 "Purple Rain")....4-6 84
(Black vinyl.)
W.B. (29174 "Purple Rain")....8-12 84
(Purple vinyl.)
W.B. (29216 "Let's Go Crazy")....4-6 84
W.B. (29286 "When Doves Cry")....4-8 84
(Black vinyl.)
W.B. (29286 "When Doves Cry")....8-10 84
(Colored vinyl.)
W.B. (29503 "Delirious")....4-6 83
W.B. (29548 "Let's Pretend We're Married")....4-8 84
W.B. (29746 "Little Red Corvette")....5-10 83
W.B. (29896 "1999")....10-15 82
W.B. (49050 "I Wanna Be Your Lover")...10-20 79
W.B. (49178 "Why You Wanna Treat Me So Bad")....10-15 80
W.B. (49226 "Still Waiting")....15-25 80
W.B. (49559 "Uptown")....10-15 80
W.B. (49638 "Dirty Mind")....10-15 81
W.B. (49808 "Controversy")....10-15 81

Picture Sleeves

PAISLEY PARK....4-8 85-89
W.B. (22757 "Arms of Orion")....4-6 89
W.B. (22814 "Partyman")....3-6 89
W.B. (22824 "Scandalous")....3-6 89
W.B. (22924 "Batdance")....3-6 89
W.B. (29079 "Take Me with U")....4-6 85
W.B. (29121 "I Would Die 4 U")....4-6 84
W.B. (29174 "Purple Rain")....4-6 84
W.B. (29216 "Let's Go Crazy")....4-6 84
W.B. (29286 "When Doves Cry")....4-6 84
W.B. (29503 "Delirious")....15-25 83
(Poster sleeve.)
W.B. (29548 "Let's Pretend We're Married")....4-8 84
W.B. (29896 "1999"/"1999")....15-20 82
(Promotional issue only.)
W.B. (29896 "1999"/"How Come U Don't Call Me Anymore")....10-15 82

W.B. (49178 "Why You Wanna Treat Me So Bad") 15-25 80
W.B. (49559 "Uptown") 10-15 80
LPs: 10/12-inch
HOT PINK (3223 "Minneapolis Genuis 94 East") 10-15 85
PAISLEY PARK (726 "Interruptus Collectus") 8-12 93
(Two discs.)
PAISLEY PARK (25286 "Around the World in a Day") 5-10 85
PAISLEY PARK (25395 "Parade") 5-10 86
PAISLEY PARK (25577 "Sign O' the Times") 8-12 87
(Two discs.)
PAISLEY PARK (25720 "Lovesexy") 5-8 88
(Tracks not banded.)
PAISLEY PARK (25720 "Lovesexy") 10-15 88
(Tracks are banded for easy selection.)
PAISLEY PARK (27493 "Graffiti Bridge") ... 5-10 88
W.B. (2896 "Yulesville") 40-60 78
(Colored vinyl. Promotional issue only.)
W.B. (3150 "For You") 10-15 78
W.B. (3328 "Winter Warnerland") 30-50 79
(Two colored vinyl discs; one red, one green. Promotional issue only.)
W.B. (3366 "Prince") 10-15 79
W.B. (3478 "Dirty Mind") 5-10 80
W.B. (3601 "Controversy") 10-15 81
(Includes poster.)
W.B. (3601 "Controversy") 5-10 81
(Without poster.)
W.B. (23720 "1999") 10-15 82
(Two discs.)
W.B. (25110 "Purple Rain") 8-10 84
(Black vinyl. Includes poster.)
W.B. (25110 "Purple Rain") 10-15 84
(Purple vinyl. Includes poster.)
W.B. (25110 "Purple Rain") 25-35 84
(Purple vinyl. Includes poster. With gold sticker. Promotional issue only.)
W.B. (25677 "Black Album") 3000-4000 87
(Blank cover. Reportedly contains four different mixes of *Batdance*.)
W.B. (25936 "Batman") 5-10 89
Note: Designate promotional copies – as indicated by a gold sticker – of any albums *not* listed separately, are in the $10 to $20 range.
Session: Lisa Coleman; Levi Seacer; Eric Leeds; Tony M.; Tommy Barbarella; Kirk Johnson; Damon Dickson; Sonny Thompson; Michael B.; Rosie Gaines; Dez Dickerson.
Also see LEWIS CONNECTION
Also see REVOLVER

PRINCE & SHEENA EASTON *P&R '87*
Singles: 7-inch
PAISLEY PARK (28289 "U Got the Look") ... 3-5 87
W.B. (22757 "The Arms of Orion") 3-5 89
Picture Sleeves
PAISLEY PARK (28289 "U Got the Look") ... 3-5 87
W.B. (22757 "The Arms of Orion") 3-5 89
Also see PRINCE

PRINCE, Al, & His Orchestra
Singles: 78 rpm
SWING TIME (319 "Don't Love a Married Woman") 20-40 52
Singles: 7-inch
RONN (39 "New Orleans") 5-10

PRINCE, Bobby
(With Al Smith's Orchestra)
Singles: 78 rpm
CHANCE 25-75 52-54
EXCELLO 15-25 54
MGM 10-15 54
Singles: 7-inch
CHANCE (1128 "Tell Me, Why? Why? Why?") 250-350 52
CHANCE (1158 "Better Think It Over") 250-350 54
EXCELLO (2039 "Too Many Keys") 25-50 54
MGM)11828 "One Sweet Kiss") 15-25 54

PRINCE, Dolph
Singles: 78 rpm
KING 10-15 57
Singles: 7-inch
KING (5077 "Blues Don't Call My Name") 15-25 57
STRAND (25006 "My Own True Love") 8-12 59

TIVOLI (1719 "No More") 5-10 65

PRINCE, Dorothy
Singles: 7-inch
M-PAC (7202 "I Lost a Love") 10-20 63
M-PAC (7206 "Seek and You'll Find") 10-20 63
M-PAC (7208 "I Lost a Love") 10-15 63

PRINCE, Jack
Singles: 78 rpm
SPADE (1934 "Rock Um Beat") 15-25 56
Singles: 7-inch
SPADE (1934 "Rock Um Beat") 75-125 56

PRINCE, Peppy
(With His Sugar Men; with Christine Chatman)
Singles: 78 rpm
HOLLYWOOD 10-20 54
MERCURY 5-10 51
MILLION 5-10 54
SELECTIVE 5-10 50
Singles: 7-inch
DOOTONE (430 "Dance Party") 10-20 58
HOLLYWOOD (1013 "Work Man Work") . 20-30 54
MILLION 10-20 54
LPs: 10/12-inch
DOOTO 30-40 56
Also see CHATMAN, Christine

PRINCE, Rod
Singles: 7-inch
COMET (2140 "Rainbow of Love") 35-45 61

PRINCE & PAUPERS
Singles: 7-inch
JRJ (2115 "Shoulder of a Giant") 60-80 65

PRINCE ARKY
Singles: 7-inch
NEW STAR ("Ten-Horned Devil") 100-200
(Selection number not known.)

PRINCE BUSTER *P&R/R&B '67*
(With the Sea Busters; Buster Campbell)
Singles: 7-inch
AMY (906 "Everybody Ska") 5-10 64
ATLANTIC (2231 "Don't Make Me Cry") 5-10 64
PHILIPS (40427 "Ten Commandments") . 10-15 67
RCA (9114 "Ain't That Saying a Lot") 5-10 67
STELLAR (1501 "Madness") 5-10 64
LPs: 10/12-inch
RCA (3792 "Ten Commandments") 10-20 67

PRINCE CHARLES
(With the Charmers)
Singles: 7-inch
CLASS (301 "Good Luck Charm") 15-25 62
JET STREAM (715 "Sick") 10-15 64
JIN (127 "Cheryl Ann") 10-20 60

PRINCE PAUL & SWINGIN' IMPERIALS
Singles: 7-inch
PARKER (9298 "In the Beginning") 125-150

PRINCE PHILLIP
Singles: 7-inch
SMASH (2152 "Keep On Talking") 15-25 68

PRINCE PRESTON
(With the Barnells)
Singles: 7-inch
CONGRESSIONAL (113 "She Belongs to Me") 100-200 62
CONGRESSIONAL (115 "Dancing Girl") 100-200 62

PRINCETON FIVE
Singles: 7-inch
PRINCETON (711 "Summertime Blues") . 15-25 64

PRINCETONS
Singles: 7-inch
COLPIX (793 "Georgianna") 10-15 65
PHILIPS (40379 "You're My Love") 15-25 66
PRINCETON (1465 "Georgianna") 20-30 65
WAND (193 "Little Miss Sad") 8-12 65

PRINCETONS FIVE
Singles: 7-inch
BECE (1001 "Goin' Nowhere") 10-20 61
BECE (1203 "Deadman") 10-20 61

PRINDER, Shad
Singles: 7-inch
INFINITY (009 "Here Goes a Fool") 40-50 61

PRINZ, Rosemary "Penny"
("TVs Penny")
Singles: 7-inch
PHAROS (103 "Penny") 5-10 64
LPs: 10/12-inch
PHAROS (10001 "Rosemary Prinz") 25-40

PRISCILLA
(Priscilla Paris)
Singles: 7-inch
YORK (405 "He Noticed Me") 5-10 67
LPs: 10/12-inch
HAPPY TIGER 8-12
YORK (4005 "Priscilla Sings Herself") 20-30 67
Session: Davie Allan.
Also see ALLAN, Davie
Also see PARIS SISTERS

PRISCO, Mike
Singles: 7-inch
ZIP (101 "I Love You Baby") 100-200 57

PRISCO, Tommy
(With Frank Hunter & Orchestra)
Singles: 78 rpm
KING (1178 "Now I Know") 5-10 53
WING (90071 "Lovers in Love") 5-10 56
Singles: 7-inc
EPIC (9219 "Maybe Someday") 10-20 57
EPIC (9239 "Hasty Words") 10-20 57
EPIC (9267 "Chewin' Gum") 10-20 58
EPIC (9302 "Till There Was You") 10-20 59
EPIC (9315 "Stingaree") 10-20 59
KING (1178 "Now I Know") 10-20 53
WING (90071 "Lovers in Love") 10-20 56
Picture Sleeves
EPIC 20-25 59
(We're not certain which of the Epic singles had a sleeve.)
Also see HUNTER, Frank

PRISM *P&R/LP '77*
Singles: 7-inch
ARIOLA AMERICA 4-6 77-79
CAPITOL 3-5 82
Picture Sleeves
CAPITOL 3-5 82
LPs: 10/12-inch
ARIOLA AMERICA (Except 50034) 10-15 77-79
ARIOLA AMERICA (50034 "Live Tonite") 15-25 78
(Promotional issue only.)
CAPITOL 5-10 80-82

PRISONAIRES
("Confined to the Tennessee State Prison Nashville, Tennessee")
Singles: 78 rpm
SUN (186 "Just Walkin' in the Rain") 100-200 53
SUN (189 "Softly & Tenderly") 100-150 53
SUN (191 "I Know") 75-125 53
SUN (207 "What'll You Do Next") 300-500 54
Singles: 7-inch
SUN (186 "Just Walkin' in the Rain") 200-300 53
(Black vinyl.)
SUN (186 "Just Walkin' in the Rain") 2500-3500 53
(Red vinyl.)
SUN (189 "Softly & Tenderly") 500-600 53
SUN (191 "I Know") 200-300 53
(Black vinyl.)
SUN (191 "I Know") 2500-3500 53
(Red vinyl.)
SUN (207 "There Is Love") 7500-8500 54
SUN (500 series) 5-10 76
Members: Johnny Bragg; John Drew; Marcell Andess; William Stewart.
Also see BRAGG, Johnny

PRITCHETT, Dub
Singles: 7-inch
DONA (1003 "I Don't Know How to Cook") 15-25
DONA (1001 "I Ain't Gonna Do It") 40-60
PEACEFUL VALLEY (402 "Five O'Clock Hop") 200-300

PRITCHETT, Jimmy
Singles: 7-inch
CRYSTAL (503 "That's the Way I Feel") 200-300 58

PRIVATE PARTY
Singles
MASQUE (8911 "Living on the Edge") 15-20 89
(Guitar pick-shaped picture disc. 100 made.)

PRIVATE PROPERTY OF DIGIL
Singles: 7-inch
TARGET (109/110 "Look At Me"/"To My Friends") 30-50 67
TEE PEE (23/24 "Sunshine Flames"/"Princess") 30-50 67
TEE PEE (35/36 "Jewelry Lady"/"I'm Looking At You") 30-50 67
TEE PEE (115/116 "Destination Nowhere"/"Patch of Brick") 30-50 67
Members: Doug Yankus; Chuck Posniak; Dan Jacklyn; Steve Gertch; Gary Schibilski; Dave Faas.

PROBY, P.J. *P&R '64*
Singles: 7-inch
IMPERIAL (66079 "Rocking Pneumonia") . 5-10 64
LIBERTY 8-15 61-68
LONDON (9688 "Hold Me") 10-15 64
LONDON (9705 "Together") 5-10 64
SURFSIDE (714 "I Need Love") 8-12 65
Picture Sleeves
LIBERTY (55974 "Work with Me Annie") . 10-20 67
LPs: 10/12-inch
LIBERTY 20-30 65-68
Also see POWERS, Jett

PROCOL HARUM *P&R/R&B/LP '67*
Singles: 7-inch
A&M 4-8 67-72
CHRYSALIS 4-6 73-77
DERAM (7507 "Whiter Shade of Pale") ... 10-15 67
Picture Sleeves
A&M (1347 "Conquistador") 4-8 72
CHRYSALIS 4-8 73
LPs: 10/12-inch
A&M (Except 4294 & 8053) 8-12 68-73
A&M (4294 "Broken Barricades") 12-15 71
(With die-cut gatefold cover.)
A&M (4294 "Broken Barricades") 10-12 72
(With standard cover.)
A&M (8053 "Procol Harum Lives") .... 30-40 '70s
(Promotional issue only.)
CHRYSALIS 8-10 73-77
DERAM (16008 "Procol Harum") 50-75 67
(Monaural. With bonus poster, which represents $15 to $20 of the value.)
DERAM (18008 "Procol Harum") 50-75 67
(Stereo. Includes bonus poster which represents $15 to $20 of the value.)
Members: Gary Brooker; Bobby Harrison; Matthew Fisher; Dave Knights; Ray Royer; Robin Trower; Diz Derrick.
Also see PARAMOUNTS
Also see TROWER, Robin

PRODIGALS
Singles: 7-inch
ABNER (1011 "Judy") 15-25 58
ABNER (1015 "Won't You Believe") 75-100 58
COLLECTABLES .... 3-5 '80s
FALCON (1011 "Judy") 20-30 58
TOLLIE (9019 "Judy") 5-10 64

PROFESSIONALS
Singles: 7-inch
GROOVE CITY (101 "That's Why I Love You") .... 150-250 '60s

PROFESSOR BUG
Singles: 7-inch
BEETLE (1600 "Beatlemania Beetle") 15-20 64

PROFESSOR HAMILTON & SCHOOL BOYS
(Robert Hamilton)
Singles: 7-inch
CONTOUR (0001 "Back to School") 10-20 61

PROFESSOR LONGHAIR
(With the Clippers; with His Blues Scholars; with His Shuffling Hungarians; with His New Orleans Boys)
Singles: 78 rpm
ATLANTIC (897 "Mardi Gras in New Orleans") 75-125 50
ATLANTIC (906 "Walk Your Blues Away") 75-125 50
ATLANTIC (1020 "In the Night") 40-60 53
EBB (101 "Cry Pretty Baby") 50-75 57
EBB (106 "Misery") 50-75 57
EBB (121 "Looka No Hair") 50-75 57

STAR TALENT (808 "Mardi Gras in New Orleans")....150-200 49
STAR TALENT (809 "She Ain't Got No Hair")....150-200 49

Singles: 7-inch

ATLANTIC (1020 "In the Night")....100-200 53
EBB (101 "Cry Pretty Baby")....75-125 57
EBB (106 "Misery")....75-125 57
EBB (121 "Looka No Hair")....50-100 57
RIP (155 "I Believe I'm Gonna Leave")....30-40 62
RON (326 "Cuttin' Out")....10-15 58
(Yellow label.)
RON (326 "Cuttin' Out")....35-45 58
(White label. Promotional issue.)
RON (329 "Goin' to the Mardi Gras")....10-15 59
(Yellow label.)
RON (329 "Goin' to the Mardi Gras")....25-35 59
(Pink and black label.)
RON (Red label)....5-10
SPECIALTY....4-6 '70s
WATCH (1900 "Big Chief")....8-12 65
WATCH (1904 "Third House from the Corner")....8-12 65
WATCH (6000 series)....15-20 63

EPs: 7-inch

MERCURY....75-100
(1970s promotional EP, issued without special cover. Has two Professor Longhair tracks and two by other artists.)

LPs: 10/12-inch

ALLIGATOR....5-8 80
ATLANTIC....10-15 72-82
HARVEST....8-12 78
J.S.P.....8-12
NIGHTHAWK....5-10 82
MARDI GRAS....8-12
Also see BOYD, Robert
Also see BYRD, Roy

PROFESSOR MARCELL & COLLEGIANS

Singles: 7-inch

MAYHAMS (214 "Surfin' On a Swingin' Soiree")....15-25 64
Also see BISCAYNE BAY SURFERS

PROFESSOR MORRISON'S LOLLIPOP P&R '68

Singles: 7-inch

WHITE WHALE (275 "You Got the Love").5-10 68
WHITE WHALE (288 "Angela")....5-10 69
WHITE WHALE (293 "Oo-Poo-Pah Susie")....5-10 69
Members: Jeff Travis; Craig Perkins, Kelly Kotera, Frank Elia; Bruce Watson.
Session: Layng Martine Jr.
Also see COACHMEN
Also see MARTINE, Layng

PROFESSORS

Singles: 7-inch

FAMAS (59002 "Look at Her")....50-75 59

PROFFITT, Randy, & Beachcombers
(With the Jordanaires)

Singles: 7-inch

Bett-Coe (103 "Check That Baby Out One Time")....25-35 62
Also see JORDANAIRES

PROFILES

Singles: 7-inch

GOLDIE (1103 "Take a Giant Step")....20-30 62

PROFILES

Singles: 7-inch

GAIT (1444 "Never")....100-200 65
MUSICLAND USA (20004 "Raindrops")....8-12 66

PROFITS

Singles: 7-inch

SIRE (353 "The Wind")....5-10 71
(Black vinyl.)
SIRE (353 "The Wind")....10-20 71
(Red vinyl. Promotional issue.)

PROFONIX, The

Singles: 7-inch

DAVEY-PAUL (4023 "Ain't No Sun")....10-20

PROMINENTS

Singles: 7-inch

LUMMTONE (116 "Just a Little")....15-25 65

PRONTO, Dennie, & Colonials

Singles: 7-inch

DEBLYN (717 "It's No Secret"/"Destiny").30-40
DEBLYN (7337 "It's No Secret"/"Little One")....30-40
(Also shows the number: "45-1." It's not clear which is the preferred selection number.)

PROPHET, Billy

Singles: 7-inch

MERRIMAC (1001 "Puppet on a String").10-20 62
SUE (133 "What Can I Do")....40-60 65

PROPHET, Johnny

Singles: 7-inch

CATHAY (105 "Find a Penny")....10-20 60
DITTO (107 "I Was Born Last Monday")..15-25 57
J&P (150 "More")....8-12 '60s
J.J. (2267 "I Didn't Mean to Love You")....10-15
RCA (7282 "Banana")....10-15 58

LPs: 10/12-inch

J&H (1001 "At Harold's Club")....15-20 67

PROPHETS

Singles: 7-inch

JAIRICK (201 "Sha-La-La")....75-100 63

PROPHETS

Singles: 7-inch

TWIN-SPIN (3000 "Yes I Know")....15-25 66

PROPHETS

Singles: 7-inch

CHESS (2006 "Dance Dance Dance")....5-10 67
SHELL (1005 "I Still Love You")....10-20 '60s
STEPHAYNE (335 "My Kind of Girl")....10-20 66

PROPHETS

Singles: 7-inch

BSP....4-6 79
DELPHI ("Don't You Think It's Time")....15-25 67
(Selection number not known.)
DELPHI (007 "Talk Don't Bother Me")....15-25 67
ERIC....4-6 '70s
JUBILEE (5565 "Talk Don't Bother Me")..15-25 66
JUBILEE (5596 "Don't You Think It's Time")....15-25 67
JUBILEE....10-15 66-67
RIPETE....3-5 83
SMASH (2161 "I Got the Fever")....5-10 68
Members: Tommy Witcher; Pete Pendleton; Barbara Pendleton; Fred Williamson; Billy Scott; Jim Campbell; Walter Stanley.

PROVERBIAL KNEE HIGHS

Singles: 7-inch

BEACHCOMBER (11 "Watch Out")....10-20 '60s

PROVISOR, Denny

Singles: 7-inch

20TH FOX (506 "Mickey Mouse")....5-10 64
VALIANT (717 "Little Girl Lost")....8-12 65
VALIANT (728 "She's Not Mine Anymore")....8-12 65
Also see GRASS ROOTS
Also see HOOK

PROW, Jimmy Lee

Singles: 78 rpm

KING (4929 "Shopping List")....10-15 56

Singles: 7-inch

KING (4929 "Shopping List")....15-25 56

PROWLERS

Singles: 7-inch

ARAGON (302 "Rock Me Baby")....100-150
ARAGON (303 "Get a Move On")....50-75

PRUITT, Lewis C&W '59

Singles: 7-inch

DECCA (31038 "Timbrook")....10-15 60
DECCA (31095 "Softly and Tenderly")....10-15 60
DECCA (31201 "Crazy Bullfrog")....30-50 61
DECCA (31295 "This Little Girl")....10-15 61
GREAT (1135 "Big Wheel from Boston")....5-8 68
MUSIC TOWN (020 "We're Going Down Together")....4-8 69
PEACH (703 "Pretty Baby")....150-175 58
PEACH (710 "This Little Girl")....50-75 58
PEACH (725 "Timbrook")....15-25 59
VEE-JAY (502 "Thanks a Lot")....5-10 63
VEE-JAY (601 "I'd Rather Say Goodbye").5-10 64
Also see SMITH, Carl

PRUITT, Major

Singles: 7-inch

D.W.A. (104 "Trouble in Mind")....30-40 64

PRUITT, Ralph

Singles: 7-inch

B.B. (226 "Louise")....75-100
GOLD CIRCLE (211 "Louise")....50-75
LARK (1506 "Hey Mr. Porter")....450-550
MERIDIAN (1506 "Hey Mr. Porter")....200-300 58

PRYOR, Cactus, & His Pricklypears C&W '50

Singles: 78 rpm

4 STAR....5-10 50

Singles: 7-inch

4 STAR (1459 "Cry of the Dying Duck in a Thunder-Storm")....15-25 50

PRYOR, Snooky
(With His Trio)

Singles: 78 rpm

J.O.B. (101 "Boogy Fool")....200-300 50
J.O.B. (115 "I'm Getting Tired")....200-300 52
PARROT (807 "Crosstown Blues")....100-200 54
VEE-JAY (215 "Someone to Love Me")...25-50 56

Singles: 7-inch

J.O.B. (1014 "Cryin' Shame")....450-550 53
J.O.B. (1126 "Uncle Sam, Don't Take My Man")....450-550 63
PARROT (807 "Crosstown Blues")....350-450 54
(Black vinyl.)
PARROT (807 "Crosstown Blues")....550-650 54
(Red vinyl.)
VEE-JAY (215 "Someone to Love Me")....100-200 56

LPs: 10/12-inch

BLUESWAY (6076 "Do It If You Want To")....8-12 73
TODAY (1012 "And the Country Blues")..35-45
Session: Sunnyland Slim; Eddie Taylor.
Also see SNOOKY & MOODY
Also see SUNNYLAND SLIM
Also see TAYLOR, Eddie
Also see YOUNG, Johnny

PRYSOCK, Arthur R&B '52

Singles: 78 rpm

DECCA....5-10 52-54
MERCURY....5-10 54-55
PEACOCK....5-10 57
WING....5-10 55

Singles: 7-inch

BETHLEHEM....4-6 72
DECCA (25000 series)....5-10 65
DECCA (27000 thru 29000 series)....10-20 52-54
DECCA (31000 series)....5-10 64-65
GUSTO....4-6 79
KING....4-8 69-71
MCA....4-6 78
MGM....4-6 70
MERCURY....10-20 54-55
OLD TOWN (100 series)....4-6 73-76
OLD TOWN (1000 series)....10-20 58-60
(Light blue label.)
OLD TOWN (1000 series)....4-6 76-78
(Dark blue or black label.)
OLD TOWN (1100 series)....8-12 61-66
PEACOCK....10-20 57
VERVE....5-10 66-69
WING (90016 "Come Home")....10-20 55

EPs: 7-inch

OLD TOWN (9 "Double Header")....8-10 65

LPs: 10/12-inch

DECCA....15-20 64-65
KING....8-12 69-71
MCA....5-10 78
OLD TOWN (100 series)....20-30 60-62
OLD TOWN (2000 series)....15-25 62-65
OLD TOWN (12000 series)....5-10 73-77
POLYDOR....5-10 77
VERVE....10-20 66-69
Also see ECKSTINE, Billy / Arthur Prysock
Also see JOHNSON, Buddy

PRYSOCK, Arthur, & Count Basie LP '66

Singles: 7-inch

VERVE (10396 "I Worry 'Bout You")....4-8 66

LPs: 10/12-inch

VERVE (8646 "Arthur Prysock / Count Basie")....15-20 66
Also see BASIE, Count

PRYSOCK, Red
(With the His House Rockers; Reo Prysock; Red Proysock)

Singles: 78 rpm

MERCURY....5-15 54-57
RED ROBIN (107 "Wiggles")....25-50 52
RED ROBIN (117 "Hard Rock")....15-25 53
RED ROBIN (139 "Hammer")....15-25 55
WING (90070 "Fruit Boots")....8-12 56

Singles: 7-inch

CHESS (2042 "Groovy Sax")....5-10 68
GATEWAY (735 "Wildcat")....5-10 64
JUNIOR (1015 "Groovy Sax")....5-10 67
KING (5595 "Hand Clappin' ")....5-10 62
KING (5644 "Quick As a Flash")....5-10 62
KING (5669 "Hideaway '62")....5-10 62
KING (5704 "Here We Go")....5-10 62
MERCURY (30117 "Hand Clappin' ")....5-10 64
MERCURY (70367 thru 71786)....10-20 54-61
RED ROBIN (107 "Wiggles")....75-100 52
RED ROBIN (117 "Hard Rock")....50-75 53
RED ROBIN (139 "The Hammer")....50-75 55
WING (90070 "Fruit Boots")....15-25 56

EPs: 7-inch

MERCURY....40-60 56

LPs: 10/12-inch

FORUM CIRCLE (9083 "The Big Sound of Red Prysock")....10-20 64
MERCURY (20088 "Rock 'N Roll")....75-100 56
MERCURY (20307 "The Beat")....50-75 56
MERCURY (20512 "Swing Softly")....20-30 61
(Monaural.)
MERCURY (60188 "Swing Softly")....25-35 61
(Stereo.)
SAXOPHONOGRAPH (502 "Cryin' My Heart Out")....5-10 83
WING (12007 "Fruit Boots")....35-50 57
Also see GRIMES, Tiny
Also see PLATTERS / Red Prysock / Dinah Washington

PSYCHOTICS

Singles: 7-inch

ACID (24975 "If You Don't Believe Me, Don't")....40-60 60

PSYCHOTICS

Singles: 7-inch

UPTOWN (7666 "I'm Determined")....40-60 67

Picture Sleeves

UPTOWN (7666 "I'm Determined")....50-75 67

PUBLIO & VALIANTS

Singles: 7-inch

IRISH (6255 "Lonely Guy")....200-300 62
MENARD (6252 "Image of Love")....500-750 63

PUCKETT, Dennis
(Dennis "The Rocket" Puckett)

Singles: 7-inch

EMERALD (2018 "Rockin' Teens")....75-100 58
EMERALD (2551 "Jungle Jive")....5-10
(Suggested price indicates this must be a recent issue, probably of 1958 tracks.)

Picture Sleeves

EMERALD (2018 "Rockin' Teens")....150-200 58

PUCKETT, Gary P&R '67
(With the Union Gap; Union Gap Featuring Gary Puckett)

Singles: 7-inch

COLUMBIA....4-8 67-72
COLUMBIA HALL of FAME....4-6 '70s
GUSTO....3-5 81-83

Picture Sleeves

COLUMBIA....5-10 67-70

LPs: 10/12-inch

BACK-TRAC....5-8 85
CSP....8-10 72
COLUMBIA (Except 10171)....10-20 68-71
COLUMBIA (10171 "Young Girl")....5-10
COLUMBIA HOUSE (6272/3 "Fillin' the Gap")....20-30 75
(Three-discs; one double and one single LP set.)
51 WEST....5-10 82
GUSTO....5-8 83
HARMONY....8-12 72
Members: Gary Puckett; Paul Wheatbread; Gary Withem; Kerry Chater; Dwight Bement.
Also see FRANKLIN, Aretha / Union Gap / Blood, Sweat & Tears / Moby Grape

PUDDIN' HEADS
Singles: 7-inch
CATCH (111 "Now You Say We're Through")....15-25 64

PUDDLE JUMPERS
Singles: 7-inch
FEDERAL (12336 "Snake Charmer")....15-25 58
FEDERAL (12343 "Headin' South")....15-25 58

PUGSLEY MUNION
Singles: 7-inch
J&S (2 "Just Like You")....15-25 69
LPs: 10/12-inch
J&S (001 "Just Like You")....60-80 69
Member: John Schuller.

PULLEN, Dwight
Singles: 7-inch
CARLTON (455 "Sunglasses After Dark")....100-200 61
SAGE (279 "By You, by the Bayou")....15-25 59
Also see PULLEN, Whitey

PULLEN, Whitey
(Dwight Pullen)
Singles: 7-inch
SAGE (238 "You'll Get Yours")....50-75 59
SAGE (274 "Walk My Way Back Home")....100-150 59
SAGE (294 "Let's All Go Wild Tonight")....100-150 59
SAGE (303 "I'm Beggin' Your Pardon")....25-50 60
SAGE (313 "Tuscaloosa Lucy")....100-150 60
SAGE (372 "Crazy in Love")....50-75 63
SAGE & SAND (372 "Crazy in Love")....20-30 64
Also see PULLEN, Dwight

PULLENS, Vern
Singles: 78 rpm
SPADE (1927 "Bop Crazy Baby")....150-200 56
Singles: 7-inch
ROCK IT (105 "Jitterbuggin' Baby")....4-8 79
SPADE (1927 "Bop Crazy Baby")....400-500 56
SPADE (1930 "It Took One Moment")....100-200 57
SPADE (11975 "Rock On Mabel")....5-10 75
LPs: 10/12-inch
ROCK IT (1003 "Rockin' Again")....8-12 79

PULLINS, Leroy *C&W/P&R '66*
Singles: 7-inch
KAPP....4-8 66
LPs: 10/12-inch
KAPP (3488 "I'm a Nut")....20-30 66
KAPP (3557 "Funny Bones and Hearts")....15-25 68

PULLUM, Joe
Singles: 78 rpm
SWING TIME (267 "My Woman, Part 1")....20-30 48

PULSE
Singles: 7-inch
ATCO (6530 "Burritt Bradley")....10-15 67
POISON RING (711 "Another Woman")....5-10 69
LPs: 10/12-inch
POISON RING (2237 "Pulse")....15-25 69
Members: Carl Donnell; Paul Rosano; Peter Neri; Jeff Potter; Rich Bednarzyck; Benet Segal.
Also see BRAM RIGG SET
Also see SHAGS

PUMA, Larry
(With the Triotones)
Singles: 7-inch
INTRASTATE (43 "Valerie Jo")....50-75 59

PURCELL BROTHERS
Singles: 7-inch
TAMANGO (252 "So They Tell Me")....100-125

PURDY, Steve, & Studs
Singles: 7-inch
VESTA (200 "The Weed")....100-150 62
(1000 copies made.)
VESTA (201 "I Cried")....125-175 62
(500 copies made.)

PURIFY, James & Bobby *P&R/R&B '66*
Singles: 7-inch
BELL....5-10 65-69
CASABLANCA....4-6 74-75
MERCURY....4-6 76-77
SPHERE SOUND....5-10 66
LPs: 10/12-inch
BELL....10-20 66-67
MERCURY....8-12 77
Members: James Purify; Bobby Dickey; Ben Moore.

PURKISS, D., & Fi-Dells
Singles: 7-inch
UNITED SOUNDS (110 "Alone Without Love")....40-50 64

PURPLE UNDERGROUND
Singles: 7-inch
BOSS (010 "Count Back")....15-25 '70s
BOSS (0095 "On Broadway")....15-25 72

PUSSYCATS
(Pussy Cats)
Singles: 7-inch
COLUMBIA (43272 "I Want Your Love")....8-12 65
COLUMBIA (43587 "You Can't Stop Loving Me")....8-12 66
KEETCH (6003 "You May Be Holding My Baby")....10-15 64
KEYMAN (6000 "Anniversary of Love")....50-75 63

PUZZLES
Singles: 7-inch
FAT BACK (216 "I Need You")....10-15 68
Also see FOUR PUZZLES

PYPES
Singles: 7-inch
PRISM (1942 "Tunnel of Love")....20-30 65

PYRAMIDERS
Singles: 7-inch
SCOTT (1205 "Don't Ever Leave Me")....750-1200 58

PYRAMIDS
(With Fletcher Smith's Band)
Singles: 78 rpm
C NOTE (108 "Someday")....500-750 55
FEDERAL (12233 "Deep in My Heart for You")....100-200 55
(Green label.)
FEDERAL (12233 "Deep in My Heart for You")....100-200 55
(White bio label. Promotional issue only.)
HOLLYWOOD (1047 "Someday")....250-350 55
Singles: 7-inch
C NOTE (108 "Someday")....4000-5000 55
FEDERAL (12233 "Deep in My Heart for You")....300-400 55
(Green label.)
FEDERAL (12233 "Deep in My Heart for You")....400-500 55
(White bio label. Promotional issue only.)
HOLLYWOOD (1047 "Someday")....750-1000 55
Members: Sidney Correia; Joe Dandy; Melvin White; Kenneth Perdue; Lionel Cobbs; Tom Williams.
Also see TEMPO-MENTALS

PYRAMIDS
Singles: 78 rpm
DAVIS....10-15 57
Singles: 7-inch
DAVIS (453 "At Any Cost")....20-30 57
DAVIS (457 "Why Did You Go")....40-50 57
Members: Roland Douglas; Joe Stallings; Richard Foster; Hubie Saulsberry.
Also see WHITAKER, Ruby, & Pyramids

PYRAMIDS
(With Billy Mure Orchestra)
Singles: 7-inch
COLLECTABLES....3-5 '80s
SHELL (711 "Ankle Bracelet")....40-50 58
(Gray label. Pictures two sea shells.)
SHELL (711 "Ankle Bracelet")....15-25 64
(White label. No sea shells shown.)
Also see MURE, Billy
Also see ORIGINAL PYRAMIDS

PYRAMIDS
Singles: 7-inch
CUB (9112 "I'm the Playboy")....8-12 62
SONBERT ("I'm the Playboy")....40-50 62
(No selection number used.)
VEE-JAY (489 "What Is Love")....5-10 63
Also see SATINTONES

PYRAMIDS *P&R/LP '64*
Singles: 7-inch
BEST (1 "Pyramid's Stomp")....20-25 63
BEST (102 "Penetration")....25-35 63
BEST (13001 "Pyramid's Stomp")....8-12 63
BEST (13002 "Penetration")....8-12 63
CEDWICKE (13005 "Midnight Run")....20-30 64
CEDWICKE (13006 "Contact")....20-30 64
SUNDAZED....5-10 90s
(Colored vinyl.)
Picture Sleeves
BEST (13002 "Penetration")....20-30 63
LPs: 10/12-inch
BEST (1001 "Penetration")....100-200 63
(Monaural.)
BEST (16501 "Penetration")....75-125 64
(Monaural.)
BEST (36501 "Penetration")....100-200 64
(Stereo.)
WHAT (2404 "Penetration")....5-8 83

PYTHON LEE JACKSON *P&R/LP '72*
(With Rod Stewart)
Singles: 7-inch
EUROGRAM (5001 "In a Broken Dream")....10-15
GNP (449 "In a Broken Dream")....4-8 72
LPs: 10/12-inch
GNP (2066 "In a Broken Dream")....10-15 72
Also see SMALL FACES
Also see STEWART, Rod

Q

QUAD, Bill, & Ravens
Singles: 7-inch
FLING (712 "Oh Susie Darling")....15-25 59
SAHARA (108 "Listen to Me")....5-10 65

QUADDELLS
Singles: 7-inch
VIDA ("Meatball")....10-15 62
(Selection number not known.)

QUADRANGLE
Singles: 7-inch
PHILIPS (40408 "She's Too Familiar Now")....15-25 66

QUADRELLS
Singles: 78 rpm
WHIRLIN' DISC....20-30 56
Singles: 7-inch
WHIRLIN' DISC (103 "Come to Me")....75-125 56

QUADS
Singles: 7-inch
VAULT (907 "Surfin' Hearse")....15-25 63

QUADS / Grand Prix / Customs
LPs: 10/12-inch
VAULT (104 "Hot Rod City")....25-35 63
Also see CUSTOMS
Also see GRAND PRIX
Also see QUADS

QUAIL, Rex
Singles: 7-inch
APACHE (1836 "Good Rockin' Tonight")....50-75 60

QUAILS
Singles: 78 rpm
DELUXE....25-35 55
Singles: 7-inch
DELUXE (6085 "The Things She Used to Do")....50-75 55
Also see ROBINSON, Bill, & Quails

QUAILS
Singles: 7-inch
HARVEY (116 "My Love")....15-25 62
HARVEY (120 "I Thought")....10-20 63
Also see FIVE QUAILS

QUAKER CITY BOYS *P&R '58*
Singles: 7-inch
SWAN (4023 "Teasin' ")....10-20 58
SWAN (4026 "Love Me Tonight")....10-20 59
SWAN (4045 "Goodbye '50s, Hello '60s")....10-20 59
Member: Tommy Reilly.

QUAL, Rex
Singles: 7-inch
APACHE (1836 "Going Rocking Tonight")....400-600

QUARRYMEN
Singles: 7-inch
SARA (6624 "Don't Try Your Luck")....10-20 66

QUARTA, George, Jr.
Singles: 7-inch
COOL (118 "Get Loose")....250-350

QUARTER NOTES *P&R '59*
(Quarter-Notes)
Singles: 78 rpm
DOT (15685 "Like You Bug Me")....15-25 57
Singles: 7-inch
BISON (757 "Frantic Flip")....15-20 60
DELUXE (6116 "Loneliness")....10-15 57
DELUXE (6129 "My Fantasy")....10-15 57
DOT (15685 "Like You Bug Me")....20-30 57
GLENN (2550 "The Shock")....10-20 62
(First issued as *Guitar Bass Boogie*, by Gary Vallet. Has sound effects added.)
GUYDEN (2083 "Pretty Preity Eyes")....10-15 63
IMPERIAL (5647 "Frantic Flip")....10-15 60
LITTLE STAR (112 "Baby")....500-750 62
RCA (7327 "Punkanilla")....10-20 58
WIZZ (715 "Record Hop Blues")....15-25 59
Also see VALLET, Gary

QUARTERMAN, Joe *R&B '72*
(Sir Joe Quarterman & Free Soul)
Singles: 7-inch
GSF....5-10 72-74
MERCURY....4-6 74-75
LPs: 10/12-inch
GSF (1009 "Sir Joe Quarterman and Free Soul")....100-150 73

QUARTETTE TRÉS BIEN
Singles: 7-inch
ATLANTIC (2295 "Three O'Clock in the Morning")....5-10 65
DECCA (31904 "Love Theme from *Madame X*")....5-10 66
GASLIGHT (402 "Always on Sunday")....10-20 62
NORMAN (526 "Ramblin' Rose")....20-25 62
NORMAN (534 "Secretly")....20-25 63
NORMAN (541 "Boss Tres Bien")....20-25 63
NORMAN (559 " Three O'Clock in the Morning")....20-25 65
LPs: 10/12-inch
DECCA (4822 "Where It's At")....10-15 67
DECCA (4893 "Here It Is")....10-15 67
NORMAN (102 "Quartette Tres Bien")....10-20 62
NORMAN (107 "Kilimanjaro")....10-20 63

QUATERMASS
LPs: 10/12-inch
HARVEST (314 "Quatermass")....15-20 70

QUATTLEBAUM, Doug
Singles: 78 rpm
GOTHAM (519 "Don't Be Funny, Baby")....25-50 53
Singles: 7-inch
GOTHAM (519 "Don't Be Funny, Baby")....50-75 53
LPs: 10/12-inch
PRESTIGE BLUESVILLE (1065 "Softee Man Blues")....100-150 62

QUEEN *LP '73*
Singles: 12-inch
CAPITOL....4-8 84-86
ELEKTRA (11401 "Fat Bottom Girls and Bicycle Race")....10-20 78
(Promotional issue only.)
Singles: 7-inch
CAPITOL....3-5 84-89
ELEKTRA....3-6 74-82
HOLLYWOOD....3-5 92
Picture Sleeves
CAPITOL....3-5 84-89
ELEKTRA (Except 45478)....4-8 77-82
ELEKTRA (45478 "It's Late")....10-20 78
LPs: 10/12-inch
CAPITOL....5-10 84-89
ELEKTRA (101 thru 564)....10-15 77-81
ELEKTRA (702 "Live Killers")....15-20 79
(Two discs.)
ELEKTRA (1026 "Sheer Heart Attack")....10-15 74
ELEKTRA (1053 "A Night at the Opera")....10-15 75

ELEKTRA (60128 "Hot Space") 8-12 82
ELEKTRA (EKS-75064 "Queen")............ 10-15 73
(Gold foil title stamped on cover.)
ELEKTRA (EKS-75064 "Queen")...............5-10 73
(Title printed on cover.)
ELEKTRA (EQ-75064 "Queen").............. 20-30 73
(Quadraphonic.)
ELEKTRA (75082 "Queen II") 10-15 74
HOLLYWOOD..5-8 91-92
MFSL (067 "A Night at the Opera")......... 40-60 82
MFSL (211 "The Game")..................... 25-35 94
WARNER SPECIAL PRODUCTS..............5-10 84
Members: Freddie Mercury; John Deacon; Brian May; Roger Taylor.
Also see MERCURY, Freddie
Also see SMILE

QUEEN & DAVID BOWIE P&R '81

Singles: 7-inch

ELEKTRA (47235 "Under Pressure") 3-5 81

Picture Sleeves

ELEKTRA (47235 "Under Pressure") 3-5 81
Also see BOWIE, David
Also see QUEEN

QUEEN, Bee Bee

Singles: 78 rpm

HULL.. 10-15 56-57

Singles: 7-inch

HULL (714 "Queen Bee") 20-30 56
HULL (719 "Wanna Be Loved")................ 20-30 57

QUEEN'S NECTARINE MACHINE

LPs: 10/12-inch

ABC (666 "Mystical Powers of Roving Tarot Gamble") 30-40 69

QUEENSRŸCHE LP '83

Singles: 7-inch

EMI..3-5 83-86

LPs: 10/12-inch

CAPITOL (30711 "Promised Land")...........8-10 90s
EMI (Except 48640) 5-10 83-90
EMI (SPRO-01436 "Operation: Mindcrime")... 70-80 88
(Promotional only picture disc. 500 made.)
EMI (04194 "Speak the Word") 10-20 88
(Promotional only interview.)
EMI (19006 "Queensryche")................... 20-30
(Promotional issue only. Issued in metal film can with photo.)
EMI (48640 "Operation: Mindcrime") 20-25 88
Members: Geoff Tate; Chris DeGarmo; Michael Wilton; Eddie Jackson; Scott Rockenfield.

QUEST

Singles: 7-inch

GRAMAPHONE (1270 "The Last Days"). 20-30 70

QUESTELL, Connie

Singles: 7-inch

DECCA (31783 "Straighten Up")............. 20-30 65
DECCA (31855 "Give Up Girl") 20-30 65

? & THE MYSTERIANS P&R/LP '66

(Question Mark & the Mysterians)

Singles: 7-inch

ABKCO...3-5 '80s
CAMEO (428 "96 Tears") 15-25 66
(No mention of "MGM" on label.)
CAMEO (428 "96 Tears") 12-20 68
(Label reads: "Marketed By MGM.")
CAMEO (441 "I Need Somebody") 8-10 66
CAMEO (467 "Can't Get Enough of You Baby") 8-10 67
CAMEO (479 "Girl")................................8-10 67
CAMEO (496 "Do Something to Me") 8-10 67
CAPITOL (2162 "Make You Mine")..............8-12 68
CHICORY (410 "Talk Is Cheap") 10-20 67
LUV (159 "Hot 'N' Groovin' ") 5-8 72
MILLION SELLER 3-5
NORTON 3-5 98
PA-GO-GO (102 "96 Tears")............... 300-400 66
(First issue.)
PEACOCK ("Time Is on My Side").............5-10 66
(Selection number not known.)
SUPER K (102 "Hang In") 5-10 69
TANGERINE (392 "Ain't It a Shame")........5-10

LPs: 10/12-inch

CAMEO (2004 "96 Tears") 50-100 66
CAMEO (2006 "Action")......................... 50-100 67

Members: Rudy Martinez; Robert Martinez; Frank Rodriguez; Larry Borjas; Frank Lugo; Bob Balderamma.
Also see MYSTERIONS

QUESTION MARKS

Singles: 7-inch

FIRST (102 "Ballad of a Boy and a Girl")..30-40 59
MONEY (105 "Doin' the Thing")..................8-12 64

QUESTS

(Quest's)

Singles: 7-inch

FENTON (2032 "Psychic") 50-75 66
FENTON (2086 "Shadows in the Night")..40-60 66
FENTON (2174 "Shadows in the Night")..15-25 67

QUICK

Singles: 7-inch

EPIC (10516 "Ain't Nothin' Gonna Stop Me")...10-15 69
Member: Eric Carmen.

QUICKSILVER LP '68

(Quicksilver Messenger Service)

Singles: 7-inch

CAPITOL..4-8 68-76

LPs: 10/12-inch

CAPITOL (120 "Happy Trails")..................20-30 69
CAPITOL (288 "Quicksilver Messenger Service") 30-50 69
CAPITOL (391 thru 819)...........................10-25 69-71
CAPITOL (2904 "Quicksilver Messenger Service")...20-30 68
CAPITOL (11000 series).........................10-15 72-75
CAPITOL (16000 series)...........................5-10 80
Members: John Cipollina; Dave Freiberg.
Also see BROGUES
Also see FANKHAUSER, Merrell
Also see JEFFERSON AIRPLANE
Also see MILLER, Steve / Band / Quicksilver Messenger Service
Also see VALENTI, Dino

QUILLS

Singles: 7-inch

CASINO (106 "Whose Love, But Yours").. 750-1000 59

QUINN, Bottie

Singles: 7-inch

REED (1016 "Teenage Bop")....................50-75 57

QUINNS

Singles: 7-inch

CYCLONE (111 "Oh Starlight")..............75-125 57
(Black vinyl. No address shown on label.)
CYCLONE (111 "Oh Starlight")............150-200 57
(Blue vinyl. No address shown on label.)
CYCLONE (111 "Oh Starlight")................30-40 57
(Company address shown under label name.)
LOST NITE...4-8

QUINSTRELLS

Singles: 7-inch

MOXIE (105 "I Got a Girl")........................20-30 65
Also see DEARLY BELOVEDS

QUINTEROS, Eddie

Singles: 7-inch

BRENT (7009 "Come Dance with Me") 8-12 60
BRENT (7012 "Lookin' for My Baby") 8-12 60
BRENT (7014 "Lindy Lou")........................8-12 60
DEL-FI (4156 "Pretty Baby, I Love You") .10-20 61
ED-DAR (102 "Come on Little Girl") 10-20 61
M&K (102 "Come on Little Girl")................15-25 60

QUINTETTE PLUS

Singles: 7-inch

SVR (1004 "Work Song") 20-30 65
SVR (4392 "Grits 'N' Grease") ....10-20 '60s

QUINTONES

Singles: 78 rpm

GEE (1009 "I'm Willing").......................300-400 56

Singles: 7-inch

GEE (1009 "I'm Willing").................. 2000-2500 56

QUINTONES

Singles: 78 rpm

JORDAN (1601 "Just a Little Loving")... 500-1000 56

QUINTONES

Singles: 7-inch

CHESS (1685 "I Try So Hard") 20-30 58

PARK (112 "More Than a Notion").......400-500 57
Also see WITHERSPOON, Jimmy, & Quintones

QUIN-TONES P&R/R&B '58

(QuinTones)

Singles: 78 rpm

HUNT (321 "Down the Aisle of Love")....75-125 58

Singles: 7-inch

COLLECTABLES...3-5 '80s
HUNT (321 "Down the Aisle of Love")......20-30 58
HUNT (322 "What Am I to Do")................15-25 58
RED TOP (108 "Down the Aisle of Love")..40-60 58
(First issue. Blue label)
RED TOP (108 "Down the Aisle of Love")..10-20 59
(Red label)
RED TOP (116 "Oh, Heavenly Father") ...50-75 59
Members: Roberta Haymon; Phylis Carr; Carolyn Holmes; Ronnie Scott; Jeannie Crist; Ken Sexton.

QUINTONES

Singles: 7-inch

LEE (1113 "Liverlips")...............................15-25 61
Also see FOSTER, Pat, & Quintones

QUINTONES

Singles: 7-inch

PHILLIPS INT'L (3586 "Times Sho' Gettin' Ruff")..10-15 63

QUIN-TONES

Singles: 7-inch

VO (5172 "Fool That I Am")......................20-30

QUIVER

LPs: 10/12-inch

W.B. (1939 "Quiver") 10-15 71
W.B. (2630 "Gone in the Morning") 10-15 72

QUOTATIONS

Singles: 7-inch

POPULAR REQUEST (104 "Imagination") ..3-5 94
RELIC (1025 "Imagination") 3-5 73
VERVE (10245 "Imagination") 20-30 61
VERVE (10252 "This Love of Mine") 30-40 62
VERVE (10261 "See You in September") 20-30 62

LPs: 10/12-inch

ON THE CORNER (134 "Time Was '59-'63")..15-20 90
(Black vinyl. 1000 made.)

QUOTATIONS

Singles: 7-inch

ADMIRAL (300 "It's a Shame") 150-200 61
ADMIRAL (753 "In the Night")..............150-200 64

R

R. ROGUES

Singles: 7-inch

WASP (102 "The Sound") ....25-35 '60s

R.B.

Singles: 7-inch

TOMAHAWK (674 "I Am a Roller")...........50-75

R DELLS

(R-Dells)

Singles: 7-inch

ADMIRAL (4014 "Drag Race")..................20-30 '60s
DADE (1806 "You Say")...........................15-25 60
GONE (5128 "Candy Stick Twist")...........10-15 62
Also see ARDELLS

R.E.M. P&R '83

Singles: 7-inch

EVA-TONE (105900 "Dark Globe") 5-10 90
(Promotional issue, *Sassy* magazine insert. Add $3 to $5 if accompanied by the appropriate issue of *Sassy*.)
HIBTONE ("Radio Free Europe")..............50-75 81
(Selection number not known.)
I.R.S. 3-8 82-87
MCA..3-5 85
W.B. 3-6 88-93

Picture Sleeves

HIBTONE ("Radio Free Europe")...........75-100 81
I.R.S. 4-8 82-88
W.B. 3-5 89

EPs: 7-inch

I.R.S. 5-10 82

LPs: 10/12-inch

I.R.S. 5-10 82-88
MFSL (231 "Murmur") 25-35 94
(Half-speed mastered.)
W.B. 5-8 88-93
Members: J. Michael Stipe; Bill Berry; Peter Buck; Mike Mills.

R.E.O. SPEEDWAGON LP '74

Singles: 7-inch

EPIC (Except 10000 & 11000 series)..........3-6 75-90
EPIC (10000 & 11000 series).....................4-8 72-74

Picture Sleeves

EPIC...3-5 80-88

EPs: 7-inch

CSP..4-8 81
(Nestles candy promotional issue.)

LPs: 10/12-inch

EPIC (643 "Nine Lives")...........................15-20 '80s
EPIC (31089 "R.E.O. Speedwagon") 10-20 71
(Yellow label.)
EPIC (31089 "R.E.O. Speedwagon") 8-12 73
(Orange label.)
EPIC (31745 "R.E.O./T.W.O.") 10-15 72
EPIC (32378 "Ridin' the Storm Out")..........8-12 73
EPIC (32948 "Lost in a Dream")..................8-12 74
EPIC (33338 "This Time We Mean It").........8-12 75
EPIC (34143 "R.E.O.")................................8-12 76
EPIC (34494 "Live/You Get What You Play For")..10-15 77
(Two discs.)
EPIC (35082 "You Can Tune a Piano, But You Can't Tuna Fish")...8-12 78
EPIC (35988 "Nine Lives")...........................8-12 79
EPIC (36444 "A Decade of Rock and Roll")..10-15 80
(Two discs.)
EPIC (36844 "Hi Infidelity")........................5-10 80
EPIC (36844 "Hi Infidelity").......................50-75 81
(Picture disc, made for Western Merchandisers. All copies mistakenly have music by unknown artists. 100 made.)
EPIC (38100 "Good Trouble") 5-10 82
EPIC (39593 "Wheels Are Turnin' ")............5-10 84
EPIC (40444 "Life As We Know It")............5-10 87
EPIC (44202 "The Hits") 5-10 88
EPIC (45082 "You Can Tune a Piano, But You Can't Tuna Fish")...10-20 82
(Half-speed mastered.)
EPIC (45246 "The Earth, a Small Man, His Dog and a Chicken")..5-10 90
EPIC (46844 "Hi Infidelity")......................10-20 81
(Half-speed mastered.)
Members: Kevin Cronin; Neal Doughty; Bruce Hall; Al Gratzer; Terry Luttrell.
Also see SUBURBAN 9 TO 5

R.J. & RIOTS

Singles: 7-inch

J (101 "Little Honda") ....20-30 '60s

RPMs

(RPM's)

Singles: 7-inch

AMBASSADOR (214 "White Lightnin' ") ..15-20 66
P.B.D. (102 "White Lightnin' ")..................15-20 66

RABBITT, Eddie C&W '74

Singles: 7-inch

DATE (1599 "The Bed") 4-8 68
ELEKTRA (Except 378).................................3-6 74-83
ELEKTRA (378 "Song of Ireland") 5-10 78
(Green vinyl. With green insert. Promotional issue only.)
RCA...3-5 85-89
20TH FOX (474 "Six Nights and Seven Days")..5-10 64
UNIVERSAL...3-5 89
W.B. 3-5 83-85

Picture Sleeves

DATE (1599 "The Bed") 10-15 68
ELEKTRA (47174 "Step By Step") 3-6 81

LPs: 10/12-inch

ELEKTRA..5-10 75-82
RCA..5-8 86
W.B. 5-8 84-85
Also see FRICKE, Janie

RABBITT, Eddie, & Crystal Gayle C&W/P&R '82
Singles: 7-inch
ELEKTRA (69936 "You and I")....................3-5 82
Also see GAYLE, Crystal

RABBITT, Eddie, & Juice Newton C&W '86
Singles: 7-inch
RCA (14377 "Both to Each Other")..............3-5 86
Picture Sleeves
RCA (14377 "Both to Each Other")..............3-5 86
Also see RABBITT, Eddie

RABBITT, Jimmy C&W '76
(With Renegade; with Karats; Jimmy Rabbit)
Singles: 7-inch
ATCO (6950 "Everybody Needs Somebody That They Can Talk To")....................................4-6 72
CAPITOL (4257 "Ladies Love Outlaws")......4-6 76
JOSIE (947 "My Girl")..................................8-12 65
KNIGHT (1049 "Pushover")........................20-30 65
KNIGHT (1052 "My Girl")...........................20-30 65
SOUTHERN SOUND (200 "Pushover")... 15-25 65
Session: Waylon Jennings.
Also see JENNINGS, Waylon
Also see POSITIVELY 13 O'CLOCK

RABBLE
Singles: 7-inch
AQUARIUS (5012 "Time Is on My Side").. 15-25 '60s
RCA (3409 "I'm a Laboundy Bam")........... 10-20 '60s
TRANSWORLD (1675 "Golden Girl")...... 15-25 67
TRANSWORLD (1683 "Please Set Me Free").. 15-25 67
TRANSWORLD (1692 "Rising of the Sun").. 15-25 67
TRANSWORLD (1703 "Miss Money Green").. 15-25 68
LPs: 10/12-inch
ROULETTE (42010 "The Rabble")........... 25-50
TRANSWORLD (6700 "The Rabble Rabble")..................................... 100-150 67
TRANSWORLD (6707 "Give Us Back Elaine")..................................... 100-150 68
Note: All Rabble releases listed are Canadian.

RACE MARBLES
Singles: 7-inch
CAPITOL (72312 "Like a Dribbling Fram").. 10-20 '60s
TOWER (194 "Like a Dribbling Fram").... 15-25 65

RACERS
Singles: 7-inch
RSVP (1115 "Skate Board")..................... 15-25 65

RACHEL & ORIGINALS
Singles: 7-inch
NITE STAR (010 "I'll Always Remember")... 75-125 62
Member: Rachel Legerretta.

RACHEL & REVOLVERS
Singles: 7-inch
DOT (16392 "The Revo-Lution")......... 250-300 62
DOT (16392 "The Revo-Lution")......... 200-250 62
(White label. Promotional issue only.)
Also see WRIGHT, Betty

RACHELL, Yank
Singles: 78 rpm
BLUEBIRD (8732 "It Seems Like a Dream")... 50-100 48

RACKET SQUAD
(Fenways)
Singles: 7-inch
JUBILEE (5591 "Higher than High")......... 15-25 67
JUBILEE (5601 "Romeo & Juliet")........... 10-15 67
JUBILEE (5613 "Loser")............................ 10-15 68
JUBILEE (5623 "Higher Than High")....... 10-15 68
JUBILEE (5628 "That's How Much I Love My Baby").. 10-15 68
JUBILEE (5638 "Loser")........................... 10-15 68
JUBILEE (5657 "I'll Never Forget You Love").. 10-15 69
JUBILEE (5682 "In Your Arms").............. 10-20 69
LPs: 10/12-inch
JUBILEE (8015 "Racket Squad")............ 25-50 68
JUBILEE (8026 "Corners of Your Mind"). 25-50 69
Member: Joey Covington.
Also see FENWAYS
Also see JEFFERSON AIRPLANE

Also see VIBRA-SONICS

RADAR, Don
(Don Rader)
Singles: 7-inch
STRATE 8 (1501 "Rock n' Roll Blues") ..75-125 58
STRATE 8 (1507 "Rock n' Roll Grandpa")..100-200 59
STRATE 8 (1508 "She Sure Can Rock Me")..100-200 60

RADARS
Singles: 78 rpm
ABBEY (3025 "You Belong to Me") 200-300 51
PRESTIGE (478 "I Want a Little Girl") ..100-150 52
RHYTHM AND BLUES (478 "I Want a Little Girl")..150-250 52
(Promotional issue only.)

RADCLIFFE, Jimmy
(With Steve Karmen's Band)
Singles: 7-inch
AURORA (154 "My Ship Is Comin' In").....15-25 65
MUSICOR (1016 "Don't Look My Way")...10-15 62
MUSICOR (1024 "Forgotten Man")...........10-15 62
MUSICOR (1033 "Moment of Weakness")...10-15 63
MUSICOR (1042 "What I Want I Can Never Have")..10-15 64
RCA (0138 "Lay a Little Lovin' On Me")......5-10 69
SHOUT (202 "So Deep")...........................8-12 66
U.A. (50451 "Breakaway")........................5-10 68

RADHA KRISHNA TEMPLE
Singles: 7-inch
APPLE (Commercial issues.).....................5-10 69-70
APPLE (Promotional issues.)..................25-35 70
Picture Sleeves
APPLE..8-12 70
LPs: 10/12-inch
APPLE (3376 "Radha Krishna Temple") ..15-20 71

RADIANTS
(With Art Gordon & Music Maestro Orchestra)
Singles: 7-inch
WIZZ (713 "Ra Cha Cha")....................200-300 58

RADIANTS P&R '62
(Maurice McAlister & Radiants; Maurice & Radiants)
Singles: 7-inch
CHESS (1832 "Father Knows Best")........10-15 62
CHESS (1849 "Heartbreak Society")..........8-12 63
CHESS (1865 "I Got a Girl").......................8-12 63
CHESS (1872 "Shy Guy")...........................8-12 63
CHESS (1887 "Dance to Keep My Baby") .8-12 64
CHESS (1904 "Voice Your Choice")...........8-12 65
CHESS (1925 "It Ain't No Big Thing").........8-12 65
CHESS (1939 "Tomorrow")........................5-10 65
CHESS (1986 "Feel Kind of Bad")..............5-10 66
CHESS (2021 "The Clown Is Clever")........5-10 67
CHESS (2037 "Hold On")............................8-12 68
CHESS (2057 "Tears of a Clown")..............5-10 68
CHESS (2066 "Choo Choo")........................5-10 69
CHESS (2078 "Book of Love").....................5-10 69
CHESS (2083 "Shadow of a Doubt")...........5-10 69
ERIC (231 "It Ain't No Big Thing")................4-6 73
TWINIGHT (153 "My Sunshine Girl")............4-6 71
Members: Maurice McAlister; Victor Caston; Wallace Sampson; Elzie Butler; Leonard Caston Jr.; Green McLauren; Frank McCollum; James Jameson; Mitchell Bullock.
Also see GREATER HARVEST BAPTIST CHURCH CHOIR
Also see MAURICE & MAC
Also see McALISTER, Maurice

RADIANTS
Singles: 7-inch
SOMA (1422 "Special Girl").......................25-35 65

RADLEY, Raunch
(Hank Davis)
LPs: 10/12-inch
DUCKTAIL (502 "Alive Since '55")............10-15 79
REDITA..10-15
Also see DAVIS, Hank

RAE, Donna, & Sunbeams
Singles: 7-inch
SATELLITE (103 "Little Fool")...................15-25 60

RAE, Linda
Singles: 7-inch
MIKE (4002 "Tweenager").........................15-25 66
MIKE (4010 "The Time to Love Is Now")..25-50 66

RAE, Nora
Singles: 7-inch
OUR (305 "Real Cool Kitty") 50-100 58

RAE, Penny
Singles: 7-inch
INFINITY (026 "Shame, Shame, Shame")..10-15 62

RAELETTES P&R/R&B '67
(Raeletts; Raelets)
Singles: 7-inch
TRC..4-6 70
TANGERINE...4-6 67-73
LPs: 10/12-inch
TRC..8-12 71-72
TANGERINE...8-12 72
Members: Clydie King; Mable John; Vernita Amoss; Merry Clayton; Margie Hendrix; Earl Jean McCree; Pat Lyles; Minnie Riperton; Alexandra Brown; Gwendolyn Berry; Susaye Green; Estella Yarbrough; Odia Coates.
Also see CHARLES, Ray
Also see CLAYTON, Merry
Also see EARL-JEAN
Also see JOHN, Mable
Also see KING, Clydie
Also see TURNER, Ike & Tina

RAFEY, Susan
Singles: 7-inch
JUBILEE (5468 "Just Another Pretty Face")..5-10 64
JUBILEE (5504 "Right On Time")..............5-10 65
VERVE (10366 "Big Hurt").........................5-10 65
VERVE (10390 "Hurt So Bad")....................5-10 66
VERVE (10413 "I'm Telling You Now").......5-10 66
VERVE (10498 "If I Can't Have Your Love")..5-10 67
LPs: 10/12-inch
VERVE (8636 "Hurt So Bad")..................15-20 65

RAFFERTY, Gerry P&R/LP '78
Singles: 12-inch
U.A. (171 "Baker Street")............................5-10 78
Singles: 7-inch
BLUE THUMB..4-6 72
LIBERTY..3-5 82
SIGNPOST...4-6 72
U.A. 3-6 77-80
Picture Sleeves
U.A. (1233 "Right Down the Line")..............4-6 78
LPs: 10/12-inch
BLUE THUMB..8-10 73-78
LIBERTY..5-8 82
MFSL...30-50 81
U.A. 8-10 78-80
VISA..5-10 78

RAG DOLLS P&R '64
Singles: 7-inch
MALA (493 "Dusty")..................................10-15 64
MALA (499 "Baby's Gone")........................8-12 65
MALA (506 "Little Girl Tears")....................8-12 65
Member: Jean Thomas.
Also see ANGIE & CHICKLETTES

RAG DOLLS / Caliente Combo
Singles: 7-inch
PARKWAY (921 "Society Girl"/"Ragen")..10-15 64
Also see RAG DOLLS

RAGING STORMS
Singles: 7-inch
FLAMES (1019 "High Octane")...............25-35 '60s
TRAN ATLAS (691 "So Hard to Take") 10-15 62
WARWICK (677 "The Dribble")................10-15 62

RAGLAND, Lou
(With the Bandmasters)
Singles: 7-inch
AMY (988 "Travel Alone")....................100-200 67
WAY OUT (2605 "Never Let Me Go") ..400-500 64

RAICEVIK, Nik Pascal
(Nik Pascal)
LPs: 10/12-inch
NARCO (102 "Beyond the End") 20-30 71
NARCO (123 "Zero Gravity")....................10-20 75
NARCO (321 "Magnetic Web")..................10-20 73
NARCO (666 "Sixth Ear")..........................15-25 72

RAIDERS
Singles: 7-inch
ANDEX (4015 "Hocus Pocus") 75-100 59

ATCO (6125 "Castle of Love")...............75-100 58
BRUNSWICK (55090 "My Steady Girl")...20-30 58

RAIDERS
Singles: 7-inch
VAN (00262 "Stick Shift")..........................25-50 62
VAN (00663 "On a Straight Away")............15-25 63
VAN (00763 "Supercharged")....................15-25 63
VAN (01064 "Raisin' Cain").......................15-25 64
VEE-JAY (504 "Stick Shift").......................10-15 63

RAIDERS
Singles: 7-inch
SPRING DALE (102 "Raider's Rhythm")..40-50 64

RAIK'S PROGRESS
Singles: 7-inch
LIBERTY (55930 "Why Did You Rob Us, Tank")..15-25 66

RAILBACK, Willie
Singles: 78 rpm
RECORDED IN HOLLYWOOD (212 "Tree Top Blues")..10-20 52

RAIN
Singles: 7-inch
A.P.I. (336 "E.S.P.")...................................20-30 66
A.P.I. (337 "Here You Cry") 20-30 67
LONDON (107 "E.S.P.")..............................15-25 66
LONDON (111 "Here You Cry")................20-30 67

RAIN
Singles: 7-inch
BELL (45142 "Out of My Mind")....................4-6 71
BELL (45206 "Stop Me from Believing in You")..4-6 72
MGM (13622 "Take It Away") 10-20 66
PARAMOUNT (0087 "Show Me the Road Home")..10-15 71
LPs: 10/12-inch
WHAZOO (3046 "Live Xmas Night")....100-150 68
Also see DARTELLS

RAIN DROPS
(With Ernie Freeman Orchestra)
Singles: 78 rpm
SPIN-IT 10-15 56
Singles: 7-inch
SPIN-IT (104 "Heaven in Love"/"I Prayed for Gold")..100-200 56
SPIN-IT (106 "Little One").......................75-125 56
SPIN-IT (111 "Heaven in Love"/"Little One")..10-20 60
Member: Henry Houston.
Also see FREEMAN, Ernie

RAIN DROPS / Jay & Americans / Empires / Clusters
EPs: 7-inch
THEY SANG IN BROOKLYN (1 "Rain Drops / Jay & Americans / Empires / Clusters")..............5-10 92
(Black vinyl. 500 made.)
Also see CLUSTERS
Also see EMPIRES
Also see JAY & AMERICANS
Also see RAIN DROPS

RAINBEAUS
Singles: 7-inch
WORLD PACIFIC (810 "Maybe It's Wrong")..15-25 60
Members: Louis Faison; Hasker Nelson; James Jackson; Nate Thomas.
Also see FOUR PALMS

RAINBO
Singles: 7-inch
ROULETTE (7030 "John, You Went Too Far This Time")..10-20 69
Member: Sissy Spacek.

RAINBOW
LPs: 10/12-inch
GNP (2049 "After the Storm")..................15-20 69

RAINBOW PRESS
Singles: 7-inch
MR. G (817 "There's a War On")................8-12 68
MR. G (821 "Last Platoon").........................8-12 69
LPs: 10/12-inch
MR. G (9003 "There's a War On")...........20-30 69
MR. G (9004 "Sunday Funnies") 20-30 69
Members: Joe Groff; Dave Troup; Larry Milton; Charles Osborn; Marc Ellis. Bill Vergin.

RAINBOW PROMISE
LPs: 10/12-inch
NEW WINE (1 "Rainbow Promise") 200-300 70

RAINBOWS
("Featuring Sonny Spencer")
Singles: 78 rpm
PILGRIM (703 "Mary Lee") 10-20 56
PILGRIM (711 "Shirley") 50-100 56
RAMA (209 "They Say") 100-150 56
RED ROBIN (134 "Mary Lee") 100-200 55
Singles: 7-inch
ARGYLE (1012 "Shirley") 10-15 62
FIRE (1012 "Mary Lee") 10-20 60
MELLO (555 "Mary Lee") 8-12 65
PILGRIM (703 "Mary Lee") 20-30 56
PILGRIM (711 "Shirley") 300-400 56
RAMA (209 "They Say") 400-500 56
RED ROBIN (134 "Mary Lee") 200-300 55
Note: Red Robin 141, originals of *Shirley/Stay*, do not exist – only bootlegs.)
Members: Sonny Spencer; Ron Miles; Don Covay; John Berry; Henry Womble; Don Watts; Frank Hardy; Jim Knowland; Chester Simmons.
Also see COVAY, Don
Also see MELLO-MOODS / Rainbows
Also see SPENCER, Sonny

RAINBOWS
Singles: 7-inch
MGM (13058 "Ole Man's Twist") 20-25 62

RAINBOWS
Singles: 7-inch
DAVE (908 "I Know") 10-20 63
DAVE (909 "It Wouldn't Be Right") 20-30 63
GRAMO (5508 "Till Tomorrow") 20-30 64
Members: Duval Potter; Joe Walls; Layton McDonald; Victor English; Alvin Saunders.

RAINDROPS
(With the Foxes of Marrow Orchestra)
Singles: 7-inch
VEGA (105 "Dim Those Lights") 100-200 58

RAINDROPS
Singles: 7-inch
STARDAY (368 "I Don't Want a Sweetheart") 100-200 58
STARDAY (374 "Raindrops") 75-125 58

RAINDROPS
Singles: 7-inch
CAPITOL (4136 "Rain") 10-20 59
HAMILTON (50021 "Oh Why") 15-25 59

RAINDROPS
Singles: 7-inch
CORSAIR (104 "Maybe") 40-60 60
(First issue.)
DORE (561 "Maybe") 10-20 60

RAINDROPS
Singles: 7-inch
IMPERIAL (5785 "[I Remember] In the Still of the Night") 15-25 61
Also see JUMPIN' TONES

RAINDROPS *P&R/R&B '63*
Singles: 7-inch
JUBILEE (5444 "What a Guy") 10-20 63
JUBILEE (5455 "The Kind of Boy You Can't Forget") 10-20 63
JUBILEE (5466 "That Boy John") 10-20 63
JUBILEE (5469 "Book of Love") 10-20 64
JUBILEE (5475 "Let's Go Together") 10-20 64
JUBILEE (5487 "One More Tear") 10-20 64
JUBILEE (5497 "Don't Let Go") 10-20 65
VIRGO 4-6 73
LPs: 10/12-inch
JUBILEE (J-5023 "Raindrops") 40-60 63
(Monaural.)
JUBILEE (SJ-5023 "Raindrops") 50-80 63
(Stereo.)
MURRAY HILL ..... 8-10 '80s
Members: Jeff Barry; Ellie Greenwich. (The third person pictured on the Roulette LP cover, Ellie's sister, Laura, is not heard on their records.)
Also see BARRY, Jeff
Also see GREENWICH, Ellie

RAINDROPS
Singles: 7-inch
SOTOPLAY (0028 "I Still Love You") 20-30 64

RAINE, Lorry
Singles: 78 rpm
ADVANCE 5-10 56
DOT 5-10 56
Singles: 7-inch
ADVANCE (3011 "Tell My Love Goodbye") 15-25 56
ADVANCE (3017 "Escape") 15-25 57
DOT (15493 "A Casual Look") 15-25 56

RAINER, Chris, & Elrods
Singles: 7-inch
RED HED (1005 "Kathy Spanish") 75-100 60
Also see SPEEKS, Ronnie

RAINES, Jerry
Singles: 7-inch
DREW-BLAN (1001 "Dangerous Redhead") 30-50 61
DREW-BLAN (1011 "The Darkest Night") 20-30 62
MERCURY (71585 "Dangerous Redhead") 15-25 60
MERCURY (71708 "No More") 15-25 60

RAINEY, Ma *P&R '25*
(Gertrude Rainey)
Singles: 78 rpm
PARAMOUNT (12000 series) 500-1000 24-38
LPs: 10/12-inch
BIOGRAPH 8-12 67-69
MILESTONE 8-12 67-74
RIVERSIDE (108 "Ma Rainey") 100-200 56
RIVERSIDE (137 "Ma Rainey, Vol. 2: Broken Hearted Blues") 50-100 60
Also see ARMSTRONG, Louis / Ma Rainey / Trixie Smith
Also see SMITH, Bessie / Ma Rainey / Ida Cox / Chippie Hill

RAINMAKERS
Sngles: 7-inch
DISCOTHEQUE ..... 10-15 '60s
LEE (9178 "Do You Feel It") ..... 15-25 '60s
PHALANX (1029 "Tell Her No") 15-25 67

RAINSFORD, Billy
Singles: 7-inch
HERMITAGE (803 "Starry Eyes") 50-100 63

RAINVILLE, Doris
Singles: 7-inch
BLUE RIVER (207 "Thirteen") 5-10 63

RAINWATER, Marvin *C&W/P&R '57*
Singles: 78 rpm
CORAL 5-10 55
MGM (Except 12240 & 12370) 5-15 55-57
MGM (12240 "Hot and Cold") 10-15 56
MGM (12370 "Get off the Stool") 10-15 56
Singles: 7-inch
BRAVE 5-10 63-67
CORAL (61342 "I Gotta Go Get My Baby") 8-12 55
HILLTOP ..... 5-10 '70s
MGM (12000 & 12100 series) 10-20 55
MGM (12240 "Hot and Cold") 30-40 56
MGM (12313 "Why Did You Have to Go and Love Me") 15-20 56
MGM (12370 "Get off the Stool") 30-40 56
MGM (12412 thru 12938) 10-15 57-60
NU TRAYL 4-6 76
U.A. 5-10 65-66
W.B. 4-8 69-70
WARWICK (666 "Boo Hoo") 5-10 61
WARWICK (674 "Tough Top Cat") 5-10 62
(With Patty Rainwater.)
WESCO (2105 "Talk to Me") 5-10
EPs: 7-inch
MGM (1464/1465/1466 "Songs by Marvin Rainwater") 15-25 57
(Price is for any of three volumes.)
LPs: 10/12-inch
CROWN ..... 5-10 '60s
GUEST STAR 5-10
MARK IV 8-12
MGM (3534 "Songs by Marvin Rainwater") 50-100 57
MGM (3721 "With a Heart With a Beat") 50-100 58
MGM (4046 "Gonna Find Me a Bluebird") 50-100 62
MOUNT VERNON 8-10
SPINORAMA ..... 8-10 '60s
Also see DEAN, Jimmy / Marvin Rainwater
Also see FRANCIS, Connie, & Marvin Rainwater

RAINY DAY PEOPLE
Singles: 7-inch
HBR (512 "Junior Executive") 15-25 67

RAINY DAYS
Singles: 7-inch
PANIK (7542 "Turn on Your Lovelight") 15-25 66
PANIK (7566 "I Can Only Give You Everything") 15-25 66

RAINY DAZE *P&R '67*
(With King Toke)
Singles: 7-inch
CHICORY (404 "That Acapulco Gold") 10-15 67
I.P. (100 "That Acapulco Gold") 25-35 66
UNI (55002 "That Acapulco Gold") 5-10 67
UNI (55011 "Discount City") 5-10 67
UNI (55026 "Stop Sign") 5-10 67
WHITE WHALE (279 "Make Me Laugh") 5-10 68
LPs: 10/12-inch
UNI (73002 "That Acapulco Gold") 15-25 67
Members: Tim Gilbert; Bob Heckendorf; Mac Ferris; Kip Gilbert; Sam Fuller.

RAITT, Bonnie *LP '72*
Singles: 7-inch
CAPITOL 3-5 89-91
W.B. 3-6 72-86
Picture Sleeves
W.B. 4-8 72-79
LPs: 10/12-inch
CAPITOL 5-8 89-91
W.B. 6-12 71-86
Session: Van Dyke Parks.
Also see MULDAUR, Geoff, & Bonnie Raitt
Also see ORBISON, Roy
Also see PARKS, Van Dyke

RAITT, Bonnie / Gilley's "Urban Cowboy" Band
Singles: 7-inch
FULL MOON/ASYLUM 3-5 80
Picture Sleeves
FULL MOON/ASYLUM 3-5 80
Also see RAITT, Bonnie

RAJAHS
(Nutmegs)
Singles: 7-inch
KLIK (1019 "You're Crying") 4-8 73
(Previously unissued.)
KLIK (7805 "I Fell in Love") 300-400 57
Also see NUTMEGS

RALKE, Don *P&R '59*
(Don Ralke Quintet; "Big Sound of Don Ralke;" with Jackie Weston; with Cheerettes; with Frank Lauria)
Singles: 78 rpm
CROWN 4-8 55
VITA 5-10 56-57
Singles: 7-inch
CROWN 5-15 55
DRUM BOY 4-6 66
REAL 5-15 56
VITA 15-25 56-57
W.B. 5-10 59-64
LPs: 10/12-inch
CROWN 10-20 55
W.B. 10-20 59-60
Also see BYRNES, Edward
Also see CHAPMAN, Grady
Also see COOKE, Sam
Also see DEUCES WILD
Also see DICK & DEEDEE
Also see DON, DICK 'N JIMMY
Also see JAN & ARNIE
Also see MARQUEES
Also see RALKE-TALKIES / Speedy Gonzalez
Also see SOMMERS, Joanie
Also see THREE DIMENSIONS

RALKE-TALKIES / Speedy Gonzalez
Singles: 7-inch
W.B. (5369 "Hurry Up-a-Baby") 5-10 63
Also see RALKE, Don

RALLY PACKS
Singles: 7-inch
IMPERIAL (66036 "Move Out Little Mustang") 40-50 64
Members: Phil Sloan; Steve Barri. Session: Jan Berry; Dean Torrence.
Also see FANTASTIC BAGGYS
Also see JAN & DEAN

RALPH
Singles: 7-inch
CANDIX (321 "I've Got It") 75-125 61
GREEN LEAF ("I've Got It") 250-350 61
(First issue. Selection number not known.)

RALSTON, Dick
Singles: 7-inch
NU-CLEAR (4 "Brand New Rules") 20-30 57
NU-CLEAR (14 "Sharin' Lockers") 50-75 58

RAM, Buck
(Buck Ram Platters; Buck Ram All Stars)
Singles: 78 rpm
SAVOY 10-15 44
Singles: 7-inch
AVALANCHE (224 "Sunday with You") 4-6 73
PERSONALITY (3507 "Soran Song") 10-15 63
EPs: 7-inch
CAMDEN 10-20 57
LPs: 10/12-inch
MERCURY (20392 "Magic Touch") 20-30 59
(Monaural.)
MERCURY (60067 "Magic Touch") 30-40 59
(Stereo.)
Also see PLATTERS

RAMADAS
Singles: 7-inch
NEW WORLD (2000 "Walking Down the Hall") 10-15 64
PHILIPS (40097 "Teenage Dream") 15-20 63
PHILIPS (40117 "Summer Steady") 15-20 63

RAMAL, Bill
Singles: 7-inch
HARVARD (811 "Rock Lamonde") 10-15 59
Also see CAPP, Bill
Also see GOODMAN, Dickie
Also see LEGENDS
Also see SHIEKS
Also see VIRGINIANS

RAMBEAU, Eddie *P&R/LP '65*
Singles: 7-inch
BELL (847 "Solitary Man") 5-8 69
BELL (873 "Don't Leave Me") 4-8 70
DYNO VOICE (207 "I Just Need Your Love"/"My Name Is Mud") 5-10 65
DYNO VOICE (211 "Train") 5-10 65
DYNO VOICE (217 "I Just Need Your Love"/"I'm the Sky") 5-10 66
DYNO VOICE (221 "I Miss You") 5-10 66
DYNO VOICE (225 "If I Were You") 5-10 66
DYNO VOX (204 "Concrete and Clay") 5-10 65
SWAN (4077 "Toni") 5-10 61
SWAN (4105 "My Four Leaf Clover Love") 10-15 62
SWAN (4112 "Summertime Guy") 5-10 62
SWAN (4145 "Car Hop and the Hard Top") 5-10 63
20TH FOX (491 "Come Closer") 5-10 64
VIRGO 4-6 73
LPs: 10/12-inch
DYNO VOICE (9001 "Concrete and Clay") 15-25 65
Also see MARCY JO & EDDIE RAMBEAU

RAMBLERS
Singles: 78 rpm
JAX (319 "Search My Heart") 50-75 53
Singles: 7-inch
JAX (319 "Search My Heart") 500-750 53
(Red vinyl.)

RAMBLERS
Singles: 78 rpm
MGM (11850 "Vadunt-Un-Va-Da Song") 75-125 54
MGM (55006 "Bad Girl") 50-75 55
Singles: 7-inch
MGM (11850 "Vadunt-Un-Va-Da Song") 300-400 54
MGM (55006 "Bad Girl") 100-150 55

RAMBLERS
Singles: 78 rpm
FEDERAL (12286 "Heaven and Earth") ... 20-30 56

Singles: 7-inch
FEDERAL (12286 "Heaven and Earth") 50-150 56

RAMBLERS *P&R '60*
Singles: 7-inch
ADDIT (1257 "Rambling")........................ 20-30 60
Members: Chuck Kenney; Michael Burke; Michael Anthony; Kip Martin.

RAMBLERS
Singles: 7-inch
LARKWOOD (1104 "I Need You So")...... 15-25 63

RAMBLERS
("Little" Preston)
Singles: 7-inch
TRUMPET (102 "Come On Back") 400-500 63

RAMBLERS *P&R '64*
Singles: 7-inch
ALMONT (300 "Birdland Baby").............. 15-25 63
ALMONT (311 "Father Sebastian")......... 15-25 64
ALMONT (313 "School Girl")................... 15-25 64
ALMONT (315 "Silly Little Boy") 15-25 64
SIDEWINDERS.. 10-20 64
Members: John Herbert; Sal Nastasi.

RAMBLERS
Singles: 7-inch
CORA (101 "Bye Bye Bye")................. 400-600 64

RAMBLERS
Singles: 7-inch
SUNRISE (101 "Buzzin' Bee")................ 50-75

RAMBLERS THREE
LPs: 10/12-inch
MGM (4072 "Make Way")........................ 15-25 62

RAMBLIN' EVERETT
Singles: 78 rpm
FABLE (546 "Cincinnati Woman")........... 25-50 56
Singles: 7-inch
FABLE (546 "Cincinnati Woman")......... 50-100 56

RAMBO, Ted, & Shades
Singles: 7-inch
PEAK (1201 "Sorority Girl")................... 75-100 57

RAMIREZ, Joe
(Joe Ramirez Combo)
Singles: 7-inch
GYRO (100 "Run You Down")................ 50-75
Also see STAR COMBO
Also see SUMMERS, Gene

RAMISTELLA, Johnny
(Johnny Rivers)
Singles: 7-inch
SUEDE (1401 "Little Girl")................... 550-650 57
Also see RIVERS, Johnny

RAMJET, Rodger, & American Eagles
(Gary Owens)
LPs: 10/12-inch
CAMDEN (1075 "Roger Ramjet and the American Eagles")... 15-25 66

RAMONES *LP '76*
Singles: 7-inch
RSO..3-6 80
SIRE...5-10 76-80
Picture Sleeves
SIRE...8-15 77-79
EPs: 7-inch
SIRE (605 "Rock 'N Roll High School") ... 12-18 79
(Promotional issue only.)
LPs: 10/12-inch
RADIOACTIVE (10615 "Mondo Bizarro")...8-10 92
RADIOACTIVE (10913 "Acid Eaters") 8-10 93
RADIOACTIVE (11273 "Adios Amigos") 8-10 95
SIRE (Except 3571, 6063 & 7528)...............5-8 76-89
SIRE (3571 "Pleasant Dreams") 8-12 81
SIRE (6042 "Rocket to Russia").............. 10-15 77
SIRE (6063 "Road to Ruin") 10-20 78
(Black vinyl.)
SIRE (6063 "Road to Ruin") 25-35 78
(Yellow vinyl.)
SIRE (6077 "End of the Century")........... 10-15 80
SIRE (7520 "Ramones")......................... 15-25 76
SIRE (7528 "Leave Home")..................... 15-25 77
(Has *Carbona Not Glue*, which is not on reissues.)
SIRE (7528 "Leave Home")..................... 10-20 77
(Has *Sheena Is a Punk Rocker*, instead of *Carbona Not Glue*.)
SIRE (23800 "Subterranean Jungle") 8-12 83
SIRE (25187 "Too Tough to Die")..............8-12 84
SIRE (25483 "Animal Boy").........................8-12 86
SIRE (25641 "Halfway to Sanity")..............8-12 87
SIRE (25709 "Ramones Mania")..............10-15 88
(Two discs.)
SIRE (25905 "Brain Drain").........................8-12 89

RAMP
LPs: 10/12-inch
BLUE THUMB (6028 "Come into Knowledge")..75-125 77

RAMPAGES
Singles: 7-inch
WEDGE (1011 "Alligator Stomp") 40-60 64

RAMRODS *P&R '61*
Singles: 7-inch
AMY (813 "Riders in the Sky") 15-25 60
AMY (817 "Take Me Back to My Boots and Saddle")..10-20 61
AMY (846 "War Cry")...............................10-20 61
BARCLAY (13127 "War Party") ....8-12 '60s
QUALITY (1256 "Riders in the Sky") 15-25 60
(Canadian.)
QUEEN (24014 "Slee-Zee") 8-12 62
Members: Vincent Lee Bell; Eugene Morrow; Richard Lane; Claire Lane.
Also see RANGERS

RAMRODS *R&B '72*
Singles: 7-inch
R&H (1001 "Night Ride")..........................15-25 63
RAMPAGE (1000 "Soultrain").......................4-6 72
(First issued as *Hot Potato*, by the Rinky Dinks.)
Member: King Curtis.
Also see KING CURTIS
Also see RINKY DINKS

RAMRODS
Singles: 7-inch
PLYMOUTH (2965 "Flowers in My Mind")...10-15 67
Also see ROCKIN' RAMRODS

RAMRODS
Singles: 7-inch
FENTON (2014 "You Know I Love You") .15-25 66

RAMS
(Flairs)
Singles: 78 rpm
FLAIR (1066 "Sweet Thing") 30-50 55
Singles: 7-inch
FLAIR (1066 "Sweet Thing") 100-150 55
Also see FLAIRS
Also see MAYE, Arthur Lee

RAMSEY, Gloria
(With the Sound Dealers Orchestra)
Singles: 7-inch
HAP (1894 "My Love")..........................400-600 60
Session: Impressions.
Also see IMPRESSIONS

RANADO, Chuck, & Electronaires
Singles: 7-inch
COUNT (508 "My Baby's Gone") 50-75 59
Also see ELECTRONAIRES

RANCHEROS
Singles: 7-inch
DOT (16572 "Linda's Tune") 10-15 63
LONNIE (5005 "Linda's Tune") 25-35 63
(First issue.)

RAND, Bobby
Singles: 7-inch
DOT (15580 "Don't Make My Poor Heart Weep")..15-25 57

RAND, D.C., & Jokers
Singles: 7-inch
CANDY (003 "Shake It Up") 75-125 59

RAND, Joey
Singles: 7-inch
BLUEGRASS (1001 "Long Blond Curls")..200-300

RAND, Johnny
Singles: 7-inch
HERALD (560 "Still in My Heart") 10-20 61
KENO (928 "I'm Yours") 5-10 65
Also see J.R. & ATTRACTIONS

RAND, Lincoln
Singles: 7-inch
ADONA (1444 "Long Tall Sally")..............50-75

RAND, Tony
(With Vinny Parlay's Orchestra & Chorus)
Singles: 7-inch
COLUMBIA (40925 "Seven Come Eleven")..20-40 57
7-11 (2001 "The Whole World Is Talking")...10-15 '50s

RANDALL, Jay
(With the Epics)
Singles: 7-inch
KHOURY'S (713 "Never Have I") 20-30 59
KHOURY'S (717 "My Girl") 20-30 59
LANOR (532 "Hamburger") 10-15
LANOR (544 "Garden of Eden") 10-15
LANOR (548 "Oh, Darling") 10-15
LANOR (549 "One Night of Sin") 10-15
LANOR (552 "Stand By Me") 10-15
LANOR (554 "Captain Sam") 10-15
LANOR (558 "Crazy Face") 10-15
LANOR (563 "Keep Her Guessing") 10-15

RANDALL, Rory
Singles: 7-inch
LUCK (101 "Summer Time Love")............20-30 59

RANDALL, Todd
(With the Blue Notes)
Singles: 78 rpm
JOSIE (814 "Letters")..............................30-40 57
Singles: 7-inch
GLORY (298 "Monkey Chambo")...............5-10 59
JOSIE (814 "Letters") 50-100 57
Also see BLUE NOTES

RANDAZZO, Jimmy
Singles: 7-inch
WINGATE (009 "Hungry for Love") 150-250 66

RANDAZZO, Teddy *P&R '58*
(With All 6)
Singles: 7-inch
ABC-PAR 8-12 59-62
COLPIX..5-10 62-63
DCP...5-10 64-66
MGM..5-10 66-67
VERVE FOLKWAYS (5050 "Just One More Time") 5-10 67
VIK...8-12 57-58
LPs: 10/12-inch
ABC-PAR...20-30 61-62
MGM (4410 "Girl from U.N.C.L.E.") 15-20 66
VIK (1121 "I'm Confessing").....................30-50 58
Also see THREE CHUCKLES

RANDELL, Buddy
(With the Knickerbockers; Buddy Randall)
Singles: 7-inch
CHALLENGE (59268 "All I Need Is You")..40-60 64
UNI (55209 "Randi Randi") 4-8 70
LPs: 10/12-inch
CHALLENGE (621 "Jerk & Twine Time").25-35 65
Also see KNICKERBOCKERS
Also see ROCKIN' SAINTS
Also see ROYAL TEENS

RANDELL, Johnny
Singles: 7-inch
COLONIAL (606 "Do Right") 10-20 64
COLONIAL ("How About That")................10-20 65
(Selection number not known.)

RANDELL, Lynne
Singles: 7-inch
EPIC (10147 "Stranger in My Arms") 10-20 67
Picture Sleeves
EPIC (10147 "Stranger in My Arms") 20-30 67

RANDELL, Rick
Singles: 7-inch
APT (25038 "More of the Same") 5-10 60
APT (25048 "Mr. Butterfingers") 5-10 60
DECCA (31634 "Debbie")..........................5-10 64
MGM (13521 "I'm Not Laughing") 5-10 66
U.A. (405 "Young at Heart") 5-10 62
U.A. (448 "Stars")....................................20-30 62

RAN-DELLS *P&R/R&B '63*
Singles: 7-inch
RSVP (1104 "Beyond the Stars") 10-15 64
CHAIRMAN (4403 "Martian Hop")...........15-20 63
CHAIRMAN (4407 "Come On and Love Me Too") 10-15 63
Picture Sleeves
CHAIRMAN (4403 "Martian Hop")...........30-40 63
Members: Steve Rappaport; John Sprit; Robert Rappaport.

RANDLE, Chester
("Chester Randle's Soul Sender's;" "Vocal By Scottie & Soul Dip's")
Singles: 7-inch
ANLA (102 "Soul Brother's Testify")........15-25 '60s
ANLA (105 "Take a Little Nip") ....15-25 '60s

RANDLE, Johnny
Singles: 7-inch
CRICKET (2207 "By My Side")................15-25 60
JAYREE (2205 "My One and Only One") 15-25 61

RANDLES, Robert
LPs: 10/12-inch
PRS (1005 "Portfolio of Film Music")........30-40
(Picture disc. 400 made.)
PRS (1005 "Portfolio of Film Music")........50-75
(Picture disc. Includes special plastic cover.)

RANDOLPH, Barbara
Singles: 7-inch
SOUL (35038 "I Got a Feeling") 10-20 67
SOUL (35050 "Can I Get a Witness") 10-20 68

RANDOLPH, Boots *P&R/R&B/LP '63*
(With Richie Cole; Homer Randolph)
Singles: 7-inch
MONUMENT (Except 443 thru 1038).........4-6 68-81
MONUMENT (443 thru 1038) 5-10 61-67
PAJ (7041 "Yakety Sax") 4-8
PALO ALTO 4-6
RCA (7611 "Sweet Talk")..........................8-12 59
RCA (7721 "Red Light") 8-12 60
RCA (7835 "Big Daddy") 15-20 61
(With "37" prefix. Compact 33 Single.)
RCA (7835 "Big Daddy") 8-10 61
(With "47" prefix.)
Picture Sleeves
MONUMENT (804 "Yakety Sax") 20-25 64
(Text-only sleeve reads: "Dance the 'Lorenzo Stomp' to Yakety Sax By Boots Randolph."
MONUMENT (852 "Mickey's Tune") 8-12 64
EPs: 7-inch
MONUMENT (002 "Boots Randolph")......10-20 63
(Promotional issue only.)
MONUMENT (361 "Boots and Stockings") 5-10 69
(Promotional issue only.)
MONUMENT (514 "More Yakety Sax")......5-10 '60s
(Promotional issue only.)
LPs: 10/12-inch
CAMDEN (825 "Yakin' Sax Man") 10-20 64
GUEST STAR 5-10 64
MONUMENT (Except 8000 & 18000 series)..6-12 71-82
MONUMENT (8000 & 18000 series).......10-20 63-71
PALO ALTO..5-8
RCA (LPM-2165 "Yakety Sax") 20-30 60
(Monaural.)
RCA (LSP-2165 "Yakety Sax") 30-40 60
(Stereo.)
TEXIZE (1 "Nashville Sound") 10-15 68
(Promotional issue only.)
Also see ANN-MARGRET
Also see ATKINS, Chet, Floyd Cramer & Boots Randolph
Also see FRANCIS, Connie
Also see HOLLY, Buddy
Also see HORTON, Jamie
Also see LEE, Brenda
Also see NASHVILLE ALL-STARS
Also see PRESLEY, Elvis
Also see RANDOLPH, Randy
Also see TILLOTSON, Johnny
Also see VELVETS

RANDOLPH, Boots / Bill Haley
Singles: 7-inch
LOGO (7005 "Yakety Sax") 8-12 61
Also see HALEY, Bill
Also see RANDOLPH, Boots

RANDOLPH, Randy
(Homer Randolph)
Singles: 7-inch
RCA (7395 "Yakety Sax") 10-20 59
RCA (7515 "Blue Guitar").........................10-15 59

Also see RANDOLPH, Boots

RANDY & CANDYMEN

Singles: 7-inch

BIG SOUND (6427 "Little Sister") 15-25 64

Members: Randy Rybicki; Eddie Farah; Jim Hanna; Jim Jandrain; Andy Pigeon.

RANDY & RAINBOWS P&R/R&B '63

Singles: 7-inch

AMBIENT SOUND (451 "Happy Teenager")..4-6 85

AMBIENT SOUND (02872 "Try the Impossible") 4-6 82

B.T. PUPPY (535 "I'll Be Seeing You")..... 10-15 67

CRYSTAL BALL (106 "I Wonder Why")........4-8 77

(500 made.)

CRYSTAL BALL (161 "It's Christmas Once Again") 4-6 93

(500 made.)

MIKE (4001 "Lovely Lies") 8-12 66

MIKE (4004 "Quarter to Three") 8-12 66

MIKE (4008 "Can It Be") 8-12 66

RUST (5059 "Denise") 15-25 63

(Blue label.)

RUST (5059 "Denise") 8-12 63

(Rust and white label.)

RUST (5073 "Why Do Kids Grow Up") 8-12 64

RUST (5080 "Dry Your Eyes") 8-12 64

RUST (5091 "Little Star") 8-12 64

RUST (5101 "Joy Ride") 5-10 65

STOOP SOUNDS (100 "In Your Letter") 100-150 96

(Limited edition. Estimates range from less than 10 to a few dozen made.)

LPs: 10/12-inch

AMBIENT SOUND (37715 "C'mon Let's Go") 8-12 82

AMBIENT SOUND/ROUNDER 8-10 84

MAGIC CARPET (1001 "Joyride") 15-20 91

(1st cover, white.)

MAGIC CARPET (1001 "Joyride") 25-35 91

(1st cover, white. Red vinyl. 10 made.)

MAGIC CARPET (1001 "Joyride") 10-15 91

(2nd cover, pink.)

MAGIC CARPET (1001 "Joyride") 8-12 91

(3rd cover, blue.)

MAGIC CARPET (1001 "Joyride") 5-10 91

(4th cover, maroon.)

MAGIC CARPET (1001 "Joyride") 40-50 91

(Picture disc. No cover. 25 made.)

Members: Dominick "Randy" Safuto; Frank Safuto; Mike Zero; Sal Zero; Ken Arcipowski.

Also see DIALTONES

RANDY & RAINBOWS / Four Pennies

Singles: 7-inch

LAURIE (110 "Denise"/"My Block") 4-6 78

(Double Gold reissue series.)

Also see FOUR PENNIES

RANDY & REST

Singles: 7-inch

JADE (767 "Confusion") 10-15 67

SSS INT'L (720 "The Vacuum") 15-25 67

RANDY & ROCKETS

Singles: 7-inch

ATWELL (102 "Rattlesnakin' Daddy")...... 50-75

AZALEA (138 "Over the Waves") 10-15 61

JIN (161 "Rocket's Twist") 10-15 62

N-JOY (1003 "Doggin' ") 5-10 64

VIKING (1000 "Genevieve") 10-20 59

Member: Gene Sledge.

RANEY, Dall, & Umbrellas

(Znydall Raney)

Singles: 7-inch

HOLLYWOOD (1105 "Fastback") 15-25 61

RANEY, Jimmy, & His Rhythmaires

Singles: 7-inch

MUSIC CITY (815 "Bolivia") 20-30 57

RANEY, Wayne C&W '45

Singles: 78 rpm

KING 8-12 48-55

Singles: 7-inch

DECCA (30212 "Shake Baby Shake") 50-75 57

KING 10-15 50-55

POOR BOY (109 "Everybody's Going Crazy") 60-75

LPs: 10/12-inch

KING 20-30

NASHVILLE 10-15

RIMROCK 5-10

STARDAY 15-20

RANGERS

Singles: 7-inch

FTP (404 "Riders in the Sky"/"Four on the Floor") 30-40 61

(Though not credited, the A-side is by the Ramrods.)

Also see RAMRODS

RANGLIN, Ernest

Singles: 7-inch

STUDIO (1 "Surfing") 20-25

RANK, Ken / Jades

Singles: 7-inch

FENTON (2194 "Twin City Saucer") 25-30 68

Also see JADES

RANKIN, Kenny LP '72

(Ken Rankin)

Singles: 7-inch

ABC-PAR (10268 "Go Home Little Girl") 8-12 61

COLUMBIA 5-10 63-65

DECCA 10-15 58-60

LITTLE DAVID 4-6 73-77

MERCURY 5-10 68-69

Picture Sleeves

COLUMBIA (42881 "Soft Guitar") 8-12 63

MERCURY (72768 "Peaceful") 8-12 68

LPs: 10/12-inch

ATLANTIC 5-10 80

LITTLE DAVID 8-10 72-77

MERCURY 10-15 67-69

Also see KENNY & YVONNE

Also see RANKINS, Kenneth, & Spars

RANKINS, Kenneth, & Spars

Singles: 78 rpm

GROOVE (0148 "Say a Prayer") 10-15 56

Singles: 7-inch

GROOVE (0148 "Say a Prayer") 25-50 56

Member: Kenny Rankin.

Also see RANKIN, Kenny

RANNELS

Singles: 7-inch

BOSS (2122 "Blue Island") 500-1000 63

RAPER BROTHERS

Singles: 7-inch

STARLIGHT (1004 "Rock Hop Bop") 75-150 58

RAPHAEL, Johnny

Singles: 7-inch

ALADDIN (3409 "We're Only Young Once") 10-20 57

MERCURY (71587 "School of Love") 10-25 60

RAPIDTONES

Singles: 78 rpm

RAPID (1002 "Sunday Kind of Love") 50-75 56

Singles: 7-inch

RAPID (1002 "Sunday Kind of Love")...100-150 56

Also see HARPTONES

RARE BIRD LP '70

Singles: 7-inch

ABC 4-6 72

POLYDOR 4-6 73

PROBE (477 "Sympathy") 4-8 70

LPs: 10/12-inch

ABC 8-10 72

POLYDOR 10-15 73-74

PROBE (4514 "Rare Bird") 15-25 70

RARE BREED

(Ohio Express)

Singles: 7-inch

ATTACK (1401 "Beg, Borrow & Steal") 20-30 66

(Reissued, with a different flip side, and shown as by the Ohio Express.)

ATTACK (1403 "Come and Take a Ride in My Boat") 10-20 66

Also see OHIO EXPRESS

RARE EARTH LP '69

Singles: 7-inch

MOTOWN 3-5 81

PRODIGAL 4-6 77-78

RARE EARTH (Black vinyl) 4-6 69-76

RARE EARTH (Colored vinyl) 4-8 72

(Promotional issue only.)

VERVE (10622 "Mother's Oats") 5-10 68

Picture Sleeves

RARE EARTH 4-6 71-73

LPs: 10/12-inch

MOTOWN 5-8 81

PRODIGAL 5-8 77-78

RARE EARTH (Except 507) 8-12 70-76

RARE EARTH (507 "Get Ready") 8-12 69

(With standard, square cover.)

RARE EARTH (507 "Get Ready") 30-40 69

(With rounded-top cover. Promotional issue.)

VERVE (5066 "Dreams – Answers") 10-20 68

Members: Peter Hoorelbeke; Gil Bridges; Pete Rivera; Ray Monette; Mark Olson; John Persh; Michael Urso; Edward Guzman; Ken James.

Also see SUNLINERS

RASCALS P&R '65

(Young Rascals)

Singles: 7-inch

ATLANTIC (Except 2428) 5-10 65-70

ATLANTIC (2428 "Groovin" [in Italian]") ... 10-20 67

(Backed with *Groovin'* in Spanish.)

ATLANTIC OLDIES ....4-6 '70s

COLUMBIA 4-6 71-72

PHILCO (18 "A Girl Like You"/"I've Been Lonely Too Long") 10-20 67

("Hip Pocket" flexi-disc.)

Picture Sleeves

ATLANTIC (Except 2401) 5-10 66-70

ATLANTIC (2401 "Groovin' ") 15-25 67

EPs: 7-inch

ATLANTIC (190 "Time Peace") 10-15 68

(Promotional issue only.)

LPs: 10/12-inch

ATLANTIC (137 "Freedom Suite") 20-30 69

(Promotional issue only.)

ATLANTIC (901 "Freedom Suite") 20-30 69

(Without cut corner or BB holes.)

ATLANTIC (901 "Freedom Suite") 10-20 69

(With cut corner or BB holes.)

ATLANTIC (8123 thru 8148) 15-25 66-67

ATLANTIC (8169 thru 8276) 10-15 68-71

COLUMBIA 8-12 71-72

PAIR 8-10 86

RHINO 5-8 87

W.F.O. (1000 "The Rascals") 8-12 72

Members: Felix Cavaliere; Ed Brigati; Dino Danelli; Gene Cornish; David Brigati.

Also see CORNISH, Gene

Also see DEE, Joey

Also see SWEET INSPIRATIONS

Also see UNBEATABLES

(YOUNG) RASCALS / Buggs / Four Seasons / Johnny Rivers

LPs: 10/12-inch

CORONET (283 "The Young Rascals") ...20-30 66

Also see BUGGS

Also see 4 SEASONS

Also see RIVERS, Johnny

(YOUNG) RASCALS / Isley Brothers

LPs: 10/12-inch

DESIGN (253 "Young Rascals and the Isley Brothers") ....15-25 '60s

Also see ISLEY BROTHERS

Also see RASCALS

RASH, Curley

Singles: 7-inch

CBR (124 "Bubble Gum Boogie") 200-300

RASPBERRIES P&R/LP '72

Singles: 7-inch

CAPITOL 4-8 72-74

Picture Sleeves

CAPITOL 6-10 73

LPs: 10/12-inch

CAPITOL (11036 thru 11329) 20-30 72-74

CAPITOL (11524 "Raspberries' Best") 8-12 76

CAPITOL (16095 "Raspberries' Best") 5-10 80

Members: Eric Carmen; Wally Bryson; Jim Bonfanti; John Aleksic; Dave Smalley.

Also see CHOIR

Also see YELLOW HAIR

RASPUTIN & MONKS / Octet

LPs: 10/12-inch

TRANS RADIO (200836 "Sum of My Soul") 250-350 66

(One side of the LP by each group.)

Member: Bob "Rasputin" Raymond.

RAT, Billy, & Finks

Singles: 7-inch

IGL (122 "Little Queenie") 25-35 67

Also see SHOOP, Wally, & Zombies

RATIONALS P&R '66

Singles: 7-inch

A² (101 "Look What You're Doin' ") 15-25 65

A² (103 "Feelin' Lost") 10-20 66

A² (103/4 "Feelin' Lost"/"Respect") 10-20 66

A² (104 "Respect"/"Leavin' Here") 10-20 66

A² (107 "I Need You") 10-20 68

A² (402 "I Need You") 10-20 68

(Different song than on #107.)

CAMEO (437 "Respect") 10-15 66

CAMEO (455 "Hold on Baby") 10-15 67

CAMEO (481 "Leavin' Here") 10-15 67

(Re-recorded version.)

CAPITOL (2124 "I Need You") 8-12 68

CREWE (340 "Guitar Army") 5-10 70

DANBY'S (125850 "Turn On") 30-40 66

(Promotional issue made for Danby's clothier. Identification number shown since no selection number is used.)

GENESIS (1 "Guitar Army") 8-12 69

LPs: 10/12-inch

ALIVE/TOTAL ENERGY 5-10 95

(10-inch LP.)

CREWE (1334 "Rationals") 25-35 69

Also see SRC / Rationals

RATLIFF, Bo

Singles: 7-inch

KARL (3009 "Hey, Hey, Don't Tease Me") 100-200

RATLIFF, Bozo

Singles: 7-inch

SPACE (100 "Let Me In") 300-400 58

RATS

Singles: 7-inch

BLACK CAT (502 "Rat's Revenge") 50-100 66

Also see MYSTICS

RATTLES

Singles: 7-inch

MERCURY (72554 "Dance") 5-10 66

LPs: 10/12-inch

MERCURY (21127 "Greatest Hits") 30-40 67

(Monaural.)

MERCURY (61127 "Greatest Hits") 40-60 67

(Stereo.)

Also see SEARCHERS / Rattles

RATTRAY, Duke

Singles: 7-inch

FAR-GO (107 "Just Walk Right In") 100-200

GALLIO (106 "Whirlpool of Love") 10-20 65

RAVEL, Joe

Singles: 7-inch

COUNSEL (120 "Bye Bye Love") 15-25 63

GOAL (701 "The House of the Cool") 15-25 64

RAVELL, Jackie, & Bandits

Singles: 7-inch

JORDAN (118 "Moonshine") 5-10 60

RAVELLES

Singles: 7-inch

MOBIE (3430 "Psychedelic Movement") .. 15-25 68

Members: John Richtig; Tom Lucas; Raymond Broullire; Rand Alquist; Carmella Altobelli.

RAVELS

Singles: 7-inch

DIAMOND (143 "Gonna Have Some Fun") 10-15 63

Also see SHERIFF & RAVELS

RAVEN, Eddy C&W '74

(Eddie Raven)

Singles: 7-inch

ABC 4-6 74-75

ABC/DOT 4-6 75-76

CAPITOL 3-5 89-90

COSMOS ("Ladies' Man") ... 50-75 62
(Selection number not known.)
DIMENSION ... 3-6 79-81
ELEKTRA ... 3-5 81-82
LA LOUISIANNE (77 "Pictures") ... 10-20
LA LOUISIANNE (8040 "O! Christina") ... 10-20 63
MONUMENT ... 3-5 78
RCA ... 3-5 84-88
UNIVERSAL ... 3-5 89

LPs: 10/12-inch

ABC/DOT ... 5-10 75-76
DIMENSION ... 5-8 80
ELEKTRA ... 5-8 81
LA LOUISIANNE ... 10-15
RCA ... 5-8 84-88

RAVENAIRS

Singles: 7-inch

ALGONQUIN (718 "Together Forever") ... 50-100 58
(First issued as by the Rivieras.)

RAVENETTES

Singles: 7-inch

MOON (103 "Too Young to Know") ... 50-75 59

RAVENETTES

Singles: 7-inch

VERTIGO (8002 "Baby Pull My Heart Strings") ... 25-35 59

RAVENS *P&R '47*

("Featuring Jimmy Ricks")

Singles: 78 rpm

ARGO ... 10-20 56-57
CHECKER ... 15-25 57
COLUMBIA ... 25-35 50-51
HUB (3032 "Out of a Dream") ... 50-100 46
HUB (3033 "Bye Bye Baby Blues") ... 50-100 46
KING (4234 "Bye Bye Baby Blues") ... 50-75 48
JUBILEE ... 15-25 55-56
MERCURY ... 25-50 51-55
NATIONAL (9034 "For You") ... 20-30 47
NATIONAL (9035 "Ol Man River") ... 20-30 47
NATIONAL (9038 "Write Me a Letter") ... 20-30 47
NATIONAL (9039 "Searching for Love") ... 20-30 47
NATIONAL (9040 "Fool That I Am") ... 20-30 47
NATIONAL (9042 Together") ... 20-30 48
NATIONAL (9045 "Until the Real Thing Comes Along") ... 20-30 48
NATIONAL (9053 "September Song") ... 20-30 48
NATIONAL (9056 "It's Too Soon to Know") ... 20-30 48
NATIONAL (9059 "I Don't Know Why") ... 20-30 48
NATIONAL (9062 "White Christmas") ... 20-30 48
NATIONAL (9064 "Always") ... 20-30 48
NATIONAL (9065 "Deep Purple") ... 20-30 49
NATIONAL (9073 "The House I Live In") ... 20-30 49
NATIONAL (9085 "Careless Love") ... 20-30 49
NATIONAL (9089 "Someday") ... 20-30 49
NATIONAL (9098 "I'm Afraid of You") ... 20-30 49
NATIONAL (9101 "I've Been a Fool") ... 20-30 49
NATIONAL (9111 "Count Every Star") ... 20-30 50
NATIONAL (9131 "Phantom Stage Coach") ... 20-30 50
NATIONAL (9148 "Lilacs in the Rain") ... 20-30 51
OKEH (6825 "Whiffenpoof Song") ... 20-30 51
OKEH (6843 "That Old Gang of Mine") ... 20-30 51
OKEH (6888 "Mam'selle") ... 20-30 52
RENDITION (5001 "Write Me a Letter") ... 50-100 51

Singles: 7-inch

ARGO (5255 "Kneel and Pray") ... 25-35 56
ARGO (5261 "A Simple Prayer") ... 40-50 56
(Rigid disc.)
ARGO (5261 "A Simple Prayer") ... 20-30 56
(Flexible disc.)
ARGO (5276 "That'll Be the Day") ... 20-30 57
ARGO (5284 "Here Is My Heart") ... 20-30 57
CHECKER (871 "That'll Be the Day") ... 15-25 57
COLUMBIA (1-903 "Time Takes Care of Everything") ... 750-1000 50
(Compact 33 Single.)
COLUMBIA (6-903 "Time Takes Care of Everything") ... 300-400 50
COLUMBIA (1-925 "I'm So Crazy for Love") ... 750-1000 50
(Compact 33 Single.)
COLUMBIA (6-925 "I'm So Crazy for Love") ... 300-400 50
COLUMBIA (39112 "You Don't Have to Drop a Heart to Break It") ... 300-400 51
COLUMBIA (39194 "You're Always in My Dreams") ... 300-400 51
COLUMBIA (39408 "You Foolish Thing") ... 500-750 51
JUBILEE (5184 "Bye Bye Baby Blues") ... 25-35 55
JUBILEE (5203 "Green Eyes") ... 25-35 55
JUBILEE (5217 "On Chapel Hill") ... 35-45 55
JUBILEE (5237 "I'll Always Be in Love with You") ... 40-50 55
MEDIA ("Sixty Minute Man") ... 3-5 93
(Colored vinyl. Selection number not known.)
MERCURY (5764 "There's No Use Pretending") ... 75-125 51
MERCURY (5800 "Begin the Beguine") ... 100-150 52
MERCURY (5853 "Why Did You Leave") ... 75-100 52
MERCURY (8291 "Write Me One Sweet Letter") ... 50-75 52
MERCURY (8296 "Too Soon") ... 50-75 52
MERCURY (70060 "Don't Mention My Name") ... 50-75 52
MERCURY (70119 "Come a Little Bit Closer") ... 50-75 53
MERCURY (70213 "Who'll Be the Fool") ... 50-75 53
MERCURY (70240 "Without a Song") ... 50-75 53
MERCURY (70307 "September Song") ... 40-50 54
MERCURY (70330 "Lonesome Road") ... 100-150 54
MERCURY (70413 "Love Is No Dream") ... 100-150 54
(Pink label.)
MERCURY (70413 "Love Is No Dream") ... 40-50 54
(Black label.)
MERCURY (70505 "White Christmas") ... 75-125 54
(Pink label.)
MERCURY (70505 "White Christmas") ... 40-50 54
(Black label.)
MERCURY (70554 "Write Me a Letter") ... 50-75 55
(Pink label.)
MERCURY (70554 "Write Me a Letter") ... 30-40 55
(Black label.)
NATIONAL (9111 "Count Every Star") ... 1500-2000 50
OKEH (6825 "Whiffenpoof Song") ... 300-400 51
OKEH (6843 "That Old Gang of Mine") ... 300-400 51
OKEH (6888 "Mam'selle") ... 300-400 52
SAVOY (1540 "White Christmas") ... 20-30 58
TOP RANK (2003 "Into the Shadows") ... 15-25 59
TOP RANK (2016 "Solitude") ... 15-25 59
VIRGO ... 4-6 72

Picture Sleeves

MEDIA ("Sixty Minute Man") ... 3-5 93
(Selection number not known.)

EPs: 7-inch

KING (310 "The Ravens Featuring Jimmy Ricks") ... 500-750 54
RENDITION (104 "Four Great Voices") ... 750-1000 52

LPs: 10/12-inch

HARLEM HIT PARADE (007 "The Ravens") ... 10-20 75
REGENT (6062 "Write Me a Letter") ... 100-150 57
(Green label.)
REGENT (6062 "Write Me a Letter") ... 50-100 '50s
(Red label.)
SAVOY (2227 "The Greatest Group of Them All") ... 15-25 78
(Two discs.)
Members: Warren Suttles; Ollie Jones; Maithe Marshall; Joe Van Loan; Jimmy Ricks; Leonard Puzey; Joe Medlin; Louis Heyward; Paul Van Loan; James Stewart; David Bowers; James Van Loan; Tom Evans; Willis Sanders; Rich Cannon; Louis Frazier; Bob Kornegay; Willie Ray.
Also see BELLS
Also see COBB, Arnett
Also see CUES
Also see DREAMERS
Also see KING ODOM
Also see KINGS
Also see MARSHALL BROTHERS
Also see PLAYBOYS
Also see RICKS, Jimmy
Also see VAN LOAN, Joe

RAVENS & DINAH WASHINGTON

Singles: 78 rpm

MERCURY ... 25-35 51

Singles: 7-inch

MERCURY (8257 "Hey Good Lookin'") ... 75-100 51
Also see WASHINGTON, Dinah

RAVENS / Three Clouds

Singles: 78 rpm

KING (4260 "Out of a Dream") ... 30-50 48
KING (4272 "Honey") ... 30-50 49
KING (4293 "My Sugar Is So Refined") ... 30-50 49
Also see RAVENS

RAVENS

Singles: 7-inch

SARA (6383 "The Shuck") ... 15-25 63
Members: Mark Strauss; Mike McCabe; Merlin Wield; Dennis Thompson; Don Wendt.

RAVENS

Singles: 7-inch

HAVEN (197 "Sleepless Nights") ... 15-25 65

RAVENSCROFT, Thurl

(With the Jeff Alexander Quartet; with Sky Boys; with Ranger Chorus; with Skip Martin Orchestra; Thurl Ravenscroft Singers)

Singles: 78 rpm

FABOR (4005 "Never Doubt My Love") ... 25-50 55

Singles: 7-inch

AARDELL (1005 "Dr. Geek") ... 10-20 '60s
BALLY (1008 "Oh You Sweet One") ... 10-15 56
FABOR (4005 "Never Doubt My Love") ... 100-150 55
O-1 (1 "Cool Cool Bottle") ... 10-15
BUENA VISTA (364 "Ten Who Dared") ... 8-12 60

LPs: 10/12-inch

DOT (3430 "Great Hits") ... 15-25 62
(Monaural.)
DOT (25430 "Great Hits") ... 25-35 62
(Stereo.)
Also see ANDREWS SISTERS & THURL RAVENSCROFT
Also see DE CASTRO SISTERS
Also see STORM, Gale

RAVE-ONS

Singles: 7-inch

RE-CAR (9016 "Baby Don't Love Me") ... 20-30 65
TWIN TOWN (702 "Everybody Tells Me") ... 20-30 65
TWIN TOWN (710 "Whenever") ... 20-30 65
Also see JOKERS WILD
Also see SOUTH 40

RAVES

Singles: 7-inch

SWADE (104 "Tell Me One More Time") ... 30-40 59

RAVET, Kerney

Singles: 7-inch

MERCURY (71431 "Tyrone") ... 20-30 59

RAVIN' BLUE

Singles: 7-inch

MONUMENT (968 "Love") ... 15-25 66
MONUMENT (1034 "Colors") ... 5-10 67

RAVONS

(Rav-ons)

Singles: 7-inch

ARROW (734 "Teenage Hop") ... 10-20 58
DAVIS (464 "Don't Ever Break Your Baby's Heart") ... 25-35 58

RAVONS

Singles: 7-inch

BANGAR (621 "Hey Little Girl") ... 40-60 64
Also see FIVE KEEYS

RAVONS

("Vocal by Jenny Johnson")

Singles: 7-inch

YUCCA (145 "Everybody's Laughing at Me") ... 400-600 62
(Identification number is "D-10" and is on left side of label.)
YUCCA (145 "Everybody's Laughing at Me") ... 50-75 62
(Identification number is "LH-14201" and is on right side of label.)
Member: Jenny Johnson.

RAW MEAT

Singles: 7-inch

BLUE HOUR (12661 "Stand By Girl") ... 4-8 '70s
CAPITOL (2984 "Make Love to Me") ... 4-8 70
MUSICOR (1326 "Run for Your Life") ... 5-10 68
Members: Gene Peranich; Don Gruender; Mike Jablonski.

RAW SOUL EXPRESS

Singles: 7-inch

CAT ... 4-6 76-77
TURNSTILE (001 "Gimme a Place to Dance") ... 30-50 80

RAW SPITT

Singles: 7-inch

U.A. (50813 "Song to Sing") ... 8-12 71

LPs: 10/12-inch

U.A. (6795 "Maybe You Ain't Black") ... 15-25 71

RAWLS, Lou *LP '63*

Singles: 12-inch

PHILA. INT'L ... 4-8 79

Singles: 7-inch

ARISTA (0103 "Baby You Don't Know How Good You Are") ... 4-6 75
BELL (45608 "She's Gone") ... 4-6 74
BELL (45616 "Who Can Tell Us Why") ... 4-6 74
CANDIX (305 "In My Little Black Book") ... 8-12 60
CANDIX (312 "80 Ways") ... 8-12 61
CAPITOL ... 4-8 61-70
EPIC ... 3-5 82-86
GAMBLE & HUFF (310 "I Wish You Belonged to Me") ... 3-5 87
GAMBLE & HUFF (314 "When Love Walked in the Door") ... 3-5 87
MGM ... 4-6 71-73
PHILA. INT'L ... 3-6 76-81
SHAR-DEE (705 "Kiddio") ... 8-12 60

Picture Sleeves

CAPITOL (5824 "Trouble down Here Below") ... 4-8 67
EPIC (05831 "Are You with Me") ... 4-6 86

EPs: 7-inch

CAPITOL ... 5-10 '60s
(Includes Juke box issues and 33 Compacts.)

LPs: 10/12-inch

ALLEGIANCE ... 5-8 84
BELL ... 8-10 74
CAPITOL (Except 1700 thru 2900 series) ... 5-12 69-77
CAPITOL (1700 thru 2900 series) ... 12-25 63-68
EPIC ... 5-8 82-83
MGM ... 8-10 71-73
PHILA. INT'L ... 5-10 76-80
PICKWICK ... 5-10 69
POLYDOR ... 8-10 76
Also see COOKE, Sam
Also see SEEKERS / Lou Rawls

RAWLS, Lou, & Les McCann Ltd.

Singles: 7-inch

CAPITOL (4803 "Stormy Monday") ... 5-10 62

LPs: 10/12-inch

CAPITOL ... 5-10 75
(With "SM" prefix.)
CAPITOL (1714 "Stormy Monday") ... 20-30 62
(With "T" or "ST" prefix.)
Also see McCANN, Les
Also see RAWLS, Lou

RAY, Ada "Cry Baby"

Singles: 7-inch

ZELLS (252/253 "Give Our Love a Chance") ... 15-25 62
ZELLS (260/261 "I Cried to Be Free") ... 50-75 62

RAY, Anita

(With the Nature Boys; Annita Ray)

Singles: 7-inch

AVA (171 "Slow Glow") ... 5-10 65
CHOREO (108 "I'm in Love with Jim") ... 5-10 62
DREAM (1300 "Elvis Presley Blues") ... 10-20 58
JAMIE (1131 "Someday I'm Comin' Home") ... 8-12 59
ZEPHYR (17 "Letter to a Soldier") ... 15-25 57

RAY, Billy

Singles: 7-inch

KENT (367 "Texas Queen") ... 10-15 62
OKEH (18009 "I Couldn't Sleep") ... 25-50 54
OKEH (18016 "Darling Don't Pity Me") ... 25-50 54
OKEH (18030 "I've Waited So Long") ... 25-50 54
TITAN (1709 "Story of Susie") ... 10-15 60

RAY, Bobby, & Cadillacs

Singles: 7-inch

CAPITOL (4935 "La Bamba") ... 8-12 63
Also see CADILLACS

RAY, Buddy

Singles: 7-inch

SMILE (110 "Hello to You") ... 15-25

RAY, Burch, & Walkers

Singles: 7-inch

LAVENDER (2306 "Well' Alright") ... 20-25 '60s
RUFF (1017 "Love Question") ... 25-35 66
SULLY (915 "Love Question") ... 25-35 '60s
YELLOWSTONE (1632 "Banks of the Yellowstone") ... 4-8 71
YELLOWSTONE (1802 "Montana Trapper") ... 4-8 72

Picture Sleeves

YELLOWSTONE (1802 "Montana Trapper") ... 5-10 72

LPs: 10/12-inch

YELLOWSTONE (1719 "Woman On My Mind") ... 8-12 72
Also see WALKERS

RAY, Danny

Singles: 7-inch

VIN (1025 "Love Me") ... 100-150 60
(Bright green label.)
VIN (1025 "Love Me") ... 15-25 60
(Olive green label.)

RAY, Dave

LPs: 10/12-inch

ELEKTRA (284 "Snaker's Here") ... 10-20 65
ELEKTRA (319 "Fine Soft Land") ... 10-20 67

RAY, David

Singles: 7-inch

KLIFF (101 "Lonesome Baby Blues") .. 350-450 58
KLIFF (102 "Jitterbuggin' Baby") ... 400-500 58
Also see SMITH, Ray

RAY, Dessa
(With Jewell Grant & His Band)

Singles: 78 rpm

7-11 (2103 "Ain't Gonna Tell") ... 15-20 53

Singles: 7-inch

7-11 (2103 "Ain't Gonna Tell") ... 40-50 53

RAY, Diane *P&R '63*

Singles: 7-inch

MERCURY (72117 "Please Don't Talk to the Lifeguard") ... 10-15 63
MERCURY (72223 "Snowman") ... 10-15 63
MERCURY (72248 "No Arms Can Ever Hold You") ... 8-12 64
MERCURY (72276 "That Boys' Gonna Be Mine") ... 8-12 64

Picture Sleeves

MERCURY (72117 "Please Don't Talk to the Lifeguard") ... 15-20 63
MERCURY (72223 "Snowman") ... 15-20 63

LPs: 10/12-inch

MERCURY (20903 "The Exciting Years") ... 30-60 64
MERCURY (60903 "The Exciting Years") ... 50-100 64

RAY, Don

Singles: 7-inch

ARWIN (1004 "Roly Poly") ... 10-15 59
RCA (9170 "I Feel Love Coming On") ... 25-50 67
RCA (9438 "Born a Loser") ... 25-50 68
RODEO (129 "Those Rock and Roll Blues") ... 150-250 58
RODEO (130 "Doncha' Baby My Baby") ... 100-200 58

RAY, Don, & Hornets

Singles: 7-inch

HORNET (501 "I Dreamed of You") ... 30-40 59

RAY, Donald, & Solid Sound

Singles: 7-inch

BEE & TEE (68005 "I Think About Love") ... 25-35

RAY, Donna

Singles: 7-inch

SATELLITE (103 "Little Fool") ... 100-200

RAY, Gene

Singles: 7-inch

CLASS (311 "Slauson U.S.A.") ... 8-12 64
COWTOWN (802 "I'm Going to Hollywood") ... 100-200

EPs: 7-inch

COWTOWN (677 "Gene Ray") ... 150-250

RAY, James *P&R '61*
(With the Hutch Davie Orchestra)

Singles: 7-inch

CAPRICE (110 "If You Gotta Make a Fool of Somebody") ... 20-30 61
CAPRICE (114 "Itty Bitty Pieces") ... 15-25 62
CAPRICE (117 "Things Are Gonna Be Different") ... 8-12 62
CONGRESS (109 "Marie") ... 10-20 63
CONGRESS (201 "Do the Monkey") ... 10-20 63
CONGRESS (203 "One By One") ... 10-20 64
CONGRESS (218 "On That Day") ... 10-20 64
DYNAMIC (503 "I've Got My Mind Set on You") ... 10-20 62

LPs: 10/12-inch

CAPRICE (LP-1002 "James Ray") ... 75-100 62
(Monaural.)
CAPRICE (SLP-1002 "James Ray") ... 100-150 62
(Stereo.)
Also see DAVIE, Hutch
Also see GRANT, Janie

RAY, Johnnie *P&R '51*
(With the Four Lads; with Maurice King & His Wolverines; with Percy Faith & His Orchestra; with Ray Conniff Orchestra & Chorus)

Singles: 78 rpm

COLUMBIA ... 5-10 52-58
OKEH ... 8-12 51

Singles: 7-inch

CADENCE (1387 "In the Heart of a Fool") ... 5-10 60
COLUMBIA ... 10-15 52-60
DECCA ... 5-8 63-64
GROOVE (0044 "One Life") ... 5-8 64
LIBERTY (55404 "Lover's Question") ... 5-10 62
LIBERTY (55431 "Cry") ... 5-10 62
OKEH (6809 "Whiskey and Gin") ... 15-25 51
OKEH (6840 "Cry") ... 10-20 51
OKEH RHYTHM & BLUES (6840 "Cry") .. 15-25 51
U.A. (341 "How Many Nights, How Many Days") ... 5-10 61

Picture Sleeves

COLUMBIA (40803 "You Don't Owe Me a Thing") ... 10-20 57

EPs: 7-inch

COLUMBIA ... 10-20 52-59
EPIC ... 10-20 52-54

LPs: 10/12-inch

COLUMBIA (961 "The Big Beat") ... 30-50 57
COLUMBIA (1093 thru 1227) ... 20-40 57-59
COLUMBIA (1385 "On the Trail") ... 15-25 59
(Monaural.)
COLUMBIA (2510 "I Cry for You") ... 30-50 56
(10-inch LP.)
COLUMBIA (6199 "Johnnie Ray") ... 35-55 51
(10-inch LP.)
COLUMBIA (8180 "On the Trail") ... 20-30 59
(Stereo.)
EPIC (1120 "Johnnie Ray") ... 30-50 55
(10-inch LP.)
HARMONY ... 5-10 71
SUNSET (1125 "Mr. Cry") ... 10-15 66
(Monaural.)
SUNSET (5125 "Mr. Cry") ... 15-20 66
(Stereo.)
Also see CONNIFF, Ray
Also see DAY, Doris, & Johnnie Ray
Also see FAITH, Percy, Orchestra
Also see FOUR LADS
Also see KING, Maurice

RAY, Johnnie, & Timi Yuro

Singles: 7-inch

LIBERTY (55400 "I Believe") ... 8-12 61
Also see RAY, Johnnie
Also see YURO, Timi

RAY, Kai

Singles: 7-inch

BRITE STAR (2267 "I Want Some of That") ... 5-10 58
SHOOTING STAR (2267 "I Want Some of That") ... 40-60

RAY, Laverne
(With the Raytones)

Singles: 78 rpm

JUBILEE (5022 "Rock and Roll") ... 10-20 49
OKEH (7091 "I'm in Love Again") ... 15-25 57

Singles: 7-inch

OKEH (7091 "I'm in Love Again") ... 15-25 57

RAY, Little Jimmy

Singles: 7-inch

GALLIANT (1001 "Make Her Mine") ... 15-25 59

RAY, Nelson

Singles: 7-inch

PHILLIPS INT'L (3568 "You've Come Home") ... 10-15 61
REBEL (104 "Walkin' Shoes") ... 200-300

RAY, Ricardo *P&R '68*
(With the Hutch Davie Orchestra)

Singles: 7-inch

ALEGRE (4024 "Nitty Gritty") ... 5-10 68
Also see DAVIE, Hutch

RAY, Robbin

Singles: 7-inch

COMBO (142 "Strolling") ... 15-25 58
COMBO (143 "It's a Lonesome Old World") ... 15-25 58
COMBO (145 "Love My Baby") ... 50-75 58

RAY, Ronnie, & Playboys

Singles: 7-inch

CIRCLE DOT (1002 "Mean Mama Blues") ... 200-300 60

RAY, Sherry

Singles: 7-inch

PANICS (101 "Telephone Please Ring") .. 30-40 63

RAY, Spider, & Velveteens

Singles: 7-inch

BOSS (102 "Maria") ... 50-75 61

RAY & BOB *P&R '62*

Singles: 7-inch

LEDO (1151 "Air Travel") ... 10-20 62
LEDO (2110 "Our Last Night") ... 10-20 62
Members: Ray Swayne; Bob Appleberry.

RAY & DARCHAES

Singles: 7-inch

ALJON (1249 "Carol") ... 50-75 62
BUZZY (202 "Darling Forever") ... 75-100 62
(Black vinyl.)
BUZZY (202 "Darling Forever") ... 100-200 62
(Blue vinyl.)
DOWNSTAIRS (1002 "Carol") ... 4-6 73
Member: Ray Dahrouge.

RAY & LINDY

Singles: 7-inch

ATCO (6150 "Jimmy's Got a Girl") ... 10-20 59
ROCKET ... 10-20 57
STARDAY (333 "Hey Doll Baby") ... 50-75 57
U.A. (171 "Yes, That's Love") ... 10-20 59

RAY & STRAYS
(Ray Stankes & His Orchestra)

Singles: 7-inch

LARRIC (101 "How Will I Know My Love") ... 30-40 62
Member: Ray Stankes.

RAY BEATS

Singles: 7-inch

Z (8 "Calhoun Surf") ... 10-20 '60s

RAY MEN

Singles: 7-inch

DIAMOND (186 "Baby What You Want Me to Do") ... 8-10 65
Also see WRAY, Link

RAY DOTS

Singles: 78 rpm

VIBRO (1651 "I Need Someone") ... 100-200 56

Singles: 7-inch

VIBRO (1651 "I Need Someone") ... 400-600 56

RAYBURN, Rick

Singles: 7-inch

EVANA (0002 "You're Number One") ... 50-100

RAYBURN, Margie *P&R '57*

Singles: 78 rpm

ALMA ... 5-10 54
LIBERTY ... 5-10 56-57
S&G ... 5-10 54

Singles: 7-inch

ALMA ... 10-15 54
CAPITOL (5396 "Are You Sure") ... 4-8 65
CHALLENGE (9110 "Here I Am") ... 5-10 61
DOT ... 4-8 62-66
LIBERTY (Except 55102) ... 5-10 56-60
LIBERTY (55102 "I'm Available) ... 10-15 57
S&G ... 10-15 54

Picture Sleeves

LIBERTY (55072 "Freight Train") ... 10-15 57

LPs: 10/12-inch

LIBERTY (3126 "Margie") ... 20-25 59
(Monaural.)
LIBERTY (7126 "Margie") ... 25-35 59
(Stereo.)
Also see SUNNYSIDERS

RAYE, Anthony

Singles: 7-inch

IMPACT (1009 "On the Edge of Sorrow") ... 20-30 66
IMPACT (1030 "Hold on to What You Got") ... 50-100 67

RAYE, Cal
(With the Class-Airs; with the Sweettones; with Sweet-Teens)

Singles: 7-inch

COQUETTE (364 "Lovely Lies") ... 10-20
COQUETTE (3212 "We Belong Together") ... 10-15
DEVILLE ("Lovely Lies") ... 20-30
(Selection number not known.)
FLEETWOOD ("Lovely Lies") ... 15-25
(Selection number not known.)
LAURIE (3626 "Sensuous Woman") ... 4-6 75
PHAROAH ... 5-10
PROVIDENCE (412 "Lovely Lies") ... 10-15 65
SUPER (101 "My Tears Start to Fall") ... 5-10 66

RAYE, Dina

Singles: 7-inch

CAMEO (195 "Little White Diamond") ... 10-20 61

RAYE, Jackie

Singles: 78 rpm

ARCADE (114 "Crazy Cool") ... 10-20 53

Singles: 7-inch

ARCADE (114 "Crazy Cool") ... 20-30 53

RAYE, Jerry
(With Fenwyck; with New Trend)

Singles: 7-inch

DEVILLE (202 "Pray for Me") ... 10-15 68
(Red vinyl.)
DEVILLE (207 "State of Mind") ... 10-15 68
(Blue vinyl.)
DEVILLE (208 "I Cry") ... 8-12 68
PERSPECTIVE (6005 "The Simple Things of Life") ... 10-15 '60s

LPs: 10/12-inch

DE VILLE (101 "The Many Sides of Jerry Raye Featuring Fenwyck") ... 450-650 67
(Red vinyl.)
Members: Jerry Raye; Pat Robinson; Pat Maroshek; Keith Knighter.
Also see FENWYCK
Also see RAYE, Jerry

RAYE, Jimmy
(Jimmie Raye)

Singles: 7-inch

MOONSHOT (6708 "It's Written All Over Your Face") ... 5-10 68
NIAGARA (185 "You Don't Want My Love") ... 20-30 63
TUFF (401 "I Tried") ... 15-25 64

RAYLENE & BLUE ANGELS
(With Dairylanders)

Singles: 7-inch

CUCA (1141 "Sentenced") ... 25-35 63
CUCA (6633 "Shakin' All Over") ... 25-35 66
Members: Raylene Loos; Roger Loos; Tom Loos; Tom Reischl.
Also see RICKY & RAYLENE

RAYLOV, Bobby

Singles: 7-inch

LOVINN (200 "If We Can't Be Lovers") ... 20-30

RAYMOND, Litte Doc

Singles: 7-inch

COLEMAN ("It Looks Plumb Silly to Me") ... 50-100
(No selection number used.)

RAYONS

Singles: 7-inch

DECCA (32521 "Do You Love Me") ... 20-30 69
FORTE ... 10-20 '60s

RAY-O-VACS R&B '49
Singles: 78 rpm
ATCO.......10-20 57
COLEMAN (100 "I'll Always Be in Love with You")......10-15 49
DECCA.......5-10 50-53
JOSIE.......10-15 54-55
JUBILEE.......10-15 52-53
KAISER.......10-15 56
Singles: 7-inch
ATCO (6085 "Crying All Alone")......10-20 57
DECCA.......15-25 50-53
JOSIE (763 "Ridin' High")......15-25 54
JOSIE (781 "I Still Love You")......15-25 55
JUBILEE (5098 "What Can I Say")......15-25 52
JUBILEE (5124 "You Know")......15-25 53
KAISER (384 "Crying All Alone")......15-25 56
SHARP (103 "I'll Always Be in Love with You")......20-30 60
Members: Lester Harris; Herb Milliner.

RAYS P&R/R&B '57
Singles: 78 rpm
CAMEO (117 "Silhouettes")......10-20 57
CAMEO (128 "Triangle")......10-20 58
CHESS.......15-35 55-57
XYZ (100 "My Steady Girl")......40-60 57
XYZ (102 "Silhouettes")......50-100 57
Singles: 7-inch
ABKCO.......3-5 '80s
ARGO (1074 "How Long Must I Wait")......15-25 57
CAMEO (117 "Silhouettes")......20-30 57
(Yellow label.)
CAMEO (117 "Silhouettes")......10-20 57
(Orange label.)
CAMEO (128 "Triangle")......10-20 58
CAMEO (133 "Rags to Riches")......15-25 58
CHESS (1613 "Tippity Top")......20-30 55
CHESS (1678 "Second Fiddle")......20-30 57
PERRI (1004 "Are You Happy Now")......15-25 62
(With Frankie Valli.)
XYZ (2 "Silhouettes")......200-300 57
(Alternative take. Promotional issue only.)
XYZ (100 "My Steady Girl")......50-100 57
XYZ (102 "Silhouettes")......100-200 57
(Gray label.)
XYZ (102 "Silhouettes")......50-75 57
(Blue label.)
XYZ (106 "Souvenirs of Summertime")......40-60 58
XYZ (600 "Why Do You Look the Other Way")......40-60 59
XYZ (604 "Tender Words")......300-500 59
XYZ (605 "Mediterranean Moon")......30-40 59
XYZ (607 "Magic Moon")......30-40 60
(Blue label.)
XYZ (607 "Magic Moon")......15-25 60
(Red label.)
XYZ (608 "Old Devil Moon")......15-25 60
XYZ (2001 "Souvenirs of Summertime")......35-45 58
(First issued in 1958 on XYZ 106.)
EPs: 7-inch
CHESS (5120 "The Rays")......200-300 58
Members: Harold "Hal" Miller; Walter Ford; David Jones; Harry James.
Also see MILLER, Hal

RAY-VONS
Singles: 7-inch
LAURIE (3248 "Judy")......100-200 64

RAZOR'S EDGE P&R '66
Singles: 7-inch
POW (101 "Let's Call It a Day, Girl")......10-15 66
POW (103 "Night and Day")......10-15 66
POW (105 "Baby's On His Way")......10-15 67
POWER (4932 "Get Yourself Together")......15-25 67
Members: Bill Ande; Tom Condra; Dave Hieronymous; Jim Tolliver; Vic Gray.
Also see AMERICAN BEETLES
Also see ARDELLS

RAZOR'S EDGE
Singles: 7-inch
KINGSTON (196716 "Gotta Find Her")......10-20 67
Member: Pat Farrell.
Also see FARRELL, Pat, & Believers
Also see TRIUMPHS

RE & RO
Singles: 7-inch
SOUTH SEA (101 "Pink Pedal Pushers")......50-75

REACTIONS
Singles: 7-inch
CLOUD (501 "Just a Little Love")......5-10 65
COOL SOUND (701 "Just a Little Love")......8-12 64
(Black vinyl.)
COOL SOUND (701 "Just a Little Love")......10-20 64
(Blue vinyl.)
MUTUAL (509 "Our Wonderful Love")......10-15 65
ROCK (5810 "In My Grave")......30-40 '60s
TASSEL.......10-20

READ, Ed
Singles: 7-inch
VERSATILE (106 "Charm Bracelet")......40-60 60

READ, Otis
Singles: 7-inch
GANLON (412 "I'm the Only One")......75-125
(At least one source reports this issue as being credited to Mojo Watson. We don't yet know if it exists as by both Mojo [K.C] Watson and Otis Read.)
NANC.......20-30 61
(Title and selection number not known.)
Also see WATSON, K.C.

READING, Bertice
Singles: 78 rpm
GROOVE (0022 "I Wash My Hands")......5-10 54
Singles: 7-inch
GROOVE (0022 "I Wash My Hands")......15-25 54

READY, Lynn
Singles: 7-inch
COWTOWN (809 "Jeremiah Peabody's Poly Unsaturated Quick Dissolving, Fast Acting, Pleasant Tasting Green & Purple Pills")......10-15 61
SPIN (78 "Teen Age Kid")......10-15 60

READYMEN
Singles: 7-inch
BANGAR (00655 "Surfer's Blues")......50-100 65
Picture Sleeves
BANGAR (00655 "Surfer's Blues")......75-100 65

REAGAN, Jimmy, & Rhythm Rockers
Singles: 7-inch
G&G (128 "Lonely Lonely Heart")......75-100 59
MONA-LEE (128 "Lonely Lonely Heart")......30-50 58

REAL GEORGE
Singles: 7-inch
GLOVER (1001 "Flip, Flop-Flop")......25-50

REAL LIST
Singles: 7-inch
C.P. (102 "Pick Up the Marbles")......30-50

REAL McCOYS
("Lead Vocal by George Holmes")
Singles: 7-inch
PICO (523 "I Must Forget About You")......400-500 61

REAL ORIGINAL BEATLES
Singles: 7-inch
DOT (16655 "Beatles Story")......10-20 64

REAR EXIT
Singles: 7-inch
MTA (132 "Excitation")......20-30 67

REAR EXIT
Singles: 7-inch
NIGHT OWL (1527 "Thinking of You")......10-20 70
Members: Ken Burhop; Gary Leistikow; John Frederickson; Bill Preuss; Peter Bloom; Scott Yeager.

REARDON, Eddie
Singles: 7-inch
BRUNSWICK (55062 "Who Is Eddie")......15-25 58
Session: Three Friends.
Also see FONTAINE, Eddie
Also see THREE FRIENDS

REASONS WHY
Singles: 7-inch
SOUND TRACK (2000 "Melinda")......25-35 66
Also see LAVENDER HILL EXPRESS

REASONS WHY
Singles: 7-inch
AMY (962 "Why Pack Up")......10-15 66
AMY (970 "Try and See Me")......10-15 66
AMY (980 "Same Old Worries")......10-15 67
CHA CHA (780 "The Game of War")......30-40 '60s
KM (727 "All I Really Need Is Love")......20-30 67

REAVES, Pearl, & Concords
Singles: 78 rpm
HARLEM.......40-60 55
Singles: 7-inch
HARLEM (2332 "You Can't Stay Here")......250-300 55
PEARLSFAR (108 "Change Me")......15-25
Session: Tracy & Tracynettes.
Also see CONCORDS

REBB, Johnny, & Rebels
Singles: 7-inch
BULLSEYE (1027 "Rock On")......400-500 59

REBECCA
Singles: 7-inch
LAMP (2011 "Take Care of My Heart")......10-20 57
W.B. (5278 "Please Be Kind")......5-10 62

REBECCA & SUNNY BROOK FARMERS
LPs: 10/12-inch
MUSICOR (3176 "Rebecca and the Sunny Brook Farmers")......15-25 69
Members: Kiki; Ilene Novog; Ilene Rapaport; Cliff Mandell; Mark Kapner.
Also see COUNTRY JOE & FISH

REBEL, Johnny
Singles: 7-inch
PEPPER (914 "What Will You Give in Return")......100-200 60
REBEL.......10-20 67-68

REBELAIRES
Singles: 7-inch
B&K (103 "Once We Loved")......100-200 57

REBELAIRES FEATURING SAMMY SMITH
Singles: 7-inch
WEE REBEL (102 "Satellite Rock")......300-400 58

REBEL ROUSERS
Singles: 7-inch
HELENE (3 "War Paint")......50-75 60
HITT (102 "Peter Gunn Twist")......8-12 62
JAN (11959 "Red-Headed Woman")......250-350
LOUIS (1006 "Swanee Twist")......8-12 62
MEMPHIS (107 "Thunder")......10-15 64
MEMPHIS (113 "Zombie Walk")......10-15 64

REBELS
Singles: 7-inch
DORE (510 "Marathon Walk")......15-25 58

REBELS
Singles: 7-inch
KINGS-X (3362 "In the Park")......500-1000 59

REBELS P&R '62
Singles: 7-inch
MARLEE (0094 "Wild Weekend")......75-100 60
QUALITY (1024 "Wild Weekend")......25-50 60
(Canadian.)
SWAN (4125 "Wild Weekend")......10-20 62
(White label with red print.)
SWAN (4125 "Wild Weekend")......10-20 62
(White label with black print.)
Note: Most Swan issues credit the Rockin' Rebels.
Members: Tom Gorman, Paul Balon, Mickey Kipler, Jim Kipler.
Also see BUFFALO REBELS
Also see ROCKIN' REBELS

REBELS
Singles: 7-inch
GASLIGHT (558 "Run Little Sheba")......400-500 61
(Previously issued as by the Twisters.)
Also see SMITH, Bob
Also see TWISTERS

REBELS
Singles: 7-inch
REBEL (1070 "The Rebel Beat")......25-35 '60s
(Reissued as by John & Ed Strickland.)
Also see STRICKLAND, Jon & Ed

REBENNACK, Mac
(With the Soul Orchestra)
Singles: 7-inch
A.F.O. (309 "The Point")......15-25 62
ACE (611 "Good Times")......15-25 61
REX (1008 "Storm Warning")......30-50 59
Also see ANDERSON, Elton

REBS
(Rockin' Rebs)
Singles: 7-inch
FREDLO (6014 "Grandpa Rock")......100-200
LPs: 10/12-inch
FREDLO (6830 "A.D. Break Through")......400-600 68
(Reportedly 200 to 250 copies made.)

RECALLS
Singles: 7-inch
ARROW (2002 "No Reason")......50-75

RECTOR, Hank
Singles: 7-inch
STARLITE (713 "I'm Gonna Let You Go")......150-250

RED & BLUE
Singles: 7-inch
HERALD (525 "Rockin' Red Riding Hood")......25-35 58

RED & FLAMES
Singles: 7-inch
RMP (1027 "Little Cinderella")......10-20 64
Also see GARRISON, Red, & Zodiacs

RED COATS
Singles: 7-inch
DEL-CO (4002 "I Never Knew")......15-25 59
(Reissued as by the Colts.)
Member: Joe Grundy.
Also see COLTS

RED COATS
Singles: 7-inch
KITE (2003 "Perkin'")......10-20 61
Also see ALAIMO, Steve

RED CRAYOLA
LPs: 10/12-inch
INT'L ARTISTS (2 "Parable of Arable Land")......60-100 67
(Does NOT have "Masterfonics" stamped in the vinyl trail-off.)
INT'L ARTISTS (7 "God Bless the Red Crayola")......30-45 68
(Does NOT have "Masterfonics" stamped in the vinyl trail-off.)
INT'L ARTISTS.......10-20 79
(Reissues. With "Masterfonics" stamped in the vinyl trail-off.)
Members: Mayo Thompson; Danny Schact; Steve Cunningham; Rick Barthelme; Bonnie Emerson.
Also see THOMPSON, Mayo

RED HOT CHILI PEPPERS LP '87
Singles: 12-inch
EMI AMERICA.......4-6 85
Singles: 7-inch
EMI AMERICA.......3-5 84-85
EMI RECORDS GROUP.......4-6
("For Juke boxes Only!" series.)
W.B.......3-5 91
LPs: 10/12-inch
CAPITOL (29665 "Out in L.A.")......8-10 '90s
EMI AMERICA.......5-8 84-85
EMI MANHATTAN.......5-8 87
W.B. (Except 5170)......5-8 91
W.B. (5170 "Blood Sugar Sex Magic")......15-25 91
(Double LP "Radio Ready" [censored] issue. Promotional issue only.)
Members: Anthony Kiedis; Jack Irons; Hillel Slovak; Mike Balzary; John Frusciante; Chad Smith.
Also see WILSON, Nancy / Red Hot Chili Peppers

RED POWER BAND
EPs: 7-inch
UA (1499 "Red Power Band")......5-10 '60s

RED RIVER DAVE P&R '60
(Dave McEnery)
Singles: 78 rpm
TNT (Except 9006)......10-20 53-56
TNT (9006 "James Dean")......20-30 56
Singles: 7-inch
COPYRIGHT (41 "Spanish Guitar")......5-10 61
D (1243 "Moon Over the Wall")......8-12 63
LONGHORN (452004 "Pine Tarred Bat")......4-6 83
(George Brett baseball song.)
SAVOY (1627 "Ballad of Viet Nam")......5-10 65
SAVOY (3020 "There's a Star Spangled Banner Waving #2")......10-15 60

SAVOY (3023 "Trial of Francis Powers"). 10-15 60
(Above two releases are about Francis Powers, the U-2 pilot shot down in Russia in 1960.)
TNT (1003 "Red Deck of Cards")............ 15-25 53
TNT (1017 "When Davy Crockett Met the San Antonio Rose")................................ 15-25 55
TNT (9003 "Maria Elena")...................... 15-25 55
TNT (9005 "Truck Driver's Special")........ 15-25 56
TNT (9006 "James Dean")....................... 40-60 56
TNT (9010 "The Ballad of Don Larsen").. 15-25 57

EPs: 7-inch

TNT (1 "James Dean Album")................. 50-75 56
VARSITY 5-10

LPs: 10/12-inch

BLUEBONNET.. 10-20 '60s
CONTINENTAL... 10-20 62
PLACE... 10-20 '60s
SUTTON.. 10-20 '60s

RED RIVER DAVE / Davis Sisters

Singles: 78 rpm

TNT... 10-20 54

Singles: 7-inch

TNT (1011 "Truck Driver's Special"/"Midnight Mare").. 15-25 54
Also see DAVIS SISTERS
Also see RED RIVER DAVE

RED TOPS
(Original Red Tops Featuring Rufus McKay)

Singles: 7-inch

SKY (703 "Swanee River Rock")............ 15-25 60
Also see McKAY, Rufus

REDBONE *P&R/LP '70*

Singles: 7-inch

EPIC...4-6 70-74
RCA...3-5 78

LPs: 10/12-inch

ACCORD...5-10 82
EPIC...8-15 70-75
RCA...5-10 77
Members: Pat Vegas; Lolly Vegas; Tony Bellamy.
Also see VEGAS, Pat & Lolly

REDBONE, Leon *LP '76*

Singles: 78 rpm

W.B. 5-10 78
(Promotional only.)

Singles: 7-inch

EMERALD CITY..3-8 81
W.B. 5-12 77-78

LPs: 10/12-inch

ACCORD... 10-15 82
EMERALD CITY.. 10-15 81
W.B. 15-30 77-78

REDCAPS

Singles: 7-inch

HUNT (326 "Cheryl Lee")........................ 20-30 59

REDCOATS

Singles: 7-inch

MAE (1002 "Cobra")................................ 20-30

REDD, Alton, & His Down Blues Band

Singles: 78 rpm

BEL-TONE.. 15-25 46
BLACK & WHITE....................................... 15-25 45-46

REDD, Barbara

Singles: 7-inch

S.P.Q.R. (3311 "Dancing Teardrops")..... 20-30 63

REDD, Johnny

Singles: 7-inch

CARELLEN (11 "I Flipped My Top")...... 50-100 60
CARELLEN (106 "Rockin' Peg")........... 300-400 60
HORIZON (1002 "Take a Ride with Me")... 300-400

REDD, Vi
(Vi Redd Sextet)

LPs: 10/12-inch

ATCO (157 "Lady Soul")......................... 20-30 63
SOLID STATE... 10-15 69

REDDING, Otis *P&R/R&B '63*
(With the Pinetoppers; with Pinetones; with Shooters)

Singles: 7-inch

ATCO (Except 7069)...............................5-15 68-72
ATCO (7069 "White Christmas")...............4-6 77
ATCO (7321 "White Christmas")...............3-5 81
ATCO (99955 "White Christmas")..............3-5 82
BETHLEHEM (3083 "Shout Bamalama") 10-15 64
CONFEDERATE (135 "Shout Bamalama")..20-40 62
FINER ARTS (2016 "She's All Right")......30-50 61
(Previously issued as by the Shooters.)
KING (6149 "Shout Bamalama")................5-10 68
ORBIT (135 "Shout Bamalama")...........200-400 61
PHILCO (13 "Shake"/"Fa-Fa-Fa-Fa-Fa")..10-20 67
("Hip Pocket" flexi-disc.)
STONE (209 "You Left the Water Running")..4-8 76
VOLT (103 thru 121).................................10-20 62-64
VOLT (124 thru 163).................................10-15 65-68

EPs: 7-inch

VOLT (70413 "The Soul Album")..............20-30 66
(Juke box issue only. Includes title strips.)

LPs: 10/12-inch

ATCO (33-161 "Pain in My Heart")...........50-70 64
(Monaural.)
ATCO (SD-33-161 "Pain in My Heart")....60-80 64
(Stereo.)
ATCO (200 series).....................................10-15 68-69
ATCO (300 series).......................................8-12 70
ATCO (801 "The Best of Otis Redding") ..10-20 72
(Reissues available with same selection number.)
ATLANTIC...5-10 82
VOLT (Except 411)...................................20-35 65-68
VOLT (411 "Soul Ballads").......................35-55 65
(Monaural.)
VOLT (411 "Soul Ballads").......................40-60 65
(Stereo.)
Members: Steve Cropper; Booker T. Jones; Isaac Hayes; Donald "Duck" Dunn; Lewis Steinberg; Al Jackson Jr. Session: Wayne Cochran; Johnny Jenkins; William Bell; Tommie Lee Williams; Veltones; Drapels.
Also see BOOKER T. & MGs
Also see COCHRAN, Wayne
Also see HAYES, Isaac
Also see JENKINS, Johnny
Also see SHOOTERS

REDDING, Otis / Little Joe Curtis

LPs: 10/12-inch

ALSHIRE (5082 "Here Comes Some Soul")..8-12 68
SOMERSET...8-12 68

REDDING, Otis / Jimi Hendrix *LP '70*

LPs: 10/12-inch

REPRISE (2029 "Otis Redding"/"The Jimi Hendrix Experience")..10-15 70
(Disc reads: "Historic Performances Recorded At The Monterey International Pop Festival.")
REPRISE (2029 "Otis Redding"/"The Jimi Hendrix Experience")..15-25 70
(White label. Promotional issue only.)
REPRISE (93371 "Otis Redding"/"The Jimi Hendrix Experience")..15-20 70
(Different front cover than 2029. Disc reads: "Music from the Monterey Pop Soundtrack.")
Also see HENDRIX, Jimi

REDDING, Otis / King Curtis

LPs: 10/12-inch

ATCO (265/266 "Promotional LP for Record Department-in-Store Play").......................15-20 68
(Promotional issue only.)
Also see KING CURTIS

REDDING, Otis / Carla Thomas / Sam & Dave / Eddie Floyd

LPs: 10/12-inch

STAX (722 "Stax/Volt Revue, Vol. 2").......15-25 67
Also see FLOYD, Eddie
Also see OTIS & CARLA
Also see REDDING, Otis
Also see SAM & DAVE
Also see THOMAS, Carla

REDDLEMEN

Singles: 7-inch

CUSTOM (131 "I Can't Go On This Way")..20-30 66

REDELL, Teddy

Singles: 7-inch

ATCO (6162 "Judy")..................................25-50 60
HI (2024 "Pipeliner")...............................15-25 60
RAZORBACK (105 "Poor Ole Me")..........15-25 59
RIMROCK (215 "I See the Moon")............10-20 63
VADEN (110 "Knocking on the Backside")..75-125 60
VADEN (115 "Corinne Corinna")............75-125 60
VADEN (116 "Judy")...............................75-125 60
(First issue.)
VADEN (117 "Pipeliner").........................75-125 60
(First issue.)
VADEN (301 "Pipeliner")........................50-100 60
VADEN (305 "Don't Grow Old Alone")......25-50 60
Session: Otis Williams & Charms.
Also see CHARMS

REDEYE *P&R/LP '70*

Singles: 7-inch

PENTAGRAM (204 "Games")......................4-6 70
PENTAGRAM (206 "Red Eye Blues")..........4-6 71

LPs: 10/12-inch

PENTAGRAM...10-15 70-71
Members: Doug "Red" Mark; David Hodgkins; Bobby Bereman; Bill Kirkham.
Also see SUNSHINE COMPANY

REDJACKS *P&R '58*

Singles: 7-inch

APT (25006 "Big Brown Eyes")................15-25 58
OKLAHOMA (5005 "Big Brown Eyes").....40-50 58
(First issue.)

REDMAN, Nicki

Singles: 7-inch

CAMP (1278 "Cop's Rock").......................40-60 63

REDMAN, Terry

Singles: 7-inch

CUB (9042 "The Dreamer").......................10-20 59
DIXIE (1154 "What Is Forever")................25-35 '60s
HURON (22005 "Stomp")..........................10-20 61
MGM (12735 "Come On Back")................25-35 58

REDMOND, Frankie
(With the Channings)

Singles: 7-inch

ESCO (500 "Make Believe World")...........10-20 60
IMPERIAL (5718 "Anytime Anywhere")......8-12 61
IMPERIAL (8718 "Make Believe World")....8-12 '60s
LOWERY (003 "No Man Is an Island").....30-40 63

REDNOW, Eivets *P&R '68*
(Stevie Wonder)

Singles: 7-inch

GORDY (7076 "Alfie")...............................10-20 68

LPs: 10/12-inch

GORDY (932 "Eivets Rednow")................25-35 68
Also see WONDER, Stevie

REDWOODS
(Jeff Barry)

Singles: 7-inch

EPIC (9447 "Shake Shake Sherry").........15-25 61
(Also issued as by the Flairs.)
EPIC (9473 "Never Take It Away")...........10-20 61
EPIC (9505 "Where You Used to Be").....20-30 62
JONNY-A (205 "Bad Boy Baby")..............10-20
Also see BARRY, Jeff
Also see FLAIRS

REE, Mamie

Singles: 78 rpm

COMBO (93 "You Lied")............................20-30 55

Singles: 7-inch

COMBO (93 "You Lied")............................40-60 55

REED, A.C.
(With the Earlettes)

Singles: 7-inch

AGE (29103 "Come On Home")...............10-20 61
AGE (29112 "Mean Cop").........................10-20 62
AGE (29123 "I Stay Mad").......................10-20 63
COOL (5001 "Ma Baby Is Fine")...............15-25
ICE CUBE (5926 "I Am Fed Up with This Music")..4-8 81
(Labeled "X-Rated Blues.")
NIKE (2002 "Talkin' 'Bout My Friends")......5-10 66

LPs: 10/12-inch

ICE CUBE ("Take These Blues and Shove 'Em")...8-10 81
(Selection number not known.)
Also see HOOKER, Earl, & A.C. Reed

REED, Al

Singles: 78 rpm

POST (2013 "Drops of Rain")...................10-15 55

Singles: 7-inch

AXE (103 "Sorry About That")....................5-10 67
DOT (15720 "I Love Her So")..................40-60 58
INSTANT (3231 "Magic Carpet")...............8-10 61
INSTANT (3238 "Ring the Ding Dong Bells")...8-10 62
POST (2013 "Drops of Rain")...................20-30 55
TNT (150 "I Love Her So").......................75-85 58

REED, Bob
(With Lucky Ivory)

Singles: 7-inch

CREATIONS (1226 "They Don't Know")..20-30
DENA..10-20 61
MAR-VEL (333 "Choctaw Boogie").........50-75 56
MELATONE...10-15
Also see TAYLOR, Ted

REED, Bobby

Singles: 7-inch

BELL (888 "The Time Is Right for Love").30-50 70
BRUNSWICK (55282 "You Are")..............10-20 65
CLAY TOWN (17700 "You Are")..............50-75 65
(First issue.)
CYCLONE (501 "High School USA").......15-25 '60s
DOT (16113 "Johnny on the Spot")..........10-15 60
LOMA (2089 "I'll Find a Way")....................5-10 68

REED, Chuck

Singles: 78 rpm

DECCA...10-15 56
MERCURY...10-15 54-55

Singles: 7-inch

CHOCTAW (101 "Just Plain Hurt")...........40-60 62
DECCA (30170 "Another Love Has Ended")...15-20 56
HIT (101 "Just Plain Hurt").......................40-60 61
JAMIE (1194 "So Long")............................8-12 61
MERCURY (70316 "Second Choice")......15-25 54
MERCURY (70343 "Call Me Baby").........15-25 54
MERCURY (70411 "Don't Put Your Heart Up for Sale")..15-25 54
MERCURY (70433 "My Journey")............15-25 54
MERCURY (70486 "You're Out of My Sight")..15-25 54
MERCURY (70527 "Cry Like a Baby").....15-25 54
MERCURY (70593 "End of My Stairway")..15-25 55
MERCURY (70667 "Cold, Cold, Colder").15-25 55
MERCURY (70701 "Love, Love, Love")...25-35 55
MINARET (107 "Mark My Word")...............5-10 63
MINARET (110 "Lots of Happiness")..........5-10 64
MINARET (119 "Conscience")....................5-10 65
ROULETTE (4020 "Sugar Corsage").......15-25 57
ROULETTE (4058 "No School Tomorrow")..15-25 58
U.A. (50017 "After the Heartache")..............4-8 65
U.A. (50091 "Kiss the Hurt Away")...............4-8 65

REED, D., & Swinging Reeds

Singles: 7-inch

UNITED (215 "Why Don't You Believe Me")..50-75 58

REED, Dean *P&R '59*

Singles: 7-inch

CAPITOL (4121 "The Search")..................10-20 59
CAPITOL (4198 "I Kissed a Queen").......10-20 59
CAPITOL (4273 "I Ain't Got You")............10-20 59
CAPITOL (4438 "Pistolero").......................25-35 60
CAPITOL (4608 "Female Hercules")........10-15 61
IMPERIAL (5733 "Once Again")..................8-12 61

REED, Denny *P&R '60*

Singles: 7-inch

ASPIRE..3-5 77
DOT (16400 "Lamp of Love").....................8-12 62
MCI (1024 "A Teenager Feels It Too").....30-50 60
(First issue.)
TREY (3007 "A Teenager Feels It Too")..15-25 60
TREY (3014 "Lonely Little Bluebird")........10-15 61
TOWER (143 "In This Town Called Heartbreak")..4-8 65
U.A. (377 "I'm Comin' Home")....................8-12 61

REED, Don
(With Orchestra)

Singles: 78 rpm

GILT-EDGE (22 "You Are My Heart") 8-12 54

Singles: 7-inch

A&R (5001 "Lonely King of Rock and Roll")..15-25 61
DOT (15902 "San Francisco Beat")..........10-15 59
GARDENA (120 "Nature Boy")..................10-15 61
GILT-EDGE (22 "You Are My Heart")......15-25 54
SKORA (3222 "Mean Woman Blues").....50-75
UNITED (215 "Why Don't You")...............15-25 57

REED, Earl, & His Rhythm Rockers
(Featuring Johnny Scoggins)
Singles: 7-inch
CHEROKEE (778 "Drink Wine") 300-500 58
CHEROKEE (779 "Flat Foot Sam") 200-300 58

REED, James
Singles: 78 rpm
BIG TOWN 50-75 54
FLAIR 50-75 54
MONEY 50-75 54
RHYTHM (1775 "Tin Pan Alley") 300-400 54
Singles: 7-inch
BIG TOWN (117 "Things Ain't What They Used to Be") 75-100 54
FLAIR (1034 "My Mama Told Me") 100-150 54
FLAIR (1042 "Dr. Brown") 100-150 54
MONEY (201 "Oh People") 100-150 54

REED, Jerry P&R '62/C&W '67
(With the Hully Girlies; with Seldina; with Friends)
Singles: 78 rpm
CAPITOL 5-15 55-56
Singles: 7-inch
CAPITOL 10-20 55-56
COLUMBIA 10-20 61-63
COLUMBIA (42417 "Goodnight Irene") ... 20-30 62
(Red vinyl. Promotional issue only. Same song on both sides.)
NRC (014 "Have Blues Will Travel") 10-20 59
NRC (032 "Just Right") 10-20 59
NRC (5008 "Little Lovin' Liza") 10-20 59
(Same number used for a Frankie Calen issue.)
RCA (Except 8500 thru 9700) 3-8 69-85
RCA (8500 thru 9700) 5-10 65-69
Picture Sleeves
COLUMBIA (42533 "Hully Gully Guitars") 10-20 61
RCA 3-6 72-85
LPs: 10/12-inch
CAMDEN 5-10 72-74
HARMONY 8-12 71
PICKWICK/HILLTOP 5-10
RCA (Except "LPM" & "LSP" series) 5-10 73-83
RCA ("LPM" & "LSP" series) 10-20 67-73
Also see HART, Freddie / Sammi Smith / Jerry Reed
Also see JENNINGS, Waylon, & Jerry Reed
Also see JUSTIS, Bill / Jerry Reed
Also see NELSON, Willie
Also see PRESLEY, Elvis

REED, Jerry, & Chet Atkins
LPs: 10/12-inch
RCA 10-20 72
Also see ATKINS, Chet
Also see REED, Jerry

REED, Jimmie, Jr.
Singles: 7-inch
MERCURY (72668 "I Ain't Going Nowhere") 10-20 67

REED, Jimmy R&B '55
("With His Trio")
Singles: 78 rpm
CHANCE (1142 "High and Lonesome") 75-125 53
VEE-JAY (100 thru 253) 20-40 53-57
VEE-JAY (270 thru 298) 30-50 53-57
VEE-JAY (304 "I Told You Baby") 50-100 59
VEE-JAY (314 "Take Out Some Insurance") 75-125 59
VEE-JAY (326 "I Wanna Be Loved") ... 100-150 59
VEE-JAY (333 "Baby What You Want Me to Do") 150-200 59
Singles: 7-inch
ABC 4-6 73
ABC-PAR (10887 "Got Nowhere to Go") 4-8 66
BLUESWAY 4-8 67-69
CANYON 4-6 70
CHANCE (1142 "High & Lonesome") 500-1000 53
(Reissue of Vee-Jay 100.)
COLLECTABLES .... 3-5 '80s
EXODUS (2005 "Knockin' at Your Door") ... 5-10 66
EXODUS (2008 "Cousin Peaches") 5-10 66
MAGIC 8-12
OLDIES 45 .... 4-8 64
RRG 4-8
TRIP .... 4-6 '70s
VEE-JAY (100 "High & Lonesome") 150-200 53
(Black vinyl.)
VEE-JAY (100 "High & Lonesome") 500-750 53
(Red vinyl.)
VEE-JAY (105 "I Found My Baby") 100-150 53
(Black vinyl.)
VEE-JAY (105 "I Found My Baby") 300-400 53
(Red vinyl.)
VEE-JAY (119 "You Don't Have to Go") ... 50-75 54
(Black vinyl.)
VEE-JAY (119 "You Don't Have to Go") 200-300 54
(Red vinyl.)
VEE-JAY (132 "Pretty Thing") 50-75 55
VEE-JAY (153 "I Don't Go For That") 50-100 55
VEE-JAY (168 "Ain't That Lovin' You Baby") 20-40 56
VEE-JAY (186 "Can't Stand to See You Go") 30-50 56
VEE-JAY (203 "I Love You Baby") 20-40 56
VEE-JAY (226 "You've Got Me Dizzy") 20-40 56
VEE-JAY (237 "Little Rain") 20-30 57
VEE-JAY (248 "The Sun Is Shining") 20-30 57
VEE-JAY (253 "Honest I Do") 20-30 57
VEE-JAY (270 "You're Something Else") . 15-25 58
VEE-JAY (275 "Go on to School") 20-30 58
VEE-JAY (287 "Down in Virginia") 15-25 58
VEE-JAY (298 "I'm Gonna Get My Baby") 15-25 58
VEE-JAY (304 "I Told You Baby") 15-25 59
VEE-JAY (314 "Take Out Some Insurance") 15-25 59
VEE-JAY (326 "I Wanna Be Loved") 20-30 59
VEE-JAY (333 "Baby What You Want Me to Do") 20-30 59
VEE-JAY (347 "Found Love") 15-25 60
VEE-JAY (357 "Hush Hush") 15-25 60
VEE-JAY (373 "Close Together") 15-25 61
VEE-JAY (380 "Big Boss Man") 15-25 61
VEE-JAY (398 "Bright Lights, Big City") ... 15-25 61
VEE-JAY (425 "What's Wrong Baby") 10-20 61
VEE-JAY (449 "Tell Me You Love Me") 10-20 62
VEE-JAY (459 "Too Much") 10-20 62
VEE-JAY (473 "Let's Get Together") 10-20 62
VEE-JAY (509 "Shame Shame Shame") .. 10-20 63
VEE-JAY (552 "Mary Mary") 10-20 63
VEE-JAY (570 "St. Louis Blues") 10-20 63
VEE-JAY (584 "Wee Wee Baby") 10-20 64
VEE-JAY (593 "Help Yourself") 10-20 64
VEE-JAY (616 "Down in Mississippi") 20-30 64
VEE-JAY (622 "I'm Going Upside Your Head") 10-20 64
VEE-JAY (642 "I Wanna Be Loved") 10-20 65
VEE-JAY (702 "Left Handed Woman") 10-20 65
VEE-JAY (709 "When Girls Do It") 10-20 65
EPs: 7-inch
VEE-JAY (1050 "Just Jimmy Reed") 15-25 62
(Stereo. Juke box issue only. Includes title strips.)
LPs: 10/12-inch
ANTILLES 10-20
BLUES ON BLUES (10001 "Let the Bossman Speak") 8-10
BLUESWAY (6004 "The New Jimmy Reed Album") 10-30 67
BLUESWAY (6009 "Soulin' ") 10-30 67
BLUESWAY (6015 "Big Boss Man") 10-30 68
BLUESWAY (6024 "Down in Virginia") 10-30 69
BLUESWAY (6054 "I Ain't From Chicago") 10-30 73
BLUESWAY (6067 "The Ultimate") 10-30 73
BLUESWAY (6073 "At Carnegie Hall") 10-30 73
(Two discs.)
BUDDAH (4003 "Just Jimmy Reed") 10-15 69
EVEREST (234 "Jimmy Reed") 5-10 69
EXODUS (307 "At Carnegie Hall") 10-15 66
(Two discs.)
EXODUS (308 "The Best Of") 10-15 66
EXODUS (310 "Just Jimmy Reed") 10-15 66
EXODUS (311 "Jimmy Reed Sings the Best of the Blues") 10-15 66
GNP (10006 "The Best Of") 8-10 74
(Two discs.)
KENT 8-12 69-71
RRG 10-20
ROKER (4001 "As Jimmy Is") 5-10
SUNSET 10-15 68
TRADITION (2069 "Wallin' the Blues") 8-12 68
TRIP (16-47 "16 Greatest Hits") 8-15 78
TRIP (9515 "The History of Jimmy Reed, Vol. 2") 8-15 74
(Two discs.)
UPFRONT 8-12
VEE-JAY (1004 "I'm Jimmy Reed") 150-250 58
(Maroon label.)
VEE-JAY (1004 "I'm Jimmy Reed") 50-100 59
(Black label.)
VEE-JAY (1008 "Rockin' with Reed") ... 150-250 59
(Maroon label.)
VEE-JAY (1008 "Rockin' with Reed") 50-100 59
(Black label.)
VEE-JAY (1022 "Found Love") 150-250 60
(Maroon label.)
VEE-JAY (1022 "Found Love") 40-60 60
(Black label.)
VEE-JAY (1025 "Now Appearing") 40-60 60
VEE-JAY (1035 "At Carnegie Hall") 40-60 61
VEE-JAY (1039 "Best Of") 25-50 62
VEE-JAY (1050 "Just Jimmy Reed") 25-50 62
VEE-JAY (1067 "T'Ain't No Big Thing...But He Is") 25-50 63
VEE-JAY (1072 "Sings the Best of the Blues") 25-50 63
VEE-JAY (1073 "Plays the 12 String Guitar Blues") 25-50 63
VEE-JAY (1080 "More of the Best of Jimmy Reed") 25-50 63
VEE-JAY (1095 "At Soul City") 25-50 65
VEE-JAY (8501 "The Legend, the Man") . 20-30 65
VERSATILE 8-10 78
Also see DIXON, Willie
Also see MAYFIELD, Curtis
Also see TAYLOR, Eddie
Also see UPCHURCH, Phil

REED, Jimmy / Peppermint Harris
EPs: 7-inch
LUNAR (2009 "Tells It Like It Is") 5-10 81
Also see PEPPERMINT HARRIS
Also see REED, Jimmy

REED, Johnny
Singles: 7-inch
FORE (41 "Darling Please") 10-20
MAJOR (100 "A Thousand Miles Away") . 15-25 58
Also see ORIOLES

REED, Larry, & Shados
Singles: 7-inch
ARLEN (515 "Little Miss Surfer") 15-25 63

REED, Lou LP '72
(With the Velvet Underground)
Singles: 12-inch
RCA 4-8 84
Singles: 7-inch
ARISTA 4-6 76
RCA 4-8 73-86
LPs: 10/12-inch
ARISTA 5-10 76-80
PRIDE 8-12 73
RCA ("AFL1" series) 5-10 80-83
RCA ("ANL1" series) 5-10 77
RCA ("APL1" series) 6-12 73-77
RCA ("AYL1" series) 5-8 80-83
RCA ("CPL1" series) 8-12 74
RCA ("LSP" series) 8-12 72
SIRE 5-8 89-90
Also see ALL NIGHT WORKERS
Also see BEACH NUTS
Also see DION
Also see JADES
Also see PRIMITIVES
Also see VELVET UNDERGROUND

REED, Lou, & John Cale LP '90
LPs: 10/12-inch
SIRE (26140 "Songs for Drella") 5-10 90
Also see REED, Lou

REED, Lula
(With the Teeners; with Harmonaires; with Pastels; Lulu Reed)
Singles: 78 rpm
KING 15-25 52-56
Singles: 7-inch
ARGO (5298 "Anything to Say You're Mine") 10-15 58
ARGO (5333 "Come On Home") 10-15 59
ARGO (5355 "Lovin' ") 10-15 59
FEDERAL (12407 "I'm a Woman") 15-25 61
FEDERAL (12416 "I Got a Notion") 15-25 61
FEDERAL (12426 "Know What You're Doing") 15-25 61
FEDERAL (12440 "Ain't No Cotton' Pickin' Chicken") 15-25 61
GUSTO .... 3-5 '80s
KING (4578 "Let Me Be Your Love") 25-35 52
KING (4590 "Heavenly Road") 50-75 53
KING (4630 "My Poor Heart") 25-35 53
KING (4649 "Don't Make Me Love You") . 25-35 53
KING (4688 "Your Key Don't Fit No More") 25-35 53
KING (4703 "Troubles on Your Mind") 25-35 54
KING (4712 "I Ain't No Watch Dog") 25-35 54
KING (4714 "If the Sun Isn't Shining in Your Window") 25-35 54
KING (4718 "I'm Beggin' and Pleadin' ") ... 25-35 54
KING (4726 "Wonderful Love") 25-35 54
KING (4737 "What Could I Do But Believe in Jesus") 20-30 54
KING (4748 "Sick and Tired") 25-35 54
KING (4767 "Rock Love") 25-35 55
KING (4796 "Caught Me When My Love Was Down") 25-35 55
KING (4811 "Why Don't You Come On Home") 25-35 55
KING (4969 "Three Men") 25-35 56
KING (4996 "Waste No More Tears") 25-35 56
TANGERINE 5-10 62-67
LPs: 10/12-inch
KING (604 "Blue and Moody") 500-750 59
Session: Sonny Thompson; Isaac Cole; Bill Johnson.
Also see KING, Freddy, & Lula Reed
Also see KING, Freddy, / Lula Reed / Sonny Thompson
Also see PASTELS
Also see THOMPSON, Sonny

REED, Roray
Singles: 7-inch
CHRISTY (135 "Mad Lovin' ") 50-75

REED, Smokey
Singles: 7-inch
DIXIE (1127 "Country Yodel") 50-75

REED, Tawny
Singles: 7-inch
CONGRESS (270 "Can't Take It Away") 5-10 66
RED BIRD (044 "Needle in a Haystack") . 20-30 65

REED, Ursula
(With the Solitaires; with Joe Morris & Orchestra)
Singles: 78 rpm
HERALD (440 "All Gone") 10-15 54
OLD TOWN (1001 "You're Laughing Cause I'm Crying") 50-100 54
Singles: 7-inch
HERALD (440 "All Gone") 20-30 54
OLD TOWN (1001 "You're Laughing Cause I'm Crying") 200-300 54
Also see JOE & URSULA
Also see MORRIS, Joe, & His Orchestra
Also see SOLITAIRES

REEDER, Bill
Singles: 7-inch
FERNWOOD (121 "You're My Baby") 50-75 60
HI (2037 "Till I Waltz Again with You") 50-75 61
HI (2041 "Judy") 10-20 61
VOLL (100 "Till I Waltz Again with You") 100-200 61
VOLL (101 "Remember You're Mine") . 100-200 61

REEDER, Eskew
(S.Q. Reeder; Esquerita; Eskew Reeder Jr.)
Singles: 7-inch
CROSSTONE (1007 "You Better Believe It") .... 40-50 '60s
EVEREST (2025 "A Tear") 8-12 63
INSTANT (3258 "Undivided Love") 8-12 63
INSTANT (3268 "I Woke Up") 5-10 65
MINIT (648 "Green Door") 8-12 62
MINIT (658 "Never Again") 8-12 63
OKEH (7239 "I Want to Know") 5-10 66
Also see ESQUERITA
Also see RIO ROCKERS

REEDS, Ensenada, Orchestra
Singles: 7-inch
M&P (001 "Summertime") 30-40

REEGAN, Vala, & Valarons
Singles: 7-inch
ATCO (6412 "Fireman") 20-30 66

REE-GENTS
Singles: 7-inch
CONBIE (1000 "Downshiftin' ") 15-20 65

REEKERS

Singles: 7-inch

RU-JAC (13 "Grindin' ")........................ 20-30 64

Also see HANGMEN

REES, Jerry, & Monarcks

Singles: 7-inch

SOMA (1184 "Streak of Lightning")......... 20-25 62

Picture Sleeves

SOMA (1184 "Streak of Lightning")......... 30-50 62

REESE, Bill

(Bill Reese Quintet & Coronets; with His Rhythm Kings, vocal by Tommy Malone)

Singles: 78 rpm

PENNANT 40-60 55
STERLING.. 100-200 55

Singles: 7-inch

PENNANT (334 "Whiskey, Ol' Whiskey").. 100-150 55
STERLING (903 "Don't Deprive Me") .. 250-350 55

REESE, Danny

Singles: 7-inch

CHARTWHEEL (101 "Country Mama Boogie") 10-15 77

REESE, Della P&R '57

(With the Meditation Singers; with Jimmie Hamilton & Orchestra; with Sid Bass Orchestra; Glenn Osser & Orchestra; with Joya Sherrill)

Singles: 78 rpm

GREAT LAKES (1203 "Yes Indeed")....... 10-20 54
JUBILEE...8-15 55-57

Singles: 7-inch

ABC..4-8 67-73
ABC-PAR..5-10 65-66
AVCO EMBASSY.................................4-8 69-72
CHI-SOUND 4-6 77
GREAT LAKES (1203 "Yes Indeed")....... 20-30 54
JUBILEE (5000 series) 10-20 55-59
(Monaural.)
JUBILEE (9007 "Stormy Weather")......... 20-25 58
(Stereo.)
LMI..4-6 73
RCA 8-15 59-64
VIRGO 4-6 72

Picture Sleeves

AVCO EMBASSY.................................4-8 69-72
RCA 10-20 60-63

EPs: 7-inch

RCA 10-20 61

LPs: 10/12-inch

ABC..5-10 76
ABC-PAR.. 15-20 65-67
APPLAUSE...5-8 83
DESIGN...5-10
HURRAH (1026 "Della Reese & Joya Sherrill") 5-10
JUBILEE (1000 & 5000 series) 20-30 57-63
JUBILEE (6000 series) 10-15 69
LMI..5-10 73
PICKWICK..5-8 78
RCA (2000 thru 4600 series)................. 10-25 60-72
SUNSET...5-10 71

Also see ANN-MARGRET / Kitty Kalen / Della Reese
Also see ARMSTRONG, Louis / Della Reese / Wild Bill Davison
Also see LIMELITERS / Della Reese /Mario Lanza / Norman Luboff Choir

REESE, Reatha

Singles: 7-inch

DOT (16630 "Only Lies")...................... 100-200 64

REESE, Slim

Singles: 78 rpm

SITTIN' IN WITH (581 "Got the World in a Jug").. 20-50 51

REEVES, Barbara, & Pageants

Singles: 7-inch

BEACON (559 "It's Been So Long")......... 15-25 64

Also see PAGEANTS

REEVES, Danny

Singles: 7-inch

D (1206 "Bell Hop Blues") 200-300 61
SAN ("Spunky Monkey")....................... 150-250
(Selection number not known.)

REEVES, Del C&W '61

(With the Goodtime Charlies)

Singles: 7-inch

CHART (5082 "Stand In")............................4-6 70
COLUMBIA (43044 "Talking to the Night Lights")...4-6 64
DECCA...5-10 61-62
KOALA...3-5 80-82
LAS VEGAS (1440 "Because You Love Me")..15-25 59
PEACH (739 "I Watched You Walk Away")..10-20 60
PEACH (746 "Time After Time") 10-20 61
PLAYBACK..3-5 86
REPRISE (20158 "Love She Offered Me")...4-8 63
REPRISE (20228 "Once a Fool")..................4-8 63
U.A. 4-8 66-78

Picture Sleeves

KOALA..3-5 80
U.A. (50157 "The Private")......................4-6 67

LPs: 10/12-inch

KOALA..5-8 79-80
STARDAY 5-8
SUNSET...5-10 69-70
U.A. (200 thru 600 series) 5-10 73-76
U.A. (3000 & 6000 series)........................10-20 65-71

REEVES, Del, & Penny DeHaven C&W '72

Singles: 7-inch

U.A. (50829 "Crying in the Rain") 4-6 72

REEVES, Del, & Bobby Goldsboro C&W '68

Singles: 7-inch

U.A. 4-6 65-71

LPs: 10/12-inch

U.A. 10-20 68

Also see GOLDSBORO, Bobby

REEVES, Del / Red Sovine

LPs: 10/12-inch

EXACT...5-8 80

Also see SOVINE, Red

REEVES, Del, & Billie Jo Spears C&W '76

Singles: 7-inch

U.A. (797 "On the Rebound")......................4-6 76
U.A. (832 "Teardrops Will Kiss the Morning Dew")..4-6 76

LPs: 10/12-inch

LIBERTY...5-8 82
U.A. 5-10 76

Also see REEVES, Del

REEVES, Eddie

(With the Vox Poppers)

Singles: 7-inch

ASCOT (2155 "Heartbreakin' ") 15-25 64
KAPP (2164 "Tulsa Turnaround")..................4-8 72
WARWICK (667 "Talk, Talk"/"Cry Baby") .10-15 61
WARWICK (681 "Talk, Talk"/"In My Heart of Hearts")..10-15 62

Picture Sleeves

WARWICK (667 "Cry Baby")......................15-25 61

REEVES, Glenn

Singles: 78 rpm

ATCO...20-30 56
REPUBLIC 5-10 55
TNT...20-30 55

Singles: 7-inch

ATCO (6080 "Rockin' Country Style").......30-50 56
DECCA (30589 "Rock-A-Boogie Lou") 20-30 58
DECCA (30780 "Tarzan").........................20-30 58
REPUBLIC (7121 "That'll Be Love") 8-12 55
TNT (120 "I'm Johnny on the Spot") 50-75 55
TNT (129 "I Ain't Got Room to Rock") 50-75 56

REEVES, Harriet

Singles: 7-inch

EON (103 "Just Friends")..........................30-40 61

REEVES, Jim C&W '53

(With His Circle O Ranch Boys)

Singles: 78 rpm

ABBOTT (Black plastic)...........................15-25 53-55
ABBOTT (Colored plastic)........................25-50 53-55
MACY'S (115 "Teardrops of Regret")...400-500 50
MACY'S (132 "I've Never Been So Blue") 400-500 51
QUALITY (1177 "Bimbo")..........................15-25 53
(Canadian.)
RCA...10-20 55-57

Singles: 7-inch

ABBOTT (115 "Wagon Load of Love") 15-25 53
(Black vinyl.)
ABBOTT (115 "Wagon Load of Love") 35-50 53
(Colored vinyl.)
ABBOTT (116 "Mexican Joe") 15-25 53
(Black vinyl.)
ABBOTT (116 "Mexican Joe") 35-50 53
(Colored vinyl.)
ABBOTT (137 "Butterfly Love")..................15-25 53
(Black vinyl.)
ABBOTT (137 "Butterfly Love")..................35-50 53
(Colored vinyl.)
ABBOTT (143 "El Rancho Del Rio").........15-25 53
(Black vinyl.)
ABBOTT (143 "El Rancho Del Rio") 35-50 53
(Colored vinyl.)
ABBOTT (148 "Bimbo")..............................15-25 53
(Black vinyl.)
ABBOTT (148 "Bimbo")..............................35-50 53
(Colored vinyl.)
ABBOTT (160 thru 186) 10-20 54-56
ABBOTT (3000 series)..............................10-20 55
ABBOTT (4000 series)...............................4-8
QUALITY (1177 "Bimbo")..........................35-50 53
(Canadian.)
RCA (0135 thru 0963) 4-8 69-74
RCA (6200 thru 7557) 10-20 55-59
RCA (7643 "He'll Have to Go") 8-12 59
RCA (7643 "He'll Have to Go") 150-250 59
(Single-sided. Promotional issue only.)
RCA (7756 thru 9969) 4-10 60-71
RCA (10133 thru 13693).............................3-6 75-84

Picture Sleeves

RCA (7756 "I'm Gettin Better")..................10-15 60
RCA (7800 "Am I Losing You")..................10-15 60
RCA (8080 "I'm Gonna Change Everything")..8-12 62
RCA (8127 "Is This Me") 8-12 63
RCA (8193 "Guilty")..................................8-12 63
RCA (8252 "Señor Santa Claus")............15-20 63
RCA (8625 "Is It Really Over")...................5-10 65

EPs: 7-inch

RCA (133 "Tall Tales & Short Tempers") .20-30 61
(Compact 33 Double.)
RCA (757 "Singing Down the Lane")........20-30 56
RCA (1256 "Singing Down the Lane")....50-100 56
(Two discs.)
RCA (1410 "Bimbo").................................15-25 57
RCA (1576 "Jim Reeves").........................15-25 57
RCA (2487 "A Touch of Velvet")................10-20 62
(Stereo. Juke box issue only. Includes title strips.)
RCA (3793 "Jim Reeves").........................10-15 66
RCA (4062 "Four Walls")..........................15-25 57
RCA (4357 "He'll Have to Go") 15-25 57
RCA (5124 "Jim Reeves Hits") 10-20 59
RCA (5145 "Am I Losing You")..................10-20 60

LPs: 10/12-inch

ABBOTT (5001 "Jim Reeves Sings") .800-1200 56
CMF (008 "Live at the Opry")......................5-10
CAMDEN (Except 583 thru 686).................5-15 64-73
CAMDEN (583 thru 686)............................10-20 60-63
CANDLELIGHT ("Jim Reeves") 15-25 83
(Boxed five-disc set. Selection number not known.)
GUEST STAR (1471 "I Love You")...........10-15 64
HISTORY OF COUNTRY MUSIC...............6-10 72
PAIR...6-12 82
PICKWICK 5-10 72
PICKWICK/HILLTOP................................5-10 74
RCA (0039 thru 5044) 5-10 73-84
(With "AHL," "ANL," "APL," "AYL" or "CPL" prefix.)
RCA (0126 "Jim Reeves Collection") 10-15 75
(Special Products issue, Two discs.)
RCA (0246 "Take My Hand, Precious Lord")..10-15
(Special Products issue. Two discs.)
RCA (479 "Somethin' Special")............125-150 67
(Promotional issue only.)
RCA (0587 "Golden Collection")..............30-35
(Special Products issue, five-disc set.)
RCA (LPM-1256 "Singing Down the Lane")..100-200 56
RCA (LPM-1410 "Bimbo")........................40-60 57
RCA (LPM-1576 "Jim Reeves") 30-50 57
RCA (LPM-1685 "Girls I Have Known")....25-50 58
RCA (LPM-1950 "God Be with You")........20-40 58
(Monaural.)
RCA (LSP-1950 "God Be with You") 20-40 58
(Stereo.)
RCA (LPM-2001 thru LPM-2339) 15-25 59-61
(Monaural.)
RCA (LSP-2001 thru LSP-2339)..............20-30 59-61
(Stereo.)
RCA (LPM-2487 thru LPM-3903) 10-20 62-67
RCA (LSP-2487 thru LSP-3903)..............10-25 62-67
RCA (LPM-3987 "A Touch of Sadness")..25-35 68
(Monaural.)
RCA (LSP-3987 "A Touch of Sadness") .. 10-15 68
(Stereo.)
RCA (LSP-4062 thru LSP-4749)..................8-15 68-72
RADIANT 5-10
READER'S DIGEST/RCA (210 "Unforgettable Jim Reeves")..25-35 76
(Boxed, six-disc set.)
TAMPA/RCA SPECIAL PRODUCTS (0126 "Jim Reeves")..8-10 75

Also see BLUE BOYS
Also see CRAMER, Floyd
Also see JORDANAIRES
Also see KERR, Anita
Also see PRESLEY, Elvis / Hank Snow / Eddy Arnold / Hank Snow
Also see WRIGHT, Ginny

REEVES, Jim, & Deborah Allen C&W '79

Singles: 7-inch

RCA..3-5 79-80

REEVES, Jim, & Patsy Cline C&W '81

(Patsy Cline & Jim Reeves)

Singles: 7-inch

MCA..3-5 82
RCA..3-5 81

LPs: 10/12-inch

MCA..5-10 82
RCA..5-10 81

Also see CLINE, Patsy

REEVES, Jim / Alvadean Coker

Singles: 78 rpm

ABBOTT (184 "Are You the One")...........10-20 55

Singles: 7-inch

ABBOTT (184 "Are You the One")...........15-25 55

Also see COKER, Al

REEVES, Jim / Hugi & Luigi Chorus

Singles: 7-inch

U.S.A.F. (89 "In a Mansion Stands My Love")..20-30 '60s
(Promotional issue only.)

REEVES, Jim, & Dottie West

Singles: 7-inch

RCA (8324 "Look Who's Talking")................4-8 64

Also see REEVES, Jim
Also see WEST, Dottie

REEVES, Steve

Singles: 7-inch

COOL (104 "Come Along with Me") 25-50 58
FRONTIER CITY (104 "Come Along with Me")..50-100 58
(First issue.)

REFFUSE, Glenn

Singles: 7-inch

CONTINENTAL ("Love's No Game") ...100-200
(Selection number not known.)

REFLECTIONS

(With the Pete Bennett Orchestra)

Singles: 7-inch

CROSSROADS (401 "Maybe Tomorrow")..30-40 61
CROSSROADS (402 "Rocket to the Moon")...50-75 62
MALONE..10-15 '60s

REFLECTIONS P&R '64

Singles: 7-inch

ABC-PAR (10794 "Like Adam and Eve"). 15-25 66
ABC-PAR (10822 "You're Gonna Find Out You Need Me")..20-30 66
ADAM & EVE (1 "Helpless")......................3-5 '80s
(Black vinyl. 500 made.)
ERIC (277 "Romeo & Juliet")......................3-6 79
FLAX...4-8
GOLDEN WORLD (9 "Romeo & Juliet") .. 10-15 64
(Flip, *Can't You Tell By the Look in My Eyes*, is Golden World 8.)
GOLDEN WORLD (12 "Like Columbus Did")...10-15 64
GOLDEN WORLD (19 "You Are My Baby")..10-15 64
GOLDEN WORLD (20 "Poor Man's Son")..10-15 65
GOLDEN WORLD (22 "Deborah Ann").... 10-15 65
GOLDEN WORLD (29 "Girl in the Candy Store")..10-15 65

JANELL (824 "Sweet Days") ... 4-6 '70s
KAY•KO (1003 "Helpless") ... 40-60 63
LANA (140 "Romeo & Juliet") ... 4-8 '60s
TIGRE (602 "In the Still of the Night") ... 20-30 62
LPs: 10/12-inch
GOLDEN WORLD (300 "[Just Like] Romeo & Juliet") ... 50-75 64
Members: Tony Micale; John Dean; Phil Castrodale; Dan Bennie; Ray Steinberg.
Also see GRAY, Dobie / Reflections
Also see LARADOS
Also see MICHAELS, Tony

REFLECTIONS — P&R/R&B '75
Singles: 7-inch
CAPITOL (4078 "3 Steps from True Love") ... 10-15 75
CAPITOL (4137 "Love On Delivery") ... 10-15 75
CAPITOL (4222 "Day After Day") ... 5-10 76
CAPITOL (4358 "Gift Wrap My Love") ... 5-10 76
Members: Herman Edwards; Josh Pridgen; Edmund "Butch" Simmons; John Simmons.

REGAL, Mike
(With the Quotations)
Singles: 7-inch
KAPP (506 "Too Young") ... 20-30 63

REGAL-AIRS
Singles: 7-inch
STAR-X (504 "It") ... 10-20 57

REGALS
Singles: 78 rpm
ALADDIN ... 15-25 54
ATLANTIC ... 10-20 55
MGM ... 10-15 54
Singles: 7-inch
ALADDIN (3266 "Run Pretty Baby") ... 75-125 54
ATLANTIC (1062 "I'm So Lonely") ... 15-25 55
MGM (11869 "When You're Home") ... 15-25 54
Members: Harold Wright; Billy Adams; Jerry Holman; Al Russell.
Also see DIAMONDS
Also see METRONOMES
Also see ORIOLES

REGALS
Singles: 7-inch
JAM-CHA (303 "Lonely Guy") ... 50-75

REGAN, Eddie
Singles: 7-inch
ABC-PAR (10795 "Playin' Hide & Seek") 20-30 66

REGAN, Keray
Singles: 78 rpm
LONDON (17012 "Vibratin' ") ... 10-20 50
Singles: 7-inch
LONDON (17012 "Vibratin' ") ... 50-75 50

REGAN, Lonnie
Singles: 7-inch
FERN (801 "She's Gone") ... 50-75 61

REGAN, Tommy
Singles: 7-inch
ALL-STAR ("Twistin' Santa") ... 10-20
(Selection number not known.)
COLPIX (725 "I'll Never Stop Loving You") ... 40-60 64
WORLD ARTISTS (1049 "9 to 5") ... 5-10 65
Also see MARCELS

REGENT CONCERT ORCHESTRA
LPs: 10/12-inch
REGENT (6091 "Amor") ... 25-50 58
(Cover pictures Jayne Mansfield, although she is not heard on the disc.)
Also see MANSFIELD, Jayne

REGENTS
Singles: 7-inch
KAYO (101 "No Hard Feelings") ... 20-30 60
(Label reads "Distributed by Clark & Sons.")
KAYO (101 "No Hard Feelings") ... 10-15 60
(Label reads "Distributed by Stroll Records.")
PEORIA (8 "Summertime Blues") ... 8-12 '60s
Also see FIVE SPENDERS

REGENTS — P&R/R&B '61
Singles: 7-inch
ABC ... 4-6 73
APEX (76753 "Barbara-Ann") ... 15-25 61
(Canadian.)
COUSINS (1002 "Barbara-Ann") ... 350-450 61
GEE (1065 "Barbara-Ann") ... 20-30 61
GEE (1071 "Runaround") ... 20-30 61
GEE (1073 "Don't Be a Fool") ... 15-25 61
GEE (1075 "Lonesome Boy ") ... 15-25 61
ROULETTE ... 4-6 '70s
LPs: 10/12-inch
CAPITOL (KAO-2153 "Live at the AM-PM Discotheque") ... 35-45 64
(Monaural.)
CAPITOL (SKAO-2153 "Live at the AM-PM Discotheque") ... 45-55 64
(Stereo.)
EMUS ... 5-10 79
GEE (GLP-706 ("Barbara-Ann") ... 75-100 61
(Monaural.)
GEE (SGLP-706 ("Barbara-Ann") ... 100-125 61
(Stereo.)
MURRAY HILL ... 5-8 85
Members: Guy Villari; Sal Cuomo; Chuck Fassert; Don Jacobucci; Tony Gravagna.
Also see CARDBOARD ZEPPELIN
Also see DEE, Sonny
Also see DESIRES
Also see HARPER, Chuck
Also see LYNDON, Frank
Also see MARTY
Also see RUNAROUNDS
Also see TREMONTS
Also see VILLARI, Guy

REGENTS
Singles: 7-inch
REPRISE (0430 "When I Die, Don't You Cry") ... 15-25 65
Member: Michael McDonald.
Also see McDONALD, Michael

REGENTS
Singles: 7-inch
SOLID GOLD (6401 "Albino Bat") ... 50-75

REID, Clarence — P&R/R&B '69
(With the Delmiras; Clarence Reed)
Singles: 7-inch
ALSTON ... 4-8 68-79
ATCO (7025 "I Bet You Believe Me Now") ... 4-6 75
DEEP CITY (2372 "Cadillac Baby") ... 10-20 67
DIAL (3018 "I Got My Share") ... 8-12 64
DIAL (4019 "I Refuse to Give Up") ... 8-12 65
DIAL (4040 "Part of Your Love") ... 8-12 66
PHIL-L.A. OF SOUL (301 "Tired Blood") ... 5-10 67
REID (2744 "I Refuse to Give Up") ... 20-30 '60s
SELMA (4002 "Sooner Or Later") ... 35-45 63
TAY-STER (6013 "I'm Sorry Baby") ... 5-10 67
TAY-STER (6022 "Along Came a Woman") ... 5-10 69
WAND (1106 "Somebody Will") ... 10-20 65
WAND (1121 "I'm Your Yes Man") ... 20-30 65
LPs: 10/12-inch
ATCO (307 "Dancin' with Nobody But You Babe") ... 15-25 69

REID, Eddie
Singles: 7-inch
TWIRL (2010 "One Summer's Love") ... 5-10 61

REID, Gerri
(With the Valalades)
Singles: 7-inch
SLA-MON (304 "No Fool No More") ... 15-25
SLA-MON (305 "Crazy Crazy Baby") ... 15-25

REID, Matthew
Singles: 7-inch
ABC-PAR (10259 "Jane") ... 15-25 61
ABC-PAR (10305 "Through My Tears") ... 15-25 62
DECCA (31662 "One More Minute") ... 5-10 64
PHILIPS (40634 "Outward Bound") ... 5-10 69
SCEPTER (1238 "Faded Roses") ... 10-20 62
TOPIX (6006 "Cry Myself to Sleep") ... 15-25 62
Session: 4 Seasons.
Also see 4 SEASONS
Also see VALLI, Frankie

REINER, Carl, & Mel Brooks — LP '73
Singles: 7-inch
WORLD PACIFIC (825 "2000 Year Old Man") ... 5-10 61
LPs: 10/12-inch
CAPITOL (1529 "2000 Years with Carl Reiner and Mel Brooks") ... 15-25 61
CAPITOL (1618 "2000 and One Years with Carl Reiner and Mel Brooks") ... 15-25 61
CAPITOL (2981 "Best of the 2000 Year Old Man") ... 10-15 68
W.B. (2741 "2000 & Thirteen") ... 5-10 73
W.B. (2744 "2000 Years with Carl Reiner and Mel Brooks") ... 15-25 73
(Three-disc set.)
WORLD PACIFIC (1401 "2000 Years with Carl Reiner and Mel Brooks") ... 25-35 60

REITZ, Ken
Singles: 7-inch
SARA (65112 "Willing Consent") ... 10-20 65

REJECTS
Singles: 7-inch
AUDIO ART (5813 "Wild One") ... 25-35 65
STARLITE (6440 "Yogi") ... 8-12

REJECTS
Singles: 7-inch
BIG SOUND (305 "Hey Girl") ... 30-50 66

REJECTS
Singles: 7-inch
CABELL (107 "All My Life") ... 8-12

REL YEAS
Singles: 7-inch
KAYE (101 "Good Good Lovin' ") ... 50-100
WILDCAT (0044 "Round Rock Boogie") ... 20-40 60
WILDCAT (0056 "Country Boy") ... 20-40 61

RELATIONS
Singles: 7-inch
KAPE (504 "Until We Two Are One") ... 10-15 63
KAPE (703 "What Did I Do Wrong") ... 4-8 72
MICHELE (506 "All Nite Long") ... 10-20 60
REENA (1033 "Stack-Up") ... 4-8 68
UTOPIA ... 10-15 '60s
ZELL'S (712 "Say You Love Me") ... 10-20 63

RELATIONS
Singles: 7-inch
DAVY JONES PRESENTS (664 "Back to the Beach") ... 15-20 67
DEMAND (501 "Back to the Beach") ... 25-35 67
Picture Sleeves
DAVY JONES PRESENTS (664 "Back to the Beach") ... 20-30 67

RELATIVES
Singles: 7-inch
ALMONT (303 "I'm Just Looking for Love") ... 20-30 63
ALMONT (306 "I'm Just Looking for Love") ... 10-20 64
MUSICOR (1063 "Eternally") ... 5-10 65
WOW (711 "She's Got Soul") ... 5-10 68

RELF, Bobby
(With the Laurels; with Ernie Freeman Combo; Bob Relf)
Singles: 78 rpm
CASH (1019 "Our Love") ... 8-12 56
DOT (15510 "Little Fool") ... 10-20 56
FLAIR (1063 "Yours Alone") ... 100-200 55
Singles: 7-inch
CASH (1019 "Our Love") ... 15-25 56
DEE DEE (103 "I'm a Big Wheel") ... 10-20 59
DOT (15510 "Little Fool") ... 30-40 56
(Maroon label.)
DOT (15510 "Little Fool") ... 10-15
(Black label.)
FLAIR (1063 "Yours Alone") ... 1000-1500 55
TRANS-AMERICAN (0010 "Girl, You're My Kind of Wonderful") ... 10-15 68
Also see ANGELLE, Bobby
Also see BOB & EARL
Also see FREEMAN, Ernie
Also see LAURELS
Also see VALENTINO, Bobby

RELF, Keith
("Keith Relf of the Yardbirds")
Singles: 7-inch
EPIC (10044 "Mr. Zero") ... 20-30 66
(Black vinyl.)
EPIC (10044 "Mr. Zero") ... 50-75 66
(Colored vinyl. Promotional issue only.)
EPIC (10110 "Shapes in My Mind") ... 20-30 66
(Black vinyl.)
EPIC (10110 "Shapes in My Mind") ... 50-75 66
(Colored vinyl.)
MCCM (002 "Together Now") ... 3-5 89
(Black vinyl.)
MCCM (002 "Together Now") ... 4-8 89
(Colored vinyl. Promotional issue only.)
Picture Sleeves
EPIC (10110 "Shapes in My Mind") ... 40-50 67
MCCM (002 "Together Now") ... 3-5 89
Also see RENAISSANCE
Also see YARDBIRDS

RELIABLES
Singles: 7-inch
ANDERSON (22532 "Dreams That We Once Knew") ... 40-50 '60s

REMAINING FEW
Singles: 7-inch
ASKEL (112 "Painted Air") ... 15-25 67

REMAINDERS
(With J. Parker & Accents)
Singles: 7-inch
VICO ("Pen in Hand") ... 100-200
(No selection number used.)

REMAINS
Singles: 7-inch
EPIC (9783 "Why Do I Cry") ... 40-80 65
EPIC (9842 "I Can't Get Away") ... 40-80 65
EPIC (10001 "Diddy Wah Diddy") ... 40-80 66
(Black vinyl.)
EPIC (10001 "Diddy Wah Diddy") ... 50-100 66
(Colored vinyl.)
EPIC (10060 "Don't Look Back") ... 40-80 66
SPOONFED ... 4-8 78
(Colored vinyl.)
Picture Sleeves
EPIC (10001 "Diddy Wah Diddy") ... 40-50 66
LPs: 10/12-inch
EPIC (24214 "The Remains") ... 150-250 66
(Monaural.)
EPIC (26214 "The Remains") ... 200-300 66
(Stereo.)
SPOONFED (3205 "The Remains") ... 8-12 78
(Black vinyl.)
SPOONFED (3205 "The Remains") ... 15-25 78
(Colored vinyl.)

REMARKABLE MARQUIS
Singles: 7-inch
DAWN (108568 "In Love with Yourself") ... 10-20 '60s

REMARKABLES
Singles: 7-inch
CHASE (1600 "Write Me") ... 250-350 64

REMINISCENTS
(With the Goldtones)
Singles: 7-inch
CLEOPATRA (104 "For Your Love") ... 100-150 63
DAY (1000 "Zoom Zoom Zoom") ... 50-75 63
(Blue label. Colored vinyl.)
DAY (1000 "Zoom Zoom Zoom") ... 40-50 63
(Yellow label. Blue or red vinyl.)
DAY (1000 "Zoom Zoom Zoom") ... 10-20 63
(Black vinyl.)
MARCEL (1000 "Cards of Love") ... 50-75 62
(Blue or red vinyl.)
MARCEL (1000 "Cards of Love") ... 40-50 62
(Black vinyl.)

REMUS, Eugene
(With the Rayber Voices)
Singles: 7-inch
MOTOWN (1001 "You Never Miss a Good Thing"/"Hold Me Tight") ... 300-400 61
MOTOWN (1001 "You Never Miss a Good Thing"/"Gotta Have Your Lovin' ") ... 250-350 61
Also see HOLLAND, Eddie

RENAE, Eddie, & Titans
Singles: 7-inch
PINE (1001 "Snake Leg") ... 50-100 60

RENAISSANCE — LP '73
Singles: 7-inch
I.R.S. ... 3-5 82
SIRE (Except 1022) ... 4-6 74-79
SIRE (1022 "Northern Lights") ... 10-20 78
(Picture disc. Promotional issue only.)
LPs: 10/12-inch
CAPITOL ... 8-12 72-78
ELEKTRA (74068 "Renaissance") ... 15-25 69

I.R.S. 5-8 81-83
MFSL (099 "Scheherazade and Other Stories") 30-50 82
SIRE 8-10 74-79
SINGCORD 8-10 76-77
SOVEREIGN 8-12 73
Members: John Tout; Mike Dunford; Annie Haslam; Jim McCarty; Keith Relf; Jon Camp; Terry Sullivan; Louis Cennamo; Jane Relf.
Also see RELF, Keith

RENAISSANCE FAIR
Singles: 7-inch
ASTRAL PROJECTION (170 "She's a Woman") ....15-25 '60s

RENALDO, Don
Singles: 78 rpm
SOUND (132 "Far Away") 15-25 56
Singles: 7-inch
SOUND (132 "Far Away") 30-40 56

RENAULTS
Singles: 7-inch
CHICORY (1600 "10 Questions") 10-20 63
WAND 10-15 61-62
W.B. (5094 "Stella") 15-20 59

RENAULTS
Singles: 7-inch
BRYTE (306 "Rockin' with Joe") 35-50 62

RENAY, Diane P&R/LP '64
Singles: 7-inch
ATCO (6240 "Falling Star") 5-10 62
ATCO (6262 "Dime a Dozen") 5-10 63
D MAN (101 "Can't Help Lovin'") 15-25
DICE (8018 "Navy Blue") 15-20 87
ERIC (175 "Navy Blue") 4-6 73
FONTANA (1679 "Yesterday") 8-15 69
MGM (13296 "Billy Blue Eyes") 10-20 64
MGM (13335 "I Had a Dream") 10-20 65
NEW VOICE (800 "Words") 5-10 65
NEW VOICE (803 "Happy Birthday, Broken Heart") 5-10 65
REX (293 "Maybe") 15-25
20TH FOX (456 "Navy Blue") 10-15 63
20TH FOX (477 "Kiss Me Sailor") 10-15 64
20TH FOX (514 "Growin' Up Too Fast") ..10-15 64
20TH FOX (533 "It's in Your Hands") 10-15 64
U.A. (50048 "Please Gypsy") 10-15 66
LPs: 10/12-inch
20TH FOX (TF-3133 "Navy Blue") 25-40 64
(Monaural.)
20TH FOX (TFS-3133 "Navy Blue") 30-50 64
(Stereo.)

RENAY, Marsha, & Don Juans
Singles: 7-inch
HI-Q (5017 "It's Nice") 30-40 60

RENAY, Rita
Singles: 7-inch
LIBERTY (55073 "Every Night") 10-15 57

RENBOURN, John
LPs: 10/12-inch
REPRISE 10-15 70-73
Also see PENTANGLE

RENDEZVOUS
Singles: 7-inch
REPRISE (20089 "Congratulations Baby") 40-50 62
RUST (5041 "It Breaks My Heart") 40-50 61

RENDEZVOUS STOMPERS
Singles: 7-inch
DORE (626 "Gremmies Unite") 15-25 62

RENDITIONS
Singles: 7-inch
KISKI (2046 "That's When I Cried") 15-25 64

RENE, Googie R&B '60
Singles: 78 rpm
CLASS 8-15 56-58
Singles: 7-inch
CLASS 5-15 56-66
KAPP (449 "Look At Your Girl") 5-10 62
NEW BAG 5-10 67
REED 10-15 60
RENDEZVOUS (134 "The Slide") 10-15 60
RENDEZVOUS (144 "April Is Her Name") .8-12 61
RENDEZVOUS (157 "Ez-Zee") 8-12 61
Picture Sleeves
RENDEZVOUS (134 "The Slide") 15-20 60
LPs: 10/12-inch
CLASS 15-30 59-63

RENÉ, Henri, & His Orchestra P&R '40
Singles: 78 rpm
RCA 3-5 48-56
STANDARD 3-5 52-53
VICTOR 3-6 40-47
Singles: 7-inch
DECCA 4-6 62
IMPERIAL 5-10 59
RCA 5-10 51-56
STANDARD 5-10 52-53
Picture Sleeves
RCA 8-12 55
EPs: 7-inch
CAMDEN 5-10 54-57
RCA 5-10 53-56
LPs: 10/12-inch
CAMDEN 10-20 54-57
KAPP 5-10 67
RCA (Except 1046 & 3000 series) 10-20 56-61
RCA (1046 "Music for Bachelors") 50-75 54
(Cover pictures Jayne Mansfield, although she is not heard on the disc.)
RCA (3049 "Serenede to Love") 15-25 53
(10-inch LP.)
RCA (3076 "Listen to René") 15-25 53
(10-inch LP.)
Also see HONEYDREAMERS
Also see MANSFIELD, Jayne
Also see STEVENS, April

RENE & RAY P&R '62
Singles: 7-inch
DONNA (1360 "Queen of My Heart") 15-25 62
DONNA (1368 "Too Late") 15-25 62

RENE & RENE P&R '64
Singles: 7-inch
ABC 4-6 73
ABC-PAR (10699 "Chantilly Lace") 4-8 65
ARU 4-8 64
CERTRON (10011 "My Amigo José") 4-6 70
COBRA (212 "Crei") 4-8 65
COLUMBIA 4-8 64
EPIC 4-6 69
FALCON 4-8 68
JOX 8-12 64-66
WHITE WHALE 4-8 68-69
Picture Sleeves
COLUMBIA (43045 "Angelito") 15-25 64
LPs: 10/12-inch
CERTRON 8-10 70
EPIC 10-15 69
WHITE WHALE 10-15 68
Members: Rene Ornelas; J. Ramirez.

RENEGADES
Singles: 7-inch
AMERICAN INT'L 15-25 59-62
Also see GAMBLERS

RENEGADES
Singles: 7-inch
DORSET (5007 "Stolen Angel") 15-25 61

RENEGADES
Singles: 7-inch
CITATION (5005 "Istanbul") 15-25 63
Members: Mickey Slutzky; Richard Schurk; Paul Rubitzky; Keith Dreher; Bob Barian; Denny Sachse; Kurt Kronhelm; Denny Scheuneman; Louie Friedman.
Also see WALKING STICKS

RENEGADES
Singles: 7-inch
POLARIS (501 "Waiting for You") 15-25 65

RENEGADES
Singles: 7-inch
CHARDO ....10-20 '60s
CONGRESS (241 "Cadillac") 15-25 65

RENEGADES
Singles: 7-inch
CAMBRIDGE (12110 "Raving Blue") 50-100
CAMBRIDGE ("She's Your Find") 50-75
(Selection number not known.)

RENEGADES IV
Singles: 7-inch
FENTON (945 "Greensleeves") 15-25 64

RENEGADES V
Singles: 7-inch
DUBONAY (982 "Wine, Wine, Wine") 50-100

RENEGAIDS
Singles: 7-inch
GNP (193 "Surfin' Tragedy") 10-15 63
Member: Bob Vaught.
Also see VAUGHT, Bob

RENES
Singles: 7-inch
RIBA (1001 "Shy Guy") 15-20 65

RENFRO, Anthony R&B '76
(Anthony C. Renfro Orchestra)
Singles: 7-inch
RENFRO (43 "Gloria's Theme") 4-6 76
RENFRO (122 "This Is Our Moment of Love") 30-40 76

RENFRO BROTHERS
Singles: 7-inch
DIXIANA ("Just Over a Girl") 50-75
(Selection number not known.)

RENI, Chet, & Kings
Singles: 7-inch
GEORGIE (101 "What's Wrong with Me") 75-125 59

RENILLI, Vincent
Singles: 7-inch
INJUN (101 "Baby Doll") 50-75

RENN, Kathy
Singles: 7-inch
HANOVER (4545 "Billy Jim") 10-15 60

RENNE, Betty
Singles: 7-inch
NEW ART (1001 "Darling Bless You") 10-15 62

RENNER, Dianne
Singles: 7-inch
ACCENT (1088 "Quicksand") 30-50 63

RENO, Al
(With the Dials)
Singles: 7-inch
KAPP (432 "Cheryl") 50-75 61
Also see CHESTERFIELDS

RENO, Frank
Singles: 7-inch
DIAMOND (118 "I Want My Love") 10-20 62

RENO, Jack C&W '67
Singles: 7-inch
DOT 4-8 68-70
EUREKA (33 "Moon Won't Tell") 50-75
JAB 4-8 67-68
TARGET 4-6 71-72
U.A. 4-6 73-74
LPs: 10/12-inch
ATCO 10-15 68
DERBYTOWN 5-10 78
DOT 10-15 68-69
TARGET 8-12 72

RENO, Johnny
Singles: 7-inch
VALLEY (105 "Naughty Mama") 50-75

RENO, Nick
Singles: 7-inch
GES (0100 "I Had a Dream") 50-75 59

RENO, Tony, & Sherwoods
Singles: 7-inch
JOHNSON (123 "Maria Elena") 10-20 63
Also see SHERWOODS

RENO & SMILEY C&W '61
(With the Tennessee Cut-Ups; Don Reno - Red Smiley)
Singles: 78 rpm
KING 5-10 52-57
Singles: 7-inch
DOT (15588 thru 15835) 8-12 57-58
KING (1235 thru 5169) 10-20 53-58
KING (5184 thru 6082) 5-12 59-67
EPs: 7-inch
KING 10-15 58-62
LPs: 10/12-inch
ATTEIRAM 5-10
DOT (3490 "Bluegrass Hits") 10-20 63
GUSTO 5-8
KING (550 thru 693) 25-40 58-59
KING (701 thru 1091) 10-25 61-70
NASHVILLE 10-15 69
STARDAY 5-10 73-75
STARDAY/KING 5-8
Members: Don Reno; Red Smiley.
Also see RENO, Don
Also see SMILEY, Red

RENOLDS, Mike, & Infants of Soul
Singles: 7-inch
FROG DEATH (3 "When Will I Find Her") 15-25 64

RENOWNS
Singles: 7-inch
EVEREST (19396 "My Mind's Made Up") 30-40 61
Member: Marjorie Lake.

RENRUT, Icky
("Vocal by Jimmy Thomas"; Ike Turner)
Singles: 7-inch
STEVENS (104 "Jack Rabbit") 100-150 59
STEVENS (107 "Ho - - - Ho") 150-200 59
Also see THOMAS, Jimmy
Also see TURNER, Ike

REO, Walt, & Bishops
Singles: 7-inch
BRIDGES (1106 "Twist with Mary Lou") 100-150 62
Also see BISHOPS & MELLOWTONES

REPARATA P&R '65
(With the Delrons; Mary Aiese)
Singles: 7-inch
BELL (573 "I Believe") 8-12 67
BELL (589 "Captain of Your Ship") 8-12 68
BIG TREE (114 "Just You") 4-8 71
KAPP (989 "Bowery") 5-10 69
KAPP (2010 "San Juan") 5-10 69
KAPP (2050 "Walking in the Rain") 5-10 70
LAURIE (3589 "Octopus' Garden") 4-6 72
MALA (12000 "Saturday Night Didn't Happen") 8-12 68
MALA (12016 "Weather Forecast") 8-12 68
MALA (12026 "Summer Laughter") 8-12 68
NORTH AMERICAN MUSIC 4-6 74
POLYDOR (14271 "Shoes") 4-6 75
RCA (8721 "I Can Tell") 10-15 65
RCA (8820 "I'm Nobody's Baby Now") 10-15 66
RCA (8921 "Mama's Little Girl") 10-15 66
RCA (9123 "Boys & Girls") 10-15 67
RCA (9185 "I Can Hear the Bells") 10-15 67
WORLD ARTISTS (1036 "Whenever a Teenager Cries") 8-12 64
WORLD ARTISTS (1051 "Tommy") 8-12 65
WORLD ARTISTS (1057 "He's the Greatest") 8-12 65
WORLD ARTISTS (1062 "The Boy I Love") 8-12 65
LPs: 10/12-inch
AVCO EMBASSY (33008 "1970 Rock & Roll Revolution") 10-20 70
WORLD ARTISTS (2006 "Whenever a Teenager Cries") 40-60 65
(Monaural.)
WORLD ARTISTS (3006 "Whenever a Teenager Cries") 60-80 65
(Stereo.)
Members: Mary Aiese; Sheila Reilly; Carol Drobnicki; Nanette Licari; Lorraine Mazzola; Cookie Sirico.
Also see DEL-RONS

REPLACEMENTS LP '86
Singles: 7-inch
SIRE 3-5 85-90
TWIN TONE 3-5 82-84
Picture Sleeves
SIRE 3-5 89
LPs: 10/12-inch
SIRE 5-10 85-90
TWIN/TONE 5-10 84
Promotional LPs
SIRE ("Interview with Paul Westerberg") .20-25 85
Members: Paul Westerberg; Tom Stinson; Chris Mars.

REPTILES
Singles: 7-inch
MBM (60724 "Ballad of Mrs. George Wallace") 10-20 60
RESEARCH
Singles: 7-inch
FLICK CITY (3005 "I Don't Walk There No More") 10-15 67
FLICK CITY (3007 "Can You Baby") 10-15 67
LPs: 10/12-inch
FLICK CITY (5001 "In Research") 35-55 67
RESIDENTS
Singles: 12-inch
RALPH (8006 "Diskomo") 6-12 80
(Black vinyl.)
RALPH (8006 "Diskomo") 10-15 80
(Colored vinyl.)
RALPH (8721 "Hit the Road Jack [Dance Mix]") 5-8 87
Singles: 7-inch
CRYPTIC (1SP-1 "Earth vs. The Flying Saucers") 25-50 86
(Green vinyl. Bonus single, packaged with collector's edition of *The Cryptic Guide to the Residents*.)
RALPH ("17 X 7") 80-120 87
(Boxed set. Includes *It's a Man's, Man's, Man's World* picture disc.)
RALPH (0577 "Beatles Play the Residents"/"Residents Play the Beatles") 100-200 77
RALPH (0776 "Satisfaction") 250-350 76
RALPH (1272 "Santa Dog") 1000-2000 72
(Two-disc set titled *Santa Dog.*. Includes *Fire/Aircraft Damage* and *Lightning/Explosion*. Selection number represents release date: i.e. 12/72.)
RALPH (7803 "Satisfaction") 3-5 78
(Reissue.)
RALPH (7812 "Santa Dog '78") 40-60 78
(Selection number is transposed release date: i.e. 12/78.)
RALPH (8422 "It's a Man's, Man's, Man's World") 3-5 87
(Black vinyl.)
RALPH (8422 "It's a Man's, Man's, Man's World") 10-15 87
(Picture disc.)
RALPH (8621 "Kaw-Liga") 10-15 86
(Picture disc.)
RALPH (8622 "Kaw-Liga") 3-5 86
(Black vinyl.)
RALPH (8622 "Kaw-Liga") 5-10 86
(Colored vinyl.)
RALPH (8721 "Hit the Road Jack") 3-5 87
RALPH (8721 "Hit the Road Jack") 10-15 87
(Picture disc.)
RALPH/EVA-TONE ("Meet the Residents Sampler") 40-50 74
(5-inch, Eva-Tone soundsheet. Issued in a 9-inch, paper, gatefold jacket.)
REFLEX/EVA-TONE (10371900-1 "Diskomo Live") 5-10 88
(Soundsheet. Promotional issue only.)
Picture Sleeves
RALPH (1272 "Santa Dog") 50-100 72
RALPH (0577 "Beatles Play the Residents"/"Residents Play the Beatles") 30-50 77
RALPH (7812 "Santa Dog '78") 10-15 78
EPs: 7-inch
RALPH (0377 "Babyfingers") 350-450 79
(Issued in paper sleeve. Reportedly 35 to 40 made.)
RALPH (0377 "Babyfingers") 800-1200 79
(Sleeve is similar to Ralph 7812, *Santa Dog '78*. Reportedly 8 to 10 made.)
RALPH (0377 "Babyfingers") 25-30 85
(Pink vinyl.)
RALPH (1177 "Duck Stab") 10-15 78
RALPH (1177 "Duck Stab") 200-250 78
(EP "Combo Pack.")
RALPH (8007 "Buy Or Die #5") 15-25 80
(Promotional issue only.)
RALPH (8050 "Buy Or Die #6") 15-25 80
(Promotional issue only.)
RALPH (11271 "Buy Or Die #14") 15-25 87
(Promotional issue only.)
RALPH (11271 "Buy Or Die #14.5") 15-25 87
(Promotional issue only.)
W.E.I.R.D. (1 "Babyfingers") 40-60 81
LPs: 10/12-inch
CRYPTIC (2 "For Elsie") 50-75 87
(Green vinyl. Single-sided pressing.)
EPISODE (21 "Census Taker") 15-25 85
(Black vinyl. Soundtrack.)
EPISODE (21 "Census Taker") 35-45 85
(Colored vinyl. Soundtrack.)
RALPH (001 "Mole Show") 15-25 83
RALPH (002A "Mole Show") 20-30 83
(Picture disc.)
RALPH (011 "Freak Show") 15-20 91
(Black vinyl. Promotional issue only.)
RALPH (011 "Freak Show") 10-15 91
(Picture disc.)
RALPH (0274 "Meet the Residents") 100-150 74
RALPH (0278 "Duck Stab/Buster Glen") 15-20 78
(Green title box on back of cover.)
RALPH (0278 "Duck Stab/Buster Glen") 10-15 78
(Yellow title box on back of cover.)
RALPH (0677 "Meet the Residents") 10-15 77
RALPH (1075 "Third Reich & Roll") 125-150 76
(Cover indicates "First Pressing, 1000 Copies." Selection number represents final recording date: i.e. 10/75.)
RALPH (1075 "Third Reich & Roll") 10-15 77
(No mention of "first pressing.")
RALPH (1075 "Third Reich & Roll") 2500-3500 80
(Colored vinyl in a wooden box, enclosed in a drawstring bag. Labels and cover silkscreened. Includes lithographs of cover art. 25 made.)
RALPH (1075 "Third Reich & Roll") 10-15 80
(With swastikas pasted on cover.)
RALPH (1174 "Not Available") 25-50 78
(Orange label.)
RALPH (1174 "Not Available") 10-15 78
(Yellow label.)
RALPH (1276 "Fingerprince") 75-100 77
(Cover indicates "First Pressing.")
RALPH (1276 "Fingerprince") 25-30 77
(Brown cover.)
RALPH (1276 "Fingerprince") 10-15 77
(Full-color cover.)
RALPH (7707 "Meet the Residents") 20-30 85
(Picture disc. Special 13th Anniversary Edition.)
RALPH (7901 "Please Don't Steal It") 50-75 79
(Promotional issue only.)
RALPH (7906 "Eskimo") 15-20 79
(Black vinyl. Gatefold cover.)
RALPH (7906 "Eskimo") 5-10 79
(Black vinyl. Standard cover.)
RALPH (7906 "Eskimo") 20-30 79
(White vinyl. Two single-side discs.)
RALPH (7906 "Eskimo") 20-30 80
(Picture disc.)
RALPH (8052 "Commercial Album") 20-25 80
(Purple Ralph logo. Contents printed incorrectly on cover.)
RALPH (8052 "Commercial Album") 5-10 80
(Green Ralph logo. Contents printed correctly.)
RALPH (8052 "Commercial Album") 10-15 80
(Colored vinyl.)
RALPH (8152 "Mark of the Mole") 10-15 81
(Black vinyl.)
RALPH (8152 "Mark of the Mole") 50-75 81
(Brown vinyl. Silkscreen cover. Signed collector's edition with lyrics.)
RALPH (8202 "Tunes of Two Cities") 8-12 82
RALPH (8252 "Intermission") 8-12 82
RALPH (8302 "Residue of the Residents") 5-10 83
RALPH (8315 "Title in Limbo") 10-20 83
(As Renaldo & Loaf.)
RALPH (8402 "George & James") 5-10 84
(Black vinyl.)
RALPH (8402 "George & James") 10-20 84
(Clear vinyl.)
RALPH (8452 "Whatever Happened to Vileness Fats") 5-10 84
(Black vinyl.)
RALPH (8452 "Whatever Happened to Vileness Fats") 40-50 84
(Red vinyl.)
RALPH (8552 "The Big Bubble") 5-10 85
(Black vinyl.)
RALPH (8552 "The Big Bubble") 75-100 85
(Marbled pink vinyl.)
RALPH (8602 "Thirteenth Anniversary Show") 5-10 86
(Black vinyl.)
RALPH (8602 "Thirteenth Anniversary Show") 10-20 86
(White vinyl.)
RALPH (8652 "Stars & Hank Forever") 10-20 86
(Blue vinyl.)
RALPH (82761 "Fingerprince") 5-8 82
(Black vinyl.)
RALPH (82761 "Fingerprince") 8-10 82
(Purple vinyl.)
RALPH (87521 "Duck Stab!"/"Buster Glen") 5-8 87
(Black vinyl.)
RALPH (87521 "Duck Stab!"/"Buster Glen") 10-15 87
(Colored vinyl.)
RALPH (88521 "Meet the Residents") 5-8 88
(Black vinyl.)
RALPH (88521 "Meet the Residents") 10-15 88
(Colored vinyl.)
RYKO (0044 "God in 3 Persons") 5-10 88
(Clear vinyl.)
RYKO (0045 "God in 3 Persons Instrumental") 5-10 88
(Clear vinyl. Soundtrack.)
UWEB (0011 "Stranger Than Supper") 5-9 91
Members: Phil Lithman; Pamela Zeibak; Peggy Honeydew; Chris Cutler; Don Jackovich; Don Preston.
Also see SCHWUMP
RESOLUTIONS
Singles: 7-inch
VALENTINE (1001 "January 1, 1962") 40-60 62
(Same number used on an Ultimates release.)
Member: Billy Vera (plus members from the Passions and Mystics).
Also see MYSTICS
Also see PASSIONS
Also see VERA, Billy
RESONETS
Singles: 7-inch
LINDA LEE (002 "Surf Carnival") .... 10-20 '60s
RESONICS
Singles: 7-inch
LIL-LARRY (1005 "With Your Love to Guide Me") .... 30-40 '60s
LUCKY TOKEN (108 "I'm Really in Love") 50-75 64
UNITY (101 "Split Personality") 15-25 63
RESTIVO, Johnny *P&R '59*
Singles: 7-inch
CAMEO (416 "Suzanne") 5-10 66
EPIC (9537 "My Reputation") 10-15 62
RCA (47-7559 "The Shape I'm In") 10-15 59
(Monaural.)
RCA (61-7559 "The Shape I'm In") 25-50 59
(Stereo.)
RCA (7601 "Dear Someone") 10-15 59
RCA (7636 "Come Closer") 10-15 59
RCA (7697 "High School Play") 10-15 60
RCA (7758 "I Can't Take It") 10-15 60
RCA (7818 "Two Crazy Kids") 10-15 60
20TH FOX (260 "Sweet Lovin'") 10-15 61
20TH FOX (279 "Doctor Love") 10-15 61
Picture Sleeves
RCA (7559 "The Shape I'm In") 30-40 59
RCA (7601 "Dear Someone") 20-25 59
20TH FOX (279 "Doctor Love") 15-25 61
LPs: 10/12-inch
RCA (LPM-2149 "Oh Johnny") 40-60 59
(Monaural.)
RCA (LSP-2149 "Oh Johnny") 50-100 59
(Stereo.)
Session: King Curtis.
Also see KING CURTIS
RESTLESS HEARTS
Singles: 7-inch
GREEN SEA 15-25 66
RESTRICTIONS
Singles: 7-inch
IGL (147 "She's Gone Away") 10-20 68
RESTUM, Willie
Singles: 7-inch
CAPITOL 8-10 55
COLUMBIA 5-8 65
EPs: 7-inch
CAPITOL (688 "Honkin'") 10-20 55
LPs: 10/12-inch
GONE (5011 "At the Dream Lounge") 75-100 60
ROULETTE (25152 "Dream Bar") 30-40 61
REUBEN & CHAPTERS
Singles: 7-inch
SURFSIDE (3 "Cara Mia") 10-20 79
REUNION *P&R '74*
Singles: 7-inch
MR. G. (816 "People Gettin' Younger") 5-10 68
RCA (10056 "Life Is a Rock") 4-6 74
RCA (10150 "Disco-Tekin") 4-6 75
RCA (10252 "They Don't Make 'Em Like That Anymore") 4-6 75
Members: Joey Levine; Marc Bellack, Paul DiFranco; Norman Dolph.
Also see OHIO EXPRESS
REVALONS
Singles: 7-inch
COLLECTABLES .... 3-5 '80s
PET (802 "Dreams Are for Fools") 100-150 58
REVEL, Joe
Singles: 7-inch
ABC-PAR (10261 "Things Didn't Work Out") 5-10 61
REVELAIRES
(With the Ross Dristy Orchestra)
Singles: 78 rpm
BURGUNDY 40-60 54
Singles: 7-inch
BURGUNDY (1001 "Only the Angels Know") 100-200 54
REVELERS
(With Jacques Belasco & Orchestra)
Singles: 7-inch
MASQUERADE (22459 "Give Me a Second Chance") 40-50 58
REVELIERS
Singles: 7-inch
G-CLEF (702 "Hangin' Five") 15-25 63
LAWN (237 "Maureen") 10-15 64
REVELIERS 4
Singles: 7-inch
TROY (227 "It's Not Right") 15-25 63
REVELLES
Singles: 7-inch
JIM-KO (41105 "Out of Sight") 20-30 66
JIM-KO (41106 "Little Girl") 20-30 66
REVELLS
LPs: 10/12-inch
REPRISE (R-6160 "The Go Sound of the Slots") 40-60 65
(Monaural.)
REPRISE (RS-6160 "The Go Sound of the Slots") 40-60 65
(Stereo.)
Members: Chuck Girard; Joe Kelly; Richard Podolor; Richard Burns; Bill Cooper.
Also see PODOLOR, Dickie
RE'VELLS
Singles: 7-inch
ROMAN PRESS (201 "Let It Please Be You") 50-75 63
RE-VELS *P&R/R&B '59*
(Revels; Re-Vels Quartette; with Gene Kutch & the Butch Ballard Orchestra; "Orch. Con. by Sid Bass")
Singles: 78 rpm
ATLAS (1035 "My Lost Love") 200-300 54
SOUND 15-25 56
Singles: 7-inch
ANDIE (5007 "Please") 10-20 59
ANGLE TONE (1035 "My Lost Love") 3-5
ATLAS (1035 "My Lost Love") 3000-4000 54
CHESS (1708 "False Alarm") 150-200 58
(Promotional issue only.)
CHESS (1708 "False Alarm") 100-150 58
(Blue label.)
CHESS (1708 "False Alarm") 10-15 63
MASTERPIECE (303 "Dream My Darling Dream") 3-5
NORGOLDE (103 "Dead Mans' Stroll") 50-75 59
NORGOLDE (103 "Midnight Stroll") 10-15 59
NORGOLDE (104 "Foo Man Choo") 10-20 59
NORGOLDE (106 "[Money] Is All I Need") 30-40 60
NORGOLDE (218 "The Greatness of Love") 75-100 60
SOUND (129 "You Lied to Me") 100-150 56

SOUND (135 "Dream My Darling Dream")....75-125 56
TEEN (122 "So in Love")....600-700 58

REVELS
(With Barbara Adkins)
Singles: 7-inch
CT (1 "Church Key")....25-50 60
DOWNEY (123 "Intoxica")....8-10 64
IMPACT (1 "Church Key")....20-30 60
(Black vinyl.)
IMPACT (1 "Church Key")....40-60 60
(Colored vinyl.)
IMPACT (3 "Intoxica")....8-12 61
(Black vinyl. Colored vinyl possible but not yet confirmed.)
IMPACT (7 "Rampage")....8-12 62
(Black vinyl.)
IMPACT (7 "Rampage")....15-25 62
(Colored vinyl.)
IMPACT (13 "Party Time")....10-15 63
(Black vinyl. Colored vinyl possible but not yet confirmed.)
IMPACT (22 "Revellion"/"Conga Twist")....8-12 64
(Black vinyl.)
IMPACT (22 "Revellion"/"Conga Twist")..15-25 64
(Colored vinyl.)
IMPACT (22 "Revellion"/"Monkey Bird")....8-12 64
(Black vinyl.)
IMPACT (22 "Revellion"/"Monkey Bird")..15-25 64
(Colored vinyl.)
LYNN (1302 "Six Pak")....40-50 59
PALETTE (5074 "Oh How I Love You")...15-25 61
SWINGIN' (620 "Six Pak")....15-25 60
WESTCO (3 "It's Party Time")....5-10 63
(Black vinyl.)
WESTCO (3 "Party Time")....15-25 63
(Colored vinyl.)
WESTCO (4 "Soft Top")....25-35 63
LPs: 10/12-inch
IMPACT (1 "On a Rampage")....75-125 64
SUNDAZED....5-10 '90s
(Colored vinyl.)
Members: Brian English; Dan Darnold Dave Davis; Jim McRae; Norman Knowles; Sam Eddy; Dean Sorenson; Paul Sorenson.
Also see EDDY, Sam, & Revels
Also see SENTINELS

REVELS, Don
Singles: 7-inch
LUPINE ("The Return of Stagger Lee")...15-25 60
(First issue. Selection number not known.)
U.A. (277 "The Return of Stagger Lee")..10-15 60

REVENS
Singles: 7-inch
NIGHT OWL (67116 "For You")....15-25 67

REVERE, Paul, & Raiders *P&R '61*
(Raiders; "Featuring Mark Lindsay")
Singles: 7-inch
("The Judge")....20-30 69
(Promotional 33 rpm for Pontiac GTO. No label name or selection number used.)
APEX (106 "Beatnik Sticks")....50-100 60
(First issue.)
COLUMBIA (10126 "Your Love")....5-8 75
COLUMBIA (42814 "Louie Louie")....10-20 63
COLUMBIA (43008 "Louie – Go Home")..10-20 64
COLUMBIA (43114 "Over You")....10-20 64
COLUMBIA (43273 "Oh Poo Pah Doo")..10-20 65
COLUMBIA (43375 "Steppin' Out")....5-10 65
(Black vinyl – commercial or promo.)
COLUMBIA (43375 "Steppin' Out")....25-35 65
(Colored vinyl. Promotional issue only.)
COLUMBIA (43461 "Just Like Me")....5-10 65
(Black vinyl – commercial or promo.)
COLUMBIA (43461 "Just Like Me")....25-35 65
(Colored vinyl. Promotional issue only.)
COLUMBIA (43556 "Kicks")....5-10 66
(Black vinyl – commercial or promo.)
COLUMBIA (43556 "Kicks")....25-35 66
(Colored vinyl. Promotional issue only.)
COLUMBIA (43678 "Hungry")....5-10 66
(Black vinyl – commercial or promo.)
COLUMBIA (43678 "Hungry")....25-35 66
(Colored vinyl. Promotional issue only.)
COLUMBIA (43810 "The Great Airplane Strike")....5-10 66
(Black vinyl – commercial or promo.)
COLUMBIA (43810 "The Great Airplane Strike")....25-35 66
(Colored vinyl. Promotional issue only.)
COLUMBIA (43907 "Good Thing")....5-10 67
(Black vinyl – commercial or promo.)
COLUMBIA (43907 "Good Thing")....15-25 67
(Colored vinyl. Promotional issue only.)
COLUMBIA (44018 "Ups & Downs")....5-8 67
COLUMBIA (44094 "Him Or Me, What's It Gonna Be")....5-8 67
COLUMBIA (44227 "I Had a Dream")....5-8 67
COLUMBIA (44335 "Peace of Mind")....5-8 67
COLUMBIA (44444 "Too Much Talk")....5-8 68
COLUMBIA (44553 "Don't Take It So Hard")....5-8 68
COLUMBIA (44655 "Cinderella Sunshine")....5-8 68
COLUMBIA (44744 "Mr. Sun, Mr. Moon")....5-8 69
COLUMBIA (44854 "Let Me")....5-8 69
COLUMBIA (44970 "We Gotta All Get Together")....5-8 69
COLUMBIA (45082 thru 45898)....4-6 70-74
COLUMBIA (105499 "SS 396"/"Corvair Baby")....10-20 66
(Promotional issue only.)
DRIVE (6248 "Ain't Nothin' Wrong")....4-8 76
GARDENA (106 "Beatnik Sticks")....20-30 60
GARDENA (115 "Paul Revere's Ride")....20-30 60
GARDENA (116 "Like Long Hair")....20-30 61
GARDENA (118 "Midnight Ride")....15-25 61
GARDENA (124 "All Night Long")....15-25 62
GARDENA (127 "Like, Bluegrass")....15-25 62
GARDENA (131 "Shake It Up")....15-25 62
GARDENA (137 "Tall Cool One")....15-25 63
JERDEN (807 "So Fine")....15-25 63
RAIDER AMERICA....5-10 82
SANDE (101 "Louie Louie")....25-35 63
TEEN SCOOP ("Interview")....15-25 67
(Square cardboard picture disc. Included in magazine.)
20TH FOX (2281 "The British Are Coming")....4-6 76
Picture Sleeves
COLUMBIA (10126 "Your Love")....10-15 75
COLUMBIA (43678 "Hungry")....5-10 66
COLUMBIA (43810 "The Great Airplane Strike")....15-20 66
COLUMBIA (43907 "Good Thing")....5-10 67
COLUMBIA (44018 "Ups & Downs")....5-10 67
COLUMBIA (44094 "Him Or Me, What's It Gonna Be")....5-10 67
COLUMBIA (44227 "I Had a Dream")....5-10 67
COLUMBIA (44335 "Peace of Mind")....5-10 67
COLUMBIA (44444 "Too Much Talk")....5-10 68
COLUMBIA (44553 "Don't Take It So Hard")....5-10 68
COLUMBIA (44655 "Cinderella Sunshine")....5-10 68
COLUMBIA (44744 "Mr. Sun, Mr. Moon")..5-10 69
COLUMBIA (45601 "Powder Blue Mercedes Queen")....10-15 72
EPs: 7-inch
JERDEN (JRLS-7004 "In the Beginning")....40-60 66
(Juke box issue only. Includes title strips.)
LPs: 10/12-inch
BACK-TRAC....5-8 85
COLUMBIA (12 "Two All-Time Great Selling LPs")....15-20 69
COLUMBIA (462 "Greatest Hits")....20-25 67
(Monaural.)
COLUMBIA (2307 "Here They Come")....25-40 65
(Monaural.)
COLUMBIA (2451 "Just Like Us")....25-40 66
(Monaural.)
COLUMBIA (2508 "Midnight Ride")....25-40 66
(Monaural.)
COLUMBIA (2595 "Spirit of '67")....25-40 66
(Monaural.)
COLUMBIA (2662 "Greatest Hits")....25-40 67
(Monaural.)
COLUMBIA (2721 "Revolution")....25-40 67
(Monaural.)
COLUMBIA (2755 "Christmas Present and Past")....40-60 67
(Monaural.)
COLUMBIA (2805 "Goin' to Memphis")....20-30 68
(Monaural.)
COLUMBIA (9107 "Here They Come")....25-40 65
(Stereo.)
COLUMBIA (9251 "Just Like Us")....25-40 66
(Stereo.)
COLUMBIA (9308 "Midnight Ride")....25-40 66
(Stereo.)
COLUMBIA (9395 "Spirit of '67")....25-40 66
(Stereo.)
COLUMBIA (9462 "Greatest Hits")....25-40 67
(Stereo.)
COLUMBIA (9521 "Revolution")....25-40 67
(Stereo.)
COLUMBIA (9555 "Christmas Present and Past")....40-60 67
(Stereo.)
COLUMBIA (9605 "Goin' to Memphis")....20-25 68
(Stereo.)
COLUMBIA (9665 "Something Happening")....10-20 68
COLUMBIA (9753 "Hard 'N' Heavy")....10-20 69
(Black and white cover.)
COLUMBIA (9753 "Hard 'N' Heavy")....15-25 69
(Color cover.)
COLUMBIA (9905 "Alias Pink Puzz")....10-20 69
COLUMBIA (9905 "Alias Pink Puzz")....10-20 69
COLUMBIA (9964 "Collage")....10-20 70
COLUMBIA (30386 "Greatest Hits, Vol. 2")....10-20 71
COLUMBIA (30768 "Indian Reservation")....10-20 71
COLUMBIA (31196 "Country Wine")....30-50 71
COLUMBIA SPECIAL PRODUCTS (141714 "The Judge")....150-200 69
(Promotional issue only.)
HARMONY (30089 "Paul Revere & the Raiders Featuring Mark Lindsay")....10-15 70
HARMONY (30975 "Good Thing")....10-15 71
HARMONY (31183 "Movin' On")....10-15 72
HOLLYWOOD (66012 "Paul Revere & Raiders")....50-75 65
(Red vinyl. Only *You Can't Sit Down* and *Some Times* are by Paul Revere & Raiders. Other 10 tracks are uncredited.)
GARDENA (1000 "Like Long Hair")....500-750 61
JERDEN (7004 "In the Beginning")....75-125 66
PICKWICK (3176 "Paul Revere and the Raiders")....10-15 '70s
RAIDER....10-15 82
SANDE (1001 "Paul Revere and the Raiders")....300-400 63
SEARS....40-50 '60s
(Special Products Sears promotional issue.)
Members: Mark Lindsay; Freddy Weller; Paul Revere; Keith Allison; Joe Correro Jr; Danny Krause; Omar Martinez; Carl Driggs; Drake Levin; Doug Heath; Ron Foos; Mike Smith; Philip Volk; Mike Holiday.
Also see ALLISON, Keith
Also see CYRKLE / Paul Revere & Raiders
Also see JOYRIDE
Also see LINDSAY, Mark
Also see LOVE, Mike, & Dean Torrance / Paul Revere & Raiders
Also see VALLEY, Jim
Also see WELLER, Freddy

REVERE, Paul, & Raiders / Simon & Garfunkel / Byrds / Aretha Franklin
EPs: 7-inch
COLUMBIA SPECIAL PRODUCTS (546 "The Moving Crowd")....25-30 66
(Promotional issue only. Made for National Shoes & Mary Jane Shoe Stores)
Also see BUCKINGHAMS / Byrds / Aretha Franklin / Paul Revere & Raiders
Also see BYRDS
Also see FRANKLIN, Aretha
Also see REVERE, Paul, & Raiders
Also see SIMON & GARFUNKEL

REVERES
Singles: 7-inch
VALIANT (6041 "Big T")....15-25 64

REVERES / Honeystrollers
Singles: 7-inch
GLORY (272 "Leonore"/"Honeystrollin' ").10-20 58

REVIERAS
(With Cliff Parman & Orchestra)
Singles: 7-inch
VICTORIA (103 "Walk Away")....15-25 64

REVLONS
Singles: 7-inch
CAPITOL (4739 "Dry Your Eyes")....20-30 62
RAE COX (105 "I Promise Love")....10-20 61

REV-LONS
Singles: 7-inch
GARPAX (44168 "Boy Trouble")....10-20 62

REVLONS
(With Little Martin & Mustangs)
Singles: 7-inch
VRC (112 "Bye Bye Baby")....10-15 '60s
Also see MARTIN'S MUSTANGS

REVLONS
Singles: 7-inch
PARKWAY (107 "It Could Happen to You")....10-20 66
REPRISE (251 "After Last Night")....8-12 64
REPRISE (20200 "I Can't Forget About You")....8-12 63
SHURFINE (006 "Sugaree")....15-25 65
STARBURST (123 "I Can't Forget About You")....10-20 '60s
TOY (101 "Did I Make a Mistake")....10-20 62

REVLONS
Singles: 7-inch
CRYSTAL BALL (138 "Moonlight Angel")....4-8 81
(Black vinyl. 500 made.)
CRYSTAL BALL (138 "Moonlight Angel")..8-12 81
(Red vinyl. 25 made.)
CRYSTAL BALL (138 "Moonlight Angel") 30-40 81
(Multi-colored vinyl. Five made.)

REVOLVER
Singles: 7-inch
FUTURE (30488 "Little Miss Hip")....40-60 '70s
Member: Dez Dickerson.
Also see PRINCE

REVOLVERS
Singles: 7-inch
JL (101 "The Pounding of My Heart")....4-8 93
(Colored vinyl.)
TY TEX (127 "Like Me")....20-30 65
TY TEX (128 "Good Lovin' Women")....20-30 65
TY TEX (131 "I Like Lovin' You")....20-30 65

REVS
Singles: 7-inch
SPEEDWAY (2578 "Go Or Blow Twist")..10-20 62

REX & HERB
Singles: 7-inch
JANET (202 "Come Back Big Bertha")....50-75

REY, Rayner
Singles: 7-inch
JERDEN (781 "Whiplash")....15-25 66

REY, Tony
Singles: 7-inch
KING BEE (101 "Something On Your Mind")....15-25 63

REYNOLDS, Big Jack, & His Blues Men
Singles: 7-inch
HI-Q (5036 "You Won't Treat Me Right").25-50 63
MAH'S (10 "You Don't Treat Me Right")...25-50 62
(Note title difference.)

REYNOLDS, Debbie *P&R '57*
Singles: 78 rpm
CORAL....5-10 57
MGM....4-8 55-57
Singles: 7-inch
ABC....4-6 74
ABC-PAR....4-8 65
BEVERLY HILLS....4-6 72
CORAL....5-10 57-58
DOT....4-8 59-63
JANUS....4-6 70
MCA....3-5 '80s
MGM (11000 & 12000 series)....5-10 55-59
MGM (13000 series)....4-8 63-66
PARAMOUNT....4-6 73
Picture Sleeves
DOT....5-10 59-60
MGM....8-15 58-66
EPs: 7-inch
CORAL....10-20 58
MGM....10-20 55

LPs: 10/12-inch
DOT (Except 25295) ... 15-20 59-63
DOT (25295 "Am I That Easy to Forget") 15-25 60
(Black vinyl.
DOT (25295 "Am I That Easy to Forget") 50-75 60
(Colored vinyl.
MGM ... 15-25 60-66
METRO ... 10-15 65
Also see FISHER, Eddie, & Debbie Reynolds

REYNOLDS, Eddie
Singles: 7-inch
DIXIE (819 "Teen Lover") ... 50-60
DIXIE (838 "What Was It") ... 50-75 58
TIME (460 "Fe, Fi, Fo, Fum") ... 5-10 59

REYNOLDS, Jo Ann
Singles: 7-inch
BANNER (111 "Ring a Ding Dong Daddy") ... 75-85 66

REYNOLDS, Jody *P&R/R&B '58*
Singles: 78 rpm
DEMON (1507 "Endless Sleep") ... 50-75 58
Singles: 7-inch
ABC ... 4-6 73
BRENT (7042 "Raggedy Ann") ... 5-10 63
COLLECTABLES ... 3-5 '80s
DEMON (1507 "Endless Sleep") ... 15-25 58
DEMON (1509 "Fire of Love") ... 10-20 58
DEMON (1511 "Elope with Me") ... 10-20 58
DEMON (1515 "Golden Idol") ... 20-30 59
DEMON (1519 "The Storm") ... 20-30 59
DEMON (1523 "Whipping Post") ... 10-20 60
DEMON (1524 "Stone Cold") ... 10-20 60
PULSAR (2419 "Endless Sleep") ... 5-10 69
SMASH (1810 "Don't Jump") ... 5-10 63
TITAN (1734 "Devil Girl") ... 5-10 66
LPs: 10/12-inch
TRU-GEMS (1002 "Endless Sleep") ... 8-12 78
Also see CASEY, Al
Also see CLARK, Sanford

REYNOLDS, Jody, & Bobbie Gentry
Singles: 7-inch
TITAN (1736 "Requiem for Love") ... 5-10 66

REYNOLDS, Jody / Olympics
Singles: 7-inch
LIBERTY (54514 "Endless Sleep"/"Western Movies") ... 5-10 63
("All-Time Hits" series.)
TITAN (1801 "Endless Sleep"/"Western Movies") ... 10-20 61
Picture Sleeves
TITAN (1801 "Endless Sleep"/"Western Movies") ... 25-35 61
Also see OLYMPICS

REYNOLDS, Jody, & Storms
Singles: 7-inch
INDIGO (127 "Thunder"/"Tarantula") ... 15-25 61
(Remake of both sides of Sundown 114, shown as by the Storms.)
Also see CASEY, Al
Also see REYNOLDS, Jody
Also see STORMS

REYNOLDS, Joey / Joey & Danny
Singles: 7-inch
SWAN (4276 "Santa's Got a Brand New Bag"/"Rats in My Room") ... 15-25 67
Also see 4 SEASONS
Also see JOEY & DANNY

REYNOLDS, Teddy
(With the Twisters)
Singles: 78 rpm
SITTIN' IN WITH (517 "Walkin' the Floor Baby") ... 20-40 49
SITTIN' IN WITH (558 "Why Baby Why") 20-40 50
SITTIN' IN WITH (586 "You Put a Voodoo Spell on Me") ... 20-40 51
SITTIN' IN WITH (594 "Strange Mysterious Woman") ... 20-40 51
SITTIN' IN WITH (613 "Waitin' at the Station") ... 20-40 51
Singles: 7-inch
KENT (371 "Do You Wanna Twist") ... 5-8 62
MERCURY (71281 "Puppy Dogs") ... 20-30 58
NEWMAN ... 5-8 66
SPECIALTY (695 "Ain't That Soul") ... 4-6 72

LPs: 10/12-inch
CROWN (247 "The Twist") ... 25-50 62
Also see WILEY, Ed

REYNOLDS, Timmy
(Tim Reynolds)
Singles: 7-inch
OPERATORS (2008 "Duke of Earl") ... 5-10 62
TWIN HITS (5018 "This Little Girl") ... 15-25 61
Also see LYNN, Sandy / Timmy Reynolds

REYNOLDS, Tony
Singles: 7-inch
BATON (242 "King of the Stars") ... 15-25 57

REYNOLDS, Wesley
(Wes Reynolds)
Singles: 7-inch
ANCHOR (183 "Helpless") ... 5-10 70
BISMARK ... 10-15 65
D (1164 "Hey Little Boy Blue") ... 15-25 60
ROSE (108 "Trip to the Moon") ... 75-100 57
ROSE (117 "Rag Mop") ... 60-80 57
VALOR ("Shut Down") ... 10-15
(Selection number not known.)

RHAMBO, Bo
("Tenor Sax with Rhythm Accomp.")
Singles: 78 rpm
CASH ... 8-12 55-57
Singles: 7-inch
CASH (1001 "Jump Time") ... 15-20 55
CASH (1037 "Move It on Out") ... 15-20 56
CASH (1047 "Dianne") ... 15-20 57
CASH (1050 "Indian Love Call") ... 15-20 57
IMPERIAL (5552 "Indian Love Call") ... 10-15 58
IMPERIAL (5657 "Two for the Blues") ... 8-12 60
Also see TILLIS, Clyde

RHODES, Darrell
Singles: 7-inch
DEL PAR (103 "Red Sails in the Sunset") ... 100-200
WINSTON (1026 "Four O'Clock Baby") ... 150-250 58
WINSTON (1029 "Lou Lou") ... 300-400 58
WINSTON (1041 "Runnin' & Chasin'") . 150-250 59
WONDER (1976 "Burgers from Heaven") .. 5-10 76

RHODES, Jimmy
Singles: 7-inch
CUPID (5005 "I Wanna Go") ... 60-75 58
JASON (111 "I Wanna Go") ... 60-75 59

RHODES, Red
Singles: 7-inch
BLUE RIVER (231 "Steelin' Uptown") ... 5-10 68
COUNTRYSIDE ... 4-6 73
LPs: 10/12-inch
COUNTRYSIDE ... 8-10 73
CROWN (555 "Steel Guitar Rag") ... 10-15 66
Also see NESMITH, Michael

RHODES, Slim
(Featuring Sandy Brooks; with Brad Suggs; with Dusty & Dot)
Singles: 78 rpm
GILT-EDGE (5026 "Memphis Bounce") ... 15-25 50
GILT-EDGE (5034 "Hot Foot Rag") ... 15-25 51
GILT-EDGE (5044 "Ozark Boogie") ... 15-25 51
SUN (216 "Uncertain Love") ... 25-75 55
SUN (225 "House of Sin") ... 25-75 55
SUN (238 "Gonna Romp and Stomp") ... 50-75 56
SUN (256 "Do What I Do") ... 15-25 56
Singles: 7-inch
RHODES (101 "Brothers Frank and Jesse James") ... 15-25
SUN (216 "Uncertain Love") ... 75-100 55
SUN (225 "House of Sin") ... 200-300 55
SUN (238 "Gonna Romp and Stomp") . 100-125 56
SUN (256 "Do What I Do") ... 50-75 56
Also see SUGGS, Brad

RHODES, Texas Red
Singles: 7-inch
ECHO (1001 "Go Cats Go") ... 200-300

RHODES, Todd *R&B '48*
Singles: 78 rpm
KING ... 15-35 48-54
MODERN ... 10-15 49
SENSATION (Except 6) ... 10-20 47-49
SENSATION (6 "Blues for the Red Boy") . 25-35 47
VITACOUSTIC ... 10-20 47

Singles: 7-inch
KING (4469 "Gin Gin Gin") ... 50-75 51
KING (4486 "Good Man") ... 40-60 51
(Black vinyl.)
KING (4486 "Good Man") ... 200-300 51
(Green vinyl.)
KING (4509 "Your Daddy's Doggin' Around") ... 40-60 51
(Black vinyl.)
KING (4509 "Your Daddy's Doggin' Around") ... 150-175 51
(Blue-green vinyl.)
KING (4528 "Rocket 69") ... 50-75 52
KING (4556 "Trying") ... 75-125 52
KING (4566 "Blue Autumn") ... 75-125 52
KING (4583 "Must I Cry Again" ... 75-125 52
KING (4601 "Lost Child") ... 75-125 53
(Lavern Baker is the vocalist on one side of each of the four King issues in the 4556-4601 series)
KING (4648 "Feathers") ... 20-30 53
KING (4666 "Let Down Blues") ... 40-60 53
KING (4736 "Silver Sunset") ... 20-30 54
KING (4755 "Echoes") ... 20-30 54
EPs: 7-inch
KING ... 30-40 52-54
LPs: 10/12-inch
KING (88 "Todd Rhodes Plays the Hits") ... 75-100 53
KING (658 "Dance Music") ... 35-55 60
Session: Lavern Baker; Kitty Stevenson; Sadie Madison.
Also see ALLEN, Connee
Also see BAKER, Lavern
Also see BARTHOLOMEW, Dave
Also see HARRIS, Wynonie

RHODES, Walter
Singles: 7-inch
MASCOT (129 "I Worship the Ground You Walk On") ... 20-30 60

RHOMBERG, Dude
Singles: 7-inch
COULEE (111 "Your Broken Heart's Starting to Show") ... 15-25 65

RHOTON, Howard
Singles: 7-inch
CANARY (1008 "I'll Skip School") ... 20-30

RHULE, John Rocky
Singles: 7-inch
MARK (212 "Rock the Joint") ... 250-350

RHYS, John, & Lively Set
Singles: 7-inch
IMPACT (1024 "Nothing But Love") ... 10-20 67

RHYTHM, J.T.
Singles: 7-inch
PALMER (5021 "My Sweet Baby") ... 5-10 67

RHYTHM, Johnny
(With the Audios)
Singles: 7-inch
MGM (13043 "Wouldn't It Be Nice") ... 40-60 61

RHYTHM ACES
Singles: 78 rpm
ACE ... 10-20 56
VEE-JAY ... 50-100 54-55
Singles: 7-inch
ACE (518 "Look What You've Done") ... 20-25 56
VEE-JAY (124 "I Wonder Why") ... 150-250 54
(Black vinyl.)
VEE-JAY (124 "I Wonder Why") ... 1000-2000 54
(Red vinyl.)
VEE-JAY (138 "Whisper to Me") ... 150-250 55
(Black vinyl.)
VEE-JAY (138 "Whisper to Me") ... 1000-2000 55
(Red vinyl.)
VEE-JAY (160 "That's My Sugar") ... 75-100 55

RHYTHM ACES / Chantels
Singles: 7-inch
OLDIES 45 (93 "I Wonder Why"/"Look in My Eyes") ... 4-6
Also see CHANTELS

RHYTHM ACES / Harptones
Singles: 7-inch
OLDIES 45 (103 "Flippity Flop"/"Life Is But a Dream") ... 4-6
Also see HARPTONES

RHYTHM ACES / Willows
Singles: 7-inch
OLDIES 45 (107 "That's My Sugar"/"Church Bells May Ring") ... 4-6
Also see RHYTHM ACES
Also see WILLOWS

RHYTHM ACES
("Gil Haas, Vocalist")
Singles: 78 rpm
KAMPUS ... 5-10 55
Singles: 7-inch
KAMPUS (1001 "The Blues Are Here") ... 10-15 55
KAMPUS (1002 "Well, Waddaya Know") . 10-15 55

RHYTHM ACES
Singles: 7-inch
MARK-X (8004 "Crazy Jealousy") ... 8-12 60
Members: Lou Fallo; Herb Glazer; John D'Amaro; Steve Freeman; Vinnie Fiore.

RHYTHM ACES
Singles: 7-inch
ROULETTE (4268 "Mohawk Rock") ... 8-12 60
ROULETTE (4426 "Raunchy Twist") ... 5-10 62
SIOUX (82260 "Allan's Rock") ... 10-15 60
SIOUX (102261 "What'd I Say Twist") ... 10-20 61
UNIVERSAL ARTISTS (3160 "Mohawk Rock") ... 20-30 60

RHYTHM ACES
Singles: 7-inch
STARLITE (61 "Wherever You May Go") 50-75
STARLITE (66 "Oh My Darling") ... 30-50

RHYTHM ADDICTS
Singles: 7-inch
CEE-GEE (701 "If You're Square") ... 100-150
RADDIX (7530 "Hey! Whatcha Say Babe!") ... 150-250

RHYTHM CADETS
("Featuring George Singleton")
Singles: 7-inch
VESTA (501 "Dearest Doryce") ... 2000-2500 57
(100 made.)
Member: George "Bebo" Singleton.
Also see SINGLETON, Bebo

RHYTHM CASTERS
Singles: 78 rpm
EXCELLO (2115 "Oh My Darling") ... 50-100 57
Singles: 7-inch
EXCELLO (2115 "Oh My Darling") ... 250-300 57

RHYTHM CATS
Singles: 78 rpm
SPECIALTY (496 "Blue Saxophone") ... 10-15 54
Singles: 7-inch
SPECIALTY (496 "Blue Saxophone") ... 10-20 54

RHYTHM DEVILS
LPs: 10/12-inch
PASSPORT ... 10-20 80
Members: Mickey Hart; Phil Lesh; Mike Hinton; Jordan Amarantha; Jim Lovelace; Greg Errico; Bill Kruetzmann; Airto Moreira.
Also see HART, Mickey

RHYTHM FIVE
Singles: 7-inch
TIFCO (829 "Baby Please Don't Go") ... 10-15 62

RHYTHM GENTS
Singles: 7-inch
MERRI (6008 "Linda") ... 15-25 64

RHYTHM HEIRS
Singles: 7-inch
YUCCA (105 "Strange World") ... 50-75 59

RHYTHM JESTERS
Singles: 78 rpm
RAMA (213 "Rock to the Music") ... 15-25 56
Singles: 7-inch
LECTRA (501 "Please Be Mine") ... 20-30 62
(No group credited.)
LECTRA (501 "Please Be Mine") ... 15-25 62
(Credits the Rhythm Jesters.)
RAMA (213 "Rock to the Music") ... 50-75 56
Also see DAVIES, Bob

RHYTHM KINGS
Singles: 78 rpm
APOLLO (1171 "Merry Christmas One and All") ... 25-50 50

APOLLO (1181 "Why My Darling, Why"). 25-50 51
IVORY (751 "Night After Night")............. 40-60 49
(Various artists EPs on Ivory are bootlegs.)
EPs: 7-inch
LLOYDS (707 "Rhythm Kings")........... 200-300 54

RHYTHM KINGS
Singles: 7-inch
ACEMGA..3-5
BROOKE (118 "Boppin' Guitar")............ 10-20 60
CHALLENGE (9178 "Bordertown")......... 10-20 62
CUCA ("Maj") 10-20 60
(Selection number not known.)
GNP (196 "Exotic") 8-12 63
TOLLIE (9014 "Latin Ska") 5-10 64
VELPA...3-5
Members: Al Garcia; Fred Mendoza; Vince Bumatay; Art Rodriguez.
Also see CHARADES
Also see LINK - EDDY COMBO
Also see MYERS, Dave, & Surftones / Rhythm Kings

RHYTHM MAKERS
("Music By the Cannibals")
Singles: 7-inch
ARROW (1007 "I Wanna Be the One").... 20-30 58

RHYTHM MASTERS
Singles: 78 rpm
FLIP (314 "Baby We Two").................. 100-200 56
Singles: 7-inch
FLIP (314 "Baby We Two")............. 1000-2000 56

RHYTHM MASTERS
Singles: 7-inch
ACE (610 "Holding My Savior's Hand") 8-12 61
MOBILE FIDELITY (1001 "Little Lisa") 20-30 64

RHYTHM OUTLAWS
Singles: 7-inch
CO (430 "Steel Guitar Rag")........................8-12
KALOX (1028 "Walking to Kansas City"). 10-20 60

RHYTHM PLAYBOYS
Singles: 7-inch
SS (16210 "Rhythm Playboys Stomp").......8-12

RHYTHM RASCALS
(With Bebbie Boy Butch)
Singles: 7-inch
ROULETTE (4696 "Girl By My Side").........5-10 66
SONIC (117 "Girl By My Side") 10-20 66

RHYTHM RASCALS
Singles: 7-inch
JAR (402 "Long Way Home")................... 10-20 '60s

RHYTHM RIDERS
Singles: 7-inch
RYDER (1000 "Cajun Baby") 15-25 62
SOUTH SEA (112 "Knockout")....................8-12 '60s

RHYTHM ROCKERS
(Rythm Rockers)
Singles: 78 rpm
CROSS COUNTRY 75-100 56
SUN 50-75 56
Singles: 7-inch
CROSS COUNTRY (524-35 "Juke box, Help Me Find My Baby"") 150-250 56
(First issue.)
SUN (248 "Juke box, Help Me Find My Baby") 75-100 56
Members: Hardrock Gunter; Buddy Durham.
Also see GUNTER, Hardrock

RHYTHM ROCKERS
("Featuring Chet Atkins")
Singles: 78 rpm
RCA (6919 "Martinique") 8-10 57
Singles: 7-inch
RCA (6808 "Tricky").................................. 20-30 57
RCA (6919 "Martinique") 20-30 57
Also see ATKINS, Chet

RHYTHM ROCKERS
Singles: 7-inch
GONE (5073 "Madness") 15-25 59
OASIS (104 "Thinkin' About You") 100-150 59
SATIN (921 "Oh Boy"/"We Belong Together") 50-75 60
(B-side by Johnny & Bob.)
SQUARE (505 "Oh, Oh Honey") 50-75 59
SQUARE (506 "Madness") 50-75 59

Picture Sleeves
SATIN (921 "Oh Boy"/"We Belong Together")..75-100 60

RHYTHM ROCKERS
(Mike Patterson & Rhythm Rockers)
Singles: 7-inch
CHALLENGE (9196 "Rendezvous Stomp")..10-15 63
WIPE OUT (1001 "Foot Cruising")...........15-25 63
LPs: 10/12-inch
CHALLENGE (617 "Soul Surfin'") 75-100 63
Members: Mike Patterson; Mike Moran; John; Steve; Dave; Tracy.
Also see PATTERSON, Mike

RHYTHM ROCKERS
Singles: 7-inch
FENTON (944 "Three Strikes")..................15-25 64

RHYTHM ROCKERS
Singles: 7-inch
GAITY (6105 "Twang") ....50-75 '60s

RHYTHM ROCKERS
Singles: 7-inch
JOREL ("Giving Everything Away") 300-500
(Selection number not known.)

RHYTHM ROCKERS
Singles: 7-inch
MAG-NA-TONE ("Maggie") 50-100
(Selection number not known.)

RHYTHM ROCKETS
Singles: 7-inch
GULFSTREAM (6654 "My Shadow") ...200-300

RHYTHM ROUSERS
Singles: 7-inch
ROUSER (7423 "Just Because")...........75-125 58

RHYTHM STARS
Singles: 7-inch
CLOCK (1007 "Lynn") 50-75 58
CORSICAN (0057 "My Girl Babe").........75-100 59

RHYTHM STEPPERS
Singles: 7-inch
SPINNING (6010 "Hey Little Lola")..........10-20 59

RHYTHM SURFERS
Singles: 7-inch
DAYTONE (6301 "502") 25-35 63

RHYTHM TEENS
Singles: 7-inch
BURGER ("True Lover")............................50-75
(Selection number not known.)

RHYTHM TONES
Singles: 7-inch
VEST (828 "Something Wrong Upstairs")..75-125 59

RHYTHM WILLIE
(With His Gang)
Singles: 78 rpm
OKEH ....10-20 '40s
PREMIUM (866 "I Got Rhythm") 30-40 50

RHYTHMAIRES
Singles: 78 rpm
SWAN..15-25 46

RHYTHMAIRES
Singles: 7-inch
RHYTHM (113 "Screw Driver") 30-40 57

RHYTHMERES
Singles: 7-inch
BRUNSWICK (55083 "Elaine") 40-50 58

RHYTHMETTES
Singles: 78 rpm
BRUNSWICK...5-10 57
MANHATTAN..5-10 56
RCA..5-10 55-56
Singles: 7-inch
BRUNSWICK...5-10 57
CORAL (62186 "High School Lovers") 10-15 60
MANHATTAN (501 "Innocent Eyes").......10-15 56
RCA (6089 "Only You") 10-15 55
RCA (6244 "Bridge of Love")....................10-15 55
RCA (6349 "Take My Hand, Show Me the Way")..10-15 55
RCA (6539 "Boom Boom") 10-15 56

Picture Sleeves
RCA (6539 "Boom Boom") 20-30 56
("This Is Their Life" sleeve makes no reference to this particular release. Promotional issue only.)
Members: Donna Watkins; Nadine Small; Jo Craig.

RIA
(With the Reasons; with Revellons)
Singles: 7-inch
AMY (888 "Memories Linger On") 10-15 63
(Black vinyl.)
AMY (888 "Memories Linger On") 100-200 63
(Blue vinyl.)
RSVP (1110 "He's Not There") 10-15 65

RIALTOS
Singles: 7-inch
PIKE (5907 "Like Thunder") 15-25 61
Also see HOLLISTER, Bobby, & Rialtos

RIALTOS
Singles: 7-inch
CB (5009 "Let Me In")..........................400-500 64

RIBBONS *P&R '63*
Singles: 7-inch
ERA (012 "Ain't Gonna Kiss Ya")..................4-6 72
MARSH (202 "Ain't Gonna Kiss Ya")........15-25 63
MARSH (203 "After Last Night") 10-20 63
PARKWAY (912 "They Played a Sad Song")..5-10 64

RIC & RAY & BOSSMEN
Singles: 7-inch
BOSS (2113 "One Look").........................30-40 63

RICARDOS
("Music by the Regal-Airs")
Singles: 7-inch
STAR-X (512 "Mary's Little Lamb").........75-125 58

RIC-A-SHAYS
Singles: 7-inch
LOLA (002 "Turn On") 10-20 65
Members: Ron Story; Harry Nilsson.
Also see NILSSON, Harry
Also see TRAVELERS

RICE, Eldon
Singles: 7-inch
EL-RIO (413 "Don't Let Love Break Your Heart")..500-750 61

RICE, Mack *R&B '65*
(Sir Mack Rice)
Singles: 7-inch
ATCO (6645 "Coal Man")..............................5-10 69
ATCO (7065 "I Can Never Be Satisfied") 4-6 76
BLUE ROCK (4014 "Mustang Sally") 5-10 65
CAPITOL..15-20
LU PINE (119 "My Baby") 5-10 64
LU PINE (125 "The Whip")..........................5-10 64
MAX DAY 5-10
MERCURY (72541 "It's All Right")............20-30 66
STAX 5-10 67-78
TRUTH 4-8 78
Also see FALCONS
Also see FIVE SCALDERS
Also see OLLIE & NIGHTINGALES

RICE, Ronnie
(With the Gents; with Silvertones; with Dalmatians)
Singles: 7-inch
IRC (6910 "Over the Mountain") 10-15 62
IRC (6912 "Maybe It's Because I Love You")..15-25 63
IRC (6917 "Come Back, Little Girl") 5-10 64
IRC (6931 "Tell Her")..................................5-10 66
LIMELIGHT (3029 "She's Not Yours")......15-25 64
MGM (13153 "I Know") 15-25 63
MGM (13228 "Bitter Tears").....................10-15 64
QUILL (106 "Warm Baby") 5-10 66
Also see NEW COLONY SIX

RICE, Tony
(With the Overtones)
Singles: 7-inch
ACTION (100 "My Darling You")..............10-20 60
PRINCETON (101 "Summer's Love").......50-75 60
RAE COX (106 "Little School Girl") 10-15 61

RICH, Buddy *LP '66*
(Buddy Rich Band)
Singles: 78 rpm
CLEF 4-8 54
NORGRAN..4-8 55-56
Singles: 7-inch
ARGO (5384 "Makin' Whoopee") 4-8 61
CLEF 5-10 54
EVEREST 4-6 71
GROOVE MERCHANT (1031 "The Bull")....4-6 75
LIBERTY (56188 "Keep the Customer Satisfied") 4-6 70
MCA 3-5 81
NORGRAN 5-10 55-56
PACIFIC JAZZ..4-6 66-67
RCA...4-6 76
EPs: 7-inch
NORGRAN 20-40 54-56
LPs: 10/12-inch
ARGO (676 "Playtime").............................35-45 61
CLEF (684 "Gene Krupa & Buddy Rich")..100-150 56
EMARCY..10-20 65-76
GREAT AMERICAN GRAMOPHONE..5-8 78
GROOVE MERCHANT...............................5-10 74-75
GRYPHON..5-10 79
LIBERTY 8-12 70
MCA...5-8 81
MERCURY (126 "Buddy Rich Story") 10-20 69
MERCURY (20448 "Rich vs. Roach")......50-75 59
(Monaural.)
MERCURY (20451 "Richcraft") 50-75 60
(Monaural.)
MERCURY (20461 "The Voice Is Rich")..40-60 60
(Monaural.)
MERCURY (60133 "Rich vs. Roach")......60-85 59
(Stereo.)
MERCURY (60136 "Richcraft") 60-85 60
(Stereo.)
MERCURY (60144 "The Voice Is Rich")..45-65 60
(Stereo.)
NORGRAN (26 "Swingin'")....................75-125 54
NORGRAN (1031 "Sing and Swing").......60-80 55
NORGRAN (1038 "Buddy Rich and Sweets Edison") 60-80 55
NORGRAN (1052 "Swingin'")..................60-80 55
NORGRAN (1078 "Wailing")....................50-75 56
NORGRAN (1086 "One for Basie") 50-75 56
PACIFIC JAZZ (Except 10000 series)........8-18 66-70
PACIFIC JAZZ (10000 series)....................5-8 81
PAUSA...5-8 '80s
RCA...8-12 72-77
ROOST 10-20 66
TRIP 8-10 76
VSP 10-15 67
VERVE (2009 "Buddy Rich Sings Johnny Mercer") 50-75 57
VERVE (8129 "Buddy Rich and Sweets Edison") 50-75 57
VERVE (8142 "Swingin'")........................50-75 57
VERVE (8168 "Wailin'")...........................50-75 57
VERVE (8176 "One for Basie")................50-75 57
VERVE (8285 "In Miami") 50-75 58
VERVE (8425 "Blue Caravan")................30-40 62
VERVE (8471 "Burnin' Beat") 30-40 62
(Monaural.)
VERVE (8484 "Drum Battle: Gene Krupa & Buddy Rich")..25-40 62
VERVE (68471 "Burnin' Beat") 35-45 62
(Stereo.)
VERVE (68778 "Super Rich") 10-15 69
VERVE (68824 "Monster")........................10-15 73
WHO'S WHO in JAZZ.................................5-10 78
WING 8-12 69
WORLD PACIFIC......................................10-15 68
Also see DAVIS, Sammy, Jr., & Buddy Rich
Also see TORME, Mel
Also see YOUNG, Lester, Nat "King" Cole & Buddy Rich

RICH, Charlie *P&R '60/C&W '68*
Singles: 7-inch
COLUMBIA..3-5 82
EPIC...3-6 70-81
ELEKTRA..3-6 78-81
GROOVE (0020 "She Loved Everybody But Me")...8-12 63
GROOVE (0025 "Big Boss Man")..............8-12 63
GROOVE (0032 "Lady Love") 8-12 64
GROOVE (0035 "My Mountain Dew")........8-12 64
GROOVE (0041 "Nice 'N' Easy")...............8-12 64
HI (2116 "Pass On By")...............................5-10 66
HI (2123 "My Heart Would Know") 5-10 67
HI (2134 "Only Me") 5-10 67
MERCURY..4-6 73-74

MONUMENT 4-6
PHILLIPS INT'L (3532 "Whirlwind") 25-35 58
PHILLIPS INT'L (3542 "Rebound") 25-35 59
PHILLIPS INT'L (3552 "Lonely Weekends") 20-30 59
PHILLIPS INT'L (3552 "Lonely Weekends") 20-30 60
PHILLIPS INT'L (3560 "Gonna Be Waiting") 20-30 60
PHILLIPS INT'L (3562 "On My Knees") ... 15-25 60
PHILLIPS INT'L (3566 "Who Will the Next Fool Be") 15-25 61
PHILLIPS INT'L (3572 "Just a Little Bit Sweet") 15-25 61
PHILLIPS INT'L (3576 "Easy Money") 15-25 62
PHILLIPS INT'L (3582 "Sittin' and Thinkin' ") 15-25 62
PHILLIPS INT'L (3584 "There's Another Place I Can't Go") 15-25 63
RCA (Except 8000 series) 4-6 74-77
RCA (8464 "It's All Over Now") 5-10 64
RCA (8468 "It's All Over Now") 5-10 64
RCA (8536 "There Won't Be Any More") 5-10 65
RCA (8817 "Nice 'N' Easy") 5-10 65
SSS/SUN .... 4-6 '70s
SMASH (1993 "Mohair Sam") 8-12 65
SMASH (2012 "Dance of Love") 8-12 65
SMASH (2022 "Something Just Came Over Me") 8-12 66
SMASH (2038 "No Home") 8-12 66
SMASH (2060 "That's My Way") 8-12 66
U.A. 3-6 78-80

Picture Sleeves

GROOVE (0020 "She Loved Everybody But Me") 10-20 63
EPIC (AE7-1065 "Big Boss Man") 4-8 73
(Promotional bonus only)
MONUMENT 4-6

EPs: 7-inch

EPIC (1099 "Silver Linings") 8-12 76
(Promotional issue only.)

LPs: 10/12-inch

BUCKBOARD .... 8-10 '70s
CAMDEN 8-10 70-74
CELEBRITY INT'L 5-8 91
EPIC (Except 139) 6-12 68-78
EPIC (139 "Everything You Wanted to Hear by Charlie Rich") 15-20 76
(Promotional issue only.)
ELEKTRA 5-10 80
51 WEST 5-10
GROOVE (G-1000 "Charlie Rich") 20-30 64
(Monaural.)
GROOVE (GS-1000 "Charlie Rich") 30-40 64
(Stereo.)
HARMONY 8-10 73
HI (Except 32037) 8-10 74-77
HI (32037 "Charlie Rich") 15-25 67
HILLTOP .... 8-10 '70s
MERCURY 10-15 74
PHILLIPS INT'L (1970 "Lonely Weekends") 500-800 60
PHONORAMA 5-8 83
PICKWICK .... 5-10 '70s
POWER PAK 8-10 74-75
RCA (Except 3000 series) 8-10 73-77
RCA (3000 series) 15-25 65-66
SSS/SUN 5-10 69-79
SMASH 15-25 65-66
SUNNYVALE 5-10 77
TIME-LIFE 5-10 81
TRIP 8-10 74
U.A. 5-10 78-79
WING 15-25 69

Session: Jordanaires; David Wills; Anita Kerr Singers; Gene Lowery Singers.
Also see CASH, Johnny
Also see HARRIS, Ray
Also see JORDANAIRES
Also see KERR, Anita
Also see LEWIS, Jerry Lee, Carl Perkins & Charlie Rich
Also see POWERS, Johnny
Also see SHERIDAN, Bobby
Also see TUBB, Ernest

RICH, Charlie, & Janie Fricke C&W '78

Singles: 7-inch

EPIC (50616 "On My Knees") 3-6 78
Also see FRICKE, Janie
Also see RICH, Charlie

RICH, Teddy, & Rockets
("Vocal by Kenny Hodge")

Singles: 7-inch

TEENAGE (501 "Gotta Rock, Gotta Roll") .... 20-30 '50s

RICH & RAYS

Singles: 7-inch

RICHLY (101 "My Heart") 50-75

RICHARD, Cliff P&R '59
(With the Drifters; with Shadows)

Singles: 12-inch

EMI AMERICA 4-8 83

Singles: 7-inch

ABC-PAR (10042 "Living Doll") 15-25 59
ABC-PAR (10066 "Dynamite") 20-30 59
ABC-PAR (10093 "Don't Be Mad at Me") .10-20 60
ABC-PAR (10109 "Fall in Love with You") 10-20 60
ABC-PAR (10136 "Please Don't Tease") .10-20 60
ABC-PAR (10175 "Catch Me, I'm Falling") 10-20 61
ABC-PAR (10195 "Mumblin' Mosie") 10-20 61
BIG TOP (3101 "Young Ones") 10-15 62
CAPITOL (4154 "Livin' Lovin' Doll") 10-20 59
DOT (16399 "Wonderful to Be Young") 5-10 62
EMI AMERICA 3-5 79-84
EPIC 4-8 63-67
MONUMENT 4-6 70-72
ROCKET 4-6 76-79
SIRE 4-6 73
STRIPED HORSE 3-5 87
UNI 5-10 68-69
W.B. 4-6 69

Picture Sleeves

EMI AMERICA 3-5 80-81
EPIC 8-15 63-66
STRIPED HORSE 3-5 87

LPs: 10/12-inch

ABC-PAR (ABC-321 "Cliff Sings") 40-60 60
(Monaural.)
ABC-PAR (ABCS-321 "Cliff Sings") 60-80 60
(Stereo.)
ABC-PAR (ABC-391 "Listen to Cliff") 35-50 61
(Monaural.)
ABC-PAR (ABCS-391 "Listen to Cliff") 50-75 61
(Stereo.)
EMI AMERICA 5-10 79-83
EPIC 15-25 63-65
ROCKET 5-10 76-78
Also see NEWTON-JOHN, Olivia, & Electric Light Orchestra
Also see NEWTON-JOHN, Olivia, & Cliff Richard
Also see SHADOWS

RICHARD, Robert

Singles: 78 rpm

KING (4274 "Wigwam Woman") 75-125 48
Also see RICHARD BROTHERS

RICHARD, Robert / Joseph Von Battle

Singles: 78 rpm

JVB (75828 "Cadillac Woman") 100-150 48
Also see RICHARD, Robert

RICHARD & SHELLS

Singles: 7-inch

TURNTABLE (150/1 "Something Different") 10-20 65

RICHARD & YOUNG LIONS P&R '66

Singles: 7-inch

PHILIPS (40381 "Open Up Your Door") ... 40-60 66
PHILIPS (40414 "Nasty") 5-10 66
PHILIPS (40438 "You Can Make It") 5-10 67

Picture Sleeves

PHILIPS (40381 "Open Up Your Door") ... 15-25 66
Members: Richard Tepp; Bob Freedman; Norm Cohen; Marc Lees; Jerry Raff; Freddy Randall; Ricky Rackin; Lou Vlahakas; Mark Greenberg.

RICHARD BROTHERS

Singles: 7-inch

RICHLAND (22 "Gonna Work") 100-150
STRATE 8 (1500 "Stolen Property") 30-50 59
Members: Robert Richard; Howard Richard.
Also see RICHARD, Robert

RICHARD'S COMBO

Singles: 7-inch

CARRIE (011 "Double Bad") 10-20 70

RICHARDS, Dick
(With Eddie Zack & Dude Ranchers)

Singles: 78 rpm

COLUMBIA (40957 "Blue-Jean Baby") 20-30 57

Singles: 7-inch

COLUMBIA (40957 "Blue-Jean Baby") 25-35 57
Also see ZACK, Eddie, & Cousin Richie

RICHARDS, Donald

Singles: 7-inch

CHEX (1003 "Hello Operator") 10-20 62

RICHARDS, Jack, & Falcons

Singles: 7-inch

DAWN (233 "Pretty Baby") 40-50 57

RICHARDS, Jay

Singles: 7-inch

GOLDBAND (1101 "Reach for a Moment") 10-20 60
GOLDBAND (1111 "Johnny Get Your Gun") 10-20 61
HOLLYWOOD (1099 "Gosh Dog Baby") 75-125 59
HOLLYWOOD (1100 "Echoes on My Mind") 40-60 59

RICHARDS, Jimmy

Singles: 7-inch

A&M 4-8 68-69
COLUMBIA (41083 "Cool As a Moose") .. 15-25 58
LAVETTE (1006 "I'm Blue") 40-50 64

RICHARDS, Joey

Singles: 7-inch

ASTRA (303 "Summer Love") 15-25 63

RICHARDS, Keith LP '88

Singles: 7-inch

ROLLING STONES (316 "Before They Make Me Run") 5-10 78
ROLLING STONES (39311 "Run Rudolph, Run") 4-6 79
VIRGIN (99287 "Take It So Hard") 3-5 88

Picture Sleeves

ROLLING STONES (316 "Before They Make Me Run") 10-15 78
VIRGIN (99287 "Take It So Hard") 4-6 88
(Promotional issue only.)

LPs: 10/12-inch

VIRGIN 5-8 88
Also see ROLLING STONES

RICHARDS, Penny

Singles: 7-inch

MOONGLOW (201 "I'll Be Yours") 40-50 61
Session: Paramours.
Also see PARAMOURS

RICHARDS, Tony
(With the Twilights)

Singles: 7-inch

CARLTON (572 "Wind-Up Toy") 5-10 62
COLPIX (178 "Please Believe in Me") 75-100 61
COLPIX (199 "Summer Is Comin' ") 20-30 61

RICHARDS, Trig

Singles: 7-inch

FALCON (205 "Hollywood Cat") 35-45

RICHARDS, Val

Singles: 7-inch

SCENE (601 "My Oh My") 30-45

RICHARDSON, Bobby, & Creations

Singles: 7-inch

EMBER (1076 "This Is Love") 15-25 61

RICHARDSON, Del
(With Herb Buchanan & Orchestra)

Singles: 7-inch

CORAL (62374 "All of Me") 5-10 63
MGM (13088 "Boys Night Out") 10-15 62
SMASH (1729 "Don't Cry Linda") 15-25 62
STELLAR (1010 "You Pass This Way Only Once") 15-25 62
STELLAR (1729 "Don't Cry Linda") 25-35 61
(First issue.)

RICHARDSON, George

Singles: 7-inch

SANDY (1031 "Close to You") 50-75 61

RICHARDSON, Gwen, & Cotillions

Singles: 7-inch

CB (5002 "That's My Baby") 30-40 63

RICHARDSON, Henry

Singles: 7-inch

ELOIS (303 "Dancing Girl") 15-25 67

RICHARDSON, Jape
(With His Japettes)

Singles: 78 rpm

MERCURY 15-25 57

Singles: 7-inch

MERCURY (71219 "Beggar to a King") ... 30-50 57
MERCURY (71312 "Teenage Moon") 25-50 58
Also see BIG BOPPER

RICHARDSON, Jimmy

Singles: 7-inch

HOLLYWOOD (1102 "The Drive") 5-10 60
NASHVILLE (5033 "Freeway") 10-15 61

LPs: 10/12-inch

STARDAY (126 "Sweet with a Beat") 10-15 60

RICHARDSON, Murle

Singles: 7-inch

CARON (6103 "Mean & Cruel") 200-300 58

RICHARDSON, Richie

Singles: 7-inch

GALAXY (103 "The Jump") 150-250 60

RICHARDSON, Rudi

Singles: 78 rpm

SUN (271 "Fools Hall of Fame") 25-50 57

Singles: 7-inch

SUN (271 "Fools Hall of Fame") 25-50 57

RICHARDSON, Rudy, Trio

Singles: 78 rpm

MANOR 15-25 46
MIRACLE (1057 "Hick-Botham") 30-40 48

RICHARDSON, Skeet

Singles: 7-inch

VIBRATONE (3075 "To My Baby") 300-500 63

RICHIE

Singles: 7-inch

KIP (241 "Cherie") 15-25 61

Picture Sleeves

KIP (241 "Cherie") 25-50 61

RICHIE, Darris

Singles: 7-inch

HARVEST (721 "Shake This Town") 50-75

RICHIE, Joe

Singles: 7-inch

BUDDY (122 "Across the Bay") 60-75 59

RICHIE & REBELS

Singles: 7-inch

BARCLAY (13348 "Rebel Rock") .... 15-25 '60s

RICHIE & REKNOWNS
(Richie & Renowns)

Singles: 7-inch

STREKE (247 "Please Say You Want Me") 40-50 63
(Shown as Richie & Renowns.)
STREKE (247 "Please Say You Want Me") 50-75 63
(Shown as Richie & Reknowns.)

RICHIE & ROYALS

Singles: 7-inch

GOLDEN CREST (573 "Be My Girl") 30-40 62
RELLO (1 "And When I'm Near You") 30-40 61
RELLO (3 "Be My Girl") 100-150 62
(First issue.)

RICHMOND, Faye

LPs: 10/12-inch

DAVIS (108 "For Men Only") 25-40 57

RICHMOND, Pat, & Fire Balls

Singles: 7-inch

VULCO (1500 "Don't Stop the Rockin' ") 100-150 58

RICHMOND GROUP / Earl Preston's Realms / Michael Allen Group

LPs: 10/12-inch

CAPITOL (T-2544 "Where It All Began") .. 20-25 66
(Monaural.)
CAPITOL (ST-2544 "Where It All Began") 25-30 66
(Stereo.)

RICHY, Paul
Singles: 7-inch
RICHWOOD (1000 "Framed")...10-15 59
SUN (338 "Legend of the Big Steeple")...15-25 60

RICK & FAIRLANES
Singles: 7-inch
TAP ("Liberty Bell Rock")...15-25 59
(Selection number not known.)

RICK & ISLANDERS
Singles: 7-inch
H&G (185 "Just for You")...15-25

RICK & KEENS P&R '61
Singles: 7-inch
AUSTIN (303 "Peanuts")...40-50 61
JAMIE (1219 "Your Turn to Cry")...10-15 62
LE CAM (133 "Darla")...15-25 61
LE CAM (721 "Peanuts")...40-50 61
SMASH (1705 "Peanuts")...15-20 61
SMASH (1722 "Popcorn")...10-15 61
TOLLIE (9016 "Darla")...10-15 64
TROY...20-30 63

RICK & LANCE
Singles: 7-inch
BIG TOP (3105 "Good Buddy")...10-15 62
BIG TOP (3133 "Laura Lee")...10-15 63
BIG TOP (3157 "Roses and Orchids")...10-15 63

RICK & LEGENDS
Singles: 7-inch
JD (155 "Diary of a Teenage Bride")...10-15 65
JD (162 "I Wonder Why")...10-15 65
U.A. (50093 "I Wonder Why")...10-15 66
Members: Rick Palmer; Jean Palmer; Jerry Nolan; Charles "Buz" Rose.
Also see PALMER, Rick

RICK & MASTERS
Singles: 7-inch
CAMEO (226 "Flame of Love")...20-30 62
CAMEO (247 "Let It Please Be You")...30-40 63
HARAL (778 "Bewitched, Bothered, Bewildered")...50-100 63
TABA (101 "Flame of Love")...100-200 62
Members: Tony Tromdetta; Frank Condo; Rick Finizo; Mike Silenzio.
Also see LYNN, Billy
Also see RYDELL, Bobby
Also see YOUNG, Bobby

RICK & RAVENS
(Featuring Ray Daniels)
Singles: 7-inch
AURA (4506 "Henrietta")...40-50 64
AURA (4511 "Soul Train")...30-40 65
POSAE (101 "Big Bucket T")...40-50 '60s
Member: Ray Daniels.
Also see MANZAREK, Ray

RICK & RICK-A-SHAYS
Singles: 7-inch
REPRISE (20,226 "The Drag")...10-15 63
(First issued by Eddie Ford. First reissue is by the Mar-Villes.)
Also see FORD, Eddie
Also see MAR-VILLES

RICK & RONNIE
Singles: 7-inch
SPRITE (5001 "Don't Do Me This Way"). 15-25 66

RICKELS, Rick
(With His Wild Guitar)
Singles: 7-inch
BISHOP (1001 "I'm Gone")...4-6 80
MH (2 "I'm Gone")...200-300

RICKIE & HALLMARKS
Singles: 7-inch
AMY (877 "Wherever You Are")...20-30 63
Member: Rick Lisi.

RICKIE & JENNELL
Singles: 78 rpm
FLAIR (1033 "This Time It's Real")...10-20 54
Singles: 7-inch
FLAIR (1033 "This Time It's Real")...25-40 54
Members: Richard Berry; Jennell Hawkins.
Also see BERRY, Richard
Also see HAWKINS, Jennell

RICKMAN, Joe
Singles: 7-inch
WESTWOOD (204 "Lonely Heart")...300-400

RICKOCHETS
Singles: 7-inch
BON BON (1313 "Monkey Scratch")...10-20 63
Also see COYNE, Ricky, & His Guitar Rockers

RICKS, Jimmy
(James Ricks; with the Rickateers; with Raves; with Surburbans)
Singles: 78 rpm
JOSIE...10-20 56
MERCURY...20-30 54
PARIS...10-20 57
Singles: 7-inch
ARNOLD (1011 "Canadian Sunset")...8-12 63
ATCO (6193 "Young At Heart")...10-15 61
ATCO (6220 "Daddy Rollin' Stone")...20-40 62
ATLANTIC (2246 "Romance in the Dark")..8-12 64
BATON (236 "I'm a Fool to Want You")...10-20 57
DECCA (30443 "Lazy Mule")...15-25 57
FELSTED (8560 "Secret Love")...15-25 59
FELSTED (8582 "Here Come the Tears Again")...15-25 59
FELSTED (8694 "Anytime")...15-25 64
FESTIVAL (703 "Ol Man River")...50-75 66
FESTIVAL (25004 "Daddy Rollin' Stone")...15-25 62
FURY (1070 "I Wonder")...10-15 62
JOSIE (796 "She's Fine, She's Mine")...30-40 56
JUBILEE (5559 "Lonely Man")...5-10 67
JUBILEE (5561 "Wigglin' and Gigglin'")...5-10 67
JUBILEE (5619 "Snap Your Fingers")...5-10 68
MERCURY (8296 "Too Soon")...40-60 52
PARIS (504 "Do You Promise")...10-15 57
SIGNATURE (12013 "At Sunrise")...10-20 59
SIGNATURE (12040 "I Needed Your Love")...10-20 60
LPs: 10/12-inch
JUBILEE (8021 "Tell Her You Love Her")...10-20 69
MAINSTREAM (6050 "Vibrations")...15-25 65
SIGNATURE (1032 "Jimmy Ricks")...150-250 60
Also see BAKER, LaVern, & Jimmy Ricks
Also see RAVENS
Also see SUBURBANS

RICKS, Travis
Singles: 78 rpm
FLAIR (1033 "This Time It's Real")...10-15 54
Singles: 7-inch
FLAIR (1033 "This Time It's Real")...30-40 54
ORDELL (502 "No Need to Cry")...10-15 63

RICKY, Ron, & Semi-Tones
Singles: 7-inch
SEMI-TONE (1 "There's a Girl in My Heart")...150-250

RICKY & HITCH-HIKERS
Singles: 7-inch
DORE (690 "Undertow")...10-20 63
(Reissued as by Billy Joe & Checkmates.)

RICKY & LEXINGTONS
Singles: 7-inch
SATELLITE...10-15 '60s
Member: Rick Nichols.
Also see NICHOLS, Rick

RICKY & RAYLENE
Singles: 7-inch
TEE PEE (17/18 "It Must Be Love"/"Light of Day")...10-20 67
Members: Ricky Leigh Smolinski; Raylene Loos; Roger Loos; Tom Loos.
Also see RAYLENE & BLUE ANGELS

RICKY & STOMPERS
Singles: 7-inch
PRINCETON (102 "Wild One")...50-75 58

RICKY & VACELS
Singles: 7-inch
EXPRESS (711 "Lorraine")...15-25 62
FARGO (1050 "His Girl")...30-40 63
(Black vinyl.)
FARGO (1050 "His Girl")...50-75 63
(Blue vinyl.)
Also see VACELS

RICO & RAVENS
Singles: 7-inch
AUTUMN (6 "Don't You Know")...8-12 64
COLLECTABLES...3-5 '80s
RALLY (1601 "Don't You Know")...15-25 65

RICOCHETTES
(Ar Stevens & Ricochettes)
Singles: 7-inch
DESTINATION (629 "I Don't Want You")..15-25 67
CONTINENTAL (500 "Find Another Boy")...10-20 66
MEAN MT. (1424 "Rock On")...3-5 82
QUILL (102 "Losing You")...25-50 66
RAYNARD (10030 "I'll Be Back")...5-10 65
UNIVERSAL ("I'll Be Back")...15-25 '60s
(Promotional issue only. No selection number used.)
Picture Sleeves
MEAN MT. (1424 "Rock On")...3-6 82
Members: Ar Stevens; Jerry Wollenzien; Herb Hohnke; John Galobich; Bob Heuhofer; Mick Milewski; Bruce Cole.

RIC-SHAWS
Singles: 7-inch
DELMA (111 "Sometimes I Have to Cry")...15-25

RIDDELL, Allan C&W '60
Singles: 7-inch
FLING (723 "Moon Is Crying")...100-200 61
PLAID (1001 "Moon Is Crying")...150-250 60

RIDDLE, Don
(Don Riddle 5)
Singles: 7-inch
GENERAL AMERICAN (723 "Don't Be Cruel")...30-40 65

RIDDLE, George
(Georgie Riddle)
Singles: 7-inch
KNOX (2 "Tell Me Truly Baby")...100-200
STARDAY...5-10 65-67
U.A....8-12 61-64

RIDDLE, Ricky, & His Band
Singles: 78 rpm
DECCA...15-25 56
MGM...10-20 54
TENNESSEE (758 "Cold Icy Feet")...25-35 51
Singles: 7-inch
DECCA (29813 "I'm a Whip-Crackin' Daddy")...15-25 56
MGM (11741 "Steamboat Boogie")...20-30 54

RIDDLE, Tommy
Singles: 7-inch
STAIRCASE ("Rayford Line")...100-200
(No selection number used.)

RIDERS OF THE MARK
Singles: 7-inch
20TH FOX (6694 "The Electronic Insides and Metal Complexion That Make Up Herr Doktor Kreig")...15-25 67

RIDERS OF THE PURPLE SAGE
EPs: 7-inch
ROYALE (191 "Riders of the Purple Sage")...10-20 '50s
Members: Foy Willing; Eddie Dean.
Also see DEAN, Eddie
Also see WILLING, Foy, Eddie Dean & His Riders Of The Purple Sage

RIDGLEY, Tommy
Singles: 78 rpm
DECCA...20-40 51
HERALD...10-20 56-57
IMPERIAL...20-40 50-53
Singles: 7-inch
ATLANTIC (1009 "Oh Lawdy")...35-45 53
ATLANTIC (1039 "Jam Up")...15-25 54
ATLANTIC (2000 series)...5-10 62
DECCA (48226 "Anything But Love")...40-60 51
HEP'ME...5-8
HERALD...10-20 57-59
IMPERIAL (5198 "I Live My Life")...50-100 52
IMPERIAL (5203 "Looped")...50-100 52
IMPERIAL (5214 "Monkey Man")...50-100 53
IMPERIAL (5223 "Good Times")...50-100 53
INTERNATIONAL CITY...5-10
JOHEN...5-10 64
MAISON DE SOUL...4-8
ORBIT...10-15
RIC...10-15 60-63
RONN...4-8 69
SANSU...5-10
WHITE CLIFFS...4-8 67
LPs: 10/12-inch
ROUNDER...5-8

RIDLEY, Jimmy, & the Sentinels
Singles: 7-inch
HEM (101 "Rock-A-Bye Baby")...100-125 58

RIENZI, Nino
Singles: 7-inch
TRANS ATLAS (699 "Persian King")...50-75 62

RIFF, Eddie
(Mickey Baker)
Singles: 7-inch
DOVER (102 "My Baby's Gone Away")200-300 57
Also see BAKER, Mickey

RIFFS
Singles: 7-inch
JAMIE (1296 "Tell Her")...8-12 65
LUBEE (1296 "Tell Her")...15-25 64
OLD TOWN (1179 "Tell Tale Friends")...50-75 65
SUNNY (22 "Little Girl")...100-200 64
Also see CHIMES

RIGHTEOUS BROTHERS P&R '63
(With the Righteous Brothers Band; with Mike Patterson Band; with Paramours)
Singles: 7-inch
COLLECTABLES...3-5 '80s
ERIC...3-5 '80s
HAVEN (800 "Hold On")...4-8 76
HAVEN (7002 "Rock and Roll Heaven")...4-8 74
HAVEN (7004 "Give It to the People")...4-8 74
HAVEN (7006 "Dream On")...4-8 74
HAVEN (7011 "Never Say I Love You")...4-8 75
HAVEN (7014 "Substitute")...4-8 75
MGM (507 "You've Lost That Lovin' Feelin'")...4-6 78
MGM (541 "Unchained Melody")...4-6 79
MICROGROOVE (167 "The Righteous Brothers with Patricia Crowley – Open-End Interview") 10-20 67
(Promotional issue only.)
MOONGLOW (215 "Little Latin Lupe Lu")...10-20 62
(Black vinyl.)
MOONGLOW (215 "Little Latin Lupe Lu")...100-150 62
(Red vinyl. Promotional issue only.)
MOONGLOW (223 "My Babe")...10-15 63
MOONGLOW (224 "Koko Jo")...10-15 63
MOONGLOW (231 "Try to Find Another Man")...10-15 64
MOONGLOW (234 "Bring Your Love to Me")...10-15 64
MOONGLOW (235 "This Little Girl of Mine")...10-15 64
MOONGLOW (238 "Bring Your Love to Me")...10-15 65
MOONGLOW (239 "You Can Have Her")...10-15 65
MOONGLOW (242 "Justine")...10-15 65
MOONGLOW (243 "For Your Love")...10-15 65
MOONGLOW (244 "Georgia on My Mind")...10-15 66
MOONGLOW (245 "Bring Your Love to Me")...10-15 66
PHILLES (124 "You've Lost That Lovin' Feelin'")...10-20 64
(Colored vinyl pressings are 1979 bootlegs.)
PHILLES (127 "Just Once in My Life")...10-20 65
PHILLES (129 "Unchained Melody")...10-20 65
(Colored vinyl pressings are 1979 bootlegs.)
PHILLES (130 "Ebb Tide")...1000-1500 65
(Custom label. Has Phil Spector's picture on the label. Promotional issue only.)
PHILLES (130 "Ebb Tide")...10-20 65
(No picture on label.)
PHILLES (132 "White Cliffs of Dover")...15-25 66
POLYDOR BAND OF GOLD (507 "You've Lost That Lovin' Feelin'")...3-6
STARDUST (1295 "Unchained Melody")...3-5 '90s
VERVE (10383 "Soul and Inspiration")...5-10 66
VERVE (10406 "He")...5-10 66
VERVE (10430 "Go Ahead and Cry")...5-10 66
VERVE (10449 "On This Side of Goodbye")...5-10 66

VERVE (10479 "Along Came Jones") 8-12 67
VERVE (10507 "Melancholy Music Man")..5-10 67
VERVE (10520 "Go Ahead and Cry") 5-10 67
VERVE (10521 "Hold On, I'm Coming") 5-10 67
VERVE (10522 "Melancholy Music Man")..5-10 67
VERVE (10523 "Island in the Sun") 5-10 67
VERVE (10524 "Something You Got") 5-10 67
VERVE (10551 "Stranded in the Middle of Noplace") 5-10 67
VERVE (10577 "Here I Am") 8-12 67
VERVE (10637 "You've Lost That Lovin' Feeling") 4-8 69
VERVE (10648 "Woman, Man Needs Ya") ..4-8 69
(With Jimmy Walker instead of Bill Medley.)
VERVE (10649 "Po Folks") 4-8 69
(With Jimmy Walker instead of Bill Medley.)
VERVE CELEBRITY SCENE (8 "Righteous Brothers") 50-75 66
(Boxed set of five singles – 10520 through 10524 – with bio insert. Some sets include juke box title strips.)
VERVE FORECAST (871882 "Unchained Melody") 3-5 90
VERVE SOUNDS OF FAME (138 thru 142) 4-8 68

Picture Sleeves

PHILLES (127 "Just Once in My Life") 25-35 65
PHILLES (130 "Ebb Tide") 15-25 65
PHILLES (132 "White Cliffs of Dover") 15-25 66
VERVE (10383 "Soul and Inspiration") 8-12 66
VERVE (10406 "He") 8-12 66
VERVE (10430 "Go Ahead and Cry") .. 100-200 66
VERVE (10551 "Stranded in the Middle of Noplace") 8-12 67

EPs: 7-inch

MGM (002 "Righteous Brothers") 10-20 67
MOONGLOW (71004 "Best of the Righteous Brothers") 10-20 66
(Juke box issue.)

LPs: 10/12-inch

CHADWICK (1020 "Righteous Brothers") 10-15 84
(Two discs. Mail-order offer.)
HAVEN (9201 "Give It to the People") 10-15 74
HAVEN (9203 "Sons of Mrs. Righteous") 15-25 75
MGM (4885 "History of the Righteous Brothers") 10-15 73
MOONGLOW (1001 "Right Now") 20-30 63
MOONGLOW (1002 "Some Blue Eyed Soul") 20-30 64
MOONGLOW (1003 "This Is New") 20-30 65
MOONGLOW (1004 "The Best of the Righteous Brothers) 20-30 66
PHILLES (4007 "You've Lost That Lovin' Feeling") 35-45 64
PHILLES (4008 "Just Once in My Life") .. 35-45 65
PHILLES (4009 "Back to Back") 35-45 66
PHILLES (90677 "Back to Back") 30-40 66
(Capitol Record Club issue.)
PHILLES (90692 "You've Lost That Lovin' Feelin' ") 30-40 66
(Capitol Record Club issue.)
VERVE (5001 "Soul and Inspiration") 15-25 66
VERVE (5004 "Go Ahead and Cry") 15-25 66
VERVE (5010 "Sayin' Something") 15-25 67
VERVE (5020 "Greatest Hits") 15-25 67
VERVE (5031 "Souled Out") 15-25 67
VERVE (5051 "Standards") 15-25 68
VERVE (5058 "One for the Road") 15-25 68
VERVE (5071 "Greatest Hits, Vol. II") 15-25 69
VERVE (5076 "Re-Birth") 15-25 69
(With Jimmy Walker instead of Bill Medley.)
VERVE (90669 "Soul and Inspiration") 15-25 66
(Capitol Record Club issue.)
VERVE (91057 "Sayin' Somethin' ") 15-25 67
(Capitol Record Club issue.)
VERVE (91298 "Greatest Hits") 15-25 67
(Capitol Record Club issue.)
Members: Bill Medley; Bobby Hatfield.
Also see HATFIELD, Bobby
Also see MEDLEY, Bill
Also see NEWELL, Skip, & Mustangs
Also see PARAMOURS
Also see PEPPERS
Also see PREACHERS
Also see RIGHTEOUS BROTHERS BAND
Also see WALKER, Jimmy

RIGHTEOUS BROTHERS / Ronnie Baxter

Singles: 7-inch

LAKE (2000 "Don't Give Up On Me"/"Someone to Love Me") 8-12
Also see BAXTER, Ronnie

RIGHTEOUS BROTHERS BAND

Singles: 7-inch

VERVE (10403 "Rat Race") 10-15 66
Also see RIGHTEOUS BROTHERS

RIGUEZ, Rod

Singles: 7-inch

IMPACT (1031 "You'd Like to Admit It") ...15-25 67
SUSSEX 10-20 71-72

RIKI & RIKATONES

Singles: 7-inch

MANHATTAN (201 "TNT") 200-250

RILEY, Billy Lee — P&R '72

(With His Little Green Men; Bill Riley)

Singles: 78 rpm

SUN 25-75 56-57

Singles: 7-inch

ATLANTIC (2525 "Happy Man") 5-10 68
BRUNSWICK (55085 "Rockin' on the Moon") 150-250 58
ENTRANCE 4-8 72
GNP (371 "That's the Bag I'm In") 5-10 66
GNP (377 "Way I Feel") 5-10 66
HIP (8006 "Family Portrait") 5-10 68
HIP (8011 "Show Me Your Soul") 5-10 69
HOME OF THE BLUES (233 "Flip Flop and Fly") 20-30 61
MERCURY (72314 "Bo Diddley") 8-12 64
MERCURY (72385 "Charlene") 5-10 65
MOJO (1933 "Southern Soul") 5-10 67
MOJO (3611 "Valley of the Dolls") 8-12 67
RITA (1013 "That's What I Want") 10-20 61
SUN (245 "Rock with Me Baby") 50-100 56
SUN (260 "Flying Saucers Rock & Roll") 50-100 57
(Counterfeits exist of this release.)
SUN (277 "Red Hot") 35-55 57
SUN (289 "Wouldn't You Know") 15-25 58
SUN (313 "No Name Girl") 15-25 58
SUN (322 "Got the Water Boiling") 50-75 59
SSS/SUN 4-8 69-70

LPs: 10/12-inch

CROWN (5277 "Harmonica & the Blues") 50-100 63
GNP (2020 "Funk Harmonica") 15-20 66
GNP (2028 "Billy Lee Riley in Action") 15-20 66
MERCURY (20965 "Big Harmonica Special") 15-25 64
(Monaural.)
MERCURY (20974 "Harmonica Beatlemania") 25-35 64
(Monaural.)
MERCURY (20985 "Whiskey-A-Go-Go Presents Billy Lee Riley") 15-25 65
(Monaural.)
MERCURY (60965 "Big Harmonica Special") 20-30 64
(Stereo.)
MERCURY (60974 "Harmonica Beatlemania") 40-60 64
(Stereo.)
MERCURY (60985 "Whiskey-A-Go-Go Presents Billy Lee Riley") 20-30 65
(Stereo.)
MOJO (1933 "Southern Soul") 30-50 79
Also see ALTON & JIMMY
Also see DONN, Larry
Also see HOOPER, Jess, & Daydreamers
Also see JANES, Roland
Also see LEE, Daaron
Also see LIGHTNIN' LEON
Also see MEGATONS
Also see ROCKIN' STOCKINGS
Also see WILEY, Skip

RILEY, Bob

(With Jack Hansen Orchestra & Chorus; "Bob Riley and His Magic Guitar")

Singles: 78 rpm

VIKIM (7661 "Too Late") 5-10 56

Singles: 7-inch

COFFEE HOUSE (3001 "Sylvie") 10-20
CORAL (62002 "Mr. Bluebird") 10-15 58
CORAL (62125 "I Think It's a Shame") 10-20 59
DOT (15625 "Without Your Love") 15-25 57
MGM (12612 "Wanda Jean") 75-100 58
ST. CLAIR (1003 "Case O' the Blues") 5-10 66
TIBOR (4500 "Weekend Vacation") 8-12 61
VIKIM (1333 "The Strange Little Girl") 8-12
VIKIM (7661 "Too Late") 10-20 56
YORK (805 "Big Dog") 75-125 59

EPs: 7-inch

CORAL (81186 "Bruce Morrow's Musical Museum") 25-50 59
Also see MORROW, Bruce

RILEY, Otis

(With the Losers)

Singles: 7-inch

KAPPA (208 "Rock & Roll Riley") 100-150 58
KAPPA (209 "Little Miss Bibbity Bobbity") 60-75 58
SPHINX (6108 "Goodbye Love") 15-25 61

RILEY, Pat

(With His Tin Pan Alley Trio & Orchestra)

Singles: 7-inch

REED (1201 "Little Bop-a-Little") 75-100 60
TIN PAN ALLEY (175 "Without You to Love") 125-150 57
TIN PAN ALLEY (185 "No Regrets Have I") 100-125 57

RILEY, Russ, & Five Sounds

(With Al Browne's Orchestra)

Singles: 7-inch

ALJON (115 "Tonight Must Live On") ...300-400 61
ARCADE (1005 "Tonight Must Live On") ...5-10 77

RINCON SURFSIDE BAND

Singles: 7-inch

DUNHILL (1 "Surfing Songbook") 10-20 65
(Promotional issue only. Excerpts from the LP *Surfing Songbook*.)

Picture Sleeves

DUNHILL (1 "Surfing Songbook") 20-30 65
(Promotional issue only.)

LPs: 10/12-inch

DUNHILL (50001 "Surfing Songbook") 50-75 65
Also see FANTASTIC BAGGYS

RINGLEADERS

Singles: 7-inch

M-PAC (7232 "Let's Start Over") 50-100 66

RINGO, Eddie

Singles: 7-inch

TWIN STAR (1016 "Full Racing Cam") ..75-125 60

RINGO, Jimmy

Singles: 7-inch

DOT (15787 "I Like This Kind of Music") ..15-25 58

RINGO, Ron, & Originals

Singles: 7-inch

JUGGY (701 "Queen of the Jerk") 15-25 64

RINKY-DINKS — P&R/R&B '58

(Featuring Bobby Darin)

Singles: 7-inch

ATCO (6121 "Early in the Morning") 25-50 58
(Previously issued as by the Ding Dongs. Later issued as by "Bobby Darin & the Rinky Dinks.")
Also see DARIN, Bobby

RINKY DINKS

Singles: 7-inch

ENJOY (1010 "Hot Potato") 10-15 62
(Reissued as *Soultrain*, by the Ramrods.)
EVERLAST (5029 "Hot Potato") 5-10 65
Member: King Curtis.
Also see KING CURTIS
Also see RAMRODS

RIO, Bobby

(With the Revelles; Bobby "King" Rio)

Singles: 7-inch

ABC-PAR (10656 "Boy Meets Girl") 10-15 65
LENOX (5569 "I Got You") 10-15 63
MERCURY (72221 "Don Diddley") 10-15 63
MIO INT'L (100 "My Kind of Jungle") 15-25 63

RIO, Chuck

(Chuck "Tequila" Rio & Originals; with Individuals; with Kreshendos; Danny Flores)

Singles: 7-inch

CHALLENGE 10-20 58-60
FLAIR (103 "Big Boy") 15-25 62
JACKPOT (48016 "Margarita") 15-25 59
KENT (308 "Bye Bye Baby") 15-25 58
SATURN (402 "Kreschendo Stomp") 15-25 63
TEQUILA (103 "If You Were the Only Girl in the World") 400-500 60
Also see CHAMPS
Also see CONTENDERS
Also see CRESCHENDOES
Also see FLORES, Danny
Also see INDIVIDUALS
Also see ORIGINALS
Also see PERSUADERS
Also see ROSS, Johnny

RIO, Chuck, & Delaney

Singles: 7-inch

TOPPA (1976 "Doin' the Bossa Nova") 8-12 62
Members: Chuck Rio; Delaney Bramlett.
Also see RIO, Chuck

RIO & LITTLE RED RYDERS

Singles: 7-inch

LANJO (7780 "You Better Believe It") 75-125 60

RIO ROCKERS

Singles: 7-inch

CAPITOL (3884 "Mexican Rock & Roll")..40-60 58
Members: Don Cole; Paul Smith; Rusty Isabell; Sam Babcock; Eskew Reeder.
Also see COLE, Don
Also see ISABELL, Rusty
Also see REEDER, Eskew

RIOS, Augie — P&R '58

(With the Notations)

Singles: 7-inch

MGM 10-15 60-64
METRO 10-20 58-59
SHELLEY (Except 181) 10-20 63-64
SHELLEY (181 "I've Got a Girl") 40-50 63

RIOS, Johnny

Singles: 7-inch

SPANORAMIC ("I Go Wild") 50-75
(Selection number not known.)

RIP CHORDS — P&R '63

Singles: 7-inch

COLUMBIA (42687 "Here I Stand") 10-15 63
COLUMBIA (42812 "Gone") 10-15 63
(Black vinyl.)
COLUMBIA (42812 "Gone") 20-30 63
(Green vinyl. Promotional issue only.)
COLUMBIA (42921 "Hey Little Cobra") 10-15 63
(Black vinyl.)
COLUMBIA (42921 "Hey Little Cobra") 20-30 63
(Red vinyl. Promotional issue only.)
COLUMBIA (43035 "Three Window Coupe") 10-15 64
(Black vinyl.)
COLUMBIA (43035 "Three Window Coupe") 20-30 64
(Red vinyl. Promotional issue only.)
COLUMBIA (43093 "One-Piece, Topless Bathing Suit") 10-15 64
COLUMBIA (43221 "Don't Be Scared") ...10-15 64
COLUMBIA (3-42000 series) 10-20 63
(Compact 33 singles.)

Picture Sleeves

COLUMBIA (42687 "Here I Stand") 15-25 63
(Promotional issue only.)
COLUMBIA (42812 "Gone") 15-25 63

LPs: 10/12-inch

COLUMBIA (2151 "Hey Little Cobra") 25-35 64
(Monaural.)
COLUMBIA (2216 "Three Window Coupe") 30-40 64
(Monaural.)
COLUMBIA (8951 "Hey Little Cobra") 25-35 64
(Stereo.)
COLUMBIA (9016 "Three Window Coupe") 30-40 64
(Stereo.)
Members: Bruce Johnston; Terry Melcher; Phil Stewart; Ernie Bringas; Steve Barri; Phil Sloan; Glen Campbell; Hal Blaine; Tommy Tedesco.
Also see BRUCE & TERRY
Also see CAMPBELL, Glen
Also see FANTASTIC BAGGYS
Also see MIKE & DEAN
Also see ROGUES
Also see TEDESCO, Tommy

RIP TIDES

Singles: 7-inch

CHALLENGE (59058 "Deep Blue") 15-25 59

RIP-CHORDS

Singles: 78 rpm

ABCO 100-200 56

Singles: 7-inch

ABCO (105 "I Love You the Most") ... 750-1000 56
(Black vinyl.)
ABCO (105 "I Love You the Most") .. 2000-3000 56
(Red vinyl.)

RIP-CHORDS

Singles: 7-inch

M.M.I. (1236 "I Laughed So Hard") ... 100-150 58

RIPLEY COTTON CHOPPERS

Singles: 78 rpm

SUN (190 "Silver Bells") ... 1000-2000 53

RIPPLES

Singles: 7-inch

BOND (1479 "Please Let Me Love You") ... 500-750 60

RIPPLES & WAVES PLUS MICHAEL

(Jackson Five)

Singles: 7-inch

STEELTOWN (688 "Let Me Carry Your School Books") ... 35-50 69
(Mono. "Steeltown" is in all upper case letters on label.)
STEELTOWN (688 "Let Me Carry Your School Books") ... 50-75 69
(Stereo. "Steeltown" is in upper and lower case letters.)
Also see JACKSONS

RISERS

LPs: 10/12-inch

IMPERIAL (9269 "She's a Bad Motorcycle") ... 20-30 64
(Monaural.)
IMPERIAL (12269 "She's a Bad Motorcycle") ... 20-30 64
(Stereo.)

RISING SONS

Singles: 7-inch

AMY (931 "Talk to Me Baby") ... 5-10 65

RISING SONS

Singles: 7-inch

COLUMBIA (43534 "Candy Man") ... 15-25 66
Members: Taj Mahal; Ed Cassidy; Ry Cooder; Kevin Kelly; Gary Marker; Jesse Lee Kincade.
Also see COODER, Ry
Also see MAHAL, Taj
Also see SPIRIT

RISING SONS

Singles: 7-inch

UPSTATE (600 "I'm Feeling Down") ... 10-15 66

RISING STORM

LPs: 10/12-inch

ARF ARF (007 "Alive in Anover Again") 75-100 83
(Numbered edition of 1,000 copies.)
REMNANT (3571 "Calm Before . . .the Rising Storm") ... 1000-1500 66
STANTON PARK (001 "Calm Before . . .the Rising Storm") ... 8-10 91
(Reissued using original cover art.)
Members: Tony Thompson; Todd Cohen; Bob Cohan; Tom Scheft; Charlie Rockwell; Rich Weinberg.

RITA & TIERRAS

Singles: 7-inch

DORE (783 "Gone with the Wind Is My Love") ... 75-125 67

RITCHIE, John

Singles: 7-inch

20TH FOX (269 "Gone, Gone, Gone") ... 20-30 61

RITCHIE, Little Joe

LPs: 10/12-inch

BRUNSWICK ... 10-15 68

RITCHIE & RUNAROUNDS

Singles: 7-inch

ASCOT (2136 "Lost in the Crowd") ... 15-25 63
Members: Lou Christie; Kripp Johnson.
Also see CHRISTIE, Lou
Also see JOHNSON, Kripp

RITENOUR, Lee — LP '77

Singles: 7-inch

ELEKTRA ... 3-5 81-82
EPIC ... 3-6 76-80

Picture Sleeves

ELEKTRA ... 3-5 81

LPs: 10/12-inch

ELEKTRA ... 5-8 78-84
EPIC ... 5-10 76-80
GRP ... 5-8 85
JVC ... 5-10 78
MFSL (147 "Captain Fingers") ... 25-35 85
MUSICIAN ... 5-8 82

RITES OF SPRING

Singles: 7-inch

PARKWAY (109 "Why") ... 15-25 66

RITTER, Tex — C&W/P&R '44

(With the Texans; with Plainsmen)

Singles: 78 rpm

CAPITOL ... 5-10 44-57
CHAMPION ... 10-20 '30s
CONQUEROR ... 10-20 '30s
DECCA ... 5-10 35-41
U.A. ("High Noon Ballad—Do Not Forsake Me") ... 30-40 52
(Single-sided disc. Promotional issue only.)

Singles: 7-inch

CAPITOL (1100 thru 3900 series) ... 10-20 50-58
(Purple labels.)
CAPITOL (2000 thru 4000 series) ... 4-8 68-76
(Orange labels.)
CAPITOL (4000 thru 5900 series) ... 5-15 58-67
CAPITOL (10485 "High Noon") ... 25-35 52
(Single-sided disc. Promotional issue only.)

Picture Sleeves

CAPITOL ... 5-10 68

EPs: 7-inch

CAPITOL (Except 431) ... 10-20 59-60
CAPITOL (431 "Tex Ritter Sings") ... 20-40 53

LPs: 10/12-inch

ALBUM GLOBE ... 5-8 '80s
BUCKBOARD ... 5-8 '80s
CAPITOL (213 thru 467) ... 8-12 69-71
CAPITOL (971 "Songs from the Western Screen") ... 25-40 58
CAPITOL (1100 "Psalms") ... 20-30 59
CAPITOL (T-1292 "Blood on the Saddle") ... 15-25 60
(Monaural.)
CAPITOL (ST-1292 "Blood on the Saddle") ... 15-30 60
(Stereo.)
CAPITOL (SM-1292 "Blood on the Saddle") ... 5-10 78
CAPITOL (1623 thru 2800) ... 10-20 61-68
CAPITOL (W-1562 "The Lincoln Hymns") ... 25-30 61
(Monaural.)
CAPITOL (SW-1562 "The Lincoln Hymns") ... 30-35 61
(Stereo.)
CAPITOL (4004 "Cowboy Favorites") ... 50-75 53
(10-inch LP.)
CORONET ... 8-12 '60s
HILLTOP ... 10-15 '60s
LA BREA (8036 "Jamboree") ... 30-40 62
PICKWICK/HILLTOP ... 6-12 66-68
PREMIER ... 5-10
SHASTA ... 8-12 '60s
SPIN-O-RAMA ... 8-12 '60s
Session: Rio Grande River Boys; Spud Goodall.
Also see KENTON, Stan, & Tex Ritter

RITTER, Tex / Merle Travis

Singles: 7-inch

CAPITOL (40143 "Fort Worth Jail"/"Sioux City Sue") ... 20-35 '50s
(One 45 from *Cowboy Hit Parade*, Capitol album ADF-4000, a multi-disc set. At this time, we lack the titles and artists for the other records in what we presume to be a boxed set. Probably also issued on 78 rpm.)
Also see RITTER, Tex
Also see TRAVIS, Merle

RITUAL

Singles: 7-inch

HASTLE (1306 "Speed Freak") ... 25-35 69

RITUALS

Singles: 7-inch

ARWIN (120 "Girl in Zanzibar") ... 10-20 59
ARWIN (127 "This Is Paradise") ... 15-25 64
ARWIN (128 "Surfer's Rule") ... 10-20 64
Member: Arnie Ginsburg.
Also see JAN & ARNIE

RIVALS

Singles: 78 rpm

APOLLO (1166 "Don't Say You're Sorry Again") ... 25-50 50

RIVALS

Singles: 7-inch

DARRYL (722 "I Must See You Again") ... 40-50 57
JUNIOR (990 "I Must See You Again") ... 400-500 63
PUFF (1001 "Love Me") ... 40-50 62
PUFF (3912 "She's Mine") ... 20-30 62
TREYCO (401 "I'll Never Walk Alone") ... 20-30 63

RIVALS

(With T.J. Fowler's Band)

Singles: 7-inch

LU PINE (118 "It's Gonna Work Out Fine") ... 15-25 64

RIVER ROVERS

Singles: 78 rpm

APOLLO (432 "Bald Headed Daddy") ... 40-60 51

Singles: 7-inch

APOLLO (432 "Bald Headed Daddy") .. 100-200 51

RIVERA, Little Bobby, & Hemlocks

Singles: 78 rpm

FURY (1004 "Cora Lee") ... 75-125 57

Singles: 7-inch

FURY (1004 "Cora Lee") ... 75-125 57
(Maroon label.)
FURY (1004 "Cora Lee") ... 10-20 62
(Yellow label.)

RIVERA, Lucy

Singles: 7-inch

END (1041 "Make Me Queen") ... 20-30 59

RIVERA, Ray

Singles: 7-inch

COTIQUE (101 "El Rey") ... 5-10 66
DAYHILL (2009 "Troubles, Troubles") ... 8-12 62
DECCA (31049 "Let Me Kiss You Goodnight") ... 10-15 60
FORD (139 "I Walked Up the Mountain") ... 5-10 65
MERCURY (72783 "Love Is Blue") ... 5-10 68
NEAL (101 "There's No Return from Love") ... 5-10 64
OKLAHOMA (5003 "Come Back") ... 50-75 58
RCA (8372 "Joanie") ... 5-10 64

LPs: 10/12-inch

FORD (716 "Ray Rivera Tonight in Person") ... 15-25 63
MERCURY (61182 "Latin Workout") ... 10-15 68

RIVERS, Candy, & Falcons

Singles: 78 rpm

FLIP (302 "You Are the Only One") ... 50-75 54

Singles: 7-inch

FLIP (302 "You Are the Only One") ... 250-350 54
Also see FALCONS
Also see WOODMAN, Brother

RIVERS, Chuck

Singles: 7-inch

CENLA (222 "All Alone at Night") ... 50-75

RIVERS, Cliff

(Joey Castle)

Singles: 7-inch

THANKS (1201 "True Lips") ... 100-150 63
Also see CASTLE, Joey

RIVERS, Jack — C&W '48

Singles: 78 rpm

CAPITOL (15169 "Dear Oakie") ... 10-20 48

Singles: 7-inch

RON-MAR (1001 "Call On Me") ... 100-200

RIVERS, Johnny — P&R/LP '64

(Johnny Ramistella)

Singles: 7-inch

ATLANTIC (3011 "Sitting in Limbo") ... 4-6 74
ATLANTIC (3028 "Six Days on the Road") .. 4-6 74
ATLANTIC (3230 "John Lee Hooker '74") ... 4-6 74
BIG TREE (16094 "Swayin' to the Music [Slow Dancin']") ... 4-6 77
(Previously issued as "Slow Dancin' " on Soul City.)
BIG TREE (16106 "Curious Mind") ... 4-6 77
CAPITOL (4850 "Long Black Veil") ... 10-20 62
CAPITOL (4913 "If You Want It, I've Got It") ... 10-20 63
CAPITOL (5232 "Long Black Veil") ... 10-20 64
CHANCELLOR (1070 "Knock Three Times") ... 10-20 61
CHANCELLOR (1096 "Blue Skies") ... 10-20 61
CHANCELLOR (1108 "To Be Loved") ... 10-20 62
CORAL (62425 "That's My Babe") ... 15-25 64
CUB (9047 "Everyday") ... 25-35 59
CUB (9058 "Answer Me, My Love") ... 25-35 60
DEE DEE (239 "Your First and Last Love") ... 50-75 59
EPIC/SOUL CITY ... 4-6 75-76
GONE (5026 "Baby Come Back") ... 30-50 58
GUYDEN (2003 "You're the One") ... 20-30 58
GUYDEN (2110 "You're the One") ... 8-10 64
IMPERIAL (66032 thru 66453) ... 6-12 64-70
MCA ... 3-5 84
MGM (13266 "Answer Me My Love") ... 8-10 64
RSO ... 4-6 80
ROULETTE (4565 "Baby Come Back") ... 40-60 64
ROWE/AMI ... 5-10 66
("Play Me" Sales Stimulator promotional issue.)
SOUL CITY (007 "Ashes and Sand") ... 4-6 76-77
SOUL CITY (008 "Slow Dancing") ... 8-10 77
(First issue.)
SOUL CITY (010 "Little White Lie") ... 4-6 80
U.A. (198 thru 310) ... 4-6 73
U.A. (741 "Knock Three Times") ... 8-12 64
U.A. (769 "Dream Doll") ... 8-12 64
U.A. (50778 thru 50960) ... 4-8 71-72

Picture Sleeves

EPIC/SOUL CITY (50121 "Help Me Rhonda") ... 5-10 75
IMPERIAL (66056 thru 66386) ... 8-15 64-69
U.A. (50778 "Sea Cruise") ... 5-10 71

LPs: 10/12-inch

ATLANTIC (7301 "Road") ... 8-12 74
BIG TREE (76004 "Outside Help") ... 8-12 77
CAPITOL (T-2161 "Sensational Johnny Rivers") ... 35-50 64
(Monaural.)
CAPITOL (ST-2161 "Sensational Johnny Rivers") ... 50-75 64
(Stereo.)
COLUMBIA (FE-38429 "Not a Through Street") ... 8-10 83
COLUMBIA (PE-38429 "Not a Through Street") ... 5-8 85
CUSTOM ... 8-12 '60s
EPIC (33681 "New Lovers & Old Friends") ... 8-12 75
IMPERIAL (9264 thru 9341) ... 10-20 64-67
(Monaural.)
IMPERIAL (12264 thru 12341) ... 10-20 64-67
IMPERIAL (12372 thru 16001) ... 8-12 68-70
KOALA ... 5-10 79
LIBERTY ... 5-8 81-82
MCA (917 "Greatest Hits") ... 5-10 85
PICKWICK (3022 "Johnny Rivers") ... 10-12 68
PICKWICK (3191 "If You Want It, I Got It") ... 10-12 70
PRIORITY ... 5-8 83
RSO (3082 "Borrowed Time") ... 8-10 80
SEARS (417 "Mr. Teenage") ... 20-30 '60s
(Special Products issue for Sears stores)
SOUL CITY (1007 "Greatest Hits") ... 15-25 98
(Reportedly 500 made, each one autographed.)
SUNSET ... 8-12 67-69
U.A. (075 "Blue Suede Shoes") ... 8-12 73
U.A. (93 "Superpak") ... 15-20 72
(Two discs.)
U.A. (253 "Very Best of Johnny Rivers") .. 10-12 74
U.A. (387 "Very Best of Johnny Rivers") ... 8-10 75
U.A. (486 "Wild Night") ... 8-12 76
U.A. (3386 "Go Johnny Go") ... 20-25 64
(Monaural.)
U.A. (6386 "Go Johnny Go") ... 20-30 64
(Stereo.)
U.A. (5532 "Homegrown") ... 10-15 71
U.A. (5650 "L.A. Reggae") ... 10-15 72
UNART (007 "The Great Johnny Rivers") .. 8-12 67
Also see 4 SEASONS / Neil Sedaka / J Brothers / Johnny Rivers
Also see JONES, Tom / Freddie & Dreamers / Johnny Rivers
Also see RAMISTELLA, Johnny
Also see RASCALS / Buggs / Four Seasons / Johnny Rivers
Also see SIMON, Paul
Also see WILSON, Brian

RIVERS, Johnny / Steve Alaimo
LPs: 10/12-inch
CUSTOM....8-12 '60s
Also see ALAIMO, Steve

RIVERS, Johnny / Jerry Cole
LPs: 10/12-inch
CROWN.... 10-20 64
Also see COLE, Jerry

RIVERS, Johnny / 4 Seasons / Jerry Butler / Jimmy Soul
LPs: 10/12-inch
GLADWYNNE (2004 "Shindig Hullabaloo Spectacular")....10-20 65
Also see BUTLER, Jerry
Also see 4 SEASONS
Also see SOUL, Jimmy

RIVERS, Johnny / Ronnie Frost
LPs: 10/12-inch
GUEST STAR (1482 "Johnny Rivers").... 10-15 64
(Three cuts by Rivers; seven by Frost.)

RIVERS, Johnny / Trini Lopez
LPs: 10/12-inch
CUSTOM....8-12 '60s
Also see LOPEZ, Trini

RIVERS, Johnny / Ricky Nelson / Randy Sparks
LPs: 10/12-inch
MGM (E-4256 "Johnny Rivers, Ricky Nelson, Randy Sparks")....20-25 64
(Monaural.)
MGM (SE-4256 "Johnny Rivers, Ricky Nelson, Randy Sparks")....20-30 64
(Stereo.)
Also see NELSON, Ricky
Also see SPARKS, Randy

RIVERS, Johnny / Tremonts / Luke Gordon / Charlie Francis
LPs: 10/12-inch
CORONET (246 "Swingin' Shindig")........ 10-20 64
PREMIER (P-9037 "Swingin' Shindig").... 10-20 64
(Monaural.)
PREMIER (PS-9037 "Swingin' Shindig"). 15-25 64
(Stereo.)
Also see RIVERS, Johnny

RIVERS, Johnny
Singles: 7-inch
ERA (3037 "Call Me")....8-12 61
RIVERAIRE (1001 "Don't Bug Me Baby")....10-20 59

RIVERS, Little Jimmy, & Tops
Singles: 7-inch
SWAN (4091 "Puppy Love")....10-15 61
Also see LITTLE JIMMY & TOPS

RIVIARES
Singles: 7-inch
ADEN (101 "The Bug")....15-25 64

RIVIERAS
Singles: 7-inch
ALGONQUIN (718 "A Night to Remember")....200-300 58
(Reissued as by the Ravenairs.)

RIVIERAS *P&R '58*
Singles: 7-inch
COED (503 "Count Every Star")....30-40 58
(Red label.)
COED (503 "Count Every Star")....10-15 61
(Black label.)
COED (508 "Moonlight Serenade")....30-40 58
COED (513 "Our Love")....25-35 59
COED (522 "Since I Made You Cry")....25-35 59
COED (529 "Moonlight Cocktails")....15-25 60
COED (538 "My Friend")....15-25 60
COED (542 "Easy to Remember")....15-25 60
COED (551 "Eldorado")....15-25 61
COED (592 "Moonlight Cocktails")....5-10 64
COLLECTABLES....3-5 '80s
ERIC (285 "California Sun")....3-5 79
HOUSE OF SOUNDS....4-8 '60s
LOST NITE....4-8 '70s
LPs: 10/12-inch
POST....10-15 '70s
Members: Ronald Cook; Homer Dunn; Andy Jones; Charles Allen.
Also see DUPREES / RIVIERAS
Also see FIVE BOB-O-LINKS

RIVIERAS *P&R/LP '64*
Singles: 7-inch
DELTA (3211 "California Sun")....10-20 63
(Canadian.)
LANA....4-6 '60s
RIVIERA (1401 "California Sun"/"H.B. Goose Step")....5-10 63
RIVIERA (1401 "California Sun"/"Played On")....15-25 63
(1,000 made. Note different flip.)
RIVIERA (1402 "Little Donna")....8-10 64
RIVIERA (1403 "Rockin' Robin")....8-10 64
RIVIERA (1405 "Rip It Up"/"Whole Lotta Shakin'")....8-10 64
RIVIERA (1405 "Whole Lotta Shakin'"/ "Lakeview Lane")....10-15 64
(Has a different take of *Lakeview Lane* than found on 1406.)
RIVIERA (1406 "Let's Go to Hawaii"/"Lakeview Lane")....8-10 65
RIVIERA (1407 "Somebody New")....8-10 65
(Credited to Rivieras, but actually by Bobby Whiteside.)
RIVIERA (1409 "Bug Juice")....10-15 65
LPs: 10/12-inch
RIVIERA (701 "Campus Party")....50-100 64
USA (102 "Let's Have a Party")....50-100 64
Members: Marty Fortson; Paul Dennert; Otto Nuss; Doug Gean; Joe Pennell.
Also see WHITESIDE, Bobby

RIVIERAS
Singles: 7-inch
RILEY'S (369 "You Counter Feit Girl")....15-25 '60s
Members: Joey King Fish; Jim Riley.

RIVILEERS
Singles: 78 rpm
BATON....15-50 54-57
Singles: 7-inch
BATON (200 "A Thousand Stars")....75-125 54
BATON (201 "Forever")....75-125 54
BATON (205 "Eternal Love")....100-150 54
BATON (207 "For Sentimental Reasons")....20-30 54
(Has "Record No. 45-207" on left side.)
BATON (207 "For Sentimental Reasons")....10-20 54
(Has "Record No. 45-207" on right side.)
BATON (209 "Little Girl")....40-50 55
BATON (241 "A Thousand Stars")....15-25 57
(Has small print.)
BATON (241 "A Thousand Stars")....10-15
(Has large print.)
DARK (241 "A Thousand Stars")....10-15 57
Members: Gene Pearson; Herb Crosby; Milt Edwards; Errol Lennard; Al Delaney; Pete LeMonier; Mel Dancey.
Also see EMBERS

RIVINGTONS *P&R '62*
Singles: 7-inch
A.R.E. AMERICAN (100 "All That Glitters")....10-15 64
BATON MASTER....5-10 67
COLUMBIA....5-10 66
J.D. (122 "Don't Hate Your Father")....10-20
LADERA (6400 "Don't Hate Your Father")....20-30
LIBERTY (55427 "Papa Oom Mow Mow")....15-25 62
LIBERTY (55513 "Kickapoo Joy Juice")...10-15 62
LIBERTY (55528 "Mama Oom Mow Mow")....10-15 63
LIBERTY (55553 "The Bird's the Word")..15-20 63
LIBERTY (55585 "The Shaky Bird")....10-15 63
LIBERTY (55610 "Cherry")....30-50 63
LIBERTY (55671 "Fairy Tales")....5-10 64
NEWMAN (605 "Just Got to Be Mine")....10-20 67
QUAN (1379 "You're Gonna Pay")....5-10 67
RCA....5-10 69
REPRISE (293 "One Monkey")....5-10 64
VEE-JAY....5-10 64-65
WAND....4-6 73
Picture Sleeves
LIBERTY (55553 "The Bird's the Word")..15-20 63
LPs: 10/12-inch
LIBERTY (3282 "Doin' the Bird")....50-60 63
(Monaural.)
LIBERTY (7282 "Doin' the Bird")....50-75 63
(Stereo.)
LIBERTY (10184 "Papa-Oom-Mow-Mow")....5-10 82
Members: Carl White; Al Frazier; Sonny Harris; Turner Wilson; Darryl White.
Also see CRENSHAWS
Also see EBBTIDES
Also see ELL, Carl, & Buddies
Also see LAMPLIGHTERS
Also see MELLOMOODS
Also see SHARPS
Also see TENDERFOOTS

RIZZO, Johnny, & Tri-Lites
Singles: 7-inch
LE HARVE (1027 "I Need Her")....50-100

ROACH, Freddie
Singles: 7-inch
PRESTIGE (429 "One Track Mind")....5-10 66
PRESTIGE (454 "My People")....5-10 67

ROACH, Little Bobby, & Combo
Singles: 7-inch
FIRE (1013 "Mush")....10-20 60

ROAD
Singles: 7-inch
BLUE ONION (106 "You Rub Me the Wrong Way")....15-25 69
LEMON LIME (101 "You Rub Me the Wrong Way")....10-20 69

ROAD RUNNERS
(Roadrunners)
Singles: 7-inch
CHALLENGE (9197 "Dead Man")....8-10 63
FELSTED (8692 "Quasimoto")....15-25 64
FOOTNOTE (701 "El Skid")....20-30 '60s
LONDON (5208 "Cute Little Colt")....15-25 64
MIRAMAR (116 "I'll Make It Up to You")..10-15 65
MOROCCO (001 "Goodbye")....10-15 66
REPRISE (0418 "I'll Make It Up to You")..10-15 65
LPs: 10/12-inch
LONDON (381 "New Mustang")....50-75 64
(Monaural.)
LONDON (3381 "New Mustang")....60-80 64
(Stereo.)
Members: John Youngblood; Charles Casper; Dave Scheilbach; Jerry Schillinger; Gary Usher.
Also see PAXTON, Gary
Also see USHER, Gary

ROAD RUNNERS
Singles: 7-inch
CHAN (111 "Little Pig")....25-35 64
COMMERCE (560 "Little Pig")....15-25 64

ROAD RUNNERS
Singles: 7-inch
MICHIGAN NICKEL (003 "Roadrunner Walk")....10-20 65

ROAD RUNNERS
Singles: 7-inch
CHAMP (3402 "It's So Hard")....10-20 65
RAYNARD (10031 "It's So Hard")....10-20 65
Members: Jimmy Dentici; Kenny Jablonski; Rudy Villasenor; Dave Frashenski; Richie Rendzik; Mike Kowaleski; Tom Fabre; Kenny Rogers; Doug Schanning.
Also see BOGIS CHIMES

ROAN, Jimmy
Singles: 7-inch
DESK (1002 "The Sun Will Shine")....50-75

ROADSTERS
Singles: 7-inch
DONNA (1390 "Mag Rims")....15-25 64
20TH FOX (486 "Drag")....10-15 64

ROAMERS
Singles: 78 rpm
SAVOY....10-15 55
Singles: 7-inch
SAVOY (1147 "I'll Never Get Over You") .20-30 55
SAVOY (1156 "Never Let Me Go")....20-30 55
Also see DILLARD, Varetta
Also see HARRISON, Wilbert

ROAMIN' TOGAS
Singles: 7-inch
LIGHTNING (101 "Bar the Door")....20-30 67

ROAVE, Johnny
Singles: 7-inch
WAGON (1004 "Drag Strip Baby")....600-700

ROB & RHYTHM ACES
Singles: 7-inch
SWALLOW (101 "You've Gone Too Far")....50-75

ROBBE, Warren
Singles: 7-inch
MYSTIC (730 "My Chicken Pen")....300-400 58
MYSTIC (811 "Single Man")....200-300 58

ROBBINS, Eddie
Singles: 7-inch
DAVID (1001 "Janice")....10-20 61
DOT (15702 "Dear Parents")....10-20 58
POWER (214 "Dear Parents")....75-100 57

ROBBINS, James / Roy Wright
Singles: 7-inch
MICA (2016 "I Can't Please You")....25-35 '60s
Also see ROBINS, James
Also see WRIGHT, Roy

ROBBINS, Marty *C&W '52*
(With the Ray Conniff Orchestra & Chorus)
Singles: 78 rpm
COLUMBIA (20925 thru 21324)....20-30 52-54
COLUMBIA (21351 thru 21545)....30-40 54-56
COLUMBIA (40000 thru 41000 series)....20-50 56-58
Singles: 7-inch
COLUMBIA (02000 & 03000 series)....3-5 81-83
COLUMBIA (10305 thru 11425)....3-6 76-81
COLUMBIA (20925 "Tomorrow You'll Be Gone")....30-40 52
COLUMBIA (20965 "Crying Cause I Love You")....30-40 52
COLUMBIA (21022 "I'll Go On Alone")....30-40 52
COLUMBIA (21032 "My Isle of Golden Dreams")....30-40 53
COLUMBIA (21075 "I Couldn't Keep from Crying")....30-40 53
COLUMBIA (21111 "A Halfway Chance with You")....30-40 53
COLUMBIA (21145 "Sing Me Something Sentimental")....30-40 53
COLUMBIA (21172 "Blessed Jesus Should I Fall")....30-40 53
COLUMBIA (21176 "It's a Long Long Ride")....30-40 53
COLUMBIA (21213 "Aloha Oe")....30-40 54
COLUMBIA (21246 "Pretty Words")....30-40 54
COLUMBIA (21291 "Call Me Up")....30-40 54
COLUMBIA (21324 "Time Goes By")....30-40 54
COLUMBIA (21351 "That's All Right")....40-50 55
COLUMBIA (21352 "God Understands") .30-40 55
COLUMBIA (21388 "Daddy Loves You")....30-40 55
COLUMBIA (21414 "It Looks Like I'm Just in the Way")....30-40 55
COLUMBIA (21446 "Maybellene")....40-50 55
COLUMBIA (21461 "Pretty Mama")....40-50 55
COLUMBIA (21477 "Tennessee Toddy").40-50 56
COLUMBIA (21508 "Singing the Blues") .30-40 56
COLUMBIA (21545 "Singing the Blues") .20-30 56
COLUMBIA (30511 "El Paso")....30-40 59
(Compact 33.)
COLUMBIA (30589 "Big Iron")....30-40 60
(Compact 33.)
COLUMBIA (31749 "Little Rich Girl")....20-40 62
(Compact 33 stereo.)
COLUMBIA (31751 "Kinda Halfway Feel")....20-40 62
(Compact 33 stereo.)
COLUMBIA (33013 "El Paso")....20-40 61
(Compact 33 stereo.)
COLUMBIA (40679 "Long Tall Sally")....30-50 56
COLUMBIA (40706 "Respectfully Miss Brooks")....30-50 56
COLUMBIA (40815 "Knee Deep in the Blues")....20-30 57
COLUMBIA (40864 "A White Sport Coat")....20-30 57
COLUMBIA (40969 "Please Don't Blame Me")....20-30 57
COLUMBIA (41013 "The Story of My Life")....20-30 57
COLUMBIA (41143 "Just Married")....20-30 58
COLUMBIA (41208 "She Was Only Seventeen")....20-30 58

COLUMBIA (41282 "Ain't I the Lucky One") ... 20-30 58
COLUMBIA (41325 "The Hanging Tree") 20-30 59
COLUMBIA (41408 "Cap and Gown") ... 20-30 59
COLUMBIA (41511 "El Paso [4:37]"/"El Paso [2:58]") ... 20-30 59
(Long/short version "Special Radio Station Edition." Promotional issue only.)
COLUMBIA (41589 "Big Iron") ... 15-25 60
COLUMBIA (41686 "Is There Any Chance") ... 15-25 60
COLUMBIA (41771 "Five Brothers") ... 15-25 60
COLUMBIA (41809 "Ballad of the Alamo") ... 15-25 60
COLUMBIA (41922 "Don't Worry") ... 10-20 61
COLUMBIA (42008 "Jimmy Martinez") ... 10-20 61
COLUMBIA (42065 "It's Your World") ... 10-20 61
COLUMBIA (42246 "Sometimes I'm Tempted") ... 10-20 61
COLUMBIA (42375 "Love Can't Wait") ... 10-20 62
COLUMBIA (42486 "Devil Woman") ... 10-20 62
COLUMBIA (42614 "Ruby Ann") ... 10-20 62
COLUMBIA (42701 "Cigarettes and Coffee Blues") ... 10-20 63
COLUMBIA (42749 "Little Rich Girl") ... 20-40 63
COLUMBIA (42751 "Kinda Halfway Feel") ... 20-40 63
COLUMBIA (42781 "I'm Not Ready Yet") ... 8-12 63
COLUMBIA (42831 "Not So Long Ago") ... 8-12 63
COLUMBIA (42890 "Begging to You") ... 8-12 63
COLUMBIA (42968 thru 43770) ... 6-12 64-66
COLUMBIA (43845 thru 45775) ... 4-8 67-73
DECCA ... 4-6 72
MCA ... 4-6 73-75
PALOMINO ... 100-200 72
(Title and selection number not known.)

Picture Sleeves

COLUMBIA (40864 "A White Sport Coat") ... 20-30 57
COLUMBIA (41013 "The Story of My Life") ... 20-30 57
COLUMBIA (41208 "She Was Only Seventeen") ... 20-30 57
COLUMBIA (41325 "The Hanging Tree") 15-25 59
COLUMBIA (41511 "El Paso") ... 10-20 59
(Pictures Marty Robbins.)
COLUMBIA (41511 "El Paso") ... 30-40 59
(Text only, no picture. For "Special Radio Station Edition." Promotional issue only.)
COLUMBIA (41589 "Big Iron") ... 10-20 60
COLUMBIA (41809 "Ballad of the Alamo") ... 10-20 60
COLUMBIA (41922 "Don't Worry") ... 10-20 61
COLUMBIA (42008 "Jimmy Martinez") ... 10-20 61
COLUMBIA (42065 "It's Your World") ... 10-20 61
COLUMBIA (42246 "I Told the Brook") ... 10-20 61
COLUMBIA (42375 "Love Can't Wait") ... 10-15 62
COLUMBIA (42486 "Devil Woman") ... 10-15 62
COLUMBIA (42614 "Ruby Ann") ... 10-15 62
COLUMBIA (42701 "Cigarettes and Coffee Blues") ... 10-15 63
COLUMBIA (42781 "No Sign of Loneliness Here") ... 10-15 63

EPs: 7-inch

COLUMBIA (1785 "Marty Robbins") ... 50-100 56
COLUMBIA (2116 "Singing the Blues") . 50-100 56
COLUMBIA (2134 "A White Sport Coat") 25-50 57
COLUMBIA (2153 "Marty Robbins") ... 25-50 56
COLUMBIA (2808 "Marty Robbins") ... 20-40 57
COLUMBIA (2814 "Marty Robbins") ... 20-30 58
COLUMBIA (9020 "R.F.D.") ... 10-20 64
(Stereo juke box issue.)
COLUMBIA (9761/9762/9763 "The Song of Robbins") ... 15-25 57
(Price is for any of three volumes.)
COLUMBIA (10871 "Song of the Islands") ... 20-40 57
COLUMBIA (11891 "Marty Robbins") ... 15-25 58
COLUMBIA (13491/13492/13493 "Gunfighter Ballads and Trail Songs") ... 10-20 59
(Price is for any of three volumes.)
COLUMBIA (14811/14812/14813 "Gunfighter Ballads and Trail Songs, Vol. 2") ... 10-20 60
(Price is for any of three volumes.)

LPs: 10/12-inch

ARTCO (110 "Best of Marty Robbins") ... 40-50 73
(Covers shows 110 but label has 644.)
CBS (19738 "Cause I Love You") ... 5-10 84
CANDLELITE ... 8-12 77
COLUMBIA (15 "Marty's Country") ... 10-15 69
COLUMBIA (31 "Open-End Columbia Artists Interviews") ... 35-50 '60s
(Promotional issue only.)
COLUMBIA (32 "Columbia Artists Interviews with Frank Jones") ... 50-75 59
(Includes 42-page booklet. Promotional issue only.)
COLUMBIA (237 "Saddle Tramp") ... 25-35 66
(Columbia Record Club issue.)
COLUMBIA (445 "Bend in the River") ... 35-45 68
(Columbia Record Club issue.)
COLUMBIA (890 "Marty Robbins Gold") ... 8-10 75
COLUMBIA (976 "Song of Robbins") ... 25-45 57
COLUMBIA (1087 "Song of the Islands") . 25-45 57
COLUMBIA (1189 "Marty Robbins") ... 25-45 58
COLUMBIA (1256 "Return of the Gunfighter") ... 15-20 69
(Columbia "Country Star" series.)
COLUMBIA (1325 "Marty's Greatest Hits") ... 15-25 59
(Monaural.)
COLUMBIA (1349 "Gunfighter Ballads and Trail Songs") ... 15-25 59
(Monaural.)
COLUMBIA (1481 "More Gunfighter Ballads and Trail Songs") ... 15-25 60
(Monaural.)
COLUMBIA (1599 "Marty's Greatest Hits") ... 15-20 69
(Columbia "Country Star" series issue.)
COLUMBIA (1635 "More Greatest Hits") ... 15-25 61
(Monaural.)
COLUMBIA (1666 "Just a Little Sentimental") ... 15-25 61
(Monaural.)
COLUMBIA (1801 "Marty After Midnight") ... 40-50 62
(Monaural.)
COLUMBIA (1855 "Portrait of Marty") ... 25-35 62
(With bonus portrait of Marty. Monaural.)
COLUMBIA (1855 "Portrait of Marty") ... 15-25 62
(Without bonus portrait of Marty. Monaural.)
COLUMBIA (1918 "Devil Woman") ... 15-20 62
(Monaural.)
COLUMBIA (2016 "The Heart of Marty Robbins") ... 80-100 69
(Columbia "Country Star" series issue.)
COLUMBIA (2040 "Hawaii's Calling Me") ... 20-30 62
(Monaural.)
COLUMBIA (2072 "Return of the Gunfighter") ... 15-20 63
(Monaural.)
COLUMBIA (2167 "Island Woman") ... 25-35 64
(Monaural.)
COLUMBIA (2220 "R.F.D.") ... 25-35 64
(Monaural.)
COLUMBIA (2304 "Turn the Lights Down Low") ... 20-40 65
(Monaural.)
COLUMBIA (2448 "What God Has Done") ... 15-20 65
(Monaural.)
COLUMBIA (2527 "The Drifter") ... 10-20 66
(Monaural.)
COLUMBIA (2563 "What God Has Done") ... 15-20 69
(Columbia "Country Star" series issue.)
COLUMBIA (2601 "Rock'n Roll'n Robbins") ... 500-750 56
(10-inch LP.)
COLUMBIA (2645 "My Kind of Country") . 15-20 67
(Monaural.)
COLUMBIA (2725 "Tonight Carmen") ... 10-20 67
(Monaural.)
COLUMBIA (2735 "Christmas with Marty Robbins") ... 20-30 67
(Monaural.)
COLUMBIA (2762 "More Gunfighter Ballads and Trail Songs") ... 15-20 69
(Columbia "Country Star" series issue.)
COLUMBIA (2817 "By The Time I Get to Phoenix") ... 20-30 68
(Monaural.)
COLUMBIA (3557 "The Drifter") ... 15-20 69
(Columbia "Country Star" series issue.)
COLUMBIA (3867 "My Kind of Country") . 15-20 69
(Columbia "Country Star" series issue.)
COLUMBIA (5489 "Tonight Carmen") ... 15-20 69
(Columbia "Country Star" series issue.)
COLUMBIA (5498 "Christmas with Marty Robbins") ... 15-20 69
(Columbia "Country Star" series issue.)
COLUMBIA (5812 "Marty") ... 20-40 72
(Five-disc set. Columbia Special Products issue.)
COLUMBIA (6994 "I Walk Alone") ... 15-20 69
(Columbia "Country Star" series issue.)
COLUMBIA (CS-8158 "Gunfighter Ballads and Trail Songs") ... 15-25 59
(Stereo.)
COLUMBIA (PC-8158 "Gunfighter Ballads and Trail Songs") ... 5-10
COLUMBIA (CS-8272 "More Gunfighter Ballads and Trail Songs") ... 15-25 60
(Stereo.)
COLUMBIA (PC-8272 "More Gunfighter Ballads and Trail Songs") ... 5-10
COLUMBIA (CS-8435 "More Greatest Hits") ... 15-20 61
(Stereo.)
COLUMBIA (PC-8435 "More Greatest Hits") ... 5-10
COLUMBIA (8466 "Just a Little Sentimental") ... 15-25 61
(Stereo.)
COLUMBIA (8601 "Marty After Midnight") ... 25-35 62
(Stereo.)
COLUMBIA (8639 "Marty's Greatest Hits") ... 15-25 62
(Stereo.)
COLUMBIA (8655 "Portrait of Marty") ... 25-35 62
(With bonus portrait of Marty. Stereo.)
COLUMBIA (8655 "Portrait of Marty") ... 15-25 62
(Without bonus portrait. Stereo.)
COLUMBIA (8718 "Devil Woman") ... 15-20 62
(Stereo.)
COLUMBIA (8840 "Hawaii's Calling Me") ... 20-30 62
(Stereo.)
COLUMBIA (8872 "Return of the Gunfighter") ... 15-20 63
(Stereo.)
COLUMBIA (8976 "Island Woman") ... 35-40 64
(Stereo.)
COLUMBIA (CS-9020 "R.F.D.") ... 25-35 64
(Stereo.)
COLUMBIA (CSRP-9020 "R.F.D.") ... 8-10
(Columbia Special Products issue.)
COLUMBIA (9104 "Turn the Lights Down Low") ... 20-40 65
(Stereo.)
COLUMBIA (CS-9248 "What God Has Done") ... 15-20 65
(Stereo.)
COLUMBIA (ACS-9248 "What God Has Done") ... 5-10
(Columbia Special Products issue.)
COLUMBIA (9327 "The Drifter") ... 10-20 66
(Stereo.)
COLUMBIA (9421 "Song of Robbins") ... 30-40 67
(Stereo.)
COLUMBIA (9445 "My Kind of Country") . 15-25 67
(Stereo.)
COLUMBIA (9525 "Tonight Carmen") ... 10-20 67
(Stereo.)
COLUMBIA (9535 "Christmas with Marty Robbins") ... 10-20 67
(Stereo.)
COLUMBIA (9617 "By the Time I Get to Phoenix") ... 10-15 68
(Stereo.)
COLUMBIA (9725 "I Walk Alone") ... 10-15 68
COLUMBIA (9811 "It's a Sin") ... 20-30 69
COLUMBIA (9978 "My Woman, My Woman, My Wife") ... 8-12 70
COLUMBIA (10022 thru 10579) ... 8-10 73-75
(Columbia's Limited Edition series. All Have an "LE" prefix.)
COLUMBIA (10980 "Christmas with Marty Robbins") ... 15-20 70
(Columbia Special Products issue.)
COLUMBIA (11221 "By the Time I Get to Phoenix") ... 5-10 '80s
(Columbia Special Products issue.)
COLUMBIA (11222 "Marty's Greatest Hits") ... 5-10 75
COLUMBIA (11311 "By the Time I Get to Phoenix") ... 5-10 70
(Columbia Special Products issue.)
COLUMBIA (11513 "By the Time I Get to Phoenix") ... 15-20 71
(Columbia Special Products issue.)
COLUMBIA (12416 "Marty Robbins' Own Favorites") ... 12-15 74
(Special Products issue for Vaseline Hair Tonic.)
COLUMBIA (13358 "Christmas with Marty Robbins") ... 5-10 72
(Columbia Special Products issue.)
COLUMBIA (14035 "Legendary Music Man") ... 8-12 77
(Columbia Special Products issue.)
COLUMBIA (14613 "Best of Marty Robbins") ... 5-10 78
(Columbia Special Products issue.)
COLUMBIA (15594 "Number One Cowboy") ... 5-10 81
(Columbia Special Products issue.)
COLUMBIA (15812 "Marty Robbins' Best") ... 5-10 82
(Columbia Special Products issue.)
COLUMBIA (16561 "Reflections") ... 5-10 82
(Columbia Special Products issue.)
COLUMBIA (16578 "Classics") ... 15-20 83
(Three-disc set. Columbia Special Products issue.)
COLUMBIA (16914 "Country Classics") ... 5-10 83
(Columbia Special Products issue.)
COLUMBIA (17120 "Sincerely") ... 5-10 83
(Columbia Special Products issue.)
COLUMBIA (17136 "Forever Yours") ... 5-10 83
(Columbia Special Products issue.)
COLUMBIA (17137 "That Country Feeling") ... 5-10 83
(Columbia Special Products issue.)
COLUMBIA (17138 "Banquet of Songs") ... 5-10 83
(Columbia Special Products issue.)
COLUMBIA (17159 "The Great Marty Robbins") ... 5-10 83
(Columbia Special Products issue.)
COLUMBIA (17206 "The Legendary Marty Robbins") ... 5-10 83
(Columbia Special Products issue.)
COLUMBIA (17209 "Country Cowboy") ... 5-10 83
(Columbia Special Products issue.)
COLUMBIA (17367 "Song of the Islands"). 5-10 83
(Columbia Special Products issue.)
COLUMBIA (17730 "Great Love Songs") .. 5-10 '80s
(Columbia Special Products issue.)
COLUMBIA (30000 thru 40000 series) ... 5-12 70-86
DECCA ... 8-12 72
GUSTO/COLUMBIA ... 8-10 81
HARMONY (Except 31258) ... 8-15 69-72
HARMONY (31258 "Song of the Islands") ... 20-25 72
K-TEL ... 8-10 77
MCA ... 6-12 73-74
ORBIT ... 8-10 84
PICKWICK ... 5-10 '70s
READER'S DIGEST (054 "Greatest Hits") ... 20-30 83
(Boxed, five-disc set.)
SUNRISE MEDIA ... 5-10 81
TIME-LIFE ... 5-10 81
WORD ... 5-10

Session: Ray Conniff Singers; Jordanaires; David Briggs; Bobby Braddock; Grady Martin; Bob Bishop; Bill Pursell; Buddy Spicher; Arlene Harden; Bobby Sykes.

Also see BISHOP, Bob
Also see CONNIFF, Ray
Also see EMERSON, Lee, & Marty Robbins
Also see JORDANAIRES
Also see SMITH, Carl / Lefty Frizzell / Marty Robbins
Also see TUBB, Ernest

ROBBINS, Marty / Johnny Cash / Ray Price

LPs: 10/12-inch

COLUMBIA ... 8-10 70
Also see CASH, Johnny
Also see PRICE, Ray

ROBBINS, Mel

(Mel "Pigue" Robbins)

Singles: 7-inch

ARGO (5340 "Save It") ... 75-100 59
MR. PEACOCK (103 "Fidgety") ... 10-20 62
WILDCAT (1001 "Go Ahead On") ... 10-20 61

LPs: 10/12-inch
SMASH (27012 "Hully Gully to the Hits") ... 15-20 62
(Monaural.)
SMASH (67012 "Hully Gully to the Hits") ... 20-25 62
(Stereo.)

ROBBINS, Randy
Singles: 78 rpm
FLASH (103 "Sticky Stuff") ... 10-15 56
Singles: 7-inch
FLASH (103 "Sticky Stuff") ... 15-25 56

ROBBINS, Robbie
Singles: 7-inch
HEP (2001 "Hurry") ... 75-100 '60s

ROBBS *LP '68*
Singles: 7-inch
ABC ... 4-8 70-71
ATLANTIC (2511 "Castles in the Air") ... 5-10 68
ATLANTIC (2578 "Changin' Winds") ... 5-10 68
DUNHILL (4208 "Movin' ") ... 5-10 69
DUNHILL (4233 "Last of the Wine") ... 5-8 70
MERCURY ... 5-10 66-67
Picture Sleeves
ABC (11270 "I'll Never Get Enough") ... 5-10 70
MERCURY (72641 "Bittersweet") ... 8-12 67
LPs: 10/12-inch
ABC (719 "Cherokee") ... 10-20 71
MERCURY (21130 "The Robbs") ... 20-25 67
(Monaural.)
MERCURY (61130 "The Robbs") ... 20-30 67
(Stereo.)
Members: David Donaldson; Dennis Sachse; Robert Donaldson; George Donaldson; Dick Gonia; Teddy Peplinski; Craig Krampf.
Also see ROBBY & ROBINS
Also see TONY'S TYGERS / Skunks / Robbs

ROBBY & ROBINS
Singles: 7-inch
TODD (1089 "Surfer's Life") ... 15-25 63
Also see ROBBS

ROBERSON BRO'S
Singles: 7-inch
VERL ("Wishing") ... 50-75 62
(Blue vinyl. No selection number used.)
VERL ("Wishing") ... 20-30 62
(Black vinyl. No selection number used. First issued as by Walt, Percy & the Tracers.)
Members: Walt Roberson; Percy Roberson.
Also see WALT, PERCY & TRACERS

ROBERT & JOHNNY *P&R/R&B '58*
Singles: 78 rpm
OLD TOWN ... 15-25 56-57
Singles: 7-inch
ATLANTIC OLDIES SERIES ... 4-6 '70s
BARRY (1015 "Hear My Heartbeat") ... 5-10 63
COLLECTABLES ... 3-5 '80s
COTILLION (44116 "You're Mine") ... 4-6 71
HI-OLDIES (463 thru 468) ... 3-5
JANUS (718 "We Belong Together") ... 4-6
MEMORIES OF THE PAST (2504 "We Belong Together") ... 3-5
OLD TOWN ... 12-25 56-62
SUE (792 "A Perfect Wife") ... 15-20 62
Members: Robert Carr; Johnny Mitchell.

ROBERT & JOHNNY / Fiestas
Singles: 7-inch
ATCO ... 3-5 '80s
Also see FIESTAS
Also see ROBERT & JOHNNY

ROBERTA
Singles: 7-inch
LU-CEE (103 "I'll Try") ... 50-75

ROBERTO
(Roberto Ketally)
Singles: 7-inch
CORAL ... 4-6
DEESON (103 "Rockin' with Roberto") ... 15-25 58

ROBERTS, Allen
Singles: 7-inch
CHEVELL (1003 "Song On the Juke Box") ... 5-10 64
KNIGHT (2009 "Angel in My Life") ... 15-25 59

ROBERTS, Bobby
(With the Ravons; Ravons with Bobby Roberts)
Singles: 7-inch
CAMEO (339 "How Can I Make Her Mine") ... 5-10 64
GMA (10 "How Can I Make Her Mine") ... 50-75 64
(First issue.)
GMA (13 "I Want You to Be") ... 15-25
GMA (15 "Jenny Jenny") ... 15-25
GMA (3309 "Little Flirt") ... 15-25
HUT (881 "Hop, Skip & Jump") ... 150-250 58
KING (4837 "Gonna Comb Your Outta My Hair") ... 50-75 55
SKY (101 "Big Sandy") ... 1500-2000 58

ROBERTS, Buddy, & HiLiters
Singles: 7-inch
BONANZA (689 "Ding Dong") ... 20-30 60
GONE (5017 "Strange Sensation") ... 30-40 57

ROBERTS, Dave
Singles: 7-inch
PL (14 "Wonderous") ... 100-150 58
REV (3518 "Honolulu Holiday") ... 20-30 58

ROBERTS, Don "Red"
Singles: 7-inch
CHART (643 "Only One") ... 30-50 57
RAMA (230 "Only One") ... 30-50 57

ROBERTS, Gary, & 5 Stars
Singles: 7-inch
STERLING (681 "You Made Me a Prisoner of Love") ... 30-40

ROBERTS, Gip
Singles: 7-inch
J.V.B. (29 "No One Monkey Goin' Ruin My Show") ... 30-50 58

ROBERTS, Jerry
Singles: 7-inch
ABC-PAR (10130 "Madonna") ... 8-12 60
APT (25070 "Little Bitty Lover") ... 20-30 62

ROBERTS, Jerry, & Toppers
Singles: 7-inch
GAITY (165 "Hopelessly") ... 40-60 59
KAY BEE (2037 "Rendezvous") ... 30-50 '60s

ROBERTS, Johnny
Singles: 7-inch
STYLO (2107 "My Lovin' Arms") ... 50-100

ROBERTS, Lance
(With the Gene Lowery Singers)
Singles: 7-inch
DECCA (30891 "You've Got Everything") ... 15-25 59
DECCA (30955 "Gonna Have Myself a Ball") ... 15-25 59
SUN (348 "The Time Is Right") ... 10-20 60

ROBERTS, Lee, & Echoes
Singles: 7-inch
SPOTLIGHT (101 "School Days") ... 60-80

ROBERTS, Lou
Singles: 7-inch
GENIE (101 "Rattle Snake Shake") ... 75-125 65

ROBERTS, Lou, & Marks
Singles: 7-inch
MGM (13347 "Gettin' Ready") ... 15-25 65

ROBERTS, Lucy
Singles: 78 rpm
VIK (0201 "Leap Year Red") ... 5-10 56
Singles: 7-inch
VIK (0201 "Leap Year Red") ... 15-25 56
Also see DUPREE, Champion Jack, & His Combo / Lucy Roberts with Neal Hefti & His Orchestra

ROBERTS, Lynn
(With the Phantoms)
Singles: 78 rpm
ORIOLE (101 "I'll Be Around") ... 50-100 56
UNIQUE ... 5-10 56
Singles: 7-inch
ORIOLE (101 "I'll Be Around") ... 200-300 56
(Black vinyl.)
ORIOLE (101 "I'll Be Around") ... 500-750 56
(Red vinyl.)
ROULETTE (4320 "Johnny, Wait for Me") ... 8-12 61
UNIQUE (336 "While the City Sleeps") ... 10-20 56

ROBERTS, Marty
(With Saxons)
Singles: 7-inch
ARC (8003 "Your Feets Too Big") ... 40-60 57
FLAME ("Tangle-Weed") ... 10-20 60
(Selection number not known.)

ROBERTS, Pernell
LPs: 10/12-inch
RCA (2662 "Come All Ye Fair and Tender Ladies") ... 15-25 63

ROBERTS, Pete
Singles: 7-inch
CAPE (201 "Missing You") ... 40-60
RENDEZVOUS (124 "Hold Me") ... 8-12 60
(First issued as by Larry Bright.)
Also see BRIGHT, Larry

ROBERTS, Rocky
(With the Airedales)
Singles: 7-inch
BRUNSWICK (55357 "To Much") ... 5-10 67
BRUNSWICK (55368 "Tell Me") ... 5-10 68
ROULETTE (4506 "T-Bird") ... 15-25 63
ROULETTE (4595 "T-Bird") ... 10-15 65
LPs: 10/12-inch
BRUNSWICK (54133 "Rocky Roberts and the Airedales") ... 10-20 68

ROBERTS, Roy
Singles: 7-inch
NINANDY (1011 "The Legend of Otis Redding") ... 20-30 68

ROBERTS, Skippy
Singles: 7-inch
LARK (7 "Holy Mack'ral, Andy") ... 10-20 59

ROBERTS, Sonny & Echoes
Singles: 7-inch
IMPALA (1001 "I'll Never Let You Go") ... 500-600 58

ROBERTS, Vivian
Singles: 7-inch
VAULT (921 "Don't Say Goodbye") ... 10-20 65

ROBERTSON, Nat
Singles: 7-inch
NU-KAT (118 "Country Boy") ... 50-75 59

ROBERTSON, Texas Jim *C&W '46*
(With the Panhandle Punchers)
Singles: 78 rpm
RCA ... 5-10 46-50
Singles: 7-inch
RCA (48-0133 "Revenge") ... 10-20 50
(Green vinyl.)
RCA (48-0217 "Cowboy Fun, Pt. 1") ... 10-20 50
(Yellow vinyl. Children's series.)
RCA (48-0398 "Army Life") ... 10-20 50
(Green vinyl.)
EPs: 7-inch
CAMDEN ... 8-12
LPs: 10/12-inch
DESIGN ... 10-20 '60s
GRAND PRIX ... 10-20 '60s
INT'L AWARD ... 10-20 '60s
STRAND (1016 "Texas Jim Robertson [Tales and Songs of the Old West]") ... 25-35 61

ROBERTSON, Walter
(Walter Robinson)
Singles: 78 rpm
FLAIR ... 50-75 55
Singles: 7-inch
FLAIR (1053 "Sputterin' Blues") ... 150-200 55
Also see ROBINSON BROTHERS

ROBIN, Richie
Singles: 7-inch
GOLDISC (3002 "Sugar Love") ... 8-12 60
GONE (5083 "Strange Dreams") ... 15-25 59

ROBIN, Ruth
Singles: 7-inch
TITAN (1725 "Lonely Eyes") ... 30-40 62

ROBIN, Tina *P&R '61*
Singles: 78 rpm
CORAL ... 5-10 57
Singles: 7-inch
CAMEO (193 "First Kiss") ... 5-10 61
CORAL ... 10-15 57-59
MERCURY (Except 71852) ... 5-10 61-63
MERCURY (71852 "Dear Mr. K.J. Play It Again") ... 15-25 61
Picture Sleeves
CORAL (61822 "My Mammy") ... 20-25 57

ROBIN & BATMEN
Singles: 7-inch
DJ (670 "The Riddler") ... 10-20 67
SARA ("6614 "Batskinner") ... 10-20 66

ROBIN & COOL CATS
Singles: 7-inch
PUSSY CAT (501 "Give Me Your Love") ... 400-600
(No selection number used.)

ROBIN & THREE HOODS
Singles: 7-inch
FAN JR. (1003 "I Wanta Do It") ... 15-25 66
(First issued as by Marrell's Marauders.)
FAN JR. (5678 "We the Living") ... 10-20 66
FAN JR (5680 "I Wanna Do It") ... 10-15 66
(Reissue of #1003.)
HOLLYWOOD (1110 "I Wanna Do It") ... 5-10 66
Members: Dave Reed; Jim Schwartz; Bob Bernhagen; Bruce Benson; Mike Warner.
Also see MARRELL'S MARAUDERS

ROBIN HOOD & MERRI MEN
Singles: 7-inch
DELSEY (303 " We Had a Quarrel") ... 10-15 65
MOHAWK (130 "Ellen") ... 20-30 62

ROBINS *R&B '50*
(Robbins; with Maggie Hathaway)
Singles: 78 rpm
ALADDIN (3031 "Don't Like the Way You're Doing") ... 200-300 49
ATCO (6059 "Smokey Joe's Café") ... 15-25 55
CROWN ... 50-75 54
QUALITY ... 30-50 54
(Canadian.)
RCA ... 50-75 53
RECORDED IN HOLLYWOOD (112 "Bayou Baby Blues") ... 300-400 50
RECORDED IN HOLLYWOOD (121 "Falling Star") ... 150-250 50
RECORDED IN HOLLYWOOD (150 "School Girl Blues") ... 50-75 51
SAVOY (726 "If It's So Baby") ... 50-75 50
SAVOY (732 "Turkey Hop") ... 50-75 50
SAVOY (738 "Our Romance Is Gone") ... 50-75 50
SAVOY (752 "There's Rain in My Eyes") ... 50-75 50
SAVOY (762 "I'm Through") ... 50-75 50
SAVOY (975 "I Found Out") ... 4-8
(Previously unreleased.)
SCORE (4010 "Around About Midnight") ... 100-200 49
SPARK (103 "Wrap It Up") ... 50-75 54
SPARK (107 "Framed") ... 30-50 54
SPARK (110 "If Teardrops Were Kisses") ... 75-125 55
SPARK (113 "One Kiss") ... 30-50 55
SPARK (116 "I Must Be Dreaming") ... 30-50 55
SPARK (122 "Smokey Joe's Cafe") ... 75-125 55
WHIPPET ... 30-50 56-57
Singles: 7-inch
ARVEE (5001 "Just Like That") ... 10-20 60
ARVEE (5013 "Oh No!") ... 10-20 60
ATCO (6059 "Smokey Joe's Cafe") ... 15-25 55
CROWN (106 "I Made a Vow") ... 400-500 54
CROWN (120 "Key to My Heart") ... 100-200 54
GONE (5101 "Baby Love") ... 15-25 61
KNIGHT (2001 "Quarter to Twelve") ... 15-25 58
KNIGHT (2008 "It's Never Too Late") ... 50-75 58
QUALITY (1269 "Riot in Cell Block No. 9") ... 200-300 54
(Canadian.)
RCA (5175 "A Fool Such As I") ... 400-500 53
RCA (5271 "All Night Baby") ... 100-200 53
RCA (5434 "How Would You Know") ... 300-400 53
RCA (5486 "My Baby Done Told Me") ... 200-300 53
RCA (5489 "Ten Days in Jail") ... 75-125 53
RCA (5564 "Don't Stop Now") ... 75-125 53
SPARK (103 "Riot in Cell Block No. 9") ... 200-300 54
(Red label with silver print. Copies with yellow and black labels are '70s counterfeits.)
SPARK (107 "Framed") ... 200-300 54
(Any Spark colored vinyl issues are bootlegs.)
SPARK (110 "If Teardrops Were Kisses") ... 200-300 55

SPARK (113 "One Kiss")....................... 200-300 55
SPARK (116 "I Must Be Dreaming")..... 100-200 55
SPARK (122 "Smokey Joe's Cafe")..... 200-300 55
WHIPPET (100 "Cherry Lips")................ 75-100 56
WHIPPET (200 "Cherry Lips").................. 50-75 56
WHIPPET (201 "Hurt Me")........................ 50-75 56
WHIPPET (203 "Since I First Met You").. 50-75 56
WHIPPET (206 "A Fool in Love")............ 50-75 57
WHIPPET (208 "Every Night")................. 50-75 57
WHIPPET (211 "In My Dreams")............ 50-75 57
WHIPPET (212 "You Wanted Fun")......... 50-75 58
LPs: 10/12-inch
GNP...8-10 75
WHIPPET (703 "Rock 'N' Roll with the Robins").. 500-750 58
Members: Ty Terrell; Bobby Nunn; Grady Chapman; Carl Gardner; Bill Richards; H.B. Barnum; Roy Richards; Richard Berry.
Also see BARNUM, H.B.
Also see BERRY, Richard
Also see CHAPMAN, Grady
Also see COASTERS
Also see LITTLE RICHARD
Also see NIC NACS
Also see NUNN, Bobby
Also see OTIS, Johnny, Quintette, with Little Esther & Robins

ROBINS / Mel Walker & Bluenotes
(With the Johnny Otis Orchestra)
Singles: 78 rpm
REGENT (1016 "Cry Baby")..................... 40-60 50
Also see OTIS, Johnny
Also see ROBINS
Also see WALKER, Mel

ROBINS
Singles: 7-inch
TEXAS FILM (1 "Zombie")........................ 10-20 60

ROBINS
Singles: 7-inch
LAVENDER (001 "White Cliffs of Dover") 10-20 61
LAVENDER (002 "Magic of a Dream").... 15-25 61

ROBINS
Singles: 7-inch
NEW HIT (3010 "Johnny")........................ 10-15 63
SWEET TAFFY (400 "Johnny")............... 15-20 62

ROBINS, Jimmy R&B '67
(James Robbins; James Robins)
Singles: 7-inch
ALA (1173 "Repossessing My Love")...........4-6
FEDERAL (12504 "I'll Be There")...............8-12 63
JERHART (207 "I Can't Please You")...... 10-20 66
(Previously issued as by James Robbins, with Roy Wright on the flip.)
KENT (487 "It's Real")..................................4-8 68
TANGERINE (995 "Lonely Street")............5-10 '60s
20TH FOX (6661 "Shine It On")..................5-10 66
Also see ROBBINS, James / Roy Wright

ROBINS, Webb
Singles: 7-inch
REED (1063 "Why Was I Blue")........... 200-300

ROBINSON, Alvin P&R/R&B '64
Singles: 7-inch
ATCO (6581 "Let Me Down Easy")............5-10 68
BLUE CAT (104 "Searchin' ")....................8-12 65
BLUE CAT (108 "How Can I Get Over You")...8-12 65
BLUE CAT (113 "Bottom of My Soul")........8-12 65
JOE JONES (1 "Whatever You Had You Ain't Got It No More")..8-12 66
RED BIRD (010 "Fever")..............................8-12 64
TIGER (104 "Something You Got")......... 15-20 64

ROBINSON, Bill, & Quails
Singles: 78 rpm
DELUXE... 50-75 54-55
Singles: 7-inch
AMERICAN..5-10 63
DATE (1620 "Do I Love You").......................4-6 68
DELUXE (6030 "Lonely Star")............. 150-200 54
(Black label. No High Fidelity on label.)
DELUXE (6030 "Lonely Star")................ 15-25
(Black label. High Fidelity on label.)
DELUXE (6030 "Lonely Star")................. 10-15
(Yellow label.)
DELUXE (6047 "I Know She's Gone"). 150-200 54
DELUXE (6057 "Little Bit of Love")...... 150-200 54
DELUXE (6059 "Why Do I Wait")......... 150-250 54
DELUXE (6074 "Love of My Life")..........75-125 55
Also see QUAILS

ROBINSON, Billy, & Burners
Singles: 7-inch
CRAZY HORSE (1305 "I'm a Lonely Black Boy")...25-50 68

ROBINSON, Claude
Singles: 7-inch
STUDIO (1002 "Cotton Pickin' Mama")....40-60 59

ROBINSON, Cleveland
Singles: 7-inch
ASCOT (2132 "These Are the Hands")....10-15 63
NOSNIBOR (1010 "Loving Time")...........15-20 '60s

ROBINSON, Danny
Singles: 7-inch
GUYDEN (2057 "I Got a Big Cadillac")....15-25 61
SKYROCKET (107 "I Got a Big Cadillac")..100-200 56

ROBINSON, Dick
Singles: 78 rpm
MCI (1006 "Boppin' Martian")...................40-60 56
Singles: 7-inch
MCI (1006 "Boppin' Martian")..................75-100 56

ROBINSON, Eddie
Singles: 78 rpm
CLASS (204 "Suez Canal")......................10-15 56
Singles: 7-inch
CLASS (204 "Suez Canal").......................15-20 56

ROBINSON, Faithe
Singles: 7-inch
DOLPHIN (792 "My Birthday Wish").....400-500 60

ROBINSON, Fat Man R&B '49
Singles: 78 rpm
MOTIF (2001 "Lavender Coffin")..............30-40 49
REGENT (1005 "Bye Bye Roberta").........40-50 49

ROBINSON, Fenton
(With His Dukes; with His Castle Rockers; Fention Robinson)
Singles: 7-inch
DUKE (191 "Mississippi Steamboat").......15-25 58
DUKE (312 "School Boy").........................10-20 59
DUKE (329 "Tennessee Woman")...........10-20 60
GIANT..8-12 '60s
METEOR (5041 "Tennessee Woman")...150-250 57
PALOS (1200 "Somebody").......................10-20
SEVENTY SEVEN (122 "She's a Wiggler") .4-6 72
SOUND STAGE 7 (2654 "Leave You in the Arms of Your Other Man")...4-8 70
USA (842 "From My Heart").........................5-10 66
LPs: 10/12-inch
ALLIGATOR...5-10 74-78
SEVENTY-7..8-12 72

ROBINSON, Fenton / David Dean's Combo
Singles: 7-inch
DUKE...5-10 58
Also see DEAN, David
Also see ROBINSON, Fenton

ROBINSON, Floyd P&R/R&B '59
Singles: 7-inch
DOT...5-10 61-62
GROOVE (0040 "Suppose").........................5-10 64
JAMIE (1186 "Mother Nature")....................5-10 61
RCA..10-20 59-60
U.A...5-10 63-66
EPs: 7-inch
RCA (4350 "Makin' Love").........................50-75 59
LPs: 10/12-inch
RCA (LPM-2162 "Floyd Robinson")..........30-60 60
(Monaural.)
RCA (LSP-2162 "Floyd Robinson") 50-100 60
(Stereo.)

ROBINSON, Freddy P&R/R&B/LP '70
Singles: 7-inch
CHECKER...10-15 66
LIBERTY (56214 "Carmelita").......................4-6 70
LIMELIGHT (3005 "Not Like Now")...........10-15 63
MERCURY...10-15 58
PACIFIC JAZZ...4-6 69-70
QUEEN (24005 "The Hawk").......................8-12 61
WORLD PACIFIC..4-6 70
LPs: 10/12-inch
ENTERPRISE..8-12 71
PACIFIC JAZZ...10-15 69-70
Also see LITTLE WALTER
Also see HOWLIN' WOLF

ROBINSON, Hubert
(With His Yardbirds)
Singles: 78 rpm
EDDIE'S...15-25 49
JADE...10-20 51
MACY'S...15-25 50

ROBINSON, Jessie Mae
(With Little Fry & Monroe Tucker's Orchestra; Jessie Mae Robertson)
Singles: 78 rpm
DISCOVERY...15-25 46
RECORDED IN HOLLYWOOD (175 "Rompin' and Stompin' ")...15-25 51
Singles: 7-inch
BLAZE (111 "Rock 'Em & Roll 'Em") ....15-25 '50s
(Identification number shown since no selection number is used.)
MELIC (4135 "I Had a Wish").......................5-10 63
Also see TUCKER, Monroe

ROBINSON, Jim
Singles: 78 rpm
EPIC (9234 "Whole Lot of Lovin' ") 100-200 57
Singles: 7-inch
BRILL (2 "Man From Texas")..................75-125 59
EPIC (9234 "Whole Lot of Lovin' ") 150-200 57
Session: Buddy Holly (lead guitar); Joe B. Mauldin; Jerry Allison; Roses.
Also see HOLLY, Buddy
Also see JACK & JIM
Also see ROSES

ROBINSON, Jimmy Lee
Singles: 7-inch
BANDERA (2510 "Twist It Baby")............20-30 61
Also see JIMMY LEE
Also see LONESOME LEE

ROBINSON, Joey
Singles: 7-inch
MONT (1007 "Stood Up")........................75-125 62

ROBINSON, Johnny
Singles: 7-inch
EPIC...5-10 69-70
MERCURY...10-15 65
OKEH (7307 "Gone But Not Forgotten")..50-75 68
OKEH (7317 "Poor Man")..........................10-15 68
OKEH (7328 "Green Grass of Home").......8-12 68
LPs: 10/12-inch
EPIC...10-20 70

ROBINSON, L.C.
Singles: 7-inch
RHYTHM (1772 "If I Lose You Baby")....50-100 54
LPs: 10/12-inch
ARHOOLIE..8-10 72
BLUESWAY (6082 "House Cleanin' Blues")..8-10 74
Also see ROBINSON BROTHERS

ROBINSON, L.C. "Good Rockin'" / Lafayette "Thing" Thomas / Dave Alexander
LPs: 10/12-inch
WORLD PACIFIC...10-15 69
Also see ROBINSON, L.C.
Also see THOMAS, Lafayette

ROBINSON, Lucius "Mushmouth"
Singles: 78 rpm
BLACK & WHITE..15-25 45
CHIEF (700 "Hey, Pretty Mama!") 75-100
CHIEF (701 "Take It Out in the Alley") .100-125

ROBINSON, Mark
(With Duane Eddy)
Singles: 7-inch
JAMIE (1103 "Pretty Jane").......................40-60 58
TEE GEE (104 "Pretty Jane")..................75-100 58
(First issue.)
Also see EDDY, Duane

ROBINSON, Mike
Singles: 7-inch
VIBRO (4000 "Red Light")...........................10-15 60

ROBINSON, Othello
Singles: 7-inch
BABY LUV (35 "So in Luv")....................75-125 67
(First issue.)
ERA (3179 "So in Luv")...............................50-75 67

ROBINSON, Rev. Cleophus
Singles: 7-inch
BATTLE (45923 "Consecrated")..................5-10 63
LPs: 10/12-inch
BATTLE (6124 "You've Got to Love Everybody")...15-25 63

ROBINSON, Rudy
Singles: 7-inch
C.J. (633 "Bachelor Blues") 5-10 64
WHEEL CITY (40 "Mustang")...................15-25 65

ROBINSON, Shawn
Singles: 7-inch
MINIT (32013 "My Dear Heart")...............35-55 66

ROBINSON, Smokey P&R/R&B/LP '73
(William Robinson)
Singles: 7-inch
TAMLA..3-8 73-86
MOTOWN...3-5 87-88
Picture Sleeves
MOTOWN...3-5 87-88
LPs: 10/12-inch
MOTOWN..5-10 82-90
TAMLA..8-12 73-86
Also see MIRACLES
Also see ROSS, Diana, Stevie Wonder, Marvin Gaye & Smokey Robinson
Also see TEMPTATIONS

ROBINSON, Smokey, & Barbara Mitchell P&R/R&B '83
Singles: 7-inch
TAMLA (1684 "Blame It On Love")..............3-5 83
Also see ROBINSON, Smokey

ROBINSON, Stan P&R '59
Singles: 7-inch
AMY (810 "Rhinoceros")..............................5-10 60
AMY (818 "North, South, East, West").......5-10 61
MONUMENT..5-10 59
TOTSY (601 "Start to Jump")..................75-100 59

ROBINSON, Sugar "Chile" R&B '49
Singles: 78 rpm
CAPITOL..20-30 49-50
Singles: 7-inch
CAPITOL (1259 "Christmas Boogie").......50-75 50
LPs: 10/12-inch
CAPITOL (589 "Boogie Woogie")...........75-125 55

ROBINSON, Sugar "Chile" / Harry Belafonte
Singles: 78 rpm
CAPITOL (70037 "Numbers Boogie") 15-25 49
(Promotional issue only.)
Singles: 7-inch
CAPITOL (70037 "Numbers Boogie") 25-50 49
(Promotional issue only.)
Also see BELAFONTE, Harry
Also see ROBINSON, Sugar "Chile"

ROBINSON BROTHERS
Singles: 78 rpm
BLACK & WHITE (107 "I Got to Go") 75-100 45
BLACK & WHITE (108 "L.C. Boogie")....75-100 45
Members: L.C. Robinson; Walter Robinson.
Also see ROBINSON, L.C.
Also see ROBERTSON, Walter

ROBISON, Carson C&W '45
(With His Pleasant Valley Boys; with His Old Timers)
Singles: 78 rpm
CLARION...5-15 '40s
COLUMBIA..5-15 55
MGM (except 12266).....................................5-10 47-54
MGM (12266 "Rockin' & Rollin' with Grandma")...20-30 56
VICTOR...5-15 45
Singles: 7-inch
COLUMBIA..10-20 55
MGM (except 12266)...................................10-20 52-54
MGM (12266 "Rockin' & Rollin' with Grandma")..50-100 56
EPs: 7-inch
MGM...10-20 52-58
RCA...10-20 53
LPs: 10/12-inch
COLUMBIA (2551 "Square Dance")..........25-35 55
(10-inch LP.)
COLUMBIA (6029 "Square Dance").........25-35 49
(10-inch LP.)
GLENDALE..8-10

MGM (13 "Call Your Own Square Dances") 25-35 52
(10-inch LP.)
MGM (557 "Square Dances") 25-35 52
(10-inch LP.)
MGM (3258 "Square Dances") 10-20 55
MGM (3594 "Life Gets Tee-Jus, Don't It") 15-20 58
METRO (504 "Square Dance Calls") .... 10-20 '60s
RCA (3030 "Square Dances") 25-35 53
(10-inch LP.)
Also see DALHART, Vernon, & Carson Robison

ROBISON, Fabor

Singles: 78 rpm

FABOR 10-15 56

Singles: 7-inch

FABOR (4010 "Stop the Clock") 15-25 56
FAVOR (4012 "Why Am I Falling") 15-25 56

ROCCO, Lenny

Singles: 7-inch

DELSEY (301"Sugar Girl") 750-1000 65

ROCCO, Tommy
(With the Cavaliers)

Singles: 7-inch

E&M (3264 "Midnight Train") 30-40 60
RAZORBACK (102 "Back to School") 15-25 58

ROCHELL & CANDLES P&R/R&B '61

Singles: 7-inch

CHALLENGE (9158 "Each Night") 50-60 62
CHALLENGE (9191 "Let's Run Away and Get Married") 10-15 62
COLLECTABLES .... 3-5 '80s
SWINGIN' (623 "Once Upon a Time") 15-25 60
SWINGIN' (634 "So Far Away") 10-20 61
SWINGIN' (640 "Peg O' My Heart") 10-20 62
SWINGIN' (652 "Long Time Ago") 15-25 63
Members: Rochell Henderson; Johnny Wyatt; T. C. Henderson; Mel Sasso.
Also see WYATT, Johnny

ROCHELLES

Singles: 7-inch

SPACEY (201 "Teardrops") 40-50

ROCK, Jimmy
(With the Royal Lancers)

Singles: 7-inch

HI MAR (503/504 "Summer Love"/ "Mama") 10-20 63
TODD (1024 "The Drag") 10-15 59
Session: Otis Blackwell; Paul Gottschall; Bobby Gregg; Pete Bennett; Roy Buchanan.
Also see BLACKWELL, Otis
Also see BUCHANAN, Roy
Also see GREGG, Bobby
Also see ROYAL LANCERS
Also see THOMAS, Paul

ROCK FLOWERS P&R '72

Singles: 7-inch

WHEEL 4-8 71-73

Picture Sleeves

WHEEL (282 "Number Wonderful") 20-40 71

LPs: 10/12-inch

WHEEL 10-15 71-72
Members: Ardie Tillman; Debbie Clinger; Rindy; Jacquie Wiseman.

ROCK-A-BOUTS

Singles: 7-inch

CHANCELLOR (1030 "She's a Fat Girl") 10-20 59
Also see STARGLOWS / Rock-A-Bouts / Cecil Young Quartet

ROCK-A-FELLAS

Singles: 7-inch

ABC-PAR (9923 "Red Lips") 10-20 58
COED (505 "High School Girl") 15-25 58
COED (517 "Super Chick") 15-25 59
DEVERE (313 "Red Lips") 50-75 58
(First issue.)
Also see BELL, Eddie
Also see NICHOLS, Joey, & Rock-A-Fellas

ROCKAFELLAS
(Rocka-Fellas)

Singles: 7-inch

SCA (18003 "Strike It Rich") 10-20 63
SOUTHERN SOUND (112 "Strike It Rich") 30-40 62

ROCK-A-FELLERS

Singles: 7-inch

CUCA (1039 "Reaction") 15-20 61
Members: Bob Merkt; Del Stralo; Miles Merkt; Ken Berdoll; Jim Sessody.

ROCK-A-TEENS P&R '59

Singles: 7-inch

APEX (76591 "Woo-Hoo") 10-20 59
(Canadian.)
DORAN (3515 "Woo-Hoo") 40-60 59
ROULETTE (4192 "Woo-Hoo") 15-20 59
ROULETTE (4217 "Doggone It Baby") 15-20 60

LPs: 10/12-inch

MURRAY HILL .... 5-10 '80s
ROULETTE (R-25109 "Woo-Hoo") 75-125 60
(Monaural.)
ROULETTE (SR-25109 "Woo-Hoo") 100-200 60
(Stereo.)
ROULETTE (SR-25109 "Woo-Hoo") 5-10 84
(Label shows year as 1984.)

ROCKATEERS

Singles: 78 rpm

STARS, INC. (544 "Rock Bottom") 10-15 57

Singles: 7-inch

STARS, INC. (544 "Rock Bottom") 15-25 57

ROCK-A-TONES

Singles: 7-inch

JUDY TONE (369 "Please Don't Talk About Me") 100-150
WHAMMY (7450 "One More Chance") 75-85 61

ROCKATUNES

Singles: 7-inch

COLUMBIA (2613 "Tomorrow") 50-100
(Canadian.)

ROCKATUNES

Singles: 7-inch

ROCK-A-TUNES (1010 "Woman Fever") 75-125

ROCKAWAYS

Singles: 7-inch

NASH (600 "Rampage") 20-40
Member: Cliff Nash.
Also see NASH, Cliff, & Rockaways

ROCKER, Johnny
(With the Cheques)

Singles: 7-inch

FEDERAL (12425 "Queen") 10-15 61
LARK (4514 "Song of the Lonely Guitar") 200-300 61
(Blue vinyl.)

ROCKERS
(With Emmet Carter Combo)

Singles: 78 rpm

CARTER (3029 "Tell Me Why") 200-300 55
FEDERAL (12267 "What Am I to Do") 50-75 56
FEDERAL (12273 "Why Don't You Believe Me") 25-50 56

Singles: 7-inch

CARTER (3029 "Tell Me Why") 1000-1500 55
(Maroon label.)
CARTER (3029 "Tell Me Why") 50-75
(Blue label.)
FEDERAL (12267 "What Am I to Do") 150-250 56
(Green label.)
FEDERAL (12267 "What Am I to Do") 200-300 56
(White label with bio. Promotional issue only.)
FEDERAL (12273 "Why Don't You Believe Me") 75-125 56
Member: Art Larson.
Also see FANANDOS

ROCKERS

Singles: 7-inch

ARVIS (104 "I Got That Queen") 300-400
Member: Arnold Blevins.

ROCKERS

Singles: 7-inch

MARK (135 "Rock, Rock Rocketship") 100-200 59

ROCKERS

Singles: 7-inch

ROCK (101 "Mean Mean Woman") 400-500

ROCKET TONES

Singles: 7-inch

OPERATORS (2015 "Fireball") 75-85 62

ROCKETEERS

Singles: 78 rpm

HERALD 75-100 53

Singles: 7-inch

HERALD (415 "Foolish One") 400-500 53
(Black vinyl.)
HERALD (415 "Foolish One") 1000-1500 53
(Red vinyl.)

ROCKETEERS

Singles: 78 rpm

MODERN 15-25 56

Singles: 7-inch

MODERN (999 "Talk It Over Baby") 40-50 56

ROCKETEERS

Singles: 7-inch

GLAD HAMP (2017 "Drag Strip") 15-25 63
VAL-UE (1002 "Rippin' and Rockin'") 10-20 60

ROCKETEERS

Singles: 7-inch

FIREFLY (326 "My Reckless Heart") 3-5 74
(Black vinyl.)
FIREFLY (326 "My Reckless Heart") 4-6 74
(Red vinyl.)
M.J.C. (501 "My Reckless Heart") 800-1200 58
Also see CADETS
Also see CLASS-NOTES

ROCKETONES

Singles: 78 rpm

MELBA (113 "Mexico") 50-75 57

Singles: 7-inch

MELBA (113 "Mexico") 50-75 57
(Small print.)
MELBA (113 "Mexico") 10-15 57
(Large print.)
Members: Bill Witt; Arthur Blackman; Ron Johnson; Al Days; Harold Chapman.

ROCKET-TONES

Singles: 7-inch

3 SONS (928 "Too Many Loves") 75-125 62

ROCKETS

Singles: 78 rpm

MODERN (992 "You Are the First One") 10-20 56

Singles: 7-inch

MODERN (992 "You Are the First One") 40-50 56
Also see BEASLEY, Jimmy
Also see JACKS

ROCKETS
("Vocal by Gene Watson")

Singles: 7-inch

TRI-DEC (8357 "My Rockin' Baby") 300-400 58
(Also issued as by Gene Watson.)
Also see WATSON, Gene

ROCKETS

Singles: 7-inch

COOL (712 "Always Alone") .... 20-30 '50s
COOL (9035 "Movin' & Groovin'") 15-25 58
Also see LEE, Lois

ROCKETS

Singles: 7-inch

WHITE WHALE (270 "Hole in My Pocket") 4-8 68

LPs: 10/12-inch

WHITE WHALE 15-20 68
Members: Ralph Molina; Danny Whitten; Bob Notkoff; Billy Talbot; Leon Whitsell; George Whitsell.

ROCKETS

Singles: 7-inch

LO-NEL (2002 "Little Drummer") 300-350

ROCKETS, Stan D.

Singles: 7-inch

CLIX (812 "Satan's Angels") 75-125 58

ROCKETTES

Singles: 78 rpm

PARROT (789 "I Can't Forget") 200-400 53

Singles: 7-inch

PARROT (789 "I Can't Forget") 1000-1500 53

ROCKETTS

Singles: 7-inch

JANET (203 "Moonlight Rock") 75-125
Also see DOTSON BROTHERS

ROCK-FELLERS

Singles: 7-inch

VALOR (2004 "Ours") 25-35 59

ROCKIN' BRADLEY
(With His Rockers)

Singles: 7-inch

FIRE (1007 "Lookout") 100-150 59
HULL (729 "She's Mine Not Yours") 50-75 58

ROCKIN' CHAIRS

Singles: 7-inch

RECORTE (402 "Rockin' Chair Boogie") 75-100 58
RECORTE (404 "Come On Baby") 30-50 58
RECORTE (412 "Memories of Love") 30-50 59
Members: Lenny Dean; Bob Gerardi; Carmine Ray; Rick Baxter; Joe Cary.
Also see DEAN, Lenny, & Rockin' Chairs
Also see WINCHELL, Danny

ROCKIN' CONTINENTALS

Singles: 7-inch

CASINO (1007 "The 309") 600-900 62
CASINO (1009 "Cobra 289") 20-30 63
Members: Johnny Thompson; Melvin Ralston; Chuck Smith; Bill Doyle.

ROCKIN' DEVILS

Singles: 7-inch

ORFEON (1699 "Wooly Bully") .... 15-25 '60s
ORFEON (1752 "Gloria") .... 15-25 '60s

ROCKIN' DUKES
(Rockin Dukes)

Singles: 7-inch

OJ (1007 "Angel and a Rose") 250-300 58

ROCKIN' DUKES

Singles: 7-inch

SHELLEY (128 "Cross Current") 15-25 61
(Also issued as by Sterly Singleton.)
Also see SINGLETON, Sterly

ROCKIN' FOO

Singles: 7-inch

HOBBIT (42001 "Rochester River") 5-10 69

Picture Sleeves

HOBBIT (42001 "Rochester River") 8-10 69

LPs: 10/12-inch

HOBBIT (5001 "Rockin Foo") 15-25 69
UNI 8-12 71

Singles: 7-inch

MARK (114 "Hey, Maryann") 75-125 57

ROCKIN' HORSES

Singles: 78 rpm

GRAND (139 "House Rocker") 15-25 56

Singles: 7-inch

GRAND (139 "House Rocker") 30-50 56

ROCKIN' JESTERS

Singles: 7-inch

HEBRA (128 "I Was Too Blind") 100-150
OKLAHOMA (5004 "I Was Too Blind") 75-100 58

ROCKIN' R's P&R '59

Singles: 7-inch

STEPHENY (1842 "Walking You to School") 25-35 60
TEMPUS (1507 "Heat") 15-20 59
TEMPUS (7541 "The Beat") 20-30 59
VEE-JAY (334 "I'm Still in Love with You") 10-20 60
VEE-JAY (346 "Hum Bug") 10-20 60
Also see VOLZ, Ron, & Rockin' R's

ROCKIN' RAMRODS
(Ramrods)

Singles: 7-inch

BON-BON (1315 "She Lied") 20-30 64
CLARIDGE (301 "Don't Fool with Fu Manchu") 5-10 65
CLARIDGE (317 "Play It") 15-25 66
EXPLOSIVE (101 "Jungle Call") 15-25 63
PLYMOUTH (2961 "I Wanna Be Your Man") 15-25 64
PLYMOUTH (2963 "Bright Lit Blue Skies") 10-20 66
SOUTHERN SOUND (205 "Wild About You") 10-15 65

Picture Sleeves

PLYMOUTH (2961 "I Wanna Be Your Man") 20-30 64
Also see RAMRODS

ROCKIN' REBELLIONS
Singles: 7-inch
GOLD GROOVE (111 "Anyway the Wind Blows") ... 20-30 67

ROCKIN' REBELS — P&R '62
Singles: 7-inch
ABC ... 4-6 73
ERIC (108 "Wild Weekend") ... 4-6 73
ITZY (8 "Wild Weekend") ... 10-15 66
REO ... 10-20 62-63
(Canadian.)
REO GOLDEN TREASURES ... 4-8 67
(Canadian.)
STORK (3 "Bongo Blue Beat") ... 10-15 64
SWAN (4125 "Wild Weekend") ... 8-12 62
SWAN (4140 "Rockin' Crickets") ... 10-15 63
(Previously issued as by the Hot Toddys.)
SWAN (4150 "Another Wild Weekend") ... 8-12 63
SWAN (4161 "Monday Morning") ... 8-12 63
SWAN (4248 "Wild Weekend") ... 10-20 66
(Though not credited, the flip of 4248, *Donkey Twine*, is by Kathy Lynn & Playboys.)
LPs: 10/12-inch
SWAN (509 "Wild Weekend") ... 50-100 63
Members: Tom Gorman; Paul Balon; Mickey Kipler; Jim Kipler.
Also see BUFFALO REBELS
Also see HOT TODDYS
Also see LYNN, Kathy
Also see REBELS

ROCKIN' REBELS
Singles: 7-inch
SENECA (11008 "Study Hall Blues") ... 300-400

ROCKIN' ROADRUNNERS
Singles: 7-inch
LEE C (696 "Go Away") ... 15-25 66
LEE C (970 "King of the Jungle") ... 10-15 66
TENER (1015 "Down") ... 15-25 67

ROCKIN' RONALD & REBELS
Singles: 7-inch
END (1043 "Kansas City") ... 15-25 59
ORCHID (5005 "Kansas City") ... 30-50 58
Member: Ronnie Hawkins.
Also see HAWKINS, Ronnie

ROCKIN' SAINTS
Singles: 7-inch
DECCA (30990 "Alright Baby") ... 20-25 59
DECCA (31144 "Cheat On Me, Baby") ... 50-75 60
Member: Buddy Randell.
Also see RANDELL, Buddy

ROCKIN' SID
Singles: 7-inch
AVENUE (1926 "Misery") ... 150-250 57

ROCKIN' STOCKINGS
Singles: 7-inch
SUN (350 "Rockin' Lang Syne") ... 50-100 60
SUN (1960 "Rockin' Lang Syne") ... 20-30 60
Member: Billy Lee Riley.
Also see RILEY, Billy Lee

ROCKING BROTHERS
Singles: 78 rpm
ELKO (901 "Play Boy Hop") ... 25-50 55
IMPERIAL ... 10-15 55
POST (2015 "Teen Time Theme") ... 10-15 55
R&B (1309 "Rock It") ... 15-20 55
SAVOY (1144 "Play Boy Hop") ... 10-20 55
Singles: 7-inch
ELKO (901 "Play Boy Hop") ... 150-200 55
(First issue.)
IMPERIAL (5333 "Rock It") ... 20-30 55
IMPERIAL (5341 "Blow Torch") ... 20-30 55
(Black vinyl.)
IMPERIAL (5341 "Blow Torch") ... 100-200 55
(Purple vinyl.)
POST (2015 "Teen Time Theme") ... 20-30 55
R&B (1309 "Rock It") ... 30-40 55
(First issue.)
SAVOY (1144 "Play Boy Hop") ... 20-40 55
WHIPPET (207 "Yeah! Yeah!") ... 15-25 57
Members: Jason; Wilbur.

ROCKING GHOSTS
Singles: 7-inch
MOD (1001 "Belinda") ... 10-20 66

ROCKING MARTIN
Singles: 7-inch
STARDAY (658 "All Because of You") .250-500 58
(Promotional issue only. This same number is also used on a 1963 Cowboy Copas release.)
Also see COPAS, Cowboy

ROCKING REBELS
Singles: 7-inch
TRIO (849 "Tom-Tom, Pt. 1"/"Tom-Tom, Pt. 2") ... 15-25 60
(Also issued as by Carl Newman.)
Also see NEWMAN, Carl

ROCKING RICHARD
Singles: 7-inch
CORE ("I Had to Cry") ... 15-25
(No selection number used.)

ROCK-ITS
Singles: 7-inch
SPANGLE (2010 "It's L-o-v-e") ... 75-100 58
Also see WRIGHT, Dale

ROCK'N ROLLERS
Singles: 7-inch
VEN (100 "For You") ... 100-200 58

ROCKS
Singles: 7-inch
GOLD MASTER (1003 "Rock Pretty Baby") ... 15-25 '60s

ROCKY & MILLIONAIRES
Singles: 7-inch
ORCHESTRA (102 "Remember Me") .. 500-750 63

ROCKY & RIDDLERS
Singles: 7-inch
PANORAMA (28 "Flash & Crash") ... 15-25 66
Member: Rocky Rhoades.
Also see IMPERIALS

ROCKY & ROCKY FELLOWS
Singles: 7-inch
GOLDWATER (424 "Paint the Town Red") ... 150-200 58

ROCKY FELLERS — P&R '63
Singles: 7-inch
DONNA (1383 "Don't Sit Down") ... 10-20 63
PARKWAY (836 "Long Tall Sally") ... 10-20 62
SCEPTER ... 10-20 62-64
W.B. ... 8-12 64-65
Picture Sleeves
SCEPTER (1254 "Like the Big Guys Do") ... 10-20 63
LPs: 10/12-inch
SCEPTER (SP-512 "Killer Joe") ... 25-35 63
(Monaural.)
SCEPTER (SPS-512 "Killer Joe") ... 30-40 63
(Stereo.)
Members: Eddie; Albert; Tony; Junior; Pop.

ROD & TERRY
Singles: 7-inch
CUCA (1206 "That's All Right") ... 75-100 65
Also see LAVENDERS

ROD TWISTERS
Singles: 7-inch
ZULU (100 "Speed Limit") ... 25-30

RODANS
Singles: 7-inch
VEST (825 "Time Is Passing") ... 150-200 58

RODENTS
Singles: 7-inch
PEQUOD ("And Your Bird Can Sing") ... 50-100 66
Members: David Lindley; Mark Freedman.
Also see KALEIDOSCOPE

RODERICK, Judy
LPs: 10/12-inch
COLUMBIA ... 10-15 64
VANGUARD ... 10-15 65

RODGERS, Buck
Singles: 7-inch
STARDAY (245 "Little Rock Rock") ... 150-250 56

RODGERS, Hank & Ramona
Singles: 7-inch
RUBY (610 "Hop, Skip, and Jump") ... 50-75 58

RODGERS, Jack
Singles: 7-inch
SPRY (105 "Train Whistle Blues") ... 20-30 57
STAFF (101 "Take Me Back") ... 50-75

RODGERS, Jimmie — C&W '55
Singles: 78 rpm
BLUEBIRD ... 40-80 '30s
ELECTRADISK (1830 "Moonlight & Skies") ... 250-500 32
ELECTRADISK (1966 "Looking for a New Mama") ... 200-400 32
ELECTRADISK (1983 "Whisper Your Mother's Name") ... 200-400 33
ELECTRADISK (1999 "Whippin' That Old T.B.") ... 200-400 33
ELECTRADISK (2008 "Mother, the Queen of My Heart") ... 200-400 33
ELECTRADISK (2009 "You and My Old Guitar") ... 200-400 33
ELECTRADISK (2042 "Mississippi Moon") ... 200-400 33
ELECTRADISK (2060 "Waiting for a Train") ... 200-400 33
ELECTRADISK (2109 "In the Jailhouse Now") ... 200-400 33
ELECTRADISK (2155 "Jimmie Rodgers' Last Blue Yodel") ... 200-400 33
MONTGOMERY WARD ... 50-100 '30s
SUNRISE (3104 "Moonlight & Skies") .. 200-300 33
SUNRISE (3131 "Looking for a New Mama") ... 200-300 33
SUNRISE (3142 "Whisper Your Mother's Name") ... 200-300 33
SUNRISE (3157 "Whippin' That Old T.B.") ... 200-300 33
SUNRISE (3167 "Mother, the Queen of My Heart") ... 200-300 33
SUNRISE (3168 "Down the Old Road to Home") ... 200-300 33
SUNRISE (3169 "Why Should I Be Lonely") ... 200-300 33
SUNRISE (3170 "You and My Old Guitar") ... 200-300 34
SUNRISE (3171 "Let Me Be Your Side Track") ... 200-300 34
SUNRISE (3172 "Blue Yodel") ... 200-300 34
SUNRISE (3217 "Mississippi Moon") ... 200-300 34
SUNRISE (3244 "Waiting for a Train") .200-300 34
SUNRISE (3306 "In the Jailhouse Now") ... 200-300 34
SUNRISE (3362 "Jimmie Rodgers' Last Blue Yodel") ... 200-300 34
SUNRISE (3418 "Lullaby Yodel") ... 200-300 34
VICTOR (20864 thru 23574) ... 25-75 27-33
VICTOR (23580 thru 24456) ... 50-100 '30s
VICTOR (4000 series) ... 15-25
VICTOR (5000 & 6000 series) ... 5-15 49-56
VICTOR (18-6000 "Cowhand's Last Ride") ... 1500-2500 33
(Picture disc.)
Note: Many of Jimmie Rodgers' releases in the early '30s were made by Victor/Bluebird specifically for sale in department store chains: Elektradisk (Woolworth's), Sunrise (W.T. Grant, Kress, McCrory), and Montgomery Ward, with its own label.
Albums: 78 rpm
RCA (244 "Yodelingly Yours") ... 100-150 52
(Includes three 78 rpm singles.)
RCA (282 "Yodelingly Yours, Vol. 2") ... 100-150 52
(Includes three 78 rpm singles.)
RCA (318 "Yodelingly Yours, Vol. 3") ... 100-150 52
(Includes three 78 rpm singles.)
RCA (3035 "Yodelingly Yours, Vol. 4") .100-150 52
(Includes three 78 rpm singles.)
Singles: 7-inch
RCA (0017 thru 6408) ... 10-20 49-56
EPs: 7-inch
RCA (6 "Immortal Performances By Jimmie Rodgers") ... 35-50 50
RCA (10 "Jimmie Rodgers, Vol. 1") ... 35-50 51
RCA (21 "Jimmie Rodgers Memorial Album, Vol. 1") ... 35-50 52
RCA (22 "Jimmie Rodgers Memorial Album, Vol. 2") ... 35-50 52
RCA (23 "Jimmie Rodgers Memorial Album, Vol. 3") ... 35-50 52
RCA (409 "Jimmie Rodgers Memorial Album, Vol. 4") ... 35-50 52
RCA (410 "Jimmie Rodgers Memorial Album, Vol. 5") ... 35-50 52
RCA (411 "Jimmie Rodgers Memorial Album, Vol. 6") ... 35-50 52
RCA (793 "Never No Mo' Blues") ... 25-35 56
(Two EPs)
RCA (1232 "Never No Mo' Blues") ... 35-55 55
(Two EPs)
RCA (3073 "Travelin' Blues") ... 50-100 52
(Two EPs)
RCA (5097 "Legendary Jimmie Rodgers") ... 20-30 58
LPs: 10/12-inch
ANTHOLOGY OF COUNTRY MUSIC (11 "Unissued Jimmie Rodgers") ... 15-25 83
PICKWICK ... 6-12 76
RCA (0075 "Legendary Jimmie Rodgers") ... 10-20 74
(Mail order offer.)
RCA (LPM-1232 ("Never No Mo' Blues") . 20-30 55
RCA (AHM1-1232 "Never No Mo' Blues") .. 5-10 '70s
RCA (LPM-1640 "Train Whistle Blues") ... 20-30 57
RCA (AHM1-1640 "Train Whistle Blues") .. 5-10 '70s
RCA (LPM-2112 "My Rough and Rowdy Ways") ... 15-25 60
RCA (ANL1-2112 "My Rough and Rowdy Ways") ... 5-10 75
RCA (LPM-2213 "Jimmie the Kid") ... 15-25 61
RCA (AHM1-2213 "Jimmie the Kid") ... 5-10 '70s
RCA (2504 "A Legendary Performer") ... 6-12 78
RCA (AHM1-2531 "Country Music Hall of Fame") ... 5-10 '70s
RCA (LPM-2531 "Country Music Hall of Fame") ... 15-25 62
RCA (LPM-2634 "The Short But Brilliant Life of Jimmie Rodgers") ... 15-25 55
RCA (AHM1-2634 "The Short But Brilliant Life of Jimmie Rodgers") ... 5-10 '70s
RCA (LPM-2865 "My Time Ain't Long") ... 15-25 64
RCA (AHM1-2865 "My Time Ain't Long") ... 5-10 '70s
RCA (3037 "Jimmie Rodgers Memorial Album, Vol. 1 – Yodelingly Yours") ... 150-250 52
(10-inch LP.)
RCA (3038 "Jimmie Rodgers Memorial Album, Vol. 2 – Yodelingly Yours") ... 150-250 52
(10-inch LP.)
RCA (3039 "Jimmie Rodgers Memorial Album, Vol. 3 – Yodelingly Yours") ... 150-250 52
(10-inch LP.)
RCA (3073 "Travelin' Blues") ... 150-250 53
(10-inch LP.)
RCA (LPM/LSP-3315 "Best of the Legendary Jimmie Rodgers") ... 10-15 65
RCA (AHL1-3315 "Best of the Legendary Jimmie Rodgers") ... 5-10 '70s
RCA (6091 "This Is Jimmie Rodgers") ... 8-12 73

RODGERS, Jimmie — P&R/C&W/R&B/LP '57
("With Michele")
Singles: 78 rpm
ROULETTE ... 20-40 57
Singles: 7-inch
A&M ... 4-8 67-70
ABC ... 4-6 73
DOT ... 5-10 62-67
EPIC ... 4-6 71-72
PEAK (7011 " Ring-A-Ling-A-Lario") ... 5-10 62
RCA ... 4-6 73-75
ROULETTE (4015 thru 4045) ... 15-25 57-58
(Red or orange labels.)
ROULETTE (4015 thru 4045) ... 10-15 58
(White label, colored lines.)
ROULETTE (4070 thru 4439) ... 6-12 58-62
ROULETTE (SSR-4158 "Ring-A-Ling-A-Lario") ... 20-30 59
(Stereo.)
ROULETTE (SSR-4218 "T.L.C.") ... 20-30 60
(Stereo.)
ROULETTE (SSR-8001 "Bo Diddley") ... 20-30 59
(Stereo.)
ROULETTE (SSR-8007 "Froggy Went A-Courtin' ") ... 20-30 59
(Stereo.)
ROULETTE (SSR-8010 "St. James Infirmary") ... 20-30 59
(Stereo.)
SCRIMSHAW (1318 "Secretly") ... 3-5 78
Picture Sleeves
DOT (16378 "No One Will Ever Know") ... 8-12 62
PEAK (7011 " Ring-A-Ling-A-Lario") ... 8-12 62
ROULETTE (4070 "Secretly") ... 10-20 58

ROULETTE (4090 "Are You Really Mine") 10-20 58
ROULETTE (4158 "Ring-A-Ling-A-Lario") 10-20 59
ROULETTE (4293 "Woman from Liberia") 10-20 60

EPs: 7-inch

ROULETTE 15-25 57-60

LPs: 10/12-inch

A&M 8-15 67-70
DOT 10-25 62-67
FORUM 15-25 60
HAMILTON 10-25 64-65
RCA 8-12 73-75
ROULETTE (25020 thru 25057) 20-30 57-59
ROULETTE (R-25071 thru R-25199) 15-30 59-63
(Monaural.)
ROULETTE (SR-25071 thru SR-25199) .. 20-35 59-63
(Stereo.)
ROULETTE (42000 series) 5-10
SCRIMSHAW 5-10 78

RODGERS, Jimmie / Lampliters

LPs: 10/12-inch

GUEST STAR (1405 "Songs America Sings") 10-15 63

RODGERS, Morris, & Continentals

Singles: 7-inch

DELTA (601/602 "Wonders of Love") 75-125 63

RODNEY & BLAZERS

Singles: 7-inch

CHAN (110 "It's All Over But the Crying") 30-40 61
DORE (572 "Teenage Cinderella") 20-30 60
DORE (588 "Tell Me Baby") 10-15 61
KAMPUS (100 "Teenage Cinderella") ... 50-100 60
(First issue.)
KAMPUS (561 "Summer Love") 20-40 60
KAMPUS (812 "Blue School") 20-40 61
KAMPUS (880 "Warpaint") 20-40 61
KAMPUS (6264 "Short Fat Fannie") 15-25 64
Members: Rodney Lay; Bob York; Bob Scott; Pete Williams; Don Downing; Gene Bongiorni; Sam Beck; Skip Knape; Chan Romero; Dennis Winton.

ROE, Tex, & Ramblers

Singles: 7-inch

STERLING (1839 "Rocketship to the Moon") 100-150 57

ROE, Tommy P&R/R&B/LP '62
(With the Satins; with Flamingos; with Roemans)

Singles: 7-inch

ABC 4-8 66-71
ABC-PAR 5-10 62-66
AERTAUN (1108 "Wendy") 5-10 67
AWESOME (104 "First Things First") 3-5 84
AWESOME (108 "Sittin' in a Mood") 3-5 84
BGO (1003 "She Do Run Run") 3-5 82
CURB/MCA 3-5 85-86
JUDD (1018 "Caveman") 15-25 60
JUDD (1022 "Sheila") 25-45 60
MCA (1447 "Dizzy") 3-5 84
MGM/SOUTH 4-6 72-73
MARK IV (001 "Caveman") 25-50 60
MERCURY 3-5 86-87
MONUMENT 4-6 72-77
ROULETTE (119 "Everybody") 4-6 71
ROULETTE (120 "Jam Up and Jelly Tight") .4-6 71
TRUMPET (1401 "Caveman") 40-60 60
W.B./CURB 3-6 78-80

Picture Sleeves

ABC 4-8 66-70
ABC-PAR (10362 "Susie Darlin'") 8-12 62

LPs: 10/12-inch

ABC (594 thru 762) 10-15 67-72
ABC-PAR (ABC-423 thru ABC-574) 20-35 62-66
(Monaural.)
ABC-PAR (ABCS-423 thru ABCS-575) ... 25-40 62-66
(Stereo.)
ACCORD 5-10 82
GUSTO .... 5-10 '80s
MCA 5-10 82
MONUMENT 8-12 76-77

ROE, Tommy / Bobby Rydell / Gene Pitney

LPs: 10/12-inch

INT'L AWARD .... 10-15 '60s
Also see PITNEY, Gene

ROE, Tommy / Bobby Rydell / Ray Stevens

LPs: 10/12-inch

DESIGN (178 "Young Lovers") 15-20 63
Also see RYDELL, Bobby
Also see STEVENS, Ray

ROE, Tommy / Bobby Lee Trammell

LPs: 10/12-inch

CROWN 15-20 63
Also see ROE, Tommy
Also see TRAMMELL, Bobby Lee

ROGER & TEMPESTS

Singles: 7-inch

NU RECORDS (4268 "Bad Bad Way") 100-200

ROGER & TRAVELERS

Singles: 7-inch

CRYSTAL BALL (128 "Smile") 4-8 78
(Black vinyl. 500 made.)
CRYSTAL BALL (128 "Smile") 8-12 78
(Red vinyl. 25 made.)
EMBER (1079 "You're Daddy's Little Girl") 75-100 61
(Multi-color label with "logs" logo.)
EMBER (1079 "You're Daddy's Little Girl") 50-75 62
(Black label with "flames" logo.)
SCATT (128 "Smile") 4-6 88
Member: Roger Koob; Billy Koob; John Roddy; Joe Vece.
Also see PREMIERS

ROGERS, Dan

Singles: 7-inch

ERA (3131 "Lost Without You") 40-60 64

ROGERS, Frantic Johnny
(Al Casey)

Singles: 7-inch

CINDY (3010 "Ramrod") 30-40 58
Also see CASEY, Al

ROGERS, Jesse, & His 49ers C&W '49
(Jesse Rodgers)

Singles: 78 rpm

BLUEBIRD 10-25 35-49
COWBOY 8-10

Singles: 7-inch

RCA (48-0350 "Great Big Needle") 10-20 50
(Green vinyl.)
RCA (48-0359 "Finders Keepers") 10-20 50
(Green vinyl.)
RCA (48-0389 "Plain Old Lovin' ") 10-20 50
(Green vinyl.)

ROGERS, Jesse

Singles: 7-inch

ARCADE (143 "You Can't Hang That Monkey on My Back") 10-20 57
ARCADE (162 "Nightwind") 10-20 61
ARCADE (169 "Jump Cats, Jump") 50-100 62

ROGERS, Jimmy R&B '57
(With His Trio; with His Rocking Four)

Singles: 78 rpm

CHESS (1435 "That's All Right") 50-100 50
CHESS (1442 "Going Away Baby") 50-100 50
CHESS (1453 "The World Is in a Tangle") 50-100 51
CHESS (1476 "Chance to Love") 25-50 51
CHESS (1506 "I Used to Have a Woman") 75-100 51
CHESS (1519 thru 1721) 20-40 52-59

Singles: 7-inch

CHESS (1506 "I Used to Have a Woman") 100-150 52
CHESS (1519 "The Last Time") 50-100 52
CHESS (1543 "Left Me with a Broken Heart") 50-75 53
CHESS (1574 "Chicago Bound") 50-75 54
CHESS (1616 "You're the One") 40-60 55
CHESS (1643 "Walking By Myself") 40-60 56
CHESS (1659 "One Kiss") 40-60 57
CHESS (1721 "My Last Meal") 20-30 59

LPs: 10/12-inch

CHESS (207 "Jimmy Rogers") 15-25 76
(Two discs.)
CHESS (407 "Chicago Bound") 8-12 74
Session: Muddy Waters; Big Crawford; Little Walter; Elgin Evans; Willie Dixon; J.T. Brown; Otis Spann; Big Walter Horton; Fred Below.
Also see BROWN, J.T.
Also see DIXON, Willie
Also see HORTON, Big Walter
Also see LITTLE WALTER
Also see SPANN, Otis
Also see SUNNYLAND SLIM
Also see WATERS, Muddy
Also see WILLIAMSON, Sonny Boy

ROGERS, Jimmy, & Freddy King

LPs: 10/12-inch

SHELTER (8921 "Gold Tailed Bird") 8-12 73
Also see KING, Freddy
Also see ROGERS, Jimmy

ROGERS, Joey
(With the All Americans)

Singles: 7-inch

ABC-PAR (10110 "Don't Go Away Mad") ... 5-10 60
NU-CLEAR (1 "Bumble Bee") 15-25 57
NU-CLEAR ("Jeannine") 15-25 57

ROGERS, Johnny

Singles: 78 rpm

RONEL (106 "Madly in Love") 8-12 55

Singles: 7-inch

CINDY (3010 "Ramrod") 8-12 58
RONEL (106 "Madly in Love") 20-30 55

ROGERS, Juanita, & Lynn Hollings
(With Mr. V's Five Joys)

Singles: 7-inch

PINK CLOUDS (333 "Teenager's Letter of Promises") 400-500 58
PINK CLOUDS (334 "Teenager's Love Letter") 50-75 58

ROGERS, Kenny C&W '75
(Kenneth Rogers; with Linda Davis)

Singles: 7-inch

CARLTON (454 "That Crazy Feeling") 50-75 58
CARLTON (468 "For You Alone") 40-50 58
EVA-TONE/READER'S DIGEST ("His Greatest Hits") 10-15 83
(Single-sided, square, cardboard soundsheet. Promotional issue only.)
JOLLY ROGERS 4-6 73-74
KEN-LEE (102 "Jole Blon") 50-100 58
LIBERTY 3-5 80-86
MERCURY 5-10 66
RCA 3-5 84-89
REPRISE 3-5 89-91
U.A. 3-6 76-80

Picture Sleeves

LIBERTY 3-5 80-83
RCA 3-5 84-86
U.A. 4-6 79-80

LPs: 10/12-inch

BREAKAWAY 5-8 84
JOLLY ROGERS (5001 "Backroads") .. 100-200 75
(Promotional picture disc.)
LIBERTY (Except 8344) 5-10 80-85
LIBERTY (8344 "HBO Presents Kenny Rogers Greatest Hits") 15-20 83
(Promotional only picture disc.)
MFSL (044 "The Gambler") 30-40 80
MFSL (049 "Greatest Hits") 30-40 80
MASTERS 5-10
PICKWICK 5-10 79
QSP 5-10 84
RCA 5-8 84-87
REPRISE 5-8 89
U.A. (Except 934) 5-8 76-80
U.A. (934 "The Gambler) 5-10 78
(Black vinyl.)
U.A. (934 "The Gambler) 50-100 78
(Picture disc. Promotional issue only. One of a four-artist, four-disc set.)
Session: Bill Medley.
Also see CAMPBELL, Glen / Anne Murray / Kenny Rogers / Crystal Gayle
Also see DOYLE, Bobby
Also see MEDLEY, Bill

ROGERS, Kenny, & Kim Carnes C&W/P&R '80

Singles: 7-inch

U.A. 3-5 80

Picture Sleeves

U.A. 3-5 80
Also see CARNES, Kim

ROGERS, Kenny, Kim Carnes & James Ingram C&W/P&R/R&B '84

Singles: 7-inch

RCA 3-5 84

Picture Sleeves

RCA 3-5 84
Also see ROGERS, Kenny, & Kim Carnes

ROGERS, Kenny, & Holly Dunn C&W '90

Singles: 7-inch

REPRISE 3-5 90

ROGERS, Kenny, & Sheena Easton C&W/P&R '83

Singles: 7-inch

LIBERTY 3-5 83

Picture Sleeves

LIBERTY 3-5 83

LPs: 10/12-inch

LIBERTY 5-10 84

ROGERS, Kenny, & First Edition P&R/C&W/LP '69

Singles: 7-inch

JOLLY ROGERS 4-6 72-73
REPRISE 4-8 68-72

LPs: 10/12-inch

JOLLY ROGERS 8-12 72-73
REPRISE 10-25 69-72
Members: Kenny Rogers; Mike Settle; Mickey Jones; Terry Williams; Kin Vassy; Mary Arnold.
Also see FIRST EDITION

ROGERS, Kenny, & Dolly Parton P&R '83

Singles: 7-inch

RCA 3-5 83-85
REPRISE 3-5 90

Picture Sleeves

RCA 3-5 83
Also see PARTON, Dolly

ROGERS, Kenny, & Nickie Ryder C&W '86

Singles: 7-inch

RCA 3-5 86

ROGERS, Kenny, & Dottie West C&W '78

Singles: 7-inch

LIBERTY 3-5 81-84
U.A. 4-6 78-79

LPs: 10/12-inch

U.A. 5-10 78-80
Also see ROGERS, Kenny
Also see WEST, Dottie

ROGERS, Lee R&B '65

Singles: 7-inch

DIAMOND JIM (1006 "Sweetest Woman Ever Born") 5-10
DIAMOND JIM (1008 "Sex Appeal") 5-10
D-TOWN (1029 "Sad Affair") 10-20 64
D-TOWN (1035 "I Want You to Have Everything") 10-20 64
D-TOWN (1041 "Cream of the Crop") 10-20 64
D-TOWN (1050 "Boss Love") 10-20 64
D-TOWN (1062 "You Won't Have to Wait Til Christmas") 10-20 65
D-TOWN (1067 "I'm a Practical Guy") 10-20 65
LOADSTONE 4-6 72
MAH'S (0009 "Walk on By") 15-25 62
PLATINUM SOUND 3-6 79
PREMIUM STUFF (4 "Jack the Playboy") 15-25 67
WHEELSVILLE (121 "Love for a Love") ... 60-80 66

ROGERS, Lelan

Singles: 7-inch

LYNN (502 "Hold It") 20-30 60

ROGERS, Pauline

Singles: 78 rpm

ATCO 5-10 55
FLAIR-X 10-15 56

Singles: 7-inch

ATCO (6050 "Up Till Now") 15-25 55
ATCO (6071 "Round and Round") 15-25 55
FLAIR-X (5001 "I've Been Pretending") ... 20-30 56

ROGERS, Rock
(Leon Payne)

Singles: 78 rpm

STARDAY (245 "That Ain't It") 25-50 56

Singles: 7-inch

STARDAY (245 "That Ain't It") 75-100 56
Also see PAYNE, Leon

ROGERS, Rod

Singles: 7-inch

B-ATLAS (900 "My Honey Bee") ... 8-12 66
FILM CITY (1027 "Tick Tock") ... 15-25 64
FILM CITY (1052 "I Can't Decide") ... 15-25 '60s
FILM CITY (3024 "Move Along Surfing Girl") ... 20-30 '60s
LUTONE (900 "I've Been Missing Someone") ... 10-20 '60s

ROGERS, Roy P&R '38/C&W '46
(With Dale Evans; with Sons Of The Pioneers; with Pat Brady; with Ranch Hands; with Mitch Miller Orchestra)

Singles: 78 rpm

DECCA ... 10-20 40-44
GOLDEN ... 4-8 '50s
RCA ... 5-15 50-57
VICTOR ... 8-15 45-48
VOCALION ... 20-30 38

Singles: 7-inch

CAPITOL ... 4-6 70-71
GOLDEN ... 5-10 '50s
MCA ... 3-5 80
NEW DISC ... 8-12 56
RCA (48-0008 thru 48-0204) ... 10-20 49-50
(Green vinyl.)
RCA (48-0255 thru 48-0293) ... 10-20 50
(Yellow vinyl. Children's series.)
RCA (48-0399 "Yellow Bonnets and Polka-Dot Shoes") ... 10-20 50
(Green vinyl.)
RCA (Except 215) ... 5-15 51-52
RCA (215 "Souvenir Album") ... 20-40 49
(Boxed set of three green vinyl 45s.)
RCA (253 "Round-Up") ... 20-40 51
(Boxed set of three green vinyl 45s.)
RCA (286 "Hymns of Faith") ... 20-40 51
(Boxed set of three green vinyl 45s.)
RCA (388 "Lore of the West") ... 10-20 51
(Boxed set of two yellow vinyl 45s.)
RCA (389 "Pecos Bill") ... 10-20 51
(Boxed set of two yellow vinyl 45s.)
RCA (413 "Roy Roger's Rodeo") ... 10-20 52
(Boxed set of two yellow vinyl 45s.)
20TH CENTURY ... 4-6 74-75

Picture Sleeves

GOLDEN ... 5-10 '50s

EPs: 7-inch

BLUEBIRD ... 10-20 '50s
RCA (Except 3041) ... 12-25 50-57
RCA (3041 "Souvenir Album") ... 25-50 52
THREE ON ONE (324 "Roy Rogers' Cowboy Songs") ... 20-30 '50s
(Yellow vinyl.)

LPs: 10/12-inch

BLUEBIRD ... 15-25 59
CAMDEN ... 10-20 60-75
CAPITOL ... 10-30 62-72
GHOST TOWN ... 10-20
GOLDEN ... 15-30 62
NOSTALGIA MERCHANT ... 8-10
PICKWICK ... 5-10 '70s
RADIOLA ... 8-10
RCA (1439 "Sweet Hour of Prayer") ... 20-30 57
RCA (3041 "Souvenir Album") ... 40-60 52
(10-inch LP.)
RCA (3168 "Hymns of Faith") ... 30-50 54
(10-inch LP.)
20TH FOX ... 5-10 74
WORD ... 4-8 73-77
Also see SONS OF THE PIONEERS

ROGERS, Roy, & Clint Black C&W '91

Singles: 7-inch

RCA (62061 "Hold On Partner") ... 3-5 91

ROGERS, Roy, with Spade Cooley's Buckle Busters

Singles: 78 rpm

CORAL (8004 "Square Dances") ... 15-25 50
(Boxed, three-disc set.)

Singles: 7-inch

CORAL (8004 "Square Dances") ... 25-50 50
(Boxed, three-disc set.)
Also see COOLEY, Spade
Also see ROGERS, Roy

ROGERS, Shorty
(With the Giants; Mickey Shorty Rogers)

Singles: 7-inch

HBR (442 "Theme from *Jonny Quest*") ... 5-10 65
TAMPA (154 "Big Boy") ... 15-25 58

LPs: 10/12-inch

RCA (1428 "Plays Richard Rodgers") ... 10-15 57
Also see BROWN, Boots
Also see COOL, Calvin
Also see SHANK, Bud
Also see PETERSON, Ray

ROGERS, Timmie P&R '57
(Timmie "Oh Yeah" Rogers; with Excelsior Hep Cats; with Stomp Russell Trio; Timmy Rogers; Timmie Rodgers; Super Soul Brother Alias Clark Dark.)

Singles: 78 rpm

CAMEO ... 10-25 57-58
CAPITOL ... 5-10 53
EXCELSIOR ... 10-20 45
MAJESTIC ... 10-20 46
MERCURY ... 10-20 54
REGIS ... 10-20 45
VARSITY ... 10-20 '50s

Singles: 7-inch

CADET (5685 "Super Soul Brothers") ... 4-6 71
CAMEO (116 "Back to School Again") ... 10-20 57
CAMEO (131 "Take Me to Your Leader") ... 10-20 57
CAPITOL ... 10-20 53
EPIC ... 5-8 65-66
MERCURY (70451 "If I Give My Heart to You") ... 25-35 54
PARKWAY ... 10-15 60
PARTEE ... 4-6 73
PHILIPS ... 5-8 62
SIGNATURE ... 8-12 60

LPs: 10/12-inch

EPIC ... 15-20 65
PARTEE ... 10-15 73
PHILIPS ... 15-20 63

ROGERS, Wayne

Singles: 7-inch

S&S (473 "Wayne Boogie") ... 75-125

ROGERS, Weldon

Singles: 78 rpm

IMPERIAL (5451 "So Long, Good Luck and Goodbye"/"Tryin to Get to You") ... 50-75 57
JE-WEL (104 "Women Drivers") ... 25-50 56

Singles: 7-inch

IMPERIAL (5451 "So Long, Good Luck and Goodbye"/"Tryin to Get to You") ... 50-100 57
(This track of *Trying to Get to You* was previously issued as by the Teen Kings on Je-Wel.)
JE-WEL (104 "Women Drivers") ... 100-150 56
PEACH (759 "As Long As You Are Mine") ... 10-20 63
Also see TEEN KINGS

ROGERS, Weldon, & Wanda Wolfe
(Weldon & Wanda Rogers)

Singles: 78 rpm

JE-WEL ... 50-100 56

Singles: 7-inch

JE-WEL (103 "Everybody Wants You") ... 200-300 56
(With Glen Campbell.)
PEACH (744 "Lying Lips and Cheating Heart") ... 10-20 61
PEACH (763 "I'm Hanging Up the Phone") ... 8-12 64
Also see CAMPBELL, Glen
Also see ROGERS, Weldon

ROGUES

Singles: 78 rpm

OLD TOWN ... 10-30 56-57

Singles: 7-inch

OLD TOWN (300 "If You Love Me") ... 30-40 56
OLD TOWN (304 "Puppy Love") ... 30-40 57
OLD TOWN (1056 "I've Been Dreaming") ... 15-25 58

ROGUES

Singles: 7-inch

BING (4900 "Barracuda") ... 20-30 64

ROGUES

Singles: 7-inch

COLUMBIA (43190 "Everyday") ... 10-20 64
COLUMBIA (43253 "Come on Let's Go") ... 10-20 65
Members: Bruce Johnston; Terry Melcher; Phil Stewart; Ernie Bringas.
Also see BRUCE & TERRY
Also see RIP CHORDS

ROGUES

Singles: 7-inch

MBM (2002 "Put You Down") ... 15-25 65

ROGUES

Singles: 7-inch

PEYTON (1001 "It's the Same All Over the World") ... 50-100 66
Members: Mike Bouyea; Tom Flanigan; John Folcik; Kurt Robinson.
Also see SQUIRES

ROGUES

Singles: 7-inch

AUDITION (6110 "Train Kept A-Rollin'") ... 150-250 66

ROGUES

Singles: 7-inch

KAPAN (713 "It's Gonna Work Out Fine") ... 15-25 66
KAPAN (999 "Tell Me No Lies") ... 15-25 67

ROGUES

Singles: 7-inch

MIRAGE (601 "Something Beautiful Is Dying") ... 15-25 67

ROGUES

Singles: 7-inch

LA LOUISIANNE (8094 "Tonight") ... 15-25 67

ROGUES

Singles: 7-inch

NIGHT OWL (67102 "The Secret") ... 15-25 67
Members: John Castellano; Larry Krzeminski; Rick Rebstock; Casey Dutcavich; Ron Olenik.

ROGUES

Singles: 7-inch

WELHAVEN (9582 "Sam") ... 40-60 67

ROGUES

Singles: 7-inch

TALENT ASSOCIATES ("Good Lovin'") ... 20-30 '60s
(No selection number used. "Talent Associates" name and address is on the label, but may not be a label name. However, there is no other indication of a label name. Sold at the group's concerts.)

ROGUES

Singles: 7-inch

BOSS CITY (160 "No Lies") ... 10-20 68
BOSS CITY (166 "Tobacco Road") ... 10-20 68

ROK

Singles: 7-inch

MARK VII (1012 "Transparent Day") ... 15-25 66

ROKES

Singles: 7-inch

RCA (9199 "Let's Live for Today") ... 5-10 67
RCA (9546 "When the Wind Arises") ... 5-10 67

LPs: 10/12-inch

RCA INT'L (185 "Che Mondo Strano") ... 30-50 67

ROLEY, Hank

Singles: 7-inch

D (1253 "Anna Anna") ... 50-75 64

ROLLER, Lonesome Long John / Ned Mullan

Singles: 7-inch

FLAGPOLE (28 "Blue Am I") ... 100-150 '50s
FLAGPOLE (301 "Long John's Flagpole Rock") ... 300-400 '50s
Session: Al Casey.
Also see CASEY, Al

ROLLERS P&R/R&B '61

Singles: 7-inch

LIBERTY (55303 "Got My Eye on You") ... 10-15 61
LIBERTY (55320 "The Continental Walk") ... 15-20 61
LIBERTY (55357 "The Bounce") ... 10-15 61
Member: Al Wilson; Don Sampson; Eddie Wilson; Willie Willingham.
Also see WILSON, Al

ROLLETTES

Singles: 7-inch

MELKER (103 "An Understanding") ... 800-1000 60

ROLLETTES ORCHESTRA

Singles: 7-inch

CINCH (2004 "Why Oh Why") ... 30-50 58
CINCH (2025 "Venus Rock") ... 50-100 58
CINCH ("Satellite Boogie") ... 30-50 59
(Selection number not known.)
Member: Raymond Ojeda; Leroy Titzi; Floyd Jester; Ray Titzi; Gerry Bartelmas.
Also see NIGHT BEATS

ROLLING CREW
("With Orchestra")

Singles: 78 rpm

ALADDIN (3301 "Crying Emma") ... 25-35 55

Singles: 7-inch

ALADDIN (3301 "Crying Emma") ... 100-200 55

ROLLING STONES P&R/LP '64

Singles: 12-inch

ATCO (4616 "Miss You") ... 10-20 79
ROLLING STONES (70 "Hot Stuff") ... 50-100 76
(Promotional issue only.)
ROLLING STONES (119 "Miss You") ... 25-50 78
(Promotional issue only.)
ROLLING STONES (253 "If I Was a Dancer") ... 25-50 79
(Promotional issue only.)
ROLLING STONES (367 "Emotional Rescue") ... 20-40 80
(Promotional issue only.)
ROLLING STONES (397 "Start Me Up") ... 20-40 81
(Promotional issue only. Price includes special cover.)
ROLLING STONES (574 "She Was Hot") ... 20-40 84
(Promotional issue only.)
ROLLING STONES (685 "Undercover of the Night") ... 25-40 83
(White label. Promotional issue only.)
ROLLING STONES (685 "Undercover of the Night") ... 20-40 83
(Yellow label. Promotional issue only.)
ROLLING STONES (692 "Too Much Blood") ... 20-40 85
(Promotional issue only. Price includes special cover.)
ROLLING STONES (2275 "Harlem Shuffle") ... 10-15 86
(Price includes special cover.)
ROLLING STONES (2275 "Harlem Shuffle") ... 10-20 86
(Promotional issue only. Price includes special cover.)
ROLLING STONES (2340 "One Hit") ... 10-15 86
(Price includes color cover.)
ROLLING STONES (2340 "One Hit") ... 20-30 86
(Price includes black and white cover. Promotional issue only.)
ROLLING STONES (4609 "Miss You") ... 10-15 78
(Price includes special cover.)
ROLLING STONES (4616 "Miss You"/"Hot Stuff") ... 15-25 78
ROLLING STONES (96902 "Too Much Blood") ... 10-15 85
(Price includes special cover.)
ROLLING STONES (96978 "Undercover of the Night") ... 10-15 83
(Price includes special cover.)

Singles: 7-inch

ABKCO (4701 "I Don't Know Why") ... 5-10 75
ABKCO (4702 "Out of Time") ... 5-10 75
COLUMBIA ... 3-5 90-91
LONDON (901 thru 910) ... 10-15 66-69
LONDON (9641 "Stoned") ... 5000-7500 64
LONDON (9657 "Not Fade Away") ... 10-20 64
(Purple and white label.)
LONDON (9657 "Not Fade Away") ... 8-10 65
(Blue and white swirl label.)
LONDON (9682 "Tell Me") ... 10-20 64
(Purple and white label.)
LONDON (9682 "Tell Me") ... 8-10 65
(Blue and white swirl label.)
LONDON (9687 "It's All Over Now") ... 10-20 64
(Purple and white label.)
LONDON (9687 "It's All Over Now") ... 8-10 65
(Blue and white swirl label.)
LONDON (9708 "Time Is on My Side") ... 20-30 64
(Purple and white label.)
LONDON (9708 "Time Is on My Side") ... 25-50 64
(Purple label with silver print. Canadian.)
LONDON (9708 "Time Is on My Side") ... 8-10 65
(Blue and white swirl label.)
LONDON (9725 "Heart of Stone") ... 10-20 65
(Purple and white label.)
LONDON (9725 "Heart of Stone") ... 25-50 65
(Purple label with silver print. Canadian.)

LONDON (9725 "Heart of Stone")..............5-10 65
(Blue and white swirl label.)
LONDON (9741 "The Last Time")........... 15-25 65
(Purple and white label.)
LONDON (9741 "The Last Time")..............5-10 65
(Blue and white swirl label.)
LONDON (9766 "Satisfaction")..................5-10 65
LONDON (9766 "Satisfaction")................ 25-50 65
(Purple label with silver print. Canadian.)
LONDON (9792 "Get Off of My Cloud")......5-10 65
LONDON (9808 "As Tears Go By")...........5-10 65
LONDON (9823 "19th Nervous
Breakdown")...5-10 66
ROLLING STONES (Except 99724)............3-8 71-86
ROLLING STONES (99724 "Miss You"/"Too
Tough").. 10-15 78
VIRGIN (38448 "Love Is Strong").................3-5 94
WMEE 97FM (001 "The Stones on 97").......4-8
Note: The three Canadian purple label with silver print issues are the only ones we have confirmed so far with that label – the same as used by London in the '50s and early '60s. If any other early Stones singles came on this label, we would like to know of them.

Promotional Singles

ABKCO (4701 "I Don't Know Why")...........8-12 75
ABKCO (4702 "Out of Time")......................8-12 75
COLUMBIA...5-10 90
LONDON (901 thru 910)......................... 20-30 66-69
LONDON (9641 "Stoned")............... 1000-2000 64
LONDON (9657 "Not Fade Away")........ 50-100 64
LONDON (9682 "Tell Me")..................... 25-50 64
LONDON (9687 "It's All Over Now")........ 25-50 64
LONDON (9708 "Time Is on My Side").... 25-50 64
LONDON (9725 "Heart of Stone")........... 25-50 65
LONDON (9741 "The Last Time")........... 25-50 65
LONDON (9766 "Satisfaction")............... 15-25 65
LONDON (9792 "Get Off of My Cloud")... 15-25 65
LONDON (9808 "As Tears Go By")......... 15-25 65
LONDON (9823 "19th Nervous
Breakdown").. 15-25 66
ROLLING STONES (228 "Time Waits for No
One").. 15-25 76
ROLLING STONES (316 "Before They Make Me
Run")... 15-25 78
ROLLING STONES (05000 series)...........5-15 86
ROLLING STONES (19000 thru 21301, except
19307)...5-15 71-82
ROLLING STONES (19307 "Miss You"/"Far Away
Eyes")...5-15 78
ROLLING STONES (19307 "Far Away Eyes"/"Far
Away Eyes")... 50-100 78
ROLLING STONES (90000 series, except
99724)...5-10 82-85
ROLLING STONES (99724 "Miss You"/"Miss
You").. 15-25 78

Picture Sleeves

LONDON (901 "Paint It Black")............... 30-40 66
LONDON (902 "Mother's Little Helper")... 15-25 66
LONDON (903 "Have You Seen Your Mother Baby,
Standing in the Shadows")...................... 15-25 66
LONDON (904 "Ruby Tuesday")............. 15-25 67
LONDON (905 "Dandelion")................ 200-250 67
LONDON (906 "She's a Rainbow").......... 15-25 67
LONDON (908 "Jumpin' Jack Flash")...... 10-20 68
LONDON (909 "Street Fighting
Man")... 8000-12000 68
(Thus far, approximately 12 copies are known to exist.)
LONDON (910 "Honky Tonk Women").... 10-20 69
LONDON (9657 "Not Fade Away")...... 200-300 64
LONDON (9682 "Tell Me")................... 75-125 64
LONDON (9687 "It's All Over Now")...... 75-125 64
LONDON (9708 "Time Is on My Side").. 75-125 64
LONDON (9725 "Heart of Stone")........ 550-650 65
LONDON (9741 "The Last Time")........... 25-50 65
LONDON (9766 "Satisfaction")............. 50-100 65
LONDON (9792 "Get Off of My Cloud")... 25-35 65
LONDON (9808 "As Tears Go By")......... 30-40 65
LONDON (9823 "19th Nervous
Breakdown").. 25-45 66
ROLLING STONES (Except 228, 316 and
19309)...3-6 78-86
ROLLING STONES (228 "Time Waits for No
One")... 15-25 76
(Promotional issue only.)
ROLLING STONES (316 "Before They Make Me
Run").. 15-25 78
(Promotional issue only.)
ROLLING STONES (19309 "Beast of
Burden").. 1000-2000 78
ROLLING STONES......................................3-6 71-81
(For generic, die-cut paper sleeves with Rolling Stones tongue logo. Not for any specific release.)
VIRGIN (38448 "Love Is Strong")................3-5 94

EPs: 7-inch

ATLANTIC (900 "Exile on Main Street")...50-75 72
(Juke box issue only.)
ATLANTIC (5901 "Goats Head Soup").....50-75 73
(Juke box issue only.)
DECCA (8590 "Five By Five")..............300-400 63
(Canadian.)
LONDON (34 "Rolling Stones Now")....200-300 64
(Juke box issue only.)
LONDON (37 "Out of Our Heads").......200-300 64
(Juke box issue only.)
LONDON (43 "December's Children")..200-300 64
(Juke box issue only.)
LONDON (54 "Their Satanic Majesties
Request")...250-350 64
(Juke box issue only.)
ROLLING STONES (287 "The Rolling
Stones")..50-100 77
(Promotional issue only.)
ROLLING STONES (73133 "Rock and a Hard
Place")..20-25 89
(12-inch.)

LPs: 10/12-inch

ABKCO (1 "Metamorphosis")...................10-15 75
ABKCO (1 "Songs of the Rolling
Stones").. 2500-3000 75
(Promotional issue only.)
ABKCO (0268 "Greatest Hits").................20-25 '70s
(TV mail-order offer.)
ABKCO (1077 "30 Greatest Hits")...........20-25 77
(Canadian.)
ABKCO (1089 "Greatest Hits, Vol. II")......20-25 77
ABKCO (1218 "Singles Collection")..........15-25 89
(Four-disc set.)
CAPITOL (61755 "Voodoo Lounge")........10-15 '90s
CAPITOL (7527 "Stripped")......................10-15 '90s
CRAWDADDY ("Rolling Stones Tour
Special")..150-200 76
(Promotional issue to college radio stations only.)
D.I.R. (312 "King Biscuit Flower
Hour")..150-200 80
(Promotional issue only.)
D.I.R. (325 "King Biscuit Flower
Hour")..150-200 80
(Promotional issue only.)
INS RADIO (1003 "It's Here Luv")..........75-125 65
LONDON (NP-1 "Big Hits")............. 5000-7500 66
(Monaural. Full title printed on one line on cover. Artist credit on second line.)
LONDON (NP-1 "Big Hits")......................40-60 66
(Monaural. Title on three lines on cover. Artist credit on two lines.)
LONDON (NPS-1 "Big Hits")....................30-40 66
(Stereo.)
LONDON (NP-2 "Their Satanic Majesties
Request")..150-200 67
(Monaural. Has 3-D cover.)
LONDON (NPS-2 "Their Satanic Majesties
Request")..40-60 67
(Stereo. Has 3-D cover.)
LONDON (NPS-2 "Their Satanic Majesties
Request")..10-15 70
(Stereo. Standard cover.)
LONDON (NPS-3 "Through the Past
Darkly")..10-15 69
LONDON (NPS-4 "Let It Bleed")..............15-25 69
(With bonus poster.)
LONDON (NPS-4 "Let It Bleed")..............10-15 69
(Without poster.)
LONDON (NPS-5 "Get Yer Ya-Yas
Out")..10-15 70
LONDON (RSD1 "The Promotional
Album")... 800-1000
LONDON (375 "Rolling Stones")..............40-50 64
(Stereo. Add $75 to $100 if accompanied by a 12" x 12" bonus, color photo. Cover has printed note about photo at lower left. With "Full Frequency Range Recording" label.)
LONDON (375 "Rolling Stones")..............10-15 65
(No mention of photo on cover. Does not have "Full Frequency Range Recording" on label.)
LONDON (402 "12 x 5")...........................40-50 64
(Stereo. With "Full Frequency Range Recording" label.)
LONDON (402 "12 x 5")...........................10-15 65
(Does not have "Full Frequency Range Recording" on label.)
LONDON (420 "Rolling Stones Now")......30-50 65
(Stereo. With "Full Frequency Range Recording" label.)
LONDON (420 "Rolling Stones Now")......10-15 65
(Does not have "Full Frequency Range Recording" on label.)
LONDON (429 "Out of Our Heads").........30-50 65
(Stereo. With "Full Frequency Range Recording" label.)
LONDON (429 "Out of Our Heads").........10-15 65
(Does not have "Full Frequency Range Recording" on label.)
LONDON (451 "December's Children")....30-50 65
(Stereo. With "Full Frequency Range Recording" label.)
LONDON (451 "December's Children")....10-15 65
(Does not have "Full Frequency Range Recording" on label.)
LONDON (476 "Aftermath")......................10-15 66
(Stereo.)
LONDON (493 "Got Live If You Want It").10-15 66
(Stereo.)
LONDON (499 "Between the Buttons")....10-15 67
(Stereo.)
LONDON (509 "Flowers")..........................8-10 67
(Stereo.)
LONDON (539 "Beggars Banquet")...........8-12 68
(All songs are shown as written by Jagger & Richard.)
LONDON (539 "Beggars Banquet")...........8-12 '60s
(*Prodigal Son* is shown as written by Rev. Wilkins.)
LONDON (606/7 "Hot Rocks")..................10-20 71
LONDON (626/7 "More Hot Rocks")..........10-20 72
LONDON (3375 "The Rolling Stones")...75-100 64
(Monaural. With "Full Frequency Range Recording" label. Add $75 to $100 if accompanied by a 12" x 12" bonus, color photo. Cover has printed note about photo at lower left.)
LONDON (3375 "The Rolling Stones").....30-40 65
(Does not have "Full Frequency Range Recording" on label.)
LONDON (3375 "The Rolling
Stones")...800-1200 64
(White label, monaural. Promotional issue only.)
LONDON (3402 "12 x 5").......................50-100 64
(Monaural. With "Full Frequency Range Recording" label.)
LONDON (3402 "12 x 5")..........................30-40 65
(Does not have "Full Frequency Range Recording" on label.)
LONDON (3420 "Rolling Stones Now")..50-100 65
(Monaural. With "Full Frequency Range Recording" label.)
LONDON (3420 "Rolling Stones Now")....30-40 65
(Does not have "Full Frequency Range Recording" on label.)
LONDON (3429 "Out of Our Heads").....50-100 65
(Monaural. With "Full Frequency Range Recording" label.)
LONDON (3429 "Out of Our Heads").......30-40 65
(Does not have "Full Frequency Range Recording" on label.)
LONDON (3451 "December's
Children")..50-100 65
(Monaural. With "Full Frequency Range Recording" label.)
LONDON (3451 "December's
Children")...30-40 65
(Does not have "Full Frequency Range Recording" on label.)
LONDON (3476 "Aftermath")...................25-50 66
(Monaural.)
LONDON (3493 "Got Live If You Want
It")..25-50 66
(Monaural.)
LONDON (3499 "Between the Buttons")..25-50 67
(Monaural.)
LONDON (3509 "Flowers").......................25-50 67
(Monaural.)
LONDON (9134 "Big Hits, High Tide & Green
Grass")...1000-1500 69
(Test picture disc. Some have photo of the group Ten Years After on one side. All have music from *Thru the Past Darkly.*)
LONDON/ABKCO (66671 "Hot Rocks")...15-20 96
LONDON/ABKCO (62671 "Fazed
Cookies")..15-20 96
LONDON/ABKCO (70,000 series)...........10-15 96
LONDON/ABKCO (80,000 series)...........10-15 96
MFSL (1 "Rolling Stones")...................300-400 85
(11-LP boxed set, includes booklet, postcard and alignment tool.)
MFSL (060 "Sticky Fingers")....................40-60 82
MFSL (087 "Some Girls").........................40-60 82
MUTUAL BROADCASTING SYSTEM ("Rolling Stones: Past and Present")............................800-1200 84
(Boxed, 12-disc set, issued only to radio stations. Price includes programming sheets.)
ROLLING STONES (2900 "Exile on Main
St.")..10-15 72
(Add $3 to $5 if accompanied by sheet of 12 bonus postcards.)
ROLLING STONES (9001 "Love You
Live")..10-15 77
ROLLING STONES (16015 "Emotional
Rescue")...5-10 80
ROLLING STONES (16028 "Sucking in the
Seventies")...5-10 81
ROLLING STONES (16052 "Tattoo You").5-10 81
ROLLING STONES (39108 "Some
Girls")...10-15 78
(With all girls' faces shown.)
ROLLING STONES (39108 "Some Girls").5-10 78
(Not all girls' faces shown. Cover is "Under Construction.")
ROLLING STONES (39113 "Still Life")......5-10 82
ROLLING STONES (39114 "Still Life")....40-50 82
(Picture disc.)
ROLLING STONES (40250 "Dirty Work")..5-10 86
ROLLING STONES (45333 "Steel
Wheels")..5-10 89
ROLLING STONES (47456 "Flashpoint")..8-10 91
ROLLING STONES (59100 "Sticky
Fingers")...8-10 71
(Yellow label.)
ROLLING STONES (59100 "Sticky
Fingers")..150-250 71
(White label. Promotional issue only.)
ROLLING STONES (59101 "Goats Head
Soup")..8-10 73
ROLLING STONES (79101 "It's Only Rock &
Roll")..8-10 74
ROLLING STONES (79102 "Made in the
Shade")...8-10 75
ROLLING STONES (79104 "Black and
Blue")..8-10 76
ROLLING STONES (90120
"Undercover")..5-10 83
ROLLING STONES (90176 "Rewind").......5-10 84
SILHOUETTE (10005 "Precious
Stones")...10-15 81
(Picture disc.)
VIRGIN...8-10 94
Members: Mick Jagger; Keith Richards; Bill Wyman; Brian Jones; Charlie Watts; Mick Taylor; Ron Wood.
Also see BEACH BOYS
Also see FAITHFUL, Marianne
Also see JAGGER, Mick
Also see JAMESON, Bobby
Also see JONES, Brian
Also see RICHARDS, Keith
Also see WOOD, Ron
Also see WYMAN, Bill

ROLLINS, Bird

(With the Jersey Burners)

Singles: 7-inch

CALLA (178 "Do It to It")..............................4-6 71
CALLA (182 "She Needs Lovin' ")...............4-6 72
HARVARD (805 "I'll Love You Forever")..40-50 59
HARVARD (810 "Betty Lou")..................20-30 59
JOHNSON (105 "Pretty Little School
Girl")..20-30 57
SKYMAC (1006 "Answer My Prayer")......10-15 64
STRAND (25034 "Just Let Me Be")...........8-12 61
VANGUARD (35003 "You Are My
Angel")..75-125 58

ROMA, Teena

Singles: 7-inch

ARTEEN (1002 "Just for You")................15-25 61

ROMAINES

Singles: 78 rpm

GROOVE (0035 "Your Kind of Love")......10-15 54

Singles: 7-inch

GROOVE (0035 "Your Kind of Love")......30-40 54

ROMAN, Danny
Singles: 7-inch

AD LIB ... 10-15 60
TAZ (1005 "Let's Cut Out") ... 25-35 57

ROMAN, Don
Singles: 7-inch

DAANI ... 20-30 63
Also see ZAPPA, Frank

ROMAN, Murray
Singles: 7-inch

U.A. ... 4-6 72
LPs: 10/12-inch
EVEREST ... 15-25 60
NERO ... 20-30 60
TETRAGRAMMATON ... 10-15 68-69
U.A. (5595 "Busted") ... 15-20 72
(Promotional issue only. With bonus single and bio insert.)

ROMAN, Net
(Nap Roman)
Singles: 7-inch

SAHARA (102 "Tears from My Eyes") ... 1000-1500 63
(Credits Net Roman.)
SAHARA (102 "Tears from My Eyes") ... 500-1000 63
(Credits "Nap" Roman.)

ROMAN, Nip
Singles: 7-inch

FLASH (121 "With These Words") ... 15-25 57

ROMAN, Rich
Singles: 7-inch

C.G. (5003 "Truly, Baby") ... 40-60 60
X ... 10-15 60

ROMAN NUMERALS
Singles: 7-inch

COLUMBIA (44314 "The Come On") ... 8-12 67
Picture Sleeves
COLUMBIA (44314 "The Come On") ... 15-25 67

ROMANAIRES
Singles: 7-inch

D&J (100 "Is It Too Late") ... 50-100 '60s

ROMANCERS
Singles: 78 rpm

DOOTONE ... 20-30 56
Singles: 7-inch
BAY TONE (101 "You Don't Understand") ... 30-40 58
DOOTONE (381 "I Still Remember") ... 50-75 56
(Red label.)
DOOTONE (381 "I Still Remember") ... 40-50 56
(Maroon label.)
Members: Al Thomas; Bob Freeman; Woody Blake; Tyrone French; James Shelbourne.

ROMANCERS
Singles: 7-inch

BEACON (701 "No Greater Love") ... 20-30 61
CELEBRITY (701 "No Greater Love") ... 40-60 61
(First issue.)

ROMANCERS
Singles: 7-inch

LINDA (117 "Don't Let Her Go") ... 10-15 65
LINDA (119 "My Heart Cries") ... 10-15 65
LINDA (120 "Do You Cry") ... 10-15 65
LINDA (123 "She Gives Me Love") ... 15-20 66
LINDA (124 "That's Why I Love You") ... 15-20 66
MEDIEVAL (202 "It Only Happens with You") ... 5-10 64
PALETTE (5067 "Moody") ... 15-25 60
PALETTE (5075 "It Only Happens with You") ... 15-25 61
PALETTE (5085 "That Lucky Old Sun") .. 15-25 61
PALETTE (5095 "What About Love") ... 15-25 62

ROMANCERS
("Featuring Wilbert Burleson")
Singles: 7-inch

MARQUEE (701 "Meet Me at the Altar") . 20-30 62
Member: Wilbert Burleson.

ROMANS
Singles: 78 rpm

HAVEN (111 "Honey Love") ... 15-25 57
Singles: 7-inch
HAVEN (111 "Honey Love") ... 20-30 57
Members: Tony Leone; Chick Leone; Joe Apuzzo; Chick Ciccolallo; Stan Dortch.
Also see FIVE SATINS

ROMANS
Singles: 7-inch

JUNO (014 "You Are My Only Love") ... 600-800 58
M.M.I. (1238 "Wild Ideas") ... 100-150 58

ROMANS
Singles: 7-inch

DB (41765 "The Drag") ... 15-25 65
(Number is also release date, 4-17-65.)
PANIC (100 "Doin' the Drag") ... 10-15 66
(*Doin' the Drag* is a rerecording of *The Drag*.)
Members: Richard Reisinger; Tom Henry; Tom Elicker; Barry Leach.

ROMANS
Singles: 7-inch

MY (2905 "I'll Find a Way") ... 10-20 66
MY (2908 "I Just Had to Fall") ... 10-20 66
Picture Sleeves
MY (2905 "I'll Find a Way") ... 20-30 66

ROMANS
Singles: 7-inch

DOME (1000 "Magic") ... 50-75

ROME, Billy
Singles: 7-inch

CARD (377 "Donna") ... 40-50 61
SULTAN ... 15-25 60-62
Also see CAMEOS Featuring Billy Rome

ROMEOS
Singles: 78 rpm

APOLLO (461 "Love Me") ... 150-200 54
APOLLO (466 "Rags") ... 40-50 54
Singles: 7-inch
APOLLO (461 "Love Me") ... 400-500 54
APOLLO (466 "Rags") ... 75-125 54
Also see JUMPIN, JACKS

ROMEOS
(With George Braxton Band; with Lucky Lee Band)
Singles: 78 rpm

ATCO (6107 "Moments to Remember") ... 20-30 57
Singles: 7-inch
ATCO (6107 "Moments to Remember") ... 40-50 57
FOX (748/9 "Gone Gone Get Away") ... 100-200 57
(Cream color label.)
FOX (748/9 "Gone Gone Get Away") ... 40-50 57
(Yellow label.)
FOX (845/6 "Moments to Remember") . 400-600 58
(Cream color label.)
FOX (845/6 "Moments to Remember") ... 75-100 58
(Yellow label.)
Members: Lamont Dozier; Ty Hunter; Gene Dyer; Ken Johnson; Don Davenport; Leon Ware.
Also see DOZIER, Lamont
Also see HUNTER, Ty
Also see LARADO
Also see VOICE MASTERS

ROMEOS — P&R/R&B '67
Singles: 7-inch

MARK II (101 "Precious Memories") ... 8-12 67
MARK II (103 "Searching") ... 5-10 67
LPs: 10/12-inch
MARK II (1001 "Precious Memories") ... 15-25 67
Members: Kenny Gamble; Thom Bell; Roland Chambers; Winnie Walford; Karl Chambers; Leon Huff.
Also see GAMBLE, Kenny

ROMERO, Chan
Singles: 7-inch

CHALLENGE (59285 "It's Not Fine") ... 8-12 65
DEL-FI (4119 "Hippy Hippy Shake") ... 50-75 59
DEL-FI (4126 "My Little Ruby") ... 40-60 59
PHILIPS (40391 "Humpy Bumpy") ... 5-10 66
Also see RODNEY & BLAZERS

ROMMELS
Singles: 7-inch

TREND (4104 "Those Wedding Bells") ... 400-500 60

ROMMY & CENTURIES
Singles: 7-inch

LUNA (3076 "Mister Mirror") ... 25-35 62

RON & BILL
Singles: 7-inch

ARGO (5350 "It") ... 35-45 59
TAMLA (54025 "It") ... 50-75 59
(First issue.)
Members: Ron White; Bill "Smokey" Robinson.
Also see MIRACLES

RON & CONTINENTALS
Singles: 7-inch

CUCA (1156 "Rolling Stone") ... 15-25 63

RON & JON
Singles: 7-inch

SICK (50 "Hawaii Strikes Back") ... 25-35 59
Members: Ron Jacobs; Jon Demarco.
Also see CHILD'S GARDEN OF GRASS

RON & MOTIONS
Singles: 7-inch

REDBUG (6 "Last Night's Dream") ... 50-75 62

RONDELLS
Singles: 7-inch

PIKE ("Demo Derby") ... 15-25 64
(No selection number used.)

RONDELLS
(Ron-Dells; Rondels)
Singles: 7-inch

ABC-PAR (10690 "Don't Say That You Love Me") ... 8-10 65
CARLTON (467 "Dreamy") ... 10-15 58
DOT (16593 "On the Run") ... 8-12 64
XPRESS ... 5-10 '60s

RON-DELS — P&R '65
(Rondels; Ron-Dells)
Singles: 7-inch

ARLEN (723 "Slow Down") ... 15-25 63
BILLIE FRAN (101 "Matilda") ... 15-25 '60s
BROWNFIELD (2 "Hey Baby '66") ... 10-15 66
BROWNFIELD (13 "100 Pounds of Honey") ... 10-15 66
BROWNFIELD (16 "Just When You Think You're Somebody") ... 10-20 65
BROWNFIELD (18 "If You Really Want Me to, I'll Go") ... 10-20 65
BROWNFIELD (23 "Lost My Love Today") ... 10-20 65
BROWNFIELD (33 "Cryin' Over You") ... 10-15 66
BROWNFIELD (303 "I Know She Knows") ... 10-20 64
BROWNFIELD (1037 "You Made Me Cry") ... 8-12 67
CHARAY (75 "100 Pounds of Honey") ... 4-6
DOT (17323 "Matilda") ... 4-6 70
LE CAM (130 "Matilda") ... 25-35 63
(First issue.)
LE CAM (130 "Matilda") ... 4-6 73
SHAH (980 "I Ain't Never") ... 15-25 63
SHALIMAR (104 "Matilda") ... 15-25 63
SMASH (1986 "If You Really Want Me to, I'll Go") ... 8-12 65
SMASH (2002 "She's My Girl") ... 8-12 65
SMASH (2014 "Lose Your Money") ... 8-12 65
Members: Delbert McClinton; Billy Sanders; Jerry Foster; Jimmy Rodgers; Ronnie Kelly; Mike Clark; Darrell Norris; Carl Tanner; Ray Torres. Session: Ray Hildebrand; Bruce Channel.
Also see CHANNEL, Bruce
Also see CURTIS, Mac
Also see DAWSON, Ronnie
Also see JESTER, Charlie
Also see JOHNNY & MARK V / Ron-Dels
Also see McCLINTON, Delbert
Also see MILBURN, Amos, Jr.
Also see PAUL / Ron-Dels
Also see UPTOWNERS / Ron-Dels
Also see WATSON, Phil / Ron-Dels

RONETTES — P&R/R&B '63
(Ronnettes; "Featuring Veronica")
Singles: 7-inch

A&M (1040 "You Came, You Saw, You Conquered") ... 8-12 69
COLPIX (646 "I'm Gonna Quit While I'm Ahead") ... 20-30 62
DIMENSION (1046 "He Did It") ... 10-15 65
MAY (114 "Silhouettes") ... 40-50 62
MAY (138 "The Memory") ... 40-50 63
PAVILLION ... 4-6 82
PHILLES (116 "Be My Baby") ... 15-25 63
PHILLES (118 "Baby I Love You") ... 15-25 63
PHILLES (120 "Breakin' Up") ... 15-25 64
PHILLES (121 "Do I Love You") ... 15-25 64
PHILLES (123 "Walking in the Rain") ... 30-50 64
(Same selection number previously used for a Darlene Love release.)
PHILLES (126 "Born to Be Together") ... 15-25 65
PHILLES (128 "Is This What I Get for Loving You") ... 15-25 65
PHILLES (133 "I Can Hear Music") ... 15-25 66
Promotional Singles
A&M (1040 "You Came, You Saw, You Conquered") ... 10-15 69
COLPIX (646 "I'm Gonna Quit While I'm Ahead") ... 30-40 62
DIMENSION (1046 "He Did It") ... 10-15 65
MAY (114 "Silhouettes") ... 30-40 62
MAY (138 "The Memory") ... 30-40 63
PAVILLION ... 5-10 82
PHILLES (116 "Be My Baby") ... 30-40 63
PHILLES (118 "Baby I Love You") ... 30-40 63
PHILLES (120 "Breakin' Up") ... 35-45 64
PHILLES (121 "Do I Love You") ... 30-40 64
PHILLES (123 "Walking in the Rain") ... 30-40 64
PHILLES (126 "Born to Be Together") ... 40-50 65
PHILLES (128 "Is This What I Get for Loving You") ... 40-50 65
PHILLES (133 "I Can Hear Music") ... 35-45 66
Picture Sleeves
PHILLES (123 "Walking in the Rain") ... 100-200 64
PHILLES (126 "Born to Be Together") . 150-250 65
PHILLES (128 "Is This What I Get for Loving You") ... 75-125 65
LPs: 10/12-inch
COLPIX (486 "The Ronettes, Featuring Veronica") ... 50-100 65
(Blue label. Monaural.)
COLPIX (486 "The Ronettes, Featuring Veronica") ... 75-150 65
(Gold label. Monaural.)
COLPIX (486 "The Ronettes, Featuring Veronica") ... 60-75 65
(Blue label. Stereo.)
COLPIX (486 "The Ronettes, Featuring Veronica") ... 100-200 65
(Gold label. Stereo.)
COLPIX (486 "The Ronettes, Featuring Veronica") ... 75-100 65
(White label. Promotional issue only.)
PHILLES (4006 "Presenting the Fabulous Ronettes") ... 100-200 64
(Blue label. Monaural.)
PHILLES (4006 "Presenting the Fabulous Ronettes") ... 75-150 64
(Yellow label. Monaural.)
PHILLES (4006 "Presenting the Fabulous Ronettes") ... 200-300 64
(Yellow label with red print. Stereo.)
PHILLES (4006/T-90721 "Presenting the Fabulous Ronettes") ... 200-300 64
(Capitol Record Club issue.)
MURRAY HILL ... 5-10 86
Members: Veronica Bennett-Spector; Estelle Bennett; Nedra Talley-Ross.
Also see DEE, Joey
Also see ESTELLE
Also see LOVE, Darlene / Ronettes
Also see RONNIE & RELATIVES
Also see SPECTOR, Ronnie

RONETTES / Crystals / Darlene Love
Singles: 7-inch

PAVILLION (1354 "Phil Spector's Christmas Medley") ... 4-8 81
(Promotional issue only.)

RONETTES / Crystals / Darlene Love / Bob B. Soxx & Blue Jeans
EPs: 7-inch

PHILLES ("Christmas EP") ... 30-50 63
(Issued with paper sleeve. Promotional issue only.)
LPs: 10/12-inch
APPLE (3400 "Phil Spector's Christmas Album") ... 25-35 72
PASSPORT (3604 "Phil Spector's Christmas Album") ... 8-10 85
PAVILLION ... 8-12 81
PHILLES (4005 "A Christmas Gift for You") ... 75-125 63
(Blue label.)
PHILLES (4005 "A Christmas Gift for You") ... 50-75 63
(Yellow and red label.)
W.B./SPECTOR ... 8-12

Also see BOB B. SOXX & BLUE JEANS
Also see CRYSTALS
Also see HARVEY, Phil
Also see LOVE, Darlene
Also see RONETTES

RONNIE & COMETS
Singles: 7-inch
SOMA (1172 "Memories") 15-20 61
Also see MIDNIGHTERS

RONNIE & CRAYONS
Singles: 7-inch
COUNSEL (102 "Birchard's Bread") 10-15 64
(First issue.)
DOMAIN (1402 "Birchard's Bread") 8-10 64
Also see CRAYONS

RONNIE & DELAIRES
Singles: 7-inch
CORAL (62404 "Drag") 20-25 64
Members: Ronny Linares; John Becker; Bob Osborne; Garry Jones.
Also see DEL-AIRES

RONNIE & HI-LITES *P&R '62*
Singles: 7-inch
ABC-PAR (10685 "High School Romance") 10-15 65
COLLECTABLES ....3-5 '80s
ERIC (117 "I Wish That We Were Married").4-6 73
JOY (260 "I Wish That We Were Married") 15-25 62
JOY (265 "Send My Love") 15-25 62
RAVEN (8000 "Valerie") 10-15 63
(Black label.)
RAVEN (8000 "Valerie") 15-25 63
(White label. Promotional issue only.)
U.G.H.A. (16 "For Lovers") 4-8 82
WIN (250 "A Slow Dance") 15-25 63
WIN (251 "The Fact of the Matter") 15-25 63
WIN (252 "High School Romance") 20-30 63
Picture Sleeves
U.G.H.A. (16 "For Lovers") 5-10 82

RONNIE & HOP KATS
Singles: 7-inch
COUGAR (101 "Persian Melon & Passion Pink") .... 10-20 '60s

RONNIE & MARLENE
Singles: 7-inch
WESTPORT (144 "I Wanna Love You").. 30-40 59

RONNIE & PARLEYS
Singles: 7-inch
KERWOOD (1001 "Am I in Love") 30-40

RONNIE & POMONA CASUALS
Singles: 7-inch
DONNA (1400 "Casual Blues") 5-10 64
DONNA (1402 "Sloopy") 5-10 64
MUSTANG (3005 "We're Gonna Do the Freddie") 5-10 65
LPs: 10/12-inch
DONNA (2112 "Everybody Jerk") 15-25 65

RONNIE & PREMIERS
Singles: 7-inch
HIGHLAND (1014 "Sharon") 15-25 61

RONNIE & RED CAPS
Singles: 7-inch
REB (105 "Conquest") 150-250 58
(Reportedly 500 made.)
Members: Ronnie James Dio; Billy De Wolf; Nick Pantas; Tom Rogers; Jack Musci.
Also see DIO, Ronnie

RONNIE & RELATIVES
(Ronettes)
Singles: 7-inch
COLPIX (601 "I Want a Boy") 20-30 61
MAY (111 "My Guiding Angel") 75-125 61
Also see RONETTES

RONNIE & RENEGADES
Singles: 7-inch
SULTAN (1003 "Blue Guitar") 10-20 60

RONNIE & ROBYN
(Ronnie & Robin)
Singles: 7-inch
HBR (489 "Cradle of Love") 10-15 66
SIDRA (9001/9002 "Cradle of Love"/"Dreamin' ") 15-25 66
SIDRA (9006 "Each Time") 15-25 67
SIDRA (9007 "Sidra's Theme") 15-25 67
SIDRA (9011 "As Long As You Love Me") 15-25 67

RONNIE & ROCKIN' KINGS
Singles: 7-inch
RCA (7248 "Rock 'N Roll Sal") 25-35 58

RONNIE & ROY
Singles: 7-inch
CAPITOL (4192 "Big Fat Sally") 25-35 59
(Monaural.)
CAPITOL (4192 "Big Fat Sally") 35-55 59
(Stereo.)
CAPITOL (4246 "Get Up and Dance") 10-20 59

RONNIE & SCHOOLMATES
Singles: 7-inch
COED (605 "Just Born") 10-15 65
COLLECTABLES ....3-5 '80s
Session: Billy Dawn Smith.
Also see DAWN, Billy

RONNIE & SENSASHUNS
Singles: 7-inch
WHAM (99041 "Laugh It Up Baby") ....20-30 '60s

RONNY & DAYTONAS *P&R/LP '64*
Singles: 7-inch
BARRY (562 "G.T.O.") 5-10 67
(Canadian.)
BARRY (3272 "G.T.O.") 10-20 64
(Canadian.)
BARRY (3349 "Beach Boy") 5-10 64
(Canadian.)
MALA 6-12 64-66
RCA 5-10 66-68
SHOW-BIZ 8-12 68
Picture Sleeves
BARRY (562 "G.T.O.") 10-15 66
(Generic "Golden Treasures on Wax" sleeve, with title imprint at top. Canadian.)
RCA (8896 "Dianne, Dianne") 15-25 66
LPs: 10/12-inch
MALA (4001 "G.T.O.") 50-100 64
MALA (4002 "Sandy") 20-35 66
(Monaural.)
MALA (4002-S "Sandy") 75-100 66
(Stereo.)
Members: Ronny Dayton; John "Bucky" Wilkin; Buzz Cason.
Also see BUZZ & BUCKY

RONNY & JOHNNY
Singles: 7-inch
LUCKY (1001 "Massacre") 150-200 60
Members: Ronny Roach; Johnny Coons.
Also see FOLEY, Jim

RONNY & SATELLITES
(With the Raiders; Ronny & Satelites)
Singles: 7-inch
DOLLY (22254 "Bunny Lee") 40-50 60
ROSE (1001 "Dream of You") 100-150 59

RONSTADT, Linda *P&R '68/C&W '74*
(With the Stone Poneys; with Nelson Riddle Orchestra)
Singles: 7-inch
ASYLUM 3-8 73-85
CAPITOL (2110 "Up to My Neck in High Muddy Water") 10-15 68
CAPITOL (2195 "Some of Shelly's Blues") 10-15 68
CAPITOL (2438 "Dolphins") 5-10 69
CAPITOL (2767 "Lovesick Blues") 4-8 70
CAPITOL (2846 thru 4050) 4-6 70-75
CAPITOL (5838 "All the Beautiful Things") 8-12 67
CAPITOL (5910 "Evergreen") 5-10 67
ELEKTRA 4-6 75-78
Picture Sleeves
ASYLUM 3-6 78-82
CAPITOL (2110 "Up to My Neck in High Muddy Water") 15-25 68
LPs: 10/12-inch
ASYLUM (Except 401 & 60489) 5-10 73-86
ASYLUM (401 "Living in the USA") 10-15 78
(Picture disc.)
ASYLUM (60489 "'Round Midnight") 10-15 86
CAPITOL (208 thru 635) 10-15 69-72
CAPITOL (2000 series) 12-18 68
CAPITOL (11000 series) 8-12 74-77
CAPITOL (16000 series) 5-10 80
ELEKTRA 5-10 80-87
MFSL (158 "What's New") 25-35 85
NAUTILUS (26 "Simple Dreams") 15-25 81
PICKWICK (3298 "Stoney End") 8-12 72
REALISTIC (7002 "For Country Lovers") .15-25
(Capitol Special Products. Made for Radio Shack.)
Session: Davie Allan; Nelson Riddle.
Also see ALLAN, Davie
Also see AXTON, Hoyt
Also see CASH, Johnny / Roy Clark / Linda Ronstadt
Also see CHRISTMAS SPIRIT
Also see EAGLES
Also see NEWMAN, Randy
Also see NITTY GRITTY DIRT BAND & LINDA RONSTADT
Also see PARTON, Dolly, Linda Ronstadt, & Emmylou Harris
Also see SHILOH
Also see STONE PONEYS
Also see THOMAS, David Clayton / Linda Ronstadt

RONSTADT, Linda, & Emmylou Harris
Singles: 7-inch
ASYLUM (45295 "The Sweetest Gift") 4-6 75
Also see HARRIS, Emmylou

RONSTADT, Linda, & Aaron Neville *LP '89*
LPs: 10/12-inch
ELEKTRA 5-8 89
Also see NEVILLE, Aaron

RONSTADT, Linda, & J.D. Souther *C&W '82*
Singles: 7-inch
ASYLUM 3-5 82
Also see RONSTADT, Linda

ROOFTOP SINGERS *P&R/C&W/R&B/LP '63*
Singles: 7-inch
ATCO (6526 "Kites") 4-6 67
VANGUARD 4-8 62-65
Picture Sleeves
VANGUARD 5-10 63
LPs: 10/12-inch
VANGUARD 10-20 63-65
Members: Erik Darling; Lynne Taylor; Bill Svanoe.
Also see TARRIERS

ROOKS
Singles: 7-inch
ETIQUETTE (14 "I'll Be the One") 5-10 65
JO-WAY (5000 "Ice & Fire") 5-10 67
MERCURY (72644 "Empty Heart") 10-15 67
MUSTANG (3008 "Gimme a Break") 15-25 65

ROOMATES *P&R '61*
(Roommates)
Singles: 7-inch
ADDIT (2211 "Making Believe") 10-20 60
BAN (691 "A Place Called Love") 3-5 85
CAMEO (233 "A Sunday Kind of Love")...15-25 62
CANADIAN AMERICAN (166 "My Heart") 10-15 64
CANADIAN AMERICAN (215 "Someone to Watch over Me") 3-5 99
(Gold vinyl. Shown as by the "Roommates.")
COLLECTABLES ....3-5 '80s
PHILIPS (40105 "Gee") 10-15 63
PHILIPS (40153 "The Nearness of You").30-40 63
PROMO (2211 "Making Believe") 5-10 64
VALMOR (008 "Glory of Love") 10-15 61
VALMOR (010 "Band of Gold") 10-15 61
VALMOR (013 "My Foolish Heart") 10-20 61
LPs: 10/12-inch
RELIC ....5-10 '80s
Members: Jack Carlson; Steve Susskind; Felix Alvarez; Bob Minsky; George Rodriguez.
Also see CATHY JEAN & ROOMATES

ROOMFUL OF BLUES
Singles: 7-inch
ROOMTONE (1001 "You Rascal, You")...10-20 75
ROOMTONE (1002 "Reelin' & Rockin' ")....5-10 82
LPs: 10/12-inch
ANTILLES (7071 "Let's Have a Party") 10-20 79
BLUE FLAME (1001 "Hot Little Mama") ...15-25 81
ISLAND (9474 "Roomful of Blues") 15-25 77
VARRICK 5-10 84-87
Members: Duke Robillard; Al Copley; Preston Hubbard; John Rossi; Greg Piccolo; Richard Latailie; Doug James; Ronnie Earl; Ron Levy; Jimmy Wimpfheimer; Porky Cohen; Danny Motta; Bob Enos; Rory MacLeod; Curtis Salgado; Chris Vachon; Carl Querfurth; Matt McCabe; Ken Grace; Sugar Ray Norcia.
Also see TURNER, Joe, & Roomful Of Blues
Also see VINSON, Eddie "Cleanhead," & Roomful Of Blues

ROONEY, Mickey
Singles: 78 rpm
KING (1296 "Alimony Blues") 5-10 54
Singles: 7-inch
KING (1296 "Alimony Blues") 10-20 54

ROONEY, Teddy
Singles: 7-inch
IMPERIAL (5644 "Bite Your Tongue") 20-30 60

ROOSEVELT, Franklin D.
Singles: 78 rpm
COLUMBIA (36516 "President Roosevelt's War Message to Congress and the Nation, December 8, 1941") 5-15 42
NATIONAL VOICE LIBRARY ("Fireside Chats") 200-300 45
(Five cardboard picture discs with mailer envelope. No selection numbers used.)
NATIONAL VOICE LIBRARY ("Fireside Chat on Defense 12-29-40") 40-60 45
NATIONAL VOICE LIBRARY ("Report of Nazi Attack") 40-60 45
NATIONAL VOICE LIBRARY ("Declaration of War 12-8-41") 40-60 45
NATIONAL VOICE LIBRARY ("State of Union 1-6-42") 40-60 45
NATIONAL VOICE LIBRARY ("D-Day Proclamation 6-6-44") 40-60 45

ROOSTERS
Singles: 7-inch
EPIC (9487 "Let's Try Again") 5-10 62
FELSTED (8642 "Chicken Hop") 5-10 62
PHILIPS (40559 "Good Good Lovin' ") 5-8 68
SHAR-DEE (704 "Chicken Hop") 10-15 59

ROOSTERS
Singles: 7-inch
ENITH (125 "Ain't Gonna Cry Anymore")...8-12 67
PROGRESSIVE SOUNDS (11032 "One of These Days") 25-30 66

ROOTS
Singles: 7-inch
BROWNFIELD (22 "Lost One") 20-30 65
Also see WYLD

ROSALLE & DONELL
Singles: 78 rpm
FLIP (307 "Shame on You") 5-10 55
Singles: 7-inch
FLIP (307 "Shame on You") 15-25 55
Members: Trudy Williams; Donald Woods.
Also see WILLIAMS, Trudy
Also see WOODS, Donald

ROSANOVA, Joe, & Vineyard
LPs: 10/12-inch
ASTRO SONIC (4000 "In Dedication to the Ones We Love") 50-75 67

ROSCO & BARBARA
Singles: 7-inch
OLD TOWN (1175 "It Ain't Right") 8-12 65
Member: Roscoe Gordon.
Also see GORDON, Roscoe

ROSCOE & LITTLE GREEN MEN
Singles: 7-inch
FOUR WINDS 20-25 61
(Title and selection number not known.)
GOLDEN WING 10-20 62
PONTIAC (105 "Roll Over Beethoven") ...40-60 59
RGM 40-60
(Title and selection number not known.)
RSVP (116 "I'll Cry") 20-25 63
20TH FOX (166 "Weird") 10-15 59
Members: Roscoe Wharton; Tommy Lee; Danny Stuckenberg.
Also see GREEN, Johnny, & Greenmen
Also see KIT KATS
Also see LAURENCE, T., & Sherwood Greens
Also see ORBITS

ROSE, Andy *P&R '58*
(With the Thorns; with Exotics)
Singles: 7-inch
AAMCO (100 "Just Young") 20-30 58

AAMCO (103 "My Devotion") 50-75 58
CORAL (62109 "Dance On Pretty Clown") 10-20 59
CORAL (62142 "With Feeling") 10-20 59
CORAL (62189 "Undecided") 10-20 60
CORAL (62227 "A Rose and a Thorn") ... 10-20 60
CORAL (62254 "I Can't Forget You") 10-20 61
CORAL (62271 "Crazy for You") 40-50 61
CORAL (62284 "Don't Ask Me to Be Lonely") 50-60 61
CORAL (62297 "I Was the One") 10-20 61
EMBER (1112 "Everybody But You") 8-12 64
GOLDEN CREST (590 "Hey Scooter") 5-10 64
SHELLEY (190 "The Harem") 8-12 64
Also see EXOTICS

ROSE, Dave, & Continentals

Singles: 7-inch

EVENT (502 "Take This Heart") 50-75 60

ROSE, David, & His Orchestra *P&R '43*

Singles: 78 rpm

MGM 3-5 50-57
VICTOR 4-6 43-44

Singles: 7-inch

CAPITOL 4-6 66-69
MGM 5-15 50-67
MGM (158 "The Stripper") 4-8 64
(Golden Circle reissue series.)

Picture Sleeves

MGM (12243 "Forbidden Planet") 15-25 56
MGM (13086 "Wonderful World of the Brothers Grimm") 8-12 62

EPs: 7-inch

KAPP 5-10 59
MGM 5-10 51-58
ROYALE .... 5-10 '50s

LPs: 10/12-inch

CAPITOL 8-15 66-69
DINO 5-10 72
KAPP 10-25 59-61
LION 10-20 59
MCA 5-8 83
MGM 10-30 51-70
METRO 5-15 65-66
SPIN-O-RAMA .... 5-10 '60s
Also see PREVIN, Andre

ROSE, Lester

Singles: 7-inch

ARLEN (1014 "Wino Blues") 50-75 63

ROSE, Tim

Singles: 7-inch

COLUMBIA (43563 "I'm Bringing It Home") 5-10 66
COLUMBIA (43648 "Hey Joe") 5-10 66
(Commercial issue.)
COLUMBIA (43648 "Hey Joe") 15-25 66
(Red vinyl. Includes "Unique Situation" insert. Promotional issue only.)
COLUMBIA (43722 "Where Was I") 5-10 66
COLUMBIA (43958 "I'm Gonna Be Strong") 5-10 67
COLUMBIA (44031 "Morning Dew") 5-10 67
COLUMBIA (44387 "Long Time Man") 5-10 67
PLAYBOY 4-6 72

LPs: 10/12-inch

CAPITOL 8-12 70
COLUMBIA 10-15 68-69
PLAYBOY 8-12 72
Also see BIG THREE

ROSE GARDEN *P&R '67*

Singles: 7-inch

ATCO 5-10 67-68

LPs: 10/12-inch

ATCO (255 "Rose Garden") 15-25 68
Members: Diana DiRose; James Groshong; John Noreen; Bill Fleming; Bruce Boudin.

ROSEBUDS

Singles: 7-inch

GEE (1033 "Dearest Darling") 15-25 57
LANCER (102 "Kiss Me Goodnight") 15-25 59

ROSEBUDS

Singles: 7-inch

BOBWIN (148 "South Side High") 15-25 62

ROSELLA, Carmela

Singles: 7-inch

NANCY (1004 "Oh! It Was Elvis") 10-20 61

ROSEMARY & ROSEBUDS

Singles: 7-inch

LARKWOOD (1101 "What Do I Mean to You") 30-40 62

ROSENTHAL, Rochelle, & Kickball Queen

Singles: 7-inch

SUPER BOLT (33170 "Lottery") .... 20-30 '60s

ROSES

Singles: 7-inch

DOT (15816 "Almost Paradise") 15-25 58
Also see DON & HIS ROSES
Also see GUESS, Don
Also see IVAN
Also see ROBINSON, Jim

ROSIE *P&R '60*

(With the Originals; Rosie "Formerly with the Originals"; Rosalie Hamlin)

Singles: 7-inch

ABC 4-6 73
HIGHLAND (1011 "Angel Baby") 20-30 60
HIGHLAND (1025 "Angel from Above") 10-20 61
HIGHLAND (1032 "Lonely Blue Nights") .. 20-30 62
BRUNSWICK (55205 "Lonely Blue Nights") 15-25 61

LPs: 10/12-inch

BRUNSWICK (54102 "Lonely Blue Nights") 60-80 61
(Monaural.)
BRUNSWICK (754102 "Lonely Blue Nights") 75-100 61
(Stereo.)
Also see TEEN QUEENS / Rosie & Originals

ROSIE'S BABY DOLLS

Singles: 7-inch

FARGO (1017 "I Should Have Known") ... 10-20 60
Also see BABY DOLLS

ROSS, Bibby

Singles: 7-inch

LYRIC (2002 "Beach Party Tonight") 40-50 57

ROSS, Bob

Singles: 7-inch

GLOBAL (719 "Stingy Daddy") 50-75

ROSS, Charles

Singles: 7-inch

CLAT-RO (8529 "Little Bit Lonesome") 300-400

ROSS, Danny

Singles: 7-inch

MINOR (107 "Look At You Go") 150-200 57
STONEWAY (1057 "St. Louis Blues") 10-15
STONEWAY (1072 "Carroll County Blues") 10-15

ROSS, Diana *P&R/R&B/LP '70*

Singles: 12-inch

MOTOWN 5-10 78-80

Singles: 7-inch

MCA 3-5 88
MOTOWN (Black vinyl) 3-6 70-89
MOTOWN (Colored vinyl) 5-15 70-81
(Promotional only.)
RCA (Black vinyl) 3-5 81-87
RCA (Colored vinyl) 5-10 81-87
(Promotional only.)

Picture Sleeves

MOTOWN 3-6 70-91
RCA 3-5 82-87

EPs: 7-inch

MOTOWN (7588 "Sneak Preview from Lady Sings the Blues") 30-50 72
(Promotional issue only.)
MOTOWN (PR-3 "Last Time I Saw Him") 25-35 74
(Promotional issue only.)

LPs: 10/12-inch

DORAL (104 "Diana Ross") .... 150-200 '60s
(Promotional mail-order issue, from Doral cigarettes.)
KORY 8-10 77
MOTOWN (100 series) 5-10 81-83
MOTOWN (711 thru 907) 8-12 70-78
MOTOWN (923 "The Boss") 5-10 79
(Black vinyl.)
MOTOWN (923 "The Boss") 10-20 79
(Colored vinyl. Promotional issue only.)
MOTOWN (951 thru 960) 6-12 81
MOTOWN (5000 series) 5-15 83
MOTOWN (6000 series) 6-12 83-89
(Black vinyl.)
MOTOWN (6381 "Remixes") .... 10-12 '90s
(Colored vinyl. Promotional issue only.)
PARAMOUNT (181/182 "Lady Sings the Blues") 35-50 72
(An "MRA Multiple Record Album, serving the requirements of both radio and TV stations," this LP has a 15-minute interview with Diana Ross. Includes scripts. Promotional issue only.)
RCA 5-10 81-87
Also see DENVER, John / Diana Ross
Also see GAYE, Marvin, & Diana Ross
Also see SUPREMES
Also see TEMPTATIONS

ROSS, Diana, & Bill Cosby / Diana Ross & Jackson Five

Singles: 7-inch

MOTOWN 10-15 70

Picture Sleeves

MOTOWN 10-15 70
Also see COSBY, Bill
Also see JACKSONS

ROSS, Diana, & Michael Jackson *P&R/R&B '78*

Singles: 7-inch

MCA (40947 "Ease On Down the Road") 3-5 78

Picture Sleeves

MCA (40947 "Ease On Down the Road") 3-5 78
Also see JACKSON, Michael

ROSS, Diana, & Lionel Richie *P&R/R&B '81*

Singles: 7-inch

MOTOWN (1519 "Endless Love") 3-5 81
POLYGRAM ("Dreaming of You") 10-15 81
(Promotional issue only. No number given.)

ROSS, Diana, Stevie Wonder, Marvin Gaye, Smokey Robinson *P&R/R&B '79*

Singles: 7-inch

MOTOWN (1455 "Pops, We Love You") 3-5 79
(Black vinyl.)
MOTOWN (1455 "Pops, We Love You") 5-10 79
(Heart shaped disc. Red vinyl.)
MOTOWN (1455 "Pops, We Love You") .. 10-20 79
(Green vinyl. Promotional issue only.)

LPs: 10/12-inch

MOTOWN 5-10 79
Also see DIAMOND, Neil / Diana Ross & Supremes
Also see GAYE, Marvin
Also see ROBINSON, Smokey
Also see ROSS, Diana
Also see WONDER, Stevie

ROSS, Doctor

(With His Jump & Jive Boys; with His Orbits; Charles Ross)

Singles: 78 rpm

CHESS (1504 "Country Clown") 100-200 52
SUN (193 "Come Back Baby") 100-200 54
SUN (212 "Boogie Disease") 150-250 54

Singles: 7-inch

D.I.R. (101 "Industrial Boogie") 25-50 58
FORTUNE (857 "Cat Squirrel") 15-20 59
HI-Q (5027 "Cannonball") 10-20 62
HI-Q (5033 "Call the Doctor") 10-20 63
SUN (193 "Come Back Baby") 400-600 54
SUN (212 "Boogie Disease") 500-1000 54

LPs: 10/12-inch

FORTUNE (3011 "Harmonica Boss") 15-25 71
TESTAMENT (2206 "Dr. Ross") 10-15

ROSS, Jack, & Meadowlarks

Singles: 78 rpm

CHANCE (1125 "Close to You") 50-75 53

Singles: 7-inch

CHANCE (1125 "Close to You") 100-200 53

ROSS, Jack *P&R '62*

Singles: 7-inch

DOT 6-12 61-63
ROMAL (770 "Happy Jose") 15-20 61

LPs: 10/12-inch

DOT (3429 "Cinderella") 15-25 62

ROSS, Jackie *P&R/R&B '64*

(Jacki Ross)

Singles: 7-inch

BRUNSWICK 5-10 67-68
CAPITOL 4-6 76
CHESS 5-10 64
FOUNTAIN 5-10 69
GSF 4-6 72-73
MERCURY 4-6 70-71
SAR (129 "Hard Times") 10-20 62
SCEPTER 4-6 72
USA (103 "Man Is Born") 5-10 67

LPs: 10/12-inch

CHESS (1489 "Full Bloom") 15-25 64

ROSS, Jerry

Singles: 7-inch

APEX (7763 "Out'er Drive") 15-25 61
FALCON (1003 "You Got MyBaby") 100-150
MURCO (1016 "Ever'body's Tryin' ") 200-300 59

ROSS, Johnny

("Directed by Chuck Tequila Rio"; "A&R Man Chuck Tequila Rio")

Singles: 7-inch

CADET (5686 "Chi-Ca-Go") 4-8 72
CORVETTE (1006 "That's What You Mean to Me"/"My Dreams Have Gone") 750-1250 58
(Some discs with these labels play *Fame and Fortune* backed with *Starry Eyed*, by Milt Kilpatrick [Magnet 2006]; however, these show a Hollywood, Calif. address for the company. Actual Johnny Ross discs have no address for Corvette on the label.)
Also see KILPATRICK, Milt
Also see RIO, Chuck

ROSS, Lanny, with Stephen Kisley & His Orchestra & Amory Brothers

Singles: 78 rpm

MAJESTIC (1195 "Whiffenpoof Song") 8-12 47
(The Amory Brothers are believed to be the Ames Brothers.)
Alsc see AMES BROTHERS

ROSS, Macy

Singles: 7-inch

VEEP ("Big Chief Buffalo Nickel") 100-200
(Selection number not known.)

ROSS, Patty, & Jaguars

Singles: 78 rpm

AARDELL 5-10 56

Singles: 7-inch

AARDELL (0002 "Rock It, Davy, Rock It") 20-30 56
Also see JAGUARS

ROSS, Stan

Singles: 7-inch

DEL-FI (4200 "One Man's Family") 8-12 63
REPRISE 15-25 62
WORLD PACIFIC (813 "Please Don't Tease") 40-60 60

LPs: 10/12-inch

DEL-FI (DF-1233 "My Son the Copy Cat") 20-30 63
(Monaural.)
DEL-FI (DFS-1233 "My Son the Copy Cat") 30-40 63
(Stereo.)
Also see ARBOGAST & ROSS

ROSS, Stefan

Singles: 7-inch

INTRO (001 "Please Be My Love") 200-300 60

ROSSI, Frankie, & Dreams

Singles: 78 rpm

MARK (7001 "Dream Boy") 10-20 57

Singles: 7-inch

MARK (7001 "Dream Boy") 15-25 57

ROTARY CONNECTION *LP '68*

Singles: 7-inch

CADET CONCEPT 5-10 68-70

LPs: 10/12-inch

CADET CONCEPT 15-25 68-70
Members: Minnie Riperton; Sidney Barnes.
Also see ALIOTTA, HAYNES & JEREMIAH
Also see BARNES, Sidney

ROTATIONS

Singles: 7-inch

ORIGINAL SOUND (41 "Crusher") 8-12 63
Members: Paul Buff; David Aerni.
Also see LORD, Brian, & Midnighters

ROTATIONS

Singles: 7-inch

FRANTIC (200 "D - 9") 100-150 65
FRANTIC (202 "Changed Man") 50-100 67
MALA (576 "Misty Roses") 15-25 67

ROUBIAN, Bob

Singles: 78 rpm

CAPITOL ... 5-10 56
PREP ... 10-25 57

Singles: 7-inch

CAPITOL (3373 "Blue Suede Shoes") ... 5-10 56
PREP (101 "Rocket to the Moon") ... 15-25 57
PREP (109 "Cracker Stacker") ... 15-25 57

ROUBIK, Jack

Singles: 7-inch

LINDY (741 "Live It Up") ... 100-200

ROUGES

Singles: 7-inch

WAVERLEY (108 "The Next Guy") ... 20-30 66

ROUGH RIDERS

Singles: 7-inch

HANOVER (4527 "Stampede") ... 8-12 59
Members: Dick Hyman, Milt DeLugg.
Also see HYMAN, Dick

ROULETTE, Freddie

LPs: 10/12-inch

JANUS (3053 "Sweet, Funky Steel") ... 20-30 73
Also see HOOKER, Earl

ROULETTES
("Singing Roulettes")

Singles: 7-inch

SCEPTER (1204 "Hasten Jason") ... 400-600 59

ROULETTES
(With the Al Browne Band)

Singles: 7-inch

CHAMP (102 "I See a Star") ... 25-35 59
EBB (124 "You Don't Care Anymore") ... 50-75 57
(Promotional issue. Shown as by the Five Orleans.)
EBB (124 "You Don't Care Anymore") ... 15-25 57
Also see BROWNE, Al
Also see GALLANT, Billy

ROULETTES

Singles: 7-inch

ANGLE (1001 "Surfer's Charge") ... 8-12 63
(Also issued as *Invasion* by the Invaders.)
Also see INVADERS

ROUND ROBIN P&R '64

Singles: 7-inch

CAPITOL ... 5-10 67
DOMAIN ... 8-12 63-65
SHOT ... 5-10 66

LPs: 10/12-inch

CHALLENGE (620 "Land of 1000 Dances") ... 15-25 65
DOMAIN (101 "Greatest Dance Hits Slauson Style") ... 25-35 64

ROUND UP BOYS

Singles: 7-inch

HARK (504 "Rock and Roll Baby") ... 100-200

ROUNDERS

Singles: 7-inch

JORA (1001 "Small Town Girl") ... 75-100
(Reissued as by Jimmy Tig & Rounders.)
Also see TIG, Jimmy

ROUTERS P&R '62

Singles: 7-inch

MERCURY (73418 "Superbird") ... 4-6 73
W.B. ... 8-12 62-64

LPs: 10/12-inch

MERCURY ... 10-15 73
W.B. (1490 "Let's Go") ... 30-50 63
W.B. (1524 "1963's Great Instrumental Hits") ... 20-30 63
W.B. (1559 "Charge!") ... 20-30 64
W.B. (1595 "Chuck Berry Songbook") ... 20-30 65
Members: Joe Saraceno; Rene Hall; Ed Kay; Mike Gordon.

ROVERS

Singles: 78 rpm

CAPITOL ... 10-15 55
MUSIC CITY ... 25-50 55

Singles: 7-inch

CAPITOL (3078 "Why Oh-h") ... 20-30 55
MUSIC CITY (750 "Why, Oh-h") ... 40-50 54
(Black vinyl.)
MUSIC CITY (750 "Why, Oh-h") ... 100-200 54
(Green vinyl.)
MUSIC CITY (750 "Why, Oh-h") ... 50-150 54
(Red or blue vinyl.)
MUSIC CITY (780 "Salute to Johnny Ace") ... 40-50 55
(Black vinyl.)
MUSIC CITY (780 "Salute to Johnny Ace") ... 100-200 55
(Purple vinyl.)
MUSIC CITY (780 "Salute to Johnny Ace") ... 50-150 54
(Blue vinyl.)
Also see 5 ROVERS
Also see GAYLARKS / Rovers

ROVIN' FLAMES

Singles: 7-inch

BOSS (002 "I Can't") ... 15-25 66
DECCA (32191 "How Many Times") ... 10-15 67
FULLER (2627 "Gloria") ... 25-35 65
TAMPA BAY (1111 "Seven Million People") ... 15-25 66

ROVIN' GAMBLERS

Singles: 7-inch

MAVERICK (614 "Do the Fly") ... 10-15 61

ROVIN' KIND
(With Barney Pip)

Singles: 7-inch

COUNTERPOINT (9006 "Everybody") ... 10-20 65
DUNWICH (146 "My Generation") ... 10-15 66
DUNWICH (154 "She") ... 10-15 67
ROULETTE (4687 "Night People") ... 8-12 66
SMASH (2102 "You Can't Sit Down") ... 5-10 67
Members: Paul Cotton; Kal David; Frank Bartoli; Mike Anthony; Fred Page.

ROWANS P&R '76

Singles: 7-inch

ASYLUM ... 4-6 75-76
COLUMBIA ... 4-8 72-73

LPs: 10/12-inch

ASYLUM ... 8-10 75-77
COLUMBIA ... 10-15 72
Members: Peter Rowan; Chris Rowan; Lorin Rowan.
Also see GARCIA, Jerry
Also see OLD AND IN THE WAY

ROWE, Lynn

Singles: 7-inch

HITT (181 "Red Rover") ... 50-75 58

ROWE, Steve

Singles: 7-inch

(21304 "Minor Chaos") ... 100-125 '60s
(No label name used.)

ROWLAND, Roc
(With the Cineramas)

Singles: 7-inch

RHAPSODY (71987 "Playing for Keeps") ... 30-40 60
Also see CINERAMAS

ROWLAND, Steve
(With the Ring Leaders; with Family Dogg)

Singles: 78 rpm

LIBERTY ... 5-10 56

Singles: 7-inch

BELL (863 "Moonshine Mary") ... 4-8 70
CROSS COUNTRY (1818 "Out Ridin'") ... 8-12 63
LIBERTY (55030 "Flat Wheel Train") ... 8-12 56
VIRGO (1003 "How Would You Like It") ... 10-20 59

Picture Sleeves

CROSS COUNTRY (1818 "Out Ridin'") ... 10-20 63

ROWLAND, Will

Singles: 78 rpm

GOLD STAR (657 "Reefer Blues") ... 25-50 47
MODERN ... 15-25 46-47

ROWLES, Jimmy

LPs: 10/12-inch

TAMPA (8 "Let's Get Acquainted with Jazz") ... 40-60 55

ROXSTERS

Singles: 7-inch

ART (175 "Goodbye Baby") ... 300-400 58
Members: Butch Watts; Wesley Hardin; Don Ward; Dave Hieronymus; Keith MacKendrick.
Also see CHAMPS
Also see HARDIN, Wesley, & Roxsters
Also see THINK

ROXY & DAYCHORDS

Singles: 7-inch

CANDLELITE (430 "I'm So in Love") ... 5-10 64
CLIFTON (24 "Mary Lou") ... 4-6 77
DON-EL (116 "Mary Lou") ... 150-200 62
Also see DAYCHORDS

ROXY MUSIC LP '73

Singles: 12-inch

W.B. (2033 "Avalon") ... 5-8 82

Singles: 7-inch

ATCO ... 3-6 75-81
REPRISE ... 4-8 72
W.B. (Except 7779) ... 3-5 82-83
W.B. (7779 "Do the Strand") ... 4-8 73

Promotional Singles

ATCO ... 5-10 75-80
W.B. ... 3-5 82-83

Picture Sleeves

W.B. ... 3-5 82-83

LPs: 10/12-inch

ATCO (Except 106 & 8114) ... 8-15 74-83
ATCO (106 "Country Life") ... 20-35 75
(Cover pictures two women in their underwear.)
ATCO (106 "Country Life") ... 8-15 75
(The two women are not pictured on cover.)
ATCO (38114 "Manifesto") ... 25-30 75
(Picture disc. Promotional issue only.)
ATLANTIC ... 8-10 74
REPRISE (2114 "Roxy Music") ... 15-25 72
W.B. (Except 2696) ... 5-10 82-83
W.B. (2696 "For Your Pleasure") ... 15-25 73
Member: Bryan Ferry.

ROY, Bobby, & Chord-A-Roys

Singles: 7-inch

JDS (5001 "Little Girl Lost") ... 20-30 59

ROY, Doty

Singles: 7-inch

TRIBE (8309 "He's My Idea") ... 5-10 65

ROY, Jackie, & Collegians

Singles: 78 rpm

OKEH ... 5-10 53

Singles: 7-inch

OKEH (6970 "You Made a Fool Out of Me") ... 20-30 53
OKEH (6987 "My Heart Knows") ... 15-25 53

ROY, Lee
(Bro. Lee Roy & His Band; "Featuring Brother Lee Roy on Baritone Sax")

Singles: 78 rpm

EPIC ... 5-10 53-54

Singles: 7-inch

EPIC (9001 "Man on the Beat") ... 10-20 53
EPIC (9011 "The Creep") ... 10-20 54
EPIC (9014 "The Bunny Hop") ... 10-20 54
EPIC (9027 'Rollin' Rock") ... 10-20 54
EPIC (9043 "Hop-Scotch") ... 10-20 54
EPIC (9061 "Mexican Hat Dance") ... 10-20 54
EPIC (9067 "Who Dat") ... 10-20 54
EPIC (9073 "Believe Me") ... 10-20 54
EPIC (9081 "South Rampart Street Blues") ... 10-20 54
SANWAYNE (1140 "Skoobie Doo") ... 8-12 62

EPs: 7-inch

EPIC (7027 "Teen-Age Party Dances") ... 15-25 54
EPIC (7037 "Sock Hop") ... 15-25 54
EPIC (7044 "Bro. Lee Roy") ... 15-25 54

LPs: 10/12-inch

EPIC (1011 "Teenage Party Dances") ... 25-50 54
EPIC (1014 "Sock Hop") ... 25-50 54

ROY, Ricky

Singles: 7-inch

MERCURY (71230 "Because You're Mine") ... 10-20 57
SPANN (416 "Screamin' Mimi") ... 40-60 59

ROY & GLORIA

Singles: 78 rpm

DELUXE ... 8-12 57

Singles: 7-inch

DELUXE (6145 "We Fell in Love") ... 10-20 57
DELUXE (6153 "You Know My Love Is True") ... 10-20 57
Members: Roy Gaines; Gloria Hawkins.
Also see GAINES, Roy

ROY - SARAH & TRAITS

Singles: 7-inch

LORI (9551 "You'll Never Make Me Blue") ... 10-20 65
(Same song as *Treat Me Right*, the title track of Roy Head's Scepter LP.)
Member: Roy Head.
Also see HEAD, Roy

ROYAL, Bill

Singles: 7-inch

ODESSA (504 "Caffeine, Nicotine, Gasoline") ... 150-250 58

ROYAL, Billy Joe P&R/LP '65

Singles: 7-inch

ALL WOOD (401 "If It Wasn't for a Woman") ... 5-10 62
ATLANTIC (2300 series) ... 4-8 66
ATLANTIC (87000 thru 89000 series) ... 3-5 85-91
ATLANTIC AMERICA ... 3-5 85-89
COLUMBIA (43305 "Down in the Boondocks") ... 4-8 65
(Black vinyl.)
COLUMBIA (43305 "Down in the Boondocks") ... 10-20 65
(Colored vinyl. Promotional issue only.)
COLUMBIA (43390 "I Knew You When") ... 4-8 65
(Black vinyl.)
COLUMBIA (43390 "I Knew You When") ... 10-20 65
(Colored vinyl. Promotional issue only.)
COLUMBIA (43465 thru 45620) ... 4-8 65-72
FAIRLANE (21009 "Never in a Hundred Years") ... 20-30 61
FAIRLANE (21013 "Dark Glasses") ... 8-12 61
KAT FAMILY ... 3-5 81
MGM/SOUTH ... 4-6 73
MERCURY ... 3-5 80
PLAYER'S ... 5-10 65
PRIVATE STOCK ... 4-6 78-79
SCEPTER (12419 "All Night Rain") ... 4-6 76
TOLLIE (9011 "Mama Didn't Raise No Fools") ... 5-10 64

Picture Sleeves

ATLANTIC AMERICA ... 3-6 '80s
TOLLIE ... 8-12 64

LPs: 10/12-inch

ATLANTIC AMERICA ... 5-10 86-89
BACK-TRAC ... 5-8 85
BRYLEN ... 5-10
COLUMBIA (Except 45063) ... 15-25 65-69
COLUMBIA (45063 "Greatest Hits") ... 5-8 89
51 WEST ... 5-10 83
KAT FAMILY ... 5-10 81
MERCURY ... 5-10 80
Also see SOUTH, Joe / Billy Joe Royal
Also see WINE, Toni, & Billy Joe Royal

ROYAL, Chuck

Singles: 7-inch

BELLA (2210 "My Baby Is Gone") ... 60-75 59
BLUE MOON (406 "You're Like a Butterfly") ... 40-60 58

ROYAL AIRCOACH

Singles: 7-inch

FLYING MACHINE (8868 "Wondering Why") ... 15-25 68

ROYAL BOYS

Singles: 7-inch

TROPELCO (1007 "Darling Angel") ... 2000-3000 60

ROYAL COACHMEN

Singles: 7-inch

CHALLENGE (59251 "Loophole") ... 10-20 64
COACHMEN (200,915 "Bama-Lama") ... 40-60 '60s
GE GE (102 "Tidal Wave") ... 15-25 62

ROYAL DEMONS

Singles: 7-inch

RHYTHM (5004 "What's the Matter Baby") ... 200-300 59

ROYAL DEMONS

Singles: 7-inch

PEK (8101 "Trembling Hand") ... 200-300 61

ROYAL DRIFTERS

Singles: 7-inch

'TEEN (506 "Little Linda") ... 150-250 59
'TEEN (508 "To Each His Own") ... 100-150 59

ROYAL FIVE
(Royal-Five)

Singles: 7-inch

ARCTIC (160 "Peace of Mind") 5-10 69
P and L (317 "Over the Rainbow") 400-600 66
TYLER (200 "Say It to My Face") 50-75 67
Members: Reggie Marshall; Jerome Marshall; Billy Stokes; Ronnie Stokes; Ben Durr.

ROYAL FLAIRS

Singles: 7-inch

MARINA (503 "Suicide") 50-75 65
SAM (119 "Dream Angel") 20-40 63
Also see UNLIMITED

ROYAL GALAXIES

Singles: 7-inch

CAPITOL (4488 "Over and Done With") .. 15-25 60

ROYAL GUARDSMEN P&R '66

Singles: 7-inch

LAURIE (3359 "Baby Let's Wait") 10-15 66
LAURIE (3366 "Squeaky Vs. the Black Knight") 30-50 66
(Re-recorded as *Snoopy Vs. the Red Baron.* Canadian. We have yet to verify a US issue of this title.)
LAURIE (3366 "Snoopy Vs. the Red Baron") 5-10 66
LAURIE (3374 "Snoopy Vs. the Black Knight") 5-10 67
LAURIE (3379 "Return of the Red Baron") .5-10 67
LAURIE (3391 "Airplane Song") 5-10 67
LAURIE (3397 "Wednesday") 5-10 67
LAURIE (3416 "Snoopy's Christmas") 5-10 68
LAURIE (3428 "I Say Love") 5-10 68
LAURIE (3451 "Snoopy for President") 5-10 68
LAURIE (3461 "Baby Let's Wait") 5-10 68
LAURIE (3494 "Mother, Where's Your Daughter") 5-10 69
LAURIE (3590 "Snoopy for President") 4-6 72
LAURIE (3646 "Snoopy for President") 3-5 76

LPs: 10/12-inch

AUDIO FIDELITY (1913 "Snoopy's Christmas") 10-15 83
(Picture disc.)
LAURIE (2038 "Snoopy Vs. the Red Baron") 15-20 67
LAURIE (2039 "Return of the Red Baron") 15-20 67
LAURIE (2042 "Snoopy & His Friends, the Royal Guardsmen") 15-20 67
LAURIE (2046 "Snoopy for President") ... 15-20 68
Members: Chris Nunley; Barry Winslow; Bill Balough; Tom Richards.
Also see WINSLOW, Barry

ROYAL HALOS

Singles: 7-inch

ALADDIN (3460 "My Love Is True") 50-75 59

ROYAL HARMONY QUARTET R&B '42

Singles: 78 rpm

KEYNOTE 5-10 42
Members: Julius Ginyard; Ted Brooks; Bill Johnson; John Jennings; George McFadden.
Also see JUBALAIRES

ROYAL HAWK
(Roy Hawkins)

Singles: 78 rpm

FLAIR (1013 "The Royal Hawk") 20-40 53

Singles: 7-inch

FLAIR (1013 "The Royal Hawk") 50-100 53
Also see HAWKINS, Roy

ROYAL HOLIDAYS

Singles: 7-inch

CARLTON (472 "I'm Sorry") 10-15 58
HERALD (536 "Rockin' at the Bandstand") 200-250 59
(Original has a multi-color label.)
PENTHOUSE (9357 "I'm Sorry") 100-150 58

ROYAL HOST

Singles: 7-inch

AT (684 "Whatever Happened to Joey") .. 10-20 68
Also see LEE, Robin

ROYAL JACKS
(With Vince Catalano & Orchestra)

Singles: 7-inch

AMY (865 "Anticipation") 10-15 62
DANCO (503 "You'll Never Be Mine") 8-12 64
OPERATORS SPECIAL (001 "Who What Where When and Why") 40-60 61
STUDIO (9903 "Who What Where When and Why") 50-75 59
20TH FOX (100 "I'm in Love Again") 15-25 58
Also see CATALANO, Vinny

ROYAL JESTERS
("Vocal with orch. by Charlie & the Jives")

Singles: 7-inch

HARLEM (105 "My Angel of Love") 500-600 60
Also see CHARLIE & JIVES

ROYAL JESTERS
(With the Casuals; with Memphis III)

Singles: 7-inch

COBRA (2222 "Love Me") 10-20 62
COBRA (7777 "I Want to Be Loved") 20-30 63
COBRA (611025 "Ask Me to Move a Mountain") 20-30 61
JESTER (102 "Wisdom of a Fool") 15-25 62
JESTER (103 "My Love, My Love") 10-20 62
JESTER (104 "We Go Together") 10-20 62
JESTER (106 "Let There Be You") 10-20 62
JESTER (108 "I'm So Sorry") 10-20 62
JOX (029 "Please Say You Want Me Too") 5-10 65
JOX (036 "Wishing Ring") 5-10 65
JOX (046 "Look for a Star") 5-10 66

ROYAL JOKERS P&R '55

Singles: 78 rpm

ATCO 10-20 55-56
HI-Q 15-25 57

Singles: 7-inch

ATCO (6052 "You Tickle Me Baby") 40-50 55
ATCO (6062 "Don't Leave Me, Fanny") 25-35 55
ATCO (6077 "She's Mine, All Mine") 20-30 57
FORTUNE (560 "You Tickle Me Baby") ...10-15 63
FORTUNE (840 "Sweet Little Angel") 40-50 57
HI-Q (5004 "September in the Rain") 30-40 57
Also see MUSKETEERS

ROYAL JOKERS

LPs: 10/12-inch

DAWN (1119 "Rock and Roll Spectacular") 50-100 57

ROYAL JOKERS

Singles: 7-inch

MURCO (1015 "Beatnik") 15-25 58

ROYAL KINGS

Singles: 7-inch

LANCE (1035 "My Last Song") 20-30 57

ROYAL KINGS
(With the Cashmers)

Singles: 7-inch

CANDLELITE (410 "Peter-Peter") 8-12 63
FORLIN (502 "Peter-Peter") 40-60 61

ROYAL KNIGHTS

Singles: 7-inch

FIREBALL (104 "Knight-Mare") 75-125 64
SHADOW (108 "Midnight Drag") 20-30 67
SNAP (005 "I Don't Want to Go") ....25-35 '60s

ROYAL KNIGHTS

Singles: 7-inch

NITE (1005 "I Wanna Know") 15-25 66

Picture Sleeves

NITE (1005 "I Wanna Know") 25-35 66

ROYAL KNIGHTS

Singles: 7-inch

RENDEZVOUS (01 "Have You Heard") ...10-20 '60s
Members: Benny Williams; Charles Hills.
Also see DESCIPLES OF SOUL

ROYAL LANCERS

Singles: 7-inch

ABC-PAR (10751 "Baby, I Love You") 15-25 65
HI MAR (501/502 "Good Good Lovin' "/"This Time") 10-20 63
HI MAR (6049/6050 "Be My Girl"/"Hey Little Girl") 10-20 65
LAWN (205 "Oh Little Girl") 25-35 63
(Also issued as by the Lancers.)
LAWN (215 "Hey Little One") 10-20 63
Members: Keith "Corky" Weiss; John Mader; Bruce Carscadon; Larry Borrell; Bill Weaver.
Also see CRAIG, Vilas & Royal Lancers / Badgers
Also see LANCERS
Also see PREMIER, Ronnie
Also see ROCK, Jimmy
Also see STEFAN, Paul
Also see TYLER, Chuck, & Royal Lancers

ROYAL LANCERS

Singles: 7-inch

RIZE (100 "Is This the Place") 150-200

ROYAL MASTERS

Singles: 7-inch

GUYDEN (2078 "You're the One") 50-75 63

ROYAL NOTES / Phil Johnson & Duvals
(With Floyd Williams & Orchestra)

Singles: 7-inch

KELIT (7034 "You Are My Love"/"Wee Small Hours") 500-600 58
Also see JOHNSON, Phil, & Duvals
Also see JOHNSON, Phil, & Duvals / Royal Notes

ROYAL PLAY BOYS

Singles: 7-inch

IMPERIAL (5782 "Walking On") 15-25 61

ROYAL PLAYBOYS

LPs: 10/12-inch

WALDORF MUSIC HALL (136 "Spirituals and Jubilees") 50-75 53
(10-inch LP.)

ROYAL PLAYBOYS

Singles: 7-inch

DO DE (101 "Happy Hours") 15-25 64
DO DE (111 "Arabia") 50-100 64

ROYAL RAVENS

Singles: 7-inch

MAH'S (0015 "All Over You") 50-75 63

ROYAL REBELS

Singles: 7-inch

KISKI (2067 "Drive-in") 20-30 65

ROYAL REVERES

Singles: 7-inch

JUMP-UP (114 "Such a Fool") ....40-50 '60s

ROYAL RHYTHMS

Singles: 7-inch

ROYAL (5070 "Lovey Dovey") ....50-80 '50s
ROYAL (7825 "Wayward Wind") ....50-75 '50s

ROYAL SONS QUINTET
(Five Royales)

Singles: 78 rpm

APOLLO (253 "Bedside of a Neighbor") 100-200 52
APOLLO (266 "Come Over Here") 50-100 52
Members: Johnny Tanner; Lowman Pauling; Clarence Pauling; William Samuels; Otto Jeffries; Clarence Pauling; Johnny Holmes.
Also see CASHMERES
Also see COSYTONES
Also see FIVE ROYALES
Also see KING & SHARPETTES

ROYAL SPADES

Singles: 7-inch

MARQUEE (702 "I'm Gonna Voodoo You") 10-20 62

ROYAL TEENS P&R/R&B '58
("Joey Villa & Royal Teens")

Singles: 78 rpm

ABC-PAR (Except 9882) 20-50 57-58
ABC-PAR (9882 "Short Shorts") 75-100 57
POWER (215 "Short Shorts") 75-100 57

Singles: 7-inch

ABC 4-6 73
ABC-PAR (9882 "Short Shorts") 20-30 57
ABC-PAR (9918 "Big Name Button") 20-30 58
ABC-PAR (9945 "Harvey's Got a Girlfriend") 20-30 58
ABC-PAR (9955 "My Kind of Dream") 20-30 58
ALLNEW (1415 "Royal Twist") 10-20 62
ASTRA (1012 "Mad Gass") 5-10 65
CAPITOL (4261 "Believe Me") 25-35 59
(Promotional issue only.)
CAPITOL (4261 "Believe Me") 20-30 59
(Capitol dome logo at top.)
CAPITOL (4261 "Believe Me") 10-20 59
(Capitol dome logo at left side.)
CAPITOL (4335 "Was It a Dream") 10-20 60
CAPITOL (4402 "With You") 10-20 60
JUBILEE (5418 "Royal Twist") 5-10 62
MIGHTY (110 "Royal Blue") 10-20 58
MIGHTY (112 "Cave Man") 20-30 59
MIGHTY (200 "My Memories ofYou") 20-30 61
MUSICOR (1398 "Smile a Little Smile for Me") 5-8 70
POWER (113 "Mad Gass") 20-30 59
POWER (215 "Short Shorts") 75-100 57
SPARTON (534 "Short Shorts") 25-50 58
(Canadian. Runs 2:39. That's 27 seconds longer than ABC-Paramount single, which fades out at 2:12.)
SWAN (4200 "I'll Love You") 75-125 65
(Previously issued on Bluejay as by the Bluetones.)
TCF (117 "Bad Girl") 5-10 65

LPs: 10/12-inch

DEMAND (010 "Believe Me") 10-20
MUSICOR (3186 "Newies But Oldies") 10-20 70
TRU-GEMS (101 "Music Gems") 8-12 74
Members: Bob Gaudio; Al Kooper; Buddy Randell; Joey Villa; Billy Crandall; Tom Austin; Tony Grochowski.
Also see BENNETT, Joe, & Sparkletones / Royal Teens
Also see BLUETONES
Also see DISENTRI, Turner
Also see 4 SEASONS
Also see RANDELL, Buddy
Also see VILLA, Joey

ROYAL TONES

Singles: 7-inch

EMPIRE (1001 "Creeping Thunder") 20-30 60
JUBILEE (5362 "Little Bo") 20-30 59
TITANIC (5014 "Black Lightnin' ") 15-25 64

ROYAL TONES

Singles: 7-inch

ATHENA (201 "Come Dance with Me") 300-400
ATHENA (729 "Come to My House Rock") 400-500
Members: Bill Logsdon; Pat Logsdon.

ROYAL VIKINGS

Singles: 7-inch

METROPOLIS (7001 "Surfin' Mary") 15-25 63

ROYAL-AIRES
(With the Lee Clark Orchestra)

Singles: 7-inch

GALLO (108 "Friendship Ring") 20-30 57
GALLO (110 "You're in Love") 20-30 57

ROYALAIRES

Singles: 7-inch

QUEEN (30001 "Frying Chicken") 10-20 61

ROYALE MONARCHS

Singles: 7-inch

DELL (101 "Sombrero Stomp") 15-25 62
DELL STAR (102 "Surfs Up") 15-25 62
DELL STAR (104 "Teen Scene") 15-25 64
Member: Roger Stafford.

ROYALETTES P&R/R&B '65

Singles: 7-inch

CHANCELLOR (1133 "Yesterday's Lovers") 10-15 63
CHANCELLOR (1140 "Blue Summer") 10-15 63
MGM (13283 "He's Gone") 10-15 64
MGM (13327 "Poor Boy") 10-15 65
MGM (13366 "It's Gonna Take a Miracle") 10-15 65
MGM (13405 "I Want to Meet Him") 10-15 65
MGM (13451 "Only When You're Lonely") 10-15 66
MGM (13507 "It's a Big Mistake") 10-15 66
MGM (13544 "Affair to Remember") 10-15 66
MGM (13588 " When Summer's Gone") ..10-15 66
MGM (13627 "Take My Love") 10-15 66
ROULETTE (4768 "River of Tears") 5-10 67
W.B. (5439 "Come to Me") 5-10 64

LPs: 10/12-inch

MGM (4332 "It's Gonna Take a Miracle") 15-25 65
MGM (4366 "Elegant Sound of the Royalettes") 15-25 66
Members: Anita Ross; Sheila Ross; Terry Jones; Ronnie Brown.

ROYALITES

Singles: 7-inch

MOJAK (5265 "Harlem Nocturne") 15-25 65

ROYALS
Singles: 78 rpm
OKEH (6832 "If You Love Me") 200-300 51
Singles: 7-inch
OKEH (6832 "If You Love Me") 2000-2500 51
Also see WILLIS, Chuck

ROYALS R&B '53
Singles: 78 rpm
FEDERAL (12064 "Every Beat of My Heart") 100-200 52
FEDERAL (12077 "Starting from Tonight") 100-200 52
FEDERAL (12088 "Moonrise") 100-200 52
FEDERAL (12098 "Love in My Heart") .. 50-100 52
FEDERAL (12113 "Are You Forgetting") . 40-60 52
FEDERAL (12121 "The Shrine of St. Cecilia") 100-150 53
FEDERAL (12133 "Get It") 40-60 53
FEDERAL (12150 "Hello Miss Fine") ... 150-200 53
FEDERAL (12160 "That's It") 40-60 53
FEDERAL (12169 "Work with Me Annie") 40-60 54
Singles: 7-inch
FEDERAL (12064 "Every Beat of My Heart") 500-1000 52
(Black vinyl.)
FEDERAL (12064 "Every Beat of My Heart") 2500-3500 52
(Blue vinyl.)
FEDERAL (12077 "Starting from Tonight") 1000-2000 52
FEDERAL (12088 "Moonrise") 1000-2000 52
FEDERAL (12098 "Love in My Heart") 750-1000 52
FEDERAL (12113 "Are You Forgetting") 300-400 52
FEDERAL (12121 "The Shrine of St. Cecilia") 500-1000 53
FEDERAL (12133 "Get It") 200-300 53
FEDERAL (12150 "Hey Miss Fine") 150-250 53
FEDERAL (12160 "That's It") 150-250 54
FEDERAL (12169 "Work with Me Annie") 150-250 54
FEDERAL (12177 "Give It Up") 200-300 54
(White label. Test pressing only. Commercial copies credit: "The Midnighters, Formally Known as the Royals.")
GUSTO .... 3-5 '80s
Note: Federal titles reissued as by the Midnighters are in the Midnighters' section.
Members: Henry Booth; Hank Ballard; Charles Sutton; Lawson Smith; Alonzo Tucker; Sonny Woods. Session: Wynonie Harris.
Also see BALLARD, Hank
Also see BOOTH, Henry
Also see HARRIS, Wynonie
Also see MIDNIGHTERS

ROYALS
Singles: 78 rpm
VENUS 50-100 54
Singles: 7-inch
VENUS (103 "Someday We'll Meet Again") 200-300 54
Also see SCOOTERS

ROYALS
Singles: 7-inch
PENGUIN (1008 "Thunder Wagon") 15-25 59

ROYALS
Singles: 7-inch
ADIRONDACK (1096 "Back in Town") 20-30 60

ROYALS
Singles: 7-inch
MONUMENTAL 5-8 64
VAGABOND (134 "Surfin' Lagoon") 10-20 62
VAGABOND (444 "Christmas Party") 10-20 63
(Black vinyl.)
VAGABOND (444 "Christmas Party") 30-50 63
(Colored vinyl.)

ROYALS
Singles: 7-inch
CORI (31002 "I'm All Alone") 10-20 65
CROYDON ("Slow Down Boy") 10-20 67
(No selection number used.)
CROYDON ("Summertime in Maine") 10-20
(No selection number used.)
ODYSSEY (711 "Comin' & Goin'") .... 25-35 '60s

ROYALS
Singles: 7-inch
COPELAND (2130 "Say You Love Me") .. 25-35

ROYALTONES
Singles: 78 rpm
OLD TOWN 25-35 56
Singles: 7-inch
OLD TOWN (1018 "Crazy Love") 40-50 56
OLD TOWN (1028 "Latin Love") 50-75 56
Also see McFADDEN, Ruth

ROYALTONES P&R '58
Singles: 78 rpm
JUBILEE (5338 "Poor Boy") 40-60 58
Singles: 7-inch
ABC 4-6 73
GOLDISC 10-20 60-62
JANUS GOLD 4-6
JUBILEE (5338 "Poor Boy") 15-25 58
JUBILEE (5362 "Little Bo") 10-20 59
JUBILEE (5418 "Royal Twist") 8-12 62
MALA (473 "Our Faded Love") 5-10 64
MALA (482 "Lonely World") 5-10 64
MALA (487 "Misty Sea") 5-10 64
PENTHOUSE (777 "Clip Clop") 25-35 59
PORT (70037 "Poor Boy") 8-12 64
ROULETTE 4-6 71
TWIRL (2007 "Boss Limbo") 8-10 62
VIRGO 4-6 72

ROYER, Luke
Singles: 7-inch
BEE JAY (1375 "One's All the Law Will Allow") 25-35

ROYSTER, Jimmy
Singles: 7-inch
SKY (1 "They May Not Like Me") 100-150 58
(Red vinyl.)
SKY (45 "Rock") 50-75

ROZZI, Little Sammy, & Guys
Singles: 7-inch
PELHAM (722 "Christine") 200-300 61
(Reissued as by Little Sammy & the Tones.)
Also see LITTLE SAMMY & TONES

RUBBER BAND
(Tommy Stuart & Rubber Band)
Singles: 7-inch
ABC (10849 "Let's Sail Away") 5-10 66
COLUMBIA 5-10 66-67
1-2-3 (1725 "Peeking Through Your Window") 4-6 70
REPRISE (637 "I'm Gonna Make It") 5-8 67
LPs: 10/12-inch
GREENWOOD (1650 "The Band That Wouldn't Die") 15-20 85
Members: Johnny Wyker; Tippy Armstrong; Tommy Stuart; John Townsend; Lou Mullinix; Brook Clement; Bill Connell.
Also see ALLMAN JOYS
Also see SAILCAT

RUBBER BAND
Singles: 7-inch
COULEE (122 "My Baby Left Me") 10-15 68

RUBBER MAZE
Singles: 7-inch
RUFF (1098 "Mrs. Griffith") 15-25 68
TOWER (351 "Mrs. Griffith") 8-12 67

RUBBER MEMORY
LPs: 10/12-inch
RPC (69401 "Welcome") 200-250 66

RU-BEE-ELS
Singles: 7-inch
FLIP (359 "I'll Try") 15-25 62

RUBEN & JETS
(Mothers Of Invention)
Singles: 7-inch
VERVE (10632 "Any Way the Wind Blows") 20-30 68
VERVE (10632 "Deseri") 20-30 68
LPs: 10/12-inch
VERVE (5055 "Crusin' with Ruben and the Jets") 30-40 68
(Issued with three paper inserts, any of which can add $15 to $25 to the value.)
Also see MOTHERS OF INVENTION

RUBEN & JETS
Singles: 7-inch
MERCURY (73381 "Wedding Bells") 10-20 73
LPs: 10/12-inch
MERCURY 15-25 73
Members: Ruben Guevara; Johnny Martinez; Tony Duran; Robert Zamora; Bob Roberts; Robert Camarena; Jim Sherwood.
Also see GUEVARA, Ruben

RUBIES
Singles: 78 rpm
TNT 10-15 53
Singles: 7-inch
TNT (101 "Zing Went the Strings of My Heart") 15-25 53

RUBIES
Singles: 78 rpm
VERNE (103 "Someday") 10-15 54
Singles: 7-inch
VERNE (103 "Someday") 30-40 54

RUBIES
Singles: 7-inch
DISTRICT (301 "Loaded with Goodies") .. 20-30 61
Also see FOUR JEWELS

RUBIES
Singles: 7-inch
EMPRESS (103 "He Was an Angel") 10-20 61
EMPRESS (103 "He Was an Angel") 15-25 61
(Single-sided. Promotional issue only.)
VEE-JAY (596 "Spanish Boy") 8-12 64
Picture Sleeves
EMPRESS (103 "He Was an Angel") 15-25 61
VEE-JAY (596 "Spanish Boy") 15-25 64
(Promotional issue only.)

RUBIN
Singles: 7-inch
KAPP (869 "You've Been Away") 25-50 68

RUBY
Singles: 7-inch
ABC 10-20
GOLDEN TOKEN (100 "Feminine Ingenuity") 100-125

RUBY, Don
Singles: 7-inch
CUB (9012 "Rockin' Piano, Outta Tune Guitar") 50-75 58

RUBY & ROMANTICS P&R/R&B/LP '63
Singles: 7-inch
A&M 4-6 69
ABC 4-8 67-68
KAPP 5-10 62-67
MCA (60052 "Our Day Will Come") 4-6 73
Picture Sleeves
KAPP 5-10 63-64
LPs: 10/12-inch
ABC 10-20 68
KAPP 15-25 63-67
MCA .... 5-10 '80s
PICKWICK .... 8-10 '70s
Members: Ruby Nash; Edward Roberts; Ronald Mosley; Leroy Fann; George Lee.

RUBY J. & MILLIONAIRES
Singles: 7-inch
PLEDGE (108 "Stop Wasting Your Tears") 100-150 62

RUDD, Lawson
Singles: 7-inch
HARVEST (709 "Shake This Town") 75-100
STARDAY (711 "Blues on the Run") 100-150

RUDD, Norma
Singles: 7-inch
SURE SHOT (5009 "He's Mine") 5-10 65

RUDOLPH, Lorri
Singles: 7-inch
JET STREAM (817 "Keep Coming Back for More") 35-45
TRI-PHI (1003 "Don't Let Them Tell Me") 10-20 61
Also see LOE & JOE

RUDOLPH, Randy
Singles: 7-inch
PREVIEW (1507 "Little Surfer Teen") ...... 15-25 '60s

RUDY & TRADEWINDS
Singles: 7-inch
ANGLETONE (543 "Careless Love") 40-50 62

RUDY & WHEELS
Singles: 7-inch
CURTIS (751 "It's Not for Me") 300-400 59

RUE-TEENS
(Ru-Teens)
Singles: 7-inch
LOUIS (6805 "Lucky Boy") 15-20 64
OLD TIMER (612 "Come a Little Bit Closer") 8-12 65

RUFF, Bill
Singles: 78 rpm
GATEWAY (1163 "Juke Box Baby") 10-15 56
Singles: 7-inch
GATEWAY (1163 "Juke Box Baby") 20-30 56

RUFF, Ray
(With the Checkmates; Ray Ruffin)
Singles: 7-inch
BOLO (741 "Pledge of Love") 35-45 63
KIXZ (101 "The KIXZ Twist") 100-125 62
(Promotional issue only. Approximately 200 made.)
LIN (5034 "Beatle Maniacs") 45-65 64
LIN (5035 "Angel Blue") 45-65 64
LIN (5036 "In Dreamland") 35-45 64
LONDON (9889 "I Took a Liking to You") 45-65
NORMAN (503 "Half-Pint Baby") 50-70 61
NORMAN (508 "My Wish Is You") 65-75 61
NORMAN (513 "Angel Blue") 45-65 62
NORMAN (524 "My Gift to You") 45-65 62
NORMAN (528 "Lonely Hours") 45-65 63
NORMAN (539 "I'm Qualified") 75-100 63
STORME (101 "Ummm Oh Yeah") 100-125
SULLY (100 "Pretty Blue Eyes") 75-100

RUFFIN, David P&R/R&B/LP '69
Singles: 7-inch
ANNA (1127 "I'm in Love") 20-30 61
CHECK MATE (1003 "You Can Get What I Got") 15-25 61
CHECK MATE (1010 "Mr. Bus Driver") 15-25 62
MOTOWN 4-6 69-78
W.B. 3-6 79-80
LPs: 10/12-inch
MOTOWN (100 & 200 series) 5-10 82
MOTOWN (600 series) 10-15 69
MOTOWN (700 & 800 series) 8-10 73-76
W.B. 8-10 77-80
Also see BUSH, Little David
Also see HALL, Daryl, John Oates, David Ruffin & Eddie Kendrick
Also see TEMPTATIONS
Also see VOICE MASTERS

RUFFIN, David, & Eddie Kendricks R&B '87
Singles: 7-inch
RCA 3-5 87-88
Picture Sleeves
RCA (6925 "One More for the Lonely Hearts Club") 4-6 88

RUFFIN, David & Jimmy P&R/R&B '70
(Ruffin Brothers)
Singles: 7-inch
SOUL (35076 "Stand By Me") 4-6 70
SOUL (35082 "Stepping Out of a Dream") ... 4-6 71
LPs: 10/12-inch
MOTOWN 5-10 80
SOUL (728 "My Brother's Keeper") 10-20 70
Also see RUFFIN, David
Also see RUFFIN, Jimmy

RUFFIN, Jimmy P&R/R&B '66
Singles: 12-inch
EPIC 4-8 77
Singles: 7-inch
ATCO (6926 "Goin' Home") 4-6 73
EPIC 4-6 77
MIRACLE (1 "Heart") 50-100 61
MOTOWN (1329 "What Becomes of the Broken Hearted") 4-6 74
RSO 3-5 80
SOUL (Except 35002 & 35022) 8-15 65-72
SOUL (35002 "Since I've Lost You") 15-25 64
SOUL (35022 "What Becomes of the Broken Hearted") 5-10 66
(Black vinyl.)

SOUL (35022 "What Becomes of the Broken Hearted")...15-25 66
(Colored vinyl. Promotional issue only.)

EPs: 7-inch

SOUL (69704 "Top Ten")...15-25 66

LPs: 10/12-inch

RSO...5-8 80
SOUL (704 "Sings Top Ten")...20-30 66
SOUL (708 "Ruff 'N Ready")...20-30 67
SOUL (727 "Groove Governor")...15-25 70
Also see FOUR HOLLIDAYS
Also see RUFFIN, David & Jimmy

RUFFIN, Kenneth

Singles: 7-inch

CARNIVAL (536 "I'll Keep Holding On")..20-30 68

RUFFIN, Riff
(Mr. Ruffin; with Rifftones)

Singles: 78 rpm

CASH...8-12 56-57
EBB...10-15 57
MAMBO (109 "Darkest Hour")...10-15 55
SPARK (115 "Touch of Heaven")...8-12 55

Singles: 7-inch

BALL (501 "I'm Confessin' ")...10-15 57
CASH...10-20 56-57
DUKE (403 "Thunder & Lightnin' ")...4-8 66
EBB (103 "No More")...10-20 57
EBB (116 "Combination")...10-20 57
ENJOY...5-10 64-65
FIRE (1019 "All My Life")...10-15 60
FURY (1043 "Dig That Rock & Roll")...10-15 61
MAMBO (109 "Darkest Hour")...20-30 55
OLD TOWN (1054 "All the Way")...5-10 58
SPARK (115 "Touch of Heaven")...10-20 55

RUFUS R&B/LP '73
("Featuring Chaka Khan")

Singles: 12-inch

W.B. ...4-8 83-84

Singles: 7-inch

ABC...4-6 73-78
ATLANTIC...4-6 74
BEARSVILLE...3-5 75
EPIC...4-6 70-71
MCA (Except picture discs)...3-6 79-81
MCA (9162 "Party 'Til You're Broke")...20-25 81
(Dollar-shaped picture disc. Promotional issue only. Includes picture cover.)
MCA (9288 "Do You Love What You Feel")...15-25 81
(Strawberry-shaped picture disc. Promotional issue only. Includes strawberry scented picture cover. 1000 made.)
W.B. ...3-5 83-84

LPs: 10/12-inch

ABC (Except picture discs)...8-10 73-78
ABC (AA-1049 "Street Player")...25-30 78
(Picture disc. Promotional issue only.)
ABC (AA-1098 "Numbers")...20-25 79
(Picture disc. Promotional issue only. 100 made.)
ABC/COMMAND (40023 "Rufusized")...15-25 75
(Quadraphonic.)
ABC/COMMAND (40024 "Rags to Rufus")...15-25 75
(Quadraphonic.)
MCA...5-10 79-82
W.B. (23679 "Stompin' at the Savoy")...8-12 83
(Two discs.)
W.B. (23753 "Seal in Red")...5-10 83
Members: Paulette McWilliams; Chaka Khan.
Also see AMERICAN BREED

RUFUS & CARLA
(Carla & Rufus)

Singles: 7-inch

ATCO (6177 "Cause I Love You")...15-20 60
SATELLITE (102 "Cause I Love You")...20-25 60
(First issue.)
STAX (151 "That's Really Some Good")..10-15 64
STAX (176 "We're Tight")...10-15 65
STAX (184 "Birds and Bees")...10-15 66
Members: Rufus Thomas; Carla Thomas.
Also see THOMAS, Carla
Also see THOMAS, Rufus

RUFUS & FRIEND

Singles: 7-inch

ATCO (6199 "I Didn't Believe")...15-20 61
Also see THOMAS, Rufus

RUGBYS P&R '69

Singles: 7-inch

AMAZON (Except 1)...5-10 69-70
AMAZON (1 "You, I")...5-8 69
(Black vinyl.)
AMAZON (1 "You, I")...10-15 69
(Colored vinyl. Promotional issue only.)
SMASH (1997 " 'Til the Day I Die")...5-10 65
TOP DOG (2315 "Endlessly")...10-15 66

LPs: 10/12-inch

AMAZON (1000 "Hot Cargo")...15-20 70
Members: Steve McNicol; Jim McNicol; Chris Hubbs; Ed Vernon; Mike Morner; Glen Howerton.

RUGOLO, Pete, & His Orchestra

Singles: 78 rpm

COLUMBIA...5-10 54-55
MERCURY (71004 "Snowfall")...4-8 56

Singles: 7-inch

COLUMBIA...10-15 54-55
MERCURY (71004 "Snowfall")...8-12 56
MERCURY (71447 "Richard Diamond Theme")...5-10 59
MERCURY (71499 "Teen Age Rock")...5-10 59
MERCURY (71957 "Ben Casey")...5-10 62
RCA (7694 "Jack the Ripper")...5-10 60
TIME (1033 "Theme from *Thriller*")...5-10 61

Picture Sleeves

RCA (7694 "Jack the Ripper")...20-30 60

LPs: 10/12-inch

CAPITOL (2132 "Artistry in Voices and Brass")...8-12 64
EMARCY...10-20 59
MERCURY...10-20 58-62
RCA (2199 "Jack the Ripper")...25-30 60
(Monaural.)
RCA (2199 "Jack the Ripper")...45-50 60
(Stereo.)
TIME (52034 "Thriller")...20-30 61
(Monaural.)
TIME (2034 "Thriller")...35-45 60
(Stereo.)
20TH FOX (4198 "Sweet Ride")...15-20 68
W.B. (1371 "Behind Brigitte Bardot")...20-30 60
Session: Nino Tempo.
Also see BARDOT, Brigitte
Also see DIAMONDS, & Pete Rugolo
Also see TEMPO, Nino

RUMBLERS P&R '63

Singles: 7-inch

DOT...10-15 63-64
DOWNEY...20-30 62-66
HIGHLAND (1026 "Intersection")...25-35 62

LPs: 10/12-inch

DOT (3509 "Boss")...20-25 63
(Monaural.)
DOT (25509 "Boss")...25-30 63
(Stereo.)
DOWNEY (DLP-1001 "Boss")...40-60 63
(Monaural.)
DOWNEY (DLPS-1001 "Boss")...50-75 63
(Stereo.)
Members: Adrian Lloyd; Johnny Kirkland; Bob Jones; Wayne Matteson; Mike Kelishes; Greg Crowner.
Also see ADRIAN & SUNSETS
Also see LITTLE JOHNNY & RUMBLERS
Also see NYLONS

RUMBLES LTD.
(Rumbles)

Singles: 7-inch

CAPITOL (2903 "Hey Lenora")...5-10 70
DAD'S (101 "Everybody's Talkin' ")...30-40 65
DAD'S (103 "Wildest Christmas")...15-25 68
GNP (430 "Try a Little Harder")...5-10 69
LEMON (101 "Try a Little Harder")...8-12 69
MAGIC (10034 "Wipe Out")...4-6 80
(At least one source gives 102 as the selection number.)
MERCURY...8-15 66-68
RUMBLES (210032 "Wildest Christmas")...3-5 82
SIRE (4110 "First to Know")...10-15 69

Picture Sleeves

DAD'S (101 "Everybody's Talkin")...60-80 65
DAD'S (103 "Wildest Christmas")...25-35 68
RUMBLES (210032 "Wildest Christmas")...4-6 82

LPs: 10/12-inch

MAGIC (28124 "How Can This Be")...10-20 80
RUMBLES (30765 "Rumbles Live")...10-20 83
RUMBLES (304009 "The Rumbles 1964-1970")...30-50 83
(Only 500 made.)
Members: Rich Clayton; Bud Phillips.
Also see CLAYTON, Rich, & Rumbles
Also see FABULOUS RUMBLES

RUMORS

Singles: 7-inch

GEMCOR (5002 "Hold Me Now")...15-25 66

RUNABOUTS
(With Johnny Hammer)

Singles: 7-inch

HI JINX (9661 "Swampwater")...15-25 61
KEM (2766 "Lobo")...10-20 61

RUNABOUTS

Singles: 7-inch

GAMA (699 "Surfer's Fright")...15-25 63

RUNABOUTS

Singles: 7-inch

VOX ("The Chase")...20-30 65
(No selection number used.)

RUN-A-BOUTS

Singles: 7-inch

KAY-GEE (4817 "Hi Hat")...20-30 65

RUNABOUTS

Singles: 7-inch

C&W (114 "The Prom")...50-75

RUNAROUNDS
(Emotions)

Singles: 7-inch

JASON SCOTT (13 "The Nearest Thing to Heaven")...3-5 81
(500 made.)
PIO (107 "The Nearest Thing to Heaven")...150-200 61
Also see EMOTIONS

RUNAROUNDS
(Run-A-Rounds)

Singles: 7-inch

CAPITOL (5644 "Perfect Woman")...8-12 66
FELSTED (8704 "Carrie")...20-30 64
KC (116 "Unbelievable")...10-15 63
(Black vinyl.)
KC (116 "Unbelievable")...20-30 63
(Brown vinyl.)
MGM (13763 "You Lied")...8-12 67
TARHEEL (065 "Are You Looking for a Sweetheart")...20-30 63
Also see MARENO, Lee
Also see REGENTS

RUNAROUNDS / Regents

LPs: 10/12-inch

CRYSTAL BALL (123 "Runarounds AKA the Regents")...10-15 85
(Black vinyl. 1000 made.)
Also see REGENTS

RUN-A-ROUNDS

Singles: 7-inch

MANEL (100 "I Can't Take You Back")...15-25 66

RUN-AROUNDS

Singles: 7-inch

HYLAND (3018 "Oh Why")...50-100

RUNAWAYS

Singles: 7-inch

TEENSOUND (1924 "Teenage Style")...40-60 '60s

RUNAWAYS LP '76

Singles: 7-inch

MERCURY...5-10 76-77

LPs: 10/12-inch

MERCURY (1090 "Runaways")...15-25 76-77
MERCURY (1126 "Queens of Noise")...15-25 77
MERCURY (3705 "Waiting for the Night")...15-25 77
RHINO (250 "Little Lost Girls")...5-10 82
RHINO (250 "Little Lost Girls")...25-30 82
(Picture disc.)
Members: Joan Jett; Cherie Currie; Lita Ford; Sandy West; Micki Steele; Jackie Fox; Vickie Blue.
Also see JETT, Joan

RUNDGREN, Todd LP '71
(Todd Rundgren's Utopia)

Singles: 7-inch

BEARSVILLE (Except 0003)...3-6 72-83
BEARSVILLE (0003 "I Saw the Light")...5-10 72
(Black vinyl.)
BEARSVILLE (0003 "I Saw the Light")...10-15 72
(Blue vinyl.)

LPs: 10/12-inch

BEARSVILLE (524 "Todd Rundgren Radio Show")...40-50 '70s
(Promotional issue only.)
BEARSVILLE (597 "Radio Interview")..120-130 81
(Promotional issue only.)
BEARSVILLE (788 "Todd Rundgren Radio Sampler")...25-40 79
(Promotional issue only.)
BEARSVILLE (2066 "Something"/ "Anything")...10-12 72
BEARSVILLE (2066 "Something"/ "Anything")...150-200 72
(Colored vinyl. Price includes lyrics insert.
BEARSVILLE (2133 "A Wizard"/"A True Star")...5-10 73
BEARSVILLE (3522 "Healing")...8-10 81
(Price includes the bonus single, *Time Heals*.)
BEARSVILLE (6952 "Todd")...12-15 74
(Price includes bonus poster.)
BEARSVILLE (6957 "Initiation")...8-10 75
BEARSVILLE (6961 "Another Live")...10-12 75
BEARSVILLE (6963 "Faithful")...8-10 76
BEARSVILLE (6965 "Ra")...10-12 77
BEARSVILLE (6970 "Oops, Wrong Planet")...10-12 77
BEARSVILLE (6981 "Hermit of Mink Hollow")...5-8 78
BEARSVILLE (6986 "Back to the Bars")...8-10 78
BEARSVILLE (23732 "Ever Popular Tortured Artist Effect")...5-8 83
MFSL (225 "Something Anything")...35-40 94
RHINO (71109 "Back to the Bars")...8-12 '90s
Also see NAZZ
Also see RUNT

RUNT P&R '70
(Featuring Todd Rundgren)

Singles: 7-inch

AMPEX (31001 "We Gotta Get You a Woman")...5-10 70
BEARSVILLE...4-8 71-74

LPs: 10/12-inch

AMPEX (10105 "Runt")...100-150 70
(With *Say No More* and a full-length version of *Baby Let's Swing*.)
AMPEX (10105 "Runt")...50-100 70
(Does not have *Say No More*. Has *Baby Let's Swing* as part of a medley.)
AMPEX (10116 "The Ballad of Todd Rundgren")...50-100 71
W.B. ...5-8 85-91
Also see RUNDGREN, Todd

RUNYON, Al

Singles: 7-inch

KENTUCKY ("I'm Moving On")...50-75
(Selection number not known.)
STARDAY (676 "Baby Please Come Home")...100-200

RUSH LP '74

Singles: 7-inch

MERCURY...3-5 75-87
MOON (001 "Not Fade Away")...500-1000 73

Picture Sleeves

MERCURY...3-5 81-85

EPs: 7-inch

MERCURY...5-10 80

LPs: 10/12-inch

ATLANTIC...5-8 89-93
MERCURY (1000 thru 4000 series, except 1300)...5-12 74-82
MERCURY (1300 "Hemispheres")...35-45 78
(Picture disc.)
MERCURY (7001 "Exit ... Stage Left")...8-12 81
(Two discs.)
MERCURY (7508 "All the World's a Stage")...10-12 76
(Two discs.)
MERCURY (9200 "Archives")...10-15 78
(Three discs.)
MERCURY (800000 series)...5-10 84-88

MERCURY/POLYGRAM ("Rush 'N' Roulette")................................ 15-25 81
(Has six edited tracks which play randomly, "Russian Roulette" style. Promotional issue only.)
Members: Geddy Lee; Neil Peart; Alex Lifeson.

RUSH, Hazel

Singles: 7-inch

VEE-EIGHT (8000 "Salvation Is Free").... 20-25 64

RUSH, Neil, & Aztecs

Singles: 7-inch

TERRY (103 "Does It Really Mean That Much")................................ 15-25 60

RUSH, Otis *R&B '56*

Singles: 78 rpm

COBRA................................ 10-20 56-57

Singles: 7-inch

BLUESTOWN (777 "Sit Down Baby")...... 15-25 '60s
BLUESTOWN (778 "Three Times a Fool")................................ 15-25 '60s
CHESS (1751 "So Many Roads, So Many Trains")................................ 10-20 60
CHESS (1775 "Can't Stop Baby")........... 10-20 60
CHIEF (8000 "Sit Down Baby")............... 20-30 61
COBRA (5000 "Sit Down Baby")............. 50-60 56
COBRA (5005 "Violent Love")................ 50-60 56
COBRA (5010 "Groaning the Blues")...... 25-35 57
COBRA (5015 "Love That Woman")........ 25-35 57
COBRA (5023 "Three Times a Fool")...... 25-35 58
COBRA (5027 "It Takes Time")............. 25-35 58
COBRA (5030 "Double Trouble")............ 25-35 59
COBRA (5032 "All Your Love")............... 25-35 59
COTILLION................................5-10 69
DUKE (356 "Home Work")..................... 15-25 62

LPs: 10/12-inch

BLUE HORIZON................................ 10-15 68-70
BULLFROG................................8-10 77
COTILLION................................ 10-20 69
DELMARK................................ 10-20 75-79
Session: Bob Neely; Lafayette Leake; Matt Murphy; Willie Dixon; Odie Payne; Ike Turner.
Also see DIXON, Willie
Also see KING, Albert, & Otis Rush
Also see TURNER, Ike

RUSHING, Jimmy
(Little Jimmy Rushing; "Mr. 5 x 5")

Singles: 78 rpm

COLUMBIA................................ 15-25 46
EXCELSIOR................................ 15-25 46
GOTHAM................................ 20-30 53
KING................................ 25-50 51-52
PARROT................................ 100-150 54

Singles: 7-inch

BLUESWAY................................4-8 67
COLPIX................................5-10 63
COLUMBIA................................ 10-20 58
GOTHAM (230 "Lotsa Poppa")............... 50-75 53
GOTHAM (247 "Hey Miss Bessie")......... 50-75 53
KING (4502 "I'm So Lonely")................. 75-100 51
KING (4564 "Go Get Some More")........ 75-100 51
KING (4588 "In the Moonlight")............. 75-100 52
KING (4606 "She's Mine, She's Yours") 75-100 52
PARROT (797 "Mr. Five By Five")....... 250-350 54
U.A. 10-15 62

EPs: 7-inch

COLUMBIA (11521 "Little Jimmy Rushing")................................ 25-35 58
KING (305 "Jimmy Rushing").................. 30-40 54

LPs: 10/12-inch

BLUESWAY................................ 10-20 67-73
CAMDEN................................ 15-25 60
COLPIX................................ 20-30 63
COLUMBIA................................ 30-60 57-61
JAZZTONE................................ 25-35
MJR................................8-10 '70s
RCA................................8-12 71
VANGUARD (2008 "If This Ain't the Blues")................................ 40-60 58
VANGUARD (8011 "Jimmy Rushing Sings the Blues")................................75-100 55
(10-inch LP.)
VANGUARD (8500 series)...................... 30-45 55-58
Note: Jimmy Rushing may be shown with such artists as Buddy Tate, Dave Brubeck, Coleman Hawkins, Count Basie, Buck Clayton, Frank Culley, and Zoot Sims.
Also see BRUBECK, Dave, Quartet
Also see CHARLES, Ray / Ivory Joe Hunter / Jimmy Rushing
Also see CULLEY, Frank
Also see OTIS, Johnny

RUSHING, Jimmy / Jack Dupree

LPs: 10/12-inch

AUDIO LAB (1512 "Two Shades of Blues")................................40-50 59
Also see DUPREE, Champion Jack

RUSHING, Jimmy / Al Hibbler

LPs: 10/12-inch

GRAND PRIX (407 "Big Boy Blues")........15-25 '60s
Also see RUSHING, Jimmy
Also see HIBBLER, Al

RUSHING, Jimmy, Ada Moore & Buck Clayton

LPs: 10/12-inch

COLUMBIA (778 "Cat Meets Chick")........50-75 55
Also see MOORE, Ada
Also see RUSHING, Jimmy

RUSS, Irvin

Singles: 7-inch

BONNIE BEE (501 "Silly Old Man")...........8-12 63
FELCO (201 "Crazy Alligator").............250-350 59

Picture Sleeves

FELCO (201 "Crazy Alligator").............300-400 59

RUSS, Lonnie *P&R '62*
(Lonn Russ)

Singles: 7-inch

4J (501 "My Wife Can't Cook")..................10-15 62
4J (504 "Flip Flop")................................10-15 62
4J (507 "We Belong Together")..................5-10 63
4J (510 "Lil Evett")................................5-10 63
KERWOOD................................8-12

RUSS & STING-RAYS

Singles: 7-inch

CAROL (102 "Do the Surf").......................20-30 66

RUSSELL, Al, Trio
(With the Do-Re-Me Trio)

Singles: 78 rpm

COLUMBIA................................50-75 51
EXCELSIOR................................5-15 '50s
OKEH................................30-50 51
QUEEN (4162 "Holiday Blues")................20-40 47

Singles: 7-inch

COLUMBIA (39385 "No More Dreams")................................200-250 51
OKEH (6806 "How Can You Say You Love Me")................................100-150 51
OKEH (6831 "I'll Be Waiting")................75-125 51
OKEH (6845 "I Love Each Move You Make")................................100-150 51
Also see DO-RE-ME TRIO

RUSSELL, Barbara

Singles: 7-inch

U.A. (222 "Last Dance")............................8-12 60
U.A. (223 "He's My Guy")...........................8-12 60

LPs: 10/12-inch

U.A. (3088 "Barbara Russell")...................15-20 60
(Monaural.)
U.A. (6088 "Barbara Russell")...................20-25 60
(Stereo.)

RUSSELL, Bonnie

Singles: 7-inch

HAMMOND (104 "Too High Class") 20-30 59

RUSSELL, C.J.

Singles: 7-inch

MERCURY (72139 "The Girl I Lost in the Rain")................................5-10 63

RUSSELL, Gene, Trio

Singles: 7-inch

DOT (16995 "Norwegian Wood").............10-20 67
KRIS (106 "Doin' the Snake Hips")............8-12 '60s

RUSSELL, George

Singles: 7-inch

A-OK ("Cherokee Stomp").........................10-20 65
(Selection number not known.)

RUSSELL, Harvey
(With the Rogues)

Singles: 7-inch

HANDS (1001 "Keep a Knockin' ")............15-25 '60s
ROULETTE (4697 "Shake Sherry")............5-10 66

RUSSELL, Jimmy
(Jimmy Russell Combo)

Singles: 7-inch

CUCA (1167 "Find Me a Job")..................10-20 64
CUCA (1233 "Moo Moo")..........................10-20 65
ODESSA (2001 "Come Here My Love")...10-20 61
TYLJA (1111 "Nursery Rhyme Rock and Roll")................................10-20 '60s

RUSSELL, Johnnie

Singles: 7-inch

RADIO (125 "Rome Wasn't Built in a Day")................................10-20 59
10-15................................70

RUSSELL, Lee
(Leon Russell)

Singles: 7-inch

BATON (264 "Rich Poor Man")..................10-15 59
ROULETTE (4049 "Honky Tonk Woman")................................10-20 58
Also see RUSSELL, Leon

RUSSELL, Leon *LP '70*
(With the Shelter People; with New Grass Revival)

Singles: 7-inch

A&M (734 "Cindy")..................................10-15 64
A&M (1200 series)................................4-6 71
ABC................................4-6 78
COLUMBIA................................4-6 '70s
DOT (16771 "It's Alright with Me")..............8-12 65
MCA................................3-5
PARADISE................................3-6 76-81
SHELTER................................4-8 70-76

Picture Sleeves

PARADISE (8667 "Elvis and Marilyn").......5-10 78
SHELTER (40210 "If I Were a Carpenter")..4-8 74

LPs: 10/12-inch

MCA................................5-10 79
OLYMPIC................................8-12 73
PARADISE................................5-10 78-81
SHELTER (1000 & 2000 series)...............10-20 70-75
SHELTER (8000 series, except 8917).....10-15 71-73
SHELTER (8917 "Leon Live")...................10-20 73
SHELTER (52000 series)..........................8-10 76
Also see ADAMS, Jerry
Also see BLACK GRASS
Also see CAMPBELL, Glen, & Leon Russell
Also see CATALINAS
Also see CLAPTON, Eric
Also see COCKER, Joe
Also see DAVID & LEE
Also see HARRISON, George
Also see IN-GROUP
Also see JAN & DEAN
Also see KING, Freddie
Also see KNIGHTS
Also see LEGENDARY MASKED SURFERS
Also see LEWIS, Gary, & Playboys
Also see MASON, Dave
Also see NELSON, Willie, & Leon Russell
Also see PICKETT, Bobby
Also see RUSSELL, Lee
Also see VEGAS, Pat, & Lolly

RUSSELL, Nathan
(With the Honeydreamers; "Orchestra & Vocal Under Direction of Ray Ellis")

Singles: 78 rpm

BALLY (1035 "Similau")............................10-15 57
FOREST (5603 "His Name Was Dean")..10-15 56

Singles: 7-inch

BALLY (1035 "Similau")............................15-25 57
FOREST (5603 "His Name Was Dean")..20-30 56
HUX (601 "Cheer Up Baby").....................10-20
Also see ELLIS, Ray, Orchestra

RUSSELL, Red Hot

Singles: 7-inch

PORTER (5012 "Stop")...............................40-60 58

RUSSELL, Rick

Singles: 7-inch

POPLAR (120 "My Angel")........................20-30 63

RUSSELL, Saxy
(With the Casey Jones Band)

Singles: 7-inch

AGE (29107 "I'll Be Loving You")..............20-30 62

RUSSELL, Sonny

Singles: 7-inch

BAND BOX (332 "50 Megatons")...........75-125 63

RUSSELL, Ted
(With the Rhythm Rockers)

Singles: 7-inch

GLEE (0568 "Real Cool")..........................20-30 60
TEROCK (1000 "Bright Lights")...........100-200 61

RUSSO, Mike

Singles: 7-inch

AMERICAN AUDIOGRAPHICS ("She Lets Me Watch Her Mom & Dad Fight")............................10-15
(Square picture disc included with a Mad Magazine issue. No selection number used.)
CROSLEY (218 "I'm Gonna Knock on Your Door")................................25-35 60
Also see DELLWOODS / Mike Russo / Jeanne Hayes

RUST, Lee

Singles: 7-inch

ROFRAN (1003 "Scramble")......................15-25

RUSTILS

Singles: 7-inch

YE OLD KING (1000 "Can't Get You Out of My Heart")................................20-40 65
Also see FAINE JADE

RUSTIX *LP '69*

Singles: 7-inch

CADET (5628 "When I Get Home")...........5-10 68
RARE EARTH (5011 "I Guess This Is Goodbye")................................5-8 69
RARE EARTH (5014 "Free Again")............4-8 70
RARE EARTH (5034 "My Peace of Heaven")................................4-8 71
RARE EARTH (5037 "Down Down")...........4-8 71

LPs: 10/12-inch

RARE EARTH (508 "Bedlam") 8-12 69
(Standard cover.)
RARE EARTH (508 "Bedlam") 20-40 69
(Rounded-top cover. Promotional issue.)
RARE EARTH (513 "Come On People")....8-12 69

RUSTY & DOUG *C&W '55*

Singles: 78 rpm

HICKORY................................5-15 55-57

Singles: 7-inch

HICKORY (1000 & 1100 series)..............10-25 55-62
MERCURY (72451 "I Haven't Found It Yet")................................5-10 65
PRINCESS (4054 "Little Papoose")...........5-10 66
RCA................................5-10 63-64

LPs: 10/12-inch

HICKORY (103 "Favorites").....................30-50 60
Members: Rusty Kershaw; Doug Kershaw.

RUTH, Babe
(George Herman Ruth)

Singles: 78 rpm

PATHE ACTVELLE (022443 "Babe Ruth's Home Run Story")................................40-60 27
Also see BABE & LOU

RUTHANNE & INVICTAS

Singles: 7-inch

MAVIS (220 "Little Angel")........................15-25 63
Also see INVICTAS

RUTHERFORD, Nellie

Singles: 7-inch

HICKORY (1172 "Turn Me On")..............30-40 60

RUTLEDGE, Bob

Singles: 7-inch

ZIPP (7007 "Waitin' in Line")....................25-50 '50s
ZIPP (11216 "Go Slow Fatso")............300-400 56

RUTLES *LP '78*

Singles: 12-inch

W.B. (723 "The Rutles")...........................15-20 78
(Colored vinyl. Promotional issue only.)

Singles: 7-inch

PASSPORT................................4-6 '70s
W.B. 3-5 78

LPs: 10/12-inch

W.B. (3151 "Meet the Rutles")..................10-15 78
(Add $4 to $6 if accompanied by bonus booklet.)
Members: Neil Innes; Rick Fataar; Eric Idle; John Hasley.
Also see BONZO DOG BAND
Also see FLAME
Also see MONTY PYTHON

RYAL, Ricky
Singles: 7-inch
SOUND LABS ("Sycamore Lane")....... 200-300
(Selection number not known.)

RYAN, Allen
(With Rikki Dawn & His Orchestra)
Singles: 7-inch
SONIC (1600 "You Left Me")............... 250-350 57

RYAN, Buck
(Charlie Ryan)
Singles: 7-inch
GILT EDGE (5088 "West Virginia Express").. 10-20 61
Also see RYAN, Charlie

RYAN, Cathy
(With Four Fellows)
Singles: 78 rpm
KING 10-15 55-56
Singles: 7-inch
KING (1495 "24 Hours a Day")................ 50-75 55
KING (4848 "Come Home")..................... 15-25 55
KING (4890 "Only a Dream") 15-25 56
KING (4916 "Love You with All My Might")... 15-25 56
Also see FOUR FELLOWS

RYAN, Charlie *C&W/P&R '60*
(With the Timberline Riders; with Livingston Brothers)
Singles: 78 rpm
SOUVENIR (101 "Hot Rod Lincoln")........ 10-20 55
Singles: 7-inch
4 STAR 15-20 60-63
LINCOLN (1812 "Rocket Race")............. 50-75 63
SOUVENIR (101 "Hot Rod Lincoln")........ 20-40 55
Picture Sleeves
4 STAR (1745 "Side Car Cycle")............. 15-25 60
LPs: 10/12-inch
KING (751 "Hot Rod")........................... 100-200 61
Also see RYAN, Buck

RYAN, Ricky
Singles: 7-inch
SATURN (1001 "Running Back to You") . 15-25 '60s

RYDELL, Bobby *P&R/R&B '59*
Singles: 7-inch
ABKCO..4-6 '70s
CAMEO ("Steel Pier") 15-25 63
(No selection number used. Single-sided, promotional issue from the Steel Pier in Atlantic City.)
CAMEO (160 "Please Don't Be Mad")..... 50-75 59
CAMEO (164 "All I Want Is You")............ 20-30 59
CAMEO (167 thru 186)............................ 15-25 59-61
CAMEO (190 thru 228)............................ 10-20 61-62
CAMEO (242 "Butterfly Baby")................ 15-25 63
CAMEO (252 thru 361)............................ 10-15 63-65
CAMEO (1070 "Forget Him"/"A Message from Bobby") 10-20 63
(Packaged as a bonus single with *Top Hits of 1963.*)
CAPITOL 5-10 64-66
P.I.P. (6515 "Sway") 4-6 76
P.I.P. (6521 "You're Not the Only Girl for Me")..4-6 76
P.I.P. (6531 "It's Getting Better")....................4-6 76
PERCEPTION 4-6 74
RCA..4-6 70
REPRISE (656 "Lovin' Things") 4-8 68
VEKO (731 "Fatty Fatty")........................ 50-100 58
VENISE (201 "Fatty Fatty") 35-50 62
Picture Sleeves
CAMEO (167 thru 175)............................ 20-30 59-60
CAMEO (179 thru 361)............................ 10-20 60-65
CAPITOL 8-12 64
EPs: 7-inch
CAPITOL 10-20 65
LPs: 10/12-inch
CAMEO (1006 "We Got Love") 50-100 59
CAMEO (1007 "Bobby Sings, Bobby Swings")... 35-50 60
CAMEO (1009 "Bobby's Biggest Hits").... 40-60 61
(Gatefold cover. With 12 x 12 photo insert.)
CAMEO (1009 "Bobby's Biggest Hits").... 30-35 61
(Gatefold cover. Without 12 x 12 photo.)
CAMEO (1009 "Bobby's Biggest Hits").... 15-25 62
(Standard cover. Some copies with 1009 on the cover may have Cameo 1008 on the disc.)
CAMEO (1010 "Bobby Rydell Salutes the Great Ones").. 20-30 61
CAMEO (1011 "Rydell at the Copa") 20-30 61
(Monaural.)
CAMEO (SC-1011 "Rydell at the Copa")..25-35 61
(Stereo.)
CAMEO (1019 "All the Hits")....................20-30 62
CAMEO (1028 "Bobby's Biggest Hits, Vol. 2") 25-35 62
CAMEO (1040 "All the Hits, Vol. 2").........20-30 62
(Monaural.)
CAMEO (SC-1040 "All the Hits, Vol. 2")...25-35 62
(Stereo.)
CAMEO (1043 "Bye Bye Birdie") 25-30 63
(Monaural.)
CAMEO (SC-1043 "Bye Bye Birdie")........30-35 63
(Stereo.)
CAMEO (1055 "Wild [Wood] Days") 20-30 63
(Monaural.)
CAMEO (1070 "Top Hits of 1963 Sung by Robby Rydell") 25-35 63
(Monaural. With bonus single *Forget Him/A Message from Bobby.*)
CAMEO (1070 "Top Hits of 1963 Sung by Robby Rydell") 15-25 63
(Monaural. Without bonus single.)
CAMEO (SC-1070 "Top Hits of 1963 Sung by Robby Rydell") 30-40 63
(Stereo. With bonus single *Forget Him/A Message from Bobby.*)
CAMEO (SC-1070 "Top Hits of 1963 Sung by Robby Rydell") 20-30 63
(Stereo. Without bonus single.)
CAMEO (1080 "Forget Him") 20-30 64
CAMEO (2001 "18 Golden Hits") ....20-30 '60s
CAMEO (4017 "An Era Reborn") 20-30 64
(Monaural.)
CAMEO (SC-4017 "An Era Reborn")........25-35 64
(Stereo.)
CAPITOL (2281 "Somebody Loves You") 15-25 65
DESIGN..10-20 '60s
P.I.P. 8-12 76
SPINORAMA...10-20 '60s
STRAND (1120 "Bobby Rydell Sings").....35-45 60
Session: Rick & the Masters; Georgie Young & Rockin' Bocs.
Also see CHECKER, Chubby, & Bobby Rydell
Also see CHRISTIE, Lou / Len Barry & Dovells / Bobby Rydell / Tokens
Also see RICK & MASTERS
Also see ROE, Tommy / Bobby Rydell / Gene Pitney
Also see ROE, Tommy / Bobby Rydell / Ray Stevens
Also see YOUNG, Georgie

RYDELL, Bobby / Barry Norman / Steve Garrick
LPs: 10/12-inch
VENISE (7035 "Twistin'") 15-20 62
Also see RYDELL, Bobby

RYDER, Junior, & Peacocks
(With the Johnny Otis Orchestra)
Singles: 78 rpm
DUKE (119 "Sad Story")...........................15-25 54
DUKE (139 "Don't Tell Nobody")..............10-20 55
Singles: 7-inch
DUKE (119 "Sad Story")...........................50-75 54
DUKE (139 "Don't Tell Nobody")..............30-40 55
Also see OTIS, Johnny

RYDER, Mitch *P&R '65*
(With the Detroit Wheels)
Singles: 7-inch
ABC 4-6 73
AVCO EMBASSY 4-6 70
DOT...4-6 69
DYNO VOICE..4-8 67-69
ERIC (186 "Devil with a Blue Dress & Good Golly Miss Molly") 4-6 74
ERIC (187 "Sock It to Me")..............................4-6 74
ERIC (188 "Jenny Take a Ride")......................4-6 74
NEW VOICE (Except 820) 4-8 65-68
NEW VOICE (820 "Sock It to Me Baby")....5-10 67
(With "Feels like a punch" lyrics.)
NEW VOICE (820 "Sock It to Me Baby")......4-6 67
(With "Hits me like a punch" lyrics.)
PHILCO (4 "Jenny Take a Ride"/"Sock It to Me Baby") 10-20 67
("Hip Pocket" flexi-disc.)
RIVA 3-5 83
VIRGO 4-6 73
Picture Sleeves
NEW VOICE..4-8 67
LPs: 10/12-inch
CREWE...12-15
DOT..12-15 69
DYNO VOICE 10-20 67
NEW VOICE...20-30 66-68
RIVA 5-8 83
ROULETTE...5-10
SEEDS & STEMS.......................................5-10 78-80
VIRGO..8-10 73
Members: Mitch Ryder; Joe Kubert; Jim McCallister; Jim McCarty; Johnny Badanjek.
Also see LEE, Billy, & Rivieras

RYE, Forrest
Singles: 78 rpm
FORTUNE (172 "Wild Cat Boogie")..........15-25 53
Singles: 7-inch
FORTUNE (172 "Wild Cat Boogie")..........50-75 53

RYLAND, Little Sir
Singles: 7-inch
U.S.A. (1214 "My Worried Lover")...........15-25 '60s

One would surely think this record to be *One for the Money* by the Whispers (1976), but it is far from it. Both sides play Elvis Presley's *Don't'cha Think It's Time* (1958). RCA made this bizarre disc while testing a process where all label information is actually stamped right into the vinyl itself — rather than printed on paper and affixed to the disc during the stamping procedure.

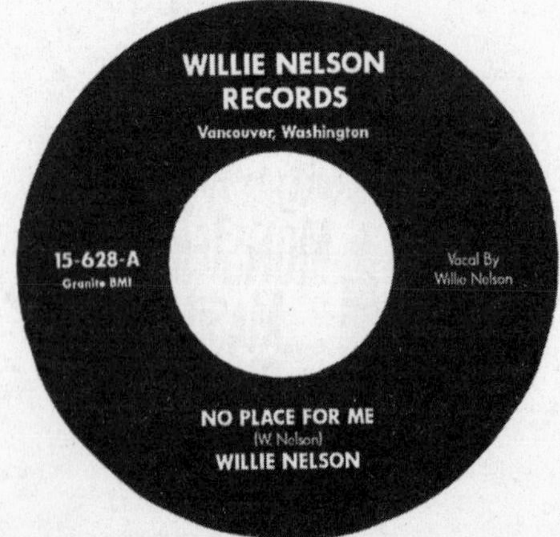

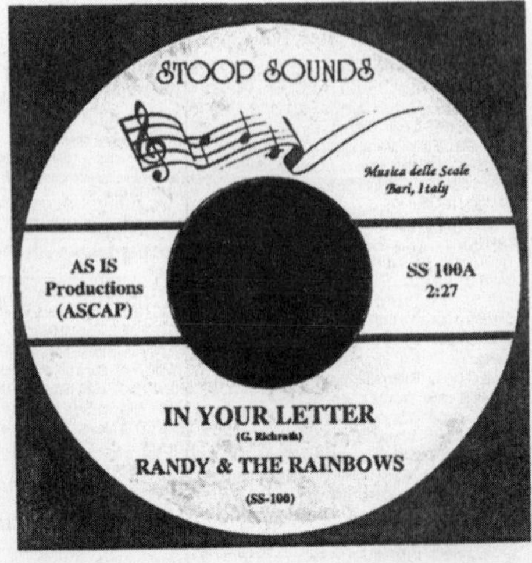

S

S&H SCAMPS
Singles: 7-inch
GREGMARK (1 "Sassy")........................ 10-20 61
GREGMARK (3 "Punjab")........................ 10-20 61
Members: Lee Hazlewood, Lester Sills.

S.J. & CROSSROADS
Singles: 7-inch
DEUCE (101 "Darkest Hour")................... 15-25 '60s
MARK VII (1019 "Play Your Game")........ 15-25 '60s
SALMAR (100 "Darkest Hour") 15-25 66
SALMAR (101 "Ooh Poo Pah Doo")........ 15-25 66
SALMAR (103 "London Girl")................... 15-25 66
SALMAR (105 "In the Beginning") 15-25 68

SRC LP '68
(Scott Richard Case)
Singles: 7-inch
A^2 (301 "I'm So Glad")............................ 10-20 67
BIG CASINO (1001 "Born to Love")............5-10 71
CAPITOL 5-10 68-69
Picture Sleeves
BIG CASINO (1001 "Born to Love")......... 10-15 71
LPs: 10/12-inch
CAPITOL (134 "Milestones")................... 30-40 69
CAPITOL (273 "Travelers Tale")............. 15-25 69
CAPITOL (2991 "SRC")........................... 40-60 68
Members: Scott Richardson; Steve Lyman; Glen Quackenbush; Gary Quackenbush; Robin Dale.
Also see FUGITIVES

SRC / Rationals
Singles: 7-inch
A^2 (402 "Get the Picture") 10-20 67
Also see RATIONALS
Also see SRC

SABER, Johnny
Singles: 7-inch
ADONIS (103 "Wish It Could Be Me") . 100-200 59
HITSVILLE (1137 "The Note That I Wrote")... 40-50 62
Session: Passions.
Also see PASSIONS

SABER, Sonny
Singles: 7-inch
ARCADE (151 "Little Daisy").................... 25-35 59
MALA (437 "Shadow of My Mind")........... 15-25 61
MYERS (107 "Pretty Little Girl") 10-15 60

SABERS
Singles: 78 rpm
BULLSEYE.. 50-75 55
Singles: 7-inch
BULLSEYE (101 "You Can Depend on Me")... 200-300 55

SABERS
Singles: 78 rpm
CAL-WEST... 100-150 55
Singles: 7-inch
CAL-WEST (847 "Cool, Cool Christmas") 300-400 55
Member: Billy Storm.
Also see STORM, Billy

SABLAN, Johnny, & Blends
Singles: 7-inch
SKYLARK (105 "Big Fat Lie").............. 100-150 60

SABRES
Singles: 78 rpm
RCA 8-12 57
Singles: 7-inch
RCA 8-12 57
EPs: 7-inch
RCA (979/980/981 "Ridin' High with the Sabres") 10-15 56
(Price is for either volume.)
RCA (1979/1980/1981 "Rockin' with the Sabres") 10-20 57
(Price is for either volume.)
RCA (4102 "Rockin' with the Sabres")..... 20-30 57
LPs: 10/12-inch
RCA (1376 "Ridin' High with the Sabres") 25-50 56
Members: Jerry Wright; Dick Henson; Fritz Weybright.

SABRES
(Featuring Lou Gittins)
Singles: 7-inch
KAT (100 "My Hot Mama") 1500-2500 58

SABRES
Singles: 7-inch
LIBERTY (55128 "Lulu")...........................10-15 58

SABRES
("Vocals – Jimmy Stringer")
Singles: 7-inch
DIAL (102 "Bounty Hunter") 10-20 59
FOX (105 "Rustler") 10-20 60
GALA (114 "Hot Rod Kelly")..................150-250 60
KILMAC (1412 "Take Up the Slack, Daddy-O")...75-100 59

SABRES
Singles: 7-inch
SCOTTIE (1316 "Sabre Dance Rock")......10-20 60

SABRES
Singles: 7-inch
PRINCE (101 "Gonna Leave")..................40-50 '60s

SABY & ORIENTALS
Singles: 7-inch
MEL-PAR (1114 "Little Girl") 50-75

SACCA, Jimmy
Singles: 78 rpm
DOT..5-10 54
Singles: 7-inch
DOT (15130 "You're All That I Need")......10-15 54
DOT (15163 "Alone with My Heart").........10-15 54
Also see HILLTOPPERS

SACCO
(Lou Christie)
Singles: 12-inch
LIFESONG (81775 "People Theme") 8-10 78
Singles: 7-inch
LIFESONG (1775 "People Theme") 30-50 78
Also see CHRISTIE, Lou

SACRED MUSHROOM
Singles: 7-inch
MINARET (131 "Breakaway Girl") 10-15 67
LPs: 10/12-inch
PARALLAX (4001 "Sacred Mushroom")...100-150 69
Members: Larry Goshorn; Danny Goshorn; Joe Stewart; Rusty York.
Also see PURE PRAIRIE LEAGUE

SADDLE-LITE DAN & ORBITS
Singles: 7-inch
SOMA (1103 "Don't Go Away")..............75-125 58

SADINA
Singles: 7-inch
SMASH (1979 "I Want That Boy") 20-30 65

SADLER, Barry P&R/C&W/LP '66
(S/SGT. Barry Sadler)
Singles: 7-inch
GAS 3-5 78
RCA 4-6 66-67
VETERAN 4-6 74
Picture Sleeves
RCA..5-10 66-67
LPs: 10/12-inch
RCA...10-20 66-67
VETERAN 8-12 74
Also see ANN-MARGRET

SADLER, Haskell, & His Orchestra
Singles: 78 rpm
FLASH (103 "Do Right Mind")..................20-40 55
Singles: 7-inch
FLASH (103 "Do Right Mind")..................50-75 55
MELODIA...10-20

SAFARIS P&R '60
(With Phantoms Band)
Singles: 7-inch
DEE JAY (203 "My Image of a Girl")............3-5 89
(Red vinyl.)
ELDO (101 "Image of a Girl") 15-25 60
ELDO (105 "Girl With a Story in Her Eyes")..15-25 60
ELDO (110 "Shadows")...........................10-20 60
ELDO (113 "Garden of Love")..................10-20 61
OLD HIT 3-5
QUALITY (1034 "Image of a Girl")...........20-30 60
(Canadian.)
LPs: 10/12-inch
IMAGE (1001 "Image of a Girl")................10-15 91
(Only 1000 made.)
Members: Jimmy Stephens; Sheldon Breier; Marv Rosenberg.
Also see ANGELS
Also see STEVENS, Jimmy
Also see SUDDENS

SAFARIS
Singles: 7-inch
VALIANT (6036 "Kick Out")......................20-30 63

SAGITTARIUS P&R '67
Singles: 7-inch
COLUMBIA 5-10 67-69
TOGETHER...5-10 68-69
LPs: 10/12-inch
BACK-TRAC 5-10 85
COLUMBIA (9644 "Present Tense").........20-30 68
TOGETHER (1002 "Blue Marble")............25-35 69
Members: Gary Usher; Glen Campbell; Bruce Johnston; Terry Melcher; Curt Boetcher; Mike Fennelly; Lee Mallory; Ron Edgar.
Also see BRUCE & TERRY
Also see CAMPBELL, Glen
Also see USHER, Gary

SAHARAS
Singles: 7-inch
FENTON (2016 "I'm Free") 15-25 66

SAHARAS
Singles: 7-inch
UNITED (1033 "They Play It Wild") ....50-75 '60s

SAHM, Doug LP '73
(With the Mex Trip; with Texas Tornados; with Markays; with Pharaohs)
Singles: 7-inch
ABC/DOT 4-6 76
ATLANTIC...5-10 73
CASABLANCA (0828 "Roll with the Punches")...10-20 75
CHRYSALIS...3-5 81
COBRA (116 "Just a Moment")................40-50 61
CRAZY CAJUN...4-6 74
HARLEM (107 "Why, Why, Why") 100-150 60
HARLEM (108 "Baby, Tell Me") 20-30 60
(Black vinyl.)
HARLEM (108 "Baby, Tell Me") 40-60 60
(Colored vinyl. Promotional issue only.)
HARLEM (113 "Slow Down") 40-50 61
HARLEM (116 "Just a Moment") 40-50 61
PERSONALITY (260 "Baby, What's on Your Mind")..30-40 59
PERSONALITY (3504 "Baby What's on Your Mind")..15-25 62
RENNER (212 "Big Hat") 20-30 61
(Black vinyl.)
RENNER (212 "Big Hat") 50-75 61
(Colored vinyl. Promotional issue only.)
RENNER (215 "Baby, What's on Your Mind")..20-30 61
(Black vinyl.)
RENNER (215 "Baby, What's on Your Mind")..50-75 61
(Colored vinyl. Promotional issue only.)
RENNER (226 "Just Because") 20-30 62
RENNER (232 "Cry")................................20-30 63
RENNER (240 "Lucky Me").......................20-30 63
RENNER (247 "Mr. Kool").........................20-30 64
SATIN (100 "Crazy Daisy") 75-125 59
SOFT (1031 "Cry") 20-30 65
SWINGIN' (625 "Why, Oh Why") 15-25 60
TEXAS RECORD (108 "Henrietta")..........10-20 76
W.B. (7819 "Groovers Paradise") 4-6 74
WARRIOR (507 "Crazy Daisy") 75-125 58
Picture Sleeves
CHRYSALIS...3-5 81
LPs: 10/12-inch
ANTONE'S 5-8 88
ATLANTIC...8-12 73
HARLEM 8-10 79
MERCURY 10-20 73
TAKOMA..5-10 80
W.B. 10-20 74
Also see DYLAN, Bob
Also see FENDER, Freddy, & Sir Douglas
Also see LITTLE DOUG
Also see NELSON, Willie
Also see SIR DOUGLAS QUINTET

SAHM, Doug, & Augie Meyers
Singles: 7-inch
TEARDROP...3-5 83
Picture Sleeves
TEARDROP...3-5 83
Also see MEYERS, Augie
Also see SAHM, Doug

SAIGONS
Singles: 78 rpm
DOOTONE (375 "You're Heavenly")......50-100 55
Singles: 7-inch
DOOTONE (375 "You're Heavenly")....200-300 55

SAILCAT P&R/LP '72
Singles: 7-inch
ELEKTRA...4-6 72-73
LPs: 10/12-inch
ELEKTRA...10-15 72
Members: Johnny Wyker; Court Pickett.
Also see RUBBER BAND

SAILES, Jesse, & Waves
Singles: 7-inch
FELSTED (8690 "Monkey Drums") 10-15 63
Also see SALLES, Jessie, & Crypt-Kickers

SAILOR BOY
(Alex Spearman)
Singles: 78 rpm
DIG (126 "What Have I Done Wrong").....20-40 56
Singles: 7-inch
DIG (126 "What Have I Done Wrong").....50-75 56

SAILOR BOY / Preston Love
Singles: 78 rpm
DIG (116 "Country Home") 20-40 56
Singles: 7-inch
DIG (116 "Country Home") 50-75 56
Also see LOVE, Preston
Also see SAILOR BOY

SAINT, Cathy
Singles: 7-inch
DAISY (501 "Big Bad World") 25-35 63

SAINT, Del, & Devils
Singles: 7-inch
CHECKER (897 "Rock Yea")....................25-35 58

SAINT CLAIR, Bobby
Singles: 7-inch
PHILIPS (40358 "Fool That I Am") 10-20 66

ST. CLAIR, Butch
Singles: 7-inch
IMPRA (2005 "Get a Little") 100-150

ST. CLAIR, Nicky, & Five Trojans
(Nicky St. Claire & Five Trojans)
Singles: 7-inch
EDISON INT'L (410 "I Hear Those Bells") 50-60 59
Also see FIVE TROJANS

ST. CLAIRE, Sylvia
Singles: 7-inch
BRUNSWICK (55276 "Bring Back Yesterday")..25-35 65
BRUNSWICK (55279 "Just Love Me")..10-20 65

ST. CLOUD, Endle
Singles: 7-inch
INT'L ARTISTS (129 "Tell Me One More Time") 10-20 68
INT'L ARTISTS (139 "She Wears It Like a Badge")..10-20 70
LPs: 10/12-inch
INT'L ARTISTS (12 "Thank You All Very Much") 35-55 68

ST. GERMAIN, Ray
Singles: 7-inch
CHATEAU (107 "She's a Square").........75-125

ST. JAMES, Bobby
Singles: 7-inch
WATTS (901 "I Was Taken for a Ride")...20-30 68

ST. JAMES, Holly
Singles: 7-inch
ABC (10996 "That's Not Love") 100-125 68
ABC (11042 "Magic Moments")...............25-50 68

ST. JOHN, Dick
Singles: 7-inch
DOT (17080 "Childhood")...5-10 68
DOT (17140 "Brand New Season")...5-10 68
LIBERTY (55380 "Gonna Stick By You")...8-12 61
PHILIPS (40256 "Believe Me Baby")...5-10 65
PHILIPS (40325 "You Know What I Mean")...5-10 65
POM POM...10-15 61
ROMA (1001 "Hey, Little Gal")...10-15 60
Also see DICK & DEEDEE

ST. JOHN, Marcel
Singles: 7-inch
TEENAGE (101 "Big Black Jacket")...75-125

ST. JOHN, Rose, & Wonderettes
Singles: 7-inch
U.A. (997 "Mend My Broken Heart")...10-15 66
VEEP (1231 "I Know the Meaning")...10-20 66
Also see WONDERETTES

ST. JOHN & CARDINALS
Singles: 7-inch
SHURFINE (010 "Rampage")...15-25 66

ST. JOHN'S FLEA CIRCUS
Singles: 7-inch
WR (4720 "Good Day")...20-30 '60s

ST. JOHN GREEN
LPs: 10/12-inch
FLICK CITY ("Live")...20-40 70
(Selection number not known.)
FLICK CITY (001 "St. John Green")...50-100 67
Members: Mike Baxter; Ed Bissot; Shel Scott; Vic Sabino; William Kirkland.

ST. LOUIS JIMMY
(James Oden; with Red Saunders Band)
Singles: 78 rpm
ARISTOCRAT (7001 "Florida Hurricane")...50-75 48
DUKE (110 "Drinkin' Woman")...40-60 53
HERALD (407 "Hard Luck Boogie")...40-60 53
HERALD (408 "Whiskey Drinkin' Woman")...25-50 53
J.O.B. (101 "Mother's Day")...20-40 49
MIRACLE (134 "Biscuit Roller")...20-40 48
OPERA (4 "Coming Up Fast")...20-40 53
PARROT (823 "Goin' Down Slow")...40-60 56
Singles: 7-inch
DUKE (110 "Drinkin' Woman")...75-125 53
HERALD (407 "Hard Luck Boogie")...150-200 52
HERALD (408 "Whiskey Drinkin' Woman")...150-200 52
PARROT (823 "Goin' Down Slow")...150-200 56
LPs: 10/12-inch
PRESTIGE/BLUESVILLE (1028 "Goin' Down Slow")...25-35 61
Also see POOR BOY
Also see SAUNDERS, Red

ST. PETERS, Crispian P&R '66
Singles: 7-inch
JAMIE...5-10 65-68
LPs: 10/12-inch
JAMIE (3027 "The Pied Piper")...20-30 66

ST. PIERRE, Alan
Singles: 7-inch
DMO (2001 "Footsteps")...15-20 67
Also see UNBELIEVABLE UGLIES

ST. ROMAIN, Kirby P&R '63
Singles: 7-inch
IMCO...5-10 64
INETTE...8-12 63-64
KARSONG...5-10 63
TEARDROP...5-10 64
Also see BUDDY & HEARTS
Also see SHUT DOWNS

ST. SHAW, Mike
(With Thee Neon; with Prophets; Mike St. Shaw Trio)
Singles: 7-inch
ATCO (6648 "Joint Meeting")...4-8 69
REPRISE (0273 "Take This Hammer")...5-10 64
REPRISE (0282 "Mike's Mid-Nite Special")...5-10 64
REPRISE (0325 "Send Me Some Lovin'")...8-12 64
LPs: 10/12-inch
REPRISE (6128 "Mike St. Shaw Trio")...10-20 64
Members: Mike St. Shaw; Ray Garcia; Harold Logan; Danny Taylor; Chuck Hatfield.
Also see ESQUIRES / Mike Shaw & Prophets / Thunder Frog Ensemble

SAINT STEVEN
Singles: 7-inch
PROBE (463 "Louisiana Home")...10-15 69
LPs: 10/12-inch
PROBE (4506 "Over the Hills – The Bastich")...40-60 69

SAINTE ANTHONY'S FYRE
Singles: 7-inch
ZONK (001 "Sainte Anthony's Fyre")...50-100 71

SAINTE-MARIE, Buffy LP '66
Singles: 7-inch
ABC...4-6 76
MCA...4-6 74-75
VANGUARD...4-8 65-72
LPs: 10/12-inch
ABC...5-10 76
MCA...5-10 74-75
VANGUARD...8-15 64-74

SAINTS
Singles: 7-inch
CUE (7934 "Will You")...10-20 57

SAINTS
Singles: 7-inch
PRESCOTT (1570 "Snap Dragon")...15-20 58

SAINTS
Singles: 7-inch
INFINITY (1001 "My Only One")...250-350 '50s
Members: C. Lundback; E. Williams; X. Ramos; A. Barksdale; M. Ridley.

SAINTS
Singles: 7-inch
A-B-S (114 "What's Her Name")...100-150 61

SAINTS
Singles: 7-inch
KENT (480 "The Sun Don't Shine")...5-10 67
RAYDIN (101 "Girl Forgive Me")...20-25 67
REVUE (11069 "Mirror Mirror on the Wall")...4-8 70

SAINTS
Singles: 7-inch
FORMAT (57 "Leaving You Baby")...10-15
SALEM (1012 "Rock & Roll Ruby")...50-75
Picture Sleeves
FORMAT (57 "Leaving You Baby")...10-15

SAINTS FIVE
Singles: 7-inch
PENTAGON (2001 "Mercy Mercy")...15-25 66
Members: Santo Cincotta; Kenny Rogers; Brad Mckay; Jim Nowicki; Stu Moebus; Gordy Elliot; Gary Lane; John Grignon; Mike Fitzpatrick; John Dombeck.

SAITH
Singles: 7-inch
GOLI (501 "Bad Days Walk")...20-30 '60s

SAKAMOTO, Kyu P&R/R&B/LP '63
Singles: 7-inch
CAPITOL...4-8 63-64
EMI...4-6 75
LPs: 10/12-inch
CAPITOL...10-20 63

SAKI, Mia
Singles: 78 rpm
BRUCE (2001 "Deed I Do")...10-15 55
Singles: 7-inch
BRUCE (2001 "Deed I Do")...15-20 55

SAL & CONTINENTALS
Singles: 7-inch
441 (34 "I'm Goin' Away")...15-25 64

SALADIN
Singles: 7-inch
CARICATURE (101 "Honey Do")...50-75 62
CARICATURE (102 "Tough 'N Rough")...50-75 62
Picture Sleeves
CARICATURE (101 "Honey Do")...50-75 62

SALADOS
Singles: 7-inch
TSM (9623 "Spider Walk")...20-25 66

SALE, Georgie, & Escapades
Singles: 7-inch
HI-Q (5014 "I'll Love You Forever")...40-50 60

SALEM MASS
LPs: 10/12-inch
SALEM MASS (101 "Witch Burning")...250-300 '70s

SALEMS
Singles: 7-inch
EPIC (9480 "Maria")...10-15 61
MERCURY (71754 "My Precious Love")...15-20 61

SALES, Mac
Singles: 78 rpm
METEOR (5022 "Yakety Yak")...40-60 55
Singles: 7-inch
METEOR (5022 "Yakety Yak")...150-250 55

SALES, Soupy P&R/LP '65
Singles: 7-inch
ABC-PAR (10646 "The Mouse")...8-10 65
ABC-PAR (10681 "Hey Pearl")...8-10 65
ABC-PAR (10747 "I'm a Bird Watching Man")...8-10 65
CAPITOL (5752 "Spanish Flea")...5-10 66
CAPITOL (5766 "Use Your Noggin")...5-10 66
MOTOWN (1141 "Muck-Arty Park")...15-25 69
REPRISE (244 "Santa Claus Is Surfin' to Town")...10-15 62
REPRISE (368 "Pie in the Face")...8-10 65
REPRISE (20041 "White Fang")...8-12 61
REPRISE (20064 "Soupy's Theme")...8-12 62
REPRISE (20108 "My Baby's Got a Crush on Frankenstein")...8-12 62
REPRISE (20189 "Hill Billy Ding Dong Choo Choo")...8-12 63
WIZDOM...3-5
Picture Sleeves
CAPITOL (5752 "Spanish Flea")...10-15 66
LPs: 10/12-inch
ABC-PAR (503 "Spy with a Pie")...20-30 64
ABC-PAR (517 "Do the Mouse")...15-25 65
MOTOWN (686 "A Bag of Soup")...25-35 69
REPRISE (6010 "Soupy Sales Show")...20-30 61
REPRISE (6052 "Up in the Air")...20-30 62

SALISBURY, Sandy
Singles: 7-inch
TOGETHER...10-20 68-69
Also see MILLENNIUM

SALMAS BROTHERS
Singles: 78 rpm
IMPERIAL...10-15 56
POST...10-15 55
Singles: 7-inch
ERA (1029 "Go Let Her Go")...15-25 57
IMPERIAL (3001 "Spark of Love")...20-30 56
KEEN (2002 "Circle Rock")...10-20 58
KEEN (2017 "Things I Love")...10-20 59
KEEN (2108 "Kissin' Bug")...10-20 59
KEEN (82116 "Lolita")...10-20 60
POST (2005 "I Don't Care")...20-30 55

SALT WATER TAFFY
Singles: 7-inch
BUDDAH...5-10 68-70
METROMEDIA...4-8 71
LPs: 10/12-inch
BUDDAH...10-20 68-70
Member: Tommy West.

SALTY PEPPERS
Singles: 7-inch
CAPITOL (2433 La, La, Time")...25-35 69
TEC (1014 "La, La, Time")...30-40 69
Members: Maurice White; Wade Flemons.
Also see EARTH, WIND & FIRE
Also see FLEMONS, Wade

SALVADOR, Pat
Singles: 7-inch
HOUMA (113 "Sleep Walk")...10-20 59

SALVADORE, Bobby
Singles: 7-inch
IPG (1012 "Stick 'Em Up Santa")...10-20 63

SALVATION
Singles: 7-inch
ABC (11025 "Think Twice")...5-10 67
U.A. (50695 "Someday the Gray Will Come")...4-8 70
LPs: 10/12-inch
ABC (623 "Salvation")...10-20 67
ABC (653 "Gypsy Carnival Caravan")...10-20 68
Members: Al Linde; Joe Tate; Rick Levin; Art McLean; Art Resnick.
Also see THIRD RAIL

SALVO, Sammy P&R '58
Singles: 78 rpm
RCA...10-20 57
Singles: 7-inch
DOT (16135 "It's the After")...10-15 60
HICKORY...5-10 61-63
IMPERIAL (5616 "Marble Heart")...8-12 59
IMPERIAL (5636 "Leave Me No More")...10-20 60
MARK V...10-20 58
RCA (7097 "Oh Julie")...10-20 57
RCA (7190 "Julie Doesn't Love Me Anymore")...10-20 58
RCA (7272 "Lovin' at Night")...10-20 58
RCA (7350 "Here I Go Again")...10-20 58
RCA (7516 "My Perfect Love")...10-20 59

SAM & BILL P&R/R&B '65
Singles: 7-inch
JODA (100 "For Your Love")...5-10 65
JODA (104 "Fly Me to the Moon")...5-10 65
KARATE (508 "For Your Love")...10-15 65
Members: Sam Gary; Bill Johnson.
Also see SOUL BROTHERS

SAM & BOB & SOULMEN
LPs: 10/12-inch
SABO (1001 Mississippi Mud")...200-225 '60s
(Approximately 400 made.)
Members: Sam Mosley; Bob Johnson.
Session: Doris Badie.

SAM & DAVE P&R/R&B/LP '66
Singles: 7-inch
ATLANTIC...4-8 68-71
ROULETTE...5-10 62-66
STAX...5-10 65-68
U.A. ...4-6 74-75
LPs: 10/12-inch
ATLANTIC (8205 "I Thank You")...15-20 68
ATLANTIC (8218 "Best of Sam & Dave")...8-12 69
GUSTO...5-10
ROULETTE (25323 "Sam & Dave")...15-25 66
STAX (708 "Hold On I'm Coming")...20-30 66
STAX (712 "Double Dynamite")...20-30 66
STAX (725 "Soul Men")...20-30 67
U.A. ...8-12 74-75
Members: Sam Moore; Dave Prater.
Also see PICKETT, Wilson / Sam & Dave
Also see REDDING, Otis / Carla Thomas / Sam & Dave / Eddie Floyd

SAM & DAVE / Don Covay
Singles: 7-inch
TRIP (121 "Hold On I'm Comin'"/"Mercy Mercy")...3-5
Also see COVAY, Don
Also see SAM & DAVE

SAM & WESTSIDERS
Singles: 7-inch
INTEGRITY (692 "Let's Go Surfing")...50-75 64
Session: Marquerite Cockins.

SAM THE SHAM & PHARAOHS
(Sam the Sham Revue; Sam; Sam Samudio) P&R/R&B/LP '65
Singles: 7-inch
DINGO (001 "Haunted House")...150-200 64
FRETONE (048 "The Wookie")...4-6 77
MGM (13000 series, except 13972)...5-10 64-69
MGM (13972 "I Couldn't Spell !!*@!")...10-15 69
MGM (14000 series)...4-6 73
PHILCO (3 "Ju Ju Hand"/"Wooly Bully")...10-20 67
("Hip Pocket" flexi-disc.)
POLYDOR...3-5 '80s
TUPELO (2982 "Betty & Dupree")...200-250 63
WARRIOR...20-30 '60s
XL (905 "Signifyin' Monkey")...50-100 64
XL (906 "Wooly Bully")...200-250 65
Picture Sleeves
MGM (13364 "Ju Ju Hand")...30-40 65
MGM (13397 "Ring Dang Doo")...10-15 65
MGM (13581 "The Hair on My Chinny Chin Chin")...10-15 66
MGM (13649 "How Do You Catch a Girl")...10-15 66

LPs: 10/12-inch
MGM 15-25 65-68
Session: David Martin.
Also see SUMMERS, Gene

SAMMY
Singles: 7-inch
REB ("Sally Mae") 50-75
(No selection number used.)

SAMMY & DEL LARKS
Singles: 7-inch
CLIFTON (29 "I Never Will Forget") 4-6 78
EA-JAY (100 "I Never Will Forget") 50-75 61
Session: Teacho Wiltshire.
Also see SAMMY & DEL-LARDS
Also see WILTSHIRE, Teacho

SAMMY & PARLIAMENTS
Singles: 7-inch
ARNOLD (1001 "No Hard Feelings") 30-40 60

SAMPSON, Phil
(Sam Chatman)
Singles: 7-inch
BEA & BABY (114 "It's So Hard") 10-20 60
Also see CHATMAN, Sam
Also see SINGIN' SAM

SAMS, The
Singles: 7-inch
EBONY (4551 "Please Come on Back").. 40-60 66
EBONY (4553 "My Guardian Angel") 40-60 67

SAMUELS, Bill — R&B '46
(With the Cats 'N' Jammer Three; Cats 'N' Jammers)
Singles: 78 rpm
MERCURY 20-50 46-53
Singles: 7-inch
MERCURY (70205 "I Cover the Waterfront") 50-75 53

SAMUELS, Bill
Singles: 7-inch
NORTH STAR (2062 "I Cried for You") ...... 8-12 '60s
SOMA (1150 "I'm Glad There Is You") 8-12 61

SAMUELS, Clarence
Singles: 78 rpm
ARISTOCRAT (1001 "Boogie Woogie Blues") 20-30 48
DELUXE (3219 "Gimmie") 15-25 50
EXCELLO 10-20 56
FREEDOM (1533 "Lost My Head") 15-25 49
FREEDOM (1541 "She Walk, She Walk, She Walk") 15-25 49
FREEDOM (1544 "Hey Joe") 15-25 49
LAMP (8004 "Crazy with the Heat") 20-40 54
LAMP (8005 "Lightnin' Struck Me") 20-40 54
SWING TIME (131 "Household Troubles") 15-25 48
SWING TIME (149 "Deep Sea Diver") 15-25 48
Singles: 7-inch
APT (25028 "We're Goin' to the Hop") 15-25 59
EXCELLO (2093 "Chicken Hearted Woman") 20-40 56
LAMP (8004 "Life Don't Mean a Thing") .. 25-50 54
LAMP (8005 "Cryin' 'Cause I'm Troubled") 25-50 54
SHARON ("Cryin' 'Cause I'm Troubled") 8-12 66
Also see CARTER, Goree / Clarence Samuels

SAMUELS, Jerry
Singles: 78 rpm
VIK (0197 "Puppy Love") 10-15 56
Singles: 7-inch
J.E.P. (1175 "Who Are You to Tell Me Not to Smoke Marijuana") .... 8-12 '60s
SILVER BLUE (813 "Can You Dig It") 5-10
VIK (0197 "The Chosen Few") 15-25 56
Also see NAPOLEON XIV

SAN FRANCISCO LTD.
LPs: 10/12-inch
CRYSTAL CLEAR (5004 "San Francisco Ltd.") 10-20 76
(White vinyl, limited edition, direct to disc. Magic record, with two separate vocal tracks. When played at 45 rpm, vocalist is Willow Wray. When played at 33 rpm, vocalist is Terry Garthwaite.)
Members: Terry Garthwaite; Willow Wray; Philip G. Smith; Robert Earl Smith; Brian Atkinson; David Austin; Chuck Metcalf; Kent Middleton; John Stafford; Bill Schwartz.

SAN REMO GOLDEN STRINGS — P&R '65
Singles: 7-inch
GORDY (7060 "Festival Time") 10-20 67
RIC-TIC 8-15 65-66
LPs: 10/12-inch
GORDY (923 "Hungry for Love") 25-35 67
GORDY (928 "Swing") 15-25 68
RIC-TIC (901 "Hungry for Love") 30-60 66

SANCHEZ, Mike
Singles: 7-inch
MAYTE (24 "Wicked") 75-125 60

SANDALS — LP '67
Singles: 7-inch
WORLD PACIFIC (415 "Theme from *Endless Summer*) 10-15 64
WORLD PACIFIC (421 "Always") 15-25 64
WORLD PACIFIC (77000 series) 8-12 65-67
LPs: 10/12-inch
WORLD PACIFIC (WP-1832 "Endless Summer") 25-30 66
(Monaural. Soundtrack.)
WORLD PACIFIC (ST-1832 "Endless Summer") 35-40 66
(Stereo. Soundtrack.)
WORLD PACIFIC (21884 "Last of the Ski Bums") 50-75 69
Members: John Blakely; Danny Brawner; John Gibson; Gaston Georis; Walter Georis.
Also see SANDELLS
Also see STONEGROUND

SANDELLS
Singles: 7-inch
AURA (4501 "School's Out!") 10-15 65
WORLD PACIFIC (405 "Scrambler") 10-20 64
LPs: 10/12-inch
WORLD PACIFIC (WP-1818 "Scrambler") 30-40 64
(Monaural.)
WORLD PACIFIC (ST-1818 "Scrambler") 50-70 64
(Stereo. Black vinyl.)
WORLD PACIFIC (1818 "Scrambler") 75-125 64
(Stereo. Red vinyl.)
Also see SANDALS

SANDERS, Andy
Singles: 7-inch
DOTTIE (1010 "Rock and Roll Baby") 40-60

SANDERS, Arlen
(With the Pacifics)
Singles: 7-inch
FARO (616 "Hopped-Up Mustang") 15-25 64

SANDERS, Bobby
(With the Performers; with Toughtones; Bobby Saunders)
Singles: 7-inch
KAYBO (618 "I'm On My Way") 50-75 61
KENT (382 "Maybe I'm Wrong") 1000-1500 62
PICK-A-HIT .... 10-15 '60s
SOUND-O-RAMA (117 "Cleopatra") 40-60 63
Also see BOBBY & VELVETS

SANDERS, Curly
(With the Sanitones; Ray Sanders)
Singles: 78 rpm
IMPERIAL (8226 "Too Much Lovin' ") 10-20 54
JAMBOREE (590 "Brand New Rock n' Roll") 100-200 56
JAMBOREE (1833 "Heartsick & Blue") 15-25 56
Singles: 7-inch
CONCEPT (897 "Dynamite") 75-100 57
CONCEPT (898 "This Time") 25-50 57
IMPERIAL (8226 "Too Much Lovin' ") 20-30 54
JAMBOREE (590 "Brand New Rock n' Roll") 600-800 56
JAMBOREE (1833 "Heartsick & Blue") .. 75-100 56
Also see SANDERS, Ray

SANDERS, Ed, & Hemptones
(Ed Saunders)
LPs: 10/12-inch
REPRISE (2105 "Beer Cans on the Moon") 20-25 73
REPRISE (6374 "Sanders Truckstop") 20-25 69
Also see FUGS

SANDERS, Fred, & His Pearl House Rockers
("Featuring Roy Tipton")
Singles: 7-inch
SPIN (111 "Another Fool in Love") 300-400 61
(50 made.)
Members: Fred Sanders; Roy Tipton.

SANDERS, Hank
Singles: 7-inch
CREST (1039 "How Much") 75-125 58

SANDERS, Rabon
Singles: 7-inch
LOGAN (3113 "Tore Your Playhouse Down") 100-150

SANDERS, Ray — C&W '60
Singles: 7-inch
GNP 4-6 67-68
HILLSIDE 3-5 80
IMPERIAL 4-6 69
LIBERTY (Except 56202) 5-10 60-63
LIBERTY (56202 "Blame It On Rosie") 4-6 70
REPUBLIC 3-5 77-78
SHEB (001 "You're Puttin' Me On") 4-8
STADIUM (134 "Lonesome & Me") 4-8 64
TOWER 4-8 65-66
U.A. 4-6 70-73
LPs: 10/12-inch
IMPERIAL 10-15 69
REPUBLIC 8-10 77
U.A. 8-12 72
Also see SANDERS, Curly

SANDERS, Willis
(With the Fabulous Embers; with Embers; with Duprees; with Art Harris & Orchestra; Will Sanders)
Singles: 7-inch
CORAL (62146 "Time Out for Tears") 40-60 59
JUNO (213 "Your Souvenir") 600-700 57
JUNO (215 "I'll Be with You") 1500-2000 57
JVPITER (213 "Your Souvenir") 700-800 57
(First issue. From Jupiter Record Co., though label mistakenly reads "Jvpiter.")
MILLIONAIRE (775 "Loveable You") 100-200 58
REGATTA (2000 "Summertime") 25-35 61
REGATTA (2003 "Living Truth") 15-25 61
UNART (2004 "Lovable You") 30-40 58
Also see EMBERS

SANDETTS
Singles: 7-inch
SMOKEY (109 "Without You") 50-75 60

SANDLIN, Billy
Singles: 7-inch
GALA (110 "She's Mean") 50-75 60
GALA (115 "Teenager's Dream") 15-25 61
MEGA (0107 "You Are Love") 4-8 73
VIM (1006 "She's Mean") 75-125 59

SANDMEN
Singles: 78 rpm
OKEH 15-25 55
Singles: 7-inch
OKEH (7052 "When I Grow Too Old to Dream") 30-40 55
Member: Brook Benton.
Also see BENTON, Brook
Also see WILLIS, Chuck

SANDMEN
Singles: 7-inch
BLUE JAY (5002 "Searching for a New Love") 20-30 65

SANDOVAL, Serafin
Singles: 7-inch
DEL NORTE (725 "Hey Baby") 75-125

SANDPAPERS
Singles: 7-inch
CHARGER (114 "Ain't Gonna Kiss Ya") ... 20-30 65

SANDPIPERS
Singles: 7-inch
GIANT (705 "Lonely Too Long") 100-200 68

SANDRA & HIGHLANDERS
Singles: 7-inch
HIGHLAND (1015 "Written in the Stars") . 50-75 61

SANDS
Singles: 7-inch
CAPRI (522 "Open Your Eyes") 15-25 67

SANDS
Singles: 7-inch
JCP (1042 "Little Things") 15-25 65

SANDS, Bobby, & Royal Teentones
Singles: 7-inch
NUGGET (1003 "Secret Lover") 75-125 59

SANDS, Jeri Lynn
Singles: 7-inch
ARCADE (148 "Crazy in Love") 20-30 58
ARCADE (153 "As Long As I") 15-25 59
ARCADE (156 "Walking Beat") 10-20 60
BIG TOP (3015 "If") 15-25 59
Session: Bill Haley's Comets.
Also see HALEY, Bill

SANDS, Jim
(With the 5 Dollars)
Singles: 7-inch
HI-Q (5009 "Dreamboat Rock") 50-60 58
HI-Q (5010 "We're Gonna Rock") 20-30 58

SANDS, Jodie — P&R '57
(With the Peter DeAngelis Orchestra)
Singles: 78 rpm
BERNLO 8-12 57
CHANCELLOR 5-10 57
TEEN 5-10 55
Singles: 7-inch
ABC 4-6 74
ABC-PAR (10337 "We Had Words") 8-12 62
ABC-PAR (10376 "Hello, Heartache") 8-12 62
ABC-PAR (10451 "Time to Love") 8-12 63
BERNLO (1003 "Love Me Always") 10-20 57
CHANCELLOR (1003 "With All My Heart") 10-20 57
CHANCELLOR (1005 "If You're Not Completely Satisfied") 10-20 58
CHANCELLOR (1023 "Someday") 10-20 59
PARIS (551 "Give Me a Break") 10-15 60
SIGNATURE (12015 "Turnabout Heart") . 10-15 59
TEEN (109 "Love Me Always") 15-25 55
TEEN (115 "Let Me Show You Around My Heart") 15-20 55
THOR (101 "Hold Me") 10-15 59
THOR (103 "Turnabout Heart") 10-15 59

SANDS, Tommy — P&R/R&B/LP '57
(With the Raiders)
Singles: 78 rpm
CAPITOL 10-25 57
RCA 8-12 54-56
Singles: 7-inch
ABC-PAR 4-8 63-64
CAPITOL ("Graduation Day") 15-25 57
(No selection number used, though *Steady Date* LP number [T-848] is shown. Promotional issue only.)
CAPITOL (3639 thru 4082) 10-15 57-58
CAPITOL (4160 thru 4580) 5-10 59-61
IMPERIAL 4-8 66-67
LIBERTY (55807 "Love's Funny") 4-8 65
LIBERTY (55842 "The Statue") 4-8 65
RCA 10-20 54-56
SUPERSCOPE 4-6 69
Picture Sleeves
CAPITOL 10-20 58-59
EPs: 7-inch
CAPITOL (1-2-3 848 "Steady Date with Tommy Sands") 15-25 57
(Price is for any of three volumes.)
CAPITOL (851 "Teen-Age Crush") 20-30 57
CAPITOL (1-2-3 929 "Sing Boy Sing") 15-25 58
(Price is for any of three volumes.)
CAPITOL (1123 "This Thing Called Love") 15-20 59
LPs: 10/12-inch
BRUNSWICK 8-10 78
CAPITOL (848 "Steady Date") 35-50 57
CAPITOL (929 "Sing Boy Sing") 35-50 58
CAPITOL (1081 "Sands Storm") 30-50 58
CAPITOL (T-1123 "This Thing Called Love") 30-40 59
(Monaural.)
CAPITOL (ST-1123 "This Thing Called Love") 35-45 59
(Stereo.)
CAPITOL (T-1239 "When I'm Thinking of You") 30-40 59
(Monaural.)

CAPITOL (ST-1239 "When I'm Thinking of You") 35-45 59
(Stereo.)
CAPITOL (T-1364 "Sands at the Storm") 30-40 60
(Monaural.)
CAPITOL (ST-1364 "Sands at the Sands") 35-45 60
(Stereo.)
CAPITOL (T-1426 "Dream with Me") 30-40 60
(Monaural.)
CAPITOL (ST-1426 "Dream with Me")..... 35-45 60
(Stereo.)
Also see ANNETTE & TOMMY SANDS
Also see BLAINE, Hal
Also see VINCENT, Gene / Tommy Sands / Sonny James / Ferlin Husky

SANDS OF TIME
Singles: 7-inch
STERLING AWARD (1082 "Red Light") .. 15-25 66

SANDS OF TIME
Singles: 7-inch
STEARLY (8167 "Come Back Little Girl") 15-25 67

SANDY, Frank, & Jackals
Singles: 7-inch
MARK (138 "Shamrock") 10-20 59
MGM (12626 "Tarrentella Rock.......... 25-50 58
MGM (12678 "Let's Go Rock and Roll") 75-100 58

SANDY & BEACHCOMBERS
Singles: 7-inch
SPAR (760 "2 + 2") 15-20 65

SANDY & STY-LETTES
Singles: 7-inch
REM (101 "Wishing Star") 40-50 60

SANSHERS
Singles: 7-inch
KWEEK ("Gonna Git That Man").......... 15-25 64

SANTANA P&R/LP '69
(Carlos Santana)
Singles: 12-inch
COLUMBIA.......... 4-6 85
Singles: 7-inch
COLUMBIA.......... 3-8 69-90
Picture Sleeves
COLUMBIA.......... 3-8 70-85
LPs: 10/12-inch
COLUMBIA (Except "CQ" and "HC" series) 5-15 69-90
COLUMBIA (CQ-30130 "Abraxas").......... 15-25 75
(Quadraphonic.)
COLUMBIA (CQ-31610 "Caravanserai"). 15-25 74
(Quadraphonic.)
COLUMBIA (CQ-32900 "Illuminations")... 15-25 74
(Quadraphonic.)
COLUMBIA (HC-40130 "Abraxas").......... 40-60 81
(Half-speed mastered.)
Members: Devadip Carlos Santana; Armando Peraza; Graham Lear; David Margen; Richard Baker; Alex Ligertwood; Orestes Vilato; Raul Rekow.
Also see BOOKER T. & MGs
Also see FRANKLIN, Aretha
Also see HANCOCK, Herbie

SANTANA TRIO
Singles: 7-inch
TITANIC (5013 "Land of Odin").......... 20-25 63

SANTO & JOHNNY P&R/R&B '59
Singles: 7-inch
CANADIAN AMERICAN.......... 5-12 59-67
ERIC.......... 4-6 '70s
IMPERIAL.......... 4-8 67-68
PAUSA.......... 4-6 76
U.A. 4-8 66
Picture Sleeves
CANADIAN AMERICAN.......... 8-15 60-65
LPs: 10/12-inch
CANADIAN AMERICAN 20-40 59-64
IMPERIAL.......... 10-20 67-69
Members: Santo Farina; Johnny Farina.

SANTO & JOHNNY / Linda Scott
Singles: 7-inch
CANADIAN AMERICAN (132 "Twistin' Bells"/"Christmas Day") 5-10 61
Also see SCOTT, Linda
Also see SANTO & JOHNNY

SANTOS, Larry P&R '76
Singles: 7-inch
ATLANTIC (2250 "Someday").......... 10-15 64
CASABLANCA.......... 4-6 76-77
EVOLUTION 5-15 69-71
LPs: 10/12-inch
CASABLANCA.......... 8-10 77
EVOLUTION 10-20 69
Session: 4 Seasons.
Also see 4 SEASONS
Also see MADISONS
Also see TONES

SAPPHIRE THINKERS
Singles: 7-inch
HOBBIT.......... 5-10 69
LPs: 10/12-inch
HOBBIT (5003 "From Within") 15-25 69
Members: Peggy Richmond; Bill Richmond; Steve Richmond; Tim Lee.

SAPPHIRES P&R/R&B '64
Singles: 7-inch
ABC.......... 4-6 73
ABC-PAR (10559 "Hearts Are Made to Be Broken").......... 8-12 64
ABC-PAR (10590 "Our Love Is Everywhere").......... 8-12 64
ABC-PAR (10639 "Gotta Have Your Love").......... 10-15 65
ABC-PAR (10693 "Evil One").......... 8-12 65
ABC-PAR (10753 "Gonna Be a Big Thing").......... 8-12 65
ABC-PAR (10778 "Slow Fizz").......... 5-10 66
CASINO (102 "Who Do You Love").......... 4-8
(Yellow label.)
COLLECTABLES.......... 3-5 '80s
ERIC.......... 4-6 '70s
ITZY (5 "Who Do You Love").......... 8-12 66
SWAN (4143 "Where Is Johnny Now")..... 10-20 63
SWAN (4162 "Who Do You Love").......... 10-20 63
SWAN (4177 "I Found Out Too Late")...... 10-20 64
SWAN (4184 "Gotta Be More Than Friends") 10-20 64
LPs: 10/12-inch
SWAN (513 "Who Do You Love") 150-250 64
Members: Carol Jackson; George Gainer; Joe Livingston.

SARATOGAS
Singles: 7-inch
IMPERIAL (5738 "I'll Be Loving You") 10-20 61

SARAZEN, Ronnie
Singles: 7-inch
ROULETTE (4275 "Confessions of Love"). 5-10 61

SARDAMS
Singles: 7-inch
JCP (1038 "Somethin' You Got") 10-20 64

SARDO, Frank
(Frankie Sardo)
Singles: 7-inch
ABC-PAR (9963 "Fake Out").......... 20-30 58
ABC-PAR (10003 "Oh Linda").......... 15-25 59
LIDO (602 "The Girl I'm Gonna Dream About") 15-25 59
MGM (12621 "May I").......... 15-25 58
NEWTOWN (5005 "Mr. Make Believe").... 15-25 60
RAYNA (5005 "Ring of Love").......... 10-20 62
SG (1 "Ring of Love").......... 15-25 60
STUDIO (9910 "Just You Watch Me")...... 20-30 61
20TH FOX (208 "I Know Why and So Do You").......... 10-20 60
20TH FOX (221 "Dream Lover").......... 10-20 60
Also see FRANKIE & JOHNNY

SARDO, Johnny
Singles: 7-inch
CHOCK FULL O' HITS (104 "Take a Ride with Me").......... 100-200 58
VIVID (108 "I Can Understand").......... 5-10 64
W.B. (5044 "Late to School").......... 15-25 59
Also see FRANKIE & JOHNNY

SARGENT, Chuck, & Ambassadors
Singles: 7-inch
CUCA (1079 "Don't You Ever Go").......... 30-50 62
Also see KENNEDY, Dave

SARGENT, Don
(With the Buddies)
Singles: 7-inch
CATALINA (4514 "Leadfoot") 10-20 59
GOLDEN MELODY (72530 "Ole Rex") 8-12 61
MECCA (101 "Rockin' Chair Roll") 40-60 53
RCA (7128 "Red Ruby Lips").......... 30-40 58
RCA (7241 "10 Minutes to Heaven") 30-40 58
WORLD PACIFIC (806 "Gypsy Boots").... 50-75 59
Picture Sleeves
CATALINA (4514 "Leadfoot") 25-35 59
(Die-cut sleeve which displays record label.)
Session: Four Palms.
Also see FOUR PALMS.

SARGENT, Lou
(Lou Sargent's Band)
Singles: 78 rpm
CHESS (1465 "Ridin' the Boogie") 15-25 51

SA-SHAYS
Singles: 7-inch
ALFI (1 "Boo Hoo Hoo").......... 20-30 61
ZEN (101 "Boo Hoo Hoo") 8-12 61
ZEN (110 "On That Beautiful Day") 8-12 63

SATAN, Jimmy
Singles: 7-inch
MALTESE (102 "Look at the Clock") 25-50 66

SATAN & DISCIPLES
Singles: 7-inch
GOLDBAND (1188 "Mummies Curse") 15-25 69
LPs: 10/12-inch
GOLDBAND (7750 "Underground").......... 15-25 69

SATAN'S BREED
Singles: 7-inch
A-L-M (201,130 "Laugh Myself to the Grave") 15-25 66

SATANS
LPs: 10/12-inch
("Raisin' Hell") 50-100 62
(No label name is shown.)

SATANS
Singles: 7-inch
SATAN ("Say It Again") 10-20 63
(Selection number not known.)

SATANS
Singles: 7-inch
MANHATTAN (801 "Making Deals")........ 15-20 66

SATELLITES
Singles: 7-inch
CLASS (234 "Heavenly Angel") 30-40 58
(First issue.)
MALYNN (234 "Heavenly Angel").......... 20-30 58
Members: David Ford; Earl Nelson; Curt Williams; Curley Dinkins.
Also see DAY, Bobby
Also see HOLLYWOOD FLAMES
Also see NELSON, Earl

SATELLITES
Singles: 7-inch
U.A. (141 "I Found a Girl").......... 25-35 58

SATELLITES
Singles: 7-inch
CHECKER (891 "Blast Off") 15-25 58
CHESS (1789 "Blast Off") 10-20 62
RONNIE (204 "Blast Off").......... 35-50 58
(First issue.)

SATELLITES
Singles: 7-inch
ABC-PAR (10038 "Linda Jean") 25-35 59
CUPID (5004 "Linda Jean") 40-60 58
D-M-G (4001 "Each Night").......... 30-40 60
(With the High Seas.)
PALACE (102 "Buzz Buzz") 20-30 60
3 SONS (102 "Buzz Buzz") 10-15 63
Member: Mickey Brazell.
Also see HIGH SEAS

SATIN, Sonny
Singles: 7-inch
CASTLE (1051 "My Baby Put Me Down").......... 20-30 65
(First issue.)
GNP (352 "My Baby Put Me Down") 10-15 65

SATIN LADIES
Singles: 7-inch
STAGEDOOR ("You'll Always Be Mine") .... 200-300 '60s
(Selection number not known.)

SATINTONES
Singles: 7-inch
MOTOWN (1000 "My Beloved") 200-300 60
(Without strings. ID number is MT-12345.)
MOTOWN (1000 "My Beloved") 150-250 60
(Strings added. ID number is 1000-G3.)
MOTOWN (1006 "Tomorrow and Always") 100-200 61
(Without strings.)
MOTOWN (1006 "Tomorrow and Always") 100-200 61
(Strings added.)
MOTOWN (1006 "Angel") 600-800 61
(Male lead vocal. Serial number is H-625.)
MOTOWN (1006 "Angel") 400-500 61
(Male/Female duet. Serial number is H-55596.)
MOTOWN (1010 "My Kind of Love").... 100-150 61
MOTOWN (1020 "Zing Went the Strings of My Heart") 100-150 62
TAMLA (54026 "Going to the Hop") 300-400 60
Members: Charles "Chico" Leverette; Freddie Gorman; Brian Holland; James Ellis; Sonny Sanders; Robert Bateman; Vernon Williams; Sammy Mack; Joe Charles.
Also see FIVE MASTERS
Also see GORMAN, Freddie
Also see HOLLAND, Brian
Also see HOLLAND, Eddie
Also see LEVERETTE, Chico
Also see LOE & JOE
Also see PYRAMIDS

SATISFACTIONS
Singles: 7-inch
CHESAPEAKE (610 "We Will Walk Together").......... 40-50 62

SATISFACTIONS
Singles: 7-inch
LEE (3735 "Bad Times") 45-65 66
LEE (3736 "Only Once") 40-50 66

SATISFACTIONS
Singles: 7-inch
TWIN TOWN (714 "Bad Times") 10-20 66
Also see MARAUDERS

SATISFACTIONS
Singles: 7-inch
IMPERIAL (66170 "Bring It All Down") 10-15 66
1-2-3 (1716 "Gonna Get Right Tonight").... 5-10 69
SMASH (2059 "Give Me Your Love") 10-15 66
SMASH (2098 "Take It Or Leave It") 15-25 67
SMASH (2131 "Keep on Tryin") 10-15 67

SATURDAY KNIGHTS
(Saturday Nights)
Singles: 7-inch
NOCTURNE (1030 "Sea Mist") .... 30-50 '60s
SWAN (4075 "Ticonderoga") 10-15 61
(Credited to Saturday Nights.)
SWAN (4075 "Ticonderoga") 5-10 61
(Credited to Saturday Knights.)
SWAN (4081 "Texas Tommy") 5-10 61
Member: Van Trevor.
Also see SHELDON, Rick, & Saturday Knights
Also see TREVOR, Van

SATURDAY KNIGHTS
Singles: 7-inch
JET (101 "Dum Diddly Dum") .... 15-20 '60s

SAUCERS
(Frank Jordan & the Saucers)
Singles: 7-inch
FELCO (104 "Why Do I Dream") 200-300 59
(Identification number is "ZTSC-10407.")
FELCO (104 "Why Do I Dream") 50-150 59
(Identification number is "TB-155.")
KICK (516 "Flossie Mae") 200-300 58
(Black label.)
KICK (516 "Flossie Mae") 50-75 58
(Yellow and red label.)
LYNNE (101 "Hello Darling") 100-200 64
NRM (901 "Why Do I Dream") 10-15
LPs: 10/12-inch
GULF COAST.......... 5-10 89

Members: Frank Jordan; Leonard Allen; Jim Beacham; Charles Beacham; James Stanley; Verdie Lee Thomas.

SAUL, Hender
Singles: 7-inch
LIBERTY (104 "I Ain't Gonna Rock Tonight") 500-600 '50s

SAUNDERS, Jay
Singles: 78 rpm
CLUB 10-20 56
Singles: 7-inch
CLUB (1012 "I'm Still in Love with You") 40-50 56

SAUNDERS, Little Butchie
(Little Butchie Saunders & His Buddies)
Singles: 78 rpm
HERALD 15-25 56
Singles: 7-inch
HERALD (485 "Lindy Lou") 30-40 56
HERALD (491 "Great Big Heart") 30-40 56
Also see ELCHORDS
Also see LITTLE BUTCH & VELLS

SAUNDERS, Red
(With His Orchestra; "Featuring Delores Hawkins")
Singles: 78 rpm
BLUE LAKE (101 "Riverboat") 5-10 53
OKEH (Except 6862) 5-10 46-55
OKEH (6862 "Hambone") 15-25 52
(With Dee Clark.)
SAVOY 10-15 45
SULTAN 10-15 46
SUPREME 5-10 49
Singles: 7-inch
BLUE LAKE (101 "Riverboat") 35-50 53
(Colored vinyl.)
OKEH (6801 thru 6856) 15-25 51-52
OKEH (6862 "Hambone") 40-60 52
(With Dee Clark.)
OKEH (6884 thru 6953) 15-25 52-53
OKEH (7061 "Mistreatin' Woman Blues") 10-20 55
OKEH (7166 "Hambone") 10-15 63
Picture Sleeves
OKEH (7166 "Hambone") 15-25 63
Also see CLARK, Dee
Also see MERCURY ALL-STARS
Also see ST. LOUIS JIMMY

SAUNDERS, Slim
Singles: 78 rpm
CHESS 15-25 54
LAMP 10-20 57
Singles: 7-inch
CHESS (1563 "Let's Have Some Fun") 35-55 54
LAMP (2004 "No One Can Love You Like I Do") 15-25 57

SAVAGE, Al
(With Joe Morris & His Orchestra; with Kirkland Singers)
Singles: 78 rpm
HERALD 10-15 55-57
Singles: 7-inch
HERALD (417 "I Had a Notion") 20-30 53
(Black vinyl.)
HERALD (417 "I Had a Notion") 50-75 53
(Red vinyl.)
HERALD (421 "Love Is a Funny Thing") 15-25 54
(Black vinyl.)
HERALD (421 "Love Is a Funny Thing") 50-100 54
(Red vinyl.)
HERALD (430 "Take Your Time") 20-30 54
HERALD (437 "Don't Tell Me") 20-30 54
HERALD (441 "You Told Me So") 20-30 54
HERALD (445 "Dream Girl") 20-30 55
HERALD (460 "My Sweetie's Gone") 20-30 55
HERALD (468 "Teenage Romance") 20-30 55
HERALD (482 "Bridge of Love") 15-25 56
HERALD (494 "Happy Tears") 15-25 57
HERALD (505 "A Fool Was I") 15-25 57
LIDO (605 "I Need") 10-20 59
Also see MORRIS, Joe

SAVAGE, Duke, & Arribins
Singles: 7-inch
ARGO (5346 "Your Love") 30-40 59

SAVAGE, Gene
Singles: 7-inch
BIG WEST (1109 "Big Machine") 50-75

SAVAGES
Singles: 7-inch
RED FOX (111 "Cheating On Me") 10-20 66

SAVAGES
Singles: 7-inch
DUANE (1043 "No No No") 10-20 66
DUANE (1049 "Roses Are Red") 10-20 66
DUANE (1054 "The World Ain't Round, It's Square") 30-50 66
LPs: 10/12-inch
DUANE (1047 "Live and Wild") 300-400 66
(Counterfeits exist, using same label and number.)

SAVAGES
Singles: 7-inch
LAURIE (3328 "Little Miss Sad") 15-25 66

SAVOY, Jules, & Chromatics
("Singing Discovery of Hesperia Inn, Hesperia, Calif.")
Singles: 7-inch
REAL (1320 "Would You") 1800-2000 57
REAL (1321 "Lonesome Heart") 400-500 57
REAL (1322 "Give Me the Will") 400-500 57
REAL (1323 "Clap Clap") 200-300 57

SAVOY, Ronnie P&R '61
(With the Cliff Parman Orchestra)
Singles: 7-inch
CANDELO (381 "Challenge") 8-12 59
EPIC (9619 "I Hear Violins") 5-10 63
EPIC (9708 "Sally Blue") 5-10 64
GONE (5079 "Ooh, What a Girl") 8-12 59
MGM (12950 "And the Heavens Cried") 10-20 60
MGM (13001 "Bewitched") 10-20 61
MGM (13042 "Jungle Love Call") 10-20 61
PHILIPS (40032 "Big Hand, Little Hand") 5-10 62
PHILIPS (40071 "Moonlight to Sunlight") 5-10 63
TUFF (416 "Pitfall") 20-30 65
WINGATE (001 "Loving You") 10-20 65
Also see NITECAPS

SAVOY BROWN P&R/LP '69
(Savoy Brown Blues Band)
Singles: 7-inch
LONDON 4-6 74-75
PARROT 4-6 69-73
TOWN HOUSE 3-5 81
LPs: 10/12-inch
LONDON (600 & 700 series) 8-10 74-77
LONDON (50000 "Best of Savoy Brown") 5-8 77
PARROT 10-15 68-73
TOWN HOUSE (Except 7562) 8-12 81
TOWN HOUSE (7562 "Prime Cuts") 10-15 81
(Promotional issue only.)

SAVOYS
Singles: 78 rpm
COMBO 20-30 55
Singles: 7-inch
COMBO (75 "Darling Stay with Me") 100-150 55
(Purple label. Has "Combo Records, Hollywood, Calif." at top.)
COMBO (75 "Darling Stay with Me") 30-50 55
(Red label, or purple label with only "Combo" at top.)
Also see WOODMAN, Brother

SAVOYS / Jack McVea
Singles: 78 rpm
COMBO (90 "Chop Chop Boom") 20-30 55
Singles: 7-inch
COMBO (90 "Chop Chop Boom") 50-75 55
Also see McVEA, Jack
Also see SAVOYS

SAVOYS
Singles: 78 rpm
SAVOY (1188 "Say You're Mine") 10-20 56
Singles: 7-inch
SAVOY (1188 "Say You're Mine") 20-30 56
Members: Jimmy Jones; Bill Walker; Bobby Moore; Ken Saxton; Melvin Walton.
Also see JONES, Jimmy
Also see PRETENDERS

SAVOYS
(With the Bella Tones)
Singles: 7-inch
BELLA (18 "I Love My Baby") 15-25 59
BELLA (58 "Mortal Monster Man") 50-75 59
CHRISTY (130 "You're the Beating of My Heart") 75-125 60

SAVOYS
Singles: 7-inch
NRM (904 "Slappin' Rods & Leaky Oil") 50-75 66
PDQ ("Slappin' Rods & Leaky Oil") 75-100 60
(Selection number not known.)

SAVOYS
Singles: 7-inch
SUMMIT (403 "Can It Be") 20-30 66

SAWYER, Henry, & Jupiters
("Music by Mike Tam")
Singles: 7-inch
PLANET X (9621 "It Takes Two") 4000-5000 57

SAWYER, J.C.
Singles: 7-inch
DIXIE (692 "Going Steppin' ") 2000-2500

SAWYER, Ray P&R/C&W '76
Singles: 7-inch
CAPITOL 4-6 76-79
SANDY (1030 "Bells in My Heart") 150-250 60
SANDY (1037 "I'm Gonna Leave") 50-75 61
LPs: 10/12-inch
CAPITOL 8-12 76

SAWYER, Virgil
Singles: 7-inch
YALE (202 "You're Gonna Grieve When I Leave") 50-75 60

SAX, Bobby
Singles: 7-inch
DE PLACE (2826 "Taste of Soul") 8-12 64
RU-JAC (0015 "Soul at Last") 15-25 59

SAXON, Eddie
(With the Paramounts)
Singles: 7-inch
EMPRESS (106 "Blues No More") 150-200 62
(Single-sided disc. Promotional issue only.)
EMPRESS (106 "Blues No More") 100-150 62
FORD (104 "What a Night") 10-20 61

SAXON, Sky
(Sky Saxon Blues Band)
Singles: 7-inch
CONQUEST (777 "They Say") 15-25 64
LPs: 10/12-inch
GNP (2040 "Full Spoon of Seedy Blues") 20-30 67
(Originals have the logo, "GNP Crescendo," on a horizontal line. Reissues have the name in a circular pattern.)
VOXX 5-10
Also see MARSH, Ritchie
Also see SEEDS
Also see YA HO WA 13 & SKY SAXON

SAXONS
Singles: 7-inch
OUR ("Please Be My Love Tonight") 300-500 57
(Selection number not known.)

SAXONS
Singles: 7-inch
CONTENDER (1313 "Is It True") 40-50 58
RELIC (1011 "Is It True") 5-10 65
TAMPA (139 "Tryin' ") 40-50 58
Also see HOLLYWOOD SAXONS

SAXONS
Singles: 7-inch
SHO-BIZ (1003 "Camel Walk") 15-25 59

SAXONS
Singles: 7-inch
MIRASONIC 5-10 65
LPs: 10/12-inch
MIRASONIC (A-1017 "Saxons") 30-40 66
(Monaural.)
MIRASONIC (AS-1017 "Saxons") 40-50 66
(Stereo.)

SAXONS
Singles: 7-inch
YORKSHIRE (101 "Everybody Puts Her Down") 5-10 64
YORKSHIRE (127 "Things Have Been Bad") 15-25 66

SCAFFOLD P&R '68
Singles: 7-inch
BELL (701 "Thank U Very Much") 10-15 68
BELL (724 "Do You Remember") 10-15 68
BELL (747 "Lily the Pink") 10-15 68
BELL (821 "Charity Bubbles") 10-15 69
BELL (849 "Liver Birds") 10-15 69
W.B. (8001 "Liverpool Lou") 4-8 74
LPs: 10/12-inch
BELL (6018 "Thank U Very Much") 25-35 68
Members: Mike McGear; Roger McGough; John Gorman; Mike Vickers; Lol Creme; Zoot Money; Andy Roberts.
Also see MONEY, Zoot

SCAGGS, Boz P&R/LP '71
Singles: 12-inch
COLUMBIA 4-8 81
Singles: 7-inch
ATLANTIC 5-10 69
COLUMBIA 3-8 71-88
FULL MOON 3-6 81
Picture Sleeves
COLUMBIA 3-6 76-88
EPs: 7-inch
COLUMBIA 5-10 76
LPs: 10/12-inch
ATLANTIC (8239 "Boz Scaggs") 10-15 69
ATLANTIC (19166 "Boz Scaggs") 5-8 78
COLUMBIA (Except 40000 series) 5-10 71-80
COLUMBIA (40463 "Other Roads") 5-8 88
COLUMBIA (43920 "Silk Degrees") 15-20 80
(Half-speed mastered.)
Promotional LPs
COLUMBIA (A2S-71 "Boz Scaggs KSAN Live Concert") 200-300 74
(Promotional issue only. Two discs.)
COLUMBIA (203 "The Boz Scaggs Sampler") 10-20 76
Also see MILLER, Steve
Also see MOTHER EARTH

SCAGGS, Boz / Kris Kristofferson
EPs: 7-inch
PLAYBACK/COLUMBIA (1001 "Boz Scaggs Live]") 20-40 74
Also see KRISTOFFERSON, Kris
Also see SCAGGS, Boz

SCALES, Alonzo
Singles: 78 rpm
ABBEY 25-45 '50s
WING 60-80 55-56
Singles: 7-inch
WING (90020 "She's Gone") 75-125 55
WING (90049 "Hard Luck Child") 75-125 56

SCALESE, Jack
Singles: 7-inch
SENATOR (715 "Make Love to Me") 100-200

SCALE-TONES
Singles: 78 rpm
JAY-DEE (810 "Everlasting Love") 40-60 56
Singles: 7-inch
JAY-DEE (810 "Everlasting Love") 200-300 56
Members: Tom Gardner; Cleveland Still; James Montgomery; James Miller; Don Archer.
Also see DUBS
Also see 5 WINGS
Also see MARVELS

SCALLYWAGS
(Skallywags)
Singles: 7-inch
SOLA (5 "Surfin' Mickey") 20-30 63

SCAMPS
Singles: 78 rpm
PEACOCK (1655 "Yes, My Baby") 20-30 55
Singles: 7-inch
PEACOCK (1655 "Yes, My Baby") 75-100 55

SCARLET HENCHMEN
Singles: 7-inch
NIGHT OWL (6835 "Ring Dreams") 10-20 68
NIGHT OWL (6913 "Crystal Palace") 10-20 69
Picture Sleeves
NIGHT OWL (6835 "Ring Dreams") 20-25 68
NIGHT OWL (6913 "Crystal Palace") 20-25 69
Members: Carl Trieloff; Jim Johnson; James Gardner; John Schaller.

SCARLETS
("With Rhythm Accompaniment")
Singles: 78 rpm
RED ROBIN 50-75 54-55
Singles: 7-inch
EVENT (4287 "Dear One") 8-12 58

LOST NITE....................4-8
OLDIES....................4-6
RED ROBIN (128 "Dear One")....................75-125 54
RED ROBIN (133 "Darling, I'm Yours")....................200-300 54
RED ROBIN (135 "True Love")....................100-150 55
RED ROBIN (138 "Kiss Me")....................200-300 55
Members: Fred Parris; Nat Mosley; Silvester Hopkins; Al Denby; Bill Powers.

LPs: 10/12-inch

LOST NITE (143 "Greatest Hits")....................8-12 '70s
(Red vinyl.)
Also see FIVE SATINS
Also see 4 SEASONS / Scarlets

SCARLETS

Singles: 7-inch

DOT (16004 "Stampede")....................10-15 59
PRINCE (1207 "Stampede")....................25-35 59
(First issue.)

SCARLETS

Singles: 7-inch

FURY (1036 "Truly Yours")....................15-25 60

SCAVENGERS

Singles: 7-inch

FENTON (987 "Curfew")....................20-30 64
MOBILE FIDELITY (1005 "The Angels Listened In")....................15-25 63
MOBILE FIDELITY (1212 "Devil's Reef")....................15-25 64
STARS OF HOLLYWOOD (1210 "Shotgun"/"Cream Puff")....................20-30 63
STARS OF HOLLYWOOD (1211 "Shotgun"/"Zip Code")....................15-25 63
(1210 and 1211 have the same B-side track, but with different titles.)
STARS OF HOLLYWOOD (1212 "Devil's Reef")....................15-25 63

SCAVENGERS

Singles: 7-inch

SUEMI (4552 "Bogus")....................10-20 65

SCHAEFER, Freddy

Singles: 7-inch

KING (5621 "Zoom Zoom Zoom")....................30-40 62

SCHAEFER, Hal
(Hal Schaefer & His Orchestra; Hal Schaefer Trio; "with Alvin Stoller on Drums and Joe Mondragon on Bass")

Singles: 7-inch

U.A. (130 "March of the Vikings")....................8-12 58

Picture Sleeves

U.A. (130 "March of the Vikings")....................15-25 58

EPs: 7-inch

RCA (626 "Hal Schaefer Trio")....................10-15 55

SCHAFF, Murray
(With the Aristocrats)

Singles: 78 rpm

JOSIE (788 "Unfinished Rock")....................10-15 56
SOUND (101 "Believe Me")....................15-25 54

Singles: 7-inch

JOSIE (788 "Unfinished Rock")....................20-30 56
SOUND (101 "Believe Me")....................30-40 54

SCHARMEERS / Jive Chords

Singles: 7-inch

VINTAGE (1017 "I've Waited So Long"/"Traveling Stranger")....................10-15 74
(Gold vinyl.)

SCHEEREN, Frank
(With Joe Hintz & Orchestra)

Singles: 7-inch

STYLE (101 "I Got Trouble")....................25-35 61

SCHENZEL, Roger, & Flav-o-rites
(Robin Lee)

Singles: 7-inch

PFAU ("We Are Meant to Be")....................25-35 57
(Selection number not known.)
Also see LEE, Robin

SCHILLING, Johnny, & Sherwoods

Singles: 7-inch

C&A (507 "King of the World")....................150-200 63
(May also be credited to Little John & the Sherwoods.)
Also see LITTLE JOHN & SHERWOODS

SCHMERDLEY, Herman

Singles: 7-inch

FREEWAY ("Mona Lisa")....................250-350
(Selection number not known.)

SCHMIDLING, Tyrone

Singles: 7-inch

ANDEX (4022 "You're Gone, I'm Left")....................150-250 58

SCHOLARS

Singles: 78 rpm

CUE....................10-15 56
DOT....................5-10 56

Singles: 7-inch

CUE (7927 "What Did I Do Wrong")....................20-30 56
CUE (7931 "Spin the Wheel")....................20-30 56
(First issue.)
DOT (15498 "Spin the Wheel")....................10-15 56
DOT (15519 "If You Listen with Your Heart")....................10-15 56
PIC (026 "Women Drivers")....................10-15 '50s

SCHOLARS

Singles: 78 rpm

IMPERIAL....................10-20 57

Singles: 7-inch

IMPERIAL (5449 "Beloved")....................15-25 57
IMPERIAL (5459 "Eternally Yours")....................10-15 57

SCHOLARS

Singles: 7-inch

RUBY RAY (1 "I Need Your Lovin' ")....................20-30 '60s

SCHOLARS / Perennials

Singles: 7-inch

RUBY RAY (2 "Please Please")....................75-125 '60s

SCHOOLBOY CLEVE
(School Boy Cleve; Cleve White)

Singles: 78 rpm

FEATURE (3013 "She's Gone")....................75-100 54

Singles: 7-inch

CHERRIE....................4-6 74
FEATURE (3013 "She's Gone")....................200-300 54

SCHOOLBOYS P&R/R&B '57

Singles: 78 rpm

OKEH....................15-30 56-57

Singles: 7-inch

BIM BAM BOOM (107 "Angel of Love")....................4-6 72
JUANITA (103 "Angel of Love")....................75-100 58
(Black vinyl.)
JUANITA (103 "Angel of Love")....................40-50 '60s
(Red vinyl.)
OKEH (7076 "Shirley")....................20-30 56
(Purple label.)
OKEH (7076 "Shirley")....................10-15 57
(Yellow label.)
OKEH (7085 "Mary")....................15-25 57
OKEH (7090 "Carol")....................20-30 57
(Purple label.)
OKEH (7090 "Carol")....................30-40 57
(White label. Promotional issue only.)
OKEH (7090 "Carol")....................10-15 57
(Yellow label.)

EPs: 7-inch

MAGIC CARPET (511 "Schoolboys")....................10-15 90
(Black vinyl. Issued with paper sleeve. 500 made.)
Members: Les Martin; Jim Edwards; Roger Hayes; Jim McKay; Renaldo Gamble.
Also see CADILLACS
Also see KODOKS

SCHOOLBOYS

LPs: 10/12-inch

PALACE (777 "Beatle Mash")....................35-45 64
(Also issued as by the Liverpool Kids.)
Also see LIVERPOOL KIDS

SCHOONERS

Singles: 7-inch

EMBER (1041 "Schooner Blues")....................50-75 58
PEEK-A-BOO (106 "No Letter Today")....................25-50 58

SCHORY, Dick LP '59
(Dick Schory's Percussion Pops Orchestra)

LPs: 10/12-inch

RCA....................10-20 59-63

SCHRAIER, Don

Singles: 7-inch

ORBIT (510 "Pigtail")....................15-25 58

SCHUMACHER, Christine, & Supremes

Singles: 7-inch

MOTOWN ("Mother You, Smother You")....................200-250 68
(In a radio contest, Christine won the chance to record with the Supremes – thus this disc.)
Also see SUPREMES

SCHURB, Duane

Singles: 7-inch

ENTERPRISE (1226 "Roly Poly")....................50-100 59
PRESENTING DUANE SCHURB ("Roly Poly")....................150-250 58
(Selection number not known.)

SCHUYLER BROTHERS

Singles: 7-inch

SUNBEAM (110 "The Snake")....................10-20 58

SCHWUMP
(Residents)

Singles: 7-inch

RALPH (0766 "Aphids in the Hall")....................20-30 76

Picture Sleeves

RALPH (0766 "Aphids in the Hall")....................40-60 76
Also see RESIDENTS

SCOGGINS, Hoyt

Singles: 7-inch

STARDAY (563 "Tennessee Rock")....................100-200

SCOOBY DOO ALL STARS

Singles: 78 rpm

ZEPHYR (006 "Ernie's Journey")....................10-15 56

Singles: 7-inch

ZEPHYR (006 "Ernie's Journey")....................20-30 56

LPs: 10/12-inch

ZEPHYR....................40-60 '50s
(No title or selection number used. Though not a title, cover reads "Good Rock & Roll for Dancing.")
Session: Ernie Freeman; Plas Johnson; Jerry Leiber.
Also see FREEMAN, Ernie
Also see JOHNSON, Plas
Also see LEIBER, Jerry

SCOOTERS
("Featuring Alexander Ames")

Singles: 78 rpm

DAWN....................50-100 57

Singles: 7-inch

DAWN (224 "Someday We'll Meet Again")....................200-300 57
ERA (1065 "Everybody's Got a Girl")....................15-25 58
ERA (1072 "Everybody's Got a Girl")....................10-20 58
Member: Alexander Ames.
Also see ROYALS

SCORPIO TUBE

Singles: 7-inch

VITA (001 "Yellow Listen")....................15-25 67

SCORPION

LPs: 10/12-inch

TOWER (5171 "Scorpion")....................30-40 69

SCOTCHTONES

Singles: 7-inch

RUSTONE (1402 "Do You Have the Right")....................400-600 60

SCOTSMEN

Singles: 7-inch

PANORAMA (22 "Tuff Enough")....................10-20 66

SCOTSMEN

Singles: 7-inch

SCOTTY (65 "Beer Bust Blues")....................50-75
SCOTTY (1803 "Beer Bust Blues")....................15-25 '60s

SCOTT, Albert

Singles: 7-inch

ACE (533 "I Feel So Good")....................10-15 57
VIN (1005 "Hey Hey Baby Come Home")....................10-15 58

SCOTT, Allan

LPs: 10/12-inch

TOWER (5164 "When I Needed a Woman")....................10-15 69

SCOTT, Andre

Singles: 7-inch

SUNFLOWER (101 "One Girl")....................10-20

SCOTT, Beverley, Trio

Singles: 78 rpm

MURRAY (503 "Shakin' the Boogie")....................50-100 48
Members: Beverley Scott; Louis Jackson; Ernest McCoy.

SCOTT, Billy P&R '58

Singles: 78 rpm

CAMEO....................10-20 57

Singles: 7-inch

CAMEO (103 "The Secret")....................15-25 57
CAMEO (121 "You're the Greatest")....................15-25 57
CAMEO (143 "A Million Boys")....................15-25 58
EVEREST (19315 "Carole")....................10-20 59

SCOTT, Bob

Singles: 7-inch

MILO (102 "Rita")....................10-20 59
REF (100 "Moon Up Above")....................15-25 62
REF (107 "Fast Suds")....................15-25 62

SCOTT, Bobby P&R '56
(With Don Costa & Orchestra)

Singles: 78 rpm

ABC-PAR (Except 9658)....................5-10 56
ABC-PAR (9658 "Chain Gang")....................10-15 55

Singles: 7-inch

ABC....................4-6 73
ABC-PAR (Except 9658)....................8-12 56-57
ABC-PAR (9658 "Chain Gang")....................15-20 55
COLUMBIA....................4-8 69
GOLDIES 45 (1478 "Chain Gang")....................3-6 73
MERCURY....................5-10 62-63
PLAYBOY....................4-6 72
VERVE (2007 "Danny Boy")....................5-10

LPs: 10/12-inch

COLUMBIA....................5-15
MERCURY....................15-20 63
Also see COSTA, Don, Orchestra

SCOTT, Brian

Singles: 7-inch

IGL (145 "Run for Your Life")....................10-20 '60s

SCOTT, Cindy

Singles: 7-inch

VEEP (1253 "I Love You Baby")....................20-30 67
VEEP (1268 "Time Can Change a Love")....................10-20 67
Also see SIGLER, Bunny, & Cindy Scott

SCOTT, Clifford
(With the 6 Stars)

Singles: 7-inch

AURA (409 "Beach Bunny")....................5-10 64
KING....................5-10 62-64
OMEGA (501/2 "Beach Bunny")....................5-10 64

LPs: 10/12-inch

WORLD PACIFIC (1811 "Clifford Scott Plays the Big Ones")....................20-30 63
(Black vinyl.)
WORLD PACIFIC (1811 "Clifford Scott Plays the Big Ones")....................50-75 63
(Colored vinyl.)
WORLD PACIFIC (1825 "Lavender Sax")....................35-45 63
Also see DOGGETT, Bill

SCOTT, Dexter

Singles: 7-inch

RO-CAL (1001 "Tasty Lips")....................20-30 60

SCOTT, Earl C&W '62

Singles: 7-inch

D....................5-10 61
DECCA....................4-6 64-68
HAP (1018 "Opal Lee")....................100-150
KAPP....................4-8 62
MERCURY....................4-8 63
SKY (113 "Stop Your Knocking")....................150-250

SCOTT, Frank, & Scottsmen

Singles: 7-inch

CASA BLANCA (5563 "She Said")....................15-25 59
(First issue.)
KAPP (164 "She Said")....................10-15 59
Session: Bill Haley's Comets.
Also see HALEY, Bill

SCOTT, Freddie P&R/R&B '63
(With the Symphonics; with Shytone 5 Orchestra; with Teddy McRae Orchestra)

Singles: 78 rpm

J&S (1761 "Running Home")....................8-12 56

Singles: 7-inch

ABC....................4-6 74
BOW (307 "Tell Them for Me")....................5-10
COLPIX (692 "Hey, Girl")....................8-12 63
COLPIX (709 "I Got a Woman")....................8-12 63
COLPIX (724 "Where Does Love Go")....................8-12 64
COLPIX (752 "If I Had a Hammer")....................5-10 64
COLUMBIA (43112 "One Heartache Too Many")....................10-15 64
COLUMBIA (43199 "Lonely Man")....................10-15 65
COLUMBIA (43316 "Don't Let It End")....................10-15 65

ELEPHANT V LTD. 4-6
ENRICA (1002 "Come On Honey") 5-10 64
ERIC 4-6 68
J&S (1761 "Running Home") 30-40 56
JOY (250 "Lost the Right") 10-15 61
JOY (255 "I Gotta Stand Tall") 10-15 61
JOY (280 "I Gotta Stand Tall") 10-15 63
MAINSTREAM (5562 "You're So Hard to Forget") 4-6 74
P.I.P. (8932 "Deep in the Night") 4-6 72
PROBE (481 "Girl I Love You") 4-8 70
SHOUT 4-8 66-71
SOLID GOLD 4-6 73
VANGUARD (35137 "Please Listen") 4-6 71

Picture Sleeves

COLPIX (692 "Hey, Girl") 5-10 '90s

LPs: 10/12-inch

COLPIX (CP-461 "Freddie Scott Sings") 40-80 64
(Gold label. Monaural.)
COLPIX (SCP-461 "Freddie Scott Sings") 50-100 64
(Gold label. Stereo.)
COLPIX (CP-461 "Freddie Scott Sings") 30-40 64
(Blue label.)
COLPIX (SCP-461 "Freddie Scott Sings") 35-50 64
(Blue label.)
COLUMBIA (2258 "Everything I Have Is Yours") 10-20 64
(Monaural.)
COLUMBIA (2660 "Lonely Man") 10-20 67
(Monaural.)
COLUMBIA (9058 "Everything I Have Is Yours") 10-20 64
(Stereo.)
COLUMBIA (9460 "Lonely Man") 10-20 67
(Stereo.)
PROBE (451 "I Shall Be Released") 10-15 70
SHOUT (501 "Are You Lonely for Me") 10-20 67
Also see CHIMES
Also see SYMPHONICS

SCOTT, Gary

Singles: 7-inch

TITANIC (5010 "Beverly") 30-40 63

SCOTT, Glenn

Singles: 7-inch

RUBY (200 "Katy Bar the Door") 25-35 57
SHERMAN (930 "The Show Must Go On") 15-25

SCOTT, Greg, & Embers

Singles: 7-inch

DELOSS (101 "Cheryl") 75-125 '60s
RIVERA (4911 "Movin', Twistin' Around") 25-35 '60s
SOMA (1162 "When I Say Goodbye") 200-300 '60s
Also see SCOTT, Mumbles, & Esquires

SCOTT, Jack — *P&R/R&B '58*

(With the Chantones)

Singles: 78 rpm

ABC-PAR 50-100 57
SPARTON 50-100 57

Singles: 7-inch

ABC (10843 "Before the Bird Flies") 5-10 66
ABC-PAR (9818 "Baby, She's Gone") 50-100 57
(Black label.)
ABC-PAR (9818 "Baby, She's Gone") 50-75 57
(White label. Promotional issue only.)
ABC-PAR (9860 "Two Timin' Woman") 50-100 57
(Black label.)
ABC-PAR (9860 "Two Timin' Woman") 50-75 57
(White label. Promotional issue only.)
CAPITOL (4554 "A Little Feeling") 15-25 61
CAPITOL (4597 "My Dream Come True") 10-20 61
CAPITOL (4637 "Steps 1 & 2") 10-20 61
CAPITOL (4689 "Cry, Cry, Cry") 10-20 62
CAPITOL (4738 "The Part Where I Cry") 8-12 62
CAPITOL (4796 "I Can't Hold Your Letters") 8-12 62
CAPITOL (4855 "If Only") 8-12 62
CAPITOL (4903 "Laugh and the World Laughs with You") 8-12 63
CAPITOL (4955 "All I See Is Blue") 8-12 63
CAPITOL (6077 "What in the World's Come over You") 4-8 65
(Starline Series.)
CARLTON (462 "My True Love") 10-15 58
CARLTON (483 "With Your Love") 10-15 58
CARLTON (493 "Goodbye Baby") 10-15 58
CARLTON (504 "I Never Felt Like This Before") 10-15 59
(Beige label.)
CARLTON (504 "I Never Felt Like This Before") 20-30 59
(Red label. Promotional issue only.)
CARLTON (514 "The Way I Walk") 10-15 59
CARLTON (519 "There Comes a Time") 10-20 59
(Monaural.)
CARLTON (ST-519 "There Comes a Time") 30-50 59
(Stereo.)
COLLECTABLES 3-5 '80s
CURB (76820 "Cooper, Cagney & Gable") 3-5 90
DOT 4-6 73
ERIC 4-6 '70s
GRT (35 "Billy Jack") 4-8 70
GROOVE (0027 "There's Trouble Brewin' ") 10-15 63
GROOVE (0031 "I Knew You First") 5-10 64
GROOVE (0037 "Wiggle on Out") 10-15 64
GROOVE (0042 "Thou Shalt Not Steal") 10-15 64
GROOVE (0049 "Flakey John") 10-15 64
GUARANTEED (209 "What Am I Living For") 10-20 60
GUARANTEED (211 "Go Wild Little Sadie") 15-25 60
GUSTO (810 "Burning Bridges") 4-6 79
JUBILEE (5606 "My Special Angel") 5-10 67
PONIE (563 "Apple Blossom Time") 4-6
PONIE (6083-20 "Country Witch") 4-6 '70s
RCA (8505 "I Don't Believe in Tea Leaves") 8-12 65
RCA (8685 "Looking for Linda") 8-12 65
RCA (8724 "Don't Hush the Laughter") 8-12 65
SPARTON (438 "Baby, She's Gone") 75-100 57
(Canadian.)
SPARTON (509 "Two Timin' Woman") 75-100 57
(Canadian.)
TOP RANK (2028 "What in the World's Come Over You") 15-25 59
TOP RANK (2041 "Burning Bridges") 15-25 60
(Monaural.)
TOP RANK (2041 "Burning Bridges") 35-55 60
(Stereo.)
TOP RANK (2055 "It Only Happened Yesterday") 15-25 60
TOP RANK (2075 "Patsy") 15-25 60
TOP RANK (2093 "Is There Something on Your Mind") 15-25 60

Picture Sleeves

CAPITOL (4554 "A Little Feeling") 25-35 61
CAPITOL (4597 "My Dream Come True") 25-35 61
CAPITOL (4637 "Steps 1 & 2") 25-35 61
CAPITOL (4689 "Cry Cry Cry") 25-35 62
CAPITOL (4738 "The Part Where I Cry") 25-35 62
CARLTON (483 "With Your Love") 25-35 58
CARLTON (493 "Goodbye Baby") 25-35 58
TOP RANK (2041 "Burning Bridges") 25-35 60
TOP RANK (2093 "Is There Something on Your Mind") 25-35 60

EPs: 7-inch

CARLTON (1070 "Jack Scott") 50-100 58
CARLTON (1071 "Presenting Jack Scott") 50-100 58
CARLTON (1072 "Jack Scott Sings") 50-100 59
TOP RANK (1001 "Jack Scott") 50-100 60

LPs: 10/12-inch

CAPITOL (2035 "Burning Bridges") 100-150 64
CAPITOL (8-2035 "Burning Bridges") 100-150 64
(Capitol Record Club issue.)
CARLTON (LP-107 "Jack Scott") 100-200 58
(Monaural.)
CARLTON (STLP-12 107 "Jack Scott") 150-250 58
(Stereo.)
CARLTON (LP-122 "What Am I Living For") 100-200 60
(Monaural.)
CARLTON (STLP-12 122 "What Am I Living For") 200-300 60
(Stereo.)
JADE 10-15
PONIE 8-10 74-77
SESAC (4201 "Soul Stirring") 75-100 59
TOP RANK (348 "The Spirit Moves Me") 75-125 60
TOP RANK (319 "I Remember Hank Williams") 75-125 60
(Monaural.)
TOP RANK (619 "I Remember Hank Williams") 100-150 60
(Stereo.)
TOP RANK (326 "What in the World's Come Over You") 100-150 61
(Monaural.)
TOP RANK (626 "What in the World's Come Over You") 150-200 61
(Stereo.)
Also see CHANTONES

SCOTT, Jay & Tommy

Singles: 7-inch

FIDELITY (4060 "Angela") 15-25 63

SCOTT, Jim, & Crusaders

Singles: 7-inch

7 TEEN (17-101 "Betty") 40-50 63

SCOTT, Jimmy

(Little Jimmy Scott)

Singles: 78 rpm

CORAL 5-10 52
KING 5-10 57
ROOST 5-10 50-51
SAVOY 5-10 55

Singles: 7-inch

ANTONIO 8-12
BRUNSWICK (84000 "Something of a Fool") 10-20 52
CORAL (60650 "Wheel of Fortune") 10-20 52
CORAL (60668 "They Saw You Cry") 10-20 52
CORAL (60825 "You Never Miss the Water") 10-20 52
EARWAX (776 "Love Language") 4-6
EASTBOUND 8-12
GIANT (706 "Do You Get the Message") 5-10 68
KING (5086 "When Day Is Done") 15-25 57
KING (5104 "Home") 15-25 58
KING (5150 "Somehow") 10-15 58
KING (5168 "Please") 10-15 58
KING (5201 "I'm Falling for You") 10-15 59
KING (5834 "Somewhere Down the Line") 5-10 64
ROYAL ROOST (603 "Why Do You Cry") 10-20 55
ROYAL ROOST (613 "It's the Talk of the Town") 10-20 55
SAVOY (1100 series) 10-20 55-56
SAVOY (1593 "My Romance") 8-12 61
SHARP (100 "I'm Afraid the Masquerade Is Over") 10-20 60
SHARP (109 "An Evening in Paradise") 10-20 60

LPs: 10/12-inch

SAVOY (1100 series) 5-10
SAVOY (12027 "Very Truly Yours") 50-75 55
SAVOY (12150 "Fabulous Songs") 25-40 61
SAVOY (12300 "Soul of Little Jimmy Scott") 10-20 69
SAVOY (14003 "If You Only Knew") 20-30 58
TANGERINE (1501 "Falling in Love Is Wonderful") 15-20 63

SCOTT, Joan

Singles: 78 rpm

IMPERIAL 30-40 54

Singles: 7-inch

IMPERIAL (5328 "My Wedding Day") 75-125 54

SCOTT, Joel

Singles: 7-inch

PHILLES (101 "Here I Stand") 20-30 62

SCOTT, Lee, & Windsors

Singles: 7-inch

BACK BEAT (506 "My Gloria") 4000-5000 58
(Possibly on promo only. Commercial copies not yet known to exist. Colored vinyl pressings are counterfeits.)

SCOTT, Linda — *P&R/R&B '61*

Singles: 7-inch

CANADIAN AMERICAN 10-20 61-62
CONGRESS 8-15 62-64
ERIC 4-6 '70s
KAPP 5-10 64-66
RCA 5-8 68

Picture Sleeves

CANADIAN AMERICAN (123 "I've Told Every Little Star") 5-10 '90s

EPs: 7-inch

CONGRESS (1005 "Starlight Starbright") 25-35 62
CONGRESS (3001 "Linda Scott") 25-35 62
(Promotional issue only. Issued with picture insert, but not with cover.)

LPs: 10/12-inch

CANADIAN AMERICAN (CALP-1005 "Starlight Starbright") 35-55 61
(Monaural.)
CANADIAN AMERICAN (SCALP-1005 "Starlight Starbright") 50-75 61
(Stereo.)
CANADIAN AMERICAN (CALP-1007 "Great Scott") 35-45 62
(Monaural.)
CANADIAN AMERICAN (SCALP-1007 "Great Scott") 40-50 62
(Stereo.)
CONGRESS (3001 "Linda") 25-35 62
KAPP (3424 "Hey Look at Me Now") 25-35 65
Also see SANTO & JOHNNY / Linda Scott

SCOTT, Lizabeth

LPs: 10/12-inch

VIK (1130 "Lizabeth") 30-40 57

SCOTT, Mabel — *R&B '48*

Singles: 78 rpm

BRUNSWICK 5-10 52
CORAL 5-10 51-52
EXCELSIOR 8-12 47-48
EXCLUSIVE 8-12 48
FESTIVAL 5-10 55
HOLLYWOOD 5-10 54
HUB 10-15 46
KING 5-10 50-51
PARROT 15-25 53-54

Singles: 7-inch

BRUNSWICK (84001 "Wailin' Daddy") 15-25 52
CORAL 15-25 51-52
FESTIVAL 15-25 55
HOLLYWOOD (1023 "Boogie Woogie Santa Claus") 15-25 54
PARROT (780 "Mr. Fine") 25-50 53
(Black vinyl.)
PARROT (780 "Mr. Fine") 100-150 53
(Colored vinyl.)
PARROT (794 "Fool Burro") 25-50 54
Also see BROWN, Charles

SCOTT, Mumbles, & Esquires

Singles: 7-inch

APPLAUSE (1005 "Searchin") 40-60 64
Also see SCOTT, Greg, & Embers

SCOTT, Neil — *P&R '61*

(With the Concords; Neal Scott; Neil Bogart)

Singles: 7-inch

CAMEO (476 "Let Me Think It Over") 5-10 67
COMET (2151 "Tomboy") 10-15 62
HERALD (581 "One Piece Bathing Suit") 15-25 63
PORTRAIT (102 "Bobby") 10-15 61
PORTRAIT (106 "It Happened All Over Again") 10-15 62
Also see CONCORDS

SCOTT, Ray

(With the Demens; with Scottsmen)

Singles: 7-inch

ANTLER (1104 "Let's Be Friends") 30-40 59
DECCA (32068 "Right Now") 10-20 66
ERWIN (507 "Train's Done Gone") 50-75
ERWIN (700 "Boppin' Wigwam Willie") 200-300 57
GOLDBAND (1222 "I'm Your Boogie Man") 8-12 62
RAN DEE (102 "Joy") 8-12 62
SATELLITE (104 "You Drive Me Crazy") 1000-1500 59
STOMPER TIME (1161 "Boy Meets Girl") 50-75 61
TRIESS (1001 "We Need Love") 15-25 60

SCOTT, Ricky

Singles: 7-inch

CUB (9079 "Darling, Darlin' ") 10-15 60
X-CLUSIVE (1001 "Darling, Darlin' ") 40-50 60
(First issue.)

SCOTT, Rodney

Singles: 7-inch

CANON (225 "Granny Went Rockin' ") 200-300 61

CANON (231 "You're So Square") 100-150 61
MR. PEEKE (119 "You're So Square") 50-75 62
MR. PEEKE (126 "That's The Way It Goes") 15-25 63

SCOTT, Roy
Singles: 7-inch
TRIBUTE (218 "Beautiful Girl") 8-12 64
EPs: 7-inch
ESSGEE (663 "Roy Scott") 50-100

SCOTT, Sandy
Singles: 7-inch
CHOICE (5605 "Mister Big") 50-75 57
CHOICE (5606 "Shake It Up") 50-75 57

SCOTT, Seaphus, & Five Masqueraders
(With the Billy Gale Orchestra)
Singles: 7-inch
JOYCE (303 "Summer Sunrise") 400-500 58

SCOTT, Sherree
(With Her Melody Rockers & Thompson Sisters)
Singles: 7-inch
ROBBINS (101 "Whole Lotta Shakin' Going On") 40-60 59
ROBBINS (105 "Twinkle Toes") 10-15 59
ROCKET (1036 "Fascinating Baby") ... 300-400 59
(With photo insert.)
ROCKET (1036 "Fascinating Baby") ... 100-150 59
(Without photo insert.)
SHERREE HEART (1479 "Easy Payments") 75-125
Picture Sleeves
ROBBINS (101 "Whole Lotta Shakin' Going On") 50-75 59

SCOTT, Shirley
(Shirley Scott Trio; with Soul Saxes; with Clark Terry)
Singles: 7-inch
ATLANTIC (2699 "It's Your Thing") 5-10 69
IMPULSE 5-10 66-67
PRESTIGE 5-15 58-67
LPs: 10/12-inch
ATLANTIC (1515 "Soul Song") 10-15 69
ATLANTIC (1532 "Shirley Scott and the Soul Saxes") 10-15 69
IMPULSE (51 "For Members Only") 20-30 63
IMPULSE (67 "Great Scott") 20-30 64
IMPULSE (93 "Latin Shadows") 10-20 66
IMPULSE (9109 "On a Clear Day") 10-20 66
IMPULSE (9119 "Roll 'Em") 10-20 66
IMPULSE (9133 "Soul Duo") 10-20 67
IMPULSE (9141 "Girl Talk") 10-20 67
MOODSVILLE (5 "Shirley Scott Trio") 30-50 60
MOODSVILLE (19 "Like Cozy") 30-50 60
PRESTIGE (7143 "Great Scott") 30-50 58
(Yellow label.)
PRESTIGE (7155 "Scottie") 30-50 59
(Yellow label.)
PRESTIGE (7163 "Shirley Scott Plays the Duke") 30-50 59
(Yellow label.)
PRESTIGE (7173 "Soul Searching") 30-50 59
(Yellow label.)
PRESTIGE (7182 "Mucho Mucho") 30-50 60
(Yellow label.)
PRESTIGE (7205 "Hip Soul") 30-50 61
(Yellow label.)
PRESTIGE (7205 "Hip Soul") 15-25 65
(Blue label.)
PRESTIGE (7240 "Shirley Scott Plays Horace Silver") 30-40 61
(Yellow label.)
PRESTIGE (7262 "Happy Talk") 30-40 62
(Yellow label.)
PRESTIGE (7283 "Satin Doll") 30-40 63
(Yellow label.)
PRESTIGE (7305 "Drag 'Em Out") 30-40 64
(Yellow label.)
PRESTIGE (7328 "Travelin' Light") 25-35 65
PRESTIGE (7376 "Blue Seven") 10-20 66
PRESTIGE (7392 "Soul Sister") 10-20 67
PRESTIGE (7424 "Workin' ") 10-20 67
PRESTIGE (7440 "Now's the Time") 10-20 68
Members (Trio): Shirley Scott; George Duvivier; Arthur Edgehill. Session: King Curtis; Hank Crawford; David "Fathead" Newman.
Also see CRAWFORD, Hank
Also see KING CURTIS
Also see NEWMAN, David "Fathead"
Also see TERRY, Clark

SCOTT, Shirley, / Stanley Turrentine
Singles: 7-inch
PRESTIGE (210 "Hip Twist") 5-10 62
LPs: 10/12-inch
IMPULSE (73 "Everybody Loves a Lover") 25-35 65
IMPULSE (81 "Queen of the Organ") 25-35 65
PRESTIGE (7226 "Hip Twist") 30-50 61
(Yellow label.)
PRESTIGE (7226 "Hip Twist") 15-25 65
(Blue label.)
PRESTIGE (7267 "The Soul Is Willing") ... 30-40 62
(Yellow label.)
PRESTIGE (7267 "The Soul Is Willing") ... 15-25 65
(Blue label.)
PRESTIGE (7312 "Soul Shoutin' ") 30-40 64
(Yellow label.)
PRESTIGE (7312 "Soul Shoutin' ") 15-25 65
(Blue label.)
PRESTIGE (7338 "Blue Flames") 30-40 65
PRESTIGE (7707 "The Best of Shirley Scott / Stanley Turrentine") 5-10 69
Also see SCOTT, Shirley
Also see TURRENTINE, Stanley

SCOTT, Tom
Singles: 7-inch
HEP (2140 "Record Hop") 200-300 58

SCOTT, Tommy
(Ramblin' Tommy Scott)
Singles: 78 rpm
FEDERAL (Except 10003) 10-15 51
FEDERAL (10003 "Rockin' & Rollin' ") 30-50 51
KING 15-25 52
Singles: 7-inch
FEDERAL (10003 "Rockin' & Rollin' ") ... 75-100 51
FEDERAL (10011 "Tennessee") 30-50 51
FEDERAL (10026 "Everything Reminds Me of You") 30-50 51
FEDERAL (10030 "It's You") 30-50 51
KATONA (1167 "Love Sick & Lonesome") 75-125
KATONA (1270 "Thibodaux") 50-75
KING (1129 "What Do You Know") 50-75 52

SCOTT, Walt
Singles: 7-inch
RUBY (100 "A Little Love") 15-25 57
RUBY (160 "Mother and Dad") 15-25 57
RUBY (240 "One Life to Live") 50-75 57

SCOTT, Walter
(With the Kapers)
Singles: 7-inch
EAGLE (1003 "On the Way Out") 15-25 58
IVANHOE (5018 "I Want to Thank You") .. 10-15 65
MUSICLAND USA 5-15 66-67
PZAZZ (026 "Soul Stew Recipe") 5-10 69
VANESSA 4-6 74
WHITE WHALE (259 "Silly Girl") 10-20 67
LPs: 10/12-inch
MUSICLAND USA 15-25 67
WHITE WHALE 15-20 70
Also see KUBAN, Bob

SCOTTIE, Lue & Don
Singles: 7-inch
CORNER (7232 "Beyond Those City Lights") 15-25 59
(Identification number shown since no selection number is used.)

SCOTTIES
Singles: 7-inch
SCOTTIE (1305 "Let Me Love You Tonight") 25-35 59

SCREAMERS
("Vocal, Dan and Jer")
Singles: 7-inch
KAY BANK (1519 "I Dig") 100-200
Members: Bob Dawdy; Danny Matousek; Jerry De Mers; Don Bourret.
Also see VELAIRES

SCREAMING GYPSY BANDITS
LPs: 10/12-inch
BRBQ (004 "The Dancer Inside You") 25-35 74
BRBQ (22185 "In the Eye") 40-50 73
Members: Tina Lane; Mark Bingham; Bruce Anderson; Bob Lucas.

SCUDERI, Ron
Singles: 7-inch
KIMLEY (924 "Swanee River Shake") .. 100-200

SCURVY KNAVES
Singles: 7-inch
TWELVE HANDS ("Gypsy Baby") 15-25 66
(Selection number not known.)

SEA SHELLS
Singles: 7-inch
GOLIATH (1357 "Love Those Beach Boys") 20-30 64
JUBILEE (5587 "Hit the Surf") 10-15 67
VILLAGE (1000 "Quiet Home") 40-60

SEABURY, Levi
Singles: 7-inch
BLUES BOYS KINGDOM (101 "Boogie Beat") 100-125 57

SEAFOOD MAMA
(Quarterflash)
Singles: 7-inch
WHITEFIRE (808-24 "Harden My Heart") 15-25 80
(Identification number shown since no selection number is used.)
Picture Sleeves
WHITEFIRE ("Harden My Heart") 30-40 80

SEALS, Jimmy
Singles: 7-inch
CARLTON (470 "Sneaky Pete") 50-100 58
CHALLENGE (9153 "Runaway Heart") .. 50-100 62
CHALLENGE (9200 "Lady Heartbreak") 50-100 64
CHALLENGE (59270 "Everybody's Doin' the Jerk") 50-100 64
CHALLENGE (59299 "She's Not a Bad Girl") 100-150 65
Also see SEALS & CROFTS
Also see UNCLE SOUND

SEALS, Wayland
Singles: 7-inch
WINSTON (1016 "When I'm Gone") 100-200 57

SEALS & CROFTS
LP '70
Singles: 7-inch
T.A. 4-8 69-71
W.B. 3-6 71-80
Picture Sleeves
W.B. (8190 "Get Closer") 4-8 76
W.B. (8405 "My Fair Share") 4-8 77
LPs: 10/12-inch
T.A. 20-25 69-70
W.B. (Except 2809) 6-12 71-80
W.B. (2809 "Seals & Crofts I & II") 10-15 74
Members: Jimmy Seals; Dash Crofts. Session: Louie Shelton; Jack Lenz; Ed Green; Wilton Felder; Jim Horn; Carolyn Willis.
Also see CHAMPS
Also see SEALS, Jimmy

SEARCH
Singles: 7-inch
ERA (3181 "Everybody's Searchin' ") 5-10 67
IN-SOUND (404 "Climate") 25-30 67

SEARCH PARTY
LPs: 10/12-inch
("Montgomery's Chapel") 1500-2500 69
(Approximately a dozen made. No label name or selection number used.)

SEARCHERS
(With the Kayos)
Singles: 7-inch
MAC (351 Yvonne") 400-500 61
Also see PETS / Searchers

SEARCHERS
P&R/LP '64
Singles: 7-inch
ERIC 3-5
KAPP 10-15 64-67
LIBERTY (55646 "Sugar & Spice") 15-25 63
LIBERTY (55689 "Sugar & Spice") 10-15 64
MERCURY (72172 "Sweets for My Sweet") 5-10 63
RCA 4-6 71-72
SIRE 3-5 80-81
SOUND CLASSICS 3-5
Picture Sleeves
KAPP (577 "Needles and Pins"/"Saturday Night Out") 15-20 64
KAPP (577 "Needles and Pins"/"Ain't That Just Like Me") 50-100 64
(Black and white "Special Rush Release!" sleeve. Promotional issue only.)
KAPP (577 "Needles and Pins"/"Ain't That Just Like Me") 20-30 64
(Red and white.)
KAPP (609 "Some Day We're Gonna Love Again") 15-20 64
LPs: 10/12-inch
KAPP 20-30 64-66
MERCURY (20914 "Hear! Hear!") 25-35 64
(Monaural. Red label.)
MERCURY (20914 "Hear! Hear!") 40-60 64
(White label. Promotional issue only.)
MERCURY (60914 "Hear! Hear!") 25-35 64
(Stereo. Red label.)
MERCURY (60914 "Hear! Hear!") 40-60 64
(White label. Promotional issue only.)
PYE 10-12 76
RHINO 5-8 85
SIRE 8-10 80-81

SEARCHERS / Rattles
LPs: 10/12-inch
MERCURY (20994 "The Searchers Meet the Rattles") 35-45 65
(Monaural. Red label.)
MERCURY (20994 "The Searchers Meet the Rattles") 50-75 65
(White label. Promotional issue only.)
MERCURY (60994 "The Searchers Meet the Rattles") 35-45 65
(Stereo. Red label.)
MERCURY (60994 "The Searchers Meet the Rattles") 50-75 65
(White label. Promotional issue only.)
Also see RATTLES
Also see SEARCHERS

SEARS, Al
(With His Rock 'N' Rollers; with Herb Cooper; Big Al Sears; Al Sears Orchestra)
Singles: 78 rpm
CORAL 10-15 55
GROOVE 10-15 56
HERALD 10-20 54
JUBILEE 10-15 57-58
KING 10-15 51
RCA 10-15 52
Singles: 7-inch
BLUE FLAME ("Montreal Express") 40-60
(Selection number not known.)
CORAL (61427 "Come Dance with Me") .. 10-20 55
CORAL (61558 "Come a Runnin' ") 10-20 55
DERRICK (501 "Castle-Rock") 10-20 61
GATOR 10-20 61
GROOVE (0151 "Love Call") 10-20 56
GROOVE (0166 "Here's the Beat") 10-20 56
HERALD (448 "Tweedle Dee") 15-25 55
JUBILEE (5293 "Fascination") 10-20 57
JUBILEE (5303 "So Glad") 10-20 57
JUBILEE (5327 "Peacock Strut") 10-20 58
KING (4489 "Baltimore Bounce") 10-20 51
KING (4499 "Groove Station") 10-20 51
KING (4520 "Very Well") 10-20 52
PRESTIGE (192 "Record Hop") 10-15 61
RCA (5131 "Huffin' and Puffin' ") 15-25 52
RCA (5272 "Easy Ernie") 15-25 52
Picture Sleeves
BLUE FLAME ("Montreal Express") 60-80
EPs: 7-inch
KING (270 "Al Sears' All Stars, Vol. 1") 20-40 54
KING (271 "Al Sears' All Stars, Vol. 2") 20-40 54
Also see COOPER, Herb
Also see DUNGAREE DARLINGS
Also see DUNGAREE DOLLS

SEARS, Kelly
Singles: 7-inch
QUINTET (104 "Barnyard Rock") 100-200

SEATON, Dick, & Mad Lads
Singles: 7-inch
K-ARK (302 "Juke Box Rock") 400-600

SEBASTIAN

Singles: 7-inch

BROWN DOG (9008 "Wasted Days and Wasted Nights") 4-6 75
COLT (302 "The Best Man Cried") 10-15 63
DECCA (32655 "Elaine") 5-10 70
MR. MAESTRO (801 "Darling I Do") 30-40 59
(First issue.)
TAKE 3 (2002 "Darling I Do") 15-25 59

LPs: 10/12-inch

MCA 10-15 70

SEBASTIAN, Joel

Singles: 7-inch

MIRACLE (9 "Blue Cinderella") 30-50 61

SEBASTIAN, John — *P&R '69*

Singles: 7-inch

KAMA SUTRA 4-6 68-70
MGM 4-6 68-70
REPRISE 4-6 70-77

Picture Sleeves

KAMA SUTRA 4-8 69

LPs: 10/12-inch

KAMA SUTRA 10-15 70
MGM 10-15 69-70
REPRISE 8-12 70-76
Also see LOVIN' SPOONFUL
Also see MUGWUMPS

SECOND SUMMERS

Singles: 7-inch

CONN (202,079 "Sad Vibrations") 25-35 68

SECRETS

Singles: 7-inch

DECCA (30350 "See You Next Year") 10-20 57
(Previously issued as by the Five Secrets.)
Also see FIVE SECRETS
Also see LOUNGERS

SECRETS

Singles: 7-inch

SWAN (4097 "Twin Exhaust") 10-15 62

SECRETS — *P&R '63*

Singles: 7-inch

DCP (1139 "Shy Guy") 8-12 65
OMEN (15 "Here I Am") 8-12 66
PHILIPS (40146 "The Boy Next Door") 10-15 63
PHILIPS (40173 "Hey Big Boy") 8-12 63
PHILIPS (40196 "Here He Comes Now") ...8-12 64
PHILIPS (40222 "He's the Boy") 8-12 64

Picture Sleeves

PHILIPS (40173 "Hey Big Boy") 10-20 64
Members: Jackie Allen; Pat Miller; Karen Gray; Carol Raymont.

SECRETS

Singles: 7-inch

RAYNARD (10047 "I Don't Know") 10-20 66
Members: Larry Fenlon; Pat Noel; Bob Pitton; Tom Bertrand; Dave Krieger.

SECTION 5

Singles: 7-inch

AUDIO DYNAMICS (105 "Pusher's Route") 15-25 67

SEDAKA, Neil — *P&R '58*

(With the Marvels; with Cookies)

Singles: 12-inch

CURB 4-8
ELEKTRA ....4-8 '70s

Singles: 7-inch

CURB 3-5
DECCA (30520 "Laura Lee") 50-75 57
(We have yet to confirm U.S. 78 rpms of this, or any of Neil's singles, though they may exist – especially the Decca and first RCAs.)
ELEKTRA 3-6 77-80
GUYDEN (2004 "Ring-a-Rockin' ") 40-60 58
KIRSHNER 4-6 71-72
LEGION (133 "Ring-a-Rockin' ") 50-75 58
MCA 3-6 75-84
MGM 4-6 73
RCA (96 "Special DJ Spots") 25-50 60
(Promotional issue only.)
RCA (7408 "The Diary") 15-25 58
(Black label.)
RCA (7408 "The Diary") 30-40 58
(White, photo label. Promotional issue only.)
RCA (7473 "I Go Ape") 35-45 59
RCA (7530 "Crying My Heart Out for You") 15-25 59
RCA (47-7595 "Oh Carol") 10-20 59
(Monaural.)
RCA (61-7595 "Oh Carol") 35-50 59
(Stereo.)
RCA (47-7709 "Stairway to Heaven") 10-20 60
(Monaural.)
RCA (61-7709 "Stairway to Heaven") 35-50 60
(Stereo.)
RCA (47-7781 "Run Sampson Run") 10-20 60
(Monaural.)
RCA (61-7781 "Run Sampson Run") 25-50 60
(Stereo.)
RCA (37-7829 "Calendar Girl") 25-50 60
(Compact 33 Single.)
RCA (47-7829 "Calendar Girl") 10-15 60
(Monaural.)
RCA (61-7829 "Calendar Girl") 25-50 60
(Stereo.)
RCA (37-7874 "Little Devil") 25-50 61
(Compact 33 Single.)
RCA (47-7874 "Little Devil") 10-15 61
RCA (37-7922 "Sweet Little You") 15-25 61
(Compact 33 Single.)
RCA (47-7922 "Sweet Little You") 10-15 61
RCA (37-7957 "Happy Birthday Sweet Sixteen") 25-50 61
(Compact 33 Single.)
RCA (47-7957 "Happy Birthday Sweet Sixteen") 10-15 61
RCA (37-8007 "King of Clowns") 25-50 62
(Compact 33 Single.)
RCA (47-8007 "King of Clowns") 10-15 62
RCA (37-8007 "King of Clowns") 25-50 62
(Compact 33 Single.)
RCA (8046 "Breaking Up Is Hard to Do") .10-15 62
RCA (8086 "Next Door to an Angel") 10-15 62
RCA (8137 "Alice in Wonderland") 10-15 63
RCA (8169 "Let's Go Steady Again") 10-15 63
RCA (8209 "The Dreamer") 10-15 63
RCA (8254 "Bad Girl") 10-15 63
RCA (8341 "The Closest Thing to Heaven") 10-15 64
RCA (8382 "Sunny") 10-15 64
RCA (8453 "I Hope He Breaks Your Heart") 10-15 64
RCA (8511 "Let the People Talk") 10-15 65
RCA (8637 "The World Through a Tear") .10-15 65
RCA (8737 "The Answer to My Prayer") ..10-15 66
RCA (8844 "Grown-Up Games") 10-15 66
RCA (9004 "We Can Make It if We Try) ...10-15 66
RCA GOLD STANDARD 3-8 62-89
RSO 4-6
ROCKET 4-6 74-76
S.G.C. 5-8 68-69

Picture Sleeves

RCA (7781 "Run Sampson Run") 10-20 60
RCA (7829 "Calendar Girl") 10-20 60
RCA (7874 "Little Devil") 10-20 61
RCA (8007 "King of Clowns") 10-20 62
RCA (8046 "Breaking Up Is Hard to Do") 10-15 62
RCA (8086 "Next Door to an Angel") 10-15 62
RCA (8137 "Alice in Wonderland") 10-15 63
RCA (8169 "Let's Go Steady Again") 10-15 63
RCA (8209 "The Dreamer") 10-15 63
RCA (8511 "Let the People Talk") 10-15 65
RCA (8637 "The World Through a Tear") .10-15 65

EPs: 7-inch

RCA (105 "Neil's Best") 30-50 61
(Compact 33 Double.)
RCA (135 "Little Devil") 30-50 61
(Compact 33 Double.)
RCA (4334 "I Go Ape") 30-50 59
RCA (4353 "Oh Carol") 30-50 59

LPs: 10/12-inch

ACCORD (7152 "Singer, Songwriter, Melody Maker") 5-10 81
CAMDEN (7006 "Breaking Up Is Hard to Do") ....8-12 '60s
CROWN ....10-20 '60s
CURB 5-10
ELEKTRA (102 "A Song") 8-10 77
ELEKTRA (161 "All You Need Is Music") ...8-10 78
ELEKTRA (348 "Neil Sedaka") 8-10 81
ELEKTRA (259 "In the Pocket") 8-10 80
51 WEST ....5-8 '80s
GUEST STAR ....10-20 '60s
INTERMEDIA 5-8 85
KIRSHNER (111 "Emergence") 10-15 71
KIRSHNER (117 "Solitaire") 10-15 72
MCA 5-10 84
ORBIT (17196 "Bravo!") 5-10 83
PICKWICK ....10-15 '70s
POLYDOR 5-10
RCA (0149 "Original Hits") 10-15 75
(Two discs. Mail order offer.)
RCA (0879 "Oh, Carol") 8-10 75
RCA (0928 "Greatest Hits") 8-10 75
RCA (1314 "Pure Gold") 8-10 76
RCA (1540 "Live in Australia") 8-10 76
RCA (1789 "Emergence") 8-10 76
RCA (1790 "Solitaire") 8-10 76
RCA (LPM-2035 "Neil Sedaka") 40-60 59
(Monaural.)
RCA (LSP-2035 "Neil Sedaka") 75-100 59
(Stereo.)
RCA (2254 "The '50s & '60s") 8-10 77
RCA (LPM-2317 "Circulate") 25-35 61
(Monaural.)
RCA (LSP-2317 "Circulate") 35-45 61
(Stereo.)
RCA (LPM-2421 "Little Devil") 25-35 61
(Monaural.)
RCA (LSP-2421 "Little Devil") 35-45 61
(Stereo.)
RCA (2524 "Many Sides") 8-10 78
RCA (LPM-2627 "Greatest Hits") 25-35 62
(Monaural.)
RCA (LSP-2627 "Greatest Hits") 35-45 62
(Stereo.)
RCA (3465 "Greatest Hits") 5-8 79
RCA (10181 "Smile") 15-20 66
ROCKET (463 "Sedaka's Back") 8-10 74
ROCKET (2157 "Hungry Years") 8-10 75
ROCKET (2195 "Steppin' Out") 8-10 76
ROCKET (2297 "Greatest Hits") 8-10 77
Session: King Curtis; Graham Gouldman; Lol Creme; Kevin Godley.
Also see ANKA, Paul / Sam Cooke / Neil Sedaka
Also see COOKE, Sam / Rod Lauren / Neil Sedaka / Browns
Also see COOKIES
Also see 4 SEASONS / Neil Sedaka / J Brothers / Johnny Rivers
Also see JOHN, Elton
Also see KING CURTIS
Also see SIMON, Paul
Also see 10CC
Also see WILLOWS

SEDAKA, Neil / Ann-Margret / Browns / Sam Cooke

EPs: 7-inch

RCA (33-149 "Headline Hits") 10-20 61
(Promotional issue, made for Nestlé's.)
Also see ANN-MARGRET
Also see BROWNS
Also see COOKE, Sam

SEDAKA, Neil & Dara — *P&R '80*

Singles: 7-inch

ELEKTRA 3-6 80
MCA 3-5 84

SEDAKA, Neil / Marvels

Singles: 7-inch

PYRAMID (623 "Oh Delilah"/"Neil's Twist") 15-20 62
Also see CATTIVA, Savina / Marvels

SEDAKA, Neil, & Tokens

LPs: 10/12-inch

GUEST STAR (1448 "Neil Sedaka and the Tokens") ....10-20 '60s
VERNON (518 "Neil Sedaka with the Tokens") ....10-20 '60s

SEDAKA, Neil, & Tokens / Coins

LPs: 10/12-inch

CROWN (366 "Neil Sedaka") 10-20 63

SEDAKA, Neil, & Tokens / Angels / Jimmy Gilmer & Fireballs

LPs: 10/12-inch

ALMOR (105 "Teen Bandstand") ....15-25 '60s
Also see ANGELS
Also see GILMER, Jimmy
Also see SEDAKA, Neil
Also see TOKENS

SEDATES

Singles: 7-inch

MRB (171 "Please Love Me Forever") 25-35 58
PORT (70004 "Please Love Me Forever") 10-20 58
TWENTIETH CENTURY (1212 "Please Love Me Forever") 10-15 61

SEDATES

Singles: 7-inch

TRANS ATLAS (692 "Girl of Mine") 400-500 62

SEDLAR, Jimmy

Singles: 7-inch

BIG M (1000 "Shorty's Got to Go") 25-50

EPs: 7-inch

RCA Victor (4075 "Teenagers Dance the Rockabilly") 50-75 57

SEEDS — *P&R '66*

(Featuring Sky Saxon)

Singles: 7-inch

GNP (354 "Can't Seem to Make You Mine"/"Daisy Mae") 10-15 65
GNP (354 "Can't Seem to Make You Mine"/"I Tell Myself") 5-10 67
GNP (364 "You're Pushing Too Hard"/"Out of the Question") 10-15 65
GNP (370 "The Other Place") 5-10 66
GNP (372 "Pushin' Too Hard"/"Try to Understand") 8-12 66
("Crescendo" in script at top.)
GNP (372 "Pushin' Too Hard"/"Try to Understand") 5-10 66
(GNP Crescendo logo in box at top.)
GNP (383 "Mr. Farmer") 5-10 67
GNP (394 "A Thousand Shadows") 5-10 67
GNP (398 "Six Dreams") 5-10 67
GNP (408 "Satisfy You") 5-10 68
GNP (422 "Fallin' Off the Edge of My Mind") 5-10 69
MGM (14163 "Bad Part of Town") 8-12 69
MGM (14190 "Love Is a Summer Basket") 8-12 70

Picture Sleeves

GNP (354 "Can't Seem to Make You Mine"/"I Tell Myself") 10-20 67
GNP (383 "Mr. Farmer") 10-20 67
GNP (394 "A Thousand Shadows") 10-20 67

LPs: 10/12-inch

GNP (2023 thru 2043) 20-30 66-67
(All Seeds LPs, except 2043, *Raw and Alive*, were reissued with original selection numbers. First issue, red label, 1960s LPs have the logo, "GNP/Crescendo," on a horizontal line. Reissues have the label name in a circular manner on the label.)
GNP (2100 series) 5-10 77
Also see SAXON, Sky

SEEDS OF EUPHORIA

Singles: 7-inch

TMP-TING (120 "Let's Send Batman to Viet Nam") 10-20 66

SEEGER, Pete — *LP '63*

(Peter Seeger & His Five String Banjo; with Ernst Busch)

Albums: 78 rpm

FOLKWAYS (3 "Darling Corey") 50-100 50

Singles: 7-inch

COLUMBIA 5-10 63-67
FOLKWAYS (202 "Skip to My Lou") 10-15 59
PIONEER (202 "Skip to My Lou") 8-12 60

LPs: 10/12-inch

ARAVEL 10-20 63-64
ARCHIVE OF FOLK MUSIC 10-15 65
BROADSIDE 10-20 63
CAPITOL 10-20 64-67
COLUMBIA 10-20 63-72
DISC 10-20 64
FOLKWAYS (3 "Darling Corey") 50-100 50
(10-inch LP.)
FOLKWAYS (Black vinyl) 10-25 59-75
FOLKWAYS (7610 "Animal Folk Songs") 25-35
(Colored vinyl.)
HARMONY 5-10 68-70
ODYSSEY 8-12 68
OLYMPIC 5-10 73
PHILIPS 10-20 63
STINSON (57 "Pete Seeger Concert") 20-30 54
(10-inch LP.)
STINSON (90 "Pete") 5-10 70
TRADITION 5-10 73
VANGUARD 6-12 78

VERVE FOLKWAYS....10-20 65
VOX....5-10 72
W.B....5-10 79
Also see ALMANAC SINGERS
Also see BROONZY, Big Bill, & Pete Seeger
Also see SEEGERS
Also see WEAVERS

SEEGER, Pete, & Arlo Guthrie *LP '75*
LPs: 10/12-inch
REPRISE....8-12 75
W.B. 5-10 81

SEEGER, Pete, with Pacific Gas & Electric
LPs: 10/12-inch
COLUMBIA (3540 "Tell Me That You Love Me, Junie Moon")....10-15 70
(Soundtrack.)
Also see PACIFIC GAS & ELECTRIC

SEEGERS
LPs: 10/12-inch
PRESTIGE (7375 "Folk Songs with the Seegers")....10-20 65
Members: Pete; Peggy; Mike; Barbara; Penny.
Also see SEEGER, Pete

SEEKERS *P&R/LP '65*
Singles: 7-inch
ATMOS (711 "Wild Rover")....5-10 65
CAPITOL....5-10 65-68
MARVEL (1060 "Chilly Winds")....5-10 65
Picture Sleeves
CAPITOL (5430 "A World of Our Own")....8-12 65
LPs: 10/12-inch
CAPITOL (100 series)....8-12 69
CAPITOL (2000 series)....10-20 65-67
CAPITOL (16000 series)....5-10 80
MARVEL (2060 "The Seekers")....15-20 65
Members: Judy Durham; Keith Potger.
Also see JAMES, Sonny / Seekers
Also see NEW SEEKERS

SEEKERS / Lou Rawls
Singles: 7-inch
CAPITOL (50 "Island of Dreams")....5-10 67
(Promotional issue, made for Frito-Lay.)
Picture Sleeves
CAPITOL (50 "Island of Dreams")....5-10 67
(Paper sleeve with die-cut hole. Promotional issue, made for Frito-Lay.)
Also see SEEKERS
Also see RAWLS, Lou

SEGER, Bob *P&R '68*
(With the Last Heard; with Silver Bullet Band; Bob Seger System)
Singles: 12-inch
CAPITOL (8433 "Travelin' Man")....10-15 75
(Promotional issue.)
CAPITOL (9085 "Old Time Rock & Roll")....8-10 83
(Promotional issue.)
Singles: 7-inch
ABKCO....4-6 72-75
CAMEO (438 "East Side Story")....15-25 66
CAMEO (444 "Sock It to Me Santa")....20-30 66
CAMEO (465 "Persecution Smith")....15-25 67
CAMEO (473 "Vagrant Winter")....15-25 67
CAMEO (494 "Heavy Music")....10-20 67
CAPITOL (2297 thru 3187)....5-10 68-71
CAPITOL (4116 thru 5658)....3-6 71-86
CAPITOL (57797 "Old Time Rock & Roll")....3-5 '90s
HIDEOUT (1013 "East Side Story")....25-50 66
HIDEOUT (1014 "Persecution Smith")....25-50 66
MCA (53094 "Shakedown")....3-5 87
PALLADIUM....4-6 71-74
REPRISE....4-6 72
Promotional Singles
CAPITOL (4653 "We've Got Tonight")....4-8 78
(Colored vinyl.)
CAPITOL (9878 "Shame on the Moon")....4-6 82
(Edited version [4:22], not the promo that runs 4:55.)
Picture Sleeves
CAPITOL (4653 thru 4904)....3-8 78-80
CAPITOL (4951 "Horizontal Bop")....30-50 80
CAPITOL (5042 thru 5623)....3-6 81-80
MCA (53094 "Shakedown")....3-5 87
LPs: 10/12-inch
CAPITOL (ST-172 "Ramblin' Gamblin' Man")....15-25 69
CAPITOL (SM-172 "Ramblin' Gamblin' Man")....8-10 75
CAPITOL (ST-236 "Noah")....50-70 69
CAPITOL (SKAO-499 "Mongrel")....15-25 70
CAPITOL (SM-499 "Mongrel")....8-10 75
CAPITOL (ST-731 "Brand New Morning")....30-50 71
CAPITOL (8433 "Live Bullet, Consensus Cuts")....20-30 75
(Promotional issue only.)
CAPITOL (11000 series, except 11557 & 11904)....6-12 75-78
CAPITOL (ST-11557 "Night Moves")....5-10 78
CAPITOL (ST-11557 "Night Moves")....25-35 78
(Picture disc. Promotional issue only. 800 made.)
CAPITOL (SW-11904 "Stranger in Town")....5-10 78
CAPITOL (SEAX-11904 "Stranger in Town")....15-20 79
(Picture disc.)
CAPITOL (12000 series)....6-10 80-86
CAPITOL (16000 series)....5-8 80
CAPITOL (30334 "Greatest Hits")....10-15 '90s
CAPITOL (91124 "Fire Inside")....8-10 91
INNER VIEW ("Demonstration Record: Bob Seger")....15-25 76
(Promotional issue only.)
MFSL (034 "Night Moves")....40-60 79
MFSL (127 "Against the Wind")....30-40 85
PALLADIUM (1006 "Smokin' O.P.'s")....15-25 72
PALLADIUM (2126 "Back in '72")....50-75 73
REPRISE....10-15 72-74
Members: Alto Reed; Robyn Robbins; Charlie Martin; Drew Abbott; Chris Campbell. Session: Glenn Frey; Don Henley; Timothy B. Schmit.
Also see BEACH BUMS
Also see BROWN, Doug
Also see NEWMAN, Randy
Also see ORMANDY

SEGURA, Allen
Singles: 7-inch
ROME (769 "My Suzie Q")....50-75

SEIDEL, Barry
Singles: 7-inch
BELINDA (102 "Wonders of Love")....15-25 62

SELAH JUBILEE QUARTETTE
(Selah Jubilee Singers)
Singles: 78 rpm
SAVOY (4069 "Gospel Train")....5-10 56
Singles: 7-inch
SAVOY (4069 "Gospel Train")....10-15 56
LPs: 10/12-inch
REMINGTON (1023 "Spirituals")....50-100 51
(10-inch LP.)
Also see LARKS
Also see MURPHY, Rose

SELBY, Dayton
(Dayton Selby Trio; with Wilene Barton)
Singles: 7-inch
ABC-PAR (10030 "Do a Little")....5-10 59
EPs: 7-inch
RCA Victor (4055 "Teenagers Dance the Tonky Honk")....20-30 57

SELECTIONS
(With the Electras)
Singles: 7-inch
ANTONE (101 "Guardian Angel")....250-350 58
MONA-LEE (129 "Guardian Angel")....30-40 58
Members: Ernie Karilikins; George; Butch; Jose.

SELENA *P&R '95*
Singles: 7-inch
EMI LATIN....3-5 95
FREDDIE (451 "No Puedo Estar Sin Ti")....50-100 79
(Reportedly 100 made.)
Members: Selena Quintanilla; Abraham Quintanilla; A.B. Quintanilla; Suzette Quintanilla; Rena Dearman; Rodney Pyeatt.

SELF, Alvie
Singles: 7-inch
ACCENT....3-5 81-86
DON RAY (5960 "Let's Go Wild")....75-125 60
FORD (1015 "Rain Dance")....50-75 60

SELF, G.
Singles: 7-inch
ACME (1290 "Roll On Big Mama")....200-300

SELF, Jimmy
Singles: 7-inch
CORAL (62009 "Oh Babe")....20-30 58

SELF, Mack
Singles: 7-inch
BLAKE....5-10 66
SABRE....4-6 76
SUN (273 "Easy to Love")....10-20 57
ZONE (1062 "Mexican Limbo")....15-25 62
ZONE (1085)....5-10 65
(Title not known.)

SELF, Mack, & Charlie Feathers
Singles: 7-inch
PHILLIPS INT'L (3548 "Mad at You")....10-15 59
Also see FEATHERS, Charlie
Also see SELF, Mac

SELF, Ronnie *P&R '58*
Singles: 78 rpm
ABC-PAR....25-50 56
COLUMBIA....25-50 57
Singles: 7-inch
ABC-PAR (9714 "Pretty Bad Blues")....75-100 56
ABC-PAR (9768 "Sweet Love")....50-75 56
AMY (11009 "High On Life")....5-10 68
COLUMBIA (40875 "Flame of Love")....30-50 57
COLUMBIA (40989 "Ain't I'm a Dog")....30-50 57
COLUMBIA (41101 "Bop-A-Lena")....30-50 58
COLUMBIA (41166 "Big Blon Baby")....30-50 58
COLUMBIA (41241 "Petrified")....75-125 58
DECCA (30958 "Big Town")....15-25 59
DECCA (31131 "I've Been There")....15-25 60
DECCA (31351 "Instant Man")....15-25 62
DECCA (31431 "Oh Me, Oh My")....15-25 62
KAPP (546 "Houdini")....8-12 63
EPs: 7-inch
COLUMBIA (2149 "Ain't I'm a Dog")....500-600 57

SELF, Stewart
(With the Gents)
Singles: 7-inch
ERMINE (46 "Mary Ellen")....10-15 63
ERMINE (49 "Lady Loneliness")....10-15 63
ERMINE (53 "Drivin' On")....10-15 64
STARRETT (5709 "Mary Ellen")....30-40 63
(First issue.)

SELLERS, Johnny
(Brother John Sellers; with King Kolax Orch.)
Singles: 78 rpm
CHANCE....25-50 52-53
CINCINNATI....15-25 45
DECCA....15-25 45
GOTHAM....15-25 48
KING....15-25 46-51
MIRACLE....15-25 47
RCA....15-25 47
SOUTHERN....15-25 45
Singles: 7-inch
CHANCE (1120 "Josie Jones")....100-150 52
CHANCE (1123 "Mighty Lonesome")....100-150 52
CHANCE (1138 "Mirror Blues")....100-150 53
(Black vinyl.)
CHANCE (1138 "Mirror Blues")....450-550 53
(Red vinyl.)
LPs: 10/12-inch
LONDON (1705 "In London")....35-50 57
MONITOR (335 "Baptist Shouts")....15-25 60
MONITOR (505 "Big Beat Up the River")....25-30 59
VANGUARD (7022 "Jack of Diamonds")....25-45 55
VANGUARD (8005 "Folk Songs and Blues")....25-45 54
VANGUARD (9036 "Blues and Folk Songs")....25-45 58
Session: Doc Bagby; Mickey Baker; Willie Dixon; Sonny Terry.
Also see BAGBY, Doc
Also see BAKER, Mickey
Also see DIXON, Willie
Also see TERRY, Sonny

SELPH, Jimmy
Singles: 7-inch
COIN (106 "Tom Cattin' Around")....25-35 57

SEMINOLES
(Featuring Joey Finaro)
Singles: 7-inch
CHECK MATE (1012 "I Can't Stand It")....50-75 62
GO-GEE (287 "Open Your Eyes")....50-75 61
HI-LITE (109 "Meant to Be")....50-75 60
HI-LITE (80043 "I Can't Stand It")....150-200
MID TOWN (101 "Forever")....50-75 65
(Previously issued as by the Embers.)
Also see EMBERS

SENA, Tommy
(With the Val-Monts)
Singles: 7-inch
ADORE (903 "I Can't Get Up")....15-25 61
VALMONT (904 "Let It Be Me")....40-60 61
VALMONT (905 "Onions")....20-30 62
(Reads "Valmont Records" at top.)
VALMONT (905 "Onions")....10-20 62
(Reads only "Valmont" at top.)

SENATOR BOBBY *P&R '67*
(Senator Bobby & Bobby Sockers)
Singles: 7-inch
RCA....10-20 67-68
Member: Bill Minkin.

SENATORS
Singles: 7-inch
ABNER (1031 "Julie")....75-125 59
GOLDEN CREST (514 "Poor Little Puppet")....250-300 58

SENATORS
(With John Dickerson & Orchestra)
Singles: 7-inch
BRISTOL (1916 "Scheming")....300-400 59
WINN (1917 "Wedding Bells")....150-250 62
(Artist credit handwritten – not printed – on label.)
WINN (1917 "Wedding Bells")....75-125 62
(Artist credit printed on label.)
Also see MARVELS

SENDERS
Singles: 7-inch
ENTRA (711 "Pretty Little Girl")....200-300 61
(Black label.)
ENTRA (711 "Pretty Little Girl")....20-30 61
(Red label.)
KENT (320 "I Dream of You")....30-40 59
KENT (324 "One More Kiss")....100-200 59
LEOPARD (201 "Party Line")....200-300

SENIORS
Singles: 7-inch
EXCELLO (2130 "Why Did You Leave Me")....25-35 58
LOST NITE....4-8
TETRA (4446 "Evening Shadows Falling")....150-200 56

SENIORS
Singles: 7-inch
DECCA (31112 "Hello Mr. Robin")....8-12 60
DECCA (31244 "When I Fall in Love")....8-12 61
KENT (342 "Pitter Patter Heart")....10-15 60
TAMPA (163 "It's Been a Long Time")....40-50 59

SENIORS
(With Daniel Monroe Orchestra)
Singles: 7-inch
E S V (1016 "Rock and Rolly")....10-20 60

SENNS, Charles
(Chuck Senns)
Singles: 7-inch
OJ (1013 "Gee Whiz Liz")....100-200 58
(Shown as by Chuck Senns.)
OJ (1014 "Gee Whiz Liz")....100-200 58

SENORS
Singles: 7-inch
SUE (756 "May I Have This Dance")....40-50 62
(Promotional issue only. Old style logo.)
SUE (756 "May I Have This Dance")....25-35 62
(Orange and black label.)

SENSATIONAL DELLOS
Singles: 7-inch
MIDA (106 "So Shy")....50-75 58
MIDA (109 "Lost Love")....50-75 58
Also see SHAW, John, & Dell-Os

SENSATIONAL MANHATTANS
Singles: 7-inch
YOUR (1988 "I Guess That's Love")....50-75

SENSATIONAL SLEEPERS
Singles: 7-inch
MAAD (32468 "Hey Girl")....25-35 68
Member: Dennis Morgan.

SENSATIONS *R&B '56*
(Yvonne Mills & Sensations; Yvonne Baker & Sensations)
Singles: 78 rpm
ATCO....15-25 55-56

Singles: 7-inch
ARGO (5391 "Music Music Music") 15-20 61
ARGO (5405 "Let Me In") 10-15 61
(Black label.)
ARGO (5405 "Let Me In") 5-10 61
(Brown label.)
ATCO (6056 "Yes Sir, That's My Baby") . 20-30 55
ATCO (6067 "Please Mr. Disc Jockey")... 20-30 56
ATCO (6075 "My Heart Cries for You") ... 20-30 56
ATCO (6083 "Such a Love")................... 20-30 57
ATCO (6090 "My Debut to Love")........... 20-30 57
ATCO (6115 "Romance in the Dark") 20-30 58
CHESS 4-6 73
JUNIOR (1002 "We Were Meant to Be"). 15-25 62
JUNIOR (1005 "You Made a Fool Out of Me") 10-20 63
JUNIOR (1006 "Baby") 15-25 63
JUNIOR (1010 "I Can't Change") 10-20 63
JUNIOR (1021 "We Were Meant to Be")....8-12 64
LOST NITE (255 "Let Me In") 10-15
(Red vinyl.)
TOLLIE (9009 "You Made a Fool of Me") 10-15 64
Picture Sleeves
TOLLIE (9009 "You Made a Fool of Me") 30-40 64
(Promotional issue only.)
LPs: 10/12-inch
ARGO (4022 "Let Me In") 150-250 63
Also see BAKER, Yvonne

SENSATIONS
Singles: 7-inch
RIVER (228 "The Price of Love") 25-35 62

SENSATIONS
Singles: 7-inch
DRAEGER (01 "Wild Cat 401") 10-20 63
Members: Ray Plauske; Harry Voss; Dave Villo; Jeff Gertanbach; Pete Ruffalo.

SENSATIONS
Singles: 7-inch
LA LOUISIANNE (805 "Bo-Time") 20-40

SENTIMENTAL REASONS
Singles: 7-inch
DEBRA (1008 "Let It Please Be You")..... 20-25 96
(Colored vinyl.)

SENTIMENTALISTS
(Four Tunes)
Singles: 78 rpm
MANOR (1049 "I'd Rather Be Safe Than Sorry") 20-30 46
MANOR (8002 "Silent Night")................... 20-30 46
MANOR (8003 "White Christmas") 20-30 46
Also see FOUR TUNES

SENTIMENTALS
Singles: 78 rpm
CHECKER... 10-20 57
Singles: 7-inch
CHECKER (875 "I Want to Love You").... 10-20 57
KNAP TOWN (0010 "I Know You Too Well")...5-10 70
MINT (801 "I Want to Love You") 40-50 57
(First issue.)
MINT (802 "Wedding Bells")..................... 50-75 57
(Has straight horizontal lines.)
MINT (802 "Wedding Bells")..................... 10-20 57
(Has waxy horizontal lines.)
MINT (803 "I'm Your Fool")...................... 30-40 58
MINT (805 "You're Mine")........................ 20-30 59
MINT (807 "I'll Miss These Things")......... 10-20 68
MINT (808 "I Want to Love You") 5-10 72
Also see CARTER, James
Also see YORK, Patti

SENTIMENTALS
Singles: 7-inch
CORAL (62100 "We Three") 15-25 59
CORAL (62172 "Two Different Worlds").. 15-25 60
VANITY (589 "Love Is a Gamble") 40-50 59

SENTINALS
(Sentinal Six; Sentinels)
Singles: 7-inch
ADMIRAL (900 "Roughshod") 15-25 61
DEL-FI (4197 "Big Surf")......................... 10-15 63
ERA (3082 "Latin'ia") 10-15 62
ERA (3097 "Latin Soul") 10-15 63
POINT (5100 "The Bee") 20-30 60
(Reissued as by Kenny Hinkle.)
POINT (5101 "Bony Maronie") 20-30 61
(Reissued as by Kenny Karter.)
WCEB (23 "Latin'ia")................................20-30 62
(First issue.)
WESTCO (12 "I've Been Blue") 10-20 63
WESTCO (14 "Tell Me")............................10-20 63
LPs: 10/12-inch
DEL-FI (DFLP-1232 "Big Surf")................40-60 63
(Monaural.)
DEL-FI (DFST-1232 "Big Surf") 50-75 63
(Stereo.)
DEL-FI (DLF-1232 "Big Surf") 10-12 98
("Thick, hard wax" reissue.)
DEL-FI (DFLP-1241 "Surfer Girl")............40-60 63
(Monaural.)
DEL-FI (DFST-1241 "Surfer Girl")............50-75 63
(Stereo.)
DEL-FI (DLF-1241 "Surfer Girl") 10-12 98
("Thick, hard wax" reissue.)
SUTTON (SU-338 "Vegas Go Go") 30-35 64
(Monaural.)
SUTTON (SSU-338 "Vegas Go Go")........35-40 64
(Stereo.)
Members: Norman Knowles; Tommy Nunes; Lee Michales; Kenny Hinkle; Johnny Barbata; Merrell Fankhauser.
Also see BARBATA, Johnny
Also see FANKHAUSER, Merrell
Also see HINKLE, Kenny
Also see KARTER, Kenny

SEOMPI
Singles: 7-inch
YIN YANG (101 "Summer's Comin' on Heavy") ....30-50 '60s

SEPIANAIRES
Singles: 78 rpm
SPINIT (0101 "All I Can Do Is Dream") 20-30 50

SEPTORS
Singles: 7-inch
DOME (4005 "Den of Thieves") 25-50

SEQUENCE, The
("Music by The Pharaohs")
Singles: 7-inch
PEGASO (552 "Nite Owl")....................400-500

SEQUINS
Singles: 78 rpm
RED ROBIN 50-100 56
Singles: 7-inch
RED ROBIN (140 "Why Can't You Treat Me Right") 200-300 56

SEQUINS
Singles: 7-inch
RENFRO (112 "A Case of Love") ....25-50 '60s

SEQUINS / Lefty Bates
Singles: 7-inch
BOXER (203 "Lullaby of Birdland"/"Say Whoa") 15-25 59
Also see JESSIE & SEQUINS

SERATT, Howard
Singles: 78 rpm
SUN (198 "Troublesome Waters")........100-150 54
Singles: 7-inch
SUN (198 "Troublesome Waters") 250-350 54

SERENADERS
Singles: 78 rpm
CORAL (60720 "It's Funny") 100-200 52
CORAL (65093 "Misery")......................200-300 52
DELUXE 75-100 53
J.V.B. (2001 "Tomorrow Night") 750-1000 52
RED ROBIN 150-200 53
SWING TIME...300-400 54
Singles: 7-inch
DELUXE (6022 "Please, Please Forgive Me")..400-500 53
RED ROBIN (115 "Will She Know")......500-600 53
SWING TIME (347 "M-a-y-b-e-l-l-e") 1000-1500 54

SERENADERS
Singles: 7-inch
CHOCK FULL O' HITS (101 "I Wrote a Letter") 100-200 57
CHOCK FULL O' HITS (103 "Give Me a Girl") 50-100 57
MGM (12623 "I Wrote a Letter")...............30-40 58
MGM (12666 "Give Me a Girl") 40-50 58
MOTOWN (1046 "I'll Cry Tomorrow") 750-1000 63
RAE COX (101 "Gotta Go to School")......20-30 59
RIVERSIDE (4549 "Adios My Love")........30-50 63
STARFIRE (115 "Nite Owl")..........................5-8 80
(Colored vinyl.)
V.I.P. (25002 "I'll Cry Tomorrow") 40-60 64
Picture Sleeves
STARFIRE (115 "Nite Owl") 5-8 80
Members: Sidney Barnes; Luke Gross; George Kerr; Timothy Wilson.
Also see BARNES, Sidney
Also see WILSON, Timothy

SERENADERS
(With Hal Gordon & Orchestra)
Singles: 7-inch
TEEN LIFE (9 "Gates of Gold")...........800-1000 58
Member: Nick Forrest.

SERENADES
Singles: 78 rpm
CHIEF (7002 "Sinner in Love") 75-125 57
Singles: 7-inch
CHIEF (7002 "Sinner in Love") 150-200 57

SERENADETTES
Singles: 7-inch
ENRICA (1008 "Boy Friend") 8-12 61

SERENDIPITY SINGERS *P&R/LP '64*
Singles: 7-inch
PHILIPS...5-10 64-66
U.A. 4-8 67-69
Picture Sleeves
PHILIPS (40236 "Same Old Reason") 5-10 64
PHILIPS (40246 "Little Brown Jug") 5-10 64
PHILIPS (40356 "The Phoenix Love Theme") 5-10 66
LPs: 10/12-inch
PHILIPS...10-20 64-65
WING...8-12 68

SERFMEN
Singles: 7-inch
NEMFRES (101 "Back Again") 15-20 65

SERGENT, Shorty
Singles: 7-inch
JET (501 "Record Hop")...........................40-60 58

SERPENT POWER
LPs: 10/12-inch
VANGUARD (9252 "Serpent Power") 75-125 67
(Monaural.)
VANGUARD (79252 "Serpent Power") 50-75 67
(Stereo.)
Members: Tina Meltzer; David Meltzer; Denny Ellis; Clark Coolidge; Bob Cuff.
Also see MELTZER, David & Tina
Also see MYSTERY TREND

SERTIFIED SOUND
Singles: 7-inch
TEE PEE (25/26 "Love Is Strange"/"Everday")...10-15 67

SERVICEMEN
Singles: 7-inch
CHARTMAKER (408 "Connie") 100-200 66
PATHWAY (101/102 "My Turn"/"Helping Hand")..75-125 67
WIND HIT (100 "Are You Angry") 250-500 65

SESAME STREET DO WAS
Singles: 7-inch
SESAME STREET (22112 "Counting the Days") 25-50

SESSIONS, Don
Singles: 7-inch
VERTICO (1001 "You're a Cheater")......50-100

SETTLE, Mike
(With the Settlers)
Singles: 7-inch
AMOS (155 "I See America")........................4-6 71
FOLK SING 4-8 62-63
RCA..4-8 65
UNI 4-6 71-72
LPs: 10/12-inch
FOLK SING 15-25 62-63
REPRISE...15-20 65
Also see FIRST EDITION
Also see SUGAR BEARS

SEVEN BLENDS
LPs: 10/12-inch
ROULETTE (R-25172 "Twistin' at the Miami Beach Peppermint Lounge") 15- 20 62
(Monaural.)
ROULETTE (SR-25172 "Twistin' at the Miami Beach Peppermint Lounge") 20- 25 62
(Stereo.)

7 DWARFS
Singles: 7-inch
IDEAL (1168 "Stop Girl") 15-25 67

SEVEN OF US
Singles: 7-inch
RED BIRD (069 "How Could You") 10-20 66
RED BIRD (080 "It's Not Easy to Forget")..10-20 66
Members: Frankie Gadler; Terry Adams; Jody Stampanato.
Also see NRBQ

SEVEN RAINDROPS
Singles: 7-inch
WORLD (800 "You're Gonna Cry So Many Tears") ....100-200 '60s

SEVEN SONS
Singles: 7-inch
DYNAR (121568 "And You Would Know"). 8-12 67
IGL (110 "House of the Rising Sun")........20-25 65
SOMA (1462 "House of the Rising Sun"). 15-20 67
STANAL (7308 "Product of Time") 10-20 67
VTI (20671 "Baby Please Come Back")... 10-20 67

SEVEN SOULS
Singles: 7-inch
OKEH (7289 "I Still Love You")................35-50 67
VENTURE (614 "Got to Find a Way") 8-12 68

SEVEN TEENS
Singles: 7-inch
GOLDEN CREST (503 "Steady Guy") 30-40 58

SEVENS, Sammy
Singles: 7-inch
SWAN (4146 "Here Comes the Bride")....15-25 63
SWAN (4159 "Everybody Crossfire") 15-25 63

7TH AVENUE AVIATORS
Singles: 7-inch
CONGRESS (255 "You Should 'O Held On") 30-50 65

SEVERSON, John
LPs: 10/12-inch
CAPITOL (1915 "Sunset Surf")................15-25 63

SEVILLE, David *P&R '56*
(Ross Bagdasarian)
Singles: 78 rpm
LIBERTY (55041 thru 55124) 8-15 56-58
LIBERTY (55132 "Witch Doctor") 50-75 58
Singles: 7-inch
LIBERTY (55041 thru 55124) 10-20 56-58
LIBERTY (55132 "Witch Doctor")............15-25 58
LIBERTY (55140 thru 55314) 10-15 58-61
Picture Sleeves
LIBERTY (55079 "Gotta Get to Your House")..15-25 57
EPs: 7-inch
LIBERTY (1003 "Witch Doctor") 35-50 57
(Issued with paper sleeve.)
LPs: 10/12-inch
LIBERTY (3073 "The Music of David Seville") 50-75 57
LIBERTY (3092 "Witch Doctor") 50-75 58
Also see ALFI & HARRY
Also see BAGDASARIAN, Ross
Also see CHIPMUNKS

SEVILLES *P&R '61*
Singles: 7-inch
CAL-GOLD (172 "Don't You Know I Care") 8-12 62
GALAXY (717 "Treat You Right")..............8-12 63
GALAXY (721 "Charlena") 8-12 63
GALAXY (727 "Baby")................................8-12 64
J.C. (116 "Charlena") 25-35 60
J.C. (118 "Louella") 15-20 61
J.C. (120 "Fat Sally")...............................10-15 61

SEVILLES
Singles: 7-inch
REN-CO (1056 "Burnell Blues") 10-20 62

Members: Joe Zampach; Jack Abuya; Virgil Herder; Jerry Crocker; Ronnie Lalich; Charlie Lewondowski; Mel Lewondowski.

SEVILLES
(With the Chick Morris Five)
Singles: 7-inch
VAGABOND (103 "Beverly") 50-100
Also see MORRIS, Chick

SEWARD, Alec
LPs: 10/12-inch
BLUE LABOR.. 20-30
PRESTIGE/BLUESVILLE (1076 "Creepin' Blues").. 20-40 65

SEWARD, Slim, & Fat Boy Hayes
(Alec Seward; Louis Hayes)
Singles: 78 rpm
MGM (10306 "Travelin' Boy's Blues") .. 100-150 47
MGM (10770 "Railroad Blues") 100-150 47
Also see BACK PORCH BOYS
Also see BLUES BOY
Also see BLUES KING
Also see JELLY BELLY & SLIM SEWARD
Also see SEWARD, Alec

SEX PISTOLS LP '77
Singles: 7-inch
W.B. (8516 "Submission").............................4-6 78
Picture Sleeves
W.B. (8516 "Submission") 4-6 78
LPs: 10/12-inch
W.B. (3147 "Never Mind the Bollocks, Here's the Sex Pistols") 15-20 77
(With cover sticker which reads: "Includes Submission.")
W.B. (3147 "Never Mind the Bollocks, Here's the Sex Pistols") 10-15 77
(Without "Submission" cover sticker.)
W.B. (72256 "Swindle Continues")..............8-10 '90s
W.B. (72511 "Live at Chelmsford Prison")..8-10 '90s

SEXTON, Orden
Singles: 7-inch
CAMELLIA (100 "Rock-A-Way") 100-150

SHA NA NA LP '69
Singles: 78 rpm
KAMA SUTRA (20 "Rock and Roll Is Here to Stay").. 30-40 '70s
Singles: 7-inch
KAMA SUTRA...4-8 70-75
SUTRA...4-6 74
Picture Sleeves
KAMA SUTRA...4-6 71
LPs: 10/12-inch
ACCORD...5-10 81-83
BUDDAH 5-10 77
CSP...8-12 78
EMUS..5-10 78
K-TEL..5-10 81
KAMA SUTRA.. 10-15 69-76
NASHVILLE...5-10 80
Members: Lennie Baker; Jon "Bowzer" Bauman; Johnny Contardo; Denny Green; Henry Gross; Jocko Marcellino; Danny McBride; Scott Powell; David-Allan "Chico" Ryan; "Screamin' Scott Simon; Donny York.

SHACKLEFORDS P&R '63
Singles: 7-inch
CAPITOL...4-6 66
LHI...4-6 67-68
MERCURY (72112 "A Stranger in Your Town")..5-10 63
LPs: 10/12-inch
CAPITOL... 10-20 66
MERCURY 15-25 63
Members: Lee Hazlewood; Marty Cooper; Al Stone; Garcia Nitzsche.
Also see MOMENTS

SHADDEN & KING LEARS
Singles: 7-inch
ARBET (1016 "All I Want Is You")............ 15-25 67
ARBET (1017 "Knock on Wood")............ 15-25 67
BELL (717 "Goodbye Little Girl")................8-12 68

SHADDOWS
Singles: 7-inch
UNITED AUDIO (80245 "Stormy Weather")... 50-100

SHADEMEN
Singles: 7-inch
VERANN (501 "That's Tuff") 15-25 66

SHADES
Singles: 7-inch
ALADDIN (3453 "Dear Lori")................400-500 59
(Black label.)
ALADDIN (3453 "Dear Lori")................450-550 59
(White label. Promotional issue only.)

SHADES
Singles: 7-inch
MAYPOLE (504 "Walkin' Wanda")...........40-60 61
SCOTTIE (1309 "Splashing")...................10-15 59

SHADES
Singles: 7-inch
TIMES SQUARE (16 "Voodoo Woman")..15-25 63

SHADES
Singles: 7-inch
SIGN (1001 "California")................................4-8
SOMA (1437 "Please, Please, Please")...25-35 65
WELHAVEN (4957 "I Feel So Fine") 25-35 65
Also see MIDWEST

SHADES
Singles: 7-inch
A-OK (1028 "Gingerbread Man") 15-25 67

SHADES
Singles: 7-inch
CADET (5608 "Ballot Bachs")...................10-20 68
PRINCETON (7012 "Ballot Bachs")..........15-25 68
(First issue.)

SHADES
Singles: 7-inch
RAPA ("Cry Over You")..........................15-25 '60s
(No selection number used.)

SHADES
Singles: 7-inch
FRANCE...10-15 '60s
METROPOLIS (7003 "Denny") 25-45

SHADES OF BLUE P&R/R&B '66
Singles: 7-inch
COLLECTABLES..3-5 '80s
IMPACT (1007 "Oh How Happy") 10-15 66
IMPACT (1014 "Lonely Summer") 10-15 66
IMPACT (1015 "Happiness")....................10-15 66
IMPACT (1026 "All I Want Is Love") 10-15 67
IMPACT (1028 "Penny Arcade")..............10-15 67
SHADES (1030 "You Must Believe Me")....5-10 67
LPs: 10/12-inch
IMPACT (101 "Happiness Is")..................30-50 66
(Monaural.)
IMPACT (101 "Happiness Is")..................50-75 66
(Stereo.)
Members: Linda Kerr; Robert Kerr; Ernest Dernai; Nick Marinelli.

SHADES OF BROWN
Singles: 7-inch
CADET (5657 "Little Girl")...........................5-10 69
CADET (5666 "Man's Worst Enemy").........5-10 70
CADET (5673 "Garbage Man")...................5-10 70
LPs: 10/12-inch
CADET (843 "Shades of Brown") 40-60 70

SHADES OF NIGHT
Singles: 7-inch
ALAMO AUDIO (111 "Fluctuation") 15-25 67

SHADES OF RHYTHM
(Featuring Bob Williams)
Singles: 78 rpm
CADDY (102 "Gumbo") 20-30 56
Singles: 7-inch
CADDY (102 "Gumbo") 75-125 56

SHADES OF SOUL
Singles: 7-inch
SURE-FIRE...8-12

SHADLE, Bobby
Singles: 7-inch
BLUE BONNET (334 "Come On Baby") 150-250

SHADOW
Singles: 7-inch
CLEAN (60002 "I'm Drifting") ....10-20 '60s

SHADOW CASTERS
Singles: 7-inch
J.R.P. (002 "Going to the Moon")..............15-25 68
J.R.P. (003 "Cinnamon Snowflake")..........15-25 68

SHADOWS R&B '50
Singles: 78 rpm
LEE (200 "I've Been a Fool") 20-30 49
LEE (202 "I'd Rather Be Wrong Than Blue") 15-25 50
LEE (207 "Don't Blame My Dreams").......15-25 50
Members; Jasper Edwards; Ray Reed; Sam McClure; Scott King; Bobby Buster.

SHADOWS
Singles: 78 rpm
DECCA..30-50 53-54
HUB..15-25 53
SITTIN' IN WITH..15-25 50-52
Singles: 7-inch
DECCA (28765 "Stay")..........................75-125 53
DECCA (48307 "Tell Her")...................150-200 54
DECCA (48322 "Big Mouth Mama") 150-200 54
Also see FOUR TUNES / Shadows

SHADOWS
Singles: 7-inch
DELTA (1509 "Bop-A-Lena") 200-300 57

SHADOWS
Singles: 7-inch
DEL-FI (4109 "Under Stars of Love") 55-65 58
(Has multi-colored balloons on label.)
DEL-FI (4109 "Under Stars of Love") 15-25 59
(Green label.)

SHADOWS
Singles: 7-inch
EL-GEE-BEE (101 "I Love You") 200-300 58

SHADOWS
Singles: 7-inch
FRATERNITY (795 "You Make My Heart Sing Ah!")..20-30 58
Member: Elroy Peace.
Also see PEACE, Elroy Shadow

SHADOWS
Singles: 7-inch
ABC-PAR (10073 "Saturday Dance").......10-15 60
ABC-PAR (10138 "Apache")....................10-15 60
ATLANTIC...8-12 61-64
EPIC 10-15 65-66
LPs: 10/12-inch
ATLANTIC (8089 "Surfing with the Shadows") 35-45 63
(Monaural.)
ATLANTIC (SD-8089 "Surfing with the Shadows") 45-55 63
(Stereo.)
ATLANTIC (8097 "The Shadows Know") .25-30 64
(Monaural.)
ATLANTIC (SD-8097 "The Shadows Know") 30-40 64
(Stereo.)
Members: Jet Harris; Bruce Welch; Hank Marvin; Tony Meehan.
Also see FOUR JETS
Also see MARVIN & FARRAR
Also see RICHARD, Cliff

SHADOWS
Singles: 7-inch
USA (106 "No Other Love") ....20-30 '60s
WOODRICH (18507 "If You Love Me")....10-20 '60s

SHADOWS
Singles: 7-inch
JAM (110 "Shake Sherry") 10-15 64

SHADOWS FIVE
Singles: 7-inch
PEACOCK (1912 "Twistin' Shadows") 8-12 62
SULLY (45111 "Dynamic Drums")............10-20 61
TECH (4836 "Gathers No Moss") ....10-20 '60s
Members: Leon Sanders; Rich Grissom; Gary Sullivan.
Also see CHAMPS

SHADOWS FOUR
Singles: 7-inch
D-M-E (200,964 "I'm Beggin' You") 15-25 65
FLEETWOOD (4553 "Heart of Wood").....20-30 65

SHADOWS OF KNIGHT P&R/LP '66
Singles: 7-inch
ATCO (6634 "Gloria '69")...............................8-12 68
ATCO (6776 "I Am the Hunter")....................5-10 70
COLUMBIA/AURAVISION ("Shadows of Knight Sing Potato Chip")..75-100 66
(Square 5-inch cardboard picture disc. Included in boxes of Fairmont Potato Chips.)
DUNWICH (116 "Gloria") 15-25 66
(Gold label. No reference to distribution by Atco.)
DUNWICH (116 "Gloria") 10-20 66
(Yellow label. Has "Distributed by Atco" at top.)
DUNWICH (116 "Gloria") 8-12 66
(Multi-color label. Has "Distributed by Atco" at bottom.)
DUNWICH (122 "Oh Yeah") 10-20 66
DUNWICH (128 "Bad Little Woman").......10-20 66
DUNWICH (141 "I'm Gonna Make You Mine") 10-20 66
DUNWICH (151 "Willie Jean") 10-20 67
DUNWICH (167 "Someone Like Me") 10-20 67
SUPER K (108 "Taurus") 8-12 69
TEAM (520 "Shake") 8-12 68
Picture Sleeves
DUNWICH (122 "Oh Yeah") 15-20 66
DUNWICH (128 "Bad Little Woman").......20-30 66
LPs: 10/12-inch
DUNWICH (666 "Gloria") 50-100 66
DUNWICH (667 "Back Door Men") 50-100 66
SUNDAZED ....5-10 '90s
SUPER K (6002 "The Shadows of Knight")..15-25 69

SHADRACK
Singles: 7-inch
SONIC (202 "I Wonder Why")..................10-20 '60s
LPs: 10/12-inch
IGL (132 "Chameleon") 250-350 71

SHADY DAYS
Singles: 7-inch
RPR (104 "Little Girl")...............................15-25 69

SHADY DAZE
Singles: 7-inch
IT'S A GASS (6831 "You Don't Know Like I Know")..15-25 68
USA (883 "I'll Make You Pay")..............100-150 67
Members: Gregg Owen; Breg Biela; Mark Drzewiecki.

SHAFTO, Bobby P&R '64
Singles: 7-inch
RUST 5-10 64-66

SHAG
Singles: 7-inch
CAPITOL (5995 "Stop & Listen")............. 15-25 67
Also see SHAGS

SHAGGS
LPs: 10/12-inch
MCM (6311 "Wink")..........................1000-2000 67
Members: Geoff Gillette; Franklin Krakowski; Rick Medich; Ted Poulos; Ray Wheatley.

SHAGGS
LPs: 10/12-inch
ROUNDER..8-12 82
THIRD WORLD (3001 "Philosophy of the World")..1200-1500 72
(Reportedly 2,000 made.)
Members: Betty Wiggin; Dorothy Wiggin; Helen Wiggin.

SHAGNASTY, Boliver
Singles: 7-inch
FUN (10000 "Tapping That Thing") .... 10-15 '60s
QUARTERCASH (70 "Tapping That Thing")..40-60 '60s

SHAGS
(Shag)
Singles: 7-inch
RAYNARD (10034 "Dance Woman")........15-25 65
Members: John Sahli; Mike Lamers; Don Luther; Paul Greenwald.
Also see SHAG

SHAGS
Singles: 7-inch
CONCERT (1-78-65 "Louis Louis") 40-60 65

SHAGS
Singles: 7-inch
CAMEO (470 "As Long As I Have You")....5-10 67
KAYDEN (407 "As Long As I Have You") 10-15 67

KAYDEN (408 "Breathe in My Ear")........ 10-15 67
LAURIE (3353 "I Call Your Name")......... 10-15 66
NUTTA (101 "Wait and See").....................8-12 65
PALMER (5010 "The Way I Care")............8-12 66
SAMMY (102 "By My Side").......................8-12 65
TAURUS (1881 "Don't Press Your Luck").. 20-30 66
Members: Carl Donnell; Aaron Perkins; Tommy Roberts; Johnny Stanton; Lance Gardner; Bill Hall.
Also see PULSE

SHAGS

Singles: 7-inch

EAGLE (123 "Smiling Fenceposts")........ 25-35

SHAKERS

Singles: 7-inch

ABC (10960 "Love, Love, Love") 5-10 67
AUDIO FIDELITY (119 "Ticket to Ride")....5-10 66

LPs: 10/12-inch

AUDIO FIDELITY (2155 "The Shakers Break It All").. 30-40 66
(Monaural.)
AUDIO FIDELITY (6155 "The Shakers Break It All").. 35-45 66
(Stereo.)

SHAKEY JAKE

(With the All Stars; James Harris)

Singles: 7-inch

ARTISTIC (1502 "Roll Your Money Maker").. 15-25 58
PRESTIGE BLUESVILLE (807 "My Foolish Heart").. 10-15 60
VIVID (100 "Roll Your Money Maker")..... 25-35 64

LPs: 10/12-inch

PRESTIGE BLUESVILLE (1008 "Good Times").. 75-100 60
PRESTIGE BLUESVILLE (1027 "Mouth Harp Blues").. 30-40 61
WORLD PACIFIC.................................... 25-35 '60s

SHALIMARS

Singles: 7-inch

BRUNSWICK (55281 "Montezuma")..........8-12 65
VERVE (10388 "Baby")........................... 15-25 66

SHALLOWS

Singles: 7-inch

RAE COX (108 "Wrecking My Life")........ 15-25 61

SHALLOWS

Singles: 7-inch

FORLIN (503 "I Wonder")....................... 20-30 62

SHALOMARS

Singles: 7-inch

STAR SATELLITE (1016 "Today, Tomorrow and Forever").. 20-30 '60s

SHAMANS

(With the William Powell Group)

Singles: 7-inch

KAYHAM (1/2 "Valley of Tears")........... 75-125 59
KAYHAM (3/4 "I'll Wait Forever")........... 75-125 59

SHAMES

Singles: 7-inch

RFT (1001 "The Special Ones").............. 15-25 66

SHAM-ETTES

(Shamettes)

Singles: 7-inch

GOLD DUST ("Wasting Your Time") 75-125
(Selection number not known.)
MGM (13618 "Big Bad Wolf")......................8-12 66
MGM (13798 "He'll Come Back")................8-12 67

SHAMROCKS

Singles: 7-inch

54 (5424 "Danny Boy")........................ 150-200 59

SHAMROCKS

Singles: 7-inch

ANDIE (5021 "Scrappy")............................8-12 61
(First issued as by the Check-Mates.)
Member: Jim Ford.
Also see CHECK-MATES
Also see FORD, Jim

SHAMROCKS

Singles: 7-inch

LIBERTY (55460 "Lonely Island")........... 10-20 62
Members: Dorsey and Johnny Burnette.
Also see BURNETTE, Johnny & Dorsey

SHANDELLS

Singles: 7-inch

BANGAR (0659 "Gorilla")......................100-125 64
STUDIO CITY (1037 "Here Comes the Pain")..25-35 66
Members: Jeff Gottheardt; Grant Gilbertson; Mick Zirngible; Jim Coggins.

SHAN-DELLS

Singles: 7-inch

BRIDGE SOCIETY (112 "Chimes")........50-100
BRIDGE SOCIETY (114 "I've Got to Love Her")..100-150

SHANDELLS / Fab Four

Singles: 7-inch

SIZZLE (5130 "Mary Mary"/"Caroline").....25-35 67

SHANDELS

Singles: 7-inch

MUSIC TOWN (113 "Stop Your Cryin'")...15-25 66

SHANGRI-LAS — P&R/R&B '64

(Shangra-Las)

Singles: 7-inch

COLLECTABLES......................................3-5 '80s
ERIC..4-6 '70s
LANA...4-8 '60s
MERCURY (72645 "Sweet Sounds of Summer")..5-10 66
MERCURY (72670 "Take the Time")..........5-10 67
RED BIRD (008 "Remember")..................8-12 64
RED BIRD (014 "Leader of the Pack").......8-12 64
RED BIRD (018 "Give Him a Great Big Kiss")..8-12 64
RED BIRD (019 "Maybe")........................8-12 64
RED BIRD (025 "Out in the Streets")........8-12 65
RED BIRD (030 "Give Us Your Blessing") .8-12 65
RED BIRD (036 "Right Now and Not Later")..8-12 65
RED BIRD (043 "I Can Never Go Home Anymore")..8-12 65
RED BIRD (048 "Long Live Our Love")......8-12 66
RED BIRD (053 "He Cried")......................8-12 66
RED BIRD (068 "Past, Present & Future").8-12 66
SSS INT'L..3-5 '80s
SCEPTER (1291 "Wishing Well")..............8-12 65
SMASH (1866 "Simon Says")..................10-20 63
SPOKANE (4006 "Wishing Well")............10-15 64
TRIP..4-6 '70s

LPs: 10/12-inch

BACK-TRAC 5-10 85
COLLECTABLES (5011 "At Their Best")....5-10 82
(Black vinyl.)
COLLECTABLES (5011 "At Their Best")..10-15 82
(Picture disc.)
MERCURY (21099 "Golden Hits of the Shangri-las")..20-30 66
(Monaural.)
MERCURY (21099 "Golden Hits")...........50-75 66
(Shown as monaural but plays in true stereo.)
MERCURY (61099 "Golden Hits")...........25-35 66
(Stereo.)
POST...10-12
RED BIRD (101 "Leader of the Pack").....30-50 65
RED BIRD (104 "Shangri-Las '65")........60-100 65
RED BIRD (104 "I Can Never Go Home Anymore")..50-85 65
Members: Mary Weiss; Marge Ganser; Mary Ann Ganser.

SHANK, Bud — P&R/LP '66

(With Clare Fischer)

Singles: 78 rpm

GOOD TIME JAZZ....................................4-6 54

Singles: 7-inch

GOOD TIME JAZZ....................................5-10 54
PACIFIC JAZZ...4-8 61-70
WORLD PACIFIC......................................4-6 64-68

EPs: 7-inch

NOCTURNE (3/4 "The Bud Shank Quintet")..50-75 53
(Price is for either volume.)
PACIFIC JAZZ.......................................20-30 54-58

LPs: 10/12-inch

CONCORD JAZZ.......................................5-8 76
CROWN...10-20 63
KIMBERLY...10-20 63
NOCTURNE (2 "The Bud Shank Quintet")..150-200 53
(10-inch LP.)
PACIFIC JAZZ (14 "Bud Shank with Three Trombones")..75-125 54
(10-inch LP.)
PACIFIC JAZZ (20 "Bud Shank and Bob Brookmeyer")..75-125 55
(10-inch LP.)
PACIFIC JAZZ (4 thru 89)......................15-25 60-65
(12-inch LPs.)
PACIFIC JAZZ (404 "Jazz Swings Broadway")..40-60 57
PACIFIC JAZZ (411 "The Swing's to TV")..40-60 57
PACIFIC JAZZ (1205 "Bud Shank and Shorty Rogers")..40-60 55
PACIFIC JAZZ (1213 "Strings and Trombones")..40-60 56
PACIFIC JAZZ (1215 "The Bud Shank Quartet")..40-60 56
PACIFIC JAZZ (1219 "Jazz at Cal-Tech")..40-60 56
PACIFIC JAZZ (1226 "Flute 'N Oboe")..40-60 57
PACIFIC JAZZ (1230 "The Bud Shank Quartet")..40-60 57
PACIFIC JAZZ (10000 & 20000 series).....5-15 66-81
SUNSET..8-12 66
WORLD PACIFIC (1000 thru 1200 series)..20-40 58-60
WORLD PACIFIC (1400 series)...............15-30 61-63
WORLD PACIFIC (1800 series)...............15-20 64-67
WORLD PACIFIC (21000 series).............10-20 66-68
Also see FOLKSWINGERS
Also see LONDON, Julie, & Bud Shank Quintet
Also see ROGERS, Shorty

SHANK, Junior, & Jesters

Singles: 7-inch

MADISON (127 "Be Bop-a-Lulu")............15-25 60

SHANKAR, Ravi — LP '67

(With Yehudi Menuhin)

Singles: 7-inch

APPLE (1838 "Joi Bangla")......................5-10 71
DARK HORSE..4-6 74
PACIFIC...4-8 '60s
WORLD PACIFIC......................................4-8 59-68

Picture Sleeves

APPLE (1838 "Joi Bangla").....................20-25 71

LPs: 10/12-inch

ANGEL..10-20 67
APPLE (3384 "Raga")............................12-18 71
APPLE (3396 "In Concert 1972")............40-50 73
CAPITOL...10-20 67-72
COLUMBIA..10-20 66-68
DARK HORSE...8-12 74-76
FANTASY...5-10 73
PRESTIGE..10-20 68
SPARK...5-10 73
WORLD PACIFIC....................................10-20 59-69
Also see BEATLES
Also see HARRISON, George

SHANNON, Bobby

(Bobby Gregory)

Singles: 7-inch

ADAIRE ("Your Last Goodbye Sounded Different")..40-50
(Selection number not known.)
Also see GREGORY, Bobby, & Cardinals

SHANNON, Del — P&R/R&B '61

Singles: 7-inch

AMY..5-10 64-66
BERLEE...8-12 63-64
BIG TOP (3067 "Runaway")....................10-20 61
BIG TOP (3075 "Hats Off to Larry").........10-20 61
BIG TOP (3083 "So Long Baby")............10-20 61
BIG TOP (3091 "Hey, Little Girl")...........10-20 61
BIG TOP (3098 "I Won't Be There").........10-20 62
BIG TOP (3112 "Cry Myself to Sleep").....10-20 62
BIG TOP (3117 "Swiss Maid")................10-20 62
BIG TOP (3131 "Little Town Flirt")...........10-20 62
BIG TOP (3143 "Two Kinds of Teardrops")..10-20 63
BIG TOP (3152 "From Me to You") 30-35 63
COLLECTABLES......................................3-5 '80s
DUNHILL..4-8 69
ERIC..4-6 '70s
ISLAND..4-6 75
LANA...4-8 '60s
LIBERTY...5-10 66-68
NETWORK...4-6 81-82
TERRIFIC...3-5
TRIP...3-6
TWIRL..4-8 '60s
W.B..3-5 85

Picture Sleeves

LIBERTY (56018 "Thinkin' It Over") 8-12 68

LPs: 10/12-inch

AMY (8003 "Handy Man")........................30-50 64
(Monaural.)
AMY (S-8003 "Handy Man")....................40-60 64
(Stereo.)
AMY (8004 "Del Shannon Sings Hank Williams")..30-50 65
(Monaural.)
AMY (S-8004 "Del Shannon Sings Hank Williams")..40-60 65
(Stereo.)
AMY (8006 "1,661 Seconds")..................30-50 65
(Monaural.)
AMY (S-8006 "1,661 Seconds")..............40-60 65
(Stereo.)
BIG TOP (1303 "Runaway")................150-250 61
(Monaural.)
BIG TOP (1303 "Runaway")................550-650 61
(Stereo.)
BIG TOP (1308 "Little Town Flirt")...........40-60 63
BUG...5-10 85
DOT (3834 "Best of Del Shannon")..........25-45 67
(Monaural.)
DOT (25834 "Best of Del Shannon")........25-45 67
(Stereo.)
LIBERTY...20-30 66-68
NETWORK/ELEKTRA................................8-10 81
PHOENIX 20..8-10 80
PICKWICK..8-10 '70s
POST..10-15
SIRE..10-15 75
SUNSET...10-15 70
U.A. 10-15 73
Also see HONDELLS / Del Shannon / Martha & Vandellas
Also see MAXIMILLIAN

SHANNON, Jackie

(Cajuns with Jacquie Shannon; Jackie DeShannon)

Singles: 7-inch

DOT (15928 "Just Another Lie")..............20-25 59
FRATERNITY (836 "Just Another Lie")......15-25 59
P.J. (101 "Trouble")................................50-75 59
SAGE (290 "Just Another Lie")...............20-40 59
SAND (330 "Trouble")............................20-40 59
Also see DE SHANNON, Jackie

SHANNON, Linda, & Deckers

Singles: 7-inch

LINDA (107 "No More Love")....................20-30 57

SHANNON, Pat

(With the Anita Kerr Singers & Owen Bradley Orchestra)

Singles: 7-inch

AMOS (152 "I Ain't Got Time Anymore")..... 4-8 70
AMOS (163 "Liar")...................................4-8 71
DECCA (Except 30666)...........................8-12 58-60
DECCA (30666 "You're So Wild")...........15-25 58
UNI..4-6 69
W.B...4-8 68

LPs: 10/12-inch

UNI..10-15 69
Also see KERR, Anita
Also see BRADLEY, Owen

SHANTEERS

Singles: 7-inch

RORI (708 "You're Gone").......................15-25 62

SHANTONES

Singles: 7-inch

TRILYTE (5001 "Come to Me") 3000-5000 56

SHANTONS

(With Billy Mure & His Orchestra)

Singles: 7-inch

JAY-MAR (165 "Triangle Love")...........300-400 59
(Identification number shown since no selection number is used.)
JAY-MAR (182 "Christmas Song") 75-125 60
(Identification number shown since no selection number is used.)
JAY-MAR (241 "Lucille")...................1000-1200 59
(Identification number shown since no selection number is used.)
Also see BROWN, Skip, & Shantons
Also see JACKSON, Skip

Also see MURE, Billy

SHANZ, Bob
Singles: 7-inch
BOULDER (015 "One Soda")... 40-50 60

SHARELL, Jerry
(With Mark III)
Singles: 7-inch
ALANNA (560 "Everybody Knows")... 15-25 60
FUZZY (1-1 "Centerpiece")... 15-25 66
(First issue.)
MAIN LINE (1365 "It'll Never Happen Again")...5-10 67
VERVE (10453 "Centerpiece")...5-10 66
Session: Valerie Simpson.
Also see SIMPSON, Valerie
Also see VELVETS

SHARKS
Singles: 7-inch
SAPIEN (1003 "Big Surf")... 20-25 63
Also see VEGAS, Pat & Lolly

SHARLETS
Singles: 7-inch
EXPLOSIVE (2 "Gleam in His Eye")... 15-25 66
Session: Davie Allan.
Also see ALLAN, Davie

SHARMEERS
Singles: 7-inch
CLIFTON (09 "A School Girl in Love")...4-6 74
RED TOP (109 "A School Girl in Love")... 350-400 58

SHARON & BITS O' HONEY
Singles: 7-inch
PENTHOUSE (1003 "Don't Push My Love Aside")... 40-60

SHARON, Ralph
(Ralph Sharon Quartet and Friend; Ralph Sharon Quartet)
Singles: 7-inch
ARGO (5315 "Time")...8-12 58
DUCHESS (1017 "Just Because")...5-10 62
DUCHESS (1019 "Night Prowler")...5-10 62
EPs: 7-inch
ARGO (1077 "Ralph Sharon Quartet")... 10-15 58
LPs: 10/12-inch
ARGO... 10-20 58
GORDY (903 "Modern Innovations on C&W Themes")... 75-100 63
Also see BENNETT, Tony

SHARON MARIE
(Sharon Pomeroy)
Singles: 7-inch
CAPITOL (5064 "Runaround Lover")... 50-75 63
CAPITOL (5195 "Thinkin' 'Bout You Baby")... 50-75 64
Also see BOB & SHERI
Also see HONEYS
Also see SHARPEES

SHARP, Billy, & Sharptones
Singles: 7-inch
KUDO (668 "Stars in My Eyes")... 200-300

SHARP, Davey
Singles: 7-inch
YORK (113 "Let's Go Steady, Baby")... 30-50 57

SHARP, Dee Dee — *P&R/R&B/LP '62*
(Dee Dee Sharp Gamble; with David Sigler)
Singles: 7-inch
ABKCO...3-5 83-84
ATCO (6445 "Bye Bye Baby")...5-10 66
ATCO (6502 "Baby, I Love You")...5-10 67
ATCO (6576 "You're Just a Fool in Love") .5-10 68
ATCO (6587 "This Love Won't Run Out")...5-10 68
CAMEO (212 "Mashed Potato Time")...8-12 62
CAMEO (219 "Gravy")...8-12 62
CAMEO (230 "Ride!")...8-12 62
CAMEO (244 "Do the Bird")...8-12 63
CAMEO (260 "Rock Me in the Cradle of Love")...8-12 63
CAMEO (274 "Wild!")...8-12 63
CAMEO (296 "Where Did I Go Wrong")...8-12 64
CAMEO (329 "He's No Ordinary Guy")...8-12 64
CAMEO (335 "Good")...8-12 64
CAMEO (347 "To Know Him Is to Love Him")...8-12 65
CAMEO (357 "Let's Twine")...8-12 65
CAMEO (375 "I Really Love You")...8-12 65
CAMEO (382 "It's a Funny Situation")...8-12 65
FAIRMOUNT (1004 "The Love I Feel for You")...5-10 66
GAMBLE (219 "What Kind of Lady")...8-12 68
GAMBLE (4005 "The Bottle Or Me")...8-12 69
PHILA. INT'L...3-6 71-81
TSOP...4-6 76
Picture Sleeves
CAMEO (219 "Gravy")...10-20 62
CAMEO (230 "Ride!")...10-20 62
CAMEO (244 "Do the Bird")...10-20 63
CAMEO (260 "Rock Me in the Cradle of Love")...10-20 63
CAMEO (274 "Wild!")...10-20 63
CAMEO (296 "Where Did I Go Wrong")...10-20 64
CAMEO (329 "He's No Ordinary Guy")...10-20 64
CAMEO (335 "Good")...10-20 64
CAMEO (375 "I Really Love You")...10-20 65
LPs: 10/12-inch
CAMEO (C-1018 "It's Mashed Potato Time")...20-30 62
CAMEO (C-1022 "Songs of Faith")...20-30 62
(Monaural.)
CAMEO (SC-1022 "Songs of Faith")...30-40 62
(Stereo.)
CAMEO (C-1032 "All the Hits")...20-30 63
(Monaural.)
CAMEO (SC-1032 "All the Hits")...20-30 63
(Stereo.)
CAMEO (C-1050 "Do the Bird")...20-30 63
(Monaural.)
CAMEO (SC-1050 "Do the Bird")...20-30 63
(Stereo.)
CAMEO (C-1062 "Biggest Hits")...20-30 63
(Monaural.)
CAMEO (SC-1062 "Biggest Hits")...20-30 63
(Stereo.)
CAMEO (C-1074 "Down Memory Lane") .20-30 63
(Monaural.)
CAMEO (SC-1074 "Down Memory Lane")...20-30 63
(Stereo.)
CAMEO (C-2002 "18 Golden Hits")...20-30 '60s
(Monaural.)
CAMEO (SC-2002 "18 Golden Hits")...20-30 '60s
(Stereo.)
PHILA. INT'L...8-10 75-81
Session: Orlons; Dreamlovers.
Also see CHECKER, Chubby, & Dee Dee Sharp
Also see DREAMLOVERS
Also see KING, Ben E., & Dee Dee Sharp
Also see ORLONS

SHARP TONES
Singles: 78 rpm
POST...50-100 55
Singles: 7-inch
POST (2009 "Since I Fell for You")...200-300 55
Members: Andre Goodwin; Charles Fitzpatrick; Willie Roland; Berlin Carpenter; Al Williams.
Also see TURBANS

SHARPE, Buddy
(With the Shakers)
Singles: 78 rpm
FEE BEE (230 "Linda Lee")...10-15 56
Singles: 7-inch
BISHOP (1000 "Dry Your Eyes")...5-10
BISHOP (1007 "Sleep All Day, Shake All Night")...10-15
(Reportedly 250 made.)
FEE BEE (230 "Linda Lee")...30-40 56
FEE BEE (901 "Fat Mama Twist")...50-75
RAMBLE ("The Shake")...10-15 62
(Selection number not known.)
SPEAR (2 "Please Please Please")...50-100 '50s
STAR (312 "Tooth Ache")...50-75 57

SHARPE, Cathy
Singles: 7-inch
GLOBAL (723 "North Pole Rock")...50-75 59

SHARPE, Henry
Singles: 7-inch
GLOBAL (717 "Shortnin' Rock and Roll")...100-200 59

SHARPE, Ray — *P&R/R&B '59*
(With the Blues Whalers; with Soul Set)
Singles: 7-inch
A&M...4-8 71
ATCO (6402 "Help Me")...5-10 66
ATCO (6437 "I Can't Take It")...5-10 66
DOT (15974 "That's the Way I Feel")...10-15 59
FLYING HIGH...3-5
GAREX (104 "I'm in Misery")...5-10 63
GREGMARK (14 "Linda Lu")...5-10 63
HAMILTON (50002 "Oh, My Baby's Gone")...10-20 58
JAMIE (1128 "Linda Lu"/"Monkey's Uncle")...15-25 59
JAMIE (1128 "Linda Lu"/"Red Sails In the Sunset")...10-20 59
JAMIE (1138 "T.A. Blues")...8-12 59
JAMIE (1149 "Bermuda")...8-12 60
JAMIE (1155 "Red Sails In the Sunset") ...8-12 60
JAMIE (1164 "Kewpie Doll")...8-12 60
LHI (1215 "Linda Lu")...5-10 68
MONUMENT (874 "Let's Go, Let's Go, Let's Go")...5-10 65
PARK AVENUE...5-8 '60s
SOCK & SOUL...5-8 70
TREY (3011 "Justine")...8-12 60
LPs: 10/12-inch
AWARD (711 "Welcome Back")...25-50
FLYING HIGH...5-10
Session: Duane Eddy; Al Casey; Jim Horn; King Curtis.
Also see CASEY, Al
Also see EDDY, Duane
Also see KING CURTIS

SHARPEES — *P&R '66*
Singles: 7-inch
ONE-DERFUL (4835 "Do the 45")...10-15 65
ONE-DERFUL (4839 "Tired of Being Lonely")...10-15 66
ONE-DERFUL (4843 "I've Got a Secret") 10-15 66
ONE-DERFUL (4845 "The Sock")...10-15 66
Members: Herbert Reeves; Benny Sharp; Vernon Guy; Horise O'Toole; Stacy Johnson.
Also see GUY, Vernon
Also see JOHNSON, Stacy
Also see LITTLE HERBERT & ARABIANS

SHARPS
Singles: 78 rpm
ALADDIN...20-40 57
JAMIE...20-40 57
TWO MIKES (101 "Heaven Only Knows")...300-500 54
Singles: 7-inch
ALADDIN (3401 "What Will I Gain")...30-40 57
COMBO (146 "All My Love")...50-75 58
(First issue.)
DOT (15806 "All My Love")...10-15 58
JAMIE (1040 "Sweet Sweetheart")...20-30 57
JAMIE (1103 "Look at Me")...10-20 58
(With Duane Eddy.)
JAMIE (1114 "Here's My Heart")...10-20 59
LAMP (2007 "Our Love Is Here to Stay")..10-20 57
WIN (702 "We Three")...75-125 58
Members: Carl White; Al Frazier; Sonny Harris; Turner Wilson; Joe Green.
Also see CRENSHAWS
Also see DON & DEWEY
Also see EDDY, Duane
Also see ELL, Carl, & Buddies
Also see FRAZIER, Ray
Also see HARRIS, Thurston
Also see KEY, Troyce
Also see MELLOMOODS
Also see RIVINGTONS
Also see STAFFORD, Billy

SHARPS
Singles: 7-inch
DARROW (511 "Cruisin'")...20-30 60
STAR HI (10460 "Double Clutch")...20-30 60
Also see FOUR SHARPS

SHARPS / Jack McVea
Singles: 7-inch
CHESS (1690 "Six Months, Three Weeks")...10-20 58
TAG (2200 "Six Months, Three Weeks")...200-300 58
Also see McVEA, Jack
Also see SHARPS

SHARPTONES
Singles: 7-inch
KUDO (668 "Stars in My Eyes")...100-200 58

SHARPTONES
(With Steve Pulliam & Orchestra)
Singles: 7-inch
ACE (133 "I'll Always Remember")...250-350 59

SHARRON, Ralph
LPs: 10/12-inch
GORDY (903 "Modern Innovations on C&W")...50-100 63

SHATNER, William
Singles: 7-inch
DECCA (32399 "Transformed Man")...10-15 68
LPs: 10/12-inch
DECCA (75043 "Transformed Man")...40-60 69
K-TEL (494 "Captain of the Starship")...40-60
(Two discs.)
LEMLI...10-15

SHATTOES
Singles: 7-inch
STUDIO CITY (1010 "Surf Fever")...100-200 64
(Reportedly 400 to 500 made.)
Also see CHATEAUX

SHAUL, Lawrence
Singles: 7-inch
REED (1049 "Hey Little Mama")...350-450 60

SHAVER, Elliot
(With the Blazers; Elliot Shavers)
Singles: 7-inch
BLAUN...5-10
ELLEN (502 "Shake 'Em Up")...10-15 62
(Black vinyl.)
ELLEN (502 "Shake 'Em Up")...20-30 62
(Colored vinyl.)
IMCO (101 "Lincoln Continental")...10-20 61
IMCO (102 "Scratch That Itch")...10-20 61
(First issue.)
KING (5546 "Scratch That Itch")...5-10 61
MAGNUM (718 "Fool, Fool, Fool")...8-12
MAGNUM (738 "Soulin' Back")...8-12
RAJA...5-10 65
SWINGIN' (630 "Do You Think I Care")...5-10 61
ZAN-DAN...5-10

SHAW, Buddy
Singles: 7-inch
STARDAY (618 "No More")...100-150
STARDAY (642 "Don't Sweep That Dirt On Me")...100-150

SHAW, Carol
Singles: 7-inch
ATCO (6278 "Jimmy Boy")...5-10 63
TALENT (1005 "I'm in Love")...15-25 63

SHAW, Cecil
Singles: 7-inch
BIL-MAR (800 "All I Want Out of Life")...10-15 73

SHAW, Eddie
Singles: 7-inch
CJ (647 "Ridin' High")...10-20 64
COLT (647 "Ridin' High")...10-20 64

SHAW, Jim
Singles: 7-inch
C&W (115 "Rockin' Boppin' Teenager")...60-75

SHAW, Jimmy
Singles: 7-inch
CONCEPT (1001 "Take a Chance on Me")...40-60 58
IMPERIAL (5603 "Take a Chance on Me")...10-15 59

SHAW, Joan
Singles: 78 rpm
ABC-PAR...5-10 56
GEM...5-10 53
JAGUAR...5-10 54-55
Singles: 7-inch
ABC-PAR (9724 "Broken Heart")...10-15 56
ABC-PAR (9751 "Just Kiss Me")...10-15 56
COLPIX 625 "You Made Me Love You")...5-10 62
GEM (209 "Baby Come On")...10-20 53
GEM (212 "You Make Me Cry Myself to Sleep")...10-20 53
GEM (213 "Regretful")...10-20 53
JAGUAR (3008 "I've Waited So Long")...10-20 54
JAGUAR (3010 "Most of All")...10-20 55
JAGUAR (3013 "Ten Commandments of Love")...10-20 55

SUE (116 "Make Someone Happy")..........5-10 65
Also see SINGER, Hal

SHAW, Joan, & Billy Ford
Singles: 78 rpm
ABBEY (3030 "Rock My Soul")............... 10-15 51
Singles: 7-inch
ABBEY (3030 "Rock My Soul")............... 20-30 51
Also see FORD, Billy
Also see SHAW, Joan

SHAW, John, & Dell-Os
(John Shaw & Dell-O's; with Billy Cooke & Orchestra)
Singles: 7-inch
U-C (5002 "Why Did You Leave Me")..............................1500-2500 58
Also see SENSATIONAL DELLOS

SHAW, Johnny, & Jaywalkers
Singles: 7-inch
JUBILEE (5511 "Wild Surfer's Call")....... 10-20 65

SHAW, Joyce, & Teasers
Singles: 78 rpm
SHOW TIME.. 10-15 55
Singles: 7-inch
SHOW TIME (1110 "Daddy You Lied to Me")..75-100 55

SHAW, Mike
Singles: 7-inch
GONE (5098 "Coal Mine")....................... 15-25 61
PERFECT (111 "Long Gone Baby").... 200-250 57

SHAW, Ricky
(With Mandarins; with Billy Mure & Orchestra)
Singles: 7-inch
CAMPUS (105 "Martian Chant")............ 15-25 57
(Colored vinyl.)
CLOUD (502 "Ups and Downs")............ 10-15 65
PRESIDENT (822 "A Fool's Memory").... 20-30 62
PRESIDENT (830 "Don't Waste Your Time").. 15-25 63
Also see MURE, Billy

SHAW, Ronnie / Grays
Singles: 7-inch
BELL (154 "Diamonds and Pearls"/"Don't Be Cruel").. 10-15 60

SHAW, Sandie — P&R '64
Singles: 7-inch
MERCURY (72315 "As Long As You're Happy")..5-10 64
RCA..5-10 68-70
REPRISE...5-10 64-67
LPs: 10/12-inch
REPRISE... 15-25 65-66

SHAW, Sandy
Singles: 7-inch
MOONGLOW (5006 "Rock Is Here to Stay")... 15-25 57

SHAW, Timmy — P&R/R&B '64
(With the Sternphones)
Singles: 7-inch
AUDREY (3740 "A Taste of the Blues")... 10-20
JAMIE (1204 "Throw It Out of Your Mind")... 10-15 61
JAMIE (1215 "This I Know").................. 10-15 62
SCEPTER...5-10 73
WAND (146 "Gonna Send You Back to Georgia")... 10-15 63
WAND (151 "If I Catch You")................ 10-15 64

SHAW, Timmy, & Little Melvin
Singles: 7-inch
PREMIUM STUFF................................ 10-20 '60s
Also see LITTLE MELVIN
Also see SHAW, Timmy

SHA-WEEZ
Singles: 78 rpm
ALADDIN (3170 "No One to Love Me").. 400-500 52
Singles: 7-inch
ALADDIN (3170 "No One to Love Me")....................................... 2000-3000 52
Members: Edgar Myles; Warren Myles; James Crawford; Irving Banister.
Also see MYLES, Big Boy

SHAY, Janet
(With the Four Jacks; with Don Neal & Playboys)
Singles: 7-inch
ALCAR (1502 "Busy Bee").......................20-30 60
LIN (1003 "At the Sock Hop")..................50-75 58
PELPAL...10-15
Also see FOUR JACKS

SHAYDE
(Shaydes)
Singles: 7-inch
INT'L ARTISTS (132 "Search the Sun")...15-25 68
INT'L ARTISTS (137 "Third Number")......15-25 69

SHAYNES
Singles: 7-inch
PEE VEE (140 "You Tell Me Girl")...........20-30 66
PEE VEE (142 "From My Window").......75-125 66
PEE VEE (5000 "Valarie")........................50-60 67
X-BAT (2000 "You Tell Me Girl"/"From My Window")...10-20 99
(Green vinyl. 250 made.)
Members: Barry Bruce; Corky Irwin; Mike Kahler; Joe Huxta; Don Haus; Mike Fritsch; Sylvester "Butch" King.

SH-BOOMS
(Chords)
Singles: 78 rpm
CAT...10-20 55
VIK...15-25 57
Singles: 7-inch
ATCO (6213 "Sh-Boom")..........................8-12 61
ATLANTIC (2074 "Blue Moon")...............10-20 60
CAT (117 "Could It Be")..........................30-40 55
TEEN (2 "Blue Moon")...............................3-5
VIK (0295 "I Don't Want to Set the World on Fire")..20-30 57
Also see CHORDS

SHEARING, George, Quintet — LP '56
Singles: 78 rpm
CAPITOL..3-5 55-57
MGM..3-6 50-56
Singles: 7-inch
CAPITOL..4-8 55-67
DISCOVERY (106 "Cotton Top")............30-50 50
(Red vinyl.)
LONDON..4-6 63
MGM..6-12 50-56
SHEBA..4-6 71
EPs: 7-inch
CAPITOL..5-15 55-60
MGM..5-15 51-55
LPs: 10/12-inch
ARCHIVE OF FOLK MUSIC.......................6-12 68
BASF..5-10 73
CAPITOL (Except 648 thru 1628).............5-20 62-77
CAPITOL (648 thru 1628).......................20-40 55-61
CONCORD JAZZ......................................5-8 80-82
CORONET...5-10 '60s
DISCOVERY (3002 "George Shearing Quintet")..50-75 50
(10-inch LP.)
EVEREST...5-10 69
LION..10-20 59
MGM (90 "A Touch of Genius")...............20-40 51
(10-inch LP.)
MGM (155 "I Hear Music")......................20-40 52
(10-inch LP.)
MGM (226 "When Lights Are Low").........20-40 53
(10-inch LP.)
MGM (252 "An Evening with George Shearing")...20-40 55
(10-inch LP.)
MGM (100 series).....................................5-10 70
MGM (3000 series)..................................15-25 55-60
MGM (4000 series)..................................10-20 62-63
MPS...5-10 74-75
METRO..10-15 65
MOSAIC (157 "Complete Capitol Live Recordings")..90-100 '90s
(Boxed, seven-disc audiophile set. 7500 made.)
PAUSA..5-8 79-82
PICKWICK...5-8
SAVOY (12093 "Midnight on Cloud 69")..15-25 57
SAVOY (15003 "Piano Solo")..................30-50 51
(10-inch LP.)
SHEBA..5-10 71-76
VSP...10-15 66-67
Members: Marjorie Hyams; Chuck Wayne; Denzil Best; John Levy.
Also see COLE, Cozy
Also see COLE, Nat "King," & George Shearing
Also see COLE, Natalie
Also see LEE, Peggy, & George Shearing

SHEARING, George, & Montgomery Brothers
Singles: 7-inch
JAZZLAND..4-8 62
LPs: 10/12-inch
JAZZLAND (55 "George Shearing & Montgomery Brothers")...25-40 61
(Cover pictures Shearing with the three brothers.)
JAZZLAND (55 "George Shearing & Montgomery Brothers")...15-25 62
(Cover pictures a woman.)
RIVERSIDE..5-10 82
Also see MONTGOMERY BROTHERS
Also see SHEARING, George, Quintet
Also see WILSON, Nancy, & George Shearing

SHEATHER, Sonny
Singles: 7-inch
BEAVER (101 "Orbit with Me")................50-75 63
BEAVER (102 "Mississippi Ride")...........10-20 63

SHEELY, Jerry, & Versatiles
Singles: 7-inch
STAR (220 "Love Only Me")................350-450 '60s

SHEELY, Ted
Singles: 7-inch
J-V-B (5003 "Eagle Shuffle")....................15-25 59

SHEEN, Bobby — R&B '75
Singles: 7-inch
CAPITOL (2507 "I Don't Have to Dream")..10-20 69
CAPITOL (5672 "Sweet Sweet Love").....10-20 66
CAPITOL (5827 "I Shook the World").......10-20 67
CAPITOL (5984 "Way of Love")...............10-20 67
CHELSEA (3034 "Love Stealing")...............4-6 75
DIMENSION (1043 "My Shoes Keep Walking Back to You")...8-12 65
LIBERTY (55459 "How Many Nights – How Many Days")..5-10 62
W.B. (7662 "May Not Be What You Want")..10-15 72
Also see ALLEY CATS
Also see BOB B. SOXX & BLUE JEANS

SHEEP — P&R '66
Singles: 7-inch
BOOM (60000 "Hide & Seek")..................15-25 66
BOOM (60007 "Dynamite").......................15-25 66
Members: Bob Feldman; Jerry Goldstein; Richie Gottehrer. Session: Tom Kobus; Jack Raczka; John Shine; Richie Lauro.
Also see STRANGELOVES

SHEER COINCIDENCE
Singles: 7-inch
WRIGHT (6951 "I Didn't Lie")....................10-20 69

SHEETS, Sonny
Singles: 7-inch
D (1015 "Wheels")...................................50-100
SATURN (1200 "Skippin' Class")..............25-35

SHEFFIELD, Charles
(Mad Dog Sheffield)
Singles: 7-inch
EXCELLO (2200 "Rock N' Roll Train").....10-20 61
EXCELLO (2205 "Kangaroo")...................10-20 61
GOLDBAND (1045 "Mad Dog")..............75-100 57
(First issue.)
HOLLYWOOD (1079 "Mad Dog")..............50-75 57
ROCKO (509 "Never No More")...............10-15 60
ROCKO (515 "Shoo, Shoo Chicken").......10-15 61

SHEFFIELDS
Singles: 7-inch
DESTINATION (613 "Please Come Back to Me")..8-12 66
DESTINATION (621 "Do You Still Love Me")..8-12 66
FENTON (980 "Nothing I Can Do")..........20-30 65
FENTON (2118 "Fool Minus a Heart").....15-25 66

SHEFFIELDS
Singles: 7-inch
SSEXX (672 "This Road")..........................5-10 '60s

SHEIKS
Singles: 78 rpm
CAT (116 "Walk That Walk")....................10-15 55
EF-N-DE (1000 "Give Me Another Chance")..200-300 55
FEDERAL (12237 "So Fine")....................20-30 55
Singles: 7-inch
CAT (116 "Walk That Walk")....................20-30 55
EF-N-DE (1000 "Give Me Another Chance")..2000-3000 55
FEDERAL (12237 "So Fine")..................50-150 55
Also see BELVIN, Jesse

SHEIKS
Singles: 7-inch
JAMIE (1147 "Candlelight Cafe").............10-20 59
Also see GILMORE, Geoff / Sheiks

SHEIKS
Singles: 7-inch
SULTAN (1001 "Ya-Habibi")......................10-20 59

SHEIKS
Singles: 7-inch
AMY (807 "Come On Back")................200-300 60

SHEILA
LPs: 10/12-inch
PHILIPS (200144 "Sheila")......................10-15 64
(Monaural.)
PHILIPS (600144 "Sheila")......................15-20 64
(Stereo.)

SHEKERYK, Pete, & Delua-Tones
Singles: 7-inch
UKEY (101 "Believe in Me").................500-750

SHELBY, Jim
Singles: 7-inch
BARTON (409 "Long Gone Daddy")........50-75

SHELDON, Doug
Singles: 7-inch
CONGRESS (266 "It's Because of You")...5-10 66
MGM (13261 "Lonely Boy")........................5-10 64

SHELDON, Rick, & Saturday Knights
Singles: 7-inch
MANSION (18883 "Why Does My Baby Cry")..50-75 '60s
Also see SATURDAY KNIGHTS

SHELDON, Sandi
Singles: 7-inch
OKEH (7277 "Baby You're Mine")...........15-25 67
Session: Van McCoy.
Also see McCOY, Van

SHELLS — P&R '60
Singles: 78 rpm
END (1022 "Pretty Little Girl")..............100-200 58
JOHNSON (104 "Baby, Oh Baby"/"Angel Eyes")..50-100 57
Singles: 10-inch
CANDLELITE (436 "Baby Oh Baby").........8-12 72
(Gold vinyl.)
Singles: 7-inch
ABC (2733 "Baby, Oh Baby")......................4-6 75
BOARDWALK (17 "Oh, What a Night")........4-6 70
CLIFTON (22 "On My Honor").....................4-6 77
COLLECTABLES..3-5 '80s
END (1022 "Pretty Little Girl")..............200-300 58
END (1050 "Whispering Winds")..............50-75 59
GONE (5103 "Pretty Little Girl")...............20-30 61
JOHNSON (099 "My Cherie")......................4-8 73
JOHNSON (104 "Baby, Oh Baby"/"Angel Eyes")...35-55 57
(Has selection number [104] centered between the horizontal lines.)
JOHNSON (104 "Baby, Oh Baby"/"What's in an Angel Eyes")...15-25 60
(Has two sets of parallel lines, one thinner than the other. These lines are both the same thickness on the '57 issue. Most 1957 issues have the shorter flip side title, whereas those with the longer title are 1960 issues.)
JOHNSON (106 "Pleading No More")..100-150 58
JOHNSON (107 "Explain It to Me").........10-20 61
JOHNSON (109 "Better Forget Him")......10-20 61
JOHNSON (110 "In the Dim of the Dark")..10-20 61
JOHNSON (112 "Sweetest One")...........15-25 61
JOHNSON (119 "Deep in My Heart").......20-30 63
JOHNSON (120 "A Toast on Your Birthday")..30-40 63
JOHNSON (127 "On My Honor")..............50-75 63
JOHNSON (332 "Explain It to Me").........15-25 61

JOSIE (912 "Deep in My Heart")... 15-25 63
ROULETTE (4156 "She Wasn't Meant for Me")... 15-25 59
SELSOM (334 "A Toast on Your Birthday")... 10-15 65
SNOWFLAKE (1959 "If You Were Gone from Me"/"Misty")... 10-20 64
(Blank, orange labels.)
SOUNDS FROM THE SUBWAY... 4-6 77
(Colored vinyl.)

LPs: 10/12-inch

CANDLELITE... 10-15 '70s
COLLECTABLES... 5-8 '80s
GRECO... 5-8 '80s
JUBILEE... 10-20
SNOWFLAKE (1000 "Acappella Session with the Shells")... 25-35
Members: Nathaniel Bouknight; Shade Alston; Bobby Nurse; Danny Small; Gus Geter; Roy Jones.
Also see DUBS / Shells
Also see FIVE SATINS / Youngtones / Youngsters / Shells
Also see LITTLE NAT & ETIQUETTES
Also see LITTLE NATE & CHRYSLERS

SHELLS
(With Bob Gross & Orchestra)

Singles: 7-inch

GENIE (100/101 "Same Old Thing")... 100-200 58

SHELLS

Singles: 7-inch

CONLO (879 "Whiplash")... 15-25 '60s

SHELLY & KIM

Singles: 7-inch

COULEE (107 "We Love Them All")... 8-12 64

Picture Sleeves

COULEE (107 "We Love Them All")... 10-20 64
Members: Shelly Hutchins; Kim Statler.

SHELTON, Bobbie

Singles: 7-inch

W.B. (5463 "Juke Box Blue Boy")... 10-20 64

SHELTON, Curley

Singles: 7-inch

FALCON (609 "Have You Seen My Baby")... 40-60

SHELTON, Gary
(Gary Schelton; Troy Shondell; with Toneblenders)

Singles: 7-inch

ALPINE (56 "Til the End of the Line")... 50-75 60
MARK (143 "Goodbye Little Darlin' Goodbye")... 800-1200 59
MARK (145 "A Prayer & a Jukebox")... 200-300 59
MERCURY (71310 "Kissin' at the Drive-In")... 100-200 58
REGIS (1001 "The Trance")... 100-200 59
SMASH (200 "My Hero")... 100-200 58
Also see SHONDELL, Troy
Also see TONEBLENDERS

SHELTON, Gil

Singles: 7-inch

GILLY-BOY (100 "I'm Afraid to Love You")... 10-15
(Colored vinyl.)
LUTE (6004 "Shirley My Love")... 10-20 61
VALIANT (6062 "Not Now")... 5-10 65

SHELTON, Johnny, & His Rockabillies

Singles: 7-inch

SCENIC (806 "Groovy Joe's")... 100-125

SHELTON, Roscoe R&B '65

Singles: 7-inch

BATTLE (45905 "Yesterday's Mistakes") 10-15 62
BATTLE (45913 "My Best Friend")... 10-15 63
EXCELLO (2167 "Pleadin' for Love")... 15-25 59
EXCELLO (2170 "It's My Fault")... 15-25 60
EXCELLO (2176 "We've Been Wrong").. 15-25 60
EXCELLO (2181 "Miss You")... 15-25 60
EXCELLO (2192 "It's Too Late Baby")... 15-25 61
EXCELLO (2198 "Baby, It's True Love"). 15-25 61
SIMS (156 "Love Is the Key")... 8-12 63
SIMS (190 "Love Comes and Goes")... 8-12 64
SIMS (217 "Question")... 8-12 64
SIMS (240 "Wedding Cake")... 8-12 65
SIMS (245 "Fire Still Burns")... 8-12 65
SOUND PLUS (2106 "Running for My Life")... 5-10
SOUND STAGE 7... 5-10 65-68

LPs: 10/12-inch

EXCELLO (8002 "Roscoe Shelton Sings")... 50-75 61
SOUND STAGE 7 (5002 "Soul in His Music, Music in His Soul")... 15-25 66

SHEMWELL, Sylvia

Singles: 7-inch

PHILIPS (40149 "Funny What Time Can Do")... 10-15 63
Also see SWEET INSPIRATIONS

SHEP & LIMELITES P&R/R&B '61
(Featuring James Sheppard)

Singles: 7-inch

ABC (2486 "Daddy's Home")... 4-6 73
HULL (740 "Daddy's Home")... 15-25 61
HULL (742 "Ready For Your Love")... 15-20 61
HULL (747 "Three Steps from the Altar"). 15-20 61
HULL (748 "Our Anniversary")... 15-20 62
HULL (751 "What Did Daddy Do")... 15-20 62
HULL (753 "Gee Baby, What About You")... 15-20 62
HULL (756 "Remember Baby")... 15-20 63
HULL (757 "Stick By Me")... 15-20 63
HULL (759 "Steal Away")... 15-20 63
HULL (761 "Easy to Remember")... 15-20 64
HULL (767 "Why Did You Fall For Me")... 15-20 64
HULL (770 "A Party for Two")... 20-30 65
HULL (772 "In Case I Forget")... 15-20 65
ROULETTE (102 "Ready For Your Love")... 4-6 73

LPs: 10/12-inch

HULL (1001 "Our Anniversary")... 400-600 62
ROULETTE (25350 "Our Anniversary")... 35-45 67
Also see ALSTON, Shirley
Also see HEARTBEATS
Also see HEARTBEATS / Shep & Limelites
Also see SHEPPARD, Shane

SHEPARD, Jean C&W/P&R '53

Singles: 78 rpm

CAPITOL... 4-8 53-57

Singles: 7-inch

CAPITOL... 5-10 53-61
(Purple labels.)
CAPITOL... 4-8 61-72
(Orange, orange/yellow, or red labels.)
MERCURY... 4-6 72
SCORPION... 3-5 78
U.A.... 4-6 73-77

EPs: 7-inch

CAPITOL... 5-10 56-61

LPs: 10/12-inch

CAPITOL (100 thru 800 series)... 10-20 69-71
CAPITOL (700 thru 1200 series)... 15-25 56-59
(With a "T" prefix.)
CAPITOL (1500 thru 2900 series)... 10-15 61-68
CAPITOL (11000 series)... 5-10 72-79
FIRST GENERATION... 5-10 81
MERCURY... 5-10 71
PICKWICK/HILLTOP... 5-12 67-68
POWER PAK... 5-8 75-80
U.A.... 5-10 73-76
Session: Justin Tubb; Red Sovine.
Also see TUBB, Justin
Also see YOUNG, Faron / Jean Shepard

SHEPARD, Jean, & Ferlin Huskey C&W/P&R '53

Singles: 78 rpm

CAPITOL... 10-15 53-54

Singles: 7-inch

CAPITOL (2502 "A Dear John Letter")... 20-25 53
CAPITOL (2586 "Forgive Me John")... 20-25 53
CAPITOL (2706 "Let's Kiss and Try Again")... 20-25 54
Also see HUSKY, Ferlin

SHEPARD, Jean, & Ray Pillow C&W '66

Singles: 7-inch

CAPITOL (5633 "I'll Take the Dog")... 4-8 66
CAPITOL (5769 "Mr. Do-It-Yourself")... 4-8 66

LPs: 10/12-inch

CAPITOL (2537 "I'll Take the Dog")... 10-15 66
Also see SHEPARD, Jean

SHEPARD, Joe

Singles: 7-inch

END (1024 "What's the Matter Baby")... 20-40 58

SHEPARD, Kenny

Singles: 7-inch

MAXX (332 "What Difference Does It Make")... 40-60 64

SHEPEL, Milan

Singles: 7-inch

FALCON (501 "Rip It Up")... 100-200

SHEPHERD, Buddy

Singles: 7-inch

PLAY ME (3517 "I'm Hypnotized")... 10-15 59
PLAY ME (3520 "Who Do I Know Like This")... 15-25 59

Picture Sleeves

PLAY ME (3517 "I'm Hypnotized")... 20-30 59

SHEPHERD, Johnnie

Singles: 7-inch

ABC (10548 "I Really Love You")... 10-20 64
COLUMBIA (44057 "Diddily Dee")... 10-15 67
TILDEN (3001 "How Blue My Heart")... 15-25 61
Session: Dedications.
Also see DEDICATIONS

SHEPHERD, Wyatt "Big Boy"

Singles: 7-inch

U.A. (216 "You Don't Want Me No More")... 40-60 60

SHEPHERD SISTERS P&R '57
(Sheppard Sisters; Shepard Sisters; Shephard Sisters)

Singles: 78 rpm

LANCE... 5-10 57
MELBA... 5-10 56
MERCURY... 5-10 57

Singles: 7-inch

ABC... 4-6 73
ATLANTIC (2176 "Don't Mention My Name")... 5-10 63
ATLANTIC (2195 "Talk Is Cheap")... 5-10 63
BIG TOP (3066 "Hapsburg Serenade")... 10-15 61
COLLECTABLES... 3-5 '80s
LANCE (125 "Alone")... 10-15 57
MGM (12766 "Heart and Soul")... 5-10 59
MELBA (101 "Rock and Roll Cha Cha")... 10-15 56
MELBA (108 "I Walked Beside the Sea"). 10-15 57
MERCURY (71244 "Gettin' Ready for Freddie")... 5-10 57
MERCURY (71350 "Is It a Crime")... 5-10 58
PRIVATE STOCK... 4-6 75
20TH FOX (468 "Finders Keepers")... 5-10 64
U.A. (350 "I'm Still Dancin' ")... 5-10 61
U.A. (456 "Lolita Ya Ya")... 5-10 62
WARWICK (511 "I Think It's Time")... 5-10 59
WARWICK (530 "Alone")... 5-10 60
WARWICK (548 "How Softly a Heart Breaks")... 5-10 60
YORK... 5-10 65

EPs: 7-inch

MERCURY (3369 "Sheppard Sisters")... 20-30 57
Members: Mary Lou; Judy; Martha; Gayle.

SHEPPARD, Buddy, & Holidays

Singles: 7-inch

SABINA (506 "My Love Is Real")... 50-60 62
SABINA (510 "Now It's All Over")... 50-60 63
SABINA (510 "Now It's All Over")... 100-200 63
(White label promotional issue.)
Also see BELMONTS
Also see TONY & HOLIDAYS

SHEPPARD, Shane
(With the Limelites; Shane Shep)

Singles: 7-inch

APT (25039 "Too Young To Wed")... 30-40 60
APT (25046 "I'm So Lonely")... 30-40 60
Also see SHEP & LIMELITES

SHEPPARD, Zeke

Singles: 7-inch

PRESIDENT (831 "Snow Surfin'")... 15-25 64

SHEPPARDS

Singles: 78 rpm

THERON (112 "Love")... 50-100 55
UNITED (198 "Sherry")... 50-75 56

Singles: 7-inch

ABC (10758 "Let Yourself Go")... 5-10 66
ABNER (7006 "Loving You")... 8-12 62
APEX (7750 "Island of Love")... 15-25 59
APEX (7752 "Just Like You")... 15-25 59
APEX (7755 "Meant to Be")... 15-25 60
APEX (7759 "Society Girl")... 15-25 60
APEX (7760 "Just Like You")... 15-25 60
APEX (7762 "Tragic")... 15-25 60
B&F (198 "Sherry")... 10-15 60
BUNKY (7764 "Island of Love")... 5-10 69
BUNKY (7766 "I'm Not Wanted")... 5-10 69
CONSTELLATION (123 "Island of Love").. 5-10 64
CONSTELLATION (176 "Island of Love").. 5-10 66
KING TUT (168 "Devil Eyes")... 4-8 76
OKEH (7173 "Pretend You're Still Mine"). 10-15 63
OWL (330 "Queen of Hearts")... 4-6 74
PAM (1001 "Never Let Me Go")... 10-15 61
SHARP (6039 "Glitter in Your Eyes")... 5-10 69
UNITED (198 "Sherry")... 100-200 56
VEE-JAY (406 "Every Now and Then")... 10-20 61
VEE-JAY (441 "Tragic")... 15-25 62
WES... 10-15 61

LPs: 10/12-inch

CONSTELLATION (4 "The Sheppards").. 25-50 64
SOLID SMOKE... 5-10 80
Members: Mill Edwards; Oscar Boyd; James Dennis Issac; George "Sonny" Parker; John Pruitt; Nate Tucker; Kent McGhee; Murrie Eskridge; Kermit Chandler.

SHEPPARDS

Singles: 7-inch

IMPACT (1018 "Poor Man's Thing")... 20-30 67
Also see ESQUIRES

SHERIDAN, Bobby
(Charlie Rich)

Singles: 7-inch

SUN (354 "Sad News")... 10-20 61
Also see RICH, Charlie

SHERIDAN, Mike, & Nightriders

Singles: 7-inch

LIVERPOOL SOUND (902 "Please Mr. Postman")... 60-80 64
Also see IDLE RACE

SHERIDONS

Singles: 7-inch

UP-BEAT ("Unchained Melody")... 75-100
(No selection number used.)

SHERIFF & RAVELS

Singles: 7-inch

VEE-JAY (306 "Shombalor")... 20-30 58
Also see RAVELS

SHERMAN, Allan LP '62
(With Friends; with Boston Pops Orch.; with Lou Busch & Orchestra)

Singles: 7-inch

RCA... 4-8 68
W.B.... 5-10 63-66

Picture Sleeves

W.B.... 8-15 63-64

LPs: 10/12-inch

JUBILEE... 10-20 62
RCA (Except 310)... 10-15 64
RCA (310 "Allan Sherman and You")... 20-30 64
(Promotional issue only. Includes 25-page script, letter from Allan and a comments postcard.)
RHINO... 5-8 85-86
W.B.... 15-25 62-66
Also see BOSTON POPS ORCHESTRA

SHERMAN, Bobby P&R/LP '69

Singles: 7-inch

CAMEO (403 "Happiness Is")... 5-10 66
CAMEO (403 "Happiness Is")... 10-15 66
(Single-sided. Promotional issue only.)
CONDOR... 5-8 69
DECCA... 8-15 64-65
DOT... 5-10 63
EPIC... 5-10 67
GRT... 4-6 76
JANUS... 4-6 75
METROMEDIA... 4-6 69-73
PARKWAY... 5-10 66
STARCREST... 5-10 62

Picture Sleeves

DECCA (31741 "It Hurts Me")... 8-15 65
METROMEDIA... 4-6 69-72

EPs: 7-inch

METROMEDIA ("Bobby Sherman")... 5-10 70
(Cardboard cutout picture discs from cereal boxes. Four different pictures made, each listing five songs. The song actually on the disc is stamped into the label area. 20 different picture/song variations exist.)

LPs: 10/12-inch

METROMEDIA...5-10 69-73

SHERMAN & DARTS

Singles: 7-inch

FURY (1014 "Remember")...75-125 58

SHERMAN & NOTATIONS

Singles: 7-inch

KIT (1012 "Conscience")...75-125

SHERRILL, Billy

(Bill Sherrell)

Singles: 7-inch

ABC-PAR (10465 "Drag Race")...10-15 63
EPIC...3-5 78
MERCURY (71679 "Rules of the Game")...10-15 60
SEE (1005 "Hear Her Rave On")...30-50
TYME (101 "Don't You Rock Me Daddy-O")...75-125 57
TYME (102 "Cadillac Baby")...75-125 58
TYME (103 "Rock On, Baby")...75-125 58
TYME (104 "Kool Kat")...150-250 58
TYME (106 "Rock and Roll Teenager")...50-100 58
Also see VANDELLS

SHERRY, Ruby

Singles: 7-inch

TAKE 6 (1002 "Feminine Ingenuity")...75-125 '60s

SHERRY LEE

(With Shorty Ashford & Country Music Boys; "Sixteen-Year-Old Miss Country Music"; Jackie De Shannon)

Singles: 78 rpm

MAR-VEL (903 "I'm Crazy Darlin' ")...40-60 56

Singles: 7-inch

MAR-VEL (903 "I'm Crazy Darlin' ")...50-100 56
RENDEZVOUS (147 "Unwritten Law")...20-30 61
Also see DE SHANNON, Jackie

SHERRY SISTERS

Singles: 7-inch

CINDY (3000 "The Prize")...20-30 57

SHERRYS P&R/R&B '62

Singles: 7-inch

GUYDEN (2068 "Pop Pop Pop – Pie")...15-20 62
GUYDEN (2077 "Slop Time")...15-20 62
GUYDEN (2084 "Saturday Night")...10-20 63
GUYDEN (2094 "That Boy of Mine")...10-20 63
MERCURY (72256 "No No Baby")...5-10 64
ROBERTS...5-10 '60s

LPs: 10/12-inch

GUYDEN (503 "At the Hop")...100-200 62
GUYDEN (503 "At the Hop")...200-300 62
(White label. Promotional issue only.)

SHERWIN, Ben

Singles: 7-inch

GOLD ARROW (210 "Little Girl")...15-25 62
LIBERTY (55281 "Johnny Goofed")...8-12 60

SHERWOOD, Fred

Singles: 7-inch

BROOKE (110 "Dream Boat")...50-75

SHERWOODS

Singles: 7-inch

JOHNSON...10-15 61-63
MAGGIE (101/2 "Nanette")...8-12 61
Member: Tony Reno.
Also see RENO, Tony, & Sherwoods

SHERWOODS

(Concords)

Singles: 7-inch

DOT (16540 "Cold and Frosty Morning")...20-30 63
Also see CONCORDS

SHERWOODS

Singles: 7-inch

EASTWOOD...10-15 '60s
EXETER (123 "Tickler")...150-250 64
KAPP (679 "Come On")...5-10 65
MAGNIFICO (103 "Monkey See, Monkey Do")...5-10 61
MAGNIFICO (105 "Happy Holiday")...10-15 61
MERCURY (72042 "Recipe for Going Steady")...15-25 62
V-TONE (506 "Uncle Sam")...10-15 63

SHEVELLES

Singles: 7-inch

WORLD ARTISTS (1023 "Do Poo Pa Doo")...5-10 64
WORLD ARTISTS (1025 "I Could Conquer the World")...5-10 64

SHIBLEY, Arkie C&W '50

(With His Mountain Dew Boys; "Vocal by Leon Kelly")

Singles: 78 rpm

GILT-EDGE (8)...10-20 50
(Title not known.)
GILT-EDGE (5021 "Hot Rod Race")...50-60 51
GILT-EDGE (5030 "Hot Rod Race No. 2")...50-60 51
GILT-EDGE (5036 "Arkie Meets the Judge")...50-60 51
GILT-EDGE (5078 "Arkie's Talking Blues")...30-50 53
MAE-MAE (77)...35-50
(Title not known.)

Singles: 7-inch

4 STAR (1737 "Pickin' My Guitar")...40-60 59
GILT-EDGE (101 "Hot Rod Race")...25-50 '50s
(Reissue of Gilt-Edge 5021. Exact year of issue not yet known.)
GILT-EDGE (5021 "Hot Rod Race")...75-125 50
GILT-EDGE (5030 "Hot Rod Race No. 2")...75-125 51
GILT-EDGE (5036 "Arkie Meets the Judge")...75-125 51
GILT-EDGE (5078 "Arkie's Talking Blues")...75-125 53

SHIEKS

(Sheiks)

Singles: 7-inch

MGM (12876 "Baghdad Rock")...10-20 60
TRINE (1101 "Baghdad Rock")...25-35 59
Member: Bill Ramal.
Also see RAMAL, Bill

SHIELDS P&R/R&B '58

Singles: 78 rpm

TENDER (513 "You Cheated")...300-400 58
(Makes no mention of distribution by Dot.)
TENDER (513 "You Cheated")...100-200 58
(Label reads: "Distributed Exclusively By Dot Records.")

Singles: 7-inch

DOT (136 "You Cheated")...5-10 66
(Black vinyl.)
DOT (136 "You Cheated")...20-30 66
(Colored vinyl. Promotional issue only.)
DOT (15805 "You Cheated")...20-30 58
DOT (15856 "I'm Sorry Now")...30-40 58
DOT (15940 "Play the Game Fair")...15-25 59
FALCON (100 "The Girl Around the Corner")...150-200 60
TENDER (513 "You Cheated")...50-100 58
(Makes no mention of distribution by Dot.)
TENDER (513 "You Cheated")...20-30 58
(Label reads: "Distributed Exclusively By Dot Records.")
TENDER (518 "I'm Sorry Now")...20-30 59
(Same number used on a Capris release.)
TENDER (521 "Play the Game Fair")...20-30 59
TENDER (567 "You Cheated")...10-15
TRANSCONTINENTAL (1013 "The Girl Around the Corner")...400-500 60
(First issue.)

LPs: 10/12-inch

BRYLEN...5-10
Members: Frankie Ervin; Jesse Belvin; Charles Wright; Nathaniel Wilson; Johnny "Guitar" Watson; Mel Williams. Session: Tony Allen.
Also see ALLEN, Tony
Also see BELVIN, Jesse
Also see ERVIN, Frankie
Also see WATSON, Johnny
Also see WRIGHT, Charles

SHIELDS

Singles: 7-inch

CONTINENTAL (4072 "You Told a Lie")...1500-2500 61

SHIELDS, Billy

(Tony Orlando)

Singles: 7-inch

HARBOUR (304 "I Was a Boy")...10-15 69
Also see ORLANDO, Tony

SHIELDS, Bobby

(With the Street Singers & Orchestra)

Singles: 78 rpm

DAWN...25-35 55
MELBA...15-25 56

Singles: 7-inch

DAWN (211 "I Was Dreaming")...75-100 55
MELBA (105 "Land of Rock and Roll")...30-40 56

SHIELDS, Charles K.

Singles: 7-inch

FARRIS (1280 "Go Alabama Girl")...50-75
SHERWOOD (1281 "Go Alabama Girl")...75-100

SHIELDS, Johnny

Singles: 7-inch

ARMOUR (4466 "Crying in the Chapel")...50-75 63

SHILOH

Singles: 7-inch

AMOS (140 "Jennifer")...5-10 71
AMOS (162 "Down on the Farm")...5-10 71

LPs: 10/12-inch

AMOS (7015 "Shiloh")...200-300 71
LAMB & LION...8-12
Members: Al Perkins; Don Henley; Jim Norman; Mike Bowden; Richard Bowden.
Also see RONSTADT, Linda

SHINALL, Joe

Singles: 7-inch

GALA (122 "No Alimony")...50-75
ATTEIRAM...4-6 74

SHIN-DIG SMITH & SOUL SHAKERS

Singles: 7-inch

PITTER - PAT (101 "Through Fooling Around")...5-10 '60s

SHINDIGS

(Bobby Fuller Four)

Singles: 7-inch

MUSTANG (3003 "Wolfman")...10-15 65
Also see FULLER, Bobby

SHINDOGS P&R '66

Singles: 7-inch

VIVA (601 "Who Do You Think You Are")...5-10 66
W.B. (5665 "Someday, Someday")...5-10 65
Members: Delaney Bramlett; Joey Cooper; Chuck Blackwell; James Burton.

SHINES, Johnny

Singles: 78 rpm

J.O.B. (116 "Ramblin' ")...100-200 52
J.O.B. (1010 "Evening Sun")...100-200 53

Singles: 7-inch

J.O.B. (1010 "Evening Sun")...500-1000 53
JOLIET (206 "Skull & Crossbone Blues")...4-6

LPs: 10/12-inch

ADVENT...8-10 74
BLUE HORIZON...10-15
BLUE LABOR...8-10 77
CHESS...8-10
ROUNDER...5-10 84

SHINES, Johnny, & Big Walter Horton

LPs: 10/12-inch

TESTAMENT...10-20 '60s
Also see HORTON, Big Walter
Also see SHINES, Johnny

SHIPLEY, Reese

Singles: 78 rpm

VALLEY (106 "Catfish Boogie")...10-20 53

Singles: 7-inch

VALLEY (106 "Catfish Boogie")...25-35 53

SHIPMAN, Jerry

Singles: 7-inch

RIDGECREST (1206 "Rock & Roll Queen")...30-40 59

SHIPPELL, Bob

(With the Royals)

Singles: 7-inch

CHARM (9572 "The Chicken and the Bop")...25-35 59
TRANS ATLAS (689 "What Happened to Me")...10-20 62

SHIRA

Singles: 7-inch

JAMIE (1400 "Krishna")...10-15 71
JAMIE (1413 "Frank's Ant Farm")...10-15 73

SHIRELLES P&R '58

(With Luther Dixon & Orchestra)

Singles: 7-inch

COLLECTABLES...3-5 '80s
BLUE ROCK (4051 "Sweet Lovin' ")...5-10 68
BLUE ROCK (4066 "Call Me")...5-10 68
DECCA...10-25 58-61
ERIC...4-6 '70s
GUSTO...3-5
RCA...5-10 71-73
SCEPTER (1203 "Dedicated to the One I Love")...20-25 58
(White label.)
SCEPTER (1203 "Dedicated to the One I Love")...15-20 58
(Red label.)
SCEPTER (1205 thru 1208)...15-20 59-60
(White label.)
SCEPTER (1205 thru 1208)...10-15 59-60
(Red label.)
SCEPTER (1211 "Tomorrow")...20-30 60
SCEPTER (1211 "Will You Love Me Tomorrow")...10-15 60
(Note longer title.)
SCEPTER (1217 thru 1296)...8-12 61-65
SCEPTER (12000 series)...5-10 65-68
TIARA (6112 "I Met Him On a Sunday")...100-150 57
U.A....4-8 70-71

Picture Sleeves

SCEPTER (1248 "Foolish Little Girl")...10-20 63
SCEPTER (1255 "Don't Say Goodnight and Mean Goodbye")...10-20 63

LPs: 10/12-inch

BACK-TRAC...5-10 85
EVEREST...5-10 81
GUSTO...5-10 '80s
PHOENIX...5-10 81
PRICEWISE...15-25 '60s
RCA...10-15 71-72
RHINO...5-8 85
SCEPTER (M-501 "Tonight's the Night")...60-80 61
(Monaural.)
SCEPTER (S-501 "Tonight's the Night")...75-100 61
(Stereo.)
SCEPTER (M-502 "Shirelles Sing to Trumpets & Strings")...25-50 61
(Monaural.)
SCEPTER (S-502 "Shirelles Sing to Trumpets & Strings")...40-60 61
(Stereo.)
SCEPTER (M-504 "Baby It's You")...25-50 62
(Monaural.)
SCEPTER (S-504 "Baby It's You")...40-60 62
(Stereo.)
SCEPTER (M-507 "Greatest Hits")...25-50 63
(Monaural.)
SCEPTER (S-507 "Greatest Hits")...40-60 63
(Stereo.)
SCEPTER (M-511 "Foolish Little Girl")...25-50 63
(Monaural.)
SCEPTER (S-511 "Foolish Little Girl")...40-60 63
(Stereo.)
SCEPTER (M-514 "It's a Mad, Mad, Mad, Mad World")...20-40 63
(Monaural.)
SCEPTER (S-514 "It's a Mad, Mad, Mad, Mad World")...25-50 63
(Stereo.)
SCEPTER (M-516 "Golden Oldies")...20-40 64
(Monaural.)
SCEPTER (S-516 "Golden Oldies")...25-50 64
(Stereo.)
SCEPTER (560 "Greatest Hits, Vol. 2")...20-40 67
SCEPTER (562 "Spontaneous Combustion")...20-40 67
SCEPTER (599 "Remember When")...15-20 72
SPRINGBOARD...8-10 72
U.A....10-15 71-75
Members: Shirley Jackson-Alston; Beverly Lee; Doris Coley-Jackson; Addie "Micki" Harris-McFadden.
Also see ALSTON, Shirley
Also see DIXON, Luther
Also see JAN & DEAN / Roy Orbison / 4 Seasons / Shirelles
Also see KING, Carole
Also see SHIRLEY & SHIRELLES
Also see VALLI

SHIRELLES & KING CURTIS

LPs: 10/12-inch

SCEPTER (M-505 "A Twist Party")......... 25-50 62
(Monaural.)
SCEPTER (S-505 "A Twist Party") 40-60 62
(Stereo.)
SCEPTER (569 "Eternally Soul") 25-35 68
Also see KING CURTIS

SHIRELLES / Don Julian & Larks

Singles: 7-inch

ORIGINAL SOUND (4514 "Soldier Boy"/"I Want You Back")..4-6 '80s
Also see LARKS
Also see SHIRELLES

SHIRLEE MAY
(Shirley Ellis)

Singles: 7-inch

MERCURY (71969 "Lonely Birthday")........8-12 62
Also see ELLIS, Shirley

SHIRLEY, Danny C&W '84

Singles: 7-inch

AMOR..4-6 84-88

LPs: 10/12-inch

AMOR (1003 "Local Legend")............ 50-100 84

SHIRLEY, Danny, & Piano Red C&W '85

Singles: 7-inch

AMOR (1006 "Yo Yo") 5-10 85
Also see PIANO RED
Also see SHIRLEY, Danny

SHIRLEY, Dell, & Joe Brown
(With the Playetts)

Singles: 7-inch

LOGAN (3118 "Cliff's Rocket")................ 40-60 60

SHIRLEY, SHIRLEY

Singles: 7-inch

TIME (1069 "The Last of Larry's Goodbyes")... 10-15 63

SHIRLEY & JESSIE

Singles: 7-inch

WAND (1116 "You Can't Fight Love")...... 10-15 66
WAND (1131 "Oh Baby")........................ 10-15 66

SHIRLEY & LEE P&R '52
(With the Dave Bartholomew Orchestra; with Halos; with Jimmy Mundy & Orchestra)

Singles: 78 rpm

ALADDIN.. 20-40 52-57

Singles: 7-inch

ABC..4-6 73
ALADDIN (3153 "I'm Gone") 75-100 52
ALADDIN (3173 "Baby")........................ 50-100 53
ALADDIN (3192 "Shirley's Back") 50-100 53
ALADDIN (3205 "Two Happy People")..... 25-40 53
ALADDIN (3222 "Why Did I") 25-40 53
ALADDIN (3244 "Confessin' ")................ 25-40 54
ALADDIN (3258 "Comin' Over")............... 25-40 54
ALADDIN (3289 "Feel So Good") 30-40 55
ALADDIN (3302 "Lee's Dream") 15-25 55
ALADDIN (3313 "That's What I'll Do") 20-30 55
ALADDIN (3325 "Let the Good Times Roll").. 20-30 56
ALADDIN (3338 "I Feel Good")................ 20-30 56
ALADDIN (3362 "When I Saw You")........ 10-20 57
ALADDIN (3369 "I Want to Dance")......... 10-20 57
ALADDIN (3380 "Rock All Nite") 10-20 57
ALADDIN (3390 "Rockin' with the Clock")... 10-20 57
ALADDIN (3405 "I'll Thrill You") 10-20 57
ALADDIN (3418 "Everybody's Rockin' ").. 10-20 58
ALADDIN (3432 "All I Want to Do Is Cry").. 10-20 58
ALADDIN (3455 "True Love").................. 10-20 59
IMPERIAL (5818 "The Joker")..................5-10 62
IMPERIAL (5854 "My Last Letter").............5-10 62
IMPERIAL (5868 "A Little Thing")..............5-10 62
IMPERIAL (5922 "Hey Little Boy") 5-10 63
IMPERIAL (5970 "I'm Gone") 5-10 63
IMPERIAL (5979 "The Brink of Disaster") ..5-10 63
LIBERTY...3-5 '80s
U.A. (0087 "Let the Good Times Roll") 4-6 73
WARWICK (535 "Like You Used to Do"). 10-15 60
WARWICK (581 "Let the Good Times Roll").. 10-15 60
WARWICK (609 'Two Peas in a Pod")..... 10-15 61
WARWICK (664 "Well-A Well-A") 10-15 61
WARWICK (679 "Let's Live It Up").......... 10-15 62

LPs: 10/12-inch

ALADDIN (807 "Let the Good Times Roll") 1000-1500 56
IMPERIAL (9179 "Let the Good Times Roll") 100-150 62
SCORE (4023 "Let the Good Times Roll") 100-150 57
U.A. (340 "Legendary Masters") 20-25 74
WARWICK (2028 "Let the Good Times Roll") 100-150 61
Members: Shirley Goodman; Leonard Lee.
Also see ADAMS, Faye / Little Esther / Shirley & Lee
Also see BARTHOLOMEW, Dave
Also see GENE & EUNICE / Shirley & Lee
Also see HEART-THROBS
Also see KING, Ben E.

SHIRLEY & SHIRELLES
(Featuring Shirley Alston)

Singles: 7-inch

BELL (760 "Look What You've Done to My Heart")...8-12 69
BELL (787 'Looking Glass") 8-12 69
BELL (815 "Never Give You Up") 8-12 69
Also see ALSTON, Shirley
Also see SHIRELLES

SHIRLEY & SQUIRES

Singles: 7-inch

CONSTELLATION (107 "Drip Drop") 40-50 63

SHIRLEY & SWEETHEARTS

Singles: 7-inch

TWIRL (2011 "Tony")................................10-20 64

SHIVA'S HEADBAND

Singles: 7-inch

ARMADILLO 8-12 71-76
IGNITE (681 "Kaleidoscopic") 15-25 67

Picture Sleeves

ARMADILLO (3 "Country Boy")................15-25 '70s
ARMADILLO (6-1 "Extension") 15-25 76

LPs: 10/12-inch

APE (1001 "Yesterdays") 10-15 78
ARMADILLO ("Coming to a Head") 75-125 70
(No selection number used.)
CAPITOL (538 "Take Me to the Mountains")...40-60 70
MOONTOWER...8-10 85
Members: Spencer Perskin; Shawn Siegel; Bob Tonreid; Susan Perskin; Kenny Parker; Robert Gladwin; Richard Finnell.

SHOCK

Singles: 7-inch

DOWNTOWN (502 "We Were That Noise") 25-50 78
(Blue vinyl.)

Picture Sleeves

DOWNTOWN (502 "We Were That Noise") 25-50 78

EPs: 7-inch

IMPACT (501 "This Generation's On Vacation") 75-100 78
(Red vinyl. Gatefold sleeve. Counterfeits exist but can be identified by the label logo printed in silver. Originals have that logo in white.)
Members: Paul Lesperance; Steve Reiner; Kip Brown; Gaylord.
Also see LITTLE GIRLS

SHOCKETTES

Singles: 7-inch

SYMBOL (914 "Hold Back the Tears") 20-30 61

SHOCKING BLUE P&R '69

Singles: 7-inch

BUDDAH 4-6 71
COLOSSUS 4-8 70-71
MGM..4-6 72-73
POLYDOR...4-6 74
21...3-5 '80s

Picture Sleeves

COLOSSUS 4-8 70

LPs: 10/12-inch

COLOSSUS 10-20 70
Members: Robby Van Leevwen; Klassje Van Der Wal; Mariska Veres; Cornelis Van Der Beek.

SHOFFNER, Rufus
(With Joyce Songer)

Singles: 7-inch

AMERICAN ARTISTS (7317 "Orbit Twist") 200-400 62

HI-Q (17 "Every Little Raindrop") 20-30 61

SHONDELL, Troy P&R '61
(Troy Shondel; Gary Shelton)

Singles: 7-inch

AVM (5-14 "Lookin' for Some New Blue Jeans")...3-5 88
BEAR (2002 "Still Loving You") ....3-6 '80s
BEAR (2003 "No One Knows").....................3-6 '80s
BRITE STAR ("Deeper & Deeper")..............4-6 73
(Selection number not known.)
BRITE STAR (2459 "Rip It Up-Oh Boy Medley")..4-6 73
BRITE STAR (4691 "Love Stuff")...............4-6 74
CINDA (71070 "Tonight It Might Work Out")...4-8 73
CLOUD 9 (135 "My Girl") 4-8 74
COLLECTABLES..3-5 '80s
COMMERCIAL (00031 "So Close")..............4-6 78
COMMERCIAL (00038 "The Tender Side of Me") 4-6 78
COMMERCIAL (00044 "Rip It Up-Oh Boy Medley")...4-6 78
DECCA (31712 "You Can't Catch Me") 8-12 64
EVEREST (2015 "Gone") 8-12 62
EVEREST (2018 "No Fool Like an Old Fool") 8-12 62
EVEREST (2041 "Little Miss Tease").........8-12 62
GOLDCREAST (161 "This Time") 100-150 61
(Label name is misspelled. 1000 made.)
GOLDCREST (161 "This Time")............50-100 61
(No mention of distribution by Liberty Records.)
GOLDCREST (161-A "This Time")...........35-55 61
(Label indicates "Distributed By Liberty Records Sales Corp.")
ITCC ("Imitation Woman") 4-8 72
(No selection number used.)
LIBERTY (54529 "This Time"/"Tears from an Angel") 5-10 63
(Back-to-Back Hits series.)
LIBERTY (55353 "This Time") 10-20 61
LIBERTY (55398 "Tears from an Angel"). 10-20 61
LIBERTY (55445 "Na-Ne-No") 10-20 62
LUCKY (133 "Take Me, Woman") 4-8 75
MASTER ("C'mon Everybody")....................8-12 65
(No selection number used.)
MASTER (101 "High School Dance").........8-12 65
RIC (174 "Just a Dream")...........................5-10 65
RIC (184 "Big Windy City")........................5-10 65
SOUND 90 (283 "This Time") 4-6 83
SPECTRE SOUND (102 "She'll Remember Me") 5-10 65
STAR-FOX (8-10 "The Way It Used to Be"). 4-6 77
STAR-FOX (77-2 "I Wonder Who's Kissing Her Now") 4-6 78
STAR-FOX (77-5-1 "He Took Her")..............4-6 79
STAR-FOX (101 "This Time") 4-6 81
STAR-FOX (479 "Hang on to Me")..............4-6 79
SUN CITY (1301 "Hello Josephine") 4-6 85
SUNSHINE (317 "That Same Mistake Again") 4-8 76
TRX (5001 "A Rose and a Baby Ruth")......5-10 67
TRX (5003 "Head Man")..............................5-10 67
TRX (5015 "Let's Go All the Way") 5-10 68
TRX (5019 "Something's Wrong in Indiana") 5-10 69
TELESONIC (804 "Lovin' You") 4-6 80
TELESONIC (806 "Good Times")..................4-6 81
3 RIVERS (007 "Money Honey") 5-10 66
(Identification number shown since selection number is not yet known.)
3 RIVERS (0333 "Baby Don't Do It") 5-10 66
(Identification number shown since selection number is not yet known.)
WRITERS & ARTISTS (001 "This Time") ....4-8 '70s

LPs: 10/12-inch

CHURCHILL (67243 "Wanted Dead Or Alive")... 10-15 80
COMMERCIAL (783 "An Ordinary Man"). 10-15 81
EVEREST (1206 "Many Sides of Troy Shondell") 30-50 63
(Monaural.)
EVEREST (5206 "Many Sides of Troy Shondell") 30-50 63
(Stereo.)
STAR-FOX (1020 "Still Loving You")..........8-12 79
SUN CITY (1300 "Class Reunion")..............8-12 85
SUNSET (1174 "This Time")....................15-20 67
(Monaural.)
SUNSET (5174 "This Time")....................15-20 67
(Stereo.)
Session: Jordanaires; Jerry Hedges.
Also see JIANTS
Also see JORDANAIRES
Also see SHELTON, Gary
Also see SHUNDELL, Troy

SHONDELLS
("Vocal By Novella Simmons, Shirley Brooks and the Shondells")

Singles: 7-inch

KING (5597 "Don't Cry My Soldier Boy") . 10-15 62
KING (5656 "Wonderful One")................. 10-15 62
KING (5705 "Special Delivery") 10-15 62
KING (5755 "Ooo Sometimes") 10-15 63

SHONDELLS

Singles: 7-inch

LA LOUISIANNE (8042 "San Antone") 25-50 63

SHONDELLS / Rod Bernard / Warren Storm / Skip Stewart

LPs: 10/12-inch

LA LOUISIANNE (109 "At the Saturday Hop")...50-75 64
Also see BERNARD, Rod
Also see SHONDELLS
Also see STEWART, Skip
Also see STORM, Warren

SHONDELLS
(Featuring Tommy James)

Singles: 7-inch

RED FOX (110 "Hanky Panky")...............15-25 66
SELSOM (102 "Why Do Fools Fall in Love") 10-20 65
SNAP (101 "Pretty Little Red Bird").........25-45 63
SNAP (102 "Hanky Panky")......................50-75 63
(No mention of distribution by Red Fox.)
SNAP (102 "Hanky Panky")......................20-25 65
(Reads: "Distributed by Red Fox Records.")
Also see JAMES, Tommy

SHOOP, Wally
(With the Zombies; with Fubur)

Singles: 7-inch

AJS NEW HORIZON (1001 "Evening in the City")..40-60 71
SOMA (1409 "Memphis") 40-60 64
STUDIO FIVE (1004 "Choo Choo Jenny")... 4-8 '70s
Also see BILLY RAT & FINKS

SHOOTERS
(Featuring Otis Redding)

Singles: 7-inch

TRANS-WORLD (6908 "She's All Right")...50-100 60
(Reissued on Finer Arts as by Otis Redding & the Shooters.)
Also see REDDING, Otis

SHOOTING STARS

Singles: 7-inch

RANDOLPH (10001 "I Love Her Anyway") 15-25 66

SHORE, Dinah P&R '40
(With Dick Todd; with Woody Herman)

Singles: 78 rpm

BLUEBIRD...5-10 40-42
COLUMBIA...4-8 46
RCA...3-6 50-57
VICTOR..4-8 40-46

Singles: 7-inch

CAPITOL..4-8 60-62
CAPITOL CUSTOM (3793 "Purex Presents Dinah Shore") 5-10 61
(Single-sided promotional issue, made for Purex.)
DECCA...4-6 69
MERCURY...4-6 74
PROJECT 3 ....4-6 67-68
RCA...8-15 50-57

Picture Sleeves

CAPITOL CUSTOM (3793 "The Purex Dinah Shore Special") 5-10 61
(Promotional issue, made for Purex.)
RCA (5335 "Marriage Type Love")........... 15-25 53
RCA (6077 "Whatever Lola Wants")......... 15-25 53
("This Is Her Life" sleeve. Promotional issue only.)

EPs: 7-inch

CAMDEN 5-10 56
CAPITOL...4-8 59
CAPITOL CUSTOM ("Season's Greetings: Dinah Shore") ....5-10 '50s
COLUMBIA..4-8 59

RCA 5-15 51-57

LPs: 10/12-inch

BAINBRIDGE 5-8 82
CAMDEN 5-10 59-60
CAPITOL (1200 series) 10-20 59-60
CAPITOL (1354 "Dinah Sings Some Blues with Red Norvo") 20-30 60
CAPITOL (1600 & 1700 series) 10-20 62
COLUMBIA (6000 series)........................ 20-40 50-51
(10-inch LPs.)
COLUMBIA (34000 series)........................5-10 77
DECCA 5-10 69
HARMONY 5-10 59-60
NABISCO (001 "Nabisco Invitational")..... 30-40 83
(Picture disc. Promotional issue only.)
PROJECT 3....................................5-10 68
RCA (11 "Tangos") 25-35 51
RCA (1100 & 1200 series)....................... 20-30 55-56
RCA (3000 series) 20-30 53-54
(10-inch LPs.)
REPRISE.................................... 10-15 65
S&H GREEN STAMPS (1 "Dinah")......... 10-20 62
(TV show preview LP. Promotional issue only.)
Also see CUGAT, Xavier, & Dinah Shore
Also see DAY, Doris, & Dinah Shore
Also see KINGSTON TRIO / Dinah Shore
Also see MARTIN, Dean

SHORE, Dinah, & Tony Martin

Singles: 78 rpm

RCA 5-10 51

Singles: 7-inch

RCA 10-15 51

SHORE, Dinah, Tony Martin, Betty Hutton & Phil Harris

Singles: 78 rpm

RCA 5-10 51

Singles: 7-inch

RCA 10-15 51
Also see HARRIS, Phil
Also see HUTTON, Betty
Also see MARTIN, Tony

SHORE, Dinah, & Red Norvo Quintet

LPs: 10/12-inch

CAPITOL (1354 "Dinah Sings Some Blues with Red") 15-25 60

SHORE, Dinah, & André Previn

LPs: 10/12-inch

CAPITOL (1422 "Dinah Sings, Previn Plays") 15-25 60
Also see PREVIN, André
Also see SHORE, Dinah

SHORR, Mickey, & Cutups — P&R '62

Singles: 7-inch

ELDO (120 "Twistovitz") 5-10 62
TUBA (8001 "Ben Basey")........................ 10-15 62
Also see SPENCER & SPENCER

SHORT, Bill, & Shocks

Singles: 7-inch

RESCUE (21011 "Here We Go Again")... 50-75
TOWN (1965 "Here We Go Again")......... 20-30 60

SHORT CROSS

LPs: 10/12-inch

GRIZLY (16013 "Arising")..................... 200-250 70
Members: Velpo Robertson; Gray McCalley; Burch Owens; Bird Sharp.

SHORTER, Wayne — LP '75

LPs: 10/12-inch

BLUE NOTE.................................... 20-30 62
(Label reads "Blue Note Records Inc. - New York, USA.")
BLUE NOTE.................................... 15-20 66
(Label shows Blue Note Records as a division of either Liberty or United Artists.)
COLUMBIA....................................5-10 75
VEE-JAY (Maroon label)........................... 30-40 60
VEE-JAY (Black label)............................ 20-30 61-62

SHOTGUN EXPRESS

Singles: 7-inch

UPTOWN (747 "I Could Feel the Whole World") 10-20 67
Members: Rod Stewart; Peter Bardens; Beryl Marsden.
Also see STEWART, Rod

SHOW STOPPERS — P&R '68

(Showstoppers)

Singles: 7-inch

AMBER (212 "Doctor of Love")..............50-100 63
COLLECTABLES....................................3-5 '80s
COLUMBIA (43914 "Turn On Your Lovelight") 10-15 67
COLUMBIA (44184 "Once More with Love") 10-15 67
GUYDEN (2131 "Ain't Nothin' But a House Party") 5-10 67
HERITAGE (800 "Ain't Nothin' But a House Party") 5-10 68
HERITAGE (802 "How Easy Your Heart Forgets") 5-10 68
SHOWTIME (101 "Ain't Nothin' But a House Party") 8-12 67

LPs: 10/12-inch

COLLECTABLES....................................5-10

SHOWCASES

Singles: 7-inch

FALCO (308 "This Love Is Real") ....5-10 '80s
GALAXY (732 "This Love Was Real") 2500-3000 64

SHOWMEN — P&R '61

Singles: 7-inch

AIRECORDS (334 "Valley of Love").........10-15 63
AMY (11036 "Action")..............................5-10 68
BB (4015 "In Paradise")............................15-20 65
(First issue.)
IMPERIAL (66033 "It Will Stand")..............8-12 64
IMPERIAL (66071 "Country Fool").............8-12 64
JOKERS THREE (100 "A Little Bit of Your Love") 75-100
LIBERTY....................................4-8 70-81
MINIT (632 "It Will Stand").........................15-25 61
(Orange label.)
MINIT (632 "It Will Stand").........................10-15 '60s
(Black label.)
MINIT (643 "The Wrong Girl")...................40-50 62
MINIT (647 "Comin' Home").......................10-15 62
MINIT (654 "True Fine Mama")..................10-15 62
MINIT (662 "39-21-46") 10-15 63
(Orange label.)
MINIT (662 "39-21-46") ....8-12 '60s
(Black label.)
MINIT (32007 "39-21-46") 5-10 66
SWAN (4213 "In Paradise") 10-15 65
SWAN (4219 "You're Everything")............10-20 65
SWAN (4241 "Please Try to Understand") 10-20 66
Member: General Johnson.
Also see THOMAS, Irma / Ernie K-Doe / Showmen / Benny Spellman.

SHOWMEN

Singles: 7-inch

SAM (114 "Slowly")..................................15-25 63

SHOWMEN & BOBBY LEE

Singles: 7-inch

COULEE (113 "Alright")............................15-25 65
Members: Bobby Lee; Mike Gutch; Bob Smith; Terry Hoepner; Dave Preston.

SHOWTIME, INC.

Singles: 7-inch

BLACK CIRCLE (6006 "Take This Heart of Mine") 12-15

SHOWTIME PARTS I & II

Singles: 7-inch

CANDY FLOSS (103 "Showtime")...........20-25 68

SHUNDELL, Troy

Singles: 7-inch

GAYE (2010 "This Time").........................10-15 66
(This is not Troy Shondell, as was once thought. The singer was once a member of a band that once backed Troy Shondell.)
Also see SHONDELL, Troy

SHUFFLERS

Singles: 78 rpm

OKEH 20-30 54

Singles: 7-inch

OKEH (7040 "Ain't Nothin' Wrong with That") 50-75 54

SHUFFLERS

Singles: 7-inch

J.A.G. 10-20

PENNINGTON (01 "Thick Syrup")............10-20 64
Also see JAY & SHUFFLERS

SHUFFLES

Singles: 7-inch

RAY-CO (508 "Do You Remember My Darling") 200-300 63

SHUT DOWNS

Singles: 7-inch

DIMENSION (1016 "Four on the Floor")...10-20 63
KARSONG (101 "Four on the Floor").......20-40 63

LPs: 10/12-inch

CROWN (5393 "The Deuce Coupes")......15-25 63
Member: Kirby St. Romain.
Also see ST. ROMAIN, Kirby

SHUTTERS, Harold & His Rocats

Singles: 78 rpm

GOLDEN ROD....................................100-200 56

Singles: 7-inch

GOLDEN ROD (204 "Rock & Roll, Mister Moon") 750-1000 56
GOLDEN ROD (300 "Bunny Honey")...400-600 56

SHY GUYS

Singles: 7-inch

BURGER (504 "The Burger Song")..........10-15 66
PALMER (5005 "We Gotta Go")..............10-15 66
PALMER (5008 "A Love So True")...........10-15 66
PANIK (5111 "We Gotta Go") 10-15 66

SHY GUYS

Singles: 7-inch

LITTLE FORT (9663 "Rockin' Pneumonia and the Booga Loo Flu") 20-30 67
SHAMLEY (44001 "Payin' My Dues")........10-15 68
UNI (55035 "Rockin' Pneumonia and the Booga Loo Flu") 10-15 67
Also see JOHNNY & SHY GUYS

SHY GUYS

Singles: 7-inch

MU ("Goodbye to You")............................20-30 '60s

SHYRES

Singles: 7-inch

CORI (31001 "Where Is Love")................15-25 67

SHY-TONES

(With Sammy Fields Orchestra)

Singles: 7-inch

GOODSPIN (401 "Lover's Quarrel").....100-150 60
(Reissued as *Lovers Quarrel*, and credited to the Hi-Tones.)
Members: Sal Covais; Graham True; Bill Scarpa; Al Seavozzo; Fred Alverez.
Also see EMOTIONS
Also see HI-TONES
Also see TRENTONS

SHYTONES

Singles: 7-inch

SPOT (14 "White Bucks")......................100-200 61
SPOT (15 "Annette") 100-200 61

SIDEBOTTOM, Charles

Singles: 7-inch

EXCELLENT (221 "Your Love Is the Key") 50-75

SIDEWALK SKIPPER BAND

Singles: 7-inch

CAPITOL (2127 "Strawberry Tuesday").....5-10 68
CAPITOL (2205 "It's Raining Flowers in My House") 5-10 68
TEEN TOWN (113 "Sidewalk Skipper") 5-10 69
Members: Brian Balestrieri; Dave McDowell; Rick Novac; Joe Balestrieri; Tom Youkam; Barry Biehoff; Tom Janovic.

SIDEWALK SOUNDS

Singles: 7-inch

SIDEWALK ....10-20 '60s
TOWER (352 "Billy Jack's Theme").........10-20 67
TOWER (480 "Let's Go")..........................10-20 69
Members: Mike Curb, Bob Summers.
Also see CURB, Mike
Also see SUMMERS, Bob

SIDEWALK SURFERS

Singles: 7-inch

JUBILEE (5496 "Skate Board")................15-25 65
Member: Bruce Johnston.
Also see JOHNSTON, Bruce

SIDEWINDERS

Singles: 7-inch

LOOK (5006 "Get Out of My Life")...........15-25 67

SIDNEY & CHIMPS

Singles: 7-inch

FARO (586 "Blah") 15-25 58

SIEFERT, Jerry

Singles: 7-inch

NOTE (10018 "Dirty White Bucks") 50-75 59

SIEGEL - SCHWALL BAND

Singles: 7-inch

DEUTSCHE GRAMMOPHON 4-6 73
WOODEN NICKEL....................................4-6 72-73

LPs: 10/12-inch

VANGUARD 12-25 66-70
WOODEN NICKEL....................................15-30 72-74
Members: Corky Siegel; Jim Schwall.

SIEGLING & LARRABEE

LPs: 10/12-inch

LOOK 10-15 70

SIERRAS

Singles: 7-inch

BLISS (1001 "The Donkey Call")..............30-40 60
DORIAN (1001 "Donkey Call") ....5-10 '60s

SIERRAS

(With Bob Cox Orchestra; Sierra's; "Vocal by: Richard Jarvis")

Singles: 7-inch

KNOX (102 "So Many Sleepless Nights") 100-150 62

SIERRAS

Singles: 7-inch

CHAM (101 "Then I'll Still Love You") 10-20 64
DOT (16569 "Then I'll Still Love You") 8-12 64
GOLDISC (G-4 "I Should Have Loved You") 15-25 63

SIERRAS

Singles: 7-inch

MAIL CALL (2333 "Stormy Weather")..150-200 63

SIERRAS

Singles: 7-inch

BANGAR (644 "Party at Taco Towne")....40-60 '60s

SIGGERS, Ruben, & His Fabulous Kool Kats

("Vocal By Ephraim Siggers")

Singles: 7-inch

SPINKS (600 "Those Love Me Blues") 500-750 57
Members: Ruben Siggers; Ephraim Siggers.

SIGLER, Bunny — P&R/R&B '67

("Mr. Emotions"; with Cruisers)

Singles: 12-inch

GOLD MIND 4-6 78-79
SALSOUL 4-6 80

Singles: 7-inch

BAMBOO (521 "Oh Wind") 8-12 62
BEE (1113 "Laddy Daddy")......................50-75 59
CRAIG (501 "Come On Home") 10-20 61
DECCA....................................15-25 65-67
GOLD MIND 4-6 77-79
HI LO (102 "Promise Me")......................15-25 58
PARKWAY....................................5-10 66-68
PHILA. INT'L....................................8-15 71-76
PHIL-L.A. OF SOUL (314 "I Can Give You Love") 5-10 68
SALSOUL 4-6 80
V-TONE (500 "Hold On") 10-20 59

EPs: 7-inch

PARKWAY (6000 "Bunny Sigler") 10-15 67
CAMEO/PARKWAY (6000 "Bunny Sigler") 5-10 68

LPs: 10/12-inch

GOLD MIND 5-10 78-79
PARKWAY (50,000 "Let the Good Times Roll") 10-20 67
SALSOUL 5-10 80
Also see ELLIS, Don, & Royal Dukes
Also see MASON, Barbara, & Bunny Sigler

SIGLER, Bunny, & Cindy Scott

Singles: 7-inch

NEPTUNE (24 "We're Only Human")..........4-8 70
Also see SCOTT, Cindy
Also see SIGLER, Bunny

SIGNALS
Singles: 7-inch
LEONEAL (1483 "Show Me the Way") 50-75

SIGNATURES
Singles: 7-inch
NORMAN (210 "Julie Is Her Name") 50-100 57
(First issue.)
WHIPPET (210 "Julie Is Her Name") 20-30 57
W.B. (5055 "Cling to Me") 10-20 59

SIGNIFICANT OTHER
Singles: 7-inch
CRITIQUE .... 10-20 '60s

SIKES, Bobby, & Rhythm Rebels
Singles: 7-inch
REBEL (101 "Rolling Stone") 50-100 62
Also see BEARD, Dean
Also see SIKES, Rick, & Rhythm Rebels

SIKES, Rick, & Rhythm Rebels
Singles: 7-inch
NVILLE (144 "Country DJ") 50-100 67
REBEL (20 "Give Me a Little") 100-150 62
REBEL (101 "Rolling Stone") 50-100 62
SIMS (305 "Den of Sin") 75-125 66
(Orange label.)
SIMS (305 "Den of Sin") 100-150 66
(White label. Promotional issue only.)
Also see BEARD, Dean
Also see SIKES, Bobby, & Rhythm Rebels

SILHOUETTES *P&R/R&B '58*
(With Dave McRae Orchestra; with King Twigg & His Orchestra)
Singles: 78 rpm
EMBER 50-75 57
JUNIOR 50-100 57
Singles: 7-inch
ABC 4-6 73
ACE (552 "I Sold My Heart to the Junkman") 10-20 58
COLLECTABLES .... 3-5 '80s
EMBER (1029 "Get a Job") 25-35 58
(Red or orange label.)
EMBER (1029 "Get a Job") 10-20 60
(Black label.)
EMBER (1032 "Headin' for the Poorhouse") 10-20 58
EMBER (1037 "Bing Bong") 50-75 58
(Glossy red label.)
EMBER (1037 "Bing Bong") 15-25 58
(Flat red label.)
FLASHBACK 4-8 65
GRAND (142 "Wish I Could Be There") 100-200 61
IMPERIAL (5899 "The Push") 8-12 62
JUNIOR (391 "Get a Job") 400-500 57
(Maroon label. Does not state "Junior Record Co." on label.)
JUNIOR (391 "Get a Job") 100-150 57
(Maroon label. Only "Junior" on label.)
JUNIOR (391 "Get a Job") 50-100 57
(Blue label.)
JUNIOR (396 "I Sold My Heart to the Junkman") 75-125 58
JUNIOR (400 "Evelyn") 500-750 59
JUNIOR (993 "Your Love") 50-75 63
20TH FOX (240 "Never") 30-40 61
Picture Sleeves
EMBER (1029 "Get a Job") .... 5-10 '90s
LPs: 10/12-inch
GOODWAY (100 "Get a Job") 100-150 68
Members: Bill Horton; Richard Lewis; Earl Beal; Ray Edwards.
Also see HORTON, Bill, & Silhouettes
Also see INVICTORS
Also see TERMITES
Also see KING, Ben E.

SILK *LP '69*
Singles: 7-inch
ABC 5-10 69
DECCA 4-6 71
LPs: 10/12-inch
ABC (694 "Smooth As Raw Silk") 15-25 69
Members: Michael Stanley Gee; Chris Jones; Randy Sabo; Courtney Johns.
Also see STANLEY, Michael, Band

SILK WINGED ALLIANCE
Singles: 7-inch
ACCENT (1277 "Hometown") .... 20-30 '60s

SILKIE *P&R '65*
Singles: 7-inch
FONTANA 5-10 65-66
LPs: 10/12-inch
FONTANA (27548 "You've Got to Hide Your Love Away") 20-30 65
(Monaural.)
FONTANA (67548 "You've Got to Hide Your Love Away") 25-35 65
(Stereo.)
Also see BEATLES

SILKY & SHANTUNGS
Singles: 7-inch
MUSICOR (1035 "Bazooki") 15-25 63

SILLER, Bob
LPs: 10/12-inch
DUNHILL (50045 "This Is Siller's Picture") 10-15 68

SILLS, Billy
Singles: 7-inch
CHAIRMAN (4404 "I'll Love You More Tomorrow") 5-10 63
COLPIX (169 "Billy's Love Song") 10-15 60
COLPIX (193 "Bom Didi Bom") 15-25 61
DECCA (30701 "Dippy-Do") 10-15 58
MOTION (3001 "It's a Brand New Term") ... 5-10 62

SILLY SURFERS
LPs: 10/12-inch
MERCURY (20977 "Sounds of the Silly Surfers") 20-30 65
(Monaural.)
MERCURY (60977 "Sounds of the Silly Surfers") 25-35 65
(Stereo.)

SILLY SURFERS / Weird-Ohs
LPs: 10/12-inch
HAIRY (101 "Sounds of the Silly Surfers") 75-125 65
(One side of LP is by each group.)
Members: Gary Usher; Chuck Girard; Richard Burns; Shary Richards.
Also see HONDELLS
Also see SILLY SURFERS
Also see WEIRD-OHS

SILVA, Bob, & Silva-Tones
Singles: 7-inch
DEBBIE (1409 "I'll Hold You in My Heart") 100-150 59
Also see SILVA-TONES

SILVA, Margie, & Bossa Novas
Singles: 7-inch
RENDEZVOUS (203 "Bailar") 5-10 63

SILVAR JETS
Singles: 7-inch
SILVAR JETS (7881 "Roberta") 50-75

SILVA-TONES *P&R '57*
Singles: 78 rpm
ARGO 20-30 57
MONARCH 25-50 57
Singles: 7-inch
ARGO (5281 "Roses Are Blooming"/"That's All I Want from You") 30-40 57
(Silver and black label with "ship" logo.)
ARGO (5281 "Chi-Wa-Wa"/"That's All I Want from You") 10-20 57
(Black label, silver print. No "ship" logo.)
MONARCH (615 "That's All I Want from You") 50-60 57
(Yellow label.)
MONARCH (615 "That's All I Want from You") 15-25 57
(Black label.)
Also see SILVA, Bob, & Silva-Tones

SILVER, Horace, Quintet *LP '65*
Singles: 78 rpm
BLUE NOTE 4-8 54-57
Singles: 7-inch
BLUE NOTE (300 thru 1000 series) 4-6 73-77
BLUE NOTE (1600 & 1700 series) 10-15 54-61
BLUE NOTE (1800 & 1900 series) 5-10 61-69
LPs: 10/12-inch
BLUE NOTE (1518 "Horace Silver Quintet") 50-75 56
(Label gives New York street address for Blue Note Records.)
BLUE NOTE (1518 "Horace Silver Quintet") 25-50
(Label gives New York street address for Blue Note Records.)
BLUE NOTE (1520 "New Faces") 50-75 56
(Label gives New York street address for Blue Note Records.)
BLUE NOTE (1520 "New Faces") 25-50
(Label reads "Blue Note Records Inc. - New York, U.S.A.")
BLUE NOTE (1562 "Stylings") 50-75 57
(Label gives New York street address for Blue Note Records.)
BLUE NOTE (1562 "Stylings") 25-50
(Label reads "Blue Note Records Inc. - New York, U.S.A.")
BLUE NOTE (1562 "Stylings") 15-25
(Label shows Blue Note Records as a division of Liberty.)
BLUE NOTE (1589 "Further Explorations") 50-75 58
(Label gives New York street address for Blue Note Records.)
BLUE NOTE (1589 "Further Explorations") 25-50
(Label reads "Blue Note Records Inc. - New York, U.S.A.")
BLUE NOTE (1589 "Further Explorations") 15-25
(Label shows Blue Note Records as a division of Liberty.)
BLUE NOTE (4000 series) 30-50 59-60
(Label gives New York street address for Blue Note Records.)
BLUE NOTE (4000 series) 20-30 59-65
(Label reads "Blue Note Records Inc. - New York, U.S.A.")
BLUE NOTE (4000 series) 15-20 66-68
(Label shows Blue Note Records as a division of either
BLUE NOTE (5018 "New Faces") 100-150 53
(10-inch LP.)
BLUE NOTE (5034 "Horace Silver Trio") 100-150 54
(10-inch LP.)
BLUE NOTE (5058 "Horace Silver Quintet") 100-150 55
(10-inch LP.)
BLUE NOTE (5062 "Horace Silver Quintet") 100-150 55
(10-inch LP.)
BLUE NOTE (84000 series) 30-40 59-60
(Label gives New York street address for Blue Note Records.)
BLUE NOTE (84000 series) 20-30 59-65
(Label reads "Blue Note Records Inc. - New York, U.S.A.")
BLUE NOTE (84000 series) 10-20 66-80
(Label shows Blue Note Records as a division of either
EPIC (3326 "Silver's Blue") 75-125 57
EPIC (16006 "Silver's Blue") 60-80 58
Also see DAVIS, Miles
Also see STITT, Sonny, Kai Winding & Horace Silver

SILVER, Horace, Quintet, & Stanley Turrentine
LPs: 10/12-inch
BLUE NOTE (84277 "Serenade to a Soul Sister") 10-15 68
Also see SILVER, Horace, Quintet
Also see TURRENTINE, Stanley

SILVER, Sid
Singles: 7-inch
BAKERSFIELD (510 "Bumble Rumble") 150-250

SILVER APPLES *LP '68*
Singles: 7-inch
KAPP 5-10 68-69
LPs: 10/12-inch
KAPP (3562 "Silver Apples") 50-60 68
KAPP (3584 "Contact") 15-25 69

SILVER FLEET
(10CC)
Singles: 7-inch
UNI (55271 "Look Out World") 10-20 71
Also see 10CC

SILVER SHADOW
LPs: 10/12-inch
MAJOR PACIFIC (1006 "Silver Shadow") 10-20 83
(Picture disc.)

SILVER SISTERS
Singles: 7-inch
CAN-DEE (92 "Baby, Baby") 10-15 59
SHELL (718 "When a Boy Meets a Girl") 10-15 60

SILVERLETTES
Singles: 7-inch
DESTINY (1203 "I Miss You") 40-50

SILVERSTEIN, Shel *LP '73*
Singles: 7-inch
COLUMBIA 4-6 71-75
ELEKTRA 8-12 60
RCA 4-8 69-70
EPs: 7-inch
COLUMBIA (31119 "Shel Silverstein") 5-10 72
(Special coin operator release. Cover shows *Freakin' at the Freakers Ball* since same number is used on LP release.)
LPs: 10/12-inch
ATLANTIC (8072 "Inside Folk Songs") 20-30 63
(Monaural.)
ATLANTIC (SD-8072 "Inside Folk Songs") 25-35 63
(Stereo.)
ATLANTIC (8200 series) 10-15 70
CBS (39611 "Where the Sidewalk Ends") .. 8-12 84
(Picture disc.)
CADET 15-25 65-66
COLUMBIA 5-12 72-84
CRESTVIEW (804 "Stag Party") 15-25 63
ELEKTRA (176 "Hairy Jazz") 30-40 59
(Monaural.)
ELEKTRA (7-176 "Hairy Jazz") 40-50 59
(Stereo.)
FLYING FISH 5-8 80
JANUS 8-12 73
PARACHUTE (Except 20512) 5-10 78
PARACHUTE (20512 "Selected Cuts from *Songs and Stories*") 15-20 78
(Promotional issue only.)
RCA 10-15 69

SILVERTON SINGERS
Singles: 7-inch
U-C (5004 "Soldiers in the Army") 75-125 58

SILVERTONES
Singles: 7-inch
ELGIN (006 "My Only Love") 50-75 59
SILVER SLIPPER (1000 "Sentimental Memories") 10-15 60

SILVERTONES
Singles: 7-inch
GOLIATH (1355 "Get It") 30-40 63
SWEET (16 "Seven Piece Bathing Suit"). 15-25 '60s
VALIANT (704 "Get It") 10-15 65
VALIANT (6045 "Get It") 15-20 64

SILVERTONES
Singles: 7-inch
JOEY (302 "Thinking of You") 75-125 63

SILVERTONES
Singles: 7-inch
WEST COAST (451 "Louise Louise") ...... 20-30 '60s
Also see FABULOUS SILVER TONES

SIMIELE, Ernie, & Eratics
Singles: 7-inch
KIND A ROUND (11765 "Special Girl") 400-500 61
(Also shows "RB 105." It's not clear which is the correct selection number.)

SIMIEN, Sidney
Singles: 7-inch
CARL ("I'm Never Right") 40-60
(No selection number used.)

SIMMONS, Al, & Slim Green
(With the Cats from Fresno)
Singles: 78 rpm
DIG 15-25 56

Singles: 7-inch

DIG (138 "Old Folks' Boogie") ... 40-50 56
DIG (142 "You Ain't Too Old") ... 30-40 56
Also see GREEN, Slim
Also see MAIDEN, Sidney / Al Simmons

SIMMONS, Fay
(With the Royals; with "Michelle on Organ"; Faye Simmons)

Singles: 78 rpm

GRAND ... 10-20 54
PINEY ... 8-12 55

Singles: 7-inch

GONE (5029 "Rockin', Rollin' and A' Strollin' ") ... 15-25 58
GRAND (111 "Whim, Wham, Whop") ... 25-50 54
JORDAN (120 "Secret Love") ... 10-20 60
JORDAN (122 "Shake It Up") ... 10-20 60
JORDAN (124 "He's Got the Whole World in His Hands") ... 10-20 61
JORDAN (126 "Bells") ... 10-20 61
PALM (300 "It's a Sin to Tell a Lie") ... 10-15 62
(First issue.)
PINEY (110 "I'll Always Call Your Name") ... 20-30 55
POP-SIDE (8 "Just to Hold My Hand") ... 8-12 62
PORT (5002 "I Can See Through You") .. 15-25 57
RUTHIE (1038 "Rain") ... 5-10 62
SENCA (126 "Lonely Girl") ... 10-20 61
V-TONE (237 "It's a Sin to Tell a Lie") ... 8-12 62

SIMMONS, Gene P&R/LP '64
(Jumpin' Gene Simmons; Morris Gene Simmons)

Singles: 7-inch

A.G.P. (119 "Back Home Again") ... 8-10 69
CHECKER (948 "Goin' Back to Memphis") ... 20-30 60
EPIC ... 4-6 70
DELTUNE ... 4-6 77-78
HI (2034 "Teddy Bear") ... 10-20 61
HI (2039 "No Other Guy") ... 10-20 61
HI (2050 "Caledonia") ... 8-12 62
HI (2076 "Haunted House") ... 8-12 63
(May be credited to "Gene Simmons" or "Jumpin' Gene Simmons." We have yet to learn of a price difference between the two.)
HI (2080 "The Dodo") ... 8-12 64
HI (2086 "Skinny Minnie") ... 5-10 65
HI (2092 "Mattie Rae") ... 5-10 65
HI (2102 "The Batman") ... 5-10 66
HI (2113 "Keep the Meat in the Pan") ... 5-10 66
HURSHEY ... 4-6 73
JUDD (1008 "Sharlene") ... 20-30 59
MALA (12012 "I'm Just a Loser") ... 5-10 68
SANDY (1027 "Shenandoah Waltz") ... 10-20 59
SANDY (1056 "Waiting Game") ... 10-20 61
STATUE (7005 "Call Sam [Phillips]") ... 50-75 66
SUN (299 "Drinkin' Wine") ... 200-300 58
TUPELO (2981 "Little Rag Doll") ... 100-200 63

LPs: 10/12-inch

HI (2018 "Jumpin' Gene Simmons") ... 20-40 64
(Monaural.)
HI (32018 "Jumpin' Gene Simmons") ... 25-50 64
(Stereo.)

SIMMONS, Gene P&R/LP '78

Singles: 7-inch

CASABLANCA ... 3-5 78-79

LPs: 10/12-inch

CASABLANCA (7120 "Gene Simmons"). 15-25 78
(With poster.)
CASABLANCA (7120 "Gene Simmons") ... 8-12 78
(Without poster.)
CASABLANCA (PIX-7120 "Gene Simmons") ... 50-60 79
(Picture disc.)
Also see KISS

SIMMONS, Jimmy

Singles: 7-inch

ATCO (6102 "The Land of Love") ... 15-20 57
ATCO (6113 "Too Hot to Handle") ... 15-20 58
EVEREST (19349 "Unchained Melody") . 10-15 60
7 STAR (901 "Everyday Lady") ... 4-6 79
7 STAR (0001 "You Gotta Love People") ... 5-10 74

SIMMONS, Joe

Singles: 7-inch

COMET (2149 "All Aboard") ... 10-15 62
EPIC (9335 "The Dance") ... 10-20 59

SIMMONS, Little Maxine

Singles: 7-inch

VARBEE (117 "Since I Lost You") ... 100-150

SIMMONS, Lonnie, Quartet

Singles: 78 rpm

PARROT (790 "Black Orchid") ... 25-50 54

Singles: 7-inch

PARROT (790 "Black Orchid") ... 50-100 54
(Black vinyl.)
PARROT (790 "Black Orchid") ... 200-300 54
(Red vinyl.)

SIMMONS, Max, VI

Singles: 7-inch

ROSE (122 "You Are the One") ... 15-25 57

SIMMS, Jean, & Jimmy Griffin Orchestra

Singles: 78 rpm

DOT (15223 "A Love Like You") ... 10-15 54

Singles: 7-inch

DOT (15223 "A Love Like You") ... 50-60 54

SIMMS, Jerry

Singles: 7-inch

DUAL (501 "Good Luck Orville") ... 5-10 61

SIMMS, Jimmy

Singles: 7-inch

LAMP (2017 "Mystery of Love") ... 15-25 58
PEPPERMINT LOUNGE (8527 "Twisting on the Beach") ... 100-200 62

SIMMS, Johnny

Singles: 7-inch

ALITE (101 "Talk to Me") ... 20-30 63

SIMON, Carly P&R/LP '71

Singles: 7-inch

ARISTA ... 3-5 86-90
COLUMBIA ... 4-6 73
ELEKTRA ... 4-6 71-79
EPIC ... 3-5 85-86
MIRAGE ... 3-5 82
W.B. ... 3-5 80-83

Picture Sleeves

ARISTA (Except 9525) ... 3-5 86-89
ARISTA (9525 "Coming Around Again") ... 4-8 86
(Pictures Meryl Streep and Jack Nicholson.)
ARISTA (9525 "Coming Around Again") ... 3-5 86
(Pictures Carly Simon.)
ELEKTRA ... 4-6 75-79
W.B. ... 3-5 80-83

LPs: 10/12-inch

ARISTA ... 5-8 86-90
ELEKTRA (Except EQ-1048) ... 5-15 71-79
ELEKTRA (EQ-1048 "Best of Carly Simon") ... 25-35 75
EPIC ... 5-8 85-86
W.B. ... 5-10 80-83
Also see JAGGER, Mick
Also see SIMON SISTERS

SIMON, Carly, & James Taylor P&R '74

Singles: 7-inch

ELEKTRA ... 4-6 74-78
Also see SIMON, Carly
Also see TAYLOR, James

SIMON, Freddie, Quintet

Singles: 78 rpm

COMBO (33 "Cool Soup") ... 10-20 53
RECORDED IN HOLLYWOOD (190 "Hollywood Bound") ... 10-20 52

Singles: 7-inch

COMBO (33 "Cool Soup") ... 20-30 53
Also see SIMON, Maurice

SIMON, Joe R&B '65
(With the Checkmates; with Mainstreeters; with Johnny Heartsman's Band; with Golden Tones)

Singles: 7-inch

COMPLEAT ... 4-6 '70s
DOT (16570 "Only a Dream") ... 10-20 64
GEE BEE (077 "Say") ... 20-30
HUSH (103 "It's a Miracle") ... 15-25 60
HUSH (104 "Call My Name") ... 15-25 61
HUSH (106 "Pledge of Love") ... 15-25 61
HUSH (107 "Troubles") ... 15-25 61
HUSH (108 "Land of Love") ... 15-25 62
IRRAL (778 "Only a Dream") ... 15-25 63
MONUMENT ... 4-8 70-72
POSSE ... 3-5 81-82
SOUND STAGE 7 (Except 2634) ... 5-10 66-76
SOUND STAGE 7 (2634 "Don't Let Me Lose the Feeling") ... 10-15 69
SPRING ... 4-8 69-77
VEE-JAY (609 "My Adorable One") ... 10-20 64
VEE-JAY (663 "When I'm Gone") ... 10-20 65
VEE-JAY (694 "Let's Do It Over") ... 10-20 65

Picture Sleeves

GEE BEE (077 "Say") ... 25-50
SPRING ... 5-10 71-73

LPs: 10/12-inch

BUDDAH ... 10-20 69
POSSE ... 5-10 81-82
SOUND STAGE 7 ... 10-20 67-75
SPRING ... 10-20 71-78
Also see GOLDEN TONES
Also see HEARTSMAN, Johnny
(With the Pie Men; with Freddie Simon; Maurice Simmons)

Singles: 78 rpm

DOWN BEAT ... 10-20 49
RECORDED IN HOLLYWOOD ... 10-15 53

Singles: 7-inch

CARNIVAL (525 "The Git-Go") ... 5-10 67
FLASH (113 "Flashy") ... 10-20 56
RECORDED IN HOLLYWOOD (404 "Big Apple Hop") ... 40-60 53
Also see SIMON, Freddie

SIMON, Paul P&R/LP '72
(With Urubamba; with Los Incas)

Singles: 12-inch

W.B. ("Late in the Evening") ... 4-8 80
(Promotional issue only. Selection number not known.)
W.B. (2503 "You Can Call Me Al") ... 4-8 86
(Promotional issue only.)
W.B. (2652 "Boy in the Bubble") ... 4-8 86
(Promotional issue only.)

Singles: 7-inch

COLUMBIA ... 4-6 72-77
W.B. ... 3-5 80-90

Picture Sleeves

COLUMBIA ... 4-8 73-77
W.B. ... 3-5 80-87

LPs: 10/12-inch

COLUMBIA (Except C5X & 43000 series) . 6-12 72-77
COLUMBIA (C5X-37581 "Paul Simon's Collected Works") ... 30-40 81
(Boxed, five-disc set.)
COLUMBIA (43000 series) ... 15-20 81
(Half-speed mastered.)
DMG (1 "Songs of Paul Simon – Hits Collection") ... 15-25 75
(Promotional issue only. Also includes tracks by: Simon & Garfunkel; Aretha Franklin; Yes; Crykle; and Booker T. & MGs.)
DMG (2 "Songs of Paul Simon – Easy Listening Collection") ... 10-20 75
(Promotional issue only. Also includes tracks by other artists.)
MCP (8027 "Paul Simon Plus") ... 15-25 '70s
(Promotional issue only. Also includes tracks by: Tony Orlando; Neil Sedaka; Johnny Rivers; and 4 Seasons.)
W.B. (140 ""Interview Show") ... 20-30 86
(Promotional issue only. Two discs with interview and *Graceland* songs.)
W.B. (3472 "One-Trick Pony") ... 5-10 80
W.B. (23942 thru 26098) ... 5-10 80-90
Also see BOOKER T. & MGs
Also see CORDELL, Richie
Also see CYRKLE
Also see DION
Also see 4 SEASONS
Also see FRANKLIN, Aretha
Also see GARFUNKEL, Art, James Taylor & Paul Simon
Also see GREGORY, Harrison
Also see KANE, Paul
Also see LANDIS, Jerry
Also see ORLANDO, Tony
Also see RIVERS, Johnny
Also see SEDAKA, Neil
Also see SIMON & GARFUNKEL
Also see TAYLOR, True
Also see TICO & TRIUMPHS
Also see VALERY, Dana
Also see YES

SIMON, Paul, & Phoebe Snow P&R '75
(With the Jessy Dixon Singers)

Singles: 7-inch

COLUMBIA (10197 "Gone At Last") ... 4-6 75

SIMON & GARFUNKEL P&R '65

Singles: 7-inch

ABC-PAR (10788 "That's My Story") ... 10-20 66
COLUMBIA (10000 series) ... 4-6 75
COLUMBIA (11669 "Seven O'clock News – Silent Night") ... 10-15 66
COLUMBIA (33000 series) ... 3-6 66-75
COLUMBIA (43396 "The Sounds of Silence") ... 5-10 65
COLUMBIA (43396 "The Sounds of Silence") ... 30-40 65
(Colored vinyl. Promotional issue only.)
COLUMBIA (43511 "Homeward Bound") ... 5-10 66
COLUMBIA (43511 "Homeward Bound") . 30-40 66
(Colored vinyl. Promotional issue only.)
COLUMBIA (43617 "I Am a Rock") ... 5-10 66
COLUMBIA (43617 "I Am a Rock") ... 30-40 66
(Colored vinyl. Promotional issue only.)
COLUMBIA (43728 "The Dangling Conversation") ... 5-10 66
COLUMBIA (43873 "A Hazy Shade of Winter") ... 5-10 66
COLUMBIA (44046 "At the Zoo") ... 5-10 67
COLUMBIA (44232 "Fakin' It") ... 5-10 67
COLUMBIA (44465 "Scarborough Fair") ... 5-10 68
COLUMBIA (44511 "Mrs. Robinson") ... 5-10 68
COLUMBIA (44785 "The Boxer"/"Baby Driver") ... 5-8 69
COLUMBIA (44785 "The Boxer"/"The Boxer") ... 8-12 69
COLUMBIA (44785 "Baby Driver"/"Baby Driver") ... 8-12 69
COLUMBIA (45079 "Bridge Over Troubled Water") ... 4-8 70
COLUMBIA (45133 "Cecilia") ... 4-8 70
COLUMBIA (45237 "El Condor Pasa") ... 4-8 70
COLUMBIA (45663 "For Emily, Whenever I May Find Her") ... 4-6 72
TEEN SCOOP/Columbia ("Exclusive Interview") ... 20-35 65
(Square cardboard picture disc issued in premier issue of *Teen Scoop* magazine. Includes magazine with disc intact.)
TEEN SCOOP/Columbia ("Exclusive Interview") ... 15-20 65
(Square cardboard picture disc issued in premier issue of *Teen Scoop* magazine. No selection number used.)
TEEN SCOOP (789 "Visits with Simon & Garfunkel") ... 15-20 66
(*Teen Scoop* magazine bonus soundsheet.)
W.B. ... 3-5 82

Picture Sleeves

COLUMBIA ... 5-15 66-75

EPs: 7-inch

COLUMBIA ... 10-20 68-69
(Juke box issues only.)

LPs: 10/12-inch

COLUMBIA (CL-2249 "Wednesday Morning 3 A.M.") ... 10-20 64
(Monaural.)
COLUMBIA (CL-2469 "Sounds of Silence") ... 10-20 66
(Monaural.)
COLUMBIA (CL-2563 "Parsley, Sage Rosemary and Thyme") ... 10-20 66
(Monaural.)
COLUMBIA (KCL-2729 "Bookends") ... 15-25 68
(Monaural. Includes poster.)
COLUMBIA (OS-3180 "The Graduate") ... 12-15 68
(Soundtrack.)
COLUMBIA (3654 "Concert in Central Park") ... 8-12 82
COLUMBIA (CS-9049 "Wednesday Morning 3 A.M.") ... 10-15 64
(Stereo.)
COLUMBIA (PC-9049 "Wednesday Morning 3 A.M.") ... 5-10
COLUMBIA (CS-9269 "Sounds of Silence") ... 10-15 66
(Stereo.)
COLUMBIA (CS-9363 "Parsley, Sage Rosemary and Thyme") ... 10-15 66
(Stereo.)
COLUMBIA (PC-9363 "Parsley, Sage Rosemary and Thyme") ... 5-10
COLUMBIA (KCS-9529 "Bookends") ... 10-15 68
(Stereo. Includes poster.)
COLUMBIA (PC-9529 "Bookends") ... 5-10
COLUMBIA (9914 "Bridge over Troubled Water") ... 10-15 70
COLUMBIA (30995 "Bridge over Troubled Water") ... 10-20 71
(Quadraphonic.)
COLUMBIA (31350 "Greatest Hits") ... 5-10 72

COLUMBIA (37587 "Simon & Garfunkel's Collected Works") 30-40 81
(Boxed, five-disc set.)
COLUMBIA (41350 "Greatest Hits") 10-15 81
(Half-speed mastered.)
COLUMBIA (49914 "Bridge over Troubled Water") 40-60 80
(Half-speed mastered.)
MFSL (173 "Bridge over Troubled Water") 30-40 85
OFFSHORE 10-15
PICKWICK (3059 "Hit Sound of Simon & Garfunkel") 50-75 66
SEARS (435 "Simon & Garfunkel") 20-30
W.B. 5-8 82
Members: Paul Simon; Art Garfunkel.
Also see CLARK, Dave, Five / Simon & Garfunkel / Yardbirds / New Christy Minstrels
Also see GARFUNKEL, Art
Also see REVERE, Paul, & Raiders / Simon & Garfunkel / Byrds / Aretha Franklin
Also see SIMON, Paul
Also see TOM & JERRY

SIMON & PIEMEN

Singles: 7-inch

CARNIVAL (525 "Git-Go") 8-12 66
CHARTBOUND (007 "Cut It Out") .... 15-25 '60s

SIMON SISTERS P&R '64

Singles: 7-inch

COLUMBIA (02600 series) 3-5 82
COLUMBIA (45000 series) 4-6 73
KAPP (43 "Blowin' in the Wind") 5-10 65
KAPP (586 "Winkin', Blinkin' and Nod") 5-10 64
KAPP (624 "Cuddlebug") 5-10 64

LPs: 10/12-inch

COLUMBIA (21525 "Lobster Quadrille") .. 10-15 69
COLUMBIA (21539 "Simon Sisters Sing for Children") 10-12 73
COLUMBIA (24506 "Lobster Quadrille") .. 15-20 69
(Special childrens' book edition.)
COLUMBIA (37000 series) 5-10 82
KAPP (1359 "Simon Sisters") 15-20 64
(Monaural.)
KAPP (1397 "Cuddlebug") 20-25 64
(Stereo.)
KAPP (3359 "Simon Sisters") 15-20 64
(Monaural.)
KAPP (3397 "Cuddlebug") 20-25 64
(Stereo.)
W.B. 5-10 80
Members: Carly Simon; Lucy Simon.
Also see DOOBIE BROTHERS / Kate Taylor & Simon-Taylor Family
Also see SIMON, Carly

SIMPLICITIES

Singles: 7-inch

HULL (1204 "Make Him Love Me") 75-125 68

SIMPSON, Big Daddy Melvin

Singles: 7-inch

M-PAC (7224 "What Can I Do") 5-10 65
M-PAC (7226 "Give Me Back My Ring") 5-10 65

SIMPSON, Bill

Singles: 7-inch

LIN (100 "Jelly Roll Man") 10-15
SUNN (1 "Elvis-the Music Machine") 4-8

SIMPSON, Carl

Singles: 7-inch

VALLI (304 "Baby Blues Rock") 75-85 60

SIMPSON, Donald, & Rockenettes

Singles: 7-inch

MAJOR (1002 "Woe-Oh Baby") 100-125 58

SIMPSON, Hoke
(With Billy Mure Orchestra)

Singles: 7-inch

ABC-PAR (9876 "Gi-Gi") 10-15 58
COLONIAL (530 "Mountain Dew Rock") . 50-75

SIMPSON, James, Band

Singles: 7-inch

PENCO (7001 "On the Money") 20-40 80

SIMPSON, Jimmy

Singles: 78 rpm

HIDUS 10-15 55

Singles: 7-inch

CAPROCK (113 "I'm an Oilfield Boy") 10-20 59
HIDUS (2005 "Honky Tonk Spree") 50-75 55
JIFFY (210 "Blue As I Can Be") 100-150 58
SIMS (233 "I'm an Oilfield Boy") 5-10 65

SIMPSON, Valerie LP '71

Singles: 7-inch

TAMLA (Black vinyl) 4-6 71-73
TAMLA (Colored vinyl) 8-10 71-73
(Promotional issue only.)

LPs: 10/12-inch

TAMLA 10-15 71-77
Also see ASHFORD & SIMPSON
Also see SHARELL, Jerry

SIMPSON SISTERS

Singles: 7-inch

DCP (1115 "I Tore Up My Diary") 5-10 64

SIMS, Al
(Al Sims Trio)

Singles: 78 rpm

CHANCE (1102 "Moody Woman") 10-20 51

Singles: 7-inch

CHANCE (1102 "Moody Woman") 25-50 51
LISTEN (681 "Party") .... 150-200 '50s
LISTEN (690 "Little Red Caboose") .... 125-150 '50s
YUCCA (104 "Green Gatorater") 40-60 58

SIMS, Babe

Singles: 7-inch

SONGS & RECORDS (2 "Haddie Call Boogie") .... 75-125 '50s

SIMS, Charles

Singles: 7-inch

ALADDIN (3466 "Take a Bath") 75-85 60

SIMS, Chuck

Singles: 7-inch

SPANGLE (2005 "Little Pigeon") 15-25 58
(First issue.)
TREND (30000 "Little Pigeon") 10-15 58

SIMS, Frankie Lee

Singles: 78 rpm

ACE 10-15 57
BLUE BONNET (147 "Home Again, Blues") 100-150 48
BLUE BONNET (148 "Don't Forget Me, Baby") 100-150 48
SPECIALTY 40-50 53

Singles: 7-inch

ACE (524 "Misery Blues") 30-40 57
ACE (527 "Hey Little Girl") 30-40 57
ACE (539 "I Warned You Baby") 30-40 57
SPECIALTY (459 "Lucy Mae Blues") 25-35 53
SPECIALTY (478 "I'm Long, Long Gone") 20-30 53
SPECIALTY (487 "I'll Get Along Somehow") 20-30 53
VIN (1006 "She Likes to Boogie Real Low") 15-25 58

LPs: 10/12-inch

SPECIALTY (2124 "Lucy Mae Blues") 25-35 65

SIMS, Gerald

Singles: 7-inch

OKEH (7183 "Cool Breeze") 10-20 63
OKEH (7199 "Little Echo") 10-20 64
Also see DAYLIGHTERS

SIMS, Marvin
(Marvin L. Sims)

Singles: 7-inch

KAREN (1547 "Sweet Thang") 5-10 69
MELLOW (1002 "What Can I Do") 8-12 66
MELLOW (1004 "Have You Seen My Baby") 8-12 67
MELLOW (1005 "Hurting Inside") 8-12 67
MERCURY (73288 "Dream a Dream") 4-6 72
MERCURY (73340 "You Gotta Go") 4-6 72
REVUE (11024 "Talkin' 'Bout Soul") 5-10 68
REVUE (11038 "Get Off My Back") 5-10 68
RIVERTOWN (498 "Love Is on the Way") 4-6 80
UNI (55217 "It's Your Love") 4-8 70

SIMS, Syl

Singles: 7-inch

N-JOY (1002 "Landslide") 10-20 64

SIMS TWINS P&R/R&B '61
(Simms Twins)

Singles: 7-inch

ABKCO .... 4-6 '70s
CROSSOVER (975 "It's All Over") 4-6 74
KENT (4556 "Bring It On Home Where You Belong") 4-6 71
OMEN (8 "You've Got to Do the Best You Can") 5-10 65
OMEN (17 "A Losing Battle") 5-10 66
PARKWAY (6002 "Baby It's Real") 5-10 68
SAR 10-15 61-63
SPECIALTY (731 "Something Hanging On Your Mind") 4-6 74
Members: Bobby Sims; Kenneth Sims.

SIN SAY SHUNS

Singles: 7-inch

AMERICAN (3367 "You Said to Me") 10-15 66
(Selection number not known.)
VENETT (106 "I'll Be There") 10-15 66
VENETT (108 "All My Lonely Waiting") 10-15 66

LPs: 10/12-inch

VENETT (940 "I'll Be There") 20-25 66
Members: Bill Edison; Tony Visco; Bob Cottle.

SINATRA, Frank P&R '42
(With Harry James & His Orchestra; with Axel Stordahl & His Orchestra; with Big Dave's Music; with Les Baxter's Orchestra; "Tommy Dorsey Orchestra Featuring Frank Sinatra")

Singles: 78 rpm

BLUEBIRD (10726 "East of the Sun") 50-75 42
BLUEBIRD (10771 "Whispering") 50-75 42
BLUEBIRD (11463 "Night & Day") 50-75 42
BLUEBIRD (11515 "The Song Is You") 50-75 42
BRUNSWICK (8443 "From the Bottom of My Heart") 600-750 39
(Credited to Harry James & His Orchestra.)
CAPITOL (1699 thru 3900) 15-25 53-58
COLUMBIA (7492 "Soliloquy") 20-30 47
(12-inch disc.)
COLUMBIA (35209 thru 41133) 5-15 39-58
COLUMBIA (50003 thru 50079) .... 4-8 '50s
COLUMBIA (55037 "Ol Man River") 15-25 44
(12-inch disc.)
RCA (1522 thru 3500) 5-10 43-49
RCA (13247 "Oh Look at Me Now") 40-60 82
(Single-sided. Promotional issue only. 1000 numbered copies made.)
RCA (36396 "Without a Song") 15-25 42
(12-inch disc.)
VICTOR (26500 thru 27974) 5-10 40-43
(Some in this series may be shown as "RCA Victor.")

Albums: 78 rpm

COLUMBIA (112 "The Voice of Frank Sinatra") 25-50 46
(Four discs.)
COLUMBIA (117 "All Time Favorites By Harry James") 25-50 46
(Four discs. *Ciribiribin* is by Sinatra.)
COLUMBIA (117 "All Time Favorites By Harry James") 15-25 46
(Four discs. *Ciribiribin* is by Harry James.)
COLUMBIA (124 "Songs By Sinatra") 25-50 47
(Four discs.)
COLUMBIA (167 "Christmas Songs By Sinatra") 25-50 48
(Four discs.)
COLUMBIA (185 "Frankly Sentimental") .. 25-50 49
(Four discs.)
COLUMBIA (197 "Dedicated to You") 25-50 50
(Four discs.)
COLUMBIA (218 "Sing and Dance with Frank Sinatra") 25-50 50
(Four discs.)
COLUMBIA (455 "Young at Heart") 25-50 51
(Four discs.)
COLUMBIA (637 "Frank Sinatra Conducts the Music of Alec Wilder") 100-150 46
(Three 12-inch Masterworks discs.)
RCA (80 "Getting Sentimental") 20-40 40
(Four discs.)
RCA (150 "Starmaker") 20-40 41
(Four discs.)
RCA (163 "All Time Hits") 20-40 42
(Four discs.)
RCA (247 "And the Band Sang Too") 20-40 43
(Three discs)

Singles: 12-inch

QUEST (2216 "Mack the Knife") 10-20 84
(Promotional issue only.)
REPRISE (674 "Night & Day") 50-75 77
(Promotional issue only. Only 647 made.)
REPRISE (865 "New York, New York") 25-50 80
(Promotional issue only.)

Singles: 7-inch

CAPITOL ("No One Ever Tells You") 35-45 56
(No selection number used. Promotional issue only. Add $4 to $6 if accompanied by Capitol "Rush" paper sleeve.)
CAPITOL (596 "All the Way") 250-350 58
(Promotional issue only. 101 made.)
CAPITOL (1069 "Come Dance with Me") 50-75 59
(Five singles in a paper sleeve. For juke box use. With "XE" prefix.)
CAPITOL (1417 "Nice 'N' Easy ") 50-75 60
(Five singles in a paper sleeve. For juke box use. With "XE" prefix.)
CAPITOL (1491 "Sinatra's Swingin' Session") 50-75 61
(Five singles in a paper sleeve. For juke box use. With "XE" prefix.)
CAPITOL (1594 "Come Swing with Me") . 50-75 62
(Five singles in a paper sleeve. For juke box use. With "XE" prefix.)
CAPITOL (1676 "Point of No Return") 50-75 63
(Five singles in a paper sleeve. For juke box use. With "XE" prefix.)
CAPITOL (1699 "I've Got the World on a String") 20-30 51
CAPITOL (1729 "Sinatra Sings of Love and Things") .... 50-75 '60s
(Five singles in a paper sleeve. For juke box use. With "XE" prefix.)
CAPITOL (1707/8 "Mistletoe & Holly") ... 75-100 60
(Promotional issue for Christmas Seals.)
CAPITOL (2450 "Lean Baby") 15-25 53
CAPITOL (2505 thru 4070) 10-20 53-58
CAPITOL (4103 "To Love and Be Loved"). 8-12 58
CAPITOL (4103 "To Love and Be Loved") 150-250 58
(White label. Promotional issue only.)
CAPITOL (4155 "French Foreign Legion"). 8-12 59
CAPITOL (4214 "High Hopes") 8-12 59
(Purple label.)
CAPITOL (4214 "High Hopes") 50-100 60
(Red label. Promotional issue only.)
CAPITOL (4284 thru 4815) 6-12 59-62
CAPITOL (6019 thru 6195) 4-6 62
(Starline reissue series.)
COLUMBIA (112 "The Voice of Frank Sinatra") 50-75 46
(Four discs.)
COLUMBIA (167 "Christmas Songs By Sinatra") 50-75 48
(Four discs.)
COLUMBIA (197 "Dedicated to You") 50-75 50
(Four discs.)
COLUMBIA (218 "Sing and Dance with Frank Sinatra") 50-75 50
(Four discs.)
COLUMBIA (673 "If I Ever Love Again") .. 40-60 67
(Promotional issue only.)
COLUMBIA (1-106 thru 1-936) 40-60 48-51
(Microgroove 33 singles.)
COLUMBIA (6-718 thru 6-936) 15-25 50-51
(45 rpm.)
COLUMBIA (3842 "I Guess I'll Have to Dream the Rest") 40-60 71
(Promotional issue only.)
COLUMBIA (12194 "All Or Nothing at All") 30-40 55
(Promotional issue only.)
COLUMBIA (33000 series) .... 4-8 '60s
(Hall of Fame series. With "13" prefix.)
COLUMBIA (33011 thru 39213) .... 40-60 '50s
(Microgroove 33 singles. With "3" prefix.)
COLUMBIA (36814 thru 41133) 15-30 50-58
(45 rpm. With "4" prefix.)
COLUMBIA (50003 thru 50079) 10-15 55-59
(Hall of Fame series. With "4" prefix.)
COLUMBIA (116427 "White Christmas") . 40-60 63
(Promotional issue only.)
"HIGH HOPES with JACK KENNEDY"/"Jack Kennedy All the Way" 150-250 60
(Presidential campaign promotional issue only. No label name or artist shown. Reportedly 1,000 made.)
LATIMER 50-75 64
(Interview with Frank Sinatra on both sides.) Private issue only, by the 500 Club.)
LATIMER 50-75 64
(Frank's farewell to the Dorsey Orchestra. Includes introduction of Dick Haymes and award presentation from the City of Philadelphia. Private issue only, by the 500 Club.)

RCA (15 "Getting Sentimental") 35-50 50
(Boxed, four-disc set.)
RCA (20 "All Time Hits") 35-50 51
(Boxed, four-disc set.)
RCA GOLD STANDARD 4-8 60-70
(With "447" prefix.)
REPRISE ("A Special Message to You from Frank Sinatra") 750-1000 61
(Single-sided. Made as a Reprise sales and promotional tool. No selection number used. Two different pressings exist.)
REPRISE (45 "Frank Sinatra reads from Gunga Din") 450-650 66
(Promotional issue only.)
REPRISE (PRO-162 thru PRO-406)........ 25-50 63-69
(White label, promotional issues only.)
REPRISE (0243 thru 0380) 5-10 63-65
REPRISE (396 "Radio Spot for *Watertown*") 15-25 70
(Promotional issue only.)
REPRISE (0398 thru 1386) 4-8 65-77
REPRISE (20001 thru 20151) 5-10 61-63
REPRISE (20157 "California") 150-250 77
(Promotional issue only. Reportedly 1000 made.)
REPRISE (20184 "Come Blow Your Horn") 5-10 63
REPRISE (20184 "Come Blow Your Horn") 50-75 63
(White label. Promotional issue only.)
REPRISE (20209 "A New Kind of Love") ...5-10 63
REPRISE (20209 "A New Kind of Love") 50-75 63
(White label. Promotional issue only.)
REPRISE (20235 "Tangerine") 5-10 63
REPRISE (28000 & 29000 series) 3-5 82
REPRISE (40001 thru 40050) ....8-10 '60s
(33 rpm. Juke box issues.)
REPRISE (40063 thru 40092) 5-10
(33 rpm. Juke box issues.)
REPRISE (49000 series) 3-5 80-83
REPRISE/CAL NEVADA LODGE (101 "Ring-A-Ding-Ding") 50-75 63
(Promo souvenir, available from the lodge.)

Picture Sleeves

CAPITOL (596 "All the Way") 250-350 58
(Promotional issue only. 101 made.)
CAPITOL (4103 "To Love and Be Loved") 250-350 58
(Promotional issue only.)
CAPITOL (4214 "High Hopes") 250-350 60
(Promotional issue only.)
REPRISE (0429 "It Was a Very Good Year") 10-20 65
REPRISE (0531 "That's Life") 10-20 66
REPRISE (20010 "Granada") 10-20 61
REPRISE (20063 "Everybody's Twistin'") 10-20 62
REPRISE (20157 "California") 300-400 77
(Promotional issue only. Reportedly 1000 made.)
REPRISE (20184 "Come Blow Your Horn") 100-150 63
(Promotional issue only.)
REPRISE (20209 "A New Kind of Love") 100-150 63
(Promotional issue only.)
REPRISE (29903-7 "To Love a Child") 8-12 82
(Dedicated to Mrs. Nancy Reagan. With the Reprise Children's Chorus featuring Nikka Costa. Promotional issue only.)
REPRISE (49233 "New York, New York") 3-5 80
REPRISE/CAL NEVADA LODGE (101 "Ring-A-Ding-Ding") 100-150 63
(Promo souvenir, available from the lodge.)
SINATRA 4-6 75

EPs: 7-inch

CAPITOL (3 "Vocal Standards") ....5-15 '60s
(33 rpm.)
CAPITOL (100 "Special 1981 Birthday Tribute") 75-125 81
(33 rpm. Promotional issue only. Includes "Thank You" insert.)
CAPITOL (280 "Disc Jockey Interview Record for the film *High Society*") 125-175 56
(Promotional issue only.)
CAPITOL 426: see SINATRA, Frank / Roger Wagner / Hollywood Bowl Symphony
CAPITOL (434 "Selections from *Pal Joey*.) 125-175 57
(Promotional issue only.)
CAPITOL (488 thru 1594) 8-18 53-62
(Single-disc EPs, with "EAP" prefix.)
CAPITOL (488 thru 855) 12-25 53-57
(Two-disc EPs, with "EBF" prefix.)
CAPITOL (SU-581 "In the Wee Small Hours") ....5-15 '60s
(33 rpm.)
CAPITOL (DU-653 "Songs for Swingin' Lovers") ....5-15 '60s
(33 rpm.)
CAPITOL (DU-768 "This Is Sinatra") ....5-15 '60s
(33 rpm.)
CAPITOL (SU-920 "Come Fly with Me") ....5-15 '60s
(33 rpm.)
CAPITOL (1069 "Come Dance with Me").15-25 59
(Promotional issue only.)
CAPITOL (1549 "Selections from *Can-Can*") 300-500 60
(Promotional issue only.)
CAPITOL (1762 "The Great Years") ....5-15 '60s
(Stereo 33 Compact.)
Capitol (1864 "Come Swing with Capitol - New Albums for August 1961") 30-50 61
(Promotional issue only.)
CAPITOL (11583 "Frank Sinatra") ....10-15 '60s
(33 rpm.)
COLUMBIA (112 thru 455) 40-60 50-54
(Two discs.)
COLUMBIA (1524 thru 2641) 10-25 50-59
(Single-disc EPs.)
COLUMBIA (7431 thru 9533) 10-20 55-57
(Single-disc EPs.)
COLUMBIA (10321/10322 "Christmas Dreaming") 10-15 57
(Price is for either volume.)
COLUMBIA (28595 "Nancy") 75-100 58
(Promotional issue, made for B.T. Babbit and attached to their soap boxes. With custom cover.)
RCA (102 "Tommy Dorsey Originals") 10-20 60
(Compact 33 Double.)
RCA (3005 "This Is Tommy Dorsey") 25-50 50
(Two discs.)
RCA (3028 "Getting Sentimental") 25-50 50
(Two discs.)
RCA (3030 "All Time Hits") 25-50 51
(Two discs.)
RCA (3063 "Fabulous Frankie") 25-50 52
(Two discs.)
RCA (5007 thru 5147) 12-25 58-60
RCA (6038 "This Is Tommy Dorsey") ....10-15 '60s
(Juke box issue only.)
REPRISE 10-15 62-74
(Juke box issues.)

LPs: 10/12-inch

CAMDEN (650 thru 800) 5-15 61-73
CAMDEN (9027 I'm Getting Sentimental Over You") 8-12 72
CAPITOL ("Radio/TV Sampler") 200-250 58
(Number unknown. Yellow label. Promotional issue only.)
CAPITOL (200 & 300 series, except LS-308) 8-15 69
CAPITOL (LS-308 "Sinatra: The Works") 75-125 71
(Boxed, 10-disc set. Includes booklet. Add $75 to $100 if accompanied by the bonus LP, *Sinatra*.)
CAPITOL (H-488 thru H-581) 30-50 54-55
(10-inch LPs.)
CAPITOL (488 thru 1164, except 735) 20-30 54-59
(With "T" or "W" prefix.)
CAPITOL (W-735 "Frank Sinatra Conducts Tone Poems of Color") 75-100 56
CAPITOL (581 thru 1676) 5-15 61-78
(With "DT," "DW," "SM," "STBB," "SW," or "W" prefix.)
CAPITOL (T-1221 thru T-1676) 10-20 59-62
(Monaural.)
CAPITOL (ST-1221 thru ST-1676) 10-20 59-62
(Stereo.)
CAPITOL (PRO-1624 "The Best of Sinatra") 75-100 61
(Promotional issue only. Issued with paper sleeve.)
CAPITOL (1729 "Love & Things") 10-20 62
CAPITOL (1762 "Sinatra: The Great Years") 20-30 62
(Three-disc set.)
CAPITOL (1825 thru 2700) 15-30 62-68
(With "T" or "W" prefix. Monaural.)
CAPITOL (1825 thru 2700) 10-20 62-68
(With "DT" or "DW" prefix. Reprocessed stereo.)
CAPITOL (2814 "Deluxe Set") 40-60 67
(Boxed, six-disc set.)
CAPITOL (2974 "Frank Sinatra Minute Masters") 100-150 65
CAPITOL (7630 "The Sinatra Touch") 50-75 68
(Boxed, six-disc set. Includes booklet.)
CAPITOL (11000 & 12000 series) 5-10 74-80
CAPITOL (16000 series) 5-8 80-82
CAPITOL (89611 "Duets") ....8-10 '90s
CAPITOL (90000 thru 94000 series) 20-40 64-74
(Capitol Record Club issues.)
COLUMBIA (6 "The Frank Sinatra Story") 15-25 58
COLUMBIA (S3S-42 "Essential Frank Sinatra") 20-30 67
(Boxed, three-disc set. Stereo.)
COLUMBIA (S3S-842 "Essential Frank Sinatra") 10-20
(Boxed, three-disc set. Reissue.)
COLUMBIA (S3S-842 "Essential Frank Sinatra") 10-20
(Boxed, three-disc set. Reissue.)
COLUMBIA (606 "Frankie") 25-40 55
(Cover pictures Sinatra wearing a hat and alone.)
COLUMBIA (606 "Frankie") ....15-25 '50s
(Cover pictures Sinatra not wearing a hat and with two other people.)
COLUMBIA (743 "The Voice of Sinatra") .25-35 55
COLUMBIA (902 "That Old Feeling") 20-30 56
COLUMBIA (842 "Essential Frank Sinatra") 30-50 67
(Three-disc set. Includes booklet.)
COLUMBIA (953 "Adventures of the Heart") 15-25 57
COLUMBIA (1032 "Christmas Dreaming") 15-25 57
COLUMBIA (1130 thru 1359) 20-40 58-59
COLUMBIA (1448 "Reflections") 30-60 60
COLUMBIA (CL-2474 "Greatest Hits: The Early Years, Vol. 1") 10-15 66
(Monaural.)
COLUMBIA (2521 "Get Happy") 25-40 55
(10-inch LP.)
COLUMBIA (2539 "I've Got a Crush on You") 25-40 55
(10-inch LP.)
COLUMBIA (2542 "Christmas with Frank Sinatra") 25-40 55
(10-inch LP.)
COLUMBIA (CL-2572 "Greatest Hits: The Early Years, Vol. 2") 10-15 66
(Monaural.)
COLUMBIA (2475 "The Voice, Sampler") 10-15 86
(Samples tracks from C6X-40343.)
COLUMBIA (CL-2739 thru CL-2913) 10-15 66-69
(Monaural.)
COLUMBIA (4271 "Frank Sinatra Conducts the Music of Alec Wilder") 125-175 50
(Green Masterworks label.)
COLUMBIA (6001 "The Voice of Sinatra") 75-100 48
(10-inch LP.)
COLUMBIA (6059 "Frankly Sentimental") 50-75 49
(10-inch LP.)
COLUMBIA (6087 "Songs By Sinatra, Vol. 1") 50-75 50
(10-inch LP.)
COLUMBIA (6096 "Dedicated to You") 50-75 50
(10-inch LP.)
COLUMBIA (6143 "Sing and Dance with Frank Sinatra") 50-75 50
(10-inch LP.)
COLUMBIA (6290 "I've Got a Crush on You") 50-75 52
(10-inch LP.)
COLUMBIA (6339 "Young at Heart") 50-75 54
(10-inch LP.)
COLUMBIA (CS-9274 "Greatest Hits: The Early Years, Vol. 1") 8-15 66
(Stereo.)
COLUMBIA (CS-9372 "Greatest Hits: The Early Years, Vol. 2") 8-15 66
(Stereo.)
COLUMBIA (CS-9539 thru CS-9541) 8-15 66-67
(Stereo.)
COLUMBIA (10000 series) 5-10 73
COLUMBIA (30000 thru 45000 series, except 31358 & 40343) 5-12 73-87
COLUMBIA (31358 "In the Beginning") 8-12 72
(Two-disc set.)
COLUMBIA (40343 "The Voice") 30-50 86
(Boxed, six-disc set.)
EARTH NEWS 50-100 80
(Radio show on disc. Includes cue sheet/script.)
HARMONY 10-20 66-71
KATWHISKER ("Frank Sinatra: Biography in Song") 750-1000 75
(Boxed, eight-disc set. Includes cue sheets. Promotional issue only. Reportedly only 25 made.)
MFSL (1 "Frank Sinatra") 400-600 85
(Boxed, 16-disc set. Includes booklet and alignment tool. Numbered edition of 25,000 made.)
MFSL (086 "Nice 'N' Easy") 40-60 82
MFSL (130 "Swing Easy") 30-40 85
MFSL (131 "In the Wee Small Hours") 30-40 85
MFSL (132 "Close to You") 30-40 85
MFSL (133 "A Swingin Affair") 30-40 85
MFSL (134 "Where You Are") 30-40 85
MFSL (2-135 "A Jolly Christmas") 40-50 85
MFSL (136 "Come Fly with Me") 30-40 85
MFSL (137 "Only the Lonely") 30-40 85
MFSL (138 "Come Dance with Me") 30-40 85
MFSL (139 "Look at Your Heart") 30-40 85
MFSL (140 "No One Cares") 30-40 85
MFSL (141 "Sinatra's Swingin") 30-40 85
MFSL (142 "All the Way") 30-40 85
MFSL (143 "Come Swing with Me") 30-40 85
MFSL (145 "Sinatra Swings") 30-40 85
MFSL (146 "Songs for Swingin' Lovers") .30-40 85
NARWOOD ("U.S. Army Reserve Presents William B. & Company") 150-200 76
(Two-LP, public service radio show. Has Sinatra interview. Promotional issue only.)
ODYSSEY 10-20 68
PICKWICK ....5-10 '70s
RCA (10 "Getting Sentimental") 35-50 50
(10-inch LP.)
RCA (15 "All Time Hits") 35-50 51
(10-inch LP.)
RCA (017 "I'll See You in My Dreams") .....8-12 '70s
RCA (050 "What'll I Do") 5-8
RCA (474 "The Radio Years") 5-10 74
RCA (0497 "What'll I Do") 8-10 74
RCA (583 "This Love of Mine") 8-12
RCA (1569 "Frankie & Tommy") 20-40 57
RCA (1586 "Frank Sinatra with the Tommy Dorsey Orchestra") 5-8 75
RCA (1632 "We Three") 20-40 57
RCA (3005 "This Is Tommy Dorsey") 25-50 50
(10-inch LP.)
RCA (3063 "Fabulous Frankie") 25-50 52
(10-inch LP.)
RCA (4334 "The Dorsey/Sinatra Sessions, Vols. 1 & 2") 8-10 82
RCA (4335 "The Dorsey/Sinatra Sessions, Vols. 3 & 4") 8-10 82
RCA (4336 "The Dorsey/Sinatra Sessions, Vols. 5 & 6") 8-10 82
RCA (6003 "The Sentimental Gentleman") 20-40 53
(10-inch LP.)
RCA (4700 series) 5-8 83
RCA/PAIR 5-10 84
REPRISE (R-1001 thru R-1010) 10-15 61-63
(Monaural.)
REPRISE (R9-1001 thru R9-1010) 10-20 61-63
(Stereo.)
REPRISE (F-1001 thru F-1010) ....5-10 '60s
(Monaural reissues.)
REPRISE (FS-1001 thru FS-1010) ....8-12 '60s
(Stereo reissues.)
REPRISE (1011 thru 1015) 8-12 64-65
REPRISE (1016 "A Man and His Music") 10-15 66
(Two discs.)
REPRISE (1016 "A Man and His Music, Part II") 300-400 66
(Promotional issue, made for Budweiser Beer distributors. About 1,000 made.)
REPRISE (FS4-1029 thru FS4-2207) ...... 15-25 '70s
(Quadraphonic.)
REPRISE (1018 thru 1034) 8-15 66-72
REPRISE (2013 thru 2022) 20-40 62-64
REPRISE (2155 thru 2275) 5-15 73-78
REPRISE (2300 "Trilogy") 15-25 80
(Three-disc set.)
REPRISE (2305 "She Shot Me Down") 5-8 81
REPRISE (5230 "Songbook, Vol. 1") 25-35 71
REPRISE (5267 "Songbook, Vol. 2") 50-100 72
(Two-disc set.)
REPRISE (6000 series) 15-25 61-72

SINATRA 5-10 75
Session: Nuggets.
Also see ALI, Muhammad, & Frank Sinatra
Also see ANTHONY, Ray
Also see BAXTER, Les
Also see BLOCH, Ray, & Orchestra
Also see CROSBY, Bing / Grace Kelly / Frank Sinatra / Celeste Holm
Also see DAY, Doris & Frank Sinatra
Also see DORSEY, Tommy, Orchestra
Also see HAYMES, Dick
Also see JAMES, Harry
Also see KINGSTON TRIO / Frank Sinatra
Also see NUGGETS
Also see PRESLEY, Elvis / Frank Sinatra / Nat King Cole
Also see VINCENT, Gene / Frank Sinatra / Sonny James / Ron Goodwin
Also see ZENTNER, Si

SINATRA, Frank, & Charioteers

Singles: 78 rpm

COLUMBIA (36854 "Don't Forget Tonight Tomorrow") 5-15 45
Also see CHARIOTEERS

SINATRA, Frank, & Count Basie *LP '63*

EPs: 7-inch

REPRISE (1012 "It Might As Well Be Swing") 8-12 63
(Promotional issue only.)

LPs: 10/12-inch

REPRISE 10-20 63-66
Also see BASIE, Count

SINATRA, Frank / Nat "King" Cole

EPs: 7-inch

CAPITOL (500 "Witchcraft") 35-55 58
(Promotional issue only.)
Also see COLE, Nat "King"

SINATRA, Frank, Bing Crosby & Russ Columbo

Singles: 7-inch

RCA (5 "Immortal Performances") 50-75 50
(Boxed three-disc set, one by each artist. Includes bio/booklet.)

LPs: 10/12-inch

RCA (5 "Immortal Performances") 50-75 50
(10-inch LP.)

SINATRA, Frank, Bing Crosby & Dean Martin

Singles: 7-inch

REPRISE (20,217 "The Oldest Established [Permanent Floating Crap Game in New York]) 15-25 62

Picture Sleeves

REPRISE (20,217 "The Oldest Established [Permanent Floating Crap Game in New York]) 100-125 62

SINATRA, Frank, Bing Crosby, & Fred Waring

LPs: 10/12-inch

REPRISE (2020 "America, I Hear You Singing") 10-20 64
Also see CROSBY, Bing
Also see CROSBY, Bing, & Grace Kelly / Bing Crosby & Frank Sinatra
Also see WARING, Fred

SINATRA, Frank, Sammy Davis Jr. & Dean Martin *P&R '62*
(Frankie, Dino & Sammy)

Singles: 7-inch

REPRISE (20,128 "Me and My Shadow"/ "Sam's Song") 5-10 62

Picture Sleeves

REPRISE (20,128 "Me and My Shadow"/ "Sam's Song") 15-25 62

LPs: 10/12-inch

LATIMER (247-17 "Summit Meeting at the 500, Atlantic City, N.J.") 250-350 64
(Private issue only, by the 500 Club. Three different paste-on covers exist for this LP.)

SINATRA, Frank, & Duke Ellington *LP '68*

Singles: 7-inch

REPRISE (677 "How Old Am I") 4-8 68

EPs: 7-inch

REPRISE (1024 "Francis A. Sinatra and Edward K. Ellington") 8-12 68

LPs: 10/12-inch

REPRISE (1024 "Francis A. Sinatra and Edward K. Ellington") 10-20 68
Also see ELLINGTON, Duke

SINATRA, Frank / Fontaine (sic) Sisters / Glenn Miller & His Orchestra
(With the Modernaires & Ray Eberle)

EPs: 7-inch

RCA (1031/1032 "Selections from RCA Records Vault") 10-15
(Three of the four tracks are versions of *I Guess I'll Have to Dream the Rest*. Promotional issue only.)
Also see FONTANE SISTERS
Also see MILLER, Glenn, & His Orchestra

SINATRA, Frank, & Antonio Carlos Jobim *LP '67*

EPs: 7-inch

REPRISE (297-62 "Francis Albert Sinatra & Antonio Carlos Jobim") 10-15 67

LPs: 10/12-inch

REPRISE (297-62 "Francis Albert Sinatra & Antonio Carlos Jobim") 15-20 67
Also see JOBIM, Antonio Carlos

SINATRA, Frank / Jonah Jones

Singles: 7-inch

CAPITOL (4214 "High Hopes") 50-100 60
(Promotional issue only.)

Picture Sleeves

CAPITOL (4214 "High Hopes") 300-400 60
(Promotional issue only.)

SINATRA, Frank, with Quincy Jones & His Orchestra *LP '84*

Singles: 12-inch

QWEST (2216 "Mack the Knife") 25-50 84

Singles: 7-inch

QWEST (29223 "L.A. Is My Lady") 3-5 84

LPs: 10/12-inch

QWEST (25145 "L.A. Is My Lady") 5-10 84
Also see JONES, Quincy

SINATRA, Frank, Dean Martin, Sammy Davis Jr., & Bing Crosby

LPs: 10/12-inch

REPRISE (5031 "Summit") 500-1000 64
(British issue only.)
Also see CROSBY, Bing
Also see DAVIS, Sammy, Jr.
Also see MARTIN, Dean

SINATRA, Frank, & Pied Pipers

Singles: 78 rpm

RCA 5-10 41
Also see PIED PIPERS

SINATRA, Frank, & Keely Smith *P&R '58*

Singles: 78 rpm

CAPITOL (3952 "Nothing in Common") 15-25 58
(This is the last commercially-issued Sinatra 78 rpm.)

Singles: 7-inch

CAPITOL (3952 "Nothing in Common") 5-10 58
Also see SMITH, Keely

SINATRA, Frank / Roger Wagner Chorale / Hollywood Bowl Symphony

EPs: 7-inch

CAPITOL (426 "Christmas Around the World") 75-100 57
(Promotional issue only.)

SINATRA, Frank & Nancy *P&R '67*
(Sinatra Family)

Singles: 7-inch

REPRISE 4-8 66-71

LPs: 10/12-inch

REPRISE (1026 "The Sinatra Family Wishes You a Merry Christmas") 10-20 67
Members: Sinatra Family included Frank Sinatra, Frank Jr., Nancy and Tina.
Also see SINATRA, Nancy

SINATRA, Nancy *P&R '65*

Singles: 7-inch

ELEKTRA 3-5 80
PRIVATE STOCK 4-6 75-77
RCA 4-6 72-73
REPRISE 5-10 61-71

Picture Sleeves

REPRISE (620 "Lightning's Girl") 8-12 67
REPRISE (20017 "Cuff Links and a Tie Clip") 10-15 67

EPs: 7-inch

REPRISE 10-12 66
(Juke box issue only.)

LPs: 10/12-inch

RCA 8-10 72
REPRISE 15-30 66-72
Also see MARTIN, Dean
Also see PRESLEY, Elvis
Also see SINATRA, Frank & Nancy
Also see TILLIS, Mel, & Nancy Sinatra

SINATRA, Nancy, & Lee Hazlewood *P&R/LP '68*

Singles: 7-inch

PRIVATE STOCK 4-6 76
RCA 4-6 72
REPRISE 5-8 67-68

LPs: 10/12-inch

RCA 8-10 72
REPRISE 10-15 68
Also see SINATRA, Nancy

SINBAD, Paul

Singles: 7-inch

HYPE (1003/1004 "I'm Uptight") .... 10-20 '60s
HYPE (1007/1008 "Do Whatcha Wanna Do") .... 10-20 '60s
KNOX .... 5-10 '60s
LAP (1214 "I'm Up Tight") 5-10 65
POWERTREE ("I Was a Fool") 30-50
(Selection number not known.)

SINCERELY YOURS

Singles: 7-inch

IMPACT (1020 "Little Girl") 25-50 67

SINCERES
(With L. Bergo & Orchestra)

Singles: 7-inch

JORDAN (117 "You're Too Young") 100-150 60
RICHIE (545 "Please Don't Cheat on Me") 250-350 61
(No mention of Roulette distribution on label.)
RICHIE (545 "Please Don't Cheat on Me") 50-75 61
(White label. Promotional issue only. Label indicates "Distributed by Roulette.)
RICHIE (545 "Please Don't Cheat on Me") 40-60 61
(Label indicates "Distributed by Roulette.)
SIGMA (1004 "Darling") 250-350 60
Member: Jay Proctor.
Also see JAY & TECHNIQUES

SINCERES

Singles: 7-inch

COLUMBIA (43110 "Sincerely") 8-12 64
EPIC (9583 "Our Winter Love") 8-12 63
TAURUS (377 "Magic of Love") 8-12 65

SINCERES

Singles: 7-inch

PZAZZ (007 "Girl, I Love You") 30-40 68

SINCLAIR, Terry

Singles: 7-inch

D.P.G. (1006 "Clown Suit") 10-20 64

SING-A-LONG WITH THE BEATLES

LPs: 10/12-inch

TOWER (5000 "Sing-A-Long with the Beatles") 50-100 65
(Instrumental tracks of Beatles tunes. Listed by title since no artist is credited.)

SINGER, Hal
(Hal "Cornbread" Singer; with Charlie Shavers; with His Orchestra and Joan Shaw)

Singles: 78 rpm

CORAL 30-40 51
SAVOY 10-20 48-56

Singles: 7-inch

CORAL (65070 "Buttermilk and Beans") 40-50 51
CORAL (65086 "Lonesome and Blue") 40-50 51
CORAL (65098 "Please Doctor Jive") 40-50 51
PRESTIGE (134 "Blue Stompin' ") 8-12 59
SAVOY (861 "The Frog Hop") 15-25 52
SAVOY (890 "Hometown") 15-25 53
SAVOY (1179 "Hot Rod") 15-25 55
SAVOY (1194 "Hound's Tooth") 15-25 56
TIME (1001 "Hula Hoop Rock") 10-20 58

LPs: 10/12-inch

PRESTIGE (7153 "Blue Stompin' ") 25-35 59
Also see SHAW, Joan

SINGER, Johnny

Singles: 7-inch

C&W (216 "Talk Back Trembling Lips") .... 10-20 '60s
C&W (240 "Shotgun Boogie") 50-75

SINGIN' SAM
(Sam Chatman)

Singles: 7-inch

MISS (115 "My Story") 10-20 60
Also see CHATMAN, Sam
Also see SAMPSON, Phil

SINGING BELLES *P&R '60*

Singles: 7-inch

MADISON (126 "Someone Loves You") 8-12 60
MADISON (132 "High Noon") 8-12 60

SINGING NUN *P&R/LP '63*
(Soeur Sourire; Jeanine Deckers)

Singles: 7-inch

PHILIPS 4-8 63-64

Picture Sleeves

PHILIPS 5-10 63-64

LPs: 10/12-inch

PHILIPS 8-12 63-69

SINGING SAM & SPARKS

Singles: 7-inch

DEE DEE (2223 "Messin' ") 15-20 66
DEE DEE (2231 "I Can't Believe It") 20-25 66
HONEY (1472 "I Know My Baby Loves Me") 8-12
Also see CHATMAN, Sam, & Sparks

SINGING WANDERERS

Singles: 78 rpm

DECCA (29230 "Say Hey, Willie Mays") 10-20 54
DECCA (29298 "Three Roses") 30-40 54

Singles: 7-inch

DECCA (29230 "Say Hey, Willie Mays") 50-75 54
DECCA (29298 "Three Roses") 200-300 54
Also see WANDERERS

SINGLETON, Bebo
(With Jeff & Notes)

Singles: 7-inch

STENTOR (101 "The Shrine of the Echoes") 800-1000 59
(White promotional issue only. 25 made.)
STENTOR (101 "The Shrine of the Echoes") 400-600 59
VIM (508 "Dreams of Dreams") 50-75 60
Also see RHYTHM CADETS

SINGLETON, Charlie
(With the All Stars; Charlie "Hoss" Singleton)

Singles: 78 rpm

APOLLO 10-20 49
ATLAS 10-15 52-53
ATLANTIC 10-15 54
DECCA 20-30 51
FAITH .... 10-15 '50s
LEE .... 10-15 '50s
RAINBOW 10-15 50
ROBIN (103 "Earthquake") 40-60 51
SATURN 10-20 52
STAR 10-15 50
SUNSET 10-20 54-55

Singles: 7-inch

ATLANTIC (1032 "Boardwalk") 25-40 54
ATLAS (1029 "Pony Express") 40-50 53
DECCA (48193 "Alligator Meat") 50-100 51
RED ROBIN (103 "Earthquake") 20-30 52
SUNSET 20-40 54-55

LPs: 10/12-inch

CAMDEN (713 "Big Twist Hits") 15-25 62
Also see CHARLIE & ROSIE
Also see HOSS, Charlie, & Ponies

SINGLETON, Eddie
(With the Chromatics)

Singles: 7-inch

AMSCO (3701 "Too Late") 100-150 57
GLOVER (211 "Let Me Know") 10-15 60
JOKER (1001 "It's Not My Fault") 10-15 62

SINGLETON, Eddie, & Chromatics / Augie Austin & Chromatics

Singles: 7-inch

BRUNSWICK (55080 "Too Late") 40-50 58
Also see AUSTIN, Augie
Also see CHROMATICS
Also see SINGLETON, Eddie

SINGLETON, Jimmy, & Royal Satins
(With the Hi-Fis)
Singles: 7-inch
DEVERE (006 "Sally") ... 400-500 60
MARK (148 "Sally") ... 100-200 60
Also see HI-FIs

SINGLETON, Sterly
Singles: 7-inch
SHELLEY (128 "Cross Current") ... 15-25 61
(Also issued as by the Rockin' Dukes.)
Also see ROCKIN' DUKES

SINKS, Earl
Singles: 7-inch
CAPITOL (4885 "Be Good") ... 15-25 62
CAPITOL (4985 "Looking for Love") ... 15-25 63
HICKORY (1315 "Language of Love") ... 5-10 65
W.B. (5197 "Look for Me") ... 5-10 61

SINNERS
(With the Jack Nitzsche Orchestra)
Singles: 7-inch
EDEN (1 "Could This Be Love") ... 150-200 62
Also see NITZSCHE, Jack

SINNERS
Singles: 7-inch
MERCURY (72453 "Goin' Out of My Mind") ... 10-20 65
Session: Davie Allan.
Also see ALLAN, Davie

SINNERS
LPs: 10/12-inch
PENTAGON (141 "Rocky Road") ... 50-100 65
(Canadian.)
Members: Darek Middleton; Myles Devine; Bob Burns; Larry Goguen; Roy Feener.

SIPES, Leonard, & Rhythm Oakies
Singles: 78 rpm
MORGAN (106 "Campus Boogie") ... 400-800
Member: Tommy Collins.
Also see COLLINS, Tommy

SIR ALBERT
Singles: 7-inch
ROZAN (1101 "For Your Love") ... 10-15 68

SIR CHAUNCEY P&R '60
(With His Exciting Strings; Ernie Freeman)
Singles: 7-inch
PATTERN (603 "Beautiful Obsession") ... 10-15 60
(First issue.)
W.B. (5150 "Beautiful Obsession") ... 5-10 60
W.B. (5185 "Beyond Our Love") ... 5-10 60
Also see FREEMAN, Ernie

SIR DOUGLAS QUINTET P&R '65
(Sir Douglas Band)
Singles: 7-inch
ATLANTIC ... 4-8 73
CASABLANCA (0828 "Roll with the Punches") ... 5-15 75
MERCURY ... 4-6 71
PACEMAKER (260 "Sugar Bee") ... 15-20 66
PHILIPS ... 4-8 70-71
SMASH ... 5-10 68-70
TRIBE (No Indian on label.) ... 8-12 65
TRIBE (Label pictures Indian.) ... 5-10 65-67
Picture Sleeves
PHILIPS ... 4-8 70-71
LPs: 10/12-inch
ACCORD ... 5-10 82
ATLANTIC ... 10-15 73
MERCURY ... 10-15 72
PHILIPS ... 15-25 70-71
SMASH ... 15-25 68-70
TAKOMA ... 5-10 80-83
TRIBE (47001 "Best of Sir Douglas Quintet") ... 50-75 66
Members: Doug Sahm; Augie Meyers; Jack Barber; Leon Baetty; John Perez; Frank Morin; Jim Stallings.
Also see CASCADES / Sir Douglas Quintet
Also see DEVONS
Also see LONG, Joey
Also see MEYERS, Augie
Also see SAHM, Doug

SIR FROG & TOADS
Singles: 7-inch
DOWNEY (131 "The Frog") ... 10-20 66

SIR GUY & ROCKING CAVALIERS
Singles: 7-inch
D.P.G. (1009 "My Sweet Baby") ... 5-10 69
(One source shows this number as 801. We're not yet sure which is correct.)
S.P.Q.R. (1104 "The Frog") ... 5-10 67

SIR JOE & MAIDENS
Singles: 7-inch
LENOX (5563 "Jivin' Jean") ... 10-15 63

SIR LAWRENCE & CRESCENTS
Singles: 7-inch
TWIN TOWN (723 "Flip Me Over") ... 50-75 '60s

SIR RALEIGH
(With the Cupons)
Singles: 7-inch
A&M (757 "Somethin' Or Other") ... 5-10 64
A&M (764 "While I Wait") ... 5-10 64
JERDEN (760 "Tomorrow's Gonna Be Another Day") ... 10-20 65
Also see ARTHUR

SIR WINSTON & COMMONS
Singles: 7-inch
NAUSEATING BUTTERFLY (2207 "Not in the Spirit of India") ... 25-35 67
SOMA (1454 "Come Back Again") ... 50-75 66

SIREN
Singles: 7-inch
MIDSONG INT'L ... 3-5 79
LPs: 10/12-inch
ELEKTRA (74087 "Locomotion") ... 10-20 71
DANDELION ... 10-15 70

SISCO, Bobby
Singles: 78 rpm
MAR-VEL (111 "Honky Tonkin' Rhythm") ... 50-100 56
Singles: 7-inch
BRAVE (1006 "Not Like I Used To") ... 5-10 64
CHESS (1650 "Go, Go, Go") ... 250-350 57
GLENN (011 "I'm Sure") ... 5-10 60
GLENN (012 "Blue Lights") ... 5-10 61
MAR-VEL (111 "Honky Tonkin' Rhythm") ... 100-200 56
VEE-JAY (544 "Are You the Type") ... 5-10 63

SISCO, Gene
(With Ramblin' Ramblers)
Singles: 7-inch
B&4 (817 "Ladder of Love") ... 100-200 '60s
BAY SHORE (1 "Somebody to Love") ... 10-20 62
DESS (7001 "Grandma Rock and Roll") ... 450-550
DESS (7003 "Turning the Tables") ... 100-150

SISNEROS, Gilbert, & Saints
("Gilbert Sisneros Meets the Saints")
Singles: 7-inch
DANT (101 "Little Girl of My Dreams") ... 50-75

SISTER FOSTER
Singles: 78 rpm
BIG TOWN (104 "What to Do When Trouble Comes") ... 15-25 53
Singles: 7-inch
BIG TOWN (104 "What to Do When Trouble Comes") ... 25-50 53

SIVARTSEN, Sam
Singles: 7-inch
SWEET SHOPPE (218 "Doo-Wopps Are Forever") ... 10-15 89

SIX PAK
("Lead Vocal by Stevie")
Singles: 7-inch
GORDO (701 "Tombstone Shadow") ... 15-25 '60s
GORDO (704 "Weep No More") ... 15-25 '60s

SIX PENTS
Singles: 7-inch
KIDD (1335 "She Lied") ... 20-35 '60s

SIX SHOOTERS
Singles: 7-inch
CUCA (1011 "Don't You Just Know It") ... 15-25 60
Member: Vilas Craig.

SIX TEENS P&R '56
("Featuring 13-Year-Old Trudy Williams"; "Featuring Trudy Williams"; "Featuring Trudy & Louise")
Singles: 78 rpm
FLIP (315 thru 326) ... 15-25 56-57
FLIP (329 "My Secret") ... 25-50 58
Singles: 7-inch
FLIP (315 "A Casual Look") ... 15-25 56
FLIP (317 "Send Me Flowers") ... 15-25 56
FLIP (320 "My Special Guy") ... 15-25 56
FLIP (322 "Arrow of Love") ... 15-25 57
FLIP (326 "My Surprise") ... 15-25 57
FLIP (329 "My Secret") ... 15-25 58
FLIP (333 "Danny") ... 15-25 58
FLIP (338 "Baby-O") ... 30-40 58
FLIP (346 "Why Do I Go to School") ... 15-25 59
FLIP (350 "That Wonderful Secret of Love") ... 15-25 60
FLIP (351 "A Little Prayer") ... 15-25 60
Members: Trudy Williams; Louise Williams; Ed Wells; Beverly Pecot; Kenneth Sinclair; Darryl Lewis.
Also see ELEMENTS
Also see ELGINS
Also see TRUDY & LOUISE
Also see WILLIAMS, Trudy

SIX TEENS / Donald Woods / Richard Berry
LPs: 10/12-inch
FLIP (1001 "12 Flip Hits") ... 100-125 59
Also see BERRY, Richard
Also see WOODS, Donald

SIXPENCE
(Thee Sixpence)
Singles: 7-inch
ALL AMERICAN (313 "Fortune Teller") ... 20-30 66
ALL AMERICAN (333 "Hey Joe") ... 15-25 67
ALL AMERICAN (353 "Fortune Teller") ... 15-25 67
DOT (16959 "Fortune Teller") ... 10-20 66
Members: Randy Seol; Ed King; Lee Freeman; George Bunnel; Gary Loverto; Mark Weitz.
Also see STRAWBERRY ALARM CLOCK

SIXPENCE
Singles: 7-inch
IMPACT (1025 "You're the Love") ... 15-25 67

SIXPENTZ
Singles: 7-inch
BRENT (7062 "Please Come Home") ... 10-20 67
BRENT (7064 "Don't Say You're Sorry") .. 10-20 67
Also see FUN & GAMES

1619 BAD ASS BAND
LPs: 10/12-inch
GRAXAM INT'L ("1619 Bad Ass Band") ... 250-300

6680 LEXINGTON
Singles: 7-inch
MGM (14280 "Can't You See") ... 5-10 71
LPs: 10/12-inch
MGM (4783 "6680 Lexington") ... 10-20 71
Members: Bill Medley; Mike Patterson; Art Munson; Darlene Love; Chris Morgan.
Also see LOVE, Darlene
Also see MEDLEY, Bill
Also see MORGAN, Chris
Also see PATTERSON, Mike

SIZEMORE, Gordon
Singles: 7-inch
ALVIC (8852 "Waddlin' Mama") ... 50-75

SKAGGS, Ricky C&W '80
(With Tony Rice; with Sharon White)
Singles: 7-inch
EPIC ... 3-5 81-90
ROUNDER ... 3-6 80
SUGAR HILL (3700 series) ... 3-6 80
SUGAR HILL (04000 series) ... 3-5 83-84
LPs: 10/12-inch
EPIC ... 5-10 81-86
REBEL (1550 "That's It") ... 10-15 75
ROUNDER ... 5-10 82
SUGAR HILL ... 5-10 79-80
WEL DUN ... 10-15 78
Also see COUNTRY GENTLEMEN
Also see FRICKE, Janie
Also see HARRIS, Emmylou
Also see NITTY GRITTY DIRT BAND
Also see PARTON, Dolly
Also see SCRUGGS, Earl

SKAGGS, Ricky, & Keith Whitley
LPs: 10/12-inch
REBEL ... 10-15 71-72
Also see SKAGGS, Ricky

SKAPEGOAT
Singles: 7-inch
ALCEE (1001 "Good Times, Bad Times") ... 15-25 '60s

SKARLETTONES
Singles: 7-inch
EMBER (1053 "Do You Remember") ... 100-150 59

SKAVENGERS
Singles: 7-inch
MAYN (200758 "Lend Me Your Love") ... 15-25 '60s

SKEE BROTHERS
Singles: 7-inch
EPIC (9275 "Big Deal") ... 50-75 58
OKEH (7108 "That's All She Wrote") ... 25-35 59
ROULETTE (4164 "Romeo Joe") ... 10-15 59

SKEENE, Danny, & Ricquettes
Singles: 7-inch
VALEX (105/106 "Over the Rainbow") . 100-150

SKEENS, Bill
Singles: 7-inch
HOLIDAY (256 "I Just Can't Stop") ... 50-75

SKELTON, Eddie
Singles: 7-inch
CHART (5077 "Colorado Queenie") ... 10-15 70
DIXIE (2011 "Gotta Keep Swinging") ... 1000-1500 58
DIXIE (2015 "Rebel's Retreat") ... 25-50 59
DIXIE (2025 "Curley") ... 25-50 59
STARDAY (294 "My Heart Gets Lonely") ... 100-150 57
STARDAY (315 "That's Love") ... 50-100 57

SKEPTICS
Singles: 7-inch
KAMPUS (814 "Ride Child") ... 15-25 '60s
KAMPUS (815 "Certain Kind of Girl") ... 15-25 '60s
SCRATCH (7823 "East Side Tenement House") ... 15-25 '60s
SHO-BOAT (106 "Turn It On") ... 15-25 '60s
SPRING (80330 "I'm Lonely Again") ... 15-25 '60s
Also see WAUGH, Jerry, & Skeptics

SKI, Gene, & Troubadours
Singles: 7-inch
SARA (6632 "Six Foot Down") ... 75-125 66
TEE PEE (1004 "To Hell with Love") ... 8-12 69

SKILES, Johnny
Singles: 7-inch
HONEY B (102 "After Tonight") ... 15-25 59
RUMAC (301 "Rockin' and Rollin'") ... 200-300 59
RURAL RHYTHM (518 "Is My Baby Comin' Back") ... 100-200 59

SKILLET & LEROY
LPs: 10/12-inch
LAFF (131 "2 or 3 Times") ... 25-35
LAFF (141 "Burglar in the Bedroom") ... 25-35
Also see OTIS, Johnny

SKINNER, Jimmie C&W '49
(Jimmie Skinner / Jimmie Logsdon)
Singles: 78 rpm
CAPITOL ... 4-8 51-54
DECCA ... 4-8 53-55
MERCURY ... 4-8 57
RADIO ARTIST ... 5-10 49
Singles: 7-inch
CAPITOL ... 5-10 51-54
DECCA ... 5-10 53-55
MERCURY ... 4-8 57-63
SIMS (300 "Let's Call It a Day") ... 4-6 66
(With Paula Ellis.)
STARDAY ... 5-10 58-64
EPs: 7-inch
MERCURY ... 5-10 61
LPs: 10/12-inch
COUNTRY CORNER ("Jimmie Skinner") ... 100-150
(Selection number not known.)
DECCA (4132 "Country Singer") ... 35-45 61
MERCURY (20352 "Songs That Make the Juke Box Play") ... 30-50 57
MERCURY (20700 "Jimmie Skinner Sings Jimmie Rodgers") ... 15-25 62
(Monaural.)
MERCURY (60700 "Jimmie Skinner Sings Jimmie Rodgers") ... 25-35 62
(Stereo.)

QCA....5-10 '70s
RICH-R-TONE....5-10
STARDAY (240 "Jimmie Skinner, the Kentucky Colonel")....30-40 63
STARDAY (988 "#1 Bluegrass")....5-10 '60s
VETCO....10-15 76
WEL DUN....10-15 78
WING....10-15 64

SKIP & CREATIONS

LPs: 10/12-inch

JUSTICE ("Mobam")....150-200 '60s
(Selection number not known.)

SKIP & ECHOTONES

Singles: 7-inch

DR (1001 "Born to Love")....10-20 59
WARWICK (634 "Born to Love")....8-12 61

SKIP & FLIP *P&R '59*
(With Clyde Gary & His Orchestra)

Singles: 7-inch

BRENT (7002 "It Was I")....10-20 59
BRENT (7005 "Fancy Nancy")....10-20 59
BRENT (7010 "Cherry Pie")....10-20 60
BRENT (7013 "Teenage Honeymoon")....10-20 60
BRENT (7017 "Green Door")....10-20 60
BRENT (7028 "Over the Mountain")....4-8 62
COLLECTABLES....3-5 '80s
ERIC....4-6 '70s
TIME (1031 "Betty Jean")....10-15 61
Members: Clyde "Skip" Battin; Gary Paxton.
Also see BATTIN, Skip
Also see GARY, Clyde, & His Orchestra
Also see GARY & CLYDE
Also see PAXTON, Gary
Also see PLEDGES

SKIP & HUSTLERS

Singles: 7-inch

INVICTA (9001 "In the Soup")....15-25 57

SKIP & 102's

Singles: 7-inch

KAY BEE (106 "Gotta Pay the Price")....30-40 63

SKIPPER, Macy

Singles: 7-inch

LIGHT (2020 "Who Put the Squeeze on Eloise")....50-75
STAX (111 "Goofin' Off")....10-15 62

SKIPPY & HI-LITES

Singles: 7-inch

ELMOR (1027 "Old Man River")....100-150 62
(First issue.)
STREAM-LITE (1027 "Old Man River")....75-125 62

SKOODLE DUM DOO & SHEFFIELD
(Seth Richard)

Singles: 78 rpm

MANOR (1056 "Broome Street Blues")....75-125 43
REGIS (107 "Tampa Blues")....75-125 43
Members: Seth Richard; Sheffield.

SKULL SNAPS

Singles: 7-inch

GRILL (301 "Ain't That Lovin' You")....5-10 75

LPs: 10/12-inch

GSF (1011 "The Skull Snaps")....250-350 73

SKUNKS

Singles: 7-inch

QUILL (120 "Don't Ask Why")....10-20 66
QUILL (121 "Little Angel")....10-20 66
SHERI (100 "Heart Teaser")....8-12 69
TEEN TOWN (103 "I Need No One")....10-15 68
TEEN TOWN (106 "Small Town Girl")....10-15 68
TEEN TOWN (110 "Doing Nothing")....10-15 69
USA (865 "Elvira")....8-12 67
WATER STREET....5-10 '60s
WHITE WHALE (322 "Doing Nothing")....8-12 69
WHITE WHALE (325 "Doing Nothing")....5-10 69
WORLD PACIFIC (77889 "I Need No One")....5-10 67

LPs: 10/12-inch

TEEN TOWN (101 "Getting Started")....25-50 68
Members: Larry Lynne Ostricki; Duane Lundy; Rick Allen Sutherland; Tony Kolp; Randy Klein; Paul Fredericks; Jack Tappy; Teddy Paplinski.
Also see BONNEVILLES
Also see TONY'S TYGERS / Skunks / Robbs
Also see UNBELIEVABLES

SKUNKS

Singles: 7-inch

SKUNKS (4 "The Racket")....40-50

Picture Sleeves

SKUNKS (4 "The Racket")....50-75

SKYLAR, Norm

Singles: 7-inch

CREST (1044 "Rock and Roll Blues")....75-100 58

SKYLAR, Rick

Singles: 7-inch

CARLTON (594 "Crying in My Cherry Soda")....5-10 63
CARLTON (604 "Playboy")....5-10 64

SKYLARKS

Singles: 78 rpm

DECCA....75-125 51

Singles: 7-inch

DECCA (48241 "Glory of Love")....400-500 51

SKYLARKS

Singles: 7-inch

EVERLAST (5022 "Everybody's Got Somebody")....15-25 63

SKYLARKS

Singles: 7-inch

ADMIRAL (500 "How Many Times")....15-20 65

SKYLIGHTERS

Singles: 7-inch

EMJAY (6152 "How Foolish Am I")....40-50
PEN (110 "Hold On")....5-10 62

SKYLINERS *P&R '59*
(Jimmy Beaumont & Skyliners; with Lenny Martin Orchestra.)

Singles: 12-inch

TORTOISE INT'L (11345 "Love Bug")....8-10 76
(Promotional issue only.)

Singles: 7-inch

ATCO (6270 "Since I Fell for You")....10-20 63
CALICO (103 "Since I Don't Have You")....30-40 59
CALICO (106 "This I Swear")....20-30 59
CALICO (109 "It Happened Today")....20-30 59
CALICO (114 "How Much")....15-25 60
CALICO (117 "Pennies from Heaven")....20-30 60
CALICO (120 "Believe Me")....15-25 60
CAMEO (215 "Three Coins in the Fountain")....15-25 62
CAPITOL (3979 "I Could Have Loved You")....15-25 75
CLASSIC ARTISTS (123 "You're My Christmas Present")....5-8 90
(Black vinyl. 1000 made.)
CLASSIC ARTISTS (123 "You're My Christmas Present")....8-10 90
(Red vinyl. 1000 made.)
COAST (100 "Since I Fell for You")....3-5
COLPIX (188 "I'll Close My Eyes")....15-25 61
COLPIX (613 "Close Your Eyes")....10-20 61
JUBILEE....10-15 65-66
OLD HIT (5003 "This I Swear")....4-6
ORIGINAL SOUND (35 "Since I Don't Have You")....5-10 63
ORIGINAL SOUND (36 "Pennies from Heaven")....5-10 63
ORIGINAL SOUND (37 "This I Swear")....5-10 63
ORIGINAL SOUND (4500 series)....3-5 84
TORTOISE INT'L....4-8 77
VIRGO....4-6 73
VISCOUNT (104 "Comes Love")....15-25 62

LPs: 10/12-inch

CALICO (3000 "Skyliners")....350-450 59
KAMA SUTRA (2026 "Once Upon a Time")....15-25 71
ORIGINAL SOUND (5010 "Since I Don't Have You")....15-25 63
(Monaural.)
ORIGINAL SOUND (8873 "Since I Don't Have You")....20-30 64
(Stereo.)
ORIGINAL SOUND (8873 "Greatest Hits")....5-10 87
(Reissued using same number, but with 20 tracks.)
RELIC (5051 "Pre Flight")....5-10 85
TORTOISE INT'L....8-10 78
Members: Jimmy Beaumont; Janet Vogel; Wally Lester; Jack Taylor; Joe Verscharen.
Also see BEAUMONT, Jimmy
Also see DEANE, Janet

SKYLINERS / Preston Epps

Singles: 7-inch

OLDIES 45....5-10 '60s
Also see EPPS, Preston

SKYLINERS / Wade Flemons

Singles: 7-inch

OLDIES 45....5-10 '60s
Also see FLEMONS, Wade
Also see SKYLINERS

SKYLINERS / Tune weavers

Singles: 7-inch

CLASSIC ARTISTS (116 "What Are You Doing New Year's Eve")....10-20 89
(Black vinyl. Promotional issue only. 1000 made.)
Also see SKYLINERS
Also see TUNE WEAVERS

SKYLITERS

Singles: 7-inch

SCOTTE (2666 "Tidal Wave")....15-25 63

SKYLITES
(With Mike Joseph & Orchestra)

Singles: 7-inch

TA-RAH (101 "My Only Girl")....50-75 61
Also see JOSEPH, Mike

SKYSCRAPERS

Singles: 78 rpm

MIRACLE (119 "Last Call")....10-20 47
MERCURY....5-10 56
RAMA....10-15 53

Singles: 7-inch

MERCURY (70795 "I Thought You'd Care")....15-25 56
RAMA (16 "Lost in the Shuffle")....40-50 53
Also see FATS JR. & SKYSCRAPERS
Also see GUY, Browley, & Skyscrapers

SKYTONES

Singles: 7-inch

GAYLO (101 "Mr. Moon")....50-75 59

SLADE *P&R/LP '72*

Singles: 7-inch

CBS ASSOCIATED....3-5 84-85
COTILLION....5-10 71-72
POLYDOR....4-8 72-73
REPRISE....4-8 73
W.B.....4-8 73-76

LPs: 10/12-inch

CBS ASSOCIATED....5-8 84-85
COTILLION....10-15 70
POLYDOR....8-12 72-73
REPRISE....8-12 73
W.B.....8-12 74-76
Also see AMBROSE SLADE

SLADE, Carol

Singles: 7-inch

DOMINO (1010 "Eavesdropping")....15-20 62
DOMINO (1015 "I Wanna Know Right Now")....10-15 62
HIGHLAND (1034 "I Wanna Know Right Now")....8-12 63
MAYLINN (9000 "I Wanna Know Right Now")....8-12 63

SLADE, Prentis

Singles: 7-inch

FLICK (011 "My Lonely Heart")....15-25 60
HAMILTON (50020 "Scrap Iron")....10-15 59
KING (5555 "I Can Tell")....5-10 61
KING (5630 "Love Talk")....5-10 62
KING (5653 "Everything's Gonna Be Alright")....5-10 62

SLADES *P&R '58*

Singles: 7-inch

DOMINO (500 "You Cheated")....40-50 58
(Add $50 to $75 if accompanied by photo/bio insert.)
DOMINO (800 "You Gambled")....20-30 58
DOMINO (901 "Just You")....20-30 59
DOMINO (906 "It's Your Turn")....15-25 61
DOMINO (1000 "You Must Try")....10-20 61

Picture Sleeves

DOMINO (901 "Just You")....50-60 59
Member: Don Burch.
Also see WEBB, Joyce

SLAUGHTER, Chuck / Roxie Williams
(With Buddy Ray & the Shamrocks)

Singles: 7-inch

LUCKY 11 ("Lucky 11 Rock")....75-100 '60s

SLAUGHTERS, Lee

EPs: 7-inch

JAY (2159 "Lee Slaughters")....75-125

SLAVIN, Slick

Singles: 7-inch

COMMANDER (1003 "Hey, Mr. Krushchev")....8-12 61
DEL-FI (4157 "Albert the Astronaut")....5-10 61
GRAVEYARD (3000 "Dr. Finkenstein's Castle")....10-20
IMPERIAL (5540 "Speed Crazy")....20-30 58

SLAY, Emitt
(Emitt Slay Trio; Emitt Slay's Slayriders with Sweetie Dolores)

Singles: 78 rpm

SAVOY....10-15 53

Singles: 7-inch

CHECKER (898 "Honey Bun")....25-50 58
J.V.B. (5002 "Don't Blame It On Me")....8-12 59
SAVOY (886 "My Kind of Woman")....15-25 53
SAVOY (892 "I've Learned My Lesson")....15-25 53

SLAY, Frank, & His Orchestra *P&R '61*

Singles: 7-inch

SCA (18002 "Bullfight")....5-10 63
SWAN (4085 "Flying Circle")....8-12 61
SWAN (4101 "Irish Rose")....5-10 61
Also see ANDREWS, Lee
Also see CANNON, Freddy
Also see LARSEN, Key
Also see LY-DELLS

SLED, Bob & Toboggans

Singles: 7-inch

CAMEO (400 "Here We Go")....50-75 66
Also see JOHNSTON, Bruce

SLEDGE, Nat

Singles: 7-inch

BLUJAY (1000 "Cry'n Baby")....100-150 61
Also see BLUE JAYS

SLEDGE, Percy *P&R/LP '66*

Singles: 7-inch

ATLANTIC....5-10 66-72
CAPRICORN....4-6 74-77
MONUMENT....3-5 83
PHILCO (12 "When a Man Loves a Woman"/"Baby Help Me")....10-20 67
("Hip Pocket" flexi-disc.)
RIPETE....3-5 89

EPs: 7-inch

ATLANTIC (8180 "Take Time to Know Her")....20-30 68

LPs: 10/12-inch

ATLANTIC (8125 "When a Man Loves a Woman")....15-20 66
ATLANTIC (8132 "Warm and Tender Soul")....15-20 66
ATLANTIC (8146 "The Percy Sledge Way")....12-18 67
ATLANTIC (8180 "Take Time to Know Her")....12-18 68
ATLANTIC (8210 "Best of Percy Sledge")....10-15 69
ATLANTIC (80212 "Percy Sledge")....5-10 87
CAPRICORN (0147 "I'll Be Your Everything")....8-10 74
MONUMENT (38532 "Percy")....5-10 83

SLEEPERS

Singles: 7-inch

MARVY ("I Want a Love")....15-25 66
(No selection number used.)

SLEEPLESS KNIGHTS

Singles: 7-inch

JERROC (1000 "You're Drivin' Me Crazy")....15-25 '60s

SLICK, Grace *LP '68*
(With the Great Society)

Singles: 7-inch

GRUNT....4-6 72-74
RCA....3-5 80-81

Picture Sleeves

RCA....3-5 80

LPs: 10/12-inch
COLUMBIA (CS-9624 "Conspicuous Only") 20-30 68
COLUMBIA (PC-9624 "Conspicuous Only") 5-10
COLUMBIA (CS-9702 "How It Was")....15-20 68
COLUMBIA (30459 "Collector's Item")....10-15 71
GRUNT....8-12 74
HARMONY....10-15 71
RCA....5-10 80-83
Promotional LPs
RCA ("*Dreams* Interview")....25-30 80
RCA (3922 "*Wrecking Ball* Interview")....20-30 81
RCA (3923 "Special Radio Series")....10-15 81
RCA (13708 "Interview LP")....5-10 '80s
Also see GREAT!! SOCIETY!!
Also see JEFFERSON AIRPLANE

SLIDERS
Singles: 7-inch
CHEVRON (012 "Love Is Like a Mountain")....40-50 '60s
STRAND (25033 "Blue Nights")....10-15 61
Members: Joe Gordon; Quitmann Dennis.

SLIP & DELL
Singles: 7-inch
MODERN ARTIST (100 "Don't Take a Chance")....100-200

SLLEDNATS
(Standells)
Singles: 7-inch
TOWER (312 "Don't Tell Me What to Do")....15-20 67
Also see STANDELLS

SLO, Audry
Singles: 7-inch
SWAN (4262 "Gonna Find the Right Boy")....10-20 66

SLOAN, Chuck
Singles: 7-inch
COWTOWN (806 "Too Old to Rock n' Roll")....100-200

SLOAN, Flip
(P.F. Sloan)
Singles: 7-inch
ALADDIN (3461 "All I Want Is Loving")....10-20 59
Also see SLOAN, P.F.

SLOAN, P.F. P&R '65
(Phil Sloan; Phillip "Flip" Sloan)
Singles: 7-inch
ATCO (6663 "Star Gazin' ")....5-10 69
DUNHILL (4007 "The Sins of a Family")....5-10 65
DUNHILL (4016 "I'd Have to Be Out of My Mind")....5-10 65
DUNHILL (4024 "Patterns Seg. 4")....5-10 66
DUNHILL (4037 "City Women")....5-10 66
DUNHILL (4054 "I Found a Girl")....5-10 66
DUNHILL (4064 "Sunflower, Sunflower")....5-10 67
DUNHILL (4106 "Karma")....5-10 67
MART (802 "She's My Girl")....50-75 60
MUMS (6010 "Let Me Be")....4-6 72
Picture Sleeves
DUNHILL (4064 "Sunflower")....8-12 67
LPs: 10/12-inch
ATCO (268 "Measure of Pleasure")....10-15 68
DUNHILL (50004 "Songs of Our Times")....10-20 65
DUNHILL (50007 "Twelve More Times")....10-20 66
MUMS (31260 "Raised on Records")....8-10 72
RHINO....5-8 86
Also see FANTASTIC BAGGYS
Also see GRASS ROOTS
Also see IMAGINATIONS
Also see INNER CIRCLE
Also see SLOAN, Flip
Also see STREET CLEANERS

SLOANE, Carol
Singles: 7-inch
COLUMBIA (43307 "Stay")....20-30 65

SLY
(Sly Stone; Sly Stewart)
Singles: 7-inch
AUTUMN (14 "Buttermilk")....10-15 65
AUTUMN (26 "Temptation Walk")....10-15 65
Also see SLY & FAMILY STONE
Also see STONE, Sly
Also see STEWART, Sly

SLY & FAMILY STONE P&R/LP '68
Singles: 12-inch
EPIC....4-8 79
Singles: 7-inch
EPIC....4-6 67-75
W.B.....3-5 79-85
Picture Sleeves
EPIC....4-6 68-70
EPs: 7-inch
EPIC....15-20 '60s
(Juke box only.)
LPs: 10/12-inch
EPIC (264 "Everything You Always Wanted to Hear")....10-20 76
(Promotional issue only.)
EPIC (26000 series)....10-15 67-69
EPIC (KE-30325 "Greatest Hits")....8-12 70
EPIC (PE-30325 "Greatest Hits")....5-10 '70s
EPIC (EQ-30325 "Greatest Hits")....15-25 73
(Quadraphonic. Has some true stereo tracks that were rechanneled on earlier issues.)
EPIC (30335 thru 37071)....5-10 70-81
W.B.....5-10 79-83
Members: Sylvester "Sly Stone" Stewart; Rose Stone; Larry Graham; Fred Stone; Gregg Errico; Jerry Martini.
Also see SLY
Also see STEWART, Sly
Also see STEWART BROTHERS
Also see STONE, Sly

SLY FOX
Singles: 78 rpm
SPARK (108 "Hoo-Doo Say")....25-50 54
SPARK (112 "My Four Women")....25-50 55
Singles: 7-inch
SPARK (108 "Hoo-Doo Say")....75-125 54
SPARK (112 "My Four Women")....75-125 55

SMACK
LPs: 10/12-inch
AUDIO HOUSE ("Smack")....1500-2000 67
(Reportedly 200 made.)

SMACKS
Singles: 7-inch
ALEAR (109 "I've Been Foolin' Around")..15-25 66
ALEAR (116 "Reckless Ways")....15-25 66

SMALL, Karen
Singles: 7-inch
VENUS (1066 "Boys Are Made to Love").10-15 66
Session: Larks.
Also see LARKS

SMALL, Millie P&R/LP '64
("The Blue Beat Girl")
Singles: 7-inch
ATCO (6384 "Tongue Tied")....5-10 65
ATLANTIC (2266 "Bring It On Home to Me")....5-10 64
BRIT (7002 "Mixed Up")....5-10 65
SMASH (1893 "My Boy Lollipop")....5-10 64
SMASH (1920 "Sweet William")....5-10 64
SMASH (1940 "Bring It On Home to Me")..5-10 64
SMASH (1946 "Don't You Know")....5-10 64
LPs: 10/12-inch
SMASH (27055 "My Boy Lollipop")....15-20 64
(Monaural.)
SMASH (67055 "My Boy Lollipop")....20-25 64
(Stereo.)

SMALL, Roy
Singles: 7-inch
KIN (2178 "I'm a Loser")....40-60 69

SMALL FACES P&R '67
Singles: 7-inch
COLLECTABLES....3-5
IMMEDIATE....5-10 67-69
PRESS....8-12 65-68
RCA (8949 "All or Nothing")....8-12 66
RCA (9055 "I Can't Dance with You")....8-12 66
W.B.....4-8 70-75
Picture Sleeves
IMMEDIATE (5003 "Tin Soldier")....10-20 68
RCA (8949 "All or Nothing")....15-25 66
W.B. (7681 "Cindy Incidentally")....5-10 73
LPs: 10/12-inch
ABKCO....8-12 73
ACCORD....5-10 82
ATLANTIC....8-10 77-78
COMPLEAT....5-8 86
IMMEDIATE (002 "There Are But Four Small Faces")....20-30 68
IMMEDIATE (008 "Ogden's Nut Gone Flake")....20-30 68
IMMEDIATE (4225 "Ogden's Nut Gone Flake")....10-15 73
MGM....10-15 74
PRIDE....10-15 72-73
SIRE....10-15
W.B.....10-15 70
Members: Steve Marriott; Ronnie Lane; Kenny Jones; Ian McLagen.
Also see PYTHON LEE JACKSON
Also see WHO

SMALLEY, Leroy
Singles: 7-inch
GOLDEN WORLD (7 "Girls Are Sentimental")....10-20 64
GOLDEN WORLD (107 "Girls Are Sentimental")....20-30 62

SMALLING, Eddie
Singles: 7-inch
DELTA (555 "Jeanie")....50-100

SMART TONES
Singles: 7-inch
HERALD (529 "Bob O Link")....75-100 58
(Yellow label.)
HERALD (529 "Bob O Link")....40-50 58
(Multi-color label.)

SMASHING PUMPKINS LP '91
Singles: 12-inch
AUDIODISC ("The End Is the Beginning of the End")....10-20 97
(No selection number used. Includes picture sleeve.)
VIRGIN (38541 "1979")....10-20 95
(Contains four remixes of *1979*. Includes picture sleeve.)
W.B. (8928 "The End Is the Beginning of the End")....100-200 97
(Two-disc set. Includes picture sleeve. Promotional issue only.)
Singles: 7-inch
VIRGIN ("Tonight Tonight")....15-25 95
(No selection number used.)
VIRGIN (38522 "Bullet with Butterfly Wings")....10-20 95
(Promotional issue only.)
Picture Sleeves
VIRGIN ("Tonight Tonight")....15-20 95
(No selection number used.)
VIRGIN (38522 "Bullet with Butterfly Wings")....4-8 95
(Promotional issue only.)
LPs: 10/12-inch
CAROLINE (1705 "Gish")....10-20 91
CAROLINE (1767 "Pisces Iscariot")....20-30 '90s
(Colored vinyl.)
CAROLINE (61740 "Siamese Dream")....10-20 '90s
Members: Darcy Wretzky; James Iah; Billy Corgon; Jimmy Chamberlain.

SMILE
Singles: 7-inch
MERCURY (72977 "Step on Me")....30-40 69
LPs: 10/12-inch
PICKWICK (3288 "Smile")....25-35 73
Members: Brian May; Roger Taylor.
Also see QUEEN

SMILEY, Austin
Singles: 7-inch
BRUNSWICK (55061 "Pretty Baby-O")....10-20 58

SMILEY, Red
Singles: 7-inch
JIN (107 "Take a Ride")....50-75
Also see RENO & SMILEY

SMILEY BROTHERS
Singles: 7-inch
DOCTOR SHINY-TEETH (9 "Do the Brush")....150-200

SMITH P&R/LP '69
Singles: 7-inch
DUNHILL....4-8 69-70
GOLDIES 45....3-6 73
ROULETTE....4-6 '70s
Picture Sleeves
DUNHILL....4-8 69
LPs: 10/12-inch
DUNHILL....10-15 69-70
Member: Gayle McCormick.
Also see McCORMICK, Gayle

SMITH, Al
("Al Smith & Band"; Al Smith's Progressive Jazz)
Singles: 78 rpm
CHANCE (1124 "Slow Mood")....50-100 52
FALCON (1007 "Road House")....20-30 58
METEOR....25-50 53-56
Singles: 7-inch
ABNER (1020 "One Two Cha-Cha-Cha")..5-10 59
CHANCE (1124 "Slow Mood")....150-200 52
FALCON....10-20 57-59
METEOR (5013 "Beale Street Stomp")....100-150 53
METEOR (5026 "Chop Chop Boogie")...75-125 56
(Same track as *Beale Street Stomp.*)
Also see BLACKWELL, Lou
Also see DIXON, Dizzy
Also see EL DORADOS (on Vee-Jay)
Also see FALCONS
Also see HENDERSON, Big Bertha, & Al Smith Orchestra
Also see MOROCCOS
Also see PRINCE, Bobby

SMITH, Al, & Savoys / Jack McVea with Al Smith & Savoys
Singles: 78 rpm
COMBO (90 "Chop Chop Boom")....50-75 55
Singles: 7-inch
COMBO (90 "Chop Chop Boom")....75-100 55
Also see McVEA, Jack
Also see SAVOYS
Also see SMITH, Al

SMITH, Al
(With the Angels)
Singles: 7-inch
IRMA (105 "Leaving You Baby")....200-300 57
PRESTIGE....10-15 59-60
PRESTIGE BLUESVILLE....8-12 60
LPs: 10/12-inch
PRESTIGE BLUESVILLE (1001 "Hear My Blues")....20-30 60
PRESTIGE BLUESVILLE (1013 "Midnight Special")....20-30 61

SMITH, Alvin
(Al King)
Singles: 78 rpm
MUSIC CITY (743 "On My Way")....10-20 54
Singles: 7-inch
MUSIC CITY (743 "On My Way")....25-50 54
Also see KING, Al

SMITH, Arlene
Singles: 7-inch
BIG TOP (3073 "Love, Love, Love")....8-12 61
END (1120 "Mon Cherie Au Revoir")....8-12 63
SPECTORIOUS (150 "Everything")....8-12 63
Session: Chantels.
Also see CHANTELS
Also see WILSON, Willie, & Tunemasters

SMITH, Arthur C&W/P&R '48
(Arthur "Guitar Boogie" Smith; with Crossroads Quartet)
Singles: 78 rpm
MGM....5-10 48-57
SUPER DISC (1004 "Guitar Boogie")....20-30 48
Singles: 7-inch
MGM (10229 thru 12791)....5-15 49-60
STARDAY....4-8 63
EPs: 7-inch
DOT (600 "Original Guitar Boogie")....8-12 64
(Stereo. Juke box issue only.)
MGM....10-20 51-56
LPs: 10/12-inch
ABC-PAR (441 "Guitar & Voices")....15-25 63
DOT....10-15 64-66
FOLKWAYS....10-15 64
HAMILTON (134 "Arthur Smith Show")....10-15 64
(Monaural.)
HAMILTON (12134 "Arthur Smith Show")....15-20 64
(Stereo.)
MGM (236 "Foolish Questions")....25-50 54
(10-inch LP.)
MGM (533 "Fingers on Fire")....25-50 51
(10-inch LP.)
MGM (3301 "Specials")....25-50 56

MONUMENT 6-12 70-75
NASHVILLE 8-12 68
STARDAY (186 thru 415) 15-30 62-68
Also see HAMILTON, George, IV / Arthur Smith

SMITH, Bessie *P&R '23*
Singles: 78 rpm
COLUMBIA (3000 & 4000 series) 25-50 23
COLUMBIA (13000 & 14000 series) 25-50 23-33
OKEH (8000 series) 20-30 31
Singles: 7-inch
OKEH (6893 "Gimmie a Pig Foot") 20-30 52
LPs: 10/12-inch
COLUMBIA 10-15 70-72

SMITH, Bessie / Ma Rainey / Ida Cox / Chippie Hill
LPs: 10/12-inch
RIVERSIDE (121 "Great Blues Singers") 100-200 57
Also see RAINEY, Ma
Also see SMITH, Bessie

SMITH, Betty *P&R '58*
(Betty Smith Group)
Singles: 7-inch
ECHO (584 "Oh Yeah") 40-60
LONDON (1787 "Bewitched") 10-15 58

SMITH, Bill
(Bill Smith Combo; with Jeanette; Tom Toms)
Singles: 7-inch
CHESS (1773 "Heartbreak Hotel") 10-20 60
CHESS (1780 "Raunchy") 10-20 60
LE BILL (303 "Tough") 15-25 60
LE BILL (305 "Heartbreak Hotel") 15-25 60
LE BILL (306 "Ptomaine") 15-25 60
(Also issued as by the Tom Toms.)
ROULETTE (4517 "Tough") 5-10 63
Members: Tommy Brown; Eddie Hill; Leonard Walters; Joel Colbert; Joe Donnell; David Martin.
Also see BROWN, Tom, & Tom Toms
Also see MR. SAKS & BLUE STRINGS
Also see SUMMERS, Gene
Also see TOM TOMS

SMITH, Bill
Singles: 7-inch
RED HED (4511 "Tell Me Baby") 200-300

SMITH, Bob
(Bobby Smith)
Singles: 7-inch
BUZZ (105 "Coffee Break") 15-25 59
FOX (104 "Bevy Mae") 400-600 60
R.R.E (1006 "I'll Make Believe") 8-12 63
YONAH 10-20 63
Also see REBELS
Also see TWISTERS

SMITH, Bob
LPs: 10/12-inch
KENT (551 "The Visit") 50-75 70
(Add $10 to $15 if accompanied by bonus poster.)
Also see THORNDIKE PICKLEDISH

SMITH, Bob C.
Singles: 7-inch
CLET (1001 "Honky Tonkin' Baby") 100-150 63
CLET (1003 "Tavern Outside of Town") 10-20 63

SMITH, Bobbie
(With the Dream Girls)
Singles: 7-inch
AMERICAN ARTS (2 "Miss Stronghearted") 15-25 64
BELL (628 "I'll Be Around") 8-12 65
BIG TOP (3085 "Mr. Fine") 15-25 61
BIG TOP (3100 "Duchess of Earl") 20-30 62
BIG TOP (3111 "Here Comes Baby") 20-30 62
BIG TOP (3129 "Now He's Gone") 15-25 62
Also see DREAM GIRLS

SMITH, Bobby
(With the Shades, with Neat Beats)
Singles: 7-inch
CUCA (1071 "Be My Baby") 10-20 62
CUCA (1126 "Come Back, Laurie") 10-20 62

SMITH, Bobby
(With the Spinners)
Singles: 7-inch
TRI-PHI (1018 "She Don't Love Me") 15-25 62
Also see SPINNERS

SMITH, Buster
(With His Heat Waves; "Vocal by Sir Harding Taylor")
Singles: 78 rpm
BIG TOWN 10-15 55
METEOR 15-25 53
TORCH (6900 "Boogie Daddy") 75-100 52
Singles: 7-inch
BIG TOWN (127 "That's Your Lovin' Baby") 15-25 55
METEOR (5010 "Crying in the Chapel") ...25-35 53
LPs: 10/12-inch
ATLANTIC (1323 "The Legendary Buster Smith") 30-50 60

SMITH, Carl *C&W '51*
(With the Tunesmiths)
Singles: 78 rpm
COLUMBIA 5-10 51-57
Singles: 7-inch
ABC/HICKORY 4-6 76-78
COLUMBIA (20000 & 21000 series) 8-15 51-56
COLUMBIA (40823 thru 42858) 4-10 57-63
COLUMBIA (42949 thru 45923) 4-8 64-73
HICKORY 4-6 74-76
Picture Sleeves
COLUMBIA 5-10 59
EPs: 7-inch
COLUMBIA (2801 thru 10223) 8-15 57-58
COLUMBIA (10964 "Taste of Country") 5-10 72
(Juke box issue.)
COLUMBIA (11721) 8-15 58
LPs: 10/12-inch
ABC/HICKORY 10-15 77-78
COLUMBIA (31 "Anniversary Album") 8-12 70
COLUMBIA (DS-341 thru DS-517) 5-15
(Record club issues.)
COLUMBIA (900 thru 1100 series) 25-50 57-58
COLUMBIA (1500 thru 2600 series) 10-20 60-69
COLUMBIA (2579 "Carl Smith") 50-75 56
(10-inch LP.)
COLUMBIA (8300 thru 9800 series) 10-20 60-72
COLUMBIA (9023 "Sentimental Songs") ..50-75 54
(10-inch LP.)
COLUMBIA (9026 "Softly and Tenderly") .50-75 54
(10-inch LP.)
COLUMBIA (10000 series) 5-10 73
COLUMBIA (30000 series) 10-20 70-84
COLUMBIA SPECIAL PRODUCTS (8000 series) 10-15
COUNTRY CLASSICS 5-10
GUSTO 5-8 80
HICKORY 5-10 75
HARMONY 5-15 64-72
LAKE SHORE 5-10
Session: Lewis Pruitt.
Also see PRICE, Ray / Lefty Frizzell / Carl Smith
Also see PRICE, Ray / Johnny Horton / Carl Smith / George Morgan
Also see PRUITT, Lewis
Also see TUNESMITHS

SMITH, Carl / Lefty Frizzell / Marty Robbins
LPs: 10/12-inch
COLUMBIA (2544 "Carl, Lefty & Marty") 150-250 56
(10-inch LP.)
Also see FRIZZELL, Lefty
Also see ROBBINS, Marty
Also see SMITH, Carl

SMITH, Chester
Singles: 7-inch
DECCA (30603 "You Gotta Move") 25-50 58
POPPY (2004 "Tennessee Saturday Night") 100-150

SMITH, Connie *C&W '64*
Singles: 7-inch
COLUMBIA 4-6 73-77
EPIC 3-5 85
MONUMENT 3-5 77-83
RCA 4-8 64-74
Picture Sleeves
RCA (9214 "Cincinnati, Ohio") 4-8 67
LPs: 10/12-inch
CAMDEN 10-15 67-72
COLUMBIA 10-20 73-77
MONUMENT 5-8 77-78
RCA (0100 thru 1200 series) 5-10 73-75
RCA (3300 thru 4800 series) 10-20 65-73

SMITH, Connie, & Nat Stuckey *C&W '69*
Singles: 7-inch
RCA 4-8 69-70
Also see SMITH, Connie
Also see STUCKEY, Nat

SMITH, Cool Papa, & His Orchestra
Singles: 78 rpm
UPTOWN (202 "Christmas Blues") 75-125 49

SMITH, Dappa
Singles: 7-inch
PEACH (709 "China Doll") 200-300 58

SMITH, Dayton
Singles: 7-inch
WARRIOR (501 "What Will the Answer Be") 75-125

SMITH, Dennis
Singles: 7-inch
LYNDAN (500 "This Little Heart") 50-100

SMITH, Dickie
(With Don Gardner & His Sonotones)
Singles: 78 rpm
BRUCE (103 "New Kind of Love") 10-20 54
Singles: 7-inch
BRUCE (103 "New Kind of Love") 30-50 54
Also see FIVE KEYS
Also see GARDNER, Don

SMITH, Don
Singles: 7-inch
ROSE BETH ("Money, Money, Money") 75-125
(Selection number not known.)

SMITH, Earl
Singles: 7-inch
LOVELADY (201 "Blackwater Bay") 50-75

SMITH, Earl Dean
Singles: 7-inch
COLISEUM (603 "Go Home Cheater") 15-25 63
COLISEUM (2700 "Untie Me") 15-25 63
LIBERTY (55808 "Odds and Ends") 5-10 65

SMITH, Effie
(With the Squires)
Singles: 78 rpm
ALADDIN 10-20 46-53
G&G 10-20 45
GEM 10-20 45
MILTONE (218 "It's Been So Long") 15-25 47
VITA (117 "Guiding Angel") 15-25 55
VITA (124 "Champagne Mind with a Soda Water Income") 5-10 56
Singles: 7-inch
ALADDIN (3302 "Dial That Telephone") ...30-40 53
ALADDIN (3303 "Standing in the Doorway") 30-40 53
DUO DISC (107 "Dial That Telephone") 5-10 65
DUO DISC (111 "Me and My Kids") 5-10 65
DUO DISC (115 "Teenage World") 5-10 65
EEE CEE (100 "Harper Valley P.T.A. Gossip") 5-10 68
SPOT (103 "Dial That Telephone") 10-20 59
VITA (117 "Guiding Angel") 75-125 55
VITA (124 "Champagne Mind with a Soda Water Income") 15-25 56
LPs: 10/12-inch
JUBILEE (2057 "Dial That Telephone") 15-25 66
Also see CARPENTER, Ike
Also see SQUIRES

SMITH, Evelyn
Singles: 7-inch
MAGIC TOUCH (2006 "Don't Make Me No Promises") 10-20 67

SMITH, Floyd
(With the Montclairs)
Singles: 7-inch
DAKAR (604 "Getting Nowhere Fast") 8-12 69
FORTUNE (540 "Grandpa's Gully Rock") 50-75 60
Also see MONTCLAIRS

SMITH, Fraser, with Dumb Blondes & Malibu Mudhens
Singles
CRUSHED TOY (KLOS "Cool Patrol") 20-30 82
(Picture disc. Promotional issue only.)

SMITH, Gary
(Gary Smith's Blues Band)
EPs: 7-inch
MESSAROUND (001 "Gary Smith's Blues Band") 15-20 74
Members: Gary Smith; John Garcia; Steve Gomes; Johny Moon; Jim Gordon.
Session: Jack Gusto; Lynn; Gary Horsman; Louie; Marilyn; Green Street Winos.

SMITH, Geechie
(Vernon Smith)
Singles: 78 rpm
CAPITOL 5-10 46-47
KICKS (5 "Geneva Sue") 10-15 54
Singles: 7-inch
KICKS (5 "Geneva Sue") 20-30 54

SMITH, Gene
(Gene Smith's 4 Notes)
Singles: 78 rpm
BLUE KEY 25-50 52
Singles: 7-inch
BLUE KEY (1001 "I Didn't Mean to Be So Mean") 100-150 52
Members: Gene Smith; Ted Queen; Roy Magee; Earl Thomas.

SMITH, Gene
Singles: 7-inch
REM (440 "Rubber Legs") 75-100 65
REM (458 "I'm Gone") 50-75 65

SMITH, George
(George "Harmonica" Smith; Little George Smith)
Singles: 78 rpm
RPM 25-50 55-56
Singles: 7-inch
BARBARY COAST (1002 "Bess You Is My Woman") 5-10 59
CUCA (6343 "Frog Liver Quiver") 5-10 63
LAURIE (3263 "Born Again") 5-10 64
RPM (434 "Telephone Blues") 40-60 55
RPM (442 "Blues Stay Away") 40-60 55
RPM (456 "Love Life") 40-60 56
RPM (478 "You Don't Love Me") 40-60 56
TURNTABLE (713 "I've Had It") 20-30 65
LPs: 10/12-inch
BLUESWAY (6029 "Of the Blues") 10-15 69
DERAM 8-12 71
WORLD PACIFIC 10-15 69
Also see ALLEN, George
Also see HARMONICA KING
Also see SPANN, Otis

SMITH, Grace
Singles: 78 rpm
NATIONAL (9046 "Competition Blues") ...50-75 48

SMITH, Hagen
Singles: 7-inch
SWELL ("Among the Unloved") 20-40 65
(No selection number used.)

SMITH, Hank
(George Jones; with Nashville Playboys; Hank Smith / Bud Roman & Toppers / "Scat" Benny / Sue Richards / Bob Sandy)
Singles: 78 rpm
GILMAR ....30-40 '50s
EPs: 7-inch
HOLLYWOOD HIT CLUB (280 "Heartbreak Hotel") 50-100 56
TOPS (280 "Heartbreak Hotel") 30-40 56
Also see JONES, George

SMITH, Helene
Singles: 7-inch
DEEP CITY (2375 "Sure Thing"/"True Love Don't Grow On Trees") 10-20 67
DEEP CITY (2380 "Sure Thing"/"Wrong Or Right He's My Baby") 10-20 67
PHIL-L.A. OF SOUL (Except 300) 5-10 68-69
PHIL-L.A. OF SOUL (300 "Like a Baby") .10-15 67
LPs: 10/12-inch
DEEP CITY (1001 "Sings Sweet Soul") ...15-25 67

SMITH, Henry, & His Blue Flames
Singles: 78 rpm
DOT 25-40 54
Singles: 7-inch
DOT (1220 "Good Rocking Mama") 75-125 54
Also see POSEY, Clarence / Henry Smith

SMITH, Herbie
Singles: 7-inch
DO RE MI (1406 "Baby Moon") 50-75
SAND (275 "So Wild Over You") 50-75
WILDCAT (824 "Sampson & Delilah") . 100-200

SMITH, Huey *P&R '57*
(With His Band; with Clowns; with Pitter Pats; Huey "Piano" Smith)
Singles: 78 rpm
ACE 10-25 56-58
SAVOY (1113 "You Made Me Cry") 30-50 53
Singles: 7-inch
ABC 4-6 73
ACE (521 thru 571) 20-30 56-59
ACE (584 thru 672) 10-15 60-63
ACE (8000 series) 5-10 62-63
COLLECTABLES .... 3-5 '80s
CONSTELLATION (102 "He's Back Again") 5-10 63
COTILLION 4-6 72
GOLDISC (3063 "Don't You Just Know It") .... 8-12 '60s
IMPERIAL (5772 "More Girls") 8-12 61
INSTANT 5-8 66-72
OLDIES 45 .... 5-10 64
VIN (1024 "I Didn't Do It") 10-15 60
EPs: 7-inch
ACE (104 "Having Fun") 50-75 59
ACE (639 "Huey 'Piano' Smith") 30-40 61
LPs: 10/12-inch
ACE (1004 "Having a Good Time") 100-150 59
ACE (1015 "For Dancing") 100-150 61
ACE (1027 "Twas the Night Before Christmas") 100-200 62
ACE (2021 "Rock & Roll Revival") 25-35 74
GRAND PRIX .... 10-20 '60s
Members (Clowns): Bobby Marchan; Curley Smith.
Session: Lee Allen.
Also see ALLEN, Lee
Also see CRAWFORD, James
Also see FORD, Frankie
Also see GORDON, Junior
Also see HUEY & JERRY
Also see KING, Earl
Also see MARCHAN, Bobby
Also see SUPREMES

SMITH, Jack C.
Singles: 7-inch
LIBERTY (55257 "Honeysuckle Rose") ... 15-25 60

SMITH, Jan
Singles: 7-inch
DELTA (1401 "It'd Surprise You") 50-75

SMITH, Jennie
Singles: 7-inch
CANADIAN AMERICAN (Except 135) 5-10 62-63
CANADIAN AMERICAN (135 "Murder for Roberta") 30-40 62
TOP RANK (2077 "Suspicion") 5-10 60
EPs: 7-inch
RCA (1523 "Jennie") 10-15 57
LPs: 10/12-inch
CANADIAN AMERICAN (1010 "Nightly Yours on the Steve Allen Show") 15-25 63
COLUMBIA (1242 "Love Among the Young") 20-30 58
(Monaural.)
COLUMBIA (8028 "Love Among the Young") 30-40 58
(Stereo.)
DOT (3586 "Jennie") 10-15 64
(Monaural.)
DOT (25586 "Jennie") 15-20 64
(Stereo.)
RCA (1523 "Jennie") 20-30 57

SMITH, Jerry *C&W/P&R/LP '69*
(With His Pianos)
Singles: 7-inch
ABC 5-8 69
AD 8-12 59-61
CHART (1440 "Annette") 5-8 67
DECCA 4-6 70-72
RANWOOD 4-6 73-78
RICE (5029 "Shaky's Theme") 5-8 67
SOUND STAGE 7 .... 5-10 65
LPs: 10/12-inch
ABC 8-12 69
DECCA 8-12 70-72
RANWOOD 5-10 73-75
Also see CORNBREAD & JERRY
Also see DIXIEBELLES
Also see JOHNSTON, Colonel Jubilation B., & His Mystic Knights Band & Street Singers

SMITH, Jerry Lee
Singles: 7-inch
SANDY (1500 "Girl Can't Help It") 50-75

SMITH, Jimmie
(Gene Autry)
Singles: 78 rpm
TIMELY TUNES (1554 "I'm a Truthful Fellow") 25-75
TIMELY TUNES (1555 "I'm Blue and Lonesome") 25-75
TIMELY TUNES (1556 "Bear Cat Mama from Horner Corner") 25-75
TIMELY TUNES (1557 "She's a Hum Dinger") 25-75
Also see AUTRY, Gene

SMITH, Jimmie
(Jimmy Smith)
Singles: 7-inch
FLIP (347 "I Cry and Cry Every Night") ... 20-30 59
WONDER (110 "Pinch Me Quick") 100-200 59

SMITH, Jimmy *P&R/LP '62*
Singles: 7-inch
BLUE NOTE 8-15 56-63
MGM 4-6 78
MERCURY 4-6 77
PRIDE 4-6 74
VERVE 5-10 62-73
LPs: 10/12-inch
BLUE NOTE 40-80 56-60
(Label gives New York street address for Blue Note Records.)
BLUE NOTE 20-30 61-63
(Label reads "Blue Note Records Inc. - New York, USA.")
BLUE NOTE 10-20 66-73
(Label shows Blue Note Records as a division of either Liberty or United Artists.)
COBBLESTONE 6-12 72
ELEKTRA 5-10 82-83
GUEST STAR 8-12 64
INNER CITY 5-10 81
MGM 8-12 70
MERCURY 5-10 77-78
METRO 8-15 67
MOJO 5-10 75
PRIDE 5-10 74
SUNSET 5-10 70
VERVE 10-25 63-72
(Reads "MGM Records - A Division of Metro-Goldwyn-Mayer, Inc." at bottom of label.)
VERVE 5-10 73-84
(Reads "Manufactured By MGM Record Corp.," or mentions either Polydor or Polygram at bottom of label.)
Also see BURRELL, Kenny, & Jimmy Smith

SMITH, Jimmy, & Wes Montgomery *LP '67*
LPs: 10/12-inch
VERVE 10-20 66-69
Also see MONTGOMERY, Wes
Also see SMITH, Jimmy

SMITH, Jo Ann
Singles: 7-inch
CENTURA (101 "Dear Calendar") 5-10 63
COLUMBIA (43330 "Call Me Anything") 5-10 65

SMITH, John Gary
Singles: 7-inch
LEVEE (705 "I Miss My Baby") .... 25-50 '50s

SMITH, Johnny
(With the Jubalaires)
Singles: 78 rpm
CAPITOL 10-15 50
ROYAL ROOST 5-10 54-56
Singles: 7-inch
ARROW (732 "Imagination") 8-12 58
CAPITOL (821 "Blue Ribbon Baby") 30-40 50
ROYAL ROOST 10-15 54-60
Also see JUBALAIRES

SMITH, Jojo
Singles: 7-inch
STATURE (1103 "Find This Woman") .... 8-12 '60s
Members: Peter Steinberg; Jim Johnson.
Also see UNDERBEATS

SMITH, Juanita, & Vanguards
Singles: 7-inch
VANGUARD (767 "Sometimes I Wonder") .... 400-500 '50s

SMITH, Keely *LP '58*
Singles: 78 rpm
CAPITOL 3-8 56-58
Singles: 7-inch
ATLANTIC 4-6 67
CAPITOL 5-15 56-58
DOT 5-10 59-62
RCA 4-6 66-71
REPRISE 4-8 63-66
Picture Sleeves
CAPITOL ("Capitol Introduces a New Capitol Artist") 4-8 56
(Generic Capitol "New Artist" sleeve. Includes Kelly Smith bio/picture insert.)
DOT 8-12 60
EPs: 7-inch
CAPITOL 10-15 58-59
DOT 8-12 60
LPs: 10/12-inch
CAPITOL 10-25 58-75
DOT 10-15 59-62
HARMONY 5-10 69
REPRISE 8-15 63-65
Also see PRIMA, Louis, & Keely Smith
Also see SINATRA, Frank, & Keely Smith

SMITH, Kenny
Singles: 7-inch
CHESS (1947 "Keep on Walkin' Baby") 8-12 65
FRATERNITY (907 "Dee Dee Darlin' ") 8-12 63
FRATERNITY (934 "Deep in My Heart"/"Money Talks") 75-125 64
FRATERNITY (934 "Deep in My Heart"/"Let's Get Together") 40-50 64
FRATERNITY (993 "Night Beat") 8-12 67
GAR .... 10-20 '60s
RURAL RHYTHM (507 "Walking by My Lonesome") 50-75
TELECOM (1 "Deep in My Heart") 5-10 92
TOPPER (281 "I'm So Lonesome Baby") . 50-75

SMITH, L.C.
(With the Southern Playboys)
Singles: 7-inch
WANGO (104 "Radio Boogie") 200-300
WANGO (106 "Lonesome Road Blues") 100-150
WEDGE (1020 "Corrine, Corrina") 25-35

SMITH, Lendon, & Jesters
Singles: 78 rpm
METEOR (5030 "Lost Love") 10-15 56
Singles: 7-inch
METEOR (5030 "Lost Love") 20-30 56

SMITH, Leon
(With the Basics; with Ponsonby Sisters; with Orbit Rockers)
Singles: 7-inch
EPIC (9326 "Little '40 Ford") 25-35 59
LAVENDAR (1851 "Jailer, Bring Me Water") 15-20 65
WILLAMETTE (101 "Little '40 Ford") 75-125 59
(First issue.)
WILLAMETTE (105 "Honey Honey") 10-15 59
WILLAMETTE (109 "Flip, Flop and Fly") .. 10-15 60
Also see ORBIT ROCKERS

SMITH, Leroy
Singles: 78 rpm
HERALD (426 "Big Pile of Love") 15-20 54
Singles: 7-inch
HERALD (426 "Big Pile of Love") 20-30 54

SMITH, Lester, Jr., & Upnilons
("Lester [Smith] Jr. & the Upnilons")
Singles: 7-inch
LUMMTONE (115 "Grow Up Romeo") 15-25 64
Also see GEE GEE & UPNILONS

SMITH, Liza
Singles: 7-inch
BIG TOP (3045 "Follow Me") 10-20 60
METRO (20035 "Follow Me") 15-25 60
(First issue.)
Also see JONES, Willie

SMITH, Lloyd "Fat Man"
(With Caldonia's Boys Orchestra)
Singles: 78 rpm
OKEH 15-25 56
PEACOCK 10-20 53
Singles: 7-inch
OKEH (7073 "Where You Been") 50-75 56
PEACOCK (1593 "Giddy-Up, Giddy-Up") 25-35 53
PEACOCK (1611 "My Clock Stopped") 25-35 53

SMITH, Lloyd, & Tru-Tones
Singles: 7-inch
K/B (6037 "Soldier's Last Letter") .... 10-15 '50s
Session: Harold K. Moderhack; Joe Havens; Russ Van Fleet.
Also see TRU-TONES

SMITH, Lonnie *LP '70*
Singles: 7-inch
BLUE NOTE 4-6 69-70
GROOVE MERCHANT 4-6 75
LRC 4-6 78-79
LPs: 10/12-inch
BLUE NOTE 8-15 68-70
COLUMBIA 10-15 67
GROOVE MERCHANT 5-10 75-76
KUDU 5-10 71
LRC 5-10 78

SMITH, Lorenzo
Singles: 7-inch
C.J. (603 "Moose On the Loose") 5-10 59
MAR-VEL (2701 "Shindig") 8-12 64
Also see PARKER, Little Willie

SMITH, Mack Allen
Singles: 7-inch
ACE (3011 "King of Rock & Roll") 50-75 74
ACE (3014 "Baby, When I'm Gone") 15-25 74
CYNTHIA (1961 "Lonely Weekends") 15-25
DELTA SOUNDS (1 "I See the Want in Your Eyes") .... 8-12 '60s
JAB (9001 "Big Silver Tears") 15-25 67
MARITEEN (6602 "Big Silver Tears") .... 50-75 '60s
STATUE (602 "Such a Night") .... 40-60 '60s
STATUE (603 "It's Only Make Believe") ... 40-60 '60s
STATUE (607 "Mean Ol' Frisco") .... 40-60 '60s
VEE-EIGHT (1006 "I'm a Hobo Man") 50-75 64

SMITH, Marvin
Singles: 7-inch
BRUNSWICK (55299 "Time Stopped") 5-10 66
BRUNSWICK (55314 "I Want") 5-10 67
BRUNSWICK (55348 "Hold On") 5-10 67
MAYFIELD 4-8 71
Session: Artistics.
Also see ARTISTICS
Also see FOUR EL DORADOS

SMITH, Maurice
LPs: 10/12-inch
MAINSTREAM (56085 "Bitter Acid") 10-15 66
(Monaural.)
MAINSTREAM (6085 "Bitter Acid") 15-20 66
(Stereo.)

SMITH, Melvin
(With the Night Riders)
Singles: 78 rpm
GROOVE 5-10 54
RCA 5-10 52-54
Singles: 7-inch
CAMEO (135 "Open the Door, Richard") . 15-20 58
CHIME 8-12 62
GROOVE (0010 "No Baby") 10-20 54
METRO (20023 "Oh Promise Me") 10-15 59
RCA 15-25 52-54
SMASH (1775 "Nobody's Fault") 8-12 62
Also see NIGHTRIDERS

SMITH, Moses
Singles: 7-inch
DIONN (508 "Hey Love") 25-50 68

SMITH, Myrna
Singles: 7-inch
VERVE (10497 "Sound of Tears") 5-10 67
Also see SWEET INSPIRATIONS

SMITH, O.C. *P&R/LP '68*
(With Joe Lipman & Orchestra; Ocie Smith)
Singles: 78 rpm
CADENCE 5-10 56-57
MGM 5-10 56

Singles: 7-inch

BIG TOP (3039 "Well, I'm Dancin' ") 8-12 60
BROADWAY 10-20
CADENCE (1304 "Forbidden Fruit") 10-20 56
CADENCE (1312 "If You Don't Love Me") 10-20 57
CADENCE (1329 "Too Late") 10-20 57
CARIBOU 4-6 76-77
CITATION 10-15 59
COLUMBIA 4-8 66-74
FAMILY 3-5 80
GORDY 3-5 82
MGM (12321 "At Last My Baby's Comin' Home") 10-20 56
MOTOWN 3-5 82
RENDEZVOUS 3-5 86-87
SHADYBROOK 3-5 78
SOUL WEST 4-6 72
SOUTH BAY 3-5 82

Picture Sleeves

COLUMBIA 5-8 69

LPs: 10/12-inch

CARIBOU 5-10 79
COLUMBIA 8-12 67-74
HARMONY 8-10 71
MGM 8-10 72
MOTOWN 5-10 82
SOUTH BAY 5-8 82

SMITH, Patti ***LP '75***
(Patti Smith Group)

Singles: 7-inch

ARISTA 4-6 76-79
MER (601 "Hey Joe") 50-75 74
SIRE (1009 "Hey Joe") 4-6 77

Picture Sleeves

ARISTA 4-8 78-79

LPs: 10/12-inch

ARISTA 6-12 75-88
Members: Patti Smith; Ivan Kral; Lenny Kaye; Jay Dee Daugherty; Allen Lanier; Andy Paley; Richard Sohl.

SMITH, Phyllis

Singles: 7-inch

J&M (1000 "I Need Somebody to Love") 5-10 69
YEW (1003 "I Need Somebody to Love") ... 5-10 69

SMITH, Ralph

Singles: 7-inch

COLLIER (2502 "Twister") 5-10 61
LIBERTY BELL (9016 "Could It Be") 10-15 57

SMITH, Ray ***P&R '60***
(David Ray Smith)

Singles: 7-inch

ABC (2595 "Nice Guy") 4-6 73
ABC (2576 "Robbin' the Cradle") 4-6 73
ADAIRE (90 "It's Love") 10-20 61
AREA (10 "Letter from Home") 10-20
B-C (351 "I Guess I Better Move Along") 5-10
(Reissue from the Ray Smith Fan Club of Joliet, Illinois.)
B-C (7130 "Let the Four Winds Blow") ....8-12 '60s
(Canadian.)
CELEBRITY CIRCLE (6901 "I Walk the Line") 5-10 64
CINNAMON (755 "I've Traded Better for Worse") 4-6 73
CINNAMON (760 "It Wasn't Easy") 4-6 73
CINNAMON (773 "The First Lonely Weekend") 4-6 73
CINNAMON (795 "Because of Losing You") 4-6 74
COLLECTABLES .... 3-5 '80s
CORONA (222 "Thank You Love") 4-6 75
CORONA (226 "Kaw-Liga") 4-6 76
CORONA (228 "Danny Boy") 4-6 76
CORONA (230 "Light That Candle") 4-6 77
HEART (250 "Gone Baby, Gone") ... 1500-2000 '50s
INFINITY (003 "After This Night Is Through") 30-40 61
INFINITY (007 "Let Yourself Go") 10-20 61
JUDD (1016 "Rockin' Little Angel") 20-30 59
JUDD (1017 "Put Your Arms Around Me Honey") 20-30 60
JUDD (1019 "One Wonderful Love") 20-30 60
JUDD (1021 "Blonde Hair, Blue Eyes") ... 20-30 60
NATIONAL (5016 "When the Day Rolls Around") 10-20
NATIONAL (5019 "Born to Lose") 10-20
NATIONAL (5020 "I'm a Fool to Care") ... 10-20
SMASH (1787 "These Four Precious Years") 5-8 62
SSS INT'L .... 4-8 '70s
SSS/SUN .... 4-8 '70s
SUN (298 "Right Behind You Baby") 50-75 58
SUN (308 "Why Why Why") 20-30 59
(Some copies mistakenly have *Sorry I Lied* by Cliff Thomas on the B-side.)
SUN (319 "Rockin' Bandit") 20-30 59
SUN (372 "Traveling Salesman") 20-30 61
SUN (375 "Candy Doll") 20-30 62
TOLLIE (9029 "Did We Have a Party") 8-10 64
VEE-JAY (579 "Robbin' the Cradle") 5-10 64
W.B. (5371 "I'm Snowed") 5-10 63
WIX (101 "Room Full of Roses") 4-6 78
WIX (102 "Whole Lot of Shakin' ") 4-6 78

LPs: 10/12-inch

BOOT (7182 "The Country Side of Ray Smith") 5-10 78
JUDD (701 "Travelin' with Ray") 200-300 60
T (56062 "Best of Ray Smith") .... 20-30 '70s
(Repackage of Judd 701.)
WIX (1000 "I'm Gonna Rock Some More") 10-15
Also see DONNER, Ral / Ray Smith / Bobby Dale
Also see RAY, David
Also see THOMAS, Cliff

SMITH, Ray / Pat Cupp

LPs: 10/12-inch

CROWN (5364 "Ray Smith and Patt Cupp") 50-75 63
(Cover shows "Patt" Cupp; label has "Pat.")
Also see CUPP, Pat

SMITH, Ray / Harold Dorman

Singles: 7-inch

GOLDIES 45 (2595 "Nice Guy"/"Mountain of Love") 4-6 74
Also see DORMAN, Harold

SMITH, Ray / That Rockin' Band

Singles: 7-inch

DIAMOND (193 "Everybody's Goin' Somewhere"/"Au-Go-Go-Go") 5-10 65
Also see SMITH, Ray

SMITH, Ray

Singles: 7-inch

NU-TONE (1182 "She's Mine") 5-10 64
TOPPA (1071 "Almost Alone") 5-10 62

LPs: 10/12-inch

COLUMBIA (1937 "Ray Smith's Greatest Hits") 20-30 63
(Monaural.)
COLUMBIA (8737 "Ray Smith's Greatest Hits") 30-40 63
(Stereo.)

SMITH, Robert

Singles: 7-inch

CAMELIA (100 "Traveling Sam") 75-100

SMITH, Robert Curtis
(R.C. Smith)

Singles: 7-inch

ARHOOLIE (502 "Please Don't Drive Me Away") 5-10 61

LPs: 10/12-inch

PRESTIGE BLUESVILLE (1064 "Blues of Robert Curtis Smith") 20-30 63

SMITH, Robert T.

Singles: 7-inch

BOBBIN (118 "Workin' Again") 15-25 60

SMITH, Roger ***P&R '59***

Singles: 7-inch

W.B. (5068 "Beach Time") 5-10 59
W.B. (5106 "Love of Two") 5-10 59

Picture Sleeves

W.B. (5068 "Beach Time") 10-15 59

LPs: 10/12-inch

W.B. (1305 "Beach Romance") 30-40 59

SMITH, Roger

Singles: 7-inch

AIR (5001 "Be Bop Boogie") 100-150

SMITH, Ronnie

Singles: 7-inch

BRUNSWICK (55137 "Lookie Lookie Lookie") 30-50 59
HAMILTON (50003 "My Babe") 10-20 58
IMPERIAL (5667 "Long Time No Love") .. 15-25 60
IMPERIAL (5679 "I Hear You Knocking") . 15-25 60

SMITH, Roy

Singles: 7-inch

ADAIRE (1777 "It's Love") 150-200
ASCOT (2239 "Don't Go Away") 50-75 67
CANTOR (707 "He's Not Your Type") 40-60 63
CUTLASS 40-60
LIBERTY (55975 "It Happens to the Best of Us") 40-60 67
U.A. (50679 "Soul Control") 40-60 70
Session: Brian Hyland.
Also see GEORGIA PROPHETS
Also see HYLAND, Brian

SMITH, Roy

Singles: 7-inch

PRESTIGE (2301 "Love Me Long") 20-30
VANGUARD (35194 "For the Love of Her") 10-15 75

SMITH, Roy, & Hilites

Singles: 7-inch

NU-TONE (1182 "She's Fine") 30-40 61

SMITH, Ruby

Singles: 78 rpm

RCA (2152 "Port Wine Blues") 30-40 47

SMITH, Sammy

Singles: 7-inch

MONA (101 "Bobby Soxer's Dream") 15-25 59

SMITH, Savannah

Singles: 7-inch

END (1077 "Anytime, Anyplace, Anywhere") 30-40 60

SMITH, Shelby

Singles: 7-inch

REBEL (728 "Rockin' Mama") 100-200 62
REBEL (729 "Big Boss Man") 25-50 62
SMITTY (55783 "What's on Your Mind") 500-750

SMITH, Shorty, & His Rhythm
(Arthur Smith)

Singles: 78 rpm

LENOX (510 "Wiggle Round") 15-25 48
Also see SONNY BOY & LONNIE
Also see SONNY BOY & SAM

SMITH, Shuggy
(Shuggy Ray Smith)

Singles: 7-inch

IMPERIAL (5918 "Hustlin' Man") 5-10 63
KAMMY (621 "Cause I'm Cryin' ") 5-10 62
PZAZZ (014 "My Mama Didn't Raise No Fool") 5-10 68
PZAZZ (019 "Hitchhiking Hippie") 5-10 69
PZAZZ (028 "Hitchhiking Hippie"/"My Mama Didn't Raise No Fool") 5-10 69
TOWER (187 "Little Tommy's Letter") 5-10 65

SMITH, Smiley

Singles: 7-inch

APOLLO (533 "Voo Doo Woman") 40-60 59

SMITH, Smiley

Singles: 7-inch

SPS (368 "Stand Up for America") 5-10 68
(Issued in support of the Presidential campaign of Alabama Gov. George Wallace.)

Picture Sleeves

SPS (368 "Stand Up for America") 5-10 68
(Pictures Gov. George Wallace.)

SMITH, Smokey

Singles: 7-inch

CARDINAL (501 "Bayou Boogie") 20-30
SIMS (270 "Too Late to Be Sorry") 4-8 66

SMITH, Smoochie

Singles: 7-inch

CASTAWAYS (1000 "It's All Your Fault") . 15-25

SMITH, Somethin,' & Redheads ***P&R '55***

Singles: 78 rpm

EPIC 4-8 54-57

Singles: 7-inch

EPIC 5-10 54-59
MGM 4-6 61

Picture Sleeves

EPIC 10-15 58

EPs: 7-inch

EPIC 10-20 59

LPs: 10/12-inch

EPIC 15-25 59
MGM 10-20 61

SMITH, Tab ***P&R '51***
(With His Band; with His Orchestra; with Robie Kirk & the Ruppert-Aires)

Singles: 78 rpm

ARCO 5-10 48
ATLANTIC 10-15 52
CHESS 5-10 52
DECCA 5-10 44
HARLEM 5-10 46
HUB 5-10 45-46
KING 5-10 46
MANOR 5-10 44-48
QUEEN 5-10 46
REGIS 5-10 44
SOUTHERN 5-10 46
20TH CENTURY 5-10 45
UNITED 5-15 51-57

Singles: 7-inch

ARGO (5323 "My Happiness") 10-20 59
ATLANTIC (961 "Echo Blues") 15-25 52
B&F (1348 "Pickin' Up the Tab") 10-15 61
CHECKER (933 "Because of You") 10-15 59
CHESS (1501 "Slow and Easy") 20-40 52
EBONY (1008 "Romance Time") 100-200 58
KING (4000 series) 20-40 52
KING (5000 series) 10-15 60-61
UNITED (Black vinyl) 15-25 51-58
UNITED (Red vinyl) 25-50 51

EPs: 7-inch

KING (263 "Tab Smith") 15-25 54

LPs: 10/12-inch

CHECKER (2971 "Keeping Tab") 50-100 59
(Black vinyl.)
CHECKER (2971 "Keeping Tab") 200-400 59
(Multi-color vinyl. Promotional issue only.)
UNITED (001 "Music Styled by Tab Smith") 75-125 52
UNITED (003 "Red Hot and Cool Blue Moods") 75-125 53
Also see POMUS, Doc

SMITH, Thunder
(Wilson Smith)

Singles: 78 rpm

ALADDIN (166 "L.A. Blues") 75-100 46
GOLD STAR (615 "Cruel Hearted Woman") 50-75 47
GOLD STAR (644 "Sante Fe Blues") 50-75 49
Session: Lightnin' Hopkins.
Also see HOPKINS, Lightnin,' & Thunder Smith
Also see STONEHAM, Luther
Also see THOMAS, Andrew

SMITH, Thunder, & Rockie

Singles: 78 rpm

DOWN TOWN (2011 "Thunder's Unfinished Boogie") 40-60 48
DOWN TOWN (2012 "New Worried Life Blues") 40-60 48
DOWN TOWN (2013 "West Coast Blues") 40-60 48
Members: Wilson Smith; Luther Stoneham.
Also see SMITH, Thunder

SMITH, Verdelle ***P&R '66***

Singles: 7-inch

CAPITOL 5-10 66-67
COLUMBIA (43296 "Juanita") 5-10 65
JANUS 4-6 75

Picture Sleeves

COLUMBIA (43296 "Juanita") 5-10 65

LPs: 10/12-inch

CAPITOL (2476 "In My Room") 150-250 66
JANUS 8-12 75

SMITH, Walter (Tang)

Singles: 78 rpm

J-B (606 "High Tone Mama") 100-200 52

SMITH, Warren ***P&R '57/C&W '60***

Singles: 78 rpm

QUALITY 50-100 56
(Canadian.)
SUN 50-100 56-57

Singles: 7-inch

LIBERTY 8-12 59-64
MERCURY (72825 "Lie to Me") 4-8 68

QUALITY (1493 "Rock & Roll Ruby") 75-125 56
(Canadian.)
QUALITY (1558 "Ubangi Stomp") 50-75 56
(Canadian.)
SUN (239 "Rock 'M' Roll Ruby") 100-125 56
(With slight title misprint.)
SUN (239 "Rock 'N' Roll Ruby") 50-100 56
(Title is correct.)
SUN (250 "Ubangi Stomp") 50-75 56
SUN (268 "So Long I'm Gone") 30-50 57
SUN (286 "I've Got Love if You Want It"). 30-50 58
SUN (314 "Sweet Sweet Girl") 15-25 59
SSS/SUN 3-5 80
W.B. (5125 "Dear Santa") 10-20 59

LPs: 10/12-inch

LIBERTY (3199 "First Country Collection") 35-45 61
(Monaural.)
LIBERTY (7199 "First Country Collection") 40-60 61
(Stereo.)
ROCK IT (1004 "Back in Action") 8-12 79

SMITH, Warren, & Shirley Collie *C&W '61*

Singles: 7-inch

LIBERTY (55361 "Why, Baby, Why") 10-15 61
Also see COLLIE, Shirley
Also see SMITH, Warren

SMITH, Whistling Jack *P&R '67*

Singles: 7-inch

DERAM (85005 "I Was Kaiser Bill's Batman") 5-10 67
DERAM (85041 "Early One Morning") 5-10 69

LPs: 10/12-inch

DERAM 10-15 67

SMITHSON, Lonnie

Singles: 7-inch

STARDAY (330 "Me and the Blues") 75-125
STARDAY (359 "Quarter in the Jukebox") 50-75

SMITTY & STORIES

Singles: 7-inch

ELF (102 "Before You Go") 75-100 62

SMITTY & VISCOUNTS

Singles: 7-inch

LYNN (1301 "Midnight Hop") 10-20 59

SMOKE

LPs: 10/12-inch

SIDEWALK (5912 "The Smoke") 30-40 68
Member: Michael Lloyd.
Also see CANNED HEAT

SMOKE
(John Orvis & Smoke)

Singles: 7-inch

UNI (55154 "Choose It") 5-10 69

LPs: 10/12-inch

UNI 15-25 69-70
Also see NOMADS

SMOKE RING *P&R '69*

Singles: 7-inch

BUDDAH (77 "No, Not Much") 5-10 69
BUDDAH (112 "Portrait of My Love") 5-10 69
CERTRON (10008 "First Reaction") 4-8 70
GOLD DUST (317 "No, Not Much") 5-10 68
MALA (568 "Her Love's a Lie") 5-10 67
SHUE (1988 "Triangle") 4-6
Members: Joe Hupp; Nick Hupp; Bob Hupp; Jim Casey, Chuck Asmuss; John Schrad; Gary Benjamin.
Also see LITTLE JOE & RAMRODS

SMOKE RINGS

Singles: 7-inch

DOT (16975 "Love's the Thing") 10-15 66
PROSPECT (101 "Love's the Thing") 20-30 66

SMOKE RISE

Singles: 7-inch

ATCO (6851 "I Need a Woman") 4-8 71
PARAMOUNT (0113 "I'm Here") 4-8 71

LPs: 10/12-inch

PARAMOUNT (9000 "Survival of St. Joan") 10-20 71
(Includes 10-page booklet.)

SMOKESTACK LIGHTNIN' *LP '69*

Singles: 7-inch

BELL 4-8 69-70
WHITE WHALE 5-10 67

LPs: 10/12-inch

BELL 10-15 69

SMOKEY & HIS SISTER

Singles: 7-inch

COLUMBIA (43995 "In a Dream of Silent Seas") 5-10 67
COLUMBIA (44207 "Lot of Lovin' ") 5-10 67
W.B. (7284 "Sheridan Square") 5-10 69

LPs: 10/12-inch

W.B. (1763 "Smokey & His Sister") 10-15 68

SMOKEY JOE
(Smokey Joe Baugh)

Singles: 78 rpm

FLIP 40-75 55
SUN 30-60 55

Singles: 7-inch

FLIP (228 "The Signifying Monkey") 100-150 55
SUN (228 "The Signifying Monkey") 75-125 55
SUN (393 "The Signifying Monkey") 25-50 64
Also see EMERSON, Billy "The Kid" / Smokey Joe
Also see TAYLOR, Bill, & Smokey Joe

SMOKY & FABULOUS BLADES

Singles: 7-inch

DORE (723 "Jerk, Baby, Jerk") 25-35 65

SMOOTHIES

Singles: 7-inch

DECCA (31105 "Joanie") 8-12 60
DECCA (31159 "Ride Ride Ride") 8-12 60
Members: John Phillips; Scott McKenzie.
Also see McKENZIE, Scott
Also see PHILLIPS, John

SMOOTHTONES
(With the Walt Harper's Orchestra)

Singles: 78 rpm

JEM 25-35 55
OKEH 15-25 57

Singles: 7-inch

JEM (412 "Bring Back Your Love") 75-125 55
OKEH (7078 "Little Cupid") 15-25 57

SMOOTHTONES

Singles: 78 rpm

EMBER (1001 "Dear Diary") 15-25 56

Singles: 7-inch

COLLECTABLES .... 3-5 '80s
EMBER (1001 "Dear Diary") 40-60 56
(Red label.)
EMBER (1001 "Dear Diary") 15-25 60
(Multi-color label.)

SMOTHERS, Dick

Singles: 7-inch

MERCURY (72717 "Saturday Night at the World") 10-20 67

Picture Sleeves

MERCURY (72717 "Saturday Night at the World") 15-25 67

LPs: 10/12-inch

MERCURY (21134 "Saturday Night at the World") 10-15 67
(Monaural.)
MERCURY (61134 "Saturday Night at the World") 15-20 67
(Stereo.)
Also see SMOTHERS BROTHERS

SMOTHERS, Smokey

Singles: 7-inch

FEDERAL (12385 "Crying Tears") 15-25 60
FEDERAL (12395 "I Ain't Gonna Be No Monkey Man No More") 15-25 60
FEDERAL (12405 "Come On, Rock Little Girl") 15-25 61
FEDERAL (12420 "Honey, I Ain't Teasin' ") 15-25 61
FEDERAL (12441 "Blind and Dumb Man") 15-25 61
FEDERAL (12466 "Twist with Me Annie") 10-20 60
FEDERAL (12488 "Give It Back") 10-20 63
FEDERAL (12503 "The Case Is Closed") 10-20 63

LPs: 10/12-inch

KING (779 "Backporch Blues") 500-800 62

SMOTHERS BROTHERS *LP '62*

Singles: 7-inch

MERCURY 5-10 62-65
SMOTHERS INCORPORATED ("The Christmas Bunny") 25-35 69
(No selection number used. Promotional issue only.)

Picture Sleeves

MERCURY (72483 "Three Song") 8-12 64
MERCURY (72519 "The Toy Song") 8-12 65
SMOTHERS INCORPORATED ("The Christmas Bunny") 25-50 69
(Promotional issue only.)

EPs: 7-inch

MERCURY (104 "Comedy Hour") 10-15 68
(Promotional issue only.)
MERCURY (628 "Two Sides") 10-20 62

LPs: 10/12-inch

MERCURY (20 "Best of the Smothers Brothers") 25-35 64
(Promotional issue only.)
MERCURY (25 "Brothers Smothers Month") 25-35 64
(Promotional issue only. Open-end interview.)
MERCURY (20000 series, except 20904) 10-20 61-68
(Monaural.)
MERCURY (20904 "It Must Have Been Something I Said") 15-20 64
(Commercial issue.)
MERCURY (20904 "It Must Have Been Something I Said") .... 20-30 '60s
(White label. Promotional issue. Has some different material than on commercial copies.)
MERCURY (60000 series) 12-25 61-68
(Stereo.)
Members: Dick Smothers; Tom Smothers.
Also see SMOTHERS, Dick
Also see TOM & DICK
Also see WILLIAMS, Mason / Smothers Brothers

SNAP SHOTS

Singles: 7-inch

CALJO (502 "I Still Love You") 15-25 62

SNEAKERS

Singles: 7-inch

DELTA (1868 "You Belong to Me") 10-15
DELTA (1910 "Till I Find My Girl") 15-25
DELTA (2141 "It's Just Not Funny Anymore") .... 15-25 '60s

SNEAKY PETE & SNEAKERS
(Pete Kleinow)

Singles: 7-inch

ALWAYS IN SOUNDS (200 "One Part of the Human Race") 15-25 67

LPs: 10/12-inch

SHILO (4086 "Sneaky Pete") 20-30 79

SNEED, Grady

Singles: 7-inch

REPRISE (20164 "Skippin' School") 10-15 63
Also see GRADY & BRADY

SNEED, Roy

Singles: 7-inch

VALLEY (102 "That Same Old Dream") ... 30-50 58

SNEEKERS

Singles: 7-inch

COLUMBIA (43438 "Soul Sneeker") 5-10 65

Picture Sleeves

COLUMBIA (43438 "Soul Sneeker") 10-15 65

SNEEZER, Ebe, & Epidemics
(Featuring John D. Loudermilk)

Singles: 7-inch

COLONIAL (436 "That's All I Got") 50-75 57
Also see LOUDERMILK, John D.

SNEL, Billy

Singles: 7-inch

WILD (100 "One Too Many Heads") 50-75 60

SNIDER, Tony

Singles: 7-inch

WESTWOOD (203 "They Call It Puppy Love") 75-100 60

SNOOKY & MOODY

Singles: 78 rpm

MARVEL ("Stockyard Blues") 75-100 47
(Selection number not known.)
OLD SWINGMASTER (18 "Boogie") 40-60 48
OLD SWINGMASTER (22 "Stockyard Blues") 40-60 48
PLANET (101 "Boogie") 75-100 48
Members: James Edward Pryor; Floyd Jones.
Also see PRYOR, Snooky

SNOOPY & OTHERS

Singles: 7-inch

HICKORY (1432 "You Better Take Me Home") 10-15 67

SNOW, Connie

Singles: 7-inch

MIDAS (04 "Walkin' in My Sleep") 50-75

SNOW, Eddie

Singles: 78 rpm

SUN (226 "Ain't That Right") 50-75 55

Singles: 7-inch

SUN (226 "Ain't That Right") 150-250 55

SNOW, Glenn

Singles: 7-inch

KANGAROO (21 "I Wonder What the Future Holds for Me") 10-15 61
KANGAROO (22 "Which Way Did You Come In") 10-15 62

SNOW, Hank *C&W '49*
(The Singing Ranger & His Rainbow Ranch Boys; with Kelly Foxton)

Singles: 78 rpm

BLUEBIRD .... 15-30 '40s
RCA 5-10 49-57

Singles: 7-inch

RCA (48-0056 thru 48-0400) 20-40 49-51
(Green vinyl.)
RCA (0100 & 0900 series) 4-8 69-74
(Orange labels.)
RCA (0300 & 0400 series) 15-25 50-51
(Green or gray labels.)
RCA (4346 thru 7748) 10-20 52-60
RCA (7803 thru 9907) 5-10 61-70
RCA (10000 & 11000 series) 3-6 74-80

Picture Sleeves

RCA (8151 "The Man Who Robbed the Bank at Santa Fe") 10-15 63

EPs: 7-inch

RCA (295 thru 1113) 12-25 54-56
RCA (1156 "Old Doc Brown") 35-45 55
RCA (1200 series) 20-30 55
RCA (1400 series) 15-25 57
RCA (3000 series) 30-50 52-54
RCA (4000 series) 15-20 58
RCA (5000 series) 12-25 58-60

LPs: 10/12-inch

CAMDEN 8-15 59-74
DETOUR 5-10
HANK SNOW SCHOOL OF MUSIC (1149/50 "The Guitar") 250-300 58
(Special issue from the Hank Snow School of Music. Includes guitar instruction booklet.)
PICKWICK 5-10 75-76
RCA (0134 "Living Legend") 100-125 78
(RCA Special Products issue.)
RCA (0162 thru 0908) 5-10 73-75
RCA (1004 "I'm Movin' On") 15-20 82
(RCA Special Products issue.)
RCA (1052 thru 3987) 5-10 75-81
(With ""AHL1, "ANL1," "AYL1" or "APL1" prefix.)
RCA (1113 "Just Keep-A-Movin' ") 25-35 55
(With "LPM" prefix.)
RCA (1156 "Old Doc Brown") 150-175 55
RCA (1233 thru 1861) 25-50 55-58
RCA (2043 thru 4708) 10-25 60-72
RCA (3026 "Country Classics") 75-150 52
(10-inch LP.)
RCA (3070 "Hank Snow Sings") 75-150 52
(10-inch LP.)
RCA (3131 "Hank Snow Salutes Jimmie Rodgers") 50-100 53
(10-inch LP.)
RCA (3192 "Tennessee Jamboree") 50-100 53
(10-inch LP.)
RCA (3220 "Country Western Caravan") 50-100 54
(10-inch LP.)
RCA (3267 "Country Guitar") 50-100 53
(10-inch LP.)
RCA (6014 "This Is My Story") 20-30 66
(Two discs.)
RCA SPECIAL PRODUCTS/KRAFT FOODS 10-20 64-67
(TV mail-order offer.)
RCA SPECIAL PRODUCTS/TEE VEE 10-15 74-78

READER'S DIGEST (216 "I'm Movin' On")... 125-150
(Boxed, six-disc set.)
Session: Jordanaires; Anita Kerr Singers; Jimmy Snow.
Also see JORDANAIRES
Also see KERR, Anita
Also see MARTIN, Janis / Hank Snow
Also see PRESLEY, Elvis / Hank Snow / Eddy Arnold / Hank Snow

SNOW, Hank, & Chet Atkins

Singles: 78 rpm

RCA (5995 "Silver Bell")... 4-8 55

Singles: 7-inch

RCA (5995 "Silver Bell")... 10-20 55

LPs: 10/12-inch

RCA (2952 "Reminiscing")... 25-35 64
RCA (4254 "By Special Request")... 20-30 70
Also see ATKINS, Chet

SNOW, Hank, & Anita Carter *C&W '51*

(Anita Carter & Hank Snow; with the Rainbow Ranch Boys)

Singles: 78 rpm

RCA... 4-8 51-56

Singles: 7-inch

RCA... 10-20 51-56

LPs: 10/12-inch

RCA (2580 "Together Again")... 20-30 62
Also see CARTER, Anita

SNOW, Hank / Hank Locklin / Porter Wagoner

LPs: 10/12-inch

RCA (2723 "Three Country Gentlemen"). 15-25 63
Also see LOCKLIN, Hank
Also see SNOW, Hank
Also see WAGONER, Porter

SNOW, Hap, & Whirlwinds

Singles: 7-inch

FLEETWOOD (1005 "Banshee")... 30-50 58

SNOW, Valaida

Singles: 78 rpm

BEL-TONE... 10-15 45
CHESS... 25-50 53
DERBY... 20-30 51

Singles: 7-inch

CHESS (1555 "I Ain't Gonna Tell")... 50-100 53
DERBY (735 "Coconut Head")... 50-100 51
(Colored vinyl.)

SNOW MEN

Singles: 7-inch

CHALLENGE (59227 "Ski Storm")... 10-15 64
DIMENSION (1045 "Skiing U.S.A.")... 5-10 65
Members: Ed Medora; Vince Hozier; Marty DiGiovanni; Davey Holt.
Also see HOLT, Davey, & Hubcaps
Also see SUNRAYS

SNOWMEN

(Concords)

Singles: 7-inch

HERALD (597 "Cold & Frosty Morning")... 8-12 64
(Issued in 1963 on Herald 578, shown as by the Concords.)
ROULETTE (4578 "Sugar Daddy")... 5-10 64
Also see CONCORDS

SNYDER, James B.

Singles: 78 rpm

VITA (144 "Don't Slam the Door")... 10-15 56

Singles: 7-inch

VITA (144 "Don't Slam the Door")... 20-30 56

SOCIAL OUTCASTS

Singles: 7-inch

SULTAN (1003 "Mad")... 20-30

SOCIETY

Singles: 7-inch

MARK VII (1005 "High & Mighty")... 15-25 66
(One source shows this number as 105. We're not yet sure which is correct.)

SOCIETY

Singles: 7-inch

FEATURE (112 "For Me")... 15-25 66
Members: Kevin Kohl; Roger Jerry; Kenny Rogers; Mike Dennis; John Blarjeske.

SOCIETY'S CHILDREN

Singles: 7-inch

ATCO (Except 6618)... 5-10 67-68
ATCO (6618 "Tribute to the 4 Seasons")... 10-20 69
CHA CHA... 10-20 '60s

SOCIETY'S PEOPLE

Singles: 7-inch

SMILE (432 "That's the Way of Our Day")... 50-75 67

SOCRATES

LPs: 10/12-inch

PI... 10-15 73

SODAMAN

LPs: 10/12-inch

VISUAL VINYL (1005 "Adventures of Sodaman")... 30-40 83
(Picture disc. Canadian.)

SODER, Skip, Band

Singles: 7-inch

ARTEEN (1019 "Begin the Beguine")... 10-20 62
CANDIX (336 "Begin the Beguine")... 8-12 62

SOFFOS, Phil

Singles: 7-inch

MEM (103 "Rock All Night")... 75-100 61

SOFT BOYS

LPs: 10/12-inch

TWO CRABS... 10-15
Member: Kimberley Rew.

SOFT MACHINE *LP '68*

Singles: 7-inch

PROBE (452 "Joy of a Toy")... 5-10 68

LPs: 10/12-inch

ACCORD... 5-10 82
COLUMBIA... 8-12 70-73
COMMAND (964 "Soft Machine")... 15-20 73
(Two discs.)
PROBE (4500 "Soft Machine")... 20-30 68
(With movable parts cover.)
PROBE (4500 "Soft Machine")... 15-20 69
(With standard cover.)
PROBE (4505 "Soft Machine, Vol. 2")... 15-25 69
RECKLESS... 5-10 88

SOFT TONES

Singles: 78 rpm

SAMPSON... 15-25 55

Singles: 7-inch

SAMPSON (103 "My Mother's Eyes")... 50-75 55
(Rigid – or thicker – disc.)
SAMPSON (103 "My Mother's Eyes")... 20-30 55
(Flexible – or thinner – disc.)

SOFT WHITE UNDERBELLY

LPs: 10/12-inch

ELEKTRA ("Soft White Underbelly")... 35-45 69
(Selection number not known.)
Also see BLUE OYSTER CULT

SOF-TONES

Singles: 7-inch

CEEBEE (1062 "Oh Why")... 3000-4000 57
Also see DELMIRAS / Sof-Tones

SOFTWINDS

Singles: 7-inch

HAC (105 "Cross My Heart")... 10-15 61

SOHL, Don

(With the Roadrunners)

Singles: 7-inch

DREEM (728 "Voo-Doo")... 50-100 59
DREEM (1005 "Knockout")... 50-75 60
DREEM (1667 "Paper Doll")... 40-60 61
DREEM (2349 "Twin City Bues")... 50-75 61
PALMS (728 "Voo-Doo")... 25-50 61
SHUE (1970 "Something You Want to Try")... 5-10 72
SHUE (1973 "Love What You Do")... 5-10 72

SOLDIER BOYS

Singles: 7-inch

SCEPTER (1230 "I'm Your Soldier Boy")... 75-125 62
Session: Don Covay; Wally Roker.
Also see COVAY, Don

SOLE SURVIVORS

Singles: 7-inch

CORI (31008 "There Were Times")... 10-20 '60s

SOLEY, Chuck

Singles: 78 rpm

TRUMPET... 10-20 55

Singles: 7-inch

TRUMPET (236 "I Just Want to Be Yours")... 15-25 55

SOLITAIRES

Singles: 78 rpm

OLD TOWN (Except 1000)... 50-100 54-57
OLD TOWN (1000 "Blue Valentine")... 250-350 54

Singles: 7-inch

ARGO (5316 "Walking Along")... 10-15 58
FINE ("Rose Mary")... 50-100 61
(No selection number used.)
MGM (13221 "Fool That I Am")... 15-25 64
OLD TOWN (1000 "Blue Valentine")... 150-250 54
(Black vinyl.)
OLD TOWN (1000 "Blue Valentine")... 600-800 54
(Red vinyl.)
OLD TOWN (1003 "If I Loved You")... 4-8 78
(Previously unreleased. Recorded in 1954.)
OLD TOWN (1006/1007 "Please Remember My Heart")... 400-500 54
(Black vinyl.)
OLD TOWN (1006/1007 "Please Remember My Heart")... 3000-4000 54
(Red vinyl.)
OLD TOWN (1006/1006 "Please Remember My Heart")... 75-100 54
(Note different flip side number.)
OLD TOWN (1008 "Chances I've Taken")... 400-500 54
(Black vinyl.)
OLD TOWN (1008 "Chances I've Taken")... 2000-3000 54
(Red vinyl.)
OLD TOWN (1008 "Please Remember My Heart")... 15-25 '60s
(Blue label.)
OLD TOWN (1010 "I Don't Stand a Ghost of a Chance")... 200-300 55
OLD TOWN (1012 "What Did She Say")... 100-150 55
(Logo in Old English typestyle.)
OLD TOWN (1012 "What Did She Say").. 50-75 56
(Logo in block typestyle.)
OLD TOWN (1014 "Wedding")... 50-75 55
OLD TOWN (1015 "Magic Rose")... 50-75 55
OLD TOWN (1019 "Honeymoon")... 50-75 56
OLD TOWN (1026 "You've Sinned"/"You're Back with Me")... 200-300 56
OLD TOWN (1026 "You've Sinned"/"The Angels Sang")... 40-60 56
OLD TOWN (1032 "Give Me One More Chance")... 100-150 56
OLD TOWN (1034 "Walking Along")... 50-75 57
(Yellow label.)
OLD TOWN (1034 "Walking Along")... 10-20 '60s
(Blue label.)
OLD TOWN (1044 "I Really Love You So")... 100-200 57
OLD TOWN (1049 "Walking and Talking")... 50-100 58
OLD TOWN (1059 "Please Remember My Heart")... 30-50 58
OLD TOWN (1066 "Embraceable You")... 40-60 59
OLD TOWN (1071 "Light a Candle in the Chapel")... 25-35 59
OLD TOWN (1096 "Lonesome Lover")... 10-15 61
OLD TOWN (1139 "The Time Is Here")... 10-15 63

LPs: 10/12-inch

MURRAY HILL... 5-10 84
Members: Herman Curtis; Monte Owens; Bobby Williams; Bobby Baylor; Buzzy Willis; Milton Love; Pat Gaston; Fred Barksdale; Reggie Barnes; Wally Roker; Cecil Holmes.
Also see CADILLACS
Also see McFADDEN, Ruth
Also see REED, Ursula
Also see SOLITAIRES

SOLLEY, Jim

(With the Lubocs.)

Singles: 7-inch

DEB (8791 "Yes I Do")... 15-20 59
LUBOC... 8-12
NRC (5011 "Yes I Do")... 10-15 60
RCA (9193 "Momma and Poppa")... 5-10 67
STESO... 4-8

SOLOMON, Ed

Singles: 7-inch

DIAMOND (160 "Beatle Flying Saucer").. 10-15 64

SOLOMON, King

(With the Lad Teens Band; King Soloman; Solomon King; Ellis Solomon)

Singles: 78 rpm

BIG TOWN (102 "Mean Train")... 20-30 53

Singles: 7-inch

ASHANTI (003 "I Got a Sweet Tooth")... 5-10 '60s
BIG TOWN (102 "Mean Train")... 50-100 53
CADILLAC (503 "Louisiana Groove")... 5-10 '60s
CHECKER (980 "Non-Support Blues")... 15-25 61
DON-J... 5-10 '60s
FRANKLIN... 5-10
HIGHLAND... 5-10 69
KENT (446 "Mr. Bad Luck")... 5-10 66
KENT (451 "S.K. Blues")... 5-10 66
LE BAM (1201 "Something's Wrong with Me")... 15-25
MADER-D (302 "Little Dab Will Do It")... 10-15 '60s
MAGNUM... 4-6
RESIST... 4-8 66
STANSON (003 "If I Were a Strong Man")... 5-8
TOMSEY... 4-8 '60s
WORLD'S... 4-6
U.A. (967 "It's a Good Thing")... 5-10 66

SOLOTONES

Singles: 78 rpm

EXCELLO (2060 "Pork & Beans")... 20-30 55

Singles: 7-inch

EXCELLO (2060 "Pork & Beans")... 75-125 55

SOLUTION

Singles: 7-inch

IGL (166 "Love's Where You Find It")... 10-20 '60s

SOMEBODY'S CHYLDREN

Singles: 7-inch

UPTOWN (727 "Shadows")... 5-10 66
Also see WHITCOMB, Ian

SOMETHING WILD

Singles: 7-inch

PSYCHEDELIC (1691 "Trippin' Out")... 25-50 '60s

SOMETHING YOUNG

Singles: 7-inch

FONTANA (1556 "Oh, Don't Come Crying Back to Me")... 10-20 66

SOMMERS, Joanie *P&R '60*

(With Don Ralke & His Orchestra)

Singles: 7-inch

ABC (12323 "Peppermint Engineer")... 3-5 78
CAPITOL (5936 "Trains & Boats & Planes")... 4-8 67
COLUMBIA (43731 "Never Throw Your Dreams Away")... 4-8 66
COLUMBIA (43950 "It Doesn't Matter Anymore")... 4-8 66
HAPPY TIGER (522 "Step Inside Love")... 4-6 70
HAPPY TIGER (537 "Tell Him")... 4-6 70
W.B. (107 "Sommers' Hot, Sommers' Here")... 10-15 60
(Promotional issue only.)
W.B. (5157 "One Boy")... 10-15 60
(Black vinyl.)
W.B. (5157 "One Boy")... 30-40 60
(Gold vinyl. Promotional issue only.)
W.B. (5177 "Be My Love")... 10-15 60
W.B. (5183 "Ruby-Duby-Du")... 10-15 60
W.B. (5201 "I Don't Want to Walk Without You")... 10-15 61
(Black vinyl.)
W.B. (5201 "I Don't Want to Walk Without You")... 30-40 61
(Gold vinyl. Promotional issue only.)
W.B. (5226 thru 5629)... 8-12 61-65
W.B. (7251 "The Great Divide")... 4-8 68

Picture Sleeves

W.B. (107 "Sommers' Hot, Sommers' Here")... 20-30 60
(Promotional issue only.)
W.B. (5157 "One Boy")... 10-15 60
(Die-cut center hole. Promotional issue only.)

EPs: 7-inch

W.B. (1504 "Sommers' Seasons")... 10-20 63
(Juke box issue.)
W.B. (5507 "Joannie Sommers")... 10-20 61

LPs: 10/12-inch
COLUMBIA (2495 "Come Alive")............ 10-20 66
(Monaural.)
COLUMBIA (9295 "Come Alive")............ 10-20 66
(Stereo.)
DISCOVERY..5-10 83
W.B. (W-1346 "Positively the Most")........ 20-30 60
(Monaural.)
W.B. (WS-1346 "Positively the Most")..... 25-35 60
(Stereo.)
W.B. (W-1412 "Voice of the Sixties")....... 20-30 61
(Monaural.)
W.B. (WS-1412 "Voice of the Sixties")..... 25-35 61
(Stereo.)
W.B. (W-1436 "For Those Who Think Young").. 20-30 62
(Monaural.)
W.B. (WS-1436 "For Those Who Think Young").. 25-35 62
(Stereo.)
W.B. (W-1470 "Johnny Get Angry")......... 20-30 62
(Monaural.)
W.B. (WS-1470 "Johnny Get Angry") 25-35 62
(Stereo.)
W.B. (W-1474 "Let's Talk About Love")... 20-30 62
(Monaural.)
W.B. (WS-1474 "Let's Talk About Love"). 25-35 62
(Stereo.)
W.B. (W-1504 "Sommers' Seasons")....................................... 20-30 63
(Monaural.)
W.B. (WS-1504 "Sommers' Seasons").... 25-35 63
(Stereo.)
Also see BYRNES, Edd "Kookie," with Joanie Sommers & Mary Kaye Trio
Also see NELSON, Rick / Joanie Sommers / Dona Jean Young
Also see RALKE, Don

SOMMERS, Joanie, & Laurindo Almeida
LPs: 10/12-inch
W.B. (W-1575 "Softly, the Brazilian Sound").. 20-30 64
(Monaural.)
W.B. (WS-1575 "Softly, the Brazilian Sound").. 25-35 64
(Stereo.)
Also see ALMEIDA, Laurindo
Also see SOMMERS, Joanie

SOMMERS, Ronny
(Sonny Bono)
Singles: 7-inch
SAWMI (1001 "Don't Shake My Tree").... 25-35 61
(Label name misspelled. Should be "Swami.")
SWAMI (1001 "Don't Shake My Tree").... 15-25 61
(Label name spelled correctly.)
Also see SONNY

SONARS
Singles: 7-inch
VULCO (2 "Who's That Knockin' ") 50-75 60
Picture Sleeves
VULCO (2 "Who's That Knockin' ") 60-80 60

SONGCRAFTERS
(Joseph S. Powe's Songcrafters)
Singles: 7-inch
ANTON (106 "Please Tell Me")........... 150-200 61

SONGSPINNERS
Singles: 7-inch
LEILA (1602 "Bobbie")........................... 75-100 58

SONIC YOUTH — LP '90
LPs: 10/12-inch
DGC..5-8 90
ENIGMA..5-10 '80s
HOMESTEAD..5-10 '80s
MFSL (257 "Goo")................................. 25-35 96
SST..5-10 '80s
W.B. (71591 "Made in the USA") ....8-12 '90s
(Colored vinyl.)
Members: Thurston Moore; Kim Gordon; Lee Ranaldo; Steve Shelley.

SONICS
Singles: 78 rpm
GROOVE (0112 "As I Live On")............... 40-50 55
Singles: 7-inch
GROOVE (0112 "As I Live On")........... 200-250 55

SONICS
Singles: 7-inch
GAITY (113 "Marlene").................... 2000-3000 59

SONICS
(With the Bill Fontaine Orchestra)
Singles: 7-inch
NOCTURNE (110 "Triangle Love")...........30-40 59
RKO UNIQUE (411 "Triangle Love") 15-25 57

SONICS
("Featuring Donald Sheffield")
Singles: 7-inch
AMCO (001 "It's You")...........................100-200 62
CANDLELITE (416 "Once in a Lifetime")....5-10 63
(Black vinyl.)
CANDLELITE (416 "Once in a Lifetime")....8-12 63
(Red vinyl.)
CHECKER (922 "This Broken Heart") 10-15 59
CLIFTON (12 "Once in a Lifetime")..............4-6 75
HARVARD (801 "This Broken Heart") ..250-350 59
HARVARD (922 "This Broken Heart") 30-40 59
JAMIE (1235 "Sugaree") 10-15 62
X-TRA (107 "Once In a Lifetime").... 1500-2000 58
Members: Donald Sheffield; Kenny "Butch" Hamilton.
Also see 5 WINGS

SONICS
Singles: 7-inch
ARMONIA (102 "Funny").......................150-200 62

SONICS
Singles: 7-inch
LITTLE MARK (1939 "Two Degrees North")...10-20 62

SONICS
Singles: 7-inch
BYRON...5-10 64
Members: Myles Reese; Bobby White; Marty Markiewicz; Harry Jeroleman; Ginter Schatz; Bob Short.
Also see CHOSEN FEW

SONICS
Singles: 7-inch
BURDETTE (106 "Dirty Old Man")..............4-8 75
ETIQUETTE (11 "Keep a Knockin' ") 20-30 64
ETIQUETTE (ET-11 "Psycho"/"The Witch") 30-50 65
ETIQUETTE (16 "Hustler")........................20-30 65
ETIQUETTE (18 "Shot Down") 20-30 65
ETIQUETTE (23 "Louie Louie") 20-30 65
GREAT NORTHWEST MUSIC........................3-5 79
JERDEN (809 "Love Lights").......................8-12 66
JERDEN (810 "The Witch")..........................8-12 66
JERDEN (811 "Psycho") 8-12 66
PICCADILLY (244 "Lost Love")..................10-20 67
PICCADILLY (255 "Love-Itis")..................15-25 67
UNI (55039 "Lost Love")..............................5-10 67
Note: Sold in an online auction, for $127, is a picture sleeve for *Johnny B. Goode/Louie Louie*. Not given is the label name and number. We would appreciate more information on this release.
LPs: 10/12-inch
BOMP (4011 "Sinderella").........................10-15 80
BUCKSHOT (001 "Explosives")...........150-175 73
ETIQUETTE (024 "Here Are the Sonics")..100-150 66
ETIQUETTE (024 "Here Are the Sonics") ..5-10 84
(Reissues the 1984 date on back cover.)
ETIQUETTE (027 "The Sonics Boom")..100-150 67
ETIQUETTE (1184 "Full Force")..................8-12 85
FIRST (7719 "The Sonics")......................10-15 78
FIRST AMERICAN (7719 "Unreleased")..10-15 80
FIRST AMERICAN (7779 "Fire and Ice") .10-15 83
JERDEN (7007 "Introducing the Sonics")..100-150 67
Members: Gerry Roslie; Andy Parypa; Larry Parypa; Rob Lind; Bob Bennett; Jim Brady; Randy Haitt; Steve Mosier; Ron Foos.

SONICS / Wailers
Singles: 7-inch
ETIQUETTE (22 "Don't Believe in Christmas")..10-15 65

SONICS / Wailers / Galaxies
LPs: 10/12-inch
ETIQUETTE (ETALB-025 "Merry Christmas")......................................100-150 66
ETIQUETTE (025 "Merry Christmas")........5-10 84
(Reissues the 1984 date on back cover.)
ETIQUETTE (028 "The Northwest Collection")...125-150
(Six-disc boxed set.)
Also see GALAXIES
Also see SONICS
Also see WAILERS

SONNETS
Singles: 78 rpm
HERALD..10-15 56
Singles: 7-inch
GUYDEN (2112 "Forever for You") 20-30 64
HERALD (477 "Why Should We Break Up")..50-75 56
LANE (501 "Angel of My Dreams").......100-125 58
Also see DEL VIKINGS / Sonnets

SONNETTES
Singles: 7-inch
'KO' KNOCKOUT (1 "I've Gotton [sic] Over You")...50-100 63
'KO' KNOCKOUT (2 "Hit and Run Lover")..50-100 63

SONNY — P&R '65
(Sonny Bono)
Singles: 7-inch
ATCO 5-10 65-67
HIGHLAND 5-10 63
MCA...4-6 72-74
SPECIALTY 4-8 65-72
LPs: 10/12-inch
ATCO (229 "Inner Views") 15-20 67
Also see CARTER, Prince
Also see CHRISTY, Don
Also see JACKSON, Roddy
Also see SOMMERS, Ronny
Also see SONNY & CHER

SONNY & CHER — P&R/LP '65
Singles: 7-inch
ATCO (6345 "Just You") 5-10 65
ATCO (6359 "I Got You Babe") 5-10 65
ATCO (6381 "But You're Mine") 5-10 65
ATCO (6395 "What Now My Love")............5-10 65
ATCO (6420 "Have I Stayed Too Long")....5-10 66
ATCO (6440 "Little Man")...........................5-10 66
ATCO (6449 "Living for You").....................5-10 66
ATCO (6461 "The Beat Goes On").............5-10 67
ATCO (6480 "A Beautiful Story")................5-10 67
ATCO (6486 "Plastic Man")........................5-10 67
ATCO (6507 "It's the Little Things")...........5-10 67
ATCO (6541 "Good Combination")..............5-10 67
ATCO (6555 "I Would Marry You Today")..5-10 68
ATCO (6605 "You Gotta Have a Thing of Your Own")...5-10 68
ATCO (6683 "You're a Friend of Mine") 5-10 69
ATCO (6758 "Get It Together")...................5-10 70
KAPP (2141 "Real People")..........................4-8 71
KAPP (2151 "All I Ever Need Is You")..........4-8 71
KAPP (2163 "A Cowboy's Work Is Never Done")..4-8 72
KAPP (2176 "When You Say Love") 4-8 72
MCA (40026 "Mama Was a Rock & Roll Singer, Papa Used to Write All Her Songs") 4-8 73
MCA (40083 "The Greatest Show on Earth")..4-8 73
PHILCO (8 "I Got You Babe"/"The Beat Goes On")...10-20 67
("Hip Pocket" flexi-disc.)
REPRISE (309 "Baby Don't Go"/"Walkin' the Quetzal")...10-15 64
REPRISE (392 "Baby Don't Go"/"Walkin' the Quetzal")..8-12 65
REPRISE (392 "Baby Don't Go"/"Love Is Strange")..5-10 65
(Note different flip side.)
VAULT (916 "The Letter"/"Spring Fever") 10-15 65
(Previously issued as by Caesar & Cleo.)
W.B. (8341 "You're Not Right for Me") 4-8 77
Picture Sleeves
VAULT (916 "The Letter") 10-20 65
EPs: 7-inch
ATCO 8-12 65
(Juke box issues only.)
REPRISE (6177 "Baby Don't Go")............15-25 65
LPs: 10/12-inch
ATCO (177 "Look At Us")..........................15-20 65
ATCO (183 "The Wondrous World of Sonny and Cher")..15-20 66
ATCO (203 "In Case You're in Love")......15-20 67
ATCO (214 "Good Times") 15-20 67
ATCO (219 "The Best of Sonny & Cher") 15-20 67
ATCO (804 "The Two of Us")....................15-20 72
(Two discs.)
ATCO (5178 "Greatest Hits")....................15-25 67
(Two discs.)
ATCO (11000 "The Beat Goes On").........15-20 67
KAPP (3654 "Sonny & Cher Live") 10-20 71
KAPP (3660 "All I Ever Need Is You")......10-20 72
MCA (2009 "Sonny & Cher Live")...............8-12 73
MCA (2021 "All I Ever Need Is You") 8-12 73
MCA (2102 "Mama Was a Rock & Roll Singer, Papa Used to Write All Her Songs")...................8-12 73
MCA (2117 "Greatest Hits")........................8-12 73
MCA (8004 "Live in Las Vegas, Vol. 2")......8-12 73
(Two discs.)
TVP 8-10 77
Members: Salvatore Bono; Cher LaPiere; Cher Bono.
Also see CAESAR & CLEO
Also see CHER
Also see HALE & HUSHABYES
Also see SONNY

SONNY & CHER / Bill Medley / Lettermen / Blendells
LPs: 10/12-inch
REPRISE (6177 "Baby Don't Go")............25-35 65
(Shown as by "Sonny & Cher and Friends.")
Also see BLENDELLS
Also see LETTERMEN
Also see MEDLEY, Bill
Also see SONNY & CHER

SONNY & DEMONS
LPs: 10/12-inch
U.A. (3316 "Drag Kings") 25-35 64
(Monaural.)
U.A. (6316 "Drag Kings") 30-40 64
(Stereo.)
Also see DRAG KINGS

SONNY & DIANE
Singles: 7-inch
EPIC (50280 "Love Trap") 10-15 76

SONNY & DUKES
Singles: 7-inch
REVERB (611 "My Love")..........................30-40 63

SONNY & EAGLES
Singles: 7-inch
GOLD EAGLE (1800 "Whadda Ya Some Kinda Nut")..5-10 61
U.A. (645 "Surfin' Monkey") 5-10 63
LPs: 10/12-inch
U.A. (3311 "Everybody Monkey") 10-15 63
(Monaural.)
U.A. (6311 "Everybody Monkey") 15-20 63
(Stereo.)

SONNY & JAYCEE
Singles: 7-inch
EMBER (1034 "Mister Froggie")..................8-12 58
Members: Sonny Terry; J.C. Burris.
Also see TERRY, Sonny

SONNY & PHYLLIS
(With the Danes; Sunny & Phyllis)
Singles: 7-inch
SOFT...8-12 67
UNI (55064 "I've Been Lost") 5-10 68
UNI (55091 "When I Look Into Your Eyes")..5-10 68
Members: Sonny Threatt; Phyllis Brown-Threatt.
Also see JOHNNY & MARK V
Also see NOMADS
Also see PAUL & PAULA
Also see THREATT, Sonny

SONNY & PREMIERS
Singles: 7-inch
CHIPHAM (100 "You Send Me") 15-25

SONNY & SATELLITES
Singles: 7-inch
NOCTURN (1003 "You Shouldn't") 10-15 64

SONNY BOY & LONNIE
Singles: 78 rpm
CONTINENTAL..15-25 47
LPs: 10/12-inch
CONTINENTAL..30-35 61
Members: Arthur Smith; Lonnie Johnson.

Also see SMITH, Shorty, & His Rhythm

SONNY BOY & SAM

Singles: 78 rpm

CONTINENTAL........ 20-40 47
Members: Arthur Smith; Sam Bradley.
Also see SMITH, Shorty, & His Rhythm
Also see SONNY BOY & LONNIE

SONNY V & VELVETS

Singles: 7-inch

ZENETTE (2010 "Baby")........ 100-150

SONODA, Harry

Singles: 7-inch

HANA HO (1022 "You Don't Need A Mind, Just Soul")........5-10 68

LPs: 10/12-inch

HANA HO (1 "You Don't Need A Mind, Just Soul")........ 10-15 68

SONS

Singles: 7-inch

COASTLINE (101 "I'm Gone")........ 30-40 66
Also see MAGIC MUSHROOM

SONS OF ADAM

Singles: 7-inch

ALAMO ("Take My Hand")........ 25-30 66
(First issue. Selection number not known.)
ALAMO (5473 "Feathered Fish")........ 20-30 66
DECCA (31887 "Take My Hand")........ 15-20 66
DECCA (31995 "You're a Better Man Than I")........ 15-25 66
PENTACLE (104 "Brown Eyed Woman") 10-20

EPs: 7-inch

MOXIE (1032 "Sons of Adam")........5-10 80
Members: Craig Tawater; Mike Port; Michael Stuart; Joe Cookin; Marcus David.
Also see OTHER HALF

SONS OF ADAM

Singles: 7-inch

PENTACLE (101 "Thinking Animal")........ 15-25 '60s

SONS OF BARBEE DOLL

Singles: 7-inch

CODE (1 "Psychedelic Seat")........ 10-20

SONS OF CHAMPLIN *LP '69*
(Sons)

Singles: 7-inch

ARIOLA AMERICA........4-6 75-77
CAPITOL........4-8 69-70
COLUMBIA........4-6 73
GOLDMINE........8-12
VERVE (10500 "Fat City")........5-10 67

LPs: 10/12-inch

ARIOLA AMERICA........8-10 75-77
CAPITOL (200 "Loosen Up Naturally")........ 30-40 69
(Two discs.)
CAPITOL (332 "Sons Minus Seeds and Stems")........ 15-25 69
COLUMBIA (32341 "Welcome to the Dance")........ 10-15 73
MILL VALLEY ("Sons Minus Seeds and Stems")........ 20-30 94
(Selection number not known. Reportedly 1000 made.)
SONS OF CHAMPLIN ("Sons Minus Seeds and Stems")........ 300-400 69
(Selection number not known. Reportedly 100 made.)
Members: Bill Champlin; Geoff Palmer; Bill Bowen; Al Strong; Jim Myers; Tim Caine.

SONS OF MOURNING

Singles: 7-inch

MIDGARD (204 "Come on Everybody")........ 25-35 67

SONS OF THE PIONEERS *P&R '34/C&W '45*

Singles: 78 rpm

DECCA........5-10 34-44
RCA........4-8 45-56

Singles: 7-inch

BLUEBIRD (105 "Sugarfoot")........5-10 58
CORAL........5-10 54
DECCA (29000 series)........5-10 56
RCA (0100 thru 0400 series)........5-10 50-51
(Black vinyl.)
RCA (0100 thru 0400 series)........ 10-20 50-51
(Colored vinyl.)
RCA (2000 thru 6000 series)........5-10 50-56
RCA (8000 series)........4-6 '60s

Picture Sleeves

RCA (68 "Wagon Train")........15-25 57
(Pictures TV series star Ward Bond.)
RCA (105 "Sugarfoot")........10-20 58
(Pictures TV series star Will Hutchins.)

EPs: 7-inch

RCA (103 "Tumbling Tumbleweeds")........8-15 61
RCA (168 "Cowboy Classics")........25-40 52
(Boxed set of three colored discs.)
RCA (400 thru 1400 series)........5-15 55-57
RCA (3000 series)........15-25 52-53
RCA (4000 series)........8-12 58
RCA (5000 series)........5-10 59

LPs: 10/12-inch

AMERICAN FOLK MUSIC........6-12 81
CAMDEN........8-18 58-73
COLUMBIA........5-8 82
GRANITE........6-10 76
HARMONY........10-15 64
J.E.M.F........8-10
LONG........10-15
MCA........4-8 83
PICKWICK........5-10 75
RCA (1092 "Cool Water")........5-10 76
RCA (1130 thru 2957, except 1431)........20-40 55-64
(With "LPM" or "LSP" prefix.)
RCA (1431 "How Great Thou Art")........30-40 57
RCA (2332 thru 2808)........5-10 77-78
RCA (3032 "Cowboy Classics")........30-50 52
(10-inch LP.)
RCA (3095 "Cowboy Hymns and Spirtuals")........30-50 52
(10-inch LP.)
RCA (3162 "Western Classics")........30-50 53
(10-inch LP.)
RCA (3351 thru 4119)........10-20 65-68
(With "LPM" or "LSP" prefix.)
RCA (3468 "Best of the Sons of the Pioneers")........5-10 79
RCA (4000 series)........4-8 81
VOCALION........8-12 64
Members: Roy Rogers; Bob Nolan; Tommy Doss; Tim Spencer; Ken Curtis; Hugh Farr; Karl Farr; Lloyd Perrymen; Shug Fisher; Pat Brady.
Also see ALLEN, Rex, Jr., & Sons Of The Pioneers
Also see CURTIS, Ken / Rex Allen & Arizona Wranglers
Also see ROGERS, Roy

SONYA
(With the Sensations)

Singles: 7-inch

DOT (16235 "Little Red Rooster")........8-12 61
DOT (16356 "For Your Love")........8-12 62
GEND (31 "Oh Lonesome Heart")........15-25 63

SONYA & CAPRIS

Singles: 7-inch

SCARLET (104 "Extra Extra")........100-150

SOOTHERS

Singles: 7-inch

PORT (70041 "Little White Cloud")........10-20 64
(Black vinyl.)
PORT (70041 "Little White Cloud")........20-30 64
(Colored vinyl.)
Members: Hank Jernigan; Fred Taylor; Nicky Clark; Bill Dempsey; Curt Cerebin.
Also see HARPTONES

SOOTHSAYERS
(Higher Elevation)

Singles: 7-inch

ACROPOLIS (6601 "Please Don't Be Mad")........15-25 66
ACROPOLIS (6612 "Do You Need Me")........15-25 66

Picture Sleeves

ACROPOLIS (6601 "Please Don't Be Mad")........25-35 66
ACROPOLIS (6612 "Do You Need Me")........25-35 66
Also see DIAMOND, Dave

SOOTZ, Manny, & Thieves

Singles: 78 rpm

PIRATE (841 "Cape Canaveral")........10-20 57

Singles: 7-inch

PIRATE (841 "Cape Canaveral")........20-30 57

SOPHOMORES

Singles: 78 rpm

DAWN........10-15 56-58

Singles: 7-inch

CHORD (1302 "Charades")........50-75 57
DAWN (216 "Every Night About This Time")........20-30 56
DAWN (218 "Linda")........20-30 56
DAWN (223 "Ocean Blue")........20-30 56
DAWN (225 "Is There Someone for Me")........10-20 57
DAWN (228 "If I Should Lose Your Love")........10-20 57
DAWN (237 "Each Time I Hold You")........10-20 58
EPIC (9259 "Charades")........10-20 57

LPs: 10/12-inch

SEECO (451 "The Sophomores")........50-75 58

SOPWITH CAMEL *P&R '66*

Singles: 7-inch

KAMA SUTRA (217 "Hello Hello")........4-8 66
KAMA SUTRA (224 "Postcard from Jamaica")........4-8 67
KAMA SUTRA (236 "Saga of the Low Down Let Down")........4-8 67
REPRISE........4-6 73

Picture Sleeves

KAMA SUTRA (224 "Postcard from Jamaica")........5-10 67

LPs: 10/12-inch

KAMA SUTRA........15-20 67-73
REPRISE........15-20 73
Members: Peter Kraemer; Terry MacNeil; William Sievers; Martin Beard; Norman Mayell.

SORENSEN, Roy, Group

Singles: 7-inch

COLD WART (78 "If You Could Read Me")........40-50 '60s

SORENSEN BROS.

Singles: 7-inch

MARLINDA (7507 "They've Landed")........35-50

SOTOLONGO, Edward
(With Leroy Kirkland & Orchestra)

Singles: 7-inch

3D (374 "When in the World")........100-200 58
Session: Crystal Chords.
Also see MONTALVO, Lenny, & Crystal Chords

SOUL, Billy
(Billy T. Soul)

Singles: 7-inch

KING (5904 "She's Gone")........10-15 64
KING (5929 "Big Balls of Fire")........10-15 64
MUSICOR (1248 "Call On Billy")........10-20 67

SOUL, David *P&R/LP '77*

Singles: 7-inch

MGM (13510 "Covered Man")........5-10 66
MGM (13589 "Before")........5-10 66
MGM (13842 "No One's Gonna Cry")........5-10 67
PARAMOUNT (0021 "This Train")........4-8 70
PRIVATE STOCK........3-5 76-77

LPs: 10/12-inch

PRIVATE STOCK........8-10 77

SOUL, Jimmy *P&R '62*
(With the Chants; James McCleese)

Singles: 7-inch

S.P.Q.R. (3300 "Twistin' Matilda")........8-12 62
S.P.Q.R. (3302 "When Matilda Comes Back")........8-12 62
S.P.Q.R. (3304 "Guess Things Happen That Way")........8-12 63
S.P.Q.R. (3305 "If You Wanna Be Happy")........8-12 63
S.P.Q.R. (3310 "Treat 'Em Tough")........8-12 63
S.P.Q.R. (3312 "Everybody's Gone Ape")........8-12 63
S.P.Q.R. (3313 "Go Away Christina")........8-12 63
S.P.Q.R. (3314 "Change Partners")........8-12 63
S.P.Q.R. (3315 "My Girl, She Sure Can Cook")........8-12 64
S.P.Q.R. (3318 "Take Me to Los Angeles")........8-12 64
S.P.Q.R. (3319 "Twistin' Matilda")........5-10 64
S.P.Q.R. (3321 "My Little Room")........8-12 64
20TH FOX (413 "Respectable")........5-10 63

Picture Sleeves

S.P.Q.R. (3302 "When Mathilda Comes Back")........15-25 62
S.P.Q.R. (3305 "If You Wanna Be Happy")........15-25 63

LPs: 10/12-inch

S.P.Q.R. (2000 "Greatest Hits")........15-25
S.P.Q.R. (16001 "If You Wanna Be Happy")........50-100 63
Session: Bill Deal.
Also see BENTON, Brook / Chuck Jackson / Jimmy Soul
Also see CHANTS
Also see DEAL, Bill
Also see McCLEESE, James
Also see RIVERS, Johnny / 4 Seasons / Jerry Butler / Jimmy Soul

SOUL, Jimmy / Belmonts / Connie Francis

LPs: 10/12-inch

SPINORAMA (125 "Jimmy Soul & the Belmonts")........20-25 63
Also see BELMONTS
Also see FRANCIS, Connie
Also see SOUL, Jimmy

SOUL, Johnny

Singles: 7-inch

FEDERAL (12557 "I Want Some")........10-20 70
SSS INT'L (763 "I Almost Called Your Name")........8-15 69
SSS INT'L (785 "Come and Get It")........8-15 69

SOUL, Sharon

Singles: 7-inch

CORAL (62487 "Let Me Get to Know You")........10-20 66
CORAL (62505 "Just How Long Can I Go On")........10-20 66
WILD DEUCE (1001 "How Can I Get to You")........15-25 65

SOUL AGENTS

Singles: 7-inch

CAMEO (350 "Seventh Son")........10-15 65
INTERPHON (7702 "Mean Woman Blues")........10-15 64

SOUL BENDERS

Singles: 7-inch

MALA (596 "Seven and Seven Is")........5-10 68
PHANTASM (2530 "Hey Joe")........10-15 67
PHANTASM (2568 "Seven and Seven Is")........10-15 67

Picture Sleeves

PHANTASM (2530 "Hey Joe")........30-40 67
Member: Aris Hampers.

SOUL BROTHERS

Singles: 7-inch

TARX (1004 "Love at First Sight")........40-60 63

SOUL BROTHERS

Singles: 7-inch

BLUE CAT (107 "Keep It Up")........10-20 65
BRUNSWICK (55397 "She Put a Hurtin' on Me")........5-10 69
D-TOWN (1069 "Heartaches")........5-10 '60s
MERCURY (72575 "Good Lovin' Never Hurt")........8-12 66
MERCURY (72632 "My Only Reason for Living")........8-12 66
SEG-WAY (101 "Tell It Like It Is")........15-20 61
WAND (125 "Notify Me")........10-20 62
Member: Sam Gary.
Also see SAM & BILL

SOUL BROTHERS INC.
(Soul Bros. Inc.)

Singles: 7-inch

GOLDEN EYE (1001 "Pyramid")........200-225
COMMONWEALTH UNITED (3012 "That Love Feeling")........5-10 70
SALEM (500 "Teardrops")........25-35
S.B.I........10-15
Member: George Brown.

SOUL BROTHERS SIX *P&R '67*

Singles: 7-inch

ATLANTIC (2406 "Some Kind of Wonderful")........25-35 67
ATLANTIC (2456 "You Better Check Yourself")........15-25 67
ATLANTIC (2535 "Your Love Is Such a Wonderful Love")........15-25 68
ATLANTIC (2592 "Somebody Else Is Loving My Baby")........15-25 69
ATLANTIC (2645 "Drive")........15-25 69
GRT (116 "Can You Feel the Vibrations")........5-10 76
(Canadian.)
FINE ("Stop Hurting Me")........200-300 65
(Selection number not known.)
LYDELL (746 "Don't Neglect Your Baby")........100-150 66

PHIL-L.A. OF SOUL (360 "You Gotta Come a Little Closer") ... 5-10 73
PHIL-L.A. OF SOUL (365 "Lost the Will to Live") ... 5-10 74
Members: John Ellison; Von Elle Benjamin; Sam Armstrong; Charles Armstrong; Lester Peleman; Moses Armstrong.

SOUL CHILDREN
P&R/LP '69

Singles: 12-inch

STAX ... 4-8 78-79

Singles: 7-inch

EPIC ... 4-6 75-76
STAX ... 4-8 68-74

LPs: 10/12-inch

EPIC ... 8-10 76
STAX ... 10-25 69-79
Members: Anita Louis; Shelbra Bennett; John Colbert; Norman West.
Also see BLACKFOOT, J.D.

SOUL CITY

Singles: 7-inch

GOODTIME (801 "Everybody Dance") ... 10-20 66
MERCURY (72735 "I Shot for the Moon") ... 10-20 67

SOUL CLAN
P&R '68

Singles: 7-inch

ATLANTIC (2530 "Soul Meeting") ... 8-12 68

Picture Sleeves

ATLANTIC (2530 "Soul Meeting") ... 10-15 68

LPs: 10/12-inch

ATCO ("Soul Meeting") ... 15-25 68
(Selection number not known.)
Members: Solomon Burke; Arthur Conley; Don Covay; Ben E. King; Joe Tex.
Also see BURKE, Solomon
Also see CONLEY, Arthur
Also see COVAY, Don
Also see KING, Ben E.
Also see TEX, Joe

SOUL EXPRESS

Singles: 7-inch

EXPRESS (8843 "Jeanette") ... 25-35 68

SOUL FINDERS

LPs: 10/12-inch

CAMDEN (2170 "Soul Music") ... 10-20 67
CAMDEN (2239 "Soul Man") ... 10-20 68

SOUL 4

Singles: 7-inch

RINGO (4321 "Misery") ... 10-15 65

SOUL GENTS
(Soul Generation)

Singles: 7-inch

EBONY SOUNDS ... 5-10 72-74
FROS RAY (Except 2707) ... 8-15 68-71
FROS-RAY (2707 "If I Should Win Your Love") ... 30-40 69

LPs: 10/12-inch

EBONY SOUNDS ... 10-15 72

SOUL IMPACTS

Singles: 7-inch

ECCO ... 10-15
S.I.M. (32669 "Here's Some Dances") ... 10-15 '60s

SOUL INCORPORATED

Singles: 7-inch

JOLI (075 "It Really Doesn't Matter Now") ... 40-60 65
SOCK (1002 "Funky Lady") ... 8-10 68
Also see SULLIVAN, Niki

SOUL INCORPORATED
(Soul Inc.)

Singles: 7-inch

BOSS (9920 "60 Miles High") ... 15-25 67
COUNTERPOINT ("Love Me When I'm Down") ... 10-20 68
FRATERNITY (962 "Don't You Go") ... 8-12 66
LAURIE (3430 "Love Me When I'm Down") ... 5-10 68
RONDO ... 5-10 69
Members: Jimmy Orton; Wayne Young; Frank Bugbee; Jim Settle; Marvin Maxwell.

SOUL INCORPORATED
(Soul Inc.)

Singles: 7-inch

EMBLEM (101 "What Goes Up Must Come Down") ... 300-400

LPs: 10/12-inch

EMBLEM (106 "Live! at the Cellar, Charlotte, N.C.") ... 250-350
Members: Eddie Zommerfeld; Freddie Pugh; Pete Tolio; Edgar Smith; Skip Davis; Robbie Robinson.

SOUL MESSENGERS

Singles: 7-inch

PHIL'S (1020 "That Girl") ... 75-125

SOUL NOTES

Singles: 7-inch

WAY OUT (1001 "How Long Will It Last") ... 10-20 68
WAY OUT (1006 "I Got Everything I Need") ... 15-25 69

SOUL PLEASERS

Singles: 7-inch

LIVING LEGEND (102 "I Found a Love") ... 15-25 65

SOUL PROCEDURES

Singles: 7-inch

FIVE-O (505 "Caution") ... 15-25 69
FIVE-O (506 "But What Is This Feeling") ... 100-150 69

SOUL RUNNERS
(Charles Wright & Watts 103rd Street Rhythm Band)

Singles: 7-inch

MO SOUL (101 "Grits n' Cornbread") ... 30-40 66
Also see WRIGHT, Charles, & Watts 103rd Street Rhythm Band

SOUL SEARCHERS

Singles: 7-inch

POLYDOR ... 4-6 75
SUSSEX ... 5-8 72-74

LPs: 10/12-inch

SUSSEX (7020 "We the People") ... 15-25 73
SUSSEX (8030 "Salt of the Earth") ... 40-50 74
Members: Chuck Brown; John Ewell; Frank Wellman.

SOUL SEEKERS

Singles: 7-inch

REVELATION ... 10-15
WESTCHESTER (266 "Boom Boom") ... 10-20 67
WESTCHESTER (272 "Glitter & Gold") ... 10-20 67

SOUL SET

Singles: 7-inch

BB (4012 "Flunky-Flunky") ... 5-10 67
BI-ME (7683 "Will You Ever Learn") ... 35-45
GOODTIME (1 "Call On Me") ... 10-20 66
JOHNSON (737 "Love Love Love") ... 5-10 67
JOHNSON (738 "For You Love") ... 5-10 67

LPs: 10/12-inch

JOHNSON (1001 "Soul Set") ... 15-25 67

SOUL SETTERS

Singles: 7-inch

ONACREST (503 "Out O' Sight") ... 15-25 66

SOUL SHAKERS

Singles: 7-inch

LOMA (2027 "Cold Letter") ... 10-20 66
LOMA (2047 "It's Love") ... 20-30 66

SOUL SISTERS
P&R '64

Singles: 7-inch

GUYDEN (2066 "Warm-Up") ... 10-20 62
KAYO (5101 "I Can't Let Him Go") ... 10-20 63
SUE (5 "Foolish Dreamer") ... 8-10 68
SUE (10-005 "Good Time Tonight") ... 10-15 64
SUE (107 "Loop De Loop") ... 10-15 64
SUE (111 "Just a Moment Ago") ... 10-15 64
SUE (130 "The Right Time") ... 10-15 65
SUE (140 "Some Satisfaction") ... 10-15 66
SUE (148 "So Much Love") ... 10-15 67
SUE (799 "I Can't Stand It") ... 10-20 64
VEEP (1291 "You Got 'Em Beat") ... 8-10 68

LPs: 10/12-inch

SUE (1022 "I Can't Stand It") ... 35-50 64
Members: Theresa Cleveland; Ann Gissendanner.

SOUL SOCIETY

Singles: 7-inch

DOT (17136 "Sidewinder") ... 5-10 68
SHOWCO ("What Cha Gonna Do") ... 8-12 67
(Selection number not known.)
SHOWCO (001 "Knock on Wood") ... 8-12 67

LPs: 10/12-inch

DOT (25842 "Satisfaction") ... 10-20 68

SOUL SOUNDS

Singles: 7-inch

JUNE (21228 "Lost in a Dream") ... 10-20 66

LPs: 10/12-inch

SUNSET (5249 "Best of the Soul Hits") ... 10-15 69

SOUL STIRRERS

Singles: 78 rpm

ALADDIN ... 15-25 53
SPECIALTY (300 series) ... 10-20 50-51

Singles: 7-inch

CHECKER ... 4-8 65-71
SAR ... 5-10 59-64
SPECIALTY (800 series) ... 15-25 51-56
(Black vinyl.)
SPECIALTY (800 series) ... 25-45 '50s
(Red vinyl.)

LPs: 10/12-inch

CHESS (10063 "Tribute to Sam Cooke") ... 8-12 71
SPECIALTY (Except 2106) ... 6-12 69-75
SPECIALTY (2106 "Soul Stirrers") ... 15-25 59
Members: Sam Cooke; Johnnie Taylor; James Carr; James Phelps.
Also see CARR, James
Also see COOKE, Sam
Also see PHELPS, James
Also see TAYLOR, Johnnie

SOUL SUPERIORS

Singles: 7-inch

SOUL BEAT (107 "Trust in Me Baby") ... 10-20

SOUL STOPPERS

Singles: 7-inch

CAPP-MATT (601 "Let's Sit Down") ... 30-50 66
(Reportedly, 500 made.)
Members: Johnny Matthews; Lenny Goldberg.

SOUL SURFERS / Delicates

Singles: 7-inch

CHALLENGE (59267 "Home from Camp") ... 10-15 63
Also see DELICATES
Also see JAN & DEAN / Soul Surfers
Also see WALLACE, Jerry / Soul Surfers

SOUL SURVIVORS

Singles: 7-inch

DOT (16793 "Look at Me") ... 20-30 65
DOT (16830 "Snow Man") ... 10-20 66
(Same number used on a Twigs release.)
Members: Gene Chalk; Pat Shanahan; Allen Kemp; Bob Webber.
Also see NELSON, Rick
Also see SUGARLOAF

SOUL SURVIVORS
P&R/LP '67

Singles: 7-inch

ATCO ... 5-10 68-70
CRIMSON ... 5-10 67-68
DECCA (32080 "Shakin' with Linda") ... 40-60 67
PHILA. INT'L ... 4-6 76
TSOP ... 4-6 74-75

LPs: 10/12-inch

ATCO (277 "Take Another Look") ... 15-20 69
CRIMSON (502 "When the Whistle Blows") ... 20-25 67
TSOP ... 8-10 75
Members: Richard Ingui; Charles Ingui; Kenny Jeremiah; Chuck Trois; Paul Venturini.

SOUL TRIPPERS

Singles: 7-inch

PROVIDENCE (415 "King Bee") ... 15-25 66
Also see OUTSIDERS

SOUL TWINS

Singles: 7-inch

BACK BEAT (599 "She's the One") ... 8-12 69
KAREN (1531 "Mr. Pitiful") ... 25-35 67
KAREN (1533 "Quick Change Artist") ... 25-35 67
KAREN (1535 "Just One Look") ... 10-20 67

SOUL TWISTERS

Singles: 7-inch

ROMAT (1002 "Swinging on a Grapevine") ... 15-25 '60s

SOULATIONS

Singles: 7-inch

CEI (126 "Will You Be Mine") ... 75-125 '60s

SOULBENDERS

Singles: 7-inch

MALA (596 "7 and 7 Is") ... 8-12 67
PHANTASM (2530 "Hey Joe") ... 15-25 67
PHANTASM (2568 "7 and 7 Is") ... 15-25 67

Picture Sleeves

PHANTASM (2530 "Hey Joe") ... 20-30 67
Also see PEDESTRIANS / Association / Five Americans / Soulbenders

SOULFUL STRINGS
LP '67

Singles: 7-inch

CADET (5540 "Message to Michael") ... 4-8 66
CADET (5559 "Paint It Black") ... 4-8 67
CADET (5576 "Burning Spear") ... 4-8 67
CADET (5607 "The Stripper") ... 4-8 68
CADET (5617 "Jericho") ... 4-8 68
CADET (5633 "Listen Here") ... 4-8 69
CADET (5654 "A Love Song") ... 4-8 69

LPs: 10/12-inch

CADET ... 5-10 67-73

SOULS OF SLAIN

Singles: 7-inch

RICKSHAW (101 "7 and 7 Is") ... 15-25 '60s

SOULTONES

Singles: 7-inch

VALISE (1900 "You & Me Baby") ... 10-20

SOUND APPARATUS

Singles: 7-inch

BLACK & BLUE (901 "Travel Agent Man") ... 15-20 69

SOUND BARRIER

Singles: 7-inch

ZOUNDS (1004 "My Baby's Gone") ... 30-50 67
UNITED AUDIO (90411 "Greasy Heart") ... 10-20 69

Picture Sleeves

UNITED AUDIO (90411 "Greasy Heart") ... 20-30 69

SOUND BREAKERS

Singles: 7-inch

RADIANT (1502 "Lover's Beach") ... 15-25 61

SOUND DEPARTMENT

Singles: 7-inch

CITE (68102 "Plain Girl") ... 15-25 68

SOUND SANDWICH

Singles: 7-inch

VIVA (615 "Apothecary Dream") ... 10-20 67
VIVA (625 "Mr. Sunshine Man") ... 10-20 67

SOUND SYSTEM

Singles: 7-inch

ROMAT (1001 "Take a Look at Yourself") ... 15-25 67

SOUND VENDOR

Singles: 7-inch

LIQUID STEREO (25 "Mister Sun") ... 10-15 69

SOUNDALIKES

Singles: 7-inch

LITTLE SISTER ("Broken Hearted") ... 20-30
(Selection number not known.)

SOUND-MASTERS

Singles: 7-inch

JULET (102 "I Want You to Be My Baby") ... 50-75 '60s

SOUNDS

Singles: 78 rpm

MODERN ... 10-15 55

Singles: 7-inch

MODERN (975 "So Unnecessary") ... 40-50 55
(Red or maroon label.)
MODERN (975 "So Unnecessary") ... 25-35 55
(Blue label.)
MODERN (981 "Sweet Sixteen") ... 40-50 55
(Maroon label.)
MODERN (981 "Sweet Sixteen") ... 10-20 55
(Black label.)
Also see BYRD, Bobby
Also see DEL-VIKINGS / Sonnets

SOUNDS

Singles: 7-inch

HOP-TEL (1002 "Billy Boy Hop") ... 10-12 59
QUEEN (24008 "Judy, I Love You So") ... 8-12 61
SARG (172 "Life") ... 15-25 60
SARG (181 "My Pillow of Dreams") ... 15-25 61

SOUNDS
Singles: 7-inch
SUNGLOW (126 "Little Joe") 20-30 67

SOUNDS FOUR
Singles: 7-inch
SAINTMO (203 "Hey Girl") 30-40 68

SOUNDS, INC.
(Sounds Incorporated)
Singles: 7-inch
LIBERTY... 10-20 64-65
UA 5-10 70-71

SOUNDS LIKE US
Singles: 7-inch
FONTANA (1570 "Outside Chance")....... 40-60 67
JILL ANN (101 "Outside Chance")........... 40-60 66
SOMA (8108 "It Was a Very Good Year") 20-25 67

SOUNDS OF TIME
Singles: 7-inch
ENGLISH ("Tranquility") .... 10-20 '60s
(Selection number not known.)
Picture Sleeves
ENGLISH ("Tranquility") .... 15-25 '60s

SOUNDS ORCHESTRAL *P&R/LP '65*
Singles: 7-inch
JANUS...4-8 '60s
PARKWAY...5-8 65-67
LPs: 10/12-inch
PARKWAY.. 10-15 65-67

SOUNDS UNLIMITED
Singles: 7-inch
ABC-PAR (10803 "Nobody But You")...... 10-15 66

SOUNDS UNLIMITED
Singles: 7-inch
DUNWICH (157 "A Girl As Sweet As You") 10-20 67
Also see MASON PROFFIT

SOUNDS UNLIMITED
Singles: 7-inch
SOLAR (101 "Keep Your Hands Off")...... 10-20 '60s

SOUNDTRACKS
Singles: 7-inch
PENTHOUSE (101 "Wise Men").............. 40-50

SOUNDTRIP
Singles: 7-inch
PIECE (1011 "Someday")......................... 15-25 67

SOUP
Singles: 7-inch
TARGET (1005 "Big Boss Man") 10-20 69
LPs: 10/12-inch
ARF ARF (1 "Soup") 75-100 70
BIG TREE.. 10-20 71
Members: Doug Yankus; Dave Faas; Rob Griffith; Roger Jerry.
Also see WHITE DUCK

SOUP GREENS
Singles: 7-inch
GOLDEN RULE (5000 "Like a Rolling Stone") 15-25 65

SOURCE, Pete
(With the Driftwoods; with Good Intentions; Pete Sorce)
Singles: 7-inch
COUNT (1002 "I'm Too Young for Love") 20-30 59
FAN JR. (5080 "I'm Too Young for Love")... 10-20 63
Also see CATALINAS
Also see DRIFTWOODS

SOUTH, Joe *P&R '58*
(With the Believers)
Singles: 7-inch
A&M (922 "Yo Yo")...................................5-10 68
ALL WOOD (402 "Just Remember You're Mine").. 10-20 62
APT (25084 "Deep Inside Me")................8-12 65
CAPITOL..4-8 67-75
COLUMBIA (43893 "Backfield in Motion")..8-12 67
COLUMBIA (44218 "Fool in Love")............8-12 67
FAIRLANE (21006 "You're the Reason"). 10-20 61
FAIRLANE (21010 "Masquerade")........... 10-20 61
FAIRLANE (21015 "Slippin' Around") 10-20 62
ISLAND...4-6 75
MGM (13145 "Same Old Song")................8-12 63
MGM (13196 "Concrete Jungle")................8-12 63
MGM (13276 "Little Queenie")....................8-12 64
NRC (002 "I'm Snowed").........................50-100 58
NRC (022 "What a Night").......................10-20 59
NRC (041 "Little Bluebird")......................10-20 60
NRC (053 "Tell the Truth") 10-20 60
NRC (065 "Let's Talk It Over") 10-20 61
NRC (5000 "The Purple People Eater Meets the Witch Doctor")...................................15-25 58
NRC (5001 "One Fool to Another")...........15-25 58
SOUTHERN TRACKS (2018 "River Dog")...3-5 90
LPs: 10/12-inch
ACCORD..5-10 81
CAPITOL..8-15 68-72
ISLAND..8-12 75
MINE..8-12 70
Also see CHIPS

SOUTH, Joe / Dells
LPs: 10/12-inch
APPLE (3377 "Come Together")..............15-25 71
Also see DELLS

SOUTH, Joe / Billy Joe Royal
LPs: 10/12-inch
NASHVILLE (2092 "You're the Reason") ...5-10 '70s
Also see ROYAL, Billy Joe
Also see SOUTH, Joe

SOUTH 40
Singles: 7-inch
METROBEAT (4450 "Good Lovin' ") 15-20 67
METROBEAT (4457 "Goin' Someplace Else")...15-20 68
LPs: 10/12-inch
METROBEAT (1000 "Live at Someplace Else")...30-50 68
Member: David Waggoner.
Also see AARDVARKS
Also see CROW
Also see RAVE-ONS

SOUTHBOUND FREEWAY
Singles: 7-inch
RED ROOSTER (67001 "Psychedelic Used Car Lot Blues") 15-25 67
ROULETTE (4739 "Psychedelic Used Car Lot Blues") 10-15 67
SWAN (4272 "Crazy Shadows")................8-12 67
TERA SHIRMA (67001 "Psychedelic Used Car Lot Blues")...20-30 67
(First issue.)

SOUTHERN COMFORT *LP '71*
Singles: 7-inch
CAPITOL..4-8 71-72
COTILLION 5-8 69
LPs: 10/12-inch
BRYLEN 5-8
CAPITOL...10-12 71
COLUMBIA...10-12 70
SIRE 12-15 69
Also see MATTHEWS' SOUTHERN COMFORT

SOUTHERN HARMONAIRES
(Larks)
Singles: 78 rpm
APOLLO (200 series) 10-20 50
Singles: 7-inch
APOLLO (529 "I'm So Glad") 20-30 58
Also see LARKS

SOUTHERN NEGRO QUARTETTE
(Southern Quartet)
Singles: 78 rpm
COLUMBIA...25-50 21-24

SOUTHERN SONS QUARTET
Singles: 78 rpm
TRUMPET..30-50 50-52
Members: Roscoe Robinson; David Smith; Earl Ratliff; Cliff Givens.

SOUTHERN SOUL
Singles: 78 rpm
TRUMPET..15-25 53
Singles: 7-inch
TRUMPET (206 "Rock in a Dreamy Land")..25-35 53

SOUTHERN TORNADOES
Singles: 78 rpm
UNITED 5-10 52
Singles: 7-inch
UNITED (117 "Satisfied") 10-20 52
UNITED (123 "How About You")...............10-20 52

SOUTHERN TRAVELERS
Singles: 78 rpm
BIG TOWN...15-25 54
Singles: 7-inch
BIG TOWN (112 "Peace in the Land") 25-50 54

SOUTHLANDERS
Singles: 7-inch
CASTLE (503 "The Wiggle")......................50-75

SOUTHWEST F.O.B. *P&R '68*
Singles: 7-inch
GPC (1945 "Smell of Incense")................10-20 68
HIP (8002 "Smell of Incense") 5-10 68
HIP (8009 "Nadine") 5-10 69
HIP (8015 "As I Look At You") 5-10 69
HIP (8022 "Feelin' Groovy")........................5-10 69
LPs: 10/12-inch
HIP (7001 "Smell of Incense") 25-35 69
Members: Dan Seals; John Ford Coley; Shane Keister.
Also see THESE FEW

SOUTHWIND
Singles: 7-inch
BLUE THUMB..4-8 69-71
VENTURE (616 "Get On Board the Train")..5-10 68
VENTURE (621 "You've Been On My Mind")..5-10 68
LPs: 10/12-inch
BLUE THUMB..10-15 69
VENTURE...10-15 68

SOUTHWINDS
Singles: 7-inch
FURY (1017 "Build Me a Cabin")..............10-15 58

SOUVENIRS
Singles: 78 rpm
DOOTO (412 "So Long Daddy")...............20-30 57
Singles: 7-inch
DOOTO (412 "So Long Daddy")...............30-40 57

SOUVENIRS
(With the Larry Lucie Orchestra)
Singles: 7-inch
INFERNO (2001 "I Could Have Danced All Night")..50-75 62

SOVINE, Red *C&W '55*
(With the Girls)
Singles: 78 rpm
DECCA (Except 30239) 5-10 54-57
DECCA (30239 "Juke Joint Johnny") 10-15 57
MGM...5-10 50-53
Singles: 7-inch
CHART...4-6 71-75
DECCA (Except 29825 & 30239) 5-10 54-66
DECCA (29825 "If Jesus Came to Your House")..10-20 56
DECCA (30239 "Juke Joint Johnny") 20-30 57
GUSTO...3-6 77-80
MGM..8-15 50-53
RCA..4-8 62
RIC...4-6 64-65
STARDAY (Except 500 thru 800 series) 4-6 70-78
STARDAY (500 thru 800 series)...............4-8 60-70
EPs: 7-inch
MGM...10-20 57
LPs: 10/12-inch
CMI...5-10 77
CHART...5-10 72-74
DECCA (4445 "Red Sovine")...................15-25 64
DECCA (4736 "Country Music Time")......10-20 66
GUSTO/STARDAY.......................................5-10 78
LAKE SHORE...8-12
MGM (3465 "Red Sovine")......................30-40 57
METRO (618 "Farewell, So Long, Goodbye")..10-15 67
NASHVILLE..6-12 70
POWER PAK ....5-10 '80s
RIC..10-15 65
SOMERSET/ STEREO FIDELITY 8-12 63
STARDAY (Except 100 series) 10-20 65-76
STARDAY (100 series) 15-25 61-62
VOCALION...8-12 68
Also see BEAVERS, Clyde, & Red Sovine
Also see FELTS, Narvel / Red Sovine / Mel Tillis
Also see MULLICAN, Moon / Cowboy Copas / Red Sovine
Also see REEVES, Del / Red Sovine
Also see SHEPARD, Jean

SOVINE, Red, & Goldie Hill *C&W '55*
Singles: 78 rpm
DECCA (29411 "Are You Mine") 5-10 55
Singles: 7-inch
DECCA (29411 "Are You Mine") 10-20 55

SOVINE, Red, & Webb Pierce *C&W '56*
Singles: 78 rpm
DECCA..5-10 56
Singles: 7-inch
DECCA (29755 "Why Baby Why") 10-20 56
DECCA (29876 "Little Rosa"/"Hold Everything")..10-20 56
Also see PIERCE, Webb
Also see SOVINE, Red

SOWARDS, Don
Singles: 7-inch
RENA (2004 "Gonna Get Tough")............50-75

SPACEMEN *P&R '59*
(Space Men)
Singles: 7-inch
ALTON (254 "The Clouds").......................15-20 59
ALTON (300 "Movin' Up") 10-15 60
FELSTED (8578 "Blast Off").....................10-15 59
JAMECO (2005 "Space Walkin' ")..............5-10 65
JUBILEE (5368 "Round Up")....................10-15 59
LPs: 10/12-inch
ROULETTE...15-25 64-66

SPACEMEN
Singles: 7-inch
BIG SOUND (303 "Modman")...................25-50 66
BIG SOUND (309 "Same Old Grind") 25-50 66
GEMINI (5566 "Spacewalk")......................25-50 65
Picture Sleeves
BIG SOUND (309 "Same Old Grind") 40-60 66
Members: Gene Fondow; Bob Jilek; Tom McMahon; John Schuster; Loren Skaare.

SPADACHENE, Smith
Singles: 7-inch
L&Q (100 "Beatle Twist")..........................15-25 64

SPADE, Tony, & His Band
Singles: 7-inch
BACK BEAT (505 "What's Gwyne [sic] On") 50-100 58

SPADES
Singles: 7-inch
DOMINO (100 "You Mean Everything to Me") 100-150 57
LIBERTY (55118 "You Mean Everything to Me") 15-25 57

SPADES
Singles: 7-inch
MAJOR (1007 "Close to You")..................40-50 58

SPADES
(Thirteenth Floor Elevators)
Singles: 7-inch
ZERO (10001 "I Need a Girl")...............100-200 65
ZERO (10002 "You're Gonna Miss Me")..200-300 65
(A different recording than later issued by the Thirteenth Floor Elevators.)
Also see THIRTEENTH FLOOR ELEVATORS

SPADES
Singles: 7-inch
REBEL (500 "Hey Hey").............................75-125

SPAIN, Dick, & Rogue Valley Boys
Singles: 7-inch
OASIS (1001 "Straw Broom Boogie") ..100-200 '50s

SPAIN, Johnny, & Flames
Singles: 7-inch
BACK BEAT (516 "I'm in Love") 40-60 58

SPAK, Emil, & Encores
Singles: 7-inch
WGW (3004 "Stuck Up").........................75-100 61

SPANGLER, Randy
Singles: 7-inch
MART (112 "Rock 'N Roll Baby")..........100-200 58

SPANIELS P&R '57
(Spanials)

Singles: 78 rpm

CHANCE (1141 "Baby It's You")........... 50-100 53
VEE-JAY (101 "Baby, It's You") 100-200 53
VEE-JAY (103 "Bells Ring Out") 50-100 53
VEE-JAY (107 "Goodnite Sweetheart, Goodnite").. 75-100 54
(Mistakenly credits the "Spanials.")
VEE-JAY (107 "Goodnite Sweetheart, Goodnite").. 50-75 54
(Properly credits the "Spaniels.")
VEE-JAY (116 thru 200 series)............... 25-75 54-58

Singles: 7-inch

BUDDAH (153 "Maybe")..................................5-8 69
CALLA (172 "Fairy Tales") 5-10 70
CANTERBURY (101 "Peace of Mind") 4-6 74
CHANCE (1141 "Baby It's You")......... 200-300 53
(Black vinyl.)
CHANCE (1141 "Baby It's You")......... 600-800 53
(Red vinyl.)
CLASSIC ARTISTS (138 "All the Places I've Been")..5-8 95
(Black vinyl. 300 made.)
CLASSIC ARTISTS (138 "All the Places I've Been")..8-10 95
(Yellow vinyl. Promotional issue only. 100 made.)
COLLECTABLES..3-5 '80s
ERIC ....4-6 '70s
JUKEBOX TREASURES (409 "Bells Ring Out")...3-5 93
LOST NITE...4-6
NORTH AMERICAN (101 "Fairy Tales") 5-8 70
(First issue.)
NORTH AMERICAN (102 "Stand in Line")...4-6 70
NORTH AMERICAN (3114 "Money Blues") .4-8 '70s
OWL (328 "Little Joe") 4-6 74
SKYLARK (582 "So Deep Within")..............5-10 79
(Black or red vinyl.)
TRIP...4-6
VEE-JAY (101 "Baby It's You") 500-750 53
(Black vinyl. Maroon label.)
VEE-JAY (101 "Baby It's You") 3000-4000 53
(Red vinyl.)
VEE-JAY (101 "Baby It's You") 10-15 61
(Black label.)
VEE-JAY (103 "Bells Ring Out") 200-300 53
(Black vinyl.)
VEE-JAY (103 "Bells Ring Out") 750-1000 53
(Red vinyl.)
VEE-JAY (107 "Goodnite Sweetheart, Goodnite").. 125-150 54
(Black vinyl. Credited to the Spanials.)
VEE-JAY (107 "Goodnite Sweetheart, Goodnite").. 50-75 54
(Black vinyl. Credited to Spaniels.)
VEE-JAY (107 "Goodnite Sweetheart, Goodnite").. 300-400 54
(Red vinyl. No "Trade Mark Reg." on label.)
VEE-JAY (107 "Goodnite Sweetheart, Goodnite")..8-12 93
(Red vinyl, Vee-Jay commemorative issue. Has "Trade Mark Reg." on label.)
VEE-JAY (116 "Play It Cool") 50-75 54
(Black vinyl.)
VEE-JAY (116 "Play It Cool") 500-750 54
(Red vinyl.)
VEE-JAY (131 "Do-Wah") 40-60 55
(Black vinyl.)
VEE-JAY (131 "Do-Wah") 500-750 55
(Red vinyl.)
VEE-JAY (154 "You Painted Pictures") ... 50-75 55
(First pressing has incorrect title.)
VEE-JAY (154 "Painted Pictures") 25-35 55
(Mistakenly credits the "Spanials." Shows corrected title.)
VEE-JAY (178 "False Love")................. 75-125 56
VEE-JAY (189 "Dear Heart").................. 75-125 56
VEE-JAY (201 "Red Sails in the Sunset")... 200-300 '60s
(40 made.)
VEE-JAY (202 "Since I Fell for You")... 100-200 56
VEE-JAY (229 thru 328) 30-50 56-58
VEE-JAY (342 "People Will Say We're in Love").. 75-125 59
VEE-JAY (350 "I Know")......................... 30-40 60

Picture Sleeves

VEE-JAY (107 "Goodnite Sweetheart, Goodnite")...2-4 93
(Commemorative issue with this title although no specific artist or titles are shown.)

LPs: 10/12-inch

LOST NITE (19 "The Spaniels")...............10-20 81
(10-inch LP. Red vinyl. 1000 made.)
LOST NITE (137 "The Spaniels") ....15-20 '70s
VEE-JAY (1002 "Goodnite, It's Time to Go")...200-300 59
(Maroon label.)
VEE-JAY (1002 "Goodnite, It's Time to Go")...75-100 61
(Black label.)
VEE-JAY (1024 "Spaniels")..................200-250 60
(Back cover has liner notes, but does not picture other Vee-Jay LPs.)
VEE-JAY (1024 "Spaniels")..................100-125 63
(Back cover pictures 15 other Vee-Jay LPs.)
UPFRONT...10-20
Members: Pookie Hudson; Jerry Gregory; Ernest Warren; Willie Jackson; Opal Courtney; James Cochran; Carl Rainge; Don Porter; Andy Magruder; Bill Carey.
Also see HUDSON, Pookie

SPANKY & OUR GANG P&R/LP '67

Singles: 7-inch

EPIC 4-6 75-76
MERCURY 5-8 67-69
PHILCO (19 "Making Every Minute Count"/"Bird Avenue")...10-20 67
("Hip Pocket" flexi-disc.)

Picture Sleeves

MERCURY 8-12 67-68

EPs: 7-inch

MERCURY (90 "Like to Get to Know You")..10-20 67
(Promotional issue only. Issued with paper sleeve.)

LPs: 10/12-inch

EPIC 8-10 75
MERCURY 10-20 67-71
RHINO...5-8 86
Members: Elaine "Spanky" McFarlane; Lefty Baker; Malcolm Hale; Nigel Pickering; John Seiter.

SPANN, Otis

Singles: 7-inch

CHECKER (807 "It Must Have Been the Devil")..500-600 55
EXCELLO (2329 "Blues for Hippies").........5-10 73

LPs: 10/12-inch

ARCHIVE OF FOLK MUSIC 10-15 68
BARNABY 10-12 70
BLUE HORIZON..10-12 70
BLUES TIME..10-12 70
BLUESWAY 10-20 67-73
CANDID (9001 "Otis Spann Is the Blues") 75-100 61
CRY...10-15
LONDON 10-15 68-69
PRESTIGE 8-10 69
VANGUARD..8-10 70
Also see CLAPTON, Eric
Also see COTTON, James
Also see DIDDLEY, Bo
Also see DIXON, Willie
Also see GUY, Buddy
Also see PAGE, Jimmy
Also see ROGERS, Jimmy
Also see SMITH, George
Also see WATERS, Muddy
Also see WELLS, Junior
Also see WILLIAMSON, Sonny Boy

SPANN, Otis, & Fleetwood Mac

Singles: 7-inch

BLUE HORIZON (304 "Walkin' ")...............8-12 70

LPs: 10/12-inch

BLUE HORIZON (4802 "Biggest Thing Since Colossus") 15-25 70
Also see FLEETWOOD MAC

SPANN, Otis, & Robert Lockwood Jr.

LPs: 10/12-inch

BARNABY...10-20 72
Also see LOCKWOOD, Robert, Jr.
Also see SPANN, Otis

SPARK PLUGS

LPs: 10/12-inch

SUTTON..10-15 '60s

SPARKELS

Singles: 7-inch

OLD TOWN (1160 "Try Love")...............50-100 64

SPARKLERS

Singles: 7-inch

TAMPA (124 "Dreamy Eyes") 100-150 57

SPARKLERS FOUR

Singles: 7-inch

RUBU ("My Heart Still Remembers").........8-12 62
(No selection number used.)
Members: George Nauman; John Christmas; Jay Riness; Jim Passell.

SPARKLES

Singles: 7-inch

POPLAR (119 "We Got It").......................15-20 63

SPARKLES

Singles: 7-inch

CARON (94 "The U.T.") 10-15 62
HICKORY (1364 "The Hip")......................10-20 65
HICKORY (1390 "Something That You Said") 10-20 66
HICKORY (1406 "Jack and the Beanstalk")..10-20 66
HICKORY (1443 "No Friend of Mine")......10-20 67
HICKORY (1474 "Hipsville 29 BC").........10-20 67

SPARKLETONES

Singles: 7-inch

PAGEANT (604 "Just One Chance")........30-40 63

SPARKLETTES

Singles: 7-inch

BELMONT (4007 "Doodling Around") 10-15 62

SPARKS

Singles: 78 rpm

HULL (723 "Danny Boy").......................300-400 57
HULL (724 "Adreann")..............................50-75 57

Singles: 7-inch

HULL (723 "Danny Boy").......................500-750 57
HULL (724 "Adreann")..............................50-75 57

SPARKS

Singles: 7-inch

ARWIN (114 "Robin Redbreast").............10-15 58
CARLTON (522 "The Genie")....................8-12 59
DECCA (30378 "Ol' Man River")..............10-15 57
DECCA (30509 "A Cuddle and a Kiss") ...10-15 57
DECCA (30974 "La Macarena") 8-12 59
PETAL (1610 "Do Me, Do Me Right").........5-10 64

SPARKS LP '74

Singles: 12-inch

ATLANTIC...4-6 84
ELEKTRA..5-10 79

Singles: 7-inch

ATLANTIC...3-5 82-84
BEARSVILLE (0006 "Wonder Girl").............4-6 72
COLUMBIA 3-5 78
ELEKTRA..3-5 79
FINE ARTS 3-5 88
ISLAND 4-6 73-76
RCA..3-5 81

Picture Sleeves

ATLANTIC...3-5 82-83

LPs: 10/12-inch

ATLANTIC...5-10 82-84
BEARSVILLE 12-15 72-73
COLUMBIA (Black vinyl) 8-10 77
COLUMBIA (Colored vinyl) 12-15 77
ELEKTRA..8-10 79
ISLAND 8-10 74-76
RCA...5-10 81
Members: Ron Mael; Russell Mael.

SPARKS, Ernie

Singles: 7-inch

LAKE (710 "Vacation Twist") 8-12 62

SPARKS, Milton
(With Sammy Lowe & Orchestra)

Singles: 7-inch

HUNT (320 "A Certain Smile") 20-30 58
VULCAN (137 "A Certain Smile") 200-300 58
(First issue.)
Session: Delroys.
Also see DELROYS
Also see LOWE, Sammy, Orchestra

SPARKS, Randy
(Randy Sparks Three)

Singles: 7-inch

AIR 3-5
COLUMBIA (43138 "At the End of the Rainbow")..5-10 64
MGM...4-6 71
VERVE (10177 "Make Her Mine")..............5-10 59
VERVE (10196 "Big Night") 5-10 60
VERVE (10225 "Julianne") 5-10 60
VERVE (10240 "Fly By Night")....................5-10 61

Picture Sleeves

COLUMBIA (43138 "At the End of the Rainbow")..5-10 64

LPs: 10/12-inch

BUBBLE UP (25339 "Music to Drink Bubble Up By") 30-50 61
(Promotional issue only.)
DISNEYLAND (1332 "Hang Your Hat on the Wind")..8-10 69
MGM...8-10 71
VERVE (2126 "Walkin' the Low Road") ...20-25 60
VERVE (2143 "Randy Sparks Three") 20-25 60
Also see NEW CHRISTY MINSTRELS
Also see RIVERS, Johnny / Ricky Nelson / Randy Sparks

SPARKS OF RHYTHM

Singles: 78 rpm

APOLLO...50-75 55

Singles: 7-inch

APOLLO (479 "Don't Love You Anymore")..150-200 55
APOLLO (481 "Stars Are in the Sky") ..150-200 55
APOLLO (541 "Handy Man") 30-40 60
Member: Jimmy Jones.
Also see JONES, Jimmy

SPARROW, Johnny R&B '50
(With His Bows & Arrows)

Singles: 78 rpm

GOTHAM 10-15 53-54
MELFORD (253 "Sparrow's Flight") 15-20 49
"X"..5-10 55

Singles: 7-inch

GOTHAM (7282 "Sparrow in the Barrel"). 15-25 53
GOTHAM (7292 "Paradise Rock") 20-30 54
(Colored vinyl.)
"X" (0103 "Sparrow's Nest").....................10-15 55

SPARROWS

Singles: 78 rpm

DAVIS..75-100 56
JAY-DEE 100-150 53

Singles: 7-inch

DAVIS (456 "Love Me Tender")...........250-300 56
JAY-DEE (783 "Tell Me Baby")............400-500 53
JAY-DEE (790 "I'll Be Loving You")..300-400 54
Also see BLENDERS / Sparrows

SPARROWS

LPs: 10/12-inch

ELKAY (3009 "Mersey Sound")................25-35 64

SPARROWS
(Jack London & the Sparrows; The Sparrow)

Singles: 7-inch

CAPITOL (72203 "If You Don't Want My Love") 25-35 65
(Canadian.)
CAPITOL (72210 "Dream on Dreamer")..25-35 65
(Canadian.)
CAPITOL (72229 "Sparrows & Daisys")...25-35 65
(Canadian.)
CAPITOL (72257 "Hard Times with the Law")..25-35 65
(Canadian.)
COLUMBIA (43755 "Tomorrow's Ship")... 15-25 66
(Credits "The Sparrow.")
COLUMBIA (43960 "Down Goes Your Love")..10-20 67
LAURIE (3285 "If You Don't Want My Love") 10-15 66

Picture Sleeves

COLUMBIA (43755 "Tomorrow's Ship")...25-50 66
(Credits "The Sparrow.")

LPs: 10/12-inch

CAPITOL (6115 "Jack London and the Sparrows")..550-650 65
(Canadian.)

Members: Jack London; Jerry Edmonton; Dennis Edmonton; Nick St. Nicholas; Goldy McJohn; Art Ayre; John Kay.
Also see STEPPENWOLF

SPARTANS
(With Banjo Bill & His Rhythm Kings)
Singles: 78 rpm
CAPRI....100-200 54
Singles: 7-inch
CAPRI (7201 "Faith, Hope and Charity")....750-1250 54

SPARTANS
Singles: 7-inch
AUDIO INT'L (102 "One More Chance").. 15-25 61

SPARTANS
Singles: 7-inch
PRINCESS (53 "Mr. Moto")....15-25 63

SPARTANS
Singles: 7-inch
WEB (1 "Can You Waddle")....10-20 63

SPATS P&R '64
("Featuring Dick Johnson")
Singles: 7-inch
ABC-PAR (10585 "Gator Tails and Monkey Ribs"....10-15 64
ABC-PAR (10600 "She Kissed Me Last Night"....5-10 64
ABC-PAR (10640 "Billy, the Blue Grasshopper")....5-10 65
ABC-PAR (10711 "Go Go Yamaha")....5-10 65
ABC-PAR (10790 "Scoobee Doo")....5-10 66
ENITH (1268 "Gator Tails and Monkey Ribs")....20-25 64
(First issue.)
JANO (1550 "Sleepy Hollow Mama")....10-20 67
LPs: 10/12-inch
ABC-PAR (502 "Cookin' with the Spats") 20-25 65
Member: Dick Johnson.

SPEARS, Merle, & Treats
Singles: 7-inch
ATLANTIC (2243 "I Want to Know")....5-10 64
WHIT (711 "Gonna Move")....100-200

SPEARS, Russell
Singles: 7-inch
YOLK ("Beggin' Time")....150-250
(Selection number not known.)

SPECIALS
Singles: 7-inch
MARC (103 "Kissin' Like Lovers")....15-25 63

SPECIALS
Singles: 7-inch
SATCH (512 "You Stood Me Up")....100-150 '60s

SPECK, Darrell
Singles: 7-inch
ALVIC (500 "That's How Much I Love You")....100-200

SPECK & DOYLE – THE WRIGHT BROTHERS
Singles: 7-inch
SYRUP BUCKET (1000 "Big Noise, Bright Lights")....600-800
Members: Speck Wright; Doyle Wright.

SPECKULATIONS
Singles: 7-inch
SPECK (6129 "Hula Hoop")....100-200 58

SPECTACLE
(Cellophane Spectacle)
Singles: 7-inch
FISH (2353 "Going Back to Miami")....5-10 68
SPECTACULAR (61968 "It's Not Unusual")....5-10 68
(At least one source gives 9006 as the selection number.)

SPECTOR, Phil
Singles: 7-inch
PHILLES ("Thanks for Giving Me the Right Time")....250-350 65
(No selection number used. Promotional issue for dee jays only.)
Also see HARVEY, Phil
Also see SPECTORS THREE

SPECTOR, Ronnie P&R '71
(With the Ronettes; with E Street Band)
Singles: 12-inch
EPIC/CLEVELAND INT'L (350 "Say Goodbye to Hollywood")....10-15 77
(Promotional issue only.)
Singles: 7-inch
ALSTON (3738 "It's a Heartache")....5-10 78
APPLE (1832 "Try Some, Buy Some")....10-20 71
BUDDAH (384 "Lover Lover")....8-12 73
BUDDAH (408 "I Wonder What He's Doing")....8-12 74
EPIC/CLEVELAND INT'L (50374 "Say Goodbye to Hollywood")....5-10 77
COLUMBIA....3-5 87
POLISH....4-6 80
TOM CAT (10380 "You'd Be Good for Me")....5-10 76
(Black vinyl.)
TOM CAT (10380 "You'd Be Good for Me")....10-20 76
(Colored vinyl. Promotional issue only.)
W.B./SPECTOR (0409 "When I Saw You")....5-10 76
Picture Sleeves
APPLE (1832 "Try Some, Buy Some")....15-20 71
COLUMBIA....4-6 87
EPIC/CLEVELAND INT'L (50374 "Say Goodbye to Hollywood")....20-25 77
LPs: 10/12-inch
POLISH (808 "Siren")....10-15 80
Also see MONEY, Eddie, & Ronnie Spector
Also see RONETTES
Also see SPRINGSTEEN, Bruce
Also see VERONICA

SPECTORS THREE
Singles: 7-inch
TREY (3001 "I Know Why")....25-35 59
TREY (3005 "My Heart Stood Still")....25-35 60
Member: Phil Spector.
Also see SPECTOR, Phil
Also see TEDDY BEARS

SPECTRES
Singles: 7-inch
N-JOY (1020 "High Stepper")....8-12 67
SALEM (004 "So Near to Me")....10-20 '60s

SPECTRUM
Singles: 7-inch
DCR (10203 "For You")....10-20 '60s
RCA (0295 "Glory")....5-10 69
RCA (9593 "London Bridge Is Coming Down")....5-10 68
UDELL (61219 "Bald Headed Woman")...10-20 '60s

SPECTRUM
Singles: 7-inch
SOMETHIN' GROOVY (500 "Confetti")....30-40 67

SPECTRUMS
Singles: 7-inch
KNIGHT (4969 "Wine Wine Wine")....15-25 '60s
MERCURY (72438 "Our Meeting Place")...5-10 65

SPEEDO & CADILLACS
(Cadillacs)
Singles: 7-inch
JOSIE (876 "Tell Me Today")....30-40 60
Members: Earl Carroll; Roland Martinez; Kirk Davis; Ronnie Bright.
Also see CADILLACS

SPEEDO & IMPALAS
(Impalas)
Singles: 7-inch
CUB (9066 "All Alone")....10-15 60
Also see IMPALAS

SPEEDO & PEARLS
Singles: 7-inch
JOSIE (865 "Who Ya Gonna Kiss")....15-25 59
Member: Earl Carroll.
Also see CADILLACS
Also see SPEEDO & CADILLACS

SPEEDY
(With the Alka-Seltzers)
Singles: 7-inch
FEATURE (501 "Donna")....15-25 65
TEE PEE (47/48 "Cathy Lost Her Love Today"/"I Wonder What She's Doing Tonight")....15-25 68

Members: Jerry Lariden; Bob Kenison; Bruce Benson; Jim Donovan; Jim Bisbee; Bob Bellard; Jim Lombard; Lance Massey.

SPEEDY & REVERBS
Singles: 7-inch
REVERB (51 "100 Proof")....15-25 '60s

SPEEKS, Ronnie C&W '81
(With His Elrods)
Singles: 7-inch
DIMENSION....3-5 81
KING (5548 "What Is Your Technique")...40-50 61
PALETTE (5094 "Mister Glenn")....25-35 62
RED HED (1004 "If You Tell a Lie")....75-100 60
RED HED (1006 "Lover's Express")....75-100 60
Also see RAINER, Chris, & Elrods

SPEIDELS
("Vocal by Bill Bagby"; Spidels)
Singles: 7-inch
CROSLEY (201 "Dear Joan")....50-75 58
(Has "Crosley" all in same size letters.)
CROSLEY (201 "Dear Joan")....25-35 58
(Has "Crosley" in letters of different sizes.)
MINARET (112 "I'll Catch a Rainbow")....15-20 63
(Credits: "Spidels.")
MINARET (112 "I'll Catch a Rainbow")....10-15 63
(Credits: "Speidels.")
MONTE CARLO (101 "Oh Baby")....150-200 60
PROVIDENCE (418 "Dream Girl")....5-10 65

SPEKTRUM
Singles: 7-inch
SOMETHIN' GROOVY (500 "I Was a Fool")....15-25 '60s

SPELLBINDERS P&R '65
Singles: 7-inch
COLUMBIA (43384 "For You")....5-10 65
COLUMBIA (43522 "Chain Reaction")....5-10 66
COLUMBIA (43611 "Long Lost Love")....5-10 66
COLUMBIA (43830 "Help Me")....5-10 66
DATE (1556 "I Believe")....10-15 67
MIRAMAR (115)....10-15 65
(Exact title not known.)
LPs: 10/12-inch
COLUMBIA (2514 "Magic of the Spellbinders")....15-25 66
(Monaural.)
COLUMBIA (9314 "Magic of the Spellbinders")....15-25 66
(Stereo.)
Members: Bob Shivers; Jimmy Wright; Ben Grant; McArthur Munford; Elouise Pennington.

SPELLMAN, Benny P&R '62
Singles: 7-inch
ACE (630 "Roll on Big Wheel")....10-20 61
ALON....5-10 65-66
ATLANTIC (2291 "I Feel Good")....5-10 65
MINIT....10-20 60-63
SANSU (462 "But If You Love Her")....5-10 67
WATCH (6332 "Please Mr. Genie")....5-10 64
LPs: 10/12-inch
BANDY (70018 "Benny Spellman")....10-15 '70s
Also see K-DOE, Ernie
Also see THOMAS, Irma / Ernie K-Doe / Showmen / Benny Spellman

SPELLMAN, Jimmy
Singles: 78 rpm
DOT....15-25 57
VIV....10-20 56
Singles: 7-inch
DOT (15564 "Here I Am")....15-25 57
DOT (15607 "Doggonit")....15-25 57
REV (3521 "Ladder of Love")....15-25 58
VIK (0320 "Deep Love")....15-25 58
VIV (1000 "Give Me Some of Yours")....15-25 56
VIV (1002 "It's You, You, You")....15-25 56
VIV (1004 "No Escape")....15-25 56

SPENCE, Alexander "Skip"
Singles: 7-inch
SUNDAZED (153 "All My Life")....3-5 2000
LPs: 10/12-inch
COLUMBIA (9831 "Oar")....50-100 69

SPENCE, Cornell
("Music by The Play Boys; Background Vocal – The Elites")
Singles: 7-inch
HOWARD (505 "Beams of Heaven")....50-75 60

SPENCER, Bob
Singles: 78 rpm
EPIC....5-10 55-56
Singles: 7-inch
APOLLO (531 "Open Arms")....10-15 59
EPIC (9139 "Roll, Hotrod, Roll")....10-20 55
EPIC (9176 "Rock and Roll Lullabye")....10-20 56

SPENCER, Carl
(With the Mellows; with Sammy Lowe Orchestra)
Singles: 7-inch
CANDLELIGHT (1012 "Farewell, Farewell")....75-125 57
RUST (5104 "Cover Girl")....25-50 66
SOUTHSIDE (1001 "Till My Ship Comes In")....15-25 62
SOUTHSIDE (1002 "Prayer")....40-50 62
WREN (306 "One Last Kiss")....15-25 60
Also see MELLOWS

SPENCER, Don
Singles: 7-inch
20TH FOX (440 "XL5")....10-20 63

SPENCER, Richard, & Winstons
Singles: 7-inch
METROMEDIA (166 "Say Goodbye to Daddy")....5-10 69
Also see WINSTONS

SPENCER, Sammy, & Tilts
Singles: 7-inch
TOWNHOUSE (3 "Sweet Love")....10-20 59
TOWNHOUSE (10 "Happy Jack")....50-75

SPENCER, Sonny P&R '59
Singles: 7-inch
MEMO (17984 "Gilee")....15-25 59
MUSIC HALL (24002 "Hold My Hand")....15-25
ONDA (111 "Bessie Lou")....15-25
Session: Rainbows.
Also see RAINBOWS

SPENCER & SPENCER P&R '59
(With the Sonia Pryor Choir)
Singles: 7-inch
ARGO (5331 "Russian Bandstand")....15-25 59
GONE (5053 "Stagger Lawrence")....15-25 59
Members: Dickie Goodman; Mickey Shorr.
Also see GOODMAN, Dickie
Also see SHORR, Mickey, & Cutups

SPERRY, Steve P&R '77
Singles: 7-inch
CUCA (1008 "Our Summer Love")....40-50 60
MERCURY (73905 "Flame")....4-6 77
Also see LANGDON, Jim, Trio

SPIC & SPAN
Singles: 7-inch
LEN....10-15 61
V-TONE (218 "Slippin' & Slidin' ")....10-15 61

SPICES
Singles: 7-inch
CARLTON (480 "Tell Me Little Girl")....500-600 59

SPIDELLS
Singles: 7-inch
CORAL (62508 "Pushed Out of the Picture")....25-50 66
CORAL (62531 "Don't You Forget That You're My Baby")....15-25 67
MONZA (1112 "Find Out What's Happening")....10-20 64
MONZA (1123 "Hmmm, with Feeling")....10-20 65

SPI-DELLS
Singles: 7-inch
SPI-DELLS/LITTLE TOWN (575 "Never Ever")....20-30 66

SPI-DELLS
Singles: 7-inch
TYME (263 "Take Me As I Am")....30-40

SPIDELS
Singles: 7-inch
CHAVIS (1035 "You Know I Need You")..10-20 62

SPIDER & CRABS
Singles: 7-inch
VERITAS (42168 "Some Kind of Magic")...5-10 68
(Some copies shown as by the Rye; some show both artists.)

SPIDER SAM

Singles: 78 rpm

ATLANTIC (980 "After Midnight")............ 25-35 50

Members: Van Walls; Brownie McGhee.

Also see McGHEE, Brownie

Also see WALLS, Van

SPIDER, SNAKE & EEL

Singles: 7-inch

L.A. BEAT (6054 "Only a Boy")............... 15-25 '60s

SPIDERS *R&B '54*

Singles: 78 rpm

IMPERIAL.. 25-75 54-57

Singles: 7-inch

IMPERIAL (5265 "I Didn't Want to Do It") 40-50 53

IMPERIAL (5280 "Tears Began to Flow").. 75-100 54

IMPERIAL (5291 "I'm Searching")........... 40-50 54

IMPERIAL (5305 "Real Thing")............... 30-40 54

IMPERIAL (5318 "She Keeps Me Wondering").. 30-40 54

IMPERIAL (5331 "That's Enough")......... 30-40 55

IMPERIAL (5344 "Am I the One")........... 30-40 55

IMPERIAL (5354 "Bells in My Heart")...... 50-75 55

(Red label.)

IMPERIAL (5354 "Bells in My Heart")...... 10-15 57

(Black label.)

IMPERIAL (5366 "Is It True").................. 50-75 55

(Blue label.)

IMPERIAL (5366 "Is It True").................. 15-25 55

(Red label.)

IMPERIAL (5376 "Don't Pity Me")........... 15-25 56

IMPERIAL (5393 "Dear Mary")................ 30-40 56

IMPERIAL (5405 "Goodbye").................. 30-40 56

IMPERIAL (5423 "Honey Bee")............... 30-40 56

IMPERIAL (5618 "I Didn't Want to Do It").. 15-25 59

IMPERIAL (5714 "You're the One")......... 10-15 60

IMPERIAL (5739 "Witchcraft")................ 10-15 61

OWL.. 4-6 73

LPs: 10/12-inch

IMPERIAL (9142 "I Didn't Want to Do It").. 250-500 61

Members: Hayward "Chuck" Carbo; Leonard "Chick" Carbo; Joe Maxon; Matthew West; Oliver Howard.

Also see CARBO, Chick

Also see CARBO, Chuck

Also see CARBO, Leonard

SPIDERS

Singles: 7-inch

MASCOT (112 "Why Don't You Love Me").. 750-1000 65

SANTA CRUZ (003 "Don't Blow Your Mind").. 350-400 66

Members: Vince "Alice Cooper" Furnier; John Speer; Glen Buxton; Dennis Dunaway; Mike Bruce.

Also see COOPER, Alice

SPIDERS

Singles: 7-inch

LAWN (234 "Run Boy Run")........................ 8-10 64

Also see WRAY, Link

SPIEDELS

Singles: 7-inch

CROSLEY (201 "Dear Joan")................. 50-75 58

(Original issue has grainy vinyl.)

CROSLEY (201 "Dear Joan")................. 10-20 58

PROVIDENCE (418 "Dream Girl")............. 5-10 66

SPIKE DRIVERS

Singles: 7-inch

OM 1000 (1676 "High Time")................. 20-30 66

REPRISE (0535 "High Time").................. 10-15 66

REPRISE (0558 "Strange Mysterious Sounds")... 10-15 67

SPINDLES

Singles: 7-inch

ABC-PAR (10802 "To Make You Mine").. 10-20 66

ABC-PAR (10850 "Ten Shades of Blue") 15-25 66

SPINDRIFTS

(Featuring Freddy Cannon; with the Downbeats)

Singles: 7-inch

ABC-PAR (9904 "Cha Cha Doo")........... 25-35 58

HOT (1000 "Cha Cha Doo").................. 50-100 58

Also see CANNON, Freddy

SPINNER, Alice

Singles: 7-inch

HUGO (11722 "Sweet Promises")........... 10-20 65

SPINNERS

("Vocal Don Barksdale")

Singles: 7-inch

RHYTHM (125 "Marvella")...................400-600 58

SPINNERS

Singles: 7-inch

CAPITOL (3955 "Love's Prayer")............15-25 58

END (1045 "Bird Watchin'")...................75-125 58

(Gray label.)

END (1045 "Bird Watchin'").....................30-40 59

(Multi-Color label.)

Member: Don Barksdale.

SPINNERS

Singles: 7-inch

CRYSTALETTE (736 "Boomerang").........15-25 60

(Reissued as *Surf Stomp*, by the Crestriders and as *The Lion*, by Duke Mitchell.)

Also see CRESTRIDERS

Also see MITCHELL, Duke

SPINNERS *P&R '61*

(Spinners / Harvey)

Singles: 7-inch

ATLANTIC...3-6 72-85

MOTOWN (1067 thru 1136)......................8-15 64-68

MOTOWN (1155 "In My Diary")......... 500-1000 69

MOTOWN (1235 "Bad Bad Weather")..........4-6 73

TRI-PHI (1001 "That's What Girls Are Made For")..20-30 61

TRI-PHI (1004 "Love [I'm So Glad] I Found You")..15-25 61

TRI-PHI (1007 "What Did She Use")........15-25 62

TRI-PHI (1013 "I've Been Hurt")..............15-25 62

V.I.P. (25050 "In My Diary")...................10-20 69

V.I.P. (25054 "Message from a Black Man")..10-20 70

V.I.P. (25057 "It's a Shame")....................5-10 70

V.I.P. (25060 "We'll Have It Made")...........5-10 71

(Black vinyl.)

V.I.P. (25060 "We'll Have It Made").........15-25 71

(Red vinyl. Promotional issue only.)

LPs: 10/12-inch

ATLANTIC (Except QD-18141)..................5-15 73-84

ATLANTIC (QD-18141 "Pick of the Litter")..25-35 75

MOTOWN (Except 639)...........................5-10 73-82

MOTOWN (639 "Original Spinners").........20-40 67

PICKWICK..8-10 76

V.I.P. (405 "Second Time Around").........20-40 70

Members: Bobby Smith; Henry Fambrough; Bill Henderson; Pervis Jackson; G.C. Cameron; Philippe Wynne; Reese Palmer; Jim Knowland; Ed Edwards; Chester Simmons.

Also see ABBA / Spinners / Firefall / England Dan & John Ford Coley

Also see HARVEY

Also see LOE & JOE

Also see MARQUEES

Also see SMITH, Bobby

Also see WARWICK, Dionne, & Spinners

SPINNERS

LPs: 10/12-inch

TIME (52092 "Party – My Pad [After Surfin']")..20-30 63

SPINNERS

Singles: 7-inch

LAWSON (324 "Beetle Mania")................10-20 64

SPINNING WHEEL

Singles: 7-inch

CENTURY (36668 "Funky Alien")..............5-10 '60s

SPIRAL STARECASE *P&R/LP '69*

Singles: 7-inch

COLUMBIA..4-8 69-70

LPs: 10/12-inch

COLUMBIA (9852 "More Today Than Yesterday")..15-20 69

COLUMBIA (10172 "More Today Than Yesterday")..8-12

Members: Pat Upton; Dick Lopes; Vinny Parello; Bob Raymond; Harvey Kaplan.

SPIRALS

Singles: 7-inch

CAPITOL (4084 "The Rockin' Cow")........15-20 58

SPIRALS

Singles: 7-inch

INDIGO (500 "Baby You Just Wait").....300-600 60

SPIRALS

Singles: 7-inch

ADMIRAL (913 "Forever and a Day").500-1000 61

(First issue.)

SMASH (1719 "Forever and a Day")......50-100 61

SPIRALS

Singles: 7-inch

END (1112 "Hungry for You")..................10-15 62

SPIRALS

Singles: 7-inch

LUXOR (1012 "My Humble Prayer").....150-250 62

SPIRES, Big Boy

(With His Trio; Arthur Spires)

Singles: 78 rpm

CHANCE...300-500 53

Singles: 7-inch

CHANCE (1137 "About to Lose My Mind")..800-1200 53

(Colored vinyl. With John Lee Henley.)

Also see JOHN LEE

SPIRES OF OXFORD

Singles: 7-inch

MY (2923 "But You're Gone")..................15-25 67

SPIRIT *LP '68*

Singles: 12-inch

MERCURY...4-6 84

Singles: 7-inch

EPIC...4-6 70-74

MERCURY...4-6 75-76

ODE..4-8 68-69

POTATO...3-5 78

RHINO...3-5 81

Picture Sleeves

EPIC...4-8 74

POTATO...3-5 78

LPs: 10/12-inch

EPIC...8-12 70-73

MERCURY (Except 818514)....................10-15 75-77

MERCURY (818514 "Spirit of '84")............5-8 84

ODE (44003 "Spirit").............................20-25 68

(Monaural.)

ODE (44004 "Spirit").............................15-20 68

(Stereo.)

ODE (44014 "The Family That Plays Together")...10-20 68

ODE (44016 "Clear")..............................10-15 69

POTATO...10-15

RHINO...5-8 81

Members: Jay Ferguson; Randy California; Ed Cassidy; Mark Andes; John Locke; John Arliss.

Also see HEART

Also see RISING SONS

Also see YELLOW BALLOON

SPIRIT OF MEMPHIS

Singles: 78 rpm

KING...10-20 49-53

Singles: 7-inch

AUDIO LAB (22 "The 10 Commandments")....................................20-40 59

KING (4538 "That Awful Day")...............50-100 52

KING (4562 "Just to Behold His Face")..50-100 52

KING (4575 "God's Amazing Grace").....50-100 52

KING (4576 "Lord Jesus").....................50-100 52

KING (4614 "There's No Sorrow")...........50-75 53

PEACOCK (1710 thru 1847)...................20-40 58-62

SPIRITS & WORM

Singles: 7-inch

A&M (1104 "Fanny Firecracker").............15-25 69

LPs: 10/12-inch

A&M (4229 "Spirits & Worm")..............150-250 69

SPIRITS OF BLUE LIGHTNING

Singles: 7-inch

LAVENDER (2009 "Love Muscle")..........10-20 '60s

SPIRITS OF RHYTHM

Singles: 78 rpm

BLACK & WHITE (23 "She Ain't No Saint")..15-25 45

Members: Georgie Vann; Leo Watson; Leonard Feather; Teddy Bunn; Ulysses Livingstone; Red Callender.

SPIRITUAL HARMONIZERS

Singles: 7-inch

GLORY (4004 "Do You Know Him")........15-25

SPIRITUAL TRAVELERS

Singles: 78 rpm

EXCEL (103 "Remember Me")................15-20 55

Singles: 7-inch

EXCEL (103 "Remember Me")................25-50 55

SPITFIRES

Singles: 7-inch

JARO (77004 "Catfish")..........................10-15 59

SPIVEY, Joyce, & Melvettes

Singles: 7-inch

OLIMPIC (254 "Angel")...........................10-15 65

SPIVEY, Ken

Singles: 7-inch

SMOKE (100 "Woke Up This Morning")....40-60 59

SPIVEY, Victoria

Singles: 7-inch

QUEEN VEE SOUVENIR (1 "Brown Skin Warmup")...10-20 62

Also see JOHNSON, Lonnie

Also see THREE KINGS & A QUEEN

SPLASHERS

Singles: 7-inch

KAYO (928 "The Girl in the Bikini").........40-50 58

(Same number used on a Debutantes release.)

SPLENDORS

Singles: 7-inch

LOVE MUSIC (1003 "Golden Years").........3-5 83

TAURUS (101 "Golden Years")............150-200 60

TAURUS (102 "Who Can It Be")..............30-50 61

SPLENDORS

Singles: 7-inch

JANO (004 "Puddin' Tain")......................40-60 62

KARATE (520 "Please Don't Go")............50-75 66

SPLIT ENDS

Singles: 7-inch

CFP (4 "Rich with Nothin'")......................25-50 66

SPLIT ENZ *P&R/LP '80*

Singles: 7-inch

A&M (Except 2339 & AMS-8128)................3-5 80-84

A&M (2339 "One Step Ahead")..................4-6 82

("Laser Etched Single.")

A&M (AMS-8128 "Shark Attack")...........75-100 82

(Laser etched, shaped picture disc. Promotional issue only.)

Picture Sleeves

A&M...3-5 80-82

EPs: 7-inch

A&M (4848 "I Don't Want to Dance")........15-25 81

(Picture disc. Promotional issue only.)

LPs: 10/12-inch

A&M...5-10 80-84

CHRYSALIS...8-10 77

Members: Tim Finn; Neil Finn.

SPOKES

Singles: 7-inch

SCORPIO (401 "Mini-Bike")....................20-25 '60s

SPOKESMEN *P&R '65*

Singles: 7-inch

DECCA...5-10 65-66

WINCHESTER (1001 "Mary Jane")............5-10 67

LPs: 10/12-inch

DECCA (4712 "Dawn of Correction").......25-30 65

Members: Johnny Madara; David White; Roy Gilmore.

Also see MADARA, Johnny

SPONGY & DOLLS

Singles: 7-inch

BRIDGEVIEW (7001 "It Looks Like Love")..20-30 66

SPONTANEOUS COMBUSTION

Singles: 7-inch

HARVEST...4-6 72-73

ROD (103 "Love Comes & Goes")...........10-15 68

LPs: 10/12-inch

CAPITOL..10-12 72

FLYING DUTCHMAN (102 "Come and Stick Your Head In")..12-15 69

HARVEST...10-12 72

SPONTANES

Singles: 7-inch

BEAVER...4-6 '60s

CASINO (4797 "Share My Name")...........15-20 '60s

ECLIPSE...5-10 '60s

U.A. (50269 "Ain't No Big Thing")................5-10 68
LPs: 10/12-inch
HIT ATTRACTIONS (7999 "Solid Soul").. 100-150 '60s
(Selection number not known.)

SPOOKY TOOTH *LP '69*
(Gary Wright's Spooky Tooth)
Singles: 7-inch
A&M (1110 "Feelin' Bad")...........................5-10 69
A&M (1144 "That Was Only Yesterday")....5-10 69
MALA (587 "Sunshine Help Me")................5-10 68
MALA (12013 "Love Really Changed Me")..5-10 68
MALA (12022 "Do Right People") 5-10 68
ISLAND...4-6 72
LPs: 10/12-inch
A&M 10-15 69-73
ACCORD..5-10 82
BELL (6019 "Spooky Tooth") 15-20 68
ISLAND...8-10 73-74
Members: Gary Wright; Mike Harrison; Luther Grosvenor.
Also see WRIGHT, Gary

SPORTCOATS
Singles: 7-inch
SPC ("Starfire") 40-60
(No selection number used.)
TIBER (5657 "Fluorescent Sea") 50-75

SPORTSMEN
(With Pep Boys: Manny, Moe & Jack; with Bob Bain's Music)
Singles: 78 rpm
KEY (503 "Hot Rod Hop")........................ 10-15 55
KEY (513 "Me & My Shadow")................. 15-25 56
Singles: 7-inch
A (104 "Dreaming").................................. 10-20 59
KEY (503 "Hot Rod Hop")........................ 20-30 55
KEY (513 "Me and My Shadow")............ 20-30 56
RONROY (1004 "Santa's Toy Express")....5-10 62

SPORTTONES
("With Rhythm Acc.")
Singles: 7-inch
MUNICH (101 "In My Dreams").......... 750-1000 59

SPOTLIGHTERS
(With Bob Thompson & Band)
Singles: 78 rpm
IMPERIAL (5342 "It's Cold")..................... 40-60 55
Singles: 7-inch
ALADDIN (3436 "Please Be My Girlfriend")... 150-200 58
ALADDIN (3441 "This Is My Story")......... 40-50 58
IMPERIAL (5342 "It's Cold").................. 75-125 55
(Black vinyl.)
IMPERIAL (5342 "It's Cold")................ 300-400 55
(Purple vinyl.)
Also see THOMPSON, Bob, Orchestra

SPOTLITES
Singles: 7-inch
CATALINA (1001 "All Kinds of Dancing Going On") 50-75 59

SPOTLYTERS
Singles: 7-inch
CROWN CITY (101 "If I Didn't Care")....... 50-75

SPOTNICKS
Singles: 7-inch
ATCO (6261 "Orange Blossom Special") ...5-10 63
FELSTED (8649 "Old Spinning Wheel").. 20-30 62
LAURIE (3241 "I'm Goin' Home")................5-10 64
LAURIE (3260 "Endless Sleep")..................5-10 65
LAURIE (3297 "Just Listen to My Heart")...5-10 65
LAURIE (3333 "Drum Diddley")...................5-10 66

SPRIGGS, Walter
(Walter Spreegs; with Five Echoes)
Singles: 78 rpm
APOLLO (445 "I Don't Want You").......... 10-15 53
ATCO (609 "I'm Gonna Love You") 10-20 56
BLUE LAKE (109 "I'm Not Your Fool Anymore") 20-30 55
Singles: 7-inch
APOLLO (445 "I Don't Want You").......... 15-30 53
ATCO (609 "I'm Gonna Love You") 10-20 56
ATCO (6112 "You're Movin' Me")............ 10-15 58
BLUE LAKE (109 "I'm Not Your Fool Anymore") 100-150 55
Also see FIVE ECHOES
Also see SPRINGER, Walter
Also see WILSON, Wally

SPRING
Singles: 7-inch
GAMBLE (4017 "Fever") 5-8 71
U.A. (50848 "Now That Everything's Been Said")...10-15 71
U.A. (50907 "Good Time")........................25-30 72
LPs: 10/12-inch
U.A. 15-25 72
Members: Marilyn Wilson; Diane Rovell.
Also see AMERICAN SPRING
Also see HONEYS

SPRINGER, Walter
Singles: 7-inch
KAISER (398 "The Sunshine of Your Smile")..30-40 59
KAISER (401 "Everything")......................30-40 59
Also see SPRIGGS, Walter

SPRINGERS
Singles: 7-inch
UES-THAD (423 "Every Night and Day") .15-25 66
WAY OUT (2799 "Last Heartbreak") 20-30 66

SPRINGFIELD, Dusty *P&R/LP '64*
Singles: 7-inch
ATLANTIC...4-8 68-71
CASABLANCA...3-5 82
DUNHILL...4-6 73
PHILIPS (40162 "I Only Want to Be with You")..8-12 63
PHILIPS (40180 "Stay Awhile")..................8-12 64
PHILIPS (40207 "Wishin' and Hopin' ") 8-12 64
PHILIPS (40229 thru 40553)....................5-10 64-68
20TH FOX...3-5 80
U.A. 4-6 77-79
Picture Sleeves
PHILIPS...5-10 64-67
ATLANTIC..5-10 68
EPs: 7-inch
PHILIPS (2700 "The Look of Love") 5-10 67
("Stereo Compact 6.")
LPs: 10/12-inch
ATLANTIC..10-15 69-70
CASABLANCA..5-8 82
DUNHILL...8-10 73
PHILIPS...12-20 64-67
U.A. 5-10 78-79
WING..10-15 68
Also see HONDELLS / Dusty Springfield
Also see PET SHOP BOYS & DUSTY SPRINGFIELD
Also see SPRINGFIELDS

SPRINGFIELD, Rick *P&R/LP '72*
Singles: 12-inch
RCA..4-6 83-84
Singles: 7-inch
CAPITOL...4-6 72-73
CHELSEA...4-6 76
COLUMBIA...4-6 74
MERCURY...3-5 84-85
RCA..3-5 81-85
Picture Sleeves
CAPITOL...4-8 72
MERCURY...3-5 84
RCA..3-5 81-88
LPs: 10/12-inch
CAPITOL (11000 series) 15-20 72-73
CAPITOL (16000 series) 5-10 81
CHELSEA..8-12 76
COLUMBIA (KC-32000 series) 10-15 73
COLUMBIA (PC-32000 series) 5-8
MERCURY...5-8 84
RCA..5-10 80-88

SPRINGFIELD, Rick, & Randy Crawford *P&R '84*
Singles: 7-inch
RCA..3-5 84
Picture Sleeves
RCA..3-5 84
Also see SPRINGFIELD, Rick

SPRINGFIELD RIFLE
(Springfield Rifles)
Singles: 7-inch
ABC (10878 "Bears")...................................5-10 66
BURDETTE..5-10 68-69
JERDEN...5-10 68-69
TOWER (455 "I Love Her") 5-10 68
LPs: 10/12-inch
BURDETTE (5159 "Springfield Rifle") 15-25 69
Members: Terry Afdem; Jeff Afdem; Harry Wilson; Bob Perry; Joe Cavender.
Also see AFDEM, Jeff, & Springfield Flute
Also see DYNAMICS

SPRINGFIELDS *C&W/P&R '62*
Singles: 7-inch
PHILIPS...8-12 62-63
LPs: 10/12-inch
PHILIPS...15-25 62-63
Members: Dusty Springfield; Tom Springfield; Tim Field.
Also see SPRINGFIELD, Dusty

SPRINGS, Kenneth
(Kenny Springs & Scat Cats)
Singles: 7-inch
COLUMBIA (41999 "Please Tell Me Now") 10-20 61
SPOT...10-20
ZOOM (203 "Please Tell Me Now")..........10-20

SPRINGSTEEN, Bruce *P&R/LP '75*
(With the E Street Band)
Singles: 12-inch
COLUMBIA (1332 "Santa Claus Is Comin' to Town")...30-40 81
(White label. Includes sleeve. Promotional issue only.)
COLUMBIA (2007 "I'm on Fire") 20-25 85
(Red label. Black and white cover. Promotional issue only.)
COLUMBIA (2082 "Glory Days") 20-25 85
(Red label. Black and white cover. Promotional issue only.)
COLUMBIA (2174 "I'm Goin' Down")..........20-25 85
(Red label. Black and white cover. Promotional issue only.)
COLUMBIA (2233 "My Hometown")..........20-25 85
(Red label. Black and white cover. Promotional issue only.)
COLUMBIA (2543 "Bruce Springsteen & E Street Band Live, 1975-85")...................................20-25 86
(Eight track sampler. Promotional issue only.)
COLUMBIA (05028 "Dancing in the Dark")..5-8 84
COLUMBIA (05028 "Dancing in the Dark")..20-30 84
(With black and white cover. Promotional issue only.)
COLUMBIA (05028 "Dancing in the Dark")..15-25 84
(Promotional issue with color cover and gold promo stamp.)
COLUMBIA (05087 "Cover Me")...................5-8 84
COLUMBIA (05147 "Born in the USA")........4-6 84
COLUMBIA (05147 "Born in the USA")....15-20 84
(White label. Promotional issue only.)
COLUMBIA (44445 "Chimes of Freedom")..5-8 88
Singles: 7-inch
COLUMBIA (03243 "Hungry Heart")............3-5 84
COLUMBIA (04463 "Dancing in the Dark")..3-5 84
COLUMBIA (04561 "Cover Me")...................3-5 84
COLUMBIA (04680 "Born in the USA")........3-5 84
COLUMBIA (04772 "I'm on Fire")..................3-5 85
COLUMBIA (04924 "Glory Days")..................3-5 85
COLUMBIA (05603 "I'm Goin' Down")...........3-5 85
COLUMBIA (05728 "My Hometown")............3-5 85
COLUMBIA (06432 "War")...............................3-5 86
COLUMBIA (06657 "Fire")...............................3-5 87
COLUMBIA (07595 "Brilliant Disguise").......3-5 87
COLUMBIA (07663 "Tunnel of Love")............3-5 87
COLUMBIA (07726 "One Step Up")...............3-5 88
COLUMBIA (08400 series)............................3-5 88
(Columbia Hall of Fame series.)
COLUMBIA (10209 "Born to Run")...........10-15 75
COLUMBIA (10274 "Tenth Avenue Freeze-Out")...8-12 75
COLUMBIA (10763 "Prove It All Night").....8-12 78
COLUMBIA (10801 "Badlands")...................4-6 78
COLUMBIA (11391 "Hungry Heart")............3-5 80
COLUMBIA (11431 "Fade Away"/"To Be True")...15-25 81
COLUMBIA (11431 "Fade Away"/"Be True")..3-5 81
COLUMBIA (33323 "Born to Run")............8-10 76
(Red label. Columbia Hall of Fame series.)
COLUMBIA (33323 "Born to Run")..............3-5 84
(Gray label. Columbia Hall of Fame series.)
COLUMBIA (45805 "Blinded By the Light")...150-250 73
COLUMBIA (45864 "Spirit in the Night")..300-500 73
COLUMBIA (74354 "57 Channels")............3-5 92
Promotional Singles: 7-inch
COLUMBIA (2557 "War")..........................10-15 86
(Has 1:55 spoken intro on one side.)
COLUMBIA (04463 "Dancing in the Dark")..8-10 84
COLUMBIA (04561 "Cover Me") 6-10 84
COLUMBIA (04680 "Born in the USA")......6-10 84
COLUMBIA (04772 "I'm on Fire")..............6-10 85
COLUMBIA (04924 "Glory Days")..............6-10 85
COLUMBIA (05606 "I'm Goin' Down") 6-10 85
COLUMBIA (05728 "My Hometown").........6-10 85
COLUMBIA (06432 "War")..........................5-8 86
COLUMBIA (07595 "Brilliant Disguise").......5-8 87
COLUMBIA (07663 "Tunnel of Love")..........5-8 87
COLUMBIA (07726 "One Step Up")..............5-8 88
COLUMBIA (10209 "Born to Run")...........30-35 75
(With large letters on label.)
COLUMBIA (10209 "Born to Run")...........20-25 75
(With small letters on label.)
COLUMBIA (10274 "Tenth Avenue Freeze-Out")...15-20 75
COLUMBIA (10763 "Prove It All Night")...15-20 78
COLUMBIA (10801 "Badlands")...............15-20 78
COLUMBIA (11391 "Hungry Heart") 15-20 80
COLUMBIA (11431 "Fade Away")............10-15 81
COLUMBIA (45805 "Blinded By the Light")..45-55 73
COLUMBIA (45864 "Spirit in the Night")..35-45 73
Picture Sleeves
COLUMBIA (1329 "Santa Claus Is Comin' to Town")...15-20 81
(Promotional issue only.)
COLUMBIA (2557 "War")..........................10-15 86
(Sleeve for spoken intro promo.)
COLUMBIA (04463 "Dancing in the Dark")..5-10 84
COLUMBIA (04561 "Cover Me") 5-10 84
COLUMBIA (04680 "Born in the USA")..5-10 84
COLUMBIA (04772 "I'm on Fire")..............5-10 85
COLUMBIA (04924 "Glory Days")..............5-10 85
COLUMBIA (05606 "I'm Goin' Down") 5-10 85
COLUMBIA (05728 "My Hometown").........5-10 85
COLUMBIA (06432 "War")..........................4-8 86
COLUMBIA (07595 "Brilliant Disguise").......4-8 87
COLUMBIA (07663 "Tunnel of Love")..........4-8 87
COLUMBIA (07726 "One Step Up")..............4-8 88
COLUMBIA (11391 "Hungry Heart")............4-8 80
COLUMBIA (11431 "Fade Away")................4-8 81
COLUMBIA (45805 "Blinded By the Light") 300-500 73
LPs: 10/12-inch
COLUMBIA (KC-31903 "Greetings from Asbury Park")..15-20 73
COLUMBIA (PC-31903 "Greetings from Asbury Park")..8-12 75
COLUMBIA (JC-31903 "Greetings from Asbury Park")..5-8 78
COLUMBIA (KC-32432 "The Wild Innocent and the E Street Shuffle")...15-18 73
COLUMBIA (PC-32432 "The Wild Innocent and the E Street Shuffle")...10-15 73
COLUMBIA (JC-32432 "The Wild Innocent and the E Street Shuffle")..5-8 78
COLUMBIA (PC-33795 "Born to Run") 25-30 75
(Credits show Jon Landau as "John.")
COLUMBIA (PC-33795 "Born to Run") 15-20 75
(Has "Jon" correction strip applied to cover.)
COLUMBIA (PC-33795 "Born to Run") 8-12 75
(Has "Jon" correction printed on cover.)
COLUMBIA (JC-33795 "Born to Run")........5-8 78
COLUMBIA (JC-35318 "Darkness on the Edge of Town") 5-8 78
COLUMBIA (36854 "The River") 10-15 80
COLUMBIA (38358 "Nebraska")..................5-8 82
COLUMBIA (38653 "Born in the USA")........5-8 84
COLUMBIA (40558 "Bruce Springsteen & E Street Band Live, 1975-85")..................................30-40 86
(Includes 36-page booklet.)
COLUMBIA (40999 "Tunnel of Love")..........5-8 87
COLUMBIA (HC-43795 "Born to Run")....25-35 80
(Half-speed mastered.)
COLUMBIA (HC-45318 "Darkness on the Edge of Town") 40-60 81
(Half-speed mastered.)
COLUMBIA (67060 "Greatest Hits").........10-15 95
COLUMBIA (67484 "The Ghost of Tom Joad") 8-10 96

Promotional LPs
COLUMBIA (978 "As Requested Around the World") 30-40 81
COLUMBIA (1957 "Born in the USA") 20-30 84
COLUMBIA (31903 "Greetings from Asbury Park") 35-45 73
(White label.)
COLUMBIA (32432 "The Wild Innocent and the E Street Shuffle") 35-45 73
(White label.)
COLUMBIA (33795 "Born to Run") 750-1000 75
(With "script" title cover.)
COLUMBIA (33795 "Born to Run") 40-50 75
(White label.)
COLUMBIA (JC-35318 "Darkness on the Edge of Town") 30-40 78
(White label.)
COLUMBIA (PAL-35318 "Darkness on the Edge of Town") 100-150 78
(Picture disc. 200 made. Add $15 to $25 if lyric sheet is included.)
COLUMBIA (36854 "The River") 25-35 80
(White label.)
COLUMBIA (38358 "Nebraska") 15-25 82
(White label.)
COLUMBIA (38653 "Born in the USA") ... 15-20 84
(White label.)
Session: Bobby Hatfield.
Also see ADDEO, Nicky
Also see BONDS, Gary "U.S."
Also see HATFIELD, Bobby
Also see ORBISON, Roy
Also see PARKER, Graham
Also see SPECTOR, Ronnie

SPRINGSTEEN, Bruce / Jackson Browne

Singles: 12-inch
ASYLUM (11442 "Medley") 40-50 79
(45 rpm. Has plain sleeve with info sticker.)
Also see BROWNE, Jackson

SPRINGSTEEN, Bruce / Andy Pratt

Singles: 7-inch
COLUMBIA/PLAYBACK (AS-45 "Blinded By the Light") 75-100 73
(Add $40 to $50 if accompanied by booklet.)
Picture Sleeves
COLUMBIA/PLAYBACK (AS-45 "Blinded By the Light") 5-10 73

SPRINGSTEEN, Bruce / Loudon Wainwright III / Taj Mahal / Albert Hammond

Singles: 7-inch
COLUMBIA/PLAYBACK (AS-52 "The Circus Song [Recorded Live]") 75-100 73
(Add $40 to $50 if accompanied by booklet.)
Picture Sleeves
COLUMBIA/PLAYBACK (AS-52 "The Circus Song") 5-10 73
Also see MAHAL, Taj
Also see WAINWRIGHT, Loudon, III

SPRINGSTEEN, Bruce / Johnny Winter / Hollies

Singles: 7-inch
COLUMBIA/PLAYBACK (AS-66 "Rosalita") 75-100 73
(Add $40 to $50 if accompanied by booklet.)
Picture Sleeves
COLUMBIA/PLAYBACK (AS-66 "Rosalita") 5-10 73
Also see HOLLIES
Also see SPRINGSTEEN, Bruce
Also see WINTER, Johnny

SPRITES

Singles: 7-inch
PATIENCE (100 "My Picture") 25-35 62
TURRENT (103 "My Picture") 5-10 72
Members: Bobby Hendricks; Bill Pinkney; Andrew Thrasher; Gerhart Thrasher.
Also see DRIFTERS

SPROTT, Horace

LPs: 10/12-inch
FOLKWAYS (654 "Take Rocks and Gravel to Make a Solid Road") 20-30 54

SPROUTS

Singles: 7-inch
MERCURY (71727 "Why Did You Go") ... 15-20 60
RCA (7172 "Every Little Once in a While") .8-12 57
SPANGLE (2002 "Goodbye, She's Gone") 15-25 57
SPROUTS (1007 "Merciful Tears") 5-10 61

SPRUILL, Wild Jimmy

(Jimmy "Wildman" Spruill; James Spruill & His Band)
Singles: 7-inch
CEE-JAY (581 "Jumping In") 8-12 61
ENJOY (2006 "Cut and Dried") 8-12 64
EVERLAST (5004 "Jumping In") 10-15 57
EVERLAST (5017 "Scratch and Twist") 8-12 62
FIRE (1006 "Hard Grind") 15-25 59
VIM (521 "Scratchin'") 5-10 64
Also see COOPER, Horace
Also see HARRISON, Jim & Bob
Also see WALKER, Charles, & Band

SPRYTES

Singles: 7-inch
MORTICIAN (104 "Land of 1,000 Dances") 10-20 66

SPURLIN, Tommy

Singles: 7-inch
ART (131 "Heart Throb") .... 75-125 '70s
(First issue of tracks made in the mid-'50s.)
PERFECT (109 "Hang Loose") 150-250 56

SPURLING, Charles

Singles: 7-inch
KING (6077 "You'd Be Surprised") 10-15 65

SPURLING, Hank

Singles: 7-inch
HI-LITE (501 "Box Car Blues") 100-150

SPUTNIKS

Singles: 78 rpm
CLASS (217 "My Love Is Gone") 20-30 58
Singles: 7-inch
CLASS (217 "My Love Is Gone") 20-30 58
CLASS (222 "Wait a Little Longer") 15-25 58
PAM MAR (601 "My Love Is Gone") 200-300 57

SPYDELS

(Spydells)
Singles: 7-inch
ADDIT (1220 "We're in Love") 10-15 60
ASSAULT (1859/1860 "Peace of Mind"/"Change Your Mind") 5-10 63
CRACKERJACK (4001 "We'll Be Together") 8-12 61
MZ (112 "No More Teasin'") 15-25 61
Also see DOW, Johnny
Also see FINN, Gar, & Spydels

SPYRES Featuring Mark Prewitt

Singles: 7-inch
VIX (1001 "Baby, Let Me Take You Home") .... 15-25 '60s

SPYRO GYRA — P&R/LP '78

Singles: 7-inch
AMHERST (730 "Shaker Song") 3-5 78
INFINITY (50011 "Morning Dance") 3-5 79
INFINITY (50041 "Jubilee") 3-5 79
MCA 3-5 80-85
Picture Sleeves
INFINITY (50011 "Morning Dance") 3-5 79
EPs: 7-inch
INFINITY (1011 "Live Spyro Gyra") 5-10 79
(Promotional issue only. With insert. Not issued with cover.)
LPs: 10/12-inch
AMHERST 5-10 78
GRP 5-8 90-91
INFINITY 5-10 79
MCA (5000 series) 5-10 80-86
MCA (6000 series) 8-10 84-89
MCA (9004 "Morning Dance") 40-60 79
(Picture disc. Promotional issue only.)
MCA (42000 series) 5-8 87
Members: Chet Catallo; Jay Beckenstein.

SQUARE ROOT OF TWO

Singles: 7-inch
BAJA (4504 "Turned On") 30-40

SQUARES

Singles: 7-inch
BRISTOL (10001 "Davey's Drag") 15-25 59
(First issue.)
TEL (1003 "Davey's Drag") 10-15 59
Member: Dave Sanderson.

SQUEEZE — LP '80

(U.K. Squeeze)
Singles: 7-inch
A&M 3-5 79-87
Picture Sleeves
A&M 3-5 80-87
LPs: 10/12-inch
A&M (Except 3413 & 4687) 5-10 79-89
A&M (3413 "Squeeze") 10-20 72
A&M (4687 "U.K. Squeeze") 10-15 78
I.R.S. 5-8 90
Members: Chris Difford; Glenn Tilbrook; Jools Holland; Gilson Lavis; Keith Wilkinson; Andy Metcalfe.

SQUEEZER

LPs: 10/12-inch
NOW 10-12 74

SQUEEZY, John Cameron

Singles: 7-inch
PRINCESS (4022 "The Bearded Leader" [Fidel Castro]) 15-25 63

SQUIDDLY DIDDLY

LPs: 10/12-inch
HBR (2043 "Squiddly Diddly's Surfin' Surfari") 75-100 65

SQUIRES

Singles: 78 rpm
COMBO (35 "Let's Give Love a Try") 75-125 53
COMBO (42 "Oh Darling") 75-125 54
Singles: 7-inch
COMBO (35 "Let's Give Love a Try") ... 400-500 53
(Red label.)
COMBO (42 "Oh Darling") 350-450 54
(Red label.)
Members: Delmar Wilburn; Ethel Brown; Otis White; James Richardson; James Myles; Maudice Giles.

SQUIRES

Singles: 78 rpm
GUYDEN (714 "Bobby Sox Jamboree") 8-12 55
Singles: 7-inch
GUYDEN (714 "Bobby Sox Jamboree") ... 15-25 55
Also see ESQUIRE BOYS

SQUIRES

(Blue Jays; with Jackie Kelso & Orchestra)
Singles: 78 rpm
ALADDIN (3360 "Dreamy Eyes") 40-50 57
KICKS (1 "A Dream Come True") 100-200 54
MAMBO (105 "Sindy") 35-50 55
VITA 20-40 55-56
Singles: 7-inch
ALADDIN (3360 "Dreamy Eyes") 40-50 57
KICKS (1 "A Dream Come True") 500-1000 54
MAMBO (105 "Sindy") 100-150 55
(Maroon label.)
MAMBO (105 "Sindy") 50-75 55
(Black label.)
VITA (105 "Sindy") 50-75 55
VITA (113 "Sweet Girl") 50-75 55
VITA (116 "Heavenly Angel") 50-100 55
VITA (128 "Breath of Air") 50-100 56
Members: Don Bowman; Dewey Terry; Leon Washington; Chester Pipkin; Bob Armstrong; Lee Goudeau.
Also see BLUE JAYS
Also see DON & DEWEY
Also see KELSO, Jackie
Also see SMITH, Effie

SQUIRES

Singles: 7-inch
V (109 "The Sultan") 50-75 61
Also see YOUNG, Neil

SQUIRES

Singles: 7-inch
CHAN (102 "Movin' Out") 10-15 61
(First issue.)
MGM (13044 "Movin' Out") 5-10 61

SQUIRES

Singles: 7-inch
GEE (1082 "Don't Accuse Me") 40-50 62
HERALD (580 "Why Should I Suffer") 10-20 63

SQUIRES

Singles: 7-inch
BOSS (2120 "It's Time") 100-200 63

SQUIRES

Singles: 7-inch
CONGRESS (223 "Joyce") 40-60 64
STARLITE (1 "Movin'") 15-25 64

SQUIRES

Singles: 7-inch
LEAF (6581 "Dear Jan") 10-15 65

SQUIRES

Singles: 7-inch
ATCO (6442 "Going All the Way") 15-25 66
LPs: 10/12-inch
CRYPT (008 "Going All the Way with the Squires") 15-25 86
Members: Mike Bouyea; Tom Flanigan; John Folcik; Kurt Robinson; Jim Lynch.
Also see ROGUES

SQUIRES

Singles: 7-inch
NORTHWESTERN 10-20
PENGUIN (161 "Batmobile") .... 10-20 '60s

S'QUIRES

Singles: 7-inch
BARRY (3312 "Green Surf") .... 8-12 '60s
(Canadian.)
BARRY (3398 "Remember") .... 8-12 '60s
(Canadian.)

SQUIRES V

Singles: 7-inch
BLUE SAINT (1002 "Bucket of Tears") 10-15 66

STACCATOS

Singles: 7-inch
CAPITOL 8-15 65-68
(Canadian.)
SYNCRO (661 "Gypsy Girl") 15-25 66
TOWER (277 "Face to Face") 10-20 67
Member: Les Emmerson.
Also see GUESS WHO / Staccatos

STACCATOS

(Staccato's)
Singles: 7-inch
KANDY KANE (1004 "Moondog") .... 20-30 '60s

STACEY, Carl, Trio

Singles: 7-inch
CADEL (4501 "The Big Gass") 25-50
(Identification number shown since no selection number is used.)
Members: Carl Stacey; El Gassaway; Don Dunckon.

STACEY, Clint

Singles: 7-inch
JET (514 "Who Is The Girl") 15-25 62

STACKS, Gene

Singles: 7-inch
COOPER (2059 "I Know My Baby Loves Me") 150-250

STACY, Clarence

Singles: 7-inch
CAROL (4114 "Jack the Ripper") 15-25 61
GLORY (301 "Forget Me") 10-20 60
SPARKLE (101 "Lonely Guy") 15-25 58

STACY, Clyde — P&R '57

(With the Nitecaps)
Singles: 7-inch
ARGYLE (1001 "So Young") 15-25 59
BULLSEYE (1004 "Baby Shame") 15-25 58
BULLSEYE (1008 "Honky Tonk Hardwood Floor") 75-125 58
BULLSEYE (1014 "You Want Love") 15-25 58
CANDLELIGHT (1015 "Hoy Hoy") 30-40 57
CANDLELIGHT (1018 "Dream Boy") 30-40 57
G&H (101 "You Want Love") 40-60 58
(First issue.)
LEN (1015 "You're Satisfied") 25-35 61

STACY, Homer

Singles: 7-inch
GALAHAD (545 "For Better Or Worse") ... 15-25 61

STADLER, Dave

Singles: 7-inch
BAY TONE (410 "Bony Maronie") 50-75

STAFFORD, Billy

Singles: 78 rpm
JAB (104 "Pappa Shotgun") 20-30 56

Singles: 7-inch
JAB (104 "Pappa Shotgun") 100-150 56
Session: Sharps.
Also see SHARPS

STAFFORD, Jo *P&R '44*
(With Paul Weston & His Orchestra; "Piano, George Greeley")
Singles: 78 rpm
CAPITOL 5-15 43-50
COLUMBIA.. 5-10 50-57
COLUMBIA/SNOWY BLEACH (22270/22271 "I Only Have Eyes for You"/"St. Louis Blues") .... 8-12 '50s
(7-inch 78 rpm. Promotional issue for Snowy Bleach and Glass Wax. No actual label name shown.)
Singles: 7-inch
CAPITOL (800 thru 1100 series)............ 15-20 50
COLPIX.. 5-10 62
COLUMBIA.. 15-25 50-60
COLUMBIA/SNOWY BLEACH (22500/22501 "I Only Have Eyes for You"/"St. Louis Blues") .... 15-25 '50s
(Promotional issue for Snowy Bleach and Glass Wax. No actual label name shown.)
DECCA.. 4-8 68
DOT.. 5-10 65-66
REPRISE.. 5-10 63
Picture Sleeves
COLUMBIA (40143 "Make Love to Me") . 40-50 53
EPs: 7-inch
CAPITOL.. 10-20 50-57
COLUMBIA.. 10-20 50-59
LPs: 10/12-inch
BAINBRIDGE 5-8 82
CAPITOL (H-75 thru H-435)............ 25-50 50-53
(10-inch LPs.)
CAPITOL (T-197 thru T-435)............ 20-40 55
CAPITOL (T-1653 thru T-2166)............ 15-25 62-64
(Monaural.)
CAPITOL (ST-1653 thru ST-2166)............ 15-30 62-64
(Stereo.)
CAPITOL (9014 "Songs of Faith")............ 25-50 54
(10-inch LP.)
CAPITOL (11000 series) 5-8 79
COLUMBIA (584 thru 1339)............ 20-40 54-59
(Monaural.)
COLUMBIA (1561 "Jo Plus Jazz")............ 40-50 60
(Monaural.)
COLUMBIA (2500 series)............ 20-40 55
(10-inch LPs.)
COLUMBIA (6000 series)............ 25-50 50-54
(10-inch LPs.)
COLUMBIA (8080 "I'll Be Seeing You")... 30-40 59
(Stereo.)
COLUMBIA (8139 "Ballad of the Blues"). 30-40 59
(Stereo.)
COLUMBIA (8361 "Jo Plus Jazz")............ 40-60 60
(Stereo.)
DECCA.. 10-15 68
DOT.. 10-15 66
TRIBUTE.. 5-10 71
VOCALION.. 8-12 68-69
Also see EDWARDS, Jonathan & Darlene
Also see INGLE, Red, & Natural Seven
Also see LAINE, Frankie, & Jo Stafford
Also see MacRAE, Gordon, & Jo Stafford
Also see MERCER, Johnny, Jo Stafford & Pied Pipers
Also see PIED PIPERS
Also see WESTON, Paul

STAFFORD, Sonny
Singles: 7-inch
BLUE MOON (416 "Record Hop Blues") . 50-75 60

STAFFORD, Terry *P&R/LP '64*
Singles: 7-inch
A&M (707 "Heartaches on the Way")............ 8-12 63
ATLANTIC (4006 "Amarillo By Morning")..... 4-8 73
ATLANTIC (4015 "Captured") 4-8 74
ATLANTIC (4026 "Stop If You Love Me")..... 4-8 74
CASINO (113 "It Sure Is Bad to Love Her") .4-6 77
COLLECTABLES ("Suspicion")............ 3-5 '80s
(Selection number not known.)
CRUSADER (101 "Suspicion")............ 8-12 64
CRUSADER (105 "I'll Touch a Star")............ 8-12 64
CRUSADER (109 "Follow the Rainbow") ...8-12 64
CRUSADER (110 "Hoping")............ 8-12 64
ERIC ("Suspicion"/"I'll Touch a Star") .... 3-6 '70s
(Selection number not known.)
FIRSTLINE (710 "Everybody Loves a Love Song")............ 3-6 81
LANA (139 "Suspicion")............ 4-8 '60s
MGM (14232 "Mean Woman Blues")............ 4-6 71
MELODYLAND (6009 "I Can't Find It")........ 4-6 75
MERCURY (72538 "Forbidden")............ 5-10 66
PLAYER (134 "Lonestar Lonesome")............ 3-5 89
SIDEWALK (902 "Soldier Boy")............ 5-10 66
SIDEWALK (914 "Joke's On Me")............ 5-10 67
TERRIFIC ("Suspicion")............ 3-6
(Selection number not known.)
W.B. (7286 "Big in Dallas")............ 5-10 69
Picture Sleeves
ERIC ("Suspicion"/"I'll Touch a Star") .... 8-12 '70s
(Selection number not known. Labeled "Demo Not For Sale.")
LPs: 10/12-inch
ATLANTIC (7282 "Say, Has Anybody Seen My Sweet Gypsy Rose")............ 10-15 73
CRUSADER (1001 "Suspicion!")............ 25-35 64
(Monaural)
CRUSADER (1001 "Suspicion!")............ 35-50 64
(Stereo)
Session: Davie Allan.
Also see ALLAN, Davie

STAFFS
Singles: 7-inch
PA-GO-GO (118 "Another Love")............ 15-25 66

STAGE MEN
Singles: 7-inch
CUCA (6472 "Fallout")............ 35-50 64
Members: Wally Messner; Bob King; Ed Lenop; Eric Henry.

STAGEHANDS
Singles: 7-inch
T.A. (101 "You Started It")............ 15-25 64

STAGEMASTERS
Singles: 7-inch
HIT KINGDOM (1801 "Baby, I'm Here Just to Love You")............ 25-35 66
SLIDE (2101 "Baby, I'm Here Just to Love You")............ 15-25 66

STAGG, Tommy
(With Rocky G. Braiter & Orchestra)
Singles: 7-inch
BAMBI (802 "Memories of Love")............ 50-100 61

STAGS
Singles: 7-inch
M&S (502 "Sailor Boy")............ 100-150 58

STAINS
Singles: 7-inch
LOTUS (1000 "Now and Then")............ 25-35 '60s

STAIRCASES
Singles: 7-inch
SOUND CITY (001 "Lost in the World of a Dream")............ 15-25 '60s

STAIRWAY TO STARS
Singles: 7-inch
BRITE STAR (17910 "Cry")............ 20-30 67

STALLCUP, James, & Flairs
Singles: 7-inch
LE CAM (724 "Baby Let's Make Love") 15-25 61

STALLINGS, Jimmy
Singles: 7-inch
PAXLEY (101 "I Played the Fool")........ 100-150 61

STAMPEDERS *P&R/LP '71*
Singles: 7-inch
BELL.. 4-6 71-73
CAPITOL.. 4-6 73
FLASHBACK.. 4-6 74
MGM.. 4-8 68
QUALITY.. 4-6 76
LPs: 10/12-inch
BELL.. 10-15 71
CAPITOL.. 8-12 73-74
PRIVATE STOCK/QUALITY............ 8-10 76
Also see WOLFMAN JACK

STAMPLEY, Joe *C&W '71*
Singles: 7-inch
ABC.. 3-5 77
ABC/DOT.. 4-6 75-76
CHESS (1798 "Creation of Love") 100-150 63
DOT.. 4-6 70-74
EPIC.. 3-6 75-86
EVERGREEN.. 3-5 88-89
IMPERIAL (5617 "We're Through") 15-25 59
PARAMOUNT (0025 "All the Good Is Gone")............ 4-6 70
PAULA (403 "Groovin' Out")............ 4-6 74
LPs: 10/12-inch
ABC.. 5-10 77
ABC/DOT.. 8-12 74-76
ACCORD.. 5-10 82
DOT.. 8-12 73
EPIC.. 5-10 75-85
PHONORAMA.. 5-8 83
Also see BANDY, Moe, & Joe Stampley
Also see UNIQUES

STAN & DOUG
(Stan Boreson & Doug Setterberg)
Singles: 7-inch
GOLDEN CREST (531 "Swedish Rock and Roll")............ 5-10 59
GOLDEN CREST (550 "Christmas Goose")............ 4-8 70
(Parody of Anne Murray's *Snowbird*. Year is correct.)
GOLDEN CREST (587 "Skvitt Skvatt") 4-8 61
LPs: 10/12-inch
GOLDEN CREST (3079 "Yust Try to Sing Along in Swedish")............ 8-12 61
Members: Stan Boreson; Doug Setterberg.

STANBACK, Jean
Singles: 7-inch
PEACOCK (1958 "I Still Love You")......... 15-25 68

STANDARDS
Singles: 7-inch
AMOS (134 "When You Wish upon a Star")............ 5-10 69
CHESS (1869 "Hello Love")............ 10-20 63
DEBRO (3178 "Tears Bring Heartaches")............ 100-200 63
GAMBIT (1102 "The Girl Across the Way")............ 15-25 63
GLENDEN (1315 "It Isn't Fair")............ 15-25 64
MAGNA (1314 "Hello Love")............ 50-75 63
MAGNA (1315 "It Isn't Fair")............ 40-50 63
MAGNA (1869 "Hello Love")............ 20-30 63
ROULETTE (4487 "Tears Bring Heartaches")............ 10-15 63

STANDELLS *P&R/LP '66*
Singles: 7-inch
COLLECTABLES.. 3-5 '80s
LIBERTY (55680 "Peppermint Beatles") .. 10-20 64
LIBERTY (55722 "Help Yourself") 10-20 64
LIBERTY (55743 "Linda Lou") 10-20 64
MGM (13350 "Some Day You'll Cry")....... 10-20 65
SUNSET (61000 "Help Yourself")............ 10-20 66
TOWER (185 "Dirty Water")............ 10-20 66
TOWER (257 "Sometimes Good Guys Don't Wear White")............ 10-20 66
TOWER (282 "Why Pick On Me")............ 10-20 66
TOWER (310 "Try It")............ 10-20 67
TOWER (314 "Riot on Sunset Strip") 10-20 67
TOWER (348 "Ninety-Nine and a Half")... 10-20 68
TOWER (398 "Animal Girl") 10-20 68
VEE-JAY (643 "The Boy Next Door") 10-20 65
VEE-JAY (679 "Don't Say Goodbye")......... 10-20 65
Picture Sleeves
TOWER (310 "Try It")............ 15-25 67
TOWER (314 "Riot on Sunset Strip") 15-25 67
VEE-JAY (643 "The Boy Next Door") 15-25 65
LPs: 10/12-inch
LIBERTY (3384 "In Person at P.J.'s")....... 40-50 64
(Monaural.)
LIBERTY (7384 "In Person at P.J.'s")....... 50-60 64
(Stereo.)
RHINO.. 5-8
SUNSET (1136 "Live and Out of Sight") .. 15-25 66
(Monaural.)
SUNSET (5136 "Live and Out of Sight") .. 20-30 66
(Stereo.)
TOWER (T-5027 "Dirty Water") 40-50 66
(Monaural.)
TOWER (ST-5027 "Dirty Water")............ 50-60 66
(Stereo.)
TOWER (T-5044 "Why Pick On Me") 40-50 66
(Monaural.)
TOWER (ST-5044 "Why Pick On Me")..... 50-60 66
(Stereo.)
TOWER (T-5049 "Hot Ones") 40-50 66
(Monaural.)
TOWER (ST-5049 "Hot Ones")............ 50-60 66
(Stereo.)
TOWER (T-5098 "Try It")............ 40-50 66
(Monaural.)
TOWER (ST-5098 "Try It")............ 50-60 66
(Stereo.)
Members: Dick Dodd; Larry Tamblyn; Gary Lane; Tony Valentino; Dave Burke.
Also see DODD, Dick
Also see SLLEDNATS
Also see TAMBLYN, Larry

STANDLEY, Johnny *P&R '52*
(With Horace Heidt & His Musical Knights)
Singles: 78 rpm
CAPITOL.. 5-10 52-56
MAGNOLIA (1063 "It's in the Book")........ 25-50 52
(First issue.)
Singles: 7-inch
CAPITOL (2249 "It's in the Book")............ 15-25 52
CAPITOL (2569 "Clap Your Hands")........ 15-25 53
CAPITOL (3544 "Get Out and Vote") 10-20 56
MAGNOLIA (1003 "Rock & Roll Must Go")............ 40-60 60
(Definitely a 1960 issue on 45 rpm; however, the number indicates a 1949 release. If not for the title, one might think this a reissue on 45 of an old 78. Can anyone explain?)
EPs: 7-inch
CAPITOL (697 "It's in the Book")............ 25-45 52

STANFIELD, Lee
Singles: 7-inch
AMBER (204 "Lee's Blues")............ 10-15 61

STANFORD, Dick, & Teenbeats
Singles: 7-inch
DODE (104 "Money Honey") 15-25

STANFORD, Doug
Singles: 7-inch
D (1034 "Won't You Tell Me")............ 150-300 58

STANGE, Howie
Singles: 7-inch
JENN (101 "Real Gone Daddy")............ 200-300 59

STANGIS, Linda
Singles: 7-inch
EDISON INT'L (413 "Too Young")............ 10-15 59

STANLEY, Earl, & Stereos
Singles: 7-inch
PITASSY (210 "Midnight in New Orleans")............ 10-20 62

STANLEY, Michael, Band *LP '75*
Singles: 7-inch
ARISTA.. 3-5 78-79
EMI AMERICA.. 3-5 80-83
EPIC.. 3-5 77
TUMBLEWEED.. 4-6 72-73
LPs: 10/12-inch
ARISTA.. 5-8 78-79
EMI AMERICA.. 5-8 80-83
EPIC.. 8-12 75-76
MCA.. 10-12 73
TUMBLEWEED.. 8-12 73
Also see CIRCUS
Also see SILK
Also see TREE STUMPS

STANLEY, Paul *P&R/LP '78*
Singles: 7-inch
CASABLANCA.. 3-5 78
LPs: 10/12-inch
CASABLANCA (7123 "Paul Stanley") 15-25 78
(With poster.)
CASABLANCA (7123 "Paul Stanley") 8-12 78
(Without poster.)
CASABLANCA (PIX-7123 "Paul Stanley")............ 50-60 79
(Picture disc.)
Also see KISS

STANLEY, Ray
Singles: 78 rpm
ARGO.. 10-15 57
CAPITOL.. 8-12 56
ZEPHYR.. 15-20 57
Singles: 7-inch
ARGO (5280 "I Can't Wait")............ 10-15 57
CAPITOL (3451 "Let's Get Acquainted").. 15-25 56
ZEPHYR (011 "Pushin'") 30-50 57
ZEPHYR (022 "Love Charms") 30-50 57
Also see ADAMS, Alicia

Also see COCHRAN, Eddie
Also see TERRIFICS

STANLEY, Skip

Singles: 7-inch

SATELLITE (92 "Satellite Baby") 50-75
SPOTLIGHT (399 "Satellite Baby") 25-35 59

STANLEY & ROBERT

Singles: 7-inch

LANCE (126 "Big Guitar") 15-25 57

STANLEY BROTHERS C&W '60

Singles: 78 rpm

COLUMBIA 4-8 51-52
KING 4-8 58
MERCURY 4-8 53-55
RICH-R-TONE 5-10 47

Singles: 7-inch

COLUMBIA 5-10 52
KING 4-8 58-65
MERCURY 5-10 53-58

EPs: 7-inch

COLUMBIA 10-15 58
KING 5-10 61-62
STARDAY 8-12 59

LPs: 10/12-inch

CABIN CREEK (1 "Stanley Series, Vol. 1") 30-40
(Four individual LPs.)
CABIN CREEK (2 "Stanley Series, Vol. 2") 5-10
(Single LP.)
CABIN CREEK (203 "Bluegrass Gospel Favorites") 40-60 66
COLLECTOR'S CLASSICS 5-10
COOPER CREEK 5-10
COUNTY 6-12 73
GTO (103-108) 50-75 83
(Six individual LPs, packaged as a set.)
GUSTO 5-10 80
GUSTO/KING 6-12 75-76
HARMONY 12-25 61-66
KING (645 thru 1013) 15-30 59-67
MELODEON 5-10
MERCURY (20349 "Country Pickin' and Singin' ") 30-50 58
MERCURY (20384 "Hard Times") 25-35 63
(Monaural.)
MERCURY (60384 "Hard Times") 30-40 63
(Stereo.)
NASHVILLE 8-12 70
OLD HOMESTEAD 5-10
POWER PAK .... 5-10 '80s
REBEL 5-10
RIMROCK 5-10
ROUNDER 5-10
STARDAY (106 "Mountain Song") 25-35 59
STARDAY (122 "Sacred Songs") 25-35 60
STARDAY (201 "Mountain Music") 20-30 62
STARDAY (384 "Jacob's Vision") 15-25 66
STARDAY (834 "Folk Concert") 6-12 76
STARDAY (3003 "16 Hits") 5-10
STARDAY/KING 5-10
VINTAGE COLLECTOR'S CLUB (002 "Live at Antioch College") 50-75 61
WANGO 6-12 76
WING 15-20 66
Members: Ralph Stanley; Carter Stanley.

STANTER, Patrinell

Singles: 7-inch

SEPIA (8201 "Little Love Affair") 15-25

STANTON, Larry, & Charlettes

Singles: 7-inch

SAPIEN (1004 "Love Notes") 30-40 61

STANTON, Sandy

Singles: 78 rpm

FABLE (556 "Sadie Lou") 25-35 57

Singles: 7-inch

FABLE (556 "Sadie Lou") 30-40 57
Also see GERROIR, Carol
Also see WAITS, Carolyn

STAPLE SINGERS P&R '67
(The Staples)

Singles: 78 rpm

UNITED (165 "It Rained, Children") 50-100 54
VEE-JAY (870 "I'm Leaning") 40-60 59

Singles: 7-inch

ABC 4-6 73
CURTOM 4-6 75-77
D-TOWN 4-6
EPIC 5-10 64-71
PRIVATE I 3-5 84-86
RIVERSIDE 5-10 62-63
SHARP (603 "This May Be My Last Time") 8-10 60
STAX 4-8 68-74
20TH FOX 3-5 81
UNITED (165 "It Rained, Children") 200-300 54
VEE-JAY 10-15 59-62
W.B. 3-6 76-80

LPs: 10/12-inch

BUDDAH 5-10 69
CREED 5-10 73
CURTOM 5-10 76
EPIC 8-12 65-71
EVEREST 8-12 68-69
FANTASY 5-10 73
51 WEST .... 5-8 '80s
GOSPEL 5-15 59
HARMONY 5-10 72
MILESTONE 5-10 75
PRIVATE I 5-8 84-86
RIVERSIDE 10-15 62-65
STAX 5-10 68-81
20TH FOX 5-10 81
TRIP 5-10 71-77
VEE-JAY 10-15 59-63
W.B. 5-10 76-78
Members: Mavis Staples; Roebuck Staples; Cleo Staples; Yvonne Staples.

STAPLES, Gordon, & Motown Strings

Singles: 7-inch

MOTOWN (1180 "Strung Out") 10-20 71
(Black vinyl.)
MOTOWN (1180 "Strung Out") 15-25 71
(Colored vinyl. Promotional issue only.)

LPs: 10/12-inch

MOTOWN (722 "Strung Out") 15-25 71

STAPLETON, Eddie

Singles: 7-inch

FORTUNE (559 "I Want Your Love") 15-25 64

STAR, Chuck

Singles: 7-inch

ATLANTIC (2178 "Shirley") 10-15 63

STAR, Linda, & Starlets

Singles: 7-inch

JOEY (104 "Find a Star") 10-15 63

STAR COMBO
("Vocal Frankie Mann"; Joe Ramirez Combo)

Singles: 7-inch

SKIPPY (102 "Mister Rock and Roll") 75-125 58
Members: Joe Ramirez; Frankie Mann.
Also see RAMIREZ, Joe

STAR FIRES
(Starfires)

Singles: 7-inch

HARAL (777 "Each Night at Nine") 75-100 63
LAURIE (3332 "You Done Me Wrong") 5-10 66
Also see STARFIRES

STAR STEPPERS

Singles: 7-inch

AMY (801 "You're Gone") 50-75 60

STAR TONES

Singles: 7-inch

BAND BOX (354 "The Chase") 10-20 64

STAR TREK

Singles: 7-inch

POWER (25 "Passage to Moauv") 10-20 75
POWER (26 "Crier In Emptiness") 10-20 75

STARBOYS

Singles: 7-inch

CRIMINAL (822 "Pennies in a Jar") 10-20 75

EPs: 7-inch

DISH ("Hey Mama") 10-20 69
(Selection number not known.)
Members: John Sieger; Gregg Kishline; Frank Niccolai; Phil Clark; Ken Vanderpoel; Mike Sieger; Cy Costabile.
Also see STUDEBAKER BROTHERS

STARBUCK & RAINMAKERS

Singles: 7-inch

VALIANT (744 "I Who Have Nothing") 10-20 66

STARCASTLE LP '76

Singles: 7-inch

EPIC 4-6 76-78

LPs: 10/12-inch

EPIC (Except PAL-34935) 5-10 76-79
EPIC (PAL-34935 "Citadel") 50-75 79
(Picture disc. Promotional issue only.)

STARCHER, Buddy C&W '49

Singles: 78 rpm

4 STAR (Except 1145) 4-8 49-50
4 STAR (1145 "I'll Still Write Your Name in the Sand") 10-20 49

Singles: 7-inch

BOONE (1038 "History Repeats Itself") 5-10 66
(Black vinyl.)
BOONE (1038 "History Repeats Itself") ... 20-30 66
(Orange vinyl.)
DECCA (31975 "Day of Decision") 4-8 66
DECCA (32012 "Fall of a Nation") 4-8 66
4 STAR .... 10-15 '50s
HEARTWARMING (5069 "When Payday Comes") 4-8 67
STARDAY 5-15 59-66

EPs: 7-inch

4 STAR .... 5-10 '50s
STARDAY 5-10 61

LPs: 10/12-inch

BLUEBONNET 10-20
DECCA (4796 "History Repeats Itself") 10-20 66
HEARTWARMING 5-10 68
STARDAY 10-20 62-66

STARCHER, Larry

Singles: 7-inch

BOHEMIA (112 "You Want My Baby") 50-75

STARCROST

LPs: 10/12-inch

FABLE ("Starcrost") 250-300 75
(Selection number not known.)

STAR-DRIFTS

Singles: 7-inch

GOLDISC (G-3 "An Eye for an Eye") 15-25 63

STARDUSTERS

Singles: 7-inch

BLUE RIBBON (101 "Cy Boogie") 8-12
EDISON INT'L (404 "Love Story") 10-20 58
JIM SIM (119 "Because You're Mine") 10-20 59
JO-RAY-ME (001 "Rockin' Boat") 10-20 62
LOVE LOCK (109 "Playing on Wood") 50-75

STARFIRES

Singles: 7-inch

BERNICE (201 "Yearning for Love") 200-300 58
BERNICE (202 "You Are Mine") 100-200 58
DECCA (30730 "Three Roses") 20-30 58
DECCA (30916 "Love Is Here to Stay") ... 30-40 58

STARFIRES
(Original Starfires)

Singles: 7-inch

APT (25030 "Fender Bender") 15-20 59
PACE (101 "Fender Bender") 25-35 59
(First issue.)
Member: Jim Ford.

STARFIRES

Singles: 7-inch

ATOMIC (1912 "Love Will Break Your Heart") 15-25 61
BARGAIN (5001 "You're the One") 30-40 61
BARGAIN (5003 "Love Will Break Your Heart") 20-30 61
(First issue.)
D&H (200 "These Foolish Things") 50-75 61

STARFIRES

Singles: 7-inch

PAMA (117 "Billy's Blues") 30-40 61
Members: Bill Bruno; Tom King; Rickey Baker; Merdin Madsen.
Also see OUTSIDERS

STARFIRES

Singles: 7-inch

ACCENT (1132 "All I Do Is Cry") 5-10 64
COLLEGE (501 "Twistin' Strings") 8-12 62
DUEL (518 "Fools Fall in Love") 20-30 62
TRIUMPH (61 "Fink") 10-25 65

EPs: 7-inch

OHIO RECORDING SERVICE 10-15 64

LPs: 10/12-inch

OHIO RECORDING SERVICE 15-20 64

STARFIRES

Singles: 7-inch

ROUND (1016 "Space Needle") 10-15 62

Picture Sleeves

ROUND (1016 "Space Needle") 20-30 62

STARFIRES

Singles: 7-inch

SONIC (7163 "Re-Entry") 15-25 63
Members: Joe Santiloni; Henry Rice; Pete Tabili; Stan Wojtym; Ronnie Barret.

STARFIRES

Singles: 7-inch

ROMCO (104 "Something Else") 50-75 63

STARFIRES

Singles: 7-inch

SARA (6363 "Nervous Breakdown") 15-25 63
Members: Tommy Lee Lindermann; Bill Orr; Rick Sherman; Kip Maercklein; Bill Kucharet; Mickey Abrams.

STARFIRES

Singles: 7-inch

G.I. (4001 "Linda") 150-250 65
G.I. (4002 "Rockin' Dixie") 25-35 65
G.I. (4004 "Cry for Freedom") 25-35 65
YARDBIRD (4005 "Unchain My Heart") ... 10-20 66
YARDBIRD (4006 "The Hardest Way") 10-20 66

LPs: 10/12-inch

LA BREA (8018 "Teenbeat A Go Go") 25-35 64
Members: Chuck Butler; Dave Anderson; Jack Emerick; Freddy Fields; Sonny Lathrop.

STARFIRES

Singles: 7-inch

BIG SOUND (301 "Please Go Away") 25-35 65
Members: Forrest Jehn; Gary Van Sleet; Mike Reinecke; Wayne Leitermann; Dick Sternberg.

STARFIRES

Singles: 7-inch

STARFIRE (200, 597 "She's Long and Tall") 50-75 65

STARFIRES

Singles: 7-inch

B&V (101 "You're My Only Love") .... 50-75 '60s

STARGLOWS

Singles: 7-inch

ATCO (6272 "Let's Be Lovers") 10-15 63
Member: Nate Nelson.
Also see FLAMINGOS

STARGLOWS / Rock-A-Bouts / Cecil Young Quartet

EPs: 7-inch

SPINNING (7 "Let's Be Lovers") 4-8
Also see ROCK-A-BOUTS
Also see YOUNG, Cecil

STARK, Johnny

Singles: 7-inch

CRYSTALETTE 15-25 57-58
POP (1106 "Broken Heart") 8-12 59

STARK NAKED
(With the Car Thieves)

Singles: 7-inch

ATTRACK/MGM .... 5-10 '60s
ORO .... 5-10 '60s
RCA (0588 "Done") 4-8 71
SUNBURST (774 "Look Back in Love") 5-10 68

LPs: 10/12-inch

RCA 10-15 71

STARKS, Blackie

Singles: 7-inch

J.W. ENTERPRISE (1279 "Running Wild") 100-200

STARKS, Doc, & Nite Riders
(With the Night Riders; with Nightriders; Doc Starkes & Niteriders)

Singles: 78 rpm

CAPITOL 8-12 55

Singles: 7-inch

BERNLO 15-25 57
CAPITOL (3236 "Night Ridin'") 15-25 55
LINDA (109 "Love Me Like Crazy") 50-75 58

MODERN SOUND (6908 "Rockin' to School")........ 50-75 58
SOUND (119 "Night Ridin' ")........ 35-50 55
(First issue.)
SOUND (128 "Never")........ 35-50 55
SWAN (4003 "Apple Cider")........ 10-20 58
TEEN (114 "Apple Cider")........ 25-35 57
Also see NITE RIDERS

STARKS, Glenn

Singles: 7-inch

J.W. ENTERPRISE ("Gonna Have a Party")........ 100-200
(Selection number not known.)

STARLARKS
(Featuring Wes Forbes)

Singles: 7-inch

ANCHO (102 "My Dear")........ 100-200 57
COLLECTABLES........ 3-5 '80s
ELM (001 "The Fountain of Love")... 1000-1200 57
EMBER (1013 "The Fountain of Love")... 25-35 57
RELIC (508 "My Dear")........ 5-10 64
Member: Wes Forbes.
Also see FIVE SATINS

STARLARKS

Singles: 7-inch

ASTRA (100 "Darling, Please Love Me"). 50-75 64
(Reportedly 1,000 made.)
THEME (108 "Dear Heart")........ 8-10

STARLETS

Singles: 7-inch

ASTRO (202 "P.S. I Love You")........ 10-20 60
ASTRO (204 "Romeo & Juliet")........ 10-20 60
Also see ANGELS

STARLETS P&R '61

Singles: 7-inch

LUTE (5909 "I'm So Young")........ 15-25 60
PAM (1003 "Better Tell Him No")........ 15-25 61
PAM (1004 "My Last Cry")........ 10-20 61
PEAK (5000 "Missing You")........ 150-250 57
Members: Maxine Edwards; Bernice Williams; Liz Walker; Mickey McKinney; Jane Hall.
Also see BLUE BELLES

STARLETS

Singles: 7-inch

TOWER (115 "Multiply By Three")........ 5-10 65
TOWER (144 "You Don't Love Me")........ 5-10 65
Session: Davie Allan.
Also see ALLAN, Davie

STARLETS

Singles: 7-inch

CHESS (1997 "My Baby's Real")........ 10-20 67
CHESS (2038 "I Wanna Be Good to You")........ 10-20 68

STARLETS

Singles: 7-inch

MIDDLE C (100 "You Don't Seem to Want Me")........ 10-15

STARLETTES

Singles: 7-inch

CHECKER (895 "Please Ring My Phone")........ 75-125 58

STARLIGHTERS

Singles: 78 rpm

IRMA (101 "Love Cry")........ 250-450 56
Also see STARLITERS with Jonesy's Combo

STARLIGHTERS

Singles: 7-inch

INTRO........ 25-35 58

STARLIGHTERS

Singles: 7-inch

LAMP (2014 "Rocking Too Much")........ 8-12 58

STARLIGHTERS

Singles: 7-inch

SUNCOAST (1001 "Until You Return")........ 2000-3000 58

STARLIGHTERS

Singles: 7-inch

END (1031 "It's Twelve O'Clock")........ 150-200 58
END (1049 "I Cried")........ 50-75 59
END (1072 "A Story of Love")........ 150-200 60
HALO (1004 "It's Twelve O'Clock")........ 3-5

STARLIGHTERS

Singles: 7-inch

NUGGET (1002 "A Fool's Understanding")........ 200-300 59

STARLIGHTERS

Singles: 7-inch

HI-Q (5016 "Zoom")........ 30-40 60
WHEEL (1004 "Creepin' ")........ 10-20 60

STARLIGHTERS

Singles: 7-inch

RADIO (103 "Wicked Ruby")........ 75-125

STARLIGHTS

Singles: 7-inch

CLIMAX (107 "Starfire")........ 10-15 59

STARLIGHTS

Singles: 7-inch

KAY BANK (223 "In Paradise")........ 10-15 '60s

STARLIGHTS

Singles: 7-inch

PREMIUM (101 "Searching for Love")........ 15-20

STARLINERS

Singles: 7-inch

NO-NEE (101 "Gotz")........ 20-30 '60s
REED (1066 "Thunder")........ 8-12
ULTRACON (101 "Kooknik")........ 10-20 '60s
VISCOUNT (101 "Watusi Time")........ 10-15 61

LPs: 10/12-inch

LEJAC (1001 "Live at Papa Joe's") . 1000-1500 '60s

STARLINGS
("Featuring: Bill and Johnny")

Singles: 78 rpm

DAWN........ 100-200 55
JOSIE........ 100-200 54

Singles: 7-inch

DAWN (212 "I'm Just a Crying Fool")... 400-500 55
DAWN (213 "I Gotta Go Now")........ 200-300 55
JOSIE (760 "My Plea for Love")........ 500-600 54
Member: Larry Gales.
Also see SUPREMES
Also see TWILIGHTERS

STARLINGS

Singles: 7-inch

WORLD PACIFIC (809 "All I Want")........ 20-30 59

STARLITERS

Singles: 7-inch

GALA (106 "Teenage Bop")........ 100-150 60

STARLITERS

Singles: 7-inch

4 SONS (4107 "Don't Ever Leave Me")........ 100-200

STARLITERS with Jonesy's Combo

Singles: 78 rpm

COMBO (73 "Arline")........ 75-125 55

Singles: 7-inch

COMBO (73 "Arline")........ 400-500 55
(Red label.)
COMBO (73 "Arline")........ 50-75 56
(Purple label.)
Also see STARLIGHTERS

STARLITES
(With Al Browne & Band)

Singles: 78 rpm

PEAK (5000 "Missing You")........ 75-100 57

Singles: 7-inch

PEAK (5000 "Missing You")........ 100-150 57
Also see BROWNE, Al
Also see DREAMS
Also see EDDIE & STARLITES
Also see ESQUIRE, Kenny, & Starlites

STARLITES

Singles: 7-inch

QUEEN (5000 "My Darling")........ 50-100 60

STARLITES

Singles: 7-inch

EVERLAST (5027 "Valarie")........ 8-12 64
(Shown as "Vararie.")
FLASHBACK (8 "Valarie")........ 5-10 65
FURY (1034 "Valarie")........ 15-25 60
(Multi-color label.)
FURY (1034 "Valarie")........ 10-15 60
(Yellow label with lines.)
FURY (1034 "Valarie")........ 5-10 62
(Black vinyl. Horse in logo.)
FURY (1034 "Valarie")........ 15-25 62
(Blue vinyl. Horse in logo.)
FURY (1045 "Silver Lining")........ 10-20 61
RELIC (1001 "Joannie")........ 5-10 65
SPHERE SOUND (705 "Seven Day Fool")........ 25-35 65
Also see JACKIE & STARLITES
Also see KODOKS / Starlites

STARLITES

Singles: 7-inch

BARCLAY (15016 "Stagger Lee")........ 15-25 66
BARCLAY (17134 "I Can't See You")........ 15-25 67
Also see BEATIN' PATH

STARLITES

Singles: 7-inch

STARLITE (6298 "Starlite Rock")........ 8-12 '60s

STARNOTES
(With the Al Hogan Combo)

Singles: 7-inch

CAPER (101 "Say the Word")........ 30-40 62

STARO, Frankie
(Frank Staro)

Singles: 7-inch

ELMOR (305 "You I Like")........ 10-20 62
TEMPOTONE (100 "Operator Please")........ 5-10 62
UP (112 "Edge of a Star")........ 5-10 60

STARR, Andy
(Frank "Andy" Starr; with Casinos)

Singles: 78 rpm

ARCADE (115 "I Love You Baby")........ 50-75 53
KAPP (190 "Do It Right Now")........ 15-25 57
MGM (12263 "Rockin' Rollin' Stone")........ 50-75 56

Singles: 7-inch

ARCADE (115 "I Love You Baby")........ 200-300 53
KAPP (190 "Do It Right Now")........ 20-30 57
LIN (1009 "Dig Them Squeaky Shoes")........ 100-200 55
LIN (1013 "Tell Me Why")........ 25-50 55
LIN (5033 "Me and the Fool")........ 15-25 64
MGM (12263 "Rockin' Rollin' Stone")... 100-200 56
MGM (12315 "She's a Going, Jessie").. 100-200 56
MGM (12264 "Round and Round")........ 100-200 57
MGM (12421 "One More Time")........ 100-200 57
VALIANT (101 "Just A-Walkin' ")........ 300-500
Also see STARR, Frank, & His Rock-Away Boys

STARR, Berde

Singles: 7-inch

AZTEC (111 "What My Heart's Too Blind to See")........ 8-12 62

STARR, Betty Jo & Johnny

Singles: 7-inch

ALASKA (1279 "Eskimo Boogie")........ 50-75
ALASKA (1410 "Son of a Sourdough")........ 15-25
Also see STARR, Johnny

STARR, Bill
(With the Rhythm Jesters; with Rock Brooks; with Students)

Singles: 7-inch

APPLAUSE (1235 "Love for a Year")... 100-150 60
BANA (1964 "The Wanderer")........ 15-25 60
SCHOCK (8-11 "Grizzly Bear")........ 300-500 58

STARR, Billy

Singles: 7-inch

TWI-LITE (751 "Every Little Wrong")........ 75-125

STARR, Bob

Singles: 7-inch

ACCENT (1066 "Flat Foot Susie")........ 15-25 60
BEN-HUE (1001 "I Want to Rock and Roll")........ 25-50
FABLE (712 "Hound Dog")........ 5-10 61
ROCKIN (603 "One Tank of Gas")........ 5-8 74

STARR, Bobby
(Tony Allen)

Singles: 7-inch

RADIO (120 "Please Give Me a Chance")........ 50-75 59
Session: Chimes.
Also see ALLEN, Tony
Also see CHIMES

STARR, David

Singles: 7-inch

ABBOTT (2030 "Shake a Hand")........ 15-25 57
CANON (226 "Teen Doll")........ 100-200

STARR, Edwin P&R '65

Singles: 12-inch

20TH FOX........ 5-8 77-80

Singles: 7-inch

A.S.R. (29116 "Hit Me with Your Love")........ 4-6 '70s
CASABLANCA........ 3-5 84
GRANITE........ 4-6 75-76
GORDY (Black vinyl)........ 5-10 67-71
GORDY (Colored vinyl)........ 10-20 69-70
(Promotional issues only.)
MONTAGE........ 3-5 82
MOTOWN........ 4-6 73-74
RIC-TIC (103 "Agent Double-O Soul")........ 10-15 65
RIC-TIC (107 "Back Street")........ 10-15 66
RIC-TIC (109 "Stop Her On Sight [S.O.S.]")........ 10-15 66
RIC-TIC (109X "Scott's on Swingers [S.O.S.]")........ 40-50 66
(Promotional issue only.)
RIC-TIC (114 "Headline News")........ 10-15 66
RIC-TIC (118 "It's My Turn Now")........ 10-15 67
RIC-TIC (120 "You're My Mellow")........ 25-50 67
SOUL (35100 "Don't Tell Me I'm Crazy")........ 4-6 72
SOUL (35103 "There You Go")........ 4-6 73
20TH FOX........ 3-6 77-84

LPs: 10/12-inch

GORDY (931 "Soul Master")........ 15-25 68
GORDY (940 "25 Miles")........ 15-25 69
GORDY (948 "War & Peace")........ 10-20 70
GORDY (956 "Involved")........ 10-15 71
GRANITE........ 8-10 75
MOTOWN........ 8-10 73-82
20TH FOX........ 8-10 77-81
Also see FUTURETONES
Also see HOLIDAYS

STARR, Edwin, & Blinky

Singles: 7-inch

GORDY (7090 "Oh How Happy")........ 5-10 69

LPs: 10/12-inch

GORDY (945 "Just We Two")........ 10-20 69
Also see BLINKY
Also see STARR, Edwin

STARR, Frank, & His Rock-Away Boys
(Andy Starr; Frankie Starr)

Singles: 7-inch

HOLIDAY INN (104 "Knees Shaking")... 50-100 62
HOLIDAY INN (108 "Little Bitty Feeling"). 25-50 62
Session: Boots Randolph; Floyd Cramer; Bob Moore; Jordanaires; Murray Harman; Ray Edenton.
Also see CRAMER, Floyd
Also see JORDANAIRES
Also see MOORE, Bob
Also see RANDOLPH, Boots
Also see STARR, Andy

STARR, Frankie

Singles: 7-inch

SIMS (212 "Elevator Baby")........ 15-25 64
STAR-WIN (7003)"Elevator Boogie")........ 50-75 64
STAR-WIN (7008)"Elevator Baby")........ 50-75 64
(First issue.)

STARR, Harry

Singles: 7-inch

END (1129 "Another Time, Another Place")........ 20-40 64

STARR, J. T.

Singles: 7-inch

COAST (9017 "Rattlesnake Boogie")........ 50-75

STARR, Jerry
(With the Clippers)

Singles: 7-inch

PIC-ONE (104 "Teenage Tangle")........ 10-20 59
(First issue.)
ROCKO (521 "High Ride")........ 10-20 61
RON (321 "Teenage Tangle")........ 10-20 59
ZINN (1012 "Side Steppin")........ 10-20 59
ZINN (1015 "Love Dreams")........ 10-20 59

STARR, Jimmy
(With the Palis Royals)

Singles: 7-inch

DEBBIE (1408 "All I Ever Do")........ 15-20 59
ESTATE (1001 "All I Ever Do")........ 8-12 61
LAUREL (1015 "Adele")........ 10-15 60
LAUREL (1018 "All I Ever Do")........ 10-15 60
NASHVILLE (5118 "Blind Date")........ 5-8 63
RIDER (106 "All I Ever Do")........ 8-12 61

STARR, Johnny

Singles: 7-inch

EASTERN (01 "Don't Hold Back") 15-25 64
MALA (10219 "Do Re Mi Fa So La Ti Do") 10-20 68
OLYMPIA (7006 "Marizinia") 40-60
Also see STARR, Betty Jo & Johnny

STARR, Johnny / McAfees

Singles: 7-inch

C&B (101 "Sleep Tight"/"There'll Be an Angel") 15-25 '60s
Also see STARR, Johnny

STARR, Kay — P&R '48

(With the Crystalette All Stars)

Singles: 78 rpm

CAPITOL 5-10 48-57
CRYSTALETTE 10-15 50
JEWEL (1000 "I Ain't Gonna Cry") 20-40 45
MODERN 15-25 49
RCA 4-8 55-57

Singles: 7-inch

ABC 4-6 67-68
CAPITOL (811 thru 2887) 15-25 50-54
CAPITOL (4000 & 5000 series) 10-20 58-64
CRYSTALETTE (101/102/103/104 "Kay Starr Sings Starlight Starbright") 30-40 50
(Four red vinyl discs.)
CRYSTALETTE (632 "Where Or When") 15-25 50
(Black vinyl.)
CRYSTALETTE (632 "Where Or When") 20-40 50
(Red vinyl.)
DOT 4-8 68
GNP 4-6 74-75
HAPPY TIGER 4-6 70
RCA (0100 series) 4-6 73
RCA (6000 & 7000 series) 10-20 55-59

Picture Sleeves

CAPITOL (4835 "Four Walls") 10-20 62

EPs: 7-inch

CAPITOL 10-20 50-61
RCA 10-15 55-58

LPs: 10/12-inch

ABC 5-15 68
ALLEGRO 5-10
CAMDEN 10-20 60-61
CAPITOL (With "DT" or "SM" prefix) 5-15 63-75
(Reissue series including reprocessed stereo.)
CAPITOL (H-211 "Songs by Kay Starr") 50-100 50
(10-inch LP.)
CAPITOL (T-211 "Songs by Kay Starr") 30-40 55
CAPITOL (H-363 "Kay Starr Style") 50-75 53
(10-inch LP.)
CAPITOL (T-363 "Kay Starr Style") 30-40 55
CAPITOL (H-415 "Hits of Kay Starr") 50-75 53
(10-inch LP.)
CAPITOL (T-415 "Hits of Kay Starr") 30-40 55
(10-inch LP.)
CAPITOL (T-580 "In a Blue Mood") 30-40 55
CAPITOL (1254 thru 1681) 25-40 59-62
(With "T" or "ST" prefix.)
CAPITOL (1795 thru 2100 series) 15-30 62-64
(With "T" or "ST" prefix.)
CAPITOL (11000 series) 5-10 74-79
CORONET 10-20 63
CRYSTALETTE (4500 "Kay Starr Sings") 50-100 52
(10-inch LP.)
EVON 10-15 '50s
GNP 5-10 74-75
GALAXY 5-10
LIBERTY (3280 "Swingin' with the Starr") 15-25 63
LIBERTY (9001 "Swingin' with the Starr") 35-45 56
RCA (1100 thru 1700 series) 20-30 55-57
RONDO-LETTE (3 "Them There Eyes") 20-30 58
SUNSET 8-12 '60s
TOPS (9760 "Kay Starr Sings") 20-30 57
Also see WILLIAMS, Tex

STARR, Kay, & Count Basie

LPs: 10/12-inch

MCA 5-10 83
PARAMOUNT 10-15 69
Also see BASIE, Count

STARR, Kay, & Tennessee Ernie Ford

Singles: 78 rpm

CAPITOL 4-8 50-56

Singles: 7-inch

CAPITOL 10-20 50-56

EPs: 7-inch

CAPITOL 5-15 56
Also see FORD, Tennessee Ernie

STARR, Kay / Erroll Garner

LPs: 10/12-inch

CROWN (5003 "Singin' & Swingin'") 30-40 57
MODERN (1203 "Singin' & Swingin'") 50-75 56
Also see GARNER, Erroll
Also see STARR, Kay

STARR, Kenny

Singles: 7-inch

SAGE (278 "Rock Me") 25-35 59

STARR, Kenny — C&W '73

Singles: 7-inch

MCA 4-6 73-78
SRO (0001 "The Blind Man in the Bleachers") 20-30 82
(Orange-yellow vinyl. "Limited Collectors Series" star-shaped disc.)
S.S. TITANIC 3-5 81

LPs: 10/12-inch

MCA 5-10 75
SRO 5-10 82
Also see LYNN, Loretta

STARR, Leon

Singles: 7-inch

VU (101 "Little Live Wire") 50-75

STARR, Lucille — P&R '64

Singles: 7-inch

A&M 5-10 66
ALMO 5-10 64-65
EPIC 5-10 67-69

LPs: 10/12-inch

A&M 20-30 66
EPIC 20-30 69
Also see BOB & LUCILLE
Also see CANADIAN SWEETHEARTS

STARR, Lucky

Singles: 7-inch

BIG TOP (3123 "Cuddle Closer") 10-15 62
DOT (16544 "Blistered") 20-30 63

STARR, Mack

(With the Mellows)

Singles: 7-inch

CHENE (101 "Bundle of Joy") 8-12 64
CUB (9117 "Drifting Apart") 10-15 62
Also see PARAGONS

STARR, Martha

Singles: 7-inch

THELMA (111 "No Part Time Love for Me") 25-35 65
THELMA (112 "Love Is the Only Solution") 75-125 65
THELMA (113 "I Wanna Be Your Girl") 50-75 65

STARR, No No

Singles: 7-inch

MIDAS (301 "Pull Yourself Together") 10-20 '60s

STARR, Randy — P&R '57

Singles: 78 rpm

DALE 10-20 57

Singles: 7-inch

DALE (100 "After School") 15-25 57
DALE (102 "Double Date") 10-20 57
DALE (103 "The Prettiest Girl in School") 10-20 57
DALE (104 "Pink Lemonade") 10-20 57
DALE (110 "All About Me") 10-20 58
LAURIE (3231 "Do You Remember the Day") 5-10 64
MAYFLOWER (17 "You're Growing Up") 10-15 59
Also see ISLANDERS

STARR, Randy, & Frank Metis

LPs: 10/12-inch

MAYFLOWER (632 "Pittsburgh") 20-30 59
Also see METIS, Frank
Also see STARR, Randy

STARR, Ray

Singles: 7-inch

FEDERAL (12393 "Three Hearts in a Tangle") 10-15 60
KING (5652 "I Have to Laugh to Keep from Crying") 5-10 62
LEE (505 "Billy Jo") 50-100 58
MUSIC TOWER 3-5 78

STARR, Richard

Singles: 7-inch

CAMEO (340 "Singing the Blues") 8-12 65

STARR, Richie

(With the Bel-Larks)

Singles: 7-inch

HAMMER (6314 "I've Got It Bad") 75-100 63
Also see BEL-LARKS

STARR, Ricki & His All Stars

Singles: 7-inch

RCA (7640 "Shooting Star") 10-15 59

STARR, Ringo — P&R/LP '70

Singles: 12-inch

ATLANTIC (93 "Drowning in the Sea of Love") 25-30 77
(Promotional issue only.)

Singles: 7-inch

APPLE (1831 "It Don't Come Easy") 4-8 71
APPLE (1849 "Back Off Boogaloo") 40-60 72
(With a blue apple on the label.)
APPLE (1849 "Back Off Boogaloo") 4-6 73
(With a green apple on the label.)
APPLE (1865 "Photograph") 4-6 73
APPLE (1870 "You're Sixteen") 5-8 73
(With standard apple label.)
APPLE (1870 "You're Sixteen") 4-6 73
(With five-point star label.)
APPLE (1872 "Oh My My") 5-8 74
(With standard apple label.)
APPLE (1872 "Oh My My") 4-6 74
(With five-point star label.)
APPLE (1876 "Only You") 4-6 74
APPLE (1880 "No No Song") 4-6 75
APPLE (1882 "It's All Down to Goodnight Vienna") 4-6 75
APPLE (2969 "Beaucoups of Blues") 4-8 70
ATLANTIC (3361 "Dose of Rock 'N' Roll") 8-12 76
ATLANTIC (3371 "Hey Baby") 10-20 76
ATLANTIC (3412 "Drowning in the Sea of Love") 75-100 77
ATLANTIC (3429 "Wings") 10-20 77
BOARDWALK (130 "Wrack My Brain") 3-5 81
BOARDWALK (134 "Private Property") 3-5 82
CAPITOL (1831 "It Don't Come Easy") 25-35 76
(Orange label.)
CAPITOL (1849 "It Don't Come Easy") 3-5 78
(Purple label.)
CAPITOL (1849 "It Don't Come Easy") 3-5 83
(Black label.)
CAPITOL (1849 "Back Off Boogaloo") 25-35 76
(Orange label.)
CAPITOL (1849 "Back Off Boogaloo") 3-5 78
(Purple label.)
CAPITOL (1865 "Photograph") 3-5 78
(Purple label.)
CAPITOL (1865 "Photograph") 3-5 83
(Black label.)
CAPITOL (1870 "You're Sixteen") 25-35 76
(Orange label.)
CAPITOL (1870 "You're Sixteen") 3-5 78
(Purple label.)
CAPITOL (1870 "You're Sixteen") 3-5 83
(Black label.)
CAPITOL (1880 "No No Song") 3-5 78
(Purple label.)
CAPITOL (1880 "No No Song") 3-5 83
(Black label.)
CAPITOL (2969 "Beaucoups of Blues") 25-35 76
(Orange label.)
CAPITOL (2969 "Beaucoups of Blues") 3-5 78
(Purple label.)
PORTRAIT (70015 "Lipstick Traces") 10-15 78
PORTRAIT (70018 "Heart on My Sleeve") 10-15 78
RIGHT STUFF (18178 "In My Car") 6-8 94
(Orange vinyl. Made "For Jukeboxes Only.")
RIGHT STUFF (18179 "Wrack My Brain") 6-8 94
(Red vinyl. Made "For Jukeboxes Only.")

Picture Sleeves

APPLE (1826 "Beaucoups of Blues") 25-35 70
(Selection number 2969 mistakenly shown as Apple 1826.)
APPLE (1831 "It Don't Come Easy") 15-20 71
APPLE (1849 "Back Off Boogaloo") 20-25 72
APPLE (1865 "Photograph") 8-12 73
APPLE (1870 "You're Sixteen") 8-12 73
APPLE (1876 "Only You") 5-10 74
APPLE (1882 "It's All Down to Goodnight Vienna") 8-10 75
APPLE (2969 "Beaucoups of Blues") 35-45 70
(Selection number correctly shown.)
BOARDWALK (130 "Wrack My Brain") 3-5 81
MERCURY (195 "La De Da") 20-25 98
(Promotional issue only.)

Promotional Singles

APPLE (1849 "Back Off Boogaloo") 100-150 72
(White label.)
APPLE (1865 "Photograph") 30-35 73
APPLE (1870 "You're Sixteen") 30-35 73
APPLE (1872 "Oh My My") 30-35 74
APPLE (1876 "Only You") 30-35 74
APPLE (1880 "No No Song") 30-35 75
APPLE (1882 "It's All Down to Goodnight Vienna") 30-35 75
APPLE (1882 "Oo-Wee") 40-50 75
ATLANTIC (3361 "Dose of Rock 'N' Roll") 60-75 76
(White label.)
ATLANTIC (3361 "Dose of Rock 'N' Roll") 10-15 76
(Blue label.)
ATLANTIC (3371 "Hey Baby") 20-30 76
(White label.)
ATLANTIC (3371 "Hey Baby") 10-15 76
(Red-white and blue labels.)
ATLANTIC (3412 "Drowning in the Sea of Love") 10-20 77
ATLANTIC (3429 "Wings") 60-75 77
(White label.)
ATLANTIC (3429 "Wings") 10-12 77
(Red-white and blue labels.)
BOARDWALK (130 "Wrack My Brain") 8-12 81
BOARDWALK (134 "Private Property") 10-15 82
MERCURY (195 "La De Da") 20-25 98
PORTRAIT (70015 "Lipstick Traces") 10-15 78
PORTRAIT (70018 "Heart on My Sleeve") 10-15 78

LPs: 10/12-inch

APPLE (3365 "Sentimental Journey") 15-20 70
APPLE (3368 "Beaucoups of Blues") 15-20 70
APPLE (3413 "Ringo") 15-20 73
(Includes 20-page booklet. Has 5:26 version of *Six O'Clock* listed, but plays the 4:05.)
APPLE (3417 "Goodnight Vienna") 10-15 75
APPLE (3422 "Blast from Your Past") 10-15 75
ATLANTIC (18193 "Ringo's Rotogravure") 10-15 76
(With uncut cover.)
ATLANTIC (18193 "Ringo's Rotogravure") 8-10 76
(With cut cover.)
ATLANTIC (19108 "Ringo the 4th") 8-12 77
BOARDWALK (33246 "Stop and Smell the Roses") 10-15 81
(With uncut cover.)
BOARDWALK (33246 "Stop and Smell the Roses") 8-10 81
(With cut cover.)
CAPITOL (3365 "Sentimental Journey") 35-45 78
CAPITOL (16114 "Ringo") 10-15 80
CAPITOL (16218 "Sentimental Journey") 15-25 80
CAPITOL (16219 "Goodnight Vienna") 15-25 80
CAPITOL (16235 "Beaucoups of Blues") 10-20 80
CAPITOL (16236 "Blast from Your Past") 10-15 80
PORTRAIT (35378 "Bad Boy") 8-10 78
RHINO (70135 "Starr Struck") 20-25 89

Promotional LPs

APPLE (3413 "Ringo") 400-450 73
(Includes 20-page booklet. Has 5:26 version of the *Six O'Clock*, noticeably the largest band on Side 2. Label mistakenly lists the song at 4:05. Promo indicated only by hole punched in top corner of cover. Disc is identical to commercial issue.)
ATLANTIC (18193 "Ringo's Rotogravure") 10-20 76
(With programming sticker on front cover.)
ATLANTIC (19108 "Ringo the 4th") 10-20 77
(With programming sticker on front cover.)
PORTRAIT (35378 "Bad Boy") 75-100 78
(Labels reads "Advance Promotion.")
PORTRAIT (35378 "Bad Boy") 20-30 78
(Labels reads "Demonstration, Not For Sale.")
Session: Van Dyke Parks.
Also see BEATLES
Also see CLAPTON, Eric
Also see FRAMPTON, Peter

Also see JOHN, Elton
Also see LOMAX, Jackie
Also see NILSSON
Also see OWENS, Buck, & Ringo Starr
Also see PARKS, Van Dyke
Also see THOMAS, Guthrie

STARR, Rocky

Singles: 78 rpm
CROWN....10-20 53
MERCURY....5-10 53
Singles: 7-inch
CROWN (3588 "Rock-a-Bye Boogie")....25-30 53
(First issue.)
MERCURY (70192 "Rock-a-Bye Boogie")....10-20 53

STARR, Sally

Singles: 7-inch
ARCADE (157 "Rocky the Rockin' Rabbit")....20-30 60
CLYMAX (103 "Rockin' in the Nursery")..30-40 59
EPs: 7-inch
CLYMAX (1001/2/3 "Our Gal Sal")....75-125 59
(Three discs in gatefold cover.)
LPs: 10/12-inch
ARCADE (1001 "Our Gal Sal")....40-60 60
CLYMAX (1001 "Our Gal Sal")....100-150 59

STARR, Sid

Singles: 7-inch
MAYAN (365 "For You")....50-75

STARR, Suzy

Singles: 7-inch
MORGIL (102 "Lover's Quarrel")....20-30 61

STARR, Tommy

Singles: 7-inch
LOMA (2095 "Love Wheel")....5-10 68

STARR, Winnie

Singles: 7-inch
WINNIE HUNT (1206 "Baby by Rock")....25-35

STARR BROTHERS
(With Ted Sieber)

Singles: 7-inch
CORTLAND (104 "Don Juan"/"Don Juan")....20-30 62
(Promotional issue only.)
CORTLAND (104 "Don Juan"/"Down on My Knees")....10-20 62
CORTLAND (106 "Beautiful Woman")....8-12 63
CORTLAND (108 "Mother Goose")....8-12 63
Member: Donald Jenkins.
Also see DONALD & DELIGHTERS

STARR SISTERS

Singles: 7-inch
LUTE (6003 "Love's a Funny Little Game")....10-15 60
STARR (12 "Show Me the Way")....20-25 59

STARS

Singles: 7-inch
VEGA (001 "Let's Cuddle Again")....10-15 59
VEGA (002 "No Letter from You")....10-15 60

STARS OF BETHEL

Singles: 78 rpm
R&B (1307 "There Is a Fountain")....10-20 54
Singles: 7-inch
R&B (1307 "There Is a Fountain")....20-30 54

STARSHIP P&R/LP '85
(Jefferson Starship)

Singles: 12-inch
GRUNT (14226 "We Built This City")....5-10 85
Singles: 7-inch
ELEKTRA (69349 "Wild Again")....3-5 88
GRUNT....3-5 85-87
RCA....3-5 87-89
Picture Sleeves
ELEKTRA (69349 "Wild Again")....10-20 88
GRUNT....3-5 85-87
RCA....3-5 87-89
LPs: 10/12-inch
GRUNT....5-8 85-89
Also see JEFFERSON STARSHIP

STARTONES
(Carnations)

Singles: 78 rpm
RAINBOW....10-15 56
Singles: 7-inch
RAINBOW (341 "Forever My Love")....40-60 56
Also see CARNATIONS

STARTONES

Singles: 7-inch
BILLIE FRAN (001 "One Rose")....200-300 65

STAR-TREKS

Singles: 7-inch
VEEP (1254 "Gonna Need Magic")....20-30 67

STATE OF MICKY & TOMMY

Singles: 7-inch
MERCURY (72712 "With Love from One to Five")....15-25 67

STATEN, Little Mary

Singles: 7-inch
GME (1329 "Helpless Girl")....10-20 64

STATENS

Singles: 7-inch
CRYSTAL BALL (115 "Valentine")....4-8 78
(Black vinyl. 500 made.)
CRYSTAL BALL (115 "Valentine")....8-12 78
(Red vinyl. 25 made.)
CRYSTAL BALL (127 "Didn't Mean to Fall in Love")....4-8 78
(Black vinyl. 500 made.)
CRYSTAL BALL (127 "Didn't Mean to Fall in Love")....8-12 78
(Red vinyl. 25 made.)
MARK-X (8011 "Summertime Is the Right Time for Love")....50-100 61
LPs: 10/12-inch
CRYSTAL BALL (109 "Test of Time")....15-20 82
(Black vinyl. 1000 made.)
CRYSTAL BALL (109 "Test of Time")....30-40 82
(Colored vinyl. 25 made.)
CRYSTAL BALL (109 "Test of Time")....60-70 82
(Picture disc. No cover. 25 made.)

STATESMEN

Singles: 7-inch
BRADLEA (200 "Rampage")....8-12 61
JAMIE (1230 "A Matter of Who")....5-10 62
TEMA (137 "Stop and Get a Ticket")....5-10 68
TEMA (171 "Lollypop")....5-10
Picture Sleeves
TEMA (137 "Stop and Get a Ticket")....10-15 68
TEMA (171 "Lollypop")....10-15

STATESMEN

Singles: 7-inch
RAYNARD (014 "Teen Theme")....10-20 65

STATICS

Singles: 7-inch
EVENT (4279 "The Day You Left Me")....10-20 58

STATICS

Singles: 7-inch
MANTIS (102 "Shanghaied")....25-50 61
Also see DEE, Lynn, & Statics

STATICS & TINY TONY

Singles: 7-inch
CAMELOT (110 "Harlem Shuffle")....10-20 61
Also see TINY TONY & STATICS

STATLER BROTHERS C&W/P&R '65

Singles: 7-inch
COLUMBIA....4-8 64-69
MERCURY....3-6 70-90
Picture Sleeves
MERCURY....3-5
LPs: 10/12-inch
CBS....5-10 82-85
COLUMBIA (CL-2000 series)....15-25 66-67
(Monaural.)
COLUMBIA (CS-9000 series)....15-25 66-69
(Stereo.)
COLUMBIA (PC-9000 series)....5-8 '80s
COLUMBIA (31000 series)....8-10 '70s
51 WEST....5-8 '80s
HARMONY....6-12 71-73
MERCURY....5-15 71-90
PRIORITY....5-8 82
REALM....5-10
TIME-LIFE....5-8 81
Members: Harold Reid; Don Reid; Lew DeWitt; Phil Balsley; Jimmy Fortune. Session: Carl Perkins; Ernest Tubb.
Also see CASH, Johnny
Also see PERKINS, Carl
Also see TUBB, Ernest

STATLERS

Singles: 7-inch
LITTLE STAR (108 "Gone")....75-125 62

STATON, Candi P&R '69

Singles: 7-inch
FAME....4-8 69-73
L.A....3-5 81
SUGAR HILL....3-5 82
UNITY (711 "Now That You Have the Upper Hand")....75-125
W.B....3-6 74-80
LPs: 10/12-inch
FAME....8-12 70-72
SUGAR HILL....5-8 82
W.B....8-10 74-80

STATON, Dakota LP '58

Singles: 78 rpm
CAPITOL....4-8 55-63
Singles: 7-inch
CAPITOL....5-15 55-63
GROOVE MERCHANT....4-6 72
EPs: 7-inch
CAPITOL....5-15 58-60
LPs: 10/12-inch
CAPITOL (800 thru 1600 series)....30-45 58-63
HALF MOON....5-8 83
LONDON....10-15 67
U.A....10-20 63-64
VERVE....8-12 71

STATON, Johnny, & Feathers / Jaguars

Singles: 7-inch
CLASSIC ARTISTS (117 "More Than Enough for Me")....8-10 89
(Red vinyl. 1000 made.)
Also see FEATHERS
Also see JAGUARS

STATUES P&R '60

Singles: 7-inch
LIBERTY (55245 "Blue Velvet")....15-25 60
LIBERTY (55292 "White Christmas")....10-20 60
LIBERTY (55363 "Love at First Sight")....10-20 61
Members: James "Buzz" Cason (a.k.a. Garry Miles); Richard Williams; Hugh Jarrett.
Also see MILES, Garry

STATUS QUO

Singles: 7-inch
GRANT (690 "They All Want Her Love")..15-25 '60s

STAUDT, Bernie

Singles: 7-inch
VAR-BEE (114 "I Lost My Girl Last Night")....15-25

STAVIS, George

LPs: 10/12-inch
VANGUARD....8-12 69

STAYTON, Jimmy
(James Stayton)

Singles: 7-inch
BLUE HEN (220 "Hot Hot Mama")....200-300 56
BLUE HEN (224 "You're Gonna Treat Me Right")....400-600 57
20TH FOX (310 "More Than You'll Ever Know")....40-60 62

STEALERS

Singles: 7-inch
TORRID (101 "It Must Be Love")....10-20

STEAM P&R '69

Singles: 7-inch
FONTANA (1667 " Na Na Hey Hey Kiss Him Goodbye")....5-10 69
MERCURY....4-8 69-76
Picture Sleeves
MERCURY (30160 "Na Na Hey Hey Kiss Him Goodbye")....10-15 76
(Promotional Chicago White Sox sleeve.)
LPs: 10/12-inch
MERCURY....12-18 69

STEAMHAMMER

Singles: 7-inch
EPIC....4-8 69-70
LPs: 10/12-inch
EPIC....15-20 69-70

STEEL, Danny

Singles: 7-inch
SOLAR (1013 "Chinese Twist")....10-15 62

STEEL, Tracy
(With the Outlaws; Tracy Steele)

Singles: 7-inch
C-WAY (227 "Take Me with You")....50-75 '60s
DELAWARE (1705 "A Letter to Paul")....20-30 64

STEEL BREEZE

Singles: 7-inch
BRAND X....10-20 '60s

STEEL GLASS

Singles: 7-inch
LAMARR (245 "I Told My Baby")....10-20 '60s

STEEL IMAGE

Singles: 7-inch
FONTANA (1678 "Hey Jude")....5-10 69
LPs: 10/12-inch
FONTANA....10-15 70

STEELE, Bette Anne

Singles: 78 rpm
ABC-PAR (9744 "Is This the Way")....8-12 56
Singles: 7-inch
ABC-PAR (9744 "Is This the Way")....20-25 56

STEELE, Don
("The Real Don Steele")

Singles: 7-inch
CAMEO (399 "Tina Del Gado Is Alive")...10-15 66
PATCHES (102 "Cecil, the Unwanted French Fry")....5-10 69
WHITE WHALE (366 "Judy, Judy, Judy")..5-10 70

STEELE, Don / Willie Nelson

LPs: 10/12-inch
CATHOLIC COMMUNITY SERVICES (1986 "Renegade Heart")....5-10 86
(Promotional, C.C.S. benefit issue only. Has only one Nelson track, *Healing Hands of Time.*)
Also see STEELE, Don
Also see NELSON, Willie

STEELE, Julia

Singles: 7-inch
AJ (901 'Why Did He Make the Rainbow")....10-15 62
TELLA (1000 "What's in It for Me")....10-20

STEELE, Larry C&W '66
(With the Wranglers)

Singles: 7-inch
AIR STREAM (004 "Daylight Losing Time").4-8 74
ASSAULT (1847 "I Can't Help It")....5-10 63
K-ARK (648 "Baby Workout")....5-10 65
K-ARK (659 "I Ain't Crying Mister")....5-10 65
K-ARK (802 "Hard Times")....5-8 68
K-ARK (875 "How About It, Young Lady")...5-8 68

STEELE, Little Joe

Singles: 7-inch
ABC-PAR (10577 "Too Young")....5-10 64
KC (114 "I'm So Hurt")....10-15 63

STEELE, Sonny

Singles: 7-inch
REPUBLIC (2020 "Sweet Ways About You")....100-150 61
Picture Sleeves
REPUBLIC (2020 "Sweet Ways About You")....200-250 61

STEELE, Tommy

Singles: 7-inch
BUENA VISTA (457 "Fortuosity")....5-10 67
LONDON....8-12 58-60
RCA (8602 "Half a Sixpence")....5-10 65
WAM (1 "Elevator Rock")....10-20 '60s
Picture Sleeves
BUENA VISTA (457 "Fortuosity")....10-15 67
(Two different sleeves. Same value for both.)
LPs: 10/12-inch
LIBERTY (3426 "Everything's Coming Up Broadway")....10-20 65
(Monaural.)
LIBERTY (7426 "Everything's Coming Up Broadway")....20-30 65
(Stereo.)

STEELERS

Singles: 7-inch
CRASH (428 "The Flame Remains")....10-20

GLOW STAR (815 "Walk Alone") 10-20

STEELEYE SPAN LP '75

Singles: 7-inch

CHRYSALIS 4-6 72-78

LPs: 10/12-inch

BIG TREE 12-15 71
CHRYSALIS 8-12 72-78
MFSL (027 "All Around My Hat") 40-60 79
TAKOMA 8-10 81
Also see PRIOR, Maddy, & June Taylor

STEELS, L.C.

Singles: 7-inch

K (14 "Come Back Betty") 10-20
STEELS (101 "I Always Will Love You") 100-200

STEELY DAN P&R/LP '72

Singles: 7-inch

ABC 4-8 72-78
MCA 3-6 78-81

EPs: 7-inch

ABC ("Pretzel Logic") 10-20 74
(Quadraphonic. Juke box "Special Promotional Record." Includes title strips.)
ABC (779 "Countdown to Ecstasy") 5-10 73
(Juke box issue. Includes title strips.)
ABC (12003 "Steely Dan") 5-10 77
(Juke box issue. Includes title strips.)

LPs: 10/12-inch

ABC 6-12 72-78
ABC/COMMAND (40009 "Can't Buy a Thrill") 30-40 74
(Quadraphonic.)
ABC/COMMAND (40010 "Countdown to Ecstasy") 30-40 74
(Quadraphonic.)
ABC/COMMAND (40015 "Pretzel Logic") 30-40 74
(Quadraphonic.)
MCA 5-10 79-82
MFSL (007 "Katy Lied") 50-75 79
MFSL (033 "Aja") 50-75 79
Members: Donald Fagen; Walter Becker; Jim Hodder; Jeff Baxter. Session: Bernard Purdie; Chuck Rainey; Victor Feldman; Larry Carlton; Tom Scott.
Also see BEAD GAME
Also see FAGEN, Donald
Also see JAY & AMERICANS
Also see McDONALD, Michael
Also see ULTIMATE SPINACH

STEEPLECHASE

Singles: 7-inch

POLYDOR 4-8 70

LPs: 10/12-inch

POLYDOR 10-12 70

STEFAN, Paul
(With Royal Lancers; with Apollos; Paul Steffen.)

Singles: 7-inch

CITATION (5003 "I Fought the Law") 50-75 62
(Black vinyl.)
CITATION (5003 "I Fought the Law") .. 100-150 62
(Blue vinyl.)
CITATION (5004 "Baby I Don't Care") 10-20 62
CITE (5007 "Hey Lonely One") 15-25 63
CITE (5008 "You") 15-25 64
DOT (16573 "Hey Lonely One") 8-12 64
Also see PAUL & PACK / Mad Doctors
Also see CRAIG, Vilas, & Royal Lancers / Badgers
Also see PEIL, Danny
Also see PREMIER, Ronnie
Also see ROYAL LANCERS
Also see STONE, Roland
Also see VALIANTS

STEGALL, Bob

Singles: 78 rpm

ABBOTT (139 "Strong Coffee") 10-15 53

Singles: 7-inch

ABBOTT (139 "Strong Coffee") 15-25 53

STEIN, Frank N., & Tombstones

Singles: 7-inch

MARCO (003 "Mess Around") 25-35 62

STEIN, Frankie, & His Ghouls

Singles: 7-inch

POWER (338 "Goon River") 8-10 64

Picture Sleeves

POWER (338 "Goon River") 10-15 64

LPs: 10/12-inch

POWER 15-25 64-65

STEINBERG, Wilbur

Singles: 7-inch

HUT (4401 "Mop Bop Boogie") 150-250 58

STEINWAYS

Singles: 7-inch

OLIVER (2002 "My Heart's Not in It Anymore") 15-25 66
OLIVER (2007 "Call Me") 15-25 66

STEMMONS EXPRESS

Singles: 7-inch

KARMA (201 "Woman, Love Thief") 25-50 69
WAND (1198 "Woman, Love Thief") 10-20 69

STEPHANIE & GOTHICS

Singles: 7-inch

SHELLEY (126 "I'll String Along with You") 10-20 61

STEPHENS, Barbara

Singles: 7-inch

STAX (113 "I Don't Worry") 10-20 61

STEPHENS, Big Will

Singles: 7-inch

CORVET (1013 "Saturday Night") 40-60

STEPHENS, Buddy

Singles: 7-inch

MANCO (1007 "No One Will Know") 10-15 60
MANCO (1033 "Our Star of Love") 10-15 62
MANCO (1050 "If That's What You Want") 10-15 63
YUCCA (109 "What Good Are Memories") 10-20 59
YUCCA (112 "I'm in Love with You") 10-20 59
YUCCA (123 "I Want a True Love") 10-20 60

STEPHENS, Leigh

Singles: 7-inch

PHILIPS (40628 "Red Weather") 5-10 69

LPs: 10/12-inch

PHILIPS (600294 "Red Weather") 30-50 69
Also see BLUE CHEER

STEPHENS, Steve
(With Stevedores)

Singles: 7-inch

REBEL (1314 "Weird Session") 10-20 59
UNITED SOUTHERN ARTISTS (103 "Pizza Pete") 20-40 61

STEPHENS, Tommy

Singles: 7-inch

ABC-PAR (9842 "Camel's Jump") 15-25 57

STEPHENS, Von

Singles: 7-inch

KARL (3006 "Huckleberry Junction") 100-200

STEPHENSON, N.A., & Four Kings

Singles: 7-inch

ROCK IT (103 "Boogie Woogie Country Girl") 4-8 79
WESTWOOD (201 "Boogie Woogie Country Girl") 500-700 59

STEPIN FETCHIT
(Stepin' Fetchit; Stepin Fetchit & Orchestra)

Singles: 78 rpm

FERRIS (904 "Jet-Zoom") 8-10 56
HOLLYWOOD 10-15 55

Singles: 7-inch

FERRIS (904 "Jet-Zoom") 10-15 56
HOLLYWOOD (1037 "Davy Crockett Boogie") 15-25 55
VEE-JAY (382 "The Flight") 5-10 61

LPs: 10/12-inch

VEE-JAY (1032 "Stepin' Fetchit") 25-35 61

STEPPENWOLF P&R/LP '68

Singles: 7-inch

ABC 4-6 70
DUNHILL 5-10 67-71
MCA .... 3-5 '80s
MUMS 4-6 74-75
ROULETTE .... 4-6 '70s

Picture Sleeves

DUNHILL 5-10 71
MUMS 5-10 74

EPs: 7-inch

DUNHILL 5-10 68
(Juke box issues only.)

LPs: 10/12-inch

ABC 8-12 75-76
ALLEGIANCE 5-8
DUNHILL (Except 50053) 10-20 68-73
DUNHILL (50053 "At Your Birthday Party") 20-30 69
EPIC 8-12 75-76
MCA 5-10 79
MUMS 8-10 74
PICKWICK (3603 "The Best of Steppenwolf") 5-10 78
Members: John Kay; Goldy McJohn; Michael Monarch; Jerry Edmonton; Nick St. Nicholas.
Also see HARD TIMES
Also see SPARROWS
Also see T.I.M.E.

STEPPING STARS

Singles: 7-inch

J.C.D.T. (1 "Making Love") 75-125

STEPPING STONES

Singles: 7-inch

DIPLOMACY .... 10-15 '60s
FLAIR (200 "Walk On By") 5-10 68
PHILIPS (40108 "I Got My Job Through the New York Times") 5-10 63

STEREO SHOESTRINGS

Singles: 7-inch

ENGLISH (1302 "Tell Her No") 50-75 68

STEREOPHONICS

Singles: 7-inch

APT (25003 "No More Heartaches") 15-20 58

STEREOS

Singles: 7-inch

MINK (22 "Memory Lane") 50-75 59
(*Memory Lane* was reissued later in 1959, showing the group as the Tams. The same track was again issued in 1963, shown as by the Tams and then by the Hippies.)
Also see HIPPIES / Reggie Harrison
Also see TAMS

STEREOS

Singles: 7-inch

AFS (306 "Hot Rod") 200-300 59

STEREOS P&R '61

Singles: 7-inch

CADET (5577 "Stereo Freeze") 5-10 67
CADET (5626 "I Can't Stop These Tears") 5-10 68
COLLECTABLES 3-5 86
CUB (9095 "I Really Love You") 15-25 61
CUB (9103 "Big Knock") 10-15 61
CUB (9106 "Do You Love Me") 10-15 62
(Black vinyl.)
CUB (9106 "Do You Love Me") 40-50 62
(Yellow vinyl.)
GIBRALTAR (105 "Love for Only You") ... 20-30 59
(Dark blue label.)
GIBRALTAR (105 "Love for Only You") 8-12 59
(Light blue label.)
HYDE (101 "Stereo Freeze") .... 5-10 '60s
WORLD ARTISTS (1012 "Good News") .. 10-15 63
Members: Bruce Robinson; Ronnie Collins; Sam Profit; George Otis; Nathaniel Hicks.

STEREOS

Singles: 7-inch

COLUMBIA (42626 "Echo in My Heart") 600-800 62
(Without promotional stickers.)
COLUMBIA (42626 "Echo in My Heart") 750-1000 62
(With promotional stickers.)
Also see BUCKEYES

STEREOS

Singles: 7-inch

ROBIN NEST (101 "My Heart") 15-25 62
ROBIN NEST (1588 "Don't Cry Darling") . 15-25 62

STEREOS
("Vocals by Tommy Knight")

EPs: 7-inch

MARTINIQUE (17 "The Martinique Nite Club Presents the Sensational Stereos") 20-30 63

STEREOS

Singles: 7-inch

HYDE (101 "Stereo Freeze") 15-25 67
(Reportedly 1000 made.)

STEREOS

Singles: 7-inch

IDEAL ("Life") 10-15
(No selection number used.)

STERLING, Don

Singles: 7-inch

CORVETTE (1008 "Wonderful Someone") 25-35

STERLING, Gee Nee

Singles: 7-inch

LIBERTY (55247 "Mama Don't Tell Me") ... 5-10 59

STERLING, Spencer

Singles: 7-inch

BIG TOP (3104 "Jilted") 10-20 62
JAM .... 10-20 '60s

STERLING BROTHERS

Singles: 7-inch

HERALD (579 "What Is This Thing Called Love") 10-20 63

STERLING GUITARS

Singles: 7-inch

SAX 5TH AVE. (209 "Go Kart") 15-25 63

STERN, Carol, & Companions

Singles: 7-inch

DOVE (236 "Love at First Sight") 10-20 58

STERN, Nina

Singles: 7-inch

JERDEN (759 "Take It from Me") 8-12 65

STEVE / Cookie

Singles: 7-inch

PRESIDENT (431 "I Won't Cry"/"I Won't Cry") 8-12 61
Also see COOKIE

STEVE & DONNA / Steve Venet

Singles: 7-inch

LIBERTY (55192 "All the Better to Love You"/ "Ever Since the World Began") 8-12 59
Also see VENET, Steve

STEVE & DYNAMICS

Singles: 7-inch

RAYCO (101 "Down Payment") 10-15 62
RAYCO (520 "I Wanna Love Somebody") 10-15 62
STERLING (101 "Down Payment") 15-25 62
(First issue.)

STEVE & EMPERORS

Singles: 7-inch

BEST (103 "The Breeze and I") 15-25 64
Also see EMPERORS

STEVE & YOUNGER SET

Singles: 7-inch

SOUND CORE (1001 "After Dark") .... 15-25 '60s

STEVE, BOB, & RICH

Singles: 7-inch

BAT (42484 "Balls") 50-100 84
(Reportedly 2000 made.)

STEVENS, April P&R '51
(With Henri Rene & His Orchestra; April)

Singles: 78 rpm

LAUREL ("No No Not That") 8-12 50
(Selection number not known.)
RCA 5-10 51-52
SOCIETY 10-15 50-51

Singles: 7-inch

A&M 4-6 72-75
ATCO (6346 "Teach Me Tiger '65") 5-8 65
ATCO (6380 "Lovin' Valentine") 5-8 65
CONTRACT (429 "Love Kitten") 5-10 61
IMPERIAL 5-15 59-65
KING (5826 "Soft Warm Lips") 5-10 63
PALACE 3-5 84
RCA 10-20 51-52
SOCIETY (10 "Don't Do It") 20-30 50
SOCIETY (13 "The Envelope and the Rope") 20-30 50
VERVE 4-6 71

EPs: 7-inch
KING (300 "April Stevens")........................ 15-25 54
LPs: 10/12-inch
IMPERIAL (9118 "Teach Me Tiger")........ 20-30 61
(Monaural.)
IMPERIAL (12055 "Teach Me Tiger")...... 25-35 64
(Stereo.)
LIBERTY...5-10 83
Also see RENÉ, Henri & His Orchestra
Also see TEMPO, Nino, & April Stevens

STEVENS, April / Marg Phelan
LPs: 10/12-inch
AUDIO LAB 15-20 59
Also see STEVENS, April

STEVENS, Bob, & His Orchestra
(With Marvin Moran & the Chorus)
Singles: 7-inch
ERRO (102 "Go Get Em Braves")........... 10-20 58

STEVENS, Bobby, & Checkmates Ltd.
LPs: 10/12-inch
RUSTIC 10-15 71
Also see CHECKMATES LTD.

STEVENS, Carol Ann
Singles: 7-inch
CAROL (4111 "Lonely Hearted") 75-125 61

STEVENS, Cat P&R/LP '71
Singles: 12-inch
A&M..5-8 77
Singles: 7-inch
A&M...4-6 70-79
DERAM..4-6 66-72
Picture Sleeves
A&M...4-6 71-78
EPs: 7-inch
A&M...8-10 70
(Juke box issue only.)
LPs: 10/12-inch
A&M...5-10 69-84
DERAM... 10-15 67-72
LONDON..5-10 78
MFSL (035 "Tea for the Tillerman")....... 75-100 79
MFSL (UHQR 035 "Tea for the Tillerman").. 100-125 79
(Boxed set.)
MFSL (244 "Teaser & the Firecat").......... 25-35 95
MFSL (254 "Izitso")............................. 25-35 96

STEVENS, Connie P&R '60
Singles: 7-inch
BELL...4-8 70-72
FARO (596 "Between the Devil and the Deep Blue Sea")...5-10 59
(With Ed Davis.)
MGM (13906 "Wouldn't It Be Nice [To Have Wings and Fly]")... 10-15 68
PARAMOUNT ("Why Can't He Care for Me").. 35-50 58
(Promotional issue only. No actual label name or number is shown, but this may have been distributed by Paramount to promote the film, *Rock-A-Bye Baby*, in which Connie starred.)
W.B. (Except 5092).................................8-12 59-66
W.B. (5092 "Apollo")............................ 15-20 59
Picture Sleeves
W.B. (5159 "Too Young to Go Steady").. 15-25 60
LPs: 10/12-inch
HARMONY.. 10-20 69
W.B. (1208 "Conchetta")...................... 40-50 58
W.B. (1335 thru 1460)......................... 20-40 59-62
Also see BYRNES, Edward

STEVENS, Debbie
(With the Deltones)
Singles: 7-inch
ABC-PAR (10034 "I Sit and Cry") 5-10 59
APT (25027 "If You Can't Rock Me") 50-75 59
ROULETTE (4081 "Jerry") 15-25 58

STEVENS, Dodie P&R '59
(Geraldine Stevens)
Singles: 7-inch
CRYSTALETTE (724 "Pink Shoe Laces")... 10-20 59
CRYSTALETTE (728 "Yes-Sir-ee") 10-20 59
DOLTON (83 "I Wore Out Our Record").....8-12 63
DOT (146 "Pink Shoe Laces"/"Yes-Sir-ee")..4-8 63
DOT (15975 "Miss Lonely Hearts")........... 10-15 59
DOT (16002 "Steady Eddy")..................... 10-15 59
DOT (16067 "Candy Store Blues")........... 10-15 60
DOT (16103 "No").......................................10-15 60
DOT (16139 "Am I Too Young")...............10-15 60
DOT (16167 "Yes, I'm Lonesome Tonight")...10-15 60
DOT (16200 "I Fall to Pieces").....................8-12 61
DOT (16259 "Let Me Tell You About Johnny")...8-12 61
DOT (16279 "In Between Years") 8-12 61
DOT (16339 "I Cried") 5-10 62
DOT (16389 "Pink Shoe Laces"/"Yes-Sir-ee")..5-10 62
IMPERIAL (5908 "Don't Send Me Roses").8-12 63
IMPERIAL (5930 "Hello Stranger") 8-12 63
Picture Sleeves
CRYSTALETTE (724 "Pink Shoe Laces")...30-50 59
LPs: 10/12-inch
DOT (3212 "Dodie Stevens") 30-40 60
(Monaural.)
DOT (3323 "Over the Rainbow")..............30-40 60
(Monaural.)
DOT (3371 "Pink Shoe Laces")................30-40 61
(Monaural.)
DOT (25212 "Dodie Stevens") 40-50 60
(Stereo.)
DOT (25323 "Over the Rainbow")............40-50 60
(Stereo.)
DOT (25371 "Pink Shoe Laces") 40-50 61
(Stereo.)
Session: Billy Vaughn Orchestra.
Also see VAUGHN, Billy, Orchestra

STEVENS, Duke
Singles: 7-inch
LANOR (504 "I've Been Your Fool")........10-15 61
LANOR (506 "I've Been Your Fool") 5-10 61
(Re-recording of 504.)
OKEH (7132 "Yeah Yeah") 40-60 60

STEVENS, Eddie
Singles: 7-inch
CARLTON (556 "Teenage Bachelor")........8-12 61

STEVENS, Hoyt, & Tennessee Ramblers
Singles: 7-inch
LOG CABIN (6171 " '55 Chevy")..........400-500

STEVENS, Hunt
Singles: 7-inch
U.A. (107 "Johnny on the Spot") 10-20 58
U.A. (121 "My Melody") 10-20 58
Picture Sleeves
U.A. (107 "Johnny On the Spot") 20-30 58

STEVENS, Jesse
Singles: 7-inch
BLUEGRASS (712 "Mama Mama")......150-250

STEVENS, Jim
Singles: 7-inch
PROCESS (154 "I'm Gonna Rock Away My Worries")...75-125

STEVENS, Jimmy
(Jimmy Stephens)
Singles: 7-inch
ELDO (112 "Congratulations") 5-10 61
VALIANT (6033 "That's Where the Difference Lies")..40-60 63
VITAPHONIC 15-25
Session: Safaris.
Also see SAFARIS

STEVENS, Johnny
Singles: 7-inch
FORD (123 "Oh Yeah").............................15-25 63
PARKWAY (805 "Hm-Mm-Baby-Hm-Mm")...50-60 59

STEVENS, Julie
(With the Premiers; Julie Stephens)
Singles: 78 rpm
DIG (115 "Blue Mood")..................................8-12 56
Singles: 7-inch
DIG (115 "Blue Mood")............................15-25 56
DIG (129 "Take My Heart") 10-15 57
DORE (547 "True Deep Love")..................20-30 60
DORE (614 "What Makes Little Girls Cry")...15-25 61
DORE (603 "Evening Star") 10-15 61
ELDO (107 "Blue Mood")..............................8-12 61
SURE (104 "Don't Worry About Me") 10-15 60
Also see PREMIERS

STEVENS, Kenny
Singles: 7-inch
JONI (916 "Teen-Age Blues") 5-10 60
OLD TOWN (1158 "Echo in My Heart")....10-15 64

STEVENS, Larry
(With the Three Dolls)
Singles: 7-inch
EPIC (9358 "Wait for Me")......................10-20 60
FINER ARTS (1003 "Just Think of Me").....5-10 61

STEVENS, Mark, & Charmers
Singles: 7-inch
ALLISON (921 "Magic Rose")..................40-50 62
ALLISON (921 "Magic Rose") 4-6 92
(Yellow vinyl. 500 made.)

STEVENS, Matt
Singles: 7-inch
CAMEO (172 "Jimmy's Girl") 8-12 60

STEVENS, Michael
Singles: 7-inch
HANOVER (4512 "Suzanne").......................8-12 58

STEVENS, N., & Dee Vines
Singles: 7-inch
BRUNSWICK (55096 "More and More")..10-20 58

STEVENS, Neil
(With the Temptations; with Dee-Vines)
Singles: 7-inch
BRUNSWICK (55095 "What Could Be Better")...15-25 58
GOLDISC (319 "Ballad of Love")..............10-20 61
GONE (5067 "Ballad of Love")..................15-25 59
Also see TEMPTATIONS

STEVENS, Niki
(With Jack Stern & His Orchestra)
Singles: 7-inch
RIDGEWAY (113 "The Bop")....................10-20 '50s
Session: Buddy Cole; Alvino Rey; Nick Fatool; Clint Neagley; Don Whitaker; Jack Stern.

STEVENS, Randy
Singles: 7-inch
LOMA (301 "All My Love") 20-30 58

STEVENS, Ray P&R '61/C&W '69
(With the Merry Melody Singers)
Singles: 7-inch
BARNABY...4-6 70-76
CAPITOL (3967 "Chickie Chickie Wah Wah")..15-25 58
CAPITOL (4030 "Cat Pants").....................15-25 58
CAPITOL (4101 "The Clown") 15-25 59
CAPITOL/CURB (79430 "Help Me Make It Through the Night")..4-6 90
(Promotional issue only.)
JOY'S LIMITED EDITIONS (74 "The Streak")..10-20
(Promotional issue only.)
MCA (52451 thru 53423)................................3-5 85-88
MCA (53661 "I Saw Elvis in a UFO")...........8-10 89
MERCURY (66 "Butch Barbarian")...........15-25 64
(Promotional issue only.)
MERCURY (71843 "Jeremiah Peabody's Polyunsaturated Quick Dissolving Fast Acting Pleasant Tasting Green and Purple Pills")..............10-15 61
MERCURY (71888 "Scratch My Back")...10-15 61
MERCURY (71966 "Ahab, the Arab") 10-15 62
MERCURY (72039 "Further More")...........10-15 62
MERCURY (72058 "Santa Claus Is Watching You")..10-15 62
MERCURY (72098 "Funny Man")..............10-15 63
MERCURY (72125 "Harry the Hairy Ape")...10-15 63
MERCURY (72189 "Speed Ball") 10-15 63
MERCURY (72255 "Butch Barbarian").....10-15 64
MERCURY (72307 "Bubble Gum the Bubble Dancer")..5-10 64
MERCURY (72382 "Rockin' Teenage Mummies") 8-12 65
MERCURY (72430 "Mr. Baker the Undertaker")...8-12 65
MERCURY (72816 "Funny Man")...............5-10 68
MERCURY (812 496 thru 818 057 series)...3-5 83
MONUMENT..5-10 65-70
NRC (031 "High School Yearbook") 20-30 59
NRC (042 "My Heart Cries for You") 20-30 59
NRC (057 "Sergeant Preston of the Yukon")..15-25 60
NRC (063 "Happy Blue Year") 15-25 60
PREP (108 "Silver Bracelet")....................30-50 57
PREP (122 "Five More Steps")..................30-50 57
PRIORITY...3-5 '80s
RCA...3-6 80-82
W.B./AHAB 4-6 76-79
Picture Sleeves
BARNABY (2024 "Bridget the Midget")........4-8 70
MCA..3-5 86
MERCURY (71843 "Jeremiah Peabody's Polyunsaturated Quick Dissolving Fast Acting Pleasant Tasting Green and Purple Pills")................15-25 61
MERCURY (71888 "Scratch My Back")...15-25 61
MERCURY (71966 "Ahab, the Arab") 15-25 62
MERCURY (72058 "Santa Claus Is Watching You")..15-25 62
MERCURY (72125 "Harry the Hairy Ape")..15-25 63
MERCURY (72307 "Bubble Gum the Bubble Gum Dancer")..15-25 64
W.B./AHAB (8785 "I Need Your Help Barry Manilow")...3-5 79
EPs: 7-inch
MERCURY (85 "Ray Stevens")...............10-20 62
(Promotional issue only. Not issued with cover.)
LPs: 10/12-inch
BARNABY...10-15 70-78
MCA..5-8 85-89
MERCURY (16377 "The Best of Ray Stevens")...10-15 68
MERCURY (20732 "1,837 Seconds of Humor")..50-75 62
MERCURY (20732 "Ahab the Arab") 20-25 62
(Reissue of *1,837 Seconds of Humor.*)
MERCURY (20828 "This Is Ray Stevens")...20-30 63
MERCURY (60732 "1,837 Seconds of Humor")..60-80 62
MERCURY (60732 "Ahab the Arab") 25-35 62
(Reissue of *1,837 Seconds of Humor.*)
MERCURY (60828 "This Is Ray Stevens")...25-35 63
MERCURY (61272 "The Best of Ray Stevens")...10-15 70
MERCURY (810000 series).......................5-8 83
MONUMENT..10-15 66-69
PICKWICK...5-10 71-79
PRIORITY..5-8 82
RCA..5-10 80-82
W.B. 5-10 76-79
Session: Minnie Pearl; Jerry Clower.
Also see ARCHIES
Also see BENTON, Brook
Also see 4 SEASONS / Ray Stevens
Also see MINNIE PEARL
Also see PRESLEY, Elvis
Also see ROE, Tommy / Bobby Rydell / Ray Stevens
Also see VELVETS

STEVENS, Ray / Hal Winters
LPs: 10/12-inch
CROWN..15-20 63
Also see STEVENS, Ray

STEVENS, Rosie, & Suedes
Singles: 7-inch
SPINNING (6011 "Everybody's Trying to Be My Baby")..10-15 60

STEVENS, Scott
(With the Cavaliers)
Singles: 7-inch
ABC-PAR (10054 "I Found a Girl")..........10-20 59
APT (25031 "Sunday in May") 15-25 59
APT (25044 "Too Long Ago") 10-20 60
Also see CAVALIERS

STEVENS, Tari
(With Hugo Winterhalter & His Orchestra; with Joe Leahy's Orchestra; Terri Stevens)
Singles: 78 rpm
DOUBLE AA..5-10 55
RCA...5-10 55-57
Singles: 7-inch
DOUBLE AA (101 "Unsuspecting Heart") 10-20 55
DOUBLE AA (109 "Just Wonderful").......10-20 55
FAIRMONT (1001 "False Alarm")............20-30 66
FELSTED (8538 "All Alone")........................8-12 59
FELSTED (8586 "Adonis")............................8-12 59
RCA (6165 "Why Am I to Blame") 5-10 55
RCA (6393 "Dood-Ly Dood-Ly")...................5-10 56
RCA (7014 "Pin-Up Girl")........................10-15 57
RPC (506 "The Boy Next Door")..............15-25 62

LPs: 10/12-inch
EVEREST (1088 "It's Been a Long, Long Time")....15-20 60
(Monaural.)
EVEREST (5088 "It's Been a Long, Long Time")....20-25 60
(Stereo.)
Also see LEAHY, Joe
Also see WINTERHALTER, Hugo, & His Orchestra

STEVENS, Tracy
Singles: 7-inch
LORD BINGO (106 "My Golden One")....15-25 63

STEVENSON, Scotty, & Edmonton Eskimos
Singles: 78 rpm
RCA BLUEBIRD (3309 "Red Hot Boogie")....50-100 '50s
(Canadian.)
Singles: 7-inch
RCA BLUEBIRD (3309 "Red Hot Boogie")....150-250 '50s
(Canadian.)

STEVENSON, Sonny
Singles: 7-inch
ONDA (111 "Bessie Lou")....15-25 59

STEWARD, Jimmy, Jr.
Singles: 7-inch
CORAL (62514 "Listen Fool")....10-20 67
CORAL (62530 "Convince Me")....40-50 67
HONOR (101 "I Surrender Dear")....15-25 61

STEWART, Al LP '74
Singles: 7-inch
ARISTA....3-6 78-82
ENIGMA....3-6 88
JANUS....4-8 74-77
Picture Sleeves
JANUS....4-8 74
LPs: 10/12-inch
ARISTA (Except 40)....5-10 78-81
ARISTA (40 "Live Radio Concert")....25-35 80
(Promotional issue only.)
ENIGMA....5-8 88
EPIC....20-25 70
JANUS....10-15 74-77
MFSL (009 "Year of the Cat")....50-75 78
MFSL (082 "Time Passages")....30-40 82
Also see PAGE, Jimmy

STEWART, Amii P&R/LP '79
Singles: 12-inch
ARIOLA (Black vinyl)....4-8 79
ARIOLA (7736 "Knock on Wood"/"When You Are Beautiful")....8-12 79
(Picture disc.)
ARIOLA (7736 "Knock on Wood"/"Knock on Wood")....15-25 79
(Picture disc.)
ARIOLA (7736 "Knock on Wood"/"Light My Fire")....20-30 79
(Picture disc. Promotional issue only.)
EMERGENCY....4-6 85
Singles: 7-inch
ARIOLA....3-5 79
EMERGENCY....3-5 85
LPs: 10/12-inch
ARIOLA AMERICA....5-10 79
HANDSHAKE....5-8 81

STEWART, Amii, & Johnny Bristol P&R '80
Singles: 7-inch
HANDSHAKE....3-5 80
Also see STEWART, Amii

STEWART, Andy P&R '61
Singles: 7-inch
CAPITOL (4809 "Take Me Back")....4-8 62
EPIC (2219 "Donald Where's Your Troosers")....4-8 64
TOP RANK (2088 "Scottish Soldier")....8-12 60
WARWICK (627 "Scottish Soldier")....8-15 61
WARWICK (665 "Donald Where's Your Troosers")....15-20 61
WARWICK (676 "Take Me Back")....5-10 62
LPs: 10/12-inch
CAPITOL....5-15 62-72
EPIC....5-15 64-68
GREEN LINNET....4-8 83
WARWICK (2043 "Scottish Soldier")....15-25 61

STEWART, Ben (Queenie)
Singles: 7-inch
A.E.A. (3301 "I Wish I Didn't Love You")..10-20

STEWART, Billy P&R '62
(With the Marquees)
Singles: 78 rpm
ARGO (5256 "Billy's Blues")....10-20 56
CHESS (1625 "Billy's Blues")....20-30 56
OKEH (7095 "Baby, You're My Only Love")....75-100 57
Singles: 7-inch
ARGO (5256 "Billy's Blues")....30-40 56
CHESS (1625 "Billy's Blues")....50-75 56
(Reissued three months later on Argo.)
CHESS (1820 "Reap What You Sow")....8-12 62
CHESS (1835 "Wedding Bells")....8-12 62
CHESS (1852 "Scramble")....8-12 63
CHESS (1868 "Strange Feeling")....8-12 63
CHESS (1888 "Count Me Out")....8-12 64
CHESS (1905 "Tell It Like It Is")....8-12 64
CHESS (1922 "I Do Love You")....5-10 65
CHESS (1932 "Sitting in the Park")....5-10 65
CHESS (1941 "How Nice It Is")....5-10 65
CHESS (1948 "Because I Love You")....5-10 65
CHESS (1960 "Love Me")....5-10 66
CHESS (1966 "Summertime")....10-15 66
(Maroon label.)
CHESS (1966 "Summertime")....5-10 66
(Blue label.)
CHESS (1978 "Secret Love")....5-10 66
CHESS (1991 "Every Day I Have the Blues")....5-10 67
CHESS (2002 "Cross My Heart")....5-10 67
CHESS (2053 "Tell Me the Truth")....5-10 68
CHESS (2063 "I'm in Love")....5-8 69
CHESS (2080 "By the Time I Get to Phoenix")....5-8 69
CHESS (9000 series)....4-6 73
ERIC....4-6 '70s
OKEH (7095 "Baby, You're My Only Love")....75-100 57
U.A. (340 "Young in Years")....15-25 61
LPs: 10/12-inch
CADET (50059 "Cross My Heart")....8-10 74
CHESS (1496 "I Do Love You")....100-125 65
(Red cover. Black label.)
CHESS (1496 "I Do Love You")....50-100 65
(Blue cover. Blue label.)
CHESS (1499 "Unbelievable")....20-40 65
CHESS (1513 "Billy Stewart Teaches Old Standards New Tricks")....15-25 67
CHESS (1547 "Billy Stewart Remembered")....10-15 70
CHESS (50059 "Cross My Heart")....10-15
Session: Four Jewels.
Also see FOUR JEWELS
Also see MARQUEES
Also see STEWART, Billy

STEWART, Bobby
Singles: 7-inch
M.B.S. (1650 "Troubles")....15-25 63

STEWART, Charlie
Singles: 7-inch
QUEEN (24003 "Hey! Castro")....10-20 61
SOLID GOLD (779 "Old Age and Rough Treatment")....150-250

STEWART, D., & Juliettes
Singles: 7-inch
SAGINAW (500 "Got Your Love in My Heart")....30-40

STEWART, Danny
(Danny [Sly] Stewart)
Singles: 7-inch
LUKE (1008 "Long Time Alone")....500-600 61
(Reissued as by Sylvester Stewart.)
PHILLIPS INT'L (3561 "I'll Change My Ways")....20-30 60
Also see STEWART, Danny
Also see STEWART, Sly

STEWART, Darryl
Singles: 7-inch
WAND (11209 "Name It and Claim It")....15-25 69

STEWART, Del
Singles: 7-inch
WATCH (6331 "Let My Lover Go")....10-20 63

STEWART, Don, & Fendermen
Singles: 7-inch
DAB (103 "More Than Words Can Tell")..25-50 59
Also see FENDERMEN

STEWART, Franklin
Singles: 7-inch
JAXON (500 "That Long Black Train").300-400 57
LU (501 "That Long Black Train")....500-750 57
(First issue.)

STEWART, Gary C&W '73
(With the Nashville Edition; with Dean Dillon)
Singles: 7-inch
CORY (101 "Walk On Boy")....10-20 64
DECCA....4-6 71
HIGHTONE....3-5 88-89
KAPP....4-8 68-70
MCA....4-6 75
RCA....3-8 73-83
RED ASH....3-5 84
Picture Sleeves
RCA (10351 "Flat Natural Born Good-Timin' Man")....4-6 75
RCA (13049 "Brotherly Love")....3-5 82
LPs: 10/12-inch
MCA....5-10 75
RCA....5-10 75-83
Also see HARRIS, Emmylou

STEWART, Gene
Singles: 7-inch
KING (5124 "O Baby Dance with Me")....10-15 58

STEWART, James
(Harmonica Cat)
Singles: 78 rpm
FOLK STAR (1192 "Sweet Woman")....10-15 54
Singles: 7-inch
FOLK STAR (1192 "Sweet Woman")....35-45 54

STEWART, Janet
Singles: 7-inch
SUBURBAN (2030 "What Can I Do")....10-15

STEWART, Jimmy
Singles: 7-inch
CRYSTAL ("Rock on the Moon")....150-250 58
(Selection number not known.)
EKO ("Rock on the Moon")....600-700 58
(No selection number used.)
HANOVER (4521 "Crazy Dream")....15-25 59
TRUMP (817 "Livin' Doll")....15-25 59

STEWART, Jimmy, & Night Hawks
Singles: 7-inch
NIGHTHAWK (635 "Nothin' But a Nothin' ")....1000-2000
Members: Jimmy Stewart; Smilin' Roger Perry; Eddy Taylor; Grady Montague.

STEWART, John P&R/LP '69
Singles: 7-inch
ALLEGIANCE....3-5
CAPITOL....5-8 69
RCA....4-6 73-75
RSO....4-6 78-80
W.B.....4-6 71
Picture Sleeves
RCA....5-10 '70s
LPs: 10/12-inch
ALLEGIANCE....5-8 '80s
CAPITOL....10-20 69-70
RCA....5-10 73-75
RSO....5-10 77-80
SHIP....5-10 87
W.B.....8-12 71
Also see CUMBERLAND THREE
Also see KINGSTON TRIO
Also see NICKS, Stevie
Also see STEWART, Johnny, & Furies

STEWART, John, & Buffy Ford
LPs: 10/12-inch
CAPITOL (2975 "Signals Through the Glass")....30-50 68

STEWART, John, & Nick Reynolds
LPs: 10/12-inch
TAKOMA....5-10
Also see KINGSTON TRIO
Also see STEWART, John

STEWART, Johnny
Singles: 7-inch
SHELLEY (128 "Whole Lot of Lovin' ")....10-15 61
START (642 "C'mon and Monkey with Me")....5-10 63

STEWART, Johnny, & Furies
Singles: 7-inch
VITA (169 "Rockin' Anna"/"Lorraine")...400-500 57
Also see STEWART, John

STEWART, Judy, & Her Beatle Buddies
Singles: 7-inch
DIPLOMAT (0101 "Who Can I Believe")....8-12 64
Also see BEATLE BUDDIES

STEWART, Marlow
(With His Four Guitars; with Illusions)
Singles: 7-inch
SOUVENIR (102 "Riptide")....10-20 63
VP (201 "Earthquake")....10-20 '60s
Picture Sleeves
SOUVENIR (102 "Riptide")....25-50 63
(One source shows this label as "Variety" instead of "Souvenir." We're not yet sure which is correct.)

STEWART, Mike
Singles: 7-inch
DWAIN (817 "Kiss By Kiss")....5-10 60

STEWART, Rex, & Vernon Story
Singles: 78 rpm
DIAL....10-15
Also see COLE, Cozy

STEWART, Rod LP '69
(With Faces)
Singles: 12-inch
W.B.....5-10 78-82
Singles: 7-inch
ENIGMA....3-5 88
GEFFEN....3-5 87
GNP....4-6 73
MERCURY....5-8 70-76
POLYDOR....3-5 92
PRESS (8722 "Good Morning Little Schoolgirl")....15-25 65
PRIVATE STOCK....4-6 76
W.B.....3-6 75-93
Picture Sleeves
GEFFEN....3-5 87
MERCURY....8-15 72-73
POLYDOR....3-5 92
W.B.....3-6 78-93
LPs: 10/12-inch
ACCORD....5-8 81
MERCURY (Except 61000 series)....8-12 71-76
MERCURY (61000 series)....10-20 69-70
MFSL (054 "Blondes Have More Fun")....40-60 81
PRIVATE STOCK....8-10 77
SPRINGBOARD....8-12 72
TRIP....8-10 77
W.B. (Except BSP-3276)....5-10 75-88
W.B. (BSP-3276 "Blondes Have More Fun")....10-15 79
(Picture disc. Has Rod Stewart on both sides.)
W.B./RCA (3276 "Blondes Have More Fun")....500-1000 79
(Picture disc. Pictures Rod Stewart and a woman on one side; Elvis Presley – from NBC-TV Special – on reverse. Experimental pressing only.)
Also see BECK, Jeff, & Rod Stewart
Also see G.T.O.
Also see PYTHON LEE JACKSON
Also see SHOTGUN EXPRESS

STEWART, Rod, & Ronald Isley P&R '90
Singles: 7-inch
W.B. (19983 "This Old Heart of Mine")....3-5 90

STEWART, Rod, & Ronnie Wood
Singles: 7-inch
W.B.....3-5 93
Picture Sleeves
W.B.....3-5 93
Also see STEWART, Rod
Also see WOOD, Ron

STEWART, Sandy P&R '53
Singles: 78 rpm
EPIC....5-10 54
OKEH....5-10 53
20TH CENTURY....5-10 54
"X"....5-10 55

Singles: 7-inch
ATCO (6118 "A Certain Smile") 10-15 58
ATCO (6137 "Playmates") 10-15 59
COLPIX (669 "My Coloring Book") 5-10 62
COLPIX (681 "My Favorite Song") 5-10 63
COLPIX (704 "Don't Fall in Love with Me Again") 5-10 63
DCP (1004 "Little Child") 5-10 64
DCP (1122 "I'll Never Go There Anymore") 5-10 64
EAST WEST (122 "To My Love") 8-12 58
EPIC (9016 "The One I Want") 10-20 54
EPIC (9039 "I Understand") 10-20 54
EPIC (9070 "Mama Mama") 10-20 54
OKEH (6941 "Since You Went Away from Me") 10-20 53
OKEH (6967 "If My Heart Had a Window") 10-20 53
OKEH (6991 "Loved and Lost") 10-20 53
OKEH (7000 "The Petals Drop") 10-20 53
20TH CENTURY (5014 "Saturday Night") 10-20 54
U.A. (232 "Indoor Sport") 8-12 60
U.A. (287 "Past the Age of Innocence") 8-12 61
U.A. (332 "Nice Guy") 8-12 61
"X" (0126 "No More Love") 10-20 55
"X" (0156 "In Nuevo Laredo") 10-20 55
"X" (0176 "Could It Be") 10-20 55
Picture Sleeves
COLPIX (669 "My Coloring Book") 10-20 62
LPs: 10/12-inch
COLPIX (441 "My Coloring Book") 15-25 63

STEWART, Sandy / Dave Garroway
Singles: 7-inch
DICK CHARLES ("May You Always") 8-12 63
(Promotional issue only. No selection number used.)

STEWART, Skip
Singles: 7-inch
PAULA (224 "16 Candles") 5-10 65
TAMM .... 4-8 '60s
Also see SHONDELLS / Rod Bernard / Warren Storm / Skip Stewart

STEWART, Sly
Singles: 7-inch
AUTUMN (3 "I Just Learned to Swim") 10-20 64
Also see SLY
Also see SLY & FAMILY STONE
Also see STEWART, Danny
Also see STEWART BROTHERS
Also see STONE, Sly

STEWART, Sylvester
Singles: 7-inch
G&P (901 "Long Time Alone") 100-200 61
(First issued as by Danny [Sly] Stewart.)
Also see STEWART, Danny
Also see STEWART, Sly

STEWART, Ty, & Jokers
Singles: 7-inch
AMY (828 "Young Girl") 10-20 61

STEWART, Vernon — C&W '63
Singles: 7-inch
CHART (501 "The Way It Feels to Die") .. 10-15 63
PEACH (740 "I'll Still Love You") 40-60 60
PEACH (751 "Mean Mean Baby") 50-100 61

STEWART, Wynn — C&W '56
(With the Tourists; Win Stewart)
Singles: 78 rpm
CAPITOL 5-10 56-57
INTRO (6088 "I've Waited a Lifetime"/"After All") 50-100 54
INTRO (6090 "Throw a Little Wood on the Fire"/"Castaway Heart") .... ? ?
(We have yet to confirm any "Win" Stewart Intro 45s. We do not know of any releases of 6090, 78 or 45, though both sides are now on CD.)
Singles: 7-inch
ATLANTIC 4-6 74
CAPITOL (2000 series) 4-8 67-71
CAPITOL (3408 "Waltz of the Angels") 15-25 56
CAPITOL (3515 "Keeper of the Keys") 15-25 56
CAPITOL (3596 "You Took Her Off My Hands") 15-25 56
CAPITOL (3651 "A New Love") 15-25 57
CAPITOL (3803 "I Wish I Could Say the Same") 15-25 57
CAPITOL (5000 series) 5-10 62-67
CHALLENGE 10-15 59-64
4 STAR (8001 "Inflation Blues") 3-6 80
JACKPOT (48005 "Come On") 200-300 58
JACKPOT (48019 "Above and Beyond") .. 20-30 59
PHONORAMA 3-6 83
PLAYBOY 5-10 75-76
PRETTY WORLD 3-6 85
RCA 5-10 72-73
WIN (126 "Eyes Big As Dallas") 4-8 78
WINS (127 "Could I Talk You Into Loving Me Again") 4-8 79
Picture Sleeves
CAPITOL (2012 "Love's Gonna Happen to Me") 5-10 67
CAPITOL (2137 "Something Pretty") 5-10 66
CAPITOL (2240 "In Love") 5-10 68
CAPITOL (5721 "Half of This, Half of That") 10-15 64
CAPITOL (5937 "Cause I Have You") 8-10 67
LPs: 10/12-inch
CAPITOL 10-20 67-75
PICKWICK/HILLTOP 5-12 67
PLAYBOY 5-10 76
STARDAY 8-12 68
WRANGLER (1006 "Wynn Stewart") 30-40 62
Session: Bobby Austin; Bobby Bare; Glen Campbell; Eddie Cochran; Tommy Collins; Hank Garland; Lloyd Green; Merle Haggard; Anita Kerr Singers; Skeet McDonald; Ralph Mooney; Bob Moore; Roy Nichols; Buck Owens; Hargus "Pig" Robbins; Beverly Stewart.
Also see BARE, Bobby
Also see CAMPBELL, Glen
Also see COCHRAN, Eddie
Also see COLLINS, Tommy
Also see GARLAND, Hank
Also see GREEN, Lloyd
Also see HAGGARD, Merle
Also see KERR, Anita
Also see MAPHIS, Joe
Also see McDONALD, Skeets
Also see MOONEY, Ralph
Also see MOORE, Bob
Also see MOORE, Merrill
Also see OWENS, Buck
Also see PIERCE, Webb / Wynn Stewart

STEWART, Wynn, & Jan Howard — C&W '60
Singles: 7-inch
CHALLENGE (9017 "Wrong Company") .. 10-20 60
JACKPOT (48014 "How the Other Half Lives") 15-25 59
LPs: 10/12-inch
CHALLENGE (611 "Sweethearts of Country Music") 40-50 60
STARDAY (421 "Their Hits") 15-25 68

STEWART, Wynn, & Johnny Paycheck
Singles: 7-inch
PRETTY WORLD (008 "The Wild Side of Life") 3-6 85
Also see PAYCHECK, Johnny
Also see STEWART, Wynn

STEWART BROTHERS
Singles: 7-inch
ENSIGN (4032 "The Rat") 75-125 59
KEEN (82113 "Sleep on the Porch") 15-25 60
Picture Sleeves
KEEN (82113 "Sleep on the Porch") 35-50 60
Members: Sly Stewart; Danny Stewart.
Also see STEWART, Danny
Also see STEWART, Sly

STEWART SISTERS
Singles: 7-inch
SPECIALTY (653 "Movie Magazine") 10-15 58

STEWART TWINS
Singles: 7-inch
BATON (259 "Ho Hum") 10-15 58
BATON (263 "Daddy O") 10-15 58

STICK LEGS
("Stick Leg's & the Butchering Persian's" [sic])
Singles: 7-inch
HARD-TIMES (3002 "The Wedding") ... 300-400 62

STICK SHIFTS
Singles: 7-inch
CHISWICK (118 "Paramatta Road") .... 8-12 '60s

STICKS & BRICKS
Singles: 7-inch
JOSIE (839 "Kiss the Pretty Girl Twice") .. 15-25 58

STIDHAM, Arbee
Singles: 78 rpm
ABCO 20-30 56
CHECKER 25-50 52
RCA 10-20 47-52
SITTIN' IN WITH 15-25 51
STATES 10-20 57
Singles: 7-inch
ABCO (100 "I'll Always Remember") 40-60 56
ABCO (107 "When I Find My Baby") 40-60 56
BLUES CITY (1113 "Mighty Long Time") .20-30 '50s
CHECKER (778 "Don't Set Your Cap for Me") 50-100 53
RCA (50-0003 "I Found Out for Myself") .. 50-75 49
(Cherry red vinyl.)
RCA (50-0024 "What the Blues Will Do") .50-75 49
(Cherry red vinyl.)
RCA (50-0037 "Send My Regrets") 50-75 49
(Cherry red vinyl.)
RCA (50-0083 "Let My Dreams Come True") 50-75 50
(Cherry red vinyl.)
RCA (50-0093 "Feel Like I'm Losing You") 50-75 50
(Cherry red vinyl.)
RCA (50-0101 "You'll Be Sorry") 50-75 49
(Cherry red vinyl.)
RCA (4951 "I Found Out for Myself") 50-75 52
STATES (164 "Look Me Straight in the Eyes") 20-30 57
LPs: 10/12-inch
FOLKWAYS (31033 "There's Always Tomorrow") 15-25
MAINSTREAM 8-10 72
PRESTIGE BLUESVILLE (1021 "Tired of Wandering") 50-100 61
Also see CHARLES, Ray / Arbee Stidham / Li'l Son Jackson / James Wayne.
Also see MILLINDER, Lucky

STIERLE, Wayne
Singles: 7-inch
CANDLELITE 4-6 70
LPs: 10/12-inch
CANDLELITE 10-25 70-73
(Black vinyl.)
CANDLELITE 25-35 70-73
(Colored vinyl.)
Also see PHANTOM OF ROCK

STILLINGER, Buzz
Singles: 7-inch
NANCY (1002 "My First Love") 10-15 61

STILLMAN-DAVIS BAND
Singles: 7-inch
COLLEGETOWN (3006 "Orange Bowl Reflections") 10-15 81
(Tiger paw-shaped picture disc. Tribute to Clemson University Tigers Orange Bowl appearance.)
Singles: 7-inch
SP (0102 "We Are Vandy") 8-12 82
(Picture disc.)
LPs: 10/12-inch
BULLDAWG (1001 "Bulldawg Boogie") 10-15 82
(Picture disc. Tribute to University of Georgia football team.)
COLLEGETOWN (3001 "Hoosier High NCAA Champs") 10-15 81
(Picture disc. Tribute to Indiana University basketball team.)
COLLEGETOWN (3002 "Orange Breakout") 10-15 81
(Picture disc. Tribute to Clemson University basketball team.)
COLLEGETOWN (3003 "Carolina Fever") 10-15 81
(Picture disc. Tribute to North Carolina Tar Heels football team.)
GAMECOCK ROCK (1001 "Gamecock Rock") 10-15 81
(Picture disc. Tribute to South Carolina football team.)
SPORT SONG (1002 "Gator Jaws") 10-15 82
(Picture disc. Tribute to University of Florida football team.)
SPORT SONG (1003 "Wolfpack Tracks") 10-15 83
(Picture disc. Tribute to North Carolina State University basketball.)
SPORT SONG (1004 "Hawkeye Boogie") 10-15 83
(Picture disc. Tribute to Iowa University Hawkeyes.)
SPORT SONG (6006 "Illinois Rose") 10-15 83
(Picture disc. Tribute to Illinois University football team.)

STILLROVEN
Singles: 7-inch
AUGUST (101 "Little Picture Playhouse") 20-25 68
AUGUST (102 "Have You Seen Me") 20-25 68
AUGUST (102 "Come in the Morning") .. 80-120 68
(Same selection number used twice.)
FALCON (69 "Hey Joe") 30-50 67
FALCON (7296 "She's My Woman") 150-175 66
ROULETTE (4748 "Hey Joe") 20-25 67

STILLS, Stephen — P&R/LP '70
(With Manassas; with Michael Finnigan)
Singles: 7-inch
ATLANTIC 3-8 70-84
COLUMBIA 4-6 75-78
Picture Sleeves
ATLANTIC (2806 "Change Partners") 4-8 71
ATLANTIC (89633 "Stranger") 3-5 84
EPs: 7-inch
ATLANTIC (77206 "Stephen Stills Two") ... 6-12 71
LPs: 10/12-inch
ATLANTIC 5-10 70-84
COLUMBIA (Except PCQ-33575) 5-10 75-78
COLUMBIA (PCQ-33575 "Stills") 10-20 75
(Quadraphonic.)
Also see AU GO-GO SINGERS
Also see BLOOMFIELD, Mike, Al Kooper & Steve Stills
Also see BUFFALO SPRINGFIELD
Also see CROSBY, STILLS & NASH
Also see JEFFERSON AIRPLANE

STIMULATORS
Singles: 7-inch
SOUND O RIFFIC (2 "Warm Summer Night") .... 150-200 '60s

STING RAYS
Singles: 7-inch
COIN (1511 "Sting Ray Stomp") .... 15-25 '60s
HITT (07 "Run on Home") 10-20 63
L&M (201 "Fast Track") 15-25 61
RAY (3473 "Mad Surfer") 10-20 64
ROSE (101 "Hot Sausage") 10-20 63

STING REYS
Singles: 7-inch
CRAZY TOWN (101 "When You Wish Upon a Star") 20-30 64

STINGERS
LPs: 10/12-inch
CROWN (476 "Guitars a Go Go") 15-25 63

STINGRAYS
Singles: 7-inch
JOBEL (100 "Dynamite") 10-20 65
VAN (04567 "Girl, You Said Again") .... 50-75 '60s
VERMILLION (107 "I Need Her") 10-15 65

STINGRAYS
Singles: 7-inch
WELLHAVEN (8852 "Shaggy Dog") 40-60 67

STING-RAYS
Singles: 7-inch
LAWN (252 "Hey Girl, What'cha Gonna Do") 10-20 65

STING-RAYS OF NEWBURGH
Singles: 7-inch
COLUMBIA (44085 "Fool") 10-20 67
COLUMBIA (44235 "Friday's Gone") 10-20 67

STING-RAYS OF SPRINGFIELD
Singles: 7-inch
RAY (877 "Surfer's Walk") 20-30 67

STINSON BROTHERS
(Ray Stinson; Stinson Trio)
Singles: 7-inch
CANADIAN AMERICAN (192 "Going Back to Birmingham") 10-15 66
EVEREST (19405 "Make Me Know You Love Me") 10-20 61

RKO (1224 "Diggin' That Rock and Roll") 250-350 '60s
RKO (1225 "Everyone's Got Rainbows in Their Eyes") 20-30 '60s
SOMA (1153 "Joker") 15-25 61
SOMA (1183 "Jenny Twist") 50-75 62

LPs:10/12-inch

CANADIAN AMERICAN (1012 "Live in Las Vegas") 15-25 67

STITCH IN TIME

Singles: 7-inch

YORKVILLE 15-20 66

STITES, Gary *P&R '59*

Singles: 7-inch

CARLTON (508 "Lonely for You") 15-20 59
CARLTON (516 "A Girl Like You") 15-20 59
CARLTON (521 "Starry Eyed") 15-20 59
CARLTON (525 "Lawdy Miss Clawdy") 15-20 60
EPIC (10064 "Thinking of You") 5-10 66
MADISON (138 "Young Love") 10-15 60
MADISON (155 "Honey Girl") 10-15 61
MALA (474 "Find Yourself Another Fool") 5-10 64
MR. PEEKE (122 "You Doubted Me") 8-12 62

LPs: 10/12-inch

CARLTON (STLP-120 "Lonely for You") 50-100 60
(Monaural.)
CARLTON (STLP-120 "Lonely for You") 100-200 60
(Stereo.)

STITH, Bill
(With the Corvairs; "Featuring Little Joe & Joyce")

Singles: 7-inch

JAMIE (1417 "Big Bruce") 4-6 73
TWIN (19671 "I'm Gonna Marry You") 30-40 62
Members: Bill Stith; Little Joe Williams.
Also see CORVAIRS

STITT, Sonny *LP '67*
(With Bennie Green)

Singles: 78 rpm

PRESTIGE 5-10 '50s
ROYAL ROOST 5-10 54

Singles: 7-inch

ARGO 5-10 61-65
ATLANTIC 4-6 63
CADET (5701 "Mr. Bojangles") 4-6 74
CADET (5705 "Will You Love Me Tomorrow") 4-6 74
CADET (5708 "Theme from Godfather II") 4-6 74
CATALYST 3-5 77
ENTERPRISE 4-6 69
IMPULSE 4-8 64
PRESTIGE 5-10 63-69
ROULETTE 4-8 66-67
ROYAL ROOST 5-10 54
WINGATE 8-15 65-66
WORLD PACIFIC 4-6 63

EPs: 7-inch

PRESTIGE 10-25 53

LPs: 10/12-inch

ARGO 20-50 58-65
ATLANTIC 15-30 62-64
CADET 10-25 65-74
CATALYST 5-10 76-77
CHESS 8-12 76
COLPIX 10-20 66
EVEREST 5-8 82
FLYING DUTCHMAN 5-10 75-76
IMPULSE 15-25 63-64
JAMAL 8-12 71
JAZZLAND 20-40 62
MUSE 5-10 73-82
PACIFIC JAZZ 20-30 63
PAULA 5-10 74
PRESTIGE (060 "Kaleidoscope") 5-10 83
PRESTIGE (103 "Sonny Stitt Plays") 100-200 51
(10-inch LP.)
PRESTIGE (111 "Mr. Saxophone") 100-200 51
(10-inch LP.)
PRESTIGE (126 "Favorites") 100-200 52
(10-inch LP.)
PRESTIGE (148 "Favorites") 100-200 53
(10-inch LP.)
PRESTIGE (7000 series) 25-75 56-64
(Yellow label.)
PRESTIGE (7000 series) 10-25 65-70
(Blue labels.)
PRESTIGE (10000 series) 8-12 71-74
PRESTIGE (20000 series) 8-15 74
ROOST (418 "At the Hi Hat") 150-250 52
(10-inch LP.)
ROOST (1200 series) 30-50 56
ROOST (2200 series) 15-35 57-66
ROULETTE 10-25 65-70
SAVOY (9006 "Be-Bop") 100-200 53
(10-inch LP.)
SOLID STATE 10-15 69
TRIP 8-12 73
UPFRONT 5-10 77
VERVE 40-80 57-59
(Reads "Verve Records, Inc." at bottom of label.)
VERVE 12-25 62-72
(Reads "MGM Records - A Division Of Metro-Goldwyn-Mayer, Inc." at bottom of label.)
VERVE 5-10 73-84
(Reads "Manufactured By MGM Record Corp." or mentions either Polydor or Polygram at bottom of label.)
Also see MARR, Hank / Sonny Stitt

STITT, Sonny, & Kai Winding

LPs: 10/12-inch

JAZZTONE (1231 "Early Modern") 70-100 56
JAZZTONE (1263 "Early Modern") 50-75 57

STITT, Sonny, Kai Winding & Horace Silver

LPs: 10/12-inch

ROOST (415 "From the Pen of Johnny Richards") 150-250 52
(10-inch LP.)
Also see AMMONS, Gene, & Sonny Stitt
Also see SILVER, Horace
Also see STITT, Sonny
Also see WINDING, Kai

STOCKING HEADS

LPs: 10/12-inch

ROADSIDE (1 "Stocking Heads") 10-15 83
(Picture disc.)

STOECKLEIN, Val

Singles: 7-inch

DOT (17200 "Sounds of Yesterday") 10-15 69
DOT (17234 "All the Way Home") 10-15 69

LPs: 10/12-inch

DOT (25904 "Grey Life") 25-35 68
Also see BLUETHINGS

STOGNER, George

Singles: 78 rpm

DELUXE (2000 "Hardtop Race") 15-25 53

Singles: 7-inch

DELUXE (2000 "Hardtop Race") 75-125 53

STOICS

Singles: 7-inch

BRAMS (101 "Hate") 40-60 67
Also see CHILDREN

STOKER, Billy

Singles: 7-inch

BETTY (1212 "Miami") 15-25 64
Also see CAMPBELL, Dick

STOKES

Singles: 7-inch

II BROS (1 "My Sandra's Jump") 10-20 62

STOKES

Singles: 7-inch

ALON (9019 "Whipped Cream") 8-12 65
ALON (9023 "Fat Cat") 8-12 65
ALON (9026 "Bump Bump") 8-12 65
ALON (9029 "One Mint Julep") 8-12 66
ALON (9032 "Crystal Ball") 8-12 66
Members: Allen Toussaint; Billy Fayard; Al Fayard.
Also see TOUSSAINT, Allen
Also see YOUNG ONES

STOKES, Simon *P&R '69*
(With the Nighthawks; Simon T. Stokes)

Singles: 7-inch

CASABLANCA (0004 "Captain Howdy") 4-6 74
ELEKTRA 4-8 69-70
HBR (487 "Big City Blues") 5-10 66
IN SOUND (406 "Big City Blues") 5-10 68
U.A. 4-6 77

Picture Sleeves

CASABLANCA (0004 "Captain Howdy") 4-8 74

LPs: 10/12-inch

MGM 10-15 70
SPINDIZZY 8-12 73
U.A. 5-10 77

STOKES, Tiny

Singles: 7-inch

BIG T (235 "Blackfoot Boogie") 50-75

STOLTZ BROTHERS

Singles: 7-inch

RODEO ("Rock and Roll Riot") 250-350
(Selection number not known.)

STOMPERS

Singles: 7-inch

SOUVENIR (1003 "I Miss You So") 40-60 60

STOMPERS

Singles: 7-inch

GONE (5120 "Stompin' Round the Xmas Tree") 150-200 61

STOMPERS *P&R '62*

Singles: 7-inch

LANDA (684 "Quarter to Four Stomp") 20-30 62
MERCURY (72111 "Frump") 8-12 63
Members: Bobby Pickett; Leonard Capizzi; Bill Capizzi; Ron Deltorto; Lou Toscano; Don Squire.
Also see CORDIALS
Also see PICKETT, Bobby

STOMPERS

Singles: 7-inch

STOMP (5477 "I Still Love You") 25-35 65
STUDIO CITY (1028 "Hey Baby") 40-60 65

STOMPERS / Dick Dale

LPs: 10/12-inch

CLOISTER (6301 "Sounds of the Silver Surf") 75-125 63
Also see DALE, Dick

STONE, Albert

Singles: 7-inch

KHAWAM (2201 "Ballad from Watts" ["Official Theme Song of the Watts Festival"]) 200-300 65
(Given out at a Watts Festival. Reportedly 1000 made.)
REPRISE (404 "Don't Believe Him, Donna") 5-10 65

STONE, Charlie

Singles: 78 rpm

ARCADE 5-10 52-54
PALACE (105 "Frankie and Johnnie") 10-15 52

Singles: 7-inch

ARCADE (102 "Wanted") 10-20 52
ARCADE (113 "The Boys Are All Gone from My Corner") 10-20 53
ARCADE (129 "Wreck of Old 97") 10-20 54
PALACE (105 "Frankie and Johnnie") 50-75 52

STONE, Cherry

Singles: 7-inch

DIAL (4032 "My Cup Runneth Over") 5-10 66

STONE, Cliffie, & His Orchestra *C&W '47*
(With His Barn Dance Band; Cliffie Stone Singers; Cliffie Stone's Country Hombres)

Singles: 78 rpm

CAPITOL (Except 2910) 3-6 47-57
CAPITOL (2910 "Blue Moon of Kentucky") 4-8 54

Singles: 7-inch

CAPITOL (Except 2910) 4-10 50-69
CAPITOL (2910 "Blue Moon of Kentucky") 10-20 54
TOWER (361 "Del Rio") 4-6 67

LPs: 10/12-inch

CAPITOL (100 thru 300 series) 5-10 68-69
CAPITOL (1000 thru 1600 series) 20-40 58-62
CAPITOL (2100 series) 10-20 64
TOWER 10-15 67
Also see ADAMS, Kay
Also see FORD, Tennessee Ernie

STONE, Daniel A.
(With Jack Nitzsche Orchestra & Chorus)

Singles: 7-inch

CAPITOL (4590 "Little Miss Cool") 10-15 61
SMASH (1757 "Stay in My Heart") 10-15 62
Also see NITZSCHE, Jack

STONE, Doug

Singles: 7-inch

CEE DEE (101 "Memphis Yodel Blues") 50-75

STONE, George

Singles: 7-inch

MUSICOR (1122 "My Beat") 8-12 65

LPs: 10/12-inch

MUSICO 10-15 69

STONE, Jeff

Singles: 7-inch

SARG (151 "Everybody Rock") 75-100 57

STONE, Jesse

Singles: 78 rpm

ATCO 10-15 55
ATLANTIC 10-15 54
RCA 15-25 47-49

Singles: 7-inch

ATCO (6051 "Night Life") 20-30 55
ATLANTIC (1028 "Oh, That'll Be Joyful") 20-30 54
POPLAR (109 "The Stash") 15-25 59
RCA (50-0010 "Cole Slaw") 50-75 49
(Cherry red vinyl.)
Also see FOUR LOVERS

STONE, Jim & Evelyn

Singles: 7-inch

OKIE (1002 "Mustang Twist") 50-75

STONE, Jimmy

Singles: 7-inch

CROSS COUNTRY (523 "Found") 100-200 56
GONE (5001 "Found") 75-125 57

STONE, John
(Johnny Stone)

Singles: 78 rpm

EBB (118 "First Love") 8-12 57

Singles: 7-inch

ACE (579 "Together") 10-20 60
EBB (118 "First Love") 10-20 57
JERDEN (104 "My Blue Heaven") 10-15 60
SPECIALTY (663 "Be Sure") 10-20 59

STONE, Kirby, Four *P&R/LP '58*
(Kirby Stone Quartet)

Singles: 78 rpm

CADENCE (1328 "S' Wonderful") 4-8 57
COLUMBIA 4-8 57

Singles: 7-inch

CADENCE (1328 "S' Wonderful") 8-12 57
COLUMBIA 8-12 57-65
MGM 5-10 67
W.B. 5-10 63-64

LPs: 10/12-inch

ACORN (671 "Show Time") 10-15 62
CADENCE 10-15
COLUMBIA 15-25 58-62
CORONET 8-12 '60s
GOLDEN TONE 8-12
RONDO 8-12 '60s
TOPS (1582 "Kirby Stone Four") 10-20 57
W.B. 10-20 63-64
Members: Kirby Stone; Edward Hall; Michael Gardner; Larry Foster.
Also see FOUR FRESHMEN / Kirby Stone Four / University Four
Also see U.S. DOUBLE QUARTET

STONE, Lawrence

Singles: 78 rpm

DIG (130 "Everytime") 8-12 57
VITA (115 "Dark of Night") 20-25 55

Singles: 7-inch

DIG (130 "Everytime") 10-20 57
VITA (115 "Dark of Night") 30-35 55

STONE, Lee

Singles: 7-inch

CORAL (62077 "A Prayer and a Penny") 5-10 59
CORAL (62129 "Oh, What a Feeling") 15-25 59
R.R.E. (1003 "Black Night") 5-10 63
ROYAL CREST (201 "Black Night") 5-8 68
SANDURA (712 "Wait for Me") 5-10 64

STONE, Roland

Singles: 7-inch

U.S.A. (1212 "Lost Love") 10-20 59
Also see STEFAN, Paul

STONE, Roland

Singles: 7-inch

ACE (593 "Desert Winds") 10-15 60
ACE (629 "Just a Moment") 10-15 61
ACE (643 "I Was a Fool") 10-15 62
ACE (656 "My Mother's Eyes") 10-15 62
SPINNET (1002 "Preacher's Daughter") 10-20 60

LPs: 10/12-inch

ACE 25-35 61

STONE, Sly LP '75
(Sylvester "Sly Stone" Stewart; with Biscaynes)
Singles: 12-inch
EPIC....4-8 80
Singles: 7-inch
A&M....3-5 86
EPIC....4-6 75-79
SUBBARO (489 "Oh What a Night")....10-15 76
LPs: 10/12-inch
EPIC....5-10 79
Also see SLY & FAMILY STONE
Also see STEWART, Sly

STONE CIRCUS
Singles: 7-inch
MAINSTREAM (694 "Mister Grey")....10-15 69
LPs: 10/12-inch
MAINSTREAM (6119 "Stone Circus")....50-75 69
Members: Ronnie Page; Jonathan Caine; Sonny Haines; Mike Burns; Dave Keeler.

STONE COUNTRY
Singles: 7-inch
RCA (9472 "Magnolias")....5-10 68
RCA (9534 "Wheels On Fire")....5-10 68
LPs: 10/12-inch
RCA (3958 "Stone Country")....10-15 68

STONE PILLOW
LPs: 10/12-inch
LONDON (44123 "Eleazar's Circus")....10-15 69

STONE PONEYS P&R/LP '67
(Featuring Linda Ronstadt)
Singles: 7-inch
CAPITOL (2004 "Different Drum")....10-15 67
SIDEWALK (937 "So Fine")....100-150 68
(Same number used on an Unforscene release.)
LPs: 10/12-inch
CAPITOL (2600 & 2700 series)....15-25 67
Also see RONSTADT, Linda

STONED HINGE
Singles: 7-inch
CANDID (2805 "Janis")....15-25 '60s

STONEGROUND
Singles: 7-inch
FLAT-OUT....4-6 76
W.B. 4-6 70-78
LPs: 10/12-inch
FLAT OUT....8-10 76
W.B. (1895 "Stoneground")....10-15 71
W.B. (1956 "Stoneground Family Album")....15-20 71
W.B. (2645 "Stoneground 3")....10-15 72
W.B. (3187 "Hearts of Stone")....8-10 78
Members: Sal Valentino; Tim Barnes; Annie Sampson; Pete Sears; Deirdre La Porte; Lynne Hughes; Luther Bildt; Cory Lerios; Steven Price.
Also see JEFFERSON STARSHIP
Also see PABLO CRUISE
Also see SANDALS
Also see VALENTINO, Sal

STONEHAM, Luther
Singles: 78 rpm
MERCURY....25-40 51
Also see SMITH, Thunder

STONEHENGE
Singles: 7-inch
BOZO ("King Snake")....20-30
(Selection number not known.)
RENEGADE....4-8 70

STONEMANS C&W '66
(With the Tracy Schwartz Band; Stoneman Family)
Singles: 7-inch
GULF REEF (1010 "White Lightning")....5-10 62
MGM....4-8 66-68
STARDAY (599 "That Pal of Mine")....5-10 62
WORLD PACIFIC (413 "Take Me Home")....4-8 64
LPs: 10/12-inch
CMH....5-12 76-82
FOLKWAYS....10-20
MGM....10-20 66-70
NASHVILLE (2063 "Stonemans")....8-12 68
RCA....6-12 70-71
STARDAY (393 "White Lightning")....15-25 65
SUNSET (5203 "Live")....10-15 68
WORLD PACIFIC (1828 "Stoneman Family")....15-20 64
Members: Pop; Donna; Scott; Van; Roni.

STONEMEN
Singles: 7-inch
BIG TOPPER (1017 "No More")....10-15 66

STONEY & MEAT LOAF P&R '71
Singles: 7-inch
RARE EARTH (5027 "What You See Is What You Get")....4-6 71
RARE EARTH (5033 "It Takes All Kinds of People")....4-6 71
LPs: 10/12-inch
PRODIGAL....5-10 78
RARE EARTH....10-15 71
Also see MEAT LOAF

STOOGES LP '69
(Featuring Iggy Pop)
Singles: 7-inch
ELEKTRA....5-10 69-70
LPs: 10/12-inch
BOMP (114 "Jesus Loves the Stooges")....8-12 78
(10-inch LP. With 3-D cover and 3-D glasses.)
ELEKTRA....15-25 69-70
Also see POP, Iggy

STOOKEY, Paul P&R/LP '71
Singles: 7-inch
ERIC....4-6 '70s
W.B. 4-6 71-72
LPs: 10/12-inch
NEWPAX....5-8
W.B. 10-15 71
Also see PETER, PAUL & MARY

STOPPERS
Singles: 7-inch
JUBILEE (5528 "The La La Song")....15-25 66

STORCH, Larry
(With Leroy Holmes & Orchestra)
Singles: 78 rpm
ROULETTE....8-12 57
Singles: 7-inch
JUBILEE (5462 "Valachi Sings")....5-10 63
MGM (12711 "Pooped")....5-10 58
ROULETTE (4014 "I'm Walkin' ")....8-12 57
ROULETTE (4024 "Goody Goody")....8-12 57
LPs: 10/12-inch
PRESTIGE (30005 "Larry Storch Reads Philip Roth's *Epstein*")....8-12 62

STOREY, Dean, & Dukes
Singles: 7-inch
SURF (1521 "Ring-a Ding Ding")....50-100 58
Members: Dick Sherman; Robert Sherman.

STOREY, Denny
Singles: 7-inch
SONIC (219 "Kind of a Hush")....5-10 '60s
Also see DEE JAY & RUNAWAYS
Also see CHEVELLES
Also see JERRY & CASUALS / Rockin' Tones

STOREY SISTERS P&R '58
Singles: 7-inch
BATON (255 "Cha Cha Boom")....10-20 58
CAMEO (126 "Bad Motorcycle")....20-30 58
MERCURY (71457 "Lost Love")....10-15 59
Members: Lillian Storey; Ann Storey.
Also see TWINKLES

STORIES P&R/LP '72
(Ian Lloyd & Stories)
Singles: 7-inch
ERIC....4-8 '70s
KAMA SUTRA (Except 545)....4-6 72-74
KAMA SUTRA (545 "I'm Coming Home")....5-10 72
(Cardboard cover.)
RADIOACTIVE GOLD....4-6 74
LPs: 10/12-inch
KAMA SUTRA....8-12 72-73
Members: Michael Brown; Ian Lloyd; Bryan Madey; Steve Love.
Also see LEFT BANKE

STORM, Billy P&R '59
(With the Valiants; "Orchestra Directed by Neely Plumb")
Singles: 7-inch
ATLANTIC (2076 "Chapel in the Moonlight")....10-15 60
ATLANTIC (2098 "Dear One")....10-15 61
ATLANTIC (2112 "Honey Love")....10-15 61
BARBARY COAST (1001 "The Way to My Heart")....75-125 58
BUENA VISTA (403 "Puppy Love Is Here to Stay")....15-20 62
BUENA VISTA (413 "Love Theme from El Cid")....15-20 62
BUENA VISTA (415 "Double Date")....15-20 63
BUENA VISTA (418 "Deed I Do")....15-20 63
BUENA VISTA (424 "Motherless Child")....15-20 63
BUENA VISTA (429 "Since I Fell for You")....15-20 63
COLUMBIA (41356 "I've Come of Age")....10-20 59
COLUMBIA (41431 "Easy Chair")....10-20 59
COLUMBIA (41494 "Emotion")....10-20 59
COLUMBIA (41545 "Enchanted")....10-20 59
EARLY BIRD (1001 "This Is the Nite")....4-6 95
(Orange vinyl.)
EARLY BIRD (1003 "Please Wait My Love")....4-6 95
(Dark green vinyl.)
ENSIGN (4035 "We Knew")....10-20 59
GREGMARK (9 "3,000 Tears")....10-20 61
HBR (474 "Please Don't Mention Her Name")....10-15 66
INFINITY (013 "Don't Let Go")....10-15 62
INFINITY (018 "A Million Miles from Nowhere")....10-15 63
INFINITY (023 "Educated Fool")....10-15 63
LOMA (2001 "I Never Want to Dream Again")....8-12 64
LOMA (2009 "Goldfinger Theme")....8-12 65
ODE (120 "Coal Mine")....5-10 69
Picture Sleeves
HBR (474 "Please Don't Mention Her Name")....15-25 66
LPs: 10/12-inch
BUENA VISTA (3315 "Billy Storm")....30-40 63
FAMOUS (504 "This Is the Night")....100-200 69
Also see CHARADES
Also see CHAVELLES
Also see ELECTRAS
Also see SABERS
Also see VALIANTS

STORM, Gale P&R '55
(With Billy Vaughn's Orchestra)
Singles: 78 rpm
DOT....8-15 55-56
Singles: 7-inch
CONFIDEO....5-10
DOT (15412 "I Hear You Knocking")....15-20 55
DOT (15436 "Memories Are Made of This")....10-20 55
DOT (15448 "Why Do Fools Fall in Love")....10-20 56
DOT (15458 "Ivory Tower")....10-20 56
DOT (15474 "Tell Me Why")....10-20 56
DOT (15492 "Now Is the Hour")....10-20 56
DOT (15515 "My Heart Belongs to You")....10-20 56
DOT (15528 "I Need You So")....10-20 56
DOT (15539 "On Treasure Island")....10-20 57
DOT (15558 "Dark Moon")....10-20 57
DOT (15606 "Love By the Jukebox Light")....10-20 57
DOT (15666 "Go Way from My Window")....10-20 57
DOT (15691 thru 16111)....8-15 58-60
DOT (100 series)....5-8 63
REO (8140 "I Need You So")....10-20 56
(Canadian.)
Picture Sleeves
DOT (15734 "You")....20-30 58
EPs: 7-inch
DOT (1050/1051/1052 "Gale Storm")....15-25 56
(Price is for any of three volumes.)
DOT (1074 "Gale's Great Hits")....15-25 58
LPs: 10/12-inch
DOT (3011 "Gale Storm")....50-100 56
DOT (3017 "Sentimental Me")....50-75 56
DOT (3098 "Gale Storm Hits")....50-75 58
DOT (3197 "Softly and Tenderly")....30-50 59
(Monaural.)
DOT (3209 "Gale Storm Sings")....30-50 59
DOT (25197 "Softly and Tenderly")....40-60 59
(Stereo.)
HAMILTON (171 "I Don't Want to Walk Without You")....10-20 66
(Monaural.)
HAMILTON (12171 "I Don't Want to Walk Without You")....10-20 66
(Stereo.)
MCA....5-10 82
Session: Thurl Ravenscroft.
Also see RAVENSCROFT, Thurl
Also see VAUGHN, Billy, Orchestra

STORM, Rocky
(With the Twinkletones)
Singles: 7-inch
JOSIE (847 "Should I")....15-25 58
RENDEZVOUS (109 "Blue Wind")....10-20 59
RENDEZVOUS (198 "Blue Wind")....5-10 63

STORM, Rory, & Hurricanes / Faron's Flamingos
Singles: 7-inch
COLUMBIA (43018 "I Can Tell")....20-30 64

STORM, Tom, & Peps
Singles: 7-inch
GE GE ("That's the Way Love Is")....20-30 65
(No selection number used.)
Also see PEPS

STORM, Warren P&R '58
Singles: 78 rpm
NASCO (6015 "Prisoner's Song")....20-30 58
NASCO (6025 "Troubles Troubles")....25-45 59
Singles: 7-inch
ATCO (6577 "Nobody Would Know")....5-8 68
DOT (16272 "Gotta Go Back to School")....10-15 61
DOT (16344 "It's Hard But It's Fair")....10-15 62
KINGFISH....4-8
NASCO (6015 "Prisoner's Song")....15-25 58
NASCO (6025 "Troubles Troubles")....15-25 59
NASCO (6028 "So Long So Long")....15-25 59
NASCO (6031 "Birmingham Jail")....15-25 60
ROCKO (512 "Oh Oh Baby")....15-20 61
ROCKO (520 "I'm Such a Fool")....15-20 61
SINCERE (102 "Love Me Cherry")....20-40 57
SINCERE (107 "Honky Tonk Song")....20-40 58
SOUTH STAR....3-5 83
STARFLITE....4-6 79
TOP RANK (2086 "No No")....10-15 60
ZYNN (1019 "Kansas City")....10-20 62
ZYNN (1021 "This Should Go On Forever")....10-20 62
ZYNN (1024 "Let Me Know")....10-20 62
Also see LIGHTNIN' SLIM
Also see SHONDELLS / Rod Bernard / Warren Storm / Skip Stewart

STORM TRIO
Singles: 78 rpm
THERON....20-30 55
Singles: 7-inch
JUBILEE (5306 "Wonderful Lover")....10-15 57
KIETH (5177 "Wonderful Lover")....40-50 57
(First issue.)
THERON (107 "You're Mine Again")....100-150 55

STORMS
Singles: 7-inch
SUNDOWN (114 "Thunder"/"Tarantula")....35-45 59
(Both sides were rerecorded in 1961 [Indigo 127] as by Jody Reynolds & the Storms.)
Members: Al Casey; Jody Reynolds; Billie Ray; Plas Johnson; Noel Stutte; Ray Martinez.
Also see CASEY, Al
Also see REYNOLDS, Jody, & Storms

STORMS
Singles: 7-inch
IMPALA (212 "Thunder")....10-20 60
(Despite identical title, this is a different band and music than the Storms on Sundown.)

STORMS (CARL GROVES)
Singles: 7-inch
MUSICALE (116 "Canteen Baby")....35-50 59

STORMY HERMAN & HIS MIDNIGHT RAMBLERS
Singles: 78 rpm
DOOTONE (358 "The Jitterbug")....8-12 55
Singles: 7-inch
DOOTONE (358 "The Jitterbug")....25-35 55

STORY, Allen
(Allen Bo Story)
Singles: 7-inch
ANNA (1118 "Blue Moon")....25-35 60
CHECK MATE (1014 "Why Oh Why")....15-25 62

STORY TELLERS
Singles: 7-inch
$TACK (500 "You Played Me a Fool")....250-350 59

STORY TELLERS
Singles: 7-inch
TRYSTERO (101 "Cry with Me") 20-30 67

STORYBOOK
Singles: 7-inch
SIDEWALK (940 "Psych-Out") 5-10 68

STORYBOOK PEOPLE
Singles: 7-inch
DUNHILL (4100 "Do You Believe") 5-10 67
DUNHILL (4130 "No Return") 5-10 68

STORYTELLERS
Singles: 7-inch
CAPITOL (5042 "I Don't Want an Angel") 15-25 63
CLASSIC ARTISTS (118 "Please Remember My Love") 5-8 90
(Black vinyl. 1000 made.)
CLASSIC ARTISTS (118 "Please Remember My Love") 8-10 90
(Red vinyl. 1000 made.)
CLASSIC ARTISTS (133 "Heart for Heart") .4-6 92
(Red vinyl. 1000 made.)
COLUMBIA (42930 "Engagement Party") ..8-12 63
DIMENSION (1014 "When Two People") 15-25 63
RAMARCA (501 "When Two People") 25-35 63
Members: Steve Barri; Carol Connors.
Also see BARRI, Steve
Also see CONNORS, Carol

STOUT, Bernie
Singles: 7-inch
BAR BEE ("It's Too Bad for Me") 10-20
(Selection number not known.)

STOVALL, LaVerne
Singles: 7-inch
FELSTED (8516 "Left Behind") 1500-2500 58
FELSTED (8516 "Left Behind") 500-750 58
(Yellow label. Canadian.)
KIP (400 "Your Love") 250-350 59
(500 made.)

STOVALL, Percy
Singles: 7-inch
BLUE ROCK (4006 "Lisa") 5-10 64

STOWAWAYS
LPs: 10/12-inch
JUSTICE (148 "Stowaways") 350-450 68

STRAGGLERS
Singles: 7-inch
BRISTOL (6005 "Girl of My Dreams") 50-75 64

STRAIGHT A's
Singles: 7-inch
KAPP (2017 "Blue Moon") 5-10 69
KAPP (2057 "Too Big to Hide") 5-10 69
LPs: 10/12-inch
KAPP (3604 " Straight A's") 10-15 69

STRAIT, George *C&W '81*
Singles: 7-inch
D 15-25 76
MCA 3-5 81-91
LPs: 10/12-inch
MCA 5-10 81-91

STRAITJACKETS
Singles: 7-inch
U.A. (453 "Gigolo") 15-25 62
Members: Delbert McClinton; Ronnie Kelly; Bob Jones; Billy Cox; Ray Torres.
Also see CHANNEL, Bruce
Also see CLINTON, Mac, & Straitjackets

STRANDS
Singles: 7-inch
FIREFLY (331 "How Will I Know") 100-125 60
TRI-ODE (101 "Never") 25-35 62

STRANGE
(With "Narration by Edmond Good")
Singles: 7-inch
OUTER GALAXY (11229 "Jimi") 15-25 73
OUTER GALAXY (11229-A "Color My World") 15-25 73
OUTER GALAXY (11250-A "My Sweet Daddy's Home") 15-25 74
OUTER GALAXY (11250-2-A "I Dreamt I Love You") 20-40 74
OUTER GALAXY (305322 "Jimi") 15-25 73
OUTER GALAXY (321570 "Annihilation") 15-25 73
Note: On some releases, label name may be shown as "Outer Galaxie." As is shown, their numbering pattern is indeed strange.
LPs: 10/12-inch
OUTER GALAXY (1000 "Translucent World") 75-100 73
OUTER GALAXY (1001 "Raw Power") ..75-100 76
Members: Terry Brooks; Don Haste; John Kotch; Donnie Capetta; Jim Chapman; Don Hall; Brian Leary.

STRANGE, Billy *P&R/LP '64*
(With the Telstars; with Transients)
Singles: 78 rpm
CAPITOL 5-10 54-55
DECCA 5-10 55
ERA 5-10 56
Singles: 7-inch
BUENA VISTA (406 "I'll Remember April") 15-20 62
BUENA VISTA (417 "Johnny Shiloh") 15-20 63
CAPITOL 10-15 54-55
COLISEUM (605 "A Lotta Limbo") 5-10 63
DECCA (29551 "Gamblin' Hall") 10-15 55
ERA (1014 "Buddy's Girl") 10-15 56
ERA (1030 "Big Man") 10-15 56
GNP 5-10 64-65
LIBERTY 5-10 61-62
TOWER 4-6 69
LPs: 10/12-inch
COLISEUM (100 "Limbo Rock") 10-20 62
GNP 8-20 63-75
HORIZON (1633 "Funky Twelve String") .10-15 63
SUNSET (5209 "Mr. Guitar") 8-10 68
SURREY (1001 "The Best of Billy Strange") 10-15 65
TRADITION (2080 "Strange Country") 8-12 68
Also see AVALANCHES
Also see CAMPBELL, Glen, & Billy Strange
Also see CATALINAS
Also see JOHNSON, Sweetpea
Also see NELSON, Willie
Also see PETERSEN, Paul
Also see TRANSIENTS

STRANGE, Billy, & Challengers
Singles: 7-inch
GNP (380 "Milord") 5-10 66
LPs: 10/12-inch
GNP (2030 "Billy Strange and the Challengers") 15-20 66
Also see CHALLENGERS
Also see STRANGE, Billy

STRANGE, Tommy
Singles: 7-inch
ERA (3157 "Two Steps Forward") 5-10 65
RAMCO (1986 "Piano Man from Louisiana") 5-10 67
RAMCO (1995 "One More Time") 5-10 67
ROCKO (504 "Nervous and Shakin' All Over") 100-200 60

STRANGE FATE
Singles: 7-inch
CAR (2002 "Hold Me Baby") 15-25 67

STRANGELOVES *P&R/LP '65*
Singles: 7-inch
BANG (501 "I Want Candy") 10-15 65
BANG (508 "Cara-Lin") 8-12 65
BANG (514 "Night Time") 8-12 65
BANG (524 Hand Jive") 8-12 66
BANG (544 "Quarter to Three") 8-12 67
SIRE (4102 "I Wanna Do It") 5-8 68
SWAN (4192 "I'm on Fire") 10-20 64
LPs: 10/12-inch
BANG (BLP-211 "I Want Candy") 35-55 65
(Monaural.)
BANG (BLPS-211 "I Want Candy") 55-65 65
(Stereo.)
Members: Bob Feldman; Jerry Goldstein; Richie Gottehrer. Session: Tom Kobus; Jack Raczka; John Shine; Richie Lauro; George Young; Joe Piazza; Ken Jones.
Also see HUMBLE MUD
Also see McCOYS
Also see SHEEP

STRANGERS
Singles: 78 rpm
KING 50-125 54-56
Singles: 7-inch
KING (4697 "My Friends") 100-200 54
(Does not have "High Fidelity" on label.)
KING (4697 "My Friends") 25-35 54
(With "High Fidelity" on label.)
KING (4709 "Blue Flowers") 500-750 54
(Does not have "High Fidelity" on label.)
KING (4709 "Blue Flowers") 40-50 54
(With "High Fidelity" on label.)
KING (4722 "Hoping You'll Understand") 200-300 54
(Does not have "High Fidelity" on label.)
KING (4722 "Hoping You'll Understand") .25-35 54
(With "High Fidelity" on label.)
KING (4745 "Drop Down to My Place") ..75-125 54
KING (4766 "How Long Must I Wait") ...200-300 54
(Blue label.)
KING (4766 "How Long Must I Wait") ...250-350 54
(White bio label. Promotional issue only.)
KING (4821 "Without a Friend") 50-150 55
(Does not have "High Fidelity" on label.)
KING (4821 "Without a Friend") 20-30 56
(With "High Fidelity" on label.)
Members: William Clarke; John Grant; Pringle Sims; Woodrow Jackson; Seifert Brizant; Al Brizant.

STRANGERS
Singles: 7-inch
CHRISTY (107 "We're in Love") 10-15 59
CHRISTY (108 "Song About Judy") 20-30 59

STRANGERS *P&R '59*
Singles: 7-inch
TITAN (1701 "Caterpillar Crawl") 15-25 59
TITAN (1702 "Hill Stomp") 15-25 59
TITAN (1704 "Boogie Man") 15-25 60
TITAN (1711 "Navajo") 15-25 60
Member: Joel Hill.
Also see HILL, Joel

STRANGERS
Singles: 7-inch
KCM (3703 "Honky Tonk Women") 50-75 59

STRANGERS
Singles: 7-inch
CHOICE (5 "Bret Maverick") 10-15 60

STRANGERS
Singles: 7-inch
CHECKER (1010 "Darlin' ") 5-10 62
MASKE (101 "I'm Feeling Sad") 25-35 60

STRANGERS
Singles: 7-inch
CUCA (1172 "Runaway") 40-60 64
LIBERTY (55481 "Loco") 8-12 62
LIBERTY (55550 "Card Shark") 8-12 63
Members: Bill Velline; Dick Dunkirk; Bob Korum; Ken Harvey.
Also see DUNKIRK, Dick, & Strangers
Also see JOHNSON, Dave, & Shadows
Also see TORNADOES
Also see VEE, Bobby

STRANGERS
Singles: 7-inch
KL (115 "Land of Music") 15-25 66
LINDA (118 "Tell Me") 15-25 65
W.B. (5438 "Night Winds") 10-20 64

STRANGERS
Singles: 7-inch
CHATTAHOOCHEE (710 "Like a Stranger") 8-10 66
JUBILEE (5514 "What's the Matter Baby") 8-10 65

STRANGERS
Singles: 7-inch
ORIEL (341 "What a Life") .... 10-20 '60s

STRANGERS IN TOWN
Singles: 7-inch
DATE (1531 "Inside Outside") 5-10 66
TOY TIGER (1003 "You'll Never Know") ..10-20 67

STRASSMAN, Marcia
Singles: 7-inch
UNI (55006 "Flower Children") 5-10 67
UNI (55023 "Flower Shop") 5-10 67
Picture Sleeves
UNI 8-12 67

STRATEGICS
Singles: 7-inch
LYNDELL (773 "I Am Looking Too") 20-30

STRATFORDS
("Music by the Ambassadors")
Singles: 7-inch
UNIVERSAL ARTISTS (1215 "Promise Her Anything") 75-100 61

STRATO-JACS
Singles: 7-inch
PARROT (45003 "Sunset Surfer") 10-20 64

STRAT-O-LITES
Singles: 7-inch
TEL (1008 "Hot Foot") 10-20 59

STRAUSS, Sharon
Singles: 7-inch
ABC-PAR (10349 "Don't Keep Our Friends Away from Me") 5-10 62
Picture Sleeves
ABC-PAR (10349 "Don't Keep Our Friends Away from Me") 8-12 62

STRAWBERRY ALARM CLOCK *P&R/LP '67*
Singles: 7-inch
ALL AMERICAN (373 "Incense and Peppermints") 100-150 67
MCA 3-6 73-80
UNI (Except 55218) 5-15 67-70
UNI (55218 "California Day") 10-20 70
LPs: 10/12-inch
BACK-TRAC 5-10 85
UNI (73014 "Incense and Peppermints") .20-40 67
UNI (73025 "Wake Up, It's Tomorrow") ...20-40 67
UNI (73035 "The World in a Seashell") ...20-40 68
UNI (73054 "Good Morning Starshine") ...20-40 69
UNI (73074 "The Best of the Strawberry Alarm Clock") 20-40 70
VOCALION (73915 "Changes") 15-20 71
Members: George Munford; Randy Seol; Ed King; Lee Freeman; George Bunnel; Jimmy Pitman; Gary Loverto; Gene Gunnels; Mark Weitz.
Also see GOLDTONES
Also see IRIDESCENTS
Also see LYNYRD SKYNYRD
Also see SIXPENCE
Also see WHO / Strawberry Alarm Clock

STRAWBERRY CHILDREN
Singles: 7-inch
SOUL CITY (758 "Love Years Coming") .. 10-20 67
Member: Jimmy Webb.

STRAWBS *LP '72*
Singles: 7-inch
A&M 4-8 68-75
ARISTA 3-5 78
OYSTER 4-6 76-77
LPs: 10/12-inch
A&M 8-15 71-78
ARISTA 5-10 78
OYSTER 8-12 76-77
Also see WAKEMAN, Rick

STRAWN, Ron, & Bucks
Singles: 7-inch
EKO (503 "Drivin' ") 100-150 58

STREAMERS
Singles: 7-inch
DOT (16648 "Blue Mountain") 8-12 64
Session: Davie Allan.
Also see ALLAN, Davie

STREAPLERS
Singles: 7-inch
CENTURY (0007 "Yes Tonight, Josephine") .... 15-20 '60s

STREET
Singles: 7-inch
TRAFFIC (1001 "Why Concern Yourself") . 5-10 69
VERVE FORECAST (5103 "It's Hard to Live On Promises") 4-8 69
LPs: 10/12-inch
VERVE FORECAST (3057 "Street") 10-15 68

STREET, Richard, & Distants
Singles: 7-inch
HARMON (1002 "Answer Me") 50-75 62
Members: Richard Street; Eddie Kendricks; Paul Williams.

Also see DISTANTS
Also see TEMPTATIONS

STREET CLEANERS
Singles: 7-inch
AMY (916 "Garbage City")........................ 10-20 64
Members: Phil Sloan; Steve Barri.
Also see FANTASTIC BAGGYS

STREET SINGERS
Singles: 7-inch
TUXEDO (899 "Tonight Was Like a Dream")... 100-125 56

STREISAND, Barbra LP '63
Singles: 12-inch
COLUMBIA (White label)........................ 15-25 79-85
(Promotional issues only.)
COLUMBIA (39909 "Emotion") 20-30 85
(Picture disc.)
COLUMBIA (99-1791 "The Way He Makes Me Feel").. 30-40 85
(Picture disc. Promotional issue only.)
Singles: 7-inch
ARISTA (123 "More Than You Know") 4-6 75
COLUMBIA (02065 thru 05680)...................3-5 83-85
COLUMBIA (10450 thru 11364)...................3-6 76-80
COLUMBIA (3-42648 "My Coloring Book") 20-30 62
(Compact 33 Single.)
COLUMBIA (4-42648 "My Coloring Book") 8-12 62
COLUMBIA (42631 "Happy Days Are Here Again")..5-10 63
COLUMBIA (42965 thru 43469)...................4-6 64-65
COLUMBIA (43518 thru 46024)...................4-6 66-74
COLUMBIA (80826 "All I Ask of You").........4-8 88
Promotional Singles
COLUMBIA (02065 thru 05680)...................4-8 83-85
COLUMBIA (10450 thru 11364)...................4-8 76-80
COLUMBIA (4-42648 "My Coloring Book") 20-30 62
COLUMBIA (42631 "Happy Days Are Here Again") 15-25 63
COLUMBIA (42965 thru 43469).............. 10-20 64-65
(Black vinyl.)
COLUMBIA (42965 "People") 40-60 64
(Red vinyl.)
COLUMBIA (43248 "Why Did I Choose You") 40-60 65
(Blue vinyl.)
COLUMBIA (43469 "Second Hand Rose") 40-60 65
(Red vinyl.)
COLUMBIA (43518 thru 46024).................6-12 66-74
COLUMBIA (79581 "People – Special Open-End Interview") 15-25 64
(Promotional issue only. Compact 33.)
COLUMBIA (80826 "All I Ask of You")........5-10 88
Picture Sleeves
COLUMBIA (Except 43896 & 79581) 3-6 73-85
COLUMBIA (43896 "Ave Maria") 5-8 66
COLUMBIA (79581 "People – Special Open-End Interview") 15-25 64
(Promotional issue only.)
EPs: 7-inch
CAPITOL (2636 "Complete Solo Tracks from the Capitol Original Broadway Cast Album *Funny Girl*") 15-25 64
LPs: 10/12-inch
ARISTA..8-10 75
CAPITOL (2059 "Funny Girl") 10-20 64
COLUMBIA (1779 "The Legend of Barbra Streisand") 35-45 83
(Promotional, one-hour interview program.)
COLUMBIA (CL-2007 thru CL-2682)....... 15-25 63-67
(Monaural. Black vinyl.)
COLUMBIA (2054 "The Second Barbra Streisand Album") 100-200 63
(Colored vinyl. Promotional issue only.)
COLUMBIA (2478 "Color Me Barbra"). 100-200 66
(Colored vinyl. Promotional issue only.)
COLUMBIA (3220 "Funny Girl").............. 10-15 68
COLUMBIA (CS-8807 thru CS-9557) 15-25 63-68
(Stereo. Black vinyl.)
COLUMBIA (8854 "The Second Barbra Streisand Album") 100-200 63
(Colored vinyl. Promotional issue only.)
COLUMBIA (9278 "Color Me Barbra"). 100-200 66
(Colored vinyl. Promotional issue only.)
COLUMBIA (9710 thru 9968).................. 10-15 68-70
COLUMBIA (PC-8000 & PC-9000 series)....5-8
COLUMBIA (JC-9000 series).......................5-8
COLUMBIA (30086 thru 39480)..................5-15 70-84
With "FC," "JC," "KC," "M" or "PC" prefix.)
COLUMBIA (30378 thru 33815)..............20-40 73-75
(Quadraphonic. With "PCQ" prefix.)
COLUMBIA (40092 thru 45369)..................5-10 85-89
COLUMBIA (42801 thru 47678)...............15-30 82
(Half-speed mastered. With "HC" prefix.)
20TH FOX..10-15 69
Also see ARLEN, Harold, & "Friend"
Also see BLOOD, SWEAT & TEARS

STREISAND, Barbra, & Kim Carnes P&R '84
Singles: 7-inch
COLUMBIA (04695 "Make No Mistake, He's Mine")..3-5 84
Picture Sleeves
COLUMBIA (04695 "Make No Mistake, He's Mine")..3-5 84
Also see CARNES, Kim

STREISAND, Barbra / Marilyn Cooper
Singles: 7-inch
COLUMBIA..5-10
(Promotional issue only.)

STREISAND, Barbra / Doris Day / Jim Nabors / Andre Kostelanetz
LPs: 10/12-inch
COLUMBIA (1075 "Season's Greetings from Barbra Streisand & Friends")..............................15-25
(Special products issue for Maxwell House Coffee Co.)
Also see DAY, Doris

STREISAND, Barbra, & Neil Diamond P&R/C&W '78
Singles: 7-inch
COLUMBIA..3-5 78
Also see DIAMOND, Neil

STREISAND, Barbra, & Barry Gibb P&R '80
Singles: 7-inch
COLUMBIA (11390 "Guilty") 3-5 80
COLUMBIA (11430 "What Kind of Fool") 3-5 80
Also see GIBB, Barry

STREISAND, Barbra, & Don Johnson P&R '88
Singles: 7-inch
COLUMBIA..3-5 88
Picture Sleeves
COLUMBIA..3-5 88

STREISAND, Barbra, & Donna Summer P&R '79
Singles: 12-inch
COLUMBIA/CASABLANCA 8-10 79
(Promotional issue only. With special cover.)
Singles: 7-inch
COLUMBIA..3-5 79
Picture Sleeves
COLUMBIA..3-5 79
Also see STREISAND, Barbra
Also see SUMMER, Donna

STRENGTH, Bill
("Texas" Bill Strength)
Singles: 78 rpm
CAPITOL...5-10 52-54
CORAL 5-10 52
Singles: 7-inch
CAPITOL (2294 "It Ain't Much, But It's Home")..10-20 52
CAPITOL (2701 "Six Fools").....................10-20 54
CORAL (64133 "Paper Boy Boogie") 10-20 52
GOLDEN RING (3024 "Tears in My Beers")..5-10 62
STARDAY (9272 "Hillbilly Hades") ....10-20 '60s
SUN (346 "I Guess I'd Better Go")............10-20 60

STREYS
Singles: 7-inch
BWM (635 "She Cools My Mind")............20-30 '60s

STRICKLAND, Jan
("With the Shadows Orchestra Conducted by Preston Standiford")
Singles: 78 rpm
HUB...50-75 55
"X"..10-15 54-55
Singles: 7-inch
HUB (556 "Love Me, Baby")..................100-200 55
"X" (0080 "Come to Me My Little Darling")..25-50 54
"X" (0122 "Something to Remember You By") 25-50 55

STRICKLAND, Jimmy
Singles: 7-inch
ARLINGWOOD (8608 "Gonna Buy Me a Record That Cries")..5-10 64
DAVCO (104 "Touch of Heaven")...............8-12 61
DAVCO (107 "Ring in My Pocket")..............8-12 61
DOT (16956 "Don't Get Your Hopes Up")..5-10 66
SAM (109 "Funny Feeling").........................8-12 62
WAYSIDE...5-10 68

STRICKLAND, Johnny
Singles: 7-inch
ROULETTE (4119 "She's Mine")..............25-50 59
ROULETTE (4147 "I've Heard That Line Before")..15-20 59
ROULETTE (4221 "Sweet Talkin' Baby").10-15 60
ROULETTE (4335 "Fool's Hall of Fame")...10-15 61

STRICKLAND, Jon & Ed
Singles: 7-inch
REBEL (2665 "The Rebel Beat") ....8-12 '60s
(First issued as by the Rebels.)
Also see REBELS

STRICKLAND, Van
Singles: 7-inch
JUDSON (7001 "Gotta Get a Date").........10-15 60
PALETTE (5050 "Awkward Stage")............8-12 60

STRIDEL, Gene
Singles: 7-inch
ATLANTIC...5-10 68-69
COLUMBIA (42998 "One More Mountain") 5-10 64
COLUMBIA (43115 "My Town")...................5-10 64
FORD (101 "Hearts Were Never Meant to Be Broken")...8-12 61
VERVE (10247 "Let Her Go") 5-10 62
LPs: 10/12-inch
COLUMBIA (2115 "This Is Gene Stridel") 15-20 64
(Monaural.)
COLUMBIA (8915 "This Is Gene Stridel") 20-25 64
(Stereo.)

STRIDERS
Singles: 78 rpm
APOLLO...50-75 55
CAPITOL..20-40 48
DERBY...50-75 54
Singles: 7-inch
APOLLO (480 "Hesitating Fool")..........100-200 55
DERBY (857 "Come Back to Me")........100-200 54
Also see CHURCHILL, Savannah, & Striders
Also see MARTIN, Dolores, & Striders
Also see McLAURIN, Bette

STRIDERS
Singles: 7-inch
COLUMBIA (43738 "Sorrow") 10-20 66
COLUMBIA (43948 "Am I On Your Mind")..10-20 66
COLUMBIA (44143 "When You Walk in the Room")...10-15 67
DELTA (2137 "Give Me a Break") 15-25 66
LAVETTE (5007 "When You Walk in the Room")... 15-25 66

STRIDES
Singles: 7-inch
M-S (202 "I Can Get Along") 20-30 67

STRIGO, Bobby, & Blue Notes
Singles: 7-inch
RENOWN (109 "The Pad") 40-50 59

STRIKE
LPs: 10/12-inch
BUDDAH (5044 "Strike")..........................10-15 69

STRIKE FORCE
EPs: 12-inch
MASQUE (8914 "Strike Force") 8-12 89
(Picture disc. Promotional issue only.)

STRIKES
(With the Three Pelves)
Singles: 7-inch
IMPERIAL (5433 "If You Can't Rock Me") 25-50 57
IMPERIAL (5446 "Rockin' ").....................25-50 57
LIN (5006 "If You Can't Rock Me")...........50-75 57
Members: A.B. Cornelius; Willie Jacobs; Paul Kunz; Don Alexander; Walter Parsons; Ken Scott.
Also see TERRY, Don

STRING & BEANS
Singles: 7-inch
FAT CITY (6130 "Come Back to Me") 15-25 66

STRING CHEESE
LPs: 10/12-inch
WOODEN NICKEL....................................10-20 71
Member: John Maggi.
Also see TURNQUIST REMEDY

STRING KINGS
Singles: 7-inch
GAITY (144 "Blood Shot").....................400-500 64
Also see TRASHMEN

STRING-A-LONGS P&R '61
Singles: 7-inch
ATCO (6694 "Popi") 10-15 69
(Reportedly recorded by the Fireballs but credited to the String-A-Longs.)
DOT...5-10 62-65
WARWICK (603 "Wheels"/"Tell the World")...10-15 60
WARWICK (603 "Wheels"/"Am I Asking Too Much") 8-10 60
WARWICK (606 "Tell the World")............10-15 60
WARWICK (625 thru 675)..........................8-12 61-62
LPs: 10/12-inch
ATCO (241 "World Wide Hits") 15-25 68
(Reportedly recorded by the Fireballs but credited to the String-A-Longs.)
DOT...15-25 62-66
WARWICK (W-2036 "Pick-A-Hit") 40-50 61
(Monaural.)
WARWICK (WST-2036 "Pick-A-Hit").........50-75 61
(Stereo.)
Members: Keith McCormick; Jimmy Torres; Don Allen; Richard Stephens; Aubrey Lee de Cordova.
Also see BOYD, Mickey, & Plain Viewers
Also see FIREBALLS
Also see NEW STRING-A-LONGS

STRINGBEANS
Singles: 7-inch
GINA (7001 "Starbright")........................300-500 63

STRINGS
Singles: 7-inch
FLEETWOOD (1013 "Drive in Movie"). 100-200 60
(Has commercial intro for theaters.)
FLEETWOOD (1013 "Drive in Movie")...50-150 60
(Without theater intro.)

STRINGS
Singles: 7-inch
MELLOW TOWN (1006 "Love You")......50-100 '60s

STRIPES
Singles: 7-inch
ARAGON (301 "Hot Rod") 200-300

STROBEL, Joey
(With the Runaways)
Singles: 7-inch
BEAR (1973 "Sax Shuffle")........................8-12 66
REGALIA (11-15 "Tell Me That You Love Me Tonite")..10-15 '60s
SAT. SAINT (705 "It's True") ....8-12 '60s

STROGIN, Henry
(With the Crowns; with Crown)
Singles: 7-inch
AMAZON (1001 "I'll Tag Along")..............15-25 61
BALL (1012 "I Wanna Love") 20-30 61
BALL (1015 "Why Did You Go Away"/"I'll Tag Along")..40-50 63
DYNAMIC (1002 "Why Did You Go Away") 100-150 60
HANK (5001 "Misery")..............................20-30 63
HANK (5002 "Why Did You Go Away")....15-25 63

STROLL KINGS
Singles: 7-inch
CORAL (61989 "I'll Always Be in Love with You") 10-15 58

STROLLERS
Singles: 7-inch
ZEBRA (22 "You're the Only One for Me") 100-200 57

STROLLERS
(With the Lefty Bates Band)
Singles: 78 rpm
STATES 100-150 57
Singles: 7-inch
STATES (163 "In Your Dreams") 250-300 57
(Same number used for a Five Palms release.)
Also see BATES, Lefty Guitar

STROLLERS
Singles: 7-inch
WARNER RECORDS (1018 "Crowded Classroom") 10-20 58

STROLLERS
Singles: 7-inch
ALADDIN 10-20 58-59

STROLLERS
Singles: 7-inch
CUB (9060 "Favors") 20-30 60
DART (1017 "That Look in Your Eye") 8-12 60
20TH FOX (226 "One Summer Love") 20-30 60

STROLLERS P&R '61
Singles: 7-inch
CARLTON (546 "Come On Over") 30-40 61

STROLLERS
Singles: 7-inch
JUBILEE (5449 "Ever Since You Kissed Me, Joey") 10-15 63

STRONG, Barrett P&R '60
(With the Rayber Voices)
Singles: 78 rpm
ANNA (1111 "Money") 100-200 60
Singles: 7-inch
ANNA (1111 "Money") 35-45 60
(Black label.)
ANNA (1111 "Money") 15-25 60
(Gold label.)
ANNA (1116 "Yes No, Maybe So") 15-25 60
ATCO (6225 "Seven Sins") 25-35 62
CAPITOL 4-6 75
EPIC 4-6 73
MOTOWN 3-5
TAMLA (54022 "Let's Rock") 800-1200 60
TAMLA (54027 "Money") 35-55 60
(Horizontal lines on label.)
TAMLA (54027 "Money") 15-25 60
(Tamla globe logo on label.)
TAMLA (54029 "Yes No, Maybe So") 30-50 60
TAMLA (54033 "Whirlwind") 30-50 60
TAMLA (54035 "Money and Me") 30-50 61
TAMLA (54043 "Misery") 30-50 61
TOLLIE (9023 "I Better Run") 15-25 64
Picture Sleeves
ANNA (1111 "Money") .... 5-10 '90s
EPIC (11011 "Stand Up and Cheer for the Preacher") 4-6 73
LPs: 10/12-inch
CAPITOL 8-10 74
Also see HOLLAND, Eddie

STRONG, Elsie
Singles: 7-inch
FINALLY (1000 "Just Ask Me") .... 10-20 '60s
HIT TIME (183 "Baby Oh Baby") 75-125 60
LEGRAND (1000 "Workin' for You, Baby") 10-20 59
SOUNDS INTER (640 "Ask the Lonely") . 10-20

STRONG, Nolan
Singles: 7-inch
FORTUNE 8-12 66-69
Some Fortune releases before 1966 credit just Nolan Strong – without the Diablos – but they are still found in the Diablo's section.
Also see DIABLOS

STRONG, Ray
Singles: 7-inch
ROCKET (754 "You're Gonna Reap What You Sow") 300-500

STRONG, Zeke
(Zeke Strong Combo)
Singles: 7-inch
MISS ADY 10-15
FARO (604 "Times Square") 5-10 60
PROGRESS (531 "All By Myself") 10-15 63
PROWLING (406 "Cry, You Cry Alone") .. 10-15 '60s
PROWLING (2602 "North Beach") .... 10-15 '60s
Also see UNDERWOOD, Carl

STROUGHT, Keith
Singles: 7-inch
PAMA (103 "Lorie") 20-30 60
PAMA (104 "Till I Die") 20-30 60

STRYPER LP '85
Singles: 7-inch
ENIGMA (Except 1135) 3-5 84-89
ENIGMA (1135 "Reason for the Season") .. 5-10 84
(Picture disc.)
Picture Sleeves
ENIGMA 3-5 87-88
LPs: 10/12-inch
ENIGMA (Except 73277) 5-8 84-90
ENIGMA (73277 "Stryper") 10-20 86
(Picture disc.)
Members: Michael Sweet; Oz Fox; Tim Gaines; Robert Sweet.

STUART, Alice
LPs: 10/12-inch
ARHOOLIE (4002 "Alice Stuart") 10-15 64

STUART, Bobby
Singles: 7-inch
VALMOR (019 "Go On and Cry") 10-15 62

STUART, Chad
Singles: 7-inch
SIDEWALK (944 "Paxton's Song") 5-10 68
Also see CHAD & JEREMY

STUART, Chad & Jill
Singles: 7-inch
COLUMBIA (43467 "The Cruel War") 5-10 66
Picture Sleeves
COLUMBIA (43467 "The Cruel War") 8-12 66
Also see STUART, Chad

STUART, Glen
(Glen Stuart Orchestra)
Singles: 7-inch
ABEL (235 "Ruby Baby") 10-20 60
LAURIE (3255 "Just Loafin' ") 5-10 64
LAURIE (3267 "Forever True") 5-10 64
Also see CARLO
Also see COMO, Nicky

STUART, Jeb
(With the Reflextions; Soulful Jeb Stuart; with Gene Lowery Singers; with Chippers)
Singles: 7-inch
BINGO .... 15-25 '60s
EUREKA (435 "Dreamer's Hall of Fame") 10-20 66
GREAT AMERICAN 5-10 69
KENT (4559 "Can't Count the Days") 4-6 71
KING (6033 "I've Got to Cut You Loose") .. 5-10 66
MAESTRO (1004 "You Forgot About") .... 10-20 '60s
PHILIPS INT'L (3557 "Sunny Side of the Street") 10-20 60
PHILIPS INT'L (3567 "Dream") 10-20 61
PHILIPS INT'L (3575 "Little Miss Love") .. 10-20 62
PHILIPS INT'L (3580 "I Ain't Never") 20-30 62
PURE GOLD (316 "Whole Lot of Tears") . 10-20 65
SHAR (2 "What a Beautiful Face") 150-200 60

STUART, Scottie
Singles: 7-inch
MMC (006 "Nightmare") 150-250 60
Also see HONEY & DEW DROPS

STUBBS, Joe
Singles: 7-inch
LU-PINE (120 "Keep on Lovin' Me") 100-200 64
(Lu Pine [not hyphenated] 120 is also a Primettes single.)
Session: L.A. Dolls.
Also see CONTOURS
Also see FALCONS
Also see 100 PROOF Aged in Soul
Also see ORIGINALS

STUCKEY, Nat C&W '66
Singles: 7-inch
MCA 3-5 76-78
PAULA 5-10 65-70
RCA 4-8 68-75
SIMS (206 "Leave the Door Open") 5-10 64
Picture Sleeves
PAULA (243 "Sweet Thang") 5-10 66
LPs: 10/12-inch
CAMDEN 5-10 74
MCA 5-10 76
PAULA 10-20 66-67
RCA (Except "APD" series) 8-12 69-74
RCA (APD1-0080 "Nat Stuckey") 15-25 73
(Quadraphonic.)
Also see SMITH, Connie, & Nat Stuckey

STUDEBAKER BROTHERS
Singles: 7-inch
LITTLE FORT (010 "Lie'n in the Grave") .. 15-25 '60s
Member: Greg Kishline.
Also see STARBOYS

STUDEBAKER "7"
Singles: 7-inch
COOKHOUSE (7325 "In the Still of the Night") 15-25 70
COULEE (142 "One Fine Day") 15-25 72

STUDENT NURSES
Singles: 7-inch
RCA (8482 "Kiss Me Goodnight") 10-20 64

STUDENTS
Singles: 7-inch
RED TOP (100 "My Heart Is an Open Door") 150-250 57
(Blue label. Long version.)
RED TOP (100 "My Heart Is an Open Door") 75-125 57
(Blue label. Short version.)
RED TOP (100 "My Heart Is an Open Door") 20-30 58
(Red label.)
RED TOP (131 "Bye Bye Truly") 4-8 75
(Previously unreleased.)
Members: Emerson "Rocky" Brown; Colly Williams; Lamont Frisby; Larry Pindera; Clarence Smith.
Also see BROWN, Rocky

STUDENTS R&B '61
(With Jimmy Coe & Orchestra)
Singles: 78 rpm
CHECKER (902 "I'm So Young") 50-75 58
Singles: 7-inch
ARGO (5386 "I'm So Young") 10-20 61
BRASS RING 4-6 71
CHECKER (902 "I'm So Young") 30-40 58
CHECKER (1004 "My Vow to You") 8-12 62
CHESS 4-6 73
COLLECTABLES .... 3-5 '80s
NOTE (10012 "I'm So Young") 300-400 58
NOTE (10019 "My Vow to You") 200-300 59
Members: Leroy King; Rich Havens.
Also see JEWELS

STUFF
Singles: 7-inch
PREMIUM (1 "Why Are You Blowing My Mind") .... 20-30 '60s

STUMP & STUMPY
Singles: 78 rpm
MGM (11444 "Loud Woman") 10-15 53
Singles: 7-inch
MGM (11444 "Loud Woman") 15-20 53

STUMPS
Singles: 7-inch
BOYD (159 "My Generation") 15-25 67

STURGIS, Rodney
(With Louis Jordan's Elks Rendezvous Band)
Singles: 78 rpm
DECCA 10-15 38
Also see JORDAN, Louis

STYLE KINGS
Singles: 7-inch
SOTOPLAY (011 "Kissing Behind the Moon") 40-50 61
SOTOPLAY (014 "House Party") 15-25 62

STYLE SISTERS
(With the Camarata Orchestra)
Singles: 7-inch
COLISEUM (601 "Should I") 5-10 62
Picture Sleeves
COLISEUM (601 "Should I") 8-12 62
Members: Joan; Deanna; Deanda.
Also see CAMARATA

STYLERS
Singles: 78 rpm
KICKS(2 "Gentle As a Teardrop") 50-100 54
Singles: 7-inch
KICKS (2 "Gentle As a Teardrop") 250-350 54

STYLERS P&R '56
(With the Panama Francis Orchestra; Dick Thomas & Stylers)
Singles: 78 rpm
GOLDEN CREST 15-25 57
JUBILEE 10-15 54-57
Singles: 7-inch
GOLDEN CREST (1181 "You Tell Me") ... 15-25 57
GOLDEN CREST (1291 "Kiss and Run Lover") 15-25 57
GOLDEN CREST (1292 "Sweetheart of All My Dreams") 15-25 58
GORDY (7018 "Going Steady Anniversary") 15-25 63
JUBILEE (Except 5253) 10-20 54-57
JUBILEE (5253 "Confession of a Sinner") 30-40 56

STYLES
Singles: 7-inch
JOSIE (920 "School Bells to Chapel Bells") 30-40 64
PARK AVENUE (39635 "Scarlet Angel") 5-8 95
SERENE (1501 "Scarlet Angel") 75-125 61
TORCH (953 "Trying") 25-35

STYLES
Singles: 7-inch
MODERN (1048 "Baby You're Alive") 5-10 68
SWAN (4258 "I Do Love You") 15-29 66

STYLES, Johnny
Singles: 7-inch
GUYDEN (2058 "Baby Come Back to Me") 30-40 61

STY-LETTS
Singles: 7-inch
PILLAR (515 "Hello My Darling") 20-30 62

STYLISTICS P&R/LP '71
Singles: 7-inch
AMHERST 3-5 85
AVCO 5-8 70-76
H&L 4-6 76-79
MERCURY 3-5 79
PHILA. INT'L 3-5 82
SEBRING (8370 "You're a Big Girl Now") 15-25 70
STREETWISE 3-5 84-86
TSOP 3-5 80-84
Picture Sleeves
AVCO 4-6 76
LPs: 10/12-inch
AVCO 5-10 71-75
H&L 5-10 76-79
MERCURY 5-10 78-79
PHILA. INT'L 5-10 82
STREETWISE 5-8 84-86
TSOP 5-10 80-81
Members: Russell Thompkins, Jr.; Airrion Love; Herb Murrell; James Dunn; James Smith.

STYLISTS
Singles: 7-inch
JAY WING (5807 "Move It Over, Baby") 75-125 59
SAGE (317 "I've Been Waiting for You") .. 15-20 60

STYLISTS
(With Al Browne's Orchestra)
Singles: 7-inch
BIM BAM BOOM (120 "I Wonder") 4-6 74
(Black vinyl.)
BIM BAM BOOM (120 "I Wonder") 5-8 74
(Red vinyl.)
ROSE (16 "I Wonder") 40-50 60
Also see BROWNE, Al

STYLISTS
Singles: 7-inch
V.I.P. (25066 "What Is Love")................. 10-20 71

STYNER, Jerry
Singles: 7-inch
PALOMAR (2206 "Lonely Little Girl")..........8-12 65

STYNER, Ronnie
Singles: 7-inch
CAPA (101 "Love Me Faithfully") 10-20 62
CAPA (109 "Hey, Hey, Hey") 10-20 62

STYX
Singles: 7-inch
ONYX (2208 "Puppetmaster")................. 15-25 67
Also see ENGLE, Butch, & Styx

STYX *P&R '72*
Singles: 7-inch
A&M..3-8 76-84
PARAMOUNT (0104 "Soul Flow") 5-10 71
RCA..4-6 76
WOODEN NICKEL 4-8 72-78
Picture Sleeves
A&M..3-8 77-84
LPs: 10/12-inch
A&M (Except 3719, 4604 & PR-4724) 5-10 75-84
A&M (3719 "Paradise Theater")..................5-10 81
(Black vinyl on both sides.)
A&M (3719 "Paradise Theater")..................5-10 81
(Holographic image but no label on one side, standard black vinyl and label on reverse.)
A&M (4604 "Crystal Ball").......................... 20-30 76
A&M (4637 "Grand Illusion")...................... 10-20 77
(Canadian. Gold vinyl special edition.)
A&M (PR-4724 "Pieces of Eight") 10-15 79
(Picture disc.)
MFSL (026 "Grand Illusion").................... 40-60 79
NAUTILUS (27 "Cornerstone")................ 20-30 81
RCA..6-12 72-82
WOODEN NICKEL 8-12 72-77
Promotional LPs
A&M (8431 "Styx Radio Special") 15-25 77
(Two-disc set.)
A&M (17053 "Styx Radio Special") 35-40 78
(Three-disc set.)
A&M (17222 "Radio Sampler")................. 10-20 83
JIM LADD HOSTS (26-5 "Innerview").........8-12 76
ROLLING STONE (82-46 "Continuous History of Rock & Roll") 10-15 81
Members: Dennis De Young; James Young; Tommy Shaw; John Panozzo; Chuck Panozzo.

SUADES
Singles: 7-inch
SPINNING (6011 "Everybody's Trying to Be My Baby") 15-25 61

SUBURBAN 9 TO 5
Singles: 7-inch
GOLDEN VOICE (2630 "Sunshine Becomes You") 20-30 68
GOLDEN VOICE (5778 "I Wanna Be There") 20-30 68
LEDGER (18810 "Walk Away")................ 20-25 68
Member: Gary Richrath.
Also see R.E.O. SPEEDWAGON

SUBURBANS
Singles: 78 rpm
BATON 10-15 56-57
Singles: 7-inch
BATON (227 "I Remember") 15-25 56
BATON (240 "Leave My Gal Alone") 20-30 57
Also see COLE, Ann, & Suburbans
Also see RICKS, Jimmy, & Suburbans

SUBURBANS
Singles: 7-inch
PORT (70011 "Alphabet of Love") 40-50 59
GEE (1076 "Love Me") 15-25 62
KIP (221 "Little Bird")............................. 15-20 60
SHELLEY (184 "Walk Beside Me")........ 75-100 63
Also see FIVE CLASSICS

SUBURBANS
Singles: 7-inch
FLAMINGO (539 "Love Me")................... 10-15 61
(Reissued as by the Five Classics, then again by the Suburbans on Gee.)

SUBURBANS
Singles: 7-inch
VERMILLION (268 "Love That I Had") 10-15 65

SUBWAY RIDERS
Singles: 7-inch
MOONSHOT (6706 "Adam")....................10-20 67

SUBWAY SERENADERS
Singles: 7-inch
AVENUE D (4 "White Christmas") 15-25 80
(Black vinyl. 500 made.)
AVENUE D (4 "White Christmas") 10-20 80
(Green vinyl. 400 made.)
AVENUE D (4 "White Christmas") 15-25 80
(Red vinyl. 300 made.)
CLIFTON (53 "That's My Girl").....................3-5 80
Members: Rich Peritora; Bob Emrick; John Blewitt; Chris Mahoney; Rick Nocolini.
Also see DECADES

SUCCEED, La Ronda, & Three Dolls
Singles: 7-inch
MAGNIFICENT (111 "After Effect of Love")..30-40 61

SUDDENS
(Safaris)
Singles: 7-inch
SUDDEN (103 "China Love") 50-75 61
Also see SAFARIS

SUDELLS
Singles: 7-inch
AMERICAN ARTS (12 "Suzuki")..............10-20 65

SUE & DYNAMICS
Singles: 7-inch
FENTON (948 "Love in My Eyes")...........15-25 64

SUE & HER ELM VALLEY BOYS
Singles: 7-inch
RS (1 "West Virginia Boogie")................75-125

SUE & SUNNY
Singles: 7-inch
DERAM (85074 "Freedom") 4-8 71
EPIC (10545 "Stop Messing Around with My Heart")..5-10 69

SUEDES
Singles: 7-inch
DART (117 "Don't Be Shy")......................10-15 59

SUEDES
Singles: 7-inch
PSYCHEDELIC (113 "13 Stories High")...25-50 66

SUGAR & HONEYCOMBS
Singles: 7-inch
DORE (699 "Out of Sight")......................10-20 64

SUGAR & SPICE
Singles: 7-inch
FRANKLIN..8-12 '60s
KAPP (954 "Dreams") 5-10 68
KAPP (973 "In Love Forever") 5-10 69
WHITE WHALE (295 "Not toReturn") 8-12 69
Picture Sleeves
FRANKLIN...10-20 '60s

SUGAR 'N SPICE
Singles: 7-inch
CHATTAHOOCHEE (651 "Chapel of My Heart")...5-10 64

SUGAR & SPICES
Singles: 7-inch
STACY (968 "Bye Bye Baby").....................5-10 63
SWAN (4208 "Have Faith in Me") 5-10 65
TOLLIE (9013 "Come On Over to My House")...5-10 64
VEE-JAY (607 "Come On Over to My House")...5-10 64

SUGAR & SPICES
Singles: 7-inch
20TH FOX (618 "Duck Walk")..................10-20 65
Members: Rene Hall, Bobby Womack.
Also see HALL, Rene
Also see WOMACK, Bobby

SUGAR & SWEET
Singles: 78 rpm
EXCELLO..15-20 56
Singles: 7-inch
EXCELLO (2087 "Baby Come Back Home")...25-35 56

SUGAR & SWEET
Singles: 7-inch
FOREMOST (786 "I'll Never Be Free").......5-10 63
MORTON 10-20
PEP (103 "You Don't Have to Cry") 5-10 66
S.S.J. (1000 "You Don't Have to Cry") 5-10 65
S.S.J. (1001 "Every Minute of the Night")...5-10 65

SUGAR BEARS *P&R '72*
Singles: 7-inch
BIG TREE..4-6 72
LPs: 10/12-inch
BIG TREE...10-20 71
Members: Michael McGinnis; Kim Carnes; Baker Knight; Mike Settle; Mitch Murray.
Also see CARNES, Kim
Also see KNIGHT, Baker
Also see SETTLE, Mike

SUGAR BEATS
Singles: 7-inch
A&M (795 "First Love")...............................5-10 66
Members: Al Candaleria; Darron Stankey; Larry Knew.
Also see INNOCENTS

SUGAR BOY & HIS CANE CUTTERS
(James Crawford)
Singles: 78 rpm
CHECKER...25-50 53-54
Singles: 7-inch
CHECKER (783 "I Don't Know What I'll Do")..50-100 53
CHECKER (787 "Jock-O-Mo")................50-100 53
CHECKER (795 "No More Heartaches")...50-100 54
Also see CRAWFORD, James

SUGAR BOY & SUGAR LUMPS
Singles: 7-inch
PEACOCK (1925 "Mama Won't You Turn Me Loose") 10-15 63

SUGAR BUNS
Singles: 7-inch
W.B. (5046 "Pajama Party")......................10-15 59

SUGAR CANES
Singles: 7-inch
FEDERAL (12326 "Charleston Rock") 10-15 58
KING (5157 "Sioux Rock") 10-15 58

SUGAR CANYON
Singles: 7-inch
BUDDAH (58 "On Top of the World")..........5-10 68

SUGAR CREEK
LPs: 10/12-inch
METROMEDIA (1020 "Please Tell a Friend")..40-60 69

SUGAR PIE & PEE WEE
Singles: 7-inch
ALADDIN (3416 "One, Two, Let's Rock").40-60 58
RHYTHM (104 "Let's Get Together")........20-30 58
RHYTHM (117 "Beautiful Love")...............20-30 58
RHYTHM (1001 "A Few Lil' Words")........20-30 57
Members: Umpeylia Balinton; Pee Wee Kingsley (Parham).
Also see DE SANTO, Sugar Pie

SUGAR PLUMS
Singles: 7-inch
TROY (1005 "Doing What I Have To") 10-15 63

SUGAR RAY & BLUETONES
(Featuring Little Ronnie)
EPs: 7-inch
BARON...5-10 79
Member: Sugar Ray Norcia.
Also see ROOMFUL OF BLUES

SUGAR SHOPPE
Singles: 7-inch
CAPITOL (2233 "Skip-a-Long Sam") 5-10 68
CAPITOL (2326 "Poor Papa")......................5-10 68
EPIC (10517 "Easy to Be Hard") 5-10 69
LPs: 10/12-inch
CAPITOL (2959 "Sugar Shoppe") 10-15 68

SUGAR TONES
("With Orchestral Acc."; Sugartones; Enchanters)
Singles: 78 rpm
BENIDA (5021 "Scandal")..........................50-75 54
OKEH 50-100 51-52
ONYX (2007 "Anabelle") 40-60 51
ONYX (2008 "They Said It Couldn't Happen") 40-60 51
Singles: 7-inch
BENIDA (5021 "Scandal").....................100-150 54
CANNON (391 "How Can I Pretend") 15-25 60
CANNON (392 "Baby") 15-25 61
OKEH (6814 "You Fool Again") 200-300 51
OKEH (6837 "It's Over").........................200-300 51
OKEH (6877 "Today Is Your Birthday")..250-350 52
OKEH (6992 "I Just Want to Dream") ..200-300 52
Also see ENCHANTERS

SUGARCANE & HIS VIOLIN
(Don Harris)
Singles: 7-inch
ELDO (103 "Elm Stole My Baby")............10-20 60

SUGARHILL FOUR
Singles: 7-inch
LIMELIGHT (3034 "My Lonely Life") 5-10 64

SUGARHILL GANG *P&R '79*
Singles: 12-inch
SUGAR HILL (Except 542).........................5-10 80-85
SUGAR HILL (542 "Rapper's Delight").....20-30 79
Singles: 7-inch
SUGAR HILL 3-5 79-85
LPs: 10/12-inch
SUGAR HILL 5-10 80-85

SUGARLOAF *P&R/LP '70*
(With Jerry Corbetta)
Singles: 7-inch
BRUT 4-8 73-74
CLARIDGE...4-8 74-76
LIBERTY 5-10 70
U.A. 4-8 74
Picture Sleeves
BRUT (815 "I Got a Song") 5-10 73
LIBERTY (56218 "Tongue in Cheek")........5-10 71
LPs: 10/12-inch
BRUT 8-10 73
CLARIDGE..8-10 75
LIBERTY 10-15 70-71
Members: Jerry Corbetta; Bob Webber; Bob Raymond; Bob MacVittie; Robert Yeazel; Myron Pollock.

SUGARMAN
Singles: 78 rpm
SITTIN' IN WITH (609 "Which Woman Do I Love") 25-35 51

SUGARMINTS
Singles: 7-inch
BRUNSWICK (55042 "You'll Have Everything")..15-25 57

SUGGS, Brad
(With the Swingsters)
Singles: 78 rpm
METEOR..50-100 56
Singles: 7-inch
METEOR (5034 "Charcoal Suit")..........300-400 56
PHILLIPS INT'L (3545 "Low Outside").......15-25 59
PHILLIPS INT'L (3549 "Ooh Wee")...........15-25 59
PHILLIPS INT'L (3554 "Cloudy")...............15-25 60
PHILLIPS INT'L (3563 "Sam's Tune").......15-25 60
PHILLIPS INT'L (3571 "Elephant Walk")..15-25 61
Also see RHODES, Slim

SUHR, John
Singles: 7-inch
WEE REBEL (101 "Hey Hey Sugar Baby")..150-250 58

SUITER, Jeri
Singles: 7-inch
LIMELIGHT (3006 "How Is It Possible")...10-15 63

SULIK, Eddie
(With the Echoes)
Singles: 7-inch
HARD ROCK HATTIE (002 "Sweet Memories – Eddie Sulik") 15-18 2001
(Gatefold cover. Contains a red vinyl 45 of *Do I Love You/Bye-Bye My Baby*. Also includes a 15-track CD and a poster insert. Price is for complete set.)

HARD ROCK HATTIE (05 "Do I Love You") 5-10 2001
(Red vinyl. Limited edition of several hundred made for inclusion in the *Sweet Memories* set. Price is for record only.)
HARD ROCK HATTIE (06 "Ecstasy") 5-10 2001
(Blue vinyl. Limited edition of several hundred made.)
Also see ECHOES

SULL, Eddie
Singles: 7-inch
RENEE ("I'm Looking for My Baby") .... 10-20 '60s
(Selection number not known.)

SULLIVAN, Jerry
Singles: 78 rpm
VEE (100 "Curly Headed Baby") 20-40 56
Singles: 7-inch
VEE (100 "Curly Headed Baby") 50-60 56

SULLIVAN, Niki
Singles: 7-inch
DOT (15751 "It's All Over") 75-100 58
JOLI (073 "Do the Dive") 40-60
Also see CRICKETS
Also see HOLLY, Buddy
Also see HOLLYHAWKS
Also see SOUL INCORPORATED

SULLIVAN, Othell
Singles: 7-inch
WONDER (106 "Call Me Baby") 50-100 58

SULLIVAN, Paul
Singles: 7-inch
WHIRL-O-WAY ("Juke Joint Boogie") .. 100-200
(Selection number not known.)

SULLIVAN, Phil *C&W '59*
Singles: 7-inch
STARDAY (437 "Hearts Are Lonely") 15-25 59
STARDAY (462 "You Get a Thrill") 50-100 59

SULLIVAN, Romeo
Singles: 7-inch
TOP NOTCH ("Haunting Rhythm") 300-500
(Selection number not known.)

SULLIVAN FAMILY
Singles: 7-inch
SANDY (1006 "Happy On My Way") 10-20 58

SULTANS
Singles: 78 rpm
JUBILEE (5054 "Lemon Squeezing Daddy") 100-200 51
Singles: 7-inch
JUBILEE (5077 "Don't Be Angry") 750-1000 52

SULTANS
Singles: 78 rpm
DUKE 30-40 54
Singles: 7-inch
DUKE (125 "Good Thing Baby") 75-100 54
DUKE (133 "I Cried My Heart Out") 75-100 54
DUKE (135 "What Makes Me Feel This Way") 50-75 54
DUKE (178 "If I Could Tell") 50-75 57
Members: Richard Beasley; James Farmer; Willie Barnes; Wesley Devereaux; Eugene McDaniels.
Also see ADMIRALS
Also see BARNES, Billy
Also see McDANIELS, Gene

SULTANS
Singles: 7-inch
KNOWLES (105 "Say Hey Girl") 50-60 61
(Indicates "Shelton" in dead wax.)
KNOWLES (105 "Say Hey Girl") 10-15 61

SULTANS
Singles: 7-inch
DECADE (101 "I Always Will") 50-100
GUYDEN (2079 "Christina") 10-15 63
JAM (103 "Tossin' in My Sleep") 15-25 62
JAM (107 "Mary Mary") 10-15 63
JAM (113 "Poor Boy") 10-15 63
TILT (782 "It'll Be Easy") 50-100 61
(Yellow label.)
TILT (782 "It'll Be Easy") .... 5-10 '70s
(Black label.)
Also see BOYD, Donnie

SULTANS
Singles: 7-inch
ASCOT (2228 "I Wanna Know") 15-25 67

SULTANS
Singles: 7-inch
BACKSTAGE (1101 "She's Got It") .... 50-150 '60s

SULTANS
Singles: 7-inch
GLEN (0072 "Sultan's Groove") 10-15

SULTANS FIVE
Singles: 7-inch
ENTERPRISE THIRTEEN (1066 "You Know, You Know") 8-12 67
RAL (1754-03 "Tonight Is the Night") 10-20 64
RAL (7934 "Walk with Me") 10-20 64
RAYNARD (10052 "Tonight Is the Night") 10-20 65
RAYNARD (10053 "Daisy") 15-25 65
Picture Sleeves
RAYNARD (10052 "Tonight Is the Night") 10-20 65
(Die-cut sleeve which displays record label.)
Members: Ray Plauske; Len Juliano; Ken Allen; Tim Michna; Vic Weinfurter Jr.; Tom Zager; Butch Kieffer.

SUM PEAR
LPs: 10/12-inch
EUPHORIA (1 "Sum Pear") 20-25 71

SUMAC, Yma
Singles: 78 rpm
CAPITOL 8-12 51-56
Singles: 7-inch
CAPITOL 10-20 51-56
CAPITOL (244 "Voice of the Xtabay") 50-75 52
(Boxed set of four discs.)
CORAL (8058 "Presenting Yma Sumac") 50-75 54
(Boxed set of four discs.)
Picture Sleeves
CAPITOL (1819 "Birds") 30-40 51
EPs: 7-inch
CAPITOL (244 "Voice of the Xtabay") 50-75 52
(Double EP.)
CORAL (81050/51"Presenting Yma Sumac") 25-35 54
(Price is for either of two volumes.)
CAPITOL (1-299/2-299 "Legend of the Sun Virgin") 25-35 55
(Price is for either of two volumes.)
CAPITOL (FBF-299 "Legend of the Sun Virgin") 50-75 55
(Double EP.)
CAPITOL (FBF-423 "Inca Taqui") 50-75 53
(Double EP.)
CAPITOL (1-564/2-564 "Mambo") 25-35 54
(Price is for either of two volumes.)
CAPITOL (1-770/2-770/3-770 "The Legend of Jivaro") 10-20 56
(Price is for any of three volumes.)
CORAL (81050 "Presenting Yma Sumac") 35-45 54
LPs: 10/12-inch
CAPITOL (H-244 "Voice of the Xtabay") 50-100 52
(10-inch LP.)
CAPITOL (W-244 "Voice of the Xtabay") .40-60 55
CAPITOL (L-299 "Legend of the Sun Virgin") 50-100 52
(10-inch LP.)
CAPITOL (T-299 "Legend of the Sun Virgin") 40-60 55
CAPITOL (L-423 "Inca Taqui") 40-60 53
CAPITOL (H-564 "Mambo") 50-100 54
(10-inch LP.)
CAPITOL (T-564 "Mambo") 40-60 55
CAPITOL (T-770 "The Legend of Jivaro") 40-60 56
CAPITOL (T-1169 "Fuego Del Ande") 35-45 59
(Monaural.)
CAPITOL (T-1169 "Fuego Del Ande") 40-60 59
(Stereo.)
CAPITOL ("M" & "SM" series) 5-10 75-80
CORAL (56058 "Presenting Yma Sumac") 50-100 54
(10-inch LP.)
LONDON (608 "Miracles") 8-10 72

SUMMER, Donna *P&R/LP '75*
Singles: 12-inch
CASABLANCA 5-8 78-80
GEFFEN 4-8 80-87
MERCURY 4-8 83
OASIS 5-10 75-76
Singles: 7-inch
ATLANTIC 3-5 89
CASABLANCA 3-6 75-80
GEFFEN 3-5 80-87
MERCURY (812-370-7 "She Works Hard for the Money") 3-5 83
OASIS 4-6 75-76
Picture Sleeves
ATLANTIC 3-5 89
GEFFEN 3-5 80-87
MERCURY (812-370-7 "She Works Hard for the Money") 4-8 83
OASIS 4-6 76
LPs: 10/12-inch
ATLANTIC 5-8 89
CASABLANCA (Except NBPIX-7119 & 20110) 5-10 75-80
CASABLANCA (NBPIX-7119 "The Best of Live and More") 10-20 78
(Picture disc.)
CASABLANCA (20110 "Once Upon a Time") 12-15 77
(Promotional issue only.)
GEFFEN 5-10 80-87
MERCURY 5-10 83
OASIS 6-12 75-76
Also see STREISAND, Barbra, & Donna Summer

SUMMER SNOW
Singles: 7-inch
CAPITOL (2031 "Flying on the Ground") .20-25 67

SUMMERS, Bob
(Bobby Summers; Sleepy Summers)
Singles: 7-inch
CAPITOL 8-12 59-60
CHALLENGE 5-10 62-65
CHEVRON (201 "Take the "A" Train") 8-12 62
CRUSADER (107 "Organization") 8-12 64
GOLD LEAF 10-15 61
LIBERTY (55739 "After Dark") 5-10 64
VOGUE INT'L 10-15
EPs: 7-inch
4 STAR 8-12
Member: Jerry Lefors.
Also see SIDEWALK SOUNDS

SUMMERS, Gene
(With His Rebels; with Tom Toms; Jac & Jay; with Platinum Fog; with Dea Summers)
Singles: 78 rpm
JAN (100 "School of Rock 'n' Roll") 200-300 58
(100 copies made for 78 rpm juke boxs.)
JANE (102 "Nervous") 150-250 58
Singles: 7-inch
ALTA (104 "You Said You Loved Me") 10-15 62
ALTA (106 "Dance Dance Dance") 10-15 62
APEX (76278 "School of Rock 'n' Roll") ... 25-50 58
(Canadian.)
CAPRI (502 "Blue Diamond") 10-20 64
CAPRI (507 "Alabama Shake") 20-30 64
CAPRI (513 "Jack & Jill's New House") ... 10-15 65
CHARAY (47 "The Clown") 10-20 66
(First issue.)
CHARAY (100 "Hot Pants") 4-8 71
COUNTRY DISCO (1221 "Do You Think I'm Sexy") 4-6 79
(Reissue of Le Cam 34.)
DOMINO (101 "Who Stole the Marker") 5-10 68
DOMINO (104 "Young Voices of Children") . 4-8 70
DOMINO (106 "The Loser") 4-8 71
DOMINO (111 "A Man Can Cry") 4-8 75
DONNYBROOK (556 "Blue Diamond") 30-40 63
DONNYBROOK (557 "My Picture") 15-25 66
JAMIE (1273 "Big Blue Diamonds") 8-10 64
JAN (100 "School of Rock 'n' Roll") 25-50 58
JAN (102 "Nervous") 20-30 58
(First issue.)
JAN (106 "Twixteen") 15-25 58
JANE (102 "Nervous") 8-12 58
JUBILEE (102 "Nervous") 20-30 58
(Canadian.)
LAFAYETTE (1001 "Almost 12 O'Clock") 15-25 62
LE CAM (34 "The Clown"/"Do You Think I'm Sexy") 4-8 79
(First issue of *Do You Think I'm Sexy.*)
MARIDENE (106 "Big Blue Diamonds") 5-10 71
(Rerecorded version. Though credited to Gene Summers and Platinum Fog, the flip side, *The Waltz You Saved for Me*, is actually by Tom Brown and the Tom Toms.)
MERCURY (72606 "The Clown") 5-10 66
RM (1025 "School of Rock 'n' Roll") 5-10 77
(Reissue of Jan 100.)
TEAR DROP (3211 "Cloudy Day") 5-10 66
TEAR DROP (3405 "Goodbye Priscilla [Bye Bye Baby Blue]") 5-10 77
TEAR DROP (3405 "Goodbye Priscilla [Bye Bye Blue Baby]") 10-15 77
(Single-sided disc. Label mistakenly shows subtitle as "Bye Bye Blue Baby." Promotional issue only.)
EPs: 7-inch
NORTON (061 "A Gene Summers Record Date") 4-8 97
ROXY (4 "School of Rock 'n' Roll") 5-10 92
LPs: 10/12-inch
LAKE COUNTY (502 "Southern Cat Rocks On") 10-15 78
LAKE COUNTY (504 "Mister Rock 'n' Roll") 10-15 78
Members: Gene Summers; James McClung; Gary Moon; Benny Williams; Charlie Mendias; C.B. Williams; Ernest Walker; Jesse Lopez. Session: Rene Hall; Earl Palmer; Plas Johnson; Sid King; Red Callender; Five Masks; Freddy Powers; David Martin; Melvin Robinson; Glenn Keener; Joe Ramirez Combo; Guy Parnell; Bobby Clark; Lightcrust Doughboys; Ronnie Dawson; Joe Cook; Dan Edwards; Buddy Stevens; Larry Jannasch.
Also see CALLENDER, Red
Also see DAWSON, Ronnie
Also see FIVE MASKS
Also see JAC & JAY
Also see JOHNSON, Plas
Also see KING, Sid
Also see PARNELL, Guy, & Nite Beats
Also see POWERS, Freddy, & Powerhouse IV
Also see RAMIREZ, Joe
Also see RINGSIDE RICKY
Also see SAM THE SHAM & PHARAOHS
Also see SMITH, Bill

SUMMERS, Johnny
Singles: 7-inch
YORKTOWN (1007 "Prove It to Me") ... 200-400

SUMMERS, Ronnie
Singles: 7-inch
BAMBOO (514 "Girl of My Dreams") 5-10 61
LOCKET (103 "Freeze") 5-10 61
R.R.E. (1022 "I'm Sorry for You") 5-10 63
RADIO (124 "Salt and Pepper") 15-25 59

SUMMIT, Clark
Singles: 7-inch
MAY (104 "Why Not") 10-20 61

SUMMITS
Singles: 7-inch
CLIFTON (01 "Times Square Stomp") 4-6 72
DC INTERNATIONAL 4-6
HARMON (1017 "He's an Angel") 20-30 63
LA SALLE (504 "Let's Love Now") 50-75 57
RUST (5072 "He's an Angel") 8-12 64
TIMES SQUARE (422 "Times Square Stomp") 40-50 61

SUMMITS
Singles: 7-inch
RAMPART (651 "Hey Joe") 10-20 66

SUMNER, J.D., & Stamps Quartet
Singles: 7-inch
HEART WARMING 4-6 72
QCA (461 "Elvis Has Left the Building") 3-5 77
Picture Sleeves
QCA (461 "Elvis Has Left the Building") 5-10 77
LPs: 10/12-inch
BLUE MARK (373 "Memories of Our Friend Elvis") 10-20 78
HEART WARMING 4-8 71-74
QCA (362 "Elvis' Favorite Gospel Songs"). 8-10 77
Members: J.D. Sumner; Ed Enoch; Donnie Sumner; Richard Sturbin; Bill Baise; Kenny Parker; Nick Bruno; Phil Johnson.
Also see FOWLER, Wally

Also see OAK RIDGE BOYS
Also see PRESLEY, Elvis

SUMPIN' ELSE
Singles: 7-inch
LIBERTY (55873 "Baby You're Wrong").. 10-15 66
LIBERTY (55900 "You're Bad")............... 10-15 66

SUN, Jimmy, & Radiants
Singles: 7-inch
CUCA (1046 "Cocaine Blues")................ 15-20 61
CUCA (6636 "Rockpile")....................... 10-15 66
Members: Jimmy Sundquist; Don Phillips; Tom Gress; John Christanovich; Johnny Zolinski; Dave Vasser; Shorty DeLongchamp; Cliff Johnson; Ray Peters; Bob Edmondson.
Also see FENDERMEN

SUN FERRY AID
Singles: 12-inch
PROFILE 10-15 87
(Commercial issues.)
PROFILE 30-40 87
(Promotional issues.)
Singles: 7-inch
PROFILE (5147 "Let It Be").......................4-8 87
Picture Sleeves
PROFILE (5147 "Let It Be").........................4-8 87
Also see BUSH, Kate
Also see McCARTNEY, Paul

SUN LIGHTNING INCORPORATED
Singles: 7-inch
WHAP (319 "Quasar 45")........................ 10-15 69
Member: Philip R. Armstrong.

SUNBEAMS
Singles: 78 rpm
HERALD (451 "Tell Me Why")............... 50-100 55
Singles: 7-inch
ACME (719 "Please Say You'll Be Mine")... 1000-1500 57
COLLECTABLES...3-5 '80s
HERALD (451 "Tell Me Why")............. 200-300 55
Members: Al Mickens; Bobby Lee Hollis; Robert Colman; James Davis; Johnny Cumbo; William Edwards.
Also see ORIENTS

SUNDAE SERVANTS
Singles: 7-inch
DAD'S 15-25 66

SUNDAE TRAIN
Singles: 7-inch
B.T. PUPPY (550 "Sing Sweet Barbara")...5-10 68
20TH FOX (6693 "Wake Up")..................5-10 67

SUNDANCERS
Singles: 7-inch
BREAK OUT (111 "Devil Surf")............... 25-35 '60s

SUNDAY, Salty, & Stags
Singles: 7-inch
NO PAL ("So Lonely")......................... 200-300
(Selection number not known.)

SUNDAY & MENN
Singles: 7-inch
SIDEWALK (922 "You Cheated")............ 10-15 67

SUNDAY FUNNIES
Singles: 7-inch
CAPITOL (5614 "Headlines").....................5-10 66
HIDEOUT (1070 "Heavy Music")............ 15-25
MERCURY (72571 "Wonder Woman").......5-10 66
RARE EARTH (5035 "It's Just a Dream").....4-8 71
VALHALLA (671 "A Pindaric Ode")......... 20-30 67
LPs: 10/12-inch
RARE EARTH 8-12 71-72
Members: Richard Fidge; Ron Aitken; Richard Mitchell; Richard Kosinski.

SUNDAY GROUP
Singles: 7-inch
DOWNEY (129 "Pink Grapes")............... 10-20 65

SUNDAY SERVANTS
Singles: 7-inch
WORLD PACIFIC (77825 "I'm Puttin' You On").. 10-20 66

SUNDIALS
Singles: 7-inch
GUYDEN (2065 "Chapel of Love")....... 250-300 62

SUNDOWN PLAYBOYS
Singles: 7-inch
APPLE (1852 "Saturday Night Special") ..10-20 72

SUNDOWNERS
Singles: 7-inch
CIRCLE C (711 "Rockin' Spot") 100-200 59
Member: Curley Coldiron.

SUNDOWNERS
Singles: 7-inch
CHIP (1008 "Never Let You Go").............20-30 61

SUNDOWNERS
Singles: 7-inch
WINK (1009 "Rumble")..............................10-20 61

SUNDOWNERS
Singles: 7-inch
FARGO (1051 "Someone to Care").........30-40 64
Session: Del Satins.
Also see DEL SATINS

SUNDOWNERS
Singles: 7-inch
COED (603 "Leave Me Never") 8-12 65
JAMIE (1271 "Come On In") 15-25 64

SUNDOWNERS
Singles: 7-inch
TRC (2839 "Live It Up")..........................75-125 '60s

SUNDOWNERS
Singles: 7-inch
SUNRISE (1 "Snake-Eyed Woman")....150-200

SUNGLOWS P&R/LP '63
(Sunny & Sunglows; Sunny & Sunliners; Sunny Ozuna & Sunliners)
Singles: 7-inch
DISCO GRANDE (1021 "Peanuts")..........15-20 65
KEY LOC' (1001 "Lagrimas del Alma").......5-10 66
KEY LOC' (1002 "Hopeless Case") 10-15 66
KOOL (1006 "Just a Moment")..................8-12 60
LONDON 5-10
LYNN (511 "Just a Moment")....................8-12 61
OKEH (7143 "Golly Gee")..........................8-12 61
RPR (102 "Hip Huggin' Mini")....................5-10 69
RPR (105 "If I Could See You Now")..........5-10 69
SUNGLOW (Except 107) 8-12 62-66
SUNGLOW (107 "Love Me"/"Peanuts")....10-20 65
SUNGLOW (107 "Peanuts"/"Happy Hippo")...8-12 65
TEAR DROP (Except 3014).......................8-12 63-64
TEAR DROP (3014 "Talk to Me")..............20-30 63
WHITE WHALE (324 "It's Okay")...............5-10 69
LPs: 10/12-inch
SIESTA (101 "Original Peanuts")..............20-30 65
SUNGLOW (103 "Peanuts").......................25-35 65
TEAR DROP (2000 "Talk to Me") 30-50 63
Also see LOS STARDUSTERS

SUNLIGHT'S SEVEN
Singles: 7-inch
ENTRA (1082-3 "Judy in Disguise") 5-10 69
WINDI ....4-8 '60s
Member: G.C. Prophet.
Also see CREATION OF SUNLIGHT

SUNLINERS
Singles: 7-inch
GOLDEN WORLD (31 "All Alone")..........15-25 65
HERCULES (182 "Sweet Little Girl") 30-40 62
HERCULES (183 "Hit It")..........................30-40 62
HERCULES (184 "So in Love")..................30-40 62
MGM (13809 "Land of Nod").....................10-20 67
Also see RARE EARTH

SUNLOVERS
Singles: 7-inch
MUTT-JEFF (18 "This Love of Ours").......15-25

SUNNY & HIS GANG
Singles: 7-inch
PORT (70003 "I'm a Rollin' ") 10-15 58
Member: Sunny Skylar.

SUNNY & HORIZONS
Singles: 7-inch
LUXOR (1016 "Nature's Creation").......150-200 62
(Yellow label.)
LUXOR (1016 "Nature's Creation")...........50-75 62
(Red label.)

SUNNY BOYS
Singles: 7-inch
MR. MAESTRO (805 "For the Rest of My Life")..15-25 59
MR. MAESTRO (806 "Chapel Bells") 25-35 59
TAKE 3 (2001 "Chapel Bells") 15-25 59
(First issue.)

SUNNY FOUR
Singles: 7-inch
EPIC (10519 "Why Not") 5-10 69

SUNNY FUNNY CO.
Singles: 7-inch
STANAL (712 "Alone") ....30-50 '60s

SUNNY LADS
Singles: 7-inch
JAX (103 "That's My Desire")...................15-25 59

SUNNYLAND SLIM
(With His Playboys; with His Sunny Boys; with His Sunnyland Boys; with Lefty Bates Combo; Albert Luandrew)
Singles: 78 rpm
APOLLO..20-30 50
BLUE LAKE (105 "Goin' Back to Memphis") 50-75 54
BLUE LAKE (107 "Shake It Baby")..........50-75 54
CLUB 51 (C-106 "Be Mine Alone")..........30-50 55
COBRA (5006 "It's You, Baby") 20-30 56
HYTONE 20-30 49
MERCURY 20-30 49-51
REGAL 15-25 51
SUNNY (101 "Back to Korea Blues") 50-75 50
TEMPO TONE (1001 "Blue Baby").........75-100 48
J.O.B...25-50 50-54
Singles: 7-inch
AIRWAY (4743 "See My Lawyer")...........15-25
BLUE LAKE (105 "Goin' Back to Memphis") 150-250 54
(Black vinyl.)
BLUE LAKE (105 "Goin' Back to Memphis") 400-500 54
(Red vinyl.)
BLUE LAKE (107 "Shake It Baby").......150-250 54
(Black vinyl.)
BLUE LAKE (107 "Shake It Baby").......300-400 54
(Red vinyl.)
CLUB 51 (C-106 "Be Mine Alone").........75-125 55
COBRA (5006 "It's You, Baby") 175-200 56
J.O.B. (1101 "Woman Trouble") 75-125 54
J.O.B. (1105 "Shake It, Baby")...............75-125 54
J.O.B. (1108 "That Woman")..................75-125 55
MISS (117 "Worried About My Baby")......15-20 61
PRESTIGE BLUESVILLE (811 "Baby, How Long") 10-20 60
LPs: 10/12-inch
BLUE HORIZON.......................................10-15
BLUESWAY (6068 "Sunnyland Slim Plays the Ragtime Blues") 8-12 73
JEWEL 8-10 73
PRESTIGE..5-10 69
PRESTIGE BLUESVILLE.........................25-45 61
WORLD PACIFIC 20-30 69
Session: King Curtis.
Also see BABY FACE
Also see BRIM, John
Also see DELTA JOE
Also see HORTON, Big Walter
Also see HUTTO, J.B., & Sunnyland Slim
Also see KING CURTIS
Also see LENOIR, J.B.
Also see LITTLE WALTER
Also see MONTGOMERY, Little Brother
Also see PRYOR, Snooky
Also see ROGERS, Jimmy
Also see TAYLOR, Eddie

SUNNYLAND SLIM & MUDDY WATERS
Singles: 78 rpm
ARISTOCRAT 25-50 47-48
TEMPO TONE (1002 "Blue Baby")...........50-75 48
Also see WATERS, Muddy

SUNNYLAND TRIO
Singles: 78 rpm
J.O.B...25-50 52
Singles: 7-inch
PREP..5-10 57-58
Members: Sunnyland Slim; Billy Howell; Robert Lockwood Jr.
Also see BABY FACE
Also see LOCKWOOD, Robert, Jr.

Also see SUNNYLAND SLIM

SUNRAYS
Singles: 7-inch
SUN (293 "Lonely Hours") 25-35 58

SUNRAYS P&R '65
Singles: 7-inch
CAPITOL (72275 "I Live for the Sun")......15-25 65
(Canadian.)
TOWER (101 "Car Party")...........................8-12 64
TOWER (148 "I Live for the Sun") 8-12 65
TOWER (191 "Andrea") 8-12 66
TOWER (224 "Still") 8-12 66
TOWER (256 "Don't Take Yourself Too Seriously") 8-12 67
TOWER (290 "Hi, How Are You")...............8-12 66
TOWER (340 "Loaded with Love ")............8-12 67
W.B. (5253 "Talk to Him") 10-20 62
Picture Sleeves
TOWER (340 "Loaded with Love")........... 15-25 67
LPs: 10/12-inch
TOWER (5017 "Andrea")........................50-100 66
Members: Rick Henn; Bryon Case; Vince Hozier; Ed Medora; Marty DiGiovanni.
Also see ALLAN, Davie / Eternity's Children / Main Attraction / Sunrays

SUNRISERS
Singles: 7-inch
PATTY (101 "I Saw Her Yesterday")........15-25 66

SUNSETS
(With the Eddie Wilcox Orchestra)
Singles: 7-inch
RAE COX (102 "How Will I Remember") . 15-25 59
Also see WILCOX, Eddie, Orchestra

SUNSETS
Singles: 7-inch
CHALLENGE (9198 "Lonely Surfer Boy") 40-60 63
CHALLENGE (9208 "My Little Beach Bunny")..20-30 63
PETAL (1040 "Lydia") 50-75 63
LPs: 10/12-inch
PALACE..30-35 63
Members: Gary Usher; Richard Burns.

SUNSHINE
Singles: 7-inch
BUMPSHOP ("Sunshine")......................25-35
(Selection number not known.)
CAPITOL..4-6 71
KIRSHNER (4254 "There's a Road") 4-6 74
PHIL-L.A. OF SOUL (359 "Going Home to an Empty House")..4-8 72
ROULETTE (7210 "Reach Out") 4-6 77
ROULETTE (7212 "Dance Romance") 4-6 77
SCEPTER (12350 "Only in My Dreams")..... 4-8 72
LPs: 10/12-inch
BACK BEAT.. 10-12 70

SUNSHINE BOYS
Singles: 7-inch
SCOTTIE (1307 "If You Still Want Me") ... 10-20 59

SUNSHINE COMPANY P&R/LP '67
Singles: 7-inch
IMPERIAL 4-8 67-68
LPs: 10/12-inch
IMPERIAL 10-20 67-68
Members: Doug "Red" Mark; Maury Manseau; Larry Sims; Merle Brigante; Mary Nance.
Also see REDEYE

SUNSTONE LOLLIPOP
Singles: 7-inch
KEL (8515 "People of Today")................. 10-20 68
KEL (8516 "Never Sad") 10-20 68
KEL (8518 "Mr. Keat")............................. 10-20 68
Picture Sleeves
KEL (8515 "People of Today")................. 15-25 68
Members: Keith Diciani; David Diciani; Tom Hansen.

SUPER STOCKS
Singles: 7-inch
CAPITOL (2643 "Midnight Run") 5-10 64
(Bonus promotional single, packaged with an LP by Mr. Gasser and the Weirdos.)
CAPITOL (5153 "Thunder Road") 5-10 64
LPs: 10/12-inch
CAPITOL (T-2060 "Thunder Road").........40-60 64
(Monaural.)

CAPITOL (ST-2060 "Thunder Road")...... 50-75 64
(Stereo.)
CAPITOL (T-2113 "Surf Route 101")..... 50-100 64
(Monaural.)
(Includes bonus single by Mr. Gasser & Weirdos. Deduct $5-$10 if this 45 is missing.)
CAPITOL (ST-2113 "Surf Route 101"). 100-150 64
(Stereo.)
(Includes bonus single by Mr. Gasser & Weirdos. Deduct $5-$10 if this 45 is missing.)
CAPITOL (T-2190 "School Is a Drag")..... 40-60 64
(Monaural.)
CAPITOL (ST-2190 "School Is a Drag").. 50-75 64
(Stereo.)
Members: Gary Usher; Jerry Cole.
Also see COLE, Jerry
Also see DALE, Dick / Jerry Cole / Super Stocks / Mr. Gasser & Weirdos
Also see GHOULS
Also see MR. GASSER & WEIRDOS
Also see USHER, Gary

SUPER STOCKS / Hot Rod Rog (Roger Christian) / (Steve) Shutdown Douglas

LPs: 10/12-inch

CAPITOL (T-1997 "Hot Rod Magazine Rally")................................ 25-35 63
(Monaural. Special *Hot Rod Magazine* edition)
CAPITOL (T-1997 "Hot Rod Rally")........ 15-25 63
(Monaural.)
CAPITOL (ST-1997 "Hot Rod Rally")...... 20-30 63
(Stereo.)
Also see CHRISTIAN, Roger
Also see DOUGLAS, Steve
Also see SUPER STOCKS

SUPERBS *P&R '64*

Singles: 7-inch

ALTEEN (3004 "You Don't Care")........... 10-20
COLLECTABLES.......................................3-5 '80s
DT (107 "In and Out of Love")................. 10-20 '60s
DORE 15-30 64-67
HERITAGE (103 "Rainbow of Love")...... 40-50 61

SUPERBS

Singles: 7-inch

MELMAR (121 "My Love for You")....... 100-150

SUPERBS / Rialtos

Singles: 7-inch

STOOP SOUNDS (511 "Never Again"/"It Hurts").. 75-100 98

SUPER-CHILDS

Singles: 7-inch

ROULETTE (7033 "Broadway Joe")..........5-10 69

SUPERFINE DANDELION

Singles: 7-inch

MAINSTREAM 5-10 67

LPs: 10/12-inch

MAINSTREAM (6102 "Superfine Dandelion").. 15-25 67
Members: Mike McFadden; Mike Collins; Ed Black; Rick Anderson.

SUPERIOR ANGELS

Singles: 7-inch

SKYLARK (0023 "Crying in the Chapel"). 10-15 64

SUPERIORS

Singles: 78 rpm

ATCO (6106 "Lost Love")......................... 15-25 57

Singles: 7-inch

ATCO (6106 "Lost Love")........................ 15-25 57
MAIN LINE (104 "Lost Love")............... 100-200 58
(Shows "1510 Fairmount Ave., Philadelphia, Pa" address on label.)
MAIN LINE (104 "Lost Love").................. 20-30 62
(Has only "Philadelphia, Pennsylvania" address on label.)

SUPERIORS
(With the Modernistics)

Singles: 7-inch

FAL (301 "What Is Love")........................ 50-75 61
FEDERAL (12436 "Dance of Love")........ 15-25 61

SUPERIORS

Singles: 7-inch

REAL FINE (837 "Eternal Dream")...... 500-600 63
Members: Billy Thedford; Eddie Curtis.

SUPERLATIVES

Singles: 7-inch

DYNAMICS (1011 "Do What You Want to Do")..8-12 '60s
DYNAMICS (1012 "Won't You Please").....8-12 '60s
DYNAMICS (1016 "Lonely in a Crowd").....8-12 '60s
DYNAMICS (1017 "Don't Let True Love Die")..8-12 '60s
UPTITE (250 "I Still Love You")....................4-8 66
WALLY 5-10
WESTBOUND (154 "She's My Wonder Woman")...4-6 69

SUPER-PHONICS

Singles: 7-inch

LINDY (102 "Teenage Partner")...............40-50 59
Members: Ronnie Hanson; Pete Larkin; George Eberdt; Al Banasik; Gary Wolfe.
Session: Dave Kennedy.
Also see KENNEDY, Dave, & Super-Phonics / Super-Phonics
Also see VINCENT, Gene / Super-Phonics

SUPERSAX *LP '73*

LPs: 10/12-inch

CAPITOL 8-12 73-74
MFSL (511 "Play Bird")...........................25-35 '80s

SUPER-SONICS *P&R '53*
(With Third Dimension Sound)

Singles: 78 rpm

RAINBOW 10-20 53

Singles: 7-inch

RAINBOW (214 "New Guitar Boogie Shuffle")...10-25 53
(Black vinyl.)
RAINBOW (214 "New Guitar Boogie Shuffle")...25-35 53
(Colored vinyl.)
RAINBOW (214 "Guitar Boogie Shuffle") .15-25 55
(Note title change.)
RAINBOW (217 "Tabu")..........................15-25 55
RAINBOW (222 "New Cherokee Boogie")..15-25 55

SUPERTONES

Singles: 7-inch

EVEREST (19325 "Slippin' & Sloppin' ") ..10-15 60
Member: Billy Mure.
Also see MURE, Billy

SUPERTRAMP *LP '74*

Singles: 12-inch

A&M...4-6 82-85

Singles: 7-inch

A&M...3-8 71-85

Picture Sleeves

A&M...3-6 77-85

LPs: 10/12-inch

A&M (Except 3730 & 17236)......................8-12 70-87
A&M (3730 "Breakfast in America")......400-600 79
(Picture disc. Promotional issue only.)
A&M (17236 "Supersampler")..................10-15 83
(Promotional issue only.)
MFSL (005 "Crime of the Century")..........60-80 78
MFSL/UHQR (005 "Crime of the Century")..100-150 78
(Boxed set.)
MFSL (045 "Breakfast in America")..........50-75 80
Members: Rick Davies; Roger Hodgson; Doug Thomson; Bob Benberg; John Helliwell.

SUPREMES

Singles: 78 rpm

OLD TOWN (1024 "Tonight"/"She Don't Want Me No More")..40-80 56
OLD TOWN (1024 "Tonight"/"My Babe") .30-50 56
(Note different flip.)

Singles: 7-inch

OLD TOWN (1024 "Tonight"/"She Don't Want Me No More")..100-150 56
OLD TOWN (1024 "Tonight"/"My Babe")...75-100 56
(Note different flip.)
Members: Larry "Lonnie" Gales; Ed "Sonny" Jordan; Waldo "Champ Rollow" Champen; Billy Baines.
Also see STARLINGS

SUPREMES

Singles: 78 rpm

KITTEN...100-150 56

Singles: 7-inch

KITTEN (6969 "Could This Be You")....500-600 56

Members: Ralph Murphy; Jace Murphy; Archie Moore; Bill Perry; Claude Brown; Lee Murphy; John Brown.

SUPREMES
(Featuring Huey Smith)

Singles: 78 rpm

ACE (534 "Just for You and I") 15-25 57

Singles: 7-inch

ACE (534 "Just for You and I") 40-50 57
Members: Forrest Porter; Jay Robinson; Ed Jackson; Bob Isbell; Ed Dumas; Eddie Jackson.
Also see FOUR PHAROAHS
Also see SMITH, Huey

SUPREMES

Singles: 7-inch

MARK (129 "Nobody Can Love You")..1000-1200 58

SUPREMES

Singles: 7-inch

MASCOT (126 "Little Sally Walker").......75-125 60

SUPREMES

Singles: 7-inch

APT (25055 "Another Chance to Love")...40-50 61

SUPREMES
(Supremes 4)

Singles: 7-inch

SARA (1032 "I Love You, Patricia")..1200-2000 61
(Credits "Supremes")
SARA (1032 "I Love You, Patricia")..1000-1800 61
(Credits "Supremes 4")
Members: Lovelace Redmond; Homer Walton; Carl Campbell; Phillips Green.

SUPREMES *P&R '62*
(Diana Ross & Supremes)

Singles: 12-inch

MOTOWN 8-10 79-81

Singles: 7-inch

AMERICAN INT'L PICTURES ("Dr. Goldfoot and the Bikini Machine")..30-40 66
(Single-sided disc, used to promote the film of the same name.)
GEORGE ALEXANDER INC. (1079 "The Only Time I'm Happy")...30-40 65
(Special premium record. Has a Supremes interview on the flip.)
COLGEMS ("Snatches from the Soundtrack: *The Happening*")..50-100 67
(No selection number used. Promotional issue only.)
EEOC ("Things Are Changing")............50-100 65
(Equal Employment Opportunity Center promotional issue.)
MOTOWN (400 series)...............................3-5
MOTOWN (1008 "I Want a Guy").......500-1000 61
MOTOWN (1027 "Your Heart Belongs to Me")...20-30 62
MOTOWN (1034 "Let Me Go the Right Way")...30-40 62
MOTOWN (1040 "My Heart Can't Take It No More")..30-40 63
MOTOWN (1044 "A Breath Taking, First Sight Soul Shaking, One Night Love Making, Next Day Heart Breaking Guy")....................................150-250 63
(Blue label.)
MOTOWN (1044 "A Breath Taking, First Sight Soul Shaking, One Night Love Making, Next Day Heart Breaking Guy")......................................75-125 63
(White label. Promotional issue only.)
MOTOWN (1044 "A Breath Taking Guy")...20-30 63
(Reissue, with much shorter title.)
MOTOWN (1051 "When the Lovelight Starts Shining Through His Eyes")...............................20-30 63
MOTOWN (1054 "Run Run Run).............20-30 64
MOTOWN (1060 "Where Did Our Love Go")..15-20 64
MOTOWN (1066 "Baby Love")................15-20 64
MOTOWN (1068 "Come See About Me")..15-20 64
MOTOWN (1074 "Stop! In the Name of Love")..10-15 65
MOTOWN (1074 "Stop! In the Name of Love")..20-25 65
(Single-sided. Promotional issue only.)
MOTOWN (1075 "Back in My Arms Again")..10-15 65
MOTOWN (1080 "Nothing But Heartaches")...10-15 65

MOTOWN (1083 "I Hear a Symphony")..... 8-12 65
(Black vinyl.)
MOTOWN (1083 "I Hear a Symphony")...20-30 65
(Colored vinyl. Promotional issue only.)
MOTOWN (1085 "Children's Christmas Song")..15-25 65
(Colored vinyl. Promotional issue only.)
MOTOWN (1089 "My World Is Empty Without You")..8-12 66
MOTOWN (1094 "Love Is Like an Itching in My Heart")...8-12 66
MOTOWN (1097 "You Can't Hurry Love").8-12 66
MOTOWN (1101 "You Keep Me Hangin' On")..8-12 66
MOTOWN (1103 "Love Is Here and Now You're Gone")...8-12 67
MOTOWN (1107 "The Happening")...........8-12 67
MOTOWN (1111 "Reflections")...............5-10 67
MOTOWN (1116 "In and Out of Love").......5-10 67
MOTOWN (1122 "Forever Came Today") .5-10 68
MOTOWN (1126 "Some Things You Never Get Used To")..5-10 68
MOTOWN (1135 "Love Child")...............5-10 68
MOTOWN (1139 "I'm Livin' in Shame")......5-10 69
MOTOWN (1146 "The Composer")...........5-10 69
MOTOWN (1148 "No Matter What Sign You Are")...5-10 69
(Black vinyl.)
MOTOWN (1148 "No Matter What Sign You Are")...15-25 69
(Red vinyl. Promotional issue only.)
MOTOWN (1148 "The Young Folks")...... 15-25 69
(Red vinyl. Promotional issue only.) (Motown issued each side of 1148 on colored vinyl as separate DJ releases.)
MOTOWN (1156 "Someday We'll Be Together")..5-10 69
MOTOWN (1488 "Medley of Hits")...............4-6 80
MOTOWN (1523 "Medley of Hits")..............3-5 81
MOTOWN/TOPPS (1 "Baby Love").........50-75 67
MOTOWN/TOPPS (2 "Stop in the Name of Love")..50-75 67
MOTOWN/TOPPS (3 "Where Did Our Love Go") 50-75 67
MOTOWN/TOPPS (15 "Come See About Me")...50-75 67
MOTOWN/TOPPS (16 "My World Is Empty Without You")...50-75 67
(Motown 1 through 16 are Topps Chewing Gum promotional, single-sided, cardboard, flexi, picture discs. Issued with generic sleeves.)
TAMLA (54038 "I Want a Guy")...........100-150 61
TAMLA (54045 "Buttered Popcorn").......50-100 61

Picture Sleeves

EEOC ("Things Are Changing").............50-100 65
(Equal Employment Opportunity Center promotional issue.)
MOTOWN (1027 "Your Heart Belongs to Me") 75-125 62
MOTOWN (1060 "Where Did Our Love Go") 20-40 64
MOTOWN (1066 "Baby Love")................20-40 64
MOTOWN (1074 "Stop in the Name of Love")..20-40 64
MOTOWN (1075 "Back in My Arms Again")..20-40 65
MOTOWN (1080 "Nothing But Heartaches") 20-40 65
MOTOWN (1085 "Children's Christmas Song")..20-40 65
MOTOWN (1097 "You Can't Hurry Love")... 15-25 66
MOTOWN (1101 "You Keep Me Hanging On") 15-25 66

EPs: 7-inch

MOTOWN (60621 "Where Did Our Love Go") 25-50 64
MOTOWN (60623 "A Little Bit of Liverpool")..25-50 64
MOTOWN (60627 "More Hits")................25-50 65
MOTOWN (60649 "A Go Go")..................20-40 66

LPs: 10/12-inch

MOTOWN (100 & 200 series).....................5-10 80-82
MOTOWN (606 "Meet the Supremes") 1000-1200 63
(Front cover pictures each member sitting on a stool. Label has red star, indicating Detroit, in upper right.)
MOTOWN (606 "Meet the Supremes")....50-75 65
(Front cover pictures the head of each group member. Label has red star, indicating Detroit, in upper left.)

MOTOWN (621 "Where Did Our Love Go") 20-40 64
MOTOWN (623 "A Little Bit of Liverpool") 20-30 64
MOTOWN (625 "Country Western and Pop") 20-30 65
MOTOWN (627 "More Hits") 15-25 65
MOTOWN (629 "We Remember Sam Cooke") 20-30 65
MOTOWN (636 "At the Copa") 20-30 65
MOTOWN (638 "Merry Christmas") 25-35 65
MOTOWN (643 thru 708) 15-25 66-70
MOTOWN (794 "Anthology") 15-20 74
(Three-disc set. Includes 12-page booklet.)
MOTOWN (900 series) 5-10 75
MOTOWN (5000 series, except 5381) 5-12 83-84
MOTOWN (5381 "25th Anniversary") 15-20 86
(Three-disc set. Includes 12-page booklet.)
NATURAL RESOURCES 8-10 78
PICKWICK (3383 "Baby Love") 8-10 74
Members: Diana Ross; Mary Wilson; Florence Ballard; Cindy Birdsong.
Note: For Supremes Motown releases without Diana Ross see SUPREMES section below.
Also see BALLARD, Florence
Also see DIAMOND, Neil / Diana Ross & Supremes
Also see HORTON, Willie
Also see McKENZIE, Don
Also see PRIMETTES
Also see ROSS, Diana
Also see SCHUMACHER, Christine, & Supremes

SUPREMES & FOUR TOPS — P&R '70

Singles: 7-inch

MOTOWN (400 series) 3-5
MOTOWN (1173 "River Deep – Mountain High") 4-8 70
MOTOWN (1181 "You Gotta Have Love in Your Heart") 4-8 71

EPs: 7-inch

MOTOWN (717 "Magnificent Seven") 5-15 70
(Juke box issue.)

LPs: 10/12-inch

MOTOWN (100 series) 5-10 82
MOTOWN (700 series) 10-15 70-71
Also see FOUR TOPS

SUPREMES & TEMPTATIONS — P&R/LP '68

Singles: 7-inch

MOTOWN (400 series) 3-5
MOTOWN (1137 "I'm Gonna Make You Love Me") 4-8 68
MOTOWN (1142 "I'll Try Something New") 4-8 69
MOTOWN (1153 "The Weight") 4-8 69

Picture Sleeves

MOTOWN (1137 "I'm Gonna Make You Love Me") 10-20 68

LPs: 10/12-inch

MOTOWN (100 series) 5-10 82
MOTOWN (600 series) 10-15 68-69
Also see SUPREMES
Also see TEMPTATIONS

SUPREMES — P&R/LP '70

Singles: 7-inch

MOTOWN (400 series) 3-5
MOTOWN (1162 thru 1415) 4-8 70-77
(Black vinyl.)
MOTOWN (1172 "Stoned Love") 10-15 70
(Colored vinyl. Promotional issue only.)

LPs: 10/12-inch

MOTOWN (102 "Touch") 15-20 71
(Open-end interview LP. Price includes script. Promotional issue only.)
MOTOWN (702 thru 904) 6-12 70-78
Members: Jean Terrell; Mary Wilson; Cindy Birdsong.

SUR ROYAL DA COUNT & PARLIAMENTS

Singles: 7-inch

VILLA YORE (606 "Scream Mother Scream") 15-25 66

SURF, Adam, & Pebble Beach Band

Singles: 7-inch

PALADIN (3 "Fun, Fun, Fun") 10-20 64

SURF BOYS

Singles: 7-inch

KARATE (526 "Da Doo Ron Ron") 5-10 66
SCEPTER (12180 "I Told Santa I Want You") 10-20 66

SURF BREAKERS

Singles: 7-inch

MERCURY (72174 "Hang Ten") 10-20 63

SURF BUNNIES

Singles: 7-inch

DOT (16523 "Our Surfer Boys") 10-20 63
GOLIATH (1352 "Our Surfer Boys") 25-35 63
GOLIATH (1353 "Surf City High") 25-35 63
Members: Pat; Donna; Patty.

SURF DWELLERS

Singles: 7-inch

SWIFT (102 "Wave Breaker") .... 10-20 '60s

SURF KNIGHTS

Singles: 7-inch

TIKI (1001 "Midnight Surf") 20-30 67

SURF RIDERS

Singles: 7-inch

NASCO (6008 "I'm Out") 75-100 58

SURF RIDERS

Singles: 7-inch

DECCA (31477 "The Birds") 10-20 63

SURF SIDE FIVE

LPs: 10/12-inch

INTERMOUNTAIN ("Surf Side Five Recorded Live") .... 150-200 '60s
(Selection number not known.)

SURF STOMPERS
(Bruce Johnston)

Singles: 7-inch

DEL-FI (4202 "The Original Surfer Stomp") 25-35 63
(Promotional issue only. Reissued commercially as by Bruce Johnston.)
DONNA (1354 "Do the Surfer Stomp") 30-40 62
(Promotional issue only. Reissued commercially as by Bruce Johnston.)

LPs: 10/12-inch

DEL-FI (DFLP-1236 "The Original Surfer Stomp") 40-50 63
(Monaural.)
DEL-FI (DFST-1236 "The Original Surfer Stomp") 50-60 63
(Stereo.)
DEL-FI (DLF-1236 "Original Surfer Stomp") 10-15 98
("Thick, hard wax" reissue.)
Also see JOHNSTON, Bruce

SURF TEENS

LPs: 10/12-inch

SUTTON (SU-339 "Surf Mania") 40-50 63
(Monaural.)
SUTTON (SSU-339 "Surf Mania") 50-60 63
(Stereo.)

SURFARIS — P&R/LP '63

Singles: 7-inch

ABC (2703 "Wipe Out") 3-6 74
DFS (11 "Wipe Out"/"Surfer Joe") 1000-2000 63
(Has original version of *Surfer Joe*, which has additional verses, not heard on Dot release, and runs 3:39.)
DECCA (31538 "Point Panic") 10-20 63
DECCA (31561 "Santa's Speed Shop") 10-20 63
DECCA (31581 "Scatter Shield") 10-20 63
DECCA (31605 "Murphy the Surfie") 10-20 64
DECCA (31641 "Boss Barracuda") 10-20 64
DECCA (31682 "Hot Rod High") 10-20 64
DECCA (31731 "Beat '65") 10-20 65
DECCA (31784 "Somethin' Else") 10-20 65
DECCA (31835 "Don't Hurt My Little Sister") 10-20 65
DOT (144 "Wipe Out") 5-10 66
(Black vinyl.)
DOT (144 "Wipe Out") 25-30 66
(Colored vinyl. Promotional issue only.)
DOT (16479 "Wipe Out") 8-12 63
DOT (16757 "Surfer Joe"/"Early in the Evening") 8-12 65
DOT (16966 "Show Biz") 5-10 66
DOT (17008 "Shake") 5-10 67
KOINKIDINK (101 "Scatter Shield") 3-5 82
MCA (2703 "Wipe Out") 3-5
MCA (60055 "Wipe Out") 3-5
PRINCESS (50 "Wipe Out") 150-200 63
(Short version, same as Dot issue. Has "RE-1" etched in the vinyl trail-off.)
PRINCESS (50 "Wipe Out") 200-250 63
(Long version. Does not have "RE-1" etched in the vinyl trail-off.)
UNIVERSAL (965 "Wipe Out") 20-40 63

Picture Sleeves

KOINKIDINK (101 "Scatter Shield") 3-5 82

EPs: 7-inch

DECCA (2765 "Wipe Out") 20-40 63

LPs: 10/12-inch

DECCA (4470 "The Surfaris Play") 25-45 64
(Monaural.)
DECCA (4487 "Hit City '64") 25-45 64
(Monaural.)
DECCA (4560 "Fun City U.S.A.") 25-45 64
(Monaural.)
DECCA (4614 "Hit City '65") 25-45 65
(Monaural.)
DECCA (4683 "It Ain't Me, Babe") 25-45 65
(Monaural.)
DECCA (74470 "The Surfaris Play") 30-50 64
(Stereo.)
DECCA (74487 "Hit City '64") 30-50 64
(Stereo.)
DECCA (74560 "Fun City U.S.A.") 30-50 64
(Stereo.)
DECCA (74614 "Hit City '65") 30-50 65
(Stereo.)
DECCA (74683 "It Ain't Me Babe") 30-50 65
(Stereo.)
DOT (3535 "Wipe Out") 35-45 63
(Monaural. Front cover reads "The Original Hit Version, Wipe Out.")
DOT (3535 "Wipe Out") 25-35 63
(Monaural. Front cover reads "Wipe Out and Surfer Joe and Other Popular selections By Other Instrumental Groups." The Surfaris are heard only on *Wipe Out* and *Surfer Joe*. Remaining tracks are by the Challengers.)
DOT (25535 "Wipe Out") 40-50 63
(Stereo. Front cover reads "The Original Hit Version, Wipe Out.")
DOT (25535 "Wipe Out") 35-45 63
(Stereo. Front cover reads "Wipe Out and Surfer Joe and Other Popular selections By Other Instrumental Groups." The Surfaris are heard only on *Wipe Out* and *Surfer Joe*. Remaining tracks are by the Challengers.)
PICKWICK 10-15 78
SUNDAZED .... 5-10 '90s
Members: Ron Wilson; Jim Fuller; Jim Pash; Pat Connolly; Bob Berryhill; Ken Forssi. Session: Richie Podolor; Chuck Girard; Gary Usher.
Also see DALE, Dick / Surfaris / Fireballs
Also see HONEYS
Also see PODOLOR, Dickie
Also see SURFARIS / Challengers
Also see USHER, Gary

SURFARIS / Challengers

Singles: 7-inch

DOT (16757 "Surfer Joe"/"You Can't Sit Down") 8-12 65
Also see CHALLENGERS
Also see SURFARIS

SURFARIS
(Original Surfaris)

Singles: 7-inch

CHANCELLOR (1143 "Midnight Surf") 20-30 63
DEL-FI (4219 "Surfari") 20-30 63
FELSTED (8688 "Psyche-Out") 15-25 63
REGANO (201 "Surfin' 63") 20-25 63
(First issued as *Steppin' Out*, credited to the Customs.)
SURFARI (301 "Gum Dipped Slicks") 25-35 64

LPs: 10/12-inch

DIPLOMAT (2309 "Wheels, Shorts, Hot Rods") 15-25 63
Members: Larry Weed; Doug Weisman; Mike Biondo; Jim Tran; Chuck Vehle.
Also see CUSTOMS
Also see DALE, Dick / Surfaris / Surf Kings (Beach Boys)
Also see ORIGINAL SURFARIS
Also see SURFARIS / Biscaynes

SURFARIS / Biscaynes

Singles: 7-inch

NORTHRIDGE (1001 "Moment of Truth") 15-25 63
REPRISE (20180 "Moment of Truth") 10-15 63
Also see SURFARIS (Original Surfaris)
Also see WALKER, Gary

SURFER GIRLS

Singles: 7-inch

COLUMBIA (43001 "Draggin' Wagon") 15-25 64

SURFERS

Singles: 7-inch

ORBIT (526 "Blue Hawaii") 5-10 58
(Monaural.)
ORBIT (526 "Blue Hawaii") 15-25 58
(Stereo.)
ORBIT (538 "Mambo Jambo") 5-10 58

SURFERS

Singles: 7-inch

DRA (318 "Widgit") 15-25 62

SURFERS

LPs: 10/12-inch

HI-FI (408 "The Surfers") .... 75-125 '60s
HI-FI (411 "The Surfers at High Tide") .... 75-125 '60s

SURFERS

Singles: 7-inch

(260 "Wherever There's a Will") .... 10-20 '60s
(No label name used.)

SURFERS

LP: 10/12-inch

DAYBREAK (2001 "Live & Well at Hop Louie's Latitude 20°") 10-20 71
STEREO SOUNDS (10 "Hawaii a Go Go") .... 15-25 '60s
Members: Clayton Naluai; Alan Naluai; Buddy Naluai; Pat Sylva; Ray Pader; Joe Stevens.

SURFETTES
(Carol Connors)

Singles: 7-inch

MUSTANG (3001 "Sammy, the Sidewalk Surfer") 15-25 65
Also see CONNORS, Carol

SURFMEN

Singles: 7-inch

TITAN (1723 "Extacy") 15-25 62
TITAN (1723 "Paradise Cove") 10-20 62
(Same track as *Extacy*.)
TITAN (1727 "Malibu Run") 15-25 62
TITAN (1729 "The Breakers") 15-25 63
Members: Jim Masoner; Ron Griffith; Tim Fitzpatrick; Ed Chiaverini.
Also see EXPRESSOS
Also see LIVELY ONES

SURFRIDERS

Singles: 7-inch

BRASS (172 "Island in the Sun") .... 10-20 '60s
CENTURY (1027 "Radiation") .... 10-20 '60s

SURFRIDERS

LPs: 10/12-inch

VAULT (105 "Surfbeat, Vol. 2") 30-50 63
Also see CHALLENGERS

SURFSIDE FOUR

Singles: 7-inch

CLOISTER (6202 "Surfboard") 10-20 62

Picture Sleeves

CLOISTER (6202 "Surfboard") 30-40 62

SURFSIDE SIX

Singles: 7-inch

PALISADES (20 "South Bay") .... 15-25 '60s

SURFSIDERS

Singles: 7-inch

20TH FOX (298 "My Friend the Sea") 5-10 62

SURFSIDERS

Singles: 7-inch

ASTRO (101 "Chug-a-Lug Charlie") 15-20 64

SURFSIDERS

LPs: 10/12-inch

DESIGN (208 "Beach Boys Songbook") 10-20 65

SURPRISE PACKAGE

Singles: 7-inch

COLUMBIA (43922 "Out of My Mind") 8-12 66
COLUMBIA (44292 "The Other Me") 8-12 67
COLUMBIA (44460 "I'll Run") 8-12 68
LHI (10 "Free Up") 5-10 69
LHI (15 "New Way Home") 5-10 69

LPs: 10/12-inch

LHI (12006 "Free Up") 15-25 69

Members: Mike Rogers; Fred Zenfeldt; Rob Lowery; Greg Beck.
Also see VICEROYS

SURREALISTIC PILLAR
Singles: 7-inch
TAMM (2027 "I Like Girls") 15-25 67

SURVIVORS
Singles: 7-inch
CAPITOL (5102 "Pamela Jean") 100-200 64
Members: Brian Wilson; Dave Nowlen; Bob Norberg; Rich Peterson.
Also see BEACH BOYS
Also see BOB & SHERRY
Also see NODAENS

SUSAN & DYNAMICS
Singles: 7-inch
DOT (16476 "Letter to an Angel") 15-25 63

SUSAN MARIE
Singles: 7-inch
TEE PEE (61/62 "The Moon Won't Tell"/"Warm in the Summertime") 10-20 68

SUSIE
Singles: 7-inch
REQUEST (2008 "I'm Kissing You Goodnight") 10-20 59

SUSIE & FOUR TRUMPETS
Singles: 7-inch
U.A. (471 "Starry Eyes") 50-100 62

SUTHERLAND, David
Singles: 7-inch
STARK (005 "Leave My Baby Alone") 50-75

SUTTER, Hub
Singles: 7-inch
COLUMBUS (103 "Gone Goslin") 75-100 57

SUTTON, Danny
Singles: 78 rpm
FEDERAL (14003 "Is It True") 15-25 52

SUTTON, Glenn C&W/P&R '79
Singles: 7-inch
ABC 4-6 73
ACE (658 "Ring on Your Finger") 10-15 62
EPIC (10163 "Too Many Honky Tonks") 5-10 67
MGM (13273 "Karate Sam") 5-10 64
MGM (13333 "Clarence the Cross-Eyed Lion") 5-10 65
MGM (13352 "Gee-Whopper") 5-10 65
M.O.C. (653 "Long Tall Texan") 5-10 64
MERCURY 3-6 78-86
LPs: 10/12-inch
MERCURY 5-10 79
Also see KELLUM, Murray / Glenn Sutton

SUTTON, Jess "88"
Singles: 78 rpm
TIFFANY (1314 "I Ain't Got Nobody") 10-15 55
Singles: 7-inch
TIFFANY (1314 "I Ain't Got Nobody") 15-25 55

SUTTON, Ronnie
Singles: 7-inch
MAR-VEL (5000 "Country Rock") 10-20 64

SUZANNE
(With Full House; with Band-Aides)
Singles: 7-inch
LIBERTY (55313 "You May Never Know") . 8-12 61
TRUMP (002 "You May Never Know") 15-20 61
TRUMP (005 "Cryin' Room") 10-15 61
Member: Suzanne Mullins.

SUZETTES / John Van Horn
Singles: 7-inch
MOONGLOW (225 "Sky High"/"Somewhere") 8-12 63
Also see VAN HORN, John

SUZUKI, Pat
Singles: 7-inch
CAPITOL (4653 "When You Want Me") 8-12 61
RCA (7458 "I Enjoy Being a Girl") 10-20 59
RCA (7551 "Dreamsville") 10-20 59
VIK (0329 "Daddy") 10-20 58
VIK (0339 "Roar, Lion, Roar") 10-20 58
VIK (0340 "The Victors") 10-20 58
VIK (0341 "The Eyes of Texas") 10-20 58
VIK (0342 "Bow Down to Washington") ... 10-20 58
EPs: 7-inch
RCA (45-60 "Your Studebaker Dealer Presents Pat Suzuki") 15-25 60
(Promotional issue only. Issued with paper sleeve.)
LPs: 10/12-inch
RCA (1965 "Broadway '59") 15-25 59
RCA (2005 "Many Sides") 15-25 59
RCA (2030 "Pat Suzuki") 15-25 59
RCA (2186 "Looking at You") 15-25 60
VIK (1127 "Many Sides") 25-35 58
VIK (1147 "Pat Suzuki") 25-35 58

SUZY & COPYCATS
Singles: 7-inch
BRENT (7020 "Come Back to Me") 10-15 61

SUZY & RED STRIPES P&R '77
(Linda McCartney & Wings)
Singles: 12-inch
CAPITOL (15244 "Seaside Woman") 10-20 86
EPIC (361 "Seaside Woman") 20-30 77
(Promotional issue only.)
Singles: 7-inch
CAPITOL (5608 "Seaside Woman") 3-6 86
(Remixed version.)
EPIC (50403 "Seaside Woman") 4-8 77
Promotional Singles
CAPITOL (5608 "Seaside Woman") 10-15 86
EPIC (50403 "Seaside Woman") 30-40 77
(Colored vinyl.)
EPIC (50403 "Seaside Woman") 35-45 77
(Black vinyl. White label, states "Advance Promotion")
EPIC (50403 "Seaside Woman") 40-50 77
(Black vinyl. White label, no mention of "Advance Promotion")
Also see McCARTNEY, Paul

SWADE, Del
Singles: 7-inch
PRODUCTION (65212 "Better Get Ready, Betty") 100-200

SWAGGART, Jimmy
LPs: 10/12-inch
JIM (24-141 "25th Anniversary") 30-40 81
(Picture disc.)
L (3364 "Homeward Bound") 50-60
(Picture disc. Promotional issue only.)

SWAGS
Singles: 7-inch
DEL-FI (4143 "Rockin' Matilda") 10-15 60
WESTWIND (1003 "Rockin' Matilda") 10-20 60
Picture Sleeves
WESTWIND (1003 "Rockin' Matilda") 20-30 60
Members: Gailen Ludtke; Allen Barr; Wayne Morisett; Chet Dow; George Johnson; Bruce Reddick.

SWALLOWS R&B '51
Singles: 78 rpm
AFTER HOURS (104 "My Baby") 200-300 54
KING (4458 "Will You Be Mine") 100-200 51
KING (4466 "Since You've Been Away") 150-250 51
KING (4501 "Eternally") 100-200 51
KING (4515 "Tell Me Why") 150-250 51
KING (4525 "Beside You") 50-100 52
KING (4533 "I Only Have Eyes for You") 50-100 52
KING (4579 "Where Do I Go from Here") 50-100 52
KING (4612 "Laugh") 50-100 53
KING (4632 "Nobody's Lovin' Me") 75-125 53
KING (4656 "Trust Me") 75-125 53
KING (4676 "I'll Be Waiting") 50-100 53
Singles: 7-inch
AFTER HOURS (104 "My Baby") 2000-3000 54
GUSTO .... 3-5 '80s
KING (4458 "Will You Be Mine") 1000-1200 51
KING (4501 "Eternally") 300-500 51
(Black vinyl.)
KING (4501 "Eternally") 750-1000 51
(Blue vinyl.)
KING (4515 "Tell Me Why") 400-600 51
(Black vinyl.)
KING (4515 "Tell Me Why") 2500-3500 51
(Green vinyl.)
KING (4525-AA "Beside You") 200-300 52
KING (4525 "Beside You") 50-75 52
(Does not have "AA" on label.)
KING (4533 "I Only Have Eyes for You") 400-500 52
KING (4579 "Where Do I Go from Here") 200-300 52
KING (4612 "Laugh") 150-250 53
KING (4632 "Nobody's Lovin' Me") 100-200 53
KING (4656 "Trust Me") 100-200 53
KING (4676 "I'll Be Waiting") 100-200 53
Members: Junior Denby; Ed Rich; Earl Hurley; Fred Johnson; Norris Mack; Dee Bailey; Buddy Bailey; Irving Turner; Al France; Cal Kollette.
Also see DENBY, Junior

SWALLOWS P&R '58
Singles: 7-inch
FEDERAL (12319 "Angel Baby") 30-40 58
FEDERAL (12328 "We Want to Rock") 20-30 58
FEDERAL (12329 "Beside You") 30-40 58
FEDERAL (12333 "Itchy Twitchy Feeling") 50-75 58

SWALLOWS
(Guides)
Singles: 7-inch
GUYDEN (2023 "How Long Must a Fool Go On") 75-125 59
(By the Guides, but credited to the Swallows on some promotional copies.)
Also see GUIDES

SWAMP RATS
Singles: 7-inch
CO & CE (245 "It's Not Easy") 10-20 67
ST. CLAIR (69 "Louie Louie") 25-50 66
ST. CLAIR (2222 "Psycho") 100-200 66
ST. CLAIR (3333 "Two Tymes Two") 25-50 66
ST. CLAIR (711,711 "It's Not Easy") 25-50 66
LPs: 10/12-inch
KEYSTONE (39 "Disco Sucks") 10-15 79
Members: Bob Hocko; Dick Newton; Denny Nicholson.
Also see FANTASTIC DEE-JAYS
Also see GALACTUS

SWAN, Dottie
Singles: 7-inch
DIXIE (889 "Blue News") 50-100

SWAN, Jimmy
(With the Sons of the South; with Plummer Davis & Orchestra)
Singles: 78 rpm
MGM 10-20 56
PEACOCK 10-20 53
TRUMPET 15-25 52-53
Singles: 7-inch
CHECKER (946 "Little Fine Healthy Thing") 15-20 60
DECCA (31043 "Don't Conceal Your Wedding Ring") 10-20 60
JB (105 "Rattle Shakin' Daddy") 30-40 57
MGM (12348 "Country Cattin' ") 25-35 56
PEACOCK (1622 "Hey No Baby, Hey") ... 40-60 53
TRUMPET (176 "Juke Joint Mama") 50-75 52
TRUMPET (177 "Triflin' On Me") 25-50 52
TRUMPET (197 "Mark of Shame") 25-50 53
TRUMPET (198 "One More Time") 25-50 53

SWAN, Mary
Singles: 7-inch
SWAN (4009 "Love Could Be Like This"). 10-20 58
SWAN (4016 "I'll Wait for You") 10-20 58
SWAN (4028 "Prisoner of Love") 10-20 59
UNART (2019 "Crying in the Chapel") 10-20 59

SWAN SILVERTONES
Singles: 78 rpm
KING 10-20 51
SPECIALTY 5-10 52-54
VEE-JAY 5-10 57-58
Singles: 7-inch
HOB 4-6 74
KING (4542 "Grant It Lord") 50-100 51
SPECIALTY 15-25 52-54
VEE-JAY (100 & 200 series) 15-25 56
VEE-JAY (800 & 900 series) 5-15 57-64
LPs: 10/12-inch
HOB 5-10 74
VEE-JAY (5052 "The Best of the Swan Silvertones") 15-25 64
VEE-JAY INT'L 5-10 74
Members: Claude Jeter; Paul Owens; Louis Johnson; Azell Monk; Lonwood Hargrove.

SWANEE & ROCK-A-BILLIES
Singles: 7-inch
CLIX (825 "Thrill Happy") 150-250
HAPPY HEARTS (121 "I'll Prove It One Day") 8-12 61

SWANEE SPIRITUAL SINGERS
Singles: 7-inch
DUKE (200 "God Spoke to Me") 25-50 58

SWANGER, Sandy
Singles: 7-inch
CONNIE (1002 "School Bus Ride") 10-20 59

SWANKS
Singles: 7-inch
JAGUAR (3027 "Little Angel") 75-100 59

SWANKS
Singles: 7-inch
CHARM (6081 "Ghost Train") 5-10 65

SWANN, Bettye P&R '67
Singles: 7-inch
A-BET 4-8 72-74
ATLANTIC 4-8 72-76
BIG TREE .... 4-8 '70s
CAPITOL 5-8 68-70
FAME 4-8 71
MONEY 8-12 65-68
Picture Sleeves
CAPITOL (2382 "Don't Touch Me") 8-12 69
LPs: 10/12-inch
A-BET 10-12 72
ATLANTIC 10-12 72-75
CAPITOL 10-15 69
MONEY 15-20 67

SWANS
Singles: 78 rpm
RAGE (101 "Fools Fall in Love") 50-100 54
Singles: 7-inch
RAGE (101 "Fools Fall in Love") 300-500 54
(Also issued as by Mel Williams & Montclairs.)
Also see WILLIAMS, Mel

SWANS
(With Gene Nero Orchestra)
Singles: 78 rpm
BALLAD (1000/1001 "For Dreams Come True"/"Happy") 100-200 53
BALLAD (1003/1006 "It's a Must"/"Night Train") 50-75 54
BALLAD (1007 "Santa Claus Boogie") 50-75 55
FORTUNE 100-150 55
RAINBOW 100-200 53
Singles: 7-inch
BALLAD (1003/1006 "It's a Must"/"Night Train") 200-300 54
BALLAD (1007 "Santa Claus Boogie Song") 100-200 55
FORTUNE (822 "I'll Forever Love You") 500-1000 55
LOST NITE 4-8
RAINBOW (233 "My True Love") 1000-1200 53
(Red vinyl.)
STEAMBOAT (101 "Believe in Me"). 1000-1200 57
Also see LEWIS, Paul, & Swans

SWANS P&R '64
Singles: 7-inch
CAMEO (302 "The Boy with the Beatle Hair") 30-40 64
KAPP (488 "Indian Summer") 8-12 62
PARKWAY (881 "The Promise") 8-12 63
SWAN (4151 "He's Mine") 10-15 63
Also see ALICE WONDER LAND

SWANSON, Benice
Singles: 7-inch
CHESS (1927 "Baby, I'm Yours") 8-12 65

SWANSON, Bob, & Bee Jays
Singles: 7-inch
R.S.P. (101 "Will You Be There") 5-10 66
R.S.P. (114 "Ain't-Not Tree") 5-10 66
R.S.P. (120 "Toys of Love") 5-10 67
R.S.P. (131 "Richard Cory") 5-10 67
Also see BEE JAYS

SWANSON, Bobby
(With His Sonics)
Singles: 7-inch
DONNA (1326 "Tom and Suzy") 20-30 60
DONNA (1336 "Janie's Face") 10-20 61
DONNA (1356 "Hello There Lover Doll").. 10-20 62
IGLOO (16 "Angel") 50-75 61
IGLOO (1003 "Rockin Little Eskimo") ... 400-600 59

SWANSON, Earl

Singles: 7-inch

LEGRAND (1002 "Tiger Rock")............... 20-30 60

SWANSON, Joe

Singles: 78 rpm

RECORDED IN HOLLYWOOD (221 "Forgive Me")... 10-20 52

SWATLEY, Hank

Singles: 7-inch

AARON (101 "Oakie Boogie")................ 50-75

SWAYDES

Singles: 7-inch

ACCOLADE (1 "Remember Me")............ 20-30 65

SWAYDES

Singles: 7-inch

PARIS TOWER (108 "Anymore")............ 15-25 67
(Add $15 to $25 if accompanied by 5" x 8" photo insert.)
Members: Jack Chastain; Jim Adams; Pat Rooney; Billy Ayo; Barry Crook.

SWEATHOG *P&R '71*

Singles: 7-inch

COLUMBIA (45492 "Hallelujah")..................4-6 71

LPs: 10/12-inch

COLUMBIA..8-12 71-72
Members: Lenny Lee Goldsmith; Robert "B.J." Morris; Dave Johnson; Barry Eugene Frost.

SWEATHOG / Free Movement / Bob Dylan / Edgar Winter's White Trash

EPs: 7-inch

COLUMBIA/PLAYBACK (31 "Hallelujah") 25-35 72
Also see DYLAN, Bob
Also see SWEATHOG
Also see WINTER, Edgar

SWEATT, Al
(With Johnnie Cale & Valentines)

Singles: 7-inch

ALVERA (94 "Moochin' Smoochin'") 25-35
KEEN (289 "I Hate Myself")................... 100-200

SWEENEY, Jimmy
(With the Varieteers; Jim Sweeney)

Singles: 78 rpm

CHIC (1002 "The Question").......................5-10 56
HICKORY (1004 "I've Got a Woman's Love").. 100-150 54
TENNESSEE (714)................................ 50-100 50
(Title not known.)

Singles: 7-inch

BUCKLEY (1101 "She Wears My Ring")....5-10 62
CHIC (1002 "The Question").................... 10-20 56
CHIC (1007 "Tica Boo")........................... 10-20 57
COLUMBIA (41262 "Afraid")...................... 10-20 58
COLUMBIA (41454 "I'll Follow You") 10-20 59
DATE (1001 "The Midnight Hour").......... 10-20 58
HICKORY (1004 "I've Got a Woman's Love").. 250-300 54
HICKORY (1136 "She Wears My Ring") . 20-30 54
Also see FOUR BARS
Also see VARIETEERS

SWEENEY TODD *P&R '76*

Singles: 7-inch

LONDON 4-8 76

LPs: 10/12-inch

LONDON (694 "If Wishes Were Horses") 20-25 77
Members: Nick Gilder; James McCulloch; Bryan Guy Adams.
Also see ADAMS, Bryan

SWEET

Singles: 7-inch

SMASH (2116 "You Can't Win at Love") . 10-15 67
SMASH (2136 "Don't Do It")................... 10-15 67

SWEET *P&R '71*

Singles: 7-inch

BELL..4-6 71-74
CAPITOL...4-6 75-79
PARAMOUNT 5-10 71

LPs: 10/12-inch

BELL 10-20 73
CAPITOL (Except 16000 series)................8-10 75-79
CAPITOL (16000 series) 5-8 80-82
KORY...8-10 77

Promotional LPs

CAPITOL (8849 "Short & Sweet")........... 20-30 78
CAPITOL (11129 "Cut Above the Rest")..45-55 79
(Boxed set, containing the LP, 8-track and cassette issues of *Cut Above the Rest*, plus a group photo and biography.)
Members: Brian Connolly; Steve Priest; Andy Scott; Mick Tucker.

SWEET, Don, & Hesitations

Singles: 7-inch

D-TOWN (1040 "Wild Little Willie")...........50-75 65

SWEET, Sammy J.

Singles: 7-inch

HI-Q (5039 "Baby Just You & Me")..........10-15 64

SWEET & SASSY

Singles: 7-inch

DEL PAT (207 "Don't Leave Me")............10-20 59

SWEET INSPIRATIONS *P&R '67*
(With the Richie Rome Orchestra)

Singles: 12-inch

RSO...4-8 79

Singles: 7-inch

ATLANTIC..5-10 67-71
CARIBOU (9022 "Black Sunday")...............4-6 77
RSO...3-5 79
STAX 4-6 73-74

Picture Sleeves

ATLANTIC (2686 "A Brand New Lover")....8-12 70
(Promotional issue only.)

EPs: 7-inch

ATLANTIC (1016 "What the World Needs Now Is Love")...8-12 69
(Promotional issue only.)

LPs: 10/12-inch

ATLANTIC..10-15 68-70
RSO...5-10 79
STAX 8-10 73
Members: Cissy Houston; Sylvia Shemwell; Myrna Smith; Estelle Brown.
Also see FRANKLIN, Aretha
Also see HOUSTON, Cissy
Also see PRESLEY, Elvis
Also see RASCALS
Also see SHEMWELL, Sylvia
Also see SMITH, Myrna

SWEET LINDA DIVINE
(Linda Divine)

Singles: 7-inch

COLUMBIA (44954 "Good Day Sunshine") 5-10 69

LPs: 10/12-inch

COLUMBIA (9771 "Sweet Linda Divine").10-15 69

SWEET MAMA LOVE

SWEET MARQUEES

Singles: 7-inch

APACHE (1516 "You Lied") 750-1000 57

SWEET NUTHINS

Singles: 7-inch

SWAN (4195 "I Don't Love Him").............10-15 64

SWEET PAIN

Singles: 7-inch

U.A. 4-6 71

LPs: 10/12-inch

MERCURY (61231 "Sweet Pain")............10-12 69
U.A. 8-10 71

SWEET PANTS

LPs: 10/12-inch

(1141 "Fat Peter Presents Sweet Pants")...150-200 69
(No label name used.)
Members: Mike Mulloney; Mike Carr; Tony Molla.

SWEET PIE & BILL MALONEY

LPs: 10/12-inch

RIG ESP 15-25

SWEET SICK TEENS

Singles: 7-inch

RCA (37-7940 "The Pretzel") 50-75 62
(Compact 33 Single.)
RCA (47-7940 "The Pretzel") 40-50 62

SWEET SMOKE

Singles: 7-inch

AMY (11042 "Morning Dew") 10-15 68
AMY (11053 "You've Got to Hide Your Love Away")...10-15 69
JAN-GI (101 "Morning Dew") 10-20 68
JAN-GI (102 "Baby Sweet Baby")............10-20 68
Also see TRACERS
Also see TRY CERZ

SWEET SOUL GENERATION

Singles: 7-inch

PARIS TOWER (134 "Knock On Wood") .15-25 67

SWEET SOULS

Singles: 7-inch

RPR (112 "Your Baby")..............................5-10 69
Members: Johnny Fortune; Glen Campbell.
Also see CAMPBELL, Glen
Also see FORTUNE, Johnny

SWEET TEENS

Singles: 78 rpm

FLIP (311 "Forever More").......................20-30 55
GEE (1030 "With This Ring")....................25-35 57

Singles: 7-inch

FLIP (311 "Forever More") 40-50 55
GEE (1030 "With This Ring") 30-40 57

SWEET THINGS

Singles: 7-inch

DATE (1504 "You're My Lovin' Baby") 10-20 66
DATE (1522 "Baby's Blue").......................15-25 66

Picture Sleeves

DATE (1504 "You're My Lovin' Baby") 15-25 66
Member: Francine Barker.
Also see PEACHES & HERB

SWEET THREE

Singles: 7-inch

CAMEO (463 "Don't Leave Me Now") 10-20 67
DECCA (31938 "Spring Fever")..................8-12 66
DECCA (32005 "That's the Way It Is") 8-12 66

SWEET THURSDAY

Singles: 7-inch

GREAT WESTERN GRAMAPHONE 4-6 72
TETRAGRAMMATON (1512 "Getting It Together")...5-10 68

LPs: 10/12-inch

COLUMBIA (32039 "Sweet Thursday")....10-15 69
GREAT WESTERN GRAMAPHONE 8-10 72
TETRAGRAMMATON 10-20 69
Member: Jon Mark.
Also see MARK, Jon

SWEET TOOTHE

LPs: 10/12-inch

DOMINION (7360 "Testing")................200-300 71
Member: Michael Hopkins.

SWEETARTS

Singles: 7-inch

SONOBEAT (101 "Without You") 15-25 67
VANDAN (8195 "So Many Times")...........10-20 66

Picture Sleeves

SONOBEAT (101 "Without You") 25-35 67

SWEETHEARTS

Singles: 7-inch

BRUNSWICK (55237 "In Between Kisses")...5-10 62
BRUNSWICK (55240 "What Did I Do") 5-10 63
BRUNSWICK (55255 "What Will Mother Say")..5-10 63
BRUNSWICK (55265 "No No")..................5-10 64
COMO (451 "Come On, Make Love to Me")..5-10 68
D&H (500 "My Baby")..............................20-30 61
DISCOTEK (3019 "Come and Go with Me")...10-15 67
HARRIS (1001 "You'll Always Know")......30-40
HI-III (116 "They Talk Too Much") 30-40 61
HI-III (117 "Summer Days")......................15-25 61
KENT (428 "Eddie My Love")......................8-12 65
KENT (442 "No More Tears")......................8-12 66
RAY STAR (778 "Sorry Daddy") 50-60 61
(White label. Promotional issue only.)
RAY STAR (778 "Sorry Daddy") 40-50 61
(Yellow label.)
RAY STAR (778 "Sorry Daddy") 20-30 61
(Blue label.)
SEEBURG (3019 "Come Go with Me") 5-10 66
SEEBURG (3020 "Heatwave") 5-10 66

SWEETIES

Singles: 7-inch

END (1110 "After You")............................ 10-15 62

SWEETS

Singles: 7-inch

VALIANT (711 "Mama Saw Me")...............5-10 65
Member: Felice Taylor.
Also see TAYLOR, Felice

SWENDEL, Johnny

Singles: 7-inch

GAMETIME (109 "You Went Rockin' Tonight")...50-75 57

EPs: 7-inch

GAMETIME (106 "Johnny Swendel")........15-25
(We do not yet know if this EP came with a cover.)

SWENSON, Inga

LPs: 10/12-inch

LIBERTY (3379 "I'm Old Fashioned") 20-25 64
(Monaural.)
LIBERTY (7379 "I'm Old Fashioned") 25-30 64
(Stereo.)

SWENSONS

Singles: 7-inch

X-TRA (100 "Remember Me to My Darling")...15-25 '50s

SWIFT, Allen

Singles: 78 rpm

JUBILEE...5-10 55

Singles: 7-inch

JUBILEE (5222 "Johnny Podres Has a Halo 'Round His Head") 10-15 55
LEADER (815 "Are You Lonesome Tonight")..10-15 61

SWIFT, Allen, Pat Bright & Herb Duncan

Singles: 7-inch

MAD ("Gall in the Family Fare")...................4-8 73
(Plastic 33 rpm soundsheet.)
Also see SWIFT, Allen

SWIFT, Basil, & Seegrams

Singles: 7-inch

MERCURY (72386 "Farmer's Daughter") 15-25 65
Also see HUTTON, Danny

SWIFT, Joe
(With the Internationals)

Singles: 78 rpm

EXCLUSIVE...10-15 48

Singles: 7-inch

ONACREST (501 "Bell Bottoms")..............5-10 66
Also see OTIS, Johnny

SWIFT, Tom
(With the Electric Grandmothers; with Electric Bag)

Singles: 7-inch

DAWN (235 "High School Ring")............. 10-20 58
SOUND TEX..15-20 '60s

LPs: 10/12-inch

CUSTOM (1115 "Are You Experienced").20-25 '60s

SWING, Bill

Singles: 7-inch

BURTON (816 "Messed Up")................200-300

SWING BROTHERS
(Eddie Burns)

Singles: 78 rpm

PALDA ("Papa's Boogie") 75-100 48
(Selection number not known.)
Also see BURNS, Eddie

SWING KINGS

Singles: 78 rpm

METEOR (5016 Mary Jane").................. 15-25 54

Singles: 7-inch

METEOR (5016 Mary Jane").....................25-50 54
Member: Skeet Williams.

SWINGIN' MEDALLIONS *P&R/LP '66*

Singles: 7-inch

CAPITOL (2338 "Hey, Hey, Baby") 5-10 68
COLLECTABLES ....3-5 '80s
DOT (16721 "I Want to Be Your Guy").......5-10 65
4 SALE (002 "Double Shot")....................20-30 66
1-2-3...4-8 70-71
SMASH 5-10 66-67

LPs: 10/12-inch

SMASH (27083 "Double Shot") 25-35 66
(Monaural.)
SMASH (67083 "Double Shot") 25-35 66
(Stereo.)
Also see PIECES OF EIGHT

SWINGIN' SENSATIONS

Singles: 7-inch

SOUND SENSATION (8616 "There Is a Girl") 15-25

SWINGING BLUE JEANS P&R/LP '64

Singles: 7-inch

CAPITOL (72143 "The Hippy Hippy Shake") 10-20 64
(Canadian.)
CAPITOL (72152 "Good Golly Miss Molly") 10-20 64
(Canadian.)
IMPERIAL 8-15 64-67

LPs: 10/12-inch

IMPERIAL (9261 "The Hippy Hippy Shake") 50-75 64
(Monaural.)
IMPERIAL (12261 "The Hippy Hippy Shake") 30-50 64
(Stereo.)
LIBERTY (10191 "Swinging Blue Jeans") ..5-10 82
Members: Ray Ennis; Ralph Ellis; Les Braid; Norman Kuhlke; Terry Sylvester.
Also see HOLLIES

SWINGING BRIDGETTES

Singles: 7-inch

BRONZE (1016 "Please Come Back to Me") 10-15 66

SWINGING EMBERS

Singles: 7-inch

ACE (644 "Winter Wonderland") 10-15 61
Member: Jackie Hamilton Gore.
Also see EMBERS

SWINGING HEARTS

Singles: 7-inch

DIAMOND (162 "Please Say It Isn't So"). 10-15 64
(Black vinyl.)
DIAMOND (162 "Please Say It Isn't So"). 15-25 64
(Brown vinyl. Promotional issue only.)
LUCKY FOUR (1011 "Please Say It Isn't So") 75-100 61
MAGIC TOUCH (2001 "You Speak of Love") 15-25 65
NRM (1002 "How Can I Love You") 200-300 63
620 (1002 "How Can I Love You") 75-100 63
(Black vinyl.)
620 (1002 "How Can I Love You") 400-500 63
(Multi-colored vinyl.)
620 (1005 "Something Made Me Stop Shopping Around") 40-50 63
620 (1009 "You Speak of Love") 75-125 64

SWINGING HEARTS

Singles: 7-inch

MAGIC TOUCH (2001 "You Speak of Love") 10-20 67

SWINGING MACHINE

Singles: 7-inch

S.P.Q.R. (1101 "Do You Have to Ask") ... 15-25 66

SWINGING PHILLIES

Singles: 7-inch

DELUXE (6171 "L-o-v-e") 150-200 58
Members: Charles Cosome; Phillip Hurt; Richard Hill; Ronald Headin; Al Hirt.

SWINGING STINGRAYS

Singles: 7-inch

FUJIMO (6017 "Teen Queen") 10-20 63

SWINGING TIGERS

Singles: 7-inch

TAMLA (54024 "Snake Walk") 100-200 60
(Same number used on a Chico Leverett release.)

SWINGSTERS

Singles: 7-inch

DIXIETONE (5856 "Southern Drums") 15-25 66
Member: J.D. Wyatt.
Also see WYATT, J.D. & Thunderbolts

SWINGTONES

Singles: 7-inch

ABC-PAR (9902 "You Know Baby") 10-15 58
RHYTHM (5001 "You Know Baby") 40-60 58
(First issue.)

SWISHER, Debra

Singles: 7-inch

BOOM (60001 "You're So Good to Me") 5-10 66
Also see ANGELS
Also see PIXIES THREE

SWISS MOVEMENT

Singles: 7-inch

CASABLANCA 4-8 74
PERKY (101 "Spoonful") 20-30 68
RCA 4-6 73

LPs: 10/12-inch

RCA 8-12 73

SWORDS, Howard, & Blue Light Boys

Singles: 78 rpm

METEOR 40-50 55

Singles: 7-inch

METEOR (5019 "I'm Lonely As I Can Be") 100-200 55

SWORDSMEN

Singles: 7-inch

SEMAC (2114 "Kathi, Please Don't Cry").25-35 61

SYCAMORES

Singles: 78 rpm

GROOVE 50-75 55

Singles: 7-inch

GROOVE (0121 "I'll Be Waiting") 100-200 55

SYDELLS

Singles: 7-inch

BELTONE (2032 "In the Night") 10-15 63
(Black vinyl.)
BELTONE (2032 "In the Night") 20-30 63
(Brown vinyl.)

SYKES, Bobby

Singles: 7-inch

COLUMBIA (41946 "Memphis Address") .15-25 62
DECCA (30573 "Touch of Loving") 25-50 58
JMI (33 "Sugarfoot Rag") 8-12
RIC (170 "Hey Bo") 5-10 65
RIC (185 "World Wide Distributor") 5-10 66
Also see BISHOP, Bob
Also see MARTIN, Benny, & Bobby Sykes

SYKES, Keith LP '80

Singles: 7-inch

BACKSTREET 3-5 80

LPs: 10/12-inch

BACKSTREET 5-10 80
MEMPHIS (928 "I'm Not Strange, I'm Just Like You") 8-12 79
MIDLAND INT'L 8-10 77
VANGUARD 10-12 70-71

SYKES, Roosevelt
(With the Honeydrippers; "The Honey Dripper")

Singles: 78 rpm

BLACK & WHITE 15-25 45
BLUEBIRD 20-50 44-46
BULLET 15-25 49
HOUSE OF SOUND 50-75 57
IMPERIAL 15-25 55
RCA 15-25 46-49
REGAL 15-25 50-51
UNITED 25-35 51-53

Singles: 7-inch

BEA & BABY (116 "Pinewoods") 5-10 60
HOUSE OF SOUND (505 "She's Jail Bait") 50-75 57
IMPERIAL (5367 "Crazy Fox") 25-35 55
KENT (384 "Slave for Your Love") 8-12 62
KENT (434 "Out on a Limb") 5-10 65
RCA (50-0025 "I Know How You Feel") ...50-75 49
(Cherry red vinyl.)
RCA (50-0040 "Southern Blues") 50-75 49
(Cherry red vinyl.)
UNITED (101 "Fine and Brown") 30-40 51
UNITED (120 "Raining in My Heart") 25-35 52
UNITED (129 "Walking This Boogie") 25-35 52
UNITED (139 "Four O'Clock Blues") 25-35 53
(Black vinyl.)
UNITED (139 "Four O'Clock Blues") 50-75 53
(Colored vinyl.)
UNITED (152 "Come Back Baby") 25-35 53

LPs: 10/12-inch

BARCLAY 20-30
BLIND PIG 5-10 78
BLUE LABOR 20-30
BLUESVILLE 10-20
BLUESWAY (6077 "Double Dirty Mother") 8-12 73
CROWN 15-25 62
DELMARK 8-15 66-73
INNER CITY 8-15
JEWEL 8-12 73
PRESTIGE 8-12 69
PRESTIGE BLUESVILLE 25-35 60-61
UNITED 8-12
Also see GILLUM, Jazz
Also see MEMPHIS SLIM & ROOSEVELT SYKES
Also see THREE KINGS & A QUEEN
Also see WASHBOARD SAM

SYKES, Roosevelt, & Little Brother Montgomery

LPs: 10/12-inch

FANTASY 8-12 73
Also see MONTGOMERY, Little Brother
Also see SYKES, Roosevelt

SYLLABLES

Singles: 7-inch

IMPERIAL (5619 "It's You for Me") 10-15 59

SYLTE SISTERS

Singles: 7-inch

ASCOT (2135 "Summer Magic") 5-10 63
COLISEUM (601 "Should I") 5-10 62
COLISEUM (604 "Cinderella Jones") 5-10 63
COLISEUM (2701 "Summer Magic") 5-10 63

SYMBOLS

Singles: 7-inch

STANSON (502 "Blue Autumn") 50-75 58

SYMBOLS

Singles: 7-inch

DORE (666 "Last Year About This Time") 20-30 63
(Yellow label.)

SYMBOLS

Singles: 7-inch

JCP (1040 "Give Me Time") 10-20 65

SYMBOLS

Singles: 7-inch

VINTAGE (1007 "Bye Bye") 10-15 73
(Green vinyl.)

SYMPHONICS

Singles: 7-inch

ENRICA (1002 "Come on Honey") 10-15 59
Member: Freddy Scott.
Also see SCOTT, Freddie

SYMPHONICS

Singles: 7-inch

ABC (11068 "Boy") 5-10 68
BRUNSWICK 5-10 66-67
DEE-JON (001 "All Roads Lead to Heartbreak") 10-15 64
TRU-LITE (116 "Our Love Will Grow") 10-20 63

SYMPHONICS

Singles: 7-inch

BOCK (5001 "She's My Girl") 20-30

SYMS, Sylvia P&R '56

Singles: 78 rpm

ATLANTIC 3-6 52-53
DECCA 3-6 56-57

Singles: 7-inch

ATLANTIC 10-20 52-53
COLUMBIA 5-15 59-65
DECCA 5-15 56-64
PRESTIGE 4-8 67
RORI 5-10 62

EPs: 7-inch

ATLANTIC 10-15 56
DECCA 10-15 55

LPs: 10/12-inch

A&M 5-10 78
ATLANTIC (137 "Songs By Sylvia Syms") 50-100 53
(10-inch LP.)
ATLANTIC (1243 "Songs By Sylvia Syms") 20-40 56
(Has Atlantic logo at top of label.)
ATLANTIC (1243 "Songs By Sylvia Syms") 15-25 60
(Has Atlantic logo on side of label.)
ATLANTIC (18000 series) 5-10 76
COLUMBIA 20-30 60
DECCA (8188 "Sylvia Sings") 35-45 55
DECCA (8639 "Song of Love") 30-40 58
KAPP 15-25 61
MOVIETONE 10-15 67
PRESTIGE 15-25 65-67
REPRISE 5-10 82
20TH FOX 10-20 64
VERSION (103 "After Dark") 40-50 54
(10-inch LP.)

SYN

Singles: 7-inch

DERAM (7510 "Grounded") 10-15 67

SYNCAPATES

Singles: 7-inch

TIMES SQUARE (7 "Your Tender Lips").. 15-25 63
(Green vinyl.)

SYNCOPATERS

Singles: 78 rpm

NATIONAL (9093 "Mule Train") 50-75 49
NATIONAL (9095 "River, Stay Away from My Door") 50-75 49

SYNDICATE

Singles: 7-inch

DORE (743 "My Baby's Barefoot") 20-40 65
DOT (16807 "Egyptian Thing") 20-40 66

SYNDICATE
(Cobblers)

Singles: 7-inch

TEE PEE (45/46 "Next 21st of May"/"My Baby Kicked the Bucket") 10-20 68
Members: Ron Spanbauer; Bob Misky; Mike Meidl; Pat Nugent; Bob Weisapple; Nick Christas.
Also see COBBLERS

SYNDICATE OF SOUND P&R/LP '66

Singles: 7-inch

BELL 5-10 66-67
BUDDAH 4-8 70
CAPITOL 5-8 69
DEL-FI (4304 "Prepare for Love") 10-20 65
HUSH (228 "Little Girl") 20-30 66
SCARLET (5-3 "Prepare for Love") 15-25 65

LPs: 10/12-inch

BELL (LP-6001 "Little Girl") 25-35 66
(Monaural.)
BELL (SLP-6001 "Little Girl") 30-45 66
(Stereo.)
PERFORMANCE 5-8 88
Members: Jim Sawyers; Bob Gonzalez; Barrie Thompson; John Sharkey; Don Baskin; Larry Roy; John Duckworth; Carl Scott; Dennis Tracy.

SYNDICATES

Singles: 7-inch

MELLO (552 "The Duke") 10-15 65

SYSTEM

Singles: 7-inch

VINEYARD (444 "One in a Million") .... 20-30 '60s

SZABO, Gabor LP '67

Singles: 7-inch

BLUE THUMB 4-8 70
BUDDAH 4-8 70
CTI 4-6 73
IMPULSE 5-10 66-68
MERCURY 4-6 76-77
REPRISE 4-6 73
SKYE 5-8 68-70

LPs: 10/12-inch

BLUE THUMB 8-12 70
BUDDAH 8-12 70
CTI 8-12 73-74
IMPULSE 10-20 66-70
MCA 5-8 82
MERCURY 5-10 76
SALVATION 5-10 75
SKYE 8-12 68-70
Also see HORNE, Lena, & Gabor Szabo
Also see McFARLAND, Gary, & Gabor Szabo
Also see WOMACK, Bobby, & Gabor Szabo

SZABO, Peter

Singles: 7-inch

SKIP (149141 "Susie Rock") 15-25 59

SZABO, Sandor

Singles: 78 rpm

HAMMERLOCK (101 "Take Me in Your Arms") .... 10-20 '50s

Singles: 7-inch
HAMMERLOCK (101 "Take Me in Your Arms") .... 25-35 '50s

SZIGETI, Sandy
("Produced By Rick Nelson")
Singles: 7-inch
DECCA (32862 "America's Sweetheart") 4-8 71
LPs: 10/12-inch
DECCA (75270 "America's Sweetheart") 10-15 71
Also see NELSON, Rick

T

T BONES P&R '65
(T-Bones)
Singles: 7-inch
LIBERTY 5-10 64-67
EPs: 7-inch
LIBERTY 8-12 65
(Juke box issues only.)
LPs: 10/12-inch
LIBERTY 20-30 64-66
SUNSET 10-20 66
Members: Dan Hamilton; Joe Frank Carollo; Tom Reynolds; Gene Pello; Judd Hamilton; Richard Torres; George Dee.

T.P. & INDIANS
Singles: 7-inch
DELLWOOD (3239 "Ally or Enemy") 15-25 67

T. REX P&R/LP '71
(Tyrannosaurus Rex)
Singles: 7-inch
A&M 5-10 68
BLUE THUMB 4-8 71-72
CASABLANCA 4-6 75
REPRISE 4-6 71-74
LPs: 10/12-inch
A&M (3000 series) 10-15 72
A&M (4000 series) 15-20 68
BLUE THUMB (7 "Unicorn") 10-20 71
BLUE THUMB (18 "Beard of Stars") 10-20 72
(Add $5 to $10 if accompanied by the bonus single *Ride a White Swan.*)
CASABLANCA 8-10 74
REPRISE 8-12 71-73
W.B. (25333 "T. Rexstasy – Best of 1970-1973") 15-20
Members: Marc Bolan; Steve Peregrine Took; Mickey Finn; Bill Legend; Dino Dines; Steve Currie; Jack Green; Gloria Jones. Session: Howard Kaylan; Marc Volman.
Also see BOLAN, Marc

T.C. ATLANTIC
Singles: 7-inch
AESOP'S LABEL (6044 "Once Upon a Melody") 25-35 65
B SHARP (272 "Mona") 40-60 66
CANDY FLOSS (101 "20 Years Ago") 30-40 68
PARAMOUNT (0098 "Judgment Train") .. 10-20 71
PARROT (330 "20 Years Ago") 20-25 68
PARROT (338 "Faces") 20-25 68
TURTLE (1103 "Faces") 150-175 66
TURTLE (1105 "Shake") 25-35 66
LPs: 10/12-inch
DOVE (4459 "T.C. Atlantic") 15-25 67
(Price reduced since recent boot availability.)
Members: Bob Wells; Rod Eaton; Fred Freeman; Joe Kanan.
Also see MARSHALL, Eric, & Chimes

T.I.M.E.
(Trust in Men Everywhere)
Singles: 7-inch
LIBERTY (56020 "Take Me Along") 5-10 68
LIBERTY (56060 "Tripping into Sunshine") 5-10 68
Picture Sleeves
LIBERTY (56020 "Take Me Along") 10-15 68
LPs: 10/12-inch
LIBERTY 12-15 68-69
Members: Larry Byrom; Pat Couchois; William Richardson; Richard Tepp.
Also see HARD TIMES
Also see NEW PHOENIX
Also see STEPPENWOLF

TJ'S
Singles: 7-inch
LINDY (740 "Party Party") 200-300 57
LINDY (741 "I Got a Baby") 75-100 57
LINDY (1124 "Baby Doll") 50-75 58
Members: Tom Terry; Duane Schroeder; Jack Roubik; Bill Weigel; Ronnie Hagaland; Guy Buchalou.
Also see CARAVANS

T.P. & INDIANS
Singles: 7-inch
DELLWOOD (3239 "Goodbye Good Times") 15-25 67

T.R. & YARDSMEN
Singles: 7-inch
HIDEOUT (1105 "I Tried") 15-25 65

T.S.U. TORONADOS P&R/R&B '69
(Tornados)
Singles: 7-inch
ATLANTIC 5-10 68-69
OVIDE (227 "You're Mine") 15-25 67
OVIDE (250 "Nothing Can Stop Me") 10-20 68
VOLT 4-6 69-70
Note: We're told there is a connection between this group and Archie Bell & the Drells.
Also see BELL, Archie

T2
LPs: 10/12-inch
LONDON (583 "It's All Work Out in Boomland") 20-30 71
Members: Keith Cross; Peter Dunton; Bernard Jinks.

T.V. & TRIBESMEN
LPs: 10/12-inch
HBR (8507/9507 "Barefootin' ") 10-20 66

T.V. SLIM
(With His Heartbreakers; with His Bluesmen; with His Good Rocking Band; Oscar Wills; Oscar "TV" Wills)
Singles: 78 rpm
CHECKER (870 "Flat Foot Sam") 15-25 57
CLIFF (103 "Flat Foot Sam") 50-100 57
Singles: 7-inch
CHECKER (870 "Flat Foot Sam") 15-25 57
CLIFF (103 "Flat Foot Sam") 200-300 57
(First issue.)
EXCELL (104 "TV Man") 30-40 66
IDEEL (581 "You Won't Treat Me Right") ... 8-12 '60s
PZAZZ 5-10 68-69
SPEED (703 "Don't Reach 'Cross My Plate") 20-30 59
SPEED (704 "Flat Foot Sam Met Jim Dandy") 20-30 59
SPEED (705 "My Ship Is Sinking") .... 10-20 '60s
SPEED (706 "My Baby Is Gone") .... 10-20 '60s
SPEED (708 "Mean Woman Blues") .... 10-20 '60s
SPEED (710 "Dancing Senorita") .... 10-20 '60s
SPEED (711 "My Baby Is Gone") .... 10-20 '60s
SPEED (714 "Dream Girl") .... 10-20 '60s
SPEED (715 "Gravy Around Your Steak") .... 10-20 '60s
SPEED (803 "The Big Fight") .... 10-20 '60s
SPEED (807 "Boogie Woogie Guitar Twist") .... 10-20 '60s
SPEED (808 "Hen Peck Joe") .... 10-20 '60s
SPEED (810 "Hold Me Close to Your Heart") .... 10-20 '60s
SPEED (6865 "To Prove My Love") 40-60 58
TIMBRE (510 "Can't Be Satisfied") 8-12 66
USA (739 "Hold Me Close to Your Heart") .8-12
Also see WILLS, Oscar (With Fats Domino's Band) / Paul Gayten

TABB, Jimmy, & Little Boppers
Singles: 7-inch
TIFCO (828 "Pink Scarf") 15-25 62

TABBY & HIS MELLOW, MELLOW MEN
(Tabby Thomas)
Singles: 78 rpm
DELTA (416 "Thinking Blues") 25-50 53
Singles: 7-inch
DELTA (416 "Thinking Blues") 75-100 53
Also see THOMAS, Tabby

TABBYS
Singles: 7-inch
TIME (1008 "My Darling") 30-50 59
(Blue label.)
TIME (1008 "My Darling") 15-25 59
(Red label.)

TABBYS
Singles: 7-inch
CLEOPATRA (1 "Hong Kong Baby") 5-10 63
METRO INT'L (2 "Hong Kong Baby") 10-15 63
(First issue.)

TABLE TOPPERS
Singles: 7-inch
KLONDIKE (1010 "Talk to Me Baby") .. 200-300

TABOOS
Singles: 7-inch
LA SALLE (382 "So Sad") 15-25

TABOR, Gene
Singles: 7-inch
STARDAY (198 "I'm Hot to Trot") 50-75

TABS
Singles: 7-inch
DOT (15887 "First Star") 8-12 59
GARDENA (110 "Never Forget") 20-30 60
NASCO (6016 "Still Love You Baby") 15-20 58
NOBLE (719 "Never Forget") 150-250 59
(First pressed crediting the Marquis.)
NOBLE (720 "Oops") 1000-1500 59
VEE-JAY (418 "Dance Party") 8-12 61
VEE-JAY (446 "Mash Dem Taters") 8-12 61
WAND (130 "Two Stupid Feet") 5-10 63
WAND (139 "I'm with You") 5-10 63
Members: Bill Gardner; John Johnson; Jim Tanlin; Herb Northern; Ted Forbes.
Also see MARQUIS

TACKER, Dick
Singles: 7-inch
KINGSTON (443 "Heartaches Waiting 'Round the Bend") 15-25
KINGSTON (1364 "Rock All Night with Me") 300-400 59

TAD & SMALL FRY
Singles: 7-inch
LE CAM (956 "Checkered Continental") ... 15-25 62

TADS
(With the Jimmy Wilcox Band)
Singles: 78 rpm
DOT 10-15 56
LIBERTY BELL 30-50 56
Singles: 7-inch
DOT (15518 "Your Reason") 15-25 56
LIBERTY BELL (9010 "Your Reason") . 100-150 56
REV (3513 "She Is My Dream") 20-30 57

TAFFYS
Singles: 7-inch
AMY (933 "Game Called Love") 5-10 65
FAIRMOUNT (610 "Everybody South Street") 10-15 63
PAGEANT (608 "Can't We Just Be Friends") 15-20 63
PARKWAY (872 "Can't We Just Be Friends"/ "Everybody South Street") 10-15 63
(First issue.)

TAFT, Gene
Singles: 7-inch
TOPIC ("Make These Blues Go Away") 150-250
(Selection number not known.)

TAG & EFFIE
Singles: 7-inch
SUMMIT (106 "You Done Flubbed Your Dub") 150-250

TAGES
Singles: 7-inch
VERVE (10626 "Halcyon Days") 10-20 68
Also see FRAMPTON, Peter

TAIL FEATHERS
Singles: 7-inch
UPTITE (252 "Now Ain't That Love") 15-25 67

TAK TIKS
Singles: 7-inch
GUYDEN (2130 "Nut Rocker") 5-10 67
Also see KIT KATS

TALBOT, Johnny
(With De-Thangs)
Singles: 7-inch
JASMAN (2 "Pickin Cotton") .... 10-15 '60s

MODERN (1002 "Never Make Your Baby Cry") 5-10 65
RED FIRE (1002 "What You Want to Do"). 8-12 64

TALBURT, Gus
Singles: 7-inch
PINE (1001 "I'm in Love") 75-100

TALISMEN
Singles: 7-inch
AMERICAN ARTS (22 "Masters of War") .. 5-10 65
DOT (16068 "Surfin' Man") 8-12 60
PRESTIGE (357 "Off to the Sea") 5-10 65
LPs: 10/12-inch
BLUE STAR (6323 "Treasury of American Railroad Songs and Ballads") 10-20 64
PRESTIGE (7406 "Talismen") 10-20 65

TALISMEN
Singles: 7-inch
RAMPRO (115 "Glitter & Gold") 15-25 66
Members: Paul Beneke; Bill Sherek; John Javorsky; Russ Loniello.
Also see TIKIS

TALISMEN
Singles: 7-inch
HIDEOUT (1226 "Vintage NSU") 10-20 67
JULIAN (105 "She Was Good") 8-12
RAIO & RAIO (1005 "Good Bye My Love") 50-75

TALISMEN
Singles: 7-inch
UA (570 "I Get Carried Away") .... 8-12 '60s

TALKABOUTS
Singles: 78 rpm
REGENCY (792 "Sweet Lovin' Baby") 50-75 59
(Canadian.)
Singles: 7-inch
POPLAR (117 "Sweet Lovin' Baby") 10-20 59
REGENCY (792 "Sweet Lovin' Baby") 20-30 59
(Canadian.)

TALKING HEADS LP '77
Singles: 12-inch
SIRE 4-8 79-86
Singles: 7-inch
SIRE 3-5 77-88
Picture Sleeves
SIRE 3-5 78-86
LPs: 10/12-inch
SIRE (Except 23771) 5-10 77-88
SIRE (23771 "Speaking in Tongues") 20-30 83
(Promotional issue only.)
W.B. (104 "Live on Tour") 25-45 79
(Promotional issue only.)
Members: David Byrne; Jerry Harrison; Robert Fripp; Tina Weymouth; Chris Frantz; Brian Eno.
Also see MODERN LOVERS

TALL, Tom C&W '64
Singles: 78 rpm
FABOR (Except 132) 10-15 54-56
FABOR (132 "Hot Rod Is Her Name") 30-50 56
Singles: 7-inch
CHART 4-8 64-74
CREST (1038 "Stack-a-Records") 50-100 57
CREST (1052 "High School Love") 15-25 58
FABOR (Except 132 & 139) 10-15 54-56
FABOR (132 "Hot Rod Is Her Name") 30-50 56
FABOR (139 "Don't You Know") 20-30 56
(With Ruckus Tyler.)
PETAL 5-10 63
SAGE (305 "This Island") 10-15 59
SUNDOWN (133 "Yukon Trail") 5-10 60
Also see CREEL SISTERS & TOM TALL
Also see TYLER, Ruckus
Also see WRIGHT, Ginny, & Tom Tall

TALLEY, Johnny T.
Singles: 78 rpm
MERCURY 15-20 56
Singles: 7-inch
MERCURY (70902 "Lost My Wild Wild Mind") 40-50 56

TALLY, Bill, & Envoys
Singles: 7-inch
CANADIAN AMERICAN (104 "Summer Sun") 15-25 59

TALLYSMEN
Singles: 7-inch
TALLY (200,688 "Little By Little")............ 15-25 65

TAMANEERS
("Featuring Harvey Lee Everhardt Big 4 Orch.")
Singles: 7-inch
BRAMLEY (102 "Searching").............. 200-300 60

TAMBLYN, Larry
(With the Standells)
Singles: 7-inch
FARO (601 "Dearest")............................. 20-30 60
FARO (603 "My Bride to Be").................. 40-50 60
FARO (612 "This Is the Night")............... 30-40 61
(Purple & silver label.)
FARO (612 "This Is the Night")............... 15-25 61
(Green label.)
LINDA (112 "The Girl in My Heart")......... 40-50 63
STEEL CITY (105 "This Is the Night")..... 10-15
Also see STANDELLS

TAMBLYN, Russ
Singles: 7-inch
BOSCO/MGM (225 "Tom Thumb's Tune").8-12 58
(Promotional issue made for Bosco.)
METRO (20012 "Tom Thumb's Tune").......5-10 58
Picture Sleeves
BOSCO/MGM (225 "Tom Thumb's Tune")................................. 15-20 58
(Promotional issue made for Bosco.)

TAMIKO
(Tamiko Jones)
Singles: 7-inch
ATCO (6298 "Don't Laugh if I Cry at Your Party")................................. 20-30 64
CHECKER (1041 "It's a Sin").................. 10-15 63

TAMMY & BACHELORS
Singles: 7-inch
BANGAR (00610 "My Summer Love")..... 15-25 64

TAMMY & CAROLINAS
Singles: 7-inch
LARSON (707 "You Took Me For Granted")......................................5-10 61

TAMMYS
Singles: 7-inch
U.A. (632 "Part of Growing Up")................8-12 63
U.A. (819 "Gypsy").......................................8-12 65
(First issue.)
VEEP (1210 "Gypsy")...............................5-10 65
VEEP (1220 "Blues Sixteen")....................5-10 65

TAMPA RED *P&R '36*
(Hudson Whittaker)
Singles: 78 rpm
BLUEBIRD... 25-50 44-45
RCA... 20-40 45-54
Singles: 7-inch
RCA (50-0019 "Come On, If You're Coming")... 100-150 49
(Cherry red vinyl.)
RCA (50-0027 "It's a Brand New Boogey")... 100-150 49
(Cherry red vinyl.)
RCA (50-0041 "That's Her Own Business").. 100-150 49
(Cherry red vinyl.)
RCA (50-0056 "Please Try to See It My Way").. 100-150 49
(Cherry red vinyl.)
RCA (50-0084 "1950 Blues")................ 100-150 50
(Cherry red vinyl.)
RCA (50-0094 "It's Good Like That")... 100-150 50
(Cherry red vinyl.)
RCA (50-0107 "Sweet Little Angel")....... 75-125 50
RCA (50-0112 "Midnight Boogie").......... 75-125 50
RCA (50-0123 "She's Dynamite")........... 75-125 51
RCA (50-0136 "Pretty Baby Blues")........ 75-125 51
RCA (4275 "Boogie Woogie Woman")... 50-100 51
RCA (4399 "She's a Cool Operator")..... 50-100 51
RCA (4722 "I'm Gonna Put You Down")... 50-100 52
RCA (4898 "True Love")........................ 50-100 52
RCA (5134 "Too Late Too Long")........... 50-100 52
RCA (5273 "I'll Never Let You Go")........ 50-100 52
RCA (5523 "So Much Trouble")............. 50-100 53
RCA (5594 "If She Don't Come Back")... 50-100 54
LPs: 10/12-inch
BLUEBIRD (2-5501 "Guitar Wizard")........15-25 75
(Two discs.)
BLUES CLASSICS (25 "Guitar Wizard")....5-10
PRESTIGE BLUESVILLE (1030 "Don't Tampa with the Blues")......................................25-50 61
PRESTIGE BLUESVILLE (1043 "Don't Jive Me")..25-50 62
YAZOO (1039 "Bottle Neck Guitar").........10-15
Also see BIG MACEO
Also see EAGER, Jimmy

TAMRONS
Singles: 7-inch
PYRAMID (7381 "Wild Man")...................20-30 67

TAMS
Singles: 7-inch
MINK (22 "Memory Lane").......................40-50 59
(Memory Lane was first issued in 1959, showing the group as the Stereos. The same track was reissued in 1963, shown first as by the Tams and then by the Hippies.)
PARKWAY (863 "Memory Lane")............10-15 63
Also see HIPPIES / Reggie Harrison
Also see STEREOS

TAMS *P&R/R&B '62*
Singles: 7-inch
ABC (10825 thru 11358)............................5-10 68-73
ABC-PAR (10502 "What Kind of Fool")....10-15 63
ABC-PAR (10533 "You Lied to Your Daddy")...10-15 64
ABC-PAR (10573 "Hey Girl Don't Bother Me")...10-15 64
ABC-PAR (10601 "Silly Little Girl")..........10-15 64
ABC-PAR (10635 "Unlove You")................8-12 65
ABC-PAR (10702 "Concrete Jungle").......8-12 65
ABC-PAR (10741 "I've Been Hurt")...........8-12 65
ABC-PAR (10779 "Got to Get Used to a Broken Heart")..8-12 66
APT/ABC (26010 "Numbers").......................4-6 72
ARLEN (7-11 "Untie Me").........................10-20 62
ARLEN (717 "Deep Inside Me")...............10-15 62
ARLEN (720 "You'll Never Know")...........10-15 63
ARLEN (729 "Find Another Love")...........10-15 63
CAPITOL..4-6 71
COLLECTABLES..3-5 '80s
COMPLEAT...3-5 83
DAISY..5-10 '60s
DUNHILL (4290 "Hey Girl Don't Bother Me")..4-6 71
GENERAL AMERICAN (714 "Find Another Love")..5-10 62
GUSTO..3-5 80
HERITAGE (101 "Vacation Time")........150-250 61
KING (6012 "Untie Me")...............................5-10 65
MCA (2400 "What Kind of Fool")..................3-5 83
MGM SOUTH (7023 "Alley Oop")..................4-6 73
1-2-3 (1726 "How Long Love")......................5-8 70
RIPETE..3-6 82
ROULETTE GOLDEN GOODIES................4-6 '70s
SOUTH..4-6 73
SWAN (4055 "Sorry").................................20-30 60
WONDER..3-5 82
Picture Sleeves
DUNHILL (4290 "Hey Girl Don't Bother Me")..15-25 71
(Promotional issue only.)
LPs: 10/12-inch
ABC..10-20 67-69
ABC-PAR (481 "The Tams").....................20-30 64
ABC-PAR (499 "Hey Girl Don't Bother Me")..20-30 64
BRYLEN...5-10 84
CAPITOL..5-10 79
COMPLEAT..5-8 83
1-2-3...8-12 70
SOUNDS SOUTH...8-10 77
Members: Joe Pope; Charles Pope; Lee Smith; Floyd Ashton; Albert Cottle; Robert Horace Key.

TANDELLS
Singles: 7-inch
JAM-TRA (302 "Is It Love, Baby")............40-50

TANDI & TEAMATES
Singles: 7-inch
EMBER (1068 "Weekend Lover")............10-15 60

TANEGA, Norma *P&R '66*
Singles: 7-inch
ABC..4-6 73
ERIC...4-6 '70s
NEW VOICE..5-10 66-67
VIRGO...4-6 73
LPs: 10/12-inch
NEW VOICE..15-20 66

TANGEERS
Singles: 7-inch
OKEH (7319 "Let My Heart and Soul Be Free")..20-30 69

TANGENTS
(With the Rene Hall Orchestra)
Singles: 7-inch
FRESH (1 "I Can't Live Alone")................15-25 60
FRESH (2274 "Never Leave Again")........20-30 60

TANGENTS
Singles: 7-inch
U.A. (201 "The Wiggle")...........................10-15 60
Also see HALL, Rene

TANGENTS
Singles: 7-inch
MASTERTONE..5-10 64
Members: Sonny Threatt; Andy McKinney; Tony Compton; Murry Judy; Ross Bolin; Land Ligon.
Also see NOMADS
Also see THREATT, Sonny

TANGENTS
Singles: 7-inch
IMPRESSION (111 "Hey Joe")................15-25 66

TANGERINE ROOF
Singles: 7-inch
ROOF (1 "Back in My Arms")...................15-25 68

TANGERINE ZOO
Singles: 7-inch
MAINSTREAM (682 "One More Heartache")...10-15 68
MAINSTREAM (690 "Like People")..........10-15 68
LPs: 10/12-inch
MAINSTREAM (6107 "Tangerine Zoo")...25-35 68
MAINSTREAM (6116 "Outisde Looking In")...35-55 69
Members: Tony Tavares; Don Smith; Robert Benevides; Ron Medeiros; Wayne Gagnon.
Also see EBB TIDES

TANGERINES
Singles: 7-inch
GINA (7002 "Jim That's Him")..................20-30 64
WILDCAT (603 "The Answer Is Always You")..10-15 61

TANGIERS
(Hollywood Flames)
Singles: 78 rpm
DECCA...30-40 55-56
Singles: 7-inch
A-J (905 "The Plea")..................................15-25 62
(Blue label.)
A-J (905 "The Plea")..................................10-15 62
(Green label.)
CLASS (224 "Don't Try")...........................10-20 58
DECCA (29603 "I Won't Be Around").....50-100 55
DECCA (29971 "Remember Me")..........50-100 56
Also see HOLLYWOOD FLAMES

TANGIERS
Singles: 7-inch
STRAND (25039 "Ping Pong").................15-25 61

TANN, Roy
(Roy Tan)
Singles: 7-inch
DOT (15551 "Isabella")..............................20-30 57
DOT (16585 "Isabella")................................8-12 64
TAN (3002 "Isabella")................................50-75 57
(First issue.)

TANNER, Joe
Singles: 7-inch
COLONIAL (7017 "Lover's Holiday")..........5-10 61
Also see DEE, Johnny

TANNER, Kid
Singles: 78 rpm
MODERN (889 "Wino")..............................10-20 53
Singles: 7-inch
MODERN (889 "Wino")..............................25-35 53

TANNER, Sammy
Singles: 7-inch
KCM (3702 "No One")..............................10-15 59

TANNER, William V.
Singles: 7-inch
LIN (5031 "Lonely Rhapsody")...................5-10 63

TANNO, Marc
Singles: 7-inch
PRESIDENT (718 "Someday")................10-15 62
20TH FOX (185 "One Moan, One Sigh, One Kiss")..10-20 60
WHALE (501 "Dear Abby").......................50-75 61

TANNY, Ric
Singles: 7-inch
TARGET (852 "Have Love Will Treasure") 8-12 60

TANTONES
Singles: 78 rpm
LAMP..40-50 57
Singles: 7-inch
LAMP (2002 "No Matter What").............75-100 57
LAMP (2008 "Tell Me")...........................75-100 57

TANYET
LPs: 10/12-inch
VAULT (117 "Tanyet")...............................10-15 68

TANZY, Jan
Singles: 7-inch
COLUMBIA (43219 "Are You Proud")......10-15 65

TAPIA, Larry
Singles: 7-inch
TALENT (101 "Hey Pretty Baby")...........10-15 59

TAPP, Demetriss *C&W '73*
Singles: 7-inch
ABC (11383 "Skinny Dippin' ")......................4-6 73
BRUNSWICK (55251 "Lipstick Paint a Smile on Me")..10-15 63
BRUNSWICK (55257 "Let Go of My Heart")..10-20 64
BRUNSWICK (55274 "Ring Dang Doo")..10-15 65
COLUMBIA (42362 "Am I the Keeper")....10-20 62
NASCO (015 "Just Out of Reach")..............4-6 71

TAPP, Dora
Singles: 7-inch
ARROW (733 "Sad and Broken Heart")...15-25 58

TARANTULAS
Singles: 7-inch
ATLANTIC (2102 "Tarantula")..................15-20 61
(Without "fan" logo.)
ATLANTIC (2102 "Tarantula")..................10-15 61
(With "fan" logo.)
FERNWOOD (131 "Kawliga")......................5-10 62
SILVER DOLLAR (1001 "Herky Jerky").50-100 61
STOP (102 "Herky Jerky")..........................5-10 64
Member: Bob Tucker.
Also see TUCKER, Bob

TARBUTTON, Jim
Singles: 7-inch
GEAR (100 "Stinger")...............................10-20 66

TARGETS
Singles: 7-inch
KING (5538 "It Doesn't Matter")...............40-50 61

TARHEEL SLIM & LITTLE ANN
(Slim & Ann; Slim & Little Ann; Tarheel Slim & Li'l Annie) *R&B '59*
Singles: 78 rpm
FIRE (1000 "Don't Ever Leave Me").......75-125 59
Singles: 7-inch
ATCO (6259 "TwoTime Loser").................8-12 63
BOB BOB (102 "It's Too Late")....................4-8
COLLECTABLES (1641 "It's Too Late")......3-5 '80s
ENJOY (2014 "You Make Me Feel So Good")..8-12 65
FIRE (503 "It's a Sin")...............................15-25 61
FIRE (506 "Forever I'll Be Yours")...........15-25 62
FIRE (1000 "It's Too Late")........................30-40 59
FIRE (1009 "Much Too Late").....................25-35 59
FIRE (1017 "Can't Stay Away")..................25-35 60
FIRE (1021 "Forever I'll Be Yours")............25-35 60
FIRE (1030 "Security")................................25-35 60
FURY (1016 "Number 9 Train")............100-200 58
(Maroon label.)
FURY (1016 "Number 9 Train")................50-75 58
(Yellow label.)

FURY (1068 "I Love You Because")........ 15-25 62
PORT (3001 "I Submit to You")..................5-10 65
Also see BUNN, Allen
Also see LITTLE ANN
Also see LOVERS

TARO, Frankie

Singles: 7-inch

G&G (111 "Suzy Ann")........................ 100-150 58

TARRIERS *P&R '56*

Singles: 78 rpm

GLORY..8-12 56

Singles: 7-inch

DECCA..5-10 63-64
GLORY.. 10-20 56-58
U.A. 8-12 59

LPs: 10/12-inch

ATLANTIC.. 15-25 60
DECCA.. 10-20 62-64
GLORY (1200 "The Tarriers")................. 40-60 57
KAPP 10-20 63
U.A. 15-25 59
Members: Erik Darling; Alan Arkin; Bob Carey.
Also see BRAND, Oscar, & Tarriers
Also see MARTIN, Vince
Also see ROOFTOP SINGERS
Also see WEISSBERG, Eric

TARRYTONS

Singles: 7-inch

DOT (16537 "Rough Surfin' ")....................5-10 63
EXCLUSIVE (2270 "Rough Surfin' ")......... 10-15 63
(First issue.)

TARTANS
(With the Kaddo Strings)

Singles: 7-inch

IMPACT (1010 "Nothing But Love")......... 10-20 66

TARTANS OF LAVENDER LAND

Singles: 7-inch

CAPITOL (2019 "Lovers of the World
Unite").. 20-25 67

TARVER, Leon
(With the Chordones; Leon D. Tarver)

Singles: 78 rpm

BLUE LAKE (118 "Somebody Help
Me")... 20-30 56
CHECKER (791 "I'm a Young
Rooster")... 75-125 54

Singles: 7-inch

BLUE LAKE (118 "Somebody Help
Me")... 50-75 56
CHECKER (791 "I'm a Young
Rooster")... 400-500 54

TASMANIANS

Singles: 7-inch

CONDA (101 "Baby").............................. 20-30 66
POWER (4933 "I Can't Explain This
Feeling")... 10-20 67

TASSELS *P&R '59*

Singles: 7-inch

AMY (946 "To a Soldier Boy")....................8-12 66
MADISON (117 "To a Soldier Boy")......... 15-25 59
MADISON (121 "My Guy and I")............. 10-20 59
Members: John Gaudet; Rochelle Gaudet; Leo Joyce; Joe Intelisano.

TASSO, Vicki

Singles: 7-inch

COLPIX (638 "Foolish Me").........................8-12 62
JEFFREY (401 "Dear Rickey")................ 10-15 61

TASSO THE GREAT

Singles: 78 rpm

UNITED..8-12 53

Singles: 7-inch

B&F (1338 "Ebony After Midnight")......... 10-15 60
UNITED (150 "Ebony After Midnight")..... 15-25 53
Also see KAIN, Tasso

TASTE *LP '69*

Singles: 7-inch

ATCO...4-6 69-70

LPs: 10/12-inch

ATCO.. 10-15 69-70
Members: Rory Gallagher; Richard McCracken; John Wilson.

TATE, Billy

Singles: 78 rpm

IMPERIAL...40-60 54
PEACOCK...10-15 56

Singles: 7-inch

IMPERIAL (5337 "Single Life").............250-350 54
(Blue vinyl.)
IMPERIAL (5337 "Single Life").............100-200 54
(Black vinyl. With script style logo.)
PEACOCK (1671 "Don't Call My Name") .15-25 56

TATE, Blind Bill

Singles: 78 rpm

HERALD..15-20 53

Singles: 7-inch

HERALD (411 "Love Is a Crazy Thing") ...20-30 53

TATE, Buddy
(Buddy Tate Orchestra)

Singles: 78 rpm

BATON 8-12 54

Singles: 7-inch

BATON (202 "Blue Buddy")......................20-30 54
BATON (206 "Jackie")..............................20-30 54
Also see DILLARD, Varetta

TATE, Howard *P&R/R&B '66*

Singles: 7-inch

ATLANTIC..4-6 71-72
EPIC 4-6 74
TURNTABLE...5-10 69-70
UTOPIA (510 "Half a Man").....................15-25 66
VERVE 8-12 66-68

LPs: 10/12-inch

ATLANTIC...10-20 71
TURNTABLE...8-10 70
VERVE 10-20 67-68
Also see DOGGETT, Bill
Also see GAINORS

TATE, Joe

Singles: 7-inch

ROULETTE (4059 "Satellite Rock")..........75-85 58

TATE, Laurie
(With the Joe Morris Blues Cavalcade)

Singles: 78 rpm

ATLANTIC..25-35 52

Singles: 7-inch

ATLANTIC (965 "Rock Me Daddy") 50-75 52
Also see MORRIS, Joe, & His Orchestra

TATE, Paul

Singles: 78 rpm

CHART..5-10 55

Singles: 7-inch

CHART (603 "You Know I Tried")............10-20 55
FALCON (1012 "Dance On")....................10-15 58

TATE, Tommy *R&B '72*

Singles: 7-inch

ABC-PAR (10626 "What's the Matter").....15-25 65
JACKSON SOUND 8-10 70
KOKO 4-6 72-76
OKEH (7242 "Are You from Heaven") 8-12 66
OKEH (7253 "Big Blue Diamonds") 8-12 66

TAURUS

Singles: 7-inch

TOWER...5-10 69
Member: Johnny Cymbal.
Also see CYMBAL, Johnny

TAVENER, John

LPs: 10/12-inch

APPLE (3369 "The Whale") 10-15 72

TAWNEY, Jerry

Singles: 7-inch

BELL...4-6 71-73
LIBERTY (55892 "Run to the Door") 5-10 66
Also see PORTRAITS
Also see YELLOW HAND

TAXPAYERS

Singles: 7-inch

POVERTY ("Wiped Out")..........................15-25 '60s
(No selection number used.)

Picture Sleeves

POVERTY ("Wiped Out") ....15-25 '60s
(Die-cut sleeve which displays record label.)

TAXXI *LP '82*

Singles: 7-inch

FANTASY..3-5 82

LPs: 10/12-inch

FANTASY (9617 "States of Emergency") 20-30 82
MCA..10-15 85

TAYLES

Singles: 7-inch

AGE OF AQUARIUS (1548 "She Made Me That
Way") ....10-15 '70s
AGE OF AQUARIUS (1549 "It's High
Time") ....10-15 '70s

Picture Sleeves

AGE OF AQUARIUS ....10-20 '70s
(1548 and 1549 were both issued in same gatefold picture sleeve.)

LPs: 10/12-inch

CINEVISTA (1001 "Who Are These
Guys")...100-150 72
Members: Scott Eakin; Rick Markstrom; Bob Schmidtke; Jeremy Wilson; Paul Petzold.

TAYLOR, Adam

Singles: 7-inch

ATCO (6886 "My How You've Grown") 4-6 72
LE HARVE (1028 "Yvonne")...................75-125

TAYLOR, Al, & Orbits

Singles: 7-inch

FIVE-FOUR (5436 "I'll Never Love
Again") 15-25 63

TAYLOR, Andrew

Singles: 7-inch

GONE (5109 "That's How I Feel About
You")...400-500 61
Also see BLACKWELL, Joe, & Individuals / Andrew Taylor & Individuals

TAYLOR, Austin *P&R '60*

Singles: 7-inch

LAURIE (3067 "Push Push")....................10-15 60
LAURIE (3082 "Lovin' Hands") 10-15 61
LAURIE (3095 "Together Forever")..........10-15 61
Also see TAYLOR, Ted

TAYLOR, Bert

Singles: 78 rpm

ESSEX (396 "Soldier Boy").......................10-15 55

Singles: 7-inch

ESSEX (396 "Soldier Boy").......................15-25 55

TAYLOR, Big John

Singles: 7-inch

RAM (1107 "Money, Money")...................15-25 59
TRI DEC (8457 "Stompin' ")......................50-75
Also see JOY, Benny

TAYLOR, Bill

Singles: 7-inch

CITATION (5002 "Income Taxes and
You") 10-15 62

TAYLOR, Bill, & Smokey Jo
(With Clyde Leoppard's Snearly Ranch Boys)

Singles: 78 rpm

FLIP (502 "Split Personality")................200-300 55

Singles: 7-inch

EASTWOOD (121 "You Hold My
Letters") 75-125
FLIP (502 "Split Personality")................500-700 55
JET ("Please Tell Me") 50-100
(Selection number not known.)
Members: Bill Taylor; Stan Kesler; Smokey Joe Baugh; Clyde Leoppard; Buddy Holobaugh.
Also see SMOKEY JOE

TAYLOR, Billy
(With the Teardrops; Billy Taylor Trio; Bill Taylor; with David Frost)

Singles: 7-inch

BELL (950 "House of Christmas") 4-6 71
FELCO (101 "Wombie Zombie")...........100-150 59
FELSTED (8564 "Bandstand Baby") 10-15 59
TOWER (421 "Sunny")...............................5-10 68
TROPHY (500 "Nelda Jane")....................20-30 58

LPs: 10/12-inch

ABC-PAR (112 "Evergreens")...................40-60 55
ARGO (650 "Taylor Made Jazz") 25-40 59
BELL (6049 "OK Billy")..............................8-12 70
BELL (6053 "Merry Christmas from Billy Taylor & David
Frost") 8-12 70
PRESTIGE (7762 "Today") 8-12 70
Also see MITCHELL, Willie

TAYLOR, Bobby
(With Charlie & the Jives; Bob Taylor & Counts)

Singles: 7-inch

ASTRA (1016 "Seven Steps to an Angel"). 8-12 65
BARBRA 962640 "You Are My Heart") ..75-150 62
CALDWELL (402 "Frankie & Johnny") 20-30 60
CHYTOWN (104 "A Stranger") ....50-100 '60s
DO-RA-ME (1432 "Samson & Delilah")....10-20 63
GUYDEN (2031 "Night Express")............15-25 60
HOUR (102 "Seven Steps to an Angel") ..20-30 62
KAJO (2201 "It's Funny") 40-50 61
STACY (953 "After Hours").......................10-15 62
YUCCA (102 "Taylor's Rock")..................10-20 58
YUCCA (110 "Don't Be Unfair")..............75-125 59
Also see CHARLIE & JIVES
Also see FULLER, Bobby

TAYLOR, Bobby *P&R/R&B '68*
(With the Vancouvers)

Singles: 7-inch

GORDY (Black vinyl, except 7088) 10-20 68-69
GORDY (7088 "Oh I've Been
Blessed") 300-400 69
GORDY (Colored vinyl)...........................10-20 68
(Promotional issue only.)
HOUR..10-15
INTEGRA (103 "This Is My Woman").......50-75 68
MOWEST (5006 "Hey Lordy") 4-8 71
PLAYBOY (6046 "Why Play Games")..........4-6 75
SUNFLOWER (126 "There Are Roses Somewhere in
This World")...15-25 72
TOMMY..4-6 73
V.I.P. (25053 "Blackmail").......................10-20 69
(Same track on both sides. Promotional issue only.)
V.I.P. (25053 "Oh I've Been Blessed") 10-20 69
(Black vinyl.)
V.I.P. (25053 "Oh I've Been Blessed") 20-40 69
(Colored vinyl. Promotional issue only.)

LPs: 10/12-inch

GORDY (930 "Bobby Taylor & the
Vancouvers")..40-60 68
GORDY (942 "Taylor Made Soul") 40-60 69
Members: Bobby Taylor; Wes Henderson; Ted Lewis; Eddie Patterson; Robbie King; Tommy Chong.
Also see CHEECH & CHONG
Also see COLUMBUS PHARAOHS
Also see FOUR PHARAOHS

TAYLOR, Burt

Singles: 78 rpm

ESSEX 8-12 54-55

Singles: 7-inch

EAST WEST (105 "I Can't Help It") 10-20 58
EAST WEST (118 "Long Lost Love") 10-20 58
ESSEX (378 "Anything")..........................15-25 54
ESSEX (396 "Soldier Boy").......................15-25 55
Also see FAITH, Percy, Orchestra

TAYLOR, Carmen
(With the Boleros; with Orchestra; "Billboard's 1954 Disc-Jockey Poll Winner")

Singles: 78 rpm

APOLLO (489 "Oh Please").......................15-25 56
ATLANTIC (Except 1041) 10-20 53
ATLANTIC (1041 "Freddie") 30-50 54
GUYDEN...10-15 54
TIN PAN ALLEY 10-15 54

Singles: 7-inch

APOLLO (489 "Oh Please").......................40-50 56
ATLANTIC (1002 "Lovin' Daddy")............20-40 53
ATLANTIC (1015 "Big Mamou Daddy") ...20-40 53
ATLANTIC (1041 "Freddie") 75-125 54
EL TORO (501 "Willie 'B' ")......................50-75
GUYDEN (100 "Let Me Go Lover") 15-25 54
KAMA SUTRA (206 "My Son") 5-10 66
KING (5085 "Why Did You Leave Me
Alone") 15-25 57
TIN PAN ALLEY (130 "Love Is
Everything")..15-25 54

TAYLOR, Carmol *C&W '75*

Singles: 7-inch

ELEKTRA..4-6 75-77
SHERBA (1501 "Street of Broken
Hearts") 10-20 59
TAGG (504 "Free As a Breeze")..............50-75 59

TAYLOR, Cathie

Singles: 7-inch

CAPITOL (4565 "Bobby Boy") 8-12 61
TOPPA (1006 "Tree Near My House")......10-15 59

Picture Sleeves

CAPITOL (4565 "Bobby Boy")..................10-20 61

LPs: 10/12-inch

CAPITOL (1359 "Little Bit of Sweetness") 15-25 60
CAPITOL (1448 "Tree Near My House"). 15-25 60

TAYLOR, Chip C&W '75
(With Ghost Train)

Singles: 7-inch

BUDDAH (325 "Angel of the Morning")........4-6 72
BUDDAH (344 Londonderry Co.") 4-6 73
CAPITOL 3-5 79
COLUMBIA..4-6 69-77
EPIC (10567 "It's Such a Lonely Time of Year") 5-10 69
MGM (12993 "Foolin' Around") 5-10 61
MGM (13040 "Sad Songs") 5-10 61
MALA (476 "Joanie's Blues").......................5-10 64
MALA (489 "Suzannah")..............................5-10 64
MALA (507 "Young Love").........................5-10 65
RAINY DAY (6002 "I'll Never Be Alone Again") 5-10 67
W.B. (5314 "Here I Am")............................5-10 62
W.B. (7700 series) 4-6 73-76

LPs: 10/12-inch

BUDDAH (5118 "Gasoline")........................8-12 72
CAPITOL..5-10 79
COLUMBIA...5-10 76
W.B. 8-10 73-75
Also see JUST US

TAYLOR, Chuck

Singles: 7-inch

COLUMBIA...4-6 76
DECCA (31099 "Little Lover") 10-15 60
VEE-JAY (388 "The Burning of Atlanta") 8-12 61

TAYLOR, Danny "Run Joe"
(With the Louis Payne Orchestra)

Singles: 78 rpm

BRUCE... 10-15 55
RCA.. 10-15 53
SAXONY.. 10-15 53

Singles: 7-inch

BRUCE (118 "Bad Bad Draws").............. 15-20 55
RCA (5558 "You Look Bad") 20-30 53
SAXONY (101 "I Know What I Want") 20-30 55
WHEELER.. 30-35 '50s
Also see PAYNE, Louis, Orchestra

TAYLOR, Debbie R&B '68

Singles: 7-inch

ARISTA...4-6 75-76
DECCA..5-10 68
GWP...8-12 69
POLYDOR..4-6 74
TODAY 4-8 72

LPs: 10/12-inch

TODAY 10-15 72

TAYLOR, Eddie

Singles: 78 rpm

VEE-JAY.. 20-40 55-56

Singles: 7-inch

VEE-JAY (149 "Bad Boy") 75-125 55
VEE-JAY (185 "Ride Em On Down") 75-125 55
VEE-JAY (206 "You'll Always Have a Home") 50-75 56
VEE-JAY (267 "I'm Gonna Love You") 30-50 57
VIVID (104 "I'm Sitting Here") 15-25 64
Session: Jimmy Reed.
Also see PRYOR, Snooky
Also see REED, Jimmy
Also see SUNNYLAND SLIM

TAYLOR, Elaine, & Mastertones

Singles: 7-inch

BAND BOX (233 "Baby, Won't You Please Come Home") 30-50 60
Also see SCOTTY & BOBO WITH THE MASTERTONES

TAYLOR, Faith, & Sweet Teens

Singles: 7-inch

BEA & BABY (104 "I Need Him to Love Me") 15-25 59
BEA & BABY (105 "I Love You Darling"). 15-25 59
FEDERAL (12334 "Your Candy Kisses") 100-200 58

TAYLOR, Faron

Singles: 7-inch

COLUMBIA (44428 "Blue Eyed Soul")........5-10 68

TAYLOR, Felice P&R/R&B '67

Singles: 7-inch

KENT (483 "Good Luck")............................5-10 67
KENT (488 "New Love") 5-10 68
MUSTANG (3024 "It May Be Winter Outside") 10-15 66
MUSTANG (3026 "Love Theme") 5-10 67
Also see SWEETS

TAYLOR, Gene

Singles: 7-inch

KENT (417 "Cut Me Loose") 5-10 65
MINIT (32073 "Don't Go Away") 5-10 69
STARDAY (190 "I'm Not the Marrying Kind") 50-75

TAYLOR, Gerri

Singles: 7-inch

CONSTELLATION (154 "Empty Arms and Bitter Tears") 10-20 65

TAYLOR, Glenn

Singles: 78 rpm

ARCADE 5-10 54-55

Singles: 7-inch

ARCADE (118 "Wastin' Time")..................10-20 54
ARCADE (125 "Without You")...................10-20 55

TAYLOR, Gloria P&R/R&B '69
(Gloria Ann Taylor)

Singles: 7-inch

COLUMBIA...4-6 74
GLO-WHIZ (601 "Freedom") 5-10 69
KING SOUL (493 "Poor Unfortunate Me") 15-25 68
SELECTOR SOUND (0352 "World That's Not Real") ....4-6 '70s
SILVER FOX (14 "You Got to Pay the Price") 5-10 69
SILVER FOX (19 "Grounded") 5-10 69

TAYLOR, Guy, & Phantoms / Rick Neri

Singles: 7-inch

LOOP (800 "Lesa"/"You Made My Heart Cry") 75-100 58

TAYLOR, Hound Dog
(With the Houserockers)

Singles: 7-inch

BEA & BABY (112 "Take Five") 15-25 60
CJ (626 "Christine") 15-25 62
FIRMA (626 "Christine") 10-20 62
KEY (112 "Take Five") 10-20 62
MARJETTE (1102 "Baby's Coming Home") 20-25

LPs: 10/12-inch

ALLIGATOR (Except 4701)........................8-12 74-82
ALLIGATOR (4701 "Hound Dog Taylor & the Houserockers") 10-20 71
(Alligator's first LP release.)
Also see WILLIAMS, Willie

TAYLOR, Hound Dog / Robert Nighthawk / John Littlejohn / Earl Hooker

LPs: 10/12-inch

CHICAGO SLIDE (005 "Slide Guitar Classics") 10-15
Also see HOOKER, Earl
Also see NIGHTHAWK, Robert
Also see TAYLOR, Hound Dog

TAYLOR, James P&R/LP '70
(With the Original Flying Machine)

Singles: 7-inch

APPLE (1805 "Carolina in My Mind"/"Taking It In") 200-300 69
APPLE (1805 "Carolina in My Mind"/ "Something's Wrong") 5-10 70
(Note different flip side.)
APPLE (PRO-1805 "Carolina on My Mind) 25-35 70
(Note title variance. Promotional issue only.)
APPLE (4675 "More Apples, Radio Co-Op Ads") 150-200 69
(Single-sided disc. Promotional issue only.)
CAPITOL..4-6 76
COLUMBIA...3-6 77-88
EUPHORIA...4-6 71
W.B. 4-6 70-76

Picture Sleeves

COLUMBIA...3-5 81-88

LPs: 10/12-inch

APPLE 20-30 69-70
COLUMBIA 5-10 77-88
EUPHORIA 12-15 71
SPRINGBOARD ....5-10 '70s
TRIP 8-10 73
W.B. (Except MS4-2866)............................8-10 70-77
W.B. (BS4-2866 "Gorilla") 30-60 75
(Quadraphonic.)
Also see DOOBIE BROTHERS, JAMES HALL & JAMES TAYLOR
Also see DOOBIE BROTHERS / Kate Taylor & Simon-Taylor Family
Also see GARFUNKEL, Art, James Taylor & Paul Simon
Also see SIMON, Carly, & James Taylor

TAYLOR, James, & J.D. Souther P&R '81

Singles: 7-inch

COLUMBIA 3-5 81
Also see TAYLOR, James

TAYLOR, Joanie, & Tabs

Singles: 7-inch

HERALD (568 "You Lied") 10-15 62

TAYLOR, Joe, & Dominoes

Singles: 7-inch

HMF (2002 "You Don't Love Me")............30-50 '60s

TAYLOR, Joe, & Hitch Hikers

Singles: 7-inch

MARBLE ("The Big Bad Wolf") 40-60 67
(Selection number not known.)

TAYLOR, Johnnie P&R/R&B '63
(Johnny Taylor; the "Soul Philosopher")

Singles: 78 rpm

HOLLYWOOD 10-20 54

Singles: 7-inch

BEVERLY GLEN 3-5 82
COLUMBIA 4-8 76-80
DERBY (101 "Dance What You Wanna") 10-20 63
DERBY (1006 "Baby We've Got Love") ...10-20 63
DERBY (1010 "I Need Lots of Love") 10-20 64
HOLLYWOOD (1011 "Over the Hill") 50-100 54
HOLLYWOOD (1018 "She Wouldn't Lay Down") 50-100 54
MALACO 3-6 83-87
RCA...4-8 77
SAR (114 "Whole Lotta Woman") 15-25 61
SAR (131 "Never, Never") 10-20 61
SAR (156 "Oh, How I Love You") 5-10 65
STAX (186 thru 253).....................................5-10 66-68
STAX (0009 thru 3201) 4-8 68-77

LPs: 10/12-inch

BEVERLY GLEN (10001 "Just Ain't Good Enough") 5-10 82
COLUMBIA (PC-33951 "Eargasm") 8-12 76
COLUMBIA (PCQ-33951 "Eargasm") 15-25 76
(Quadraphonic.)
COLUMBIA (PC-34401 "Rated Extraordinaire") 8-12 77
COLUMBIA (PCQ-34401 "Rated Extraordinaire") 15-25 77
(Quadraphonic.)
COLUMBIA (35340 "Ever Ready") 8-12 77
COLUMBIA (36061 "She's Killing Me") 6-10 79
COLUMBIA (36548 "New Day")..................6-10 80
COLUMBIA (37127 "The Best of Johnnie Taylor") 6-10 81
MALACO...5-10 83-86
RCA (2527 "Reflections") 8-12 77
STAX (715 "Wanted: One Soul Singer") ..15-25 67
STAX (2005 "Who's Making Love") 15-25 68
STAX (2008 "Raw Blues") 10-20 69
STAX (2012 "Rare Stamps").....................10-20 69
STAX (2023 "The Johnnie Taylor Philosophy Continues") 10-20 69
STAX (2030 "One Step Beyond") 10-20 71
STAX (2032 "Greatest Hits")......................10-20 70
STAX (3014 "Taylored in Silk") 10-15 73
STAX (5509 "Super Taylor") 10-15 74
STAX (5522 "The Best of Johnnie Taylor") 10-15 75
STAX (8520 "Super Hits") 6-10 83
STAX (88001 "Chronicle")..........................10-15 77
(Two discs.)
Also see FIVE ECHOES
Also see SOUL STIRRERS

TAYLOR, Johnnie, & Carla Thomas

Singles: 7-inch

STAX (0042 "Just Keep On Loving Me")....5-10 69
Also see TAYLOR, Johnnie
Also see THOMAS, Carla

TAYLOR, Johnny

Singles: 78 rpm

BLUE (129 "Mr. Monkey Man")...............50-100 52

Singles: 7-inch

BAKERSFIELD ("Mixed Up Rhythm and Blues") ....200-300 '50s
(Selection number not known.)

TAYLOR, Josephine

Singles: 7-inch

MAR-V-LUS (6011 "Good Lovin' ")...........10-20 66
MAR-V-LUS (6013 "What Is Love")..........10-20 66
MAR-V-LUS (6017 "Ordinary Girl") 10-20 67
TWINIGHT (122 "Is It Worth a Chance")....5-10 69

TAYLOR, Joyce
(With the Jack Halloran Singers and David Carroll Orchestra)

Singles: 78 rpm

MERCURY...5-10 54

Singles: 7-inch

LIBERTY (55090 "How Will I Know")........10-15 57
MERCURY (70461 "Your Mind, Your Lips, Your Heart") 10-20 54
Also see HALLORAN, Jack, Singers

TAYLOR, Kirk
(With the Belltones)

Singles: 7-inch

BANDERA (2507 "You Didn't Learn That in School") 30-40 60
SALEM (11084 "It's So Hard") 5-10 65
TEK (2634 "Been So Long") 25-35 58

TAYLOR, Koko P&R/R&B '66
(Cocoa Taylor; Ko Ko Taylor)

Singles: 7-inch

CHECKER 8-15 66-68
USA (745 "Like Heaven to Me") 10-20 63
YAMBO (107/108 "A Mighty Love").........10-15 69

LPs: 10/12-inch

ALLIGATOR...8-15 76-89
CHESS..10-15 69-72
Session: Willie Dixon; Walter Horton; Buddy Guy; Lafayette Leake; Robert Nighthawk; Jack Meyers; Clifton James.
Also see DIXON, Willie
Also see GUY, Buddy
Also see HORTON, Big Walter
Also see NIGHTHAWK, Robert

TAYLOR, Leroy
(With the Four Kays)

Singles: 7-inch

BRUNSWICK (55345 "Oh Linda")............10-15 67
COLPIX (739 "Dr. Fix-It") 8-12 64
COLUMBIA (42258 "Dooley Walk")...........8-12 62
SHRINE (101 "Taking My Time")..........200-300 65

TAYLOR, Linwood

Singles: 7-inch

JAMECO (2003 "Sweet Little Girl") 10-15 64

TAYLOR, Little Eddie

Singles: 7-inch

PEACOCK (1949 "I Had a Good Life").....50-75 67

TAYLOR, Little Johnny P&R/R&B/LP '63
(With Paul Clifton & His Band)

Singles: 7-inch

GALAXY..8-15 63-67
RONN..4-6 71-79
SWINGIN' (624 "Looking at the Future")..15-25 60
SWINGIN' (639 "One More Chance").......25-35 62

LPs: 10/12-inch

BEVERLY GLEN 5-8 87
ICHIBAN...5-10
GALAXY (203 "Little Johnny Taylor").......25-45 63
RONN..5-10 72-79
Also see CLIFTON, Paul

TAYLOR, Little Johnny, & Ted Taylor

Singles: 7-inch

RONN (75 "Cry It Out Baby")........................4-6 73
RONN (89 "Pretending Love") 4-6 74

LPs: 10/12-inch

RONN (7533 "Super Taylors")....................5-10 73
Also see TAYLOR, Little Johnny
Also see TAYLOR, Ted

TAYLOR, Livingston LP '70

Singles: 7-inch

CAPRICORN 4-6 71-74

CRITIQUE....3-5 88
EPIC....3-5 78-80

LPs: 10/12-inch

ATCO....8-12 70
CAPRICORN....5-10 70-79
EPIC....5-10 78
Also see DOOBIE BROTHERS / Kate Taylor & Simon-Taylor Family

TAYLOR, Livingston, & Leah Kunkel *C&W '88*

Singles: 7-inch

CRITIQUE....3-5 88
Also see TAYLOR, Livingston

TAYLOR, Lynn, & Peachettes

Singles: 7-inch

BLACKHAWK (12102 "The Bells of St. Mary's")....5-10 65
CLOCK (1033 "The Bells of St. Mary's").. 10-20 60

TAYLOR, Mad Man

Singles: 7-inch

EAST WEST (117 "Rumble Tumble")..... 50-60 58

TAYLOR, Mark
(With the Markees; with Kaye Golden)

Singles: 7-inch

HI (2006 "Linda Lou").... 15-25 58
(First issue.)
JUDD (1006 "Linda Lou").... 10-15 59
JUDD (1011 "I'm Waiting Just for You") .. 10-15 59

TAYLOR, Mel
(With the Darts; with Magics)

Singles: 7-inch

AVALANCHE (36008 "Bandolero")....4-6 72
RENDEZVOUS (187 "Drumstick")....8-10 62
TOPPA....8-10 62
W.B. 5-10 65-66

LPs: 10/12-inch

W.B. (1624 "In Action").... 15-25 65
Also see VENTURES

TAYLOR, Mike

Singles: 7-inch

DREAM ("He's a Lover").... 150-200 66
(No selection number used. Both 1959 and 1962 have also been offered as the year of issue.)
Session: Camerons.
Also see CAMERONS

TAYLOR, Monroe

Singles: 7-inch

CHESAPEAKE (617 "Proud Guy").... 10-15 63
Session: Soul Masters.

TAYLOR, Montana

Singles: 78 rpm

CIRCLE 15-25 46-47

TAYLOR, Montana, & Clarence Lofton

LPs: 10/12-inch

RIVERSIDE.... 15-25 61
Also see TAYLOR, Montana

TAYLOR, Morris

Singles: 7-inch

KEY (5718 "Look-a-What").... 50-100 58
MASTERS MUSIC (2 "Running Back to You") 50-100

TAYLOR, R. Dean *P&R '70*

Singles: 7-inch

AUDIO MASTER (1 "At the High School Dance").... 100-150 60
BARRY (3023 "At the High School Dance").... 75-125 60
(Canadian.)
CLASSIC (6728 "At the High School Dance") .... 50-75 '60s
FARR....4-6 76
JANE....4-6 77
MALA (444 "I'll Remember").... 25-50 62
MOTOWN....4-6
RAGAMUFFIN....4-6 79
RARE EARTH (Black vinyl)....4-8 70-72
RARE EARTH (Colored vinyl)....6-12 70-71
STRUMMER....3-5 83
20TH FOX 3-5 81
V.I.P. 10-20 65-68

Picture Sleeves

RARE EARTH (5023 "Ain't It a Sad Thing")....5-10 71

LPs: 10/12-inch

RARE EARTH (522 "I Think, Therefore I Am")....10-15 70

TAYLOR, Ray

Singles: 7-inch

CLIX (801 "Clocking My Card")....250-350 57
CLIX (802 "My Hamtrack Baby")....500-750 57
CLIX (803 "I'll Never Let You Weary My Mind Any More")....100-200 57
CLIX (2207 "Connie Lou")....100-200

TAYLOR, Robert
(With the Soul Exciters; with HPJ'S)

Singles: 7-inch

SONIC (33075 "Memories of Yesterday"/"Memories of Yesterday")....20-30 '60s
(Promotional issue only.)
SONIC (111776 "Somebody Have Mercy")....15-25 '60s
SONIC (121974 "Let Me Love You")....15-25 '60s
SONIC (478486 "A Change Gonna Come")....15-25 '60s

EPs: 7-inch

SONIC (33075 "Memories of Yesterday")....30-50 '60s

TAYLOR, Ronnie

Singles: 7-inch

REVILOT (212 "I Can't Take It")....10-20 67

TAYLOR, Sam "The Man"
(With Claude Cloud & His Thunderclaps)

Singles: 78 rpm

ABBEY....10-20 49
MGM....10-15 54-56

Singles: 7-inch

BIG TOP (3043 "Any Time")....10-15 60
MGM....10-20 54-60

EPs: 7-inch

MGM (293 "Music with the Big Beat")....25-50 56
(Two discs. "Produced Under the Supervision of Alan Freed.")
MGM (1181/1182/1183 "Blue Mist")....15-25 55
(Price is for any of three volumes.)
MGM (1272/1273/1274 "Out of This World")....15-25 56
(Price is for any of three volumes.)
MGM (1417/1418/1419 "Music for Melancholy Babies")....15-25 57
(Price is for any of three volumes.)
MGM (1484/1485/1486 "Rockin' Sax & Rollin' Organ")....15-25 57
(Price is for either volume.)
MGM (1515/1516/1517 "Prelude to Blues")....15-25 57
(Price is for any of three volumes.)

LPs: 10/12-inch

MGM (293 "Music with the Big Beat")....50-100 56
(10-inch LP. "Produced Under the Supervision of Alan Freed.")
MGM (3292 "Blue Mist")....30-60 55
MGM (3380 "Out of This World")....30-60 56
MGM (3473 "Music with the Big Beat")....50-75 56
MGM (3482 "Music for Melancholy Babies")....30-60 57
MGM (3553 "Rockin' Sax & Rollin' Organ")....30-60 57
MGM (3573 "Prelude to Blues")....30-60 57
Also see FREED, Alan
Also see MR. BEAR

TAYLOR, Sam "The Man," & Dick Hyman

Singles: 78 rpm

MGM....5-10 56

Singles: 7-inch

MGM....10-15 56
Also see HYMAN, Dick
Also see TAYLOR, Sam "The Man

TAYLOR, Sam

Singles: 7-inch

BIG TOP (3043 "Anytime")....10-15 60

TAYLOR, Sammy
(With the Trailers)

Singles: 7-inch

ATLANTIC (2209 "She Rocks My Soul")....8-12 63
ENJOY (2028 "Your Precious Love")....8-12 65
JALYNNE (109 "Switchin' in the Kitchen")....10-15 61
MAY (123 "Friday the 13th")....10-15 62

TAYLOR, Sean

Singles: 7-inch

MAGIC TOUCH (2008 "Put Me Down Easy")....8-12 67
Also see ESQUIRES

TAYLOR, Shelly

Singles: 7-inch

SOUND STAGE 7 (2525 "My Song Is You")....5-10 64

TAYLOR, Sherri

Singles: 7-inch

GLORECO (1002 "I've Got a Crush")....30-50 '60s
Also see TAYLOR TONES

TAYLOR, Sherri, & Singin' Sammy Ward

Singles: 7-inch

MOTOWN (1004 "That's Why I Love You So Much")....25-35 60
Also see TAYLOR, Sherri
Also see WARD, Singin' Sammy

TAYLOR, Ted *P&R/R&B '65*
(With the Bob Reed Orchestra; Ted Taylor Combo)

Singles: 7-inch

ALARM (112 "Steal Away")....4-6 76
APT (25063 "Ltle Things Mean a Lot")....10-20 62
ATCO (6388 "Dancing Annie")....5-10 65
ATCO (6408 "Long Distance Love")....5-10 66
ATCO (6434 "Help the Bear")....5-10 66
ATCO (6481 "Feed the Flame")....5-10 67
DADE (5000 "I Lost the Best Thing I Ever Had")....8-12 63
DUKE (304 "Be Ever Wonderful")....30-40 59
DUKE (308 "Count the Stars")....15-25 59
EBB (113 "Everywhere I Go")....15-25 57
EBB (132 "Keep Walkin' On")....15-25 58
EBB (151 "Very Truly Yours")....15-25 58
EPIC (2241 "Be Ever Wonderful")....5-10 66
EPIC (2249 "Daddy's Baby")....5-10 66
GOLD EAGLE (1805 "My Darling")....10-15 61
GOLD EAGLE (1808 "Bandstand Drag") .10-15 61
GOLD EAGLE (1810 "I Don't Care")....10-15 61
GOLD EAGLE (1812 "Never in My Life") .10-15 61
JEWEL....5-10 65-66
LAURIE (3076 "You've Been Crying")....10-20 60
MELATONE (1003 "I'm Leaving You")....8-12 '60s
OKEH....10-15 62-65
RONN....5-10 67-73
SONCRAFT (400 "Anytime, Anyplace, Anywhere")....10-20 61
TOP RANK (2011 "I'm Saving My Love").20-30 59
TOP RANK (2048 "I Need You So")....15-20 60
TOP RANK (2076 "Darling, Take Me Back")....15-20 60
TOP RANK (3001 "Someday")....10-15 61
(First issue.)
U.A. (452 "Pretending Love")....8-12 62
WARWICK (628 "Someday")....8-12 61
WATTS CITY (1003 "I'm Leaving You")....4-6 83

LPs: 10/12-inch

OKEH....20-40 63-66
MCA....5-10 78
RONN....8-15 69-72
Also see CADETS
Also see REED, Bob
Also see TAYLOR, Austin
Also see TAYLOR, Little Johnny & Ted Taylor

TAYLOR, Tommy, & Five Knights

Singles: 7-inch

MINIT (636 "I Want Somebody")....10-20 61
Also see FIVE KNIGHTS

TAYLOR, True
(Paul Simon)

Singles: 7-inch

BIG (614 "Teenage Fool")....30-50 58
Also see SIMON, Paul

TAYLOR, Ty, & Cameos

Singles: 7-inch

DESIGN (834 "The Beginning of Love")...10-15 60

TAYLOR, Vernon

Singles: 78 rpm

DOT (15632 "I've Got the Blues")....50-75 57

Singles: 7-inch

DOT (15632 "I've Got the Blues")....50-75 57
DOT (15697 "Satisfaction Guaranteed") ..50-75 57
SUN (310 "Today Is Blue Day")....15-20 58
SUN (325 "Mystery Train")....15-20 59

TAYLOR, William Tell

Singles: 7-inch

D (1051 "I Like It")....25-50 59
D (1080 "Uh Huh")....20-30 59

TAYLOR, Zola

Singles: 78 rpm

RPM (405 "Make Love to Me")....100-200 54

Singles: 7-inch

RPM (405 "Make Love to Me")....150-250 54
Also see GUNTER, Shirley
Also see PLATTERS

TAYLOR TONES

Singles: 7-inch

C&T (0001 "Too Young to Love")....40-50 '60s
STAR MAKER (1926 "Poor Little Girl")....15-25 61
Members: Sherri Taylor; Clara Taylor.
Also see TAYLOR, Sherri

TAYLORTOPS

Singles: 7-inch

ALTON (2000 "I'll See You Somewhere") 30-40 59

TAZMEN
("Guitar Solo By Joe Rumoro")

Singles: 78 rpm

TAZ (9121 "Easy Pickin' ")....20-30 57
(Identification number shown since no selection number is used.)

Singles: 7-inch

ABC-PAR (9812 "Easy Pickin' ")....10-15 57
TAZ ("Gobo")....30-40 57
(No selection number used.)
TAZ (1003 "Crackajack")....15-25 57
TAZ (9105 "Easy Pickin' ")....20-30 58
(Identification number shown since no selection number is used. Same track as *Gobo.*)
Member: Joe Rumoro.

T-BIRDS

Singles: 7-inch

CASTLE (641 "Thunder Rock")....15-25 59
NEW TALENT (101 "Thunder Rock")....15-25 59
(Canadian.)

T-BIRDS

Singles: 7-inch

CHESS (1778 "Green Stamps")....8-12 61
GONE (5141 "Wild Stomp")....8-12 62
T-BIRD (101 "Green Stamps")....25-35 61
(First issue.)
VEGAS (720 "Nobody But Me")....25-35 67
Members: Jimmy Norman; Jesse Belvin.
Also see BELVIN, Jesse
Also see NORMAN, Jimmy

TEA COMPANY

Singles: 7-inch

SMASH (2176 "Come and Have Some Tea with Me")....5-10 68

LPs: 10/12-inch

SMASH (67105 "Come and Have Some Tea")....15-20 68

TEACHO & STUDENTS

Singles: 7-inch

FELSTED (8517 "Rock-et").... 15-25 58
OKEH (7234 "Chills & Fever").... 15-25 65
Member: Teacho Wilshire.
Also see WILTSHIRE, Teacho

TEAGARDEN, Jack
(With the Five Keys)

LPs: 10/12-inch

CAPITOL (820 "Swing Low, Sweet Spirtual")....150-250 54
Also see FIVE KEYS

TEAM-BEATS

Singles: 7-inch

MUTUAL (503 "Riverside Shake")....10-20 64

TEAM MATES
(Teamates)

Singles: 7-inch

ABC-PAR (10760 "You Must Pay")....8-12 66
LE CAM (701 "Sooner Or Later")....15-20 59
(Released with two different B-sides.)
LE CAM (706 "You Must Pay")....10-15 59
LE CAM (707 "Once There Was a Time")....15-25 60
(Released with three different B-sides.)
LE CAM (709 "Sylvia")....20-30 60
LE-MANS (003 "Calendar of Love")....10-15 64

PAULA (220 "Most of All") 50-75 65
PHILIPS (40029 "Once There Was a Time") 10-15 62
SOFT (104 "Most of All") 75-100 62
(First issued as by the Danes.)
TWINKLE (503 "In My Dreams") 40-50
Also see DANES

TEARDROPS

Singles: 78 rpm

SAMPSON (634 "Come Back to Me") 50-75 52

TEARDROPS

Singles: 78 rpm

JOSIE (766 "The Stars Are Out Tonight") 75-100 54
JOSIE (771 "My Heart") 50-75 55

Singles: 7-inch

JOSIE (766 "The Stars Are Out Tonight") 150-250 54
JOSIE (771 "My Heart") 300-400 55
(800 series issues are by a different group and are listed below.)
PORT (70019 "The Stars Are Out Tonight") 10-15 60

TEARDROPS

Singles: 78 rpm

KING 10-20 56-57

Singles: 7-inch

KING (5004 "My Inspiration") 15-25 56
KING (5037 "After School") 10-15 57

TEARDROPS

Singles: 78 rpm

DOT (15569 "Bridge of Love") 10-15 57

Singles: 7-inch

DOT (15569 "Bridge of Love") 10-15 57
RENDEZVOUS (102 "Sugar Baby") 5-10 58
Members: Tony; Paul.

TEARDROPS

Singles: 7-inch

JOSIE (856 thru 873) 15-25 59-60
(700 series issues are by a different group and are listed above.)

TEARDROPS

Singles: 7-inch

COLVIN (777 "I Know") 75-150 59

TEARDROPS

LPs: 10/12-inch

20TH FOX (5011 "At Trinchi's") 15-25 63

TEARDROPS

Singles: 7-inch

MUSICOR (1139 "Tears Come Tumbling") 5-10 65
MUSICOR (1218 "I Will Love You Dear Forever") 5-10 66
SAXONY (1007 "Tonight I'm Gonna Fall in Love Again") 15-20 64
SAXONY (1008 "I'm Gonna Steal Your Boyfriend") 10-15 65
SAXONY (1009 "Tears Come Tumbling") 10-15 65
SAXONY (2002 "I Will Love You Dear Forever") 4-6 93
SAXONY (2009 "Tears Come Tumbling") 4-6 98
SAXONY (3003 "Here Comes Loneliness") .4-6 2002
Members: Dorothy Dyer; Pat Strunk; Linda Schroeder; Wanda Sheriff

TEARDROPS

Singles: 7-inch

004 (101 "Armfull of Teddy Bear") .... 10-15 '60s
004 (102 "You Go Your Way") .... 10-15 '60s

Picture Sleeves

004 (101 "Armfull of Teddy Bear") .... 15-25 '60s
004 (102 "You Go Your Way") .... 15-25 '60s

TEARS

Singles: 78 rpm

DIG (112 "Nothing But Love") 15-25 56

Singles: 7-inch

DIG (112 "Nothing But Love") 30-40 56

TEARS

Singles: 7-inch

ASTRONAUT (5001 "Hurt") 40-50 61

TEARS

Singles: 7-inch

SMASH (1981 "Good Luck, My Love") 15-25 65

TEARS

Singles: 7-inch

EMBASSY (1005 "In the Palm of My Hand") 15-25

TEASERS

Singles: 78 rpm

CHECKER 100-150 54

Singles: 7-inch

CHECKER (800 "How Could You Hurt Me So") 400-500 54
(Black vinyl.)
CHECKER (800 "How Could You Hurt Me So") 2000-3000 54
(Red vinyl.)
Also see BINKLEY, Jimmy

TECHNICS

Singles: 7-inch

CHEX (1012 "Cause I Really Love You") . 10-15 63
CHEX (1013 "Hey Girl Don't Leave Me").. 10-15 63
Also see TONY & TECHNICS

TECHNIQUES P&R '57

Singles: 78 rpm

ROULETTE 10-15 57

Singles: 7-inch

ROULETTE (4030 "Hey! Little Girl") 20-30 57
ROULETTE (4048 "Let Her Go") 10-15 58
ROULETTE (4097 "The Wisest Man You Know") 10-15 58
STARS (551 "Hey! Little Girl") 40-50 57

TECHNIQUES

Singles: 7-inch

VENUS ("Dream Theme") .... 10-15 '60s
(No selection number used. Identification number, shown on label, is 8540.)

TED & JOHNNY

Singles: 7-inch

PEACH (565 "Teenage Party") 10-15 59

TEDDER, Randy

Singles: 7-inch

TWIN ROSE (101 "Nancy") 100-200

TEDDY & CONTINENTALS

Singles: 7-inch

PIK (235 "Tick Tick Tock") 10-15 61
RICHIE (445 "Do You") 75-125 61
(Label makes no reference to distribution by Roulette.)
RICHIE (445 "Do You") 20-30 61
(Label indicates distribution by Roulette.)
RICHIE (453 "Crying Over You") 40-60 61
RICHIE (1001 "Tick Tick Tock") 50-75 60
Member: Teddy Henry.

TEDDY & CONTINENTALS / Teen Kings

Singles: 7-inch

RAGO (201 "Tick Tick Tock"/"Wild Christening Party") 30-40 62
Also see TEDDY & CONTINENTALS
Also see TEEN KINGS

TEDDY & DARREL

Singles: 7-inch

MIRA (235 "Wild Thing") 5-10 67

LPs: 10/12-inch

MIRA (10000 "These Are the Hits, You Silly Savage") 10-20 66

TEDDY & FINGERPOPPERS

Singles: 7-inch

ARCTIC (143 "Soul Groove") 5-10 68

TEDDY & HIS PATCHES

Singles: 7-inch

CHANCE (101 "Suzy Creemcheese") 30-40 67
CHANCE (669 "Haight Ashbury") 30-40 67

TEDDY & PANDAS

Singles: 7-inch

CORISTINE 8-12 66
MUSICOR (1176 "Once Upon a Time") 8-12 66
MUSICOR (1190 "We Can't Go On This Way") 8-12 66
MUSICOR (1212 "Sunny Side Up") 8-12 66
TIMBRI 8-12 67
TOWER (433 "Childhood Friends") 5-10 68

LPs: 10/12-inch

TOWER (5125 "Basic Magnetism") 10-20 68

TEDDY & ROUGH RIDERS

Singles: 7-inch

HURON (22002 "Dream Come True") 10-15 61
HURON (22008 "Money & Gold") 10-15 61
MEAN MT. (1420 "Thunderhead") 3-5 82
TILT (778 "Thunderhead") 15-25 61

Picture Sleeves

MEAN MT. (1420 "Thunderhead") 3-5 82

TEDDY & TWILIGHTS P&R '62

Singles: 7-inch

SWAN (4102 "Woman Is a Man's Best Friend") 15-25 62
SWAN (4115 "Running Around Town") 15-20 62
SWAN (4126 "I'm Just Your Clown") 10-20 62
Also see TIFFANYS

TEDDY BEARS P&R/R&B '58

Singles: 78 rpm

DORE (503 "To Know Him Is to Love Him") 50-100 58
(Canadian.)

Singles: 7-inch

COLLECTABLES .... 3-5 '80s
DORE (503 "To Know Him Is to Love Him") 25-30 58
DORE (520 "Wonderful Loveable You") 25-30 59
IMPERIAL (5562 "Oh Why") 15-25 58
IMPERIAL (5581 "You Said Goodbye") 10-15 59
IMPERIAL (5594 "Don't Go Away") 10-15 59
(Black vinyl.)
IMPERIAL (5594 "Don't Go Away") 15-25 59
(Yellow vinyl.)

Picture Sleeves

DORE (503 "To Know Him Is to Love Him") .... 5-10 '90s

LPs: 10/12-inch

IMPERIAL (9067 "The Teddy Bears Sing") 200-300 59
(Monaural.)
IMPERIAL (12010 "The Teddy Bears Sing") 450-650 59
(Stereo.)
Members: Phil Spector; Annette Kleinbard; Marshall Leib.
Also see CONNORS, Carol
Also see HARVEY, Phil
Also see NELSON, Sandy

TEDDY BOYS

Singles: 7-inch

NORTHLAND (7005 "Jody") 25-50 58
Members: Don Uglow; Leo Weidenfeld; Allen Bauman; Glen Zastrow; Ron Bass.

TEDDY BOYS

Singles: 7-inch

(1616 "Don't Mess with Me") 20-30 65
(No label name used.)
CAMEO (433 "La La") 10-15 66
CAMEO (448 "Mona") 10-15 66
MGM (13515 "Jezebel") 10-15 66
Also see MORTIMER

TEDDY BOYS

Singles: 7-inch

RICKY DOG 10-20 81

LPs: 10/12-inch

RICKY DOG 10-15 82

TEDESCO, Tommy

Singles: 7-inch

IMPERIAL (66141 "La Montana") 5-10 65

LPs: 10/12-inch

DISCOVERY 5-10
DOT (3449 "Twangin' Twelve Great Hits") 15-25 62
(Monaural.)
DOT (25449 "Twangin' Twelve Great Hits") 20-30 62
(Stereo.)
IMPERIAL (9295 "Guitars of Tom Tedesco") 15-20 65
(Monaural.)
IMPERIAL (9321 "Calypso Soul") 15-20 66
(Monaural.)
IMPERIAL (12295 "Guitars of Tom Tedesco") 20-25 65
(Stereo.)
IMPERIAL (12321 "Calypso Soul") 20-25 66
(Stereo.)
TREND 5-10 79
Also see ANNETTE
Also see AVALANCHES
Also see CATALINAS
Also see FIREBALLS
Also see KNIGHTS
Also see LEWIS, Gary, & Playboys
Also see MARKETTS
Also see MONTEZ, Chris
Also see NELSON, Rick
Also see RIP CHORDS

TEE, Willie P&R/R&B '65
(Wilson Turbinton)

Singles: 7-inch

A.F.O. (307 "All for One") 15-25 62
A.F.O. (311 "Why Lie") 15-25 63
ATLANTIC (2273 "Teasin' You") 8-10 65
ATLANTIC (2302 "You Better Say Yes") 8-10 65
CAPITOL 5-8 68-70
CINDERELLA (1202 "Foolish Girl") 20-30
GATOR (509 "First Taste of Love") 10-20
GATOR (701 "She Really Did Surprise Me") 20-30 71
GATOR (8001 "Get Up") 10-20
HOT LINE 4-8
NOLA (708 "Teasin' You") 30-40 65
NOLA (737 "Please Don't Go") 100-200 67
U.A. 4-6 76

LPs: 10/12-inch

CAPITOL 10-15 69
U.A. 5-10 76

TEE & CARA

LPs: 10/12-inch

U.A. 8-12 69
Members: Tee Sapoff; Cara Beckenstein.

TEE SET P&R/LP '70

Singles: 7-inch

COLLECTABLES .... 3-5 '80s
COLOSSUS 4-6 69-71

Picture Sleeves

COLOSSUS 4-6 69

LPs: 10/12-inch

COLOSSUS 10-15 70

TEEGARDEN & VAN WINKLE P&R '70

Singles: 7-inch

ATCO 5-10 68
PLUMM (68102 "God, Love & Rock & Roll") 8-12 70
WESTBOUND 5-8 69-72

Picture Sleeves

WESTBOUND 4-6 70

LPs: 10/12-inch

ATCO 10-15 68
WESTBOUND 8-12 69-72
Members: David Teegarden; Skip Knape.

TEEMATES

Singles: 7-inch

AUDIO FIDELITY (104 "Dream on Little Girl") 8-12 64
AUDIO FIDELITY (105 "Night Fall") 8-12 64

Picture Sleeves

AUDIO FIDELITY (105 "Night Fall") 15-20 64

LPs: 10/12-inch

AUDIO FIDELITY (7042 "Jet Set Dance Discotheque") 30-50 64

TEEN, Sandra

Singles: 7-inch

IMPACT (4 "Angel Baby") 10-20 60

TEEN BEATS

Singles: 7-inch

ORIGINAL SOUND (07 "Slop Beat") 10-20 59
ORIGINAL SOUND (16 "Night Surfing") .. 15-25 61
ORIGINAL SOUND (46 "Big Bad Boss Beat") 10-20 64

TEEN BEATS

LPs: 10/12-inch

LONDON (83 "Guitar Boogie") 20-30 61
(Canadian.)

TEEN BEATS

Singles: 7-inch

CHAIN (5315 "I Guess That's Why You're Mine") 50-75
PEERLESS (5132 "Rock-a-Beatin' Boogie") 100-200

TEEN BUGS

Singles: 7-inch

BLUE RIVER (208 "Yes, You Can Hold My Hand") ... 15-20 64

TEEN DREAMS
(Debbie & Teen Dreams)

Singles: 7-inch

VERNON ("The Time") ... 35-45 62
(No selection number used. Credits the Teen Dreams.)
VERNON (101 "The Time") ... 15-20 62
(Credits Debbie & Teen Dreams.)
Members: Dorothy Yutenkas; Joan Yutenkas; Marie Broncotti.
Also see DEBBIE & DARNELS

TEEN KINGS

Singles: 78 rpm

JE-WEL (101 "Ooby Dooby") ... 500-750 56

Singles: 7-inch

JE-WEL (101 "Ooby Dooby") ... 2500-3500 56
(May read "Vocal Roy Oribson," instead of "Orbison," on some labels. Beware since some counterfeits exist that are difficult to identify. Consult an expert if in doubt.)
Members: Roy Orbison; Johnny "Peanuts" Wilson; Billy Par Ellis; James Monroe; Jack Kennelly.
Also see ORBISON, Roy
Also see ROGERS, Weldon

TEEN KINGS

Singles: 7-inch

WILLETT (118 "Don't Just Stand There") ... 100-200 59
Also see TEDDY & CONTINENTALS / Teen Kings

TEEN KINGS

Singles: 7-inch

SARA (6342 "It's Too Late") ... 50-75 63
Members: Tom Shills; Richie Ehler; Darrell Mand; Mike Mellenhoeft; Wayne Ehler; Bob Castellan; Tom Kuck.

TEEN NOTES

Singles: 7-inch

DEB (121 "Precious Jewel") ... 10-20 60
DEB (127 "Hi-Fi Sweetie") ... 10-20 61

TEEN QUEENS *P&R/R&B '56*
("Betty and Rosie")

Singles: 78 rpm

RPM ... 15-25 56-57

Singles: 7-inch

ANTLER (4014 "There's Nothing on My Mind") ... 10-20 60
ANTLER (4015 "I'm a Fool") ... 10-20 60
ANTLER (4016 "Donny") ... 10-20 61
ANTLER (4017 "I Heard Violins") ... 10-20 61
COLLECTABLES ... 3-5 '80s
KENT (14 "Eddie My Love") ... 4-6
KENT (348 "Eddie My Love") ... 10-20 60
KENT (359 "Eddie My Love") ... 10-15 61
RCA (7206 "Dear Tommy") ... 15-25 58
RCA (7396 "First Crush") ... 15-25 58
RPM (453 "Eddie My Love") ... 40-50 56
RPM (460 "So All Alone") ... 25-35 56
RPM (464 "Billy Boy") ... 25-35 56
RPM (470 "Red Top") ... 25-35 56
RPM (480 "My First Love") ... 25-35 56
RPM (484 "My Heart's Desire") ... 25-35 56
RPM (500 "I Miss You") ... 25-35 57

Picture Sleeves

ANTLER (4016 "Donny") ... 30-50 61

LPs: 10/12-inch

BEST/AMERICAN INT'L (5022 "Eddie My Love") ... 50-75 '50s
(May have American Int'l stickers covering Crown name on cover.)
CROWN (5022 "Eddie My Love") ... 100-200 56
CROWN (5373 "Teen Queens") ... 30-40 63
UNITED ... 8-12
Members: Rose Collins; Betty Collins.

TEEN QUEENS / Rosie & Originals

Singles: 7-inch

TRIP (125 "Eddie My Love"/"Angel Baby") ... 3-5
Also see ROSIE
Also see TEEN QUEENS

TEEN ROCKERS

Singles: 7-inch

COOL (146 "Road Block") ... 10-15 60
DELTONE (5015 "Rinky-Dink Blues") ... 10-15 60
ELDO (116 "Rattlesnake") ... 10-15 61

TEEN STARLETS

Singles: 7-inch

RPC (505 "Children's Picnic Song") ... 10-15 61
Also see LEAHY, Joe

TEEN TONES
("Lead Vocal Gerald Powers")

Singles: 7-inch

NU-CLEAR (2 "Faded Love") ... 40-50 57
WYNNE (107 "Faded Love") ... 15-25 59

TEEN TONES
(Teen-Tones; Teentones)

Singles: 7-inch

DANDY DAN (2 "Darling I Love You") ... 100-200 63
DEB (132 "Susan Ann") ... 20-30 60
DECCA (30895 "Yes You May") ... 20-30 59
DON & MARIE ("Poison Ivy") ... 10-20
(Selection number not known.)
GONE (5061 "Rockin' Rumble") ... 20-30 59
SWAN (4040 "My Little Baby") ... 25-35 59
T&T (2488 "Do You Wanna Dance") ... 5-10 65

TEEN TONES

Singles: 7-inch

TRI DISC (102 "I Feel So Happy") ... 15-25 61

TEEN TONES

Singles: 7-inch

CUCA (1160 "Be Careful") ... 10-15 63
SONIC ... 10-15

TEEN TURBANS

Singles: 7-inch

LOMA (2066 "Didn't He Run") ... 10-20 66

TEEN'S MEN

Singles: 7-inch

CUCA (1021 "Spin Out") ... 15-25 60

TEENAGE MOONLIGHTERS

Singles: 7-inch

MARK (134 "Sorry, Sorry") ... 2500-3500 59

TEENAGE REBELS

Singles: 7-inch

REELFOOT ... 15-25 '60s

TEENAGERS

Singles: 78 rpm

GEE (1046 "Flip-Flop") ... 10-20 57

Singles: 7-inch

END (1071 "Crying") ... 40-50 60
END (1076 "Can You Tell Me") ... 50-75 60
GEE (1046 "Flip-Flop") ... 10-20 57
ROULETTE (4086 "My Broken Heart") ... 40-50 58
Members: Billy Lobrano; Herman Santiago; Sherman Garnes; Jim Merchant; Joe Negroni.
Also see JOEY & TEENAGERS
Also see LYMON, Frankie

TEENAGERS

Singles: 7-inch

CRYSTAL BALL (142 "I Hear the Angels Cry") ... 4-8 81
(Black vinyl. 500 made.)
CRYSTAL BALL (142 "I Hear the Angels Cry") ... 8-12 81
(Red vinyl. 25 made.)
CRYSTAL BALL (142 "I Hear the Angels Cry") ... 30-40 81
(Multi-colored vinyl. Five made.)
CRYSTAL BALL (144 "He's No Lover") ... 4-8 81
(Black vinyl. 500 made.)
CRYSTAL BALL (144 "He's No Lover") ... 8-12 81
(Red vinyl. 25 made.)
CRYSTAL BALL (144 "He's No Lover") ... 30-40 81
(Multi-colored vinyl. Five made.)

Picture Sleeves

CRYSTAL BALL (142 "I Hear the Angels Cry") ... 15-20 81
(200 made.)
CRYSTAL BALL (144 "He's No Lover") ... 20-25 81
(200 made.)

TEENANGELS

Singles: 7-inch

SUN (388 "Tell Me My Love") ... 25-35 64
(Promotional issue only.)

TEENBEATS

Singles: 7-inch

TEENBEAT ("Surf Bound") ... 25-35 63
(No selection number used. Also issued as *Russian Roulette* by the Nevegans.)
Also see NEVEGANS

TEEN-CLEFS

Singles: 7-inch

DICE (98/99 "Hiding My Tears"/"Sputnik") ... 150-250 59

TEENERS

Singles: 7-inch

VISCOUNT (532 "Don't Mess Around") ... 15-25 58

TEENETTES

Singles: 7-inch

BRUNSWICK (55125 "I Want a Boy with a Hi-Fi") ... 10-20 59
GOAL (704 "Story") ... 50-100 64
JOSIE (830 "My Lucky Star") ... 15-25 58
SANDY (250 "Bye Bye Baby") ... 10-20 63

TEEN-KINGS

Singles: 7-inch

BEE (1114/1115 "Tell Me if You Know"/"That's a Teen-Age Love") ... 2500-3500 59
(Black vinyl.)
BEE (1114/1115 "Tell Me if You Know"/"That's a Teen-Age Love") ... 4-6 96
(Red vinyl.)

TEENOS

Singles: 7-inch

DUB (2839 "Love Only You") ... 20-30 58
RELIC (506 "Love Only You") ... 5-10 64

TEENTONES
("Featuring Arnold Malone with Larry Luple Orchestra")

Singles: 7-inch

REGO (1004 "Love Is a Vow") ... 400-500 58
Also see LEVEE SONGSTERS
Also see MELLOHARPS

TEIFER, Jerry
(With Chuck Sagel & His Orchestra)

Singles: 78 rpm

WING (90029 "Lady Love") ... 5-10 55

Singles: 7-inch

WING (90029 "Lady Love") ... 10-20 55

TEIG, Dave

Singles: 7-inch

SIGNATURE (12042 "Splish Splash") ... 10-15 60

TEJUNS

Singles: 7-inch

100-PROOF (144 "Girl") ... 500-750

TELEGRAMS

Singles: 7-inch

CREOLE (163 "Oh Baby Please") ... 40-50 78

TELLERS

Singles: 7-inch

FIRE (1038 "Tears Fell from My Eyes") ... 20-30 61

TELSTARS

Singles: 7-inch

GUIDE ... 5-10
IMPERIAL (5905 "Continental Mash") ... 10-15 62
TEEN (510 "Continental Mash") ... 15-25 62
TEEN (513 "Pow Wow") ... 15-25 63
TEEN (516 "Topless") ... 15-25 64
TEEN (51 "Tough George") ... 15-25 64

TELSTARS

Singles: 7-inch

COLUMBIA ... 10-15 67

TEMPESTS

Singles: 7-inch

WILLAMETTE (103 "Never Let You Go") ... 50-100 59

TEMPESTS

Singles: 7-inch

CENTURY (605 "My World") ... 10-15 61

TEMPESTS

Singles: 7-inch

FUJIMO (6946 "Look Away") ... 15-25 63
FUJIMO (7701 "Love I'm In") ... 15-25 '60s
FUJIMO (8126 "Looking Out the Window") ... 15-25 '60s

TEMPESTS

Singles: 7-inch

POLYDOR ... 4-6 71
SMASH ... 4-8 67-68
SOUTHERN WING ... 4-6 74

LPs: 10/12-inch

SMASH ... 15-25 66
Members: Roger Branch; Mike Branch; Mike Williams; Bill Lynch; Ken Baker; Manny Rojas; Rick White; Hazel Martin; Otis Adams.
Also see ARP, James, & Tempest
Also see WILLIAMS, Mike
Also see WARNER, Sonny

TEMPESTS

Singles: 7-inch

PANORAMA (30 "Our Lovin' Ways") ... 15-25 '60s

TEMPESTS

Singles: 7-inch

LIFETIME (1010 "Rockin' Rochester") ... 300-500

TEMPLE, Bob

Singles: 78 rpm

FRATERNITY ... 8-12 57
KING ... 10-15 56

Singles: 7-inch

FRATERNITY (762 "Gonna See My Baby") ... 10-20 57
KING (4958 "Vim Vam Vamoose") ... 20-30 56

TEMPLE, Joan

Singles: 7-inch

PREP (124 "Promise") ... 15-20 57
PREP (130 "The Heart You Break") ... 15-20 58

TEMPLE, Johnny

Singles: 78 rpm

KING ... 15-25 46
MIRACLE (156 "Sit Right on It") ... 20-30 49

TEMPLE, Pick

LPs:10/12-inch

PRESTIGE (13008 "Pick of the Crop") ... 20-30 '60s

TEMPLES

Singles: 7-inch

DATE (1004 " Whispering Campaign") ... 30-40 58

TEMPLET, Doyle
(With the Del Royals Orchestra)

Singles: 7-inch

ALART (501 "You Know What to Do") ... 15-25 '50s
MINIT (605 "Betty Jane") ... 10-20 60
Also see DEL ROYALS

TEMPLETON, Joe

Singles: 7-inch

AMY (843 "Lover Be Fair") ... 10-20 62
Session: Centuries.

TEMPO, Nick

LPs: 10/12-inch

LIBERTY (3023 "Rock N' Roll Beach Party") ... 30-40 58

TEMPO, Nino *P&R '73*
(With 5th Ave. Sax)

Singles: 7-inch

A&M ... 4-6 73-74
RCA ... 6-12 59-60
TOWER ... 4-6 67
U.A. ... 5-10 60

LPs: 10/12-inch

A&M ... 8-10 74
ATCO ... 10-15 66
Also see ARCHIES
Also see CANO, Eddie, & Nino Tempo
Also see CORCORAN, Noreen
Also see RUGOLO, Pete, & His Orchestra

TEMPO, Nino, & April Stevens *P&R '62*

Singles: 7-inch

A&M ... 4-6 72-75
ABC ... 4-6 73
ATCO ... 5-10 62-66
ATCO (6897 "She's My Baby") ... 4-6 72
BELL ... 4-6 69
CHELSEA ... 4-6 76
DADDY SAM ... 4-6 70
HORN ... 3-5 80
MGM ... 4-6 67-71
MARINA ... 4-6 72
NIAGARA ... 4-6 76
U.A. (272 "High School Sweetheart") ... 8-12 60
WHITE WHALE ... 5-10 66-68

LPs: 10/12-inch

ATCO ... 10-20 63-66
CAMDEN ... 10-15 64
WHITE WHALE ... 10-15 69

Also see PEWTER, Jim
Also see STEVENS, April
Also see TEMPO, Nino

TEMPO TOPPERS
(Featuring Little Richard)
Singles: 78 rpm
PEACOCK.......30-40 53-54
Singles: 7-inch
PEACOCK (1616 "Fool at the Wheel") 100-150 53
PEACOCK (1628 "Always")........75-125 54
Members: Richard Penniman; Jimmy Swan; Barry Gilmore; Bill Brooks.
Also see DUCES OF RHYTHM & TEMPO TOPPERS
Also see LITTLE RICHARD

TEMPOMEN
Singles: 7-inch
S-K-E (517 "Midnight on Pier 13")........ 20-30 '60s

TEMPO-MENTALS
Singles: 78 rpm
EBB (112 "Dearest").......30-40 57
Singles: 7-inch
EBB (112 "Dearest").......30-40 57
Also see PYRAMIDS

TEMPOS
Singles: 7-inch
RHYTHM (121 "Promise Me").......500-750 58
RHYTHM (129 "To Love Again")........4-6 84
Members: Marvin Smith; Jewel Jones; James Maddox; Louis Bradley; Dick Nichens.
Also see EL DORADOS
Also see SMITH, Marvin

TEMPOS P&R '59
(With the Billy Mure Orchestra)
Singles: 7-inch
CLIMAX (102 "See You in September") .. 15-20 59
CLIMAX (105 "Crossroads of Love") 10-15 59
KAPP (178 "Kingdom of Love")........ 10-15 57
KAPP (199 "Prettiest Girl in School")....... 10-15 57
KAPP (213 "I Got a Job")........ 10-15 58
PARIS (550 "Look Homeward Angel")..... 10-15 59
ROULETTE GOLDEN GOODIES........4-6 '70s
Members: Mike Lazo; Gene Schachter; Jim Drake; Tom Minoto.
Also see MURE, Billy

TEMPOS
Singles: 7-inch
HI-Q (100 "It's Tough")........ 25-50 59
HI-Q (5005 "I'm Laughing at You")........ 20-30 58
(First issued as by the Gardenias.)
OASIS (105 "It's Tough")........ 25-50 59

TEMPOS
Singles: 7-inch
FREDLO (6202 "Only One")........ 100-200 '50s

TEMPOS
Singles: 7-inch
ASCOT (2167 "When You Loved Me").......8-12 64
ASCOT (2173 "I Wish It Were Summer") ...8-12 65
BOFUZ (1106 "Why Don't You Write Me")........ 100-150 63
CANTERBURY (504 "Here I Come").........5-10 67
MONTEL (955 "It Was You")........ 10-20 66
RILEY'S (5 "Don't Act That Way")........ 10-20 66
RILEY'S (8781 "I Need You")........ 10-20 66
RILEY'S (8782 "Lonely One")........ 15-25 66
USA (810 "Why Don't You Write Me") 15-25 64

TEMPOS
LPs: 10/12-inch
CRYPT (10 "The Tempos")........ 10-15 87
JUSTICE (104 "Speaking of the Tempos")........ 450-550 66

TEMPO-TONES
(Featuring Richard Lanham; Tempo Tones; Tempotones)
Singles: 7-inch
ACME (713 "Get Yourself Another Fool")........ 100-150 57
(Small print on label.)
ACME (713 "Get Yourself Another Fool")........ 50-75 57
(Large print on label.)
ACME (715 "In My Dreams")........ 250-350 57
ACME (718 "Come Into My Heart")...... 250-350 57
Also see LANHAM, Richard
Also see LEE, Nancy

TEMPTATIONS
Singles: 7-inch
KING (5118 "Standing Alone")........150-250 58
Also see VAN DKYES

TEMPTATIONS
Singles: 7-inch
SAVOY (1532 "Mad at Love")........10-15 58
SAVOY (1550 "Don't You Know")........10-15 58

TEMPTATIONS
Singles: 7-inch
COTTON (1005 "Peppermint Cane")......10-15 62
DAISY (502 "Trophy Run")........40-50 63
(Also released as by Bob Moore & Temps.)
P&L (0001 "Blue Surf")........15-25 63
PARKWAY (803 "Birds 'N' Bees")........15-25 59
Also see MOORE, Bob, & Temps

TEMPTATIONS P&R '60
Singles: 7-inch
GOLDISC (3001 "Barbara")........20-30 60
(Black label.)
GOLDISC (3001 "Barbara")........8-12 60
(Multi-color label.)
GOLDISC (3007 "Fickle Little Girl")........10-20 60
Members: Neil Stevens; Larry Curtis; Artie Sands; Artie Marin.
Also see DUCANES / Temptations
Also see STEVENS, Neil

TEMPTATIONS R&B '62
Singles: 7-inch
ATLANTIC........4-6 77-78
GORDY (1631 thru 1933)........3-6 82-88
GORDY (7001 "Dream Come True")......30-40 62
GORDY (7010 "Paradise")........25-35 62
GORDY (7015 "I Want a Love I Can See")........15-25 63
GORDY (7020 "Farewell My Love")........15-25 63
GORDY (7028 thru 7081)........10-15 64-68
GORDY (7082 "Rudolph the Red-Nosed Reindeer")........10-20 68
GORDY (7084 thru 7115)........5-10 69-72
GORDY (7119 "Flunky Music Sho Nuff Turns Me On")........5-10 72
(Black vinyl.)
GORDY (7119 "Flunky Music Sho Nuff Turns Me On")........10-20 72
(Red vinyl. Promotional issue only.)
GORDY (7121 thru 7213)........4-8 72-81
MIRACLE (5 "Oh Mother of Mine")........50-75 61
MIRACLE (12 "Check Yourself")........20-30 62
MOTOWN........3-5 84-87
MOTOWN/TOPPS (4 "My Girl")........50-75 67
MOTOWN/TOPPS (13 "The Way You Do the Things You Do")........50-75 67
(Topps Chewing Gum promotional item. Single-sided, cardboard flexi, picture disc. Issued with generic paper sleeve.)
STOOP SOUNDS (104 "You Can Depend on Me")........100-150 96
Picture Sleeves
GORDY (7038 "My Girl")........25-50 65
GORDY (7055 "Beauty Is Only Skin Deep")........10-20 66
GORDY (7099 "Ball of Confusion")........10-20 70
EPs: 7-inch
GORDY (60914 "Tempting Temptations")........15-25 65
GORDY (60918 "Getting Ready")........15-25 66
GORDY (60919 "Greatest Hits")........15-25 66
MOTOWN (2004 "Temptations")........15-25 '60s
MOTOWN (2010 "It's the Temptations")...15-25
Note: All are juke box EPs.
LPs: 10/12-inch
ATLANTIC........5-10 77-78
GORDY (911 "Meet the Temptations").....30-40 64
GORDY (S-911 "Meet the Temptations") .40-50 64
GORDY (912 "The Temptations Sing Smokey")........20-30 65
GORDY (914 "The Tempting Temptations")........20-30 65
GORDY (918 "Gettin' Ready")........20-30 66
GORDY (919 Greatest Hits)........15-25 66
GORDY (921 "Live")........15-25 67
GORDY (922 "With a Lot O' Soul")........15-25 67
GORDY (924 "In a Mellow Mood")........15-25 67
GORDY (927 "Wish It Would Rain")........15-25 68
GORDY (933 thru 1006)........8-18 69-80
GORDY (6000 series)........5-8 82-86
KORY........8-10 77
MOTOWN (100 & 200 series)........5-10 81-82
MOTOWN (782 "Anthology")........20-25 73
(Three-disc set. Includes 12-page booklet.)
MOTOWN (998 "Give Love at Christmas")........15-20 80
(Promotional issue only.)
MOTOWN (5389 "25th Anniversary")......10-15 86
(Includes 8-page booklet.)
MOTOWN (6246 "Together Again")........5-8 87
NATURAL RESOURCES........5-10 78
Members: David Ruffin; Eddie Kendricks; Melvin Franklin; Otis Williams; Paul Williams; Damon Harris; Dennis Edwards.
Also see DISTANTS
Also see FOUR TOPS / Temptations
Also see LANDS, Liz, & Temptations
Also see PIRATES
Also see ROBINSON, Smokey
Also see ROSS, Diana
Also see RUFFIN, David
Also see STREET, Richard, & Distants
Also see SUPREMES & TEMPTATIONS

TEMPTATIONS & FOUR TOPS
LPs: 10/12-inch
MOTOWN (134 "Battle of the Champions")........10-20
(Promotional issue only.)
SILVER EAGLE (1052 "T N T")........10-15 87
(Three-disc set.)
Also see FOUR TOPS

TEMPTATIONS / Finis Henderson
Singles: 12-inch
MOTOWN (119 "Surface Thrill")........4-8
(Promotional issue only.)

TEMPTATIONS & RICK JAMES R&B '82
Singles: 12-inch
GORDY........4-6 82
Singles: 7-inch
GORDY........3-5 82

TEMPTATIONS / Stevie Wonder
LPs: 10/12-inch
GORDY/TAMLA/MOTOWN (100 "The Sky's the Limit")........15-25 71
(Promotional issue only.)
Also see TEMPTATIONS
Also see WONDER, Stevie

TEMPTATIONS
Singles: 7-inch
CUCA (1094 "Call of the Wind")........15-25 62
Members: Ricky Lee Smolinski; Roger Loos.

TEMPTATIONS
Singles: 7-inch
MOON (8687 "Hey Bo Diddley")........30-40 '60s

TEMPTERS
Singles: 78 rpm
EMPIRE (105 "I'm Sorry Now")........10-20 56
Singles: 7-inch
EMPIRE (105 "I'm Sorry Now")........40-50 56
Also see YOUNGSTERS

TEMPTERS
Singles: 7-inch
LINK (708 "I Will Go")........20-30 '60s

TEMPTONES
Singles: 7-inch
ARCTIC (130 "Girl I Love You")........10-20 67
ARCTIC (136 "Say These Words of Love")........10-20 67
Member: Daryl Hall.

TEMPTORS
Singles: 7-inch
HALL OF FAME (101 "Wooley Bully Soul")........10-20 '60s
Member: Terry Klein.
Also see DEE JAY & RUNAWAYS

10CC P&R '73
Singles: 7-inch
MERCURY........4-6 75-77
POLYDOR........3-5 78
UK........4-6 72-74
Picture Sleeves
MERCURY........5-8 75-77
LPs: 10/12-inch
MERCURY........10-15 75-77
POLYDOR........5-8 78-79
UK........10-15 73-75
W.B.........8-10 80
Members: Kevin Godley; Lol Creme; Graham Gouldman; Eric Stewart; Paul Burgess; Rick Fenn; Tony O'Malley; Stuart Tosh.
Also see GOULDMAN, Graham
Also see MOCKINGBIRDS
Also see OHIO EXPRESS
Also see SEDAKA, Neil
Also see SILVER FLEET

TEN BROKEN HEARTS
Singles: 7-inch
DIAMOND (123 "Ten Lonely Guys")........25-35 62
Member: Neil Diamond.
Also see DIAMOND, Neil

10,000 MANIACS LP '87
Singles: 7-inch
ELEKTRA........3-5 87-89
Picture Sleeves
ELEKTRA........3-5 88-89
LPs: 10/12-inch
ELEKTRA........5-10 87-90
MARK (20247 "Human Conflict No. 5")........100-150 82
MARK (20389 "Secrets of the I Ching") .75-100 83
(Includes lyrics/print insert.)
Members: Natalie Merchant; Robert Buck; John Lombardo; Dennis Drew; Jerome Augustyniak; Steven Gustafson; Robert Wachter.

TEN WHEEL DRIVE P&R/LP '70
(With Genya Ravan)
Singles: 7-inch
CAPITOL........4-6 73
POLYDOR........4-6 69-71
LPs: 10/12-inch
CAPITOL........8-10 73
POLYDOR........10-12 69-71
Member: Genya Ravan.

TENDER SLIM P&R '60
Singles: 7-inch
GREY CLIFF (723 "Teenage Hayride")......8-12 59
HERALD (571 "I'm Checkin' Up")........5-10 62

TENDER TONES
Singles: 7-inch
DUCKY (713 "Just for a Little While")...600-800 59

TENDER TOUCH
Singles: 7-inch
PARAMOUNT (0252 "You Were Never Mine to Begin With")........10-20

TENDERFOOTS
Singles: 78 rpm
FEDERAL........20-30 55
Singles: 7-inch
FEDERAL (12214 "Kissing Bug")........50-100 55
FEDERAL (12219 "My Confession")......50-100 55
FEDERAL (12225 "Those Golden Bells")........50-100 55
FEDERAL (12228 "Sindy")........75-125 55
Members: Carl White; Al Frazier; Sonny Harris; Matt Nelson; Harold Lewis.
Also see LAMPLIGHTERS
Also see RIVINGTONS

TENNANT, Barbara
Singles: 7-inch
KUDO (665 "Rock, Baby, Rock")........25-35 58

TENNANT, Jimmy
(Jimmy Tenant; with Buddy Lucas & Dynatones)
Singles: 7-inch
AMP (790 "Heartbreak Avenue")........10-20 59
THUNDER (1000 "The Witness")........30-50 59
WARWICK (533 "Salute")........10-15 60
Also see VELVET, Jimmy

TENNESSEE DRIFTERS
Singles: 78 rpm
DOT........5-10 52-54
Singles: 7-inch
DOT (1098 "Boogie Beat Rag")........15-25 52
DOT (1166 "Boogie Woogie Baby")........20-40 54
MAID (1000 "The Drifter")........250-350 '50s

TENNESSEE JIM
Singles: 7-inch
CHOICE (852 "My Baby, She's Rockin'")........150-250 57

CHOICE ("Hangin' Out My Tears") 150-250
(Selection number not known.)
Also see McDONALD, Jim

TENNESSEE SLIM
Singles: 7-inch
SPEED (106 "I'm an Old Wolf") 50-75

TENNESSEE TWO & FRIEND
Singles: 7-inch
COLUMBIA 10-20 60-61
Session: Jerry Lee Lewis.
Also see LEWIS, Jerry Lee

TENNESSEE THREE
Singles: 7-inch
COLUMBIA 8-12 65-67

TENNYSON, Bill
Singles: 7-inch
PET (805 "Even Now") 15-25 58

TENSIONETTES
Singles: 7-inch
HITT (102 "You Made Me Cry") 10-15

TEO, Roy
Singles: 7-inch
NASCO (6027 "Mama Doll") 8-12 59

TERENCE
LPs: 10/12-inch
DECCA 10-15 69

TERESE, Claire
Singles: 7-inch
CORSAIR (100 "Just for You") 30-40 60

TERMITES
("Featuring Barry Boswell")
Singles: 7-inch
BEE (B-1825 "Carrie Lou"/"Give Me Your Heart") 150-250 64
BEE (BGX-1825 "Carrie Lou"/"Give Me Your Heart") 5-10 98
Members (on "Carrie Lou"): Barry Boswell; Ray Edwards; Bill Yuhas; Robert Rohrbach; Gene Yuhas.
("Give Me Your Heart" is by a different group of Termites.)
Also see INVICTORS
Also see SILHOUETTES

TERRACE, Ray
Singles: 7-inch
JUBILEE (5515 "Ray's Beat") 8-12 65
LPs: 10/12-inch
TOWER 10-20 68

TERRACETONES
Singles: 7-inch
APT (25016 "Words of Wisdom") 40-50 58
Members: Andy Cheatham; Len Walker; Pat Johnson; Ed Johnson; James Ashley; Carl Foushee.

TERRAIN, Moss
Singles: 7-inch
USA (112 "Together") .... 5-10 '60s

TERRANS
Singles: 7-inch
GRAHAM (801 "Moonrise"/"Soap Soap") 75-125 63
(Reissued as by Rene Harris & Terrans.)
Also see HARRIS, Rene, & Terrans

TERRELL, Clyde
Singles: 7-inch
EXCELLO (2151 "My One Desire") 10-20 59

TERRELL, Phil
Singles: 7-inch
CARNIVAL (513 "I'll Just Erase You") 20-30 65
CARNIVAL (523 "Don't You Run Away"). 20-30 66

TERRELL, Tammi *P&R/R&B '66*
Singles: 7-inch
MOTOWN (1086 thru 1138) 8-12 65-69
LPs: 10/12-inch
MOTOWN (200 series) 5-10 82
MOTOWN (652 "Irresistible") 40-60 66
Also see GAYE, Marvin, & Tammi Terrell
Also see JACKSON, Chuck, & Tammi Terrell
Also see MONTGOMERY, Tammy

TERRI & JAY
Singles: 7-inch
TARCO (100 "Tomorrow's Another Day") 40-50 60

TERRI & KITTENS
Singles: 7-inch
IMPERIAL (5728 "Wedding Bells") 15-25 61

TERRI & TRITONES
Singles: 7-inch
KAY BEE (6009 "Patty") .... 10-20 '60s

TERRI & VELVETEENS
Singles: 7-inch
ARC (6534 "I'm Waiting") 10-20 63
KERWOOD (711 "Bells of Love") 40-50 62

TERRIFICS
Singles: 7-inch
BELL (88 "Little Star") 15-25 58
DEMON (1516 "I Don't Care How You Do It") 10-20 59
VALOR 10-20 58
Member: Ray Stanley.
Also see STANLEY, Ray

TERRIFICS
Singles: 7-inch
FIG (301 "Lover's Plea") 40-60 68

TERRIGAN BROTHERS
Singles: 7-inch
FORTUNE (207 "Little Love") 15-25 59

TERRI-TONES
Singles: 7-inch
CORTLAND (105 "Go") 10-20 62

TERRY, Clark
(With Bob Brookmeyer; with His Jolly Giants; with Jesper Thilo; Clark Terry Five; Clark Terry Quartet; Clark Terry Quintet)
Singles: 7-inch
CAMEO (262 "More") 5-10 63
CAMEO (281 "East Side Drive") 5-10 63
MAINSTREAM (610 "Blind Man, Blind Man") 5-10 65
MAINSTREAM (642 "The Mumbler Strikes Again") 5-10 66
VANGUARD (35186 "Mumbles") 4-6 75
LPs: 10/12-inch
JAZZ MAN (5046 "Color Changes") 5-10 82
MAINSTREAM (56066 "Mumbles") 10-15 66
(Monaural.)
MAINSTREAM (6066 "Mumbles) 15-20 66
(Stereo.)
MATRIX (1002 "Funk Dumplins") 5-10 80
PABLO 6-12 79-80
PAUSA (7131 "Wham") 5-10 82
RIVERSIDE (066 "Serenade to a Bus Seat") 5-10 83
STORYVILLE (4072 "Tribute to Frog") 5-10 82
TRIP (5528 "Swahili") 8-12 74
VANGUARD 8-12 75-77
Also see McFARLAND, Gary, & Clark Terry
Also see PETERSON, Oscar
Also see SCOTT, Shirley

TERRY, Dan, Band
Singles: 78 rpm
COLUMBIA 5-10 54
Singles: 7-inch
COLUMBIA (40211 "Lazy Alley") 10-20 54
COLUMBIA (40212 "Terry's Tune") 10-20 54
COLUMBIA (40231 "White Buck Special") 10-20 54
COLUMBIA (40232 "Levi Leap") 10-20 54
COLUMBIA (40263 "Mr. Flamingo") 10-20 54
COLUMBIA (40312 "Teen Ager") 10-20 54
DEVERE (317 "Coca-Cola Rock") 10-15 58
RITA (1008 "Wail-Tale") 10-20 55
EPs: 7-inch
COLUMBIA (414 "Teen-Age Dance Session") 15-25 54
COLUMBIA (1853 "Teen-Age Dance Session") 15-25 54
LPs: 10/12-inch
COLUMBIA (6288 "Teen-Age Dance Session") 40-60 54
(10-inch LP.)

TERRY, Dewey
LPs: 10/12-inch
TUMBLEWEED 10-15
Also see DON & DEWEY

TERRY, Don
(With the Strikes; Don Alexander)
Singles: 7-inch
LIN (5018 "Knees Shakin' ") 75-125 59
Also see STRIKES

TERRY, Dossie
(Dossie "Georgia Boy" Terry)
Singles: 78 rpm
CHICAGO 15-25 45
KING (5072 "Thunderbird") 25-35 57
RCA 10-20 51
Singles: 7-inch
AMP 3 (2113 "Skinny Ginny") 20-30 58
BONUS (101 "No Other Love") .... 20-30 '50s
KING (5072 "Thunderbird") 20-40 57
RCA (4474 "Didn't Satisfy You") 20-40 51
RCA (4684 "When I Hit the Number") 20-40 51
RCA (4864 "Lost My Head") 20-40 51
X-TRA (103 "Railroad Section Man") 20-40 57

TERRY, Flash
Singles: 7-inch
KENT (310 "One Thing We Know") 50-75 61
INDIGO (135 "Cool It") 75-100 61
LAVENDER (5 "Cool It") 75-100 61

TERRY, Gene
(With His Down Beats; with His Kool Kats)
Singles: 7-inch
GOLDBAND (1066 "Cindy Lou") 75-100 58
GOLDBAND (1081 "No Mail Today") 10-15 59
GOLDBAND (1088 "Cinderella, Cinderella") 15-20 59
ROCK-IT (598 "Woman I Love") 1000-2000
SAVOY (1559 "Fine Fine") 10-15 59

TERRY, George
Singles: 7-inch
SPHERE SOUND (711 "Dreamy Eyes") .. 10-15 65
Also see GEORGE, Terry

TERRY, Gordon *C&W '70*
(With the Tennessee Guitars; with Tennessee Fiddles)
Singles: 78 rpm
CADENCE 5-10 57-58
COLUMBIA 5-10 55-56
Singles: 7-inch
CADENCE 5-10 57-58
CAPITOL (2792 "Untanglin' My Mind") 4-8 70
CHART (1014 "Easy Way Out") 5-10 67
CHART (1030 "That's What Tears Me Up") 5-10 68
CHART (1049 "Little Bit") 5-10 68
CHART (5005 "Charlie's Pride") 5-10 69
CHART (5028 "Day of the Gun") 5-10 69
COLUMBIA 5-10 55-56
LIBERTY 5-10 62-63
RCA (Except 7632) 10-20 58-62
RCA (7632 "Lotta Lotta Woman") 30-40 59
LPs: 10/12-inch
CHART 10-15 68
LIBERTY 10-20 62
PLANTATION 5-10 77-81
RCA 10-20 62

TERRY, Larry
Singles: 7-inch
TESTA (106 "Hep Cat") 750-1000 61
(Label also shows the number 006.)

TERRY, Lynn
Singles: 7-inch
RUST (5109 "When You Walk in the Room") 10-20 66

TERRY, Mark
Singles: 7-inch
JANARD (1052 "All Dressed Up") 10-20 63
KEN (2746 "Nobody's Darlin' ") 150-250

TERRY, Maureen
Singles: 7-inch
MARIA (102 "There's a Boy") 20-30 64

TERRY, Nat
Singles: 78 rpm
IMPERIAL (5150 "Take It Easy") 50-75 51

TERRY, Sonny
(Sonny "Hootin'" Terry & His Night Owls; with His Buckshot Five)
Singles: 78 rpm
ASCH 15-25 45
CAPITOL 15-40 47-50
GOTHAM 15-25 51
GRAMERCY 15-25 52
GROOVE 15-25 54-55
HARLEM 15-25 54
JACKSON 25-50 52
JOSIE 15-25 56
OLD TOWN 15-25 56
RCA 30-60 53
RED ROBIN 25-50 52
SAVOY 15-25 48
SOLO 20-40 49
Singles: 7-inch
CAPITOL (931 "Telephone Blues") 50-100 50
CHESS (1860 "Dangerous Woman") 10-15 63
CHOICE (15 "Hootin' ") 10-15 61
GOTHAM (517 "Baby, Let's Have Some Fun") 20-30 51
GOTHAM (518 "Harmonica Rumbo") 20-30 51
GRAMERCY (1004 "Hootin' Blues") 25-35 52
(Black vinyl.)
GRAMERCY (1004 "Hootin' Blues") 50-75 52
(Colored vinyl.)
GROOVE (0015 "Lost Jawbone") 25-35 54
GROOVE (0135 "Ride & Roll") 25-35 56
HARLEM (2327 "Dangerous Woman") 40-50 54
JACKSON (2302 "That Woman Is Killing Me") 50-100 52
(Red vinyl.)
JAX (305 "I Don't Worry") 200-300 53
(Red vinyl.)
JOSIE (828 "Fast Freight Blues") 15-25 57
OLD TOWN (1023 "Uncle Bud") 20-30 56
RCA (5492 "Hootin' & Jumpin' ") 50-100 53
RCA (5577 "Sonny Is Drinkin' ") 50-100 53
RED ROBIN (110 "Harmonica Hop") 75-125 52
LPs: 10/12-inch
ARCHIVE OF FOLK MUSIC (106 "Sonny Terry") 15-25 65
(Monaural.)
ARCHIVE OF FOLK MUSIC (206 "Sonny Terry") 20-30 65
(Stereo.)
EVEREST .... 5-10 '70s
FOLKWAYS (35 "Harmonica and Vocal Solos") 50-100 51
(10-inch LP.)
PRESTIGE BLUESVILLE (1025 "Sonny's Story") 20-30 61
RIVERSIDE (644 "Sonny Terry and His Mouth Harp") 50-100 57
STINSON (55 "Sonny Terry and His Mouth Harp") 100-200 53
(10-inch LP.)
WASHINGTON (702 "Talkin' About the Blues") 25-35 61
Session: Mickey Baker; Brownie McGhee.
Also see BAGBY, Doc
Also see BAKER, Mickey
Also see DAVIS, Blind Gary, & Sonny Terry
Also see HOPKINS, Lightnin,' & Sonny Terry
Also see LEADBELLY / Josh White / Sonny Terry
Also see McGHEE, Brownie, & Sonny Terry
Also see SELLERS, Johnny
Also see SONNY & JAYCEE
Also see WALTON, Square

TERRY, Tex
(With the Big Jim DeNoon Band; Ferlin Husky)
Singles: 78 rpm
4 STAR ("Ozark Waltz") 15-25
(Selection number not known.)
Also see HUSKY, Ferlin

TERRY, Wiley
Singles: 7-inch
USA (793 "Follow the Leader") 8-12 65
USA (804 "Shake It Baby") 8-12 65

TERRY & BELLES
Singles: 7-inch
DUCKY (711 "I'll Always Be Nearby") 50-75 59
HANOVER (4505 "I'm Alone Because I Love You") 10-20 58

TERRY & FLIPPERS

Singles: 7-inch

RSVP (1116 "Ready-Aim-Fire") 10-20 65

Also see FABULOUS FLIPPERS

TERRY & JERRY

Singles: 7-inch

CLASS (226 "Mama Julie") 10-15 58
CLASS (240 "What Is Love") 10-15 59

TERRY & MELLOS

(Terry Corin)

Singles: 7-inch

AMY (812 "Bells of St. Mary's") 10-20 60
RIDER (108 "Why Did You Do It") 15-25 61

Also see CORIN, Terry

TERRY & PIRATES

Singles: 7-inch

CHESS (1696 "What Did He Say") 20-30 58
VALLI (100 "What Did He Say") 50-75 58
(First issue.)

TERRY & TAGS

Singles: 7-inch

SYLVESTER (100 "Rampage") 15-25 62

TERRY & TOPICS

Singles: 7-inch

CORAL (62509 "Just a Gigolo") 15-25 67

TERRY & TUNISIANS

Singles: 7-inch

SEVILLE (131 "The Street") 40-50 64

TERRY & TOMMY

Singles: 7-inch

A-OK (1030 "I'm No Fool") 15-25 67

TERRYS

Singles: 7-inch

GOLDWAX (319 "Stormy Love Affair") 5-10 67
GOLDWAX (325 "Stay Away From Brenda") 5-10 67
RIC (101 "Never Never Land") 5-10 64
RIC (110 "Don't Tell Me Now") 5-10 64

TESTA, Jimmy

Singles: 7-inch

DARROW (513 "Yeh Yeh No No") 30-40 59
DARROW ("Mama Done Told Me") 20-30 59
(Selection number not known.)

TEX, Joe P&R '64

(With the Class Mates; with Vibrators)

Singles: 78 rpm

KING 20-50 55-57

Singles: 12-inch

EPIC 4-8 77

Singles: 7-inch

ACE (544 "Cut It Out") 40-60 58
ACE (550 "You Little Baby Face Thing") . 50-75 58
ACE (559 "Charlie Brown Got Expelled") 20-30 59
ACE (572 "Yum, Yum, Yum") 20-30 59
ACE (591 "Boys Will Be Boys") 20-30 60
ACE (674 "Boys Will Be Boys") 15-25 63
ANNA (1119 "All I Could Do Was Cry") ... 15-25 60
ANNA (1124 "I'll Never Break Your Heart") 15-25 60
ANNA (1128 "Ain't It a Mess") 15-25 61
ATLANTIC 4-6 72
CHECKER (1055 "You Keep Her") 10-15 63
CHECKER (1104 "All I Could Do Was Cry") 8-10 65
(Maroon and silver label. "Checker" at left.)
CHECKER (1104 "All I Could Do Was Cry") 5-10 65
(Multi-color label. "Checker" at top.)
DIAL (1000 series) 4-6 71-76
DIAL (2800 series) 3-5 78
DIAL (3000 series) 5-10 61-64
DIAL (4000 series) 5-10 64-69
EPIC 3-5 77-79
HANDSHAKE 3-5 81
JALYNNE (105 "Goodbye My Love") 5-10 61
KING (4840 "Come in This House") 40-60 55
KING (4884 "My Biggest Mistake") 25-50 56
KING (4980 "Pneumonia") 25-50 56
KING (4911 "She's Mine") 25-50 65
KING (5064 "Ain't Nobody's Business") ... 25-50 57
KING (5981 "Come in This House") 5-10 65
PARROT (45012 "Say Thank You") 5-10 69

EPs: 7-inch

ATLANTIC (1017 "Happy Talk") 8-12 69
(Promotional issue only.)
ATLANTIC (8115 "The New Boss") 8-12 65
(Juke box issue only. Includes title strips.)

LPs: 10/12-inch

ACCORD 5-10 82
ATLANTIC 10-15 65-72
CHECKER 20-30 64
DIAL 8-10 72-79
EPIC 5-10 77-78
KING 15-25 65
LONDON 5-10 79
PARROT 15-25 65
PRIDE 8-10 73

Members: Mike Appell; Rod Bristow.
Also see KELLY, Paul
Also see SOUL CLAN

TEX & CHEX

Singles: 7-inch

ATLANTIC (2116 "I Do Love You") 40-50 61
(Red and black label.)
ATLANTIC (2116 "I Do Love You") 25-35 61
(White label. Promotional issue only.)
ATLANTIC (2116 "I Do Love You") 5-10
(Red and black label with pinwheel.)
NEWTOWN (5010 "Be On the Lookout for My Girl") 8-12 63
20TH FOX (411 "Love Me Now") 10-15 63

Also see MAGICIANS

TEXANS P&R '61

Singles: 7-inch

GOTHIC (001 "Rockin' Johnny Home") 15-25 61
INFINITY (001 "Green Grass of Texas") ..20-30 61
JOX (001 "Rockin' Johnny Home") 10-15 63
VEE-JAY (658 "Green Grass of Texas") 8-12 65

Members: Dorsey Burnette; Johnny Burnette.
Also see BURNETTE, Johnny & Dorsey

TEXANS

Singles: 7-inch

BLUE STAR (1578 "Walk Don't Run") ......10-20 '60s

TEXAS "GUITAR" SLIM

(Johnny Winter)

Singles: 7-inch

JIN (174 "Broke and Lonely") 30-50 62
(This same number was used for *Something's Wrong*, by Rockin' Sidney.)
MOON-LITE 75-100 60

Also see GUITAR SLIM
Also see WINTER, Johnny

TEXAS RAY

(Texas-Ray)

Singles: 7-inch

KAYDEE (3001 "Mary Ann") 15-25 60
LAURIE (3072 "Hackensack") 10-15 60
(Previously issued this same year as by "Gene Franklin, Vocal By Texas Ray.")

Also see FRANKLIN, Gene

TEXAS RED

(With the Contours; Texas Red & Jimmy)

Singles: 78 rpm

BULLSEYE 10-15 56
CHECKER 10-20 57
VICEROY 10-20 57

Singles: 7-inch

BULLSEYE (1009 "Turn Around") 10-20 56
CHECKER 10-20 57
VICEROY 10-20 57

TEXAS SLIM

(John Lee Hooker)

Singles: 78 rpm

KING (4283 "Black Man Blues") 50-75 50
KING (4329 "Heart Trouble Blues") 50-75 50
KING (4366 "Don't You Remember Me") .50-75 50
KING (4377 "Moaning Blues") 75-125 50

Also see HOOKER, John Lee

TEXIERA, John

Singles: 7-inch

G&G (100 "Strike It Rich") 50-75

THACKER, Rudy

Singles: 7-inch

LUCKY (0012 "Black Train") 100-150
WHIRL ("Mountain Guitar") 75-100
(Selection number not known.)

THACKERAY ROCKE

Singles: 7-inch

CASTALIA (268 "Tobacco Road") 10-20 67
CASTALIA (671 "Bawling") 10-20 67

THANO

Singles: 7-inch

VERVE (10399 "Gimme Something") 10-20 66

THAQUER, Carrie

Singles: 7-inch

LAUREL-LI (401 "Tennessee Mama") 75-125

THARP, Chuck

(With the Fireballs)

Singles: 7-inch

JARO (77029 "Long, Long Ponytail") 75-100 60
KAPP (248 "I Don't Know") 150-200 58
LUCKY (012 "Long Long Ponytail") 75-100 60

Also see FIREBALLS

THARPE, Sister Rosetta

Singles: 78 rpm

DECCA 15-25 45-56
MERCURY 10-15 56

Singles: 7-inch

DECCA 20-30 51-56
MGM (12915 "Light a Candle") 5-10 60
MERCURY (70910 "When the Saints Go Marching In") 15-20 56
MERCURY (70982 "Home in the Sky") 15-20 56
MERCURY (71133 "Let It Shine") 15-20 57
VERVE (10249 "That's All") 5-10 62

LPs: 10/12-inch

DECCA (5382 "The Wedding Ceremony of Sister Rosetta Tharpe") 350-450 52
(10-inch LP.)
MGM (3821 "Sister Rosetta Tharpe") 40-60 60
MERCURY (20412 "Gospel Truth") 15-20 59
(Monaural.)
MERCURY (60080 "Gospel Truth") 20-25 59
(Stereo.)
OMEGA DISK (31 "Sister Rosetta Tharpe") 20-25 60
(Stereo.)
OMEGA DISK (1031 "Sister Rosetta Tharpe") 15-20 60
(Monaural.)
VERVE (3005 "Sister On Tour") 15-20 61
VERVE (8439 "Gospel Truth") 15-20 62
WING (12235 "Gospel Train") 15-20 63
(Monaural.)
WING (12235 "Gospel Train") 20-25 63
(Stereo.)

Session: Rosette Gospel Singers.
Also see LITTLE RICHARD / Sister Rosetta

THARPE, Sister Rosetta, & Marie Knight

Singles: 78 rpm

DECCA 5-10 54

Singles: 7-inch

DECCA 8-12 54

Also see KNIGHT, Marie
Also see THARPE, Sister Rosetta

THAXTER, Jim, & Travelers

Singles: 7-inch

ARIEL (73060 "Sally-Jo") 350-400 60
(500 made.)

Also see TRASHMEN

THAXTON, Lloyd

Singles: 7-inch

CAPITOL (4982 "Image of a Surfer") 5-10 63
DECCA (31689 "Chug-A-Lug") 5-10 64

LPs: 10/12-inch

DECCA (4594 "Lloyd Thaxton Presents") 20-30 64
(Monaural.)
DECCA (7-4594 "Lloyd Thaxton Presents") 25-35 64
(Stereo.)

Also see CHALLENGERS
Also see KNICKERBOCKERS

THAYER, Frank

(With the Lyonals)

Singles: 7-inch

OUTLAW (1 "Long Gray Highway") 75-100

EPs: 7-inch

OUTLAW 5-8 80

LPs: 10/12-inch

OUTLAW 8-10 80

THEE MIDNITERS P&R '65

Singles: 7-inch

CHATTAHOOCHEE (666 "Land of 1000 Dances") 8-12 65
CHATTAHOOCHEE (674 "Sad Girl") 8-12 65
CHATTAHOOCHEE (675 "Sad Girl") 8-12 65
CHATTAHOOCHEE (684 "Whitter Boulevard") 8-12 65
CHATTAHOOCHEE (693 "I Need Someone") 8-12 65
CHATTAHOOCHEE (694 "It's Not Unusual") 8-12 65
CHATTAHOOCHEE (695 "Heat Wave") 8-12 65
CHATTAHOOCHEE (706 "Are You Angry") 8-12 66
UNI (55170 "I've Come Alive") 5-10 69
WHITTIER (200 "Sad Girl") ....15-25 '60s
WHITTIER (201 "That's All") ....15-25 '60s
WHITTIER (202 "I Need Someone") ....15-25 '60s
WHITTIER (500 thru 509) 10-20 66-67
WHITTIER (511 "You're Gonna Make Me Cry") 100-200 68
WHITTIER (512 "The Ballad of Cesar Chavez") 5-10 68
WHITTIER (513 "Chicano Power") 5-10 68
WHITTIER (674 "Sad Girl") 5-10 68

LPs: 10/12-inch

CHATTAHOOCHEE (C-1001 "Thee Midniters") 25-35 65
(Monaural.)
CHATTAHOOCHEE (CS-1001 "Thee Midniters") 35-50 65
(Stereo.)
RHINO 5-10 83
WHITTIER (W-1001 "Thee Midniters") 20-30 66
(Monaural.)
WHITTIER (WS-1001 "Thee Midniters") ..25-45 66
(Stereo.)
WHITTIER (5000 "Special Delivery") 15-25 66
WHITTIER (5001 "Unlimited") 15-25 66
WHITTIER (5002 "Giants") 15-25 67

THEE MUFFINS

LPs: 10/12-inch

("Pop Up") 100-150
(Fan club issue only. No selection number used.)

THEE PROPHETS P&R/LP '69

Singles: 7-inch

KAPP 5-8 68-70
TEE PEE (29/30 "To Be with You"/"If You Would Leave Me") 5-10 67

LPs: 10/12-inch

KAPP (3596 "Playgirl") 15-20 69

Members: Brian Lake; Jim Anderson; Dave Leslie; Chris Michaels; Mark Sandusky; Tony Gazzana; Joe Kopecky; Jerry George; Jose Salazar; Dave Maciolek; Lee Johnson.

THEM P&R/LP '65

(Featuring Van Morrison)

Singles: 7-inch

HAPPY TIGER (525 "Lonely Weekends") .5-10 69
LOMA (2051 "Gloria's Dream") 5-10 66
LONDON ....4-6 '70s
PARROT (365 "Gloria") 4-8 72
PARROT (3003 "Don't You Know") 10-15 66
PARROT (3006 "Don't Start Crying Now") 10-15 66
PARROT (9702 "Don't Start Crying Now") 20-30 64
(Polystyrene.)
PARROT (9702 "Don't Start Crying Now") 35-50 64
(Vinyl. Promotional issue only.)
PARROT (9727 "Gloria") 10-15 65
PARROT (9749 "Here Comes the Night") 10-15 65
PARROT (9784 "Gonna Dress in Black") 10-15 65
PARROT (9796 "Mystic Eyes") 10-15 65
PARROT (9819 "Call My Name") 10-15 66
RUFF (1088 "Walking in the Queen's Garden") 10-15 67
SULLY (1021 "Dirty Old Man") ....15-25 '60s
TOWER (384 "Walking in the Queen's Garden") 5-10 67
TOWER (407 "But It's Alright") 5-10 68
TOWER (461 "We've All Agreed to Help") .5-10 69
TOWER (493 "Corinna") 5-10 69

Picture Sleeves
TOWER (384 "Walking in the Queen's Garden") 15-25 67
LPs: 10/12-inch
HAPPY TIGER (1004 "Them") 20-30 69
HAPPY TIGER (1012 "In Reality") 20-30 71
LONDON 5-10 77
PARROT (61005 "Them") 50-100 65
(Cover does not highlight *Gloria*.)
(Monaural.)
PARROT (61005 "Them") 30-35 65
(Cover highlights *Gloria*.)
(Monaural.)
PARROT (61008 "Them Again") 25-30 66
(Monaural.)
PARROT (71005 "Them") 50-100 65
(Cover does not highlight *Gloria*.)
(Stereo.)
PARROT (71005 "Them") 40-50 65
(Cover highlights *Gloria*.)
(Stereo.)
PARROT (71008 "Them Again") 40-50 66
(Stereo.)
PARROT (71053 "Them Featuring Van Morrison") 10-15 72
TOWER (5104 "Now and Them") 25-35 68
TOWER (5116 "Time Out") 25-35 68
Members: Van Morrison; Billy Harrison; Alan Henderson; Peter Bardens; J. McAuley; John Stark.
Also see MORRISON, Van

THEM / Marvelettes
Singles: 7-inch
A&M (1201 "Baby, Please Don't Go") 3-5 88
Picture Sleeves
A&M (1201 "Baby, Please Don't Go") 3-5 88
Also see MARVELETTES
Also see THEM

THEM FEATURING HIM
Singles: 78 rpm
HEG (501 "I'm Sorry Now") 10-15 56
Singles: 7-inch
HEG (501 "I'm Sorry Now") 40-50 56

THEMES
Singles: 7-inch
EXCELLO (2152 "The Magic of You") 30-40 59
FIDELITY ("Cross My Heart") 15-25 59
(No selection number used.)

THEMES
Singles: 7-inch
MINIT (32009 "Bent Out of Shape") 5-10 66
STORK (001 "There's No Moon Tonight") 15-25 64

THEMES
Singles: 7-inch
IDEAL (21 "A Sunday Kind of Love") 10-15

THEMES, INC.
Singles: 7-inch
VEE-JAY (635 "Paula's Percussion") 5-10 65
Members: Phil Sloan; Steve Barri.
Also see FANTASTIC BAGGYS

THEOBALD, Jack & Mike
LPs: 10/12-inch
SHILOH (4087 "With Bluegrass Country") 10-15 79

THERRIEN, Joe
(Joe Therrien Jr. & His Rockets, with the Eckos; Joe Therrien Jr. & Sully Trio; with Rhythm Four)
Singles: 78 rpm
BRUNSWICK 20-30 57
LIDO 75-125 57
Singles: 7-inch
BRUNSWICK (55005 "Hey Babe, Let's Go Downtown") 20-30 57
BRUNSWICK (55017 "You're Long Gone") 50-75 57
JAT (101 "I Ain't Gonna Be Around") 50-75 59
LIDO (505 "Hey Babe, Let's Go Downtown") 75-125 57
SENTINEL (8905 "Tell Me") 1000-1500 61
(Reportedly 1000 made.)

THERRY, Nick
(With the Nickabobs & Orchestra; with Four Wheels)
Singles: 78 rpm
SPIN-IT (107 "If You Should Go") 10-15 56
Singles: 7-inch
SPIN-IT (107 "If You Should Go") 15-25 56
SPIN-IT (108 "Grateful") 40-50 57

THESE FEW
Singles: 7-inch
BLACKNIGHT (901 "Dynamite") 15-25 66
Also see SOUTHWEST F.O.B.

THESE TRAILS
LPs: 10/12-inch
SINERGIA ("These Trails") 100-150 73
(Selection number not known.)

THESE VIZITORS
Singles: 7-inch
CAPITOL (2163 "For Mary's Sake") 8-12 68

THIBADEAUX, R.B.
Singles: 78 rpm
PEACOCK 15-25 49

THIELEMANS, Toots
(With Svend Asmussen; Toots Thielemans Harmonization)
Singles: 7-inch
ABC-PAR (10500 "Bluesette") 5-8 63
BELL (773 "Father O'Conner") 4-8 69
COLUMBIA (44960 "Tippy-Toe") 4-8 69
COMMAND (4089 "Big Boy") 4-8 66
COMMAND (4102 "Continental") 4-8 67
COMMAND (4107 "Sleigh Ride") 4-8 67
SIGNATURE (12039 "Secret Love") 5-10 60
WORLD PACIFIC (375 "I'll Be Around") 5-8 63
LPs: 10/12-inch
A&M (3613 "Yesterday & Today") 5-10 74
ABC-PAR (482 "Whistler and His Guitar") 8-12 64
CHOICE (1007 "Captured Alive") 5-10 74
COMMAND (906 "Contrasts") 8-10 66
COMMAND (918 "Guitar & Strings") 8-10 67
COMMAND (930 "Toots") 8-10 68
COMMAND (978-2 "The Salient One") 8-12 73
MGM (4014 "Romantic Sound Of") 10-15 62
PHILIPS (200188 "Too Much") 8-12 65
(Monaural.)
PHILIPS (600188 "Too Much") 10-15 65
(Stereo.)
SIGNATURE (6006 "Soul Of") 10-15 60
Also see JONES, Quincy

THIEVES
Singles: 7-inch
BROADWAY (405 "I'm Not the One") 20-30 65

THIGPEN, Amanda
Singles: 7-inch
DOT (16196 "My Baby Loves His Guitar Better Than Me") 8-12 61

THIN LIZZY — P&R/LP '76
Singles: 12-inch
W.B. 4-8 78
(Promotional only.)
Singles: 7-inch
LONDON 4-6 73
MERCURY 4-6 76-77
VERTIGO 4-6 75
W.B. 3-5 78-79
Picture Sleeves
VERTIGO 4-6 75
LPs: 10/12-inch
LONDON (500 & 600 series) 10-15 71
LONDON (20000 series) 8-12 72
LONDON (50000 series) 5-10 77
MERCURY 8-12 76-77
VERTIGO 10-12 74-75
W.B. 5-10 78-84
Members: Philip Lynott; Gary Moore; Brian Robertson.
Also see MOORE, Gary

THINGIES
Singles: 7-inch
CASINO (2305 "It's a Long Way Down") 15-25 66
SONOBEAT (104 "Mass Confusion") 15-25 68

THINGS TO COME
Singles: 7-inch
STARFIRE (103 "Sweet Gina") 20-30 66
W.B. (7164 "Come Alive") 5-10 68
W.B. (7228 "Hello") 5-10 68
Members: Bryan Garofalo; Russ Ward.

THINGS TO COME
Singles: 7-inch
DUNWICH (124 "I'm Not Talkin'") 10-15 66
Members: Ken Ashely; Keith MacKendrick.
Also see CHAMPS
Also see ROXSTERS

THIRD AVENUE BLUES BAND
Singles: 7-inch
REVUE (11028 "If You Don't Love Me") 5-10 68
REVUE (11051 "Pipedream") 5-10 69
REVUE (11067 "Rose Garden") 15-25 69

THIRD BOOTH
Singles: 7-inch
INDEPENDENCE (86 "I Need Love") 5-10 68
THUNDER (8346 "Sound Inc.") 15-25 68
(Different title, but same song as *I Need Love*, on Independence.)

THIRD EAR BAND
LPs: 10/12-inch
HARVEST 10-15 69

3RD EVOLUTION
Singles: 7-inch
DAWN (306 "Don't Play with Me") 15-25 66
DAWN (312 "Everybody Needs Somebody") 5-10 67

THIRD POWER — LP '70
Singles: 7-inch
BARON (626 "Snow") 10-20 68
VANGUARD 4-8 70
LPs: 10/12-inch
VANGUARD (6554 "Believe") 15-20 70
Members: Jim Craig; Drew Abbott.

THIRD RAIL — P&R '67
Singles: 7-inch
CAMEO (445 "Train Rush Hour Stomp") 5-10 66
EPIC 5-10 67-69
LPs: 10/12-inch
EPIC 20-30 67
Members: Joey Levine; Kris Resnik; Art Resnik.
Also see SALVATION

THIRTEENTH COMMITTEE
Singles: 7-inch
MANHATTAN (810 "Sha La La") 5-10 67
Session: Davie Allan.
Also see ALLAN, Davie

THIRTEENTH FLOOR ELEVATORS — P&R '66
Singles: 7-inch
CONTACT (5269 "You're Gonna Miss Me") 50-75 66
(First issue of *You're Gonna Miss Me.*)
HBR (492 "You're Gonna Miss Me") 50-75 66
(Third issue of *You're Gonna Miss Me.*)
INT'L ARTISTS (107 "You're Gonna Miss Me") 10-20 66
(Second issue of *You're Gonna Miss Me.* May be found with: a) two tone light blue label; b) solid dark blue label [which exists with both "IA" and "AI" at top]; c) green and yellow label; d) white label, promotional issue. We have yet to learn of a noteworthy price difference between these.)
INT'L ARTISTS (111 through 130) 10-20 66-68
LPs: 10/12-inch
INT'L ARTISTS (1 "Psychedelic Sounds") 100-200 67
(Does NOT have "Masterfonics" stamped in the vinyl trail-off.)
INT'L ARTISTS (5 "Easter Everywhere") 500-750 67
(Does NOT have "Masterfonics" stamped in the vinyl trail-off.)
INT'L ARTISTS (8 "Live") 40-60 68
(Does NOT have "Masterfonics" stamped in the vinyl trail-off.)
INT'L ARTISTS (9 "Bull of the Woods") 40-60 68
(Does NOT have "Masterfonics" stamped in the vinyl trail-off.)
INT'L ARTISTS 10-20 79
(Reissues. With "Masterfonics" stamped in the vinyl trail-off.)
INT'L ARTISTS (White label) 150-225 67-68
(Promotional issues only.)
TEXAS ARCHIVE 8-10 85
Members: Roky Erickson; Tommy Hall; Stacy Sutherland; John Ike Walton; Benny Thurman.
Also see ERICKSON, Roky
Also see YA HO WA 13
Also see SPADES

13TH HOUR
Singles: 7-inch
TARGET (10/11 "All Right and About Time"/"Badger Beat") 10-20 66
Members: Ricky Lee Smolinski; Jimmy Van Hoof; Bill Vandenburgt.

13TH HOUR GLASS
Singles: 7-inch
FORMAT ("Do I Have to Come Right Out and Say It") 20-30 '60s
(Selection number not known.)
FORMAT (5003 "Keep on Running") 20-30 '60s
PRESTIGE ("Try") 20-30 '60s
(Selection number not known.)

13TH POWER
Singles: 7-inch
DYNO VOICE (227 "Captain Hassel") 10-20 66
SIDEWALK (927 "Captain Hassel") 5-10 67

13TH PRECINCT
Singles: 7-inch
TRX (5005 "You Gotta Be Mine") 15-25 67

31ST OF FEBRUARY
(Allman Brothers Band)
Singles: 7-inch
VANGUARD 5-10 68-69
LPs: 10/12-inch
VANGUARD (6503 "31st of February") 20-25 68
Members: Butch Truchs; Scott Boyer; Dave Brown.
Also see ALLMAN BROTHERS BAND
Also see TIFFANY SYSTEM

THOMAS, Al
Singles: 7-inch
JOHNSON (734 "I Have But One Heart") 5-10 65
PACEMAKER (235 "Jealousy (Little Green Man") 10-15 66
(First issue.)
SCEPTER (12155 "Jealousy (Little Green Man") 5-10 66
VIRTUE (2500 "I Had a Good Thing") 5-10 68

THOMAS, Alexander "Mudcat"
Singles: 7-inch
NRC (062 "12th Street Rag") 10-20 60
LPs: 10/12-inch
SMASH 15-25 64

THOMAS, Andrew
(Andy Thomas)
Singles: 78 rpm
GOLD STAR 25-50 48-49
SWING WITH THE STARS (1039 "I Love My Baby") 50-75 49
Singles: 7-inch
STARWAY 10-20 60-61
Also see HOPKINS, Lightnin'
Also see SMITH, Thunder

THOMAS, Arthur
Singles: 7-inch
CAPA (126 "A Bee Sticks to Honey") 50-75 65
JAMIE (1250 "Hey Mabel") 15-25 63
RAVEN (1105 "Hey Mabel") 40-60 63
(First issue.)

THOMAS, B.J. — P&R '66
(With the Triumphs)
Singles: 7-inch
ABC 4-6 75
BRAGG (103 "Billy & Sue") 20-30 66
CLEVELAND INT'L 3-5 83-84
COLLECTABLES 3-5 '80s
COLUMBIA 3-5 83-86
HICKORY 6-12 66
JOED (119 "Keep It Up") 10-15 65
LORI (9547 "Hey Judy") 8-10 63
LORI (9561 "For Your Precious Love") 8-10 64
MCA 3-6 77-82
MYRRH 3-6 77-81
PACEMAKER (227 "I'm So Lonesome I Could Cry") 10-15 64
PACEMAKER (231 "M-a-m-a") 10-15 65
PACEMAKER (234 "Bring Back the Time") 10-15 65
PACEMAKER (239 "Tomorrow Never Comes") 10-15 65
PACEMAKER (247 "Plain Jane") 10-15 65
PACEMAKER (253 "Baby Cried") 10-15 65
PACEMAKER (256 "I Can't Help It") 10-15 65

PACEMAKER (259 "Pretty Country Girl") ... 10-15 66
PARAMOUNT ... 4-6 73-74
SCEPTER (12100 series) ... 5-10 66-67
SCEPTER (12200 thru 12379) ... 4-6 68-73
SCEPTER (21000 series) ... 4-6 73-74
VALERIE ... 5-10 '60s
W.B. (5491 "Billy & Sue") ... 15-20 64

Picture Sleeves

MCA ... 3-5 79

LPs: 10/12-inch

ABC ... 5-10 74-77
ACCORD ... 5-10 81-82
BUCKBOARD ... 5-10
CLEVELAND INT'L ... 5-10 83
COLUMBIA ... 5-8 86
DORAL ... 15-25 '60s
(Promotional mail-order issue, from Doral cigarettes.)
EXACT ... 5-10 80
EXCELSIOR ... 5-10 80
EVEREST ... 5-10 81
51 WEST ... 5-10 79
HICKORY (133 "Very Best") ... 20-30 66
MCA ... 5-10 77-82
MCA/SONGBIRD ... 5-10 80
MYRRH ... 5-8 78-83
PACEMAKER (3001 "B.J. Thomas and the Triumphs") ... 40-50 66
PARAMOUNT ... 5-10 73-74
PHOENIX 20 ... 5-10 81
PICKWICK ... 5-8 78
PRIORITY ... 5-8 83
SCEPTER (535 thru 561) ... 10-20 66-67
SCEPTER (586 thru 597) ... 8-12 70-71
SCEPTER (5101 "Billy Joe Thomas") ... 8-12 72
SCEPTER (5108 "Country") ... 8-12 72
SCEPTER (5112 "Greatest All-Time Hits") ... 10-15 73
SPRINGBOARD ... 5-10 73-79
STARDAY ... 5-10 77
TRIP ... 5-10 76
U.A. ... 5-10 74
Also see CHARLES, Ray, & B.J. Thomas
Also see EDDY, Duane
Also see TRIUMPHS

THOMAS, B.J. / Smiley Lewis

Singles: 7-inch

OLDIES 45 ... 3-5
Also see LEWIS, Smiley
Also see THOMAS, B.J.

THOMAS, Ba Ba

Singles: 7-inch

KING (5858 "Leave It Alone") ... 40-60 64
KING (5889 "Miss Shake It") ... 40-60 64

THOMAS, Bennie

Singles: 7-inch

RCA ... 5-10 65
Also see MARCH, Little Peggy, & Bennie Thomas

THOMAS, Bill
(With Carolyn Sherrard)

Singles: 7-inch

CULLMAN (6402 "Shakedown") ... 200-300 58

THOMAS, Bob

Singles: 7-inch

ABEL (232 "My Day") ... 20-30 60
KINGSTON (430 "My Friends") ... 5-10 63
Session: Belmonts.
Also see BELMONTS

THOMAS, Burt, & His Band

Singles: 78 rpm

JADE ... 15-25 51

THOMAS, Carl
(With the Fitones)

Singles: 7-inch

CUPID ... 5-10 70
O-GEE (1004 "I Love You Judy") ... 10-20 59
STROLL (101 "I Love You Judy") ... 50-75 59
Also see FITONES

THOMAS, Carla — P&R/R&B '61

Singles: 7-inch

ATLANTIC ... 10-15 60-65
SATELLITE (104 "Gee Whiz, Look at His Eyes") ... 40-60 60
STAX ... 8-12 65-72

Picture Sleeves

STAX (188 "Let Me Be Good to You") ... 10-15 66

EPs: 7-inch

STAX ... 10-15 66
(Juke box issues only.)

LPs: 10/12-inch

ATLANTIC (8057 "Gee Whiz") ... 25-35 61
ATLANTIC (8232 "Best of Carla Thomas") ... 15-20 69
STAX ... 15-25 66-71
Also see OTIS & CARLA
Also see REDDING, Otis / Carla Thomas / Sam & Dave / Eddie Floyd
Also see RUFUS & CARLA
Also see TAYLOR, Johnnie, & Carla Thomas

THOMAS, Charles

Singles: 7-inch

LOMA (2031 "Lookin' for Love") ... 10-20 66

THOMAS, Cheri

Singles: 7-inch

RAYNARD (10069 "Glory Girl") ... 15-25 66

THOMAS, Chuck
(With the Hitchhikers)

Singles: 7-inch

BAND BOX (360 "Why Baby") ... 5-10 64
BAND BOX (365 "What Happened Baby") . 5-10 64

THOMAS, Cliff
("With Ed & Barbara")

Singles: 7-inch

PHILLIPS INT'L (3521 "Treat Me Right") .. 20-30 58
PHILLIPS INT'L (3531 "Sorry I Lied") ... 20-30 58
PHILLIPS INT'L (3538 "All Your Love") ... 20-30 59
SUN ... 4-6 '70s
Session: Ed Thomas; Barbara Thomas.
Also see SMITH, Ray

THOMAS, Cliff & Ed

Singles: 7-inch

ACE (613 "Do You No Wrong") ... 5-10 61
Also see THOMAS, Cliff

THOMAS, Dale

Singles: 7-inch

AD (0573 "I Can't Help Myself") ... 10-20
DOT (16343 "Hello, Lonesome") ... 10-20 62
SKY (12837 "Crocodile Hop") ... 40-60
WAHOO (52 "Fools Gold") ... 5-10 67
WAHOO (225 "Brella Girl") ... 5-10 68
WAHOO (1103 "Silent Sea") ... 5-10 68

THOMAS, Danny

Singles: 78 rpm

DECCA ... 3-5 55-56
RCA ... 3-5 53-57

Singles: 7-inch

DECCA ... 5-10 55-56
MYRRH ... 4-6 73
RCA ... 4-10 53-67

Picture Sleeves

RCA ... 4-6 67

LPs: 10/12-inch

COLUMBIA (60818 "An Evening with Danny Thomas") ... 15-25 '50s
(Promotional issue for Post Cereals.)
MGM (200 series) ... 20-40 53
(10-inch LP.)
MYRRH ... 5-10 74
Also see DAY, Doris, & Danny Thomas
Also see MARTIN, Dean

THOMAS, David Clayton — LP '69
(With the Shays; with the Fabulous Shays; with Bossmen; with His Quartet; David Clayton-Thomas)

Singles: 7-inch

ATCA (6901 "Boom Boom") ... 30-40 64
(Canadian.)
ATCA (6904 "Barby Lee") ... 25-35 64
(Canadian.)
ATCO (6347 "Hey Hey Hey") ... 15-25 65
COLUMBIA (45569 "Sing a Song") ... 4-6 72
COLUMBIA (45603 "Magnificent Sanctuary Band") ... 4-6 72
COLUMBIA (45675 "Yesterday's Music") ... 4-6 72
DECCA (32556 "Say Boss Man") ... 5-10 69
EPIC (03792 "Some Hearts Get All the Breaks") ... 3-5 83
RCA (74-0966 "Harmony Junction") ... 4-6 73
RCA (APBO-0078 "Prof. Longhair") ... 4-6 73
RCA (APBO-0216 "Yolanda") ... 4-6 74
RCA (APBO-0296 "Anytime...Babe") ... 4-6 74
RED LEAF (65001 "Hey Hey Hey") ... 100-150 65
ROMAN (1101 "Take Me Back") ... 75-100 66
(Black label. Canadian.)
ROMAN (1102 "Out of the Sunshine") ... 50-100 66
(Black label. Canadian.)
ROMAN (1105 "Brain Washed") ... 75-100 66
(Black label. Canadian.)
ROMAN (Blue label) ... 25-75 67
ROULETTE (7048 "No No No") ... 5-10 69
TOWER (263 "Born with the Blues") ... 15-25 66

LPs: 10/12-inch

ABC ... 5-10 78
COLUMBIA ... 10-15 72
DECCA (75146 "David Clayton-Thomas") ... 10-20 69
(Remixed rechanneled reissue of Roman tracks. Incorrectly hyphenates "Clayton" and "Thomas.")
RCA ... 8-12 73-74
ROMAN (101 "David Clayton Thomas and the Shays a Go Go") ... 75-125 67
(Canadian.)
ROMAN (102 "Tell It Like It Is") ... 75-125 68
(Canadian.)
Members ("Quartet"/Shays): Fred Keeler; Scott Richards; John Wetherell; Ritchie Oates; Gord Fleming.
Also see BLOOD, SWEAT & TEARS

THOMAS, David Clayton / Paupers / Shays

LPs: 10/12-inch

ROMAN (103 "David Clayton Thomas / Paupers / Shays") ... 50-100 68
(Canadian.)
Also see PAUPERS

THOMAS, David Clayton / Linda Ronstadt

LP: 10/12-inch

CAPITOL ("Back on the Streets") ... 15-25 69
(Selection number not known.)
PICKWICK (3245 "Back on the Streets") . 10-15 70
Also see RONSTADT, Linda
Also see THOMAS, David Clayton

THOMAS, Dee, & Versatiles

Singles: 7-inch

COASTER (800 "In the Garden of Love") 15-25 60

THOMAS, Dick — C&W '45
(With His Nashville Ramblers)

Singles: 78 rpm

DECCA ... 10-15 48-49
NATIONAL ... 15-20 45-46

LPs: 10/12-inch

VIKING ... 10-15

THOMAS, Dick

Singles: 7-inch

KAREN (1010 "Number One Doll") ... 10-15 60
Also see TOPPERS

THOMAS, Don

Singles: 7-inch

CORAL (62380 "Hey There, You in the Mirror") ... 5-10 64
CORAL (62418 "Hey Little Dancing Girl") ... 25-35 64
MINUTEMAN (200 "Do You Wanna Know") ... 5-10 65
PROBE (466 "Ain't It a Shame") ... 4-8 69

THOMAS, Eddie

Singles: 7-inch

SPINNING (6001 "Frankenstein Rock") ... 25-50 58
STEPHENY (1837 "Eight Slow Freights") ... 25-50 59

THOMAS, Ella
(With the Starlets)

Singles: 7-inch

FLAG (101 "Ain't That the Truth") ... 8-12 63
GEDINSON'S (101 "If You Leave Me") ... 30-40 62
TRIAD (502 "Understanding") ... 8-12 64

THOMAS, Gene — P&R '61

Singles: 7-inch

HICKORY ... 4-6 71-72
TRX (5023 "Destiny's Children") ... 5-10 69
U.A. ... 8-12 61-65
VENUS (1439 "Sometime") ... 20-30 61
VENUS (1441 "Lamp of Love") ... 10-20 62
VENUS (1444 "Down the Road") ... 40-60 62
VENUS (1445 "Wrong") ... 30-50 62
Also see GENE & DEBBE

THOMAS, Gerri

Singles: 7-inch

WORLD ARTISTS (1059 "It Could Have Been Me") ... 10-20 65

THOMAS, Guthrie

LPs: 10/12-inch

CAPITOL (11435 "Guthrie Thomas One") . 8-12 75
CAPITOL (11519 "Lies and Alibis") ... 8-12 76
EAGLE ("Kidnapped") ... 10-20 77
(1000 made.)
EAGLE ("The Poisonous Beauty") ... 25-50 79
(500 made.)
EAGLE ("Buffalo") ... 8-12 82
SINGING FOLKS ("Sitting Crooked") ... 50-100 74
(500 made.)
SINGING FOLKS ("Dear Ginny, Dear Ginny") ... 50-100 74
(500 made.)
TAXIM ("This One's for Sarah") ... 8-12 78
Session: Ramblin' Jack Elliott; David Foster; David Paich; Marc Edelstein; Ringo Starr; John Hartford; Jimmie Keltner; Waddy Wachell; Ron Wood; Mark Dawson.
Also see FOSTER, David
Also see STARR, Ringo
Also see WOOD, Ron

THOMAS, Henry

Singles: 78 rpm

VOCALION (1094 "Cornfield Blues") ... 200-400 27

LPs: 10/12-inch

ORIGIN ... 8-10

THOMAS, Irma — R&B '60

Singles: 78 rpm

RON (328 "Set Me Free") ... 50-75 59

Singles: 7-inch

BANDY ... 5-10 '60s
BUMPA ... 10-20
CANYON ... 4-6 70
CHECKER ... 5-10
CHESS ... 4-6 68
COTILLION ... 4-6 71-72
FUNGUS ... 4-6 73
IMPERIAL (Except 66080) ... 5-10 64-66
IMPERIAL (66080 "He's My Guy") ... 10-15 65
MAISON DE SOUL ... 4-6
MINIT ... 8-12 61-63
RCS ... 3-5 79-81
ROKER ... 4-8 71
RON (328 "Set Me Free") ... 10-20 59
RON (330 "Good Man") ... 10-20 59
ROUNDER ... 3-5 84

LPs: 10/12-inch

BANDY (70003 "Irma Thomas") ... 10-15 '70s
FUNGUS ... 8-10 73
IMPERIAL (266 "Wish Someone Would Care") ... 20-30 64
IMPERIAL (302 "Take a Look") ... 15-20 66
RCS ... 5-10 80
Also see BROWN, Maxine / Irma Thomas

THOMAS, Irma / Ernie K-Doe / Showmen / Benny Spellman

LPs: 10/12-inch

MINIT (0004 "New Orleans, Home of the Blues, Vol. 2") ... 30-40 64
Also see HILL, Jessie / Aaron Neville / Lee Diamond / Ernie K-Doe
Also see K-DOE, Ernie
Also see SHOWMEN
Also see SPELLMAN, Benny

THOMAS, Jake

Singles: 7-inch

DIXIE (987 "What'll I Do") ... 300-400
DIXIE (1112 "Meanest Blues") ... 100-150 '60s

THOMAS, Jamo — P&R '66
(With the Party Brothers; with Party Brothers Orchestra)

Singles: 7-inch

CHESS (1971 "I'll Be Your Fool") ... 5-10 66
DECCA (32293 "Education Is Where It's At") ... 5-10 68
DECCA (32406 "Bahama Mama") ... 5-10 68
SOUND STAGE 7 (2584 "Nassau Daddy") ... 5-10 67
SOUND STAGE 7 (2596 "Bahama Mama") ... 5-10 67
THOMAS (303 "I Spy") ... 5-10 66
THOMAS (304 "Arrest Me") ... 5-10 66

Picture Sleeves
THOMAS (303 "I Spy") 8-12 66

THOMAS, Jeannie
(Jean Thomas)
Singles: 7-inch
CADENCE (1419 "Moon River") 8-12 62
CADENCE (1435 "Seven Roses") 8-12 63
CADENCE (1438 "The Boy That I Want Doesn't Want Me") 8-12 63
FELSTED (8590 "Honey") 10-20 59
FELSTED (8599 "I Long to Be Loved") 10-20 60
GENIE (7816 "Believing") 10-15 60
MGM (13263 "Don't Make Me") 5-10 64
MINUTEMAN (206 "All You Had to Do Was Love Me") 5-10 66
SEECO (6018 "Needless to Say") 10-20 59
STRAND (25026 "Say Something Sweet to Me") 5-10 61
LPs: 10/12-inch
RELIABLE (101 "His 'N' Hers") 15-25 62
STRAND (1030 "For the Boys") 15-25 61

THOMAS, Jerry
Singles: 7-inch
ASCOR (2212 "It's So Strange") 10-15 66
KHOURY'S (708 "Baby Please") 25-35 58
ORCHID (274 "Jungle Dan") 50-75 60
ORCHID (945 "We Won't Be Sorry") 10-15 60

THOMAS, Jerry
LPs: 10/12-inch
STRAND (1082 "Organ Moods") 15-25 63

THOMAS, Jesse
(The Blues Troubador)
Singles: 78 rpm
CLUB ("I Wonder Why") 75-100 48
(No selection number used.)
CLUB ("You Are My Dreams") 75-100 48
(No selection number used.)
ELKO (107 "Another Fool Like Me") 75-100 53
FREEDOM (1513 "Guess I'll Walk Alone") 25-50 49
HOLLYWOOD (1072 "Long Time") 200-300 57
MILTONE (232 "Same Old Stuff") 75-100 48
MILTONE (233 "Zepher Blues") 75-100 48
MODERN (710 "Texas Blues") 25-50 49
SPECIALTY (419 "Jack O'Diamonds") 25-50 52
SWING TIME 25-50 51
Singles: 7-inch
ACE (5001 "That'll Get It") 40-60 58
HOLLYWOOD (1072 "Long Time") 75-125 57
SPECIALTY (419 "Jack O'Diamonds") ..50-100 52

THOMAS, Jimmy
(With the Ike & Tina Revue)
Singles: 7-inch
B&F (1349 "I Wanna Cry") 10-15 61
MIRWOOD (5522 "Just Tryin' to Please You") 5-10 66
SIRE (4121 "White Dove") 4-8 70
SONJA ....5-10 '60s
SPUTNIK ....5-10 '60s
SUE (778 "You Can Go") 5-10 63
Also see RENRUT, Icky

THOMAS, Joe R&B '49
(Joe Thomas Orchestra)
Singles: 78 rpm
KING 10-20 49-51
MERCURY 10-20 51
Singles: 7-inch
KING (4299 "Page Boy Shuffle") 25-35 49
KING (4460 "Jumpin' Joe") 20-30 51
KING (4474 "You're Just My Kind") 20-30 51
MERCURY (8268 "Everybody Loves My Baby") 20-30 51
Also see BRENSTON, Jackie / Joe Thomas

THOMAS, Joe
Singles: 7-inch
COBBLESTONE (714 "Comin' Home Baby") 15-25 68
SUE (807 "I Don't Want Nobody") 10-15 64

THOMAS, Joe, & Bill Elliott
Singles: 7-inch
SYMBOL (200 "Speak Your Piece") 5-10 64
LPs: 10/12-inch
SUE (1025 "Speak Your Piece") 15-25 64
Also see THOMAS, Joe

THOMAS, Joey
Singles: 78 rpm
DECCA (48210 "There Ain't Enough Room Here to Boogie") 15-25 51

THOMAS, Jon P&R/R&B '60
(John Thomas; Jon Thomas & Orchestra)
Singles: 78 rpm
CHECKER 10-20 55
MERCURY 10-20 57
NOTE 15-25 55
Singles: 7-inch
ABC-PAR 10-15 60-61
CHECKER (809 "Rib Tips") 15-20 55
JUNIOR (1003 "Feeling Good") 8-12 64
MERCURY (71078 "Hard Head") 15-25 57
MERCURY (71151 "Fatback") 15-25 57
NOTE (1001 "Rib Tips") 30-40 55
(First issue.)
VEEP 5-15 67-68
LPs: 10/12-inch
ABC-PAR (351 "Heartbreak") 20-30 60
(Monaural.)
ABC-PAR (S-351 "Heartbreak") 30-40 60
(Stereo.)
WING 10-20 63

THOMAS, Judy
Singles: 7-inch
1-2-3 (1711 "It Was Worth It All") 5-10 69
PHILIPS (40011 "Welcome Home") 5-10 62
REPRISE (20186 "Little Rag Doll") 5-10 63
REPRISE (20229 "Tall, Dark Handsome Stranger") 5-10 63
TOLLIE (9021 "Golden Records") 10-15 64
TOWER (131 "I Don't Know You") 5-10 65
TOWER (167 "He's My Hero") 5-10 65
U.A. (518 "Devil Woman") 5-10 62
U.A. (564 "Little Rag Doll") 5-10 63

THOMAS, L.J.
Singles: 78 rpm
CHESS (1493 "Baby, Take a Chance with Me") 50-100 52

THOMAS, Lafayette
Singles: 78 rpm
JUMPING 8-12 55
Singles: 7-inch
JUMPING (5000 "Cockroach Run") 15-25 55
SAVOY 10-15 59
Also see JUMPIN' JUDGE & HIS COURT / Lafayette Thomas
Also see ROBINSON, L.C. / Lafayette 'Thing' Thomas / Dave Alexander

THOMAS, Lee
(With the Don Juans)
Singles: 7-inch
JAGUAR (3020 "Baby, Don't You Care") .40-50 57

THOMAS, Mamie
Singles: 78 rpm
MGM (55009 "Daddy on My Mind") 10-15 55
Singles: 7-inch
MGM (55009 "Daddy on My Mind") 25-35 55

THOMAS, Marcellus, & His Rhythm Rockets
Singles: 7-inch
AJAX (104 "Breather Blues") 20-40
Also see MERCY DEE

THOMAS, Mary Ann
Singles: 7-inch
20TH FOX (162 "Dreamin' Fool") 10-20 59

THOMAS, Milton, & Escorts
Singles: 7-inch
BI-MI (101 "Angel of My Dreams") 75-125 61

THOMAS, Minnie
(With Slim Waters & Lagoons)
Singles: 78 rpm
METEOR 25-50 56
Singles: 7-inch
METEOR (5036 "What Can the Matter Be") 50-75 56

THOMAS, Mona
Singles: 7-inch
USA (776 "There He Goes") 15-25 64

THOMAS, Mule
Singles: 7-inch
HOLLYWOOD (1091 "Take Some and Leave Some") 75-125 58

THOMAS, Nancy
Singles: 7-inch
CUB (9087 "Nighty Night") 8-12 61
MALA (455 "Kiss 'n' Tell") 8-12 62

THOMAS, Pat P&R '62
Singles: 7-inch
MGM 4-6 62-63
VERVE 4-6 62-64
Picture Sleeves
MGM 4-6 62
LPs: 10/12-inch
MGM 10-20 62-64
STRAND 10-20 61

THOMAS, Paul
(Paul Gottschall Jr.)
Singles: 7-inch
GUYDEN (2086 "Come Right Out and Say It") 5-10 63
HI MAR (101/102 "He's Thinking of You"/"Long Black Veil") 10-15 62
Also see ADMIRAL TONES
Also see ROCK, Jimmy

THOMAS, Philip-Michael R&B '85
Singles: 7-inch
ATLANTIC 4-6 85
LPs: 10/12-inch
ATLANTIC (90468 "Living the Book of My Life") 15-25 85

THOMAS, Playboy
Singles: 78 rpm
PARROT 50-75 53
SWING TIME 50-75 53
Singles: 7-inch
PARROT (785 "Too Much Pride") 75-125 53
(Black vinyl.)
PARROT (785 "Too Much Pride") 200-300 53
(Red vinyl.)
SWING TIME (340 "Too Much Pride") ...75-125 53
SWING TIME (344 "End of the Road") ...75-125 53

THOMAS, Priscilla
Singles: 7-inch
WINNER (7-11 "Step Aside") ....10-20 '60s

THOMAS, Ramblin'
LPs: 10/12-inch
BIOGRAPH 10-15 70

THOMAS, Randy
Singles: 7-inch
FARO (622 "Are You Ready") 10-15 65

THOMAS, Ray LP '75
Singles: 7-inch
THRESHOLD 4-6 75
LPs: 10/12-inch
THRESHOLD (16 "From Mighty Oaks") ...10-15 75
(Gatefold cover.)
THRESHOLD (17 "Hopes, Wishes and Dreams") 10-15 76
THRESHOLD (102 "Ray Thomas Discusses *From Mighty Oaks*") 15-25 75
(Promotional issue only.)
Also see MOODY BLUES

THOMAS, Rita, & Fats Gaines Band
Singles: 7-inch
BAY-TONE (118 "Take Care of My Heart") 8-12 65
Also see GAINES, Fats, Band

THOMAS, Rufus R&B '53
(Rufus "Bearcat" Thomas; Rufus Thomas Jr.)
Singles: 12-inch
A.V.I. 4-8 78
Singles: 78 rpm
CHESS (1466 "Night Walkin' Blues") 15-25 52
CHESS (1492 "No More Doggin' Around") 15-25 52
CHESS (1517 "Juanita") 15-25 52
STAR TALENT (807 "I'm So Worried") 20-30 50
SUN (181 "Bear Cat [Answer to Hound Dog]") 75-125 53
(With subtitle.)
SUN (181 "Bear Cat") 50-75 53
(Without subtitle.)
SUN (188 "Tiger Man") 50-100 53
Singles: 7-inch
A.V.I. 3-5 77-78
ARTISTS OF AMERICA (126 "Blues in the Basement") 5-10 76
ERWIN (184 "How Far Will You Go") 5-10 78
HI (78520 "I Ain't Got Time") 4-8 78
METEOR (5039 "I'm Steady Holdin' On") 100-150 56
STAX (100 & 200 series) 5-10 62-68
STAX (0010 thru 0236) 4-8 68-75
SUN (181 "Bear Cat [Answer to Hound Dog]") 100-200 53
(With subtitle.)
SUN (181 "Bear Cat") 75-125 53
(Without subtitle.)
SUN (188 "Tiger Man") 100-150 53
LPs: 10/12-inch
A.V.I. 5-10 77-78
ARTISTS OF AMERICA 8-10 76
GUSTO 5-10 80
STAX (Except 704) 6-15 70-79
STAX (704 "Walking the Dog") 25-50 63
Also see RUFUS & CARLA
Also see RUFUS & FRIEND

THOMAS, Rusty
Singles: 7-inch
CLUB (265 "Maybellene") 75-100

THOMAS, Tabby
(Tab Thomas; Rockin' Tabby Thomas)
Singles: 7-inch
EXCELLO 5-10 61-65
FEATURE (3007 "Tomorrow") 25-35 54
GUTTER 3-5 85
ROCKO 10-15 61
ZYNN 10-15 61
Also see TABBY & HIS MELLOW, MELLOW MEN

THOMAS, Taffy
Singles: 7-inch
COLUMBIA (41644 "Say Something Nice to Me") 10-20 60
NEWPORT (130 "I'm Comin' On Back") ..10-15 '60s
Also see THOMPSON, Sue

THOMAS, Tony, & Tartans
Singles: 7-inch
SMASH (2000 "Old Enough to Know") 40-60 58

THOMAS, Tracy, & Tru-Sonics
Singles: 7-inch
BOLO (729 "Twist Around the Puget Sound") 10-15 62
Also see TRU-SONICS

THOMAS, Vic
(With the 4-Evers)
Singles: 7-inch
APPLAUSE (1240 "You're Gonna Change") 20-30 60
PHILIPS (40183 "Marianne") 10-15 64
PHILIPS (40228 "Village of Love") 10-15 64
PHILIPS (40265 "Love My Baby") 10-15 65
PREMIUM ("Rock and Roll Tonight") ...200-300
(Selection number not known.)

THOME, Henry
Singles: 7-inch
VIV (3 "Scotch & Soda") 5-10 62
(Era reissue.)
VIV (5 "Brandy") 5-10 62
VIV (6 "Scarlet") 5-10 62
VIV (305 "Scotch & Soda") 10-15 62
(First issue.)

THOMPSON, Al
Singles: 7-inch
DEBONAIRE 15-25

THOMPSON, Billy
Singles: 7-inch
COLUMBUS (1043 "Black-Eyed Girl") .100-150 66
WAND (1108 "Black-Eyed Girl") 50-75 66

THOMPSON, Bob
Singles: 78 rpm
ZEPHYR (004 "Goodbye Old Girl") 10-15 56
Singles: 7-inch
ZEPHYR (004 "Goodbye Old Girl") 20-30 56

THOMPSON, Bob, Orchestra
LPs: 10/12-inch
RCA (2357 "Wildcat") 10-20 61

Also see SPOTLIGHTERS

THOMPSON, Buddy
(With Sid Bass & Orchestra)
Singles: 78 rpm
ATCO (6095 "This Is the Night") ... 20-30 57
RCA ... 5-15 55-56
Singles; 7-inch
ATCO (6095 "This Is the Night") ... 20-30 57
GREENWICH (409 "Sweet Love") ... 15-20 58
RCA ... 15-25 55-56

THOMPSON, Cheryle
Singles: 7-inch
CORAL (62493 "Mansion of Tears") ... 5-10 66
DECCA (32066 "Wall to Wall Heartaches") ... 5-10 66
DECCA (32144 "Something to Think About") ... 5-10 67
VEE-JAY (695 "It's the End") ... 10-15 65

THOMPSON, Chuck
(With Avis Thompson)
Singles: 7-inch
GRANITE (560 "I'm Tired of Fooling Around") ... 50-100
JAX (109 "Baby") ... 50-100
ON THE BALL (108 "Why So") ... 100-150 62

THOMPSON, Claudia
(With Barney Kessel)
Singles: 7-inch
EDISON INT'L (408 "Goodnight My Pet") ... 5-10 59
LPs: 10/12-inch
EDISON INT'L ... 15-20 60
Also see KESSEL, Barney / Grant Green / Oscar Moore / Mundell Lowe

THOMPSON, Cotton
Singles: 78 rpm
GOLD STAR ... 10-20 49
Also see MULLICAN, Moon / Cotton Thompson

THOMPSON, Del
Singles: 7-inch
HOPE (554 "The Love Waiting for Me") ... 10-15

THOMPSON, Dickie
Singles: 78 rpm
HERALD ... 10-15 54
Singles: 7-inch
HERALD (424 "I'm Innocent") ... 15-25 54
HERALD (431 "Jockin' ") ... 15-25 54
WINLEY (239 "Real Zan Zee") ... 10-20 59

THOMPSON, Don
Singles: 7-inch
MAVERICK (618 "Don't Let Me Go") ... 50-75
LPs: 10/12-inch
SUNDAY ... 8-10

THOMPSON, Donnie
(Donnie Thompson Combo, Donnie Thompson Quintet)
Singles: 7-inch
DOT (16082 "Cheeze Blintzes") ... 10-20 60
V-TONE (209 "Chicken Hop") ... 10-20 60

THOMPSON, Ed
Singles: 7-inch
AUDIO HOUSE (12667 "That Girl Needed Kissin' ") ... 40-50

THOMPSON, Ernestine
Singles: 7-inch
BLAST (212 "Just One More Time") ... 10-15 64

THOMPSON, Fred
Singles: 7-inch
JIM DANDY (4501 "Please Be Fair") ... 100-200

THOMPSON, Gene, & Counts
Singles: 7-inch
ACE (673 "You Don't Love Me") ... 10-15 62

THOMPSON, Hank *C&W '48*
(With the Brazos Valley Boys)
Singles: 78 rpm
BLUE BONNET ... 25-50 47
(Title and selection number not known.)
CAPITOL ... 10-25 47-57
GLOBE (124 "Whoa Sailor") ... 100-200 46
Singles: 7-inch
ABC ... 4-6 75-79
ABC/DOT ... 4-6 74-77
CAPITOL (1000 & 2000 series) ... 15-30 50-54
CAPITOL (3000 & 4000 series) ... 10-20 55-63
CAPITOL (5000 series) ... 8-12 63-66
CHURCHILL ... 3-5 81-83
DOT ... 5-10 68-74
MCA ... 3-5 79-80
W.B. ... 5-10 66-67
Picture Sleeves
CAPITOL (4649 "Lost John") ... 15-25 61
EPs: 7-inch
CAPITOL ... 15-25 53-59
LPs: 10/12-inch
ABC ... 5-10 78
ABC/DOT ... 5-10 74-77
CAPITOL (H-418 "Songs of the Brazos Valley") ... 75-100 53
(10-inch LP.)
CAPITOL (T-418 "Songs of the Brazos Valley") ... 50-75 55
(Green label.)
CAPITOL (T-618 "North of the Rio Grande") ... 40-60 55
(Green label.)
CAPITOL (T-729 "New Recordings") ... 30-50 55
CAPITOL (T-826 "Hank!") ... 30-40 57
CAPITOL (T-975 "Dance Ranch") ... 30-40 58
CAPITOL (T-1111 thru T-2154) ... 15-30 59-64
(Monaural.)
CAPITOL (ST-1111 through ST-2154) ... 20-40 59-64
(Stereo.)
CAPITOL (SM-2000 series) ... 5-8 75
CAPITOL (T-2274 thru T-2800) ... 10-20 65-67
(Monaural.)
CAPITOL (ST-2274 through ST-2826) ... 10-25 65-67
(Stereo.)
CAPITOL (H-9111 "Favorites") ... 50-100 52
(10-inch LP.)
CAPITOL (11000 series) ... 5-8 79
CHURCHILL ... 5-8 84
DOT ... 5-15 68-74
GUSTO ... 5-8 80
MCA/DOT ... 5-8
PICKWICK/HILLTOP ... 5-15 67-68
PROVINCIA ... 5-8
SEARS (135 "How Many Teardrops Will It Take") ... 10-15 '60s
STEP ONE ... 5-8 87
TOWER ... 8-15 68
WACO (101 "Hank Thompson Sings and Plays Bob Wills") ... 30-50
W.B. ... 10-20 66-67

THOMPSON, Hank, & Merle Travis *C&W '55*
(With the Brazos Valley Boys)
Singles: 78 rpm
CAPITOL ... 5-10 55
Singles: 7-inch
CAPITOL ... 8-12 55
Also see THOMPSON, Hank
Also see TRAVIS, Merle

THOMPSON, Hayden
(Haydon Thompson)
Singles: 78 rpm
VON ... 50-100 54
Singles: 7-inch
ARLEN (728 "Queen Bee") ... 10-20 63
B.E.A.T. (1011 "Dream Love") ... 15-25 60
BRAVE (1015 "If It's Alright") ... 5-10 67
EXTREMELY BRAVE ... 4-6 73
H.T. ... 4-6 75
KAPP (763 "And She Cried") ... 5-10 66
KAPP (795 "Present for Mommy") ... 5-10 66
NASHVILLE NORTH ... 4-6 70-73
PHILLIPS INT'L (3517 "Love My Baby") ... 100-200 57
PROFILE (4015 "Whatcha Gonna Do") ... 50-75 61
VON (1001 "Whatcha' Gonna Do") ... 400-500 54
LPs: 10/12-inch
KAPP (1507 "Here's Hayden Thompson") ... 12-15 66
(Monaural.)
KAPP (3507 "Here's Hayden Thompson") ... 15-20 66
(Stereo.)

THOMPSON, Helen
(With the Street Singers & Orchestra)
Singles: 78 rpm
DAWN ... 20-30 54
STATES ... 10-20 53-55
Singles: 7-inch
DAWN (210 "Oh Baby") ... 75-100 54
STATES (126 "All by Myself") ... 30-40 53
(Black vinyl.)
STATES (126 "All by Myself") ... 75-125 53
(Colored vinyl.)
STATES (138 "My Baby's Love") ... 25-35 55
(Black vinyl.)
TRAIL (102 "Chattanooga Drummer Man") ... 100-200 '50s

THOMPSON, Howard, & Upsetters
Singles: 7-inch
MAJOR (1037 "Can't Go on This Way") ... 30-50

THOMPSON, Jimmy
Singles: 78 rpm
VITA (143 "Now Hear This") ... 10-15 56
Singles: 7-inch
VITA (143 "Now Hear This") ... 20-30 56

THOMPSON, Junior
(With the Meteors)
Singles: 78 rpm
METEOR ... 100-200 56
Singles: 7-inch
ATCO (6500 "Jungle Girl") ... 5-10 67
BADD (1001 "Big Black Spider") ... 100-200
J.J.'S (Except 006) ... 15-25
J.J.'S (006 "Oobie Doobie") ... 100-125
METEOR (5029 "Mama's Little Baby") ... 350-450 56
TUNE ("How Come You Do Me?") ... 150-250
(No selection number used.)

THOMPSON, Kid Guitar / Darnell Johnson
Singles: 7-inch
DORE (581 "My Baby Done Me Wrong"/"Comic Papers") ... 50-75 61

THOMPSON, Leroy
Singles: 7-inch
MIK-ER-PHONE (1165 "Walkin' and a-Talkin' ") ... 50-75

THOMPSON, Loretta
Singles: 78 rpm
UNITED ... 25-35 57
Singles: 7-inch
SKOOP (1050 "Square from Nowhere") ... 40-50 59
UNITED (214 "Hi-De-Ho Rock & Roll") ... 25-35 57

THOMPSON, Lucky
Singles: 78 rpm
ABC-PAR ... 25-35 57
DECCA ... 8-12 53
SWING BEAT ... 10-15 49
LPs: 10/12-inch
ABC-PAR (171 "Lucky Thompson") ... 35-55 57
DAWN (1113 "Lucky Thompson") ... 25-50 57
DECCA (28871 "Flamingo") ... 30-40 53
URANIA (1206 "Accent on the Tenor") ... 25-50 57
Also see DAVIS, Miles

THOMPSON, Marie
Singles: 7-inch
J.C.D. (101 "Missing You So") ... 10-15 59

THOMPSON, Mayo
LPs: 10/12-inch
MUSIC LANGUAGE ... 10-15 76
TEXAS REVOLUTION (2270 "Corky's Debt") ... 20-25 69
Also see RED CRAYOLA

THOMPSON, Paul
Singles: 7-inch
VOLT (4042 "Special Kind of Woman") ... 15-25 70

THOMPSON, Peggy
Singles: 7-inch
GIANT (1010 "I Sold My Heart to the Junkman") ... 10-15 62

THOMPSON, Ray
Singles: 7-inch
ON THE SQUARE (315 "Little Eva") ... 30-40 59

THOMPSON, Richie, & Jesters
Singles: 7-inch
DIAMOND (103 "Too Late to Worry") ... 30-40 61

THOMPSON, Rocky
(Goree Carter)
Singles: 78 rpm
JADE (207 "My Wish") ... 25-50 51
Also see CARTER, Goree

THOMPSON, Ron, & Broughams
Singles: 7-inch
SOMA (1108 "Switchblade") ... 100-125 59
Also see ALLISON, Dick, & Broughams

THOMPSON, Sonny *P&R/R&B '48*
Singles: 78 rpm
CHART ... 10-15 56
KING ... 5-15 50-57
MIRACLE ... 10-15 48
Singles: 7-inch
CHART (612 "Slow Rock, Pt. 1") ... 15-25 56
CHART (633 "Juke Joint, Pt. 1") ... 15-25 56
CHART (637 "Drive In") ... 15-25 57
CHART (642 "Candy, Pt. 1") ... 15-25 57
CHART (645 "Hi-Ho") ... 15-25 57
CHART (648 "Night Watch") ... 15-25 57
KING (4400 thru 5300 series) ... 5-15 51-60
KNIGHT ... 5-10 61
EPs: 7-inch
KING ... 20-40 52-54
LPs: 10/12-inch
KING (568 "Moody Blues") ... 100-150 58
KING (655 "Mellow Blues") ... 50-100 59
Also see KING, Freddie / Lula Reed / Sonny Thompson
Also see REED, Lula

THOMPSON, Sue *P&R '61/C&W '72*
(With Hank Penny; with David Carroll Orchestra)
Singles: 78 rpm
DECCA ... 5-10 55-57
MERCURY ... 5-10 50-54
Singles: 7-inch
DECCA (29314 "Walkin' in the Snow") ... 10-20 55
DECCA (29545 "Day Dreaming") ... 10-20 55
DECCA (30435 "Walkin' to Missouri") ... 10-20 57
GUSTO ... 3-5 '80s
HICKORY (308 thru 370) ... 4-6 73-76
HICKORY (1144 "Angel Angel") ... 10-15 61
HICKORY (1153 "Sad Movies") ... 5-10 61
HICKORY (1159 "Norman") ... 5-10 61
HICKORY (1166 "Two of a Kind") ... 15-25 62
(With picture insert. Promotional issue only.)
HICKORY (1166 "Two of a Kind") ... 5-10 62
(Without insert.)
HICKORY (1174 thru 1488) ... 5-10 62-67
HICKORY (1493 thru 1669) ... 5-8 67-73
MERCURY (6416 "Red Hot Henrietta Brown") ... 15-25 52
MERCURY (70066 "How Many Tears") ... 10-20 52
MERCURY (70084 "Take Care, My Love") ... 10-20 53
MERCURY (70089 "You and Me") ... 10-20 53
MERCURY (70152 "I'm Not That Kind of Girl") ... 10-20 53
MERCURY (70309 "Gee But I Hate to Go Home Alone") ... 10-20 54
Picture Sleeves
HICKORY (1204 "What's Wrong Bill") ... 10-15 64
HICKORY (1217 "True Confessions") ... 10-15 64
LPs: 10/12-inch
HICKORY (104 "Meet Sue Thompson") ... 25-30 62
HICKORY (107 "Two of a Kind") ... 15-25 62
HICKORY (111 "Golden Hits") ... 15-25 63
HICKORY (121 "Paper Tiger") ... 15-25 65
HICKORY (130 "Sue Thompson with Strings Attached") ... 10-20 66
HICKORY (148 "This Is Sue Thompson") ... 10-15 69
HICKORY/MGM (4500 series) ... 8-10 74-75
WING (12317 "Country Side") ... 10-15 66
(Monaural.)
WING (16317 "Country Side") ... 10-15 66
(Stereo.)
Also see GIBSON, Don, & Sue Thompson
Also see MARTIN, Dude
Also see PENNY, Hank
Also see THOMAS, Taffy
Also see LUMAN, Bob, & Sue Thompson

THOMPSON, Sue, & Bob Luman
Singles: 7-inch
HICKORY (1221 "I Like Your Kind of Love") ... 5-10 63
Also see LUMAN, Bob
Also see THOMPSON, Sue

THOMPSON, Tennessee
Singles: 7-inch
RTC (703 "Slippin' and Slidin' ") ... 400-600

THOMPSON BROTHERS
Singles: 7-inch
DOT (17072 "Walk Away") ... 5-10 68

IVANHOE (5022 "Walk Away") 10-20 67

THOR-ABLES

Singles: 7-inch

TITANIC ("Our Love Song") 350-400 62
(No selection number used.)
TITANIC (1002 "My Reckless Heart").. 300-350 62
Members: Lloyd McCraw; Willie Davis.
Also see CADETS

THOR-ABLES / Aaron Collins

Singles: 7-inch

TITANIC (1001 "Our Love Song")......... 75-125 62
Also see THOR-ABLES

THORINSHIELD

Singles: 7-inch

PHILIPS (40492 "Life Is a Dream")............5-10 67
PHILIPS (40521 "Family of Man")..............5-10 68

Picture Sleeves

PHILIPS (40492 "Life Is a Dream")............8-12 67

LPs: 10/12-inch

PHILLIPS (200251 "Thorinshield")........... 10-20 67
(Monaural.)
PHILLIPS (600251 "Thorinshield")........... 10-20 67
(Stereo.)

THORNDIKE PICKLEDISH

(Thorndike Pickledish Choir; Thorndike Pickledish Pacifist Choir; Bob Smith)

Singles: 7-inch

ABSURD (304 "Viet Nama Mama") 5-10 66
LO-FI..5-10 67-68
MTA (114 "Ballad of Walter Wart")..............5-10 66
MTA (126 "Lonely Bullfrog") 5-10 67

EPs: 7-inch

PICCADILLY (247 "Imperial Grand Mother S.F. Bound") 8-12 67
Also see SMITH, Bob

THORNE, Del

Singles: 78 rpm

EXCELLO... 20-30 52

Singles: 7-inch

EXCELLO (2006 "I Let Him Move Me")... 40-60 52
EXCELLO (2017 "Fly Chicken Blues")...... 40-60 52

THORNE, Roscoe

Singles: 78 rpm

ATLAS (1033 "Peddler of Dreams")..... 200-300 53

Singles: 7-inch

ATLAS (1033 "Peddler of Dreams"). 3000-4000 53

THORNE, Woody

Singles: 7-inch

GNP (169 "Teenagers in Love")............. 10-20 61

THORNTON, Teri

Singles: 7-inch

COLUMBIA (42896 "Open Highway" [Route 66 Theme])..8-12 63
COLUMBIA (42958 "Day I Stop Lovin' You") 8-12 64
COLUMBIA (43002 "Cold, Cold Heart")......8-12 64
COLUMBIA (43027 "Why Don't You Love Me")...8-12 64
COLUMBIA (43151 "Secret Life")...............8-12 64
DAUNTLESS (036 "Somewhere in the Night" [Naked City Theme]) 8-12 64

LPs: 10/12-inch

COLUMBIA (2094 "Open Highway")........ 10-15 63
COLUMBIA (8894 "Open Highway")........ 15-20 63
DAUNTLESS (4306 "Somewhere in the Night") 10-15 63
DAUNTLESS (6306 "Somewhere in the Night") 15-20 63

THORNTON, Willie Mae — R&B '53

(Big Mama Thornton)

Singles: 78 rpm

PEACOCK... 25-50 51-57

Singles: 7-inch

ABC...4-6 73
ARHOOLIE...4-6 68
BAY TONE (107 "You Did Me Wrong") ... 15-25 61
GALAXY (749 "Life Goes On")....................8-12 66
IRMA (13 "Don't Talk Back") .... 50-100 '50s
KENT (424 "Before Day")...........................5-10 65
MERCURY (72981 "Hound Dog")................5-10 69
PEACOCK (1567 "Partnership Blues").. 50-100 51
PEACOCK (1603 "Mischievous Boogie") 50-100 52
PEACOCK (1612 "Hound Dog")........... 100-150 53
PEACOCK (1621 "Cotton Picking Blues") 50-75 53
PEACOCK (1626 "I Ain't No Fool Either") 50-75 53
PEACOCK (1632 "I've Searched the World Over") 50-75 54
PEACOCK (1642 "Stop Hoppin' on Me")..50-75 54
PEACOCK (1647 "Walking Blues")...........35-50 55
PEACOCK (1650 "The Fish")...................35-50 55
PEACOCK (1654 "Tarzan and the Dignified Monkey") 35-50 55
(White label issues of this or earlier numbers are reissues, which Peacock continued carrying in their catalog through the '70s.)
PEACOCK (1681 "Just Like a Dog") 15-25 57
ST. CAROLYN ....4-8 '70s
SOTOPLAY (0033 "Summertime") 8-12 65
SOTOPLAY (0039 "Tomcat").......................8-12 65

LPs: 10/12-inch

ARHOOLIE..10-15 66-67
BACK BEAT 20-25 70
MERCURY 10-15 69-70
PENTAGRAM 12-25 71
ROULETTE...10-15 70
VANGUARD..8-10 74-75
Session: Don Johnson; Johnny Otis; George Washington; Pete Lewis; Devonia Williams.
Also see ACE, Johnny, & Willie Mae Thornton
Also see HARLEM STARS
Also see OTIS, Johnny

THORNTON, FRADKIN & UNGER

(With Paul McCartney)

Singles: 7-inch

ESP-DISK...8-12 71
Also see McCARTNEY, Paul

THOROGOOD, George — LP '78

(With the Destroyers)

Singles: 12-inch

EMI (Black vinyl) 4-6 83-85
EMI (9293 "Rock & Roll Christmas")...........5-10 83
(Colored vinyl. Promotional issue only.)

Singles: 7-inch

EMI (Except 17517)..3-5 82-94
EMI (17517 "Get a Haircut")...........................5-10 94
(White label, black vinyl. Reads: "For Juke boxes Only!")
EMI (17517 "Get a Haircut")......................10-15 94
(White label, colored vinyl. Reads: "For Juke boxes Only!")
MCA..3-5 79
ROUNDER 3-5 78-80

Picture Sleeves

ROUNDER (4536 "Bottom of the Sea")........3-5 80

LPs: 10/12-inch

EMI 5-8 82-91
MCA..5-10 79
ROUNDER...6-12 77-80

THORPE, Billy — P&R/LP '79

Singles: 7-inch

CAPRICORN...3-5 79
POLYDOR..3-5 79
PASHA (Except "Retail Teaser")...................3-5 85
PASHA ("Retail Teaser")................................4-8 85
(Selection number not known.)

LPs: 10/12-inch

CAPRICORN...15-20 79
ELEKTRA..5-8 80
PASHA..8-12 82-85
POLYDOR...5-8 79

THORPE, Lionel

(Carl "Lionel" Thorpe)

Singles: 7-inch

ROULETTE (4144 "More, More, More")...15-25 59
ROULETTE (4222 "She Was Love") 10-15 60
Also see CHORDS

THOSE BOYS

Singles: 7-inch

FED (1012 "Never Go Away").................20-30 66
FED (1016 "No Good Girl") 20-30 66

THOSE FIVE

Singles: 7-inch

PARIS TOWER (117 "Sidewalks")...........10-15 67

THOSE FOUR ELDORADOS

(El Dorados)

Singles: 7-inch

ACADEMY (8138 "A Lonely Boy")..... 750-1000 58
Members: Juell Jones; Louis Bradley; Marvin Smith; James Maddox.
Also see EL DORADOS
Also see SMITH, Marvin

THOSE GUYS

Singles: 7-inch

BLACK SHEEP ....10-20 '60s
IGL (129 "Love Is a Beautiful Thing") ....15-25 '60s

THOSE OF US

Singles: 7-inch

IGL (124 "Without You") 25-35 67
Also see GREGORY, Dale, & Shouters

THOUGHTS

Singles: 7-inch

PLANET (118 "All Night Stand") 10-20 66

THRASHER, Tommy

Singles: 7-inch

TOM TOM (102 "My Baby Knows") 50-75 61
TOPPA (1081 "Endless Hours") 10-15 63

THRASHERS

(With Joe Ruffin Band)

Singles: 7-inch

CANDLELITE (421 "Jeannie") 5-10 64
MASON'S (178-062 "Jeannie").........1000-1200 57
(Black vinyl. Reads: "Mason's Recording Co. 1630 Amsterdam Ave. N.Y.C.")
MASON'S (178-062 "Jeannie")............100-150 61
(Red vinyl. Reads: "Mason's Records 267 Franklin Ave. Brooklyn 5, N.Y.")

THREATT, Sonny

Singles: 7-inch

SOFT...5-10 68
Also see SONNY & PHYLLIS
Also see TANGENTS

THREE ACES & JOKER

Singles: 7-inch

GRC (104 "Booze Party")......................250-350

THREE BARONS

(Three Riffs)

Singles: 78 rpm

SAVOY 15-25 45
Also see THREE RIFFS

THREE BEAUS & A PEEP

Singles: 78 rpm

ALADDIN..5-10 57
COLUMBIA 5-10 53

Singles: 7-inch

ALADDIN..8-12 57
COLUMBIA 8-12 53
Also see VALLO, Rick

THREE BITS OF RHYTHM

Singles: 78 rpm

DECCA...15-25 41
MODERN MUSIC 15-25

THREE BLAZES

Singles: 78 rpm

MONEY 10-15 54

Singles: 7-inch

MONEY (205 "What Makes a Man Fool Around")...40-50 54

THREE BLONDE MICE

Singles: 7-inch

ATCO (6324 "Ringo Bells")....................10-15 64
ATCO (6353 "What'd I Say")....................5-10 65

THREE CHEERS

Singles: 7-inch

GLORY (291 "Broken Dream") 10-15 59
GLORY (296 "To Be in Love") 10-15 59
KEYS (2 "Broken Dream") 20-30 59
PHILIPS (40036 "Hallelujah, I Love Her So") 5-10 62

THREE CHIMES

Singles: 7-inch

CROSSWAY (444 "Tears and Pain") 75-125 64
Also see CHIMES

THREE CHUCKLES — P&R '54

(Featuring Teddy Randazzo)

Singles: 78 rpm

BOULEVARD (100 "Runaround")............10-20 53
VIK...5-10 56
"X"...8-12 54-56

Singles: 7-inch

BOULEVARD (100 "Runaround")............40-60 53
CLOUD (507 "Runaround")..........................5-8 66
VIK (0186 "Anyway") 10-15 56
VIK (0194 "And the Angels Sing") 10-15 56
VIK (0216 "Gypsy in My Soul") 10-15 56
VIK (0232 "Midnight Till Dawn")...............10-20 56
VIK (0244 "Won't You Give Me a Chance")...10-20 56
"X" (0066 "Runaround") 15-20 54
"X" (0095 "Foolishly") 15-20 55
"X" (0134 "So Long")................................15-20 55
"X" (0150 "Realize") 15-20 55
"X" (0162 "Times Two, I Love You").........15-20 55
"X" (0186 "Anyway")................................15-20 55
"X" (0194 "And the Angels Sing") 15-20 56
"X" (0216 "Gypsy in My Soul")..................15-20 56

EPs: 7-inch

RCA (192/193/194 "Three Chuckles")......15-25 55
(Price is for any of three volumes.)
VIK (4 "Three Chuckles") 20-40 57
(Promotional issue only. Not issued with cover.)

LPs: 10/12-inch

VIK (1067 "Three Chuckles")...............100-150 55
Members: Teddy Randazzo; Phil Benti; Tom Romano; Russ Gilberto.
Also see RANDAZZO, Teddy

THREE CLICKS

Singles: 7-inch

DEVERE (500 "Rockin' Along") 200-300

THREE COQUETTES

Singles: 7-inch

HOPE (1002 "I Wonder") 10-15 60

THREE Ds

Singles: 78 rpm

PILGRIM 5-10 56

Singles: 7-inch

BRUNSWICK (55152 "Happiest Boy and Girl")..8-12 59
PARIS..8-12 57-58
PILGRIM (719 "Broken Dreams") 8-12 56
SQUARE (502 "Squeeze")........................50-75
SQUARE (503 "High School Love") 50-75
Also see GINSBURG, Arnie

THREE Ds

Singles: 7-inch

CAPITOL (5188 "Sinner Man")...................5-10 64
CAPITOL (5249 "Crayon Box")...................5-10 64

LPs: 10/12-inch

CAPITOL (2171 "New Dimensions in Folk Songs") 15-25 64
CAPITOL (2314 "I Won't Be Worried Long") 15-25 65

THREE Ds

Singles: 7-inch

AMBER (4401 "Love Letters") 8-12 66

THREE Ds

Singles: 7-inch

LOWELL (212 "My Fraternity Dance") 10-20

THREE DEBS

Singles: 78 rpm

CROWN 10-15 55

Singles: 7-inch

CROWN (153 "If You Were Here Tonight") 15-25 55

THREE DEES

Singles: 7-inch

DEAN (521 "Broken Hearted")..................20-30 61

THREE DEGREES — P&R '65

Singles: 7-inch

ARIOLA AMERICA.......................................3-5 78-80
EPIC...4-6 76
ICHIBAN..3-5 89
METROMEDIA 4-6 69
NEPTUNE...4-6 70
PHILA. INT'L...4-6 73-76
ROULETTE...4-6 70-72
SWAN 6-12 65-67
W.B. 5-10 68

LPs: 10/12-inch

ARIOLA AMERICA.......................................5-10 78-81
EPIC...8-10 77
PHILA. INT'L...8-10 74-76
ROULETTE...10-20 70-75

THREE DIMENSIONS
(With the Don Ralke Orchestra)
Singles: 7-inch
CASCADE (5903 "Nightfall") 40-50 59
Also see RALKE, Don

THREE DOG NIGHT P&R/LP '69
(3 Dog Night)
Singles: 7-inch
ABC 4-6 70-76
DUNHILL (Except 4168) 6-8 69-75
DUNHILL (4168 "Nobody") 8-10 68
PASSPORT 3-5 83
Picture Sleeves
DUNHILL (4168 "Nobody") 20-30 68
(Promotional issue only.)
DUNHILL (4239 "Mama Told Me") 4-6 70
EPs: 7-inch
ABC (40014 "Hard Labor") 10-20 74
(Quadraphonic. Juke box "Special Promotional Record." Includes title strips.)
DUNHILL (PRO-50158 "Cyan") 8-12 73
(Promotional only issue.)
LPs: 10/12-inch
ABC (888 "Coming Down Your Way") 8-12 75
ABC (928 "American Pastime") 8-12 76
ABC/COMMAND (40014 "Hard Labor") ... 15-25 74
(Quadraphonic.)
ABC/COMMAND (40018 "Dog Style") 15-25 74
(Quadraphonic.)
ABC/COMMAND (40019 "Coming Down Your Way") 15-25 75
(Quadraphonic.)
DUNHILL (50048 thru 50068) 10-15 68-69
DUNHILL (50078 "It Ain't Easy") 50-100 70
(Cover pictures nude people.)
DUNHILL (50078 "It Ain't Easy") 10-12 70
(Cover doesn't show nudes.)
DUNHILL (50088 thru 50158) 10-15 70-73
DUNHILL (50168 "Hard Labor") 15-20 74
(With baby delivery cover.)
DUNHILL (50168 "Hard Labor") 10-12 74
(With Band-Aid cover.)
DUNHILL (50178 "Joy to the World") 8-10 74
K-TEL 5-10
MCA 5-8 82
PASSPORT 5-8 83
PICKWICK 5-8 79
Members: Danny Hutton; Cory Wells; Chuck Negron; Mike Allsup; Jimmy Greenspoon; Joe Schermie; Floyd Sneed.
Also see HUTTON, Danny

THREE DONS & GINNY
(Three Dons & Ginny Greer)
Singles: 78 rpm
ALLIED (5000 "Tutti Frutti Baby") 10-15 53
Singles: 7-inch
ALLIED (5000 "Tutti Frutti Baby") 20-30 53
BLUE RIVER (205 "Tutti Frutti Baby") 5-10 63

THREE DOTS
Singles: 7-inch
BUZZ (104 "Tip Toe") 10-15 59
RICH (1003 "White Silver Sands") 5-10 60

THREE DOTS AND A DASH & BIG JAY MCNEELY & HIS ORCHESTRA
Singles: 78 rpm
IMPERIAL (5164 "I'll Never Love Again") 75-125 51
Singles: 7-inch
IMPERIAL (5164 "I'll Never Love Again") 500-750 51
Also see McNEELY, Big Jay

THREE EMOTIONS
Singles: 7-inch
FURY (1026 "The Night We Met") 30-40 59

THREE FLAMES P&R/R&B '47
Singles: 78 rpm
COLUMBIA 15-25 47-51
GOTHAM 15-25 46
HARMONY 10-20 49
MGM 10-20 50
LPs: 10/12-inch
MERCURY (20239 "At the Bon Soir") 25-50 57
Members: Tiger Haynes; Rill Pollard; Roy Testamark.
Also see BARNES, Mae

3 FRIENDS
Singles: 78 rpm
LIDO 20-40 56-57
Singles: 7-inch
BRUNSWICK (55032 "Jinx") 10-15 57
LIDO (500 "Blanche") 75-100 56
(Gray label. With straight horizontal lines.)
LIDO (500 "Blanche") .... 45-65 '50s
(Gray label. With wavy horizontal lines.)
LIDO (500 "Blanche") 30-50 57
(Blue label.)
LIDO (502 "Jinx") 15-25 57
LIDO (504 "Now That You're Gone") 15-25 57
RELIC (1021 "Blanche") 3-5 73
Members: Joey Villa; Frankie Starro; Tony Grochowski; Dom Bartolomeo; Joe Buono. Session: Mickey Baker.
Also see BAKER, Mickey
Also see EMANONS
Also see HEARTBEATS
Also see ILLUSIONS
Also see REARDON, Eddie

3 FRIENDS P&R '61
(Three Friends)
Singles: 7-inch
CAL-GOLD (169 "Blue Ribbon Baby") .. 100-200 61
IMPERIAL (5763 "Dedicated [To the Songs I Love]") 20-30 61
IMPERIAL (5773 "Go on to School") 10-15 61

THREE Gs P&R '58
Singles: 7-inch
COLUMBIA (Except 41175) 5-10 58-61
COLUMBIA (41175 "Let's Go Steady for the Summer") 10-20 58
Members: Jerry Glasser; Ted Glasser; Robert Glasser.

THREE GRACES
Singles: 7-inch
GOLDEN CREST 8-12 59-60

THREE GRACES / Wailers
EPs: 7-inch
GOLDEN CREST (88601/2 "Four Songs on 45 rpm") 75-125 60
(With paper sleeve-mailer. Both sides have label pictures.)
Also see THREE GRACES
Also see WAILERS

THREE HAIRCUTS
Singles: 78 rpm
RCA (6149 "Goin' Crazy") 5-10 55
Singles: 7-inch
RCA (6149 "Goin' Crazy") 10-15 55
Members: Sid Caesar; Carl Reiner; Howie Morris.

THREE HONEYDROPS
Singles: 7-inch
MUSIC CITY (813 "Honeydrops") 40-50 57
MUSIC CITY (814 "Rockin' Satellite") 40-50 57

THREE JAYS
Singles: 7-inch
RCA (6692 "Memory of You") 10-15 56
(Tribute to James Dean.)

THREE JOKERS
Singles: 7-inch
MERCURY (72345 "He's a Bum") 10-20 64

THREE KEYS
Singles: 78 rpm
BRUNSWICK 15-25 32-43
COLUMBIA 15-25 32
VOCALION 15-25 33-34

THREE KINGS & A QUEEN
LPs: 10/12-inch
SPIVEY .... 10-20 '60s
Members: Lonnie Johnson; Roosevelt Sykes; Big Joe Williams; Victoria Spivey.
Also see DYLAN, Bob
Also see JOHNSON, Lonnie
Also see SPIVEY, Victoria
Also see SYKES, Roosevelt
Also see WILLIAMS, Big Joe

THREE MAN ARMY
LPs: 10/12-inch
KAMA SUTRA (2044 "Third of a Lifetime") 12-15 71
(Pink label. Gatefold cover.)
KAMA SUTRA (2044 "Third of a Lifetime") 10-12 72
(Blue label. Standard cover.)
REPRISE 10-12 73-74
Members: Ginger Baker; Adrian Gurvitz; Paul Gurvitz.

THREE NOTES
(3 Notes)
Singles: 7-inch
HAMILTON (50008 "Honeymoon") 10-20 58
TALLY (116 "I've Been Thinking It Over") 15-25 58
TEE GEE (106 "Bertha, My Girl") 50-100 58

THREE OF US
Singles: 7-inch
KAPP (756 "One Golden Day") 10-15 66

THREE OF US
Singles: 7-inch
PAM (1000 "Big Sid") 50-75

THREE PEPPERS
Singles: 78 rpm
DECCA 15-25 39-47
GOTHAM 10-20 49
VARIETY 15-25 37
VOCALION 15-25 37

THREE PLAYMATES P&R '58
Singles: 7-inch
SAVOY (1528 "Sugah Wooga") 10-20 58
SAVOY (1537 "I Dreamed") 10-15 58

THREE RAMBLERS
Singles: 7-inch
OZARK (716 "Walkin' Talkin' Baby Doll") 50-100
Member: Jerald Boykin.

THREE RAYS
Singles: 78 rpm
CORAL (61370 "The Wallflower") 10-15 55
Singles: 7-inch
CORAL (61370 "The Wallflower") 15-25 55

THREE REASONS
(With the Highlanders)
Singles: 7-inch
CARNIVAL (551 "Go Right On") .... 8-12 '60s
JRE (224 "No Regrets") 15-25 62

THREE RIFFS
Singles: 78 rpm
APOLLO 15-25 50
ATLANTIC 15-25 48-49
DECCA 20-30 39
Members: Joe Seneca; Eddie Parton.
Also see THREE BARONS

THREE SHARPS & FLAT
(Three Sharps & the Flats)
Singles: 78 rpm
DECCA 15-25 39
HAMP-TONE 15-25 39
OKEH 15-25 40-41
TOWER 15-25 47

3 SOULS
Singles: 7-inch
ARGO (5313 "Night Theme") 10-20 58
ARGO (5369 "The Horse") 10-20 60
ARGO (5472 "Hi Heel Sneakers") 10-15 64
ARGO (5514 "You're No Good") 10-15 65
NOTE (10020 "Night Theme") 5-10 59
NOTE (10030 "Sinful") 5-10 60
LPs: 10/12-inch
ARGO 15-25 64-65
Member: Sonny Cox.

THREE SOUNDS
Singles: 7-inch
BLUE NOTE 5-10 58-64
LIMELIGHT (3059 "Justerini") 5-10 65
LIMELIGHT (3068 "Hot Cha") 5-10 65
LIMELIGHT (3075 "Downtown") 5-10 66
LPs: 10/12-inch
BLUE NOTE 15-25 59-64
LIMELIGHT 10-20 65
Members: Gene Harris; Bill Dowdy; Andrew Simpkins.

THREE STOOGES
Singles: 7-inch
COLPIX (120 "Have Rocket Will Travel") ... 8-12 59
LPs: 10/12-inch
CORAL (57289 "Nonsense Song Book") . 20-30 59
(Monaural.)
CORAL (757289 "Nonsense Song Book") 30-40 59
(Stereo.)
MCA (909 "Nonsense Song Book") 5-10 84
RHINO (808 "Madcap Musical Nonsense") 8-12 82
(Picture disc.)

THREE VALES
Singles: 7-inch
CINDY (3007 "Blue Lights") 100-200 57

THREETEENS
Singles: 7-inch
REV (3516 "Dear 53310761") 10-20 58
REV (3522 "X + Y = Z") 10-20 59
TODD (1021 "X + Y = Z") 5-10 59

THRESHOLD OF SOUNDS
Singles: 7-inch
NETTIE (101 "She's Mine") .... 15-25 '60s

THRILLERS
Singles: 78 rpm
BIG TOWN (109 "The Drunkard") 50-100 53
HERALD (432 "Lizabeth") 50-75 54
THRILLER (170 "The Drunkard") 150-200 53
(First issue.)
THRILLER (3530 "I'm Going to Live My Life Alone") 200-300 53
Singles: 7-inch
BIG TOWN (109 "The Drunkard") 250-350 53
HERALD (432 "Lizabeth") 100-150 54
(Original has block letters.)
Members: Bill Davis; Carl Stewart; Joe Murphy; John Dorsey.
Also see FIVE JETS
Also see FIVE STARS
Also see WILSON, Jimmy / Thrillers / Little Caesar

THUNDER, Johnny P&R '62
Singles: 7-inch
ABC 4-6 74
BELL 4-6 73
CALLA (161 "I'm Alive") 5-10 69
DIAMOND 5-15 62-68
EPIC (9329 "Ever You Man") 10-20 59
U.A. 4-6 70
Picture Sleeves
DIAMOND (132 "The Rosy Dance") 10-20 63
LPs: 10/12-inch
DIAMOND (D-5001 "Loop De Loop") 35-50 63
(Monaural.)
DIAMOND (SD-5001 "Loop De Loop") 50-75 63
(Stereo.)
REAL RECORDS 10-15
Also see ARCHIES / Johnny Thunder

THUNDER, Johnny, & Ruby Winters P&R/R&B '67
Singles: 7-inch
DIAMOND (218 "Make Love to Me") 5-10 67
DIAMOND (238 "Teach Me Tonight") 5-10 68
Also see THUNDER, Johnny
Also see WINTERS, Ruby

THUNDER & ROSES
Singles: 7-inch
U.A. (50536 "Country Life") 5-10 69
LPs: 10/12-inch
U.A. (6709 "King of the Black Sunrise") ... 15-25 69
Members: Chris Bond; Tom Schaffer.

THUNDER HEADS
Singles: 7-inch
CARTWHEEL (100 "Thunder Head") 20-25 66

THUNDER ROCKS
Singles: 7-inch
ROSELAWN (501 "What's the Word") .... 15-25 '60s
SABRE (100 "Warpath") 15-25 60
SABRE (104 "Oh My Linda") 50-75 60

THUNDERBIRDS
(With Art Harris & His Orchestra)
Singles: 78 rpm
DELUXE (6075 "Pledging My Love") 30-50 55
G.G. (518 "Love Is a Problem") 25-40 55
Singles: 7-inch
DELUXE (6075 "Pledging My Love") 100-150 55
G.G. (518 "Love Is a Problem") 50-100 55

THUNDERBIRDS

Singles: 78 rpm

HOLIDAY.......50-100 57

Singles: 7-inch

HOLIDAY (2609 "In My Thunderbird"). 100-150 57
(Glossy red label.)
HOLIDAY (2609 "In My Thunderbird")..... 15-25 '60s
(Flat red label.)

THUNDERBIRDS

Singles: 7-inch

BUFFALO ("Flying Saucers").............. 200-400 59
(No selection number used. Only promo copies made.)

THUNDERBIRDS

Singles: 7-inch

DELTA.......5-10 62
MELBOURNE (1499 "Wild Weekend").......5-10 63
UNITED SOUTHERN ARTISTS (115 "T-Bird Rock")....... 10-15 62

LPs: 10/12-inch

RED FEATHER (1 "Meet the Fabulous Thunderbirds")....... 150-200 64

THUNDERBIRDS

Singles: 7-inch

CORTLAND (51 "Steel")....... 10-20 64
DELAWARE (1706 "Take a Look at Me")....... 10-20 65
DELAWARE (1710 "Is It Wrong")....... 10-20 66
IVANHOE (50000 "Cindy, Oh Cindy")...... 10-20
ERMINE (51 "Stalking the Thunderbird"). 20-30 63
ERMINE (54 "Simmering")....... 20-30 64
ERMINE (56 "Crater Soda")....... 20-30 64

THUNDERBOLTS
(Thunder Bolts)

Singles: 7-inch

RONDACK (7546 "Thunder Head")......... 15-25 60
RONDACK (9768 "I'm Sorry")....... 15-25 61

Picture Sleeves

RONDACK (9768 "I'm Sorry")....... 25-50 61

THUNDERKLOUD, Billy, & Chieftones *C&W/P&R '75*

Singles: 7-inch

POLYDOR.......3-5 76-78
STABLE.......4-6 75
SUPERIOR.......4-6 74
20TH FOX.......4-6 74-75
YOUNGSTOWN.......8-12 68

LPs: 10/12-inch

SUPERIOR.......8-12 74
20TH FOX.......6-12 74-75
Members: Jack Wolf; Barry Littlestar; Richard Grayowl.
Also see CHIEFTONES

THUNDERMEN
(Al & Gerry Jay & Thundermen)

Singles: 7-inch

CUCA (6372 "Night Train")....... 10-15 63
SOMA (1194 "Flyin' High").......5-10 62
THUNDERMEN.......3-5 82-89

LPs:10/12-inch

THUNDERMEN.......5-10 82-86
Members: Rick Hoehn; Al Fremstad; Rick Gerry Johnson; Mickey Lynnes; Mike Marx; Chuck Solberg.

THUNDERMEN

Singles: 7-inch

KISKI (2066 "Thunderbeat")....... 10-15 63

THUNDERPUSSY

LPs: 10/12-inch

MRT (31748 "Documents of Captivity")....... 100-150 73
Members: Steven Jay Morris; Ben Russell; George Tutko.

THUNDERTONES

Singles: 7-inch

DOT (16137 "Jungle Fever")....... 15-25 60
Member: Lenny Drake.
Also see BROWN, Doug
Also see LENNY & THUNDERTONES

THUNDERTONES

Singles: 7-inch

DONNA (1343 "Thunder Rhythm")......... 15-25 61

THUNDERTONES

LPs: 10/12-inch

AURORA (920 "Cloudburst")....... 75-125 '60s

THUNDERTREE

LPs: 10/12-inch

ROULETTE (42038 "Thundertree")..........30-50 70
Members: Bill Hallquist; Rick Liabraaten; John Miesen; Terry Tilley; Devin Wallin.

THURMAN, Jimmy, & Cavaliers

Singles: 7-inch

SPARKETTE (1006 "Pretty Baby")..........40-60 59

THURMOND, Duff

Singles: 7-inch

NEW VOICE (816 "Now That You Left Me").......10-20 66

THURSDAY'S CHILDREN

Singles: 7-inch

INT'L ARTISTS (110 "Air Conditioned Man").......40-60 66
INT'L ARTISTS (115 "Help, Murder, Police").......40-60 67
KIDD (1334 "You'll Never Be My Girl").....30-50 66
PARADISE (1022 "You'll Never Be My Girl").......20-30 66

THYME

Singles: 7-inch

A^2 (201 "Somehow").......25-40 '60s
A^2 (202 "Time of the Season").......25-40 '60s
BANG (546 "Love to Love").......10-20 67

TIARAS

Singles: 7-inch

3D (378 "Mr. Wise Guy").......30-40 58

TIARAS

Singles: 7-inch

VALIANT (6027 "You Told Me").......8-12 63
VALIANT (6030 "Don't Believe a Word")....8-12 63
Member: Don Cole.
Also see COLE, Don

TIARAS

Singles: 7-inch

ALLIANCE (1934 "Mexican Rock")............5-10 64
Also see DALLAS, Jackie

TIARAS

Singles: 7-inch

DORE (783 "Wild Times").......10-20 67
RUFF (1019 "Southern Love").......10-20 66

TIATT, Lynn, & Comets

Singles: 7-inch

PUSSY CAT (1 "Dad Is Home")....... 1200-1500

TIBBS, Andrew *R&B '49*
(With the Dozier Boys)

Singles: 78 rpm

ARISTOCRAT.......15-25 47-49
PEACOCK.......10-20 52

Singles: 7-inch

M-PAC (7228 "I Made a Mistake").............5-10 66
PEACOCK (1597 "Mother's Letter") 25-35 52
Also see DOZIER BOYS
Also see TIBBS BROTHERS

TIBBS, Kenny
(With the Jokers; Kenneth Tibbs)

Singles: 7-inch

FEDERAL (12335 "Darling I Want Your Love").......15-25 58
VIKING (1009 "I'm Still Alone")................10-15 60
Also see TIBBS BROTHERS

TIBBS BROTHERS

Singles: 78 rpm

ATCO (6074 "I'm Going Crazy")..............10-20 56

Singles: 7-inch

ATCO (6074 "I'm Going Crazy")..............25-50 56
Members: Andrew Tibbs; Kenneth Tibbs.
Also see TIBBS, Andrew
Also see TIBBS, Kenny

TIBOR BROTHERS *C&W '76*

Singles: 7-inch

ARIOLA AMERICA.......4-6 76
JOMAR.......4-6 74

LPs: 10/12-inch

JOMAR (10830 "Rock & Roll Gold")........10-20 74
(Two discs.)
Members: Larry; Kurt; Harvey; Francis; Gerard.
Also see MAVERICKS

TIC TOCS
("Featuring Johnny Williams")

Singles: 78 rpm

BACK BEAT.......10-20 57

Singles: 7-inch

BACK BEAT (502 "Zola").......15-25 57
RUSH (1042 "True By You").......10-15 62

TICKER TAPES

Singles: 7-inch

GO GO (103 "Her Own Imagination").......10-20 67

TICKLERS

Singles: 7-inch

MUSTANG (3007 "Millie the Ghoul").........5-10 65

TICO & TRIUMPHS *P&R '62*
(Featuring Paul Simon)

Singles: 7-inch

AMY (835 "Motorcycle").......50-75 61
AMY (845 "Wild Flower").......30-40 62
AMY (860 "Cry Little Boy").......40-50 62
AMY (876 "Cards of Love").......75-100 62
JASON SCOTT (14 "Cards of Love")...........3-5 81
(500 made.)
MADISON (169 "Motorcycle")..............100-200 61
(First issue.)
Also see SIMON, Paul

TIDAL WAVES

Singles: 7-inch

HBR (482 "Farmer John").......8-12 66
HBR (501 "Big Boy Pete").......8-12 66
HBR (515 "Action").......8-12 67
PLYMOUTH (2968 "Little Boy Sad").........15-20 67
RIGHT (6607 "Farmer John").......15-25 66
SVR (1007 "Farmer John").......15-25 66
(We're not sure which of the above two came first, but both probably preceded the HBR.)
STRAFFORD (6503 "You Name It").........15-25 65

TIDE

Singles: 7-inch

MOUTH (513 "Cowboy Song").......5-10 71
MOUTH (875 "I'm in a Dancing Mood")......5-10 72

LPs: 10/12-inch

MOUTH (7237 "Almost Live").......30-45 71

TIDES
(With the Merry Melody Singers; with the Jerry Kennedy Orchestra)

Singles: 7-inch

DORE.......15-30 59-61
MERCURY.......5-10 62

LPs: 10/12-inch

MERCURY.......20-25 62-63
WING (12265 "Surf City/Surfin' USA and Other Surfin' Favorites").......40-60 63
(Monaural.)
WING (16265 "Surf City/Surfin' USA and Other Surfin' Favorites").......50-75 63
(Stereo.)
Also see KENNEDY, Jerry

TIDES

Singles: 7-inch

WARWICK (653 "Stranger").......10-15 61

TIDES

Singles: 7-inch

620 (1007 "Bring It on Home").......25-35 64
Member: Willie Sullivan.
Also see UNIQUES

TIDE'S IN

Singles: 7-inch

SANFRIS (18 "Trip with Me").......20-30 67

TIDWELL, Billy

Singles: 7-inch

KO CO BO (1009 "Folsom Prison Blues").......50-75

TIDWELL, Bobby

Singles: 7-inch

SKIPPY (108 "Cherokee Stomp")............40-60 59

TIDWELL, Harold

Singles: 7-inch

CJ (605 "Sweet Suzie").......15-25 59

TIEKEN, Freddie, & Rockers

Singles: 7-inch

IT (2302 "Humpty Jump").......10-20 57

LPs: 10/12-inch

IT (2301 "By Popular Demand")..............30-50 57
IT (2304 "Live").......30-50 58
Also see GIPSON, Wild Child
Also see GONN
Also see ILMO SMOKEHOUSE

TIENO, Al

Singles: 7-inch

RUST (5033 "Getting Nowhere with My Baby").......15-25 61

TIFANOS

Singles: 7-inch

TIFCO (822 "It's Raining").......30-40 60
(Label name takes up about half the top portion of the label—between hole and edge of disc.)
TIFCO (822 "It's Raining").......10-20 60
(Label name takes up about 2/3 the top portion of the label—between hole and edge of disc.)

TIFFANY SHADE

Singles: 7-inch

MAINSTREAM.......8-12 68

LPs: 10/12-inch

MAINSTREAM (6105 "Tiffany Shade")....20-30 68
Members: Michael Barnes; Bob Leonard.

TIFFANY SYSTEM

Singles: 7-inch

MINARET (128 "Let's Get Together")...... 10-15 '60s
Members: Scott Boyer; Dave Brown.
Also see 31ST of FEBRUARY

TIFFANYS
(Tiffany's)

Singles: 7-inch

ROCKIN-ROBIN (1 "I've Got a Girl")....400-600 63

TIFFANYS

Singles: 7-inch

SWAN (4104 "The Pleasure of Love")..... 15-25 62
Also see TEDDY & TWILIGHTS

TIFFANYS

Singles: 7-inch

ATLANTIC (2240 "Please Tell Me")..........5-10 64
MRS (777 "Please Tell Me").......20-30 64

TIFFANYS
(Tiffanies)

Singles: 7-inch

ARCTIC (101 "Love Me").......10-20 64
JOSIE.......5-15 65-66
KR (120 "He's Good for Me").......10-20 67
RKO.......5-10 '60s

TIG, Jimmy
(With the Rounders; with Louise & Co.)

Singles: 7-inch

BELL (708 "Who Can I Turn To")..........5-10 68
SPAR (779 "Small Town Girl").......40-50
(First released as by the Rounders.)
Also see ROUNDERS

TIGERMEN

Singles: 7-inch

BUFF (1005 "Close That Door")............15-25 65
BUFF (1006 "Tiger Girl").......15-25 65

TIGERS

Singles: 7-inch

COLPIX (773 "GeeTO Tiger"/"The Prowl").......15-20 65
COLPIX (773 "GeeTO Tiger"/"Big Sounds of the GeeTO Tiger").......20-25 65
(Promotional issue only.)

Picture Sleeves

COLPIX (773 "GeeTO Tiger"/"The Prowl").......20-30 65
COLPIX (773 "GeeTO Tiger"/"Big Sounds of the GeeTO Tiger").......30-40 65
(Promotional issue only.)
Members: Barry Hockenberger; Neal Moser; Jerry Cervenka; Enzo Piazza; John Anderson.

TIGERS

Singles: 7-inch

SUMTHIN' ELSE (3929 "I See the Light").......15-25 65
Also see PEIL, Danny

TIGERS

Singles: 7-inch

ZIMBY (301 "There She Goes").......8-12 '60s

TIGRE, Terry
Singles: 7-inch
GUSTO-STARDAY ... 4-8 77-78
LPs: 10/12-inch
GUSTO-STARDAY ... 10-15 77
Session: Scotty Moore; D.J. Fontana; Bob Moore; Jordanaires.
Also see JORDANAIRES
Also see MOORE, Bob
Also see MOORE, Scotty

TIGRO, Al
(With the Tigers)
Singles: 7-inch
CUPPY (112 "Yvonne") ... 75-100

TIJUANA BEATLES
LPs: 10/12-inch
ALSHIRE ... 10-15 69

TIKIES
Singles: 7-inch
WRIGHT SOUND (0001 "Steam") ... 40-60 62

TIKIS
Singles: 7-inch
FUJIMO (6139 "Show You Love") ... 15-25 66

TIKIS
Singles: 7-inch
ASCOT (2186 "Stop-Look-Listen") ... 5-10 65
ASCOT (2204 "Whole Lotta Soul") ... 5-10 66
DIAL ... 5-10 66
MINARET (115 "One More Chance") ... 5-10 63
MINARET (116 "Popsicle") ... 5-10 64
W.B. ... 5-10 66
Also see OTHER TIKIS
Also see WADE, Len

TIKIS
Singles: 7-inch
SARA (6641 "We're on the Move") ... 15-25 66
Members: Hugh Pearl; Bill Sherek.
Also see TALISMEN

TIKIS & FABULONS
Singles: 7-inch
PANORAMA (13 "Take a Look") ... 8-12 65
REX ... 8-12 '60s
TOWER (181 "Take a Look") ... 5-10 65
Members (Tikis): Dale Colama; Ollie Smith. (Fabulons): Ron Ferrante; Mike Roholt; Terry McKinley; John Chassaign; John Goldman; Dan Shillings; John Duval; Jim Wilson; Gary Welk; Bill Higginbotham.

TIL, Sonny
(With Buddy Lucas Orchestra; with Sid Bass Orchestra; Sonny Till)
Singles: 78 rpm
JUBILEE ... 50-75 52-53
Singles: 7-inch
CLOWN (3061 "I Gave It All Up") ... 5-10 '60s
HARLEM SOUND (1001 "Lonely Christmas") ... 5-10
JUBILEE (5066 "For All We Know") ... 150-200 52
(Black vinyl.)
JUBILEE (5066 "For All We Know") ... 500-650 52
(Red vinyl.)
JUBILEE (5076 "Proud of You") ... 150-200 52
JUBILEE (5112 "Have You Heard") ... 150-200 52
(Black vinyl.)
JUBILEE (5112 "Have You Heard") ... 500-650 52
(Red vinyl.)
JUBILEE (5118 "Congratulations to Someone") ... 100-200 53
RCA ... 5-10 69-72
ROULETTE (4079 "Shy") ... 15-25 58
LPs: 10/12-inch
DOBRE ... 5-10 78
RCA ... 10-20 70-71
Also see McGRIFF, Edna, & Sonny Til
Also see ORIOLES

TILGHMAN, Dick
Singles: 7-inch
ELSAN (1006 "You Cheated On Me") ... 60-80

TILL, Johnny
Singles: 7-inch
SAN LEON (500 "Dreamy Eyes") ... 100-150 '50s

TILL, Sonny / Sonny & Virgil
Singles: 7-inch
DADE (5002 "Someone Up and Told Me") ... 10-20
Also see TIL, Sonny

TILLERY, Linda, & Loading Zone
Singles: 7-inch
RCA (9620 "No More Tears") ... 5-10 68
Also see LOADING ZONE

TILLIS, Big Son, & D.C. Bender
Singles: 78 rpm
ELKO (821 "Rocks Is My Pillow") ... 50-100 53
ELKO (822 "When I Get in This House, Woman") ... 50-100 53
ELKO (823 "Dayton Stomp") ... 50-100 53

TILLIS, Clyde
(Clyde "Thin Man" Tillis; with Harmony Kings)
Singles: 7-inch
CASH (1045 "It Makes No Difference") ... 75-100 56
CASH (1054 "It Makes No Difference") ... 50-75 57
CASH (1064 "It Makes No Difference") ... 30-40 58
MILMART (112 "You Can Do What You Wanta Do") ... 30-40 59
Session: Bo Rhambo Combo.
Also see RHAMBO, Bo

TILLIS, Mel C&W '58
(With the Statesiders; with Sue York)
Singles: 78 rpm
COLUMBIA (40944 "Juke Box Man") ... 10-20 57
COLUMBIA (41000 series except 41026) ... 8-12 57
COLUMBIA (41026 "Hearts of Stone") ... 15-25 57
Singles: 7-inch
COLUMBIA (40845 "It Takes a Worried Man to Sing a Worried Song") ... 10-20 57
COLUMBIA (40904 "Case of the Blues") ... 10-20 57
COLUMBIA (40944 "Juke Box Man") ... 10-20 57
COLUMBIA (41026 "Hearts of Stone") ... 15-25 57
COLUMBIA (41115 "Teen Age Wedding") ... 15-25 58
COLUMBIA (41189 thru 41863) ... 10-20 58-61
COLUMBIA (3-41986 "Hearts of Stone") ... 20-30 61
(Compact 33 Single.)
COLUMBIA (4-41986 "Hearts of Stone") ... 10-15 61
COLUMBIA (4-42262 "Party Girl") ... 10-15 62
ELEKTRA ... 3-6 79-82
GUSTO ... 3-5 '80s
KAPP ... 5-8 65-71
MCA ... 3-6 73-84
MGM ... 4-8 70-76
RCA ... 3-5 85-86
RADIO ... 3-5 89
RIC ... 5-10 65
LPs: 10/12-inch
COLUMBIA (1724 "Heart Over Mind") ... 15-25 62
(Monaural.)
COLUMBIA (1724 "Heart Over Mind") ... 25-35 62
(Stereo.)
COLUMBIA (30253 "Heart Over Mind") ... 8-12 70
CORAL ... 5-10 73
ELEKTRA ... 5-10 79-83
GUSTO ... 5-8 '80s
HARMONY ... 10-20 66-72
KAPP ... 10-20 66-71
MCA ... 5-12 73-84
MGM ... 5-12 70-78
PICKWICK ... 5-10 73
POWER PAK ... 5-8
STARDAY ... 8-10 72
TEE VEE ... 8-10 '70s
VOCALION ... 5-10 70-72
Also see FELTS, Narvel / Red Sovine / Mel Tillis
Also see PIERCE, Webb, & Mel Tillis
Also see WILLS, Bob, & Mel Tillis

TILLIS, Mel, & Sherry Bryce C&W '71
Singles: 7-inch
MGM ... 4-6 71-75
LPs: 10/12-inch
MGM ... 6-12 71-74

TILLIS, Mel, & Glen Campbell C&W '84
Singles: 7-inch
MCA ... 3-5 84
Also see CAMPBELL, Glen

TILLIS, Mel, & Bill Phillips C&W '59
Singles: 7-inch
COLUMBIA ... 10-15 59-60
Also see PHILLIPS, Bill

TILLIS, Mel, & Nancy Sinatra C&W '81
Singles: 7-inch
ELEKTRA ... 3-5 81
LPs: 10/12-inch
ELEKTRA ... 5-10 81
Also see SINATRA, Nancy
Also see TILLIS, Mel

TILLISON, Roger
Singles: 7-inch
ATCO (6831 "Old Cracked Looking Glass") ... 4-8 71
WORLD PACIFIC (77856 "Nobody's Lover") ... 5-10 66
Also see LEATHERCOATED MINDS

TILLMAN, Art
Singles: 7-inch
TNT (166 "I'm a King") ... 10-15 59

TILLMAN, Bertha P&R '62
Singles: 7-inch
BRENT (7029 "Oh My Angel") ... 15-20 62
BRENT (7032 "I Wish") ... 20-25 62
JOCKO (599 "What Am I Trying to Prove") ... 10-15 '60s

TILLMAN, Charlotta
Singles: 7-inch
JOSIE (953 "Baby, I'm Serious") ... 10-15 66

TILLMAN, Lee
Singles: 7-inch
MONTEL (953 "Kiss Tomorrow Goodbye") ... 5-10 66
RON (341 "Will Travel") ... 10-15 61
SONORA (211 "Here I Go Again") ... 75-125 66

TILLMAN, Mickey
Singles: 7-inch
VEE-JAY (296 "Dear Mom and Dad") ... 15-25 58
Session: Sheppards.

TILLOTSON, Johnny P&R '58
Singles: 7-inch
AMOS ... 4-6 69-70
ATLANTIC (87978 "Bim Bam Boom") ... 5-10 90
BARNABY ... 4-6 76
BUDDAH ... 4-8 71-73
CADENCE (1300 series) ... 15-20 58-60
CADENCE (1400 series) ... 10-15 61-63
COLUMBIA ... 4-6 73-75
ERIC ... 4-6 '70s
MGM ... 5-10 63-68
REWARD ... 3-5 82-84
ROWE/AMI ... 5-10 66
("Play Me" Sales Stimulator promotional issue.)
U.A. ... 4-6 76-77
Picture Sleeves
CADENCE (1377 "Earth Angel") ... 15-25 60
CADENCE (1391 "Jimmy's Girl") ... 15-25 60
MGM ... 6-12 63-66
EPs: 7-inch
CADENCE (114 "Dreamy Eyes") ... 25-35 60
CADENCE (33-1 "This Is Johnny Tillotson") ... 15-25 61
("Cadence Little LP." With cardboard insert in clear cover.)
CADENCE (33-2 "Music by Johnny Tillotson") ... 15-25 61
("Cadence Little LP." With cardboard insert in clear cover.)
LPs: 10/12-inch
ACCORD (7194 "Scrapbook") ... 5-10 82
AMOS (7006 "Tears on My Pillow") ... 10-15 69
BACK-TRAC ... 5-8 85
BARNABY (4007 "Greatest") ... 8-10 77
BUCKBOARD ... 5-10 '80s
BUDDAH (5112 "Johnny Tillotson") ... 10-15 72
CADENCE (3052 "Johnny Tillotson's Best") ... 35-45 61
(Monaural.)
CADENCE (3058 "It Keeps Right On a-Hurtin' ") ... 30-40 62
(Monaural.)
CADENCE (3067 "You Can Never Stop Me Loving You") ... 30-40 63
(Monaural.)
CADENCE (25052 "Johnny Tillotson's Best") ... 40-60 61
(Stereo.)
CADENCE (25058 "It Keeps Right On a-Hurtin' ") ... 35-45 62
(Stereo.)
CADENCE (25067 "You Can Never Stop Me Loving You") ... 35-45 63
(Stereo.)
EVEREST (4113 "Greatest Hits") ... 5-8 82
METRO (561 "Sings Tillotson") ... 10-20 66
MGM ... 12-25 64-71
U.A. ... 8-10 77
Session: Boots Randolph.
Also see GENEVIEVE
Also see RANDOLPH, Boots

TILLOTSON, Johnny / J.D. Souther
Singles: 7-inch
BUDDAH ... 4-6 71
Also see TILLOTSON, Johnny

TILTON, Muriel
Singles: 7-inch
BERTRAM INT'L (224 "Bird Dog") ... 15-20 63
Also see TILTON SISTERS

TILTON SISTERS
Singles: 7-inch
BERTRAM INT'L (214 "Why Won't He Call Me") ... 15-20 59
BERTRAM INT'L (217 "He Knows") ... 15-20 60
BERTRAM INT'L (220 "Yellow Bird") ... 15-20 61
DOT (15939 "Why Why Why") ... 25-35 59
Members: Sheila; Gwen; Muriel.
Also see TILTON, Muriel

TILTON SISTERS & LAWRENCE BROTHERS COMBO
Singles: 7-inch
BERTRAM INT'L (211 "Why Why Why") ... 10-20 58
Also see LAWRENCE BROTHERS COMBO
Also see TILTON SISTERS

TIM
(Tim Smith)
Singles: 7-inch
CELTEX (102 "My Side of the Track") ... 10-20

TIM DAWE
LPs: 10/12-inch
STRAIGHT ... 10-15 69

TIM TAM & TURN-ONS P&R '66
Singles: 7-inch
PALMER (5002 "Wait a Minute") ... 15-25 65
PALMER (5003 "Cheryl Ann") ... 10-15 66
PALMER (5006 "Kimberly") ... 15-25 66
PALMER (5014 "Don't Say Hi") ... 10-15 67
Members: Rick Wiesend; Dan Wiesend; John Ogen; Don Gunderson; Earl Rennie; Nick Butsicaris.

TIMBERLAND FOUR
Singles: 7-inch
JAMIE (1236 "Hummingbird") ... 10-15 62
Members: Robert Gunerare; Fred Gunerare; Steve Young; Charles Peterson; Ronald Stoddard.

TIMBERLANES
Singles: 7-inch
DRAGON (101 "Sweet Dreams Sweetheart") ... 10-20

TIMBERLINE
LPs: 10/12-inch
EPIC (34681 "Timberline") ... 8-12 77
(Black vinyl.)
EPIC (34681 "Timberline") ... 10-15 77
(Colored vinyl.)

TIMBERS
Singles: 7-inch
CUPID (1002 "Stop Crying") ... 10-20 60
TEE GEE (101 "Stop Crying") ... 40-50 58

TIME OF YOUR LIFE
Singles: 7-inch
IONIC (101 "Ode to a Bad Dream") ... 20-30 67

TIME PIECE
Singles: 7-inch
GREAT NORTHERN (1001 "Can't Be So Bad") ... 15-25 '60s

TIMERS
Singles: 7-inch
REPRISE (231 "Competition Coupe") ... 50-75 63
Members: Gary Usher; Brian Wilson; Chuck Girard.
Also see USHER, Gary
Also see WILSON, Brian

TIMESTOPPERS
Singles: 7-inch
HBR (516 "I Need Love") ... 10-20 67

TIMETAKERS
Singles: 7-inch
AUDIO DYNAMICS (190 "At Least I'll Try") ... 10-20 67

TIMETONES P&R '61
(Time Tones)
Singles: 7-inch
ATCO (6201 "I've Got a Feeling") ... 15-25 61
GREENE STONE ... 4-8
LOST NITE (406 "I've Got a Feeling") ... 4-8
RELIC ... 5-10 65-66
TIMES SQUARE (26 "Sunday Kind of Love") ... 25-35 64
TIMES SQUARE (34 "House Where Lovers Dream") ... 40-60 64
TIMES SQUARE (421 "Here in My Heart") ... 50-75 61
TIMES SQUARE (421 "In My Heart") ... 20-30 61
(Note shortened title.)
Member: Slim Rose.
Also see SLIM FROM TIMES

TIMMONS, Terry
Singles: 78 rpm
UNITED (161 "My Last Cry") ... 5-10 53
Singles: 7-inch
UNITED (161 "My Last Cry") ... 15-20 53

TIMMY & PERSIANETTES
Singles: 7-inch
OLYMPIA (100 "Timmy Boy") ... 10-15 63
OLYMPIA (101 "Summertime Is Near") ... 10-15 63
Member: Timmy Carr.
Also see CARR, Timmy, & Persianettes
Also see PERSIANETTES

TIMOTHY
Singles: 7-inch
TEE PEE (200/201 "What Good Will Crying Do Me Now"/"Live Once") ... 10-15 69

TINA LOUISE
Singles: 7-inch
U.A. (127 "I'll Be Yours") ... 10-15 58
Picture Sleeves
U.A. (127 "I'll Be Yours") ... 25-35 58
Also see LIGHT, Enoch, & His Orchestra

TINDLEY, George R&B '69
(With the Modern Red Caps; George Tinley)
Singles: 7-inch
DOO-WOP ... 4-8
EMBER (1060 "Wedding Bells") ... 15-25 60
HERALD (558 "Close Your Eyes") ... 10-15 61
ROWAX (801 "They Can Dream") ... 10-15 63
PARKWAY (834 "Fairy Tales") ... 8-12 62
SMASH (1768 "I Couldn't Care Less") ... 8-12 62
WAND ... 5-10 69-70
Also see DREAMS
Also see ESQUIRE, Kenny, & Starlites
Also see MODERN RED CAPS

TINGLING MOTHERS' CIRCUS
Singles: 7-inch
MUSICOR (1335 "Positively Negative") ... 8-12 68
ROULETTE (4758 "Face in My Mind") ... 10-15 67
LPs: 10/12-inch
MUSICOR (3167 "Circus of the Mind") ... 15-25 68

TINO
(Tino & Revlons)
Singles: 7-inch
DEARBORN (525 "Rave On") ... 10-20 65
DEARBORN (530 "I'm Coming Home") ... 10-20 65
DEARBORN (540 "Lotta Lovin'") ... 10-20 66
MARK (154 "Story of Our Love") ... 50-75 60
MAY (103 "Rave On") ... 40-60 61
PIP (4000 "Wedding Bells Will Ring") ... 15-25 63
LPs: 10/12-inch
DEARBORN (1004 "By Request at the Sway-Zee") ... 100-200 66

TINO, Babs
Singles: 7-inch
CAMEO (114 "My Honeybun") ... 10-20 57
KAPP (388 "If Only for Tonight") ... 8-12 61
KAPP (458 "Too Late to Worry") ... 8-12 62
KAPP (472 "Forgive Me") ... 8-12 62
KAPP (498 "Call Off the Wedding") ... 8-12 62
KAPP (517 "My First Love") ... 8-12 63
KAPP (561 "Dr. Jekyll or Mr. Hyde") ... 10-15 63

TINO, Freddie, & Twisting Cyclones
Singles: 7-inch
RIC (988 "Shoestring Twist") ... 10-20 62

TINO, Johnny
Singles: 7-inch
CROSBY (16 "I Want Some Lovin'") ... 50-75

TINO, Val
(With Herb Buchanan & Orchestra)
Singles: 7-inch
SURE (120 "Loving Tree") ... 10-20

TINORY, Rick
Singles: 7-inch
AMY (856 "Toy Man") ... 8-12 62
FEDERAL (12323 "Cha Cha Sue") ... 15-20 58
SEQUEL (1001 "Claire Lorraine") ... 10-15 61
VENTURE (6003 "Poor Chimp") ... 8-12

TINSLEY, Slim
Singles: 78 rpm
RECORDED IN HOLLYWOOD (167 "Big Shot Mama") ... 10-20 51

TINSON, Paul
Singles: 7-inch
FEDERAL (12418 "Crazy Sadie") ... 50-75 61

TINY CHEROKEE
LPs: 10/12-inch
UA (1009 "The Happy Hour Presents Live – Tiny Cherokee") ... 8-12 '60s

TINY JOE
Singles: 7-inch
DANBAR (223 "Evil Woman Blues") ... 8-12 63

TINY & TIM
Singles: 7-inch
OKEH (7105 "Bo-a-Diddy Do") ... 15-25 58

TINY TIM
(With the Tornados)
Singles: 7-inch
DELUXE (6184 "Face to Face") ... 15-25 59
TEEN'S CHOICE (8 "My One Desire") ... 300-400 60

TINY TIM P&R/LP '68
(Herbert Khaury; with Miss Vicki)
Singles: 7-inch
BLUE CAT (127 "Little Girl") ... 8-12 65
CLOUDS ... 4-6 79
NLT ... 3-5 88
REPRISE ... 5-10 68-71
SCEPTER ... 4-8 72
VIC TIM ... 4-8 71
LPs: 10/12-inch
BOUQUET ... 10-12
REPRISE ... 10-20 68

TINY TIM / Michelle Ramos / Bruce Haack
LPs: 10/12-inch
RA-JO INT'L ... 5-8 86
Also see TINY TIM

TINY TIM & HITS
Singles: 7-inch
ROULETTE (4123 "Wedding Bells") ... 30-40 58

TINY TIM & TORNADOES
Singles: 7-inch
TEEN'S CHOICE (8 "I've Gotta Find Someone") ... 100-200 57

TINY TIP & TIP-TOPS
("Tiny Tip [14 yrs. Old]")
Singles: 7-inch
CHESS (1822 "Matrimony") ... 10-15 62
SCARLET (4129 "I Said a Prayer") ... 100-200 60
(Number 1002 also shown on label.)

TINY TONY & STATICS
Singles: 7-inch
BOLO (734 "I Wanna Hold Your Hand") ... 10-20 62
Members: "Tiny" Tony Smith; Merrilee Rush.
Also see GALLAHADS
Also see RUSH, Merrilee
Also see STATICS

TINY TOPSY
Singles: 7-inch
ARGO (5383 "How You Changed") ... 10-15 61
FEDERAL (12302 "Miss You So") ... 20-30 57
FEDERAL (12309 "Come On, Come On") ... 20-30 57
FEDERAL (12315 "Waterproof Eyes") ... 20-30 57
FEDERAL (12357 "Just a Little Bit") ... 10-15 59
Session: Charms.
Also see CHARMS

TIP TOES
Singles: 7-inch
KAPP (726 "Rama Lama") ... 10-20 65

TIP TOP BAND
Singles: 7-inch
TIP TOP (725 "Doctor & the Monks") ... 15-20 59

TIP TOPS
Singles: 7-inch
PARKWAY (868 "He's Braggin'") ... 5-10 63
Also see BLACKMAN, Hank / Tip Tops

TIP TOPS
Singles: 7-inch
ROULETTE (4684 "A Little Bit More") ... 10-15 66

TIPPIE & CLOVERMEN
Singles: 7-inch
STENTON (7001 "Please Mr. Sun") ... 25-35 62
Member: Roosevelt "Tippie" Hubbard.
Also see CLOVERS

TIPPIE & CLOVERS
Singles: 7-inch
TIGER (201 "Bossa Nova, Baby") ... 30-50 62
Member: Roosevelt "Tippie" Hubbard.
Also see CLOVERS
Also see TIPPIE & CLOVERMEN

TIPS
Singles: 7-inch
AHP (15568 "If I Say") ... 200-300 68
(Blue vinyl. Reportedly 50 made.)

TIRCUIT, Billy
Singles: 7-inch
BONATEMP (802 "I Was a Fool") ... 10-20
PONTCHARTRAIN (400 "Face the Facts") ... 50-75

TISDOM, James
Singles: 78 rpm
UNIVERSAL-FOX (100 "Model-T Boogie") ... 75-125 48
UNIVERSAL-FOX (101 "Throw This Dog a Bone") ... 75-125 48
UNIVERSAL-FOX (102 "I Feel So Bad") ... 75-125 48

TITANS
Singles: 78 rpm
SPECIALTY (614 "Sweet Peach") ... 20-30 57
SPECIALTY (625 "Don't You Just Know It") ... 25-50 58
SPECIALTY (632 "Arlene") ... 50-100 58
VITA (148 "So Hard to Laugh") ... 60-80 57
VITA (158 "Look What You're Doing Baby") ... 40-60 57
Singles: 7-inch
CLASS (244 "No Time") ... 15-25 59
FIDELITY (3016 "What Have I Done") ... 30-40 60
SPECIALTY (614 "Sweet Peach") ... 20-30 57
SPECIALTY (625 "Don't You Just Know It") ... 20-30 58
SPECIALTY (632 "Arlene") ... 25-35 58
VITA (148 "So Hard to Laugh") ... 75-100 57
VITA (158 "Look What You're Doing Baby") ... 40-50 57
Also see DON & DEWEY

TITANS
Singles: 7-inch
NOLTA (351 "A-Rab") ... 10-20 61

TITANS
LPs: 10/12-inch
MGM (3992 "Today's Teen Beat") ... 15-25 61
Also see DAVIS, Danny
Also see TOKYO BOYS / Titans

TITANS
(Titens)
Singles: 7-inch
BANGAR (611 "Motivation") ... 20-25 64
DUFFS (111 "Little Girl") ... 8-12 67
DUFFS (112 "Ode to Billy Martin") ... 8-12 67
METROBEAT (4452 "Mountain of Love") 15-20 67
SOMA (1402 "Summer Place") ... 10-20 63
SOMA (1411 "Noplace Special") ... 10-20 64
SOUND OF MUSIC (12186 "Fun Seekers") ... 8-12 67
STUDIO CITY (1008 "Noplace Special") .. 15-25 63
Picture Sleeves
SOUND OF MUSIC (12186 "Fun Seekers") ... 40-60 67
Member: Rick Colburn.
Also see ALLEN, Dale, & Rebel Rousers

TITO & SILHOUETTES
Singles: 7-inch
RIVAL (03 "Baby Doll") ... 50-75 '50s

TITONES
Singles: 7-inch
SCEPTER (1206 "Symbol of Love") ... 40-50 59
(White label.)
SCEPTER (1206 "Symbol of Love") ... 10-15 60
(Red label.)
WAND (105 "Symbol of Love") ... 8-12 60

TITUS, Bud
Singles: 7-inch
SAGE (244 "Hocus Pocus") ... 50-75

TITUS, Libby
LPs: 10/12-inch
COLUMBIA ... 8-10 77
HOT BISQUIT ... 10-15 68

TITUS OATES
LPs: 10/12-inch
LIPS ("Jungle Lady") ... 100-200 74
Members: Rick Jackson; Lou Tielli; Bill Beaudet; Chris Eigenmann.

TJADER, Cal LP '63
(With Vince Guaraldi; with Paul Horn; with John Marabuto; with Jerome Richardson; with Sonny Clark; with Joe Silva; with Tony Terran; with Lonnie Hewitt; with Red Callender; with Buddy Motsinger; Cal Tjader Trio)
Singles: 78 rpm
FANTASY ... 3-5 54-57
SAVOY ... 3-5 53-54
Singles: 7-inch
FANTASY ... 5-15 54-71
GALAXY ... 5-10 61
SAVOY ... 10-15 53-54
SKYE ... 4-8 68
VERVE ... 5-10 61-66
EPs: 7-inch
FANTASY (4021 "Ritmo Caliente") ... 25-35 54
FANTASY (4022 "Ritmo Caliente") ... 25-35 54
FANTASY (4049 "Tjader Plays Tjazz") ... 25-35 55
FANTASY (4050 "Tjader Plays Tjazz") ... 25-35 55
FANTASY (4057 "Ritmo Caliente") ... 40-50 56
(Red vinyl.)
FANTASY (4067 "Latin Kick") ... 25-35 57
FANTASY (4069 "Jazz at the Blackhawk") ... 25-35 57
SAVOY (8100 "Cal Tjader Quartet") ... 25-35 54
SAVOY (8111 "Cal Tjader Quartet") ... 25-35 54
LPs: 10/12-inch
BUDDAH ... 8-12 70
CLASSIC JAZZ ... 5-8 80
CONCORD JAZZ ... 5-8 80-82
FANTASY (3-9 "Cal Tjader Trio") ... 75-125 54
(10-inch LP.)
FANTASY (3-17 "Ritmo Caliente") ... 75-125 54
(10-inch LP.)
FANTASY (3211 "Tjader Plays Tjazz") ... 50-75 55
FANTASY (3216 "Ritmo Caliente") ... 50-75 56
FANTASY (3241 "Jazz at the Blackhawk") ... 40-60 57
FANTASY (3250 "Latin Kick") ... 40-60 57
FANTASY (3271 "San Francisco Moods") ... 30-50 58
FANTASY (3279 "Latin for Lovers") ... 30-50 58
(Monaural.)
FANTASY (3283 "Night at the Blackhawk") ... 30-50 59
(Monaural.)
FANTASY (3295 "Concert by the Sea") ... 30-50 59
(Monaural.)
FANTASY (3299 "Concert on the Campus") ... 30-40 60
(Monaural.)
FANTASY (3309 "Demasado Caliente") .. 30-40 60
(Monaural.)
FANTASY (3310 "West Side Story") ... 30-40 60
(Monaural.)

FANTASY (3315 "Live & Direct") 25-35 61
(Monaural.)
FANTASY (3330 "Cal Tjader Plays Harold Arlen") 25-35 61
(Monaural.)
FANTASY (3341 "Concert by the Sea, Vol. 2") 25-35 61
(Monaural.)
FANTASY (3366 "Greatest Hits") 20-30 65
(Monaural.)
FANTASY (8016 "Latin for Lovers") 40-60 58
(Stereo.)
FANTASY (8017 "San Francisco Moods") 40-60 58
(Stereo.)
FANTASY (8026 "Night at the Blackhawk") 40-60 59
(Stereo.)
FANTASY (8030 "Tjader Goes Latin) 75-125 59
(Stereo. Red vinyl.)
FANTASY (8035 "Concert by the Sea")... 40-60 59
(Stereo.)
FANTASY (8044 "Concert on the Campus") 40-50 60
(Stereo.)
FANTASY (8053 "Demasado Caliente") 40-50 60
(Stereo.)
FANTASY (8054 "West Side Story") 40-50 60
(Stereo.)
FANTASY (8059 "Live & Direct") 35-45 61
(Stereo.)
FANTASY (8072 "Cal Tjader Plays Harold Arlen") 35-45 61
(Stereo.)
FANTASY (8098 "Concert by the Sea, Vol. 2") 35-45 61
(Stereo.)
FANTASY (8366 "Greatest Hits") 25-35 65
(Stereo.)
FANTASY (8400 series) 8-15 71-72
FANTASY (9000 series) 6-12 72-77
GALAXY 5-10 78-79
METRO 10-15 67
PRESTIGE 5-10 73
SAVOY (9036 "Cal Tjader Quartet") 75-125 54
(10-inch LP.)
SAVOY (12054 "Vib-Rations") 50-100 56
SAVOY (12000 series) 20-40 56
SKYE 8-12 68-69
VERVE 10-30 61-69
(Reads "MGM Records - A Division of Metro-Goldwyn-Mayer, Inc." at bottom of label.)
VERVE 5-12 73-84
(Reads "Manufactured By MGM Record Corp.," or mentions either Polydor or Polygram at bottom of label.)
Also see BRUBECK, Dave, Quartet
Also see CALLENDER, Red
Also see GUARALDI, Vince
Also see O'DAY, Anita, & Cal Tjader

TJADER, Cal, & Stan Getz
(With Vince Guaraldi)

LPs: 10/12-inch

FANTASY (3266 "Cal Tjader and Stan Getz") 40-60 58
(Monaural.)
FANTASY (3348 "Cal Tjader and Stan Getz") 15-25 65
(Monaural.)
FANTASY (8005 "Cal Tjader and Stan Getz") 50-75 58
(Stereo.)
FANTASY (8348 "Cal Tjader and Stan Getz") 20-30 65
(Stereo.)
Also see GETZ, Stan
Also see GUARALDI, Vince
Also see TJADER, Cal

TOADS

Singles: 7-inch

CREWE (342 "A Little at a Time") 4-8 70
DECCA (31847 "Leaving It All Behind") 8-12 65

LPs: 10/12-inch

RITE 20-35
WIGGINS (64021 "The Toads") 50-75 65

TOADS / Golden Boys

Singles: 7-inch

BRENT (7050 "Backaruda") 10-15 65
Also see GOLDEN BOYS
Also see TOADS

TOBY & RAY WITH THE MARGILATORS

Singles: 7-inch

BLUE MOON (411 "Boom Do Wa") 75-100 59

TOBY BEAU — P&R/LP '78

Singles: 7-inch

RCA 3-5 78-80

LPs: 10/12-inch

RCA (Except 2994) 5-10 78-81
RCA (2994 "Three You Missed, One You Didn't") 10-15 78
(Promotional issue only.)

TOBY BEN BLUES BAND

Singles: 7-inch

COLUMBIA (43898 "I Don't Want You")... 10-15 66

TODAY

Singles: 7-inch

BURDETTE (488 "That's What I'm For") 5-10 69

TODAY & TOMORROW

Singles: 7-inch

NOOSE (812 "Dooley Swings") 20-30 59

TODAY'S TOMORROW

Singles: 7-inch

BANG (577 "Witchi Tai To") 8-12 70
TEEN TOWN (118 "You've Gone Away") 10-20 71
TEEN TOWN (125 "Smile Away") 10-20 72
Members: Chuck Holzer; Alex Campbell; Ralph Russell; Eric Melby; Mark Melby; Randy Taylor; Clare Troyanek.
Also see LADDS

TODD, Art & Dotty — P&R/R&B '58

Singles: 78 rpm

ABBOTT 10-15 55
DIAMOND 5-10 56
LONDON (17040 "Chanson d'Amour") 15-25 58
(Canadian.)

Singles: 7-inch

ABBOTT (3006 "Busy Signal") 15-25 55
CAPITOL (4778 "Sweet Someone") 5-10 62
COLLECTABLES .... 3-5 '80s
DAKAR (6301 "12th Street Rag") 5-10 63
DART 5-15 59-67
DECCA (31227 "Ca C'est La Vie") 5-10 61
DECCA (31329 "Your Cheatin' Heart") 5-10 61
DIAMOND (3002 "Button Up Your Overcoat") 10-20 56
DIAMOND (3003 "But Only for Me") 15-25 56
DOT 5-10 66
ERA 15-25 58-59
LONDON (17040 "Chanson d'Amour") 15-25 58
(Canadian.)
M.O.L. 5-10 68
SIGNET 5-10 65

LPs: 10/12-inch

BEVERLY HILLS 8-10 73
DART (444 "Black Velvet Eyes") 25-50 60
DOT (3742 "Chanson d'Amour") 20-30 66
REPRISE 10-20 65

TODD, Dylan

Singles: 78 rpm

RCA 10-15 56

Singles: 7-inch

RCA (6463 "Ballad of James Dean") 15-25 56

Picture Sleeves

RCA (6463 "Ballad of James Dean") 40-60 56

TODD, Fuller

Singles: 78 rpm

KING 10-20 57

Singles: 7-inch

KING (5048 "Old Fashioned") 10-20 57
KING (5075 "Real True Love") 10-20 57
KING (5111 "Jeannie Marie") 10-20 58

TODD, Greg, & Jacks

Singles: 7-inch

HOLIDAY INN (2202 "Love") 8-12 68
HOLIDAY INN (2217 "Garden of Delights") 8-12 69

TODD, Johnny

Singles: 78 rpm

MODERN (1003 "Pink Cadillac") 25-50 56

Singles: 7-inch

MODERN (1003 "Pink Cadillac") 50-100 56

TODD, Nick — P&R '57

Singles: 78 rpm

DOT 10-20 57

Singles: 7-inch

DOT 10-20 57-60

TODD, Shane

Singles: 7-inch

DUTCH (1061 "Today") 15-25 61
Also see CORVETTES & TODDETTES

TODD, Sharkey, & Monsters

Singles: 7-inch

CAPITOL (4234 "Horror Show") 10-15 59

TODD & DEVIN

Singles: 7-inch

BRAGG (208 "You Make the Decisions"). 10-20 '60s

TODDS

Singles: 7-inch

TODD (1064 "May We Always") 10-15 61
TODD (1076 "Popsicle") 10-15 62

TODDS

Singles: 7-inch

TODDLIN' TOWN (102 "I Want Her Back") 10-20 67

TODES

Singles: 7-inch

EMANON (102 "Good Things") 15-25 66

TOE FAT

Singles: 7-inch

RARE EARTH (5019 "Just Like Me") 4-6 70
(Black vinyl)
RARE EARTH (5019 "Just Like Me") 4-8 70
(Colored vinyl. Promotional issue only.)

LPs: 10/12-inch

RARE EARTH 10-15 70-71
Members: Cliff Bennett; Ken Hensley; Lee Kerslake; Joe Konas.
Also see BENNETT, Cliff, & Rebel Rousers

TOGAS

Singles: 7-inch

CHALLENGE (59309 "Hurry to me") 5-10 65
Also see MORGAN, Chris

TOKAYS

Singles: 7-inch

BONNIE (102 "Lost and Found") 75-125 62

TOKAYS

Singles: 7-inch

BRUTE (1 "Baby, Baby, Baby") 50-100 67
SCORPIO (403 "Now") 10-15 65
TO-KAY (273 "Out of Hand") .... 10-15 '60s

TOKENS — P&R '61
(With Sammy Lowe & Orchestra)

Singles: 12-inch

DOWNTOWN (103 "The Lion Sleeps Tonight") 8-12 88
(Issued with cover.)

Singles: 78 rpm

MELBA (104 "While I Dream") 10-15 56

Singles: 7-inch

ABC 4-6 73
ATCO (7009 "Penny Whistle Band") 4-6 74
B.T. PUPPY (500 "A Girl Named Arlene").. 8-12 64
B.T. PUPPY (502 "He's in Town") 5-10 64
B.T. PUPPY (504 "You're My Girl") 5-10 64
B.T. PUPPY (505 "Mr. Cupid") 5-10 65
B.T. PUPPY (505 "Mr. Cupid") 10-15 64
(Promotional issue.)
B.T. PUPPY (507 "Sylvie Sleepin' ") 5-10 65
B.T. PUPPY (512 "Only My Friend") 5-10 65
B.T. PUPPY (513 "Just One Smile") 5-10 66
B.T. PUPPY (516 "Three Bells") 5-10 66
B.T. PUPPY (518 "I Hear Trumpets Blow") 5-10 66
B.T. PUPPY (519 "Breezy") 5-10 66
B.T. PUPPY (525 "Saloogy") 5-10 67
B.T. PUPPY (552 "Get a Job") 5-8 69
BELL (45190 "You and Me") 4-6 72
BUDDAH (151 "She Lets Her Hair Down") 5-10 69
BUDDAH (159 "Don't Worry Baby") 5-8 70
BUDDAH (174 "Both Sides Now") 5-8 70
BUDDAH (187 "Listen to the Words") 5-8 70
COLLECTABLES 3-5 84
LAURIE (3180 "Please Write") 10-15 63
MELBA (104 "While I Dream") 15-20 56
RCA (37-7896 "When I Go to Sleep at Night") 30-40 61
(Compact 33 Single.)
RCA (47-7896 "When I Go to Sleep at Night") 10-15 61
RCA (37-7925 "Sincerely") 25-35 61
(Compact 33 Single.)
RCA (47-7925 "Sincerely") 10-20 61
RCA (37-7954 "The Lion Sleeps Tonight") 25-35 61
(Compact 33 Single.)
RCA (47-7954 "The Lion Sleeps Tonight") 10-20 61
RCA (37-7991 "B'Wa Nina") 25-35 62
(Compact 33 Single.)
RCA (47-7991 "B'Wa Nina") 10-15 62
RCA (37-8018 "The Riddle") 20-30 62
(Compact 33 Single.)
RCA (47-8018 "The Riddle") 8-12 62
RCA (8052 "La Bomba") 10-15 62
RCA (8089 "I'll Do My Crying Tomorrow") . 8-12 62
RCA (8114 "A Bird Flies Out of Sight") 8-12 63
RCA (8148 "Tonight I Met an Angel") 8-12 63
RCA (8210 "Hear the Bells") 10-15 63
RCA (8309 "Two Cars") 8-12 64
RCA (8749 "Re-Doo-Wopp") 3-5 88
RCA GOLD STANDARD (0702 "The Lion Sleeps Tonight"/"B'Wa Nina") .... 5-10 '60s
RADIO ACTIVE GOLD 3-5
W.B. 5-10 67-69
WARWICK (615 "Tonight I Fell in Love") . 20-30 61

Picture Sleeves

B.T. PUPPY (518 "I Hear Trumpets Blow") 20-30 66
B.T. PUPPY (591 "Greatest Moments in a Girl's Life") 10-15 66
RCA (7896 "When I Go to Sleep at Night") 20-30 61
RCA (7991 "B'Wa Nina") 20-30 62
(Orange sleeve. No mention of *The Lion Sleeps Tonight* LP.)
RCA (7991 "B'Wa Nina") 10-15 62
(Orange and white sleeve. Plugs *The Lion Sleeps Tonight* LP.)
RCA (8018 "The Riddle") 20-30 62
RCA (8052 "La Bomba") 15-25 62
RCA (8089 "I'll Do My Crying Tomorrow") 30-40 62
RCA (8114 "A Bird Flies Out of Sight") 20-30 63
RCA (8148 "Tonight I Met an Angel") 20-30 63
RCA (8210 "Hear the Bells") 20-30 63
RCA (8309 "Two Cars") 20-30 64
W.B. (5900 "Portrait of My Love") 15-25 67

LPs: 10/12-inch

B.T. PUPPY 15-25 66-78
BUDDAH (5059 "Both Sides Now") 15-20 70
DOWNTOWN 5-8 88
RCA (LPM-2514 "The Lion Sleeps Tonight") 30-50 61
(Monaural.)
RCA (LSP-2514 "The Lion Sleeps Tonight") 50-75 61
(Stereo.)
RCA (LPM-2631 "We The Tokens Sing Folk") 20-40 62
(Monaural.)
RCA (LSP-2631 "We The Tokens Sing Folk") 25-50 62
(Stereo.)
RCA (LPM-2886 "Wheels") 30-50 64
(Monaural.)
RCA (LSP-2886 "Wheels") 40-60 64
(Stereo.)
RCA (LPM-3685 "The Tokens Again") 20-40 66
(Monaural.)
RCA (LSP-3685 "The Tokens Again") 20-40 66
(Stereo.)
RCA (8534 "Re-Doo-Wopp") 5-8 88
W.B. (1685 "It's a Happening World") 15-25 67
Members: Jay Siegel; Mitchell Margo; Philip Margo; Henry Medress.
Also see BUDDIES
Also see CHRISTIE, Lou / Len Barry & Dovells / Bobby Rydell / Tokens

Also see COEDS
Also see CONCEPTS /Tokens
Also see DARRELL & OXFORDS
Also see FOUR WINDS
Also see KEITH
Also see LOWE, Sammy
Also see SEDAKA, Neil
Also see U.S. DOUBLE QUARTET

TOKENS / Happenings *LP '67*
LPs: 10/12-inch
B.T. PUPPY 15-25 67
Also see HAPPENINGS
Also see TOKENS

TOKENS
Singles: 7-inch
DATE (2737 "Oh What a Night") 100-150 61
(No distributor shown on label.)
DATE (2737 "Oh What a Night") 10-20 61
(Distributed by Eldo on label.)
GARY (1006 "Come Dance with Me") ... 75-125 61
(Company address is shown as on Broadway.)
GARY (1006 "Come Dance with Me") 30-40 61
(Company address is shown as on W. 49th St.)
GARY (1006 "Come Dance with Me") 10-20
(No address on label.)
MUSIC MAKERS (110 "Arlene") 10-15 62
MUSICTONE (1113 "Come Dance with Me") 8-12 63
RUST (5094 "Arlene") 8-12 65

TOKYO BOYS / Titans
Singles: 7-inch
MGM (13207 "Midnight in Tokyo"/"Yojimbo") 5-10 64
Also see DAVIS, Danny
Also see TITANS

TOLEDOS
Singles: 7-inch
DOWN (2003 "This Is Our Night") 10-20 61
(First issue.)
END (1094 "This Is Our Night") 5-10 61

TOLIVER, Bo, & Timers
Singles: 7-inch
AIRWAY (105 "Beggin' ") 100-200 58

TOLIVER, Donny, & Renegades
Singles: 7-inch
IMPACT (16 "Little Boy Blue") 15-25 63

TOLIVER, Jimmy
(With His California Blues Men)
Singles: 78 rpm
CHIMES .... 25-50 '50s
Singles: 7-inch
T&T (102 "Breaking Out") 15-25 63

TOLIVER, Mickey, & Capitols
Singles: 7-inch
CINDY (3002 "Rose-Marie") 250-350 57

TOLLESON, Johnny
Singles: 7-inch
CHANCE (31761 "You're in Love with Yourself") 150-250

TOLLESON, Tommie
Singles: 7-inch
GULF COAST (102 "Gulf Coast Twist"). 75-125
GULF COAST (1550 "Carla Blues") 100-200
KOOL (1005 "To the Dance") 75-125 60

TOLLEY, Jo Ann
Singles: 7-inch
JUBILEE (5268 "Kissin' Tim") 10-20 57

TOM & DICK
Singles: 7-inch
MERCURY (72573 "Lark Day") 8-10 66
(May have been promotional only.)
Members: Tom Smothers; Dick Smothers.
Also see SMOTHERS BROTHERS

TOM & JERRIO *P&R/R&B '65*
Singles: 7-inch
ABC-PAR (10638 "Boo-Ga-Loo") 5-10 65
ABC-PAR (10704 "Great Goo-Ga Moo-Ga") 5-10 65
ABC-PAR (10787 "Bacardi") 5-10 66
JERRY-O (110 "Boo-Ga-Loo") 20-30 65
(First issue.)
Members: Robert Tharp; Jerry Murray.

TOM & JERRY *P&R '57*
Singles: 78 rpm
BIG (613 "Hey, Schoolgirl") 300-400 57
Singles: 7-inch
ABC-PAR (10363 "Surrender, Please Surrender") 15-25 62
ABC-PAR (10788 "This Is My Story") 10-15 66
BIG (613 "Hey, Schoolgirl") 30-40 57
BIG (616 "Two Teenagers") 30-40 58
BIG (618 "Don't Say Goodbye") 30-40 58
BIG (621 "Baby Talk") 30-40 59
EMBER (1094 "I'm Lonesome") 25-35 63
HUNT (319 "Don't Say Goodbye") 40-50 58
KING (5167 "Hey, Schoolgirl") 40-50 58
Members: Paul Simon; Art Garfunkel.
Also see SIMON & GARFUNKEL

TOM & JERRY / Ronnie Lawrence
Singles: 7-inch
BELL (120 "Baby Talk") 20-30 60
Picture Sleeves
BELL (120 "Baby Talk") 30-50 60
Also see TOM & JERRY

TOM & JERRY
Singles: 7-inch
MERCURY 5-10 61-63
LPs: 10/12-inch
MERCURY (Except 842) 20-25 61-62
MERCURY (842 "Surfin' Hootenanny") 50-75 63
WING 10-15 67
Members: Tommy Tomlinson; Jerry Kennedy.
Also see KENNEDY, Jerry
Also see TOMLINSON & BAKER

TOM & TEMPESTS
Singles: 7-inch
ALCO (1004 "Play It Cool") .... 15-25 '60s

TOM & TORNADOS
Singles: 7-inch
NORTHWAY SOUND (1007 "Long Pony Tail") 200-300
Also see JAMES, Tommy

TOM & WAYNE
Singles: 7-inch
GAMA (707 "I Have Some Love") 10-20

TOM CAT & FISHCAKES
Singles: 7-inch
OUTHOUSE (717 "She's Got Freckles on Her But--") 10-20

TOM, PAUL, & JONES
Singles: 7-inch
ADVENTURE (285 "Dance Little Girl") 15-25

TOM TOMS
Singles: 7-inch
LAUREL (1011 "Pandemonium") 15-25 59

TOM TOMS
(Bill Smith Combo)
Singles: 7-inch
LE CAM (715 "Ptomaine") 15-25 60
(Also issued as by the Bill Smith Combo.)
Also see BROWN, Tom, & Tom Toms
Also see SMITH, Bill

TOM TONES
Singles: 7-inch
DEE DEE .... 15-25 '60s

TOMANGOES
Singles: 7-inch
WASHPAN (3125 "I Really Love You") 100-200

TOMBSTONES
Singles: 7-inch
GRAVE (1001 "I Want You") .... 10-20 '60s

TOMCATS
Singles: 7-inch
TERRY (103 "Saxy Boogie") 10-20 61
Member: Tommy Wills.
Also see WILLS, Tommy

TOMKOS
(Tomko Trio)
Singles: 7-inch
ARTISTIQUE (607 "Get with It") 6-12 62
ARTISTIQUE (5003 "Spook"/"Spook Pt. 2") 5-10 63
ARTISTIQUE (5003 "Spook"/"Carol") 5-10 63
(Issued with different flip side.)

TOMMY & DEL-NOTES
Singles: 7-inch
CHARTER (1001 "Why Can't I Have You") 60-80

TOMMY & DEL ROYALS
Singles: 7-inch
DESTINY (101 "Trust in Love") 200-300 63
(Reportedly 100 made.)

TOMMY & EDDIE
Singles: 7-inch
FINCH (2001 "Be My Girlfriend") 10-20 59
MONEY (124 "I Love My Baby") 5-10 66

TOMMY & MIGHTY FOUR
Singles: 7-inch
MOONBOW (1003 "In Love with Me and My Honda") 100-150

TOMMY & RIVIERAS
Singles: 7-inch
CAMEO (461 "Messing with the Kid") 10-20 67
P'ZAZZ 5-10 66
Members: Tommy Dee; Johnny Ferrari; Dennis Dean; Buddy Tinari; Pete Ream; Ellie DeLieto; Cathy DeSanto; Sue Johnson.

TOMMY & TWISTERS
Singles: 7-inch
REGENT (205 "Mr. Twist") 5-10 62
LPs: 10/12-inch
REGENT (6104 "Let's All Do the Twist") .. 20-40 61

TOMMY "T"
Singles: 7-inch
EVEREST (19330 "The Funeral") 15-25 60
TIVOLI (1718 "I Cried in the Chapel") 75-125

TOMMY T'S FEDERAL RESERVE
Singles: 7-inch
CADET (5584 "Grow Up Someday") 5-10 67
CADET (5622 "Let's Go Down to the Park") 5-10 68
R-JAY (6856 "Get It Together") 10-20 68
Member: Tommy Tucker.

TOMORROW'S CHILDREN
Singles: 7-inch
BROOKMONT (555 "Take a Good Look") .... 20-30 '60s
RAYNARD (10065 "In the Midnight Hour") 40-60 66

TOMPALL & GLASER BROS. *P&R '69*
(Tompall & Glasers; Tompall Glaser)
Singles: 7-inch
DECCA 5-10 59-65
ELEKTRA 3-5 80-82
MGM 5-8 66-71
RICH (1004 "Yakety-Yak") 10-15 61
ROBBINS (1006 "I Want You") 50-75 58
LPs: 10/12-inch
DECCA (DL-4041 "This Land") 20-40 60
(Monaural.)
DECCA (DL7-4041 "This Land") 30-50 60
(Stereo.)
ELEKTRA 5-10 81
MGM 10-20 67-75
U.A. (3540 "Ballad of *Namu the Killer Whale* and Others") 25-35 66
(Monaural.)
U.A. (6540 "Ballad of *Namu the Killer Whale* and Others") 30-40 66
(Stereo.)
VOCALION (3807 "Country Folk") 8-12 67
Members: Tompall; Jim; Chuck.
Also see GLASER, Jim

TOMS
(The Toms)
LPs: 10/12-inch
BLACK SHEEP (10903 "Yawning for Pleasure") 5-10 86
BLACK SHEEP (11177 "The Toms") 20-30 79
Member: Thomas J. Marolda.

TOMSCO, George, & Dots
Singles: 7-inch
DOT (16691 "Mexican Fun") 5-10 65
Also see FIREBALLS
Also see GEORGE & BABS

TONE TWINS
Singles: 7-inch
ATLANTIC (1064 "Hey Pretty Girl") 25-35 55

TONEBLENDERS
("Featuring Ernestine with the Highlights")
Singles: 7-inch
MAD (1014 "When You're Hurting") 30-40 59
PLAY (1002 "I Thank Heaven") 150-200 58
(Same number used on a Miles & Andrew release.)
Also see SHELTON, Gary

TONES
(With the Al Cailoa Orchestra)
Singles: 7-inch
BATON (265 "We") 10-15 59
Also see CAIOLA, Al
Also see SANTOS, Larry

TONES
Singles: 7-inch
ELMOR (6001 "Paula Is Mine") 10-20 63
Also see ARDELLS

TONETTES
(With Sammy Lowe Orchestra)
Singles: 78 rpm
MODERN 10-15 56
Singles: 7-inch
ABC-PAR (9905 "Oh What a Baby") 10-20 58
DOE (101 "Oh What a Baby") 75-100 58
(First issue.)
DOE (103 "Uh-Oh") 75-100 58
DYNAMIC (103 "I Gotta Know") 20-30 59
MODERN (997 "Tonight You Belong to Me") 20-30 56
VOLT (101 "Please Don't Go") 10-20 62
VOLT (104 "Stolen Angel") 10-20 63
Also see CASTRO, Vince

TONEY, Oscar, Jr. *P&R/R&B/LP '67*
Singles: 7-inch
ATCO (6933 "Everything I Own") 10-15 74
BELL 5-10 67-69
CAPRICORN 10-20 70-72
CONTEMPO (7702 "Is It Because I'm Black") 5-10 74
KING (5906 "You Are Going to Need Me") 10-20 64
LPs: 10/12-inch
BELL 10-20 67

TONGUE
Singles: 7-inch
HEMISPHERE (101 "Keep On Truckin' ") 4-8 70
TEKTRA (1811 "Hotel Arbutus") 4-6
LPs: 10/12-inch
HEMISPHERE 15-20 70

TONGUE & GROOVE
Singles: 7-inch
FONTANA 5-10 69
LPs: 10/12-inch
FONTANA 15-20 69
Members: Michael Ferguson; Lynne Hughes.

TONGUES OF TRUTH / Grodes
Singles: 7-inch
CURRENT (112 "Let's Talk About Girls"). 15-25 66
Also see GRODES

TONI
Singles: 7-inch
MUSICTONE (6124 "If I Were Ready for Love") 15-20 64

TONI
Singles: 7-inch
CHERRY (1006 "I Want You to Be My Baby") 150-250

TONI & SHOWMEN
Singles: 7-inch
TEN STAR (103 "Beware") 20-30 65

TONTO & RENEGADES
(Tonto & Renigades)
Singles: 7-inch
SOUND OF THE SCEEN (2178 "Easy Way Out") 10-20 67
SOUND OF THE SCEEN (2212 "Little Boy Blue") 15-25 67

TONTO'S EXPANDING HEAD BAND
LPs: 10/12-inch
ATLANTIC (18123 "Zero Time")..................5-10 75
(First issued in the U.K. as Atlantic 40251, in 1971.)
EMBRYO (0732 "Zero Time") 10-15 71

TONY & DAYDREAMS
Singles: 7-inch
PLANET (1008 "Why Don't You Be Nice")...................................... 50-75 59
PLANET (1054 "Christmas Lullabye") . 150-200 61
Member: Tony Carmen.
Also see CARMEN, Tony, & Spitfires

TONY & DEL-FI'S
Singles: 7-inch
NEW GROUP (6001 "Goin' to Miami"). 100-150

TONY & HOLIDAYS
Singles: 7-inch
ABC-PAR (10295 "There Goes My Heart Again") 100-150 62
ABC-PAR (10295 "There Goes My Heart Again") 50-100 62
(West Coast. Styrene.)
Member: Buddy Sheppard.
Also see SHEPPARD, Buddy, & Holidays

TONY & JOE *P&R '58*
Singles: 7-inch
DORE (619 "Twist and Freeze") 5-10 61
DORE (688 "The Freeze")...........................5-10 63
ERA (1075 "The Freeze")......................... 10-15 58
FLYTE (106 "Fairytale Love")......................8-12 59
GARDENA (103 "Instant Love")....................8-12 60
Members: Tony Savonne; Joe Saraceno.
Also see BEACH BOYS / Tony & Joe

TONY & JOHNNY
(With the Rextones)
Singles: 7-inch
MILO (105 "I Pray")................................. 10-20 58
Members: Tony Passarella; Johnny Moccia.

TONY & KNIGHTS
Singles: 7-inch
USA (720 "Twist'in Mary Jane") 10-15 62
USA (728 "Bacon Fat")............................ 10-15 62

TONY & MASQUINS
Singles: 7-inch
RUTHIE (1000 "My Angel Eyes")........... 75-125 61

TONY & MONSTROSITIES
Singles: 7-inch
CRYPT (107 "Igor's Party") 10-20 60
INDIGO (148 "Igor's Party")........................5-10 61

TONY & RAINDROPS
Singles: 7-inch
CHESAPEAKE (609 "While Walking")...... 50-75 62
CROSLEY (340 "My Heart Cried")....... 500-750 62

TONY & TECHNICS
Singles: 7-inch
CHEX (1010 "Work Out")........................ 10-15 63
Also see TECHNICS

TONY & TWILIGHTERS
(Anthony & Sophmores)
Singles: 7-inch
COLLECTABLES...3-5 '80s
JALYNNE (106 "Be My Girl") 50-75 60
RED TOP (127 "Key to My Heart") 150-175 60
Member: Anthony "Tony" Maresco.
Also see ANTHONY & SOPHOMORES
Also see DYNAMICS Featuring Tony Maresco

TONY & TYRONE
Singles: 7-inch
ATLANTIC (2458 "Please Operator") 15-25 67
COLUMBIA (43292 "Fool Am I") 8-12 65
COLUMBIA (43432 "Turn It On") 8-12 65
STON-ROC 12-18
Members: Tony Johnson; Tyrone Pickens.

TONY & VELVETS
Singles: 7-inch
ZOOM (9606 "Sunday")......................... 75-125 63

TONY & VIZITORS
Singles: 7-inch
SIDEWALK (915 "Nite Owl") 10-20 67
Session: Davie Allan.
Also see ALLAN, Davie

TONY, BOB & JIMMY
Singles: 7-inch
CAPITOL (4760 "4760 "Dutchman's Gold")..5-10 62
Members: Tony Butala; Bob Engemann; Jim Pike.
Also see LETTERMEN

TONY'S TYGERS
(Tygers)
Singles: 7-inch
A&M (921 "Little By Little") 5-10 68
JAMIE (1378 "Resurrection") 5-10 69
TEEN TOWN (102 "Little By Little")............8-10 68
TEEN TOWN (105 "I Can't Believe") 8-10 68
TEEN TOWN (107 "Debbie on My Mind")..8-10 68
Members: Tony Dancy; Dave Kuck; Craig Fairchild; Joe Turano; Lanny Hale; Fred Euler; Dennis Duchrow.

TONY'S TYGERS / Skunks / Robbs
EPs: 7-inch
WRIT RADIO (1340 "WRIT Sampler")......15-25 68
Also see ROBBS
Also see SKUNKS
Also see TONY'S TYGERS

TOOL
LPs: 10/12-inch
ZOO (11052 "Undertow") 40-50 93
(Gray vinyl. Promotional issue only.)
ZOO (31027 "Opiate") 15-25 92
ZOO (31052 "Undertow") 20-30 93
(Two discs.)

TOOLEY, Johnny
Singles: 7-inch
STARDAY (696 "Looking-Glass Heart")...50-75

TOOMBS, Jackson
Singles: 78 rpm
EXCELLO (2083 "Kiss-A Me Quick")........10-20 56
Singles: 7-inch
EXCELLO (2083 "Kiss-A Me Quick")........35-50 56

TOOMBS, Wayne
Singles: 7-inch
YOUNGSTOWN (603 "I Found My Dreams in You") 150-200

TOOMORROW
Singles: 7-inch
KIRSHNER (5005 "Going Back")..............15-25 70
Member: Olivia Newton-John.
Also see NEWTON-JOHN, Olivia

TOONE, Gene
Singles: 7-inch
ANNETTE (1001 "You're My Baby")........10-20 64
SIMCO...8-12 '60s

TOOTIE & BOUQUETS
Singles: 7-inch
PARKWAY (887 "The Conqueror")...........15-25 63

TOOTSIE & VERSATILES
Singles: 7-inch
ELMOR (6000 "I've Got a Feeling")..........10-20 62

TOP DRAWER
LPs: 10/12-inch
WISHBON (207 "Solid Oak")................300-400 69
Members: Steve Geary; John Baker; Alan Berry; Ray Herr; Ron Linn.

TOP HATS
Singles: 7-inch
CANE...10-20 '60s
REED (1039 "A Fool in Love") 15-20 60

TOPHATTERS
(With Morton Craft & Orchestra)
Singles: 78 rpm
CADENCE...5-10 56
Singles: 7-inch
CADENCE (1289 "I'll Never Stand in Your Way") 10-15 56
CADENCE (1290 "My Isle of Golden Dreams")...10-15 56
EXCLUSIVE (01 "I Owe a Kiss")..................8-12 59
JUBILEE (5295 "Don't You Know")............8-12 57
MGM (12642 "Candy Baby")........................8-12 58
Also see FOUR TOPHATTERS

TOP HITS
Singles: 7-inch
JAGUAR (5055 "Love No One") ....3-5 '90s
NORMAN (504 "Love No One")...........400-500 61

TOP NOTES
Singles: 78 rpm
JUBILEE (5088 "For Love of All") 20-30 52
Singles: 7-inch
JUBILEE (5088 "For Love of All") 200-300 52

TOP NOTES
("Derek Ray, Guy Howard & Co."; Topnotes)
Singles: 7-inch
ABC-PAR (10399 "I Love You So Much")..5-10 63
ATLANTIC (2066 "Wonderful Time")..........10-15 60
ATLANTIC (2080 "Say Yes") 10-15 60
ATLANTIC (2097 "Hearts of Stone") 10-15 61
ATLANTIC (2115 "Twist & Shout") 15-25 61
FESTIVAL (1021 "Come Back, Cleopatra") 10-20 62
Members: Derek Ray; Guy Howard.

TOPICS
Singles: 7-inch
CROSS COUNTRY (102 "In a Little While") 15-25 59

TOPICS
(4 Seasons)
Singles: 7-inch
PERRI (1007 "The Girl in My Dreams")....40-50 62
Also see DIXON, Billy, & Topics
Also see 4 SEASONS

TOPICS
Singles: 7-inch
CARNIVAL (520 "She's So Fine") 20-30 66
CHADWICK (102 "Hey Girl")....................50-75 67
HEAVY DUTY..5-10 '60s
TOPIC (100 "The Devil") ....10-15 '60s
LPs: 10/12-inch
TOPIC ("Living Evidence") ....15-25 '60s
(Selection number not known.)
VANCO (1002 "Topics for Tonight").........15-25 '60s

TOPPERS
Singles: 78 rpm
REGENT..10-20 48
SAVOY 10-20 48
Members: Steve Gibson; Dave Patillo; Emmett Matthews; Romaine Brown.
Also see GIBSON, Steve

TOPPERS
Singles: 78 rpm
AVALON (63707 "I Love You") 10-20 54
Singles: 7-inch
AVALON (63707 "I Love You") 20-30 54

TOPPERS
(With Orchestra)
Singles: 78 rpm
JUBILEE..25-35 54
Singles: 7-inch
JUBILEE (5136 "Let Me Bang Your Box") 50-100 54
Members: Sam Fickling; Fred Williams; Vernon Britton; Jerry Half Hide; Henry Austin.
Also see HURRICANES

TOPPERS
Singles: 7-inch
STACY (927 "Tell Me Why") 10-15 61

TOPPERS
(Dick Thomas & Toppers)
EPs: 7-inch
TOPS (61 "Once Upon a Time")..............30-40 61
(Not issued with cover.)
Also see THOMAS, Dick

TOPPS
Singles: 78 rpm
RED ROBIN 50-75 54
Singles: 7-inch
RED ROBIN (126 "What Do You Do")....50-150 54
RED ROBIN (131 "I Got a Feeling") 100-200 54

TOPS
Singles: 78 rpm
SINGULAR..50-75 58
Singles: 7-inch
SINGULAR (712 "An Innocent Kiss") ...100-125 58
V-TONE (102 "Puppy Love")................400-500 59
(Repressed as by Little Jimmy & Tops.)
Also see LITTLE JIMMY & TOPS

TOPSIDERS
Singles: 7-inch
JOSIE (907 "Heartbreak Hotel") 5-10 63
LPs: 10/12-inch
JOSIE (4000 "Rock Goes Folk")..............15-25 63

TORAN, Rex
Singles: 7-inch
REX (101 "Memphis Rockin' ") 150-250

TORCHES
Singles: 7-inch
RING-O (302 "Darn Your Love")..............15-25 65

TOREADORS
Singles: 7-inch
PAWN (1202 "Ring-a-Leevio")..................10-15 63

TOREADORS
Singles: 7-inch
MIDAS (1001 "Do You Remember") ....50-75 '60s

TORKAYS
Singles: 7-inch
STACY (960 "Karate")...................................8-10 63
Member: Keith Murphy.
Also see O'CONNER, Keith

TORKAYS
Singles: 7-inch
COULEE (112 "Linda, I'm Worried So").....8-12 65
Members: Ken Cunningham; Jerry Upson.

TORME, Mel *P&R '45*
(With the Meltones)
Singles: 78 rpm
BETHLEHEM...5-10 56-57
CAPITOL (1000 & 2000 series)....................4-8 50-53
MGM (10584 "Gone with the Wind") 5-10 49
Singles: 7-inch
ATLANTIC (2165 "Comin' Home Baby")..10-15 62
(With the Cookies.)
ATLANTIC (2183 thru 2219).......................5-10 63-64
BETHLEHEM...10-15 56-58
CAPITOL (1000 & 2000 series)...............10-20 50-53
(Purple labels.)
CAPITOL (2000 series) 4-6 69-70
(Orange labels.)
COLUMBIA..4-8 64-67
CORAL...10-15 53-56
LIBERTY (56022 "Day in the Life of Bonnie and Clyde")..4-8 68
LIBERTY (56066 "Didn't We") 4-8 68
MGM (30354 "Mel Torme Sings")............20-30 50
(Four discs. Boxed set.)
VERVE..10-15 59-61
EPs: 7-inch
CAPITOL..5-15 50
P.R.I. (9 "The Touch of Your Lips") 5-10
LPs: 10/12-inch
ATLANTIC (8000 series)..........................12-25 62-64
ATLANTIC (18000 series)...........................5-10 75
ATLANTIC (80000 series)............................5-8 83
BETHLEHEM (34 "It's a Blue World") 25-50 55
BETHLEHEM (52 "Mel Torme")...............25-50 56
BETHLEHEM (4000 series)......................10-20 65
BETHLEHEM (6000 series)......................20-40 58-60
(Maroon labels.)
BETHLEHEM (6000 series).........................5-10 77-78
(Gray labels.)
CAPITOL (200 "California Suite")...........50-100 50
(10-inch LP.)
CAPITOL (300 & 400 series).....................8-12 69-70
COLUMBIA (2000 series) 10-20 64-66
(Monaural.)
COLUMBIA (9000 series) 10-20 64-66
(Stereo.)
CONCORD JAZZ 5-8 82
CORAL (57012 "At the Crescendo") 50-100 54
CORAL (57044 "Musical Sounds").........50-100 54
EVEREST...5-10 76
GLENDALE...5-8 78-79
GRYPHON..5-8 79
HALO (50243 "Mel Torme Sings")...........25-50 57
LIBERTY (7560 "Day in the Life of Bonnie and Clyde")..10-15 68
MGM (552 "Songs by Mel Torme").........50-100 52
(10-inch LP.)
MAYFAIR 25-35 58
METRO...10-20 65
MUSICRAFT...5-8 83
STRAND 12-25 60
TOPS..10-20 56

VERVE....................20-35 58-60
(Reads "Verve Records, Inc." at bottom of label.)
VERVE....................10-20 61-72
(Reads "MGM Records - A Division of Metro-Goldwyn-Mayer, Inc." at bottom of label.)
VERVE....................5-10 73-84
(Reads "Manufactured By MGM Record Corp.," or mentions either Polydor or Polygram at bottom of label.)
VOCALION....................5-10 70
Also see COOKIES
Also see CROSBY, Bing, & Mel Torme
Also see LEE, Peggy, & Mel Torme
Also see RICH, Buddy
Also see WHITING, Margaret

TORME, Mel, & Ray Eberle
LPs: 10/12-inch
TOPS (1595 "Mel Torme & Ray Eberle"). 10-20 57

TORMENTORS
Singles: 7-inch
KERWOOD (712 "Didn't It Rain")............ 15-25 '60s
ROYAL (002 "She's Gone")............ 10-20 67
ROYAL (003 "Merry-Go-Round")............ 10-20 67
ROYAL (003-1 "Sounds of Summer")...... 10-20 67
TSA (100 "Bye Bye")............ 100-150
LPs: 10/12-inch
EVA (12055 "Hanging 'Round")............8-10 88
ROYAL (111 "Hanging 'Round")......... 100-200 67
Members: Tim Daley; Dan Davis; Mark Davis; Lee Harper.

TORNADOES
Singles: 7-inch
ABC-PAR (10174 "Like a Frog")............ 10-15 60

TORNADOES
Singles: 7-inch
AERTAUN (100 "Bustin' Surfboards")...... 20-30 62
AERTAUN (101 "The Gremmie")............ 10-20 62
AERTAUN (102 "Shootin' Beaver"/"Phantom Surfer")............ 15-25 63
AERTAUN (102 "Lightnin'"/"Phantom Surfer")............ 10-20 64
(Issued with different flip side.)
LPs: 10/12-inch
JOSIE (4005 "Bustin' Surfboards")........ 50-100 63
Members: Gerald Sanders; Norman Sanders; Jesse Sanders; George White; Leonard Delany.
Also see BEACH BOYS / Tornadoes
Also see HOLLYWOOD TORNADOES

TORNADOES
Singles: 7-inch
CUCA (1099 "Loneliest Guy in Town").... 15-25 62
Members: Bill Velline; Terry Erdman; Richie Wynn; Chet Priewe; Al Johnson; Mark Rowe; Freddie Swenson.
Also see STRANGERS
Also see WYNN, Richie, & Tornadoes

TORNADOES ***P&R/R&B '62***
Singles: 7-inch
LONDON............5-10 62-63
TOWER (152 "Early Bird")............5-10 65
TOWER (171 "Stingray")............5-10 65
LPs: 10/12-inch
LONDON (3279 "Telstar")............ 50-75 62
LONDON (3293 "Sounds Of")............ 25-35 63
Members: Heinz Burt; Alan Caddy; Clem Cattini; George Bellamy.

TORNADOS
Singles: 7-inch
BUMBLE BEE (503 "Love in Your Life").. 30-40 59

TORNADOS
Singles: 7-inch
CUCA (1104 "Hey There")............ 15-25 62
(Not sure if this is the same as Tornados group below.)

TORNADOS
Singles: 7-inch
CUCA (1092 "Scalping Party")............ 15-25 62
CUCA (6361 "Last Date")............ 15-25 63
Members: Gordy Hastreiter; Bob Olson; Teddy Vernick; Denny Hastreiter; Dan Peterson; Dick Saykally; Cookie Bushar.

TORNADOS
Singles: 7-inch
VOX (269 "Time Goes By")............8-12 '60s

TORNADOS
Singles: 7-inch
NEW WORLD (100 "A World That's Free")............10-20 '60s

TORNADOS
Singles: 7-inch
PHALANX (1004 "Alone")............50-100 66
PHALANX (1014 "Rainy Day Fairy Tales")............50-100 66

TORNADOS
Singles: 7-inch
HEAD (2001 "The Hawk")............8-12 68
TORNADO (975 "Riot")............40-60

TORONADOES
Singles: 7-inch
VULCO (2 "Ramblin' Man")............10-15 62

TORONADOS
Singles: 7-inch
DATE (1519 "Next Stop, Kansas City")....10-20 66

TORNAY, Sue, & Four Kings
Singles: 7-inch
CESSNA (478 "Tell Me")............20-30 60
DORE (594 "Tell Me")............10-15 61

TOROK, Mitchell ***C&W/P&R '53***
(With the Louisiana Hayride Band; with Matches; with Ramona Redd; Mitch Torok)
Singles: 78 rpm
ABBOTT............10-20 53-54
DECCA............5-15 57-58
FBC (102 "Nacogdoches County Line")...15-25 48
FBC (115 "Piney Woods Boogie")............15-25 49
Singles: 7-inch
ABBOTT (136 "Judalina")............20-30 53
ABBOTT (140 "Caribbean")............30-40 53
ABBOTT (150 "Hootchy Kootchy Henry") 20-30 53
ABBOTT (156 "Living on Love")............15-25 54
ABBOTT (162 "Dancerette")............15-25 54
CALICO............4-6
CAPITOL (4846 "Fools Disguise")............5-10 62
CAPITOL (4946 "Mighty Mighty Man")......5-10 63
DECCA (30230 "Pledge of Love")............10-20 57
DECCA (30424 "Two Words")............10-20 57
DECCA (30599 "Be Kind to Me")............10-20 58
DECCA (30661 "Sweet Revenge")............10-20 58
DECCA (30742 "Date with a Teardrop")..10-20 58
DECCA (30859 "Go Ahead and Be a Fool")............10-20 59
DECCA (30901 "P.T.A. Rock and Roll")...10-20 59
GUYDEN (2018 "Caribbean")............10-20 59
GUYDEN (2028 "Mexican Joe")............10-20 59
GUYDEN (2032 "Guardian Angel")............20-30 60
GUYDEN (2034 "Pink Chiffon")............10-20 60
GUYDEN (2040 "Happy Street")............10-20 60
INETTE (105 "Are You Tryin' to Tell Me Somethin' ")............5-10 63
MERCURY (71816 "Eating My Heart Out")............8-12 61
RCA (8646 "I Need All the Help I Can Get")............5-10 65
RCA (8703 "Caribbean")............5-10 65
REPRISE (541 "Instant Love")............5-10 66
REPRISE (568 "Baby, Baby, Baby")............5-10 68
Picture Sleeves
GUYDEN (2032 "Guardian Angel")............20-30 60
GUYDEN (2034 "Pink Chiffon")............20-30 60
LPs: 10/12-inch
CALICO............10-15
GUYDEN (502 "Caribbean")............25-45 60
(Monaural.)
GUYDEN (ST-502 "Caribbean")............50-75 60
(Stereo.)
REPRISE (6233 "Guitar Course")............10-15 66
Also see GREAT PRETENDER & TENNESSEE TWO AND A HALF
Also see MITCH & GAIL

TORQUAYS
Singles: 7-inch
GEE GEE CEE (8163 "Escondido")............15-25 63

TORQUAYS
Singles: 7-inch
AERTAUN (103 "Phantom Surfer")............15-25 64

TORQUAYS
Singles: 7-inch
COLPIX (782 "Image of a Girl")............8-12 65

TORQUAYS
Singles: 7-inch
GYPSY (265 "Busting Point")............15-25 67
ORIGINAL SOUND (66 "Harmonica Man")............10-20 67

TORQUAYS
Singles: 7-inch
TEE PEE (43/44 "I'll Never Forget"/"Even the Wind")............15-25 68
Members: Jim Chase; Paul Smith; Al Ives; Tom Guenther.

TORQUAYS
Singles: 7-inch
HIDEOUT (1002 "Shake It Tail Feather").20-30 '60s

TORQUAYS
Singles: 7-inch
ROCK-IT............15-20 '60s

TORQUAYS
(Torquay's)
Singles: 7-inch
HOLLY (4701 "Pineapple Moon")............40-50 '60s

TORQUES
Singles: 7-inch
CHESTERFIELD............10-15 63
LEMCO (890 "Bumpin' ")............10-15 65
LPs: 10/12-inch
LEMCO (604 "Live")............50-75 66
WIGGINS (64010 "Zoom")............50-75 67

TORQUETTS
Singles: 7-inch
SANTA CRUZ (002 "Any More")............10-20 65
TORQUETT (005 "Feedback")............15-25 '60s
TORQUETT (007 "Side Swiped")............15-25 '60s

TORRANCE, George ***P&R/R&B '68***
(With the Naturals; with Dippers)
Singles: 7-inch
DUO DISC............5-10 66
EPIC............5-10 61
KING (5376 "Go Away")............5-10 60
SHOUT............4-6 68

TORREES
Singles: 7-inch
ICL (114 "Didn't You Know")............25-40 '60s

TORRELL, Jack
Singles: 7-inch
DUDE ("I'm Gonna Look")............150-250
(Selection number not known.)

TORRELLS
Singles: 7-inch
SOMA (1186 "Lost Love")............25-35 63

TORRENCE, Georgie
(With the Dippers; with Caribbeans)
Singles: 7-inch
DUO DISC (117 "Fine Foxy Frame")........10-15 65
EPIC (9453 "Such a Fool Was I")............40-50 61
GALLIANT (1003 "Too Soon")............40-50 59

TORRENCE, Johnny
(With the Jewels; Johnny Torrance)
Singles: 78 rpm
IMPERIAL (5230 "Sad Day")............25-50 53
R&B (1306 "Rosalie")............50-75 54
Singles: 7-inch
IMPERIAL (5230 "Sad Day")............100-200 53
IMPERIAL (5897 "Your Lover Man")........10-20 62
R&B (1306 "Rosalie")............100-200 54
Also see JEWELS

TORRENCE, Lionel
Singles: 7-inch
EXCELLO (2218 "Flim Flam")............10-15 62
ZYNN (1008 "Rockin' Jole Blon")............25-45 61
ZYNN (1023 "Rooty Tooty")............15-25 61

TORRENS, George
Singles: 7-inch
TERRY (801 "Mary Lou")............50-75
TERRY (802 "TR-3")............50-75

TORRENT, Shay
Singles: 7-inch
HEARTBEAT (1 "Rock-a-Boogie")............15-25 59
HEARTBEAT (32 "You Can't Be True Dear")............10-15 60

TORRES, Edwin
Singles: 7-inch
VITERECT (7011 "Goodbye Adios, Roberto Clemente")............10-15

TORRES, Jim, & Sidemen
Singles: 7-inch
ALLIED (6341 "Wheels")............10-20 61
(Canadian.)

TORRIE, Bill
Singles: 7-inch
ABC-PAR (10188 "If You Let Me")............5-10 61
ALTON (302 "If You Let Me")............10-20 60

TORRIES
(Torres)
Singles: 7-inch
IGL (114 "Play Your Games")............10-20 66
SOMA (1438 "I've Had It")............10-20 '60s
SOMA (1463 "Ride On")............10-20 '60s

TORTILLA, Pete
Singles: 7-inch
IMPERIAL (5502 "Corrido Rock")............15-25 58

TOSH, Peter ***LP '76***
Singles: 12-inch
EMI AMERICA............4-6 83
Singles: 7-inch
COLUMBIA............4-6 76-77
EMI AMERICA............3-5 81-84
ROLLING STONES............3-5 78-79
Picture Sleeves
ROLLING STONES............4-6 78
EPs: 7-inch
COLUMBIA............4-8 76
(Promotional issue only.)
LPs: 10/12-inch
COLUMBIA............5-12 76-77
EMI AMERICA............5-8 81-84
ROLLING STONES............5-10 79

TOSH, Peter, & Mick Jagger
Singles: 7-inch
ROLLING STONES (19308 "Don't Look Back")............4-6 78
(With "Rolling Stones" at top of label.)
ROLLING STONES (19308 "Don't Look Back")............3-5 78
(Without "Rolling Stones" at top of label.)
Promotional Singles
ROLLING STONES (130 "Don't Look Back")............10-20 78
ROLLING STONES (7500 "Don't Look Back")............5-10 78
LPs: 10/12-inch
ROLLING STONES............5-10 78
Also see JAGGER, Mick
Also see MARLEY, Bob, & Wailers

TOSTI, Dick
Singles: 7-inch
DA-MAR (2004 "I'm Gonna Love You So")............15-25 62

TOTAL ECLIPSE
LPs: 10/12-inch
IMPERIAL............10-15 67

TOTO ***P&R/LP '78***
(With the Vienna Symphony Orchestra; with Jean-Michel Byron)
Singles: 12-inch
COLUMBIA............4-8 78-85
Singles: 10-inch
COLUMBIA (168065 "Gift with the Golden Gun"/"Goodbye Elenore")............5-10 81
(Two discs, songs from *Turn Back*.)
Picture Disc Singles
COLUMBIA (6784 "Hold the Line")............15-25 78
(Picture disc. Has same picture on both sides. Includes card insert autographed by band member.)
COLUMBIA (ZSS-165008 "Hold the Line")............10-15 78
(Licorice Pizza logo picture disc.)
COLUMBIA (ZSS-165008 "Hold the Line")............15-20 78
(KRBE logo picture disc.)
COLUMBIA (ZSS-165009 "Hold the Line")............15-20 78
(Roxy Invitation picture disc.)

COLUMBIA (ZSS-165009 "Hold the Line") 15-20 78
(Licorice Pizza or Wherehouse logo picture disc.)
COLUMBIA (165 792 "Georgy Porgy") 25-30 79
(Octagon picture disc. Promotional issue only.)
COLUMBIA (166 516/7 "Hydra") 80-100 79
(Square picture disc. Promotional issue only. 100 made. Includes folder. Some have KORL Channel 65 logo.)
COLUMBIA (166 518/19 "St. George and the Dragon") 80-100 80
(Square picture disc. Promotional issue only.)
COLUMBIA (169-156/109 "Africa"/"We Made It") 15-20 82
(Africa-shaped picture disc. Promotional issue only.)
COLUMBIA (169-156/157 "Africa"/"Good for You") 15-20 82
(Africa-shaped picture disc. Promotional issue only.)
COLUMBIA (8C8-38685 "Africa"/ "Rosanna") 15-20 82
(Africa-shaped picture disc.)

Singles: 7-inch

COLUMBIA 3-5 78-88

Picture Sleeves

COLUMBIA 3-6 82-88

LPs: 10/12-inch

COLUMBIA (30000 series) 5-10 78-86
(Black viny—no picture discs.)
COLUMBIA (9C9-39911 "Isolation") 12-18 84
(Picture disc.)
COLUMBIA (PJC-35317 "Toto") 25-35 79
(Picture disc. Same value for promotional issue. Add $10 if with die-cut cover.)
COLUMBIA (37928 "Toto IV") 20-30 82
(Picture disc. Promotional issue only.)
COLUMBIA (37928 "Toto IV") 25-35 82
(Picture disc. Promotional issue only with *Strawberries*, with WBCN logo.)
COLUMBIA (37928 "Toto IV") 30-40 82
(Picture disc. Promotional issue only, with "Turtles Annual Getaway" logo.)
COLUMBIA (PD-36813 "Turn Back") 35-45 79
(Picture disc. Promotional issue only. Includes calendar insert. 400 made.)
COLUMBIA (47728 "Toto IV") 10-15 83
(Half-speed mastered.)
MFLS (250 "Toto IV") 15-25
POLYDOR 5-8 84
Members: Steve Porcaro; David Paich; Steve Lukather; David Hungate; Jeffrey Porcaro; Bobby Kimball.

TOUCH

Singles: 7-inch

MAINLINE ("Light My Fire") 100-200 69
(Selection number not known.)
MAINLINE ("Stormy Monday Blues") ... 100-200 69
(Selection number not known.)

LPs: 10/12-inch

MAINLINE (2001 "Street Suite") 1000-1500 69
(Reportedly 100 made.)
Members: Ray Stone; Jerry Schulte.

TOUCH — R&B '77

Singles: 12-inch

BRUNSWICK 4-6 77

Singles: 7-inch

ATCO 3-5 80
BRUNSWICK 3-5 77
COLISEUM (2712 "Miss Teach") 5-10 69
LECASVER 5-10 69
PUBLIC (103 "No Shame") .... 5-10 '60s

LPs: 10/12-inch

ATCO 5-10 80
COLISEUM (51004 "20-20 Sound") 15-20 68
Members: Don Gallucci; Jeff Hawks; Joe Newman; Bruce Hauser; John Bordonaro.
Also see DON & GOODTIMES

TOUCHSTONE

Singles: 7-inch

SOUND MACHINE (10051 "Walk Out in the Rain") 8-12 68

TOUCHSTONE

Singles: 7-inch

COULEE (131 "Sweet 'N Tender") 10-15 69
TRANSACTION (708 "The Show") 10-15 69

Picture Sleeves

COULEE (131 "Sweet 'N Tender") 10-20 69
Members: Janet Evans; Tom Schmidt; Dave Schwandt; Bill Menke; George Swan.

TOUSSAINT, Allen

(Al Tousan)

Singles: 7-inch

ALON (9021 "Go Back Home") 8-12 65
BELL 5-10 68-69
CAYENNE 5-10
RCA (7192 "Happy Times") 15-25 58
REPRISE (1334 "When the Party's Over") .5-10 75
SCEPTER (12317 "From a Whisper to a Scream") 5-10 71
SCEPTER (12334 "Working in a Coal Mine") 4-6 71
SEVILLE (103 "Sweetie-Pie") 8-12 60
SEVILLE (110 "Naomi") 8-12 60
SEVILLE (113 "Blue Mood") 8-12 61
SEVILLE (124 "20 Years Later") 8-12 63
TIFFANY (9015 "From a Whisper to a Scream") 5-10 70

LPs: 10/12-inch

ART (26 "Live at La Fin") .... 15-25 '60s
BANDY (70017 "Allen Toussaint Sings with Billy Fayard & the Stokes") .... 10-15 '70s
RCA (1767 "The Wild Sounds of New Orleans") 150-200 58
REPRISE 10-15 72
SCEPTER 10-15 71
W.B. 5-10 78
Also see STOKES
Also see YOUNG ONES

TOWER OF POWER — LP '71

Singles: 7-inch

COLUMBIA 4-6 76-78
SAN FRANCISCO 5-8 64-73
W.B. 4-8 72-75

EPs: 7-inch

SAN FRANCISCO (7-204 "East Bay Grease") 15-25 71
(Promotional issue only.)

LPs: 10/12-inch

COLUMBIA 5-10 76-79
SAN FRANCISCO (204 "East Bay Grease") 10-20 71
W.B. 8-15 72-76
Members: Greg Adams; Mic Gillette; Steve Kupka; Emilio Castillo; Lenny Pickett; Chester Thompson; Francis Prestia; Edward McGhee; Rufus Miller; Lenny Williams.
Also see LITTLE FEAT

TOWERS

Singles: 7-inch

STUART (427 "Sham-Rock") 15-25 58

TOWERS

Singles: 7-inch

ERA (3106 "Friday Night Dance") 10-15 63

TOWERS, Bobby

Singles: 7-inch

STYLO (2108 "Gone Gone Gone Dreams") 30-40 60

TOWN, Chris

(With the Townsmen; Chris Town's Unit)

Singles: 7-inch

COTILLION 8-15 68-69
DECANTER (912 "So Many Days") 10-15
PORT (3021 "Turn to Me") 10-20 67

TOWN, Julie / Larry Mc Ginnis

Singles: 7-inch

BELL (94 "Tears on My Pillow"/"Tea for Two Cha Cha") 30-40 58

TOWN THREE

Singles: 7-inch

DE LUXE (6176 "Midnight Blues") 15-25 58
Member: Wes Voight.
Also see VOIGHT, Wes

TOWNES, Jerry

Singles: 7-inch

PENNY (108 "You Are My Sunshine") 8-12 69
Session: Cheers.
Also see CHEERS

TOWNES, Tobi

Singles: 7-inch

MICHELE (601 "His Buddy's Girl") 10-15

TOWNLEY, John, & Apostolic Family

Singles: 7-inch

VANGUARD (35122 "Just Another Day") ... 5-10 69
Also see FAMILY OF APOSTOLIC

TOWNSEND, Ed — P&R/R&B '58

Singles: 7-inch

ALADDIN (3373 "Love Never Dies") 15-25 57
CAPITOL (3926 "For Your Love") 15-25 58
CAPITOL (4048 "When I Grow Too Old to Dream") 10-20 58
CAPITOL (4104 "Richer Than I") 10-20 58
CAPITOL (4171 "Lover Come Back to Me") 10-20 59
CAPITOL (4240 "Hold On") 10-20 59
CAPITOL (4314 "Be My Love") 10-20 59
CAPITOL STARLINE (3926 "For Your Love") 5-10 63
CHALLENGE (9118 "Ed Townsend's Boogie Woogie") 8-12 61
CHALLENGE (9129 "And Then Came Love") 10-15 61
CHALLENGE (9144 "I Love to Hear That Beat") 8-12 62
DOT (15596 "My Need for You") 10-20 57
DYNASTY (643 "I Can't Leave You Alone") 10-15 60
GLO-TOWN (1008 "Don't Lead Me On") 5-10 66
KT (502 "Get Myself Together") .... 5-10 '60s
LIBERTY (55516 "Tell Her") 10-15 62
LIBERTY (55542 "There's No End") 10-15 63
MGM 5-10 67
MAXX (325 "I Love You") 10-20 64
POLYDOR 4-6 70
W.B. (5174 "I Love Everything About You") 10-20 60
W.B. (5174 "I Love Everything About You") 30-40 60
(Gold vinyl. Promotional issue only.)
W.B. (5200 "Dream World") 10-15 61

EPs: 7-inch

CAPITOL (985 "New in Town") 20-40 58
(Promotional issue only.)
CAPITOL (1091 "Ed Townsend") 20-40 58

LPs: 10/12-inch

CAPITOL (1140 "New in Town") 40-60 59
CAPITOL (1214 "Glad to Be Here") 40-60 59
CURTOM 8-12 76

TOWNSEND, Henry

Singles: 78 rpm

COLUMBIA (14491 "Mistreated Blues") 100-200 29

LPs: 10/12-inch

PRESTIGE BLUESVILLE 25-35 62

TOWNSEND, Honey

Singles: 7-inch

MALA (540 "Technicolor Dream") 8-12 66

TOWNSEND, Jerry

Singles: 7-inch

MASTER (1012 "Cold Cold Day") 15-25

TOWNSEND, Sherrell

Singles: 7-inch

GONE (5135 "He Thinks I Still Care") 10-20 62
LITTLE STAR (115 "Summer Days Are Here") 20-30 62
LUTE (6015 "Summer Days Are Here") ... 15-25 61

TOWNSHEND, Pete — LP '72

Singles: 7-inch

ATCO 3-5 80-85

Picture Sleeves

ATCO 3-5 85

LPs: 10/12-inch

ATCO 5-12 80-87
ATLANTIC 5-8 89
DECCA/TRACK 10-12 72
Also see WHO

TOWNSHEND, Pete, & Ronnie Lane — LP '77

Singles: 7-inch

MCA 3-6 77-78

LPs: 10/12-inch

MCA 8-10 77
Also see CLAPTON, Eric
Also see TOWNSHEND, Pete
Also see WOOD, Ron, & Ronnie Lane

TOWNSMEN

Singles: 7-inch

EVENT (503 "You're Having the Last Dance with Me") 50-75 60
VANITY 10-15 60
W.B. (5190 "You're Having the Last Dance with Me") 8-12 61

TOWNSMEN

Singles: 7-inch

COLUMBIA (43207 "Gotta Get Moving") ... 5-10 65
HERALD (585 "Is It All Over") 10-15 63
JOEY (6202 "I'm in the Mood for Love") .. 10-15 63

TOWNSMEN / Louie Lymon

Singles: 7-inch

P.J. (1340/1341 "I Can't Go"/"That's All I'll Ever Need") 200-300 63
Also see LYMON, Lewis, & Teenchords

TOWNSMEN

LP: 10/12-inch

COULEE (1009 "I Believe") .... 10-15 '70s
Also see JERRY & SILVERTONES

TOY DOLLS — P&R '62

Singles: 7-inch

ERA (3093 "Little Tin Soldier") 10-15 62

TOY FACTORY

Singles: 7-inch

JUBILEE (5668 "Sunny Sunny Feeling") ... 5-10 69
Member: Eric Olson.
Also see NEXT FIVE

TOYS — P&R/R&B '65

Singles: 7-inch

ABC 4-6 73
DYNO VOICE 4-8 65-66
ERIC .... 4-6 '70s
GUSTO .... 3-5 '80s
MUSICOR 5-10 68
PHILIPS 5-10 67
VIRGO 4-6 72

LPs: 10/12-inch

DYNO VOICE (9002 "A Lover's Concerto"/ "Attack") 25-35 66
(Monaural.)
DYNO VOICE (9002-S "A Lover's Concerto"/ "Attack") 20-30 66
(Stereo.)
SECTET 5-10 81
Members: Barbara Harris; June Montiero; Barbara Parritt.

TRACERS

Singles: 7-inch

SOLLY (928 "She Said Yeah") 10-20 66
(Label name misspelled.)
SULLY (928 "She Said Yeah") 10-20 66
(Label name correct.)
Also see SWEET SMOKE
Also see TRY CERZ

TRACES

Singles: 7-inch

LAURIE (3493 "What Am I to Do") 5-10 69
LAURIE (3515 "Runaround Sue") 5-10 69
Member: Sal Corrente.
Also see CORRENTE, Sal

TRACEY, Wreg

Singles: 7-inch

ANNA (1105 "All I Want Is You") 15-25 59
ANNA (1126 "Take Me Back") 15-25 60

TRACEY & TROY

Singles: 7-inch

ROULETTE (4509 "The Buffalo Walk") 5-10 63

TRACEY TWINS

(With Wendell Tracy & Orchestra; with Wendell Tracy Quartet)

Singles: 78 rpm

RESERVE 5-10 56-57

Singles: 7-inch

EAST WEST (108 "Heartbreak Hill") 10-20 58
RESERVE (102 "Flip Flop") 10-20 56
RESERVE (104 "Every Little Now and Then") 10-20 56
RESERVE (108 "Give Me Love") 10-20 56
RESERVE (110 "Tonight You Belong to Me") 15-25 56
RESERVE (114 "Do You Ever Think of Me") 10-20 57
(Same number also used for a Metrotones release.)
Also see METROTONES
Also see TRACY, Wendell

TRACI

Singles: 7-inch

INSTANT (3278 "The Loser")....5-10 66
SHRINE ("Take It From Me")....50-100 66
(Selection number not known.)

TRACKERS

Singles: 7-inch

LANDA (101 "You Are My World")....15-25 66
WHIP....10-20 65

TRACY, Bill
(Billy Tracy; Bill Tracey)

Singles: 78 rpm

RPM (489 "Kiss at Daybreak")....20-30 57

Singles: 7-inch

DEL-FI (4124 "You're My Girl")....10-15 59
DEL-FI (4132 "I'm So Happy")....10-15 59
DOT (15797 "One Chance")....25-50 58
RPM (489 "Kiss At Daybreak")....20-30 57
RADIANT (1504 "High School Hero")....8-12 61
STARFIRE....8-12

TRACY & TRACYNETTES

Singles: 7-inch

PEARLSFAR (108 "How Can I Tell")....15-25 58

TRADE WINDS *P&R '65*

Singles: 7-inch

BACK BEAT (590 "What's Love About")....4-6 68
ERIC....4-6 '70s
KAMA SUTRA (212 "Mind Excursion")....10-15 66
KAMA SUTRA (218 "Catch Me in the Meadow")....10-15 66
KAMA SUTRA (234 "Mind Excursion")....8-12 67
RED BIRD (020 "New York's a Lonely Town")....15-25 65
RED BIRD (028 "The Girl from Greenwich Village")....10-20 65
RED BIRD (033 "Summertime Girl")....40-50 65

LPs: 10/12-inch

KAMA SUTRA....25-35 67
Members: Pete Anders; Vinnie Poncia.
Also see ANDERS & PONCIA
Also see BEACH BOYS / Trade Winds

TRADEMARKS

Singles: 7-inch

JUBAL (100 "Baha-Ree-Ba")....10-20 63

TRADEMARKS

Singles: 7-inch

PALMER (5018 "If I Was Gone")....10-20 67

TRADEWINDS *P&R '59*

Singles: 7-inch

RCA (7511 "Twins")....8-12 59
RCA (7553 "Furry Murray")....15-20 59
Members: Ralph Rizzoli; Angel Cifelli; Sal Capriglione; Phil Mehill.

TRADEWINDS

Singles: 7-inch

UNITED SOUTHERN ARTISTS (104 "Boy Named Jerry")....8-12 61

TRADEWINDS

Singles: 7-inch

DAWN CORY (1005 "Gotcha")....20-30 64

TRADEWINDS

Singles: 7-inch

BRANDYWINE (1001 "Jump")....8-12
BRANDYWINE (1004 "Raw-Hide")....30-40 65
DAN-TONE (1001 "Congo Beat")....8-12 62
TRIUMPH (301 "Strange")....8-12

TRADEWINDS 5
(Tradewinds Five, Inc.)

Singles: 7-inch

ARIOLA (14098 "Get Down with It")....8-12
FOX (421 "It Must Be Love")....8-12 66
FRANKLIN (617 "Get Down with It")....12-18 68
FRANKLIN (623 "Be Sure")....12-18 68
REACTION (1006 "Come On...You're Alright")....25-35 67

Picture Sleeves

ARIOLA (14098 "Get Down with It")....10-15
Members: Rick Miller; Vern Peterson; Richard Torrance; Pat Majors; Rip Cullins; Tom Weiser; Mark Van Horn; Ken Weisman.

TRADITIONS

Singles: 7-inch

BELL (616 "Forever and Always")....15-25 65
DAWN (301 "Once in a While")....8-12 65
(Blue vinyl.)
FELLATIO (102 "Once in a While")....8-12 65

TRADITIONS / Ditalians

Singles: 7-inch

SAXONY (2004 "Forever and Always"/"I Gotta Go")....4-6 96
Also see TRADITIONS

TRAFALGAR SQUARE

Singles: 7-inch

USA (890 "Till the End of the Day")....15-25 67
Members: Tim Eifler; Steve Grim; John Marselli.

TRAFFIC *P&R '67*
(Traffic Etc.)

Singles: 7-inch

ASYLUM....4-6 74
ISLAND....4-6 72-73
U.A.....5-10 67-72

Picture Sleeves

U.A.....8-10 67

LPs: 10/12-inch

ASYLUM....10-15 74
ISLAND (Except 9000 series)....5-8 83
ISLAND (9000 series)....10-15 71-75
MFSL (209 "The Low Spark of High Heeled Boys")....25-35 94
(Half-speed mastered.)
U.A.....10-20 68-75
Members: Jim Capaldi; Dave Mason; Steve Winwood; Chris Wood.
Also see MASON, Dave
Also see WINWOOD, Steve

TRAIL, Buck

Singles: 7-inch

ART (103 "Knocked Out Joint on Mars")....5-10
TRAIL (100 "Honky Tonk on 2nd Street")....300-400
TRAIL (103 "Knocked Out Joint on Mars")....2000-2500
TRAIL (105 "Chattanooga Drummer Man")....300-400

TRAIL BLAZERS

Singles: 7-inch

ABC-PAR (10187 "Deserted Street")....10-15 61

TRAILBLAZERS

Singles: 7-inch

WATSON (500 "Grandpa's Rock")....150-250

TRAIN

Singles: 7-inch

FULLTONE (1002 "I Want Sunshine")....60-80 '60s

TRAITS *P&R '66*

Singles: 7-inch

ASCOT (2108 "Linda Lou")....10-20 62
GARRISON (3007 "Too Good to Be True")....10-15 67
PACEMAKER (254 "Too Good to Be True")....15-20 65
RENNER (221 "Linda Lou")....15-25 62
RENNER (229 "Got My Mojo Working")....10-20 62
(Black vinyl.)
RENNER (229 "Got My Mojo Working")....20-30 62
(Colored vinyl. Promotional issue only.)
SCEPTER (12169 "Harlem Shuffle")....5-10 66
TNT (164 "Don't Be Blue")....75-125 59
TNT (175 "Live It Up")....50-75 59
TNT (177 "My Baby's Fine")....50-75 60
TNT (181 "Your Turn to Cry")....50-75 61
TNT (185 "Walkin' All Day")....50-75 61
UNIVERSAL....10-15 66
Member: Roy Head.
Also see HEAD, Roy

TRAITS

Singles: 7-inch

CONTACT (4058 "Some Day, Some Way")....25-30
QUEEN'S CITY (101 "Nobody Loves the Hulk")....10-20 68

TRAMMELL, Bobby Lee *C&W '72*

Singles: 7-inch

ABC-PAR (9890 "Shirley Lee")....50-75 58
ALLEY (1001 "Arkansas Twist")....15-25 62
ALLEY (1004 "Come On Baby")....15-25 63
ALLEY (1050 "If You Ever Get It Once")....15-25 67
ATLANTA....15-25 62
ATLANTIC....5-10 66
CAPITOL (3718 "Love")....4-6 73
CAPITOL (3801 "You Mostest Girl")....5-8 73
CINNAMON (797 "Warmth of Your Love")....4-6 74
CONFEDERATE (125 "Shake Me Baby")....30-40
COUNTRY....5-10 66
FABOR (127 "You Mostest Girl")....10-15 64
FABOR (4038 "Shirley Lee")....75-125 58
HOT (101 "Shimmy Lou")....20-30 59
HOT (102 "Betty Jean")....20-30 59
RADIO (102 "You Mostest Girl")....30-40 58
RADIO (114 "My Susie Jane")....30-40 58
SANTO....10-20
SIMS (183 "Good Lovin' ")....5-10 64
SIMS (195 "Come On and Love Me")....5-10 64
SIMS (225 "24 Hours")....5-10 65
SIMS (241 "I Tried")....5-10 65
SIMS (254 "Lone Tall Sally")....5-10 65
SKYLA (1107 "You Mostest Girl")....10-20 61
(Also issued as by Bob Lee.)
SOUNCOT....4-8 71-72
VADEN (304 "Been a Walking")....50-100 60
WARRIOR (1554 "Woe Is Me")....50-75 59

LPs: 10/12-inch

ATLANTA (1503 "Arkansas Twist")....75-100 62
SOUNCOT....10-20 71-72
Session: Sonny Burgess; Ace Cannon.
Also see BURGESS, Sonny
Also see CANNON, Ace
Also see LEE, Bob
Also see ROE, Tommy / Bobby Lee Trammell

TRAMMELL, Bobby Lee, & Jean Steakley

Singles: 7-inch

SOUNCOT....4-6 72
Also see TRAMMELL, Bobby Lee

TRAMPS

Singles: 7-inch

ARVEE (1 "I'm So Glad")....400-500 58
ARVEE (548 "Ride On")....10-20 59
ARVEE (570 "Your Love")....15-25 59

TRANA, Raul, & Nicaraguans

Singles: 7-inch

ENSIGN (2009 "Soy Sentimental")....40-50 58

TRANELLS

Singles: 7-inch

CHELTEN (090 "Come on and Tell Me")....40-50 '60s

TRANQUILS

Singles: 7-inch

HAMILTON (50005 "You're Such a Much")....15-25 58

TRANSACTIONS

Singles: 7-inch

BRC (3294 "Spooky")....10-20 67

TRANS-ATLANTIC SUBWAY

Singles: 7-inch

LIGHTFOOT (100,333 "Servent of the People")....10-20 68

TRANSIENTS

LPs: 10/12-inch

HORIZON....15-25 63
Member: Billy Strange.
Also see STRANGE, Billy

TRAN-SISTERS

Singles: 7-inch

IMPERIAL (5952 "Somebody's Blue")....10-15 63
IMPERIAL (5983 "Your Love")....10-15 63
PICKWICK CITY....5-10 '60s

TRANSPLANT

Singles: 7-inch

LEJAC (1942 "With Her Head Tucked Underneath Her Arm")....15-25 '60s

TRANTHAM, Carl

Singles: 7-inch

LINCOLN (643 "Where There's a Will")....400-500
STARDAY (361 "Deedle Deedle Dum")....100-200 58

TRAPE, Mary Jo

Singles: 7-inch

SHERRY (537 "What Would Johnny Say")....10-15 60

TRAPEZE *LP '74*

Singles: 7-inch

PAID....3-5 81
THRESHOLD....4-8 71-72
W.B.....4-6 74-75

LPs: 10/12-inch

PAID....5-10 81
POLYDOR ("Medusa")....50-100 71
(Selection number not known.)
SHARK....8-10
THRESHOLD (2 "Trapeze")....25-50 71
THRESHOLD (4 "Medusa")....75-100 71
THRESHOLD (8 "You Are the Music, We're Just the Band")....25-50 72
THRESHOLD (11 "Final Swing")....25-50 72
W.B.....8-10 74-75
Also see DEEP PURPLE

TRASH

Singles: 7-inch

APPLE (1804 "Road to Nowhere")....75-100 69
APPLE (1811 "Golden Slumbers")....15-20 69
APPLE (4671 "Road to Nowhere")....60-80 69
(Promotional issue only.)

TRASHMEN *P&R '63*

Singles: 7-inch

APEX (76894 "Surfin' Bird")....15-25 63
APEX (76904 "Bird Dance Beat")....15-25 64
APEX (76916 "Bad News")....15-25 64
APEX (76925 "Peppermint Man")....25-35 64
APEX (76942 "Whoa Dad!")....25-35 64
APEX (76973 "Keep Your Hands Off My Baby")....25-35 65
ARGO (5516 "Bird '65")....50-75 65
BEAR (1966 "Lost Angel")....10-20 66
ERA....4-8 72
ERIC....4-6 '70s
GARRETT (4002 "Surfin' Bird")....10-20 63
(Red label.)
GARRETT (4002 "Surfin' Bird")....10-20 63
(Orange label.)
GARRETT (4003 "Bird Dance Beat")....10-20 64
GARRETT (4005 "Bad News")....10-20 64
GARRETT (4010 "Peppermint Man")....10-20 64
GARRETT (4012 "Whoa Dad!")....10-20 64
GARRETT (4013 "Dancin' with Santa")....10-20 64
LANA....5-10 '60s
METROBEAT (4448 "Green Green Backs Back Home")....15-20 68
TERRIFIC (5003 "Surfin' Bird")....4-6
TRIBE (8315 "Same Lines")....25-35 66

Picture Sleeves

GARRETT (4012 "Whoa Dad!")....60-80 64
GARRETT (4013 "Dancin' with Santa")....100-125 64

LPs: 10/12-inch

SOMA/GARRETT (GA-200 "Surfin' Bird")....100-150 64
(Monaural.)
SOMA/GARRETT (GAS-200 "Surfin' Bird")....150-200 64
(Stereo.)
SUNDAZED....5-10 '90s
Members: Tony Andreason; Bob Reed; Dal Winslow; Steve Wahrer; Gary Nielsen.
Also see STRING KINGS
Also see THAXTER, Jim, & Travelers

TRASHMEN / Castaways

Singles: 7-inch

SOMA (1469 "Surfin' Bird"/"Liar Liar")....5-10 '60s
Also see TRASHMEN

TRAVEL AGENCY

Singles: 7-inch

HILLPORT (1002 "Until the Day")....8-12
TANQUERAY (20102 "Time")....10-20 67
VIVA (637 "What's a Man")....8-12 69
ZORDAN (107 "Jailbait")....10-20

LPs: 10/12-inch

VIVA (36017 "Travel Agency")....15-25 68
Member: Frank Davis.
Also see FEVER TREE

TRAVELERS
(Frank Lopez & Travelers)

Singles: 78 rpm

ATLAS (1086 "Betty Jean")....50-100 57

Singles: 7-inch

ANGLE TONE (1086 "Betty Jean")....3-5
ATLAS (1086 "Betty Jean")....100-150 57

ATLAS (1086 "Betty Jean") 10-20
(Has Atlas at 11:00.)
Member: Frank Lopez.

TRAVELERS

Singles: 7-inch

ANDEX (2011 "I'll Be Home for Christmas") 25-35 57
ANDEX (4006 "Why") 25-35 58
ANDEX (4012 "He's Got the Whole World in His Hands") 15-25 58
ANDEX (4033 "I Go for You") 25-35 59

TRAVELERS

Singles: 7-inch

ABC-PAR (10119 "June, July, August") .. 10-15 60
DECCA (31215 "Ivy On the Old School Wall") 10-20 61
DECCA (31282 "Oh My Love") 30-40 61
DON RAY (5965 "Traveler") 8-12 62
GASS (1000 "In the Pines") 10-20 63
KNIGHT (2763 "Spanish Moon") 5-40 63
KNIGHT (2864 "Everywhere I Go") 5-10 64
MG (928 "Rock Me Baby") 10-15 59
MAGIC LAMP (516 "Goin' Home") 5-10 64
PRINCESS (52 "Spanish Moon") 15-25 63
VAULT (911 "Spanish Moon") 5-10 64
YELLOW SAND 8-12 63-65
Member: Ron Story.
Also see RIC-A-SHAYS

TRAVELERS

Singles: 7-inch

WORLD-WIDE (8511 "Too Young") 75-125 62

TRAVELERS

Singles: 7-inch

GLAD-HAMP (2024 "My Baby Doesn't Love Me Anymore") 15-25 65

TRAVELERS IV

Singles: 7-inch

ROX (1001 "A Message for You") .... 10-20 '60s

TRAVELING SALESMEN

Singles: 7-inch

RCA (9167 "Days of My Years") 10-15 67

TRAVELING WILBURYS *P&R/LP '88*

Singles: 7-inch

WILBURY (27732 "Handle with Care") 4-8 88
(Commercial issue.)
WILBURY (27732 "Handle with Care") 10-20 88
(Promotional issue.)
WILBURY (27637 "End of theLine") 10-15 88
(Commercial issue.)
WILBURY (27637 "End of theLine") 10-20 88
(Promotional issue.)

Picture Sleeves

WILBURY (27732 "Handle with Care") 4-8 88
WILBURY (27637 "End of the Line") 10-20 88

LPs: 10/12-inch

WILBURY 8-15 88-90
Members: George Harrison; Bob Dylan; Roy Orbison; Tom Petty; Jeff Lynne.
Also see DYLAN, Bob
Also see HARRISON, George
Also see LYNNE, Jeff
Also see ORBISON, Roy
Also see PETTY, Tom, & Heartbreakers

TRAVELLERS

Singles: 7-inch

IMAGE (5003 "The Bomb") 8-12 61
Also see CATES, Ronnie

TRA-VELLES

Singles: 7-inch

DEBONAIR (101 "Can't Go for That") 50-100

TRAVERS, Mary *P&R/LP '71*

Singles: 7-inch

CHRYSALIS 3-5 78-79
W.B. 4-6 71-73

LPs: 10/12-inch

CHRYSALIS 5-10 78
W.B. 6-12 71-74
Also see DENVER, John
Also see PETER, PAUL & MARY

TRAVIS, Bob

Singles: 7-inch

ALMATA (101 "Hey Ho Hey Ho Ho Baby Baby") 100-200

TRAVIS, Danny

Singles: 7-inch

BENN-X (54 "Ever Since") 150-200 62

TRAVIS, Dave

Singles: 7-inch

BAGDAD (108 "I Don't Like Him") 100-200 63
U.S.P. (101 "She's Gone") 10-15 66

TRAVIS, Merle *C&W/P&R '46*

Singles: 78 rpm

CAPITOL 4-10 46-57

Singles: 7-inch

CAPITOL (1100 thru 3100 series) 5-15 50-55
CAPITOL (5600 series) 4-6 66

EPs: 7-inch

CAPITOL 10-20 56-57

LPs: 10/12-inch

CMH 8-15 79-81
CAPITOL (T-650 "Guitar") 50-80 56
CAPITOL (SM-650 "Guitar") 5-10 75
CAPITOL (891 "Back Home") 50-60 57
CAPITOL (1391 "Walkin' the Strings") 50-60 60
CAPITOL (1664 "Travis") 30-40 62
CAPITOL (1956 "Songs of the Coal Mine") 50-60 57
CAPITOL (T/ST-2662 "Best of Merle Travis") 15-25 67
CAPITOL (SM-2662 "Best of Merle Travis") 5-10 75
CAPITOL (2938 "Strictly Guitar") 20-30 69
PICKWICK/HILLTOP 10-15 66
PREMIER 5-8
SHASTA 10-15
SPIN-O-RAMA .... 8-12 '60s
Also see CAMPI, Ray, & Merle Travis
Also see RITTER, Tex / Merle Travis
Also see THOMPSON, Hank, & Merle Travis

TRAVIS, Merle, & Johnny Bond

LPs: 10/12-inch

CAPITOL (249 "Great Songs of the Delmore Brothers") 10-20 69
Also see BOND, Johnny

TRAVIS, Merle, & Joe Maphis

LPs: 10/12-inch

CMH 8-12
CAPITOL (T-2102 "Merle Travis & Joe Maphis, Two Great Guitars") 40-50 64
(Monaural.)
CAPITOL (ST-2102 "Merle Travis & Joe Maphis, Two Great Guitars") 50-60 64
(Stereo.)
CAPITOL (SM-2102 "Merle Travis & Joe Maphis, Two Great Guitars") 5-10 78

TRAVIS, Merle, & Mac Wiseman

LPs: 10/12-inch

CMH 8-12 82
Also see TRAVIS, Merle
Also see WISEMAN, Mac

TRAVIS & BOB *P&R/R&B '59*

Singles: 78 rpm

BARREL (601 "Tell Him No") 100-200 59
(Canadian.)

Singles: 7-inch

BARREL (601 "Tell Him No") 10-20 59
(Canadian.)
BIG TOP (3054 "Pocahontas") 10-15 60
MERCURY (71797 "Give Your Love to Me") 5-10 61
SANDY (1017 "Tell Him No") 15-25 59
(No "Distributed By Dot" on label.)
SANDY (1017 "Tell Him No" 10-15 59
(Has "Distributed By Dot" on label)
SANDY (1019 "Little Bitty Johnny") 10-15 59
SANDY (1024 "Oh Yeah") 10-15 59
SANDY (1029 "That's How Long") 10-15 60
Members: Travis Pritchett; Bob Weaver.

TRAYLOR, Pearl
(With Chuck Thomas & His All Stars)

Singles: 78 rpm

OKEH (6822 "Come On Daddy") 10-20 51

Singles: 7-inch

OKEH (6822 "Come On Daddy") 25-50 51

TRAYNOR, Jay

Singles: 7-inch

ABC-PAR (10809 "Come On") 20-30 66
ABC-PAR (10845 "Up and Over") 20-30 66
(According to Jay Traynor, DCP issues of this are unauthorized.)
CORAL (62396 "I Rise, I Fall") 30-40 64
CORAL (62420 "Little Sister") 30-40 64
ROARING (800 "Dusty Said Goodbye") ... 10-15 67
Also see JAY & AMERICANS

TRAYWICK, Randy *C&W '79*

Singles: 7-inch

PAULA (429 "Dreamin' ") 8-12 78
PAULA (431 "She's My Woman") 10-20 78

TREADWAY, Dicky

Singles: 7-inch

T.S.M. (8321 "Party Crasher") 5-10 67
Also see SCOTT, Mark, & Dicky Treadway

TREASURERS

Singles: 7-inch

CROWN (005 "I Walk with an Angel") .. 150-250 61
(Reportedly 100 made.)

TREASURES

Singles: 7-inch

VALOR (5534 "Lean Jean") .... 20-30 '60s
(With the Aaron Brothers.)
VALOR (47900 "Minor Chaos") 50-75 64
(Black vinyl. 250 made.)
VALOR (47900 "Minor Chaos") 75-125 64
(Green vinyl. 250 made.)
Member: Paul M. Hubbard.

TREASURES

Singles: 7-inch

SHIRLEY (500 "Hold Me Tight") 50-75 64
Members: Pete Anders; Vinnie Poncia.
Also see ANDERS & PONCIA

TREBELAIRES

Singles: 78 rpm

NESTOR 20-30 54

Singles: 7-inch

NESTOR (16 "There Goes That Train") 150-200 54

TREBELS

Singles: 7-inch

VIKING (1021 "Oh Darlin' ") 10-20 61

TREBLE CHORDS

Singles: 7-inch

DECCA (31015 "Teresa") 40-50 59

TREBLE TONES

Singles: 7-inch

B-ATLAS (260 "The Crawl") 10-20 60
SOUVENIR (1010 "Little Laurie") 10-20 62

TREBUS, Bob, & Fender Benders

Singles: 7-inch

SOMA (1450 "Sadie") 8-12 66
Also see FENDERBENDERS

TREE

Singles: 7-inch

BARVIS (7010 "No Good Woman") 15-25 67

LPs: 10/12-inch

GOAT FARM (580 "Tree") 40-60 70
Member: Chris Roach.

TREE STUMPS
(Tree-Mendous-Stumps)

Singles: 7-inch

RECORD (20013 "Listen to Love") 15-25 66

Picture Sleeves

RECORD (20013 "Listen to Love") 15-25 66
Member: Michael Stanley.
Also see SILK
Also see STANLEY, Michael, Band

TREE SWINGERS *P&R '60*

Singles: 7-inch

BIG TOP (3058 "Only Forever") 10-15 60
GUYDEN (2036 "Kookie Little Paradise") .. 8-12 60
Members: Art Polhemus; Terry Byrnes; Kenny Bolognese.
Also see CHANDLER, Kenny

TREE TOPS
(Featuring Jerry Doell)

Singles: 7-inch

ZERO (108 "The Fastest Gun") 15-20 60
ZERO (109 "Tree Top") 50-75 60

TREES

Singles: 7-inch

BALI-HI (808 "Your Life") .... 15-25 '60s
MUM .... 10-20 '60s

TREEZ

Singles: 7-inch

HARLEQUIN (72566 "You Lied to Me Before") 15-25 66

TREETOP, Bobby

Singles: 7-inch

TUFF (415 "So Sweet") 25-35 65
TUFF (417 "Wait Till I Get to Know Ya") .. 25-35 65

TRE-J'S

Singles: 7-inch

TEE GEE 10-20 58

TRELLS
(With the Soulful Saxons)

Singles: 7-inch

PORT CITY (1112 "Bad Weather") .... 50-75 '60s

TREMAIN, Willy
(Willy Tremain's Thunderbirds; Willie Tremain's Thunderbirds)

Singles: 7-inch

CUCA (1001 "Midnight Express") 25-50 59
(Credits "Willie." 500 made.)
SWASTIKA (1001 "Midnight Express") 200-300 59
(First issue. Credits "Willy." 500 made.)
Members: Frank Cunningham; Williams Tremain; Dick Scully; Joe Schumacher.

TREMAINES
(With "Orchestra")

Singles: 7-inch

CASH (100 "Moon Shining Bright") 750-1000 58
(First issue.)
CASH (100 "Moon Shining Bright") 400-600 58
(Copies with Val label steamed off.)
KANE (008 "Heavenly") 100-200 62
(First issue. Black vinyl.)
KANE (008 "Heavenly") 200-300 62
(First issue. Red vinyl.)
OLD TOWN (1051 "Moon Shining Bright") 50-60 58
VAL (101 "Moon Shining Bright") 100-150 58
V-TONE (507 "Heavenly") 10-20 63

TREMBLE, Tommy

Singles: 7-inch

SOUND TEX ("She Said") 100-200
(Selection number not known.)

TREMELOES *P&R/LP '67*

Singles: 7-inch

DJM 4-6 76
EPIC 5-10 66-70

Picture Sleeves

EPIC (10184 "Silence Is Golden") 5-10 67
EPIC (10233 "Even the Bad Times Are Good") 5-10 67

EPs: 7-inch

EPIC (26388 "The Tremeloes") 8-12 68
(Juke box issue.)

LPs: 10/12-inch

DJM 8-10 76
EPIC 15-25 67-68
Also see POOLE, Brian

TREMELOES / Hollies

Singles: 7-inch

EPIC (10184 "Silence is Golden"/"Carrie-Anne") 50-100 67
(Red vinyl. Promotional issue only.)

Picture Sleeves

EPIC (10184 "Silence is Golden"/"Carrie-Anne") 50-100 67
Also see HOLLIES
Also see TREMELOES

TREMELOES

Singles: 7-inch

ROCKLAND (102 "Jaguar") .... 15-25 '60s

TREM-LOS

Singles: 7-inch

NOLTA (350 "Silly Affair") 30-40 61

Picture Sleeves

NOLTA (350 "Silly Affair") 50-75 61

TREMOLONS

Singles: 7-inch

WILDWOOD 10-20 65

TREMONTS

("Featuring Joe Dee"; with Joe Dee & Top Hands)

Singles: 7-inch

BRUNSWICK (55217 "Legend of Love") 10-20 61
PAT RICCIO (101 "Legend of Love") 50-75 61
(First issue.)
Also see CHICAGO, Artie
Also see CURTISS, Jimmy
Also see DEE, Joe, & Top Hands
Also see JOYCE & PRIVATEERS
Also see REGENTS
Also see RIVERS, Johnny / Tremonts / Luke Gordon / Charlie Francis

TREMORS

Singles: 7-inch

LODE (2005 "Yucatan") 10-15 58

TRENAY, Joey

Singles: 7-inch

MAGENTA (05 "Why Walk Alone") 50-75 61

TRENCHMEN

Singles: 7-inch

IMPACT SOUND (236678 "Chains on My Heart") 25-35 '60s

TREN-DELLS

(Trend-els)

Singles: 7-inch

BOSS (9919 "Love") 15-25 65
BOSS (9921 "That's My Desire") 15-25 65
CAPITOL (4852 "Night Owl") 8-12 62
JAM (100 "Night Owl") 10-20 62
JAM (111 "Hey Da-Da-Dow") 8-12 62
SOUND STAGE 7 (2508 "Ain't That Funny") 10-15 63
SOUTHTOWN (22001 "Everyday") 5-10 64
TILT (779 "I'm So Young") 30-40 61
(Black label.)
TILT (779 "I'm So Young") 10-20 61
(Yellow label.)
TILT (788 "I Miss You So") 50-75 62
(Yellow label.)
Members: Johnny Hourigan; Joe Bergman; Bill Summit; Bill Mathley.

TRENDS

Singles: 7-inch

ARGO (5341 "I'll Be True") 8-12 59
CLOVER (1002 "I'll Be True") 15-25 59
(First issue.)
RCA (7733 "The Beard") 10-15 60
SCOPE (102 "Once Again") 30-40 59

TRENDS

Singles: 7-inch

RECORD CENTER (1101 "Tell Me") 8-12 63

TRENDS

Singles: 7-inch

ABC (10731 "Not too Old to Cry") 15-25 65
ABC (10817 "A Night for Love") 15-25 66
ABC (10881 "No One There") 15-25 66
ABC (10993 "Thanks for a Little Lovin'") 10-20 67
ABC (11091 "Soul Clap") 10-20 68
ABC (11150 "Not Another Day") 20-30 68
ABC-PAR (10731 "Not Too Old to Cry") 25-35 65
SMASH (1914 "Dance with Me Baby") 10-20 64
SMASH (1933 "Get Something Going") 10-20 64

TREND-TONES

Singles: 7-inch

SUPERB (100 "This Is Love") 50-75 61
(First issued as by the Paradons.)
Also see PARADONS

TRENIER, Milton

(Milt Trenier; with Gene Gilbeaux Quartet)

Singles: 78 rpm

GROOVE 5-10 54
RCA 5-10 53

Singles: 7-inch

DOT (15922 "Gonna Catch Me a Rat") 15-25 59
GROOVE 10-20 54-63
RCA 10-20 53
Also see TRENIERS

TRENIER, Milton, & Micki Lynn

LPs: 10/12-inch

CADET 10-15 67

TRENIER TWINS

(With the Jimmie Lunceford Orchestra)

Singles: 78 rpm

CORAL 10-20 49
MERCURY 15-25 47-48
Members: Claude Trenier; Cliff Trenier.
Also see TRENIERS

TRENIERS R&B '51

(With Gene Gilbeaux)

Singles: 78 rpm

BRUNSWICK 10-20 57-58
EPIC 5-15 54-56
LONDON 10-15 50
OKEH 10-15 51-55
VIK 8-12 56

Singles: 7-inch

BRUNSWICK 10-20 57-58
DOM 5-10 68
DOT (Except 15882) 8-12 58-59
DOT (15882 "Never, Never") 10-20 58
EPIC 10-20 54-56
LONDON (30080 "Everybody Get Together") 20-30 50
OKEH 15-30 51-55
VIK 10-20 56

EPs: 7-inch

EPIC (7014 "Go Go Go") 35-50 56
EPIC (7103 "On TV") 35-50 56
EPIC (7014 "Go Go Go") 35-50 57

LPs: 10/12-inch

DOT (3257 "Souvenir Album") 50-75 60
EPIC (3125 "On TV") 100-150 56
Members: Milt; Cliff; Claude.
Also see MAYS, Willie, & Treniers
Also see TRENIER, Milt
Also see TRENIER, Skip, & Fabulous Treniers
Also see TRENIER TWINS

TRENT, Barbara

Singles: 7-inch

RED LABEL (38 "One Child") 10-15 '60s
TERRY (108 "Come On Home") 10-15 61

TRENT, Buck

Singles: 7-inch

BOONE (1076 "Five String General") 5-10 68

TRENT, Charles

Singles: 7-inch

DEL-FI (4134 "Ol' Man Mose") 8-12 60
DEL-FI (4154 "Ol' Man Mose") 5-10 61
TENDER (519 "No Kiss") 30-40 59
TIDE (010 "Blue Stamp Blues") 10-15 60

TRENT, Jackie

Singles: 7-inch

A&M (1022 "Don't Send Me Away") 5-10 69
KAPP (583 "If You Love Me, Really Love Me") 5-10 64
KAPP (630 "I Heard Someone Say") 5-10 64
NASCO (6012 "What's He Got") 10-20 58
PARKWAY 8-12 65-66
W.B. 5-10 65-68

TRENT, Kenneth

Singles: 7-inch

VEEDA (4008 "The Way I Feel About You") 40-60 '60s

TREN-TEENS

Singles: 7-inch

CARNIVAL (501 "My Babys [sic] Gone") 50-75 64

TRENTONS

Singles: 7-inch

SHEPHERD (2204 "All Alone") 100-150 62
Also see HI-TONES
Also see SHY TONES

TRES FEMMES

Singles: 7-inch

PHIL-L.A. OF SOUL (333 "Listen to Your Mama") 5-10 69
20TH FOX (6702 "You Better Get Back") 5-10 68

TRESPASSERS

Singles: 7-inch

SILVER SEAL (1020 "Come with Me") 15-25 '60s

TRETONES

Singles: 7-inch

B-W (604 "Blind Date") 10-20 60

TREVOR, Van C&W '66

(With the Saturday Knights)

Singles: 7-inch

ATLANTIC (2175 "I Want to Cry") 10-15 63
BAND BOX 8-15 66-67
CANADIAN AMERICAN (181 "Louisiana Hot Sauce") 5-10 64
CANADIAN AMERICAN (188 "For This Girl") 5-10 65
CLARIDGE (305 "Melting Snow") 5-10 65
CORSICAN 10-15 61
DATE 5-10 67-68
MALA (478 "Dirty Lies") 5-10 64
VIVID (1004 "C'mon Now Baby") 15-20 63
(With the 4 Seasons.)
ROYAL AMERICAN 5-8 69-71

LPs: 10/12-inch

BAND BOX 10-15 67
DATE 10-15 67
ROYAL AMERICAN 8-12 70
Also see 4 SEASONS
Also see SATURDAY KNIGHTS

TREXLER, Gary

Singles: 78 rpm

REV (3507 "Teen Baby") 10-15 57

Singles: 7-inch

REV (3507 "Teen Baby") 10-15 57

TREY TONES

Singles: 7-inch

B-W (603 "Blind Date") 10-15 60
SUNLINER (101 "Nonymous") 15-25 64

TRIADS

Singles: 7-inch

RINGO (111 "Bacon Fat") 10-20 60

TRIADS

Singles: 78 rpm

ENCINO (1002 "One More Kiss") 10-15 56

Singles: 7-inch

ENCINO (1002 "One More Kiss") 30-40 56

TRIANGLE

Singles: 7-inch

FUN ("Why") 15-25 67
(No selection number used.)

TRIANGLE

Singles: 7-inch

AMARET (108 "Magic Touch") 8-12 69
AMARET (113 "Lucille") 8-12 69

LPs: 10/12-inch

AMARET (5001 "How Now Blue Cow") 15-25 69
Members: Michael Carelli; Ty Grimes.
Also see CAPTAIN BEEFHEART

TRIANGLES

Singles: 7-inch

FARGO (1023 "Dance the Magoo") 8-12 62
FIFO (107 "Really I Do") 200-300 61
HERALD (549 "Savin' My Love") 150-250 60

TRIBBLE, TNT, & King Bees

Singles: 7-inch

FRANDY (600 "Crazy to the Bone") 20-30 61

TRIBBLE, TNT, with Frank Motley & His Crew

Singles: 78 rpm

GOTHAM 10-15 53-54
RCA 10-20 52

Singles: 7-inch

CHART (638 "T.N.T.") 15-25 57
EAST WEST (125 "Madison Beat") 15-25 59
GOTHAM (288 "Twin-H Jump") 20-30 53
GOTHAM (294 "Hamburger") 20-30 54
GOTHAM (300 "Hot Heat!") 20-30 54
RCA (4460 "T.V. Boogie Blues") 25-50 52
Also see MOTLEY, Frank

TRIBE

Singles: 7-inch

FENTON (2088 "Try Try") 20-30 67
PLANET (108 "Gamma Goochie) 10-20 66

TRIBU TERRYS

Singles: 7-inch

PRISM (1951 "Leavin' to Stay") 15-20 '60s

TRIBULATIONS

Singles: 7-inch

IMPERIAL (66416 "Mama's Love") 15-25 69

TRIBUNES

Singles: 7-inch

DERRICK (502 "Now That You're Gone") 30-40 62
TEEN (1008 "Hearts Are Not Made") 30-40

TRIBUTES

Singles: 7-inch

DONNA (1391 "Here Comes Ringo") 10-15 64

TRICKLES

Singles: 7-inch

GONE (5078 "With Each Step a Tear") 50-100 59
POWER (250 "With Each Step a Tear") 150-250 58

TRICKS

Singles: 7-inch

JANE (108 "My One Desire") 10-20 59

TRICKS

Singles: 7-inch

ELCO (0627 "You're the One") 100-150

TRI-COUNTS

Singles: 7-inch

BRB (1001 "You've Got It") 30-50 '60s

TRICYCLE

LPs: 10/12-inch

ABC (674 "Tricycle") 10-15 69

TRI-DELLS

Singles: 7-inch

ELDO (104 "Baby I Love You So") 10-15 60

TRIDELS

Singles: 7-inch

SAN-DEE (1009 "Land of Love") 30-40 64

TRIDER, Larry

Singles: 7-inch

AMY (11023 "Goin' Away") 6-12 68
CORAL (62362 "Note Under My Door") 25-35 63
CORAL (62391 "Carbon Copy") 50-75 64
CORAL (62440 "Make It Do") 25-35 64
DOT (16727 "New Orleans") 15-25 65
ROULETTE (4362 "Don't Stop") 15-20 61

TRI-FIVE

Singles: 7-inch

DAMARK (2400 "Like Chop") 10-20 62

TRI-GERIANS

Singles: 7-inch

MARLO (1529 "Kingdom of Love") 75-125 63

TRI-LADS

Singles: 7-inch

BULLSEYE (1003 "Cherry Pie") 20-30 58

TRI-LITES

Singles: 7-inch

ENITH INT'L (721 "Hot Dog! Here He Comes") 8-12 63
Session: Gaynel Hodge.

TRILOGY

Singles: 7-inch

G.W.P. 4-6 '60s
MERCURY 4-6 70
SUSSEX 4-6 71

LPs: 10/12-inch

G.W.P. (2031 "It Starts Again") 10-20 '60s
MERCURY 10-15 70

TRILONS

Singles: 7-inch

TAG (449 "Forever") 10-15 62

TRILYTERS

Singles: 78 rpm

TRILYTE (100) 25-50 56
(Title not known.)

TRINIDADS

(Trinadads; with the Frank Derrick Orchestra)

Singles: 7-inch

FORMAL (1005 "Don't Say Goodbye") 1500-3500 60
FORMAL (1006 "When We're Together") 400-500 60
Member: Charles Davis.
Also see CHANCE, Nolan

TRINITY RIVER BOYS
LPs: 10/12-inch
PROSPECTOR (1 "Trinity River Boys")... 30-40 64
Also see NESMITH, Michael

TRINKETS
Singles: 7-inch
CORTLAND (111 "Nobody But You") 8-12 62
IMPERIAL (5497 "Little Boy") 10-15 58

TRIOLO, Frank
(With the Shipmates Orch.)
Singles: 7-inch
FLAGSHIP (106 "Ice Cream Baby")..... 150-250 58

TRIOTONES
("Vocal Larry Puma with Chuck Ray & His Gang")
Singles: 7-inch
INTRASTATE (43 "Valerie Jo") 100-200 58

TRIPPERS
Singles: 7-inch
FULLTONE (9260 "Watch Yourself") 20-25 68
MILLTOWN (101 "Have You Ever") 20-25 69

TRIPPS
Singles: 7-inch
SOUNDSVILLE 8-12
VICTORIA (1003 "Give It Back") 8-12 67

TRIPSICHORD MUSIC BOX
Singles: 7-inch
SAN FRANCISCO (115 "Times and Season") 8-12 70
LPs: 10/12-inch
JANUS (3016 "San Francisco Sound") 150-250 71

TRIPTIDES
Singles: 7-inch
OFFICIAL (1001 "Lonely Beachcomber") 75-85 '60s

TRITONES
Singles: 78 rpm
GRAND (126 "Blues in the Closet") 15-25 54
JAMIE (1035 "Blues in the Closet") 15-25 57
Singles: 7-inch
GRAND (126 "Blues in the Closet") 40-50 54
JAMIE (1035 "Blues in the Closet") 15-25 57

TRI-TONES
Singles: 7-inch
RANGER (9650 "Chicken in the Basket") 50-100 57

TRI-TONES
Singles: 7-inch
RAYCRAFT ("Hum Waa") 75-125 58
(Selection number not known.)
TWILIGHT (406 "Surf-A-Nova") 15-20 63
(First issued on Twilight 405, as by the Parallels.)
Also see PARALLELS

TRI-TONES
Singles: 7-inch
MISS JULIE (6501 "Teardrops") 100-150 64

TRIUMPH P&R/LP '79
Singles: 12-inch
MCA (1240 "Spellbound") 5-8 84
(Promotional issue only.)
Singles: 7-inch
MCA (Black vinyl) 3-5 85-86
MCA (Colored vinyl) 4-8 85-86
RCA 3-6 78-84
Picture Sleeves
MCA 3-6 85-86
RCA 4-8 79
LPs: 10/12-inch
ATTIC (1036 "Rock and Roll Machine") .. 30-50 77
(Silver vinyl. Reportedly 100 made. Canadian.)
ATTIC (1036 "Rock and Roll Machine") 8-12 77
(Black vinyl. Canadian.)
MCA 5-8 85-87
RCA 5-10 78-84
Members: Mike Levine; Gil Moore; Rik Emmett.

TRIUMPHS
Singles: 7-inch
DANTE (1788 "The Lazy Man") 5-10 62
DANTE (3002 "The Lazy Man") 10-15 61
DANTE (3011 "You're Mine Tonight") 10-15 62
GENUINE (152 "It's So Easy") 10-20 67
GENUINE (163 "The Walk") 10-20 67
JOED (117 "Garner State Park") .... 15-25 '60s
KAB 5-10 63
OKEH (7272 "Workin'") 8-12 67
OKEH (7273 "Memories") 8-12 67
OKEH (7291 "I'm Comin' to Your Rescue") 15-25 67
SWAN (4130 "Joust About") 5-10 63
TRIUMPH (1001 "Fender Bender") 20-25 61
VERVE (10422 "Walkin' the Deck") 5-10 66

TRIUMPHS
Singles: 7-inch
VOLT (100 "Burnt Biscuits") 10-20 61
Member: Booker T.
Also see BOOKER T. & MGs
Also see MAR-KEYS

TRIUMPHS
Singles: 7-inch
IFF (151 "Surfside Date") 75-85 63
Members: Jim Peterson; Tom Runte; Jerry George; Mike Prescott; Bob Hahm; Tony Gazzana; Bruce Cole.

TRIUMPHS
Singles: 7-inch
BARCLAY 10-15 64
Member: Pat Farrell.
Also see FARRELL, Pat, & Believers
Also see RAZOR'S EDGE

TRIUMPHS
Singles: 7-inch
PACEMAKER (238 "Better Come Get Her") 5-10 65
Also see THOMAS, B.J.

TRODDEN PATH
Singles: 7-inch
NIGHT OWL (6711 "Don't Follow Me") 15-25 67
Members: Tim Urban; Mike Frommer; Steve Turner; Tom Szymarek.

TROGGS P&R/LP '66
Singles: 7-inch
ATCO (6415 "Wild Thing"/"With a Girl Like You") 15-20 66
(Writer credited is [Reg] "Presley.")
ATCO (6415 "Wild Thing"/"With a Girl Like You") 8-10 66
(Writer credited is [Chip] "Taylor.")
ATCO (6415 "I Want You") 5-10 66
(Same number used twice.)
ATCO (6444 "I Can't Control Myself") 5-10 66
BELL 4-6 73
FONTANA 8-12 66-68
PAGE ONE 5-8 69-70
PRIVATE STOCK 4-6 76
PYE 4-6 75-76
LPs: 10/12-inch
ATCO (33-193 "Wild Thing") 35-45 66
(Monaural.)
ATCO (SD-33-193 "Wild Thing") 25-35 66
(Stereo.)
FONTANA (27556 "The Troggs") 25-35 66
(Monaural.)
FONTANA (67556 "The Troggs") 20-30 66
(Stereo.)
FONTANA (67576 "Love Is All Around") ..20-30 68
LIBERTY (3472 "You're Gonna Hear from Me") 25-35 66
(Monaural.)
LIBERTY (7472 "You're Gonna Hear from Me") 25-35 66
(Stereo.)
MKC 8-10 80
PRIVATE STOCK 10-15 76
PYE 10-15 75
RHINO 5-8 84
SIRE 10-15 76
Members: Reg Presley; Chris Britton; Pete Staples; Ronnie Bullis.

TROGGS / Brook Benton
Singles: 7-inch
MILLER BEER (621 "Radio Spots") ....5-10 '60s
Picture Sleeves
MILLER BEER (621 "Radio Spots") ....10-15 '60s
Also see BENTON, Brook
Also see TROGGS

TROIS, Chuck
(With the Amazing Maze)
Singles: 7-inch
A&M 5-10 69
SOCK & SOUL 10-20 70

TROJANS
(With Ike Turner & Orch.)
Singles: 78 rpm
RPM 40-60 55
Singles: 7-inch
FELSTED (8534 "Make It Up") 10-15 59
RPM (446 "As Long As I Have You") ...200-300 55
Members: Art Lassiter; George Green; Murrey Green; Douglas Martin.
Also see LASSITER, Art

TROJANS
Singles: 7-inch
TENDER (516 "Don't Ask Me to Be Lonely") 50-75 58
(Previously issued as by the 5 Trojans.)
Also see 5 TROJANS

TROJANS
Singles: 7-inch
TRIANGLE (51317 "All Night Long") 100-150 60

TROJANS
(Mighty Trojans)
Singles: 7-inch
AIR TOWN ....5-10 '60s
DODGE (804 "Just About Daybreak") 8-12 61
JOED (711 "Just About Daybreak") 5-10 62
TRIANGLE (51317 "All Night Long") 15-25 60

TROJANS OF EVOL
Singles: 7-inch
T.O.E. (125970 "Through the Night") 20-30 67
(Identification number shown since no selection number is used.)

TROLINDER, Delbert
Singles: 7-inch
MIST (1012 "So We Walked") 20-30

TROLL, The
Singles: 7-inch
SMASH (2208 "Satin City News") 5-10 69
LPs: 10/12-inch
SMASH (67114 "Animated Music") 20-30 69
Members: Richard Gallagher; Richard Clark; Max Jordan; Ken Cortese.
Also see TROLLS

TROLLEY
Singles: 7-inch
PICCADILLY (246 "Toy Shop") 10-15 67

TROLLS
Singles: 7-inch
PEATLORE (23267 "Walkin' Shoes") 10-20 66

TROLLS
Singles: 7-inch
RUFF (1010 "That's the Way Love Is") 20-30 66
WARRIOR (173 "Stupid Girl") 5-10 67
Picture Sleeves
WARRIOR (173 "Stupid Girl") 10-20 67

TROLLS P&R '66
Singles: 7-inch
ABC (10823 "Every Day and Every Night") 5-10 66
ABC (10884 "Something Here Inside") 5-10 66
ABC (10916 "They Don't Know") 5-10 67
ABC (10952 "Who Was That Boy") 5-10 67
USA (905 "Don't Come Around") 10-20 68
Also see CARNIVAL OF SOUND
Also see TROLL

TRONICS
Singles: 7-inch
LANDA (676 "Pickin' & Stompin'") 8-12 61
LANDA (680 "The Big Scroungy") 8-12 61
Members: Baker Knight, Rene Hall.
Also see HALL, Rene
Also see KNIGHT, Baker
Also see PAYMENTS

TROOPERS
Singles: 7-inch
LAMP (2009 "My Resolution") 50-75 57

TROPAY, Mary Jo
Singles: 7-inch
WORLD ARTISTS (1005 "Blind Date") 5-10 63

TROPHIES
Singles: 7-inch
CHALLENGE (9133 "Desire") 50-75 61
CHALLENGE (9149 "Peg o' My Heart") ...20-30 62
CHALLENGE (9170 "Felicia") 10-15 62
Members: Dave Burgess; Glen Campbell; Jerry Fuller; Ricky Nelson.
Session: Champs.
Also see BURGESS, Dave
Also see CAMPBELL, Glen
Also see CHAMPS
Also see FLEAS
Also see FULLER, Jerry
Also see NELSON, Rick

TROPHIES
Singles: 7-inch
KAPP 5-10 65-66
NORK (79907 "Walkin' the Dog") 10-15 65
Member: Richard Eriksen.
Also see BUSTERS

TROPICS
Singles: 7-inch
COLUMBIA (43976 "Time") 5-10 67
COLUMBIA (44248 "This Must Be the Place") 5-10 67
FREEPORT ....5-10 '60s
KNIGHT (102 "I Want More") 10-15 65
LAURIE (3330 "You Better Move") 5-10 66
MALACO ....5-10 '60s
THAMES (103 "For a Long Time") 10-15 66
TOPIC (551 "Happy Hour") 25-35

TROUP, Bobby
Singles: 7-inch
BETHLEHEM (11006 "Jamboree Jones") .. 8-12 58
LIBERTY (55121 "Tangerine") 8-12 58
LPs: 10/12-inch
BETHLEHEM ("Bobby Troup Sings Johnny Mercer") 10-15 58
(Selection number not known.)
LIBERTY (3078 "Here's to My Lady") 15-25 57

TROUPERS
Singles: 7-inch
CLIFTON (08 "Peter Pumpkin Eater") 4-6 74
RED TOP (118 "Peter Pumpkin Eater") ...40-50 59

TROUT, Glen
Singles: 7-inch
DORE (717 "I Didn't Have the Sense to Go") 5-10 64
Also see VAL-JEENS

TROWBRIDGE, Cliff
Singles: 7-inch
ELLEN (1074 "Don't Try to Get Away") ..75-100

TROWER, Robin LP '73
Singles: 12-inch
GNP (2 "No Time") 5-8 87
(Promotional issue only.)
Singles: 7-inch
CHRYSALIS 4-6 72-78
LPs: 10/12-inch
ATLANTIC 5-8 88
CHRYSALIS 5-12 73-82
GNP 5-8 83-87
PASSPORT 5-10 85
Also see PROCOL HARUM

TROY
Singles: 7-inch
ALHAMBRA (001 "Amnesia") 10-20 69
WHITE WHALE (356 "Then Go") 5-8 70

TROY, Benny R&B '75
(With Maze; Ben E. Troy)
Singles: 7-inch
AMPEX (11011 "The Girl with San Francisco in Her Eye") 4-8 71
DE-LITE (1566 "I've Always Had You") 4-6 75
DE-LITE (1572 "I Wanna Give You Tomorrow") 4-6 75
DE-LITE (1580 "Stranger in Paradise") 4-6 76
DE-LITE (1587 "Ecstasy, Passion & Pain") . 3-5 77
DE-LITE (1593 "I'm Gonna Love You All Over") 3-5 77
EPIC (10595 "I Miss You") 4-8 70
20TH FOX 4-6
LPs: 10/12-inch
DE-LITE (2024 "Tearin' Me to Pieces") 10-15 77

TROY, Bo, & His Hot Rods / Dick Dale
LPs: 10/12-inch
DIPLOMAT (2304 "Wild Hot Rod Wails") 20-30 63
(Cover gives Dick Dale top billing, but LP has only two Dale tracks.)
Also see DALE, Dick

TROY, Doris P&R/R&B '63
Singles: 7-inch
APPLE (1820 "Ain't That Cute") 5-10 70
APPLE (1824 "Get Back") 5-10 70
ATLANTIC 10-15 63-65
CALLA (114 "Heartaches") 10-20 66
CAPITOL (2043 "He's Qualified") 5-10 67
MIDLAND INT'L (10806 "Lyin' Eyes") 4-6 76
LPs: 10/12-inch
APPLE (3371 "Doris Troy") 15-20 70
ATLANTIC (8088 "Just One Look") 20-30 64

TROY, J.B.
Singles: 7-inch
MUSICOR (1188 "Ain't It the Truth") 5-10 66
MUSICOR (1210 "Live On") 10-20 66

TROY, Kelly
(With the 3 Jays)
Singles: 7-inch
CORVETTE (100 "Remember When") 10-15 60
HARVEY ("You're Lucky in Love") 4-8
(Selection number not known.)
TAD (101 "You're Lucky in Love"/"Pretty Little Pigeon") 125-175 61
TAD (102 "You're Lucky in Love"/"Rockaway Playland") 100-150 62

TROY, Lou
Singles: 7-inch
MARKIE (105 "Kathy") 10-15 63

TROY, Riki
Singles: 7-inch
CEVETONE (511 "Linda") 15-25 63

TROYANO, Joyce
Singles: 7-inch
TRIBUTE (104 "Tall Boy, Short Girl") 5-10 63
20TH FOX (542 "He's a Big Deal") 10-15 64

TROYES
Singles: 7-inch
PHALANX (1008 "Rainbow Chaser") 25-35 66
SPACE (7001 "Rainbow Chaser") 10-20 66
SPACE (7002 "Love Comes Love Dies") 10-20 67

TROYS
Singles: 7-inch
HI-HAT (147 "I Was Dreaming") 50-75 58
OKEH (7120 "Ding-A-Ling-A-Ling-Ding-Dong") 40-50 59
Also see DELL, Dickey & Bing Bongs

TROYS
Singles: 7-inch
TOWER (406 "Gotta Fit You Into My Life") 5-10 68
Member: Mark Gallagher.
Also see LITTER

TRUANTS
Singles: 7-inch
ROCK-IT (1002 The Truant") 15-25 63
Members: Eddie Rea; Dick Zeiner; Ed Puchalski; Larry Taylor.

TRUDY & LOUISE
Singles: 7-inch
FLIP (362 "My Special Guy") 10-15 63
Members: Trudy Williams; Louise Williams.
Session: Six Teens.
Also see SIX TEENS

TRUE, Andrea P&R/R&B/LP '76
(Andrea True Connection)
Singles: 7-inch
BUDDAH 4-6 76-78
ERIC 4-6 78
Picture Sleeves
BUDDAH (515 "More More More") 10-15 76
LPs: 10/12-inch
BUDDAH 5-10 76-78

TRUE LADS
Singles: 7-inch
PEACH ("Pretty Baby") 100-150
(Selection number not known.)

TRUELOVES
(Lovenotes)
Singles: 7-inch
PREMIUM (611 "A Love Like Yours") 200-300 57
(Previously issued as by the Lovenotes. May have a "Trueloves" sticker covering "Lovenotes" label credit.)
Member: David Haywood.
Also see LOVENOTES

TRUETONES
(True Tones)
Singles: 7-inch
FELSTED (8625 "Blushing Bride") 50-100 61
JOSIE (950 "That's Love") 15-25 66
JOSIE (1003 "That's Love") 10-15 69
SOULVILLE (2871-53 "That's Love") 50-75 65
(First issue.)

TRUETONES
(With Jimmy Griffin & His Orch.)
Singles: 7-inch
MONUMENT (4501 "Honey, Honey") 75-125 58

TRUITT, Johnny
(Little Johnny Truitt)
Singles: 7-inch
A-BET 10-15 66-69

TRUJILLO, Orlie
Singles: 7-inch
DEL-FI (4171 "Let's Dance the Corrido") 10-20 62

TRUMAININS
Singles: 7-inch
RCA (11117 "Mr. Magic Man") 10-20 77

TRUMPETEERS R&B '48
Singles: 78 rpm
KING 10-15 50
SCORE 10-25 48
LPs: 10/12-inch
GRAND 25-40
SCORE (4021 "Milky White Way") 100-150 56

TRUMPETEERS P&R '59
Singles: 7-inch
SPLASH (800 "String of Trumpets") 10-15 59
Member: Billy Mure.
Also see MURE, Billy

TRUNZO, Phil, & Counts
Singles: 7-inch
EUPHON ("Teardrops in My Heart") 25-35
(No selection number used.)

TRU-SONICS
Singles: 7-inch
BOLO (724 "Forgotten Love") 10-15 61
Also see THOMAS, Tracy, & Tru-Sonics

TRUSTIN' HOWARD
Singles: 7-inch
REPRISE 15-20 62

TRUTH
Singles: 7-inch
ABC-PAR (10765 "Girl") 5-10 66
W.B. (7214 "Momentarily Gone") 5-10 68

TRUTH
Singles: 7-inch
DERAM (7503 "Hey Gyp") 10-20 67
Also see KENNY & KASUALS

TRUTH
Singles: 7-inch
CADET (5627 "I Can") 8-12 68

TRUTH
Singles: 7-inch
DRIVING WHEEL (7302 "Around and Around") 5-10 73
LPs: 10/12-inch
PEOPLE (5002 "Truth") 20-30 70

TRUTH & JANEY
Singles: 7-inch
SOUND (81472 "Under My Thumb") 8-10 72
LPs: 10/12-inch
MONTROSS (376 "No Rest for the Wicked") 40-60 76
Member: Bill Janey.

TRUTHS
Singles: 7-inch
CIRCLE (953 "Pending") 8-12 65

TRU TONES
Singles: 7-inch
SPOT (1115 "Never Had a Chance") 10-20 64
SPOT (1121 "Little Hit and Run Darling") 10-20 65

TRU-TONES
(True Tones)
Singles: 78 rpm
CHART 40-50 56
Singles: 7-inch
CHART (634 "Tears in My Eyes") 400-500 56

TRU-TONES
Singles: 7-inch
DEN RIC (4527 "I'm the Guy") 10-15 '50s
Members: Harold Moderhack; Gene Lewis
Also see SMITH, Lloyd, & Tru-Tones

TRU-TONES
Singles: 7-inch
TRU ("Darling I'm Sorry") 75-100
(Selection number not known.)

TRUTONES
Singles: 7-inch
STARLA (14 "2 A.M. on Mulholland Drive") 10-15 59

TRY CERZ
Singles: 7-inch
JAN-GI (91 "Almost There") 10-20 66
Also see SWEET SMOKE
Also see TRACERS

TUBB, Ernest P&R '41/C&W '44
(With the Texas Troubadours; with "Friends")
Singles: 78 rpm
BLUEBIRD (6693 "The Passing of Jimmie Rodgers") 400-500 '30s
BLUEBIRD (7000 "T.B. Is Whipping Me") 300-400 '30s
BLUEBIRD (8899 "Married Man Blues") 300-400 '30s
BLUEBIRD (8966 "Right Train to Heaven") 300-400 '30s
DECCA 10-20 40-57
Singles: 7-inch
CACHET 3-5 79
DECCA (28067 thru 30872) 10-20 52-59
DECCA (30952 thru 33014) 5-10 59-72
DECCA (46000 series) 10-20 50-52
FIRST GENERATION 3-5 77
MCA 4-6 73
RHINO (74415 "Walking the Floor Over You") 3-5 91
(Gold vinyl.)
RHINO (74415 "Walking the Floor Over You") 4-6 91
(Blue vinyl.)
RHINO (74415 "Walking the Floor Over You") 8-12 91
(Black vinyl.)
Picture Sleeves
RHINO (74415 "Walking the Floor Over You") 4-6 91
EPs: 7-inch
DECCA 15-30 51-65
LPs: 10/12-inch
ACM 8-12
CACHET 8-12 79
CASTLE 5-10
CORAL 5-10 73
DECCA (159 "Ernest Tubb Story") 30-50 58
(Two discs. Monaural. Includes booklet.)
DECCA (7-159 "Ernest Tubb Story") 40-60 58
(Two discs. Stereo. Includes booklet.)
DECCA (4042 thru 5006) 20-40 60-68
DECCA (5301 "Ernest Tubb Favorites") 50-75 51
(10-inch LP.)
DECCA (5334 "Old Rugged Cross-Favorite Sacred Songs") 50-75 51
(10-inch LP.)
DECCA (5336 "Jimmie Rodgers Songs Sung by Ernest Tubb") 50-75 51
DECCA (5497 "Sing a Song of Christmas") 40-60 54
(10-inch LP.)
DECCA (8291 "Ernest Tubb Favorites") 40-60 56
DECCA (8553 "Daddy of 'Em All") 35-55 56
DECCA (8834 "The Importance of Being Ernest") 35-55 59
(Monaural.)
DECCA (74042 thru 75006) 25-45 60-68
DECCA (75072 thru 75388) 10-20 68-72
DECCA (78834 "The Importance of Being Ernest") 40-60 59
(Stereo.)
FIRST GENERATION (001 "Living Legend") 8-12 77
FIRST GENERATION (0002 "The Legend and the Legacy") 75-125 79
(Back cover mentions "Ernest Tubb's Record Shop," "Gray Line Tours" and "Grand Ole Opry Tickets.")
FIRST GENERATION (0002 "The Legend and the Legacy") 70-90 79
(Back cover mentions "Ernest Tubb's Record Shop," but not "Gray Line Tours" and "Grand Ole Opry Tickets.")
FIRST GENERATION (0002 "The Legend and the Legacy") 60-80 79
(No mention on back cover of "Ernest Tubb's Record Shop," "Gray Line Tours" or "Grand Ole Opry Tickets.")
MCA 5-12 72-84
PICKWICK/HILLTOP 8-12
RADIOLA 5-10 83
RHINO (70902 "Live") 5-10 91
ROUNDER 5-10 82
TV (1033 "The Legend and the Legacy") 40-50 79
(TV mail order offer.)
VOCALION 10-25 60-69
Session: Cal Smith; Jack Greene; Waylon Jennings; Willie Nelson; Merle Haggard; Chet Atkins; Charlie Daniels; Jordanaires; Loretta Lynn; Vern Gosdin; Johnny Paycheck; Marty Robbins; Wilburn Brothers; George Jones; Johnny Cash; Ferlin Husky/Simon Crum; Charlie Rich; Conway Twitty; Justin Tubb; Charlie McCoy; Jerry Kennedy; Grady Martin; Billy Grammer; Billy Byrd; Buddy Emmons; Pete Mitchell; Pete Drake; Kitty Wells; Webb Pierce; Patsy Cline.
Also see ANDREWS SISTERS & ERNEST TUBB
Also see ATKINS, Chet
Also see CASH, Johnny
Also see CLINE, Patsy
Also see DANIELS, Charlie
Also see FOLEY, Red, & Ernest Tubb
Also see GRAMMER, Billy
Also see GREENE, Jack
Also see HAGGARD, Merle
Also see HUSKY, Ferlin
Also see JENNINGS, Waylon
Also see JORDANAIRES
Also see MARTIN, Grady
Also see McCOY, Charlie
Also see NELSON, Willie
Also see PAYCHECK, Johnny
Also see RICH, Charlie
Also see ROBBINS, Marty
Also see STATLER BROTHERS
Also see TWITTY, Conway
Also see WELLS, Kitty

TUBB, Ernest, & Loretta Lynn C&W '69
Singles: 7-inch
DECCA 5-10 65-69
LPs: 10/12-inch
DECCA 15-25 65-69
MCA 8-12 73
Also see LYNN, Loretta

TUBB, Ernest, & Loretta Lynn / Tubb, Ernest, & George Jones
Singles: 7-inch
FIRST GENERATION (006 "Thanks a Lot"/"Half a Mind") 3-5 81
Also see JONES, George

TUBB, Ernest / Justin Tubb
EPs: 7-inch
DECCA (2422 "Jimmie Rodgers Favorites") 20-30 57
Also see TUBB, Justin

TUBB, Ernest, & Wilburn Brothers C&W '58
Singles: 7-inch
DECCA 5-10 58
EPs: 7-inch
DECCA 10-15 59
Also see TUBB, Ernest
Also see WILBURN BROTHERS

TUBB, Glenn Douglas
Singles: 7-inch
LIMELIGHT (3024 "I'm So Happy I Could Cry") 5-10 64

TUBB, Justin C&W '55
(With Norma Gallant)
Singles: 78 rpm
DECCA....5-15 53-57
Singles: 7-inch
CHALLENGE....5-10 60
CUTLASS....4-6 72-73
DECCA....5-15 53-59
DOT....4-6 69
FIRST GENERATION....3-6 78-81
GROOVE....5-10 63-64
HILLTOP....4-6 75
RCA....5-10 65-67
2ND GENERATION....4-6 77
STARDAY....5-10 60-62
EPs: 7-inch
DECCA....10-20 57
LPs: 10/12-inch
CUTLASS (123 "Travelin' Singin' Man")..20-30 72
(Interestingly, reissued circa 1983 on cassette only, which credits Justin but pictures Ernest Tubb.)
DECCA (8644 "Country Boy in Love")....30-50 57
DOT....15-20 69
FIRST GENERATION (01 "Justin Tubb")...8-10 81
HILLTOP (102 "Hilltop Country Presents Justin Tubb")....5-8
(Mail order repackage of Hilltop 209.)
HILLTOP (209 "A New Country Heard From")....8-12 74
PHONORAMA (5565 "What's Wrong with the Way We're Doing It Now")....5-8 83
(Repackage of First Generation 01.)
RCA....15-25 65
STARDAY (160 "Star of the Grand Ole Opry")....20-30 62
STARDAY (198 "Modern Country Music Sound")....20-30 62
STARDAY (334 "Best of Justin Tubb")....20-30 65
VOCALION....10-15 65-67
Also see TUBB, Ernest, & Justin Tubb

TUBB, Justin, & Lorene Mann C&W '65
Singles: 7-inch
RCA....4-6 65-66
LPs: 10/12-inch
RCA (3591 "Together & Alone")....20-30 66
Also see MANN, Lorene

TUBB, Justin / Roger Miller
Singles: 7-inch
DECCA....5-10 58
Also see MILLER, Roger
Also see TUBB, Justin

TUBB, Mack, & Shades
Singles: 7-inch
HUB (1 "You Keep Me Going")....20-30

TUCKER, Anita
Singles: 78 rpm
CAPITOL....5-10 55-56
GUYDEN....5-10 54
Singles: 7-inch
CAPITOL (3277 "Slow, Smooth and Easy")....10-15 55
CAPITOL (3376 "Trying to Get to You")..10-15 56
CAPITOL (3452 "Handcuffed Heart")....10-15 56
GUYDEN (602 "Ring-Aling-Aling")....10-15 54
Session: Cues.
Also see CUES

TUCKER, Billy Joe
Singles: 7-inch
DOT (16240 "Boogie Woogie Bill")....50-75 61
MAHA (103 "Boogie Woogie Bill")....100-200 61
MID WAY (2013 "Tiny Tears")....10-20

TUCKER, Bob
Singles: 7-inch
SILVER-DOLLAR (1002 "Down & Dirty") 10-20 61
Also see TARANTULAS

TUCKER, Bobby
Singles: 7-inch
MALA (12006 "Your Love Is All I Need")....8-12 68

TUCKER, Ernie
(With the Operators; Ernest Tucker; Little Ernest Tucker)
Singles: 7-inch
EARTH (501 "I'm That Someone")....10-20 60
FORTUNE (843 "Too Small to Dance")....150-250 58
JUBILEE (5340 "Have Mercy, Uncle Sam")....10-20 58
JUBILEE (5360 "Cowboy Hop")....10-20 59
MUSICOR (1005 "Betty & Bobby")....8-12 61

TUCKER, Frankie
Singles: 78 rpm
BATON (234 "Hey Hester!")....5-10 56
Singles: 7-inch
BATON (234 "Hey Hester!")....10-15 56
DECCA (30707 "Fools Will Be Fools")....15-25 58

TUCKER, Gabe
Singles: 78 rpm
TNT (114 "Trip to the City")....10-15 54
Singles: 7-inch
TNT (114 "Trip to the City")....15-25 54

TUCKER, Jack
Singles: 78 rpm
"X" (0093 "First On Your List")....5-10 55
Singles: 7-inch
BEL-AIRE....5-10
FOUR STAR (1719 "Big Door")....50-75 58
IMPERIAL (5623 "Lonely Man")....10-20 59
OZARK (960 "Honeymoon Trip to Mars").50-75 58
OZARK (962 "Lonely Man")....30-40 59
(First issue.)
TOPPA....5-10 '60s
"X" (0093 "First On Your List")....10-15 55
YOUNG....5-10 '60s

TUCKER, Joe
Singles: 7-inch
RKO UNIQUE (410 "Who Knows")....10-15 57

TUCKER, Johnny, & Pastels
Singles: 7-inch
SONIC (30864 "Mr. Kennedy")....10-15 64
Picture Sleeves
SONIC (30864 "Mr. Kennedy")....15-20 64

TUCKER, Les
Singles: 7-inch
HEP (2144 "Wrong Kinda Lovin'")....30-50 58

TUCKER, Mark, & Beach
Singles: 7-inch
TETRAPOD SPOOLS (99752 "Sultry Summer Siren")....4-6 79
(Orange vinyl.)
LPs: 10/12-inch
BALKIN....10-12 72
DOWNEY....10-15 76
(Promotional issues only.)
RPC....12-15 68-71
TETRAPOD....8-10 75-83

TUCKER, Mickey
Singles: 7-inch
ATLANTIC (2264 "Hi Heel Sneakers")....5-10 64

TUCKER, Monroe
(Monroe Tucker's Orchestra)
Singles: 78 rpm
IMPERIAL (5109 "Kinfolks")....25-50 51
Singles: 7-inch
IMPERIAL (5109 "Kinfolks")....75-100 51
Also see GUNTER, Shirley
Also see HAYES, Linda

TUCKER, Orrin
Singles: 7-inch
WHITE ROCK (1115 "Been Lookin' for Love")....60-80 58

TUCKER, Rick C&W '89
Singles: 78 rpm
COLUMBIA (41041 "Patty Baby")....50-100 57
Singles: 7-inch
COLUMBIA (41041 "Patty Baby")....50-100 57
HITSVILLE (6035 "I Heard a Song")....4-6 76
OAK (1066 "Honey I'm Just Walking Out the Door")....3-5 88
VEEDA (4005 "I'll Be There")....30-50 60
LPs: 10/12-inch
HITSVILLE....5-10 76
Session: Rick Tucker; Roy Orbison; Buddy Holly; Don Guess; Bo Clark; Bill Pickering & Picks.
Also see PICKS

TUCKER, Tommy P&R/R&B '64
(With the Two Timers; Tee Tucker)
Singles: 7-inch
ATCO (6208 "My Girl")....10-20 61
CADET (5584 "Take the Midnight Train")..5-10 67
CADET (5622 "Someday")....5-10 68
CHECKER (1067 "Hi-Heel Sneakers")....5-10 64
CHECKER (1075 "Long Tall Shorty")....5-10 64
CHECKER (1112 "Alimony")....5-10 65
CHECKER (1133 "I've Been a Fool")....5-10 66
CHECKER (1178 "I'm Shorty")....5-10 67
CHECKER (1186 "A Whole Lot of Fun")....5-10 67
ELBAM (70 "I'll Be Gone")....5-10 66
FESTIVAL (704 "That's Live")....5-10 66
HI (2014 "Man in Love")....20-30 59
HI (2020 "Miller's Cave")....15-25 60
MARK (120 "Backtrack")....25-35 58
(Add $8 to $12 if a promo and accompanied by "Tommy Tucker Flash" postcard insert.)
PEACH (760 "Johnny Boy")....5-10 64
SUNBEAM (128 "Man That Comes Around")....15-25 59
LPs: 10/12-inch
CHECKER (2990 "Hi-Heel Sneakers")....40-60 64
Also see DUSTERS

TUCKER, Tommy
Singles: 7-inch
RCA (47-7838 "Return of the Teenage Queen")....5-10 61
RCA (37-7838 "Return of the Teenage Queen")....10-20 61
(Compact 33 Single.)
RCA (68-7838 "Return of the Teenage Queen")....15-25 61
(Stereo Compact 33 Single.)

TUCKER, Tommy, & Esquires
Singles: 7-inch
IGL (108 "Peace of Mind")....30-40 66
IGL (121 "Don't Tell Me Lies")....15-25 66

TUCKER, Tommy, & Lullabyes
(With Peter Daniels & Orchestra)
Singles: 7-inch
EMBASSY (204 "You Belong to Me")....75-100 62
KELWAY (111 "Oh Baby")....5-10 75
(Green vinyl.)

TUCKY BUZZARD
Singles: 7-inch
PASSPORT....4-6 74
LPs: 10/12-inch
CAPITOL....10-15 71
PASSPORT....10-15 73-74

TUDOR MINSTRELS
Singles: 7-inch
LONDON (1012 "The Family Way")....30-40 67
(Promotional issue only.)
Also see McCARTNEY, Paul

TUESDAY CLUB
Singles: 7-inch
PHILIPS (40478 "Only Human")....5-10 67

TUESDAY'S CHILDREN
Singles: 7-inch
COLUMBIA (43860 "I'll Be Back")....8-12 66
COLUMBIA (44149 "What Is Love")....8-12 67
KIDD (1334 "Try Girl")....8-12 66
PARADISE (1022 "Try Girl")....8-12 66

TUFANO & GIAMMARESE P&R '73
Singles: 7-inch
ODE....4-6 73-76
LPs: 10/12-inch
EPIC/ODE....8-10 76-77
ODE....10-15 73-74
Members: Dennis Tufano; Carl Giammarese.
Also see BUCKINGHAMS

TUFFS
(With Kay Bell)
Singles: 7-inch
DORE (757 "I Only Cry Once a Day Now")....20-30 66
DOT (16304 "Surfer's Stomp")....10-20 61
Also see BELL, Kay

TULSA, Johnny
Singles: 7-inch
KING (5505 "No One But Me")....10-15 61

TULU BABIES
Singles: 7-inch
TEMA (125 "Debbie")....10-15 65
TEMA (817 "The Hurtin' Kind")....10-15 65
(Copies on Mar—crediting the "Talula Babies"—are bootlegs.)
Also see BASKERVILLE HOUNDS

TUMBLERS
Singles: 7-inch
POCONO (4 "Scream")....40-60 65

TUMBLEWEEDS
Singles: 7-inch
TEE PEE (1001 "Truck Driver's Wife")....10-20 69

TUNE BLENDERS
Singles: 78 rpm
FEDERAL....20-30 54
Singles: 7-inch
FEDERAL (12201 "Oh Yes I Know")....50-75 54

TUNE ROCKERS P&R '58
Singles: 7-inch
PET (804 "No Stoppin' This Boppin'")....20-30 58
U.A. (139 "Green Mosquito")....15-25 58
Members: Gene Strong; Tim Nolan; Fred Patton; Mickey Vanderlip.

TUNE SHARKS
Singles: 7-inch
SO-RE-CO (501 "Party Time")....10-20 64

TUNE TAILORS
(With the Pete Pecorara Qunitet)
Singles: 7-inch
CENTURY (4158 "Beverly")....15-25 58

TUNE TIMERS
Singles: 7-inch
OKEH (7081 "Thinking")....15-25 57

TUNE TONES
Singles: 7-inch
HERALD (524 "Please Baby, Please")....15-25 58
HERALD (539 "She's Right with Me")....10-15 59

TUNE WEAVERS P&R/R&B '57
(Margo Sylvia & Tune Weavers; with Paul Gayten Orchestra; Tune Weavers / Paul Gayten & Tone Weavers; Tune-Weavers with Frank Paul's Orcestra)
Singles: 78 rpm
CASA GRANDE....20-30 57
CHECKER (872 "Happy, Happy Birthday Baby")....35-45 57
CHECKER (880 "Ol Man River")....10-15 57
Singles: 7-inch
CASA GRANDE (101 "Little Boy")....30-40 59
CASA GRANDE (3038 "My Congratulations Baby")....20-30 60
CASA GRANDE (4037 "Happy, Happy Birthday Baby")....50-75 57
CASA GRANDE (4038 "I Remember Dear")....15-25 57
CASA GRANDE (4040 "There Stands My Love")....20-30 58
CHECKER (872 "Happy, Happy Birthday Baby")....30-40 57
(Checkerboard top label. Can be found with either of two flips: *Ol Man River* or *Yo Yo Walk.*)
CHECKER (872 "Happy, Happy Birthday Baby")....8-12 58
(No Checkerboard at top.)
CHECKER (880 "Ol Man River")....15-20 57
(Flip side credits Paul Gayten & the Tone [sic] Weavers.)
CHECKER (1007 "Congratulations on Your Wedding")....10-15 62
CHESS....4-6 73
CLASSIC ARTISTS (104 "Come Back to Me")....5-8 88
(Black vinyl. 1000 made.)
CLASSIC ARTISTS (107 "Merry Merry Christmas Baby")....5-8 88
(Black vinyl. 1000 made.)
COLLECTABLES....3-5 '80s
ERIC....4-6 '70s
LPs: 10/12-inch
CASA GRANDE....10-15 73
Members: Margo Sylvia; Charlotte Davis; Gil Lopez; John Sylvia.
Also see GAYTEN, Paul
Also see SKYLINERS / TUNE WEAVERS

TUNEDROPS
(Tune Drops)
Singles: 78 rpm
GONE (5003 "Rosie Lee")....10-20 57

Singles: 7-inch
GONE (5003 "Rosie Lee") 20-30 57
GONE (5072 "Smoothie") 10-20 59
METRO (20028 "Smoothie") 30-40 59
(First issue.)
Also see DODDS, Malcolm

TUNEMASTERS
Singles: 78 rpm
MARK 100-200 57
Singles: 7-inch
ASKEL (2 "Down the Line") 100-200
MARK (7002 "Sending This Letter") 200-300 57
TUNE (203 "Lover's Paradise") 30-40 57
Also see WILSON, Willie, & Tunemasters

TUNES
Singles: 7-inch
PEL (101 "Only Time Will Tell") 10-15 59
SWADE (102 "Close the Door") 20-25 59

TUNESMITHS WITH ROSEMARY CLOONEY & DON CHERRY
EPs: 7-inch
COLUMBIA (8941 "Carl Smith's Tunesmiths") 10-20 56
Also see CHERRY, Don
Also see CLOONEY, Rosemary
Also see SMITH, Carl
Also see TUNESMITHS

TUNESTERS
Singles: 7-inch
CORDON (1201 "Wicki Up") .... 8-12 '60s

TURBANS
Singles: 78 rpm
MONEY 40-50 55
Singles: 7-inch
MONEY (209 "Tick Tock Awoo") 75-125 55
Members: Andre Goodwin; Charles Fitzpatrick; Willie Roland; Berlin Carpenter; Al Williams.
Also see SHARP TONES

TURBANS / Jet Aces
Singles: 78 rpm
MONEY 10-20 55
Singles: 7-inch
MONEY (211 "When I Return"/"Do It Yourself") 30-50 55
Also see JET ACES

TURBANS / Turks
Singles: 78 rpm
MONEY 10-20 55
Singles: 7-inch
MONEY (211 "When I Return"/"Emily") ... 30-40 55
(Orange label.)
MONEY(211 "When I Return"/"Emily") .... 10-15 '60s
(Yellow label.)
Also see TURBANS
Also see TURKS / Seniors

TURBANS *P&R/R&B '55*
Singles: 78 rpm
HERALD 25-50 55-57
Singles: 7-inch
ABC 4-6 73
COLLECTABLES .... 3-5 '80s
FLASHBACK 5-10 65
HERALD (458 "When You Dance") 50-75 55
(Script print/flag logo.)
HERALD (458 "When You Dance") 10-15 57
(Block print logo.)
HERALD (469 "Sister Sookey") 15-25 56
HERALD (478 "I'm Nobody's") 20-30 56
HERALD (486 "All of My Love") 15-25 56
HERALD (495 "Valley of Love") 15-25 57
(Black vinyl.)
HERALD (495 "Valley of Love") 40-50 57
(Brown vinyl.)
HERALD (510 "Congratulations") 30-40 57
(Script print/flag logo.)
HERALD (510 "Congratulations") 15-25 57
(Block print logo.)
HERALD (510 "Congratulations") 25-35 57
(Single sided. Promotional issue only.)
HI-OLDIES .... 3-5 '80s
IMPERIAL (5807 "Six Questions") 10-20 61
IMPERIAL (5828 "This Is My Story") 15-25 62
IMPERIAL (5847 "I Wonder") 10-20 62
PARKWAY (820 "Golden Rings") 10-20 61
RED TOP (115 "I Promise You Love") 30-40 59
ROULETTE (4281 "Diamonds & Pearls") ... 8-12 60
ROULETTE (4326 "I'm Not Your Fool Anymore") 8-12 61
LPs: 10/12-inch
COLLECTABLES 5-8 84
LOST NITE (25 "The Turbans") 10-20 81
(10-inch LP. Red vinyl. 1000 made.)
RELIC .... 10-15 '70s
Members: Al Banks; Matt Platt; Andrew Jones; Charles Williams.

TURBO-JETS
Singles: 7-inch
FEDERAL (12349 "Bingo") 5-10 59
(Monaural.)
FEDERAL (12349 "Bingo") 10-15 59
(Stereo.)
FEDERAL (12353 "So Sassy") 5-10 59

TURFITS
Singles: 7-inch
CAPITOL (2018 "If It's Love You Want") .. 20-25 67

TURGEN, Hank
Singles: 7-inch
BOSS (101 "I've Got to Hand It to You") .. 10-15 61

TURKS
Singles: 78 rpm
BALLY (1017 "This Heart of Mine") 8-12 56
CASH (1042 "It Can't Be True") 8-12 56
MONEY (215 "I'm a Fool") 10-15 56
Singles: 7-inch
BALLY (1017 "This Heart of Mine") 15-25 56
CASH (1042 "It Can't Be True") 15-25 56
CLASS (256 "Rockville U.S.A.") 10-15 59
IMPERIAL (5783 "It Can't Be True") 5-10 61
KEEN (4016 "Father Time") 15-25 58
KNIGHT (2005 "It Can't Be True") 10-20 58
MEMORY PAIN 3-5
MONEY (215 "I'm a Fool") 30-40 56
Members: Gaynel Hodge; Delmer Wilburn; Alex Hodge; Carl Green; Jody Jefferson.
Also see CARR, Wynona
Also see HOLLYWOOD FLAMES
Also see TURBANS / Turks

TURKS / Seniors
Singles: 7-inch
BALL (001 "Emily"/"My Soul") 15-20 59
Also see TURBANS / Turks

TURKS / Sonny Harper
Singles: 7-inch
BALL (101 "Emily"/"Going Back Home") .. 10-15 60
Also see TURKS

TURKS
Singles: 7-inch
D.J.O. (113 "Let It Flame") 10-20 70
DARAN 5-10 69

TURKS
Singles: 7-inch
P.B.D. (112 "Baja") 15-25 64
P.B.D. (113 "Wipe Out") 15-25 64

TURLEY, Duane, & Tads
Singles: 7-inch
VIV (103 "Devil's Den") 10-20 58

TURLEY, Richard
(With the All American Boy's Orchestra)
Singles: 7-inch
DOT (16231 "I Wanna Dance") 25-35 61
FRATERNITY (845 "Makin' Love with My Baby") 25-35 59

TURMAN, Don
(With the Vibra Sonics)
Singles: 7-inch
CANDY (101 "Ram Charger '64") 15-25 64
HART (101 "Rock & Roll Blues") 10-15 61

TURN AROUNDS
Singles: 7-inch
ERA (3137 "Ain't Nothin' Shakin' ") 15-25 64

TURNABOUTS
Singles: 7-inch
PRANN (5002 "Cott'n Pick'n' ") 10-15 63
Member: Ike Turner.
Also see TURNER, Ike

TURNER, Baby Face
Singles: 78 rpm
MODERN (882 "Blue Serenade") 100-150 52
Singles: 7-inch
MODERN (882 "Blue Serenade") 500-1000 52
Session: Ike Turner.
Also see BLAIR, Sunny
Also see TURNER, Ike

TURNER, Benny
(With the Armourettes; Bernie Turner)
Singles: 7-inch
M-PAC (7215 "Love Me") 8-12 64
M-PAC (7219 "Good to Me") 8-12 65
ONE-DERFUL (4807 "When I'm Gone") .. 10-15 62
SKYMAC (1003 "No More Crying") 5-10 63
SKYMAC (1005 "I Want to Know") 30-40 64

TURNER, Betty
(With the Chevelles)
Singles: 7-inch
CRESCENT (631 "Blue Star") 10-20 63
CRESCENT (637 "The Wind Kept Laughing") 100-200 63
CRESCENT (6501 "Tell Yourself a Lie") .. 10-20 65
INFINITY (008 "I Believe in You") 20-30 61
INFINITY (019 "Stay Away from Jim") 10-20 63
LIBERTY (55861 "Be Careful Girl") 20-30 66
Also see CHEVELLES

TURNER, Billy
Singles: 7-inch
ROULETTE (4489 "For You") 10-15 63
TACIT (111 "I Know, I Know") 10-15 62

TURNER, Bobby
Singles: 7-inch
DECCA (31367 "I Miss You So") 10-15 62

TURNER, Bonnie & Ike
Singles: 78 rpm
RPM (362 "Looking for My Baby") 15-25 52
Singles: 7-inch
RPM (362 "Looking for My Baby") 50-75 52

TURNER, Cile
Singles: 7-inch
COLONIAL (7004 "Crap Shootin' Sinner") . 8-12 59

TURNER, Dale
Singles: 7-inch
COLUMBIA (44300 "Luckiest Girl") 5-10 67
COLUMBIA (44391 "Daddy Won't Be Home Anymore") 5-10 67

TURNER, Dave
Singles: 78 rpm
DREXEL 10-15 55
Singles: 7-inch
DREXEL (906 "I'm All Yours, Sugar") 20-30 55
DYNO VOICE (234 "I") 5-10 67

TURNER, Dennis
Singles: 7-inch
LOUIS (2002 "Lover Please") 15-25 61
LOUIS (6800 "Little Miss Heartbreak") 15-25 62

TURNER, Denny
Singles: 7-inch
DIAMOND (202 "Rockin' Little Angel") 10-20 66

TURNER, Duke
(With the Chi-Towns)
Singles: 7-inch
CRAJON (48301 "Give Me Some Sugar") . 5-10 '70s
OMEGA (1101 "Put Soul in Your Dance") 10-20
OMEGA SOUND (23147 "Put Some Soul In Your Dance") 10-20
SPINNING TOP (22174 "Give Me Some Sugar") 5-10 74
SPINNING TOP (42170 "Let Me Be Your Babysitter") 20-30

TURNER, Dwight
Singles: 7-inch
CHATOK (1001 "You're Alone") .... 50-75 '60s
Also see TURNER, Spyder

TURNER, Ernest
Singles: 7-inch
HOLLYWOOD (1136 "I Still Love You") 5-10 68

TURNER, Grant *C&W '64*
Singles: 7-inch
CHART (1130 "The Bible in Her Hand") 10-15 64
CHART (1275 "Old North Star") 10-15 65

TURNER, Horace
Singles: 7-inch
CARD (557 "I Got to Have You") 50-75 61

TURNER, Houston, & Dixielanders
Singles: 7-inch
DO-RA-ME (1416 "Uncle John's Bongos") 20-30 60

TURNER, Ike
(With the Kings of Rhythm; with His Orchestra; with Dee Dee Johnson; "Vocal Tommy Hodge"; with Ben Burton Orchestra)
Singles: 78 rpm
CHESS (1459 "Heartbroken & Worried") . 20-40 51
COBRA (5033 "Box Top") 25-35 59
FEDERAL (12297 "Do You Mean It") 20-30 57
FEDERAL (12304 "Rock-A-Bucket") 25-75 57
FLAIR 20-40 54-55
RPM (356 "You're Driving Me Insane") 25-50 52
RPM (446 "I Wanna Make Love to You") . 15-25 55
Singles: 7-inch
ARTISTIC (1504 "Down & Out") 10-20 59
COBRA (5033 "Box Top") 10-20 59
FEDERAL (12297 "Do You Mean It") 50-75 57
FEDERAL (12304 "Rock-A-Bucket") 20-40 57
FLAIR (1040 "Cubano Jump") 40-60 54
FLAIR (1059 "Cuban Getaway") 40-60 55
INNIS (3002 "The Drag") 4-6
KING (5553 "Big Question") 10-15 61
LIBERTY (56194 "Love Is a Game") 4-6 70
RPM (356 "You're Driving Me Insane") 50-75 52
RPM (446 "I Wanna Make Love to You") . 25-35 55
ROYAL AMERICAN (105 "I Know You Don't Love Me") 10-15 62
SUE (722 "My Love") 15-20 59
U.A. 4-6 71-74
LPs: 10/12-inch
CROWN (367 "Ike Turner Rocks the Blues") 50-100 63
POMPEII 10-15 69
U.A. 6-12 72-73
Also see BERRY, Richard
Also see BLAND, Bobby, & Ike Turner
Also see BRENSTON, Jackie
Also see EMERSON, Billy 'The Kid'
Also see HOWLIN' WOLF
Also see JOHNSON, Ike & Dee Dee
Also see KING, B.B.
Also see KING, Willie
Also see RENRUT, Icky
Also see RUSH, Otis
Also see TURNABOUTS
Also see TURNER, Baby Face
Also see TURNER, Bonnie & Ike
Also see WRIGHT, Johnny

TURNER, Ike & Tina *P&R/R&B '60*
(With the Ikettes; with Home Grown Funk; "Featuring Tina")
Singles: 7-inch
A&M (1118 "River Deep – Mountain High") 5-10 69
A&M (1170 "A Love Like Yours") 5-10 69
BLUE THUMB (101 "I've Been Loving You Too Long") 5-10 69
BLUE THUMB (102 "The Hunter") 5-10 69
BLUE THUMB (104 "Bold Soul Sister") 5-10 69
BLUE THUMB (202 "I've Been Loving You Too Long") 4-6 71
CENCO (112 "You Weren't Ready") 5-10 65
COLLECTABLES .... 3-5 '80s
FANTASY 3-5 80
INNIS (6666 "Betcha Can't Kiss Me") 5-10 67
INNIS (6667 "So Fine") 10-15 68
INNIS (6668 "I Better Get Ta Steppin' ") .. 10-15 68
KENT (34 "Please Please Please") 3-5
KENT (44 "Goodbye, So Long") 3-5
KENT (402 "I Can't Believe What You Say") 10-15 64
KENT (409 "Please Please Please") 5-10 64
KENT (418 "Chicken Shack") 5-10 65
KENT (457 "I Wish My Dream Would Come True") 5-10 66
KENT (4514 "Please Please Please") 4-6 70
LIBERTY 4-6 70-71
LOMA (2011 "Tell Her I'm Not Home") 10-15 65
LOMA (2015 "Just to Be with You") 10-15 65
MINIT (32060 "I'm Gonna Do All I Can") 5-10 69
MINIT (32068 "I Wish It Would Rain") 5-10 69
MINIT (32077 "I Wanna Jump") 5-10 69

MINIT (32087 "Come Together") 4-8 70
MODERN (1007 "Goodbye, So Long") 10-15 65
MODERN (1012 "Gonna Have Fun") 10-15 65
PHILLES (131 "River Deep – Mountain High") 10-15 66
PHILLES (134 "A Man Is a Man Is a Man") 10-20 66
PHILLES (135 "I'll Never Need More Than This") 10-20 67
PHILLES (136 "A Love Like Yours") 10-20 67
POMPEII 5-8 68-70
SONJA (2001 "If I Can't Be First") 8-10 63
SONJA (2005 "You Can't Miss Nothin' That You Never Had") 8-10 64
SONJA (5000 "We Need an Understanding") 8-10 64
SUE (135 "Two Is a Couple") 5-10 65
SUE (138 "New Breed") 5-10 65
SUE (139 "Stagger Lee & Billy") 5-10 65
SUE (146 "Dear John") 5-10 66
SUE (730 "A Fool in Love") 15-20 60
SUE (734 "Fool Too Long") 10-15 60
SUE (735 "I Idolize You") 10-15 60
SUE (740 "You're My Baby") 10-15 61
SUE (749 "It's Gonna Work Out Fine") 10-15 61
SUE (753 "Poor Fool") 10-15 61
SUE (757 "Tra La La La La") 10-15 62
SUE (760 "It's Gonna Work Out Fine") 8-10 62
SUE (765 "You Should'a Treated Me Right") 8-12 62
SUE (768 "I Idolize You") 8-12 62
SUE (772 "Mind in a Whirl") 8-12 62
SUE (774 "Please Don't Hurt Me") 8-12 62
SUE (784 "Don't Play Me Cheap") 8-12 63
TRC 4-6 71
TANGERINE (963 "Beauty Is Only Skin Deep") 5-10 66
TANGERINE (967 "I'm Hooked") 5-10 66
TANGERINE (1019 "Anything You Wasn't Born With") 4-6 71
TUNETOWN (501 "Boxtop") 4-6
U.A. 4-6 71-75
W.B. (5433 "A Fool for a Fool") 5-10 64
W.B. (5461 "It's All Over") 5-10 64
W.B. (5493 "Ooh-Poo-Pah-Doo") 5-10 64

Picture Sleeves

MINIT 5-10 69
POMPEII 5-10 69
W.B. (5433 "A Fool for a Fool") 10-20 64

LPs: 10/12-inch

A&M (3179 "River Deep – Mountain High") 8-12 82
A&M (4178 "River Deep – Mountain High") 15-25 69
ABC ....8-10 '70s
ACCORD 5-10 81
BLUE THUMB 8-12 69-73
CAPITOL (500 series) 5-10 75
(With "SM" prefix.)
CAPITOL (500 series) 10-15 69
(With "ST" prefix.)
CENCO .... 15-20 '60s
COLLECTABLES 5-8 88
FANTASY 5-10 80
HARMONY (11000 series) 10-12 69
HARMONY (30000 series) 8-10 71
KENT (519 "Soul of Ike & Tina") 25-35 61
KENT (538 "Festival of Live Performances") 25-35 62
KENT (550 "Please Please Please") 25-35 62
KENT (5014 "Ike & Tina Revue") 15-25 64
LIBERTY (7000 series) 10-12 70
LIBERTY (51000 series) 5-8 85
LOMA 10-20 66
MINIT 10-15 69
PHILLES (4011 "River Deep – Mountain High") 5000-10000 66
(Covers for a U.S. pressing on Philles are not known to exist. British pressings [London/ Philles SHU-8298] do exist with covers.)
PICKWICK ....5-10 '70s
POMPEII 10-15 68-69
SUE (2001 "The Sound of Ike & Tina Turner") 200-300 61
SUE (2003 "Dance with Ike & Tina Turner's Kings of Rhythm") 100-200 62
(Instrumentals by Ike & Tina Turner's band.)
SUE (2004 "Dynamite") 250-350 63
SUE (2005 "Don't Play Me Cheap") 100-200 63
SUE (2007 "It's Gonna Work Out Fine") 100-200 63
SUE (1038 "Greatest Hits") 35-45 65
SUNSET 8-12 69-70
UNART ....5-10 '70s
U.A. 8-12 71-78
UNITED SUPERIOR 8-10
W.B. 10-20 65-69
Session: Vernon Guy; Stacy Johnson.
Also see BLAND, Bobby, & Ike Turner
Also see GUY, Vernon
Also see IKETTES
Also see JOHNSON, Stacy
Also see RAELETTES
Also see TURNER, Ike
Also see TURNER, Tina

TURNER, Ike, Carlson Oliver & Little Ann

Singles: 7-inch

TUNE TOWN (501 "Boxtop") 400-500
(Reportedly Little Ann is Tina Turner and this is supposedly her first record.)

TURNER, Jack

(With His Granger Gang)

Singles: 78 rpm

HICKORY 40-60 56
RCA 10-15 53-55

Singles: 7-inch

HICKORY (1050 "Everybody's Rockin' But Me") 50-100 56
MGM 10-20 58
RCA 15-25 53-55

TURNER, Jesse Lee — P&R '59

Singles: 7-inch

CARLTON (496 "Shake, Baby, Shake") ...40-50 59
CARLTON (509 "Baby Please Don't Tease") 10-20 59
FRATERNITY (855 "Teenage Misery") 10-20 59
GNP (184 "All You Gotta Do") 5-10 62
GNP (188 "Shotgun Boogie") 40-60 62
IMPERIAL (5635 "Slippin' Around") 8-12 60
IMPERIAL (5649 "I'm the Little Space Girl's Father") 8-12 60
SUDDEN 4-6
TOP RANK (2064 "Do I Worry") 8-12 60

Picture Sleeves

CARLTON (509 "Baby Please Don't Tease") 15-25 59
FRATERNITY (855 "Teenage Misery") 35-50 59

TURNER, Joe — R&B '46

(With His Blues Kings; with Pete Johnson & His Orchestra; with Van "Piano Man" Walls & His Orchestra; with Freddie Slack; Big Joe Turner)

Singles: 78 rpm

ALADDIN (3013 "Morning Glory") 50-100 49
ALADDIN (3070 "Back Breaking Baby") .50-100 50
ATLANTIC 10-30 51-57
BAYOU 10-20 53
COLONY (108 "Little Bitty Baby") 10-20 52
CORAL (65004 "Blues on Central Avenue") 30-40 48
DECCA 10-20 41-56
DOOTONE (305 "I Love Ya, I Love Ya, I Love Ya") 50-100 51
DOWN BEAT 10-20 48
EXCELSIOR 10-20 49
FIDELITY 10-20 51-52
FREEDOM 10-20 50
IMPERIAL 10-20 50
MGM 10-20 48-50
NATIONAL 10-20 46-51
RPM 25-50 51
SWING BEAT 10-20 49
VOCALION 15-25 39

Singles: 7-inch

ATLANTIC (939 "Chains of Love") 150-200 51
ATLANTIC (949 "The Chill Is On") 150-200 51
ATLANTIC (960 "Sweet Sixteen") 100-150 52
ATLANTIC (970 "Don't You Cry") 50-100 52
ATLANTIC (982 "Still in Love") 50-100 52
ATLANTIC (1001 "Honey Hush") 50-100 53
ATLANTIC (1016 "TV Mama") 50-100 53
ATLANTIC (1026 "Shake Rattle & Roll") ..30-40 54
ATLANTIC (1040 "Well All Right") 30-40 54
ATLANTIC (1053 "Flip Flop and Fly") 30-40 55
ATLANTIC (1069 "Hide & Seek") 30-40 55
ATLANTIC (1080 "Morning Noon and Night") 30-40 56
ATLANTIC (1088 "Corrine Corrina") 20-30 56
ATLANTIC (1100 thru 1184) 20-40 56-58
ATLANTIC (2000 series) 10-20 59-60
BAYOU (015 "The Blues Jumped a Rabbit") 200-300 53
BLUESTIME (45001 "Two Loves Have I") 25-50
BLUESWAY (61009 "Big Wheel") 5-10 67
CORAL (62408 "I Walk a Lonely Mile") 10-15 64
CORAL (62429 "Shake, Rattle & Roll") 10-15 64
DECCA (29711 "Got a Gal for Every Day of the Week") 30-40 55
DECCA (29924 "Corrine Corrina") 30-40 55
KENT 5-8 69-72
RPM (331 "Roll 'Em Blues") 100-150 51
RPM (345 "Ridin' Blues") 100-150 51
RONN 4-6 69

EPs: 7-inch

ATLANTIC (536 "Joe Turner Sings") 50-75 55
ATLANTIC (565 "Joe Turner") 50-75 56
ATLANTIC (586 "Joe Turner") 50-75 56
ATLANTIC (606 "Rock with Joe Turner") .50-75 56
EMARCY (6132 "Joe Turner and Pete Johnson") 50-75 56

LPs: 10/12-inch

ARHOOLIE 15-25 62
ATCO 8-12 71
ATLANTIC (1234 "Boss of the Blues") .100-150 58
ATLANTIC (1332 "Big Joe Rides Again") .50-75 60
ATLANTIC (8005 "Joe Turner") 100-200 57
(Black label.)
ATLANTIC (8005 "Joe Turner") 50-100 59
(Red label.)
ATLANTIC (8023 "Rockin' the Blues") ..100-150 58
(Black label.)
ATLANTIC (8023 "Rockin' the Blues") 50-75 59
(Red label.)
ATLANTIC (8033 "Big Joe Is Here") 100-150 59
(Black label.)
ATLANTIC (8033 "Big Joe Is Here") 50-75 59
(Red label.)
ATLANTIC (8081 "Best of Joe Turner") 30-50 63
ATLANTIC (8812 "Boss of the Blues") 5-10 81
BIG TOWN 5-10 78
BLUES SPECTRUM 10-12
BLUESTIME (9002 "The Real Boss of the Blues") ....20-30 '60s
BLUESWAY (6006 "Singing the Blues") 8-12 67
BLUESWAY (6060 "Roll 'Em") 8-12 73
CHIARDSCURO 8-10 76
CLASSIC JAZZ 5-10 79
EMARCY (36014 "Joe Turner with Pete Johnson") 100-200 56
INTERMEDIA 5-10 83-84
KENT ....8-12 '70s
LMI 8-10 74
MCA 5-10 80
PABLO 5-10 76-83
SAVOY (14012 "Blues Can Make You Happy") 100-150 58
SAVOY (14106 "Carless Love") 50-75 64
SAVOY (2223 "Big Joe Is Here") 5-10 77
UNITED 8-10
Session: King Curtis.
Also see BIG VERNON
Also see JOHNSON, Pete
Also see KING CURTIS
Also see WILLIAMS, Dootsie

TURNER, Joe / Jimmy Nelson

LPs: 10/12-inch

CROWN 15-25 62
Also see NELSON, Jimmy

TURNER, Joe, & Roomful Of Blues

LPs: 10/12-inch

MUSE (5293 "Blues Train") 5-10 83
Also see ROOMFUL OF BLUES
Also see TURNER, Joe

TURNER, Johnny

Singles: 7-inch

JAKE LEG 15-20
(Compact 33 single.)

TURNER, Ken

Singles: 7-inch

FARRALL (690 "Loving Man") 300-400

TURNER, Kylo

Singles: 7-inch

ANDEX (4027 "Where There's a Will There's a Way") 15-20 58
SAR (102 "Wildest Girl in Town") 10-15 60

TURNER, Marie

Singles: 7-inch

QUEEN (24004 "What's He Got") 5-10 61

TURNER, Maurice

Singles: 7-inch

STUDIO CITY (1013 "On the Street Where You Live") 8-12 64
UA (417 "Just a Little Blue") ....5-10 '60s

Picture Sleeves

STUDIO CITY (1013 "On the Street Where You Live") 10-20 64

TURNER, Mickey

Singles: 7-inch

REVOLVO (46 "Honest I Do") 15-25 60
VELLEY (1403 "Rock with a Redhead") .50-100 58

TURNER, Odelle

Singles: 78 rpm

ATLANTIC 50-75 52

Singles: 7-inch

ATLANTIC (964 "Alarm Clock Boogie") 100-125 52

TURNER, Pete, & His Blues Band

Singles: 78 rpm

HAVEN 15-25 47

TURNER, Rex, & Westerners

Singles: 7-inch

ROYALE (45268 "Moanin' the Blues") 10-15

TURNER, Rocky

Singles: 7-inch

PROGRESS (101 "Slow Jerkin'") 10-15 65
(First issue.)
W.B. (5603 "Slow Jerkin'") 5-10 65

TURNER, Sammy — P&R/R&B '59

(With the Twisters)

Singles: 7-inch

BIG TOP (3007 "Sweet Annie Laurie") 10-15 59
BIG TOP (3016 "Lavender Blue") 15-20 59
(Monaural.)
BIG TOP (3016 "Lavender Blue") 30-40 59
(Stereo.)
BIG TOP (3029 "Always") 15-20 59
(Monaural.)
BIG TOP (3029 "Always") 20-30 59
(Stereo.)
BIG TOP (3032 "Paradise") 15-20 60
BIG TOP (3038 "I Want to Be Loved") 10-15 60
BIG TOP (3049 "Fools Fall in Love") 10-15 60
BIG TOP (3061 "Things I Love") 10-15 61
BIG TOP (3065 "Love Keeps Calling") 10-15 61
BIG TOP (3070 "Starlight, Starbright") 10-15 61
BIG TOP (3082 "Fool of the Year") 10-15 61
BIG TOP (3089 "Falling") 10-15 61
ERIC ....4-6 '70s
MILLENNIUM (616 "Do You Know") 4-6 78
MOTOWN (1055 "Only You") 15-25 64
PACIFIC (3016 "Lavender Blue") 30-40 58
PACIFIC (3029 "Always") 20-30 59
S.S.I. (1022 "When There's Only Two of Us") 4-6 70
(With Gloria Henry.)
20TH FOX (6610 "The House I Live In") 5-10 65
VERVE (10465 "A Child Is Born") 12-25 66

EPs: 7-inch

BIG TOP (101 "Lavender Blue Moods") ...40-60 60
(Not issued with standard cover. Plain paper 45-type sleeve has rubber stamped on both sides: A Special Promotional EP for D.J. use only.")

LPs: 10/12-inch

BIG TOP (1301 "Lavender Blue Moods") .30-50 60
(Monaural.)
BIG TOP (ST-1301 "Lavender Blue Moods") 40-60 60
(Stereo.)
Session: King Curtis.
Also see KING CURTIS

TURNER, Sammy / Ivory Joe Hunter

Singles: 7-inch

GOLD SOUL 3-5
Also see HUNTER, Ivory Joe
Also see TURNER, Sammy

TURNER, Smiley

Singles: 78 rpm

MERCURY 15-25 49

Singles: 7-inch
VISTONE (2029 "Judge & Jury") 10-15 62

TURNER, Sonny, & Sound Ltd.
LPs: 10/12-inch
SONNY (1000 "Standing Ovation")......... 10-15 74
Members: Sonny Turner; Leonard Veal; Paul; Jay; Terry; Jeff; Joe.
Also see HESITATIONS
Also see PLATTERS

TURNER, Spyder P&R/R&B '66
(Dwight Turner)
Singles: 7-inch
KWANZA..4-6 73
MGM..5-15 66-71
POLYDOR..3-5 84
WHITFIELD..3-5 78-79
LPs: 10/12-inch
MGM.. 15-20 67
WHITFIELD..5-10 78-79
Also see TURNER, Dwight

TURNER, Tina R&B/LP '75
Singles: 12-inch
CAPITOL..4-6 84-87
Singles: 7-inch
CAPITOL..3-5 84-89
POMPEII..5-10 68
U.A...4-6 75-78
WAGNER..3-5 79
Picture Sleeves
CAPITOL..3-5 84-89
LPs: 10/12-inch
AUDIO FIDELITY (100 "Tina Turner")..... 25-35 84
(Picture disc.)
CAPITOL..5-8 84-89
FANTASY..5-10
SPRINGBOARD..8-10 72
U.A. (Except 200)..8-10 75-78
U.A. (200 "Tina Turner Turns the Country On")... 10-15 67
WAGNER..5-8 79
Also see ADAMS, Bryan, & Tina Turner
Also see BASS, Fontella, & Tina Turner / Tina Turner
Also see BOWIE, David
Also see CLAPTON, Eric, & Tina Turner
Also see JOHN, Elton / Tina Turner
Also see TURNER, Ike & Tina

TURNER, Titus P&R/R&B '59
Singles: 78 rpm
ATLANTIC.. 15-25 57
OKEH.. 10-20 52-54
WING.. 15-25 55-56
Singles: 7-inch
ATCO (6310 "Baby Girl")..........................5-10 64
ATLANTIC (1127 "A-Knocking at My Baby's Door")... 15-25 57
BELL (620 "Sportin' Tom")..........................5-10 65
COLUMBIA (42873 "Goodbye Rose")........5-10 63
COLUMBIA (42947 "Make Someone Love You")..5-10 64
DART (102 "Sodom & Gomorrah")............5-10 59
ENJOY (1005 "My Darkest Hour")............8-12 62
ENJOY (1015 "My Darkest Hour")............5-10 64
ENJOY (2010 "Bow Wow")..........................5-10 64
GLOVER (200 "Run Home Little Girl")..... 10-15 59
GLOVER (201 "Taking Care of Business")... 10-15 59
GLOVER (202 "When the Sergeant Comes Marching Home").. 15-20 60
GLOVER (206 "Cool Down")...................... 10-15 60
JAMIE (1174 "Sound Off")..........................8-12 60
JAMIE (1177 "Pony Train")..........................8-12 61
JAMIE (1184 "Hey Doll Baby")................ 10-15 61
JAMIE (1189 "Horsin' Around")................8-12 61
JAMIE (1202 "Shake the Hand of a Fool") .8-12 61
JAMIE (1213 "Twistin' Train")....................5-10 62
JOSIE..5-10 68-69
KING (Except 5213).......................... 10-25 57-61
KING (5213 "Fall Guy")........................ 10-20 59
(Monaural.)
KING (5213 "Fall Guy")........................... 25-35 59
(Stereo.)
MAGGIE (609 "Your Lovin' Is Killin' Me Baby")... 10-20
MURBO (1001 "Hoop Hoop Hoop a Hoopa Doo")..5-10 65
OKEH (6844 "The Same Old Feeling").... 20-40 52
OKEH (6883 "What'cha Gonna Do")........ 20-40 52
OKEH (6907 "Jambalaya")...................... 20-40 52
OKEH (6929 "Be Sure You Know").........20-40 52
OKEH (6938 "My Plea")..........................20-40 53
OKEH (6961 "Big Mary")..........................20-40 53
OKEH (7027 "Over the Rainbow")............20-40 54
OKEH (7038 "Hello Stranger")..................20-40 54
OKEH (7244 "Eye to Eye")..........................5-10 66
PHILIPS (40445"Mary Mack")......................5-10 67
WING (90006 "Around the World")...........15-25 55
WING (90033 "Sweet and Low")...............15-25 55
WING (90058 "Get on the Right Track, Baby")..15-25 56
LPs: 10/12-inch
JAMIE (3018 "Sound Off")........................25-50 61
Session: Mickey Baker.
Also see BAKER, Mickey

TURNER, Tommy
Singles: 7-inch
BELL (736 "Wish I Knew")..........................5-10 68
ELBAM (70 "Lady")..........................15-25 66

TURNER, Velvert, Group
LPs: 10/12-inch
FAMILY..10-12 72

TURNER, Windy
Singles: 7-inch
CAPITOL (4988 "Joannie")......................10-15 63

TURNER, Zeb C&W '49
Singles: 78 rpm
KING..5-15 49-53
Singles: 7-inch
KING (950 "Chew Tobacco Rag")............20-30 51
KING (1176 "Jersey Rock")......................20-30 53
LPs: 10/12-inch
AUDIO LAB (1537 "Country Music in the Zeb Turner Style")..30-40 59

TURNER BROTHERS
Singles: 7-inch
CARNIVAL..5-10 68
MB (572-19 "Let's Go Fishing")................15-25

TURNPIKES
Singles: 7-inch
CAPITOL (2234 "Cast a Spell")..............30-40 66

TURNQUIST REMEDY
LPs: 10/12-inch
PENTAGRAM (10004 "Turnquist Remedy")..15-20 70
Members: Scott Harder; John Maggi; Michael Woods.
Also see STRING CHEESE

TURNSTALL, Arkey
Singles: 7-inch
BRAND X (00 "Is the King Dead")..............8-12 78

TURRENTINE, Stanley LP '67
Singles: 7-inch
BLUE NOTE..5-8 61-69
CTI..4-6 72
ELEKTRA..3-6 79-81
FANTASY..4-6 74-78
IMPULSE..4-8 67
LPs: 10/12-inch
BAINBRIDGE..5-8 81
BLUE NOTE..25-50 60-61
(Label gives New York street address for Blue Note Records.)
BLUE NOTE..15-30 62-65
(Label reads "Blue Note Records Inc. - New York, U.S.A.")
BLUE NOTE..8-18 65-85
(Label shows Blue Note Records as a division of either Liberty or United Artists.)
CTI..8-12 71-75
ELEKTRA..5-8 79-81
FPM..5-8 75
FANTASY..8-12 74-78
IMPULSE..8-15 67-78
MAINSTREAM..15-25 65
PRESTIGE..6-12 70-71
SUNSET..8-12 69
TIME..25-50 62-63
UPFRONT..6-12 72
Also see BYRD, Donald
Also see FULSON, Lowell
Also see HUBBARD, Freddie, & Stanley Turrentine
Also see SCOTT, Shirley, / Stanley Turrentine
Also see SILVER, Horace, Quintet, & Stanley Turrentine

TURSSO, Wayne
Singles: 7-inch
PERRY (802 "Won't You Hold Me")........20-25 '60s
TWAYNE (802 "Hootchy-Koo")................20-25 '60s
Picture Sleeves
TWAYNE (802 "Hootchy-Koo")................25-35 '60s

TURTLES
Singles: 78 rpm
RCA (6356 "Mystery Train")......................5-10 55
Singles: 7-inch
RCA (6356 "Mystery Train")......................10-20 55

TURTLES P&R/LP '65
Singles: 7-inch
BUCCANEER (3002 "Happy Together")....5-10 '60s
COLLECTABLES..3-5 '80s
LOST NITE..3-5
RHINO..3-5 84
WHITE WHALE..5-15 65-70
Picture Sleeves
WHITE WHALE (Except 244)..................10-15 66-69
WHITE WHALE (244 "Happy Together") .15-25 67
EPs: 7-inch
RHINO (RNPD-901 "Turtles 1968")...........8-10 83
(Picture disc.)
LPs: 10/12-inch
RHINO..5-8 82-86
SIRE..10-15 74
TRIP..5-10 '70s
WHITE WHALE..15-30 65-71
Members: Howard Kaylan; Mark Volman; John Barbata; Chuck Portz; Al Nichol; Jim Pons; Don Murray; Jim Tucker; John Seiter; Chip Douglas.
Also see CHRISTMAS SPIRIT
Also see CROSSFIRES
Also see LEAVES
Also see MODERN FOLK QUARTET

TURZY, Jane
Singles: 78 rpm
DECCA..3-6 51-54
Singles: 7-inch
B&F..10-20 59
CORAL..5-10 58
DECCA..5-10 51-54

TU-TONES
Singles: 7-inch
CABOT (114 "Don't Say We're Through")..30-40 57
LIN (5021 "Still in Love with You")...........40-50 59
Members: Larry Mackey; Joe Whitfield; Ronnie Goodrich; Mike Post.

TUTT, Bill
Singles: 78 rpm
GILT-EDGE (5082 "Salty Dog")..................5-10 53
Singles: 7-inch
GILT-EDGE (5082 "Salty Dog")...............15-25 53

TUTTLE, Wesley, & His Texas Stars C&W '45
(With Marilyn Tuttle)
Singles: 78 rpm
CAPITOL..4-8 45-54
Singles: 7-inch
CAPITOL..6-12 52-54
SACRED..10-20

TUXEDO JUNCTION P&R/LP '78
Singles: 12-inch
BUTTERFLY..4-8 78-80
Singles: 7-inch
BUTTERFLY (Black vinyl)..........................3-6 78-80
BUTTERFLY (Colored vinyl)......................4-6 78
LPs: 10/12-inch
BUTTERFLY (Black vinyl)..........................5-10 77-79
BUTTERFLY (Colored vinyl)....................10-12 77
(Promotional issues only.)

TUXEDOS
Singles: 7-inch
FORTÉ (1414 "Yes It's True")................75-125 60
(Gold label.)
FORTÉ (1414 "Yes It's True")..................15-25 60
(Yellow label.)
Also see HOLLYWOOD SAXONS
Also see PORTRAITS

TWANGY REBELS
Singles: 7-inch
GENERAL AMERICAN (719 "Rebel Rouser 65")..5-10 65
Member: Frank Virtuoso.
Also see VIRTUOSO, Frank

TWANS
Singles: 7-inch
DADE (1903 "I Can't See Him Again").150-250 '60s

TWAS BRILLIG
Singles: 7-inch
DATE (1550 "Dirty Old Man")....................40-60 67
SCOTTY (6620 "Dirty Old Man")...............60-80 66
Members: Earl Bulinski; Bill Bulinski; Jerry Fink; Gary Omerza; Tim Elving.
Also see ELECTRAS

TWEETERS
Singles: 7-inch
DECCA (30725 "Mascara Mama")...........15-25 58

12 A.M.
Singles: 7-inch
GROOVY (102 "The Way I Feel")............15-25 67

TWENTIE GRANS
Singles: 7-inch
COLUMBIA (44239 "Giving Up Your Love")..15-25 67
(Also issued as by the Players.)
Member: Herman Griffin.
Also see GRIFFIN, Herman
Also see PLAYERS

TWENTIETH CENTURY ZOO
Singles: 7-inch
CAZ (103 "You Don't Remember")............8-12 67
VAULT..5-10 69-70
LPs: 10/12-inch
VAULT (122 "Thunder on a Clear Day") .. 15-25 68

24 CARAT BLACK
Singles: 7-inch
ENTERPRISE..5-10 73
LPs: 10/12-inch
ENTERPRISE (1030 "Ghetto – Misfortune's Wealth")..75-100 73

27th SUBMARINE AIRBORNE
Singles: 7-inch
WESTCHESTER (268 "I'll Never Leave") .. 8-12 67

$27 SNAP-ON FACE
LPs: 10/12-inch
HETRODYNE (001 "Hetrodyne State Hospital")..35-55 77
(Colored vinyl.)

TWIGGY
Singles: 7-inch
CAPITOL (5903 "Over and Over")..............5-10 67
MERCURY..4-6 76
Picture Sleeves
CAPITOL (5903 "Over and Over")..............5-10 67
LPs: 10/12-inch
MERCURY..8-12 76

TWIGS
Singles: 7-inch
DOT (16830 "I Need Your Love Babe") 5-10 66
(Same number used on a Soul Survivors release.)

TWILETTES
Singles: 7-inch
DARCEY (5002 "Boss Town Shuffle") 10-15 65

TWILIGHT STRINGERS
Singles: 7-inch
VALE (1 "Pale Face Twist")....................10-15 62
VALE (2 "Cherokee Twist")....................10-15 62

TWILIGHTERS
(With "Frank Motley [Dual Trumpeter] & His Crew")
Singles: 78 rpm
MARSHALL..75-125 53
Singles: 7-inch
MARSHALL (702 "Please Tell Me You're Mine")..10-15 '70s
(Black vinyl.)
MARSHALL (702 "Please Tell Me You're Mine")..1000-1500 53
(Dark red vinyl.)
MARSHALL (702 "Please Tell Me You're Mine")..100-150 '60s
(Light red vinyl.)
Members: Melvin Jennings; Earl Williams; DeRoy Green; Robert Richardson; William Pierce.
Also see MOTLEY, Frank

TWILIGHTERS

Singles: 78 rpm

SPECIALTY (548 "It's True")....................25-35 55

Singles: 7-inch

SPECIALTY (548 "It's True")..................75-125 55

Also see ALLEN, Tony

TWI-LIGHTERS

Singles: 78 rpm

GROOVE..10-15 56

Singles: 7-inch

GROOVE (0154 "Sittin' in a Corner").......30-40 56

Also see CHILDS, Lillian

TWILIGHTERS

(Twi-Lighters)

Singles: 78 rpm

DOT (15526 "Eternally")...........................10-20 56

EBB (117 "Pride and Joy").......................20-30 57

MGM (55011 "Little Did I Dream")...........40-60 55

MGM (55014 "Lovely Lady")....................50-75 55

Singles: 7-inch

ARCADE (1003 "The Key to My Heart").....5-10 77

BUBBLE (1334 "My Silent Prayer")..........15-25 62

CHESS (1803 "She Needs a Guy").........10-15 61

COLLECTABLES..3-5 '80s

DOT (15526 "Eternally")...........................40-50 56

EBB (117 "Pride and Joy").......................20-30 57

ELDO (115 "Do You Believe")..................40-50 61

IMPERIAL (66201 "Shake a Tail Feather")...5-10 66

J-V-B (83 "How Many Times")..........1000-2000 57

MGM (55011 "Little Did I Dream")........250-300 55

MGM (55014 "Lovely Lady")................200-250 55

PICO (2801 "Eternally")...........................40-50 60

PLA-BAC (1113 "Eternally")..................75-125 57

RED TOP (127 "The Key to My Heart")..100-200 60

RICKI (907 "Help Me")............................15-25 61

SUPER (1003 "Please Come Home").....30-40 60

Also see STARLINGS

TWILIGHTERS / Leon Brooks

Singles: 7-inch

CHOLLY (712 "Let There Be Love"/"Money Talks")...2000-3000 58

TWILIGHTERS / Little Cholly Wright

Singles: 7-inch

CADDY (103 "Eternally"/"I Believe")....300-400 57

Also see TWILIGHTERS

Also see WRIGHT, Little Cholly

TWI-LIGHTERS

Singles: 7-inch

FRATERNITY (889 "Beginning of Love") 10-15 61

SAXONY (2003 "Beginning of Love")...........4-6 94

TWILIGHTERS

Singles: 7-inch

BETHLEHEM (3002 "Just Like Before")..15-25 61

BETHLEHEM (3004 "It Hurts Me So").....15-25 62

TWILIGHTERS

Singles: 7-inch

SARA (1048 "Can't You Stay a Little Longer")...8-12 61

TWILIGHTERS

Singles: 7-inch

MORGIL (105 "Carrie-Jo").........................40-50 62

TWILIGHTERS

Singles: 7-inch

BELL (624 "Be Faithful")............................10-15 65

BELL (631 "Boo's Blues")..........................10-15 65

MARK VII..5-10 68

TWILIGHTERS

Singles: 7-inch

LATIN (101 "The Stomp").........................10-15 '60s

TWILIGHTERS Featuring Donald Richards

Singles: 7-inch

SPIN (1 "Yes You Are")........................200-300 60

TWILIGHTS

Singles: 78 rpm

TUXEDO..20-30 56

Singles: 7-inch

TUXEDO (917 "I'm Falling for You")....100-150 56

TWILIGHTS

Singles: 7-inch

FINESSE (1717 "My Heart Belongs to Only You")..15-25 59

TWILIGHTS

Singles: 7-inch

AQUA...5-10 '60s

FELICE (713 "Believe It Or Not").............30-40 63

(Red vinyl.)

HARTHON (134 "It's Been So Long").......15-25 64

HARTHON (135 "Shipwreck")...................15-25 64

PARKWAY (128 "Shipwreck")....................8-12 67

PARROT (45013 "She's There")................5-10 65

SELECT (742 "I Have the Right")..............5-10 65

6 STAR (1001 "Little Richard")................10-15 63

TWILIGHT (1028 "It Could Be True").......10-15 62

TWILIGHTS

Singles: 7-inch

BANGAR (634 "Tears")............................10-20 64

CUCA (6531 "007")..................................10-20 65

Members: Gene Frazier; Dan Dernbach; Bob Grizb; Donnie Winget.

TWI-LIGHTS

Singles: 7-inch

SPENADA (101 "Just Can't Let Her Go")..75-125

TWILIGHTS Featuring Tony Richards

(With the Richard Wolfe Orchestra)

Singles: 7-inch

COLPIX (178 "Paper Boy")....................75-125 60

TWILITERS

Singles: 7-inch

FLIPPIN' (106 "Infatuation").....................10-15 61

NIX (102 "Hey There")..............................40-50 61

NIX (103 "Back to School").......................15-25 61

TWILITERS

Singles: 7-inch

SARA (1048 "Restless Love")................50-100 61

TWILITERS

(With Bill Kennedy)

Singles: 7-inch

EMPIRE (6 "The Girl from Liverpool")..250-350 63

TWILITERS

Singles: 7-inch

PALOMA (100 "You Better Make It")........15-25 64

TWILITERS

Singles: 7-inch

ROULETTE (4546 "Sweet Lips")..............10-20 64

TWILITERS

Singles: 7-inch

EDGEWOOD (137 "There in the Night")..30-40 '70s

(Recorded in the fifties. Previously unreleased.)

TWI-LITES

Singles: 7-inch

KING (5461 "Pony Time")..........................8-12 61

TWIN TUNES QUINTET

Singles: 78 rpm

SOUND 8-12 55

Singles: 7-inch

RCA (7091 "The Love Nest")...................10-15 57

RCA (7225 "Dream Face").......................10-15 58

SOUND (115 "I'll Make You Mine")...........10-15 55

SOUND (125 "Feel So Good")..................15-20 55

TWIN-DELLS

Singles: 7-inch

TWIN DELL (201,022 "Nancy")................15-25 66

Members: Charlie Basile; Paul Basile; Bobby Pano.

TWINETTES

Singles: 7-inch

VEE-JAY (284 "Let the People Talk").......15-25 58

TWINKLE

Singles: 7-inch

AURORA (163 "What Am I Doing Here with You")..5-10 67

TOLLIE (9040 "Terry")................................5-10 65

TOLLIE (9047 "Ain't Nobody Home But Me")..5-10 65

Picture Sleeves

TOLLIE (9040 "Terry")..............................15-25 64

TWINKLES

(With Al Browne & His Band)

Singles: 7-inch

MUSICOR (1031 "Oh Little Star")..............5-10 63

PEAK (5001 "Bad Motorcycle")................40-50 58

Also see BROWNE, Al

Also see STOREY SISTERS

TWINKLETONES

Singles: 7-inch

JOSIE (847 "Should I")............................15-25 58

Also see HOMBS, Jimmie / Twinkletones

TWINN CONNEXION

LPs: 10/12-inch

DECCA..10-15 68

TWINS

(Twin Tones)

Singles: 7-inch

LANCER (106 "Buttercup").......................10-15 59

MONTE CARLO 10-15 57

RCA (7148 "Flip Skip")............................10-15 58

RCA (7235 "Jo-Ann's Sister")..................10-15 58

RCA (7382 "Classroom Rock")...............10-15 58

Picture Sleeves

LANCER (106 "Buttercup").......................10-20 59

RCA (7235 "Jo-Ann's Sister")..................15-25 58

EPs: 7-inch

RCA (4107 "Jim & John").........................20-30 58

RCA (4237 "Teenagers Love the Twins") 20-30 58

LPs: 10/12-inch

RCA (1708 "Teenagers Love the Twins") 40-60 58

Members: Jim; John.

TWINTONETTES

Singles: 7-inch

TITAN (1721 "School Bells")....................20-30 61

TWIST, Johnny

Singles: 7-inch

CHECKER (1139 "Go Go Baby")..............5-10 66

TWISTER, Big Bill, & His Minters

LPs: 10/12-inch

INT'L AWARD (187 "Do the Twist").........10-15 62

TWISTER, Eddie

Singles: 7-inch

PHILIPS (40009 "Double Twist")...............8-12 62

TWISTERS

Singles: 7-inch

APT (25045 "Come Go with Me")............15-20 60

CAMPUS (125 "Elvis Leaves Sorrento")..10-15 61

CAPITOL (4451 "Dancing Little Clown")..10-15 60

FELCO (103 "Speed Limit").......................5-10 59

HULL (741 "Little Carousel")......................5-10 61

TWISTERS

("Music by: The Shades")

Singles: 7-inch

SUN-SET (501 "This Is the End")........700-800 61

TWISTERS

Singles: 7-inch

DUEL (502 "Peppermint Twist")..................8-10 61

Also see JOEY & TWISTERS

TWISTERS

(Bobby Smith Combo)

Singles: 7-inch

GEMINI (101 "Run Little Sheba")..........100-200 61

(Reissued as by the Rebels.)

Also see REBELS

Also see SMITH, Bob

TWISTERS

LPs: 10/12-inch

TREASURE...15-25 62

TWISTIN' KINGS

Singles: 7-inch

MOTOWN (1022 "Xmas Twist")...............20-30 61

MOTOWN (1023 "Congo")........................20-30 62

LPs: 10/12-inch

MOTOWN (601 "Twistin' Around the World")..50-100 61

TWITTY, Conway P&R '57/C&W '66

Singles: 78 rpm

MGM (12677 "It's Only Make Believe")...100-150 58

(Canadian.)

MERCURY..25-75 57

Singles: 7-inch

ABC-PAR (10507 "Go On & Cry")...........15-25 63

ABC-PAR (10550 "My Baby Left Me").....20-30 64

CONWAY TWITTY FAN CLUB ("It's Only Make Believe")..10-20

(Promotional, fan club issue only.)

DECCA...5-10 65-72

ELEKTRA..3-5 82-83

MCA 3-6 73-92

MGM (500 series)...4-6 78

MGM (12677 "It's Only Make Believe")....15-25 58

MGM (12748 "Story of My Love")............15-25 59

MGM (12785 "Hey Little Lucy")...............15-25 59

MGM (12804 "Mona Lisa").......................15-25 59

MGM (12826 "Danny Boy").......................15-25 59

MGM (12857 "Lonely Blue Boy")..............15-25 59

MGM (12886 "What Am I Living For")......10-20 60

MGM (12911 "Is a Blue Bird Blue")..........10-20 60

MGM (12918 "What a Dream")..................10-20 60

MGM (12943 "I Need You So")..................10-20 60

MGM (12962 "Whole Lot of Shakin' Going On")..10-20 60

MGM (12969 "C'est Si Bon")....................10-20 60

MGM (12998 "The Next Kiss")..................10-20 61

MGM (13011 "I'm in a Blue, Blue Mood").10-20 61

MGM (13034 "It's Drivin' Me Wild")..........10-20 61

MGM (13050 "Portrait of a Fool")............10-20 61

MGM (13072 "Little Piece of My Heart")..10-20 62

MGM (13089 "Unchained Melody")..........10-20 62

MGM (13112 "The Pickup")......................10-20 62

MGM (13149 "Got My Mojo Working")......10-20 63

MGM (14000 series)....................................4-6 71-72

MGM (50107 "It's Only Make Believe")....40-60 58

(Stereo.)

MGM (50115 "Story of My Love")............30-50 59

(Stereo.)

MGM (50130 "Danny Boy").......................30-50 59

(Stereo.)

MGM GOLDEN CIRCLE..............................3-5

MERCURY (71086 "I Need Your Lovin'")...30-40 57

MERCURY (71148 "Shake It Up")............30-40 57

MERCURY (71384 "Why Can't I Get Through to You")..30-40 58

MUSIGRAM...4-6

(Flexi-disc.)

POLYDOR ....3-5 '80s

W.B. 3-5 83-86

Picture Sleeves

ELEKTRA (47302 "The Clown")...................4-6 82

MGM (12886 "What Am I Living For")......20-30 60

MGM (12911 "Is a Blue Bird Blue")..........20-30 60

MGM (12969 "C'est Si Bon")....................20-30 60

MGM (12998 "The Next Kiss")..................20-30 61

MGM (13034 "It's Drivin' Me Wild").........20-30 61

EPs: 7-inch

DECCA (34437 "Look Into My Teardrops")...10-20 66

(Juke box issue only. Includes title strips.)

MGM (1623 "It's Only Make Believe")......30-50 58

MGM (1640/1641/1642 "Conway Twitty Sings")..20-30 59

(Price is for any of three volumes.)

MGM (1678/1679/1680 "Saturday Night with Conway Twitty")..20-30 59

(Price is for any of three volumes.)

MGM (1701 "Lonely Blue Boy")...............20-30 60

LPs: 10/12-inch

ACCORD 5-10 82

ALLEGIANCE...5-8 84

CT (1001 "Solid Gold")..............................8-12

CANDLELITE ("Living Legend")...............30-50 '70s

(No selection number used.)

CONWAY TWITTY/MCA (1002 "Conway Twitty")..8-10

CORAL..5-8 73

CUTLASS 40-50 72

(Title and selection number not known.)

DECCA...8-18 66-72

DEMAND 8-12 72

ELEKTRA..5-8 82-83

MCA 5-15 73-85

MGM (110 "Conway Twitty")....................15-20 70

MGM (3744 "Conway Twitty Sings").......50-100 59

MGM (E-3786 "Saturday Night with Conway Twitty")..50-75 59

(Monaural.)

MGM (SE-3786 "Saturday Night with Conway Twitty")..75-100 59

(Stereo.)

MGM (E-3818 "Lonely Blue Boy")........... 50-75 60
(Monaural.)
MGM (SE-3818 "Lonely Blue Boy") 75-100 60
(Stereo.)
MGM (E-3849 "Conway Twitty's Greatest Hits").. 50-75 60
(Monaural. Black label. With gatefold cover and poster.)
MGM (SE-3849 "Conway Twitty's Greatest Hits")...................................... 75-100 60
(Stereo. With gatefold cover and poster.)
MGM (3849 "Conway Twitty's Greatest Hits").. 15-20 68
(Blue and yellow label. With standard cover.)
MGM (E-3907 "Rock and Roll Story")...... 50-75 61
(Monaural.)
MGM (SE-3907 "Rock and Roll Story") . 75-100 61
(Stereo.)
MGM (E-3943 "Conway Twitty Touch") ... 30-40 61
(Monaural.)
MGM (SE-3943 "Conway Twitty Touch"). 35-50 61
(Stereo.)
MGM (E-4019 thru E-4217)..................... 20-40 62-64
(Monaural.)
MGM (SE-4019 thru SE-4217)................ 25-50 62-64
(Stereo.)
MGM (4650 thru 4884) 10-20 69-73
METRO... 15-25 65
OPRYLAND (12636 "Conway Twitty, Then and Now").. 75-100
(Six-disc set. Promotional issue only.)
PICKWICK... 10-15 72
SUNRISE MEDIA......................................5-10 81
TEE VEE..5-10 78
TROLLY CAR..5-10
TWITTY BIRD (1001 "Solid Gold")........... 10-12 82
(Two-discs.)
W.B. 5-10 83-86
Session: Fred Carter Jr.; Anthony Armstrong Jones; Joni Lee.
Also see LYNN, Loretta, & Conway Twitty
Also see MARTIN, Dean
Also see McDOWELL, Ronnie
Also see MILLER, Buddy
Also see TUBB, Ernest

TWO ACES

Singles: 7-inch

GARY (1009 "Flame in My Heart")........... 10-15 58

TWO B'S

Singles: 7-inch

ARGO (5349 "Angel That Lied")..................8-12 59

TWO BITS

Singles: 7-inch

BIG DEAL (6601 "Things Must Change")...5-10 66

TWO BROTHERS

Singles: 7-inch

IMPERIAL (5748 "Lonely Boy")...................8-12 61
IMPERIAL (5810 "Blue Monday") 8-12 62
IMPERIAL (5887 "Tell Her") 8-12 62

TWO CHAPS

Singles: 7-inch

ATLANTIC (1195 "Forgive Me").............. 10-20 59
Member: Jay Black.
Also see BLACK, Jay

TWO FRIENDS

Singles: 7-inch

HPC (1001 "Just Too Much to Hope For").. 40-60 60
Members: Clyde Wilson (a.k.a. Steve Mancha); Wilbert Jackson.
Also see MANCHA, Steve

TWO GOSPEL KEYS & THRASHER WONDERS

Singles: 78 rpm

RED ROBIN 5-10 52

Singles: 7-inch

RED ROBIN (106 "Motherless Child") 10-15 52

TWO GUITARS

LPs: 10/12-inch

KING (2029 "Time for Two Guitars")........ 15-25 61

TWO NOTES

Singles: 7-inch

CORAL (62153 "Sandy, Sandy") 8-12 59

2 OF CLUBS P&R '67

Singles: 7-inch

FRATERNITY..5-10 66-67

TWO PLUS TWO

Singles: 7-inch

DITTO (108 "High Rise") 50-75 68
RCA (8948 "Strangers in the Night") 15-20 66

TWO SWEETHEARTS

Singles: 78 rpm

GROOVE (0122 "True Love Is Missing")....5-10 55

Singles: 7-inch

GROOVE (0122 "True Love Is Missing")..10-15 55

TWOVOICE, Johnny
(With the Medallions)

Singles: 78 rpm

DOOTONE..10-20 55

Singles: 7-inch

DOOTONE (373 "My Pretty Baby") 40-50 55
SPECIALTY (676 "You and Your Lovin' Ways")..15-25 59
SPECIALTY (685 "Superman")................10-20 60
Also see GREEN, Vernon, & Medallions

TWYLIGHTS

Singles: 7-inch

ROCK'N (102 "Darling Lets [sic] Fall in Love")...50-75 61
Session: Van McCoy
Also see McCOY, Van

TY, Jimmy

Singles: 7-inch

BELLA (607 "Mary Jane") 25-35 62

TYCE, Napoleon

Singles: 7-inch

NORWOOD (105 "Sitting Here")..........150-200 60

TYFER, Jerry
(With the Jack Halloran Singers, Carl Stevens & His Orchestra)

Singles: 78 rpm

WING..8-12 55-56

Singles: 7-inch

WING (90029 "Lady Love").......................15-20 55
WING (90061 "I'm So Sorry")....................15-20 56
Also see HALLORAN, Jack, Singers

TYGH & CRITERIONS

Singles: 7-inch

FLITE (101 "To Be Mine") 40-60 63

TYLE, Teddy
(With His Saxophone & Orchestra)

Singles: 7-inch

GOLDEN CREST (500 "Drifting and Dreaming")...10-20 58
GOLDEN CREST (504 "Wabash Blues") .10-20 58
GOLDEN CREST (549 "Way Out Upon the Swanee River") 10-20 60

TYLER, Alvin "Red"
(Red Tyler & Gyros)

Singles: 7-inch

ACE (556 "Snake Eyes")...........................10-20 59
ACE (576 "Happy Sax").............................10-20 59

LPs: 10/12-inch

ACE (1006 "Rockin' & Rollin' ")...................50-75 60
Also see GAYTEN, Paul

TYLER, Big T.

Singles: 78 rpm

ALADDIN 25-50 56

Singles: 7-inch

ALADDIN (362 "Looking for a Baby") 50-100 56
ALADDIN (3384 "King Kong") 100-150 57

TYLER, Charles

Singles: 7-inch

LANOR (517 "Let's Stick Together")...........5-10 63
LANOR (520 "Lonely, Lonely Nights") 5-10 64
LANOR (521 "My Lonely Life")....................5-10 64

TYLER, Chip

Singles: 7-inch

CHICORY (401 "I Love You Yvonne").....15-25 66

TYLER, Chuck, & Royal Lancers

Singles: 7-inch

FENWAY (7004 "She's All Mine")...........75-100 61
Also see GRECCO, Tony
Also see PREMIER, Ronnie
Also see ROYAL LANCERS

TYLER, Frankie
(Frankie Valli)

Singles: 7-inch

OKEH (7103 "I Go Ape")...........................50-75 58

Promotional Singles

OKEH (7103 "I Go Ape")...........................40-60 58
Also see VALLI, Frankie

TYLER, George

Singles: 7-inch

CANYON (252 "I'm Going Back to Texas") 100-200

TYLER, Gladys

Singles: 7-inch

ASCOT (2130 "Pack Up") 10-15 63
BROOKS (101 "One Man's Woman").......15-25 64
CORAL (62389 "I'm in the Mood for Love")..10-15 63
DECCA (31991 "Little Bitty Girl") 5-10 66
DECCA (32135 "That Man of Mine") 5-10 67

TYLER, Jim

LPs: 10/12-inch

TIME (2053 "Twist")..................................15-25 62
(Stereo.)
TIME (52053 "Twist")................................10-20 62
(Monaural.)

TYLER, Jimmy

Singles: 78 rpm

FEDERAL (12080 "Take It Away") 20-30 52
FEDERAL (12100 thru 12200 series).......10-25 54-57

Singles: 7-inch

FEDERAL (12080 "Take It Away") 50-75 52
FEDERAL (12100 thru 12200 series).......15-25 54-57

TYLER, Jimmy

Singles: 7-inch

ORIGINAL SOUND 8-12 62-63

TYLER, Joey

Singles: 7-inch

REPRISE (269 "All the Good Times Are Over")...5-10 64

TYLER, Johnny

Singles: 78 rpm

DECCA (29180 "Just Out of Reach") 5-10 54
EKKO (1000 "Devil's Hot Rod")................20-40 55
EKKO (1001 "Where You Gonna Hide") ..15-25 55
LIBERTY (55007 "Heads Up") 8-12 55
STARDAY (263 "Lie to Me Baby")............20-30 56

Singles: 7-inch

DECCA (29180 "Just Out of Reach") 10-15 54
EKKO (1000 "Devil's Hot Rod") 50-100 55
EKKO (1001 "Where You Gonna Hide") ..25-50 55
LIBERTY (55007 "Heads Up") 10-20 55
RURAL RHYTHM (515 "Lie to Me Baby")...75-125 59
STARDAY (263 "Lie to Me Baby")............50-75 56
(Black vinyl.)
STARDAY (263 "Lie to Me Baby")........150-250 56
(Red vinyl.)

TYLER, Kip
(With the White Fronts; with Flips)

Singles: 7-inch

CHALLENGE (1014 "She's Got Eyes") 15-25 58
CHALLENGE (59008 "Jungle Hop").........25-35 58
EBB (154 "Rumble Rock") 25-35 58
EBB (156 "Oh Linda")...............................15-25 59
GYRO DISC...10-15 63

Picture Sleeves

GYRO DISC...15-25 63
Members: Kip Tyler; Steve Douglas.
Also see DOUGLAS, Steve
Also see TYLER & FLIPS

TYLER, Ruckus

Singles: 78 rpm

FABOR (135 "Rockin' & Rollin' ") 25-45 56

Singles: 7-inch

FABOR (135 "Rockin' & Rollin' ") 50-75 56
Also see TALL, Tom

TYLER, T. Texas C&W '46
(With His Oklahoma Melody Boys)

Singles: 78 rpm

DECCA...4-8 53-54
4 STAR..5-10 46-54

Singles: 7-inch

DECCA...5-10 53-54
4 STAR..10-20 53-54
KING..5-10 59-60
RCA...5-10 53-54

LPs: 10/12-inch

CAPITOL..15-25 62-65
DESIGN 10-20 62
INTERNATIONAL AWARD ....8-12 '60s
KING (664 "T. Texas Tyler").....................30-50 59
KING (689 "The Great Texan")..................25-40 60
KING (721 "T. Texas Tyler") 15-25 61
KING (734 "Songs Along the Way") 20-30 61
NASHVILLE..5-10 72
PICKWICK/HILLTOP..................................10-15 67
SOUND (607 "Deck of Cards") 35-55 58
STARDAY (379 "The Man with a Million Friends")..20-30 66
WRANGLER (1002 "T. Texas Tyler").......10-20 62
Also see CLINE, Patsy / T. Texas Tyler / Bill Taylor / Eddie Marvin
Also see PIERCE, Webb / Patsy Cline / T. Texas Tyler

TYLER, Terry

Singles: 7-inch

LANDA (679 "Answer Me") 5-10 61
SUNLAND (101 "Beginning of the End")....5-10 62

TYLER, Tod

Singles: 7-inch

DITTO (129 "Inside a Teardrop")..............30-60

TYLER & FLIPS

Singles: 7-inch

STARLA (2 "Let's Monkey Around").........15-25 57
Members: Kip Tyler, Sandy Nelson.
Also see NELSON, Sandy
Also see TYLER, Kip

TYMES P&R/R&B/LP '63

Singles: 7-inch

ABKCO..4-6 74
COLUMBIA...5-10 68-70
MGM (13536 "Pretend")..............................8-12 66
MGM (13531 "A Touch of Baby") 8-12 66
PARKWAY (871 "So in Love")..................15-20 63
PARKWAY (871 "So Much in Love").......10-15 63
PARKWAY (884 "Wonderful, Wonderful")..10-15 63
PARKWAY (891 "Somewhere")...............10-15 63
PARKWAY (908 "To Each His Own") 10-15 64
PARKWAY (919 "The Magic of Our Summer Love") 10-15 64
PARKWAY (924 "Here She Comes")........10-15 64
PARKWAY (933 "The Twelfth of Never")...8-12 64
PARKWAY (7039 "Isle of Love") 8-12 64
RCA..4-6 74-77
WINCHESTER (1002 "These Foolish Things") 8-10 67

Picture Sleeves

PARKWAY 10-20 63-64

LPs: 10/12-inch

ABKCO (4228 "Best of the Tymes")...........8-10 74
COLUMBIA (9778 "People")......................10-15 69
PARKWAY (7032 "So Much in Love")......40-60 63
(Cover has silhouette drawing of couple walking, with group's picture over the drawing.
PARKWAY (7032 "So Much in Love")......20-40 63
(Cover pictures only the group, checking the "time" on their watches.)
PARKWAY (7038 "Sound of the Wonderful Tymes")...20-40 63
PARKWAY (7039 "Somewhere")..............35-45 64
(With bonus single: *Isle of Love.*)
PARKWAY (7039 "Somewhere")..............20-30 64
(Without bonus single.)
RCA (0727 "Trustmaker") 8-12 74
RCA (1835 "Turning Point") 8-10 77
WYNCOTE...10-20 '60s
Members: George Williams Jr; Donald Banks; Al Berry; Norman Burnett; George Hilliard.
Also see MAESTRO, Johnny, & Tymes

TYNER, McCoy LP '75
(McCoy Tyner Trio)

Singles: 7-inch

COLUMBIA..3-5 82
IMPULSE 5-10 65
MILESTONE 4-6 77

LPs: 10/12-inch

BLUE NOTE..8-15 66-76
COLUMBIA..5-8 82
ELEKTRA (60350 "Dimensions")................5-10 84
FPM..5-10 75
IMPULSE 10-30 62-78

MCA.....5-10 81
MILESTONE.....5-12 72-82
PAUSA.....5-8 82

TYNES, Maria
Singles: 7-inch
UPTOWN (743 "Change My Mind").....10-20 67
Session: Blossoms.
Also see BLOSSOMS

TYRANNIES
Singles: 7-inch
WATCH (1903 "Little Girl").....15-25 65

TYRELL, Danny, & Cleeshays
Singles: 7-inch
EASTMAN (784 "You're Only 17").....15-25 58
Also see KNIGHT, Sonny

TYRELL, Steve
Singles: 7-inch
ALL BOY (8506 "Greatest Love").....8-12 63
PHILIPS (40150 "Young Boy Blues").....10-15 63

TYRONE, Janice
Singles: 7-inch
PZAZZ (041 "Meet Me Baby").....10-20 70

TYRONE (The Wonder Boy)
(Tyrone Davis)
Singles: 7-inch
4 BROTHERS (447 "Try Me").....10-15 65
4 BROTHERS (450 "Good Company").....10-15 66
FOUR BROTHERS (453 "Please Consider Me").....10-15 67
(Note slight change in how label name is shown.)

TYRONE & NU PORTS
(With the Joseph Ricci Orchestra)
Singles: 7-inch
DARROW (20 "Feel Like a Million").....30-40 60
(Maroon label. First issued as by the Mystery Men.)
DARROW (20 "Feel Like a Million").....10-20
(Red label.)
DARROW (71 "Look at Her Eyes").....75-125 63
Also see GERRY & GEMS / Tyrone & Nu Ports
Also see MYSTERY MEN

TYRONES
Singles: 78 rpm
MERCURY.....10-15 56-57
WING.....10-15 56
Singles: 7-inch
DAHLIA (1001 "My Love").....40-50 59
DECCA (30559 "Giggles").....10-15 58
DECCA (30643 "Blast Off").....10-15 58
MERCURY (70939 "My Rock and Roll Baby").....10-15 56
MERCURY (71104 "Pink Champagne").....10-15 57
WING (90072 "Campus Rock").....10-15 56

TYROS
Singles: 7-inch
RONDACK (9780 "Torquay").....15-25 63
(Colored vinyl.)

TYSON, Clay
Singles: 7-inch
KING (6209 "Man on the Moon").....5-10 69
WINLEY (246 "Beatniks").....5-10 60
EPs: 7-inch
WINLEY (254 "Clay Tyson").....8-12 60

TYSON, J.J.
Singles: 7-inch
THUNDERHEAD (7012 "Dirty, Dirty Feeling").....10-15

TYSON, Roy
Singles: 7-inch
DOUBLE L (723 "Oh What a Night for Love").....40-50 63
(White label. Promotional issue only.)
DOUBLE L (723 "Oh What a Night for Love").....30-40 63
(Yellow label.)
DOUBLE L (723 "Oh What a Night for Love").....15-25 63
(Black label.)
DOUBLE L (733 "The Girl I Love").....40-50 64

TYTONES
Singles: 7-inch
NORTHWOOD ("I Cried a River").....75-125
(Selection number not known.)

U

UFO — LP '75
Singles: 7-inch
CHRYSALIS (Black vinyl).....3-6 73-86
CHRYSALIS (2157 "Too Hot to Handle").....4-6 77
(Colored vinyl.)
Picture Sleeves
CHRYSALIS (2157 "Too Hot to Handle").....4-6 77
CHRYSALIS (2239 "Cherry").....4-6 78
LPs: 10/12-inch
CHRYSALIS.....5-12 74-86
RARE EARTH.....10-15 71

U.S. BEATLEWIGS
Singles: 7-inch
ORBIT (531 "She's No Innocent").....8-12 64

U.S. DOUBLE QUARTET
(United States Double Quartet)
Singles: 7-inch
B.T. PUPPY (524 "Life Is Groovy").....5-10 66
B.T. PUPPY (547 "Walking Along").....5-10 67
B.T. PUPPY (551 "Do Re Me").....5-10 67
LPs: 10/12-inch
B.T. PUPPY (1005 "Life Is Groovy").....10-15 69
Members: Tokens; Kirby Stone Four.
Also see STONE, Kirby, Four
Also see TOKENS

U.S. FOUR
Singles: 7-inch
HERITAGE (110 "Please Don't Stay Away Too Long").....5-10 62

U.S. GROUP
Singles: 7-inch
UPTOWN (736 "Just a Year Ago Today").....10-15 66

U.S. KIDS
Singles: 7-inch
REX (2629 "I Love the Rain").....8-12 67

U.S. MALE
Singles: 7-inch
MGM (13838 "Boys Can Be Hurt").....5-10 67
SPECIAL DELIVERY (1005 "I Don't Want to Know").....15-20 '60s
UNITED AMERICAN PRODUCTS (1002 "It's Gonna Be So Hard").....5-10 67

U.S. MALES
Singles: 7-inch
BRITANIA (101 "Open Up Your Heart").....10-15 68
(Gold vinyl.)
Also see COASTLINERS

U2 — LP '81
Singles: 12-inch
ISLAND.....4-6 83
Singles: 7-inch
ISLAND.....3-5 81-93
Picture Sleeves
ISLAND.....3-8 81-93
EPs: 7-inch
ISLAND (99385 "Joshua Tree").....5-10 87
LPs: 10/12-inch
ISLAND (Except 314-510347).....5-10 81-91
ISLAND (314-510347 "Achtung Baby").....15-20 91
(With "naked" cover.)
ISLAND (314-510347 "Achtung Baby").....5-10 91
(Without "naked" cover.")
MFSL (207 "The Unforgettable Fire").....25-35 94
POLYDOR.....8-10 '90s
Members: Paul "Bono Vox" Hewson; David "The Edge" Evan; Adam Clayton; Larry Mullen.

U2 & B.B. KING — P&R '89
Singles: 12-inch
ISLAND.....4-6 89
Singles: 7-inch
ISLAND.....3-5 89
Picture Sleeves
ISLAND.....3-5 89
Also see KING, B.B.
Also see U2

UBANS
Singles: 7-inch
RADIANT (102 "Gloria").....150-200 64

UGLY DUCKLINGS
Singles: 7-inch
RAZOR (2 "Pain Is Alright").....3-5 80
YORKTOWN (45001 "Nothin'").....50-75 66
(Black and silver label. Canadian)
YORKTOWN (45001 "Nothin'").....20-30 66
(Multi-color label. Canadian)
YORKTOWN (45002 "10:30 Train").....25-40 66
(Canadian.)
YORKTOWN (45003 "Just in Case You Wonder").....25-40 66
(Canadian.)
YORKTOWN (45005 "Postman's Fancy").....20-30 67
(Canadian.)
YORKVILLE (45013 "Gaslight").....15-25 67
(Canadian.)
YORKVILLE (45017 "I Know What to Say").....15-25 67
(Canadian.)
Picture Sleeves
RAZOR (2 "Pain Is Alright").....3-5 80
LPs: 10/12-inch
YORKTOWN (50001 "Somewhere Outside").....175-225 67
(Canadian.)

ULTIMATE SPINACH — LP '68
Singles: 7-inch
MGM.....5-10 68-69
LPs: 10/12-inch
MGM (4518 "Ultimate Spinach").....20-30 68
MGM (4570 "Behold & See").....20-30 68
MGM (4600 "Ultimate Spinach").....15-25 69
Members: Barbara Hudson; Richard Nese; Ian Bruce Douglas; Jeff Baxter; Ted Myers; Tony Scheuren; Mike Levine; Russ Levine.
Also see CHAMAELEON CHURCH
Also see STEELY DAN

ULTIMATES
Singles: 7-inch
ENVOY (2302 "I Can Tell You Love Me Too").....15-25 61
Also see EXCELLENTS

ULTIMATES
Singles: 7-inch
VALENTINE (1001 "Why I Love You").....30-50 62
(Same number used on a Resolutions release.)

ULTIMATES
Singles: 7-inch
ULTIMA (707 "Autumn Wind").....10-15 64
Also see MESSINA, Jim

ULTIMATES
Singles: 7-inch
BR. ROMA (101 "Girl I've Been Trying to Tell You").....10-15
LAVENDER (2001 "Little Girl").....15-25 '60s

ULTRATONES
(Ultra Tones)
Singles: 7-inch
CARY (2001 "Locomotion").....40-50 62
COMPARE (0000 "Traffic").....30-40 '60s
SAN TANA (101 "Chain Reaction").....10-20 60

ULTTMATTONS
Singles: 7-inch
MAR-V-LUS (6020 "Would I Do It Over").....10-20

ULYSSES
LPs: 10/12-inch
20TH FOX (Except 101).....10-12 78
20TH FOX (101 "Greek Suite").....25-30 79
(Picture disc. Promotional issue only.)

UMEKI, Miyoshi
Singles: 7-inch
MERCURY (71215 "Ooh What Good Company We Could Be").....10-15 57
MERCURY (71216 "Sayonara").....10-20 57
MERCURY (71243 "Sayonara").....10-15 58

UMILIANI, Piero — P&R '69
(Sweden Heaven & Hell Soundtrack)
Singles: 7-inch
ARIEL (500 "Mah-Na, Mah-Na").....5-8 69
LPs: 10/12-inch
ARIEL (15000 "Sweden, Heaven & Hell").....8-12 69

UNBEATABLES
("Gene Cornish & His Orchestra")
Singles: 7-inch
DAWN (552 "I Love Paris").....15-25 64
LPs: 10/12-inch
DAWN (5050 "Live at Palisades Park").....50-100 64
(May have local dee jay imprint at top of front cover. Issued on both Dawn and Fawn.)
FAWN (5050 "Live at Palisades Park").....50-100 64
(May have local dee jay imprint at top of front cover. Issued on both Dawn and Fawn.)
Member: Gene Cornish.
Also see CORNISH, Gene
Also see RASCALS

UNBELIEVABLE UGLIES
(Uglies)
Singles: 7-inch
CARDINAL (0071 "Off My Hands").....20-30 65
INDEPENDENCE (42767 "Spiderman").....80-120 67
LIBERTY (55935 "Get Straight").....10-20 66
MUSIC MASTERS (72164 "Judy Angel").....20-30 64
SOMA (1451 "Keep Her Satisfied").....10-20 65
SOUND.....20-25 69-70
UGLIES.....12-18 78
UA.....20-25 68-69
Members: Alan St. Pierre; Bob (Robbie Jay) Evesloge; Dave (Winston Fink) Hoffman; Mike Vanata.
Also see FRIENDSHIP
Also see JAY, Robbie
Also see ST. PIERRE, Alan

UNBELIEVABLES
Singles: 7-inch
ERA (3155 "Ring Rang Roo").....5-10 65
Also see SKUNKS

UNCALLED FOR
Singles: 7-inch
DOLLIE (509 "Do Like Me").....10-20 67
LAURIE (3394 "Do Like Me").....8-12 67

UNCHAINED MYNDS
Singles: 7-inch
BUDDAH (111 "We Can't Go on This Way").....5-10 69
BUDDAH (119 "Everyday").....5-10 70
BUDDAH (140 "Everyday").....5-10 70
TEEN TOWN (109 "We Can't Go on This Way").....15-25 69
TRANSACTION (705 "We Can't Go on This Way").....5-10 69
TRANSACTION (707 "Hole in My Shoe").....5-10 69
Picture Sleeves
TRANSACTION (705 "We Can't Go on This Way").....50-75 69
Members: Randy Purdy; Wayne Bentzen; Clare Troyanek; Dan Hansen; Doug Krupinski.

UNCLAIMED
Singles: 7-inch
PHILIPS (40430 "Jingle Jangle").....5-10 67

UNCLE ALVIS
Singles: 7-inch
AW (4501 "Hey Hey Pussycat").....200-300

UNCLE HIX
Singles: 7-inch
TEEPEE (1071 "Big Man Blues").....250-350

UNCLE LAR' & LI'L TOMMY
(Larry Lujack)
LPs: 10/12-inch
WLS (890 "Animal Stories, Vol. II").....15-25 82
WLS (847 "Animal Stories, Vol. III").....15-25 83
WLS (1001 "Animal Stories").....15-25 81

UNCLE NED
Singles: 7-inch
HOT TODDY (1002 "Two Eggs Over").....100-150

UNCLE SAM & WAR MACHINE
Singles: 7-inch
BLUE ONION (103 "Spy Girl").....15-25 67

UNCLE SOUND
Singles: 7-inch
W.B......5-10 68
Member: Jimmy Seals.
Also see SEALS, Jimmy

UNDECIDED
Singles: 7-inch
DEARBORN (542 "Make Her Cry")......... 20-30 66

UNDERBEATS
Singles: 7-inch
APEX (76915 "Foot Stompin' ")............... 20-25 64
APEX (76937 "Annie Do the Dog")........... 20-25 64
BANGAR (0632 "Annie Do the Dog")...... 30-60 65
BANGAR (0657 "Little Romance")........... 30-60 66
GARRETT (4004 "Foot Stompin' ")........... 15-25 64
GARRETT ("Annie Do the Dog")............. 10-15 64
(Selection number not known.)
METROBEAT (4449 "It's Gonna Rain Today")............... 15-25 67
SOMA (1449 "Darling Lorraine")............. 10-15 66
SOMA (1458 "I Can't Stand It")............... 40-60 66
TWIN TOWN (706 "Our Love")............... 20-30 65
Picture Sleeves
SOMA (1449 "Darling Lorraine")............. 25-35 66
Also see SMITH, Jojo

UNDERDOGS
Singles: 7-inch
HIDEOUT (1001 "Man in the Glass")....... 25-35 65
(First issue.)
HIDEOUT (1004 "Little Girl").................... 25-35 66
(First issue.)
HIDEOUT (1011 "Surprise, Surprise")..... 25-35 66
REPRISE (0422 "Man in the Glass")....... 10-15 65
REPRISE (0446 "Little Girl")..................... 10-15 66
V.I.P. (25040 "Love's Gone Bad")........... 15-25 67
(Black vinyl.)
V.I.P. (25040 "Love's Gone Bad")........... 25-35 67
(Colored vinyl. Promotional issue only.)

UNDERGRADS
Singles: 7-inch
AUDIO SPECTRUM..................................5-10 64

UNDERGROUND
Singles: 7-inch
MAINSTREAM 10-15 66
LPs: 10/12-inch
WING (12337 "Psychedelic Visions")...... 15-20 67
(Monaural.)
WING (16337 "Psychedelic Visions")...... 20-25 67
(Stereo.)

UNDERGROUND BALLOON CORPS.
Singles: 7-inch
SCOPE (1/2 "Made of Soul")................... 15-25 '60s

UNDERGROUND LITE BULB CO.
Singles: 7-inch
RED LITE (118 "Happy People")............ 10-20 68

UNDERGROUND SUNSHINE *P&R/LP '69*
Singles: 7-inch
EARTH (100 "Birthday")............................8-12 69
INTREPID..5-10 69-70
LPs: 10/12-inch
INTREPID 15-25 69
Members: Rex Rhode; Jane Little Whirry; Bert Hohl; Frank Kohl; Mike Hollihan; Dave Wayne; Chris Connors.
Also see CHALLENGERS

UNDERPRIVILEGED
Singles: 7-inch
SMASH (2051 "You Hurt Me") 10-20 66

UNDERTAKERS
Singles: 7-inch
PARKWAY (909 "Just a Little Bit")............8-10 64

UNDERTAKERS
Singles: 7-inch
PINE HILLS (110 "Searching")................ 15-25 67
PINE HILLS (115 "Love So Dear").......... 15-25 67

UNDERTAKERS
Singles: 7-inch
STUDIO 7 (101 "Unchain My Heart")....... 15-25 67

UNDERTAKERS / Spirits
Singles: 7-inch
SCENE ("Rosalyn")................................. 15-25 66
(No selection number used.)

UNDERWOOD, Carl
(With Zeke Strong Band; with Dealia Copeland)
Singles: 7-inch
CEE JAM (90053 "The Hurt Is On")...........8-12 65
CELESTE (320 "Don't Ever Stop")........... 10-15 64
KUJINGA (101 "Every Woman Has a Right")...8-12
NORTH AMERICAN (101 "The Hurt Is On")..15-25 65
PROGRESS (320 "Don't Ever Stop") 10-20 63
Also see STRONG, Zeke

UNDERWOOD, Charles, Glide Band
Singles: 7-inch
LOMA (2046 "Doggin' Around") 5-10 66
LOMA (2050 "Let's Go Get Stoned") 5-10 66

UNDERWORLD
Singles: 7-inch
REGENCY (979 "Bound") 100-150 68
(Canadian.)

UNDISPUTED TRUTH *P&R/R&B/LP '71*
Singles: 12-inch
WHITFIELD..4-8 77-79
Singles: 7-inch
GORDY (Black vinyl).....................................4-8 71-75
GORDY (Colored vinyl) 10-15 71-72
MOTOWN...4-6
WHITFIELD..4-6 76-79
LPs: 10/12-inch
GORDY 10-20 71-75
WHITFIELD..8-12 77-79
Members: Joe Harris; Brenda Evans; Tyrone Berkley; Billie Calvin; Carl Smalls; Virginia McDonald; Tyrone Douglas; Calvin Stevens; Melvin Stuart; Marcy Thomas; Taka Boom; Hershel Kennedy.
Also see DRAMATICS
Also see LITTLE JOE & MOROCCOS
Also see MAGIC TONES
Also see OHIO PLAYERS
Also see PEPS
Also see SWEAT BAND

UNFOLDING
LPs: 10/12-inch
AUDIO FIDELITY (6184 "How to Blow Your Mind")...50-75 68
Members: David Dalton; Andrea Ross; Victoria Sackville; Steve Kapovitch.

UNFORGETTABLES
Singles: 7-inch
COLPIX (192 "It Hurts")..............................8-12 61
PAMELA (204 "Oh, Wishing Well").......150-200 61
(Black vinyl.)
PAMELA (204 "Oh, Wishing Well").......400-500 61
(Blue vinyl.)
TITANIC (5012 "Oh There He Goes") 30-40 63

UNFORSCENE
Singles: 7-inch
MOMENTUM (674 "You and Me").............5-10 67
SIDEWALK (926 "Happiness Is You")..........5-10 67
SIDEWALK (937 "Roses and Rainbows")..5-10 67
(Same number used on a Stone Poneys release.)

UNIFICS *P&R/R&B '68*
Singles: 7-inch
FOUNTAIN...4-6 71
KAPP...5-10 68-69
MCA..4-6 73
Picture Sleeves
KAPP (957 "The Beginning of My End").....8-12 68
KAPP (985 "It's a Groovy World")..............8-12 69
LPs: 10/12-inch
KAPP 10-15 68
Members: Al Johnson; Michael Ward; Greg Cook; Harold Worthington; Tom Fauntleroy; Marvin Brown.

UNION
Singles: 7-inch
RADEL (108 "I Sit and Cry").....................10-15

UNION, Johnny, & Pickets
Singles: 7-inch
IMPERIAL (66100 "Do the Freddy") 5-10 65

UNION JACKS
Singles: 7-inch
RAMPRO (116 "I Gotta Go")....................25-35 66

UNIQUE ECHOES
Singles: 7-inch
SOUTHERN SOUND (108 "Zoom").........30-40 61

UNIQUE TEENS
Singles: 7-inch
DYNAMIC (110 "Run Fast")......................50-75 59
HANOVER (4510 "Jeannie")....................30-40 58
IVY (112 "Jeannie") 10-20 60
(Both yellow and green labels.)
RELIC (518 "Run Fast") 5-10 64

UNIQUES
(With the John W. Pate Orchestra)
Singles: 7-inch
PEACOCK (1677 "Somewhere") 30-40 57
PEACOCK (1695 "Picture of My Baby")...15-25 60
Members: Earl King; Johnny Taylor; Charles Jordan; Leonard Garr; Bob Morland.
Also see KING, Earl
Also see PATE, Johnny

UNIQUES
Singles: 7-inch
GLORY (289 "The Rocking Toy Soldier") 10-20 58

UNIQUES
(With the Outlaws)
Singles: 7-inch
C-WAY (2676-01 "Let Me Weep, Let Me Cry")..15-25 59

UNIQUES
Singles: 7-inch
WORLD PACIFIC (808 "That's Love")..500-750 59

UNIQUES
("Uneeks Featuring Tiny Valentine")
Singles: 7-inch
BLISS (1004 "I'm So Unhappy") 2000-2500 60
(First issue.)
END (1012 "Tell the Angels")...............150-200 58
FLIPPIN' (202 "Come Marry Me")............20-30 59
GONE (5113 "I'm So Unhappy"/"I'm Confessin' ")...150-200 61
(Has playing time on right side.)
GONE (5113 "I'm So Unhappy"/"I'm Confessin' ")...100-150 61
(Has playing time on left side.)
GONE (5113 "I'm So Unhappy"/"It's Got to Come")...50-75 61
(Note different flip.)
MR. CEE (100 "Look at Me") 100-200 60
PRIDE (1018 "I'm So Unhappy") 75-100 60
TEE KAY (112 "A Million Miles Away").....15-25 62
(Black vinyl.)
TEE KAY (112 "A Million Miles Away").....40-50 62
(Brown vinyl.)
TOLEDO (1501 "Look at Me") 2000-3000 60
(First issue.)
Also see ADDEO, Nicky
Also see LEWIS, Sabby

UNIQUES
Singles: 7-inch
AMBER (2004 "Taboo") 15-25 61
UNITED SOUTHERN ARTISTS (104 "Renegade") 15-25 61

UNIQUES
Singles: 7-inch
LUCKY FOUR (1024 "Silvery Moon")...250-350 62
620 (1003 "Pretty Baby")....................50-100 63
Member: Willie Sullivan.
Also see EUNIQUES
Also see GLIDERS / Uniques

UNIQUES
("Vocal by Stuffy")
Singles: 7-inch
DEMAND (2936 "Merry Christmas Darling")...30-40 63
(First issue.)
DEMAND (2940 "Times Change")............40-50 64
DEMAND (3950 "Merry Christmas Darling")...20-30 63
DOT (16533 "Merry Christmas Darling")..10-20 63
Picture Sleeves
DEMAND (2936 "Merry Christmas Darling")...20-30 63
Member: Stuffy.

UNIQUES
Singles: 7-inch
CAPITOL (4949 "Loving You")...................5-10 63
ROULETTE (4528 "This Little Boy of Mine")..8-12 63

UNIQUES
Singles: 7-inch
ASTRA (1022 "I'm Confessin' ") 5-10 66

UNIQUES
Singles: 7-inch
BANGAR (609 "Baby Don't Cry") 50-75 63

UNIQUES *P&R '65*
(With the University of Utah Chamber Choir)
Singles: 7-inch
PARAMOUNT...4-6 70-72
PAULA 4-8 65-76
LPs: 10/12-inch
PAULA 12-25 66-70
Members: Joe Stampley; Bobby Stampley; Jim Woodfield; Mike Love; Ray Mills; Bobby Sims; Ronnie Weiss.
Also see MOUSE
Also see STAMPLEY, Joe

UNIQUES
Singles: 7-inch
DBC (1233 "Hey, Senorita")..................400-500 59

UNIQUES
Singles: 7-inch
LEE ("Never Let Me Go").........................15-25
(No selection number used.)

UNIT 4+2 *P&R '65*
Singles: 7-inch
LONDON...5-10 65-66
LPs: 10/12-inch
LONDON (427 "Unit 4+2")........................25-35 65
(Monaural.)
LONDON (3427 "Unit 4+2").......................25-40 65
(Stereo.)
Member: Russ Ballard.

UNITED FOUR
Singles: 7-inch
HARTHON (139 "Go On")........................20-30 64
HARTHON (143 "One More Year")..........20-30 65

UNITED FRUIT CO.
Singles: 7-inch
LAURIE (3408 "Sunshine Street")..............5-10 68
YORK (403 "Ain't It Babe").........................5-10 67

UNITED STATES OF AMERICA *LP '68*
LPs: 10/12-inch
COLUMBIA (9619 "United States of America")..20-30 68
(With stenciled title brown wrapper.)
COLUMBIA (9619 "United States of America")..10-20 68
(Without wrapper.)
Members: Dorothy Moskowitz; Rand Forbes; Joseph Byrd; Gordon Marron; Craig Woodson.
Also see BYRD, Joe, & Field Hippies

UNITED TRAVEL SERVICE
Singles: 7-inch
RUST (5120 "Wind and Stone") 10-20 67

UNITONES
Singles: 7-inch
CANDY (005 "Judy") 10-20 60

UNIVERSAL JONES
Singles: 7-inch
MGM/VERVE ("Feeling That Glow") 15-25
Member: Gene McDaniels.
Also see McDANIELS, Gene

UNIVERSALS
("With Rhythm Acc.")
Singles: 7-inch
ASCOT (2124 "Dear Ruth") 75-125 63
CORA-LEE (501 "He's So Right") 20-30 58
FESTIVAL (1601 "[I'll Just Have to Go On] Dreaming")..40-50 61
FESTIVAL (25001 "Dreaming")................10-15 61
(Note shorter title and number change.)
JUKE BOX (511 "Dreaming")......................5-8
KERWOOD (712 "Never Was a Girl")..500-600 62
MARK-X (7004 "Again")..........................75-150 57
(Label shows 45 RPM designation.)
MARK-X (7004 "Again")...........................25-35 57
(45 RPM not shown on label.)
SHEPHERD (2200 "A Love Only You Can Give")..50-100 62
V-TONE (236 "You Always Remain")....... 15-25 62
LPs: 10/12-inch
RELIC..8-12 73
Members: Earl Worsham; Roosevelt Simmons; Kent Peeler; John Christian; James Williams.
Also see WATKINS, Sis

UNIVERSOULS
Singles: 7-inch
TENER (1053 "New Generation")................8-12 '60s

UNKNOWN, The
(Jimmy Fields)
Singles: 7-inch
AUTOGRAPH (206 "I Have Returned")... 20-30 60
SVR (1008 "Shake a Tail Feather") 20-30

UNKNOWN IV
Singles: 7-inch
JCP (1017 "I Want You to Be Mine") 15-25 64
JCP (1019 "Give Me a Chance")............. 50-75 64

UNKNOWN KIND
Singles: 7-inch
STAR TREK (3405 "Who Cares") 10-15

UNKNOWNS
Singles: 7-inch
X-TRA (102 "One More Chance") 600-800 57
SHIELD (7101 "One More Chance")........ 30-40 62

UNKNOWNS
Singles: 7-inch
HI-HAT (142 "Crazy Daisy") 50-100 58

UNKNOWNS
Singles: 7-inch
FELSTED (8535 "Oh, Summer Love")..... 15-25 59

UNKNOWNS *P&R '66*
Singles: 7-inch
MARLIN (16008 "Tighter").................... 10-15 67
PARROT (307 "Melody for an Unknown Girl") 8-12 66
Members: Keith Allison; Mark Lindsay; Steve Alaimo
Also see ALAIMO, Steve
Also see ALLISON, Keith
Also see LINDSAY, Mark

UNLIMITED
Singles: 7-inch
MARINA (504 "Gone Away")................... 20-30 66
Also see ROYAL FLAIRS

UNLIMITED FOUR
Singles: 7-inch
CHANSON (1178 "Calling")..................... 10-20
CHANSON (1180 "Walk Away Lover").... 10-20
CHANSON (1811 "Somebody Help Please")... 10-20
Member: Mel Hueston.
Also see HUESTON, Mel

UNLUV'D
Singles: 7-inch
MGM (13903 "I Got It Bad")........................5-10 68
PARKWAY (138 "Exception to the Rule")...5-10 67

UNRELATED SEGMENTS
Singles: 7-inch
HBR (514 "Story of My Life").................... 10-15 67
LIBERTY (55992 "Where You Gonna Go").. 10-15 67
LIBERTY (56052 "Cry, Cry, Cry") 15-25 68

UNTOUCHABLES
(Chavelles)
Singles: 7-inch
LIBERTY (55335 "You're the Top")......... 15-20 61
LIBERTY (55423 "Medicine Man").............5-10 62
MADISON (128 "Poor Boy Needs a Preacher").. 15-20 60
MADISON (134 "Goodnight Sweetheart") 10-15 60
MADISON (139 "Sixty Minute Man")........ 10-15 60
MADISON (147 "Raisin' Sugar Cane") 5-10 61
Also see CHAVELLES
Also see GOEFIELD, Brice

UNTOUCHABLES
Singles: 7-inch
HUNT (450 "Church Key")...................... 10-20 66
LAWN (211 "Deacon's Walk") 8-12 63
LAWN (212 "Swingin' Flute").......................8-12 63
RELLO (2 "Benny the Beatnik") 10-20 61
RELLO (5 "Deacon's Walk")..................... 10-20 62
Member: Al Huntzinger.
Also see AL'S UNTOUCHABLES

UNTOUCHABLES
Singles: 7-inch
ALAN K (6901 "Funny What a Little Kiss Can Do")...200-300 62
(Reissued as by Little John & Unforgettables.)
Also see LITTLE JOHN & UNFORGETTABLES

UNTOUCHABLES
Singles: 7-inch
DOT (16306 "Blues in the Night") 5-10 62
FAAP (26579 "Dragster Boy")..................15-25 '60s
NAU-VOO (809 "Blue Chip Bounce") 5-10 60

UNTOUCHABLES
Singles: 7-inch
WASP (105 "Don't Go I'm Beggin' ")...........15-25 67

UNUSUALS
Singles: 7-inch
MAINSTREAM (653 "Summer Is Over")...10-20 66
PANORAMA (23 "I'm Walkin' Baby")........15-25 65
Members: Pat Jerns; Laurie Vitt; Bill Capp; Vic Bundy; Harvey Redman; Kathi McDonald; Gary Ramsey.

UNWANTED CHILDREN
Singles: 7-inch
MURBO (1031 "Without You") 15-25 69

UP, The
Singles: 7-inch
RAINBOW (22191 "Free John Now") ...125-150 71
SUNDANCE (22190 "Just Like an Aborigine")..50-75 '60s
(Colored vinyl.)
Picture Sleeves
SUNDANCE (22190 "Just Like an Aborigine")..75-125 '60s
LPs: 10/12-inch
ALIVE/TOTAL ENERGY.............................5-10 95
(10-inch LP.)

UPBEATS *P&R '58*
Singles: 7-inch
JOY..10-15 58-59
PREP (119 "I Don't Know") 10-20 57
PREP (131 "Will You Be Mine")................10-20 58
SWAN (4010 "Just Like in the Movies")....10-20 58

UPCHURCH, Phil *P&R '61*
(Phil Upchurch Combo)
Singles: 7-inch
BOYD (329 "You Can't Sit Down")...........10-15 61
(Indicates distribution by United Artists.)
BOYD (1026 "You Can't Sit Down")...........5-10 66
BOYD (3398 "You Can't Sit Down")...........10-20 61
(No mention of U.A. distribution on label.)
CADET (5661 "I Don't Know").......................4-8 70
CADET (5675 "Softly") 4-8 70
GOLDEN FLEECE...4-6 74
MARLIN 3-5 79
U.A. (329 "You Can't Sit Down")..............10-15 61
U.A. (355 "Pink Lollipop")..........................10-15 61
U.A. (385 "Hog") 10-15 61
U.A. (417 "Organ Grinders' Twist") 10-15 62
U.A. (488 "Flap Jack") 10-15 62
LPs: 10/12-inch
BLUE THUMB (59 "Lovin' Feeling")............8-10 73
BOYD (B-398 "You Can't Sit Down") 25-35 61
(Monaural.)
BOYD (BS-398 "You Can't Sit Down")......40-50 61
(Stereo.)
CADET (826 "Phil Upchurch")...................10-15 69
MARLIN (2209 "Phil Upchurch") 8-12 78
MILESTONE...5-8
U.A. (3162 "You Can't Sit Down") 15-25 61
(Monaural.)
U.A. (3175 "Big Hit Dances")....................15-25 62
(Monaural.)
U.A. (6162 "You Can't Sit Down") 25-35 61
(Monaural.)
U.A. (6175 "Big Hit Dances")....................25-35 62
(Stereo.)
Also see CLARK, Dee
Also see REED, Jimmy

UPCHURCH, Terry, & Upchurch Brothers
EPs: 7-inch
JEWEL (401 "Terry Upchurch and the Upchurch Brothers")..8-12 61

UPCHURCH BROTHERS
EPs: 7-inch
ARK (205 "The Upchurch Brothers") 5-10 62
Also see UPCHURCH, Terry, & Upchurch Brothers

UPFRONTS
Singles: 7-inch
LUMMTONE (103 "It Took Time") 75-100 60
LUMMTONE (104 "Too Far to Turn Around")..30-40 60
LUMMTONE (106 "Little Girl") 100-150 61
LUMMTONE (107 "Send Me Someone to Love")..50-60 61
(White label.)
LUMMTONE (107 "Send Me Someone to Love")..30-40 62
(Black label.)
LUMMTONE (107 "I Stopped the Duke of Earl") 400-500 62
LUMMTONE (108 "It Took Time")...........10-20 62
LUMMTONE (114 "Do the Beetle") 200-300 64

UPPER CLASSMEN
Singles: 7-inch
CHATTAHOOCHEE (648 "Dancing on the Ceiling") 8-12 64

UPPER DIVISION & TRUE DON BLEU
LPs:10/12-inch
U-D ("Back to the '50s Rock and Roll Revue")...20-30 '70s
(Fewer than 100 pressed.)

UPSETS
("Henny, Sam & Joe. Lead: Dave")
Singles: 7-inch
HARWOOD (7 "Mom & Dad")............750-1000 62

UPSETTERS
(Little Richard's band)
Singles: 7-inch
FALCON (1010 "The Upsetter")...............10-20 58
FIRE (1029 "Jaywalking")..........................10-15 60
GEE (1055 "Rolling On") 10-15 60
LEE...10-15 '60s
PALM..10-15 60
ZANETTE..10-15 '60s

UPSETTERS Featuring Little Richard
Singles: 7-inch
LITTLE STAR (118 "Let's Get a Thing Going")...10-20 62
LITTLE STAR (123 "I'm in Love Again")...10-20 63
LITTLE STAR (128 "Freedom Ride") 10-20 63
Also see LITTLE RICHARD
Also see UPSETTERS

UPSETTERS
Singles: 7-inch
AUTUMN (4 "Draggin the Main") 15-25 64

UPSETTERS
Singles: 7-inch
ABC (11081 "Tossin' and Turnin' ") 5-10 68
ABC (11120 "Don't Be Cruel") 5-10 68
LPs: 10/12-inch
ABC (651 "We Remember Otis") 10-15 68

UP-STAIRS
Singles: 7-inch
CUCA (1309 "Operator Please")................5-10 67
Also see JAGUARS

UPSTARTS
Singles: 78 rpm
APOLLO (468 "Feed Me Baby") 15-25 55
Singles: 7-inch
APOLLO (468 "Feed Me Baby") 50-75 55

UPSTARTS
Singles: 7-inch
TOP TEN (7000-2 "Get It Together").........15-25 69
Members: Jack Calvert; Jon Battle; Bobby Carrol; Rusty Rutledge.

UPTIGHTS
Singles: 7-inch
COLUMBIA (44243 "Shy Guy") 20-30 67
MALA (528 "Academy Awards of Love")..15-20 66

UPTITES
Singles: 7-inch
RA-SEL (2 "Philly Bound") ....50-75 '60s

UPTON, Peggy
Singles: 7-inch
ROSE (129 "Your Smallest Tear")...........50-75 57

UPTONES
Singles: 7-inch
COLLECTABLES..3-5 '80s

LUTE (6225 "No More") 20-30 62
(Black label.)
LUTE (6225 "No More") 10-15 62
(Multi-color label.)
LUTE (6229 "Be Mine")............................30-40 62
MAGNUM (714 "Wear My Ring")...............5-10 63
WATTS (1080 "Wear My Ring") 10-15 63
(First issue.)
Also see DANDEVILLES
Also see GUIDES

UPTOWNS
Singles: 7-inch
LAURIE (3204 "Asiatic Flu") 10-20 63
SHANGRI-LA...8-12 65

UPTOWNERS
Singles: 7-inch
CAPTOWN (4030 "From Lovers to Friends")...50-100 69
LE CAM (123 "The Search Is Over")........15-20 64
LE CAM (126 "Vicki") 10-15 64
MAJOR (132 "And Then Some") 5-10 68
RAGE (59 "What's the Matter")..................8-12 59
TIRIS (707 "She's Mine") 15-25 65

UPTOWNERS / Ron-Dels
Singles: 7-inch
CHARAY 58 ("She's Mine") 5-10
CHARAY 86 ("She's Mine") 5-10
Also see RON-DELS
Also see UPTOWNERS

UP-TUNES
Singles: 7-inch
GENIE (103 "I Wanna Love Just You").... 10-20 66
GENIE (107 "Little Blue Tears")................ 10-20 66

URBAN, Al
Singles: 7-inch
FANG (1001 "Lonely Life").........................20-30 59
SARG (148 "Lookin' for Money") 100-150 57
SARG (158 "Won't Tell You Her Name")..100-150 58
SARG (174 "Last Heartache") 20-30 60

URBAN RENEWAL
Singles: 7-inch
PARAMOUNT...4-8 70
ST. GEORGE INT'L (202,270 "Love Eyes") 10-20 68

URNESS, Harvey
Singles: 7-inch
STUDIO CITY (1018 "Never Been Blue") 25-35 64

US
Singles: 7-inch
ERA (3201 "Delicious") 5-10 68
PATTY...10-15 64

US
("Those Li'l Ole Music Makers")
Singles: 7-inch
FEATURE (102 "Summertime")................15-25 65

US
Singles: 7-inch
HOUR (31137 "Somewhere in the Morning")..15-25 67
Picture Sleeves
HOUR (31137 "Somewhere in the Morning")...25-50 67

US FOUR
Singles: 7-inch
RISING SONS (701 "By My Side")...........15-25 67

US TOO GROUP
(Us Too)
Singles: 7-inch
HI (2133 "I'll Leave You Crying") 8-12 67
JYNX ("I'll Leave You Crying")..................15-25 66
(No selection number used.)

USHER, Gary
(With the Usherettes)
Singles: 7-inch
CAPITOL (5128 "Jody") 15-25 64
CAPITOL (5193 "Sacramento")................25-30 64
CAPITOL (5403 "Jody") 15-25 65
DOT (16158 "Three Surfer Boys")............50-75 63
LAN-CET (144 "Tomorrow") 30-50 61
TITAN (1716 "You're the Girl")................75-100 61
(With Ginger Blake.)
Also see DEVONS

Also see FOUR SPEEDS
Also see GINGER
Also see HONDELLS
Also see HONEYS
Also see KICKSTANDS
Also see KNIGHTS
Also see ROAD RUNNERS
Also see SAGITTARIUS
Also see SUNSETS
Also see SUPER STOCKS
Also see SURFARIS
Also see WHEEL MEN

UTAH CARL
(Carl Beach)
Singles: 7-inch
STARDAY (301 "Sometime") 50-75

UTMOSTS
Singles: 7-inch
PAN-OR (1123 "I Need You") 50-75 62
Member: Oma Heard.
Also see HEARD, Oma

UTOPIA
LPs: 10/12-inch
KENT (566 "Utopia") 30-50 73

UTOPIANS
Singles: 7-inch
IMPERIAL (5861 "Dutch Treat") 10-15 62
IMPERIAL (5876 "Along My Lonely Way") 150-250 62
IMPERIAL (5891 "Let Love Come Later") ..8-12 62

UTOPIAS
Singles: 7-inch
FORTUNE (568 "Sally Bad") 10-20 64
HI-Q (0103 "Maybe") .... 25-35 '60s
LA SALLE (0072 "Girls Are Against Me") .... 200-300 '60s
Picture Sleeves
FORTUNE (568 "Sally Bad") 15-25 64

V

V & B.B.
Singles: 7-inch
J&S (1623/1624 "They're Just Rocking and Rolling"/"Let's Begin Again") 20-30 58

V.I.P.s
(V.I.P.'s)
Singles: 7-inch
CARMEL (44 "Fall Guy") 500-750 63

V.I.P.s
Singles: 7-inch
BIG TOP (518 "Flashback") 10-15 64
BIG TOP (521 "I'm On to You Baby") 10-15 64
BIG TOP (100 "Don't Pass Me By") 10-15 65
CONGRESS (211 "My Girl Cried") 20-30 64
DARROW (16013 "Den Yen") 8-12
GUITARSVILLE (2123 "Don't Turn Around") 8-12

V - NOTES
Singles: 7-inch
VOLK (102 "Get a Baby Like Mine") 50-100 58

VAC, Ricky, & Rock-A-Ways
Singles: 7-inch
HILLTOP (1871 "Colleen") 75-125 61

VACANT LOT
Singles: 7-inch
LTD (0004 "Don't You Just Know It") .... 10-20 '60s
ROULETTE (4740 "I Blew It") 5-10 67
STUDIO 5 (1003 "I'd Like to Wish Her Well") 5-10 70
Also see ORIGINAL PLAYBOYS

VACCO, Bobby
Singles: 7-inch
IMPALA (208 "Kissin' Fresh") 10-20 60
LATIMER 500 (1000 "Copy Cat Love") 10-20 64

VACELS P&R '65
Singles: 7-inch
KAMA SUTRA (200 "You're My Baby") 10-15 65
KAMA SUTRA (204 "I'm Just a Poor Boy") 10-15 65
Also see RICKY & VACELS

VADEN, Butch
Singles: 7-inch
FORTUNE (552 "Harem Girl") 5-10 63
Also see NITE SOUNDS

VADEN, Clark, & Crescents
Singles: 7-inch
DOLLY (5578 "You Can Make It if You Try") 750-1000 61
(Identification number shown since no selection number is used.)

VAGABONDS
Singles: 78 rpm
RKO UNIQUE 5-10 57
Singles: 7-inch
RKO UNIQUE (380 "I Wish I Could Shimmy Like My Sister Kate") 8-12 57
VIVA (62 "Baby Face") 5-10 59
LPs: 10/12-inch
RKO UNIQUE (112 "The Vagabonds") 15-25 57
Members: Attilio Risso; Dom Germano; Al Torriere; Pete Peterson.

VAGABONDS & JIMMIE HINES / Jimmie Hines
Singles: 7-inch
VIVA (65 "Jimmie's Blues, Pt."/"Jimmie's Blues, Pt. 2") 5-10 60
Also see VAGABONDS

VAGABONDS
Singles: 7-inch
ABCO (1001 "Night Drag") 10-20 64
(Also issued as by the Lincolns.)
Also see LINCOLNS

VAGRANTS
Singles: 7-inch
ATCO (6473 "Respect") 5-10 67
ATCO (6513 "Beside the Sea") 5-10 67
ATCO (6552 "And When It's Over") 5-10 68
SOUTHERN SOUND (204 "Oh, Those Eyes") 15-25 66
VANGUARD (35038 "Young Blues") 10-15 66
VANGUARD (35042 "Final Hour") 10-20 66
Picture Sleeves
VANGUARD (35038 "Young Blues") 15-25 66
LPs: 10/12-inch
ARISTA (8459 "Great Lost Album") 10-20 87

VAILON, Bobby
Singles: 7-inch
CAMELOT (118 "Surfin' Alone") .... 15-25 '60s

VAILS
Singles: 7-inch
BELMONT (4002 "Great Somewhere") 20-30 60
BELMONT (4004 "There'll Come a Time") 20-30 61

VAL, Frankie
Singles: 7-inch
FEE (1002 "Mister Echo") 50-100 62

VAL, Joe
Singles: 7-inch
JOC (100 "Baby of Mine") 50-75

VAL, Johnny
Singles: 7-inch
SOMA (1140 "Blue Mama") 20-25 60

VAL, Tommy
Singles: 7-inch
ABS (100 "Summer Is Over") 5-10 67

VALA QUONS
(Valaquons; Vala-Quons)
Singles: 7-inch
LAGUNA (102 "Teardrops") 150-200 64
RAYCO (516 "Jolly Green Giant") 40-50 65
TANGERINE (951 "I Want a Woman") 15-25 65

VALADIERS P&R '61
Singles: 7-inch
GORDY (7003 "While I'm Away") 20-30 62
GORDY (7013 "I Found a Girl") 20-30 63
MIRACLE (6 "Greetings") 40-50 61
MIRACLE (6 "Greetings [This Is Uncle Sam]") 10-20 61
(Note longer title.)
Member: Paul Kelly.
Also see KELLY, Paul

VALAIRES
(With Tom Everett & Orchestra; Val-Aires)
Singles: 7-inch
CORAL (62177 "Launie, My Love") 40-50 60
WILLETT (114 "Launie, My Love") 400-500 59
Also see VOGUES

VALAIRES
Singles: 7-inch
RAMCO (1983 "It's Over") 5-10 67

VAL-CHORDS
("Vocal Featuring Tommy Drumgoole")
Singles: 7-inch
GAMETIME (104 "Candy Store Love") 100-150 57
(Double horizontal lines – one thick and one thin – on label.)
GAMETIME (104 "Candy Store Love") 50-75 57
(Single straight horizontal line.)
GAMETIME (104 "Candy Store Love") 15-25 57
(Wavy horizontal line.)
Member: Tommy Drumgoole. Session: Raymond Brown.

VALDELER, Pat
Singles: 78 rpm
MERCURY (70201 "Baby, Rock Me") 5-10 53
Singles: 7-inch
MERCURY (70201 "Baby, Rock Me") 15-25 53

VALDONS
Singles: 7-inch
TWIN CITY MOVEMENT (S8-121 "All Day Long") .... 10-15 '60s

VAL DOROS Featuring Charles Pryor
("With Gene Preston & His Band Featuring Erwin Kalcks")
Singles: 78 rpm
SILHOUETTE 15-25 56
Singles: 7-inch
SILHOUETTE (517 "Don't Open the Grave") 40-50 56

VALE, Barbara
Singles: 7-inch
KYRA (1005 "Little Dream Boy") 10-20 65

VALE, Blacky
Singles: 7-inch
HURRICANE (100 "If I Had Me a Woman") 500-600 58

VALE, Bobby
Singles: 7-inch
LAWN (209 "Two Fast Guns") 10-20 63

VALE, Dick
Singles: 7-inch
CORAL (61844 "Rockabilly Blues") 30-50 57

VALE, Jerry P&R '53
(With Mary Mayo)
Singles: 78 rpm
COLUMBIA 3-8 51-57
Singles: 7-inch
BUDDAH 3-5 78
COLUMBIA (39000 thru 41373) 10-20 51-59
COLUMBIA (41423 thru 43774) 5-10 59-66
COLUMBIA (43895 thru 45992) 4-8 66-74
COLUMBIA (10000 series) 3-6 74
Picture Sleeves
COLUMBIA 8-12 64-65
EPs: 7-inch
COLUMBIA 5-15 56-59
LPs: 10/12-inch
COLUMBIA 5-20 58-75
HARMONY 5-10 69-74
Also see CLARK, Dave, Five / New Christy Minstrels / Bobby Vinton / Jerry Vale
Also see MATHIS, Johnny / Tony Bennett / North Carolina Ramblers / Ray Conniff & Jerry Vale with Eugene Ormandy
Also see MAYO, Mary

VALE, Pat
Singles: 7-inch
CURIO (20 "Ride") 10-20 62

VALE, Ricky, & His Surfers
LPs: 10/12-inch
STRAND (1104 "Everybody Surfin' ") 20-25 63
Members: Ricky Vale; Mark Pastner; Benjie Lipman.

VALE, Sandy
(With the Valiants)
Singles: 7-inch
DECCA (30941 "Suntan Tattoo") 10-15 59
INTERNATIONALE (278 "You Don't Love Me Anymore") 5-10 63

VALENS, Ritchie P&R/R&B '58
Singles: 12-inch
DEL-FI (1287 "La Bamba") 15-25 87
Singles: 78 rpm
APEX (76402 "Donna") 100-200 58
(Canadian.)
Singles: 7-inch
ABC 4-6 74
APEX (76402 "Donna") 15-30 58
(Canadian.)
DEL-FI (1287 "La Bamba '87") 3-5 87
DEL-FI (4106 "C'mon Let's Go") 20-30 58
(Green label.)
DEL-FI (4106 "C'mon Let's Go") 100-150 58
(Orange label.)
DEL-FI (4110 "Donna") 20-30 58
(Solid green label with black print.)
DEL-FI (4110 "Donna") 10-20 58
(Has rows of circles on label.)
DEL-FI (4110 "Donna") 8-12 61
(Black label with sawtooth circle.)
DEL-FI (4111 "Fast Freight") 15-25 59
(First issued as by Arvee Allens.)
DEL-FI (4114 "That's My Little Suzie") 15-25 59
DEL-FI (4117 "Little Girl") 15-25 59
(Del-Fi "Limited Valens Memorial Series.")
DEL-FI (4128 "Stay Beside Me") 20-30 60
DEL-FI (4133 "Paddiwack") 15-25 60
ERIC .... 4-6 '70s
GOODIES 3-5
KASEY (7040 "Donna") 5-10
LANA .... 4-8 '60s
LOST NITE 4-8
Picture Sleeves
DEL-FI (4114 "That's My Little Suzie") 25-50 59
DEL-FI (4117 "Little Girl") 40-60 59
(With explanatory "Concerning This Record" insert.)
DEL-FI (4117 "Little Girl") 25-35 59
(Without insert.)
DEL-FI (4128 "Stay Beside Me") 20-30 60
DEL-FI (4133 "Cry, Cry, Cry") 20-30 60
KASEY (7040 "Donna") 5-10
EPs: 7-inch
DEL-FI (1 "Ritchie Valens") 50-75 59
(Promotional issue only.)
DEL-FI (101 "Ritchie Valens") 50-75 59
DEL-FI (111 "Ritchie Valens Sings") 50-75 59
LPs: 10/12-inch
DEL-FI (1201 "Ritchie Valens") 150-200 59
(Back cover shows *That's My Little Suzie* as "I Got a Gal Named Sue.")
DEL-FI (1201 "Ritchie Valens") 50-100 59
(Back cover properly shows *That's My Little Suzie.*)
DEL-FI (1206 "Ritchie") 50-100 59
DEL-FI (1214 "Ritchie Valens in Concert at Pacoima Jr. High") 100-200 61
DEL-FI (1225 "Greatest Hits") 50-100 63
DEL-FI (1247 "Greatest Hits, Vol. 2") 50-100 65
GUEST STAR (1484 "The Original La Bamba") 15-25 64
GUEST STAR (1489 "The Original Ritchie Valens") 15-25 64
MGM (117 "Ritchie Valens") 10-20 70
RHINO (200 "Best of Ritchie Valens") 5-8 81
RHINO (2798 "History of Ritchie Valens") 20-30 81
(Boxed, three-disc set.)
Also see ALLENS, Arvee

VALENS, Ritchie / Jerry Kole
LPs: 10/12-inch
CROWN (5336 "Ritchie Valens & Jerry Kole") 20-30 63
Also see COLE, Jerry

VALENTE, Dino
Singles: 7-inch
ELEKTRA (45012 "Don't Let It Down") 5-10 64
LPs: 10/12-inch
EPIC (26335 "Dino") 15-20 68
Also see QUICKSILVER

VALENTINE, Billy
(Billy Valentine Trio)
Singles: 78 rpm
CAPITOL 5-15 55-56
DECCA 5-10 51-52
MERCURY 8-12 49
PRESTIGE 5-10 53
Singles: 7-inch
CAPITOL 15-25 55-56
DECCA 15-25 51-52
DORSET (5004 "Don't You Cry") 10-15 60
FEDERAL (12346 "Wasted Tears") 10-15 59
PRESTIGE 15-25 53
Session: Mickey Baker.
Also see BAKER, Mickey
Also see WASHBOARD BILL

VALENTINE, Bobby
Singles: 7-inch
LITA (1003 "Special Delivery") 25-35 62

VALENTINE, Cal, & Texas Rockers
Singles: 7-inch
LYONS (108 "The Boogie Twist") 8-12 62
Also see FIVE MASKS

VALENTINE, Don
Singles: 7-inch
U.T. (4003 "Being Together") 30-50 59

VALENTINE, Floyd, & His Orchestra
Singles: 78 rpm
VEE-JAY (113 "Fussin and Lovin") 10-20 54
Singles: 7-inch
VEE-JAY (113 "Fussin and Lovin") 20-30 54
(Black vinyl.)
VEE-JAY (113 "Fussin and Lovin") 40-60 54
(Red vinyl.)

VALENTINE, Hilton
LPs: 10/12-inch
CAPITOL (330 "All in Your Head") 10-20 69
Also see ANIMALS

VALENTINE, Jimmy
Singles: 7-inch
CUB (9024 "Just Keep Walkin' ") 10-20 59

VALENTINE, Joe
Singles: 7-inch
RONN (14 "One Night of Satisfaction") 5-10 67
RONN (30 "Woman's Love") 5-10 69

VALENTINE, Judy
Singles: 78 rpm
DOT (15259 "Have Fun Baby") 5-10 54
EPIC (9004 "She Was Five and He Was Ten") 5-10 53
Singles: 7-inch
ABC-PAR (10057 "Gum Drop") 10-15 59
DOT (15259 "Have Fun Baby") 10-20 54
EPIC (9004 "She Was Five and He Was Ten") 10-20 53
LPs: 10/12-inch
MGM (504 "Mother Goose Nursery Rhymes") 8-12 63
MGM (510 "Babes in Toyland") 8-12 63

VALENTINE, Lezli R&B '68
Singles: 7-inch
ALL PLATINUM (2305 "I Won't Do Anything") 5-10 68

VALENTINE, Louie
Singles: 7-inch
GREAT (1160 "I've Gotta Stay High") 5-10 68

VALENTINE, Marty
Singles: 7-inch
MALA (415 "Dream Book") 10-15 60
MALA (421 "Growing Boy") 10-15 60

VALENTINE, Patience
Singles: 7-inch
SAR (111 "In the Dark") 10-20 61
SAR (119 "I Miss You So") 10-20 61
SAR (142 "Ernestine") 10-20 63
SAR (157 "Lost and Lookin' ") 10-20 64
Also see FLAIRS

VALENTINE, Patty
(With the Jack Marshall Orchestra)
Singles: 7-inch
R-DELL (102 "If You're Old Enough") 20-30 58

VALENTINE, Penny
Singles: 7-inch
LIBERTY (55774 "I Want to Kiss Ringo Goodbye") 8-12 65

VALENTINE, Rose
Singles: 7-inch
RCA (9276 "When the Heartaches End") .15-25 67

VALENTINE, T.
Singles: 7-inch
BEA & BABY (110 "Teenage Jump") 10-15 60

VALENTINE, Tony
Singles: 7-inch
GOOD LUCK (600 "Don't Bother Me") 5-10 64

VALENTINE & SWEETHEARTS
Singles: 7-inch
BIG TOP (3147 "Lipstick and High-Heel Shoes") 10-15 63

VALENTINES
(With Jimmy Wright & His Orchestra)
Singles: 78 rpm
OLD TOWN 100-200 54
RAMA 50-100 55-57
Singles: 7-inch
OLD TOWN (1009 "Tonight Kathleen") 400-500 54
RAMA (171 "Lily Maebelle") 40-50 55
(Blue label.)
RAMA (171 "Lily Maebelle") 15-25 57
(Red label.)
RAMA (181 "I Love You, Darling") 50-75 56
RAMA (186 "Christmas Prayer") 400-500 56
(Blue label.)
RAMA (186 "Christmas Prayer") 30-40 57
(Red label.)
RAMA (196 "Woo Woo Train") 50-75 56
(Blue label.)
RAMA (196 "Woo Woo Train") 15-25 57
(Red label.)
RAMA (201 "Twenty Minutes") 50-75 56
RAMA (208 "Nature's Creation") 40-50 56
RAMA (228 "Don't Say Goodnight") 50-75 57
ROULETTE ....4-6 '70s
Members: Richard Barrett; Mickey Francis; Ray Briggs; Ron Bright; Don Raysor; Ed Edgehill; Dave "Baby" Cortez; Carl Hogan.
Also see BARRETT, Richard
Also see CORTEZ, Dave "Baby"
Also see WRIGHT, Jimmy

VALENTINES
Singles: 7-inch
LUDIX (102 "Johnny One Heart") 10-15 63

VALENTINES
Singles: 7-inch
BETHLEHEM (3055 "I'll Forget You") 10-15 62
KING (5338 "Please Don't Leave, Please Don't Go") 10-15 60
KING (5433 "Hey Ruby") 10-15 60
KING (5830 "I Have Two Loves") 5-10 63
U.A. (764 "Alone in the Night") 5-10 64

VALENTINES
Singles: 7-inch
LEE (5465 "Beautyful [sic]") 15-25 65

VALENTINES
Singles: 7-inch
SOUND STAGE 7 (2646 "Gotta Get Yourself Together") 5-15 69
SOUND STAGE 7 (2663 "If You Love Me") 5-15 70

VALENTINES
Singles: 7-inch
KING BEE (103 "This Is My Story") 25-35

VALENTINO
Singles: 7-inch
PINKY (201 "If You're Mine") 5-10 59

VALENTINO, Anna
Singles: 78 rpm
VITA (132 "I Wasn't Fooling") 8-12 56
VITA (162 "Easy Kisses") 8-12 57
Singles: 7-inch
DOT (15543 "Calypso Joe") 10-20 57
VITA (132 "I Wasn't Fooling") 10-20 56
VITA (162 "Easy Kisses") 10-20 57

VALENTINO, Bobby
Singles: 7-inch
LITA (1003 "Special Delivery") 5-10 62
Also see RELF, Bobby

VALENTINO, Danny P&R '60
Singles: 7-inch
CONTRAST (600 "Name of the Game Is Lonely") 5-10 67
MGM (12835 "Stampede") 10-20 59
MGM (12881 "Biology") 10-20 60
MGM (12952 "Pictures from the Past") 10-20 60

VALENTINO, Mark P&R '62
Singles: 7-inch
SWAN (4121 "Push and Kick") 10-15 62
SWAN (4135 "Do It") 10-15 63
SWAN (4142 "Part Time Job") 10-15 63
(Shown as "Mark Valentinon" on some labels.)
LPs: 10/12-inch
SWAN (508 "Mark Valentino") 40-60 63

VALENTINO, Sal
(With the Valentines)
Singles: 7-inch
FALCO (1006 "I Wanna Twist") 15-25 62
W.B. (7268 "An Added Attraction") 5-10 69
W.B. (7289 "Friends and Lovers") 5-10 69
Also see BEAU BRUMMELS
Also see STONEGROUND

VALENTINO, Tony
Singles: 7-inch
SWAN (4093 "Gee") 10-15 62
SWAN (4109 "Good Time Flo") 10-15 62

VALENTINO & LOVERS
Singles: 7-inch
DONNA (1345 "One Teardrop Too Late") 100-150 61

VALENTINOS
Singles: 7-inch
BRUNSWICK (55171 "A Kiss from Your Lips") 40-50 60
(Same number used on an Originals release.)

VALENTINOS P&R/R&B '62
Singles: 7-inch
ABKCO ....4-6 '70s
ASTRA (1026 "Looking for a Love") 5-10 66
CHESS (1952 "Do It Right") 5-10 66
CHESS (1977 "Let's Get Together") 5-10 66
CLEAN 5-10 73
JUBILEE (5636 "Death of Love") 5-10 68
JUBILEE (5650 "You've Got the Kind of Love That's for Real") 5-10 69
SAR (132 "Looking for a Love") 10-20 62
SAR (137 "Darling Come Back Home") 10-20 62
SAR (144 "She's So Good to Me") 10-20 63
SAR (152 "It's All Over Now") 10-15 64
SAR (155 "Bitter Dreams") 10-15 64
Members: Bobby Womack; Curtis Womack.
Also see WOMACK, Bobby
Also see WOMACK BROTHERS

VALENTYNE, Rudy
(Rudy Valentine)
Singles: 7-inch
REGALIA (20 "Evening Star") 5-10 61
ROULETTE (4611 "Don't Ever Leave Me") 5-10 65
ROULETTE (4613 "Girls") 5-10 65
ROULETTE (4618 "When I Fall in Love") ..5-10 65
ROULETTE (4619 "And Now") 5-10 65
ROULETTE (4620 "More Than This I Cannot Give") 5-10 65
LPs: 10/12-inch
ROULETTE (25299 "And Now...Rudy Valentyne") 15-25 65

VALERIE & NICK
Singles: 7-inch
GLOVER (3000 "Lonely Town") 10-15 64
Members: Valerie Simpson; Nick Ashford.
Also see ASHFORD & SIMPSON

VALERY, Dana P&R '76
Singles: 7-inch
ABC 5-10 68-69
COLUMBIA (44004 "Having You Around") 15-25 67
LIBERTY (56156 "Clinging Vine") 4-6 70
LIBERTY (56209 "Point of No Return") 4-6 70
PHANTOM 4-6 75
SCOTTI BROS 4-6 79
Picture Sleeves
PHANTOM 4-6 75
LPs: 10/12-inch
BRUNSWICK 5-10
PHANTOM 5-10 75
Also see SIMON, Paul

VALETS
(With the Sammy Lowe Orchestra)
Singles: 7-inch
JON (4025 "I Need Someone") 100-125 59
JON (4219 "Sherry") 10-15 59
VULCAN (135 "Sherry") 125-150 58
Also see LOWE, Sammy, Orchestra

VALHALLA
LPs: 10/12-inch
U.A. (6730 "Valhalla") 10-15 69

VALIANT TRIO
Singles: 7-inch
EV (97500 "You Left Me") 10-20 65

VALIANTS P&R '57
(With the Bumps Blackwell Orchestra; Featuring Billy Storm)
Singles: 78 rpm
KEEN 20-40 57
Singles: 7-inch
ANDEX (4026 "Please Wait My Love") 50-75 58
(First issue.)
EARLY BIRD (001 "This Is the Night") 3-5 95
(Orange vinyl.)
EARLY BIRD (003 "Please Wait My Love") . 3-5 95
(Green vinyl.)
KEEN (4008 "Temptation of My Heart") ...30-40 58
KEEN (4026 "Please Wait My Love") 40-50 58
KEEN (34004 "This Is the Nite") 15-20 58
KEEN (34007 "Lover Lover") 10-15 58
KEEN (82120 "This Is the Night") 8-12 60
SHAR-DEE (703 "Dear Cindy") 150-200 59
(Reads: "Made in U.S.A." at bottom. No mention of distribution by London.)
SHAR-DEE (703 "Dear Cindy") 15-25 59
(Reads "Distributed by London Records, Inc." at bottom)
Also see CHAVELLES
Also see STORM, Billy

VALIANTS
Singles: 7-inch
SPECK (1001 "Wedding Bells") 3000-4000 58
STAR VILL (1004 "Wedding Bells") ....3-5 '90s

VALIANTS
(Dixieaires)
Singles: 7-inch
JOY (235 "Let Me Go Lover") 8-12 60
Also see BELLS
Also see DIXIEAIRES
Also see VAN LOAN, Joe

VALIANTS
Singles: 7-inch
NEW PHOENIX (102 "I Had a Dream") ...40-60 60
Members: Paul Stefen; Jim Bing; Tony Kern; Gene Stankowski; Ralph Stevens; Paul Yopps.
Also see STEFAN, Paul

VALIANTS
Singles: 7-inch
FAIRLANE (21007 "See-Saw") 10-15 61
IMPERIAL (5843 "Love Comes in Many Ways") 8-12 62
IMPERIAL (5915 "Living in Paradise") 8-12 63
KC (108 "Are You Ready") 8-12 62
VANCE (102 "Are You Ready") 10-15

VALIANTS
Singles: 7-inch
FREDLO (6208 "Twistin' Til the End") 20-30 62

VALIANTS
Singles: 7-inch
ROULETTE (4510 "Johnny Lonely") 8-12 63

VALIANTS
Singles: 7-inch
SABRE (103 "Wild Party") 10-20 63

VALIANTS
Singles: 7-inch
AMCAN (404 "Moonflight"/"Star of Hawaii") 10-20 64

AMCAN (404 "Moonflight") 15-25 64
(Single-sided. Promotional issue only.)
DOT (16884 "I'll Return to You") 5-10 66

VALIANTS

Singles: 7-inch

CORTLAND (114 "Come On Let's Go") .. 10-15 64

VALIANTS

Singles: 7-inch

VALOR (101 "The Valiant") .... 10-15 '60s

VALIANTS

Singles: 7-inch

ALLSTAR (3677 "Jack the Ripper") 8-12
EV 8-12
FIDELITY (4057 "Slogian") 8-12
RIDGE (1091 "Jack the Ripper") 8-12
VB (2 "Dawn") 8-12

VALIDS

Singles: 7-inch

AMBER (853 "Hey Senorita") 5-10 66
AMBER (855 "Congratulations") 5-10 66

LPs: 10/12-inch

AMBER (802 "Accapella") 15-25 66

VALIENTS

Singles: 7-inch

BANGAR (00601 "Jail Bird") 15-25 63
GARRETT (4006 "Jail Bird") 10-20 64

VALINO, Joe — P&R '56

(With the Gospelaires)

Singles: 78 rpm

U.A. 8-12 57
VIK 5-10 56

Singles: 7-inch

BANDBOX (261 "Now") 5-10 61
CLEARVIEW 5-10
CROSLEY (216 "Hidden Persuasion") 5-10 59
CROSLEY (219 "Game of Fools") 5-10 60
DEBUT (138 "Sinner or Saint") 4-6 67
DEBUT (144 "Vicki") 4-6 68
RCA (7535 "Out of the Darkness") 8-12 60
RCA (7723 "Caravan") 8-12 60
U.A. 10-15 57-58
VIK 10-20 56

Picture Sleeves

U.A. (101 "Legend of the Lost") 20-30 57
U.A. (119 "God's Little Acre") 20-30 58
(Pictures film's cast on one side, Joe Valino on other.)

LPs: 10/12-inch

DEBUT (7505 "Saint or Sinner") 8-12 67

VALJEAN — P&R/LP '62

(Valjean Johns)

Singles: 7-inch

CARLTON (573 "Theme from Ben Casey") 5-10 62
CARLTON (576 "Till There Was You") 5-10 62
CARLTON (582 "Mewsette") 5-10 62
CARLTON (586 "For the Birds") 5-10 63

Picture Sleeves

CARLTON (573 "Theme from Ben Casey") 5-10 62

LPs: 10/12-inch

CARLTON (143 "Theme from Ben Casey") 15-25 62
CARLTON (146 "Mashin' the Classics") .. 15-25 63

VAL-JEENS

("Vocal Jim Young")

Singles: 7-inch

PEE VEE (141 "Darlene") 50-75 66
(500 made.)
Members: Jim Young; Jack Zeager; Byron Wright; Ravic "Rags" Ringlaben; Mike English; Gene Stillwagon; Marty Valle; Glen Trout.
Also see TROUT, Glen

VALKYRIES

Singles: 7-inch

CORI (31003 "Love You Like I Do") 10-20 65

VALLA, Tony

(With the Alamos)

Singles: 7-inch

FORTUNE (858 "La Bamba") 20-30 61
FORTUNE (859 "Love") 20-30 61
HI-Q (5030 "Donkey Walk") 8-12 63

VALLANDEERS

Singles: 7-inch

PLEASANT ("Mexican Hop") 100-150
(Selection number not known.)

VALLET, Gary

Singles: 7-inch

BISON ("Guitar Bass Boogie") 20-25 60
(Selection number not known. Later issued as *The Shock*, by the Quarter Notes.)

VALLEY, Jim

(Jim "Harpo" Valley; with Don & Goodtimes)

Singles: 7-inch

DUNHILL (4096 "Invitations") 5-10 67
DUNHILL (4103 "Maintain") 5-10 67
JERDEN (814 "I'm Real") 5-10 67

Picture Sleeves

DUNHILL 4-6 67

LPs: 10/12-inch

PANORAMA (104 "Harpo") 20-30 68
Also see DON & GOODTIMES
Also see REVERE, Paul, & Raiders
Also see VICEROYS

VALLEY, Jim, & Steve Schurr

LPs: 10/12-inch

LIGHT 10-15
Also see VALLEY, Jim

VALLEY YOUTH CHORALE

Singles: 7-inch

FELSTED (8693 "Little Bell") 5-10 64

VALLI

(With the Shirelles)

Singles: 7-inch

SCEPTER (1233 "Hurry Home to Me") 10-15 62
SPOKANE (4002 "I Sit At My Window") ... 10-15 63
Also see SHIRELLES

VALLI, Frankie — P&R '66

(With the Travelers; Frankie Valle; Frankie Vally; Frankie Valley; with Romans; with Valli Boys)

Singles: 78 rpm

MERCURY 50-75 54

Singles: 10/12-inch

MOTOWN (124-10 "Just Look What You Have Done") 15-20 73
(10-inch single.)
PRIVATE STOCK (5101 "Boomerang") ... 10-15 77
(12-inch single.)

Singles: 7-inch

BOB CREWE PRESENTS (1 "The Girl I'll Never Know") 25-35 69
(Promotional issue only.)
CINDY (3012 "Real") 150-200 58
COLLECTABLES .... 3-5 '80s
CORONA (1234 "My Mother's Eyes") ... 300-500 53
DECCA (30994 "Please Take a Chance") 75-125 59
DECCA (30994 "Please Take a Chance") 100-150 59
(Promotional issue only.)
DECCA (30994 "Please Take a Chance") 4-6 75
(Shown as by the Four Lovers.)
MAGIC CARPET (503 "My Mother's Eyes") 10-15
(Black vinyl. 475 made.)
MAGIC CARPET (503 "My Mother's Eyes") 30-35
(Colored vinyl. 25 made.)
MERCURY (70381 "Forgive & Forget") 100-150 54
(Maroon label.)
MERCURY (70381 "Forgive & Forget") 50-75 54
(Black label.)
MERCURY (70381 "Forgive & Forget") 50-75 54
(Promotional issue only.)
MOTOWN (1251 "You've Got Your Troubles") 8-12 73
MOTOWN (1279 "The Scalawag Song") 8-12 73
MOWEST (5011 "Love Isn't Here") 5-10 72
MOWEST (5025 "The Night") 5-10 72
MOWEST (5025 "The Night") 10-15 72
(Promotional issue only.)
PHILIPS (40407 "The Proud One") 5-10 66
PHILIPS (40446 "Can't Take My Eyes Off You") 5-10 67
PHILIPS (40484 "I Make a Fool of Myself") 5-10 67
PHILIPS (40500 "Donnybrook") 20-40 67
PHILIPS (40510 "To Give") 5-10 67
PHILIPS (40622 "The Girl I'll Never Know") 5-10 69
PHILIPS (40661 "You've Got Your Troubles") 10-15 69
PHILIPS (40680 "Circles in the Sand") 10-15 70
PRIVATE STOCK (45003 "My Eyes Adored You") 4-6 74
PRIVATE STOCK (45021 "Swearin' to God") 4-6 75
PRIVATE STOCK (45043 "Our Day Will Come") 4-6 75
PRIVATE STOCK (45074 "Fallen Angel") 4-6 76
PRIVATE STOCK (45098 "We're All Alone") 4-6 76
PRIVATE STOCK (45109 "Boomerang") 4-6 76
PRIVATE STOCK (45140 "Easily") 4-6 77
PRIVATE STOCK (45154 "Second Thoughts") 4-6 77
PRIVATE STOCK (45169 "I Need You") 4-6 77
PRIVATE STOCK (45180 "I Could Have Loved You") 4-6 78
RSO (897 "Grease") 4-6 78
SEASONS 3-5
SMASH (1995 "The Sun Ain't Gonna Shine") 5-10 65
SMASH (2015 "Hurt Yourself") 5-10 65
SMASH (2037 "You're Ready Now") 5-10 66
W.B./CURB (8670 "No Love At All") 4-6 78
W.B./CURB (8734 "Fancy Dancer") 4-6 79

Picture Sleeves

PHILIPS (40407 "The Proud One") 10-20 66
PHILIPS (40446 "Can't Take My Eyes Off You") 10-20 67
PHILIPS (40484 "I Make a Fool of Myself") 10-20 67
PHILIPS (40510 "To Give") 10-20 67
PHILIPS (40622 "The Girl I'll Never Know") 10-20 69

LPs: 10/12-inch

MCA (3198 "Very Best") 5-10 79
MCA (5134 "Heaven Above Me") 5-10 80
MOTOWN (104 "Superstar Series") 5-8 81
MOTOWN (852 "Inside You") 8-12 75
PHILIPS (200247 "Solo") 30-40 67
(Monaural.)
PHILIPS (600247 "Solo") 20-25 67
(Stereo.)
PHILIPS (600274 "Timeless") 20-25 68
PRIVATE STOCK (2000 "Closeup") 8-12 75
PRIVATE STOCK (2001 "Gold") 8-12 75
PRIVATE STOCK (2006 "Our Day Will Come") 8-12 75
PRIVATE STOCK (2017 "Valli") 8-12 76
PRIVATE STOCK (7002 "Lady Put the Light Out") 8-12 77
PRIVATE STOCK (7012 "Frankie Valli Hits") 8-12 78
W.B. (3233 "Frankie Valli Is the Word") 8-12 78
Also see BEACH BOYS with FRANKIE VALLI & 4 SEASONS
Also see FOUR LOVERS
Also see 4 SEASONS
Also see HARTFORD, Ken
Also see LEE, Larry
Also see NOLAN, Frankie
Also see REID, Matthew
Also see TYLER, Frankie

VALLI, Frankie, & Chris Forde — P&R '80

Singles: 7-inch

MCA/CURB (41253 "Where Did We Go Wrong") 3-5 80

VALLI, Frankie, & Cheryl Ladd

Singles: 7-inch

CAPITOL (5115 "Can't Say No to You") 3-5 82
Also see VALLI, Frankie

VALLI, June — P&R '52

(With Joe Reisman's Orchestra)

Singles: 78 rpm

RCA 5-10 52-56

Singles: 7-inch

ABC-PAR (10442 "Gather Your Dreams") . 5-10 63
ABC-PAR (10467 "Silly Girl") 5-10 63
DCP (1120 "Empty Rooms") 5-10 64
MERCURY 8-15 58-61
RCA 10-20 52-56
U.A. (466 "I'm Afraid") 5-10 62
U.A. (490 "Is It Right or Wrong") 5-10 62

Picture Sleeves

MERCURY (71750 "Tell Him for Me") 10-20 61

EPs: 7-inch

RCA 5-10 55-56

LPs: 10/12-inch

AUDIO FIDELITY (6214 "Today") 5-10 69
MERCURY (20463 "Do It Yourself Wedding Album") 8-15 60
RCA 12-25 55-56
Also see PIANO RED / June Valli
Also see ZABACH, Florian

VALLIER, Geneva

Singles: 78 rpm

CASH (1009 "Geneva's Blues") 15-20 55

Singles: 7-inch

CASH (1009 "Geneva's Blues") 25-35 55

VALLO, Rick

(With Three Beaus & a Peep; Ricky Vallo)

Singles: 78 rpm

MGM 4-6 53

Singles: 7-inch

MGM 5-10 53
VERVE (10148 "Rockin' River") 10-15 58
VERVE (10149 "Could I Love You More") 10-15 58
Also see THREE BEAUS & A PEEP

VALLONE, Alan

(Alan Vallone Group)

Singles: 7-inch

ABC (10837 "She Won't Kiss Me Goodnight") 10-15 66
AUDICON (113 "Mambo Twist") 10-20 61
LAURIE (3459 "Lazy Love") 8-12 68
PHILIPS (40144 "Our Love Will Grow") ... 10-20 63
VCB (0941 "Just a Friend") 10-20 61

VALOR, Tony

(Tony Valor Sounds Orchestra)

Singles: 7-inch

MUSICTONE (1119 "There's a Story in My Heart") 75-100 63
PAULA (432 "Opus 22") 4-6 78
PAULA (436 "Midnight Affair") 4-6 78
PAULA (1243 "Opus 22") 5-8 70

VALQUINS

Singles: 7-inch

GAITY (162 "Falling Star") 1000-1500 59
(Black vinyl. Approximately 300 made.)
GAITY (162 "Falling Star") 2500-3500 59
(Gold vinyl. 500 made)

VALRAYS

Singles: 7-inch

PARKWAY (880 "Get a Board") 10-15 63
PARKWAY (904 "Yo Me Pregunto [I Ask Myself]") 15-20 64

VAL-RAYS

Singles: 7-inch

U.A. (50145 "I'm Walkin' Proud") 5-10 67

VALS

Singles: 7-inch

UNIQUE LABORATORIES/THERON ("The Song of a Lover") 3000-4000 61
(No selection number used. 200 made.)
Members: Bill Gibson; David Wilkerson Jr.; Ernie Morris; Bill Taylor; Clarence Green.
Also see JOHNSON, Vicki

VALS

Singles: 7-inch

ASCOT (2163 "Too Late") 8-12 64

VALTAIRS

Singles: 7-inch

SELSOM (101 "Soul") 10-20 64
SELSOM (106 "Moonlight in Vermont") ... 10-20 65

VALTONE BAND

Singles: 7-inch

BOSS (103 "Norma's Blues") 15-25 63
VALTONE (103 "Norma's Blues") 10-20 65
(Rerecorded version.)
VALTONE (106 "Norma's Blues") 10-20 65
(Reissued with different flip side.)

VAL-TONES

Singles: 78 rpm

DELUXE 40-60 55

Singles: 7-inch
DELUXE (6084 "Tender Darling") 100-150 55

VALTONES

Singles: 78 rpm
GEE (1004 "You Belong to My Heart") 50-75 56
Singles: 7-inch
GEE (1004 "You Belong to My Heart") 300-400 56

VALUES

Singles: 7-inch
INVICTA (1002 "Return to Me") 15-20 62
INVICTA (9007 "Return to Me") 5-10 65

VALUMDEARS

Singles: 7-inch
MART (3517 "King Bee") 15-25 59

VAMPIRE STATE BUILDING

Singles: 7-inch
ROULETTE (7056 "Barnabas") 5-10 69

VAMPIRES

LPs: 10/12-inch
U.A. (3378 "At the Monster Ball") 25-35 64
(Monaural.)
U.A. (6378 "At the Monster Ball") 30-50 64
(Stereo.)

VAMPIRES

Singles: 7-inch
CARROLL (104 "Why Didn't I Listen to Mother") 200-300 64
(Reissued as by the Bentleys.)
Also see BENTLEYS

VAN, Billy
(Billy Van Four)

Singles: 7-inch
DRA (317 "When You're in Love") 8-10 62
RODEO (274 "I Miss You") 8-10 61
LAGREE (705 "I Miss You") 10-20 60

VAN, Gary

Singles: 7-inch
INTRO (9000 "Rockin' Too Much") 50-75 58

VAN, Gloria

Singles: 7-inch
NORMAN (536 "Raindrops") 5-10 63

VAN, Harvie June
(Harvey June Van)

Singles: 7-inch
BRIAR (121 "Dasher") 5-10 61
RCA (7668 "When You Are Here") 5-10 60
RCA (7778 "Johnny Darling") 5-10 60
TODD (1078 "Biggest Broken Heart in Town") 5-10 62

VAN, Ila
(Ila Vann)

Singles: 7-inch
ARNOLD (1008 "It Must Be Love") 10-20 63
(First issue.)
LIBERTY (55595 "It Must Be Love") 5-10 63
ROULETTE (4733 "I've Got the Feeling")...5-15 67
ROULETTE (4772 "Your Love") 5-15 67
ROULETTE (7036 "Keep on Laughin' Baby") 5-15 69

VAN, Steve & Bernie

Singles: 7-inch
VAN (107 "Dream Train") 10-15 61

VAN, Trudy, & Realm

Singles: 7-inch
VJV (301 "Surf Is Up") .... 15-25 '60s

VAN & GRACE

Singles: 7-inch
SSS INT'L (765 "Set Me Free") 5-10 69

VAN & TITUS *R&B '68*

Singles: 7-inch
ELF (90016 "Cry Baby Cry") 10-15 68

VAN BECK, Doug
(Doug Van Beck Trio)

Singles: 7-inch
FARGO (1064 "Surfin' Little Girl") 10-20 64
JUDI (6500 "Sweet Lucy's Kiss") 15-25 64

VAN BROTHERS
(Norman Walton & Van Brothers; Arnold & Lee)

Singles: 7-inch
POOR BOY (111 "Servant of Love").... 500-750 60

WALTON (2500 "Uncle Jim Riggs Will") 50-75 65
EPs: 7-inch
WALTON (7848 "Sweet Marie"/"Servant of Love"/"Take That Lock"/"Too Many Women") 150-250 62
(Not issued with cover.)
Members: Arnold Van Winkle; Lee Van Winkle; Norman Walton.
Also see WINKLE, Arnold Van

VANCE, Al

Singles: 7-inch
GOLDWAX (116 "Every Woman I Know") 20-30 65

VANCE, Beverly

Singles: 7-inch
IMPERIAL (7002 "Will I") 15-25 57

VANCE, Billy

Singles: 7-inch
AUGUST 5-10
KAYO (926 "Innocent") 25-35 58
MAP (502 "Drop Me a Line") 8-12

VANCE, Chico
(With the Nocturnals)

Singles: 7-inch
REVIVE 10-15 63
STACY (967 "Why Wait for Winter") 8-12 63
Also see CHEEK-O-VASS
Also see NOCTURNALS

VANCE, Dick

Singles: 7-inch
SOR VA (500 "Nuthin' Man Nuthin' ") 20-30
SOR VA (503 "Bobbi") 20-30

VANCE, Joel

Singles: 7-inch
CADET CONCEPT (7022 "Slippin' and Slidin' ") 5-10 69
LPs: 10/12-inch
CADET CONCEPT 10-15 69

VANCE, Kenny

Singles: 7-inch
ATLANTIC (3259 "Looking for an Echo") ...8-12 75
W.B. (8348 "Looking for an Echo") 5-8 77
LPs: 10/12-inch
ATLANTIC (18135 "Vance 32") 10-15 75
(Two discs.)
GOLD CASTLE (171011 "Short Vacation")..5-8 88
ROCK-A-WAY (1457 "Short Vacation")....10-15
Also see HARBOR LIGHTS
Also see JAY & AMERICANS

VANCE, Paul *P&R '66*

Singles: 7-inch
ROULETTE (4420 "Cleopatra") 5-10 62
SCEPTER (12164 "Sexy") 5-10 66
SCEPTER (12175 "Ma Vie") 5-10 66
SCEPTER (12191 "Julie Knows") 5-10 67
SCEPTER (12197 "Don't Go") 5-10 67
LPs: 10/12-inch
SCEPTER (557 "Dommage Dommage") .10-20 66
Also see PAUL'S HIGH SCHOOL BAND

VANCE, Sammy

Singles: 7-inch
EBB (134 "Guilty of Love") 15-25 58

VANCE BROTHERS

Singles: 78 rpm
MACY'S (144 "Draftwood Blues") 10-15 50
Singles: 7-inch
MACY'S (144 "Draftwood Blues") 15-25 50

VANDAGRIFF, Earney

Singles: 78 rpm
FLAIR 8-12 53
Singles: 7-inch
FLAIR (1006 "Guest Star in Heaven") 10-20 53

VANDALL, Glenn

Singles: 7-inch
ACE (645 "Closer to You") 5-10 62
DIAL (4037 "Dit-Dat") 5-10 66

VANDALS

Singles: 7-inch
PAROLE ("Mystery") 20-30 65
(No selection number used.)

GOLDEN GATE (011 "Wet & Wild"/"Mustang Georgie") 15-25 67
(Promotional issue, made for 7-Up and Ford.)
TIARA (200 "I Saw Her in a Mustang") 15-25 66
Picture Sleeves
GOLDEN GATE (0011 "Wet & Wild"/"Mustang Georgie") 20-30 67
(Promotional issue, made for 7-Up and Ford.)
Members: George Terry; Johnny Sambataro; Augie Bucci; Richie Kutcher; Bill Cosford; Russ Septilli.

VANDALS

Singles: 7-inch
PARKWAY (136 "You Captivate Me") 8-12 67
PARKWAY (156 "Don't Fight It") 8-12 67

VANDALS

Singles: 7-inch
G.A.R. (105 "You Lied to Me") 200-300 67
Members: Jim Walden; Bob Liles; Craig Strong; Charlie Dionisio.
Also see NORSEMEN

VAN DELLOS

Singles: 7-inch
CARD (558 "Bring Back") 500-750 61

VAN DELLES

Singles: 7-inch
BOLO (731 "Time After Time") 15-25 62

VANDELLS

Singles: 7-inch
ABC-PAR (10535 "Touch") 5-10 64

VAN-DELLS
(Booker T's MGs)

Singles: 7-inch
STAX (145 "The Honeydripper") 10-15 64

VANDELLS

Singles: 7-inch
BAY TOWN 10-20
Member: Billy Sherrill.
Also see SHERRILL, Billy

VANDELS
(Vandel's)

Singles: 7-inch
USA (758 "A Small Silver Ring") 150-200 63

VAN DER GRAAF GENERATOR

Singles: 7-inch
MERCURY (72979 "Necromancer") 4-6 70
LPs: 10/12-inch
CHARISMA (1051 "Pawn Hearts") 10-15 72
DUNHILL (50097 "'H' to He Who Am the Only One") 10-15 71
MERCURY (1069 "Godbluff") 8-10 76
MERCURY (1096 "Still Life") 8-10 76
MERCURY (1116 "World Record") 8-10 76
MERCURY (61238 "Aerosol Grey Machine") 15-18 70
PROBE (4515 "The Least We Can Do Is Wave to Each Other") 10-15 70

VANDERGRIFT BROTHERS

Singles: 7-inch
COZY (447 "Still Here A-Cryin' ") 100-200

VAN DOREN

Singles: 7-inch
HICKORY (1262 "Surfin' Liza") 10-15 64

VAN DOREN, Mamie

Singles: 12-inch
CORNER STONE (3003 "State of Turmoil") 5-10 84
Singles: 7-inch
CORNER STONE 3-5 84
DOT (15883 "Lifetime of Love") 10-20 59
DOT (15970 "Beat Generation") 10-20 59
PREP (100 "Go, Go, Calypso!") 10-20 57
EPs: 7-inch
PREP (1 "Untamed Youth") 50-75 57
LPs: 10/12-inch
CHURCHILL (67323 "Mamie") 8-12 77

VAN DOREN, Mamie, & June Wilkinson

Singles: 7-inch
JUBILEE (5483 "Bikini with no Top on the Top") 5-10 64
Also see VAN DOREN, Mamie

VAN DORN SISTERS

Singles: 7-inch
PHILTONE (4765 "Baby Roo") 8-10 62

VAN DYKE, Connie
(With Steve Norman; Conny Van Dyke)

Singles: 7-inch
BARNABY (5007 thru 5026) 4-6 72-73
MOTOWN (1041 "Oh Freddy") 25-35 62
WHEELSVILLE (112 "Don't Do Nothing I Wouldn't Do") ....75-125 '60s
LPs: 10/12-inch
BARNABY (15005 "Conny Van Dyke") 5-10 73

VAN DYKE, Dick
(With the Jack Halloran Singers)

Singles: 7-inch
BUENA VISTA (441 "Chim Chim Cheree") 5-10 65
JAMIE (1178 "Three Wheels on My Wagon") 10-15 60
JAMIE (1256 "Three Wheels on My Wagon") 5-10 63
U.A. (50486 "Hushabye Mountain") 5-10 68
Picture Sleeves
BUENA VISTA (441 "Chim Chim Cheree") 5-10 65
JAMIE (1178 "Three Wheels on My Wagon") 15-20 60
JAMIE (1256 "Three Wheels on My Wagon") 10-15 63
LPs: 10/12-inch
COMMAND (860 "Songs I Like") 10-20 64
Also see ANDREWS, Julie, & Dick Van Dyke

VAN DYKE, Earl
(With the Soul Brothers; with Motown Brass)

Singles: 7-inch
RENAISSANCE (5000 "September Song") 50-75
SOUL (Except 35009) 10-20 64-69
SOUL (35009 "All for You") 100-200 65
LPs: 10/12-inch
MOTOWN (631 "Motown Sound") 20-40 65
SOUL (715 "Earl of Funk") 25-50 69
Also see WALKER, Junior

VAN DYKE, Leroy *P&R '56/C&W '57*

Singles: 78 rpm
DOT (Except 15561) 10-15 56-57
DOT (15561 "Honky Tonk Song") 20-30 57
Singles: 7-inch
ABC 4-6 74-75
ABC/DOT 4-6 75-77
DECCA 4-6 70-72
DOT (Except 15561 & 15698) 10-20 56-57
DOT (15561 "Honky Tonk Song") 25-35 57
DOT (15698 "Leather Jacket") 50-75 58
DOT (125 "Auctioneer") 5-10 63
KAPP 4-6 68-70
MCA 4-6 73
MERCURY 5-10 62-64
MOUNTAIN DEW 5-10
PLANTATION 3-5 78
SUN 3-5 79
W.B. 4-6 65-67
Picture Sleeves
MERCURY (72232 "Night People") 5-10 64
LPs: 10/12-inch
DECCA 8-10 72
DOT (16299 "Auctioneer") 20-30 61
DOT (3693 "Auctioneer") 8-15 66
HARMONY (11308 "I've Never Been Loved") 8-12 69
KAPP (3571 "Lonesome Is") 8-15 68
KAPP (3605 "Greatest Hits") 8-15 69
KAPP (3607 "Just a Closer Walk with Thee") 8-15 69
MCA 5-10 73
MERCURY 12-25 61-64
PLANTATION 5-10 77-79
SUN 5-8 74
W.B. 10-15 65-66
WING 8-15 65-66

VAN DYKES

Singles: 7-inch
DECCA (30654 "Run Betty, Run") 20-30 58
DECCA (30762 "Come On Baby") 50-75 58
DECCA (31036 "Better Come Back to Me") 20-30 60
FELSTED (8565 "Once Upon a Dream"). 10-15 59

VAN DYKES P&R '61
Singles: 7-inch
DELUXE (6193 "Bells Are Ringing") 15-25 61
DONNA (1333 "Gift of Love") 30-40 61
KING (5158 "Bells Are Ringing") 50-75 58
(Blue label. Small print.)
KING (5158 "Bells Are Ringing") 15-25 58
(Blue label. Large print.)
KING (5158 "Bells Are Ringing") .... 10-15 '60s
(Yellow label.)
SPRING (1113 "Gift of Love") 150-200 59
Also see TEMPTATIONS

VAN DYKES
(Calvin & Van Dykes)
Singles: 7-inch
ATLANTIC (2161 "King of Fools") 30-40 62

VAN DYKES
(Van Dyke Five)
Singles: 7-inch
CO-OP (515 "Rich Girl") 5-10 67
CO-OP (516 "I'll Get By") 5-10 67
CORNER CLOSET 5-10 67
GREEN SEA 15-25 65-67
Members: Frank Ruggiero; Bob Picagli; Russ Griffith; Tom Juliano; Art DeNicholas.
Also see CATALINAS

VAN DYKES P&R/R&B '66
Singles: 7-inch
HUE (6501 "No Man Is an Island") 15-25 65
MALA (520 "No Man Is an Island") 10-15 65
MALA (530 "What Will I Do") 5-10 66
MALA (539 "Never Let Me Go") 5-10 66
MALA (549 "You're Shakin' Me Up") 5-10 66
MALA (566 "A Sunday Kind of Love") 5-10 67
MALA (584 "Tears of Joy") 10-20 68
LPs: 10/12-inch
BELL (6004 "Tellin' It Like It Is") 15-25 67
Members: Ron Tandy; Wenzon Mosley; Jimmy May.

VAN EATON, Jimmy, & Untouchables
Singles: 7-inch
NITA (1004 "Bo Diddley") 10-20 62
RITA (1004 "Beat-Nik") 10-20 60

VANELL, Charles
Singles: 7-inch
ORIOLE (1319 "Knowing the Part") 35-50 59

VANELLI, Johnny
Singles: 7-inch
KENT (4539 "Alone We Have Nothing At All") 4-6 71
LITTLE APPLES (2801 "Phroomf") 8-12 65
NAME (4 "Something Made You Cry") 15-25 61

VAN GIVENS
Singles: 7-inch
PAULA (271 "Sunday School Beginners") ..5-10 67
PAULA (284 "I Want to Go Home") 5-10 67
PAULA (286 "Daddy's Baby Boy") 5-10 67

VANGUARDS
Singles: 78 rpm
DERBY (854 "So Live") 50-75 54
Singles: 7-inch
DERBY (854 "So Live") 100-200 54
DOT (15791 "Baby Doll") 10-15 58

VANGUARDS
(With B.B. Butler & Orchestra)
Singles: 7-inch
COLLECTABLES ....3-5 '80s
IVY (103 "Moonlight") 100-150 58
(White label. Promotional issue only.)
IVY (103 "Moonlight") 50-75 58
(Also credits Billy Butler's Orchestra.)
IVY (103 "Moonlight") 15-25 58
(No mention of Butler's Orchestra.)

VANGUARDS
Singles: 7-inch
REGENCY (743 "I Love You Darling"). 100-200 '50s
(Canadian.)
RUTH (439 "Last Night") 50-75

VANGUARDS
Singles: 7-inch
ENSIGN (1753 "Rear View Mirror") 5-10 62
W.B. (5800 "Girl") 5-10 66

VANGUARDS R&B '69
Singles: 7-inch
INDIE (91 "Woman Come Home") 6-10
LAMP (80 "It's Too Late for Love") 8-12 70
LAMP (81 "Girl Go Away") 6-10 70
LAMP (652 "It's To [sic] Late for Love") 6-10 70
WHIZ MASTERS (612 "Somebody Please") 8-12 69

VANGUARDS IV
Singles: 7-inch
CHARIOT, INC ("Blue Skies") ....5-10 '60s
(No selection number used.)

VAN HALEN P&R/LP '78
Singles: 12-inch
W.B. (Commercial issues.) 4-6 83-84
W.B. (Promotional issues.) 6-12 83-84
Singles: 7-inch
PALM TREE 4-8
W.B. 3-5 78-90
Promotional Singles
W.B. 5-10 78-90
Picture Sleeves
W.B. (Except 8556 & 8823) 3-8 79-88
W.B. (8556 "Running with the Devil") 20-30 78
W.B. (8823 "Dance the Night Away") 8-12 79
LPs: 10/12-inch
W.B. 5-10 78-90
W.B./LOONEY TUNES (705 "Van Halen") 10-20 78
(Colored vinyl. Promotional issue only.)
Members: David Lee Roth; Edward Van Halen; Alex Van Halen; Michael Anthony; Sammy Hagar.

VAN HOOK, Bobby
Singles: 7-inch
JEWEL (7601 "Mama Luce") 50-75
VLM (1098 "Down in Alabama") 50-75

VAN HORN, John
Singles: 7-inch
MERCURY 4-6 72
MOONGLOW (207 "Happy Jose") 5-10 62
(With Jack Collier.)
RUMBLE (1958 "Eyes Afire") 3-5 84
LPs: 10/12-inch
MERCURY 8-12 72
Also see SUZETTES / John Van Horn

VANILLA FUDGE P&R/LP '67
Singles: 7-inch
ATCO 5-10 67-70
LPs: 10/12-inch
ATCO (224 "Vanilla Fudge") 20-30 68
ATCO (237 "The Beat Goes On") 15-25 68
ATCO (244 "Renaissance") 15-25 68
ATCO (278 "Near the Beginning") 15-25 69
ATCO (303 "Rock 'N' Roll") 15-25 69
ATCO (90006 "Best of Vanilla Fudge") 8-10 82
Members: Mark Stein; Tim Bogert; Vinnie Martell; Carmine Appice.
Also see CREAM / Vanilla Fudge
Also see Pigeons

VANITY FARE P&R '69
Singles: 7-inch
BRENT (7067 "Peter Who") 5-10 67
DJM 4-6 75
PAGE ONE 5-10 68-70
SOMA (5000 "Hitchin' a Ride") 8-12 68
20TH FOX 4-6 73
LPs: 10/12-inch
PAGE ONE 10-15 70

VAN LOAN, Jamie
Singles: 7-inch
BLUE BELL (501 "Ask") 15-25 60

VAN LOAN, Joe
(Joe Van Loan Quartet; Joe VanLoan; with Duke Ellington Orchestra)
Singles: 78 rpm
CARVER (1402 "Trust in Me") 50-75 54
COLUMBIA (30195 "Joog Joog") 10-20 50
Singles: 7-inch
FORD (122 "Autumn Leaves") 10-20 63
PARKWAY (828 "Hurricane") 15-25 61
SUDAJA ....5-10 '60s
V-TONE (200 "Forever") 100-150 59
Also see BACHELORS
Also see BELLS
Also see BROWN, Wini
Also see COBB, Arnett
Also see DIXIEAIRES
Also see DU DROPPERS
Also see ELLINGTON, Duke
Also see INK SPOTS
Also see KINGS
Also see POWELL, Chris, & Five Blue Flames
Also see RAVENS
Also see VALIANTS

VANN, Dickie
Singles: 7-inch
CHEROKEE (501 "The Girl Next Door") ..40-60 59

VANN, Joey
(Joe Canzano)
Singles: 7-inch
CHUBBY 3-5 82
COED (606 "Try to Remember") 10-20 65
Also see DUPREES

VANN, Nikki
Singles: 7-inch
FAME (703 "Jade") ....10-20 '60s

VANN, Teddy P&R '61
(With Orchestra & Chorus)
Singles: 7-inch
CAPITOL (5878 "Theme from Coloredman") 5-10 67
COLUMBIA (41996 "The Lonely Crowd") 10-15 61
END (1059 "Sweetheart") 10-20 59
JUBILEE (5424 "River Keep Moving") 10-15 62
ROULETTE (4300 "Do You Love Me") 10-15 60
TRIPLE-X (101 "Cindy") 15-25 60
Also see WHEELS

VANN, Tommy
(With the Echoes; with Professionals)
Singles: 7-inch
ACADEMY (118 "Too Young") 8-12 66
ACADEMY (120 "Pretty Flamingo") 8-12 66
ACADEMY (123 "Is This Love") 10-15 67
CAPITOL (2168 "For Goodness Sake") 5-10 68
CONGRESS (6001 "I'm So Alone") 5-10 69
HOLLYWOOD (101 "I'm Hopin' You'll Be Mine") 10-20 66
REO (8942 "Pretty Flamingo") 8-12 66
(Canadian.)
Members: Tommy Vann; George Dochterman.

VANNELL, Charles
Singles: 7-inch
ORIOLE (1319 "Classmates") 10-20 59

VAN RONK, Dave
(With the Hudson Dusters)
Singles: 7-inch
VERVE FORECAST 5-10 67
LPs: 10/12-inch
MERCURY (20908 "Just Dave Van Ronk") 10-20 64
(Monaural.)
MERCURY (60908 "Just Dave Van Ronk") 15-25 64
(Stereo.)
VERVE FORECAST 10-15 67-68

VANSMEN
Singles: 7-inch
SIMS (125 "Do I Find Me in Your Plan") 5-10 62

VAN-TELS
Singles: 7-inch
CITE (5009 "Baby, What You Want") 40-60 64
RAYNARD (1085 "Ain't Too Proud to Beg") 10-20 68
Members: Jerry Trado; Joey Piccolo; Gary Jay; Chris King; Skip Kamrath; Bruce Cole; Brad Craig; Steve Fromm; Bob Hershley; Gene Recob; Dennis Pleskechek; Carl Biancuzzo; Dave Zylka.

VAN VALEN, Ellen
Singles: 7-inch
BIG TOP (3026 "I Wish I Didn't Love You") 10-15 59

VAN VOOREN, Monique
EPs: 7-inch
RCA (1553 "Mink in Hi-Fi") 10-15 57
LPs: 10/12-inch
RCA (1553 "Mink in Hi-Fi") 20-30 57

VAN WINKLE, Arnold
(With Rainbow Rhythmaires)
Singles: 7-inch
RUBY (540 "An Old Rusty Dime") 50-100 57
Also see VAN BROTHERS

VAN ZANDT, Ed / Bill Murphy
Singles: 7-inch
HIT (28 "Little Diane"/"Devil Woman") 10-20 62

VAN ZANDT, Townes
Singles: 7-inch
B.T. PUPPY 5-10 68
POPPY 4-8 69-73
TOMATO 4-6 78
LPs: 10/12-inch
POPPY 8-12 69-73
TOMATO 5-10 77-78

VAPORS
Singles: 7-inch
BELL (607 "Jump Out") 10-15 65

VAQUEROS
Singles: 7-inch
AUDITION (6102 "Desert Wind") 10-20 64

VAQUEROS
Singles: 7-inch
BANGAR (647 "Birds & Bees") 25-50 64
STUDIO CITY (1049 "Growing Pains") 25-50 66
STUDIO CITY (1059 "Mustang Sally") ...75-100 66

VARE, Ronnie, & Inspirations
(Ronnie Vare & Inspirators with Silver String Trio)
Singles: 7-inch
DELL (5202 "Let's Rock Little Girl") 50-100 59
(Has label's Hartford address under name.)
DELL (5202 "Let's Rock Little Girl") 30-40 59
(No address shown on label.)
GLO (5201 "Let Me Be Your Love") 75-100 60
(Reportedly 5000 made.)

VAREEATIONS
Singles: 7-inch
DIONN (506 "Time") 10-15 68
DIONN (510 "Foolish One") 10-15 68

VARETTA
Singles: 7-inch
BRENT (7040 "Fly by Night") 10-15 63

VARIATIONS
Singles: 7-inch
AMOUR ....4-8 '70s
BON-JOY 8-12
JUSTICE ....50-75 '60s
(Title and selection number not known.)
MTA (121 "Will You Be Mine") 50-75 67
OKEH (7324 "Empty Words") 5-10 69
POW! 4-8
VEE 4-8
LPs: 10/12-inch
JUSTICE (212 "Dig 'Em Up") ....300-400 '60s

VARIATONES
Singles: 7-inch
FIRE (1010 "I'll Keep Lovin' You") 150-250
(Another Fire 1010 exists, by Mary Ann Fisher, but it is from a different company.)
Also see FISHER, Mary Ann

VARIETEERS
("Vocal by Jimmy Sweeney")
Singles: 78 rpm
HICKORY 50-75 54-55
MGM (10888 "I'll Try to Forget I Loved You") 75-100 51
Singles: 7-inch
HICKORY (1014 "I Pay with Every Breath") 200-300 54
HICKORY (1025 "Call My Gal, Miss Jones") 150-200 55
Member: Jimmy Sweeney.
Also see SWEENEY, Jimmy

VARIETY BOYS
("Featuring Jimmy Brown")
Singles: 78 rpm
DECCA 15-25 41
RAINBOW 10-15 53
Singles: 7-inch
RAINBOW (235 "Shame") 30-40 53
(Red vinyl.)

VARNELLS
Singles: 7-inch
ARNOLD (1003 "Who Created Love") ... 40-50 61
ARNOLD (1006 "All Because") ... 20-30 61
Also see VERNALLS

VARNER, Don
Singles: 7-inch
QUINCY (8002 "Tear-Stained Face") .. 150-250 69
VEEP (1296 "Tear-Stained Face") ... 100-200 69

VARNEY, Bob
Singles: 7-inch
BLUE GRASS (641 "Stone Mountain Boogie") ... 200-300

VARSITY MEN
Singles: 7-inch
STAFF (86536 "Please Don't Cry") ... 50-75 62
(Identification number shown since no selection number is used.)

VARTAN, Sylvie
Singles: 12-inch
RCA (11594 "I Don't Want the Night to End") ... 10-15 79
Singles: 7-inch
RCA (8520 "I Made My Choice") ... 8-12 65
RCA (11578 "I Don't Want the Night to End") ... 3-5 79
LPs: 10/12-inch
RCA (3015 "I Don't Want the Night to End") ... 10-15 79

VASEL, Marianne, & Erich Storz *P&R '58*
Singles: 7-inch
MERCURY (71286 "The Little Train") ... 10-15 58
LPs: 10/12-inch
DANA (8017 "Songs of Germany") ... 15-25 59

VASHONETTES
Singles: 7-inch
CHECKER (1195 "Love") ... 10-20 68

VASSER, Dave
(With the Muleskinners)
Singles: 7-inch
SARA (63102 "New Orleans") ... 15-25 63
Also see MULESKINNERS

VAUGHAN, Dale, & Starnotes
Singles: 7-inch
VON (480 "High Steppin'") ... 200-300

VAUGHAN, Frankie *P&R '58*
Singles: 7-inch
COLUMBIA ... 8-12 59-60
EPIC ... 8-12 58
MALA (578 "There Must Be a Way") ... 5-10 67
MALA (588 "If I Didn't Care") ... 5-10 68
MALA (12004 "Nevertheless") ... 5-10 68
PHILIPS ... 5-10 62-66
LPs: 10/12-inch
COLUMBIA (1405 "At the Palladium") ... 15-20 60
(Monaural.)
COLUMBIA (8201 "At the Palladium") ... 20-25 60
(Stereo.)
PHILIPS ... 10-20 62

VAUGHAN, Malcolm
(With Frank Cordell's Orchestra)
Singles: 7-inch
CAPITOL (3797 "Guardian Angel") ... 10-20 57

VAUGHAN, Sarah *P&R '47*
(With Hal Mooney & Orchestra)
Singles: 78 rpm
ATLANTIC ... 5-10 53
COLUMBIA ... 5-10 49-53
CONTINENTAL ... 10-15 45
MGM ... 5-10 50-51
MERCURY ... 5-10 53-57
MUSICRAFT ... 8-12 47-48
Singles: 7-inch
ATLANTIC (1012 "It Might As Well Be Spring") ... 15-25 53
ATLANTIC (3835 "Fool on the Hill") ... 3-5 81
COLUMBIA (38000 & 39000 series) ... 10-20 51-53
MGM (71 "Sarah Vaughan Sings") ... 50-75 51
(Boxed, four-disc set.)
MGM (165 "Tenderly") ... 50-75 52
(Boxed, four-disc set.)
MGM (10000 & 30000 series) ... 10-20 50-51
MAINSTREAM ... 4-6 71-74
MERCURY (10020 "Smooth Operator") ... 15-25 59
(Stereo.)
MERCURY (70299 thru 71519) ... 10-20 54-59
MERCURY (71562 thru 72588) ... 6-12 60-66
ROULETTE ... 6-12 60-65
W.B. (49890 "Love Theme from Sharky's Machine") ... 3-5 81
Picture Sleeves
MERCURY (72300 "Sole Sole Sole") ... 8-12 65
EPs: 7-inch
ATLANTIC (527 "Sarah Vaughan Sings") ... 40-60 55
COLUMBIA ... 10-20 50-56
EMARCY (6000/6001 "Images") ... 20-40 54
(Price is for either volume.)
MGM (1020 "Tenderly") ... 20-40 52
MERCURY ... 10-20 53-61
REMINGTON ... 5-10
ROULETTE (1003 "Dreamy") ... 15-25 60
ROULETTE (1026/1027/1028 "The Divine One") ... 15-25 60
(Price is for any volume.)
ROYALE ... 5-10 '50s
LPs: 10/12-inch
ALLEGRO ... 5-10
ATLANTIC (16037 "Songs of the Beatles") ... 5-10 81
COLUMBIA (660 "After Hours") ... 50-75 55
COLUMBIA (745 "Sarah in Hi-Fi") ... 50-75 55
COLUMBIA (914 "Linger Awhile") ... 40-60 57
COLUMBIA (6133 "Sarah Vaughan") ... 75-125 50
(10-inch LP.)
COLUMBIA (37000 series) ... 5-8 82
CONCORD ... 15-25 56
CORONET ... 8-10 '60s
EMARCY (400 series) ... 8-12 77
EMARCY (1009 "Sarah Vaughan") ... 5-10 81
EMARCY (26005 "Images") ... 50-100 54
(10-inch LP.)
EMARCY (36004 "Sarah Vaughan") ... 50-75 54
EMARCY (36058 "In the Land of Hi-Fi") ... 50-75 55
EMARCY (36089 "Sassy Sarah") ... 50-75 56
EMARCY (36109 "Swingin' Easy") ... 50-75 57
(Repackage of *Images*.)
EVEREST ... 5-10 70-76
FORUM ... 8-12
GALAXY ... 8-12
GUEST STAR ... 8-12
HARMONY ... 5-15 59-69
MGM (165 "Tenderly") ... 75-125 51
(10-inch LP.)
MGM (544 "Sarah Vaughan Sings") ... 75-125 54
(10-inch LP.)
MGM (3274 "My Kinda Love") ... 50-100 55
MAINSTREAM ... 6-12 71-75
MERCURY (100 "Great Songs") ... 25-35 57
MERCURY (101 "Gershwin Songs") ... 25-35 57
MERCURY (1000 series) ... 5-8 82
MERCURY (20383 thru 20941) ... 20-40 58-64
(Monaural.)
MERCURY (21000 series) ... 15-25 65-67
(Monaural.)
MERCURY (25188 "Divine Sarah") ... 75-125 53
(10-inch LP)
MERCURY (60041 thru 60941) ... 20-40 59-64
(Stereo.)
MERCURY (61000 series) ... 15-25 65-67
(Stereo.)
METRO (539 "Tenderly") ... 8-15 65
MUSICO ... 10-15 69
MUSICRAFT ... 5-8 83-84
PABLO ... 5-10 78-82
PALACE ... 5-10
REMINGTON (1024 "Hot Jazz") ... 50-100 53
(10-inch LP.)
RIVERSIDE (2511 "Sarah Vaughan Sings") ... 40-60 55
RONDO (35 "Sarah Vaughan Sings") ... 20-40 59
RONDOLETTE (835 "Sarah Vaughan Sings") ... 20-40 59
ROULETTE (100 series) ... 8-15 71
ROULETTE (52046 "Dreamy") ... 20-40 60
ROULETTE (52060 "The Divine One") ... 20-40 60
ROULETTE (52070 "After Hours") ... 20-40 61
ROULETTE (52082 "You're Mine") ... 20-30 62
(Black vinyl.)
ROULETTE (52082 "You're Mine") ... 40-60 62
(Colored vinyl.)
ROULETTE (52091 "Snowbound") ... 20-30 62
ROULETTE (52092 "The Explosive Side of Sarah Vaughan") ... 20-30 63
ROULETTE (52100 "Star Eyes") ... 20-30 63
ROULETTE (52104 "Lonely Hours") ... 15-25 64
ROULETTE (52109 "The World of Sarah Vaughan") ... 15-25 64
ROULETTE (52112 "Sweet 'N' Sassy") ... 15-25 64
ROULETTE (52116 "Soulfully") ... 15-25 65
ROULETTE (52123 "Sarah Slightly Classical") ... 15-25 67
SCEPTER ... 5-10 74
SPIN-O-RAMA ... 8-12 '60s
SUTTON ... 5-10 '70s
TRIP ... 5-10 74-76
WING ... 5-15 63-68
Also see BASIE, Count, & Sarah Vaughan
Also see ECKSTINE, Billy, & Sarah Vaughan
Also see DIAMONDS / Georgia Gibbs / Sarah Vaughan / Florian Zabach
Also see LEGRAND, Michel
Also see WASHINGTON, Dinah / Joe Williams / Sarah Vaughan

VAUGHAN, Sarah, & Quincy Jones
LPs: 10/12-inch
MERCURY (20370 "Vaughan & Violins") . 20-30 59
(Monaural.)
MERCURY (60038 "Vaughan & Violins") . 30-40 59
(Stereo.)
Also see JONES, Quincy
Also see VAUGHAN, Sarah

VAUGHAN, Stevie Ray *LP '83*
(With Double Trouble)
Singles: 12-inch
EPIC ... 8-12 84-89
Singles: 7-inch
COLUMBIA ... 3-5 87
EPIC ... 4-8 83-95
LPs: 10/12-inch
EPIC (Except 8E8-39609) ... 10-15 83-95
EPIC (8E8-39609 "Couldn't Stand the Weather") ... 100-150 84
(Picture disc.)
Members: Stevie Ray Vaughan; Tommy Shannon; Chris Layton; Reese Wynans.
Also see CAST OF THOUSANDS
Also see CLARK, W.C., & Cobras
Also see COBRAS Featuring Stevie Ray Vaughan

VAUGHAN, Stevie Ray, & Dick Dale
Singles: 12-inch
COLUMBIA (2759 "Pipeline") ... 10-15 87
Singles: 7-inch
COLUMBIA (07340 "Pipeline") ... 4-6 87
Picture Sleeves
COLUMBIA (07340 "Pipeline") ... 4-8 87
Also see DALE, Dick

VAUGHN, Billy, Orchestra *P&R '54*
(With the Billy Vaughn Singers)
Singles: 78 rpm
DOT ... 3-5 54-57
Singles: 7-inch
ABC ... 4-6 74
DOT ... 5-15 54-70
PARAMOUNT ... 4-6 70-72
Picture Sleeves
DOT ... 5-15 58-67
EPs: 7-inch
DOT ... 5-10 55-59
LPs: 10/12-inch
ABC ... 5-8 74
DOT ... 10-25 55-70
HAMILTON ... 5-10 65-66
MCA ... 5-8 83
MISTLETOE ... 5-8 76
MUSICOR ... 5-8 77
PARAMOUNT ... 5-8 70-74
PICKWICK ... 5-10 68
RANWOOD ... 5-8 83
Also see BOONE, Pat
Also see BRENNAN, Walter
Also see FONTANE SISTERS
Also see HILLTOPPERS
Also see NORDINE, Ken
Also see STEVENS, Dodie
Also see STORM, Gale

VAUGHN, Bobby
Singles: 7-inch
WHIZ (503 "Good Good Lovin'") ... 25-35 57

VAUGHN, Dell
Singles: 7-inch
FORTUNE (205 "Rock the Universe") .. 400-500 60
HI-Q (5034 "Let Me Be Loved") ... 15-25 64

VAUGHN, Denny *P&R '56*
Singles: 78 rpm
KAPP (143 "Walk Hand in Hand") ... 5-10 56
Singles: 7-inch
GLORY (251 "If You Believe") ... 10-15 57
GLORY (256 "Since You Went Away") ... 10-15 57
GLORY (261 "Once Again") ... 10-15 57
GLORY (278 "My Lost Love") ... 10-15 58
GLORY (293 "Lovers Lament") ... 10-15 59
KAPP (143 "Walk Hand in Hand") ... 10-15 56

VAUGHN, Sammy, & Star Marks
Singles: 7-inch
STARDOM (0012 "Always Be Mine") ... 100-200

VAUGHN, Shirley
Singles: 7-inch
DOUBLE RR (246 "Watch Out Mr. Lonely") ... 10-20 66
FAIRMOUNT (1010 "You Don't Know") ... 10-20 66
FAIRMOUNT (1023 "Stop and Listen") ... 10-20 66

VAUGHN, Walter
Singles: 7-inch
DUCHESS (1001 "Down on My Knees") .. 10-15 61
(First issue.)
DUCHESS (1011 "White Silver Sands") ... 5-10 61
LIBERTY (55330 "Down on My Knees") ... 5-10 61

VAUGHN, Yvonne
Singles: 7-inch
DOT (16751 "Lonely Little Girl") ... 100-150 65
FABOR (132 "How Could They Know") ... 20-30 64

VAUGHT, Bob
(With the Renegades; with Renegaids; with Wheels)
Singles: 7-inch
BAMBOO (520 "Church Key Twist") ... 10-15 62
FELSTED (8682 "Doin' the Surf") ... 10-20 64
GNP ... 10-15 63
IMPACT (24 "Church Key Twist") ... 15-20 64
LPs: 10/12-inch
GNP (GNP-83 "Surf Crazy") ... 20-25 63
(Monaural.)
GNP (GNPS-83 "Surf Crazy") ... 25-30 63
(Stereo.)
Members: Bob Vaught; Dave Vaught; Jerry Feliciello; J. Gordon Smith; Neal Nissenson.
Also see RENEGADES

VEAL, Anita
Singles: 7-inch
SKY (201 "Daddy Let Me Go") ... 150-250

VECTORS
Singles: 7-inch
STANDARD (700 "One Day") ... 75-100 58

VEE, Bobby *P&R '59*
(With the Shadows; with Eligibles; with Strangers; with Crickets; with Johnny Mann Singers; Robert Thomas Velline)
Singles: 7-inch
COGNITO ... 4-6 81
LIBERTY (3331 "How Many Tears") ... 30-40 61
(Stereo Compact 33 Single.)
LIBERTY (55208 "Suzie Baby") ... 20-30 59
LIBERTY (55234 "What Do You Want") ... 10-20 60
LIBERTY (55251 "One Last Kiss") ... 10-20 60
LIBERTY (55270 "Devil Or Angel") ... 10-15 60
LIBERTY (55287 "Rubber Ball") ... 10-15 60
LIBERTY (55296 "Stayin' In") ... 10-15 61
LIBERTY (55325 "How Many Tears"/"Baby Face") ... 10-15 61
LIBERTY (55331 "How Many Tears"/"Bashful Bob") ... 10-15 61
LIBERTY (55354 "Take Good Care of My Baby") ... 10-15 61
LIBERTY (55388 "Run to Him") ... 10-15 61
LIBERTY (55419 "Please Don't Ask About Barbara") ... 10-15 62
LIBERTY (55451 "Sharing You") ... 10-15 62
LIBERTY (55517 "A Not So Merry Christmas") ... 10-15 62
LIBERTY (55521 "The Night Has a Thousand Eyes") ... 10-15 62
LIBERTY (55530 "Charms") ... 10-15 63
LIBERTY (55581 "Be True to Yourself") ... 8-12 63
LIBERTY (55636 "Yesterday and You") ... 8-12 63

LIBERTY (55654 "Stranger in Your Arms")....................5-10 63
LIBERTY (55670 "I'll Make You Mine").......5-10 64
LIBERTY (55700 "Hickory, Dick & Doc")....5-10 64
LIBERTY (55726 "Where Is She") 15-25 64
LIBERTY (55751 "Ev'ry Little Bit Hurts").....5-10 64
LIBERTY (55761 "Cross My Heart") 5-10 65
LIBERTY (55790 "Keep On Trying")...........5-10 65
LIBERTY (55828 "Take a Look Around Me")....................5-10 65
LIBERTY (55843 "The Story of My Life")....5-10 65
LIBERTY (55854 "Gone")........................5-10 65
LIBERTY (55877 "Look At Me Girl"/"Save a Love")....................5-10 66
LIBERTY (55877 "Butterfly"/"Save a Love")....................5-10 66
LIBERTY (55921 "Before You Go") 5-10 66
LIBERTY (55964 "Come Back When You Grow Up"/ "Swahili Serenade")....................5-10 67
LIBERTY (55964 "Come Back When You Grow Up"/ "That's All There Is to That") 5-10 67
LIBERTY (55982 "Come Back When You Grow Up"/ "Growing Pains")....................5-10 67
LIBERTY (55982 "Come Back When You Grow Up"/ "That's All There Is to That")....................5-10 67
LIBERTY (56009 "Beautiful People").........5-10 67
LIBERTY (56014 "Maybe Just Today").......5-10 68
LIBERTY (56033 "Hey Girl – My Girl")........5-10 68
LIBERTY (56057 "Do What You Gotta Do")....................5-10 68
LIBERTY (56080 "I'm into Lookin' for Someone to Love Me")....................5-10 68
LIBERTY (56096 "Santa Cruz") 5-10 68
LIBERTY (56124 "Let's Call It a Day Girl") .5-10 69
LIBERTY (56149 "In and Out of Love") 5-10 69
LIBERTY (56178 "No Obligations").............5-10 69
LIBERTY (56208 "Sweet Sweetheart")........5-10 70
SHADYBROOK....................4-8 75-77
SOMA (1110 "Suzie Baby")................. 100-150 59
U.A. 4-8 71-78

Picture Sleeves

LIBERTY (55270 "Devil Or Angel")......... 10-20 60
LIBERTY (55287 "Rubber Ball").............. 10-20 60
LIBERTY (55296 "Stayin' In").................. 10-20 61
LIBERTY (55325 "How Many Tears"/"Baby Face")....................10-20 61
LIBERTY (55419 "Please Don't Ask About Barbara")....................10-20 62
LIBERTY (55530 "Charms").................... 10-20 63
LIBERTY (55581 "Be True to Yourself").. 10-15 63
LIBERTY (55654 "Stranger in Your Arms") 10-15 63
LIBERTY (56014 "Maybe Just Today")........8-12 68

EPs: 7-inch

LIBERTY (1006 "Devil Or Angel")........... 25-35 60
LIBERTY (1010 "Bobby Vee's Hits")........ 25-35 61
LIBERTY (1013 "Bobby Vee").................. 25-35 62
U.A. (85 "Nothin' Like a Sunny Day")....... 10-12 72

LPs: 10/12-inch

LIBERTY (3165 "Bobby Vee Sings Your Favorites")....................25-35 60
(Monaural.)
LIBERTY (3181 "Bobby Vee")................. 25-35 61
(Monaural.)
LIBERTY (3186 "With Strings & Things") 25-35 61
(Monaural.)
LIBERTY (3205 "Hits of the Rockin' '50s") 25-35 61
(Monaural.)
LIBERTY (3211 "Take Good Care of My Baby") 25-35 61
(Monaural.)
LIBERTY (3232 "Bobby Vee Recording Session")....................25-35 62
(Monaural.)
LIBERTY (3245 "Golden Greats")............ 25-35 62
(Monaural.)
LIBERTY (3267 "Merry Christmas")......... 25-35 62
(Monaural.)
LIBERTY (3285 "The Night Has a Thousand Eyes")....................25-35 63
(Monaural.)
LIBERTY (3336 "I Remember Buddy Holly")....................25-35 63
(Monaural.)
LIBERTY (3352 "The New Sound from England") 25-35 64
(Monaural.)
LIBERTY (3385 "30 Big Hits from the '60s")....................20-30 64
(Two discs. Monaural.)
LIBERTY (3393 "Live On Tour") 20-25 65
(Monaural.)
LIBERTY (3448 "30 Big Hits from the '60s")....................20-25 66
(Two discs. Monaural.)
LIBERTY (3464 "Golden Greats, Vol. 2") .20-25 66
(Monaural.)
LIBERTY (3480 "Look At Me Girl") 15-25 66
(Monaural.)
LIBERTY (3534 "Come Back When You Grow Up") 15-25 67
(Monaural.)
LIBERTY (7165 "Bobby Vee Sings Your Favorites") 35-45 60
(Stereo.)
LIBERTY (7181 "Bobby Vee")..................35-45 61
(Stereo.)
LIBERTY (7186 "With Strings & Things") .35-45 61
(Stereo.)
LIBERTY (7205 "Hits of the Rockin' '50s")....................35-45 61
(Stereo.)
LIBERTY (7211 "Take Good Care of My Baby") 35-45 61
(Stereo.)
LIBERTY (7232 "Bobby Vee Recording Session")....................30-40 62
(Stereo.)
LIBERTY (7245 "Golden Greats")............30-40 62
(Stereo.)
LIBERTY (7267 "Merry Christmas")..........30-40 62
(Stereo.)
LIBERTY (7285 "The Night Has a Thousand Eyes")....................30-40 63
(Stereo.)
LIBERTY (7336 "I Remember Buddy Holly")....................30-40 63
(Stereo.)
LIBERTY (7352 "The New Sound from England") 25-35 64
(Stereo.)
LIBERTY (7385 "30 Big Hits from the '60s")....................25-35 64
(Two discs. Stereo.)
LIBERTY (7393 "Live On Tour") 20-30 65
(Stereo.)
LIBERTY (7448 "30 Big Hits from the '60s")....................20-30 66
(Two discs. Stereo.)
LIBERTY (7464 "Golden Greats, Vol. 2") .20-30 65
(Stereo.)
LIBERTY (7480 "Look At Me Girl") 15-25 66
(Stereo.)
LIBERTY (7534 "Come Back When You Grow Up")....................15-25 67
(Stereo.)
LIBERTY (7554 "Just Today")..................10-20 68
LIBERTY (7592 "Do What You Gotta Do")....................10-20 68
LIBERTY (7612 "Gates, Grills and Railings")....................10-20 69
LIBERTY (10223 "I Remember Buddy Holly")....................5-10 84
SUNSET (1162 "A Forever Kind of Love")....................10-20 67
(Monaural.)
SUNSET (1186 "Christmas Album").........10-20 67
(Monaural.)
SUNSET (5162 "A Forever Kind of Love")....................10-20 67
(Stereo.)
SUNSET (5186 "Christmas Album").........10-20 67
(Stereo.)
U.A. (25-G2 "Legendary Masters").......250-350 73
(Includes bound-in booklet. Withdrawn before release, with only two or three copies surviving.)
U.A. (332 "Very Best")....................8-10 73
U.A. (1008 "Golden Greats")....................5-10 80
Members (Shadows): Bill Velline; Bob Korum; Jim Stillman; Dick Dunkirk; Ken Harvey.
Session: Johnny Mann Singers.
Also see ASSOCIATION / Bobby Vee / Mike Love / Mary MacGregor
Also see DE SHANNON, Jackie / Bobby Vee / Eddie Hodges
Also see DUNKIRK, Dick, & Strangers
Also see MANN, Johnny, Singers
Also see STRANGERS
Also see VELINE, Bill, & Shadows

VEE, Bobby / Johnny Burnette / Fleetwoods

LPs: 10/12-inch

LIBERTY (5503 "Teensville")....................20-30 61
Also see BURNETTE, Johnny
Also see FLEETWOODS

VEE, Bobby, & Crickets LP '62

Singles: 7-inch

LIBERTY (55479 "Punish Her") 15-20 62

Picture Sleeves

LIBERTY (55479 "Punish Her") 15-25 62

LPs: 10/12-inch

LIBERTY (3228 "Bobby Vee Meets the Crickets")....................20-25 62
(Monaural.)
LIBERTY (7228 "Bobby Vee Meets the Crickets")....................25-30 62
(Stereo.)
Also see CRICKETS

VEE, Bobby / Diamonds / Drifters

Singles: 7-inch

MINDSCAPE ("Mindscape and Rock'n'roll Are Here to Stay")....................5-10 84
(Soundsheet. Promotional issue only.)
Also see DIAMONDS
Also see DRIFTERS

VEE, Bobby, & Ventures LP '63

LPs: 10/12-inch

LIBERTY (3289 "Bobby Vee Meets the Ventures")....................20-25 63
(Monaural.)
LIBERTY (7289 "Bobby Vee Meets the Ventures")....................25-30 63
(Stereo.)
Also see VEE, Bobby
Also see VENTURES

VEE, Cee

Singles: 7-inch

CARROLTON (800 "Lonely Street").......75-100

VEE, George, & Nephews

Singles: 7-inch

PINK (1012 "Please Be Mine") 15-25

VEE, Joey, & Raiders

Singles: 7-inch

CORDE (1240 "Place Called Love").....150-250
PROMOTIONAL (102 "Acts of Love") 50-75 62

VEE, Rickey

Singles: 7-inch

JET STREAM (723 "Pretty Girls")..............5-10 65

VEE-JAYS

Singles: 7-inch

RICHIE (456 "Don't Let Me Go")..............40-50 61

VEERS, Russ

Singles: 7-inch

TREND (30010 "Warm As Toast")........300-400 58

VEGA, Carol

Singles: 7-inch

ARGO (5490 "One Little Thing")...............10-15 65
CONSTELLATION (121 "I Need You Around")....................10-15 64

VEGAS, Lolly

Singles: 7-inch

AUDIO INTERNATIONAL (202 "It's Love")....................25-35 61
Also see VEGAS, Pat & Lolly

VEGAS, Pat

Singles: 7-inch

LUTE (6014 "I Wanna Be a Movie Star") .10-20 61
UNITY....................10-20
Also see PAT & WILDCATS
Also see REDBONE
Also see SHARKS
Also see VEGAS, Pat & Lolly

VEGAS, Pat, & Lolly

Singles: 7-inch

APOGEE (101 "The Robot Walk")...........10-20 64
MERCURY (72509 "Let's Get It On") 8-12 65
REPRISE (20199 "Boom Boom Boom")...10-15 63

LPs: 10/12-inch

MERCURY (21059 "Pat & Lolly Vegas at the Haunted House")....................25-35 66
(Monaural.)
MERCURY (61059 "Pat & Lolly Vegas at the Haunted House")....................30-40 66
(Stereo.)
Members: Pat Vasquez; Lolly Vasquez.
Session: Leon Russell.
Also see AVANTIES
Also see INDIVIDUALS
Also see REDBONE
Also see RUSSELL, Leon
Also see SHARKS
Also see VEGAS, Lolly
Also see VEGAS, Pat

V-EIGHTS
(V-8's)

Singles: 7-inch

ABC-PAR (10201 "My Heart") 8-12 61
AURA (101 "Chasin' the Blues")..............15-25 58
MOST (713 "Please Come Back").........75-125 59
VIBRO (4005 "My Heart") 100-200 60
VIBRO (4006 "Everything That You Said")....................150-250 61
Also see JACKSON, Stoney

VEJTABLES P&R '65

Singles: 7-inch

AUTUMN (15 "I Still Love You") 8-12 65
AUTUMN (23 "Mansion of Tears") 8-12 65
UPTOWN (741 "Feel the Music") 5-10 67

VEL-AIRES
(Bel-Aires)

Singles: 78 rpm

FLIP (303 "This Paradise") 10-15 54

Singles: 7-inch

FLIP (303 "This Paradise") 20-30 54
Also see BEL-AIRES
Also see WOODS, Donald

VEL AIRES

Singles: 7-inch

DINO (100 "Forever Always")..............400-500 61

VELAIRES P&R '61

Singles: 7-inch

JAMIE (1198 "Roll Over Beethoven"/ "Brazil")....................10-20 61
(First issued as by the Flairs.)
JAMIE (1198 "Roll Over Beethoven"/"Frankie & Johnny") 10-20 61
JAMIE (1203 "Dream")............................10-15 61
JAMIE (1211 "Ubangi Stomp") 8-12 62
JAMIE (1223 "Memory Tree")..................10-15 62
MERCURY (72924 "Yes, I Love You").......5-10 69
PALMS (730 "Summertime Blues")..........30-60 61
RAMCO (1983 "I Found a Love") 5-10 67
Members: Bob Dawdy; Danny Matousek; Jerry De Mers; Don Bourret.
Also see FLAIRS
Also see SCREAMERS

VELAIRES

Singles: 7-inch

HI MAR (9173/9174 "Yes It Was Me"/"I Could Have Cried")....................10-15 65
Members: Denny Sweigart; Terry Gehman; Bob Peachy; Berry Shelly.

VELAIRS

Singles: 7-inch

MGM (12667 "Don't Tell Tales Out of School")....................10-15 58

VELEZ, Martha LP '76

Singles: 7-inch

MCA....................3-5 80
POLYDOR....................4-6 73
SIRE....................4-6 69-77

LPs: 10/12-inch

SIRE (6040 "American Heartbeat")............8-10 76
SIRE (7000 series)....................8-10 74-76
SIRE (97008 "Friends & Angels")............10-12 69

VELEZ, Martha, & Pete Wingfield

Singles: 7-inch

SIRE (722 "Mockingbird") 4-6 75

VELIA, Tania

Singles: 7-inch

WARWICK (528 "Ja-Ma-I-Ca")..................5-10 60

VELLA, Tony
Singles: 7-inch
HI-Q (5047 "Danny's Polka")........5-10 65

VELLINE, Bill, & Shadows
Singles: 7-inch
VEE (1001 "Leave Me Alone")........50-75 60
Also see VEE, Bobby

VELLO, Lee
Singles: 7-inch
UNIVERSAL ARTISTS (2562 "Teenagers Love")........10-15 58

VELLS
(Vandellas)
Singles: 7-inch
MEL-O-DY (103 "There He Is")........30-40 62
Members: Gloria Williamson; Martha Reeves; Annette Beard; Rosalind Ashford.
Also see DEL-PHIS
Also see MARTHA & VANDELLAS

VEL-MARS
Singles: 7-inch
CONTINENTAL ARTS........5-10 64

VELONS
Singles: 7-inch
BJM (6568 "Summer Love")........5-10 68
BJM (6569 "That's All Right")........5-10 68
BLAST (216 "From the Chapel")........40-60 64
Members: Patsy Bello; Tom Scott; Ray Vitolo; Ron Auriemma; Paul Auriemma.

VELOURS *P&R '57*
(With the Sammy Lowe Orchestra)
Singles: 78 rpm
ONYX........50-100 56-57
Singles: 7-inch
CLASSIC ARTISTS (136 "I Apologize")........3-5 94
(Red vinyl. 900 made.)
CLASSIC ARTISTS (136 "I Apologize")........8-10 94
(Red vinyl. Promotional issue only. 100 made.)
CUB (9001 "Can I Walk You Home")........10-15 58
CUB (9014 "I'll Never Smile Again")........10-15 58
CUB (9029 "Blue Velvet")........10-15 59
END (1090 "Lover Come Back")........10-15 61
GOLDISC (3012 "Sweet Sixteen")........10-20 60
GONE (5092 "Can I Come Over Tonight")........10-15 60
ONYX (501 "My Love Come Back")........200-300 56
ONYX (508 "Romeo")........750-1000 57
ONYX (512 "Can I Come Over Tonight")........75-150 57
ONYX (515 "This Could Be the Night")........40-60 57
ONYX (520 "Can I Walk You Home")........75-125 58
(Promotional issue only.)
ONYX (520 "Can I Walk You Home")........40-60 58
(Black and orange label.)
ONYX (520 "Can I Walk You Home")........50-75 58
(Green label.)
ORBIT (9001 "Can I Walk You Home")........25-35 58
(Green or red label.)
RELIC (502 "Romeo")........5-10 64
RELIC (503 "My Love Come Back")........5-10 64
RELIC (504 "Can I Come Over Tonight")........5-10 64
RELIC (516 "This Could Be the Night")........5-10 64
ROULETTE........4-6 '70s
STUDIO (9902 "I Promise")........25-35 59
Members: Jerome Ramos; Pete Winston; John Pearson; Don Heywoode; John Cheatdom; Charles Moffett; Keith Williams; Troyce Key.
Also see KEY, Troyce
Also see LOWE, Sammy, Orchestra

VELOURS
Singles: 7-inch
MGM (13780 "Don't Pity Me")........20-30 67
RONA (010 "Woman for Me")........10-20 66

VELS
(With the Tim Whitsett Imperials)
Singles: 7-inch
TREBCO (702 "Please Be Mine")........100-150 61
Also see WHITSETT, Tim, & Imperials

VELS
Singles: 7-inch
AMY (881 "Do the Walk")........20-30 63

VEL-TONES
Singles: 7-inch
FEE BEE (1 "Broken Heart")........4-6 '80s
GOLDWAX (301 "Darling")........10-15
VEL (9178 "Broken Heart")........1000-2000 58
(Identification number shown since no selection number is used.)

VEL-TONES
(With the Blue Shields)
Singles: 7-inch
COY (101 "Playboy")........100-200 58
KAPP (268 "Playboy")........40-50 59

VELTONES
Singles: 7-inch
JIN (107 "Take a Ride")........5-10 59
JIN (115 "I'm Your Fool")........5-10 59

VELTONES
Singles: 7-inch
MERCURY (71526 "Fool in Love")........20-30 59
SATELLITE (100 "Fool in Love")........125-175 59
(First issue.)

VELTONES
(With Al Brown & His Band; Vel-Tones)
Singles: 7-inch
LOST NITE (103 "Now")........20-30 61
(First issue.)
LOST NITE (103 "Now")........40-50 61
(Red vinyl.)
ZARA (901 "Now")........40-50 61
Also see BROWNE, Al

VELTONES
Singles: 7-inch
WEDGE (1013 "I Want to Know")........100-200 64

VELUZAT, Renaud
Singles: 7-inch
DIXIE (880 "Race Track Boogie")........50-75
SUNDOWN (1001 "Surf Zone")........10-20 '60s

VELVATEENS
Singles: 7-inch
VELVET (1001 "Please Don't Let Me Go")........15-25

VELVATONES
Singles: 7-inch
METEOR (5042 "Real Gone Baby")........100-200 57

VELVATONES
(With Richmond's Lil Walters Band)
Singles: 7-inch
NU KAT (110 "Impossible")........40-50 59

VELVATONES / Continentals
Singles: 7-inch
CANDLELITE (412 "Impossible")........5-10 63
(Black vinyl.)
CANDLELITE (412 "Impossible")........8-12 63
(Red vinyl.)
Also see VELVATONES
Also see CONTINENTAL 5

VELVATONES FIVE
Singles: 7-inch
KODIAK (1601 "Freeloader")........10-20 63

VELVEDERES
Singles: 7-inch
COBRA (1601 "Daiquiri")........8-12 63

VELVELETTES *P&R/R&B '64*
Singles: 7-inch
I.P.G. (1002 "There He Goes")........50-75 63
SOUL (35025 "These Things Will Keep Me Loving You")........10-20 66
V.I.P. (25007 "Needle in a Haystack")........10-25 64
V.I.P. (25013 "He Was Really Saying Something")........10-25 64
V.I.P. (25017 "Lonely, Lonely Girl Am I")........10-25 65
V.I.P. (25021 "Bird in the Hand")........300-500 66
V.I.P. (25030 "Bird in the Hand")........15-25 66
V.I.P. (25034 "These Things Will Keep Me Loving You")........15-25 66
Members: Carolyn Gill, Sandra Tilley; Betty Kelly; Bertha McNeal; Mildred Gill; Norma Barbee.
Also see BARBEES
Also see MARTHA & VANDELLAS

VELVET, Chuck
Singles: 7-inch
U.S.A. (1224 "Red Lipstick")........8-12 60

VELVET, Jimmy *P&R '63*
(Jimmy Velvet Five; James Velvet; Jimmy Velvit; Jimmy Tennant)
Singles: 7-inch
ABC-PAR (10488 "We Belong Together")........10-20 63
ABC-PAR (10528 "To the Aisle")........10-20 64
ABNAK (108 "Donna")........8-12 65
BELL (692 "A Woman in Bloom")........5-10 67
CAMEO (464 "Take Me Tonight")........15-25 67
CAMEO (488 "Roses Are Blue")........10-15 67
CORREC-TONE (502 "When I Needed You")........50-100 62
CUB (9100 "Look at Me")........10-15 61
CUB (9105 "We Belong Together")........10-15 61
CUB (9111 "Bouquet of Flowers")........10-15 62
DIVISION (102 "Look at Me")........20-30 61
(First issue.)
MUSIC CITY........4-8 70
NOSTALGIA (102 "Shop Around")........4-6 73
PHILIPS (40285 "It's Almost Tomorrow")........10-15 65
PHILIPS (40314 "Young Hearts")........10-15 65
ROYAL AMERICAN (286 "It's You")........5-10 69
ROYAL AMERICAN (291 "Missing You")........5-10 69
SUNDI........4-6 71
TOLLIE (9037 "Teen Angel")........10-15 64
U.A. (50272 "Good, Good Lovin' ")........10-20 68
U.A. (50279 "Candy Heart")........10-20 68
VELVET (201 "We Belong Together")........50-75 61
VELVET TONE (101 "Teen Angel")........15-25 64
VELVET TONE (102 "It's Almost Tomorrow")........15-25 64
(First issue.)
VELVET TONE (112 "Candy Heart")........10-20 67
VELVET TONE (114 "Good, Good Lovin' ")........10-20 68
WITCH (115 "We Belong Together")........10-20 63
EPs: 7-inch
VELVET TONE (201 "Golden Hits")........15-25 '60s
LPs: 10/12-inch
MUSIC CITY (502 "Jimmy Velvet with Kathy Scott")........10-15 73
U.A. (6653 "A Touch of Velvet")........15-25 68
VELVET TONE (501 "A Touch of Velvet")........20-30 68
Note: Though the artist shown on Bi, Blue, and Teardrop releases is Jimmy Velvet, the singer is actually Jimmy Velvit. Those issues are in his section.
Also see TENNANT, Jimmy
Also see VELVET VIEW
Also see VELVIT, Jimmy

VELVET ANGELS
Singles: 7-inch
CO-OP (201 "I'm in Love")........5-10 65
MEDIEVAL (201 "I'm in Love")........8-12 64
MEDIEVAL (207 "Baby I Wanna Know")........8-12 64
LPs: 10/12-inch
RELIC........10-15

VELVET CREST
Singles: 7-inch
BOLD (8732 "Na Na Song")........15-20
HARBOUR (303 "Song of the Rain")........5-10 69
LIBERTY (56141 "Gotta Make You Mine')........5-10 69

VELVET HAMMER
Singles: 7-inch
EPIC (10617 "Sun")........4-8 70
EPIC (10664 "Didn't It Rain")........4-8 70
PACEMAKER (752 "Hey Joe Soul")........10-15

VELVET ILLUSIONS
(Georgy & Velvet Illusions)
Singles: 7-inch
METRO MEDIA (307 "Acid Head")........25-30 67
METRO MEDIA (308 "Town of Fools")........15-25 67
METRO MEDIA (309 "Velvet Illusions")........20-25 67
METRO MEDIA (311 "Mini Shimmy")........20-25 67
TELL INT'L (700 "Acid Head")........30-40 67

VELVET KEYS
Singles: 7-inch
KING (5090 "My Baby's Gone")........50-60 57
KING (5109 "The Truth About Youth")........40-50 58

VELVET NIGHT
Singles: 7-inch
METROMEDIA (110 "Velvet Night")........4-6 69
LPs: 10/12-inch
METROMEDIA (1026 "Velvet Night")........10-15 70

VELVET SATINS
Singles: 7-inch
GENERAL AMERICAN (006 "Nothing Can Compare to You")........30-50 65
GENERAL AMERICAN (716 "Cherry")........15-25 64
GENERAL AMERICAN (720 "Angel Adorable")........20-30 64
Also see CAPRI, Bobby

VELVET SOUNDS
(With the Cosmopolites; "Featuring Oliver Johnson & Earl Robbins")
Singles: 78 rpm
COSMOPOLITAN........250-500 53
Singles: 7-inch
COSMOPOLITAN (101 "Silver Star")........1500-2500 53
(Red vinyl.)
COSMOPOLITAN (105 "Pretty Darling")........1000-2000 53
COSMOPOLITAN (530 "Sing a Song of Christmas Cheer")........1000-2000 53
Members: Oliver Johnson; Earl Robbins.

VELVET UNDERGROUND *LP '68*
Singles: 12-inch
POLYGRAM........5-10 85
Singles: 7-inch
ASPEN ("Loop")........20-40 66
(Single-sided soundsheet. Promotional issue only.)
COTILLION (44107 "Who Loves the Sun")........20-40 71
INDEX ("Interview")........30-50 67
(Single-sided picture disc soundsheet. Promotional issue only.)
MGM (14057 "What Goes On")........25-50 69
VERVE (10560 "White Light"/"White Heat")........150-250 68
(Blue label.)
VERVE (10560 "White Light"/"White Heat")........100-150 68
(White label. Promotional issue only.)
LPs: 10/12-inch
COTILLION (9034 "Loaded")........15-20 70
COTILLION (9500 "Live")........15-20 70
MGM (131 "Velvet Underground")........8-10 71
MGM (4617 "Velvet Underground")........15-25 69
MGM (4617 "Velvet Underground")........250-350 69
(White label. Promotional issue only.)
MGM (4950 "Archetypes")........10-15 74
MERCURY (7504 "Velvet Underground")........12-15 72
PRIDE........10-15 73
VERVE (5046 "White Light"/"White Heat")........30-40 67
VERVE (800000 series)........5-10 84-85
Members: Lou Reed; John Cale; Sterling Morrison; Maureen Tucker; Doug Yule.
Also see REED, Lou

VELVET UNDERGROUND & NICO *LP '67*
Singles: 7-inch
VERVE (10427 "All Tomorrow's Parties")........300-400 66
(Blue label.)
VERVE (10427 "All Tomorrow's Parties")........100-150 66
(White label. Promotional issue only.)
VERVE (10466 "Sunday Morning")........150-250 66
(Blue label.)
VERVE (10466 "Sunday Morning")........75-100 66
(Promotional issue only.)
Picture Sleeves
VERVE (10427 "All Tomorrow's Parties")........4500-5000 66
(Promotional issue only.)
LPs: 10/12-inch
VERVE (5008 "Velvet Underground & Nico")........500-1000 67
(Monaural. With banana sticker on front cover. Back cover pictures an upside-down torso of a man behind the photo of Andy Warhol. Thus far, all copies meeting this description have been mono.)
VERVE (5008 "Velvet Underground & Nico")........50-100 67
(Stereo. With adhesive banana sticker on front cover. If a stereo copy with the upside-down male torso photo behind Andy Warhol exists, its value would approximately double.)
VERVE (5008 "Velvet Underground & Nico")........100-150 67
(With banana sticker on front cover. Back cover has a

sticker above the photo of the group on stage, which reads: "The Velvet Underground & Nico.")
VERVE (5008 "Velvet Underground & Nico")....................30-60 '60s
(With adhesive banana sticker on front cover. Does not picture the upside-down male torso.)
VERVE (5008 "Velvet Underground & Nico")....................40-60 67
(No banana sticker on front cover.)
VERVE (800000 series)....................5-10 84
Also see NICO
Also see VELVET UNDERGROUND

VELVET VIEW

Singles: 7-inch

VELVET TONE (444 "We Belong Together")....................5-10 69
Member: Jimmy Velvet.
Also see VELVET, Jimmy

VELVETEENS
("Ronnie Baker with Monty & the Specialties")

Singles: 7-inch

GOLDEN ARTISTS....................5-10 65
LAURIE (3126 "I Thank You")....................8-12 62
STARK (102 "Teen Prayer")....................20-30 61
(Has only "Stark" at top. *Teen Prayer* is *Please Holy Father* retitled.)
STARK (102 "Teen Prayer")....................15-20 61
(Reads: "Stark Records" at top.)
STARK (102 "Teen Prayer")....................10-15 61
(Reads: "Stark Distributed By Triway Record Co." at top.)
STARK (105 "I Thank You")....................15-25 61
STARK (12591 "Please Holy Father")....................50-75 60
(First issue.)
VELVET (1001 "Please Don't Let Me Go")....................10-20 63

VELVETEERS

Singles: 78 rpm

MANOR (1190 "Fine Like Wine")....................75-125 49
SPITFIRE (15 "Tell Me You're Mine")..300-400 56

Singles: 7-inch

SPITFIRE (15 "Tell Me You're Mine")....................3000-4000 56

VELVETIERS

Singles: 7-inch

RIC (958 "Oh Baby")....................100-200 58

VELVETONES

Singles: 78 rpm

COLUMBIA (30206 "How I Miss You")....25-35 50
COLUMBIA (30224 "I'm Disillusioned")...25-35 50
CORONET (1 "One Day")....................20-30 46
CORONET (2 "Sweet Lorraine")....................20-30 46
CORONET (3 "Swing Out, It Don't Cost Nothing")....................20-30 46
CORONET (4 "Don't Say You're Sorry Again")....................20-30 46
CORONET (5 "Singing River")....................20-30 46
RONDO (1554 "Can You Look Me in the Eyes")....................15-25 49
SAVOY (991 "Don't Say You're Sorry")........4-8
(Previously unreleased.)
SONORA (2014 "Ask Anyone Who Knows")....................20-30 47
SONORA (2015 "Can You Look Me in the Eyes")....................20-30 47
SONORA (3010 "It's Written All Over Your Face")....................20-30 46
SONORA (3012 "It Just Ain't Right")........20-30 46
SUPER DISC (1055 "Find My Baby Blues")....................15-25 48

VELVETONES
(With Tommy Hudson & Savoys)

Singles: 78 rpm

ALADDIN....................100-200 57

Singles: 7-inch

ALADDIN (3372 "Glory of Love")..........75-125 57
(Address shows Beverly Hills, Ca.)
ALADDIN (3372 "Glory of Love")..........30-40 57
(Address shows Los Angeles, Ca.)
ALADDIN (3372 "Glory of Love")..........15-25 57
(Black label.)
ALADDIN (3391 "I Found My Love")......75-125 57
ALADDIN (3463 "My Every Thought").100-150 60
(Black label.)
D (1049 "Come Back")....................50-75 59
D (1072 "Worried Over You")....................40-50 59
DEB (1008 "Who Took My Girl")..........150-200 59
IMPERIAL (5878 "Glory of Love")..........10-15 62
IMPERIAL (66020 "Glory of Love")..........5-10 64
Member: J.R. Bailey.

VELVETONES

Singles: 7-inch

ASCOT (2117 "Yes I Will")....................8-12 62
ASCOT (2126 "Starry Eyes")....................10-15 63

VELVETONES

Singles: 7-inch

GLENN (309 "Doheny Run")....................15-25 63
VELVET (101 "Doheny Run")....................20-30 63

VELVETONES

Singles: 7-inch

G.A.R.P. (102 "Mister X")....................15-25 65
(Black vinyl.)
G.A.R.P. (102 "Mister X")....................30-50 65
(Colored vinyl.)

VELVETONES

Singles: 7-inch

VERVE (10514 "What Can the Matter Be")....................5-10 67

VELVETONES

Singles: 7-inch

JAC-OBE ("Beetle Walk")....................10-20 '60s
(Selection number not known.)

VELVETONES

Singles: 7-inch

VANDA (0001 "Reaching for a Rainbow")....................15-25

VELVETS

Singles: 78 rpm

FURY....................25-50 58
PILGRIM....................15-25 56
RED ROBIN....................20-50 53-54

Singles: 7-inch

EVENT (4285 "At Last")....................8-12 58
FURY (1012 "I-I-I")....................20-30 58
PILGRIM (706 "At Last")....................10-15 56
PILGRIM (710 "I Cried")....................10-15 56
RED ROBIN (120 "They Tried")..........75-125 53
RED ROBIN (122 "At Last")..........75-125 53
RED ROBIN (127 "I Cried")..........50-100 54
Members: Charles Sampson; Berle Ashton; Don Raysor; Joe Raysor. Session: Ray Stevens; Boots Randolph.

VELVETS / Wade Flemmons

Singles: 7-inch

OLDIES 45 (119 "I"/"Woops Now")..........4-6 '60s
Also see FLEMONS, Wade
Also see VELVETS

VELVETS P&R '61
("Featuring Virgil Johnson")

Singles: 7-inch

MONUMENT (435 "That Lucky Old Sun")....................20-30 61
MONUMENT (441 "Tonight")....................10-20 61
MONUMENT (448 "Laugh")....................20-30 61
MONUMENT (458 "The Love Express")..10-15 62
MONUMENT (464 "The Lights Go On, the Lights Go Off")....................10-15 62
MONUMENT (500 series)....................5-8 63
(Oldies reissue series.)
MONUMENT (810 "Crying in the Chapel")....................20-30 63
MONUMENT (836 "Nightmare")..........15-25 64
MONUMENT (861 "If")....................5-10 64
MONUMENT (961 "Let the Fool Kiss You")....................5-10 66
PLAID (101 "Everybody Knows")..........30-40 59
(Features Jerry Sharell. Reissued the following year by Jerry Sharell.)
20TH FOX (165 "Happy Days Are Here Again")....................15-25 59
Members: Virgil Johnson; Will Soloman; Mark Prince; Bob Thursby; Clarence Rigby; Jerry Sharell; Steve Novosel.
Also see SHARELL, Jerry

VEL-VETS

Singles: 7-inch

DORE (774 "Ride in a Rocket")..........8-12 66
20TH FOX (6676 "What Now My Love")..15-25 67

VELVIT, Jimmy
(Jimmy Velvet; James Mullins)

Singles: 7-inch

ALTA....................10-20 62
BI....................5-10 '60s
BLUE....................5-10 '60s
SHANE....................5-10 '60s
STARTIME (103 "Wisdom of a Fool")......10-20 61
TEARDROP....................5-10 '60s

LPs: 10/12-inch

TEARDROP....................15-25 '60s
Note: Though shown as Jimmy Velvet on Bi, Blue, and Teardrop, the singer is James Mullins a.k.a. Jimmy Velvit.
Also see HENDRICKS, Bobby
Also see VELVET, Jimmy

VELVITONES

Singles: 7-inch

MILMART (113 "Little Girl I Love You So")....................200-300 59

VENABLE, Ray
(With the Ray Gregory Orchestra)

Singles: 7-inch

KELTONE INT'L (1001 "Monorail Holiday")....................8-10 63

VENDORS

Singles: 7-inch

VICTORIO (128 "Where All Lovers Meet")....................450-650 63
(Actually a '62 Invictors' issue [TPE 8221] but with the Victorio/Vendors label on top.)
Also see INVICTORS

VENDORS

Singles: 7-inch

MGM (13133 "Stepping Stones")..........5-10 63

VENEERS

Singles: 7-inch

PRINCETON (102 "Believe Me")..........30-40 60
TREYCO (402 "With All My Love")..........20-30 63
Also see CHANTELS

VENET, Nick

Singles: 7-inch

DECCA (31939 "Theme from Out of Sight")....................5-10 66
IMPERIAL (5522 Love in Be-Bop Time").30-50 58

EPs: 7-inch

RCA (4100 "Flippin' ")....................20-30 57

LPs: 10/12-inch

DECCA (4751 "Out of Sight")..........15-20 66
MIRA (3004 "Skatedater")..........15-20 66

VENET, Steve

Singles: 7-inch

DORE (557 "Teen Age Prayer")..........10-15 60
Also see STEVE & DONNA / Steve Venet

VENOM

Singles: 7-inch

IOM (1 "Acid Queen")....................15-20 83
(Picture disc.)

VENSON, Darlene

Singles: 7-inch

SOMA (1195 "I've Got a Secret")..........8-12 '60s

VENTRILLS

Singles: 7-inch

IVANHOE (5000 "Confusion")..........15-25 67
(First issue.)
LITTLE FORT....................10-20 65-67
PARKWAY (141 "Confusion")..........8-12 67
Members: Frank Vale Ellefson; Jan Hassman; Dave Lexington Hansen; Bob Bellard; Tommy Lee; Donnie Ray Rousch.
Also see LITTLE KIDS

VENTSHA, Ralph
(With the Red Julian Quartet)

Singles: 7-inch

VISTONE (2019 "Listen to Me")..........10-20 61

VENTURA, Ben, with Guys & Doll

Singles: 7-inch

STARDUST (1002 "Head & Shoulders")..10-20

VENTURA, Carol

Singles: 7-inch

CAPITOL (4782 "Mr. Muscles")..........5-10 62
CAPITOL (4840 "I Am")..........5-10 62
PRESTIGE (410 "You've Got Possibilities")....................5-10 66
ROULETTE (4396 "I Wish You Love").......5-10 61

LPs: 10/12-inch

PRESTIGE (7405 "I Love to Sing")..........10-15 66

VENTURA, Jesse

Singles: 12-inch

RHINO (6000 "The Body")..........10-20 '80s
(Picture disc.)
TWIN TONE (8442 "Body Rules")..........10-20 84
(Picture disc.)

VENTURAS

Singles: 7-inch

DONNA (1352 "Corrido Twist")..........10-20 62
SUGAR (223 "Corrido Twist")..........15-25 61

VENTURAS

Singles: 7-inch

DRUM BOY (107 "Ram-Charger")..........15-25 64

LPs: 10/12-inch

DRUM BOY (DB-1003 "Here They Are").50-75 64
(Monaural.)
DRUM BOY (DBS-1003 "Here They Are")....................100-150 64
(Stereo.)
Members: Ken Ciezek; Jim Radomski; Roman Woprych; Roger Weir.

VENTURES P&R/R&B/LP '60

Singles: 12-inch

TRIDEX (1245 "Surfin' & Spyin' ")..........5-10 81
(Vocals by Charlotte Caffey and Jane Weidlin.)

Singles: 78 rpm

REO (8497 "Walk – Don't Run")..........50-100 60
(Canadian.)

Singles: 7-inch

BLUE HORIZON (100 "Real McCoy")..100-200 59
BLUE HORIZON (101 "Walk Don't Run")....................500-750 60
(300 made.)
DOLTON (25 "Walk – Don't Run"/ "Home")....................20-30 60
DOLTON (25-X "Walk – Don't Run"/"The McCoy")....................10-15 60
DOLTON (28 "Perfidia")..........10-20 60
DOLTON (32 "Ram-Bunk-Shush")..........10-20 61
DOLTON (41 Lullaby of the Leaves")......10-20 61
DOLTON (44 "Silver City")..........10-20 61
DOLTON (47 "Blue Moon")..........10-20 61
DOLTON (50 "Yellow Jacket")..........10-20 62
DOLTON (55 "Instant Mashed")..........10-20 62
DOLTON (60 "Lolita Ya-Ya")..........10-20 62
DOLTON (67 "2,000 Pound Bee")..........10-20 62
DOLTON (68 "Skip to M'Limbo")..........10-20 63
DOLTON (78 "The Ninth Wave")..........10-20 63
DOLTON (85 "The Savage")..........10-20 63
DOLTON (91 "Journey to the Stars")......10-20 64
DOLTON (94 "Scratchin' ")..........10-15 64
DOLTON (96 "Walk – Don't Run '64")......10-15 64
DOLTON (300 "Slaughter on Tenth Avenue")....................10-15 64
DOLTON (303 "Diamond Head")..........10-15 65
DOLTON (306 "The Swingin' Creeper")....8-12 65
DOLTON (308 "Bird Rockers")..........8-12 65
DOLTON (311 "Gemini")..........8-12 65
DOLTON (312 "Sleigh Ride")..........8-12 65
DOLTON (316 "Secret Agent Man")..........8-12 65
DOLTON (320 "Blue Star")..........8-12 66
DOLTON (321 "Arabesque")..........8-12 66
DOLTON (323 "Green Hornet Theme")......8-12 66
DOLTON (325 "Penetration")..........8-12 66
DOLTON (327 "The Wild Angels")..........8-12 66
EMI (18212 "Jingle Bell Rock")..........5-8 '90s
(Red vinyl. Juke box issue only.)
LIBERTY....................5-10 67-70
QUALITY ("Walk – Don't Run")..........8-12 '60s
(Canadian. Reissue of Reo 8497. Selection number not known.)
REO (8497 "Walk – Don't Run")..........15-25 60
(Canadian.)
TRIDEX....................4-6 81
U.A. 4-8 70-78

Picture Sleeves

DOLTON (28 "Perfidia")..........10-20 60
DOLTON (96 "Walk – Don't Run '64")......10-20 64
DOLTON (300 "Slaughter on Tenth Avenue")....................10-20 64
DOLTON (320 "Blue Star")..........10-20 66
DOLTON (323 "Green Hornet Theme")...10-20 66
DOLTON (325 "Penetration")..........10-20 66

TRIDEX....................................4-8 81
U.A. (52800 "Indian Sun") ....
EPs: 7-inch
DOLTON (503 "Walk – Don't Run") 30-40 60
LPs: 10/12-inch
AWARD 8-12 84
DOLTON (2003 "Walk Don't Run") 40-50 60
(Light blue label. Monaural.)
DOLTON (2003 "Walk Don't Run") 20-30 61
(Dark blue label. Monaural.)
DOLTON (2004 thru 2050)...................... 25-50 61-67
(Monaural.)
DOLTON (8003 "Walk Don't Run") 50-60 60
(Light blue label. Stereo.)
DOLTON (8003 "Walk Don't Run") 25-35 61
(Dark blue label. Stereo.)
DOLTON (8004 thru 8050)...................... 25-50 61-67
(Stereo.)
DOLTON (16500 series)......................... 25-50 '60s
DOLTON (17000 series)......................... 15-25 65-66
LIBERTY (2000 & 8000 series)............... 10-20 67-70
LIBERTY (10000 series).............................5-10 81-84
LIBERTY (35000 series)......................... 10-15 70
SUNSET.. 10-15 66-71
TRIDEX...5-10 81-83
U.A. 10-15 71-77
Members: Don Wilson; Bob Bogle; Mel Taylor; Nokie Edwards; Jerry McGee; Skip Moore; Howie Johnson; John Durrill.
Also see JAN & DEAN / Ventures
Also see LOPEZ, Trini, with the Ventures & Nancy Ames
Also see MARKSMEN
Also see McGEE, Jerry
Also see MOON STONES
Also see TAYLOR, Mel
Also see VEE, Bobby, & Ventures
Also see WILSON, Don

VENTURIE "5"
Singles: 7-inch
VENTURIE (1001 "Good 'N Bad").......... 10-20 '60s

VENUS, Vik *P&R '69*
Singles: 7-inch
BUDDAH (118 "Moonflight").......................5-10 69
BUDDAH (138 "Moonjack").........................5-10 69

VENUS FLYTRAP
Singles: 7-inch
JAGUAR ("103 "Have You Ever")........... 15-20 66
MIJJI ("3005 "Have You Ever") 10-20 67

VENUTI, Nick
Singles: 7-inch
IMPALA (5522 "Love in Be-Bop Time") ... 20-30 61

VERA, Billy *P&R '67*
(With the Contrasts; with Beaters; with Blue Eyed Soul)
Singles: 7-inch
ALFA (7002 "I Can Take Care of Myself") 4-8 81
ALFA (7005 "At This Moment") 5-10 81
ALFA (7020 "We Got It All") 4-8 82
ALFA (7126 "Hopeless Romantic")...............4-8 82
ATLANTIC (2526 "With Pen in Hand")........5-10 68
ATLANTIC (2555 "I've Been Loving You Too Long")...5-10 68
ATLANTIC (2586 "Julie")...........................5-10 68
ATLANTIC (2628 "The Bible Salesman") ...5-10 69
ATLANTIC (2654 "Tell It Like It Is")............5-10 69
ATLANTIC (2700 "J.W.'s Dream") 5-10 70
FLAVOR 10-20 64
MACOLA 3-5 87
MIDLAND INT'L (10639 "Back Door Man") ..4-6 76
MIDLAND INT'L (10909 "Private Clown")......4-6 77
MIDLAND INT'L (11042 "Something Like Nothing Before")..4-6 77
MIDSONG (72014 "She Ain't Loni")..............4-6 80
ORANGE..4-8 73
RHINO (74403 "At This Moment") 3-5 86
RUST (5051 "All My Love") 10-15 62
Picture Sleeves
ALFA (7005 "At This Moment") 5-10 81
LPs: 10/12-inch
ALFA (10001 "Billy & the Beaters")............8-12 81
ATLANTIC (8197 "With Pen in Hand")..... 10-15 68
CAPITOL 5-8 88
MACOLA 5-8 87
MIDSONG INT'L (2219 "Out of the Darkness") 8-12 77
RHINO (70858 "By Request") 5-10 86
Also see BLUE EYED SOUL
Also see KNIGHT RIDERS
Also see RESOLUTIONS

VERA, Billy & Judy Clay *P&R/R&B '67*
Singles: 7-inch
ATLANTIC (2445 "Storybook Children").....5-10 67
ATLANTIC (2480 "Country Girl – City Man")..5-10 68
ATLANTIC (2515 "When Do We Go") 5-10 68
LPs: 10/12-inch
ATLANTIC (8174 "Storybook Children")...10-20 68
Also see CLAY, Judy

VERA, Ricky
(With George Cates & Orchestra)
Singles: 78 rpm
CORAL..5-10 53
Singles: 7-inch
CORAL (61106 "Dragnet Goes to Kindergarten"/"Rosita Red Riding Hood") 10-15 53
Session: Laurindo Almeida.
Also see ALLEN, Steve, & Ricky Vera
Also see ALMEIDA, Laurindo

VERA & THREE JAYS
Singles: 7-inch
EL BEE (162 "Fire in Your Heart")...........15-25 57

VERBATIM
Singles: 7-inch
METROMEDIA (108 "Hieronymous Bosch") 5-10 69

VERDELL, Jackie
Singles: 7-inch
CORAL (62555 "Call On Me")....................5-10 68
DECCA (32118 "I'm Your Girl")................10-15 67
PEACOCK (1921 "Hush") 8-12 63
PEACOCK (1930 "Come Let Me Love You") 8-12 64

VERDI, Joe
Singles: 7-inch
KP (1002 "Arlene")...................................20-40 59

VERDI, Liz
Singles: 7-inch
COLUMBIA (43154 "You Let Him Get Away")..10-15 64

VERDICTS
(With Al Browne's Orchestra)
Singles: 7-inch
EAST COAST (103 "My Life's Desire")..250-300 61
O'DELL...10-15 '60s
RELIC (507 "My Life's Desire") 5-10 64
VINTAGE (1009 "Never Let Me Go")........10-15 73
(Yellow vinyl.)
Also see BROWNE, Al

VERITY, John
(John Verity Band)
LPs: 10/12-inch
DUNHILL..15-20 74
Also see ARGENT

VERLIN, Chico
Singles: 78 rpm
STAR (1007 "Braveland Boogie")..............5-10 55
Singles: 7-inch
STAR (1007 "Braveland Boogie") 10-20 55
Also see HOLIDAY, Chico

VERNALLS
(Varnells)
Singles: 7-inch
RU LU (6753 "Why Can't You Be True")..400-500 58
Also see VARNELLS

VERNE, Bobby
Singles: 7-inch
DOC HOLIDAY (101 "Red Hot Car") 100-200

VERNE, Larry *P&R/R&B '60*
Singles: 7-inch
COLLECTABLES..3-5 '80s
ERA 10-15 60-64
Picture Sleeves
ERA (3034 "Mr. Livingston")...................10-20 60
EPs: 7-inch
ERA (104 "Hi-Lites from Mister Larry Verne")..15-25 60
(Promotional issue only. Not issued with special cover.)
LPs: 10/12-inch
ERA (104 "Mister Larry Verne")................25-35 60

VERNEE, Yvonne
Singles: 7-inch
CORREC-TONE (3178 "Does He Love Me Anymore")..20-30 '60s
SONBERT (3475 "It's Been a Long Time") ....25-35 '60s
SONBERT (5842 "Just Like You Did Me") ....500-750 '60s

VERNITA / Five Jets
Singles: 7-inch
J.V.B. (2000/01 "There's No Doubt About You"/"I'm Not Leaving You Alone") 20-30 57
Also see FIVE JETS

VERNON
(With the Gil Baca Combo)
Singles: 7-inch
GUYDEN (2074 "Pledging My Love").........8-12 62

VERNON, Babs
Singles: 7-inch
DOT (16623 "Lover Boy").........................10-20 64

VERNON, Lynn
Singles: 7-inch
COVER (5932 "Moon Rocket")................15-25 59
Also see B-B / Lyn Vernon

VERNON, Millie
Singles: 7-inch
ARGO (5348 "That Old Feeling")............10-20 59
COLPIX (627 "Look No Further")...............8-12 62
COLPIX (677 "Somebody to Love")............8-12 63

VERNON, Paul
Singles: 7-inch
LOVE (821 "Keeps My Mind a Wonderin' ") ....10-20 '60s

VERNON, Ray
(With the Raymen; Vernon Wray)
Singles: 7-inch
CAMEO (109 "Evil Angel"/"I'll Take Tomorrow")...15-25 57
CAMEO (109 "Evil Angel"/"Remember You're Mine")...15-25 57
(Note different flip side.)
CAMEO (115 "Terry")..............................15-25 57
CAMEO (136 "Window Shopping")..........15-25 58
LAWN (245 "Gotta Go Get My Baby")........8-12 64
LIBERTY (55201 "My Sugar Plum") 10-20 59
MALA (456 "Hold It") 8-12 62
MARK...10-20 58
RUMBLE (1349 "Evil Angel")..................50-75 61
SCOTTIE (1320 "Rough Shod") 10-20 60
SWAN (4215 "Indian Love Call") 8-12 65
VERNON (100 "Here Was a Man") 15-25 60
Also see WRAY BROTHERS

VERNON & CLIFF
Singles: 7-inch
DOOTO (443 "You Came Along") 20-30 59
Members: Vernon Green; Cliff Chambers.
Also see CHAMBERS, Cliff
Also see GREEN, Vernon, & Medallions

VERNON & JEWELL
(Vernon & the Jewels; Vernon & Jewel)
Singles: 7-inch
BAY-TONE (111 "I Love You") 10-15 63
BAY-TONE (112 "It Hit Me Where It Hurts")...10-15 63
IMPERIAL (5722 "You're Gonna Be Paid") 10-15 61
KAYO (5104 "The Thought of You"/"Baby, You Got What It Takes")..10-15 63
KENT (405 "That's a Rockin' Good Way")...10-20 64
KENT (430 "Hold My Hand")..................10-20 65
NETWORK (101 "You're Gonna Be Paid")..20-30 61
(First issue.)
PAM MAR (611 "My Every Thought"/"You've Got What It Takes") ....10-15 '60s
(Identical to tracks on Kayo, though titles differ slightly. We don't know yet which disc came first. This one is credited to "Vernon & Jewell," whereas Kayo credits "Vernon & the Jewels.")
Members: Vernon Garrett; Jewell.
Also see GARRETT, Vernon
Also see JACQUET, Russell, Orchestra, & Vernon Garrett

VERNON GIRLS
(Vernon's Girls)
Singles: 7-inch
CHALLENGE (59234 "We Love You Beatles")..15-25 64
CHALLENGE (59261 "Stupid Little Girl")...15-25 64
Members: Lyn Cornell; Betty Prescott.
Also see CAREFREES

VERONICA
(Veronica "Ronnie" Spector)
Singles: 7-inch
PHIL SPECTOR (1 "So Young")..............25-50 64
PHIL SPECTOR (2 "Why Don't They Let Us Fall in Love") 40-60 64
Also see NITZSCHE, Jack
Also see SPECTOR, Ronnie

VERSAILLES
Singles: 7-inch
HARLEQUIN (401 "Teenager's Dream").. 10-15 57
(Red vinyl.)

VERSAILLES
Singles: 7-inch
OLD TIMER (607 "Lorraine")......................8-12 65
(Black vinyl.)
OLD TIMER (607 "Lorraine") 10-15 65
(Blue vinyl.)
Member: Joey Spano.

VERSALES & TORQUAYS
Singles: 7-inch
MENTOR (4 "Drop Out").....................100-200 62

VERSALETTES
Singles: 7-inch
WITCH (116 "Shining Armor") 8-12 63
WITCH (120 "Don Juan in Town").............8-12 64

VERSATILE FOUR
Singles: 7-inch
U.A. (476 "Every Other Night") 5-10 62

VERSATILES
Singles: 7-inch
ATLANTIC (2004 "Passing By") 10-20 58
PEACOCK (1910 "White Cliffs of Dover") 10-15 62
RO-CAL (1002 "Lundee Dundee")............50-75 60
Members: Rick Cordo; Ron Gathers; Gene Glass; Della Moore; Frank Trout.

VERSATILES
Singles: 7-inch
KIN-GAR (104 "Summer Date")...............10-20 64

VERSATILES
Singles: 7-inch
BRONCO (2050 "Bye Bye Baby") 5-10 66
RICH TONE (18643 "Easy to Say")............5-10 67
SEA CREST (6001 "Lonely Boy") 10-20 64

VERSATILES
Singles: 7-inch
CHEECO (779 "Oh Yeh").........................25-30 '60s

VERSATILES
Singles: 7-inch
STAFF (210 "Cry Like a Baby") 20-30

VERSATILES
Singles: 7-inch
COASTER (800 "In the Garden of Love") 25-35

VERSATILES & MIKE METKO COMBO
Singles: 7-inch
MARIE (101 "Blue Feelin' ") 4-8 77
RAMCO (3717 "Blue Feelin' ")..........150-250 62
Also see VICEROYS

VERSATONES
Singles: 78 rpm
RCA...5-10 57
Singles: 7-inch
RCA...5-10 57
EPs: 7-inch
RCA...15-20 57
LPs: 10/12-inch
RCA (1538 "The Versatones")................30-40 57

VERSATONES

Singles: 7-inch

ALL STAR (501 "Tight Skirt & Sweater") . 30-40 58
ATLANTIC (2211 "Tight Skirt & Sweater")..5-10 63
FENWAY (7001 "Tight Skirt & Sweater"). 10-15 60
LOST NITE (115 "Tight Skirt & Sweater") 4-8 64
MAGIC CITY (004 "Rockin' & Rollin' ")..... 40-60

VERSA-TONES

Singles: 7-inch

KENCO (5015 "Cobra")........................... 10-15 61
TIFCO (831 "Heartbeat")........................ 10-15 62

VERSATONES

Singles: 7-inch

RICHIE (4081 "Will She Return")......... 300-400 63

VERSITILES

Singles: 7-inch

AMAKER (417 "Don't Go")...................... 10-15 62
AMAKER (418 "Strange")........................ 10-15 62

VERTUES FOUR

Singles: 7-inch

SEA SEVEN (22 "Angel Baby")............... 30-40 63

VERY-ATIONS

Singles: 7-inch

RINK (542 "I'm So Lonely")................... 10-20 '60s

VESPERS

Singles: 7-inch

SWAN (4156 "Mr. Cupid")....................... 30-40 63
Also see FOUR EPICS

VESTEE, Russ

Singles: 7-inch

AMY (833 "Well Alright")........................ 10-20 61
AMY (866 "A Touch of Venus")............... 15-25 62
NERO (17000 "Shy Guy")....................... 15-25 61

VESTELLES

Singles: 7-inch

DECCA (30733 "Come Home")................ 10-20 58

VESTELLS

Singles: 7-inch

BO JO (1 "Won't You Tell Me")............... 10-20 67

VETS

Singles: 7-inch

SWAMI (551 "Natural Born Lover").......... 20-30 61

VETTES

Singles: 7-inch

MGM.. 10-20 63

LPs: 10/12-inch

MGM (E-4193 "Rev-Up")......................... 60-80 63
(Monaural.)
MGM (SE-4193 "Rev-Up")...................... 75-125 63
(Stereo.)
Members: Bruce Johnston; Steve Douglas.
Also see DOUGLAS, Steve
Also see JOHNSTON, Bruce

VIBES
("Formerly the Vibranaires")

Singles: 78 rpm

AFTER HOURS 200-300 54
CHARIOT.. 300-400 54

Singles: 7-inch

AFTER HOURS (105 "Stop Torturing Me!")...................................... 1500-2000 54
CHARIOT (105 "Stop Torturing Me!")...................................... 2500-3500 54
Also see VIBRANAIRES

VIBES

Singles: 78 rpm

ABC-PAR (9810 "Darling")..................... 20-30 57

Singles: 7-inch

ABC-PAR (9810 "Darling")..................... 20-30 57

VIBES
("Vocal By Ronnie Franklin")

Singles: 7-inch

PERSPECTIVE (5858 "Pretty Baby") .. 100-125 58
Member: David Gates as Ronnie Franklin.
Also see GATES, Ronnie

VIBES

Singles: 7-inch

ALLIED (10006 "What's Her Name") 50-75 58
ALLIED (10007 "Misunderstood") 40-50 59

VIBES

Singles: 7-inch

RAYNA (103 "You Got Me Crying").........15-25

VIBRAHARPS
(Vibra-Harps)

Singles: 78 rpm

BEECH (713 "Walk Beside Me")..............25-50 56

Singles: 7-inch

ATCO (6134 "It Must Be Magic") 10-20 59
BEECH (713 "Walk Beside Me")...........75-125 56
FURY (1022 "The Only Love of Mine").300-400 59
Also see ELBERT, Donnie

VIBRANAIRES
(With Eddie Swanston Quintette; Vibes)

Singles: 78 rpm

AFTER HOURS 200-300 54
CHARIOT..200-300 54

Singles: 7-inch

AFTER HOURS (103 "Doll Face") ... 2000-3000 54
(Red vinyl.)
CHARIOT (103 "Doll Face")............ 2000-3000 54

LPs: 10/12-inch

LIRRA (500 "Vibranaires Live")................20-30 82
(10-inch LP.)
Members: Bobby Thomas; Jimmy Roache; Cleveland Dickerson; Dornell Chavous; Matthew McKnight.
Also see VIBES

VIBRANAIRES

Singles: 7-inch

KELLY-PHONE ("My Sweet Little Johnny")...50-75
(Selection number not known.)

VIBRANTS
(Vibrents)

Singles: 7-inch

TRIUMPH (101 "Wildfire").........................10-20 62
Also see VIBRENTS

VIBRA-SONICS

Singles: 7-inch

IDEAL ("Thunder Storm")..........................15-25 64
(No selection number used.)
Members: George Tweedy; Bob Tweedy; Bill Sabo; Joe Colner; Joey Covington.
Also see FENWAYS
Also see JEFFERSON AIRPLANE
Also see RACKET SQUAD

VIBRASONICS

Singles: 7-inch

MARJON (511 "Don't Go") 10-20 66

VIBRATIONS P&R/R&B '61

Singles: 7-inch

ABC...4-6 74
AMY (11006 "A Shot of Love")....................5-10 68
ATLANTIC (2204 "Between Hello and Goodbye")...8-12 63
ATLANTIC (2221 "My Girl Sloopy") 10-20 64
BET (0001 "So Blue") 200-300 60
CHECKER (954 "So Blue") 20-30 60
CHECKER (961 "Feel So Bad")................10-15 60
CHECKER (967 "Doing the Slop")............10-15 60
(Same number used on a Neptunes release.)
CHECKER (969 "Watusi")..........................15-25 61
CHECKER (974 "Continental") 10-15 61
CHECKER (982 "Don't Say Goodbye") 10-15 61
CHECKER (987 "All My Love Belongs to You")..15-20 61
(Maroon label.)
CHECKER (987 "All My Love Belongs to You")..20-25 61
(White label. Promotional issue only.)
CHECKER (990 "Let's Pony Again") 10-15 61
CHECKER (1002 "Oh Cindy")...................10-15 61
CHECKER (1011 "New Hully Gully").........10-15 62
CHECKER (1022 "Hamburgers on a Bun")...10-15 62
CHECKER (1038 "Since I Fell for You")...10-15 63
CHECKER (1061 "Dancing Danny")...........8-12 63
CHESS (2151 "Make It Last").......................4-6 74
EPIC (10418 "Cause You're Mine") 10-20 68
MANDALA (2511 "Wind Up Toy")..................4-6 72
NEPTUNE (19 "Expressway to Your Heart")..5-10 69
NEPTUNE (21 "Smoke Signals")..................4-8 70
NEPTUNE (28 "Right On Brother")...............4-6 70
NORTH BAY (307 "Sneakin' ")...................5-10
OKEH 10-15 64-68

LPs: 10/12-inch

CHECKER (2978 "Watusi").......................50-75 61
MANDALA (3006 "Taking a New Step")...10-15 72
OKEH (12111 "Shout")............................25-40 65
(Monaural.)
OKEH (12112 "Misty")..............................25-40 66
(Monaural.)
OKEH (12114 "New Vibrations")..............25-40 66
(Monaural.)
OKEH (14111 "Shout")..............................25-40 65
(Stereo.)
OKEH (14112 "Misty")...............................25-40 66
(Stereo.)
OKEH (14114 "New Vibrations")..............25-40 66
(Stereo.)
OKEH (14129 "Greatest Hits")..................35-50 69
Also see JAYHAWKS
Also see MARATHONS
Also see NEPTUNES

VIBRA-TONES

Singles: 7-inch

CANDI (1025 "I'm Begging You") 15-25 62

VIBRATONES

Singles: 7-inch

CUCA (1073 "Side-Winder")........................8-12 62
RAYNARD (10032 "Eventually")..................8-12 65
RAYNARD (10044 "I Remember Yesterday")..8-12 65
Members: Jim Maas; Jerry Schroeder; Roger Bader; Reggie Roznowski; Dickie Leigh; Gary Van Sistine.

VIBRATONES

Singles: 7-inch

MASTERTONE (3075 "Moanin' Bass")....50-75 '60s

VIBRATORS

Singles: 7-inch

BROOKE (106 "Way Out")..........................8-12 59

VIBRATOS

Singles: 7-inch

SPECTOR (0 "Something Else") 20-30 66

VIBRENTS
(Vibrants)

Singles: 7-inch

BAY TOWNE (409 "Fuel Injection")..........10-15 63
Also see VIBRANTS

VIC & GENTS

Singles: 7-inch

DORANA (1170 "Lydia") 100-150 64

VIC & VICKY

Singles: 7-inch

IMPERIAL (5506 "Never Let You Go").....10-20 58

VICE-ROYS

Singles: 78 rpm

ALADDIN...50-75 55

Singles: 7-inch

ALADDIN (3273 "Please Baby, Please")...100-200 55

VICEROYS
(With the Mike Metko Combo; Vice-Roys)

Singles: 7-inch

LITTLE STAR (107 "I'm So Sorry").........75-100 61
ORIGINAL SOUND (15 Dreamy Eyes") ...15-25 61
RAMCO (3715 "My Heart")...................500-750 62
SMASH (1716 "I'm So Sorry")..................15-20 61
Also see VERSATILES
Also see PENGUINS

VICEROYS

Singles: 7-inch

E'DEN (9001 "Don't Let Go") 75-85 62

VICEROYS
(Vice-Roys)

Singles: 7-inch

BETHLEHEM 8-15 62-65
DVC...5-10 '60s
U.S.A. (761 "Liverpool") 5-10 64
Members: Richard P. Giannini; Larry Holmes; Rick Emerson; Harry Kawolski; Ron Emerson; Jon Ehlers; Frank Giannini; William Morales.
Also see BALLARD, Hank, & Midnighters / Viceroys

VICEROYS

Singles: 7-inch

BOLO 10-15 63-65
DOT...8-12 63

LPs: 10/12-inch

BOLO (8000 "At Granny's Pad")...............50-75 63
Member: Jim Valley.
Also see SURPRISE PACKAGE
Also see VALLEY, Jim
Also see WINK & JUDY with the Viceroys Five

VICEROYS

Singles: 7-inch

IMPERIAL (66058 "Earth Angel")...............5-10 64

VICKERS, Vic
(Mac Vickery)

Singles: 7-inch

JAMIE (1278 "Actions Speak Louder Than Words")...15-25 64
Also see VICKERY, Mack

VICKERY, Mack C&W '77
(Mac Vickery)

Singles: 7-inch

AFCO (520 "Bell Bottom Jeans")................8-12 66
GONE (5075 "Lover's Plea")....................10-20 59
GONE (5085 "I'll Never Love Again").......10-20 60
GONE (5093 "Fantasy")...........................10-20 60
PLAYBOY 4-6 77
PRINCETON (101 "High School Blues")..50-100 60

LPs: 10/12-inch

MEGA (1002 "Live at the Alabama Women's Prison")..10-15 70
Also see VICKERS, Vic

VICKY
(Vicky Leandros)

Singles: 7-inch

PHILIPS (40546 "Dance with Me Until Tomorrow")...10-15 68
VICKY...5-10 68

LPs: 10/12-inch

PHILIPS 8-12 68

VI-COUNTS

Singles: 7-inch

ACE (587 "The Loser")................................5-10 60
DONICK (100 "Passion") 5-10 59
VI-COUNTS 5-10

VI-COUNTS

Singles: 7-inch

SALESMAKER (5-5760 "Good Bye")......10-15 65

VICT, Ray, & His Bop Rockers

Singles: 7-inch

GOLDBAND (1042 "Bop Stop Rock") 50-80 57
ZIP (1042 " Bop Stop Rock") 100-150 57

VICTIMS OF CHANCE

LPs: 10/12-inch

CRESTVIEW (3052 "Victims of Chance")...35-55 '60s

VICTOR

Singles: 7-inch

DORSET (5011 "Stop A-Knockin' ") 30-40 62

VICTORIALS

Singles: 78 rpm

IMPERIAL (5398 "I Get That Feeling").....25-40 56

Singles: 7-inch

IMPERIAL (5398 "I Get That Feeling").....50-75 56

VICTORIANS

Singles: 78 rpm

SPECIALTY (411 "I Guess You're Satisfied")...75-100 51
SPECIALTY (420 "Naturally Too Weak for You")...250-500 52

Singles: 7-inch

SPECIALTY (411 "I Guess You're Satisfied") 750-1000 51

VICTORIANS

Singles: 78 rpm

SAXONY (103 "Heartbreaking Moon"). 150-250 56

Singles: 7-inch

SAXONY (103 "Heartbreaking Moon"). 700-800 56
SELMA (1002 "Wedding Bells")............ 100-200 58
Members: Cas Bridges; Bobby Thompson; Bill Carey; Donny Miles.
Also see CLEFFTONES

VICTORIANS

Singles: 7-inch

HERCULES (101 "Catrina")................... 10-20 60
ROWENA (994 "Side By Side").............. 15-25

VICTORIANS
Singles: 7-inch
END (1033 "Cowbell Rock") 10-15 58

VICTORIANS
Singles: 7-inch
ANCHOR (138 "Mr. Alone") 15-25 63
Member: Mike Ester.

VICTORIANS
Singles: 7-inch
LIBERTY (55574 "What Makes Little Girls Cry") 10-15 63
LIBERTY (55656 "You're Invited to a Party") 10-15 64
LIBERTY (55693 "Happy Birthday Blue") 10-15 64
LIBERTY (55728 "If I Loved You") 10-15 64

VICTORIANS
Singles: 7-inch
BANG (550 "Merry-Go-Round") 10-15 67
REPRISE 10-15 66
Member: Nick Massi.

VICTORIANS
Singles: 7-inch
ARNOLD J (571 "Lovin' ") 5-10 68

VICTORS
Singles: 7-inch
DOT (16558 "Bird Walk") 5-10 63
JACKPOT (48015 "Mi Amor") 10-15 59

VICTORS
Singles: 7-inch
ALPHA (603 "We Struck a Match") 10-20 66

VICTORS
Singles: 7-inch
PHILIPS (40475 "Hurt") 20-30 67

VICTORY FIVE
Singles: 7-inch
TERP (101 "I Never Knew") 1000-1500 57
(Red vinyl.)

VIDALTONES
Singles: 7-inch
JOSIE (900 "Forever") 30-40 62

VI DELS
Singles: 7-inch
FARGO (1062 "Walkin' Down the Street") 50-75 64

VIDELS
Singles: 7-inch
DUSTY DISC (473 "I Wish") 5-10 64
EARLY (702 "I Wish") 1000-1500 60

VIDELS *P&R '60*
(With Joe Sherman & His Orchestra; with Frank Spino & His Orchestra; Vi-Dels; Videls')
Singles: 7-inch
COLLECTABLES .... 3-5 '80s
JDS (5004 "Mister Lonely") 15-20 60
(Gray label. Reads: "Distributed by United Telefilm Records.")
JDS (5004 "Mister Lonely") 8-12 60
(Multi-color label. No mention of distribution by United Telefilm.)
JDS (5005 "She's Not Coming Home") 10-15 60
(Gray label. Reads: "Distributed by United Telefilm Records.")
JDS (5005 "She's Not Coming Home") 15-25 60
(Yellow label. Reads: "Distributed by United Telefilm Records.")
JDS (5005 "She's Not Coming Home") 8-12 60
(Multi-color label. No mention of distribution by United Telefilm.)
KAPP (361 "Streets of Love") 15-25 61
KAPP (405 "A Letter from Ann") 40-50 61
MEDIEVAL (203 "Be My Girl") 8-12 59
MUSICNOTE (117 "We Belong Together") 50-60 63
(Black vinyl.)
MUSICNOTE (117 "We Belong Together") 100-150 63
(Multi-colored vinyl.)
RHODY (2000 "Be My Girl") 30-40 59
(First issue.)
TIC-TAC-TOE (5005 "Now That Summer Is Here") 30-40 62
LPs: 10/12-inch
MAGIC CARPET (1005 "A Letter from the Videls") 8-12 91
(Black vinyl. 2000 made.)
MAGIC CARPET (1005 "A Letter from the Videls") 25-30 91
(Red vinyl. 10 made.)
MAGIC CARPET (1005 "A Letter from the Videls") 40-50 91
(Picture disc. No cover. 25 made.)
Members: Pete Anders; Vinnie Poncia.
Also see ANDERS & PONCIA

VIDEOS
Singles: 7-inch
BIM BAM BOOM (101 "Love Or Infatuation") 4-8 72
CASINO (102 "Trickle, Trickle") 50-60 58
(Label name in shadow print. Does not have six ace playing cards. No mention of distribution by Gone.)
CASINO (102 "Trickle, Trickle") 10-15 58
(Has six ace playing cards.)
CASINO (102 "Trickle, Trickle") 15-25 61
(Label name in block, shadowless print. Does not have six ace playing cards. Indicates distribution by Gone.)
CASINO (105 "Love Or Infatuation") 100-200 59
Members: Ron Woodall; John Jackson; Ron Cuffey; Clarence Bassett; Charles Baskerville.
Also see FIVE SHARPS

VIDONE, Bob
(With the Rhythm Rockers)
Singles: 7-inch
FLEETWOOD (1008 "Going My Way") 150-250 59
SENTRY (7066 "Untrue") 200-300 59

VIGILANTES
Singles: 7-inch
CUCA (1042 "Ramblin' On") 10-20 61
CUCA (1042 "Travelin' On") 10-20 61
(Retitled reissue.)
CUCA (1064 "Highland Fling") 20-30 61
HER MI (001 "Warm Wind") 10-20 62
Members: James Brogan; Don Hermanson; Greg Coby; Don Kaekala; Jay Mihelich; Lee Sterbenz; John Mitchell; Lloyd Hugo.

VIGILANTES
Singles: 7-inch
JCP (1010 "Notice Me") 15-25 67

VI-KINGS
Singles: 7-inch
DEL-MANN (544 "Rock a Little Bit") 50-75 60
VI-KINGS (318 "She's Cool") 75-125

VIKINGS
Singles: 7-inch
ALTA (105 "Big Squeaky") 10-20 62
LIBERTY (55295 "Cliff Dweller") 10-20 61
NATIONWIDE (11 "The Viking Twist") 10-20 62
MONUMENT (839 "Tradewinds") 10-20 64
Members: Leon Halverson; Cliff Hanson; Carl Hintz; Bob Hinze; Tom Stubler.

VIKINGS
Singles: 7-inch
ATHENS (201 "Nicotine") 20-30 62

VIKINGS
Singles: 7-inch
SALEM (007 "You Can't Do That") 15-25 65

VIKINGS
Singles: 7-inch
CUCA (1096 "Rawhide") 10-20 65

VIKINGS
Singles: 7-inch
VALHALLA (661 "Boo Hoo Hoo") 100-200 66
(Originally issued as by the Atlantics.)
VIKING (1000 "Come on and Love Me") 20-30 66
Also see ATLANTICS

VILADOS
Singles: 7-inch
STREN (102 "Wild Party") 50-75 63

VILLA, Claudio
Singles: 7-inch
4 CORNERS (140 "Non Dirme Addio") 4-6 67
LPs:10/12-inch
CORAL (57281 "Sings") 20-30 58
CORAL (57373 "Romantic Moods Italiano") 20-30 58

VILLA, Danny
Singles: 7-inch
DANCO (501 "Baby") 5-10 64
DANCO (502 "Water Under the Bridge") 5-10 65

VILLA, Joey
(Joe Villa; Joey & the Original 3 Friends)
Singles: 7-inch
CAPITOL (4484 "All American Girl") 10-15 60
CHEVRON (500 "Blanche") 5-10 62
DE-LITE (501 "Chloe") 8-12 67
DE-LITE (504 "Magic of Your Love") .... 8-12 '60s
MF (101 "Blanche") 15-25 62
(First issue.)
Also see BLUETONES
Also see ROYAL TEENS

VILLA, Pancho
(With the Bandits; Pancho Villa Orchestra)
Singles: 7-inch
ARLISS (1010 "Bobby's Guitar") 10-15 61
CAPRICORN (1001 "Baby Cakes Hunch") 15-25 60
CHANCELLOR (1058 "Baby Cakes") 10-20 60
MAIN LINE (101 "After School Rock") 20-30 57
PEE VEE (100 "Ain't That Bad") 10-20 63
SYMBOL (202 "Ain't That Bad") 5-10 64
WAND (134 "Non Stop") 8-12 63

VILLA, Pepe, & Mariachi Jalosco
LPs: 10/12-inch
EPIC (18018 "Pasodobles") 10-20 62
(Monaural.)
EPIC (19018 "Pasodobles") 10-20 62
(Stereo.)
KING (660 "Music of Mexico") 15-25 59

VILLAGE PEOPLE *LP '77*
Singles: 12-inch
CASABLANCA 4-8 78-79
Singles: 7-inch
CASABLANCA 3-5 78-79
RCA 3-5 81
Picture Sleeves
CASABLANCA 3-5 78-79
RCA 3-5 81
LPs: 10/12-inch
CASABLANCA (Except NBPIX series) 5-12 77-80
CASABLANCA (NBPIX series) 15-25 78
(Picture discs.)
RCA 5-10 81
Members: Victor Willis; Alexander Briley; Felipe Rose; Randy Jones; David Hodo; Glenn Hughes.

VILLAGE SOUL CHOIR *P&R/R&B '70*
Singles: 7-inch
ABBOTT 4-6 69-70
SCM (1000 "Talk to Me Sometimes") .... 8-12 '60s

VILLAGE SOUND
Singles: 7-inch
HIP (8003 "Sally's Got a Good Thing") 5-10 68
HIP (8013 "Hey Jack") 5-10 69
HIP (8021 "Truth Or Consequences") 5-10 69
ONYX (102 "These Windows") .... 30-40 '60s

VILLAGE STOMPERS *P&R/R&B/LP '63*
Singles: 7-inch
CAMEO (2000 "Sing All Together") 5-10 67
EPIC 5-10 63-67
Picture Sleeves
EPIC 8-12 63-65
LPs: 10/12-inch
EPIC 10-20 63-67
Also see VINTON, Bobby, & Village Stompers

VILLAGE VOICES
Singles: 7-inch
TOPIX (6000 "Red Lips") 30-40 61
(Yellow and black label.)
TOPIX (6000 "Red Lips") 20-30 61
(Yellow, black and white label.)
Also see 4 SEASONS

VILLAGERS
Singles: 7-inch
ATCO (6517 "Every Saturday") 5-10 67
ATCO (6568 "Thank You Baby") 5-10 68
FAME (1005 "You're Gonna Lose That Girl") 10-20 66
PETAL (110 "To Be Redeemed") 5-10 63

VILLAGERS
Singles: 7-inch
JCP (1005 "C.C. Rider") 10-20 64
JCP (1012 "I Won't Cry") 10-20 64

VILLARI, Guy
Singles: 7-inch
COUSINS (1004 "I'm All Alone") 40-50 61
(Same number used on a Consorts release.)
Also see REGENTS

VILLERAL, Don
Singles: 7-inch
CORSAIR (219 "Somewhere") 10-20

VILLETTE SISTERS
Singles: 7-inch
MGM (12928 "I Gave Him Back His Ring") 10-20 60

VILLIAN, Jesse
Singles: 7-inch
HI-LITE (8598 "Strange Feeling") 50-75

VILLIANS
Singles: 7-inch
BULLETS (136 "Don't Ever Leave Me") 5-10 66

VILONS
Singles: 7-inch
ALJON (1259 "Mother Nature") 50-75 63
(Thick wax.)
BIM BAM BOOM (104 "Angel Darling") 4-6 72
LAKE (713 "What Kind of Fool Am I") 15-25 62
RELIC (524 "Mother Nature") 5-10 64
VINTAGE (1011 "Tears On My Pillow") 10-15 73
(Orange vinyl.)
Member: Bob Alveray.

VINA, Joe
Singles: 7-inch
ALLIED (7778 "That's Alright") 5-10 59
WEBBER (5001 "Take This Heart") 5-10 60

VINCE & JIM
Singles: 7-inch
SOUTHERN SOUND (203 "April Day") 15-25 63

VINCE & VICTORS
Singles: 7-inch
JERDEN 5-10 65
Member: Vince Gerber.
Also see GERBER, Vince

VINCE & WAIKIKI RUMBLERS
Singles: 7-inch
BIG BEN (1003 "Waikiki Rumblers") 15-25 65
ZODIAC (1004 "Waikiki Rumblers") 20-30 65

VINCENT, Danny
Singles: 7-inch
ROULETTE (4334 "Carolyn") 5-10 61

VINCENT, Darryl
Singles: 7-inch
SANDY (1016 "Mercy Me") 50-75 58
SANDY (1020 "Wild Wild Party") 75-85 59

VINCENT, Gene *P&R/R&B/C&W/LP '56*
(With His Blue Caps)
Singles: 78 rpm
CAPITOL 100-150 56-57
Promotional Singles: 78 rpm
CAPITOL (3450 "Be-Bop-a-Lula") 150-175 56
("Be-Bop-a-Lula" exists as a white label promo 78. We're not yet sure which others were made.)
Singles: 7-inch
CAPITOL (3450 "Be-Bop-a-Lula") 30-40 56
CAPITOL (3450 "Be-Bop-a-Lula") 100-200 56
(White label. Promotional issue. An insert exists for the promo copy. Reads: "Introducing on Capitol Gene Vincent and His Blue Caps." Price range for insert is $500 to $1000.)
CAPITOL (3530 "Race with the Devil") 30-40 56
CAPITOL (3558 "Bluejean Bop") 30-40 56
CAPITOL (3617 "Crazy Legs") 30-40 57
CAPITOL (3678 "B-I-Bickey-Bi, Bo-Bo-Go") 30-40 57
CAPITOL (3763 "Lotta Lovin' ") 30-40 57
CAPITOL (3763 "Lotta Lovin' ") 75-125 57
(White label. Promotional issue. An insert exists for the promo copy. Reads: "Gene Vincent Is Getting the Most Out of Lotta Lovin'." Price range for insert is $500 to $1000.)
CAPITOL (3839 "Dance to the Bop") 30-40 57

CAPITOL (3874 "Walkin' Home from School") ... 20-30 58
CAPITOL (3959 "Baby Blue") ... 20-30 58
CAPITOL (4010 "Rocky Road Blues") ... 20-30 58
CAPITOL (4051 "Little Lover") ... 20-30 59
CAPITOL (4105 "Say Mama") ... 20-30 59
CAPITOL (4153 "Who's Pushin' Your Swing") ... 20-30 59
CAPITOL (4153 "Who's Pushin' Your Swing") ... 50-75 59
(White label. Promotional issue.)
CAPITOL (4237 "Right Now") ... 20-30 60
CAPITOL (4313 "Wild Cat") ... 20-30 60
CAPITOL (4442 "Pistol Packin' Mama") .. 15-25 60
CAPITOL (4525 "Mister Loneliness") ... 40-50 61
CAPITOL (4665 "Lucky Star") ... 50-75 61
CAPITOL STAR LINE (6042 "Be-Bop-a-Lula") ... 5-10 '60s
CHALLENGE (59337 "Bird Doggin'") ... 15-20 66
CHALLENGE (59347 "Lonely Street") ... 15-20 66
CHALLENGE (59365 "Born to be a Rolling Stone") ... 15-20 67
FOREVER (6001 "Story of the Rockers") 10-20 69
KAMA SUTRA (514 "Sunshine") ... 8-12 70
KAMA SUTRA (518 "High on Life") ... 8-12 71
PLAYGROUND (100 "Story of the Rockers") ... 150-175 68

Promotional Singles: 7-inch

CAPITOL ... 50-100 56-61
(White or yellow labels.)

Picture Sleeves

CAPITOL (3450 "Be-Bop-a-Lula") ... 5-10 '90s
CAPITOL (4237 "Right Now") ... 800-1000 60

EPs: 7-inch

CAPITOL (438 "Dance to the Bop") ... 150-200 57
(Promotional issue only. Not issued with cover.)
CAPITOL (764 "Bluejean Bop") ... 75-125 57
(Price is for any of three volumes.)
CAPITOL (811 "Gene Vincent & His Blue Caps") ... 75-125 57
(Price is for any of three volumes.)
CAPITOL (970 "Gene Vincent Rocks & Bluecaps Roll") ... 75-125 58
(Price is for any of three volumes.)
CAPITOL (985 "Hot Rod Gang") ... 450-650 58
(Green label. Soundtrack.)
CAPITOL (985 "Hot Rod Gang") ... 500-750 58
(Promotional issue.)
CAPITOL (1059 "Record Date") ... 75-125 58
(Price is for any of three volumes.)

LPs: 10/12-inch

CAPITOL (DKAO-380 "Gene Vincent's Greatest") ... 15-25 69
CAPITOL (SM-380 "Gene Vincent's Greatest") ... 5-10 78
CAPITOL (764 "Bluejean Bop") ... 200-300 56
CAPITOL (811 "Gene Vincent & His Blue Caps") ... 200-300 57
CAPITOL (970 "Gene Vincent Rocks") 200-300 58
CAPITOL (1059 "Gene Vincent Record Date") ... 200-300 58
CAPITOL (1207 "Sounds Like Gene Vincent") ... 200-300 59
CAPITOL (T-1342 "Crazy Times") ... 150-250 60
(Monaural.)
CAPITOL (ST-1342 "Crazy Times") ... 250-350 60
(Stereo.)
CAPITOL (11000 series) ... 8-12 74
CAPITOL (16000 series) ... 5-10 81
COLUMBIA HOUSE (516208 "Gene Vincent's Greatest") ... 8-12
DANDELION ... 10-20 70
KAMA SUTRA ... 10-20 70-71
ROLLIN' ROCK ... 5-10 80-81
Session: Cliff Gallup.
Also see BATTIN, Skip
Also see CHAMPS
Also see FACENDA, Tommy
Also see MERRITT, Jerry
Also see MEYERS, Augie
Also see PRESLEY, Elvis
Also see SUPER-PHONICS / Gene Vincent

VINCENT, Gene / Tommy Sands / Sonny James / Ferlin Husky

LPs: 10/12-inch

CAPITOL (1009 "Teen Age Rock") ... 50-100 58
Also see HUSKY, Ferlin
Also see SANDS, Tommy

VINCENT, Gene / Frank Sinatra / Sonny James / Ron Goodwin

EPs: 7-inch

CAPITOL (437 "Special Hit Pressing") ... 75-100 57
(Promotional issue only. Not issued with cover.)
Also see JAMES, Sonny
Also see SINATRA, Frank

VINCENT, Gene / Super-Phonics

Singles: 7-inch

MEAN MT. (1425 "Interview with Gene Vincent"/"Teenage Partner") ... 5-10 82

Picture Sleeves

MEAN MT. (1425 "Interview with Gene Vincent"/"Teenage Partner") ... 8-12 82
Also see SUPER-PHONICS
Also see VINCENT, Gene

VINCENT, Joey

Singles: 7-inch

SUE (779 "Drip Drop") ... 8-12 63

VINCENT, Larry
(With the Feilden Foursome; with His Look Out Boys; with the Jenadoos; Prof. Vincent; Pearl Boys; Pearl Trio)

Singles: 78 rpm

PEARL (Except 57) ... 5-10 46-50
PEARL (57 "Larry's Barnyard Boogie") ... 25-35 50

Singles: 7-inch

PEARL (57 "Larry's Barnyard Boogie") 100-200 50

VINCENT, Ronnie

Singles: 7-inch

FM (9004 "Why Did You Have to Go") ... 5-10 64

VINCENT, Rudy, Jr., & His Rockin' Crickets

Singles: 7-inch

END (1042 "Rockin' Crickets") ... 10-15 59
Also see HOT TODDYS

VINCENT, Stan
(Stanley Vincent; Stan Vincent Thing; with the Dwains)

Singles: 7-inch

BEE (302 "Breakup Night") ... 15-25 61
BUDDAH (190 "What Have They Done to My Song, Ma") ... 5-8 70
DWAIN (809 "The Shark") ... 15-25 60
DWAIN (818 "Five") ... 15-25 60
FELICE (711 "Hot Fudge Sundaes and Pizza Pies") ... 30-40 63
GOLD (101 "Runnin' Scared") ... 20-30 60
MGM (13220 "Hi-Lili, Hi Lo") ... 8-12 64
MARLU (7003 "Little Teardrops") ... 30-40 61
POPLAR (112 "Amazon Trail") ... 15-25 62
(This same number was also used for a Voxpoppers release.)
Also see PARAMOUNTS

VINCENT, Stan, & Del Satins

Singles: 7-inch

COMET (915 "She's So Wonderful") ... 4-8 95
(Clear vinyl. 500 made.)
COMET (2147 "She's So Wonderful") ... 75-125 63
Also see DEL SATINS

VINCENT, Tami

Singles: 7-inch

RCA (8853 "When I Fall in Love") ... 10-15 66

VINCENT, Vinnie

Singles: 7-inch

ALJA (1022 "Wailin' and Scalin'") ... 50-75

VINCENT, Walter
(With Chatman's Mississippi Hot Footers)

Singles: 78 rpm

BRUNSWICK (7190 "Mississippi Yodelin' Blues") ... 500-750 30

VINCENTE, Vin

Singles: 7-inch

SWINGIN' (644 "Little Cutie") ... 20-30 63

VINE, Joe

Singles: 7-inch

HERCULES (103 "Down & Out") ... 10-15 65

VINE, Marty

Singles: 7-inch

EPIC (9382 "Cheryl") ... 15-25 60
MASTERMADE (101 "Cheryl") ... 10-15 61

Picture Sleeves

EPIC (9382 "Cheryl") ... 20-30 60

VINE STREET BOYS

Singles: 7-inch

ERA (3105 "That Certain Someone") ... 8-12 63

VINES

Singles: 7-inch

CEE=JAY (582 "Love So Sweet") ... 20-30 61

VINNIE & SUE

Singles: 7-inch

SPRING (1111 "Your Name and Mine") ... 25-35 60

VINNY & KENNY

Singles: 7-inch

FIRE (1005 "Schooltime") ... 15-25 59

VINNY & NITELITES

Singles: 7-inch

KC (107 "Poppin' Popcorn") ... 10-15 62

VINSON, Don

Singles: 7-inch

MGM (12734 "Livin' with the Blues") ... 10-20 58
RISING SONS (706 "Don't Shoot") ... 5-10 67

VINSON, Eddie *R&B '47*
(Eddie "Cleanhead" Vinson)

Singles: 78 rpm

KING ... 15-25 50-52
MERCURY ... 10-25 46-55

Singles: 7-inch

BETHLEHEM (3016 "Sweet Lovin' Baby") . 8-12 61
BETHLEHEM (11097 "Cherry Red") ... 8-12 61
BLUESWAY ... 5-10 67
KING (4563 "Good Bread Alley") ... 100-150 52
KING (4582 "Lonesome Train") ... 100-150 52
MERCURY (70334 "Old Man Boogie") ... 50-100 54
MERCURY (70525 "Anxious Heart") ... 50-75 54
MERCURY (70621 "Anxious Heart") ... 50-75 55
RIVERSIDE (4512 "Back Door Blues") ... 5-10 62

LPs: 10/12-inch

AAMCO (312 "Eddie "Cleanhead" Vinson Sings") ... 25-35
BETHLEHEM (5005 "Eddie "Cleanhead" Vinson Sings") ... 50-100 57
BETHLEHEM (6000 series) ... 5-10 78
BLUES TIME ... 10-15 69
BLUESWAY (6007 "Cherry Red") ... 10-20 67
DELMARK ... 5-10 80
KING (1087 "Cherry Red") ... 10-15 69
MUSE ... 5-10 78-83
REGGIES ... 5-10 81
RIVERSIDE (3502 "Backdoor Blues") ... 30-40 62
Also see BROWN, Roy
Also see HARRIS, Wynonie / Roy Brown / Eddie Vinson
Also see WILLIAMS, Cootie
Also see WITHERSPOON, Jimmy / Eddie Vinson

VINSON, Eddie "Cleanhead," & Roomful Of Blues

LPs: 10/12-inch

MUSE ... 5-10 82
Also see ROOMFUL OF BLUES

VINSON, Eddie / Jimmy Witherspoon

LPs: 10/12-inch

KING (634 "Battle of the Blues, Vol. 3") ... 500-750 59
Also see VINSON, Eddie
Also see WITHERSPOON, Jimmy

VINSON, Smith

Singles: 7-inch

STATUE (20 "The Trials of a Flower Child") ... 50-75 71

LPs: 10/12-inch

PLAYBOY ... 15-20 '70s

VINTAGE

Singles: 7-inch

CATAMOUNT (117 "Harbor Lights") ... 5-10 66

VINTON, Bobby *P&R/R&B/LP '62*
(Bobby Vinton Orchestra)

Singles: 7-inch

ABC ... 4-6 74-77
ALPINE (50 "First Impression") ... 10-20 59
ALPINE (59 "The Freshman and a Sophomore") ... 10-20 60
AURAVISION (6722 "Rain, Rain Go Away") ... 8-12 64
(Cardboard flexi-disc, one of six by six different artists. Columbia Record Club "Enrollment Premium." Set comes in custom paper sleeve.)
CURB ... 3-5 88-89
ELEKTRA ... 4-6 78
EPIC (2207 "Roses Are Red"/"Rain Rain Go Away") ... 5-10 63
EPIC (9417 "Tornado") ... 10-15 60
EPIC (9440 "Little Lonely One") ... 10-15 61
EPIC (9469 "Well I Ask Ya") ... 10-15 61
EPIC (9509 "Roses Are Red") ... 5-10 62
(Black vinyl.)
EPIC (9509 "Roses Are Red") ... 15-25 62
(Red vinyl. Promotional issue.)
EPIC (9532 "Rain Rain Go Away") ... 5-10 62
EPIC (9561 "Trouble Is My Middle Name") ... 5-10 62
(Black vinyl.)
EPIC (9561 "Trouble Is My Middle Name") ... 15-25 62
(Red vinyl.)
EPIC (9577 "Faded Pictures") ... 5-10 63
EPIC (9593 "Blue on Blue") ... 5-10 63
(Black vinyl.)
EPIC (9593 "Blue on Blue") ... 5-10 63
(Blue vinyl. Promotional issue.)
EPIC (9614 thru 9705) ... 5-10 63-64
EPIC (9730 "Mr. Lonely") ... 5-10 64
(Black vinyl.)
EPIC (9730 "Mr. Lonely") ... 15-25 64
(Red vinyl. Promotional issue only.)
EPIC (9741 thru 9894) ... 5-10 64-65
EPIC (10014 thru 10305) ... 5-10 66-68
EPIC (10350 "Halfway to Paradise"/"Kristie") ... 4-6 68
EPIC (10350 "Halfway to Paradise"/"[My Little] Christie") ... 8-10 68
(Note alternative B-side title.)
EPIC (10397 thru 50169) ... 4-6 66-75
EPIC MEMORY LANE ... 3-6 66-87
LARC ... 3-5 83
MELODY ... 15-25 59
TAPESTRY ... 3-6 79-82

Picture Sleeves

EPIC (9509 "Roses Are Red") ... 8-12 62
(Has an angle head shot of Bobby. No hand shown.)
EPIC (9509 "Roses Are Red") ... 8-12 62
(Has a front shot of Bobby, with hand under chin.)
EPIC (9532 "Rain Rain Go Away") ... 8-12 62
EPIC (9561 "Trouble Is My Middle Name") ... 8-12 62
(Color sleeve.)
EPIC (9561 "Trouble Is My Middle Name") ... 10-20 62
(Black-and-white. Promotional issue only.)
EPIC (9577 thru 9705) ... 8-12 63-64
EPIC (9730 "Mr. Lonely") ... 8-12 64
(Pictures Bobby.)
EPIC (9730 "Mr. Lonely") ... 10-20 64
(Text-only sleeve. Promotional issue only.)
EPIC (9741 "Dearest Santa") ... 10-15 64
(Pictures Bobby.)
EPIC (9741 "Dearest Santa") ... 10-20 64
(Text-only sleeve. Promotional issue only.)
EPIC (9768 thru 10305) ... 5-10 65-68
EPIC (10350 "Halfway to Paradise"/"Kristie") ... 5-10 68
EPIC (10350 "Halfway to Paradise"/"[My Little] Christie") ... 8-12 68
(Note alternative B-side title.)
EPIC (10397 thru 10936) ... 5-8 68-72
TAPESTRY ... 3-5 80

EPs: 7-inch

EPIC ... 6-12 63-65
(Juke box issues.)

LPs: 10/12-inch

ABC ... 8-10 74-77
CSP ... 5-10 '80s
COLUMBIA ... 8-10 73
EPIC (579 "Dancing at the Hop") ... 20-25 60
(Monaural.)
EPIC (597 "Bobby Vinton") ... 20-25 61
(Monaural.)
EPIC (3727 "Dancing at the Hop") ... 25-35 60
(Stereo.)
EPIC (3780 "Bobby Vinton") ... 20-30 61
(Stereo.)
EPIC (24020 "Roses Are Red") ... 10-20 62
(Monaural.)
EPIC (24035 "The Big Ones") ... 10-20 62
(Monaural.)

EPIC (24049 "Greatest Hits of the Golden Groups") ... 10-20 63
(Monaural.)
EPIC (24068 "Blue Velvet") ... 10-20 63
(Black vinyl. Monaural.)
EPIC (20468 "Blue Velvet") ... 40-60 63
(Blue vinyl. Monaural. Promotional issue only.)
EPIC (24081 thru 24382) ... 10-20 64-68
(Monaural.)
EPIC (26020 "Roses Are Red") ... 10-20 62
(Stereo.)
EPIC (26035 "The Big Ones") ... 10-20 62
(Stereo.)
EPIC (26049 "Greatest Hits of the Golden Groups") ... 10-20 63
(Stereo.)
EPIC (26068 "Blue Velvet") ... 10-20 63
(Stereo.)
EPIC (26081 thru 26540) ... 10-20 64-70
(Stereo.)
EPIC (30000 series) ... 5-10 72-79
HARMONY ... 5-10 70
TAPESTRY ... 5-10 80
Also see CLARK, Dave, Five / Roy Meriwether Trio / Bobby Vinton / Bob Dylan
Also see CLARK, Dave, Five / New Christy Minstrels / Bobby Vinton / Jerry Vale
Also see JAN & DEAN / Bobby Vinton / Andy Williams

VINTON, Bobby / Chuck & Johnny

Singles: 7-inch

DIAMOND (121 "I Love You the Way You Are") ... 8-10 62

VINTON, Bobby, & Village Stompers

LPs: 10/12-inch

EPIC ... 10-20 66
Also see VILLAGE STOMPERS
Also see VINTON, Bobby

VIOLATIONS

Singles: 7-inch

DOT (16868 "You Sure Have Changed") ... 5-10 66

VIOLETTES

Singles: 7-inch

HERALD (594 "What Makes the World Go Round") ... 10-15 64

VIOLETTS

Singles: 7-inch

DIAMOND (243 "I Won't Cry") ... 5-10 68

VIOLINAIRES

("Voilinaires")

Singles: 78 rpm

DRUMMOND ... 75-125 54

Singles: 7-inch

CHECKER (5013 "Old Time Religion") ... 5-10 66
CHECKER (5063 "Salt of the Earth") ... 5-10 66
DRUMMOND (4000 "Another Soldier Gone") ... 450-650 54
(Group name is misspelled on label as: "Voilinaires.")

LPs: 10/12-inch

CHECKER (10017 "The Fantastic Violinaires") ... 10-15 66
Also see GALES

VIOLINS

(With Al Browne's Orchestra)

Singles: 7-inch

LAKE (713 "What Kind of Fool Am I") ... 40-60 62
Also see BROWNE, Al

VIOT, Russ

Singles: 7-inch

NOSE ... 5-10 67
Session: Davie Allan.
Also see ALLAN, Davie

VIPERS

Singles: 7-inch

DUCHESS (102 "Little Miss Sweetness") ... 40-50 '60s

VIPERS SKIFFLE GROUP

Singles: 7-inch

CAPITOL (3673 "Don't You Rock Me Daddy-O") ... 25-35 57
(With "Capitol Introduces" insert. Promotional issue only.)
CAPITOL (3673 "Don't You Rock Me Daddy-O") ... 10-20 57
(Without insert.)

Members: Johnny Martyn; Walt Whyton; Jean Van Den Basch. (Insert pictures four men but only names three.)

VIRG, MURF & PROF.

Singles: 7-inch

DECCA (30612 "Way Out") ... 10-15 58

VIRGIL & 4 CHANELS

Singles: 7-inch

DEB (508 "Waiting") ... 20-30 59
Also see CHANELS

VIRGIL BROTHERS

Singles: 7-inch

RARE EARTH (5006 "Look Away") ... 5-10 69

VIRGIN INSANITY

LPs: 10/12-inch

FUNKY (71411 "Illusions of the Maintaince Man") ... 75-100 '60s

VIRGIN SLEEP

Singles: 7-inch

DERAM ("Love") ... 10-20 67

VIRGINIA FOUR

Singles: 78 rpm

DECCA (7662 "Dig My Jelly Roll") ... 50-75 39
DECCA (7808 "I'd Feel Much Better") ... 50-75 39
VICTOR (23376 "Don't Leave Me Behind") ... 50-75 30
VICTOR (38569 "Since I Been Born") ... 50-75 30

VIRGINIA WOLVES

Singles: 7-inch

ABC (10972 "I Can't Believe That You're in Love with Me") ... 5-10 67
AMY (966 "Stay") ... 5-10 66

VIRGINIANS

Singles: 7-inch

DIAMOND (120 "There Goes My Baby") .. 10-20 62
Member: Bill Ramal.

VIRGINIANS

Singles: 7-inch

CUCA (6523 "Lonesome As Me") ... 8-12 65

VIRGINIANS

Singles: 7-inch

EPIC ... 5-10 66-67
Member: Bill Swofford.
Also see OLIVER

VIRGOS

Singles: 7-inch

PIONEER (16621 "You're a Stranger") ... 10-15 64
PIONEER (16624 "Cost of Love") ... 10-15 65

VIRTUE, Frank

(Frank Virtue Combo; Frank Virtuoso)

Singles: 78 rpm

ARCADE (135 "Ooh You Gotta") ... 5-10 55

Singles: 7-inch

ARCADE (135 "Ooh You Gotta") ... 10-15 55
JOY (275 "Midnight Hassle") ... 5-10 63
Also see VIRTUES
Also see VIRTUOSO, Frank

VIRTUES — P&R/R&B '59

(Frank Virtuoso & Virtues; Frank Virtuoso & His Quintet; Fantastic Virtues)

Singles: 7-inch

ABC ... 4-6 73
ABC-PAR (10071 "Vaya con Dios") ... 5-10 59
ARCADE ... 8-12 '50s
B.V.D. ... 5-10
FAYETTE (1626 "Guitar Shuffle") ... 5-10 64
HIGHLAND (2505 "Happy Guitar") ... 10-15 60
HUNT (Monaural) ... 5-10 59
HUNT (Stereo) ... 15-25 59
RHYTHM ... 8-12 '50s
SURE (500 series) ... 8-12 59
SURE (1700 series) ... 5-10 62
VIRNON (603 "Guitar Shimmy") ... 5-10 60
VIRTUE (190 "Cotton Candy") ... 5-10 66
VIRTUE (2503 "Guitar On the Wild Side") .. 5-10 69
WYNNE (123 "Highland Guitar") ... 5-10 60

LPs: 10/12-inch

FAYETTE ... 25-35 64
STRAND (1061 "Guitar Boogie Shuffle") .. 20-30 63
WYNNE (111 "Guitar Boogie Shuffle") ... 30-40 60
Members: Frank Virtuoso; Jimmy Bruno; John Renner; Joe Vespe.
Also see VIRTUE, Frank
Also see VIRTUOSO, Frank

VIRTUOSO, Frank

Singles: 7-inch

LIBERTY (55706 "Move On") ... 10-20 64
REFRESHMENT (1 "Mountaineer Mashed Potatoes") ... 25-50 '60s
RHYTHM (13 "Rollin' & Rockin'") ... 20-30
TONE-CRAFT (206 "San Antonio Rose") ... 10-20 '50s
TONE-CRAFT (207 "Rollin' & Rockin'") ... 50-75 '50s
Also see VIRTUE, Frank
Also see VIRTUES

VIRVA, Dan, & Flying "D" Ramblers

Singles: 7-inch

MARATHON (5002 "Duck Tail Cat") ... 250-350 '50s

VISAS

Singles: 7-inch

TIMELY (904 "Night Train") ... 10-20 65

VISCAYNES

Singles: 7-inch

TROPO (101 "Stop What You Are Doing") ... 150-200 61
(Credits "The Viscaynes and the Ramblers.")
TROPO (101 "Stop What You Are Doing") ... 50-100 61
(Credits only "The Viscaynes.")

VISCAYNES

Singles: 7-inch

VPM (1006 "Heavenly Angel") ... 15-25 61
(Same number used on a Biscaynes release.)
VEEP (1221 "Pauline") ... 5-10 65
Also see BISCAYNES
Also see WOODS, Jasper, & Viscaynes

VISCOS

Singles: 7-inch

JCP (103 "Midnight in Madrid") ... 8-12 '60s

VISCOUNT V

Singles: 7-inch

LAVETTE (5003 "Cherry Red Vette") ... 10-20 '60s
LAVETTE (5010 "She Doesn't Know") ... 10-20 '60s

VISCOUNTS

Singles: 78 rpm

MERCURY (71073 "My Girl") ... 10-15 57

Singles: 7-inch

MERCURY (71073 "My Girl") ... 10-15 57
RESERVE (123 "Rejoice") ... 10-15 57
VEGA (1003 "Saki-Laki-Waki") ... 8-12 59

VISCOUNTS

Singles: 7-inch

STAR-FAX (1002 "Wandering") ... 1000-1200 63

VISCOUNTS — P&R '59

(Vicounts)

Singles: 7-inch

AMY (940 "Harlem Nocturne") ... 5-10 65
AMY (949 "Night Train") ... 5-10 66
CORAL ... 5-10 66-67
MADISON (123 "Harlem Nocturne") ... 10-15 59
MADISON (129 "The Touch") ... 10-15 60
MADISON (133 "Night Train") ... 10-15 60
MADISON (140 "Wabash Blues") ... 10-15 60
MADISON (152 "Shadrack") ... 10-15 61
MADISON (159 "Opus 1") ... 10-15 61
MADISON (165 "Sophisticated Lady") ... 10-15 61
MR. PEACOCK ... 8-12 61-62
MR. PEEKE ... 5-10 62-63
REO (8435 "Harlem Nocturne") ... 10-15 59
(Canadian.)

LPs: 10/12-inch

AMY (8008 "Harlem Nocturne") ... 20-30 65
MADISON (1001 "Viscounts") ... 50-100 60
Members: Bobby Spievak; Joe Spievak; Harry Haller; Larry Vecchio; Clark Smith; Mike De Stefano.

VISCOUNTS

Singles: 7-inch

TEEN TUNES (200 "Long Tall Sally") ... 75-125
Member: Dave McQuitty.
Also see McQUITTY, Dave

VISIONS

Singles: 7-inch

WARWICK (108 "Darling Dear") ... 20-30 59

VISIONS

Singles: 7-inch

R&R (3002 "It's You I Love") ... 500-1000 60

VISIONS

Singles: 7-inch

BIG TOP (3092 "Tell Me You're Mine") ... 15-25 62
BIG TOP (3119 "Secret World of Tears"). 15-25 62
BRUNSWICK (55206 "There'll Be No Next Time") ... 5-10 61
COED (598 "Tell Her Now") ... 5-10 64
CORAL (65575 "Vision of Love") ... 10-15 63
ELGEY (1003 "Teenager's Life") ... 15-25 60
LOST NITE (102 "Teenager's Life") ... 10-15 61
MERCURY (72188 "Oh Boy What a Girl") ... 5-10 63
ORIGINAL SOUND (32 "Look at Me Now") ... 15-20 63

VISIONS

Singles: 7-inch

TRIODEX (115 "Peace of Mind") ... 5-10 62

VISIONS

Singles: 7-inch

VIMCO (20 "Take Her") ... 30-50 65
VIMCO (20 "Route 66") ... 75-125 65
(Same number used twice.)
VIMCO (21 "Humpty Dumpty") ... 30-50 66

VISIONS

Singles: 7-inch

UNI (55031 "How Can I Be Down") ... 5-10 67
UNI (55042 "Small Town Commotion") ... 5-10 67
W.B. (5898 "Bulldog Cadillac") ... 5-10 67

VISIONS OF A NEW 'OUR

Singles: 7-inch

CAPITOL (2554 "Everything I Am") ... 5-10 69

VISITORS

Singles: 7-inch

TOWER (268 "The Wild Angels") ... 8-10 66
Session: Davie Allan.
Also see ALLAN, Davie

VISTAS

Singles: 7-inch

REBEL (77755 "Ghost Wave") ... 15-25 63
VENPRO (1000 "Ghost Wave") ... 25-35 63
(First issue.)

VISTAS

Singles: 7-inch

TUFF (990 "No Return") ... 15-25 64

VISUALS

Singles: 7-inch

JASON SCOTT (11 "Please Don't Be Mad at Me") ... 4-6 81
(500 made.)
POPLAR (115 "Maybe You") ... 10-20 62
POPLAR (117 "My Juanita") ... 15-25 63
POPLAR (121 "Please Don't Be Mad at Me") ... 250-350 63

VITALE, Don

Singles: 7-inch

CONQUEST (4501 "Please Tell Her") ... 8-12 62

VITALE, Jo Jo

Singles: 7-inch

COUNSELLOR (6209 "Teenage Dream") ... 10-20 62
MAY (127 "My Little Cinderella") ... 15-25 62

Picture Sleeves

COUNSELLOR (6209 "Teenage Dream") ... 25-35

VITA-MEN

Singles: 7-inch

CHALLENGE (59327 "Frog Legs") ... 5-10 66

VITELLS

Singles: 7-inch

DECCA (31362 "Shirley") ... 30-40 62

VITO, Gene

(With the Playboys)

Singles: 7-inch

BLAST (213 "Playboy") ... 8-12 64
DECCA (32140 "With the Dawn") ... 5-10 67
DECCA (32198 "You Knew About Her All the Time") ... 5-10 67

VITO, Sonny

Singles: 7-inch

ABC-PAR (9958 "Teenage Blues") ... 15-25 58
APRIL (1100 "Hush") ... 15-25 59

CHANCELLOR (1112 "I Remember the Night") 10-20 62
STRAND (25045 "Mister Groovy") 10-20 61

VITO & SALUTATIONS P&R '63

Singles: 7-inch

APT (25079 "Walkin' ") 40-50 65
BOOM (60020 "Bring Back Yesterday") .. 10-15 66
CRYSTAL BALL (104 "Unchained Melody") 4-8 77
(Black vinyl. 500 made.)
CRYSTAL BALL (104 "Unchained Melody") 8-12 77
(Red vinyl. 25 made.)
HAROLD (5009 "Gloria") 8-12 62
HERALD (583 "Unchained Melody") 20-30 63
HERALD (586 "Extraordinary Girl") 20-30 64
KRAM (1202 "Your Way") 30-40 62
(First issue. Reissue label is "Kran.")
KRAN (5002 "Your Way") 10-15 62
RAYNA (5009 "Gloria") 20-30 62
(No reference to a distributor.)
RAYNA (5009 "Gloria") 10-15 62
(Label reads: "Nat'l dist. By Seg-Way Record Corp.")
RED BOY (1001 "So Wonderful") 15-25 66
RED BOY (5009 "Gloria") 5-10 66
REGINA (1320 "Get a Job") 10-15 64
RUST (5106 "Can I Depend on You") 5-10 66
SANDBAG (103 "So Wonderful") 8-12 68
STOOP SOUNDS (103 "Be My Girlfriend") 100-150 96
(Limited edition. Estimates range from fewer than 10 to several dozen made.)
STOOP SOUNDS (107 "Over the Rainbow") 100-150 97
(Limited edition. Estimates range from fewer than 10 to several dozen made.)
STOOP SOUNDS (108 "Gloria") 100-150 97
(Limited edition. Estimates range from fewer than 10 to several dozen made.)
STOOP SOUNDS (109 "I Believe") 100-150 97
(Limited edition. Estimates range from fewer than 10 to several dozen made.)
WELLS (1008 "Can I Depend on You") ... 10-20 64
(Black vinyl.)
WELLS (1008 "Can I Depend on You") ... 40-50 64
(Yellow vinyl. Reportedly 20 made.)

LPs: 10/12-inch

KAPE (1002 "Greatest Hits") 10-15 73
RED BOY (200/201 "Greatest Hits") 20-30 81
(Two-disc set, each with a different number.)
ROYAL-T (404 "Unchained Memories") . 10-15 89
Members: Vito Balsamo; Bobby DiPaolo; Bobby Mitchell; Johnny Venero; Shelly Buchansky; Ray Russell; Randy Silverman; Len Citron; Frank Fox; Alan Messenger.
Also see KELLOGS
Also see POSSESSIONS

VI-TONES

Singles: 7-inch

ARTEEN (1007 "Stop What You Are Doing") 50-100 61

VI-TONES

Singles: 7-inch

TIMES SQUARE (105 "The Storm") 10-15 64
(Black vinyl.)
TIMES SQUARE (105 "The Storm") 15-25 64
(Yellow vinyl.)

VITRONES

Singles: 7-inch

AUDITION (6104 "London Fog") 10-20 65

VIVATONES

Singles: 7-inch

BRIAN INT'L (112 "The Vivatones Are Rocking") 75-100

VIVIENNE

Singles: 7-inch

VIP (1003 "Light a Candle") .... 10-20 '60s

VIXEN

LPs: 10/12-inch

AZRA (64 "Made in Hawaii") 250-350 83
(Blue vinyl.)
AZRA (64 "Made in Hawaii") 50-100 83
(Picture disc. Issued in boxed set with photo and bio. 150 made.)
Members: Marty Friedman; Kim La Chance; Jeff Graves; Kimo.

VOCAL LORDS

Singles: 7-inch

ABLE ("At Seventeen") 150-200 59
(First issue. No selection number used.)
TAURUS (2968 "At Seventeen") 50-100 59
(Identification number shown since no selection number is used.)

VOCAL TONES

Singles: 7-inch

BIM BAM BOOM (117 "Walkin' with My Baby") 4-6 73
(Black vinyl.)
BIM BAM BOOM (117 "Walkin' with My Baby") 5-8 73
(Green vinyl.)
JUANITA (100 "Walkin' with My Baby") 50-80 58
Members: Roland Martinez; Bobby Moore; Bobby Robinson; Irving Lee Gail.
Also see PRETENDERS
Also see VOCALTONES

VOCALAIRES

Singles: 7-inch

HERALD (573 "Dance Dance") 30-40 62
Member: Eric Nathanson.
Also see BLUE SONNETTS

VOCALAIRES / Actuals

Singles: 7-inch

RONNIE (200 "Dream Ship"/"We Built a Nest") 4-6 76
Also see DUBS / Actuals

VOCALEERS R&B '53

("Vocaleers and Joe Duncan"; "with Rhythm Accompaniment")

Singles: 78 rpm

RED ROBIN 35-75 53-54

Singles: 7-inch

OLD TOWN (1089 "This Is the Night") 15-25 60
OLDIES 45 .... 5-8 65
PARADISE (113 "Have You Ever Loved Someone") 20-25 59
RED ROBIN (113 "Be True") 100-200 53
RED ROBIN (114 "Is It a Dream") 100-200 53
RED ROBIN (119 "I Walk Alone") 100-200 53
RED ROBIN (125 "Will You Be True") .. 100-200 54
RED ROBIN (132 "Angel Face") 100-200 54
TWISTIME (11 "A Golden Tear") 10-20 62
VEST (832 "Hear My Plea") 100-150 61

LPs: 10/12-inch

RELIC (5094 "Is It a Dream") 5-10 92
Members: Joe Duncan; Curtis Dunham; Ted Williams; Mel Walton; Bill Walker; Lamarr Cooper; Joe Powell; Richard Blandon; Leo Fuller; Curtis Blandon; Caesar Williams.
Also see BLENDERS
Also see LITTLE ESTHER & JUNIOR WITH THE JOHNNY OTIS ORCHESTRA / Johnny Otis Orchestra with the Vocaleers

VOCALEERS / Mango Jones

Singles: 7-inch

OLDIES 45 .... 5-10 65
Also see VOCALEERS

VOCALS

Singles: 7-inch

TANGERINE (938 "Lonesome Mood") 5-10 64
TANGERINE (945 "I Could Make You Change Your Mind") 5-10 64

VOCAL-TEENS

Singles: 7-inch

DOWNSTAIRS (1000 "Be a Slave") 5-10 73

VOCALTONES

Singles: 78 rpm

APOLLO 30-40 56

Singles: 7-inch

APOLLO (488 "My Girl") 75-125 56
APOLLO (492 "Darling") 100-150 56
APOLLO (497 "My Version of Love") 150-200 56
CINDY (3004 "Walkin' My Baby") 30-40 57
JUANITA (100 "Walkin' My Baby") 50-150 58
Members: Roland Martinez; Eddie Quiñones; Wyndon Porter; Tom Grate; Bobby Robinson.
Also see DOVERS
Also see VOCAL TONES
Also see 5 WINGS

VO-DE-O-DOES

Singles: 7-inch

CLASS (200 "Penelope") 10-15 56

VOGT, Les

Singles: 7-inch

APT (25042 "Moon Rocketin' ") 15-25 60
IONA (1001 "Moon Rocketin' ") 35-50 60

VOGUES

Singles: 7-inch

SURF (5020 "Left Over Love") 10-15 58

VOGUES P&R '65

Singles: 7-inch

ABC 4-6 73
ABC-PAR 5-10 65
ASTRA (1029 "You're the One") 4-6 73
(Black vinyl.)
ASTRA (1029 "You're the One") 5-8 73
(Colored vinyl.)
ASTRA (1030 "Five O'Clock World") 4-6 73
BELL (991 "We're On Our Way") 4-6 71
BELL (45127 "I'll Be with You") 4-6 71
BELL (45158 "American Family") 4-6 71
BLUE STAR (229 "You're the One") 15-25 65
CASCADE (5908 "Ev'ry Day, Ev'ry Night") 15-25 59
CO & CE 5-10 65-67
COLLECTABLES .... 3-5 '80s
DOT (15798 "Love Is a Funny Little Game") 10-20 58
DOT (15859 "Try Baby Try") 10-20 58
ERA .... 4-6 '70s
GOLDIES 45 .... 3-6 73
GUSTO 3-5 81
MGM 5-10 67
MAINSTREAM 4-6 72
REPRISE (Except 0663) 4-6 68-71
REPRISE (0663 "Just What I've Been Looking For") 5-10 68
REVUE (11005 "Love Is Gone") 5-10 67
REVUE (11018 "My Baby Loves Me") 5-10 68
ROCK'N MANIA 3-5
SSS INT'L 4-6 77
SUN 4-6 77-79
20TH FOX 4-6 73-74

LPs: 10/12-inch

CSP 5-8 82
CO & CE 25-35 65-66
51 WEST .... 5-10 '80s
PICKWICK 8-10 71
PLANTATION (43 "Golden Hits") 5-8 81
REPRISE 10-15 68-70
RHINO 5-8 88
SSS INT'L (34 "Greatest Hits") 5-10 77
SEARS .... 15-20 '60s
Members: Bob Bush; Bill Burkette; Hugh Geyer; Chuck Blasko; Don Miller. SSS Int'l/Plantation/51 West/CSP line-up: Charly Tichenor; Dick Stevens; Kelly Goad; Bill Packard; Bill Davidson.
Also see VAL-AIRES

VOICE MASTERS R&B '70

Singles: 7-inch

ANNA (101 "Hope and Pray") 40-60 59
ANNA (102 "Needed") 40-60 59
BAMBOO 8-15 68-70
FRISCO (15235 "In Love in Vain") 30-50 60
(Identification number shown since no selection number is used.)
Members: Ty Hunter; C.P. Spencer; Lamont Dozier; David Ruffin; Freddie Gorman.
Also see DOZIER, Lamont
Also see HUNTER, Ty
Also see ORIGINALS
Also see ROMEOS
Also see RUFFIN, David

VOICES

Singles: 78 rpm

CASH 15-25 55

Singles: 7-inch

CASH (1011 "Why") 40-50 55
CASH (1014 "Hey Now") 30-40 55
CASH (1015 "Takes Two to Make a Home") 30-40 55
CASH (1016 ("Santa Claus Boogie") 40-50 55
Members: Earl Nelson; Bobby Byrd; Ernie Freeman.
Also see BYRD, Bobby
Also see FREEMAN, Ernie
Also see NELSON, Earl

VOIGHT, Wes

(With the Town Three; Chip Taylor)

Singles: 7-inch

DELUXE (6176 "Midnight Blues") 50-100 58
DELUXE (6180 "I Want a Lover") 35-45 58
KING (5211 "I'm Movin' In") 40-60 59
(Monaural.)
KING (S-5211 "I'm Movin' In") 100-150 59
(Stereo.)
KING (5231 "I'm Ready to Go Steady") ... 25-35 59
(Monaural.)
KING (S-5231 "I'm Ready to Go Steady") 50-80 59
(Stereo.)
Also see TOWN THREE

VOIT, Johnny

Singles: 7-inch

OXBORO (3083 "Why Wait for Winter") ..... 5-10 '60s

VOIVOD LP '89

EPs: 12-inch

COMBAT (8124 "Thrashing Rage") 15-20
(Picture disc.)

LPs: 10/12-inch

MECHANIC 5-8 89
("Too Scared to Scream") 15-25 89
(Picture disc. No label name or selection number used.)

VOLCANICS

Singles: 7-inch

PARKWAY (149 "But I Love Her") 5-10 67

VOLCANOES

Singles: 7-inch

EPIC (9490 "Shotgun") 10-15 62

VOLCANOS

Singles: 7-inch

TAILSPIN (1 "You Knock Me Out") 10-20 60

VOLCANOS R&B '65

Singles: 7-inch

ARCTIC (103 "Baby") 5-10 65
ARCTIC (106 "Storm Warning") 5-10 65
ARCTIC (111 "Help Wanted") 5-10 65
ARCTIC (115 "Laws of Love") 5-10 65
ARCTIC (125 "Lady's Man") 5-10 66
ARCTIC (128 "Make Your Move") 5-10 66
HARTHON (138 "Movin' and Groovin' ") .. 10-20 64
HARTHON (146 "Take Me Back Again") . 10-20 65
VIRTUE (2513 "No Trespassing") 4-8 70
Members: Gene Faith; Earl Young; Dennis Harris; Ron Kersey; Jimmy Ellis; John Hart; Stanley Wade; Michael Thompson.

VOLCHORDS

Singles: 7-inch

REGATTA (2004 "Bongo Love") 20-30 61

VOLK, Dennis

Singles: 7-inch

FLING (713 "You Are the One") 100-200 59

VOLK, Val

Singles: 7-inch

ROCKET (1050 "There'll Be a Rockin' Party Tonight") 100-200 59
Also see VOLK BROTHERS

VOLK BROTHERS

Singles: 7-inch

CLOVER (1003 "Ducks Flying Backward") 15-25 60
(No artist credit shown on label.)
Member: Val Volk.
Also see VOLK, Val

VOLKSWAGONS

Singles: 7-inch

DO-RE-MI (201 "The Astronaut") .... 15-20 '60s

VOLTAIRES

Singles: 7-inch

BACONE (9468 "My My Baby") 50-75

VOLTONES

Singles: 7-inch

DYNAMIC (108 "If She Should Call") 1000-1500 59

VOLUMES

(With Ben Smith's Orchestra)

Singles: 78 rpm

JAGUAR 50-100 54

Singles: 7-inch
JAGUAR (3004 "I Won't Tell a Soul") .. 500-700 54
KAREN ... 10-20
Also see WATKINS, La Cille, & Volumes

VOLUMES P&R '62
(Valume's)
Singles: 7-inch
ABC ... 4-6 73
AMERICAN ARTS (6 "Gotta Give Her Love") ... 20-30 64
AMERICAN ARTS (18 "I Just Can't Help Myself") ... 20-30 65
ASTRA (1020 "Gotta Give Her Love") ... 8-12 65
CHEX (1002 "I Love You") ... 100-200 62
(Label mistakenly credits "Valume's.")
CHEX (1002 "I Love You") ... 25-35 62
(Credits the "Volumes." No mention of distribution by Jay-Gee.)
CHEX (1002 "I Love You") ... 15-25 62
(Credits the "Volumes." Reads "Nationally Dist. by Jay-Gee Rec. Co. Inc.")
CHEX (1005 "The Bell") ... 15-25 62
IMPACT (1017 "That Same Old Feeling") ... 25-50 66
INFERNO ... 10-20 67-68
JUBILEE (5446 "Sandra") ... 10-15 63
JUBILEE (5454 "Our Song") ... 10-15 63
OLD TOWN (1154 "Why") ... 15-25 64
TWIRL (2016 "I Got Love") ... 15-25 61
VIRGO ... 4-6 73
LPs: 10/12-inch
RELIC ... 5-10 85
Also see NUTMEGS / Volumes

VOLZ, Ron, & Rockin' R's
Singles: 7-inch
TEMPUS (1515 "I'm Still in Love with You") ... 100-150 59
(First issue.)
VEE-JAY (334 "I'm Still in Love with You") ... 30-50 59
Also see ROCKIN' R's

VON, Gary
Singles: 7-inch
DOT (16730 "Heartbreaking Emily") ... 5-10 65
LTD (406 "Can You Tell Me Why") ... 5-10 66
RE-VON (101 "I Wanna Know") ... 5-10 64

VON, Tawny
Singles: 7-inch
ENTRE (1002 "Last Night") ... 10-15 66

VON & VOYAGERS
Singles: 7-inch
FLAME (7301 "Shortest Way to Wealth") 10-20 '60s

VON CARL, Jimmy
(With the June Voices, Sax Kari & Orchestra)
Singles: 7-inch
FLICK (002 "Lonely Night") ... 30-40 59
Also see KARI, Sax

VONDELLS
Singles: 7-inch
AIRTOWN ... 8-12
MARVELLO (5003 "Valentino") ... 50-75 '50s
MARVELLO (5006 "Leonora") ... 50-75 '50s

VON DRAKE, Ludwig
Singles: 7-inch
BUENA VISTA (386 "I'm Ludwig Von Drake") ... 10-15 61

VON GAYELS
Singles: 7-inch
DORE (544 "The Twirl") ... 15-25 60
U.S.A. (1221 "Loneliness") ... 30-50 59
Members: Joe Brackenridge; Stacy Steel Jr.; Jimmy Washington; Willie C. Robinson; Charles Johnson.
Also see CASCADES

VONNAIR SISTERS
Singles: 7-inch
BUENA VISTA ... 5-10 61-63
Also see ANNETTE & VONNAIR SISTERS

VONNS
Singles: 7-inch
KING (5793 "So Many Days") ... 10-15 63

VON RUDEN
(Rudy Von Ruden)
Singles: 7-inch
IVANHOE (101 "Spider & the Fly") ... 10-20 70
IVANHOE (503 "Spider & the Fly") ... 10-20 70
Also see JOHNNY & SHY GUYS

VONS
Singles: 7-inch
POP ("Rollin' Stone") ... 75-125
(Selection number not known.)

VONTASTICS P&R/R&B '66
Singles: 7-inch
CHESS (2024 "Why Must We Part") ... 5-10 67
MOONSHOT (6702 "When My Baby Comes Back Home") ... 15-20
ST. LAWRENCE (1007 "Peace of Mind") ... 8-12 65
ST. LAWRENCE (1009 "I Need You") ... 8-12 65
ST. LAWRENCE (1014 "Day Tripper") ... 8-12 66
ST. LAWRENCE (1023 "You Can Work It Out") ... 8-12 66
SATELLITE (2002 "I'll Never Say Goodbye") ... 25-35 65
TODDLIN' TOWN (115 "Let Me Down Easy") ... 5-10 69
Members: Bobby Newsome; Jose Holmes; Kenneth Golar; Raymond Penn.
Also see FANTASTIC VONTASTICS

VONTONES
Singles: 7-inch
AL KING (11011 "Bald Headed Daddy") .. 50-75 61

VOO DOO MEN
Singles: 7-inch
SOMA (1407 "MoJo Workin") ... 25-50 '60s
Also see BUFORD, Mojo

VOORHIES, Lee
Singles: 7-inch
STARDUST (671 "Load Up My Blues") ... 100-150

VOTRIAN, Pete
Singles: 7-inch
RENDEZVOUS (104 "We Have It Made") ... 15-20 59

VOWELS
Singles: 7-inch
LEBAM (156 "It's Alright") ... 10-20 '60s
LEBAM (157 "Your Lovin' Kisses") ... 15-25 '60s
Session: Andy Belvin.
Also see BELVIN, Andy

VOWS
Singles: 7-inch
BIG 3 (400 "Say You'll Be Mine") ... 10-20 '60s
(Reissued as by the Majors.)
MARKAY (103 "I Wanna a Chance") ... 500-600 62
(Black label.)
MARKAY (103 "I Wanna Chance") ... 30-40 62
(Orange label. Note slight title change.)
RAN-DEE (112 "Girl in Red") ... 8-12 63
STA-SET (402 "Say You'll Be Mine") ... 20-30 64
TAMARA (760 "Dottie") ... 15-25 64
V.I.P. (25016 "Buttered Popcorn") ... 20-30 65
(Single-sided disc. Promotional issue only.)
V.I.P. (25016 "Buttered Popcorn"/"Tell Me") ... 40-50 65

VOXMEN
Singles: 7-inch
VM (8438 "Good Things") ... 50-75 67

VOXPOPPERS P&R/R&B '58
Singles: 7-inch
AMP 3 (1004 "Wishing for Your Love") ... 15-25 58
MERCURY (71282 "Wishing for Your Love") ... 10-20 58
MERCURY (71315 "Pony Tail") ... 10-15 58
POPLAR (107 "Come Back Little Girl") ... 10-15 57
POPLAR (112 "Come Back Little Girl") ... 10-15 57
(Each of the Poplar discs has a different flip. This same number was also used for a Stan Vincent release.)
POPLAR (122 "A Love to Last a Lifetime") ... 8-12 64
VERSAILLES (200 "A Blessing After All") ... 20-30 59
EPs: 7-inch
MERCURY (3391 "Voxpoppers") ... 75-125 58

VOYAGERS
Singles: 7-inch
TITAN (1712 "I Never Loved Anyone") ... 20-30 61

VOYAGERS
Singles: 7-inch
20TH FOX (410 "The Keeper of My Heart") ... 5-10 63

VOYAGERS
Singles: 7-inch
FEATURE (101 "Can't Save This Heart") ... 15-25 65
FEATURE (111 "Away") ... 15-25 66
Members: Joey Gonzales; Jay Seger; Steve Porter; Lance Davenport; Dave King.

VOYTEK, Jimmy, & Knights
Singles: 7-inch
CAPER (1551 "Close Your Eyes") ... 50-75 59
SCOTT ... 10-20 58

VULCANES
(Vulcaines)
Singles: 7-inch
GOLIATH (1348 "Stomp Sign") ... 15-25 62
GOLIATH (1350 "Last Prom") ... 15-25 63

VULCANES
Singles: 7-inch
CAPITOL (5199 "Twilight City") ... 5-10 64
CAPITOL (5285 "Liverpool") ... 5-10 64

VULCANES
Singles: 7-inch
IMPERIAL (66204 "Green Light") ... 5-10 66
LIBERTY (55995 "Let's Go Baby") ... 5-10 67

VULCANS
Singles: 7-inch
FLICK (010 "Jambo") ... 8-12 60

VULTURES
Singles: 7-inch
JRJ (1105 "Good Lovin") ... 60-80 65
(500 copies made.)

VY-DELS
Singles: 7-inch
GARNET (101 "What I'm Gonna Do") ... 10-20 65

VYNE, Judy
Singles: 7-inch
CUCA (1005 "Hell's Bells") ... 15-25 60
Picture Sleeves
CUCA (1005 "Hell's Bells") ... 30-40 60

VYNES
Singles: 7-inch
ATHON (103 "I Might Be Free") ... 10-20

W

WADDELL, Phil
Singles: 7-inch
LUPINE (122 "Rocket Walk") ... 15-25 64

WADDY, Sandy
Singles: 7-inch
S.O.S. (1003 "Everything Is Everything") ... 8-12
WAND (1169 "Secret Love") ... 5-10 68

WADE, Adam P&R '60
(With George Paxton, His Orchestra and the Bel-Aire Singers)
Singles: 7-inch
COED ... 10-15 59-62
DALYA ... 4-6 '70s
EPIC ... 5-10 62-66
KIRSHNER ... 4-6 77
REMEMBER ... 4-6 69
W.B. ... 5-10 67-68
Picture Sleeves
COED (536 "Speaking of Her") ... 10-20 60
COED (539 "For the Want of Your Love") ... 10-20 60
COED (541 "Gloria's Theme") ... 10-20 60
COED (550 "The Writing on the Wall") ... 10-20 61
COED (553 "As If I Didn't Know") ... 10-20 61
COED (556 "Tonight I Won't Be There") .. 10-20 61
EPIC (9521 "I'm Climbin' the Wall") ... 5-10 62
EPIC (9557 "There'll Be No Teardrops Tonight") ... 5-10 62
EPIC (9609 "Theme from *Irma La Douce*") ... 5-10 63
EPs: 7-inch
COED (102 "Adam Wade") ... 10-20 60
(Promotional issue only.)
LPs: 10/12-inch
COED (902 "Adam Wade") ... 25-35 60
EPIC ... 15-20 62
KIRSHNER ... 5-10 77

WADE, Billy
(With the Third Degrees)
Singles: 7-inch
ABC (10991 "Tear It Up") ... 5-10 67

WADE, Billy
Singles: 7-inch
STAR ("Conscience Let Me Go") ... 75-125
(Selection number not known.)

WADE, Cory
Singles: 7-inch
USA (733 "Before It's Too Late") ... 8-12 62

WADE, Don
Singles: 7-inch
SAN (206 "Gone Gone Gone") ... 200-300 58
SAN (207 "Forever Yours") ... 250-350 59

WADE, Earl
Singles: 7-inch
SEVILLE (111 "Feel So Bad") ... 10-15 61
SWAN (4008 "I Dig Rock & Roll") ... 40-60 58

WADE, Elvis
Singles: 7-inch
MEMORY (244 "Memories of the King") ... 5-10 77
SAHARA (301 "Memories of the King") ... 10-15 77
(First issue.)

WADE, Iona, & Billboards
Singles: 7-inch
VISTONE (2025 "I Love You Baby") ... 200-300 62
(Yellow vinyl.)
Also see BILLBOARDS

WADE, Johnny, / Skitter Bob
Singles: 7-inch
PETAL (1280 "Please, Please Come Back") ... 8-12 62

WADE, Kenny
Singles: 7-inch
APOLLO (756 "Did You Ever") ... 8-12 61
ROULETTE (4418 "She's Got Soul") ... 8-12 62

WADE, Len
(With the Tikis)
Singles: 7-inch
DIAL (4047 "Whatcha Gonna Do") ... 5-10 66
MINARET (111 "My Bonnie") ... 5-10 63
MINARET (118 "Traveling Shoes") ... 5-10 64
U.A. (891 "Don't Put Me On") ... 5-10 65
U.A. (987 "Boss Beat") ... 5-10 66
Also see TIKIS

WADE, Lindy
Singles: 7-inch
TENDER (515 "Johnny Sorrow") ... 15-25 58

WADE, Morris
("Music by the Manhattans")
Singles: 7-inch
RANSOM (102 "It Was a Nite Like This") ... 500-700 58
Also see 4 PHARAOHS

WADE, Roger
Singles: 7-inch
HARMON (1003 "Little Girl") ... 40-50 62
THELMA (42282 "Little Girl") ... 25-35 62

WADE, Ronny
Singles: 78 rpm
KING (5099 "Annie Don't Work") ... 40-60 57
KING (5061 "Gotta Make You Mine") ... 50-75 57
Singles: 7-inch
KING (5099 "Annie Don't Work") ... 40-60 57
KING (5061 "Gotta Make You Mine") ... 50-75 57

WADE, Tommy
Singles: 7-inch
THUNDERBOLT (811 "Ain't Misbehavin' ") ... 5-10 59

WADE, Wilbert

Singles: 7-inch

LIBERTY (55780 "Come Here Girl")..........5-10 65

WADE, Willis

Singles: 7-inch

SIMS (278 "Sitting Here Thinking")............5-10 66

WADE & DICK

(With the College Kids)

Singles: 78 rpm

SUN (269 "Bop Bop Baby")..................... 30-50 57

Singles: 7-inch

SUN (269 "Bop Bop Baby")..................... 50-75 57

Members: Wade Moore; Dick Penner.

Also see PENNER, Dick

WADE & JAMIE

Singles: 7-inch

PALOMAR (2200 "Send for Me")...............8-12 63

WADOOD, Arleemah

Singles: 7-inch

WILLOW (23005 "Oh Baby")......................8-12 61

WADSWORTH, Terry

Singles: 7-inch

TOPAZ (1302 "Path of Broken Dreams") 10-15 60

WADSWORTH MANSION *P&R '70*

Singles: 7-inch

SUSSEX (209 "Sweet Mary").......................4-6 70

LPs: 10/12-inch

SUSSEX (7008 "Wadsworth Mansion")... 10-20 71

(Mistakenly shown as "Wadsworth Manison" on some issues.)

WAGGONER, Charlie

Singles: 7-inch

LINCO (503 "One-Eyed Sam")................ 75-85 58

WAGGONER, Mike, & Bops

Singles: 7-inch

DOVE (1101 "Blue Days Black Nights").. 50-75 '60s

VEE (2311 "Baby Baby")..................... 150-250

VEE (7002 "Basher #5")...................... 250-300 59

WAGNER, Bob

Singles: 7-inch

ACE (628 "A Girl Like You")......................5-10 61

ACE (669 "Blue Evening")........................5-10 62

WAGNER, Cliff

Singles: 7-inch

JEWEL (777 "Exception to the Rule")........8-12 67

JOLUM (105 "Somethings Got a Hold On Me").. 10-15 64

WAGNER, Danny, & Kindred Soul

Singles: 7-inch

IMPERIAL (66305 "I Lost a True Love").. 15-25 68

IMPERIAL (66327 "Harlem Shuffle")........ 10-15 68

LPs: 10/12-inch

IMPERIAL (12405 "Kindred Soul of Danny Wagner").. 20-30 68

WAGNER, Dick

(With the Frost)

Singles: 7-inch

DATE (1577 "Rainy Day")..........................8-12 67

DATE (1596 "Sunshine")........................ 20-30 68

Picture Sleeves

DATE (1577 "Rainy Day")...................... 10-20 67

WAGNER, Robert

Singles: 7-inch

LIBERTY (55069 "So Young")....................8-12 57

WAGNER, Ty, & Scotchmen

Singles: 7-inch

ERA (3168 "Slander").................................5-10 66

CHATTAHOOCHEE (699 "I'm a No Count")..5-10 66

WAGNER BROTHERS

Singles: 7-inch

ALLEY (1026 "Feeling Bad")......................5-10 66

WAGONER, Porter *C&W '54*

(With the Blackwood Brothers)

Singles: 78 rpm

RCA 5-10 53-57

Singles: 7-inch

RCA (0013 thru 1007).............................4-8 69-74

RCA (5086 thru 7638)......................... 10-20 53-59

RCA (7708 thru 9979)...........................5-10 60-71

RCA (10124 thru 11998)..........................4-6 74-79

W.B. 3-5 82-83

EPs: 7-inch

RCA (937 "A Satisfied Mind")..................10-20 56

RCA (938 "Company's Comin' ")..............10-20 56

LPs: 10/12-inch

ACCORD (7179 "Down Home Country")....5-10 82

CAMDEN (769 "A Satisfied Mind")..........10-20 63

CAMDEN (861 "Old Log Cabin for Sale").10-20 65

CAMDEN (942 "Your Old Love Letters")..10-20 66

CAMDEN (2116 "I'm Day Dreamin' Tonight")..10-20 66

CAMDEN (2116 "Ballads of Heart & Soul")..10-20 67

(Repackage of *I'm Day Dreamin' Tonight*.)

CAMDEN (2191 "Green Green Grass of Home")..10-15 68

CAMDEN (2321 "Country Feeling").........10-15 69

CAMDEN (2409 "Howdy Neighbor, Howdy")..10-15 70

CAMDEN (2478 "Porter Wagoner Country")..10-15 71

CAMDEN (2588 "The Silent Kind")..........10-15 73

CAMDEN (9010 "Blue Moon of Kentucky")..12-18 71

(Two discs.)

COUNTRY FIDELITY..................................5-8 82

H.S.R.D. (782 "Natural Wonder").............15-25 81

MCA/DOT...5-8 86

MUSIC MASTERS.......................................5-10

PICKWICK (7046 "Blue Moon of Kentucky")..8-12 77

(Two discs.)

PICKWICK (9010 "Blue Moon of Kentucky")...10-15 75

(Two discs.)

RCA (0142 thru 3210)..............................8-12 73-79

RCA (1358 "A Satisfied Mind")................30-40 56

RCA (2447 "A Slice of Life – Songs Happy 'N' Sad")..15-25 62

RCA (2650 "The Porter Wagoner Show")..15-25 63

RCA (2706 "Y'All Come").........................15-25 63

RCA (2840 "Porter Wagoner in Person") .15-25 64

RCA (2960 "Bluegrass Story")..................10-20 65

RCA (3389 "Thin Man From West Plains")..10-20 65

RCA (3488 "Grand Old Gospel")..............10-20 66

RCA (3509 "Live, On the Road")..............10-20 66

RCA (3560 "Best of Porter Wagoner")......10-20 66

RCA (3593 "Confessions of a Broken Man")..10-20 66

RCA (3683 "Soul of a Convict")...............10-20 67

RCA (3797 "Cold Hard Facts of Life")......10-20 67

RCA (3855 "More Grand Old Gospel").....10-20 67

RCA (3968 thru 4810).............................10-20 68-72

TUDOR (100302 "Porter Wagoner's Greatest")..5-8 84

W.B. (23783 "Viva Porter Wagoner")...........5-8 83

Also see NORMA JEAN

Also see SNOW, Hank / Hank Locklin / Porter Wagoner

WAGONER, Porter, & Skeeter Davis

LPs: 10/12-inch

RCA (2529 "Porter Wagoner and Skeeter Davis Sing Duets")..15-25 62

Also see DAVIS, Skeeter

WAGONER, Porter / David Houston

EPs: 7-inch

RCA (DJ-15 "Porter Wagoner / David Houston")..20-30 56

(Not issued with special cover.)

Also see HOUSTON, David

WAGONER, Porter, & Dolly Parton *C&W '67*

Singles: 7-inch

RCA...3-6 67-80

LPs: 10/12-inch

RCA (0248 "Love & Music").......................10-15 73

RCA (0646 "Porter 'N' Dolly")..................10-15 74

RCA (1116 "Say Forever You'll Be Mine")..8-12 75

RCA (3700 "Porter Wagoner and Dolly Parton")..5-10 80

RCA (LPM-3926 "Just Between You and Me")..30-40 68

(Monaural.)

RCA (LSP-3926 "Just Between You and Me")..10-20 68

(Stereo.)

RCA (4039 "Just the Two of Us")............10-20 68

RCA (4186 "Always, Always")..................10-20 69

RCA (4305 "Porter Wayne and Dolly Rebecca")...10-15 70

RCA (4388 "Once More")..........................10-15 70

RCA (4490 "Two of a Kind").....................10-15 71

RCA (4556 "Best of Porter Wagoner and Dolly Parton")..10-15 71

RCA (4628 "The Right Combination/Burning the Midnight Oil")..10-15 72

RCA (4761 "Together Always")................10-15 72

RCA (4841 "We Found It")........................10-15 73

Also see PARTON, Dolly

Also see WAGONER, Porter

WAIKIKIS *P&R '64*

Singles: 7-inch

KAPP...4-6 64-68

PALETTE..4-6 62-63

LPs: 10/12-inch

BOOT..5-8 78

KAPP...8-15 64-69

MCA...5-8 '80s

WAILERS

Singles: 78 rpm

COLUMBIA (40288 "Hot Love")...............25-35 54

PARADISE (102 "Guitar Shuffle").............10-15 55

Singles: 7-inch

COLUMBIA (40288 "Hot Love").............75-100 54

PARADISE (102 "Guitar Shuffle")............20-25 55

WAILERS *P&R/R&B '59*

Singles: 7-inch

BELL (694 "Thinking Out Loud")................5-10 67

ETIQUETTE..5-15 62-66

GOLDEN CREST...10-20 59

(Label pictures the group.)

GOLDEN CREST..5-10 60-64

(No group picture on label.)

IMPERIAL..5-10 64

U.A. 5-10 67

VIVA (614 "I'm Determined").......................4-6 67

LPs: 10/12-inch

BELL (6016 "Walk Thru the People").......10-15 68

ETIQUETTE (1 "The Fabulous Wailers at the Castle")...75-100 66

ETIQUETTE (022 "The Wailers and Company")..40-60 66

ETIQUETTE (023 "Wailers Wailers Everywhere")..75-100 66

ETIQUETTE (026 "Out of Our Tree").......40-60 '60s

(Reissues of Etiquette LPs have a 1980s date on back cover.)

ETIQUETTE (1100 series)............................5-8 86

ETIQUETTE (22296/97 "The Wailers and Their Greatest Hits")..10-20 79

(Two discs. Includes a note from Etiquette's GOLDEN CREST (3075 "The Fabulous Wailers")..100-150 60

(Color cover photo.)

GOLDEN CREST (3075 "The Fabulous Wailers")..40-60 60

(Black and white cover.)

GOLDEN CREST (3075 "The Wailers Wail")..25-35 '60s

IMPERIAL...15-20 64

U.A. (3557 "Outburst!")...........................25-35 67

(Monaural.)

U.A. (6557 "Outburst!")...........................35-45 67

(Stereo.)

Members: Kent Morrill; Robin Roberts; Gail Harris; Mark Marush; Rich Dangel; John "Buck" Ormsby; Mike Burk; Neil Anderson; Ron Gardner; Dave Roland.

Also see BREAKERS

Also see MORRILL, Kent

Also see SONICS / Wailers

Also see SONICS / Wailers / Galaxies

Also see THREE GRACES / Wailers

WAILING BETHEA & CAP-TANS

Singles: 7-inch

HAWKEYE (0430 "Rockin' in the Jungle")..40-60 62

Also see BETHEA & CAP-TANS

WAINER, Cherry

Singles: 7-inch

PARIS (533 "Iced Coffee").......................15-25 59

WAINWRIGHT, Happy

(With the Vi-Counts; with Shinn Bones)

Singles: 7-inch

ASTRO (107 "Dem-O-Cat")........................8-12 64

CARMA (505 "Nothin' But Love")............50-75

SANDY (1004 "Walkin' and Talkin' ")...100-200 57

WAINWRIGHT, Loudon, III *P&R/LP '73*

Singles: 7-inch

ARISTA...4-6 76-78

COLUMBIA..4-8 73

HANNIBAL (0705 "Jesse Don't Like It").......3-5 90

Picture Sleeves

HANNIBAL (0705 "Jesse Don't Like It").......4-6 90

LPs: 10/12-inch

ARISTA..5-10 76-78

ATLANTIC..10-20 70-71

COLUMBIA ("KC" series)............................10-20 72-73

COLUMBIA ("PC" series)............................5-10 75

ROUNDER..5-10 80-83

Also see SPRINGSTEEN, Bruce / Albert Hammond / Loudon Wainwright, III / Taj Mahal

WAITERS, Gene

Singles: 7-inch

HIP (123 "Nothing I Won't Do")................10-15 '60s

WAITS, Carolyn

(With the Gus Norman Singers, Sandy Stanton & Orchestra)

Singles: 7-inch

FABLE (657 "School")..............................15-20 59

Also see STANTON, Sandy

WAKEFIELD SUN

Singles: 7-inch

MGM (14028 "Get Out")...........................10-15 69

MGM (14072 "Trypt on Love")..................15-25 69

ROULETTE (7073 "Sing a Simple Song")...4-8 70

LPs: 10/12-inch

MGM (4625 "Wakefield Sun")...................20-30 69

WAKELY, Jimmy *P&R '43/C&W '44*

(With Les Baxter Chorus; with Velma Williams; with Eva Summers)

Singles: 78 rpm

CAPITOL...3-6 48-52

CORAL..3-6 53-55

DECCA..4-8 43-57

JIMMY WAKELY SOUVENIR....................5-10 '50s

STERLING...5-10 47

Singles: 7-inch

ARTCO..4-6 74

CAPITOL (1300 thru 2100 series)...........10-20 50-52

CORAL..10-20 53-55

DECCA..5-15 55-70

DOT..4-6 66

SHASTA (100 series)..................................5-10 58-67

SHASTA (200 series)...................................4-6 71

Picture Sleeves

SHASTA..10-20 58

EPs: 7-inch

CAPITOL..10-20 50-53

CORAL...10-15 54

DECCA...10-15 58

LPs: 10/12-inch

ALBUM GLOBE..5-10 81

CAPITOL (4008 "Songs of the West")......25-50 50

(10-inch LP.)

CAPITOL (9004 "Christmas on the Range")..20-40 53

(10-inch LP.)

CORAL..4-8 73

DANNY..8-10

DECCA (8400 thru 8600 series)..............20-35 56-57

DECCA (75000 thru 78000 series)............8-18 67-70

DOT...10-15 66

MCA..4-8 '80s

MCR...10-15 74

SHASTA...5-15 58-75

TOPS (1601 "Jimmy Wakely")..................15-25 57

VOCALION..5-10 68-70

Also see BARTON, Eileen, & Jimmy Wakely

Also see CHANDLER, Karen, & Jimmy Wakely

Also see WHITING, Margaret, & Jimmy Wakely

WAKEMAN, Rick *LP '73*

(With the London Symphony Orchestra & English Chamber Choir; with English Rock Ensemble)

Singles: 7-inch

A&M...4-6 73

LPs: 10/12-inch

A&M (3000 series)..5-10 74

A&M (4000 series)..5-12 73-77

A&M (QU-5000 series).................................10-20 74

(Quadraphonic.)

A&M (6000 series)..10-15 79

MFSL (230 "Journey to the Centre of the Earth") 25-35 94
Also see STRAWBS
Also see YES

WALCOES
Singles: 7-inch
DRUM (011 "Tell Me Why") 100-200 59

WALD, Jerry
Singles: 7-inch
KAPP (212 "Mesa Verde") 8-12 58
TODD (1022 "Moon over Miami") 5-10 59

WALDEN, Carl, & Humans
Singles: 7-inch
A&M (777 "My True, True Love") 5-10 65
ALMO (219 "Watusi Lucy") 5-10 65

WALDON, Bernie
Singles: 7-inch
FLOYD (104 "Mind Your Own Business") 50-75

WALDON, Cliff
Singles: 7-inch
MARK (107 "My Baby Doll") 50-75

WALDRON, Ron
Singles: 7-inch
VIBRA (101 "Witch Girl") 10-15 61

WALE, Steve
Singles: 7-inch
LUTE (6007 "Boy Meets Girl") 15-20 61

WALEEN, Johnny
(Johnny Wallin)
Singles: 7-inch
COULEE (102 "Mystery Train") 75-85 64
Picture Sleeves
COULEE (102 "Mystery Train") 40-60 64
Also see WALLIN, Johnny

WALES, Howard & Jerry Garcia
Singles: 7-inch
DOUGLAS 10-15 72
LPs: 10/12-inch
DOUGLAS (30859 "Hooteroll") 40-60 71
Also see GARCIA, Jerry
Also see WALES, Howard

WALKER, April, & Jerry Lakes
LP: 10/12-inch
DBL (3001 "All I Ever Need Is You") 10-15 74

WALKER, Billy C&W '54
Singles: 78 rpm
COLUMBIA 4-8 54-56
Singles: 7-inch
CAPRICE 3-6 79-80
CASINO 4-6 77
COLUMBIA (21000 series) 6-12 54-56
COLUMBIA (33000 series) .... 4-6 '60s
COLUMBIA (40000 series) 10-20 56-60
COLUMBIA (42000 & 43000 series) 5-10 61-65
DIMENSION 3-5 83
MCA 4-6 77
MGM 4-6 70-74
MRC 4-6 77-78
MONUMENT 4-6 66-70
PAID 3-5 80
RCA 4-6 75-76
SCORPION 4-6 78
TALL TEXAN 3-5 85-88
Picture Sleeves
COLUMBIA 5-10 63-67
LPs: 10/12-inch
COLUMBIA 10-20 63-69
FIRST GENERATION 5-10 81
GUSTO 5-8 78
H.S.R.D. 5-10 84
HARMONY 8-15 64-70
MGM 6-12 70-74
MONUMENT 8-18 66-72
RCA 5-10 75-76

WALKER, Billy, & Barbara Fairchild C&W '80
Singles: 7-inch
PAID 3-5 81
LPs: 10/12-inch
PAID 5-10 81

WALKER, Billy, & Brenda Kaye Perry C&W '77
Singles: 7-inch
MRC 4-6 77
Also see WALKER, Billy

WALKER, Bob, & Friend
Singles: 7-inch
DEE GEE (3007 "Debby") 5-10 66
Also see WALLEY, Deborah

WALKER, Boots P&R '67
Singles: 7-inch
LAURIE (3522 "Geraldine") 5-10 69
PROVIDENCE (416 "Hey Little Girl") 5-10 65
RUST 5-10 66-68

WALKER, Bryan "Legs"
Singles: 7-inch
PIPER PLATTERS (501 "I Stubbed My Toe") 50-75 59

WALKER, Buddy
Singles: 7-inch
FLOP (100 "Why Can't You Stay") 100-150 61
SANDY (1033 "Too Young") 10-20 61
SANDY (1036 "I Want You") 10-20 61

WALKER, Charles, & Band
(With the Daffodils)
Singles: 7-inch
CHAMPION (1014 "Slave to Love") 40-50 59
ENSIGN (4030 "Got My Eyes on the World") 50-100 59
FURY (3000 "You Know It Ain't Right") 25-50
HOLIDAY (2604 "Driving Home") 25-35 57
VEST (829 "It Ain't Right") 15-25 60
Member: James Spruill.
Also see SPRUILL, Wild Jimmy

WALKER, Charlie C&W '56
Singles: 78 rpm
DECCA 4-8 54-56
Singles: 7-inch
CAPITOL 4-6 74
COLUMBIA 8-15 58-63
DECCA 10-20 54-56
EPIC 4-8 64-72
RCA 4-6 72-73
LPs: 10/12-inch
COLUMBIA 15-25 61
EPIC 8-15 65-71
HARMONY 10-15 67
PLANTATION 5-10 78-81
RCA 6-12 72-73
VOCALION 10-15 67

WALKER, Clint
(With the Sunflower Serenaders; Clint Walker / Sunflower Serenaders)
Singles: 7-inch
W.B. (5133 "Silver Bells") 8-10 59
W.B. (5135 "I Believe") 8-10 59
Picture Sleeves
W.B. (5133 "Silver Bells") 15-20 59
LPs: 10/12-inch
W.B. (1343 "Inspiration") 20-25 59

WALKER, David T. R&B '69
Singles: 7-inch
ODE 4-6 73-76
REVUE (11032 "Reach Out For Me") 5-10 68
REVUE (11060 "My Baby Loves Me") 5-10 69
REVUE (11070 "Baby I Need Your Loving") 4-8 70
ZEA (50005 "Love Vibrations") 4-8 70
LPs: 10/12-inch
ODE 8-10 74-76
REVUE 10-15 68-69
ZEA (1000 "Plum Happy") 8-12 70
Also see HUMPHREY, Paul, & His Cool Aid Chemists

WALKER, Eddie
(With the Demons; Edie Walker)
Singles: 7-inch
KEET (1000 "Twistin' Your Life Away") 15-25 63
MEW (102 "I Don't Need You Anymore") 20-30
MEW (103 "Baby Angel") 20-30
RISING SONS (713 "Good Guys") 5-10 68
RISING SONS (719 "A Stop Along the Way") 5-10 69

WALKER, Gary
Singles: 7-inch
DATE (1506 "Get It Right") 5-10 66
JIN (195 "Santa's Got a Brand New Bag") 5-10 66
JIN (202 "Who Needs You So Bad") 5-10 66
Also see SURFARIS / Biscaynes
Also see WALKER BROTHERS

WALKER, Gene
Singles: 7-inch
("I Go Ape") 100-200
(No label name or selection number used.)

WALKER, Gene, & Combo
Singles: 7-inch
AROCK (1002 "Empire City") 8-12 64

WALKER, Gloria P&R/R&B '68
(With the Chevelles)
Singles: 7-inch
FEDERAL 5-10 72
FLAMING ARROW 5-10 68-69
PEOPLE (2504 "Papa's Got the Wagon") 4-6 71

WALKER, Hamilton
(Rhet Hamilton Walker)
Singles: 7-inch
JERDEN (791 "I Don't Know What It Is") 5-10 66
UNI (55010 "Graveyard Shift") 5-10 67

WALKER, Jackie
Singles: 78 rpm
IMPERIAL (8268 "Big Fat Fib") 8-12 54
Singles: 7-inch
DOT (15552 "On the Way Home") 10-20 57
EVEREST (2026 "Ready Or Not") 5-10 62
EVEREST (20004 "Take a Dream") 5-10 62
EVEREST (20010 "Dearly Beloved") 5-10 62
IMPERIAL (5473 "Peggy Sue") 15-25 57
IMPERIAL (5521 "Eternally") 15-25 58
IMPERIAL (8268 "Big Fat Fib") 10-20 54
TIDAL (1001 "These Empty Arms") 8-12 61

WALKER, Jay
(With the Pedestrians)
Singles: 7-inch
AMY (848 "Hey Now") 8-12 62
VEE-JAY (369 "Shoo Be Doobie Do") 10-15 60

WALKER, Jeri
Singles: 7-inch
SIMS (218 "Once a Day") 5-10 64

WALKER, Jerry Jeff C&W/P&R '68
Singles: 7-inch
ATCO 4-6 68-70
MCA 3-6 73-80
SOUTH COAST 3-5 81
TRIED & TRUE 3-5 89
LPs: 10/12-inch
ATCO (Except 297) 15-20 68-70
ATCO (297 "Five Years Gone") 30-50 69
DECCA 10-12 72
ELEKTRA .... 8-10 '70s
MCA 5-10 73-80
SOUTH COAST 5-10 81
VANGUARD 10-12 69

WALKER, Jimmy
Singles: 7-inch
WALKER (1001 "Detour") 5-10 65
Also see KNICKERBOCKERS
Also see RIGHTEOUS BROTHERS

WALKER, Jimmy
Singles: 7-inch
COLUMBIA (44742 "Dawn") 5-10 69

WALKER, John
Singles: 7-inch
GREAT MOUNTAIN 4-6 73
SMASH 5-10 67-69
Also see WALKER BROTHERS

WALKER, Johnnie
Singles: 7-inch
TOLLIE (9017 "You're All Mine") 5-10 64

WALKER, Johnny
Singles: 7-inch
ALMO (208 "Beginning of the End") 5-10 64
AMY (923 "Girl Named Mary") 5-10 65

WALKER, Junior P&R/R&B/LP '65
(With the All Stars; with All the Stars; Junior Walker All Stars; Jr. Walker)
Singles: 12-inch
WHITFIELD 4-8 79
Singles: 7-inch
HARVEY 10-20 62-63
MOTOWN 3-5 83
SOUL (Except 35003) 5-12 65-77
(Black vinyl.)
SOUL (35003 "Monkey Jump") 10-15 64
SOUL (Colored vinyl) 8-12 70-72
(Promotional issues only.)
WHITFIELD 3-5 79
Picture Sleeves
SOUL (35008 "Shotgun") 10-15 65
SOUL (35024 "How Sweet It Is") 8-12 65
EPs: 7-inch
SOUL (69701 "Shotgun") 15-25 66
SOUL (69702 "Soul Sessions") 15-25 66
SOUL (69703 "Road Runner") 15-25 66
LPs: 10/12-inch
MOTOWN (Except 700 series) 5-10 80-83
MOTOWN (700 series) 8-12 74
SOUL (701 "Shotgun") 20-30 66
SOUL (702 "Soul Sessions") 20-30 66
SOUL (703 "Road Runner") 20-30 66
SOUL (705 "Live") 20-30 66
SOUL (710 "Home Cookin' ") 15-20 69
SOUL (718 "Greatest Hits") 10-20 69
SOUL (721 "What Does It Take") 10-20 69
SOUL (725 thru 750) 5-15 70-78
SOUL (35073 "Jr. Walker") .... 15-25 '60s
(Colored vinyl. Promotional issue only.)
WHITFIELD 8-10 79
Members: Autry Dewalt II (Jr. Walker); Willie Woods; Vic Thomas; James Graves.
Also see FOREIGNER
Also see VAN DKYE, Earl

WALKER, Lanie
(With His Black Mountain Boys; with Bob Harmon's Band)
Singles: 78 rpm
BLUE HEN 25-50 55-56
Singles: 7-inch
BLUE HEN (123 "Drop In") 400-500 59
BLUE HEN (209 "Side Track Daddy") 50-100 55
BLUE HEN (219 "Eenie Meenie Miney Mo") 500-600 56
BLUE HEN (235 "Jumpin' the Gun") 40-60
CAMELOT (5204 "They Say an Angel Loved Me Once") 4-8 75
EPs: 7-inch
THREE STAR (999 "Lanie Walker") .... 100-150 '50s
Also see HARMON, Bob

WALKER, Lee
Singles: 7-inch
CLARA (110 "Slippin In") 20-30 65

WALKER, Lonnie
Singles: 7-inch
CUCA (1111 "I Slipped, I Stumbled, I Fell") 30-40 62
Session: Dave Kennedy & Ambassadors.
Also see KENNEDY, Dave

WALKER, Lou
Singles: 7-inch
SIMS (181 "Too Much Gossip") 5-10 64
STARDAY (657 "Rock & Roll") 200-300
STARDAY (701 "Little Bitty Man") 100-200

WALKER, Lucille
LPs: 10/12-inch
CHECKER (1428 "The Best of Lucille Walker") 30-50 57

WALKER, Martin
Singles: 7-inch
ABC-PAR (10541 "Forever and a Day") 5-10 64
PINKY (301 "Love Is Everything") 8-12 60
Picture Sleeves
PINKY (301 "Love Is Everything") 10-15 60
LPs: 10/12-inch
ABC-PAR (483 "From Scotland with Love") 10-20 64

WALKER, Mel
Singles: 78 rpm
MERCURY 10-15 53-54
Singles: 7-inch
MERCURY (70276 "Unlucky Man") 20-30 53

MERCURY (70323 "You Passed By")..... 20-30 54
MERCURY (70370 "I'd Like to Make You Mine").. 20-30 54
Also see LITTLE ESTHER & MEL WALKER
Also see OTIS, Johnny
Also see ROBINS / Mel Walker & His Bluenotes

WALKER, Missouri
Singles: 7-inch
DIXIE (916 "Lonesome Guitar") 200-300

WALKER, Patty
(Patti Walker)
Singles: 7-inch
EPIC (9679 "Shy Boy")..............................8-12 64
RONN (6 "If I Touch You")..........................5-10 67

WALKER, Peter
LPs: 10/12-inch
VANGUARD (9238 "Rainy Day Raga") ... 20-25 67

WALKER, Phillip
("And Band"; with Tracers)
Singles: 7-inch
ELKO (001 "I Want You for Myself") 200-300 58
ELKO (002 "Playing in the Dark") 100-200 58
FANTASY (673 "Hey, Hey Baby's Gone")....4-8 72
GILKEY (345 "Gorilla" [sic])..................... 10-20
JOLIET..4-8 77
PLAYBOY (50032 "I Can't Lose") 4-6 73
VAULT (959 "The Struggle") 5-10 69
LPs: 10/12-inch
ALLIGATOR (4715 "Someday You'll Have These Blues")..5-10 80
JOLIET (6001 "Someday You'll Have These Blues")... 15-25 77
PLAYBOY (118 "Bottom of the Top")....... 10-15 73
Also see CHENIER, Clifton
Also see LONESOME SUNDOWN & PHILIP WALKER
Also see PHIL & BEA BOPP

WALKER, Randolph
Singles: 7-inch
BLACK PRINCE (316 "Shindy [sic] Butterfly") 5-10
MALA (572 "Achin' All Over")......................5-10 67
SHOUT (240 "I Love Her More")..................5-10 68

WALKER, Randy
Singles: 7-inch
LUDWIG (1004 "Bouquet of Flowers")..... 50-75

WALKER, Riley
Singles: 7-inch
ATOMIC (701 "Uranium Miner's Boogie") 100-200
(Colored vinyl.)

WALKER, Robert
(With the Night Riders; with Soul Strings)
Singles: 7-inch
DETROIT SOUND (224 "Everything's Alright") 50-75 67
GNP (2027 "Excuse Me")......................... 20-30 66
RCA (9304 "Stick by Me") 10-20 67

WALKER, Ronnie
Singles: 7-inch
ABC (11215 "Precious")...............................5-10 69
BELL (651 "I'm Sayin' Goodbye") 5-10 66
NICO...5-10
PHILIPS (40470 "Ain't It Funny")..................5-10 67
PHILIPS (40501 "You're the One") 5-10 67

WALKER, Sandy
Singles: 7-inch
SAGE (227 "So Long Baby Blues")........ 75-125

WALKER, Scott
(Scott Engel)
Singles: 7-inch
PHILIPS...4-8 71
SMASH..5-10 68-69
LPs: 10/12-inch
SMASH... 15-20 68-69
Also see ENGEL, Scott
Also see WALKER BROTHERS

WALKER, Steve, & Bold
Singles: 7-inch
DYNO VOICE (232 "Train Kept a-Rollin'") 15-20 67
Also see BOLD

WALKER, T-Bone — P&R '47
(With "His Guitar")
Singles: 78 rpm
ATLANTIC...10-20 55
BLACK & WHITE..15-25 46-48
COMET..15-25 48-49
CAPITOL..15-25 45-50
IMPERIAL..15-25 50-57
MERCURY..15-25 46
POST..15-25 55
RHUMBOOGIE...15-25 45-46
Singles: 7-inch
ATLANTIC (1065 Papa Ain't Salty")........50-100 55
ATLANTIC (1074 "Play On Little Girl") ...50-100 55
BLUESWAY (61008 "Every Night I Have to Cry")..5-10 67
CAPITOL (799 "On Your Way Blues")..200-300 49
CAPITOL (944 "Too Much Trouble Blues")...100-200 50
IMPERIAL (5171 "Cold Cold Feeling") 20-30 61
(First issue of this track on 45 rpm.)
IMPERIAL (5181 "I Got the Blues Again")...300-500 52
IMPERIAL (5193 "I Got the Blues") 300-500 52
IMPERIAL (5202 "Street Walkin' Woman")...150-250 52
IMPERIAL (5216 "Blue Mood") 200-300 53
IMPERIAL (5228 "Railroad Station Blues") 200-300 53
IMPERIAL (5239 "Party Girl") 200-300 53
IMPERIAL (5247 "Everytime") 150-250 53
IMPERIAL (5261 "I'm About to Lose My Mind")..150-250 53
IMPERIAL (5264 "Pony Tail") 150-250 54
IMPERIAL (5274 "Vida Lee") 150-250 54
IMPERIAL (5284 "Bye Bye Baby")........150-250 54
IMPERIAL (5299 "Teenage Baby").......150-250 54
IMPERIAL (5311 "Love Is a Gamble")...75-125 55
IMPERIAL (5330 "I'll Understand") 75-125 55
IMPERIAL (5384 "Welcome Blues").......75-125 56
IMPERIAL (5695 "Travelin' Blues")...........20-30 60
IMPERIAL (5171 "Cold Cold Feeling") 20-30 61
IMPERIAL (5832 "Evil Hearted Woman").20-30 62
IMPERIAL (5962 "Doin' Time")..................20-30 63
JET STREAM (726 "Reconsider Baby").....8-12 66
JET STREAM (730 "T-Bone's Back") 8-12 67
JET STREAM (738 "She's a Hit") 8-12 69
MODERN (1004 "Hey Hey Baby") 8-12 65
POST (2002 "I Get So Weary")................25-50 55
EPs: 7-inch
CAPITOL (370 "Classics in Jazz") 100-150 53
LPs: 10/12-inch
ATLANTIC (8020 "T-Bone Blues")........150-250 59
(Black label.)
ATLANTIC (8020 "T-Bone Blues")........100-150 60
(Red label.)
ATLANTIC (8256 "T-Bone Blues")............10-15 70
BLUE NOTE (533 "T-Bone Walker")..........8-12
BLUESTIME (29010 "Blue Rocks") 10-15 73
BLUESWAY (6008 "Stormy Monday Blues") 10-20 67
BLUESWAY (6014 "Funky Town") 10-20 67
BLUESWAY (6058 "Dirty Mistreater") 10-20 70
BLUESWAY (6061 "Blues Classics") 10-20 73
BRUNSWICK (754126 "The Truth") 10-20 68
CAPITOL (H-370 "Classics in Jazz") 300-400 53
(10-inch LP.)
CAPITOL (T-370 "Classics in Jazz").....200-300 56
CAPITOL (1958 "Great Blues Vocals and Guitar")...50-100 63
DELMARK (633 "I Want a Little Girl").........8-10
HOMECOOKING...8-12
IMPERIAL (9098 "T-Bone Walker Sings the Blues") 100-200 59
IMPERIAL (9116 "Singing the Blues")....75-125 60
IMPERIAL (9146 "I Get So Weary")........75-125 61
IMPERIAL (12397 "Singing the Blues")....15-25 68
MOSAIC (MR-9-130 "Complete Recordings of T-Bone Walker: 1940-1954")......................300-350 90
(Boxed, nine-disc set. Numbered limited edition of 7500.)
POLYDOR (5521 "Fly Walker Airlines") ...10-15 73
REPRISE (6483 "Very Rare") 10-20 73
(Two discs.)
WET SOUL (1002 "Stormy Monday Blues")...10-20 67
Also see GLENN, Lloyd
Also see McCRACKLIN, Jimmy / T-Bone Walker / Charles Brown
Also see WITHERSPOON, Jimmy
Also see X-RAYS

WALKER, T-Bone, Jr.
Singles: 7-inch
DOT (16441 "Empty Feeling") 8-12 63
MIDNITE (101 "Empty Feeling") 10-20 62

WALKER, Troy
Singles: 7-inch
GNP (179 "Midnight in Moscow") 5-10 62
TRANS-WORLD (7003 "I'm Gettin' Hip") ...5-10 61
LPs: 10/12-inch
HI FI (1021 "Troy Walker") 10-15 64

WALKER, Van
Singles: 7-inch
MERCURY (71646 "Think It Over Baby") ..8-12 60

WALKER, Wayne
Singles: 78 rpm
ABC-PAR 15-25 56
CHESS 10-15 54
COLUMBIA 10-20 57
Singles: 7-inch
ABC-PAR (9735 "It's My Way")................35-55 56
BRUNSWICK (55133 "You've Got Me")...20-30 59
CHESS (4860 "You Got the Best of Me").15-25 54
COLUMBIA 10-15 57-58
CORAL (62328 "Reaching for the Impossible")..5-10 62
EVEREST (19380 "Love, Love")................8-12 60
RIC (155 "Nobody Knows But Me") 5-10 65
RIC (171 "When Passion Calls")................5-10 65
RIC (180 "Ever So Often")..........................5-10 65
Also see LEE, Jimmy, & Wayne Walker

WALKER, Wee Willie
Singles: 7-inch
GOLDWAX (329 "Ticket to Ride") 5-10 67

WALKER, Willie
(With the Alpacas)
Singles: 7-inch
CHECKER...5-10 68-69
FREEDOM (44006 "Money Mad Man")....20-30 59
HI 4-6 78
MOTIF (015 "Little Girl Echo") 10-15 59
PAWN...8-12

WALKER, Wilmar
Singles: 7-inch
PHILIPS (40030 "Stompin' Roaches")......10-20 62

WALKER BROTHERS
Singles: 7-inch
KAY-Y (66785 "Beautiful Brown Eyes")..75-100 60

WALKER BROTHERS — P&R '65
Singles: 7-inch
SMASH...5-10 64-66
Picture Sleeves
SMASH...8-12 65-66
LPs: 10/12-inch
SMASH...20-25 66-67
Members: Scott Engel; John Maus; Gary Leeds.
Also see ENGEL, Scott, & John Stewart
Also see WALKER, Gary
Also see WALKER, John
Also see WALKER, Scott

WALKERS
Singles: 7-inch
SOMA (1187 "Waitin' Around")................20-25 63
Also see RAY, Burch, & Walkers

WALKING STICKS
Singles: 7-inch
RAYNARD (10042 "Why") 15-25 65
Members: Bob Barian; Keith Dreher; Kurt Kronhelm; Dick Schurk; Paul Spencer; Gary Josing; Mike Welch; J.D. Harper; Norm Drifka; Denny Schuenemann.
Also see RENEGADES

WALL, Bobby
Singles: 7-inch
ALADDIN..10-20 58

WALL OF SOUND
Singles: 7-inch
BIG BIRD (127 "Hang On")......................10-15 67
TOWER (363 "Hang On")............................5-10 67

WALLACE, Billy
Singles: 78 rpm
BLUE HEN 25-50 55
MERCURY...25-50 56
Singles: 7-inch
BLUE HEN 100-150 55
DEB (882 "Wolf Call")..............................100-150 57
DEB (1003 "Don't Flirt with My Baby") ...75-100 59
MERCURY (70876 "Mean Mistreatin' Baby")..75-125 56
MERCURY (70957 "What'll I Do") 75-125 56
PACE ("Gotta Keep Ridin'")......................50-75 59
(Selection number not known.)

WALLACE, Christine
Singles: 7-inch
GOWEN (1402 "Feeling") 10-15 61

WALLACE, Esko
Singles: 7-inch
GRAHAM (802 "Triple Zero").......................5-10 63

WALLACE, Fonda
Singles: 7-inch
WINSTON (1014 "Lou Lou Knows").......75-100 57

WALLACE, Jerry — P&R '54
(With the Jewels; with Jay Rand Orchestra & Chorus)
Singles: 78 rpm
ALLIED..5-15 51-54
ALPHA 4-8
CHALLENGE..10-20 57
CLASS 5-10 53
MERCURY...5-10 55-56
TOPS..5-10 53
VOGUE 5-10 52
WING 5-10 56
Singles: 7-inch
ALLIED..10-20 54
BMA...4-6 77-78
CHALLENGE (1003 "Blue Jean Baby") ...20-25 57
CHALLENGE (9047 "Primrose Lane") 20-30 59
CHALLENGE (9107 "Life's a Holiday") 5-10 61
CHALLENGE (9117 "Eyes") 5-10 61
CHALLENGE (9130 "Rollin' River")............5-10 61
CHALLENGE (9139 "Mr. Lonely") 5-10 62
CHALLENGE (9152 "Here I Go") 5-10 62
CHALLENGE (9171 "Shutters & Boards") .5-10 62
CHALLENGE (9185 "Move Over") 5-10 63
CHALLENGE (9195 "Just Walking in the Rain")...5-10 63
CHALLENGE (9205 "Empty Arms Again").5-10 63
CHALLENGE (59000 "The Other Me")......10-20 58
CHALLENGE (59013 "How the Time Flies")...10-20 58
CHALLENGE (59027 "Diamond Ring")....10-20 58
CHALLENGE (59040 "A Touch of Pink"). 10-20 59
CHALLENGE (59047 "Primrose Lane") ... 10-20 59
CHALLENGE (59060 "Little Coco Palm") 10-20 59
CHALLENGE (59082 "Swingin' down the Lane")..10-20 60
CHALLENGE (59098 "There She Goes")..10-20 60
CHALLENGE (59223 "Auf Wiedersehn")...5-10 63
CHALLENGE (59246 "In the Misty Moonlight"/"Even the Bad Times Are Good") 5-10 64
(Reissue with same number has Soul Surfers track, *Cannon Ball*, on B-side.)
CHALLENGE (59278 "Helpless") 5-10 65
CHALLENGE (59265 "Even the Bad Times Are Good") 5-10 65
CLASS (502 "Taj Mahal").........................10-20 53
DECCA..4-6 71-72
DOOR KNOB...3-6 79-80
ERIC..4-6 '70s
4-STAR 4-6 78-79
GLENOLDEN..4-6 68
GUSTO ....3-5 '80s
LIBERTY..4-6 67-70
MCA 4-6 73-74
MGM..4-6 75-76
MERCURY (70000 series)......................10-20 55-56
MERCURY (72000 series).........................5-10 64-66
SUNSET..5-10
TOPS..10-20 53
U.A. 4-6 72-75
VOGUE 10-20 52
WING (90065 "Eyes of Fire, Lips of Wine")..10-15 56
Picture Sleeves
CHALLENGE (59013 thru 59098) 10-20 58-60
CHALLENGE (59200 series) 5-10 63-65
EPs: 7-inch
CHALLENGE..15-25 60
LPs: 10/12-inch
BMA...8-10 77

CHALLENGE (606 "Just Jerry") 30-35 59
CHALLENGE (612 "There She Goes") 20-25 61
CHALLENGE (616 "Shutters & Boards"). 15-25 63
CHALLENGE (619 "In the Misty Moonlight") 15-25 64
CHALLENGE (2002 "Greatest Hits") 10-15 69
DECCA 8-12 71-72
4-STAR 5-8 83
LIBERTY 10-12 68
MCA 8-10 73-74
MGM 8-10 75
MERCURY 10-20 66
PICKWICK .... 5-10 '70s
U.A. 8-12 72-75
WING 10-12 68
Also see BARE, Bobby / Donna Fargo / Jerry Wallace

WALLACE, Jerry / Soul Surfers
Singles: 7-inch
CHALLENGE (59249 "In the Misty Moonlight"/"Cannonball") 5-10 64
Also see SOUL SURFERS / Delicates
Also see WALLACE, Jerry

WALLACE, Jimmy
Singles: 7-inch
DON-EL (109 "If I Were Free") 10-20 61
DON-EL (115 "Please Don't Say No") 10-20 62

WALLACE, Joe
Singles: 7-inch
MOON (304 "Leopard Man") 40-60 59

WALLACE, John & Bill
Singles: 7-inch
A-B-S (133 "Blinded By Your Love") 5-10 62
Also see WALLACE BROTHERS

WALLACE, Pat
(With the Rock'n Ravens)
Singles: 7-inch
ASTERISK 10-15
BISHOP (1004 "Angel Baby") 5-8 80
BISHOP (1009 "Switchblade") 5-8 81
BISHOP (1011 "Goin' Cattin' ") 5-8 81
ST. CLAIR (007 "Fill the Hole") 15-25

WALLACE, Richard
(Richie Wallace; with Stars Of Bethlehem)
Singles: 7-inch
ENSIGN (3001 "Nobody Knows") 75-100 61
FEDERAL (12485 "Darling You Done Me Wrong") 15-20 63
FEDERAL (12511 "Bernice") 10-15 63

WALLACE, Sonny
Singles: 7-inch
YUCCA (127 "Black Cadillac") 50-100 61

WALLACE BROTHERS *P&R '64*
Singles: 7-inch
JEWEL 5-10 68-77
SIMS (158 "Faith") 10-15 63
SIMS (174 "Precious Words") 10-15 64
SIMS (189 "Lover's Prayer") 10-15 64
SIMS (220 "One Way Affair") 8-12 65
SIMS (229 "I'll Step Aside") 8-12 65
SIMS (248 "No More") 8-12 65
SIMS (304 "Stepping Stone") 8-12 66
SIMS (311 "These Arms of Mine") 8-12 67
SIMS (316 "Thanks a Lot") 8-12 67
LPs: 10/12-inch
SIMS (128 "Soul, Soul & More Soul") 25-35 65
Members: John Wallace; Ervin Wallace; John Simon. Session: Jimmy Simon; David Briggs; Wallace Cosby; Jack Martin; Larry Daniel.
Also see WALLACE, John & Bill

WALLER, Carole
Singles: 7-inch
USA (863 "This Love of Mine") 15-25 67

WALLER, Fats
(With His Buddies; with His Rhythm)
Singles: 78 rpm
BLUEBIRD 5-15 38-43
COLUMBIA (14593 "I'm Crazy 'Bout My Baby") 40-60
VICTOR (20000 thru 25000 series) 5-15 26-38
VICTOR (38050 "Harlem Fuss") 30-50 29
VICTOR (38086 "Lookin' Good but Feelin' Bad") 30-50 29
VICTOR (38110 "When I'm Alone") 30-50 30
VICTOR (38119 "Ridin' but Walkin' ") 30-50 30
VICTOR (38508 "Numb Fumblin' ") 30-50 30
VICTOR (38554 "Valentine Stomp") 30-50 30
VICTOR (38568 "Turn On the Heat") 30-50 31
VICTOR (38613 "Smashing Thirds") 30-50 31
Singles: 7-inch
RCA VICTOR .... 10-20 '50s
EPs: 7-inch
RCA (14 "Waller Favorites") 10-20 50
RCA (802 "Ain't Misbehavin' ") 10-20 56
RCA (1001 "Waller Plays and Sings") 10-20 53
RCA (1246 "Ain't Misbehavin' ") 20-30 56
(Two discs.)
RCA (3024 "Your Feet's Too Big") 10-20 53
(Two discs.)
RCA (3040 "Swingin' the Organ") 10-20 53
(Two discs.)
RCA (5140 "Your Feet's Too Big") 10-20 60
RCA (6001 "Fats Waller") 10-20 55
RIVERSIDE (105 "Rediscovered Solos") . 10-20 56
LPs: 10/12-inch
CAMDEN (473 "Real Fats Waller") 15-25 59
CAPITOL (10258 "Fats Waller in London") 15-25 61
RCA (14 "Waller Favorites") 40-60 50
(10-inch LP.)
RCA (516 "1934-1935) 10-20 65
RCA (525 "Valentine Stomp") 10-20 66
RCA (537 "Fractious Fingering") 10-20 67
RCA (1001 "Waller Plays and Sings") 25-35 53
RCA (1246 "Ain't Misbehavin' ") 25-35 56
RCA (3040 "Swingin' the Organ") 30-40 53
(10-inch LP.)
RCA (6001 "Fats Waller") 20-30 55
RIVERSIDE (103 "Early Solos") 20-30 56
RIVERSIDE (109 "The Amazing Mr. Waller") 20-30 56
RIVERSIDE (1010 "Rediscovered Solos") 30-40 53
RIVERSIDE (1021 "The Amazing Mr. Waller") 30-40 53
(Two discs.)
"X" (3035 "Young Fats Waller") 20-30 56
Session: Orlando Roberson; Four Wanderers; Harry Dial.

WALLER, Gordon
Singles: 7-inch
BELL 5-8 69-70
CAPITOL 5-10 67-68
LPs: 10/12-inch
ABC (749 "And Gordon") 10-15 72
Also see PETER & GORDON

WALLER, Jerry
Singles: 7-inch
SIMS (323 "One Way Street") 5-10 67

WALLER, Jim, & Deltas
Singles: 7-inch
ARVEE (5072 "Surfin' Wild") 15-25 64
CAMBRIDGE (124 "Goodnight My Love") 20-30 64
TRAC (502 "I've Been Blue") 30-40 61
LPs: 10/12-inch
ARVEE (A-432 "Surfin' Wild") 125-175 63
(Monaural.)
ARVEE (AS-432 "Surfin' Wild") 175-225 63
(Stereo.)
Members: Jim Waller; Roy Carlson; Ed Atkinson; Jeff Christensen; Terry Christofferson.
Also see JAY & DELTAS
Also see BREAKERS

WALLEY, Deborah
Singles: 7-inch
DEE GEE (3006 "So Little Time") 8-10 66
Also see WALKER, Bob, & Friend

WALLIN, Johnny
(Johnny Waleen)
Singles: 7-inch
SOMA (1120 "Road of Heartaches") 20-30 59
Also see WALEEN, Johnny

WALLIS, Jack
Singles: 7-inch
PENNY (1486 "Sheet Board Down") 50-75

WALLIS, Ruth *P&R '53*
(With the Deluxe Rhumba Band)
Singles: 78 rpm
DE-LUXE 5-10 47
KING 5-10 52-53
MONARCH 5-10 53-54
WALLIS ORIGINAL 5-10 55-57
Singles: 7-inch
DECCA (30560 "Butterfly Heart") 10-15 58
DE-LUXE 15-25 51
KING 15-25 52-53
MONARCH 15-25 53-54
WALLIS ORIGINAL 15-25 55-57
(Some – or all – in this series are red vinyl.)
EPs: 7-inch
DE-LUXE (215/216/217 "House Party") ... 25-40 52
(Price is for any of three volumes.)
LPs: 10/12-inch
KING (6 "Rhumba Party") 75-100 52
(10-inch LP.)
KING (9 "House Party") 75-100 52
(10-inch LP.)
KING (507 "House Party") 50-100 56
WALLIS ORIGINAL (2 "Ruth Wallis") 20-30 57

WALLS, Ann, & Ernie Fields
Singles: 7-inch
RENDEZVOUS (148 "Fallin' ") 5-10 61
Also see FIELDS, Ernie

WALLS, Bill
Singles: 7-inch
ACCENT (1157 "Rockin' & Reelin' ") 5-10 65

WALLS, Jimmy
Singles: 7-inch
WALTON (010 "What a Little Kiss Can Do") .... 75-125 '60s
WALTON (1500 "Look Me in the Eyes") ... 40-60 '60s

WALLS, Van
(Van "Piano Man" Walls & His Orchestra; with Rockets)
Singles: 78 rpm
ATLANTIC (980 "After Midnight") 25-50 52
ATLANTIC (988 "Open the Door") 50-75 53
Singles: 7-inch
ATLANTIC (980 "After Midnight") 75-100 52
ATLANTIC (988 "Open the Door") 100-150 53
Also see BROWN, Clarence "Gatemouth"/ Camille Howard / Bill Johnson Quartet / Van "Piano Man" Walls
Also see SPIDER SAM
Also see TURNER, Joe

WALLY & DON
Singles: 7-inch
SAGE (308 "Please Don't") 50-75

WALLY & KNIGHTS
Singles: 7-inch
VEEP (1259 "I Need You") 5-10 67

WALLY & RIGHTS
Singles: 7-inch
GM (113 "Hey Now Little Girl") 15-25 66

WALSH, Andy
Singles: 78 rpm
SOMA (1013 "Guitar Boogie") 10-20 56
Singles: 7-inch
FM (338 "Guitar Boogie") 40-60 56
(First issue.)
SOMA (1013 "Guitar Boogie") 25-50 56

WALSH, George
Singles: 7-inch
ALADDIN (3438 "Don't Let Me Down") 50-75 58

WALSH, Joe *LP '72*
Singles: 7-inch
ABC 4-6 75-78
ASYLUM 3-6 78-81
DUNHILL 4-8 73-75
FULL MOON 3-5 80-83
MCA 4-6 79
Picture Sleeves
FULL MOON 4-6 80-83
EPs: 7-inch
ABC/COMMAND (40016 "The Smoker You Drink, the Player You Get") 10-20 74
(Quadraphonic. Juke box "Special Promotional Record." Includes title strips.)
LPs: 10/12-inch
ABC 5-10 76-78
ABC/COMMAND (40016 "The Smoker You Drink, the Player You Get") 15-25 74
(Quadraphonic.)
ABC/COMMAND (40017 "So What") 15-25 75
(Quadraphonic.)
ASYLUM 5-10 78-81
DUNHILL 8-12 72-74
MCA 5-10 79
W.B. 5-8 83-87
Also see EAGLES

WALSH, Johnny
Singles: 7-inch
BUENA VISTA (350 "My Darling, Why") 5-10 59
COLUMBIA (43532 "Lovey Kravezit") 5-10 66
COLUMBIA (43936 "Green Trees") 5-10 66
DOT (16118 "Forgive Me Again") 5-10 60
W.B. (5196 "Beautiful Obsession") 5-10 61
W.B. (5252 "Bleached Blonde") 5-10 62
EPs: 7-inch
W.B. (5503 "Don't Knock It") 10-15 61

WALT & SATANS
Singles: 7-inch
EMKAY (106 "Maybe One Day") 15-25 65
FORD (106 "Maybe One Day") 20-30 61

WALT, PERCY & TRACERS
Singles: 7-inch
THREE RIVERS ("Wishing") 500-750 61
(No selection number used. Reissued as by the Roberson Bro's.)
Also see ROBERSON BRO'S

WALTER & FANCY
Singles: 7-inch
MAGIC LAMP (612 "Campaign Train") 8-12 64
Members: Walter Crankcase; Fancy Flickerson.

WALTERS, Bucky & Jukes
Singles: 7-inch
NU-PHI ("Cruisin' ") .... 20-30 '60s
(Selection number not known.)

WALTERS, Denny
(With the Braxton Combo; with Braxton Knighthawks)
Singles: 7-inch
MASTER (1015 "A Brand New Fool") 10-20
MASTER (1018 "I Met Her in a Tavern") .. 10-20
MASTER (1050 "I Miss You") 10-20

WALTERS, Tommy
Singles: 7-inch
BARDELL (775 "Church Bells in the Park") 15-20 63
LIMELIGHT (771 "That's Love") 10-15
Picture Sleeves
LIMELIGHT (771 "That's Love") 15-25

WALTERS, Marshall
Singles: 7-inch
MINOR (115 "Willie, Willie, Willie") 200-300 59

WALTERS, Muddy
Singles: 7-inch
FEDERAL (12409 "Baby, Look at You") .. 10-20 61

WALTON, Charles
Singles: 7-inch
SKY (114 "Teenage Blues") 200-300

WALTON, J.
(James Walton & His Blues Kings)
Singles: 7-inch
BIG STAR (003 "Tell Me What You Got") 15-25 64
HI-Q (5029 "Leaving Blues") 10-15 63

WALTON, Jimmy
Singles: 78 rpm
FLAIR (1008 "Always & Always") 10-20 53
Singles: 7-inch
FLAIR (1008 "Always & Always") 25-35 53

WALTON, Square
(With Sonny Terry)
Singles: 78 rpm
RCA 25-50 54
Singles: 7-inch
RCA (5584 "Bad Hangover") 75-100 54
RCA (5493 "Gimme Your Bank Roll") 75-100 54
Also see TERRY, Sonny

WALTON, Wade
Singles: 7-inch
ARHOOLIE (1005 "Rooster Blues") 10-15 60
LPs: 10/12-inch
PRESTIGE BLUESVILLE (1060 "Shake "Em on Down") 20-40 62

WALTON & SILVER LAKE BOYS
Singles: 7-inch
LAEL (1137 "Man, What a Party") 150-200

WALTON BROTHERS
Singles: 7-inch
BIG HIT (300 "Funky Soul")...10-15

WAMMACK, Travis *P&R '64*
Singles: 7-inch
ARA...5-10 64-65
ATLANTIC...5-10 66
CAPRICORN...4-6 75-76
CONGRESS (6005 "Wolverton Mt.")...4-6 69
CONGRESS (6018 "Twanging My Thang")...4-6 70
FAME...4-6 72-73
FERNWOOD (103 "Rock and & Blues")...75-100 58
LPs: 10/12-inch
CAPRICORN...5-10 75
FAME...8-12 72
PHONORAMA...5-10
U.A. (1801 "Travis Wammack")...8-12 72

WANDERER
Singles: 7-inch
FLAIR-X (5003 "The Man in the Telephone Booth – Hello Baby")...20-30 57

WANDERER'S REST
Singles: 7-inch
NIGHT OWL (6771 "The Boat That I Row")...10-20 67
WRIGHT (6813 "Temptation")...10-20 68
WRIGHT (67101 "You'll Forget")...10-20 67
Members: Richard Podraza; Michael Podraza; Michael Milonszyk; Stanley Starich.

WANDERERS *P&R '61*
(With the Sammy Lowe Orchestra)
Singles: 78 rpm
ONYX (518 "Thinking of You")...30-50 57
SAVOY (1109 "We Could Find Happiness")...50-100 53
Singles: 7-inch
CUB (9003 "Teenage Quarrel")...10-15 58
CUB (9019 "Collecting Hearts")...20-30 58
CUB (9023 "Please")...10-15 58
CUB (9035 "I'm Not Ashamed")...10-15 59
CUB (9054 "I Walked Through a Forest")...10-15 59
CUB (9075 "I Need You More")...10-15 60
CUB (9089 "For Your Love")...20-30 61
CUB (9094 "I'll Never Smile Again")...10-15 61
CUB (9099 "She Wears My Ring")...20-30 61
CUB (9109 "There Is No Greater Love")...20-30 62
GONE (5005 "Mask Off")...10-20 57
MGM (13082 "There Is No Greater Love")...10-20 62
ONYX (518 "Thinking of You")...50-60 57
ORBIT (9003 "Teenage Quarrel")...30-40 58
(Green or red label.)
SAVOY (1098 "How Can I Get Along Without You")...4-6 75
SAVOY (1099 "What Do I Do")...4-6 75
SAVOY (1109 "We Could Find Happiness")...400-500 53
U.A. (570 "After He Breaks Your Heart")...10-20 63
U.A. (648 "I'll Know")...30-40 63
Members: Ray Pollard; Bob Yarborough; Sheppard Grant; Frank Joyner.
Also see COOPER, Dolly
Also see POLLARD, Ray
Also see SINGING WANDERERS

WANDERERS
Singles: 7-inch
BANNER (4601 "Delta Airlines")...10-20 '60s

WANDERERS
Singles: 7-inch
TEXAS RECORD CO. (2067 "Higher Education")...15-25 67

WANDERERS
Singles: 7-inch
CAGG ("What's Right")...10-15 67
(No selection number used.)

WANDERERS THREE
Singles: 7-inch
DOLTON...5-10 62-63
MGM...5-10 64
LPs: 10/12-inch
DOLTON...10-20 63

WANDERLEY, Walter *P&R/LP '66*
Singles: 7-inch
A&M...4-6 69
GNP...3-5 81
TOWER...4-6 66-67
VERVE...4-6 66-68
WORLD PACIFIC...4-6 66
LPs: 10/12-inch
A&M...5-10 69
CAPITOL...10-15 63
GNP...5-8 81
PHILIPS...8-12 67
TOWER...8-15 66-67
VERVE...8-15 66-68
WORLD PACIFIC...8-15 66-67

WANTED
Singles: 7-inch
DEMO (1046 "The Wanted")...10-15 66
Members: Chuck Travis; Harry Mccullough; Tony Wells; Paul Leaken; Paul Polizak.

WANTED
Singles: 7-inch
A&M...5-10 67
DETROIT SOUND (Except 222)...5-10 66-67
DETROIT SOUND (222 "Here to Stay")...15-25 66

WAR *P&R '70*
Singles: 12-inch
MCA...4-8 78-79
Singles: 7-inch
BLUE NOTE...4-6 77
COCO PLUM...3-5 85
LAX...3-5 81
MCA...3-6 77-82
PRIORITY...3-5 87
RCA...3-5 82-83
U.A....4-6 71-78
WAR...4-6 77
Picture Sleeves
MCA...4-6 77
U.A....4-6 71-75
EPs: 7-inch
U.A. (92 "The World Is a Ghetto")...10-15 72
(Promotional issue only. With paper cover.)
LPs: 10/12-inch
ABC...8-10 76
BLUE NOTE...8-10 76
MCA...8-10 77-82
PRIORITY...5-10 87
RCA...5-10 82-83
U.A. (Except 103)...8-10 71-78
U.A. (103 "Radio Free War")...15-20 74
(Colored vinyl. Promotional issue only.)
Members: Howard Scott; Lonnie Jordan; Dee Allen; B.B. Dickerson; Lee Oskar; Charles Miller; Harold Brown.
Also see BURDON, Eric, & War

WARD, Billy, & Dominoes *R&B '51*
Singles: 78 rpm
DECCA...15-30 56-57
FEDERAL...50-100 52-57
JUBILEE...10-15 54-55
KING (Except 1281)...20-30 53-57
KING (1281 "Christmas in Heaven")...30-40 53
LIBERTY...20-30 57
QUALITY/KING...50-100 53
(Canadian.)
Singles: 7-inch
ABC-PAR (10128 "You're Mine")...10-15 60
ABC-PAR (10156 "You")...10-15 60
DECCA (29933 "St. Theresa of the Roses")...20-30 56
DECCA (30043 "Will You Remember")...20-30 56
DECCA (30149 "Evermore")...20-30 56
DECCA (30199 "Rock, Plymouth Rock")...20-30 56
DECCA (30420 "To Each His Own")...20-30 57
DECCA (30514 "September Song")...20-30 57
FEDERAL (12105 "I'd Be Satisfied")...75-125 52
FEDERAL (12106 "Yours Forever")...75-125 52
FEDERAL (12114 "Pedal Pushin' Papa")...75-125 52
FEDERAL (12129 "These Foolish Things")...200-300 53
(Gold top label.)
FEDERAL (12129 "These Foolish Things")...30-50 53
(Silver top label.)
FEDERAL (12129 "These Foolish Things")...10-20 '50s
(Green label.)
FEDERAL (12139 "Where Now, Little Heart")...50-100 53
FEDERAL (12162 "My Baby's 3-D")...50-100 53
FEDERAL (12178 "Tootsie Roll")...50-75 54
(Gold top label.)
FEDERAL (12178 "Tootsie Roll")...20-30 54
(Silver top label.)
FEDERAL (12184 "Handwriting on the Wall")...150-200 54
FEDERAL (12193 "Above Jacob's Ladder")...30-50 54
FEDERAL (12209 "Can't Do Sixty No More")...50-75 55
FEDERAL (12218 "Cave Man")...30-40 55
FEDERAL (12263 "Bobby Sox Baby")...30-40 56
FEDERAL (12301 "St. Louis Blues")...30-40 57
FEDERAL (12308 "Have Mercy Baby")...30-40 57
GUSTO...3-5 '80s
JUBILEE (5163 "Come to Me, Baby")...20-30 54
JUBILEE (5213 "Sweethearts on Parade")...20-30 55
KING (1280 "Rags to Riches")...30-40 53
KING (1281 "Christmas in Heaven")...30-40 53
KING (1342 "A Little Lie")...30-40 54
KING (1364 "Three Coins in the Fountain")...30-40 55
KING (1368 "Little Things Mean a Lot")...30-40 55
KING (1492 "Learnin' the Blues")...30-40 55
KING (1502 "Over the Rainbow")...30-40 55
KING (5322 "Have Mercy Baby")...10-15 60
KING (5463 "Lay It on the Line")...10-15 61
KING (6002 "This Love of Mine")...5-10 65
KING (6016 "Oh Holy Night")...5-10 65
LIBERTY (55071 "Star Dust")...20-25 57
LIBERTY (55099 "Deep Purple")...20-25 57
LIBERTY (55111 "My Proudest Possession")...20-25 57
LIBERTY (55126 "Solitude")...15-20 58
LIBERTY (55136 "Jenny Lee")...15-20 58
LIBERTY (55181 "Please Don't Say No")...10-15 59
QUALITY/KING (4227 "These Foolish Things")...200-300 53
(Canadian.)
QUALITY/KING (4266 "My Baby's 3-D")...150-250 53
(Canadian.)
RO-ZAN (10001 "My Fair Weather Friend")...15-25 62
UNDERGROUND (6736 "Star Dust")...4-6
Picture Sleeves
LIBERTY (55071 "Star Dust")...50-75 57
EPs: 7-inch
DECCA (2549 "Billy Ward & His Dominoes")...100-200 58
FEDERAL (212 "Billy Ward & His Dominoes, Vol. 1")...200-300 55
(Silver top label.)
FEDERAL (262 "Billy Ward & His Dominoes, Vol. 2")...200-300 55
(Silver top label.)
FEDERAL (269 "Billy Ward & His Dominoes, Vol. 3")...200-300 55
(Silver top label.)
FEDERAL (212 "Billy Ward & His Dominoes, Vol. 1")...100-150 57
(Green label.)
FEDERAL (262 "Billy Ward & His Dominoes, Vol. 2")...100-150 57
(Green label.)
FEDERAL (269 "Billy Ward & His Dominoes, Vol. 3")...100-150 57
(Green label.)
LIBERTY (1/2/3-3056 "Sea of Glass")...50-100 58
(Price is for any of three volumes.)
LIBERTY (1/2/3-3083 "Yours Forever")...50-100 59
(Price is for any of three volumes.)
LPs: 10/12-inch
DECCA (8621 "Billy Ward & His Dominoes")...300-500 58
FEDERAL (94 "Billy Ward & His Dominoes")...15000-20000 54
(10-inch LP.)
FEDERAL (548 "Billy Ward & His Dominoes")...1000-1500 57
FEDERAL (559 "Clyde McPhatter with Billy Ward & His Dominoes")...1000-1500 57
KING (548 "Billy Ward & His Dominoes")...300-500 58
KING (559 "Clyde McPhatter with Billy Ward & His Dominoes")...200-400 61
KING (733 "Billy Ward & His Dominoes Featuring Clyde McPhatter & Jackie Wilson")...200-300 61
KING (952 "24 Songs")...25-50 66
KING/GUSTO...5-10
LIBERTY (3056 "Sea of Glass")...100-150 58
LIBERTY (3083 "Yours Forever")...100-150 59
LIBERTY (3113 "Pagan Love Song")...100-150 59
(Monaural.)
LIBERTY (7113 "Pagan Love Song")...200-400 59
(Stereo.)
Members: Clyde McPhatter; Jackie Wilson; Billy Ward; Gene Mumford; Milton Merle; Milton Grayson; William Lamont; Cliff Givens.
Also see DOMINOES
Also see MUMFORD, Gene
Also see WILSON, Jackie

WARD, Burt
Singles: 7-inch
MGM (13632 "Boy Wonder, I Love You")...75-125 66

WARD, Dale *P&R '63*
(With Robin Ward)
Singles: 7-inch
BIG WAY (001 "River Boat Annie")...5-10 '60s
BOYD (118 "Big Dale Twist")...10-15 62
BOYD (150 "Shake Rattle & Roll")...5-10 65
BOYD (152 "I Tried")...5-10 65
BOYD (154 "I Didn't Know")...5-10 65
DOT (247 "A Letter from Sherry")...5-10 65
DOT (16520 "A Letter from Sherry")...8-12 64
DOT (16590 "Crying for Laura")...5-10 64
DOT (16632 "I'll Never Love Again")...5-10 64
DOT (16672 "One Last Kiss Cherie")...5-10 64
DOT (16704 "Dirty Old Town")...5-10 65
DOT (16759 "Lonely Mary Ann")...5-10 65
DOT (17000 series)...4-6 71-72
MONUMENT...5-10 66-69
PARAMOUNT...4-6 70-71
Picture Sleeves
BOYD (118 "Big Dale Twist")...20-30 62
Also see WARD, Robin

WARD, Dusty
Singles: 7-inch
FABLE (517 "If You Two-Time Me")...75-125
(Red vinyl.)

WARD, Harold "Thunderhead"
Singles: 7-inch
ALLAN (108 "How Wild Can a Woman Be")...8-12 59

WARD, Herb
Singles: 7-inch
ARGO (5510 "Strange Change")...50-75 65
PHIL-L.A. OF SOUL (312 "Wrong Place at the Wrong Time")...20-30 68
RCA (9688 "Honest to Goodness")...40-60 68

WARD, Janice
Singles: 7-inch
FLORENTEEN (1001 "When a Girl Gives Her Heart")...10-20
MONUMENT (442 "When a Girl Gives Her Heart")...30-40 61

WARD, Lee
Singles: 7-inch
GAIT (407 "The Defense Rest")...40-50 62
(Also issued on the same label, by the Chev-rons.)
Also see CHEV-RONS

WARD, Little Sammy
(With Alley Kats & Kitty - Sax Kari Orchestra)
Singles: 7-inch
P-C (103 "Begging for Love")...1000-2000
Also see KARI, Sax
Also see WARD, Singin' Sammy

WARD, Lucky
Singles: 7-inch
BAND K ("Satellite Rock")...200-300
(Selection number not known.)

WARD, Richard, & Hustlers
Singles: 7-inch
DOWNEY (121 "Topless Bathing Suit")...30-40 64

WARD, Robert, & Ohio Untouchables
Singles: 7-inch
THELMA (601 "Your Love Is Real")...15-25 64
Also see OHIO UNTOUCHABLES

WARD, Robin P&R/R&B '63
Singles: 7-inch
DOT (249 "Wonderful Summer")..........5-10 66
DOT (16530 "Wonderful Summer")..........8-12 63
DOT (16578 "Winter's Here")..........8-12 64
DOT (16599 "Johnny, Come and Get Me")..........8-12 64
DOT (16624 "In His Car")..........15-25 64
SONGS UNLIMITED (33 "I Surrender Dear")..........8-12 63
SONGS UNLIMITED (37 "Loser's Lullaby")..........8-12 63
Picture Sleeves
SONGS UNLIMITED (33 "I Surrender Dear")..........10-20 63
SONGS UNLIMITED (37 "Loser's Lullaby")..........10-20 63
LPs: 10/12-inch
DOT (3555 "Wonderful Summer")..........30-40 63
(Monaural.)
DOT (25555 "Wonderful Summer")..........40-50 63
(Stereo.)
Also see BOONE, Pat
Also see MARTINDALE, Wink, & Robin Ward
Also see WARD, Dale

WARD, Sam
Singles: 7-inch
GROOVE CITY (205 "Sister Lee")..........50-100 '60s

WARD, Singin' Sammy R&B '61
(Sammy Ward)
Singles: 7-inch
SOUL (35004 "You've Got to Change")..........20-30 64
TAMLA (54030 "What Makes You Love Him")..........50-100 60
(With horizontal lines. Same number used twice.)
TAMLA (54030 "That Child Is Really Wild")..........50-100 60
(With horizontal lines.)
TAMLA (54030 "What Makes You Love Him")..........25-50 61
(With Tamla globe logo.)
TAMLA (54030 "That Child Is Really Wild")..........25-50 61
(With Tamla globe logo.)
TAMLA (54049 "What Makes You Love Him")..........20-40 61
TAMLA (54057 "Everybody Knew It")..........30-40 62
TAMLA (54071 "Part Time Love")..........25-35 62
Also see TAYLOR, Sherri, & Singin' Sammy Ward
Also see WARD, Little Sammy

WARD, Walter, & Challengers
Singles: 7-inch
MELATONE (1002 "I Can Tell")..........200-300 57
Also see OLYMPICS

WARD, Willie
(With the Warblers)
Singles: 7-inch
FEE BEE (233 "I'm a Madman")..........125-150 58
STAR (229 "Iggy Joe")..........50-75 57
(At least one source shows this release as Starr 509. We don't yet know which is correct.)

WARDELL, Roosevelt
(With Ed Wiley Orchestra)
Singles: 78 rpm
ROCKIN' (508 "Lost My Woman")..........75-125 53
Also see WILEY, ED

WARDELL & SULTANS
Singles: 7-inch
IMPERIAL (5812 "The Original Popeye")..........8-12 62
IMPERIAL (5886 "I'm Broke")..........8-12 62

WARDEN, J.W., & Jokers
Singles: 7-inch
SIMPSON (11301 "Sidewalk Rock and Roll")..........300-400 59

WARDEN & HIS FUGITIVES
Singles: 7-inch
BING (302 "The World Ain't Changed")..........15-25 65

WARE, Claude, & Werewolves
Singles: 7-inch
END (1089 "Pacing")..........8-12 61

WARE, Curtis, & Four-Do-Matics
Singles: 7-inch
KAY BEE (101 "Flame in My Heart")..........1500-2000 63

WARE, Eddie
Singles: 78 rpm
CHESS (1461 "Lima Beans")..........20-30 51
CHESS (1507 "Jealous Woman")..........20-30 52
STATES..........25-35 54
Singles: 7-inch
STATES (130 "That's the Stuff I Like")..........50-100 54

WARE, Jim
(With the Motives)
Singles: 7-inch
ATCO (6361 "Cindy's in Love")..........5-10 65
WHITE WHALE (332 "Animal Crackers")..........5-8 69

WARFIELD, Joe
Singles: 7-inch
JJ (42011 "Mama's Little Girl")..........100-200

WARFIELD, Peter
Singles: 78 rpm
MILTONE (5249 "Morning Train Blues")..........25-50 48

WARING, Fred P&R '23
(With the Pennsylvanians)
Singles: 78 rpm
CAPITOL..........3-5 57-58
DECCA..........3-6 50-57
Singles: 7-inch
CAPITOL..........5-10 57-59
DECCA..........5-15 50-68
REPRISE..........5-10 64
EPs: 7-inch
CAPITOL..........5-10 57-58
DECCA..........5-10 50-59
SHAWNEE PRESS ("Excerpts from the Fred Waring Band Book")..........10-15 '50s
(Includes 18-page "Band Book." Promotional issue only.)
LPs: 10/12-inch
CAPITOL..........5-15 57-69
DECCA..........5-20 50-68
HARMONY..........5-10 69
MCA..........5-8 77
MEGA..........5-8 71
REPRISE..........5-15 64-65
RCA..........5-10 68
Also see SINATRA, Frank, Bing Crosby, & Fred Waring

WARLOCK
Singles: 7-inch
EX-PLO (009 "In a Dream")..........10-20 69
Members: Henry Rice; Bob Lawler; Frank Pederson; Larry Threadgill.

WARLOCKS
Singles: 7-inch
DECCA (31806 "I'll Go Crazy")..........8-15 65
WASHINGTON SQUARE..........10-15 '60s

WARLOCKS
Singles: 7-inch
ARA (1015 "Another Year")..........200-300 66
(Reportedly, 500 made.)
ARA (1017 "If You Really Want Me to Stay")..........200-300 66
(Reportedly, 500 made.)
PARADISE (1021 "Life's a Misery")..........200-300 65
(Reportedly, 500 made.)
Members: Frank Beard; Dusty Hill; Rocky Hill.
Also see AMERICAN BLUES
Also see ZZ TOP

WARLORDS
Singles: 7-inch
AGR (0759 "Real Fine Lady")..........20-30 66

WARLORDS
Singles: 7-inch
NIGHT OWL (6861 "My Girl")..........10-15 68
Members: James White; Kurt Kuzalka; Steve Beau; George Barrahas; Randy Lindert; Larry Williams; Bill Shupe.

WARMER, Faron / Slim Marbles
(Gary Seger)
Singles: 7-inch
JO-REE (501 "Cruisin' Central")..........20-25 59

WARMEST SPRING
Singles: 7-inch
PARKWAY (985 "Younger Girl")..........8-12 66
PARKWAY (990 "Suddenly")..........8-12 66
Picture Sleeves
PARKWAY (990 "Suddenly")..........15-25 66

WARNER, Danny
Singles: 7-inch
REPRISE (459 "Love Is You")..........5-10 66
REPRISE (505 "It Hurts")..........5-10 66
SMASH (2110 "Bright Colors")..........5-10 67

WARNER, Danny, & Sessions
Singles: 7-inch
CHATTAHOOCHEE (675 "Big Boss Man")..........10-20 66

WARNER, Eddie
Singles: 7-inch
BERRY (7135 "Island in the Sun")..........5-10 63

WARNER, Herb & Betty
(With Bugs Bower & Orchestra)
Singles: 7-inc
DALE (109 "Slowly")..........8-10 58
DALE (111 "Mission of Love")..........8-10 59
JUBILEE (5380 "Dream Talk")..........8-12 60

WARNER, Merrill
Singles: 7-inch
TRAVEL (505 "Don't Let Me Dream Tonight")..........50-100

WARNER, Sandra
(With George Wyle & Orchestra)
Singles: 7-inch
OMYMPIA (820 "Willow Weep for Me")..........5-10 60

WARNER, Sonny
(Little Sonny Warner)
Singles: 7-inch
CHECKER (1151 "Bell Bottom Blue Jeans")..........8-12 66
CONCERTONE (220 "Nothing")..........8-12 61
FREEDOM (44015 "Riff Runner")..........10-15 59
Also see McNEELY, Big Jay
Also see TEMPESTS

WARNER, Sonny, & Marie Allen
Singles: 7-inch
BEE BEE (221 "Hand in Hand")..........5-10 61
Also see ALLEN, Little Marie
Also see WARNER, Sonny

WARNER BROTHERS
Singles: 7-inch
BALANCE..........10-15 66
DESTINATION (612 "Please Mr. Sullivan")..........10-20 65
DESTINATION (617 "Little Darlin' ")..........40-50 66
DUNWICH (131 "Lonely")..........10-15 66
EVEREST (2043 "Mairzy Doats")..........10-15 64
EVEREST (2050 "Comin' Home")..........10-15 64
EVEREST (2057 "Guitar Blue")..........10-15 65
KANDY KANE (408 "Study Hall")..........10-15 67
RAMPAGE (1702 "Beauty & the Beast")..........15-25 '60s

WARNES, Jennifer P&R/C&W/LP '77
(Jennifer Warren)
Singles: 12-inch
20TH FOX ("It Goes Like It Goes")..........5-10 79
(Shown as by Jennifer Warnes. No selection number used.)
20TH FOX (379 "It Goes Like It Goes")..........10-15 79
(Shown as by Jennifer Warren.)
Singles: 7-inch
ARISTA..........4-8 77-82
CYPRESS..........3-5 87
PARROT..........4-6 68
W.B...........3-5 83
LPs: 10/12-inch
ARISTA..........5-10 76-82
CYPRESS..........5-8 87
REPRISE..........5-10 72
Also see COCKER, Joe, & Jennifer Warnes
Also see GILLETTE, Steve, & Jennifer Warnes
Also see MEDLEY, Bill, & Jennifer Warnes
Also see ORBISON, Roy

WARNES, Jennifer, & Chris Thompson P&R '83
Singles: 7-inch
CASABLANCA..........3-6 83

WARNOCK, Cleve
Singles: 7-inch
STARS (502 "My Baby Is Gone")..........400-500

WARREN, Baby Boy
(With His Buddy [Charlie Mills]; Robert Warren)
Singles: 78 rpm
BLUE LAKE (106 "Mattie Mae")..........50-100 54
DRUMMOND..........50-100 54
EXCELLO (2211 "Sanafee")..........15-25 53
FEDERAL (12008 "Forgive Me Darling")..........50-75 51
GOTHAM (507 "Nervy Woman Blues")..........50-75 49
J.V.B. (26 "Sanafee")..........50-100 53
SAMPSON (633 "Taxi Driver")..........100-200 54
STAFF (707 "Don't Want No Skinny Woman")..........100-200 49
STAFF (709 "Forgive Me Darling")..........100-200 49
Singles: 7-inch
BLUE LAKE (106 "Santa Fe")..........200-250 54
(Colored vinyl. A completely different recording than J.V.B. 26 and Excello 2211.)
DRUMMOND (3002 "Chicken")..........250-350 54
DRUMMOND (3003 "Somebody Put Bad Luck on Me")..........250-350 54
EXCELLO (2211 "Not Welcome Anymore")..........40-60 62
(Same song as "Sanafee" as previously issued on J.V.B.)
Also see WILLIAMS, Johnny

WARREN, Beverly
Singles: 7-inch
B.T. PUPPY (521 "Would You Believe")..........5-10 66
B.T. PUPPY (526 "He's So Fine")..........5-10 67
RUST (5098 "Let Me Get Close to You")..........5-10 65
Also see CARROLL, Andrea / Beverly Warren

WARREN, Bobbie
Singles: 7-inch
PAMCO (1501 "Someone")..........5-10 60

WARREN, Bobby, Five
Singles: 7-inch
JORDAN (119 "Nite-Beat")..........15-25 61

WARREN, Dale
Singles: 7-inch
V-TONE (63111 "Follow Your Heart")..........40-50

WARREN, Doug
(With the Rays)
Singles: 7-inch
IMAGE (1011 "Around Midnight")..........15-25 60
IMAGE (1013 "Ain't That Love")..........15-25 60
SUNDOWN (136 "Troubles to Burn")..........10-15 60
Also see WARREN, Gary

WARREN, Fran
(With Hugo Winterhalter & Orchestra)
Singles: 78 rpm
MGM..........4-8 56
RCA..........5-10 51
UNIQUE..........4-8 56
Singles: 7-inch
MGM..........5-10 56
RCA..........10-15 51
UNIQUE..........5-10 56
EPs: 7-inch
MGM..........5-15 56
LPs: 10/12-inch
MGM (3394 "Mood Indigo")..........20-30 56
TOPS (1585 "Hey There")..........10-20 57
VENISE (10019 "Fran Warren")..........50-75 '50s
(Colored vinyl.)
Also see WINTERHALTER, Hugo, & His Orchestra

WARREN, Gary
Singles: 7-inch
IMAGE (1012 "Cindy")..........5-10 60
NASCO (6017 "Midnight Rain")..........5-10 58
SOUTHERN SOUND (110 "Charles Atlas")..........5-10 62
Also see WARREN, Doug

WARREN, Jerry
(With the Pets)
Singles: 7-inch
ARWIN (118 "Monkey Walk")..........8-12 59
DORSET (5002 "Rompin' ")..........5-10 60
Also see PETS

WARREN, Joel
Singles: 7-inch
KAPP (463 "Let Her Go")..........5-10 62

WARREN, Joey
Singles: 7-inch
SUPERIOR (3305 "Goatee")..........10-20 57

WARREN, Junior
Singles: 7-inch
SHERBA (1500 "Rock & Roll Fever") .. 200-300

WARREN, Lucky
Singles: 78 rpm
JAY-DEE (809 "Paradise Rock")............. 10-15 56
Singles: 7-inch
JAY-DEE (809 "Paradise Rock")............. 15-25 56
Also see LOVE NOTES

WARREN, Phil, Orchestra
Singles: 7-inch
MAY (110 "All Keyed Up")..........................5-10 61

WARREN, Randy
(With the Roland James Orchestra)
Singles: 7-inch
GOOD (002 "Little Princess").................. 10-20
Also see JANES, Roland

WARREN, Rusty LP '60
Singles: 7-inch
JUBILEE...5-10 60
EPs: 7-inch
JUBILEE... 10-15 62
LPs: 10/12-inch
GNP...5-12 74-77
JUBILEE... 10-20 60-68

WARREN, Shorty & Smokey
Singles: 7-inch
FLAME (111 "So Bad")...............................5-10 59

WARREN, Shorty / Smokey & Dottie Mae Warren
Singles: 7-inch
YALE (222 "Jersey Central Special").........5-10 60

WARREN, Smokey
Singles: 7-inch
FLAMINGO (542 "Ball of Fire")..................5-10 63
ROULETTE (7006 "Ball of Fire")............ 10-15 58
Also see WARREN, Shorty & Smokey

WARREN, Terry
Singles: 7-inch
RIC-TIC (106 "I Don't Know").................. 20-30 62

WARRIORS
Singles: 7-inch
MAYFLOWER...8-12 59
Also see ISLANDERS

WARWICK, Dee Dee P&R/R&B '65
(With the Dixie Flyers)
Singles: 7-inch
ATCO...4-8 70-71
BLUE ROCK (4008 "Happiness")..............8-12 65
BLUE ROCK (4027 "I Want to Be with You")...8-12 65
BLUE ROCK (4032 "Baby I'm Yours")........8-12 65
HURT (79 "I")..8-12 66
JUBILEE (5459 "You're No Good")......... 10-20 63
MERCURY...5-10 66-69
PRIVATE STOCK...4-6 75
SUTRA..4-6
TIGER (103 "I Don't Think My Baby's Coming Back").. 10-20 64
LPs: 10/12-inch
ATCO...8-12 70
HERITAGE SOUND.....................................5-8 83
MERCURY.. 10-20 67-69

WARWICK, Dionne P&R '62
(Dionne Warwicke)
Singles: 12-inch
ARISTA...4-6 84
Singles: 7-inch
ARISTA...3-5 79-90
COLLECTABLES..3-5 '80s
ERIC...4-6 '70s
FOREVER..3-5 '80s
MUSICOR...4-6 77
SCEPTER (1200 series)..............................5-10 62-65
SCEPTER (12000 series)............................4-8 65-73
W.B. 4-6 72-78
Picture Sleeves
ARISTA (9460 "Whisper in the Dark")..........4-6 85
SCEPTER...5-10 63-71
EPs: 7-inch
SCEPTER (9534 "In Paris").........................5-10
LPs: 10/12-inch
ARISTA...5-8 79-90
CIRCA...5-8
EVEREST..5-8 81
51 WEST...5-8 '80s
MFSL...40-60 82
MUSICOR...5-10 77
PHOENIX..5-8 81
PICKWICK...5-10 '70s
RHINO..5-8 '80s
SCEPTER (Except 200)..........................10-25 64-72
SCEPTER (200 "March Is Dionne Warwick Month")..20-30 67
(Promotional issue only.)
SCEPTER/COLUMBIA (5139/40 "Dionne")..15-25 67
(Record club issue.)
U.A. 8-10 74
TRIP...8-10 76
W.B. 8-10 72-77
Also see BROWN, Nappy
Also see CAMPBELL, Glen / Dionne Warwick / Burt Bacharach
Also see GIBB, Barry
Also see HAYES, Isaac, & Dionne Warwick
Also see MATHIS, Johnny, & Dionne Warwick
Also see WONDER, Stevie / Dionne Warwick

WARWICK, Dionne, & Howard Hewett R&B '88
Singles: 7-inch
ARISTA...3-5 88

WARWICK, Dionne, & Glenn Jones R&B '85
Singles: 7-inch
ARISTA...3-5 85

WARWICK, Dionne, & Jeffrey Osborne P&R/R&B '87
Singles: 7-inch
ARISTA...3-5 87
Picture Sleeves
ARISTA...3-5 87

WARWICK, Dionne, & Spinners P&R/R&B '74
Singles: 7-inch
ATLANTIC..4-6 74
Picture Sleeves
ATLANTIC..4-6 74
Also see SPINNERS

WARWICK, Dionne, & Luther Vandross P&R/R&B '83
Singles: 7-inch
ARISTA...3-5 83
Picture Sleeves
ARISTA...3-5 83
Also see VANDROSS, Luther
Also see WARWICK, Dionne

WASDEN, Jaybee
Singles: 7-inch
TREPUR (1011 "Elvis in the Army").....400-500 59

WASHBOARD BILL
(Bill Valentine)
Singles: 78 rpm
KING..8-12 56-57
Singles: 7-inch
KING (4983 "In the Morning")..................20-30 56
KING (5062 "Washboard Story")...............20-30 57
Session: Mickey Baker; King Curtis.
Also see BAKER, Mickey
Also see KING CURTIS
Also see VALENTINE, Billy

WASHBOARD PETE
(Pete Sanders)
Singles: 78 rpm
SAVOY...25-50 48
Member: Ralph Willis.
Also see WILLIS, Ralph

WASHBOARD SAM
(Robert Brown)
Singles: 78 rpm
BLUEBIRD...15-25 43
CHESS (1545 "Bright Eyes")......................25-50 53
RCA..10-15 47-50
Singles: 7-inch
CHESS (1545 "Bright Eyes")..................200-300 53
RCA (0023 "I'm Just Tired")....................50-100 49
(Colored vinyl.)
RCA (0048 "You Said You Love Me")....50-100 50
(Colored vinyl.)
RCA (0090 "Gamblin Man")....................50-100 50
(Colored vinyl.)
LPs: 10/12-inch
BLUES CLASSICS.......................................5-10
RCA..10-15 71
Also see BROONZY, Big Bill, & Washboard Sam
Also see DIXON, Willie
Also see SYKES, Roosevelt

WASHBOARD WILLIE & HIS SUPER SUDS OF RHYTHM
Singles: 78 rpm
J.V.B. 25-50 56
Singles: 7-inch
HERCULON...10-15 66
J.V.B. (59 "Cherry Red Blues")...............75-125 56
J.V.B. (70 "Washboard Blues")..............75-125 56
VON..10-15 64

WASHBURN, Beverly
Singles: 7-inch
SMASH (1855 "Wartime Blues")................5-10 63

WASHBURN, Billy
Singles: 7-inch
ATLANTIC (2208 "Don't It Sound Good").10-15 63

WASHBURN, Frank, & His Orchestra
LPs: 10/12-inch
PROMENADE (2052 "I'm in the Mood for Love")..25-50 57
(Cover pictures Jayne Mansfield, although she is not heard on the disc.)
Also see MANSFIELD, Jayne

WASHBURN, Perry
Singles: 7-inch
MUSTANG (300 "Pocahontas Baby")......20-30 '60s

WASHER WINDSHIELD
Singles: 7-inch
INDIGO ("Kathy Young Finds the Innocents Guilty")..30-50 61
Picture Sleeves
INDIGO ("Kathy Young Finds the Innocents Guilty")..50-75 61
(Promotional issue only.)
Members: Kathy Young; Innocents.
Also see INNOCENTS
Also see YOUNG, Kathy

WASHINGTON, Albert
(With the Kings)
Singles: 7-inch
BLUESTOWN (703 "You're Gonna Miss Me")..10-20 65
DELUXE..4-6 71
FINCH (10990 "You're Gonna Miss Me").30-50 65
(First issue.)
FRATERNITY (1002 "I'm the Man")..........10-20 67
FRATERNITY (1010 "Bring It On Up").....10-20 68
FRATERNITY (1016 "Lonely Mountain").10-20 69
FRATERNITY (1021 "Hold Me Baby").....10-20 69
FRATERNITY (1029 "Having a Good Time")..10-20 70
FRATERNITY (1032 "Crazy Legs")..........10-20 70
JEWEL...4-8 71-73
L&W...8-12
VLM (1100 "So Tired")............................15-25 64
WESTWORLD...4-6
LPs: 10/12-inch
EASTBOUND...10-15 74

WASHINGTON, Baby R&B '59
(Jeanette "Baby" Washington; Justine Washington)
Singles: 7-inch
ABC-PAR (10223 "My Time to Cry")........15-25 61
ABC-PAR (10245 "There You Go Again")..10-20 61
A.V.I. (253 "I Wanna Dance").....................4-6 78
CHECKER (918 "I Hate to See You Go")...8-12 59
CHECKER (1105 "Is It Worth It")...............5-10 65
CHESS (2099 "Is It Worth It")....................4-8 70
COLLECTABLES...3-5 '80s
COTILLION...5-10 69-70
J&S (1001 "It's Been a Long Time").........15-25 63
J&S (1604 "There Must Be a Reason")....30-40 57
J&S (1607 "Ah-Ha")...............................20-30 58
J&S (1619 "Hard Way to Go")..................20-30 58
J&S (1632 "I Hate to See You Go")..........15-25 59
J&S (1656 "Every Day")..........................15-25 57
LAWTON (1600 "Come See About Me")......3-5 81
MASTER FIVE (1001 "Crying in the Midnight Hour")..3-5 88
MASTER FIVE (1800 "Tear After Tear")......4-6 78
MASTER FIVE (3500 "Can't Get Over Losing You")..5-10 74
MASTER FIVE (3502 "Tell Me a Lie").........4-6 75
MASTER FIVE (9104 "Just Can't Get You Out of My Mind")..5-10 73
MASTER FIVE (9107 "I've Got to Break Away")..5-10 73
NEPTUNE (101 "The Time")......................15-20 58
NEPTUNE (104 "The Bells").....................15-20 59
NEPTUNE (116 "Deep Down Love")........15-20 60
NEPTUNE (120 "Medicine Man")............15-20 60
NEPTUNE (121 "Too Late")......................15-20 60
NEPTUNE (122 "Nobody Cares")............15-20 61
7L (3000 "Turn Your Boogie Loose")..........4-6 79
SIXTH AVENUE (10816 "Either You Love Me Or You Don't")..4-6 76
SUE (4 "I Know")..5-10 68
SUE (104 thru 150).....................................8-15 64-67
SUE (764 thru 794)..................................10-20 62-63
SUE (797 "Who's Going to Take Care of Me")..30-50 63
VEEP (1274 "White Christmas")..................8-12 68
VEEP (1297 "Hold Back the Dawn")..........5-10 69
LPs: 10/12-inch
A.V.I. 8-12 78
COLLECTABLES..5-8 87-88
SUE..20-40 63-65
TRIP...8-12 71
UNART...10-20 67
VEEP..10-20 68
Also see DEL PRIS
Also see HEARTS

WASHINGTON, Baby, & Don Gardner R&B '73
Singles: 7-inch
MASTER FIVE (9103 "Forever")................5-10 73
MASTER FIVE (9110 "Lay a Little Lovin' on Me")..5-10 74
LPs: 10/12-inch
MASTER FIVE...10-15 74
Also see GARDNER Don
Also see WASHINGTON, Baby

WASHINGTON, Billy
Singles: 7-inch
BETHLEHEM (3044 "Third Finger Left Hand")..5-10 62
CIGAR (001 "Our Love")............................5-10 63
D'ORO (1303 "Do You Really Love Me")...5-10 64

WASHINGTON, Booker T.
Singles: 78 rpm
BLUEBIRD..15-25
BROOME (14605 "Atlanta Exposition Address")...100-200 1909
COLUMBIA GRAMOPHONE (14605 "Atlanta Exposition Address")...........................100-200 1909

WASHINGTON, Cecil
Singles: 7-inch
PROPHONICS (2029 "I Don't Like to Lose")...100-200

WASHINGTON, Connie
Singles: 7-inch
CENTRAL (624 "Your Other Love")...........8-12 60

WASHINGTON, D.C.
(D.C. Bendy)
Singles: 78 rpm
GOLD STAR (661 "Rebob Boogie").........25-50 49
Singles: 7-inch
FELSTED (8655 "The Mohawk")................5-10 62
Also see BENDER, D.C.

WASHINGTON, Dinah R&B '48
Singles: 78 rpm
APOLLO..10-25 45-47
KEYNOTE..20-40 44
MERCURY...5-15 46-57
Singles: 7-inch
MERCURY (5488 "Harbor Lights")...........25-50 50
MERCURY (5503 "I'll Never Be Free").....25-50 50
MERCURY (5728 "Cold Cold Heart")........25-50 51
MERCURY (7200 series).........................15-25 62
(Compact 33 singles.)
MERCURY (8187 thru 8294)....................25-50 50-52
MERCURY (10008 "What a Diff'rence a Day Makes")..20-30 59
(Stereo.)
MERCURY (10015 "Unforgettable").........20-30 59
(Stereo.)

MERCURY (30091 "Unforgettable") ... 8-12 62
MERCURY (30114 "A Cottage for Sale") ... 8-12 63
MERCURY (70046 thru 71377) ... 15-30 52-58
MERCURY (71435 thru 72040) ... 10-20 59-62
MERCURY CELEBRITY SERIES ... 4-8 '60s
ROULETTE (4424 "You're Nobody 'Til Somebody Loves You") ... 8-12 62
ROULETTE (4444 "I Wouldn't Know") ... 8-12 62
ROULETTE (4455 "You're a Sweetheart") ... 8-12 62
ROULETTE (4476 "Romance in the Dark") ... 8-12 63
ROULETTE (4490 "Soulville") ... 8-12 63
ROULETTE (4520 "The Show Must Go On") ... 8-12 63
ROULETTE (4534 "That Sunday, That Summer") ... 8-12 63
ROULETTE (4538 "Call Me Irresponsible") ... 8-12 63

Picture Sleeves

MERCURY (71635 "This Bitter Earth") ... 10-20 60
MERCURY (71696 "Love Walked In") ... 10-20 60
MERCURY (71744 "We Have Love") ... 10-20 60
MERCURY (71778 "Early Every Morning") ... 10-20 61
MERCURY (71812 "Our Love Is Here to Stay") ... 10-20 61
MERCURY (71876 "September in the Rain") ... 10-20 61
MERCURY (71922 "Tears & Laughter") ... 10-20 61
MERCURY (71958 "Dream") ... 10-20 61
MERCURY (72040 "Cold, Cold Heart") ... 10-20 61

EPs: 7-inch

EMARCY ... 15-25 54-56
MERCURY (3000 thru 3200 series) ... 15-25 51-57
MERCURY (3300 series) ... 10-15 60
MERCURY (4000 series) ... 10-15 61
ROULETTE (269 "Dinah Washington") ... 8-12 64

LPs: 10/12-inch

EMARCY (400 series) ... 8-12 76
EMARCY (26032 "After Hours") ... 50-100 54
(10-inch LP.)
EMARCY (36011 "For Those in Love") ... 50-75 55
EMARCY (36028 "After Hours") ... 50-75 55
EMARCY (36065 "Dinah") ... 50-75 56
EMARCY (36073 "In the Land of Hi-Fi") ... 50-75 56
EMARCY (36119 "Dinah Sings Fats Waller") ... 50-75 57
EMARCY (36130 "Dinah Sings Bessie Smith") ... 50-75 58
EVEREST ... 8-10 75
MERCURY (103 "This Is My Story") ... 20-30 63
MERCURY (121 "Original Queen of Soul") ... 12-15 69
MERCURY (603 "This Is My Story") ... 20-30 63
MERCURY (20100 & 20200 series) ... 40-60 55-58
MERCURY (20479 thru 20928) ... 20-30 59-65
(Monaural.)
MERCURY (21119 "Dinah Discovered") ... 10-20 67
(Monaural.)
MERCURY (25060 "Dinah Washington") ... 50-100 50
(10-inch LP.)
MERCURY (25060 "Dinah Washington") 20-30 64
MERCURY (25138 "Dynamic Dinah") ... 50-100 51
(10-inch LP.)
MERCURY (25140 "Blazing Ballads") ... 50-100 51
(10-inch LP.)
MERCURY (25138 "Dynamic Dinah") ... 50-100 51
(10-inch LP.)
MERCURY (60158 thru 60928) ... 20-40 59-65
(Stereo.)
MERCURY (61119 "Dinah Discovered") ... 10-20 67
(Stereo.)
MUSICO ... 10-15 69
PICKWICK ... 5-10
ROSETTA ... 5-8 84
ROULETTE (100 series) ... 10-12 71-72
ROULETTE (25170 "Dinah '62") ... 20-30 62
ROULETTE (25100 "In Love") ... 20-30 62
ROULETTE (25183 "Drinking Again") ... 20-30 62
ROULETTE (25189 "Back to the Blues") ... 20-30 63
ROULETTE (25220 "Dinah '63") ... 20-30 63
ROULETTE (25253 "A Stranger On Earth") ... 20-30 63
ROULETTE (25244 "In Tribute") ... 20-30 64
ROULETTE (25253 "Stranger On Earth") ... 20-30 64
ROULETTE (25260 "Dinah Washington Sings Fats Waller") ... 20-30 64
ROULETTE (25269 "Dinah Washington") ... 20-30 64
ROULETTE (25289 "The Best of Dinah Washington") ... 15-25 65
TRIP ... 8-10 73-78
WING (12140 "Late Late Show") ... 20-30 59
Also see BENTON, Brook, & Dinah Washington
Also see CHAMBLEE, Eddie
Also see HAMPTON, Lionel & Dinah Washington
Also see JONES, Quincy
Also see PLATTERS / Red Prysock / Dinah Washington
Also see RAVENS & DINAH WASHINGTON

WASHINGTON, Dinah / Ink Spots

EPs: 7-inch

WALDORF ... 10-20 55
Also see INK SPOTS
Also see WASHINGTON, Dinah

WASHINGTON, Dinah / Joe Williams / Sarah Vaughan

LPs: 10/12-inch

ROULETTE (25250 "We Three") ... 15-25 64
Also see VAUGHAN, Sarah
Also see WASHINGTON, Dinah
Also see WILLIAMS, Joe

WASHINGTON, Earl

Singles: 7-inch

CHECKER (905 "Miserlou") ... 8-12 58

WASHINGTON, Ella — P&R/R&B '69

Singles: 7-inch

ATLANTIC ... 5-10 67
SOUND STAGE ... 4-6 67-72

LPs: 10/12-inch

SOUND STAGE ... 10-15 69

WASHINGTON, Ernestine

(Madame Ernestine Washington)

Singles: 78 rpm

GROOVE (0019 "Holding On") ... 5-10 54

Singles: 7-inch

GROOVE (0019 "Holding On") ... 10-20 54

WASHINGTON, Ernie

Singles: 7-inch

CHATTAHOOCHEE (673 "How About You") ... 8-12 65

WASHINGTON, Freddy, Band

Singles: 7-inch

ATLAS (1026 "8-9-10") ... 8-12 69

WASHINGTON, Geno

(With the Ramjam Band)

Singles: 7-inch

CONGRESS (269 "Water") ... 5-10 66
CONGRESS (273 "Beach Bash") ... 5-10 66
DJM (1011 "You Lovely Witch") ... 4-6 76
KAPP (796 "All I Need") ... 5-10 66

LPs: 10/12-inch

KAPP (1515 "Live") ... 10-20 67
(Monaural.)
KAPP (3515 "Live") ... 10-20 67
(Stereo.)

WASHINGTON, George

(With the Cherry Bombs; with Cherry Stompers)

Singles: 78 rpm

ACE ... 15-25 58

Singles: 7-inch

ACE ... 15-25 58
MGM ... 5-10 66
SEAELL (101 "Back Shelf of Your Mind") ... 15-25 67

WASHINGTON, Gino

Singles: 7-inch

AMON (90580 "Out of This World") ... 8-12 63
ATAC (101 "Doin' the Popcorn") ... 15-25 69
ATAC (102 "I'll Be Around") ... 25-35 69
ATAC (2743 "It's Winter") ... 8-12 71
(More picture sleeves than records made. Promotional issue only.)
ATAC (2829 "You Got Me in a Whirlpool") ... 8-12 74
ATAC (2830 "Rat Race") ... 10-20 75
ATAC (2878 "Oh Not Me") ... 8-12 76
ATAC (2930 "Could It Be I'm Falling in Love") ... 8-12 77
(Shown as by George Washington.)
ATAC (3031 "I'll Never Leave You") ... 8-12 78
ATAC (7823 "I'll Be Around") ... 25-35 69
ATAC (7825 "Doin' the Popcorn") ... 8-12 69
ATAC (7826 "Girl Here I Am") ... 8-12
ATAC (7826 "Hey I'm a Love Bandit") ... 4-8 81
(Same selection number used twice.)
ATAC (62743 "Gino the Gamanisist") ... 4-8 85
CORREC-TONE (503 "I'm a Coward") ... 35-45 62
CREED (1051 "Romeo") ... 10-20 68
DO DE RE (358 "Gino Is a Coward") ... 4-8 71
G+G (0001 "Flying High") ... 5-10 '70s
(Shown as by Sir George.)
MALA (12029 "I'll Be Around") ... 20-30 68
PERFECTA (2870 "Gino's Push & Pull") ... 5-10 71
RIC-TIC (100 "Gino Is a Coward") ... 10-15 64
SIDRA (9005 "Romeo") ... 10-20 66
SONBERT (3770 "Gino Is a Coward") ... 10-20 64
WAND (147 "Out of This World") ... 10-15 64
WAND (155 "Baby Be Mine") ... 10-15 64
WASHPAN (3122 "What Can a Man Do") ... 8-12 68
WASHPAN (32937 "Do the Frog") ... 8-12 68
WASHPAN (32943 "Rat Race") ... 8-12 '70s
WIG (9005 "Romeo") ... 10-20 71

Picture Sleeves

ATAC (2743 "It's Winter") ... 20-30 71

LPs: 10/12-inch

ATAC (2743 "Golden Hits Now") ... 71

WASHINGTON, Grover, Jr. — R&B/LP '72

Singles: 7-inch

COLUMBIA ... 3-5 87
ELEKTRA ... 3-6 79-84
KUDU ... 4-6 71-78
MOTOWN ... 3-6 78-83

Picture Sleeves

ELEKTRA ... 3-5 80-82

LPs: 10/12-inch

COLUMBIA ... 5-8 87
ELEKTRA ... 5-10 79-84
KUDU ... 8-15 71-77
MOTOWN ... 5-10 78-83
Also see COSBY, Bill
Also see LABELLE, Patti, & Grover Washington Jr.
Also see WITHERS, Bill

WASHINGTON, Jimmy

Singles: 7-inch

BACK BEAT (549 "My One Sin") ... 5-10 65

WASHINGTON, Lee

Singles: 7-inch

FAT FISH (8006 "Little Girl") ... 20-25

WASHINGTON, Leroy

Singles: 7-inch

EXCELLO (2144 "Wild Cherry") ... 50-100 58
(Counterfeits have "SHELDON" etched in the vinyl trail-off. Originals have that name mechanically stamped there.)
EXCELLO (2161 "My Chinatown Gal") ... 25-50 59
EXCELLO (2172 "Why Should I") ... 25-50 60
REO (8299 "Wild Cherry") ... 15-25 58
(Canadian.)
ROCKO (514 "Darling It Takes You") ... 10-20 61

WASHINGTON, Little Joe

Singles: 7-inch

DONNA (1359 "The Last Tear") ... 5-10 62
FEDERAL ... 8-12 63-64

WASHINGTON, Lou

(Lou D. Washington & the Professionals)

Singles: 7-inch

STEELTOWN ... 10-20 69
USA (831 "When We Meet Again") ... 200-300 66
Also see GAINES, Fats, Band

WASHINGTON, Roger

Singles: 7-inch

BEACON (563 "Unless You Let Me") ... 20-30 61
BURDETTE (1912 "Unless You Let Me") ... 10-20 66
JOE DAVIS (7121 "You're Too Much") ... 15-25 66

WASHINGTON, Sherry, & Chromatics

Singles: 78 rpm

MILLION (2016 "Honey Bug") ... 15-25 56

Singles: 7-inch

LAMP (2003 "I Got Plenty") ... 20-30 57
MILLION (2016 "Honey Bug") ... 50-75 56
Also see CHROMATICS

WASHINGTON, Toni

Singles: 7-inch

KON-TI (1063 "Dear Diary") ... 10-20 66
KON-TI (1170 "Satisfaction") ... 15-25 66

WASHINGTON D.C.s

Singles: 7-inch

DATE (1537 "Thirty-second Floor") ... 5-10 66
FLIP (363 "Where Did You Go") ... 10-15 63

WASHINGTON MERRY-GO-ROUND

Singles: 7-inch

PICCADILLY (254 "Land of Odin") ... 5-10 67

WASSON, Ben

Singles: 7-inch

NORMAN (519 "It's Springtime, Baby") ... 10-15 62

WASSON, Jimmy

Singles: 7-inch

FABLE (613 "No Idea Poor Girl") ... 15-25 '50s

WATCHBAND

Singles: 7-inch

STANAL (7137 "No Dice") ... 50-75 67

WATERFORD, Crown Prince

(With His Twistologists; Charles Waterford)

Singles: 78 rpm

ALADDIN ... 15-25 47
CAPITOL ... 10-20 48
EXCELLO ... 10-20 56
HYTONE ... 15-25 47
KING ... 10-20 49-50
TORCH ... 15-25 50

Singles: 7-inch

EXCELLO (2065 "Driftwood Blues") ... 50-75 56
ORBIT (6943 "I Don't Wanna Get Married") ... 10-15 62
Also see McSHANN, Jay
Also see MILBURN, Amos / Wynonie Harris / Crown Prince Waterford

WATERPROOF TINKERTOY

Singles: 7-inch

CAITLIN ... 10-20 68
LAURIE (3457 "Groovy Girl") ... 8-12 68
LAURIE (3469 "Workin' for My Baby") ... 8-12 68

WATERS

Singles: 7-inch

HIP (8012 "Day In and Out") ... 5-10 69

WATERS, Clear

Singles: 7-inch

ATOMIC (905 "A-Minor Cha-Cha") ... 20-30 59
LA SALLE (502 "Cool Water") ... 50-75 57

WATERS, Ethel — P&R '21

Singles: 78 rpm

BLACK SWAN ... 10-20 21-23
BRUNSWICK ... 10-15 33-34
COLUMBIA ... 10-15 25-33
CONTINENTAL ... 5-10 46-47
DECCA ... 8-12 34-38

EPs: 7-inch

CHANCEL ... 20-30 '50s
MERCURY (3245/46 "Favorites") ... 20-30 55
(Price is for either volume.)

LPs: 10/12-inch

BIOGRAPH ... 8-12 70
COLUMBIA ... 8-12 68-72
CONTINENTAL (16008 "Ethel Waters Sings") ... 20-30 62
JAY (3010 "Sings Her Best") ... 40-60 57
MERCURY (20051 "Favorites") ... 30-50 54
REMINGTON ("Shades of Blue") ... 75-100 50
(10-inch LP.)
WORD (3173 "Ethel Waters Reminisces") ... 10-15 62
"X" (1009 "Ethel Waters") ... 40-60 55

WATERS, Freddie — R&B '77

Singles: 7-inch

KARI (107 "It Has to Be Love") ... 15-30 80
OCTOBER ... 4-6 77

WATERS, Larry

Singles: 78 rpm

DIG ... 8-12 56

Singles: 7-inch

DIG (108 "Full Grown Woman") ... 10-15 56
DIG (121 "I Wonder, I Wonder") ... 10-15 56

WATERS, Muddy — R&B '48

(With His Guitar)

Singles: 78 rpm

ARISTOCRAT (406 "Sneakin' and Cryin' ") ... 100-150 50

ARISTOCRAT (412 "Rollin' and Tumblin' ")...300-400 50
ARISTOCRAT (1302 "Gypsy Woman")...100-150 48
ARISTOCRAT (1305 "I Can't Be Satisfied")...100-150 48
ARISTOCRAT (1306 "Train Fare Home")...100-150 48
ARISTOCRAT (1307 "You're Gonna Miss Me")...100-150 49
ARISTOCRAT (1310 "Streamlined Woman")...100-150 49
ARISTOCRAT (1311 "Little Geneva")..100-150 49
CHESS (1426 "Rollin' Stone")...200-300 50
CHESS (1434 "You're Gonna Need My Help I Said")...75-100 50
CHESS (1441 "Louisiana Blues")...75-100 50
CHESS (1452 "Long Distance Call")...75-100 51
CHESS (1468 "Appealing Blues")...75-100 51
CHESS (1480 "My Fault")...75-100 51
CHESS (1490 "Early Morning Blues")...75-100 51
CHESS (1509 thru 1704)...25-75 52-58
CHESS (1718 thru 1739)...75-125 59

Singles: 7-inch

CHESS (1509 "All Night Long")...400-500 52
CHESS (1514 "Looking for My Baby")...300-400 52
CHESS (1526 "Standing Around Crying")...300-400 52
CHESS (1537 "She's All Right")...150-200 53
CHESS (1542 "Who's Gonna Be Your Sweet Man")...150-200 52
CHESS (1550 "Mad Love")...125-175 53
CHESS (1560 "I'm Your Hootchie Coochie Man")...40-50 53
CHESS (1571 "Just Make Love to Me")..50-75 54
CHESS (1579 "I'm Ready")...50-75 54
CHESS (1585 "I'm a Natural Born Lover")...50-75 54
CHESS (1596 "I Want to Be Loved")...50-75 55
CHESS (1602 "Mannish Boy")...75-125 55
CHESS (1612 "Sugar Sweet")...40-60 55
CHESS (1620 "Forty Days and Forty Nights")...40-60 56
CHESS (1630 "Don't Go No Farther")...40-60 56
CHESS (1644 "I Got to Find My Baby")...40-60 56
CHESS (1652 "Rock Me")...40-60 57
CHESS (1667 "Good News")...40-60 57
CHESS (1680 "Evil")...30-50 58
CHESS (1692 "I Won't Go On")...25-50 58
CHESS (1704 "Close to You")...25-50 58
CHESS (1718 "Walkin' Thru the Park")...25-50 59
CHESS (1724 "Ooh Wee")...25-50 59
CHESS (1733 "Take the Bitter with the Sweet")...25-50 59
CHESS (1739 "Tell Me Baby")...25-50 59
CHESS (1748 "I Feel So Good")...25-50 60
CHESS (1752 "I'm Your Doctor")...25-50 60
CHESS (1758 "Love Affair")...25-50 60
CHESS (1765 "Tiger in Your Tank")...25-50 60
CHESS (1774 "Woman Wanted")...25-50 60
CHESS (1796 "Lonesome Room Blues") 20-40 61
CHESS (1819 "Going Home")...20-30 62
CHESS (1827 "You Shook Me")...20-30 62
CHESS (1839 "You Need Love")...20-30 62
CHESS (1862 "Five Long Years")...15-25 63
CHESS (1895 "You Can't Lose What You Ain't Never Had")...15-25 64
CHESS (1914 "Short Dress Woman")...15-25 64
CHESS (1921 "Still a Fool")...10-20 65
CHESS (1937 "I Got a Rich Man's Woman")...10-20 65
CHESS (1973 " I'm Your Hootchie Cootchie Man")...10-20 66
CHESS (2018 "Bird Nest on the Ground")...10-20 67
CHESS (2085 "I Feel So Good")...8-12 70
CHESS (2143 "Can't Get No Grindin' ")...8-12 73

LPs: 10/12-inch

BLUE SKY (37064 "King Bee")...8-12 81
CADET CONCEPT (314 "Electric Mud")...10-20 68
(Includes eight-page booklet.)
CADET CONCEPT (320 "After the Rain")...10-15 69
CHESS (127 "Fathers and Sons")...15-25 69
CHESS (203 "Muddy Waters")...15-25 76
(Two discs.)
CHESS (1427 "The Best of Muddy Waters")...250-350 57
CHESS (1444 "Muddy Waters Sings Big Bill")...50-100 60
CHESS (1449 "Muddy Waters at Newport")...20-30 64
CHESS (1483 "Folk Singer")...15-25 64
CHESS (1500 "Real Folk Blues of Muddy Waters")...15-20 66
CHESS (1507 "Muddy, Brass, and the Blues")...15-20 66
CHESS (1511 "More Real Folk Blues")...15-20 67
CHESS (1539 "Sail On")...15-20 69
CHESS (1553 "They Call Me Muddy Waters")...15-20 69
CHESS (8202 "Rollin' Stone")...5-10 83
CHESS (9000 series)...5-10
CHESS (50023 "Can't Get No Grindin' ")..10-15 73
CHESS (50033 "Fathers & Sons")...10-15 75
CHESS (60006 "McKinley Morganfield A.K.A. Muddy Waters")...10-15 71
CHESS (60013 "The London Muddy Waters Sessions")...10-15 72
CHESS (60031 "Unk in Funk")...10-15 74
CHESS (60035 "Muddy Waters at Woodstock")...10-15 75
MFSL (201 "Folk Singer")...25-35 94
(Half-speed mastered.)
TESTAMENT (2210 "Down on Stovall's Plantation")...10-15 '60s
Session: Little Walter; Otis Spann; Jimmy Rogers; Willie Dixon; Elgin Evans; James Cotton; Earl Hooker; Willie Smith; Pat Hare.
Also see CARTER, James "Sweet Lucy," & His Orchestra
Also see COTTON, James
Also see DIXON, Willie
Also see FOSTER, Leroy, & Muddy Waters
Also see HOOKER, Earl
Also see HORTON, Big Walter
Also see JOHNSON, Luther / Mojo Buford
Also see JONES, Little Johnny
Also see MEMPHIS SLIM / Muddy Waters / Jimmy Driftwood & Stoney Mountain Boys
Also see ROGERS, Jimmy
Also see SPANN, Otis
Also see SUNNYLAND SLIM
Also see WELLS, Junior
Also see WILLIAMSON, Sonny Boy
Also see WINTER, Johnny

WATERS, Muddy, & Howlin' Wolf

LPs: 10/12-inch

CHESS (9100 "Muddy and the Wolf")...8-10 85
CHESS (60026 "London Revisited")...10-15 74
Session: Eric Clapton.
Also see CLAPTON, Eric
Also see DIDDLEY, Bo, Howlin' Wolf & Muddy Waters
Also see HOWLIN' WOLF
Also see WATERS, Muddy

WATERS, Patty

LPs: 10/12-inch

ESP (1025 "Patty Waters Sings")...10-15 66

WATKINS, Billy

(Bill Watkins)

Singles: 7-inch

ALLIED (10000/10001 "Space Love"/"Sandman of Love")...50-100 58
ARWIN (117 "Convince Me")...15-25 58
CHALLENGE (59056 "Rendezvous")...10-15 59
CHALLENGE (59078 "Go Billy Go")...10-15 60
CHART MAKER (405 "Just for You")...8-12 66
CHART MAKER (406 "Too Many Times")..8-12 66
CHATTAHOOCHEE (712 "I'm Somebody's Love")...8-12 66
CHESS (1786 "I Wanna Know")...10-15 61
CHESS (1810 "Crackin' Up")...10-15 61
ERA (3183 "The Ice-Man")...20-30 67
IMPERIAL (66371 "Echoes")...5-10 69
KENT (411 "Just for You")...10-15 65
LUCKY (0006 "Missed the Workhouse")...300-400
ROBELL (1001 "I'm Somebody's Love")..40-50 59
TIP-TOE (14321 "I Got Troubles")...75-125 64

WATKINS, Katie / Texas Red & Jimmy

(Katie "Blue" Watkins; Katie Blue)

Singles: 78 rpm

CHECKER...10-20 57
VICEROY...15-25 57

Singles: 7-inch

CHECKER...10-20 57
VICEROY...15-25 57
Also see BLUE, Katie, & Peppermints
Also see KARI, Sax

WATKINS, La Cille

(With the Volumes; with Belltones)

Singles: 78 rpm

JAGUAR...50-100 54

Singles: 7-inch

JAGUAR (3006 "You Left Me Lonely")...250-350 54
KAPP (145 "Maybe You'll Be There")...15-25 57
Also see VOLUMES

WATKINS, Lovelace

Singles: 7-inch

GROOVE (0016 "Tender Love")...10-15 63
GROOVE (0023 "I Won't Believe It")...10-15 63
MGM (12875 "When I Fall in Love")...8-12 60
MGM (12941 "But Not for Me")...8-12 60
SUE (3 "Who Am I")...4-6 68
SUE (10-003 "Who Am I")...8-12 64
UNI (55131 "Man Without a Dream")...5-10 69

LPs: 10/12-inch

MGM (E-3831 "The Voice of Lovelace Watkins")...20-25 60
(Monaural.)
MGM (E-3831 "The Voice of Lovelace Watkins")...25-35 60
(Stereo.)
UNI (73068 "Love Is")...10-20 69

WATKINS, Sis

Singles: 7-inch

DIPLOMACY (9 "A Love Only You Can Give")...15-25 64
Session: Universals.
Also see UNIVERSALS

WATKINS, Tiny

(E. Tiny Watkins)

Singles: 7-inch

EXCELLO...10-15 67-69
RIM (4108 "All At Once")...8-12 62
RIM (4112 "Can't Take It with You")...8-12 63
SANDY (1009 "Rocking Satellite")...20-30 58
TEIA (1002 "Torturing Lover")...10-15 64

WATKINS, Viola

(With the Honey Drips; with Otis Blackwell Quintet)

Singles: 78 rpm

JUBILEE...10-20 49-52
MGM...5-15 48-49
RAMA...10-20 52
SUPER DISC...5-10 47-48

Singles: 7-inch

EBONY...10-20 58
JUBILEE (5095 "Really Real")...400-500 52
RAMA (8 "Real Fine Man")...50-75 52
(Black vinyl.)
RAMA (8 "Real Fine Man")...150-250 52
(Colored vinyl.)
Also see BLACKWELL, Otis
Also see CROWS

WATSON, Alabama

Singles: 7-inch

BLUESTOWN (704 "My Baby Left Me")...10-20 65
BLUESTOWN (706 "Mean Old Train")...10-20 65

WATSON, Bessie

Singles: 7-inch

JAY PEE (1001 "I'm in Your Corner")...20-30

WATSON, Big John

Singles: 7-inch

CAPA (106 "Everybody's Twist'n")...10-20 62
CAPA (123 "Girls Girls Girls Girls")...10-20 62

WATSON, Bill

Singles: 7-inch

COUNTRY JUBILEE (525 "You're the One for Me")...50-75

WATSON, Bobby Lee

Singles: 7-inch

MAUREEN (1002 "The Very First Time")..15-25 62

WATSON, Bruce

Singles: 7-inch

PIC-A-TUNE (1206 "I Never Realized")...5-10 62

WATSON, Buddy

Singles: 7-inch

CLOVER (301 "If I Had Me a Woman")...200-300

WATSON, Charles, & Panthers

Singles: 7-inch

VILLAGE (103 "I Found a Love")...20-30 '60s

WATSON, Clayton

Singles: 7-inch

LAVENDER (2454 "Everybody's Boppin' ")...250-350
Also see LORD DENT & INVADERS

WATSON, Dick, & Crescents

Singles: 7-inch

GONE (5144 "Groovy")...10-15 63

WATSON, Doc — C&W '73

(With Merle Watson)

Singles: 7-inch

POPPY...4-6 72-74
U.A. ...4-6 73-79

LPs: 10/12-inch

FLYING FISH...5-8 81
FOLKWAYS...10-20 63-69
LIBERTY...5-8 83
POPPY...6-12 72
U.A. ...8-15 75-76
VANGUARD...8-18 64-77
VERVE FOLKWAYS...10-15 66
Also see ATKINS, Chet, & Doc Watson
Also see FLATT, Lester, Earl Scruggs & Doc Watson

WATSON, Gene — C&W '75

(With the Farewell Party Band)

Singles: 7-inch

CAPITOL...3-6 75-80
CURB/MCA...3-5 85
DIXIE (2003 "I'll Always Love You")...20-30 58
EPIC...3-5 85-87
MCA...3-5 81-84
RESCO...4-6 75
TONKA...5-10 65
TRI-DEC (8357 "My Rockin' Baby")...300-400 58
(Also issued as by the Rockets.)
W.B. ...3-5 81-89
WIDE WORLD...4-6 69-72

LPs: 10/12-inch

CAPITOL...6-12 75-84
MCA...5-10 81-84
STONEWAY...5-10
Session: Tony Booth.
Also see ROCKETS

WATSON, Jimmy

Singles: 7-inch

BRUNSWICK (55079 "Daisy")...10-20 58

WATSON, John

Singles: 7-inch

B&4 (7465 "Gettin' Right")...75-100

WATSON, John L., & Hummelfugs

Singles: 7-inch

PARKWAY (946 "Lookin' for Love")...5-10 65

WATSON, Johnny — R&B '55

(Johnny Guitar Watson; Young John Watson; Johnny Watson Trio)

Singles: 78 rpm

FEDERAL...40-60 53-54
KEEN...20-30 57
RPM...25-40 55-56

Singles: 7-inch

ALL STAR (7167 "Darling of My Dreams")...100-150 58
ARVEE (5016 "Untouchable")...20-30 60
CACTUS (118 "Let's Rock")...350-450 59
CLASS (246 "One More Kiss")...15-25 59
DJM...3-6 76-80
ESCORT...5-10
FANTASY...4-8 73-75
FEDERAL (12120 "Highway 60")...150-250 53
FEDERAL (12131 "Motor Head Baby")...150-250 53
FEDERAL (12143 "I Got Eyes") 150-250 ... 53
FEDERAL (12157 "What's Going On").150-250 53
FEDERAL (12175 "Half Pint of Whiskey")...150-250 54
FEDERAL (12183 "Gettin' Drunk")...150-250 54
GOTH (101 "Falling in Love")...50-75 60
HIGHLAND (1151 "Wait a Minute Baby") 10-20 64
KEEN (4005 "Gangster of Love")...30-50 57
KEEN (4023 "Honey")...30-50 58
KENT (328 "Those Lonely, Lonely Nights")...10-20 59
KING (5536 "Embraceable You")...10-20 61

KING (5579 "Broke and Lonely") 10-20 61
KING (5607 "Nearness of You") 10-20 62
KING (5666 "Sweet Lovin' Mama") 10-20 62
KING (5716 "Cold Cold Heart") 10-20 62
KING (5774 "Gangster of Love") 10-20 63
KING (5833 "I Say I Love You") 10-20 64
OKEH (7263 "Keep On Lovin' You") 10-15 66
OKEH (7270 "Wolfman") 10-15 67
OKEH (7290 "Soul Food") 10-15 67
OKEH (7302 "Crazy About You") 10-15 67
RPM (423 "Hot Little Mama") 50-75 55
RPM (431 "Too Tired") 50-75 55
RPM (436 "Those Lonely, Lonely Nights") 50-75 55
RPM (447 "Oh, Baby") 50-75 55
RPM (455 "Three Hours Past Midnight") . 50-75 56
RPM (471 "She Moves Me") 50-75 56
VALLEY VUE 3-5 84

Picture Sleeves

DJM (1020 "Ain't That a Bitch") 4-6 76

LPs: 10/12-inch

A&M 5-10 81
BIG TOWN 8-10 77
CADET (4056 "I Cried for You") 10-15 67
CHESS (1490 "Blues Soul") 50-100 64
DJM 5-10 76-81
FANTASY 5-10 73-81
KING (857 "Johnny Guitar Watson") 50-100 63
OKEH 10-15 67
MCA 5-10 81
Also see BLAND, Bobby / Johnny Guitar Watson
Also see LARRY & JOHNNY
Also see OTIS, Johnny
Also see SHIELDS
Also see WILLIAMS, Larry, & Johnny Watson

WATSON, K.C.
(Mojo Watson)

Singles: 7-inch

ATLAS (1080 "All Alone") 25-50 57
GANLON (412 "I'm the Only One") 75-125
(At least one source reports this issue as being credited to Otis Read. We don't yet know if it exists as by both Mojo Watson and Otis Read.)
NANC (003 "Love Bloodhound") 75-125 61
NANC (007 "Look-a-There") 20-30 61
Also see READ, Otis

WATSON, Paula *R&B '48*

Singles: 78 rpm

MONOGRAM 5-10 49
SUPREME 5-10 48-49

WATSON, Phil / Ron-Dels

Singles: 7-inch

CHARAY (97 "Jan") 5-10 69
Also see RON-DELS

WATSON, Roberta, & Calendars

Singles: 7-inch

CORSICAN (111 "Dear Donnie") 15-25 63

WATSON, Romance

Singles: 7-inch

CORAL (62133 "Until the Real Thing Comes Along") 10-20 59
CORAL (62442 "Where Does That Leave Me") 40-60 65

WATSON & SHERLOCKS

Singles: 7-inch

SOULVILLE (1015 "Funky Walk") 15-25 69

WATTERSON, Henry, Expressway

Singles: 7-inch

TRX (5020 "Ob-La-Di, Ob-La-Da") 5-10 69

WATTLES, Dud, Orchestra

Singles: 7-inch

ROULETTE (4165 "Maverick"/"Ballad of Paladin") 5-10 59

WATTS, Alan

LPs: 10/12-inch

ASCENSION 10-20 70
TOGETHER 10-20 70

WATTS, Bette
(With the Watts)

Singles: 7-inch

WAND (103 "Big Paul Bunyan") 10-15 60
WAND (104 "Do Me a Favor") 10-15 60

WATTS, Bette, & Watts / Annie Watts

Singles: 7-inch

ELGIN (1030 "Do Me a Favor"/"Let It Be") 50-75 59
Also see WATTS, Bette

WATTS, Bob

Singles: 7-inch

CAROLINA (209 "Carolina Rock") 50-75

WATTS, Glenn

Singles: 7-inch

BUNKY (7751 "My Little Plaything") 10-15 67

WATTS, Hunter

Singles: 7-inch

HAMMOND (103 "Wild Man Rock") 75-100
PARADISE (109 "Big Daddy Rock") 100-125

WATTS, Louis

Singles: 7-inch

VAL-UE (1001 "My Foolish Heart") 10-15 60

WATTS, Maymie

Singles: 78 rpm

GROOVE (0103 "Quicksand") 5-10 55

Singles: 7-inch

GROOVE (0103 "Quicksand") 15-25 55
Session: Du Droppers.
Also see DU DROPPERS

WATTS, Noble *P&R '57*
(Noble "Thin Man" Watts & His Rhythm Sparks; Noble Watts Quintet; with Paul "Hucklebuck" Williams)

Singles: 78 rpm

BATON (246 "Easy Going") 15-25 57
BATON (249 "The Slop") 15-25 57
BATON (249 "Hard Times") 10-20 57
(Note title change.)
DELUXE 10-15 54
VEE-JAY 10-15 56

Singles: 7-inch

ARRAWAK (1006 "Leave That Little Girl Alone") 8-12 64
BATON (246 "Easy Going") 20-30 57
BATON (249 "The Slop") 20-30 58
BATON (249 "Hard Times") 15-20 58
(Note title change.)
BATON (251 "Blast Off") 10-20 58
BATON (254 "The Slide") 10-20 58
BATON (257 "The Creep") 10-20 58
BATON (266 "Hot Tamales") 10-20 59
BATON (273 "Boogie Woogie") 10-20 59
BRUNSWICK (55382 "F.L.A.") 5-10 68
CLAMIKE (500 "I Don't Wanta") 8-12 63
CLAMIKE (501 "Teen Scene") 8-12 64
CUB (9078 "The Beaver") 10-20 60
DELUXE (6066 "Mashing Potatoes") 15-25 54
JELL ("Florida Shake") 10-15 62
(No selection number used.)
SIR (273 "Mashed Potatos") 10-15 59
VEE-JAY (268 "South Shore Drive") 20-30 56
Also see COBB, Danny
Also see WILLIAMS, Paul

WATTS, Noble, & June Bateman

Singles: 7-inch

ENJOY (1008 "Jookin' ") 8-12 63
PEANUT (2002 "Georgia Mule") .... 5-10 '60s
Also see BATEMON, June
Also see WATTS, Noble

WATTS, Slim

Singles: 7-inch

STARDAY (282 "Tu La Lu") 200-300

WATTS, Tommy

Singles: 7-inch

CAPITOL (3726 "Grasshopper") 15-25 58

WATTS, Wortham

Singles: 7-inch

D (1002 "Cotton Picker") 15-25 58
(First issue.)
ORBIT (517 "Cotton Picker") 10-20 58

WATTS 103rd ST. RHYTHM BAND *P&R/R&B '67*
(Featuring Charles Wright)

Singles: 7-inch

KEYMEN (108 "Spreadin' Honey") 15-20 67
W.B. 5-10 68-71

LPs: 10/12-inch

W.B. 10-20 68-71
Also see SOUL RUNNERS
Also see WRIGHT, Charles

WATUSI WARRIORS

Singles: 7-inch

PRINCE (1206 "Wa-Chi-Bam-Ba") 10-15 59

WAUGH, Jerry, & Skeptics

Singles: 7-inch

THRUSH (1002 "For My Own") 10-15 65
Also see SKEPTICS

WAVE CRESTS

LPs: 10/12-inch

VIKING (6606 "Surftime USA") 25-35 63

WAVERIDERS

Singles: 7-inch

GUYDEN (2095 "Malibu") 10-20 63
TENER (154 "Ain't It a Shame") .... 15-25 '60s

WAY, Jerry, & Way Outs

Singles: 7-inch

COULEE (101 "Castaway of Love") 15-25 63

WAYFARERS

Singles: 78 rpm

RCA 5-10 56

Singles: 7-inch

LONDON (9510 "Whistle Down the Wind") 5-10 62
RCA 8-12 56-63

Picture Sleeves

LONDON (9510 "Whistle Down the Wind") 15-25 62
(Sleeve pictures Hayley Mills.)

LPs: 10/12-inch

RCA 10-20 63-64
Also see MILLS, Hayley

WAY-LITES

Singles: 7-inch

RON (4459 "The School Song") .... 5-10 '60s

WAYMON, Sam

Singles: 7-inch

NINANDY (1012 "You Can Count On Me") 10-15 68

WAYNE, Allen

Singles: 7-inch

CHARTBUSTER (1114 "No") 8-12 65
KAPP (553 "Walkin' My Baby") 10-15 63
TRY (503 "No") 8-12 65

WAYNE, Alvis

Singles: 78 rpm

WESTPORT (132 "Swing Bop Boogie") 100-200 56

Singles: 7-inch

WESTPORT (132 "Swing Bop Boogie") 250-350 56
WESTPORT (138 "Don't Mean Maybe Baby") 75-100 57
WESTPORT (140 "You Are the One") .150-200 58

WAYNE, Artie
(With Tony Lavello & Orchestra; with Jerry Fielding & Orchestra; Art Wayne)

Singles: 78 rpm

KEM (2718 "Rachel") 10-15 52
LIBERTY 5-10 56

Singles: 7-inch

KEM (2718 "Rachel") 15-25 52
EPIC (9288 "Ooooh! You Said the Magic Word") 15-20 58
LIBERTY (55010 "How Do I Love You") ... 10-15 56
LIBERTY (55021 "Angel") 10-15 56
LIBERTY (55625 "I Hurt That Girl") 15-25 63
RKO UNIQUE 10-15 57
SMASH (2077 "Automated Man") 5-10 67
SMASH (2125 "Rainbow Song") 5-10 67
XAVIER (8890 "Let Me Make My Own Mistakes") 10-15 61

LPs: 10/12-inch

RKO UNIQUE (123 "You're Mr. Thrill") 25-50 57
(Cover pictures Anita Ekberg.)

WAYNE, Bernie

Singles: 7-inch

EVEREST (19403 "The Heiress") 5-10 61
HANOVER (4528 "Chickie") 10-20 59
IMPERIAL (5575 "Soft Shoe Rock") 8-12 59
RUST (5063 "38-24-38") 8-12 63

LPs: 10/12-inch

ICE BLUE (670 "Music of Miss America") 15-25 63

WAYNE, Billy

Singles: 7-inch

FEDORA (1008 "Telegram") 10-20 62
HILLCREST (778 "Walking and Strollin' ") 500-700 58

WAYNE, Bobby

Singles: 7-inch

A&M (716 "Bobby's Boogie") 5-10 63
A&M (736 "Last Date") 5-10 64
BONITA (1313 "Swing Train Twist") 400-600
DEBBY (066 "Lonely Nights") 5-10 63
EPIC (9595 "Big Train") 5-10 63
JERDEN 8-12 63-66
LA VAL 5-10
LJV (101 "Sally Ann") 200-300 61
W.B. (5427 "Half Breed") 5-10 64

LPs: 10/12-inch

CROWN (607 "Big in Vegas") .... 10-20 '60s
JERDEN 15-25 64
Members: Bobby Wayne; Dennis Roberts; Vince Gerber.

WAYNE, Bobby

Singles: 7-inch

LONDON (11020 "Mother at Your Feet Is Kneeling") 5-10 63

WAYNE, Buddy
(With the Vi-Dells; Buddy Wayne Stokes)

Singles: 7-inch

CAPITOL 5-10 68-70
DORE (742 "Spotlight Dance") 8-12 65
GARDENA (132 "Heartbreak Ahead") 8-12 62
GARDENA (134 "It's Hurtin' Me") 8-12 63
GARPAX (44182 "I'd Fight for My Baby") .. 8-12 64
P.P.I. (1000 "Garden of Memory") 5-10 66
SATELLITE (101 "Road Runner") 150-250

WAYNE, Carl, & Vikings

Singles: 7-inch

ABC-PAR (10752 "My Girl") 8-12 65

WAYNE, Chuck

Singles: 78 rpm

CAVALIER (836 "Mean Mean Mean") 25-50 54

Singles: 7-inch

CAVALIER (836 "Mean Mean Mean") 50-100 54

WAYNE, Danny

Singles: 7-inch

CARD (101 "You're Wrong") 40-60

WAYNE, Dennis

Singles: 7-inch

SHADOW (7712 "Blind Date") 10-15

WAYNE, Don

Singles: 7-inch

LAURIE (3209 "Tall Dark Stranger") 5-10 63
LOOK (1002 "My Heart Is Getting Impatient") 10-15 59
MERCURY (72773 "Cut Me Loose") 5-10 68
SWAN (4024 "Head Over Heels") 50-75 58
U.A. (985 "Lois") 5-10 66

WAYNE, Francis

LPs: 10/12-inch

ATLANTIC (1263 "Warm Sound") 40-50 57
(Black & silver label.)

WAYNE, Gaylon

Singles: 7-inch

COUNTRY SOUND 4-8 70
DELTA 4-8 72-73
HARVESTER 10-15 68
SENSATION 4-6 76-77
UNIVERSAL ARTIST (7172 "I'm Gonna Love the Devil Out of You") 10-20 72
UNIVERSAL ARTIST (52071 "High School's on Fire") 50-75 71
Also see WILLIAMS, Wayne, & Sure Shots

WAYNE, Hal, & Pee Wee King

Singles: 7-inch

CUCA (1316 "Night Friends") 5-10 67
Also see KING, Pee Wee

WAYNE, Jackie
(Little Jackie Wayne)

Singles: 7-inch

REM (306 "White Felt Hat") 400-500

STANDOUT (501 "Why Must We Wait Until Tomorrow") 10-20 62

WAYNE, James R&B '51
(With the Kidds; James Waynes; Wee Willie Wayne)
Singles: 78 rpm
ALADDIN 10-20 54
IMPERIAL 15-30 51-57
MILLION 15-25 55
PEACOCK 15-25 57
SITTIN' IN WITH (573 "Gypsy Blues") 30-50 50
SITTIN' IN WITH (588 "Love Me Blues") . 30-50 51
SITTIN' IN WITH (607 "Junco Partner")... 30-50 51
SITTIN' IN WITH (622 "Please Baby Please") 30-50 52
SITTIN' IN WITH (639 "Money Blues") 30-50 52
Singles: 7-inch
ANGLE TONE (540 "This Little Letter") ... 10-20 60
ALADDIN (3234 "Cryin' in Vain") 40-60 54
IMPERIAL (5258 I'm in Love with You") .. 40-60 53
IMPERIAL (5355 "I Remember") 50-100 55
IMPERIAL (5368 "Good News") 40-60 55
IMPERIAL (5696 "Hard to Handle") 20-30 60
IMPERIAL (5725 "Travelin' Mood") 20-30 61
IMPERIAL (5737 "Woman") 20-30 61
MILLION (2009 "Junco's Return") 40-60 55
PEACOCK (1672 "Yes I Do") 25-35 57
LPs: 10/12-inch
IMPERIAL (9144 "Travelin' Mood") 200-300 61
Also see CHARLES, Ray / Arbee Stidham / Li'l Son Jackson / James Wayne
Also see EVANS, Larry

WAYNE, Jeff
(With Justin Hayward)
Singles: 7-inch
COLUMBIA 5-10 78
LPs: 10/12-inch
COLUMBIA 20-30 78
Also see HAYWARD, Justin

WAYNE, Jerry
Singles: 7-inch
GNP (157 "Half Hearted Love") 5-10 60
MGM (12622 "I Can't Forget Last Night") ... 8-12 58

WAYNE, Jimmy
Singles: 7-inch
CORWIN (6618 "You Shake Me") 100-200
ZIN-A-SPIN ("That's the Way the Mop Flops") 50-75
(Selection number not known.)

WAYNE, John LP '73
(With Hank Levine Orchestra & Chorus)
Singles: 7-inch
CASABLANCA 4-6 79
LIBERTY (55399 "I Have Faith") 5-10 61
RCA 4-6 73
LPs: 10/12-inch
RCA (3000 series) 5-10 79-81
RCA (4828 "America") 15-25 73

WAYNE, Larry
Singles: 78 rpm
ARCADE 5-10 52-54
Singles: 7-inch
ARCADE (103 "Wastin' Time") 10-20 52
ARCADE (108 "Louisiana Shuffle") 10-20 52
ARCADE (111 "Don't") 10-20 53
ARCADE (121 "Stardust and Moonlight") 10-20 54
SANTO (9001 "Tag Along") 5-10 62

WAYNE, Leonard, & Hi-Tones
(Lenny Wayne & Hi Tones)
Singles: 7-inch
ANDRE (701 "That's All I Want to Do") .. 50-100 63
SKY LINE (701 "That's All I Want to Do") 25-35 64

WAYNE, Lorrie
Singles: 7-inch
DALE (115 "Until Tomorrow") 8-10 59

WAYNE, Luther
Singles: 7-inch
TOPPA (1012 "Linda") 8-12 60

WAYNE, Mark
Singles: 7-inch
BOONE (1030 "Keeping Busy") 5-10 65
CT (2 "Miracle of Love") 10-15 60
W.B. (5256 "Tell Me It's a Lie") 5-10 62

WAYNE, Pat
Singles: 7-inch
TOWER (175 "Come Dance with Me") 5-10 65

WAYNE, Paula
Singles: 7-inch
COLGEMS 5-10 68-69
COLUMBIA (43727 "Never Less Than Yesterday") 5-10 66
COLUMBIA (43876 "Nothing Left to Do But Cry") 5-10 66
MONOCLE 4-6
Picture Sleeves
COLUMBIA (43727 "Never Less Than Yesterday") 10-15 66

WAYNE, Roy
Singles: 7-inch
CLIF (101 "Honey Won't You Listen") ... 400-500

WAYNE, Scotty
(Baldemar Huerta)
Singles: 7-inch
TALENT SCOUT (1008 "Only One") 25-35 62
Also see FENDER, Freddy

WAYNE, Susan
Singles: 7-inch
COLUMBIA (43148 "Riding On a Rainbow") 10-15 64
COLUMBIA (43237 "Think Summer") 10-15 65

WAYNE, Tammy
Singles: 7-inch
BOOM (60004 "Kissaway") 5-10 66

WAYNE, Ted
Singles: 7-inch
YOU GLO (205 "Don't Dream") 30-40 61

WAYNE, Terry
Singles: 7-inch
COLUMBIA (41377 "Go Steady with Me") 15-25 59
COTCO (66 "Dinosaur Cavern") 10-20 62
TREND (30013 "School Is Out") 20-30 58

WAYNE, Thomas P&R/R&B '59
(With the DeLons)
Singles: 7-inch
CAPEHART (5009 "Tragedy") 10-15 61
CHALET 4-6 69
COLLECTABLES .... 3-5 '80s
ERIC (160 "Tragedy") .... 4-6 '70s
FERNWOOD (106 "You're the One That Done It") 75-100 58
FERNWOOD (109 "Tragedy") 20-30 59
FERNWOOD (111 "Eternally") 15-25 59
FERNWOOD (113 "Gonna Be Waitin' ") .. 15-25 59
FERNWOOD (120 "Guilty of Love") 10-20 60
FERNWOOD (122 "Because of You") 10-20 60
FERNWOOD (128 "Tragedy") 8-12 61
MERCURY (71287 "You're the One That Done It") 30-50 58
MERCURY (71454 "You're the One That Done It") 20-30 59
OLDIES 45 (76 "Tragedy") 5-10 64
PHILLIPS INT'L (3577 "I've Got It Made") 10-15 62
RACER (3131 "Kiss Away") 10-15 65
Members [DeLons]: Sandra Brown; Nancy Reed; Carol Moss.

WAYNE, Vik
Singles: 7-inch
HAMILTON (50013 "Girl I Saw on Bandstand") 5-10 58

WAYNE, Vince
Singles: 7-inch
BANDSTAND (21631 "Judge and Jury") 5-10 62
RAVEN (8002 "Take a Chance") 10-15 63
ROULETTE (4132 "I'm All Alone Tonight") 10-15 59
ROULETTE (4155 "Fare Thee Well My Love") 10-15 59
SEECO (6012 "I Laughed at Love") 10-15 59
STARDUST (01 "Don't Give Your Heart Away") 5-10 65

WAYNE & DWAIN
Singles: 7-inch
CRUSADER (102 "Ski Surfin' Man") 10-20 64

WAYNE & RAY
Singles: 7-inch
ADONIS (109 "I've Got Your Love on My Mind") 15-25 60
ADONIS (110 "For Your Precious Love"). 15-25 60
MUTUAL (104 "Be My Honey Bee") 15-25 60
TWENTIETH CENTURY (1211 "Sweet Lou") 75-125

WAYNICK, Don
Singles: 7-inch
DIXIE (1147 "Telephone Boogie") 200-300

WAYORES / Bill Howell
Singles: 7-inch
COLT (646 "Get the Butter"/"Fat Emma") .. 5-10 67
Also see HOWELL, Bill

WAYWARD SONS
Singles: 7-inch
HOPE (1846 "How Will I Know") 20-30 61

WE FIVE P&R/LP '65
Singles: 7-inch
A&M 5-10 65-69
MGM 4-6 73
VAULT 5-10 67
VERVE 4-8 68-73
LPs: 10/12-inch
A&M 15-20 65-69
A.V.I. 5-10 77
VAULT 10-15 70
Members: Mike Stewart; Pete Fullerton; Beverly Bivens; Bob Jones; Jerry Burgan.

WE IN A NUTSHELL
Singles: 7-inch
VILLA (68017 "Never Fade Away") 15-25 68

WE TALKIES
Singles: 7-inch
EPIC (10121 "I've Got to Hold On") 5-10 67

WE THE PEOPLE
Singles: 7-inch
CHALLENGE (59333 "Mirror of Your Mind") 10-20 66
CHALLENGE (59340 "You Burn Me Up and Down") 10-20 66
CHALLENGE (59351 "In the Past") 10-20 67
DJ (251 "Point Panic") 20-25 65
HOTLINE (3680 "My Brother the Man") ... 20-30 66
RCA 8-12 67-68

WE THE PEOPLE R&B '72
Singles: 7-inch
DAVEL 4-8 75
IMPERIAL 5-10 69
LION 4-6 72-74
MAP CITY (301 "If We Can Fly to the Moon") 5-10 69
MAP CITY (305 "Cat and Mouse") 4-8 70
REENA (116 "Who Am I") 5-10 68
VERVE 4-6 71
LPs: 10/12-inch
CENTURY ADVENT (5262 "We the People") 10-15 73
Members: Terri Gonzalez; Robert Taylor; Shabi Weems; Billy McKeechun.

WE THREE
Singles: 7-inch
COURTNEY (711 "Back to School") 10-15 63
DOT (16470 "Happy Graduation Day") 10-15 63
DOT (16504 "Please Stay") 10-15 63

WE THREE
Singles: 7-inch
CUCA (6841 "Our Graduation Song") 10-15 68

WE TWO
Singles: 7-inch
ABC (10930 "Magic Moments") 10-20 67

WE WHO ARE
Singles: 7-inch
LOVE (6739 "Last Trip") 150-250 67
Members: Greg Sell; Greg Coffin; Greg Riggert; Al Herron.

WEADS
Singles: 7-inch
DUANE (1042 "Today") 10-20 65

WEASELS
LPs: 10/12-inch
WING (12282 "Liverpool Beat") 20-25 64
(Monaural.)
WING (16282 "Liverpool Beat") 25-30 64
(Stereo.)

WEATHERBEE, Alfy
Singles: 7-inch
ROULETTE (4005 "Why Am I Crying") 8-12 57

WEATHERLY, Jim P&R/LP '74
Singles: 7-inch
ABC 4-6 76-77
BUDDAH 4-6 74-75
ELEKTRA 3-6 79-80
ERIC 4-6 78
RCA 4-6 72-74
20TH FOX 5-10 65
Picture Sleeves
BUDDAH 4-6 74
LPs: 10/12-inch
ABC 5-10 77
BUDDAH 5-10 74-75
RCA 8-12 72

WEAVER, Curley
Singles: 78 rpm
SITTIN' IN WITH (547 "My Baby's Gone") 30-40 50

WEAVER, Darry
Singles: 7-inch
CAPEHART (5001 "Sweet Mary Jo") 15-20 60
Also see GAMBLERS

WEAVER, Dennis LP '72
(With the Good Time People)
Singles: 7-inch
CASCADE (5906 "Girls") 10-15 59
CENTURY CITY 4-6 69
DJM (1023 "Make Love to Live") 4-6 77
EVA (103 "Chicken Mash") 5-10 63
IM'PRESS 4-6 72
JUST GOOD (104 "World Needs Country Music") 3-5 80
OVATION 4-6 75
W.B. (5352 "Genesis Through Exodus") 5-10 63
Picture Sleeves
EVA (103 "Chicken Mash") 30-50 63
LPs: 10/12-inch
IM'PRESS 8-10 72
OVATION 5-10 75

WEAVER, Dennis & Gerry
Singles: 7-inch
JEREMIAH (1010 "Calhoun") 3-5 81
Also see WEAVER, Dennis

WEAVER, Earl
LPs: 10/12-inch
LIFESONG (8138 "Earl of Baltimore") 15-25 82
(Picture disc.)

WEAVER, Gil
Singles: 7-inch
JCP (1056 "Do Like I Do") .... 5-10 '60s

WEAVER, Jackie
Singles: 7-inch
CHESS (1797 "The Tingle") 15-20 61

WEAVER, J.C.
TURKEY (712 "Elvis, Coming on Strong") . 8-12 77

WEAVER, Joe
(With the Blue Notes; with Don Juans; with His Blue Note Orchestra)
Singles: 78 rpm
DELUXE 20-30 53
FORTUNE 15-35 56-57
JAGUAR 15-25 55
Singles: 7-inch
DACO (1307 "Farm Boy") .... 20-30 '50s
DELUXE (6006 "Soft Pillow") 50-75 53
DELUXE (6021 "J.D. Boogie") 50-75 53
FORTUNE (820 "Loose Caboose") 30-40 55
FORTUNE (825 "Baby, I Love You So") .. 40-50 56
FORTUNE (832 "Looka Here, Pretty Baby") 30-40 57
FORTUNE (852 "Too Hot to Trot") 10-15 60
JAGUAR (3011 "Lazy Susan") 40-60 55
Also see KENT, Al
Also see LAKE, Don, & Don Juans

WEAVER, Wee Willie
Singles: 7-inch
TANDY (101 "Automatic Reaction")............5-10 65

WEAVERS — P&R '50
(With Gordon Jenkins' Orchestra)
Singles: 78 rpm
DECCA............5-10 50-57
Singles: 7-inch
DECCA (27000 thru 29000 series)..........10-25 50-55
DECCA (31000 series)............5-10 62
MCA............4-6 73
NSD............3-5 82
VANGUARD............5-10 60-62
EPs: 7-inch
DECCA............10-25 51-52
LPs: 10/12-inch
DECCA (173 "Best of the Weavers")..........10-20 65
(Monaural.)
DECCA (7173 "Best of the Weavers")..........10-20 65
(Stereo.)
DECCA (5285 "Folk Songs")............25-50 51
(10-inch LP.)
DECCA (5373 "Merry Christmas")............20-40 52
(10-inch LP.)
DECCA (8893 "Best of the Weavers")..........15-25 59
DECCA (74277 "Weavers Gold")............10-15 70
VANGUARD (15-16 "Greatest Hits")............12-18 71
VANGUARD (2000 series)............15-25 59-63
VANGUARD (3000 thru 6000 series)..........8-15 67-70
VANGUARD (9000 series)............15-35 56-63
VANGUARD (9100 series)............12-25 65
Members: Pete Seeger; Lee Hays; Fred Hellerman; Ronnie Gilbert.
Also see ALMANAC SINGERS
Also see JENKINS, Gordon, & His Orchestra
Also see SEEGER, Pete

WEAVERS & TERRY GILKYSON — C&W '51
Singles: 7-inch
DECCA............4-8 51
Singles: 7-inch
DECCA............8-10 51
Also see GILKYSON, Terry
Also see WEAVERS

WEAVILS
Singles: 7-inch
LORI (9550 "We're the Weavils")............20-30 65

WEBB, Bobby
Singles: 7-inch
ACE (542 "Hear Me")............20-30 58
SAVOY (1578 "My Dream")............10-15 59
VIN (1012 "My Dream")............10-15 59
WEBB (429 "What You Need Is Me")..........8-12

WEBB, Boogie Bill
Singles: 78 rpm
IMPERIAL (5257 "Bad Dog")............50-75 53
Singles: 7-inch
IMPERIAL (5257 "Bad Dog")............150-200 53

WEBB, Dick
Singles: 7-inch
EPIC (9397 "Just One More Kiss")..........15-25 60
MADISON (114 "We Loved")............10-15 59
Picture Sleeves
EPIC (9397 "Just One More Kiss")..........15-25 60

WEBB, Don
Singles: 7-inch
BRUNSWICK (55158 "Little Bitty Baby").20-30 59

WEBB, Doris
Singles: 7-inch
AVA (141 "Kiss Goodbye")............5-10 63

WEBB, Gary
(Gary "Spider" Webb)
Singles: 7-inch
BAMBOO (504 "The Cave")............5-10 61
DONNA (1321 "Drum City")............5-10 60
Also see HOLLYWOOD ARGYLES

WEBB, Hoyt
(With Jo Webb)
Singles: 7-inch
COTTON CLUB (177 "Baby, Won't You Slow It Down")............150-250 57
DIXIE (846 "Don't Wake Me I'm Dreaming")............75-100
RUBY (320 "Baby, Won't You Slow It Down")............75-125 57

WEBB, Jack — LP '55
(With Jazz Combo; with Billy May's Orchestra)
Singles: 7-inch
W.B. (5003 "You'd Never Know the Old Place Now")............5-10 58
EPs: 7-inch
RCA (0342/3 "Christmas Story")............15-25 '50s
RCA (1126 "Pete Kelly's Blues")............20-35 55
RCA (3199 "Christmas Story")............50-100 53
LPs: 10/12-inch
RCA (1126 "Pete Kelly's Blues")............30-50 55
RCA (2053 "Pete Kelly's Blues")............20-30 59
RCA (3199 "Christmas Story")............75-125 53
(10-inch LP.)
W.B. (B-1207 "You're My Girl")............30-50 58
(Monaural.)
W.B. (BS-1207 "You're My Girl")............50-100 58
(Stereo.)
W.B. (B-1217 "Pete Kelly Lets His Hair Down")............30-50 58
(Monaural.)
W.B. (BS-1217 "Pete Kelly Lets His Hair Down")............50-100 58
(Stereo.)
Members: Jack Webb; Matty Matlock; Dick Cathcart; Nick Fatool; Elmer "Moe" Schneider; George Van Eps; Ray Sherman; Jud DeNaut.

WEBB, Jay Lee — C&W '67
(Jack Webb; with Luanne)
Singles: 7-inch
DECCA............4-8 67-71
O'BRIEN............4-6
LPs: 10/12-inch
DECCA............10-15 67-69
Also see LYNN, Loretta

WEBB, Jimmy
(Jim Webb)
Singles: 7-inch
ASYLUM............4-6 74
ATLANTIC............4-6 77
BELL (892 "Lost Generation")............4-6 70
DUNHILL............5-10 68
EPIC............5-10 68
REPRISE............4-6 70-72
LPs: 10/12-inch
ASYLUM............8-10 74
ATLANTIC............8-12 77
COLUMBIA............5-10 82
EPIC (26401 "Jim Webb Sings Jim Webb")............15-20 68
REPRISE............5-10 70-72
Also see MIDNIGHT MAIL
Also see STRAWBERRY CHILDREN

WEBB, Jody & Round Up Boys
Singles: 78 rpm
FLAIR (1007 "The Honey Jump")............8-12 53
Singles: 7-inch
FLAIR (1007 "The Honey Jump")............10-20 53

WEBB, Joyce
(With the Slades)
Singles: 7-inch
DOMINO (300 Right Here")............15-25 58
DOMINO (600 "Ain't That Just Like a Man")............15-25 58
GOLDEN WORLD (108 "Laughing to Keep from Crying")............8-12 63
LEE RAY (502 "Tears on My Pillow")..........40-60
PROBE (473 "I Believe in Love")............5-8 69
RIC-TIC (102 "You've Got a Whole Lot of Living to Do")............8-12 62
Also see SLADES

WEBB, June — C&W '58
Singles: 7-inch
HICKORY (1086 "Mansion on the Hill")....15-20 58

WEBB, Spider, & Insects
Singles: 7-inch
LUGAR (100 "Maggie")............10-15 63
SCOTTIE (1326 "Cock a Doodle Doo")....10-15 60

WEBB, Stanley
Singles: 7-inch
VANDAN (2021 "Bye Bye Dream Girl")......5-10 64

WEBB, Tamela, & George
Singles: 7-inch
LIBERTY (56102 "Hold On, I'm Comin' ")...5-10 69

WEBB, Walter, & Highlighters
Singles: 7-inch
CHESS (2091 "Your Time Is Gonna Come")............15-25 70

WEBBER, Rollie
Singles: 7-inch
COUNTRY ("Tired of Livin' ")............25-35
(Selection number not known.)
Members: Rollie Webber; Buck Owens; Don Rich.
Also see OWENS, Buck

WEBER, Joan — P&R '54
Singles: 78 rpm
COLUMBIA............3-5 54-56
Singles: 7-inch
COLUMBIA............5-10 54-56
CROSLEY............4-6 63
MAPLE............4-6 61
EPs: 7-inch
COLUMBIA............5-10 55

WEBER, Lewis
Singles: 7-inch
GOLDISC (G-9 Tempted")............8-12 63
MAGNUM (82260 "Jean")............10-20 60
SCOTTIE (1304 "Judy")............100-150 59
TATTOO (7453 "Tell Me Baby")............75-100 58
TODD (1061 "Someone")............10-20 61

WEBS
Singles: 7-inch
SOTOPLAY (006 "Do I Have a Chance")............200-300 58
(Reissued on Sotoplay's 007, credited to the Notemakers.)
Also see NOTEMAKERS

WEBS — R&B '67
Singles: 7-inch
GUYDEN (2090 "Question")............50-75 63
MGM............5-10 66
POPSIDE............8-15 67-68
VERVE............5-10 68

WEBS
Singles: 7-inch
HEART (333 "Lost")............10-20 62
HEART (335 "Dizzy Boy")............10-20 61
LITE (9004 "Lost")............15-25 62
Members: Bobby Goldsboro; John Rainey Adkins; Paul Garrison.
Also see GOLDSBORO, Bobby

WEBSTER, John T., III, & Anna
Singles: 7-inch
FREEDOM (44022 "Million Teardrops")...15-20 59

WEBSTER, Katie
(With the Songettes")
Singles: 7-inch
A-BET (9420 "My Dearest Darling")............8-12 67
ACTION (1000 "Close to My Heart")........10-20 61
DECCA (30945 "Sea of Love")............20-25 59
GOLDBAND............6-12 '60s
QUEEN (24002 "Close to My Heart").......10-20 61
ROCKO (503 "Open Arms")............15-25 60
ROCKO (513 "Goodbye Baby, I'm Still Leavin' You")............10-20 61
ROCKO (522 "If I Ask You")............10-20 61
SPOT (1000 "Glory of Love")............10-20 '60s
ZYNN (505 "Sweet Daddy")............50-100 58
Also see LAZY LESTER
Also see LIGHTNIN' SLIM

WEBSTER, Katie, & Ashton Conroy
Singles: 7-inch
KRY (100 "Baby Baby")............20-30 58

WEBSTER, Mamie
LPs: 10/12-inch
CUB (8002 "The Blues")............100-150 59

WEBTONES
Singles: 7-inch
MGM (12724 "My Lost Love")............15-25 58
Members: Louis Williams; Terry Wilson; Frank Clemens
Also see DANLEERS

WEDGWOODS
Singles: 7-inch
LIMELIGHT (3025 "September in the Rain")............10-15 64

WEDLAW, Frankie
Singles: 7-inch
SKYLA (1112 "Run Buddy Run")............10-15 61

WEE FOUR
Singles: 7-inch
NU SOUND LTD (6111 "Weird")............5-10 66

WEE THREE TRIO
Singles: 7-inch
ÄVA (181 "Shine for Me")............5-10 65

WEE WILLIE & MELLODIERS
Singles: 7-inch
WOW (110 "When")............500-750

WEEBA, Dale, & Rebels / Untouchables
Singles: 7-inch
FEE (1003 "I Love You Darling"/"Baby You Sure Look Fine")............100-150 62

WEED, Gene
Singles: 7-inch
20TH FOX (416 "Poor Poor Billy")............8-12 63
Also see BAGGYS

WEEDS
Singles: 7-inch
N.W.I. (2745 "No Good News")............10-15 69
TEENBEAT (1006 "Little Girl")............20-30 67
Picture Sleeves
N.W.I. (2745 "No Good News")............15-25 69
Members: Ron Buzzel; Bob Atkins; Edward Bowen; Fred Cole; Carl Fortina; Tim Rockson.
Also see LOLLIPOP SHOPPE

WEEKENDS
Singles: 7-inch
COLUMBIA (43597 "You're Number One with Me")............5-10 66
LE-MANS (001 "Ringo")............8-12 64

WEEMS, Ritchie, & Continental Five
Singles: 7-inch
DUNHILL (202 "Natural Born Man")..........5-10 65
SPOT (1122 "Natural Born Man")............8-12 65

WEHBA, Dale
Singles: 7-inch
KINGS X (3364 "Russian Roulette")..........5-10 59

WEIGAND, Jack
Singles: 7-inch
CAMEO (178 "Shangri-La")............5-10 60
CAMEO (185 "Sixteen Candles")............5-10 61
CAMEO (315 "Prisoner of Love")............5-10 64
LPs: 10/12-inch
WYNCOTE............10-15 64

WEIGHT, The
Singles: 7-inch
BERTRAM INT'L (230 "Flip, Flop, and Fly")............10-20 64
BERTRAM INT'L (232 "Too Much Monkey Business")............10-20 64

WEINBERG, Cheryl
Singles: 7-inch
ARGO ("Vision of Love")............200-300
(Tan label. No selection number used.)

WEINE, Sherri
Singles: 7-inch
WORLD ARTISTS (1038 "Start the World Spinning")............10-15 65

WEINRIB, Len
Singles: 7-inch
CAPITOL (4806 "Prez Conference")..........8-12 62
(With the White House Band.)
CAPITOL (4877 "Love Express")............8-12 62

WEIR, Bob — LP '72
Singles: 7-inch
ARISTA (315 "Bombs Away")............4-6 77
ARISTA (336 "I'll Be Doggone")............10-15 77
(Promotional issue only.)
W.B.............8-12 72
LPs: 10/12-inch
ARISTA............5-10 78
W.B. (2627 "Ace")............25-30 72
Also see GRATEFUL DEAD

WEIRD STREET CARNIVAL
Singles: 7-inch
COPRA (2305 "The Subterranean Edible Fungus")....20-30 '60s

WEIRD-OHS
Singles: 7-inch
MERCURY (72410 "Digger")....5-10 65
LPs: 10/12-inch
MERCURY (20976 "New Sounds")....30-50 65
(Monaural.)
MERCURY (60976 "New Sounds")....20-30 65
(Stereo.)
Also see SILLY SURFERS / Weird-Ohs

WEIRDOS
Singles: 7-inch
LAN-CET (145 "E.S.P.")....8-10 61

WEIRNAUT BROTHERS
(With Bill Baker & Orchestra)
Singles: 78 rpm
FORECAST (105 "Lost & Found")....10-15 54
Singles: 7-inch
FORECAST (105 "Lost & Found")....20-30 54

WEISE, George
Singles: 7-inch
ARGO (5270 "Married for Life")....10-15 57

WEISS, Doug
Singles: 7-inch
DINAMO (1001 "Do You Love Another")....75-100 59

WEISS, Joseph, Orchestra
Singles: 7-inch
AVA (166 "Polly's Theme")....5-10 64

WEISS, Larry
Singles: 7-inch
LAURIE (3527 "Mary Anna")....5-10 69

WEISSBERG, Eric, & Marshall Brickman
LPs: 10/12-inch
ELEKTRA (EKL-238 "New Dimensions in Banjo & Bluegrass")....15-25 63
(Monaural.)
ELEKTRA (ESK7-238 "New Dimensions in Banjo & Bluegrass")....20-30 63
(Stereo.)
Also see TARRIERS

WELCH, Bob *P&R/LP '77*
Singles: 7-inch
CAPITOL....3-6 77-81
RCA....3-5 81-83
Picture Sleeves
CAPITOL....3-6 78-81
LPs: 10/12-inch
CAPITOL (Except 16000 series)....8-10 77-80
CAPITOL (16000 series)....5-8 80-82
RCA....5-10 81-83
Promotional LPs
CAPITOL (11663 "French Kiss")....15-25 79
(Picture disc.)
Also see FLEETWOOD MAC

WELCH, Jimmy
Singles: 7-inch
ABS (146 "Searight Blues")....150-250

WELCH, Lenny *P&R/R&B '60*
(Lenny & the Storks)
Singles: 7-inch
ATCO (6894 "A Sunday Kind of Love")....4-8 72
ATCO (6915 "Fancy Meeting You Here Baby")....5-10 73
BARNABY (537 "Since I Fell for You")....4-6 76
BIG TREE....3-6 78-83
CADENCE (1373 "You Don't Know Me")....10-15 59
CADENCE (1386 "Darlin'")....10-15 60
CADENCE (1394 "I'd Like to Know")....10-15 61
CADENCE (1399 "Boogie Cha Cha")....10-15 61
CADENCE (1416 "It's Just Not That Easy")....10-15 62
CADENCE (1422 "Ebb Tide")....15-25 62
CADENCE (1428 "A Taste of Honey")....10-15 62
CADENCE (1439 "Since I Fell for You")....10-15 63
CADENCE (1446 "If You See My Love")....10-15 64
COLUMBIA (44007 "Since I Fell for You")....5-10 67
COMMONWEALTH UNITED (3004 "Breaking Up Is Hard to Do")....5-10 69
COMMONWEALTH UNITED (3011 "To Be Loved – Glory of Love")....4-8 70
DECCA (30637 "My One Sincere")....15-25 58
DECCA (30829 "Blessing of Love")....10-15 59
JASON SCOTT (25 "Congratulations Baby"/"My One Sincere")....3-5 '80s
(500 made.)
KAPP....10-15 65-67
MAINSTREAM....4-6 73-74
MERCURY (72777 "Darling Stay with Me")....8-12 68
ROULETTE (7092 "Such a Night")....4-6 70
LPs: 10/12-inch
CADENCE....15-25 64
COLUMBIA....10-20 65
KAPP....10-20 66-67

WELCH, Percy
Singles: 7-inch
FRAN (144 "Nursery Rhyme Rock")....100-200

WELCH BROTHERS
Singles: 7-inch
BO-KAY (105 "Blue Eyes and Golden Curls")....10-20 58

WELD, Tuesday
Singles: 7-inch
PLAZA (508 "Are You the Boy")....10-15 62

WELDON, Ann
Singles: 78 rpm
RCA....5-10 55
Singles: 7-inch
ANTLER (1100 "Ole Man River")....20-30 59
UNIVERSAL INT'L (7422 "Ol' Man River")....200-300 58
RCA (6226 "Pamper Me")....10-15 55

WELDON, Joe, & Whirlwinds
Singles: 7-inch
KHOURY'S (714 "Someone")....20-30 59
KHOURY'S (724 "Please Come Home")....10-15 60

WELK, Lawrence, & His Orchestra *P&R '38*
(With Eileen Barton)
Singles: 78 rpm
CORAL....3-5 50-57
DECCA....3-6 42-45
MERCURY....3-5 50-55
OKEH....3-6 41
VOCALION....3-8 38-39
Singles: 7-inch
CORAL....5-15 50-66
DOT....5-10 59-67
MERCURY....10-20 50-55
RANWOOD....4-8 68-77
EPs: 7-inch
CORAL....4-8 50-58
DOT....4-8 59-60
MERCURY....4-8 50-55
LPs: 10/12-inch
CORAL....5-15 50-65
DECCA....5-10 72
DOT....5-15 59-67
HAMILTON....4-8 64-66
HARMONY....4-8 68-70
MCA....4-8 74-76
PICKWICK....4-8
RANWOOD....4-8 68-85
SUNNYVALE....4-6 79
TRADITION....4-8 75
VOCALION....4-8 59-70
WING....4-8 60-62
Also see BARTON, Eileen
Also see FOLEY, Red
Also see HODGES, Johnny, & Lawrence Welk
Also see HOOPER, Larry
Also see LENNON SISTERS
Also see McGUIRE SISTERS
Also see PRESLEY, Elvis / Lawrence Welk

WELLER, Freddy *C&W/LP '69*
Singles: 7-inch
ABC/DOT....4-6 75
APT (25096 "Walk Away Slowly")....5-10 65
COLUMBIA....3-6 69-80
DORE....5-10 61
LPs: 10/12-inch
ABC/DOT....5-10 75
COLUMBIA....5-12 69-80
EPIC....8-12 74
51 WEST....5-8 '80s
Also see REVERE, Paul, & Raiders

WELLES, Orson *LP '70*
Singles: 7-inch
MAX ("I Know What It Is Like to Be Young")....3-6 84
(No selection number used.)
LPs: 10/12-inch
MEDIARTS....10-15 70
Also see CROSBY, Bing, & Orson Welles

WELLINGTON, Mary Sue
Singles: 7-inch
TUFF (400 "Spoiled")....10-15 64

WELLINGTON, Rusty
(With the Travelaires; with Shorty Long's Santa Fe Rangers; with Ginger)
Singles: 78 rpm
ARCADE....10-20 53-57
MGM....100-200 57
Singles: 7-inch
ARCADE (116 "Doggone It Baby, I'm in Love")....15-35 53
ARCADE (124 "I Want a Little Lovin'")....15-35 54
ARCADE (137 "Blue Ranger")....15-35 55
ARCADE (140 "Jump Jump Honey")....15-35 55
ARCADE (144 "I Ain't A-Movin' No More")....15-35 57
ARCADE (184 "The Allagash")....10-20 65
ARCADE (185 "Soft Shoulders")....10-20 65
ARCADE (189 "Echo")....10-20 66
ARCADE (191 "Lonely Lips")....10-20 67
MGM (12581 "Rocking Chair on the Moon")....15-25 57
Also see LONG, Shorty

WELLINGTONS
Singles: 7-inch
ASCOT (2217 "Go Ahead and Cry")....5-10 66
BUENA VISTA (421 "Savage Sam and Me")....15-20 63
Also see ANNETTE & TOMMY KIRK / Annette & Wellingtons

WELLS, Billy, & Crescents
Singles: 78 rpm
RESERVE (105 "Julie")....100-200 56
Singles: 7-inch
RESERVE (105 "Julie")....300-400 56

WELLS, Bobby
Singles: 7-inch
MERCURY (72272 "Dance Little Girl")....15-20 64

WELLS, Chuck
Singles: 7-inch
RICE (5018 "Good Morning Fool")....5-10 66

WELLS, Dennis
Singles: 7-inch
CREST (1068 "Lillabelle")....5-10 60

WELLS, Donnie
Singles: 7-inch
SCEPTER (12119 "A Real Love")....10-20 65

WELLS, Eddie
Singles: 7-inch
CELMAR (1001 "Congratulations")....8-12 60

WELLS, Fargo
Singles: 7-inch
RING-A-DING (703 "Camel Train")....5-10 63

WELLS, Garry
Singles: 7-inch
ARWIN (103 "Too Late for Love")....10-15 58
ARWIN (104 "Not Mine")....10-15 58
MGM (12844 "I'm Walkin' Away")....8-12 59

WELLS, Glenn, & Blends
Singles: 7-inch
HALLWAY (1903 "Is It Wrong")....8-12 62
JIN (122 "Write Me a Letter")....10-15 60
JIN (139 "As My Tears Fall")....10-15 61
U.A. (244 "Written in the Stars")....10-15 60

WELLS, James
Singles: 7-inch
COED (566 "All My Soul")....8-12 62

WELLS, Jean *R&B '67*
Singles: 7-inch
ABC-PAR (10745 "Don't Come Running to Me")....10-20 65
CALLA....5-10 67-68
CANYON (39 "Somebody's Been Lovin' You")....5-10
QUAKER TOWN....4-8
T.E.C....4-6 79
VOLARE....5-10 69

WELLS, Johnny
Singles: 7-inch
ASTOR (1001 "Lonely Moon")....10-15 59
ASTOR (1002 "For Everyone")....10-15 60

WELLS, Junior *R&B '60*
(With His Eagle Rockers; Junior Wells' Chicago Blues Band)
Singles: 78 rpm
STATES....25-50 53-55
Singles: 7-inch
ALL POINTS (2000 "Little By Little")....10-15 66
BLUE ROCK....8-12 68-69
BRIGHT STAR (146 "I'm Losing You")....10-15 66
BRIGHT STAR (149 "Up in Heah")....8-12 66
BRIGHT STAR (152 "I'm Gonna Cramp Your Style")....8-12 67
BRIGHT STAR (504 "I Found Out")....8-12 67
CHIEF (7005 "Two-Headed Woman")....20-30 57
CHIEF (7008 "I Could Cry")....15-25 58
CHIEF (7030 "I'm a Stranger")....10-20 61
CHIEF (7034 "You Sure Look Good to Me")....10-20 61
CHIEF (7035 "It Hurts Me Too")....10-20 61
CHIEF (7037 "So Tired")....10-20 61
CHIEF (7038 "I Need Me a Car")....10-20 61
HIT SOUND (223 "It's All Soul")....5-10 68
KAPP (270 "So Tired")....8-12 59
MEL....10-15
PROFILE (4005 "I Could Cry")....15-25 59
PROFILE (4011 "Come on in This House")....15-25 60
PROFILE (4013 "You Don't Care")....15-25 60
SHAD (5010 "So Tired")....15-25 59
STATES (122 "Cut That Out")....500-800 53
(Red vinyl.)
STATES (134 "Hoodo Man")....500-800 55
(Red vinyl.)
STATES (139 "Lawdy Lawdy")....400-600 55
(Red vinyl.)
STATES (143 "So All Alone")....400-600 55
(Red vinyl.)
USA (736 "Every Goodbye Ain't Gone")....10-15 63
USA (742 "She's a Sweet One")....10-15 63
USA (790 "Come On in This House")....10-15 64
VANGUARD (35049 "Shake It Baby")....5-10 67
LPs: 10/12-inch
BLUE ROCK....10-20 68
DELMARK....10-20 66-69
VANGUARD....15-25 66-68
Also see COTTON, James, Carey Bell, Junior Wells & Billy Branch
Also see DIXON, Willie
Also see HOOKER, Earl / Junior Wells
Also see LENOIR, J.B.
Also see SPANN, Otis
Also see WATERS, Muddy

WELLS, Junior, & Buddy Guy
LPs: 10/12-inch
ATCO....8-12 72
BLIND PIG....5-10 82
INTERMEDIA....5-10 84
Also see GUY, Buddy
Also see WELLS, Junior

WELLS, Karen
Singles: 7-inch
CUCA (1035 "Believe Him")....40-60 61

WELLS, Kenny
Singles: 7-inch
NEW VOICE (812 "I Can't Stop")....30-50 66

WELLS, Kitty *C&W/P&R '52*
Singles: 78 rpm
DECCA....4-10 52-57
RCA....6-12 50
Singles: 7-inch
CAPRICORN....4-6 74-76
DECCA (28000 & 29000 series)....10-20 52-56
DECCA (30000 thru 32000 series)....5-15 56-71
MCA....4-6 73
RCA (0333 "Make Up Your Mind")....25-40 50
(Colored vinyl.)
RUBOCA....3-6 79-80
Picture Sleeves
DECCA (32455 "Guilty Street")....5-10 69

EPs: 7-inch

DECCA....5-15 55-65

LPs: 10/12-inch

BULLDOG....5-10
CAPRICORN....5-10 74
CORAL/MCA....5-8 84
DECCA (174 "Kitty Wells Story")....15-25 63
(Monaural. Includes booklet.)
DECCA (7-174 "Kitty Wells Story")....20-30 63
(Stereo. Includes booklet.)
DECCA (4075 thru 4929)....10-25 61-67
(Monaural.)
DECCA (7-4075 thru 7-4929)....15-30 61-67
(Stereo.)
DECCA (7-4961 thru 7-5350)....10-15 68-72
(Stereo.)
DECCA (8293 "Country Hit Parade")....35-45 56
(Monaural.)
DECCA (7-8293 "Country Hit Parade")....15-25 68
(Stereo.)
DECCA (8552 "Winner of Your Heart")....35-45 56
DECCA (7-8552 "Winner of Your Heart") 10-15 65
DECCA (8732 "Lonely Street")....30-40 58
(Monaural.)
DECCA (7-8732 "Lonely Street")....10-15 65
(Stereo.)
DECCA (8858 "Dust on the Bible")....25-35 59
(Monaural.)
DECCA (7-8858 "Dust on the Bible")....10-15 68
(Stereo.)
DECCA (8888 "After Dark")....30-40 59
(Monaural.)
DECCA (7-8888 "After Dark")....10-15 68
(Stereo.)
DECCA (8979 "Kitty's Choice")....25-35 59
(Monaural.)
DECCA (7-8979 "Kitty's Choice")....30-40 59
(Stereo.)
EXACT....5-10 80
GOLDEN COUNTRY....5-10
IMPERIAL HOUSE....5-10 80
KOALA....5-10 79
MCA....4-8 73-83
MISTLETOE....5-8 '80s
PICKWICK/HILLTOP....5-10 '70s
ROUNDER....5-8 82
RUBOCA....8-12 79
SUFFOLK MARKETING....5-10 80
VOCALION....8-15 66-69
Also see ACUFF, Roy, & Kitty Wells
Also see JOHNNIE & JACK
Also see PIERCE, Webb, & Kitty Wells
Also see TUBB, Ernest

WELLS, Kitty / Bill Anderson

LPs: 10/12-inch

MCA (734584 "Collector's Album")....8-12
Also see ANDERSON, Bill

WELLS, Kitty, & Red Foley C&W '54

Singles: 78 rpm

DECCA....4-10 54-56

Singles: 7-inch

DECCA (29000 series)....5-15 54-56
DECCA (32000 series)....4-6 67-69

EPs: 7-inch

DECCA....8-12 59

LPs: 10/12-inch

DECCA....12-25 61-67
Also see FOLEY, Red

WELLS, Kitty / Bill Phillips / Bobby Wright / Johnny Wright

LP: 10/12-inch

DECCA (74831 "The Kitty Wells Show"). 10-20 66
Also see PHILLIPS, Bill
Also see WRIGHT, Johnny

WELLS, Kitty, & Webb Pierce C&W '57

Singles: 78 rpm

DECCA....5-10 57

Singles: 7-inch

DECCA....5-10 57-64

EPs: 7-inch

DECCA....10-15 59
Also see PIERCE, Webb

WELLS, Kitty, & Johnny Wright C&W '68

Singles: 7-inch

DECCA....4-6 68-72

LPs: 10/12-inch

DECCA....10-20 68-72
Also see WELLS, Kitty
Also see WRIGHT, Johnny

WELLS, Mary R&B '60

Singles: 12-inch

EPIC....4-8 82

Singles: 7-inch

ATCO....10-15 65-67
EPIC....3-5 82
JUBILEE....5-15 68-71
MOTOWN (1003 "Bye Bye Baby")....25-35 60
(Pink label.)
MOTOWN (1011 "I Don't Want to Take a Chance")....15-25 61
(Pink label.)
MOTOWN (1011 "I Don't Want to Take a Chance")....10-15 61
(Blue label.)
MOTOWN (1016 "Strange Love")....15-25 62
MOTOWN (1024 thru 1056)....15-25 62-64
MOTOWN (1061 "When I'm Gone")....100-200 65
MOTOWN (1065 "I'll Be Available")....15-25 65
REPRISE....5-10 71-74
20TH FOX....10-15 64-66

Picture Sleeves

MOTOWN (1011 "I Don't Want to Take a Chance")....50-75 61
MOTOWN (1016 "Strange Love")....50-75 61
MOTOWN (1024 "The One Who Really Loves You")....40-60 62
MOTOWN (1032 "You Beat Me to the Punch")....40-60 62
20TH FOX (590 "He's a Lover")....15-25 65
20TH FOX (606 "Me Without You")....15-25 65

EPs: 7-inch

MOTOWN (60616 "Greatest Hits")....25-50 64

LPs: 10/12-inch

ALLEGIANCE....5-10 84
ATCO (199 "Two Sides of Mary Wells")....15-25 66
EPIC....5-10 81
51 WEST....5-8 83
JUBILEE....10-20 68
MOTOWN (100 & 200 series)....5-10 82
MOTOWN (600 "Mary Wells")....200-300 61
(White label with blue print.)
MOTOWN (605 "The One Who Really Loves You")....150-200 62
MOTOWN (607 "Two Lovers")....75-125 63
MOTOWN (611 "On Stage")....40-60 64
MOTOWN (616 "Greatest Hits")....25-35 64
MOTOWN (617 "My Guy")....40-60 64
MOTOWN (653 "Vintage Stock")....40-60 66
MOVIETONE (71010 "Ooh!")....15-25 66
(Monaural.)
MOVIETONE (72020 "Ooh!")....15-25 66
(Stereo.)
POWER PAK....5-8
20TH FOX (3171 "Mary Wells")....20-30 65
(Monaural.)
20TH FOX (3178 "Love Songs of the Beatles")....20-30 65
(Monaural.)
20TH FOX (4171 "Mary Wells")....20-30 65
(Stereo.)
20TH FOX (4178 "Love Songs of the Beatles")....20-30 65
(Stereo.)
Also see GAYE, Marvin, & Mary Wells
Also see MARVELETTES / Mary Wells / Miracles / Marvin Gaye

WELLS, Ruby

Singles: 78 rpm

RCA....5-10 54-55

Singles: 7-inch

RCA (5944 "Hearts of Stone")....10-15 54
RCA (6131 "Rollin' Stone")....10-15 55

WELLS, Terry

Singles: 7-inch

RAMCO (3711 "Her Song")....5-10 62

WELTON, Danny

Singles: 7-inch

DOT (15559 "Calypso Melody")....15-25 57
ENITH (715 "Surf Dreamin' ")....10-20 63

WELZ, Joey
(With the Kidd Brothers; with New Century Singers; with Link Wray)

Singles: 7-inch

AUDIO FIDELITY....4-6 69
BAT (1001 "Boppin' the Stroll")....15-25 59
BAT (1002 "Mystery of Love")....5-10 63
BAT (1003 "Let's Bop and Stroll Again")....5-10 64
BAT (1004 "Maybe")....5-10 64
(Reissued in 1967 using the same number.)
BAT (4000 series)....5-10 67
CANADIAN AMERICAN....5-10 64-68
CAPRICE....3-5 86-92
GAME TIME....5-10 65
LEEDLE....5-10
LEFEVRE....5-10 66
MONUMENTAL....5-10 64
MUSIC CITY....4-6 78
PALMER....5-10 67-69
SWAN....5-10 67
TEARDROP....5-10 65-67

Picture Sleeves

CAPRICE....3-5 86-92

LPs: 10/12-inch

MUSIC CITY....5-10 78
PALMER....10-15 70
Also see HALEY, Bill
Also see WRAY, Link

WELZ, Joey, & Dew Watson

Singles: 7-inch

BOLD (888 "Somewhere Elvis Is Smiling")..3-5 92

Picture Sleeves

BOLD (888 "Somewhere Elvis Is Smiling")..3-5 92
(Wrap-around insert sleeve.)
Also see WELZ, Joey

WENCES, Señor

Singles: 7-inch

JOY (228 " 'S-All Right? – 'S-All Right!")....5-10 59

Picture Sleeves

JOY (228 " 'S-All Right? – 'S-All Right!")..15-25 59

WENDE, Friedel

Singles: 7-inch

CADENCE (1413 "Leibchen")....5-10 62

WENDEL, Will, & Aktones

Singles: 7-inch

TRANS AMERICAN (10,000 "Lonely Blue Boy")....400-500 62

WENDELL, Glen, & Epics

Singles: 7-inch

THREE RIVERS (101 "That's It")....50-75

WENDELL & DREAMERS

Singles: 7-inch

REON (1305 "That's Love")....40-60

WENDI

Singles: 7-inch

CHAMP (12148 "You're So Fine")....5-10 67

WENDY & SCHOOLGIRLS
(With Blackie Scheckner & Orchestra)

Singles: 7-inch

GOLDEN CREST (502 "My Guy")....50-100 58

WERLEY, Coy, & Blackjacks

Singles: 7-inch

SUNDOWN (122 "Black Jack")....75-85 59

WERPS

Singles: 7-inch

W.G.W. (18703 "Love's a Fire")....20-30 67

WERT, Jimmy

Singles: 7-inch

SKYLINE (752 "Bingo Blues")....150-250 59

WES, Johnny

Singles: 7-inch

ROSE (101 "Hully Gully")....10-20 62

WESLEY, Chuck

Singles: 7-inch

ARLINGTON (102 "Baby, Baby, Baby")...50-75

WESLEY, Gate

Singles: 7-inch

ATLANTIC (2319 "Do the Batman")....5-10 66

WESLEY, John
(With the 4 Tees)

Singles: 7-inch

MELIC (4170 "You Still Need Me")....15-25 65
MELIC (4195 "Love Is Such a Funny Thing")....10-20
VIVID (107 "Girl with the Red Dress On")..5-10 64

WESS, Jill

Singles: 7-inch

MARLU (7004 "I Don't Wanna Have a School Vacation")....10-15 61

WEST

Singles: 7-inch

EPIC (10335 "Baby You Been On My Mind")....5-10 68
EPIC (10378 "Step By Step")....5-10 68
EPIC (10449 "Peaceful Times")....5-10 69

LPs: 10/12-inch

EPIC (26380 "West")....10-15 68
EPIC (26433 "Bridges")....10-15 69

WEST, Adam

Singles: 7-inch

20TH FOX (6627 "Miranda")....5-10 66

Picture Sleeves

20TH FOX (6627 "Miranda")....10-20 66

WEST, Dottie C&W '63
(With Dale West)

Singles: 7-inch

ATLANTIC....5-10 62
LIBERTY....3-6 80-83
PERMIAN....3-5 84-85
RCA (Except 8000 series)....3-8 66-81
RCA (8000 series)....5-10 63-66
STARDAY (500 series)....8-12 60-61
STARDAY (700 series)....5-10 65
U.A.....3-6 76-80

Picture Sleeves

LIBERTY....3-6 80-81

LPs: 10/12-inch

CAMDEN....5-10 71-73
COLUMBIA....5-10 80
GUSTO....5-8 82
LIBERTY....5-8 81-82
NASHVILLE....8-12 '70s
PERMIAN....5-8 85
PICKWICK....5-10 75
POWER PAK....5-10 '70s
RCA....10-20 65-75
STARDAY....10-20 64-65
U.A.....5-10 73-80
Session: Jordanaires.
Also see JORDANAIRES
Also see REEVES, Jim, & Dottie West
Also see ROGERS, Kenny, & Dottie West

WEST, Dottie, & Don Gibson C&W '70

Singles: 7-inch

RCA....4-6 69-70

LPs: 10/12-inch

RCA....10-15 69
Also see GIBSON, Don

WEST, Dottie / Melba Montgomery

LPs: 10/12-inch

STARDAY (352 "Queens of Country Music")....10-20 65
Also see WEST, Dottie

WEST, Eastin

Singles: 7-inch

EVEREST (2028 "Ring Telephone")....8-12 63

WEST, Glen

Singles: 78 rpm

TRUMPET....15-25 53

Singles: 7-inch

TRUMPET (204 "I Love My Steady")....25-35 53
TRUMPET (205 "Ain't Got Time")....25-35 53

WEST, Guy

Singles: 7-inch

ERA (3160 "Devil Is Her Name")....5-10 66

WEST, Jimmy

Singles: 78 rpm

SANDEE....25-50 56

Singles: 7-inch

SANDEE (315 "Bringing Home the Bacon")....50-100 56

WEST, Jimmy

Singles: 7-inch

CHERRY (111 "Pink Alligator Rock")....50-75

WEST, Johnny

Singles: 7-inch

COUGAR (1866 "How Glad I Am")....50-75 60
SOUL (841 "Tears Baby")....15-25 61
Session: Marveliers.

Also see MARVELIERS

WEST, Keith

Singles: 7-inch

NEW VOICE (825 "Excerpts from a Teenage Opera")....5-10 67

WEST, Leslie *LP '69*

(Leslie West Band)

Singles: 7-inch

PHANTOM....4-6 75-76

LPs: 10/12-inch

PHANTOM....8-10 75-76

WINDFALL....10-15 69

Also see JAGGER, Mick

Also see MOUNTAIN

Also see WEST, BRUCE & LAING

WEST, Little Willie

Singles: 7-inch

RUSTONE (1401 "Sweet Little Girl")....5-10 60

WEST, Lynette

Singles: 7-inch

BEE 'N DEE (101 "If She Doesn't Want You")....15-20 63

(First issue.)

JOSIE (910 "If She Doesn't Want You")..10-15 63

WEST, Mae *P&R '33*

(With Somebody's Chyldren; with Lenny Marvin & Orchestra)

Singles: 78 rpm

BRUNSWICK....10-30 33

Singles: 7-inch

MGM (14491 "Great Balls of Fire")....4-8 73

PLAZA....5-10 62

TOWER....5-10 66

20TH FOX (6718 "Hard to Handle")....15-30 70

EPs: 7-inch

DECCA (838 "Fabulous Mae West")....50-75 55

(Three-disc set.)

LPs: 10/12-inch

DAGONET (4 "Wild Christmas")....10-15 66

DECCA (9016 "Fabulous Mae West")....40-60 55

DECCA (79016 "Fabulous Mae West")...10-15 70

DECCA (79176 "Original Voice Tracks from Her Greatest Movies")....10-15 70

MGM (4869 "Great Balls of Fire")....10-20 72

MEZZO TONE (1 "Mae West Songs")....25-35 '50s

(10-inch LP.)

TOWER (5028 "Way Out West")....15-25 66

WEST, Mae, & W.C. Fields

LPs: 10/12-inch

HARMONY (11405 "Side By Side")....8-12 70

PROSCENIUM (22 "Mae West and W.C. Fields")....15-20 60

Also see FIELDS, W.C.

Also see WEST, Mae

WEST, Marshall

Singles: 7-inch

PARKWAY (878 "I Hurt Myself")....5-10 63

WEST, Norm

(Norman West)

Singles: 7-inch

CHRISTY (101 "Plagued")....25-35 57

HI (2073 "Day Dreamin' ")....5-10 64

HI (2082 "Burning Bridges")....5-10 65

M.O.C. (664 "Baby Please")....10-20 66

SMASH (2100 "Let Them Talk")....10-15 67

SMASH (2123 "Words Won't Say")....10-15 67

WEST, Penny

Singles: 7-inch

OZARK (102 "Needle in a Haystack")....50-75

WEST, Red

(Red West Combo)

Singles: 7-inch

DOT (16268 "Midnight Ride")....10-15 61

JARO (77031 "F.B.I. Story")....10-20 60

SANTO (9006 "My Babe")....10-20 63

SONNET (2960 "My Thanks to You")....10-20 60

WEST, Rick

(With the Red Hots)

Singles: 7-inch

CENTRAL (314010 "Cop Car")....40-60 '60s

SOLLY (930 "Crackin' Up")....8-12 66

WEST, Rudy

Singles: 7-inch

KING (5276 "Just to Be with You")....10-20 59

KING (5305 "The Measure of My Love")..10-20 59

Also see FIVE KEYS

WEST, Sonny

(Sonee West)

Singles: 78 rpm

NOR-VA-JAK (1956 "Rock-Ola Ruby").400-500 59

Singles: 7-inch

ATLANTIC (1174 "Rave On")....40-60 58

BAND BOX (276 "Wasted Days and Wasted Nights")....10-20 61

NOR-VA-JAK (1956 "Rock-Ola Ruby")....1500-2000 59

WEST, Speedy, & Jimmy Bryant

EPs: 7-inch

CAPITOL (520 "2 Guitars Country Style")....10-20 54

LPs: 10/12-inch

CAPITOL (H-520 "2 Guitars Country Style")....45-55 54

(10-inch LP.)

CAPITOL (T-520 "2 Guitars Country Style")....30-50 54

CAPITOL (956 thru 1835)....15-25 58-62

Also see BRYANT, Jimmy

WEST, Willie

Singles: 7-inch

CHECKER (964 "Did You Have Fun")....20-30 60

DEE-SU (306 "Greatest Love")....5-10 65

DEE-SU (314 "Did You Have Fun")....5-10 66

DEE-SU (317 "Baby I Love You")....5-10 67

FRISCO (107 "Lost Love")....8-12 63

FRISCO (108 "You Told Me")....8-12 63

FRISCO (111 "Am I the Fool")....8-12 63

JOSIE (1019 "I Sleep with the Blues")....4-8 70

W.B.....4-6 75

WEST, BRUCE & LAING *LP '72*

Singles: 7-inch

COLUMBIA....4-6 73

LPs: 10/12-inch

COLUMBIA....8-10 74

COLUMBIA/WINDFALL....8-12 72-74

Members: Leslie West; Jack Bruce; Corky Laing.

Also see MOUNTAIN

Also see WEST, Leslie

WEST COAST BRANCH

Singles: 7-inch

A&M....5-10 67

VALIANT (753 "Linda's Gone")....10-20 66

WEST COAST POP ART EXPERIMENTAL BAND

Singles: 7-inch

AMOS (119 "Where's My Daddy")....8-12 69

REPRISE (0552 "1906")....15-25 67

REPRISE (0582 "Help I'm a Rock")....15-25 67

REPRISE (0776 "Smell of Incense")....15-25 68

LPs: 10/12-inch

AMOS (7004 "Where's My Daddy")....30-40 68

FIFO (101 "West Coast Pop Art Experimental Band")....200-400 66

REPRISE (6247 "West Coast Pop Art Experimental Band Vol. One")....50-100 67

REPRISE (6270 "West Coast Pop Art Experimental Band Vol. Two")....50-100 67

REPRISE (6298 "A Child's Guide to Good and Evil")....50-100 68

Members: Dan Harris; Shaun Harris; Bob Markley.

Also see MARKLEY, Bob

WEST COAST WORKSHOP

LPs: 10/12-inch

CAPITOL (T-2776 "Wizard of Oz")....15-25 67

(Monaural.)

CAPITOL (ST-2776 "Wizard of Oz")....15-25 67

(Stereo.)

WEST MINIST'R

Singles: 7-inch

MAGIC (7432 "My Life")....15-25 67

MAGIC (45001 "Sister Jane")....15-25 67

RAZZBERRY (2975 "Bright Lights, Windy City")....10-20 '60s

WEST TEXAS SLIM

(Ernest Lewis)

Singles: 78 rpm

FLAME (1007 "Little Mae Bell")....150-250 53

Also see LEWIS, Ernest

WEST WINDS

Singles: 7-inch

ENITH (1269 "You Know I'll Miss Him")....5-10 64

KAPP (588 "Oowee, Oowee, Oowee, Oowee")....5-10 64

WESTBERRY, Kent, & Shaperones

(Kent Westbury)

Singles: 7-inch

ART (172 "My Baby Don't Rock Me Now")....200-300 58

ART (174 "Turkish Doghouse Rock")...100-200 58

TRAIL (103 "My Baby Don't Rock Me Now")....400-500 57

WESTBROOK, Walter J., & His Phantom Five

Singles: 7-inch

BOBBIN (106 "Bring Your Clothes Back Home, Baby")....15-25 59

WESTBROOKS

Singles: 7-inch

MIRA (225 "Travelin' Pain")....5-10 66

WESTERFIELD, Jimmy

Singles: 7-inch

PALOMAR (2211 "Another Time")....5-10 65

WESTERN, Howard

Singles: 7-inch

WESTERN STAR ("Sawmill Boogie Blues")....100-200

(Selection number not known.)

WESTERN, Johnny

Singles: 7-inch

COLUMBIA....8-12 58

LPs: 10/12-inch

COLUMBIA (1788 "Have Gun, Will Travel")....20-25 62

(Monaural.)

COLUMBIA (8588 "Have Gun, Will Travel")....30-35 62

(Stereo.)

WESTFAUSTER

LPs: 10/12-inch

NASCO (9008 "In a King's Dream")....50-75 71

Member: C.W. Fauster

WEST-SIDERS

Singles: 7-inch

INFINITY (031 "Candy Yams")....10-20 62

WESTON, Billy

Singles: 7-inch

EP-SOM (1002 "I Need You")....10-20 62

WESTON, George

Singles: 7-inch

CHALLENGE (59066 "Dead Man")....15-25 60

GLENN (116 "Now I'm Lonely")....5-10 65

JACKPOT (48013 "Hey Little Car Hop").50-100 59

JACKPOT (48017 "Shelley, Shelley")....10-20 59

TALLY (118 "Hold Still Baby")....300-400 57

WESTON, Kim *P&R/R&B '63*

Singles: 7-inch

BANYAN TREE....5-10 69

ENTERPRISE....4-6 74

GORDY....10-20 65-66

MGM....10-20 67-68

MIKIM....4-6 71-72

NIGHTMARE....3-5 87-88

PEOPLE....6-12 69-70

PRIDE....4-6 70

RAHKIM....4-8 75

TAMLA....15-25 63-64

Picture Sleeves

MGM (13720 "I Got What You Need")....10-15 67

EPs: 7-inch

MOTOWN (2005 "Kim Weston")....15-25

MOTOWN (2015 "Rock Me a Little While")....15-25

LPs: 10/12-inch

ENTERPRISE....8-12 74

MGM....15-25 67-68

PEOPLE....8-12 70

VOLT....10-15 71

Also see GAYE, Marvin, & Kim Weston

Also see NASH, Johnny, & Kim Weston

Also see WRIGHT SPECIALS

WESTON, Kim / Marvelettes

Singles: 7-inch

TAMLA/MOTOWN (1000 "Do I Like It")....3-6 80

Also see MARVELETTES

Also see WESTON, Kim

WESTON, Paul, Orchestra *LP '55*

Singles: 78 rpm

CAPITOL....3-5 45-57

COLUMBIA....3-5 50-56

Singles: 7-inch

CAPITOL....4-8 57-60

COLUMBIA....4-8 50-56

EPs: 7-inch

COLUMBIA....5-10 50-56

LPs: 10/12-inch

CAPITOL....5-15 57-61

COLUMBIA....5-15 50-56

CORINTHIAN....4-8 78

HARMONY....4-8 72

Also see EDWARDS, Jonathan & Darlene

Also see KAYE, Danny

Also see STAFFORD, Jo

WESTPORT KIDS

Singles: 78 rpm

WESTPORT....15-25 54-56

Singles: 7-inch

WESTPORT (125 "Right or Wrong")....25-35 54

WESTPORT (126 "Three's a Crowd")....25-35 54

WESTPORT (128 "Mama, I Won't Rock It")....25-50 55

WESTPORT (130 "You Can't Take It with You")....20-35 56

WESTSIDERS

(West Siders)

Singles: 7-inch

INFINITY (031 "Candy Yams")....5-10 64

LEOPARD (5004 "Don't You Know")....30-40 63

U.A. (600 "Don't You Know")....8-12 63

Members: Edward Alston; Nelson Shields; Joe Sheppard; Ronald Judge; Prince McKnight; Bill Fiason.

Also see LEADERS

WESTWOODS

Singles: 78 rpm

KEM (2763 "Limbo")....15-25 55

Singles: 7-inch

KEM (2763 "Limbo")....30-60 55

WESTWOODS

Singles: 7-inch

A&M (763 "I Miss My Surfer Boy")....15-25 65

WET, Kevin

LPs: 10/12-inch

VISUAL VINYL (1003 "Wet")....20-30 81

(Picture disc. 1000 made.)

VISUAL VINYL (1004 "Hard Attack")....20-30 81

(Picture disc. Canadian. 1000 made.)

WET (Except 002)....8-10 81

WET (002 "Hard Attack")....20-30 81

(Picture disc.)

WETBACKS

Singles: 7-inch

WILDCAT (0047 "Jose Jimenez")....5-10 60

WHALEFEATHERS

Singles: 7-inch

NASCO (026 "It's a Hard Road")....8-12 72

LPs: 10/12-inch

NASCO (9003 "Declare")....50-100 69

NASCO (9005 "Whalefeathers")....50-100 70

Members: Lennie LeBlanc; Stephen Bacon; Michael Jones; M.E. Blackmon; Alex Spence.

WHALEN, Bobby

(With Billy Rock & Orchestra; Bob Whalen)

Singles: 7-inch

JUBILEE (5289 "Sunshine and Rain")....15-25 57

KING (5563 "Because You've Fallen in Love")....15-25 61

MUSIC NOTE (123 "Pool of Love")....15-25 64

WHALIN, Jimmy

Singles: 7-inch

ROULETTE (4142 "Lost Love")....8-12 59

WHAM! *P&R/D&D/LP '83*

(Wham! U.K.; "Featuring George Michael")

Singles: 12-inch

COLUMBIA....4-6 82-86

Singles: 7-inch
COLUMBIA....3-5 83-86
Picture Sleeves
COLUMBIA....3-5 82-86
LPs: 10/12-inch
COLUMBIA (Except 40062)....5-8 83-86
COLUMBIA (40062 "Make It Big") 15-20 84
(Picture disc.)
Members: George Michael; Andrew Ridgely.

WHAMMIES
Singles: 7-inch
BETHLEHEM (3023 "Double Whammy") 10-20 61

WHAT FOUR
(What For; Whatt Four)
Singles: 7-inch
CAPITOL (5449 "Anything for a Laugh") 5-10 65
COLUMBIA (43711 "Baby, I Dig Love")......5-10 66
COLUMBIA (43843 "Ain't No Use in Crying, Susan")....5-10 66
DESTINATION (633 "We Could Be Happy")....5-10 67
ESP (109 "Our Love Should Last Forever")....15-25 66
MERCURY (72716 "Dandelion Wine") 10-20 67
REPRISE (0387 "Gemini 4") 10-20 65
TOWER (404 "Stop in the Name of Love").5-10 68

WHAT FOURS
Singles: 7-inch
FLEETWOOD (4571 "Basement Walls"). 15-25 66

WHAT KNOTS
Singles: 7-inch
DIAL (4067 "I Ain't Dead Yet")..... 10-20 67

WHAT NOTS
Singles: 7-inch
AMBER (101 " Anybody Else")..... 15-25 66
AMBER (102 "Morning")..... 15-25 66

WHAT'S HAPPENING
Singles: 7-inch
CORECO (101 "Baby You're Hurtin'")..... 20-30 66

WHAT'S LEFT
Singles: 7-inch
CAPRI (520 "Girl Said No") 15-25 66

WHEAT, Buck
Singles: 7-inch
GOLDBAND (1093 "Texas Woman")..... 10-15 60

WHEATON, Winston
Singles: 7-inch
DONNA (1318 "Hully Gully Every Day").....5-10 60
Also see KNIGHT, Alan

WHEATSTRAW, Peetie
Singles: 78 rpm
DECCA.... 25-50 34-40
VOCALION.... 40-60 32-44

WHEATSTRAW, Peetie, & Kokomo Arnold
LPs: 10/12-inch
ARHOOLIE.... 10-20 64
BLUES CLASSICS....5-10

WHEATSTRAW, Peetie, & Rudy Ray Moore
LPs: 10/12-inch
KENT....8-12 71
Also see MOORE, Rudy Ray
Also see WHEATSTRAW, Peetie

WHEEL
LPs: 10/12-inch
COBURT (1001 "The Wheel")..... 15-25
Member: Bernie Schwartz.
Also see ATELLO, Don

WHEEL MEN
Singles: 7-inch
W.B. (5480 "Hon-Da Beach").... 30-50 64
Member: Gary Usher.
Also see USHER, Gary

WHEEL OF FORTUNE
Singles: 7-inch
JAMIE (1360 "All the World")....5-10 68

WHEEL-A-WAYS
Singles: 7-inch
AURORA (157 "Bad Little Woman") 5-10 66
AURORA (1258 "Bad Little Woman") 10-20 68

WHEELER, Art
Singles: 7-inch
CEE JAM (4 "Walk On")....15-25 66
DOT (17185 "Coming Attraction")....5-10 68
SABRINA (333 "The Plea")....15-25 59
SWINGIN' (642 "Jo Jo")....20-30 62

WHEELER, Billy Edd C&W '64
(With Rashell Richmond; with Joan Sommer; with Shelly Manne)
Singles: 7-inch
CAPITOL....4-6 75-76
KAPP....4-8 63-68
NSD....3-5 80-81
RCA....4-6 70-73
RADIO CINEMA....3-5 79
U.A. 4-6 69
Picture Sleeves
KAPP....4-8 67
LPs: 10/12-inch
AVALANCHE....8-10 73
FLYING FISH....5-10 79
KAPP....10-20 64-68
MONITOR....15-25 61-62
RCA....8-10 71
U.A.....8-15 69

WHEELER, Bobby, & His B-Bops
Singles: 7-inch
DIAMOND (101 "Rock N' Roll Baby").....75-100 61

WHEELER, Chuck
Singles: 7-inch
MARLO (1520 "Feelin' Kind of Lonesome")....50-75 60
STEVENS (103 "Cherokee Rock") 75-100 59

WHEELER, Dennis
Singles: 7-inch
KING (5898 "Rock Bottom")....5-10 64

WHEELER, Larry
Singles: 7-inch
GLORY (279 "Cry Woman Cry")....75-100 58
GLORY (282 "I Wanna Make Love") 40-60 58

WHEELER, Lin
Singles: 7-inch
ROULETTE (4096 "Too Small")....10-15 58

WHEELER, Mary
(With the Knights)
Singles: 7-inch
ATOM (701 "A Falling Tear")....40-50 '60s
CALLA (C-111-A "Prove It")....10-15 65
(Reads "Arranged by Horace Ott.")
CALLA (111-A "Prove It")....8-12 65
(Reads "Arranged by H. Ott.")

WHEELER, Onie C&W '73
Singles: 78 rpm
COLUMBIA....10-30 55-57
OKEH....5-10 52-54
ORGANA....10-15 51
Singles: 7-inch
COLUMBIA....15-30 55-57
EPIC....5-10 62
OKEH....10-20 52-54
OLE WINDMILL....4-6 73
ROYAL AMERICAN....4-6 73
SCOTTIE....5-10 60
SUN (315 "Jump Right Out of This Juke Box")....15-25 59
Picture Sleeves
EPIC....5-10 62
LPs: 10/12-inch
BRYLEN....5-10
ONIE....8-12 73

WHEELERS
Singles: 7-inch
CENCO (107 "Once I Had a Girl") 40-60 60

WHEELS
Singles: 78 rpm
PREMIUM (405 "My Heart's Desire") 15-25 56
PREMIUM (408 "Teasin' Heart")....25-50 56
PREMIUM (410 "I Can't Forget") 50-75 56
Singles: 7-inch
EARLY BIRD (006 "Where Were You")........3-5 96
(Clear vinyl.)
PREMIUM (405 "My Heart's Desire") 25-50 56
PREMIUM (408 "Teasin' Heart")....75-125 56
PREMIUM (410 "I Can't Forget") 200-300 56
TIME (1003 "Where Were You")....50-75 58
Members: Randy Anderson; Allen Bunn; Jim Pender; Ken Fox; Lorenzo Cook.
Also see BUNN, Allen
Also see FEDERALS
Also see LAKE, Arthur

WHEELS
Singles: 7-inch
FOLLY (800 "Clap Your Hands")....8-12 59
Member: Teddy Vann.
Also see VANN, Teddy

WHEELS
Singles: 7-inch
ROULETTE (4271 "No One But You").....30-40 60

WHEELS
LPs: 10/12-inch
MONTGOMERY WARD (010 "Sounds of the Hot Rods")....15-25 63

WHEELS
Singles: 7-inch
BANG (503 "Bad Little Woman")....5-10 65
BANG (507 "Gloria")....5-10 65

WHEELS
Singles: 7-inch
ARA (1913 "Rolls Royce")....8-12
IMPACT (1029 "Dancing in the Street") ...10-20 67
LAURIE (3498 "You're Playing with Fire")..5-10 69
SIDEWALK (946 "Wheels")....10-15 69

WHEELS, Burt, & Speedsters
LPs: 10/12-inch
CORONET (216 "Sounds of the Big Racers")....15-25 63

WHETHER BUREAU
Singles: 7-inch
LAURIE (3431 "Why Can't You and I")....10-15 68

WHIFFENPOOFS
LPs: 10/12-inch
CARILLON (115 "Whiffenpoofs of 1960-'61")....10-20 61

WHIGS
Singles: 7-inch
TWO PLUS TWO (103 "Heat Wave").........5-10 66

WHIPPETS
Singles: 7-inch
JOSIE (921 "Go Go with Ringo")....8-12 64

WHIPOORWILLS
(With the Joy Vendors; "Featuring Georgia Brown;" Whippoorwills)
Singles: 78 rpm
DOOTONE....10-20 54-55
Singles: 7-inch
DOOTONE (300 series)....15-25 54
DOOTONE (1201 "I Want My Love") 15-25 55
DOOTONE (1202 "Take Time to Pray")...10-20 55

WHIPPOORWILLS
Singles: 7-inch
JOSIE (892 "Deep Within'")....50-75 61

WHIPS
(Flairs)
Singles: 78 rpm
FLAIR (1025 "Pleadin' Heart") 200-300 54
Singles: 7-inch
FLAIR (1025 "Pleadin' Heart") 2000-3000 54
Also see FLAIRS

WHIPS
Singles: 7-inch
DORE (502 "Rosie's Blues")....10-15 58

WHIPS
Singles: 7-inch
MGM (13410 "First Dance Fear")....5-10 65

WHIRLERS
Singles: 7-inch
PORT (70025 "Tonight and Forever")......10-15 61
WHIRLIN' DISC (108 "Tonight and Forever")....50-75 57
Members: John Barnes; Les Cooper; Bobby Dunn; Bill Toddman.
Also see COOPER, Les
Also see EMPIRES

WHIRLWINDS
Singles: 7-inch
GUYDEN (2052 "Angel Love")....15-25 61
PHILIPS (40139 "Heartbeat")....100-150 63

WHIRLWINDS / Elgins
Singles: 7-inch
TIMES SQUARE (112 "Heartbeat"/"That's My Girl")....20-30 67

WHISK KIDS
Singles: 7-inch
REPRISE (371 "Bo-Dacious")....5-10 65

WHISNANT, Ray
Singles: 7-inch
ORBIT (4890 "I'm a Fool Over You")......75-125 62
RADCAR (326 "I'm a Fool Over You") 50-75 63

WHISPERING PIGG
Singles: 7-inch
EAST WEST (111 "Darlene")....10-20 58

WHISPERING WINDS
Singles: 7-inch
MGM (13372 "My Baby")....5-10 65

WHISPERING SMITH
Singles: 7-inch
EXCELLO (2232 "Hound Dog Twist") 10-15 62
EXCELLO (2237 "Live Jive")....10-15 62

WHISPERS
Singles: 78 rpm
APOLLO (1156 "I've Got No Time") 25-35 50

WHISPERS
Singles: 78 rpm
GOTHAM (309 "Fool Heart")....50-75 55
GOTHAM (312 "Are You Sorry") 150-200 55
Singles: 7-inch
GOTHAM (309 "Fool Heart")....75-125 55
GOTHAM (312 "Are You Sorry") 750-1000 55

WHISPERS
Singles: 7-inch
CANADIAN AMERICAN (179 "Tomorrow's on Your Side")....10-15 64
LAURIE (3344 "Here Comes Summer").....5-10 66

WHISPERS R&B '69
Singles: 12-inch
SOLAR....4-6 80-84
Singles: 7-inch
COLLECTABLES....3-5 '80s
DORE (724 "It Only Hurts for a Little While")....15-25 64
DORE (729 "Never Again")....15-25 65
(Blue label. Promotional issue.)
DORE (735 "It Hurts So Much")....10-15 65
DORE (740 "As I Sit Here")....15-25 65
(Blue label.)
DORE (751 "Doctor Love")....10-15 66
DORE (758 "I Was Born When You Kissed Me")....10-15 66
DORE (768 "Take a Lesson from the Teacher")....25-35 66
DORE (792 "You Can't Fight What's Right")....10-15 67
DORE....10-20 64-66
FONTANA....10-20 66
JANUS....4-6 70-75
SOLAR....3-6 78-88
SOUL CLOCK....5-10 69-70
SOUL TRAIN....4-6 75-77
Picture Sleeves
SOLAR (11739 "A Song for Donny")....4-6 79
SOLAR (48008 "Emergency")....4-6 82
LPs: 10/12-inch
ACCORD....5-10 81
ALLEGIANCE....5-8 84
CAPITOL....5-8 90
DORE....5-10 80
JANUS....8-10 72-75
SOLAR....5-10 78-87
SOUL TRAIN....5-10 76-77
Members: Walter Scott; Wallace Scott; Nicholas Caldwell; Marcus Hutson; Gordy Harmon; Leaveil Degree.
Also see PRESLEY, Elvis

WHITAKER, Ruby, & Pyramids
Singles: 7-inch
MARK-X (7007 "I Get the Feeling")......100-150 57

Also see PYRAMIDS

WHITAKER, Sammy, & Tribesmen

Singles: 7-inch

AFFCAN (378 "Hypo")........15-25 57

WHITBY, Gary

Singles: 7-inch

CARROLL (101 "Fools Fall in Love")........10-15 64

WHITCOMB, Ian P&R/LP '65

(With Bluesville; with Somebody's Chyldren)

Singles: 7-inch

JERDEN........8-12 64-65
TOWER........5-10 65-68
U.A. 4-6 73

Picture Sleeves

TOWER (274 "Where Did Robinson Go with Friday on Saturday Night")........5-10 66

LPs: 10/12-inch

FIRST AMERICAN........5-10 78-82
SIERRA........5-10 80
TOWER........15-20 65-68
U.A........8-10 72
Also see SOMEBODY'S CHYLDREN

WHITE, Barry P&R/R&B/LP '73

(With Love Unlimited & Love Unlimited Orchestra; with Glodean)

Singles: 12-inch

20TH FOX........4-8 73-78
UNLIMITED GOLD........4-6 83

Singles: 7-inch

A&M........3-5 87
BRONCO........5-10 67
CASABLANCA........4-6 '70s
20TH FOX........4-6 73-78
UNLIMITED GOLD........3-6 79-83

LPs: 10/12-inch

A&M........5-8 87
SUPREMACY........10-15 74
20TH FOX (Except 1)........5-10 73-81
20TH FOX (1 "Barry White Radio Special")........10-20 '70s
(Promotional issue only.)
UNLIMITED GOLD........5-10 79-82
Also see BOB & EARL
Also see BURNETT, Carl, & Hustlers
Also see JONES, Quincy, James Ingram, Al B. Sure, El DeBarge & Barry White
Also see PAGE, Gene

WHITE, Barry, & Atlantics / Atlantics

Singles: 7-inch

FARO (613 "Flame of Love"/"Tracy")........15-25 63
Also see WHITE, Barry

WHITE, Ben, & Darchaes

Singles: 7-inch

ALJON (1247 "Jocko Sent Me")........800-1000 62
CONEY ISLAND (1959 "Jocko Sent Me")........10-15 80
Also see ADDEO, Nicky

WHITE, Bergen

Singles: 7-inch

MONUMENT (1040 "Bird Song")........5-10 67
PRIVATE STOCK........4-6 75-76
SSS INT'L........4-8 70

LPs: 10/12-inch

SSS INT'L........5-10 '70s
Also see CURRY, Clifford

WHITE, Beverly R&B '43

(With Her Blues Chasers)

Singles: 78 rpm

BEACON (111 "Don't Stop Now")........25-35 43
DAVIS........20-30 46
TRUMPET (182 "I Don't Care")........10-20 52
TRUMPET (183 "Cling to Me")........10-20 52

Singles: 7-inch

PHILIPS........5-10 62
Also see WHITE, Josh, & Family

WHITE, Bill

Singles: 7-inch

AC'CENT (1058 "Leave My Gal Alone")........40-60 58

WHITE, Bob

Singles: 7-inch

CLOWN (3010 "Learning How to Love")........5-10 60

WHITE, Bob / Jane White

(With the Sunset Playboys)

Singles: 7-inch

EVANA........5-10 '60s
Also see WHITE, Bob

WHITE, Bobby

Singles: 7-inch

END (1097 "Our Last Goodbye")........50-75 61
KENT (491 "It's a Great Life")........5-10 68

WHITE, Boyd

Singles: 7-inch

MERCURY (71714 "Secret Love")........10-15 60
SONDRA (210 "To Be Loved")........8-12 60

WHITE, Buddy

(With the Bell Hops)

Singles: 7-inch

MILESTONE (2006 "Betty Jean")........10-15 61
MURCO (1017 "Teenage Ball")........50-75 59
SAN (1521 "Love Without Faith")........20-30 '60s
WHEELER DEALERS (501 "For Your Love")........50-75

WHITE, Bukka

(Booker White)

Singles: 78 rpm

VOCALION (03711 "Shake 'Em on Down")........400-600 39
VOCALION (05489 "High Fever Blues")........400-600 40
VOCALION (05526 "Strange Place Blues")........400-600 40
VOCALION (05588 "Fixin' to Die Blues")........550-650 41

Singles: 7-inch

ARHOOLIE........5-10 65
TAKOMA........5-10 63

LPs: 10/12-inch

ARHOOLIE........10-20 65
BLUE HORIZON........10-15
COLUMBIA........10-15 70
HERWIN........10-15
TAKOMA........10-15

WHITE, Butch

Singles: 7-inch

POP (1105 "Dream Girl")........15-25 59

WHITE, Charlie

(With the Clovers)

Singles: 7-inch

WINLEY (219 "Sweetie Baby")........15-25 57
WINLEY (229 "Dearest to Me")........30-50 58
Also see CLOVERS

WHITE, Clifton

(With His Royal Knights)

Singles: 7-inch

ANLA (106 "If You Love Me")........15-25 '60s
SAR (128 "Dance What You Wanna")........10-20 62

WHITE, Danny

Singles: 7-inch

ABC-PAR (10525 "One Little Lie")........8-12 64
ABC-PAR (10589 "Moonbeam")........8-12 64
ATLAS (1257 "I'm Dedicating My Life")........10-20 66
ATTERU (2001 "I'm Dedicating My Life")........20-30 66
(Much higher quality than Atlas pressing.)
DECCA (32048 "Taking Inventory")........5-10 66
DECCA (32106 "Kiss Tomorrow Goodbye")........5-10 67
DOT (16188 "Give and Take")........15-25 61
FRISCO (104 "Kiss Tomorrow Goodbye")........15-25 63
FRISCO (106 "Make Her Mine")........15-25 63
FRISCO (109 "Twitch")........15-25 63
FRISCO (110 "One Little Lie")........15-25 63
FRISCO (114 "My Living Doll")........15-25 63
KASHE (443 "Never Like This")........8-12 65
SSS INT'L (754 "Natural Soul Brother")........5-10 69

WHITE, Dave

(With the Pyramids)

Singles: 7-inch

PINK (705 "24 Hours")........20-30 60

LPs: 10/12-inch

BELL........10-15
Also see DANNY & JUNIORS

WHITE, Donnie

Singles: 7-inch

FELSTED (8619 "For an Eternity")........5-10 61
RIDGEWAY (714 "Teenage Blues")........10-15 59

WHITE, Donny

Singles: 7-inch

KING (5122 "That's My Doll")........50-60 58

WHITE, E.T., & His Great Potential Band

Singles: 7-inch

GREAT POTENTIAL (136 "Psycho")........20-30
GREAT POTENTIAL (12962 "Loosen Up")........10-15 68

WHITE, Edward "Gates"

Singles: 78 rpm

STATES (124 "Mother-in-Law")........8-12 53

Singles: 7-inch

STATES (124 "Mother-in-Law")........15-25 53

WHITE, Evelyn

Singles: 7-inch

DESS (7016 "Mind Your Own Business")........40-60

WHITE, Floyd

(With the Dealers)

Singles: 7-inch

CRITERION (1 "Cinderella")........75-100 58
TEE VEE (302 "Hey Theresa")........150-200 58

WHITE, Frankie

Singles: 7-inch

IDEAL (500 "It's All Over Now")........20-30 58

Singles: 7-inch

JUANITA (104 "Happy Heart")........10-15 59

WHITE, Jane

Singles: 7-inch

DAUNTLESS (033 "Alas, No Gas")........5-10 63
Also see WHITE, Bob / Jane White

WHITE, Jay

LPs: 10/12-inch

ESSEX (104 "I Love")........15-25 54
(10-inch LP.)

WHITE, Jim

Singles: 7-inch

GREGG (26701 "Boomerang")........5-10 67
GREGG (26702 "Just Another Broken Heart")........5-10 67

WHITE, Jim

Singles: 7-inch

UBC (1020 "Teenage Doll")........25-35

WHITE, Joe L.

Singles: 7-inch

LAWSON (333 "Stayin' Home Tonight")........250-350

WHITE, Johnny

(With His Country Rhythm Boys)

Singles: 7-inch

BROWNFIELD (15 "Don't Pity Me")........10-15 65
DEBONAIR (205 "Just a Face in the Crowd")........8-12 66
DON-MAR (4043 "Rose in the Garden")........50-75 60

WHITE, Josh

Singles: 78 rpm

ASCH........10-20 44-45
DECCA........10-20 46-47
LONDON........5-15 50-52
MAYOR........10-15 52
V-DISC........10-15 44-45
VOGUE........10-20 50

Singles: 7-inch

DECCA (25000 series)........5-10 64
LONDON........10-20 50-52
MERCURY........5-10 62-63
MIRWOOD (5506 "Jelly Jelly Blues")........5-10 65

EPs: 7-inch

DECCA........15-25 50
EMARCY........10-25 55-56
LONDON........10-25 54-55

LPs: 10/12-inch

ABC-PAR (124 "Stories")........40-50 55
ABC-PAR (166 "Stories, Vol. 2")........20-40 57
ABC-PAR (407 "Josh White Live")........15-25 62
ARCHIVE OF FOLK MUSIC........10-15 67
DECCA (5082 "Ballads & Blues")........50-100 49
(10-inch LP.)
DECCA (5247 "Ballads & Blues, Vol. 2")........50-100 50
(10-inch LP.)
DECCA (8665 "Josh White")........20-30 58
ELEKTRA (100 series)........20-30 56-58
ELEKTRA (211 "Empty Bed Blues")........15-25 62
ELEKTRA (701 "Story of John Henry")........25-35 55
ELEKTRA (75000 series)........10-15 70
EMARCY (26010 "Josh White Sings")........25-35 55
EVEREST........5-8
51 WEST........5-8 86
LONDON (341 "A Josh White Program")........25-35 54
LONDON (1057 "Josh White Sings, Vol. 2")........25-35 55
MERCURY (20203 "Josh White's Blues")........20-30 57
MERCURY (20821 "Beginning")........12-25 63
(Monaural.)
MERCURY (21022 "I'm on My Own Way")........12-25 63
(Monaural.)
MERCURY (25014 "Josh Sings")........50-100 50
(10-inch LP.)
MERCURY (60821 "Beginning")........12-25 63
(Stereo.)
MERCURY (61022 "I'm on My Own Way")........12-25 63
(Stereo.)
PERIOD (1115 "Josh Comes A-Visiting") 30-40 56
STINSON (14 "Josh White Sings the Blues")........35-55 50
(10-inch LP.)
STINSON (15 "Josh White Sings Folk Songs")........35-55 50
(10-inch LP.)
SUPER MAJESTY........8-12
TRADITION........8-10 70
Also see LEADBELLY / Josh White / Sonny Terry

WHITE, Josh & Big Bill Broonzy

LPs: 10/12-inch

Mercury (36052 "Jazz Great Folk Blues") 25-35
Also see BROONZY, Big Bill

WHITE, Josh / Leadbelly / Bill Broonzy

LP: 10/12-inch

DESIGN (903 "Three of a Kind")........10-20
Also see BROONZY, Big Bill
Also see LEADBELLY

WHITE, Josh, & Family

(Josh White, Sr; Josh White, Jr.; Beverly White)

LPs: 10/12-inch

MERCURY........15-25 62
Also see WHITE, Beverly
Also see WHITE, Josh

WHITE, Judy

Singles: 7-inch

BUDDAH........5-10 68
T-NECK........5-10 69
Also see ISLEY BROTHERS / Brooklyn Bridge

WHITE, Junior

Singles: 7-inch

DIXIE (972 "Rock N' Roll Twist")........100-150

WHITE, Margo

Singles: 7-inch

JET STREAM (740 "I'm a Lover Not a Fighter")........8-12 69
JIN (176 "You Had Your Chance")........10-15 65
JIN (187 "I've Got a Right to Lose My Mind")........10-15 65
KHOURY'S (729 "Johnny's Coming Home")........8-12 61

WHITE, Maurice P&R/R&B/D&D/LP '85

Singles: 12-inch

COLUMBIA........4-6 86

Singles: 7-inch

COLUMBIA........3-5 85-86
ELEKTRA........4-6 78
GOLD (7333 "Big Bad Wolf")........40-60 59
GOLD (7334 "Rhythm Uh-Huh")........40-60 59
PRIDE (1003 "Rhythm Uh-Huh")........15-25 60

Picture Sleeves

COLUMBIA........3-5 85-86

LPs: 10/12-inch

COLUMBIA........5-8 85-86

WHITE, Otis

Singles: 7-inch

GALA (101 "Shape Up")........200-300 59

WHITE, Roger C&W '67

Singles: 7-inch

BIG A (103 "Wild Roses")........5-10 67

BLUE GIANT (001 "Somebody's Stealing My Baby") 75-100

WHITE, Ronnie

Singles: 7-inch

BRENT (7075 "Out of Breath") 10-15 67

WHITE, Ruth, & Continentals

Singles: 7-inch

CANDI (1029 "Give Us Your Blessing") ... 10-20 63

WHITE, Sam

Singles: 7-inch

SHASTA (111 "Rock Baby Rock") 20-30 59
SHASTONE (101 "Rock Baby Rock") 50-75 58

WHITE, Sir, & His Sounds

Singles: 7-inch

REDBUG (1 "Moody Dreamer") 10-15 61

WHITE, Tony Joe P&R/LP '69
(With the Mojos; with Waylon Jennings)

Singles: 7-inch

ARISTA 4-6 79
CASABLANCA 3-5 80
COLUMBIA 3-5 83-85
J-BECK 5-8
MONUMENT 5-8 67-70
20TH FOX 4-6 76

LPs: 10/12-inch

CASABLANCA 5-10 80
COLUMBIA 5-8 83
MONUMENT 8-15 69-70
20TH FOX 5-10 77
W.B. 8-10 71-73
Session: Waylon Jennings.
Also see JENNINGS, Waylon

WHITE, Wilbur "Hi-Fi"

Singles: 7-inch

BANDERA (3301 "Don't Look Now") .... 20-30 '60s
SANDMAN 5-10

WHITE, Willie

Singles: 7-inch

IMPERIAL (5862 "Mr. Blues") 8-12 62
IMPERIAL (5888 "Good News") 8-12 62
SHAW (104 "It's Wrong") 5-10 65

WHITE, Yolanda

Singles: 7-inch

DECCA (31340 "What I Want for Christmas") 5-10 61

WHITE BUCKS

Singles: 7-inch

DOT (15905 "Get That Fly") 8-12 59

WHITE CAPS

Singles: 7-inch

BLUE RIVER (201 "Fender Vendor") .... 10-20 '60s

WHITE DUCK

Singles: 7-inch

UNI (55345 "Again") 4-6 72

LPs: 10/12-inch

UNI 10-15 71-72
Member: Doug Yankus.
Also see SOUP

WHITE FLUFF

Singles: 7-inch

EAB (1112 "Vegetable Binge") 15-25 69

Picture Sleeves

EAB (1112 "Vegetable Binge") 25-35 69

WHITE HAVEN PILLOW

Singles: 7-inch

MTA (142 "Music Man") 5-10 68

WHITE KNIGHTS

Singles: 7-inch

GAIETY (117 "Run Baby Run") .... 15-25 '60s
GAIETY (121 "Promise Her Love") .... 15-25 '60s

WHITE LIGHT

LPs: 10/12-inch

CENTURY (39955 "White Light") 200-300 69
(Front cover is identical to *After Sundown*, by the Philosophers.)
Also see PHILOSOPHERS

WHITE LIGHTING

Singles: 7-inch

ATCO (6660 "Of Paupers & Poets") 30-40 69
HEXAGON (944 "Of Paupers & Poets") .. 40-60 69
Member: Tommy "Zippy" Kaplan.
Also see LIGHTNING
Also see LITTER

WHITE PLAINS P&R/LP '70

Singles: 7-inch

DERAM 4-6 70-73
LONDON ....4-6 '70s

LPs: 10/12-inch

DERAM 10-15 70
Members: Tony Burrows; Ricky Wolff; Roger Greenaway; Robin Box; Robin Shaw; Pete Nelson; Roger Hills.
Also see FLOWERPOT MEN

WHITE WING

Singles: 7-inch

ASI (1006 "Hansa") ....5-10 '60s
POWER PAGE (2569 "Lukie's Tune") ....10-15 '60s
POWER PAGE (2570 "The Nation's At War") ....10-15 '60s

LPs: 10/12-inch

ASI (212 "White Wing") ....25-35 '70s

WHITEFACE

Singles: 7-inch

MERCURY 4-6 79

LPs: 10/12-inch

MERCURY (103 "Live at the Agora") 20-25 79

WHITEHAWK, John

Singles: 7-inch

LITTLE DARLIN' (0064 "It Shows On Your Face") 5-10 69
LITTLE DARLIN' (0071 "It Is Love") 5-10 69

WHITEHEAD, Charlie R&B '75
(With the Swamp Dogg Band; Charles Whitehead)

Singles: 7-inch

ISLAND 4-6 75

LPs: 10/12-inch

FUNGUS 10-15
WIZARD 5-10 78

WHITEHURST, F.

Singles: 7-inch

SANDY (1012 "Brand New Baby") 40-60 58

WHITEMAN, Paul, Orchestra P&R '20

Singles: 78 rpm

CAPITOL 3-5 42-43
COLUMBIA 3-6 28-32
CORAL 3-5 50-56
DECCA 3-5 38-39
VICTOR (Black Plastic) 3-8 20-36
VICTOR (39000 "Night with Paul Whiteman at the Biltmore") ....300-400 '30s
(Picture disc.)

Singles: 7-inch

CORAL 5-15 50-56
WORLD'S FAIR (82083/84 "Conducts Rhapsody 21") 20-25 62
(Picture disc. Souvenir from Seattle World's Fair.)

EPs: 7-inch

CORAL 4-8 50-56

LPs: 10/12-inch

CAPITOL 5-10 62
CORAL 10-20 50-56
DECCA (8024 "George Gershwin Music") 20-30 49
GRAND AWARD 10-20 56-59
RCA (Except 67-2000) 5-10 68-69
RCA (67-2000 "Night with Paul Whiteman at the Biltmore") ....400-600 '30s
(Picture disc.)
WESTMINSTER 4-8 74

WHITEMAN, Stark
(With His Crowns & the Veltones)

Singles: 7-inch

SHO-BIZ (1004 "We Will All Remember") 20-30 59
WHITE CLIFFS (261 "We Will All Remember") 5-10 67
Member: Henry G. Schroeder.

WHITESIDE, Bobby

Singles: 7-inch

DESTINATION (603 "Say It Softly") 5-10 65
DESTINATION (606 "You Give Me Strength") 5-10 65
DESTINATION (626 "And Then I Saw You Cry") 5-10 66
PHILIPS (40322 "Lonesome King") 5-10 65
USA (775 "I'm Goin' Your Way") 10-15 64
USA (879 "I Saw You with Him") 5-10 67

LPs: 10/12-inch

CURTOM 8-12 74
Also see RIVIERAS

WHITESIDEWALLS
(Whitesidewalls Rock'n Roll Review)

Singles: 7-inch

SPIFF-OLA (839 "Clear Lake Medley") 8-12 82

LPs: 10/12-inch

SPIFF-OLA (897 "Whitesidewalls") 15-20 82
SPIFF-OLA (4954 "Whitesidewalls") 15-20 81
(A different collection than on Spiff-Ola 897.)

WHITFIELD, David P&R '54

Singles: 78 rpm

LONDON 5-10 53-57

Singles: 7-inch

LONDON 8-12 53-63

EPs: 7-inch

LONDON 10-15 54

LPs: 10/12-inch

LONDON 10-20 54-66
Also see MANTOVANI

WHITFIELD, Smoki

Singles: 7-inch

CREST (Black vinyl) 8-10 55-56
CREST (Colored vinyl) 15-20 55-56

WHITFIELD, Wilbur, & Pleasers
(Little Wilbur & the Pleasers)

Singles: 78 rpm

ALADDIN 25-50 57

Singles: 7-inch

ALADDIN (3381 "The One I Love") 40-50 57
ALADDIN (3396 "I Don't Care") 40-50 57
ALADDIN (3402 "Heart to Heart") 30-40 57

WHITHERSPOONE

Singles: 7-inch

WHITE WHALE (336 "Jennifer Tompkins") 5-10 69

WHITING, Margaret P&R '46

Singles: 78 rpm

CAPITOL 3-8 46-56
DOT 3-8 57

Singles: 7-inch

CAPITOL 5-10 50-56
DOT 5-8 57-59
LONDON 4-6 66-70
VERVE 4-6 60

EPs: 7-inch

CAPITOL 5-10 50-56

LPs: 10/12-inch

CAPITOL 12-25 50-56
DOT 8-18 57-67
HAMILTON 5-15 59-65
LONDON 5-15 67-68
VERVE 10-20 60
Also see MARTIN, Dean, & Margaret Whiting
Also see TORME, Mel

WHITING, Margaret, & Jimmy Wakely C&W '49

Singles: 78 rpm

CAPITOL 3-8 49-51

Singles: 7-inch

CAPITOL 5-10 49-51

EPs: 7-inch

CAPITOL 8-15 53

LPs: 10/12-inch

PICKWICK 8-12 67
Also see WHITING, Margaret
Also see WAKELY, Jimmy

WHITLEY, Jackie

Singles: 7-inch

EDA (1743 "Mean Man Blues") 20-30

WHITLEY, Ray

Singles: 7-inch

APT (25086 "Runaway") 5-10 65
ATTARACK 5-10
COLUMBIA 5-10 66-67
1-2-3 (1707 "Don't Throw Your Love to the Wind") 4-6 69
TRX (5007 "Gotta Go There") 5-10 68
VEE-JAY (Except 433) 5-10 62-64
VEE-JAY (433 "Yessiree Yessiree") 10-20 62

WHITLOCK, Bobby LP '72

Singles: 7-inch

DUNHILL 4-6 72
HIP (8001 "Raspberry Rug") 5-10 68

LPs: 10/12-inch

CAPRICORN 8-10 76
DUNHILL 10-12 72
Also see DELANEY & BONNIE
Also see DEREK & DOMINOES

WHITMAN, Slim C&W/P&R '52

Singles: 78 rpm

IMPERIAL 5-15 52-57

Singles: 7-inch

CLEVELAND INT'L 3-5 80-82
EPIC 3-5 84
IMPERIAL (5000 series) 5-10 61-63
IMPERIAL (8000 thru 8200 series) 10-25 52-58
IMPERIAL (8300 series) 8-12 59-60
IMPERIAL (50000 series) 4-6 70-71
IMPERIAL (65000 & 66000 series) 5-10 61-69
LIBERTY (56199 "Shutters and Boards") 4-6 70
U.A. 4-8 70-77

EPs: 7-inch

IMPERIAL 30-50 54-65
RCA (3217 "Slim Whitman Sings and Yodels") 100-150 54
(Two discs.)

LPs: 10/12-inch

CAMDEN 8-12 66
CLEVELAND INT'L (Except AS-99875) 5-10 80-81
CLEVELAND INT'L (AS-99875 "Songs I Love to Sing") 30-35 80
(Picture disc. Promotional issue only. Reportedly 1,600 made.)
EPIC 5-8 84
IMPERIAL (3004 "America's Favorite Folk Artist") 550-650 54
(10-inch LP. Colored vinyl.)
IMPERIAL (9000 series) 35-50 56-60
(Maroon or black label with "Imperial" at top.)
IMPERIAL (9000 series) 8-15 66
(Black label with "Imperial" on left side.)
IMPERIAL (9100 series) 20-40 60-62
(Black label with "Imperial" at top.)
IMPERIAL (9100 series) 8-15 66
(Black label with "Imperial" on left side.)
IMPERIAL (9200 & 9300 series) 15-25 63-67
IMPERIAL (12100 series) 20-30 62
(Black label with "Imperial" at top.)
IMPERIAL (12100 series) 8-15 66
(Black label with "Imperial" on left side.)
IMPERIAL (12200 & 12300 series) 12-25 65-68
IMPERIAL (12400 series) 8-12 68-69
LIBERTY 5-10 80-82
PICKWICK ....5-10 '70s
RCA (3217 "Slim Whitman Sings and Yodels") 250-350 54
RCA (3700 series) 5-8 80
SUFFOLK MARKETING 8-12 79-82
SUNSET 8-12 66-70
U.A. 6-12 70-80
Also see WILLIAMS, Hank / Slim Whitman

WHITNER, Fuzzy

Singles: 7-inch

STARDAY (704 "Sugar Bugger") 200-300

WHITNEY, Jill
(With Don Costa & Orchestra)

Singles: 78 rpm

CORAL (61055 "Tennessee Wig-Walk") 8-10 53

Singles: 7-inch

CORAL (61055 "Tennessee Wig-Walk") .. 10-15 53
Also see COSTA, Don, Orchestra

WHITNEY, Marva P&R/R&B '69

Singles: 7-inch

EXCELLO (2328 "Don't Let Our Love Fade Away") 5-10 73
FEDERAL (12545 "Your Love Was Good for Me") 10-15 67
KING 5-10 67-69
T-NECK 4-6 70

LPs: 10/12-inch

KING 10-15 69
Session: Ellis Taylor.
Also see BROWN, James, & Marva Whitney

WHITNEY, Mary Lee
Singles: 7-inch
LOMA (2044 "This Could Have Been Mine")....5-10 66

WHITNEY, Ty
Singles: 7-inch
CARMEL (22 "Big Brown Eyes")....8-12 61
DENNY (4466 "Other Side of Love")....5-10 62
MGM....4-6 72
20TH FOX (447 "Move Over Darling")....5-10 63
20TH FOX (448 "Surfin' Santa Claus")....10-20 63

WHITNEY SUNDAY
LPs: 10/12-inch
DECCA (75239 "Whitney Sunday")....10-15 70
Members: Joe Hinchliffe; Doug Jacobs; Bill White; Larry Scarano; Lester Figarsky; Bill Gallagher.

WHITNEYS
Singles: 7-inch
JOSIE (948 "A Place for Me")....5-10 66

WHITSETT, Tim, & Imperials
Singles: 7-inch
ACE (665 "Monkey Man")....5-10 62
IMPERIAL (5757 "Jive Harp")....8-12 61
RIM....5-10 62-63
TREBCO (701 "Jive Harp")....10-20 61
(First issue.)
TREBCO (703 "I Don't Care")....15-25 61
Also see VELS

WHITTAKER, Roger *P&R/LP '75*
Singles: 7-inch
MAIN STREET....3-5 83-84
RCA....3-6 70-86
Picture Sleeves
RCA....3-5 80
LPs: 10/12-inch
MAIN STREET....5-8 84
RCA....5-12 70-86

WHITTINGTON, Dick, & Cats
Singles: 7-inch
ROUND (1003 "Midnight Hour")....50-60 59

WHITTLEY, Bill
Singles: 7-inch
AMBER (2672 "Fool Fool Fool")....40-60
BLUEBONNET (7453 "I'm a Rich Man")....100-150

WHIZ-HUNT
Singles: 7-inch
GUYDEN (2071 "Seaman")....5-10 62

WHIZZ KIDDS
Singles: 7-inch
HIGHLAND (2001 "Sweet Honey")....8-12 '60s

WHO *P&R '65*
Singles: 7-inch
ATCO (6409 "Substitute")....20-30 66
ATCO (6509 "Substitute")....10-15 67
DECCA (31725 "I Can't Explain")....15-20 64
DECCA (31801 "Anyway Anyhow Anywhere")....50-75 65
DECCA (31877 "My Generation")....15-25 65
DECCA (31988 "The Kids Are Alright")....15-25 66
DECCA (32058 "I'm a Boy")....15-25 66
DECCA (32114 "Happy Jack")....8-12 67
DECCA (32156 "Pictures of Lily")....8-12 67
DECCA (32206 "I Can See for Miles")....5-10 67
DECCA (32288 "Call Me Lightning")....8-12 68
DECCA (32362 "Magic Bus")....5-10 68
DECCA (32465 "Pinball Wizard")....5-10 69
DECCA (32519 "I'm Free")....5-10 69
DECCA (32670 "The Seeker")....5-10 70
DECCA (32708 "Summertime Blues")....5-10 70
DECCA (32729 "See Me, Feel Me")....5-10 70
DECCA (32737 "Young Man Blues")....50-75 70
DECCA (32846 "Won't Get Fooled Again")....5-10 71
DECCA (32888 "Behind Blue Eyes")....5-10 71
DECCA (32983 "Join Together")....5-10 72
DECCA (33041 "The Relay")....5-10 72
LIFE....20-30
MCA....4-6 74-79
POLYDOR....4-6 75-79
TRACK....4-8 72-74
W.B.....3-5 81-83
Picture Sleeves
DECCA (32114 "Happy Jack")....10-20 67
DECCA (32465 "Pinball Wizard")....8-12 69
DECCA (32729 "See Me, Feel Me")....8-12 70
DECCA (32737 "Young Man Blues")....75-125 70
POLYDOR....4-6 75-79
W.B.....3-5 81-83
Promotional Singles
ATCO (6409 "Substitute")....25-35 66
ATCO (6509 "Substitute")....10-20 67
DECCA (31725 "I Can't Explain")....20-25 64
DECCA (31801 "Anyway Anyhow Anywhere")....20-30 65
DECCA (31877 "My Generation")....20-30 65
DECCA (31988 "The Kids Are Alright")....20-30 66
DECCA (32058 "I'm a Boy")....20-30 66
DECCA (32114 "Happy Jack")....10-20 67
DECCA (32156 "Pictures of Lily")....10-20 67
DECCA (32206 "I Can See for Miles")....10-15 67
DECCA (32288 "Call Me Lightning")....10-15 68
DECCA (32362 "Magic Bus")....8-12 68
DECCA (32465 "Pinball Wizard")....5-10 69
DECCA (32519 "I'm Free")....5-10 69
DECCA (32670 "The Seeker")....10-15 70
DECCA (32708 "Summertime Blues")....10-15 70
DECCA (32729 "See Me, Feel Me")....8-12 70
DECCA (32737 "Young Man Blues")....50-75 70
DECCA (32846 "Won't Get Fooled Again")....8-12 71
DECCA (32888 "Behind Blue Eyes")....8-12 71
DECCA (32983 "Join Together")....8-12 72
DECCA (33041 "The Relay")....8-12 72
DECCA (34444 "Happy Jack")....20-30 67
DECCA ("Excerpts from *Tommy*")....25-35 69
(Boxed set for radio programming. Includes inserts. No number used.)
LIFE....20-30
MCA (Except 8559)....5-10 74-79
MCA (8559 "Long Live Rock")....90-120 79
(Picture disc. Has National Record Mart or NARM logo on back. Promotional issue only.)
MCA (8559 "Long Live Rock")....70-90 79
(Picture disc. With any logo other than NARM's on back.)
POLYDOR....5-10 75-79
TRACK....5-10 72-74
W.B.....4-8 81-83
LPs: 10/12-inch
DDL/MCA (16610 "Who Are You")....40-50 78
(Half-speed mastered.)
DWJ ("Musical Biography")....30-50 78
(Promotional issue only. Not issued with cover.)
DECCA (DL-4664 "My Generation")....50-75 66
(Monaural.)
DECCA (DL-4664 "My Generation")....75-100 66
(White label. Promotional issue only.)
DECCA (DL7-4664 "My Generation")....40-60 66
(Stereo.)
DECCA (DL-4892 "Happy Jack")....50-75 67
(Monaural.)
DECCA (DL-4892 "Happy Jack")....75-100 67
(White label. Promotional issue only.)
DECCA (DL7-4892 "Happy Jack")....40-60 67
(Stereo.)
DECCA (DL-4950 "The Who Sell Out")....30-40 67
(Monaural.)
DECCA (DL-4950 "The Who Sell Out")....50-75 67
(White label. Promotional issue only.)
DECCA (DL7-4950 "The Who Sell Out")..20-30 67
(Stereo.)
DECCA (DL-5064 "Magic Bus")....50-75 68
(Monaural. White label. Promotional issue only.)
DECCA (DL7-5064 "Magic Bus")....25-30 68
DECCA (DXW-7205 "Excerpts from Tommy")....100-150 69
(Monaural. White label. Promotional issue only. Includes 12-page booklet.)
DECCA (DXSW-7205 "Tommy")....25-35 69
(Stereo. Includes 12-page booklet.)
DECCA (79175 "Live at Leeds")....30-40 70
(Includes eight photo copies of various Who and High Numbers documents and correspondence, plus two black and white photos.)
DECCA (79175 "Live at Leeds")....15-25 70
(Without bonus materials.)
DECCA (79175 "Live at Leeds")....60-80 70
(White label. Promotional issue only. Includes eight photo copies of various Who and High Numbers documents and correspondence, plus two black and white photos.)
DECCA (79175 "Live at Leeds")....40-60 70
(White label. Promotional issue only. Without bonus materials.)
DECCA (79182 "Who's Next")....15-20 71
DECCA (79184 "Meaty Beaty Big & Bouncy")....15-20 71
MCA (1496 "Who's Greatest Hits")....5-10 83
MCA (1578 "Meaty Beaty Big & Bouncy")..5-10 80
MCA (1987 "Who Are You")....15-25 78
MCA (2000 series)....15-25 74
MCA (2161 "Who by Numbers")....8-10 75
MCA (3024 "Who's Next")....8-10
MCA (3050 "Who Are You")....8-10 78
(Black vinyl.)
MCA (3050 "Who Are You")....15-20 78
(Red vinyl.)
MCA (4067 "Happy Jack"/"The Who Sell Out")....15-25 74
MCA (4068 "My Generation"/"Magic Bus")....15-25 74
MCA (5000 series)....5-8 83-85
MCA (6000 series)....10-12 74
MCA (6895 "Quadrophenia")....8-10 80
(Does not have booklet.)
MCA (8000 series)....10-12 84
MCA (10004 "Quadrophenia")....10-12 81
MCA (10005 "Tommy")....10-12 77
MCA (11005 "The Kids Are Alright")....10-20 79
(Price includes 18-page booklet.)
MCA (12001 "Hooligans")....10-12 81
MCA (14950 "Who Are You")....12-15 79
(Picture disc.)
MCA (19501 "Join Together")....8-12 90
MCA (37000 series)....5-8 79
MFSL (115 "Face Dances")....30-40 84
POLYDOR....5-10
TRACK/MCA (2126 "Odds and Sods")....10-20 74
(Includes insert. Add $15 if accompanied by an 18" x 12" *Odds and Sods* poster.)
TRACK/MCA (4000 series)....10-12 74
TRACK/MCA (10004 "Quadrophenia")....15-20 73
(Includes 44-page booklet.)
W.B.....5-10 81-82
Members: Roger Daltrey; Pete Townshend; John Entwistle; Keith Moon; Kenny Jones.
Also see McCARTNEY, Paul / Rochestra / Who / Rockpile
Also see MOON, Keith
Also see SMALL FACES
Also see TOWNSHEND, Pete

WHO / Strawberry Alarm Clock
LPs: 10/12-inch
DECCA (734586 "The Who/Strawberry Alarm Clock")....50-75 69
(Philco-Ford Special Products promotional issue.)
Also see STRAWBERRY ALARM CLOCK
Also see WHO

WHOLE GROUP
Singles: 7-inch
S-A (929682 "Meandering Thru My Mind")....5-10 68

WHY FOUR
Singles: 7-inch
RAMPRO (118 "Hard Life")....15-25 66
Members: Drew Lund; Gerry Cain; Ken Stoneberner; Terry Lund.

WHYTE BOOTS
Singles: 7-inch
PHILIPS (40422 "Nightmare")....30-50 67

WICHITA TRAIN WHISTLE *LP '68*
Singles: 7-inch
DOT....5-10 68
LPs: 10/12-inch
DOT....15-20 68
PACIFIC ARTS....8-10 78
Member: Michael Nesmith.
Also see NESMITH, Michael

WICK, Craig, & Auto Cords
Singles: 7-inch
COOL (154 "Auto Hop")....20-30 60

WICK, Jimmy
Singles: 7-inch
LENOX (5561 "Send for Me")....5-10 63

WICKED TRUTH
Singles: 7-inch
TERV (1119 "Take a Chance")....10-15

WICKED WAY
Singles: 7-inch
PIECE (1009 "Complete Control")....15-25 '60s

WICKER, Carolyn
Singles: 7-inch
KON-TI (1158 "Prison Blues")....15-25

WICKS, Johnny, & His Swinging Ozarks
Singles: 78 rpm
UNITED....20-30 52
Singles: 7-inch
UNITED (116 "Jockey Jack Boogie")....35-50 52
UNITED (126 "Glasgow, Kentucky Blues")....35-50 52
(Black vinyl.)
UNITED (126 "Glasgow, Kentucky Blues")....50-75 52
(Red vinyl.)

WIG
Singles: 7-inch
BLACKKNIGHT (903 "Crackin' Up")....20-30 67
EMPIRE (1 "Crackin' Up")....20-30 67
(Colored vinyl.)
GOYLE (101 "Drive It Home")....20-30 66

WIGTWISTERS
Singles: 7-inch
A-RON (1001 "Wheel of Love")....50-100 57

WIG WAGS
Singles: 7-inch
ERA....5-10 60
SAMA (1002 "I'm on My Way Down the Road")....30-40 '60s

WIGFALL, William, & Lyrics
Singles: 7-inch
SKYLIGHT (202 "Got to Get Along")....2500-3500 62
Also see LYRICS

WIGGINS, Ben
Singles: 7-inch
ALMERIA (4004 "It's All Over")....8-12 78

WIGGINS, Curly
Singles: 7-inch
PLAZA (503 "Nobody to Love")....10-20 62

WIGGINS, Gerald
(Jerry Wiggins)
Singles: 7-inch
BRAD (007 "Downboy Blues")....10-20 58
LPs: 10/12-inch
DIG (102 "Wiggin' with Wig")....75-100 56
HI-FI (618 "Wiggin' Out")....25-40 61
Also see AUGUST, Art

WIGGINS, Jay
Singles: 7-inch
AMY (955 "Sad Girl")....8-10 66
ERIC....4-6 '70s
I.P.G. (1008 "Sad Girl")....15-25 63
SOLID SOUND (3001 "You're on My Mind")....10-20 '60s

WIGGINS, Percy
Singles: 7-inch
A-BET (9434 "Look What I've Done")....15-25 69
ATCO (6479 "Book of Memories")....5-10 67
ATCO (6520 "They Don't Know")....5-10 67
RCA (8915 "It Didn't Take Much")....15-25 66
RCA (9838 "Singing a Song")....8-12 70

WIGGINS, Ron
Singles: 7-inch
A.P.I. (333 "Never Let Me Go")....5-10 65
FALCON (1000 "Someday")....5-10 57

WIGGINS, Spencer *R&B '70*
Singles: 7-inch
FAME....4-8 69-70
GOLDWAX....5-10 66-69

WIGGINS, Wally
Singles: 7-inch
MERCURY (Except 71645)....5-15 60-62
MERCURY (71645 "I Need You")....50-75 60

WIGGLES & WAGGLES
Singles: 7-inch
CORAL (61943 "Rock & Roll Session")... 15-25 58

WIGS
Singles: 7-inch
GOLDEN CREST (592 "Sweeter Than Wine") ... 30-40 64

WILBURN BROTHERS *C&W '55*
Singles: 78 rpm
DECCA ... 5-15 54-57
Singles: 7-inch
DECCA (29190 thru 30428) ... 8-15 54-57
DECCA (30591 "Oo Bop Sha Boom") ... 15-25 58
DECCA (30686 thru 33027) ... 4-8 58-72
MCA ... 4-6 73
EPs: 7-inch
DECCA ... 5-15 57-62
LPs: 10/12-inch
CORAL ... 5-8 '80s
DECCA (4142 thru 4645) ... 10-20 61-65
DECCA (4721 "Wilburn Brothers Show") ... 50-75 66
(With Loretta Lynn, Ernest Tubb & Harold Morrison.)
DECCA (4817 thru 5291) ... 8-15 67-71
DECCA (8774 "Side By Side") ... 30-40 58
(Monaural.)
DECCA (78774 "Side By Side") ... 50-75 58
(Stereo.)
DECCA (8959 "Livin' in God's Country") . 20-30 59
(Monaural.)
DECCA (78959 "Livin' in God's Country") ... 30-40 59
(Stereo.)
DESIGN ... 8-12 '60s
FIRST GENERATION ... 5-10 81
KING (746 "The Wonderful Wilburn Brothers") ... 25-35 61
MCA (4011 "A Portrait") ... 15-20
(Two discs. Stereo.)
PHONORAMA ... 5-8 83
VOCALION ... 10-20 62-70
WORD ... 5-8
Members: Teddy Wilburn; Doyle Wilburn. Session: Anita Kerr Singers.
Also see KERR, Anita
Also see LYNN, Loretta
Also see PIERCE, Webb, & Wilburn Brothers
Also see TUBB, Ernest, & Wilburn Brothers

WILCO, Roger
Singles: 7-inch
MILESTONE (2007 "I Won't Love Nobody") ... 10-15 61

WILCOX, Coye
Singles: 7-inch
AZALEA (118 "You Gotta Quit Cheatin' ") ... 40-60 60

WILCOX, David
LPs: 10/12-inch
CAPITOL (6513 "Bad Reputation") ... 20-30 84
(Canadian.)
CAPITOL (48551 "Breakfast at the Circus") ... 10-20 87
(Canadian.)
FREEDOM (010 "Out of the Woods") ... 30-40 80
(Canadian.)

WILCOX, Eddie, Orchestra *R&B '52*
(Featuring Sunny Gale)
Singles: 78 rpm
DERBY ... 5-10 52
Singles: 7-inch
DERBY (45-787 "Wheel of Fortune") ... 15-25 52
(Colored vinyl.)
Also see GALE, Sunny
Also see SUNSETS

WILCOX, Harlow *C&W/P&R '69*
(With the Oakies)
Singles: 7-inch
IMPEL (002 "Groovy Grubworm") ... 15-25 68
PLANTATION ... 4-8 69-70
SSS INT'L ... 4-6 '70s
Picture Sleeves
IMPEL (002 "Groovy Grubworm") ... 25-35 68
PLANTATION (28 Groovy Grubworm") ... 5-10 69
LPs: 10/12-inch
PLANTATION ... 5-10 70-71

WILCOX, Mikki
Singles: 7-inch
PHILLIPS INT'L (3573 "I Know What It Means") ... 5-10 61

WILCOX, Nancy
Singles: 7-inch
RCA (9233 "Coming On Strong") ... 10-20 67

WILCOX THREE
LPs: 10/12-inch
CAMDEN (669 "Greatest Folk Songs Ever Sung") ... 20-30 61
Member: Chip Douglas.
Also see MODERN FOLK QUARTET

WILD AFFAIR
Singles: 7-inch
MGM (13552 "Baby, Baby") ... 5-10 66

WILD BEES
Singles: 7-inch
RCA (7275 "Doctor Rock") ... 15-25 58

WILD CHERRIES
Singles: 7-inch
KAPP (2113 "You Know What Cha Want") ... 8-12 70
KAPP (2137 "Wigwam") ... 8-12 71

WILD CHILDS
Singles: 7-inch
CASCADE (102 "Rockin' Heart") ... 100-150 59

WILD COUNTRY
Singles: 7-inch
LSI (75-12-1 "Sweet Country Woman") ... 25-35 70
("From Me to You"/"Down That Cheatin' Road Again") ... 20-30 76
(Label and selection number not known.)
LPs: 10/12-inch
LSI (0275 "Wild Country") ... 500-1000 70
Members: Randy Owen; Jeff Cook; Teddy Gentry; John B. Vartanian.
Also see ALABAMA

WILD FLOWERS
Singles: 7-inch
ASTER (01 "On a Day Like Today") ... 15-25 66
ASTER (02 "More Than Me") ... 15-25 66

WILD ONES
Singles: 7-inch
S.P.Q.R. (3316 "I've Been Crying") ... 10-20 64

WILD ONES *LP '65*
Singles: 7-inch
MAINLINE ... 5-10 65
MALA (564 "Valerie") ... 5-10 67
U.A. ... 5-10 65-66
LPs: 10/12-inch
U.A. ... 15-20 65
Also see ANTELL, Peter

WILD ONES
Singles: 7-inch
SEARS (2180 "Come on Back") ... 5-10 66
TIGAR PROD. (500 "Please") ... 5-10
Picture Sleeves
SEARS (2180 "Come on Back") ... 10-15 66

WILD ONES
Singles: 7-inch
ORLYN (66791 "Tale of a City") ... 10-20 66

WILD SILK
Singles: 7-inch
KAPP (974 "Jessica") ... 5-10 69

WILD THINGS
Singles: 7-inch
BLUE ONION (101 "Summer's Gone") ... 10-20 67
BLUE ONION (104 "Acid") ... 10-20 67

WILD THINGS
Singles: 7-inch
DAMON (12680 "Tell Me") ... 15-25 '60s

WILD TONES
Singles: 7-inch
MADISON (102 "Martian Band") ... 15-20 58
MADISON (109 "Sick Chick") ... 15-20 58
TEE GEE (105 "King Cobra") ... 20-30 58

WILD TURKEY *LP '72*
Singles: 7-inch
CHRYSALIS ... 4-6 72-73
REPRISE ... 4-6 72
LPs: 10/12-inch
CHRYSALIS ... 8-10 72-73
REPRISE ... 8-12 72
Members: Gary Pickford-Hopkins; Tweke Lewis; Jon Blackmore; Glenn Cornick; Jeff Jones; Steve Gurl.
Also see JETHRO TULL

WILDCARD, Johnny
Singles: 7-inch
GULF REEF (1002 "Rock & Roll Yodel") . 10-15 61
RADIO (108 "The Blues Showing Thru Again") ... 10-15 58

WILD-CATS *P&R '59*
Singles: 7-inch
U.A. (154 "Gazachstahagen"/"Billy's Cha Cha") ... 15-25 58
(Monaural.)
U.A. (1154 "Gazachstahagen"/"?????????????????? ?????????????????????") ... 20-30 59
(Monaural. Flip side, a novelty, has no credits – only question marks on label.)
U.A. (169 "King Size Guitar") ... 10-20 59
U.A. (1154 "Gazachstahagen") ... 20-30 58
(Stereo [reprocessed].)
LPs: 10/12-inch
U.A. (3031 "Bandstand Record Hop") ... 35-45 59
Also see MURE, Billy

WILDCATS
Singles: 78 rpm
RCA (6386 "Keep Talking") ... 10-15 56
Singles: 7-inch
RCA (6386 "Keep Talking") ... 15-25 56

WILDCATS
(Blossoms)
Singles: 7-inch
REPRISE (0253 "3625 Groovy Street") ... 10-15 64
Also see BLOSSOMS

WILDCATS
Singles: 7-inch
COUNSEL (1301 "The Swim") ... 10-20 64

WILDE, Bobby
Singles: 7-inch
SOUTHSIDE (1005 "Summer School") ... 5-10 62

WILDE, Jimmy
Singles: 7-inch
CHELSEA (1006 "Crazy Eyes for You") ... 25-35 62
Session: El Domingos.
Also see EL DOMINGOS

WILDE, Johnny
Singles: 7-inch
CORONET (1302 "Pearl of My Heart") ... 10-20 59

WILDE, Marty *P&R '60*
(With the Wild Cats)
Singles: 7-inch
BELL (45603 "All Night Girl") ... 4-6 74
EPIC ... 5-15 58-60
JAMIE (1282 "Kiss Me") ... 5-10 64
LPs: 10/12-inch
EPIC (575 "Wilde About Marty") ... 30-40 60
(Stereo.)
EPIC (3686 "Bad Boy") ... 30-40 60
EPIC (3711 "Wilde About Marty") ... 25-35 60
(Monaural.)

WILDE, Tim
Singles: 7-inch
TOWER (353 "Popcorn Double Feature") .. 5-10 67

WILDE KNIGHTS
Singles: 7-inch
MODERN (1014 "Beaver Patrol") ... 10-15 65
STAR-BRIGHT (3051 "Beaver Patrol") ... 25-35 65
LPs: 10/12-inch
VOXX ... 5-10
Also see AMERICAN CHEESE

WILDER, Farris
Singles: 7-inch
HI-Q (11 "It's All Your Fault") ... 100-200

WILDER, Vic
Singles: 7-inch
DECCA (31001 "My Love For You") ... 15-25 59
RIC (959 "Earlene") ... 50-75 59

WILDER BROTHERS
(With Jack Cathcart's Orchestra)
Singles: 78 rpm
WING ... 5-10 55
"X" ... 5-10 55
Singles: 7-inch
LEEDS (781 "Party Line") ... 10-20 59
WING (90039 "The Old Chimney") ... 10-20 55
WING (90046 "Love That Melody") ... 10-20 55
"X" (0169 "Yes and No") ... 10-20 55

WILDERNESS ROAD
Singles: 7-inch
COLUMBIA (45565 "Bounty Man") ... 4-6 72
EPs: 7-inch
REPRISE (PRO-556 "Three Genuine Transparent") ... 25-50 73
(Promotional issue only.)
LPs: 10/12-inch
COLUMBIA (31118 "Wilderness Road") .. 10-20 72
REPRISE (2125 "Sold for the Prevention of Disease Only") ... 10-20 73

WILDER BROTHERS
(With Jack Cathcart & Orchestra; with Barney Kessel & Orchestra)
Singles: 78 rpm
FORECAST ... 8-10 54
Singles: 7-inch
FORECAST (101 "Race Track Blues") ... 10-20 54
IMPERIAL (5711 "Tiger Tail") ... 5-10 60
VERVE (10055 "Teenage Angel") ... 15-25 57
Also see KESSEL, Barney / Grant Green / Oscar Moore / Mundell Lowe

WILDFLOWER
Singles: 7-inch
MAINSTREAM (659 "Baby Dear") ... 5-10 66
U.A. (50504 "Butterfly") ... 5-10 69

WILDFLOWER / Harbinger Complex / Euphoria / Other Side
LPs: 10/12-inch
MAINSTREAM (56100 "With Love: A Pot of Flowers") ... 25-35 68
(Monaural.)
MAINSTREAM (S-56100 "With Love: A Pot of Flowers") ... 25-35 68
(Stereo.)
Also see EUPHORIA
Also see OTHER SIDE

WILDING, Bobby
Singles: 7-inch
ABC-PAR (10275 "Mama") ... 15-25 61
DCP (1009 "I Want to Be a Beatle") ... 10-20 64
DCP (1106 "I Want You") ... 5-10 64
MAY (125 "Slide") ... 5-10 62

WILDING BONUS
LPs: 10/12-inch
VISA (7003 "Pleasure Signals") ... 10-15 78
(Picture disc.)

WILDROOT, Raven
Singles: 7-inch
JARO (77038 "I Love You So") ... 10-15 60

WILDWOOD TRIO
("Featuring Fred Netherton")
Singles: 7-inch
DIXIE (1 "Wildwood Rock") ... 300-400
Also see NETHERTON, Fred

WILDWOODS
Singles: 7-inch
CAPRICE (101 "When the Swallows Come Back to Capistrano") ... 75-125 61
MAY (106 "Here Comes Big Ed") ... 15-25 61
Members: Fred Parris; Johnny Seastrand; Johnny Fisko; Jerry Greenberg.
Also see FIVE SATINS
Also see FIVE SATINS / Gerry Granahan & Five Satins

WILERSON, Alvin
Singles: 7-inch
TOWNE HOUSE (1008 "My Git Up and Go Got Up and Went") ... 15-25

WIL-ETTES
Singles: 7-inch
JAMIE (1234 "Summertime Is Gone") ... 10-15 62

WILEY, Arnold
(Doc Wiley)
Singles: 78 rpm
APOLLO 15-25 47
BULLET 15-25 50
CHICAGO 20-30 45
KING 15-25 48
Singles: 7-inch
ACE (111 "It'll Be a Long Time") 15-25 59

WILEY, Chuck
(Charles Wiley)
Singles: 7-inch
CARIB 5-10 64
JAX (1004 "I Love You So Much") 50-75 59
MUSIC CENTER (3101 "Come Back Baby") 20-30 60
U.A. (113 "Tear It Up") 40-60 58
U.A. (131 "Shake It Up") 30-40 58

WILEY, Ed *R&B '50*
(With His After Hour Rhythm; with Teddy Reynolds & King Tut)
Singles: 78 rpm
ATLANTIC 15-25 51
SITTIN' IN WITH 15-25 50
Singles: 7-inch
ATLANTIC (959 "So Glad I'm Free") 100-150 51
SITTIN' IN WITH (545 "Cry, Cry Baby") 100-200 50
Members: Teddy Reynolds; King Tut.
Also see KING TUT
Also see REYNOLDS, Teddy
Also see WARDELL, Roosevelt

WILEY, Reid
Singles: 7-inch
GUYDEN (2118 "Say Girl") 10-20 65

WILEY, Shirley Jean
Singles: 7-inch
MYRL (408 "Long Tall Sally") 40-60

WILEY, Skip
Singles: 7-inch
MOJO (2169 "Fast Livin'") 25-35
Also see RILEY, Billy Lee

WILHELM
(Mike Wilhelm)
LPs: 10/12-inch
ZIG ZAG (221 "Wilhelm") 15-25 76
Also see CHARLATANS

WILKINS, Artie, & Palms
Singles: 78 rpm
STATES (157 "Darling Patricia") 50-75 56
Singles: 7-inch
STATES (157 "Darling Patricia") 400-500 56
Also see PALMS

WILKINS, Buddy
Singles: 7-inch
TRI-ESS (1000 "Private Eye") 10-20 60

WILKINS, David
Singles: 7-inch
PHILLIPS INT'L (3581 "There's Something About You") 5-10 62

WILKINS, Robert
Singles: 78 rpm
VICTOR (21741 "Rolling Stone") 800-1200 29

WILKINSON TRI-CYCLE
LPs: 10/12-inch
DATE (4016 "Wilkinson Tri-Cycle") 15-20 69

WILKS & WILKERSON
Singles: 7-inch
BAMBOO (518 "Young Lover") 5-10 62

WILLARD, Jess
Singles: 78 rpm
EKKO (1018 "Don't Hold Her So Close") 5-10 55
Singles: 7-inch
EKKO (1018 "Don't Hold Her So Close") 10-20 55

WILLETT, Slim *C&W '52*
(With the Brush Cutters; Slim Willet; Winston Moore)
Singles: 78 rpm
FOUR STAR 5-10 52-56
SLIM WILLET (133 "Four Hand Blues") .. 20-40 53
STAR TALENT 10-20 50
Singles: 7-inch
EDMORAL (1010 "I've Been a Wonderin'") 15-25 57
FOUR STAR 10-20 52-56
LPs: 10/12-inch
AUDIO LAB (1542 "Slim Willett") 30-40 60
Also see MILS, Telli .W.

WILLETTE, Baby Face
Singles: 78 rpm
RECORDED IN HOLLYWOOD (230 "Cool Blues") 15-25 52
Singles: 7-inch
ARGO (5484 "Dad's Theme") 5-10 64
ARGO (5503 "Amen") 5-10 65
LPs: 10/12-inch
ARGO (739 "Mo-Roc") 15-25 64

WILLETTE, Jo
Singles: 78 rpm
MONEY (222 "Don't Touch Me") 10-15 56
Singles: 7-inch
MONEY (222 "Don't Touch Me") 20-30 56

WILLETTE, Ken, & Blue Notes
Singles: 7-inch
RENOWN (111 "Love Is a Flame") 50-75 59

WILLETTE, Wally
(With the Telecaster Cats)
Singles: 7-inch
FLAG (118 "Eenie Meenie") 200-300 59
EPs: 7-inch
SMUDGE 5-10 80
LPs: 10/12-inch

WILLIAM & CONQUERORS
Singles: 7-inch
BIG SOUND (1001 "Nowhere to Run") .... 20-25 '60s

WILLIAM THE WILD ONE
Singles: 7-inch
FESTIVAL (701 "Willie the Wild One") 40-60

WILLIAMS, Al
Singles: 7-inch
LABEAT 8-12
PALMER (5011 "I Am Nothing") 8-12 67

WILLIAMS, Alaine
Singles: 7-inch
PARKWAY (923 "When Are We Getting Married") 5-10 64

WILLIAMS, Andre *R&B '57*
(With the Don Juans; with Five Dollars; with Diablos; with Gino Purifoy; with Joe Weaver & His Blue Note Orchestra; Andre "Bacon Fat" Williams & Inspirations; Andre "Mr. Rhythm" Williams)
Singles: 78 rpm
EPIC 10-20 57
FORTUNE 10-30 55-57
Singles: 7-inch
AVIN (103 "Rib Tips") 5-10 66
AVIN (105 "Hard Hustling") 5-10 66
CHECKER (1205 "Mrs. Mother U.S.A.") 8-12 68
CHECKER (1214 "Do the Popcorn") 5-10 69
CHECKER (1219 "Girdle Up") 5-10 69
EPIC (9196 "Bacon Fat") 20-30 56
(Different take than first issued on Fortune.)
FORTUNE (824 "Pulling Time") 40-50 55
FORTUNE (828 "It's All Over") 20-30 56
FORTUNE (831 "Bacon Fat") 30-40 56
(Blue label.)
FORTUNE (831 "Bacon Fat") 20-30 57
(Orange label. Same as version on Epic.)
FORTUNE (831 "Bacon Fat") 4-8
(Blue label. No lines.)
FORTUNE (834 "Mean Jean") 20-30 57
FORTUNE (837 "Jail Bait") 30-40 57
FORTUNE (842 "My Last Dance with You") 25-35 58
FORTUNE (856 "Jail House Blues") 40-50 60
FORTUNE (1986 "Bacon Fat [86]") 4-6 86
(Rerecorded version.)
RIC-TIC (124 "You Got It and I Want It") .. 10-20 67
RONALD (1001 "Please Give Me a Chance") .... 20-30 '50s
MIRACLE (4 "Rosa Lee") 300-500 60
SPORT (105 "Pearl Time") 10-20 67
WINGATE (014 "Loose Juice") 8-12 66
WINGATE (021 "Do It") 8-12 66
LPs: 10/12-inch
FORTUNE 5-10 86
Members: (Don Juans) Steve Gaston; Bobby Calhoun; Jay Johnson; Gino Parks.
Also see FIVE DOLLARS
Also see KAY, Gary

WILLIAMS, Andre, & Gino Parks
Singles: 7-inch
FORTUNE (839 "The Greasy Chicken"/"Come On Baby") 20-30 57
FORTUNE (839 "The Greasy Chicken"/"Please Pass the Biscuits") 20-30 57
FORTUNE (839X "Don't Touch"/"Please Pass the Biscuits") 20-30 58
FORTUNE (851 "Movin'") 20-30 60
Also see PARKS, Gino
Also see WILLIAMS, Andre

WILLIAMS, Andy *P&R '56*
Singles: 12-inch
COLUMBIA 4-6 79
Singles: 78 rpm
CADENCE 5-10 56-57
Singles: 7-inch
AURAVISION (6727 "Tammy") 5-10 64
(Cardboard flexi-disc, one of six by six different artists. Columbia Record Club "Enrollment Premium." Set came in a special paper sleeve.)
CADENCE (1288 thru 1374) 10-20 56-59
CADENCE (1378 thru 1447) 6-12 60-64
COLUMBIA (Except 42199 thru 44202) 3-8 68-79
COLUMBIA (42199 thru 44202) 8-12 61-67
Picture Sleeves
CADENCE (1374 "The Village of St. Bernadette") 10-20 59
COLUMBIA 3-5 61-76
EPs: 7-inch
CADENCE 10-15 57-59
COLUMBIA 5-10 62-66
(Juke box issues only.)
COLUMBIA/KFC (679 "Taste of Honey") ... 5-10 '60s
(Promotional issue, made for Kentucky Fried Chicken.)
COLUMBIA SPECIAL PRODUCTS .... 4-6 '60s
LPs: 10/12-inch
CADENCE 20-30 58-62
COLUMBIA 5-15 62-77
COLUMBIA SPECIAL PRODUCTS 5-10
Also see JAN & DEAN / Bobby Vinton / Andy Williams

WILLIAMS, Andy, & Cavaliers
Singles: 7-inch
OUR (305 "You Must Be Born Again") .500-750 57
(Black vinyl.)
OUR (305 "You Must Be Born Again") 800-1200 57
(Red vinyl.)

WILLIAMS, Annie
Singles: 7-inch
U.A. (374 "Playboy") 10-15 61

WILLIAMS, Arnie
Singles: 78 rpm
HERALD (479 "Margie") 10-15 56
Singles: 7-inch
HERALD (479 "Margie") 15-25 56

WILLIAMS, B.
Singles: 78 rpm
TOP TUNES (101 "You're So Near to Me") 50-75 50

WILLIAMS, Ben E.
(With the Steps Four & Del-Reys)
Singles: 7-inch
RIFF (6102 "Nay-Oy-Gwor") 1500-2000 61

WILLIAMS, Benny
Singles: 7-inch
ROBEN (1873 "Hiking for J.F.K.") 5-10 63
TODD (1099 "90 Miles") 5-10 64

WILLIAMS, Bernie
(With the Scrubs)
Singles: 78 rpm
IMPERIAL 10-15 55
Singles: 7-inch
BELL (768 "Ever Again") 100-200 69
DEL-VAL 10-20
IMPERIAL (5360 "Don't Tease Me") 40-50 55

WILLIAMS, Beverly
(With Stu Phillips Orchestra & Chorus)
Singles: 7-inch
DECCA (31912 "He's Hurtin' Me") 10-20 66
Also see PHILLIPS, Stu, & His Orchestra

WILLIAMS, Big Joe
(Joe Lee Williams)
Singles: 78 rpm
TRUMPET (169 "Whispering Blues") 10-20 52
LPs: 10/12-inch
ARCHIVE OF FOLK MUSIC 10-15 68
ARHOOLIE 8-12 70
BLUES ON BLUE 10-15
BLUESWAY (6080 "Don't Your Plum Look Mellow Hanging on Your Tree") 8-10 74
DELMARK 20-35 60-62
EVEREST .... 8-10 '70s
FOLKWAYS 15-25 62-67
MILESTONE (3001 "Classic Delta Blues") 10-20 66
PRESTIGE 25-40 62
PRESTIGE BLUESVILLE (1067 "At Folk City") 15-25 63
PRESTIGE BLUESVILLE (1083 "Studio Blues") 15-25 64
STORYVILLE 5-8 82
TESTAMENT 15-25 64
WORLD PACIFIC 10-15 69
Also see McCOY, Rube
Also see THREE KINGS & A QUEEN
Also see WILLIAMS, Joe (Joe Lee Williams)
Also see WILLIAMSON, Sonny Boy, & Big Joe Williams

WILLIAMS, Big Joe, & J.D. Short
LPs: 10/12-inch
DELMARK (609 "Stavin' Chain Blues") 10-20 66

WILLIAMS, Big Joe, & Sonny Boy Williamson
LPs: 10/12-inch
BLUES CLASSICS (21 "Big Joe Williams & Sonny Boy Williamson") .... 15-25 '60s
Also see WILLIAMSON, Sonny Boy

WILLIAMS, Big Joe, & Johnny Young
LPs: 10/12-inch
DELMARK 15-25 62
Also see YOUNG, Johnny

WILLIAMS, Big Joe, & Short Stuff Macon
LPs: 10/12-inch
FOLKWAYS 15-25 62-67
Also see MR. SHORT STUFF
Also see MR. SHORT STUFF & BIG JOE WILLIAMS
Also see WILLIAMS, Big Joe

WILLIAMS, Billy *P&R '47*
(Billy Williams Quartet)
Singles: 78 rpm
CORAL 8-12 54-56
MGM 10-15 50-52
MERCURY 10-15 52-56
RCA 10-15 47
Singles: 7-inch
CORAL (61212 thru 61751) 20-30 54-56
CORAL (61795 thru 62069) 15-25 57-59
CORAL (62101 "Red Hot Love") 25-50 59
CORAL (62140 thru 65500 series) 8-12 59-64
MCA .... 4-6 '70s
MGM (10000 & 11000 series) 20-40 50-52
MGM (12000 series) 10-15 57
MERCURY 20-30 52-57
EPs: 7-inch
CORAL 15-25 57
MGM 15-25 57
MERCURY 15-25 53-55
LPs: 10/12-inch
CORAL (57184 "Billy Williams") 35-45 57
CORAL (57251 "Half Sweet Half Beat") ... 30-40 59
CORAL (57343 "Billy Williams Revue") 30-40 60
MGM (3400 "Billy Williams Quartet") 35-45 57
MERCURY (20317 "Oh Yeah!") 35-45 58
WING (12131 "Vote for Billy Williams") 30-40 59
Members: Billy Williams; Claude Riddick; John Ball; Eugene Dixon.
Also see CHARIOTEERS

WILLIAMS, Billy, & Westerners
LPs: 10/12-inch
CROWN ("Your Cheatin' Heart") 5-10 65
(Selection number not known.)

WILLIAMS, Billy Dee
LPs: 10/12-inch
PRESTIGE (30001 "Let's Misbehave") 20-30 61

WILLIAMS, Blind Boy
(With His Blues Band; Brownie McGhee)
Singles: 78 rpm
SITTIN' IN WITH (538 "Just Drifting") 15-25 48
Also see McGHEE, Brownie

WILLIAMS, Bob

Singles: 78 rpm

VITA....................10-15 56

Singles: 7-inch

VITA (129 "Women Are So Much Smarter")....................20-30 56
VITA (142 "You")....................20-30 56

WILLIAMS, Bob
(With the Cyclones)

Singles: 7-inch

DEBONAIR (161 "My Goose Is Cooked")....................15-25
LEDO (1680 "My Goose Is Cooked")....... 25-35 60
SPIN (989 "Hot Rod Race")....................15-25 60
TROPHY (503 "You Can't Make Me Cry")....................30-40 58

WILLIAMS, Bobby
(With the Nightliters)

Singles: 78 rpm

BLEND (109 "I'll Never Change").............15-25 55

Singles: 7-inch

BLEND (109 "I'll Never Change")............40-60 55
CANDIX (323 "Wonder If My Baby's Coming Home")....................8-12 61
CORT (1314 "If Dreams Could Come True")....................40-50 58
CORT (1315 "Lost My Job")....................25-35 59
DECK (142 "Chapel of Love")....................40-50 59
SWINGIN' (619 "So Many Women")........25-35 59

WILLIAMS, Bobby R&B '76
(Bobby Williams Group)

Singles: 7-inch

CAPITOL....................5-10 68
LU PINE (111 "Tell It to My Face")..............8-12 63
ROCK 'N' ROLL....................4-6 76
SEVEN B (7018 "Boogaloo Mardi Gras")...8-12 '60s
SURE SHOT (5003 "Try Love")..............10-20 64
SURE SHOT (5005 "Keep on Loving Me")....................10-20 65
SURE SHOT (5013 "When You Play").... 10-20 65
SURE SHOT (5016 "The Last Time")...... 10-20 66
SURE SHOT (5025 "Try It Again")........... 10-20 66
SURE SHOT (5031 "I'll Hate Myself Tomorrow")....................25-50 67

WILLIAMS, Bobby, & Mystics

Singles: 7-inch

MGM (13828 "Seven Letters")....................5-10 67

WILLIAMS, Bobby, & Royal Flairs

Singles: 7-inch

SAM (119 "Let's Go")....................20-30 63

WILLIAMS, Brock

Singles: 7-inch

TOPPA (1001 "What Am I")................. 100-200

WILLIAMS, Buddy

Singles: 7-inch

CADETTE (8008 "Marry Him")................. 15-25 63
VITA (161 "Cry Angel")....................10-15 57

WILLIAMS, Buzz

EPs: 7-inch

WORTHMORE (185 "Buzz Williams")... 75-125

WILLIAMS, Calvin

Singles: 7-inch

ATCO (6399 "It Won't Matter At All")..........5-10 66

WILLIAMS, Candy

Singles: 7-inch

REQUEST (3012 "Last Night")....................8-12 62

WILLIAMS, Carol

Singles: 7-inch

RAM (101 "Just for Awhile")....................15-25

WILLIAMS, Cee Vee

Singles: 7-inch

CARROLLTON (800 "Lonely Street").. 150-250

WILLIAMS, Charles
(With Paul Gayten Orchestra)

Singles: 78 rpm

CHECKER....................10-15 57

Singles: 7-inch

CHECKER (831 "So Glad She's Mine")... 15-25 56
CHECKER (866 "Darling")....................15-25 57
(Checkerboard top label.)
Also see GAYTEN, Paul

WILLIAMS, Cheryl

Singles: 7-inch

MAXX (328 "Love Me")....................10-15 64

WILLIAMS, Chickie

Singles: 7-inch

WHEELING (1019 "Storm")....................8-12 '50s

WILLIAMS, Clarence

Singles: 7-inch

ACCENT (1280 "Sandy")....................4-8 70
CHANCELLOR (1118 "Love Me").............15-25 62
KIM (526/527 "Every Lover Has a Heartache"/"Let's Make Up")....................15-25
THRONE (318 "Love Me")....................40-50 62
THRONE (803 "Seventh Son")....................5-10 63
TINA (101 "I Know It's True")....................10-20 64

LPs: 10/12-inch

ACCENT (5057 "Magic Crystal Ball")..........8-12 70

WILLIAMS, Clyde

Singles: 7-inch

STEPHENY (1814 "Little Bit Forgetful")...10-15 58

WILLIAMS, Colly

Singles: 7-inch

POPLAR (118 "We'll Make It Someday").15-20 58
RY-AN (501 "You Know I'll Love You Tomorrow")....................10-15 61

WILLIAMS, Cootie R&B/C&W '44
(With Eddie "Cleanhead" Vinson)

Singles: 78 rpm

CAPITOL....................10-20 46
DERBY....................20-30 51
HIT....................20-30 44-45
MERCURY....................10-20 49

Singles: 7-inch

DERBY (756 "Shotgun Boogie").............50-100 51
RCA (6899 "Rinky Dink")....................20-30 57
RCA (7012 "Block Rock")....................20-30 57
WARWICK (580 "When the Saints Go Marching In")....................10-15 60

LPs: 10/12-inch

MOODSVILLE (27 "Solid Trumpet")..........20-30 62
(Monaural.)
MOODSVILLE (27-SD "Solid Trumpet")...25-35 62
(Stereo.)
RCA (1718 "In Hi-Fi")....................40-60 58
WARWICK (2027 "Do Nothing Till You Hear from Me")....................40-60 59

WILLIAMS, Cootie, & Wini Brown

Singles: 7-inch

JARO (77018 "Gone Again")....................10-15 60

LPs: 10/12-inch

JARO (5001 "Around Midnight")..............40-60 60
Also see BROWN, Wini
Also see VINSON, Eddie

WILLIAMS, Cootie / Jimmy Preston

LP: 10/12-inch

ALLEGRO (4109 "Rock 'N' Roll")..............15-25
Also see PRESTON, Jimmy
Also see WILLIAMS, Cootie

WILLIAMS, Cora, & Four Jacks / Shirley Haven & Four Jacks

Singles: 78 rpm

FEDERAL....................100-200 52

Singles: 7-inch

FEDERAL (12079 "I Ain't Coming Back Anymore")....................500-1000 52
Also see FOUR JACKS
Also see HAVEN, Shirley, & Four Jacks

WILLIAMS, Curley

Singles: 78 rpm

MODERN (1004 "This Heart of Mine")........8-12 56

Singles: 7-inch

CIRCLE G ("Movin' in a Little Closer")....75-125
(Selection number not known.)
MODERN (1004 "This Heart of Mine")......20-30 56

WILLIAMS, Curtis E.

Singles: 7-inch

SKYWAY (122 "Hula Hula Rock")..............8-12 59

WILLIAMS, Cynthia

Singles: 7-inch

ABCO (1002 "Anytime")....................5-10 65

WILLIAMS, Dan, & Freelancers

Singles: 7-inch

BETH (20 "High School Flame")..............40-50
(Also issued as by the Freelancers.)
Also see FREELANCERS

WILLIAMS, Danny P&R/R&B/LP '64
(With Russ Black Orchestra; with Don Costa & Orchestra)

Singles: 7-inch

DAWILLA (101 "My Little Black Book")....10-15 64
(Previously issued as by Alton Albright.)
PILOT (401 "Tennessee Rose")..............10-15 62
U.A. (348 "Lonely")....................8-12 61
U.A. (411 "Jeannie")....................8-12 62
U.A. (480 "Something's Gotta Give")..........8-12 62
U.A. (493 "Tears")....................8-12 62
U.A. (601 "More")....................8-12 63
U.A. (685 "White on White")....................5-10 63
U.A. (729 "Little Toy Balloon")....................5-10 64
U.A. (762 "Forget Her, Forget Her")...........5-10 64
U.A. (825 "How Soon")....................5-10 65
U.A. (860 "Masquerade")....................5-10 65
U.A. (959 "Stranger")....................5-10 65
U.A. (50020 "Blue on White")....................5-10 66

LPs: 10/12-inch

U.A. (3297 "Exciting")....................20-25 63
(Monaural.)
U.A. (3359 "White on White")....................20-25 64
(Monaural.)
U.A. (3380 "With You in Mind")................20-25 64
(Monaural.)
U.A. (3493 "Magic Town")....................20-25 66
(Monaural.)
U.A. (6297 "Exciting")....................20-30 63
(Stereo.)
U.A. (6359 "White on White")....................20-30 64
(Stereo.)
U.A. (6380 "With You in Mind")................20-30 64
(Stereo.)
U.A. (6493 "Magic Town")....................20-30 66
(Stereo.)
Also see ALBRIGHT, Alton
Also see COSTA, Don, Orchestra
Also see WILLIAMS BROTHERS

WILLIAMS, Dee, Sextet R&B '49

Singles: 78 rpm

SAVOY....................15-25 49

WILLIAMS, Deniece P&R/R&B '76

Singles: 12-inch

COLUMBIA....................4-8 77-86

Singles: 7-inch

ARC....................3-6 79-82
COLUMBIA....................3-6 76-88
TODDLIN' TOWN....................5-10 '60s

Picture Sleeves

COLUMBIA....................3-5 84-88

LPs: 10/12-inch

ARC (Except 1432)....................5-10 79-82
ARC (1432 "Niecy")....................20-25 82
(Picture disc. Promotional issue only.)
COLUMBIA....................5-10 76-88
Also see MATHIS, Johnny, & Deniece Williams
Also see WONDER, Stevie

WILLIAMS, Des, & Red Coats

Singles: 7-inch

KING (5248 "Roll Me Over Rock")..............8-12 59

WILLIAMS, Dick, Kids

Singles: 7-inch

ARGO (5491 "My Blue Heaven")................5-10 65

WILLIAMS, Dickie
(Dick Williams)

Singles: 78 rpm

RCA....................5-15 56

Singles: 7-inch

AURORA (1803 "Does It Show")................5-10 63
OLD TOWN (102 "Born to Sing")..................4-8 73
PLEDGE (108 "Heartache Hill")..................5-10 63
RCA (6384 "If This Is Sin")....................15-20 56
RCA (6523 "Rock Hearted Mama")..........15-20 56
RCA (6599 "A Fool for You")....................15-20 56
VIN (1021 "Tee-Na-Na")....................10-15 60

WILLIAMS, Dicky

Singles: 7-inch

ACE (3007 "Two Women")....................4-6 74
BAD (1003 "In the Same Motel")..................4-8

LPs: 10/12-inch

BAD (30002 "Red Negligee, White Whiskey & Blue Lights")....................10-20

WILLIAMS, Doc & Cy
(With the Border Riders)

Singles: 78 rpm

WHEELING (1002 "Silver Bell")..................8-10 50

Singles: 7-inch

WHEELING (1002 "Silver Bell")................15-25 50

WILLIAMS, Don C&W '72

Singles: 7-inch

ABC....................4-6 75-78
ABC/DOT....................4-6 74-77
CAPITOL....................3-5 86
DOT....................4-6 74
JMI....................4-8 72-74
MCA (Except 1763)....................3-6 79-85
MCA (1763 "Special Message from Don Williams for Your Radio Station")....................4-8 82
(Promotional issue only.)

LPs: 10/12-inch

ABC (Except 28 & 44)....................5-10 77-78
ABC (28 "Don Williams")....................10-15 77
(Promotional issue only.)
ABC/DOT....................8-10 74-77
CAPITOL....................5-8 86
JMI....................15-20 73-74
K-TEL....................5-8 78
MCA (Except 44)....................5-10 75-85
MCA (44 "Expressions")....................15-20 78
(Picture disc. Promotional issue only.)
Also see HARRIS, Emmylou, & Don Williams
Also see POZO SECO SINGERS

WILLIAMS, Donn

Singles: 7-inch

ROOKIE (101 "We Two Rock")............350-450

WILLIAMS, Donnie, & Bluenotes

Singles: 7-inch

VIKING (1005 "Cry Your Heart Out").......10-15 60

WILLIAMS, Dootsie, & His Orchestra

Singles: 78 rpm

COAST....................15-25 48
DOOTONE....................10-20 52-54
Also see PENGUINS
Also see TURNER, Joe

WILLIAMS, Dorothy

Singles: 7-inch

GOLDWAX (115 "Country Style")...............8-12 65
VOLT (118 "Closer to My Baby")................8-12 64

WILLIAMS, Doug, & Mell-O-Tones

Singles: 7-inch

HY-TONE (103 "Sorrow Valley")............75-125 58
HY-TONE (122 "Sorrow Valley")..............40-50 59
HY-TONE (125 "Send Me")....................40-50 59

WILLIAMS, Earl

Singles: 7-inch

ABC-PAR (9843 "Someday Sweetheart")....................15-25 57
ACE (573 "I Believe")....................10-20 59

WILLIAMS, Eddie R&B '49
(With His Brown Buddies)

Singles: 78 rpm

CRYSTAL....................15-25 50
DISCOVERY....................15-25 50
SELECTIVE....................15-25 50
SUPREME....................15-25 49
SWING TIME....................15-25 49
Also see DIXON, Floyd
Also see MOORE, Johnny

WILLIAMS, Eddie

Singles: 7-inch

BARONET (4 "Just One More")................15-25 62
CORSAIR (402 "Tears Had Fallen")..........15-25 64
DOT (16149 "Peace of Mind")..................10-20 60
EXCELLO (2158 "You Broke Your Vows")....................15-25 59
EXCELLO (2180 "It's Too Late Baby")......15-25 60
R-DELL (114 "Just One More")...............30-40 58
ROULETTE (4237 "Sad and Lonely").......10-20 60

WILLIAMS, Eddie, & Sheiks

Singles: 7-inch

CORONADO (112 "I Just Can't Help Myself")....................15-25 '60s

WILLIAMS, Eddy

Singles: 7-inch

ALCOR (2013 "Have a Heart") ... 20-30 63

WILLIAMS, Elly

Singles: 78 rpm

RAINBOW ... 5-10 54

Singles: 7-inch

RAINBOW (253 "Worry, Worry, Worry") .. 20-30 54
(Red vinyl.)

WILLIAMS, Ernie

Singles: 7-inch

SATURN (4237 "Hot Skillet Mama") 100-200

WILLIAMS, Esther *R&B '76*

Singles: 7-inch

FRIENDS & CO. ... 4-6 76-78
KENT (438 "This Life of Mine") ... 5-10 65

WILLIAMS, Fletcher

Singles: 7-inch

BULLSEYE (1001 "Mary Lou") ... 15-25 57

WILLIAMS, Floyd
(With His Alto Sax & His Band)

Singles: 78 rpm

RAINBOW (301 "Jambo Jump") ... 5-10 52

Singles: 7-inch

RAINBOW (301 "Jambo Jump") ... 15-25 52

WILLIAMS, Floyd (Horsecollar)

Singles: 7-inch

THAT'S IT (226 "Thru-Way") ... 25-35

WILLIAMS, Freddie

Singles: 7-inch

BARONET (9 "Can't You See") ... 15-25 62
HOLLYWOOD (1114 "Name in Lights") .. 10-20 67
HOLLYWOOD (1121 "Heart Can You Hear Me") ... 25-50 67
HOLLYWOOD (1129 "Sea of Love") ... 10-20 68
TOP RANK (2083 "If You Love Me") ... 15-25 60

WILLIAMS, Garrett

Singles: 7-inch

AIRWAY (104 "Little Darling") ... 100-150 58
AIRWAY (106 "Linda") ... 100-150 58
JEANNIE (101 "Motorcycle Millie") ... 100-150

WILLIAMS, Hank *C&W '47*
(With the Drifting Cowboys; Hank Williams as Luke the Drifter; with Audrey Williams)

Singles: 78 rpm

MGM ... 20-30 47-55
STERLING (201 "Calling You") ... 300-400 47
STERLING (204 "Wealth Won't Save Your Soul") ... 250-300 47
STERLING (208 "I Don't Care") ... 200-250 47
STERLING (210 "Honky Tonkin'") ... 200-250 47

Singles: 7-inch

MGM (100 series) ... 5-8 63
(Golden Hits reissue series.)
MGM (168 "Moanin' the Blues") ... 40-60 52
(Boxed, four-disc set.)
MGM (10000 & 11000 series) ... 10-20 50-55
MGM (12000 series) ... 5-15 55-59
MGM (13000 series) ... 4-6 64-67

EPs: 7-inch

ARHOOLIE ... 4-6 83
(Not issued with cover.)
MGM (100 & 200 series) ... 25-50 52-54
MGM (1000 thru 1600 series) ... 15-30 55-60

LPs: 10/12-inch

ACM ... 5-10 83
BLAINE HOUSE ... 15-20 72
BOLL WEEVIL ... 8-12 76
CMF ... 5-10
CANDLELITE ("Golden Dream of Hank Williams") ... 15-20 '70s
(Boxed, three-disc set.)
CANDLELITE ("1951-52: Golden Dream of Hank Williams") ... 8-12 76
COLUMBIA (5616 "Hank Williams Treasury") ... 35-45 '60s
(Boxed, four-disc set. Columbia House Record Club issue.)
GOLDEN COUNTRY ... 5-8 82
JAMBALAYA ... 5-10
MGM (2 "36 of Hank Williams' Greatest Hits") ... 80-100 57
(Three discs.)
MGM (4 "36 More of Hank Williams' Greatest Hits") ... 80-100 58
(Three discs.)
MGM (107 "Hank Williams Sings") ... 50-100 51
(10-inch LP.)
MGM (168 "Moanin' the Blues") ... 50-100 52
(10-inch LP.)
MGM (202 "Memorial Album") ... 50-100 53
(10-inch LP.)
MGM (203 "Hank Williams As Luke the Drifter") ... 50-100 53
(10-inch LP.)
MGM (240-2 "24 Karat Hits, Hank Williams") ... 15-20 68
MGM (242 "Honky Tonkin'") ... 50-100 54
(10-inch LP.)
MGM (243 "I Saw the Light") ... 50-100 55
(10-inch LP.)
MGM (291 "Ramblin' Man") ... 50-100 54
(10-inch LP.)
MGM (912 "Hank Williams . . . Reflections By Those Who Loved Him") ... 100-200 75
(Boxed, three-disc set. Promotional issue only. Includes guest speakers: Roy Acuff, Little Jimmy Dickens, Lefty Frizzell, Pee Wee King, George Morgan, Bill Monroe, Minnie Pearl, Wesley Rose, Ernest Tubb, Grant Turner, Audrey Williams, Faron Young, and Hank Williams Jr.)
MGM (1000 series) ... 8-10 76
(Special Products issue.)
MGM (3219 "Ramblin' Man") ... 50-75 55
(Blue "sketch" cover.)
MGM (3219 "Ramblin' Man") ... 25-45
(Yellow "suit" cover.)
MGM (3330 "Moanin' the Blues") ... 100-150 56
(Yellow label.)
MGM (E-3200 thru 3900 series) ... 25-50 55-61
(Monaural. Through 3733, first issues have a yellow label.)
MGM (SE-3200 thru 3900 series) ... 10-20 63-70
(Reprocessed stereo. Through 3733, first issues have a yellow label.)
MGM (4000 thru 4700 series, except 4267) ... 10-20 63-71
MGM (4267 "The Hank Williams Story") .. 50-75 66
(Boxed, four-disc set.)
MGM (4900 thru 5400 series) ... 5-10 75-77
METRO ... 10-15 65-67
POLYDOR ... 5-15 83-84
SUNRISE MEDIA ... 8-10 81
TIME-LIFE (Except LCW-01) ... 5-8 81-82
TIME-LIFE (LCW-01 "Hank Williams") ... 10-15 81
(Boxed, three-disc set.)
Also see PRESLEY, Elvis / Hank Williams

WILLIAMS, Hank / Roy Acuff

LPs: 10/12-inch

LAMB & LION ... 10-15
(Three discs. Two by Hank Williams, one by Roy Acuff.)
Also see ACUFF, Roy

WILLIAMS, Hank / Slim Whitman

LPs: 10/12-inch

SUNRISE MEDIA ... 8-10 81
Also see WHITMAN, Slim

WILLIAMS, Hank, & Hank Williams Jr. *LP '65*
(Hank Williams / Hank Williams Jr.; Hank Williams Jr. & Hank Williams Sr.)

Singles: 7-inch

W.B. ... 3-5 89

LPs: 10/12-inch

COLUMBIA HOUSE ("Hank's Place") ... 5-10 81
(One side by each artist. Bonus LP with boxed set below. Selection number not known.)
COLUMBIA HOUSE "Hank Williams / Hank Williams Jr.) ... 20-25 81
(Boxed, five-disc record club set. Selection number not known.)
MGM (4200 series) ... 15-25 65
MGM (4300 thru 4900 series) ... 10-15 66-74
Also see WILLIAMS, Hank
Also see WILLIAMS, Hank, Jr.

WILLIAMS, Hank, Jr. *C&W/P&R '64*
(With the Cheatin' Hearts; with Mike Curb Congregation; Luke the Drifter Jr.; with Bama Band)

Singles: 7-inch

CONSOL ... 10-20
(Promotional issue from Consolidation Coal.)
ELEKTRA/CURB ... 3-6 79-82
MGM (13000 series) ... 5-10 64-68
MGM (14000 series) ... 4-6 68-76
MGM GOLDEN CIRCLE ... 4-6 '70s
W.B./CURB (Except 8000 series) ... 3-5 82-88
W.B./CURB (8000 series) ... 4-6 77-78

Picture Sleeves

MGM (13000 series) ... 5-10 64-68

LPs: 10/12-inch

CURB ... 5-8 83-84
ELEKTRA ... 5-8 79-83
MGM (Except 5009) ... 10-20 64-76
MGM (5009 "Hank Williams Jr. and Friends") ... 25-50 75
POLYDOR ... 5-8
W.B. (Except 2092) ... 5-10 77-87
W.B. (2092 "Interview") ... 8-12 83
(Promotional issue only.)
W.B./CURB ... 5-8 85-91
Also see BOCEPHUS
Also see CASH, Johnny, & Hank Williams Jr.
Also see CHARLES, Ray, & Hank Williams Jr.
Also see CURB, Mike
Also see FRANCIS, Connie, & Hank Williams Jr.
Also see JENNINGS, Waylon, & Hank Williams Jr.
Also see JONES, George
Also see KILGORE, Merle
Also see WILLIAMS, Hank, & Hank Williams Jr.

WILLIAMS, Hank, Jr., & Lois Johnson *C&W '72*

Singles: 7-inch

MGM ... 4-6 70-72

LPs: 10/12-inch

MGM ... 6-12 70-72
Also see WILLIAMS, Hank, Jr.

WILLIAMS, Jeanette *R&B '69*

Singles: 7-inch

BACK BEAT ... 10-20 66-69

WILLIAMS, Jerry
(Jerry Williams, Jr.)

Singles: 7-inch

CALLA ... 10-20 66-67
COTILLION (44022 "Shipwrecked") ... 5-10 69
COTILLION (44039 "Come and Get It") ... 5-10 69
8730 RECORDS ... 5-10 67
LAURIE (3339 "Runaround Sue") ... 10-15 66
MUSICOR (1285 "Run Run Roadrunner" ... 5-10 68
V-TONE (501 "You Call it Love") ... 15-25 59
Also see LITTLE JERRY
Also see WILLIAMS, Little Jerry

WILLIAMS, Jerry

Singles: 7-inch

MOONGLOW (1001 "Twistin' Patricia") ... 8-12 63

WILLIAMS, Jerry, & Rockets

Singles: 7-inch

ROCKET (001 "Blueberry Lane") ... 15-25 62
Members: Jerry Van Dynhoven; Cliff Peranto; Larry Russell; Denny Noie; Bill Pable; Roger Loos; Donnie Van Dynhoven; Bob Timmers; Carol Van Dynhoven; Denny Hymmerman; Jerry Cole.

WILLIAMS, Jerry Lee

Singles: 7-inch

SOLID GOLD (778 "The Go-Tune") ... 15-20 59

WILLIAMS, Jim

Singles: 78 rpm

SUN (270 "Please Don't Cry Over Me") ... 10-20 57

Singles: 7-inch

SUN (270 "Please Don't Cry Over Me") ... 25-40 57

WILLIAMS, Jimmy

Singles: 7-inch

ABC (10471 "Half Man") ... 5-10 63
ACORN (754 "Hey Little Dreamboat") ... 50-75
ATLANTIC (2296 "I'm So Lost") ... 5-10 65
CUB (9031 "Keep Me with You") ... 10-20 59
CUB (9039 "C'mon Baby") ... 10-20 59
DON-EL (111 "Big Legged Woman") ... 50-75 61
DOT (16437 "Wishing Ring") ... 5-10 63
DRIFTER (101 "Teardrops and Memories") ... 75-125
DUB (2842 "You're Always Late") ... 50-75 58
DYNO VOICE (931 "Mushroom City") ... 5-10 69
HULL (765 "Smile") ... 5-10 64
LIMELIGHT (3038 "Mrs. Cherry") ... 5-10 64
NEIL (104 "I Knew") ... 15-25 57
ORBIT (9002 "You're the One") ... 15-25 58
ROULETTE (4303 "There Is No Doubt") .. 10-15 60

WILLIAMS, Jo Jo
(Joseph Williams)

Singles: 7-inch

ATOMIC-H (310 "Rock & Roll Boogie") ... 50-75 59
ATOMIC (917 "Afro Shake Dance") ... 5-10 72

WILLIAMS, Jody
(Joseph Leon Williams)

Singles: 7-inch

ARGO (5274 "You May") ... 15-25 57
NIKE ... 15-20 63
SMASH (1801 "Hideout") ... 10-15 63
YULANDO ... 10-20 62
Also see LITTLE PAPA JOE
Also see WILLIAMS, Sugar Boy

WILLIAMS, Joe
(Joe Lee Williams)

Singles: 78 rpm

BLUEBIRD ... 15-25 45
BULLET (337 "Jivin' Woman") ... 100-150 50
COLUMBIA ... 10-20 47-48
Also see WILLIAMS, Big Joe
Also see WILLIAMS, Po' Joe

WILLIAMS, Joe / James McCain

Singles: 78 rpm

CHICAGO (103 "Good Mr. Roosevelt") ... 50-75 45
Also see WILLIAMS, Joe (Joe Lee Williams)

WILLIAMS, Joe *R&B '52*
(Joseph Goreed)

Singles: 78 rpm

BLUE LAKE (102 "Tired of Moving") ... 50-75 53
CHECKER ... 15-25 52
ROULETTE ... 5-10 57
SAVOY ... 10-15 55
TRUMPET (150 "Delta Blues") ... 20-30 52
TRUMPET (171 Bad Heart Blues") ... 20-30 52

Singles: 7-inch

BLUE LAKE (102 "Tired of Moving") ... 150-300 53
CHECKER (762 "Every Day I Have the Blues") ... 25-50 52
RCA ... 5-10 62-66
ROULETTE ... 5-10 57-62
SAVOY ... 10-20 55
SOLID STATE ... 5-10 66
TEMPONIC ... 4-6 72

EPs: 7-inch

RCA (2762 "At Newport '63") ... 8-12 63
ROULETTE (310 "A Man Ain't Supposed to Cry") ... 10-15 57

LPs: 10/12-inch

RCA ... 10-15 63-65
REGENT (6002 "Everyday") ... 35-45 56
ROULETTE ... 15-30 58-64
SOLID STATE ... 10-15 66
Also see BASIE, Count
Also see WASHINGTON, Dinah / Joe Williams / Sarah Vaughan

WILLIAMS, Johnny
(John Lee Hooker)

Singles: 78 rpm

GOTHAM (509 "Questionnaire Blues") ... 15-25 52
GOTHAM (513 "Little Boy Blue") ... 15-25 53
PRIZE (704 "Miss Rosie Mae") ... 75-125 49
STAFF (710 "Wandering Blues") ... 50-75 50
STAFF (718 "Prison Bound") ... 50-75 50
SWING TIME (256 "Prison Bound") ... 15-25 50
Also see HOOKER, John Lee

WILLIAMS, Johnny
(Robert Warren)

Singles: 78 rpm

STAFF (717 "I Got Lucky") ... 50-100 50
SWING TIME (225 "I Got Lucky") ... 25-50 50
Also see WARREN, Baby Boy

WILLIAMS, Johnny

Singles: 7-inch

CY (001 "Don't Call for Me") ... 40-50 61
(First issued as by the Implacables.)
Also see IMPLACABLES

WILLIAMS, Johnny

Singles: 7-inch

KENT (400 "You've Got It") ... 5-10 64

WILLIAMS, Johnny *R&B/C&W '72*

Singles: 7-inch

BASHIE (100 "I Made a Mistake") ... 4-6 70
CINNAMON ... 4-6 74
CUB (9160 "I Got a Feeling") ... 5-10 68
EPIC (10845 "He Will Break Your Heart") ... 4-8 72

INT'L ARTISTS (103 "Honey Child")...........5-10 65
PHILA. INT'L (3502 "Love Don't Rub Off") ...4-6 71
PHILA. INT'L (3518 "Slow Motion")...............4-6 72
PHILA. INT'L (3530 "Put It in Motion") 4-6 73

WILLIAMS, Johnny, & Jokers
Singles: 7-inch
PIC-1 (105 "Won't You Forget") 10-15 65
PIC-1 (118 "Lonely Girl") 10-15 65
PIC-1 (122 "Last Letter")........................... 10-15 65

WILLIAMS, Johnny Lee
Singles: 7-inch
LOUIS (6801 "Teach Me How") 10-15 62

WILLIAMS, Juan
Singles: 7-inch
BLUE SOUL (101 "My Girl Has Gone")... 15-25

WILLIAMS, Juanita
Singles: 7-inch
GOLDEN WORLD (18 "Baby Boy") 10-20 64
WINGATE (008 "Some Things You Never Get Used To")... 10-20 65

WILLIAMS, Kae
Singles: 7-inch
KAISER (385 "Everybody's Blues") 15-25 58

WILLIAMS, Keith, & His Orchestra
Singles: 7-inch
COAST (714 "Jai Alai")................................ 10-15 58
EDISON INT'L (407 "Midnight Take Off") 10-15 59

WILLIAMS, Kel
Singles: 7-inch
JO-MAR (1001 "Jane")........................... 75-125

WILLIAMS, Ken
Singles: 7-inch
ARA (208 "Anytime You Want Me")............8-12 65
OKEH (7303 "Come Back")...................... 20-30 67
SARG (219 "Hey, Leroy")........................ 10-20 65

WILLIAMS, Ken / Dave Burgess / "Scat Man" Crothers / Johnny James
(With the Toppers; with Lew Raymond Orchestra)
EPs: 7-inch
TOPS (294 "4 Hits")................................ 15-25 56
(Not issued with cover.)
Also see BURGESS, Dave
Also see CROTHERS, Scatman

WILLIAMS, Kenny
Singles: 7-inch
BEN MORE (1001 "Old Fashioned Christmas") 10-20 73
CARLTON (578 "Sugar Lumps")............. 10-15 62

WILLIAMS, King
Singles: 7-inch
MGM (13259 "Patience Baby") 10-15 64

WILLIAMS, L.C. R&B '49
(With Conney's Combo)
Singles: 78 rpm
BAYOU (008 "Mean and Evil")................ 10-20 53
FREEDOM.. 10-20 49-50
GOLD STAR.. 10-20 48
IMPERIAL...8-15 52
JAX 10-20 52
MERCURY 8-15 52
SITTIN' IN WITH 10-20 52
Singles: 7-inch
BAYOU (008 "Mean and Evil").............. 50-100 53
Also see CONNEY'S COMBO
Also see LIGHTNIN' JR.
Also see McBOOKER, Connie
Also see WILLIAMS, Lightnin' Jr.

WILLIAMS, Larry P&R/R&B '57
(Larry Williams & His Band)
Singles: 78 rpm
SPECIALTY.. 20-40 57-58
Singles: 7-inch
CHESS 10-15 59-60
EL BAM (69 "Call On Me")..........................8-12 65
MERCURY (72147 "Woman")......................5-10 63
OKEH (7280 "I Am the One")......................5-10 67
OKEH (7294 "Just Because")......................5-10 67
SMASH (2035 "Call on Me")........................5-10 66
SPECIALTY (597 thru 658).................... 25-35 57-59
SPECIALTY (665 thru 682).................... 15-25 59-60
SPECIALTY (SPBX series)..................... 12-15 85
(Boxed set of six colored vinyl discs.)
VENTURE (627 "Wake Up")..........................5-10 68
Picture Sleeves
SPECIALTY (626 "Slow Down") 25-50 58
LPs: 10/12-inch
OKEH (12123 "Greatest Hits")..................10-15 67
SPECIALTY (2109 "Here's Larry Williams")..50-75 59
SPECIALTY (2109 "Here's Larry Williams")..8-10 86
(Has '80s information and copyright date on back cover.)
SPECIALTY (2158 "Unreleased Larry Williams")..8-10 86
SPECIALTY (2162 "Hocus Pocus")............8-10 86
Session: Art Neville; Rene Hall; Earl Palmer; Plas Johnson; Jewell Grant; Ted Brinson; Alvin Tyler; Roy Montrell.
Also see COOKE, Sam / Lloyd Price / Larry Williams / Little Richard
Also see JOHNSON, Plas
Also see NEVILLE, Art
Also see PALMER, Earl

WILLIAMS, Larry, & Johnny Watson P&R/R&B '67
Singles: 7-inch
BELL (813 "I Could Love You Baby") 5-10 69
OKEH (7274 "Mercy, Mercy, Mercy") 10-20 67
OKEH (7281 "Too Late") 10-20 67
OKEH (7300 "Nobody")..............................15-25 67
(With Kaleidoscope.)
LPs: 10/12-inch
OKEH (14122 "Two for the Price of One")...10-20 67
Also see KALEIDOSCOPE
Also see LARRY & JOHNNY
Also see WATSON, Johnny
Also see WILLIAMS, Larry

WILLIAMS, Lawton C&W '61
(With the Anita Kerr Singers)
Singles: 7-inch
ALLSTAR (7212 "Mama Doll")....................5-10 60
D (1120 "I Don't Care Who Knows")...........5-10 60
GROOVE (0011 "Carpetbaggers") 5-10 63
LE BILL (304 "Mama Doll") 5-10 60
MEGA (0035 "Asphalt Cowboy")..................4-6 71
MERCURY (71867 "Anywhere There's People")...8-12 61
RCA (7000 series) 5-10 58
RCA (8000 series) 5-10 64
LPs: 10/12-inch
MEGA...6-10 71
Also see KERR, Anita

WILLIAMS, Lee R&B '67
(With the Moonrays; with Cymbals; with Cupids; Lee "Shot" Williams)
Singles: 7-inch
BLACK CIRCLE..4-8
CARNIVAL 5-15 66-69
FEDERAL...10-15 63-64
GAMMA (101 "Love Now, Pay Later")......25-35
JEWEL (839 "Checking Out") 4-6 73
KING (5409 "I'm So in Love")................150-200 60
PM (101 "I Found a Love")...........................8-12
RAPDA...4-8
SHAMA (17393 "Get Some Order")............5-10 69
TALENT (1 "Shirley")...............................60-80 60
(Same number used on a Dreams release.)
TCHULA...4-8
TRUE...10-20
U.A. 4-8

WILLIAMS, Leon
Singles: 7-inch
JOSIE (868 "I Feel So Good").....................5-10 59

WILLIAMS, Lester
(With His Band)
Singles: 78 rpm
DUKE...15-20 54
IMPERIAL...15-25 56
MACY'S..10-20 49-50
SPECIALTY..25-50 52-53
Singles: 7-inch
DUKE (123 "Let's Do It")...........................20-30 54
DUKE (131 "Crazy 'Bout My Baby") 20-30 54
IMPERIAL (5402 "McDonald's Daughter") 25-40 56
SPECIALTY (422 "I Can't Lose with the Stuff I Use")..50-75 52
SPECIALTY (431 "Let Me Tell You a Thing Or Two")..75-100 52
SPECIALTY (437 "Sweet Lovin' Daddy")..75-100 52
SPECIALTY (450 "Brand New Baby")......50-75 53

WILLIAMS, Lew
Singles: 78 rpm
IMPERIAL 50-75 56
Singles: 7-inch
IMPERIAL (5394 "Cat Talk").....................75-100 56
IMPERIAL (5411 "Bop Bop Ba Doo Bop")..75-100 56
IMPERIAL (5429 "Centipede")..................75-100 57
IMPERIAL (8306 "I'll Play Your Game") .75-100 56

WILLIAMS, Lightnin', Jr.
(L.C. Williams)
Singles: 78 rpm
GOLD STAR...20-30 48
Also see WILLIAMS, L.C.

WILLIAMS, Little Cheryl
Singles: 7-inch
ELMAR (1085 "Jim")...................................20-30 62
(First issue.)
KAPP (500 "Jim").......................................10-15 62
Also see LITTLE CHERYL

WILLIAMS, Little Jerry
Singles: 7-inch
ACADEMY (113 "Hum-Baby") 40-60 65
CALLA...10-20 65-66
COTILLION 5-10 69
LOMA (2005 "I'm the Lover Man")...........10-15 64
SOUTHERN SOUND 10-20 64-65
Also see WILLIAMS, Jerry

WILLIAMS, Lonnie
Singles: 78 rpm
SITTIN' IN WITH (567 "Tears in My Heart")..15-25 50
SITTIN' IN WITH (593 "Wavin' Sea Blues") 15-25 51

WILLIAMS, Marie
Singles: 7-inch
SMART (324 "Cat Scratching")................40-60 61
Session: Mandells.
Also see MANDELLS

WILLIAMS, Mark, & Kingsmen
Singles: 7-inch
SHELBY (2 "Honey Honey") ....10-20 '60s

WILLIAMS, Mary Lou, Trio
Singles: 7-inch
SUE "715 "Chunk A Lunk") 8-12 59
SUE "724 "Night and Day")..........................8-12 60

WILLIAMS, Mason P&R/LP '68
Singles: 7-inch
W.B. 4-6 68-71
LPs: 10/12-inch
EVEREST..6-12 69
FLYING FISH 5-10 78
VEE-JAY 10-20 64
W.B. 6-12 68-71

WILLIAMS, Mason / Smothers Brothers
EPs: 7-inch
W.B./7 ARTS (283 "Scope Box") 20-40 70
(Promotional issue only.)
Also see SMOTHERS BROTHERS
Also see WILLIAMS, Mason

WILLIAMS, Maurice P&R/R&B '60
(With the Zodiacs; with Inspirations; Zodiacs)
Singles: 7-inch
ATLANTIC (2199 "Loneliness") 8-12 63
ATLANTIC (2741 "Sweetness")....................4-6 70
CANDI (1031 "Never Leave You Again") .10-20 63
COLLECTABLES..3-5 '80s
DEE-SU (304 "May I")..................................5-10 65
DEE-SU (307 "Ooo Poo Pa Doo") 5-10 65
DEE-SU (309 "Surely")...............................5-10 66
DEE-SU (311 "Don't Be Half Safe")............5-10 66
DEE-SU (318 "Stay – Live Version") 5-10 67
ERIC...4-6 '70s
FLASHBACK (7 "Stay")................................4-8 65
440/PLUS (4401 "I'd Rather Have a Memory Than a Dream") 8-10 70
HERALD (552 "Stay")...............................15-25 60
HERALD (556 "I Remember")....................10-20 60
HERALD (559 "Come Along")....................10-20 61
HERALD (563 "Someday") 10-15 61
HERALD (565 "Please")............................10-15 61
HERALD (572 "It's Alright")......................10-15 62
SCEPTER (12113 "I Know") 8-10 65
SEA HORN (503 "Return") 8-10 64
SEASIDE (115 "Shaking and Breaking") ...5-10
SELWYN (5121 "College Girl")................15-25 59
SOULTOWN (503 "May I") ....8-12 '60s
SPHERE SOUND (707 "So Fine") 10-15 65
VEE-JAY (678 "May I")..............................10-20 65
VEEP (1294 "The Four Corners")................5-10 68
LPs: 10/12-inch
COLLECTABLES 6-8 84
HERALD (1014 "Stay") 75-125 61
LOST NITE ("Maurice Williams and the Zodiacs")..10-20 81
(10-inch LP. Red vinyl. 1000 made.)
RELIC..10-15
SNYDER..25-30
SPHERE SOUND.......................................15-25 66
Also see GLADIOLAS
Also see ZODIACS

WILLIAMS, Max
Singles: 7-inch
LOGAN (3105 "Hey Mr. Moon")...........100-150

WILLIAMS, Mel
(With the Montclairs; with Gerald Wilson Orchestra)
Singles: 78 rpm
DECCA..10-15 55
DIG...10-15 56-57
FEDERAL 20-30 55-56
RAGE..50-75 54
Singles: 7-inch
BIT (4164 "Secret Love") 8-12 64
DECCA (29370 "Lessons in Love").........25-35 55
DECCA (29499 "Eternal Love")................25-35 55
DECCA (29554 "God Gave Me You") 25-35 55
DIG (107 "Talk to Me") 20-30 56
DIG (114 "Here in My Heart") 20-30 56
DIG (123 "My Love") 20-30 56
DIG (128 "All Through the Night") 20-30 57
DIG (136 "It's You")...................................20-30 57
DIG (140 "Stand There, Mountain")..........20-30 57
FEDERAL (12236 "Soldier Boy")...............50-75 55
FEDERAL (12241 "Send Me a Picture Baby")..50-75 55
FEDERAL (12245 "Come Early, Stay Late") 50-75 56
MODERN (1023 "Jet Set").........................10-20 66
RAGE (101 "Fools Fall in Love") 150-200 54
(Also issued as by the Capris.)
TASTY HASTY (4 "Fattenin' Frogs") 10-20
LPs: 10/12-inch
DIG (103 "All Through the Night") 100-200 56
Also see BARONS / Mel Williams & Montclairs
Also see OTIS, Johnny

WILLIAMS, Mike P&R/R&B '66
Singles: 7-inch
ATLANTIC...5-10 65-66
KING..5-10 66
Also see TEMPESTS

WILLIAMS, Morry, & Kids
Singles: 7-inch
CARLTON (477 "Oh Louise") 20-30 58
FIREFLY (319 "Time Runs Out")................4-6 74
(Black vinyl.)
FIREFLY (319 "Time Runs Out")................5-10 74
(Red vinyl.)
LUCK (102 "Time Runs Out")...............250-300 59
(Maroon label.)
LUCK (102 "Time Runs Out") 100-150 59
(Yellow label.)
TEE VEE (301 "Oh Louise") 150-200 58

WILLIAMS, Nat, & Mello-Tones
Singles: 7-inch
ARIES (1014 "You Excite Me")..................25-35 59

WILLIAMS, Nate
(With Gene Miller's Ink Spots)
Singles: 7-inch
BACK BEAT (536 "Smile").........................5-10 62
C/M (4523 "For the Good Times")...............4-6

WILLIAMS, Otis C&W '71
(With the Midnight Cowboys)
Singles: 7-inch
SCEPTER (12376 "When You Turn On the Love") 4-6 73
STOP (388 "I Wanna Go Country")..............4-6 71

LPs: 10/12-inch
STOP (1022 "Otis Williams & the Midnight Cowboys") 10-15 71
Note: These are country music releases. Solo R&B Deluxe releases credited either to "Otis Williams," or "Otis Williams & His New Group," are in the "Charms" section.
Also see CHARMS

WILLIAMS, Paul — R&B '48
(With His Orchestra)
Singles: 78 rpm
CAPITOL 5-10 55
CLEF 5-10 52
GROOVE 5-10 54
JOSIE 5-10 56
MERCURY 5-10
RAMA 20-30 55
SAVOY 5-10 48-57
Singles: 7-inch
ASCOT (2114 "I Can't Stand It") 8-12 62
ASCOT (2127 "Poor Paul") 8-12 63
CAPITOL (3205 "Rock It Davy Crockett") 15-25 55
CAPITOL (3255 "It's Over") 15-25 55
GROOVE (0014 "Women Are the Root of All Evil") 15-25 54
("Vocal refrain by Jimmy Brown.")
JAX (313 "Thin Man") 50-75 54
(Red vinyl.)
JOSIE (806 "Once Upon a Time") 15-25 56
RAMA (167 "Ring-A-Ling") 50-75 55
(Vocalist, though not credited, is believed to be Little Willie John.)
SAVOY 10-30 51-59
7 ARTS (713 "Back to Back") 5-10 61
VEE-JAY (234 "Give It Up") 10-20 57
VEE-JAY (268 "South Shore Drive") 10-20 57
Also see COBB, Danny
Also see DALE, Larry
Also see JOHN, Little Willie
Also see McNEELY, Big Jay / Paul Williams
Also see McPHERSON, Wyatt "Earp," & Paul Williams
Also see MOORE, Bill
Also see WATTS, Noble

WILLIAMS, Po' Joe
(Joe Lee Williams)
Singles: 78 rpm
VEE-JAY 15-25 56
Singles: 7-inch
VEE-JAY (227 "Going Back Home") 30-50 56
Also see WILLIAMS, Joe (Joe Lee Williams)

WILLIAMS, Ray
Singles: 7-inch
ALA (1171 "Tell Me Now") 4-6
LE CAM (717 "I Want to Know") 20-30 61
SPACE (1011 "Hen and Rooster") 5-10 67

WILLIAMS, Richard
(With the Flame Tones)
Singles: 7-inch
BELL (45192 "Oldies but Goodies") 10-15 72
FORWARD 5-10 69
QUAD 4-6 70

WILLIAMS, Robert
Singles: 7-inch
TIP TOP (730 "Loud Mufflers") 15-25 59

WILLIAMS, Robert Pete
LPs: 10/12-inch
AHURA MAZDA 8-10 71
ARHOOLIE 8-10 71
FOLK-LYRIC .... 10-20 '60s
PRESTIGE BLUESVILLE (1026 "Free Again") 25-35 61
TAKOMA .... 10-15 '70s

WILLIAMS, Robert Pete, & Snooks Eaglin
LPs: 10/12-inch
FANTASY 8-12
Also see EAGLIN, Snooks
Also see WILLIAMS, Robert Pete

WILLIAMS, Roberta
Singles: 7-inch
UPTOWN (707 "Maybe Tomorrow") 5-10 65

WILLIAMS, Roger — P&R '55
Singles: 78 rpm
KAPP 3-5 55-57
Singles: 7-inch
KAPP 4-8 55-72
MCA 4-6 73-78
W.B. 3-5 80
Picture Sleeves
KAPP 5-15 55-66
EPs: 7-inch
KAPP 4-8 55-58
LPs: 10/12-inch
KAPP 5-20 55-72
MCA 4-8 73-83
PICKWICK 4-8
VOCALION 4-8 71

WILLIAMS, Roger, & Jane Morgan
Singles: 78 rpm
KAPP 3-5 56
Singles: 7-inch
KAPP 5-15 56
Also see MORGAN, Jane
Also see WILLIAMS, Roger

WILLIAMS, Ron
Singles: 7-inch
IMPERIAL (5729 "On Top of Old Smokey") 15-25 61
IMPERIAL (5800 "Don't You Tell Me Maybe") 20-30 61
MERCURY (72145 "Time") 5-10 63
PASTEL (504 "Angel Girl") 5-10 64
TY-TEX (100 "Sue Sue Baby") 100-150 60
TY-TEX (106 "Wine Wine Wine") 50-75 61

WILLIAMS, Roxie
(With Buddy Ray & Shamrocks; Roxy Williams)
Singles: 7-inch
LUCKY ELEVEN (005 "Let the Horses Run") 10-20
LUCKY ELEVEN (1112 "15 Seconds") ... 75-125 61

WILLIAMS, Sam
Singles: 7-inch
TOWER (367 "Let's Talk It Over") 40-60 67
UPTOWN (742 "Miracle Worker") 10-20 67

WILLIAMS, Sandy
Singles: 7-inch
FAYETTE (101767 "He Won't Forgive Me") 8-12
4 CORNERS (137 "Anyone in the World") 10-20 66
OLIVER (2005 "California") 8-12 66

WILLIAMS, Scotty
Singles: 7-inch
JUBILEE (5602 "In the Same Old Way") .. 10-20 67
MONA LEE .... 10-20 '60s

WILLIAMS, Sebastian
(With the Soul Men)
Singles: 7-inch
COTILLION 5-10 69
OVIDE (249 "Get Your Point Over") 10-15 68
SOUND OF SOUL (102 "Too Much") 50-75 65

WILLIAMS, Sherman
Singles: 78 rpm
BULLET (823 "Red Head Blues-My Flamin' Gal") 40-60 48
FLIP (316 "I Lost My Baby") 10-20 56
Singles: 7-inch
FLIP (316 "I Lost My Baby") 20-40 56
Also see FOUR FLAMES / Sherman Williams Orchestra

WILLIAMS, Shirley
Singles: 7-inch
IMPERIAL (5640 "Larry Be True") 10-15 60

WILLIAMS, Sibelius
Singles: 7-inch
FELSTED (8680 "My Love My Love") 8-12 63

WILLIAMS, Skeet
Singles: 7-inch
HACIENDA (0001 "Mary, Mary, Mary Jane") 150-250

WILLIAMS, Sonny
Singles: 7-inch
COIN (1502 "Lucky Linda") 40-60 59
COIN (1515 "All Because of You") 10-20 59

WILLIAMS, Sonny Boy — R&B '43
(Enoch Williams)
Singles: 78 rpm
DECCA (7800 series) .... 25-35 '30s
DECCA (8500 & 8600 series) 25-35 41-45

WILLIAMS, Sugar Boy
(Joseph Leon Williams)
Singles: 7-inch
HERALD (555 "Little Girl") 15-25 60
RAINES 10-20 65
Also see WILLIAMS, Jody

WILLIAMS, Sunny, Trio
(Enoch Williams)
Singles: 78 rpm
SUPER DISC 15-25 47-48

WILLIAMS, T.J., & Two Shades Of Soul
(Timothy "T.J." Williams & Two Shades Of Soul)
Singles: 7-inch
JOSIE (995 "My Life") 10-20 68
JOSIE (1000 "Baby I Need You") 15-25 68
Member: Timmy Williams.

WILLIAMS, Teddy
Singles: 78 rpm
FEDERAL 10-15 51
Singles: 7-inch
FEDERAL (12017 "If I Didn't Love You") .. 20-30 51
FEDERAL (12025 "Heading for the River") 20-30 51

WILLIAMS, Tex — C&W '46
(With His Western Caravan; with Spade Cooley; with California Express)
Singles: 78 rpm
CAPITOL 4-8 46-51
COLUMBIA 4-8 46
DECCA 4-8 53-55
Singles: 7-inch
BOONE 5-8 65-68
CAPITOL 8-12 51-60
DECCA 8-12 53-55
DOT 5-8 66
GARU 3-5 82
GRANITE 4-6 74
LIBERTY 5-10 63-65
MONUMENT 4-6 70-72
SHASTA 5-10 60-61
EPs: 7-inch
CAMDEN 8-12 58
CAPITOL 10-15 56-57
DECCA 10-15 55
LPs: 10/12-inch
BOONE (1210 "Two Sides Of") 10-15 66
CAMDEN (363 "Tex Williams' Best") 20-40 58
CAPITOL (1463 "Smoke! Smoke! Smoke!") 20-40 60
DECCA (4295 "Country Music Time") 15-25 62
DECCA (5565 "Dance-O-Rama") 40-60 55
(10-inch LP.)
GARU (101 "California Express") 5-10 81
GRANITE 6-12 74
IMPERIAL (9309 "Voice of Authority") 10-15 66
(Monaural.)
IMPERIAL (12309 "Voice of Authority") 15-20 66
(Stereo.)
LIBERTY 15-25 63
MONUMENT 8-12 71
SHASTA 8-12
SUNSET 10-15 66
Also see COOLEY, Spade, & His Orchestra
Also see STARR, Kay

WILLIAMS, Tim
LPs: 10/12-inch
EPIC (26472 "Blues Full Circle") 10-15 69

WILLIAMS, Timmy
Singles: 7-inch
MALA (515 "Competition") 150-250 65
Also see WILLIAMS, T.J., & Two Shades Of Soul

WILLIAMS, Tom B.
Singles: 7-inch
TOPIX (6009 "Wishing Well") 20-25 62

WILLIAMS, Tommy
(With the Fingerpoppers)
Singles: 7-inch
BACK BEAT (561 "Going Crazy") 5-10 66
FORTÉ (1415 "Here I Stand") 500-600 60
SUE (747 "I'll Follow You") 10-15 61
ULTRASONIC (111 "Strange Are the Ways of Love") 5-10 61
VICA (101 "Late, Late Last Night") 15-25 59

WILLIAMS, Toni
(Tawny Williams)
Singles: 7-inch
DELUXE (110 "Precious Minutes") 5-10 69
JET STREAM (729 "Cast the First Stone") 5-10 67
TUFF (1824 "Oh Baby") 25-35 62
TUFF (1836 "Pretty Little Words") 25-35 62

WILLIAMS, Tony
Singles: 7-inch
MERCURY 10-20 57-59
PHILIPS 5-10 62-63
REPRISE 10-15 61-62
LPs: 10/12-inch
MERCURY 20-30 59
PHILIPS 15-25 62
REPRISE 20-25 61
Also see PLATTERS

WILLIAMS, Tracey
Singles: 7-inch
DORE (676 "He Loves Me") 5-10 63

WILLIAMS, Troy
Singles: 7-inch
HI (2067 "Anna Baby") 10-15 63

WILLIAMS, Trudy
Singles: 7-inch
FLIP (340 "A Foolish Little Girl") 10-20 58
Also see ROSALLE & DONELL
Also see SIX TEENS

WILLIAMS, Tug
Singles: 78 rpm
TRUMPET (103 "Sweetheart, I Wouldn't Change a Thing") 20-30 50
TRUMPET (Except 103) 10-20 53-54
Singles: 7-inch
TRUMPET (192 "Bye and Bye") 15-25 53
TRUMPET (193 "One Sided Love") 15-25 53
TRUMPET (224 "I'm Building a Castle") .. 15-25 54
TRUMPET (225 "You're Messing with My Heart") 15-25 54

WILLIAMS, Verna
Singles: 7-inch
BELINDA (100 "Wrong Number Right Girl") 10-15 62
BELINDA (101 "I'll Wait") 10-15 62
VERSAILLES (865 "Mine All Mine") 50-75

WILLIAMS, W., & Tones
Singles: 7-inch
KENNEDY (5146 "A Star") 50-75

WILLIAMS, Wanda
Singles: 7-inch
FOREST GREEN ("It's All Over") 10-15 64
(No selection number used.)

WILLIAMS, Ward, & Kents
Singles: 7-inch
LAURIE (3221 "Written in the Sky") 5-10 64
LAURIE (3264 "Incessantly") 5-10 64

WILLIAMS, Wayne, & Sure Shots
(Gaylon Wayne)
Singles: 7-inch
SURE (1001 "Red Hot Mama") 1500-2000 57
Also see WAYNE, Gaylon

WILLIAMS, Willie
(W.W. Williams)
Singles: 7-inch
ABC 6-12 66-67
RCA 5-10 69
SUPREME (777 "38 Woman") 5-10
SUPREME (778 "Black Diamond Rattler"). 5-10
SUPREME (1001 "Wine Headed Woman") 5-10 73
LPs: 10/12-inch
SUPREME (1001 "Raw Unpolluted Soul") 10-15 73
Also see TAYLOR, Hound Dog

WILLIAMS BROTHERS
Singles: 7-inch
SWINGIN' (617 "Valerie") 8-12 59

WILLIAMS BROTHERS — C&W '63
Singles: 7-inch
DELMARK (1008 "Last Minute") 5-10 63
Members: Jimmy Williams; Bobby Williams.

WILLIAMS BROTHERS

Singles: 7-inch

TREND (1017 "The First One")...8-10 66

Member: Danny Williams.

Also see WILLIAMS, Danny

WILLIAMS BROTHERS

Singles: 7-inch

DIXIE (873 "Whatcha Gonna Do Now")...75-125

WILLIAMSON, James, & His Trio

Singles: 78 rpm

CHANCE (1121 "Lonesome Ole Train")...150-250 52
CHANCE (1131 "Homesick")...150-250 53

Singles: 7-inch

CHANCE (1121 "Lonesome Ole Train")...1000-1500 52
CHANCE (1131 "Homesick")...1000-1500 53

Also see HOMESICK JAMES

WILLIAMSON, Joe

Singles: 7-inch

GNP (323 "Ninety-Nine Miles")...5-10 64

WILLIAMSON, Sonny Boy *R&B '47*

(John Lee Williamson)

Singles: 78 rpm

BLUEBIRD (0736 "Miss Stella Brown Blues")...25-50 45
BLUEBIRD (0744 "Elevator Woman")...25-50 46
RCA (0001 "Wonderful Time")...20-40 49
RCA (0021 "Little Girl")...20-40 49
RCA (0046 "Southern Dream")...20-40 49
RCA (1875 "Early in the Morning")...20-40 46
RCA (2056 "Mean Old Highway")...20-40 46
RCA (2184 "Hoodoo Hoodoo")...20-40 47
RCA (2521 "Polly Put Your Kettle On")...20-40 47
RCA (2369 "G, M & O Blues")...20-40 47
RCA (2623 "Sugar Gal")...20-40 47
RCA (2796 "I Have Got to Go")...20-40 48
RCA (2893 "Apple Tree Swing")...20-40 48
RCA (3047 "Stop Breaking Down")...20-40 48
RCA (3218 "The Big Boat")...20-40 48

Singles: 7-inch

RCA (50-0005 "Little Girl")...100-200 49
(Cherry red vinyl.)
RCA (50-0030 "Southern Dream")...100-200 49
(Cherry red vinyl.)

LPs: 10/12-inch

BLUES CLASSICS (3 "Blues Classics By Sonny Boy Williamson")...15-25 64
BLUES CLASSICS (9 "The Original Sonny Boy Williamson")...15-25 64
BLUES CLASSICS (20 "Blues Classics By Sonny Boy Williamson, Vol. 2")...15-25 64
BLUES CLASSICS (24 "Blues Classics By Sonny Boy Williamson, Vol. 3")...15-25 64

Session: Blind John Davis; Big Bill Broonzy; Al Elkins; Charles Sanders; Tampa Red; Judge Riley.

Also see WILLIAMS, Big Joe, & Sonny Boy Williamson

WILLIAMSON, Sonny Boy *R&B '55*

(Aleck "Rice" Miller; Aleck Ford)

Singles: 78 rpm

ACE...20-40 55
CHECKER (824 thru 883)...15-30 55-57
CHECKER (894 "Your Funeral & My Trial")...25-50 58
CHECKER (910 "Cross My Heart")...40-60 58
CHECKER (927 "Let Your Conscience Be Your Guide")...50-75 59
CHECKER (943 "The Goat")...50-75 60
RAM...15-20 54
TRUMPET...20-40 51-55

Singles: 7-inch

ACE (511 "Boppin' with Sonny")...50-100 55
CHECKER (824 "Don't Start Me Talkin'")...40-60 55
CHECKER (834 "Let Me Explain")...40-60 56
CHECKER (847 "Keep It to Yourself")...40-60 56
CHECKER (864 "I Don't Know")...40-60 57
CHECKER (883 "Your Funeral & My Trial")...40-60 57
CHECKER (894 "Wake Up Baby")...40-60 58
CHECKER (910 "Cross My Heart")...20-30 58
CHECKER (927 "Let Your Conscience Be Your Guide")...20-30 59
CHECKER (943 "The Goat")...20-30 60
CHECKER (956 "Lonesome Cabin")...20-30 60
CHECKER (963 "Trust Me Baby")...20-30 60
CHECKER (975 "Stop Right Now")...20-30 61
CHECKER (1003 "One Way Out")...20-30 62
CHECKER (1036 "Bye Bye Bird")...20-30 63
CHECKER (1065 "Trying to Get Back On My Feet")...20-30 63
CHECKER (1080 "My Younger Days")...10-20 64
CHECKER (1134 "Bring It On Home")...10-20 66
RAM (2501 "Mailman Mailman")...25-50 54
TRUMPET (129 "Eyesight to the Blind")...50-100 51
TRUMPET (139 "Do It if You Wanta")...50-100 51
TRUMPET (140 "Stop Crying")...50-100 51
TRUMPET (144 "I Cross My Heart")...50-100 52
TRUMPET (145 "Pontiac Blues")...50-100 52
TRUMPET (166 "Mighty Long Time")...50-100 52
TRUMPET (168 "Stop Now Baby")...50-100 52
TRUMPET (212 "Too Close Together")...50-75 53
TRUMPET (215 "She Brought Life Back to the Dead")...50-75 54
TRUMPET (216 "Red Hot Kisses")...50-75 54
TRUMPET (228 "Empty Bedroom")...50-75 54
TRUMPET (229 "No Nights By Myself")...50-75 54
TRUMPET (243 "She's Crazy")...50-75 55
TRUMPET (244 "Sonny's Rhythm")...50-75 55
TRUMPET (245 "Clowning with the World")...50-75 55

EPs: 7-inch

CHESS (1437 "Down and Out Blues)...75-125 60
(Stereo. Juke box issue only. Includes title strips.)

LPs: 10/12-inch

ARHOOLIE (2020 "King Biscuit Time")...8-12
CHESS (206 "Sonny Boy Williamson")...15-25 76
(Two discs.)
CHESS (417 "One Way Out")...10-12 74
CHESS (1437 "Down and Out Blues)...50-100 60
CHESS (1503 "Real Folk Blues")...10-20 66
CHESS (1509 "More Real Folk Blues")...10-20 66
CHESS (1536 "Bummer Road")...10-20 69
CHESS (9000 series)...5-10
CHESS (50027 "This Is My Story")...15-25 72
STORYVILLE (4016 "Portrait in Blues")...5-10 80

Session: Muddy Waters; Otis Spann; Jimmy Rogers; Fred Below; Willie Dixon.

Also see DIXON, Willie
Also see PAGE, Jimmy, & Sonny Boy Williamson
Also see ROGERS, Jimmy
Also see SPANN, Otis
Also see WATERS, Muddy
Also see YARDBIRDS

WILLIAMSON, Sonny Boy, & Memphis Slim

LPs: 10/12-inch

GNP (10003 "Sonny Boy Williamson and Memphis Slim in Paris")...8-12 74

Also see MEMPHIS SLIM
Also see WILLIAMSON, Sonny Boy

WILLIAMSON, Sonny Boy

Singles: 7-inch

RAM (2501 "Pretty Li'l Thing")...25-35 61

WILLIE & HANDJIVES

Singles: 7-inch

VEEP (1227 "Runnin' Girl")...15-25 66

WILLIE & JOKERS

Singles: 7-inch

VIKING (1007 "She Won't Hang Up")...10-15 60

WILLIE & RUTH

(Willy & Ruth)

Singles: 78 rpm

SPARK...15-35 54

Singles: 7-inch

SPARK (101 "Come a Little Bit Closer")...35-55 54
SPARK (105 "Love Me")...50-75 54

Member: Willie Egans.

Also see EGANS, Willie

WILLIE & TRAVELAIRES

Singles: 7-inch

MILKY WAY (007 "Firey Stomp")...75-100 66

WILLIE & WALKERS

Singles: 7-inch

U.A. (50249 "In My Room")...5-10 68

WILLIE & WEST

Singles: 7-inch

STANG (5001 "Watch Yourself")...5-10 69

LPs: 10/12-inch

STANG...8-12 71

WILLIE & WHEELS

Singles: 7-inch

DUNHILL (4002 "Skateboard Crazy")...10-15 65

Members: Phil Sloan; Steve Barri.

Also see FANTASTIC BAGGYS

WILLIE & ZERKONS

Singles: 7-inch

CUCA (1163 "Out of Here")...10-20 64

WILLIE B

Singles: 7-inch

HERMITAGE (806 "I Trusted in You")...5-10 63

WILLIE C.

(Willie Cobbs)

Singles: 7-inch

RULER...10-20 63

Also see COBBS, Willie

WILLIE G.

Singles: 7-inch

RIC-TIC (125 "Meet Me Halfway")...10-15 67

WILLIES

Singles: 7-inch

BLUE RIVER (211 "The Willy")...8-12 65
CO & CE (239 "The Willy")...5-10 66

WILLING, Foy, & His Riders Of The Purple Sage *C&W '44*

Singles: 78 rpm

CAPITOL...8-12 44-49
DECCA...8-12 45-46
MAJESTIC...8-12 46
VARSITY (45212 "Cool Water")...5-10 '50s

Singles: 7-inch

ROULETTE (4055 "Cowboy")...5-10 58
VARSITY (45212 "Cool Water")...10-15 '50s

LPs: 10/12-inch

ALLEGRO...5-8
BIG BOSS...8-10 77
CROWN...8-10 '60s
CUSTOM...8-10 '60s
JUBILEE...15-25 62
ROULETTE (25035 "Cowboy")...25-35 58
ROYALE (6032)...15-25
(10-inch LP.)

Session: Red River Dave.

WILLING, Foy, Eddie Dean & His Riders Of The Purple Sage

LPs: 10/12-inch

ROYALE (6987 "Foy Willing & Eddie Dean")...25-50 '50s

Also see DEAN, Eddie
Also see RIDERS OF THE PURPLE SAGE
Also see WILLING, Foy, & His Riders Of The Purple Sage

WILLING MIND

Singles: 7-inch

CUCA (6912 "Can I Get to Know You Better")...10-15 69

WILLIS, Allee

Singles

W.B. (20405 "Big Adventure")...50-100 85
(Pee Wee Herman-shaped picture disc.)

WILLIS, Bernice

Singles: 7-inch

OKEH (7335 "Confidence")...5-10 69

WILLIS, Betty

Singles: 7-inch

MOJO (102 "Gone with the Wind")...5-10 68
RENDEZVOUS (190 "Take Your Heart")...8-12 62

WILLIS, Bill

Singles: 7-inch

DIXIE (803 "Poor Man")...200-300
DIXIE (825 "Boogie Woogie All Night")...500-750
DIXIE (845 "Boogie Woogie on a Saturday Night")...50-100
ROCKET (1014 "Right Kind of Woman")...200-300

WILLIS, Chick

("The Stoop-Down Man;" Robert Willis)

Singles: 7-inch

ALTO (2009 "Twistin' on the Hospital Ward")...10-15 62
BARCLAY & THE III (9747 "The Way You're Stooping Down Baby – I Can Deal with That")...10-15
LA VAL (865 "Things I Used to Do")...8-12 64
LA VAL (871 "Stoop Down Baby")...4-6 71
LA VAL (874 "Stoop Down Shuffle")...4-6 74
STOOP DOWN (0011 "I Hear You Knocking")...8-12 '60s
STOOP DOWN (0012 "You're Gonna Miss Me")...8-12 '60s

LPs: 10/12-inch

LA VAL...15-20

Also see WILLIS, Robert

WILLIS, Chuck *R&B '52*

(With the Royals; with Sandmen; with Cookies)

Singles: 78 rpm

ATLANTIC...25-50 56-57
COLUMBIA...15-25 51
OKEH...20-30 53-56

Singles: 7-inch

ATLANTIC (1000 & 2000 series)...15-30 56-59
COLUMBIA (30238 "Can't You See")...25-50 51
OKEH (6810 "I Tried")...30-40 51
OKEH (6841 "Let's Jump Tonight")...30-40 51
OKEH (6873 "Loud Mouth Lucy")...25-35 52
OKEH (6905 "My Story")...25-35 52
OKEH (6930 "Wrong Way to Catch a Fish")...25-35 52
OKEH (6952 "Going to the River")...20-30 53
OKEH (6985 "Don't Deceive Me")...75-125 53
OKEH (7004 "My Baby's Coming Home")...20-30 53
OKEH (7015 "What's Your Name")...20-30 53
OKEH (7029 "I Feel So Bad")...20-30 54
OKEH (7041 "Change My Mind")...20-30 54
OKEH (7048 "Give and Take")...20-30 54
OKEH (7051 "Lawdy Miss Mary")...15-25 55
OKEH (7055 "I Can Tell")...15-25 55
OKEH (7062 "Search My Heart")...15-25 55
OKEH (7067 "Come on Home")...15-25 56
OKEH (7070 "Charged with Cheating")...15-25 56
REGINALD...10-15

EPs: 7-inch

ATLANTIC (591 "Chuck Willis")...50-75 57
ATLANTIC (609 "Rock with Chuck Willis")...50-75 58
ATLANTIC (612 "What Am I Living For")...50-75 58
EPIC (7070 "Sings the Blues")...50-75 56

LPs: 10/12-inch

ATCO...10-12 71
ATLANTIC (8018 "King of the Stroll")...50-100 58
(Black label.)
ATLANTIC (8018 "King of the Stroll")...25-50 59
(Red label.)
ATLANTIC (8079 "I Remember Chuck Willis")...50-100 63
COLUMBIA...5-8 80
EPIC (3425 "Chuck Willis Wails the Blues")...100-200 58
EPIC (3728 "Tribute to Chuck Willis")...100-200 58
ICHIBAN (1106 "Back to the Blues")...5-10

Also see BARGE, Gene
Also see COOKIES
Also see ROYALS
Also see SANDMEN

WILLIS, Coke, & Gleepers

Singles: 7-inch

DACO (101 "The Gleep")...40-50

WILLIS, Don

Singles: 7-inch

STYLE (1921 "Mar's Dame")...50-100
SATELLITE (101 "Boppin' High School Baby")...1500-2500 59

WILLIS, Freddie

Singles: 7-inch

DORE (538 "It's Love")...15-25 60

WILLIS, Gene

(With the Aggregation)

Singles: 7-inch

CORONADO (139 "Shing-a-Ling's the Thing")...5-10 66
HOLLYWOOD (1132 "You'll Get Yours")...5-10 68

WILLIS, Hal *C&W '64*

Singles: 78 rpm

ATLANTIC...150-200 57

Singles: 7-inch

ATHENS (704 "Crazy Little Mama")...75-125 58
ATLANTIC (1114 "Bop-A-Dee Bop-A-Doo")...100-150 57
DECCA (30949 "Poor Little Jimmy")...8-12 59
MERCURY (71933 "Bayou Pierre")...5-10 62
SIMS (207 "Dig Me a Hole")...5-10 64
SIMS (224 "What's Left of Me")...5-10 65

SIMS (235 "Klondike Mike") 5-10 65
SIMS (243 "Nopper the Topper") 5-10 65
SIMS (250 "Creole Rose") 5-10 65
SIMS (288 "Doggin' in the U.S. Mail") 8-12 66
SIMS (307 "Private Dick") 5-10 66
WAYSIDE (1027 "Everybody's Got Troubles") 5-10 69

LPs: 10/12-inch

ARC 10-15
BONANZA 10-15

WILLIS, Herman

Singles: 7-inch

B&C (100 "Forever in Love") 200-300 '50s
(Reissued in 1961 as by the Five Blacks.)
Also see FIVE BLACK

WILLIS, Little Son
(Mac Willis)

Singles: 78 rpm

SWING TIME 25-50 52-53

Singles: 7-inch

SWING TIME (304 "Bad Luck and Trouble") 50-100 52
SWING TIME (305 "Harlem Blues") 50-100 52
SWING TIME (306 "Nothing But the Blues") 50-100 52
SWING TIME (341 "Roll Me Over Slow") 50-100 53
Also see WILLIS, Mac

WILLIS, Mac

Singles: 78 rpm

ELKO (254 "Pretty Woman") 50-100 50
Also see WILLIS, Little Son

WILLIS, Pete, & Four Royals

Singles: 7-inch

R.F.H. (001 "What's Your Point of View") 400-500

WILLIS, Ralph
(With His Alabama Trio; Ralph "Bama" Willis; Ralph Willis Country Boys)

Singles: 78 rpm

ABBEY 10-20 49
JUBILEE 10-15 50-52
KING (4611 "Do Right") 25-50 53
KING (4631 "Gonna Hop on Down the Line") 25-50 53
PAR 15-25 52
PRESTIGE 10-20 51-52
REGIS 15-25 44
SIGNATURE 10-20 47-49
20TH CENTURY 10-20 46

Singles: 7-inch

KING (4611 "Do Right") 100-150 53
KING (4631 "Gonna Hop on Down the Line") 100-150 53

LPs: 10/12-inch

BLUES CLASSICS 15-25 64
Also see ALABAMA SLIM
Also see McGHEE, Brownie, & Sonny Terry
Also see WASHBOARD PETE

WILLIS, Ray

Singles: 7-inch

JANE (103 "Patricia Darling") 20-30 58

WILLIS, Robert
(Robert "Chick" Willis)

Singles: 7-inch

BAY-TONE (104 "Pleading") 20-30 60
EBB (126 "Never Let Me Go") 15-25 57
Session: Fabulous Flames.
Also see FABULOUS FLAMES
Also see WILLIS, Chick

WILLIS, Rod

Singles: 78 rpm

CHIC (1010 "Somebody's Been Rockin' My Baby") 50-75 57

Singles: 7-inch

CHIC (1010 "Somebody's Been Rockin' My Baby") 40-60 57
NRC (020 "The Cat") 300-400 59

WILLIS, Rollie, & Contenders
(With the Matadors)

Singles: 7-inch

SAXONY (1001 "Whenever I Get Lonely") 500-750 62
(Reportedly 500 made.)
SAXONY (2001 "Whenever I Get Lonely") 4-8 93
Also see CHARMS
Also see MARTIN, Fred, & Matadors

WILLIS, Ron, & His Jeeters

Singles: 7-inch

ACE (588 "Don't Come Too Late") 10-15 60

WILLIS, Slim

Singles: 7-inch

BISCAYNE (010 "Tighten Up Your Game, Baby") 5-10 65
C.J. 10-15 61-62

WILLIS, Timmy R&B '68
(Timothy Willis)

Singles: 7-inch

EPIC (10934 "Give Me a Little Sign") 20-30 72
JUBILEE (5660 "I Finally Found a Woman") 5-10 69
JUBILEE (5690 "Easy As Saying 1-2-3") 5-10 70
SIDRA (9013 "Mr. Soul Satisfaction") 10-15 67
(First issue.)
VEEP (1279 "Mr. Soul Satisfaction") 8-12 67
VEEP (1288 "Gotta Get Me Back to Georgia") 8-12 68

WILLIS, Willy

Singles: 7-inch

DOT (16018 "Catawampus") 10-20 59
RITA (1002 "Catawampus") 15-25 59
(First issue.)

WILLIS BROTHERS C&W '64

Singles: 7-inch

STARDAY 4-6 62-70

LPs: 10/12-inch

CORONET (150 "Gunfighter Ballads of the Badmen") 10-20
(The Willis Brothers are not credited on this LP, though they do one side.)
MASTERPIECES 5-10
NASHVILLE 10-15 '60s
PICKWICK/HILLTOP 10-15 65
STARDAY (163 "In Action") 20-30 62
STARDAY (229 "Code of the West") 25-35 63
STARDAY (306 thru 466) 10-25 65-70
Members: Vic Willis; Guy Willis; Charles Willis.
Also see WILLIS, Vic, Trio

WILLIS SISTERS

Singles: 7-inch

ABC-PAR (10497 "Pretty One") 5-10 63
ABC-PAR (10520 "Crystal Ball") 5-10 64
ABC-PAR (10546 "Why Don't They Understand") 5-10 64
CAMEO (180 "Do I Worry") 5-10 60
RCA (8060 "Ain't Gonna Be No Twistin'") 5-10 62
REJO (101 "Somebody Touched Me") 5-10 63
REKNOWN (126 "It's Christmas") 5-10 60
Also see LITTLE CINDY & WILLIS SISTERS

WILL-O-BEES P&R '68

Singles: 7-inch

DATE (1515 "Why Can't They Accept Us") 5-10 66
DATE (1543 "If You're Ready") 5-10 67
DATE (1583 "It's Not Easy") 5-10 67
SGC (002 "Make Your Own Kind of Music") 5-10 68
SGC (004 "The Ugliest Girl in Town") 5-10 68
SGC (007 "It's Getting Better") 5-10 69
Members: Janet Blossom; Steve Porter; Robert Merchanthouse.

WILLOUGHBY, Chuck

Singles: 7-inch

REPUBLIC (2029 "Stop the World") 30-40 60

WILLOW GREEN

Singles: 7-inch

WHIZ MASTERS (619 "Fields of Peppermint") 10-20 70

WILLOWBY SINGERS

Singles: 7-inch

EPIC (9710 "Black Stockings") 5-10 64

WILLOWS P&R/R&B '56

Singles: 78 rpm

CLUB (1014 "This Is the End") 50-75 56
MELBA (102 "Church Bells Are Ringing") 75-125 56
MELBA (102 "Church Bells May Ring) 50-75 56
(Note slight title change.)
MELBA (106 "Do You Love Me) 15-25 56
MELBA (115 "Little Darlin'") 50-75 57

Singles: 7-inch

ABC 4-6 73
CLUB (1014 "This Is the End") 75-100 56
(Orange label. Promotional issue only.)
CLUB (1014 "This Is the End") 50-75 56
(Orange or blue label.)
COLLECTABLES 4-6
MELBA (102 "Church Bells Are Ringing") 75-100 56
MELBA (102 "Church Bells May Ring) 20-30 56
(Note slight title change.)
MELBA (106 "Do You Love Me) 20-30 56
(Black label.)
MELBA (106 "Do You Love Me) 10-15 56
(Red label.)
MELBA (115 "Little Darlin'") 30-40 57
(Red label.)
MICHELE (501 "This Is the End") 10-15 59

LPs: 10/12-inch

ELDORADO (1000 "The Willows") 8-12
Members: Tony Middleton; Richard Davis; Ralph Martin; Joe Martin; John Steele; Richard Simon; Dotty Martin.
Also see FIVE WILLOWS
Also see MIDDLETON, Tony
Also see RHYTHM ACES / Willows
Also see SEDAKA, Neil

WILLOWS

Singles: 7-inch

WARWICK (524 "You") 15-25 59

WILLOWS

Singles: 7-inch

4 STAR (1753 "Now That I Have You") 50-150 61

WILLOWS / Hal Paige

Singles: 7-inch

EXCALIBUR (507 "Now That I Have You"/"Big Foot May") 3-5 88
Also see PAIGE, Hal
Also see WILLOWS

WILLOWS

Singles: 7-inch

HEIDI (103 "Tears in Your Eyes") 10-15 64
HEIDI (107 "Such a Night") 10-15 65

WILLS, Billy Jack, & His Western Swing Band

Singles: 78 rpm

MGM 15-25 54-56

Singles: 7-inch

MGM (11807 "Out of Gas") 50-75 54
MGM (11966 "There's Good Rocking Tonight") 50-75 55
MGM (12034 "Hey Lula") 50-75 55
MGM (12172 "All She Wants to Do Is Rock") 50-75 56
MGM (12559 "Not Very Long") 50-75 57

WILLS, Bob P&R '39/C&W '44
(With His Texas Playboys; with Rusty McDonald; with Tommy Duncan)

Singles: 78 rpm

ANTONES 15-25
CAPITOL 3-5 76
COLUMBIA 5-10 43-48
DECCA 4-8 55-56
MGM 5-10 47-55
OKEH 5-10 40-45
VOCALION 10-20 33-39

Singles: 7-inch

DECCA 10-20 55-56
LIBERTY 5-10 60-63
LIBERTY 33 COMPACT (77025 "Ida Red Likes the Boogie") 5-10 60
(Stereo.)
LONGHORN 5-10 64
MGM 10-20 50-55

EPs: 7-inch

COLUMBIA 10-20 57
DECCA 10-20 55
MGM 10-20 56
RHINO (284 "Greatest Hits of Texas") 15-20 84
(Texas-shaped picture disc.)

LPs: 10/12-inch

ANTONES (6000 "The Texas Playboys") 100-200
(10-inch LP. Fan club issue.)
ANTONES (6010 "The Texas Playboys") 100-200
(10-inch LP. Fan club issue.)
AUDIO/VIDEO 5-8 82
CAPITOL 10-20 76
COLUMBIA (Except 9003) 5-15 73-82
COLUMBIA (9003 "Round-Up") 50-75 50
(10-inch LP.)
CORAL (20109 "Swing Along") 5-10 73
CORONET 8-12 '60s
DECCA (5562 "Dance-O-Rama") 50-75 55
(10-inch LP.)
DECCA (DL-8727 "Bob Wills & His Texas Playboys") 35-55 57
(Monaural.)
DECCA (DL7-8727 "Bob Wills & His Texas Playboys") 15-25 66
(Reprocessed stereo.)
DELTA 5-10 81-83
ENCORE 5-8 79
HARMONY (Except 7036) 10-20 63-69
HARMONY (7036 "Bob Wills Special") 15-25 57
KAPP 8-12 66-71
KALEIDOSCOPE 5-10 82-83
LARIAT (1 "The Tiffany Transcriptions") 50-75 77
LIBERTY (3173 "Together Again") 20-25 60
(Monaural.)
LIBERTY (3182 "Living Legend") 20-25 61
(Monaural.)
LIBERTY (3303 "Sings & Plays") 20-25 63
(Monaural.)
LIBERTY (7173 "Together Again") 25-30 60
(Stereo.)
LIBERTY (7182 "Living Legend") 25-30 61
(Stereo.)
LIBERTY (7303 "Sings & Plays") 25-30 63
(Stereo.)
LONGHORN (001 "Bob Wills Keepsake Album, #1") 50-75 65
LONGHORN (007 "Bob Wills Collector's Series") 10-15
LONGHORN (011 "31st St. Blues") 10-15
MCA 6-12 73-80
MGM (91 "Ranch House Favorites") 75-100 51
(10-inch LP.)
MGM (141 "Tribute to Bob Wills") 8-12 71
MGM (3352 "Ranch House Favorites") 50-75 56
MGM (4866 "History of Bob Wills") 10-15 73
MGM (5303 "24 Great Hits") 8-12 77
METRO 10-15 67
PICKWICK 5-10 '70s
RHINO (284 "Greatest Hits of Texas") 8-12 85
(Texas-shaped, picture disc. Promotional issue only.)
STARDAY (375 "San Antonio Rose") 15-25 65
STARDAY (469 "Bob Wills Story") 8-12 70
SUNSET 8-12 66-69
TEXAS ROSE 5-10
TIME-LIFE 5-10 81
TIME-LIFE ("Bob Wills") 10-15 82
(Boxed 3-LP set.)
TISHOMINGO (1 "The Tiffany Transcriptions, 1945-1948") 30-50 78
U.A. 8-15 71-74
VOCALION (3735 "Swing Along") 10-20 65
VOCALION (3922 "San Antonio Rose") 10-20 71
WESTERN HERITAGE 5-10 76
Also see FORT WORTH DOUGHBOYS
Also see McAULIFFE, Leon
Also see WILLS, Johnnie Lee, & His Boys

WILLS, Bob, & Mel Tillis

LPs: 10/12-inch

KAPP (3523 "King of Western Swing") 15-25 67
KAPP (3639 "In Person") 15-25 68
Also see TILLIS, Mel
Also see WILLS, Bob

WILLS, Johnnie Lee, & His Boys C&W '50

Singles: 78 rpm

BULLET 5-10 49-50
RCA (5449 "Two Step Side Step") 5-10 53

Singles: 7-inch

FLYING FISH (4001 "Talking 'Bout You") 4-6 79
RCA (5449 "Two Step Side Step") 10-20 53
SIMS (129 "Blue Twist") 8-12 62
SIMS (133 "Milkcow Blues") 8-12 63
SIMS (289 "Milkcow Blues") 5-10 66

LPs: 10/12-inch

CROWN 10-15 '60s
DELTA 5-10 '80s
FLYING FISH 5-10 '80s
ROUNDER 5-10 '80s
SIMS (101 "Where There's a Wills There's a Way") 15-25 62

SIMS (108 "Johnnie Lee Willis at the Tulsa Stampede") ... 15-25 62
SIMS (129 "Blub Twist") ... 10-20 62
Also see WILLS, Bob

WILLS, Maury
(With His Base Stealers, John Roseboro & Tommy Davis)
Singles: 7-inch
DOT (16529 "Ballad of Maury Wills") ... 8-12 63
GLAD HAMP (2009 "Crawdad Hole") ... 8-12 62
Picture Sleeves
GLAD HAMP (2009 "Crawdad Hole") ... 20-30 62

WILLS, Oscar (With Fats Domino's Band) / Paul Gayten
Singles: 78 rpm
ARGO (5277 "Flat Foot Sam") ... 10-20 57
Singles: 7-inch
ARGO (5277 "Flat Foot Sam") ... 15-25 57
Also see DOMINO, Fats
Also see GAYTEN, Paul
Also see T.V. SLIM

WILLS, Tommy C&W '79
(With His Twisting Tomcats; with Marti Maes)
Singles: 7-inch
AIR TOWN (001 "Night Train '66") ... 4-8 66
CLUB MIAMI (501 "Let 'Em Roll") ... 100-200
GOLDEN MOON ... 4-6 79
GREGORY (100 "La-Dee-Dah") ... 5-10 63
NORMAN (502 "Third Man Theme") ... 5-10 61
TERRY (106 "Mr. Movin' Is Groovin' ") ... 5-10 62
TERRY (110 "Aw Shucks") ... 5-10 62
EPs: 7-inch
TERRY-GREGORY (1000 "Man with a Horn") ... 8-12 62
(Juke box issue.)
LPs: 10/12-inch
COUNTRY INT'L ... 5-10 75
GOLDEN MOON ... 5-10 78
GREGORY (1000 "Man with a Horn") ... 10-20 66
Also see TOMCATS

WILLS, Viola
Singles: 12-inch
SUGAR HILL (544 "Gonna Get Along Without You Now") ... 4-8 79
Singles: 7-inch
BRONCO (2051 "I Got Love") ... 10-15 66

WILMA LEE
(Wilma Lee Cooper)
Singles: 78 rpm
COLUMBIA ... 5-10 50-53
Singles: 7-inch
COLUMBIA ... 8-15 50-53
Also see COOPER, Wilma Lee & Stoney

WILMER & THE DUKES P&R '68
Singles: 7-inch
APHRODISIAC ... 4-6 69
LPs: 10/12-inch
APHRODISIAC ... 10-15 69
Member: Wilmer Alexander Jr.

WILSON, Adah Louise
Singles: 7-inch
ARRAWAK (1002 "Too Much") ... 10-15 62

WILSON, Al P&R/R&B '68
Singles: 7-inch
BELL ... 4-8 70
BELL GOLD ... 4-6 '70s
CAROUSEL ... 4-8 71
PLAYBOY (6076 "Baby I Want Your Body") ... 4-8 76
ROADSHOW ... 3-5 79
ROCKY ROAD ... 4-8 72-74
SOUL CITY ... 5-10 67-69
WAND (1135 "Help Me") ... 15-25 66
LPs: 10/12-inch
PLAYBOY ... 8-10 76
ROADSHOW ... 5-8 79
ROCKY ROAD ... 8-12 73-74
SOUL CITY ... 10-15 69
Also see ROLLERS

WILSON, Andy
Singles: 78 rpm
DOT ... 5-10 51-52
Singles: 7-inch
ATHENS (700 "Little Mama") ... 15-25 57
BACK BEAT (518 "Call Her Your Sweetheart") ... 10-20 58
BULLSEYE (1012 "My Love My Love") ... 50-75 58
BULLSEYE (1020 "Worry Worry") ... 10-20 58
BULLSEYE (1022 "Poor Boy") ... 10-20 58
BULLSEYE (1023 "Poor Boy") ... 10-20 58
DESTINY (506 "Don't You Know") ... 50-75 61
DOT (1061 "Let's Live a Little") ... 10-20 51
DOT (1102 "Great Speckled Bird") ... 10-20 52
DOT (1127 "Hillbilly Boogie") ... 10-20 52
REGENCY (744 "Worry Worry") ... 50-75

WILSON, Ann P&R '86
(With the Daybreaks)
Singles: 7-inch
CAPITOL ... 3-5 86
TOPAZ (1311 "Standin' Watchin' You") ... 50-100 67
(Reportedly 500 made.)
TOPAZ (1312 "Through Eyes & Glass") ... 50-100 67
(Reportedly 500 made.)
Picture Sleeves
CAPITOL ... 3-5 86
Also see HEART

WILSON, Ann, & Robin Zander P&R '88
Singles: 7-inch
CAPITOL ... 3-5 88
Also see WILSON, Ann

WILSON, Artie
Singles: 7-inch
CANNADY (300 "Tarzan") ... 75-125 59
KENT (313 "Jerry Jerry") ... 15-25 58
TALENT (102 "Oo-Wee Can't You See") ... 15-25 59

WILSON, Barbara
Singles: 7-inch
AURA (4502 "Make Me Happy") ... 5-10 64

WILSON, Barry, & Camelots
Singles: 7-inch
DOT (16462 "The Bug") ... 8-12 63

WILSON, Betty, & Four Bars
Singles: 7-inch
DAYCO (1631 "I'm Yours") ... 10-15 62
FALEW (108 "I've Got to Move") ... 10-20 64
Also see FOUR BARS

WILSON, Beverly Mae
Singles: 7-inch
IMPACT (11 "Lonesome Girl") ... 5-10 62

WILSON, Bill
Singles: 7-inch
BROOKE (122 "One") ... 8-12 60

WILSON, Billy
Singles: 7-inch
JIM-CO (1002 "Country Boy") ... 50-75
MASTER (1103 "Help Me to Forget") ... 10-20 '50s

WILSON, Bobby
Singles: 7-inch
20TH FOX (108 "Posse") ... 10-20 59

WILSON, Bobby R&B '73
Singles: 7-inch
BUDDAH (449 "Deeper & Deeper") ... 4-6 75
CHAIN (2101 "Here Is Where the Love Is") ... 5-10 73
VOLT (144 "Let Me Down Slow") ... 5-10 67

WILSON, Brian P&R '66
Singles: 7-inch
CAPITOL (5610 "Caroline, No") ... 15-20 66
SIRE (27694 "Melt Away") ... 4-6 88
SIRE (27814 "Love and Mercy") ... 4-6 88
SIRE (28350 "Let's Go to Heaven in My Car") ... 3-5 87
Promotional Singles
SIRE (27694 "Melt Away") ... 5-10 88
SIRE (27787 "Night Time") ... 5-10 88
SIRE (27814 "Love and Mercy") ... 15-20 88
SIRE (28350 "Let's Go to Heaven in My Car") ... 5-10 87
Picture Sleeves
SIRE (27787 "Night Time") ... 8-12 88
SIRE (27814 "Love and Mercy") ... 15-20 88
SIRE (28350 "Let's Go to Heaven in My Car") ... 15-20 87
LPs: 10/12-inch
SIRE (3248 "Brian Wilson: Words and Music") ... 15-20 88
SIRE (225669 "Brian Wilson") ... 5-10 88
Also see BEACH BOYS
Also see BERRY, Jan
Also see BLOSSOMS
Also see BOB & SHERI
Also see CAMPBELL, Glen
Also see CASTELLS
Also see DeSHANNON, Jackie
Also see HALE & HUSHABYES
Also see HONDELLS
Also see LEGENDARY MASKED SURFERS
Also see RIVERS, Johnny
Also see TIMERS

WILSON, Brian, & Mike Love
Singles: 7-inch
BROTHER (1002 "Gettin' Hungry") ... 15-25 67
Also see LOVE, Mike
Also see WILSON, Brian

WILSON, Brian, & Del Vues
Singles: 7-inch
STENTOR (165 "Blueberry Hill") ... 150-200 59

WILSON, Bud
Singles: 7-inch
MOHAWK (1043 "Rattle Snake Daddy") ... 25-35
(Coleman L. Wilson)
Singles: 7-inch
KING (5388 "Radar Blues") ... 10-20 60
KING (5512 "Passing Zone Blues") ... 10-20 61

WILSON, Curtis
Singles: 7-inch
CANARY (6417 "Teenage Party Line") ... 50-75 66
CHERRY (1014 "My Heart Is Made of the Blues") ... 15-25 60

WILSON, Dallas
(With His Western Troubadours)
Singles: 78 rpm
PEP (104 "You'll Never Know") ... 15-25 56
Singles: 7-inch
PEP (104 "You'll Never Know") ... 20-40 56
RODEO (127 "Hi-Steppin' Daddy") ... 40-60 57

WILSON, Dennis LP '77
Singles: 7-inch
CARIBOU (9023 "You and I") ... 4-8 77
LPs: 10/12-inch
CARIBOU (34353 "Pacific Ocean Blue") ... 10-15 77
Also see BEACH BOYS
Also see FOUR SPEEDS

WILSON, Dennis / Ram Jam / Joan Baez
EPs: 7-inch
COLUMBIA (1128 "Music for Every Ear") ... 15-25 77
(Promotional issue only.)
Also see BAEZ, Joan
Also see WILSON, Dennis

WILSON, Don
Singles: 7-inch
BLUE HORIZON (6054 "Twomp") ... 8-12 62
Also see VENTURES

WILSON, Doyle
Singles: 7-inch
LAMP (2015 "Hey Hey") ... 40-60 58

WILSON, Eddie
Singles: 7-inch
BACK BEAT ... 5-10 68-69
TOLLIE (9033 "Toast to the Lady") ... 10-20 64

WILSON, Fats
(Honorable Fats Wilson)
Singles: 7-inch
ROBBEE (116 "Quit Eatin' ") ... 75-100 61

WILSON, Faye
(With the Johnny Otis Orchestra)
Singles: 7-inch
HIP (401 "Playing Me for a Fool") ... 75-125 57
Also see OTIS, Johnny

WILSON, Frank
Singles: 7-inch
SOUL (35019 "Do I Love You") ... 7500-10000 66

WILSON, Gene, & Genies
Singles: 7-inch
KING (5568 "Come Here My Darling") ... 25-30 61
Also see GENIES

WILSON, Gloria
Singles: 7-inch
DAWN (236 "Little Boy Blues") ... 15-20 58
Session: Elise Bretton Singers.

WILSON, Glorious, & Belles
Singles: 7-inch
FAIRBANKS (2002 "Try and You'll See") ... 15-25 61

WILSON, Goodie
Singles: 7-inch
TITANIC (102 "I Stood Beneath Your Window") ... 15-25 63

WILSON, Henry
(With the Bluenotes)
Singles: 7-inch
COLONIAL (7778 "Are You Ready") ... 200-300 58
DOT (15692 "Mighty Low") ... 50-100 58

WILSON, Hop, & His Two Buddies
(With the Chickens; Harding Wilson)
Singles: 78 rpm
GOLDBAND ... 25-35 58
Singles: 7-inch
GOLDBAND (1071 "Chicken Stuff") ... 15-25 58
GOLDBAND (1078 "Broke and Hungry") ... 15-25 58
Also see POPPA HOP

WILSON, J. Frank P&R/LP '64
(With the Cavaliers)
Singles: 7-inch
ABC ... 4-6 73
APRIL (1 "Tell Laura I Love Her") ... 4-6
CHARAY (13 "Last Kiss '69") ... 4-8 69
CHARAY (80 "The Clown") ... 4-8 69
COLLECTABLES ... 3-5 '80s
ERIC ... 4-6 '70s
JAMIE ... 4-6 76
JOSIE (923 "Last Kiss") ... 8-12 64
JOSIE (926 "Hey Little One") ... 5-10 64
JOSIE (929 "Six Boys") ... 5-10 65
JOSIE (931 "Open Your Eyes") ... 5-10 65
JOSIE (938 "Forget Me Not") ... 5-10 65
JUBILEE (923 "Last Kiss") ... 5-10 64
(Blue label. Canadian – made by Quality.)
JUBILEE (923 "Last Kiss") ... 4-6 64
(Black label. Canadian – made by Phonodisc.)
LE CAM (500 series) ... 3-5 81
LE CAM (722 "Last Kiss") ... 15-25 64
(First issue. Different version than on Tamara and Josie.)
LE CAM (1015 "Kiss and Run") ... 5-10 65
LE CAM (12000 series) ... 3-5
MASTER (1005 "She's Winning") ... 10-20 '60s
QUALITY (049 "Last Kiss") ... 4-6 67
(Canadian.)
SOLLY (927 "Me & My Teardrops") ... 5-10 66
TAMARA (761 "Last Kiss") ... 15-25 64
(1,000 made.)
VIRGO (506 "Last Kiss") ... 4-6 72
LPs: 10/12-inch
DILL PICKEL ... 8-10 71
JOSIE (4006 "Last Kiss") ... 50-75 64

WILSON, Jackie P&R '57
(With Dick Jacobs & His Orchestra)
Singles: 78 rpm
BRUNSWICK ... 50-100 57-58
Singles: 7-inch
BRUNSWICK (7-38106 "Nothin' but the Blues") ... 40-50 60
(Stereo compact 33 single.)
BRUNSWICK (7-38107 "Excuse Me for Lovin' ") ... 40-50 60
(Stereo compact 33 single.)
Note: Other compact 33s may exist. If so, those titles and numbers would be appreciated.
BRUNSWICK (55024 "Reet Petite") ... 20-30 57
BRUNSWICK (55052 "To Be Loved") ... 20-30 58
BRUNSWICK (55070 "I'm Wandering") ... 30-40 58
BRUNSWICK (55086 "We Have Love") ... 20-30 58
BRUNSWICK (55105 "Lonely Teardrops") ... 15-25 58
BRUNSWICK (55121 "That's Why") ... 15-25 59
BRUNSWICK (55136 "I'll Be Satisfied") ... 15-25 59
BRUNSWICK (55149 "You Better Know It") ... 15-25 59
BRUNSWICK (55165 "Talk That Talk") ... 15-25 59
BRUNSWICK (55166 "Night") ... 10-20 60
BRUNSWICK (55167 "All My Love") ... 10-20 60
BRUNSWICK (55170 "Alone At Last") ... 10-20 60
BRUNSWICK (55201 "My Empty Arms") ... 10-20 61
BRUNSWICK (55208 "Please Tell Me Why") ... 10-20 61
BRUNSWICK (55216 "I'm Comin' On Back to You") ... 10-20 61
BRUNSWICK (55219 "Years from Now") ... 10-20 61

BRUNSWICK (55220 "The Way I Am") ... 10-20 61
BRUNSWICK (55221 "Greatest Hurt") ... 10-20 62
BRUNSWICK (55225 "Hearts") ... 10-20 62
BRUNSWICK (55229 "I Just Can't Help It") ... 10-20 62
BRUNSWICK (55233 "Forever and a Day") ... 10-20 62
BRUNSWICK (55236 "What Good Am I Without You") ... 15-25 62
BRUNSWICK (55239 "Baby Workout") ... 10-15 63
BRUNSWICK (55246 "Shake! Shake! Shake!") ... 10-15 63
BRUNSWICK (55250 "Baby Get It") ... 10-15 63
BRUNSWICK (55254 "Silent Night") ... 15-20 63
BRUNSWICK (55260 "I'm Travelin' On") ... 15-20 63
BRUNSWICK (55263 "Call Her Up") ... 15-20 63
BRUNSWICK (55266 "Big Boss Line") ... 8-12 64
BRUNSWICK (55269 "Squeeze Her, Tease Her") ... 8-12 64
BRUNSWICK (55273 "She's All Right") ... 10-15 65
BRUNSWICK (55277 "Danny Boy") ... 8-12 65
BRUNSWICK (55280 "No Pity") ... 8-12 65
BRUNSWICK (55283 "I Believe I'll Love On") ... 8-12 65
BRUNSWICK (55289 "I've Got to Get Back") ... 8-12 66
BRUNSWICK (55290 "Brand New Things") ... 8-12 66
BRUNSWICK (55294 "Be My Love") ... 8-12 66
BRUNSWICK (55300 "Whispers") ... 5-10 66
BRUNSWICK (55309 "Just Be Sincere") ... 5-10 67
BRUNSWICK (55321 "I've Lost You") ... 5-10 67
BRUNSWICK (55336 "Higher & Higher") ... 5-10 67
BRUNSWICK (55354 "Since You Showed Me How to Be Happy") ... 5-10 67
BRUNSWICK (55381 "I Get the Sweetest Feeling") ... 5-10 68
BRUNSWICK (55392 "For Once in My Life") ... 5-10 68
BRUNSWICK (55402 "I Still Love You") ... 5-10 69
BRUNSWICK (55418 "Helpless") ... 5-10 69
BRUNSWICK (55423 "With These Hands") ... 5-10 70
BRUNSWICK (55435 "Let This Be a Letter") ... 5-10 70
BRUNSWICK (55443 "This Love Is Real") ... 5-10 70
BRUNSWICK (55449 "This Guy's in Love with You") ... 5-10 71
BRUNSWICK (55454 "Say You Will") ... 5-10 71
BRUNSWICK (55461 "Love Is Funny That Way") ... 5-10 71
BRUNSWICK (55467 "You Got Me Walking") ... 5-10 72
BRUNSWICK (55475 "The Girl Turned Me On") ... 5-10 72
BRUNSWICK (55480 "You Left the Fire Burning") ... 5-10 72
BRUNSWICK (55490 "Beautiful Day") ... 5-10 73
BRUNSWICK (55495 "Because of You") ... 5-10 73
BRUNSWICK (55499 "Sing a Little Song") ... 5-10 73
BRUNSWICK (55504 "Shake a Leg") ... 5-10 73
BRUNSWICK (55536 "Nobody But You") ... 4-8 76
COLUMBIA ... 3-5 87
ERIC ... 3-5 83
GUSTO ... 4-6

Picture Sleeves

BRUNSWICK (55121 "That's Why") ... 30-40 59
BRUNSWICK (55165 "Talk That Talk") ... 20-30 59
BRUNSWICK (55166 "Night") ... 10-20 60
BRUNSWICK (55170 "Alone At Last") ... 10-20 60
BRUNSWICK (55201 "My Empty Arms") ... 10-20 61
BRUNSWICK (55220 "The Way I Am") ... 10-20 61
BRUNSWICK (55221 "Greatest Hurt") ... 10-20 62
BRUNSWICK (55236 "What Good Am I Without You") ... 15-25 62
BRUNSWICK (55435 "Let This Be a Letter") ... 5-10 70
COLUMBIA ... 3-5 87

EPs: 7-inch

BRUNSWICK (71040 "The Versatile Jackie Wilson") ... 25-50 60
BRUNSWICK (71042 "Jumpin' Jack") ... 25-50 60
BRUNSWICK (71045 "That's Why") ... 25-50 60
BRUNSWICK (71046 "Jackie Wilson – Talk That Talk") ... 25-50 60
BRUNSWICK (71047 "Mr. Excitement") ... 25-50 60
BRUNSWICK (71048 "So Much") ... 25-50 60
BRUNSWICK (71049 "Jackie Wilson") ... 25-50 60
BRUNSWICK (71101 "Greatest Hurt") ... 20-40 62
BRUNSWICK (71102 "I Just Can't Help It") ... 20-40 62
BRUNSWICK (71103 "Baby Workout") ... 20-40 63
BRUNSWICK (771045 "That's Why") ... 40-60 60
(Stereo.)

LPs: 10/12-inch

BRUNSWICK (111 "Solid Gold") ... 10-15
(Brunswick Special Products, mail-order offer.)
BRUNSWICK (54045 "Lonely Teardrops") ... 75-125 59
BRUNSWICK (54042 "He's So Fine") ... 50-100 59
BRUNSWICK (54050 "So Much") ... 40-80 60
BRUNSWICK (54055 "Jackie Sings the Blues") ... 30-50 60
BRUNSWICK (54058 "My Golden Favorites") ... 30-40 60
BRUNSWICK (54059 "A Woman, a Lover, a Friend") ... 30-40 60
BRUNSWICK (54100 "You Ain't Heard Nothin' Yet") ... 25-30 61
BRUNSWICK (54101 "By Request") ... 25-30 61
BRUNSWICK (54105 "Body and Soul") ... 25-30 62
BRUNSWICK (54106 "The World's Greatest Melodies") ... 25-30 62
BRUNSWICK (54108 "At the Copa") ... 25-30 62
BRUNSWICK (54110 thru 54130, except 54118) ... 20-25 63-67
BRUNSWICK (54118 "Soul Time") ... 30-50 66
(Beginning with 54050, Brunswick indicated stereo LPs with a "7" preceeding the selection number. Numbers after 54130 were available as stereo issues only, and are shown here as the 75000 series.)
BRUNSWICK (754138 thru 754167) ... 15-25 68-71
BRUNSWICK (754185 thru 754212) ... 10-20 72-77
COLUMBIA ... 5-8 87
DISCOVERY ... 8-10 78
EPIC ... 10-12 83
TELE-HOUSE ... 10-15
Also see FREED, Alan
Also see WARD, Billy, & Dominoes
Also see WILSON, Sonny

WILSON, Jackie, & Lavern Baker
P&R/R&B '66

Singles: 7-inch

BRUNSWICK (55287 "Think Twice") ... 10-15 66
Also see BAKER, Lavern

WILSON, Jackie, & Count Basie
P&R/R&B/LP '68

Singles: 7-inch

BRUNSWICK (1013 "For Your Precious Love") ... 3-5
BRUNSWICK (55365 "For Your Precious Love") ... 5-10 68
BRUNSWICK (55373 "Chain Gang") ... 5-10 68

LPs: 10/12-inch

BRUNSWICK ... 15-25 68
Also see BASIE, Count

WILSON, Jackie, & Chi-Lites
R&B '75

Singles: 7-inch

BRUNSWICK (55522 "Don't Burn No Bridges") ... 4-6 75
Also see CHI-LITES

WILSON, Jackie, & Linda Hopkins
P&R '62

Singles: 7-inch

BRUNSWICK (55224 "I Found Love") ... 10-15 62
BRUNSWICK (55243 "Shake a Hand") ... 10-15 63
BRUNSWICK (55278 "Yes Indeed") ... 8-12 65

EPs: 7-inch

BRUNSWICK (71104 "Shake a Hand") ... 20-30 63

LPs: 10/12-inch

BRUNSWICK ... 25-35 68
Also see HOPKINS, Linda
Also see WILSON, Jackie

WILSON, James

Singles: 7-inch

RAM (103 "Wilson Blues No. 1") ... 150-250

WILSON, Jerry

Singles: 7-inch

PRANN (5004 "Doin' the Thing") ... 5-10 63

WILSON, Jim
C&W '55
(With June Wilson)

Singles: 78 rpm

MERCURY ... 5-10 56

Singles: 7-inch

MERCURY (70635 "Daddy, You Know What") ... 10-20 56
REED (1032 "Have a Tear For Me") ... 250-350 59

WILSON, Jimmy
R&B '53
(With His All Stars; with Blues Blasters)

Singles: 78 rpm

ALADDIN ... 25-50 51-54
BIG TOWN ... 20-40 53-54
CAVATONE ... 15-25 51
CHART ... 20-40 56
IRMA ... 15-25 55
RHYTHM ... 15-25 50-54
7-11 ... 50-75 53

Singles: 7-inch

ALADDIN (3140 "Mistake in Life") ... 50-100 51
ALADDIN (3169 "Every Dog Has His Day") ... 50-100 53
ALADDIN (3241 "It's Time to Change") ... 50-100 54
BIG TOWN (101 "Tin Pan Alley") ... 40-60 53
BIG TOWN (103 "Call Me a Hound Dog") ... 40-60 53
BIG TOWN (107 "Blues at Sundown") ... 40-60 53
BIG TOWN (113 "Teardrops on My Pillow") ... 40-60 54
BIG TOWN (115 "Trouble in My House") ... 40-60 54
BIG TOWN (123 "I've Found Out") ... 40-60 54
CHART (610 "Louise") ... 40-60 56
CHART (629 "Send Me Your Key") ... 40-60 56
DUKE (331 "Easy Easy Baby") ... 10-20 61
DUKE (339 "I Don't Care") ... 10-20 61
GOLDBAND (1074 "Big Wheel Rolling") ... 20-30 58
GOLDBAND (1091 "Don't You Know") ... 20-30 59
GOLDBAND (1095 "Yanky Danky Doodle") ... 25-35 59
IMPERIAL (5549 "Big Wheel Rolling") ... 10-15 58
IRMA (108 "Blues in the Alley") ... 25-50 57
7-11 (2104 "Ethel Lee") ... 100-150 53
7-11 (2105 "Baby Don't Want Nobody But Me") ... 100-150 53
Session: Five Royales.
Also see FIVE ROYALES

WILSON, Jimmy / Thrillers / Little Caesar

LPs: 10/12-inch

BIG TOWN (1001 "Big Town Sampler") ... 150-250 53
(Promotional issue only.)
Also see LITTLE CAESAR
Also see THRILLERS
Also see WILSON, Jimmy

WILSON, Joe
(With Sabers)

Singles: 7-inch

DYNAMO ... 8-12
WILDCAT (53 "Fast-Slow") ... 10-20 60

WILSON, Johnny

Singles: 7-inch

ARNOLD (1009 "Now That School Is Out") ... 10-15 63
CORONADO (001 "Twilight Zone") ... 100-200
ENJOY (2002 "Please Be Fair") ... 10-20 63

WILSON, Joni
(Joni Wilson's Debonaries)

Singles: 7-inch

FENWAY (1712 "Holly Lynn") ... 8-12 '60s
VOLT (4070 "Loser's Seat") ... 4-6 71

WILSON, Larry, & Continentals

Singles: 7-inch

SHANE (36 "All of Your Love") ... 15-25 60

WILSON, Lloyd

Singles: 7-inch

ROULETTE (4498 "I'd Hate Myself in the Morning") ... 5-10 63

WILSON, Marie

LPs: 10/12-inch

DESIGN (76 "Gentlemen Prefer Marie Wilson") ... 25-50 57

WILSON, Marty
(With the Lover Boys; with Strat-O-Lites)

Singles: 7-inch

DECCA (30544 "I'm All Woke Up") ... 15-25 58
DECCA (30644 "Po-Go") ... 15-25 58
MASTER SOUND (1008 "Carol Ann") ... 75-100 59
TEL (1008 "Hot Foot") ... 10-20 59
TROPICAL ISLE (1008 "Carol Ann") ... 250-350 59
W.B. (5120 "Jungle Fantasy") ... 10-15 59

LPs: 10/12-inch

20TH FOX (3101 "Young America Dances to Golden Goodies") ... 15-20 63
(Monaural.)
20TH FOX (4101 "Young America Dances to Golden Goodies") ... 20-30 63
(Stereo.)

WILSON, Murry
(Murray Wilson)

Singles: 7-inch

CAPITOL (2063 "Leaves") ... 8-10 67

LPs: 10/12-inch

CAPITOL (T-2819 "Many Moods of Murry Wilson") ... 40-60 67
(Monaural.)
CAPITOL (ST-2819 "Many Moods of Murry Wilson") ... 35-50 67
(Stereo.)

WILSON, Nancy
LP '62

Singles: 12-inch

CAPITOL ... 4-6 79

Singles: 7-inch

CAPITOL (Except 4000 & 5000 series) ... 4-6 68-79
CAPITOL (4000 & 5000 series) ... 5-10 59-67
(Includes both purple and orange/yellow labels.)

Picture Sleeves

CAPITOL ... 4-6 65

LPs: 10/12-inch

ASI ... 5-8 81
CAPITOL (100 thru 800 series) ... 5-12 69-71
CAPITOL (1300 thru 1700 series) ... 15-30 59-62
CAPITOL (1800 thru 2900 series) ... 8-18 63-68
(With "T," "ST" or "SKAO" prefix.)
CAPITOL (1800 thru 2900 series) ... 5-8 78
(With "SM" prefix.)
CAPITOL (11000 & 12000 series) ... 5-10 74-80
CAPITOL (16000 series) ... 5-8 80
COLUMBIA ... 5-8 84
PICKWICK ... 5-8
Also see LEWIS, Ramsey, & Nancy Wilson

WILSON, Nancy, & Julian "Cannonball" Adderley
R&B/LP '62

Singles: 7-inch

CAPITOL ... 4-6 62

LPs: 10/12-inch

CAPITOL (1657 "Nancy Wilson & Cannonball Adderley") ... 15-25 62
(With "T" or "ST" prefix.)
CAPITOL (1657 "Nancy Wilson & Cannonball Adderley") ... 5-8 75
(With "SM" prefix.)
CAPITOL (16000 series) ... 4-8 81
Also see ADDERLEY, Cannonball

WILSON, Nancy, & George Shearing

Singles: 7-inch

CAPITOL ... 5-8 61

LPs: 10/12-inch

CAPITOL (1524 "Swingin's Mutual") ... 15-25 61
(With "T" or "ST" prefix.)
CAPITOL (1524 "Swingin's Mutual") ... 5-8 75
(With "SM" prefix.)
Also see SHEARING, George
Also see WILSON, Nancy

WILSON, Nancy / Red Hot Chili Peppers

Singles: 7-inch

WTG (68678 "All for Love"/"Taste the Pain") ... 5-10 89
(Colored vinyl.)
Also see HEART
Also see RED HOT CHILI PEPPERS

WILSON, Obrey

Singles: 7-inch

BELL (830 "Soul Satisfaction") ... 8-10 69
COLUMBIA (43944 "If You Were There") ... 8-10 66
EPIC ... 10-15 64-65
LIBERTY (55394 "Whipping Boy") ... 8-12 61
LIBERTY (55483 "Hey There Mountain") ... 8-12 62
PHILIPS (40514 "You Don't Love Me") ... 5-10 68
U.A. (567 "She's a Good Looker") ... 8-12 63

WILSON, Ormond, & Basin Street Boys

Singles: 78 rpm

MERCURY ... 15-25 48
Also see BASIN STREET BOYS

WILSON, Paul
Singles: 7-inch
PICTURE (1001 "Orchid in the Snow").... 10-20 61

WILSON, Peanuts
(Johnny Wilson)
Singles: 12-inch
BRUNSWICK (55039 "Cast Iron Arm").. 75-125 58
Also see ORBISON, Roy

WILSON, Phill P&R '61
Singles: 7-inch
HURON (22000 "Wishin' On a Rainbow") 10-20 61
HURON (22006 "Game of Love") 5-10 61

WILSON, Ralph
(Ralph Wilson Quintet; Ralph Wilson Orchestra)
Singles: 78 rpm
LUCKY.......... 10-15 48-49
Singles: 7-inch
QUINTET (101 "I'll Never Stand in Your Way").......... 75-100 '50s
TIARA (6110 "What's Shakin'")........ 10-20 58

WILSON, Reg
Singles: 78 rpm
HERALD (473 "My Love for You") 10-15 56
Singles: 7-inch
HERALD (473 "My Love for You") 15-25 56

WILSON, Robin
Singles: 7-inch
MONUMENT (426 "Close to Me")........... 15-25 60
TARHEEL (060 "Gonna Build a Mountain").......... 10-20 62

WILSON, Ron
Singles: 7-inch
COLUMBIA (44636 "I'll Keep On Loving You") 10-15 68

WILSON, Ronnie
Singles: 7-inch
KARATE (516 "Boy in a Crowd") 8-12 65
REED (1027 "You Love That Guitar More Than Me")......... 250-350 59

WILSON, Roosevelt
Singles: 7-inch
BULLS EYE (1135 "Caroline") 8-12 61

WILSON, Smiley
Singles: 7-inch
FREEDOM (44025 "Running Bear")..........5-10 60

WILSON, Sonny
("Sonny Wilson Sings – Billy Mitchell Plays"; Jackie Wilson)
Singles: 78 rpm
DEE GEE (4000 "Rainy Day Blues") 75-125 52
DEE GEE (4001 "Danny Boy").......... 75-125 52
Singles: 7-inch
DEE GEE (4000 "Rainy Day Blues") ... 300-400 52
DEE GEE (4001 "Danny Boy")........... 300-400 52
Also see MITCHELL, Billy
Also see WILSON, Jackie

WILSON, Sonny
(With the Gene Lowery Singers)
Singles: 7-inch
CANDIX (327 "Troubled Time").......... 10-15 61
PLAZA (1 "Troubled Time").......... 10-15 61
SUN (341 "The Great Pretender")........... 10-15 60
VALLEY..........3-6 85

WILSON, Stan
Singles: 78 rpm
CAVALIER (827 "Frankie and Johnny") 5-10 53
Singles: 7-inch
CAVALIER (827 "Frankie and Johnny") .. 10-20 53
LPs:10/12-inch
CAVALIER.......... 20-30
CLEF.......... 20-30
FANTASY.......... 15-25
VERVE.......... 15-25

WILSON, Stanley
Singles: 7-inch
CHARTER (13 "Dance with Me')..........5-10 63

WILSON, Steve
Singles: 7-inch
GNP (348 "Pretty Little Angel") 10-20 65
ORBY (203 "Pretty Little Angel").......... 20-30 60
PAMELA (205 "Oh-De-Dum") 50-75 61
(Black vinyl.)
PAMELA (205 "Oh-De-Dum") 100-200 61
(Blue vinyl.)

WILSON, Teddy
Singles: 78 rpm
CLEF 5-10 52-54
MERCURY 5-10
MUSICRAFT 5-10 45-47
LPs: 10/12-inch
ALLEGRO (4024 "All Star Sextet") 50-75 54
ALLEGRO (4031 "All Star Sextet") 50-75 54
COLUMBIA (1300 & 1400 series)..........20-30 59-60
(Monaural.)
COLUMBIA (8100 & 8200 series)..........25-35 59-60
(Stereo.)
COMMODORE (20029 "Town Hall Concert")..........75-125 50
(10-inch LP.)
DIAL (213 "All Stars") 75-125 50
(10-inch LP.)
MGM (129 "Runnin' Wild")..........75-125 51
(10-inch LP.)
VERVE (8200 & 8300 series)..........20-35 59-60
Also see BUSHKIN, Joe, & Teddy Wilson
Also see FITZGERALD, Ella / Teddy Wilson / Lena Horne
Also see HOLIDAY, Billie
Also see YOUNG, Lester, & Teddy Wilson

WILSON, Timothy R&B '67
Singles: 7-inch
BLUE ROCK (6 "Cross My Heart")..........10-20 69
BLUE ROCK (4087 "I Wanna Know Right Now") 10-20 69
BLUE ROCK (4090 "Cross My Heart").....10-20 69
BUDDAH (19 "Baby Baby Please") 10-20 67
BUDDAH (32 "Say It Again")..........10-20 68
BUDDAH (47 "Loving You") 10-20 68
BUDDAH (72 "My Queen of Hearts") 10-20 68
SKY DISC (638 "These Are the Things That Make Me Know Shes Gone")..........5-10 71
SKY DISC (643 "Hiding in Your Heart")......5-10 71
VEEP (1213 "Hey Girl, Do You Love Me")..........25-50 65
VEEP (1223 "He Will Break Your Heart").15-25 65
Also see SERENADERS

WILSON, Tom
Singles: 78 rpm
CREST (1007 "Can You Bop")..........15-25 55
CREST (1020 "Lonely Seagull") 15-25 56
Singles: 7-inch
CREST (1007 "Can You Bop")..........25-50 55
CREST (1020 "Lonely Seagull") 25-50 56

WILSON, Tommy
Singles: 7-inch
COOL (135 "Buzzin' ")..........100-150 62

WILSON, Wally
Singles: 78 rpm
SABRE (106 "If You Don't Love Me") ...100-200 54
Singles: 7-inch
SABRE (106 "If You Don't Love Me") ...400-500 54
Session: Five Echoes.
Also see FIVE ECHOES
Also see SPRIGGS, Wally

WILSON, Willie, & Tunemasters
(Willie & Arlene with the Tunemasters; with Soul Prospectors)
Singles: 7-inch
DAGGER..........10-20
END (1011 "I've Lied"/"Sending This Letter") 100-200 58
Also see SMITH, Arlene
Also see TUNEMASTERS

WIL-SONES
Singles: 7-inch
HIGHLAND (1020 "Let Me Help You") .150-200 61

WILTSHIRE, Teacho
(With the Clef Clubs; with Tin Pan Alley Trio; with His Piano & Orchestra)
Singles: 78 rpm
TIN PAN ALLEY..........10-15 56
Singles: 7-inch
EPIC (9830 "Tell Him")..........5-10 65
NOEL (108 "Glamour")..........20-30 '50s
SAVOY (1551 "It Don't Hurt Anymore")....10-20 58
TIN PAN ALLEY (141 "Love Your Loved One")..........20-30 56
TIN PAN ALLEY (143 "Working Overtime")..........20-30 56
Also see ADELPHIS
Also see COUSINS
Also see FERGUSON, Rudy
Also see FORTUNEERS
Also see GRAY, Wilhelmina
Also see LARKTONES
Also see MELLO MOODS
Also see MR. BEAR
Also see PITT, Eugene
Also see SAMMY & DEL LARKS
Also see TEACHO & STUDENTS

WILTSHIRE, Teacho, & Melloharps
Singles: 7-inch
TIN PAN ALLEY (159 "My Bleeding Heart")..........350-450 56
Also see MELLOHARPS
Also see WILTSHIRE, Teacho

WIMBERLY, Maggie Sue
Singles: 78 rpm
SUN (229 "How Long")..........15-25 55
Singles: 7-inch
SUN (229 "How Long")..........40-60 55

WINBURN, Anna Mae, & Sweethearts of Rhythm
Singles: 78 rpm
KING..........10-15 54
Singles: 7-inch
KING (4707 "That Knocks Me Out") 25-35 54

WINCHELL, Danny
(With Nino & Ebbtides; with Rockin' Chairs)
Singles: 7-inch
MGM (12577 "My Little Tree-House") 15-25 57
RECORTE (406 "Jeannie")..........20-30 59
RECORTE (410 "Don't Say You're Sorry")..........30-40 59
RECORTE (415 "Come Back My Baby") .25-35 59
Also see NINO & EBBTIDES
Also see ROCKIN' CHAIRS

WINCHELL, Paul
Singles: 7-inch
DORE (686 "Little Orphan Boy")..........10-15 63

WINCHELL, Paul, & Jerry Mahoney
(Jerry Mahoney – Paul Winchell)
Singles: 78 rpm
DECCA (308 "Hooray Hooray") ....5-10 '50s
Singles: 7-inch
DECCA (308 "Hooray Hooray")..........5-10 '50s
EPIC (9428 "When You Come to the End of a Lollipop")..........10-20 60
Picture Sleeves
DECCA (308 "Hooray Hooray")..........10-15 '50s
EPIC (9428 "When You Come to the End of a Lollipop")..........10-20 60

WINCHESTER, Jesse LP '72
Singles: 7-inch
AMPEX..........4-8 70-71
BEARSVILLE..........3-6 76-81
LPs: 10/12-inch
AMPEX (10104 "Jesse Winchester")........15-20 70
BEARSVILLE..........10-15 71-81
Promotional LPs
BEARSVILLE (692 "Live at the Bijou") 20-25 75
BEARSVILLE (693 "Live at the Bijou"/"Live Interview")..........30-40 75
Also see HARRIS, Emmylou
Also see MURRAY, Anne

WIND
Singles: 7-inch
BLACKNIGHT (900 "Don't Take Your Love Away")..........10-20 66

WIND P&R '69
Singles: 7-inch
LIFE (200 "Make Believe")..........4-8 69
LPs: 10/12-inch
LIFE..........15-20 69
Member: Tony Orlando.
Also see ORLANDO, Tony

WIND
Singles: 7-inch
SOUND HOUSE (417 "Road to Freedom")..........8-12 '60s
Picture Sleeves
SOUND HOUSE (417 "Road to Freedom")..........10-20 '60s

WIND IN THE WILLOWS LP '68
Singles: 7-inch
CAPITOL (2274 "Uptown Girl")..........5-10 68
LPs: 10/12-inch
CAPITOL (2956 "The Wind in the Willows")..........40-75 68
Members: Deborah Harry; Paul Klein; Peter Brittain; Anton Carysforth; Steve DePhillips.

WINDING, Kai, & His Orchestra P&R/LP '63
(With J.J. Johnson)
Singles: 7-inch
BETHLEHEM (11030 "Stolen Bass")..........5-8 59
BETHLEHEM (11031 "Gong Rock")..........5-8 59
COLUMBIA..........5-10 56-59
IMPULSE..........5-10 61
MGM..........3-6 78
VERVE (Except 10258)..........5-8 62-67
VERVE (10258 "Experiment in Terror") ... 10-15 62
EPs: 7-inch
COLUMBIA..........5-15 58-59
SAVOY..........10-20 53
LPs: 10/12-inch
A&M..........8-12 68
COLUMBIA (900 thru 1300 series)..........15-30 56-59
COLUMBIA (8100 series)..........15-25 59
GLENDALE..........5-8 76-77
IMPULSE..........15-25 61
PICKWICK..........5-10 65-70
ROOST (400 series)..........60-80 52
(10-inch LPs.)
SAVOY (9000 series)..........50-75 53
(10-inch LPs.)
VERVE..........10-25 61-67
(Reads "MGM Records - a Division of Metro-Goldwyn-Mayer, Inc." at bottom of label.)
VERVE..........5-10 73-84
(Reads "Manufactured By MGM Record Corp.," or mentions either Polydor or Polygram at bottom of label.)
VIK (1040 "Afternoon at Birdland")..........40-60 57
(With J.J. Johnson.)
WHO'S WHO IN JAZZ..........5-8 78
Also see STITT, Sonny, & Kai Winding

WINDS OF NOTRE DAME
Singles: 7-inch
FANTASY (596 "Radiation Baby")........200-300 65

WINDSORS
Singles: 7-inch
BACK BEAT (506 "My Gloria") 750-1000 58

WINDSORS
Singles: 7-inch
U.A. (128 "Saki Rock")..........15-25 58

WINDSORS
Singles: 7-inch
WIG-WAG (103 "Carol Ann")..........50-125 59

WINDSORS
Singles: 7-inch
ABC-PAR (10563 "Keep Away")..........5-10 64

WINE, Toni
Singles: 7-inch
ATCO (6736 "Take a Little Time Out for Love")..........4-8 70
ATCO (6773 "Let's Make Love Tonight") 4-8 70
ATCO (6800 "I Want to See Morning with Him")..........4-8 71
COLPIX (715 "My Boyfriend's Coming Home for Christmas")..........5-10 63
COLPIX (732 "I Love That Boy") 5-10 64
COLPIX (742 "A Boy Like You")..........5-10 64
COLPIX (756 "A Girl Is Not a Girl")..........5-10 64
ENTRANCE (7510 "Old Dependable Me")..........4-8 72
PRIVATE STOCK (032 "Maybe My Baby Will")..........4-6 75
PRIVATE STOCK (047 "Forever's Only Been a Day")..........4-6 75
SENATE (2104 "River Deep, Mountain High")..........5-10 67
Picture Sleeves
COLPIX (742 "A Boy Like You")..........10-15 64
(Includes promotional insert card.)
Also see ARCHIES

WINE, Toni, & Billy Joe Royal
Singles: 7-inch
KAT FAMILY (2074 "You Really Got a Hold on Me")....5-8 81
KAT FAMILY (2297 "Wasted Time")....5-8 81
Also see ROYAL, Billy Joe
Also see WINE, Toni

WINFORD, Sue
Singles: 7-inch
JAMIE (1207 "Love by the Juke Box Light")....10-15 61
20TH FOX (435 "If You Try to Steal My Baby")....8-12 63

WINGS
Singles: 7-inch
DUNHILL (4165 "That's Not Real")....5-10 68
LPs: 10/12-inch
DUNHILL (50046 "Wings")....10-15 68

WINGS OVER JORDAN
Singles: 78 rpm
KING....10-15 47-54
Singles: 7-inch
KING (4677 "I Cried and I Cried")....20-40 53
KING (4694 "Trying to Get Ready")....20-40 54

WINK & JUDY WITH THE VICEROYS FIVE
Singles: 7-inch
SEAFAIR (109 "I Still Love You")....5-10 63
Also see VICEROYS

WINKLE, Danny
Singles: 7-inch
VILLAGE (7779 "Don't Fall in Love")....5-10 63

WINKLE PICKERS
Singles: 7-inch
COLPIX (796 "Granny Goose")....5-10 66

WINKLER, Al
Singles: 7-inch
WINKLER (88 "Show Boat Boogie")....75-125

WINKLER, Judy
Singles: 7-inch
JDS (5003 "Another Girl")....10-20 59

WINKLY & NUTLEY
Singles: 7-inch
MK (101 "Report to the Nation")....15-25 60
(No mention of distribution by Roulette.)
MK (101 "Report to the Nation")....10-15 60
(Reads: "Dist. by Roulette Records, Inc.")
Members: Jim Stag; Bob Mitchell.

WINLEY, Paul, & Rockers
Singles: 78 rpm
PREMIUM (401 "My Confession")....15-25 55
Singles: 7-inch
PORWIN (1003 "Party with Paul")....8-12 63
PREMIUM (401 "My Confession")....40-50 55

WINMEN
Singles: 7-inch
RIC (123 "Don't Let Her See You Cry")....5-10 64

WINN, Bob
(With Jimmie Haskell & His Orchestra & Chorus)
Singles: 78 rpm
IMPERIAL....5-10 54-56
Singles: 7-inch
IMPERIAL (5410 "Goin' Home")....10-15 56
IMPERIAL (7004 "River's Edge")....10-15 54

WINN, Ricky
Singles: 7-inch
CAMPBELL (1001 "Till Eternity")....10-20

WINNERS
("With Rhythm Accomp.")
Singles: 78 rpm
DERBY (802 "To Think We're Only Friends")....20-30 52
Singles: 7-inch
DERBY (802 "To Think We're Only Friends")....50-100 52

WINNERS
Singles: 78 rpm
RAINBOW (331 "Can This Be Love")..100-150 56
Singles: 7-inch
RAINBOW (331 "Can This Be Love")..500-600 56

WINSLOW, Barry
Singles: 7-inch
BIG TREE (16000 "Get to Know Me")....4-6 73
LAURIE (3509 "Quality Woman")....5-10 69
Also see ROYAL GUARDSMEN

WINSLOW, Bobby, & Fabulons
Singles: 7-inch
FABULOUS (1001 "Miss Fabulous")....10-15

WINSTON, Hattie
Singles: 7-inch
PARKWAY (928 "Pictures Don't Lie")....5-10 64
PARKWAY (956 "Pass Me By")....5-10 65

WINSTON, Jack, & Hi Jacks
Singles: 7-inch
JAY WING (5806 "It's Rock and Roll")..300-400 58

WINSTON, Roger, & Plaids
Singles: 7-inch
NORTHLAND (7003 "Ever Ever True")....8-12 58
Also see LEE, Robin

WINSTONS *P&R/R&B/LP '69*
Singles: 7-inch
METROMEDIA (117 "Color Him Father")...5-10 69
METROMEDIA (142 "The Love of the Common People")....5-10 69
METROMEDIA (151 "The Greatest Love") 5-10 69
LPs: 10/12-inch
METROMEDIA....10-15 69
Members: Richard Spencer; Ray Martiano; Phil Tolotta; Quincy Mattison; Sonny Peckrol; G.C. Coleman.
Also see SPENCER, Richard, & Winstons

WINSTONS Featuring Bob Bartel
Singles: 7-inch
CINEMASOUND (92057 "To the Aisle")....200-400 57

WINTER, Cyril
Singles: 7-inch
M&L (5000 "Too Much of One Thing")....8-12 '60s
Session: Myron Lee; Caddies.
Also see LEE, Myron

WINTER, Edgar *LP '70*
(Edgar Winter Group; Edgar Winter's White Trash)
Singles: 12-inch
BLUE SKY....4-6 80
BODY ROCK....4-6 83
Singles: 7-inch
BLUE SKY....3-6 75-81
EPIC....4-8 70-75
LPs: 10/12-inch
BACK-TRAC....5-10 85
BLUE SKY (PZ-33483 "Jasmine Nightdreams")....8-10 75
(Stereo.)
BLUE SKY (PZQ-33483 "Jasmine Nightdreams")....15-25 75
(Quadraphonic.)
BLUE SKY (34858 "Re-Cycled")....6-10 77
BLUE SKY (35989 "Edgar Winter Album").6-10 79
BLUE SKY (36494 "Standing on Rock")....6-10 81
EPIC (26503 "Entrance")....10-20 70
EPIC (30512 "Edgar Winter's White Trash")....10-20 71
EPIC (31249 "Roadwork")....15-20 72
(Two discs.)
EPIC (KE-31584 "They Only Come Out at Night")....10-20 72
(Stereo.)
EPIC (KEQ-31584 "They Only Come Out at Night")....15-25 73
(Quadraphonic.)
EPIC (PE-32461 "Shock Treatment")....10-20 74
(Stereo.)
EPIC (PEQ-32461 "Shock Treatment")....15-25 74
(Quadraphonic.)
EPIC (33770 "Entrance"/"White Trash")...10-20 75
(Two discs.)
Also see SWEATHOG / Free Movement / Bob Dylan / Edgar Winter's White Trash
Also see WINTER, Johnny & Edgar

WINTER, Edgar, & Rick Derringer
Singles: 7-inch
BLUE SKY (2762 "Cool Dance")....4-6 75
BLUE SKY (2763 "Diamond Eyes")....4-6 76
LPs: 10/12-inch
BLUE SKY (PZ-33798 "Edgar Winter Group with Rick Derringer")....8-12 75
(Stereo.)
BLUE SKY (PZQ-33798 "Edgar Winter Group with Rick Derringer")....15-25 75
(Quadraphonic.)
Also see WINTER, Edgar

WINTER, Johnny *LP '69*
(With the Crystallers; Jimmy Winter)
Singles: 7-inch
ATLANTIC (2248 "Gangster of Love")....10-20 64
BLUE SKY (2754 "Raised on Rock")....4-6 75
BLUE SKY (2756 "Stranger")....4-6 75
COLUMBIA....4-8 69-74
FROLIC (501 "That's What Love Does")....75-125 62
FROLIC (503 "Voo Doo Twist")....75-125 62
FROLIC (509 "Gangster of Love")....75-125 64
FROLIC (512 "Gone for Bad")....75-125 64
GRT....5-10 69
IMPERIAL....5-10 69
KRCO (107 "One Night of Love")....50-100 61
MGM (13380 "Gone for Bad")....10-15 65
PACEMAKER (243 "Leavin' Home")....10-15 65
SONOBEAT (107 "Rollin' & Tumblin'")....10-15 68
TODD (1084 "Guy You Left Behind")....30-40 63
Picture Sleeves
SONOBEAT (107 "Rollin' & Tumblin'")....50-75 68
(Some sleeves picture the Vulcan Gas Co., an Austin nightclub, and those are at the high end of the price range given. Sleeves that do not picture the club are priced at the lower end.)
LPs: 10/12-inch
ACCORD (7135 "Ready for Winter")....5-10 81
ALLIGATOR....5-8 84-85
BLUE SKY (PZ-33292 "John Dawson Winter III")....8-12 74
(Stereo.)
BLUE SKY (PZQ-33292 "John Dawson Winter III")....15-25 74
(Quadraphonic.)
BLUE SKY (33944 "Captured Live")....8-12 76
BLUE SKY (34575 "White, Hot & Blue")....8-12 78
BLUE SKY (34813 "Nothin' But the Blues")....8-12 77
BLUE SKY (36343 "Raisin' Cain")....6-10 80
BUDDAH (7513 "First Winter")....15-20 69
CBS ASSOCIATED....5-8
COLUMBIA (9826 "Johnny Winter")....15-20 69
COLUMBIA (9947 "Second Winter")....20-15 69
(Two discs.)
COLUMBIA (30221 "Johnny Winter And")....10-15 70
COLUMBIA (KC-32188 "Still Alive & Well")....10-15 73
(Stereo.)
COLUMBIA (CQ-32715 "Still Alive & Well")....15-25 73
(Quadraphonic.)
COLUMBIA (KC-32715 "Saints & Sinners")....10-15 74
(Stereo.)
COLUMBIA (CQ-32715 "Saints & Sinners")....15-25 74
(Quadraphonic.)
COLUMBIA (30475 "Johnny Winter Live")....10-15 71
COLUMBIA (33651 "Johnny Winter Live"/"Johnny Winter And")....10-20 75
(Two discs.)
CRAZY CAJUN....8-10
GRT (10010 "The Johnny Winter Story").10-15 69
IMPERIAL (12431 "Progressive Blues Experiment")....15-25 69
JANUS (3008 "About Blues")....15-20 69
JANUS (3023 "Early Times")....15-20 69
JANUS (3056 "Before the Storm")....15-20 70
(Two discs.)
MCA (42241 "The Winter of '88")....5-10 88
SONOBEAT ("Progressive Blues Experiment")....150-200 68
(Limited edition, autographed issue.)
SONOBEAT ("Progressive Blues Experiment")....75-125 68
(Limited edition, NOT autographed.)
U.A. (139 "Austin, Texas")....8-12 74
Also see COLE, Junior
Also see JOHNNY & JAMMERS
Also see GREAT BELIEVERS
Also see GUITAR SLIM
Also see MIZZELL, Bobby
Also see SPRINGSTEEN, Bruce / Johnny Winter / Hollies
Also see TEXAS "GUITAR" SLIM
Also see WATERS, Muddy

WINTER, Johnny / Argent / Chambers Brothers / John Hammond
EPs: 7-inch
COLUMBIA/PLAYBACK (14 "Good Morning Little Schoolgirl")....15-25 72
Also see ARGENT
Also see CHAMBERS BROTHERS

WINTER, Johnny & Edgar *LP '76*
Singles: 7-inch
BLUE SKY (2764 "Soul Man")....4-6 76
CASCADE....35-45 64
LPs: 10/12-inch
BLUE SKY (242 "Johnny & Edgar Winter Discuss *Together*")....15-20 76
(Promotional issue only.)
BLUE SKY (34033 "Together")....8-10 76
Also see LA CROIX, Jerry
Also see WINTER, Edgar
Also see WINTER, Johnny

WINTERHALTER, Hugo, & His Orchestra *P&R '49*
Singles: 78 rpm
COLUMBIA....3-5 49-50
RCA....3-5 50-57
Singles: 7-inch
ABC-PAR....4-6 63
COLUMBIA....5-8 50
KAPP....4-6 64-65
MUSICOR....4-6 68-70
RCA....6-12 50-63
EPs: 7-inch
RCA....10-15 50-59
LPs: 10/12-inch
ABC-PAR....5-10 63
CAMDEN....4-8 69-72
KAPP....5-10 65
MUSICO....4-8 69-70
MUSICOR....5-10 68-71
RCA....5-15 50-77
TRIP....4-8 76
Also see CAREY, Bill
Also see COMO, Perry
Also see DE CASTRO SISTERS / Hugo Winterhalter & His Orchestra
Also see PETERSON, Ray
Also see STEVENS, Tari
Also see WARREN, Fran

WINTERS, Chuck
Singles: 7-inch
REGAL (7505 "Buckskin")....15-25 58

WINTERS, David
Singles: 7-inch
ADDISON (15004 "Sunday Kind of Love")....20-30 59
MERCURY (72537 "Anti-Protest Protest Song")....8-12 66
RORI (703 "Bye Bye")....10-20 62

WINTERS, Don *C&W '61*
Singles: 78 rpm
COIN (102 "Be My Baby")....20-30 56
Singles: 7-inch
COIN (102 "Be My Baby")....50-75 56
DECCA....5-10 60-62
HAMILTON (50039 "Jamaica Joe")....5-10 63
ROBBINS (2005 "You're Right")....10-20

WINTERS, Jonathan *LP '60*
(With the Martians)
Singles: 7-inch
CORAL (61988 "Nee Nee Na Na Na Na Nu Nu")....10-15 57
EPs: 7-inch
VERVE (5077 "Another Day, Another World")....8-10 62
(Promotional issue only.)
LPs: 10/12-inch
COLUMBIA....8-15 68-73
VERVE....15-30 59-60
(Reads "Verve Records, Inc." at bottom of label.)

VERVE....................10-20 61-67
(Reads "MGM Records - a Division of Metro-Goldwyn-Mayer, Inc." at bottom of label.)
VERVE....................5-10 73-84
(Reads"Manufactured By MGM Record Corp.," or mentions either Poly dor or Polygram at bottom of label.)

WINTERS, Lee
Singles: 78 rpm
CROWN (142 "The Wallflower")..............10-15 55
Singles: 7-inch
CROWN (142 "The Wallflower")..............20-30 55

WINTERS, Marsha
Singles: 7-inch
STEPHENY (1805 "Stay")..............8-12 57

WINTERS, Ron
(With the Patriots)
Singles: 7-inch
DIMENSION (1022 "Snow Girl")..............10-15 64
DIMENSION (1029 "Back in the U.S.A.")..10-15 64
DIMENSION (1033 "Red MG")..............10-15 64
SMASH (1987 "My Girl")..............10-15 65

WINTERS, Ruby *R&B '67*
(Ruby Winter)
Singles: 7-inch
CERTRON (10027 "It's Not Easy Baby")....5-10 71
DIAMOND (207 "In the Middle of a Heartache")..............20-30 66
DIAMOND (223 "Try Me")..............15-25 67
DIAMOND (230 "I Want Action")..............10-20 67
DIAMOND (255 "I Don't Want to Cry")..... 10-20 69
DIAMOND (258 "Just a Dream")..............10-20 69
DIAMOND (265 "Always David")..............10-20 69
DIAMOND (269 "Guess Who")..............10-20 69
MILLENNIUM (612 "I Will")..............4-6 78
(Rerecorded version of Polydor hit.)
MILLENNIUM (619 "Treat Me Right")..........4-6 78
PLAYBOY (6048 "Without You")..............5-10 75
POLYDOR (14202 "I Will")..............5-10 73
POLYDOR (14249 "Love Me Now")..............5-10 74
LPs: 10/12-inch
DIAMOND ("Ruby Winters")..............100-200 '60s
(Exact title and selection number not known. May have been promo only.)
MILLENNIUM..............8-10 78
Also see THUNDER, Johnny, & Ruby Winters

WINTERS, Tommy
Singles: 7-inch
DOTTIE (1007 "Stop the Clock")..............10-15 61

WINWOOD, Steve *LP '71*
Singles: 7-inch
ISLAND..............3-6 77-87
U.A...............4-8 71
VIRGIN..............3-5 88-90
Picture Sleeves
ISLAND..............3-5 80-88
VIRGIN..............3-5 88-89
LPs: 10/12-inch
ISLAND..............5-8 77-87
U.A. (5550 "Welcome to the Canteen") 8-12 71
U.A. (9950 "Winwood")..............20-30 71
(With liner notes by Bobby Abrahms.)
U.A. (9964 "Winwood")..............10-15 71
(Without liner notes.)
VIRGIN..............5-8 88-90
Also see BLIND FAITH
Also see DAVIS, Spencer
Also see McDONALD & GILES
Also see TRAFFIC

WISDOMS
Singles: 7-inch
GAITY (169 "Two Hearts Make One Love")..............1000-2000 59
(500 made.)

WISDOMS
Singles: 7-inch
PARIS TOWER (113 "Outer Limits '67").. 10-15 67

WISE, Wild Willie
Singles: 7-inch
BAJA (4507 "Soul Brother No. 1")..............5-10 68

WISEMAN, Mac *C&W '55*
(With Sonny Osborne; with Tommy Jackson; with Shenandoah Cut-ups; with Johnny Gimble; with Osborne Brothers; with "Friend")
Singles: 78 rpm
DOT..............5-10 51-57
Singles: 7-inch
CAPITOL..............5-10 62-63
CHURCHILL..............3-5 78-79
DOT..............8-12 51-59
MGM..............4-6 68
RCA..............4-6 69-73
WISE (1062 "Bringing Mary Home")..............4-6 65
EPs: 7-inch
DOT..............10-20 55
LPs: 10/12-inch
ABC..............10-15 74-77
CMH..............5-10 76-82
CAPITOL (1800 "Bluegrass Favorites")....25-40 62
DOT (3084 "Tis Sweet to Be Remembered")..............25-50 58
DOT (3135 thru 3697)..............15-30 59-66
(Monaural.)
DOT (25135 thru 25896)..............15-35 59-68
(Stereo.)
GILLEY'S..............10-20
GUSTO..............5-10
HAMILTON..............10-20 64-66
MCA..............5-10
PICKWICK/HILLTOP..............10-15 67
RCA..............6-12 70-75
RIDGE RUNNER..............5-10
RURAL RHYTHM..............10-20
VETCO..............10-20
Also see HERMAN, Woody
Also see OSBORNE BROTHERS & MAC WISEMAN

WISHBONE ASH *LP '71*
Singles: 7-inch
ATLANTIC..............4-6 77
DECCA..............4-6 71-72
MCA..............4-6 73-78
Picture Sleeves
MCA..............4-6 78
LPs: 10/12-inch
ATLANTIC..............6-10 76
DECCA (Except 1922)..............10-15 71-72
DECCA (1922 "Live from Memphis")........15-20 72
(Promotional issue only.)
FANTASY..............5-8 82
I.R.S./NO SPEAK..............5-8 '90s
MCA..............5-10 73-82
Members: Steve Upton; Andy Powel; Ted Turner; Martin Turner; Laurie Wisefield.

WISNER, Jimmy
Singles: 7-inch
CAMEO (373 "A Walk in Space")..............10-15 65
Also see BIG J.J.
Also see PARISIANS

WITCHER, Norman
Singles: 7-inch
POOR BOY (102 "Somebody's Been Rockin' My Boat")..............150-200 58

WITCHES
Singles: 7-inch
BANG (505 "My Little Baby")..............20-30 65

WITHERS, Bill *P&R/R&B/LP '71*
Singles: 12-inch
COLUMBIA..............4-6 79
Singles: 7-inch
COLUMBIA..............3-6 75-85
SUSSEX..............4-6 71-75
Picture Sleeves
SUSSEX..............4-6 72
LPs: 10/12-inch
COLUMBIA..............5-8 75-85
SUSSEX..............8-12 71-75
Also see WASHINGTON, Grover, Jr.
Also see WOMACK, Bobby, & Bill Withers

WITHERSPOON, Jimmy *R&B '49*
(With Groove Holmes; with Jay McShann & His Band; with Ben Webster; with Panama Francis & Savoy Sultans; with Wilbur de Paris.)
Singles: 78 rpm
CHECKER..............20-30 54-55
FEDERAL..............20-30 52-53
DOWN BEAT..............15-25 48-49
MODERN..............15-25 49-53
RCA..............15-25 57
SUPREME..............25-35 48-49
SWING BEAT..............15-25 49
SWING TIME..............15-25 51
Singles: 7-inch
ABC (11288 "Handbags and Gladrags")......4-6 71
BLUE NOTE..............4-6 75
BLUESWAY..............4-6 69
CAPITOL..............4-6 74
CHECKER (798 "Big Daddy")..............25-50 54
(Black vinyl.)
CHECKER (798 "Big Daddy")..............100-200 54
(Colored vinyl.)
CHECKER (810 "Time Brings About a Change")..............25-50 55
CHECKER (826 "It Ain't No Secret")........25-50 55
DISCOS RAFF (501 "When My Heart Beats Like a Hammer")..............5-10
FEDERAL (12095 "Two Little Girls")......75-100 52
FEDERAL (12099 "Lucille")..............75-100 52
FEDERAL (12107 "Corn Whiskey")........75-100 52
FEDERAL (12118 "Jay's Blues")..............75-100 53
FEDERAL (12128 "One Fine Gal")........75-100 53
FEDERAL (12138 "Back Door Blues")...75-100 53
FEDERAL (12155 "Fast Woman, Slow Gin")..............75-100 53
FEDERAL (12156 "Sad Life")..............100-125 53
FEDERAL (12173 "24 Sad Hours")......100-125 54
FEDERAL (12180 "It")..............75-100 54
FEDERAL (12189 "I Done Told You So")..............75-100 54
GNP (156 "Ain't Nobody's Business")......10-20 59
HI FI (954 "Every Time I Feel the Spirit") .10-15 60
KENT (20 "She Moves Me")..............10-20 '60s
(Stereo 33.)
KENT (23 "Boogie Woogie Woman")......10-20 '60s
(Stereo 33.)
KENT (343 "Stormy Monday Blues")........10-20 60
KENT (4551 "Ain't Nobody's Business").......4-6 71
KING (5997 "Foolish Prayer")..............15-25 65
MODERN (857 "Wind Is Blowin' ")..........40-60 52
MODERN (877 "Love My Baby")..............40-60 52
MODERN (895 "Baby Baby")..............40-60 53
MODERN (903 "Each Slip of the Way")...40-60 53
MODERN (909 "Oh Mother Dear Mother")..............75-125 53
PACIFIC JAZZ (327 "Ain't Nobody's Business")..............10-15 62
PRESTIGE (266 "Baby Baby Baby")..........8-10 63
PRESTIGE (274 "Mean Ole Frisco")..........8-10 63
PRESTIGE (341 "You're Next")..............8-10 64
PRESTIGE (355 "One Last Chance")........8-10 65
RCA (6977 "Ain't Nobody's Business").....15-25 57
RCA (7075 "All Right, Miss Moore")..........15-25 57
RCA (7377 "Ooh Wee, When the Lights Go Out")..............15-25 58
REPRISE (275 "Key to the Highway")......10-15 64
REPRISE (20013 "I Don't Know")..............10-15 61
REPRISE (20029 "Hey, Mrs. Jones")........10-15 61
RIP (126 "Endless Sleep")..............20-30 58
TRIO (711 "You Can Make It If You Try")...5-10
VEE-JAY (322 "Everything But You").......10-20 59
VERVE..............5-10 66-67
WORLD PACIFIC (327 "Ain't Nobody's Business")..............10-15 62
WORLD PACIFIC (807 "When the Lights Go Out")..............10-20 59
EPs: 7-inch
ATLANTIC (600 "New Orleans Blues") ..50-100 57
LPs: 10/12-inch
ABC..............8-12 70
ATLANTIC (1266 "New Orleans Blues")..............100-200 57
BLUE NOTE..............8-12 75
BLUESWAY (6026 "The Blues Singer").....8-15 69
BLUESWAY (6040 "Hunh!")..............8-15 70
BLUESWAY (6051 "The Best of Jimmy Witherspoon")..............8-15 70
CAPITOL..............8-10 74
CONSTELLATION..............15-25 64
CROWN (215 "Jimmy Witherspoon Sings the Blues")..............20-30 61
(Stereo. Black Vinyl.)
CROWN (215 "Jimmy Witherspoon Sings the Blues")..............50-100 61
(Stereo. Colored Vinyl.)
CROWN (5156 "Jimmy Witherspoon").....30-40 60
(Monaural selection number not known.)
CROWN (5192 "Jimmy Witherspoon Sings the Blues")..............20-30 61
(Monaural.)
FANTASY..............10-15 72
HI FI (422 "Feelin' the Spirit")..............35-50 59
HI FI JAZZ (426 "At the Renaissance")..75-100 60
INNER CITY..............5-10 81
MCA..............5-8 83
MUSE..............5-8 83
OLYMPIC..............8-10 73
PRESTIGE..............10-20 64-69
RCA (1048 "Goin' to Kansas City Blues")..8-12 75
RCA (1639 "Goin' to Kansas City Blues")..............50-100 58
REPRISE (2008 "Spoon")..............25-35 61
REPRISE (6012 "Hey, Mrs. Jones")........25-35 62
REPRISE (6057 "Roots")..............25-35 62
SURREY..............12-15 65
SUTTON..............10-20 '60s
UNITED..............8-15
VERVE (5000 series)..............12-15 66-68
VERVE (8000 series)..............8-10 74
VERVE FOLKWAYS (3011 "Blues Box").25-30 66
WORLD PACIFIC (1267 "Singin' the Blues")..............40-60 59
WORLD PACIFIC (1402 "There's Good Rockin' Tonight")..............30-40 61
Session: Lamplighters.
Also see BURDON, Eric, & Jimmy Witherspoon
Also see CHARLES, Ray, & Jimmy Witherspoon
Also see FREEMAN, Ernie
Also see HOLMES, Richard "Groove"
Also see LAMPLIGHTERS
Also see McSHANN, Jay
Also see VINSON, Eddie / Jimmy Witherspoon
Also see WALKER, T-Bone

WITHERSPOON, Jimmy, & Wilbur DeParis
LP: 10/12-inch
ATLANTIC..............10-20

WITHERSPOON, Jimmy, & Quintones
Singles: 78 rpm
ATCO (6084 "My Girl Ivy")..............30-40 57
Singles: 7-inch
ATCO (6084 "My Girl Ivy")..............30-40 57
Also see QUINTONES

WITNESS INC.
Singles: 7-inch
APEX (77063 "Not You Girl")..............20-30 68
APEX (77077 "Harlem Lady")..............8-12 68
APEX (77087 "Visions of Vanessa")........8-12 68
APEX (77093 "I've Got to Go")..............8-12 68
DECCA (32328 "Harlem Lady")..............8-12 68
Picture Sleeves
APEX (77077 "Harlem Lady")..............10-15 68

WITT, Maylon D.
Singles: 7-inch
PAULA (235 "Never Never")..............5-10 66

WITTER, Jimmy, & Shadows *P&R '61*
Singles: 7-inch
ELVIS (900 "If You Love My Woman").400-600 57
NEPTUNE (118 "My Kind of Woman").....50-75 61
U.A. (301 "Pretty Little Girl")..............10-20 61
Members: Jimmy Witter; Sidney Smith.

WIZARD
LPs: 10/12-inch
PEON (1069 "Original Wizard")..........150-200 71

WIZARDS
Singles: 7-inch
ERA (3161 "I Want to Live")..............5-10 66

WIZARDS FROM KANSAS
LPs: 10/12-inch
MERCURY (61309 "The Wizards from Kansas")..............50-100 70
Members: Robert Menadier; John Coffin; Marc Caplan; Robert Crain.

WOBBLERS
Singles: 7-inch
KING (5585 "Wobble")..............5-10 61

WOLCOTT, Charles, & MGM Orch. *P&R '60*
Singles: 7-inch
MGM (12944 "Ruby Duby Du")..............8-12 60

WOLF

Singles: 7-inch

ACADEMY ("Stompin' to the Beat") 75-125

(Selection number not known.)

WOLF, Dick

Singles: 7-inch

DALE (101 "Spine Tinglin' Love") 15-25 57

WOLF, Mike

Singles: 7-inch

(5053 "Like Magic") .... 10-20 '60s

(No label named used. Single-sided. Promotional issue only.)

WOLF, Philip

Singles: 7-inch

SIMS (252 "Little Woman") 5-10 65

WOLF MEN

Singles: 7-inch

BOBBETTE (380 "She Loves Me, She Loves Me Not") .... 100-150 '60s

WOLFE, Danny

Singles: 78 rpm

DOT 20-60 57

Singles: 7-inch

DOT (15591 "Pretty Blue Jean Baby") 20-40 57

DOT (15667 "Let's Flat Git It") 40-60 57

DOT (15715 "Pucker Paint") 20-40 57

WOLFE, Dick, & Wolverines

Singles: 7-inch

ADMIRAL (104 "Sigma 7") 30-50 63

WOLFMAN

Singles: 7-inch

OKEH (7269 "Strange") 10-20 66

WOLFMAN JACK

(Bob Smith)

Singles: 7-inch

AGC 4-8

CAVDA (333 "Free Shots"/"Something for Nothing") 5-10

(B-side by Debbie Sabusawa. Promotional issue only. Made for the Citizens Alliance for VD Awareness.)

WOODEN NICKEL 4-8 72-73

LPs: 10/12-inch

COLUMBIA 8-10 75

WOODEN NICKEL 8-12 72-73

Also see GUESS WHO

Also see STAMPEDERS

WOLFMAN JACK & WOLF PACK

Singles: 7-inch

BREAD (71 "Wolfman Boogie") 25-30 65

BREAD (73 "New Orleans") 25-30 65

LPs: 10/12-inch

BREAD (0170 "Wolfman Jack and the Wolf Pack") 300-400 65

Also see WOLFMAN JACK

WOLFORD, Jimmy

Singles: 7-inch

4 STAR (1714 "My Name Is Jimmy") 75-125 58

WOMACK, Bobby P&R/R&B/LP '68

(With the Brotherhood; with Peace)

Singles: 12-inch

ELEKTRA/WOMACK 4-6 83

Singles: 7-inch

ARISTA 3-5 79

ATLANTIC (2388 "How Does It Feel") 5-10 67

BEVERLY GLEN 3-5 81-84

CHECKER (1122 "I Found a True Love") ... 5-10 65

COLUMBIA 4-6 76-78

COLUMBIA/BROTHERHOOD 4-6 76-77

ELEKTRA/WOMACK 3-5 83

HIM 3-5

KEYMEN 3-5

LIBERTY 4-6 70

MCA 3-5 86

MINIT 5-10 67-70

SOUFFLE 3-5

U.A. 4-6 71-76

Picture Sleeves

MCA 3-5 86

EPs: 7-inch

U.A. 10-15 72

(Promotional issue only.)

LPs: 10/12-inch

ARISTA 5-8 79

BEVERLY GLEN 5-8 81-84

COLUMBIA 8-10 75-78

COLUMBIA/BROTHERHOOD 8-10 76

ELEKTRA/WOMACK 5-8 83

LIBERTY (7600 series) 8-10 70

LIBERTY (10000 series) .... 5-8 '80s

MCA 5-8 85

MINIT 10-12 68-70

U.A. 8-10 71-76

Also see SUGAR & SPICES

Also see VALENTINOS

Also see WOMACK BROTHERS

WOMACK, Bobby, & Patti Labelle P&R/R&B '84

Singles: 7-inch

BEVERLY GLEN (2012 "Love Has Finally Come At Last") 3-5 84

BEVERLY GLEN (2018 "It Takes a Lot of Strength to Say Goodbye") 3-5 84

Also see LABELLE, Patti

Also see WOMACK, Bobby

WOMACK, Bobby, & Gabor Szabo

Singles: 7-inch

BLUE THUMB (200 "Breezin' ") 4-8 71

Also see SZABO, GABOR

WOMACK, Bobby, & Bill Withers R&B '75

Singles: 7-inch

U.A. 4-6 75

Also see WITHERS, Bill

WOMACK BROTHERS

Singles: 7-inch

SAR (118 "Somebody's Wrong") 5-10 61

Members: Bobby; Cecil; Curtis; Friendly Jr.; Warris.

Also see VALENTINOS

Also see WOMACK, Bobby

WOMB

Singles: 7-inch

DOT (17250 "Hang On") 5-10 69

LPs: 10/12-inch

DOT (25933 "Womb") 10-20 69

DOT (25959 "Overdub") 10-20 69

WONDER, Dee, & Rhythm Fame

Singles: 7-inch

WARE (6003 "What You've Done") 10-20 65

WONDER, Dickie

Singles: 7-inch

SOUND OF SOUL (101 "The Story of My Love") 30-40 65

WONDER, Stevie P&R/R&B/LP '63

(Little Stevie Wonder)

Singles: 12-inch

MOTOWN 4-8

TAMLA 4-8

Singles: 7-inch

MOTOWN 3-5 84-88

(Black vinyl.)

MOTOWN 4-6 87

(Colored vinyl.)

MOTOWN/TOPPS (8 "Fingertips Part 2") 50-75 67

MOTOWN/TOPPS (10 "Uptight") 50-75 67

(Topps Chewing Gum promotional items. Single-sided, cardboard flexi, picture discs. Issued with generic paper sleeve.)

TAMLA (1600 thru 1800 series) 3-5 82-86

TAMLA (54061 "I Call It Pretty Music") 25-35 62

TAMLA (54074 "Contract on Love") 25-35 62

TAMLA (54080 "Fingertips") 5-10 63

TAMLA (54086 "Workout Stevie, Workout") 5-10 63

TAMLA (54090 "Castles in the Sand") 8-12 64

TAMLA (54096 "Hey Harmonica Man") 8-12 64

TAMLA (54103 "Happy Street") 10-20 64

TAMLA (54108 "Pretty Little Angel") 8-12 64

TAMLA (54114 "Kiss Me Baby") 8-12 65

TAMLA (54119 thru 54139) 5-10 65-66

(Black vinyl.)

TAMLA (54139 "A Place in the Sun") 10-15 66

(Colored vinyl. Promotional issue only.)

TAMLA (54142 "Some Day at Christmas") . 8-12 66

TAMLA (54147 thru 54331) 3-6 67-81

(Black vinyl.)

TAMLA (54147 thru 54331) 10-20 69-81

(Colored vinyl. Promotional issues only.)

MOTOWN 3-5 82

Picture Sleeves

MOTOWN 3-5 87

TAMLA (1639 thru 1846) 4-8 82-86

TAMLA (54061 "I Call It Pretty Music") 25-50 62

TAMLA (54080 "Fingertips") 15-25 63

TAMLA (54136 "Blowin' in the Wind") 15-25 66

TAMLA (54139 "A Place in the Sun") 15-25 66

TAMLA (54281 thru 54317) 4-8 77-80

EPs: 7-inch

MOTOWN (2006 "Stevie Wonder") .... 15-25 '60s

MOTOWN (2020 "Songs in the Key of Life") 10-15 76

TAMLA (340 "Something Extra for *Songs in the Key of Life*") 5-8 76

TAMLA (60272 "Stevie Wonder") 15-25 67

LPs: 10/12-inch

MOTOWN (100 & 200 series) 5-8 82

MOTOWN (800 series) 12-15 77

MOTOWN (6000 series) 5-8 84-91

TAMLA (232 "Tribute to Uncle Ray") 50-80 63

TAMLA (233 "The Jazz Soul of Stevie Wonder") 50-80 63

TAMLA (240 "Little Stevie Wonder") 40-50 63

TAMLA (250 "With a Song in My Heart") .. 35-55 64

TAMLA (255 "At the Beach") 35-55 64

TAMLA (268 thru 279) 15-20 66-67

TAMLA (281 "Someday at Christmas") 30-40 67

TAMLA (282 thru 371) 8-15 68-79

TAMLA (373 "Hotter Than July") 5-8 80

TAMLA (6000 series) 10-12 82-85

Promotional LPs

MOTOWN (PR-77 "Hotter Than July") 10-15 80

TAMLA (PR-61 "Stevie Wonder's Journey Through the Secret Life of Plants") 10-15 79

TAMLA (PR-98/99 "Radio Programmer's Special") .... 15-20 '80s

Session: Temptations.

Also see JACKSONS

Also see JOHN, Elton

Also see MAIN INGREDIENT

Also see MASON, Dave

Also see McCARTNEY, Paul, & Stevie Wonder

Also see REDNOW, Eivets

Also see ROSS, Diana, Stevie Wonder, Marvin Gaye & Smokey Robinson

Also see TEMPTATIONS / Stevie Wonder

Also see WILLIAMS, Deniece

WONDER, Stevie / John Denver

Singles: 7-inch

WHAT'S IT ALL ABOUT 4-8 80

(Public service, radio station issue.)

Also see DENVER, John

WONDER, Stevie, & Michael Jackson P&R '88

Singles: 7-inch

MOTOWN (1930 "Get It") 3-5 88

Picture Sleeves

MOTOWN (1930 "Get It") 3-5 88

Also see JACKSON, Michael

WONDER, Stevie, & Clarence Paul

(Little Stevie Wonder & Clarence Paul)

Singles: 7-inch

TAMLA (54070 "Little Water Boy") 25-35 62

Also see PAUL, Clarence

WONDER, Stevie / Dionne Warwick LP '84

LPs: 10/12-inch

MOTOWN (6108 "The Woman in Red") 5-10 84

Also see WARWICK, Dionne

Also see WONDER, Stevie

WONDER DOGS

Singles: 7-inch

PARIS TOWER (140 "Bo Diddley") .... 10-20 '60s

WONDER WHO? P&R '67

(4 Seasons)

Singles: 7-inch

COLLECTABLES .... 3-5 '80s

PHILIPS (40324 "Don't Think Twice") 5-10 65

PHILIPS (40380 "On the Good Ship Lollipop") 5-10 66

PHILIPS (40471 "Lonesome Road") 5-10 67

VEE-JAY (717 "Peanuts") 10-20 66

Picture Sleeves

PHILIPS (40324 "Don't Think Twice") 15-20 65

PHILIPS (40380 "On the Good Ship Lollipop") 15-20 66

PHILIPS (40471 "Lonesome Road") 15-20 67

Also see 4 SEASONS

WONDERLETTES

Singles: 7-inch

BAJA (4506 "How Soon") 10-15 68

WONDERETTES

Singles: 7-inch

ENTERPRISE 10-20 65

RUBY (5065 "I Feel Strange") 20-30 65

U.A. (944 "I Feel Strange") 10-20 65

Also see ST. JOHN, Rose, & Wonderettes

WONDERFUL ONES

Singles: 7-inch

LAURIE (3286 "I Won't Give Up") 5-10 65

WONDERLIES

Singles: 78 rpm

SHOW TIME 10-15 55

Singles: 7-inch

SHOW TIME (1108 "Pop, Potato Chip and Pickle") 30-40 55

WONDERLING, John

Singles: 7-inch

LOMA (2106 "Man of Straw") 5-10 68

PARAMOUNT (0183 "Shadows") 4-8 72

WONDERS

Singles: 78 rpm

SPACE (202 "Little Girl") 500-600 54

Also see DUNDEES

WONDERS

Singles: 7-inch

RESERVE (122 "Well Now") 15-20 57

WONDERS

Singles: 7-inch

FORWARD (601 "Be My Love") 100-125 58

Also see ALLEN, Tony

WONDERS

Singles: 7-inch

DEOWEE (6132 "Strings-A-Plenty") 10-15 61

WONDERS

Singles: 7-inch

BAMBOO (523 "With These Hands") ... 100-150 62

CHESAPEAKE (604 "I Wonder") 30-40 61

COLPIX (699 "Say There") 10-15 63

EMBER (1051 "I'll Write a Book") 15-25 59

MANCO (1024 "One Day at a Time") 10-20 61

SIANA (722 "Go Go Theme") 5-10 65

WONG, Hop A Long

Singles: 7-inch

DECCA (30462 "Goody Goody") 8-12 57

WOOD, Anita

Singles: 7-inch

ABC-PAR (9947 "Crying in the Chapel") .. 15-25 58

SANTO (9008 "Memories of You") 8-12 63

SANTO (9054 "Dream Baby") 8-12 63

SUN (361 "I'll Wait Forever") 20-30 61

WOOD, Austin

Singles: 7-inch

SURE (5015 "Theres' a Big Rock in the Road") 15-25

SURE (5102 "So Let's Rock") 50-100

WOOD, Billy, & Skylighters

Singles: 7-inch

PEN (110 "Look a Here") 10-20 62

(First issue.)

W.B. (5291 "Look a Here") 8-12 62

WOOD, Bobby P&R '64

(Bobby "Guitar" Wood)

Singles: 7-inch

CHALLENGE (9140 "Day After Forever") 10-15 62

CHALLENGE (9160 "Day After Forever") .. 8-12 62

CINNAMON 4-6 74

COLT (9322 "Mighty Nice to Know You") 4-6

JOY 8-12 63-65

LUCKY ELEVEN (361 "One Day Behind") ... 4-6 73

MALA (526 "My Special Angel") 8-12 66

MGM 5-10 67-69

SUN (369 "Everybody's Searchin' ") . 1000-2000 62

LPs: 10/12-inch

JOY (1001 "Bobby Wood") 20-30 64

Also see HALEY, Bill

Also see PRESLEY, Elvis

WOOD, Brenton *P&R/R&B/LP '67*

Singles: 7-inch

BRENT (7052 "Good Lovin' ")....................8-12 66
BRENT (7057 "Cross the Bridge")........... 10-20 66
BRENT (7068 "I Want Love")................... 10-15 67
CREAM...4-6 76-78
DOUBLE SHOT 4-6 67-71
FIRST PRESIDENT (428 "Kangaroo") 10-15 60
MR. WOOD 4-6 72-73
PROPHESY (3002 "Sticky Boom Boom Too Cold") 4-6 73
PROPHESY (3003 "Another Saturday Night")..4-6 73
WAND (145 "Mr. Schemer")................... 25-35 64
W.B. 4-6 75

LPs: 10/12-inch

CREAM...5-8 77
DOUBLE SHOT 10-20 67
Also see LITTLE FREDDY & ROCKETS

WOOD, Chuck

Singles: 7-inch

ERA (3145 "Blind Date")..............................5-10 65
MERCURY (72555 "Other Man")....................5-10 66
MERCURY (72609 "I Really Got the Business")..5-10 66
ROULETTE (4754 "Seven Days Too Long")..5-10 67
ROULETTE (7004 "Baby You Win")............5-10 68
SSS INT'L (703 "Son, Daddy Told You a Lie")..5-10 67
W.B. (5193 "Rock and Roll Waltz")............8-12 61

WOOD, Del

Singles: 7-inch

EAGLE (1000 "It Ain't Right") 40-60 58

WOOD, Eddie
(With the Bel-Aires)

Singles: 7-inch

EMBER (1064 "Girl of My Best Friend") .. 15-25 60
PALMER (5026 "Why Did You Call")..........5-10 68
PERICO (1258 "One")...................................5-10 65

WOOD, Glen

Singles: 7-inch

VANDAN (8306 "Poor Little Girl") 5-10 64

WOOD, Gloria
(With Ivan Scott & His Orchestra & Four Jewels; with Afterbeats; with Alexander Avala; with Pete Candoli & His Orchestra)

Singles: 78 rpm

CAPITOL 5-10 53
DIAMOND..8-12 56

Singles: 7-inch

BUENA VISTA (361 "Ching Ching")......... 10-15 60
CAPITOL (2471 "Hey, Bellboy!")............. 10-15 53
COLUMBIA (41070 "Back Door")............ 10-15 57
DIAMOND (3001 "The Rock and the Roll")... 15-25 56
ZEPHYR (009 "Scoundrel Blues") 10-15 57
ZEPHYR (010 "Lullaby in Blue") 10-15 57
Also see ANNETTE

WOOD, Jimmy, & Changers

Singles: 7-inch

JAMAKA (1010 "That's Why I Love You") 50-75

WOOD, Lori
(With the Belmonts)

Singles: 7-inch

AMY (842 "But That Was Long Ago") 40-50 62
ATLAS (1248 "Ain't Got No Money for Jukebox").. 10-20 60

WOOD, Natalie / Sal Mineo

Singles: 7-inch

RAINBBO ("Natalie Wood & Sal Mineo"). 30-40 57
(Cardboard picture disc. No selection number used.)
Also see MINEO, Sal

WOOD, Norman

Singles: 7-inch

TAMM (2015 "Black Lake Boogie")........ 75-125

WOOD, Ron *LP '75*
(Ronnie Wood)

Singles: 7-inch

COLUMBIA...4-6 79
W.B. 4-6 75-76

Promotional Singles

COLUMBIA...4-8 79
W.B. 4-8 75-76

LPs: 10/12-inch

COLUMBIA...5-10 79-81
W.B. 8-12 74-75
Also see BECK, Jeff
Also see ROLLING STONES
Also see STEWART, Rod, & Ronnie Wood
Also see THOMAS, Guthrie

WOOD, Ron, & Ronnie Lane
(With Pete Townshend)

LPs: 10/12-inch

ATCO (126 "Mahoney's Last Stand") 10-15 76
(Soundtrack.)
THUNDERBOLT (067 "Mahoney's Last Stand")..15-20 76
(Picture disc.)
Also see TOWNSHEND, Pete, & Ronnie Lane
Also see WOOD, Ron

WOOD, Scott

Singles: 7-inch

BEAT (1008 "Chicken Rock")......................8-12 59

WOOD, Tommy

Singles: 7-inch

D (1000 "Can't Play Hookey") 50-75 58

WOOD, Vernetta

Singles: 7-inch

AMY (873 "Keep on Dancing")....................5-10 62

WOOD SISTERS

Singles: 7-inch

PHILIPS (40294 "When I Get Over You") ..5-10 65

WOOD U BELIEVE

Singles: 7-inch

EPIC (9895 "Get Serious")...........................5-10 66

WOODALL, Boots, & Radio Wranglers

Singles: 78 rpm

KING (616 "Rattle Snakin' Daddy")...........15-25 47

WOODALL, Jimmy, & His Tarpins

Singles: 7-inch

JEM (27396 "Uncle Sam's Call")..............50-75 58
(Identification number shown since no selection number is used.)

WOODARD, Jerry
(With the Esquires; with Nuggets)

Singles: 78 rpm

FAD..20-40 '50s

Singles: 7-inch

ARGO (5435 "Boat of Love")......................10-15 63
CENTURY LIMITED (603 "You Just Wait")..15-20 63
CHANT (518 "Sweet Woman") 15-25
COLVIN (778 "You Just Wait")...................50-75 59
DIAL (3017 "I May Never Get to Heaven")..10-15 63
DIAL (3021 "Down")....................................15-20 63
FAD (301 "Where Is Judy") 25-35
FAD (901 "Six Long Weeks")..................150-200 56
FAD (902 "Downbeat") 35-45 57
FAD (903 "Pappy's Club") ....15-25 '50s
HEART (3225 "Speedway Rock")..............50-75 60
RCA (7616 "Who's Gonna Rock My Baby") 15-25 59
REED (601 "Who's Gonna Rock My Baby")..100-200 59
(First issue.)
REED (605 "Atomic Fallout").....................30-50 59
(With Bobby Mizzell.)
Also see MIZZELL, Bobby

WOODARD, Mildred

Singles: 7-inch

EXCELLO (2283 "I've Waited So Long")....5-10 67

WOODBURY, Gene

Singles: 7-inch

DEL-VAL (1005 "Ever Again")..............100-125

WOODBURY, Woody *LP '60*

LPs: 10/12-inch

STEREODDITIES 10-25 59-63

WOODCHUCKS

Singles: 7-inch

PRINCE (6514 "Angry Generation") 10-15 65
Member: Lee Hazlewood.

WOODCOCK, Clarence, & Eldorados

Singles: 7-inch

MASTER (1076 "Juke Box Baby")............15-25 '50s

WOODELL, Pat

Singles: 7-inch

COLPIX (772 "What Good Would It Do") ...8-12 65

Picture Sleeves

COLPIX (772 "What Good Would It Do") .15-25 65

WOODEN NICKELS

Singles: 7-inch

OMEN (7 "Take My Love")........................10-20 65
OMEN (14 "More Than a Friend") 10-20 66
PHILIPS (40600 "We Go Together") 5-10 69
VAULT (929 "More Than a Friend")............8-12 66
Also see COEFIELD, Brice

WOODEN TRUMPETS

Singles: 7-inch

AMY (11000 "Theme from NYPD")............5-10 67

WOODFORD, Terry

Singles: 7-inch

FAME (1002 "Hit the Ground")....................8-10 66
FAME (1004 "It's His Town").......................8-10 66
R&H (1004 "Where Is My Little Girl")........10-15 68

WOODMAN, Brother
(Brother Woodman's Combo)

Singles: 78 rpm

COMBO..50-100 54

Singles: 7-inch

COMBO (65 "Hi Ho Silver")..................100-150 54
(With Candy Rivers.)
COMBO (81 "Evil Ways").......................100-150 54
(With the Savoys.)
Also see CHANTERS
Also see RIVERS, Candy, & Falcons
Also see SAVOYS

WOODS

Singles: 7-inch

TRIUMPH (62 "Broken Marionette")...........5-10 65

WOODS, Bennie
(With 5 Dukes; with Rockin' Townies)

Singles: 78 rpm

ATLAS (1040 "I Cross My Fingers") 200-300 54
(Credits Bennie Woods 5 Dukes.)

Singles: 7-inch

ATLAS (1040 "I Cross My Fingers") .4000-5000 54
(Credits "Bennie Woods 5 Dukes.")
ATLAS (1040 "I Cross My Fingers") 300-400 60
(Credits Bennie Woods & Rockin' Townies.)

WOODS, Bill

Singles: 78 rpm

FIRE (100 "Bop") 50-100 56

Singles: 7-inch

AUDAN (119 "Rock and Roll Heaven") 10-20 61
BAKERSFIELD (125 "Phone Me Baby")...300-400 57
FIRE (100 "Bop") 150-250 56
GLOBAL (740 "Story of Susie") 15-25 60

WOODS, Billy

Singles: 7-inch

ROSE (100 "Gift from Heaven")................10-15 61
SUSSEX (213 "Let Me Make You Happy")..100-200 71
VERVE (10451 "No One to Blame")............5-10 66
VERVE (10484 "I Found Satisfaction").......5-10 67
Also see McCOY, Van

WOODS, Billy, & Emeralds

Singles: 7-inch

DOT (16053 "Falling Rain").......................40-50 60

WOODS, Bob

Singles: 7-inch

KINGSPORT (100 "Greasy Corner Boogie")..150-250
KINGSPORT (101 "Sunshine Boogie")..150-250

WOODS, Bobby

Singles: 7-inch

VIN (1009 "Kiss Me Quick") 15-25 58

WOODS, Cora

Singles: 78 rpm

FEDERAL...10-20 55-56

Singles: 7-inch

FEDERAL (12223 "Rocks in Your Head")...30-40 55
FEDERAL (12229 "Ooh La La")................30-40 55
FEDERAL (12256 "Flying Home to You Baby")..20-30 56
FEDERAL (12268 "Don't Fall in Love with Me") 20-30 56

WOODS, Chris

Singles: 78 rpm

UNITED (151 "Blues for Lew")....................8-12 53

Singles: 7-inch

UNITED (151 "Blues for Lew")..................15-25 53

WOODS, Danny

Singles: 7-inch

CORREC-TONE (1052 "You Had Me Fooled")..100-125
INVICTUS (9116 "Let Me Ride")..................5-10 72
INVICTUS (9132 "Rollercoaster")...............5-10 72
SMASH (2106 "90 Days in the County Jail")..15-25 67
SMASH (2140 "To Be Loved")...................10-20 67
SMASH (2159 "Come on and Dance").....10-15 68

LPs: 10/12-inch

INVICTUS (9808 "Aries") 8-12 72

WOODS, Darlene, & Starlings

Singles: 7-inch

DATE (2736 "All I Want") 8-12 60
WORLD PACIFIC (811 "All I Want").........30-40 59

WOODS, Debby

Singles: 7-inch

EPIC (9489 "About a Quarter to Nine")......5-10 62
EPIC (9526 "Please Be Kind")....................5-10 62
EPIC (9626 "Dream On, Little Fool")..........5-10 63

WOODS, Del

Singles: 7-inch

BIG TOP (3137 "Her Moustache")............10-15 63

WOODS, Dick, & Woodsmen

Singles: 7-inch

MADISON (122 "Theme from Just Another Hobo")...5-10 59

WOODS, Donald
(With the Vel-Aires; with Earl Palmer & Band; with Ray Johnson Combo)

Singles: 78 rpm

FLIP...20-50 55-56

Singles: 7-inch

ALADDIN (3412 "Memories of an Angel")..20-30 58
FLIP (306 "My Baby's Gone") 50-75 55
(First issue. Subtitle is *Death of an Angel.*)
FLIP (306 "Death of an Angel") 15-25 55
FLIP (309 "Stay with Me Always") 40-50 55
FLIP (312 "Heaven in My Arms")...........75-100 56
GOOD OLD GOLD..4-6
Also see BEL-AIRES
Also see PALMER, Earl
Also see ROSALLE & DONELL
Also see SIX TEENS / Donald Woods / Richard Berry
Also see VEL-AIRES

WOODS, Eddie, & Gemtones

Singles: 78 rpm

GEM (204 "Heaven Was Mine") 15-25 53

Singles: 7-inch

GEM (204 "Heaven Was Mine") 20-40 53

WOODS, Gene *C&W '60*

Singles: 7-inch

CHART (1310 "Little Bitty Heart")...............5-10 66
CHART (1380 "Crying") 5-10 66
HAP (1004 "The Ballad of Wild River") 15-25 60

WOODS, Ilene

LPs: 10/12-inch

JUBILEE (1046 "It's Late")........................25-35 57

WOODS, James
(James Wood)

Singles: 7-inch

ARROW (730 "I Cried Last Night")...........10-15 58
KID GLOVES ("Nothing Takes the Place of You")..10-15
(Selection number not known.)

WOODS, Jasper, & Viscaynes

Singles: 7-inch

VPM (1009 "Hully Gully Papa") 10-20 62
Also see VISCAYNES

WOODS, Kenni

Singles: 7-inch

PHILIPS (40112 "The Guy Is Mine") 10-15 63
PHILIPS (40156 "Back with My Baby")....10-15 63

WOODS, Little Eddie
Singles: 7-inch
COMET (2165 "Bug Killer") 8-12 64

WOODS, Lonnie, Trio
Singles: 7-inch
PEACOCK (1946 "Shakin' Sugar") 5-10 66

WOODS, Maceo R&B '69
(With the Christian Tabernacle Baptist Choir)
Singles: 78 rpm
VEE-JAY (100 series) 5-10 55-56
Singles: 7-inch
ABC 4-6 73
VEE-JAY (100 series) 5-10 55-56
VOLT (4025 "Hello Sunshine") 4-8 69
LPs: 10/12-inch
GOSPEL TRUTH 4-8 72-74
SAVOY 4-8 76-83
STAX 4-8 78
TRIP 4-8 73
VEE-JAY 5-15 60-65
VOLT 5-12 69

WOODS, Mickey
Singles: 7-inch
TAMLA (54039 "They Rode Through the Valley") 30-40 61
TAMLA (54052 "Please Mr. Kennedy") 30-40 62

WOODS, Millard
Singles: 7-inch
DEL-FI (4150 "Country Boy") 8-12 60

WOODS, Nick
Singles: 7-inch
EPIC (9685 "Plain and Simple") 5-10 64
JOEY (103 "Ballad of Billy Bud") 8-10 62

WOODS, Orville
Singles: 7-inch
LIBERTY (55669 "Darlin' ") 5-10 64

WOODS, Pearl
Singles: 78 rpm
DOT (15477 "Be My Baby") 5-10 56
Singles: 7-inch
CRACKERJACK 10-15
DAWN (100 "Right Now") 10-15 62
DOT (15477 "Be My Baby") 15-20 56
MALA (496 "I'm Gonna Stick with You") 5-10 65
MALA (505 "Let Him Go") 5-10 65
SUE (750 "Keep Your Business to Yourself") 10-15 61
WALL (551 "I'll Be a Cry Baby") 10-20 62

WOODS, Ronnie
Singles: 7-inch
EVEREST (2024 "Sugar") 5-10 61

WOODS, Sonny
(With the Four Winds; with Twigs)
Singles: 78 rpm
HOLLYWOOD 20-30 54
MIDDLE-TONE 50-75 56
Singles: 7-inch
HOLLYWOOD (1015 "Chapel of Memories") 150-200 54
HOLLYWOOD (1026 "Wonderful World") 100-150 54
MIDDLE-TONE (008 "I Promise") 250-300 56
MIDDLE-TONE (013 "Living in a Dream") 250-300 56
Also see DOWNBEATS
Also see HAYES, Linda
Also see HUGHES, Ben
Also see MOORE, Johnny

WOODS BROTHERS
Singles: 7-inch
AT LAST (1002 "Love Love Love") 10-20 72
Picture Sleeves
AT LAST (1002 "Love Love Love") 15-25 72

WOODSIDE SISTERS
(With "Vocal Quartet" [Harptones] and Instrumental Accompaniment")
Singles: 78 rpm
"X" (0049 "So Soon") 10-15 55
Singles: 7-inch
"X" (0049 "So Soon") 20-40 55
Also see HARPTONES

WOODSMEN
Singles: 7-inch
DONNA (1375 "Maybe Tomorrow") 5-10 63

WOODSON, Cash T.
Singles: 7-inch
HARVEY (201 "Maxine") 75-100

WOODSON, Johnny
Singles: 7-inch
IMPERIAL (5933 "I Want to Be Near You") 8-12 63

WOODSON, Johnny, & Crescendos
(Johnny Woodson & His Orchestra)
Singles: 7-inch
SPRY (108 "Dreamer from My Heart") .600-800 57
SPRY (1008 "Don't Say Goodbye") 300-400 60

WOODY, Don
Singles: 78 rpm
DECCA 50-100 57
Singles: 7-inch
ARCO (4623 "Not I") 75-100 58
DECCA (30277 "You're Barking Up the Wrong Tree") 150-200 57
(Black label.)
DECCA (30277 "You're Barking Up the Wrong Tree") 100-150 57
(Pink label. Promotional issue only.)

WOODY & DAVE
Singles: 7-inch
BULLSEYE (1011 "Sweet Potato") 8-12 58

WOODY WAGGERS
Singles: 7-inch
DAYTONE (6407 "Sahara Hop") 15-25 64

WOODYS
(Ozarks)
Singles: 7-inch
CALIFORNIA (304 "The Saints Go Surfin' In") 10-15 63
Previously issued as *The Saints* and shown as by the Ozarks.)

WOOFERS
LPs: 10/12-inch
WYNCOTE (9011 "Dragsville") 15-20 64

WOOL, Ed, & Nomads
Singles: 7-inch
RCA (8940 "I Need Somebody") 5-10 66
Also see WOOL

WOOLEY, Sheb P&R '55/C&W '62
Singles: 78 rpm
BLUEBONNET 20-30 54
BULLET (603 "I Can't Live Without You") .25-50 46
MGM (10436 thru 12584) 10-20 48-57
MGM (12651 "Purple People Eater") 75-100 58
Singles: 7-inch
BLUEBONNET (125 "Peepin' Thru the Keyhole") 30-60 54
BLUEBONNET (130 "Too Long with the Wrong Woman") 30-50 54
MGM (11000 series) 15-25 52-55
MGM (12000 series) 10-20 55-61
MGM (13000 series) 5-10 61-68
MGM (14000 series) 4-6 68-75
POLYDOR 4-6
Picture Sleeves
MGM (12733 "Santa and the Purple People Eater") 15-25 59
MGM (13013 "Skin Tight, Pin Striped Purple Pedal Pushers") 10-15 61
MGM (13166 "Old Rag Joe") 10-15 63
EPs: 7-inch
MGM 15-25 56-58
LPs: 10/12-inch
LAKESHORE (621-2-3 "Ben Colder and Sheb Wooley") ....10-20 '70s
MGM (3299 "Blue Guitar") 30-50 56
MGM (3904 "Days of Rawhide") 20-25 56
MGM (4136 thru 4026) 15-20 61-62
MGM (4275 thru 4615) 8-15 65-69
Also see COLDER, Ben

WOOLFOLK, Herbert
Singles: 7-inch
TATECO (446 "Strength of Love") 100-200

WOOLIES P&R '67
Singles: 7-inch
DUNHILL (4052 "Who Do You Love") 8-12 66
DUNHILL (4088 "Duncan and Brandy") 8-12 67
SPIRIT (03 "Bring It with You When You Come") 10-15 65
SPIRIT (06 "Two-Way Wishin' ") 10-15 65
SPIRIT (07 "Vandegraf's Blues") 10-15 65
SPIRIT (08 "Back for More") 10-15 65
SPIRIT (09 "Ride Ride Ride") 10-15 66
SPIRIT (13 "Who Do You Love") 15-25 66
(First issue.)
SPIRIT (14 "Can't Get That Stuff") 10-15 66
TTP (156 "Black Crow Blues") 15-20 65
LPs: 10/12-inch
SPIRIT (2001 "Basic Rock") 20-30 71
SPIRIT (2005 "Live at Lizard's") 20-30 73
Members: Stormy Rice; Ron English; Jeff Baldori; Bob Baldori.

WORDD
Singles: 7-inch
CAPRICE (4983 "You're Always Around") 10-15 66

WORDS OF LUV
Singles: 7-inch
HICKORY (1462 "Tomorrow Is a Long Time") 10-15 67

WORK, Jimmy C&W '55
Singles: 78 rpm
CAPITOL 5-10 53
DOT 5-10 55
Singles: 7-inch
ALL (503 "I Dreamed Last Night") 5-10 61
CAPITOL (2565 "Crazy Moon") 10-20 53
DOT (1221 "Making Believe") 10-20 55
DOT (1245 "That's What Makes the Juke Box Play") 10-20 55
DOT (1272 "There's Only One of You") ...10-20 55

WORKMAN BROTHERS
(Workman Twins)
Singles: 7-inch
HAMILTON (50031 "I Don't Know How to Say It") 8-12 59
POPPY (2003 "Lou Ann") 5-10 59

WORKSHOP
Singles: 7-inch
ERA (3191 "New Year's Happening") 5-10 67

WORLD
Singles: 7-inch
COBBLESTONE (744 "Laughter") 5-10 69

WORLD ARTISTS STRINGS
Singles: 7-inch
WORLD ARTISTS (1054 "Little Blonde Bombshell") 5-10 65

WORLD COLUMN
Singles: 7-inch
ATCO (6604 "Midnite Thoughts") 10-15 68
TOWER (510 "It's Not Right") 8-12 69

WORLD WONDERS
Singles: 7-inch
ALARM (21644 "Funky Washing Machine") 75-125

WORLEY, Wayne, & Worleybirds
Singles: 7-inch
BRENT (7024 "Red Headed Woman") 35-45 61
ELBRIDGE (3762 "Hully Gully Twist") ...75-125 '60s
ELBRIDGE (1102 "Just to Be Alone") ....20-30 '60s
ELBRIDGE (11016 "Red Headed Woman") 50-75 61

WORRYIN' KIND
Singles: 7-inch
TRIM (350 "Wild About You") 15-25 66

WORTH, Debby
Singles: 7-inch
TITANIC (5007 "Very Close Friend of Mine") 10-15 63
TITANIC (5011 "Poor Little Boy") 10-15 63

WORTH, Marion C&W '59
Singles: 7-inch
CHEROKEE (503 "Are You Willing, Willie") 15-25 59
COLUMBIA 10-15 60-67
DECCA 4-8 67-70
GUYDEN (2026 "Are You Willing, Willie") 10-20 59
GUYDEN (2033 "That's My Kind of Love") 10-20 60
Picture Sleeves
COLUMBIA 10-15 61-62
LPs: 10/12-inch
COLUMBIA 10-20 63-64
DECCA 8-12 67
Also see MORGAN, George, & Marion Worth

WORTHAN, Johnny
(Johnny Wortham; with Charmettes)
Singles: 7-inch
PEACH (567 "Dream Boy Dream") 20-25 59
PEACH (711 "Too Too Many") 100-150 58
PEACH (722 "Cats Were Jumpin' ") 350-450 59
PEACH (732 "Strange Woman's Love") 150-200 60
PEACH (2617 "Strange Woman's Love") .40-60 60

WORTHINGTON, Oliver
Singles: 7-inch
COMPASS (7008 "Haight-Ashbury Marketplace") 5-10 67

WOW WOWS
Singles: 7-inch
CHALLENGE (59046 "Count Down") 5-10 59
Member: Ronnie Isle.
Also see ISLE, Ronnie

WOWERS
Singles: 7-inch
CONDOR (103 "Clap Clap") 5-10 61

WOWO HOOSIER HOP GANG
Singles: 78 rpm
VOGUE (V-105 "Rural Rhythms") 400-500 47
(Two discs [R736 by Downhomers; R744 by Nancy Lee & Hilltoppers] in boxed set with sleeves.)
Also see DOWNHOMERS

WRANGLERS
Singles: 7-inch
CUCA (1049 "A Lonely Game") 15-20 61
Member: Dick Miller.
Also see MILLER, Dick, & Saddle-Ites

WRAY, Doug
Singles: 7-inch
EPIC (9322 "School Girl") 10-15 59
Also see WRAY BROTHERS

WRAY, Link P&R/R&B '58
(With His Ray Men; with His Wray Men; Link Ray)
Singles: 78 rpm
CADENCE (1347 "Rumble") 50-75 58
Singles: 7-inch
BARNABY (535 "Rumble") 4-6 76
CADENCE (1347 "Rumble") 20-30 58
EPIC (9300 "Raw-Hide") 15-25 58
EPIC (9321 Comanche") 10-20 59
EPIC (9322 "School Girl") 10-20 59
EPIC (9343 "Slinky") 10-20 59
EPIC (9361 "Golden Strings") 10-15 60
EPIC (9419 "Mary Ann") 10-15 60
EPIC (9454 "El Toro") 10-15 61
HEAVY (101 "Rumble '68") 5-10 68
KAY (3690 "I Sez Baby") 50-100 58
MALA (458 "Dancing Party") 5-10 62
MR. G (820 "Rumble '69") 5-10 69
NORTON 3-5 89
POLYDOR (14084 "Juke Box Mama") 4-6 70
POLYDOR (14096 "Juke Box Mama") 4-6 70
POLYDOR (14256 "I Got to Ramble") 4-6 74
RUMBLE (1000 "Jack the Ripper") 15-25 61
SWAN (4137 "Jack the Ripper") 15-25 63
SWAN (4154 "Week End") 10-15 63
SWAN (4163 "Run Chicken Run") 5-10 63
SWAN (4171 "The Shadow Knows") 5-10 63
SWAN (4187 "Deuces Wild") 5-10 64
SWAN (4201 "Good Rockin' Tonight") 10-15 65
SWAN (4211 "Branded") 8-12 65
SWAN (4232 "Girl from the North Country") 8-12 65
SWAN (4239 "Ace of Spades") 10-12 66
SWAN (4244 "Batman Theme") 8-10 66
SWAN (4261 "Ace of Spades") 8-10 66
SWAN (4273 "Let the Good Times Roll") ...8-10 66
SWAN (4284 "Jack the Ripper") 8-10 67
TRANS ATLAS (687 "Big City Stomp") 10-15 62

Picture Sleeves

EPIC (9343 "Slinky") 50-100 59

EPs: 7-inch

KAY (3690 "Link Wray") 200-300

LPs: 10/12-inch

EPIC (3661 "Link Wray & the Wraymen") 40-50 60
NORTON 5-10 '90s
POLYDOR (4025 "Link Wray Rumble") 8-12 73
POLYDOR (4064 "Link Wray") 8-12 73
POLYDOR (5047 "Be What You Want To") 8-12 73
RECORD FACTORY (1929 "Yesterday and Today") 20-25 74
SWAN (510 "Jack the Ripper") 50-60 63
VERMILLION (1924 "Great Guitar Hits") 20-25 75
VERMILLION (1925 "Link Wray Sings and Plays Guitar") 20-25 75
VISA (7009 "Bullshot") 5-10 79
VISA (7010 "Live at the Paradiso") 5-10 80
Session: Bobby Howard.
Also see DUDLEY, Dave / Link Wray
Also see GORDON, Robert
Also see GRAMMER, Billy / Judy Lynn / Link Wray
Also see MOON MEN
Also see RAYMEN
Also see SPIDERS
Also see WELZ, Joey
Also see WRAY, Lucky
Also see WRAY, Vernon
Also see WRAY BROTHERS

WRAY, Link / Red Saunders

Singles: 7-inch

OKEH (7166 "Rumble Mambo") 10-15 63
OKEH (7282 "Rumble Mambo") 5-10 67

WRAY, Lucky
(Link Wray)

Singles: 78 rpm

STARDAY (500 series) 10-20 56
STARDAY (608 "Teenage Cutie") 150-200 57

Singles: 7-inch

STARDAY (552 "It's Music She Says") 75-125 56
STARDAY (577 "Get Another Baby") 100-200 56
STARDAY (608 "Teenage Cutie") 150-200 57
(These 500 and 600 series numbers should not be confused with a similar series from the '60s.)

WRAY, Vernon
(With Link Wray)

LPs: 10/12-inch

VERMILLION 20-25
Also see WRAY BROTHERS

WRAY BROTHERS
(Wray Family)

Singles: 7-inch

INFINITY (033 "99 Years to Go") 8-10 64
LAWN (220 "Little Shoes") 8-10 63
Members: Link; Doug; Vernon.
Also see VERNON, Ray
Also see WRAY, Doug
Also see WRAY, Link

WRECK-A-MENDED

Singles: 7-inch

BELL (713 "Soft, Tender and Warm") 10-20 68
U.A. (50122 "Dirty Old Man") 15-25 67
U.A. (50212 "Love Is in the Air") 15-25 67

WRECKING CREW

Singles: 7-inch

O'DELL (107 "Demolition") 10-20 62
TRUTH (3214 "Bump & Boogie") 8-12

WRENS
("Featuring Bobby Mansfield")

Singles: 78 rpm

RAMA (Except 65) 50-100 55
RAMA (65 "Come Back My Love"/"Eleven Roses") 50-100 55
RAMA (65 "Come Back My Love"/"Beggin' for Love") 25-50 55

Singles: 7-inch

CLASSIC ARTISTS (131 "Why Can't You") 4-6 92
(Red vinyl. 1000 made.)
RAMA (53 "Love's Something That's Made for Two") 1000-2000 54
RAMA (65 "Come Back My Love"/"Eleven Roses") 300-500 55
RAMA (65 "Come Back My Love"/"Beggin' for Love") 75-125 55
(Blue label.)
RAMA (65 "Come Back My Love"/"Beggin' for Love") 35-45 55
(Red label.)
RAMA (65 "[Will You] Come Back My Love"/"Beggin' for Love") 50-75 55
(Blue label. Note slight title variation.)
RAMA (110 "Eleven Roses") 200-300 55
RAMA (174 "Hey Girl") 300-400 55
RAMA (184 "I Won't Come to Your Wedding") 500-750 55
(Rama 194 is in the following section for WRENS / Jimmy Wright.)
ROULETTE 4-6 72
Members: Bobby Mansfield; Frenchie Concepcion; George Magnezid; Rocky.

WRENS / Jimmy Wright

Singles: 78 rpm

RAMA (194 "C'est La Vie") 50-100 56

Singles: 7-inch

RAMA (194 "C'est La Vie") 300-500 56
Also see WRENS
Also see WRIGHT, Jimmy

WRIGHT, Betty P&R/R&B '68

Singles: 12-inch

EPIC 4-6 81
JAMAICA 4-6 84-85

Singles: 7-inch

ALSTON 4-8 68-79
ATCO 3-5 83
DEEP CITY 10-20 66
EPIC 3-5 81-83
FANTASY 3-5 82
FIRST STRING 3-5 86
JAMAICA 3-5 84-85
MS. B. 3-5 88

LPs: 10/12-inch

ALSTON 6-10 72-79
ATCO 10-15 68
COLLECTABLES 5-8 88
EPIC 5-8 81-83
MS. B. 5-8 88
Also see ALAIMO, Steve, & Betty Wright
Also see RACHEL & REVOLVERS

WRIGHT, Beverly
(With the Four Students)

Singles: 78 rpm

GROOVE 10-20 56

Singles: 7-inch

GROOVE (0153 "Shake Till I'm Shook") 20-30 56
STEPHENY (1831 "Lost Love") 10-20 58
SUE (126 "Only When You're Lonely") 5-10 65
TIME (1024 "He's Wonderful") 10-15 60
TIME (1027 "Cry Like the Wind") 10-15 61
Also see FOUR STUDENTS

WRIGHT, Bill, Sr.

Singles: 7-inch

JAMIE (1329 "Scarlet Ribbons") 5-10 67

WRIGHT, Billy R&B '49

Singles: 78 rpm

REGENT 10-20 51
SAVOY 10-20 49-52

Singles: 7-inch

CARROLLTON (801 "Have Mercy Baby") 10-20 59
CHRIS (102 "If I Didn't Love You") 10-20
SAVOY (776 "Mean Old Wine") 40-60 51
SAVOY (827 "Drinkin' and Thinkin'") 40-60 52

WRIGHT, Buddy

Singles: 7-inch

UPTOWN (723 "Foolish Things") 5-10 66

WRIGHT, Charles

Singles: 7-inch

PAN WORLD (518 "The Right Time") 30-40 60
PHILIPS (40411 "Borrowed Time") 8-12 66
PHILIPS (40690 "Borrowed Time") 5-10 70

WRIGHT, Charles, & Malibus

Singles: 7-inch

TITANIC (5003 "Latinia") 15-25 '60s

WRIGHT, Charles, & Watts 103rd Street Rhythm Band R&B/LP '69

Singles: 7-inch

ABC 4-6 75
DUNHILL 4-6 73-74
W.B. 4-6 70-71

LPs: 10/12-inch

ABC 6-10 75
DUNHILL 6-10 73-74
W.B. 10-15 70-72
Also see SHIELDS
Also see SOUL RUNNERS
Also see WATTS 103RD STREET RHYTHM BAND

WRIGHT, Chuck

Singles: 7-inch

EMBER (1087 "Dear Beloved") 10-15 62
EMBER (1091 "Don't Play That Dance") 10-15 63
EMBER (1095 "If I Promise You") 10-15 63
EMBER (1102 "It's a Lie") 10-15 64
EMBER (1110 "Heartless Tears") 10-15 64

WRIGHT, Dale P&R '58
(With the Rock-Its; with Wright Guys & the Dons; with Lew Douglas Orchestra)

Singles: 78 rpm

FRATERNITY (792 "She's Neat") 75-125 58

Singles: 7-inch

ALCAR (1503 "My Heart") 10-20 60
BOONE (1023 "Think I Really Love You") 10-15 64
FRATERNITY (761 "Lovin' Type") 50-75 57
FRATERNITY (792 "She's Neat") 20-30 58
FRATERNITY (804 "Dance with Me") 20-30 58
FRATERNITY (818 "Please Don't Do It") 15-25 58
FRATERNITY (831 "You're the Answer") 15-25 59
FRATERNITY (837 "That's My Gal") 15-25 59
FRATERNITY (850 "Forget It") 15-25 59
QUEEN-B 8-12
STARBURST (1 "Egg Beater") 50-75 '50s
Also see DOUGLAS, Lew
Also see ROCK-ITS

WRIGHT, Don

Singles: 7-inch

CADENCE (1360 "Mary, Mary") 5-10 59

WRIGHT, Don, & Housebreakers

Singles: 7-inch

BOLO (100 "Corn Bread") 8-12 '60s

WRIGHT, Duke

Singles: 7-inch

MOOLA (1002 "I Refuse to Cry") 8-12 60

WRIGHT, Earl

Singles: 7-inch

CAPITOL (5516 "Thumb a Ride") 10-20 65
CUTT-RITE (100 "Married Man Blues") 75-125

WRIGHT, Gary LP '75
(With Spooky Tooth)

Singles: 7-inch

A&M 4-6 70-72
W.B. 3-6 75-81

LPs: 10/12-inch

A&M 8-15 70-76
W.B. 5-8 75-81
Also see SPOOKY TOOTH

WRIGHT, Ginny C&W '54
(With Jim Reeves; with Jerry Rowley)

Singles: 78 rpm

ABBOTT (130 "Please Leave My Darlin' Alone") 10-15 53
FABOR (101 "I Love You") 15-20 53
FABOR (Except 101) 10-15 54-56

Singles: 7-inch

ABBOTT (130 "Please Leave My Darlin' Alone") 15-25 53
FABOR (101 "I Love You") 15-20 53
FABOR (Except 101) 10-15 54-56
Also see REEVES, Jim

WRIGHT, Ginny, & Tom Tall C&W '55

Singles: 78 rpm

FABOR 5-10 54-55

Singles: 7-inch

FABOR 10-15 54-55
ZERO (106 "Are You Mine") 5-10 60
Also see TALL, Tom
Also see WRIGHT, Ginny

WRIGHT, Hank

Singles: 7-inch

MOON (302 "Mr. Cupid") 8-12 59

WRIGHT, Jerry
(With the Domans Vocal Group & Phil Meeks Combo; with Sabres)

Singles: 7-inch

DECCA (31147 "My Baby She Don't Love Me") 10-15 60
ENSIGN (2015 "Oh Jan") 10-15 59
FREEDOM (44008 "Yes Sir, That's My Baby") 10-15 59
LANJO (2394 "Do You Remember") 15-20 60

WRIGHT, Jimmy
(Jimmy Wright Orchestra; with Merry Dee)

Singles: 78 rpm

ALADDIN 10-15 57
CASH 10-15 54
GEE (1006 "Move Over") 10-20 56
METEOR 15-25 53
RAMA 10-20 56

Singles: 7-inch

ALADDIN 10-15 57
CASH (1001 "Jimmy's Boogie") 15-25 54
GEE (1006 "Move Over") 15-25 56
LUCKY (007 "Blow Jimmy Blow") 8-12 60
METEOR (5007 "Porky Pine") 25-50 53
METEOR (5011 "Slow Down Daddy") 25-50 53
RAMA (205 "Move Over") 15-25 56
Also see ANGELS
Also see FIVE CROWNS
Also see LYMON, Frankie
Also see VALENTINES
Also see WRENS / Jimmy Wright

WRIGHT, Johnny
(With the Ike Turner Orchestra)

Singles: 78 rpm

DELUXE (6029 "I Stayed Down") 10-15 54
RPM (443 "Suffocate") 10-20 55

Singles: 7-inch

DELUXE (6029 "I Stayed Down") 25-35 54
RPM (443 "Suffocate") 30-40 55
Also see TURNER, Ike

WRIGHT, Johnny
(With Cora Bennette)

Singles: 7-inch

MAGNIFICENT (109 "Who Was") 20-30 '50s
STEVENS (1001 "Look at That Chick") 15-25 59

WRIGHT, Johnny C&W '64

Singles: 7-inch

CAPRICORN 4-6 75
DECCA 4-6 64-68

LPs: 10/12-inch

DECCA 10-20 65-68
RUBOCA 5-8
Also see JOHNNY & JACK
Also see WELLS, Kitty / Bill Phillips / Bobby Wright / Johnny Wright
Also see WELLS, Kitty, & Johnny Wright

WRIGHT, Leo
(With the El-Jays)

Singles: 7-inch

ATLANTIC (5027 "A Felicidad") 8-12 63
CB (5008 "I Wonder") 50-100 64
PERICO (1257 "I Pretend & Cry") 10-15 65
RED FOX (103 "I Wonder") 10-15 65

LPs: 10/12-inch

ATLANTIC 15-25 61-62
VORTEX 10-15 70

WRIGHT, Little Cholly

Singles: 7-inch

CHOLLY (7093 "Eternally") 3000-4000 58
Also see TWILIGHTERS / Little Cholly Wright

WRIGHT, Lonnie

Singles: 7-inch

FREE FORM (502 "Hot Rod") 15-20

WRIGHT, Marvin "Lefty"

Singles: 7-inch

BLUE STAR (1000 "Run Run Run") 5-10 64

EPs: 7-inch

X (54/55 "Boogie Woogie Piano") 10-20 54

LPs: 10/12-inch

X (3028 "Boogie Woogie Piano") 25-50 54
(10-inch LP.)

WRIGHT, Mary
(With Budd Johnson Orchestra)

Singles: 7-inch

KIM (101 "One Guy") 40-50 60

WRIGHT, Milton, & Terra Shirma Strings
Singles: 7-inch
CARLA (1902 "The Gallop") 15-25 68

WRIGHT, O.V. *P&R/R&B '65*
Singles: 7-inch
ABC 4-6 75-76
BACK BEAT 5-10 65-74
GOLDWAX 5-10 64
HI 4-6 76-79
LPs: 10/12-inch
BACK BEAT 10-20 65-72
HI 5-10 78-79

WRIGHT, Priscilla *P&R '55*
(With Don Wright & the Septette)
Singles: 78 rpm
UNIQUE 5-10 55-56
Singles: 7-inch
20TH FOX (144 "Coming of Age") 10-15 59
UNIQUE 10-20 55-57

WRIGHT, Randy *C&W '83*
Singles: 7-inch
MCA 3-5 83-84
SKIDMORE (1001 "Fifty-Fifty") 15-25
Also see MANDRELL, Barbara

WRIGHT, Rebel
Singles: 7-inch
CENTRAL (314012 "You Nearly Lose Your Mind") 100-150
LINDA (002 "Long Gone Daddy") 50-75

WRIGHT, Rena
Singles: 7-inch
TIDE (1079 "I'm Just Your Fool") 10-15 61
TIDE (2018 "This Angry World") 5-10 68
VITA (185 "Deal Me a Hand") 8-12 59

WRIGHT, Richard
(With the Star-Veils)
Singles: 7-inch
ME-O (1001 "Give Your Love to Me") 20-30 65

WRIGHT, Richard
LPs: 10/12-inch
COLUMBIA (35559 "Wet Dream") 10-15 78
Also see PINK FLOYD

WRIGHT, Rita
(Syreeta Wright)
Singles: 7-inch
GORDY (7064 "Something On My Mind") .. 5-10 67

WRIGHT, Roy
Singles: 7-inch
DREXEL 10-20 57
Also see ROBBINS, James / Roy Wright

WRIGHT, Ruben *R&B '66*
(Reuben Wright)
Singles: 7-inch
CAPITOL 5-10 64-67
LANCER (101 "Bye Bye") 10-15 59
WYNNE (119 "Love Is Gone") 8-12 60

WRIGHT, Ruby *P&R '57*
(With the Bello Larks; with Dick Pike; with Ruth Lyons)
Singles: 78 rpm
FRATERNITY 5-10 57
Singles: 7-inch
CANDEE (501 "Poor Butterfly") 10-15 59
CANDEE (502 "This Is Christmas") 10-15 59
COLUMBIA (41807 "Wasn't the Summer Short") 8-12 60
FRATERNITY (787 "Let's Light the Christmas Tree") 10-20 57
KING (1293 "Bimbo") 15-25 53
KING (4870 "Don't Take Me for Granted") 15-25 56
KING (5192 "Three Stars") 10-15 59
KING (5208 "Goodbye, Jimmy, Goodbye") 8-12 59
(Monaural.)
KING (5208 "Goodbye, Jimmy, Goodbye") 25-35 59
(Stereo.)
KING (5225 "Don't Take Me for Granted") . 8-12 59
(Monaural.)
KING (5225 "Don't Take Me for Granted") 25-35 59
(Stereo.)
KING (5261 "Sweet Night of Love") 8-12 59
KING (5297 "When You're Away") 8-12 60

WRIGHT, Sam, Group
Singles: 7-inch
BIG (17 "Telstar") 5-10 62
PEAK (7 "Green Onions") 5-10 62

WRIGHT, Sandra
Singles: 7-inch
CORAL (62559 "Gotta See My Baby") 10-15 61

WRIGHT, Steve
(With the Lin-Airs)
Singles: 7-inch
CUSTOM (13 "He Don't Love You") 5-10 64
DOT (16380 "Lucky Lips") 5-10 62
GUYDEN (2123 "He Don't Love You") 10-20 65
LIN (5022 "Wild Wild Woman") 100-200 59
LIN (5024 "Silver Bells") 15-25 60
LIN (5025 "Far and Distant Lands") 25-50 60
THUNDERBALL (136 "Back to the City") ... 5-10 67
Session: Mike Danbom.

WRIGHT, Steve
Singles: 7-inch
ATCO (6422 "Searching") 5-10 66
ATCO (7016 "Hard Road") 4-6 75
LPs: 10/12-inch
ATCO (36-109 "Hard Road") 8-10 75

WRIGHT, Tommy
Singles: 7-inch
SOUNDTRACK (1012 "We've Lost It") 10-15 66

WRIGHT, Willie
(With the Sparklers)
Singles: 7-inch
FEDERAL (12372 "Your Letter") 15-25 60
FEDERAL (12382 "What Will I Say") 15-25 60
FEDERAL (12406 "I'm Gonna Leave You") 15-25 61
HOTEL (539 "Right On for the Darkness") . 8-12 '60s
LPs: 10/12-inch
ARGO (4024 "I'm on My Way") 15-25 63
CONCERT DISC (45 "I Sing Folk Songs") 30-40 60
(Stereo.)
CONCERT DISC (1045 "I Sing Folk Songs") 20-30 60
(Monaural.)

WRIGHT SISTERS
Singles: 7-inch
CADENCE (1411 "Crazy Over You") 5-10 61

WRIGHT SOUNDS
Singles: 7-inch
KEE VEE (101 "For Sale") 75-125 64
(Reissued as by the Electrons.)
Also see ELECTRONS

WRIGHT SPECIALS
Singles: 7-inch
DIVINITY .... 8-12 '60s
Also see WESTON, Kim

WRONG NUMBERS
Singles: 7-inch
HITT CART ("I Wonder Why") 25-35 65
(No selection number used.)
PARIS TOWER (111 "I'm Gonna Go Now") 15-25 67

WYATT, Danny
Singles: 7-inch
RUBY (270 "You Broke a Date") 15-25 57
RUBY (480 "My Idle Love") 15-25 57

WYATT, Don
Singles: 7-inch
ALPAX (4 "Allright") 10-15
BRENT (7026 "I'm in Love") 8-12 61
COLPIX (164 "Tell Tale Kisses") 8-12 60
ERA (1081 "You Oughta Be in Movies") .. 40-60 58
GARPAX (44174 "I've Got Myself to Blame") 5-10 63
ROSCO (406 "When You Need Somebody") 8-12 59

WYATT, Gene *C&W '68*
Singles: 7-inch
AETNA (7030 "You Bug Me Baby") 50-75
EBB (123 "Love Fever") 50-75 57
LUCKY SEVEN (101 "Prettiest Girl at the Dance") 40-60 59
MERCURY 5-10 67-68
PAULA 4-8 68-74

WYATT, J.D. & Thunderbolts
Singles: 7-inch
G.A.R. (106 "How Do You Lose a Girl") ... 10-20 67
Also see SWINGSTERS

WYATT, Johnny
(With the Hightones)
Singles: 7-inch
BIG TIME (1927 "We Met at a Dance") 300-400 62
BRONCO 10-20 66
CHALLENGE (9172 "Be Honest with Me") 15-25 62
CHALLENGE (9207 "One, Two, Three") .. 25-35 63
CHALLENGE (59242 "Hang Up the Phone") 15-25 64
MAGNUM (736 "The Bottom of the Top") .. 5-10 65
SWINGIN' (643 "One Night with You") 10-15 63
Session: Rochell & Candles.
Also see ROCHELL & CANDLES

WYDELL, George
Singles: 7-inch
TANGERINE (953 "Do the Walk") 10-20 65

WYLD
Singles: 7-inch
CHARAY ("Know a Lot About Love") 15-25 66
(Selection number not known.)
CHARAY (28 "Lost One") 15-25 66
Also see ROOTS

WYLD, Bob
Singles: 7-inch
ACADEMY (107 "Roses Are Blooming") .. 10-15 64
FORD (124 "Midnight") 5-10 63

WYLDE HEARD
Singles: 7-inch
PHILIPS (40454 "Take It On Home") 5-10 67
Picture Sleeves
PHILIPS (40454 "Take It On Home") 10-15 67
Members: Bill; Ron; Bird; Jim.
Also see HEARD

WYLIE, Richard *R&B '71*
(Richard "Popcorn" Wylie; Popcorn Wylie & the Mohawks)
Singles: 7-inch
ABC 4-6 75
CARLA (715 "Move Over Babe") 5-10 68
EPIC (9543 "Come to Me") 15-25 62
EPIC (9575 "Brand New Man") 15-25 63
EPIC (9611 "Head Over Heels in Love") .. 15-25 63
KAREN (1542 "Rosemary, What Happened") 15-25 68
MOTOWN (1002 "Shimmy Gully") 40-50 60
MOTOWN (1009 "Money") 40-50 61
MOTOWN (1019 "Real Good Lovin'") 40-50 61
NORTHERN (3732 "Pretty Girl") .... 15-25 '60s
SOUL (35087 "Funky Rubber Band") 5-10 71
Picture Sleeves
EPIC 5-10 62
LPs: 10/12-inch
ABC 8-10 74
Also see AMES, Stewart

WYMAN, Bill *P&R '67*
Singles: 12-inch
A&M (12041 "Je Suis Un Rock Star") 6-10 81
Singles: 7-inch
A&M (2367 "Je Suis Un Rock Star") 3-5 81
ROLLING STONES 4-6 74-75
Promotional Singles
A&M (2367 "Je Suis Un Rock Star") 4-6 81
A&M (12041 "Je Suis Un Rock Star") 15-20 81
(12-inch single.)
Picture Sleeves
A&M (2367 "Je Suis Un Rock Star") 3-5 81
LPs: 10/12-inch
ROLLING STONES 8-10 74-76
(Stereo.)
ROLLING STONES (QD 79100 "Monkey Grip") 15-20 74
(Quadraphonic.)

WYMAN, Bill / Rolling Stones
Singles: 7-inch
LONDON (907 "In Another Land") 10-15 67
Promotional Singles
LONDON (907 "In Another Land") 15-20 67
Picture Sleeves
LONDON (907 "In Another Land") 25-30 67
Also see ROLLING STONES

Also see WYMAN, Bill

WYMORE, Buddy, & Knaves
Singles: 7-inch
MITCHELL (101 "Surf Mad") .... 100-125 '60s

WYNETTE, Tammy *C&W '66*
(With Ricky Skaggs; with Emmylou Harris)
Singles: 7-inch
EPIC (Except 1) 3-8 66-86
EPIC (1 "Wonders You Perform") 5-10 70
(Colored vinyl. Promotional issue only.)
Picture Sleeves
EPIC 4-6 69-76
LPs: 10/12-inch
COLUMBIA (Except "EQ" series) 5-10 72-73
COLUMBIA (EQ-30658 "We Sure Can Love Each Other") 10-15 71
(Quadraphonic.)
COLUMBIA HOUSE (5856 "Tammy Wynette") 25-35 73
(Boxed, six-disc set.)
COLUMBIA SPECIAL PRODUCTS 5-8 77-82
EPIC 5-15 68-86
HARMONY 5-10 70-71
TIME-LIFE 5-8 81
Session: Sue Richards.
Also see CASH, Johnny / Tammy Wynette
Also see HOUSTON, David, & Tammy Wynette
Also see JONES, George, & Tammy Wynette
Also see LYNN, Loretta / Tammy Wynette
Also see NEWTON, Wayne, & Tammy Wynette

WYNETTE, Tammy, & Randy Travis *C&W '91*
Singles: 7-inch
EPIC 3-5 91
Also see WYNETTE, Tammy

WYNN, Big Jim
(Big Jim Wynn's Band; with Marva Turner)
Singles: 78 rpm
MILLION 5-10 54
RECORDED IN HOLLYWOOD (108 "Hollywood Stampede") 5-10 50
Singles: 7-inch
MILLION (2004 "I'm the Boss") 20-30 54
MILLION (2006 "Cool Operation") 20-30 54

WYNN, Lee, & Chromatics
Singles: 78 rpm
MILLION 40-50 55
Singles: 7-inch
MILLION (2013 "I Couldn't Take It") 100-150 55
Also see CHROMATICS

WYNN, Richie, & Tornadoes
Singles: 7-inch
SOMA (1182 "You're Too Late") 20-25 61
Also see TORNADOES

WYNN, Roberta
Singles: 7-inch
JUBILEE (5405 "Dream Boy") 8-12 61

WYNNEWOODS
Singles: 7-inch
WYNNE (108 "Is That Wrong") 20-30 59

WYNNS, Sandy
(Edna Wright)
Singles: 7-inch
CANTERBURY (520 "Love Is Like Quicksand") 5-10 67
CHAMPION (14001 "A Lover's Quarrel") . 10-20 64
CHAMPION (14002 "Yes I Really Love You") 10-20 65
DOC (103 "A Lover's Quarrel") 20-30 64
(First issue.)

WYNTER, Mark
Singles: 7-inch
ARLEN (744 "Don't Cry") 5-10 64
GUYDEN (2115 "Answer Me") 5-10 64
SCEPTER (1299 "Can I Get to Know You Better") 5-10 65

WYNTERS, Stormy
Singles: 7-inch
MERCURY (72505 "Life Saver") 10-20 65

WYTE, Marty
Singles: 7-inch
BRUSH (7000 "Queen of the Mardi-Gras") .... 15-25 '50s

SHAMMY (501 "Queen of the Mardi-Gras")........................25-35 59

X

X LP '81

Singles: 7-inch

CURB (10538 "Wild Thing")..........3-5 84
ELEKTRA (69825 "Breathless")..........3-5 83
ELEKTRA (69885 "Blue Spark")..........3-5 82
MERCURY (Black vinyl)..........3-5 93
MERCURY (1036 "Country at War")..........3-5 93
(Colored vinyl. Promotional issue only.)

Picture Sleeves

ELEKTRA..........3-5 83
MERCURY (1036 "Country at War")..........3-5 93

LPs: 10/12-inch

ELEKTRA..........5-8 82-88
ROCSHIRE..........5-8 83
SLASH (104 "Los Angeles")..........10-20 80
SLASH (107 "Wild Gift")..........10-20 81
Members: Dave Alvin; Exene Cervenka; John Doe; D.J. Bonebrake; Tony Gilkyson.
Also see BLASTERS

X LINCOLN

Singles: 7-inch

DOT (17170 "You're Everything")..........5-10 68
TIME (1061 "Stand In for Her Past")..........5-10 62

XIT

Singles: 7-inch

CANYON..........4-8 75
MOTOWN..........4-6 74
RARE EARTH (5044 "End")..........5-10 72
RARE EARTH (5055 "Color Nature Gone")..........5-10 73

LPs: 10/12-inch

CANYON (7114 "Entrance")..........25-45 74
CANYON (7121 "Relocation")..........25-35 77
RARE EARTH (536 "Plight of the Red Man")..........15-25 72
RARE EARTH (545 "Silent Warrior")..........15-25 73
Members: Michael Martin; Lee Herrere; Mac Sauzo; R.C. Garliss, Jr.
Also see LINCOLN STREET EXIT

XLs

Singles: 7-inch

CBC..........8-12
MMC (015 "Silver Wings")..........8-12 68
SOUND ("But It's True")..........15-20 '60s
(Selection number not known.)
STRACK..........8-12
WHITE WHALE..........8-12 67-68

XL-5

Singles: 7-inch

FOUR (004 "Miserlou")..........5-10

LPs:10/12-inch

XL ("XL-5")..........5-10 69
(No selection number used.)

XL-5 MINUS 1

Singles: 7-inch

COVE (101 "Boog-A-Louie")..........5-10 67

X-CELLENTS
(E-Cellents)

Singles: 7-inch

SMASH (1996 "Hey Little Willie")..........10-15 65
SURE PLAY (0002 "And I'm Cryin'")..........25-35 66
(Mistakenly credits group as "E-Cellents.")
SURE PLAY (0003 "Hang It Up")..........15-25 66
TERRY (119 "Now That I'm Somebody")..........10-20 '60s
VOUS (11060 "Now That I'm Somebody")..........10-20 '60s

Picture Sleeves

SURE PLAY (0003 "Hang It Up")..........20-30 66

LP: 10/12-inch

PRISM..........10-20

X-CEPTIONS

Singles: 7-inch

DECEMBER (878 "Ode to Bill and Jim")..........5-10 67

XCITERS

Singles: 7-inch

JAGUAR (200 "Upsetter")..........15-25 65

X-CITERS UNLIMITED

Singles: 7-inch

ABC (11029 "Hang on Sloopy")..........5-10 68

X-CITERS VOCAL GROUP

Singles: 7-inch

CARTER (2764 "As We Dance")..........300-500 '50s

X-MEN

Singles: 7-inch

IGL (115 "Believe Me")..........5-10 66

X-RAYS R&B '49

Singles: 7-inch

SAVOY..........10-15 48-49
Also see JACQUET, Illinois
Also see WALKER, T-Bone

X-RAYS

Singles: 7-inch

KAPP (241 "Chinchilla")..........15-20 58

XTREEMS

Singles: 7-inch

STAR TREK (1221 "Substitute")..........15-25 66

Y

YA HO WA 13
(Father Yod & Spirit of '76; Yod Aquarian)

LPs: 10/12-inch

HIGHER KEY ("Principles of the Children")..........600-800 78
(Selection number not known.)
HIGHER KEY ("Contraction")..........400-500 76
HIGHER KEY ("Expansion")..........400-500 76
HIGHER KEY (3301 "Kohoutek")..........300-400 73
HIGHER KEY (3304 "All Or Nothing at All")..........300-400 74
HIGHER KEY (3306 "The Savage Sons of Ya Ho Wa")..........300-400 74
HIGHER KEY (3307 "Penetration")..........300-400 74
HIGHER KEY (3309 "I'm Gonna Take You Home")..........500-750 75
Also see THIRTEENTH FLOOR ELEVATORS

YA HO WA 13 & SKY SAXON

LPs: 10/12-inch

PSYCHO (2 "Golden Sunrise")..........15-25 82
(Colored vinyl. Reportedly 300 made.)
Also see SAXON, Sky
Also see YA HO WA 13

YACHTSMEN

Singles: 7-inch

DESTINY (402 "It's So Hard to Be Young")..........30-40 59
HAR-GLO (420 "Our Future")..........40-50 58
(Shows company address and phone.)
HAR-GLO (420 "Our Future")..........10-20 61
(No address and phone shown.)
Also see LONDON, Lloyd, & Yachtsmen

YACHTSMEN

LPs: 10/12-inch

BUENA VISTA (3310 "High and Dry with the Yachtsmen")..........20-30 61
Members: Carl Berg; Ray Gordon; Jay Huling; Bill Reed.

YAGER, Mike

Singles: 7-inch

KING (6211 "Time and Distance")..........5-10 69

YAKITY YAKS

Singles: 7-inch

SCOPE (1971 "Apart")..........30-40

Y'ALLS

Singles: 7-inch

RUFF (1016 "Run for Your Life")..........15-25 66
Also see KITCHEN CINQ

YAMA & KARMA DUSTERS

LPs: 10/12-inch

MANHOLE ("Up from the Sewers")..........100-200 70
(No selection number used.)

YANCEY, Jimmy
(With Mama Yancey)

Singles: 78 rpm

COLUMBIA..........5-10 47

Singles: 7-inch

BLACK GOLD (600 "Lion's Den")..........8-12

EPs: 7-inch

ATLANTIC (525 "At the Piano")..........15-25 51

LPs: 10/12-inch

ATLANTIC (130 "Yancey Special")..........50-100 51
(10-inch LP.)
ATLANTIC (134 "Piano Solos")..........50-100 51
(10-inch LP.)
ATLANTIC (1283 "Pure Blues")..........50-75 58
ATLANTIC (7229 "Blues Originals")..........10-15 72
PARAMOUNT (101 "Yancey Special")..........50-100 51
(10-inch LP.)
PAX (6007 "Jimmy and Mama Yancey")..........50-75 53
(10-inch LP.)
PAX (6011 "Yancey's Mixture")..........40-60 57
PAX (6012 "Evening with the Yanceys")..........40-60 57
RCA (3000 "Blues & Boogies")..........75-100 51
(10-inch LP.)
RIVERSIDE (123 "Yancey's Greeting")..........25-35 58
RIVERSIDE (124 "Yancey's Getaway")..........25-35 58
RIVERSIDE (1028 "Last Recording Date")..........50-75 54
(10-inch LP.)
RIVERSIDE (1061 "Yancey's Getaway")..........50-75 55
(10-inch LP.)

YANCEY, Jimmy / Cripple Clarence Lofton

LP: 10/12-inch

JAZZTONE (224 "Pioneers of Boogie Woogie")..........15-25 56
Also see LOFTON, Cripple Clarence

YANCEY, Mama, & Art Hodes

LPs: 10/12-inch

VERVE FOLKWAYS (9015 "Mama Yancey Sings Art Hode Plays – Blues")..........12-15 65
Also see MONTGOMERY, Little Brother, & Mama Yancey
Also see YANCEY, Jimmy

YANCEY, Vernon, Combo

Singles: 7-inch

CUCA (1146 "Crazy Rock")..........10-20 63

YANEY, "Skeets"

Singles: 78 rpm

MGM (11011 "Candy Coated Lies")..........5-10 51

Singles: 7-inch

MGM (11011 "Candy Coated Lies")..........15-25 51

YANKOVIC, "Weird Al" P&R/LP '83

Singles: 12-inch

ROCK 'N' ROLL..........4-6 84

Singles: 7-inch

CAPITOL..........4-6 79
ROCK 'N' ROLL..........3-5 83-89
SCOTTI BROS./CBS (2105 "Like a Surgeon")..........30-40 85
(Picture disc. Promotional issue only.)
T.K. (1043 "Another One Rides the Bus")..........3-5 81

Picture Sleeves

ROCK 'N' ROLL..........3-5 83-89

EPs: 7-inch

PLACEBO..........10-15 81

LPs: 10/12-inch

ROCK 'N' ROLL..........5-8 83-89

YANOVSKY, Zalman

Singles: 7-inch

BUDDAH..........5-10 67

LPs: 10/12-inch

BUDDAH..........10-15 68
KAMA SUTRA..........8-10 71
Also see LOVIN' SPOONFUL
Also see MUGWUMPS

YARBOROUGH, Lafayette

Singles: 7-inch

BART (7 "Cool Cool Baby")..........500-750 57

YARBROUGH, Glenn LP '64

Singles: 7-inch

PRIDE..........4-6 72
RCA..........5-10 64-68
STAX..........4-6 73-74
W.B...........4-6 68-71

Picture Sleeves

RCA (8498 "Baby the Rain Must Fall")..........5-10 65

LPs: 10/12-inch

ELEKTRA (135 "Here We Go, Baby")..........20-30 57
FIRST AMERICAN..........8-12 81
IM'PRESS..........8-10 71
RCA..........12-25 64-69
STACK-O-HITS..........10-20
STAX..........8-10 74
TRADITION..........8-15 67-70
W.B...........8-15 68-71
Also see LIMELITERS

YARDBIRDS P&R/LP '65

Singles: 7-inch

CAPITOL (72274 "Heart Full of Soul")..........20-40 65
(Canadian.)
EPIC (9709 "I Wish You Could")..........20-30 64
EPIC (9790 "For Your Love")..........10-20 65
EPIC (9823 "Heart Full of Soul")..........10-20 65
EPIC (9857 "I'm a Man")..........10-20 65
EPIC (9891 "Shapes of Things")..........10-20 66
EPIC (10006 "Shapes of Things")..........10-20 66
EPIC (10035 "Over Under Sideways Down")..........10-20 66
EPIC (10094 "Happenings Ten Years Time Ago")..........10-20 66
EPIC (10156 "Little Games")..........10-20 67
EPIC (10204 "Ha Ha Said the Clown")..........10-20 67
EPIC (10248 "Ten Little Indians")..........15-25 67
EPIC (10303 "Goodnight Sweet Josephine")..........20-30 68

Picture Sleeves

EPIC (9709 "I Wish You Could")..........75-125 64
(Promotional issue only.)
EPIC (9823 "Heart Full of Soul")..........25-35 65
EPIC (10035 "Over Under Sideways Down")..........20-30 66
EPIC (10094 "Happenings Ten Years Time Ago")..........20-30 66

LPs: 10/12-inch

ACCORD (7143 "For Your Love")..........5-8 81
ACCORD (7237 "Heart Full of Soul")..........5-8 83
COLUMBIA (11311 "Live Yardbirds Featuring Jimmy Page")..........25-35 72
(Columbia Special Products issue.)
COMPLEAT..........8-12 86
EPIC (24167 "For Your Love")..........50-100 65
(Monaural.)
EPIC (24177 "Having a Rave-Up")..........40-60 65
(Monaural.)
EPIC (24210 "Over Under Sideways Down")..........40-60 66
(Monaural.)
EPIC (24246 "Greatest Hits")..........30-40 66
(Monaural.)
EPIC (24313 "Little Games")..........40-60 67
(Monaural.)
EPIC (26167 "For Your Love")..........30-40 65
(Stereo.)
EPIC (26177 "Having a Rave Up")..........30-40 65
(Stereo.)
EPIC (26210 "Over Under Sideways Down")..........30-45 66
(Stereo.)
EPIC (26246 "Greatest Hits")..........30-40 66
(Stereo.)
EPIC (26313 "Little Games")..........35-50 67
(Stereo.)
EPIC (30135 "The Yardbirds Featuring Performances by Jeff Beck, Eric Clapton, Jimmy Page")..........75-100 70
EPIC (30615 "Live Yardbirds")..........50-75 71
EPIC (34490 "Yardbirds Favorites")..........8-12 77
(Orange label.)
EPIC (34490 "Yardbirds Favorites")..........5-8
(Black label.)
EPIC (34491 "Great Hits")..........8-10 77
EPIC (38455 "The Yardbirds")..........5-8 83
EPIC (48455 "The Yardbirds")..........12-15 83
(Half-speed mastered.)
MERCURY (21271 "Eric Clapton and Yardbirds Live with Sonny Boy Williamson")..........20-30 66
(Monaural.)
MERCURY (61271 "Eric Clapton and Yardbirds Live with Sonny Boy Williamson")..........30-40 66
(Stereo. Red label.)
MERCURY (61271 "Eric Clapton and Yardbirds Live with Sonny Boy Williamson")..........5-8
(Black label.)
RHINO (Black vinyl)..........6-10 82-86
RHINO (253 "Afternoon Tea")..........10-15 82
(Picture disc.)

SPRINGBOARD (4036 "Eric Clapton and the Yardbirds")....8-10 72
Members: Eric Clapton; Jeff Beck; Keith Relf; Jimmy Page; Jim McCarty; Chris Dreja.
Also see BECK, Jeff
Also see CLAPTON, Eric
Also see CLARK, Dave, Five / Simon & Garfunkel / Yardbirds / New Christy Minstrels
Also see PAGE, Jimmy
Also see RELF, Keith
Also see RENAISSANCE
Also see WILLIAMSON, Sonny Boy

YATES, Bill, & His T-Birds
Singles: 7-inch
SUN (390 "Don't Step On My Dog")....10-15 64
SUN (399 "Big, Big World")....10-15 65
EMERY....4-6 78
Also see GORGEOUS BILL

YATES, Billy
Singles: 7-inch
BETHLEHEM (3039 "Fool Around with Love")....5-10 62
1ST (101 "All I Need Is You")....5-10 61

YATES, Count
("With Orch & Chorus")
Singles: 7-inch
NEW BAG (103 "At the Soul")....5-10 67
REGIS (1 "The Golden Key")....20-30 61

YATES, Duane, & Capris
Singles: 7-inch
N-JOY (1009 "Anymore")....10-15 65
N-JOY (1010 "Here I Stand")....10-15 65

YATES, Little Sammy
Singles: 7-inch
GENIE (104 "Comic Book Crazy")....15-25 59
Also see LITTLE SAMMY

YATES, Robbie, & Elites
Singles: 7-inch
AGE (29109 "Faith")....5-10 62

YATES, Ruby, & Swinging Rocks
Singles: 7-inch
HIT PRODUCTIONS (3588 "It's Been a Long Time")....30-50 63

YATES, Tommy
Singles: 7-inch
VERVE (10556 "Darling, Something's Gotta Give")....10-20 67

YEAGER, Ray
Singles: 7-inch
TIARA ("Country Boy")....75-125
(Selection number not known.)

YEAR 2000
Singles: 7-inch
AMY (10035 "Perfect Love")....5-10 68
RAMA RAMA....5-10 69

YELLOW BALLOON P&R '67
Singles: 7-inch
CANTERBURY (508 "Yellow Balloon")....5-10 67
CANTERBURY (513 "I've Got a Feeling for Love")....5-10 67
CANTERBURY (516 "Can't Get Enough of Your Love")....5-10 67
LPs: 10/12-inch
CANTERBURY....15-20 67
Members: Alex Valdez; Don Grady; Don Braucht; Forrest Green; Paul Cannella; Darryl Dragon.
Also see CAPTAIN & TENNILLE
Also see GRADY, Don
Also see SPIRIT

YELLOW HAIR
Singles: 7-inch
BELL (856 "I Wanna Be Free")....5-10 69
PACIFIC AVENUE....5-10 '60s
Member: Scott McCarl.
Also see RASPBERRIES

YELLOW HAND
Singles: 7-inch
CAPITOL....4-6 70
LPs: 10/12-inch
CAPITOL....10-15 70
Members: Jerry Tawney; Pat Flynn; Mickey Armstrong; Kenny Trujillo; Oscar Vildasolo.
Also see TAWNEY, Jerry

YELLOW JACKETS
Singles: 7-inch
SMASH (2180 "Hi Boy")....5-10 68

YELLOW PAYGES
Singles: 7-inch
SHOWPLACE (216 "Sleeping Minds")....15-25 67
SHOWPLACE (217 "Love in the Making")....10-15 67
UNI....10-15 67-70
LPs: 10/12-inch
UNI (73045 "The Yellow Payges, Volume 1"....20-30 69
Also see NOMADS

YELVINGTON, Malcolm
(With the Star Rhythm Boys)
Singles: 78 rpm
SUN....25-50 54-56
Singles: 7-inch
SUN (211 "Drinkin' Wine Spo-Dee-O-Dee")....75-125 54
(Counterfeits exist of this release.)
SUN (246 "Rockin' with My Baby")....50-75 56

YEOMANS
Singles: 7-inch
HEIDI (113 "I'm the Guy")....10-15 65

YEOMEN
LPs: 10/12-inch
HI-TOP (6201 "Session One")....25-50 62
Members: Bob Finkenaur; Jack Otterness; Keith Critchlow; Don Bennett.

YES P&R/LP '71
Singles: 12-inch
ATCO....4-6 83-86
Singles: 7-inch
ARISTA....3-5 91
ATCO....3-5 83-87
ATLANTIC (Black vinyl)....4-6 70-78
ATLANTIC (Colored vinyl)....5-8 70-78
Picture Sleeves
ATCO....3-5 83-87
EPs: 7-inch
ATLANTIC (415 "Roundabout")....5-10 72
(Promotional issue only.)
LPs: 10/12-inch
ARISTA....5-8 91
ATCO....5-8 83-87
ATLANTIC (100 series)....10-15 73
ATLANTIC (500 series)....6-12 80
ATLANTIC (900 series)....10-15 74
ATLANTIC (7000 series)....8-12 71-72
ATLANTIC (8000 series)....10-15 69-71
ATLANTIC (16000 thru 19000 series)....5-10 74-82
MFSL (077 "Close to the Edge")....40-60 82
Promotional LPs
ATLANTIC ("Solos")....30-40 76
Members: Jon Anderson; Rick Wakeman; Steve Howe; Chris Squire; Tony Kaye; Alan White; Bill Bruford; Patrick Moraz; Geoff Downes; Trevor Rabin.
Also see ANDERSON, Jon
Also see KING CRIMSON
Also see SIMON, Paul
Also see WAKEMAN, Rick

YES IT IS
Singles: 7-inch
STUDIO CITY (1046 "Little Boy")....20-30 66
STUDIO CITY (1052 "Lonely Love")....10-15 66

YESTER, Jerry
Singles: 7-inch
DUNHILL (4042 "Sound of Summer Showers")....5-10 66
DUNHILL (4061 "Garden of Imagining")....5-10 67
Also see HENSKE, Judy, & Jerry Yester
Also see LOVIN' SPOONFUL

YESTERDAY'S CHILDREN
Singles: 7-inch
PARROT (314 "To Be Or Not to Be")....10-15 66

YESTERDAY'S CHILDREN
Singles: 7-inch
SHOWCASE (9812 "Wanna Be with You")....15-25 66

YESTERDAY'S NEWS
Singles: 7-inch
CLIFTON....3-5 80-81
LPs: 10/12-inch
ANGELA (100 "Good Old Acapella")....5-10 '80s
(Colored vinyl.)
Members: Tony Delvecchio; Vic Spina; Vinnie Gallo; Charlie Rocco; Dennis Elber.

YESTERDAY'S NEWS / Poppiti Brothers
Singles: 7-inch
CRYSTAL BALL (148 "Countdown to Love")....4-8 85
(Black vinyl. 1000 made.)
CRYSTAL BALL (148 "Countdown to Love")....8-12 85
(Red vinyl. 25 made.)
Picture Sleeves
CRYSTAL BALL (148 "Countdown to Love")....10-15 85
(500 made.)
Also see YESTERDAY'S NEWS

YESTERDAY'S OBSESSION
Singles: 7-inch
PACEMAKER (262 "Complicated Music")....15-25 66

YETTI-MEN / Uppa-Trio
LPs: 10/12-inch
KAL (4348 "The Yetti-Men")....550-650 64
(Each group has one side of the LP.)

YO YOs
(Yo-Yos)
Singles: 7-inch
CORAL (62501 "Raven")....15-25 66
GOLDWAX....10-20 66
PINCUS (100 "The Nightmare")....10-20 '60s

YOAKAM, Dwight C&W/LP '86
Singles: 7-inch
OAK....15-25 86
REPRISE....3-5 86-90
LPs: 10/12-inch
OAK (2356 "Guitars, Cadillacs, Etc.")...500-750 84
REPRISE....5-8 86-90

YOAKAM, Dwight, & Buck Owens C&W '88
Singles: 7-inch
REPRISE....3-5 88
Picture Sleeves
REPRISE (27964 "Streets of Bakersfield")..3-5 88
Also see OWENS, Buck
Also see YOAKAM, Dwight

YOCHANAN, Muck Muck
Singles: 7-inch
SATURN (4237 "Hot Skillet Momma")....25-35
WEB (1106 "My Pretty Baby")....75-125

YOHO THE PHAROAH
Singles: 7-inch
COLLECTOR (11 "Part One")....30-40 80
(Picture disc. Includes picture sleeve. Promotional issue only.)

YOKOHAMA KNIGHTS
LPs: 10/12-inch
GRT (10002 "Yokohama Knights")....8-10 69

YOKOHAMA RAMBLERS
Singles: 7-inch
TOWER (240 "Yokohama Nights")....5-10 66

YOLANDA
(With the Naturals; with Charmanes; with Castanets)
Singles: 7-inch
KIMLEY (923 "My Memories of You")....75-100 62
SMASH (1777 "Hootchy Cootchy Girl")....10-20 62
TANDEM (7002 "Meet Me After School").50-75 61

YONKER, David
Singles: 7-inch
AUDIO UNLIMITED (6359 "A Song")....15-25 67

YORE, Joseph
Singles: 7-inch
SILVERTIP (304 "Yes, Little Girl I Do")....5-10 62

YOREY, Bobby
Singles: 7-inch
SOOZEE (112 "That's What I'll Do")....5-10 62

YORGESSON, Yogi P&R '49
(With the Johnny Duffy Trio; Harry Stewart)
Singles: 78 rpm
CAPITOL....4-8 49-55
S&H (3009 "My Clam Digger Sweetheart")....10-20
Singles: 7-inch
CAPITOL (700 thru 3000 series)....5-10 49-55
EPs: 7-inch
CAPITOL....10-15 52-53
LPs: 10/12-inch
CAPITOL (336 "Family Album")....30-50 53
(10-inch LP.)
Also see KARI, Harry, & His Six Saki Sippers

YORK, Dave, & Beachcombers P&R '62
Singles: 7-inch
LANCELOT (6 "Beach Party")....30-40 62
P-K-M. (6700 "Beach Party")....15-25 62
Session: Glen Campbell; Gary Paxton; Steve Douglas; Jerry Reaple; Ray Polman.
Also see CAMPBELL, Glen
Also see DOUGLAS, Steve
Also see PAXTON, Gary

YORK, Johnny
Singles: 7-inch
BEV MAR (605 "We're True Lovers")....10-20 '60s
Also see JACK, Johnny

YORK, Laura Sue
Singles: 7-inch
PHILIPS (40201 "No Place to Go")....5-10 64
PHILIPS (40266 "You'll Thank Me Tomorrow")....5-10 65

YORK, Patti
Singles: 7-inch
MINT (806 "You Walked Away with My Heart")....15-25 58
Also see SENTIMENTALS

YORK, Rusty P&R '59
(With J.D. Jarvis)
Singles: 7-inch
CAPITOL (4663 "Just Like You")....10-15 61
CHESS (1730 "Sugaree")....20-30 59
GAYLORD (6428 "Sally Was a Good Old Girl")....5-10 63
JEWEL (700 "Sugaree '66")....50-70 66
KING (5103 "Shake 'Em Up Baby")....15-25 58
KING (5511 "Love Struck")....10-15 61
KING (5587 "Tore Up Over You")....10-15 61
NOTE (10021 "Sugaree")....50-75 60
P.J. (100 "Sugaree")....60-80 59
(First issue.)
SAGE (327 "Sadie Mae")....75-100 60
EPs: 7-inch
BLUE GRASS....10-15 61
JEWEL....10-20 61
LPs: 10/12-inch
QUEEN CITY....10-15
RURAL RHYTHM....8-12
Also see CAJUNS
Also see MACK, Lonnie, & Rusty York

YORK BROTHERS
(York Brothers / Leslie York)
Singles: 78 rpm
DECCA....20-30 57
KING....5-10 52-57
Singles: 7-inch
DECCA (30473 "Everybody's Tryin' to Be My Baby")....20-30 57
KING....10-15 52-57
EPs: 7-inch
KING....10-20 57
LPs: 10/12-inch
KING....20-40 58-63
Member: Leslie York.

YORKSHIRE PUDDING
Singles: 7-inch
DELLWOOD (1 "Black Jacket Woman")..10-20 67
DELLWOOD (3932 "Good Night Day")....10-20 67

YORKSHIRES
Singles: 7-inch
WESTCHESTER (1000 "Tossed Aside").10-20 '60s

YOST, Dennis
Singles: 7-inch
MGM....4-6 75
ROBOX....3-5 81
LPs: 10/12-inch
ACCORD....5-8 81
PHONORAMA....10-15 82
ROBOX....10-15 81
Also see CLASSICS IV

YOU & ME
Singles: 7-inch
CHARTMAKER (409 "I Got That Feeling") 10-20

"YOU KNOW WHO" GROUP *P&R '64*
Singles: 7-inch
CASUAL (94725 "Run") 8-10 65
4 CORNERS (113 "Roses Are Red My Love") 8-10 64
INT'L ALLIED (823 "This Day Love") 8-10 65
Picture Sleeves
INT'L ALLIED (823 "This Day Love") 10-15 65
LPs: 10/12-inch
INT'L ALLIED (420 "The 'You Know Who' Group") 15-20 65

YOUMANS, Bobby
Singles: 7-inch
TIFCO (827 "Teach Me Tonight") 5-10 62

YOUNG, April
Singles: 7-inch
COLUMBIA (43046 "Will You Be My Steady Boyfriend") 10-20 64
COLUMBIA (43122 "To Be Loved By You") 10-20 64
COLUMBIA (43285 "Gonna Make Him My Baby") 10-20 65
COLUMBIA (43392 "Run to My Lovin' Arms") 10-20 65

YOUNG, Barbara
Singles: 7-inch
TREND (30001 "My First Love Letter") 10-15 58

YOUNG, Barry *P&R '65*
Singles: 7-inch
A&M (747 "Ninth Street West") 5-10 64
COLUMBIA (43584 "A Heart Without a Home") 5-10 66
COLUMBIA (43723 "Cryin' Street") 5-10 66
COLUMBIA (43947 "My Future Just Passed") 5-10 66
DEVILLE 5-10 63
DOT (16756 "One Has My Name") 5-10 65
DOT (16819 "Since You Have Gone From Me") 5-10 66
EVA (102 "Come On Pretty Baby") 8-12 63
HOOKS BROTHERS (526 "My Baby Left Me") 8-12 66
Picture Sleeves
COLUMBIA (43584 "A Heart Without a Home") 5-10 66
LPs: 10/12-inch
DOT (3672 "One Has My Name") 15-25 65
(Monaural.)
DOT (25672 "One Has My Name") 15-25 65
(Stereo.)
Also see PHILLIPS, Walt, & Barry Young

YOUNG, Beamon
Singles: 7-inch
ARVEE (573 "The Love I Just Lost") 15-25 59

YOUNG, Betty
Singles: 7-inch
RISING SONS (703 "Way of Love") 5-10 67

YOUNG, Billy
Singles: 7-inch
CHESS (1961 "You Left the Water Running") 8-12 66
JOTIS (429 "Sloopy") 8-12 65
MERCURY (72693 "Nothing's Too Much") 10-15 67
MERCURY (72769 "Let Them Talk") 8-12 68
ORIGINAL SOUND (29 "Glendora") 10-20 63
SHOUT (236 "I'm Available") 8-12 68

YOUNG, Billy Joe
Singles: 7-inch
JEWEL (775 "Push") 5-10 66
JEWEL (782 "Feelin' Blue") 5-10 67
PAULA (240 "I've Got You on My Mind Again") 5-10 66

YOUNG, Bob
Singles: 7-inch
MIRA (239 "Goodbye to Yesterday") 5-10 67
PACIFIC CHALLENGER (126 "Goodbye to Yesterday") 8-12 67

YOUNG, Bobby
Singles: 7-inch
FOXIE (7009 "The Clock") 5-10 62

YOUNG, Bobby
(With Rick & the Masters)
Singles: 7-inch
GUYDEN (2087 "To Each His Own") 400-500 63
Also see RICK & MASTERS

YOUNG, Brett
Singles: 7-inch
DUEL (531 "You Can't Fool Me") 5-10 64

YOUNG, Cathy
Singles: 7-inch
MAINSTREAM (703 "Spoonful") 5-10 69
LPs: 10/12-inch
MAINSTREAM (6121 "A Spoonful of Cathy Young") 8-12 69

YOUNG, Cecil
(Cecil Young Quartet)
Singles: 78 rpm
KING 10-15 52-54
Singles: 7-inch
KING (4604 "That Old Black Magic") 20-40 53
KING (4638 "Fish Net") 20-40 53
KING (4692 "Ooh Diga-Gow") 20-40 54
KING (4749 "Who Parked the Car") 20-40 54
KING (15165 "Tea for Two") 20-40 52
KING (15174 "Night and Day") 20-40 52
KING (15175 "Rushin' on Home") 20-40 52
KING (15192 "South of the Border") 20-40 52
EPs: 7-inch
KING (247 "Cecil Young Quartet") 30-40 53
KING (277 "Cecil Young Quartet, Vol. 2") 30-40 53
KING (374 "Modern Sounds") 20-30 56
LPs: 10/12-inch
AUDIO LAB (1516 "Jazz on the Rock") 30-40 59
KING (1 "Cecil Young Quartet") 50-100 52
(10-inch LP.)
KING (505 "Concert of Cool Jazz") 40-60 56
Also see STARGLOWS / Rock-A-Bouts / Cecil Young Quartet

YOUNG, Chip
Singles: 7-inch
ESCO 15-25 60
SUE (737 "Just As You Are") 8-12 61
U.A. (50178 "Last Day in Town") 5-10 67

YOUNG, Cortez
Singles: 7-inch
GOLD (101 "Everybody's Going") 50-75

YOUNG, De De
(Dee Dee Young)
Singles: 7-inch
ASCOT (2101 "Remember You Belong to Me") 8-12 62
CHALLENGE (59225 "Tell Me Tonight") 5-10 64

YOUNG, Don
Singles: 7-inch
BANG (574 "Movin' ") 5-10 69

YOUNG, Donna Jean
Singles: 7-inch
LAD (0027 "How Sweet Your Lips") 5-10 59

YOUNG, Donny
Singles: 7-inch
AMCAN (407 "From Twelve to Seven") 100-200 64
DECCA (30881 "Old Man & the River") 10-20 59
DECCA (31077 "Shakin' the Blues") 20-25 60
DECCA (31283 "Go Ring the Bells") 10-15 61
MERCURY (71900 "On Second Thought") 10-15 61
MERCURY (71981 "Not Much I Don't") 10-15 62
TODD (1098 "I'm Glad to Have Her Back Again") 5-10 64
Also see PAYCHECK, Johnny

YOUNG, Donny, & Roger Miller
Singles: 7-inch
DECCA (30763 "On This Mountain Top") 15-25 58
Also see MILLER, Roger
Also see YOUNG, Donny

YOUNG, Faron *C&W '53*
(With the Anita Kerr Singers; with Margie Singleton; with Jordanaires)
Singles: 78 rpm
CAPITOL 5-10 53-57
Singles: 7-inch
CAPITOL (2200 thru 3900 series) 10-20 53-58
CAPITOL (4000 thru 4800 series) 5-10 58-62
MCA 3-6 79-80
MERCURY 4-8 63-78
Picture Sleeves
CAPITOL (4616 "Backtrack") 10-20 61
CAPITOL (4696 "Three Days") 10-20 61
MERCURY 5-10 62-68
EPs: 7-inch
CAPITOL 10-20 54-61
REPERTORY (1 "And Now") 10-15
LPs: 10/12-inch
ALBUM GLOBE 5-8 81
ALLEGIANCE 5-8 84
BULLDOG 5-10
CBS 5-8 83
CAPITOL (778 "Sweethearts or Strangers") 30-50 57
CAPITOL (1004 "Object of My Affection") 30-50 58
CAPITOL (1096 "This Is Faron Young") 30-50 58
CAPITOL (1185 "My Garden of Prayer") 30-50 59
CAPITOL (1245 "Talk About Hits") 30-40 59
CAPITOL (1450 thru 2536) 12-25 60-66
(With "T," "DT" or "ST" prefix.)
CAPITOL (1500 series) 5-8 75
(With "SM" prefix.)
CASTLE 5-8
EXACT 5-8 80
FARON YOUNG (001 "20 Great Hits") 25-50
FARON YOUNG (003 "Family Favorites") 25-50
FARON YOUNG (004 "Faron Young Presents the Country Deputies") 20-30
FARON YOUNG (005 "Faron Young Sings") 25-50
(Stereo.)
FARON YOUNG (4-22-82 "Fortunes in Music") 8-15 82
FARON YOUNG (101 "Most Requested") 15-25
IMPACT 5-10
K-TEL 5-10 77
MCA 4-8 79-83
MARY CARTER PAINTS (1000 "Faron Young Sings on Stage") 20-30
(Promotional issue only.)
MERCURY 5-15 63-77
MOUNTAIN DEW 5-10
PHONORAMA 5-8 82
PICCADILLY 5-10 80
PICKWICK/HILLTOP 8-12 66-68
REALM 5-8 81
SEARS 8-12
TOWER 12-15 66-68
WING 8-12 68
Session: Don Adams; Jordanaires.
Also see ATKINS, Chet, Faron Young, & Anita Kerr Singers
Also see FRANKS, Tillman
Also see JORDANAIRES
Also see KERR, Anita
Also see NELSON, Willie / Faron Young
Also see OWENS, Buck / Faron Young / Ferlin Husky

YOUNG, Faron / Carl Perkins / Claude King
LPs: 10/12-inch
PICKWICK/HILLTOP (6011 "Faron, Carl and Claude") 8-15 65
Also see KING, Claude
Also see PERKINS, Carl

YOUNG, Faron / Jean Shepard
EPs: 7-inch
CAPITOL CUSTOM (118-30 "Recorded Especially for Ballard Flour") 10-20
(Promotional issue, made for Ballard Flour.)
Also see SHEPARD, Jean
Also see YOUNG, Faron

YOUNG, Faron, & Margie Singleton *C&W '64*
Singles: 7-inch
MERCURY (72201 "Keeping Up with the Joneses"/"No Thanks I Just Had One") 8-12 64
MERCURY (72312 "Another Woman's Man – Another Man's Woman") 8-12 64
Also see YOUNG, Faron

YOUNG, Freddy
Singles: 7-inch
FRIENDLY FIVE (740 "Monkey Business") 10-15 63

YOUNG, George
Singles: 7-inch
CHORD (1301 "Wow Wow Wow") 30-40 57

YOUNG, George, & Sidemen
Singles: 7-inch
KAPP (652 "P.J.'s Party") 5-10 65

YOUNG, Georgie *P&R '58*
(With the Rockin' Bocs; George Young)
Singles: 7-inch
ARLEN (752 "Sandra") 5-10 64
CAMEO (150 "Nine More Miles") 15-25 58
CAMEO (166 "Feels So Good") 10-20 59
CAMEO (168 "Georgie Porgie") 10-20 59
CAMEO (173 "Gold Rush") 10-20 60
(First issue.)
CHANCELLOR (1066 "Indian Summer") 10-15 60
CHANCELLOR (1069 "Marie") 10-15 61
COLUMBIA (42773 "Supercar") 10-20 63
FORTUNE (524 "Buggin' Baby") 75-125 57
MERCURY (71259 "Can't Stop Me") 40-60 58
PACE SETTER 5-8
PARKWAY (809 "Gold Rush") 10-15 60
SWAN (4059 "Yogi") 10-15 60
LPs: 10/12-inch
CHANCELLOR (5021 "Veryest") 15-25 61
COLUMBIA (1881 "Greatest Saxophone in the World") 15-25 62
(Monaural.)
COLUMBIA (1929 "Gold & Satin") 15-25 63
(Monaural.)
COLUMBIA (8681 "Greatest Saxophone in the World") 20-30 62
(Stereo.)
COLUMBIA (8729 "Gold & Satin") 20-30 63
(Stereo.)
Members: Georgie Young; Bob DeNardo; Bob McGraw; Fred Bender; Pete Cozzi.
Also see RYDELL, Bobby

YOUNG, Gordon
Singles: 7-inch
FELSTED (8567 "Who's Fooling Who") 5-10 59
STRAND (25018 "Family Tree") 5-10 60

YOUNG, Greg
Singles: 7-inch
KENT (334 "Honey, Honey") 10-15 60

YOUNG, Harold
Singles: 78 rpm
ROCKIN' (511 "I Love You for Myself") 15-25 53
Also see HARRIS, Manzy

YOUNG, Inell
Singles: 7-inch
BUSY B (3 "His Love for Me") 10-20 67

YOUNG, James "Big Sambo"
Singles: 7-inch
JET STREAM (808 "You're Barkin' Up the Wrong Tree") 5-10 68

YOUNG, Jesse Colin *LP '72*
(With the Youngbloods)
Singles: 7-inch
ELEKTRA 4-6 78
REPRISE 4-6 73
W.B. 4-6 70-77
LPs: 10/12-inch
CAPITOL (2000 series) 20-25 64
CAPITOL (11000 series) 8-10 74
CAPITOL (16000 series) 5-8 80
ELEKTRA 5-8 78
MERCURY (21005 "Young Blood") 20-25 65
(Monaural.)
MERCURY (61005 "Young Blood") 20-25 65
(Stereo.)
MERCURY (61273 "Two Trips") 10-15 70
W.B. 8-10 72-77
Also see YOUNGBLOODS

YOUNG, Jimmy
(With Bob Sharples Orchestra; with Bob Sharples and His Music)
Singles: 78 rpm
EMBER (1003 "Need Your Love") ... 8-12 56
HERALD (467 "Need Your Love") ... 10-15 55
LONDON ... 5-10 56
Singles: 7-inch
EMBER (1003 "Need Your Love") ... 20-30 56
HERALD (467 "Need Your Love") ... 15-25 55
LONDON (1676 "Rich Man Poor Man") ... 10-20 56
LONDON (1723 "Lovin' Baby") ... 10-20 57

YOUNG, Johnny
(Man Young)
Singles: 78 rpm
OLD SWINGMASTER (19 "My Baby Walked Out On Me") ... 50-100 48
ORA NELLE (712 "Worried Man Blues") ... 50-100 47
PLANET (103 "My Baby Walked Out On Me") ... 100-150 48
LPs: 10/12-inch
ARHOOLIE ... 10-15
BLUE HORIZON ... 10-20
BLUESWAY (6075 "I Can't Keep My Foot from Jumping") ... 8-12 73
Also see PRYOR, Snooky
Also see WILLIAMS, Big Joe, & Johnny Young

YOUNG, Johnny, & Big Walter
LPs: 10/12-inch
ARHOOLIE ... 10-15
Also see BIG WALTER
Also see YOUNG, Johnny

YOUNG, Johnny, Trio
Singles: 78 rpm
CHANCE (1144 "Memories of You") ... 50-75 53
Singles: 7-inch
CHANCE (1144 "Memories of You") ... 100-200 53

YOUNG, Jonathan
Singles: 7-inch
ARVEE (5039 "I Don't Want to Know") ... 5-10 61

YOUNG, Kathy *P&R '60*
(With the Innocents)
Singles: 7-inch
COLLECTABLES ... 3-5 '80s
ERA (018 "Happy Birthday Blues") ... 4-6 72
ERIC ... 4-6 '70s
INDIGO (108 "A Thousand Stars") ... 15-25 60
INDIGO (115 "Happy Birthday Blues") ... 15-20 61
INDIGO (121 "Our Parents Talked It Over") ... 15-20 61
INDIGO (125 "Magic Is the Night") ... 15-20 61
INDIGO (137 "Baby Oh Baby") ... 10-15 61
INDIGO (141 "Time") ... 10-15 62
INDIGO (146 "Lonely Blue Nights") ... 10-15 62
INDIGO (147 "Send Her Away") ... 10-15 62
MONOGRAM (506 "Dream Boy") ... 8-12 62
OLDIES 45 (46 "A Thousand Stars") ... 5-10 '60s
STARFIRE (112 "Sparkle & Shine") ... 5-10 79
(Red vinyl.)
Picture Sleeves
INDIGO (115 "Happy Birthday Blues") ... 15-20 61
INDIGO (125 "Magic Is the Night") ... 15-20 61
(Both 115 and 125 have exactly the same picture and layout.)
STARFIRE ("Sparkle and Shine") ... 10-15 79
EPs: 7-inch
INDIGO (1001 ""Kathy Young") ... 50-75 61
LPs: 10/12-inch
INDIGO (504 "The Sound of Kathy Young") ... 50-100 61
STARFIRE (1000 "Our Best to You") ... 10-20 81
(Picture disc on one side, black vinyl on flip.)
Also see CHRIS & KATHY
Also see INNOCENTS
Also see WASHER WINDSHIELD

YOUNG, Kathy / Innocents
Singles: 7-inch
TRIP ... 4-6 '70s
Also see INNOCENTS
Also see YOUNG, Kathy

YOUNG, Kenneth, & English Muffins
Singles: 7-inch
DIAMOND (183 "Mrs. Green's Ugly Daughter") ... 5-10 65

YOUNG, Kenny
Singles: 7-inch
ATCO (6322 "Just a Little Bit Better") ... 5-10 64
MGM (13136 "Thumbin' ") ... 5-10 63
SHARE ... 5-10 69
U.A. (50032 "Little Sister") ... 5-10 66
W.B. ... 4-6 72
LPs: 10/12-inch
W.B. ... 8-12 72

YOUNG, Kevin
Singles: 7-inch
CHESS (1788 "Say You Will Be Mine") ... 5-10 61

YOUNG, Lennie, & Jaybirds
Singles: 7-inch
JACKPOT (48006 "Joyce") ... 10-20 58
JAY SCOTT (1001 "Joyce") ... 75-100 58

YOUNG, Leon
(With String Chorale)
Singles: 7-inch
ATCO (6274 "Spinning Jenny") ... 5-10 63
ATCO (6301 "John, Paul, George and Ringo") ... 5-10 64
LPs: 10/12-inch
ATCO (163 "Liverpool Sound") ... 15-25 64

YOUNG, Lester *R&B '44*
(With His Kansas City Five; Lester Young Quartet; Lester "Prez" Young)
Singles: 78 rpm
ALADDIN ... 5-10 46-54
KEYNOTE ... 5-10 44
MERCURY ... 5-10 44
SAVOY ... 4-8 45-46
Singles: 7-inch
ALADDIN ... 20-30 50-54
EPs: 7-inch
ALADDIN ... 35-55 53
CLEF ... 25-50 51-53
EMARCY ... 25-50 54
MERCURY ... 35-55 50
NORGRAN ... 35-55 52-54
SAVOY ... 20-40 51
LPs: 10/12-inch
ALADDIN (706 "Lester Young and His Tenor Sax") ... 150-250 53
(10-inch LP.)
ALADDIN (801 "Lester Young and His Tenor Sax, Vol. 1") ... 75-125 56
ALADDIN (802 "Lester Young and His Tenor Sax, Vol. 2") ... 75-125 56
CHARLIE PARKER (402 "Pres") ... 30-50 62
CHARLIE PARKER (405 "Pres Is Blue") ... 30-50 62
CHARLIE PARKER (409 "Just You, Just Me") ... 30-50 62
CLEF (10 "Lester Young Collates") ... 100-200 52
(10-inch LP.)
CLEF (10 "Lester Young Collates No. 2") ... 100-200 53
(10-inch LP.)
CLEF (104 "Lester Young Trio") ... 100-200 51
(10-inch LP.)
CLEF (135 "Lester Young Trio, No. 2") ... 100-200 53
(10-inch LP.)
COMMODORE (20021 "Kansas City Style") ... 100-200 50
(10-inch LP.)
COMMODORE (30014 "Kansas City Style") ... 50-75 59
EMARCY (26010 "Swinging Sounds of the '40s") ... 20-30 65
(Monaural.)
EMARCY (26021 "Pres Meets Vice-Pres") ... 100-200 54
(10-inch LP.)
EMARCY (66010 "Swinging Sounds of the '40s") ... 20-30 65
(Stereo.)
EPIC (3107 "Lester Leaps In") ... 50-100 56
EPIC (3168 "Let's Go to Prez") ... 50-100 56
EPIC (3576 "Memorial Album, Vol. 1") ... 40-60 59
EPIC (3577 "Memorial Album, Vol. 2") ... 40-60 59
EPIC (6031 "Memorial Album, Vols. 1 & 2") ... 50-100 59
(Two discs.)
IMPERIAL (9181 "Great Lester Young, Vol. 1") ... 20-30 62
(Monaural.)
IMPERIAL (9187 "Great Lester Young, Vol. 2") ... 20-30 62
(Monaural.)
IMPERIAL (12181 "Great Lester Young, Vol. 1") ... 25-35 62
(Stereo.)
IMPERIAL (12187 "Great Lester Young, Vol. 2") ... 25-35 62
(Stereo.)
INTRO (602 "Swinging") ... 50-100 57
INTRO (603 "The Greatest") ... 50-100 57
JAZZTONE (1218 "Prez & Chu") ... 50-75
MAINSTREAM (6012 "Prez") ... 25-35 65
(Stereo.)
MAINSTREAM (56012 "Prez") ... 25-35 65
(Monaural.)
MERCURY (25015 "Lester Young Quartet") ... 150-250 50
(10-inch LP.)
NORGRAN (1005 "The President") ... 50-100 54
NORGRAN (1022 "Lester Young") ... 50-100 54
NORGRAN (1043 "Pres and Sweets") ... 50-100 55
NORGRAN (1071 "Lester's Here") ... 50-75 55
NORGRAN (1072 "Pres") ... 50-75 55
NORGRAN (1074 "Lester Young and the Buddy Rich Trio") ... 50-75 55
NORGRAN (1093 "Lester Swings Again") ... 40-60 56
SAVOY (9002 "All Star Be Bop") ... 150-250 51
SAVOY (12068 "Blue Lester") ... 40-60 56
SAVOY (12071 "Master's Touch") ... 40-60 56
SAVOY (12155 "Immortal") ... 30-50 59
SAVOY (1109 "Lester Young") ... 10-15 77
SCORE (4028 "Swinging") ... 40-60 58
SCORE (4029 "The Greatest") ... 40-60 58
SUNSET (1181 "Giant of Jazz") ... 10-20 67
(Monaural.)
SUNSET (5181 "Giant of Jazz") ... 10-20 67
(Stereo.)
VSP (27 "Pres and His Cabinet") ... 20-30 66
VSP (41 "At Jazz at the Philharmonic") ... 20-30 67
VERVE (2516 "Lester Swings") ... 10-20 77
(Two discs.)
VERVE (2518 "Bird and Pres") ... 10-20 77
(Two discs.)
VERVE (6054 "Laughin' to Keep from Crying") ... 50-70 59
(Stereo.)
VERVE (8161 "Lester's Here") ... 40-60 57
VERVE (8162 "Pres") ... 40-60 57
VERVE (8164 "Lester Young and the Buddy Rich Trio") ... 40-60 57
VERVE (8181 "Lester Swings Again") ... 40-60 57
VERVE (8187 "It Don't Mean a Thing") ... 40-60 57
VERVE (8208 "Lester Young Story") ... 40-60 59
VERVE (8298 "Going for Myself") ... 40-60 59
VERVE (8303 "The Lester Young Story") 40-60 59
VERVE (8316 "Laughin' to Keep from Crying") ... 40-60 59
(Monaural.)
VERVE (8378 "In Paris") ... 40-60 59
VERVE (8398 "The Essential Lester Young") ... 30-50 61
Session: Red Callender; Howard McGhee; Paul Quinchette; Buddy Rich; Ray Brown; John Lewis; Connie Kay; Harry Edison; Chu Berry; Kenny Clarke; Roy Eldridge; Teddy Wilson; Count Basie; Coleman Hawkins.
Also see BASIE, Count
Also see CALLENDER, Red
Also see JACQUET, Illinois / Lester Young

YOUNG, Lester, & Nat "King" Cole
Singles: 78 rpm
PHILCO ... 5-10 42
EPs: 7-inch
ALADDIN ... 20-40 53
LPs: 10/12-inch
ALADDIN (705 "Lester Young Trio with Nat 'King' Cole") ... 100-200 53
(10-inch LP.)
SCORE (4019 "Lester Young Trio with Nat 'King' Cole") ... 50-75 58
Also see COLE, Nat "King"
Also see PETERSON, Oscar

YOUNG, Lester, Nat "King" Cole & Buddy Rich
LPs: 10/12-inch
VSP (30 "Giants 3") ... 20-30 66
Also see RICH, Buddy
Also see YOUNG, Lester, & Nat "King" Cole

YOUNG, Lester, & Oscar Peterson
EPs: 7-inch
NORGRAN ... 20-40 52
LPs: 10/12-inch
NORGRAN (5 "Lester Young with Oscar Peterson") ... 100-150 52
(10-inch LP.)
NORGRAN (6 "Lester Young with Oscar Peterson, No. 2") ... 100-150 52
(10-inch LP.)
NORGRAN (1054 "The President Plays with the Oscar Peterson Trio") ... 50-100 55
VERVE (8144 "The President Plays with the Oscar Peterson Trio") ... 50-75 57
Also see PETERSON, Oscar

YOUNG, Lester, / Paul Quinichette
EPs: 7-inch
MERCURY (6002 "Lester Young / Paul Quinichette") ... 10-20 57
Also see QUINICHETTE, Paul

YOUNG, Lester, & Teddy Wilson
LPs: 10/12-inch
AMERICAN RECORDING SOCIETY (8205 "Pres and Teddy") ... 50-75 57
VERVE (8205 "Pres and Teddy") ... 40-60 57
Also see WILSON, Teddy
Also see YOUNG, Lester

YOUNG, Lester
(With the California Playboys)
Singles: 7-inch
ANGLE TONE (548 "Birmingham") ... 5-10 64
ANGLE TONE (549 "Marybell") ... 5-10 64
BARRY (1009 "Stop") ... 10-15 66
BARRY (1016 "Fool in Love") ... 10-15 67
CHASE (1200 "Wobble Time") ... 5-10 63
OLD TOWN (1186 "I Got the Right") ... 5-10 65
UNITY (27004 "Funky Funky Horse") ... 5-10 68

YOUNG, Mae
Singles: 7-inch
KARATE (530 "No Ifs, No Ands, No Buts") ... 10-20 66

YOUNG, Mighty Joe
Singles: 78 rpm
JIFFY ... 10-20 56
Singles: 7-inch
FIRE (1033 "Empty Arms") ... 15-25 61
JACKLYN (1008 "Guitar Star") ... 10-15 69
JIFFY ("Broke, Downhearted and Disgusted") ... 20-40 56
(Selection number not known.)
USA (861 "Hard Times") ... 5-10 66
WEBCOR (101 "Voo Doo Dust") ... 8-12 65
WEBCOR (102 "Hey Baby") ... 8-12 65
WET SOUL (3 "The Rains Came") ... 5-10
LPs: 10/12-inch
DELMARK ... 8-12 71
OVATION ... 5-10 74

YOUNG, Neil *LP '69*
(With Crazy Horse; with Shocking Pinks; with Bluenotes)
Singles: 12-inch
GEFFEN ... 4-6 86
Singles: 7-inch
GEFFEN ... 3-5 83-86
REPRISE (0785 thru 0898) ... 4-6 68-70
REPRISE (0911 thru 1396) ... 4-6 70-79
(Black vinyl.)
REPRISE (1395 "Comes a Time") ... 250-300 78
(Picture disc. 200 numbered copies made. Promotional issue only.)
REPRISE (49000 series, except 49895) ... 3-6 79-81
REPRISE (49895 "Southern Pacific") .. 250-350 81
(Triangular picture disc. Promotional issue only. Green vinyl. 25 made.)
REPRISE (49895 "Southern Pacific") .. 250-350 81
(Auto- or train-shaped picture disc. Promotional issue only. 10 made of each shape.)
REPRISE (49895 "Southern Pacific") ... 15-25 81
(Triangular picture disc. Promotional issue only. With either red or black vinyl.)
Picture Sleeves
GEFFEN ... 3-5 83
REPRISE ... 3-6 78-81
EPs: 7-inch
REPRISE ... 10-15 72
(Juke box issue only.)

LPs: 10/12-inch
GEFFEN (Except 2018)....5-8 83-87
GEFFEN (2018 "Trans")....10-15 82
(Cover lists *If You Got Love*, which is not on LP.)
GEFFEN (2018 "Trans")....5-8 82
(Cover does not list *If You Got Love*.)
MFSL (252 "Old Ways")....20-30 95
REPRISE (2000 series, except 2257 & 2296)....5-8 72-90
REPRISE (2257 "Decade")....12-18 77
REPRISE (2296 "Live Rust")....10-15 79
REPRISE (6317 "Neil Young")....150-250 68
(Front cover does NOT have Neil Young's name.)
REPRISE (6317 "Neil Young")....10-15 68
(Front cover shows Neil Young's name.)
REPRISE (6349 "Everybody Knows This Is Nowhere")....10-15 69
REPRISE (6383 "After the Gold Rush")..10-15 70
REPRISE (6480 "Journey Through the Past")....10-15 72
REPRISE (25000 thru 46000 series)....5-12 88-96
W.B. 6-15 72-79
Session: Waylon Jennings.
Also see BUFFALO SPRINGFIELD
Also see CASCADES
Also see CROSBY, STILLS, NASH & YOUNG
Also see DANNY & MEMORIES
Also see HARRIS, Emmylou
Also see JENNINGS, Waylon
Also see SQUIRES

YOUNG, Neil, & Jim Messina
Singles: 7-inch
REPRISE....4-8 70
Also see MESSINA, Jim

YOUNG, Neil, & Graham Nash *P&R '72*
Singles: 7-inch
REPRISE (1099 "War Song")....4-8 72
Also see NASH, Graham
Also see YOUNG, Neil

YOUNG, Nelson
(With the Sandy Valley Boys)
Singles: 7-inch
LUCKY (0002 "Rock Old Sputnik")....150-200 59
MADISON (3003 "Charlie Brown's Mule")....50-100 59
RUBY (310 "Hillybilly Rock and Roll")....50-100 57
VETCO (526 "Big Pipeline")....25-50

YOUNG, Patti
Singles: 7-inch
ERNSTRAT (495 "Head and Shoulders")....100-150

YOUNG, Paul, & Versatones
Singles: 7-inch
BECK (111 "Three Idols")....8-12 63

YOUNG, Ralph
Singles: 7-inch
EVEREST (19307 "Pier 34")....5-10 59
EVEREST (19317 "Nothin' to Do")....5-10 59
EVEREST (19324 "Moonlight Gambler")....5-10 60

YOUNG, Ray
Singles: 7-inch
DELTA INT'L (1026 "La-Da-Di-Dum")....8-12 59

YOUNG, Reggie
Singles: 7-inch
M.O.C. (660 "Ebb Tide")....5-10 65
SCEPTER (12325 "Pencil")....4-6 71

YOUNG, Sonny
Singles: 7-inch
S.P.Q.R. (3320 "Judy")....5-10 64

YOUNG, Tami
Singles: 7-inch
MODERN (1049 "I Don't Wanna Lose You")....10-15 68

YOUNG, Tom, & Hippies
Singles: 7-inch
CAMEO (224 "The Wah Watusi")....5-10 62

YOUNG, Tony
Singles: 7-inch
CAMEO (224 "Mash")....5-10 62

YOUNG, Vern
(With the Ambassadors)
Singles: 7-inch
CHORDS (101 "Cindy Lou")....5-10 60

YOUNG, Vicki
(With Big Dave & His Orchestra)
Singles: 78 rpm
CAPITOL....5-10 54-56
Singles: 7-inch
BRUNSWICK (55055 "King Size Love")...10-15 57
CAPITOL (2704 "Forever Yours")....10-20 54
CAPITOL (2761 "Take Me Back")....10-20 54
CAPITOL (2865 "Honey Love")....10-20 54
CAPITOL (3008 "Hearts of Stone")....10-20 54
CAPITOL (3046 "Tweedle Dee")....10-20 55
CAPITOL (3076 "Zoom Zoom Zoom")....10-20 55
CAPITOL (3143 "Do It Now")....10-20 55
CAPITOL (3197 "Put Your Arm Around Me")....10-20 55
CAPITOL (3256 "It Makes No Difference Now")....10-20 55
CAPITOL (3308 "Steel Guitar")....10-20 55
CAPITOL (3358 "Spanish Main")....10-20 56
CAPITOL (3425 "All Shook Up")....10-20 56
EPs: 7-inch
CAPITOL (593 "Riot in Cell Block Number Nine")....20-40 54

YOUNG, Vicki, & Joe Carr
(With the Joy Riders)
Singles: 78 rpm
CAPITOL....5-10 56
Singles: 7-inch
CAPITOL (3231 "Give Me a Band and My Baby")....10-20 56
Also see CARR, Joe "Fingers"
Also see YOUNG, Vicki

YOUNG, Victor *P&R '31*
Singles: 78 rpm
BRUNSWICK....3-5 31-34
DECCA....3-5 34-57
Singles: 7-inch
DECCA....5-10 50-57
Picture Sleeves
DECCA (29433 "Theme from Medic")....15-25 55
(Pictures Richard Boone and other TV series cast.)
EPs: 7-inch
DECCA....5-15 50-57
LPs: 10/12-inch
DECCA....10-25 50-59
Also see CROSBY, Bing
Also see GARLAND, Judy

YOUNG ALLEY CATS
Singles: 7-inch
ROBIN (100 "Since You Been Gone")....10-15 66

YOUNG AMERICANS *LP '69*
Singles: 7-inch
ABC (10940 "One by One")....5-10 67
ABC (10977 "Little Girl")....5-10 67
ABC (10998 "Here I Am")....5-10 67
LPs: 10/12-inch
ABC (586 "While We're Young")....10-15 67

YOUNG ARISTOCRACY
Singles: 7-inch
ACROPOLIS (6721 "Don't Lie")....10-20 67

YOUNG AT HEART
Singles: 7-inch
FOUR WAYS (1004 "Know Love")....5-10 67

YOUNG BROTHERS
Singles: 7-inch
SOUL POWER ("What's Your Game").350-400
(Selection number not known.)

YOUNG CANADIANS
Singles: 7-inch
FILMWAYS (109 "Making My Mind Up")..15-25 66

YOUNG CHICAGOANS
Singles: 7-inch
DESTINATION (636 "Summertime Blues")....10-15 67

YOUNG ENTERPRISE
Singles: 7-inch
FONTANA (1631 "Little Imogene")....5-10 68
FONTANA (1644 "The Magician")....5-10 69
RUST (5111 "I Wanted You")....5-10 66

YOUNG EXECUTIVES
Singles: 7-inch
MERCURY (72524 "Come On in Baby")....5-10 66

YOUNG FOLK
Singles: 7-inch
MAR-V-LUS (6018 "Lonely Girl")....8-15 67

YOUNG GENERATION
Singles: 7-inch
CAPTAIN....8-12
RED BIRD (065 "Hideaway")....8-12 66
Member: Janis Siegel.
Also see MANHATTAN TRANSFER

YOUNG GENTS
Singles: 7-inch
BUDDAH (134 "Think About the Children")....5-10 69

YOUNG HEARTS *P&R/R&B '68*
(Younghearts)
Singles: 7-inch
AVCO EMBASSY (4554 "Change of Mind")....5-10 70
MINIT (32039 "Oh, I'll Never Be the Same")....5-10 68
MINIT (32049 "I've Got Love for My Baby")....20-30 68
MINIT (32057 "Girls")....5-10 69
MINIT (32066 "Count Down")....5-10 69
MINIT (32084 "Young Hearts Get Lonely Too")....5-10 70
SOULTOWN (3000 "I've Got Dancing Fever")....10-20
20TH FOX (2080 "Me and You")....4-6 74
20TH FOX (2130 "Wake Up and Start Standing")....4-6 75
LPs: 10/12-inch
MINIT....15-25 69
Members: Ronald Preyer; Earl Carter; James Moore; Charles Ingersoll; Bob Solomon.

YOUNG - HOLT UNLIMITED *P&R/R&B '66*
(Young-Holt Trio)
Singles: 7-inch
BRUNSWICK....4-6 66-69
COTILLION....4-6 70-71
ERIC....3-5 83
PAULA....4-6 73
LPs: 10/12-inch
ATLANTIC....8-10 73
BRUNSWICK....10-20 67-69
COTILLION....8-12 70-71
PAULA....5-10 73
Members: Eldee Young; Isaac Holt; Floyd Morris.
Also see LEWIS, Ramsey

YOUNG IDEA
Singles: 7-inch
CAPITOL (5875 "Just Look at the Rain")...5-10 67
CAPITOL (5943 "With a Little Help from My Friends")....5-10 67
CAPITOL (2093 "Room with a View")....5-10 68

YOUNG IDEAS
Singles: 7-inch
SWAN (4044 "Dream")....10-20 59

YOUNG IDEAS
Singles: 7-inch
ABC (11067 "Candy Street")....5-10 68
DATE (1614 "Melody")....5-10 68

YOUNG IMAGINATION
Singles: 7-inch
(S-80 142 "Your Friend")....5-10 '60s
(No label name used.)

YOUNG LADS
Singles: 78 rpm
NEIL (100 "Moonlight")....10-20 56
Singles: 7-inch
NEIL (100 "Moonlight")....40-50 56

YOUNG LADS
Singles: 7-inch
FELICE (712 "Graduation Kiss")....50-75 63

YOUNG LIONS
Singles: 7-inch
TAMPA (158 "Oh Daddy")....50-75 59

YOUNG LIONS
Singles: 7-inch
U.A. (177 "Maybe Someday")....15-25 59

YOUNG LIONS
Singles: 7-inch
DOT (16172 "Little Girl")....30-40 60

YOUNG LIONS
Singles: 7-inch
LOMA (2022 "Live and Learn")....5-10 65

YOUNG MEN
Singles: 7-inch
BOLO (742 "Walkin' Along")....8-15 64
BOLO (744 "It's Luv")....8-15 64
BOLO (748 "Backfield Beat")....8-15 64
CAMELOT....5-10
Members: Ron Wilderman; Rainier Rey; Larry Wilber; Tom Severns.

YOUNG MEN
Singles: 7-inch
VIVA (632 "Get the Message")....5-10 68

YOUNG MEN
Singles: 7-inch
MALTESE (105 "A Young Man's Problem")....15-25 '60s
MALTESE (108 "Go Away Girl")....50-75 '60s

YOUNG MONKEY MEN
Singles: 7-inch
JADE (101 "Bald Headed Woman")....15-25 66
P&M (3648 "I'm Waitin' for the Letter")....15-25 67

YOUNG ONES
(Stokes)
Singles: 7-inch
ALON (9025 "Sawdust Floor")....8-12 65
Members: Allen Toussaint; Billy Fayard; Al Fayard.
Also see STOKES

YOUNG ONES
(Youngones)
Singles: 7-inch
YUSSELS (7701 "Marie")....30-50 62
YUSSELS (7703 "I'm in the Mood for Love")....25-40 62
YUSSELS (7704 "Diamonds & Pearls")...25-40 62

YOUNG ONES
Singles: 7-inch
RELIC (540 "Gloria")....5-10 65
TIMES SQUARE (28 "Gloria")....10-15 64

YOUNG ONES / El Sierros
Singles: 7-inch
RELIC (527 "Sweeter Than"/"Picture of Love")....5-10 65
TIMES SQUARE (36 "Sweeter Than"/"Picture of Love")....10-20 64
Also see EL SIERROS
Also see YOUNG ONES

YOUNG ONES
Singles: 7-inch
COLUMBIA (43788 "Sour Grapes")....8-12 66
Picture Sleeves
COLUMBIA (43788 "Sour Grapes")....10-15 66

YOUNG ONES
Singles: 7-inch
SUPER-COOL (7337 "Too Much Lovin'")....30-40 67
Also see CYKLE

YOUNG RICHARD
Singles: 7-inch
AGE (29108 "I Can't Understand")....5-10 62

YOUNG ROX
Singles: 7-inch
ROX (2014 "Penetration")....10-20 '60s

YOUNG SAVAGES
Singles: 7-inch
DYNAMIC SOUND (2006 "The Invaders Are Coming")....15-25 67
DYNAMIC SOUND (2007 "I Love You Oh So Much")....15-25 67
Member: Doc Couty.

YOUNG SAVAGES
Singles: 7-inch
ROULETTE (4777 "Can I Be Dreaming") 10-15 67
ROULETTE (7009 "Wait a Minute")....10-15 68

YOUNG SISTERS
Singles: 7-inch
MALA (467 "Jerry Boy")....5-10 63

PHILIPS (40803 "Let's Do the Latin Hustle") 4-6 75
TWIRL (2001 "My Guy") 20-30 62
TWIRL (2008 "Playgirl") 10-20 63

YOUNG TEMPTATIONS

Singles: 7-inch

LURO (716 "What Time Is It") 100-200 65

YOUNG TURKS

Singles: 7-inch

ODYSSEY (101 "Looky, Looky") 5-10 69

YOUNG TYRANTS

Singles: 7-inch

IN (67101 "She Don't Got the Right") 10-20 67
TRY (101 "I Try") 15-25 67

YOUNG 'UNS

Singles: 7-inch

ARCADE (142 "Don't Cry on My Shoulder") 10-15 56

YOUNG VOYAGERS

Singles: 7-inch

RUST (5083 "The Angry Sea") 5-10 64

YOUNG WILLIAM & JAMAICANS

Singles: 7-inch

DIMENSION (1005 "Limbo Drum") 10-20 63

YOUNG WOLF
(Gus Jenkins)

Singles: 78 rpm

COMBO (88 "Worries & Troubles") 15-25 55

Singles: 7-inch

COMBO (88 "Worries & Troubles") 30-50 55
Also see JENKINS, Gus

YOUNG WORLD SINGERS

Singles: 7-inch

DECCA (31660 "Ringo for President") 10-20 64

YOUNGBLOOD

Singles: 7-inch

TANGERINE (962 "I Had a Dream") 5-10 66

YOUNGBLOOD, Edison

Singles: 7-inch

COMET (101 "Big Bad Betty") 25-35 60
HANOVER (4530 "Maybe Now") 5-10 59
HERALD (544 "Why Oh Why") 5-10 59

YOUNGBLOOD, Lonnie R&B '72
(Lonnie Youngblood's Combo)

Singles: 7-inch

CALLA (109 "Let My Love Bring Out the Woman in You") 4-6 76
CAMEO (374 "Come On Let's Strut") 5-10 65
EARTH ....5-10 '60s
FAIRMOUNT (1002 "Go Go Place") 5-10 66
FAIRMOUNT (1016 "Grass") 5-10 66
FAIRMOUNT (1022 "Soul Food") 5-10 67
LOMA (2081 "African Twist") 5-10 67
LOMA (2097 "Tomorrow") 5-10 68
RADIO 3-5 81
SHAKAT 4-6 74
SILVER-TONE 4-6
TURBO 4-6 71-73
VIBRATION 4-6 76

LPs: 10/12-inch

RADIO 5-8 81
TURBO (7003 "Live at the Sugar Shack") ..8-10 71
Also see HENDRIX, Jimi, & Lonnie Youngblood

YOUNGBLOOD, Tommy

Singles: 7-inch

CHATTAHOOCHEE (654 "Hello Darling") 10-20 64
CHATTAHOOCHEE (679 "Lonesome for You") 10-15 65
CHATTAHOOCHEE (699 "Lonesome for You") 5-10 66
J-R-M (004 "Caress Me My Love") 5-10 67
KENT (4516 "Hey Little Girl") 4-6 70
NEWPORT (100 "I'm a Man") 10-20 62
RAYCO (518 "Now That You're on Your Own") 10-15 64

LPs: 10/12-inch

UNITED SUPERIOR 8-10

YOUNGBLOODS P&R '66
(Featuring Jesse Colin Young)

Singles: 7-inch

MERCURY 5-10 66-69
RCA 4-8 66-71
W.B./RACCOON 4-6 70-72

Picture Sleeves

RCA 4-6 66

LPs: 10/12-inch

RCA (3000 series) 5-8 80
(With "ALY1" prefix.)
RCA (3000 series) 12-15 67
(With "LPM" or "LSP" prefix.)
RCA (4000 series) 10-15 69-71
(With "LPM" or "LSP" prefix.)
RCA (6000 series) 12-15 72
W.B./RACCOON 10-12 70-72
Members: Jesse Colin Young; Jerry Corbit; Joe Bauer; Lowell "Banana" Levinger.
Also see BOWIE, David / Joe Cocker / Youngbloods
Also see YOUNG, Jesse Colin

YOUNGER, Johnny

Singles: 7-inch

LAURIE (3068 "The Coward") 5-10 60

YOUNGER, Louis

Singles: 7-inch

FESTIVAL (707 "Here I Come") 5-10 67

YOUNGER, Scotty, & Outlaws

Singles: 7-inch

DOBROY (711 "Oh My Milinda") 5-10 61

YOUNGER BROTHERS

Singles: 7-inch

ROULETTE (7012 "I Can't Forget You") 5-10 68
SCEPTER (1279 "Harmonica Lesson") 5-10 64
SCEPTER (1297 "Harmonica Man") 5-10 65
W.B. (5386 "Somewhere") 5-10 63
W.B. (5424 "Sally's Sister") 5-10 64
WENDY (101 "Go Away") 5-10 67
Also see ORANGE COLORED SKY

YOUNGER GENERATION

Singles: 7-inch

EPIC (10549 "When the World Changes") 5-10 69

YOUNGER SOCIETY

Singles: 7-inch

SMASH (2200 "Everything") 5-10 68

YOUNG STUFF

Singles: 7-inch

CANTERBURY (514 "Poor Boy") 5-10 67

YOUNGFOLK
(Young Folk)

Singles: 7-inch

DOUBLE SHOT (107 "Lovin' Seed") 5-10 67
DOUBLE SHOT (117 In Spring") 5-10 67
DOUBLE SHOT (123 "Ferris Wheel Love") 5-10 67
MERCURY (72654 "Absence of Lisa") 5-10 67

YOUNGHEARTS

Singles: 7-inch

INFINITY (006 "Do Not Forsake Me") ...500-750 61
(White label. Promotional issue only.)
INFINITY (006 "Do Not Forsake Me") 750-1000 61
(Green label.)

YOUNGHEARTS

Singles: 7-inch

ABC 4-6 77
CANTERBURY (506 "Beginning of the End") 5-10 67
20TH FOX 4-6 73-76

LPs: 10/12-inch

ABC 5-8 77
20TH FOX 8-10 73-74

YOUNGSTERS

Singles: 78 rpm

EMPIRE 25-35 56

Singles: 7-inch

EMPIRE (104 "Shattered Dreams") 40-50 56
EMPIRE (107 "You're an Angel") 40-50 56
EMPIRE (109 "Dreamy Eyes"/"Dreamy Eyes") 50-150 56
EMPIRE (109 "Dreamy Eyes"/"I'm Sorry Now") 40-50 56
EMPIRE (109 "Dreamy Eyes"/"Christmas in Jail") 30-40 56
Members: Charles Everidge; Harold Murray; James Warren; Homer Green; Robert Johnson; Herman Pruitt.
Also see CALVANES
Also see FIVE SATINS / Youngtones / Youngsters / Shells
Also see PRELUDES
Also see TEMPTERS

YOUNGSTERS

Singles: 7-inch

APT (25021 "Sweet Talk") 10-15 58
CHECKER (917 "Lucky Sixteen") 10-15 59

YOUNGSTERS

Singles: 7-inch

CANDLELITE (428 "You Told Another Lie") 5-10 65
Also see LITTLE PETE & YOUNGSTERS

YOUNGSTERS

Singles: 7-inch

BLUE BERRY SUNSHINE (102 "Candy Apple") 8-12 69
JUBILEE (5687 "Candy Apple") 8-12 69
YOUNGSTERS (8478 "Telling Lies") 40-60 67

YOUNGSTERS

Singles: 7-inch

MELIC (4115 "Organ Grinder") 10-15 61

YOUNGSTERS / Danny Zella

Singles: 7-inch

SHOW-BIZ (555 "Zebra") ....8-12 '60s
Also see ZELLA, Danny

YOUNGTONES

Singles: 7-inch

BRUNSWICK (55089 "Come On Baby") ..50-75 58

YOUNGTONES

Singles: 7-inch

CANDLELITE (417 "You I Adore") 5-10 64
(Black vinyl.)
CANDLELITE (417 "You I Adore") 8-12 64
(Red vinyl.)
CANDLELITE (419 "Can I Come Over") 5-10 64
(Black vinyl.)
CANDLELITE (419 "Can I Come Over") 8-12 64
(Red vinyl.)
TIMES SQUARE (13 "Patricia") 10-15 63
(Black vinyl.)
TIMES SQUARE (13 "Patricia") 15-20 63
(Blue vinyl.)
X-TRA (104 "You I Adore") 100-150 57
(Titles and artists in 1/8-inch letters. Label also has double horizontal lines.)
X-TRA (110 "Patricia") 50-75 58
(Titles and artists in 1/8-inch letters. Label also has double horizontal lines.)
X-TRA (120 "Can I Come Over") 150-200 59
(Titles and artists in 1/8-inch letters. Label also has double horizontal lines.)
X-TRA (120 "Can I Come Over") 30-40 59
(Titles and artists in 1/4-inch letters.)
Member: Ron Jackson.
Also see FIVE SATINS / Youngtones / Youngsters / Shells

YOUNGTONES / Blasters

Singles: 7-inch

TIMES SQUARE (31 "I Do"/"Day Train")..10-15 64
Also see YOUNGTONES

YOUR FRIENDS

Singles: 7-inch

SOLA (14 "Sun Burned Idol") 10-15 67

YOUR GANG

LPs: 10/12-inch

MERCURY (21094 "Your Gang") 10-15 66
(Monaural.)
MERCURY (61094 "Your Gang") 15-20 66
(Stereo.)

YUKON, Johnny

Singles: 7-inch

VERSATILE (101 "Magnolia") 5-10 59
VERSATILE (104 "Thirteen Steps") 5-10 60

YUM YUM KIDS

LPs: 10/12-inch

MGM (4396 "Yummy in Your Tummy") 10-15 66
MGM (4405 "Down in Jungle Town") 10-15 66

YUM YUMS

Singles: 7-inch

ABC-PAR (10697 "Looky, Looky") 10-20 65

YUMMIES

Singles: 7-inch

SUNFLOWER (103 "Hippie Lady") ....15-25 '60s

YURO, Timi P&R/R&B/LP '61

Singles: 7-inch

FREQUENCY (101 "Nothing Takes the Place of You") ....5-10 '60s
LIBERTY (54526 "Hurt") 5-10 63
LIBERTY (54535 "Make the World Go Away") 5-10 65
LIBERTY (55343 "Hurt") 10-20 61
LIBERTY (55375 "Smile") 10-15 61
LIBERTY (55410 "Let Me Call You Sweetheart") 10-15 62
LIBERTY (55432 "I Know") 10-15 62
LIBERTY (55469 "What's a Matter Baby") 10-15 62
LIBERTY (55519 "Love of a Boy") 10-15 62
LIBERTY (55552 "Insult to Injury") 10-15 63
LIBERTY (55587 "Make the World Go Away") 10-15 63
LIBERTY (55634 "Gotta Travel On") 8-12 63
LIBERTY (55665 "Call Me") 8-12 64
LIBERTY (55701 "A Legend in My Time") .8-12 64
LIBERTY (55747 "I'm Movin' On") 8-12 64
LIBERTY (56049 "Something Bad On My Mind") 5-10 68
LIBERTY (56061 "Interlude") 5-10 68
MERCURY (72316 "If") 8-12 64
MERCURY (72355 "I Got It Bad") 8-12 64
MERCURY (72391 "You Can Have Him") 10-15 65
MERCURY (72431 "Get Out of My Life") 8-12 65
MERCURY (72478 "Big Mistake") 8-12 65
MERCURY (72515 "Once a Day") 8-12 65
MERCURY (72601 "Don't Keep Me Lonely Too Long") 8-12 66
MERCURY (72628 "Turn the World Around") 8-12 66
MERCURY (72674 "Why Not Now") 8-12 67
PLAYBOY (6050 "Southern Lady") 4-8 75

EPs: 7-inch

LIBERTY ("Timi Yuro") 10-20 61
(Juke box issue only. Selection number not known.)

LPs: 10/12-inch

COLGEMS (5007 "Interlude") 10-20 68
LIBERTY (3208 "Timi Yuro") 20-30 61
(Monaural.)
LIBERTY (3212 "Soul") 20-30 62
(Monaural.)
LIBERTY (3234 "Let Me Call You Sweetheart") 20-30 62
(Monaural.)
LIBERTY (3263 "What's a Matter Baby") .20-30 62
(Monaural.)
LIBERTY (3286 "The Best of Timi Yuro") .20-30 63
(Monaural.)
LIBERTY (3319 "Make the World Go Away") 20-30 63
(Monaural.)
LIBERTY (7208 "Timi Yuro") 25-35 61
(Stereo.)
LIBERTY (7212 "Soul") 25-35 62
(Stereo.)
LIBERTY (7234 "Let Me Call You Sweetheart") 25-35 62
(Stereo.)
LIBERTY (7263 "What's a Matter Baby") .25-35 62
(Stereo.)
LIBERTY (7286 "The Best of Timi Yuro") .25-35 63
(Stereo.)
LIBERTY (7319 "Make the World Go Away") 25-35 63
(Stereo.)
LIBERTY (7594 "Something Bad On My Mind") 10-20 68
MERCURY (20963 "Amazing Timi Yuro") 15-25 64
(Monaural.)
MERCURY (60963 "Amazing Timi Yuro") 20-30 64
(Stereo.)
SUNSET (1107 "Timi Yuro") 10-20 66
(Monaural.)
SUNSET (5107 "Timi Yuro") 10-20 66
(Stereo.)
U.A. (429 "The Very Best of Timi Yuro") 8-12 75
U.A. (631 "The Timi Yuro Album") 8-12 76

WING (16363 "Amazing Timi Yuro")........ 10-15 68
Session: Willie Mitchell.
Also see MITCHELL, Willie
Also see RAY, Johnnie, & Timi Yuro

YVETTE & LORDS

Singles: 7-inch

YVETTE (102 "Crawl Baby Crawl")............5-10 66

YVONNE & VIOLETS

Singles: 7-inch

BARRY (1004 "Cross My Heart")................8-12 '60s

Z

Z DEBS

Singles: 7-inch

ROULETTE (4544 "Changing My Life For You")..5-10 64

ZZ TOP *P&R/LP '72*

Singles: 12-inch

W.B. 4-6 84-86

Singles: 7-inch

LONDON...4-8 70-77
SCAT (500 "Salt Lick")........................ 100-200
W.B. 3-5 80-90

Picture Sleeves

LONDON...5-10 75-76
W.B. 3-5 83-90

LPs: 10/12-inch

LONDON (Except 1001)..........................8-12 71-77
LONDON (1001 "World Wide Texas Tour")... 10-20 76
(Promotional issue only.)
W.B. 5-15 79-90
Members: Bill Gibbons; Frank Beard; Dusty Hill.
Also see AMERICAN BLUES
Also see MOVING SIDEWALKS
Also see WARLOCKS

ZABACH, Florian *P&R '51*

Singles: 78 rpm

DECCA..3-5 51-54
MERCURY..3-5 56-57

Singles: 7-inch

CADENCE (1406 "Oceans of Love")..........5-10 61
DECCA..5-10 51-54
MERCURY..5-10 56-58

EPs: 7-inch

DECCA..5-10 51-54
MERCURY..5-10 56-58

LPs: 10/12-inch

DECCA..5-15 51-65
MERCURY..5-15 56-60
VOCALION...5-10 63-66
WING...5-10 63
Also see DIAMONDS / Georgia Gibbs / Sarah Vaughan / Florian Zabach
Also see VALLI, June

ZABE, Dick

Singles: 7-inch

MPA (852 "Sentimental No More")............5-10
PIO (103 "My Senior Prom").................. 10-20 61

ZACHERLE, John *P&R/R&B '58*
(Zacherle; Zacherley; John Zacherlie "Cool Ghoul")

Singles: 78 rpm

CAMEO... 25-50 58

Singles: 7-inch

ABKCO..3-5 '80s
CAMEO (130 "Igor"/"Dinner with Drac, Part 1").. 30-40 58
CAMEO (130 "Dinner with Drac, Part 1"/"Dinner with Drac, Part 2").................................. 20-30 58
CAMEO (139 "82 Tombstones").............. 10-15 58
CAMEO (145 "I Was a Teen Age Cave Man").. 20-30 58
COLPIX (743 "Monsters Have Problems Too")..5-10 64
ELEKTRA (13 "Coolest Little Monster")......5-10 60
PARKWAY..5-10 62-64

LPs: 10/12-inch

CRESTVIEW (803 "Zacherley's Monster Gallery")25-35 63
ELEKTRA (190 "Spook Along with Zacherley")..25-30 60
(Monaural.)
ELEKTRA (7190 "Spook Along with Zacherley")..30-35 60
(Stereo.)
PARKWAY..25-35 62-63
Session: Applejacks.

ZACK, Eddie, & Cousin Richie
(With His Dude Ranchers)

Singles: 78 rpm

COLUMBIA..40-60 54-55

Singles: 7-inch

COLUMBIA (21307 "You're Out of My Sight")..100-150 54
COLUMBIA (21387 "Rocky Road Blues")..100-150 55
COLUMBIA (21441 "I'm Gonna Rock and Roll")..100-150 55
Members: Eddie Zack; Dick Richards.
Also see RICHARDS, Dick

ZACK, Jimmy

Singles: 7-inch

AMERICAN (101 "Evil Ways")...............75-100

ZACK, Richie

Singles: 7-inch

SILVER STAR (1010 "It's Written in the Stars")..5-10 66
SILVER STAR (1017 "You're So Right")....5-10 66

ZACKERY, Jan

Singles: 7-inch

TOGA (1961 "Hurtin' Heart")......................8-12 61

ZADORA, Pia *C&W '79*
(With the London Symphony Orchestra)

Singles: 12-inch

MCA..4-6 83

Singles: 7-inch

CURB..3-5 83
ELEKTRA...3-5 82-83
MCA..3-5 83-84
W.B./CURB..4-6 78-80

LPs: 10/12-inch

CBS ASSOCIATED 5-8 86
ELEKTRA...5-8 82
Also see LITTLE PIA

ZADORA, Pia, & Lou Christie

Singles: 7-inch

MIDSONG (72013 "Don't Knock My Love")..15-20 80
Also see CHRISTIE, Lou
Also see ZADORA, Pia

ZAGER & EVANS *P&R/LP '69*

Singles: 7-inch

RCA (0174 "In the Year 2525")..................5-10 69
RCA (0246 "Mr. Turnkey").........................5-10 69
RCA (0299 "Listen to the People")............5-10 69
RCA (9816 "Help One Man Today")............4-8 70
TRUTH (0246 "Mr. Turnkey")..................10-15 69
TRUTH (0299 "Listen to the People").......10-15 69
TRUTH (8082 "In the Year 2525")............15-25 68
VANGUARD (35125 "Hydra 15,000").........4-8 71

Picture Sleeves

VANGUARD (35125 "Hydra 15,000").........5-10 71

LPs: 10/12-inch

RCA (1077 "In the Year 2525")..................8-10 75
RCA (4214 "2525")..................................10-20 69
RCA (4302 "Zager and Evans")...............10-20 70
VANGUARD (6568 "Food for the Mind")..10-15 71
WHITE WHALE (7123 "Early Writings")....15-20 69
Members: Denny Zager; Rick Evans.
Also see ECCENTRICS

ZAHND, Ricky, & Blue Jeaners *P&R '55*

Singles: 78 rpm

COLUMBIA..4-6 55-56

Singles: 7-inch

COLUMBIA..10-15 55-56

Picture Sleeves

COLUMBIA (263 "Nuttin for Christmas")..15-20 56

ZAKARY THAKS

Singles: 7-inch

CEE BEE (1005 "Everybody Wants to Be Somebody")..10-20 69
J-BECK (1006 "I Need You")....................20-30 66
J-BECK (1009 "Face to Face")..................20-30 67
J-BECK (1101 "Won't Come Back").........20-30 67
J-BECK (1103 "Mirror of Yesterday").......20-30 67
MERCURY (72633 "I Need You")............10-15 66
THAK (1001 "My Door")..........................15-25 68

LPs: 10/12-inch

MOXIE (2 "Texas Band")............................5-10 80
Members: Chris Gerniottis; Rex Gregory; John Lopez; Stanley Moore; Pete Stinson.

ZAKONS

Singles: 7-inch

CUCA (1033 "Trackin' ")..........................50-60 61
Members: Larry Krecowski; Bill Joswick; Tom Kropp; Ronnie Pagel; Billy Lee King; Bill Anderson; Bob Bierd.

ZAMBON, Francis, & Naturals

Singles: 7-inch

VAMALCO (503 "Our Love Will Last")......15-20 59

ZANE, Herb
(With Lee Pines & Orchestra)

Singles: 78 rpm

DELUXE..5-10 56
RAINBOW...5-10 55

Singles: 7-inch

ARROW (718 "Love, Love, Crazy Love").10-20 57
DELUXE (6099 "Let Me Be in Your Heart")..10-20 56
RAINBOW (289 " 'You Name It' Mambo")..15-20 55
20TH FOX (289 "Hokey Pokey Rock")........8-12 62
20TH FOX (405 "Laughed Till I Cried")......8-12 63

ZANETIS, Alex

Singles: 7-inch

RIC (106 "Arkansas")...............................5-10 64

ZANG, Tommy

Singles: 7-inch

CANADIAN AMERICAN (102 "Jennings St. Near Falcon Square")...................................8-12 59
HICKORY (1148 "Every Hour Every Day") 5-10 61

ZANGO, Willie

Singles: 7-inch

GIZMO (66435 "Nancy Jane")..................15-25 60
(Identification number shown since no selection number is used.)

ZANICCHI, Iva

LPs: 10/12-inch

U.A. (15502 "Cara Mio")..........................30-40

ZANIES

Singles: 7-inch

DORE (509 "Do You Dig Me Mister Pigmy")..10-20 58
DORE (515 "Mad Scientist")....................10-20 59
DORE (597 "It's Lovely")........................10-15 61
DORE (632 "Frustration")..........................8-12 62
DORE (638 "London Rock").......................8-12 62
DORE (647 "Sleepwalker").........................8-12 62
DORE (655 "Hello Jackie")........................8-12 62
DORE (658 "Russian Roulette")..................8-12 63
DORE (683 "Chicken Surfer")....................10-20 63
DORE (734 "Last Dance at the Prom")......5-10 65
DORE (823 "Clair De Looney")..................5-10 69
DORE (853 "Will the Real Frankenstein Please Stand Up")..30-40 71
DORE (875 "Mr. President to Be")..............4-8 72
DORE (889 "Let Out a Scream")..................4-8 73
DORE (900 "Let Out a Scream")..................4-8 74
DORE (979 "It's a Million Miles to Paradise")..3-5 83
ERA (1080 "The Blob")...........................10-20 58

LPs: 10/12-inch

DORE (321 "The Zanies").........................10-20 69
DORE (337 "The Zanies")..........................5-10 79
Session: Davie Allan.
Also see ALLAN, Davie

ZANN, Nicky

Singles: 7-inch

OMEGA (101 "Gina")..................................8-12 62

ZAPATA

Singles: 7-inch

ATCO (6649 "Freedom Bells")....................5-10 69
ORIGINAL SOUND (107 "Una Vez Mas")....4-6 73

ZAPATA, Rufino

Singles: 7-inch

KOOL (1019 "Give Me a Chance")............5-10 63

ZAPPA, Frank *LP '70*
(With the Mothers; Francis Vincent Zappa)

Singles: 12-inch

BARKING PUMPKIN (1114 "Goblin Girl")...20-30 79
(Picture disc. Promotional issue only.)
BARKING PUMPKIN (1115 "Baby Snakes")..40-50 82
(Picture disc.)
RHINO/DEL-FI (604 "Rare Meat")...........10-20 83
(Cover has portrait of Zappa.)
RHINO/DEL-FI (604 "Rare Meat")..............5-10 83
(Plain cover, no portrait of Zappa.)
ZAPPA (1001 "I Don't Want to Get Drafted")..8-10 80

Singles: 7-inch

BARKING PUMPKIN.................................5-10 81-82
DISCREET (1312 "Don't Eat the Yellow Snow")..8-12 74
ROTATE...5-10
U.A. (50857 "Magic Fingers")..................30-40 71
W.B. (8296 "Find Her Finer")...................20-30 76
W.B. (8342 "Disco Boy")..........................20-30 76
ZAPPA...6-12 79-80

Promotional Singles

BARKING PUMPKIN................................10-20 81-82
DISCREET (586 "Cosmik Debris")...........15-20 74
ROTATE...5-10
U.A. (50857 "Magic Fingers")..................20-30 71
W.B. (8296 "Find Her Finer")...................15-25 76
W.B. (8342 "Disco Boy")..........................15-25 76
ZAPPA...5-10 79-80

Picture Sleeves

ZAPPA...3-5 80

EPs: 7-inch

REPRISE (336 "Hot Rats")....................100-150 72
(Promotional issue only.)
U.A. ("200 Motels")..............................75-125 71
(Promotional issue only.)

LPs: 10/12-inch

BARKING PUMPKIN (37000 series)........10-15 81
BARKING PUMPKIN (38000 series)..........5-10 82-83
BARKING PUMPKIN (74000 series)..........5-10 84-88
BIZARRE (2030 "Chunga's Revenge")....15-25 70
(Blue label.)
BIZARRE (2030 "Chunga's Revenge")......5-10 '70s
(Brown label.)
BIZARRE (2094 "Waka Jawaka")............15-25 70
(Blue label.)
BIZARRE (2094 "Waka Jawaka")..............5-10 '70s
(Brown label.)
BIZARRE (6356 "Hot Rats")....................15-25 69
(Blue label.)
BIZARRE (6356 "Hot Rats")......................5-10 '70s
(Brown label.)
DEL-FI (604 "Rare Meat").........................35-45 83
DISCREET (DS-2175 "Apostrophe' ")......15-25 74
DISCREET (DS4-2175 "Apostrophe' ")....30-40 74
(Quadraphonic.)
DISCREET (DSK-2289 "Apostrophe' ")......8-10 77
DISCREET (2202 "Roxy & Elsewhere")...20-30 74
DISCREET (2216 "One Size Fits All")......15-25 75
DISCREET (2234 "Bongo Fury")...............15-25 75
DISCREET (2290 "Zappa in New York")..300-400 78
(Has *Punky's Whips* and a full-length *Titties and Beer*. May have been on test pressings only.)
DISCREET (2290 "Zappa in New York")..100-200 78
(Cover indicates *Punky's Whips* and a full-length *Titties and Beer*, though discs have neither.)
DISCREET (2290 "Zappa in New York")..20-30 78
(Omits *Punky's Whips* and has an edited *Titties and Beer*.)
DISCREET (2291 "Studio Tan")..............10-15 78
DISCREET (2294 "Orchestral Favorites")..10-15 79
EMI/ANGEL (38170 "Boulez Conducts Zappa")..10-15 84
REPRISE..8-12 72
RHINO (70907 "Beat the Boots")..........100-175 91
(Boxed, eight-disc set. Includes button and T-shirt.)
VERVE (8741 "Lumpy Gravy")................25-30 68
U.A. 20-30 71
ZAPPA (1501 "Sheik Yerbouti")...............10-20 79
ZAPPA (1502 "Joe's Garage, Acts I & III")..10-20 79
ZAPPA (1603 "Joe's Garage, Act I")........10-15 79
W.B. 5-10 76

Promotional LPs
BARKING PUMPKIN (1111 "Shut Up 'N' Play Yer Guitar")................ 15-20 81
(Mail-order LP offer.)
BARKING PUMPKIN (1112 "Shut Up 'N' Play Yer Guitar Some More")................ 15-20 81
(Mail-order LP offer.)
BARKING PUMPKIN (1113 "Return of Shut Up 'N' Play Yer Guitar")................ 15-20 81
(Mail-order LP offer.)
BIZARRE (368 "Zapped")................ 30-40 69
(Photo collage cover with title in red. Also has tracks by Alice Cooper, Captain Beefheart & His Magic Band, Judy Henske & Jerry Yester, Tim Buckley, Wild Man Fischer, Tim Dawe, Lord Buckley, Jeff Simmons, and G.T.O.
BIZARRE (368 "Zapped")................ 20-30 69
(Cover pictures only Frank Zappa. Title in black.)
BIZARRE (2030 "Chunga's Revenge").... 30-40 70
ZAPPA (78 "Sheik Yerbouti, Clean Cuts")................ 20-30 79
ZAPPA (129 "Joe's Garage, Acts I, II & III")................ 30-40 79
Session: Howard Kaylan; Marc Volman.
Also see BABY RAY & FERNS
Also see FANKHAUSER, Merrell
Also see G.T.O.
Also see GUY, Bob
Also see HOGS
Also see HEARTBREAKERS
Also see HOLLYWOOD PERSUADERS
Also see HURVITZ, Sandy
Also see LORD, Brian, & Midnighters
Also see MINTZ, Junior
Also see MR. CLEAN
Also see MOTHERS OF INVENTION
Also see NED & NELDA
Also see ROMAN, Don

ZAPPA, Frank & Moon

Singles: 12-inch
BARKING PUMPKIN (03069 "Valley Girl")...5-8 82
Singles: 7-inch
BARKING PUMPKIN (02972 "Valley Girl")...3-5 82
Picture Sleeves
BARKING PUMPKIN (02972 "Valley Girl")...3-5 82
Promotional Singles
BARKING PUMPKIN (1490 "Valley Girl").....4-6 82
Also see ZAPPA, Frank

ZARA, Michael, & Compliments
(With Bill Ramal & Orchestra)

Singles: 7-inch
SHELL (313 "Angels of Mercy")................ 10-20 63

ZARIO, Rex

Singles: 78 rpm
ARCADE................ 8-15 54-57
Singles: 7-inch
ARCADE................ 10-20 54-62
SKYROCKET (Except 1006)................ 10-20 59-60
SKYROCKET (1006 "Go Man")................ 50-75 58
Session: Bill Haley's Comets.
Also see HALEY, Bill

ZAVAL, Dave

Singles: 7-inch
SQUARE (117 "I Want to Be Wanted")......5-10 60

ZBORNIK, Layton Redell, Jr.
(King Zbornik)

Singles: 7-inch
PARADE (6929 "I Like It Like That")........ 10-15 64
USA (806 "I Like It Like That")................5-10 65
Also see MARTIN, Jerry

ZE MAJESTICS
(Ze-Majestics)

Singles: 7-inch
ABC-PAR (10318 "Sapphire")................ 10-20 62
FOX (5014 "Bobbi Ann")................ 50-100

ZEBRA

Singles: 7-inch
BLUE THUMB (109 "Christmas Morning") .5-10 69
PHILIPS (40534 "Miss Anne")................5-10 68
VORTEX (301 "Lord, Lord, Lord")................5-10 68
WHITE WHALE (305 "Bring Me to My Knees")................5-10 69

ZEBULONS

Singles: 7-inch
CUB (9069 "Falling Water")................ 50-75 60

ZEE, Ginny

Singles: 7-inch
ATCO (6218 "Bobby Baby")................10-20 62

ZEE, Kathy

Singles: 7-inch
LAURIE (3020 "Buzzin'")................10-20 58

ZEE, Lani

Singles: 7-inch
SEECO (6074 "Sea Tides")................10-20 61
Session: Caslons.
Also see CASLONS

ZEE, Tommy

Singles: 7-inch
AMY (815 "Rebecca, Remember")..........25-35 61
(At least one source says this artist is Johnny Zee, not Tommy Zee. We don't know yet who's right.)

ZEKE & GENEVA
(With the Zeke Strong Band)

Singles: 7-inch
SWINGIN' (632 "Every Woman Has a Right")................5-10 61
Member: Zeke Strong.

ZEKES

Singles: 7-inch
BEVERLY HILLS (9353 "Leaving You")...15-25 '60s

ZEKLEY, Gary

Singles: 7-inch
AVA (151 "Vagabond")................10-20 63

ZEL, Rita

Singles: 7-inch
J&S (1685 "I Need You to Help Me")........20-30 60

ZELLA, Danny
P&R '59
(With the Larados & His Zell Rocks)

Singles: 7-inch
DIAL (100 "Sapphire")................75-125 59
FOX ("Black Sax")................30-40 58
(No selection number used. First issue.)
FOX (10057 "Wicked Ruby"/"Black Sax")................30-40 58
RED ROCKET (475 "Black Sax")..........40-60 63
Also see DANNY & ZELTONES
Also see LARADOS
Also see YOUNGSTERS / Danny Zella

ZELLER, Keith, & Starliners

Singles: 7-inch
AGAR (7126 "Carry Mae")................10-15 '60s

ZEN

Singles: 7-inch
PHILIPS (40588 "Hair")................5-10 69
P.I.P. (8914 "Get Me Down")................5-10 70

ZEN IDOLS

Singles
ERIKA (18411 "Rub the Buddha")..........10-15 84
(Buddha-shaped picture disc.)

ZENTNER, Si, & His Orchestra
P&R/LP '61
(With the Johnny Mann Singers)

Singles: 7-inch
BEL CANTO................5-10 59
LIBERTY................5-10 59-67
RCA................4-6 64-66
Picture Sleeves
LIBERTY (55437 "Mississippi Mud")..........5-10 62
LIBERTY (55499 "Desafinado")................5-10 62
EPs: 7-inch
LIBERTY................5-10 59-67
LPs: 10/12-inch
BEL CANTO................10-20 59
LIBERTY................10-20 59-67
RCA................5-10 65-66
SUNSET................5-10 66
Also see CARPENTER, Ike
Also see DENNY, Martin
Also see MANN, Johnny, Singers
Also see MARTIN, Dean / Patti Page
Also see SINATRA, Frank

ZEPHYR
LP '69

Singles: 7-inch
PROBE (475 "Cross the River")................5-8 70
W.B. 4-6 70
Promotional Singles
PROBE................10-12 70
LPs: 10/12-inch
PROBE (4510 "Zephyr")................40-50 69
RED SNEAKERS................5-10 82
W.B. 25-30 71-72
Members: Candy Givens; Tommy Bolin; David Givens; John Faris; Robbie Chamberlain.

ZEPHYRS

Singles: 7-inch
AMBER (213 "Pink Rhapsody")................8-12 64
AMBER (214 "She's Mine")................8-12 65
AMBER (215 "Yes, My Love")................8-12 66
ROTATE (5006 "She Lost You")................5-10 65
ROTATE (5009 "Let Me Love You Baby") .5-10 65
Picture Sleeves
AMBER (214 "She's Mine")................10-15 65

ZEPPA, Ben
(With the 4 Jacks; with Zephers; Ben Joe Zeppa; with Pharaohs)

Singles: 78 rpm
SPECIALTY................10-20 56
Singles: 7-inch
AWARD (124 "Shame on You Miss Lindy")................40-60 59
ERA (1042 "Topsy Turvy")................40-60 57
GILMAR (278 "No Not Much")................75-100 57
HUSH (1000 "Young Heartaches")..........10-20 58
METRO (9001 "Shame on You Miss Lindy")................50-75 58
SPECIALTY (577 "Foolish Fool")............50-75 56
TOPS................15-25 56
EPs: 7-inch
TOPS (278 "Why Do Fools Fall in Love").30-50 56

ZEPPERS

Singles: 7-inch
LONGFIBER (202 "Let's Forget the Past")................40-50 66
(Reportedly 100 made.)

ZERFAS

LPs: 10/12-inch
700 WEST (730710 "Zerfas")..............350-450 73
Members: Herman Zerfas; David Zerfas; Bill Rice; Steve Newbold; Mark Tribby.

006

Singles: 7-inch
HARLEQUINN (606415 "Like What, Me Worry")................20-30 66
RED BIRD (066 "Like What, Me Worry")..10-20 66

ZEROES

Singles: 7-inch
TY-TEX (105 "Flossie Mae")................100-150 62

ZEV

Singles: 7-inch
FETISH (13 "Wipe Out")................10-20 '60s

ZEVON, Warren
LP '76
(Zevon)

Singles: 7-inch
ASYLUM................3-6 76-80
CHRYSALIS................3-5 87
Picture Sleeves
CHRYSALIS................3-5 87
LPs: 10/12-inch
ASYLUM................5-8 76-82
ELEKTRA (11386 "Werewolves of London")................70-90 78
(Picture disc. Promotional issue only.)
IMPERIAL................10-12 70
VIRGIN................5-8 87
Members: Richard Hayward; Kenny Gradney; Greg Beck; Karen Childs.
Also see LITTLE FEAT

ZIG ZAG PAPER CO.

Singles: 7-inch
BELL (748 "I Feel Free")................5-10 68
BELL (752 "Cast out the Worries")............5-10 68

ZIGGY & ZEU
(With Ena Anka)

Singles: 7-inch
ZEU (5011 "Da-Doo-Ron-Ron")................20-30 '70s
ZEU (5011 "Little Star")................20-30 '70s
(Same selection number used twice.)

ZIGGY & ZOOMERS

Singles: 7-inch
REO (1003 "Let's Do the Cha Cha")........10-15 60

ZILL, Pat
P&R '61

Singles: 7-inch
BIG C (119 "Two Empty Arms")................5-10 62
BOONE (1031 "All I Have to Do Is Wait") ..5-10 65
DOLEJO (1002 "The Fool")................10-15 60
ERA (3108 "Key's in the Mailbox")............5-10 63
INDIGO (119 "La Mirada")................8-12 61
INDIGO (126 "Hold Tight")................8-12 61
SAND (356 "La Mirada")................8-12 61
SIMS (234 "Key's in the Mailbox")............5-10 65

ZIMBALIST, Efrem, Jr. / Guitars Inc.

Singles: 7-inch
W.B. (5126 "Adeste Fidelis")................5-10 59
Picture Sleeves
W.B. (5126 "Adeste Fidelis")................10-20 59

ZIMMERAN, George, & Thrills
(With Bubby Cypers Band)

Singles: 78 rpm
JAB................50-150 56
Singles: 7-inch
JAB (103 "Whose Baby Are You").......300-400 56
Session: Bubby Cypers; L.D. Williams; Herb Adams; Guy Richard Jones; Vonnie Holte; Jimmy Nolan.

ZINE, Ben

Singles: 7-inch
PARKWAY (996 "Village of Tears").........40-60 66

ZION TRAVELERS

Singles: 78 rpm
DOOTONE................10-15 56
Singles: 7-inch
DOOTO (400 series)................5-10 59-63
DOOTONE (389 "Two Little Fishes").......15-25 56
DOOTONE (399 "Soldier of the Cross")...15-25 56
EBB (114 "Believe in Me")................5-10 57

ZIONAIRES

Singles: 78 rpm
TNT (8007 "One Morning Soon")..............10-15 55
Singles: 7-inch
TNT (8007 "One Morning Soon")..............15-25 55

ZIP, Danny
(With the Zippers)

Singles: 7-inch
MGM (13254 "Hey Hey Girl")................25-35 64
Member [Zippers]: Barney Zarzana.
Also see BAY BOPS

ZIP & ZIPPERS

Singles: 7-inch
PAGEANT (607 "Where You Goin' Little Boy")................20-30 63
Members: Shirley Brickley; Rosetta Hightower; Steve Caldwell; Marlena Davis.
Also see ORLONS

ZIP CODES

Singles: 7-inch
BETTER................8-12 '60s
LIBERTY (55703 "Run Little Mustang") ... 10-15 64
LPs: 10/12-inch
LIBERTY (3367 "Mustang")................50-75 64
(Monaural.)
LIBERTY (7367 "Mustang")................75-100 64
(Stereo.)

ZIPPERS

Singles: 7-inch
HICKORY (1252 "My Sailor Boy")..............5-10 64

ZIPPERS

Singles: 12-inch
RHINO (601 "Six Song Mini Album")........20-30 81

ZIRCONS

Singles: 7-inch
DEVILLE (120 "Frog in the Fog")..............8-12 63
DOT (15724 "Only One Love")................10-15 58
FEDERAL (12452 "No Twistin' on Sunday")................8-12 62
FEDERAL (12478 "Mr. Jones")................8-12 62
WINSTON (1020 "Only One Love")..........30-40 57
WINSTON (1022 "Crazy Crazy")..........100-150 58
Picture Sleeves
DEVILLE (120 "Frog in the Fog")..............30-40
Also see COREY, Benson, & Zircons

ZIRCONS

Singles: 7-inch
BAGDAD (1007 "Surfing in the Sunset")..15-25 63

ZIRCONS

Singles: 7-inch

AMBER (851 "One Summer Night")..........5-10 66
COOL SOUND (1030 "Silver Bells") 15-25 64
MELLOMOOD (1000 "Lonely Way") 10-15 63
OLD TIMER (603 "Sincerely")....................5-10 64
(Black vinyl.)
OLD TIMER (603 "Sincerely") 10-15 64
(Yellow or blue vinyl.)
OLD TIMER (606 "Remember Then") 10-15 64
(Yellow or red vinyl.)
RELIC (1008 "Lonely Way") 5-10 65
SIAMESE (403 "Sincerely").........................5-10 65

LPs: 10/12-inch

SNOWFLAKE (1003 "The Crown Kings of Acappella")... 45-65

ZIRCONS / Destinaires

Singles: 7-inch

OLD TIMER (602 "Silver Bells"/"Traveling Stranger")...8-12 64
Also see DESTINAIRES
Also see ZIRCONS

ZIRCONS

Singles: 7-inch

CAPITOL (2667 "Finders Keepers") 20-30 69
HEIGH-HO (607 "Where There's a Will"). 10-20 61
HEIGH-HO (608 "I Couldn't Stop Crying") 10-20 61
HEIGH-HO (646 "Go On & Cry")................8-12 67

ZITTS

Singles: 7-inch

O&W (76 "Surfin' & Sleepin' ") .... 10-20 '60s

ZODIAC

Singles: 7-inch

UNI (55138 " 'X' Rated") 5-10 69

ZODIACS

Singles: 7-inch

COLE (100 "Golly Gee").......................... 40-50 59
COLE (101 "She's Mine") 40-50 59
Also see WILLIAMS, Maurice

ZODIACS

Singles: 7-inch

VEE-JAY (678 "May I") 8-12 64

ZODIACS

Singles: 7-inch

SOMA (1410 "Lita")................................... 20-30 64
SOMA (1418 "Anything") 20-30 64

ZOLA
(Zola & His Horn)

Singles: 7-inch

CARTHAY (102 "Slide").......................... 15-20 59
(First issue.)
JARO (77011 "Slide") 10-15 59

ZOLTON, Frank
(With the Town and Country Boys)

Singles: 7-inch

DIXIE (1056 "Cats Eyes")..................... 100-200

ZOMBIES *P&R '64*

Singles: 7-inch

DATE (1604 "Time of the Season"/"I'll Call You Mine")... 10-15 68
DATE (1612 "This Will Be Our Year")...... 10-15 68
DATE (1628 "Time of the Season"/"Friends of Mine")...4-6 68
DATE (1644 "Imagine the Swan")..............5-10 69
DATE (1648 "If It Don't Work Out") 5-10 69
EPIC (11145 "Time of the Season") 4-6 72
ERIC 3-5 83
LONDON (59029 "Tell Her No")...................3-6
PARROT (3004 "Indication").......................8-10 66
PARROT (9695 "She's Not There") 8-10 64
(Black label.)
PARROT (9695 "She's Not There") 15-25 64
(Orange label. Promotional issue only.)
PARROT (9695 "She's Not There") 15-25 64
(Blue label. Canadian.)
PARROT (9695 "She's Not There") ....5-10 '60s
(Black label. Canadian.)
PARROT (9723 "Tell Her No") 8-12 65
PARROT (9769 "I Want You Back Again").8-12 65
PARROT (9747 "She's Coming Home").....8-12 65
PARROT (9786 "I Love You") 8-10 65
PARROT (9797 "Remember You")..............8-10 65
PARROT (9821 "Don't Go Away") 8-10 66

Picture Sleeves

PARROT (9723 "Tell Her No") 25-35 65
PARROT (9747 "She's Coming Home")...20-30 65

LPs: 10/12-inch

BACK-TRAC 5-8 85
DATE (4013 "Odessey & Oracle") 20-30 68
(No promotional mention of *Time of the Season* on front cover.)
DATE (4013 "Odessey & Oracle") 15-25 68
(With promo for *Time of the Season* on front cover.)
EPIC (32861 "Time of the Zombies")........15-20 74
(Two discs.)
LONDON (557 "Early Days")....................15-20 69
PARROT (61001 "The Zombies") 30-40 65
(Monaural.)
PARROT (71001 "The Zombies") 30-40 65
(Stereo.)
RHINO...5-8
Members: Colin Blunstone; Rod Argent.
Also see ARGENT

ZONE V

Singles: 7-inch

CARAVAN (21449 "Black Jacket Woman")..15-25

ZOO

Singles: 7-inch

PARKWAY (147 "She Said – Good Day Sunshine") 8-12 67
SEASCAPE (502 "Feeling") 8-12
SUNBURST 5-10 68-69

LPs: 10/12-inch

MERCURY (61300 "The Zoo").................15-25 70
SUNBURST (7500 "Chocolate Moose")...35-50 68

ZOO

Singles: 7-inch

PKC (1013 "Gonna Miss Me")..................10-20 68

ZOOFS

Singles: 7-inch

DEE-SU (310 "Not So Near")...................10-15 66

ZOOKIE & POTENTATES

Singles: 7-inch

COCONUT GROOVE (2017 "Banana Man")..15-25 68
NU-SOUND (711 "Telephony")...................8-12 '60s
Member: Gary "Zookie" Story.
Also see PLAIN BROWN WRAPPER

ZORO & ZIPS

Singles: 7-inch

SPOT (1002 "Frankie & Johnny") ....10-15 '60s
Member: Bobby McBride.

ZORRO

Singles: 7-inch

MASKE (702 "Somebody Cares")............20-30 61

ZORRO, Johnny

Singles: 7-inch

ÄVA (138 "Spinning Wheels").....................5-10 63
BRAVO ("Road Hog"/"Coesville") 15-25 59
(No selection number used.)
BRAVO (123 "Road Hog"/"Camel Train").10-20 59
(Note different flip.)
INFINITY (002 "Bongo Guitar")..................5-10 61
JOCKO 5-10 64
W.B. (5111 "Road Hog")..............................5-10 59
W.B. (5162 "The Choke") 5-10 60

ZOSER

Singles: 7-inch

HEXAGON (944S-3328 "Together").........10-15 70
(500 made.)

ZOTS

Singles: 7-inch

O.E.K. (203 "Rocka-Bongo").......................5-10 61

ZU ZU BAND
(Zu Zu Blues Band)

Singles: 7-inch

A&M (790 "Side Show")..............................5-10 66

ZUCKERMAN'S DREAM

Singles: 7-inch

COLUMBIA (44831 "Revolution's Over")....5-10 69

ZUETTA, Mary Lou, & Velveteens

Singles: 7-inch

EMMY (1007 "Oh Baby")..........................15-25 60

ZUMMO, Guy

Singles: 7-inch

EVEREST (19357 "Fantabulous") 5-10 60

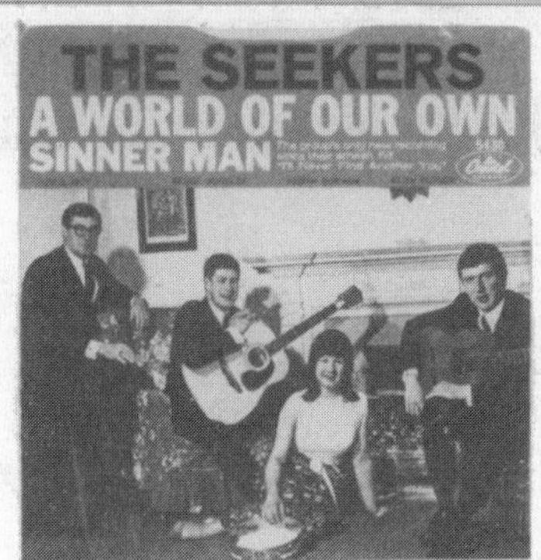

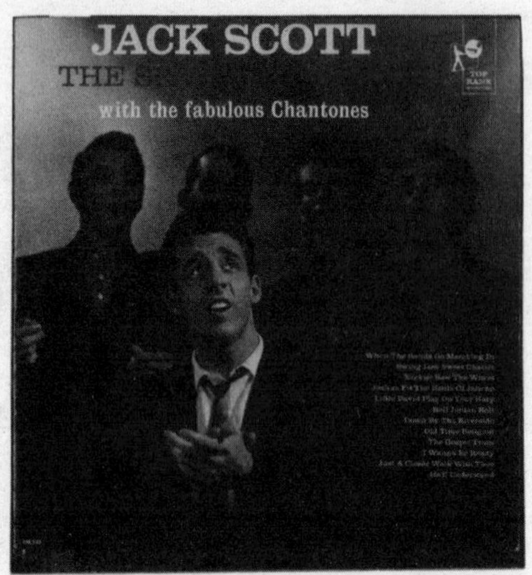
JACK SCOTT
with the fabulous Chantones

DECCA
MANUFACTURED BY DECCA RECORDS, INC., NEW YORK, U.S.A.
(70488)
Blues Singing with Piano, Bass, Guitar and Traps
WORRIED LIFE BLUES
(Merriweather-Estes)
SONNY BOY WILLIAMS
7888 A

REPRISE RECORDS • MADE IN U.S.A.
reprise:
PROMOTION COPY
NOT FOR SALE
R,20-157
(1828)
FRANK SINATRA
Orchestra Conducted by Nelson Riddle
AMERICA, THE BEAUTIFUL
(P.D.)
2:19
Manufactured for Bristol Productions

REPRISE RECORDS • MADE IN U.S.A.
reprise:
PROMOTION COPY
NOT FOR SALE
R,20-157
(1826)
FRANK SINATRA
Orchestra Conducted by Nelson Riddle
CALIFORNIA
(Cahn - Van Heusen)
Sergeant Music Co./Glorste Music, Inc./
Van Heusen Music Corp.
ASCAP
3:35
Manufactured for Bristol Productions

BUYERS–SELLERS DIRECTORY

Whether you are building a collection, selling a collection, or just maintaining a collection, the pages of our Buyers-Sellers Directory are certain to appeal to anyone with an interest in music.

Most books in the Osborne series offer an outstanding opportunity to cost-effectively spread the word of your products and services to a targeted worldwide audience.

For over 27 years, the results of the Directory have proven to be tremendous. We are especially proud of our incredibly high rate of repeat advertisers, one that far surpasses industry standards.

Look through these pages carefully. You might just find the dealer or contact you've been wanting to assist you in building your collection.

You can easily advertise in the next record guide, or any of the other books in our series. Simply contact our office and ask for complete details. We will do for you what we have done for countless others!

Osborne Enterprises
Box 255
Port Townsend WA 98368
Phone: (360) 385-1200 — Fax: (360) 385-6572
e-mail: bsd@jerryosborne.com web site: www.jerryosborne.com

Getting Better All the Time...
... Increased circulation – 35% more subscribers than last year!
... More information and diverse editorial for music lovers – addition of new writers and new columns!
... Many great advertising opportunities that target a variety of advertisers – 45 Special, Bargain Shop, R&B Special, Country & Western, Guide to Collecting on the Web.
... Friendly, personal customer service – striving to accommodate your business needs!
To Discuss A Cost-Effective Advertising Plan For Your Business, Contact
JOHN BEINBORN
1-800-480-0132 x173
Overseas: 563-588-2073 x173
Email: beinbornj@krause.com
discoveries
P.O. Box 1050 • Dubuque, IA 52004-1050
FAX: 1-800-531-0880
OVERSEAS FAX: 563-588-0888
Discoveries Print and On-Line Advertising
Connecting Collectors Worldwide at http://www.collect.com/discoveries

YOUR PAST IS OUR FUTURE!
CHALLENGE US!

RECORD-RAMA®
SOUND ARCHIVES

Celebrating 30 Years of Service 1968 - 1998
Covering 50 Years of Popular Music

"It's certainly one of the most — if not *the* most — impressive private collections I know of in existence."
— Gerald Gibson, Curator of Film, Audio & Video, U.S. Library of Congress

No Other Record Store or Collection Has More!

OVER FIVE MILLION SONG TITLES IN STOCK AT ALL TIMES
USED CDs ONLY $5.99 OR 3/$15.00 •
DJ DISCOUNTS & SUPPLIES • PHONOGRAPH NEEDLES • REFERENCE MATERIAL
PREMIUM CLEANING & STORAGE PRODUCTS
WE BUY SOUND RECORDINGS • WE MAIL ANYWHERE!

WHY SETTLE FOR LESS?

1130 Perry Highway (Route 19 North)
Pines Plaza Shopping Center
Pittsburgh, PA 15237-2132

ORDERS & INQUIRIES
(412) 367-7330
We do not answer the phones on Saturday
FAX (412) 367-7388
Retail web site: www.recordrama.com
e-mail: recrama@recordrama.com
Open daily, Monday through Saturday: 10 am – 6 pm E.S.T.
Closed Sunday

CHALLENGE US TO FIND ANY RARE, UNUSUAL OR HARD-TO-FIND RECORDING!

SEND FOR MY FREE LIST OF RECORDS
FOR SALE AT SET PRICES
RHYTHM & BLUES OUR SPECIALTY
Cool Cats
We're hep—
Specializing in the music of the 1950's, 33 1/3, 45, & 78 rpm.
Want lists filled; collections bought.
Over 100,000 records in stock at all times.
Victor Pearlin
VICTOR PEARLIN
PO Box 60299
Greendale Station
Worcester MA 01606 USA
e-mail: vpearlin@aol.com

There's more than one way
to keep track of your records...
We suggest you try ours.
Music Tracker 2.0
• Inventory & Pricing Software for Vinyl Record Collectors
• Featuring Jerry Osborne's Latest Price Guide Data
Find us online at www.bangzoom.com
or call us at 1-800-589-7333
Only
$32.99

RECORD RON'S

in cyberspace

http://www.recordron.com

E-MAIL:
recordron@recordron.com

TELL 'EM I SENT YOU! TO CYBERSPACE

EVERYTHING I COLLECTED FOR 40 YEARS IS FOR SALE!

IF IT'S RARE, OUT OF PRINT, HARD TO FIND...

I LOVE VINYL

lp's
45's
78's
posters
playbills
sheet music
lunch boxes
sound tracks
music memorabilia

KISS

Home of original
KISS Mylar Posters,
1978, by the Ball Game, 20"x 25"

$10 each plus $5.95 shipping or
$49.95 for set of 5,
domestic shipping included

239 Chartres Street · New Orleans, LA 70130
(504)522-2239 · FAX: (504)522-7305
P.O. Box 24535 · New Orleans, LA 70124
mail orders: 1-800-234-6889

WE SHIP WORLD-WIDE!

Dennis Hartman

("Dr. D")
"The Knight of the Turntable"
Dealer/D.J.
Music Freak Extraordinare

28 years experience to serve you and your sound needs

BUY • SELL TRADE

Customer satisfaction is our #1 goal. Over 40,000 records in stock! "If we don't have it, we'll find it"

Mon. - Sat.: 10 a.m. - 6:30 p.m.
e-mail vinyldr@aol.com

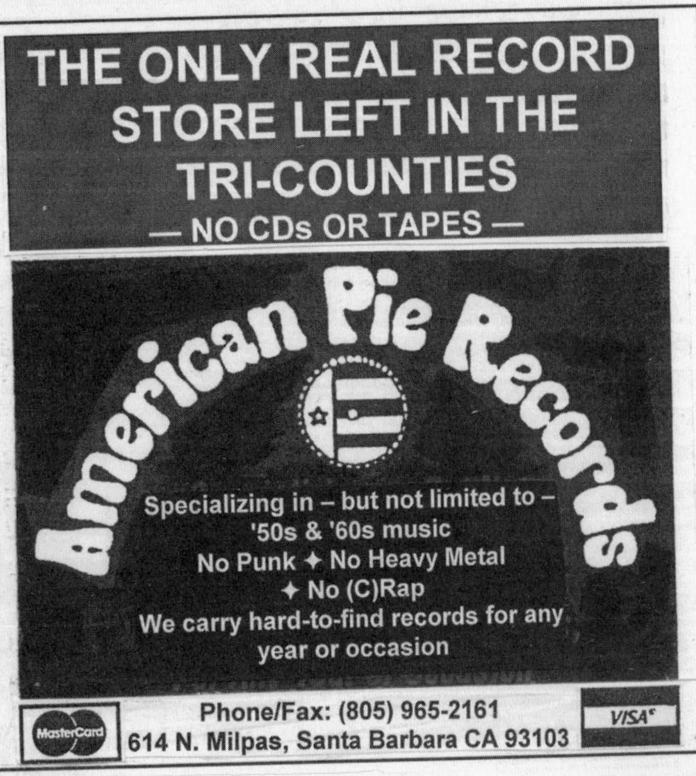

THE ONLY REAL RECORD STORE LEFT IN THE TRI-COUNTIES

— NO CDs OR TAPES —

American Pie Records

Specializing in – but not limited to –
'50s & '60s music
No Punk ✦ No Heavy Metal
✦ No (C)Rap
We carry hard-to-find records for any year or occasion

Phone/Fax: (805) 965-2161
614 N. Milpas, Santa Barbara CA 93103

VISA

"Specializing in ELVIS"

"Quality Elvis Presley collectibles at reasonable prices!"

THOUSANDS OF ITEMS FOR SALE:

Records *(LP's - 45's - EP's - 78's)*

Compact Discs *(U.S. - Imports - Promos)*

Las Vegas Memorabilia *(souvenir menus - tour books - posters - buttons - postcards - scarves - photos - rarities)*

RCA Promotional Items *(bonus photos - calendars - postcards - books - posters)*

1956 E.P.E. Memorabilia

Rare and unusual collector items!

New Address!

PO BOX 873
FRANKFORT IL 60423
Phone: (815) 464-7681
Fax: (815) 464-7682
e-mail- Sndzgood @aol.com

ROBERT ALANIZ — Owner

www.mcwonline.com

★ COLLECTING ★ MOVIE POSTERS?

Read the hobby's ★leading publication!

It's no secret that the hobby of collectible movie posters is growing rapidly. If the words "one sheet," "lobby card," or "insert" are familiar terms to you, you don't want to miss a single issue of **MOVIE COLLECTOR'S WORLD**. Regarded worldwide as the premier publication for collectors of movie posters, each issue of MCW is filled cover-to-cover with exciting offers from the world's best known dealers and collectors. You'll find something new on each page.... from posters from the 'Golden Age' of Hollywood to today's blockbuster hits. Plus, you'll find helpful features and news of the poster collecting hobby that will keep you informed and entertained. Don't be left out of this exciting and rapidly growing hobby. Start your subscription to MCW today!

OVER 570 BI-WEEKLY ISSUES PUBLISHED!
PUBLISHED EVERY OTHER WEEK!
JUST $45.00 FOR ONE YEAR (in USA)
Subscribe Online: www.mcwonline.com

ORDER BY PHONE!
Visa and Mastercard orders accepted by phone!
(800) 273-6883
or via FAX:
(313) 774-5450
Give card # & expiration date when faxing!

MOVIE COLLECTOR'S WORLD • PO BOX 309-J • FRASER, MI 48026

☐ Send the next 12 issues! Enclosed is $25.00
☐ Send the next 26 issues! (1 Year). Enclosed is $45.00
(Outside USA, 26 issues = $85.00 Surface, $200.00 Air)

Check, Money order or Visa/Mastercard accepted!

Credit card #____________________ Exp: ______

Name____________________

Address____________________

City ____________ State______ Zip ________

OSBORNE Appraisals By Mail

www.jerryosborne.com/appraise.htm

Now you can get a fast and reliable appraisal of nearly any collectible, mailed directly to you by either e-mail or postal.

- **Great for those with a few items for which you have no price guide – or when you need the very latest pricing in our files, which is often more current than a recently printed edition.**
- **Our service is for individual items only! We do not appraise entire collections. (There are other appraisers who will. Request referral.)**

Visit Osborne Appraisals web site (shown above), follow the easy instructions, fill out the form, and instantly submit your request. Though we created this service primarily for online users, anyone may use it. Describe the item as thoroughly as possible, including photos or photocopies if appropriate. Too much information is much better than too little! For records, make certain to include label name and selection number. Appraisals are for near-mint condition, so a price modification may be necessary for wear.

DIRECTORY OF ADVERTISERS

ABOUT THE AUTHOR

An avid collector of records for 45 years, Jerry Osborne has also worked full-time as an author of record price guides and reference books since 1975.

In the 27 years since work began on his first *Record Collector's Price Guide*, the number of Jerry's published works on music far exceeds 200 – including 84 books and 152 periodicals. As busy as ever, he continues to produce several books per year.

Among other music-related ventures, Jerry has, since 1986, written the popular, weekly newspaper feature, *Mr. Music.* This entertaining and informative column answers readers' questions about music and records. (*Mr. Music* is syndicated nationwide by World Features Syndicate. An online edition is now available at www.jerryosborne.com/mr.music.htm.

The rest of Osborne's past is also saturated with music. Upon graduation from high school, he began a 14-year career in radio and television (1962–1976) as an announcer, or dee jay.

Over the years, Jerry founded and published three collectors news and marketplace magazines: *Record Digest* and *Music World* and the still-popular *DISCoveries.* In the mid-'80s, he began publication of *The Osborne Report,* a monthly newsletter covering new releases.

Osborne's influence and involvement in record collecting has been chronicled in virtually every major magazine and newspaper in the country: *Reader's Digest, Life, The Wall Street Journal, USA Today, People Magazine, Esquire, Oui, National Enquirer, Money, Changing Times, Photoplay, High Fidelity, Billboard, Cash Box, Music City News, Collectibles, Kiplinger's, Woman's Day* and *Rolling Stone* – to name just a few.

Jerry has been a frequent guest on many major radio and TV talk shows, discussing the record collecting hobby. Among these are: *Good Morning America, The Today Show, The Nashville Network*, and far too many local and regional shows to enumerate.

He worked in the mid-'80s as a technical advisor and consultant for the critically acclaimed ABC-TV nostalgic news-magazine program, *Our World*, and has served as a consultant for HBO, and CBS-TV's *West 57th Street.*

More recently, Jerry worked on the music segments of the ABC-TV prime time extravaganza, *The Century*, as well as MSNBC's nightly *Headliners and Legends.*

Clearly, no one person has been more responsible – directly or indirectly – for the amazing growth in the past quarter-century of the music collecting hobby.